SPORTS
MARKET PLACE

2021
SPORTS
MARKET PLACE

GREY HOUSE PUBLISHING

PRESIDENT:	Richard Gottlieb
PUBLISHER:	Leslie Mackenzie
EDITORIAL DIRECTOR:	Laura Mars
MANAGING EDITOR, COMPOSITION:	Stuart Paterson
PRODUCTION MANAGER:	Kristen Hayes
PRODUCTION ASSISTANTS:	Krystal Dos Santos, Olivia Parsonson
MARKETING DIRECTOR:	Jessica Moody

Grey House Publishing, Inc.
4919 Route 22
Amenia, NY 12501
518.789.8700
Fax: 518.789.0545
www.greyhouse.com
books@greyhouse.com

While every effort has been made to ensure the reliability of the information presented in this publication, Grey House Publishing neither guarantees the accuracy of the data contained herein nor assumes any responsibility for errors, omissions or discrepancies. Grey House accepts no payment for listing; inclusions in the publication of any organization, agency, institution, publication, service or individual does not imply endorsement of the editors or publisher.

Errors brought to the attention of the publisher and verified to the satisfaction of the publisher will be corrected in future editions.

2021 Edition
Printed in the U.S.

Sports market place. – 2021
    v. ; 27.5 cm.
    Annual
    Continues: Sports market place

1. Sporting goods industry –United States—Directories. 2. Sporting goods industry –Canada—Directories. 3. Athletics—United States –Societies, etc. –Directories. 4. Athletics –Canada –Societies, etc. –Directories. 5. Sports—United States—Directories. 6. Sports—Canada—Directories. 7. Sports administration—United States—Directories. 8. Sports administration—Canada—Directories.

HD9992.U5 S667
381/.456887/02573
ISBN: 978-1-64265-820-0

Table of Contents

Introduction

Grey House Publishing's *Sports Market Place* is the classic sports reference work that has served the sports industry for over 50 years. Over the years, this work has grown to include more than 2,300 pages of valuable content, including professional, college and youth leagues and teams, sports media, events, facilities, sponsors, manufacturers, and professional services.

According to the article, Deloitte's "2021 Sports Industry Outlook," which is reprinted in its entirety following this introduction, here are some issues that rise to the top:

- COVID-19 continues to have a dramatic effect on the sports industry;
- Sports organizations are being forced to rethink and reshape their revenue-generating models;
- Social justice continues to be a major driver of positive change in the sports industry;
- Sports organizations are increasingly seeking new ways to keep fans engaged year-round, from streaming platforms to fully integrated social media, and more.

In addition, the front matter of this edition includes the "14th Annual Canadian Sponsorship Landscape Study."

Sports Market Place is your key to this dynamic industry. It is invaluable for media professionals, agents, athletic directors, professional & student athletes, equipment & apparel manufacturers, service providers, trainers, teachers, and job seekers. It includes full coverage of 103 sports, from Air Sports to Yachting, with statistics on the fastest growing and most popular – cycling, exercise and fitness, gymnastics, martial arts, running, swimming, and weight lifting.

Praise for previous editions:

> *"If doubts persist that sports is a major industry, this exhaustive reference volume will erase any such premise. In 10 chapters, the business of sports is documented in detail . . . Grey House continues to improve on a useful, comprehensive sports directory. For the professional involved in any aspect of the sports business, this is . . .essential . . ."*

American Reference Book Association

> *"This large reference work has served the sports industry for many years [and is] recommended [for] academic and public libraries; all levels."*

CHOICE

Arrangement

Arranged in useful, business-minded chapters, *Sports Market Place* compiles sections such as Single Sports, College Sports, Media, Professional Services, Facilities, Manufacturers, Retailers and Events. Each chapter is indexed separately, in addition to the three all-volume indexes at the back of the book, for a total of 13 indexes.

Listings are full of valuable information, including company name, address, phone, fax, web site, e-mail, description, key personnel and detailed corporate data.

This Year's Stats

Sports Market Place, 2021 has over 13,000 listings. You'll find 11,413 websites, 6,129 primary e-mail addresses, and 40,000 key executives. Here's a play-by-play:

- **Single Sports** has 2,075 sport-specific organizations, leagues and teams that comprise 103 specific sports. It includes professional, major and minor leagues, coaches, managers, and an alphabetical index.

- **Multi Sports** includes 12 specific categories, including athletic foundations, Olympic teams, halls of fame and youth sports organizations. It includes a total of 834 listings, and an alphabetical index.

- **College Sports** has 1,698 listings, with associations, conferences, degree programs, and division I, II and III schools. You'll find a comprehensive list of coaches and sports management programs, and an alphabetical index.

- **Media** includes prominent newspapers and radio and television sports programming. Listings include editors, commentators, show hosts and an alphabetical index.

- **Sports Sponsors** includes 123 sponsors that support most major sports, including college bowl games, and an alphabetical index.

- **Professional Services** comprises 13 categories, from executive search services to ticket services, for a total of 1,685 listings, and an alphabetical index.

- **Facilities** has 1,366 listings, and includes seven categories from arenas to facility concession services. You'll find stadiums, race tracks, architects, management services, and an alphabetical index.

- **Manufacturers & Retailers** include 1,929 listings, with a separate section for Software Manufacturers. Listings include valuable contact information including key executives, plus products and brands. This chapter includes a combined sport and subject index.

- **Events, Meetings & Trade Shows** include 1,345 listings, of which 152 are trade shows. Events and trade shows are listed separately by both sport and date. This section also includes two alphabetical indexes, one for trade shows and one for events.

- **Three All-Volume Indexes** are conveniently grouped in the back of the book. Entry Index is a straight alphabetical listing. Executive Index is a complete alphabetical list of all key personnel, including each executive's title and affiliated organization. Geographic Index organizes all listings by country and state.

For quick, easy access to this amazing compilation of data, *Sports Market Place* is also available online at https://gold.greyhouse.com. Subscribers have access to all of this data, and can search by Organization Name, Sport, Executive Name and Geographic Area. Plus, subscribers can download contact sheets to create their own mailing list of sales leads. Call 800-562-2139 for more information.

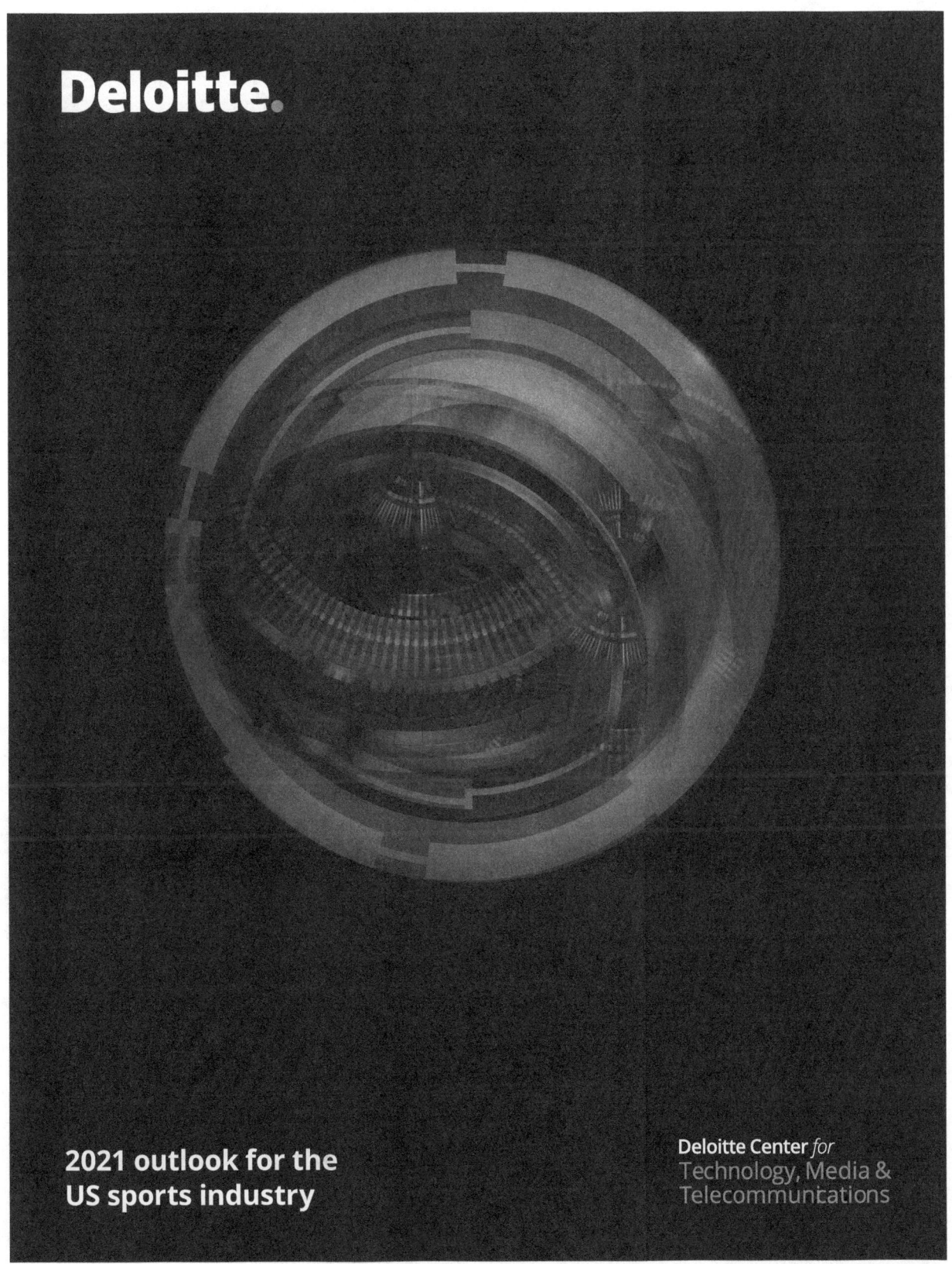

Deloitte.

**2021 outlook for the
US sports industry**

Deloitte Center *for*
Technology, Media &
Telecommunications

Interview with Pete Giorgio

During 2020, we saw two seismic shifts in sports: the pandemic and, equally as big, the social justice movement.

Because of the pandemic, there are likely to be ongoing restrictions to in-person fan attendance at US sports events extending into 2021. This will drive sports organizations to put a higher priority on identifying new ways to drive revenue and creating year-round, two-way relationships with fans. The need is dire: For example, in 2020, National Football League (NFL) teams are expected to lose an estimated $5.5 billion of stadium revenue, primarily in the form of ticket sales, concessions, sponsorships, and sales of team merchandise.[1]

Although many different diversity, equity, and inclusion issues have been perennial challenges in sports, a new urgency was created because of the events in the summer of 2020. It has become clear that US sports organizations can no longer be passive spectators around issues related to inequality and injustice. While many organizations stood behind their players during team protests and calls for action, there is still a lot of work to do across the industry.

I believe that the impacts of the events of 2020 will be felt by the US sports industry for years to come, and 2021 will be a pivotal year—challenging fans, athletes, broadcasters, teams, and leagues alike in new and unexpected ways.

Pete Giorgio
US Sports Practice leader
Deloitte Consulting LLP

Key takeaways
In 2021, sports organizations should consider three key strategic opportunities to boldly position themselves to thrive in the future:

- Leverage digital tools to drive new revenue generation models

- Be active in addressing race, gender, and LGBT+ inequality and injustice

- Explore new ways to fuel year-round fan engagement

About Deloitte's TMT industry outlook series
Deloitte's *2021 outlook for the US sports industry* seeks to identify the strategic issues that sports organizations should consider in the coming year, including their impacts, key actions to take, and critical questions to ask. The goal is to equip US sports organizations with the information needed to position themselves for a strong, resilient future.

Three critical issues for the sports industry to consider in 2021

1. **Reshaping and expanding revenue generation models**
   With many traditional revenue streams disappearing virtually overnight due to the pandemic, sports organizations are grappling with how to fill the void. Forward-looking organizations should consider a broad range of potential solutions, including monetization of data pertaining to fans, player and team performance, and sports betting; novel real estate plays; and unique partnerships with technology companies to help elevate the fan experience.

2. **Rethinking the role of sports in society**
   Although the struggle for social justice transcends sports, leagues and athletes possess powerful platforms that can fuel significant change for society as a whole. US sports organizations should consider making social justice a core component of their mission, culture, and brand.

3. **Redefining relationships with fans**
   The hollow echo of empty or partially filled stadiums highlights the critical need to establish year-round, two-way relationships with fans. With the pandemic likely to remain a major challenge throughout 2021, it is important for sports organizations to invest in multichannel digital solutions (everything from streaming platforms and augmented or virtual reality to artificial intelligence and "virtual fans") that can influence fan behavior and boost their level of year-round engagement. It's likely no longer sufficient simply to host a stand-alone app, website, or social media account; they're all important, and they should be tightly integrated across channels.

1. Reshaping and expanding revenue generation models

Even with the challenges posed by COVID-19, in-person fan attendance will undoubtedly remain a critical component of any team's business model. As such, leagues and teams should do everything possible to facilitate phased reopenings of sports venues as soon as possible. This includes taking all the steps required to make fans feel safe about returning to stadiums and arenas, along with making investments to improve the overall fan experience at games.

However, many US sports organizations are realizing that they should expand their business models beyond stadium-related sources of revenue.

With the NBA finishing its 2019–2020 regular season and playoffs in a fanless "bubble" due to the COVID-19 pandemic, the league was set to lose about $500 million,[2] making it a necessity to find ways to bring back fans to arenas and to create alternative sources of revenue in 2021.

Key opportunities for growth
One of the biggest sources of alternative revenue for US sports organizations in 2021 could be **data monetization,** particularly in the areas of fan engagement, player and team performance, and sports betting. The market for data-wranglers and aggregators is heating up as organizations increasingly employ data analytics to guide decision-making and support their marketing efforts.

In terms of fan engagement, data-driven platforms and artificial intelligence can help organizations sense the sentiment of fans, analyze the data to better understand fan behavior, and then connect with fans in ways that generate a better fan experience and new sources of revenue. This combination of sensing, analysis, and engagement can fuel monetization on an integrated e-commerce and socially active platform. Within the overall fan ecosystem, data can help organizations monetize different fan-engagement "zones" through specific value-added incentives. This can include engaging fans on social media, through the team's marketplace (website, store), via in-game offers (merchandise, refreshments), and by using hyper-personalized mobile advertising and gamification (real-time games and scoreboards with prizes).[3]

More than ever before, big data is also being used in sports to glean insights pertaining to player metrics and team performance. These data-driven insights are changing how games are played, managed, and monetized. As a result, sports data has become big business: According to Research and Markets analysts, the sports analytics industry is expected to reach nearly $4 billion by 2023 as teams, coaches, broadcasters, and rights holders harness data to improve performance and connect with fans.[4] In one recent data monetization deal, the NCAA signed a 10-year contract with a UK-based technology company to collect and distribute intercollegiate sports data, which is being packaged, licensed, and sold to media companies and other interested parties. Of course, it's important that data monetization initiatives be conducted in partnership with players' associations to help minimize the potential for foul play, such as competitors and hackers trying to use individual or league data to their advantage.

Data is likely destined to become an even hotter commodity as avenues for sports betting continue to expand across the United States. Professional sports leagues and the NCAA have a major opportunity to profit from the sale of data to sports data intelligence providers such as SportRadar, who can then repackage it for sale to sports betting operators. It's important to note that in both Tennessee and Illinois, for example, new sports betting laws require operators to purchase "official league data," enabling leagues to take advantage of a revenue stream that's already in place. As a result, leagues can cut data deals worth hundreds of millions of dollars without compromising their brands.[5] In addition, partnerships between companies with sports broadcast rights and sports betting operators may become more common in the future as they seek benefits from vertical integration and data-sharing.

Other potential revenue-generation activities include:

- **Expanding novel partnerships** that allow one or more technology companies to showcase their products while improving the fan experience.[6] Organizations should consider breaking away from traditional category management, especially in the area of technology, and develop complex stories and platforms in which multiple vendors can participate. For example, in April 2020, the NBA signed a multiyear partnership to create a direct-to-consumer platform that will use artificial intelligence (AI) and machine learning to localize experiences for the league's global fan base.[7] Capabilities will include offering games in fans' native languages, letting them chat during games, alternative audio and video feeds, real-time statistical overlays, gaming elements, and using archive footage to augment the viewing experience.

- **Attracting private equity investment** to address revenue shortfalls and working capital needs. For example, several private equity investors were considering a possible stake in Serie A, Italy's top-flight soccer league, in the summer of 2020.[8]

- **Growing the fan base** by meeting the needs of groups that have not traditionally participated in or followed the sport. For example, the NHL has a unique opportunity to increase the accessibility and visibility of ice hockey to groups it may have overlooked in the past, such as women and people of color. The league can address this challenge by establishing a presence through community outreach and promotion. One step in the right direction is the newly established Hockey Diversity Alliance (not affiliated with the NHL), which seeks to "inspire a new and diverse generation of hockey players and fans."[9]

Key challenges to overcome

While data monetization represents a significant opportunity for sports organizations, it does require a sizable infrastructure investment to generate the desired impact. These costs (for everything from data collection to potentially purchasing third-party data) can be hard to justify unless an organization truly understands the potential return on investment. Another related challenge is resolving the lingering question about who actually owns the data. Is it the team? The players' union? The league? Of course, the data owner should also abide by specific data privacy regulations (such as the GDPR in the European Union and the California Consumer Privacy Act). In addition, as data plays an ever-increasing role in management decision-making, trust will likely become an even bigger issue for athletes. How will data-sensing mechanisms be monitored to ensure that player performance data is accurate?

Although sports betting continues to expand in the United States, it poses a unique set of challenges. For one thing, it comprises a complicated ecosystem of players that is still sorting itself out. Another issue is that US sports betting regulations vary by state (some states require players to register physically rather than digitally; some allow mobile betting, while others don't). As the popularity of betting grows in the United States, leagues should adapt their officiating programs and compensation packages. Leagues are looking to take a cut of the new sports betting revenue stream with proposals like integrity fees, but there are additional considerations, such as how the leagues are already benefiting via increased viewership and attendance.

Actions companies should take now

- Prioritize investment in digital infrastructure, people, and processes pertaining to fan data.

- Build broader business acumen across your teams, along with considering nontraditional partnerships that bring outside perspectives.

- Be willing to be bold. Use today's challenging environment as an opportunity to try new things.

Strategic questions to consider

- What technologies (for example, data infrastructure technologies or in-stadium data collection) can enable new revenue opportunities?

- Do you have a coherent and comprehensive strategy for monetizing fan and athlete performance data? How could you implement that strategy more effectively?

- What learnings can you take from other sports organizations and/or other industries that have done a good job driving new revenues since the start of COVID-19?

2. Rethinking the role of sports in society

Leagues, teams, and athletes possess powerful platforms that can promote positive change for society as a whole. Sports organizations should embrace the critical role they can play in helping address race, gender, and LGBT+ inequality and injustice.

Many fans expect it—and future growth likely depends upon it.[10]

In fact, sports organizations should seriously consider the potentially adverse effects on their bottom lines of *not* addressing issues related to inequality and injustice. Now could be the time for organizations to make social justice a key tenet of their culture and brands.

In simple terms, organizations should ensure they are always aware of shifting societal dynamics and prepared to address them. The sports world has been transformed by social justice, with athletes having a stronger voice, demanding action and playing an even bigger part as role models.[11] Sports organizations' level of commitment to combating social injustice can directly affect relationships with those athletes.

Although more than 74% of the NBA's players are Black, it had just three Black general managers as of March 2019.[12]

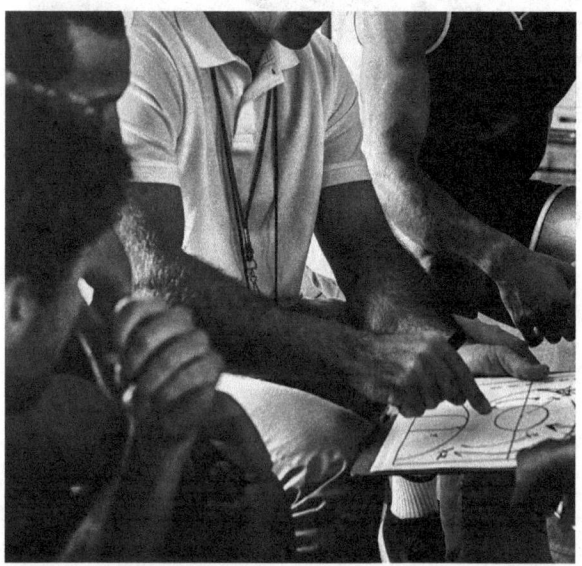

To begin to turn the tide against systemic racism, bias, and discrimination, leaders should develop six signature traits, according to Deloitte research: commitment, courage, cognizance of bias, curiosity, cultural intelligence, and collaboration.[13] By cultivating and practicing these behaviors, leaders can foster a more inclusive workplace—both today and in the long term.

When it comes to taking specific action, sports organizations should consider following the LEAD framework developed by Deloitte. The framework defines four areas on which organizations can focus when crafting the best possible response for its specific culture, values, and workforce:

- **L**isten: Be sure to gain a full understanding of the breadth of current challenges before taking action.

- **E**ngage: Use conversations to spark learning and the proper course of action.

- **A**cknowledge: Encourage frank discussions of race, ethnicity, and potential gender bias in the workplace.

- **D**o: Don't just say you're going to do something—do it, with urgency.

Key opportunities for growth

Social justice has become so critical that future growth will likely be predicated upon how authentic organizations are in responding to this challenge. Players and fans increasingly expect leagues and teams to play a proactive role in the social justice movement.[14] Deloitte's *Global Millennial Survey 2020* supports the notion that a proactive response to social injustice may be especially important to younger generations, many of whom tend to be more values-driven in how they engage with brands and businesses.

One exciting opportunity for sports organizations is to potentially capitalize on the role athletes now play as important influencers. Organizations should explore connecting their brands with athletes who demonstrate an especially strong sense of purpose (for example, women's tennis star and social justice advocate Naomi Osaka).

Another important trend to watch is the rising level of investment in women's sports. For example, the WNBA saw a 68% increase in regular-season average viewership in 2020.[15] By partnering with the right brands, generating innovative and interesting content, and collaborating with nonsporting celebrities, women's sports teams can build their own profiles and generate a large fan following. Social media represents an especially strong vehicle for women's sports and brands to gain exposure and influence fans.[16,17]

Key challenges to overcome

Despite some positive developments in 2020, the fact remains that systemic racism, bias, and discrimination will take time to overcome. A key is for sports organizations to make social justice an essential component of their culture and brand—now.

Of course, not all organizations share the same view when it comes to the social justice movement. Across college athletics and professional sports, some don't want the politics of social justice interfering with their entertainment. It may be necessary for sports organizations to find the right balance: allowing their players to express themselves on and off the field or court as they see fit, standing behind them when appropriate, but keeping the games professional and free of too much political content.

Another challenge is protecting the mental health of athletes. Mental health is a universal problem, but in the context of professional sports, the pandemic, racial injustice, and increased pressure from unique working conditions have brought the issue more to the fore. Studies have shown that historic social and economic inequality, racism, discrimination, violence, and poverty create greater mental health challenges for African-Americans.[18] "It's a miracle any African-American player turns out OK based on where we come from," NBA Hall of Famer Charles Barkley has said.[19] For professional LGBT+ athletes, there can be unique mental health pressures as well, with potential fears around coming out to teammates and fans and the repercussions for their careers.[20]

Although more players are beginning to speak out about their mental health struggles, leagues and teams should take proactive steps to address the mental strain that athletes are enduring in this pivotal time of social change and crisis. Approaches should include everything from having mental health professionals on staff to staging events dedicated to building mental health awareness.

Actions companies should take now

- Make social justice a key tenet of your organization's culture and brand.

- Thoughtfully evaluate how your organization does (or does not) support growth and pathways into leadership in an inclusive way.

- Develop a charter statement that the organization can stand behind and publicize. This can encourage sponsors and donors to make their decisions based on league and team policy rather than specific player actions.

- Develop internal and external expertise and relationships to manage mental health issues in sports.

Strategic questions to consider

- What steps can I take as a leader to personally improve working conditions within my organization?

- What processes can I put in place to ensure the recruitment, growth, promotion, and retention of all employees within my organization to ensure that league and team leadership reflects the diversity of the athletes and fans of my sports?

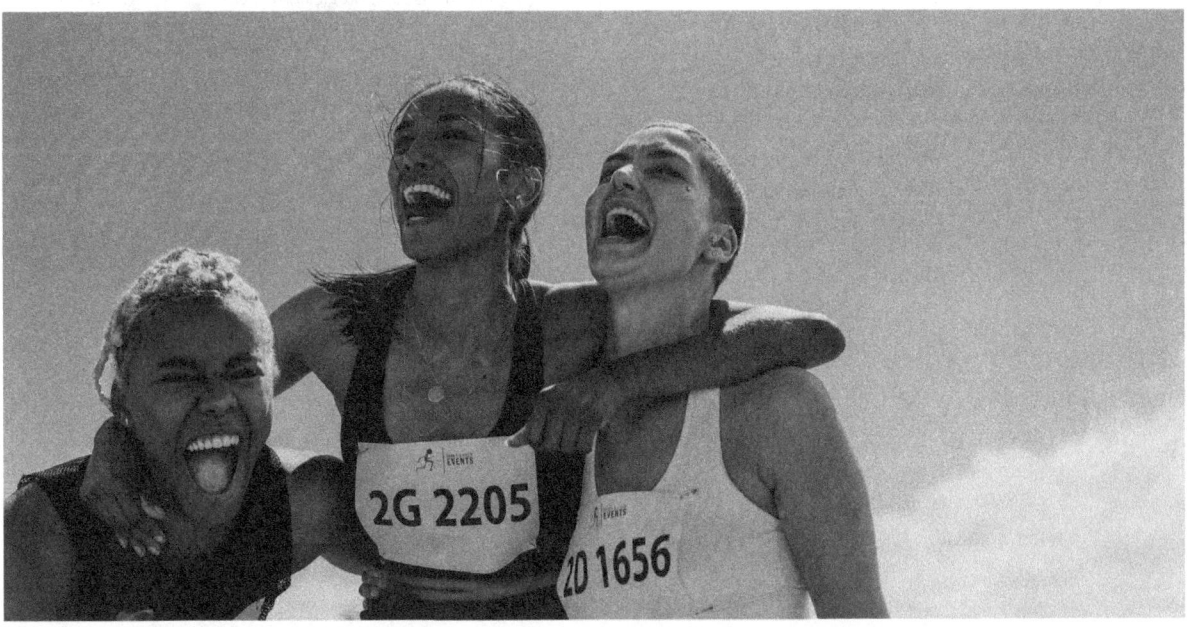

3. Redefining relationships with fans

Heading into 2021, it appears that the specter of COVID-19 will continue to haunt live sporting events across the United States—dramatically reducing fans' willingness to return to stadiums and arenas. In one recent survey conducted by Seton Hall University's Stillman School of Business, 61% of respondents who identified themselves as "sports fans" said they would not attend another live sports event until a COVID-19 vaccine has been developed and distributed.[21]

While it's been increasingly important for sports organizations to tighten fan engagement for some time, COVID-19 has amplified the critical need to reimagine the way they engage with their fan bases. Their focus should be on unlocking the power of digital technologies to build **year-round, two-way** relationships with fans.

First and foremost, those relationships should be built on a solid foundation of trust. As sports organizations attempt to navigate the COVID-19 crisis and thrive in the long term, they should focus on four dimensions of trust: **physical, emotional, financial,** and **digital:**[22]

- Can fans trust that **physical locations** (stadiums, arenas) are safe?

- Can fans trust that their **emotional** and societal needs are being safeguarded?

- Can fans trust that their economic and **financial** concerns are being served?

- Can fans trust that their **personal information** is secure?

According to the Deloitte Fan Experience survey, more than 60% of fans agreed that having a great "year-round experience" would make them more likely to become more engaged with their team in the coming season, while 55% said that it would make them more likely to purchase a ticket in the future.[23]

Once they've established a solid foundation of trust, sports organizations have an unprecedented opportunity to enhance their relationships with all fan types (from casual followers to fanatics) throughout the year.

Deloitte's fan engagement survey revealed that the more fans engage with their teams year-round, the more likely they are to purchase tickets and merchandise during the season.[24] The study also found that:

- 95% of fans currently have some form of interaction with their favorite team or league in the off-season.

- 65% of fans say they want to receive some form of content from their team at least monthly during the off-season.

- Across all fan types, those who engage just once a month in the off-season spend 40% more than fans who have no engagement during the off-season.

To truly maximize opportunities in the area of fan engagement, it's essential that sports organizations truly understand their fan bases—with the ability to segment fan groups (for example, casual fans, those "who love the game," and fanatics). This segmentation allows organizations to strategically target and incentivize different fan groups based on their level of commitment and behaviors. For example, while fanatics might desire daily social media notifications, casual fans could find them annoying. Organizations should strive to find the optimal frequency for communications based on each fan's profile.

Key opportunities for growth

First and foremost, it's critical that sports organizations invest in the infrastructure required to power digital channels, streaming platforms, and augmented and virtual reality solutions. Organizations should consider employing a wide range of channels and content types to meet varying needs across their fan bases. For example, the Deloitte Fan Experience survey found that when seeking rapid updates, fans prefer to use sports news websites, television, and social media. Fan demographics also shape their channel preferences: Deloitte's survey found that millennials are 40% more likely than baby boomers to use social media to obtain information about their favorite teams and players. In addition, 40% of fans in Deloitte's survey indicated that the presence of real-time augmented reality stats on screen would increase their likelihood of watching a live game.[25]

Sports leagues and athletes also should move beyond traditional broadcasts and start interacting directly with their fans. For example, they should encourage their athletes to become increasingly active on social media year-round to maximize fan engagement and monetization opportunities.

Recently, athletes from the NHL and NBA have leveraged leading social media platforms to provide a window into their personal lives, post workouts, host livestreams with other athletes, and even interview health experts to spread awareness about COVID-19.[26]

Athletes have also enhanced their brands and extended fan engagement by participating in live-streamed esports and casual gaming events.

In some cases, third parties are doing a better job than teams and leagues in terms of making players more accessible to fans and providing a "behind-the-scenes" look at sports. Platforms like Barstool Sports use podcasts like *Pardon My Take* and *Spittin' Chiclets* to fill gaps in the content that teams and leagues provide. Leagues and teams have the ability to offer this content and take advantage of the advertising and other revenues currently being won by third parties.

As the US sports sector continues to transform digitally, many leagues and teams are also finding innovative ways to use advanced technologies such as artificial intelligence to customize content curation, uncover interesting statistics for fans, and employ chatbots for targeted promotions and sales of subscriptions and merchandise.[27] Major League Soccer's Los Angeles FC was one of the first teams to develop an AI-powered virtual assistant (Olly) to enable preordering from concessions and messaging via mobile phones, further enhancing the fan experience.[28]

Sports organizations should consider several other vehicles to boost fan engagement:

- **Esports:** As the popularity of esports continues to skyrocket, it is helping teams, leagues, and athletes boost fan engagement. For example, the COVID-19 pandemic led the NBA's Phoenix Suns to simulate its remaining regular-season games on *NBA 2K*, streamed on Twitch. In their debut stream, set to mimic their scheduled game against the Dallas Mavericks, the Suns' Twitch stream reportedly drew 221,000 views.[29]

- **Fantasy sports:** Studies have shown that fantasy sports make fans more likely to watch games on television and attend them in-person.[30]

- **Sports betting:** Fans who participate in sports betting are increasingly watching not only their favorite teams, but also any other games on which they've placed bets.

- **Fan districts:** To help extend the in-stadium experience, teams should explore partnering with municipalities to build "fan districts," such as Ballpark Village adjacent to Busch Stadium in downtown St. Louis or the development districts around SoFi Stadium in Los Angeles.

- **In-stadium improvements:** To help bring fans back to stadiums, organizations should present a stronger sales proposition regarding the benefits of in-person attendance. Teams should consider making several improvements, including contactless technology, better in-stadium connectivity (taking full advantage of 5G wireless technology), and more player-fan engagement exclusive to the live venue.

Key challenges to overcome

Effective fan engagement relies heavily upon having the best data possible to enable highly personalized interactions with fans. As such, sports organizations should put the security of fan connections and data at the center of their digital strategies in order to maintain trust. As part of this effort, they should abide by data privacy regulations, such as the European Union's GDPR and the California Consumer Privacy Act. These regulations have led team owners to reevaluate and improve the ways they gather, process, and store confidential fan and athlete data.[31] As a result, sports organizations are emphasizing consent-based data marketing, increasing the roles and responsibilities of data controllers, and adjusting budgets to account for the cost of complying with data privacy regulations.[32]

Given the imperative to identify new revenue generation opportunities and ways of engaging with fans, sports organizations should attract and retain specialized data analytics talent. These skills are especially critical to targeting specific fan segments with personalized offers.

Traditional sports broadcasters now face stiff competition from social media and streaming video services, all of which have secured deals to stream live sports events. Sports organizations are now challenged with balancing the needs of fans who primarily view traditional broadcasts and those who prefer the digital platforms.[33]

Actions companies should take now

- Examine the actions of other industries. Explore and learn lessons from how retailers and consumer products companies have engaged customers over the past decade.

- Redevelop mobile apps, with a greater emphasis on delivering unique and added value to fans via content exclusives and personalized rewards programs.

- Experiment with content and storytelling to create strong programming around teams and athletes.

- Prioritize fan data by considering a portfolio approach to events, products, and services that meet different needs across different touchpoints throughout the year.

Strategic questions to consider

- Without new games on TV or streaming services, where are athletes and fans connecting, and which channels are most effective at fan engagement?

- How does a franchise's mobile app support a holistic, data-driven strategy across the business? How does it leverage data to deliver premium experiences to fans?

- How can teams leverage their most popular athletes to create more stories and fan touchpoints?

- How can leagues and teams take full advantage of 5G technology to boost fan engagement and the overall in-stadium experience?

Looking boldly to the future

In spring 2020, a couple of months into the COVID-19 pandemic, we stated that the US sports industry had an unprecedented opportunity to reevaluate its business models and build a new future. Success would likely require that sports organizations develop strong connections with customers, robust sensing and modeling capabilities, and the ability to continually reinvent how they think and operate.

As we prepare to enter 2021, those imperatives remain unchanged. It has never been more critical for sports organizations to acquire the digital capabilities needed to unlock innovative revenue generation possibilities and new levels of engagement with fans.

At the same time, sports organizations should make social justice an indispensable element of their culture and brand. Race, gender, and LGBT+ inequities will only hinder the progress needed to build successful sports organizations of the future.

To meet these challenges, sports organizations need bold leaders with a willingness to try new things. This includes looking beyond sports to leverage business approaches that have benefited successful companies in other industries.

Endnotes

1. Mike Ozanian, "The Stadium Revenue Each NFL Team Will Lose If Games Are Played Without Fans," *Forbes*, May 18, 2020.

2. Rob Schaefer, "Report: NBA could lose 'nearly $500 million' in ticket revenue without games," NBC Sports, March 12, 2020.

3. Mohamed Anis, "Sense, Analyze, Engage: How to Successfully Monetize Your Fan Ecosystem," Infosys, 2017.

4. Lee Rickwood, "Sports Scores, Stats and Big Data Analytics Bring Whole New Ballgame," WhatsYourTech.ca, May 23, 2018.

5. Jill R. Dorson, "Best Ways for NCAA to Monetize Sports Betting," SportsHandle, August 13, 2019.

6. Hookit, "How Technology Companies Are Leveraging Sports Sponsorships to Grow Their Brand," December 6, 2018.

7. SportBusiness, "NBA Signs Multi-faceted Technology Partnership with Microsoft," April 16, 2020.

8. Andrew Woodman, "Hard-Hit Sports World Finds New Fans: Private Equity Firms," PitchBook, July 20, 2020.

9. Hockey Diversity Alliance, "Our Purpose."

10. Ryan Barwick, "Sports Fans Are More Willing to Support Social Justice," Adweek, August 31, 2020.

11. Sam Quinn, "NBA players want owners to be proactive, not reactive, in enacting social change, per reports," CBS Sports, August 27, 2020.

12. Pete D. Camarillo, "Should the NBA Adopt the NFL's Rooney Rule?" Medium, March 10, 2019.

13. Juliet Bourke and Bernadette Dillon, "The Six Signature Traits of Inclusive Leadership," Deloitte Insights, April 14, 2016.

14. Chris Haynes, "Some NBA players remain dubious of owners' commitment to social justice initiatives," Yahoo! Sports, August 30, 2020.

15. Mechelle Voepel, "WNBA's Cathy Engelbert says 'pipeline is there' for more diversity in league," ESPN, October 1, 2020.

16. Izzy Wray, "Girls Aloud: Women's Sport Booms," Deloitte.

17. Deloitte, *2020 sports industry outlook*.

18. Monnica T. Williams, PhD, "The Link Between Racism and PTSD," *Psychology Today*, September 6, 2015.

19. Christina Similien, "NBA Stardom Isn't a Cure for Mental Health Issues," *Ebony*, October 10, 2019.

20. Alex Reimer, "Jason Collins says there's still 'fear' among closeted NBA players about coming out," Outsports, February 24, 2020.

21. Kelly Cohen, "Poll: Sports fans won't attend games without coronavirus vaccine," ESPN, April 10, 2020

22. Jennifer Lee, Bill Marquard, and Brenna Sniderman, "Embedding trust into COVID-19 recovery," Deloitte, 2020.

23. Chad Deweese, Kat Harwood, and Lee Teller, "Say Goodbye to the Off-Season: Engaging Sports Fans Year-Round," Deloitte, 2020.

24. Ibid.

25. Adam Deutsch, Kat Harwood, Lee Teller, and Chad Deweese, "The future of sports broadcasting: Enhancing digital fan engagement," Deloitte, 2019.

26. Joshua Clipperton, "NHL players, teams trying to stay connected with fans during COVID-19 pandemic," CTV News, Mar 24, 2020.

27. Venkat Viswanathan, "Why AI Is The Next Frontier In Sports Fan Engagement And Revenue," *Forbes*, August 16, 2019.

28. LAFC PR, "LAFC Partners With Satisfi Labs To Launch In-Stadium Order-Ahead On Apple Business Chat," July 18, 2019.

29. Bonneville International/KHTK Sports, "Phoenix Suns See Big Numbers As They Play Out Season On Twitch," March 20, 2020.

30. Daniel Roberts, "As live sports return to TV, so do DraftKings and FanDuel ads," Yahoo! Finance, August 4, 2020.

31. Ben Cronin, "Everton FC | Gathering fan data in the age of GDPR," SportBusiness, March 21, 2019.

32. TGSM, "3 Ways GDPR Will Affect the Data Driven Fan Experience," May 9, 2018.

33. Thomas Macaulay, "How technology is changing the sports fans' experience," *Tech Advisor*/IDG, July 31, 2019.

Get in touch

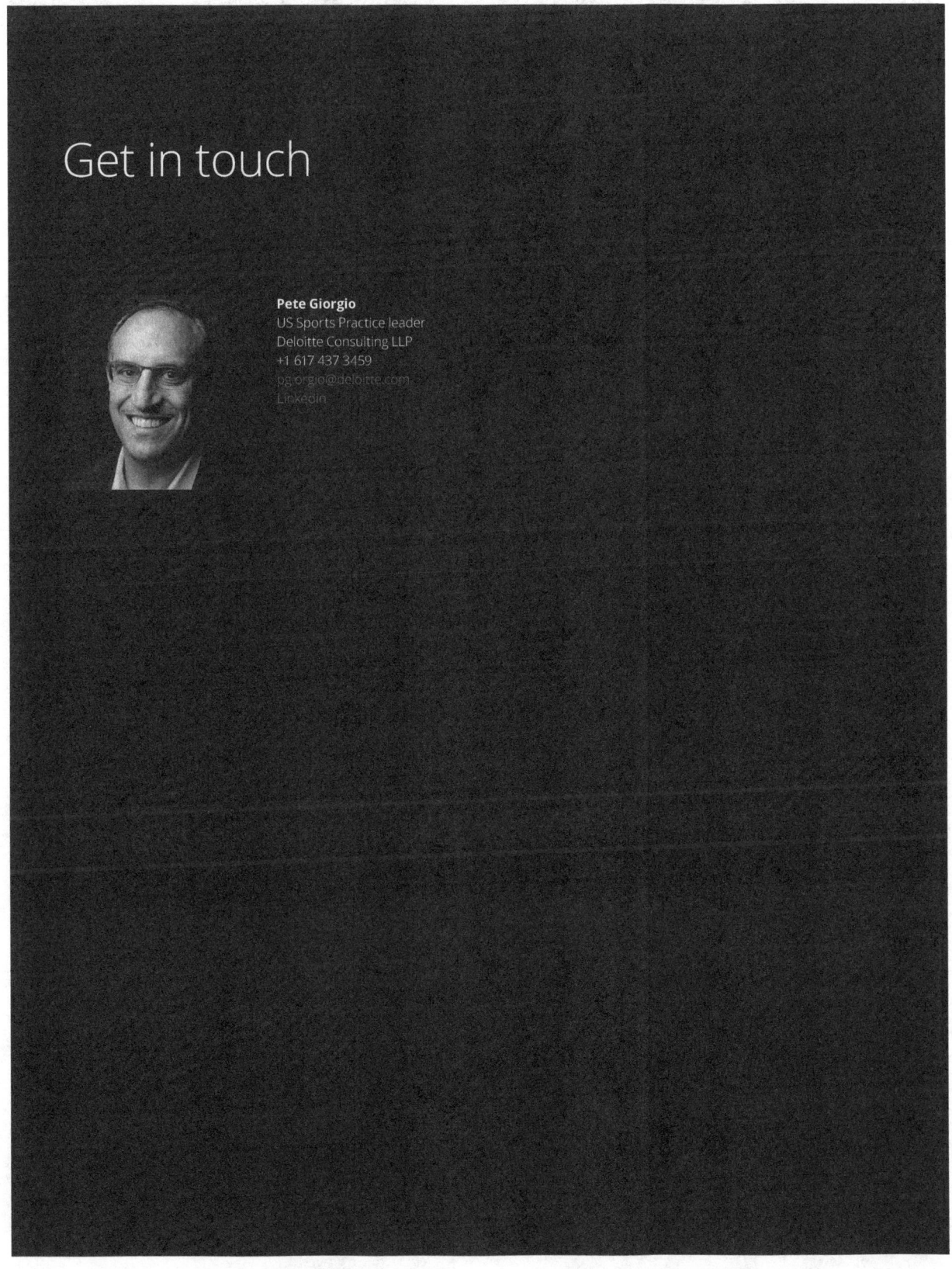

Pete Giorgio
US Sports Practice leader
Deloitte Consulting LLP
+1 617 437 3459
pgiorgio@deloitte.com
LinkedIn

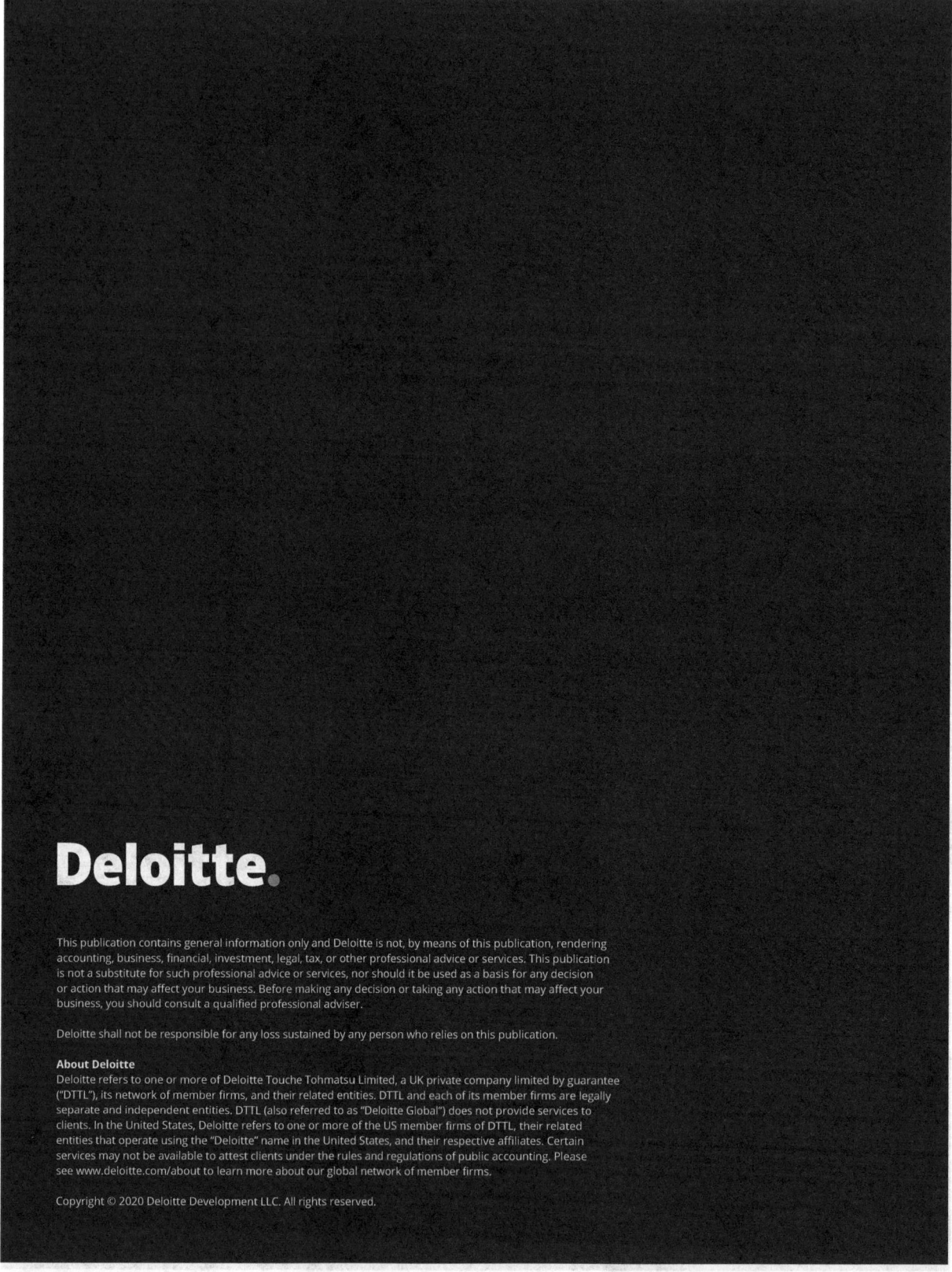

Sports Sponsorship

In 2016, the total North American sponsorship market was approximately 22 billion U.S. dollars.[1] According to ESP Properties, 106 companies allocated at least $15 million[2] to spending on properties of all types, including the arts, festivals, causes, entertainment, and sports, with professional and amateur leagues and teams, and "mega" events such as the Super Bowl,[3] accounting for 70 percent of the total, or $16 billion.

Overall, sponsorship spending continued to rise in 2016, even as many of the top spenders (including three of the top four: PepsiCo, Anheuser-Busch InBev and Coca-Cola)[4] decreased their spending, and a trend toward activation spending over fee spending strengthened.[5] Activation refers to investments—over and above rights fees—necessary to fully leverage sponsorship. In 2016, average spending on activation was more than double spending on fees for the first time.[6]

In spite of these cuts by Pepsi and other high spenders, the top ten sponsors were unchanged from 2015 (although a few companies outside the top four did trade places in the rankings). Also unchanged from 2015 were the industry categories most represented in the top 106 sponsors: beverage, auto, and banking.

In 2020, global sports sponsorship was projected to fall a whopping $17.2 billion due to the COVID-19 pandemic.[7] However, the National Football League (NFL) defied expectations with sponsorship revenue across the league soaring to $1.62 billion, a rise of 10 percent over the 2019/20 season. Naming rights deals for two new stadiums and new league-level sponsorships were key contributors to the revenue growth.[8]

---

[1] Statista. "North American sponsorship spending by property type from 2009 to 2018 (in billion U.S. dollars)." Statista.com. https://www.statista.com/statistics/196893/sponsorship-spending-by-property-type-since-2009/ (accessed March 12, 2021).

[2] IEG. "Number of companies in ESP rankings shrinks." Sponsorship.com. http://www.sponsorship.com/Report/2017/09/18/Number-Of-Companies-In-ESP-s-Top-Sponsor-Rankings-.aspx (accessed March 12, 2021).

[3] Statista. "North American sponsorship spending by property type from 2009 to 2018 (in billion U.S. dollars)." Statista.com. https://www.statista.com/statistics/196893/sponsorship-spending-by-property-type-since-2009/ (accessed March 12, 2021).

[4] ESP Properties. (2017). *Top Sponsors Report*.

[5] Ibid.

[6] IEG. "Average activation-to-fee ratio passes two-to-one for first time." Sponsorship.com. http://www.sponsorship.com/iegsr/2016/12/19/Average-Activation-To-Fee-Ratio-Passes-Two-To-One-.aspx (accessed March 12, 2021).

[7] Two Circles. "Sponsorship spend to fall $17.2bn; Financial Services by $5.7bn." Twocircles.com. https://twocircles.com/gb-en/articles/projections-sponsorship-spend-to-fall-17-2bn (accessed March 12, 2021).

[8] SportsPro. "Study: NFL defies Covid-19 as sponsorship revenue soars to US$1.62bn." Sportspromedia.com. https://www.sportspromedia.com/news/nfl-sponsorship-revenue-2020-allegiant-sofi-stadium-gambling (accessed March 12, 2021).

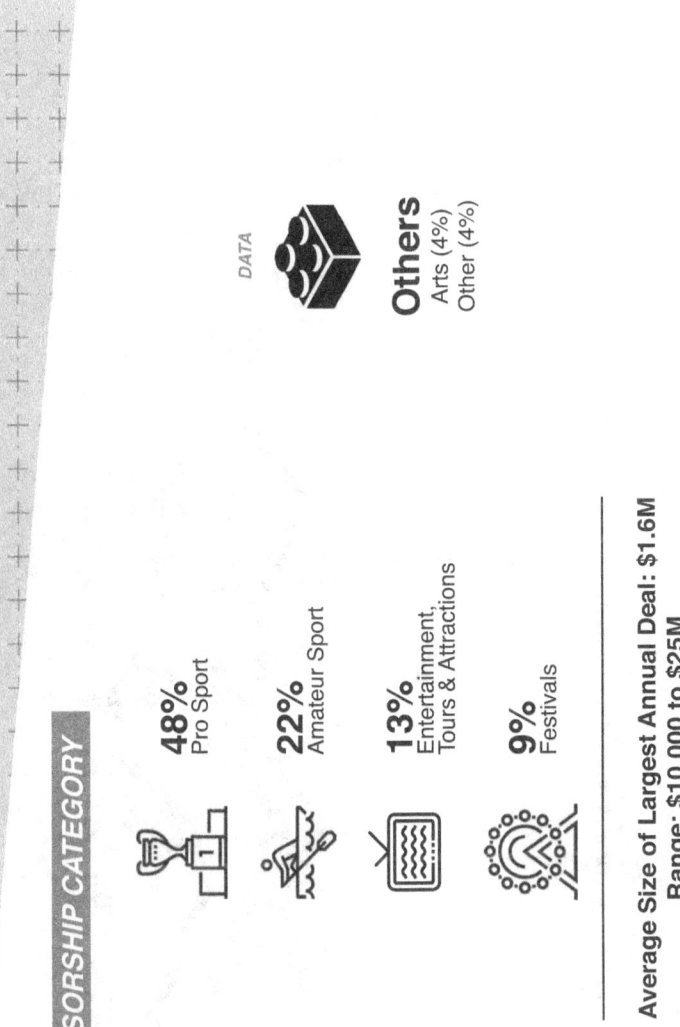

LARGEST SPONSORSHIP CATEGORY

DATA

48% Pro Sport

22% Amateur Sport

13% Entertainment, Tours & Attractions

9% Festivals

Others
Arts (4%)
Other (4%)

Average Size of Largest Annual Deal: $1.6M
Range: $10,000 to $25M

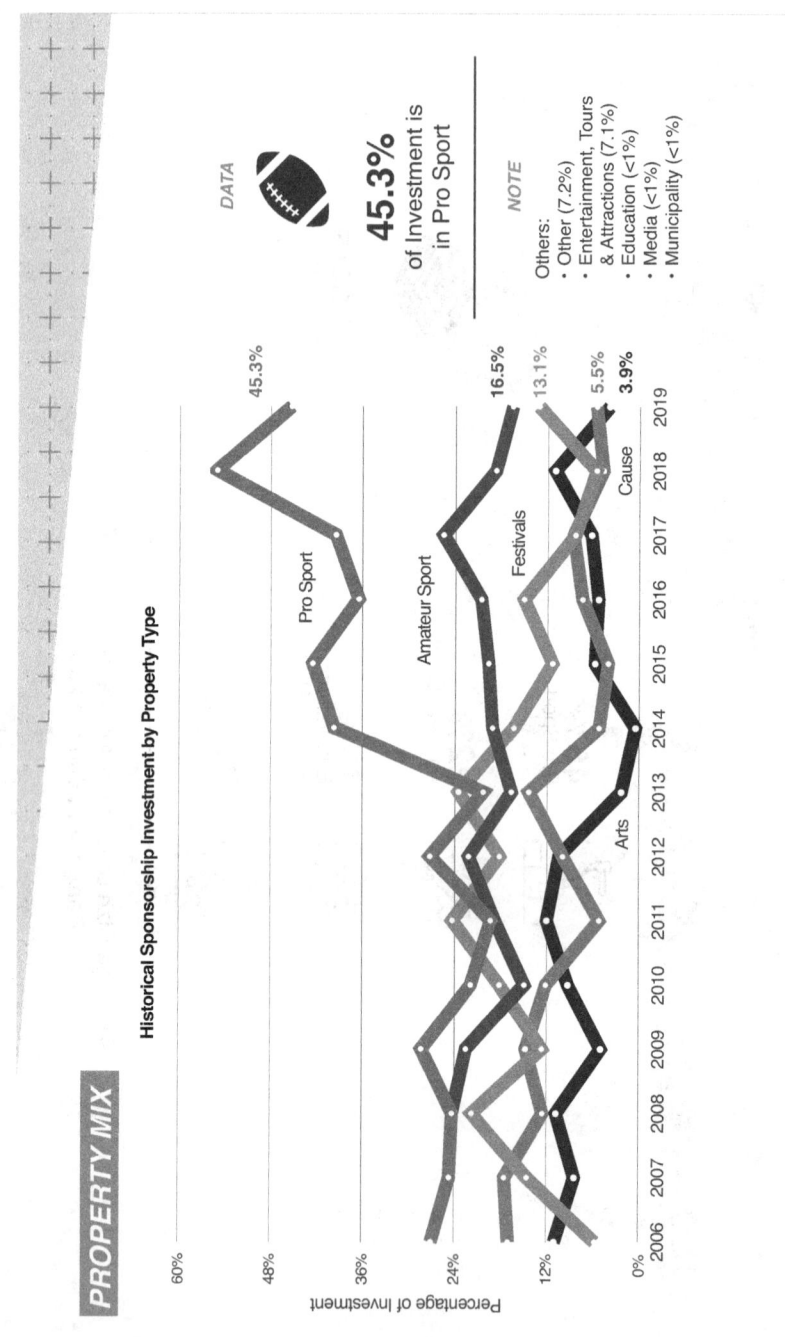

PROPERTY MIX

Historical Sponsorship Investment by Property Type

Percentage of Investment

DATA

45.3%
of Investment is
in Pro Sport

NOTE

Others:
· Other (7.2%)
· Entertainment, Tours
  & Attractions (7.1%)
· Education (<1%)
· Media (<1%)
· Municipality (<1%)

Pro Sport — 45.3%
Amateur Sport — 16.5%
Festivals — 13.1%
Arts — 5.5%
Cause — 3.9%

2006 2007 2008 2009 2010 2011 2012 2013 2014 2015 2016 2017 2018 2019

60% 48% 36% 24% 12% 0%

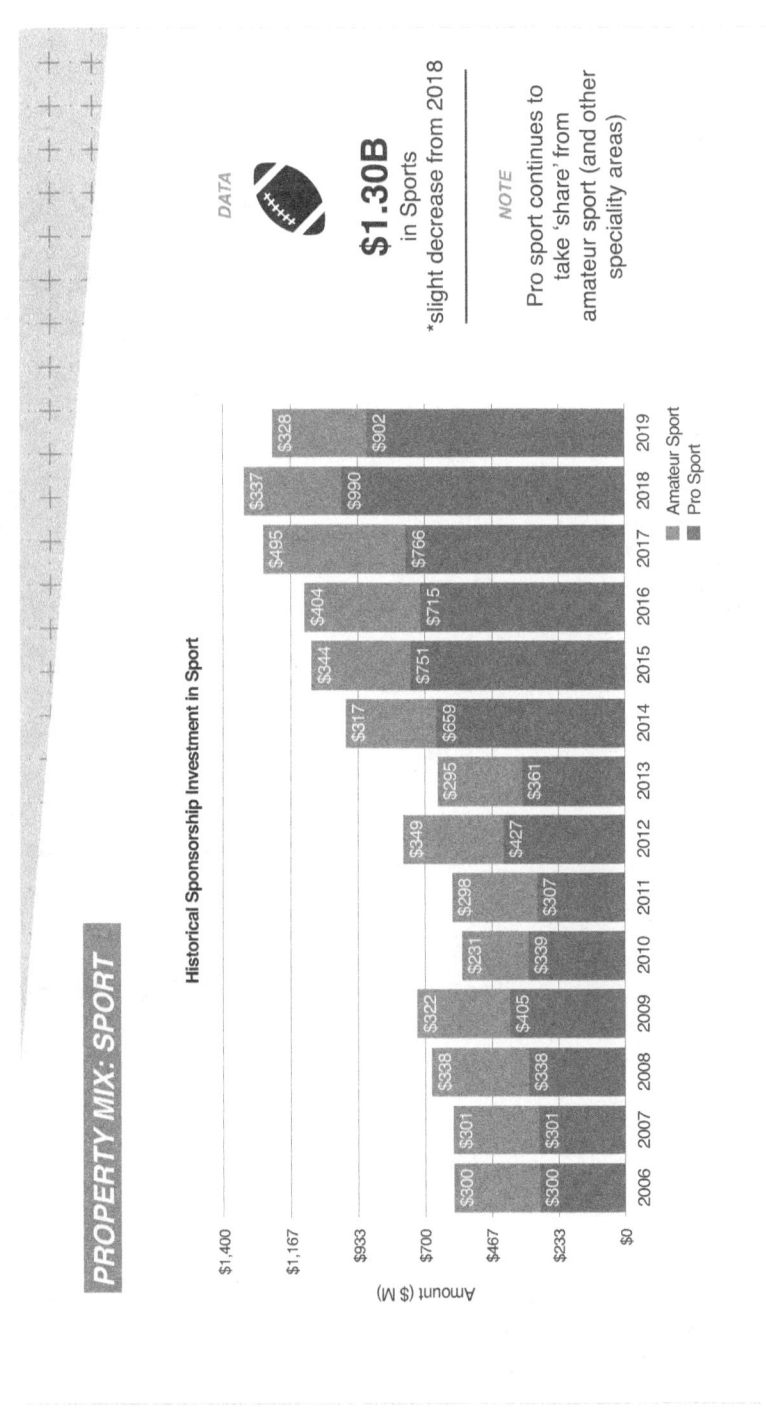

Source: O'Reilly, Norm. "14th Annual Canadian Sponsorship Landscape Study." Reproduced with permission, March 2021. https://www.sponsorshiplandscape.com/csls/

1

single sports

single sports

Air Sports Organizations

AIR SHOW NETWORK
1110 EUGENIA PLACE
SUITE 300
CARPINTERIA, CA 93013
805-553-6637
jim@airshownetwork.com
www.airshownetwork.com
• Jim J. Breen, President
jim@airshownetwork.com
• Greg Smales, Vice President
judge@airshownetwork.com
Description:
Founded in 1983, the company has served over 1,000 air shows. The Air Show Network offers numerous services to air shows across American including food concessions, production services, chalet designs and marketing services.

BALLOON FEDERATION OF AMERICA
1601 NORTH JEFFERSON
PO BOX 400
INDIANOLA, IA 50125
515-961-8809
Fax: 515-961-3537
bfaoffice@bfa.net
www.bfa.net
• Dean Carlton, President
• Cheri White, Vice President
• Tim Cloyd, Secretary
• Glen Moyer, Ballooning Editor
• Mike Shrum, Youth Program Chair
Year Founded:
1960's
Number of Members:
3,500
Member Services:
Sanctions events; products; educational materials; film library.
Publications:
BALLOONING, bimonthly magazine
Membership Requirements:
Pay dues.
Nature of Sports Service:
A non-profit association dedicated to the advancement of the sport and science of lighter-than-air aviation, both hot air and gas balloons.

CANADIAN SPORT PARACHUTING ASSOCIATION
204 - 1468 LAURIER STREET
ROCKLAND, ON, CANADA K4K 1C7
613-419-0908
Fax: 613-916-6008
office@cspa.ca
www.cspa-acps.org
• Debbie Flanagan, President
debbie.flanagan@cspa.ca
• Michelle Matte-Stotyn, Executive Director
• Judy Renaud, Executive Secretary
• Ian Flanagan, Treasurer
• John Gustafson, Media Relations
Description:
A non-profit membership association dedicated to the continuance, improvement and promotion of safe skydiving in Canada.
Publications:
CanPara, bimonthly magazine
Membership Requirements:
Pay dues.
Year Founded:
1956

INTERNATIONAL AEROBATIC CLUB, INC.
3000 POBERENZY ROAD
OSHKOSH, WI 54902-8939
920-426-4800
Fax: 920-426-6579
iac@eaa.org
www.iac.org
• Doug Sowder, President
(920) 426-4800
Sport Organization:
Membership organization that sanctions all US based aerobatic competitions.

NATIONAL AERONAUTIC ASSOCIATION
REAGAN WASHINGTON NATIONAL AIRPORT
HANGAR 7
SUITE 202
WASHINGTON, DC 20001-6015
703-416-4888
Fax: 703-416-4877
www.naa.aero
• Jonathan Gaffney, President, CEO
• Jim Albaugh, Chairman
• Durwood W. Ringo, Vice Chairman
• Roy Kiefer, Treasurer
• Elizabeth Matarese, Secretary
Year Founded:
1905
Publications:
Air & Space Magazine; World and United States Aviation & Space Records
Member Benefits:
Air & Space Magazine, a yearly copy of World and United States Aviation & Space Records, and free sporting licenses
Description:
The primary mission of NAA is the advancememnt of the art, sport, and science of aviation and space flight by fostering opportunities to participate fully in aviation activities and by promoting public understanding of the importance of aviation and space flight to the United States.

PARACHUTE INDUSTRY ASSOCIATION
6499 SOUTH KINGS RANCH ROAD
SUITE 6
GOLD CANYON, AZ 85118
480-982-6125
hq@pia.com
www.pia.com
• Roberto Montanez, President
• Mark Procos, Vice President
• Elizabeth Johnson, Secretary
• Vinny Salatino, Treasurer
• George Galloway, Executive Advisor
Description:
Comprised of companies and individuals united by a common desire to improve business opportunities in this segment of aviation.

SOARING SOCIETY OF AMERICA
5425 WEST JACK GOMEZ BOULEVARD
HOBBS, NM 88241
575-392-1177
Fax: 575-392-8154
dlayton@ssa.org
www.ssa.org
• Layton Denise, CEO, COO
dlayton@ssa.org
• Ken Sorenson, Chairman
• Phil Umphres, Treasurer
Year Founded:
1932

Number of members:
12,000 plus
Membership Requirements:
Payment of dues.
Nature of Sports Service:
Promotes and fosters all phases of soaring, both nationally and internationally.
Member Benefits:
Monthly Soaring Magazine, participation in Badge Program, Contests, Scholarships, State/National/World Records, unlimited access to SSA website, eligibility to participate in SSA Group Hull and Liability insurance program.

SPORT CLASS AIR RACING
3000 POBERENZY ROAD
OSHKOSH, WI 54902-8939
920-426-4800
Fax: 920-426-6579
iac@eaa.org
www.iac.org
• Bob Mills, President
• Vicky Benzing, Vice President
• Rick Vandam, Treasurer
• Tom McNerney, Secretary
Description:
The Sport Class Air Racing Association highlights innovative work being done with aircrafts. They host training sessions to assist new pilots learn how to air race, and host numerous races throughout the year.

STAR CREST ASSOCIATION
4509 EVE STREET
BAKERSFIELD, CA 93307
661-831-7771
• Rachael Newell
Year Founded:
1967
Number of members:
25,000
Member Services:
Permanent record of member's name and number kept in files of BBMSC; emblem; decal; certificate.
Publications:
STARCREST Magazine, bimonthly.
Membership Requirements:
Must be in a free-fall formation, complete membership form and pay one-time dues of $20. Must complete requirements for any of the SCR, SCS, NSCAR, SCSA, NSCSA or USA awards as described on the Star Crest Application sheet.
Nature of Sports Service:
Dedicated to the advancement of skydiving. Provides free-fall formation awards.

U.S. BASE ASSOCIATION/PHOTO SHOOTING
12619 MANOR DRIVE
HAWTHORNE, CA 90250
310-676-1935
Year Founded:
1981
Number of members:
5,000
Member Services:
Dissemination of information, technology, experiences, opinions; site and technique research; event organization; BASE jumper accreditation, award bestowal; video/film production and distribution. Annual plenum.
Publications:
The BASE Monitor, intermittent newsletter; USBA Curriculum and Coordination Guide;

BASEic Sport Parachuting, monograph; BASEics, preparatory guide for sky diver interested in BASE jumping.

Membership Requirements:
Extended to anyone interested in the concept of man jumping off of fixed objects. Acronym BASE is derived from the words: Building, Antenna tower (any tower or stack), Span (any bridge, arch, cable or dome), and Earth (any cliff or natural formation). Any individual making at least one jump from each category is awarded an officially recorded BASE number. Each jump must involve using parachute as life-saving device which cannot be inflated prior to jump.

Nature of Sports Service:
Dedicated to the safety, advancement and accurate positive public image of BASE jumpers and BASE jumping everywhere.

U.S. HANG GLIDING AND PARAGLIDING ASSOCIATION
1685 WEST UINTAH STREET
COLORADO SPRINGS, CO 80904
719-632-8300
800-616-6888
Fax: 719-632-6417
www.ushpa.aero
• Paul Murdoch, President
• Jamie Shelden, Vice President
• Mark Forbes, Treasurer
• Steve Rodrigues, Secretary
• Martin Palmaz, Executive Director
• Beth Van Eaton, Operations Manager
• Julie Spiegler, Program Manager

Year Founded:
1971

Member Services:
Pilot rating program, structured instructor certification program, training structure for tandem flight and aero towing, local club affiliation for the benefit of negotiated site insurance coverage, national magazine for flying, product and safety information, third party and participant liability insurance coverage for members.

Publications:
Hang Gliding & Paragliding magazine

Number of Members:
10,000

Nature of Sports Service:
A private, voluntary, membership, non-profit corporation, promotes the growth of sport flying in foot-launchable soaring aircraft.

UNITED STATES PARACHUTE ASSOCIATION
5401 SOUTHPOINT CENTRE BOULEVARD
FREDERICKSBURG, VA 22407
540-604-9740
Fax: 540-604-9741
uspa@uspa.org
www.uspa.org
• Sherry Butcher, President
• Jay Stokes, Chairman
• Randy Allison, Vice President
• Albert Berchtold, Treasurer
• Ray Lallo, Secretary
• Randy Connell, Competition and Records Coordinator

Description:
A voluntary membership organization of individuals who enjoy and support the sport of skydiving. Promotes safe skydiving through training, licensing and instructor qualification programs; ensures skydiving's rightful place on airports and in the airspace system, and promotes competition and record-setting programs.

Number of Members:
32,000

Archery Organizations

FEDERATION OF CANADIAN ARCHERS
2255 ST. LAURENT
SUITE 108
OTTAWA, ON, CANADA K1G 4K3
613-260-2113
Fax: 613-260-2114
information@archerycanada.ca
www.archerycanada.ca
• Allan R. Wills, President/VP International
• William Currie, VP Committees & Projects
• Alec Denys, VP High Performance
• Robert Tataryn, VP Administration
• Tricia Oshiro, Athlete Representative

Nature of Service:
To promote and develop the timeless sport of archery in a safe and ethical manner by providing programs that empower all participants to enjoy themselves and achieve their personal goals.

Member Services:
Coaching clinic, award systems, insurance program, rules, standardization, interprovincial club program, equipment analysis; membership and tournament software applications; archery promo video.

Number of Members:
9,000

ARCHERY SHOOTERS ASSOCIATION
PO BOX 399
KENNESAW, GA 30156
770-795-0232
Fax: 770-795-0953
info@asaarchery.com
www.asaarchery.com
• Dee Falks, Federation Director
federationdirector@asaarchery.com

Description:
Promotes archery tournaments and professional level competitions.

Publications:
ASA TOUR GUIDE.

Member Services:
Sponsor contacts, tournament/event food and lodging discounts, club insurance policy, equipment discounts. Dues: $30/year.

Number of Members:
8,000

ARCHERY TRADE ASSOCIATION
101 NORTH GERMAN
SUITE 3
NEW ULM, MN 56073
507-233-8130
866-266-2776
Fax: 507-233-8140
info@archerytrade.org
www.archerytrade.org
• Jay McAninch, President and CEO
• Teresa Johnson, Director of Communications and Public Relations
• Amy Hatfield, Director of Content Marketing
• Emily Beach, Director of Partnership and Program Development
• Mitch King, Director of Government Relations

Year Founded:
1953

Number of members:
1,200

Description:
Provides the core funding and direction for two new foundations critical to the future of archery and bowhunting: ArrowSport and the Bowhunting Preservation Alliance. Also continues to direct the industry's annual archery and bowhunting trade show.

Publications:
Inside Archery, Archery Business and ArrowTrade magazines.

Membership Requirements:
Manufacturers, distributors, retailers, sales representatives, outfitters and others serving the archery and bowhunting industry.

INTERNATIONAL BOWHUNTING ORGANIZATION
PO BOX 398
VERMILION, OH 44089
440-967-2137
Fax: 440-967-2052
www.ibo.net
• Bryan J. Marcum, President
• Gene Bihler, Vice President
• Mike Stitt, Vice President

Description:
The International Bowhunting Organization's goal is to promote, encourage, and foster the sport of bowhunting and to provide education to bowhuntners. They act as a regulatory body for bowhunters and aim to disperse essential bowhunter information to those who need it. The IBO prides itself in its ability to foster the conservation and preservation of wildlife, and to provide proactive support for wildlife management.

Year Founded:
1984

Member Benefits:
Subscription to Bowhunting World magazine, 2 window decals, official IBO rule book, accident insurance (US only) and a membership card.

NATIONAL FIELD ARCHERY ASSOCIATION
800 ARCHERY LANE
YANKTON, SD 57078
605-260-9279
Fax: 605-260-9280
www.nfaausa.com
• Bruce Cull, President
• Brian Sheffler, Vice President
• Natalie Vollmer, Executive Secretary
• Brennan Ewald, Membership Marketing Manager

Description:
A non-profit corporation dedicated to the practice of archery and is dedicated to the conservation and preservation of the game. It is resolved to foster, perpetuate and preserve the use of the bow in accordance with its ancient and honorable traditions.

Year Founded:
1939

Number of members:
50 chartered state associations and 1,100 affiliated clubs

Publications:
ARCHERY, official publication.

Membership Requirements:

Must join both state & national to be tournament member. Membership available through NFAA headquarters. Non-tournament member, join directly or through state organization.
Nature of Sports Services:
Hosts three National Championship tournaments, eight sectional indoor and eight sectional outdoor championships that draw more than 3,000.

UNITED FOUNDATION FOR DISABLED ARCHERS
20 NE 9TH AVENUE
PO BOX 251
GLENWOOD, MN 56334
320-634-3660
info@uffdaclub.com
www.uffdaclub.com
• Daniel Hendricks, President
Description:
Founded in 1994, the United Foundation for Disabled Archers aims to promote and provide a means to practice all forms of archery for the physically challenged.

USA ARCHERY
4065 SINTON ROAD
SUITE 110
COLORADO SPRINGS, CO 80907
719-866-4576
Fax: 719-632-4733
media@usarchery.org
www.teamusa.org/usa-archery
• Denise Parker, CEO
dparker@usarchery.org
• Cindy Clark, Office/Finance Manager
cclark@usarchery.org
• Cindy Tobin, Membership Manager
ctobin@usarchery.org
Description:
USA Archery is the organization recognized by the U.S. Olympic Committee for the purpose of selecting and training men's and women's teams to represent the U.S. in Olympic Games. They also select teams for the World Championships and other international competitions.

WORLD ARCHERY FEDERATION
MAISON DU SPORT INTERNATIONAL
AVENUE DE RHODANIE 54
LAUSANNE, 1007
+41-(0) 21-614-3050
Fax: +41-(0) 21-614-3055
www.worldarchery.org
• Ugur Erdener, President
erdenerugur@gmail.com
• Mario Scarzella, First Vice President
presidente@fitarco-italia.org
• Philippe Bouclet, Vice President
p.bouclet@ffta.fr
• Tom Dielen, Secretary General/Executive Director
tdielen@archery.org
• Matteo Pisani, IT Manager
• Caroline Murat, Finance Manager
• Jenny Brugger, Officer Coordinator
• Chris Marsh, Events Director
Year Founded:
1931
Description:
Promotes and regulates archery world-wide in conformity with Olympic principles and organizes international competition.
Number of members:
140

Publications:
Target magazine, published two (three in Olympic years) times a year; monthly newsletter called FITA INFO; FITA annual report.

Arm Wrestling Organizations

AMERICAN ARMSPORT ASSOCIATION
176 DEAN ROAD
MOORESBURG, TN 37811
423-272-6162
Fax: 423-272-6162
www.armsport.com
• Karen Bean, Executive Director
• Frank Bean, Executive Director
Year Founded:
1977
Number of Members:
56 U.S. armwrestling associations
Publications:
ARM BENDER, quarterly magazine.
Membership Requirements:
Payment of dues, $25 per year.
Description:
Represents the US in the WAF. Sponsors one national championship each year (Standing). Affiliate of World ArmSport Federation.

CANADIAN ARMWRESTLING FEDERATION
1635 8TH AVENUE
SASKATOON, SK, CANADA S7K 2X8
www.cawf.ca
• Rick Pinkney, President
• Ryan Espey, Vice President
• Tracey Arnold, Secretary/Treasurer
Description:
The Canadian Armwrestling Federation's purpose is to oversee organization, promotion and refereeing of the sport of armwrestling in Canada.

NEW YORK ARMWRESTLING ASSOCIATION, INC.
PO BOX 670952
FLUSHING, NY 11367-0952
718-544-4592
877-692-2767
nyawa@nycarms.com
www.nycarms.com
• Gene Camp, Founder, President
• Annette Camp, Vice President
• Bobby Buttafuoco, NY Regional Director
• Vivian Leber, NYAWA Executive Editor
nyawa@aol.com
Year Founded:
1977
Description:
The New York Arm Wresling Association is a unique property and is a NYS-registered not-for-profit organization that produces an exciting grass roots sporting event. It has drawn competition locally from the New York area and from 6 continents and 300 major cities in the USA.
Publications:
NYAWA (Call to Arms) Newsletter, quarterly.
Events:
Promotes arm wrestling events in the New York region including the Empire State Championship, N.Y.C. Junior Championships, Borough Championships,

New York Golden Arms Series (9 events); the L.I. Pro Invitational and New York Golden Arms Series.
Number of Members
1595
Nature of Service:
Production of arm wrestling championships in NYC and each of the 5 NYC boroughs, Long Island and upstate New York. Event categories include mens, womens, amateur and pro categories, age groups, and weight classes.

WORLD ARMWRESTLING FEDERATION
SOFIA PARK TRADING ZONE
BUILDING 16B
FLOOR 1, OFFICE 1-2
SOFIA, 1766
359-888-96-8541
contact@waf-armwrestling.com
www.waf-armwrestling.com
• Fred Roy, President
(306) 763-0899
fred.roy@sasktel.net
• Dave Devoto, VP North America
(707) 537-7373
• Assen Hadgitorov, VP Europe
asenhdj@mail.com
• Agzamov Mukhamedolla, VP Asia
(+73) 72 33802
fgsakz_a@mail.ru
Year Founded:
1970
Description:
Founded in 1970. Sponsors world championships. Coordinates all activities of the W.A.F. members. Solicits new W.A.F. member countries.

Auto Sports Organizations

AMERICAN AUTO RACING WRITERS AND BROADCASTERS ASSOCIATION
922 NORTH PASS AVENUE
BURBANK, CA 91505-2703
818-842-7005
Fax: 818-842-7020
www.aarwba.org
• Norma Dusty Brandel, President & Executive Director
• Kathy Seymour, Vice President
kathyseu@hotmail.com
Year Founded:
1955
Number of members:
Over 400.
Member Services:
Breakfast meetings, monthly newsletter, membership directory.
Publications:
Monthly newsletter for members only, and annual directory.
Membership Requirements:
Media who cover motorsports, public relations and advertising personnel involved with racing teams, sponsors, sanctioning bodies.
Description:
Serves to upgrade coverage of auto racing, promote coverage and the stature of racing, and to secure the best possible conditions for auto racing media. All-American auto racing team selection committee.

AMERICAN RACING DRIVERS CLUB INC./ARDC
529 OLD MILL ROAD
MILLERSVILLE, MD 21108
570-275-0649
ardcmidget.com
• Wayne Lesher, President
wlesher@centurylink.net
• Tom Grumbine, Vice President
tgrumbine@hotmail.com
Year Founded:
1939
Publications:
Monthly newsletter.
Number of members:
Average of 30 registered drivers a year.
Membership Requirements:
There are four types of annual memberships available. Four are participatory and the other is for associate members.

AMERICAN THREE QUARTER MIDGET RACING ASSOCIATION
808 WOODLANE RD
MT. HOLLY, NJ 8060
610-217-2593
Fax: 609-267-3890
atqmra.com
• Buddy Sload, President
(484) 880-0907
• Paul Dodorico, Vice President
Year Founded:
1956
Member Services:
Scheduling and organization of racing events, provision of racing insurance, newsletter. Annual meeting held during October each year.
Publications:
ATQMRA NEWSLETTER, monthly.
Membership Requirements:
Open to all persons age 18 or over; Membership categories of Driver, Car Owner, Owner-Driver, Associate.
Description:
Organization and promotion of auto racing events, specifically single-seat, open-cockpit, T.Q. Midget, race cars, in Northeastern United States.

ARCA RACING SERIES
8117 LEWIS AVENUE
TEMPERANCE, MI 48182
734-847-6726
Fax: 734-847-3137
www.arcaracing.com
• Ron Drager, President & Chief Executive Officer
(734) 847-6726
• Mark Gundrum, VP, Business Development & Corporate Partners
(734) 847-6726
mgundrum@arcaracing.com
• Joe Wells, Dirextor, Race Operations & Administration
(734) 847-6726
jwells@arcaracing.com
Year Founded:
1953
Description:
Sanctioning body for various types of auto racing in U.S. sanctions national championship series for stocks (ARCA RE/MAX Series), Trucks (ARCA Lincoln Welders Truck Series). Also sanctions Toledo and Flat Rock Speedways.
Membership Requirements:

Applications open to drivers, mechanics and car owners.
Publications:
Full line of releases to accredited members of media; newsletter to members.

DIRTCAR RACING
1 SPEEDWAY DR
WEEDSPORT, NY 13166
315-834-6606
info@dirtcar.com
www.superdirtcarseries.com
• Joe Skotnicki, Director of Competition/Track Sanctioning
• Cory Reed, Director Series/Sanctioning
Year Founded:
1976
Description:
Sanctioning body for open wheel modified dirt track racing. Races organized and sanctioned by DIRT include the Rite-Aid 100 & 200, Eastern States Weekend and Advance Auto Parts modified Super Dirt Series.

DOVER MOTORSPORTS, INC.
1131 N DUPONT HIGHWAY
PO BOX 843
DOVER, DE 19903
302-883-6500
Fax: 302-672-0100
info@dovermotorsports.com
www.dovermotorsportsinc.com
Nature of Sports Service:
Owns and operates racetracks which include Dover International Speedway, Nashville Superspeedway, Gateway International Raceway.

FAST TRACK RACING
5540 MOREHEAD ROAD
HARRISBURG, NC 28075
704-455-1700
Fax: 704-455-6603
info@fasttrackracing.com
www.fasttrackracing.com
• Andy Hillenburg, Owner
• Bill McKee, General Manager
Year Founded:
1989
Description:
The school caters to the stock racing car enthusiast. It gives the student the opportunity to get behind the wheel of a ARCA style stock car. The enthusiast has an option of the 1 day or the 3 day course, 10, and 20 lap drives, and 3 lap rides. New for 2009 is the Short Track Driver Development School, ages 14 and older, conducted on the 1/2 mile track at Rockingham Speedway, with ARCA race cars.

FELD MOTOR SPORTS
4255 MERIDIAN PARKWAY
AURORA, IL 60504
630-566-6100
webmaster@monsterjam.com
monsterjam.com
• Magnus Danielsson, Intl VP
Nature of Sports Service:
Sanctioning body for Monster Jam and Thunder Nationals, as well as motocross and quad racing.

FORMULA RACE CAR CLUB OF AMERICA
570 WEST SADDLE RIVER ROAD
RIDGEWOOD, NJ 07450
570-669-9589
frcca2014@gmail.com
www.formularacecarclubofamerica.com
• Jeff Zeller, Treasurer
(914) 584-0132
• Andy Graham, President
(914) 584-0132
Year Founded:
1980
Member Services:
Driver's Points Fund; year-end championship; trophies.
Publications:
TRANSMISSIONS, newsletter, 12 times annually.
Membership Requirements:
$125 annual membership fee.
Description:
Sanctioning body for entry-level amateur Formula Ford(older models), Formula American car racing. Issues competition licenses based upon accomplishments in the previous class. Races are held in the Northeast and Southeast. The FRCCA endeavors to put emphasis on driving ability rather than the car, in racing.

FROST MOTORSPORTS, LLC
909 SENECA ROAD
WILMETTE, IL 60091
847-853-0294
Fax: 847-853-8763
twfrost@speedwaysonline.com
www.frostmotorsports.com
• Timothy W. Frost, President
twfrost@speedwaysonline.com
Nature of Service:
Feasibility studies, market demand studies, economic impact analysis, valuation and financial consulting of motorsports facilities and motorsports industry participants

GRAND PRIX ASSOCIATION OF LONG BEACH
GRAND PRIX ASSOC OF LONG BEACH
3000 PACIFIC AVENUE
LONG BEACH, CA 90806
562-981-2600
Fax: 562-981-2616
info@gpalb.com
www.gplb.com
• Jim Michaelian, President/CEO
(562) 490-4522
• Martin Bannon, Director, Marketing
(562) 490-4512
• Gemma Bannon, Exec. Asst. to the President & CEO, Offic
(562) 490-4521
• Allison Wilson, Exec. Asst. to President & CEO/Manager of Adv
(562) 490-4522
• Dwight Tanaka, Director, Operations
(562) 490-4526
• Chris Esslinger, Director, Communications
(532) 490-4514
• Tammy Johnson, Customer Service/Ticketing Manager
(562) 490-4562

IMCA
1800 WEST D STREET
VINTON, IA 52349

319-472-2201
Fax: 319-472-2218
www.imca.com
• Brett Root, President
(319) 472-2201
broot@imca.com
• Jim Stannard, VP, Operations
• Dave Brenn, Executive Director,
Competition
Year Founded:
1915
Description:
The oldest active automobile racing
sanctioning body in the United States.
Membership Requirements:
Pay dues.
Publications:
Newsletter, 12 issues yearly
Member Services:
Competitor insurance.

IMG
200 5TH AVENUE
7TH FLOOR
NEW YORK, NY 10010
212-489-8300
Fax: 646-558-8399
www.imgworld.com
• Chuck Bennett, President, IMG Golf,
Tennis, Fashion & Events
Description:
Represents and manages leading events,
associations, tracks, teams and talent.
Clients:
Danica Patrick, Formula D Drifting, Joe
Gibbs Racing, John Force Racing, Gold
Coast 300 (featuring the V8 Supercar
Championship Series and A!GP World Cup
of Motorsports), NASCAR, NHRA, Sir Jackie
Stewart (legendary driver), World Speedway
Grand Prix, World Speedway World Cup

Other locations:

IMG MOTORSPORTS (NC)
16810 KENTON DRIVE
SUITE 300
HUNTERSVILLE, NC 28078
704-987-4080
Fax: 704-568-4116
www.imgworld.com
• Chuck Bennett, President

IMPORT DRAG RACING CIRCUIT
11231 YOUNG RIVER AVE.
FOUNTAIN VALLEY, CA 92708
714-593-0280
Fax: 714-593-0281
www.importdrag.com
• Michael Ferrara, President
mferrara@hardmediainc.com
• Richard Tran, National Director
rtran@hardmediainc.com
Description:
Founded in 1998, IDRc has established
itself as the leader in the import and sport
compact performance events arena
Membership:
DSport Magazine, Official IDRC Rulebook,
permanent competition number, etc: $45/yr.

**IMSA (INTERNATIONAL MOTOR SPORTS
ASSOCIATION)**
INTERNATIONAL MOTORSPORTS
CENTER
ONE DAYTONA BOULEVARD
DAYTONA BEACH, FL 32114

386-310-6500
info@imsa.com
www.imsa.com
• Jim France, Chairman
• Ed Bennett, CEO
• Scott Atherton, President
Membership Benefits:
Subscription to AutoWeek, decal and patch,
hat, t-shirt, lapel pin, and fan guide.
Description:
Sanctioning body for ALS, Star Mazda,
Panoz Racing Series, IMSA GT3 Cup
Challenge, and Formula BMW USA.

**INTERNATIONAL COUNCIL OF
MOTORSPORT SCIENCES**
THE ICMS
9305 CRESTVIEW DRIVE
DENTON, TX 76207
940-262-3481
Fax: 940-262-3482
info@theicms.org
www.icmsmotorsportsafety.org
• Tom Weisenbach, Executive Director
Year Founded:
1988
Membership Requirements:
Includes physicians, psychologists,
physiologists, race drivers and paramedic
personnel.
Description:
An association of medical professionals,
scientific, allied health and other interested
persons with the improvement in
performance and safety in motorsport.

**INTERNATIONAL HOT ROD
ASSOCIATION**
300 CLEVELAND ROAD
NORWALK, OH 44857
419-663-6666
Fax: 419-663-4472
comments@ihra.com
www.ihra.com
• Scott Gardner, President
Description:
Promotes racing at all levels and a racing
series in major cities in the United States
and Canada.
Founded:
1971
Publications:
Drag Review magazine, 22 issues/yr.; IHRA
Yearbook and Rulebook

INTERNATIONAL KART FEDERATION
1609 S GROVE AVE
SUITE 105
ONTARIO, CA 91761
909-923-4999
Fax: 909-923-6940
www.ikfkarting.com
• Roger Miller, President
Year Founded:
1957
Number of members:
3,000
Member Services:
Patch, decal, subscription to KARTER
NEWS. Club and track insurance, regional
point program, Grand national events.
Publications:
KARTER NEWS, monthly.
Membership Requirements:
$60.00 per year provides IKF membership
plus sprint, 4-cycle and speedway, and road
racing license. New members start at back

of grid for three races.
Description:
Governing body for kart racing. It fosters fair
and strong competition; provides reasonable
rules for a variety of competition;
administers the competition with impartiality;
and endeavors to reduce the hazards
associated with karting.

MID-AMERICA OFF ROAD ASSOCIATION
PO BOX 664
GREENUP, IL 62428
• Spencer Rising-Moore, President
Description:
Sanctioning body for off-road racing in the
United States.
Founded:
1972

**NATIONAL ASSOCIATION FOR STOCK
CAR AUTO RACING (NASCAR)**
PO BOX 2875
DAYTONA BEACH, FL 32120
386-253-0611
Fax: 386-239-2811
fanfeedback@nascar.com
www.nascar.com
• Brian France, Chairman & CEO
• Mike Helton, Vice Chairman
Description:
The National Association for Stock Car Auto
Racing oversees one of the most popular
and fastest-growing spectator sports in the
US. NASCAR runs more than 100 races
each year in three racing circuits: the
Nationwide Series, the Camping World
Truck Series and the Sprint Cup Series

NATIONAL AUTO SPORT ASSOCIATION
PO BOX 2366
NAPA VALLEY, CA 94558
510-232-6272
Fax: 510-277-0657
www.nasaproracing.com
Description:
NASA's regional divisions host a variety of
high-quality racing events for enthusiasts.
Founded:
1991

**NATIONAL CHAMPIONSHIP RACING
ASSOCIATION**
7700 N BROADWAY
WICHITA, KS 67219
316-755-1781
Fax: 316-755-0665
www.racencra.com
• Mylissa Powers, Contact
Year Founded:
1971
Description:
Sanctioning group for dirt track late model
and sprint car racing for the southwest.
Organizes 60 races annually as well as the
modifieds.
Publications:
Rule Book.

NATIONAL HOT ROD ASSOCIATION
2035 FINANCIAL WAY
GLENDORA, CA 91741
626-914-4761
Fax: 626-963-5360
nhra@nhra.com
www.nhra.com
• Peter Clifford, President

Year Founded:
1951
Description:
The largest and loudest auto racing organization. Dedicated to safety while providing millions of racing fans with The Extreme Motorsport: the fastest and most spectacular form of entertainment on wheels.
Publications:
NATIONAL DRAGSTER, weekly
Membership:
80,000

NATIONAL STREET ROD ASSOCIATION
4030 PARK AVE
MEMPHIS, TN 38111
901-452-4030
www.nsra-usa.com
• Jim Rowlett, Marketing Director
(817) 581-9915
nsra1@aol.com
Year Founded:
1970
Description:
The organizing body that made the sport what it is today, and the reason the growth of enthusiast participation has continued at a steady pace. Provides leadership, guidance, and fun events for enthusiasts who favor driving their specialty vehicles wherever and whenever they want to.
Membership Requirements:
Annual fee: $30.00.
Publications:
Monthly subscription to StreetScene Magazine; Annual copy of Fellow Pages

NATIONAL TRACTOR PULLERS ASSOCIATION
6155-B HUNTLEY RD
COLUMBUS, OH 43229
614-436-1761
Fax: 614-436-0964
www.ntpapull.com
• Gregg Randall, Executive Director
• Michaela Kramer, Publications Editor
Year Founded:
1969
Publications:
THE PULLER magazine; PULL!, yearbook
Description:
Sets the standards in the pulling industry for safety and competition rules.

RAHAL LETTERMAN LANIGAN RACING
4601 LYMAN DRIVE
HILLIARD, OH 43026
614-529-7000
Fax: 614-529-7007
www.rahal.com
• David Letterman, Co-Owner
• Bobby Rahal, Co-Owner
Sports Service Founded:
1983
Athlete Management Services:
Media exposure, product endorsements, personal appearances, guest speakers.
Event Management Services:
Organize and direct Bobby Rahal Columbus Charities Pro-Am.

RHYS MILLEN RACING
17471 APEX CIRCLE
HUNTINGTON BEACH, CA 92647
714-847-2158
Fax: 714-848-6821
sales@rmrproducts.com
www.rhys-millen-racing.myshopify.com
• Rod Millen, President/Chief Executive Officer
Sports Service Founded:
1972.
Event Management Services:
Toyota North American Touring Car and Pikes Peak Hill Climb Racing. Private design and engineering work for rally and off-road race teams. Special event (off-road) race entries for short or long-term promotions. National and international marketing campaigns. Precision driving for television commercials.

RICHARD PETTY DRIVING EXPERIENCE
6022 VICTORY LANE
CONCORD, NC 28027
704-455-9443
800-237-3889
Fax: 704-455-5595
www.drivepetty.com
• Mike Bartelli, Chief Marketing Officer
Year Founded:
1990
Description:
Offering Drive and Ride-a-Long programs. Operating over 1168 track days at 27+ tracks nationwide. 60,000 driving experiences and 70,000 Ride-Alongs
Membership Requirements:
Drivers must be 16 years old and have a valid drivers license.
Entry Fee:
$109 and up.

SKIP BARBER RACING SCHOOL LLC
5290 WINDER HIGHWAY
BRASELTON, GA 30517
866-932-1949
800-221-1131
Fax: 860-435-1321
www.skipbarber.com

SOUTHERN UNITED PROFESSIONAL RACING
12561 SOUTH CHOCTAW
BATON ROUGE, LA 70815
225-275-5040
Fax: 225-273-3166
SUPRrace@aol.com
www.suprracing.com
Year Founded:
1990
Description:
A Lousiana-based touring group that ofers area racers an affordable alternative to high-cost traveling circuits. Organizes 25 races at 14 facilities in four states
Member Services:
A point fund established for those drivers with the most accumulated points for the year.

SPEEDWAY MOTORSPORTS, INC.
5555 CONCORD PKWY S.
CONCORD, NC 28027
704-455-3239
Fax: 704-455-1268
www.gospeedway.com
• Cary Tharrington, SVP & General Counsel
• Donald Hawk, Chief Racing Development Officer
• Jerry Caldwell, EVP & General Manager

Nature of Sports Services:
A marketer and producer of motorsports entertainment in the United States. The company owns and operates six motorsports facilities including Atlanta Motor Speedway, Bristol (TN), Motor Speedway, Lowe's Motor Speedway, Las Vegas Motor Speedway, Infineon Raceway, and New Hampshire Speedway

SPORTS CAR CLUB OF AMERICA
6620 SE DWIGHT ST
TOPEKA, KS 66619-0400
785-357-7222
800-770-2055
Fax: 785-232-7228
membership@scca.com
www.scca.com
• Mike Cobb, President & CEO
Year Founded:
1944
Description:
To bring motorsports to the masses of American men and women who are passionate about automobiles, speed and competition. Exist to organize, support and develop auto racing at every level and provide an outlet for you to get out of the armchair and into the action.

SPORTSCAR VINTAGE RACING ASSOCIATION
1598 HART STREET
SUITE 100
SOUTHLAKE, TX 76092
603-640-6161
Fax: 817-953-3550
www.svra.com
• Alex Miller, National Competition Director
(610) 223-4834
• Kathy Swinford, Director, Services/Events Entry
• Kim Parella, Registrar
(850) 329-7485
Year Founded:
1976
Membership Requirements:
General Membership: $85.00 annually.
SVRA/HSR Dual Membership: $105.00 annually.
Description:
Offers tightly regulated wheel-to-wheel racing for the men and women who own and maintain their vintage and historical cars, and the venues through which they can compete

UNITED MIDGET AUTO RACING ASSOCIATION/UMRA
530 W. LOCKPORT ST, STE 200
PLAINFIELD, IL 60544
815-439-9775
Fax: 815-439-9777
Year Founded:
1985
Publications:
UMARA Newsletter, monthly.
Membership Requirements:
Driver, owner or mechanic of midget cars ($165 dues for driver, $195 car owner/driver, $35 mechanic); spectators-associate members. Drivers required to take physicals. Drivers classified as rookies for first five races and must start at back of races.
Description:

Promotes midget cars, midget racing and the thrill of the short track race.

UNITED RACING COMPANY
2109 SOUTH DUPONT HIGHWAY
DOVER, DE 19901
302-697-3273
Fax: 302-697-6548
Year Founded:
1947
Member Services:
Stages approximately 35 races each year, Season from early April to late October. Annual Awards Banquet held in November each year in Allentown, PA. Annual meetings held in March and October every year.
Publications:
Pictorial Yearbook, annual.
Membership Requirements:
83 drivers and owners. Must be a member of the United Racing Club and run Goodyear tires to participate, along with engine and wing limitations.
Affiliations:
Sprint Car Racing organization
Number of Members:
200

US LEGEND CARS
5245 NC HWY 49 SOUTH
HARRISBURG, NC 28075
704-455-3896
Fax: 704-455-3820
www.uslegendcars.com
• GE Chapman, General Manager
(704) 455-3896
gechapman@uslegendcars.com
• Chad Honeycutt, Engine Shop Manager
(704) 455-3896
chadh@uslegendcars.com
Nature of Sports Service:
Founded in 1995, INEX was developed to prmote, organize and sanction Legends Car, Bandolero and Thunder Roadster racing across the United State, Canada and Europe.
Publications:
INEX Magazine and Rulebook for Legends Cars, Bandolero and Thunder Roadster
Number of members:
3,500

WESTERN RACING ASSOCIATION
PO BOX 509
MONROVIA, CA 91017-0509
760-245-4023
www.westernracing.com
• John Wildharber, President
(626) 358-2284
• Seth Hammond, Vice President
(714) 389-9400
• Rick Turner, Race Director
(619) 449-1674
Year Founded:
1982
Member Services:
15 exhibition events are presented each year at tracks like Calistoga, El Cajon, Madera, Merced, Santa Maria, San Bernardino and Tulare.
Members:
300+
Membership Requirements:
$45 yearly fee.
Description:
A non-profit corporation, dedicated to the preservation of antique automobile racing cars and fellowship.

WORLD KARTING ASSOCIATION
6051 VICTORY LANE
CONCORD, NC 28027
704-455-1606
Fax: 704-455-1609
info@worldkarting.com
www.worldkarting.com
• Marie Borsuk, Business Manager
(704) 455-1606
marie@worldkarting.com
• Jeanne Harrison, Membership Coordinator
(704) 455-1606
members@worldkarting.com
Year Founded:
1971
Description:
A membership-owned, non-profit corporation formed to regulate and promote the sport of competitive kart racing. Over 10,000 members and 120 sanctioned race tracks.
Publications:
WKA's Karting Scene. The official publication of the World Karting Association that provides its members and subscribers schedules of events, race reports, official event results, technical reports, human-interest stories, and other related information

WORLD RACING GROUP
7575-D WEST WINDS BLVD
CONCORD, NC 28027
704-795-7223
Fax: 704-795-7229
info@dirtcar.com
www.worldracinggroup.com;
www.dirtcar.com
• Brian Carter, CEO
Description:
World Racing Group (WRG) is the world leader in the sanctioning and promotion of dirt track auto racing. WRG owns the premier national touring series for each of the top three division in dirt track racing - The Advance Auto Parts World of Outlaws Sprint Car Series, World of Outlaws Late Model Series and the Advance Auto Parts Super DIRTcar Series. WRG also sanctions weekly racing action at over 120 tracks throughout the United States and Canada under the DIRTcar Racing banner.
Year Founded:
2003

Auto Sports Racing Leagues/Teams

ARCA MENARDS SERIES EAST
www.arcaracing.com
Description:
One of two NASCAR regional developmental divisions.

Teams:

BRAD SMITH MOTORSPORTS
586-206-8298
brad@bradsmithmotorsports.com
bradsmithmotorsports.com
• Brad Smith, CEO

CHAD BRYANT RACING
press@chadbryantracing.com
chadbryantracing.com

DGR-CROSLEY
111 BYERS CREEK ROAD
MOORESVILLE, NC 28117
dgrcrosley.com
• David Gilliland, Co-Owner
• Johnny Gray, Co-Owner

VENTURINI MOTORSPORTS
571 PITTS SCHOOL ROAD NW
CONCORD, NC 28027
704-784-2500
Fax: 704-784-2575
info@venturinimotorsports.com
www.venturinimotorsports.com

WAYNE PETERSON RACING

ARCA MENARDS SERIES WEST
www.arcaracing.com
Description:
A regional stock car racing division of NASCAR.

Teams:

BILL MCANALLY RACING
916-676-0010
www.bmmaparacing.com

GMS RACING
310 AVIATION DRIVE
STATESVILLE, NC 28677
info@gmsracing.net
gmsracing.net

JERRY PITTS RACING
• Jeff Jefferson, Co-Owner/Crew Chief
• Jerry Pitts, Co-Owner/Crew Chief

VENTURINI MOTORSPORTS
571 PITTS SCHOOL ROAD NW
CONCORD, NC 28027
704-784-2500
Fax: 704-784-2575
info@venturinimotorsports.com
www.venturinimotorsports.com

FERRARI CHALLENGE NORTH AMERICA
250 SYLVAN AVENUE
ENGLEWOOD CLIFFS, NJ 07632
877-933-7727
races.ferrari.com/en/corse-clienti/north-amer
ica
• Andrea Reggiani, Communications
Andrea.Reggiani@ferrari.com
Description:
The Ferrari Challenge North America is a competition using the 458 racing model, held at several circuit locations across America.

FORMULA 1
www.formula1.com
• Stefani Domenicali, CEO

Teams:

ALFA ROMEO RACING
HINWIL
• Frederic Vasseur, Team Chief
• Jan Monchaux, Technical Chief

ALPHATAURI
SCUDERIA ALPHATAURI
VIA BOARIA, 229
FAENZA, RAVENNA, ITALY 48018
info@scuderiaalphatauri.com
www.scuderiaalphatauri.com
• Franz Tost, Team Chief
• Jody Egginton, Technical Chief

ALPINE
ENSTONE
• David Brivio, Team Chief
• Remi Taffin, Technical Chief
• Pat Fry, Technical Chief

ASTON MARTIN
SILVERSTONE
• Otmar Szafnauer, Team Chief
• Andrew Green, Technical Chief

FERRARI
MARANELLO, MO, ITALY
formula1.ferrari.com
• Mattia Binotto, Team Chief
• Enrico Cardile, Technical Chief
• Enrico Gualtieri, Technical Chief
Sponsors:
Fiat, Santander, Shell, Etihad, Acer, Mubadala,
AMD and Bridgestone

HAAS
KANNAPOLIS, NC
www.haasf1team.com
• Gene Haas, Founder/Chairman
• Guenther Steiner, Team Chief
• Simone Resta, Technical Chief

MCLAREN
MCLAREN TECHNOLOGY CENTRE
CHERTSEY ROAD
WOKING, SURREY, ENGLAND GU21 4YH
www.mclaren.com/formula1
• Zak Brown, CEO
• Andreas Seidl, Team Chief
• James Key, Technical Chief

MERCEDES
MERCEDES-AMG PETRONAS FORMULA
ONE TEAM
OPERATIONS CENTRE
BRACKLEY, NORTHANTS NN13 7BD
enquiries@mercedesamgf1.com
www.mercedesamgf1.com
• Toto Wolff, Team Chief/CEO
• James Allison, Technical Chief

RED BULL RACING
ASTON MARTIN RED BULL RACING
BRADBOURNE DRIVE
TILBROOK
MILTON KEYNES, MK7 8BJ
feedback@redbullf1.com
redbullracing.redbull.com
• Christian Horner, OBE, Team Chief
• Pierre Wache, Technical Chief

WILLIAMS
GROVE
WANTAGE, OXFORDSHIRE, ENGLAND OX12
0DQ
www.williamsf1.com
• Simon Roberts, Team Chief
• Francois-Xavier Demaison, Technical Chief
Year Founded:
1977

HISTORIC SPORTSCAR RACING LLC
PO BOX 8110
CLEARWATER, FL 33758
727-573-1340
Fax: 727-573-1350

registrar@hsrrace.com
hsrrace.com
• David Hinton, Owner/President
(727) 573-1340
david@hsrrace.com
Races:
Race Series Classes; Race Series Points
System; Endurance Series; Dash Series;
BOSS Super Cup; Historic GTP/Group C &
WSC; Championship of Makes; Historic GT;
Historic Stock Car; Jo Bonnier Cup Series;
Klub Sport Porsche Challenge Series
Year Founded:
1966
Sponsors:
RaceWatches.com; Bob Woodman Tires;
Classic Motorsports Magazine; Gene Felton
Restorations; Hector Cademartori Motor
Racing Art; HSR West; Klub Sport Racing;
Lee Chapman Racing; Moorespeed Racing;
Phelon Motorsports; R Harrington
Photography; RM Motorsports; Traqmate;
Truechoice Motorsports; Sasco Sports, Inc;
Stand 21; Vintage Motorsport Magazine;
Vintage Racing Services Inc

IMSA MICHELIN PILOT CHALLENGE
INTERNATIONAL MOTORSPORTS
CENTER
ONE DAYTONA BOULEVARD
DAYTONA BEACH, FL 32114
386-310-6500
info@imsa.com
www.imsa.com

Teams:

ATLANTA SPEEDWERKS
470 WOODSMILL ROAD
SUITE E
GAINESVILLE, GA 30501
678-971-5300
atlspeedwerks.com
• Todd Lamb, Owner

AUTOMATIC RACING
6112 HANGING MOSS ROAD
ORLANDO, FL 32807
407-230-7575
drussell@automaticracing.com
automaticracing.com
• David Russell, Team Manager
• Danimal Paskan, Chief Mechanic

AWA INC.
7353 CASTLEDERG SIDEROAD
CALEDON EAST, ON, CANADA L7C 3E4
647-588-3044
andrew@awa.team
awa.team

BGB MOTORSPORTS
6C WEST TOWER CIRCLE
UNIT 102
ORMOND BEACH, FL 32174
386-265-1979
Fax: 386-492-7817
info@teambgb.com
www.teambgb.com

BIMMERWORLD RACING
4085 PEPPERELL WAY
DUBLIN, VA 24084
877-639-9648
info@bimmerworld.com
www.bimmerworldracing.com
• James Clay, President

BRYAN HERTA AUTOSPORT
www.bryanhertaautosport.com

• Nick Franzosi, Team Manager

CARBAHN MOTORSPORTS
2232 OLD MIDDLEFIELD WAY
MOUNTAIN VIEW, CA 94043

KMW MOTORSPORTS
1800 NW 1ST AVENUE
BOCA RATON, FL 33432
561-392-3020
kmwmotorsports@aol.com
kmwmotorsports.com

KohR MOTORSPORTS
5727 EXECUTIVE DRIVE E
WESTLAND, MI 48185
734-895-1543
www.kohrmotorsports.com

L.A. HONDA WORLD RACING
DOWNEY, CA
www.lahondaworldracing.com

MOTORSPORTS IN ACTION
1016 ARTHUR SAUVÃ□ BLVD
LOCAL G
SAINT-EUSTACHE, QC, CANADA J7R 4K3
888-568-0069
info@motorsportsinaction.com
www.motorsportsinaction.com
• Carl Hermez, Team Manager

MURILLO RACING
5805 LABATH AVENUE
UNIT 4
ROHNERT PARK, CA 94928
707-280-6783
ken@murilloracing.com
www.murilloracing.com
• Ken Murillo, Team Owner

REBEL ROCK RACING
2001 INDUSTRIAL DR
DELAND, FL 32725

RILEY MOTORSPORTS
MOORESVILLE, NC

ROADSHAGGER RACING
roadshagger.com

STEPHEN CAMERON RACING
SONOMA RACEWAY
29121 ARNOLD DRIVE
BUILDING E5
SONOMA, CA 95476
707-996-1184
Fax: 707-938-1027
steve@cameronracingusa.com
www.cameronracingusa.com
• Cameron Steve, Team Manager
• Gary Rubio, Crew Chief

TEAM TGM
www.teamtgm.com
• Ted Giovanis, Owner

WINWARD RACING
HOUSTON, TX
winwardracing.com

IMSA PROTOTYPE CHALLENGE
INTERNATIONAL MOTORSPORTS
CENTER
ONE DAYTONA BOULEVARD
DAYTONA BEACH, FL 32114
386-310-6500
info@imsa.com
www.imsa.com/prototypechallenge

Teams:

ANDRETTI AUTOSPORT
7615 ZIONSVILLE RD
INDIANAPOLIS, IN 46268

CONQUEST RACING
3950 GUION LANE
INDIANAPOLIS, IN 46268
317-870-0007 EXT 34
ebachelart@conquestracing.com
conquestracing.com
• Eric Bachelart, President/CEO

FORTY 7 MOTORSPORTS
ONE MOTORSPORTS BLVD
MILLVILLE, NJ 08332
856-765-5858
info@race47.com
forty7motorsports.com

JDC MOTORSPORTS
12977 EAGLE CREEK PKWY
SAVAGE, MN 55378

ONE MOTORSPORTS
18400 STATE HIGHWAY 160
LAS VEGAS, NV 89161
702-496-2606
jeff@onemotorsports.com
www.onemotorsports.com

**PERFORMANCE TECH
MOTORSPORTS**
3000 SW 15 STREET
SUITE D
DEERFIELD BEACH, FL 33442
info@performancetechmotorsports.com
www.performancetechmotorsports.com
• Brent O'Neill, Team Owner

ROBILLARD RACING
5833 DEEP WATER DR
OXFORD, MD 21654

VOLT RACING
8800 WATSON RD
ST LOUIS, MO 63119

WIN AUTOSPORT
145 CATRON DR
RENO, NY 89512

WULVER RACING
1433 CORBETT RD
MONKTON, MD 21111

**IMSA WEATHERTECH SPORTSCAR
CHAMPIONSHIP**
INTERNATIONAL MOTORSPORTS
CENTER
ONE DAYTONA BOULEVARD
DAYTONA BEACH, FL 32114
386-310-6500
info@imsa.com
www.imsa.com/weathertech

Teams:

AF CORSE

ALEGRA MOTORSPORTS

ALLY CADILLAC RACING

BMW TEAM RLL
4601 LYMAN DRIVE
HILLIARD, OH 43026
614-529-7000
rahal.com
• Chris Mower, Team Manager
• Chris Danison, Crew Chief

CORE AUTOSPORT
283 LAKESHORE PARKWAY
ROCK HILL, SC 29730
803-325-9321
coreautosport.com
• Jon Bennett, Founder

CORVETTE RACING
www.corvetteracing.com
• Gary Pratt, Team Manager
• Dan Binks, Crew Chief

DRAGONSPEED RACING
JUPITER, FL

GRT GRASSER RACING TEAM
HAUPTSTRAÄ¡E 11
KNITTELFELD, 8720
management@grasser-racing.com
www.grasser-racing.com

JDC-MILLER MOTORSPORTS
8856 WOODHILL CIRCLE
SAVAGE, MN 55378
www.jdcmotorsport.com
• John Church, CEO
(952) 233-3075
jchurch@jdcmotorsports.com

MAGNUS RACING
4700 HIGHLAND DRIVE
SUITE B
SALT LAKE CITY, UT 84117
info@magnusracing.com
www.magnusracing.com
• John Potter, Owner

MAZDA MOTORSPORTS
1421 REYNOLDS AVENUE
IRVINE, CA 92614
800-435-2508
www.mazdamotorsports.com

**MEYER SHANK RACING W/
CURB-AGAJANIAN**
114 VENTURE DRIVE
PATASKALA, OH 43062
740-964-9998
www.michaelshankracing.com
• Mike Shank, Owner

PAUL MILLER RACING
pr@paulmillerracing.com
www.paulmillerracing.com
• Paul Miller, Principal

**PERFORMANCE TECH
MOTORSPORTS**
3000 SW 15TH STREET
SUITE D
DEERFIELD BEACH, FL 33442
info@performancetechmotorsports.com
www.performancetechmotorsports.com

• Brent O'Neill, Team Owner

PFAFF MOTORSPORTS
618 CHRISLEA ROAD
WOODBRIDGE, ON, CANADA L4L 8K9
289-596-4662
www.pfaffauto.com/motorsports
• Christopher Pfaff, CEO

PR1/MATHIASEN MOTORSPORTS
5801 E CLINTON AVENUE
FRESNO, CA 93727
559-277-1300
pr1motorsports@aol.com
pr1motorsports.com
• Bobby Oergel, Owner/Director

RISI COMPETIZIONE
6100 SOUTHWEST FREEWAY
HOUSTON, TX 77057
713-772-3868
www.risicompetizione.com
• Tony Nevotti, General Manager

SCUDERIA CORSA
7925 W ARBY AVENUE
SUITE 100
LAS VEGAS, NV 89113
888-644-0241
info@scuderiacorsa.com
www.scuderiacorsa.com

TURNER MOTORSPORT
800-280-6966
info@turnermotorsport.com
www.turnermotorsport.com/t-racing-home
• Will Turner, Owner

WHELEN ENGINEERING RACING
860-526-9504
www.whelen.com/motorsports/imsa
• Gary Nelson, Team Manager
• Bill Keuler, Crew Chief

INDY LIGHTS
10101 U.S. HIGHWAY 41 NORTH
PALMETTO, FL 34221
941-845-2500
info@roadtoindy.net
www.indylights.com
• Michelle Kish, COO
mkish@andersenpromotions.net
• Tamy Valkosky, Public Relations
pr@roadtoindy.net
Description:
The Indy Lights operates as a driver
development program for prospective
IndyCar drivers. It is the only driver
development program in the world to feature
a champion's scholarship at entry level to
advance to the next step on the ladder
system. They've produced some of the
IndyCar series biggest names.

Teams:

ANDRETTI AUTOSPORT
INDIANAPOLIS, IN
pr@andrettiautosport.com
www.andrettiautosport.com
• Michael Andretti, CEO/Chair
• J-F Thormann, President

ANDRETTI STEINBRENNER RACING
7615 ZIONSVILLE ROAD
INDIANAPOLIS, IN 46268
317-872-2700
amber.stevenson@andrettiautosport.com
www.andrettiautosport.com
• J.F. Thormann, President

CARLIN
7 COXBRIDGE BUSINESS PARK
ALTON ROAD
FARNHAM, SURREY, ENGLAND GU10 5EH
media@carlin.co.uk
www.carlin.co.uk
• Trevor Carlin, Founder
• Grahame Chilton, CEO
• Rupert Swallow, Managing Director

JUNCOS RACING
4401 GILMAN STREET
INDIANAPOLIS, IN 46224
317-552-2967
info@juncosracing.com
www.juncosracing.com/indy-lights
• Tom Vigne, Crew Chief

INDY PRO 2000
10101 U.S. HIGHWAY 41 N
PALMETTO, FL 34221
941-845-2500
info@roadtoindy.net
www.indypro2000.com
• Michelle Kish, COO
mkish@andersenpromotions.net
• Tamy Valkosky, Public Relations
pr@roadtoindy.net
  Sponsors:
  Mazda, Goodyear, Mazda Road To Indy, BBS,
  Quarter Master, Performance Friction Brakes,
  VP Racing

Teams:

ABEL MOTORSPORTS
3401 BASHFORD AVENUE COURT
LOUISVILLE, KY 40218
info@abelmotorsports.com
www.abelmotorsports.com
• Bill Abel, Contact

BN RACING
10031 VIRGINIA AVE
CHICAGO RIDGE, IL 60415
773-729-0296
bryn@bnracing.co.uk
• Bryn Nuttall, Contact

DEFORCE RACING
ONE PERFORMANCE DRIVE
ANGLETON, TX 77515
info@deforceracing.com
www.deforceracing.com
• Ernesto Martinez, Contact

EXCLUSIVE AUTOSPORT
PO BOX 32082
ERINDALE
SASKATOON, SK, CANADA S7S 1N8
www.exclusiveautosport.ca
• Michael Duncalfe, Contact

FATBOY RACING!
PO BOX 404
LOCUST VALLEY, NY 11560
brendan@fatboyracing.us
www.fatboyracing.us
• Brendan Puderbach, Contact

JAY HOWARD DRIVER DEVELOPMENT
305-915-7652
jay@jayhoward.com
www.jayhoward.com
• Jay Howard, Contact

JUNCOS RACING
4401 GILMAN STREET
INDIANAPOLIS, IN 46224
317-552-2967
info@juncosracing.com
www.juncosracing.com
• Ricardo Juncos, Contact

PABST RACING
35303 PABST ROAD
OCONOMOWOC, WI 53066
262-567-1771
information@pabstracing.com
www.pabstracing.com
• Augie Pabst, Contact

RP MOTORSPORT RACING
PIAZZA IV NOVEMBRE, 4
MILANO, ITALY, 20124
info@rpmotorsport.eu
rpmotorsportracing.com
• Fabio Pampado, Principal

INDYCAR
4551 W 16TH STREET
INDIANAPOLIS, IN 46222
317-492-6526
indycar@indycar.com
www.indycar.com
• Mark D. Miles, CEO
• Jay Frye, President
Description:
Founded 1994. Sanctions Indy 500 and
other races.

Teams:

A.J. FOYT RACING
19480 STOKES ROAD
WALLER, TX 77484
936-372-3698
info@ajfoytracing.com
www.foytracing.com
• A.J. Foyt, Owner
• Larry Foyt, President

ANDRETTI AUTOSPORT
INDIANAPOLIS, IN
pr@andrettiautosport.com
www.andrettiautosport.com
• Michael Andretti, CEO/Chair
• J-F Thormann, President
Sponsors:
DHL, Sun Drop, GoDaddy.com, Venom Energy
Drink, Window World, AirTran, Bryant Heating &
Cooling Systems, Dr. Pepper, ExactTarget,
Exel, OneAmerica, Palms, Peak Performance,
Conway, TLX, Inc., Snapple

ARROW MCLAREN SP
6803 COFFMAN ROAD
INDIANAPOLIS, IN 46268
317-209-0099
media@arrowmclarensp.com
arrowmclarensp.com
• Sam Schmidt, Co-Owner
• Ric Peterson, Co-Owner

CARLIN
7 COXBRIDGE BUSINESS PARK
ALTON ROAD
FARNHAM, SURREY, ENGLAND GU10 5EH
media@carlin.co.uk
www.carlin.co.uk
• Trevor Carlin, Founder
• Grahame Chilton, CEO

CHIP GANASSI RACING
7777 WOODLAND DRIVE
INDIANAPOLIS, IN 46278
317-802-0000
www.chipganassiracing.com
• Chip Ganassi, Owner/CEO
• Felix Sabates, Co-Owner
• Felix Sabates, Co-Owner
• Rob Kauffman, Co-Owner
• Mike Hull, Managing Director

DALE COYNE RACING
13400 S BUDLER ROAD
PLAINFIELD, IL 60544
dcrsupport@aol.com
dalecoyneracing.com
• Dale Coyne, Owner

**DALE COYNE RACING W/ VASSER
SULLIVAN**
13400 S BUDLER ROAD
PLAINFIELD, IL 60544
kdiamond@cvsindycar.com
dalecoyneracing.com
• Dale Coyne, Owner

ED CARPENTER RACING
7231 GEORGETOWN ROAD
INDIANAPOLIS, IN 46268
317-481-0195
Fax: 317-481-0322
www.edcarpenterracing.com
• Ed Carpenter, Owner
• Tim Broyles, General Manager

**MEYER SHANK RACING W/ ARROW
SPM**
114 VENTURE DRIVE
PATASKALA, OH 43062
740-964-9998
www.michaelshankracing.com
• Mike Shank, Owner
• Jim Meyer, Co-Owner

RAHAL LETTERMAN LANIGAN RACING
485 SOUTHPOINTE CIRCLE
SUITE 900
BROWNSBURG, IN 46112
317-858-3717
rahal.com
• David Letterman, Co-Owner
• Mike Lanigan, Co-Owner

TEAM PENSKE
200 PENSKE WAY
MOORESVILLE, NC 28115
www.teampenske.com
• Roger Penske, Founder/Chair

**LAMBORGHINI SUPER TROFEO NORTH
AMERICA**
VIA MODEN, 12
SANT'AGATA, BOLOGNESE, ITALY 40019
squadracorse.lamborghini.com/super-trofeo/
north-america
Description:
The Super Trofeo North America is a single
make racing series help at multiple circuits
across America.

**NASCAR (NATIONAL ASSOCIATION FOR
STOCK CAR AUTO RACING)**
DAYTONA BEACH, FL
www.nascar.com
• Jim France, Chairman/CEO
(305) 218-7839
Description:
Tracks include: Atlanta Motor Speedway,
Bristol Motor Speedway, Charlotte Motor
Speedway, Chicagoland Speedway,
Darlington Raceway, Daytona International
Speedway, Dover International Speedway,
Auto Club Speedway, Homestead-Miami
Speedway, O'Reilly Raceway Park, Iowa
Speedway, Kansas Speedwway, Kentucky
Speedway, Las Vegas Motor Speedway,
Gateway International Raceway, Michigan
International Speedway, Circuit Gilles
Villeneuve, Nashville Superspeedway, New
Hampshire Motor Speedway, Phoenix
International Raceway, Road America,

Richmond International Raceway, Talladega Superspeedway, Texas Motor Speedway, Watkins Glen International

NASCAR CUP SERIES
DAYTONA BEACH, FL
www.nascar.com/news/nascar-cup-series/series
• Jim France, Chairman/CEO

Teams:

B.J. MCLEOD MOTORSPORTS
121 GOODWIN CIRCLE
MOORESVILLE, NC 28115
www.bjmcleodmotorsports.com

CHIP GANASSI RACING
8500 WESTMORELAND DRIVE NW
CONCORD, NC 28027
704-662-9642
www.chipganassiracing.com
• Chip Ganassi, Owner

FRONT ROW MOTORSPORTS
114 MEADOW HILL CIRCLE
MOORESVILLE, NC 28117
704-873-6445
Fax: 704-873-5120
www.teamfrm.com
• Bob Jenkins, Owner

GERMAIN RACING
299 AUSTIN LANE
LEXINGTON, NC 27295
336-731-8040
contact@germainracing13.com
www.germainracing.com
• Bob Germain, Jr., Owner
• Matt Borland, Crew Chief

GO FAS RACING
www.gofasracing.com
• Archie St. Hilaire, Owner
• Ryan Sparkes, Crew Chief

HENDRICK MOTORSPORTS
4400 PAPA JOE HENDRICK BOULEVARD
CHARLOTTE, NC 28262
877-467-4890
www.hendrickmotorsports.com
• Rick Hendrick, Owner/Chair

JOE GIBBS RACING
13415 REESE BOULEVARD W
HUNTERSVILLE, NC 28078
joegibbsracing.com
• Joe Gibbs, Owner
• J.D. Gibbs, Co-Chairman
• Dave Alpern, President

JTG DAUGHERTY RACING
704-456-1221
jtgdaughertyracing.com
• Tad Geschickter, Owner
• Jodi Geschickter, Owner
• Brad Daugherty, Owner
• Gordon Smith, Owner

LEAVINE FAMILY RACING
6007 VICTORY LANE
CONCORD, NC 28027
medi@lfr95.com
www.lfr95.com
• Bob Leavine, Partner
• Matt Diliberto, Partner

MBM MOTORSPORTS
849 CONNOR STREET
STATESVILLE, NC 28677
www.mbmmotorsports.com

• Carl Long, Owner

PREMIUM MOTORSPORTS
222 RACEWAY DRIVE
MOORESVILLE, NC 28117
info@premiummotorsports.net
premiummotorsports.net
• Jay Robinson, Co-Owner
• Troy Stafford, Co-Owner
• Mark Bailey, Co-Owner
• Michael Sisk, Co-Owner

RICHARD CHILDRESS RACING
425 INDUSTRIAL DRIVE
WELCOME, NC 27374
info@rcrracing.com
www.rcrracing.com
• Richard Childress, Chairman/CEO
• Torrey Galida, President

RICHARD PETTY MOTORSPORTS
297 INDUSTRIAL DRIVE
LEXINGTON, NC 27265
richardpettymotorsports.com
• Richard Petty, Co-Owner
• Andrew Murstein, Co-Owner
• Brian Moffitt, CEO

RICK WARE RACING
111 SUNRISE CENTER
THOMASVILLE, NC 27360
wareracing.com
• Rick Ware, Owner

ROUSH FENWAY RACING
4600 ROUSH PLACE
CONCORD, NC 18027
social@roushfenway.com
www.roushfenway.com
• John Henry, Owner
• John W. Henry, Co-Owner

SPIRE MOTORSPORTS
19510 JETTON ROAD
SUITE 300
CORNELIUS, NC 28031
704-897-2880
spiresportsinc.com
• Jeff Dickerson, Co-Owner
• T.J. Puchyr, Co-Owner

STARCOM RACING
61 E WILLOW STREET
MILLBURN, NJ 07041
officeinfo@starcomracing.com
starcomracing.com
• Michael Kohler, CEO
• Matthew Kohler, President

STEWART-HAAS RACING
6001 HAAS WAY
KANNAPOLIS, NC 28081
704-652-4227
information@shracing.com
www.stewarthaasracing.com
• Tony Stewart, Co-Owner
• Gene Haas, Co-Owner

TEAM PENSKE
200 PENSKE WAY
MOORESVILLE, NC 28115
www.teampenske.com
• Roger Penske, Founder/Chairman

WOOD BROTHERS RACING
MOORESVILLE, NC
woodbrothersracing.com
• Eddie Wood, President/Co-Owner
• Glen Wood, Founder
• Len Wood, Executive VP/Co-Owner

Manufacturers:

CHEVROLET
www.chevrolet.com/motorsports/nascar

FORD
performance.ford.com/home.html

TOYOTA
www.trdusa.com/racing.html

NASCAR GANDER OUTDOORS TRUCK SERIES
DAYTONA BEACH, FL
www.nascar.com/news/gander-outdoors-truck-series
• Jim France, Chairman/CEO

Teams:

AM RACING
2268 PEACHTREE ROAD
STATESVILLE, NC 28625
pr@amracing.racing
amracingteam.com
• Tim Self, Owner/President/CEO
• Eddie Troconis, Crew Chief

B.J. MCLEOD MOTORSPORTS
121 GOODWIN CIRCLE
MOORESVILLE, NC 28115
www.bjmcleodmotorsports.com

CHAD FINLEY RACING
11349 OLD US 27
DEWITT, MI 48820
pr@chadfinleyracing.com
www.chadfinley.com
• David Gilliland, Co-Owner
• Bo LeMastus, Co-Owner/CEO
• Bruce Cook, Crew Chief

DGR-CROSLEY
111 BYERS CREEK ROAD
MOORESVILLE, NC 28117
dgrcrosley.com
• David Gilliland, Co-Owner
• Bo LeMastus, Co-Owner

GMS RACING
310 AVIATION DRIVE
STATESVILLE, NC 28677
info@gmsracing.net
gmsracing.net
• Maury Gallagher, Co-Owner
• Spencer Gallagher, Co-Owner

HALMAR FRIESEN RACING
halmarracing.com
• Chris Larsen, Co-Owner
• Stewart Friesen, Co-Owner

HATTORI RACING ENTERPRISES
161 KNOB HILL ROAD
MOORESVILLE, NC 28117
704-663-0020
hre.us.com
• Shigeaki Hattori, Owner

JENNIFER JO COBB RACING
804A PERFORMANCE ROAD
MOORESVILLE, NC 28115
info@jenniferjocobb.com
www.cobbracingteam.com
• Jennifer Jo Cobb, Owner
• Steve Kuykendall, Crew Chief

JORDAN ANDERSON RACING
2668 PEACHTREE ROAD
STATESVILLE, NC 28625
Jordan@JordanAndersonRacing.com
jordanandersonracing.com

• Jordan Anderson, Owner

KYLE BUSCH MOTORSPORTS
351 MAZEPPA ROAD
MOORESVILLE, NC 28115
web@kylebusch.com
kylebuschmotorsports.com
• Kyle Busch, Owner
Other website:
www.kylebuschfoundation.org

NEMCO MOTORSPORTS
128 S IREDELL INDUSTRIAL PARK ROAD
MOORESVILLE, NC 28115
704-664-4287
nemcomotorsports.com
• Joe Nemechek, Owner

NIECE MOTORSPORTS
330 W AVIATION DRIVE
STATESVILLE, NC 28677
media@niecemotorsports.com
www.niecemotorsports.com
• Al Niece, Owner
• Phil Gould, Crew Chief

ON POINT MOTORSPORTS
3400 DENVER DRIVE
DENVER, NC 28037
704-966-0463
hjordan@onpmotorsports.com
onpmotorsports.com
• Steven Lane, Owner

REAUME BROTHERS RACING
1519 MECKLENBURG HIGHWAY
UNIT 221
MT. MOURNE, NC 28123-0331
www.reaumebrothersracing.com
• Josh Reaume, Owner

THORSPORT RACING
312 THORSPORT WAY
SANDUSKY, OH 44870
419-621-8800
info@thorsport.com
thorsport.com
• Duke Thorson, Co-Owner
• Rhonda Thorson, Co-Owner

YOUNG'S MOTORSPORTS
604 PERFORMANCE ROAD
MOORESVILLE, NC 28115
704-658-1019
info@youngsmotorsports.com
www.youngsmotorsports.com
• Randy Young, Owner

Manufacturers:

CHEVROLET
www.chevrolet.com/motorsports/nascar

FORD
performance.ford.com/home.html

TOYOTA
www.trdusa.com/racing.html

NASCAR PINTY'S SERIES
hometracks.nascar.com/international/pintys-series
Description:
NASCAR racing series in Canada, with one race in the United States.

NASCAR WHELEN ALL-AMERICAN SERIES
1-800-630-0535
hometracks.nascar.com/local/whelen-all-american-series
Description:
NASCAR-sanctioned local racetrack series operating in the United States and Canada.

NASCAR WHELEN MODIFIED TOUR
1-800-630-0535
hometracks.nascar.com/regional/whelen-modified-tour
Description:
Only open-wheeled division of NASCAR. Races are in the Northeast and Midwest.

NASCAR XFINITY SERIES
DAYTONA BEACH, FL
www.nascar.com/news/xfinity-series
• Jim France, Chairman/CEO

Teams:

B.J. MCLEOD MOTORSPORTS
121 GOODWIN CIRCLE
MOORESVILLE, NC 28115
www.bjmcleodmotorsports.com
• B.J. McLeod, Principal
• Kevyn Rebolledo, Crew Chief

BRANDONBILT MOTORSPORTS
FREDERICKSBURG, VA
• Jerry Brown

DGM RACING
SAINT-MATHIEU-DE-BELOEIL, QC, CANADA
• Mario Gosselin, Owner

GMS RACING
310 AVIATION DRIVE
STATESVILLE, NC 28677
info@gmsracing.net
gmsracing.net
• Maury Gallagher, Co-Owner
• Spencer Gallagher, Co-Owner

JD MOTORSPORTS
1210 CHAMPION FERRY ROAD
GAFFNEY, SC 29341
864-488-1270
info@jdavismotorsports.com
www.teamjdmotorsports.com
• Johnny Davis, Co-Owner/General Manager
• Gary Keller, Co-Owner

JEREMY CLEMENTS RACING
71 COLDEN HILL ROAD
NEWBURGH, NY 12550
jeremyclements51.com
• Jeremy Clements, Co-Owner
• Tony Clements, Co-Owner

JIMMY MEANS RACING
FOREST CITY, NC
• Jimmy Means, Owner

JOE GIBBS RACING
13415 REESE BOULEVARD W
HUNTERSVILLE, NC 28078
joegibbsracing.com
• Joe Gibbs, Owner
• J.D. Gibbs, Co-Chairman
• Dave Alpern, President

JR MOTORSPORTS
349 CAYUGA DRIVE
MOORESVILLE, NC 28117
www.jrmracing.com

• Kelley Earnhardt Miller, Co-Owner/VP/Business Manager
• Dale Earnhardt, Jr., Co-Owner/President
• Rick Hendrick, Co-Owner

KAULIG RACING
PO BOX 1627
WELCOME, NC 27374
www.kauligracing.com
• Matt Kaulig, Owner
• Chris Rice, President

MBM MOTORSPORTS
849 CONNOR STREET
STATESVILLE, NC 28677
www.mbmmotorsports.com
• Carl Long, Owner

MIKE HARMON RACING
sites.google.com/view/mikeharmonracing74
• Mike Harmon, Owner

RICHARD CHILDRESS RACING
425 INDUSTRIAL DRIVE
WELCOME, NC 27374
336-731-3334 EXT 3101
info@rcrracing.com
www.rcrracing.com
• Richard Childress, Chairman/CEO
• Torrey Galida, President

RICK WARE RACING
111 SUNRISE CENTER DRIVE
THOMASVILLE, NC 27360
wareracing.com
• Rick Ware, Owner

RSS RACING
SUGAR HILL, GA
ryansiegracing.com
• Ryan Sieg, Principal

SS-GREEN LIGHT RACING
120 WILKINSON ROAD
MOORESVILLE, NC 28115
704-664-0808
www.ssgreenlight.com
• Bobby Dotter, Owner
• Ken Smith, Co-Owner
• Steve Urvan, Co-Owner

STEWART-HAAS RACING W/ BIAGI-DENBESTE
MOORESVILLE, NC
www.biagidenbesteracing.com
• Jon Hanson, Crew Chief
• Gene Haas, Co-Owner
• Fred Biagi, Co-Owner
• Greg Biagi, Co-Owner
• Bill DenBeste, Co-Owner
• Lori DenBeste, Co-Owner

TEAM PENSKE
200 PENSKE WAY
MOORESVILLE, NC 28115
www.teampenske.com
• Roger Penske, Founder/Chair

Manufacturers:

CHEVROLET
www.chevrolet.com/motorsports/nascar

FORD
performance.ford.com/home.html

TOYOTA
www.trdusa.com/racing.html

PORSCHE GT3 CUP CHALLENGE CANADA
INTERNATIONAL MOTORSPORTS CENTER
ONE DAYTONA BOULEVARD
DAYTONA BEACH, FL 32114
info@imsa.com
porschegt3cupcanada.imsa.com

PORSCHE GT3 CUP CHALLENGE USA
INTERNATIONAL MOTORSPORTS CENTER
ONE DAYTONA BOULEVARD
DAYTONA BEACH, FL 32114
info@imsa.com
porschegt3cupusa.imsa.com

Badminton Organizations

BADMINTON CANADA
700 INDUSTRIAL AVENUE
SUITE 401
OTTAWA, ON, CANADA K1G0Y9
613-569-2424
Fax: 613-748-5724
badminton@badminton.ca
www.badminton.ca
• Anil Kaul, President
• John Cowan, Vice President
• Martin Tam, Treasurer
• Mike Alexander, Director
• Jimena Gravelle, Events Manager
Membership Requirements:
Through provincial associations.
Description:
Responsible for developing world-class Canadian badminton players, coaches, officials and administrators; providing international and centralized support and/or leadership in furthering member association objectives; being the custodian, interpreter and adjudicator of the laws of Badminton in Canada.

BADMINTON PAN AM
AV. ANDRES REYES 437
OFICINA 601
LIMA, 27
51-99-422-5073
panambadminton@gmail.com
www.badmintonpanam.org
• Vishu Tolan, President
• Peter Golding, Deputy President
• Pilar Carrillo de la Fuente, Chief Operation Officer
Description:
Badminton Panam is the governing body of Badminton in the North, Central, and South Americas.

BADMINTON WORLD FEDERATION
AMODA BUILDING
22 JALAN IMBI
UNIT 17.05, LEVEL 17
KUALA LUMPUR, 55100
603-2141 7155
Fax: 603-2143 7155
bwf@bwfbadminton.org
www.bwfbadminton.org
• Thomas Lund, Chief Operating Officer
• Stuart Borrie, Director of Operations
• Darren Parks, Events Director
• Ian Wright, Development Manager
• Sharon Chan, Finance Manager

Description:
The Badminton World Federation acts as the international governing body for the sport badminton. The BWF serves to regulate, promote, develop and popularise the sport of badminton across the globe.

USA BADMINTON
ONE OLYMPIC PLAZA
COLORADO SPRINGS, CO 80909
719-866-4808
Fax: 719-866-4507
usab@usabadminton.org
www.teamusa.org/usa-badminton
• Fred Coleman, President
• Dan Cloppas, CEO/Secretary General
(719) 866-4808
dcloppas@aol.com
• Peggy Savosik, Director, Member & Financial Services
(719) 866-4808
peggy@usabadminton.org
• Mohan Subramaniam, Director, Coaching & High Performance
(719) 866-3642
mohan@usabadminton.org
Description:
USA Badminton is the organization recognized by the U.S. Olympic Committee for the purpose of selecting and training men's and women's teams to represent the U.S. in Olympic Games. They also select teams for the World Championships and other international competitions.

Bandy Organizations

USA BANDY
MINNEAPOLIS, MN 55425
952-883-0880
www.usabandy.com
• Chris Middlebrook, President
(612) 598-0966
• Andrew Knutson, Vice President
• Chris Halden, League Commissioner
• Kevin Bowen, Head Of Referees
• Scott Arundel, Rink Bandy League Commissioner
• Neal Logan, Referee Assessor
Description:
The governing body of the sport of bandy in the United States, and its representative in the International Bandy Federation.

Baseball Organizations

AMERICAN AMATEUR BASEBALL CONGRESS
100 W BROADWAY
FARMINGTON, NM 87401
505-327-3120
Fax: 505-327-3132
info@aabc.us
www.aabc.us
• Richard Neely, President
richardneely@aabc.us
• Mike Dimond, Executive Vice President
mikedimond@aabc.us
Number of members:
240,000+
Member Services:
Composed of twelve different age divisions in the United States, Puerto Rico and Canada.

Publications:
Amateur Baseball News.
Membership Requirements:
Operates on a league concept. Each league must consist of at least 4 teams playing a minimum six game league schedule.
Description:
Founded in 1935. American Amateur Baseball Congress (AABC) is the largest amateur baseball organization in the United States for players above junior baseball age and the only amateur baseball program that provides progressive and continuous organized competition - sub teens through adults.
Divisions:
Stan Musial, Connie Mack, Don Mattingly, Mickey Mantle, Ken Griffey Jr., Sandy Koufax, Nolan Ryan, Pee Wee Reese, Gil Hodges, Willie Mays, Jackie Robinson, Roberto Clemente, Rod Carew.

AMERICAN BASEBALL COACHES ASSOCIATION
4101 PIEDMONT PARKWAY
GREENSBORO, NC 27410
336-821-3140
Fax: 336-886-0000
abca@abca.org
www.abca.org
• Craig Keilitz, Executive Director
(336) 821-3145
ckeilitz@abca.org
• Jon Litchfield, Deputy Executive Director
(336) 821-3142
jlitchfield@abca.org
Nature of Service:
ABCA assists in the promotion of baseball and acts as a sounding board and spokesperson on issues concerning the various levels of baseball. Further, the Association promotes camaraderie and rapport among all baseball coaches, including that between professional and amateur levels.
Membership Requirements:
High school, junior college, college or amateur baseball coaches.
Number of members:
13,000
Membership Fees:
$75 a year for U.S. residents.
Publications:
Inside Pitch Magazine; Press Box weekly email; The Baseball Coaching Bible
Year Founded:
1945

AMERICAN BASEBALL FOUNDATION
833 SAINT VINCENT'S DRIVE
SUITE 205A
BIRMINGHAM, AL 35205
205-558-4235
Fax: 205-918-0800
abf@asmi.org
americanbaseballfoundation.com
• David Osinski, Executive Director
Description:
The American Baseball Foundation Inc. delivers educational programs in two areas: a) injury prevention in youth baseball pitching; b) redressing summer learning loss among under-served children, ages 7 through 14, through its BASIC program which combines sport skill instruction with academics in reading and math all related to sports.

single sports

AMERICAN LEGION BASEBALL
700 N PENNSYLVANIA STREET
PO BOX 1055
INDIANAPOLIS, IN 46206
317-630-1200
800-433-3318
Fax: 317-630-1223
www.legion.org
• James W. Oxford, National Commander
Teams:
Over 3,400 teams across 50 states and Canada.
Members:
55,000 players and coaches.
Publications:
The Dugout E-Newsletter; The Dispatch; and Legion Magazine.
Year Founded:
1925
Membership Requirements:
Players must be under 19 years of age.
Description:
American Legion Baseball is an amateur league that hosts over 3,400 teams. Interestingly, most major league players played in the American Legion Baseball League. The purpose of American Legion Baseball is to give young men an opportunity to develop their baseball skills.

ASSOCIATION OF PROFESSIONAL BALL PLAYERS OF AMERICA
23623 N SCOTTSDALE ROAD
SUITE 290
SCOTTSDALE, AZ 85255
480-404-9339
info@apbpa.org
apbpa.org
• Jennifer Madison, President
Nature of Service:
They provide financial assistance, educational and sobriety resources, mentors, networking, and support on multiple levels for life after baseball for professional baseball players, coaches, umpires, scouts and clubhouse men. No distinction is made between major league and minor league players. They have given out over $5 million in financial assistance since 1924.
Year Founded:
1924
Clients Include:
Indy Ball, MiLB, MLB
Membership Requirements:
Restricted to those who played or worked in professional baseball.
Membership Dues:
$150-currently on a Major League roster, $20-currently on a Minor League roster, $20-members no longer active in the game, $20-Scouts/Administrative personnel
Number of Members:
Over 101,500

BABE RUTH LEAGUE
1670 WHITEHORSE-MERCERVILLE ROAD
HAMILTON, NJ 08619
800-880-3142
Fax: 609-695-2505
www.baberuthleague.org
• Steven M. Tellefsen, President & CEO
Member Services:
Email Blasts & Bulletins; Media Guide, Rules and Regulations, Handbooks and miscellaneous materials.

Nature of Service:
Founded in 1951. Babe Ruth League, Inc., using regulation competitive baseball and softball rules, teaches skills, mental and physical development, a respect for the rules of the game, and basic ideals of sportsmanship and fair play. In all aspects, Babe Ruth League, Inc. is committed to providing its participants the very best educational sports experience possible. It is their fundamental belief that every child with a desire to play baseball or softball be afforded that opportunity. A baseball program for boys ages 13-15.
Sponsors:
Adidas, Anaconda Sports, Babe Ruth Network, DeLong Cap, David Sunflower Seeds, eFundraising, Head Down Trainers, Hershey's, K&K Insurance, Marriott, Musco Lighting, Rawlings, TSS Photography, Wisk

BASEBALL ASSISTANCE TEAM
1271 AVENUE OF THE AMERICAS
NEW YORK, NY 10020
212-931-7822
Fax: 212-949-5433
bat@mlb.com
www.mlb.com/baseball-assistance-team
Description:
The primary objective of the Baseball Assistance Team is to aid those members of the baseball family most in need. B.A.T. strives to provide a means of support to people who are unable to help themselves. Through charitable contributions from corporations, foundations and individuals, B.A.T. is there to assist those with financial, psychological or physical burdens.
Publications:
B.A.T. Newsletter, quarterly.
Year Founded:
1986

BASEBALL CANADA
2212 GLADWIN CRES
SUITE A7
OTTAWA, ON, CANADA K1B 5N1
613-748-5606
Fax: 613-748-5767
info@baseball.ca
www.baseball.ca
• Jim Baba, Executive Director
• Greg Hamilton, Head Coach & Director, National Teams
Incorporated
1964
Description:
Baseball Canada is the governing body for baseball in Canada. They are dedicated to developing and advancing baseball for all Canadians by promoting safety and ethics within the sport. Baseball Canada supports the achievement of excellence in baseball and prides itself on its focus on athletes. Baseball Canada strives to provide client programs that foster participation and involvement in baseball. Its programs allow participants to enjoy themselves and achieve their personal goals. They have also created 10 provincial associations which represent players, coaches and umpires.

BASEBALL FACTORY
9212 BERGER ROAD
SUITE 200
COLUMBIA, MD 21046

410-715-5080
800-641-4487
Fax: 410-715-1975
www.baseballfactory.com
• Steve Sclafani, Founder & Chief Executive Officer
• Rob Naddelman, President
• Steve Bernhardt, Chief Baseball Officer
Major Sponsors:
Louisville Slugger; Diamond; FBR.com, Under Armour, Eyeblack.com
Service Includes:
One day tryout at top facilities nationwide. They provide professional instruction, videotaping, pro-scout evaluations, placement counseling and targeted mail campaign to 50 colleges.
Description:
Offers a one-of-a-kind concept that provides baseball players nationwide with the very best in instruction, tournament competition, college planning and placement.
Programs:
Rookie program, B.A.T.S program, Player Development program, Exclusive program.
Member Services:
Timely recruiting information, program status information, account maintenance & transaction history and access to your pro scout evaluations.
Year Founded:
1994

CONTINENTAL AMATEUR BASEBALL ASSOCIATION
3211 HEATHLAND WAY
PO BOX 1684
MT. PLEASANT, SC 29465
843-860-1568
www.cababaseball.com
• Larry Redwine, Chief Executive Officer
(513) 677-1580
cabaredwine@gmail.com
• John Rhodes, President & COO
(843) 860-1568
diamonddevils@aol.com
Nature of Sports Service:
The Continental Amateur Baseball Association was founded in 1984. The organizations objective is to promote a love of baseball and to provide a meeting place for tournament competitions at the state, regional and the World Series.
Membership Requirements:
CABA offers competition in individual age levels 8-16 and 18 and under. The high school division is established for players 17 and under regardless of class in school, along with players 18 years of age who will be returning to school in the fall following their tournament participation (as verified by the school's administrative authority). The Collegiate division CABA series teams are made up of players that were on some college level baseball team at any accredited college or university the previous season or are 22 years of age or under. However, a player must be at least 15 years of age on the day that they play in a CABA collegiate age
Publications:
Continental News, twice annually; Rule Books.
Member Services:
Computer statistical program package. World Series.

DIXIE BOYS BASEBALL
BRIGHTLEAF COURT - OFFICE PARK
256 HONEYSUCKLE ROAD
SUITE 23
DOTHAN, AL 36305
334-793-3331
Fax: 334-793-3331
baseball.dixie.org
• J. Sandy Jones, Commissioner & CEO
Description:
Founded in 1957. Primarily a youth baseball program for boys (ages 13-14 playing in a 80' diamond) and majors (ages 15-19 playing on a 90' diamond) to meet physical development of growing boys.

DIXIE YOUTH BASEBALL
OFFICE OF THE COMMISSIONER
PO BOX 877
MONTGOMERY, AL 36109
334-265-0294
william@dixie.org
youth.dixie.org
• William Wade, Commissioner
(334) 265-0294
william@dixie.org
• Kent Bruxvoort, President
(501) 279-8663
kent_bruxvoort@cargill.com
Description:
Promoting the development of strong character, a positive attitude and a sense of responsibility and citizenship among youngsters since 1955.

DIZZY DEAN BASEBALL
PENSACOLA, FL
dizzydeanbbinc.org
• Danny Phillips, National Commissioner
(205) 514-4142
Description:
The organization is a non-profit youth group that promotes good sportsmanship and character to kids ages five through nineteen. The focus on local league play but do offer State and World series tournaments as well.
Founded:
1977

LITTLE LEAGUE BASEBALL
539 US ROUTE 15 HIGHWAY
PO BOX 3485
WILLIAMSPORT, PA 17701-0485
570-326-1921
Fax: 570-326-1074
www.littleleague.org
• Stephen D. Keener, President & CEO
• Hugh E. Tanner, Chair
Description:
A non-profit organization whose mission is to promote, develop, supervise, and voluntarily assist in all lawful ways, the interest of those who will participate in Little League Baseball and Softball.
Membership Requirements:
Must be baseball or softball league players, ages 5-18.
Publications:
Little League Magazine, Little Leaguer Newsletter, World Series Programs (8 Divisions).
Member Services:
Official Playing and Tournament Rules. Safety Program. Annual meeting each November.
Number of Members:
3.7 Million

Founded:
1939 by Carl E. Stotz

MAJOR LEAGUE BASEBALL PLAYERS ASSOCIATION
12 EAST 49TH STREET
24TH FLOOR
NEW YORK, NY 10017
212-826-0808
feedback@mlbpa.org
www.mlbplayers.com
• Tony Clark, Executive Director
Description:
Founded 1966. Serves as the labor organization representing all major league players with respect to terms and conditions of employment with major league clubs. (Also represents coaches, managers, and trainers for some purposes). In addition, the Players Association holds certain group licensing rights for all players and acts as a marketing representative for such rights.
Membership:
All players, managers, coaches and trainers who hold a signed contract with a Major League Club. Current membership includes approx. 1,200 players.

MAJOR LEAGUE BASEBALL UMPIRES ASSOCIATION
PO BOX 394
NEENAH, WI 54957
920-969-1580
Fax: 920-969-1892
www.mlbua.com
• Joe West, President
• Fieldin Culbreth, Vice President
Description:
Certified in 2000 by the National Labor Relations Board, the Major League Umpires Association (known as the World Umpires Association prior to 2018) is the bargaining agent for Major League Baseball's umpires.
Publications:
MLBUA; newsletter.

MAJOR LEAGUE BASEBALL/MLB
1271 AVENUE OF THE AMERICAS
NEW YORK, NY 10020
866-800-1275
www.mlb.com
• Rob Manfred, Commissioner of Baseball
• Dan Halem, Dep. Comm., Baseball Admin. & Chief Legal Officer
• Pat Courtney, Chief Communications Officer
Description:
Formed in 1989, Major League International is focused on the worldwide growth of baseball through game development, broadcasting, special events, sponsorship and licensing.
Additional Offices:
London, UK; Sydney, Australia; Tokyo, Japan.
Publications:
ballpark - quarterly newsletter

MINOR LEAGUE BASEBALL
9550 16TH STREET NORTH
ST. PETERSBURG, FL 33716
727-822-6937
Fax: 727-821-5819
www.milb.com
Description:
Founded in 1901. Oversees operations of minor league professional baseball teams.

Assists in increasing attendance for member clubs. Arbitrates disputes on rules and contracts. Promotes and protects the interests of players and umpires. MiLB consists of 160 teams across the United States, Canada and the Dominican Republic.
Membership Requirements:
Approved franchise in one of the member leagues.
Publications:
Minor League Baseball Information Guide; annual.
Number of members:
160 teams
Uniform Suppliers:
Diamond Sports, Jersey Express, Majestic Athletic, OT Sports, Rawlings, Russell Athletic, Wilson Sporting Goods.
Sponsors:
AMI Graphics, LLC, Baseball America, Barton Malow Design/Construction Services.
Charity Partners:
ALS Association, Big Brothers Big Sisters, Special Olympics.
Nature of Service:
Professional baseball.
Clients Include:
Esurance, Crayola, John Deere, Bush's Beans, ServiceMaster, SunRun, Gallo Wines, FIS.

NATIONAL AMATEUR BASEBALL FEDERATION
PO BOX 705
BOWIE, MD 20718
410-721-4727
Fax: 410-721-4940
nabf1914@aol.com
www.nabf.com
• Charles Blackburn, Jr., Executive Director
• Bob Mingo, President
Number of members:
103,000
Member Services:
Eight Annual World Series and Tournaments and 56 Regional Tournaments - Rookie Div (10 and under), Freshman Div (12 and under), Sophomore Div (14 and under), Junior Div (16 and under), High School Div, Senior (18 and under) Div, College Div (22 and under), Major (unlimited age) Div.
Publications:
Behind the Seams; 3 times annually. Tournament News; October annually.
Membership Requirements:
Leagues having four or more teams (amateur status); Associations that support amateur baseball and leagues.
Description:
Established in 1914, a nonprofit organization, hosts regional and national Championship tournaments held coast to coast.
Sponsors:
Baseball Warehouse, Baseball Factory, Rawlings, Louisville Slugger.

NATIONAL BASEBALL CONGRESS
110 SOUTH MAIN
SUITE 600
WICHITA, KS 67202
316-977-9400
nbcbaseball.com
• Matt Rogers, Chairman

Description:
Founded in 1934. Sanctions a series of state championships, semi-professional baseball tournaments leading to the national title tournament, the NBC World Series. Supplier of baseballs and equipment. One of the largest administering bodies for summer leagues and non-professional baseball.
Membership:
As of now there are 15 member leagues and 20 tournaments.
Publications:
Official Baseball Rule Book.

NATIONAL HIGH SCHOOL BASEBALL COACHES ASSOCIATION
PO BOX 1038
DUBLIN, OH 43017
614-764-5800
www.baseballcoaches.org
• Tim Saunders, Executive Director
Member Services:
Educational clinics; seminars; coach-of-the-year honors; hall of fame recognition; sponsor benefits; coaching enhancement exposure; annual meetings.
Membership Requirements:
Through state high school coaches' associations or directly by individual coaches.
Description:
Formed to provide services and recognition for baseball coaches and to help promote and represent high school baseball.
Sponsors:
Baseball America, Clell Wade Coaching Directory, Easton Sports, Jostens, Louisville Slugger, Miller Net Company, Reagal Awards, Turface, USA Baseball, Smushballs.
Membership Publications:
Newsletter; a coaching instructional publication; BCA directory on the website. Officially formed in 1991.

NATIONAL JUNIOR COLLEGE ATHLETIC ASSOCIATION
8801 JM KEYNES DRIVE
SUITE 4500
CHARLOTTE, NC 18262
719-590-9788
Fax: 719-590-7324
www.njcaa.org
• Chris Parker, President & CEO
cparker@njcaa.org
Description:
The program provides athletic participation in an environment that supports equitable opportunities consistent with the educational objectives of member colleges. The NCJAA is the leader in championing academic and athletic opportunities for student-athletes.

PEORIA DIAMOND CLUB
16101 N 83RD AVENUE
PEORIA, AZ 85382
623-773-8710
peoriadiamondclub.org
• Roz Shanley, General Manager
r.shanley@peoriadiamondclub.org
Year Founded:
1993
Description:
Supplies operational support for the Spring Training of the Seattle Mainers and the San Diego Padres at the Peoria Sports Complex. Formed in response to the desire of the Seattle Mariners and the San Diego Padres to have a non-profit organization handle the operation of the Complex during their Spring Training.
Members:
650

PONY BASEBALL AND SOFTBALL
1951 PONY PLACE
WASHINGTON, PA 15301
724-225-1060
Fax: 724-225-9852
info@pony.org
www.pony.org
• Abraham Key, President
• Brent Liberatore, Director of Information Technology
Description:
Founded in 1951. Sponsors international amateur youth baseball and softball programs. PONY Baseball and Softball is designed to Protect Our Nation's Youth by providing experiences in youth baseball and softball that will help young people grow into healthier and happier adults.

PROFESSIONAL BASEBALL ATHLETIC TRAINERS SOCIETY
400 COLONY SQUARE
SUITE 1750
1201 PEACHTREE STREET
ATLANTA, GA 30361
404-875-4000 EXT 203
Fax: 404-892-8560
pbats.com
• Jason Daffner, General Counsel
Number of Members:
63
Publications:
PBATS Newsletter; a semi-annual publication.
Member Services:
The mission of the Professional Baseball Athletic Trainers Society is to serve as an educational resource for the Major League and Minor League baseball athletic trainers. PBATS serves its members by providing for the continued education of the athletic trainer as it relates to the profession, helping improve his understanding of sports medicine so as to better promote the health of his constituency—professional baseball players. PBATS also serves as a resource to educate those outside the professional baseball athletic trainer community about the profession and about the athletic trainer's integral position within the sports medicine team.
Corporate Sponsorship:
EBI Sports Medicine.
Sponsors:
Major League Baseball, The James E. Olson Foundation, Cap CURE, Oral Health America's National Spit Tabacco Education Program, NATA, American Academy of Orthopaedic Surgeons.

PROFESSIONAL BASEBALL UMPIRE CORPORATION
9550 16TH STREET N
ST. PETERSBURG, FL 33716
877-799-8677
Fax: 727-456-1745
info@milbumpireacademy.com
www.milbumpireacademy.com
• Dusty Dellinger, Director
• Tim Brunswick, SVP, Baseball & Business Operations
• Jess Schneider, Manager, Umpire Operations
Year Founded:
1999
Publications:
Manual for the Two-Umpire System, Professional Baseball Umpire Program Manual
Description:
Organization is responsible for training, evaluation, and recommendations for promotions, retentions or release of all umpires in the minor league baseball system throughout the U.S. and Canada.

RANDY HUNDLEY'S FANTASY CAMPS, INC.
2118 PLUM GROVE ROAD
SUITE 285
ROLLING MEADOWS, IL 60008
847-991-9595
randy@cubsfantasycamp.com
www.cubsfantasycamp.com
• Randy Hundley, President
Requirements:
Any adult over 30 years old.
Nature of Services:
For years, Randy Hundley's Fantasy Baseball Camps have earned the highest form of praise. Our camp recreates an authentic major league experience. Randy Hundley's Fantasy Baseball Camp is the original fantasy camp.

SOCIETY FOR AMERICAN BASEBALL RESEARCH
555 N CENTRAL AVENUE
SUITE 416
PHOENIX, AZ 85004
602-496-1460
www.sabr.org
• Scott Bush, Chief Executive Officer
• Scott Carter, Executive Vice President
• Chanel Zapata, Community Engagement Manager
• Jacob Pomrenke, Director of Editorial Content
Number of members:
7,000
Member Services:
Numerous regional meetings; microfilm lending library; research exchange; research committees - Negro Leagues, Ball Parks, Biographical Research, Minor Leagues, Bibliography, Umpire and Rules, Oral History, Women in Baseball, Records, Statistical Analysis and Pictorial History. Latin America, Baseball Songs and Poems.
Publications:
The Baseball Research Journal; The National Pastime.
Membership Requirements:
Interest in professional baseball. $60 annual dues.
Description:
The purpose of SABR is to foster the research, preservation and dissemination of the history and records of baseball.
Year Founded:
1971

T-BALL USA ASSOCIATION
WEST PALM BEACH, FL 33401
teeballusa@aol.com
www.t-ballusa.org

Description:
The national not-for-profit youth sports organization dedicated to the development of the game of tee ball. They offer a broad variety of programs and services and are the center for information on how to improve existing tee ball programs and establish new ones.
Ages for Playing Tee Ball:
Recommended ages are 4 through 7

USA BASEBALL
1030 SWABIA COURT
SUITE 201
DURHAM, NC 27703
919-474-8721
Fax: 855-420-5910
info@usabaseball.com
www.usabaseball.com
• Paul Seiler, Executive Director & CEO
Description:
USA Baseball serves as the national governing body for the sport, and represents American baseball as a member of the United States Olympic Committee and the International Baseball Federation.
Publications:
USA Baseball National Team Yearbook, annual.
Member Services:
Selects official U.S.A. Baseball Teams, Sr. National Team, Jr (18-under), National Team, Youth National Team (16-under) for international competition.
Year Founded:
1978
Official Partners:
Baseball America, Franklin Sports, International Baseball Federation, Majestic Athletic, Major League Baseball, Major League Baseball Advanced Media, New Era, Palm Beach County Sports Council, Rawlings, Reebok, United States Olympic Committee, Upper Deck, Wilson Sporting Goods

WORLD BASEBALL SOFTBALL CONFEDERATION
MAISON DU SPORT INTERNATIONAL
54, AVE DE RHODAINE
LAUSANNE, SWITZERLAN CH-1007
+41-21 318 8240
Fax: +41-21 318 8241
office@wbsc.org
www.wbsc.org
• Riccardo Fraccari, President
• Beng Choo Low, Secretary General
Description:
World governing body for baseball and softball.

Baseball, Professional Leagues/Teams: Major

MAJOR LEAGUE BASEBALL/MLB
1271 AVENUE OF THE AMERICAS
NEW YORK, NY 10020
866-800-1275
customerservice@website.mlb.com
www.mlb.com
• Rob Manfred, Commissioner of Baseball
• Dan Halem, Dep. Comm., Baseball Admin. & Chief Legal Officer
• Pat Courtney, Chief Communications Officer

Nature of Service:
Administrates professional baseball. Established and enforces rules regarding franchise operation. Supervises national radio and television contracts. Handles publicity and marketing of baseball and legal matters pertaining to baseball as an industry. Operates the World Series and All-Star games.
Membership Requirements:
Teams operating in the American or National Leagues.
Year Founded:
1903

AMERICAN LEAGUE OF PROFESSIONAL BASEBALL CLUBS, THE
1271 AVENUE OF THE AMERICAS
NEW YORK, NY 10020
866-800-1275
customerservice@website.mlb.com
www.mlb.com
• Rob Manfred, Baseball Commisioner
• Dan Halem, Deputy Commisioner, Baseball Admin.
• Pat Courtney, Chief Communications Officer
  Description:
  League of professional baseball teams.
  Teams:
  15.
  Year Founded:
  1901

Teams:

BALTIMORE ORIOLES
ORIOLE PARK AT CAMDEN YARDS
333 W CAMDEN STREET
BALTIMORE, MD 21201
410-685-9800
888-848-BIRD
Fax: 410-547-6277
orioles.com
• John Angelos, Chair/Chief Executive Officer
• Mike Elias, Executive VP & General Manager
• Peter Angelos, Ownership Representative
• Eve Rosenbaum, Director of Baseball Operations
• Lou Kousouris, Senior VP. Business Development
• Michael D. Hoppes, Chief Financial Officer
• Brian Ebel, Head Athletic Trainer
• Koby Perez, Senior Director, International Scouting
• Kent Qualls, Director, Minor League Operations
• Dan Thomas, Head Groundskeeper
• Jennifer Grondahl, Senior VP, Development & Communications
• Troy Scott, VP, Ballpark Experience
Stadium:
The beautiful baseball-only facility in downtown Baltimore became the official home of the Orioles on April 6, 1992. The construction of the park was completed in essentially 33 months. Seating capacity of 48,876.

BOSTON RED SOX
FENWAY PARK
4 JERSEY STREET
BOSTON, MA 02215
617-226-6000
redsox.com
• John W. Henry, Principal Owner
• Thomas C. Werner, Chairman
• Sam Kennedy, President/CEO
• Brian O'Halloran, General Manager
• Adam Grossman, Executive VP/Chief Marketing Officer
• Tim Zue, Executive VP, Chief Financial Officer
• Pete Nesbit, Senior VP, Ballpark Operations
• Jonathan Gilula, Executive VP/COO
• Ed Weiss, Executive VP, Corporate Strategy & General Counsel
• Raquel Ferreira, Senior VP, Major/Minor

League Operations
• Gus Quattlebaum, VP, Professional Scouting
• Ben Crockett, SVP, Baseball Operations
• Jonathan Lister, VP, Facilities Management
Stadium:
Fenway Park - opened April 20, 1912. The home of the Boston Red Sox resounds with the echoes of great baseball players. Fenway Park is actually the second home for the Sox. In 1901, the Boston Americans became one of the charter members of the fledgling American League. The Americans played ball at the Huntington Avenue Grounds, now a part of Northeastern University's campus.

CHICAGO WHITE SOX
US CELLULAR FIELD
333 W 35TH STREET
CHICAGO, IL 60616
312-674-1000
866-SOX-GAME
whitesox.com
• Jerry Reinsdorf, Chairman, Board of Directors
• Howard Pizer, Senior Executive VP
• Ken Williams, Executive VP
• Rick Hahn, Senior VP/General Manager
• Tim Buzard, Senior VP, Administration
• Terry Savarise, Senior VP, Stadium Operations
• Scott Reifert, Senior VP, Communications
• Cris Quintana, Senior Director of Game Pres./Video Prod.
• Bob Grim, Senior Director, Business Development/Broadcasting
• Dan Fabian, Senior Director, Baseball Operations
• Jo Simmons, Manager, Business Development
• Christine O'Reilly-Riordan, VP, Community Relations/Executive Director
• Jeremy Haber, Assistant General Manager
• John Corvino, General Counsel/VP
• Roger Bossard, Head Groundskeeper
• Jim Willits, VP, Sales & Service
• Grace Guerrero Zwit, Senior Director, Minor League Operations
• Chris Getz, Director of Player Development
Stadium:
US Cellular Field - home of the Chicago White Sox. Opened on April 18, 1991 under the name New Comiskey Park and in 2003 was renamed to US Cellular Field.

CLEVELAND INDIANS
PROGRESSIVE FIELD
2401 ONTARIO STREET
CLEVELAND, OH 44115
216-420-4487
indians.com
• Lawrence J. Dolan, Owner
• Paul J. Dolan, Chairman/CEO
• Chris Antonetti, President, Baseball Operations
• Brian Barren, President, Business Operations
• Rich Dorffer, Senior VP, Finance and CFO
• Bob DiBiasio, Senior VP, Public Affairs
• Jim Folk, VP, Ballpark Improvements
• Joe Znidarsic, VP, General Counsel
• Paul Gillispie, VP, International Scouting
• Bart Swain, Director, Baseball Information
• Brandon Koehnke, Head Groundskeeper
• James Harris, VP, Player Development
• Tony Amato, Home Clubhouse/Equipment Manager
• Mark Schickendantz, MD, Head Team Physician
• Curtis Danburg, VP, Communications & Community Impact
• Matt Coppo, Director, Ticket Operations
• Mike Chernoff, General Manager
Stadium:
Professional baseball in Cleveland is one of the city's oldest traditions, dating back to 1869. There is a passionate connection between the city of Cleveland and the Indians, as they are a study in revival. Both are working, living examples of the power of teamwork, conviction and dedication. Progressive Field is a Cleveland landmark that offers a fan-friendly facility within an intimate environment. Opened in 1994.

DETROIT TIGERS
COMERICA PARK
2100 WOODWARD AVENUE
DETROIT, MI 48201-3470
313-962-4000
tigers.com
• Christopher Ilitch, President/CEO
• Al Avila, Executive VP, Baseball Operations/General Manager
• Bradford Keith, Senior VP, Operations & Development
• Emily Neenan, Senior VP & Chief Marketing Officer
• Chris Lawrence, VP, Park Operations
• Sam Menzin, Director, Baseball Operations & Pro Scouting
• David Chadd, VP, Assistant General Manager
• Ellen Hill-Zeringue, VP, Marketing
• Scott Bream, VP, Player Personnel
• Scott Pleis, Director, Amateur Scouting
Stadium:
Comerica Park which opened in 2000 was built around the configuration of the playing field. The design of the park was planned with the fan sight lines as the highest priority.

HOUSTON ASTROS
MINUTE MAID PARK
501 CRAWFORD STREET
HOUSTON, TX 77002
713-259-8000
astros.com
• Jim Crane, Owner/Chairman
• James Click, General Manager
• Kevin Goldstein, Special Asst. General Manager, Player Personnel
• Armando Velasco, Senior Director, Baseball Operations
• Kevin Goldstein, Special Asst. General Manager, Player Personnel
• Anita Sehgal, Senior VP, Marketing & Communications
• Marcel Braithwaite, Senior VP, Business Operations
• Michael Slaughter, Senior VP, Chief Financial Officer
• Matt Brand, Senior VP, Revenue
• Doug Seckel, VP, Finance
• Gene Dias, VP, Communications
• Creighton Kahoalii, VP, Ticket Sales & Services
• Giles Kibbe, Senior VP/General Counsel
Stadium:
2019 marks the Astros 20th season in Minute Maid Park. The first official regular-season game was played on April 7, 2000 with the Philadelphia Phillies beating the Astros 4-1. Minute Maid Park has a seating capacity of 40,950.

KANSAS CITY ROYALS
KAUFFMAN STADIUM
ONE ROYAL WAY
KANSAS CITY, MO 64129
816-921-8000
Fax: 816-921-5775
fanfeedback@royals.com
royals.com
• John Sherman, Chairman/CEO
• Dayton Moore, Senior VP, Baseball Operations/General Manager
• Scott Sharp, VP/Assistant General Manager
• Lonnie Goldberg, Assistant General Manager/Scouting
• Mike Arbuckle, Sr. Advisor To Gen. Mngr., Scouting & Player Devt.
• George Brett, VP, Baseball Operations
• Michael Bucek, VP, Marketing & Business Development
• David Laverentz, VP, Finance & Administration
• Zachary Rosenberg, Manager, Ballpark Operations
• Vincent Key, Head Team Physician
• Brian Himstedt, Senior Director, Technology
• Mike Cummings, Assistant Director, Media Relations
• Don Costante, Senior Director, Event Presentation & Production

Stadium:
Kauffman Stadium, opened on April 10, 1973, has a seating capacity of 40,785.

LOS ANGELES ANGELS OF ANAHEIM
ANGEL STADIUM OF ANAHEIM
2000 GENE AUTRY WAY
ANAHEIM, CA 92806
714-940-2000
888-796-4256
angels.com
• Arte Moreno, Owner
• Dennis Kuhl, Chairman
• John Carpino, President
• Dana Wells, Executive VP
• Perry Minasian, General Manager
• Bill Stoneman, Director, Baseball Operations
• Molly Jolly, Senior VP, Finance & Administration
Stadium:
Angel Stadium opened in April 9, 1966, and was renovated on April, 1998. Some unique features include terraced bullpens in the outfield, widened concourses, new restroom and concession areas, a large and updated press box and three full-service restaurants.

MINNESOTA TWINS
TARGET FIELD
1 TWINS WAY
MINNEAPOLIS, MN 55403
612-659-3400
800-33-TWINS
twinsbaseball.com
• Dave St. Peter, President/CEO
• Jim Pohlad, Executive Chair
• Thad Levine, Senior VP, General Manager
• Matt Hoy, Senior VP, Operations
• Deron Johnson, Senior Advisor, Scouting
• Mary Giesler, Senior VP, General Counsel
• Andy Weinstein, VP, Finance
• Victor Gonzalez, Manager, Florida Operations
• Paul Froehle, VP, Ticket Operations
• Mike Radcliff, VP, Player Personnel
Seating Capacity:
39,504 with 18,500 infield seats
Stadium Opened:
2010
Publications:
Line Drives newsletter.

NEW YORK YANKEES
YANKEE STADIUM
ONE E 161ST STREET
BRONX, NY 10451
212-926-5337
yankees.com
• Randy Levine, Esq., President
• Hal Steinbrenner, Owner/Chairman/Managing General Partner
• Jessica Steinbrenner, General Partner/Vice Chairperson
• Jennifer Steinbrenner Swindal, General Partner/Vice Chairperson
• Brian Cashman, Senior VP/General Manager
• Deborah A. Tymon, Senior VP, Marketing
• Lonn A. Trost, Esq., COO
• Anthony Bruno, Senior VP/CFO
• Irfan Kirimca, Senior Director, Ticket Operations
• Brian Smith, Senior VP, Corporate/Community Relations
• Doug Behar, Senior VP, Stadium Operations
Stadium:
The original Yankee Stadium opened in 1923, and in 2009 new Yankee Stadium opened just in time for opening day. The new stadium boasts an additional 500,000 square feet and can seat 52,325 people.
Publications:
The Final Season: The Official Retrospective, Official Opening Day Game Program, New York Yankees Official Yearbook, Yankees Magazine, Official New York Yankees Media Guides, and The Stadium Magazine Box Set
Yankee Foundation:
Founded in 1973, the New York Yankee Foundation donates funds for educational and

recreational programs to youth organizations throughout New York.

OAKLAND ATHLETICS
OAKLAND ATHLETICS
7000 COLISEUM WAY
OAKLAND, CA 94621
510-638-4900
athletics.com
• David Kaval, President
• David Forst, General Manager
• Billy Beane, Executive VP, Baseball Operations
• Eric Kubota, Director, Scouting
• Catherine Aker, VP, Marketing & Communications
• John Fisher, Managing Partner
• David Rinetti, Vice President, Stadium Operations
• Kasey Jarcik, Senior Director, Finance
• Nick Paparesta, Head Athletic Trainer
• Miguel Duarte, Chief of Staff
• Ellis D'Lonra, VP, General Counsel
• Billy Owens, Assistant GM/Director of Player Personnel
• Ed Sprague, Director, Player Development
• Steve Fanelli, VP, Sales & Business Operations
Stadium:
Oakland-Alameda Coliseum, opened on September 8, 1966 and was renovated in 1995, which added 22,000 seats, 90 luxury suites, two private clubs and two state-of-the-art scoreboards.

SEATTLE MARINERS
T-MOBILE PARK
1250 FIRST AVENUE S
SEATTLE, WA 98134
206-346-4001
fanfeedback@mariners.mlb.com
mariners.com
• John Stanton, Chair, Managing Partner, Acting President & CEO
• Tim Kornegay, Executive VP & CFO
• Jerry Dipoto, Executive VP/General Manager
• Fred Rivera, Executive VP, General Counsel
• Kevin Martinez, Senior VP, Marketing & Communications
• Andy McKay, Director, Player Development
• Trevor Gooby, Senior VP, Ballpark Events & Operations
• Kyle Torgerson, Head Athletic Trainer
• Malcolm Rogel, VP, Ticket Operations & Event Services
Stadium:
Safeco Field, which first opened on July 15 1999, has gained a widespread reputation as a great place for the game of baseball and its fans. Everything from the views of downtown Seattle's skyline to the many different angles to watch baseball creates a memorable experience for the fans. In 2013 the outfield walls were moved in for the hitter's benefit.

TAMPA BAY RAYS
TROPICANA FIELD
ONE TROPICANA DRIVE
ST. PETERSBURG, FL 33705
888-326-7297
customerservice@raysbaseball.com
raysbaseball.com
• Stuart Sternberg, Principal Owner
• Matthew Silverman, President
• Brian Auld, President
• Erik Neander, Senior VP, Baseball Operations & General Manager
• Carlos Rodriguez, VP, Player Development & International Scouting
• Eric Weisberg, VP, Marketing and Creative Services
• John Higgins, Senior VP, Administation/General Counsel
• Melanie Lenz, Chief Development Officer
• Daveid Egles, Director, Community Engagement
• Dave Haller, VP, Communications
• Jim Previtera, Senior Director, Security &

Stadium Operations
• Robert Bennett, Director, Ticket Operations
• Rob Gagliardi, VP/Chief Financial Officer
Stadium:
Tropicana Field, renovated in 1996, added 319,000 additional square feet of space and was again renovated in 2006. Various renovations included new bathrooms, lighting, fixtures, wall treatments, new premium seating club, changes to the press box and much more.

TEXAS RANGERS
GLOBE LIFE PARK
1000 BALLPARK WAY
ARLINGTON, TX 76011
817-273-5222
texasrangers.com
• Jon Daniels, President, Baseball Operations
• Ray C. Davis, Chair/Managing Partner
• Neil Leibman, President, Business Operations & COO
• Bob R. Simpson, Chair, Executive Committee
• Chris Young, Executive VP, General Manager
• Joe Januszewski, Executive VP, Chief Revenue & Marketing Officer
• Ross Fensternaker, Senior Director, International & Pro Scouting
• Travis Dillon, VP, Marketing
• Rob Matwick, EVP, Business Operations
• Kellie Fischer, Executive VP/Chief Financial Officer
• Keith Meister, Team Physician
• Chuck Morgan, EVP, Ballpark Entertainment & Productions
• Josh King, VP, Ballpark Operations & Guest Services
• Mike Lentz, Director, Ticket Operations
Stadium:
Opened in 1994, Rangers Ballpark includes a baseball museum, a children's learning center, and a four-story office building within the ballpark. The ballpark has a seating capacity of 49,115.

TORONTO BLUE JAYS
ROGERS CENTRE
1 BLUE JAYS WAY
SUITE 3200
TORONTO, ON, CANADA M5V 1J1
416-341-1000
888-654-6529
bluejays.com
• Mark A. Shapiro, President & CEO
• Edward Rogers, Chairman, Toronto Blue Jays
• Ross Atkins, Exec. VP, Baseball Operations & General Manager
• Andrew Tinnish, VP, International Scouting
• Ben Sibley, Senior Manager, Marketing & Communications
• Marnie Starkman, Executive VP, Business Operations
Stadium:
Rogers Centre, a recently renovated stadium that includes the TD Comfort Clubhouse (Club 200 VIP), Acura Executive Lounge and the 400 Summit Suite. Seating capacity 46,095.

NATIONAL LEAGUE OF PROFESSIONAL BASEBALL CLUBS, THE
MLB ADVANCED MEDIA, L.P.
1271 AVENUE OF THE AMERICAS
NEW YORK, NY 10020
212-931-7800
www.mlb.com
• Rob Manfred, Commissioner
• Dan Halem, Chief Legal Officer & Deputy Commissioner
• Tony Reagins, Chief Baseball Development Officer
• Chris Marinak, chief Operations & Strategy Officer
• Patrick Courtney, Chief Communications Officer
• Bob Starkey, Chief Financial Officer
• Noah Garden, Chief Revenue Officer
  Description:
  The National League of Professional Baseball Clubs is the older of the two leagues constituting Major League Baseball in the

United States of America and Canada. (The other major league is the American League.) Beginning with the 1903 season, the regular season champions of the two leagues have met in the World Series. (The Series was not played in either 1904 or 1994).
Year Founded:
1876

Teams:

ARIZONA DIAMONDBACKS
CHASE FIELD
401 E JEFFERSON STREET
PHOENIX, AZ 85004
602-462-6500
dbacks.com
• Derrick Hall, CEO/President
• Mike Hazen, Executive VP/General Manager
• Sam Eaton, Director , Baseball Operations
• Jason Parks, Director, Professional Scouting
• Peter Wardell, Director, International Scouting
• Kenny Farrell, VP, Marketing & Analytics
• Cullen Maxey, Executive VP, Business Ops/Chief Revenue Officer
• John Fisher, Senior VP, Ticket Sales & Marketing
• Ryan Holmstedt, VP, Ticket Sales & Events
• Tom Harris, Executive VP/Chief Financial Officer
• Ken Kendrick, Managing General Partner
• Mike Chipman, General Partner
• Jeff Royer, General Partner
• Nona Lee, EVP/Chief Legal Officer
• Bob Zweig, VP, Chief Information Officer
• Patrick O'Connell, Director, Player & Media Relations
Stadium:
Chase Field. The most notable features of Chase Field are its signature swimming pool and its retractable roof. Since March 31, 1998, nearly 18 million fans have taken advantage of the opportunity to watch the Diamondbacks without the fear of getting rained on or worrying about the Phoenix heat. Stadium capacity, 49,033.

ATLANTA BRAVES
TRUIST PARK
755 BATTERY AVENUE
ATLANTA, GA 30339
404-522-7630
braves.com
• Derek Schiller, President/CEO
• Mike Plant, President/CEO
• Terry McGuirk, Chairman
• Alex Anthopoulos, President, Baseball Operations/General Manager
• Dana Brown, VP, Scouting
• Adam Zimmerman, Senior VP, Marketing
• Anthony Esposito, Senior Director, Ticket Operations
• Jill Robinson, Executive VP/Chief Financial Officer
• Scott Wald, Senior VP, Head Of Technology Services
• Tim Griffith, Head Team Physician
• Greg Heller, Executive VP/Chief Legal Officer
• DeRetta Rhodes, PhD, Executive VP, Chief People Capital Officer
• George C. Poulis, Director, Player Health/Head Athletic Trainer
Stadium:
The Braves played their final game at Turner Field on October 2 2016. They now play at Truist Park. Truist Park features the highest percentage of seats closer to the field than any other MLB ball park. The park also has air conditioning on evert level and LEDÃ†lights to provide better quality film for TV.
Publications:
Braves Beat; ChopTalk

CHICAGO CUBS
WRIGLEY FIELD
1060 W ADDISON STREET
CHICAGO, IL 60613

773-404-2827
800-347-2827
cubs.com
• Jed Hoyer, President, Baseball Operations
• Tom Ricketts, Chairman
• Alex Sugarman, Executive VP, Business Ops./Chief Strategy Officer
• Dan Kantrovitz, VP, Scouting
• Colin Faulkner, Executive VP, Sales & Marketing
• Crane Kenney, President, Business Operations
• Jon Greifenkamp, Executive VP, Chief Financial Officer
• Michael Lufrano, EVP, Community & Govt. Affairs/Chief Legal Officer
• Jason Carr, Director, Media Relations
• Jason McLeod, Senior VP, Player Personnel
• Matt Dorey, VP, Player Development
• Steve Inman, VP, Technology
• PJ Mainville, Head Athletic Trainer
• Stephen Adams, MD, Team Physician
Stadium:
Wrigley Field, built in 1914, is the second-oldest ballpark in the Major League behind Boston's Fenway Park (1912). In 2009, Wrigley Field will be playing host to Major League Baseball for the 96th season, and to the Cubs for the 94th year. Historic moments that have taken place in Wrigley Field include: Babe Ruth's 'called shot' during Game 3 of the 1932 World Series, Ernie Banks' 500th career home run on May 12, 1970, and Kerry Wood's 20-strikeout affair in 1998. Stadium capacity, 41,160.

CINCINNATI REDS
GREAT AMERICAN BALL PARK
100 JOE NUXHALL WAY
CINCINNATI, OH 45202
513-765-7000
reds.com
• Phillip J. Castellini, President/COO
• Robert H. Castellini, CEO
• W. Joseph Williams, Jr., Chairman
• Thomas L. Williams, Vice Chair
• Nick Krall, VP & General Manager
• Mark Edwards, Manager, Baseball Operations
• Karen Forgus, Senior VP, Business Operations
• Jacob Widerschein, Senior Director, Ticket Operations
• Doug Healy, Senior VP, Finance/Chief Financial Officer
• Rob Butcher, VP, Media Relations
• Jeff Graupe, Senior Director, Player Personnel
• Timothy Kremchek, Medical Director
Stadium:
Located on the winding banks of the Ohio River in downtown Cincinnati, Great American Ball Park serves as the home of the Cincinnati Reds, baseball's first professional franchise. The stadium first opened in 2003 and seats 42,941.

COLORADO ROCKIES
COORS FIELD
2001 BLAKE STREET
DENVER, CO 80205-2000
303-292-0200
rockies.com
• Richard L. Monfort, Owner/Chairman/CEO
• Charles K. Monfort, Owner/General Partner
• Jeff P. Bridich, Executive VP/General Manager
• Rolando Fernandez, VP, International Scouting & Development
• Brian Gaffney, VP, General Counsel
• Kevin H. Kahn, VP, Chief Customer Office, Ballpark Operations
• Jill Campbell, Vice President, Communications & Marketing
• Michael J. Kent, Vice President & Chief Financial Officer
• Gregory D. Feasel, Executive VP, Chief Operating Officer
• Hal Roth, Executive VP
• Paul Egins, Senior Director, Major League Operations
• Keith Dugger, Head Athletic Trainer
Stadium:
Opened in 1995, the 76-acre ballpark has been

a league leader in attendance every year since it has been open. Most of the seats in Coors Field are green, but the upper deck's 20th row is painted purple to signify exactly one mile above sea level. Stadium capacity, 50,445.

LOS ANGELES DODGERS
DODGER STADIUM
1000 VIN SCULLY AVENUE
LOS ANGELES, CA 90012
866-363-4377
dodgers.com
- Stan Kasten, CEO/President
- Mark Walter, Chairman/Owner
- Andrew Friedman, President, Baseball Operations
- David Finley, VP, Scouting
- Lon Rosen, Executive VP/Chief Marketing Officer
- Erik Braverman, SVP, Marketing, Communications & Broadcasting
- Tucker Kain, President, Business Enterprise
- Antonio Morici, Senior VP, Ticket Sales
- Seth Bluman, VP, Ticket Operations
- Eric Hernandez, VP, Finance
- Bob Wolfe, Executive VP/COO
- William Rhymes, Director, Player Development
- Ralph Esquibel, VP, Information Technology
Stadium:
Since 1962, the beauty of Dodger Stadium has awed spectators with a breath-taking view of downtown Los Angeles to the south; green, tree-lined Elysian hills to the north and east; and the San Gabriel Mountains beyond. The stadium's seating capacity is 56,000 which extends across the 300 acres of beautiful landscaping.

MIAMI MARLINS
MARLINS PARK
501 MARLINS WAY
MIAMI, FL 33125
305-480-1300
marlins.com
- Derek Jeter, CEO
- Bruce Sherman, Principal Owner/Chairman
- Caroline O'Connor, COO
- Kim Ng, General Manager
- Adam Jones, Chief Revenue Officer
- Gary Denbo, VP, Player Development & Scouting
- Juan Martinez, Director, Events & Promotions
- Mardi Dilger, Director, Ticket Operations
- Lee Kaplan, M.D., Medical Director
- Ashwin Krishnan, VP/General Counsel
- Andre Luck, VP, Sales and Services
Stadium:
In 2012, the Marlins opened a new stadium that is owned by Miami-Dade County. It is located on the historic site of the Old Orange Bowl in Miami's Little Havana section. The new stadium has a retractable roof, air conditioning and seats 37,000.

MILWAUKEE BREWERS
MILLER PARK
ONE BREWERS WAY
MILWAUKEE, WI 53214
414-902-4400
brewers.com
- Mark Attanasio, Chairman/Principal Owner
- Rick Schlesinger, President, Business Operations
- David Stearns, President, Baseball Operations
- Matt Arnold, Senior VP & General Manager
- Tod Johnson, VP, Domestic Scouting
- Sharon McNally, VP, Marketing
- Jim Bathey, VP, Ticket Sales
- Daniel Fumai, Chief Financial Officer
- Steve Ethier, Senior VP, Stadium Operations
- Doug Melvin, Special Assistant
- Marti Wronski, Senior VP/General Counsel
- Jason Hartlund, Chief Revenue Officer
- William Raasch, Head Team Physician
- Jake McKinley, Director, Player Development
Stadium:
On April 6, 2001 the Brewers' new state-of-the-art home, Miller Park, was officially opened for business. The signature fan-shaped convertible roof, a color replay board measuring 48 feet wide and 37 feet tall on top of a matrix scoreboard measuring 76-feet by 32-feet, and four choices of front-row seats on four different levels make Miller Park one of baseball's crown jewels. Seating capacity, 41,900.

NEW YORK METS
CITI FIELD
41 SEAVER WAY
QUEENS, NY 11368
718-507-8499
fanfeedback@mets.mlb.com
mets.com
- Sandy Alderson, President
- Steve Cohen, Owner, Chair & CEO
- Zack Scott, Acting General Manager
- Sue Lucchi, VP, Ballpark Operations
- Jill Grabill, Director, Marketing
- Vacant, VP, Ticket Sales & Services
- Mark Peskin, Chief Financial Officer
- David Newman, EVP, Chief Marketing, Content & Comms. Officer
- Vacant, COO
- Jeff Deline, Executive VP/Chief Revenue Officer
- John McKay, Executive Director, Security
- Kevin Howard, Executive Director, Player Development
Stadium:
The Mets played their first game in Citi Field on April 13, 2009, and features natural grass. Seats approximately 42,000 fans.

PHILADELPHIA PHILLIES
CITIZENS BANK PARK
ONE CITIZENS BANK WAY
PHILADELPHIA, PA 19148
215-463-6000
phillies.com
- Andy MacPhail, President
- John Middleton, Managing Partner
- Matt Klentak, Strategy & Development Officer
- Sam Fuld, General Manager & VP
- Mike Ondo, Director, Professional Scouting
- Kurt Funk, VP, Marketing Programs & Events
- John Weber, Senior VP, Ticket Operations & Projects
- John Nickolas, Senior VP/Chief Financial Officer
- Bonnie Clark, VP, Communications
- Frank Bowens, Manager, Ballpark Operations
- Rick Strouse, Senior VP/General Counsel
- David Buck, Executive VP
- Josh Bonifay, Director, Player Development
- Michael G. Ciccotti, Director, Medical Services
Stadium:
The 43,500 seat, state-of-the-art Citizens Bank Park is the ultimate baseball and entertainment experience. Featuring natural grass and a dirt playing field, a scenic view of the Philadelphia skyline, an open-air atmosphere and more, the Ballpark is an exciting destination for all fans.

PITTSBURGH PIRATES
PNC PARK
115 FEDERAL STREET
PITTSBURGH, PA 15212
412-321-2827
800-BUY-BUCS
pirates.com
- Travis Williams, President
- Bob Nutting, Chairman
- Ben Cherington, Executive VP/General Manager
- Will Lawton, Director, Baseball Operations & Pro Scouting
- Steve Williams, Senior Director, Player Personnel
- Joe DelliCarri, Senior Director, Amateur Scouting
- Bryan Stroh, Senior VP, Baseball Development
- Dan Hart, Director, Media Relations
- Steve Williams, Senior Director, Player Personnel
- Todd Tomczyk, Director, Sports Medicine
- Jim Plake, Executive VP/Chief Financial Officer
- Patrick DeMeo, Medical Director
- Stephen Perkins, Executive VP, Marketing & Fan Engagement
Stadium:
PNC Park, which opened in spring 2001, is a classic-style ballpark, an intimate facility that embraces the progressiveness of Pittsburgh while saluting the spirit of early ballpark originals such as Forbes Field, Wrigley Field and Fenway Park. Seating capacity 38,496.

SAN DIEGO PADRES
PETCO PARK
100 PARK BOULEVARD
SAN DIEGO, CA 92101
619-795-5555
tickets@padres.com
padres.com
- Erik Greupner, CEO
- Peter Seidler, Chair
- Ron Fowler, Vice Chair
- A.J. Preller, President, Baseball Operations & General Manager
- Nick Ennis, Director, Baseball Operations
- Pete DeYoung, Director, Professional Scouting
- Mark Rogow, Head Athletic Trainer
- Mark Guglielmo, Senior VP, Ballpark Operations
- Chris James, VP, Finance
- Jim Kiersnowski, Senior Director, Ticket Operations
- Curt Waugh, VP, Ticket Sales & Services
- Sam Geaney, Senior Director, Player Development
- Ray Chan, VP, Information Technology
Stadium:
PETCO Park is spectacular in every way, combining the best sight lines in baseball with breathtaking views of San Diego. Architecturally magnificent, it celebrates the sea, the sky, the natural beauty, cultural diversity and unique spirit of our region. Innovative design features evoke the timeless traditions of baseball in an intimate setting, with state-of-the-art fan amenities to suit every taste and budget. Seating capacity 42,445.

SAN FRANCISCO GIANTS
ORACLE PARK
24 WILLIE MAYS PLAZA
SAN FRANCISCO, CA 94107
415-972-2000
customerservice@sfgiants.com
sfgiant.com
- Laurence Baer, President/CEO
- Bill Schlough, Senior VP/Chief Information Officer
- Scott Harris, General Manager
- Farhan Zaidi, President, Baseball Operations
- Zack Minasian, Director, Professional Scouting
- Danny Dann, VP, Marketing & Advertising
- Mario Alioto, Executive VP, Business Operations
- Russ Stanley, Senior VP, Ticket Sales & Services
- Shana Daum, SVP, Community Relations & Public Affairs
- Gene Telucci, VP, Ballpark Operations
- Lisa Pantages, Senior VP/Chief Financial Officer
- Kyle Haines, Director, Player Development
- Amy Tovar, Senior VP & General Counsel
- Maria Jacinto, Senior Director, Broadcasting Services
- Jeff Tucker, VP, Ticket Sales & Premium Seating
Stadium:
Opened in 2000, Oracle Park features a 9-foot statue of the legendary Willie Mays at the entrance, an 80-foot Coca-Cola bottle with playground slides and a mini AT&T Park that attracts children of all ages. Seating capacity 41,503.

ST. LOUIS CARDINALS
BUSCH STADIUM
700 CLARK STREET
ST. LOUIS, MO 63102
314-345-9600
guestservices@cardinals.mlb.com
cardinals.com
- William O. DeWitt, III, President
- William O. DeWitt, Jr., Chairman/CEO
- Mike Girsch, VP/General Manager
- John Mozeliak, President, Baseball Operations
- Dan Farrell, Senior VP, Sales/Marketing
- Brian Bartow, Director, Communications
- Matt Gifford, VP, Stadium Operations
- Mike Whittle, Senior VP/General Counsel
- Dan Good, VP, Business Development
- Adam Olson, Director, Medical Operations/Head Athletic Trainer
- Brad Wood, Senior VP/CFO
Stadium
On April 10, 2006, the Cardinals opened their new 46,000 seat retro-style downtown ballpark with a 6-4 win over the Milwaukee Brewers. The Cardinals also became the first team in almost 100 years to win a World Series Championship in the inaugural season of a new ballpark. The new Busch Stadium hosted the 80th MLB All-Star Game, in July 2009.

WASHINGTON NATIONALS
NATIONALS PARK
1500 SOUTH CAPITOL STREET SE
WASHINGTON, DC 20003
202-675-6287
ticketinfo@nationals.com
nationals.com
- Theodore N. Lerner, Founding Principal Owner
- Mark D. Lerner, Managing Principal Owner
- Mike Rizzo, General Manager/President, Baseball Operations
- Kris Kline, Assistant General Manager/VP, Scouting Operations
- Jacqueline Coleman, SVP, Marketing, Broadcasting & Game Presentation
- Ryan Bringger, VP, Ticket Sales & Services
- Thomas Kildahl, Senior Director, Ticket Operations
- Ted Towne, Assistant General Manager/VP, Finance
- Jennifer Giglio, Senior VP, Chief Communications Officer
- Jake Burns, Executive VP, Business Operations
- Elise Holman, Senior Vice President
- Alan Gottlieb, Chief Operating Officer, Lerner Sports
- Harvey Sharman, Executive Director, Medical Services
- Doug Harris, VP, Player Personnel/Assistant General Manager
- Lori Creasy, Chief Financial Officer/Partner
Stadium:
Opened in 2008, the new Nationals Park achieved its goal to become the first major baseball stadium in the United States accredited as LEED Certified. The ballpark is equipped with state-of-the-art technology, and the exterior was designed to reflect the architecture of Washington, D.C. Seating capacity 41,888.

Baseball, Professional Leagues/Teams: Minor

AMERICAN ASSOCIATION OF INDEPENDENT PROFESSIONAL BASEBALL
1415 HWY 54 WEST
SUITE 210
DURHAM, NC 27707
919-401-8150
Fax: 919-401-8152
www.americanassociationbaseball.com

- Miles Wolff, Commissioner
- Dan Moushon, President
- Kevin Winn, Director of Umpires
Nature of Service:
Independent Professional Baseball League
Teams: 12
Fargo-Moorhead RedHawks, Sioux Falls Canaries, St. Paul Saints, Winnipeg Goldeyes, Gary SouthShore RailCats, Kansas City T-Bones, Lincoln Saltdogs, Sioux City Explorers, Laredo Lemurs, Joplin Blasters, Wichita Wingnuts, Texas Amarillo/Grand Prairie. Founded in 2005.

APPALACHIAN LEAGUE (ADVANCED ROOKIE)
759 182ND AVENUE EAST
REDINGTON SHORES, FL 33708
727-954-4876
www.milb.com/index.jsp?sid=l120
- Lee Landers, President/Treasurer
- Bobbi Landers, League Administrator
- David Lane, Corporate Secretary
Description:
The Appalachian League was founded in 1911 with teams in Asheville, NC; Bristol, VA; Cleveland, TN; Johnson City, TN; Knoxville, TN; and Morristown, TN. After four years, the league disbanded and reformed seven years later with only six teams. Again, that league managed to last midway through 1925 before disbanding. In 1937, the league re-formed with teams in Elizabethtown, TN; Johnson City, TN; Newport, TN; and Pennington Gap, VA. Twenty years later, in 1957, the modern Appalachian League began its first year as a short-season baseball league.
Teams: 10
Currently, the Appalachian League has 10 teams.

Teams:

BLUEFIELD BLUE JAYS
BOWEN FIELD
STADIUM DRIVE
PO BOX 365
BLUEFIELD, WV 24701
304-324-1326
Fax: 304-324-1318
www.milb.com/index.jsp?sid=t517
- George McGonagle, President
Ballpark:
Bowen Field. Seating capacity, 3,000.
MLB Affiliation:
Toronto Blue Jays
Years in League:
1946-55; 1957-Present

BRISTOL PIRATES
BOYCE COX FIELD
BOX 1434
BRISTOL, VA 24203
276-206-9946
Fax: 276-669-7686
www.milb.com/index.jsp?sid=t557
- Mark Young, Vice President of Community Relations
- Edgar Varela, Manager
Ballpark:
Boyce Cox Field at Devault Memorial Stadium, built in 1969, has a seating capacity of 2,000. It is in a city sports complex that also includes an immaculate football field.
Affiliate:
Chicago White Sox
Years in League:
1921-25; 1940-55; 1969-Present

BURLINGTON ROYALS
BURLINGTON ATHLETIC STADIUM
1450 GRAHAM STREET
BURLINGTON, NC 27217
336-222-0223
Fax: 336-226-2498
info@burlingtonroyals.com
www.milb.com/index.jsp?sid=t483
- Miles Wolff, President
- Ryan Keur, General Manager
- Mikie Morrison, Director of Operations
Ballpark:
Burlington Athletic Stadium first opened in 1958 and it has a seating capacity of 3,500.
Official Charities:
Stephen K. Gates Scholarship Fund.
Affiliate:
Kansas City Royals

DANVILLE BRAVES
AMERICAN LEGION POST 325 AT DANIEL MEMORIAL PARK
302 RIVER PARK DRIVE
DANVILLE, VA 24540
434-797-3792
Fax: 423-797-3799
danvillebraves@braves.com
www.milb.com/index.jsp?sid=t429
- David Cross, General Manager
- Bob Kitzmiller, Assistant General Manager
Ballpark:
Legion Field is the second largest in the Appalachian League. With a seating capacity of 2,588, it hosted 39,063 fans last season.
Affiliate:
Atlanta Braves
Years in League:
1993 - Present

ELIZABETHTON TWINS
208 NORTH HOLLY LANE
ELIZABETHTON, TN 37643
423-547-6441
Fax: 423-547-6442
www.milb.com/index.jsp?sid=t576
- Jim Rantz, Director
- Harold Mains, President
- Mike Mains, General Manager
- Ray Smith, Manager
Ballpark:
Joe O'Brien Stadium was built in 1974 and has a seating capacity of 1,500. The field was named after O'Brien, a longtime supporter of Elizabethton baseball and the E-Twins' first board chairman, in 1980. In 1996, significant upgrades were made to the ballpark, including new locker rooms and a new reserved seating section behind the plate.
Affiliate:
Minnesota Twins
Years in League:
1937-42; 1945-51; 1974-Present

GREENEVILLE ASTROS
PIONEER PARK
135 SHILOH ROAD
PO BOX 5192
GREENEVILLE, TN 37743
423-638-0411
Fax: 423-638-9450
greeneville@astros.com
www.milb.com/index.jsp?sid=t413
- David Lane, General Manager
- Hunter Reed, Assistant General Manager
- Jim Crane, Owner and Chairman
- Reid Ryan, President, Business Operations
- Quinton McCracken, Director of Player Personnel
Ballpark:
Pioneer Park seats 2,572 fans and is owned by Tusculum College.
Affiliate:
Houston Astros
Years in League:
1988-Present

single sports

JOHNSON CITY CARDINALS
510 BERT STREET
JOHNSON CITY, TN 37601
423-461-4866
Fax: 423-461-4864
www.milb.com/index.jsp?sid=t438
• John Vuch, Director
• Tyler Parsons, General Manager
• Lee Sowers, President
• Chris Swauger, Manager
Ballpark:
Howard Johnson Field goes all the way back to 1923, although the current stadium structure went up in the 1950s. It's a city park which hosts both East Tennessee State University and the Johnson City Cardinals of the rookie-level Appalachian League. The field is a respectable size, with a right-field berm making balls to the wall very interesting (at least one fielder fell down playing the ball up the berm and off the wall).
Affiliate:
St. Louis Cardinals
Years in League:
1921-24; 1937-55; 1957-61; 1964-Present

KINGSPORT METS
HUNTER WRIGHT STADIUM
800 GRANBY ROAD
KINGSPORT, TN 37660
423-224-2626
Fax: 423-224-2625
info@kmets.com
www.milb.com/index.jsp?sid=t506
• Brian Paupeck, General Manager
• Josh Lawson, Tickets and Merchandise
Ballpark:
Hunter Wright Stadium opened in 1995 and has a 2,000 seating capacity.
Affiliate:
New York Mets
Years in League:
1921-25; 1938-52; 1957; 1960-63; 1969-82; 1984-Present

PRINCETON RAYS
H.P. HUNNICUTT FIELD
OLD BLUEFIELD RD
PRINCETON, WV 24740
304-487-2000
Fax: 304-487-8762
raysball@sunlitsurf.com
www.milb.com/index.jsp?sid=t455
• Mori Williams, President
• Jim Holland, General Manager
• Danny Scheaffer, Manager
Ballpark:
H.P. Hunnicutt Field. Seating capacity, 1,700.
Affiliate:
Tampa Bay Rays
Years in League:
1988-present

PULASKI YANKEES
CALFEE PARK
700 SOUTH WASHINGTON AVENUE
PULASKI, VA 24301
540-980-1070
Fax: 540-980-1850
info@pulaskiyankees.net
www.milb.com/index.jsp?sid=t425
• Randy Lavone, President/General Manager
• Jose Moreno, Manager
Ballpark:
Calfee Park, the ninth oldest professional minor-league Baseball Park in use in America, offers a nice, fan-friendly atmosphere for watching the game, and recent improvements are now complete. In addition to the new club house, Calfee Park features a new home team dugout, new grandstands, a new reserverd seating section with handicap accessibility, open air corporate box suite with patio tables and chairs, new lighting, underground watering and drainage system, concession area , parking lots and entrance.
Affiliate:
NY Yankees

ARIZONA FALL LEAGUE (ROOKIE LEVEL)
10201 S. 51ST ST, STE 230
PHOENIX, AZ 85044-3217
480-496-6700
Fax: 480-496-6384
mlb.com/mlb/events/afl/index.jsp
• Steve Cobb, Executive Vice President
• Joan McGrath, Office Administration
Description:
Owned and operated by the MLB and attracts many of the Minor League top prospects. The roots of the Arizona Fall League go back several years, when the Major Leagues wanted to create an easily accessible off-season league. There's a two-pronged mission to the AFL; one is for the players to accelerate, and hopefully jump a classification. The other is for the managers and umpires to develop.
Number of Teams:
6
Founded:
1992

Teams:

GLENDALE DESERT DOGS
CAMELBACK RANCH
10710 WEST CAMELBACK ROAD
PHOENIX, AZ 85037
623-302-5000
Fax: 623-877-8582
• Lance Parrish, Manager
Ballpark:
Camelback Ranch seats 10,500 fans and features a natural grass field.
MLB Affiliates:
Atlants Braves, Miami Marlins, Milwaukee Brewers, Oakland Athletics, Tampa Bay Rays.

MESA SOLAR SOX
SLOAN PARK
2330 WEST RIO SALADO PARKWAY
MESA, AZ 85201
480-668-0500
• Mark Johnson, Manager
• Steve Connelly, Pitching Coach
• Dan DeMent, Hitting Coach
Ballpark:
Sloan Park. Seating capacity, 15,000.
MLB Affiliations:
Baltimore Orioles, Chicago Cubs, Detroit Tigers, Houston Astros, Los Angeles Dodgers.

PEORIA JAVELINAS
PEORIA SPORTS COMPLEX
16101 NORTH 83RD AVENUE
PEORIA, AZ 85382
623-226-8000
Fax: 623-486-4366
• Rod Barajas, Manager
Ballpark:
Peoria Sports Complex seats 11,333 and is home to both the San Diego Padres and the Seattle Mariners.
MLB Affiliates:
San Diego Padres, Seattle Mariners, Minnesota Twins, Cincinnati Reds, Philadelphia Phillies.

SALT RIVER RAFTERS
SALT RIVER FIELDS AT TACKING STICK
7555 N. PRIMA RD
SCOTTSDALE, AZ 85258
480-270-5000
• Tripp Keister, Manager
Ballpark:
Salt River Field seats a capacity of 11,000 and features a natural grass field.
MLB Affiliates:
Arizona Diamondbacks, Chicago White Sox, Colorado Rockies, Toronto Blue Jays, Washington Nationals.

SCOTTSDALE SCORPIONS
SCOTTSDALE STADIUM
7408 EAST OSBORN ROAD
SCOTTSDALE, AZ 85251
480-941-1930
Fax: 480-941-3060
• Matt Quatraro, Manager
Ballpark:
Scottsdale Stadium is located in the middle of scenic downtown and a short walk from a wide selection of restaurants, clubs and galleries. Scottsdale Stadium is home to some of Scottsdale's most celebrated occasions including Cactus League Spring Training, Arizona Fall League, and a series of year-round meetings and events.
MLB Affiliates:
Cleveland Indians, Los Angeles Angels of Anaheim, New York Yankees, Pittsburgh Pirates, San Francisco Giants.

SURPRISE SAGUAROS
SURPRISE STADIUM
15930 NORTH BULLARD AVENUE
SURPRISE, AZ 85374
623-594-5600
• Carlos Subero, Manager
Ballpark:
Surprise Stadium seats 10,714 fans and has a natural grass field.
MLB Affiliates:
Boston Red Sox, Kansas City Royals, New York Mets, St. Louis Cardinals, Texas Rangers.

ARIZONA LEAGUE (ROOKIE)
9550 16TH STREET NORTH
ST. PETERSBURG, FL 33716
727-822-6937
Fax: 727-821-5819
www.milb.com/index.jsp?sid=l121
• Robert Richmond, President/Treasurer
• Bobby Evans, Vice President
• Ted Polakowski, Corporate Secretary
Number of Teams:
13
Publications:
Baseball AZ
Number of Games:
56
Player Eligibility:
No more than eight players 20 or older, and no more than two players 21 or older. At least 10 pitchers. No more than two years of prior service, excluding Rookie leagues outside the United States and Canada.

Teams:

ARIZONA ANGELS
TEMPE DIABLO STADIUM
2200 WEST ALAMEDA DRIVE
TEMPE, AZ 85282
480-858-7555
Fax: 480-858-7550
• Elio Sarmiento, Manager
Affiliate Team:
Los Angeles Angels of Anaheim.

ARIZONA ATHLETICS
FITCH PARK
ONE EAST 8TH STREET
MESA, AZ 85211
480-644-2711
• Webster Garrison, Manager
Affiliate Team:
Oakland Athletics

ARIZONA BREWERS
MARYVALE BASEBALL PARK
3600 NORTH 51ST AVENUE
PHOENIX, AZ 85031
623-245-5500

• Nestor Corredor, Manager
• Steve Cline, Pitching Coach
Affiliation:
MLB Milwaukee Brewers

ARIZONA CUBS
SLOAN PARK
2330 WEST RIO SOLADO PARKWAY
MESA, AZ 85201
480-668-0500
• Ricardo Medina, Manager
Affiliate Team:
Chicago Cubs

ARIZONA DIAMONDBACKS
SALT RIVER FIELDS AT TALKING STICK
7555 NORTH PIMA ROAD
SCOTTSDALE, AZ 85258
480-270-5000
• Hector de la Cruz, Manager
Ballpark:
Salt River Fields at Talking Stick.

ARIZONA DODGERS
CAMELBACK RANCH
10712 WEST CAMELBACK ROAD
PHOENIX, AZ 85037
623-302-5000
• Jack McDowell, Manager
Ballpark:
Camelback Ranch
Affiliate Team:
Los Angeles Dodgers

ARIZONA GIANTS
SCOTTSDALE STADIUM
7408 EAST OSBORN ROAD
SCOTTSDALE, AZ 85251
480-312-2586
Fax: 480-990-2349
• Mike Goff, Manager
Affiliates:
San Francisco Giants

ARIZONA INDIANS
PLAYER DEVELOPMENT COMPLEX
2601 SOUTH WOOD BOULEVARD
GOODYEAR, AZ 85338
623-302-5678
• Anthony Medrano, Manager
Affiliate:
Cleveland Indians.

ARIZONA MARINERS
PEORIA SPORTS COMPLEX
16101 NORTH 83RD AVENUE
PEORIA, AZ 85382
623-776-4818
• Darrin Garner, Manager
Affiliates:
Seattle Mariners.

ARIZONA PADRES
PEORIA SPORTS COMPLEX
16101 NORTH 83RD AVENUE
PEORIA, AZ 85382
623-412-4020
Fax: 623-487-1190
• Anthony Contreras, Manager
Affiliate Team:
San Diego Padres

ARIZONA RANGERS
SURPRISE STADIUM
15930 NORTH BULLARD AVENUE
SURPRISE, AZ 85374
623-222-2222
• Matt Siegel, Manager
Affiliate Team:
Texas Rangers

ARIZONA REDS
GOODYEAR BALLPARK
1933 SOUTH BALLPARK WAY
GOODYEAR, AZ 85338
623-882-3120
• Jose Nieves, Manager
Ballpark:
Goodyear Stadium
Affiliates:
Cincinnati Reds

ARIZONA ROYALS
SURPRISE STADIUM
15930 NORTH BULLARD AVENUE
SURPRISE, AZ 85374
623-222-2222
• Darryl Kennedy, Manager
Home Field:
Surprise Stadium

ARIZONA WHITE SOX
CAMELBACK RANCH
10712 WEST CAMELBACK ROAD
PHOENIX, AZ 85037
623-302-5000
Fax: 623-266-8032
• Tim Esmay, Manager
Affiliate Team:
Chicago White Sox

ATLANTIC LEAGUE OF PROFESSIONAL BASEBALL, THE
P.O. BOX 5190
LANCASTER, PA 17606
720-389-6992
suggestions@atlanticleague.com
www.atlanticleague.com
• Frank Boulton, Founder/Chairman
• Rick White, President
• Joe Klein, Vice President On-Field Operations
• Emily Merrill, League Administrator
Description:
The Atlantic League was created by seasoned professional baseball executives to bridge gaps in professional baseball palyer development. The atlantic League is funded by membership fees and dues. Founded in 1998, the Atlantic League has sent over 800 players to major league baseball organizations.
Number of Teams:
8
Year Founded:
1998

Teams:

BRIDGEPORT BLUEFISH
HARBOR YARD
500 MAIN STREET
BRIDGEPORT, CT 06604
203-345-4800 EXT 108
Fax: 203-345-4830
info@bridgeportbluefish.com
www.bridgeportbluefish.com
• Frank Boulton, Chief Executive Officer
• Jamie Toole, General Manager
• Drew LaBoy, Director of Ticket Sales/Operations
Ballpark:
The Bluefish are privileged to be playing baseball at The Ballpark at Harbor Yard. The $19 million ballpark was constructed in 1997-1998 and was funded though a combination of public and team contributions. It has a seating capacity of 5,500, with optional standing room admittance of 200 more for sold-out games.

LANCASTER BARNSTORMERS
CLIPPER MAGAZINE STADIUM
650 NORTH PRINCE STREET
LANCASTER, PA 17603
717-509-4487
Fax: 717-509-4486
info@lancasterbarnstormers.com
www.lancasterbarnstormers.com
• Jon Danos, President
• Kristen Simon, General Manager
• Don Pryer, Director, Stadium Operations
• Bob Ford, Director, Business Development
• Butch Hobson, Manager
Ballpark:
The stadium opened in May 2005 and is located in downtown Lancaster on a triangular plot of land bordered by North Prince Street and Harrisburg Pike.

LONG ISLAND DUCKS
BETHPAGE BALLPARK
3 COURT HOUSE DRIVE
CENTRAL ISLIP, NY 11722
631-940-3825
Fax: 631-940-3800
www.liducks.com
• Frank Boulton, Founder/CEO
• Seth Waugh, Owner
• Bud Harrelson, Owner
• Mike Pfaff, President and General Manager
Ballpark:
Opened in 2000, Bethpage Ballpark is a 6,002 seat state-of-the-art facility that is home to the Long Island Ducks. Among its many features are 20 luxury suites, spacious seating, and an indoor batting tunnel.

NEW BRITAIN BEES
NEW BRITAIN CITY HALL
27 WEST MAIN STREET
NEW BRITAIN, CT 06051
860-826-2337
info@nbbees.com
www.nbbees.com
• Frank Boulton, Principal Owner
• Katie Force, Promotions & Community Relations Coordinator
Ballpark:
The New Britain Stadium opened in 1996, and has a seating capacity of 6,146. The stadium contains skyboxes and split-level seating.

SOMERSET PATRIOTS
TD BANK BALLPARK
1 PATRIOTS PARK
BRIDGEWATER, NJ 08807
908-252-0700
Fax: 908-252-0776
patriots@somersetpatriots.com
www.somersetpatriots.com
• Steve Kalafer, Chairman
• Josh Kalafer, Vice Chairman
• Patrick McVerry, President/General Manager
• Dave Marek, Senior Vice President, Marketing
• Bryan Iwicki, Vice President of Operations
• Marc Russinoff, Vice President of Public Relations
• Matt Kopas, Vice President of Ticketing
• Kevin Fleming, Director, Sales
• Brett Jodie, Manager
Ballpark:
TD Bank Park opened its gates on June 7, 1999 for the first ever Somerset Patriots home game. The 6,100 seat ballpark is a multi-use facility that is the home of the Big East Baseball Championship Tournament and County Baseball Tournaments during the season. In the off-season, the ballpark is the site of the Big Apple Circus and the New Jersey State Fair.
Description:
Provides family affordable entertainment in a beautiful ballpark, with professional Minor League Baseball.

SOUTHERN MARYLAND BLUE CRABS
REGENCY FURNITURE STADIUM
11765 SAINT LINUS DRIVE
WALDORF, MD 20602
301-638-9788
Fax: 301-638-9877
info@somdbluecrabs.com
www.somdbluecrabs.com
• Patrick Day, General Manager
• Carlton Silverstro, Box Office Manager
• Alexandra Wohlenhaus, Office Manager
• Theresa Coffey, Finance Manager
• Candace Gick, Director of Sponsorship
• Samantha Slovik, Client Service Manager
• Stan Cliburn, Manager
Ballpark:
With a 6,000 seat capacity, Regency Furniture Stadium offers a full range of family-oriented features and attractions. A large, catered picnic area and amusement area for kids of all ages ensure a memorable experience for everyone. The ballpark also accomodates football, soccer, lacrosse and other sporting events.

SUGAR LAND SKEETERS
CONSTELLATION FIELD
101 STADIUM DRIVE
SUGARLAND, TX 77498
281-240-4487
Fax: 281-240-4550
www.sugarlandskeeters.com
• Gary Gaetti, Manager
• Miller Jay, President
Stadium:
Constellation Field seats 7,500 fans.

YORK REVOLUTION
SANTANDER STADIUM
5 BROOKS ROBINSON WAY
YORK, PA 17401
717-801-4487
Fax: 717-801-4499
ask@yorkrevolution.com
www.yorkrevolution.com
• Eric Menzer, President
(717) 801-4481
• John Gibson, General Manager
• Lori Brunson, Vice President of Finance
(717) 801-4483
lbrunson@yorkrevolution.com
• Cindy Brown, Director of Ticketing
• Mark Mason, Manager
Ballpark:
Owned by the York County Industrial Development Authority. Offers a full range of family friendly features and attractions, including a large catered picnic area overlooking the field and a fantastic amusement area for kids of all ages.
Seating Capacity:
7,312

CALIFORNIA LEAGUE (A-LEVEL)
3600 SOUTH HARBOR BOULEVARD
SUITE 122
OXNARD, CA 93035
805-985-8585
Fax: 805-985-8580
info@californialeague.com
www.californialeague.com
• Charlie Blaney, President
• Tom Volpe, Vice President
• Matt Blaney, Director of Operations and Marketing
Year Founded:
1941
League Description:
Founded by a group of Major and Pacific Coast League Clubs.
Player Eligibility:
No more than two players and one player-coach on the active list may have more than six years of experience.

Number of Teams:
10

Teams:

BAKERSFIELD BLAZE
SAM LYNN BALLPARK
4009 CHESTER AVENUE
BAKERSFIELD, CA 93301
661-716-4487
Fax: 661-322-6199
• Elizabeth Martin, General Manager
• Mike Candela, Assistant General Manager
Ballpark:
The 58-year old ballpark, Sam Lynn Ballpark, was named after Sam Lynn, the owner of the Coca-Cola bottling plant in Bakersfield during the 1930s.
Affiliate:
Cincinnati Reds

HIGH DESERT MAVERICKS
MAVERICKS STADIUM
12000 STADIUM WAY
ADELANTO, CA 92301
760-246-6287
Fax: 760-246-3197
info@hdmavs.com
• Ben Hemmen, General Manager
• Sarah Bosso, Assistant General Manager
• David Barry, Director of Tickets and Finance
• Ryan Cowan, Head Groundskeeper
Ballpark:
Stater Brothers Stadium has a seating capacity of 3,808, plus grass seating. Opened in 1991.
Affiliate:
Seattle Mariners

INLAND EMPIRE 66ERS
SAN MANUEL STADIUM
280 SOUTH EAST STREET
SAN BERNADINO, CA 92401
909-888-9922
Fax: 909-888-5251
info@ie66ers.com
www.66ers.com
• David Elmore, Co-Owner
• Donna F Tuttle, Co-Owner
• Ryan English, Assistant General Manager
• Joe Hudson, General Manager
• Ryan English, Assistant General Manager
Team History:
San Bernardino's single-A minor league baseball team in the California League, formerly known as the Stampede, has won league championships in 1995, 1999, 2000, 2003 and 2006. They became just the fourth team in California League history to win back-back titles when they won the crown in 2000
Ballpark:
San Manuel Stadium seats 5,000, with grass seating that can comfortably accomodate more fans. The ballpark boasts 12 skyboxes, each with its own private outdoor balcony, two large outdoor picnic areas and the only high-tech scoreboard featuring full-color video in the California League
Affiliate:
LA Angels

LAKE ELSINORE STORM
500 DIAMOND DRIVE
LAKE ELSINORE, CA 92531
951-245-4487
Fax: 951-245-0305
• Gary Jacobs, Owner
• Len Simon, Owner
• David Oster, Owner/President
(951) 245-4487
doster@stormbaseball.com
• Raj Narayanan, General Manager/Director of Sales
• Mark Beskid, Assistant General Manager
• Tim Arseneau, Director of Operations
Ballpark:
Lake Elsinore Diamond is a state of the art baseball park that is continually voted as one of

the finest parks in all of Minor League Baseball. The park has 6,066 fixed seats, 11 luxury suites and a grass berm seating area on the right field line - allowing over 8,000 fans to take in a night or afternoon of Storm baseball.
Affiliate:
San Diego Padres

LANCASTER JETHAWKS
THE HANGAR
45116 VALLEY CENTRAL WAY
LANCASTER, CA 93536
661-726-5400
• Jake Kerr, Owner
• Jeff Mooney, Owner
• Andy Dunn, President
• Will Thornhill, General Manager
Ballpark:
Clear Channel Stadium has a seating capacity of 4,600 and was opened in April of 1996.
Affiliate:
Houston Astros

MODESTO NUTS
JOHN THURMAN FIELD
601 NEECE DRIVE
MODESTO, CA 95351
209-572-4487
Fax: 209-572-4490
fun@modestonuts.com
• Mike Gorrasi, Executive Vice President
• Fred Ocasio, Manager
• Ed Mack, Vice President - HWS Beverage
• Chris Ganoe, Operations Manager
Ballpark:
John Thurman Field has a seating capacity of 4,000 and opened in 1955. It was renovated in 1997.
Affiliate:
Colorado Rockies.

RANCHO CUCAMONGA QUAKES
LOANMART FIELD
8408 ROCHESTER AVENUE
RANCHO CUCAMONGA, CA 91730
909-481-5000
Fax: 909-481-5005
www.rcquakes.com
• Grant Riddle, Vice President/General Manager
• Brent Miles, President
• Monica Ortega, Vice President/Tickets
• Linda Rathfon, Assistant GM/Group Sales
(909) 481-5000
lrathfon@rcquakes.com
• Bill Haselman, Manager
Ballpark:
The Epicenter has recently undergone a seating renovation project that began in September of 2008. The renovations are complete, making the stadium look brand new.
Team History:
The Rancho Cucamonga Quakes have been playing top-notch Minor League ball since 1993 the franchise has been around for over 28 years, since 1966.
Affiliate:
Los Angeles Dodgers

SAN JOSE GIANTS
588 EAST ALMA AVENUE
SAN JOSE, CA 95112
408-297-1435
Fax: 408-297-1453
info@sjgiants.com
• Daniel Orum, President/Chief Executive Officer
• Mark Wilson, General Manager, Chief Operating Officer
• Juliana Paoli, Chief Marketing Officer
juliana@sjgiants.com
• Linda Pereira, Director of Player Personnel
lindapereira@sjgiants.com
• Lance Motch, Vice President of Ballpark Operations
lancemotch@sjgiants.com
• Jacquie Stuart, Ticket Operations Manager
• Russ Morman, Manager

Ballpark:
With a seating capacity of 2,900 it was built as part of Franklin Roosevelt's Works Progress Administration (WPA), Municipal Stadium was built for a total cost of $80,000 in 1942.
Affiliate:
San Francisco Giants

STOCKTON PORTS
BANNER ISLAND BALLPARK
404 WEST FREMONT STREET
STOCKTON, CA 95203
209-644-1900
Fax: 209-644-1931
info@stocktonports.com
www.stocktonports.com
• Pat Filippone, President
• Bryan Meadows, General Manager
• Tim Pollack, Director of Tickets
• Rick Magnante, Manager
Ballpark:
Banner Island Ballpark
Affiliate:
Oakland A's.
Team History:
The Stockton Ports didn't come into play until 1941 as the Ports were one of the founding members of the California League. Over the course of the Ports 55 years as a member of the California League, they have won 10 titles and have posted the highest winning percentage in Cal League history with a .527 mark.

VISALIA RAWHIDE
RECREATION PARK
300 NORTH GIDDINGS STREET
VISALIA, CA 93291
559-732-4433
Fax: 559-739-7732
info@rawhidebaseball.com
• Kevin O'Malley, Owner
• Tom Seidler, President
• Jennifer Pendergraft, General Manager
Ballpark:
A city park named Recreation Park, the stadium itself does not have its own name. An all-wood structure stood on the current site before the existing stadium was built in 1967.
Affiliate:
Arizona Diamondbacks

CAN-AM LEAGUE
610 YOUNT DR
DAYTON, OH 45433
862-283-5935
• Miles Wolff, Commissioner
Description:
The Can-Am league, also known as the Canadian-American Association of Professional Baseball, operates in cities where the major and minor leagues do not operate.

CAROLINA LEAGUE (A-LEVEL)
1806 PEMBROKE ROAD
SUITE 2B
GREENSBORO, NC 27408
336-691-9030
Fax: 336-464-2737
office@carolinaleague.com
www.carolinaleague.com
• Steve Bryant, Executive Vice President
• Ken Young, Secretary
• Marnee Larkins, Office Assistant
Nature of Service:
Baseball Leagues.
League Description:
Over its first 59 years, the Carolina League has established itself as one of baseball's premier minor leagues, a circuit renowned for hot prospects, intense rivalries, memorable pennant races, and excellent play. Founded during World War II, the

Carolina League's inaugural 1945 season featured two Southside Virginia cites. But throughout the 40s and 50s it was known as a predominately North Carolina League.
Number of Games:
140
Teams:
8

Teams:

CAROLINA MUDCATS
1501 NC HIGHWAY 39
P.O DRAWER 1218
ZEBULON, NC 27597
919-269-2287
Fax: 919-269-4910
• Steve Bryant, President, Majority Owner
• Joe Kremer, Vice President, General Manager
• Eric Gardner, General Manager of Operations
• Yogi Brewington, Ticket & Corporate Sales Executive
• Janell Bullock, Director of Merchandise/Box Office Manager
• Patrick Ennis, Director of Stadium Operations
Stadium:
Five County Stadium.

FREDERICK KEYS
21 STADIUM DRIVE
FREDERICK, MD 21703
301-662-0013
Fax: 301-662-0018
info@frederickkeys.com
• Ken Young, President
• Dave Ziedelis, General Manager
• Bridget McCabe, Director of Marketing
• Christine Roy, Promotions Manager
• Matt Miller, Director of Group Sales
Team History:
Established in 1989, the Frederick Keys offer area families, business leaders, and civic groups a fun environment to be entertained. The fan base is wide spread averaging over 300,000 per season.
Ballpark:
Opened in 1990, Harry Grove Stadium is home to the Frederick Keys.
Affiliate:
Baltimore Orioles

LYNCHBURG HILLCATS
LYNCHBURG CITY STADIUM
3180 FORT AVENUE
LYNCHBURG, VA 24501
434-528-1144
Fax: 434-846-0768
info@lynchburg-hillcats.com
• Paul Sunwall, President/CEO
(434) 528-1144
• Ronnie Roberts, General Manager
• Darren Johnson, Director of Sales
• Ashley Stephenson, Director of Promotions
• Kyle West, Director of Broadcasting
• John Hutt, Director of Ticketing
Ballpark:
Founded in 1939 and a massive renovations project to Calvin Falwell Field was completed by Opening Day 2004, marking the dawn of a new era of baseball in Central Virginia. This grand, state of the art facility now places itself among the very elite venues in the Carolina League and in all of Class A Minor league baseball.
Affiliate:
Class A Advanced affiliate of The Atlanta Braves
Media Broadcast:
KD Country 105.5, WBRG Supertalk 1050-AM

MYRTLE BEACH PELICANS
TICKETRETURN.COM FIELD AT PELICANS BALLPARK
1251 21ST AVENUE NORTH
MYRTLE BEACH, SC 29577
843-918-6002
877-918-8499

Fax: 843-918-6001
info@myrtlebeachpelicans.com
• Chuck Greenberg, Chariman, Managing Partner
chuck@myrtlebeachpelicans.com
• Andy Milovich, President, General Manager
• Mike Snow, Assistant General Manager/Operations
• Dan Bailey, Merchandise Manager
Ballpark:
Ticketreturn.com Field at Pelicans Ballpark has 5200 fixed seats, but can accomodate 6000 with standing room.
Affiliate:
Texas Rangers

POTOMAC NATIONALS
PFITZNER STADIUM
7 COUNTY COMPLEX COURT
WOODBRIDGE, VA 22192
703-590-2311
Fax: 703-590-5716
info@potomacnationals.com
• Art Silber, Chairman/CEO
• Lani Silber Weiss, President/Chief Operating Officer
• Zach Prehn, General Manager, Vice President
• Aaron Johnson, Assistant General Manager, Dir. of Food/Beverage
• Shawna Hooke, Business Operations Manager
Years in League:
1978 - Present.
Ballpark:
G. Richard Pfitzner Stadium opened in 1984 and has a seating capacity of 6,000.
Media Sponsorships:
107.3, WMZQ 98.7-FM, Oldies 100.3
Affiliate:
Washington Nationals

SALEM RED SOX
LEWISGALE FIELD
1004 TEXAS STREET
SALEM, VA 24153
540-389-3333
Fax: 540-389-9710
• Ryan Shelton, General Manager
• Allen Lawrence, Vice President/Assistant GM
• Carlos Febles, Manager
• Steven Elovich, Director of Corporate Sponsorship
• Keegan Moody, Ticket Operations
• Samantha Barney, Marketing & Promotions Manager
Ballpark:
Lewisgale Field.
Affiliate:
Boston Red Sox
Broadcast Network:
WGMN 1240-AM, WVGM 1320-AM, WPIN 810-AM, WKEX ESPN 1430-AM, Broadcast Monsters (web streaming service), WDRL-TV UPN.

WILMINGTON BLUE ROCKS
FRAWLEY STADIUM
801 SHIPYARD DRIVE
WILMINGTON, DE 19801
302-888-2015
Fax: 302-888-2032
info@bluerocks.com
www.bluerocks.com
• Clark Minkler, Managing Partner and League Director
• Matt Minker, Honorary President
• Chris Kemple, General Manager
• Dave Heller, CEO
• Andrew Layman, Assistant General Manager
• Joe Valenti, Director of Marketing
• Steve Gold, Director of Field Operations
Ballpark:
Frawley Stadium was opened in 1993 and built by Minker Construction Company. It seats 6,532 guests.
Network Broadcast:
The Ticket 1290-AM, WDOV 1410-AM.
Affiliate:
KC Royals

WINSTON-SALEM DASH
BB&T BALLPARK
926 BROOKSTOWN AVENUE
WINSTON-SALEM, NC 27101
336-714-2287
Fax: 336-714-2288
info@wsdash.com
- Geoff Lassiter, President
- Ryan Manuel, VP - Baseball Operations
- Kurt Gehsmann, VP - Chief Financial Officer
- C.J. Johnson, VP - Ticket Sales
- Corey Bugno, VP - Corporate Partnerships
- Tim Esmay, Manager

Ballpark:
BB&T Ballpark
Affiliate:
Chicago White Sox
Network Broadcasting:
WSJS 600/1200

EASTERN LEAGUE (AA LEVEL)
30 DANFORTH STREET
SUITE 208
PORTLAND, ME 04101
207-761-2700
Fax: 207-761-7064
elpb@easternleague.com
www.easternleague.com
- Joe McEacharn, President
- Bill Rosario, Assistant to the President

League Description:
The league was formed on March 23, 1923 at the Arlington Hotel in Binghamton, New York as a six-team circuit located entirely within the states of New York and Pennsylvania. The Eastern League (EL) is now composed of two six-team divisions with teams in eight different states. The first game in league history took place in Williamsport on May 9, 1923. Since then, more than 40,000 Eastern League games have been played in front of more than seventy-five million fans. The Eastern League set the current attendance record during the 2004 season, when a total of 3,914,027 fans passed through the gates at Eastern League ballparks.

Number of Teams:
12
Publications:
The League Leader newsletter.

Teams:

AKRON RUBBERDUCKS
CANAL PARK
300 SOUTH MAIN STREET
AKRON, OH 44308-1204
330-253-5151
800-972-3767
Fax: 330-253-3300
information@akronrubberducks.com
- Ken Babby, Owner/CEO
- Jill Popov, Executive Assistant to Ken Babby
- Jim Pfander, General Manager/COO
- Dave Wallace, Manager
- Tony Mansolino, Hitting Coach

Description:
The AA affiliate of the Cleveland Indians. The Aeros play at Canal Park in downtown, Akron Ohio.
Ballpark:
Canal Park.
Ballpark Description:
The steel-framed beauty was built in 14 months, between January, 1996 and March, 1997 and has a seating capacity of 9,097
Major Team Affiliation:
Cleveland Indians.

ALTOONA CURVE
PEOPLES NATURAL GAS FIELD
1000 PARK AVENUE
ALTOONA, PA 16602
814-943-5400
877-99-CURVE
Fax: 814-943-9050
frontoffice@altoonacurve.com
- Bob Lozinak, President/Managing Director
- Joan Lozinak, President/Managing Director
- Steve Lozinak, Chief Administrative Officer
- Dave Lozinak, COO
- Rob Egan, General Manager
- Cory Homan, Director of Ticket Operations
- Mary Lamb, Director of Finance
- Doug Mattern, Ballpark Operations Manager
- Tom Prince, Manager

Ballpark:
Peoples Natural Gas Field
Ballpark Description:
The first game was on April 15, 1999 vs. Bowie. The stadium has a seating capacity of 7,210
Affiliate Team:
Pittsburg Pirates

BINGHAMTON METS
NYSEG STADIUM
211 HENRY STREET
BINGHAMTON, NY 13901
607-723-6387
Fax: 607-723-7779
bmets@bmets.com
www.bmets.com
- Bill Maines, Owner
- Michael Urda, President
- David Maines, Board of Directors
- Jim Weed, General Manager
- Richard Tylicki, Director of Stadium Operations
- Pedro Lopez, Manager

Ballpark:
NYSEG Stadium
Ballpark Description:
Originally known as Binghamton Municipal Stadium, the park was opened in 1992 and has a seating capacity of 6,000.
Media Broadcast:
WNBF-1290 AM.
Newspaper:
Binghamton Press & Sun Bulletin.
Major Team Affiliation:
New York Mets.

BOWIE BAYSOX
PRINCE GEORGES STADIUM
4101 CRAIN HIGHWAY
BOWIE, MD 20716
301-805-6000
Fax: 301-464-4911
info@baysox.com
www.baysox.com
- Brian Shallcross, General Manager
- Phil Wrye, Assistant General Manager
(301) 464-4852
- Charlene Fewer, Director of Ticket Operations
- Gary Kendall, Manager

Ballpark:
Prince George's Stadium.
Ballpark Description:
Opened in 1994. This minor league baseball stadium is the result of a cooperative venture between Maryland Baseball Limited Partnership and The Maryland-National Capital Park and Planning Commission. The stadium includes a lighted playing field, dugouts, locker rooms, 8,000 box and general admission seats, club seats, 9 skyboxes, a grass overflow area for 2,000 spectators, the concourse, concession stands, souvenir shops, ticket offices, administrative offices, a restaurant, a carousel, group picnic areas, a children's play area, and parking lots.
Publications:
Cyber Club newsletter.
Major Team Affiliation:
Baltimore Orioles.

ERIE SEAWOLVES
JERRY UHT PARK
110 EAST 10TH STREET
ERIE, PA 16501
814-456-1300
Fax: 814-456-7520
seawolves@seawolves.com
- Greg Coleman, President
- Mike Pirrello, Assistant GM/Sales
- Justin Cartor, Ticket Operations Manager
- Greg Gania, Assistant GM/Communications
- Chris McDonald, Director of Operations
- Lance Parrish, Manager

Ballpark:
Jerry Uht Park.
Ballpark Description:
Historic Jerry Uht Park celebrated its 10th year anniversary following the 2004 season. The home of the SeaWolves since 1995
Major Team Affiliation:
Detroit Tigers.

HARRISBURG SENATORS
FNB FIELD
245 CHAMPIONSHIP WAY
HARRISBURG, PA 17101
717-231-4444
Fax: 717-231-4445
information@senatorsbaseball.com
- Mark Butler, Principal Owner
- Kevin Kulp, President
- Randy Whitaker, General Manager
rwhitaker@senatorsbaseball.com
- Tim Foreman, Facility Manager
tforeman@senatorsbaseball.com

Ballpark:
FNB Field
Team History:
Baseball in Harrisburg dates back to 1907, when the local team played in the class D Tri-State League. After the 1952 season, the then Harrisburg Senators and the class B league they played in at the time called it quits.
Years in League:
1924-35, 1987-present.
Affiliation:
Washington Nationals (2005).
Media Broadcast:
WKBO 1230-AM.

HARTFORD YARD GOATS
DUNKIN' DONUTS PARK
1214 MAIN STREET
HARTFORD, CT 06103
860-246-4628
Fax: 860-247-4628
info@yardgoatsbaseball.com
- Tim Restall, General Manager
- Mike Abramson, Assistant General Manager
- Josh Montinieri, Executive Director, Tickets
- Jeff Dooley, Director, Broadcasting & Media Relations
- Pat Kennedy, Director, Stadium Operations
- Darin Everson, Manager

Ballpark:
Dunkin' Donuts Park.
Ballpark Description:
Dunkin' Donuts Park is planned to open on April 2016, and will seat 6,000.
Major Team Affiliation:
Colorado Rockies.

NEW HAMPSHIRE FISHER CATS
NORTHEAST DELTA DENTAL STADIUM
ONE LINE DRIVE
MANCHESTER, NH 03101
603-641-2005
Fax: 603-641-2055
info@nhfishercats.com
- Art Solomon, Owner
- Steve Pratt, VP, Business Operations
- Rick Brenner, President/General Manager
rbrenner@nhfishercats.com
- Tom Gauthier, Executive Director, Broadcast & Media Relations
- Bobby Meacham, Manager

Ballpark:
Northeast Delta Dental Stadium

single sports

PORTLAND SEA DOGS
271 PARK AVENUE
PORTLAND, ME 04102
207-874-9300
Fax: 207-780-0317
seadogs@seadogs.com
• Charlie Eshbach, President
ceshbach@portlandseadogs.com
• Bill Burke, Chairman
• John Kameisha, Senior Vice President
john@portlandseadogs.com
• Geoff Iacuessa, General Manager/Executive VP
geoff@seadogs.com
• Chris Cameron, Assistant GM/Dir. of Media Relations
ccameron@portlandseadogs.com
• Dennis Meehan, Executive Director of Sales
• Dennis Carter, Ticket Office Manager
• Mike Antonellis, Director, Broadcasting
• Billy McMillon, Manager
Ballpark:
Hadlock Field.
Ballpark Description:
Hadlock Field was opened in 1994, the year the Portland Sea Dogs came to town. Hadlock Field seats 7,368 patrons and has all the amenities of the larger parks including luxury boxes, a full press box, a picnic area and a souvenir store.
Media Broadcast:
Journal Tribune , Portland Press Herald , Sun Journal , The Times Record , WCSH Channel 6 , WGME Channel 13 , WPXT Fox 51
Team Affiliate:
Boston Red Sox

READING FIGHTIN PHILS
1900 CENTRE AVENUE/RT 61 SOUTH
READING, PA 19605
610-375-8469
Fax: 610-373-5868
info@fightins.com
• Craig Stein, Managing Partner
• Scott Hunsicker, General Manager
scott@readingphillies.com
• Todd Hunsicker, Director of Educational Programs, Music
andy@readingphillies.com
• Mike Becker, Director of Tickets
• Mike Robinson, Director of Community & Fan Development
pr@readingphillies.com
• Joe Bialek, Director of Sales
jbialek@readingphillies.com
• Kevin Sklenarik, Director of Baseball Operations/Merchandise
• Dusty Wathan, Manager
Team History:
The Reading Phillies offer affordable family entertainment from early April through Labor Day weekend at FirstEnergy Stadium. The Phillies are well known for creating a festive, fan-friendly atmosphere from the time the gates open until the bottom of the ninth inning. Reading won the John H. Johnson President's Trophy in 2003. The Johnson Trophy is the top honor bestowed upon the complete franchise by Minor League Baseball. Twice in the last 15 years, Reading has been awarded the Larry MacPhail Trophy as the best promotional team in all of Minor League Baseball. In 2002 the city was dubbed Baseballtown.
Ballpark:
FirstEnergy Stadium.
Ballpark Description:
The stadium itself is one of Baseball's finest and is the oldest venue in the Eastern League. Completed in 1951, the original grandstand and exterior brick wall provide an old-time ballpark feel while the right field swimming pool and left field video board cater to the modern fan. The natural grass surface is immaculately maintained and provides the perfect accent to a classic park.
Major Team Affiliation:
Philadelphia Phillies, currently the longest affiliation in baseball (since 1976).

RICHMOND FLYING SQUIRRELS
THE DIAMOND
3001 NORTH BOULEVARD
RICHMOND, VA 23230
804-359-3866
Fax: 804-359-1373
info@squirrelsbaseball.com
• Chuck Domino, Chief Executive Manager
• Bob Parney, Vice President, Chief Operations Officer
• Marty Steele, Director of Business Development
• Steve Pump, Director of Stadium Operations
• Patrick Flower, Director of Ticket Sales
• Steve Ruckman, Director of Field Operations
• Jose Alguacil, Manager
Ballpark:
The Diamond
Team Affiliate:
San Francisco Giants

TRENTON THUNDER
ARM & HAMMER PARK
ONE THUNDER ROAD
TRENTON, NJ 08611
609-394-3300
Fax: 609-394-9666
fun@trentonthunder.com
• Jeff Hurley, Chief Operations Officer/General Manager
• Eric Lipsman, Senior VP, Corporate Sales/Sponsorships
eric@trentonthunder.com
• Joe Pappalardo, Director of Merchandising
• Matt Pentima, Director of Ticket & Baseball Operations
mattp@trentonthunder.com
• Steve Brokowsky, Director of Stadium Operations
• Adam Giardino, Broadcast & Media Relations Manager
• Al Pedrique, Manager
Ballpark:
Arm and Hammer Park.
Ballpark Description:
Built in 1994 along the banks of the Deleware River, Arm and Hammer Park has seating capacity for over 6000 fans. When Trenton joined the Eastern League in 1994, it was the first time since 1950, that this city has had a Minor League team.
Media Broadcast:
WBUD 1260-AM Radio, CN8 TV.
Team Affiliate:
New York Yankees

FLORIDA STATE LEAGUE
3000 GULF TO BAY
SUITE 219
CLEARWATER, FL 33759
727-724-6146
Fax: 727-724-6145
office@floridastateleague.com
• Ken Carson, President/Chairman/Treasurer
• John Timberlake, Executive Vice President
• Paul Taglieri, VP, South Division
• Ron Myers, VP, North Division
• Horace Smith, Secretary, General Counsel
League History:
1919-1927, 1936-1941, 1946-present

Teams:

BRADENTON MARAUDERS
MCKECHNIE FIELD
1611 9TH STREET WEST
BRADENTON, FL 34205
941-747-3031
Fax: 941-747-9442
maraudersinfo@pirates.com
• Trevor Gooby, Senior Director of Florida Operations
• Rachelle Madrigal, Director of Sales and General Manager

• AJ Grant, Director of Operations
• Michael Ryan, Manager
Team Affiliate:
Pittsburgh Pirates

BREVARD COUNTY MANATEES
5800 STADIUM PARKWAY
SUITE 101
VIERA, FL 32940
321-633-9200
Fax: 321-633-4418
• Kyle Smith, General Manager
• Tom Winters, Chairman
• Charlie Baumann, President
• Chad Lovitt, Assistant General Manager
• Kelley Wheeler, Director, Business Operations and Finance
• Joe Ayrault, Team Manager
Ballpark:
Space Coast Stadium.
Ballpark Description:
Constructed in 1993 with a capacity of 8,100, Space Coast Stadium was the first Spring Training home of the Florida Marlins. Opened in 1994.
Major Team Affiliation:
Milwaukee Brewers
Media Broadcast:
WMEL 920-AM.

CHARLOTTE STONE CRABS
CHARLOTTE SPORTS PARK
2300 EL JOBEAN ROAD
PORT CHARLOTTE, FL 33948
941-206-4487
Fax: 941-206-3599
• Jared Forma, General Manager
• Jeff Cook, Director of Ticket Operations
• Kelly Scott, Box Officer Manager
• Michael Johns, Manager
Ballpark:
Charlotte Sports Park
Team Affiliate:
Tampa Bay Rays

CLEARWATER THRESHERS
BRIGHT HOUSE FIELD
601 NORTH OLD COACHMAN ROAD
CLEARWATER, FL 33765
727-712-4300
Fax: 727-712-4498
info@threshersbaseball.com
www.threshersbaseball.com
• David Montgomery, General Partner
• John Timberlake, Director of Operations/General Manager
• Dan McDonough, Assistant GM/Sales
dmcdonough@threshersbaseball.com
• Jason Adams, Assistant General Manager/Ticketing
jason@threshersbaseball.com
• Jay Warren, Ballpark Operations Manager
jwarren@threshersbaseball.com
• Greg Legg, Manager
Ballpark:
Bright House Field.
Ballpark Description:
Opened in 2004, a fan-friendly ballpark with a capacity of 8,500 with 7,000 fixed seats. We are the Spring Training grounds for the Philadelphia Phillies.
Major Team Affiliation:
Philadelphia Phillies.

DAYTONA TORTUGAS
JACKIE ROBINSON PARK
105 EAST ORANGE AVENUE
DAYTONA BEACH, FL 32114
386-257-3172
Fax: 386-523-9490
• Tammy Devine, Director of Business Operations
• Josh Lawther, General Manager
• JR Laub, Assistant General Manager
• Paul Krenzer, Director of Ticket Operations
• Eli Marrero, Manager

Ballpark:
Jackie Robinson Ballpark. (The Jack)
Ballpark Description:
The historic ballpark opened on June 4, 1914 as Daytona City Island Ballpark. In memory of the first site hosting a racially integrated game in baseball history, the ballpark was renamed Jackie Robinson Ballpark in 1990.
Major Team Affiliation:
Cincinnati Reds.

DUNEDIN BLUE JAYS
FLORIDA AUTO EXCHANGE STADIUM
373 DOUGLAS AVENUE
DUNEDIN, FL 34698
727-733-9302
Fax: 727-734-7661
• Shelby Nelson, Director, Florida Operations/GM
(727) 738-7020
• Leon Harrell, Stadium Operations
• Jonathan Valdez, Manager of Ticket Operations/Community Relati
(727) 738-7036
• Bobby Meacham, Manager
Ballpark:
Florida Auto Exchange Stadium
Ballpark Description:
Knology Park, ranked by Sports Illustrated as one of the top 5 places to watch a Spring Training game, is a community ballpark in which Dunedin residents and visitors can enjoy Toronto Blue Jays Spring Training, Dunedin Blue Jays Minor League Baseball, Dunedin Falcons High School Baseball and various additional community events throughout the year. The park capacity is 5,491 individual seats and features include a press box level with air-conditioned skyboxes and a scoreboard with electronic message display, regulation-sized Major League playing field and lighting, half-field, batting tunnels, and full concession capabilities.
Major Team Affiliation:
Toronto Blue Jays.

FORT MYERS MIRACLE
14400 SIX MILE CYPRESS PARKWAY
FORT MYERS, FL 33912
239-768-4210
Fax: 239-768-4211
miracle@miraclebaseball.com
• Jason Hochberg, President
• Marv Goldklang, Principal Owner
• Steve Gliner, Chief Operating Officer
sgliner@miraclebaseball.com
• Andrew Seymour, General Manager
aseymour@miraclebaseball.com
• Bill Levy, Director of Ticket Operations
• John Kuhn, Director of Business Development
• Suzanne Reeves, Director of Business Operations
miracle@miraclebaseball.com
• Jeff Smith, Manager
Ballpark:
William Hammond Stadium.
Ballpark Description:
Opened in 1991 and spring home of the Minnesota Twins.
Major Team Affiliation:
Minnesota Twins.

JUPITER HAMMERHEADS
ROGER DEAN STADIUM
4751 MAIN STREET
JUPITER, FL 33458
561-775-1818
Fax: 561-691-6886
• Mike Bauer, General Manager
(561) 630-1840
m.bauer@rogerdeanstadium.com
• Alex Inman, Assistant General Manager
• Haile Urquhart, Director of Ticketing
Description:
The Jupiter Hammerheads are the Advanced-A affiliate for the Florida Marlins. We have been in existance since 1998 and were originally an affiliate of the Montreal Expos through 2001.

Beginning in 2002, we became an affiliate of the Florida Marlins organization.
Ballpark:
Roger Dean Stadium.
Ballpark Description:
The stadium was built in 1997 and opened in February 1998 for Spring Training. Roger Dean Stadium is currently the Spring Training home of the Florida Marlins and St. Louis Cardinals and the Florida State League home of the Jupiter Hammerheads and Palm Beach Cardinals. The facility is the only one in the country which serves as home for two Minor League Baseball teams.
Major Team Affiliation:
Miami Marlins

LAKELAND FLYING TIGERS
JOKER MARCHANT STADIUM
2125 NORTH LAKE AVENUE
#A
LAKELAND, FL 33805
863-686-8075
Fax: 863-688-9589
• Zack Burek, General Manager
• Ron Myers, Director of Florida Operations
• Shannon Follett, Administration and Operations Manager
• Ryan Eason, Ticket Operations
• Dave Huppert, Manager
Ballpark:
Joker Marchant Stadium.
Ballpark Description:
Marchant Stadium was named in honor of the late Joker Marchant, Lakeland's former parks and recreation director. The all-concrete grandstand of the stadium was built by the City of Lakeland at a cost of $500,000 and originally seated 4,900 spectators. Expansion projects beginning in the early 1970s brought the capacity to 7,100 and the recently completed renovation project upped the capacity to approximately 8,500. Previous renovations have included the addition of lights that allowed the first night game to be played in Lakeland in 1972 and a food and picnic court that was added in 1994 to increase the fan appeal of Joker Marchant Stadium.
Major Team Affiliation:
Detroit Tigers.

PALM BEACH CARDINALS
ROGER DEAN STADIUM
4751 MAIN STREET
JUPITER, FL 33458
561-775-1818
Fax: 561-691-6886
• Mike Bauer, General Manager, Jupiter Stadium
(561) 630-1848
joe@rogerdeanstadium.com
• Alex Inman, General Manager, Palm Beach Cardinal's
• Liz Parent, Assistant to GM, Jupiter Stadium
(561) 630-1850
c.mcateer@rogerdeanstadium.com
• Dianne Detling, Office Manager
(561) 799-1376
• Haile Urquhart, Director of Ticketing
• Oliver Marmol, Manager
Description:
The Palm Beach Cardinals are the Advanced-A affiliate for the St. Louis Cardinals. They have been in existance since 2003 and are part of the East Division of the Florida State League.
Ballpark:
Roger Dean Stadium.
Ballpark Description:
The stadium was built in 1997 and opened in February 1998 for Spring Training. Roger Dean Stadium is currently the Spring Training home of the Florida Marlins and St. Louis Cardinals and the Florida State League home of the Jupiter Hammerheads and Palm Beach Cardinals. The facility is the only one in the country which serves as home to two Minor League Baseball teams.
Major Team Affiliation:
St. Louis Cardinals.

ST. LUCIE METS
TRADITION FIELD
525 NW PEACOCK BOULEVARD
PORT ST. LUCIE, FL 34986
772-871-2100
Fax: 772-878-9802
info@stluciemets.com
• Paul Taglieri, Executive Director
• Traer Van Allen, General Manager
• Clint Cure, Assistant General Manager
• Stephen Fox, Director, Ticketing and Merchandise
• Lauren Mahoney, Manager, Sales and Corporate Partnerships
• Kyle Gleockler, Manager, Ticketing and Merchandise
• John Gallagher, Manager, Food and Beverage Operations
Ballpark:
Tradition Field
Ballpark Description:
Tradition Field is home to the New York Mets Spring Training, the St. Louis Mets Minor League Team and all the New York Mets Minor League operations. It has a seating capacity of 7,160 and is available for concerts, festivals, and much more.
Major Team Affiliation:
New York Mets.

TAMPA YANKEES
GEORGE M. STEINBRENNER FIELD
ONE STEINBRENNER DRIVE
TAMPA, FL 33614
813-673-3055
Fax: 813-673-3174
• C. Vance Smith, Director of Florida Operations/General Manager
• Matt Gess, Assistant General Manager, Marketing
• Jennifer Magliocchetti, Assistant Director of Ticket Operations
• Dave Bialas, Team Manager
Ballpark:
Steinbrenner Stadium
Ballpark Description:
Opened in 1996, Legends Field is a 31 acre complex and has a seating capacity of 10,000 seats. It was renamed to Steinbrenner Stadium in 2008.
Major Team Affiliation:
New York Yankees.

FREEDOM PRO BASEBALL LEAGUE
4301 NORTH 75TH STREET
SUITE 105
PO BOX 5403
SCOTTSDALE, AZ 85251
480-946-0211
Fax: 480-947-4099
• Tim Gross, Majority Owner
• Joe Perle, President & Minority Owner
Teams:
Goodyear Centennials; Peoria Explorers; Phoenix Prospectors; Prescott Montezuma Federals

FRONTIER LEAGUE OF PROFESSIONAL BASEBALL/INDEPENDENT LEAGUE
2041 GOOSE LAKE ROAD
SUITE 2A
SAUGET, IL 62206
618-215-4134
Fax: 618-332-2115
office@frontierleague.com
www.frontierleague.com
• Bill Lee, Commissioner
blee@frontierleague.com
• Steve Tahsler, Deputy Commissioner, Operations
stahsler@frontierleague.com
• Kevin Winn, Deputy Commissioner, Strategic Development
kwinn@frontierleague.com

League History:

In the winter of 1992-1993, several men got together and decided to start an independent professional baseball league to serve the West Virginia, eastern Kentucky and southeast Ohio areas. They believed they could bring professional baseball to areas that would never have a chance of affiliated professional baseball coming to their communities. The seed was planted and they named their project The Frontier League. In 2019, the Frontier League merged with the Canadian American Association of Professional Baseball (Can-Am League).

Teams:

EVANSVILLE OTTERS
BOSSE FIELD
23 DON MATTINGLY WAY
EVANSVILLE, IN 47711
812-435-8686
Fax: 812-435-8688
ottersbb@evansville.net
www.evansvilleotters.com
• Bix Branson, Vice President
• Jake Riffert, Director of Operations
• Joel Padfield, General Manager
• Celia Langford, Director of Community Relations
• Andy McCauley, Manager
Ballpark:
Bosse Field.
Ballpark Description:
Opening Day was on June 17 1915. Seating capacity listed is at 7,180.

FLORENCE FREEDOM
UC HEALTH STADIUM
7950 FREEDOM WAY
FLORENCE, KY 41042
859-594-4487
Fax: 859-594-3194
www.florencefreedom.com
• Clint Brown, President/Owner
(859) 594-4487
• Josh Anderson, General Manager
(859) 594-4487
• Kim Brown, Assistant General Manager of Operations
• Dennis Pelfrey, Field Manager
Description:
Champion Window Field in Northern Kentucky was recently renovated.

GATEWAY GRIZZLIES
GCS BALLPARK
2301 GRIZZLIE BEAR BOULEVARD
SAUGET, IL 62206
618-337-3000
Fax: 618-332-3625
grizzlies@accessus.net
www.gatewaygrizzlies.com
• Rich Sauget, Owner
• Steve Gomric, General Manager
• Chris Kellermannn, Director of Corporate Partnerships
• Phil Warren, Manager
pwarren@gatewaygrizzlies.com
Ballpark:
GCS Stadium.
Ballpark Description:
The Grizzlies' ballpark was built in 2002. The stadium can hold over 6,000 people and has reserved box seating, lawn seating, party suites and two hot tubs. The ballpark has been featured on digitalballparks.com as one of the best in the nation.
Corporate Sponsors:
Budweiser, GCS Federal Credit Union, GMC, Mrs. T's Pierogies, National City, Pepsi, US Bank, U.S. Cellular.

LAKE ERIE CRUSHERS
ALL PRO FREIGHT STADIUM
2009 BASEBALL BOULEVARD
AVON, OH 44011
440-934-3636
Fax: 440-934-2458
www.lakeeriecrushers.com
• Tom Kramig, President/CEO
• D.J. Saylor, Assistant Director of Stadium Operations
• Vicki Winkel, VP of Business Development
• Paul Siegwarth, VP Stadium Operations
• Kathleen Hudson, Controller

NEW JERSEY JACKALS
YOGI BERRA STADIUM
ONE HALL DRIVE
LITTLE FALLS, NJ 07424
973-746-7434
Fax: 973-655-8006
info@jackals.com
www.jackals.com
• Floyd Hall, Owner and Chairman
• Gregory L. Lockard, President
• Larry Hall, Executive Vice President
• Jennifer Fertig, VP of Finance & Operations
• Joe Calfapietra, Field Manager

NORMAL CORN BELTERS
THE CORN CRIB
1000 WEST RAAB ROAD
NORMAL, IL 61761
309-454-2255
Fax: 309-454-2287
www.normalbaseball.com
• Steve Malliet, President, General Manager
• Jeff Holtke, Assistant General Manager
• Mike Petrini, Assistant General Manager
• Deana Roberts, Business Manager

OTTAWA CHAMPIONS
RAYMOND CHABOT GRANT THORNTON PARK
300 CONVENTRY RD
OTTAWA, ON, CANADA K1K 4P5613-
• Sebastian Boucher, Manager
Note:
After the merger of the Can-Am League and the Frontier League, the Ottawa Champions were excluded from the schedule.

QUEBEC CAPITALES
STADE CANAC
100 CARDINAL MAURICE-ROY ST
QUEBEC, QC, CANADA G1K 8Z1
418-521-2255
877-521-2244
Fax: 418-521-2266
info@capitalesdequebec.com
capitalesdequebec.com
• Jean Tremblay, Owner
• Michel Laplante, President
mlaplante@capitalesdequebec.com

RIVER CITY RASCALS
T.R. HUGHES BALLPARK
900 T.R. HUGHES BOULEVARD
O'FALLON, MO 63366
636-240-2287
Fax: 636-240-7313
info@rivercityrascals.com
www.rivercityrascals.com
• Dan Dial, President/General Manager
• Lisa Fegley, Assistant General Manager
• Carrie Green, Business Manager
• Mo Stranz, Director of Food & Beverage
Ballpark:
T.R. Hughes Ballpark.
Ballpark Description:
The facility has 3,491 permanent seats and a grass berm and picnic area capable of holding an additional 1,700 fans. With clean, wholesome, family entertainment played in an intimate atmosphere, T.R. Hughes Ballpark has become the place to be every summer.

Media Broadcasting:
KSLQ 104.5-FM.

ROCKLAND BOULDERS
1 PALISADES CREDIT UNION PARK DRIVE
PALISADES CREDIT UNION PARK
POMONA, NY 10970
845-364-0009
Fax: 845-364-0001
info@rocklandboulders.com
www.rocklandboulders.com
• Ken Lehner, President
klehner@rocklandboulders.com
• Shawn Reilly, Executive Vice President/General Manager
sreilly@rocklandboulders.com
• Seth Cantor, Assistant General Manager/Voice of the Boulders
scantor@rocklandboulders.com
• Nick Barbalato, Assistant General Manager/Director of Operations
nbarbalato@rocklandboulders.com
Year Founded:
2011
Seating Capacity:
4,750

SCHAUMBURG BOOMERS
1999 SPRINGINGSGUTH ROAD
SCHAUMBURG, IL 60193
847-461-3695
Fax: 630-439-3501
info@boomersbaseball.com
www.boomersbaseball.com
• Pete Laven, President/General Manager
• Mike Kline, Assistant General Manager/Director of Sales
• Rich Essegian, Director of Food and Beverage
• Mike Tlusty, Director of Facilities

SOUTHERN ILLINOIS MINERS
RENT ONE PARK
1000 MINERS DRIVE
MARION, IL 62959
618-998-8499
Fax: 618-969-8550
info@southernillinoisminers.com
www.southernillinoisminers.com
• Jayne Simmons, Owner
• Mike Pinto, Chief Operating Officer
• Casey Petermeyer, Director of Extra Events/Stadium Op.
• Jake Holtkamp, Director of Ticket Operations

SUSSEX COUNTY MINERS
SKYLANDS STADIUM
94 CHAMPIONSHIP PLACE
AUGUSTA, NJ 07822
973-383-7644
Fax: 973-383-7522
contact@scminers.com
www.sussexcountyminers.com
• Al Dorso, Sr., Owner, President
• Al Dorso, Jr., Vice President, Operations
• Mike Dorso, Vice President, Marketing
• Dave Chase, General Manager
• Tyler Borkowski, Assistant General Manager
• Dennis Mark, Director, Creative Services
• Andrew Luftglass, Director, Broadcasting & Media Relations

TRAVERSE CITY BEACH BUMS
333 STADIUM DRIVE
TRAVERSE CITY, MI 49685
231-943-0100
Fax: 231-943-0900
sales@traversecitybeachbums.com
www.traversecitybeachbums.com
• Jason Wuerfel, Vice President/Director of Baseball Operations
• John E. Wuerfel, President
• Leslye A. Wuerfel, Chief Financial Officer
• Tom Goethel, Assistant General Manager

TROIS-RIVIERES AIGLES
1760 GILLES-VILLENEUVE AVE
TROIS-RIVIERES, QC, CANADA G9A 5K8
819-379-0404
info@lesaiglestr.com
lesaiglestr.com
• Paul Poisson, President
fish56@hotmail.com
• Rene Martin, General Manager
r.martin@lesaiglestr.com

WASHINGTON WILD THINGS
CONSOL ENERGY PARK
ONE WASHINGTON FEDERAL WAY
WASHINGTON, PA 15301
724-250-9555
Fax: 724-250-2333
www.washingtonwildthings.com
• Bob Bozzuto, Field Manager
• Ben Moore, Pitching Coach

WINDY CITY THUNDERBOLTS
STANDARD BANK STADIUM
14011 SOUTH KENTON AVENUE
CRESTWOOD, IL 60445
708-489-2255
Fax: 708-489-2999
info@wcthunderbolts.com
www.wcthunderbolts.com
• Mike Lucas, General Manager
mlucas@wcthunderbolts.com
• Mike VerSchave, Assistant General Manager
• Marissa Miller, Director of Community Relations
Team History:
Founded in the winter of 1992-1993, the Windy City ThunderBolts are a minor league professional baseball club located in Crestwood, IL. They were formally known as the Cook County Cheetahs, but in 2004 they received a new ownership group, name, mascot, and a new look at minor league baseball. They are a member of the Frontier League, the premier independent professional baseball league in the country.
Ballpark:
Standard Bank Stadium
Ballpark Description:
This state of the art stadium has a capacity of over 3,000 fans and includes full-service concession areas, three picnic areas, a beer garden, and a kids' play area. Hawkinson Ford field is also one of the only minor league ballparks to have an upper deck.

GULF COAST LEAGUE
9550 16TH ST. N.
ST. PETERSBURG, FL 33716
727-456-1734
Fax: 727-821-5819
gcl@milb.com
www.milb.com
• Tim Brunswick, Vice President, Baseball & Business Operations
• Andy Shultz, Manager, Baseball & Business Operations
Teams:
Astros; Braves; Blue Jays; Cardinals; Marlins; Mets; Nationals; Orioles; Phillies; Pirates; Rays; Red Sox; Tigers; Twins; Yankees

INTERNATIONAL LEAGUE (AAA LEVEL)
55 SOUTH HIGH STREET
SUITE 202
DUBLIN, OH 43017
614-791-9300
Fax: 614-791-9009
office@ilbaseball.com
www.ilbaseball.com
• Randy A. Mobley, President/Treasurer
• Dave Rosenfield, Vice President

• Chris Sprague, Assistant to the President
• Max Schumacher, Corporate Secretary
Years League Active:
1884-Present

Teams:

BUFFALO BISONS
COCA-COLA FIELD
ONE JAMES D. GRIFFIN PLAZA
BUFFALO, NY 14203
716-846-2000
Fax: 716-852-6530
info@bisons.com
• Robert E. Rich, Jr., Owner/President
• Michael Buczkowski, Vice President/General Manager
• Melinda R. Rich, President, Rich Entertainment Group
• William G. Gisel, Jr., Vice President/Secretary
• Joseph W. Segarra, Vice President, Chief Operating Officer
• Jonathan A. Dandes, President, Rich Baseball Operations
• Tom Sciarrino, Director of Stadium Operations
Ballpark:
Coca-Cola Park
Ballpark Description:
Praised as one of the finest ballparks in professional baseball. Dunn Tire Park opened on April 14, 1988 to a sellout crowd of 19,500. Since then, millions of fans have enjoyed great baseball action and exciting promotions.
Years in League:
1886-90, 1912-70, 1998-present.
Major Team Affiliation:
New York Mets

CHARLOTTE KNIGHTS
BB&T BALLPARK
324 SOUTH MINT STREET
CHARLOTTE, NC 28202
704-274-8300
Fax: 704-274-8330
knights@charlotteknights.com
• Dan Rajkowski, Vice President, Chief Operating Officer
• Scotty Brown, General Manager of Baseball Operations
• Julie Clark, Director of Special Programs & Events
• Chris Semmens, Vice President, Sales
• Matt Millward, Director of Ticket Operations
• Tommy Viola, Director of Public Relations
Ballpark:
BB&T Ballpark
Years in League:
1993-present.
Major Team Affiliation:
Chicago White Sox.

COLUMBUA CLIPPERS
330 HUNTINGTON PARK LANE
COLUMBUS, OH 43215
614-462-5250
Fax: 614-462-3271
info@clippersbaseball.com
• Ken Schnacke, President, General Manager
• Mark Warren, Assistant General Manager
• Bonnie Badgley, Director of Finance
• Steve Dalin, Director of Ballpark Operations
• Scott Ziegler, Director of Ticket Operations
• Mark Galuska, Director of Marketing and Sales
• Seth Rhodes, Director of Promotions & In-Game Entertainment
Team History:
When the Columbus Jets pulled up stakes and moved away after the 1970 season, it left Columbus without professional baseball for the first time in 75 years. For six years central Ohio fans did without baseball. In 1977, Cooper again pushed for a professional team and a major stadium renovation. The Columbus Clippers and Franklin County Stadium were born. The new home of the Clippers is Huntington Park in downtown Columbus.
Ballpark:

Huntington Park
Team Affiliate:
Cleveland Indians

DURHAM BULLS
DURHAM BULLS ATHLETIC PARK
409 BLACKWELL STREET
DURHAM, NC 27701
919-687-6500
Fax: 919-687-6560
info@durhambulls.com
www.durhambulls.com
• George Habel, Vice President
• Jared Sandberg, Manager
• Mike Birling, General Manager
Ballpark:
Durham Bulls Athletic Park.
Ballpark Description:
The $16-million brick ballpark opened in 1995 and was expanded to a 10,000-seat capacity for the 1998 season, the year the Bulls began playing in the Triple-A International League.
Media Broadcast:
WDNC 620-AM.
Major Team Affiliation:
Tampa Bay Rays.

GWINNETT BRAVES
2500 BUFORD DRIVE
LAWRENCEVILLE, GA 30043
678-277-0300
Fax: 678-277-0338
gwinnettinfo@braves.com
gwinnett.braves.milb.com
• North Johnson, General Manager
• Shari Massengill, Assistant General Manager
• Todd Pund, Director of Ticket Sales
• Ryan Stoltenberg, Manager of Stadium Operations
• Brian Snitker, Manager
Ballpark:
Coolray Field.
Major Team Affiliation:
Atlanta Braves.
Media Broadcast:
ESPN 950-AM.

INDIANAPOLIS INDIANS
VICTORY FIELD
501 WEST MARYLAND STREET
INDIANAPOLIS, IN 46225
317-269-3542
Fax: 317-269-3541
indians@indyindians.com
www.indyindians.com
• Max B. Schumacher, President/Chairman
(317) 269-3542
• Cal Burleson, Vice President/Administration
(317) 269-3542
burleson@indyindians.com
• Randy Lewandowski, General Manager
(317) 269-3542
burleson@indyindians.com
• Brad Morris, Director, Business Operations
(317) 269-3542
bmorris@indyindians.com
• Andrew Jackson, Operations Manager
(317) 269-3542
• Matt Guay, Director of Tickets
Ballpark:
Victory Field.
Ballpark Description:
Victory Field draws its name from the Indianapolis Indians' former home. Originally opened as Perry Stadium in 1931, that ballpark held the name Victory Field from 1942 to 1967 celebrating the United States' victory in World War II.
Media Broadcast:
Indianapolis ESPN 950-AM.
Major League Affiliate:
Pittsburgh Pirates

LEHIGH VALLEY IRON PIGS
COCA-COLA PARK
1050 IRONPIGS WAY
ALLENTOWN, PA 18109

610-841-7447
Fax: 610-841-1509
info@ironpigsbaseball.com
• Craig Stein, Owner
• Joe Finley, Owner
• Chuck Domino, Senior Advisor
• Kurt Landes, President & General Manager
• Howard Scharf, Assistant General Manager
• Michelle Perl, Finance Manager
• Scott Evans, Director of Ticket Sales
• Jason Kiesel, Director, Stadium Operations
• Dale Brundage, Manager
Team Affiliate:
Philadelphia Phillies

LOUISVILLE BATS
LOUISVILLE BATS BASEBALL CLUB
401 EAST MAIN STREET
LOUISVILLE, KY 40202
502-212-2287
Fax: 502-515-2255
info@batsbaseball.com
www.batsbaseball.com
• Gary Ulmer, President
gulmer@batsbaseball.com
• Dale Owens, Senior Vice President, Corporate
Sales
dowens@batsbaseball.com
• Greg Galiette, Senior Vice President
ggaliette@batsbaseball.com
• Scott Shoemaker, Vice President, Operations
and Technology
sshoemaker@batsbaseball.com
• Kyle Reh, Director, Business Operations
jbreeding@batsbaseball.com
• Jeff Hafling, General Manager
Ballpark:
Louisville Slugger Field.
Ballpark Description:
The stadium which opened in April of 2000 seats
over 13,131 and was built on the banks of the
Ohio River, within one block of the Waterfront
Park.
Media Broadcast:
WGTK 970-AM.
Years in League:
1998-present.
Major Team Affiliation:
Cincinnati Reds.

NORFOLK TIDES
HARBOR PARK
150 PARK AVE
NORFOLK, VA 23510
757-622-2222
Fax: 757-624-9090
receptionist@norfolktides.com
www.norfolktides.com
• Ken Young, President
(757) 622-2222
kyoung@norfolktides.com
• Joe Gregory, General Manager
• Ben Giancola, Assistant General Manager
(757) 622-2222
bgiancola@norfolktides.com
• Gretchen Todd, Director, Ticket Operations
(757) 622-2222
gtodd@norfolktides.com
• Mike Zeman, Director, Stadium Operations
(757) 622-2222
mzeman@norfolktides.com
• Ron Johnson, Manager
Team History:
Norfolk had been without professional baseball
since the Tars of the Piedmont League folded
on July 13, 1955. The team operated in the
South Atlantic League for two years, first as an
independent, the second with a Cardinal working
agreement. Granny Hamner, the former Phillie
Whiz Kid, became the first manager.
Ballpark:
Harbor Park.
Ballpark Description:
Harbor Park, with its outstanding view and
sound design, is one of the finest baseball
facilities in existence. The ballpark is located in
downtown Norfolk on the Elizabeth River, has a
seating capacity of 12,067 and was opened in
1993.

Affiliation:
Baltimore Orioles

PAWTUCKET RED SOX
MCCOY STADIUM
ONE COLUMBUS AVENUE
PAWTUCKET, RI 02860
401-724-7300
Fax: 401-724-2140
info@pawsox.com
www.pawsox.com
• Larry Lucchino, Chairman of the Board
• Mike Tamburro, Vice Chairman
• Dan Rea, SVP/General Manager
• Matt White, Vice President/Chief Operating
Officer
• Dave Johnson, Director of Warehouse
Operations
• Bill Wanless, Vice President, Public Relations
• Michael Gwynn, Vice President of Sales &
Marketing
• Kevin Boles, Manager
Ballpark:
McCoy Stadium.
Ballpark Information:
The stadium was erected in 1942 and was
named in Honor of Thomas P. McCoy, mayor of
Pawtucket from 1936-1945. The total seating
capacity is 10,031.
Team Affiliate:
Boston Red Sox

ROCHESTER RED WINGS
FRONTIER FIELD
ONE MORRIE SILVER WAY
ROCHESTER, NY 14608
585-454-1001
Fax: 585-454-1056
info@redwingsbaseball.com
www.redwingsbaseball.com
• Naomi Silver, President, CEO/COO
• Gary Larder, Chairman of the Board
• Leonard Korn, Vice President
• Dan Mason, General Manager
• Will Rumbold, Assistant General Manager
• Matt Cipro, Senior Director of Sales
• Gene Buonomo, Director, Stadium Operations
• Mike Quade, Manager
• Tim Doherty, Hitting Coach
• Marty Mason, Pitching Coach
Ballpark:
Frontier Field.
Ballpark Description:
Frontier Field's official seating capacity is 10,840
with the possibility of an additional 2,500 to
3,000 more in bleacher and standing-room-only
areas in the event of a sellout crowd.
Major League Affiliation:
Minnesota Twins

SCRANTON/WILKES-BARRE RAILRIDERS
PNC FIELD
235 MONTAGE MOUNTAIN ROAD
MOOSIC, PA 18507
570-969-2255
Fax: 570-963-6564
info@swbrailriders.com
www.swbrailriders.com
• Olerud Josh, President & General Manager
Ballpark:
PNC Field
Ballpark Description:
Opened in 1989.
Seating Capacity:
10,000
Team Affiliate:
New York Yankees

SYRACUSE CHIEFS
NBT BANK STADIUM
ONE TEX SIMONE DRIVE
SYRACUSE, NY 13208
315-474-7833
Fax: 315-474-2658
www.syracusechiefs.com

• Jason Smorol, General Manager
• Kathleen McCormick, Director of Sales and
Marketing
• Billy Gardner, Manager
• Will Commisso, Director, Ticket Sales
Ballpark:
NBT Bank Stadium.
Ballpark Description:
Built on the former third base parking lot of
MacArthur Stadium. Named on October 8 1996
and dedicated on April 2 1997. First game
played on April 3 1997.
Media Broadcast:
WFBL 1390-AM.
Major Team Affiliation:
Washington Nationals

TOLEDO MUD HENS
FIFTH THIRD FIELD
406 WASHINGTON STREET
TOLEDO, OH 43604
419-725-4367
Fax: 419-725-4368
www.mudhens.com
• Joe Napoli, President, CEO
jnapoli@mudhens.com
• Erik Ibsen, EVP, General Manager
eibsen@mudhens.com
• Kim McBroom, Chief Marketing Officer
• Lloyd McClendon, Manager
Ballpark:
Fifth Third Field.
Ballpark Description:
Toledo's new ballpark, Fifth Third Field opened
in 2002 and has a seating capacity of 10,000
Media Broadcast:
WLQR 1470-AM, WFOB 1430-AM.
Camps:
Pepsi Baseball Camp.
Major Team Affiliation:
Detroit Tigers.

Teams:

JOLIET SLAMMERS
1 MAYOR ART SCHULTZ DRIVE
SLAMMERS STADIUM
JOLIET, IL 60432
815-722-2287
Fax: 815-726-4304
info@jolietslammers.com
www.jolietslammers.com
• Nick Semaca, President/Chief Executive
Officer
• Heather Mills, General Manager
• Porscha Johnson, Manager Of Corporate Sale
• Lauren Rhodes, Account Executive
Year Founded:
2011
Seating Capacity:
6,500+

MEXICAN LEAGUE A.C. (AAA LEVEL)
INSURGENTES SUR 797
THIRD FLOOR
COL. NAPLES
BENITO JUAREZ, CP, MEXICO 03810
oficina@lmb.com.mx
LMB.com.mx
• Plinio Escalante Bolio, CEO
• Nestor Alba Brito, Director of Operations
• Patricio Perez Diego Ochoa, Player
Registration and Control
• Oscarc Neri Rojas Salazar, Director of
Administration
Description:
The Mexican League is a summer Triple
AAA baseball league with teams based all
along Mexico. The only Minor League
baseball sanctioned outside of the US, and
affiliated with Major League baseball.
Teams:
16

Teams:

AGUASCALIENTES RAILROADERS
LOPEZ MATEOS #101 TORRE A
PLAZA CRISTLA COLONIA
SAN LUIS, AGUASCALIENTES, MEXICO CP
20250
449-915 1596
www.rielerosags.com
• Marco Davalillo, Manager
Ballpark:
Parque Alberto Romo Chavez

BRONCOS DE REYNOSA
BRONCOS DE REYNOSA
ESTADIO ALDOLFO LOPEZ MATEOS
REYNOSA, TAMAULIPAS, MEXICO
• Jesus Sommers, Manager
Ballpark:
Estadio Aldolfo Lopez Mateos

CAMPECHE PIRATES
PIRATES DE CAMPECHE
ESTADIO NELSON BARRERA
CAMPECHE, MEXICO
• Dan Firova, Manager
Founded:
1980

DELFINES DEL CARMEN
www.delfinesbeisbol.com.mx
• Felix Fermin, Manager
Ballpark:
Estadio Resurgimiento

LAGUNA COWBOYS
VAQUEROS LAGUNA
ESTADIO REVOLUCION
TORREON, COAHUILA, MEXICO
• Luis Dovalina Flores, General Manager
• Jorge Luis Lechuga, Manager
Founded:
1940

MEXICO CITY RED DEVILS
MANUEL M. PONCE 87
FIRST FLOOR
COL. GUADALUPE INN
MEXICO CITY, MEXICO CP 01020
contacto@diablos-rojos.com
www.diablos.com.mx
• Roberto Mansure Galan, CEO
• Jorge Alum Kahwagi, General Manager
• Vania Ravelo, Media Manager
Founded:
1940

MONCOLVA STEELERS
ACEREROS DE MONCLOVA
ESTADIO DE BEISBOL MONCLOVA
MONCLOVA, COAHUILA, MEXICO C.P. 25750
52-866-636-2650
Fax: 52-866-636-2688
acererosdelnorte@prodigy.net.mx
• Donatian Garza Gutierrez, Managing Director
• Jorge Espinoza Lumbreras, Administrative
Manager
• Oscar Romero Shot, Sports Manager
Founded:
1974

MONTERREY SULTANS
SULTANES DE MONTERREY
ESTADIO DE BEISBOL DE MONTERREY
AV. MANUEL BARRAGAN
MONTERREY, NUEVO LEON, MEXICO C.P.
64460
52-818-351-0209
Fax: 52-818-351-8022
www.sultanes.com.mx
• Jose Maiz Garcia, President
• Roberto Magdaleno Ramirez, Director General
Founded:
1939

OAXACA WARRIORS
GUERREROS DE OAXACA
ESTADIO EDUARDO VASCONCELOS
PRIVADA DEL CHOPO #115
OAXACA, MEXICO C.P. 68050
52-951-515-5522
Fax: 52-951-515-4966
www.guerreros.mx
• Vicente Perez Avella Villa, CEO
Founded:
1940

PUEBLA PARAKEETS
CALZADA IGNACIO ZARAGOZA
#666
COL. MARAVILLAS
PUEBLA, MEXICO CP 72220
11-52-222-222-2116
Fax: 11-52-222-222-2117
info@pericosdepuebla.com.mx
www.pericosdepuebla.com.mx
• Juan E. Villarreal, CEO
• Juan Emmanuel Bello Rustrian, COO
Ballpark:
Estadio de Beisbol Hermanos Serdan
Founded:
1924

QUINTANA ROO TIGERS
TIGRES DE QUINTANA ROO
ESTADIO DE BEISBOL BETO AVILA
CANCUN, QUINTANA ROO, MEXICO
• Francisco Minjarez, General Manager
Founded:
1955

SALTILLO SARAPE USERS
ESTADIO DE BEISBOL FRANSCISCO I
MADERO
BLVD NAZARIO S. ORTIZ GARZA
SALTILLO, COAHUILA, MEXICO C.P. 25280
52-844-416-9455
Fax: 52-844-439-0550
• Juan Rodriguez, Manager
Ballpark:
Estadio de Beisbol Francisco 1. Madero

TABASCO OLMECS
ESTADIO CENTENARIO 27 DE FEBRERO
COL. ATASTA DE SERRA
VILLAHERMOSA, TABASCO, MEXICO C.P.
86100
52-993-352-2787
Fax: 52-993-352-2788
olmecastab@prodigy.net.mx
• Raul Gonzalez Rodriguez, Executive President
• CP Luis Guzman Ramos, General Manager
• Lauro Jimenez Lopez, Media Chief/Public
Relations
Ballpark:
Estadio Centenario 27 de Febrero

TIJUANA BULLS
LA CASA DE NUESTROS TOROS DE
TIJUANA
BOULEVARD AGUA CALIENTE #11720
COL. HIPODROMO
TIJUANA, BC, MEXICO 22020
www.torosdetijuana.com
• Eddy Diaz, Manager
Ballpark:
Estadio Nacional de Tijuana

VERACRUZ RED EAGLES
ROJOS DEL AGUILA DE VERACRUZ
ESTADIO UNIVERSITARIO BETO AVILA
AV. JACARANDAS #244-B ESPANA
VERACRUZ, MEXICO CP 94294
52-229-935-5004
Fax: 52-229-935-5008
rojosdelaguila@prodigy.net.mx
• Jose Antonio Mansur Beltran, Executive
President
• Jean Paul Mansur Beltran, CEO
Ballpark:
Estadio Universitario Beto Avila

YUCATAN LIONS
LEONES DE YUCATAN
CALLE 50 #402-D
COL. JESUS CARRANZA
MERIDA, YUCATAN, MEXICO CP 97109
52-999-926-3022
Fax: 52-999-926-3631
www.leones.mx
• Propasa Dunosusa, Owner
• Jose Rivero, General Manager
• Edgar Tovar, Manager
Ballpark:
Estadio de Beisbol Kukulkan Alamo
Founded:
1954

MIDWEST LEAGUE (A LEVEL)
210 SOUTH MICHIGAN STREET
5TH FLOOR - PLAZA BUILDING
SOUTH BEND, IN 46601
574-532-1221
Fax: 574-234-4220
dickn@sni-law.com
www.midwestleague.com
• George H. Spelius, President Emeritus
• Richard A. Nussbaum, II,
President/Secretary
• Holly Voss, League Administrator
League History:
The Illinois State League began operation in
1947. Six cities in Southern Illinois formed
teams and banded together as a Class D
League, the lowest among the ranks of
organized Minor League Baseball. The
League was forced to change its name to
the Mississippi-Ohio Valley (MOV) League
in 1949. During the combined nine year
history of the leagues, membership was
unstable, wavering back and forth from six
to eight teams. In 1956, the Midwest League
(MWL) name became official as teams
moved out of Southern Illinois to larger
markets.
Years in League:
1947-present.

Teams:

BELOIT SNAPPERS
2301 SKYLINE DRIVE
BELOIT, WI 53511
608-362-2272
Fax: 608-362-0418
snappy@snappersbaseball.com
www.snappersbaseball.com
• Dennis Conerton, President
• Seth Flolid, General Manager
• Crystal Bowen, Director of Ticket Operations
• Robert T. Coon, Director of Media Relations &
Marketing
• Fran Riordan, Manager
Team History:
Before the Snappers arrived in town in 1982, the
only professional baseball team in Beloit was a
team affiliated with the old Class D Wisconsin
Association in 1905. The Beloit Snappers have
been a Class A affiliate of the Milwaukee
Brewers since the club joined the Midwest
League in 1982. The team was known as the
Beloit Brewers (named after the parent club)
through the 1994 season, when the club name
then changed to the Snappers.
Ballpark:
Pohlman Field.
Ballpark Description:
Built in 1981, the Harry C. Pohlman Field
(originally named Telfer Park) is the home of the
Beloit Snappers. It's seating capacity is 3,500.
Team Affiliate:
Oakland Athletics

BOWLING GREEN HOT RODS
BOWLING GREEN HOT RODS
300 8TH AVENUE
BOWLING GREEN, KY 42102
270-901-2121
Fax: 270-901-2165
fun@bghotrods.com
• Adam Nuse, General Manager/COO
• Eric Leach, Assistant General Manager
• Stephanie Morton, Director of Finance
• Jennifer Johnson, Director of Marketing and
Community Relations
• Matt Ingram, Director of Sales
• Jordan Gracey, Director of Creative Services
• Reinaldo Ruiz, Manager
Team Affiliate:
Tampa Bay Rays

BURLINGTON BEES
2712 MOUNT PLEASANT STREET
BURLINGTON, IA 52601
319-754-5705
Fax: 319-754-5882
staff@gobees.com
www.gobees.com
• Dave Walker, President
• Chuck Brockett, General Manager
chuck@gobees.com
• Bill Dowell, Vice President
• Kim Parker, Assistant GM, Director of Group
Outings
• Chad Tracy, Manager
Ballpark:
Community Field
Ballpark Description:
Built in 1947, burned in 1971 and rebuilt and
opened in 1973, then renovated in 2005. Seats
3,200.
Team Affiliate:
Los Angeles Angels of Anaheim

CEDAR RAPIDS KERNELS
PERFECT GAME FIELD
950 ROCKFORD ROAD SW
CEDAR RAPIDS, IA 52404
319-363-3887
800-860-3609
Fax: 319-363-5631
kernels@kernels.com
www.kernels.com
• Jake Mauer, Manager
• Brian Dinkelman, Hitting Coach
• J.P. Martinez, Pitching Coach
Ballpark:
Perfect Game Field.
Ballpark Description:
One of the two new ballparks in the Midwest
League in 2002. Veterans Memorial Stadium
has a seating capacity of 5,400.
Media Broadcast:
The Zone - ESPN 1600-AM.
Major League Affiliate:
Minnesota Twins

CLINTON LUMBERKINGS
ASHFORD UNIVERSITY FIELD
537 BALLPARK DRIVE
CLINTON, IA 52732
563-242-0727
Fax: 563-242-1433
lumberkings@lumberkings.com
www.lumberkings.com
• Ted Tornow, General Manager
• Tyler Oehmen, Director of Operations
• Shaun Thomas, Head Groundskeeper
• Greg Mroz, Director of Broadcasting & Media
Relations
• Alex Swartz, Director of Concessions
Ballpark:
Ashford University Field
Ballpark Description:
Built in 1937, Riverview Stadium was the orginal
name before changing to Alliant Field.
Media Broadcast:
KCLN 1390-AM.
Years in League:
1954-present.

Team Affiliate:
Seattle Mariners

DAYTON DRAGONS
FIFTH THIRD FIELD
220 NORTH PATTERSON BOULEVARD
DAYTON, OH 45402
937-228-2287
Fax: 937-228-2284
dragons@daytondragons.com
www.daytondragons.com
• Robert Murphy, President
teampresident@daytondragons.com
• Eric Deutsch, Executive Vice President
eric.deutsch@daytondragons.com
• Gary Mayse, Executive Vice President,
General Manager
gary.mayse@daytondragons.com
• Mark Schlein, Vice President of
Accounting/Finance
mark.schlein@daytondragons.com
• Jose Nieves, Manager
• Cody Oakes, Baseball Operations Manager
• Mike Vujea, Director of Group Sales
Ballpark:
Fifth Third Field.
Ballpark Description:
Opened in April 2000 with a seating capacity of
7,230.
Team Affiliate:
Cincinnati Reds

FORT WAYNE TINCAPS
PARKVIEW FIELD
1301 EWING STREET
FORT WAYNE, IN 46802
260-482-6400
Fax: 260-471-4678
info@tincaps.com
• Mike Nutter, Team President
• David Lorenz, VP, Corporate Partnerships
• Brian Schackow, VP, Finance
• Michael Limmer, VP, Marketing/Promotions
• Patrick Ventura, Director of Ticketing
• Francisco Morales, Manager
Major Team Affiliation:
San Diego Padres.
Media Broadcast:
ESPN Radio 1380-AM WONO.

GREAT LAKES LOONS
DOW DIAMOND
825 EAST MAIN STREET
MIDLAND, MI 48640
989-837-2255
888-678-2255
www.loons.com
• Paul Barbeau, President
• Scott Litle, VP, General Manager
• Jana Chotivkova, VP, Finance
• Kevin Schunk, Director of Corporate
Partnerships
• Jay Arons, Director of Sales
• Dan Straley, Director of Operations & Facilities
• Luis Matos, Manager
Stadium:
Dow Diamond
Team Affiliate:
LA Dodgers

KANE COUNTY COUGARS
NORTHWESTERN MEDICINE FIELD
34W002 CHERRY LANE
GENEVA, IL 60134
630-232-8811
Fax: 630-232-8815
info@kanecountycougars.com
www.kccougars.com
• Cheryl Froehlich, Owner & Board of Directors
• Bob Froehlich, Owner & Board of Directors
• Curtis Haug, VP, General Manager
Ballpark:
Fifth Third Bank Ballpark
Years in League:
1991-present.
Media Broadcast:
WBIG 1280-AM.

Major Team Affiliation:
Chicago Cubs

LAKE COUNTY CAPTAINS
CLASSIC PARK
35300 VINE STREET
EASTLAKE, OH 44095
440-975-8085
Fax: 440-975-8958
• Brad Seymour, General Manager
• Neil Stein, Assistant General Manager
• Rob Demko, Director of Finance
• John Klein, Director of Food & Beverage
• Drew LaFollette, Director of Promotions &
Marketing
• Wayne Loeblein, Director of Stadium
Operations
• Shaun Larkin, Manager
Team Affiliate:
Cleveland Indians

LANSING LUGNUTS
COOLEY LAW SCHOOL STADIUM
505 EAST MICHIGAN AVENUE
LANSING, MI 48912
517-485-4500
Fax: 517-485-4518
info@lansinglugnuts.com
www.lansinglugnuts.com
• Nick Grueser, General Manager
• Heather Viele, Director of Business Operations
• Dennis Busse, Stadium Operations Manager
• Ken Huckaby, Manager
Ballpark:
Cooley Law School Stadium
Ballpark Description:
Built in 1996, construction at the park was
completed in only one year by local craftspeople
and contractors. Oldsmobile Park is owned by
the City of Lansing and was financed by six local
banking institutions.
Major Team Affiliation:
Toronto Blue Jays.
Media Broadcast:
Lansing's Sports Radio 92.1/92.7-FM, WILX-TV
10.

PEORIA CHIEFS
DOZER PARK
730 SW JEFFERSON
PEORIA, IL 61605
309-680-4000
Fax: 309-680-4080
feedback@chiefsnet.com
www.peoriachiefs.com
• Rocky Vonachen, President
(309) 680-4001
rocky@chiefsnet.com
• Brendan Kelly, General Manager
(309) 680-4002
• Nathan Baliva, Director of Media & Baseball
Operations
(309) 680-4018
nathanb@chiefsnet.com
• Ryan Sivori, Box Office Manager
(309) 680-4006
ryans@chiefsnet.com
• Jason Mott, VP, Ticket Sales & Services
• Joe Kruzel, Manager
Team History:
Professional baseball in Peoria can be traced
back to 1878, with the formation of an
independent team named the Peoria Reds. In
the 1930s the team was called the Peoria
Tractors and though they played well,
attendance figures were disturbingly low. During
the time baseball was not present in Peoria, the
United States entered World War II, which led to
a shortage of professional baseball throughout
the entire country. In the fall of 1983, the team
was bought by a local businessman and
renamed the Chiefs, after the old Three-I
League team from the 1950s.
Ballpark:
Peoria Chiefs Stadium
Ballpark Description:
A $23 million multi-use facility built in 2002 with
a 7,000 seating capacity.

Sponsors:
O'Brien Automotive Team, WM Waste Management, CEFCU, CAT, Pepsi, Bud Light, Methodist Medical Center, Heart Technologies Inc., Auto Owners Insurance.
Major Team Affiliation:
St. Louis Cardinals
Years in League:
1983-present.

QUAD CITIES RIVER BANDITS
MODERN WOODMEN PARK
209 SOUTH GAINES STREET
DAVENPORT, IA 52802
563-324-3000
Fax: 563-324-3109
bandit@riverbandits.com
www.riverbandits.com
• Andrew Chesser, General Manager
• Shawn Brown, Vice President of Sales
• Travis Painter, Assitant General Manager, Baseball Operations
• Taylor Satterly, Assistant General Manager, Special Events
• Mike Clark, Assistant General Manager of Amusements
• Seth Reeve, Stadium Operations Manager
• Josh Bonifay, Manager
Team History:
On December 13 2007, a new era in Quad Cities baseball began. The Midwest League franchise that had been known as the Swing of the Quad Cities for the previous four seasons announced the overwhelming results of a recent Name the Team contest, once again giving baseball in the Quad Cities the name the community has come to love: River Bandits.
Ballpark:
Modern Woodmen Park
Ballpark Description:
In the beginning Municipal Stadium (known then as) was dedicated May 26 1931. A crowd of 2,791 watched the Davenport Blue Sox defeat the Dubuque Tigers, 7-1. Municipal Stadium was renamed in honor of former Davenport Times-Democrat sports editor John O'Donnell on May 27 1971, following O'Donnell's death.
Major Team Affiliation:
Houston Astros
Media Broadcast:
KBOB 104.9-FM.

SOUTH BEND CUBS
FOUR WINDS FIELD
501 WEST SOUTH STREET
SOUTH BEND, IN 46601
574-235-9988
Fax: 574-235-9950
cubs@southbendcubs.com
www.silverhawks.com
• Andrew Berlin, Owner & Chairman
• Joe Hart, President
• Peter Argueta, Assistant General Manager, Operations
• Cheryl Carlson, Director of Finance and Human Resources
cherylcarlson@silverhawks.com
• Nick Brown, Vice President/Business Development
• Chris Hagstrom, Director of Creative Services and Promotions
• Jimmy Gonzalez, Team Manager
Ballpark:
Coveleski Regional Stadium.
Ballpark Description:
Opened in 1988 and has 5,000 seating capacity.
Years in League:
1988-present.
Major Team Affiliation:
Chicago Cubs.

WEST MICHIGAN WHITECAPS
FIFTH THIRD BALLPARK
4500 WEST RIVER DRIVE
COMSTOCK PARK, MI 49326
616-784-4131
Fax: 616-784-4911

playball@whitecaps-baseball.com
www.whitecaps-baseball.com
• Lew Chamberlain, CEO/Managing Partner
lchamberin@whitecapsbaseball.com
• Scott Lane, President
slane@whitecapsbaseball.com
• Denny Baxter, CFO/Director of Accounting
dbaxter@whitecapsbaseball.com
• Jim Jarecki, Vice President
jjarecki@whitecapsbaseball.com
• Steve McCarthy, VP of Sales
smccarthy@whitecapsbaseball.com
• Mickey Graham, Director of Marketing/Media Relations
• Chad Sayen, Direcotor of Ticket Sales
• Andrew Graham, Manager
Team History:
When the West Michigan Whitecaps began play in the Grand Rapids area in 1994, it was the culmination of a 10-year labor of love for local businessmen Lew Chamberlin and Dennis Baxter. The two took on the challenge of bringing a minor league team to the area in 1984 and in February of 1993. Until the West Michigan Whitecaps began their inaugural season in 1994, Grand Rapids had been without a professional baseball team for 40 years, since the Grand Rapids Chicks disbanded in 1954.
Ballpark:
Fifth Third Ballpark.
Ballpark Description:
Fifth Third Ballpark is a $10 million state-of-the-art facility built in 1994 and expanded in 1995, 1996 and 1998. The stadium currently has a capacity of 11,000.
Major Team Affiliation:
Detroit Tigers.
Media Broadcast:
WBBL 1340-AM, WHTC 1450-AM, WSCG 1380-AM, WDEE 97.3-FM, WXSP-TV.

WISCONSIN TIMBER RATTLERS
FOX CITIES STADIUM
2400 NORTH CASALOMA DRIVE
APPLETON, WI 54912
920-733-4152
info@timberrattlers.com
www.timberrattlers.com
• Rob Zerjav, President
rzerjav@timberrattlers.com
• Aaron Hahn, Vice President, Assistant GM
rzerjav@timberrattlers.com
• Ron Kaiser, Director of Stadium Operations
• Chris Mehring, Media Relations
• Cathy Spanbauer, Controller
cspanbauer@timberrattlers.com
• Matt Erickson, Manager
Sponsors:
Sports Medicine Center, Pro/Net Consulting LLC, Virchow Krause & Company, Microtel.
Major Team Affiliation:
Midwest League affiliate of the Milwaukee Brewers

NEW YORK-PENNSYLVANIA LEAGUE (A LEVEL)
204 37TH AVENUE
N366
ST. PETERSBURG, FL 33704
727-289-7112
Fax: 727-683-9691
www.newyork-pennleague.com
• Ben J. Hayes, President
• Carl Gutelius, Corporate Secretary
• Jon Dandes, Treasurer
• Laurie Hayes, League Administrator
• Makenzie Burrows, Media
Nature of Service:
Baseball League.
Year Founded:
1939
League History:
The original New York-Pennsylvania League ran between 1923 and 1938 and was the immediate predecessor of the Eastern League. The current New

York-Pennsylvania League was originally known as the PONY LEAGUE in 1939-1956 before adopting the current New York-Pennsylvania League moniker in 1957.
Teams:
14

Teams:

ABERDEEN IRONBIRDS
RIPKEN STADIUM
873 LONG DRIVE
ABERDEEN, MD 21001
410-297-9292
Fax: 410-297-6653
www.ironbirdsbaseball.com
• Cal Ripken, Jr, Owner, Chair, Founder
• Joe Harrington, General Manager
• Chris Flannery, COO
• Bill Ripken, Co-Owner, Executive Vice President
• Luis Pujols, Manager
Ballpark:
Ripken Stadium
Major League Affiliation:
Baltimore Orioles

AUBURN DOUBLEDAYS
LEO PINCKNEY FIELD AT FALCON PARK
130 NORTH DIVISION STREET
AUBURN, NY 13021
315-255-2489
Fax: 315-255-2675
info@auburndoubledays.com
www.auburndoubledays.com
• Mike Voutsinas, General Manager
• Andrew Sagarin, Operations Manager
• Paul Mullin, Sponsorship Services Manager
• Derek Wohlfarth, Accounting Manager
• Jerad Head, Team Manager
Ballpark:
Falcon Park.
Ballpark Description:
Built in 1995 with a seating capacity of 2,800
Major Team Affiliation:
Washington Nationals
Media Broadcast:
WDWN 89.1-FM.
Years in League:
1958-80, 1982-present.

BATAVIA MUCKDOGS
DWYER STADIUM
299 BANK STREET
BATAVIA, NY 14020
585-343-5454
Fax: 585-343-5620
tsick@muckdogs.com
www.muckdogs.com
• Naomi Silver, Chair/COO
• Travis Sick, General Manager
• Don Rock, Director of Stadium Grounds
• Angel Espada, Team Manager
Years in League:
1939-53, 1957-59, 1961-present.
Team History:
In 1939 professional baseball came to Batavia and Genesee County. There had been talk of a professional baseball team for Batavia as early as 1936, but lack of a proper playing field including fences and lights which were the criteria, did not exist in the city. The Batavia franchise is unique in organized baseball because it is truly a community owned and operated in the strictest sense. There are no stockholders and no stock issue. The Genesee County Baseball Club Incorporated holds legal title to the franchise; its officers and directors are elected each year.
Ballpark:
Dwyer Stadium.
Ballpark Description:
The old Dwyer Stadium was demolished and replaced with a new three million dollar facility, which opened in time for the 1996 season.
Major Team Affiliation:
Miami Marlins

Media Broadcast:
WBSU 89.1-FM.

BROOKLYN CYCLONES
MCU PARK
1904 SURF AVENUE
BROOKLYN, NY 11224
718-449-8497
Fax: 718-449-6368
info@brooklyncyclones.com
www.brooklyncyclones.com
• Steve Cohen, Vice President
steve@brooklyncyclones.com
• Kevin Mahoney, General Manager
kwvin@brooklyncyclones.com
• Vladimir Lipsman, Operations Manager
vladimir@brooklyncyclones.com
• Gary J Perone, Assistant General Manager
gary@brooklyncyclones.com
• Tom Gamboa, Team Manager
Years in League:
2000-present.
Ballpark:
MCU Park.
Ballpark Description:
Opened in 2001
Media Broadcast:
WKRB 90.9
Major Team Affiliation:
New York Mets.

CONNECTICUT TIGERS
DODD STADIUM
14 STOTT AVENUE
NORWICH, CT 06360
860-887-7962
Fax: 860-886-5996
info@cttigers.com
• C.J. Knudsen, Senior Vice President
• Eric Knighton, General Manager
• Dave Schermerhorn, Assistant General Manager
• Heather Bartlett, Director of Concessions & Merchandise
• Brent Southworth, Director of Sales
• Jack Kasten, Director of Group Sales & Operations
Description:
The New York-Penn League and Minor League Baseball granted approval to the Oneonta Athletic Corporation to relocate their professional baseball franchise from Oneonta, New York to Norwich, Connecticut.
Affiliation:
Detroit Tigers, MLB

HUDSON VALLEY RENEGADES
DUTCHESS STADIUM
1500 ROUTE 9D
WAPPINGERS FALLS, NY 12590
845-838-0094
Fax: 845-838-0014
info@hvrenegades.com
www.hvrenegades.com
• Jeff Goldklang, President
• Eben Yager, Senior Vice President & General Manager
• Rick Zolzer, Vice President
• Kristen Huss, Assistant General Manager
• Vicky DeFreese, Director of Business Operations
vdefreese@hvrenegades.com
• Tim Parenton, Manager
Team History:
The Renegades officially arrived in the Hudson Valley on November 30, 1993 when team owner Marvin Goldklang and Club President Skip Weisman announced that the Erie Sailors franchise would be relocating to Dutchess County. Since that very memorable first season, the Renegades have become an integral part of the Hudson Valley community.
Ballpark:
Dutchess Stadium.
Ballpark Description:
The stadium opened it 1994 and seats 4,494
Media Broadcast:
WBNR 1260-AM, WLNA 1420-AM.

Years in League:
1994-present.
Affiliate:
Tampa Bay Rays

LOWELL SPINNERS
LELACHEUR PARK
450 AIKEN STREET
LOWELL, MA 01854
978-459-2255
Fax: 978-459-1674
www.lowellspinners.com
• Drew Weber, Owner/Chief Executive Officer
• Tim Bawmann, President, General Manager
• Jeff Cohen, Director of Merchandising
• Justin Williams, Director of Ticket Operations
• Joe Oliver, Manager
Ballpark:
Edward A. LeLacheur Park.
Ballpark Description:
Opened in 1998 and has a seating capacity of 5,000
Major Team Affiliation:
Boston Red Sox.

MAHONING VALLEY SCRAPPERS
EASTWOOD FIELD
111 EASTWOOD MALL BOULEVARD
NILES, OH 44446-1357
330-505-0000
Fax: 303-505-9696
info@mvscrappers.com
www.mvscrappers.com
• Alan Levin, Principal Owner
• Erik Haag, Executive Vice President
• Mike Rauch, Chief Financial Officer
• Jordan Taylor, General Manager/Vice President
jtaylor@mvscrappers.com
• Brad Hooser, Assistant General Manager, Operations
• Travis Fryman, Team Manager
Team History:
The Mahoning Valley Scrappers earned their initial success during the 1999-opening season and again in 2000. The team made its way to the New York - Penn Minor League playoffs 2 years in a row, with spirit and support from the Mahoning Valley.
Ballpark:
Eastwood Field.
Ballpark Description:
Completed in 1999, Eastwood Field's 6,300 seat open-air stadium is an intimate entertainment facility. This beautifully built stadium is located in Niles, Ohio half way between Cleveland & Pittsburgh. The new stadium was built in honor of the late Cafaro Company Founder, William Cafaro.
MLB Affiliate:
Cleveland Indians

STATE COLLEGE SPIKES
LUBRANO PARK
112 MEDLAR FIELD
UNIVERSITY PARK, PA 16802
814-272-1711
Fax: 814-272-1718
frontoffice@statecollegespikes.com
www.statecollegespikes.com
• Chuck Greenburg, Chairman and Managing Partner
• Jason Dambach, President
• Scott Walker, General Manager
• Johnny Rodriguez, Manager
Team Affiliate:
St. Louis Cardinals
Ballpark:
Medlar Field at Lubrano Park

STATEN ISLAND YANKEES
75 RICHMOND TERRACE
RICHMOND COUNTY BANK BALLPARK
STATEN ISLAND, NY 10301
718-720-9265
Fax: 718-273-5763
www.siyanks.com

• Jane M. Rogers, President, General Manager
• Will Smith, Operating Partner
• Brian Levine, Vice President of Corporate Relationships
• Jay Nazzaro, Chief Financial Officer
• T.J. Jahn, Vice President of Ticket Sales
• David Percarpio, Group Sales Manager
• Pat Osborn, Manager
Years in League:
1999-present.
Ballpark:
Richmond County Bank Ballpark.
Ballpark Description:
The Richmond County Bank Ballpark at St. George is New York's premier waterfront stadium and has become one of the standard bearers in professional baseball parks across the country. Opened on June 24 2001 the 7,171 seat home of the Staten Island Yankees was the crown jewel of the borough and would soon house not only baseball but concerts, picnics and other special events.
Major Team Affiliation:
New York Yankees.
Media Broadcast:
WSIA 88.9-FM.

TRI-CITY VALLEYCATS
JOSEPH L. BRUNO STADIUM
80 VANDENBURG AVENUE
TROY, NY 12180
518-629-2287
Fax: 518-629-2299
info@tcvalleycats.com
www.tcvalleycats.com
• William L. Gladstone, President, Principal Owner
• Matt Callahan, General Manager
• Michelle Skinner, General Manager
Ballpark:
Joseph L. Bruno Stadium.
Years in League:
1989-present.
Major Team Affiliation:
Houston Astros.
Media Broadcast:
WVKZ 1240-AM.

VERMONT LAKE MONSTERS
CENTENNIAL FIELD
ONE KING STREET FERRY DOCK
BURLINGTON, VT 05401
802-655-4200
Fax: 802-655-5660
www.vermontlakemonsters.com
• Ray C. Pecor, Principal Owner/President
• Kyle Bostwick, Vice President
• Nate Cloutier, Executive Director of Sales & Marketing
• Joe Doud, General Manager
• Aaron Nieckula, Manager
Team History:
The Vermont Expos have been a member of the Montreal Expos baseball system since 1994. Over the past ten seasons, the Vermont Expos have compiled a 372 win - 391 loss record, including a 48 - 26 record and a NY-PENN League Championship in 1996.
Ballpark:
Centennial Field.
Ballpark Description:
Located on the campus of the University of Vermont in Burlington. Officially opened on April 17 1906. Since the Expos made Centennial Field their home, they've completely rebuilt the pitching mound and over 1,000 feet of warning track, creating a field that compares favorably to any in baseball.
Years in League:
1994-present.
MLB Affiliate:
Oakland A's

WEST VIRGINIA BLACK BEARS
MONONGALIA COUNTY BALLPARK
2040 GYORKO DRIVE
GRANVILLE, WV 26534

304-293-7910
wvblackbears@gmail.com
• Matthew Drayer, General Manager
• Wyatt Toregas, Manager
Team Affiliate:
Pittsburg Pirates.

WILLIAMSPORT CROSSCUTTERS
BB&T BALLPARK
1700 WEST FOURTH STREET
WILLIAMSPORT, PA 17701
570-326-3389
Fax: 570-326-3494
mail@crosscutters.com
www.crosscutters.com
• Doug Estes, VP, General Manager
• Gabe Sinicropi, VP, Marketing & Public
Relations
• Sarah Budd, Director, Ticket Operations &
Community Relations
• Bill Gehron, III, Director, Food & Beverage
• Pat Borders, Team Manager
Ballpark:
Bowman Field.
Ballpark Description:
One of baseball's oldest and most distinguished
ballparks is Williamsport's own Bowman Field.
Ground was broken for the ballpark in the fall of
1925. It was modeled after a ballpark in Johnson
City, New York. The first game played in the
new ballpark was an exhibition game between
the Williamsport Grays and the Bucknell
University baseball team on April 22 1926.
Years in League:
1923-37, 1968-72, 1994-present.
Major Team Affiliation:
Philadelphia Phillies

NORTHWEST BASEBALL LEAGUE
420 CHURCHWELL DR
SUITE 18847
PANAMA CITY BEACH, FL 32407
850-588-6205
www.milb.com/northwest
• Johnson North, President
njohnsonnwl@gmail.com
• Jeff Eiseman, Vice President
• Jerry Walker, Secretary

Teams:

BOISE HAWKS
MEMORIAL STADIUM
5600 GLENWOOD STREET
BOISE, ID 83714
208-322-5000
Fax: 208-322-6846
info@boisehawks.com
• Jeff Eiseman, President
• Bob Flannery, General Manager
• Britt Talbert, Corporate Sales Manager
• Jake Lusk, Director of Operations
• Frank Gonzales, Manager
Ballpark:
Memorial Stadium. Seating capacity, 3,452.

EUGENE EMERALDS
PK PARK
PO BOX 10911
EUGENE, OR 97440
541-342-5367
Fax: 541-342-6089
info@emeraldsbaseball.com
• Allan Benavides, General Manager
• Matt Dompe, Assistant General Manager
Ballpark:
PK Park. Seating capacity, 4,000.

EVERETT AQUASOX
EVERETT MEMORIAL STADIUM
3802 BROADWAY
EVERETT, WA 98201
425-258-3673
info@aquasox.com
www.aquasox.com

• Danny Tetzlaff, General Manager
Ballpark:
Everett Memorial Stadium. Seating capacity,
3,682.

HILLSBORO HOPS
RON TONKIN FIELD
4460 NW 229TH AVENUE
HILLSBORO, OR 97124
503-640-0887
info@hillsborohops.com
• Mike McMurray, President
• K.L. Wombacher, Executive Vice President &
General Manager
• Laura McMurray, Chief Financial Officer
• Shelley Duncan, Manager
Ballpark:
Ron Tonkin. Seating capacity, 3,534.

SALEM-KEIZER VOLCANOES
VOLCANOES STADIUM
6700 FIELD OF DREAMS NE
KEIZER, OR 97307
503-390-2225
Fax: 503-390-2227
info@volcanoesbaseball.com
• Jerry Walker, General Manager
• Tom Leip, Business Operations
• Rick Nelson, Stadium Operations
Ballpark:
Volcanoes Stadium. Seating capacity, 4,254.

SPOKANE INDIANS
AVISTA STADIUM
602 NORTH HAVANA STREET
SPOKANE, WA 99202
509-343-6886
mail@spokaneindians.com
• Bobby Brett, Managing Partner
• Andy Billig, Co-Owner & Senior Advisor
• Otto Klein, Senior Vice President
• Chris Duff, General Manager/Vice President
Ballpark:
Avista Stadium. Seating capacity, 6,803.

TRI-CITY DUST DEVILS
TRI-CITY STADIUM (GESA STADIUM)
602 BURDEN BOULEVARD
PASCO, WA 99301
509-544-8789
Fax: 509-547-9570
• Brent Miles, President
• Anthony Contreras, Manager
• Derrel Ebert, General Manager
Ballpark:
Gesa Stadium. Seating capacity, 3,654.

VANCOUVER CANADIANS
SCOTIABANK FIELD AT NAT BAILEY
STADIUM
4601 ONTARIO ST
VANCOUVER, BC, CANADA V5V 3H4
604-872-5232
Fax: 604-872-1714
staff@canadiansbaseball.com
www.milb.com/vancouver
• Andy Dunn, President
(604) 872-5232
adunn@canadiansbaseball.com
• Allan Bailey, General Manager
(604) 872-5232
abailey@canadiansbaseball.com
Baseball:
Scotiabank Field at Nat Bailey Stadium. Seating
capacity, 6,500.

PACIFIC COAST LEAGUE OF PROFESSIONAL BASEBALL CLUBS (AAA LEVEL)
ONE CHISHOLM TRAIL
SUITE 4200
ROUND ROCK, TX 78681
512-310-2900
Fax: 512-310-8300

office@pclbaseball.com
www.pclbaseball.com
• Branch B. Rickey, President
• Melanie Fiore, Director of Business
• Dwight Hall, Director of Baseball
Operations
Nature of Service:
Baseball League.
Number of Members:
16 teams.

Teams:

ALBUQUERQUE ISOTOPES
1601 AVENIDA CESAR CHAVEZ SE
ISOTOPES PARK
SECOND FLOOR
ALBUQUERQUE, NM 87106
505-924-2255
Fax: 505-242-8899
info@abqisotopes.com
• Ken Young, President
• John Traub, General Manager/Vice President
• Emmett Hammond, Vice
President/Secretary/Treasurer
• Nick LoBue, Vice President, Corporate
Development
• Glenallen Hill, Manager
Years in League:
2003-present.
Ballpark:
Isotopes Park.
Ballpark Description:
Opened in 2003. Seating Capacity: 12,215
Media Broadcast:
KNML 610 The Sports Animal.
Major Team Affiliation:
Los Angeles Dodgers

COLORADO SPRINGS SKY SOX
4385 TUTT BOULEVARD
SECURITY SERVICE FIELD
COLORADO SPRINGS, CO 80922
719-597-1449
Fax: 719-597-2491
info@skysox.com
www.skysox.com
• Tony Ensor, President/General Manager
tensor@skysox.com
• Rick Sweet, Manager
• Whitney Shellem, Dir of New Media & Fan
Communication
wshellem@skysox.com
Years in League:
1988-present.
Ballpark:
Security Service Field.
Ballpark Description:
Opened in 1988. Seating Capacity: 8500
Media Broadcast:
KRDO 1240-AM.
Major Team Affiliation:
Colorado Rockies.

EL PASO CHIHUAHUAS
SOUTHWEST UNIVERSITY PARK
1 BALLPARK PLAZA
EL PASO, TX 79901
915-242-2000
Fax: 915-242-2031
info@epchihuahuas.com
• Paul Foster, Owner/Chairman
• Brad Taylor, General Manager
• Pamela De La O, Director, Finance &
Administration
• Douglas Galeano, Director, Ballpark
Operations
Team Affiliate:
San Diego Padres
Ballpark:
Southwest University Park. Seating capacity,
7,500.

FRESNO GRIZZLIES
CHUKCHANSI PARK
1800 TULARE STREET
FRESNO, CA 93721
559-320-4487
Fax: 559-320-1216
ryoung@fresnogrizzlies.com
www.fresnogrizzlies.com
• Chris Cummings, President, Managing Partner
• Derek Franks, General Manager
• Tony DeFrancesco, Manager
Years in League:
1998-present.
Ballpark:
Chukchansi Park
Ballpark Description:
Opened in 2002. Seating capacity,
approximately 12,000.
Major Team Affiliation:
San Francisco Giants.
Media Broadcast:
KOOR 790-AM.

IOWA CUBS
PRINICIPAL PARK
ONE LINE DRIVE
DES MOINES, IA 50309
515-243-6111
Fax: 515-243-5152
www.iowacubs.com
• Michael Gartner, Chairman
mgartner@iowacubs.com
• Michael Giudicessi, Corporate Secretary
• Sam Bernabe, President/General Manager
sbernabe@iowacubs.com
• Marty Pevey, Manager
Years in League:
1998-present.
Ballpark:
Principal Park.
Ballpark Description:
Opened in 1992.
Major Team Affiliation:
Chicago Cubs.
Media Broadcast:
KXTK 940-AM.

LAS VEGAS 515
CASHMAN FIELD
850 LAS VEGAS BOULEVARD NORTH
LAS VEGAS, NV 89101
702-943-7200
Fax: 702-386-7214
info@lv51.com
www.lv51.com
• Don Logan, President/COO
• Chuck Johnson, General Manager
• Mike Rodriguez, VP, Ticket Operations
• Nick Fitzenreider, VP, Operations & Security
cjohnson@lv51.com
• Chip Vespe, Operations Manager
• Wally Backman, Manager
Years in League:
1983-present.
Ballpark:
Cashman Field.
Ballpark Description:
Opened in 1983. Seating Capacity, 9,334.
MLB Affiliate:
New York Mets

MEMPHIS REDBIRDS
198 UNION AVENUE
MEMPHIS, TN 38103
901-721-6050
Fax: 901-328-1102
www.memphisredbirds.com
• Craig Unger, General Manager
• Lisa Peterson, Manager, Group Sales
• Michael Whitty, Director of Media Relations
• Mike Shildt, Manager
Years in League:
1998-present.
Ballpark:
AutoZone Park.
Ballpark Description:
Opened in 2000.

MLB Affiliate:
St. Louis Cardinals

NASHVILLE SOUNDS
FIRST TENNESSEE PARK
19 JUNIOR GILLIAM WAY
NASHVILLE, TN 37219
615-690-4487
Fax: 615-256-5684
info@nashvillesounds.com
www.nashvillesounds.com
• Garry Arthur, General Manager, COO
• Chris Sprunger, VP, Ticket Operations
• Paul Hemingway, VP, Corporate Sales &
Marketing
• Doug Scopel, VP, Operations
• Steve Scarsone, Manager
Years in League:
1998-present.
Ballpark:
Herschel Greer Stadium.
Ballpark Description:
Opened in 1978. Seating Capacity, 10,700.
Media Broadcast:
WAMB.
MLB Affiliate:
Milwaukee Brewers

NEW ORLEANS ZEPHYRS
6000 AIRLINE DRIVE
ZEPHYR FIELD
METAIRIE, LA 70003
504-734-5155
Fax: 504-734-5118
info@zephyrsbaseball.com
www.zephyrsbaseball.com
• Donald Beaver, Owner/President
• Mike Schline, General Manager
• Donna Light, Director of Finance and
Administration
• Dave Sachs, Director of Media Relations
• Andy Haines, Manager
Years in League:
1998-present.
Ballpark:
Zephyr Field.
Ballpark Description:
Opened in 1997. Seating capacity, 11,000.
Media Broadcast:
WTIX 690-AM.
MLB Affiliate:
Miami Marlins

OKLAHOMA CITY DODGERS
TWO SOUTH MICKEY MANTLE DRIVE
CHICKASAW BRICKTOWN BALLPARK
OKLAHOMA CITY, OK 73104
405-218-1000
Fax: 405-218-1011
• Michael Byrnes, President/General Manager
• Jenna Byrnes, Senior Vice President
• Armando Reyes, Director of Ticket Operations
• Kyle Daugherty, Director of Business
Development
• Damon Berryhill, Manager
Years in League:
1963-68, 1998-present.
Ballpark:
Red Hawks Ballpark.
Ballpark:
Opened in 1998. Seating Capacity, 12,000.
MLB Affiliate:
Houston Astros

OMAHA STORM CHASERS
WERNER PARK
12356 BALLPARK WAY
PAPILLION, NE 68046
402-734-2550
Fax: 402-734-7166
info@oroyals.com
www.oroyals.com
• Gary Green, Chief Executive Officer
• Martie Cordaro, General Manager/President
• Laurie Schlender, Assistant General Manager
• Andrea Stava, Assistant General Manager of
Operations

Years in League:
1998-present.
Ballpark:
Werner Park
Ballpark Description:
Opened in 1948. Seating Capacity, 22,000.
Major Team Affiliation:
Kansas City Royals.
Media Broadcast:
KOSR 1490-AM.

RENO ACES
ACES BALLPARK
250 EVANS AVENUE
RENO, NV 89501
775-334-4700
Fax: 775-334-4701
customerservice@renoaces.com
www.renoaces.com
• Eric Edelstein, President
• Andrew Daugherty, Executive Vice President
• Brian Moss, VP, Business Development
• Sarah Bliss, Ticket Operations Manager
• Audrey Hill, Director of Marketing
• Phil Nevin, Manager
Ballpark:
Aces Ballpark. Seating capacity, 9,013.
MLB Affiliate:
Arizona Diamondbacks

ROUND ROCK EXPRESS
DELL DIAMOND
3400 EAST PALM VALLEY BOULEVARD
ROUND ROCK, TX 78665
512-255-2255
Fax: 512-255-1558
info@rrexpress.com
www.roundrockexpress.com
• Don Sanders, Principal Owner
• Chris Almendarez, President
• Lynn Nolan Ryan, Principal Owner
• Bobby Jones, Manager
• Reid Ryan, Founder
• Reese Ryan, CEO
• Chris Almendarez, General Manager
• Ryan-Sanders Baseball, Owners
• Jason Wood, Manager
Ballpark:
Dell Diamond
Ballpark Description:
As the home of the Round Rock Express, the
Dell Diamond features numerous amenities
designed for the ultimate in fan comfort and
enjoyment.
MLB Affiliate:
Texas Rangers

SACRAMENTO RIVER CATS
400 BALLPARK DRIVE
RALEY FIELD
WEST SACRAMENTO, CA 95691
916-376-4722
Fax: 916-376-4710
info@rivercats.com
www.rivercats.com
• Susan Savage, Chief Executive Officer,
Majority Owner
• Jeff Savage, President
• Chip Maxson, General Manager
• John Krivacic, Director of Ticket Operations
• Jose Alguacil, Manager
Years in League:
2000-present.
Ballpark:
Raley Field.
Ballpark Description:
Opened in 2000. Seating Capacity, 11,093.
Media Broadcast:
KSTE 650-AM. KSQR 1240-AM (Spanish).
Major Team Affiliation:
Established in 2000, Raley Field is home of the
Oakland Athletics Triple-A affiliate and two-time
PCL champions, the Sacramento River Cats.

SALT LAKE BEES
SMITHS BALLPARK
77 WEST 1300 SOUTH
SALT LAKE CITY, UT 84115
801-350-6900
Fax: 801-485-6818
www.stingersbaseball.com
• Gail Miller, Owner
• Clark Whitworth, President
• Jim Olson, Chief Operations Officer
• Marc Amicone, General Manager
• Steve Klauke, Director of Broadcasting
• Dave Anderson, Manager
Years in League:
1915-25, 1958-65, 1970-84, 1994-present.
Ballpark:
Spring Mobile Park
Ballpark Description:
Opened in 1994. Seating Capacity, 15,500.
Media Broadcast:
KJQS ESPN 1230-AM.
Major Team Affiliation:
Los Angeles Anaheim Angels

TACOMA RAINIERS
CHENEY STADIUM
2502 SOUTH TYLER STREET
TACOMA, WA 98405
253-752-7707
Fax: 253-752-7135
www.tacomarainiers.com
• Aaron Artman, President
• Jim Flavin, VP, Business Development
• Pat Listach, Manager
Years in League:
1904-05, 1960-present.
Ballpark:
Cheney Stadium.
Ballpark Description:
Opened in 1960. Seating capacity, 9,600.
Media Broadcast:
KHHO 850-AM.
MLB Affiliate:
Seattle Mariners

PECOS LEAGUE (INDEPENDENT LEAGUE)
PO BOX 271489
HOUSTON, TX 77277
575-680-2212
info@pecosleague.com
www.pecosleague.com
• Andrew Dunn, Commissioner
• Wally Anderson, Vice President of
Baseball Operations

Teams:

ALPINE COWBOYS
KOKERNOT FIELD
400 LOOP ROAD
ALPINE, TX 79830
432-386-3402
• Andrew Dunn, Commissioner
• Ryan Stevens, Manager

GARDENCITY WIND
706 EAST MAPLE
GARDEN CITY, KS 67846
620-765-4129
www.gardencitywind.com
• Andrew Dunn, Commissioner
• Bill Moore, Manager

LAS CRUCES VAQUEROS
APODOCA PARK
801 EAST MADRID
LAS CRUCES, NM 88001
575-680-2212
www.lascrucesvaqueros.com
• Andrew Dunn, Commissioner
• J.D. Droddy, League Adjudicator

ROSWELL INVADERS
2500 SE MAIN STREET
ST. ROSWELL, NM 88203
575-680-2212
www.roswellinvaders.com
• Andrew Dunn, Commissioner
• Bryan Kloppe, Manager

SANTA FE FUEGO
FORT MARCY PARK
MURALES AND WASHINGTION AVENUE
SANTA FE, NM 87504
505-216-7870
andrew.dunn@pecosleague.com
www.santafefuego.com
• Andrew Dunn, Commissioner
• Consuelo Rios, Game Day Operations

TOPEKA ROBBERS
LAKE SHAWNEE
3421 SE LEISURE LANE
TOPEKA, KS 66605
575-680-2212
www.topekarobbers.com
• Andrew Dunn, Commissioner
• Bob Fritz, Manager

TRINIDAD TRIGGERS
TRINIDAD CENTRAL PARK
TRINIDAD, CO 81082
719-859-1008
www.trinidadtriggers.com
• Andrew Dunn, Commissioner
• Royce Holder, Manager

TUCSON SAGUAROS
KINO SPORTS COMPLEX
2500 EAST AJO WAY
TUCSON, AZ 85713
520-909-5600
www.saguarosbaseball.com
• Andrew Dunn, Commissioner
• J.D. Droddy, League Adjudicator

WHITE SAND PUPFISH
GRIGGS PARK
3000 NORTH FLORIDA AVENUE
ALAMOGORDO, NM 88310
575-680-2212
• Andrew Dunn, Commissioner
• Mickey Speaks, Manager

PIONEER BASEBALL LEAGUE (ADVANCED ROOKIE LEVEL)
2607 S. SOUTHEAST BOULEVARD
BUILDING B
SUITE 115
SPOKANE, WA 99223
509-456-7615
Fax: 509-456-0136
fanmail@pioneerleague.com
www.pioneerleague.com
• Jim McCurdy, President,
Secretary-Treasurer
• Vinney Purpura, Vice President
• Mary Ann McCurdy, Executive Director
League History:
The Pioneer Baseball League, also known
as the Pioneer League, formed in 1939
under the auspices of founding president
Jack P. Halliwell. The Pioneer Baseball
League is a short-season, professional
minor league with teams in Idaho, Montana,
Utah, and Wyoming. The Billings Mustangs,
Great Falls Dodgers, Helena Brewers, and
Missoula Osprey comprise the Northern
Division. The Southern Division includes the
Casper Rockies, Idaho Falls Chukars,
Ogden Raptors, and Orem Owlz.
Requirements:
Each team is limited to 35 active players

with no more than 30 uniformed players at
each game.
Player Eligibility:
No more than 17 of the 35 active players
may be 21 and older, provided that no more
than two of the 17 are 23 or older. No active
player may have more than three years of
prior service.

Teams:

BILLINGS MUSTANGS
DEHLER PARK
2611 9TH AVENUE NORTH
BILLINGS, MT 59101
406-252-1241
Fax: 406-252-2968
mustangs@billingsmustangs.com
www.billingsmustangs.com
• Gary Roller, General Manager
(406) 252-1241
groller@billingsmustangs.com
• Chris Marshall, Director, Corporate Sales &
Partnerships
cmarshall@billingsmustangs.com
• Matt Schoonover, Director, Stadium
Operations
mschoonover@billingsmustangs.com
Ballpark:
In 2008, the Pioneer League's Billings Mustangs
moved into Dehler Park, a $12.5 million ballpark
built to replace Cobb Field. The playing field is
recessed 8 feet below street level, allowing the
seats in the ballpark to completely encircle the
playing field. The concourse features
concession stands and expanded restrooms that
are larger than those of Cobb Field.
Affiliate:
Cincinnati Reds
Years in League:
1948-63, 1969-present.

GRAND JUNCTION ROCKIES
SAM SUPLIZIO FIELD
1315 NORTH AVENUE
GRAND JUNCTION, CO 81501
970-255-7625
Fax: 970-241-2374
• Tim Ray, General Manager
• B.J. Miller, Assistant General Manager
Ballpark:
Sam Suplizio Field
Affiliate:
Colorado Rockies
Founded:
1978

GREAT FALLS VOYAGERS
CENTENE STADIUM
1015 25TH STREET NORTH
GREAT FALLS, MT 59405
406-452-5311
Fax: 406-454-0811
voyagers@gfvoyagers.com
• Scott Reasoner, General Manager
• Matt Coakley, Assistant General Manager
• Scott Lettre, Director of Sales
Ballpark:
Centene Stadium. Seating capacity, 4,000.
Affiliate:
Chicago White Sox

HELENA BREWERS
KINDRICK LEGION FIELD
1300 NORTH EWING STREET
HELENA, MT 59601
406-495-0500
Fax: 406-495-0900
info@helenabrewers.net
www.helenabrewers.net
• D.G. Elmore, Principal Owner
• Paul Fetz, President/General Manager
• Travis Hawks, Director of Ticketing & Stadium
Operations
• Tony Diggs, Manager

Ballpark:
Kindrick Field opened in 1939 and has a seating capacity of 2,010.
Affiliate:
Milwaukee Brewers
Years in League:
1977-present.

IDAHO FALLS CHUKAR
MELALEUCA FIELD
900 JIM GARCHOW WAY
IDAHO FALLS, ID 83402
208-522-8363
Fax: 208-522-9858
chukars@ifchukars.com
www.ifchukars.com
• Kevin Greene, President, General Manager
• Paul Henderson, Assistant General Manager
• Alex Groh, Director of Operations
Ballpark:
Melaleuca Field opened in 2007 and has a seating capacity of 3,400.
Years in League:
1940-42, 1946-present.
Affiliate:
Kansas City Royals.

MISSOULA OSPREY
OGREN PARK ALLEGIANCE FIELD
700 CREGG LANE
MISSOULA, MT 59801
406-543-3300
Fax: 406-543-9463
info@missoulaosprey.com
www.missoulaosprey.com
• Matt Ellis, Executive Vice President
mellis@missoulaosprey.com
• Jeff Griffin, General Manager, Vice President
• Joe Mather, Manager
Years in League:
1999-present.
Ballpark:
Ogren Park Allegiance Field has a seating capacity of 3,500.
Affiliate:
Arizona Diamondbacks

OGDEN RAPTORS
LINDQUIST FIELD
2330 LINCOLN AVENUE
OGDEN, UT 84401
801-393-2400
Fax: 801-393-2473
www.ogden-raptors.com
• Dave Baggott, President
• Joey Stein, General Manager
• John Stein, Vice President
• John Shoemaker, Manager
Ballpark:
Lindquist Field was built in 1997 and has a seating capacity of 5,001.
Years in League:
1939-42, 1946-55, 1966-74, 1994-present.
Affiliate:
Los Angeles Dodgers

OREM OWLZ
BRENT BROWN BALLPARK
970 WEST UNIVERSITY PARKWAY
OREM, UT 84058
801-377-2255
Fax: 801-377-2345
fan@oremowlz.com
www.oremowlz.com
• Rick Berry, General Manager
• Julie Hatch, Assistant General Manager
• Brett Stevens, Director of Marketing
• Dave Stapleton, Manager
Ballpark:
Brent Brown Ballpark. Seating capacity, 5,000.
Years in League:
1978-present.
Affiliate:
Los Angeles Anaheim Angels

Teams:

AUGUSTA GREENJACKETS
SRP PARK
187 RAILROAD AVE
NORTH AUGUSTA, GA 29841
803-349-9467
Fax: 803-349-9434
info@greenjacketsbaseball.com
www.greenjacketsbaseball.com
• Tom Denlinger, Vice President
• Brandon Greene, General Manager
Years in League:
1988-present
Ballpark:
SRP Park
Ballpark Description:
Seating Capacity: 4,278
Major Team Affiliation:
San Francisco Giants.

_____

SOUTH ATLANTIC LEAGUE (A LEVEL)
13575 58TH STREET NORTH
SUITE 141
CLEARWATER, FL 33760-3721
727-538-4270
Fax: 727-499-6853
office@saloffice.com
www.southatlanticleague.com
• Eric Krupa, President
Description:
Minor League Baseball League, consisting of 14 teams.

Teams:

ASHEVILLE TOURISTS
MCCORMICK FIELD
30 BUCHANAN PLACE
ASHEVILLE, NC 28801
828-258-0428
Fax: 828-258-0320
info@theashevilletourists.com
www.theashevilletourists.com
• Brian DeWine, President
• Larry Hawkins, General Manager
• Warren Schaeffer, Manager
Years in League:
1976-present
Ballpark:
McCormick Field
Ballpark Description:
Opened in 1992; Seating Capacity: 4,000
Major Team Affiliation:
Colorado Rockies

CHARLESTON RIVERDOGS
360 FISHBURNE STREET
JOSPEH P. RILEY JR. PARK
CHARLESTON, SC 29403
843-723-7241
Fax: 843-723-2641
admin@riverdogs.com
www.riverdogs.com
• Marvin Goldklang, Chairman
• Mike Veeck, President
• Dave Echols, Executive Vice President, General Manager
• Luis Dorante, Manager
Years in League:
1973-78, 1980-present.
Ballpark:
Joseph P. Riley Jr. Park
Ballpark Description:
Opened in 1997. Seating Capacity: 5,094
Media Broadcast:
WQSC ESPN 1340-AM.
Major Team Affiliation:
New York Yankees.

COLUMBIA FIREFLIES
807 GERVAIS STREET
SUITE 100
COLUMBIA, SC 29201

803-726-4487
Fax: 803-726-3126
info@columbiafireflies.com
• John Katz, President
• Brad Shank, Executive Vice President
• Jose Leger, Manager
Ballpark:
Spirit Communications Park. Seating capacity, 8,500.

DELMARVA SHOREBIRDS
6400 HOBBS ROAD
PERDUE STADIUM
SALISBURY, MD 21804
410-219-3112
Fax: 410-219-9164
info@theshorebirds.com
www.theshorebirds.com
• Chris Bitters, General Manager
• Jimmy Sweet, Assistant General Manager
• Joel Chavez, Director of Stadium Operations
• Ryan Minor, Manager
Years in League:
1996-present.
Ballpark:
Arthur W. Perdue Stadium.
Ballpark Description:
Opened in 1996. Seating Capacity: 5,200
Media Broadcast:
WVES 99.3-FM.
Major Team Affiliation:
Baltimore Orioles.

GREENSBORO GRASSHOPPERS
408 BELLEMEADE STREET
FIRST NATIONAL BANK FIELD
GREENSBORO, NC 27401
336-268-2255
Fax: 336-273-7350
www.gsohoppers.com
• Donald Moore, President/General Manager
Years in League:
1979-present.
Prior Team Name:
Greensboro Bats.
Ballpark:
NewBridge Bank Park
Ballpark Description:
Opened in 2005. Seating Capacity: 6,000
Media Broadcast:
WPET 950-AM.
Major Team Affiliation:
Miami Marlins.

GREENVILLE DRIVE
945 SOUTH MAIN STREET
FLUOR FIELD
GREENVILLE, SC 29601
864-240-4500
Fax: 864-240-4501
info@greenvilledrive.com
www.greenvilledrive.com
• Craig Brown, Co-Owner/President
• Roy Bostock, Co-Owner
• Darren Fenster, Manager
• Mike DeMaine, General Manager
Ballpark:
Fluor Field, modeled after Fenway. Seating capacity, 5,700.
Major Team Affiliaton:
Boston Red Sox

HAGERSTOWN SUNS
274 EAST MEMORIAL BOULEVARD
MUNICIPAL STADIUM
HAGERSTOWN, MD 21740
301-791-6266
Fax: 301-791-6066
info@hagerstownsuns.com
www.hagerstownsuns.com
• Bruce Quinn, President
• Brian Saddler, Assistant General Manager
• Bob Bruchey, Director of Community Affairs
Years in League:
1993-present.
Ballpark:
Municipal Stadium.

Ballpark Information:
Opened in 1931. Seating Capacity: 4,600
Media Broadcast:
WHAG 1410-AM.
Major Team Affiliation:
Washington Nationals.

HICKORY CRAWDADS
CRAWDADS STADIUM
2500 CLEMENT BOULEVARD NW
HICKORY, NC 28601
828-322-3000
Fax: 828-322-6137
crawdad@hickorycrawdads.com
www.hickorycrawdads.com
• Don Beaver, President
• Mark Seaman, General Manager
• Charlie Downs, Assistant General Manager of Operations
• Peter Subsara, Director of Promotions
• Travis Gortman, Director of Group Sales
• Spike Owen, Manager
Years in League:
1952, 1960, 1993-present.
Ballpark:
L.P. Frans Stadium.
Ballpark Description:
Opened in 1993. Seating Capacity: 5,092
Media Broadcast:
WMNC 92.1-FM.
Major Team Affiliation:
Texas Rangers

KANNAPOLIS INTIMIDATORS
2888 MOOSE ROAD
INTIMIDATORS STADIUM
KANNAPOLIS, NC 28083
704-932-3267
Fax: 704-938-7040
www.milb.com
• Brad Smith, President
• Randy Long, General Manager
• Darren Cozart, Director of Operations
• Tommy Thompson, Manager
Years in League:
1995-present.
Ballpark:
Fieldcrest Cannon Stadium.
Ballpark Description:
Opened in 1995. Seating Capacity: 4,700
Major Team Affiliation:
Chicago White Sox.

LAKEWOOD BLUECLAWS
FIRSTENERGY PARK
TWO STADIUM WAY
LAKEWOOD, NJ 08701
732-901-7000
Fax: 732-901-3967
• Chris Tafrow, General Manager
• Steve Farago, VP of Baseball Operations & Special Events
Years in League:
2001-present.
Ballpark:
FirstEnergy Park.
Ballpark Description:
Opened in 2001. Seating Capacity: 6,588
Media Broadcast:
WADB 1310-AM.
Major Team Affiliation:
Philadelphia Phillies.

LEXINGTON LEGENDS
207 LEGENDS LANE
WHITAKER BANK BALLPARK
LEXINGTON, KY 40505
859-422-7867
Fax: 859-252-4487
webmaster@lexingtonlegends.com
www.lexingtonlegends.com
• Andy Shea, CEO/President
• Shannon Kidd, Director of Stadium Operations
• Keith Elkins, Director of Broadcasting & Media Relations
• Omar Ramirez, Manager

Years in League:
2001-present.
Ballpark:
Whitaker Bank Ballpark
Ballpark Description:
Opened in 2001. Seating Capacity: Approx. 6,000
Media Broadcast:
WLXG 1300-AM.
MLB Affiliate:
Houston Astros

ROME BRAVES
755 BRAVES BOULEVARD
STATE MUTUAL STADIUM
ROME, GA 30161
706-378-5100
706-378-5144
Fax: 706-368-6525
rome.braves@braves.com
www.romebraves.com
• Michael Dunn, General Manager
• Jim Jones, Assistant General Manager
• Brad Smith, Director of Operations
• Erin Elroo, Director of Special Projects
• Randy Ingle, Manager
Years in League:
1962-63, 1980-87, 1991-present.
Ballpark:
State Mutual Stadium.
Ballpark Description:
Opened in 2003. Seating Capacity: 5,000
Media Broadcast:
WLAQ 1410, WATG Oldies 95.7
Major Team Affiliation:
Atlanta Braves.

WEST VIRGINIA POWER
601 MORRIS STREET
SUITE 201
APPALACHIAN POWER PARK
CHARLESTON, WV 25301
304-344-2287
Fax: 304-344-0083
www.wvpower.com
• Tim Mueller, General Manager
• Jeremy Taylor, Assistant General Manager
• Brian Esposito, Manager
Years in League:
1987-present.
Prior Team Name:
Charleston Alley Cats.
Ballpark:
Appalachian Power Park. Seating capacity, 4,500.
Media Broadcast:
WBES 1240-AM.
Major Team Affiliation:
Pittsburg Pirates

SOUTHERN LEAGUE OF PROFESSIONAL BASEBALL CLUBS
2551 ROSWELL ROAD
SUITE 330
MARIETTA, GA 30062
770-321-0400
Fax: 770-321-0037
office@southernleague.com
www.southernleague.com
• Lori Webb, President
• Steve Desalvo, Vice President
• Peter Webb, Media Relations
Nature of Service:
Headquarters for 10 teams in a Class Double-A Minor League Baseball league.
League History:
The Southern League originated during the outburst of athletic enthusiasm that surged across America late in the nineteenth century. In 1885, The Southern League of Professional Baseball Clubs was formed by civic leaders and baseball enthusiasts in eight southern cities.
Teams:

10
Publications:
Southern League Media Guide

Teams:

BILOXI SHUCKERS
105 CAILLAVET STREET
MGM PARK
BILOXI, MS 39530
228-233-3465
info@biloxishuckers.com
biloxishuckers.com
• Ken Young, President
• Hunter Reed, General Manager
• Garrett Greene, Media Relations Manager & Broadcaster
Description:
Franchise started in 2015 in Biloxi after relocating from Huntsville.

BIRMINGHAM BARONS
1401 FIRST AVENUE SOUTH
REGIONS FIELD
BIRMINGHAM, AL 35233
205-988-3200
Fax: 205-988-9698
barons@barons.com
www.barons.com
• Don Logan, Owner
• Stan Logan, Owner
• Jeff Logan, Owner
• Jonathan Nelson, General Manager
nelson@barons.com
• Julio Vinas, Manager
Years in League:
1964-65, 1967-75, 1981-present.
Ballpark:
Regions Park
Ballpark Description:
Opened in 1988. Seating Capacity: 10,800
Media Broadcast:
The Source 101.1-FM.
MLB Affiliate:
Chicago White Sox

CHATTANOOGA LOOKOUTS
201 POWER ALLEY
AT&T FIELD
CHATTANOOGA, TN 37402
423-267-2208
Fax: 423-267-4258
lookouts@lookouts.com
www.lookouts.com
• Rich Mozingo, President/General Manager
• Harold Craw, Assistant General Manager
• Doug Mientkiewicz, Manager
Years in League:
1964-65, 1976-present.
Ballpark:
AT&T Field
Ballpark Description:
Opened in 2000. Seating Capacity: 6,160
Media Broadcast:
WQMT 98.9-FM.
MLB Affiliate:
LA Dodgers

JACKSON GENERALS
FOUR FUN PLACE
THE BALLPARK AT JACKSON
JACKSON, TN 38305
731-988-5299
Fax: 731-988-5246
www.jacksongeneralsbaseball.com
• Jason Compton, General Manager
• Mike Peasley, VP of Sales and Marketing
• Nick Hall, Assistant General Manager of Game Operations
MLB Affiliate:
Seattle Mariners

JACKSONVILLE SUNS
301 A. PHILIP RANDOLPH BOULEVARD
BASEBALL GROUNDS OF JACKSONVILLE
JACKSONVILLE, FL 32202

904-358-2846
Fax: 904-358-2845
info@jaxsuns.com
www.jaxsuns.com
• Ken Babby, Owner/CEO
• Harold Craw, General Manager
• Dave Berg, Manager
Years in League:
1970-present.
Ballpark:
Baseball Grounds of Jacksonville.
Ballpark Description:
Opened in 2003. Seating Capacity: 11,000
Media Broadcast:
The Fox 930-AM.
MLB Affiliate:
Miami Marlins

MISSISSIPPI BRAVES
1 BRAVES WAY
TRUSTMARK PARK
PEARL, MS 39208
601-932-8788
Fax: 601-936-3567
mississippibraves@braves.com
www.mississippibraves.com
• Steve DeSalvo, General Manager
• Aaron Holbert, Manager
Years in League:
1984-present.
Stadium:
Trustmark Park
Ballpark Description:
Opened in 2005. Seating Capacity 7,416
MLB Affiliate:
Atlanta Braves

MOBILE BAYBEARS
755 BOLLING BROTHERS BOULEVARD
HANK AARON STADIUM
MOBILE, AL 36606
251-479-2327
Fax: 251-476-1147
info@mobilebaybears.com
www.mobilebaybears.com
• Mike Savit, Managing Partner
• Chris Morgan, General Manager
• Robby Hammock, Manager
Years in League:
1997-present.
Ballpark:
Hank Aaron Stadium.
Ballpark Description:
Opened in 1997. Seating Capacity: 6,000
Media Broadcast:
WABB 1480-AM.
MLB Affiliate:
Arizona Diamonbacks

MONTGOMERY BISCUITS
200 COOSA STREET
RIVERWALK STADIUM
MONTGOMERY, AL 36104
334-323-2255
Fax: 334-323-2225
www.biscuitsbaseball.com
• Greg Rauch, President
• Scott Trible, General Manager
• Staci Wilkenson, Marketing Director
• Steve Blackwell, Director of Stadium
Operations
• Brady Williams, Manager
Years in League:
2004-present.
Ballpark:
Montgomery Riverwalk Stadium.
Ballpark Description:
Opened in 2004. Seating Capacity: 7,000
Media Broadcast:
WLWI 1440-AM.
Major Team Affiliation:
Tampa Bay Devil Rays.

PENSACOLA BLUE WAHOOS
351 WEST CEDAR STREET
PENSACOLA BAYFRONT STADIUM
PENSACOLA, FL 32502

850-934-8444
Fax: 850-791-6256
info@bluewahoos.com
• Quintan Struder, Owner, Director
• Bruce Balwin, President
• Delino Deshields, Manager
MLB Affiliate:
Cincinnati Reds
Ballpark:
Pensacola Bayfront Stadium. Seating capacity,
5,038.

TENNESSEE SMOKIES
3540 LINE DRIVE
SMOKIES STADIUM
KODAK, TN 37764
865-286-2300
Fax: 865-523-9913
info@smokiesbaseball.com
www.smokiesbaseball.com
• Doug Kirchhofer, Chief Executive Officer
• Chris Allen, President, COO
• Brian Cox, General Manager
• Buddy Bailey, Manager
Years in League:
1998-present.
Ballpark:
Smokies Park
Ballpark Description:
Opened in 1998. Seating Capacity: 6,412
Media Broadcast:
WTNE 97.7-FM.
MLB Affiliate:
Chicago Cubs

TEXAS BASEBALL LEAGUE (AA LEVEL)
2442 FACET OAK
SAN ANTONIO, TX 78232
210-545-5297
Fax: 210-545-5298
texasleague@sbcglobal.net
• Tom Kayser, President/Treasurer
• Scott Sonju, Vice President
• Matt Gifford, Corporate Secretary
• John Harris, Assistant to President
Nature of Service:
Baseball League.
Years League Active:
1888-1890, 1892, 1895-1899, 1902-1942,
1946-present.

Teams:

ARKANSAS TRAVELERS
400 WEST BROADWAY
DICKEY-STEPHENS PARK
NORTH LITTLE ROCK, AR 72114
501-664-1555
Fax: 501-664-1834
travs@travs.com
www.travs.com
• Paul Allen, General Manager
• Rusty Meeks, Assistant General Manager
• Patti Clark, Director of Finance
• Bill Richardson, Manager
Years in League:
1966-present.
Ballpark:
Dickey-Stephens Park. Seating capacity, 7,200.
Media Broadcast:
KASR 92.7-FM.
MLB Affiliate:
LAA Angels

CORPUS CHRISTI HOOKS
734 EAST PORT AVENUE
WHATABURGER FIELD
CORPUS CHRISTI, TX 78401
361-561-4665
Fax: 361-561-4666
• Jim Crane, Owner and Chairman
• Ken Schrom, President
• Michael Wood, Vice President, General
Manager

• Jeremy Sturgeon, Stadium Operations
• Rodney Linares, Manager
Ballpark:
Whataburger Field
Ballpark Description:
Opened in 1990. Seating Capacity: 10,000
Media Broadcast:
KHEY 1380-AM.
MLB Affiliate:
Houston Astros

FRISCO ROUGHRIDERS
7300 ROUGHRIDERS TRAIL
DR. PEPPER BALLPARK
FRISCO, TX 75034
972-731-9200
Fax: 972-731-5355
info@ridersbaseball.com
www.ridersbaseball.com
• Chuck Greenberg, CEO, General Partner
• Jason Dambach, Executive Vice President,
General Manager
• Joe Mikulik, Manager
Years in League:
2003-present.
Ballpark:
Dr Pepper Ballpark
Ballpark Description:
Opened in 2003. Seating Capacity: 10,000
Media Broadcast:
The Ticket Sportsradio 1700-AM.
MLB Affiliate:
Texas Rangers

MIDLAND ROCKHOUNDS
5514 CHAMPIONS DRIVE
SECURITY BANK BALLPARK
MIDLAND, TX 79706
432-520-2255
Fax: 432-520-8326
rockhounds@nwol.net
www.midlandrockhounds.org
• Miles Prentice, President
• Bob Richmond, Executive Vice President
• Monty Hoppel, General Manager
• Jeff VonHolle, Assistant General Manager
Years in League:
1972-present.
Ballpark:
Security Bank Ballpark
Ballpark Description:
Opened in 2002. Seating Capacity: 6,670.
Media Broadcast:
KCRS 550-AM.
Description of Sport Organization:
We have a minor league Double A baseball
team (Midland Rockhounds) and a Premier
Development League soccer team (West Texas
United Sockers).
Teams:
Midland Rockhounds- Double A affiliate of the
Oakland A's; West Texas United Sockers- PDL
Mid-South Division of Southern Conference.

NORTHWEST ARKANSAS NATURALS
3000 SOUTH 56TH STREET
ARVEST BALLPARK
SPRINGDALE, AR 72762
479-927-4900
Fax: 479-756-8088
• Justin Cole, General Manager
• Mark Zaiger, Sales Manager
• Jeff Windle, Director of Ballpark Operations
Stadium:
Arvest Ballpark
Seating Capacity:
6,500 (plus berm and picnic areas)
Field Surface:
Patriot bermuda overseeded with rye
Owned by:
City of Springdale
MLB Affiliate:
Kansas City Royals

SAN ANTONIO MISSIONS
5757 US HIGHWAY 90 WEST
WOLFF STADIUM
SAN ANTONIO, TX 78227
210-675-7275
Fax: 210-670-0001
sainfo@samissions.com
www.samissions.com
• Dave Elmore, Owner
• Burl Yarbrough, President
• Dave Gasaway, General Manager
• Mickey Holt, Assistant General Manager
• Rod Barajas, Manager
Years in League:
1888, 1892, 1895-99, 1907-42, 1946-64, 1968-present.
Ballpark:
Nelson W. Wolff Municipal Stadium.
Ballpark Description:
Opened in 1994. Seating Capacity: 6,200
Media Broadcast:
KKYX 680-AM.
Major Team Affiliation:
San Diego Padres

SPRINGFIELD CARDINALS
955 EAST TRAFFICWAY
HAMMONS FIELD
SPRINGFIELD, MO 65802
417-863-0395
Fax: 417-863-2143
springfield@cardinals.com
www.springfieldcardinals.com
• Matt Gifford, VP/General Manager
• Scott Smulczenski, VP, Baseball & Business Operations
Stadium:
Hammons Field. Seating capacity, 10,486.
Affiliated Team:
St. Louis Cardinals

TULSA DRILLERS
201 NORTH ELGIN AVENUE
TULSA DRILLERS
TULSA, OK 74120
918-744-5998
Fax: 918-747-3267
mail@tulsadrillers.com
www.tulsadrillers.com
• Mike Melega, President/General Manager
• Jason George, Executive VP/Assistant GM
Years in League:
1933-42, 1946-65, 1977-present.
Ballpark:
Oneok Field
Ballpark Description:
Opened in 1981. Seating Capacity: 10,997.
Media Broadcast:
KTBZ 1430-AM, The Buzz.
Affiliates:
Double-A Affiliate of the Colorado Rockies

VENEZUELAN BASEBALL LEAGUE
www.lvbp.com
• Oscar Prieto Parraga, President
Founded:
1945
Teams:
Aguilas del Zulia; Bravos de Margarita; Cardenales de Lara; Caribes de Anzoategul; Leones del Caracas; Navegantes de Magallanes; Tiburones de la Guaira; Tigres de Aragua

Basketball Organizations

BIDDY BASKETBALL
2377 LEON C. SIMON DRIVE
NEW ORLEANS, LA 70122
985-630-3948
Fax: 504-283-8225

info@biddybb.com
biddybb.com
• Firmin Simms, President/National Director
• Laura Block, VP
• Jerry Simms, Assistant VP
• Carolyn Block, Assistant VP
Description:
The main focus of Biddy Basketball International is to provide the best tool for developing our youth, both boys and girls in the sport of basketball. To accomplish this goal the size of the balls, the height of the goals, and the distance of the free throws lines are modified to fit young athletes. Biddy Basketball International sponsors regional and national competitive basketball tournaments throughout the United States.

CANADA BASKETBALL
1 WESTSIDE DRIVE
SUITE 11
ETOBICOKE, ON, CANADA M9C 1B2
416-614-8037
Fax: 416-614-9570
info@basketball.ca
www.basketball.ca
• Brian Cooper, Chairman
• Rob Wright, Vice-Chair
• Glen Grunwald, President/CEO
ggrunwald@basketball.ca
• Rowan Barrett, General Manager/Executive VP, Senior Men's Program
• Andrea Driedger, Director, Finance
Description:
Canada Basketball is the National Sporting Organization for the sport of Basketball in Canada. Canada Basketball is respected throughout the world and is recognized by the International Amateur Basketball Federation (FIBA) and the Government of Canada as the sole governing body of the sport of amateur basketball in Canada. Canada Basketball oversees programs at amateur and grassroots levels throughout Canada.
Member Services:
Selection, training, competitive programs of all Canadian Men's and Women's teams entering the Olympic Games, World Championships, Pan American Games, World University Games, World Junior Championships and World Under 22 Championships for Men. Provides programs for coaching development through the National Coaching Certification Program (NCCP); supports domestic competitive opportunities through the organization of the National Junior Championships and National Senior Club Championships for Men and Women.
Official Partners:
NBA Canada, Toronto Raptors, CIS.
Founded:
1923

FEDERATION INTERNATIONALE DE BASKETBALL (FIBA)
ROUTE SUISSE 5
PO BOX 29
MIES, 1295
+41-22-545-00-00
Fax: +41-22-545-00-99
info@fiba.com
www.fiba.com
• Hamane Niang, President
• Andreas Zagklis, Secretary General

Description:
FIBA acts as the international governing body for the sport of basktball, and is comprised of 213 National Basketball associations, including the US national team.

INDEPENDENT HOOPS
AUGUSTA, GA
independenthoops.com
Description:
Independant Hoops houses both the Lineage of Champions (LOCHoops) and the National Youth Basketball League. It is the premier middle school league in North America offering a platform for teams in the US and Canada. The League is designed to improve grassroots basketball at the middle school and junior high school levels. They encourage team development in an experience that cannot be duplicated anywhere else.

INTERNATIONAL ASSOCIATION OF APPROVED BASKETBALL OFFICIALS, INC.
PO BOX 355
CARLISLE, PA 17103-0355
717-713-8129
Fax: 717-718-6164
www.iaabo.org
• Felix Addeo, Executive Director
faddeo@iaabo.org
• Donnie Eppley, Associate Executive Director
eppleyd@comcast.net
Description:
The IAABO aims to educate, train, develop and provide continuous instruction for basketball officials.
Membership Requirements:
Be a registered member of IAABO at the time of nomination whose status as an active officiating and/or active non-officiating member totals a minimum of 30 years. Be a minimum 55 years of age by December 31st of the nominating year. Have promoted and contributed to the growth, purpose and ideals of IAABO and to the welfare of the game of basketball in an outstanding way through service to their local area.

NATIONAL ASSOCIATION OF BASKETBALL COACHES
1111 MAIN STREET
SUITE 1000
KANSAS CITY, MO 64105
816-878-6222
Fax: 816-878-6223
www.nabc.com
• Craig Robinson, Executive Director (816) 878-6222
• Nate Pomeday, Associate Executive Director (816) 595-6153
• Stephanie Whitcher, Chief Finanancial Offier (816) 595-6171
stephanie@nabc.com
• Rick Leddy, Senior Director, Communications (203) 815-2437
ricknabc@gmail.com
• Troy Hilton, Senior Director, Association Affairs (816) 595-6155
troy@nabc.com

History:
The National Association of Basketball Coaches (NABC), located in Kansas City, Missouri was founded in 1927 by Phog Allen, the legendary University of Kansas basketball coach. Since its beginning, the NABC has continually worked to further the best interests of the game of basketball as well as the players and coaches who participate in the sport. In doing so, the NABC works toward integrity, sportsmanship and teamwork among men's basketball coaches and the players whom they coach.
Membership Requirements:
Basketball coaches of high schools, junior colleges, colleges or universities.

NATIONAL BASKETBALL ASSOCIATION
545 FIFTH AVENUE
NEW YORK, NY 10022
nbaglobalfeedback@dazn.com
www.nba.com
• Adam Silver, Commissioner
• Mark A. Tatum, Deputy Commissioner/COO
Description:
The premier professional basketball league in North America. Many of the world's best players play in the NBA, and the overall standard of the competition is considerably higher than any other professional competition. The NBA was founded in New York City on June 6th, 1946 as the Basketball Association of America (BAA). It adopted the name National Basketball Association in the fall of 1949 after adding several teams from the rival National Basketball League.
Founded:
1946

NATIONAL BASKETBALL PLAYERS ASSOCIATION/NBPA
1133 6TH AVENUE
NEW YORK, NY 10036
212-655-0880
800-955-6272
Fax: 212-655-0881
info@nbpa.com
www.nbpa.com
• Chris Paul, President
• Andre Iguodala, First Vice President
• Harrison Barnes, Secretary-Treasurer
• Michele Roberts, Executive Director
Description:
The NBPA is a unique labor institution. For over 40 years, the NBPA has fought to promote the best interests of NBA players both on and off the court. Whether we are negotiating a collective bargaining agreement, prosecuting a grievance on a player's behalf, or counseling a player on benefits or educational opportunities.
Year Founded:
1954

NATIONAL INVITATIONAL TOURNAMENT
700 W WASHINGTON STREET
PO BOX 6222
INDIANAPOLIS, IN 46206-6222
317-917-6222
Fax: 317-917-6888
cfallon@ncaa.org
www.ncaa.org
• Mark Emmert, President (NCAA)
Description:
The National Invitational Tournament - held in Madison Square Garden - originated from the Basketball Writers Association in 1938. After two years, the association allowed local colleges to begin administering the tournament instead. The group became known as the Metropolitan Intercollegiate Basketball Committee and in 1948 became the Metropolitan Intercollegiate Basketball Association. Today, the association is comprised of representatives from the five New York City colleges, In 2005, the NIT was taken over by the NCAA.

NATIONAL JUNIOR BASKETBALL
180 E MAIN STREET
SUITE 105
TUSTIN, CA 92780
888-623-00124
Fax: 949-769-2557
info@njbl.org
www.njbl.org
• Dennis Murphy, Commissioner
• Sean Murphy, Vice President
Description:
National Junior Basketball is a nonprofit organization that provides opportunities for youth to play in basketball leagues. The main focus of the organization is centered on the Divisional Play Program that is open for all boys and girls, from grades 2 to 8. However, they also offer a Rookie League for those in 1st and 2nd grade.

NATIONAL WHEELCHAIR BASKETBALL ASSOCIATION
1130 ELKTON STREET
SUITE A
COLORADO SPRINGS, CO 80907
719-266-4082
Fax: 719-266-4876
info@nwba.org
www.nwba.org
• Tim Fox, President
• Ryan Martin, Vice President
• Mike Godsey, Treasurer
• Bruce Fischbach, Secretary
• Will Walter, CEO
Nature of Service:
Engages in the interpretation and standardization of competitive regulations for all teams playing organized wheelchair basketball. Assists in the development of teams and educates the public in the sport.
History:
Started in 1946 by the Veterans Administration Hospitals. It later spread across the nation to VA hospitals in Boston, Chicago, Memphis, Richmond and New York. Before long, the sport had spread across the border to Canada and across the ocean to England.
Membership Requirements:
Permanent physical disability of lower extremities. Players must have functional evaluations and physical classifications.

SPOKANE HOOPFEST
421 W REVERSIDE
SUITE 115
SPOKANE, WA 99201
509-624-2414
Fax: 509-624-0868
www.spokanehoopfest.net
• Matt Santangelo, Executive Director
matt@spokanehoopfest.net
• Kristi Atkinson, Manager, Marketing & Brands

• Morgan Marum, Director, Corportate & Media Relations
morgan@spokanehoopfest.net
• Giff Marleau, Program Director
giff@spokanehoopfest.net
• Chad Smith, Director, Volunteers & Staffing
chad@spokanehoopfest.net
• Connor Walsh, Manager, Programs & Events
connor@spokanehoopfest.net
Description:
Spokane Hoopfest Association is committed to organizing and operating the best outdoor 3-on-3 basketball tournament in the country. With the effort and enthusiasm of thousands of volunteers, Hoopfest strives to create a dynamic downtown festival, transcending basketball through the celebration of athleticism, fair play and community involvement. Spokane Hoopfest Association also provides charitable support through distribution of profits to Special Olympics and basketball-related activities.

USA BASKETBALL
27 S TEJON STREET
SUITE 100
COLORADO SPRINGS, CO 80903
719-590-4800
Fax: 719-590-4811
FanMail@usabasketball.com
www.usabasketball.com
• Jim Tooley, CEO
• Craig Miller, Chief Communications Officer
• Brent Baumberger, Chief Financial Officer
Description:
USA Basketball was organized in 1974 and known as the Amateur Basketball Association of the United States of America (ABAUSA). The name change from ABAUSA to USA Basketball occurred October 12, 1989, shortly after FIBA modified its rules to allow professional basketball players to participate in international competitions.
Membership Requirements:
This membership shall be open to all national sports organizations which actively conduct a national program in Basketball as a competitive sport. Active memberships may also be open to other organizations which actively conduct national programs in basketball as a competitive sport. In addition, national basketball coaches associations for men and women shall be included, as approved by the Board of Directors of USA Basketball. Such members shall have voting representation through their chosen officers, or other representatives, at meetings of the Congress membership.

WOMEN'S BASKETBALL COACHES ASSOCIATION
4646 LAWRENCEVILLE HIGHWAY
LILBURN, GA 30047
770-279-8027
Fax: 770-279-8473
www.wbca.org
• Danielle M. Donehew, Executive Director (770) 279-8027
ddonehew@wbca.org
• Mary Ellen Gillespie, Deputy Director (770) 279-8027
meg@wbca.org
• Tess Romine-Black, Director, Marketing (770) 279-8027

tromineblack@wbca.org
• Daniella Trujillo, Senior Manager, Events & Awards
• Jack Watford, Director, Communications
• Tess Romine-Black, Director, Marketing
Nature of Service:
Professional organization that supports and provides educational opportunities for women's basketball coaches on all levels, and promotes the development of the game in all of its aspects as a sport for women and girls.
Member Services:
Select WBCA Coach of the Year, Player of the Year, All-America teams for colleges and universities. Provides annual coaching clinics, clinic manuals, camps. Announces coaching position opportunities/openings. National convention held in conjunction with Division I Women's Final Four.
Publications:
FAST BREAK ALERT, quarterly newsletter; COACHING WOMEN'S BASKETBALL, bi-monthly magazine, 8 times a year; AT THE BUZZER, newsletter, 8 times a year - for high school and AAU only, NET.NEWS, bi-monthly newsletter.
Number of Members:
3,700
Founded:
1981

YOUTH BASKETBALL OF AMERICA
ADVENTHEALTH FIELDHOUSE & CONFERENCE CENTER
210 CYPRESS GARDENS BLVD
WINTER HAVEN, FL 33880
407-363-9262
membership@yboa.org
www.yboa.org
• Joe Pickett, President
 ext 216
joepickett@yboa.org
• Jack Love, Vice President
jlove@yboa.org
Description:
Youth Basketball of America, the premier youth membership organization in the sport of basketball, strives to provide opportunities for personal growth and development of youth athletes while also reinforcing positive influences, self-confidence, self-esteem and the ability to excel on and off the court. Through participation, YBOA is dedicated to educate and motivate each member while encouraging teamwork, sportsmanship and fun through the spirit of basketball.
Membership Requirements:
Leagues, associations, departments, schools, coaches and officials, players.
Member Services:
Coaching clinics; rules; local, state, regional and national championship; tournaments and competition. International friendship tournament; now offers international tournament in various foreign countries.

Basketball, Leagues and Teams

HARLEM GLOBETROTTERS
5445 TRIANGLE PARKWAY
SUITE 300
PEACHTREE CORNERS, GA 30092

678-497-1900
info@harlemglobetrotters.com
www.harlemglobetrotters.com
• Howard Smith, President
• Jeff Munn, Chief Operating Officer
• Sunni Hickman, VP, Marketing
Description:
Competitive basketball team whose games are played primarily for entertainment.
First Game Played:
1926

NATIONAL BASKETBALL ASSOCIATION/NBA
545 FIFTH AVENUE
NEW YORK, NY 10022
nbaglobalfeedback@dazn.com
www.nba.com
• Adam Silver, Commissioner
• Mark A. Tatum, Deputy Commissioner/COO
Description:
The premier professional basketball league in North America. Many of the world's best players play in the NBA, and the overall standard of the competition is considerably higher than any other professional competition. The NBA was founded in New York City on June 6, 1946 as the Basketball Association of America (BAA). It adopted the name National Basketball Association in the fall of 1949 after adding several teams from the rival National Basketball League.

Teams:

ATLANTA HAWKS
101 MARIETTA STREET NW
SUITE 1900
ATLANTA, GA 30303
404-878-3800
866-715-1500
hawks.tickets@hawks.com
www.hawks.com
• Steve Koonin, CEO
• Tony Ressler, Principle Owner/Chair
• Travis Schlenk, General Manager/Head of Basketball Operations
• Lloyd Pierce, Head Coach
Team History:
The Hawks have played in Atlanta since 1968. They play their home games at Philips Arena, in Atlanta, Georgia. Championships, 1; Conference titles, 4; Division titles, 5.
Arena:
Philips Arena. Seating capacity, 18,047.

BOSTON CELTICS
226 CAUSEWAY STREET
FOURTH FLOOR
BOSTON, MA 02114
866-423-5849
fanrelations@celtics.com
www.celtics.com
• Wyc Grousbeck, Managing Partner/CEO
• Danny Ainge, General Manager/President, Basketball Operations
• Austin Ainge, Assistant General Manager
• Brad Stevens, Head Coach
• Jamie Young, Assistant Coach
• Frank Burke, Director, Basketball Administration
Team History:
The Celtics came into being on June 6, 1946. They have won 17 NBA Championships, tied for first along with the Los Angeles Lakers. Championships, 17; Conference titles, 9; Division titles, 31.
Arena:
TD Garden. Seating capacity, 18,624.

BROOKLYN NETS
168 39TH STREET
7TH FLOOR
BROOKLYN, NY 11232
718-933-3000
Fax: 718-942-9595
www.brooklynnets.com
• Joe Tsai, Governor
• Sean Marks, General Manager
• Steve Nash, Head Coach
• Jeff Gewirtz, COO & General Counsel
• Peter Stern, EVP & Chief Financial Officer
History:
1967-76 known as New York Nets. 1976 joined the NBA. 1977-2012 known as the New Jersey Nets. 2012-Present, known as the Brooklyn Nets. Championships, 2; Conference titles, 2; Division titles, 4.
Arena:
Barclay Center. Seating capacity, 17,732.
Media Broadcast:
Fox Sports New York; WOR-710 AM; MSG Network/Metro Channel.

CHARLOTTE HORNETS
SPECTRUM CENTER
333 EAST TRADE STREET
CHARLOTTE, NC 28202
704-688-8600
Fax: 704-973-9411
info@hornets.com
www.hornets.com
• Michael Jordan, Chairman
• Mitch Kupchak, General Manager/President, Basketball Operations
• Buzz Peterson, Assistant General Manager
• James Jordan, EVP/Chief Operating Officer
• James Borrego, Head Coach
History:
The Charlotte Hornets was established in 1988.
Arena:
Spectrum Centre. Seating capacity, 20,200.
Founded:
1994

CHICAGO BULLS
UNITED CENTER
1901 W MADISON STREET
CHICAGO, IL 60612-2459
312-455-4000
www.bulls.com
• Michael Reinsdorf, President/COO
• Jerry Reinsdorf, Chairman/Alternate NBA Governor
• Marc Eversley, General Manager
• Brian Hagen, Associate General Manager
• Billy Donovan, Head Coach
• Arturas Karnisovas, Executive VP, Basketball Operations
Team History:
The Chicago Bulls joined the NBA for the 1966-67 season. Prior to the inception of the Bulls organization, two pro-teams had failed in Chicago.Championships, 6; Conference titles, 6; Division titles, 9.
Arena:
United Center. Seating capacity, 20,917.
Media Broadcast:
WGN/WCIU-TV; Fox Sports Chicago, 1000-AM.

CLEVELAND CAVALIERS
ROCKET MORTGAGE FIELDHOUSE
ONE CENTER COURT
CLEVELAND, OH 44115
216-420-2000
800-807-2287
contactus@cavs.com
www.cavs.com
• Dan Gilbert, Chairman
• Koby Altman, General Manager
• Bickerstaff J.B., Head Coach
• Len Komoroski, CEO
• Nic Barlage, President, Business Operations
Team History:
Since the Cavaliers' inaugural 1970-71 NBA season, for more than three decades the team has been making memories for the fans of northeast Ohio. Championship titles, 1;

Conference titles, 5; Division titles, 7.
Arena:
Rocket Mortgage Fieldhouse.
Media Broadcast:
WTAM 1100-AM, WUAB-TV 43

DALLAS MAVERICKS
AMERICAN AIRLINES CENTER
2500 VICTORY AVENUE
DALLAS, TX 75219
214-747-6287
www.mavs.com
• Mark Cuban, Owner
• Donnie Nelson, General Manager/President, Basketball Ops.
• Rick Carlisle, Head Coach
• Floyd Jahner, COO
• Matt Wojciechowski, CFO
Team History:
The Dallas Mavericks joined the NBA in 1980-81 and quickly became a competitive franchise. With premium draft selections the team steadily improved through the 1980s. Championships, 1; Conference titles, 2; Division titles, 3.
Arena:
American Airlines Center.

DENVER NUGGETS
PEPSI CENTER
1000 CHOPPER CIRCLE
DENVER, CO 80204
303-405-1100
nuggetsmail@pepsicenter.com
www.nuggets.com
• E. Stanley Kroenke, Owner
• Josh Kroenke, President/Governor
• Calvin Booth, General Manager/President, Basketball Operations
• Michael Malone, Head Coach
Team History:
The Denver Nuggets franchise traces its origins to 1967-68 in the American Basketball Association. A stable ABA franchise for nine years, Denver carried its winning ways into the NBA when the two leagues merged in 1976. Division titles, 11.
Arena:
Pepsi Center.
Media Broadcast:
Fox Sports Rocky Mountain; KPXC/KTVD-TV; KKFN Radio 950

DETROIT PISTONS
LITTLE CAESARS ARENA
2645 WOODWARD AVENUE
DETROIT, MI 48201
pistons.com
• Tom Gores, Owner & CEO
• Greg Campbell, CFO
• Troy Weaver, General Manager
• Dwane Casey, Head Coach
Team History:
Automobile-piston magnate Fred Zollner launched the club in 1941 and christened it the Fort Wayne Zollner Pistons. The Pistons joined the National Basketball League, a circuit that consisted primarily of teams fielded by Midwest corporations. Championships, 3; Conference titles, 5; Division titles, 11.
Arena:
Little Caesars Arena. Seating capacity, 20,332.

GOLDEN STATE WARRIORS
ORACLE ARENA
7000 COLISEUM WAY
OAKLAND, CA 94621
415-388-0100
ticketing@warriors.com
www.warriors.com
• Peter Guber, Co-Executive Chairman
• Joe Lacob, Co-Executive Chairman/CEO
• Bob Myers, General Manager
• Steve Kerr, Head Coach
• Josh Proctor, Chief Financial Officer
Team History:
The franchise played as the Philadelphia Warriors until 1962. Today the Warriors play in

the Arena in Oakland, California, and wear jerseys of blue, white, and gold. The Philadelphia Warriors won the first championship of the Basketball Association of America (BAA), the forerunner of the NBA, in 1947. In 1956 the Warriors won their first NBA title, sparked by future Hall of Fame members Paul Arizin and Neil Johnston. Championships, 6; Conference titles, 6; Division titles, 12.
Arena:
Oracle Arena. Seating capacity, 19,596.
Media Broadcast:
Fox Sports Bay Area; KICU Ch 36; KNBR Radio 680; KIQI Radio (Spanish) 1010

HOUSTON ROCKETS
TOYOTA CENTER
1510 POLK STREET
HOUSTON, TX 77002
713-758-7200
fanear@rocketball.com
www.rockets.com
• Tilman J. Fertitta, Owner/Chairman
• Thaddeus B. Brown, CEO
• Rafael Stone, General Manager
• Stephen Silas, Head Coach
• Marcus Jolibois, Chief Financial Officer
• Larry Kaiser, VP, Finance
Team Description:
1969-71 as the San Diego Rockets. 1971-present as Houston Rockets. Championships, 2; Conference Titles, 4; Division Titles, 8.
Arena:
Toyota Center. Seating Capacity, 18,500.
Media Broadcast:
Fox Sports Southwest; WB39 KHTV; KTRH Radio 740; KLAT Radio 1010 (Spanish); KHWB-TV.

INDIANA PACERS
BANKERS LIFE FIELDHOUSE
125 S PENNSYLVANIA STREET
INDIANAPOLIS, IN 46204
317-917-2500
PacersInsider@Pacers.com
www.pacers.com
• Herbert Simon, Owner/Chairman/CEO
• Chad Buchanan, General Manager
• Nate Bjorkgren, Head Coach
• Kevin Pritchard, President, Basketball Operations
• Jim Morris, Vice Chairman
Team History:
Founded in 1967 and joined the NBA in 1976. Championships, 3; Conference titles, 1; Division titles, 9.
Arena:
Bankers Life Fieldhouse. Seating capacity, 18,165.
Media Broadcast:
Fox Sports Midwest; WTTV WIBC Radio 1070

LOS ANGELES CLIPPERS
STAPLES CENTER
1111 S FIGUEROA STREET
LOS ANGELES, CA 90015
213-204-2800
www.clippers.com
• Steve Ballmer, Chairman
• Michael Winger, General Manager
• Mark Hughes, Assistant General Manager
• Trent Redden, Assistant General Manager
• Tyronn Lue, Head Coach
• Frank Lawrence, President, Basketball Operations
History:
1970-78 known as Buffalo Braves. 1978-84 known as San Diego Clippers. 1984-present presently known as the Los Angeles Clippers. Division titles, 2.
Arena:
Staples Center. Seating Capacity of 19,060

LOS ANGELES LAKERS
STAPLES CENTER
111 S FIGUEROA STREET
LOS ANGELES, CA 90015
310-426-6000
feedback@la-lakers.com
www.lakers.com
• Jeanie Marie Buss, CEO
• Rob Pelinka, General Manager
• Frank Vogel, Head Coach
• Joe McCormack, Chief Financial Officer
• Tim Harris, COO
History:
1948-60 Known as The Minneapolis Lakers. 1960-present known now as The Los Angeles Lakers. Tied with the Boston Celtics for the record of most championships held with 17. Championships, 17; Conference titles, 19; Division titles, 33.
Arena:
Staples Center. Seating capacity, 19,060.
Media Broadcast:
Fox Sports Net; KCAL 9; KLAC Radio 570

MEMPHIS GRIZZLIES
FEDEX FORUM
191 BEALE STREET
MEMPHIS, TN 38103
901-205-1234
www.grizzlies.com
• Robert J. Pera, Owner/Chairman
• Zachary Kleiman, General Manager
• Taylor Jenkins, Head Coach
History:
Founded in 1995 in Vancouver; moved to Memphis in 2001.
Arena:
FedEx Forum. Seating capacity, 18,119.

MIAMI HEAT
AMERICAN AIRLINES ARENA
601 BISCAYNE BOULEVARD
MIAMI, FL 33132
786-777-1000
www.heat.com
• Nick Arison, CEO
• Pat Riley, President
• Andy Elisburg, General Manager
• Eric Spoeistra, Head Coach
History:
Founded in 1988 in Miami. Championships, 3; Conference titles, 6; Division titles, 14.
Arena:
American Airlines Arena. Seating Capacity: 16,500
Media Broadcast:
Sunshine Network; WAMI-TV; WINC Radio 940; WIOD 610; WACC Radio 830 Partner: Terremark.

MILWAUKEE BUCKS
FISERV FORUM
1111 VEL R PHILLIPS AVENUE
MILWAUKEE, WI 53203
414-227-0504
877-428-2825
ticket@bucks.com
www.bucks.com
• Peter Feigin, President
• Jon Horst, General Manager
• Mike Budenholzer, Head Coach
• Raven Jemioson, Executive VP, Operations
• Patrick McDonough, Chief Financial Officer
History:
Founded in 1968 in Milwaukee. Championships, 1; Conference titles, 2; Division titles, 15.
Arena:
Fiserv Forum. Seating capacity, 17,341.
Founded:
1968

MINNESOTA TIMBERWOLVES
TARGET CENTER
600 FIRST AVENUE N
MINNEAPOLIS, MN 55403
612-673-1600
www.timberwolves.com

- Glen Taylor, Owner
- Ethan Casson, CEO
- Gersson Rosas, President, Basketball Operations
- Scott Layden, General Manager
- Chris Finch, Head Coach

History:
Founded in 1989 in Minnesota. Division titles, 1.

Arena:
Target Center. Seating capacity, 19,356.

NEW ORLEANS PELICANS
SMOOTHIE KING CENTER
1501 DAVE DIXON DRIVE
NEW ORLEANS, LA 70113
504-593-4700
fanexperience@pelicans.com
www.pelicans.com
- Gayle Benson, Owner
- Dennis Lauscha, President
- Trajan Langdon, General Manager
- Stan Van Gundy, Head Coach

History:
Founded in 1988 in Charlotte. Division titles, 1.

Arena:
Smoothie King Center. Seating capacity, 18,500.

Sponsored By:
Pelicans Flex Plan presented by Delta World Tire, with 15 locations in LA and MI.

NEW YORK KNICKS
MADISON SQUARE GARDEN
TWO PENNSYLVANIA PLAZA
NEW YORK, NY 10121-0091
www.knicks.com
- Andrew Lustgarten, President & CEO
- James L. Dolan, Owner/Chairman
- Scott Perry, General Manager
- Tom Thibodeau, Head Coach
- Jamie Mattews, VP, Basketball Operations

History:
Founded in 1946 in New York. Championships, 2; Conference titles, 4; Division titles, 8.

Arena:
Madison Square Garden. Seating capacity, 19,812.

Media Broadcast:
ESPN Radio 1050-AM.

OKLAHOMA CITY THUNDER
CHESAPEAKE ENERGY CENTER
208 THUNDER DRIVE
OKLAHOMA CITY, OK 73102
405-208-4800
fans@okcthunder.com
www.okcthunder.com
- Clay Bennett, Owner
- Sam Presti, Executive VP/General Manager
- Mark Daigneault, Head Coach
- Rob Hennigan, VP, Basketball Operations
- Will Dawkins, VP, Basketball Operations

Team History:
The Oklahoma City Thunders made their home debut on October 14, 2008 against the LA Clippers. Formerly the Seattle Supersonics. Championships, 1; Conference titles, 4; Division titles, 11.

Arena:
Chesapeake Energy Arena. Seating capacity, 18,203

ORLANDO MAGIC
AMWAY CENTER
400 W CHURCH STREET
SUITE 200
ORLANDO, FL 32801
407-916-2400
tickets@orlandomagic.com
www.nba.com/magic
- Alex Martins, CEO
- Dan DeVos, Chairman
- John Hammond, General Manager
- Steve Clifford, Head Coach

History:
Founded in 1989 in Orlando, FL. Conference titles, 2; Division titles, 6.

Arena:

Amway Arena, opened in 1989 with a seating capacity of 17,248.

Media Broadcast:
Magic Television Network (MTN); Sunshine Network; WDBO Radio AM- 580; AM 1440 WPRD, AM 1400 WSDO or AM 1220 WOTS.

PHILADELPHIA 76ERS
WELLS FARGO CENTER
3601 S BROAD STREET
PHILADELPHIA, PA 19148
76ersservice@sixers.com
www.sixers.com
- Josh Harris, Managing Partner
- Daryl Morey, President, Basketball Operations
- Elton Brand, General Manager
- Doc Rivers, Head Coach
- Peter Dinwiddie, Executive VP, Basketball Operations

History:
1949-63 known as Syracuse Nationals. 1963-present known as Philadelphia 76ers. Championships, 3; Conference titles, 5; Division titles, 11.

Arena:
Wells Fargo Center. Seating capacity, 21,600.

Media Broadcast:
Comcast SportsNet, Channel 7 UPN, WIP Radio 610; WPSG-TV.

PHOENIX SUNS
TALKING STICK RESORT ARENA
201 E JEFFERSON STREET
PHOENIX, AZ 85004
602-379-2000
www.suns.com
- Jason Rowley, CEO/President
- James Jones, General Manager
- Monty Williams, Head Coach
- Jeff Bower, Senior VP, Basketball Operations
- Robert Sarver, Managing Partner

History:
Founded in 1968. Conference titles, 2; Division titles, 6.

Arena:
Talking Stick Resort Arena. Seating capacity, 18,055.

PORTLAND TRAIL BLAZERS
MODA CENTER
ONE CENTER COURT
SUITE 200
PORTLAND, OR 97227
503-234-9291
Fax: 503-736-2187
ticketservices@trailblazers.com
www.blazers.com
- Chris McGowan, CEO/President
- Jody Allen, Chair
- Neil Olshey, General Manager/President, Basketball Operations
- Terry Stotts, Head Coach

History:
Founded in 1970 in Portland. Championships, 1; Conference titles, 3; Division titles, 6.

Arena:
Moda Center. Seating capacity, 19,441.

Media Broadcast:
Trail Blazers Flag Ship Station - KXL 750-AM. MAGIA 1150-AM (Spanish).

SACRAMENTO KINGS
GOLDEN 1 CENTER
500 DAVID J STERN WALK
SACRAMENTO, CA 95814
916-928-0000
888-915-4647
kings@kings.com
www.kings.com
- Vivek Ranadive, CEO/Chairman
- Rob Blake, General Manager
- Luke Walton, Head Coach

History:
1923-44 Rochester Seagrams, 1945-57 Rochester Royals, 1957-72 Cincinnati Royals, 1972-75 Kansas City Omaha Kings, 1975-85 Kansas City Kings, 1985-present Sacramento

Kings. Championships, 1; Conference titles, 1; Division titles, 5.

Arena:
Golden 1 Center. Seating capacity, 17,608.

Media Broadcast:
KHTK 1140-AM.

Founded:
1923

SAN ANTONIO SPURS
AT&T CENTER
ONE AT&T CENTER PARKWAY
SAN ANTONIO, TX 78219
210-444-5000
www.spurs.com
- Peter J. Holt, Chair
- R.C. Buford, CEO
- Brian Wright, General Manager
- Gregg Popovich, Head Coach
- Brent Barry, VP, Basketball Operations

History:
1967-70 as the Dallas Chaparrals, 1970-71 Texas Chapparrals, 1971-73 Dallas Chaparrals, 1973-present San Antonio Spurs. 1976 joined the NBA. Championships, 5; Conference titles, 6; Division titles, 22.

Arena:
AT&T Center. Seating capacity, 18,418.

TORONTO RAPTORS
SCOTIABANK ARENA
40 BAY STREET
TORONTO, ON, CANADA M5J 2X2
416-366-3865
ticketservice@mlse.com
www.raptors.com
- Masai Ujiri, President
- Bobby Webster, General Manager
- Nick Nurse, Head Coach
- Teresa Resch, VP, Basketball Operations & Player Development

History:
Founded in 1995 in Toronto. Championship titles, 1. Conference titles, 1. Division Titles, 7.

Arena:
Scotiabank Arena. Seating capacity, 19,800.

UTAH JAZZ
VIVINT SMART HOME ARENA
301 W SOUTH TEMPLE
SALT LAKE CITY, UT 84101
801-325-2500
www.nba.com/jazz
- Ryan Smith, Owner/Chair
- Justin Zanik, General Manager
- Quin Snyder, Head Coach
- Dennis Lindsey, Executive VP, Basketball Operations

History:
1974-79 New Orleans Jazz. 1979-present Utah Jazz. Conference titles, 2; Division titles, 9.

Arena:
Vivint Smart Home Arena. Seating capacity, 19,911.

WASHINGTON WIZARDS
VERIZON CENTER
601 FRONT STREET NW
WASHINGTON, DC 20004
202-661-5000
www.nba.com/wizards
- Ted Leonsis, CEO/Chairman
- Tommy Sheppard, General Manager
- Scott Brooks, Head Coach
- Greg Kershaw, Director, Basketball Operations

History:
Championships, 1; Conference titles, 4; Division titles, 8.

Arena:
Verizon Center, opened December 1997 and has a seating capacity of 18,506.

NATIONAL BASKETBALL LEAGUE OF CANADA
info@nblcanada.ca
www.nblcanada.ca

• Audley Stephenson, Deputy Commissioner

Teams:

HALIFAX HURRICANES
2717 JOSEPH HOWE DRIVE
PO BOX 610
HALIFAX, NS, CANADA B3J 2T2
902-377-3052
info@halifaxhurricanes.ca
www.halifaxhurricanes.ca
• Amy Bragg, Owner
• Mike Leslie, Head Coach

ISLAND STORM
46 KENSINGTON RD
CHARLOTTETOWN, PE, CANADA C1A 5H7
stormbasketball.ca
• Duncan Shaw, Owner/President
• Tim Kendrick, Head Coach
• Josh Fall, Team Manager

KW TITANS
400 EAST AVENUE
KITCHENER, ON, CANADA N2H 1Z6
info@kwtitans.com
www.kwtitans.com
• Leon Martin, Owner
• Cavell Johnson, Head Coach

LONDON LIGHTNING
75 BLACKFRIARS STREET
LONDON, ON, CANADA N6H 1K8
519-433-0634
www.lightningbasketball.ca
• Vito Frijia, Owner
• Mark Frijia, General Manager
• Doug Plumb, Head Coach

MONCTON MAGIC
AVENIR CENTRE
150 CANADA STREET
MONCTON, NB, CANADA E1C 0v2
info@monctonmagic.ca
www.monctonmagic.ca
• Joe Salerno, Head Coach

SAINT JOHN RIPTIDE
99 STATION STREET
SAINT JOHN, NB, CANADA E2L 4X4
506-866-8433
Fax: 506-500-0169
sjriptide.ca
• Nelson Terroba, Head Coach/General Manager

ST. JOHN'S EDGE
MILE ONE CENTRE
50 NEW GOWER STREET
ST. JOHN'S, NL, CANADA A1C 1J3
www.sjedge.ca
• Tyrone Levingston, President
tyrone@sjedge.ca
• Steven Marcus, Head Coach

SUDBURY FIVE
240 ELGIN STREET
SUDBURY, ON, CANADA P3E 3N6
705-815-5555
Fax: 705-675-3944
info@thefive.ca
thefive.ca
• Dario Zulich, Owner
• Scott Lund, CEO
• Logan Stutz, Head Coach/General Manager

WINDSOR EXPRESS
405 VICTORIA AVENUE
WINDSOR, ON, CANADA N9A 4N1
519-800-3665
www.windsorexpress.ca

• Dartis Willis, Sr., President/CEO
• Erin Basterfield, General Manager
• Bill Jones, Head Coach

NATIONAL BASKETBALL ASSOCIATION DEVELOPMENT LEAGUE
OLYMPIC TOWER
645 FIFTH AVENUE
NEW YORK, NY 10022
212-407-8000
Fax: 212-832-3861
gleague.nba.com
• Shareef Abdur-Rahim, President
Nature of Service:
Basketball League.
League Description:
Formerly the six-team National Basketball Development League, the National Basketball Association Development League serves as the NBA's in-house minor league. Founded in 2001, the league plays almost 50 games a season and serves as a place for aspiring hoops shooters to improve their game and hopefully get called up to a big league team. The NBA G-League is currently comprised of 29 teams.

Teams:

AGUA CALIENTE CLIPPERS
TOYOTA ARENA
4000 E ONTARIO CENTER PARKWAY
ONTARIO, CA 91764
909-406-9090
info@acclippers.com
aguacaliente.gleague.nba.com
• Matt Morales, General Manager
• Paul Hewitt, Head Coach
NBA Affiliate:
LA Clippers

AUSTIN SPURS
CEDAR PARK CENTER
2100 AVENUE OF THE STARS
CEDAR PARK, TX 78613
512-236-8333
info@attcenter.com
austin.gleague.nba.com
• Tyler Self, General Manager
• Blake Ahearn, Head Coach
Arena:
Cedar Park Center
NBA Affiliate:
San Antonia Spurs

CANTON CHARGE
CANTON MEMORIAL CIVIC CENTER
1101 MARKET AVENUE N
CANTON, OH 44702
866-444-1944
canton.gleague.nba.com
• Mike Levy, President
• Mike Gansey, General Manager
• Nate Reinking, Head Coach
Arena:
Cantan Memorial Civic Center
NBA Affiliate:
Cleveland Cavaliers

DELAWARE BLUE COATS
401 GARASCHES LANE
WILMINGTON, DE 19801
302-504-7587
Fax: 302-351-5370
bluecoatsinfo@76ers.com
bluecoats.gleague.nba.com
• Larry Meli, President
• Matt Lilly, General Manager
• Connor Johnson, Head Coach
NBA Affiliate:
Philadelphia 76ers
Founded:
2007

ERIE BAYHAWKS
ERIE INSURANCE ARENA
809 FRENCH STREET
ERIE, PA 16501
814-790-5600
info@nbaerie.com
erie.gleague.nba.com
• Matt Bresee, President
• Anthony Parker, General Manager
• Ryan Pannone, Head Coach
NBA Affiliate:
New Orleans Pelicans

FORT WAYNE MAD ANTS
ALLEN COUNTY WAR MEMORIAL COLISEUM
4000 PARNELL AVENUE
FORT WAYNE, IN 46805
260-469-4667
fortwayne.gleague.nba.com
• Tim Bawmann, President
• Brian Levy, General Manager
• Tom Hankins, Head Coach
• Harrison Greenberg, Director of Basketball Operations
NBA Affiliate:
Indiana Pacers

GRAND RAPIDS DRIVE
DELTA PLEX DRIVE
2500 TURNER AVENUE NW
GRAND RAPIDS, MI 49544
844-473-7483
info@nbagrandrapids.com
grandrapids.gleague.nba.com
• Steve Jbara, President
• Jon Phelps, General Manager
• Robert Werdann, Head Coach
Affiliate:
Detroit Pistons

GREENSBORO SWARM
GREENSBORO COLISEUM FIELDHOUSE
1921 W GATE CITY BLVD
GREENSBORO, NC 27403
336-373-7400
greensboro.gleague.nba.com
• Cam Twiss, General Manager
• Jay Hernandez, Head Coach
NBA Affiliate:
Charlotte Hornets

IOWA WOLVES
WELLS FARGO ARENA
730 THIRD STREET
DES MOINES, IA 50309
515-564-8550
Fax: 515-564-8551
iowa.gleague.nba.com
• Jed Kaplan, Managing Partner
• Gianluca Pascucci, General Manager
• Sam Newman-Beck, Head Coach
NBA Affiliate:
Minnesota Timberwolves

LAKELAND MAGIC
RP FUNDING CENTER
701 W LIME ST
LAKELAND, FL 33815
863-825-3258
lakeland.gleague.nba.com
• Anthony Parker, General Manager
• Stan Heath, Head Coach
NBA Affiliate:
Orlando Magic

LONG ISLAND NETS
NASSAU VETERANS MEMORIAL COLISEUM
1255 HEMPSTEAD TURNPIKE
UNIONDALE, NY 11553
844-546-3971
info@longislandnets.com
longisland.gleague.nba.com
• Alton Byrd, VP, Business Operations
• Matt Riccardi, General Manager
• Bret Brielmaier, Head Coach

NBA Affiliate:
Brooklyn Nets

MAINE RED CLAWS
PORTLAND EXPOSITION BUILDING
239 PARK AVENUE
PORTLAND, ME 04102
207-210-6655
Fax: 207-210-6659
www.maineredclaws.com
• Dajuan Eubanks, President
• Remy Cofield, General Manager
• Scott Morrison, Head Coach
Arena:
Portland Expo
Established:
2009
Affiliation:
Boston Celtics

MEMPHIS HUSTLE
LANDERS CENTER
4560 VENTURE DR
SOUTHAVEN, MS 38671
662-470-2131
memphis.gleague.nba.com
• Brady Graber, General Manager
• Jason March, Head Coach
NBA Affiliate:
Memphis Grizzlies

NORTHERN ARIZONA SUNS
NORTHERN ARIZONA SUNS
3201 N MAIN STREET
PRESCOTT VALLEY, AZ 86314
928-772-7867
northernarizona.gleague.nba.com
• Ashley Stovall, VP, Business Operations
• Jeff Feld, General Manager
• Bret Burchard, Head Coach
NBA Affiliate:
Phoenix Suns

OKLAHOMA CITY BLUE
COX CONVENTION CENTER
1 MYRIAD GARDENS
OKLAHOMA CITY, OK 73102
405-208-4800
oklahomacity.gleague.nba.com
• Grant Gibbs, Head Coach
NBA Affiliate:
Oklahoma City Thunder

RAPTORS 905
PARAMOUNT FINE FOODS CENTRE
5500 ROSE CHERRY PLACE
MISSISSAUGA, ON, CANADA L4Z 4B6
905-501-9100
raptors905.gleague.nba.com
• Sanders Chad, General Manager
• Patrick Mutombo, Head Coach
NBA Affiliate:
Toronto Raptors

RIO GRANDE VALLEY VIPERS
BERT OGDEN ARENA
4900 SI-69 C
EDINBURG, TX 78539
956-562-7362
Fax: 956-942-1150
bballops@rgvipers.com
riograndevalley.gleague.nba.com
• Rene Borrego, President/CEO
• Travis Stockbridge, General Manager
• Mahmoud Abdelfattah, Head Coach
NBA Affiliate:
Houston Rockets

SALT LAKE CITY STARS
LIFETIME ACTIVES CENTER
4600 S REDWOOD ROAD
TAYLORSVILLE, UT 84123
801-325-2500
saltlakecity.gleague.nba.com

• Jonathan Rinehart, President
• Nathan Peavy, Head Coach
NBA Affiliate:
Utah Jazz

SANTA CRUZ WARRIORS
KAISER PERMANENTE ARENA
140 FRONT STREET
SANTA CRUZ, CA 95060
831-713-4400
Fax: 831-466-3201
questions@santacruzbasketball.com
santacruz.gleague.nba.com
• Chris Murphy, President
• Ryan Atkinson, General Manager
• Kris Weems, Head Coach
NBA Affiliate:
Golden State Warriors

SIOUX FALLS SKYFORCE
SANFORD PENTAGON
2131 S MINNESOTA AVENUE
SIOUX FALLS, SD 57105
605-332-0605
info@skyforceonline.com
siouxfalls.gleague.nba.com
• Mike Heineman, Owner/President
mike@skyforceonline.com
• Jeremy DeCurtins, General Manager
• Eric Glass, Head Coach
NBA Affiliate:
Miami Heat

SOUTH BAY LAKERS
2275 E MARIPOSA AVENUE
EL SEGUNDO, CA 90245
310-426-6000
feedback@sb-lakers.com
southbay.gleague.nba.com
• Coby Karl, Head Coach
NBA Affiliate:
LA Lakers

STOCKTON KINGS
STOCKTON ARENA
248 W FREMONT STREET
STOCKTON, CA 95203
555-KINGS-209
stockton.gleague.nba.com
• Anthony McClish, General Manager
• Darrick Martin, Head Caoch
NBA Affiliate:
Sacramento Kings

TEXAS LEGENDS
COMERICA CENTER
2601 AVENUE OF THE STARS
SUITE 300
FRISCO, TX 75034
214-469-0822
texas.gleague.nba.com
• Malcolm Farmer, President/General Manager
• George Galanopoulos, Head Coach
NBA Affiliate:
Dallas Mavericks

WESTCHESTER KNICKS
WESTCHESTER COUNTY CENTER
198 CENTRAL AVENUE
WHITE PLAINS, NY 10606
914-559-6889
westchesterknicks@msg.com
westchester.gleague.nba.com
• Leon Rose, President
• Allan Houston, General Manager
• Derrick Alston, Head Coach
NBA Affiliate:
New York Knicks

WINDY CITY BULLS
NOW ARENA
5333 PRAIRIE STONE PKWY
HOFFMAN ESTATES, IL 60192
windycity.gleague.nba.com

• Brad Seymour, President
• Josh Kreibich, General Manager
NBA Affiliate:
Chicago Bulls

WISCONSIN HERD
MENOMINEE NATION ARENA
1212 SOUTH MAIN ST
OSHKOSH, WI 54902
920-744-2035
wisconsin.gleague.nba.com
• Steve Brandes, President
• Dave Dean, General Manager
• Chase Buford, Head Coach
NBA Affiliate:
Milwaukee Bucks

WOMEN'S NATIONAL BASKETBALL ASSOCIATION
OLYMPIC TOWER
645 FIFTH AVENUE
10TH FLOOR
NEW YORK, NY 10022
www.wnba.com
• Cathy Engelbert, Commissioner
Marketing & Promotional Partners:
Adidas, AOL, Beringer, Ocean Spray Craisins, Discover, EA Sports, Gatorade, Hanns G, Kia Motors, McDonalds, Mike, Peak, Pitney Bowes, Russell, Southwest, Spalding, Toyota, T-Mobile, Wheaties
Media Partners:
IHOP, Kohler, Lamisil
Teams:
12
Founded:
1997

Teams:

ATLANTA DREAM
PHILIPS ARENA
101 MARIETTA STREET NW
SUITE 3550
ATLANTA, GA 30303
877-977-7729
Fax: 404-954-6666
dream.wnba.com
• Chris Sienko, President/General Manager
• Nicki Collen, Head Coach
History:
Founded in October of 2007
Arena:
Philips Arena

CHICAGO SKY
WINTERTRUST ARENA
200 E CERMAK ROAD
CHICAGO, IL 60616
312-828-9550
tickets@chicagosky.net
sky.wnba.com
• Michael Alter, Principal Owner
• Margaret Stender, Chairman/Minority Owner
• Adam Fox, President/CEO
• James Wade, General Manager/Head Coach
Arena:
Wintertrust Arena
History:
The Chicago Sky officially joined the Chicago sports landscape on September 20, 2005. Chicago Sky began play with the 2006 season at the UIC Pavilion, located on the campus of the University of Illinois at Chicago.

CONNECTICUT SUN
MOHEGAN SUN ARENA
ONE MOHEGAN SUN BOULEVARD
UNCASVILLE, CT 06382
tickets@connecticutsun.com
sun.wnba.com
• Tom Cantone, SVP, Sports & Entertainment
• Curt Miller, General Manager/Head Coach

History:
Founded in 1999
Arena:
Mohegan Sun Arena

DALLAS WINGS
COLLEGE PARK CENTER
601 SOUTH CENTER STREET
ARLINGTON, TX 76010
dfw.wnba.com
• Greg Bibb, President/CEO
• Vickie Johnson, Head Coach
Arena:
College Park Center

INDIANA FEVER
BUTLER UNIVERSITY HINKLE FIELDHOUSE
510 W 49TH STREET
INDIANAPOLIS, IN 46208
317-917-2500
pacersinsider@pacers.com
fever.wnba.com
• Allison Barber, President/COO
• Tamika Catchings, General Manager
• Marianne Stanley, Head Coach
History:
Founded in 1999.
Arena:
Butler University Hinkle Fieldhouse

LAS VEGAS ACES
MANDALAY BAY EVENTS CENTER
3850 LAS VEGAS BOULEVARD S
LAS VEGAS, NV 89119
210-692-2237
info@lasvegasaces.com
aces.wnba.com
• Bill Laimbeer, President/Head Coach
• Dan Padover, General Manager/VP,
Basketball Operations
Arena:
Mandalay Bay Events Center

LOS ANGELES SPARKS
STAPLES CENTER
1111 S FIGUEROA STREET
LOS ANGELES, CA 90017
sparks.wnba.com
• Natalie White, Interim President & COO
• Michael Fischer, VP, Player Personnel
• Derek Fisher, Head Coach/General Manager
Arena:
STAPLES Center
Media Broadcast:
FSN-TV West.

MINNESOTA LYNX
TARGET CENTER
600 FIRST AVENUE
MINNEAPOLIS, MN 55403
612-673-8400
lynx.wnba.com
• Glen Taylor, Owner
• Ethan Casson, CEO
• Cheryl Reeve, General Manager/Head Coach
• Pete Stene, CFO
History:
Founded in 1997. In April 1998, the WNBA
announced they would add two expansion
teams, to be managed by the Minnesota
Timberwolves and Orlando Magic, for the 1999
season. The Minnesota Lynx started their
inaugural season in 1999 with 12,000 fans in
attendance to watch the first regular-season
game, against Detroit at Target Center.
Arena:
Target Center.

NEW YORK LIBERTY
BARCLAYS CENTER
620 ATLANTIC AVE
BROOKLYN, NY 11217
718-624-7000
info@nyliberty.com
liberty.wnba.com

• Keia Clarke, CEO
• Jonathan Kolb, General Manager
• Walt Hopkins, Head Coach
History:
1996-present.
Arena:
Barclays Center

PHOENIX MERCURY
US AIRWAYS CENTER
201 E JEFFERSON STREET
PHOENIX, AZ 85004
602-514-8333
Fax: 602-379-7540
mercury.wnba.com
• Robert G. Sarver, Owner
• Jim Pitman, Gernal Manager
• Sandy Brondello, Head Coach
• Sandy Brondello, Head Coach
History:
1997-present.
Arena:
US Airways Center

SEATTLE STORM
KEYARENA
3241 THORNDYKE AVENUE W
SEATTLE, WA 98119
206-217-9622
Fax: 206-281-5817
storm.wnba.com
• Alisha Valavanis, CEO/General Manager
• Dan Hughes, Head Coach
• Tricia McLean, CFO
History:
2000-present.
Arena:
KeyArena.
Media Broadcast:
Sports Radio 950 KJR.

WASHINGTON MYSTICS
ENTERTAINMENT AND SPORTS ARENA
1100 OAK DRIVE SE
WASHINGTON, DC 20032
mystics.wnba.com
• Mike Thibault, General Manager/Head Coach
• Jim Van Stone, President, Business
Operations
Arena:
Entertainment & Sports Arena

Biathlon Organizations

BIATHLON CANADA
100-1995 OLYMPIC WAY
CANMORE, AB, CANADA T1W 2T6
403-678-4002
Fax: 403-678-3644
info@biathloncanada.ca
www.biathloncanada.ca
• Matthias Ahrens, National Team Head
Coach
(403) 678-4002
mahrens@biathloncanada.ca
• Roddy Ward, National Team Coach
(403) 609-4744
rward@biathloncanada.ca
• Andy Holmwood, General Manager
(403) 609-4746
aholmwood@biathloncanada.ca
Nature of Service:
The combination of skiing and shooting
used in the sport today is founded on a
tradition of hunting, stemming back over four
thousand years. Petroglyphs found in
Norway depict hunters, with spears,
traveling on skis in pursuit of game. Written
descriptions of hunting on skis can be traced
back to 400 B.C. and the Roman poet,
Virgil. Biathlon's military uses have been

subsequently noted by generals, writers,
geographers, and historians such as
Xenophon, Strabol, Arrian, Theophanes,
Prokopius, and Acruni who described battles
of warriors equipped with skis.
Year Founded:
1985.

INTERNATIONAL BIATHLON UNION (IBU)
PEREGRINSTRASSE 14
SALZBURG, A-5020
biathlon@ibu.at
www.biathlonworld.com
• Anders Besseberg, President
anders.besseberg@ibu.at
• Olle Dahlin, Vice President, Development
olle.dahlin@ibu.at
• James E Carrabre, Vice President,
Medical Issues
jim.carrabre@ibu.at
• Nami Kim, Vice President, Special Issues
• Ivor Lehotan, Vice President, Information
• Klaus Leistner, Vice President, Finance
klaus.leistner@ibu.at
• Victor Maygurov, First Vice President
victor.maygurov@ibu.at
• Thomas Pfuller, Vice President, Marketing
thomas.pfueller@ibu.at
• Nicole Resch, Secretary General
nicole.resch@ibu.at
• Max Cobb, Vice President, Sport
max.cobb@ibu.at
Description:
The IBU serves as the international
governing body for the sport of biathlon,
sanctioning competitions and promoting the
sport.
Number of Members:
57
Publications:
Biathlon Calander (annual), BiathlonWorld
Magazine.

U.S. BIATHLON ASSOCIATION
49 PINELAND DRIVE
SUITE 301A
NEW GLOUCESTER HALL
NEW GLOUCESTER, ME 04260
207-688-6500
800-242-8456
Fax: 207-688-6505
info@usbiathlon.org
www.teamusa.org/US-Biathlon
• Max Cobb, President & CEO
(207) 688-6500
• Per Nilsson, National Team Head Coach
per.coach@gmail.com
Year Founded:
1980
Description:
The USBA promotes the development of
biathlon in the United States by organizing
training and competition around the country.
Membership Requirements:
Annual dues

Billiards Organizations

AMERICAN CUESPORTS ALLIANCE
101 SOUTH MILITARY AVENUE
SUITE P #131
GREEN BAY, WI 54303
920-662-1705
888-662-1705
Fax: 920-662-1706

jlewis@americancuesports.org
www.americancuesports.org
• Mike Wilson, President
• Sandra Chamberlain, Vice President
• John Lewis, Executive Director
• Thomas Fankhauser, Treasurer
• Annette Wood, Graphic Designer
• Janet Ybarra, Referee Administrator
Description:
Non-profit, member-governed USA-based cue sports organization offering league-sanction services and referee and instructor certification.
Number of Members:
20,000
Year Founded:
2004

AMERICAN POOLPLAYERS ASSOCIATION, INC.
1000 LAKE SAINT LOUIS BOULEVARD
SUITE 325
LAKE SAINT LOUIS, MO 63367
636-625-8611
Fax: 636-625-2975
pbellemi@aol.com
www.poolplayers.com
• Renee Lyle, President
(636) 625-8611
• Larry Hubbart, Co-Founder
• Terry Bell, Co-Founder
Nature of Service:
The APA, also known as the Canadian Poolplayers Association in Canada, has grown to more than 250,000 and boasts more members than all other 'national' leagues combined. The League is administered locally by a network of Franchise Operators. League play is conducted weekly with both 8-Ball and 9-Ball team formats offered.
History:
The history of billiards is rich and interesting. The game we know today has evolved over centuries, morphing from games popular during different periods of history. Billiards is known to have evolved from a lawn game, similar to croquet. Play was eventually moved indoors to a wooden table with green cloth, to simulate grass. The history of the noble game of billiards is deep and vast, the table, tools for play and rules have changed century to century. Billiards enthusiasts have included Kings, Queens, commoners, Conquistadors, church officials, Presidents, up to modern day players and professionals.
Member Services:
General information and APA member services are available on our web site: www.poolplayers.com.
Membership Requirements:
Must be 18 years of age to play in APA Leagues. Membership request form available on our web site.
Number of members:
Over 250,000
Publications:
The American Poolplayers (member magazine); Billiards Buzz (member e-newsletter).

BILLIARD AND BOWLING INSTITUTE OF AMERICA
621 SIX FLAGS DRIVE
ARLINGTON, TX 76011
817-385-8441
Fax: 817-633-2940

answer@billiardandbowling.org
www.billiardandbowling.org
• Jeff Mraz, President
(800) 280-2695
jmraz@acemitchell.com
• Corey Dykstra, Vice President
(213) 725-3365
corey.dykstra@brunbowl.com
• Hank Boomershine, Secretary/Treasurer
(435) 723-9640
• Skip Nemececk, Director
(312) 733-7878
opiks@msn.com
• Joleen Lawson, Director
Nature of Service:
A not-for-profit association in Chicago to service the billiard and bowling industries. Comprised of leading bowling and billiard manufacturers, independent bowling distributors and major billiard retailers, BBIA aims to foster the growth of these two great sports throughout the world and advance of common interests of its members.
Year Founded:
1940
Membership Requirements:
Manufacturers or distributors of bowling, billiards, or related supplies as well as major billiard retailers and service firms may join.
Number of Members:
139
Publications:
Annual Directory; Newsletter BBIA NEWSLINE, quarterly; Bowling Participation Study; Billiards Participation Study. BOWLING FOR EVERYONE, instructional booklet.

BILLIARD CONGRESS OF AMERICA
10900 WEST 120 AVENUE
UNIT B7
BROOMFIELD, CO 80021
303-243-5070
866-852-0999
Fax: 719-264-0900
bca@netins.net
www.bca-pool.com
• Mike Serra, Chairman
• Chance Pack, Vice Chairman
• Jonathan Goudeau, Secretary
• Tony Stick, Treasurer
• Rob Johnson, Chief Executive Officer
Nature of Service:
Dedicated to promoting and growing cue sports worldwide through industry research and promotion. participating in the process of olympic recognition, hosting amateur, junior and professional tournaments, and supporting its business members by enhancing the image of billiards and broadening its appeal.
History:
The Billiard Congress of America was established in 1948, with early involvement by players like Willie Mosconi and Willie Hoppe. The objective was to organize the players and promote the sport through qualifying tournaments at the local, regional and national levels in Straight Pool and 3-Cushion billiards (the popular competitive disciplines of the era) and recognize those champions. Organizers were also determined to produce an official rulebook to standardize the sport and help fund the effort; and to involve billiard rooms, retailers and manufacturers in meeting these promotional goals.
Member Services:

Assists with rules, tournaments, leagues.
Number of members:
40,000
Publications:
OFFICIAL RULE BOOK, updated annually; BREAK, bimonthly newsletter; other miscellaneous informational materials.

CANADIAN BILLIARDS & SNOOKER ASSOCIATION
24 WOODSTOCK AVENUE
UNIT 6
RIVERVIEW, NB, CANADA E1B 5H5
randall.morrison@cbsa.ca
www.cbsa.ca
• Randall Morrison, President
(403) 399-1972
randall.morrison@cbsa.ca
• John White, Vice President
john.white@cbsa.ca
• Frank Kakouros, Treasurer
frank.kakouros@cbsa.ca
• Candace Campbell, Secretary
candace.campbell@cbsa.ca
Description:
The CBSA is the governing body for cue sports in Canada. It is a registered non-profit organization and has been operating this way since opening in 1974. CBSA is also recognized by the Canadian Olympic Committee.
Nature of Service:
This association is responsible for arranging the national championships across all disciplines of cue sports and qualifying Canadian players to represent their country at international events staged by the world governing bodies.

CANADIAN CUE SPORTS ASSOCIATION
87 BRIGHTONSTONE GARDENS SE
CALGARY, AB, CANADA T2Z 0C6
403-271-9221
 pplted@hotmail.com
www.cdnqsport.com
• Ted Harms, President
Description:
The Canadian Cue Sports Association contains a league system and a championship program that are managed by Canadians, for Canadians. They've partnered with the American CueSports Alliance to ensure that CCS members could compete in US National Championships. They are recognized as the official sanctioning organization for pool league play and related championships in Canada.

TAP, LLC
4315 MAGNUM STREET
SUITE D
LITTLE RIVER, SC 29566
800-984-7665
Fax: 888-870-0983
www.tapleague.com
• Loyd Schonter, Founder/CEO
• Celeste Schonter, Chief Administrative Officer
• Charlie Brocklehurt, Program Director
• Kelly Nace, Event Director
Description:
TAP aims to create an amateur pool league that brings respect to both the player and the game.

UNITED STATES BILLIARD ASSOCIATION
53 HAWTHORNE AVENUE
EAST ISLIP, NY 11730
516-238-6193
www.usba.net
• Jim Shovak, President
• Tom Paley, Secretary
tpaley@msn.com
• Merrill Hughes, Treasurer
hakey99@aol.com
Description:
The USBA acts as the governing body for all forms of carom billiards, including three-cushion billiards, in America.

VNEA
201 SOUTH HENRY STREET
BAY CITY, MI 48706
www.vnea.com
• Gregg Elliott, Executive Director
• Brian Elliott, Director of Marketing & Promotions
• James Powell, Floor Operations Manager
• Rhonda Reinarz, Administrative Assistant
Description:
Non-profit organization established to promote pool on coin operated equipment. Founded in 1979, the membership is over 100,000.

WOMEN'S PROFESSIONAL BILLIARD ASSOCIATION
416 CR 501
SUITE 108
BAYFIELD, CO 81122
855-367-9722
Fax: 704-344-8660
office1@wpba.com
www.wpba.com
• Kim White-Newsome, President
• Belinda Calhoun, Vice President
• John Newsome, Secretary
• Anne Craig, Treasurer
Nature of Service:
Originally formed under the name of the Women's Professional Billiard Alliance. The WPBA sanctions billiard events for female professionals in the sport of billiards.
Year Founded:
1976
Publications:
WPBA Newsletter

WORLD POOL BILLIARD ASSOCIATION
www.wpa-pool.com
• Ian Anderson, President/CEO
• Liwei Wang, Honorary Vice President
• Anamaria Matesic, Treasurer
• Victor Maduro, Board Member
Membership Requirements:
Recognizes the continental and national federations proven to be among the leading federations in its realm. Continental federation pays $12,500 annually to support WPA. Current continental federation members include: European Pocket Billiard Federation, Asian Pocket Billiard Union, Australasian Pool Association, Billiard Congress of America (North America), South African Pool Association, Aruban Billiard Federation, Dutch Caribbean Billiard Association.
Description:
Founded in 1987. It is the international governing body for pocket billiards. Services to promote all pocket billiard sports; to unite the continents and national pool federations and recognize and support them; delegates and supervises rules and tournament regulations for various games; approves and delegates international tournaments and players eligible to compete; acknowledges, confirms and registers results achieved at official championships. Head quarters are located in Sydney, Australia.

Boating Organizations

AMERICAN BOAT & YACHT COUNCIL
613 THIRD STREET
SUITE 10
ANNAPOLIS, MD 21403
410-990-4460
Fax: 410-990-4466
www.abycinc.org
• John Adey, President
(410) 990-4460
jadey@abycinc.org
• Kevin Scullen, Membership Manager
(410) 990-4460
kscullen@abycinc.org
• Kenneth Weinbrecht, Chairman of the Board
• Brian Goodwin, Technical Director
(410) 990-4460
bgoodwin@abycinc.org
Nature of Service:
To develop quality technical practices and engineering standards for the design, construction, maintenance and repair of small crafts with refernce to their safety.

AMERICAN BOAT BUILDERS & REPAIRERS ASSOCIATION
NEWPORT SHIPYARD
1 WASHINGTON STREET
NEWPORT, RI 02840
401-236-2466
info@abbra.org
www.abbra.org
• Graham Wright, President
• Kirk Ritter, Vice President
• Peter Sabo, Treasurer
• Ron Helbig, Secretary
Nature of Service:
Serves to strengthen and to encourage the professionalism of the marine service industry through the sharing of knowledge and the search for solutions to common problems.
Year Founded:
1943
Publication:
Capstan Newsletter - Monthly.

AMERICAN BOATBUILDERS ASSOCIATION
THE BRUMBY BUILDING
MARIETTA STATION
127 CHURCH STREET, SUITE 210
MARIETTA, GA 30060
770-792-3070
Fax: 770-792-3073
glenna@aba.com
www.ababoats.com
• Jay Patton, President
• Ed Atchley, Senior Project Manager
Nature of Service:
Through the collective buying power of its members, the ABA strives to purchase high quality materials at the lowest cost of any boat building entity in the United States. They organize as necessary to bring the united voice of the independent builder to outside influences such as vendors, government, and industry associations.
Year Founded:
1992

AMERICAN POWER BOAT ASSOCIATION
17640 EAST NINE MILE ROAD
EASTPOINTE, MI 48021-0377
586-773-9700
Fax: 586-773-6490
apbahq@apba.org
www.apba.org
• Mark Wheeler, President
president@apba.org
• Dutch Squires, Vice President
• Ryan Berlin, Director of Operations
• Linda Likert, Bookeeper
Description:
The APBA is the US governing body for power boat racing.
Year Founded:
1903
Member Services:
Various.
Membership Requirements:
Complete application, pay fee.
Number of Members:
3,500+
Publications:
PROPELLER Magazine

AMERICAN WHITEWATER
629 WEST MAIN STREET
SYLVA, NC 28779
828-586-1931
Fax: 828-586-2840
membership@americanwhitewater.org
www.americanwhitewater.org
• Chris Bell, President
• Courtney Wilton, Vice President
• Trey Coleman, Treasurer
• Susan Hollingsworth-Elliott, Secretary
Nature of Service:
American Whitewater is a non-profit organization that aims to conserve and restore America's whitewater resources. It is a membership organization that aims to enhance opportunities for whitewater enthusiasts to enjoy the water safely.
Year Founded:
1954
Membership Benefits:
Six issues of the American Whitewater magazine, monthly online electronic newsletter, 10% discount on outdoor equipment from nantahalaoutdoor center store, catalog and online. 40% off the subscription of Kayak session magazine.

ASSOCIATION OF MARINA INDUSTRIES
50 WATER STREET
WARREN, RI 02885
866 367-6622
Fax: 401-247-0074
info@marinaassociation.org
www.marinaassociation.org
• Jeff Rose, Chairman
• Brad Gross, Vice Chairman
• Joe Riley, Treasurer
• Merritt Alves, Membership Coordinator
• Kate Stanley, Direcor of Events
Description:
The Association of Marina Industries is a nonprofit organization dedicated to the

marine industry. The AMI is responsible for the International Marine Institute, including the Certified Marina Manager program and the annual International Marina & Boatyard Conference.

Membership:
Benefits include critical legislative and regulatory support; timely industry information, advice, and direction; money-saving programs including marina insurance program, fuel discount program, energy purchasing program, telecom savings program, penny wise office supplies program, personal insurance program; education, seminars and certifications; online discussion forum; and access to free internet classified postings.

BOAT OWNERS ASSOCIATION OF THE UNITED STATES (BOATUS)
880 SOUTH PICKETT STREET
ALEXANDRIA, VA 22304-4606
703-461-2878
800-283-2883
membership@boatus.com
www.boatus.com
• Margaret Podlich, President
• Adam Wheeler, VP and Director of Towing
• John Condon, AVP, Towing Operations
• Heather Lougheed, VP, Membership

Nature of Service:
Provides savings, service and representation to millions of boat owners nationwide.

Year Founded:
1966

Number of Members
650,000

BOATING WRITERS INTERNATIONAL
108 NINTH STREET
WILMETTE, IL 60091
847-736-4142
www.bwi.org
• Alan Wendt, President
• Lenny Rudow, First Vice President
• Lindsey Johnson, Second Vice President
• Zuzana Prochazka, Board of Directors
• Greg Proteau, Executive Director, Secretary and Treasurer

Description:
Boating Writers International/BWI is a non-profit professional organization consisting of writers, broadcasters, editors, photographers, public relations specialists and others in the communications profession associated with the boating industry. Members include active marine journalists across the U.S., in Canada and Europe, supporting marine manufacturers and service entities, and associates in communication roles.

CANADIAN SAFE BOATING COUNCIL
400 CONSUMERS ROAD
TORONTO, ON, CANADA M2J 1P8
416-840-8938
www.csbc.ca
• John Gullick, Chair
• Vollmer Michael, Vice Chair
• Denis Vallee, Treasurer
• Susan Daly, Secretary
• Ted Fortuna, Officer

Description:
The Canadian Safe Boating Council aims to promote safe and responsible boating throughout Canada.

INDEPENDENT BOATBUILDERS INC.
215 NORTH LOGAN STREET
SUITE B
WEST FRANKFORT, IL 62896
618-932-4476
Fax: 618-932-8132
www.ibbi.com
• Tom Broy, President
• Lindsey Dillow, Accounting Assistant
• Jodi Sanders, Controller, Secretary, Treasurer

Nature of Service:
Independent Boat Builders, Inc. was formed as a marine purchasing cooperative by a group of independent, recreational boat builders. IBBI has maintained strict standards for membership, and today, we have 23, highly-regarded shareholders, each recognized in the industry for their top-quality boats, their integrity, and their financial stability.

Year Founded:
1989

INTERNATIONAL COUNCIL OF MARINE INDUSTRY ASSOCIATIONS
MARINE HOUSE
THORPE LEA ROAD
EGHAM, SURREY, ENGLAND TW20 8BF
+44-1784-22-3702
Fax: +44-1784-27-0428
info@icomia.com
www.icomia.com
• Udo Kleinitz, Secretary General
(+44) 1784 223 7
udo@icomia.com
• Patrick Hemp, Technical Manager
(+44) 1784 223 7
patrick@icomia.com
• Barbara Fountoukos, Communications Manager
(+44) 1784 223 7
barbara@icomia.com
• Trudie Bloomfield, Office Secretary

Nature of Sports Service:
Founded in 1966. Brings together in one global organization all the national boating federations and other bodies involved in the recreational marine industry, and to represent them at international level.

INTERNATIONAL JET SPORTS BOATING ASSOCIATION
330 PURISSIMA STREET
SUITE C
HALF MOON BAY, CA 94019
714-751-8695
Fax: 714-751-8609
info@ijsba.com
www.ijsba.com
• Scott Frazier, Executive Director

Nature of Service:
International membership association for personal watercraft owners with members in 35 countries. Sanctions personal watercraft boating races.

Year Founded:
1982

Number of members:
27,000

Publications:
JET SPORTS, 9 times a year.

NATIONAL MARINE MANUFACTURERS ASSOCIATION
231 SOUTH LASALLE STREET
SUITE 2050
CHICAGO, IL 60604
312-946-6200
webmaster@nmma.org
www.nmma.org
• Thomas Dammrich, President
(312) 946-6220
tdammrich@nmma.org
• Ben Wold, Executive Vice President
(312) 946-6234
bwold@nmma.org
• Carl Blackwell, Senior VP
(312) 946-6277
cblackwell@nmma.org
• Craig Boskey, Senior VP Finance
(312) 946-6232
cboskey@nmma.org
• Thomas Marhevko, Senior VP
(312) 946-6213
tmarhevko@nmma.org

Products & Services:
Dedicated to creating, promoting and protecting an environment where members can achieve financial success through excellence in manufacturing, in selling, and in servicing their customers.

RECREATIONAL BOATING & FISHING FOUNDATION
500 MONTGOMERY STREET
SUITE 300
ALEXANDRIA, VA 22314
703-519-0013
info@takemefishing.org
takemefishing.org
• Frank Peterson Jr., President & CEO
(703) 778-5157
fpeterson@rbff.org

Nature of Service:
The Recreational Boating & Fishing Foundation is a nonprofit organization whose mission is to increase participation in recreational angling and boating and thereby increase public awareness and appreciation of the need for protecting, conserving and restoring this nation's aquatic natural resources.

Year Founded:
1998

Publications:
NewsWaves, monthly e-newsletter

SAIL AMERICA
50 WATER STREET
WARREN, RI 02885
401-289-2540
Fax: 401-247-0074
www.sailamerica.com
• Katie Kelly, Association Manager
kkelly@sailamerica.com

Sports Service Founded:
1988

Event Management Services:
Nonprofit organization, promoting SAIL EXPO & Strictly Sail, sailboat shows.

SAIL CANADA
PORTSMOUTH OLYMPIC HARBOUR
53 YONGE STREET
KINGSTON, ON, CANADA K7M 6G4
613-545-3044
Fax: 613-545-3045
sailcanada@sailing.ca
www.sailing.ca

• Todd Irving, President
• Kai Bjorn, Board Member
Description:
Established in 1931, Sail Canada is the national governing body for the sport of sailing in Canada.

SUPER BOAT INTERNATIONAL
1323 20TH TERRACE
KEY WEST, FL 33040
305-296-6166
superboatracing@gmail.com
www.superboat.com
• John Carbonell, Founder
Description:
Involved in promoting Super Boat Racing events, leading to national and world championships.
Year Founded:
1992

THUNDERBOATS UNLIMITED INC.
1342 MAIN ST
SUITE B
RAMONA, CA 92065-2127
Nature of Service:
Thunderboats Unlimited, Inc. is a non-profit corporation established by a group of committed Southern California racing enthusiasts, to promote powerboat racing in San Diego, and increase tourism in the beach area. The group was initially brought together by the late legendary hydroplane racer Bill Muncey, for whom the 2Â« mile race course is named, but soon grew to include individuals from all aspects of the community.
Year Founded:
1964
Number of members:
1,450

UNITED MARINE MANUFACTURERS ASSOCIATION
714 SOUTH NATIONAL
SPRINGFIELD, MO 65804
417-869-9602
Fax: 417-869-9653
www.umma.com
• Kent Wooldridge, President
• Sherree Johnson, Accountant
• Jane Melton, Program Implementation
Description:
To empower the marine suppliers in a highly competitive and changing industry. We provide information to our members that improve their operational efforts and help build their market share, relative to the industry.
Year Founded:
1998

WOMEN'S OCEAN RACING SAILING ASSOCIATION
PO BOX 937
DANA POINT, CA 92629
949-722-7872
Fax: 949-846-1481
info@wsaoc.org
www.worsa.org
• Valerie Rhodes, Commodore
• Gabi Schwaiger, Vice Commodore
• Wayne Wallace, Treasurer
• Brenda Highley, Secretary
• Shannon Harshman, Membership Director
Nature of Service:
Provides opportunities for women to gain

sailing knowledge on and off the water, to participate in all-female regattas, and to socialize with other women sailors. Membership includes both racers and cruisers - both males and females.
Year Founded:
1979
Member Services:
Sponsors annual women's regatta in October, racing clinics for women, annual cruise to the Isthmus at Catalina Island, and other services. Members of Southern California Yachting Association, sponsors of the annual SCYA women's sailing convention held in February of each year.
Description:
Founded in 1979. Provides opportunities for women to gain sailing knowledge on and off the water, to participate in all-female regattas, and to socialize with other women sailors. Membership includes both racers and cruisers - both males and females.
Publications:
THE WHISTLE, monthly newsletter.

Bobsledding Organizations

USA BOBSLED & SKELETON FEDERATION
1631 MESA AVENUE
COPPER BUILDING
SUITE A
COLORADO SPRINGS, CO 80906
Fax: 719-520-3212
www.teamusa.org/USA-Bobsled-Skeleton-Federation
• Darrin Steele, Chief Executive Officer
darrin.steele@usabs.com
• Lisa Carlock, Finance & Operations Director
lisa.carlock@usabs.com
• Lenny Kasten, National Team Manager
Description:
This Federation was formed to advance, encourage, improve and promote amateur bobsledding and skeleton competition in the United States. It is also the National Governing Body of hte sports of bobsled and skeleton and recognized as such by the United States Olympic Committee and the Federation Internationale De Bob Sleigh De and Tobogganing Federation.
Member Services:
Passenger Rider / Sports / Supporting Memberships
Number of members:
525
Publications:
Quarterly newsletter

Bowling Organizations

AMERICAN BLIND BOWLING ASSOCIATION
7273 SOUTH RIDGELAND
CHICAGO, IL 60649
773-255-3121
www.abba1951.org
• Robert McDonald, President
(773) 255-3121
president@abba1951.org
• Joyce Spencer, 1st Vice President
(919) 796-5090
1stvicepresident@abba1951.org

• Charles Glaser, 2nd Vice President
(678) 521-2976
2ndvicepresident@abba1951.org
Description:
ABBA's goal is to allow blind and visually impaired individuals to bowl with the assistance of special guide rails. They host numerour tournaments throughout the year in many different locations in North America.
Year Founded:
1940
Membership Requirements:
Any person 18 years of age or older, legally blind or sighted.
Publications:
INTRODUCING THE BLIND BOWLING ASSOCIATION. THE BLIND BOWLER, published three times annually with information about league and tournament activities and high score awards.

AMERICAN WHEELCHAIR BOWLING ASSOCIATION
713-849-9052
info@awba.org
www.awba.org
• Richard Carlson, Founder
• Wayne Webber, Chairman
• Eddy Hutchens, Vice Chairman
• Mark Shepherd, Treasurer
• Gary Ryan, Secretary
Description:
The American Wheelchair Bowling Association serves over 500 members throughout the United States. They've formed numeruos alliance with organizations, such as the Veterans Administration, Paralyzed Veterans of America, and some youth organizations.

BILLIARD AND BOWLING INSTITUTE OF AMERICA
615 SIX FLAGS DRIVE
ARLINGTON, TX 76011
817-385-8441
Fax: 817-633-2940
answer@billiardandbowling.org
www.billiardandbowling.org
• Jeff Mraz, President
(800) 280-2695
jmraz@acemitchell.com
• Corey Dykstra, Vice President
(213) 725-3365
corey.dykstra@brunbowl.com
• Hank Boomershine, Secretary/Treasurer
(435) 723-9640
• Skip Nemececk, Director
(312) 733-7878
opiks@msn.com
• Joleen Lawson, Director
Nature of Service:
A not-for-profit association in Chicago to service the billiard and bowling industries. Comprised of leading bowling and billiard manufacturers, independent bowling distributors and major billiard retailers, BBIA aims to foster the growth of these two great sports throughout the world and advance of common interests of its members.
Year Founded:
1940
Membership Requirements:
Manufacturers or distributors of bowling, billiards, or related supplies as well as major billiard retailers and service firms may join.
Number of Members:
139

Publications:
Annual Directory; Newsletter BBIA
NEWSLINE, quarterly; Bowling Participation
Study; Billiards Participation Study.
BOWLING FOR EVERYONE, instructional
booklet.

BOWL CANADA
250 SHIELDS COURT
UNIT 10A
MARKHAM, ON, CANADA L3R 9W7
905-479-1560
Fax: 905-479-8613
info@bowlcanada.ca
www.bowlcanada.ca
• Todd Britton, President
(204) 488-0000
todd@academylanes.ca
• Ray Brittain, Vice President
(250) 753-2341
brechinlanes@gmail.com
• Trevor Peters, Director
(204) 727-2695
t.peters@thunderbirdbowl.ca
• Rod Hennessey, Treasurer
(709) 744-2553
riverdalelanes@nl.rogers.com
• Paul Oliveira, Executive Director
paul@bowlcanada.ca
• Kevin Burns, Programs Coordinator
kevin@bowlcanada.ca
Description:
Bowl Canada is a not-for-profit association
that works to support bowling centres,
promote the benefits of the sport and
recreation of bowling to the general public,
and to create a better relationship between
the many bowling establishments across
Canada.

BOWLING PROPRIETORS' ASSOCIATION OF AMERICA
621 SIX FLAGS DRIVE
ARLINGTON, TX 76011
800-343-1329
bpaa.com
• Tom Martino, President
(732) 826-6800
ajjaguar@aol.com
• Nancy Schenk, President Elect
(910) 484-5178
nancy@bandblanes.com
• Randy Thompson, Secretary
(515) 255-1111
rt@plazalanesdm.com
• Jeff Boje, Treasurer
(813) 621-2363
jeffboje@aol.com
Nature of Service:
Perpetuates the best interest of its
members, be it for business or bowling as a
whole. Promotes better relationships among
its members. Aids in formation of and
recognizes qualified state, city, district and
regional associations. Disseminates
information to members beneficial to the
conduct of their business. Cooperates and
assists others in the furtherance of the best
interests of bowling. Obtains beneficial
publicity through all available media.
Encourages clean and ideal conditions
under which bowling shall be conducted by
bowling proprietors. Discourages any
practice contrary to the best interest of the
game.
Year Founded:
1932
Number of members:

3,300
Publications:
Bowling Center Management magazine

CANADIAN 5 PIN BOWLERS' ASSOCIATION
#206 - 720 BELFAST ROAD
OTTAWA, ON, CANADA K1G 0Z5
613-744-5090
Fax: 613-744-2217
sheila.c5pba@gmail.com
www.c5pba.ca
• Dave Post, President
• Len Isleifson, 1st Vice President
• Dave Shepherd, 2nd Vice President
• Sheila Carr, Executive Director
• Chris Henderson, Corporate
Secretary/Treasurer
Description:
The Canadian 5 Pin Bowlers' Association
aims to promote 5 pin bowling and to instill a
sense of pride among it's members. The
association provides quality programs and
services to its members, given their
participation. The association regulates 5
pin bowling, resulting in standardization
within the sport.
Year Founded:
1978
Member Services:
Awards program, lane certification program,
logo merchandising, national
championships, range of technical/coaching
programs.
Membership Requirements:
Bowlers can purchase membership card
through the provincial territorial association
in the province which they reside.
Publications:
Coast to Coast Newsletter, Rule Book,
by-laws, annually; various manuals and
booklets concerning 5 pin bowling.

THE NATIONAL BOWLING ASSOCIATION, INC
9944 READING ROAD
EVENDALE, OH 45241-3106
513-769-1985
Fax: 513-769-3596
nationaloffice@tnbainc.org
www.tnbainc.org
• Gregory P. Green, President
greg.green@tnbainc.org
• Dewann Clark, Vice President
(310) 846-4590
dewann.clark@tnbainc.org
• Annette R. Samuel, Executive Secretary,
Treasurer
(513) 769-1985
annette.samuel@tnbainc.org
• Luther Moses, National Director of
Tournaments
(303) 696-9410
luther.moses@tnbainc.org
Nature of Service:
The National Bowling Association, Inc. is a
non-profit corporation that fosters and
promotes the game of Ten Pins among both
men and women.
Year Founded:
1939
Member Services:
Awards to members according to their
achievements. Sponsor Annual
Scholarships.
Membership Requirements:
Interest in bowling.

Publications:
NBA BOWLER, five times annually; NBA
Souvenir Yearbook, annually.

NATIONAL DEAF WOMEN'S BOWLING ASSOCIATION
tazgayle@yahoo.com
• Gayle Willingham, President
tazgayle@yahoo.com
• Ali Martinez, Interim Vice President
geezam64@aol.com
• Jane Jacobson, Secretary Treasurer
ndwbast@gmail.com

PROFESSIONAL BOWLERS ASSOCIATION
55 EAST JACKSON BOULEVARD
SUITE 401
CHICAGO, IL 60604
206-332-9688
Fax: 312-341-1469
www.pba.com
• Tom Clark, Commissioner
• Kirk Von Krueger, Deputy Commissioner
Nature of Service:
Conducts tournaments on both national and
regional level with members competing for
an aggregate prize fund in excess of $6
million. National tour consists of 25
tournaments annually, with over 150
contested on a regional level.
Year Founded:
1958
Member Services:
Merchandise program. Free subscription to
Bowlers Journal International. A free
pba.com e-mail address and access to an
exclusive members only site.
Membership Requirements:
A 200 or better average in at least one
league for 66 or more games per season in
each of two years prior to applying.
Number of members:
4,300
Publications:
OFFICIAL TOUR PROGRAM; Regular
press releases to media.
Sponsors:
United States Bowling Congress, GEICO,
Pepsi-Cola, Brunswick, Bayer, Denny's
Motel 6, Ace Hardware, Etonic, Columbia
300, H&R, Discover Card.

UNITED STATES BOWLING CONGRESS
621 SIX FLAGS DRIVE
ARLINGTON, TX 76011
800-514-2695
bowlinfo@bowl.com
www.bowl.com
• Frank Wilkinson, President
• Cathy Desocio, Vice President
• Chad Murphy, Executive Director
• Neil Stremmel, Managing Director
Description:
Founded in 2005, the United States Bowling
Congress serves around two million
members in the United States. It serves as
the national governing body of bowling as
recognized by the United States Olympic
Committee.

WORLD BOWLING
2208 BROOKSIDE DRIVE
ARLINGTON, TX 76012
414-803-9188
president@worldbowling.org
www.worldbowling.org

• Kevin Dornberger, CEO World Bowling
president@worldbowling.org
• Sheikh Talal, World Bowling President
kbsclub@qualitynet.net
• Suwalai Satrulee, World Bowling 1st Vice
President
suwalaisatrulee@hotmail.com
• Addie Ophelders, ETBF President
ao@etbf.eu
Description:
World Bowling is responsible to promote
and administer bowling throughout the world
and to promote the Olympic movement.
Year Founded:
1952

YOUTH BOWL CANADA
250 SHIELDS COURT
UNIT 10A
MARKHAM, ON, CANADA L3R 9W7
905-479-1560
Fax: 905-479-8613
info@bowlcanada.ca
www.youthbowl.ca
• Todd Britton, President
(204) 488-0000
todd@academylanes.ca
• Ray Brittain, Vice President
(250) 753-2341
brechinlanes@gmail.com
• Trevor Peters, Director
(204) 727-2695
• Rod Hennessey, Treasurer
(709) 744-2553
riverdalelanes@nl.rogers.com
• Colleen Haider, Secretary
(306) 783-5183
c.haider@sasktel.net
• Kevin Burns, Program Coordinator
kevin@bowlcanada.ca

Boxing Organizations

BOXING CANADA
C/O CANADIAN OLYMPIC COMMITTEE
500, BOUL. RENE-LEVESQUE OUEST
MONTREAL, QC, CANADA H2Z 2A5
514-861-5513
1-800-861-1319
Fax: 514-819-9228
info@boxingcanada.org
boxingcanada.org
• Pat Fiacco, President
pfiacco@sasktel.net
• Ryan Savage, Vice President
• Marcel Toulouse, Treasurer
• Willie McNeil, Executive Committee
Member
• Val Ryan, Executive Committee Member
Description:
To promote, encourage & develop the
widest participation in amateur boxing in
Canada & the highest proficiency amoungst
its members in pursuit of excellence.
Nature of Services:
Development and maintenance of uniform
rules and regulations governing amateur
boxing competitions in Canada, coaching
and officials development, national and
international competitions, National Team
Programs (development, training and
competition) and international relations.

IBF/USBA
899 MOUNTAIN AVENUE
SUITE 2C
SPRINGFIELD, NJ 07081
973-564-8046
Fax: 973-564-8751
jsalazar@ibfboxing.com
www.ibfusbaregistration.com
• Daryl J. Peoples, President
• Lindsey E. Tucker, Championships
Chairman
• Randy Neurmann, Treasurer
• Louis Priluker, Secretary
Description:
Serves to rate boxers in different categories;
approves championship bouts for titles;
prepares and utilizes various safety
mechanisms to provide for the overall safety
of the industry; promulgates rules and
regulations utilized worldwide for governing
professional boxing events, and where there
are no commissions, serves as a
commission to oversee the activity in that
area. Trains and licenses referees and
judges and holds semi-annual and annual
seminars for them to sharpen their skills.
Member Services:
Established retirement and trust plan for
boxers worldwide; offers special assistance
to retired boxers (SARB) fund.

INTERNATIONAL BOXING ASSOCIATION (AIBA)
MAISON DU SPORT INTERNATIONAL
AVENUE DU RHODANIE 54
LAUSANNE, 1007
info@aiba.org
www.aiba.org
• Ching-Kuo Wu, President
• Karim Bouzidi, Executive Director
Nature of Service:
AIBA is the international governing body for
the sport of boxing, overseeing national
federations across the globe, including USA
Boxing.
Year Founded:
1946
Member Services:
Administrative services; Conduct of World
Championships.
Membership Requirements:
National Federations on subscription basis.
Publications:
Boxing! The AIBA Magazine

INTERNATIONAL BOXING ORGANIZATION
340 MINORCA AVENUE
CORAL GABLES, FL 33134
305-446-0684
president@iboboxing.com
www.iboboxing.com
• Ed Levine, President
• John W. Daddono, Chairman
• Jeremy D. Levine, Vice President
• Robert Balogh, Vice President
Description:
The IBO aims to bring honesty, integrity and
trust to the sport. They use the only
independent objective computerized
rankings in boxing today and place an
emphasis on fairness and experience.

NORTH AMERICAN BOXING FEDERATION
911 KIMBARK STREET
LONGMONT, CO 80501

303-442-0258
Fax: 303-442-0380
www.nabfnews.com
• Duane B. Ford, President
• Craig Hubble, Vice President
• Joanna Aguilar, Executive Secretary
• David Sutherland, Membership Chairmen

USA BOXING
1 OLYMPIC PLAZA
COLORADO SPRINGS, CO 80909
719-866-2300
Fax: 719-866-2132
www.teamusa.org/USA-Boxing
• Mike McAtee, Interim Executive Director
mmcatee@usaboxing.org
Nature of Service:
A non-profit organization that is responsible
for the administration, development and
promotion of Olympic-style boxing in the
United States.
Year Founded:
1888
Member Services:
Support and guidance in all facets of
amateur boxing.
Membership Requirements:
Must register in the Local Boxing Committee
that oversees their locality. Boxers must be
eligible for competition in amateur boxing.
Number of members:
30,000
Publications:
USA Boxing Technical & Competition Rules

WORLD BOXING ASSOCIATION
47 OCEAN BUSINESS PLAZA
14TH FLOOR
OFFICE 14-05
MARBELLA, PANAMA
507-203-7680
Fax: 507-203-7681
info@wbanews.com
www.wbanews.com
• Gilberto Mendoza, Executive Vice
President
• Julio Thyme, Operations
jthyme@wbanews.com
• Noryoli Gil, Operations
norygil@wbanews.com

WORLD BOXING ORGANIZATION
FIRST FEDERAL BUILDING
1056 MUNOZ RIVERA AVENUE
SUITE 711-714
SAN JUAN, 00927
787-765-4444
Fax: 787-758-9053
www.wboboxing.com
• Francisco Valcarcel, President
• Luis Batista-Salas, Founder/Chairman of
the Championship Committee
• Ramon Acevedo, Past President
• John Duggan, First Vice President
• Jacinth Bryan-Labega, Second Vice
President
• Adolfo Flores, Treasurer

Broomball Organizations

CANADIAN BROOMBALL FEDERATION
145 PACIFIC AVENUE
WINNIPEG, MB, CANADA R3B 2Z6

204-925-5656
Fax: 204-925-5792
www.broomball.ca
• George Brown, President
(613) 253-7787
president@broomball.ca
• Chris Pilon, VP Administration
vpadmin@broomball.ca
• Gerry Wever, VP Technical
(613) 445-0904
vptech@broomball.ca
• Greg Mastervick, Treasurer
(780) 459-7668
treasurer@broomball.ca
• Michelle Lechner, Secretary
secretary@broomball.ca
Description:
The role of the Canadian Broomball Federation is to provide leadership by promoting and developing broomball and by developing and coordinating programs and services designed to meet the needs of the broomball community.

INTERNATIONAL FEDERATION OF BROOMBALL ASSOCIATIONS
www.internationalbroomball.org
• Marc Desparois, VP Operations
• Conrad Morneau, VP Technical
• Alan Jabs, Secretary General
Description:
The program, beginning in 1988, was formed to promote international broomball championships.

USA BROOMBALL
PO BOX 20201
BLOOMINGTON, MN 55420
612-201-6088
www.usabroomball.com
• Kevin Denesen, President
president@usabroomball.com
• Perry, Director Of Operations
(763) 214-1789
• Perry Coonce, Director of Operations
(763) 241-1789
Nature of Service:
A non-profit organization whose purpose is to further the development of broomball in the United States. Broomball is played indoors on an ice hockey rink or outdoors on frozen ponds or lakes with rules very similar to Ice Hockey. Players wear special padded sponge rubber shoes, use a ball which is sized somewhere between a soccer ball and slow pitch softball, and use specially designed manufactured brooms which are made of wood or aluminum. The goal like hockey is to put the ball in the opposing net, a net which is larger than a hockey net but much smaller than an outdoor soccer goal.
Year Founded:
1995

Canoeing Organizations

AMERICAN CANOE ASSOCIATION
503 SOPHIA STREET
SUITE 100
FREDERICKSBURG, VA 22401
540-907-4460
Fax: 888-229-3792
aca@americancanoe.org

• Anne Maleady, President
• Peter Sloan, Treasurer
• Robin Pope, Secretary
Nature of Service:
Member-based, national nonprofit organization serving the broader paddling public by providing education related to all aspects of paddling, stewardship support to help paddling environmnents, and sanctioning of programs and events to promote paddlesport competition and recreation.

CANADIAN RECREATIONAL CANOE ASSOCIATION
446 MAIN STREET WEST
PO BOX 398
MERRICKVILLE, ON, CANADA K0G 1N0
613-269-2910
Fax: 613-269-2908
www.canoe.ca

CANOEKAYAK CANADA
2197 RIVERSIDE DRIVE
SUITE 700
OTTAWA, CANADA K1H 7X3
613-260-1818
Fax: 613-260-5137
admin@canoekayak.ca
www.canoekayak.ca
• Casey Wade, Chief Executive Officer
(613) 260-1818
cwade@canoekayak.ca
• John Edwards, Domestic Development Director
(613) 260-1818
jhedwards@canoekayak.ca
• Natalie Brett, National Team Manager
(613) 260-1818
nbrett@canoekayak.ca
• Peter Neidre, Director of Coach and Athlete Development
(613) 260-1818
• Sally Clare, Director of Finance
(613) 721-0504
sclare@canoekayak.ca
• James Cartwright, Slalom High Performance Manager
(613) 260-1818
jcartwright@canoekayak.ca
Nature of Service:
Recognized governing body responsible for promotion, growth and development of canoe racing in Canada. Represents Canada within the International Canoe Federation. Canoe disciplines include Olympic Sprint Racing, Marathon, Canoe Sailing, and White Water.
Year Founded:
1900
Number of members:
26,000
Publications:
PADDLES UP, 6 times a year - newsletter.

INTERNATIONAL CANOE FEDERATION (ICF)
AVENUE DE RHODANIE 54
LAUSANNE, SWITZERLAN CH 1007
info@canoeicf.com
www.canoeicf.com
• Jose Perurena, President
jose.perurena@canoeicf.com
• Farias Cecilia, Vice President
cecilia.farias@canoeicf.com
• Luciano Buonfiglio, Treasurer
luciano.buonfiglio@canoeicf.com

• Simon Toulson, Secretary General
Simon.toulson@canoeicf.com
Nature of Service:
The ICF acts the international governing body for canoe sport, representing national canoe organizations like USA Canoe/Kayak, and sanctioning competition.

PADDLE CANADA
613-547-3196 EXT 10
888-252-6292
Fax: 613-547-4880
info@paddlecanada.com
www.paddlecanada.com
• Graham Ketcheson, Executive Director
• Dawn Callan, Events, National Paddling Week & PaddleSmart
• Adrian Camara, Media & Marketing Manager

PROFESSIONAL PADDLESPORTS ASSOCIATION
PO BOX 10847
KNOXVILLE, TN 37939
865-558-3595
office@americaoutdoors.com
www.propaddle.com

USA CANOE/KAYAK
503 SOPHIA STREET
SUITE 100
FREDERICKSBURG, VA 22401
540-907-4460 EXT 108
membership@usack.org
www.teamusa.org/usa-canoe-kayak
• Wade Blackwood, Chief Executive Officer
(804) 814-4077
wade@usack.org
• Amy Ellis, Membership Coordinator
(540) 907-4460
membership@usack.org
• Candy Patten, Insurance Coordinator
(540) 907-4460
insurance@usack.org
• Michele Eray, Sprint High Performance Director
(405) 552-4040
michele@usack.org
• Aaron Mann, Communications & Media
(301) 325-9504
aaron@usack.org
Description:
USA Canoe/Kayak is the national governing body for the Olympic sports of Canoe Sprint and Canoe Slalom, as well as the Paralympic sport of Paracanoe. The mission of USAÃ†Canoe/Kayak is to enable United States athletes to achieve competitive excellence in Olympic, Paralympic and Pan American competitions.

Climbing Organizations

AMERICAN ALPINE CLUB
710 TENTH STREET
SUITE 100
GOLDEN, CO 80401
303-384-0110
Fax: 303-384-0111
www.americanalpineclub.org
• Doug Walker, President
• Matt Culberson, Vice President
• Clark Gerhardt, Secretary
• Paul Gagner, Treasurer

Nature of Service:
Mountaineering and climbing organization. Represents U.S. in all matters relating to climbing domestically and internationally. Sponsors expeditions, and publishes climbing books.
Year Founded:
1902
Member Services:
Annual meeting held in February each year. World-wide rescue insurance. Discounts on AAC Press and Mountaineers books titles, access to European climbing huts, operates Grand Teton climbers ranch in Grand Teton National Park, public policy advocacy.
Membership Requirements:
Annual dues, climber for minimum of two years.
Number of members:
6,682
Publications:
AMERICAN ALPINE NEWS, quarterly, AMERICAN ALPINE JOURNAL, annual; ACCIDENTS IN NORTH AMERICAN MOUNTAINEERING, annual.

AMERICAN HIKING SOCIETY
8605 SECOND AVENUE
SILVER SPRING, MD 20910
301-565-6704
1-800-972-8608
info@americanhiking.org
www.americanhiking.org
• Gregory A. Miller, President
• Peter Olsen, VP for Programs and Government Relations
• Libby Wile, Senior Director of Volunteer Stewardship
• Kim Lyons, Director of Development and Marketing
Description:
American Hiking Society promotes and protects foot trails, their surrounding natural areas, and the hiking experience.

AMERICAN MOUNTAIN GUIDES ASSOCIATION
207 CANYON BOULEVARD
SUITE 201N
BOULDER, CO 80302-4932
303-271-0984
Fax: 303-271-1377
www.amga.com
• Rob Hess, President
(307) 733-4979
rob@jhmg.com
• Silas Rossi, Vice President
(207) 949-1736
silas@alpine-logic.com
• Annie Harrington, Secretary
(303) 894-6179
AHarrington@PattonBoggs.com
• Scott Soden, Treasurer
(303) 242-5758
scottsoden@alpinacapital.com
• Alex Kosseff, Executive Director
(303) 271-0984
alex@amga.com
• Jane Anderson, Logistics Coordinator
(303) 271-0984
jane@amga.com
Nature of Service:
AMGA's goal is to raise the standard of mountain guides in the United States to the international level through education and training.
Year Founded:

1979
Number of Members:
1,000
Sponsors:
Arc'teryx, Backcountry Access, Black Diamond, Gore-Tex/Windstopper, Malden Mills/Polartec, Mammut, Marmot, Mountain Headwear, Patagonia, Petzl, The North Face

ASSOCIATION OF CANADIAN MOUNTAIN GUIDES
900 MCGILL ROAD
KAMLOOPS, BC, CANADA V2C 5N3
403-678-2885
Fax: 250-371-5845
acmg@acmg.ca
www.acmg.ca
• Marc Ledwidge, President
(403) 762-4129
pres@acmg.ca
• Peter Tucker, Executive Director
(403) 949-3587
ed@acmg.ca
• Dwayne Congdon, Program Coordinator
(250) 371-5847
dcongdon@tru.ca

THE ACCESS FUND
207 CANYON BOULEVARD
SUITE 201S
BOULDER, CO 80302
303-545-6772
Fax: 303-545-6774
info@accessfund.org
www.accessfund.org
• Brady Robinson, Executive Director
(303) 545-6772
brady@accessfund.org
• Mark Baum, President
• Kenji Haroutunian, Vice President
• Ryan Gellert, Treasurer
• Alex Kutches, Secretary
• Jim Chase, Operations Director
(303) 545-6772
jim@accessfund.org
• Michael Allen, Development Director
(303) 545-6772
michael@accessfund.org
Description:
Dedicated to keeping climbing areas open & to conserving the climbing environment.
Year Founded:
1989

Cricket Organizations

CRICKET CANADA
3 CONCORDE GATE
SUITE 301
TORONTO, ON, CANADA M3C 3N7
416-426-7209
www.gocricketgocanada.com
• Vimal Hardat, President
• Amit Joshi, Vice President
• Charles Pais, Treasurer
• Ingleton Liburd, General Manager
Description:
Cricket Canada aims to grow and develop cricket across Canada in order to compete successfully at the highest level of the international game, while operating in a professional, organized and fiscally responsible manner.

INTERNATIONAL CRICKET COUNCIL
INTERNATIONAL CRICKET COUNCIL
STREET 69, DUBAI SPORTS CITY
SH MOHAMMED BIN ZAYED ROAD
DUBAI, UNITED ARA
971-4-382-8800
Fax: 971-4-382-8600
enquiry@icc-cricket.com
www.icc-cricket.com
• David Richardson, Chief Executive Officer
• N Srinivasan, Chairman
• Walter Edwards, Director (Australia)
• Nazmul Hassan, Director (Bangladesh)
Nature of Service:
As the international governing body for cricket, the International Cricket Council promotes the game as a global sport and sacntions compeition.
Major events:
The International Cricket Council (ICC) is the governing body for Test Match and One-Day International (ODI) cricket. It is also responsible for the global expansion of the game through its Associate and Affiliate Members and a major international Development Program.
Publications:
Cricket Quarterly is the official newsletter of the International Cricket Council. It is published 4 times a year and is distributed to all ICC member countries.

USA CRICKET ASSOCIATION
8461 LAKE WORTH ROAD
SUITE B-1-185
LAKE WORTH, FL 33467
561-839-1888
ibrulport@usaca.org
www.usaca.org
• Lisa Brulport, Executive Assistant
• Gladstone Dainty, President
• Antoni Grey, First Vice President
• Sankar Renganathan, Secretary
• Shakeel Yusuf, Treasurer

Croquet Organizations

CROQUET CANADA
24 DELORAINE AVENUE
TORONTO, ON, CANADA M5M 2A7
416-483-8229
Fax: 416-254-8256
chrisloat@bell.net
www.croquet.ca
• Ian MacGregor, President
(416) 868-3421
• Chris Loat, Treasurer
(905) 685-6939
• George Dej, Secretary
(416) 551-4548
• Bill Rowat, Director
(519) 565-5838

UNITED STATES CROQUET ASSOCIATION
700 FLORIDA MANGO ROAD
WEST PALM BEACH, FL 33406
561-478-0760
Fax: 561-686-5507
usca@msn.com
www.croquetamerica.com
• Johnny Mitchell, Jr., President
(832) 725-8814
• Sara Low, 1st Vice President
(401) 447-6462

• Don Oakley, 2nd Vice President
(866) 364-8895
• Steve Mossbrook, Treasurer
(307) 851-6455
• Carla P. Rueck, Secretary
(516) 480-9930
Nature of Service:
Encourages the understanding and direct involvement of individuals and clubs ranging from school and college levels through senior citizens and retirement organizations as to the social and recreational rewards of playing croquet. Principal source of income is through tax-deductible contributions of individuals and proceeds of the Annual Fall U.S. Croquet Hall of Fame Awards Dinner, and special Croquet Balls, parties and events throughout the year by member clubs and organizations.
Year Founded:
1977
Number of Members:
3,000
Publications:
USCA Croquet News, mailed quarterly; USCA Croquet Directory; Official USCA Rulebook

Curling Organizations

CANADIAN CURLING ASSOCIATION
1660 VIMONT COURT
ORLEANS, CANADA K4A 4J4
613-834-2076
800-550-2875
Fax: 613-834-0716
media@curling.ca
www.curling.ca
• Patricia Ray, Chief Operating Officer
(613) 834-2076
• Karen Ryan, Executive Assistant
(613) 834-2076
kryan@curling.ca
• JoAnne Viau, Coordinator, Financial Services
(613) 834-2076
jviau@curling.ca
• Al Cameron, Director, Communications and Media Relations
(403) 463-5500
acameron@curling.ca
• Karen Wan, Manager, Financial Services
(613) 834-2076
• Danny Lamoureux, Director, Championship Services
(613) 834-2076
dlamoureux@curling.ca
• Glenn van Gulik, Director, Information Services and Technology
(613) 834-2076
gvangulik@curling.ca
Nature of Service:
Ongoing organization and development of all aspects of the sport of Curling in Canada.
Year Founded:
1990
Member Services:
Participation in all sanctioned events; marketing and technical development programs.
Membership Requirements:
Annual association dues.
Number of Members:
352,000 (17 provincial associations).
Publications:
EXTRA END magazine, annual.

U.S. CURLING ASSOCIATION
5525 CLEM'S WAY
STEVENS POINT, WI 54482
715-344-1199
1-888-287-5377
Fax: 715-344-2279
info@usacurl.org
www.teamusa.org/usa-curling
• Rich Lepping, Chairman of the Board
chairman@usacurl.org
• Vic Huebner, Treasurer
vichuebner@optonline.net
• Gordon Maclean, Secretary
• Rick Patzke, Secretary General

WORLD CURLING FEDERATION
3 ATHOLL CRESCENT
PERTH, PH1 5NG
info@worldcurling.org
www.worldcurling.org
• Kate Caithness, President
• Bent Ramsfjell, Vice President (Europe)
• Colin Grahamslaw, Secretary General
Description:
WCF acts as the world governing body for Olympic and Paralympic curling.

Cycling Organizations

ADVENTURE CYCLING ASSOCIATION
150 EAST PINE STREET
MISSOULA, MT 59807
406-721-1776
800-755-2453
Fax: 406-721-8754
www.adventurecycling.org
• Wally Werner, President
• Donna O'Neal, Vice President
• Andrew Huppert, Treasurer
• Andy Baur, Secretary
• Jim Sayer, Executive Director
• Teri Maloughney, Director, Sales & Marketing
• Richard Darne, Database Administrator
Nature of Service:
Continues to expand network of bicycle touring routes - now totaling more than 26,000 miles of lightly traveled rural roads and off-pavement biking routes.
Member Services:
$35 per year dues.
Publications:
ADVENTURE CYCLIST, 9 time(s) a year; THE CYCLISTS' YELLOW PAGES, annually.
Member Services:
Tours programs-six to 90 day trips; sales catalog - books, maps, products - discounts on some maps, subscription to ADVENTURE CYCLIST Magazine, Advocacy program; annual meeting normally held in January each year, in Missoula

CYCLING CANADA
2197 RIVERSIDE DRIVE
SUITE 203
OTTAWA, ON, CANADA K1H 7X3
613-248-1353
Fax: 613-248-9311
general@cyclingcanada.ca
www.cyclingcanada.ca
• Greg Mathieu, CEO/Secretary General
ext 2601
greg.mathieu@cyclingcanada.ca
• Jacques Landry, High Performance

Director/Head Coach
ext 2614
jacques.landry@cyclingcanada.ca
• Brett Stewart, Director, Finance & Administration
ext 2605
brett.stewart@cyclingcanada.ca
• Mathieu Boucher, Director, Performance Development
ext 2607
mathieu.boucher@cyclingcanada.ca
• Matthew Jeffries, Director, Marketing & Communications
ext 2609
matthew.jeffries@cyclingcanada.ca
• Gleness Lapensee, Administrative Assistant
ext 2600
gleness.lapensee@cyclingcanada.ca
Nature of Service:
Encourages and promotes cycling in Canada while safeguarding the cyclists' right to the road.
Year Founded:
1882
Member Services:
Insurance benefits.
Membership Requirements:
Payment of membership fees to provincial associations.
Number of Members:
7,200
Publications:
LEARN-TO-RACE Manual and Video; Racing Rules

INTERNATIONAL POLICE MOUNTAIN BIKE ASSOCIATION (IPMBA)
583 FREDERICK ROAD
SUITE 5B
BALTIMORE, MD 21228
410-744-2400
Fax: 410-744-5504
info@ipmba.org
www.ipmba.org
• Bernie Hogancamp, President
president@ipmba.org
• Wren Nealy, Vice President
vp@ipmba.org
• Mike Harris, Treasurer
treasurer@ipmba.org
• Craig Lepkowski, Secretary
secretary@ipmba.org
• Maureen Becker, Executive Director
maureen@ipmba.org
• Michael A. Wear, Education Director
education@ipmba.org
• Tom Harris, Conference Coordinator
conferences@ipmba.org
• James Englert, Industry Liaison
industry@ipmba.org
• Brian Gillman, EMS Coordinator
emsc@ipmba.org
• Gary Strang, Membership Director
membership@ipmba.org
Nature of Service:
Governing body for organizing activities involving police mountain biking.
Year Founded:
1992
Membership Fee:
$55.00 yearly membership fee entitles the officer to discounted Police on Bikes® Conference registration, a subscription to IPMBA News, a subscription to Bicycling Magazine.
Number of Members:
3,000

Publications:
IPMBA News

NATIONAL BICYCLE DEALERS ASSOCIATION
3176 PULLMAN STREET
SUITE 117
COSTA MESA, CA 92626
949-722-6909
info@nbda.com
www.nbda.com
• Todd Grant, President/Executive Director
todd@nbda.com
• Jeff Selzerr, Treasurer
• Mike Greehan, Secretary
• Mike Baker, Director, Marketing & Communications
• John Francis, Newsletter Editor
john@nbda.com
Nature of Service:
Promotes general welfare of retail bicycle dealers and assists dealers in promoting the sport of cycling.
Year Founded:
1946
Member Services:
Representation of bicycle dealers to public, trade and government; credit card program; customer financing program; employee group insurance; publications; seminars.
Membership Requirements:
Be a legitimate bicycle dealership or member of bicycle industry.
Publications:
OUTSPOKIN', monthly.

NATIONAL CENTER FOR BICYCLING & WALKING (NCBW)
419 LAFAYETTE STREET
7TH FLOOR
NEW YORK, NY 10003
www.bikewalk.org
• Mark Plotz, Senior Associate/Program Manager
(212) 620-5660
mark@bikewalk.org
• John Williams, CenterLines Editor
news@bikewalk.org
• Jim Johnston, Web/Systems Administrator
jimmy@bikewalk.org
Nature of Service:
Promotes the increased, safe use of bicycles. Conducts research and planning projects for government agencies. Develops brochures, posters, and video materials to promote cycling and safety. Develops and implements public relations programs to encourage cycling.
Year Founded:
1977
Publications:
CenterLines, bi-weekly electronic news bulletin.

PERIMETER BICYCLING ASSOCIATION OF AMERICA, INC.
2609 EAST BROADWAY BOULEVARD
TUCSON, AZ 85716
520-745-2033
Fax: 520-745-1992
info@perimeterbicycling.com
www.perimeterbicycling.com
• Richard DeBernardis, President
president@perimeterbicycling.com
• Sally Valenzuela, Advertising Sales
marketing@perimeterbicycling.com
• Marilyn Hall, Media/Media Sales

media@perimeterbicycling.com
• Elaine Mariolle, Public Affairs
publicaffairs@perimeterbicycling.com
Nature of Service:
Organizes the bicycling events El Tour de Tucson, El Tour de Mesa, Cochise County Cycling Classic, Indoor El Tour, Bicycle, Fitness & Health Expo, El Tour Adventure Walk/Run, and El Tour Fun Rides.
Membership Requirements:
Payment of dues ($35 for individual membership, $85 for family membership).
Publications:
TAIL WINDS, bimonthly; PERIMETER BICYCLING JOURNAL, annually.

ULTRAMARATHON CYCLING ASSOCIATION
PO BOX 18028
BOULDER, CO 80308-1028
303-545-9566
Fax: 303-545-9619
www.ultracycling.com
• Paul Carpenter, President
president@ultracycling.com
• Douglas Hoffman, Executive Director
executivedirector@ultracycling.com
• Drew Clark, Records Chairman
records@ultracycling.com
• Mark Newsome, Webmaster/Data Manager
webmaster@ultracycling.com
Nature of Service:
Serves to organize Race Across America; sanctions long distance cycling records; organizes the National Points Challenge; promotes ultra-marathon cycling. Divided into two type of races: Solo or Four-Man Relay.
Year Founded:
1980
Membership Requirements:
Payment of dues.
Publications:
ULTRA CYCLING MAGAZINE, quarterly; UMCA Manual; Membership Directory; Events Directory.

UNION CYCLISTE INTERNATIONALE (UCI)
CH DE LA MELEE 12
1860 AIGLE
AIGLE, SWITZERLAN 1860
admin@uci.ch
www.uci.ch
• Brian Cookson, President
• Mohamed Wagih, Vice President
• Tracey Gaudry, Vice President
• David Lappartient, Vice President
• Sebastien Gillot, Head of Communications
• James Carr, Head of International Relations
• Cyrille Jacobsen, Head of Marketing
Nature of Service:
Serves to foster worldwide competitive cycling.
Year Founded:
1900
Publications:
Annual Reports.

USA CYCLING
210 USA CYCLING POINT
SUITE 100
COLORADO SPRINGS, CO 80919-2215
719-434-4200
Fax: 719-434-4300

help@usacycling.org
www.usacycling.org
• Derek Bouchard-Hall, President/CEO
• Bob Stapleton, Chairman
• Alex Nieroth, Vice Chairman
• Kevin Loughery, Communications Manager
(719) 434-4277
kloughery@usacycling.org
• Steve Bitter, Digital & Social Media Manager
(719) 434-4276
sbitter@usacycling.org
• Keri Kahn, Editorial & Internal Communications Manager
(719) 434-4272
kkahn@usacycling.org
• Daniel Gillespie, Sponsorship & Member Benefits Manager
(719) 434-4281
dgillespie@usacycling.org

USA/BMX, THE AMERICAN BICYCLE ASSOCIATION
1645 WEST SUNRISE BOULEVARD
GILBERT, AZ 85233
480-961-1903
Fax: 480-961-1842
www.usabmx.com
• B.A. Anderson, CEO
• John David, Chief Operating Officer
john@usabmx.com
• Craig Barrette, Chief Communications Officer
gork@usabmx.com
• Nick Adams, Chief Marketing Officer
nick@usabmx.com
• Jon Schmieder, Executive Director
jons@usabmx.com
• Brad Hallin, Senior Track Director
brad@usabmx.com
• Maile Goldston, Receptionist
maile@usabmx.com
Nature of Service:
The ABA is the world's largest BMX sanctioning body, with over 7,000 events, 54,000, 200 local facilities, 12 TV shows and a monthly publication.
Year Founded:
1977
Sponsors:
Dan's Competition, Fly Racing, Tangent, BOX Components, Promax, KMC, FastSigns, Ciari, Staats, Answer, Nationwide
Publications:
PULL Magazine.

Cycling, Leagues/Teams

LEAGUE OF AMERICAN BICYCLISTS
1612 K STREET NORTHWEST
SUITE 308
WASHINGTON, DC 20006
202-822-1333
bikeleague@bikeleague.org
www.bikeleague.org
• Alex Doty, Executive Director
• Bill Nesper, Vice President, Programs
• Caron Whitaker, Vice President, Policy
(202) 215-3908
• Lorna Green, Director, Operations
ext 260
• Alison Dewey, National Bike Summit Director
(202) 621-5443

• Ken McLeod, Legal & Policy Specialist
(202) 621-5447
Nature of Service:
Protects rights and promotes the interests of bicyclists, provides information about bicycling for its members and others, fosters and serves a nationwide network of affiliated cycling clubs and organizations. Sponsors National Century Month; national bicycle rallies; PEDAL FOR POWER cross country rides for charity; serves as international clearing house for Bike Month.
Year Founded:
1880
Membership Requirements:
Open to anyone upon payment of dues ($40 for individual membership, $60 for family membership).
Number of Members:
300,000 cyclists including a membership of 40,000 individuals and over 600 organizations
Publications:
American Cyclist Magazine, quarterly

MAJOR LEAGUE CYCLING
PO BOX 10695
LANCASTER, PA 17605-0695
info@majorleaguecycling.com
www.majorleaguecycling.com
• David Butterworth, President
Description:
Features criterium and track racing between city-based pro cycling teams, combined with family destination weekend events featuring other extreme sports, racing, and demos, children's bicycle safety clinics, community exhibits, etc.

PRIORITY HEALTH
1231 EAST BELTLINE NORTHEAST
GRAND RAPIDS, MI 49525
616-464-8571
www.teampriorityhealth.com
• Ann Vidro, Program Director
(616) 540-5115
avidro@creativestudiopromo.com
• Amy Miller, Corporate Press Contact
(616) 443-9800
amy.miller@priorityhealth.com
• Angie Scarlato, Calendar Of Events/Social Media Captain
angiebarnes11@yahoo.com
Sponsors:
Priority Health, Advantage Benefits, First Endurance, Giordana

USA CYCLING
210 USA CYCLING POINT
SUITE 100
COLORADO SPRINGS, CO 80919-2215
719-434-4200
Fax: 719-434-4300
help@usacycling.org
www.usacycling.org
• Derek Bouchard-Hall, President/CEO
• Bob Stapleton, Chairman
• Alex Nieroth, Vice Chairman
• Kevin Loughery, Communications Manager
(719) 434-4277
kloughery@usacycling.org
• Steve Bitter, Digital & Social Media Manager
(719) 434-4276
sbitter@usacycling.org
• Keri Kahn, Editorial & Internal

Communications Manager
(719) 434-4272
kkahn@usacycling.org
• Daniel Gillespie, Sponsorship & Member Benefits Manager
(719) 434-4281
dgillespie@usacycling.org
Nature of Service:
Serves as governing body for all forms of bicycle racing, amateur cycling in America and, as such, is responsible for selecting Olympic, Pan-Am and World Championship teams. Promotes events and programs, television producer.
Year Founded:
1921
Sponsors:
Barbedo, Bike Thomson, Bonk Breaker, Chase Bicycles, CLIF Bar, CUORE, Development Foundation, Endurance Conspiracy, Felt Bicycles, Kreitler, NormaTec Recovery, Osmo Nutrition, Park Tool USA, Shimano, Sierra Nevada, Sportique, Thule, Tioga, Training Peaks, USA Cycling, Vision, Vittoria, Voler, Volkswagen

Teams:

JELLY BELLY CYCLING
1035 LAKE RIDE ROAD
SAN MARCOS, CA 92069
760-598-1138
www.jellybellycycling.com
• Dan Van Haute, Team Manager
Sponsors:
Jelly Belly, Maxxis, Fast Freddie Apparel, Argon 18

PRO CYCLING MIAMI
PO BOX 162555
MIAMI, FL 33116
786-973-5484
www.procyclingmiami.com
• Johan Ismail, President

REALITY BIKES
20 TRI COUNTY PLAZA
CUMMING, GA 30040
770-886-1175
todd@realitybikes.com
• Duncan McGuire, President
• Todd Muller, Club Coordinator
Year Founded:
1995
Sponsors:
FUJI, Atlanta Sports Medicine & Orthopaedic Center

TEAM COLAVITA
1 RUNYONS LANE
EDISON, NJ 08817
732-404-8300
usa@colavita.com
www.teamcolavita.com
• Mary Zider, Sports Director
• Andrea Smith, Head Mechanic
• Amanda Rose Shission, Team Soigneur
Sponsors:
Colavita Olive Oil, Bianchi, Vittoria, Fine Cooking, Castelli, Rudy Project, Shimano, K3, Tetra Bike, Park Tool USA, Stages Cycling, Bar Fly, Osprey, CLIF Bar, Saris Cycling Group, CycleOps Power, HeadSweats

Dart Organizations

AMERICAN DARTS ORGANIZATION
230 NORTH CRESCENT WAY
SUITE K
ANAHEIM, CA 92801-6707
714-254-0212
Fax: 714-254-0214
office@adodarts.com
www.adodarts.com
• David Hascup, President
president@adodarts.com
• Joe Hogan, Vice President
joekat325@outlook.com
• Jeff Inman, Chief Financial Officer
jjinman23@oh.rr.com
• Carolyn Camp, General Secretary
jcamp13@earthlink.net
Description:
Founded in 1976. Sanctioning, governing body for the sport of darts in the U.S. Regulates and selects U.S. teams for international competition, and selects the national champions (men's and women's).
Membership requirements:
Fee of $30.00 for one year of individual membership.
Publications:
Double Eagle, national, quarterly newsletter.
Member Services:
Travel agency, airline, hotel, and rental car discounts.

NATIONAL DART ASSOCIATION
9100 PURDUE ROAD
SUITE 200
INDIANAPOLIS, IN 46268
317-387-1299
800-808-9884
Fax: 317-387-0999
info@NDAdarts.com
www.ndadarts.com
• Leslie Murphy, Executive Director
(317) 387-1299
leslie@ndadarts.com
• Kim Paugh, Associate Executive Director
(734) 717-2855
kim@ndadarts.com
• Michelle Wells, Director of Communication
michelle@ndadarts.com
• Ashley Roy, Communication Coordinator
aroy@ndadarts.com
Member Services:
Annual team championships.
Publications:
THROWLINES.
Description:
Founded in 1985. Sanctions darts leagues, establishes rules for competition; promotes the sport of electronic darting.

NATIONAL DARTS FEDERATION OF CANADA
secretary@ndfc.ca
www.ndfc.ca
• Bill Hatter, President
(403) 548-2939
president@ndfc.ca
• Maggie LeBlanc, Vice President
(514) 637-2858
maggieleblanc417@hotmail.com
• Tammy Pottie, General Secretary
(902) 401-9650
secretary@ndfc.ca

NORTH AMERICAN PROFESSIONAL DARTS ALLIANCE
2 QUEEN STREET
LANGTON, ON, CANADA N0E 1G0
www.napda.net
• Robert Sinnaeve, President & CEO
• David Holmes, Vice President, Webmaster & Membership
• John McClellan, Treasurer & CFO
• Jay Tomlinson, Publicity Director
Description:
NAPDA was officially established in 2011 and serves as the first ranking system and professional dart tour for the North American dart player.

Diving Organizations

DIVING EQUIPMENT & MARKETING ASSOCIATION
3750 CONVOY STREET
SUITE 310
SAN DIEGO, CA 92111
858-616-6108
800-862-3483
Fax: 858-616-6495
info@dema.org
www.demashow.com
• Tim Webb, President
• Dan Orr, Senior Vice President
• Darcy Kieran, Vice President
• Tom Leaird, Treasurer
• Werner Kurn, Secretary
Number of Members:
2,000
Membership Requirements:
Must be a professional in the scuba diving industry.
Description:
Founded in 1972. Promotes growth and advancement in the diving industry; to establish continuing business education programs to aid industry members, their officers and employees; to facilitate exchange of industry information; to support the diving industry with communication services, media relations and resources; to support the industry in monitoring and communicating on legislation impacting diving; to support the industry in monitoring and protection of the environment through education and activities; and monitors state and national legislation.
Publications:
Monthly Newsletter.
Member Services:
Promote scuba diving.

DIVING PLONGEON CANADA
700 INDUSTRIAL AVENUE
SUITE 312
OTTAWA, ON, CANADA K1G 0Y9
613-736-5238
Fax: 613-736-0409
cada@diving.ca
www.diving.ca
• Penny Joyce, Chief Operating Officer
(613) 736-5238
penny@diving.ca
• Mitch Geller, Chief Technical Officer
(613) 736-5238
mitch@diving.ca
• Nancy Brawley, Director, National Officials Program
(613) 736-5238
nancy@diving.ca

• Sally Clare, Finance Manager
sally@diving.ca
• Jordanna Ostrega, Administration & Communication Coordinator
(613) 736-5238
jordanna@diving.ca
Number of Members:
5,000
Member Services:
Newsletter; Entry level program (Learn To Dive); Counseling program; Athlete program, Coaching & Official program.
Publications:
Newsletter, BI-monthly.
Membership Requirements:
Pay annual fee.
Description:
Founded in 1967. Provides all divers from entry level participants to Olympic and World Champions with the opportunity to achieve personal goals through programs and services. Also organizes two senior National Championships each year, as well as one international competition, and one Junior Nationals each year.

FEDERATION INTERNATIONALE DE NATATION (FINA)
AVENUE DE L'AVANT-POSTE 4
LAUSANNE, 1005
www.fina.org
• Julio C Maglione, President
• Husain Al Musallam, Vice President
• Cornel Marculescu, Executive Director
Year Founded:
1908
Publications:
FINA newsletter, FINA Handbook, FINA Aquatics World Magazine
Description:
Comprised of 207 national member federations, FINA holds competitions in swimming, open water swimming, diving, water polo, synchronised swimming, high diving and masters.

Equestrian Organizations

AMERICAN ASSOCIATION OF EQUINE PRACTITIONERS
4033 IRON WORKS PARKWAY
LEXINGTON, KY 40511
859-233-0147
800-443-0177
Fax: 859-233-1968
aaepoffice@aaep.org
www.aaep.org
• David Foley, Executive Director
dfoley@aaep.org
• Sally Baker, Director of Marketing & Public Relations
sbaker@aaep.org
• Brad Mitchell, Director of Finance & Operations
bmitchell@aaep.org
• Keith Kleine, Director of Industry Relations
kkleine@aaep.org
Description:
Founded in 1954. Serves to improve the health and welfare of the horse, to further the professional development of its members, and to provide resource and leadership for the benefit of the equine industry.
Membership Requirements:
Must be veterinarian in connection with

equine practice.
Publications:
AAEP REPORT, 12 times annually.
Number of members:
6,500

AMERICAN HANOVERIAN SOCIETY
4067 IRON WORKS PARKWAY
SUITE 1
LEXINGTON, KY 40511
859-255-4141
Fax: 859-255-8467
AHSoffice@aol.com
www.hanoverian.org
• Edgar Schutte, President
(916) 645-1471
edgar@rainbowequus.com
• Hugh Bellis-Jones, Executive Director
(859) 255-4141
hbjahs@aol.com
• Barbara Schmidt, Executive VP & Director
(859) 485-6000
bschmidtdvm@fuse.net
• Rick Toering, Vice President
(703) 472-9954
rick.toering@gmail.com
Number of members:
1,750
Member Services:
Horse registration, inspection for breeding approval.
Publications:
AHS YEARBOOK; AHS MEMBERS GUIDE, quarterly newsletter.
Membership Requirements:
Payment of $55 dues for associate membership, $80 for active voting membership.
Description:
Founded in 1971. Horse registration office for breed of horse originating in Germany called the Hanoverian. Dedicated to developing superior riding horse.

AMERICAN HORSE COUNCIL
1616 H STREET NW
7TH FLOOR
WASHINGTON, DC 20006
202-296-4031
www.horsecouncil.org
• James J. Hickey, Jr., President
(202) 296-4031
• Ben Pendergrass, Vice President, Government Affairs
(202) 296-4031
• Cliff Williamson, Director of Health & Regulatory Affairs
• Kara Mongello, Office Administrator
(202) 296-4031
• Ashley Furst, Director of Communications
(202) 296-4031
Publications:
Horse Owners & Breeders Tax Handbook; Horse Owners & Breeders Tax Handbook; The Economic Impact of the Horse Industry State Breakout Reports; American Horsepower; Tax Tips for Horse Owners; Horse Industry Directory
Membership Requirements:
Payment of annual dues. In addition to organizational and commercial memberships ($1,000 per year), offers individual membership categories including: Legislative ($40 per year), Congressional ($100 per year), Senatorial ($500 per year), and Cabinet ($1,000 per year) and President's Circle ($5,000 per year).

Description:
Founded in 1969. Its goal is to create the most positive environment possible for participation and investment in the horse world. Pursuing that objective, AHC is involved in all aspects of federal legislation affecting the horse business; works with federal agencies to promote equitable and realistic regulations to govern the industry; forwards the national and international growth and popularity of horse activities; encourages intelligent and humane treatment of the horse through informational and educational efforts; and maintains open lines of communication among diverse segments of the horse industry.

AMERICAN MINIATURE HORSE ASSOCIATION
5601 SOUTH INTERSTATE 35 WEST
ALVARADO, TX 76009
817-783-5600
Fax: 817-783-6403
info@amha.org
www.amha.org
• Sid Hutchcraft, President
(407) 656-4818
president@amha.org
• Al Bulgawicz, Vice President
(713) 870-1293
mini@willowcrest.com
• Clair Severson, Treasurer
(651) 437-5092
toysminis@aol.com
• Julie Good, Secretary
(717) 725-7784
azariah@meadowindfarm.com
• Harry Elder, Director
harry.james.elder@gmail.com
Number of Members:
12,000
Member Services:
Public relations and promotion of the American Miniature Horse; Production and management of the National Show and three regional shows annually; Breeders' list mailed to members; Sponsorship of 250 shows; Publishes informational booklets and the American Horse Studbook.
Publications:
THE MINIATURE HORSE WORLD, six times annually.
Membership Requirements:
Pay dues.
Description:
Founded in 1978. National and international registry. Official registry of miniature horses.

AMERICAN MORGAN HORSE ASSOCIATION
4066 SHELBURNE ROAD
SUITE 5
SHELBURNE, VT 05482
802-985-4944
Fax: 802-985-8897
www.morganhorse.com
• Jeff Gove, President
(508) 341-2263
jeffreygove@yahoo.com
• Julie Broadway, Executive Director
(802) 985-4944
• Kris Breyer, Vice President, Central Region
(847) 526-3012
• Carol Fletcher, Vice President of Finance
(425) 788-9233

Number of Members:
Approximately 8,000
Member Services:
Promotional literature; member/horse recognition programs; youth program; Regional and World Championship Horse Shows; Discounts from companies with horse-related products; trail riding; breed registry.
Publications:
THE MORGAN HORSE, monthly; Newspaper, THE NETWORK, monthly.
Description:
Registry started in 1908. Purpose of organization is for the preservation, perpetuate and promotion of the Morgan breed.
Teams:
Equestrian team - Team Morgan

AMERICAN PAINT HORSE ASSOCIATION
PO BOX 961023
FORT WORTH, TX 76161-0023
817-834-2742
Fax: 817-834-3152
askapha@apha.com
www.apha.com
• Ron Shelly, President
(512) 863-0325
rshelly@texas.net
• George Ready, Vice President
(662) 429-7088
gbready@georgebreadyattorneys.com
• Craig Wood, Senior Committee Member
(859) 608-1014
chorse.wood@gmail.com
• Billy L. Smith, Executive Director
(817) 222-6401
billy@apha.com
Publications:
APHA Connection; Paint Horse Journal.
Description:
Founded in 1962 as American Paint Stockhorse Association. Registers paint horses; sponsors national and world events for paint horses.
Number of Members:
104,000
Member Services:
Free on-line services; free member quarterly newsletter; reduced fees on transactions.
Membership Requirements:
Annual $40 member dues.

AMERICAN QUARTER HORSE ASSOCIATION
1600 QUARTER HORSE DRIVE
AMARILLO, TX 79104
806-376-4811
Fax: 806-349-6411
www.aqha.com
• Glenn Blodgett, President
• Sandy Arledge, First Vice President
• Ralph Seekins, Second Vice President
Description:
Founded in 1940. Serves to collect, record and preserve the pedigrees of American Quarter Horses. Also serves as an information center for its members and the general public on matters pertaining to shows, racing, legislative issues, contests and projects designed to improve the breed and aid the industry.
Membership Requirements:
Membership dues: $30 per year.
Publications:
THE AMERICAN QUARTER HORSE

JOURNAL, monthly; AMERICA'S HORSE, bimonthly
Number of members:
336,000

AMERICAN SADDLEBRED HORSE ASSOCIATION
4083 IRON WORKS PARKWAY
LEXINGTON, KY 40511
859-259-2742
Fax: 859-259-1628
saddlebred@asha.net
www.asha.net
• Bob Funkhouser, President
• David B. Rudder, Vice President
• Bill Whitley, Executive Director
(859) 259-3888
b.whitley@asha.net
• David Mount, Treasurer
Number of members:
7,120
Events:
Futurity competitions at the Kentucky State Fair; other prize programs at nationwide prominent horse shows.
Member Services:
Subscription to magazine; free annual directory; discount savings on registrations and transfers; free literature, visual aids.
Publications:
THE AMERICAN SADDLEBRED, bimonthly magazine; THE HAYSHAKER, quarterly youth newsletter; Membership Directory, annual.
Membership Requirements:
Seven classes of individual memberships, each one with different requirements and benefits.
Description:
Founded 1891. Serves to stimulate, promote interest in and regulate any and all matters as may pertain to the history, breeding, exhibition, publicity, use and improvement of the American Saddlebred horse.

AMERICAN VAULTING ASSOCIATION
1443 EAST WASHINGTON BOULEVARD
SUITE 289
PASADENA, CA 91104
323-654-0800
Fax: 323-654-4306
info@americanvaulting.org
www.americanvaulting.org
• Connie Geisler, President
(951) 440-4589
connie_geisler@hotmail.com
• Kelley Holly, Executive Vice President
(707) 665-9281
tambourine-farm@att.net
• Kathy Rynning, VP Competitions
(360) 888-2476
• Kathy Smith, VP Membership
(303) 434-9975
rockymtnhorsepk@yahoo.com
• Carolyn Bland, VP Education
(818) 497-2947
Number of Members:
1,200
Member Services:
Tape rental, insurance, all information relating to the sport of vaulting. Tapes and books also available for purchase.
Publications:
VAULTING WORLD, bimonthly.
Membership Requirements:
Annual individual membership of $50
Description:

Founded in 1968. Provides information and rules for sport of vaulting, which combines the sport of gymnastics and the skill of horsemanship.

ARABIAN HORSE ASSOCIATION
10805 EAST BETHANY DRIVE
AURORA, CO 80014
303-696-4500
Fax: 303-696-4599
www.arabianhorses.org
• Cynthia M. Richardson, President
(720) 480-0496
cynthia.richardson@arabianhorses.org
• Nancy Harvey, Vice President
(626) 390-8918
nancy.harvey@arabianhorses.org
• Robert Nash, Treasurer
(713) 302-9072
• Jan Decker, Secretary
(317) 861-4814
jandecker1@sbcglobal.net
Member Services:
Breed registration for purchsaed Arabian, Half-Arabian, Anglo-Arabian; awards and prize money; show recognition; national show production; world's largest database of Arabian horses.
Publications:
Arabian Horse Magazine.
Membership Requirements:
$20 lowest fee for associate membership on up.
Description:
Founded 1950. Non-profit membership organization established in 1950 for the purpose of coordinating the activities of all Arabian horse associations, and encouraging the breeding, exhibiting and perpetuation of the Arabian, Half-Arabian and Anglo-Arabian breeds.

BLOODHORSE MAGAZINE
821 CORPORATE DRIVE
LEXINGTON, KY 40503
859-278-2361
800-582-5604
Fax: 859-276-4450
admin@bloodhorse.com
http://www.bloodhorse.com
• Evan Hammond, Editorial Director
(859) 278-2361
editorial@bloodhorse.com
• Scott Carling, General Manager
admin@bloodhorse.com
• Kristi Heasley, Advertising Account Executive
advertise@bloodhorse.com
• Beth Alexander, Manager, Data Management
(859) 224-2855
• Steve Gillespie, General Manager, Operations
Description:
The Jockey Club Information Systems, Inc. (TJCIS) is a unique and diversified organization that provides instant access to information and expertise to aid decision-making and improve thoroughbred management and promotion. TJCIS is a wholly owned subsidiary of The Jockey Club and reinvests all profits in the thoroughbred industry.

BREEDERS' CUP
2525 HARRODSBURG ROAD
SUITE 500
LEXINGTON, KY 40504-4230
859-223-5444
800-722-3287
Fax: 859-223-3945
help@breederscup.com
www.breederscup.com
• Craig Fravel, President & Chief Executive Officer
craig@breederscup.com
• Robert Elliston, EVP and Chief Operating Officer
bob@breederscup.com
• Michael Newman, VP, Treasurer
michael@breederscup.com
• Tim Schram, VP, Finance & Human Resources
tim@breederscup.com
Description:
Founded in 1984. It's primary purpose is to promote the sport of thoroughbred racing, thus strengthening opportunities within the industry for horsemen worldwide. Objectives have been accomplished through Breeders' Cup Championship, and through a year-round stakes program of 85 races across the United States and Canada.

CALIFORNIA THOROUGHBRED BREEDERS ASSOCIATION
201 COLORADO PLACE
ARCADIA, CA 91007
626-445-7800
800-573-2822
Fax: 626-574-0852
www.ctba.com
• Donald Valpredo, Chair
donald@valpredofarms.com
• Harris Aurbach, Vice Chair
hdauerbach@sbcglobal.net
• Doug Burge, President
(626) 445-7800
dburge@ctba.com
• John Barr, Director
oakcrest99@aol.com
• Tim Cohen, Treasurer
tcohen@ranchotemescal.com
• Sue Green, Secretary
sueshorse@aol.com
• Loretta Veiga, Advertising Manager
(626) 445-7800
loretta@ctba.com
Member Services:
Offers breeder, owner, stallion incentive awards. Sponsors numerous horse symposiums throughout the year geared to better educate the California horseman.
Publications:
THE THOROUGHBRED OF CALIFORNIA MAGAZINE, monthly.
Membership Requirements:
California owner and breeder of thoroughbreds.
Description:
Founded in 1937. Dedicated to the advancement of thoroughbred racing and breeding in California. Serves as the official registry of all California bred thoroughbred horses.

EQUINE CANADA
308 LEGGET DRIVE
SUITE 100
OTTAWA, ON, CANADA K2K 1Y6
613-287-1515
866-282-8395

Fax: 613-248-3484
www.equinecanada.ca
• Al Patterson, President
• Eva Havaris, Chief Executive Officer
• Kalie McKenna, Director, Technical Programs
(866) 282-8395
kmckenna@equinecanada.ca
Number of members:
10,000
Publications:
Equine Canada Magazine
Membership Requirements:
Individuals are required to be members of the Canadian Equestrian Federation to compete in recognized shows and programs organized by the CEF.
Description:
Governing body of equestrian sport in Canada. Recognized by the Federation Equestre Internationale, the Canadian Olympic Association and the Federal Government. Responsible for development of all aspects of equestrian activity (excluding racing) and provides the standards under which competitions are conducted.
Year Founded:
1977

FEDERATION EQUESTRE INTERNATIONALE
HM KING HUSSEIN I BUILDING
CHEMIN DE LA JOLIETTE 8
LAUSANNE, SWITZERLAN 1006
www.fei.org
• Ingmar De Vos, President
(+41) 21 310 47
ingmar.devos@fei.org
• John Madden, 1st Vice President
(+1) 315 952 65
jms@johnmaddensales.com
• Sheik Khalid Bin Abdulla Al Khalifa, 2nd Vice President
(973) 178 361 99
feigroup7@gmail.com
Description:
The International Federation for Equestrian Sports acts as the international governing body for this group of sports, sanctioning world competitions and the Olympic and Paralympic games.

HAMBLETONIAN SOCIETY
CRANBURY GATES OFFICE PARK
109 SOUTH MAIN STREET
SUITE 18
CRANBURY, NJ 08512
609-371-2211
Fax: 609-371-8890
www.hambletonian.org
• Tom Charters, President & CEO
• Callie Davies-Gooch, Stakes Manager
callie@hambletonian.org
• Moira Fanning, Director Of Publicity
mfanning@hambletonian.org
• Mary Lou Dondarski, Office Manager
MLD@hambletonian.org
Description:
The Hambletonian Society is a non-profit organization formed in 1924 to sponsor the race for which it was named, the Hambletonian Stake. The society encourages and supports the breeding of Standardbred horses through the development, administration and promotion of harness racing stakes, early-closing races

and other special events. These include harness racing's most preeminent race, the Hambletonian for 3-year-old trotters, its filly division the Hambletonian Oaks and the sport's championship series, the Breeders Crown.

Membership Requirements:
Executives nominate a board of 25 directors.

Publications:
HAMBLETONIAN SOCIETY Newsletter, two times annually.

Member Services:
Hambletonian, annually, at Meadowlands, East Rutherford, NJ first and second Saturday in August and 11 Breeders Crown races.

HAMPTON CLASSIC HORSE SHOW
240 SNAKE HOLLOW ROAD
BRIDGEHAMPTON, NY 11932-3013
631-537-3177
Fax: 631-537-5443
www.hamptonclassic.com
• Dennis Suskind, President
• Lisa Deslauriers, Chairman
• Rosanna Braccini, Director of Special Projects and Publications
rosanna@hamptonclassic.com
• Reyna Stein, Marketing Manager
reyna@hamptonclassic.com
• Bryan Cohen, Special Projects Coordinator
bryan@hamptonclassic.com

Sports Service Founded:
1976

Services:
Implements horse shows and oversees all phases of this event, featuring world-class competition attracting approximately 3,200 riders and horses, featured on Outdoor Life Network; MSG, cause tie-ins. Celebrity participants, corporate VIP tent seats.

HARNESS HORSE YOUTH FOUNDATION
16575 CAREY ROAD
WESTFIELD, IN 46074
317-867-5877
Fax: 317-867-1886
ellen@hhyf.org
www.hhyf.org
• Marlys Pinske, President
• Nicola Abrams, Vice President
• Leah Cheverie, Secretary
• Lillie Brown, Treasurer

Member Services:
Annual bids for Kids Stallion Auction; Student Scholarships; Youth Camps; Works with local 4-H Clubs and Future Farmers chapters.

Publications:
EQUINE SCHOOL AND COLLEGE DIRECTORY; HARNESS HERO CARDS, harness racing trading cards.

Description:
Founded in 1976. National, non-profit organization dedicated to the advancement of harness racing among young people. Aims to educate youth so that they are aware of the multitude of career opportunities in the industry.

HARNESS HORSEMEN INTERNATIONAL
319 HIGH STREET
SUITE 2
BURLINGTON, NJ 08016

609-747-1000
Fax: 609-747-1012
www.harnesshorsemeninternational.com
• Tom Luchento, President
leosboanj@optonline.net
• Kim Hankins, First Vice President
• Tony Somone, Second Vice President
tsomone@harnessillinois.com
• Sal DiMario, Secretary
• Gabe Prewitt, Director at Large
gprewitt@khha.net
• Jerry Knappenberger, Director at Large
JLKnappenberger@ohha.com

Number of Members:
35,000

Member Services:
Includes insurance plan.

Publications:
Newsletter.

Membership Requirements:
Member of a horseman's association.

Description:
Founded in 1964. International trade association for harness racing industry.

HARNESS TRACKS OF AMERICA
12025 EAST DRY GULCH PL.
TUCSON, AZ 85749
520-529-2525
www.harnesstracks.com
• Paul Fontaine, President
• Hugh Mitchell, Chairman of the Board
• Brock Milstein, Vice Chairman of the Board
• Paul J. Estok, Executive Vice President

Number of Members:
38

Publications:
Newsletter, daily; WEEKLY TRACK TOPICS, weekly; reports, monthly; Directory, annually.

Membership Requirements:
Must be pari-mutuel harness track.

Description:
Founded in 1954. Helps promote the industry of pari-mutuel harness racing.

HORSE SHOWS IN THE SUN
319 MAIN STREET
SAUGERTIES, NY 12477
845-246-8833
Fax: 845-246-6371
info@hitsshows.com
www.hitsshows.com
• Kristen Vale-Mosack, Office Manager
Kristen@HitsShows.com

Number of Members:
7,500

Publications:
Prize List, annual; Official Show Program, annual.

Description:
Founded in 1982. Six-week series of international show jumping events attracting 1,600 horses and riders from more than six countries including the USA, Canada, Mexico, Japan, Ireland, and England. More than $1,000,000 in prize money offered.

HORSEMEN'S BENEVOLENT AND PROTECTIVE ASSOCIATION
870 CORPORATE DRIVE
SUITE 300
LEXINGTON, KY 40503-5419
859-259-0451
866-245-1711
Fax: 859-259-0452

racing@hbpa.org
www.nationalhbpa.com
• Leroy Gessmann, President
(515) 989-4944
• Eric J. Hamelback, CEO
(859) 259-0451
• Tom Metzen, 1st Vice President
(952) 496-6442

Member Services:
Insurance coverage; third party liability; race track negotiations; other services.

Membership Requirements:
Must be licensed owner or trainer of a race horse.

Description:
Founded in 1940. Represents horsemen in the racing industry.

JOCKEY CLUB
40 EAST 52ND STREET
NEW YORK, NY 10022
212-371-5970
Fax: 212-371-6123
www.jockeyclub.com
• Stuart S. Janney, III, Chairman
• Ogden Phipps, Honorary Chairman
• William M. Lear, Vice Chairman
• Ian D. Highet, Secretary-Treasurer
• James L. Gagliano, President & CEO
jgagliano@jockeyclub.com

Description:
Founded in 1894. National, international registry for thoroughbred horses. The Jockey Club is the breed registry for all thoroughbred horses in North America. As such, it is responsible for maintaining The American Stud Book, which includes all thoroughbreds foaled in the United States, Canada and Puerto Rico as well as thoroughbreds imported into those countries from nations around the world that maintain similar thoroughbred registries. The Jockey Club was formed on Feb. 9, 1894 in New York City by several prominent thoroughbred owners and breeders determined to bring a sense of order and authority to an increasingly chaotic sport.

JOCKEYS' GUILD
448 LEWIS HARGETT CIRCLE
SUITE 220
LEXINGTON, KY 40503
859-523-5625
866-GO-JOCKS (866-465-6257)
Fax: 859-219-9892
info@jockeysguild.com
www.jockeysguild.com
• John Velazquez, Chairman
• G.R. Carter, Vice Chairman
• Rodney Prescott, Secretary
• Joel Campbell, Treasurer

Member Services:
Health and life insurance available for jockeys and families. Annual Board of Directors meeting - December, Las Vegas, NV.

Publications:
JOCKEY NEWS, bimonthly.

Membership Requirements:
Must be licensed jockey, have won at least one race. To maintain membership, jockey must have 1 mount in twelve months for throughbred & quarter horse racing.

Description:
Founded in 1940. To promote, protect & serve the welfare & prestige of the american

professional jockey community with integrity, equity & justice.

MARYLAND MILLION
30 EAST PADONIA ROAD
SUITE 303
TIMONIUM, MD 21094
410-252-2100
Fax: 410-560-0503
info@marylandmillion.com
www.marylandmillion.com
• Cricket Goodall, Executive Director
• Jordyn Egan, Assistant Director & Sponsorship
• Barroe Reightler, Director of Publications
• Nicole Hart, Finance
Description:
Founded in 1985, Maryland Million Day is the premier thoroughbred racing event that has become one of the nation's best known single days of horse racing excitement. Envisioned as a local version of the Breeders Cup, Maryland Million was so popular with both fans and horsemen that it soon attracted imitators throughout the nation. There are now many such days in different states featuring either state-bred or state-sired horses in festival-like atmospheres.

MARYLAND THOROUGHBRED HORSEMEN'S ASSOCIATION
500 REDLAND COURT
SUITE 105
OWINGS MILLS, MD 21117
410-902-6842
Fax: 410-902-6841
info@mdhorsemen.com
www.mdhorsemen.com
• Karin M. De Francis, President
• Robert J. Lillis, Executive Director
• Harry M. Harris, M.D., Medical Director
• Rosemary Lishia, Director of Finance
• Dago Dupay, Chaplain
Description:
Founded in 1995. Promotes the establishment of a multi-state licensing program for horse racing organizations, designed to ease the burden of licensing for thoroughbred and standardbred owners and trainers involved in racing.

NATIONAL CUTTING HORSE ASSOCIATION
260 BAILEY AVENUE
FORT WORTH, TX 76107
817-244-6188
Fax: 817-244-2015
www.nchacutting.com
• Jim Bret Campbell, Executive Director
• Pam Robison, Administrative Assistant
• Carl Mullins, Director of Business Development
• Angie Highland, Treasurer
• Shana Veale, Controller
Number of Members:
11,800
Member Services:
Right to participate in NCHA events, award winning cutting horse, CHATTER subscription, annual yearbook, rules book, casebook, NCHA decal, voting privileges, NCHA merchandise discounts.
Publications:
THE CUTTING HORSE CHATTER, monthly; Media Guide; Award Yearbook; Media Guide; Six Event Programs.

Membership Requirements:
Application and membership dues of $50 per year. Youth membership available.
Description:
Founded in 1946. Governing body for sport of cutting, sanctioning some 1,400 events nationwide and running six major cuttings each year, featuring 4,000 horses, 12,000 participants and $13,000,000 in purses.

NATIONAL STEEPLECHASE ASSOCIATION
400 FAIR HILL DRIVE
ELKTON, MD 21921
410-392-0700
Fax: 410-392-0706
info@nationalsteeplechase.com
www.nationalsteeplechase.com
• Beverly R. Steinman, Chairman
• Guy J. Torsilieri, President
• P. Douglas Fout, Vice President
• W Patrick Butterfield, Secretary
• Charles W. Strittmatter, Treasurer
Description:
Founded in 1895. The National Steeplechase Association is the official sanctioning body of American steeplechase horse racing. The NSA licenses participants, approves race courses, trains officials, coordinates race entries, enforces rules, compiles an official database and oversees the national marketing and public relations efforts of the sport. Among the groups the NSA serves are owners, trainers, jockeys, members, race meetings and race tracks. The NSA headquarters is located in Fair Hill, Md., home to a world-class steeplechase course, a thoroughbred training center, and an international three-day event course.
Membership Requirements:
Payment of dues.
Publications:
AMERICAN STEEPLECHASING, annual yearbook.
Number of Members:
1,500

NATIONAL THOROUGHBRED RACING
2525 HARRODSBURG ROAD
SUITE 510
LEXINGTON, KY 40504
866-678-4289
equinebenefits@ntra.com
www.ntra.com
• Alexander M. Waldrop, President & CEO
alexwaldrop@ntra.com
• Keith Chamblin, Chief Operating Officer
(859) 422-2645
• Amber Florence, Chief Financial Officer
(859) 422-2659
• Steve Koch, Executive Director
(859) 422-2668
• Jeffrey Burch, Senior Vice President
(859) 422-1225
• Michele Ravencraft, Senior Director of Events
(859) 422-2657
Publications:
TRC MEDIA UPDATE, 33 times annually; EquineCareWatch Media Bulletin, monthly; Newsroom Guide to Thoroughbred Racing; Thoroughbred Athlete and the Racing Industry; TRC Notebook, weekly via Associated Press wire service.
Description:
Founded in 1987. National, non-profit media relations organization for the sport of

Thoroughbred racing in North America. This is the NTRA headquarters. This office handles advertising, sponsorship, publicity, television and finance.

STADIUM JUMPING, INC.
1301 SIXTH AVENUE WEST
SUITE 406
BRADENTON, FL 34205
941-744-5465
800-237-8924
Fax: 941-744-0874
www.stadiumjumping.com
• Michael Morrissey, President
michael.morrissey@stadiumjumping.com
• Matt Morrissey, Marketing & Vendor Operations
matt.morrissey@stadiumjumping.com
• Mary Silcox, Advertising & Publications
mary.silcox@stadiumjumping.com
Publications:
Media Guide.
Membership Requirements:
Automatic upon participation in an AGA event. Membership includes owners, riders, trainers, show organizers, course designers, AHSA and USET officials.
Description:
Founded in 1978. Non-profit organization which promotes the highest caliber of grand prix show jumping in the United States. Works closely with the American Horse Show Association and the U.S. Equestrian team to improve the status of the sport and increase benefits to the various show organizers at each event, horse owners, riders and trainers.

STANDARDBRED CANADA
2150 MEADOWVALE BOULEVARD
MISSISSAUGA, ON, CANADA L5N 6R6
905-858-3060
Fax: 905-858-3111
www.standardbredcanada.ca
• Caren Stockwell, Corporate Secretary & Executive Assistant
(905) 858-3060
cbrown@standardbredcanada.ca
• Rosenna So, Chief Financial Officer
(905) 858-3060
rso@standardbredcanada.ca
• Heather Reid, Sales & Stakes Manager
(905) 858-3060
hreid@standardbredcanada.ca
Publications:
TROT MAGAZINE, monthly.
Description:
Standardbred Canada is a non-profit organization that aims to promote harness racing while maintaining and distributing records on registered Standardbreds in Canada. They formed in 1998 as a result of the merging of The Canadian Trotting Association and The Canadian Standardbred Horse Society.

THOROUGHBRED CLUB OF AMERICA
3555 RICE ROAD
LEXINGTON, KY 40510
859-254-4282
Fax: 859-231-6131
lgardner@thethoroughbredclub.com
www.thethoroughbredclub.com
• Shannon Arvin, President
• Gray Lyster, Vice President
• Louis Prichard, Secretary-Treasurer
• Laura Gardener, General Manager

lgardner@thethoroughbredclub.com
• Betty Flynn, Executive Director
bflynn@thethoroughbredclub.com
Description:
Founded in 1932. The purpose of the club is to promote better business relations among Thoroughbred horse riders and to provide a venue for intelligent discussion on breeding, racing and marketing of Throughbred horses.
Member Services:
Monthly meetings; club house with full scale library.
Membership Requirements:
Members must be associated with the thoroughbred horse industry (owners, breeders, track or organizational executives) and approved by the Board of Directors.

THOROUGHBRED OWNERS AND BREEDERS ASSOCIATION
3101 BEAUMONT CENTRE CIRCLE
SUITE 110
LEXINGTON, KY 40513
859-276-2291
888-606-TOBA
Fax: 859-276-2462
toba@toba.org
www.toba.org
• Dan Metzger, President
• Carl Gough, Controller
• Andrew Schweigardt, Director of Industry Relations and Development
Number of Members:
3,300
Member Services:
International Committee. Health Committee. Owners Committee. National Awards dinner held annually to recognize top state breeders.
Publications:
THE BLOOD-HORSE, weekly.
Membership Requirements:
Dues payment of $275.
Description:
Founded in 1961. National organization devoted to improving the quality of the thoroughbred racing and breeding industry.

THOROUGHBRED RACING ASSOCIATIONS
420 FAIR HILL DRIVE
SUITE 1
ELKTON, MD 21921
410-392-9200
Fax: 410-398-1366
www.tra-online.com
• Christopher N. Scherf, Executive Vice President
(410) 392-9200
cscherf@tra-online.com
• Jane E. Murray, Director of Services
(410) 392-9200
jmurray@tra-online.com
• Margie Pollard, Executive Assistant
(410) 392-9200
margiep@tra-online.com
• Karen Darling, Administrative Assistant/Webmaster
(410) 392-9200
webmaster@tra-online.com
Description:
Founded in 1942. Trade association which serves to insure the integrity of thoroughbred racing.
Membership Requirements:
Must be racetrack or racing association.

Publications:
TRA DIRECTORY AND RECORD BOOK, annual.
Member Services:
Meetings; surveys; public and media relations; data bank.

U.S. TROTTING ASSOCIATION
6130 SOUTH SUNBURY ROAD
WESTERVILLE, OH 43081-9309
614-224-2291
877-800-USTA
Fax: 614-228-1385
webmaster@ustrotting.com
www.ustrotting.com
• Mike Tanner, Executive Vice President
webmaster@ustrotting.com
• Dan Leary, Director of Marketing and Commnications
dan.leary@ustrotting.com
Number of Members:
18,000
Publications:
HOOF BEATS, monthly magazine.
Membership Requirements:
Anyone who works and/or participates in harness racing.
Description:
Founded in 1939, the U.S. Trotting Association is a not-for-profit association of Standardbred owners, breeders, drivers, trainers, and officials, organized to provide administrative, rulemaking, licensing and breed registry services to its members and promote the sport of harness racing.

UNITED STATES DRESSAGE FOUNDATION
4051 IRON WORKS PARKWAY
LEXINGTON, KY 40511
859-971-2277
Fax: 859-971-7722
www.usdf.org
• George W. Williams, President
(937) 603-9134
• Margaret C. Freeman, Secretary
(914) 548-4242
• Steven M. Schubert, Treasurer
(978) 360-6441
treasurer@usdf.org
• Lisa J. Gorretta, Vice President
(236) 406-5475
Number of Members:
38,000
Publications:
Yearbook, annually USDF Regional Newsletter, four times annually; Calendar of Competitions, annually.
Membership Requirements:
Group membership is attained by joining one of USDF's 125 Group member organizations. Members are eligible for USDF Rider Awards. Participating membership is issued directly by USDF, not through a group. They receive a copy of all USDF publications, and upon registering their horses with USDF, they are eligible for the entire USDF awards program, and are also eligible to receive a half-price subscription to DRESSAGE & CT Magazine. Business membership is issued directly by USDF. They receive all USDF publications, and receive discounted advertising and other promotional opportunities.
Description:
Founded in 1973. Non-profit educational organization dedicated to the promotion of

dressage as a basic training for all horses, as well as a competitive sport.

UNITED STATES EQUESTRIAN FEDERATION
4047 IRON WORKS PARKWAY
LEXINGTON, KY 40511
859-258-2472
Fax: 859-231-6662
customercare@usef.org
www.usef.org
• Chrystine Tauber, President
(859) 225-2046
cjtauber@usef.org
• Chris Welton, CEO
(859) 225-6912
• Colby Connell, Chief Marketing Officer
(859) 225-2024
• Will Connell, Director, Sport
(908) 326-1154
wconnell@usef.org
• Sonja Keating, SVP, General Counsel
(859) 225-2045
skeating@usef.org
Number of Members:
80,000
Member Services:
Eligibility to compete for national awards, free member services; insurance coverage; corporate discounts; free amateur status and travel discounts.
Publications:
HORSE SHOW Magazine, monthly; Rule Book, bi-annually.
Membership Requirements:
Payment of annual fee.
Description:
Founded in 1917. National Equestrian Federation of the United States. Establishes rules and regulations for 26 different breeds and disciplines including the three Olympic disciplines: Show Jumping, Dressage and Three Day Eventing. Sanctions over 2,600 horse shows throughout the United States each year. Offers variety of sponsorship programs (national championship events, award programs, etc.) in virtually every market in the U.S. purpose is to govern equestrian sports in the United States and represent the United States internationally.

UNITED STATES EQUESTRIAN TEAM FOUNDATION
1040 POTTERSVILLE ROAD
BEDMINSTER TOWNSHIP, NJ 07934
908-234-1251
Fax: 908-234-0670
info@uset.org
www.uset.org
• Brownlee O. Currey, Jr., Chairman of the Board
• Tucker S. Johnson, President and CEO
• James McNerney, Vice President
• Philip Richter, Treasurer
Member Services:
Publication, social activities. Annual meeting held in January each year.
Publications:
USET NEWS, six times annually.
Membership Requirements:
Active team members are selected on a competitive basis. Contributing members donate to support teams.
Sports Services Founded:
1950
Description:
Established as a not-for-profit organization,

the USET Foundation's role is to help provide funding for the High Performance competition, training, coaching, travel and educational needs of America's elite and developing athletes and horses in partnership with the United States Equestrian Federation.

UNITED STATES EVENTING ASSOCIATION
525 OLD WATERFORD ROAD
NORTHWEST
LEESBURG, VA 20176
703-779-0440
Fax: 703-779-0550
info@useventing.com
www.useventing.com
• Rob Burk, Chief Executive Officer
(703) 779-9895
rburk@useventing.com
• Jo Whitehouse, Developmental Officer
(703) 669-9999
jo@useventing.com
• Sharon Gallagher, Senior Director of Competitions
(703) 669-9995
sharon@useventing.com
• Jennifer Hardwick, Director of Member Services
(703) 669-9993
jennifer@useventing.com
Description:
Founded in 1959. Concerned with education in the sport of Combined Training (also known as Eventing or Horse Trials) and development of competitions throughout the country so that horses and riders from novice through Olympic level may gain necessary experience, and, at the same time, may enjoy this equestrian sport.
Membership Requirements:
Payment of dues - Full Member ($85), Junior Member ($60), Life Member ($1,500).
Publications:
EVENTING USA, bimonthly magazine; USCTA OMNIBUS, four issues per year; RULES FOR Eventing, other books, booklets and pamphlets; mailing lists.
Number of Members:
12,000

UNITED STATES POLO ASSOCIATION
9011 LAKE WORTH ROAD
LAKE WORTH, FL 33467
800-232-8772
www.uspolo.org
• Duncan Huyler, Chief Executive Officer
dhuyler@uspolo.org
• Susan Present, Chief Financial Officer
spresent@uspolo.org
• Kris Bowman, Executive Director
kbowman@uspolo.org
• Justin Powers, Director of Club Development
jpowers@uspolo.org
Number of members:
3,488
Member Services:
USPA Yearbook with name listing and handicap, access to movies of techniques of polo and on various games; identification stickers and opportunity to play in all USPA tournaments within given handicap.
Publications:
Polo Players' Edition
Membership Requirements:
Club - must have regulation field; and

accommodations for horses and tack. Must have three registered USPA-playing members as members of the club. $200 per year. Player - must belong to a registered USPA club and must follow rules and regulations stated by USPA. $135 per year.
Description:
Founded 1890. Serves as regulatory body of polo events played in the U.S. and Canada. Overseas tournaments, assigns handicaps, promotes intercollegiate and interscholastic polo. The Polo Training Foundation, conducts polo schools across the country.

WALKING HORSE TRAINER'S ASSOCIATION
1101 NORTH MAIN STREET
SHELBYVILLE, TN 37162
931-684-5866
Fax: 931-684-5895
whtrainers@gmail.com
• Billy Young, President
• Bill Cantrell, 1st Vice President
• Jamie Hankins, 2nd Vice President
Description:
Founded in 1968. Organization of professional walking horse trainers to promote and improve their interests.
Membership Requirements:
Must be classified as a professional trainer, and must spend 100% of their working time working with horses and earn 100% of their income from working with horses. Also have A and AA licensed trainers.
Publications:
FROM THE HORSES MOUTH, newsletter; THE UPDATER.
Member Services:
Receive license free; receive newsletters; annual meeting held in December of each year.

WOODBINE ENTERTAINMENT GROUP
555 REXDALE BOULEVARD
TORONTO, ON, CANADA M9W 5L2
416-675-7223
1-888-675-7223
info@woodbineentertainment.com
www.woodbineentertainment.com
• James J. Lawson, Chief Executive Officer
• H.B. Clay Horner, Chairman
• Michelle E. DiEmanuele, President & CEO, Trillium Health Partners
Description:
Parent company of Woodbine, Ft. Erie, and Mohawk racetracks.

Equestrian, Commissions/Pari-Mutuel

AGRICULTURE AND AGRI-FOOD CANADA
960 CARLING AVENUE
CEF BUILDING 74
OTTAWA, ON, CANADA K1A 0C6
613-759-6100
1-800-268-8835
Fax: 613-759-6230
cpmawebacpm@agr.gc.ca
www.agr.gc.ca/csb/cpma-acpm/index_e.php
• Gerry Ritz, Minister Of Agriculture & Agri-Food
• Andrea Lyon, Deputy Minister Of Agriculture & Agri-Food
• Chris Forbes, Associate Deputy Minister

• Ron Nichol, Director Program Coordination & National Stan
Description:
Founded 1972. Provides supervision over pari-mutuel betting on horse races in Canada under the Criminal Code. Services provided include auditing of the tote system and betting transactions, testing horses for the presence of prohibited drugs, providing video race patrol and photo finish services, and research.
Publications:
Annual Report; Schedule of Drugs, Q&A Equine Drug control Booklet.

ALCOHOL AND GAMING COMMISSION OF ONTARIO
90 SHEPPARD AVENUE EAST
SUITE 200-300
TORONTO, ON, CANADA M2N 0A4
416-326-8700
1-800-522-2876
Fax: 416-326-5555
customer.service@agco.ca
www.agco.on.ca
• Jean Major, Chief Executive Officer
• Tom Mungham, Chief Operating Officer
• Jasmina Milanovich, Corporate Secretary & Director
• Teresa Tedesco, Chief Administrative Officer
Description:
Regulates the sale, service, and consumption of beverage alcohol to promote moderation and responsible use; ensures that casino and charitable gaming is conducted in the public interest, by people with integrity, and in a manner that is socially and financially responsible.

ARIZONA DEPARTMENT OF RACING
1110 WEST WASHINGTON
SUITE 450
PHOENIX, AZ 85007
602-364-1700
Fax: 602-364-1703
racing.az.gov
• Victoria Rogen, Licensing
(602) 364-1716
vrogen@azracing.gov
• Dan Reinertson, Chief Greyhound Steward
(520) 884-7576
dreinertson@azracing.gov
Description:
The Department of Racing regulates the Arizona pari-mutuel horse and greyhound racing industry. The Department oversees and supervises all commercial horse, greyhound, and county fair racing meetings; licenses participants; collects state revenues generated by race meetings; promotes and encourages the breeding of horses and greyhounds in the State; and enforces laws and rules related to racing and wagering to protect industry participants and the public. The Department also regulates and supervises all boxing, kickboxing, tough man, and mixed martial arts events in Arizona.

BIRMINGHAM RACING COMMISSION
1000 JOHN ROGERS DRIVE
SUITE 102
BIRMINGHAM, AL 35210
205-838-7470
Fax: 205-328-0632

- Kip W. Keefer, Executive Secretary
- Valerie Carpenter, Administrative Assistant
- Leda Dimperio, Systems Administrator
brcval@mindspring.com
- Peter McCann, Veterinarian
(205) 838-7478
Description:
The Birmingham Racing Commission was organized in 1984 pursuant to the John Rogers Act, now codified as Chapter 65 of Title 11, Code of Alabama 1975. The Commission is a unique public corporation authorized to license and regulate thoroughbred and greyhound racing pari-mutuel wagering in Birmingham.

CALIFORNIA HORSE RACING BOARD
1010 HURLEY WAY
SUITE 300
SACRAMENTO, CA 95825
916-263-6000
www.chrb.ca.gov
- Rick Baedeker, Executive Director
- Jackie Wagner, Assistant Executive Director
- Bill Westermann, Chief of Licensing and Enforcement
- Wendy Voss, Chief of Administration
Description:
Regulatory body for pari-mutuel wagering in the state of California.

COLORADO RACING COMMISSION
1881 PIERCE STREET
SUITE 108
LAKEWOOD, CO 80214
303-205-2990
Fax: 303-205-2950
www.colorado.gov/pacific/enforcement/racing-commission-0
- Sean Beirne, Chair
- Pam Inmann, Vice Chair - Business Member
- Lori Scott, Veterinarian Member
Description:
The mission of the Colorado Division of Racing is to promote and foster the public confidence in the pari-mutuel industry, protect the welfare of the participants through fair, consistent, proactive enforcement of appropriate policies, statutes and Colorado racing commission rules. The Commission is responsible for promulgating all the rules and regulations governing greyhound and horse racing in Colorado.
Number of Members:
5-member commission
Publications:
Annual Report; Rule Book

HORSE RACING ALBERTA
9707 110TH STREET NW
SUITE 720
EDMONTON, AB, CANADA T5K 2L9
780-415-5432
1-888-553-7223
reception@thehorses.com
www.thehorses.com
- Shirley McClellan, Chief Executive Officer
(780) 415-5432
- Sharon Stell, Chief Financial Officer
(780) 415-5427
- Doug Fenske, Manager, Racing
(780) 415-5432
- Jeff Robillard, Manager of Marketing and Communications
(780) 415-5432

Description:
Horse Racing Alberta (HRA), is a private not-for-profit corporation that was established with the Alberta Governments proclamation of the Racing Corporation Act in 1996. The HRA was established to lead a racing industry renewal and to manage industry self-regulation.

IDAHO STATE POLICE
DEPARTMENT OF LAW ENFORCEMENT
700 SOUTH STRATFORD DRIVE
MERIDIAN, ID 83642
208-884-7080
Fax: 208-884-7098
isp.idaho.gov/racing/
- Paul J. Schneider, Chairman of the Commission
- Ardie Noyes, Racing Executive Director
ardie.noyes@isp.idaho.gov
- Jeremy Beck, Management Assistant
jeremy.beck@isp.idaho.gov
- Brent Archibald, Investigator
Description:
Regulatory body for pari-mutuel wagering in the state of Idaho.

ILLINOIS RACING BOARD
100 WEST RANDOLPH STREET
SUITE 5-700
CHICAGO, IL 60601
312-814-2600
Fax: 312-814-5062
irb.info@illinois.gov
www.illinois.gov/irb
- Domenic Dicera, Executive Director
domenic.dicera@illinois.gov
- Vitto Ezeji-Okoye, Chief Financial Officer
vitto.okoye@illinois.gov
- Ed Mingey, Director of Security
ed.mingey@illinois.gov
- Jackie Clisham, Director of Operations
jackie.clisham@illinois.gov
- Bob Lang, Director of Mutuels
bob.lang@illinois.gov
Description:
Regulatory body for pari-mutuel wagering in the state of Illinois.

IOWA RACING & GAMING COMMISSION
DMACC CAPITOL CENTER
1300 DES MOINES STREET
SUITE 100
DES MOINES, IA 50309
515-281-7352
www.iowa.gov/irgc
- Jeff Lamberti, Commissioner
(515) 964-8777
jeff.lamberti@ankenylaw.com
- Richard Arnold, Commissioner
(641) 203-0298
rcarnold@sirisonline.com
- Carl Heinrich, Commissioner
(712) 323-7253
- Kristine Kramer, Commissioner
(641) 394-3086
kandwmotors@iowatelecom.net
- Dolores Mertz, Commissioner
(515) 395-2952
Description:
They are a State of Iowa regulatory agency that regulates the excursion boat/gambling structures casinos and pari-mutual tracks in Iowa.

KANSAS RACING AND GAMING COMMISSION
700 SOUTHWEST HARRISON
SUITE 500
TOPEKA, KS 66603
785-296-5800
Fax: 785-296-0900
krgc@krgc.ks.gov
krgc.ks.gov
- Don Brownlee, Executive Director
- Rochel Towle, Human Resources Manager
- Larry Moreland, Director
- Joe Herridge, Regional Security Manager
- Dennis Bachman, Director
- Brandi White, Director Of Administration
Description:
Dedicated to protect the integrity of these industries through enforcement of Kansas laws and is committed to preserving and instilling public trust and confidence.

KENTUCKY HORSE RACING COMMISSION
4063 IRON WORKS PARKWAY
BUILDING B
LEXINGTON, KY 40511
859-246-2040
Fax: 859-246-2039
Marc.Guilfoil@ky.gov
www.khrc.ky.gov
- Marc A. Guilfoil, Executive Director
(859) 246-2040
Marc.Guilfoil@ky.gov
- John Forgy, General Counsel
(859) 246-2040
John.Forgy@ky.gov
- Jamie Eads, Deputy Executive Director
(859) 246-2040
Jamie.Eads@ky.gov
Member Services:
Licensing of owners, trainers, jockeys, and stable employees; fingerprinting of licensees; licensing reciprocity.
Publications:
Biennial Report; Kentucky Rules of Racing.
Year Founded and Description:
Established in 1906, the KHRC is an independent government agency responsible for regulation of horse racing, wagering, and related activities in the state of Kentucky.

LOUISIANA RACING COMMISSION
320 NORTH CARROLLTON AVENUE
SUITE 2-B
NEW ORLEANS, LA 70119-5100
504-483-4000
Fax: 504-483-4898
horseracing.la.gov
- Bob F. Wright, Chairman
- Judy W. Wagner, 1st Vice Chairman
- Dion Young, 2nd Vice Chairman
- Kevin S. Delahoussaye, Commissioner
Number of Members:
9.
Publications:
Rules of Racing, Racing Calendar.
Member Services:
Enforcement/Regulation of Horse Racing Licensing.
Tradition and Excellence:
Reviews, regulates, governs and supervises all forms of horse racing and pari-mutuel wagering.

MAINE GOVERNMENT, DEPARTMENT OF AGRICULTURE, CONSERVATION & FORESTRY
22 STATE HOUSE STATION
18 ELKINS LANE
AUGUSTA, ME 04333
207-287-3200
Fax: 207-287-2400
dacf@maine.gov
www.maine.gov/dacf/index.shtml
• Walter E. Whitcomb, Commissioner
walt.whitcomb@maine.gov

MANITOBA HORSE RACING COMMISSION
PO BOX 46086
RPO WESTDALE
WINNIPEG, MB, CANADA R3R 3S3
204-885-7770
Fax: 204-831-0942
www.manitobahorsecomm.org
• Tom Goodman, Chairman
mhrc@manitobahorsecomm.org
• Brian Billeck, Vice Chairman
mhrc@manitobahorsecomm.org
• Larry Huber, Executive Director
lhuber@manitobahorsecomm.org
Description:
Provides horsemen and racing organizations with the information and forms needed to facilitate their participation in pari-mutuel horse racing in Manitoba.

MARYLAND RACING COMMISSION
300 EAST TOWSONTOWN BOULEVARD
TOWSON, MD 21286
410-296-9682
Fax: 410-296-9687
dloplmarylandracingcommission-dllr@maryland.gov
www.dllr.state.md.us/racing/comm.shtml
• Bruce Quade, Chairman
Description:
In charge of licensing all persons, associations, or corporations that hold any horse racing meet within the State where racing is permitted for any stake, purse, or reward, as well as Satellite Simulcast Betting and intertrack betting.
Year Founded:
1920

MASSACHUSETTS GAMING COMMISSION
101 FEDERAL STREET
12TH FLOOR
BOSTON, MA 02110
617-979-8400
Fax: 617-725-0258
massgaming.com
• Catherine Blue, General Counsel
• Paul Connelly, Director of Licensing
• Elaine Driscoll, Director of Communications
• John R. Glennon, Chief Information Officer
• Jill Griffin, Director of Workforce
• Alexandra Lightbown, Director of Racing
• Mark Vander Linden, Director of Research and Responsible Gaming
Description:
To ensure fair and honest pari-mutuel racing, the Commission promulgates and enforces rules and regulations, proposes legislation and develops policies to better regulate the Racing Industry (horse and greyhound).

MICHIGAN GAMING CONTROL BOARD
3062 WEST GRAND BOULEVARD
SUITE L-700
DETROIT, MI 48202-6062
313-456-4100
Fax: 313-456-4200
MGCBweb@michigan.gov
www.michigan.gov/mgcb
• Richard S. Kalm, Executive Director
Description:
The Michigan Office of the Racing Commissioner issues track, race meeting, occupational licenses, and simulcasting permits; allocates racing dates and simulcasting schedules; collects racing license and tax revenues; appoints stewards and veterinarians to represent the state; hears appeals from decisions of stewards and on other matters; approves track appointed officials; monitors the daily conduct of live and simulcast racing; conducts equine and human drug testing programs and investigates any irregularities in racing which may lead to formal hearings, administrative disciplinary actions and/or criminal prosecution.

MINNESOTA RACING COMMISSION
15201 ZURICH STREET NE
SUITE 212
COLUMBUS, MN 55025
952-496-7950
Fax: 952-496-7954
www.mrc.state.mn.us
• Thomas DiPasquale, Executive Director
(952) 496-7950
tom.dipasquale@state.mn.us
• John Flynn, Director of Security
(952) 496-7950
john.flynn@state.mn.us
• Lynn Hovda, Chief Veterinarian
(952) 496-6487
lynn.hovda@state.mn.us
• Joe Scurto, Executive Deputy Director
(952) 496-7950
joe.scurto@state.mn.us
Description:
To regulate horse racing and card playing in Minnesota; to ensure that it is conducted in the public interest, and to take all necessary steps in ensuring the integrity of racing and card playing in Minnesota thus promoting the breeding of race horses in order to stimulate agriculture and rural agribusiness.

NEBRASKA STATE RACING COMMISSION
5903 WALKER AVENUE
LINCOLN, NE 68507
402-471-4155
diane.vandeun@nebraska.gov
racingcommission.nebraska.gov
• Dennis Lee, Chairman
• Janell Beveridge, Commissioner
• Jeffrey Galyen, Commissioner
• Tom Sage, Director
tom.sage@nebraska.gov
• John Frederick, Director Of Investigations
Description:
To protect, preserve, and promote agriculture and horse racing through effective and efficient effort to prevent and eliminate corrupt practices; insure fairness in decisions affecting licenses and patrons; ensure due process in administrative proceedings; be attentive to the public and licensees and provide information

concerning the industry and commission operations.

NEVADA GAMING CONTROL BOARD
1919 COLLEGE PARKWAY
CARSON CITY, NV 89706
775-684-7750
Fax: 775-687-5817
www.gaming.nv.gov
• A.G. Burnett, Chairman
• Shawn R. Reid, Member
• Terry Johnson, Member
Nature of Services:
The State Gaming Control Board governs Nevada's gaming industry through strict regulation of all persons, locations, practices, association, and related activities. Through investigations, licensure, and enforcement of laws and regulations the Board protects the integrity and the stability of the industry and ensures the collection of gaming taxes and fees that are an essential source of State revenue.

NEW MEXICO RACING COMMISSION
4900 ALAMEDA NE
ALBUQUERQUE, NM 87113
505-222-0700
Fax: 505-222-0713
rc.info@state.nm.us
www.nmrc.state.nm.us
• Laura M. Valencia, Manager/CFO
• Rosemary Garley, Manager
• Fabian C. Lopez, IT, Licensing Manager
• April Abeita, Licensing Administrator
• Ray Mitcham, Auditor
• Rosa M. Silva, Financial Specialist
Description:
To provide regulation in an equitable manner to New Mexico's pari-mutuel horseracing industry to protect the interest of wagering patrons and the State of New Mexico in a manner which promotes a climate of economic prosperity for horsemen, horse owners and racetrack management.

NEW YORK STATE GAMING COMMISSION
PO BOX 7500
SCHENECTADY, NY 12301-7500
518-388-3300
info@gaming.ny.gov
www.gaming.ny.gov
• John A. Crotty, Commissioner
• John J. Poklemba, Commissioner
• Barry Sample, Commissioner
• Todd R. Snyder, Commissioner
• Peter J. Moschetti, Jr., Commissioner
Description:
Regulatory body for pari-mutuel wagering in the state of New York.

NH RACING AND CHARITABLE GAMING COMMISSION
14 INTEGRA DRIVE
CONCORD, NH 03301
603-271-2158
Fax: 603-271-3381
rcgc@racing.nh.gov
www.racing.nh.gov
• Paul M. Kelley, Division Director
• Sudhir Naik, Division Administrator IV
Description:
The New Hampshire Pari-Mutuel Commission oversees the regulation of pari-mutuel wagering at racetracks in New

single sports

Hampshire, including Thoroughbred Racing, Harness Racing, and Greyhound Racing under RSA 284.

NORTH DAKOTA RACING COMMISSION
500 NORTH 9TH STREET
BISMARCK, ND 58501-4509
701-328-4633
Fax: 701-328-4280
racingcommission.nd.gov
• Jim Ozbun, Chairman of the Commission
circlez@ndsupernet.com
• Ray Trottier, Commissioner
rjtrots@hotmail.com
• John Hanson, Commissioner
jhanson@loggingcampranch.com
• David Piepkorn, Commissioner
dpiepkorn@nd.gov
Description:
The regulatory body in charge of regulating live and simulcast racing in North Dakota and administers three special funds for the benefit of the horse racing industry in North Dakota.

OHIO STATE RACING COMMISSION
77 SOUTH HIGH STREET
18TH FLOOR
COLUMBUS, OH 43215-6108
614-466-2757
Fax: 614-466-1900
www.racing.ohio.gov
• Robert K. Schmitz, Chairman
• Todd Book, Commissioner
• Gary G. Koch, Commissioner
• Mark Munroe, Commissioner
• Thomas R. Winters, Commissioner
Description:
Regulatory body for pari-mutuel wagering in the state of Ohio.
Year Founded:
1933.

OKLAHOMA HORSE RACING COMMISSION
SHEPHERD MALL
2401 NW 23RD STREET
SUITE 78
OKLAHOMA CITY, OK 73107
405-943-6472
Fax: 405-943-6474
ohrc@socket.net
www.ohrc.org
• Ran Leonard, Chairman
• Keith Sanders, Vice Chair
• Mel Bollenbach, Secretary
• Mike Dixon, Director of Law Enforcement
• Kelly G. Cathey, Executive Director
Description:
Encourages agriculture, the breeding of horses, and generates public revenue through the forceful control of the highest quality Commission-sanctioned racing which maintains the appearance as well as the fact of complete honesty and integrity of horse racing in this state.

OREGON RACING COMMISSION
800 NE OREGON STREET
SUITE 310
PORTLAND, OR 97232
971-673-0207
Fax: 971-673-0213
• Jack McGrail, Executive Director
(971) 673-0209
jack.mcgrail@state.or.us
• Karen Parkman, Program and

Administrative Coordinator
(971) 673-0208
karen.parkman@state.or.us
• Mike Twiggs, State Steward
(503) 285-9144
mike.twiggs@state.or.us
• Stacy Katler, Senior State Veterinarian
(503) 285-9144
stacy.katler@state.or.us
Description:
To regulate and to facilitate all aspects of the pari-mutuel industry in the state of Oregon for the benefit of the citizenry, the licensees and participants.

PENNSYLVANIA DEPARTMENT OF AGRICULTURE
2301 NORTH CAMERON STREET
HARRISBURG, PA 17110
717-787-4737
www.agriculture.pa.gov
• Kelly King, Horse Racing Executive Assistant
(717) 787-1942
kelking@pa.gov
Description:
Regulatory body for pari-mutuel wagering on harness racing in the state of Pennsylvania.

RACING COMMISSIONERS INTERNATIONAL (ARCI)
1510 NEWTOWN PIKE
SUITE 210
LEXINGTON, KY 40511
859-224-7070
www.arci.com
• Mark Lamberth, Chair
• Edward J. Martin, President
• Judy Wagner, Secretary/Chair-Elect
• Jeff Colliton, Treasurer
Description:
To protect and uphold the integrity of the pari-mutuel sports of horse racing, dog racing and jai-alai through an informed membership, by encouraging uniform regulation and by promoting the health and welfare of the industry through various programs and projects.
Membership Requirements:
Must be racing commissioner or executive director of a commission; associate members need not be commissioners, but must be connected to the industry.
Number of members:
500
Year Founded:
1934

STATE OF DELAWARE, DEPARTMENT OF AGRICULTURE
2320 SOUTH DUPONT HIGHWAY
DOVER, DE 19901
302-698-4500
800-282-8685
Fax: 302-697-4748
dda.delaware.gov
• Ed Kee, Cabinet Secretary of Agriculture
• Austin E. Short, Deputy Secretary
• Holly Porter, Executive Assistant
• Lisa Wildermuth, Executive Secretary
Description:
The Delaware Department of Agriculture Harness Racing Commission regulates and oversees the sport of Harness racing in the state. Its primary objectives and principles are to protect, preserve, and promote agriculture and horse racing through

effective and efficient efforts to prevent and eliminate corrupt practices; ensure fairness in decisions affecting licensees and patrons; ensure due process in administrative proceedings; be attentive to the public and licensees and provide information concerning the industry and commission operations.
Delaware License Application:
Licensing Information During Live Racing: Dover Downs (302) 674-4600, Ext 3242, Harrington Raceway (302) 398-7223.

STATE OF INDIANA HORSE RACING COMMISSION
1302 NORTH MERIDIAN
SUITE 175
INDIANAPOLIS, IN 46202
317-233-3119
www.in.gov/hrc/
• Thomas Weatherwax, Chairman
• Greg Schenkel, Vice Chairman
• Deena Pitman, Assistant Executive Director
• Lea Ellingwood, General Counsel
• Wendi Samuelson-Dull, Controller
• Holly Newell, Deputy General Counsel
Description:
Supervises pari-mutuel horse race betting in Indiana.

STATE OF NEW JERSEY, DEPARTMENT OF LAW & PUBLIC SAFETY
140 EAST FRONT STREET
PO BOX 088
4TH FLOOR
TRENTON, NJ 8625
609-292-0613
Fax: 609-599-1785
www.nj.gov/oag/racing
• Pamela J. Clyne, Chair
• Francesco Zanzuccki, Executive Director
Description:
To ensure that racing is conducted in a fair and responsible manner in the state of New Jersey.

STATE OF RHODE ISLAND DEPARTMENT OF BUSINESS REGULATION
1511 PONTIAC AVENUE
CRANSTON, RI 02920
401-462-9500
Fax: 401-462-9532
www.dbr.state.ri.us
• Christina Tobiasz, Chief Licensing Examiner, Racing & Athletics
(401) 462-9525
christina.tobiasz@dbr.ri.gov
• Mary F. Bernard, Chair
• Macky McCleary, Director, Business Regulation
(401) 462-9551
macky.mccleary@dbr.ri.gov
• John Mancone, Chief Public Protection Inspector
(401) 462-9646
john.mancone@dbr.ri.gov
Description:
Responsible for supervising the enforcement of laws related to licensing and regulation of racing and athletics activities, including dog racing, jai alai, boxing, wrestling, kickboxing and simulcast wagering.

TEXAS RACING COMMISSION
8505 CROSS PARK DRIVE
SUITE 110
AUSTIN, TX 78754
512-833-6699
Fax: 512-833-6907
info@txrc.state.tx.us
www.txrc.texas.gov
• Chuck Trout, Executive Director
• Joel Speight, Deputy Executive Director
• John Perryman, Director of Administration
• Cathy Cantrell, Director Of Licensing
cathy.cantrell@txrc.texas.gov
Description:
State regulatory agency for horse and
greyhound racing in Texas.

VERMONT RACING COMMISSION
109 STATE STREET
MONTPELIER, VT 05609
802-828-3333
Fax: 802-828-3339
governor.vermont.gov/boards_and_commis
sions/racing
• Peter Shumlin, Governor
• Harlan Sylvester, Commission Chair
Description:
This commission is based upon the taxing
power and the police power of the state and
provides for the establishment, licensing,
regulation and control of the pari-mutuel
system of wagering on horse races, and is
for the protection of the public welfare and
good order of the people of the state, the
support and encouragement of agricultural
fairs and the improvement of the breed of
horses in Vermont.

VIRGINIA RACING COMMISSION
5707 HUNTSMAN ROAD
SUITE 201-B
RICHMOND, VA 23250
804-966-7400
www.vrc.virginia.gov/
• Bernard J. Hettel, Executive Secretary
(804) 966-7415
bernard.hettel@vrc.virginia.gov
• David Lermond, Deputy Executive
Secretary
• Kimberly Mackey, Office Administrator
• Rich Harden, Equine Medical Director
Description:
To grow, sustain, and control a native horse
racing industry with pari-mutuel wagering by
prescribing regulations and conditions that
command and promote excellence and
complete honesty and integrity in racing and
wagering.

**WASHINGTON HORSE RACING
COMMISSION**
6326 MARTIN WAY EAST
SUITE 209
OLYMPIA, WA 98516
360-459-6462
Fax: 360-459-6461
www.whrc.wa.gov
• Doug Moore, Executive Secretary
• Patty Brown, Confidential Secretary
Number of Members:
3 Commissioners, 4 Legislative Non-voting
Ex-officio members, 2 Senators, 2
Representatives.
Description:
To provide a regulatory foundation for all
aspects of pari-mutuel horse racing in order
to protect the public and assure the overall

health of the industry.
Year Founded:
1933
Nature of Service:
State government, regulation

WV RACING COMMISSION
900 PENNSYLVANIA AVENUE
SUITE 533
CHARLESTON, WV 25302
304-558-2150
Fax: 304-558-6319
www.racing.wv.gov
• Jack Rossi, Chairman
• Greg McDermott, Commissioner
Description:
The Commission licenses all persons,
associations, or corporations that hold any
horse racing meet within the State where
racing is permitted for any stake, purse, or
reward, as well as Satellite Simulcast
Betting and inter-track betting. The
Commission makes all regulations
governing the races and, through its
stewards and judges, officiates the conduct
of racing.

WYOMING PARI-MUTUEL COMMISSION
ENERGY II BUILDING
951 WERNER COURT
SUITE 335
CASPER, WY 82601
307-265-4015
Fax: 307-265-4279
parimutuel.state.wy.us
• Charles Moore, Executive Director
Description:
Regulatory body for pari-mutuel wagering in
the state of Wyoming.

Exercise/Fitness Organizations

**AEROBICS AND FITNESS ASSOCIATION
OF AMERICA**
1750 EAST NORTHROP BOULEVARD
SUITE 200
CHANDLER, AZ 85286-1744
800-446-2322
customerservice@afaa.com
www.afaa.com
Description:
Dedicated to teaching and promoting safety
and excellence in the fields of aerobics and
fitness. Establishes instructor certification
standards and guidelines and disseminates
consumer fitness information. They service
over 180,000 instructors in 73 countries and
have more than 2,500 workshops per year.
Membership Requirements:
Payment of dues.
Year Founded:
1983

**AMERICAN ACADEMY OF PODIATRIC
SPORTS MEDICINE**
3121 NE 26TH STREET
OCALA, FL 34470
352-620-8562
info@aapsm.org
www.aapsm.org
• Alex Kor, President
(410) 550-1511
alexkor@aapsm.org

• Amol Saxena, Department of Sports
Medicine
(650) 853-2943
asaxena@aapsm.org
• Maggie Fournier, Secretary-Treasurer
(608) 797-6010
mfournier75@gmail.com
Member Services:
Informational pamphlets, lectures.
Publications:
Newsletter, quarterly; Podiatric Sports
Information.
Membership Requirements:
A degree from an accredited college or
university in podiatric medicine, physical
education or biology.
Description:
Serves to advance the understanding,
prevention and management of lower
extremity sports and fitness injuries.
Year Founded:
1976

**AMERICAN COLLEGE OF SPORTS
MEDICINE**
401 WEST MICHIGAN STREET
INDIANAPOLIS, IN 46202-3233
317-637-9200
Fax: 317-634-7817
www.acsm.org
• Carol Ewing Garber, President
• Mark Hutchinson, First Vice President
• Carrie Jaworsk, Second Vice President
Description:
Promotes and integrates scientific research,
education and practical applications of
sports medicine and exercise science to
maintain and enhance physical
performance, fitness, health and general
quality of life.
Membership Requirements:
Must possess minimum of bachelor's
degree or be a student in a field related to
health, physical education, exercise science
or biology; or, a degree in another field and
working in one of the above areas; or, the
equivalent of one of the above degrees and
currently working in a related field.
Professional membership - $185. Student
membership - $80.
Member Services:
Certifies in the following: program director,
exercise specialist, exercise test
technologist, health/fitness director,
health/fitness instructor and exercise
leader/aerobics. Grants both Continuing
Medical Education (CME) and Continuing
Education Credits (CEC). Twelve Regional
Chapters.
Year Founded:
1954

AMERICAN COUNCIL ON EXERCISE
4851 PARAMOUNT DRIVE
SAN DIEGO, CA 92123
888-825-3636
Fax: 858-576-6564
support@acefitness.org
www.acefitness.org
• Scott Goudeseune, President & CEO
• Alex Mirnezam, Chief Financial Officer
• Cedric X. Bryant, Chief Science Officer
Year Founded:
1985
Description:
A nonprofit organization committed to
enriching quality of life through safe and

effective physical activity. As America's Authority on Fitness, ACE protects all segments of society against ineffective fitness products, programs and trends through its ongoing public education, outreach and research.

AMERICAN FITNESS PROFESSIONALS & ASSOCIATES
1601 LONG BEACH BOULEVARD
BOX 214
SHIP BOTTOM, NJ 08008
609-978-7583
1-800-494-7782
Fax: 609-978-7582
afpa@afpafitness.com
www.afpafitness.com
• Mark J. Occhipinti, President/Chief Executive Officer
Description:
Offers some of the most highly regarded health, fitness, nutrition and sports certifications, education programs and educational opportunities available in the world.
Year Founded:
1994

AMERICAN OSTEOPATHIC ACADEMY OF SPORTS MEDICINE
2424 AMERICAN LANE
MADISON, WI 53704
608-443-2477
Fax: 608-443-2474
www.aoasm.org
• Scott R. Cook, President
(610) 779-2663
• Jeff Bytomski, First Vice President
(919) 681-0868
• John J. Dougherty, Second Vice President
(816) 283-2365
• Shawn Kerger, Secretary/Treasurer
(614) 544-2092

AMERICAN PHYSICAL THERAPY ASSOCIATION
1111 NORTH FAIRFAX STREET
ALEXANDRIA, VA 23214-1488
703-684-2782
800-999-2782
Fax: 703-706-8536
www.apta.org
• Michael J. Bowers, Chief Executive Officer
• Rob Batarla, Executive Vice President
Description:
The principal membership organization representing and promoting the profession of physical therapy, is to further the profession's role in the prevention, diagnosis, and treatment of movement dysfunctions and the enhancement of the physical health and functional abilities of members of the public.

ASSOCIATION OF OLDETIME BARBELL & STRONGMEN (AOBS)
PO BOX 680
WHITESTONE, NY 11357
718-661-3195
Fax: 718-661-3195
lifttech@earthlink.net
www.weightlifting.org/aobs.htm
• Vic Boff, Founder
Membership Requirements:
Men and women who are old time barbell, fitness trainees and strength athletes. Younger devotees invited to join.

Description:
Founded in 1982.

CANADIAN PHYSIOTHERAPY ASSOCIATION
955 GREEN VALLEY CRESCENT
SUITE 270
OTTAWA, ON, CANADA K2C 3V4
613-564-5454
800-387-8679
Fax: 613-564-1577
information@physiotherapy.ca
www.physiotherapy.ca
• Linda Woodhouse, President
Member Services:
National and international event coverage; national symposia; education programs and publications.
Membership Requirements:
Member of Canadian Physiotherapy Association.
Description:
To provide leadership and direction to the physiotherapy profession, foster excellence in practice, education and research, and promote high standards of health in Canada.
Year Founded:
1972

CANADIAN SOCIETY FOR EXERCISE PHYSIOLOGY
18 LOUISA STREET
SUITE 370
OTTAWA, ON, CANADA K1R 6Y6
877-651-3755
Fax: 613-234-3565
info@csep.ca
www.csep.ca
• Mary Duggan, Manager
mduggan@csep.ca
Description:
A voluntary organization composed of professionals interested and involved in the scientific study of exercise physiology, exercise biochemistry, fitness and health.
Member Services:
Journal, professional liability insurance, newsletter.
Year Founded:
1967

COLORADO HILL CLIMB ASSOCIATION
PO BOX 687
GREEN MOUNTAIN FALLS, CO 80819
office@chcaracing.com
www.chcaracing.com
• Jay Stewart, President
(719) 641-5352
jbug0353@aol.com
• Erny Shucraft, Vice President
(719) 649-8197
• Debbie Queen, Secretary
(719) 393-5966
queendbie@live.com
• Ginger Bartley, Treasurer
Description:
Sponsors a series of Colorado hill climb racing (motorized) events annually.
Year Founded:
1971

ECA WORLD FITNESS ALLIANCE
414 EAST BEECH STREET
LONG BEACH, NY 11561
516-432-6877
www.ecaworldfitness.com

• Lilli Koppelman, Event Director
• Sydell Radner, Finance Director
• Michelle Mascari, Creative Director
• Susan Kasper, Public Relations Liaison
Description:
Dedicated to furthering the education of health and fitness professionals and the promotion of current information and trends in the rapidly changing fitness industry.
Year Founded:
1991

IDEA HEALTH & FITNESS ASSOCIATION
10455 PACIFIC CENTER COURT
SAN DIEGO, CA 92121
858-535-8979 EXT 7
(800) 999-4332
Fax: 858-535-8234
contact@ideafit.com
www.ideafit.com
• Peter Davis, President and CEO
• Kathie Davis, Executive Director
Nature of Service:
Provided health and fitness professionals with unbiased data, pertinent information, educational resources, career development and industry leadership.
Membership Categories:
Business , Program Director, Personal Trainer, Group Fitness, Health Professional, Associate and Student Dues: $45-$175.
Publications:
IDEA HEALTH & FITNESS SOURCE, 10 times annually, IDEA PERSONAL TRAINER, 10 times annually, IDEA FITNESS MANAGER, 5 times annually; IDEA FITNESS EDGE, 5 times annually.
Member Services:
Publications, insurance programs including liability, occupational accident and medical discount, special member pricing on events and educational products, discounted business services, Fax-on-Demand system, CEC opportunities and more.
Year Founded:
1982

INTERNATIONAL FEDERATION OF BODYBUILDING AND FITNESS
28232 EUROPOLIS
LAS ROZAS
MADRID, SPAIN
headquarters@ifbb.com
www.ifbb.com
• Rafael Santonja, President
Description:
Founded in 1946. Sanctions amateur and professional bodybuilding contests. IFBB has 173 nations as members. Organizes a world championship each year with an international congress in a different country.

INTERNATIONAL HEALTH, RACQUET & SPORTSCLUB ASSOCIATION (IHRSA)
70 FARGO STREET
BOSTON, MA 02210
617-951-0055
800-228-4772
Fax: 617-951-0056
www.ihrsa.org
• Joe Moore, President & CEO
• Anita Horne Lawlor, Chief Operating Officer

INTERNATIONAL SPORTS SCIENCES ASSOCIATION
1015 MARK AVENUE
CARPINTERIA, CA 93013
805-745-8111
Fax: 805-745-8119
www.issaonline.edu
• Sal Arria, Co-Founder & CEO
Description:
Provides new and improved methods and services to the sports and fitness industries as science and technology advance, and addresses the need for standardization in the club industry.
Year Founded:
1988
Member Services:
Fitness training programs, certification seminars and examinations, youth fitness certification programs, product discounts.

LIFELONG FITNESS ALLIANCE
2682 MIDDLEFIELD ROAD
SUITE Z
REDWOOD CITY, CA 94063
650-361-8282
855-361-8282
Fax: 650-529-9776
step@lifelongfitnessalliance.org
www.lifelongfitnessalliance.org
• Malinda Kaplan, Program Director
Description:
Fifty-plus lifelong fitness (formerly fifty-plus fitness association) is a twenty-six year old nonprofit organization whose mission is to promote an active lifestyle for older people. The organization started at Stanford University as an outgrowth of medical research on the value of exercise for older persons. It currently has approximately 2,000 members across the United States. Fifty-Plus publishes a newsletter, distributes books and videos, and sponsors physical activity events for mid-life and older adults.
Membership Requirements:
Anyone over the age of 50 interested in fitness.
Year Founded:
1980

NATIONAL ACADEMY OF SPORTS MEDICINE
1750 EAST NORTHROP BOULEVARD
SUITE 200
CHANDLER, AZ 85286-1744
800-460-6276
Fax: 460-656-3276
www.nasm.org
• Andrew Wyant, President/General Manager
• Brad Tucker, Vice President, Sales
• Bill Toth, Vice President, Operations

NATIONAL ATHLETIC TRAINERS' ASSOCIATION
1620 VALWOOD PARKWAY
SUITE 115
CARROLLTON, TX 75006
214-637-6282
Fax: 214-637-2206
kimmelcw@apsu.edu
www.nata.org
• Scott Sailor, President
scott_sailor@csufresno.edu
• MaryBeth Horodyski, Vice President
marybethatc@gmail.com
• Kathy Dieringer, Secretary/Treasurer

Member Services:
Placement, continuing education, public relations, government affairs.
Publications:
JOURNAL OF ATHLETIC TRAINING, quarterly; NATA NEWS, monthly newsletter.
Membership Requirements:
Involvement in the athletic training profession.
Description:
Promotes the advancement and improvement of the athletic training profession.
Year Founded:
1950

NATIONAL FITNESS TRADE SHOW
WALLY BOYKO PRODUCTIONS, INC.
PO BOX 2490
WHITE CITY, OR 97503
541-830-0400
meshelle@nationalfitnesstradejournal.com
www.nationalfitnesstradejournal.com
Description:
Established to sanction Ms Fitness contests worldwide; promotes, governs and coordinates Ms Fitness competitions; regulates judging criteria and production format for all Ms Fitness competitions.
Year Founded:
1991

NATIONAL INSTITUTE FOR FITNESS AND SPORT
250 UNIVERSITY BOULEVARD
INDIANAPOLIS, IN 46202
317-274-3432
Fax: 317-274-7408
www.nifs.org
• Jerry Taylor, CEO
(317) 274-3432
• Trudy Coler, Communications Director
(317) 274-3432
• Melanie Roberts, Fitness Center Director
(317) 274-3432
Description:
A nonprofit organization committed to enhancing human health, physical fitness, and athletic performance through research, education and service.
Year Founded:
1985

NATIONAL OPERATING COMMITTEE ON STANDARDS FOR ATHLETIC EQUIPMENT / NOCSAE
11020 KING STREET
SUITE 215
OVERLAND PARK, KS 66210
913-888-1340
Fax: 913-498-8817
mike.oliver@nocsae.org
www.nocsae.org/
• Kenneth Stephens, President
• Robert Cantu, Vice President
• Terry Schlatter, Treasurer
• Lars Fuchs, Secretary
• Mike Oliver, Executive Director/Legal Counsel
mike.oliver@NOCSAE.org
Description:
Commissions research on, and where feasible, establishes standards for protective athletic equipment.
Membership Requirements:
National associations or organizations involved with athletics and with an interest in

protective athletic equipment.
Member Services:
NOCSAE football, baseball/softball, lacrosse, helmet standards; football helmet inspection checklist.
Year Founded:
1969

NATIONAL STRENGTH AND CONDITIONING ASSOCIATION
1885 BOB JOHNSON DRIVE
COLORADO SPRINGS, CO 80906
719-632-6722
800-815-6826
Fax: 719-632-6367
nsca@nsca.com
www.nsca.com
• Gregory Haff, President
• Colin Wilborn, Vice-President
Description:
A nonprofit, educational organization that provides resources and opportunities for professionals in strength and conditioning and related fields.
Year Founded:
1978

PRESIDENT'S COUNCIL ON SPORTS, FITNESS & NUTRITION
1101 WOOTTON PARKWAY
SUITE 560
ROCKVILLE, MD 20852
240-276-9567
fitness@hhs.gov
www.fitness.gov
• Holli Richmond, Executive Director
Description:
The mission of the President's Council on Sports, Fitness & Nutrition is to increase sports participation among youth of all backgrounds and abilities and to promote healthy and active lifestyles for all Americans. Since 1956, the Council has created and promoted programs and initiatives that motivate people of all ages, backgrounds, and abilities to be active and eat healthy.
Publications:
Pamphlets and booklets for personal use and institutional use.
Year Founded:
1956

SHAPE AMERICA SOCIETY OF HEALTH AND PHYSICAL EDUCATORS
1900 ASSOCIATION DRIVE
RESTON, VA 20191
800-213-7193
Fax: 703-476-9527
www.shapeamerica.org
• Steve Jefferies, President
board@shapeamerica.org
• Paul Roetert, CEO
Description:
To promote and support creative and healthy lifestyles through high quality programs in health, physical education, recreation, dance and sport, and to provide members with professional development opportunities that increase knowledge, improve skils, and encourage sound professional practices.
Membership Requirements:
Members must be professionals in their fields.
Membership Services:
Conferences, workshops, standards,

position statements, consulting, speaker's bureau related to health education, dance, sport, physical education, fitness for all ages and recreation.
Publications:
Newsletter, periodically.
Year Founded:
1942

WELLNESS INSTITUTE OF GREATER BUFFALO
65 NIAGARA SQUARE
ROOM 607
BUFFALO, NY 14202
716-851-4052
Fax: 716-851-4309
wellness@city-buffalo.org
www.healthycommunitynetwork.com
• Philip L. Haberstro, Executive Director
Nature of Service:
Non-profit national membership association and network of state governor's councils and community coalition.
Publications:
National Employee Health and Fitness Day planning tool kit
Year Founded:
1979

WORLD NATURAL BODYBUILDING FEDERATION
inbf@epix.net
www.worldnaturalbb.com
Publications:
NATURAL BODYBUILDING AND FITNESS, quarterly.
Membership Requirements:
Must be totally drug-free for minimum 7 years; have won a qualifying event, and be willing to undergo stringent drug-testing.
Description:
Serves to reward abstinence from drug use by staging bodybuilding competitions that are drug-tested and that offer cash prizes to the best natural athletes.
Year Founded:
1989

YMCA USA
101 NORTH WACKER DRIVE
CHICAGO, IL 60606
312-977-0031
800-872-9622
fulfillment@ymca.net
www.ymca.net
• Jennie Carlson, Executive Vice President
Description:
Founded in 1851. Serves to put Christian principles into practice through programs that build healthy spirit, mind and body for all.
Membership Requirements:
Pay membership fees, scholarship assistance may be available
Publications:
Youth Sports Director's Manual; Organizing Successful YMCA Tournament; YMCA Gymnastics Manual; Rookie coaches guides in baseball, basketball, football, gymnastics, soccer, softball, tennis, volleyball, and wrestling; Basketball Players Manuals; Flag Football Players Manual; Soccer Players Manual.

YWCA USA
2025 M STREET NW
SUITE 550
WASHINGTON, DC 20036
202-467-0801
Fax: 202-467-0802
info@ywca.org
www.ywca.org
• Dara Richardson-Heron, CEO
• Casey Harden, Senior Vice President
• Jackie Sam, COO
• Paula Green Johnson, Secretary
• Dara Richardson-Heron, M.D., Chief Executive Officer
Description:
Serves women and girls and works to eliminate racism and sexism. Offers health, physical education and recreation programming and other programs which stress advocacy for social change.
Publications:
HPER programming info, Interchange, biannually. Student publications. ENCORE, YWCA Post Mastectomy Program Newsletter.
Membership Requirements:
Membership through local Associations.
Year Founded:
1858

Fencing Organizations

CANADIAN FENCING FEDERATION
44-1554 CARLING AVE
OTTAWA, ON, CANADA K1Z 7M4
647-476-2401
Fax: 647-476-2402
cff@fencing.ca
fencing.ca
• Caroline Sharp, Executive Director
(613) 323-5605
ed@fencing.ca
• Tim Stang, Technical Director
(647) 476-2401
pa@fencing.ca
• Monica Peterson, High Performance Manager
(250) 661-3542
hppc@fencing.ca
Member Services:
Governing body for fencing in Canada.
Membership Requirements:
Must join through provincial affiliates.
Description:
Promotion and development of fencing in Canada. Manages International High Performance Program; national ranking of registered fencers; elite ranking of fencers who travel abroad, facilitating elite travel arrangements, information about national and international events, funding elite athletes.
Year Founded:
1971

FEDERATION INTERNATIONALE D'ESCRIME (FIE)
MAISON DU SPORT INTERNATIONAL
AVENUE DE RHODANIE 54
LAUSANNE, 1007
+41-21 320 31 15
Fax: +41-21 320 31 16
info@fie.ch
fie.org
• Nathalie Rodriguez, Chief Executive Officer

nr@fie.ch
• Evgeni Tsoukhlo, Deputy Chief Executive Officer
tsoukhlo@mail.ru

NATIONAL INTERCOLLEGIATE WOMEN'S FENCING ASSOCIATION
www.niwfa.com
• Sharon Everson, President
sje112@frontiernet.net
• Jennette Starks-Faulkner, Vice President
jsfaulk1@sbcglobal.net
• Linda Vollkommer-Lynch, Vice President
lvollkom@stevens-tech.edu
Member Services:
Minutes, Directory, Newsletter, information on all events. Annual meetings held second weekend in December, second weekend in March.
Publications:
Newsletter. Minutes of annual meeting. Committee reports. Bylaws, rules and regulations governing competitions.
Membership Requirements:
Colleges and universities granting Bachelors Degrees. $15 annual dues.
Description:
Encourages, promotes and assists in the growth and establishment of women's fencing clubs and teams in the colleges in the U.S. It has conducted an annual team and individual championship since 1929.
Year Founded:
1929

UNITED STATES FENCING COACHES ASSOCIATION
www.usfca.org
• Peter Burchard, President
president@usfca.org
Publications:
SWORDMASTER MAGAZINE, four issues a year.
Membership Requirements:
Teaching of fencing.
Description:
Concerned with teaching and promulgation of the sport of fencing, professional development of fencing masters.
Year Founded:
1941

USA FENCING
4065 SINTON RD
SUITE 140
COLORADO SPRINGS, CO 80907
719-866-4511
Fax: 719-632-5737
information@usfencing.org
www.usfencing.org
• Kris Ekeren, Executive Director
(719) 866-3604
k.ekeren@usfencing.org

Figure Skating Organizations

ICE SKATING INSTITUTE
6000 CUSTER RD
BUILDING 9
PLANO, TX 75023
972-735-8800
Fax: 972-735-8815
www.skateisi.com

• Liz Manglesdorf, Managing Director
(972) 735-8800
liz@skateisi.org
• Elizabeth Kibat, Controller
(972) 735-8800
elizabeth@skateisi.org
• Kim Hansen, ISI National Skating Program
& Events Coordinator
(972) 735-8800
khansen@skateisi.org
• Liz Manglesdorf, ISI National Skating
Programs Coordinator
(972) 735-8800
liz@skateisi.org
• Mary Ann Mangano, Membership
Coordinator
(972) 735-8800
maryann@skateisi.org
• Jeff Anderson, Administrative Service
Manager
(972) 735-8800
Jeff@skateisi.org
Description:
A not-for-profit association that represents
all aspects of the ice arena industry and is
dedicated to providing leadership, education
and other services. They offer a
Recreational Figure Skating Program and
an educational instruction program for
hockey and figure skating instructors.
Year Founded:
1959
Membership:
Categories for membership are individual,
professional, administrative, and related
services.

INTERNATIONAL SKATING UNION
AVENUE JUSTE-OLIVIER 17
LAUSANNE, 1006
www.isu.org
• Jan Dijkema, President
• Tron Espeli, 1st Vice President - Speed
Skating
• Alexander Lakernik, 2nd Vice President -
Figure Skating

PROFESSIONAL SKATERS
ASSOCIATION
3006 ALLEGRO PARK LANE SW
ROCHESTER, MN 55902
507-281-5122
Fax: 507-281-5491
www.skatepsa.com
• Jimmie Santee, Executive Director
jsantee@skatepsa.com
Description:
An international organization that supports
ice skating professionals and skating
coaches through education and
accreditation. Over 100 educational
programs are provided each year to the
more than 6,000 members. It is also the
official coaches education, training and
certification program of US Figure Skating to
the US Olympic Committee.
Publications:
Professional Skater Magazine: Official
bi-monthly newsletter.
Year Founded:
1938

SKATE CANADA
261-1200 ST LAURENT BLVD
PO BOX 15
OTTAWA, ON, CANADA K1K 3B8

613-747-1007
Fax: 613-748-5718
info@skatecanada.ca
skatecanada.ca
• Debra Armstrong, Chief Executive Officer
• Patricia Chafe, Chief Sport Development
Officer
pchafe@skatecanada.ca
Description:
As the largest figure skating governing body
it is committed to the development of
personal excellence through participation in
skating. The organization's structure relies
heavily on volunteers and is divided into 13
sections. Each year an Annual Convention
and General Meeting is held.
Publications:
Newsletter: Above the Crowd

U.S. FIGURE SKATING
20 FIRST ST
COLORADO SPRINGS, CO 80906
719-635-5200
Fax: 719-635-9548
info@usfigureskating.org
www.usfsa.org
• Sam Auxier, President
sauxier@usfigureskating.org
• David Raith, Executive Director
draith@usfigureskating.org
Description:
National governing body for the sport of
figure skating in the U.S. Membership
organization for all Olympic eligible,
competitive athletes.
Membership Requirements:
Individual, or through sanctioned clubs.
Publications:
SKATING, 10 times annually. Rulebook,
annual; Directory, annual; Media Guide,
annual.
Member Services:
Competitions, seminars, test programs,
camps, funding and training assistance.
Year Founded:
1921

USA ROLLER SPORTS
4730 SOUTH STREET
LINCOLN, NE 68506
402-483-7551
Fax: 402-483-1465
www.teamusa.org/USA-Roller-Sports

WORLD FIGURE SKATING MUSEUM AND
HALL OF FAME
20 FIRST ST
COLORADO SPRINGS, CO 80906
719-635-5200
Fax: 719-635-9548
info@worldskatingmuseum.org
www.worldskatingmuseum.org
Description:
The international repository for the sport of
figure skating. The Museum is dedicated to
the preservation and interpretation of figure
skating's history. The U.S. and World Halls
of Fame honors the greatest names in figure
skating.

Fishing Organizations

AMERICAN SPORTFISHING
ASSOCIATION
1001 NORTH FAIRFAX ST
SUITE 501
ALEXANDRIA, VA 22314
703-519-9691
Fax: 703-519-1872
info@asafishing.org
asafishing.org
• Mike Nussman, President & CEO
(703) 519-9691
mnussman@asafishing.org
• Diane Carpenter, Vice President,
Operations & CFO
(703) 519-9691
dcarpenter@asafishing.org
Nature of Service:
The American Sportfishing Association
(ASA) is the sportfishing industry's trade
association, committed to looking out for the
interests of the entire sportfishing
community. It provides the industry with a
unified voice, speaking out out behalf of
sportfishing and boating industries, state
and federal natural resource agencies,
conservation organizations, angler advocacy
groups and outdoor journalists when
emerging laws and policies could
significantly affect sportfising business or
sportfishing itself.
Year Founded:
1921
Member Services:
Annual trade show, annual business
meeting, member discounts, advocacy,
consumer shows.
Membership Requirements:
Varies

B.A.S.S. LLC
bassmaster@emailcustomerservice.com
www.bassmaster.com
Description:
Sports marketing media firm providing an
integrated multi-media program in fishing for
marketers.
Year Founded:
1967

CATSKILL FLY FISHING CENTER &
MUSEUM
1031 OLD ROUTE 17
LIVINGSTON MANOR, NY 12758
845-439-4810
office@cffcm.com
www.cffcm.com
• Glenn Pontier, Executive Director
Description:
Fly fishing center and museum, founded in
1981.

INTERNATIONAL CASTING SPORT
FEDERATION
NOVOSUCHDOLSKA 37
PRAGUE, 16500
info@icsf-castingsport.com
www.icsf-castingsport.com
• Kurt Klamet, President
(+49) 1733910939
kurt.klamet@icsf-castingsport.com
• Helmut Hochwartner, Vice President
(+43) 676 611397
helmut.hochwartner@icsf-castingsport.com
• Josef Dolezal, Secretary General

(420) 6034180490
dr.josef.dolezal@icsf-castingsport.com
year founded
1954

INTERNATIONAL FEDERATION OF FLY FISHERS
5237 U.S. HIGHWAY 89 SOUTH
Suite 11
LIVINGSTON, MT 59047
406-222-9369
Fax: 406-222-5823
www.fedflyfishers.org
• Len Zickler, President & CEO
(406) 222-9369
Description:
Educating and conserving through Fly Fishing
Year Founded:
1965
Number of Members:
12,000
Membership Requirements:
Various types of memberships available including club, foreign association, individual, family, junior, contributing, retail shop, life and sustaining.

INTERNATIONAL GAME FISH ASSOCIATION
300 GULF STREAM WAY
DANIA BEACH, FL 33004
954-927-2628
Fax: 954-924-4299
www.igfa.org
• Rob Kramer, President
• Michael J. Myatt, Director of Corporate Relations
mmyatt@igfa.org
Publications:
World Record Game Fishes book, International Angler, Junior Angler, Offshore Tournament Program, Inshore Tournament Program.
Membership Requirements:
Open to all interested individuals, fishing clubs and organizations.
Description:
Is a nonprofit organization committed to the conservation of game fish and the promotion of responsible, ethical, angling practices through science, education, rule making and record keeping.

IZAAK WALTON LEAGUE OF AMERICA
707 CONSERVATION LANE
GAITHERSBURG, MD 20878
301-548-0150
info@iwla.org
www.iwla.org
• Jeff Deschamps, President
• Kelly Kistner, Vice President
• Jim Storer, Secretary
• Walter Lynn Jr., Treasurer
Publications:
OUTDOOR AMERICA, quarterly magazine; OUTDOOR ETHICS, quarterly newsletter; SPLASH!, quarterly newsletter of Save Our Streams program.
Description:
To conserve, maintain, protect and restore the soil, forest, water and other natural resources of the United States and other lands; to promote means and opportunities for the education of the public with respect to such resources and their enjoyment and wholesome utilization.

Year Founded:
1922

RECREATIONAL BOATING & FISHING FOUNDATION
500 MONTGOMERY ST
SUITE 300
ALEXANDRIA, VA 22314
www.takemefishing.org
• Frank Peterson Jr., President & CEO
(703) 778-5157
fpeterson@rbff.org
Nature of Service:
The Recreational Boating & Fishing Foundation is a nonprofit organization whose mission is to increase participation in recreational angling and boating and thereby increase public awareness and appreciation of the need for protecting, conserving and restoring this nation's aquatic natural resources.
Year Founded:
1998
Publications:
NewsWaves, monthly e-newsletter

TROUT UNLIMITED
1777 N KENT STREET
SUITE 100
ARLINGTON, VA 22209
703-522-0200
800-834-2419
Fax: 703-284-9400
www.tu.org
• Chris Wood, President & CEO
• Elizabeth Maclin, Executive Vice President
• Matt Renaud, Chief Financial Officer
Publications:
TROUT, quarterly magazine.
Description:
Serves to conserve, protect and restore North America's cold water fisheries and their watersheds.
Year Founded:
1959

Football Organizations

AMERICAN FOOTBALL ASSOCIATION
115 HENRY STREET
SUITE 2041
BINGHAMTON, NY 13902
877-624-4485
Fax: 801-838-0175
www.americanfootballassn.com
• Dave Burch, President
Description:
The AFA is dedicated to the advancement of semi-pro/minor league football throughout the United States and serves as the National Organization for non-professional leagues and teams from coast-to-coast.
Year Founded:
1980

AMERICAN FOOTBALL COACHES ASSOCIATION
100 LEGENDS LANE
WACO, TX 76706
254-754-9900
Fax: 254-754-7373
info@afca.com
www.afca.com
• Todd Berry, Executive Director
• Gary Darnell, Associate Executive Director

• Adam Guess, CFO
• Vince Thompson, Director of Media Relations
Publications:
Extra Point (quarterly newsletter), Convention Proceedings Manual, Summer Manual, AFCA Directory
Member Services:
Free registration for Annual Convention and publications. Members are eligible to attend the AFCA Kickoff Luncheon and Awards Luncheon. Members can attend the Coach of the Year Banquet. AFCA members have access to AFCA On-Line, the Association's World Wide Web site.
Membership Requirements:
Levels of membership: Active 1, Active 2; Allied, Foreign Allied.
Founded:
1998

AMERICAN YOUTH FOOTBALL
admin@myayf.com
www.americanyouthfootball.com
• Joe Galat, President/Founder
• Dee Grayer, Football Commissioner
• Craig Karahuta, VP, Football & Cheer Operations
Description:
An international youth football organization established to promote the wholesome development of youth through their association with adult leaders in the sport of American football. Rules and regulations are established to ensure that players play in an atmosphere of safety with a competitive balance between teams.
Year Founded:
1996

FOOTBALL CANADA
825 EXHIBITION WAY
SUITE 205
OTTAWA, ON, CANADA K1S 5J3
613-564-0003
Fax: 613-564-6309
www.footballcanada.com
• Jim Mullin, President
• Shannon Donovan, Executive Director
• Aaron Geisler, Director, Sport
Description:
National sports governing body whose purpose is to initiate, regulate and manage the programs, services and events that promote participation and excellence in Canadian Amateur Football. Membership represents Flag, Touch, and Tackle football as well as players, coaches, officials, and administrators.
Governing Bodies:
British Columbia, Football Alberta, Football Saskatchewan, Football Manitoba, Ontario Football Alliance, Football Quebec, Football Nova Scotia, Football PEI, Football QJFL, CJFL, CFOA.
Year Founded:
1884

FOOTBALL WRITERS ASSOCIATION OF AMERICA
214-870-6516
tiger@fwaa.com
www.sportswriters.net/fwaa
• Doug Lesmerises, President
• Steve Richardson, Executive Director
(214) 870-6516
tiger@fwaa.com

Description:
Consists of writers across America who cover college football. Membership organization that is open to accredited members of the media and other organizations affiliated with college football. With over 1,000 members, the FWAA works to improve communication among those involved with the game of college football; sponsors scholarships for aspiring writers; and offers many membership benefits.
Year Founded:
1941

INTERNATIONAL FEDERATION OF AMERICAN FOOTBALL
79 RUE RATEAU
LA COURNEUVE, 93120
info@ifaf.org
www.ifaf.org
• Richard MacLean, President
• Mac Kaneuji, Director, Development
• Scott Hallenbeck, Vice President
• Chris Josey, Secretary
• Kasper Linden, Director, Competitions
Description:
Currently the IFAF is composed of 64 member nations on 6 continents. Works closely with major US American Football Oragnizations (USA Football, the NFL, NCAA, etc.) with the goal of being part of the international sporting community and developing membership.
Membership:
Members are granted a membership status that is suitable for them depending on their level of development. Four levels of membership: full, associated, temporary, and IFAF Country Administrator.
Founded:
1896 in Canada

MISSOURI VALLEY FOOTBALL CONFERENCE
1818 CHOUTEAU AVENUE
ST. LOUIS, MO 63103
314-444-4360
Fax: 314-444-4361
pattyv@mvc.org
www.valley-football.org
• Patty Viverito, Commissioner
• Mike Kern, Associate Commissioner
kern@mvc.org
• Greg Walter, Associate Commissioner
gwalter@mvc.org
• William Carollo, Coordinator of Officials
carollo@bigten.org
Description:
In 2008, the nine-member Gateway Football Conference and the 10-member Missouri Valley Conference approved changing the Gateway Football Conference name to Missouri Valley Football Conference.
Year Founded:
1985
Number of Members:
10
Members:
Illinois State, Indiana State. Missouri State, North Dakota State, South Dakota State, University of Northern Iowa, University of South Dakota, Southern Illinois-Carbondale, Western Illinois-Youngstown State

NATIONAL FOOTBALL SCOUTING
317-687-8100
info@nfs-nic.com
www.nfs-nic.com
Founded:
In 1982

NFL ALUMNI ASSOCIATION
3000 MIDATLANTIC DRIVE
SUITE 130
MOUNT LAUREL, NJ 08054
877-258-6635
Fax: 862-772-0277
memberservice@nflalumni.org
www.nflalumni.org
• Tracy Porter, Chairman
• Johny Haines, Vice-Chairman
Description:
A charitable organization primarily composed of former pro-football players dedicated to volunteer efforts with the motto Caring for Kids. The organization also offers support to former pro-players experiencing financial or medical hardships. The Alumni Association is covered by a 13-member Board of Directors comprised of retired players. The organization is comprised of 35 regional chapters.
Year Founded:
1967
Membership:
Open to former major league professional team members. Associate membership is availble to those that would like to support the charitable and educational goals of the organization.

NFL INTERNATIONAL/NEW YORK
345 PARK AVENUE
NEW YORK, NY 10154
www.nfl.com
• Roger Goodell, Commissioner
Nature of Sports Service:
Designed to assist the league with its ongoing international agenda. Responds to the growing worldwide interest in the NFL. Includes licensing, sponsorship, merchandising, television distribution, American Bowls and the World League. The NFL International League has divisions in Canada, China, Japan, Mexico, UK and Latin America.

NFL PLAYERS ASSOCIATION
1133 20TH STREET NW
WASHINGTON, DC 20036
800-372-2000
800-372-5535
www.nflpa.com
• DeMaurice Smith, Executive Director
• JC Tretter, President
Description:
Professional association which represents professional football players. It assures that the rights of players are protected; represents players in matters concerning wages, hours and working conditions; provides assistance to charitable and community organizations; and provides other member services and activities.
Year Founded:
1956
Membership Requirements:
Active and retired members of NFL clubs.
Member Services:
Career counseling, investment assistance,

advice on licensing, compensation information, legal assistance.

POP WARNER LITTLE SCHOLARS
586 MIDDLETOWN BOULEVARD
SUITE C-100
LANGHORNE, PA 19047
215-752-2691
Fax: 215-752-2879
www.popwarner.com
• Jon Butler, Executive Director
• Sam Mutz, National Football Commissioner
• Beth Dietz, National Events Manager
• Kevin Allen, National Recruitment & Grant Coordinator
Description:
The largest youth football, cheer, and dance program in the US providing programs for participants aged 5 to 16, in 42 states and several countries.
Year Founded:
1959 on national basis, 1929 on local basis.
Membership Requirements:
Teams must belong to a league that is committed to national standards and rules.
Number of Teams:
13,000
Number of Members:
440,000

PRO FOOTBALL WRITERS OF AMERICA
www.pfwa.org
• Lindsay Jones, President
• Jenny Vrentas, 1st Vice President
Description:
Founded 1962. Promotes the simplification and uniformity of rules in the scoring of games. Works for the improvement of facilities for reporting on professional football and the guarantee of facilities and opportunities on par with other media.
Membership Requirements:
Active Membership - individuals who cover football for a daily newspaper or press association. Statisticians who provide professional records to daily newspapers. Sports editors, assistant sports editors and columnists. Honorary Membership - former active members for ten years before their retirement.
Annual Meetings:
Prior to Super Bowl and NFL owners meeting in March.
Number of Members:
400

PROFESSIONAL FOOTBALL ATHLETIC TRAINERS SOCIETY
2970 CLAIRMONT ROAD NE
SUITE 575
ATLANTA, GA 30329
www.pfats.com
• Reggie Scott, President
• Geoff Kaplan, Secretary
• Ryan Vermillion, Treasurer
Description:
A professional association whose members are the athletic trainers of the NFL. The members of PFATS provide, lead and manage health care for NFL athletes, club employees and members of the NFL community. PFATS is dedicated to ensuring that the highest quality health care is practiced in the NFL. PFATS is guided by the professional integrity and ethical standards of its members and by the unity

they share.
Year Founded:
1982

PROFESSIONAL FOOTBALL RESEARCHERS ASSOCIATION
pfra@profootballresearchers.org
www.profootballresearchers.org
• Mark L. Ford, Executive Director
• Ken Crippen, President
• Roy Sye, VP
• Dave Burch, Secretary
• John Grasso, Treasurer
Description:
Fosters the study of professional football as a significant social and athletic institution. Hopes to establish an accurate historical account of professional football and to disseminate research information. Founded in 1979.
Publications:
COFFIN CORNER, 6 issues per year; ANNUAL; Special publications throughout the year.
Membership Requirements:
Open to anyone with a serious interest in the history of professional football or related subjects. Membership dues are $35 a year.

UNITED STATES FLAG & TOUCH FOOTBALL LEAGUE
general@usftl.com
usftl.sportngin.com
Description:
Governing body of flag football. Hosts the National Flag Football Championships every year on MLK Day weekend in Kissimmee, FL. Partners with the NFL Flag Program for youth participants. Non-profit organization.
Members:
20,000+
Year Founded:
1988

USA FOOTBALL
45 N PENNSYLVANIA STREET
SUITE 700
INDIANAPOLIS, IN 46204
317-614-7750
877-536-6822
support@usafootball.com
www.usafootball.com
• Scott Hallenbeck, Executive Director
Description:
An independent non-profit organization that serves as the governing body of football on youth and amateur levels. It does not operate leagues or teams but serves and strengthens existing leagues through a variety of programs including hosting more than 100 annual training events and offering educational programs for coaches, game officials, youth commissioners, and young players.

Football, College Bowl/Classics

ALAMO BOWL
100 MONTANA STREET
SAN ANTONIO, TX 78203
210-226-2695
info@alamobowl.com
www.alamobowl.com

• Derrick Fox, President/CEO
• Rick Hill, VP Marketing/Communications
Description:
Founded 1991. NCAA college football bowl game in which BIG 12 Conference #4 team will play BIG 10 Conference #4 team. Held at the Alamodome in San Antonio. Previous sponsors have included Sylvania, Mastercard, and Valero.

ARMED FORCES BOWL
505 MAIN STREET
SUITE 270
FORT WORTH, TX 76102
817-810-0012
Fax: 817-810-0252
www.armedforcesbowl.com
• Brant Ringler, Executive Director
(817) 810-0506
Brant.B.Ringler@espn.com
• Monty Clegg, Associate Manager of Events
(817) 810-0016
Monty.Clegg@espn.com
• Trisha Branch, Ticket Manager
(817) 810-0012
Trisha.M.Branch@espn.com
Description:
NCAA post season bowl game in Fort Worth, Texas. Game pays tribute to the men and women of the armed forces.
Year Founded:
2003

BELK BOWL, CHARLOTTE SPORTS FOUNDATION
BANK OF AMERICA STADIUM
800 SOUTH MINT STREET
CHARLOTTE, NC 28202-1518
704-644-4047
Info@CharlotteSports.org
charlottesports.org/event/belk-bowl/
• Jerry Richardson, Owner
• Vacant, President
• Marty Hurney, General Manager
Year Founded:
2002

BIRMINGHAM BOWL
ESPN EVENTS
2 RIVERCHASE OFFICE PLAZA
SUITE 110
BIRMINGHAM, AL 35244
205-733-3776
birminghambowl.com
• Mark Meadows, Executive Director
Mark.R.Meadows@espn.com
• Missy Betres, Senior Manager, ESPN Events
missy.h.betres@espn.com
• Matt Wildt, Director of Ticketing
(205) 329-4121
matt.wildt@birminghambowl.com
• Ted Feeley, Media Relations Director
(205) 704-4147
ted.feeley@birminghambowl.com
Description:
Started in 2006, the Birmingham Bowl is one of fourteen bowl games owned and operated by ESPN Events.

BOCA RATON BOWL
FAU STADIUM
777 GLADES ROAD
BOCA RATON, FL 33431

561-362-3661
jena.lamendola@espn.com
www.cheribundibocaratonbowl.com
• Anthony Barbar, Executive Committee Chairman
Description:
Division I bowl game

CACTUS BOWL
CHASE FIELD
401 E JEFFERSON STREET
PHOENIX, AZ 85251
480-350-0900
Fax: 480-350-0915
fiestabowl.org/cactus-bowl/
• Stephen Leach, Chairman
• Randy Norton, Treasurer
• Gary Hanson, Secretary
Description:
Subdivison bowl competiion.

CAMELLIA BOWL
CRAMTON BOWL
220 HALL STREET
MONTGOMERY, AL 36104
404-862-4730
www.camelliabowl.com
• Will Pope, Sponsorship Director
wpope@camelliabowl.com
• Rusty Reed, National Sponsorship Director
Rusty.w.reed@espn.com
Description:
Division I bowl competition.

CHICK-FIL-A PEACH BOWL
3284 NORTHSIDE PARKWAY
SUITE 550
ATLANTA, GA 30327
404-586-8500
www.chick-fil-apeachbowl.com
• Matt Garvey, Vice President, Communications
mgarvey@cfabowl.com
• Dillon Faulkner, Communications Manager
Year Founded:
1968

CITRUS BOWL
FLORIDA CITRUS BOWL
1 CITRUS BOWL PLACE
ORLANDO, FL 32805
407-423-2476
www.buffalowildwingscitrusbowl.com
Description:
The Citrus Bowl presented by Overtons began as the Tangerine Bowl in 1947. The bowl hosts top teams from the Big Ten and Southeastern conferences.

COTTON BOWL CLASSIC
COWBOYS STADIUM
ONE LEGENDS WAY
FAIRPARK
ARLINGTON, TX 76011
817-892-4800
Fax: 817-892-4810
coach@attcottonbowl.com
www.attcottonbowl.com
• Rick Baker, President
• Marty MacInnis, Executive VP/CFO
• Charlie Fiss, VP Communications
charlie@attcottonbowl.com
• Michael Konradi, VP External Affairs
michael@attcottonbowl.com
• Amy Scott, Director Ticket Operations

Description:
Founded January 1, 1937. Collge bowl game between Big 12 Conference # 2 vs. Southeastern Conference. Television: FOX Network.

DETROIT BOWL (QUICK LANE BOWL)
FORD FIELD EXECUTIVE OFFICES
2000 BRUSH STREET
SUITE 200
DETROIT, MI 48226
313-262-2010
Fax: 313-262-2009
www.motorcitybowl.com
• George Perles, Chief Executive Officer
• Lloyd Carr, President
• Ken Hoffman, Executive Director
• John Perles, Director of Operations
• Gary Van Dam, Director of Corporate Relations
• Tim Moore, Director of Media Relations
Nature of Sports Service:
NCAA college football bowl game in which Mid-American Conference team will play a BIG 10 Conference team. Formerly the Motor City Bowl. Played at Ford Field.
Year Founded:
1997

EAST-WEST SHRINE GAME
TROPICANA FIELD
ONE TROPICANA DR
ST. PETERSBURG, FL 33705
813-281-8686
Fax: 813-281-8687
www.shrinegame.com
• Nick Themas, Chairman
• Harold Richardson, Executive Director
• Tom Reeves, Director of Game Operations
Description:
The East-west Shrine Game is the oldest of the post-season collegiate bowl games. Since 1925, this annual event raises money for Shriners Hospitals for Children, an international heatlh care system of 22 hospitals dedicated to providing pediatric specialty care at no charge, regardless of need.

FAMOUS POTATO IDAHO BOWL
1109 MAIN STREET
SUITE 299B
BOISE, ID 83702
208-424-1011
Fax: 208-424-1121
• Kevin McDonald, Executive Director
• Danielle Brazil, Director Marketing
• Ron Dibelius, Director Sales
Description:
Founded in 1997. ACC v WAC. Held at Bronco Stadium in Boise. Television: ESPN

FIESTA BOWL
UNIVERSITY OF PHOENIX STADIUM
7135 EAST CAMELBACK RD
SUITE 190
TEMPE, AZ 85251
480-350-0900
www.fiestabowl.org
• Duane Woods, Chairman
• John Zidich, Secretary
• Dan Lewis, Chair-Elect
• John Junker, President/CEO
Description:
NCAA college football bowl game in which a PAC 10 Conference team will play a BIG East Conference team or Notre Dame. Sun

Devil Stadium. Television: NFL Network
Year Founded:
1989

FOSTERS FARM BOWL
LEVIS STADIUM
4900 MARIE P. DEBARTOLO WAY
SANTA CLARA, CA 95054
415-972-1812
Fax: 415-947-2925
• Gary Cavalli, Executive Director
• Ryan Oppelt, Assistant Executive Director
• Doug Kelly, Media Services
• Sara M Hunt, Game Operations
Description:
A post-season college football bowl game certified by the NCAA that has been played annually in San Francisco, California, since 2002. The game matches teams from the Pac-10 and ACC conferences.

GATOR BOWL
EVERBANK FIELD
1 GATOR BOWL BLVD
JACKSONVILLE, FL 32202
904-798-1700
Fax: 904-632-2080
gba@gatorbowl.com
www.gatorbowl.com
• Daniel Kennedy Murphy, Chairman
• Stephen Tremel, Chairman-Elect/Marketing
• Heather Duncan, Secretary
Description:
The Gator Bowl Association was founded in 1945. In 1955, the Gator Bowl Classic was the first-ever coast-to-coast telecast of a Bowl game and it has been nationally televised ever since. Today, the Gator Bowl is held at Alltel Stadium in Jacksonville.
Sponsor:
Tax Slayer.com at Ever Bank Field

GODADDY BOWL
PO BOX 850909
LADD-PEEBLES STADIUM
MOBILE, AL 36685
251-635-0011
contactgmac@gmacbowl.com
www.gmacbowl.com
• Jerry Silverstein, President
• Frank Modarelli, Executive Director
• Sherrie Dyal, General Manager
• Julie Jeter, Director Marketing/Media Relations
Nature of Sports Service:
NCAA college football bowl game in which a Mid-American Conference team plays a Conference USA team, originally known as the Alabama Bowl. Played in Ladd-Peebles Stadium in Mobile. (1999)

HAWAII BOWL
SHERATON HAWAII BOWL
841 BISHOP STREET
SUITE 2100
HONOLULU, HI 96813
808-523-3688
Fax: 808-523-3712
info@hawaiibowlfoundation.org
www.sheratonhawaiibowl.com
• David Matlin, Executive Director
• Daryl Garvin, Associate Executive Director
• Derek Inouchi, Media Relations
• Brad Motooka, Game Operations
Year Founded:
2002

Nature of Sports Service:
NCAA college football bowl game in which a Conference USA team will play Western Athletic Conference team.

HEART OF DALLAS BOWL
COTTON BOWL STADIUM
5201 N. O'CONNOR BLVD
SUITE 300
IRVING, TX 75039
214-774-1300
214-389-4299
• George Ellis, Chief Financial Officer
• Jon Heidtke, General Manager
• Andrew Hunt, Chief Executive Officer

HOLIDAY BOWL
QUALCOMM STADIUM
PO BOX 601400
SAN DIEGO, CA 92160
619-285-5061
Fax: 619-281-7947
info@holidaybowl.com
www.holidaybowl.com
• Bruce Binkowski, Executive Director
(619) 283-5808
bink@holidaybowl.com
• Mark Neville, Director Communications
(619) 283-5808
mneville@holidaybowl.com
• Cheryl Tishue, Game Operations
Description:
Post-season collegiate football game, involving the third selection from the Big 12 Conference vs. the runner-up from the PAC-10 Conference. Game played at Qualcomm Stadium, San Diego, CA. Television: ESPN. In 1978 at Qualcom Stadium

INDEPENDENCE BOWL
401 MARKET STREET
SUITE 120
SHREVEPORT, LA 71101
318-221-0712
888-414-2695
Fax: 318-221-7366
www.independencebowl.org
• John Hubbard, Chairman
• Troy J. Broussard, Vice Chairman
• Kyle McInnis, First Vice Chairman
• Paul Pratt, Second Vice Chairman
Description
Founded in 1976. Currently called the PetroSun Independence Bowl, this game is held at Independence Stadium in Shreveport.

LAS VEGAS BOWL
SAM BOYD STADIUM
2140 PEBBLE RD
SUITE 200
LAS VEGAS, NV 89123
702-732-3912
Fax: 702-732-4481
www.lvbowl.com
• Dan Hanneke, Executive Director
• Mark Wallington, Media Relations
• Melissa Meacham-Grossman, Game Operations
Description:
NCAA college football bowl game in which Mountain West Conference first pick team will play PAC 12 Conference #4 or #5 team.
Year Founded:
1992

Stadium:
Sam Boyd Stadium

LIBERTY BOWL
LIBERTY BOWL MEMORIAL STADIUM
335 S HOLLYWOOD STREET
MEMPHIS, TN 38104-5923
901-729-4344
general@libertybowl.org
www.libertybowl.org
• Harold Graeter, Associate Executive
Director
hgraeter@libertybowl.org
• Ron Higgins, Media Liaison
Description:
Founded in 1959. Champion of Conference
USA vs. Champion of Southeastern
Conference. Television: ESPN.

MIAMI BEACH BOWL
MARLINS PARK
501 MARLINS WAY
MIAMI, FL 33125
305-480-1342
miamibeachbowl.com
• Blake Guthrie, VP Operations
BGuthrie@miamibeachbowl.com
• Maureen Licursi, Director,
Marekting/Ticket Sales
MLicursi@miamibeachbowl.com
Description:
Division I bowl competition.

MILITARY BOWL
NAVY-MARINE CORPS MEMORIAL
STADIUM
1742 NORTH ST. NW
ANNAPOLIS, MD 20036
202-776-2509
• Steve Beck, President/CEO
• Maureen Licursi, Marketing & Media
Director
• Bob Treseler, Director Corporate
Development & Sales
• Lauren Schweiter, Game Operations
• Josh Barr, Media
Description:
Post-season college football game.
Founded 2008. Television: ESPN
Sponsor:
Northrop; Grumman

MUSIC CITY BOWL
414 UNION STREET
SUITE 800
NASHVILLE, TN 37219
615-743-3130
Fax: 615-244-3540
generalinfo@nashvillesports.com
www.musiccitybowl.com
• Scott Ramsey, President/CEO
(615) 743-3122
• Dave Herrell, VP Marketing/Development
(615) 743-3124
DHerrell@NashvilleSports.com
• Gary Karl Alexander, Senior VP/COO
(165) 743-3132
GAlexander@NashvilleSports.com
Description:
Founded 1998. Southeastern Conference
team vs. Big Ten team. Location Coliseum
in Nashville Tennessee. Television: ESPN.

NEW ERA PINSTRIPE BOWL
YANKEE STADIUM
ONE EAST 161ST STREET
BRONX, NY 10451
646-977-8400
pinstripebowl@yankees.com
web.pinstripebowl.com
• Mark Holtzman, Executive Director
• Emily Hamel, Director
• Sarah Schuler, Senior Manager, Marketing
Founded:
2010

NEW MEXICO BOWL
UNIVERSITY STADIUM
801 UNIVERSITY SE
SUITE 104
ALBUQUERQUE, NM 87106
505-925-5999
Fax: 505-272-7131
www.gildannewmexicobowl.com
• Jeff Siembieda, Executive Director
jeffrey.c.siembieda@espn.com
• RaeAnn McKernan, Media Information
• Cary Colbert, Sup. Of Ops & Sales
Fulfillment
cary.l.colbert@espn.com
Description:
The New Mexico Bowl was first held in
2006. It takes place on the Saturday after
Christmas at University Stadium on the
University of New Mexico campus, and pits
the Mountain West Conference against the
Western Athletic Conference in the state's
only annual nationally televised sporting
event.

NEW ORLEANS BOWL
MERCEDES-BENZ SUPERDOME
2020 ST. CHARLES AVE
NEW ORLEANS, LA 70130
504-525-5678
Fax: 504-529-1622
www.neworleansbowl.org
• Alison Comeaux, Game Operations
• Allison Hjortsberg, Media Relations
• Tricia Lowe, Marketing/Sales
Stadium:
Superdome
Description:
Certified by NCAA in April 2001

DISCOVER ORANGE BOWL
14360 NW 77TH COURT
MIAMI LAKES, FL 33016
305-341-4700
Fax: 305-341-4771
www.orangebowl.org
• Eric L. Poms, CEO
• Kim Garcia, Director of Events
• Larry Wahl, VP Media & Public Relations
• Jose Braojos, Director Ticket Sales
jbraojos@orangebowl.org
Description:
NCAA postseason football bowl game
played at Pro Player Stadium. Game is part
of the Bowl Championship Series.
Television: ABC.
Publications:
ORANGE BOWL TODAY, four times
annually; Game Program; Media Guide;
Corporate Report, four times annually.
Stadium:
Sun Life

OUTBACK BOWL
4211 WEST BOY SCOUT BOULEVARD
SUITE 560
TAMPA, FL 33607
813-874-2695
Fax: 813-873-1959
info@outbackbowl.com
www.outbackbowl.com
• Jim McVay, President/CEO
• Mike Schulze, Director Communications
• Becky Weightman, Coordinator of Events
Description:
New Years Day football bowl game. Big 10
Conference vs. Southeastern Conference.
Held at Raymond James Stadium in Tampa.
Founded:
In 1986.

POINSETTIA BOWL
QUALCOMM STADIUM
9449 FRIARS ROAD, L-55
SAN DIEGO, CA 92108
619-285-5061
info@holidaybowl.com
• Bruce Binkowski, Executive Director
(619) 283-5808
bink@holidaybowl.com
• Mark Neville, Director Communications
(619) 283-5808
mneville@holidaybowl.com
• Callye Cannheim, Marketing Services
Description
The Poinsettia Bowl features a Mountain
West Conference team against one of
several naval bases in the San Diego area.
It is presented by the San Diego Credit
Union.

POPEYES BAHAMAS BOWL
11001 RUSHMORE DRIVE
CHARLOTTE, NC 28277
704-973-5077
www.popeyesbahamasbowl.com
• Richard Giannini, Executive Director
• Lea Miller, Director Of Sales/Marketing
• T.R. Hollis, Event Coordinator
Description:
DI bowl game hosted in Nassau, Bahamas
annually.

ROSE BOWL
391 SOUTH ORANGE GROVE
BOULEVARD
PASADENA, CA 91184
626-449-4100
rosepr@rosemail.org
www.tournamentofroses.com
• P. Scott McKibben, Executive Director
(626) 449-4100
• Sheri Wish, Chief Revenue Officer
(626) 449-4100
• Kevin R. Ash, Chief Administrative Officer,
Rose Bowl Game
(626) 449-4100
• Gina Chappin, Director of Media, Rose
Bowl Game
(626) 449-4100
Description:
Known as 'The Granddaddy of Them All',
the Rose Bowl Game kicked off a myriad of
college football legacies in 1902. Since then,
the game has showcased 17 Heisman
Trophy winners, produced 29 national
champions, featured 193 consesnsus
All-Americans and honored 101 college
legends by inducting them into the Rose
Bowl Hall of Fame.

Publications:
Rose Parade Program, Rose Bowl Program, Rose Bowl Media Guide.
Teams:
Big Ten Champion vs. Pac-12 Champion
Stadium:
Rose Bowl

RUSSELL ATHLETIC BOWL
1610 W CHURCH ST.
ORLANDO, FL 32805-2451
407-423-2476
800-297-2695
Fax: 407-425-8451
www.fcsports.com
• Steve Hogan, Chief Executive Officer
• Carol Herbster, Executive Assistant
• Greg Creese, Director Communications

SENIOR BOWL
151 DAUPHIN STREET
MOBILE, AL 36602
251-438-2276
888-736-2695
Fax: 251-432-0409
srbowl@seniorbowl.com
www.seniorbowl.com
• Steve Hale, President/CEO
• Chris Morgan, Director of Sales & Marketing
chris@seniorbowl.com
• Kevin McDermond, Public Relations Director
• Sonya Rayburn, Sales & Community Affairs Director
sonya@seniorbowl.com
Description:
College All-Star game featuring the best college seniors coached by NFL coaching staffs.

ST. PETERSBERG BOWL
TROPICANA FIELD
ONE TROPICANA DRIVE
ST. PETERSBURG, FL 33705
727-825-3137
888-326-7297
• Brett Dulaney, Executive Director
• Carlos Padilla II, Manages Event Sponsorship and Marketing
• Jeff Famis, Media Contact
Description:
The St. Pete Bowl is a new bowl game first played in 2008. Held at Tropicana Field in St. Petersburg, it is sponsored by magicJack.

SUGAR BOWL
MERCEDES-BENZ SUPERDOME
2020 ST. CHARLES AVE
NEW ORLEANS, LA 70130
504-525-5678
www.allstatesugarbowl.org
• Bill Ferrantie, Executive Director
• Tricia Lowe, Marketing & Sales
• Allison Hjortsberg, Media
• Alison Comeaux, Game Operations
Sponsors:
Greater New Orleans Sports Hall of Fame, The Manning Award, The College Football Hall of Fame, the local chapter of the National Football Foundation.
Description:
Known for its oustanding tradition of providing the best action that college football has to offer.

SUN BOWL
4150 PINNACLE STREET
SUITE 100
EL PASO, TX 79902-3116
915-533-4416
800-915-BOWL
Fax: 915-533-0661
kristie@sunbowl.org
www.sunbowl.org
• Bernie Olivas, Executive Director
• Joe Daubach, Special Events Director
• Ellen Hughes, Ticket Manager
• Trenten Hillburn, Director Media Relations
• Pam Carter, Financial Manager
• Jay Pritchard, Marketing Director
Description:
Founded 1934. Year-round community organization for city of El Paso, organized to achieve (1) year-round activities which draw national recognition and publicity for El Paso, and (2) put on nationally prominent college football bowl game. Games played at Sun Bowl Stadium. PAC 10 #3 vs. Big 10 #5. Television: CBS. Other events include: Sierra Sun Classic Basketball Tournament; Savane College All America Golf Classic. Hosts the 2nd oldest collegiate bowl game.
Stadium:
Sun Bowl Stadium

TEXAS BOWL
RELIANT STADIUM
2 RELIANT PARK
HOUSTON, TX 77054-1373
832-667-2000
www.thetexasbowl.com
• Jamey Rootes, Executive Director
• Davey Fletcher, Marketing/Sales
• Amy Palcic, Media
• Callye Dannheim, Game Operations

Football, Professional Leagues/Teams

CANADIAN FOOTBALL LEAGUE/CFL
50 WELLINGTON STREET E
3RD FLOOR
TORONTO, ON, CANADA M5E 1C8
416-322-9650
Fax: 416-322-9651
www.cfl.ca
• Randy Ambrosie, Commissioner
• Greg Dick, Chief Financial Officer
• David Goldstein, COO
History:
The Canadian Football League was founded in 1958, in Montreal, Quebec, after the Canadian Football Council (CFC) left the Candaian Rugby Union (CRU). Since 2010 the league has expanded stadiums and added the forthcoming Ottawa Redblacks to its rosters.
Teams:
9
Founded:
1958

Teams:

BC LIONS
BC PLACE
777 PACIFIC BLVD
VANCOUVER, BC, CANADA V6B 4Y8
604-930-5466
fanservices@bclions.com
www.bclions.com

• David Braley, Owner/Chairman
• Rick LeLacheur, President
• Neil McEvoy, Co-General Manager/Director, Football Operations
• Rick Campbell, Co-General Manager/Head Coach
Home Field:
BC Place. Seating capacity 54,320.

CALGARY STAMPEDERS
MCMAHON STADIUM
1817 CROWCHILD TRAIL NW
CALGARY, AB, CANADA T2M 4R6
403-289-0205
www.stampeders.com
• John Hufnagel, President/General Manager
• Dave Dickenson, Head Coach
Home Field:
McMahon Stadium. Seating capacity 35,650.

EDMONTON ESKIMOS
THE BRICK FIELD AT COMMONWEALTH STADIUM
11000 STADIUM ROAD
EDMONTON, AB, CANADA T5H 4E2
780-448-1525
Fax: 780-448-2531
comments@esks.com
www.esks.com
• Chris Presson, CEO/President
• Brock Sunderland, General Manager/VP, Football Operations
• Jaime Elizondo, Head Coach
Home Field:
Commonwealth Stadium. Seating capacity 60,000.

HAMILTON TIGER-CATS
TIM HORTONS FIELD
64 MELROSE AVE N
HAMILTON, ON, CANADA L8L 8C1
905-547-2287
Fax: 905-547-8423
customerservice@ticats.ca
ticats.ca
• Scott Mitchell, CEO
• Scott Mitchell, CEO
• Orlando Steinauer, Head Coach
Home Field:
Tim Hortons Field. Seating capacity 22,500.

MONTREAL ALOUETTES
PERCIVAL MOLSON MEMORIAL STADIUM
475 PINE AVE W
MONTREAL, QC, CANADA H2W 1S4
514-787-2500
Fax: 514-871-2277
info@montrealalouettes.com
www.montrealalouettes.com
• Mario Cecchini, President
• Danny Maciocia, General Manager
• Khari Jones, Head Coach
Home Field:
Percival Molson Memorial Stadium. Seating capacity 25,012.

OTTAWA REDBLACKS
TD PLACE
1015 BANK STREET
OTTAWA, ON, CANADA K1S 3W7
613-232-6767 EXT 1
Fax: 613-232-5586
info@ottawaredblacks.com
www.ottawaredblacks.com
• Marcel Desjardins, General Manager
• Paul LaPolice, Head Coach
Home Field:
TD Place. Seating Capacity 24,000.

SASKATCHEWAN ROUGHRIDERS
1734 ELPHINSTONE STREET
TICKET OFFICE
REGINA, SK, CANADA S4P 1K1
888-474-3377
www.riderville.com

- Craig Reynolds, CEO/President
- Jeremy O'Day, General Manager
- Craig Dickenson, Head Coach
Home Field:
Mosaic Stadium at Taylor Field. Seating capacity 32,848.

TORONTO ARGONAUTS
45 MANITOBA DRIVE
TORONTO, ON, CANADA M6K 3C3
416-341-2746
clientservices@argonauts.ca
www.argonauts.ca
- Bill Manning, President
- Michael Clemons, General Manager
- Ryan Dinwiddie, Head Coach
Home Field:
BMO Field.

WINNIPEG BLUE BOMBERS
INVESTORS GROUP FIELD
315 CHANCELLOR MATHESON ROAD
WINNIPEG, MB, CANADA R3T 1Z2
204-784-2583
bbombers@bluebombers.com
www.bluebombers.com
- Kyle Walters, General Manager
- Mike O'Shea, Head Coach
Home Field:
Investors Group Field. Seating capacity 33,420-40,000.

INDOOR FOOTBALL LEAGUE
1607 S LOCUST STREET
SUITE A
GRAND ISLAND, NE 68802
804-643-7277
Fax: 804-643-7278
www.goifl.com
- Todd Tryon, Commissioner
- Robert Loving, Chief Financial Officer
Description:
The Indoor Football League is a professional football league serving the purpose of entertaining communities in which we play, and promoting players to the NFL.
Teams:
17

Teams:

ARIZONA RATTLERS
201 E JEFFERSON STREET
PHOENIX, AZ 85004
602-513-8282
info@azrattlers.com
www.azrattlers.com
- Ron Shurts, Owner
- Jeff Jarnigan, General Manager
- Kevin Guy, Team President/Head Coach

BISMARCK BUCKS
618 N 3RD STREET
BISMARCK, ND 58501
701-595-0771
www.bismarckbucks.com
- Heidi Ripplinger, General Manager
- Rod Miller, Head Coach

CEDAR RAPIDS RIVER KINGS
240 33RD AVENUE SW
SUITE D
CEDAR RAPIDS, IA 52402
319-382-9339
www.goriverkings.com
- Reggie Harris, General Manager
- Victor Mann, Head Coach

COLUMBUS WILD DOGS
225 E SPRING ST
COLUMBUS, OH 43215
614-826-7120
www.columbuswilddogs.com
- Dave Whinham, President, CEO & General Manager
- Titus Donnell, VP, Finance & Administration
- Bobby Olive, Head Coach

DUKE CITY GLADIATORS
7802 MENAUL BOULEVARD NE
ALBUQUERQUE, NM 87110
505-226-8006 EXT 0
www.dukecitygladiators.com
- Gina Prieskorn-Thomas, Owner
- Scott Thomas, Owner
- Martino Theus, Head Coach

FRISCO FIGHTERS
9300 WADE BLVD
SUITE 320
FRISCO, TX 75035
469-384-2552 EXT 0
info@friscofighters.com
www.friscofighters.com
- Stephen Evans, President & General Manager
- Clint Dolezel, Head Coach

GREEN BAY BLIZZARD
788 ARMED FORCES DRIVE
GREEN BAY, WI 54304
920-499-2549
office@greenbayblizzard.com
www.greenbayblizzard.com
- Kathy Treankler, Owner
- Larry Treankler, Owner
- Corey Roberson, Head Coach

IOWA BARNSTORMERS
730 3RD STREET
DES MOINES, IA 50309
515-633-2255
www.theiowabarnstormers.com
- Jeff Lamberti, Owner/President
- Ameer Ismail, Head Coach

LOUISVILLE XTREME
1300 W MUHAMMAD ALI BLVD
SUITE 118
LOUSVILLE, KY 40203
www.louxtreme.com
- Chris Redman, Team President
- Victor Cole, General Manager
- Mark Stoute, Head Coach

MASSACHUSETTS PIRATES
50 FRANKLIN ST
SUITES 200-201
WORCHESTER, MA 01608
508-452-6277
www.masspiratesfootbball.com
- Jawad Yatim, Co-Owner/President/General Manager
- Jawad Yatim, Owner/President/General Manager
- Patrick Pass, Head Coach

NORTHERN ARIZONA WRANGLERS
3201 N MAIN ST
PRESCOTT VALLEY, AZ 86314
928-379-5581
www.nazwranglers.com
- Trey Medlock, President
- Dominic Bramante, Head Coach

OAKLAND PANTHERS
OAKLAND ARENA
7000 COLISEUM WAY
OAKLAND, CA 94621
www.oakland-panthers.com
- Roy Choi, Co-Owner
- Marshawn Lynch, Co-Owner
- Kurt Bryan, Head Coach

QUAD CITY STEAMWHEELERS
4850 COMPETITION DRIVE
BETTENDORF, IA 52722
563-888-1551
info@steamwheelersfootball.com
steamwheelersfootball.com
- Doug Bland, Owner/General Manager
- Cory Ross, Head Coach

SAN DIEGO STRIKE FORCE
3636 CAMINO DEL RIO N
SUITE 120
SAN DIEGO, CA 92108
619-340-1300
info@sdstrikeforce.com
www.sdstrikeforce.com
- Ryan Eucker, General Manager
- Burt Grossman, Head Coach

SIOUX FALLS STORM
5901 S SOUTHEASTERN AVE
SIOUX FALLS, SD 57108
605-274-6686
admin@siouxfallsstorm.com
www.siouxfallsstorm.com
- Kurtiss Riggs, General Manager/Head Coach

SPOKANE SHOCK
157 S HOWARD STREET
SUITE 100
SPOKANE, WA 99201
509-934-2255
thespokaneshock.com
- Sam Adams, Owner/CEO
- Billy Back, Head Coach

TUCSON SUGAR SKULLS
2500 E AJO WAY
KINO STADIUM
TUCSON, AZ 85726
520-573-3000
www.tucsonsugarskulls.com
- Phil Sidoti, General Manager, Business Operations
- Dixie Wooten, Head Coach

NATIONAL FOOTBALL LEAGUE/NFL
345 PARK AVENUE
NEW YORK, NY 10154
www.nfl.com
- Roger Goodell, Commissioner
- Troy Vincent, Executive VP, Football Operations
- Dawn Aponte, Chief Football Administration Officer
- Arthur McAffee, Senior VP, Player Engagement
- Tracy Perlamn, Senior VP, Football Communications & Marketing
- Alberto Riveron, Senior VP, Officiating
- Natara Holloway, VP, Business Operations & Strategy
Description:
Founded 1920. Promotes, regulates and governs 32 professional football franchises in the U.S.
Publications:
NFL RECORD & FACT BOOK, annual; GAME DAY Magazine, for each game; NFL REPORT, quarterly.

Teams:

ARIZONA CARDINALS
STATE FARM STADIUM
1 CARDINALS DRIVE
GLENDALE, AZ 85305
602-379-0101
800-999-1402
askquestions@cardinals.nfl.net
www.azcardinals.com

- Michael J. Bidwill, Owner
- Steve Keim, General Manager
- Kliff Kingsbury, Head Coach
- Terry McDonough, Senior Personnel Executive
- Chris Culmer, Director, College Scouting
- Steve Bomar, VP, Ticketing
- Lisa Manning, Senior VP, Marketing
- David Koeninger, General Counsel
- Dru Grigson, Director, Player Personnel
- Greg Lee, Chief Financial Officer
- Tom Reed, Head Athletic Trainer
- Matt Harriss, Director, Football Administration
Description:
State Farm Stadium
Founded:
1920

ATLANTA FALCONS
MERCEDES BENZ STADIUM
1 AMB DRIVE
ATLANTA, GA 30313
770-965-3115
fans@falcons.nfl.com
www.atlantafalcons.com
- Arthur Blank, Owner/Chair
- Rich McKay, President/CEO
- Terry Fontenot, General Manager
- Arthur Smith, Head Coach
Founded:
1966

BALTIMORE RAVENS
M&T BANK STADIUM
1101 RUSSELL STREET
BALTIMORE, MD 21230
410-261-7283
contact.us@ravens.nfl.net
www.baltimoreravens.com
- Stephen J. Bisciotti, Owner
- Richard W. Cass, President
- Eric DeCosta, Executive VP/General Manager
- John Harbaugh, Head Coach
- Bob Eller, Senior VP, Operations
- Corey Frazier, Professional Scout
- Baker Koppelman, Senior VP, Ticket Sales & Operations
- Brad Downs, Senior VP, Marketing
- Jeff Goering, Chief Financial Officer
- Kevin Rochlitz, Chief Sales Officer
- Roy Sommerhof, Senior VP, Stadium Operations
Founded:
1996
Description:
M&T Bank Stadium.

BUFFALO BILLS
NEW ERA FIELD
ONE BILLS DRIVE
ORCHARD PARK, NY 14127
www.buffalobills.com
- Terry Pegula, Owner/CEO
- Kim Pegula, Owner/President
- Brandon Beane, General Manager
- Sean McDermott, Head Coach
- Malik Boyd, Director, Pro Personnel
- Terrance Gray, Director, College Scouting
- Jim Overdorf, Senior VP, Football Administration
- John Polka, Executive Director, Stadium Operations
Description:
New Era Field

CAROLINA PANTHERS
BANK OF AMERICA STADIUM
800 SOUTH MINT STREET
CHARLOTTE, NC 28202
704-358-7000
feedback@panthers.nfl.com
www.panthers.com
- David A. Tepper, Owner
- Scott Fitterer, General Manager
- Matt Rhule, Head Coach
- Sean Padden, VP, Football Operations
- Jeff Morrow, Executive Director, Player Personnel

- Kristi Coleman, VP/Chief Financial Officer
- Joe LaBue, VP, Ticket Sales & Services
Description:
Bank of America Stadium
Founded:
In 1993.

CHICAGO BEARS
SOLDIER FIELD
1410 MUSEUM CAMPUS DRIVE
CHICAGO, IL 60605
www.chicagobears.com
- Ted Phillips, President/CEO
- George H. McCaskey, Chairman
- Ryan Pace, General Manager
- Matt Nagy, Head Coach
- Mark Sadowski, Director, College Scouting
- Brendan Pierce, Director, Ticket Sales & Service
- Scott Hagel, Senior VP, Marketing & Communications
- Josh Lucas, Director, Player Personnel
- Karen Murphy, Chief Financial Officer
Description:
Soldier Field

CINCINNATI BENGALS
ONE PAUL BROWN STADIUM
PAUL BROWN STADIUM
CINCINNATI, OH 45202
513-621-3550
webmaster@bengals.nfl.net
www.bengals.com
- Mike Brown, President
- Zac Taylor, Head Coach
- Duke Tobin, Director, Player Personnel
- Steven Radicevic, Director, Professional Scouting
- Bob Bedinghaus, Director, Business Development
- Johanna Kappner, Chief Financial Officer
- Duane Haring, Director, Ticket Sales & Service
Founded:
In 1967.
Stadium:
Paul Brown Stadium

CLEVELAND BROWNS
76 LOU GROZA BOULEVARD
BEREA, OH 44017
440-891-5000
www.clevelandbrowns.com
- J.W. Johnson, Owner/Executive VP
- Andrew Berry, General Manager/Executive VP, Football Ops.
- Kevin Stefanski, Head Coach
- Ken Kovash, VP, Player Personnel
- Mike Cetta, Director, Scouting Research
- David Lee, Director, Ticket Operations
- Laurie Rice, Director, Finance
Description:
Cleveland Brown Stadium
Founded:
In 1945.

DALLAS COWBOYS
AT&T STADIUM
ONE AT&T WAY
ARLINGTON, TX 76011
817-892-8000
www.dallascowboys.com
- Jerry W. Jones, Owner/President/General Manager
- Stephen Jones, COO/Director, Player Personnel
- Charlotte Jones, Executive VP/Chief Brand Officer
- Mike McCarthy, Head Coach
- Jerry Jones, Jr., Executive VP, Sales & Marketing
Description:
AT&T Stadium
Founded:
In 1960.
Seating Capacity:
100,000+

DENVER BRONCOS
MILE HIGH STADIUM
1701 BRYANT STREET
DENVER, CO 80204
303-649-9000
www.denverbroncos.com
- Pat Bowlen, Owner
- George Paton, General Manager
- Joe Ellis, President/CEO
- John Elway, President, Football Operations
- Vic Fangio, Head Coach
- Chip Conway, Senior VP, Operations
- A.J. Durso, Director, Pro Personnel
- Katie Delay, Senior Director, Ticket Operations
- Ted Santiago, Senior Director, Marketing
Description:
Mile High Stadium
Founded:
In 1960.

DETROIT LIONS
FORD FIELD
2000 BRUSH STREET
DETROIT, MI 48226
313-262-2000
www.detroitlions.com
- Sheila Ford Hamp, Owner/Chair
- Rod Wood, President & CEO
- Brad Holmes, Executive VP/General Manager
- Dan Campbell, Head Coach
- Rob Lohman, Director, Pro Scouting
- Dave Sears, Director, College Scouting
- Kelly Kozole, Senior VP, Business Development
- Emily Griffin, VP, Marketing
- Allison Maki, Chief Financial Officer
Description:
Ford Field
Founded:
In 1934.

GREEN BAY PACKERS
LAMBEAU FIELD ATRIUM
1265 LOMBARDI AVENUE
GREEN BAY, WI 54304
920-569-7500
Fax: 920-569-7301
www.packers.com
- Mark Murphy, President/CEO
- Brian Gutekunst, General Manager
- Matt LaFleur, Head Coach
- Russ Ball, Executive VP/Director, Football Operations
- Jason McDonough, Director, Ticketing & Premium Seating
- Gabrielle Valdez Dow, VP, Marketing & Fan Engagement
- Ed Policy, COO & General Counsel
- Paul Baniel, VP, Finance & Administration
Founded:
In 1919.

HOUSTON TEXANS
NRG STADIUM
TWO NRG PARK
HOUSTON, TX 77054-1573
832-667-2000
fanfeedback@houstontexans.com
www.houstontexans.com
- D. Cal McNair, Chairman/CEO
- Nick Caserio, General Manager
- Culley David, Head Coach
- Jack Easterby, Executive VP, Football Operations
- Derek Beeman, VP, Ticket Sales & Business Insights
- Jennifer Davenport, Chief Marketing Officer
- Marilan Logan, Senior VP/Chief Financial Officer
Description:
NRG Stadium
Founded:
In 2002.

INDIANAPOLIS COLTS
7001 W 56TH STREET
INDIANAPOLIS, IN 46254

317-297-2658
800-805-2658
Fax: 317-297-8971
www.colts.com
• James Irsay, Owner/CEO
• Chris Ballard, General Manager
• Frank Reich, Head Coach
• Kevin Rogers, Director, Player Personnel
• Jon Shaw, Director, Pro Scouting
• Morocco Brown, Director, College Scouting
• Jim Van Dam, VP, Ticket Sales & Service
• Mike Bluem, Director, Football Administration
• Pete Ward, COO
• Kurt Humphrey, Chief Financial Officer
• Steve Campbell, VP, Communications
• Roger VanDerSnick, Chief Sales & Marketing Officer
Description:
Lucas Oil Stadium
Founded:
In 1953, Baltimore Maryland. Relocated to Indianapolis in 1984.

JACKSONVILLE JAGUARS
TIAA BANK FIELD
ONE TIAA BANK FIELD DRIVE
JACKSONVILLE, FL 32202
904-633-2000
www.jaguars.com
• Shad Khan, Owner/CEO
• Mark Lamping, President
• Trent Baalke, General Manager
• Urban Meyer, Head Coach
• Hamzah Ahmad, Director, Football Operations
• Chris Driggers, Director, Pro Scouting
• Mark Ellenz, Director, College Scouting
• Tim Bishko, Director, Ticket Operations
• Julian Duncan, Chief Marketing Officer
• Amy Palcic, VP, Football Communications
Description:
TIAA Bank Field
Founded:
In 1995.

KANSAS CITY CHIEFS
ARROWHEAD STADIUM
ONE ARROWHEAD DRIVE
KANSAS CITY, MO 64129
www.chiefs.com
• Clark Hunt, Chair/CEO
• Mark Donovan, President
• Brett Veach, General Manager
• Andy Reid, Head Coach
• Tim Terry, Director, Pro Personnel
• Ryne Nutt, Director, College Scouting
• Tyler Kirby, VP, Ticket Sales
• Tyler Epp, Executive VP, Business Operations
• Kirsten Krug, VP, Administration
• Dan Crumb, Chief Financial Officer
Description:
Arrowhead Stadium
Founded:
In 1963.

LAS VEGAS RAIDERS
ALLEGIANT STADIUM
3333 AL DAVIS WAY
LAS VEGAS, NV 89118
510-864-5000
feedback@raiders.com
www.raiders.com
• Mark Davis, Owner
• Marc Badain, President
• Mike Mayock, General Manager
• Jon Gruden, Head Coach
• Dwayne Joseph, Director, Pro Personnel
• Jim Abrams, Director, College Scouting
• Mike Taylor, Public Affairs
Description:
Allegiant Stadium
Founded:
In 1960.

LOS ANGELES CHARGERS
DIGNITY HEALTH SPORTS PARK
18400 S AVALON BOULEVARD
CARSON, CA 90746

714-540-7100
877-242-7437
www.chargers.com
• Dean A. Spanos, Controlling Owner/Chairman
• Jeanne M. Bonk, Executive VP, COO/CFO
• Tom Telesco, General Manager
• Brandon Staley, Head Coach
• Dennis Abraham, Director, Pro Scouting
• Kevin Kelly, Director, College Scouting
• John Spanos, President, Football Operations

LOS ANGELES RAMS
LOS ANGELES MEMORIAL COLISEUM
3911 S FIGUEROA STREET
LOS ANGELES, CA 90037
www.therams.com
• E Stanley Kroenke, Owner/Chairman
• Les Snead, General Manager
• Sean McVay, Head Coach
• Sophie Luoto, Director, Football Operations
• Kevin Demoff, Chief Operating Officer
• James Gladstone, Director, Scouting Strategy

MIAMI DOLPHINS
HARD ROCK STADIUM
347 DON SHULA DRIVE
MIAMI, FL 33056
www.miamidolphins.com
• Tom Garfinkel, President/CEO
• Stephen M. Ross, Chairman/Managing General Partner
• Chris Grier, General Manager
• Brian Flores, Head Coach
• Matt Winston, Assistant Director, College Scouting
• Kyle Mockler, Senior Director, Ticket Operations
• Laura Sandall, VP, Marketing
• Michael Geraci, Senior Director, Finance Operations
Description:
Hard Rock Stadium
Founded:
In 1966.

MINNESOTA VIKINGS
US BANK STADIUM
401 CHICAGO AVENUE
MINNEAPOLIS, MN 55415
952-828-6500
customerservice@vikings.nfl.net
www.vikings.com
• Zygi Wilf, Chairman/Owner
• Mark Wilf, President/Owner
• Rick Spielman, General Manager
• Mike Zimmer, Head Coach
• Rob Brzezinski, Executive VP, Football Operations
• Ryan Monnens, Director, Professional Scouting
• Rich Wang, Director, Sales Analytics & Engagement
• Martin Nance, Executive VP/Chief Marketing Officer
• Kate Shibilski, Executive VP/Chief Financial Officer
Description:
US Bank Stadium
Founded:
In 1960.

NEW ENGLAND PATRIOTS
GILLETTE STADIUM
1 PATRIOT PLACE
FOXBOROUGH, MA 02035
508-543-8200
800-543-1776 Ticket Office
www.patriots.com
• Robert Kraft, Chairman/CEO
• Jonathan A. Kraft, President
• Bill Belichick, Head Coach
• Monti Ossenfort, Director of Player Personnel
Description:
Gillette Stadium
Founded:
In 1960.

NEW ORLEANS SAINTS
MERCEDES-BENZ SUPERDOME
1500 SUGAR BOWL DRIVE
NEW ORLEANS, LA 70112
www.neworleanssaints.com
• Gayle Benson, Owner/Chair
• Dennis Lauscha, President
• Mickey Loomis, General Manager
• Sean Payton, Head Coach
• Justin Matthews, Pro Scouting Coordinator
• Paul Zimmer, College Scouting Coordinator
• Mike Stanfield, Senior VP, Sales
• Ben Hales, Senior VP/Chief Operating Officer
• Khai Harley, Executive VP, Football Administration
• Greg Bensel, Senior VP, Communications
Description:
Mercedes-Benz Superdome
Founded:
In 1967.

NEW YORK GIANTS
METLIFE STADIUM
ONE METLIFE STADIUM DRIVE
EAST RUTHERFORD, NJ 07073
www.giants.com
• John K. Mara, President/CEO
• Steve Tisch, Chairman/Executive VP
• Dave Gettleman, Senior VP/General Manager
• Joe Judge, Head Coach
• Kevin Abrams, VP, Football Operations
• Chris Mara, Senior VP, Player Personnel
• Amy Matlins, Director, Ticketing
• Pete Guelli, Senior VP/Chief Commercial Officer
• Christine Procops, Senior VP/Chief Financial Officer
• Pat Hanlon, Senior VP, Communications
Description:
Metlife Stadium
Founded:
In 1925.

NEW YORK JETS
METLIFE STADIUM
ONE METLIFE STADIUM DRIVE
EAST RUTHERFORD, NJ 07073
973-549-4800
800-469-5387
www.newyorkjets.com
• Christopher Johnson, Vice Chair/CEO
• Hymie Elhai, President
• Joe Douglas, General Manager
• Robert Saleh, Head Coach
• Chad Alexander, Director, Player Personnel
• Evan Ardoin, Pro Scout
• Jeff Hecker, Senior Director, Ticket Operations
• Timothy Kemp, VP, Marketing
• David Szott, Director, Player Development
Description:
Metlife Stadium
Founded:
In 1960.

PHILADELPHIA EAGLES
LINCOLN FINANCIAL FIELD
ONE LINCOLN FINANCIAL FIELD WAY
PHILADELPHIA, PA 19148
215-463-2500
www.philadelphiaeagles.com
• Jeffrey Lurie, Chairman/CEO
• Don Smolenski, President
• Howie Roseman, Executive VP/General Manager
• Nick Sirianni, Head Coach
• Brandon Brown, Director, Pro Scouting
• Anthony Patch, Senior Director, College Scouting
• Laini DeLawter, VP, Ticket & Fan Services
• Jen Kavanaugh, Senior VP, Media & Marketing
• Frank Gumienny, Chief Financial Officer
Description:
Lincoln Financial Field
Founded:
In 1933.

PITTSBURGH STEELERS
HEINZ FIELD
100 ART ROONEY AVENUE
PITTSBURGH, PA 15212
412-432-6018
Fax: 412-432-7878
www.steelers.com
• Arthur J. Rooney, II, President
• Kevin Colbert, VP/General Manager
• Mike Tomlin, Head Coach
• Brandon Hunt, Pro Scouting Coordinator
• Phil Kreidler, College Scouting Coordinator
• Rick Giugliano, Director, Marketing & Events
• Bob Tyler, VP, Finance
• Ben Lentz, Director, Ticket Operations
Description:
Heinz Field
Founded:
In 1933.

SAN FRANCISCO 49ERS
LEVI'S STADIUM
4900 MARIE P DEBARTOLO WAY
SANTA CLARA, CA 95054
www.49ers.com
• Jed York, CEO
• Al Guido, President
• Denise DeBartolo York, Co-Chair
• John York, Co-Chair
• John Lynch, General Manager
• Kyle Shanahan, Head Coach
• Adam Peters, Assistant General Manager
• Ran Carthon, Director, Pro Personnel
• Ethan Waugh, Director, College Scouting
• Brad Dugan, Director, Ticketing
• Alex Chang, Chief Marketing Officer
Description:
Levi's Stadium
Founded:
In 1946.

SEATTLE SEAHAWKS
CENTURY LINK FIELD
800 OCCIDENTAL AVENUE S
SEATTLE, WA 98134
425-203-8000
888-635-4295
www.seahawks.com
• Jody Allen, Chair
• Chuck Arnold, President
• John Schneider, Executive VP/General Manager
• Pete Carroll, Head Coach/Executive VP, Football Operations
• Nolan Teasley, Director, Pro Personnel
• Matt Berry, Director, College Scouting
• Chris Lawrence, VP, Ticket Sales & Services
• Jeff Richards, VP, Marketing & Community Engagement
• Pete Fonfara, Director, Finance
Description:
Century Link Field
Founded:
In 1976.

TAMPA BAY BUCCANEERS
ADVENTHEALTH TRAINING CENTER
ONE BUCCANEER PLACE
TAMPA, FL 33607
813-870-2700
800-795-2827
www.buccaneers.com
• Bryan Glazer, Owner/Chairman
• Jason Licht, General Manager
• Bruce Arians, Head Coach
• John Spytek, Director, Player Personnel
• Rob McCartney, Director, Pro Scouting
• Mike Biehl, Director, College Scouting
• Brian Ford, Chief Operating Officer
• Shelton Quarles, Director, Football Operations
Description:
Raymond James Stadium
Founded:
In 1976.

TENNESSEE TITANS
NISSAN STADIUM
ONE TITANS WAY
NASHVILLE, TN 37213
615-565-4000
www.titansonline.com
• Burke Nihill, President/CEO
• Amy Adams Strunk, Chair
• Jon Robinson, Executive VP/General Manager
• Mike Vrabel, Head Coach
• Ryan Cowden, VP, Player Personnel
• Brian Gardner, Director, Pro Scouting
• Jon Salge, Director, College Scouting
• Brooke Ellenberger, VP, Ticketing
• Beverly Gil, SVP/Chief Marketing & Revenue Officer
Description:
Nissan Stadium
Founded:
1960 as the Houston Oilers, Tennessee Oilers in 1997, and the Tennessee Titans in 1999.

WASHINGTON
FEDEX FIELD
1600 FEDEX WAY
LANDOVER, MD 20785
www.redskins.com
• Daniel Snyder, Owner
• Ron Rivera, Head Coach
• Marty Hurney, Executive VP, Football & Player Personnel
• Don Warren, Senior Pro Scout
• Tim Gribble, Director, College Scouting
Founded:
In 1932.

UNITED STATES WOMEN'S FOOTBALL LEAGUE
289 HUDSON ROAD
PINEY FLATS, TN 37686
423-797-0014
USWFL@yahoo.com
www.uswfl.net

Teams:

FAYETTEVILLE DUCKS
REID ROSS HIGH SCHOOL
FAYATTEVILLE, NC

HAMPTON ROADS HERRICANES
OLD DOMINION UNIVERSITY POWHATAN FIELD
HAMPTON ROADS, VA

RIVER CITY STING
RICHMOND, VA
rivercitysting@gmail.com
www.rivercitysting.com

TRI-CITIES THUNDER
SULLIVAN EAST HIGH SCHOOL
BRISTOL, TN
tcthunderfootball@gmail.com
tricitiesthunder.com

TRI-CITY VIPERS
HAMPTON, VA
757-718-5739
1ladyvipers1@gmail.com
tcladyvipers.com

VIRGINIA VENOM
ALEXANDRIA, VA

WEST VIRGINIA WILDFIRE
SHAWNEE SPORTS COMPLEX
CHARLESTON, WV

WOMEN'S FOOTBALL ALLIANCE / WFA
wfaprofootball.com

• Lisa King, Commissioner
(559) 328-4321
lisa.king@wfaprofootball.com
• Wyndy Flato-Dominy, Director, Operations
(303) 993-9945
wyn.dominy@wfaprofootball.com
• Chris Miller, Director, Officials
officials@wfaprofootball.com
Description:
Women's football league and partner with Minor League Foorball Allinace (MLFA).
Year Founded:
2008
Teams:
64
Division 1:
Tampa Bay Inferno; DC Divas; Dallas Elite Mustangs; Pittsburgh Passion; Arlington Impact; Boston Renegades; Cali War; St. Louis Slam; Minnesota Vixen
Division 2:
Jacksonville Dixie Blues; Portland Fighting Shockwave; Cleveland Fusion; Columbus Comets; Detroit Dark Angels; New York Wolves; Seattle Spartans; Mile High Blaze; Austin Outlaws; Houston Energy; Miami Fury; Nevada Storm; Sin City Trojans; Orlando Anarchy; Baltimore Nighthawks
Division 3:
Utica Hellcats; Inland Empire Desert Eagles; Sioux Falls Snow Leopards; Zydeco Spice; Toledo Reign; Midwest Mountain Lions; Mifa All-Stars; Nola Hurricanes; OKC Lady Force; Sun City Stealth; Louisiana Bayou Storm Surge; Sacramento Sirens; Capital Pioneers; Huntsville Tigers; Kansas City Saints; Gulf Coast Monarchy; Memphis Sabercats; Rocky Mountain Thunderkatz; Tulsa Threat; Carolina Pheonix; Daytona Waverunners; Derby City Dynamite; Knoxville Lightning; Music City Mizfits; Columbus Vanguards; Connecticut Hawks; Grand Rapids Tidal Waves; Maine Mayhem; New York Knockout; Richmond Black Widows; Houston Power; Iowa Pheonix; Kern County Crusaders

Teams:

ARLINGTON IMPACT
1015 E BROAD
MANSFIELD, TX 76063
817-226-6359
arlingtonimpactfootball.com
• Jeanette Fuller, Owner
• Lacy Brandon, Head Coach

BOSTON RENEGADES
HARRY DELLA RUSSO STADIUM
REVERE, MA
info@bostonrenegadesfootball.com
bostonrenegadesfootball.com
• John Johnson, Head Coach

CALI WAR
LOS ANGELES, CA
caliwarteam@gmail.com
caliwar.com
• Jeff King, Head Coach

D.C. DIVAS
12240 BOND STREET
WHEATON, MD 20902
divasgm@gmail.com
www.dcdivas.com
• Rich Daniel, Owner/President
• Barry Thompson, Head Coach
• Rachel Worsham, Director, Football Operations

DALLAS ELITE MUSTANGS
817-691-5568
dallaselitewomensfootball@gmail.com
dallaselitewomensfootball.com
• Maria Spencer, Co-Owner
• LynMarie Liberty-Ellington, Co-Owner
• Mike Ellington, Head Coach

KANSAS CITY TITANS
TRUMAN HIGH SCHOOL
3301 S NOLAND RD
INDEPENDENCE, MO 64055
kansascitytitans.org
• Cadena Brim, General Manager
• Leonard Bulock, Head Coach

Frisbee Organizations

USA ULTIMATE
5825 DELMONICO DR
SUITE 350
COLORADO SPRINGS, CO 80919
719-219-8322
800-872-4384
info@hq.usaultimate.org
www.usaultimate.org
• Tom Crawford, Chief Executive Officer
(719) 219-8322
tom@hq.usaultimate.org
Year Founded:
1979
Description:
To promote and support the sport of
Ultimate in the US. Our mission is to
increase participation in the sport of Ultimate
at all levels; to uphold the Spirit of the
Game, including personal responsibility and
integrity; and to provide a framework for
players to organize and conduct competition
and other activities
Membership Requirements:
$40 regular, $20 youth, and more
membership levels.
Members:
23,700
Publications:
UPA magazine: USA Ultimate, quarterly

WORLD FLYING DISC FEDERATION
5825 DELMONICO DRIVE
SUITE 350
COLORADO SPRINGS, CO 80919
+41-(0) 6138 9020 868
Volker.Bernardi@wfdf.org
www.wfdf.org
• Robert Rauch, President
(203) 570-9221
nob.rauch@wfdf.org
• Thomas Griesbaum, Secretary
(49) 162 214 526
thomas.griesbaum@wfdf.org
• Tomas Burvall, Overall Committee Chair
tomas.burvall@wfdf.org
• Kate Begeron, Treasurer
kate.bergeron@wfdf.org
• Brian Gisel, Ultimate Committee Chair
(517) 862-3182
brian.gisel@wfdf.org
Year Founded:
1985
Description:
Responsible for hosting World
Championships and developing the Rules of
the Game for the following flying disc sports:
Ultimate, Disc Golf, Freestyle, Guts, DDC,
Field Events
Number of members:

20,000+ in 46 member countries
Membership Requirements:
$1.25 US multiplied by the number of active
players belonging to the member
organization. The minimum dues for a
Regular Member is $250 US and the
maximum is $3000 US. Associate
Membership is $250 US annually.
Publications:
Annual rule book

Golf Organizations

AMERICAN GOLF CORPORATION
6080 CENTER DRIVE
SUITE 500
LOS ANGELES, CA 90045
310-664-4000
www.americangolf.com
• Jim Hinckley, President/CEO
• Rick Rosen, Chief Financial Officer
Description:
Manages more than 110 premier private,
resort and daily fee courses in the United
States. In addition to outstanding facilities
and world-class service, we are dedicated to
helping people of all ages and backgrouns
learn and enjoy the game of golf.
Notes:
Goldman Sachs and Starwood Capital
completed acqusition of National Golf
Properties and American Golf in 2003

AMERICAN JUNIOR GOLF ASSOCIATION
1980 SPORTS CLUB DRIVE
BRASELTON, GA 30517
770-868-4200
877-373-2542
Fax: 770-868-4211
ajga@ajga.org
www.ajga.org
• James E Nugent, III, President
• Gayle Champagne, Past President
• J.R. Smith, Chairman
• Joseph E. Quirk, III, Vice President
• Lewis C. Horne, Jr., Secretary
• Jason Miller, Chief Financial Officer
(770) 868-4200
Year Founded:
1977
Description:
A nonprofit organization dedicated to the
overall growth and development of young
men and women who aspire to earn college
golf scholarships through competitive junior
golf.
Membership Requirements:
For ages 12-18. Junior Membership $215;
College Bound Student Membership(CBS)
$270; Future Player Membership $95; Junior
Plus Membership $285
Number of Members:
More than 5,500
Publications:
The AJGA Link (electronic newsletter)

**AMERICAN SINGLES GOLF
ASSOCIATION**
710 MAIN STREET
PINEVILLE, NC 28134
704-889-4600
1-888-GOLFMATE
1-888-465-3628
Fax: 888-465-3295

asganational@aol.com
www.singlesgolf.com
• Tom Alsop, Founder/Chief Executive
Officer
GolfASGA@aol.com
Year Founded
1996
Description:
To serve its members and chapter leaders
so they can fully realize the benefits of
membership. The secondary goal is to
create new chapters and spread the concept
of SinglesGolf.
Number of members:
2,200

**AMERICAN SOCIETY OF GOLF COURSE
ARCHITECTS**
125 N EXECUTIVE DRIVE
SUITE 302
BROOKFIELD, WI 53005
262-786-5960
Fax: 262-786-5919
www.asgca.org
• Lee Schmidt, President
(480) 483-1994
lslap@schmidt-curley.com
• Steve Smyers, Vice President
(863) 683-6100
ssgca@aol.com
• Greg Martin, Treasurer
(630) 482-2532
g-martin@mdpltd.com
• Rick Robbins, Immediate Past President
(919) 319-1004
rock@robbinsgolf.com
• John Sanford, Secretary
(561) 691-8601
john@sanfordgolfdesign.com
Year Founded:
1946
Description:
The first professional organization of golf
course designers in America. Its members
have designed some of the world's greatest
courses.
Membership Requirements:
Must be at least 28 years of age and been
practicing golf couse architecture for a
minimum of eight years; have designed at
least 18-hole equivalents, three of which
must have opened i the past six years; and
adhere to strict professional Code of Ethics.
Number of members:
177
Publications:
The Golf Course Development Process:
Questions & Answers; Master Planning for
Golf Courses: Questions & Answers; The
Golf Course Remodeling Process:
Questions & Answers; Selecting Your Golf
Course Architect: Questions & Answers;
Sample Request for Proposal for Golf
Course Architectural Services; Life Cycle
Chart; An Environmental Approach to Golf
Course Development; BUilding a Practical
Golf Facility

**ASSOCIATION OF GOLF
MERCHANDISERS**
PO BOX 7247
PHOENIX, AZ 85011-7247
602-604-8250
Fax: 602-604-8251
info@agmgolf.org
www.agmgolf.org

• Darcy Lyberger, President
(301) 469-2003
darcy@ccclub.org
• Tracy Moffatt, Vice President
(239) 597-8383
tracymoffatt@aol.com
Year Founded:
1989
Description:
A professional association of golf-related vendors and professional merchandisers located all over the world.
Membership Requirements:
Must be buyer/merchandiser at a recognized golf shop (merchandiser member) or a golf-related business (Affiliate member)
Members:
750
Member Services:
Educational seminars on successful golf merchandising (held throughout the country), membership rosters, job bulletins and referrals, and a reference/referral center for golf buyers and merchandisers
Publications:
The Merchandiser, bimonthly newsletter; AGM Merchandise Manual, issued to members only; Viewpoints, monthly color card w/visual display ideas

CADDIE ASSOCIATION
23 MALACOMPRA ROAD
PALM COAST, FL 32137
386-446-8721
dennis@pcahq.com
www.thecaddieassociation.com
• Dennis Cone, Founder/CEO
Description:
A membership driven organization that is open to all Caddies, independent Contractors, and those who want to support the game.

CANADIAN PROFESSIONAL GOLFERS' ASSOCIATION
13450 DUBLIN LINE
ACTON, ON, CANADA L7J 2W7
519-853-5450
800-782-5764
Fax: 519-853-5449
info@pgaofcanada.com
www.pgaofcanada.com
• Heather Bodden, Operations Manager
(519) 853-5450
heather@pgaofcanada.com
• Eilon Milman, Chief Financial Officer
(519) 853-5450
eilon@pgaofcanada.com
• Chris Fry, Managing Director of Corporate
(519) 853-5450
chris@pgaofcanada.com
• Jeff Dykeman, Chief Business Officer
(519) 853-5450
jeff@pgaofcanada.com
• Darcy Kral, Managing Director of Membership & Support Services
(549) 853-5450
darcy@pgaofcanada.com
• Adam LeBrun, Managing Director, Championships & Events
(519) 853-5450
adam@pgaofcanada.com
• Gary Bernard, Chief Executive Officer
(519) 853-5450
gary@pgaofcanada.com

Year Founded:
1911
Description:
A member based non-profit organization representing over 3,500 golf professionals across Canada.
Publications:
The Exchange - Official Publication of the CPGA produced by Score Golf

CEC BALALIS CORPORATION
1500 WEST BALBOA BOULEVARD
SUITE 201
NEWPORT BEACH, CA 92663
949-673-2282
Fax: 949-673-4286
• Paul Balalis, Chairman/President/CEO
Year Founded:
1999
Description:
Organization is engaged in the development, program and construction management, maintenance, and ownership of golf course facilities

CLINTWOOD PRODUCTIONS
www.celebritygolf.com
Year Founded:
1990
Description:
To support, promote, and help raise awareness for worthwhile charities. We provide a wide range of services to celebrity and charity events that maximize event visability year round

CLUBCORP
3030 LBJ FREEWAY
SUITE 600
DALLAS, TX 75234
972-243-6191
www.clubcorp.com
• Robert H. Dedman, Sr, Founder
• Jamie K. Walters, Executive Vice President, Sales
• Eric L. Affeldt, President & CEO, Director
• Mark Burnett, Chief Operating Officer
• Daniel Tilley, Executive Vice President & CIO
• Curt McClellan, Chief Financial Officer
• Ingrid J. Keiser, General Counsel, Secretary, & Executive VP
Year Founded:
1957
Description:
ClubCorp owns or operates nearly 200 golf courses, country clubs, private business and sports clubs, and resorts. Instrumental in the renaming of the Stonebridge Ranch to Dallas Stars Country Club
Members:
200,000

Other locations:

COLORADO SECTION PGA
6630 BEAR DANCE DRIVE
SUITE 200
LARKSPUR, CO 80118
303-681-0742
www.coloradopga.com
• Leslie Core-Drevecky, President, PGA
mcreekgolf@aol.com
• Ty Thomspon, Vice President, PGA
ty.thompson@pga.com
• Patrick Salva, Marketing & Communications Director
psalva@pgahq.com

• Eddie Ainsworth, Executive Director, PGA
eainsworth@pgahq.com

ENGLAND & WALES BLIND GOLF
STATION HOUSE
NORTH STREET
HAVANT, PO9 1QU
www.blindgolf.co.uk
• Neil Baxter, Chairman
• Barry Ritchie, Secretary
Enquiries.blindgolf@gmail.com
• Ron Tomlinson, Financial Director
FD.blindgolf@gmail.com
• Derek Field, New Members Secretary
dgfield@ntlworld.com
Year Founded:
1982
Description:
To provide visually handicapped people with the facility to train and compete in the game of golf. Training is provided by giving new members support to receive lessons from professional golfers. In addition each year the organization invites all members to attend a training weekend at which PGA professional teach the various aspects of the game. Assistance is also given to schools for the blind where pupils want to start to play golf
Fundraising/Sponsorship:
The Financial Director, 12 Nutbourne Road, Hayling Island Hampshire PO11 9RT; Tel: 023 92 460 120 Fax: 023 92 460 120
Press and Public Relations:
55a Queen Mary Rd, Upper Norwood London SE 19 3NN, Tel: 020 8761 1904 Fax: 020 8761 1904

EXECUTIVE WOMEN'S GOLF ASSOCIATION
300 AVE OF THE CHAMPIONS
SUITE 140
PALM BEACH GARDENS, FL 33418-3615
561-691-0096
www.ewga.com
• Pam Swensen, CEO, EWGA
• Sheryl Wilkerson, President
• Diana Gats, Secretary-Treasurer
• Hilary Tuohy, President-Elect
• Nona Footz, Board Member
Year Founded:
1991
Description:
To provide opportunities for women to learn, play, and enjoy the game of golf for business and for life
Number of Members:
20,000 members in over 120 Chapters across US and Canada.
Membership Requirements:
Interest in learning how to play a game of golf or desire to improve one's skills to use golf for business and career advancement, Local and Association dues apply annually (average $100.00 per year) Classic membership $155; Executive Distinction Membership $400; Seniors (65+) $125; Young Professionals (ages 18-30) $75; and Corporate Membership (10 or more) $125
Member Services:
EWGA provides opportunities for professional women to learn, play, and enjoy the game of golf for business and for life throughout 100+ local Chapters in the US and Canada
Publications:
Annual EWGA Member Handbook, Annual

EWGA Yearbook Per Excellence, Golf for Women

FERRIS STATE UNIVERSITY/PROFESSIONAL GOLF MANAGEMENT PROGRAM

119 SOUTH STREET
BIG RAPIDS, MI 49307
231-591-2480
Fax: 231-591-2839
cob@ferris.edu
www.ferris.edu
• Mark Wilson, PGA Golf Management Player Development Coordinator
MarkWilson@ferris.edu
• Aaron Waltz, PGA Golf Management Director
AaronWaltz@ferris.edu
• Annette Keyt, PGA Golf Management Secretary
AnnetteKeyt@ferris.edu
• Diane Maguire, PGA Golf Management Assistant
DianeMaguire@ferris.edu
Year Founded:
1975
Undergrad Degree:
B.S. in Business; Major in Professional Golf Management; Class A PGA Membership eligible upon graduation.

Other locations:

GEORGIA STATE GOLF ASSOCIATION

121 VILLAGE PARKWAY
BUILDING 3
MARIETTA, GA 30067
770-955-4272
800-949-4742
Fax: 770-955-1156
info@gsga.org
www.gsga.org
• Dave Ballard, President
president@gsga.org
• David Burke, President-Elect
presidentelect@gsga.org
• Matt Williams, Executive Director
(678) 324-5960
mwilliams@gsga.org
• Olivia Flanagan, Secretary/Treasurer
• Jerri Smith, Senior Director
(678) 324-5973
jsmith@gsga.org
Description:
Non-profit organization dedicated solely to serving the game of golf and its membership
Year Founded:
1916
Number of Members:
360 golf clubs, 85,000 individuals

GOLF CANADA

1333 DORVAL DRIVE
SUITE 1
OAKVILLE, ON, CANADA L6M 4X7
905-849-9700
800-263-0009
Fax: 905-845-7040
www.golfcanada.ca
• Paul McLean, President
• Doug Alexander, Past President
• Charlie Beaulieu, Secretary
• Roland Deveau, 1st Vice President
• Leslie Dunning, 2nd Vice President
• Liz Hoffman, Director At Large
• Dale Jackson, Director At Large
Year Founded:
1895
Description:
The mission, as the governing body of golf in Canada, is to promote participation in and a passion for the game while protecting its traditions and integrity.
Number of members:
1,650 golf clubs; 380,000 individual members
Member Services:
Rules of Golf; Greens Consulting; Conducting National Championships; Handicaps; Hall of Fame; Museum; Library; Amateur Status; Junior Development. Conducts Canadian Open Golf Championship, Senior Open Championships; Amateur Championships, Women's Open Championship, Handicap and Course Rating, Junior Development and International Teams. Publishes GOLF CANADA MAGAZINE
Membership Requirements:
Golf Clubs in Canada or public player programs

GOLF CLEARING HOUSE/NATIONAL GOLF SALES REPRESENTATIVES ASSOCIATION (NGSA)

PO BOX 6134
SCOTTSDALE, AZ 85261-6134
480-860-6348
Fax: 480-860-6919
• Tom Moynihan, President
• Bud Brown, Vice President
• Debbie Savona, Executive Director
• Jon Schwartz, Website Administrator
Description:
NGSA representing over 3,400 independent and Company Golf Sales Representatives. The NGSA Benefits are fully encompassing. The Sales Leader Reps Wanted a service for all Golf Manufacturers to list their need for qualified Sales Reps or to find qualified Management Personnel. The NGSA Register of 3,400 Sales Reps is available to all Company Members of the Golf Clearing House, Divsion of NSGA
Number of members:
450 Member Companies

GOLF COACHES ASSOCIATION OF AMERICA

1225 WEST MAIN STREET
SUITE 110
NORMAN, OK 73069
866-422-2669
Fax: 405-573-7888
info@collegiategolf.com
www.collegiategolf.com
• Ray Conrad, President
• Andrew Sapp, First Vice President
• Greg Sands, Second Vice President
• Mark Crabtree, Third Vice President
Year Founded:
1958
Description:
This non-profit organization is dedicated to educating, promotion and recognizing its members who participate in men's golf at all levels
Membership Requirements:
College golf coach

GOLF COURSE BUILDERS ASSOCIATION OF AMERICA

6040 S 58TH STREET
SUITE D
LINCOLN, NE 68516
402-476-4444
Fax: 402-476-4489
www.gcbaa.org
• Justin Apel, Executive Director
justin_apel@gcbaa.org
• Dennis Wagner, Vice President
• Samantha Huff, Program & Planning Manager
samantha_huff@gcbaa.org
• Lori Romano, Information & Education Coordinator
lori_romano@gcbaa.org
• Rick Boylan, President
• Scott Veazey, President-Elect
• Ellen Davis, Secretary
• Patrick Karnick, Treasurer
Year Founded:
1971
Description:
A nonprofit trade association of the world's foremost golf course builders and leading suppliers to the golf course construction insdustry.
Number of members:
19,000 (70 countries), 66 Chapters
Membership Requirements:
Builder must have constructed a minimum of three courses in the past five years. Associate: suppliers, specialty contractors, and international companies
Member Services:
Two annual meetings per year, one in conjunction with the annual PGA tournament, and one timed with the annual GCSAA Membership Directory., Newsline
Publications:
Earthshaping News, Membership Directory, Guide To Estimating Cost For Golf Course Construction

GOLFCOURSEHOME NETWORK

10 UNION STREET
PO BOX 821
VINEYARD HAVEN, MA 02568
203-270-9357
Fax: 866-424-5225
dlott@golfcoursehome.net
www.golfcoursehome.com
• David Lott, Founder & Publisher
(203) 270-9357
• Alan T. Pearce, Vice President Sales
(800) 673-0321
• Paul Stanton, Western Regional Sales Director
(916) 641-8255
• Elise Jeffress Ryan, Eastern Regional Sales Manager
(410) 433-0889
Year Founded:
1999
Description:
Provide executives who are looking for a golf or waterview home or homesite. Key information about world-class, amenity and country club communities in the U.S. and the world.

GOLF COURSE SUPERINTENDENTS ASSOCIATION OF AMERICA/GCSAA

1421 RESEARCH PARK DRIVE
LAWRENCE, KS 66049
785-841-2240
800-472-7878
Fax: 785-832-3643
www.gcsaa.org
• John J O'Keefe, President
• Peter J Grass, Vice President
• William H Maynard, Secretary/Treasurer
• J. Rhett Evans, Chief Executive Officer
• Cameron Oury, Chief Financial Officer

Year Founded:
1926
Description:
Dedicated to serving its members, advancing their profession and enhancing the enjoyment, growth and vitality of the game of golf.
Number of members:
21,000 in 75 countries
Membership Requirements:
Those persons directly participating in the production and management of fine golf turf
Publications:
GOLF COURSE MANAGEMENT MAGAZINE; GREENS & GRASS ROOTS, newsletter; GCSAA Membership Directory; EADERBOARD GOLF EXECUTIVE NEWSLETTER. Also produces Par For The Course, a 30-minute TV show

GOLF WRITERS ASSOCIATION OF AMERICA
golfwritersinc@aol.com
www.gwaa.com
• Ron Sirak, President
• Jack Berry, Secretary/Treasurer
Year Founded:
1947
Description:
Insures professional working conditions
Membership Requirements:
Must be actively writing golf
Publications:
Monthly newsletter, Membership Directory

INTERNATIONAL JUNIOR GOLF ACADEMY
55 HOSPITAL CENTER COMMON
HILTON HEAD ISLAND, SC 29926
843-686-1500
888-452-6642
www.ijga.com
• Kevin Smeltz, Director Of Instruction
• DaWayne Penberthy, Assistant Director Of Golf
• Karen Harrison, Director Of Health & Athletic Development
Year Founded:
1995
Description:
Dedicated to preparing junior golfers for success in tournament golf, academics, and life. We succeed when we instill in student athletes a sense of purpose and perspective.
Sponsors:
Nike Golf, Fitness for Golf, Promax, Champion's Golf Environments, Saegertown Beverages

INTERNATIONAL ASSOCIATION OF GOLF TOUR OPERATORS
CONCORDE HOUSE
GRENVILLE PL
LONDON, ENGLAND NW7 3SA
44-(0) 20 8906 3377
Fax: 44-(0) 20 8906 8181
info@iagto.com
www.iagto.com
• Corinne Korn, Office Manager
• Daniella Leao, Events Manager
• Peter Walton, President/Chief Executive Officer
• Carlton Carugati, General Manager
• Giles Greenwood, Golf Tourism Development Director
• Susannah Wilson, Marketing Executive &

Special Projects
• Amila Udayanga, Programmer
• Peter Ellegard, Editor in Chief & Media Advisor
Year Founded:
1997
Description:
The global trade association of the golf tourism industry and its membership includes over 500 accredited golf tour operators, golf resorts, hotels, golf courses, receptive operators, airlines and tourism boards in more than 50 countries worldwide
Membership Requirements:
Annual Dues
Number of Members:
800 members, 63 countries

INTERNATIONAL BLIND GOLF ASSOCIATION
• Derrick Sheridan, Director
• Yoshinori Ikezawa, Director
• Alistair Reid, Director
• John White, Director
• Brian MacLeod, Director
Year Founded:
1998
Description:
The governing and sanctioning body of blind golf events world wide: dedicated to promoting the sport and assisting blind golfers enjoy golf.

INTERNATIONAL GOLF FEDERATION
MAISON DU SPORT INTERNATIONAL
AVENUE DE RHADANIE 54
1007 LAU SANNE, SWITZERLAN
41-216-23-12 12
Fax: 41-41 216 01 64 77
info@igfmail.org
www.igfgolf.org
• Antony Scanlon, Executive Director
• Wilson Sibbett, Joint Chairman of the Board
• Thomas O'Toole, Joint Chairman of the Board
• Peter Dawson, President
• Patsy Hankins, Women's Chairman
Year Founded:
1958
Description:
To encourage the International development of golf and to foster friendship and sportsmanship among the peoples of the world through the conduct biennially of Amateur Team Championships for the Eisenhower Trophy and the Espirito Santo Trophy
Number of Members:
65 member organizations, the women's division includes 44 countries
Membership Requirements:
Open to any organization which constitutes the sole central authority for amateur golf in its country and has adopted and administers the Rules of Amateur Status of either the Royal and Ancient Golf Club of St. Andrews, or the United States Golf Association.
Publications:
Record book of the WAG Team Championships

INTERNATIONAL JUNIOR GOLF TOUR/IJGT
55 HOSPITAL CENTER COMMONS
HILTON HEAD ISLAND, SC 29926

843-785-2444
888-358-1267
www.ijgt.com
• Brandon Nettles, Assistant Tournament Director
Brandon.Nettles@juniorsports.com
• Leigh Blake, Tournament Operations Associate
• Ben Jaklin, Tournament Operations Associate
• Chris Schramm, Northeast Tournament Director
(843) 785-2444
christopher.schramm@juniorsports.com
• Matt Molloy, Tournament Operations Associate
Matthew.Molloy@juniorsports.com
• Kira Jones, Marketing and Communications Associate
• Patrick Hauer, Tournament Operations Associate
Patrick.Hauer@juniorsports.com
Year Founded:
1995
Number of Members:
2000
Description:
Provides exceptional junior golfers the opportunity to develop and showcase their golf skills through competitive junior tournament golf. This is provided for junior golfers ages 19 and under

INTERNATIONAL NETWORK OF GOLF
556 TETON ST
LAKE MARY, FL 32746
407-328-0500
Fax: 407-878-4928
www.inggolf.com
• John Glozek, President
• Mandy Bumgarner, Events Coordinator
• Mike Jamison, Executive Director
Year Founded:
1990
Description:
A media-based, non-profit association that has been networking the golf industry. Mission is to enhance and promote communication and education in the golf industry.

JAPANESE BLIND GOLF ASSOCIATION
YUBINBANGO 167-0053 SUGINAMI-KU NISHIOGI-MINAMI
2-18-9 HISHI-KEN BUILDING SECOND FLOOR
TOKYO, JAPAN 167-0053
info@jbga.org
www.jbga.org
• Toshu Fukami, Chairman
• Masao Matsuda, President

KEMPERLESNIK
500 SKOKIE BOULEVARD
SUITE 444
NORTHBROOK, IL 60062
847-850-1818
Fax: 847-559-0406
info@kemperlesnik.com
www.kemperlesnik.com
• Gary Binder, Executive Vice President
• Steven K. Skinner, Chief Executive Officer
• Josh W. Lesnik, President
• Brian Milligan, Chief Financial Officer
• Steve Kelley, Vice President, General Counsel

Year Founded:
1967
Clients/Events:
KitchenAid, EA Sports, McDonalds Hich School All-American Games, PGA of America, Wilson Golf, EA Sports Maui Invitational
Description:
KemperLesnik is a sports/ event marketing and public relations agency based in Chicago. KemperLesnik specializes in owning, managing, creating selling and marketing events. The agency also consults with clients on sports marketing, activates sponsorships and develops strategic marketing and communication plans for events and clients. Events include the EA SPORTS Maui Invitational, The McDonald's All American High School Basketball games and PowerAde JamFest, the Senior PGA Championship presented by KitchenAid and the Champions For Change at Harbor Shores.

LADIES PROFESSIONAL GOLF ASSOCIATION/LPGA
100 INTERNATIONAL GOLF DRIVE
DAYTONA BEACH, FL 32124-1092
386-274-6200
Fax: 386-274-1099
www.lpga.com
• Michael Whan, Commissioner
• Vicki Goetze-Ackerman, President
• Karrie Webb, Vice President
• Laura Diaz, LPGA Player Director
• Katherine Kirk, LPGA Player Director
• Paige Mackenzie, LPGA Player Director
• Karen Stupples, LPGA Player Director
Year Founded:
1950
Description:
Professional women's golf tour of events; a membership organization for women teaching and club professionals
Membership Requirements:
Must successfully complete LPGA Qualifying School, for the LPGA Tour, meet membership requirements for T&CP Division
Number of members:
43 LPGA members, 40+ LPGA Teaching and Club Professional T&CP Division members
Publications:
MEDIA GUIDE; news releases, player profiles, tournament schedule, golf statistics, LPGA GOLF, distributed at LPGA tournaments, in the February Issue of GOLF MAGAZINE

LONG DRIVERS OF AMERICA
600 HENRIETTA CREEK ROAD
SUITE 200
ROANOKE, TX 76262
682-549-2105
888-233-4654
Fax: 682-549-2112
www.longdrivers.com
• Art Sellinger, Owner/Chief Executive Officer
sellinger@longdrivers.com
• Rene Towell, Office Manager
towell@longdrivers.com
• Thomas Kemp, General Counsel
tkemp@kemp-law.com
• Steve Wiley, VP Sales and Marketing
steve@longdrivers.com

• Rod Moruss, Director of Events
• Mike Ambriss, Executive Vice President
ambriz@longdrivers.com
Year Founded:
1993
Description:
Creates and implements Long Drive Tournaments
Membership Requirements:
Pay dues of $150 per year
Publications:
LDA Newsletter, approximately 6 times per year. Offers at least one long drive competition with a purse of $250,000

Other locations:

LOUISIANA GOLF ASSOCIATION
1003 HUGH WALLIS ROAD S.
SUITE A-2
LAFAYETTE, LA 70508
337-265-3938
www.lgagolf.org
• Lew Ward, President
• John Luffey, Vice President
• Richard Hunter, Secretary/Treasurer
• Carr McCalla, Executive Director
cmccalla@lgagolf.org
• Logan Ray, Director Of Championship Operations
loganr@lgagolf.org
• Tuyen Nguyen, Director Of Member Services
tnguyen@lgagolf.org
Nature of Service:
Exists to foster the enhancement and expansion of amateur golf through the development of member and information services, the promotion of oppportunities for all who want to play, and the protection of the game's integrity and valued traditions.
Year Founded:
1920
Number of Members:
20,000

METHODIST COLLEGE PROFESSIONAL GOLF MANAGEMENT PROGRAM
5400 RAMSEY STREET
FAYETTEVILLE, NC 28311
910-630-7000
800-488-7110
webmaster@methodist.edu
www.methodist.edu/pgm
• Jerry Hogge, Director PGA Golf Management
(910) 630-7144
jhogge@methodist.edu
• Bob Bruns, Associate Director
(910) 630-7180
rbruns@methodist.edu
• Steve Conley, Assistant Director
(910) 630-7146
sconley@methodist.edu
• Steve Dockery, Golf Course Superintendent
(910) 630-7604
sdockery@methodist.edu
• Tom Inczauskis, Assistant Director PGA Golf Management
(910) 630-7608
tinczauskis@methodist.edu
• Robbie Fritz, Director of Instruction, PGA Certified
(910) 630-7689
rfritz@methodist.edu
• Krista Lee, Office of Management, Admissions
(910) 630-7148
klee@methodist.edu
• Charles Koonce, Associate Director/Internship Director

(910) 630-7145
ckoonce@methodist.edu
Description:
Prepares students for a career as a PGA professional through an understanding of the business of golf, by encouraging integrity and ethical behavior in their service to their customers. The mission is to be achieved by providing students with an accredited business program, a competent and thorough PGM curriculum, access to a golf facility for skill improvemetn, and assistance in obtaining an entry level position upon graduation.

MISSISSIPPI STATE UNIVERSITY/GOLF MANAGEMENT PROGRAM
PO BOX 6217
309 McCOOL HALL
MISSISSIPPI STATE, MS 39762
662-325-3161
Fax: 662-325-1779
jadkerson@cobilan.msstate.edu
www.msupgm.com
• Jeff Adkerson, Director, PGA Golf Management
(662) 325-3161
jadkerson@business.msstate.edu
• Adam M. Scott, Assistant Director
(662) 325-3161
ascott@business.msstate.edu
• Daniel Soehren, Program Assistant
(662) 325-3161
dsoehren@business.msstate.edu
• Angie Chrestman, Associate Director, Career Center
(662) 325-3823
achrestman@career.msstate.edu
• Tony Luczak, Director of golf
(662) 325-3028
tluczak@golfcourse.msstate.edu
Description:
Undergrad Degree: B.A. in Mktg plus Certification for 24 of 36 credits for the Class A PGA Membership

MULTICULTURAL GOLF ASSOCIATION OF AMERICA
P.O. BOX 1081
WESTHAMPTON BEACH, NY 11978-7081
mgaagolf@aol.com
www.mgaagolf.org
• John David, Founder/President
• Paul David, Co-Founder/Executive Vice President
• Richard Friedson, Treasurer
Year Founded:
1991
Description:
Mission is to make golf available and accessible to all people, with the belief that learning the game of gold leads to positive character development, self-discipline, academic achievement, self-reliance, creativity, imagination, principle, values, and a balanced approach for the youth of America.

NATIONAL GOLF COURSE OWNERS ASSOCIATION
291 SEVEN FARMS DRIVE
SECOND FLOOR
CHARLESTON, SC 29492
843-881-9956
800-933-4262
Fax: 843-881-9958
www.ngcoa.org

- Matt Galvin, President
- Rock Lucas, Vice President
- Walter Lankau, Jr., Secretary
- Frank Romano, Treasurer
- Michael K Hughes, Chief Executive Officer

Year Founded:
1979

Description:
Mission is to enhance the lives of golf course owners by making their business more profitable, more efficient, better managed and more stable.

Number of members:
6,000

Membership Requirements:
Open to existing privately owned and profit oriented golf courses that are open to the general public on a daily fee and/or annual membership basis

Member Services:
Smart Buy Purchasing Program, involving the negotiation of supplier agreements; annual convention and seminars; knowledgeline; annual trade show; tracks pertinent legislative issues; insurance program

Publications:
GOLF BUSINESS, monthly; Operations Manual; Accounting for Public and Resort Golf Courses; Marketing Plan Manual, annual; GOLF BUSINESS, monthly magazine

NATIONAL GOLF FOUNDATION
1150 SOUTH US HIGHWAY ONE
STE 401
JUPITER, FL 33477
561-744-6006
888-275-4643
Fax: 561-744-6107
general@ngf.org
www.ngf.org
- Chip Brewer, Chairman
- Joe Louis Barrow, Jr., Vice Chairman
- Dick Raskopf, Secretary/Treasurer
- Joseph F. Beditz, PhD, President & Chief Executive Officer
- Greg Nathan, Senior Vice President

Year Founded:
1936

Description:
Provides the most timely and relevant information on the golf industry with original research on every aspect of the business.

Number of members:
6,000

Membership Requirements:
Charter membership: available to major golf industry companies. Sponsor membership: for all golf industry companies. Facility membership: open to all golf facilities. Association membership: available to regional, national, and international golf associations

Member Services:
Seminars, insurance plans and discounts on all research reports

Publications:
Instructional guides for playing and teaching golf; books on all phases of building and operation of golf facilities; annual research reports on all aspects of the game

NATIONAL HOLE-IN-ONE ASSOCIATION
1840 NORTH GREENVILLE AVENUE
SUITE 178
RICHARDSON, TX 75081

972-808-9001
1 (800) 527-6944
www.hio.com
- Douglas J. Burkert, President
- Sam Schachter, Marketing Director Special Events
sschachter@hio.com

Year Founded:
1981

Description:
Offers Hole-in-One prize programs, with limits up to $1,000,000 to corporate sponsors wishing to advertise at golf events. Also offers prize programs for sporting events and promotional contests

Member Services:
National Hole-In-One Association and National Media are the world's leading provider of prize insurance coverage. National Hole-In-One Association handles prize coverage for golf tournament holes in one in the USA, Europe, South America, Africa and Australia. national Media handles prize coverage on all other sports challenge contests, as well as games of luck in the same regions

London Address:
150 Fenchurch St, London, England EC3M6BL, Phone 0800 833 863, Fax 0800 387 748, Email: nhio@btconnect.com

NATIONAL SENIOR GOLF ASSOCIATION
200 PERRINE ROAD
SUITE 201
OLD BRIDGE, NJ 08857
908-208-8691
Fax: 732-525-9590
mark@nationalseniorgolf.com
- Mark Gartenfeld
- Roger Bakos

Year Founded:
2003

Description:
Conducts regional and national golf tournaments for members and other interested persons, using group purchasing power and off-season scheduling to obtain economical rates

Number of Members:
500+

Membership Requirements:
Annual fee of $35

Publications:
Fore Seniors, semi-monthly

NGA HOOTERS PRO GOLF TOUR
550 HIGHWAY 9 EAST
UNIT B
LONGS, SC 29568
800-992-8748
Fax: 843-399-5125
www.swingthought.com
- Robin L. Waters, President
joy@swingthought.com
- Ryan Waters, Vice President, Tour
- Jeff Harlow, Tour Director
harlow@swingthought.com
- Todd Barbee, Senior Tournament Director

Year Founded:
1988

Description:
We are proud to say that we are the only developmental tour in the country to offer a full week of activities that include free practice rounds, free range balls, 72 hole tournament, pro-ams, junior clinics, and shootouts

Other locations:

NORTHERN OHIO GOLF ASSOCIATION
ONE GOLFVIEW LANE
NORTH OLMSTED, OH 44070
440-686-1070
www.noga.org
- Matt Konyesni, Communications and Tournament Manager
(440) 686-1070
mkonyesni@noga.org
- Scotte Rorabaugh, Executive Director
(440) 686-1070
scotte@noga.org
- Frank Rihtar, Charities and Foundation Director
(440) 686-1070
frank@noga.org
- Matt Duffy, Handicap Services Manager
(440) 686-1070
mduffy@noga.org

Nature of Service:
Founded as the Cleveland District Golf Association to establish interclub competition for the original eight clubs, the Northern Ohio Golf Association has grown greatly to serve both its member clubs and the remainder of the golf industry in northern Ohio.

Year Founded:
1917

Number of Members:
28,000

Publications:
NOGA Fairways, e-Newsletter distributed 4-6 time(s) per year.

PGA 20/20
100 PGA TOUR BOULEVARD
PONTE VEDRA BEACH, FL 32082
904-285-3700
www.pgatour.com
- Timothy W. Fichem, Commissioner
- David Desmond, National Sales Director
(904) 273-2379
daviddesmond@pgatourhq.com
- Edward Moorhouse, Executive VP/Co-COO

Year Founded:
1995

Services:
Exclusive domestic licensing agent for the PGA Tour.

Marketing & Consulting Services:
Exclusive domestic licensing agent for the PGA Tour

PGA OF AMERICA/PROFESSIONAL GOLFERS' ASSOCIATION OF AMERICA
100 AVE OF THE CHAMPIONS
PALM BEACH GARDENS, FL 33418
561-624-8400
www.pga.com/pga-america
- Derek Sprague, President
- Allen Wronowski, Honorary President
- Peter Bevacqua, Chief Executive Officer
- Paul Levy, Vice President
- Suzy Whaley, Secretary

Year Founded:
1916

Description:
Elevates standards of the golf professional's vocation. Promotes interest in golf. Protects mutual interests of members. Holds meetings & tournaments. Assists unemployed members in obtaining a new position. Improves economic opportunities of members. Institutes a benevolent fund for relief of members. And effects any other objective determined by the Association

Number of members:
27,000

Membership Requirements:
Must successfully complete the Professional Golf Training Program (average 2 1/2 years) and Pass Playing Ability Test
Member Services:
Golf Professional Training Program, Educational seminars, employment conferences for members in various areas of the country. Film library. Books and pamphlets. 41 Sections throughout the U.S
Publications:
PGA MAGAZINE, monthly

Other locations:

ALOHA PGA SECTIONAL OFFICE
615 PIIKOI STREET
SUITE 1812
HONOLULU, HI 96814
808-593-2230
Fax: 808-593-2234
aloha411@pgahq.com
www.aspga.com
• Steve Murphy, President
• Wesley Wailehua, Executive Director
• Kyra Chun, Executive Secretary
• Charlee Kapiioho, Communications Manager
Year Founded:
1966
Number of Members:
260

CAROLINAS PGA SECTION
6271 BRYAN PARK RD
BROWNS SUMMIT, NC 27214
336-398-2742
Fax: 336-398-2743
carolinas@pgahq.com
www.carolinas.pga.com
• Ron Schmid, Executive Director
RSchmid@pgahq.com
• Kurt Battenberg, Director of Operations and Finance
kbattenberg@pgahq.com
• Cory Armstrong, Tournament Director
CArmstrong@pgahq.com
• Mike Whitenack, Senior Tournament Official
MWhitenack@pgahq.com
• David Kullenberg, Tournmant Official, PGA
dkullenberg@pgahq.com
• Liz Muroski, Director of Media and Promotions
lmuroski@pgahq.com
• Nazmieh Kheir, Tournament Coordinator
NKheir@pgahq.com
Number of Members:
2,000
Membership Requirements:
Must be a member or apprentice with the PGA of America
Publications:
CAROLINAS PGA MAGAZINE

CENTRAL NEW YORK PGA SECTIONAL OFFICE
5011 JAMESVILLE ROAD
JAMESVILLE, NY 13078
315-446-5610
Fax: 315-446-5870
www.cny.pga.com
• Alan Seamens, Executive Director
ASEAMAN@PGAHQ.COM
• Steve Nacewicz, President
snaz@pga.com
• Richard Winstead, Vice President
richardwinsteadpga@gmail.com
• Bob Fuller, Secretary
rfgolfpro@gmail.com
• Stan Gorman, Honorary President
• Rich Chapman, Director
richsquid1@hotmail.com
• Ben Mastronardi, Tournament Director
BMASTRONARDI@PGAHQ.COM
• Trish Wheeler, Membership Director/Office Manager
TWHEELER@PGAHQ.COM

Description:
Represents the finest avenue for reaching golf enthusiasts of all ages. The CNY PGA extends from the Thousand Islands in the north to Binghamton in the southern tier. From Utica to Seneca Falls, golfers are in contact with CNY PGA professionals on a regular basis.
Number of Members:
200

CONNECTICUT PGA SECTIONAL OFFICE
931 MAIN STREET
CARRIAGE HOUSE
SOUTH GLASTONBURY, CT 06073
860-257-4653
conn@pgahq.com
www.ctpga.com
• Bill Flood, President
• Ian Marshall, Vice President
• John Steffen, Secretary
• Andrew Campbell, Director
• Ciaran Carr, Director
• Bob Clark, Director
• Don Malen, Director
• Peter Pulaski, Director
• Tom Hantke, Executive Director
thantke@pgahq.com
• Sue Bell, Business Manager & Membership Director
sbell@pgahq.com
• Joe Mentz, Operations & Tournament Director
JMentz@pgahq.com
Description:
The Connecticut Section PGA is one of 41 sections chartered that together comprise the Professional Golfer's Association of America (PGA of America)
Number of Members:
364

DIXIE PGA SECTIONAL OFFICE
1300 BALLANTRAE CLUB DRIVE
PELHAM, AL 35124
205-621-6401
Fax: 205-664-3202
dixie@pgahq.com
www.dixie.pga.com
• Bart Rottier, Executive Director
brottier@pgahq.com
• Wade Dockery, Tournament Director
wdockery@pgahq.com
• Lauren Webster, Operations Manager
lwebster@pgahq.com
• Steve Schepker, Tournament Assistant
• Steve Cutler, President, Dixie Section PGA
stevec@wynlakes.com
• Eric Eshleman, Vice President, Dixie Section PGA
eeshleman@ccbham.com
• Steve Bobe, Secretary, Dixie Section PGA
sbobe1@pga.com
Number of Members:
313

GATEWAY PGA SECTIONAL OFFICE
17269 WILD HORSE CREEK ROAD
SUITE 110
CHESTERFIELD, MO 63005
636-532-3355
Fax: 636-532-0435
sbender@pgahq.com
www.gatewaypga.org
• Nathan Charmes, President
ncharnes@winghavencc.com
• Benjamin Kent, Vice President
bckent@pga.com
• Michael Suhre, Secretary
aceon4@yahoo.com
• Josh Riley, Executive Director
jriley@pgahq.com
• Steve Finn, Assistant Executive Director
sfinn@pgahq.com
• Ali Wells, Foundation Operations Director
awells@pgahq.com
• Bob Shogren, Rules Official
shogie@prodigy.net
• Susan Bender, Membership

sbender@pgahq.com
• Michael Brown, Junior Golf Director
mbrown@pgahq.com

GEORGIA PGA SECTIONAL OFFICE
590 WEST CROSSVILLE ROAD
SUITE 204
ROSWELL, GA 30075
678-461-8600
Fax: 678-461-0500
www.georgiapga.com
• Mike Paull, Executive Director
mpaull@pgahq.com
• Scott Gordon, Assistant Executive Director/Jr. Golf Director
sgordon@pgahq.com
• Scott Gordon, Assistant Executive Director
sgordon@pgahq.com
• Pat Day, Tournament Director
pday@pgahq.com
• Eric Wagner, Operations Manager
ewagner@pgahq.com
• Mike Mongell, President
mmongell@cherokeetcc.org
• Brian Albertson, Vice President
BAMULLIGAN@bellsouth.net

GULF STATES PGA SECTIONAL OFFICE
3115 6TH STREET
SUITE 110
METAIRIE, LA 70002
504-799-2444
Fax: 888-721-4037
gulfstates@pgahq.com
www.gspga.com
• Todd Roberston, President
ttrr@msn.com
• Jeff Adkerson, Vice President
jwa4@msstate.edu
• Bryant Himes, Secretary
bhimes1839@aol.com
• Robert Brown, Executive Director/Chief Executive Officer
rbrown@pgahq.com
• Brandon Roll, Tournament Director
broll@pgahq.com
• Patrick Murphy, Director of Player Development and Communications
pmurphy@pgahq.com
Year Founded:
1969
Number of Members:
380
Description:
An association of golf professionals whose mission is to promote interest, participation, and enjoyment in the game of golf; establish and maintain professional standards of practice; and enhance the well being of golf professionals.

ILLINOIS PGA SECTIONAL OFFICE
2901 WEST LAKE AVENUE
SUITE A
GLENVIEW, IL 60025
847-729-5700
Fax: 847-729-5599
illinois@pgahq.com
www.illinoispga.com
• Michael Miller, Executive Director
(847) 729-5700
mmiller@pgahq.com
• Jim Opp, President
• Mark Labiak, Vice President
• Jim Miller, Secretary
• Chris Gumbach, Honorary President
• Bill Ibrahim, Senior Director of Operations
(847) 729-5700
bibrahim@pgahq.com
• Mike Schoaf, Director Media & Communications
(847) 729-5700
mschoaf@pgahq.com
Description:
Conducts playing opportunities for PGA members, apprentices, and amateur golfers as well as support for the local golf professionals.

Number of Members:
555

INDIANA PGA
2625 HURRICANE ROAD
FRANKLIN, IN 46131
317-738-9696
800-779-7271
Fax: 317-738-9436
indiana@indianagolf.org
www.indianagolf.org
• Keith Clark, President
• Kelly Gaughan, Communications Director
(317) 739-3015
kgaughan@indianagolf.org
• Mike David, Executive Director
(317) 739-3016
mdavid@indianagolf.org
• Ryan Lambert, Assistant Executive Director
(317) 739-3019
rlambert@indianagolf.org
• Todd Dehaven, Tournament Director
(317) 739-3013
tdehaven@indianagolf.org
• Judy Deiwert, Director of Accounting
(317) 739-3011
jdeiwert@indianagolf.org
• Roger Lundy, Director of Junior Golf
Development
(317) 739-3020
rlundy@indianagolf.org
Year Founded:
1972

IOWA PGA SECTIONAL OFFICE
3184 HIGHWAY 22
RIVERSIDE, IA 52327
319-648-0026
Fax: 319-648-0008
iowa@pgahq.com
www.iowapga.com
• Troy Christensen, Executive Director
tchristensen@pgahq.com
• David Schneider, President
• John Valliere, Vice President
• Aaron Krueger, Secretary
Description:
Non-profit association, consisting of qualified
golf professionals dedicated to promoting the
game of golf; elevating the image of the PGA
and its members, providing educational and
playing opportunities, as well ad perpetuating
employment opportunities for its members

KENTUCKY PGA SECTIONAL OFFICE
1116 ELMORE JUST DRIVE
LOUISVILLE, KY 40245
502-243-8295
800-254-2742
Fax: 502-243-9266
kentucky@kygolf.org
www.kygolf.org
• Steve McMillen, Executive Director
smcmillen@kygolf.org
• Barbara Peak, Director of Finance
bpeak@kygolf.org
• Chris Osborne, President
• Tom Cooksey, Vice Pesident
• James Wagoner, Legal Counsel
• Steve McMillen, Executive Director
(800) 254-2742
smcmillen@kygolf.org
• Barbara Peak, Director,
Finance-Administration
(800) 254-2742
bpeak@kygolf.org
Description:
An organization comprised of over 200 member
clubs and courses throughout Kentucky, and is
governed by a Board of Directors made up of
representatives from facilities from across
Kentucky.

METROPOLITAN PROFESSIONAL GOLFERS ASSOCIATION
49 KNOLLWOOD ROAD
SUITE 200
ELMSFORD, NY 10523
914-347-2325
Fax: 914-347-2014
met@pgahq.com
www.met.pga.com
• Charlie Robson, Executive Director
(914) 347-2325
crobson@pgahq.com
• Kelli Clayton, Director of Operations
(914) 347-2325
kclayton@pgahq.com
• Jeff Voorheis, Tournament Director
(914) 347-2325
jvoorheis@pgahq.com
• Paul Giordano, Communications Manager
(914) 347-2325
pgiordano@pgahq.com
• Tony Murrell, Controller
(914) 347-2325
tmurrell@pgahq.com

MICHIGAN PGA SECTIONAL OFFICE
15600 CHANDLER ROAD
BATH, MI 48808
517-641-7421
Fax: 517-641-7830
michigan@pgahq.com
www.michiganpgagolf.com
• Kevin Helm, Executive Director
khelm@michiganpga.com
• Justin Phillips, Director of
Tournaments/Operations
jphillips@michiganpga.com
• Doug White, President
• Ron Osborne, Vice President
rjosborne@ci.battle-creek.mi.us
• Kevin McKinley, Secretary
kmckinley@treetops.com
• Gary Koenes, Honorary President
GaryK@pga.com
Description:
To promote the enjoyment and involvement in
the game of golf and to contribute to its growth
by providing services to golf professionals and
the golf industry.

MIDDLE ATLANTIC PGA
1 PGA DRIVE
STAFFORD, VA 22554
540-720-7420
Fax: 540-720-7076
midatl@pgahq.com
www.mapga.com
• John Madden, President
(703) 759-2640
jmrbgcc@aol.com
• Matthew Schulze, Vice President
(757) 253-3906
mdspga@verizon.net
• J.P. Lunn, Secretary
(301) 524-3213
jplunn@comcast.net
• John Lyberger, Director at Large
(301) 469-2032
• Brian Dix, A-8 Director
(410) 409-5941
bdix1008@gmail.com
• Butch Butler, Tournament Chair
(301) 342-3597
butchbutler@pga.com
• John Malinowski, Honorary President
(410) 641-6057
jmalinowski@pga.com
• Jon Guhl, Executive Director
(540) 720-7420
jguhl@pgahq.com
• Jeremy Greiner, Tournament Director
(540) 720-7420
jgreiner@pgahq.com
Number of Members:
750 members; 350 apprentices
Member Services:
Education Seminars; Employment Services;
Grow the Game Initiatives; Tournaments; Jr Golf
Foundation; Scholarship Foundation

Publications:
MAPGA Member Handbook; Middle Atlantic
PGA Annual; MAPGA Golf Pass

MIDWEST PGA SECTIONAL OFFICE
1960 NW COPPER OAKS CIRCLE
BLUE SPRINGS, MO 64015
816-229-6565
877-625-6565
Fax: 816-220-9644
midwest@pgahq.com
midwest.pga.com
• Jay Kennedy, President
(816) 318-0004
eagles4jay@aol.com
• Chad Myers, Vice President/Treasurer
(785) 456-2649
chad@wamegogolf.com
• Julie Roberts, Secretary
(816) 942-4033
jroberts@orion-mgmt.com
• Brad Demo, Executive Director
(816) 229-6493
bdemo@pgahq.com

MINNESOTA PGA SECTIONAL OFFICE
BUNKER HILLS GOLF COURSE
12800 BUNKER PRAIRIE ROAD
COON RAPIDS, MN 55448
763-754-0820
Fax: 763-754-6682
info@minnesotapga.com
www.minnesotapga.com
• Steve Fessler, President
(763) 271-5000
• Peter Kurvers, Honorary President
(320) 587-3070
• Joel Burger, Vice President
(312) 436-7990
• Mark Foley, Secretary
(651) 766-4170
• Jon Tollette, Executive Director
jtollette@pgahq.com
• Darren DeYoung, Tournament Director
ddeyoung@pgahq.com
• Kathy Swanson, Director Of Member Services
& Player Development
kswanson@pgahq.com

NEBRASKA PGA SECTIONAL OFFICE
601 J STREET
SUITE 10
LINCOLN, NE 68508
402-489-7760
Fax: 402-489-1785
nebraska@pgahq.com
www.nebraskapga.com
• Mike Antonio, President
mikea@happyhollowclub.com
• Tony Pesavento, Vice Pesident
tpesavento@omahacc.org
• Nathan Kalin, Secretary
nathan.kalin@fremontgolfclub.com
• Greg Neujahr, Honorary President/Special
Awards Chair
gneujahr@championsomaha.com
• David Honnens, Executive Director/CEO
dhonnens@pgahq.com
• Sean O'Neill, Tournament Director
soneill@pgahq.com
Number of Members:
220

NEW ENGLAND PGA SECTIONAL OFFICE
67A SHREWSBURY STREET
PO BOX 743
BOYLSTON, MA 01505
508-869-0000
Fax: 508-869-0009
neinfo@pgahq.com
www.nepga.com
• Mike Higgins, Executive Director
(508) 869-0000
mhiggins@pgahq.com
• Larry Kelley, President
(802) 558-0756

larry@fivestargolfcars.com
• Susan Bond, Vice President
(401) 322-7870
cslcbond@aol.com
• Ron Bibeau, Secretary
(207) 809-9030
rbibeau@thefirstteemaine.org
Description:
A non-profit association dedicated to promoting the game of golf, and is one of the 41 sections that comprise the PGA of America

NEW JERSEY PGA SECTION
255 OLD NEW BRUNSWICK ROAD
SUITE 100 SOUTH
PISCATAWAY, NJ 08854
732-465-1212
Fax: 732-465-9524
newjers@pgahq.com
www.newjersey.pga.com
• Chris Bauer, Executive Director
(732) 465-1212
cbauer@pgahq.com
• Steve Bartowski, Director of Tournaments
(732) 465-1212
sbartkowski@pgahq.com
• Scott Paris, President
(908) 769-3666
scottp@plainfieldcc.com
• David Reasoner, Vice President
(201) 225-6521
dreasoner@rcc1890.com
• Joe Kelly, Secretary, Treasurer & Grievance Chairman
(973) 543-7297
jpkpga@yahoo.com

NORTH FLORIDA PGA SECTIONAL OFFICE
7593 GATHERING DRIVE
KISSIMMEE, FL 34747
386-256-1221
Fax: 386-765-1478
nflorida@pgahq.com
www.nfpga.com
• Greg Lecker, President
glecker@sawgrasscountryclub.com
• Jim Lohbauer, Vice President
jimlohbauer@gmail.com
• Anthony Vaughn, Secretary
anthony.vaughn@honoursgolf.com
• Pamela Shelley, Tournament Chair
pshelley@sawgrasscountryclub.com
• Rich Smith, Executive Director/CEO
rsmith@pgahq.com
• Jane Olier, Bookkeeping and Finances
jolier@pgahq.com
Year Founded:
1999
Number of Members:
1,500

NORTHEASTERN NEW YORK PGA SECTIONAL OFFICE
TOWN OF COLONIE GOLF COURSE
418 CONSAUL RD
SCHENECTADY, NY 12304
518-438-8645
Fax: 518-438-8670
neny@pgahq.com
www.neny.pga.com
• Tracie Warner, Executive Director
(518) 438-8645
twarner@pgahq.com
• Doug Evans, Tournament Director
(518) 438-8645
devans@pgahq.com
• Kevin Hughes, President
kevinhughes@pga.com
• Ron Ireland, Vice President
ron@saratogagolfpoloclub.org
• Mike Behan, Secretary
pgagolfcar@aol.com
Description:
The Northeastern New York PGA is one of the smallest sections in the country.
Number of Members:
178

NORTHERN CALIFORNIA SECTIONAL OFFICE
411 DAVIS STREET
SUITE 103
VACAVILLE, CA 95688
707-449-4742
Fax: 707-449-4755
ncal@pgahq.com
www.ncpgalinks.com
• Chris Thomas, Executive Director/Chief Operating Officer
csthomas@pgahq.com
• Jennifer Noel, Operations Director
jnoel@pgahq.com
• Cameron MacGregor, Tournament Director
cmacgregor@pgahq.com
• Suzy Schneider, Administrative Assistant
sschneider@pgahq.com
• Carol Pence, Employment Service Consultant
(510) 706-1583
cpence@pgahq.com
• Nancy Maul, Assistant Executive Director
nmaul@pgahq.com
Description:
An organization committed to helping others through the game of golf. The association provides support to its golf professionals in the following areas: Education, Employment, Professional Tournaments, and Marketing/PR Services
Number of Members:
1,150

NORTHERN OHIO PGA SECTIONAL OFFICE
4735 RICHMOND ROAD
WARRENSVILLE HEIGHTS, OH 44128
216-765-1214
Fax: 216-765-0639
nohio@pgahq.com
thenorthernohiopga.com
• Scott Pollack, President
• Scott Sunderstrom, Vice President
• Ron Dejacimo, Secretary
• Mike Heisterkamp, Honorary President
• David Griffith, Tournament Director
dgriffith@pgahq.com
• Dominic Antenucci, Executive Director
dantenucci@pgahq.com
• Eileen Antenucci, Junior Golf Director
eantenucci@pgahq.com
Description:
Promote the enjoyment and involvement in the game of golf within the Section, and to contribute to its growth by providing services to golf professionals and the golf industry within our Section
Number of Members:
359 members, 212 golf facilities

NORTHERN TEXAS PGA SECTIONAL OFFICE
15150 PRESTON ROAD
SUITE 250
DALLAS, TX 75248
214-420-7421
Fax: 214-420-7424
mharrison@ntpga.com
www.ntpga.com
• Mark Harrison, Executive Director
(214) 420-7421
mharrison@ntpga.com
• Philip Bleakney, Honorary President
• Paul Earnest, President
• Tony Martinez, Vice Pesident
• Jason Hase, Secretary
• Courtney Connell, At-Large Director
Description:
In addition to managing the day-to-day affairs of the Section, the headquarters operates the Northern Texas PGA Junior Golf Foundation, a tax exempt organization
Number of Members:
750

PACIFIC NORTHWEST PGA SECTIONAL OFFICE
TUMWATER, WA
360-456-6496
800-688-4653
Fax: 360-456-6745
pacnw@pgahq.com
www.pnwpga.com
• Bryan Tunstill, President
(503) 285-8354
Bryan.Tunstill@cecc.com
• Greg Manley, Vice President
(253) 857-3133
greg@meridianvalleycc.com
• Greg Morris, Secretary
(406) 863-3106
gmorris@ironhorsemt.com
• Marcus King, Honorary President
(425) 454-7971
mking@overlakecc.com
• Jeff Ellison, Chief Executive Officer
JEllison@pgahq.com
• Molly Cooper, Director Of Tournament & Member Programs
MCooper@pgahq.com
Description:
Promote the enjoyment and involvement in the game of golf and to contribute to its growth by providing services to golf professionals and the golf industry
Number of Members:
1,100

PHILADELPHIA PGA SECTIONAL OFFICE
1009 PENLLYN PIKE
LOWER GWYNEDD, PA 19002
215-886-7742
Fax: 215-646-3961
phil@pgahq.com
www.philadelphia.pga.com
• Geoffrey Surrette, Executive Director
(215) 481-9083
gsurrette@pgahq.com
• Barbara Creveling, Assistant Executive Director
(215) 481-9081
bcreveling@pgahq.com
• Ellen Berlinger, Tournament Coordinator
(215) 481-9089
eberlinger@pgahq.com
• Leila Mackie, Comm & Player Development
(215) 481-9080
lmackie@pgahq.com
• John Pillar, President
(570) 685-8102
john.pillar@woodloch.com
• Ian Dalzell, Vice President
(215) 659-1584
idalzell@hvccpa.org
• John Rogers, Secretary
(717) 816-6110
jrpga@comcast.net
• Jeff Kiddie, Director Of Section Affairs
(215) 247-6001
jkiddie@aronimink.org
Number of Members:
860

ROCKY MOUNTAIN PGA SECTIONAL OFFICE
1303 SOUTH FIVE MILE ROAD
BOISE, ID 83709
208-939-6028
Fax: 208-939-6058
www.rockymountainpga.com
• Vaughn Jenkins, Executive Director
vjenkins@pgahq.com
• Laurie Draper, Member Services & Program Director
ldraper@pgahq.com
• David Snyder, President
dsnyder@wyoming.com
• Jim Brown, Vice President
jsb.brown@yahoo.com
Year Founded:
1986
Description:

The Rocky Mountain Section PGA and its member professionals are dedicated to nurturing and improving the quality of the game of golf for the thousands of golfers using our member facilities.

SOUTH CENTRAL PGA SECTIONAL OFFICE
951 NORTH FOREST RIDGE BOULEVARD
BROKEN ARROW, OK 74014
918-357-3332
Fax: 918-357-3328
scentral@pgahq.com
www.southcentral.pga.com
• Peter Vitali, President
(405) 302-2810
• Michael Henderson, Vice President
(405) 372-3399
mhenderson@stillwater.org
• Barry Howard, Secretary
(501) 624-2661
barry@hotspringscc.com
• Brian Soerensen, Honorary President
(405) 341-5350
• Brian Davis, Executive Director
bdavis@pgahq.com
• Joyce Cherblanc, Operations Manager
jcherblanc@pgahq.com
• Cimarron Grubb, Tournament Director
(405) 388-2577
cgrubb@pgahq.com
Description:
The local delivery system for PGA of America programs and activities to promote golf in this region and to enhance the skills of its members
Number of Members:
480

SOUTHERN CALIFORNIA PGA SECTIONAL OFFICE
3333 CONCOURS ST
BLDG 2, SUITE 2100
ONTARIO, CA 91764
951-845-4653
Fax: 951-769-6733
scpga@pgahq.com
www.scpga.com
• Tom Addis, Executive Director/CEO
taddis@pgahq.com
• Jeff Johnson, Director of Operations/COO
jjohnson@pgahq.com
• Max De Spain, Tournament Director
mdespain@pgahq.com
• John McNair, President
jmcnair@jcresorts.com
• Todd Keefer, Vice President
todd@wilshirecountryclub.com
Number of Members:
1,600

SOUTHERN OHIO PGA SECTIONAL OFFICE
66 SOUTH CENTRAL AVENUE
FAIRBORN, OH 45324
937-754-4263
Fax: 937-754-4663
sohio@pgahq.com
www.thesouthernohiopga.com
• Pat Delaney, President
• Brett Slater, Vice President
• Jimmy Logue, Secretary
• Amanda Fisher, Executive Director
amfisher@pgahq.com
• Kevin Stanton, Tournament Director
kstanton@pgahq.com
Year Founded:
1921
Number of Members:
500

SOUTHERN TEXAS PGA SECTIONAL
21604 CYPRESSWOOD DRIVE
SPRING, TX 77373
832-442-2404
stexas@pgahq.com
www.stpga.com

• Mike Ray, Executive Director
mray@pgahq.com
• Jeff Giedd, Tournament Manager
jgiedd@pgahq.com
• Clayton Hromadka, Director of Business Development & Tournaments
chromadka@pgahq.com
• Jeff Strong, President
• Brad Lardon, Vice President
• Doug DeSive, Secretary
• David Altemus, Honorary President
Description:
Offers an extensive tournament program within which professionals, amateurs and junior golfers can compete
Number of Members:
800

SOUTHWEST PGA SECTIONAL OFFICE
10685 NORTH 69TH STREET
SCOTTSDALE, AZ 85254
480-443-9002
Fax: 480-443-9006
swest@pgahq.com
www.southwest.pga.com
• Greg Leicht, President
gleicht@vistalgolfclub.com
• Michael Miller, Executive Director
mmiller@pgahq.com
• Mike Martino, Tournament Director
mmartino@pgahq.com
• Joe Hobby, Junior Golf Director
jhobby@pgahq.com
• Frank Calvin, Marketing Director
fcalvin@pgahq.com
• Mike Burhans, Administration/Membership Services
mburhans@pgahq.com
Description:
Promote the game of golf in this region and to enhance the skills of its members
Number of Members:
1,400

SUN COUNTRY PGA SECTIONAL OFFICE
2316 SOUTHER BLVD SE
SUITE C
RIO RANCHO, NM 87124
505-897-0864
800-346-5319
Fax: 505-897-3494
INFO@SUNCOUNTRYGOLFHOUSE.COM
www.suncountry.pga.com
• Matt Molloy, President
• Pat Gavin, Vice President
• Jason White, Secretary
• Derek Gutierrez, Past President
• Dana Lehner, Executive Director
• Teresa Hitchcock, Director Of PGA Member Services
Year Founded:
1974
Description:
Promote participation and enjoyment in the game of golf for all levels of golfers
Number of Members:
136

TENNESSEE PGA SECTIONAL OFFICE
400 FRANKLIN ROAD
FRANKLIN, TN 37069
615-790-7600
Fax: 615-790-8600
tenn@pgahq.com
www.tennpga.com
• Jeff Abbot, Executive Director
(615) 465-6311
• Ken Crowder, President
(276) 523-0739
kcrowder1@yahoo.com
• Johnny Bridgemann, Vice President
(615) 373-9922
johnny@bccgolf.org
• Jim Vernon, Secretary
(615) 847-4001
• David Olinger, Tournament Director
(615) 465-6312

Year Founded:
1995
Number of Members:
400

TRI-STATE PGA SECTIONAL OFFICE
993 BROADHEAD RD
SUITE 204
MOON TOWNSHIP, PA 15108
724-774-2224
Fax: 412-375-7395
tristate@pgahq.com
www.tristate.pga.com
• Ed Habjan, President
(412) 793-2200
ehabjan@greenoakscc.com
• John Klinchock, Vice President
(724) 238-5438
liggolf@verizon.net
• Dennis J. Darak, Sr., Executive Director/CEO
ddarak@pgahq.com
• David Wright, Assistant Executive Director/Tournament Director
dwright@pgahq.com

UTAH PGA SECTIONAL OFFICE
580 WEST 3300 SOUTH
SALT LAKE CITY, UT 84115
801-566-1005
Fax: 801-326-8098
utah@pgahq.com
www.utahpga.com
• Chriss Stover, President
chrisstover@utah.gov
• Ryan Kartchner, Vice President
ryan@hiddenvalley.cc
• Dustin Volk, Secretary
dvolk@co.davis.ut.us
• Colby Cowan, Honorary president
colby.cowan@sgcity.com
• Scott Whittaker, Executive Director
swhittaker@pgahq.com
• Annie Fisher, Programs Director
afisher@pgahq.com
Description:
Promotes involvment in and enjoyment of the game of golf for the golfers of Utah by providing services to its members, the golf industry, and to amateurs of all ages and skill levels.

WESTERN NEW YORK PGA SECTION OFFICE
8265 SHERIDAN DRIVE
WILLIAMSVILLE, NY 14221
716-626-7095
Fax: 716-626-5308
wnewyork@pgahq.com
www.westernnewyork.pga.com
• Jeff Mietus, President
jeffmietuspga@hotmail.com
• Michael O'Connor, Vice President
mjokah@aol.com
• Rob Horak, Secretary
bhhpro@rochester.rr.com
• Kirk Stauffer, Honorary President
paccpro1@verizon.net
• Joe Bertino, Executive Director
(716) 626-7095
jbertino@pgahq.com
• Alex Wright, Tournament Director
awright@pgahq.com
• Amanda Gingerich, Junior Golf Director
agingerich@pgahq.com
Year Founded:
1925
Description:
Mission is to establish the Section as a viable, valuable and visible organization in promoting the growth of golf and the advancement of the golfing professional.
Number of Members:
195

WISCONSIN PGA SECTIONAL OFFICE
11350 W THEO TRECKER WAY
WEST ALLIS, WI 53214

414-443-3570
Fax: 414-443-0817
wisc@pgahq.com
www.wisconsin.pga.com
• Rob Elliott, President
• Joe Stadler, Executive Director
jstadler@pgahq.com
• Chris Hoel, Director of Operations
choel@pgahq.com

PGA TOUR
100 PGA TOUR BOULEVARD
PONTE VEDRA BEACH, FL 32082
904-285-3700
www.pgatour.com
• Tim Finchem, Commissioner
• Charlie Zink, Executive VP/Co-Chief
Operating Officer
• Lee Bushkil, Vice President Media Sales
• Luis Goicouria, Vice President, Digital
Media Business Develo
• David Desmond, Sales Director, Digital
Media & Entertainment
• Raef Godwin, Director, Sales & Marketing
Operations
• Chris Wandell, Director, Business
Development
• Cynthia Howard, Director, Digital Sales
• Paul Johnson, Senior Vice President,
Strategic Development
Year Founded:
1974
Description:
A tax-exempt membership organization of
professional golfers. Mission is to expand
domestically and internationally to
substantially increase player financial
benefits while maintaining its commitment to
the integrity of the game.
Membership Requirements:
Must complete qualifying requirements
Publications:
Tour Book, player bibliographies, statistics,
etc

PRAIRIE GOLF
10708 SOUTH 149TH STREET
OMAHA, NE 68138
402-896-5079
800-528-5079
Fax: 402-881-8755
www.prairiegolf.com
• Scott Kasl, New Owner
Year Founded:
1995
Description:
 Eight-event tour open to professionals and
amateurs ages 16 and over. Operates in
states of Iowa, Kansas, Missouri, and
Nebraska
Membership Requirements:
$300 membership fee
Member Services:
Discounted entry fees for packages of
event; free practice rounds; $7,200 Skins
bonus pool at end of the schedule

PROFESSIONAL CADDIES ASSOCIATION
WORLDWIDE, PCA
23 MALACOMPRA ROAD
PALM COAST, FL 32137
386-446-8721
Fax: 386-446-8721
pca@pcahq.com
www.pcahq.com
• Dennis Cone, Founder/CEO
Year Founded:
1997

Description:
Open to everyone worldwide who wants to
help the mission. Over 11,000 walking
billboards to advertise and promote the your
company or products. World recognized
Association for over 20 years and
certification programs used at many top
clubs worlwide. Helps train over 11,000
caddies/members who play golf daily with
the decision maker of the world.
Number of Members:
5,500
Membership Requirements:
Dues is $50.00
Member Services:
Health, disability, retirement and marketing
benefits and opportunities for caddies and
their families. Worldwide travel company -
health card. Available to all caddies working
or retired. Caddie certification programs and
free insurance and benefits for members.

PROFESSIONAL PUTTERS
ASSOCIATION
FORT BRAGG ROAD
PO BOX 35237
FAYETTEVILLE, NC 28303
910-485-7131
Fax: 910-485-1122
www.proputters.com
• Joe Aboid, PPA Commissioner
joe@proputters.com
• Bill Baus, Players Committee Chairman
bill@proputters.com
• Rick Rybaczek, Website Developer
rick@proputters.com
• Joe Abode, PPA Commisioner
• Bill Baus
Description:
Founded 1959.
Membership Requirements:
Two membership classifications: amateur
and pro. Amateur and pro applications must
be signed by local Putt-Putt Golf Course
managing pro or forwarded to the executive
offices for review by the Board of Advisors.

SYMETRA TOUR
100 INTERNATIONAL GOLF DRIVE
DAYTONA BEACH, FL 32124
386-274-6200
Fax: 386-274-1099
futuresfeedback@lpga.com
www.symetratour.com
• Vicki Goetze-Ackerman, Player
Director-President (LGPA)
• Karrie Webb, Player Director- Vice
President (LGPA)
• Laura Diaz, Player Director (LGPA)
• Michael Whan, Commissioner
• Mike L Nichols, Chief Business Officer of
the Symetra Tour
Year Founded:
1981, Duramed Futures Golf Tour signed an
agreement with sponsor Symetra in 2011
and became the Symetra Tour.
Description:
The Future's Golf Tour's mission has three
primary objectives: to provide an opportunity
for women professional golfers to develop
their skills and pursue their competitive
goals; for tournament host communities to
meet and embrace future LPGA stars; and
for business communities and corporate
leaders at host sites to link with local
charities to develop a proven fund raising
vehicle by which to support local projects.

Membership Requirements:
We are the developmental tour of the LPGA.
Our membership is over 300 players
representing 26 different countries
Media Notes:
1999 - Signed a 5 year deal with the LPGA
making it the official developmental tour
Sponsors:
Aruba Sport, Champ®, Eco Golf, Penske
Truck Leasing, Sun Mountain® Sports, Yes!
Golf

U.S. GOLF ASSOCIATION/USGA
77 LIBERTY CORNER ROAD
FAR HILLS, NJ 07931-0708
908-234-2300
www.usga.org
• Thomas J O'Toole, President
• Diana M Murphy, Vice President
• William Gist, IV, Vice President
• Sheila C Johnson, Secretary
• Mark E Newell, Treasurer
• Ernest J Getto, General Counsel
• Mike Davis, Executive Director
Year Founded:
1894
Description:
Governing body for the sport of amateur golf
in the United States
Number of members:
700,000 members; 9,000 courses and clubs

Other locations:

ALASKA STATE GOLF ASSOCIATION
9360 OLD SEWARD HIGHWAY
ANCHORAGE, AK 99508
907-349-4653
golfalaska@gmail.com
www.agagolf.org
• Paul Blanche, President
• Jason Kimmel, Vice President
• Stacy Pettit, Treasurer
• Marcia Petros, Secretary
• Greg Sanders, Rules/Men's USGA Rep
• Bengie Sumulong, Trophies/Awards
• Rich Teders, Competitions

ANCHORAGE WOMEN'S GOLF
ASSOCIATION
9360 OLD SEWARD HWY
ANCHORAGE, AK 99515
907-555-5555
Fax: 907-563-7552
awgaak@gmail.com
ghin.com/eClubhouse/eClubHome.aspx?cid=10
68
• Nicole Harris, President
• Jamie Berge, Treasurer
• Leslie Fleming, Secretary
• Pam Chesla, Membership Chair
golf2201@aol.com
Year Founded:
1968
Description:
Promote and maintain the best interests and
true spirit of the game of golf among women in
the state of Alaska

ARIZONA GOLF ASSOCIATION
7600 E REDFIELD RD
SUITE 130
SCOTTSDALE, AZ 85260
602-944-3035
800-458-8484
Fax: 602-944-3228
aga1923@azgolf.org
www.azgolf.org
• Edward Gowan, Executive Director
edgowan@azgolf.org
• Michelle Evens, Club Program Manager
michelle@azgolf.org

- Lorraine Thies, Assistant Executive Director
lorraine@azgolf.org
- Brian Foster, Director of Marketing & Communications
bfoster@azgolf.org
- Derek McKenzie, Director of Handicapping and Course Rating
dmckenzie@azgolf.org
Year Founded:
1923
Description:
To foster the enhancement and expansion of the game of golf by leading in the development of member and information services, the promotion of opportunities for all who want to play, and the protection of the game's integrity and valued traditions

ARIZONA WOMEN'S GOLF ASSOCIATION
141 EAST PALM LANE
SUITE 210
PHOENIX, AZ 85004-1555
602-253-5655
800-442-2942
Fax: 602-253-6210
awga@awga.org
www.awga.org
- Mary Pomroy, Executive Director
mpomroy@awga.org
- Erin Groeneveld, Programs Manager
erin@awga.org
- Melanie R. Bridges, Secretary
- Robin Cook, Officer at Large
- Ginny Zak, President
- Sally Larson, Vice President
- Mary Byrd, Treasurer
Description:
Promote and maintain the best interests and true spirit of the game of golf among women in Arizona

ARKANSAS STATE GOLF ASSOCIATION
3 EAGLE HILL COURT
SUITE B
LITTLE ROCK, AR 72210
501-455-2742
800-984-2742
Fax: 501-455-8111
info@asga.org
www.asga.org
- Cippy Smith, President
- Chris Jenkins, Vice President
- Rob McSpadden, Treasurer
- Stan Lee, Secretary
- Jay Fox, Executive Director
Jay@asga.org
- Bryant Fortin, Director of Junior Golf
Bryant@asga.org
- Terri Green, Director Of Membership
Terri@asga.org

ARKANSAS WOMEN'S GOLF ASSOCIATION
PO BOX 280
CAVE SPRINGS, AR 72718
479-619-6082
dorherren@cox.net
www.awga.us
- Norma Hartney, President
n-hartney@sbcglobal.net
- Esther Tompkins, Vice President
tompkinsestherh@uams.edu
- Rosetta Parks, Secretary
rosieparks@cox.net
- Marilyn Lenggenhager, Treasurer
(501) 580-2171
Year Founded:
1924
Description:
To serve women golfers in Arkansas, which includes conducting championship tournaments, sponsoring Junior Girls championship tournaments, promote USGA Women's State Team competitions, participate inthe prestigious Fore-State Cup matches, and provide handicap (GHIN) and course rating service

BUFFALO DISTRICT GOLF ASSOCIATION
8265 SHERIDAN DRIVE
WILLIAMSVILLE, NY 14231
716-632-0151
www.buffdga.org
- Robert Rosen, President
- Nick Amigone, III, First Vice President
- Nick Morreale, Secretary/Treasurer
- Thomas Sprague, Executive Director
- Whitey Nichols, Rules Chairman
Number of Members:
78
Member Services:
Organization/Administration of 13 District Golf Tournaments, Junior Scholarship Program, Course Measurement/Rating, Handicapping Service
Membership Requirements:
Annual Dues

CAROLINAS GOLF ASSOCIATION
140 RIDGE ROAD
SOUTHERN PINES, NC 28387
910-673-1000
Fax: 910-673-1001
www.carolinasgolf.org
- G. Jackson Hughes, President
- Jack Nance, Executive Director
- Andy Priest, Assistant Executive Director
- Jason Cox, Director of Junior Golf
- Tiffany Priest, Director of Women's Golf and Membership Services
Year Founded:
1909
Description:
Conduct championships and tournaments for amateur golfers in North and South Carolina, administer the USGA handicap system in the Carolinas
Number of Members:
720
Membership Requirements:
CGA member clubs pay annual dues of $50.00

CHICAGO DISTRICT GOLF ASSOCIATION
MIDWEST GOLF HOUSE
11855 ARCHER AVENUE
LEMONT, IL 60439
630-257-2005
Fax: 630-257-2088
www.cdga.org
- David R. Haverick, President
- Michael J Grandinetti, First Vice President
- Sheldon L. Solow, Second Vice President
- Robert Markionni, Executive Director
(630) 685-2303
rmarkionni@cdga.org
- C. Daniel Cochran, Treasurer
- Mike Nass, Secretary
- Matt Baylor, Senior Director of Communications
(630) 685-2302
mbaylor@cdga.org
- Lynn Boyd, Director of Handicapping
(630) 685-2304
lboyd@cdga.org
- Margie Lawlor, Controller
(630) 685-2320
mlawlor@cdga.org
- Denny Davenport, Foundation Consultant
(630) 272-7872
ddavenport@cdga.org
Year Founded:
1914
Description:
Promote amateur golf in the Midwest
Number of Members:
100,000

COLORADO GOLF ASSOCIATION
5990 GREENWOOD PLAZA BOULEVARD
SUITE 102
GREENWOOD VILLAGE, CO 80111
303-366-4653
800-228-4675
Fax: 303-344-8229

cga@coloradogolf.org
www.coloradogolf.org
- Edward Mate, Executive Director
- Ann Bley, Director of Finance
- Dustin Jensen, Managing Director of Operations
- Aaron Kellough, Director of Communications
- Ashley Barnhart, Junior Tournament Coordinator
Year Founded:
1915
Description:
Purpose is to represent, promote, and serve the best interests of golf in the state of Colorado, and has been throughout its history
Publications:
Colorado Golf Newsletter, the official membership publication of the CGA, 4 times year to all active members; Colorado Golf, the official guide to the Golf Courses of Colorado, mailed in April to all active members; Golf in Colorado, an independent Study of the Economic Impact and Environmental Aspects of Golf in Colorado

COLORADO WOMEN'S GOLF ASSOCIATION
6 INVERNESS CT E
ENGLEWOOD, CO 80112
303-366-7888
800-392-2942
Fax: 303-474-3007
cwga@coloradowomensgolf.org
www.coloradowomensgolf.org
- Joanie Ott, President
- Juliet Miner, Vice President
- Phyllis Jensen, Secretary
- Jeanne Surbrugg, Treasurer
- Ann Guiberson, Executive Director
- Alex Westman, Manager-Tournament Administration/Member Programs
Year Founded:
1916
Number of Members:
Approximately 18,000 individual members.
Description:
The CWGA's mission is to promote women's golf in the state of Colorado and preserve the integrity of the game.
Publications:
Colorado Golf Newsletter, the official membership publication of the CGA, four times a year to all active members; Colorado Golf, official guide to the Golf Courses of Colorado, mailed in April to all active members; Golf in Colorado, an Independent Study of the Economic Impact and Environmental Aspects of Golf in Colorado

COLUMBUS DISTRICT GOLF ASSOCIATION
1570 WEST FIRST AVENUE
COLUMBUS, OH 43212
614-487-1207
golfmaster@ohiogolf.org
www.ohiogolf.org
- Gary Price, President
- James M. Popa, Executive Director
Description:
The prime moving force behind the promotion and betterment of golf in Central Ohio is the Columbus District Golf Association

CONNECTICUT STATE GOLF ASSOCIATION
35 COLD SPRING ROAD
SUITE 212
ROCKY HILL, CT 06067
860-257-4171
Fax: 860-257-8355
info@csgalinks.org
www.csgalinks.org
- Stan McFarland, President
- Mike Moraghan, Executive Director
(860) 257-4171
mmoraghan@csgalinks.org
- Ben Briggs, Vice President Club Relations
- Shelly Guyer, Vice President Competitions

- Bill Cremins, Secretary
- Jim Healy, Jr., Treasurer
- Ryan Hoffman, Director, Operations
(860) 257-4171
rhoffman@csgalinks.org
- Brent Paladino, Director, Competitions & Communications
(860) 257-4171
bpaladino@csgalinks.org
Year Founded:
1899
Description:
Functions as an extension of the USGA and provides stewardship for amateur golf in Connecticut
Number of Members:
170

DELAWARE STATE GOLF ASSOCIATION
7234 OLD LANCASTER PIKE
SUITE 302-B
HOCKESSIN, DE 19707
302-234-3365
Fax: 302-234-3359
dsga@dsga.org
www.dsga.org
- Gary Mahoney, President
- Dick Matthias, Vice President
- Wayne Carey, Vice President
- Tim Freeh, Treasurer
- Bill Barrow, Executive Director
- Laura Heien, Tournament Operations & Communications Manager
- Cameron McDonald, Board Member
- Jeff Allen, Board Member

FLORIDA STATE GOLF ASSOCIATION
12630 TELECOM DR
TAMPA, FL 33637
813-632-3742
Fax: 813-910-2129
www.fsga.org
- Randy Briggs, President
- Chuck Phillips, Vice President
- Steve Carter, Secretary/Treasurer
- Jim Applegate, Immediate Past President
- Jim Demick, Executive Director
(813) 868-5801
- Kevin Kasubinski, Manager Of Club Services & IT
(813) 868-5803
kevin@fsga.org
- Debby Lamontagne, Controller
(813) 868-5811
debby@fsga.org
- Wally Les, GHIN Regional Manager-SE Florida
(561) 704-8355
wally@fsga.org
Year Founded:
1913
Description:
Provides a variety of services to its member clubs, their members and the general golfing community of Florida.
Number of Members:
800

GOLF ASSOCIATION OF MICHIGAN
24116 RESEARCH DRIVE
FARMINGTON HILLS, MI 48335
248-478-9242
Fax: 248-478-5536
www.gam.org
- David Graham, Executive Director
(248) 478-9242
dgraham@gam.org
- Kelly Serr, Event Coordinator/Executive Administrator
(248) 478-9242
kserr@gam.org
- Susan Smiley, Manager Of Member Services & Communications
(248) 478-9242
ssmiley@gam.org
- Ken Hartmann, Senior Director Of Rules & Competition

(248) 478-9242
khartmann@gam.org
- Thomas Bollinger, President
- Steve Braun, Vice President
- James Koepke, Treasurer
- Chris Angott, Secretary
Year Founded:
1919
Description:
Our purpose is to represent, promote, and serve the best interests in the game of golf
Membership Requirements:
Blue Card Member, annual dues $30.00 with discount golf benefits and a free subscription to Michigan Links Magazine; Gold Card Member, annual dues $35.00 with full benefits, including official gam/usga handicap index and tournament eligibility
Publications:
Michigan Links Magazine free to all active members

GOLF ASSOCIATION OF PHILADELPHIA
1974 SPROUL ROAD
SUITE 400
BROOMALL, PA 19008
610-687-2340
Fax: 610-687-2082
email@gapgolf.org
www.gapgolf.org
- Robert M. Morey, President
- Kirby V. Martin, Director Of Competitions
(610) 687-2340
kmartin@gapgolf.org
- Christopher A. Roselle, Tournament Director
(610) 687-2340
croselle@gapgolf.org
- Mark E. Peterson, Executive Director
(610) 687-2340
mpeterson@gapgolf.org
- Martin D. Emeno, Jr., Director Operations
(610) 687-2340
- Mario Machi, Director of Handicapping
(610) 687-2340
mmachi@gapgolf.org
- Justin A Reasy, Tournament Assistant
(610) 687-2340
jreasy@gapgolf.org
- Jan Garber, Programs Manager
(610) 687-2340
jgarber@gapgolf.org
Year Founded:
1897
Description:
The purpose of the association is simple: to preserve, protect and promote the game of golf. Every GAP activity is designed to do just that
Number of Members:
132

GREATER CINCINNATI GOLF ASSOCIATION
9200 MOUNTGOMERY ROAD
SUITE 24B
CINCINNATI, OH 45242
513-522-4444
Fax: 513-521-4242
www.gcga.org
- Art Plate, President
- Todd Johnson, Executive Director
tjohnson@gcga.org
- James E. Stahl, Jr., Executive Vice President
- Matt Eilers, Treasurer
- Robert Gerwin, II, Secretary
- Teresa Silvers, Handicapping & Course Rating Director
tsilvers@gcga.org
Description:
Promote interest in, enthusiasm for and support for the game of golf among all golfers in the Greater Cincinnati area

HAWAII STATE GOLF ASSOCIATION
98-025 HEKAHA ST
UNIT 204A
AIEA, HI 96701

808-589-2909
Fax: 808-589-2915
info@hawaiistategolf.org
www.hawaiistategolf.org
- Paul Ogawa, Executive Director
paul@hawaiistategolf.org
- Jay Hinazumi, President
- Gary Wild, Vice President
- Darrell Yamagata, Treasurer
- Gordon Cho, Secretary
Year Founded:
1984
Description:
Non-profit organization dedicated to the goals and traditions of golf in Hawaii. Our main objective is to unite every golfer in Hawaii under one reliable and accurate handicapping system

HAWAII STATE WOMEN'S GOLF ASSOCIATION
HONOLULU, HI 96815
www.hswga.net
- Gwen Omori, President
gcomori@hawaiiantel.net
- Barbara Schroeder, Vice President
barbara.schroeder@outlook.com
- Marcia Lee, Treasurer
- Susan Church, Corresponding Secretary
wchurch1@hawaiiantel.net
Year Founded:
1976
Description:
Promote women's golf as a competitive sport and recreational activity in the State of Hawaii. We believe the game contributes to the overall self-betterment of girls and women by enhancing physical, emotional, social and mental development, and promoting lifelong values of personal motivation, discipline, integrity, patience and teamwork

IDAHO GOLF ASSOCIATION
4696 OVERLAND RD
SUITE 120
BOISE, ID 83705
208-342-4442
Fax: 208-345-5959
www.theiga.org
- Jennifer Swindell, President
(208) 473-8811
swindelljen@gmail.com
- Kelly Park, Vice President
rpark4@silverstar.com
- Brenda Sanford, Treasurer
bsanford@dlevans.com
- Genger Fahleson, Executive Director
Year Founded:
1969
Description:
Its purpose is to represent, promote and serve the best interests of golf in our state
Number of Members:
18,200
Membership Requirements:
$20 annual fee
What IGA Membership Supports:
IGA Clubs; IGA & Member Club Tournament Calendar; Handicapping; Current USGA Course Ratings for IGA Clubs; Member Education: Rules/Course Rating; Gold Course Superintendent's Association; USGA; PGA Snake River Chapter; Pacific Northwest Golf Association; Northwest Turfgrass Research; Junior Golf Activities for Girls and Boys; Publications for IGA Members; National Exposure for Idaho & Idaho Players; IGA Championships
Publications:
Intermountain Golf Magazine; Pacific NW Golfer; Idaho Gold Journal

INDIANA GOLF ASSOCIATION
2526 HURRICANE RD
PO BOX 516
FRANKLIN, IN 46131
317-738-9696
800-779-7271

Fax: 317-738-9436
www.indianagolf.org
• Mike David, Executive Director
(317) 739-3016
mdavid@indianagolf.org
• Todd Dehaven, Tournament Director
(317) 739-3013
tdehaven@indianagolf.org
• Matt Shepherd, President
• John Watts, First Vice President
• Steve Paquin, Second Vice President
• Mark Inman, Past President
• Steve Sterrett, Secretary
ext 240
• Brad Hardin, Treasurer
ext 235
• Ryan Lambert, Assistant Executive Director
(317) 739-3019
rlambert@indianagolf.org
• Kristtini Hunt, Director of Womens Golf
(317) 739-3017
krhunt@indianagolf.org
• Roger Lundy, Junior Golf Development
(317) 739-3020
rlundy@indianagolf.org
Year Founded:
1972

IOWA GOLF ASSOCIATION
1605 N ANKENY BLVD
SUITE 210
ANKENY, IA 50023
515-207-1062
888-388-4442
Fax: 515-207-1065
www.iowagolf.org
• Tom Christensen, President
• Joe Kehoe, Past President
• Andy Burton, Vice President
• Mike Pape, Secretary
• John Matovina, Treasurer
• Bill Dickens, Executive Director
dwdickens@iowagolf.org
• Clint Brown, Director Of Communications & Marketing
clint@iowagolf.org
• Katelynn Hogenson, Director Of Membership Services & Women's Golf
katelynn@iowagolf.org
Description:
Non-profit organization that works to preserve and promote the best interests and spirit of the game of golf and to encourage harmony and cooperation among golf clubs and other related associations

KANSAS CITY GOLF ASSOCIATION
8330 MELROSE DR.
LENEXA, KS 66214
913-649-5242
doug@kcgolf.org
www.kansascitygolfer.org
• Dick Sauer, Past President
• Doug Habel, Executive Director
ext 1
doug@kcgolf.org
• Taylor McCann, President
• Carol Gillard, Vice President
• Dick Swetala, Treasurer
• Gary Hruby, Secretary
• Jacque Madison, Director of Club Services
jacque@kcgolf.org
• Todd Stice, Director Of Rules & Competitions
ext 3
todd@kcgolf.org
Year Founded:
1912
Description:
Is a full service regional golf association dedicated to the betterment of the amateur golf community of greater Kansas City

KANSAS GOLF ASSOCIATION
1201 WAKARUSA DRIVE
SUITE B5
LAWRENCE, KS 66049
785-842-4833
Fax: 785-842-3831

kga@kansasgolf.org
www.kansasgolf.org
• Gary Lucas, President
• Rusty Hilst, Tournament Administrator
rhilst@cox.net
• Brian Burris, General Counsel
• John Alefs, Director
ext 202
• Sean Thayer, Secretary/Treasurer
• Mike Grosdidier, Vice President
• Jack Simpson, Past President
• Kim Richey, Executive Director
kim@kansasgolf.org
• Casey Old, Director Of Rules & Competitions
casey@kansasgolf.org
• Tyler Cummins, Director Of Member Services & Junior Golf
tyler@kansasgolf.org
Description:
Non-profit organization dedicated to promoting and preserving the game of golf in the State of Kansas
Year Founded:
1908
Number of Members:
24,000 members, 175 golf clubs
Publications:
Kansas Golfer Magazine

KANSAS WOMEN'S GOLF ASSOCIATION
TOPEKA, KS
KWGAPres@gmail.com
www.kwga.org
• Karen Hunt-Exon, President
(785) 266-0931
KWGAPres@gmail.com
• Jayne E. Clarke, Vice President
(785) 650-9610
KWGAVP@gmail.com
• Alice Kaul, Treasurer
(316) 207-4827
KWGATreasurer@gmail.com
• Kay Watts, Secretary
(316) 733-8692
KWGASecretary@gmail.com
• Debbie Slater, Tournament Director
(316) 208-9672
KWGATD@gmail.com
Year Founded:
1915
Description:
Promote the game of golf for female golfers, to encourage sportsmanship and skill, and to provide chamionships and events for women golfers, and to engage in charitable efforts related to the game of golf.
Number of Members:
4,789

KENTUCKY GOLF ASSOCIATION
GOLF HOUSE KENTUCKY
1116 ELMORE JUST DRIVE
LOUISVILLE, KY 40245
502-243-8295
800-254-2742
Fax: 502-243-9266
kentucky@kygolf.org
www.kygolf.org
• Chris Osborne, President
• Tom Cooksey, Vice President
• Barbara Peak, Director, Finance-Administration
(800) 254-2742
bpeak@kygolf.org
• Steve McMillen, Executive Director
(800) 254-2742
smcmillen@kygolf.org
• James Wagoner, Legal Counsel
• Erin Horn, Director Communications-Membership
(800) 254-2742
ehorn@kygolf.org
Year Founded:
1911
Description:
Recognized as the governing body for amateur golf in the Commonwealth

Number of Members:
200

LADIES BIRMINGHAM GOLF ASSOCIATION
lbgaemail@gmail.com
www.lbga.org
• Sharon Kellum, President
• Lynn Glover, 1st Vice President
• Jody Atchison, 2nd Vice President
• Missy Bibb, Secretary
• Pat Heilala, Treasurer
• Debbie Atchley, Past President
Year Founded:
1971

LOUISIANA WOMEN'S GOLF ASSOCIATION
JONESVILLE, LA 71343
• Mary Edwards, President
(318) 403-0111
contrarymary_@bellsouth.net
• Paula Karam, Treasurer
(318) 623-4339
pekdent211@aol.com
• Pam Washington, Secretary
(504) 452-7044
buzznrnd@hotmail.com
• Sandra Smith, Juniors
(318) 341-0575
ssmith2454@hotmail.com

MAINE STATE GOLF ASSOCIATION
58 VAL HALLA ROAD
CUMBERLAND, ME 04021
207-829-3549
Fax: 207-829-3584
msga@mesga.org
www.mesga.org
• Lowell Watson, President
• Nancy Storey, Executive Director
(207) 829-3549
nancy@mesga.org
• Brian Bickford, Treasurer
• Marty Crowe, Vice President
• Mike Doran, Director Of Tournament Administration
(207) 829-3549
mike@mesga.org
Description:
Promote and serve the best interests of amateur golf in Maine, and to sponsor a scholarship fund

MARYLAND STATE GOLF ASSOCIATION
EMICH HOUSE, COMMERCENTRE EAST
1777 REISTERSTOWN ROAD, SUITE 145
BALTIMORE, MD 21208
410-653-5300
Fax: 410-653-8810
www.msga.org
• Thomas Whelan, President
• William K Smith, Executive Director
• Stanard T. Klinefelter, Vice President
• Kimberly M. Ferguson, Director of Operations
• John J. Pauliny, Treasurer
• J. Robert Sherwood, Secretary
Year Founded:
1921
Description:
Promote the best interests of golf in the State of Maryland

MARYLAND STATE GOLF ASSOCIATION - WOMEN'S DIVISION
1777 REISTERSTOWN ROAD
SUITE 145, COMMERCENTRE EAST
BALTIMORE, MD 21208
410-653-5300
Fax: 410-653-8810
• Deb Watkins, Treasurer
• Patsy DiMuzio, Corresponding Secretary
• William Smith, Executive Director
• Melly Tucker, President
• Joan Heiss, Vice President
• Carolyn Hudson, Recording Secretary

Year Founded:
1995
Description:
Promote the best interests of golf in the State of Maryland

MASSACHUSETTS GOLF ASSOCIATION
300 ARNOLD PALMER BOULEVARD
NORTON, MA 02766
774-430-9100
800-356-2201
Fax: 774-430-9101
www.mgalinks.org
• Clarence J. Bennett, Esq., President
• Thomas Bagley, III, First Vice President
• Stephen R Dooley, Treasurer
• Jerry R. Green, Secretary
• Jesse Menachem, Executive Director
(774) 430-9102
jmenachem@mgalinks.org
• Becky Blaeser, Director Communications
(774) 430-9104
bblaeser@mgalinks.org
• Scott B. Whitcomb, Director- Field Operations
(774) 430-9108
swhitcomb@mgalinks.org
• Peter A. Caro, General Counsel
Year Founded:
1903
Description:
Dedicated to promoting and preserving amateur golf in the Commonwealth
Number of Members:
100,000

METROPOLITAN AMATEUR GOLF ASSOCIATION
11777 CLAYTON ROAD
ST.LOUIS, MO 63131
314-576-6242
Fax: 314-261-9250
info@metga.org
www.metga.org
• Stanford S. Grossman, President Emeritus
• Curt Rohe, Executive Director
curt@metga.org
• Thomas O. Sobbe, Jr., Vice President
• Thomas J. O'Toole, Jr., Vice President
• G. Scott Engelbrecht, Treasurer
• M. Ray McCraine, Secretary
• Bill Burton, Director Communications
• Carole Waugh, Director Finance
• Francis Byron, General Counsel
Year Founded:
1992
Description:
Provide a variety of amateur golf services to its member clubs
Number of Members:
130

MIAMI VALLEY GOLF ASSOCIATION
263 REGENCY RIDGE DR
DAYTON, OH 45459
937-294-6842
Fax: 866-301-2974
www.miamivalleygolf.org
• Charles Rinehart, Jr., President
charlie_rinehart@yahoo.com
• Doug Miller, Vice President
Millersfour@woh.rr.com
• Steve Jurick, Executive Director
(937) 609-3387
steve@otgt.org
• Dan Sutherly, Treasurer
drscoinc@gmail.com
• Jeff Scohy, Secretary
scohy@woh.rr.com
• Matt Wendelken, Assistant Director
(330) 618-3023

MIDDLE ATLANTIC GOLF ASSOCIATION
PO BOX 3040
GAITHERSBURG, MD 20885

301-869-6020
Fax: 301-869-6020
magainfo1902@yahoo.com
www.middleatlanticga.org
• Timothy G. Vigotsky, President
• Tim Merry, Vice President
• Randal P. Reed, Executive Director
rreed@middleatlanticga.org
• Joseph S. Burns, Treasurer
• Edward A. Johnston, General Counsel
Year Founded:
1902
Description:
Promote and serve golf in the Middle Atlantic
Number of Members:
125

MINNESOTA GOLF ASSOCIATION
6550 YORK AVENUE SOUTH
SUITE 211
EDINA, MN 55435
952-927-4643
800-642-4405
info@mngolf.org
www.mngolf.org
• Kip Colwell, President
• Ken Gerzsenyi, Past President
• Doug Hoffman, Tournament Director
(952) 345-3963
doug@mngolf.org
• Nancy LeRoy, Accounting Manager
(952) 345-3976
nleroy@mngolf.org
• Tom Ryan, Executive Director & COO
(952) 345-3971
tom@mngolf.org
• Barb Hanson, 1st Vice President
• Tom H. Smith, Secretary/Treasurer
Year Founded:
1901
Description:
Our mission is to uphold and promote the game of golf and its values for all golfers in Minnesota
Number of Members:
93,000
Publications:
Minnesota Golfer magazine published bi-monthly

MISSISSIPPI GOLF ASSOCIATION
400 CLUBHOUSE DRIVE
PEARL, MS 39208
601-939-1131
Fax: 601-939-0773
missgolf@missgolf.org
www.missgolf.org
• Richard Reed, President
• Brother Sandifer, Vice President
• Margo Coleman, Executive Director
• Ben Snow, Secretary/Treasurer
• Don Hershfelt, Tournament Director
donhershfelt@gmail.com
• Emily Sullivan, Director Of Membership & Club Services
emily@missgolf.org
Year Founded:
1925
Description:
Promote and conserve throughout the state of Mississippi the best interests and true spirit of the game of golf as embodied in its ancient and honorable traditions, and thereby promoting the common good and general welfare of the people of the state of Mississippi

MISSISSIPPI WOMEN'S GOLF ASSOCIATION
1515 SOUTH 40TH AVENUE
HATTIESBURG, MS 39402
601-268-6680
https://www.misswomensgolf.org/
• Sheila Haynes, President
shelagger@gmail.com
• Lynn Harmount, Treasurer
lharmount@comcast.net
• Dinah Kennedy, Secretary
Dsk080892@aol.com

Year Founded:
2006

MISSOURI GOLF ASSOCIATION
1616 OIL WELL DRIVE
JEFFERSON CITY, MO 65101
573-636-8994
Fax: 573-636-4225
www.mogolf.org
• Denny Payne, President
• Scott Hovis, Executive Director
shovis@mogolf.org
• Cord Dombrowski, First Vice President
• Charlie Digges, Secretary/Treasurer
• Kent Lowry, Legal Counsel
• Karen Raithel, Director Of Membership & GHIN Services
kraithel@mogolf.org
Year Founded:
1905
Description:
Non-profit organization whose purpose is to promote the best interests and true spirit of the game of golf throughout the State of Missouri

MISSOURI WOMEN'S GOLF ASSOCIATION
1616 OILWELL DRIVE
JEFFERSON CITY, MO 65109
573-636-8994
Fax: 573-636-4225
• Nancy Sebastian, President
President@mowomensga.org
• Harriette Myers, Treasurer
Treasurer@mowomensga.org
• June Halsor, Secretary
Secretary@mowomensga.org
• Karen Shippy, Vice President
Vicepresident@mowomensga.org
• Dee Johnson, Membership Director
Membership@mowomensga.org
Year Founded:
1935
Description:
Our mission is the pursuit of amateur women's golf in the state of Missouri and Johnson County, Kansas. It takes and active interest in all phases of women's golf
Number of Members:
750

MONTANA STATE GOLF ASSOCIATION
HELENA, MT 59602
406-458-3359
www.msgagolf.com
• Steve Sherburne, President
(406) 226-4540
nniins@3rivers.net
• Gerard Poore, Treasurer
(406) 442-8125
poore@bresnan.net
• Jim Opitz, Executive Director
(406) 458-3359
• Roger Amundson, Vice President
(406) 654-1130
rkamts@yahoo.com
• Emily Hulsey, Handicap/Website Coordinator
(800) 628-3752
emily@montana.net
• Nick Dietzen, MSGA Commmunications Director
(406) 459-3459
ndietzen@gmail.com
Year Founded:
1917
Description:
Non-profit organization of member clubs, governed by amateur golfers, and dedicated to serving the game of golf in Montana
Number of Members:
21,000

NEBRASKA GOLF ASSOCIATION
6618 SOUTH 118TH STREET
OMAHA, NE 68137

402-505-4653
Fax: 402-505-4695
www.nebgolf.org
• Greg Stine, President
• Craig W. Ames, Executive Director
cames@nebgolf.org
• Justin Ahrens, Assistant Executive Director
jahrens@nebgolf.org
• Ben Vigil, Manager, Association Services
bvigil@nebgolf.org
• Mike Jenkins, Vice President
Year Founded:
1966
Description:
Provides its member clubs with the latest in
technological equipment, including the GHIN
handicapping system and tournament pairing
program and instructs the clubs on how to use
the programs
Number of Members:
27,000

NEBRASKA WOMEN'S AMATEUR GOLF ASSOCIATION
6618 SOUTH 118TH STREET
OMAHA, NE 68137
402-505-4653
Fax: 402-505-4695
nwaga@nebgolf.org
www.nwaga.org
• Michele Gill, President
(308) 340-5864
nebgal1@gmail.com
• Teresa Snoozy, Vice President
tjsnoozy@gmail.com
• Maddy Toepfer, NWAGA Executive Director
(402) 505-4653
nwaga@nebgolf.org
• Barb Muldoon, Treasurer
(402) 691-8701
bmuldoon1@cox.net
• Debbie Wilbeck, Secretary
(402) 305-6237
dwilbeck@cox.net
• Maggie Peters, Executive Secretary
(402) 727-6823
malcolm5136@aol.com
• Judy Duffy, Tee Off Time Editor
(402) 397-0742
judyduffy@aol.com
Year Founded:
1973
Description:
Is an organization of golf clubs and individuals
governed by amateur women golfers and formed
for the purpose of promotion and conserving the
best interests and true spirit of the game of golf
for all women in the State of Nebraska
Number of Members:
84

NEW HAMPSHIRE GOLF ASSOCIATION
56 S. STATE STREET
CONCORD, NH 03301
603-219-0371
Fax: 603-219-0565
membership@nhgolf.com
www.nhgolf.com
• Greg Howell, Director Of Member Services &
Junior Golf
greg@nhgolf.com
• Bill Krueger, Past President
• Matt Schmidt, Executive Director
mschmidt@nhgolf.com
• Pat Spooner, Secretary
• Joseph Kane, President
• Glenn Walton, Vice President
• Don DeNovellis, Treasurer
• John Jelley, Tournament Director

NEW HAMPSHIRE WOMEN'S GOLF ASSOCIATION
603-356-9051
info@nhwga.org
www.nhwga.org
• Dana Harrity, President
president@nhwga.org
• Chris Downall, Secretary

secretary@nhwga.org
• Rowena Wilks, Past President
pastpres@nhwga.org
• Mary Jane Cormier, 1st Vice President
1vp@nhwga.org
• Donna Harvey, 2nd Vice President
2vp@nhwga.org
• Dorene Bergeron, Treasurer
treasurer@nhwga.org
Description:
Promote, stimulate, organize, and maintain
interest and activity in golf among women in the
state of New Hampshire

NEW JERSEY STATE GOLF ASSOCIATION
3 GOLF DRIVE
SUITE 206
KENILWORTH, NJ 07033
908-241-4653
Fax: 908-245-4696
info@njsga.org
www.njsga.org
• H. Frank O-Brien, President
• William E. Frese, Secretary
• Michael F. McFadden, Treasurer
• Daniel Meehan, Vice President
• Mike McAneny, Director of Tournaments &
Media Relations
mikem@njsga.org
• Rich Kennedy, Director of Handicapping &
Membership Service
richk@njsga.org
• Mike Moretti, Director Of Communications
mmoretti@njsga.org
• Kevin Purcell, Executive Director
kevinp@njsga.org
Year Founded:
1900
Description:
Promotes, supports and ensures the quality,
traditions and development of the game of golf
for everyone throughout the State of New Jersey
Number of Members:
100,000

NEW YORK STATE GOLF ASSOCIATION
4933 JAMESVILLE ROAD
JAMESVILLE, NY 13078
315-471-6979
Fax: 315-471-1372
www.nysga.org
• Richard Galvin, President
• Bill Moore, Executive Director
bmoore@nysga.org
• Joseph Strykowski, First Vice President
• Warren Winslow, Second Vice President
• Andrew Hickey, Director, Rules &
Competitions
andrew@nysga.org
• Henry Fust, Treasurer
Year Founded:
1923
Description:
Promotes and conserve the traditions of golf
throughout New York State

NORTH DAKOTA GOLF ASSOCIATION
725 RIVERWOOD DRIVE
BISMARCK, ND 58504
701-226-5641
www.ndgolf.org
• Randy Westby, President
• Rick Kuhn, Vice President
• Tim Doppler, Executive Director
ndga2020@gmail.com
• Perry Bohl, Secretary/Treasurer
• Gary Lahr, Tournament and Course Rating
Director
gplahr@hotmail.com
Description:
Formed and exists for the general purpose of
promoting and conserving throughout the state
of North Dakota the best interests and the true
spirit of the game of golf

NORTHERN CALIFORNIA GOLF ASSOCIATION
3200 LOPEZ ROAD
PEBBLE BEACH, CA 93953
831-625-4653
Fax: 831-625-0150
www.ncga.org
• Lee Gidney, President
• Vaughn Kezirian, Executive Director
vkezirian@ncga.org
• Malinda Oliver, Executive Assistant
moliver@ncga.org
• John Ronca, Vice President
• Pat Quinn, Secretary/Treasurer
• Brian Morse, Immediate Past President
Year Founded:
1901
Description:
Provide an enjoyable and fulfilling golf
experience to all involved
Number of Members:
180

NORTHERN NEVADA GOLF ASSOCIATION
PO BOX 5607
RENO, NV 89513
775-673-4653
Fax: 775-673-1144
www.nnga.org
• Larry Greenman, President
• Rich Brashear, Vice President
• Steve Rydel, Executive Director
(775) 846-8263
• Len Caley, Treasurer
• Joe Webster, Secretary
• Jack Gilbert, Past President
Description:
Promote and serve amateur golf and protect its
traditions

NORTHERN NEVADA WOMEN'S GOLF ASSOCIATION
18124 WEDGE PARKWAY
SUITE 182
RENO, NV 89511
775-851-8102
www.nnwga.org
• Lori Elliott, President
(775) 857-1812
president@nnwga.org
• Annette Ramirez, Vice President
(775) 882-2951
vp@nnwga.org
• Darla Smyth, Webmaster
(775) 851-8102
webmaster@nnwga.org
• Gretchen Legarza, Treasurer
(775) 828-4924
treas@nnwga.org
• Pat Hiatt, Secretary
(775) 742-4999
secy@nnwga.org
Year Founded:
1961
Description:
Promote interest in the game of golf for the
women of Northern Nevada and the surrounding
areas
Number of Members:
2,200
Publications:
NNWGA Newsletter: On and Off the Course is
published 3 times a year and sent to each
member via email

OKLAHOMA GOLF ASSOCIATION
2800 COLTRANE PL
SUITE 2
EDMOND, OK 73034
405-848-0042
Fax: 405-216-5795
www.okgolf.org
• Mark Felder, Executive Director
mfelder@okgolf.org
• Joby Wood, Director
• Morri Rose, Director Of Junior Golf

mrose@okgolf.org
• Jay Doudican, Director Of Ghin Services
jdoudican@okgolf.org
• Justin Limon, Tournament Director
Description:
Promotes the game of golf within the state of Oklahoma and monitors the playing thereof as an extension of the US Golf Association

OREGON GOLF ASSOCIATION
2840 HAZELNUT DRIVE
WOODBURN, OR 97071
503-981-4653
www.oga.org
• Barb Trammell, Chief Executive Officer
• Tom Gaffney, Vice President
• Eric Schoenstein, President
• Brent Whittaker, Director Of Tournament Operations
• Ryan Wyckoff, Senior Director Of Golf Course Operations
• Katie Norquist, Director of Finance, OGA & OGA Golf Course
• Henry Childs, Communications & Membership Coordinator
• Robyn Lorain, Director of Junior Golf
• Kelly Neely, Senior Director of Handicapping & Course Rating
• Gretchen Yoder, Manager of Handicapping & Course Rating
• Aaron Breniman, Director of Marketing & Communications
Year Founded:
1924
Description:
Our goal is to foster the enhancement and expansion of the game of golf by leading in the development of member and information services, the promotion of opportunities for all that want to play, and protection of the game's integrity and valued traditions. The governing body for the sport in Oregon & SW Washington.
Number of Members:
56,000
Membership Requirements:
Must be a member of a regular or associate golf club in Oregon or SW Washington
Member Services:
Handicapping, Course and Slope Rating, Tournaments, Rules of Golf
Publications:
Calendar of Events, Newsletter, Annual Report

PUERTO RICO GOLF ASSOCIATION
PARADISE COMMERCIAL CENTER
264 AVE. MATADERO
SUITE 11
SAN JUAN, PUERTO RIC 00920
787-793-3444
Fax: 787-273-3138
info@prga.org
www.prga.org
• Sidney Wolf, President
• James J Teale, Founder
• Ginelys Dahl, Communications & Web Development
info@prga.org
• Pete Birmingham, Board Director Handicapping & Club Relationship
• Julio Soto, Executive Director & USGA/GHIN Affairs
• Fransico Rivera, Tournament Director
frivera@prga.org
• Sajo Ruiz, Vice President, Marketing & Public Relations
Year Founded:
1954
Description:
Governing body for the game of golf in Puerto Rico at the amateur level, host of the 2004 World Amateur Team Championship and proud host organization of the PGA Tour at the Puerto Rico Open, presented by seepuertorico.com.
Number of Members:
Over 5,100

RHODE ISLAND GOLF ASSOCIATION
ONE BUTTON HOLE DRIVE
PROVIDENCE, RI 02909
401-272-1350
rward@rigalinks.org
www.rigalinks.org
• Luke T Hyder, President
• Jim McKenna, Director Of Rules & Competitions
jmckenna@rigalinks.org
• Michael A. Montigny, Treasurer
• Kate McCurry, Office Manager
kmccurry@rigalinks.org
• Vincent J. Cavallaro, First Vice President
• Kevin W. Clary, Second Vice President
• Robert Ward, Executive Director
(401) 272-1350
rward@rigalinks.org
• Kevin S. McLoughlin, Secretary
• Katie DeCosta, Director of Women's Golf & Member Services
kdecosta@rigalinks.org
Number of Members:
13,000
Membership Requirements:
Member of a member club
Member Services:
Handicapping; course rating, championships, rules of golf seminars; club officers seminar
Publications:
RIGA News: quarterly newsletter

ROCHESTER DISTRICT GOLF ASSOCIATION
2024 WEST HENRIETTA ROAD
SUITE 5-H
ROCHESTER, NY 14623
585-292-5950
info@rdga.org
www.rdga.org
• Dan Overbeck, President, Assistant Rules Official
danoverbeck@rdga.org
• Tim Vangellow, Executive Director
timvangellow@rdga.org
• Fredrick Lapple, Corporate Relationship& Office Operations Chairman
fredlapple@rdga.org
• Mark Battle, Vice President, Women's Committee
markbattle@rdga.org
• Mark Little, Jr. Tournament Committee
marklittle@rdga.org
• Dave Eaton, Communications Director
daveeaton@rdga.org
Year Founded:
1929
Description:
Promotes closer relationships among member clubs, conducts tournaments for members of clubs belonging to the association, promotes and supports a USGA - approved handicap system, provides course ratings and advances the best interests of amateur golf

SAN DIEGO COUNTY WOMEN'S GOLF ASSOCIATION
SAN DIEGO, CA
858-673-1128
sdcwga@aol.com
www.sdcwga.net
• Elaine Michaels, President
emichaels760@yahoo.com
• Carolyn Hogan, Secretary
cfhogan7@cox.net
• Karen Miller, Major Tournaments
kpmiller748@roadrunner.com
• Cheryl Wohlgemuth, Executive Director
sdcwga@aol.com
Year Founded:
1934
Description:
Is a non-profit organization, chartered to promote, supervise, and conduct competitive golf for SDCWGA members

SOUTH CAROLINA GOLF ASSOCIATION
7451 CAROLINA IRMO DRIVE
COLUMBIA, SC 29212
803-732-9311
Fax: 803-732-7406
info@scgolf.org
www.scgolf.org
• John Lopez, President
• James Park, Director of Member Services
jpark@scgolf.org
• Steve Fuller, Vice President
• Happ Lathrop, Executive Director
• Ron Swinson, Treasurer
• Vic Hannon, Secretary
• Kirk Page, SCJGA Director of Competitions
• Chris Miller, Senior Director Of SCJGA
cmiller@scgolf.org
• Kent Hungerpiller, Immediate Past President

SOUTH DAKOTA GOLF ASSOCIATION
4809 WEST 41ST STREET
SUITE 202
SIOUX FALLS, SD 57106
605-338-7499
1-800-577-7342
sdga@sdga.org
www.sdga.org
• Bill Scholten, President
• Wade Merry, Executive Director
• Coralee Jorgensen, Executive Director, First Tee of South Dakota
• Kelli Sinksen, First Tee of SD Program Director
Description:
Provides USGA/GHIN handicaps, conducts ten state championships, conducts junior clinics and junior tournaments

SOUTH FLORIDA PGA
186 ATLANTIS BLVD
ATLANTIS, FL 33462
561-729-0544
Fax: 561-729-0914
sflorida@pgahq.com
www.sflorida.pga.com
• Warren Bottke, President
walkbot@aol.com
• Mark VanDyck, Vice President
markvandyck@hotmail.com
• Don Meadows, Secretary
dmeadows@quailvalleygolfclub.com
• Brian Peaper, Honorary Past President
bdppga@aol.com
• Geoff Lofstead, Executive Director
glofstead@pgahq.com
• Christopher Gilkey, Tournament Director
cgilkey@pgahq.com
• Meredith Schuler, Director of Operations
mschuler@pgahq.com
Description:
Promote interest, participation and enjoyment in the game of golf; establish and maintain professional standards or practice; and enhance the well-being of golf professionals
Year Founded:
1979
Number of Members:
1,600

SOUTH JERSEY GOLF ASSOCIATION
PO BOX 884
NORTH CAPE MAY, NJ 08204
609-760-7779
sjga1946@gmail.com
• Gail Reilly, President
(609) 760-7779
sjga1946@gmail.com
• Ralph Gonzalez, Vice President
• Jeanne Leisner, Treasurer
(609) 760-4113
jleisnersjga@gmail.com
• Joan Boyle, Secretary
• John Petronis, Tournament Director
(609) 760-4580
johnpetronis@juniorgolfers.net
• Paul Wiegand, Webmaster
webmaster@sjgolf.org

Description:
Provides services to member golfers, fifty-nine public, semi-private and private clubs in the eight county southern New Jersey area
Number of Members:
700

SOUTHERN CALIFORNIA GOLF ASSOCIATION
3740 CAHUENGA BOULEVARD
STUDIO CITY, CA 91604
818-980-3630
Fax: 818-980-2709
info@scga.org
www.scga.org
• Al Frank, President
• John Morello, Vice President
• Keenan Barber, Secretary
• Jon Bilger, Treasurer
• Ken Bien, Immediate Past President
• Kevin Heaney, Executive Director
Description:
Provides tournament results, golf expo information, membership, courses, affiliate clubs, and rules of golf

SOUTHERN GOLF ASSOCIATION
1025 MONTGOMERY HIGHWAY
SUITE 210
BIRMINGHAM, AL 35216
205-979-4653
Fax: 205-979-1602
www.sgagolf.com
• Clarke Rheney, President
• W. Cabell Moore, Jr., 1st Vice President
• James E Brown, 2nd Vice President
• Al Reynolds, Treasurer
• Buford R McCarty, Executive Secretary
• Adam Powell, Assistant Executive Secretary
• Donna Stephens, Office Manager
Year Founded:
1902
Number of Members:
500

SOUTHERN ILLINOIS GOLF ASSOCIATION
122 South Division ST
CARTERVILLE, IL 62918
618-985-9595
Fax: 618-985-9595
www.sigagolf.org
• Ralph Chapman, President
• Sarah Haas, Vice President
• Ryan Farley, Secretary
• Robin Lester, Treasurer
• Steward Gilmore, Director
Year Founded:
1924

SOUTHERN NEVADA GOLF ASSOCIATION
8010 W. SAHARA AVE.
SUITE 160
LAS VEGAS, NV 89117
702-458-4653
www.snga.org
• Tim Quinn, President
• Geno Withelder, Vice President
• Ann Sunstrum, Executive Director
(702) 458-4653
asunstrum@snga.org
• Tanner Bown, Director Of Competition
(702) 830-7972
tbown@snga.org
• Tom Khamis, Secretary
• Tom Fitzgerald, Treasurer
Year Founded:
1967
Description:
Non-profit organization founded to represent, promote and serve the best interests of golf in the state of Nevada
Number of Members:
12,000

ST. LOUIS DISTRICT GOLF ASSOCIATION
560 MALINMOR DRIVE
WELDON SPRING, MO 63304
636-928-5056
Fax: 636-244-5056
www.stldga.com
• Mel Rector, President
• Andy Frost, Vice President
• Larry Etzkorn, Secretary Emeritus
• Roy Wilson, Executive Director
• Todd Burchyett, Assistant Executive Director/ Rules Chairman
Year Founded:
1916
Description:
Provide an association of private golf clubs throughout the St. Louis Metropolitan area

SUN COUNTRY AMATEUR GOLF ASSOCIATION
2316 SOUTHERN BLVD
SUITE D
RIO RANCHO, NM 87124
505-897-0864
800-346-5319
Fax: 505-897-3494
info@suncountrygolfhouse.com
• Mike Quinlan, President
• Dick Thorpe, 1st Vice President
• Dana Lehner, Executive Director
• Jan Schermerhorn, 2nd Vice President
• Bruce Buchman, Treasurer
• Cindy Smith, Secretary
Description:
Promote and serve amateur golf and protect its traditions
Number of Members:
22,000

TENNESSEE GOLF ASSOCIATION/TGA
400 FRANKLIN ROAD
FRANKLIN, TN 37069
615-790-7600
Fax: 615-790-8600
www.tngolf.org
• Matt Vanderpool, Executive Director
mvanderpool@tngolf.org
• Lynne Howd, Director, Handicapping
lhowd@tngolf.org
• Allison Brown, Director Of Women's Golf
abrown@tngolf.org
• Aon Miller, President
• Nathaniel Hantle, Manager, Course Rating & Member Services
nhantle@tngolf.org
Year Founded:
1914
Description:
Provides numerous services to its member clubs - the most important being the handicap service
Number of Members:
40,000

TEXAS GOLF ASSOCIATION
2909 COLE AVENUE
SUITE 305
DALLAS, TX 75204
214-468-8942
Fax: 214-468-8032
info@txga.org
www.txga.org
• Bill Hanley, President
• Jim Brown, First Vice President
• Carey Schulten, Second Vice President
• Rob Addington, Executive Director
raddington@txga.org
• Jonathan Shipley, Secretary/Treasurer
• Jim Spagnolo, Communications Manager
jim@txga.org
• Mary Harrison, Senior Director, Handicapping
mary@txga.org
• Cameron Crawford, Tournament Director
ccrawford@txga.org
• Ryan Finn, Managing Director Championships
rfinn@txga.org
Year Founded:
1906

Description:
Non-profit organization licensed through the USGA that represents, promotes and serves the best interest of golf in Texas
Number of Members:
Over 70,000
Membership Reqirements:
Must belong to a member club that pays annual dues
Member Services:
Conducts 11 statewide and seven regional golf championships, course rating, handicapping and educational seminars

TOLEDO DISTRICT GOLF ASSOCIATION
5533 SOUTHWYCK BOULEVARD
SUITE 204
TOLEDO, OH 43614
419-866-4771
www.tdgagolf.org
• John Byerly, President
• Doug Dantuono, Vice President
• Cliff Siehl, Executive Director, Tournament Chairman
• Bruce DeBoer, Treasurer
• Mickey Scott, Secretary

TRANS-MISSISSIPPI GOLF ASSOCIATION
2909 COLE
SUITE 305
DALLAS, TX 75204
214-468-8942
raddington@trans-miss.org
• Billy McBee, President
• Phil Patterson, Vice President
• Rob Addington, Executive Director
raddington@trans-miss.org
• Amanda Kolb, Tournament Administration
akolb@txga.org
• Hunter Nelson, Secretary
• Leo Corrigan, IV, Treasurer
• Cameron Crawford, Tournament Director
ccrawford@txga.org
Year Founded:
1900

UTAH GOLF ASSOCIATION
4444 S. 700 E.
SUITE 105
SALT LAKE CITY, UT 84107
801-563-0400
Fax: 801-563-0632
info@usga.org
www.uga.org
• Jim Harland, President
• Reese Nielsen, Vice President
• Bill Walker, Executive Director
bill@uga.org
• Steve Brinton, Treasurer
• Denise Vilven, Secretary
• Jacob Miller, Director Of Rules & Competition
jacob@uga.org
• Kelsey Chugg, Membership Director
kelsey@uga.org
Description:
Promote and protect the interest of golf and golfers within the state
Number of Members:
30,000

VALERO TEXAS OPEN
4330 MARRIOTT PKWY
SAN ANTONIO, TX 78261
210-345-3818
Fax: 210-345-3853
www.valerotexasopen.com
• Joe Gorder, President/Chief Executive Officer
• Stephanie Sage, Director of Marketing & Community Relations
• Larson Segerdahl, Executive Director
• Dawn Wood, Finance Coordinator
• Craig Smith, Director of Business Development
• Monica Villarreal, Director of Tournament Administration

Description:
Cowboy hats, golf caps and everything in between. PGA Tournament hosted at TPC San Antonio AT&T oaks Course, designed by Greg Norman and Sergio Garcia.

VERMONT GOLF ASSOCIATION
PO BOX 1612
STATION A
RUTLAND, VT 05701-1612
802-773-7180
800-924-0418
info@vtga.org
www.vtga.org
• Herb Eddy, Secretary
• Rick Simpson, President
• Roger Schoenbeck, Vice President/Treasurer
• Dave Pfannenstein, Executive Director
• Shari Pfannenstein, Website/Communications
Description:
The purpose of the VGA is to act as the authoritative body for golf in the state of Vermont; to hold such tournaments as may be arranged; to adopt, enforce and interpret the rules of golf in accordance with the rules adopted by the USGA; to promote and regulate competitions for all ages and abilities throughout Vermont; to establish, maintain, control and regulate a handicap system and course ratings for member clubs.
Year Founded:
1902
Number of Members:
67 Clubs, 11,000 Individuals

VERMONT STATE WOMEN'S GOLF ASSOCIATION
PO BOX 8235
ESSEX, VT 05451
802-662-4947
www.vswga.org
• Kathy Allbright, President, Director at Large
(603) 469-3487
puttquilt@aol.com
• Chris Johnson, Vice President, Director at Large, Liason-NE
(802) 626-5624
cjjohnson02@yahoo.com
• Phyllis Simon, Treasurer
(802) 244-7420
simonop@aol.com
• Kathy Sikora, Secretary
(802) 434-2583
g1946olf@gmavt.net
• Nancy Murphy, Past President
(802) 773-8702
nlmgolfer@yahoo.com
Description:
Serves women golfers of all ages and abilities in Vermont

VIRGINIA STATE GOLF ASSOCIATION
2400 DOVERCOURT DRIVE
MIDLOTHIAN, VA 23113
804-378-2300
Fax: 804-378-2369
www.vsga.org
• Matt Smiley, Director of Rules And Competitions
(804) 378-2300
• Andrew Blair, Director of Communications
(804) 378-2300
• Jamie Conkling, Executive Director
(804) 378-2300
• Natasha Triplett, Director Of Finance & Administration
(804) 378-2300
• Gary Beck, Treasurer
(757) 625-8181
• Michael Millen, Secretary
(434) 295-9616
• Gib Palmer, President
(804) 354-3794
• Bruce H. Matson, Vice President
(804) 783-2003
Year Founded:
1904
Description:

Promote the game of golf and serve the needs of golf in Virginia
Publications:
Virginia Golf, published bi-monthly; VSGA Yearbook and Media Guide; VIP Member Guide; Just Fore Juniors newsletter

WASHINGTON STATE GOLF ASSOCIATION
1010 SOUTH 336TH STREET
SUITE 310
FEDERAL WAY, WA 98003
206-526-8605
800-643-6410
Fax: 206-522-0281
www.thewsga.org
• Barbara Tracy, President
• Gary Rees, Vice President (District 1)
• Cathy Kay, Vice President (District 2)
• Doug Rohner, Vice President (District 3)
• Mike Welling, Vice President (District 4)
• Robert Black, Vice President (District 5)
• Troy Andrew, Executive Director/CEO
(206) 526-8605
• Steve Kay, Treasurer
• Frank Horton, Past President
• Tom Cade, Senior Director of Communications & Marketing
(253) 214-2918
• John Saegner, Jr., Senior Director Of Handicapping & Course Rating
(253) 214-2914
• Scotty Crouthamel, Senior Director Rules & Competition
(253) 214-2924
• Shari Jacobson, Director Of Membership & Club Relations
(253) 214-2925
• Abell Smith, Web Developer & Content Manager
(253) 214-2911
• Kacie Bray, Director of Marketing
(253) 214-2916
Year Founded:
1922
Description:
Non-profit amateur golf association governed by volunteer, amateur golfers
Number of Members:
85,000

WEST VIRGINIA GOLF ASSOCIATION
2115 CHARLESTON TOWN CENTER
CHARLESTON, WV 25389
304-391-5000
Fax: 304-391-5050
www.wvga.org
• Amber Hooper, Managing Director of Membership & Finance
(304) 391-5000
ahooper@wvga.org
• Colton Dean, Tournament Coordinator
(304) 391-5000
cdean@wvga.org
• Jonathan Bartlett, Senior Director of The First Tee of WV
(304) 391-5000
jbartlett@wvga.org
• Carter Page, Senior Director Of Rules & Competitions
(304) 391-5000
cpage@wvga.org
• Chris Slack, Director of Course Rating & Competitions
(304) 391-5000
cslack@wvga.org
• Zihui (Bella) Xu, Event & Public Relations Coordinator
(304) 391-5000
zxu@wvga.org
• Brad Ullman, Executive Director
(304) 391-5000
bullman@wvga.org
• Steve Fox, Vice President
Year Founded:
1913

WESTCHESTER GOLF ASSOCIATION
49 KNOLLWOOD ROAD
SUITE 220
ELMSFORD, NY 10523
914-347-2340
Fax: 914-347-2418
info@westchestergolf.org
www.westchestergolf.org
• Michael F. McCarthy, President
• Mike Zalmalkany, Tournament Director
• Bob Thomas, Executive Director
bthomas@westchestergolf.org
• George N. Tompkins, General Counsel
• Benjamin C. Kirschenbaum, Vice President
• Robert M. Miller, Secretary/Treasurer
• Robert H.M. Ferguson, Tournament Chairman
Year Founded:
1916
Number of Members:
30,000

WESTERN GOLF ASSOCIATION/EVANS SCHOLARS FOUNDATION
1 BRIAR ROAD
GOLF, IL 60029-0301
847-724-4600
Fax: 847-724-7133
www.wgaesf.org
• John Kaczkowski, President & CEO
kaczkowski@wgaesf.org
• Dennis O'Keefe, Chairman
• David Robinson, Vice Chairman
• John Mendesh, Secretary
• James M. O'Keane, Treasurer
• Daniel Coyne, General Counsel
• Amy Fuller, Director, Communications
fuller@wgaesf.org
• Steve Prioletti, Tournament Manager
prioletti@wgaesf.org
• Patrick Timson, Director, Tournament Operations
timson@wgaesf.org
Year Founded:
1899

WESTERN PENNSYLVANIA GOLF ASSOCIATION
324 FOURTH STREET
PITTSBURGH, PA 15238
412-826-2180
Fax: 412-826-2183
info@wpga.org
www.wpga.org
• Tim Fitzgerald, President
• Ron Moehler, Vice President
• Jeff Rivard, Executive Director
jrivard@wpga.org
• Claudette Graham, Treasurer
• Mark Caliendo, Secretary
• Terry Teasdale, Handicap Director
tteasdale@wpga.org
• Matt Rusinko, Championship Director
mrusinko@wpga.org
Year Founded:
1899
Description:
To foster, promote and advance the interests and the true spirit of the game of golf throughout Western Pennsylvania

WISCONSIN STATE GOLF ASSOCIATION
11350 WEST THEO TRECKER WAY
WEST ALLIS, WI 53214
414-443-3560
Fax: 414-443-0817
support@wsga.org
www.wsga.org
• Doug Fry, President
• Chuck Heath, First Vice President
• Mark Kannenberg, Vice President
• Phil Poletti, Vice President
• Mark Reinemann, Vice President
• John Knuteson, Secretary
• Rob Jansen, Executive Director
(414) 443-3561

rob@wsga.org
• David Cohn, Director Of Member Services & Communications
(414) 443-3569
david@wsga.org
• Aimee Linneman, Director Of Women's Golf & Operations
(414) 443-3577
aimee@wsga.org
• Bill Linneman, Director Rules & Competitions
(414) 443-3565
bill@wsga.org
Year Founded:
1901
Description:
Promote and conserve throughout the State of Wisconsin, the best interests and the true spirit of the game of golf
Number of Members:
65,000
Publications:
Wisconsin Golfer Magazine available to all members with a current WSGA Number

WOMEN'S GOLF ASSOCIATION OF WESTERN PENNSYLVANIA
DELMONT, PA
412-551-8549
www.wgawp.com
• Mary Beth Morrissey, President
• Corrinne Lacich, Vice President & Tournament Chairman
• Kathy Campbell, Treasurer
• Lisa Popovich, Recording Secretary
Year Founded:
1922
Description:
Promote among women of Western Pennsylvania the best interests and true spirit of the game of golf and to regulate and govern all contests in which members participate
Number of Members:
700

WOMEN'S METROPOLITAN GOLF ASSOCIATION
49 KNOLLWOOD RD
2nd Floor
ELMSFORD, NY 10523
914-592-7888
Fax: 914-462-3229
www.wmga.com
• Valerie DePiro, President
• Nancy Early, Executive director
• Phyllis Gusick, Vice President Of Competitions
• Michele Greenfield, Vice President Of Outreach, Marketing& Initiatives
• Allison Kucinski, Treasurer
• Leanne Leonard, Secretary
Year Founded:
1899
Description:
Fosters good sportsmanship, and good fellowship and friendly rivalry while encouraging and developing skilled amateur women golfers through individual competition and team play. It is also the USGA-sanctioned course rating authority for women players throughout the metropolitan region
Number of Members:
2,500 members, 192 member clubs

WOMEN'S SOUTHERN CALIFORNIA GOLF ASSOCIATION
402 WEST ARROW HIGHWAY
SUITE 10
SAN DIMAS, CA 91773
909-592-1281
Fax: 909-592-7542
• Judy Altschuler, President
(909) 592-1281
• Sheri Hauck, First Vice President
(909) 592-1281
• Debra Moats, Second Vice President
(909) 592-1281
• Judy Anderson, Secretary
(909) 592-1281
• Mary Ann Kneist, Treasurer

(909) 592-1281
• Joanne Farmer, Rules Director
(909) 592-1281
• Pat Blalock, Executive Director
(909) 592-1281
pblalock@womensgolf.org
• Louise Wright, Advisor
(909) 592-1281
Description:
Promote and foster interest in women's amateur golf through friendly organized competition
Membership Requirements:
Membership in the Association may only be obtained through the Member Club's women's organization. Each member of a Regular Member Club's Women's Organization shall also be required to be a member of this Association. Payment of Association dues: $27.00 membership fee for an 18-hole index and/or a 9-hole index. Minimum age: 18 years; however; WSCGA will provide a courtesy handicap index for any junior playing from a WSCGA Club

WYOMING STATE GOLF ASSOCIATION
1779 EAGLECREST CT.
LARAMIE, WY 82072
307-250-3044
dsnyder@wyoming.com
www.wygolf.org
• Rolf Peterson, President
• Karen Holcombe, Secretary
• Rachelle Pearson, Treasurer
• Jim Marshall, Vice President
• Dave Snyder, Executive Director
(307) 250-3044
dsnyder@wyoming.com
• Jim Marshall, Vice President
• Curtis Starkey, PGA Professional
• Roger Sheaffer, Vice President
• Kyle Wuss, Executive Director
Year Founded:
1922
Description:
The WSGA is the governing body of amateur golf in the state of Wyoming. Since its formation in 1922, the objective of the WSGA has been to promote and maintain the game of amateur golf throughout Wyoming.
Number of Members:
9,000
Publications:
Scorecard Magazine

UNITED STATES GOLF TEACHERS FEDERATION
1295 SE PORT ST. LUCIE BOULEVARD
PORT SAINT LUCIE, FL 34952
772-335-3216
888-346-3290
Fax: 772-335-3822
info@usgtf.com
www.usgtf.com
• Geoff Bryant, President
president@usgtf.com
• Suzy Johnson, Membership Services
suzy@usgtf.com
• Bob Wyatt, Jr., National Coordinator
info@usgtf.com
• Mark Harman, Director Of Education
mark@usgtf.com
• Sam Bryant, Vice President
sam@usgtf.com
• Jennifer Russakis, Membership Services Director
info@usgtf.com
Year Founded
1989
Description:
Largest organization of golf teaching professionals in the nation. Offer seven day certification courses in all parts of the country. The USGTF establish a national and international standard in training and certification for golf teaching professionals.

In addition provides services for its members and promotes the golf teaching profession
Number of members:
17,000
Member Services:
National standard of professional training & certification, Continuous educational development, International recognition, Employment referrals, Regional member tournaments, logoed USGTF merchandise, availability of self-help books on marketing & management skills, Liaison with other golf and sport associations, Opportunity to participate in the Biennial World Golf Teachers Cup & Conference, Commissionable income opportunity and discounts on golf equipment & training aids, USGTF ownership of National Training Center, Membership retirement fund, Membership liability insurance.
Publications:
Golf Teaching Pro Magazine

USBGA GOLF ASSOCIATION
NASHVILLE, TN
info@usblindgolf.com
www.blindgolf.com
• Jim Baker, President
(615) 679-9629
president@usblindgolf.com
• Diane Wilson, Vice President
(360) 437-4025
vicepresident@usblindgolf.com
Description:
The United States Blind Golf Association is organized and operated for the purposes of benefiting blind and vision impaired persons and promoting the public good through programs that advance, and increase public awareness of, golf among the blind and vision impaired throughout the United States
Membership Requirements:
Totally blind with no light perception up to 20/200 with Ophthalmologist statement, Support members also welcomed, Yearly dues totally blind $25.00, Vision impaired (B2-B3) $15.00, Support $10.00
Member Services:
Blind and vision impaired golf tournaments, Junior Blind Golf Programs.
Publications:
The Midnight Golfer, newsletter

WESTERN AUSTRALIA BLIND GOLF ASSOCIATION
wendy@wabga.org.au
www.blindgolf.com.au; www.wabga.org.au
• Ross Thompson, President
• Wendy Davidson, Secretary
Wendy@wabga.org.au
• Gerry Brown, Vice President
• Cathy French, Treasurer
• Rod Mills, Director
• Geoff Walsh, Handicapper
Year Founded:
1987
Description:
To promote the game of golf amongst Blind and Vision Impaired Persons, and to co-ordinate blind golf between the States of Australia. We aid to represent Australian blind golf internationally and to create and maintain a register of blind golf events within Australia, players, sight classifications and handicaps.

WESTERN GOLF ASSOCIATION, EVANS SCHOLARS FOUNDATION
1 BRIAR ROAD
GOLF, IL 60029-0301
847-724-4600
Fax: 847-724-7133
www.westerngolfassociation.com
• Daniel W. Coyne, General Counsel
• Dennis M. O'Keefe, Chairman
• David M. Robinson, Vice Chairman
• John S. Mendesh, Secretary
• James M. O'Keane, Treasurer
• John Kaczkowski, President & CEO
• Steve Brueggeman, Chief Financial Officer
Year Founded:
1899
Description:
Conducts three major golf championships: the Western Open and the Western Amateur (both since 1899), the Western Junior (since 1914).Administers the Evans Scholars Foundation which sends more than 810 students to college annually on full tuition and housing scholarships
Membership Requirements:
Payment of membership fees by recognized golf clubs or course
Publications:
BMW Championship Souvenir Program

WOMEN'S GOLF ASSOCIATION OF BALTIMORE
WGA OF BALTIMORE
MCDONOGH SCHOOL
PO BOX 380
OWINGS MILLS, MD 21117
410-592-2500
Fax: 410-592-2577
www.wgabaltimore.org
• Maddy Blumberg, President
• Ann Dixon, Secretary
• Eileen Witte, Vice President
• Debbie Lane, Treasurer
• Susan Wolven, Corresponding Secretary
Year Founded:
1930
Description:
The object of the Association is to encourage better golf and friendly competition among local women players by conducting Open Day events and other tournaments. We are a non-profit organization made up of 19 affiliated golf clubs and approximately 230 individual members.
Number of Members:
230

WOMEN'S GOLF COACHES ASSOCIATION
5905 NW 54th CIRCLE
CORAL SPRINGS, FL 33067
800-381-0769
Fax: 800-381-0769
community.wgcagolf.com
• Roger M Yaffe, Executive Director
roger@wgcagolf.com
• Amy Bond, President
abond@admin.fsu.edu
• Lisa Strom, Assistant Coach Representative
strom.3@osu.edu
• Ginger Brown-Lemm, Communications Director
gbrownlemm@athletics.msstate.edu
• Kristi Knight, Vice President
ksugolf@ksstatesports.com
• Kevin Williams, Treasurer
williamsk@ecu.edu
• Trelle McCombs, Secretary
tmccombs@athletics.tamu.edu
Year Founded:
1983

Description:
Promotes participation women's collegiate golf. The vision is to encourage the playing of intercollegiate golf for women in correlation with a general objective of education and in accordance with the highest tradition o fintercollegiate competition.
Number of members:
400+ member coaches
Membership Requirements:
Division I, II, III, NAIA women's head golf coaches
Member Services:
Presents All-American, Coach Of The Year awards; Hall of Fame internship program for students
Publications:
Newsletter, quarterly

WORLD GOLF VILLAGE
TWO WORLD GOLF PLACE
ST. AUGUSTINE, FL 32092
904-940-6088
www.golfwgv.com
• Jack Peter, Chief Operating Officer
(904) 940-4029
jpeter@wghof.org
• Angela Ivey, Director of Marketing
(904) 940-4031
aivey@wghof.org
• Dave Cordero, Director of Communications
(904) 940-4009
dcordero@wghof.org
• Brodie Walters, Senior Director of Museum Operations
(904) 940-4010
bwaters@wghof.org
• Elizabeth Hall, Manager of Sales & Events
(904) 940-4021
ehall@wghof.org
Golf Sponsor:
PGA Tour - Spa at Laterra.
Description:
Home to the World Golf Hall of Fame

Greyhound Racing Organizations

ARIZONA DEPARTMENT OF RACING
1110 W WASHINGTON
SUITE 260
PHOENIX, AZ 85007
602-364-1700
Fax: 602-364-1703
www.azracing.gov/
• Rudy Casillas, Director
• Dan Reinertson, Chief Greyhound Steward
(520) 884-7576
• Victoria Rogen, Licensing
(602) 364-1716
vrogen@azracing.gov
• Joyce Cozby, Deputy Director
(602) 364-1726
jcozby@azracing.gov

ASSOCIATION OF RACING COMMISSIONERS INTERNATIONAL
1510 NEWTOWN PIKE
SUITE 210
LEXINGTON, KY 40511
859-224-7070
http://arcicom.businesscatalyst.com/

• Mark Lamberth, Chair
• Edward J. Martin, President
• Jeff Colliton, Treasurer
• Judy Wagner, Chair Elect/ Secretary
• John Ward, Immediate Past-Chair
Description:
To protect and uphold the integrity of the pari-mutuel sports of horse racing, dog racing and jai-alai through an informed membership, by encouraging forcefull and uniform regulation, by promoting the health and welfare of the industry through various programs and projects.
Membership Requirements:
Must be racing commissioner or executive director of a commission; associate members need not be commissioners, but must be connected to the industry.
Number of members:
500
Year Founded:
1934

BIRMINGHAM RACING COMMISSION
1000 JOHN ROGERS DRIVE
SUITE 102
BIRMINGHAM, AL 35210
• Charles Chrockrom, Sr., Chairman
• Jarvis Patton, Vice Chairman
• Richard Arrington, Jr., Commissioner
• Joe Knight, Commissioner
• Thomas P. Dawkins, DVM, Commissioner
• Kip W. Keefer, Executive Secretary
(205) 838-7470
• Valerie Carpenter, Administrative Assistant
(205) 838-7470
brcval@mindspring.com
Description:
The Birmingham Racing Commission was organized in 1984 pursuant to the John Rogers Act, now codified as Chapter 65 of Title 11, Code of Alabama 1975. The Commission is a unique public corporation authorized to license and regulate thoroughbred and greyhound racing pari-mutuel wagering in Birmingham.

COLORADO RACING COMMISSION
1881 PIERCE STREET
SUITE 108
LAKEWOOD, CO 80214
303-205-2990
Fax: 303-205-2950
https://www.colorado.gov/pacific/enforcement/node/37806
• Mary Sharon Wells, Chair
• Sean Beirne, Vice Chair
• Charles D. Vail, Veterinarian Member
• Pam Inmann, Business Member
• Cynthia Jane Day, Racing Industry Member
Description:
The mission of the Colorado Division of Racing is to promote and foster the public confidence in the pari-mutuel industry, protect the welfare of the participants through fair, consistent, proactive enforcement of appropriate policies, statutes and Colorado racing commission rules. The Commission is responsible for promulgating all the rules and regulations governing greyhound and horse racing in Colorado.

MASSACHUSETTS STATE RACING COMMISSION
101 FEDERAL ST.
23RD FLOOR
BOSTON, MA 02110
617-979-8400
Fax: 617-725-0258
www.mass.gov/src
• Stephen Crosby, Chairman
• Bruce Stebbins, Commissioner
• Enrique Zuniga, Commissioner
• Rick Day, Executive Director
• Catherine Blue, General Counsel
• John R. Glennon, Chief Information Officer
• Alexandra Lightbown, Interim Director of Racing
Description:
To ensure fair and honest pari-mutuel racing, the Commission promulgates and enforces rules and regulations, proposes legislation and develops policies to better regulate the Racing Industry (horse and greyhound).

NATIONAL GREYHOUND ASSOCIATION
PO BOX 543
ABILENE, KS 67410
785-263-4660
nga@ngagreyhounds.com
• Julia Ward, President
(785) 263-7272
julie@waynewardinc.com
• Frederick A. Fulchino, Vice President
(860) 963-7844
• Gary Guccione, Secretary/Treasurer
(785) 263-4660
garyg@ngagreyhounds.com
Number of members:
2,950
Publications:
GREYHOUND REVIEW—Monthly on Greyhound-racing and breeding-related activities.
Description:
The National Greyhound Association (NGA), a voluntary non-profit association operated in accordance with the laws of Kansas, is officially recognized by the entire Greyhound racing industry including, all Greyhound racetracks and individual racing jurisdictions, as well as foreign Greyhound registries and governing bodies as the sole registry for racing Greyhounds on the North American continent. Organized in 1906, it has functioned in this capacity ever since the inception of Greyhound track racing in this country of more than 4,600 Greyhound owners and breeders whose Greyhounds compete at tracks throughout the continent.
Member Services:
All registration services for Greyhounds in North America.
Membership Requirements:
Completion of two-page application, submittal of $100 initiation fee & $70 dues.

NEW HAMPSHIRE RACING AND CHARITABLE GAMING COMMISSION
21 SOUTH FRUIT STREET
CONCORD, NH 03301-2428
603-271-2158
Fax: 603-271-3381
www.racing.nh.gov/
• Paul M. Kelley, Director
RCG-director@racing.nh.gov
• Timothy J. Connors, Chairman
• Anthony B. Urban, Secretary

• Sudhir Naik, Deputy Director
RCG-director@racing.nh.gov
Description:
The New Hampshire Pari-Mutuel Commission oversees the regulation of pari-mutuel wagering at racetracks in New Hampshire, including Thoroughbred Racing, Harness Racing, and Greyhound Racing under RSA 284.
Year Founded:
1933

Gymnastics Organizations

BRITISH COLUMBIA RHYTHMIC SPORTIVE GYMNASTICS FEDERATION
828 W. 8TH AVENUE
VANCOUVER, BC, CANADA V5Z 1E3
604-333-3485
Fax: 604-909-1749
bcrsgf@rhythmicsBC.com
www.rhythmicsbc.com
• Kamena Petkova, Competitive Development Committee Chair
kamenapetkova@gmail.com
• Helena Higgs, Secretary
(250) 339-4301
hilkka.higgs@telus.net
• Sashka Gitcheva, Program Coordinator
(604) 333-3485
• Mari Mitri, Director At Large
mmitri@shaw.ca
• Adrienne Arnold, President
(604) 261-2752
adriennearnold@shaw.ca
• Monika Alde, RG Development Chair
(250) 658-8341
• Adrianna Donaldson, Treasurer
adriannabd@yahoo.com
• Diana Nerman, VP Finance
(604) 671-7577
dianazoecoop@shaw.ca
Description:
Administers and delivers a variety of programs for encouraging participation in and developing excellence in rhythmic gymnastics.

CANADIAN GYMNASTICS FEDERATION
1900 Promenade City Park Drive
SUITE 120
OTTAWA, ON, CANADA K1J 1A3
613-748-5637
Fax: 613-748-5691
www.gymcan.org/site/home.php
• Richard Crepin, Chair/President
• Jim Roycroft, Secretary
• Claude Aubertin, Director
• Richard Ikeda, Athlete Representative
• Peter Nicol, President & CEO
(613) 748-5637
pnicol@gymcan.org
• Dean Giesbrecht, Vice Chair
• Sue Ashton, Program Coordinator AG
(613) 748-5637
sashton@gymcan.org
• Chantal Clermont, Director Of Finance
(613) 748-5637
chantal@gymcan.org
• Tony Smith, National Team Director MAG
tsmith@gymcan.org
Description:
Founded 1969. Serves to lead, promote, facilitate and guide gymnastics in Canada as a sport for the pursuit of excellence and world prominence, and as an activity for

lifelong participation.
Membership Requirements:
Regular members are duly constituted Provincial and Territorial Associations and Federations. Annual meeting held each June in Ottawa, Ontario.
Number of members:
160,000

INTERNATIONAL GYMNASTICS FEDERATION (FIG)
AVENUE DE LA GARE 12
CASE POSTALE 630
LAUSANNE, SWITZERLAN 1001
info@fig-gymnastics.org
www.fig-gymnastics.com
• Nicolas Cuperus, President
Description:
International governing body for the sport of trampoline.

NATIONAL ASSOCIATION OF WOMEN'S GYMNASTICS JUDGES
EDEN PRAIRIE, MN 55346
513-829-5671
nawgjsec@gmail.com
www.nawgj.org
• Evelyn Chandler, President
presnawgj@aol.com
• Mary Lee Martin, Vice President
mlmartin77@gmail.com
• Patty Shipman, Director Of Finance
pship@aol.com
• Judy Hoefarlin, National Web Director
webmaster@nawgj.org
• Barbara Tebben, Secretary
nawgjsec@gmail.com
Number of members:
1801
Member Services:
Contracts judges; educates them through symposiums and represents judges on gymnastics boards.
Publications:
Newsletter, four times annually; State and Regional Newsletters.
Description:
Founded 1974.

NATIONAL ASSOCIATION OF COLLEGIATE GYMNASTICS COACHES - WOMEN
1627 SLEEPY HOLLOW LANE
DEKALB, IL 60115-1749
815-970-0465
• Bobbie Cesarek, President
• Mike Jacki, President
(317) 823-1097
mikej@iquest.net
• Carl Leland, Vice President
(303) 871-3395
cleland@du.edu
• Cari DuBoi, Secretary
(510) 643-0282
• Gail Goodspeed, Treasurer
(603) 862-3834
gailg@cisunix.unh.edu
Number of members:
150
Member Services:
Statistical service; All-American awards; Scholar Athletic Award; Training congress once each year, Coach of the Year.
Publications:
Newsletter, four times annually; Coaches Directory.
Membership Requirements:

Membership fees of $100 per year, Must represent a university or college or Associate member $50.00.

Description:
Founded 1973. Serves to help set direction of the sport of women's gymnastics within the NCAA.

NATIONAL GYMNASTICS JUDGES ASSOCIATION, INC.
75-25 E 210 ST
BAYSIDE, NY 11364
718-545-6368
kenach@ngja.org
www.ngja.org
• Dan Bachman, President
• Jerry Donahue, General Technical Vice President
• Mike Juszczyk, National Technical Vice President
• Dean Schott, Jr. Olympic Vice President
• Greg Kester, National Technical Secretary
• Brian Richmond, National Treasurer

Member Services:
Meetings held annually, held in conjunction with USA Gymnastics Congress and USA Championships.

Publications:
National Gymnastic Rules Interpretation Book, annually; NGJA Newsletter, biannually.

Membership Requirements:
Association dues. Must take Junior Olympic, national and international practical and written certification exams, depending on the level of certification sought. All NGJA officials are evaluated every two years. Must also hold USAG professional membership and safety certification.

Description:
Founded 1969. Certifies and trains gymnastic judges for men's artistic gymnastics. Assigns men's gymnastics officials for national, international and junior competitions, interprets rules. President of the NGJA serves on the USA Gymnastics Board of Directors and on the USA Gymnastics Independent Selection Committee.

U.S. ASSOCIATION OF INDEPENDENT GYMNASTICS CLUBS/USAIGC
450 North End Aveenue
SUITE 20 F
NEW YORK, NY 10282
Fax: 212-227-9793
www.usaigc.com
• Paul Spadaro, President
paul.spadaro@usaigc.com

Member Services:
Seminars annually held in August.

Publications:
IT'S YOUR BUSINESS, quarterly newsletter.

Description:
Founded 1972. Gymnastics association sponsoring tournaments, competitions.

U.S. SPORTS ACROBATICS/USSA
132 E. WASHINGTON ST
SUITE 700
INDIANAPOLIS, IN 46204
317-237-5050
Fax: 317-237-5069
membership@usagym.org
www.usagym.org

• Luan Peszek, Vice President Of Program Development
(317) 829-5646
lpeszek@usagym.org
• Steve Penny, President/CEO
(317) 829-5050
spenny@usagym.org
• Ron Galimore, Chief Operation Officer
(317) 829-5631
rgalimore@usagym.org
• Renee Jamison, Director Of Administration & Olympic Relations
(317) 829-5635
rjamison@usagym.org
• Katelyn Dapper, Executive Office Coordinator
(317) 237-5914
kdapper@usagym.org
• Lee Johnson, Vice President of Marketing
(317) 829-5647
ljohnson@usagym.org
• Justin Hirnisey, Director of marketing
(317) 829-5666
jhirnisey@usagym.org
• Jackie Magnuson, Event Marketing Manager
(317) 829-5623
jmagnuson@usagym.org

Number of members:
1,300

Member Services:
Publication and interpretation of rules; makes competition videotapes available for purchase; conducts international and regional competitions as well as local meets; training seminars and clinics during the off season; efforts to raise dollars to support athlete travel to international competitions; judges' training. Annual meeting of Board of Directors - President's Day weekend in February.

Publications:
ACROSPORTS, newsletter six times annually.

Membership Requirements:
Interest in sports acrobatics, payment of membership dues.

Description:
Founded 1974. Promotion of sports acrobatics; conducts competitions; publishes rules and educational materials.

Handball Organizations

CANADIAN TEAM HANDBALL FEDERATION
453, RUE JACOB-NICOL
SHERBROOKE, QC, CANADA J1J 4E5
819-563-7937
Fax: 819-563-5352
www.handballcanada.ca
• Raquel Marinho, President
(647) 700-4919
raquelpedercini@hotmail.com
• Ward Hrabi, Vice President of Officials
(204) 668-9442
whrabi@shaw.ca
• Brian Hayes, Treasurer
bhayes@mymts.net
• Francois LeBeau, Chief Operating Officer
f.lebeau@videotron.ca

Description:
Founded 1966. Amateur sports organization.

HANDBALL, INTERNATIONAL FEDERATION
PETER-MERIAN STRASSE 23
PO BOX 4002
BASLE, SWITZERLAN CH-4002
ihf.office@ihf.info
www.ihf.info/
• Hassan Moustafa, President
• Sandi Sola, Treasurer
• Miguel Roca Mas, 1st Vice President

Description:
International governing body for the sport of handball.

U.S. HANDBALL ASSOCIATION
2333 N. TUCSON BLVD
TUCSON, AZ 85716
520-795-0434
Fax: 520-795-0465
handball@ushandball.org
www.ushandball.org
• Tom Sove, Vice President
(209) 575-2758
• Matt Krueger, Development Coordinator
(520) 795-0434
• Gary Cruz, Youth Development Director
• Mike Steele, President
(503) 352-2806
• LeaAnn Martin, Vice President
(360) 650-3054
• Steve Dykes, Secretary
• Mike Driscoll, Treasurer-South West Region
(972) 235-9547
• Vern Roberts, Executive Director
(520) 795-0434

Nature of Service:
Promotes handball.

Year Founded:
1951

Membership Requirements:
Dues $40 annually.

Number of members:
8,500

Publications:
HANDBALL, bimonthly.

USA TEAM HANDBALL
2330 W CALIFORNIA AVENUE
SALT LAKE CITY, UT 84104
801-463-2000
info@usateamhandball.org
www.usateamhandball.org

Hockey, Field Hockey Organizations

FIELD HOCKEY CANADA
311 WEST 1ST STREET
NORTH VANCOUVER, BC, CANADA V7M 1B5
jsauve@fieldhockey.ca
www.fieldhockey.ca
• Jeff Sauve, Chief Executive Officer
jsauve@fieldhockey.ca
• Iann Baggott, Chair
• Robin Richardson, Treasurer
• Shaheed Devji, Creative & Communication Manager
sdevji@fieldhockey.ca
• Anthony Farry, Head Coach, Men's National Program
afarry@fieldhockey.ca
• Ian Rutledge, Head Coach,Women's National Program

irutledge@fieldhockey.ca
• Lisa Northrup, High Performance Manager
Year Founded:
1991
Description:
Amalgamation of Canadian Field Hockey Association (1961) and the Canadian Women's Field Hockey Association (1962). Objectives include the development and promotion of field hockey across the country, as well as the provision of services and programs to assist individuals to achieve their potential as athletes
Number of members:
10,271
Membership Requirements:
Member Teams (Senior), Junior Teams (under 18 or high school), Associate Members (Individuals) pay annual membership fees. Other affiliate Junior categories for nominal fee and few services
Member Services:
Insurance, group accident and liability, access to national championship, national team programs, magazine subscription, high performance program access (national teams); Certification Program for Coaches and Umpires.

FIELD HOCKEY, FEDERATION INTERNATIONALE DE HOCKEY (FIH)
RUE DU VALENTIN 61
LAUSANNE, SWITZERLAN CH-1004
info@fih.ch
• Leandro Negre, President
• Kelly Fairweather, Chief Executive Officer
• Diana Capsa, Head Of Finance
• David Luckes, Sport & Development Director
• Sarah Massey, Marketing & Events Director
Description:
International governing body for the sport of field hockey.
Publication:
BDO WorldHockey Monthly, the 26 minute programme is distributed free-of-charge director from FIH to a wide selection of global broadcasters every four weeks. The programme showcases hockey with a range of topics including highlights of major tournaments; the Sahara WorldHockey Team Rankings, news from hockey competitions around the globe, and profiles of some of hockey's international stars

U.S. FIELD HOCKEY ASSOCIATION
5540 NORTH ACADEMY
SUITE 100
COLORADO SPRINGS, CO 80918
719-866-4567
Fax: 719-632-0979
information@usafieldhockey.com
www.usfieldhockey.com
• Steve Locke, Executive Director
(719) 866-4361
slocke@usafieldhockey.com
• Simon Hoskins, Chief Operating Officer
(719) 866-4370
shoskins@usafieldhockey.com
• Janet Paden, Chief Financial & Human Resources Officer
(719) 866-4368
jpaden@usafieldhockey.com
• Kait Mitchell, Communications Manager
(719) 866-4363
kmitchell@usafieldhockey.com

• Karen Collins, Director Of Events
(719) 866-4366
kcollins@usafieldhockey.com
• Shawn Hindy, Chair of the Board
shindy@usafieldhockey.com

Hockey, Ice Hockey Organizations

AMERICAN HOCKEY COACHES ASSOCIATION/AHCA
7 CONCORD STREET
GLOUCESTER, MA 1930
781-245-4177
Fax: 781-245-2492
ahcahockey@comcast.net
www.ahcahockey.com
• Casey Jones, President
• Joe Bertagna, Executive Director
j2b2hockey@gmail.com
• Bruce Delventhal, Treasurer
Year Founded:
1947
Description:
Promotes Ice Hockey
Membership:
Dues is as follows: Active, College, Division I Men: $315.00, Division II Women $315.00, Division II-III Men $185.00, Division II-III Women $185.00; Active, Non-College: $75.00; Allied $75.00; Amateur High School $25.00
Membership Requirements:
Active - college coaches from NCAA schools. Allied - anyone interested. Honorary - people in ice hockey who made contribution to game
Publications:
Meeting minutes, fall newsletter

CANADIAN ADULT RECREATIONAL HOCKEY ASSOCIATION
1420 BLAIR PLACE
SUITE 610
OTTAWA, ON, CANADA K1J 9L8
613-244-1989
800-267-1854
Fax: 613-244-0451
www.carhahockey.ca
• Michael S. Peski, President
mpeski@carhahockey.ca
• Lori Lopez, Executive Director
llopez@carhahockey.ca
• Scott Wilson, Manager, Hockey Operations
swilson@carhahockey.ca
• Laurie Langlois, Manager, Membership Services
 ext 224
llangois@carhahockey.ca
Year Founded:
1975
Description:
Serves to promote and foster recreational hockey throughout Canada, increased recreational activity and physical fitness among Canadians through participation in recreational hockey; competitions for members in various tournaments
Membership Requirements:
Adult recreational and oldtimer hockey leagues, teams and players (19 years of age and older); Adult recreational hockey tournaments; Arenas (within Canada); Referees for adult recreation and oldtimer

hockey
Member Services:
Membership program which includes benefits such as team welcome gifts, special promotions and offerings plus a comprehensive sport protection program (insurance). Tournament programs well organized, top quality adult recreational hockey tournaments from coast to coast
Publications:
THE HOCKEY POST Magazine

HOCKEY CANADA
151 CANADA OLYMPIC ROAD SW
SUITE 201
CALGARY, AB, CANADA T3B 5R5
403-777-3636
Fax: 403-777-3635
www.hockeycanada.ca
• Scott Smith, President
• Tom Renney, CEO
Year Founded:
1914
Description:
Our mission statement reflects the commitment and dedication of Hockey Canada and the hundreds of thousands of volunteers in Canada, ensuring that hockey provides quality opportunities that both positive and fun for all participants
Number of members:
500,000
Membership Requirements:
Any amateur hockey player who registers with one of the thirteen regional CHA branch offices across Canada. Must not have signed a professional contract in the same year as he/she signs an amateur card
Publications:
CANADIAN HOCKEY Magazine, annually; BREAKAWAY, newsletter, four times annually; CHA OFFICIAL HOCKEY RULES, every second year; NATIONAL JUNIOR TEAM MEDIA GUIDE, annually

HOCKEY EAST ASSOCIATION
591 NORTH AVE
2
WAKEFIELD, MA 01880
781-245-2122
Fax: 781-245-2492
info@hockeyeastonline.com
www.hockeyeastonline.com
• Steve Metcalf, Commissioner
• Brian Smith, Associate Commissioner
• Kate McAffe, Associate Commissioner
• Tim Flynn, Director, Corporate Sales
Year Founded:
1983
Teams:
Boston College, Boston University, University of Connecticut, Holy Cross (women only), University of Maine, University of Massachusetts (men only) University of Mass-Lowell (men only), Merrimack College, University of New Hampshire, Northeastern University, Providence College and University of Vermont.
Description:
Sponsors intercollegiate hockey play between member schools, including: Boston Col., Boston U., U. of Maine, U. of Mass. at Amherst, U. of Mass. at Lowell, Merrimack Col., U. of New Hampshire, Northeastern U., Providence Col
Publications:

HOCKEY EAST YEARBOOK, annual; Championship Souvenir Program, annual

HOCKEY NORTH AMERICA/NATIONAL NOVICE HOCKEY ASSOCIATION
PO BOX 78
STERLING, VA 20167-0078
703-430-8100
800-446-2539
Fax: 703-421-9205
HockeyNorthAmerica@gmail.com
www.hna.com
Year Founded:
1980
Description:
Amateur adult hockey league operating in 24 cities in the United States, Europe, and Canada offering professional style competition for players of beginning, intermediate and advanced skill. NNHA offers instruction and competition for adult beginners
Number of members:
10,000
Membership Requirements:
Must pay registration fee of $25. Also must pay league fees in addition on a regular basis.
Member Services:
National championships held in June each year. Sponsor regional tournaments leading to national championship. Also sponsor invitational tournaments. Provides web site, comprehensive statistics reporting, newsletters, FAX on demand information services.

INTERNATIONAL ICE HOCKEY FEDERATION (IIHF)
BRANDSCHENKESTRASSE 50
POSTFACH 1817
8027
ZURICH, SWITZERLAN 8027
www.iihf.com
• Rene Fasel, President
• Kalervo Kummola, Vice President (FIN)
• Bob Nicholson, Vice President (CAN)
• Thomas Wu, Vice President (HKG)
• Horst Lichtner, General Secretary

NATIONAL HOCKEY LEAGUE ENTERPRISES
1185 AVENUE OF THE AMERICAS
15TH FLOOR
NEW YORK, NY 10036-2601
212-789-2000
Fax: 212-789-2020
• Dave McCarthy, Vice President
Description:
The NHL's use of technology combined with existing client base demonstrate the breadth of applicability and growing stature as the standard for presenting numeric data online.

NATIONAL HOCKEY LEAGUE PLAYERS' ASSOCIATION/NHLPA
20 BAY STREET
SUITE 1700
TORONTO, ON, CANADA M5J 2N8
416-313-2300
www.nhlpa.com
• Don Fehr, Executive Director
Description:
The National Hockey League Player's Association/NHLPA is a labor union whose members are the players in the National Hockey League (NHL). The NHLPA works on behalf of the players in varied disciplines.

NORTHERN COLLEGIATE HOCKEY ASSOCIATION
262-993-8884
www.nchahockey.org
• Don Olson, Commissioner
(507) 429-7229
donolson@nchahockey.org
• Chris Zills, Director, Sports Information
zills@nchahockey.org
• Brian Monahan, Director, Public Relations
(651) 368-7915
monahan@naccsports.org
Nature of Service:
Member schools: St. Scholastica, Lake Forest, St. Norbet (men only), Adrian, Aurora, Concordia Wisconsin, Finlandia (men only), Marian, Trine, Milwaukee School of Engineering (men only), Lawrence (women only).
Teams:
Men's Hockey : 10 teams; Women's Hockey : 8 teams.
Numbers of Members:
11

USA HOCKEY
1775 BOB JOHNSON DRIVE
COLORADO SPRINGS, CO 80906-4090
719-576-8724
Fax: 719-538-1160
usah@usahockey.org
www.usahockey.com
• Pat Kelleher, Executive Director
• Tony Driscoll, Exec. Dir., Marketing, Communications & Events
• Kim Folsom, Director, Member Services
• Casey Jorgensen, General Counsel
• Kelly Mahncke, Exec. Director, Finance

WESTERN COLLEGIATE HOCKEY ASSOCIATION
MINNESOTA STATE UNIVERSITY, MANKATO AT EDINA
7700 FRANCE AVENUE SOUTH
SUITE 360
EDINA, MN 55435
952-818-8869
www.wcha.com
• Bill Robertson, Commissioner (Men's)
(952) 818-8879
brobertson@wcha.com
• Jennifer Flowers, Commissioner (Women's)
• Dean Thibodeau, Assistant Commissioner
• Todd Bell, Manager, Marketing & Communications
• Greg Shepherd, Supervisor Of Officials
(651) 330-5131
gshepherdwcha@gmail.com
Year Founded:
1959
Description:
Sponsors intercollegiate ice hockey. Member schools include: Alabama Huntsville, Alaska Anchorage, Alaska, Bemidji State, Bowling Green, Ferris State, Lake Superior State, Michigan Tech, Minnesota State, Northern Michigan, Minnesota Duluth, Ohio State, St. Cloud State, Wisconsin.

Hockey, Professional Hockey (NHL)

NATIONAL HOCKEY LEAGUE/NHL
1185 AVENUE OF THE AMERICAS
15TH FLOOR
NEW YORK, NY 10036
212-789-2000
800-559-2333
Fax: 212-789-2020
nhltvsupport@nhl.com
www.nhl.com
• Gary Bettman, Commissioner
• Bill Daly, Deputy Commissioner
Year Founded:
1917
Description:
League of professional hockey teams
Membership Requirements:
Approval by NHL Board of Governors
Publications:
NHL Rule Book, annual; NHL Schedule, annual; NHL Media Directory, annual; NHL Official Guide and Record Book, annual
Additional Offices:
Toronto: 50 Bay St., 11th Floor, Toronto, ON, Canada M5J 2X8; 416-359-7900; Fax: 416-981-2779. Montreal: 1800 McGill College Ave., Ste 2600, Montreal, QC, Canada H3A 3J6; 514-841-9220; Fax: 514-841-1040.

Teams:

ANAHEIM DUCKS
HONDA CENTER
2695 E KATELLA AVENUE
ANAHEIM, CA 92806
877-945-3946
www.nhl.com/ducks
• Michael Schulman, Executive Chair
• Tim Ryan, CEO
• Bill Foltz, President & COO
• Bob Murray, Executive Vice President/General Manager
• David McNab, SVP/Hockey Operations
• Bill Pedigo, EVP/Chief Commercial Officer
• Gina Galasso, Chief Human Resources Officer
• Dallas Eakins, Head Coach
• Mark Morrison, Assistant Coach
• Marty Wilford, Assistant Coach
• Sudarshan Maharaj, Goaltending Coach
• Jeremy Bettle, Director of High Performance
Year Founded:
1993
Description:
The Anaheim Ducks are a National Hockey League team based in Anaheim, California
Home Arena:
Honda Center. Seating capacity 17,174.

ARIZONA COYOTES
9400 WEST MARYLAND AVENUE
GLENDALE, AZ 85305
623-772-3200
Fax: 623-872-2000
fanservices@arizonacoyotes.com
www.nhl.com/coyotes
• Alex Meruelo, Majority Owner, Chairman & Governor
• Andrew Barroway, Minority Owner & Alternate Governor
• Xavier Gutierrez, President, CEO & Alternate Governor
• Bill Armstrong, General Manager
• Patrick Murphy, President, Business Operations
• Lowell Heit, CFO
• Anthony Horton, Executive Vice President, Ticket Sales & Strategy
• Rich Nairn, Exec. Vice President, Communications & Broadcast

- Rick Tocchet, Head Coach
- Phil Housley, Assistant Coach
- Cory Stillman, Assistant Coach
- Corey Schwab, Goaltending Coach
- Shane Doan, Chief Hockey Development Officer
- Dave Griffiths, Director, Team Services

Year Founded:
1972

Description:
The Arizona Coyotes are a National Hockey League team based in Glendale, Arizona

Home Arena:
Gila River Arena. Seating capacity 17,125.

BOSTON BRUINS
TD GARDEN
100 LEGENDS WAY
BOSTON, MA 02114
617-624-1900
fanrelations@bostonbruins.com
www.nhl.com/bruins

- Jeremy M. Jacobs, Owner & Governor; Chair, NHL Board of Governors
- Charlie Jacobs, Chief Executive Officer & Alternate Governor
- Cam Neely, President & Alternate Governor
- Don Sweeney, General Manager & Alternate Governor
- Scott Bradley, Senior Advisor to the General Manager
- Evan Gold, Assistant General Manager
- John Ferguson, Executive Director, Player Personnel
- Jamie Langenbrunner, Director, Player Development
- Bruce Cassidy, Head Coach
- Kevin Dean, Assistant Coach
- Jay Pandolfo, Assistant Coach
- Joe Sacco, Assistant Coach
- Glen Thornborough, Chief Revenue Officer

Year Founded:
1924

Description:
The Boston Bruins are a National Hockey League team based in Boston, Massachusetts

Home Arena:
TD Garden. Seating capacity 17,850.

BUFFALO SABRES
KEYBANK CENTER
ONE SEYMOUR H. KNOX III PLAZA
BUFFALO, NY 14203-4122
716-855-4100
Fax: 716-855-4122
www.nhl.com/sabres

- Terry Pegula, Owner & Chief Executive Officer
- Kim Pegula, Owner & President
- Kevyn Adams, General Manager
- Gregg Brandon, EVP & General Counsel
- Frank Cravotta, EVP, Creative Services
- Mike McFarlane, Senior VP, Finance & Administration
- Mark Preisler, EVP, Media & Content
- Ron Raccuia, EVP, PSE
- Don Granato, Interim Head Coach
- Mike Bales, Assistant Coach

Year Founded:
1970

Description:
The Buffalo Sabres are a National Hockey League team based in Buffalo, New York

Home Arena:
KeyBank Center. Seating capacity 19,070.

CALGARY FLAMES
PO BOX 1540
STN M
CALGARY, AB, CANADA T2P 3B9
403-777-4646
customerservice@calgaryflames.com
www.nhl.com/flames

- N. Murray Edwards, Chairman & Owner
- John Bean, President & Chief Executive Officer
- Cameron Olson, Chief Financial Officer
- Gordon Norrie, VP, Sports Properties Sales & Marketing

- Rollie Cyr, EVP, Revenue Development
- Brad Treliving, General Manager
- Darryl Sutter, Head Coach
- Martin Gelinas, Assistant Coach
- Ryan Huska, Assistant Coach
- Ray Edwards, Assistant Coach

Year Founded:
1972

Description:
The Calgary Flames are a National Hockey League team based in Calgary, Alberta

Home Arena:
Scotiabank Saddledome. Seating capacity 19,289.

CAROLINA HURRICANES
PNC ARENA
1400 EDWARDS MILL ROAD
RALEIGH, NC 27607
919-467-7825
Fax: 919-462-7030
www.nhl.com/hurricanes

- Tom Dundon, Owner & CEO
- Peter Karmanos, Jr., Owner & Alternate Governor
- Don Waddell, President & General Manager
- Davin Olsen, Executive VP & General Manager, PNC Arena
- Jeff Vanderbilt, Chief Financial Officer
- Aaron Schwartz, Director, Hockey Operations
- Glenn Johnson, Vice President, Information Technology
- Rod Brind'Amour, Head Coach
- Dean Chynoweth, Assistant Coach
- Jeff Daniels, Assistant Coach

Year Founded:
1972

Description:
The Carolina Hurricanes Hockey Club is a National Hockey League team based in Raleigh, North Carolina

Home Arena:
PNC Arena. Seating capacity 18,680.

CHICAGO BLACKHAWKS
1901 WEST MADISON STREET
CHICAGO, IL 60612
312-455-7000
Fax: 312-455-7070
www.nhl.com/blackhawks

- Danny Wirtz, Chief Executive Officer
- Jay Blunk, Executive Vice President
- W. Rockwell Wirtz, Chair
- Stan Bowman, President, Hockey Operations/General Manager
- Al MacIsaac, Senior Vice President, Hockey Operations
- Jaime Faulkner, President, Business Operations
- Adam Rogowin, Vice President, Communications
- T.J. Skattum, Vice President, Finance
- Jeremy Colliton, Head Coach
- Sheldon Brookbank, Assistant Coach
- Marc Crawford, Assistant Coach
- Tomas Mitell, Assistant Coach

Year Founded:
1926

Description:
The Chicago Blackhawks are a National Hockey Legue team based in Chicago, Illinois

Home Arena:
United Center. Seating capacity 19,717.

COLORADO AVALANCHE
PEPSI CENTER
1000 CHOPPER CIRCLE
DENVER, CO 80204
303-405-1100
Fax: 303-575-1920
www.nhl.com/avalanche

- E. Stanley Kroenke, Owner & Chair
- Josh Kroenke, President & Governor
- Jean Martineau, SVP, Communications & Team Services
- Joe Sakic, Executive VP/General Manager/Alternate Governor
- Craig Billington, Assistant General Manager

- Chris MacFarland, Assistant General Manager
- Charlotte Grahame, Vice President, Hockey Administration
- Jared Bednar, Head Coach
- Ray Bennett, Assistant Coach
- Nolan Pratt, Assistant Coach
- Matthew Sokolowski, Head Athletic Trainer

Year Founded:
1972

Description:
The Colorado Avalanche are a National Hockey League team based in Denver, Colorado

Home Arena:
Pepsi Center. Seating capacity 17,809.

COLUMBUS BLUE JACKETS
NATIONWIDE ARENA
200 WEST NATIONWIDE BOULEVARD
SUITE LEVEL
COLUMBUS, OH 43215
614-246-3200
www.nhl.com/bluejackets

- John P. McConnell, Governor & Majority Owner
- Mike Priest, President & Alternate Governor
- Greg Kirstein, Senior VP & General Counsel
- Cameron Scholvin, Senior VP & Chief Operating Officer
- T.J. LaMendola, Senior VP & Chief Financial Officer
- Kathryn Dobbs, Senior VP & Chief Marketing Officer
- Jarmo Kekalainen, General Manager & Alternate Governor
- Josh Flynn, Assistant General Manager
- Basil McRae, Assistant General Manager
- John Tortorella, Head Coach
- Brad Larsen, Assistant Coach
- Kenny McCudden, Assistant Coach
- Brad Shaw, Assistant Coach
- Manny Legace, Goaltending Coach

Year Founded:
2000

Description:
The Columbus Blue Jackets are a National Hockey League team based in Columbus, Ohio

Home Arena:
Nationwide Arena. Seating capacity 18,500.

DALLAS STARS
2601 AVENUE OF THE STARS
FRISCO, TX 75034
214-387-5500
www.nhl.com/stars

- Tom Gaglardi, Owner & Governor
- Brad Alberts, President & CEO
- James R. Lites, Chairman
- Matt Bowman, Executive VP & Chief Revenue Officer
- Alana Matthews, Executive VP, Business Operations/General Counsel
- Jim Nill, General Manager
- Dan Stuchal, Senior VP, Marketing
- Tom Holy, Vice President, Communications & Broadcasting
- Rick Bowness, Head Coach
- Derek Laxdal, Assistant Coach
- Todd Nelson, Assistant Coach
- John Stevens, Assistant Coach

Year Founded:
1941

Description:
The Dallas Stars are a National Hockey League team based in Frisco, Texas

Home Arena:
American Airlines Center. Seating capacity 19,323.

DETROIT RED WINGS
JOE LOUIS ARENA
19 STEVE YZERMAN DRIVE
DETROIT, MI 48226
313-471-6606
www.nhl.com/redwings

- Marian Ilitch, Owner/Secretary-Treasurer
- Chris Ilitch, President & CEO
- Jim Devallano, SVP & Alternate Governor
- Steve Yzerman, EVP & General Manager

- Ryan Martin, Assistant General Manager
- Pat Verbeek, Assistant General Manager
- Paul MacDonald, Vice President, Finance
- Jeff Blashill, Head Coach
- Dan Bylsma, Assistant Coach
- Doug Houda, Assistant Coach
- Jeff Salajko, Goaltending Coach
- Mark Howe, Director, Pro Scouting
- Kris Draper, Director, Amateur Scouting

Year Founded:
1926
Description:
The Detroit Red Wings are a National Hockey League team based in Detroit, Michigan
Home Arena:
Joe Louis Arena. Seating capacity 20,027.
Publications:
Inside Hockeytown; 48 Hours with the Detroit Red Wings; Detroit Red Wings History Book; Heroes of Hockeytown

EDMONTON OILERS
OILERS ENTERTAINMENT GROUP
300, 10214 104 AVE NW
EDMONTON, AB, CANADA T5J 0H6
780-414-4625
www.nhl.com/oilers
- Daryl A. Katz, Owner & Governor
- Tom Anselmi, President, Business Operations & COO
- Bob Nicholson, Chairman & Alternate Governor
- Wayne Gretzky, Alternate Governor
- Kevin Lowe, Alternate Governor
- Stew MacDonald, Executive VP, Revenue
- Jason Quilley, Executive VP, Finance
- Stuart Ballantyne, Senior VP, Operations
- Adam Barrie, Senior VP, Human Resources
- Jeff Harrop, Senior VP, Marketing
- Tim Shipton, Senior VP, Communications
- Ken Holland, General Manager & President, Hockey Operations
- Keith Gretzky, Assistant General Manager
- Dave Tippett, Head Coach
- Jim Playfair, Assistant Coach
- Glen Gulutzan, Assistant Coach
- Brian Wiseman, Assistant Coach

Year Founded:
1972
Description:
The Edmonton Oilers are a National Hockey League team based in Edmonton, Alberta
Home Arena:
Rogers Place. Seating capacity 18,347.

FLORIDA PANTHERS
ONE PANTHER PARKWAY
2555 NW 136TH AVENUE
SUNRISE, FL 33323
954-835-8471
www.nhl.com/panthers
- Vincent J. Viola, Owner & Governor
- Douglas A. Cifu, Vice Chair, Partner & Alternate Governor
- Matthew Caldwell, President & CEO
- Bill Zito, General Manager
- Sean McCaffrey, Chief Operating Officer
- Shawn Thornton, Chief Commercial Officer
- Scott Levine, Chief Financial Officer
- Joel Quenneville, Head Coach
- Andrew Brunette, Assistant Coach
- Derek Mackenzie, Assistant Coach
- Ulf Samuelsson, Assistant Coach
- Robb Tallas, Goaltending Coach

Year Founded:
1993
Home Arena:
BB&T Center. Seating capacity 19,250.

LOS ANGELES KINGS
STAPLES CENTER
1111 SOUTH FIGUEROA STREET
LOS ANGELES, CA 90015
213-742-7100
888-546-4752
feedback@lakings.com
www.nhl.com/kings

- Philip F. Anschutz, Owner
- Edward P. Roski, Jr., Owner
- Dan Beckerman, President & CEO, AEG & Alternate Governor
- Luc Robitaille, President & Alternate Governor
- Rob Blake, Vice President & General Manager
- Kelly Cheeseman, Chief Operating Officer & Alternate Governor
- Jeff Solomon, Executive VP, Hockey Operations & Legal Affairs
- Michael Altieri, Senior VP, Marketing, Communications & Content
- Todd McLellan, Head Coach
- Marco Sturm, Assistant Coach
- Trent Yawney, Assistant Coach
- Bill Ranford, Goaltending Coach

Year Founded:
1967
Description:
The Los Angeles Kings are a National Hockey League team based in Los Angeles, California
Home Arena:
STAPLES Center. Seating capacity 18,230.

MINNESOTA WILD
317 WASHINGTON STREET
ST. PAUL, MN 55102
651-602-6000
Fax: 651-222-1055
info@wild.com
www.nhl.com/wild
- Craig Leipold, Owner & Governor
- Matt Majka, President & Alternate Governor
- Bill Guerin, General Manager
- Jeff Pellegrom, Chief Financial Officer & Executive VP
- Jamie Spencer, Executive VP, Business Development
- Carin Anderson, Senior VP, Corporate & Retail Management
- Mitch Helgerson, Senior VP, Marketing & Ticket Sales
- Tom Kurvers, Assistant General Manager
- Dean Evason, Head Coach
- Darby Hendrickson, Assistant Coach
- Bob Woods, Assistant Coach
- Brett McLean, Assistant Coach
- Frederic Chabot, Goaltending Coach

Year Founded:
2000
Description:
The Minnesota Wild are a National Hockey League team based in St. Paul, Minnesota
Home Arena:
Xcel Energy Center. Seating capacity 17,954.

MONTREAL CANADIENS
1275, RUE SAINT-ANTOINE OUEST
MONTREAL, QC, CANADA H3C 5L2
514-932-2582
www.nhl.com/canadiens
- Geoff Molson, Owner, President & CEO
- Marc Bergevin, Executive VP & General Manager
- France Margaret Belanger, Executive VP & Chief Commercial Officer
- Anna Martini, Executive VP & Chief Financial Officer
- Scott Mellanby, Assistant General Manager
- Trevor Timmins, Assistant General Manager
- Dominique Ducharme, Interim Head Coach
- Alex Burrows, Assistant Coach
- Luke Richardson, Assistant Coach

Year Founded:
1909
Description:
The Montreal Canadiens are one of the oldest teams in the National Hockey League. They are based in Montreal, Quebec.
Home Arena:
Centre Bell. Seating capacity 21,273.

NASHVILLE PREDATORS
BRIDGESTONE ARENA
501 BROADWAY
NASHVILLE, TN 37203
615-770-2355
Fax: 615-770-2309

predators@nashvillepredators.com
www.nhl.com/predators
- Herbert Fritch, Chair, Governor & Owner
- Sean Henry, President, CEO & Alternate Governor
- David Poile, GM, Alt. Governor & President, Hockey Operations
- Michelle Kennedy, Chief Operating Officer
- Keith Hegger, Chief Financial Officer
- Chris Junghans, Executive VP & Chief Revenue Officer
- Dave Urso, Senior VP, Operations
- Jeff Kealty, Assisant GM & Director, Scouting
- Brian Poile, Assisant GM & Director, Hockey Operations
- John Hynes, Head Coach
- Dan Hinote, Assistant Coach
- Todd Richards, Assistant Coach
- Dan Lambert, Assistant Coach
- Ben Vanderklok, Goaltending Coach

Year Founded:
1998
Description:
The Nashville Predators are a National Hockey League team basedin Nashville, Tennessee
Home Arena:
Bridgestone Arena. Seating capacity 17,159.

NEW JERSEY DEVILS
PRUDENTIAL CENTER
25 LAFAYETTE STREET
NEWARK, NJ 07102
973-757-6100
mgmt@newjerseydevils.com
www.nhl.com/devils
- Josh Harris, Managing Partner
- David Blitzer, Co-Managing Partner
- Hugh Weber, President, Harris Blitzer Sports & Entertainment
- Jake Reynolds, President, New Jersey Devils
- Scott O'Neil, CEO & Alternate Governor
- Tom Fitzgerald, Executive VP & General Manager
- Martin Brodeur, Executive VP & Advisor, Hockey Operations
- Donna Daniels, Executive VP & Prudential Center GM
- David Collins, Chief Financial Officer
- Adam Davis, Chief Commercial Officer
- Dan MacKinnon, Senior VP & Assistant General Manager
- Lindy Ruff, Head Coach
- Chris Taylor, Assistant Coach
- Rick Kowalsky, Assistant Coach
- Mark Recchi, Assistant Coach
- Dave Rogalski, Goaltending Coach

Year Founded:
1974
Description:
The New Jersey Devils are a National Hockey League team based in Newark, New Jersey
Home Arena:
Prudential Center. Seating capacity 16,514.

NEW YORK ISLANDERS
1255 HEMPSTEAD TURNPIKE
UNIONDALE, NY 11553
516-501-6700
Fax: 516-501-6762
customerservice@newyorkislanders.com
www.nhl.com/islanders
- Scott Malkin, Owner & Governor
- Lou Lamoriello, President, General Manager & Alternate Governor
- Ethan Brown, Senior VP, Marketing & Community Relations
- Mike Cosentino, Senior VP, Sales, Service & Business Intelligence
- Ryan Halkett, Senior VP, Game Presentation
- Lea del Rosario, Senior VP, Human Resources
- Barry Trotz, Head Coach
- Lane Lambert, Associate Coach
- Piero Greco, Goaltending Coach

Year Founded:
1972
Description:
The New York Islanders are a National Hockey League team based in Uniondale, New York

Home Arena:
Nassau Veterans Memorial Coliseum. Seating capacity 13,917.

NEW YORK RANGERS
2 PENNSYLVANIA PLAZA
NEW YORK, NY 10121
212-465-6000
Fax: 212-465-6000
newyorkrangers@thegarden.com
www.nhl.com/rangers
• John Davidson, President
• David Hopkinson, Executive VP, Team Business Operations
• John Cudmore, Senior VP, Sports Strategy & Administration
• Jeanine McGrory, Senior VP, Finance
• Mark Piazza, Senior VP, Sports Team Operations
• John Rosasco, Senior VP, Public Relations & Player Recruitment
• Jeff Gorton, General Manager
• Chris Drury, Associate General Manager
• David Quinn, Head Coach
• Benoit Allaire, Assistant Coach & Goaltending Coach
Year Founded:
1926
Description:
The New York Rangers are a National Hockey League team based in New York City, New York
Home Arena:
Madison Square Garden. Seating capacity 18,006.

OTTAWA SENATORS
CANADIAN TIRE CENTRE
1000 PALLADIUM DR
OTTAWA, ON, CANADA K2V 1A5
613-599-0250
www.nhl.com/senators
• Pierre Dorion, General Manager
• MacTavish Peter, Assistant General Manager
• Tim Pattyson, Director, Hockey Operations
• Jordan Silmser, Director, Team Services
• D.J. Smith, Head Coach
• Jack Capuano, Associate Coach
• Pierre Groulx, Goaltending Coach
Year Founded:
1990
Description:
The Ottawa Senators are a National Hockey League team based in Ottawa, Ontario
Home Arena:
Canadian Tire Centre. Seating capacity 18,652.

PHILADELPHIA FLYERS
WELLS FARGO CENTER
3601 S. BROAD ST.
PHILADELPHIA, PA 19148-5297
215-336-3600
www.nhl.com/flyers
• Dave Scott, Chairman & Governor
• Valerie Camillo, President, Business Operations/Alternate Governor
• Chuck Fletcher, President, Hockey Operations/GM/Alternate Governor
• Phil Weinberg, EVP, Admin./General Counsel/Alternate Governor
• Blair Listino, Chief Financial Officer
• Mike Shane, Chief Business Officer
• Alain Vigneault, Head Coach
• Kim Dillabaugh, Goaltending Coach
Year Founded:
1967
Description:
The Philadelphia Flyers are a National Hockey League team basedin Philadelphia, Pennsylvania
Home Arena:
Wells Fargo Center. Seating capacity 19,306.

PITTSBURGH PENGUINS
PPG PAINTS ARENA
1001 FIFTH AVENUE
PITTSBURGH, PA 15219

412-642-1800
Fax: 412-255-1980
www.nhl.com/penguins
• Mario Lemieux, Co-Owner & Chair
• Ron Burkle, Co-Owner
• David Morehouse, President & CEO
• Terry Kalna, Chief Revenue Officer
• Jenny Darling, Chief Financial Officer
• James Santilli, Chief Experience Officer
• Ron Hextall, General Manager
• Mike Sullivan, Head Coach
• Todd Reirden, Assistant Coach
• Mike Vellucci, Assistant Coach
• Mike Buckley, Goaltending Coach
Year Founded:
1967
Description:
The Pittsburgh Penguins are a National Hockey League team basedin Pittsburgh, Pennsylvania
Home Arena:
PPG Paints Arena. Seating capacity 18,387.

SAN JOSE SHARKS
SAP CENTER
525 WEST SANTA CLARA STREET
SAN JOSE, CA 95113
408-287-7070
Fax: 408-999-5797
www.nhl.com/sharks
• Jonathan Becher, President
• Ken Caveney, Senior VP, Finance & Administration
• Scott Emmert, Vice President, Communications
• Doug Wilson, General Manager
• Tim Burke, Assistant General Manager
• Joe Will, Assistant General Manager
• Bob Boughner, Head Coach
• Rocky Thompson, Associate Coach
• Evgeni Nabokov, Goaltending Coach
Year Founded:
1991
Description:
The San Jose Sharks are a National Hockey League team based in San Jose, California
Home Arena:
SAP Center. Seating capacity 17,562.

SEATTLE KRAKEN
CLIMATE PLEDGE ARENA
305 HARRISON ST
SEATTLE, WASHINGTON
www.nhl.com/kraken
• Tod Leiweke, Owner & CEO
• David Bonderman, Owner
• Jerry Bruckheimer, Owner
• Ron Francis, General Manager
• Norm Maciver, Director, Player Personnel
Year Founded:
2021
Description:
The Seattle Kraken is a National Hockey League team based in Seattle, Washington. It is the first professional hockey team to play in Seattle since the Seattle Totems who played their last game in 1975.
Home Arena:
Climate Pledge Arena. Seating capacity 17,100.

ST. LOUIS BLUES
ENTERPRISE CENTER
1401 CLARK AVENUE AT BRETT HULL WAY
SAINT LOUIS, MO 63103
314-622-2500
customerservice@stlblues.com
www.nhl.com/blues
• Tom Stillman, Chairman & Governor
• Doug Armstrong, President, Hockey Operations/GM/Alternate Governor
• Chris Zimmerman, President & CEO, Business Operations/Alt. Governor
• Steve Chapman, Executive VP & Chief Revenue Officer
• Phil Siddle, Executive VP & Chief Operating & Financial Officer
• Keira Emerson, Vice President, Strategy & Business Intelligence
• Dave Taylor, Vice President, Hockey

Operations
• Ryan Miller, Assistant GM, Hockey Operations
• Craig Berube, Head Coach
• David Alexander, Goaltending Coach
Year Founded:
1967
Description:
The St. Louis Blues are a National Hockey League team based in St. Louis, Missouri
Home Arena:
Enterprise Center. Seating capacity 18,096.

TAMPA BAY LIGHTNING
AMALIE ARENA
401 CHANNELSIDE DRIVE
TAMPA, FL 33602
813-301-6500
membershipservices@amaliearena.com
www.nhl.com/lightning
• Jeff Vinik, Chairman & Governor
• Steve Griggs, Chief Executive Officer
• Casey Rodgers, Chief Financial Officer
• Jarrod Dillon, Chief Marketing & Revenue Officer
• Darryl Benge, Executive VP & General Manager, Amalie Arena
• Derrick Brooks, Executive VP, Corporate & Community Development
• Brian Breseman, Senior Director, Broadcasting, Programs & Comms.
• Julien BriseBois, VP & General Manager/Alternate Governor
• Mathieu Darche, Director, Hockey Operations
• Mathieu Darche, Director, Hockey Operations
• Jon Cooper, Head Coach
• Frantz Jean, Goaltending Coach
Year Founded:
1992
Description:
The Tampa Bay Lightning is a National Hockey League team based in Tampa, Florida
Home Arena:
Amalie Arena. Seating capacity 19,092.

TORONTO MAPLE LEAFS
SCOTIABANK ARENA
40 BAY STREET
SUITE 500
TORONTO, ON, CANADA M5J 2L2
416-815-5500
www.nhl.com/mapleleafs
• Brendan Shanahan, President & Alternate Governor
• Kyle Dubas, General Manager
• Laurence Gilman, Assistant General Manager
• Brandon Pridham, Assistant General Manager
• Jim Paliafito, Senior Director, Player Evaluation
• Scott Pellerin, Senior Director, Player Development
• Brad Lynn, Director, Team Operations
• Reid Mitchell, Director, Hockey & Scouting Operations
• Dave Morrison, Director, Player Personnel
• Sheldon Keefe, Head Coach
• Steve Briere, Goaltending Coach
Year Founded:
1917
Description:
The Toronto Maple Leafs are a National Hockey League team based in Toronto, Ontario.
Home Arena:
Scotiabank Arena. Seating capacity 20,270.

VANCOUVER CANUCKS
89 WEST GEORGIA STREET
VANCOUVER, BC, CANADA V6B 0N8
604-899-7400
Fax: 604-899-7401/7490
fanservices@canucks.com
www.nhl.com/canucks
• Francesco Aquilini, Chairman & Governor
• Jim Benning, General Manager
• Trent Carroll, Chief Operating Officer & Alternate Governor
• John Weisbrod, Assistant General Manager
• Chris Gear, Assistant General Manager & Chief Legal Officer

• Todd Kobus, Executive VP, Business Operations & CFO
• Ryan Johnson, Senior Director, Player Development
• Jonathan Wall, Senior Director, Hockey Operations & Analytics
• Travis Green, Head Coach
• Ian Clark, Goaltending Coach
Year Founded:
1970
Description:
The Vancouver Canucks are a National Hockey League team based in Vancouver, British Columbia
Home Arena:
Rogers Arena. Seating capacity 18,910.

VEGAS GOLDEN KNIGHTS
T-MOBILE ARENA
3780 LAS VEGAS BOULEVARD SOUTH
LAS VEGAS, NV 89158
702-790-2663
www.nhl.com/goldenknights
• Bill Foley, Chair, CEO & Governor
• George McPhee, President, Hockey Operations & Alternate Governor
• Kerry Bubolz, President, COO & Alternate Governor
• Bryan Coy, Chief Financial Officer
• Robert Foley, Chief Business Officer
• Peter Sadowski, Executive VP & Chief Legal Officer
• Brian Killingsworth, Senior VP & Chief Marketing Officer
• Jim Frevola, Senior VP & Chief Sales Officer
• Darren Eliot, Vice President, Hockey Programming & Operations
• Kelly McCrimmon, General Manager
• Peter DeBoer, Head Coach
• Mike Rosati, Goaltending Coach
Year Founded:
2017
Description:
The Vegas Golden Knights are a National Hockey League team based in Las Vegas, NV
Home Arena:
T-Mobile Arena. Seating capacity 17,500.

WASHINGTON CAPITALS
627 NORTH GLEBE ROAD
SUITE 850
ARLINGTON, VA 22203
202-266-2350
membershipservices@washcaps.com
www.nhl.com/capitals
• Ted Leonsis, Founder, Chair, Principal Partner & CEO
• Dick Patrick, Vice Chair, Partner & President
• Brian MacLellan, Senior VP & General Manager
• Keith Burrows, Senior VP, Team Finance
• Hunter Lochmann, Chief Marketing Officer
• Sergey Kocharov, Vice President, Communications
• Patricia Maccini, Vice President, Administration
• Peter Laviolette, Head Coach
• Scott Murray, Goaltending Coach
Year Founded:
1974
Description:
The Washington Capitals are a National Hockey League team based in Washington, DC
Home Arena:
Capital One Arena. Seating capacity 18,573.

WINNIPEG JETS
345 GRAHAM AVE
WINNIPEG, MB, CANADA R3C 5S6
204-987-7825
www.nhl.com/jets
• Kevin Cheveldayoff, Executive VP & General Manager
• John Olfert, President & COO
• Scott Brown, Senior Director, Hockey Communications
• Paul Maurice, Head Coach
• Jaime Kompon, Associate Coach

Year Founded:
2011
Description:
The Winnipeg Jets are a National Hockey League team based in Winnipeg, Manitoba. The franchise was formerly known as the Atlanta Thrashers until their purchase in 2011.
Home Arena:
Bell MTS Place. Seating capacity 15,321.

Hockey, Professional, Minor Leagues

AMERICAN HOCKEY LEAGUE/AHL
ONE MONARCH PLACE
SUITE 2400
SPRINGFIELD, MA 01144
413-781-2030
theahl.com
• Scott Howson, President & CEO
• David Andrews, Chair
• Chris Nikolis, Executive VP, Business
cnikolis@theahl.com
• Michael Murray, Executive VP, Hockey Operations
• Melissa Caruso, VP, Hockey Operations & Governance
Year Founded:
1936
Description:
Professional ice hockey league that serves as the primary developmental circuit for the National Hockey League.
Membership Requirements:
Purchase of a franchise
Publications:
Official guide and record book; Rule book; Schedule; Year End Statistical Package

Teams:

BAKERSFIELD CONDORS
1001 TRUXTUN AVENUE
BAKERSFIELD, CA 93301-4799
661-324-7825
Fax: 661-324-6929
condors@bakersfieldcondors.com
www.bakersfieldcondors.com
• Daryl Katz, Owner
• Matthew Riley, President
• Justin Fahsbender, Vice President, Ticket Sales
• Jose Rivera, Vice President, Member Services
• Keith Gretzky, General Manager
• Jay Woodcroft, Head Coach
• J-F Houle, Assistant Coach
• Dave Manson, Assistant Coach
• Sylvain Rodrigue, Goaltending Coach
Home Ice:
Mechanics Bank Arena. Seating capacity, 8,751.
NHL Affiliate:
Edmonton Oilers.

BELLEVILLE SENATORS
265 CANNIFTON RD
BELLEVILLE, ON, CANADA K8N 4V8
613-967-8067
info@bellevillesens.com
bellevillesens.com
• Rob Mullowney, Chief Operating Officer
mullowneyr@bellevillesens.com
• Darren Murphy, Senior Director, Finance & Operations
murphyd@bellevillesens.com
• Dorion Pierre, General Manager
• Troy Mann, Head Coach
• Kory Cooper, Goaltending Development Coach
Home Ice:
CAA Arena. Seating capacity, 4,365.

NHL Affiliation:
Ottawa Senators.

BINGHAMTON DEVILS
ONE STUART STREET
3RD FLOOR
BINGHAMTON, NY 13905
607-722-7367
www.binghamtondevils.com
• Tom Mitchell, Executive VP, Operations
tmitchell@binghamtondevils.com
• Terrance Buczkowski, Vice President Marketing & Business Development
tbuczkowski@binghamtonsenators.com
• Marc Witt, VP of Ticket Sales
mwitt@binghamtonsenators.com
• Connor Gates, Director, Game Night Operations
• Michael Karpowich, Director, Corporate Partnerships
• Mark Dennehy, Head Coach
• Sergei Brylin, Assistant Coach
• Ryan Parent, Assistant Coach
Year Founded:
2017
Description:
Formerly the Binghamton Senators
Home Ice:
Floyd L. Maines Veterans Memorial Arena. Seating capacity, 4,710.
NHL Affiliation:
New Jersey Devils.

BRIDGEPORT SOUND TIGERS
600 MAIN STREET
BRIDGEPORT, CT 06604
203-345-2300
info@soundtigers.com
www.soundtigers.com
• Scott Malkin, Co-Owner & Governor
• Brent Rossi, President, Business Operations
• Brad Dworin, Director, Ticket Sales
• Alan Fuehring, Director, Broadcasting & Communications
• Chris Lamoriello, General Manager
• Brent Thompson, Head Coach
• Eric Boguniecki, Assistant Coach
• Matt Carkner, Assistant Coach
• Chis Terreri, Goaltending Coach
Home Ice:
Webster Bank Arena. Seating capacity, 8,412.
NHL Affiliation:
New York Islanders.

CHARLOTTE CHECKERS
201 EAST TRADE STREET
SUITE E480
CHARLOTTE, NC 28202
704-342-4423
Fax: 704-377-4595
tickets@gocheckers.com
www.gocheckers.com
• Michael A. Kahn, Owner, CEO & Governor
• Derek Wilkinson, Senior VP, Hockey Operations
• Paul Branecky, Vice President, Marketing & Communications
• Jamie Black, Director, Finance & Controller
• Geordie Kinnear, Head Coach
• Patrick Dwyer, Assistant Coach
Home Ice:
Bojangles' Coliseum. Seating capacity, 8,600.
NHL Affiliation:
Florida Panthers.

CHICAGO WOLVES
2301 RAVINE WAY
GLENVIEW, IL 60025
847-724-4625
800-843-9658
Fax: 847-724-1652
info@chicagowolves.com
www.chicagowolves.com
• Don Levin, Chairman & Governor
• Buddy Meyers, Vice Chair
• Seth Gold, Director
• Wayne Messmer, Senior EVP

- Wendell Young, General Manager
- Gene Ubriaco, Senior Advisor & Director, Hockey Operations
info@chicagowolves.com
- Ryan Warsofsky, Head Coach
- Bob Nardella, Assistant Coach
- Patrick Dwyer, Assistant Coach
- Stan Dubicki, Goaltending Coach
Home Ice:
Allstate Arena. Seating capacity, 16,692.
NHL Affiliation:
Carolina Hurricanes.

CLEVELAND MONSTERS
ONE CENTER ICE
CLEVELAND, OH 44115-4001
216-420-0000
service@clevelandmonsters.com
www.clevelandmonsters.com
- Dan Gilbert, Chairman
- Mike Ostrowski, President & COO, Francise Operations
mostrowski@clevelandmonsters.com
- Chris Clark, Director, Player Personnel/General Manager
- Bill Zito, Associate General Manager
- Mike Eaves, Head Coach
- Jim Corsi, Goaltending Development Coach
Home Ice:
Rocket Mortgage FieldHouse. Seating capacity, 18,926.
NHL Affiliation:
Columbus Blue Jackets.

COLORADO EAGLES
1625 PELICAN LAKES POINT
SUITE 100
WINDSOR, CO 80550
970-686-7468
www.coloradoeagles.com
- Martin Lind, Chief Executive Officer
- Ralph Backstrom, Founder
- Craig Billington, General Manager
- Gavin Riches, Assistant General Manager
- Chris Augusto, Executive VP, Ticketing & Marketing
- Greg Cronin, Head Coach
- Ryan Bach, Goaltending Coach
Home Ice:
Budweiser Events Center. Seating capacity, 5,289.
NHL Affiliation:
Colorado Avalanche.

GRAND RAPIDS GRIFFINS
130 WEST FULTON
SUITE 111
GRAND RAPIDS, MI 49503
616-774-4585
Fax: 616-336-5464
customerservice@griffinshockey.com
www.griffinshockey.com
- Dan DeVos, Co-Owner, CEO & Governor
- David Van Andel, Co-Owner & Chairman
- Scott Gorsline, Alternate Governor, Senior VP
- Tim Gortsema, President
(616) 774-4585
tgortsema@griffinshockey.com
- Randy Cleves, Senior Director, Public Relations
(616) 774-4585
rcleves@griffinshockey.com
- Ben Simon, Head Coach
(616) 774-4585
griff@griffinshockey.com
- Brian Mahoney-Wilson, Goaltending Development Coach
Home Ice:
Van Andel Arena. Seating capacity, 11,000.
NHL Affiliation:
Detroit Red Wings.

HARTFORD WOLF PACK
ONE CIVIC CENTER PLAZA
HARTFORD, CT 06103
860-722-9425
WolfPack-Service@SpectraXP.com
www.hartfordwolfpack.com
- Ben Weiss, General Manager
- Chris Drury, General Manager, Wolfpack
- Erik Hansen, Vice President, Business Operations
erik.hansen@spectraxp.com
- Bryan Dooley, Vice President, Corporate Sales
bdooley@global-spectrum.com
- Yasmeen Badich, Director, Marketing
yasmeen.badich@spectraxp.com
- Bob Crawford, Director, Public Relations & Broadcasting
bcrawford@global-spectrum.com
- Frank Berrian, Community Relations & Game Presentation Manager
fberrian@global-spectrum.com
- Kris Knoblauch, Head Coach
- Gord Murphy, Associate Head Coach
- Eric Raymond, Goaltending Coach
Home Ice:
XL Center. Seating capacity, 14,750.
NHL Affiliation:
New York Rangers.

HENDERSON SILVER KNIGHTS
222 SOUTH WATER STREET
HENDERSON, NV 89015
www.hendersonsilverknights.com
- Kelly McCrimmon, General Manager
- Manny Viveiros, Head Coach
NHL Affiliation:
Vegas Golden Knights.

HERSHEY BEARS
550 WEST HERSHEYPARK DRIVE
HERSHEY, PA 17033
717-508-2327
Fax: 717-534-8996
hersheybears@hersheyPA.com
www.hersheybears.com
- John Lawn, President & CEO
- Bryan Helmer, Vice President, Hockey Operations
- Dan Stuck, Manager, Wellness & Team Affairs
- Zack Fisch, Manager, Media Relations & Broadcasting
zasfisch@hersheypa.com
- Spencer Carbery, Head Coach
- Scott Allen, Assistant Coach
- Patrick Wellar, Assistant Coach
Home Ice:
Giant Center. Seating capacity, 10,500.
NHL Affiliation:
Washington Capitals.

IOWA WILD
730 THIRD STREET
DES MOINES, IA 50309
515-564-8700
www.iowawild.com
- Todd Frederickson, President & Alternate Governor
todd.frederickson@iowawild.com
- Tom Kurvers, General Manager & Alternate Governor
- Eric Grundfast, Vice President, Sales
eric.grundfast@iowawild.com
- Brent Arnold, Senior Director, Sales
- Tim Army, Head Coach
- Alex Tanguay, Assistant Coach
- Richard Bachman, Goaltending Coach
Home Ice:
Wells Fargo Arena. Seating capacity, 15,181.
NHL Affiliation:
Minnesota Wild.

LAVAL ROCKET
1950 CLAUDE-GAGNE STREET
SUITE 103
MONTREAL, QC, CANADA H7N 0E4
855-595-2200
info@rocketlaval.com
www.rocketlaval.com
- John Sedgwick, Governor & Vice President, Hockey Operations

- Marc Bergevin, General Manager
- Scott Mellanby, Assistant General Manager
- Joä€°l Bouchard, Head Coach
- Marco Marciano, Goaltending & Video Coach
Home Arena:
Place Bell. Seating capacity 10,000.
NHL Affiliation:
Montreal Canadiens.

LEHIGH VALLEY PHANTOMS
701 HAMILTON STREET
ALLENTOWN, PA 18101
610-224-4625
www.phantomshockey.com
- Jim Brooks, Co-Owner & Governor
- Rob Brooks, Co-Owner & Governor
- Chris Porreca, Executive Vice President
cporreca@phantomshockey.com
- Richard Lintker, Vice President, Ticket Sales
- Barry Hanrahan, Assistant General Manager-Philadelphia Flyers
- Scott Gordon, Head Coach
- Kerry Huffman, Assistant Coach
- Dan Meinz, Strenth & Conditioning Coach
Home Ice:
Cool Insuring Arena. Seating capacity, 4,794.
NHL Affiliation:
Philadelphia Flyers.

MANITOBA MOOSE
345 GRAHAM AVE
WINNIPEG, MB, CANADA R3C 5S6
204-987-7825
info@moosehockey.com
moosehockey.com
- Craig Heisinger, General Manager
- Brad Andrews, Senior Director, Hockey & Business Operations
- Pascal Vincent, Head Coach
- Eric Dubois, Assistant Coach
- Marty Johnston, Assistant Coach
- Rick St. Croix, Developmental Goaltending Coach
Home Ice:
Bell MTS Place. Seating capacity 15,321.
NHL Affiliation:
Winnipeg Jets.

MILWAUKEE ADMIRALS
510 WEST KILBOURN AVENUE
MILWAUKEE, WI 53203
414-227-0550
Fax: 414-227-0568
www.milwaukeeadmirals.com
- Harris Turer, Owner & CEO
- Jon Greenberg, President
jgreenberg@milwaukeeadmirals.com
- Scott Nichol, General Manager
- Mike Wojciechowski, Vice President, Business Development
wojo@milwaukeeadmirals.com
- Charlie Larson, Vice President, Communications
clarson@milwaukeeadmirals.com
- Karl Taylor, Head Coach
- Scott Ford, Assistant Coach
- Greg Rallo, Assistant Coach
- Ryan Costello, Manager, Hockey Operations
Home Ice:
UW-Milwaukee Panther Arena. Seating capacity, 9,652.
NHL Affiliation:
Nashville Predators.

ONTARIO REIGN
901 VIA PIEMONTE
SUITE 370
ONTARIO, CA 91764
909-941-7825
Fax: 909-204-5555
tickets@ontarioreign.com
www.ontarioreign.com
- Darren Abbott, President
- Richard Seeley, General Manager
- Steve Fraser, Senior Director, Business Operations
- Jasmyn Wilson, Senior Director, Ticket

Operations
jwilson@ontarioreign.com
• Zach Dooley, Manager, Communications & Content
zdooley@ontarioreign.com
• John Wroblewski, Head Coach
• Chris Hajt, Assistant Coach
• Jaroslav Modry, Assistant Coach
• Matt Millar, Goaltending Development Coach
Home Ice:
Toyota Arena. Seating capacity, 9,736.
NHL Affiliation:
Los Angeles Kings.

PROVIDENCE BRUINS
1 LA SALLE SQUARE
PROVIDENCE, RI 02903
401-273-5000
www.providencebruins.com
• Jeff Fear, CEO
• Matt Poore, President
• Jeff Hagan, Chief Operating Officer
• David DeNitto, Chief Ticketing Officer
• Nathan Roberts, Chief Marketing Officer
• John Ferguson, General Manager
• Jay Leach, Head Coach
• Trent Whitfield, Assistant Coach
• Ryan Mougenel, Assistant Coach
Home Ice:
Dunkin' Donuts Center. Seating capacity, 11,273.
NHL Affiliation:
Boston Bruins.

ROCHESTER AMERICANS
ROCHESTER AMERICANS HOCKEY CLUB
ONE WAR MEMORIAL SQUARE
ROCHESTER, NY 14614
585-454-5335
Fax: 585-454-3954
www.amerks.com
• Terrence M. Pegula, Owner
• Kim Pegula, President
• Rob Minter, Vice President, Business Operations
(585) 454-5335
rob.minter@bluecrossarena.com
• Jody Gage, Director, Strategic Planning
• Warren Kosel, Senior Director, Public Relations
(585) 545-5335
wkosel@amerks.com
• Kevin Adams, General Manager
• Seth Appert, Head Coach
• Gord Dineen, Assistant Coach
• Toby Petersen, Assistant Coach
Home Ice:
Blue Cross Arena. Seating capacity, 10,662.
NHL Affiliation:
Boston Bruins.

ROCKFORD ICEHOGS
300 ELM STREET
ROCKFORD, IL 61101
815-986-6465
icehogs@icehogs.com
www.icehogs.com
• Mike Peck, Director, Business Operations
peckm@icehogs.com
• Julia Johnson, Director, Sales
(815) 847-6371
jjohnson@smgrockford.com
• Mark Bernard, Vice President, Hockey Operaitons & Affiliates
• Joseph Zakrzewski, Broadcasting/Communications Coordinator
zakrzewskij@icehogs.com
• Derek King, Head Coach
• Anders Sorensen, Assistant Coach
• Peter Aubry, Developmental Goaltending Coach
Year Founded:
1999
Home Ice:
BMO Harris Bank Center. Seating capacity, 6,200.
NHL Affiliation:
Chicago Blackhawks.

SAN DIEGO GULLS
SAN DIEGO GULLS HOCKEY CLUB
7676 HAZARD CENTER DRIVE
SUITE 1075
SAN DIEGO, CA 92108
619-359-4700
www.sandiegogulls.com
• Matt Savant, President, Business Operations
• Bob Murray, President, Hockey Operations
• Michael Schulman, Chief Executive Officer
• Bob Ferguson, General Manager
• Kevin Dineen, Head Coach
• J.F. Labbe, Goaltending Coach
Home Ice:
Pechanga Arena. Seating capacity, 12,920.
NHL Affiliation:
Anaheim Ducks.

SAN JOSE BARRACUDA
525 WEST SANTA CLARA STREET
SAN JOSE, CA 95113
408-287-7070
800-366-4423
www.sjbarracuda.com
• Jonathan Becher, President
• Joe Will, General Manager & Alternate Governor
• Daniel Bell, Game Presentation Manager
• Nick Nollenberger, Public Relations & Broadcasting Manager
• Roy Sommer, Head Coach
• Nick Gialdini, Manager, Hockey Operations
Home Ice:
SAP Center at San Jose. Seating capacity, 17,562.
NHL Affiliation:
San Hose Sharks.

SPRINGFIELD THUNDERBIRDS
45 BRUCE LANDON WAY
SPRINGFIELD, MA 01103
413-739-4625
Fax: 413-739-3389
info@springfieldthunderbirds.com
www.springfieldthunderbirds.com
• Nathan Costa, President
• Todd McDonald, Vice President, Sales & Strategy
• Steve Kunsey, Director, Business Development
• Eric Joyce, General Manager
• Geordie Kinnear, Head Coach
• Doug Janik, Assistant Coach
Description:
Formed after the sale of the Springfield Falcons, and the relocation of the Portland Pirates.
Home Ice:
MassMutual Center. Seating capacity, 6,793.
NHL Affiliation:
St. Louis Blues.

STOCKTON HEAT
248 WEST FREMONT STREET
STOCKTON, CA 95203
209-373-1500
www.stocktonheat.com
• Jamie Cochrane, Senior Director, Business Operations
• Devon Thumwood, Director, Business Operations
• Tess Jaurigue, Director, Finance & Administration
• Chris Picher, Director, Broadcasting & Digital Content
• Joe Tichy, Director, Game Operations
• Cail MacLean, Head Coach
• Thomas Speer, Goaltending Coach
Home Arena:
Stockton Arena. Seating capacity 9,737.
NHL Affiliation:
Calgary Flames.

SYRACUSE CRUNCH
800 SOUTH STATE STREET
SYRACUSE, NY 13202
315-473-4444
info@syracusecrunch.com
www.syracusecrunch.com
• Howard Dolgon, President, CEO & Governor
• Vance Lederman, SVP, Business Operations, CFO & Alt. Governor
(315) 473-4444
vlederman@syracusecrunch.com
• Jim Sarosy, Chief Operating Officer & Alt. Governor
(315) 474-4444
jsarosy@syracusecrunch.com
• Todd Cross, Vice President, Ticket Operations
(315) 473-4444
tcross@syracusecrunch.com
• Megan Cahill, Director, Public Relations & Digital Media
(315) 473-4444
mcahill@syracusecrunch.com
• Stacy Roest, General Manager
• Ben Groulx, Head Coach
• Gilles Bouchard, Assistant Coach
• Eric Veilleux, Assistant Coach
• Joe Palmer, Goaltending & Video Coach
Home Ice:
Upstate Medical University Arena at Onondaga County War Memorial. Seating capacity, 6,159.
NHL Affiliation:
Tampa Bay Lightning.

TEXAS STARS
2100 AVENUE OF THE STARS
CEDAR PARK, TX 78613
512-467-8277
tickets@texasstars.com
www.texasstars.com
• Thomas R. Gaglardi, Owner
• Brad Alberts, President & Alternate Governor
• Michael Delay, Chief Sales & Marketing Officer
• Scott White, General Manager
• Rebecca Miller, Senior Director, Corporate Sales & Sponsorship
rmiller@texasstars.com
• John Schloffman, Director, Ticket Operations
JSchloffman@texasstars.com
• Neil Graham, Head Coach
• Travis Morin, Assistant Coach
Home Ice:
H-E-B Center at Cedar Park. Seating capacity, 6,778.
NHL Affiliation:
Dallas Stars.

TORONTO MARLIES
45 MANITOBA DR
TORONTO, ON, CANADA M6K 3C3
416-597-7825
marlies.ca
• Laurence Gilman, Governor & General Manager
• Mike Dixon, Director, Minor League Operations & Alt. Governor
• Marc Lira, Director, Business Operations & Alt. Governor
• Greg Moore, Head Coach
• Jon Elkin, Goaltending Coach
Home Arena:
Coca-Cola Coliseum. Seating capacity 7,851.
NHL Affiliation:
Toronto Maple Leafs.

TUCSON ROADRUNNERS
300 WEST PASEO REDONDO
TUCSON, AZ 85701
866-774-6253
www.tucsonroadrunners.com
• Bob Hoffman, President
Bob.Hoffman@TucsonRoadrunners.com
• Denny Adrian, Director, Communications & Broadcasting
adrian.denny@tucsonroadrunners.com
• Steve Sullivan, General Manager
• Steve Potvin, Head Coach
• John Slaney, Assistant Coach
• Steve Potvin, Assistant Coach
Home Ice:
Tucson Convention Center. Seating capacity, 8,962.

NHL Affiliation:
Arizona Coyotes.

UTICA COMETS
400 ORISKANY STREET WEST
UTICA, NY 13502
315-790-9070
info@uticacomets.com
www.uticacomets.com
• Robert Esche, President
• Michael Potrzeba, Chief Financial Officer
• Adam Pawlick, Vice President
• Adam Vogel, Senior VP, Ticketing Sales, Service & Operations
• Cecelie Pikus, Vice President, Marketing
• Lindsay Mogle, Vice President, Communications
• Ryan Johnson, General Manager
• Trent Cull, Head Coach
• Gary Agnew, Associate Coach
Home Ice:
Adirondack Bank Center at the Utica Memorial Auditorium. Seating capacity, 3,860.
NHL Affiliation:
Vancouver Canucks.

WILKES-BARRE/SCRANTON PENGUINS
40 COAL STREET
WILKES-BARRE, PA 18702
570-208-7367
Fax: 570-208-5432
webinquiry@wbspenguins.com
www.wbspenguins.com
• Jeff Barrett, Chief Executive Officer
• Greg Petorak, EVP & Chief Financial Officer
• Rob Belza, Vice President, Corporate Sales
• Brian Coe, Vice President, Operations
• Mike Vellucci, General Manager
• J.D. Forrest, Head Coach
Home Ice:
Mohegan Sun Arena at Casey Plaza. Seating capacity, 8,300.
NHL Affiliation:
Pittsburgh Penguins.

EAST COAST HOCKEY LEAGUE/ECHL
116 VILLAGE BOULEVARD
SUITE 230
PRINCETON, NJ 08540
609-452-0770
Fax: 609-452-7147
echl@echl.com
www.echl.com
• Ryan Crelin, Commissioner
• Joe Ernst, Senior VP, Hockey Operations

Teams:

ADIRONDACK THUNDER
1 CIVIC CENTER PLAZA
GLENS FALLS, NY 12801
518-480-3355
Fax: 518-480-3356
info@echlthunder.com
www.echlthunder.com
• Jeff Mead, President
jmead@echlthunder.com
• Zach Dooley, Director, Communications & Community Relations
zdooley@echlthunder.com
• Sean Driscoll, Director, Ticket Sales & Services
sdriscoll@echlthunder.com
• Bryan Florkiewicz, Director, Game Operations
bflorkiewicz@echlthunder.com
• Alex Loh, Director, Hockey Operations/Head Coach
• Josh Lyons, Manager, Operations & Administration
• Alex Loh, Assistant Coach
Home Ice:
Glens Falls Civic Center

ALLEN AMERICANS
200 EAST STACY ROAD
SUITE 1350
ALLEN, TX 75002
972-912-1000
info@allenamericans.com
www.allenamericans.com
• Jack Gulati, Owner
• Mike Waddell, President
• Mike Martin, Sr. Vice President Of Sales & Service
michaelmartin@allenamericans.com
• Tommy Daniels, Vice President Of Broadcasting & Media Relations
tommy@allenamericans.com
• Robert Fatta, Director, Ticket Operations
robert@allenamericans.com
• Steve Martinson, Head Coach & General Manager
• Tony Curtale, Assistant Coach
• Thomas Speer, Goalie Coach
• Jaime Garcia, Athletic Trainer
jgarcia@allenamericans.com
Home Ice:
Allen Event Center

ATLANTA GLADIATORS
PO BOX 957238
DULUTH, GA 30095
770-497-5100
Fax: 770-497-5101
hockey@atlantagladiators.com
www.atlantagladiators.com
• Tom P. Sapitowicz, Jr., Owner
• Toby Jeffreys, Managing Member
• Jerry James, President
• Joe Gelderman, Vice President & GM, Business Operations
jgelderman@atlantagladiators.com
• Bill Davidson, Chief Financial Officer
• Jim Hall, Director, Community Relations
jhall@atlantagladiators.com
• Christina Johnson, Sr. Director, Digital/Media/Game Operations
cjohnson@atlantagladiators.com
• Jeff Pyle, Head Coach & General Manager, Hockey Operations
• Mike Flanagan, Assistant Coach
• Roman Marakhovski, Assistant/Video Coach
Home Ice:
Infinite Energy Arena

CINCINNATI CYCLONES
100 BROADWAY STREET
CINCINNATI, OH 45202
513-421-4111
Fax: 513-333-3040
info@usbankarena.com
www.cycloneshockey.com
• Ray Harris, President
• Kristin Ropp, Vice President & General Manager
• Joe Wallach, Vice President of Operations
• Matt Thomas, Head Coach
• Cam Keith, Assistant Coach
Home Ice:
U.S. Bank Arena

FLORIDA EVERBLADES
11000 EVERBLADES PARKWAY
ESTERO, FL 33928
239-948-7825
Fax: 239-948-2248
info@floridaeverblades.com
www.floridaeverblades.com
• Craig Brush, CEO/General Manager
• Chris Palin, Executive VP, Business Development
• Chris Palin, Vice President of Sales & Marketing
chrisp@floridaeverblades.com
• Trent Ferguson, Director, Sales
trent@floridaeverblades.com
• Brad Ralph, Head Coach/Director, Hockey Operations
• Tad O'Had, Assistant Coach
• Chris Emrick, Athletic Trainer

Home Ice:
Germain Arena

FORT WAYNE KOMETS
1010 MEMORIAL WAY
SUITE 100
FORT WAYNE, IN 46805
260-483-0011
Fax: 260-483-3899
www.komets.com
• Michael Franke, President/Co-Owner
• Scott Sproat, Executive VP/Co-Owner
(260) 483-1641
scott@komets.com
• David Franke, General Manager/Co-Owner
• Gene Evans, Chief Financial Officer
• Chuck Bailey, Director, Communications
• Ben Boudreau, Head Coach/Director, Player Personnel
• Konstantin Shafranov, Assistant Coach
Home Ice:
Allen County War Memorial Coliseum

GREENVILLE SWAMP RABBITS
650 NORTH ACADEMY STREET
GREENVILLE, SC 29601
864-250-4868
Fax: 864-250-4793
info@swamprabbits.com
www.swamprabbits.com
• Todd Mackin, President
(864) 250-4959
• Megan Dotson, Vice President, Marketing/Revenue Support
(864) 250-4844
• Fran Jameson, Vice President, Business Administration
(864) 250-4869
• Andrew Lord, Head Coach
(864) 250-4921
• Alan Fuehring, Broadcaster/Media Relations Manager
(864) 250-4851
• Stacey Wise, Manager Of Ticket Operations/Customer Service
(864) 250-4804
• Troy Schwab, Assistant Coach
• Blair LaMarche, Athletic Trainer
Home Ice:
Bon Secours Wellness Arena

IDAHO STEELHEADS
251 SOUTH CAPITOL BOULEVARD
BOISE, ID 83702
208-383-0080
Fax: 208-383-0194
info@idahosteelheads.com
www.idahosteelheads.com
• Eric Trapp, President, Idaho Sports Properties
• Michael DiPalma, Vice President, Idaho Sports Properties
• Neil Graham, Director, Hockey Operations & Head Coach
• Dirk Manley, Director, New Business Development
• Ben Cottier, Director, Ticketing
• Everett Sheen, Head Coach
Home Ice:
CenturyLink Arena

INDY FUEL
1202 EAST 38TH STREET
INDIANAPOLIS, IN 46205
317-925-3835
Fax: 317-925-3850
contact@indyfuelhockey.com
www.indyfuelhockey.com
• Jim Hallett, Chairman
• Larry McQueary, President & COO
• Bill Stackhouse, CPA, Chief Financial Officer
• Doug Christiansen, Head Coach/General Manager
• Tom Callahan, Director, Communications
• Steve Kuepper, Director, Ticket Sales
• Bernie John, Assistant Coach
• Jan Jas, Assistant Coach
• Derek Edwardson, Assistant Coach

Home Ice:
Indiana Farmers Coliseum

JACKSONVILLE ICEMEN
VYSTAR VETERANS MEMORIAL ARENA
300 A PHILIP RANDOLPH BLVD
JACKSONVILLE, FL 32202
www.jacksonvilleicemen.com
• Bob Ohrablo, President
• Jason Christie, Head Coach

KALAMAZOO WINGS
3600 VANRICK DRIVE
KALAMAZOO, MI 49001
269-743-6011
Fax: 269-345-6584
www.kwings.com
• Toni Will, Governor & Business Director
• Nick Bootland, Director, Hockey
Operations/Head Coach
• Jason Kane, Sales Manager
jkane@kwings.com
• Joe Roberts, Public Relations/Broadcaster
jroberts@kwings.com
• Sam Ftorek, Assistant Coach
Home Ice:
Wings Event Center

KANSAS CITY MAVERICKS
19100 EAST VALLEY VIEW PARKWAY
INDEPENDENCE, MO 64055
816-252-7825
info@kcmavericks.com
www.kcmavericks.com
• Lamar Hunt, Jr., Owner
• Brent Thiessen, Team President & General
Manager
bthiessen@kcmavericks.com
• Tad O'Had, Head Coach & Director, Hockey
Operations
Home Ice:
Silverstein Eye Centers Arena
Founded:
2009
Description:
The Kansas City Mavericks are members of the
ECHL. The Mavericks currently are the ECHL
affiliate of the NHL's Calgary Flames and AHL's
Stockton Heat and are in their ninth season as a
franchise, fourth in the ECHL.

MAINE MARINERS
CROSS INSURANCE ARENA
1 CIVIC CENTRE SQUARE
PORTLAND, ME 04101
www.marinersofmaine.com
• Danny Briere, President & General Manager
• Riley Armstrong, Head Coach

NEWFOUNDLAND GROWLERS
MILE ONE CENTRE
50 NEW GOWER STREET
ST. JOHN'S, NL, CANADA A1C 1J3
nlgrowlers.com
• Glenn Stanford, President
• John Snowden, Head Coach

NORFOLK ADMIRALS
201 EAST BRAMBLETON AVENUE
NORFOLK, VA 23510
757-640-1212
Fax: 757-622-0552
admiralsinfo@norfolkadmirals.com
www.norfolkadmirals.com
• Patrick Cavanagh, CEO
• Joe Gregory, Vice President/Governor
jgregory@norfolkadmirals.com
• Joe Eikenbary, Director, Communications
jeikenbary@norfolkadmirals.com
• Dee DiMartino Danner, Director, Ticketing
deedee@norfolkadmirals.com
• Charlie Colon, Director, Group Sales
• Ryan McGinnis, General Manager
• Rod Taylor, Head Coach
• Ben Boudreau, Assistant Coach

Home Ice:
Scope Arena

ORLANDO SOLAR BEARS
2200 LUCIEN WAY
SUITE 400
MAITLAND, FL 32751
407-951-8200
Fax: 321-972-1924
orlandoprohockey@gmail.com
www.orlandosolarbearshockey.com
• Chris Heller, President
• Joe Haleski, General
Partner/Chairman/Governor
• Chris Heller, Chief Financial & Legal Officer
• Chris Carmichael, Vice President, Ticket
Operations
• Drake Berehowsky, Head Coach & General
Manager
• John Snowden, Assistant Coach
• John Finley, Athletic Trainer
Home Ice:
Amway Center

RAPID CITY RUSH
444 MOUNT RUSHMORE ROAD NORTH
RAPID CITY, SD 57701
605-716-7825
Fax: 605-716-6100
www.rapidcityrush.com
• Todd Mackin, President
• Daniel Tetrault, Head Coach/Director, Hockey
Operations
• Mark Binetti, Director, Media Relations
• Brandon Schumacher, Chief Business Officer
• Ashley Grable, Director, Marketing & Design
• Jennifer Durham, Director, Merchandise
• Jenna Zanter, Director, Corporate
Partnerships
• Joe Ferras, General Manager/Head Coach
• Mark Desantis, Associate Coach
• Cody Lindhorst, Head Athletic Trainer
Home Ice:
Rushmore Plaza Civic Center

READING ROYALS
SANTANDER ARENA
700 PENN STREET
READING, PA 19602
610-898-7825
Fax: 610-898-1141
info@royalshockey.com
www.royalshockey.com
• David Farrar, General Manager
(610) 898-7268
dfarrar@santander-arena.com
• Mark Wallace, Corporate Sales &
Sponsorships
(610) 898-7212
mwallace@royalshockey.com
• Heather Hefty, Vice President, Finance
(610) 989-7213
hhefty@royalshockey.com
• Kirk MacDonald, Head Coach
• Kirk MacDonald, Assistant Coach
Home Ice:
Santander Arena
Major League Affiliate:
Philadelphia Flyers

SOUTH CAROLINA STINGRAYS
3300 WEST MONTAGUE AVENUE
SUITE A-200
NORTH CHARLESTON, SC 29418
843-744-2248
Fax: 843-744-2898
www.stingrayshockey.com
• Rob Concannon, President/Alternate Governor
robconcannon@stingrayshockey.com
• Todd Halloran, Owner & Governor
• Zack Fisch, Director, Communications &
Broadcasting
zfisch@stingrayshockey.com
• Ryan Blair, Director, Hockey Operations &
Head Coach
• Brenden Kotyk, Manager, Hockey Operations

& Assistant Coach
• Rick Covard, Athletic Trainer
Home Ice:
North Charleston Coliseum

TOLEDO WALLEYE
406 WASHINGTON STREET
TOLEDO, OH 43604
419-725-9255
Fax: 419-725-4368
info@toledowalleye.com
www.toledowalleye.com
• Joe Napoli, President/CEO
jnapoli@toledowalleye.com
• Neil Neukam, Executive Vice
President/General Manager
nneukam@toledowalleye.com
• Erik Ibsen, Executive Vice President/General
Manager
eibsen@toledowalleye.com
• Kim McBroom, Chief Marketing Officer
• Dan Watson, Head Coach
• Dan Watson, Associate Head Coach
• Brad Fredrick, Athletic Trainer
Home Ice:
Huntington Center

TULSA OILERS
9128 EAST 46TH STREET
TULSA, OK 74145
918-632-7825
Fax: 918-632-0006
www.tulsaoilers.com
• Rodney Steven, Owner
• Taylor Hall, General Manager
taylor@tulsaoilers.com
• Amy Wood, Vice President Of Marketing &
Sales
amy@tulsaoilers.com
• Jessica Adams, Vice President Of Operations
jessica@tulsaoilers.com
• Shawn Watring, Vice President Of Ticket
Sales
shawn@tulsaoilers.com
• Steve Duffy, Vice President Of Corporate
Partnerships
sduffy@tulsaoilers.com
• Rob Loeber, Broadcaster & Director, Media
Relations
rob@tulsaoilers.com
• Alan Parrent, Manager, Game Day Operations
• Rob Murray, Head Coach/Director, Hockey
Operations
• Sean Garner, Strength & Conditioning Coach
Home Ice:
BOK Center

UTAH GRIZZLIES
3200 DECKER LAKE DRIVE
WEST VALLEY CITY, UT 84119
801-988-8000
www.utahgrizzlies.com
• Dave Elmore, Owner/Co-Chairman
• Donna Tuttle, Owner/Co-Chairman
• Kevin Bruder, Chief Executive Officer
kbruder@maverikcenter.com
• Jill Roberts, Vice President Of Business
Operations/CFO
jroberts@maverikcenter.com
• Jared Youngman, Vice President
jyoungman@utahgrizz.com
• Adrian Denny, Vice President Of
Communications & Broadcasting
adenny@utahgrizz.com
• Derek Stell, Community Relations Manager
(801) 988-8010
• Tim Branham, Head Coach/General Manager
• Greg Leeb, Assistant Coach
• Mike Plandowski, Head Athletic Trainer
Home Ice:
Maverik Center

WHEELING NAILERS
1315 MAIN STREET
WHEELING, WV 26003
304-234-4625
Fax: 304-233-4846

pr@wheelingnailers.com
www.wheelingnailers.com
• Don Rigby, Governor
• Brian Komowroski, Alternate Governor
• Craig Bommer, Vice President
cbommer@wheelingnailers.com
• Chris Thoburn, Director, Ticket Sales
cthoburn@wheelingnailers.com
• Mark French, Head Coach
• Seamus McKelvey, Athletic Trainer
Home Ice:
WesBanco Arena

WICHITA THUNDER
505 WEST MAPLE
SUITE 100
WICHITA, KS 67213
316-264-4625
Fax: 316-264-3037
info@wichitathunder.com
www.wichitathunder.com
• Joel T. Lomurno, General Manager
jlomurno@wichitathunder.com
• Matt Brokaw, Vice President
mbrokaw@wichitathunder.com
• Jason Mals, Director, Communications
• Bruce Ramsay, Head Coach
• Cole Libby, Athletic Trainer
• Steven Smith, Equipment Manager
Home Ice:
Intrust Bank Arena

WORCESTER RAILERS
DCU CENTER - DOOR 22
105 COMMERCIAL ST
WORCESTER, MA 01608
508-365-1750
www.railershc.com
• Susan Rucker, Owner
• Cliff Rucker, Owner
• Stephanie Ramey, President
• David Cuniff, General Manager/Head Coach

FEDERAL HOCKEY LEAGUE
SYRACUSE, NY
267-261-0887
www.federalhockey.com
• Don Kirnan, Commissioner
dlkirnan@aol.com
• Andy Richards, Vice-Commissioner
thefederalhockeyleague@yahoo.com
• Dave Smolnycki, Director, Media Relations
hockeymedia3@aol.com
• Ryan Harrison, Director, Marketing &
Corporate Sales
rharrison@federalhockey.com
• Paul Jene, Director, Officiating
pjene@federalhockey.com
• Charles Apap, Manager, Social Media
capap@federalhockey.com

Teams:

CAROLINA THUNDERBIRDS
WINSTON-SALEM FAIRGROUNDS ARENA
414 DEACON BLVD
WINSTON-SALEM, NC 27105
336-774-4625
info@carolinathunderbirds.com
www.carolinathunderbirds.com
• Barry Soskin, Owner
• Kelly Curl, General Manager
• Andre Niec, Head Coach/Director, Hockey
Operations

COLUMBUS RIVER DRAGONS
COLUMBUS CIVIC CENTRE
400 4TH ST
COLUMBUS, GA 31901
706-507-4625
dragonsden@rdragons.com
www.rdragons.com
• Scott Brand, President/General Manager
• Jerome Bechard, Head Coach

DANBURY HAT TRICKS
1 INDEPENDENCE WAY
DANBURY, CT 06810
203-794-1704
hsorcher@aol.com
www.danburyhattricks.com
• Chris Buonanno, Managing Partner
• Herm Sorcher, Managing Partner
• Jed Wilson, Vice President of Corporate
Sponsorships
• Chris Hoeler, Vice President of Hockey
Operations
• Billy McCreary, General Manager
• Anthony Bohn, Head Coach
• Tricia Coe, Assistant General Manager
Home Ice:
Danbury Ice Arena

DANVILLE DASHERS
DAVIS S PALMER ARENA
100 WEST MAIN ST
DANVILLE, IL 61832
217-213-8939
info@danvilledashers.com
www.danvilledashers.com
• Barry Soskin, Owner/Governor
• Diane Short, General Manager
• Mike Wagner, FNP, Team Medical Provider
• Gary Gill, Head Coach
• Brent Clarke, Assistant Coach
Home Ice:
David S. Palmer Arena

DELAWARE THUNDER
CENTRE ICE ARENA
644 RD 316
HARRINGTON, DE 19952
302-398-7825
delawarethunder@gmail.com
delawarethunder.com
• Charles F. Pens, Sr., CEO/President/General
Manager
• Mike Basile, Director, Hockey Operations
• Lou Santini, Associate Head Coach

ELMIRA ENFORCERS
FIRST ARENA
155 N MAIN ST
ELMIRA, NY 14901
607-734-7825
www.elmiraenforecers.com
• Robbie Nichols, Owner
• Nellie Nichols, Owner
• Matt Witt, General Manager
• Ahmed Mahfouz, Head Coach

PORT HURON PROWLERS
MCMORRAN ARENA
701 MCMORRAN BLVD
PORT HURON, MI 48060
810-966-0396
info@phprowlers.com
www.phprowlers.com
• Barry Soskin, Owner/Governor
• Allison Jaegers, Director, Business Operations
allison@phprowlers.com
• LeeAnn Baker, Director, Marketing
leeann@phprowlers.com
• Rachel Soskin, Public Relations Manager
• Joe Pace, Jr., General Manager/Head Coach
Home Ice:
McMorran Place

WATERTOWN WOLVES
WATERTOWN MUNICIPAL ARENA
5675 THOMPSON RD
SYRACUSE, NY 13214
www.watertowneolves.net
• Andreas Johansson, Owner
• Robin Johansson, Owner
• Brent Clarke, Head Coach/General Manager

NORTH AMERICAN HOCKEY LEAGUE
5151 BELT LINE RD
SUITE 877
DALLAS, TX 75254
469-252-3800
Fax: 214-975-2250
www.nahl.com
• Mark Frankenfeld,
President/Commissioner
• Denny Scanlon, Vice President, Hockey
Operations
• Alex Kyrias, Director, Communications &
Sales
• Shannon Smith, Director, Finance &
Administration
• Fraser Ritchie, Director, Hockey
Administration

Teams:

ABERDEEN WINGS
12101 386TH AVE
WESTPORT, SD 57481
605-380-5852
www.aberdeenwings.com
• Greg Odde, President
godde@aberdeenwings.com
• Chris Odde, Vice President
• Pete Sauer, Director, Business Operations
psauer@aberdeenwings.com
• Aaron Smith, Director, Marketing & Media
asmith@aberdeenwings.com
• Scott Langer, Head Coach/General Manager
• Mike Grattan, Director, Scouting/Assistant
Coach
mgrattan@aberdeenwings.com
Home Ice:
Odde Ice Center

AMARILLO BULLS
1616 S KENTUCKY
SUITE A-116
AMARILLO, TX 79102
806-242-1122
www.amarillobulls.com
• Alberto Fernandez, President/Governor
• Rick Matchett, General Manager/Vice
President
• Denis J. Puska, Director,
Broadcasting/Media/Community Relations
djpuska@amarillobulls.com
• Caleb Hubbard, Director, Ticket Sales
• Austin Sutter, Manager, Business
Development/Assistant Coach
• Rocky Russo, Head Coach/Director, Hockey
Operations
• Tony Attanucci, Assistant Coach
• Bernie McDonnell, Equipment Manager
• Cyndi Hager, Administrative Assistant
Home Ice:
Amarillo Civic Center

ANCHORAGE WOLVERINES
1600 GAMBELL ST
ANCHORAGE, AK 99501
anchoragewolverines.com
• Kai Binkley Sims, President

AUSTIN BRUINS
501 - 2ND AVE NE
AUSTIN, MN 55912
507-434-4978
Fax: 507-434-4978
www.austinbruins.com
• Craig Patrick, Co-Owner & President
craig@austinbruins.com
• Mike Cooper, Co-Owner & President
mikec@austinbruins.com
• Mike Delhanty, Director, Sales & Business
Operations
mike@austinbruins.com
• Michael Keeley, Broadcasting & Media
Relations
keeley@austinbruins.com
• Becky Earl, Office Manager

• Steve Howard, Head Coach/President, Hockey
Operations
• Keenan Kelly, Assistant Coach
keenan@austinbruins.com
Home Ice:
Riverside Arena

BISMARCK BOBCATS
1200 NORTH WASHINGTON STREET
BISMARCK, ND 58501
701-222-3300
Fax: 701-222-3335
gobobcathockey@aol.com
www.bismarckbobcats.com
• Thom Brigl, Owner/Chief Executive Officer
• Paul Teeple, Director, Broadcasting & Media
• Bunny Greig, Director, Housing & Retail
Services
• Layne Sedevie, Head Coach/General Manager
• Samantha Ziegler, Athletic Trainer
• Garrett Roth, Assistant Coach
Home Ice:
V.F.W. Sports Center

CHIPPEWA STEEL
839 1ST AVE
CHIPPEWA FALLS, WI 54729
715-861-2131
chippewasteelhockey.com
• Jake Serwe, Business Manager
• Carter Foguth, Head Coach

CORPUS CHRISTI ICERAYS
1901 NORTH SHORELINE BOULEVARD
SUITE 300
CORPUS CHRISTI, TX 78401
361-814-7825
Fax: 361-980-0003
www.goicerays.com
• Cassidy Lange, President
• Scott McClarren, Director, Special Events
• Sheryl Villere, Director, Marketing
• Nate Weossner, Head Coach
• Pat Dunn, General Manager
• Amanda Marines, Front Office Manager
• Michael Benedict, Assistant Coach
• Jeff Paluseo, Strength & Conditioning Coach
Home Ice:
American Bank Center

EL PASO RHINOS
4100 E PAISANOS
BUILDING B
EL PASO, TX
915-479-7825
www.elpasorhinos.com
• Tyler Deloach, Director, Operations
• Corey Heon, General Manager
• Vinny Bohn, Co-Head Coach
• Anthony Bohn, Co-Head Coach

FAIRBANKS ICE DOGS
139 32ND AVENUE
FAIRBANKS, AK 99707
907-452-2111
Fax: 907-452-1643
www.fairbanksicedogs.com
• Rob Proffitt, General Manager
coachproffitt@fairbanksicedogs.com
• Trevor Stewart, Head Coach
trevor@fairbanksicedogs.com
• Kim Stone, Office Manager/Game Night
Operations/Billet Coord.
kim@fairbanksicedogs.com
• Scott Deur, Assistant Coach
• Howard Beito, Assistant Coach
• Jim Kimbal, Certified Athletic Trainer
Home Ice:
Big Dipper Ice Arena

JAMESTOWN REBELS
319 W 3RD ST
JAMESTOWN, NY 14701
716-484-2624
www.rebelshockey.us
• Joe Coombs, Head Coach/General Manager

JANESVILLE JETS
20 EAST MILWAUKEE STREET
SUITE 304
JANESVILLE, WI 53545
608-752-5387
www.janesvillejets.com
• Bill McCoshen, President
(608) 444-7526
bill@janesvillejets.com
• Mason Lyttle, Director, Business Operations &
Media Relations
(919) 830-6105
mason@janesvillejets.com
• Joe Dibble, General Manager
(612) 978-0519
joe.dibble@janesvillejets.com
• Parker Burgess, Head Coach
• Cody Campbell, Assistant Coach
(719) 360-7623
cody.campbell@janesvillejets.com
Home Ice:
Janesville Ice Arena

JOHNSTOWN TOMAHAWKS
326 NAPOLEON STREET
SUITE 115
JOHNSTOWN, PA 15901-1704
814-536-4625
info@johnstowntomahawks.com
www.johnstowntomahawks.com
• Rick Bouchard, President
rbouchard@johnstowntomahawks.com
• Rick Boyd, Director, Hockey
Operations/General Manager
rboyd@johnstowntomahawks.com
• Jean Desrochers, Director, Business
Operations
jean@johnstowntomahawks.com
• Katie Saylor, Game Day Operations &
Community Relations Manager
ksaylor@johnstowntomahawks.com
• Michael Gosnell, Communications Manager
mgosnell@johnstowntomahawks.com
• Ed Sheets, Public Relations Manager
esheets@johnstowntomahawks.com
• Mike Letizia, Head Coach
mletizia@johnstowntomahawks.com
• Nick Shackford, Assistant Coach
nshackford@johnstowntomahawks.com
• Steve Emmett, Skating & Skills Coach
Home Ice:
Cambria County War Memorial Arena

KANSAS CITY SCOUTS
19900 JOHNSON DR
SHAWNEE, KS 66218
913-441-3033
www.kcscouts.com
• Lamar Hunt, Jr., Owner
• Simon Watson, Head Coach/General Manager

KENAI RIVER BROWN BEARS
538 ARENA AVE
SOLDOTNA, AK 99611
907-262-7825
Fax: 910-920-9050
www.kenairiverbrownbears.com
• Chris Hedlund, General Manager
• Kevin Murdock, Head Coach
• Josh Romano, Director, Player Personnel
• Lori Karvonen, Trainer
Home Ice:
Soldotna Sports Complex

LONE STAR BRAHMAS
8851 ICE HOUSE DRIVE
NORTH RICHLAND HILLS, TX 76180
817-336-4423
Fax: 817-336-3334
www.lonestarbrahmas.com
• Salvatore Trazzera, Owner/Chief Executive
Officer
• Frank Trazzera, Owner/Governor
• Chad Siewert, Vice President
• Nick Marek, Director, Communications
nick@nytexsports.com
• Lee Rafferty, Creative Director/Marketing

lee@nytexsports.com
• Dan Wildfong, Director, Hockey Ops & Head
Coach
dwildfong10@gmail.com
• Jeff Potter, Assistant Coach
jeff3sports@yahoo.com
Home Ice:
NYTEX Sports Centre. Seating capacity 2,400.

MAINE NORDIQUES
190 BIRCH ST
LEWISTON, ME 04240
207-783-2009
mainenordiques.com
• Eric Soltys, General Manager
• Nolan Howe, Head Coach/Director, Hockey
Operations

MARYLAND BLACK BEARS
PINEY ORCHARD ICE ARENA
8781 PINEY ORCHARD PKWY
ODENTON, MD 21113
814-440-3449
marylandblackbears.com
• Robyn Remick, President
• Clint Mylymok, Head Coach/General Manager

MINNESOTA MAGICIANS
636 EAST 66TH STREET
RICHFIELD, MN 55423
612-861-9356
info@minnesotamagicians.com
www.magicianshockey.com
• Scott Krueger, Owner/Governor
• Joe Pankratz, Owner
• Ron Beran, Owner
• Kevin Ingvalson, Vice President, Operations
kevin@minnesotamagicians.com
• Gaven Bickford, General Manager/Director,
Scouting
• Stu Bickel, Assistant General Manager/Head
Coach
• Scott Kennedy, Assistant Coach
• Nick Bydal, Assistant Coach
Home Ice:
Richfield Ice Arena

MINNESOTA WILDERNESS
1111 CLOQUET AVENUE
SUITE 1
CLOQUET, MN 55720
218-879-0910
www.wildernesshockey.com
• Chris Trapp, Board Of Governor/Owner
• Joe Dusek, Board Of Governor/Owner
• Jordan Lundgren, Director, Marketing &
Gameday Operations
• David Boitz, General Manager
• Jon Vaillancourt, Head Coach
• Ryan Peltoma, Assistant General Manager
• Joshua Petrich, Assistant Coach
• Brandon Grecinger, Athletic Trainer
Home Ice:
Northwoods Credit Union Arena.

MINOT MINOTAUROS
2501 BURDICK EXPRESSWAY
WEST MINOT, ND 58701
701-852-0101
contact@minotauroshockey.com
www.minotauroshockey.com
• Ken Oda, Director, Operations
• Charlsie Benson-Burud, Assistant Director,
Operations
• Jessica Rundall, Athletic Trainer
• Shane Wagner, Head Coach
• Nigel Dube, Assistant Coach
• Cory Lonke, Goaltending Coach
• Dawn Mattern, Team Doctor
Home Ice:
Maysa Arena

NEW JERSEY TITANS
214 HARMONY ROAD
MIDDLETOWN, NJ 07748

732-856-9700
www.njtitansnahl.com
• Craig Doremus, General Manager/Head Coach
• Patrick Dooley, Equipment Manager
• Oktay Armagan, Assistant Coach
(732) 995-0254
frihockey@aol.com
• Nick Perri, Assistant Coach/Video Coach
(845) 709-2883
nickp@njtitanshockey.com
Home Ice:
Middletown Ice World

NEW MEXICO ICE WOLVES
9530 TRAMWAY BLVD
ALBUQUERQUE, NM 87122
505-856-7595
www.nmicewolves.com
• Phil Fox, General Manager/Head Coach

NORTH IOWA BULLS
3700 4TH ST SW
MASON CITY, IA 50401
641-423-4625

NORTHEAST GENERALS
1395 COMMERCE WAY
ATTLEBORO, MA 02703
844-623-5483
www.northeastgenerals.com
• Bob Penfield, Owner/Managing Director
• Rich O'Dowd, Owner/Director, Operations
• Bryan Erikson, Head Coach/President, Hockey Operations

ODESSA JACKALOPES
4201 ANDREWS HIGHWAY
ODESSA, TX 79762
432-552-7825
www.jackalopes.org
• Rick Matchett, President
• DJ Nelson, Director, Operations
dnelson@jackalopes.org
• Nick Nollenberger, Director, Media Relations & Broadcasting
nnollenberger@jackalopes.org
• Tom Snoddy, Sales
tsnoddy@jackalopes.org
• Jason Fortier, Head Coach/General Manager
• Cody Campbell, Assistant Coach
ccampbell@jackalopes.org
• Ryan Traut, Assistant Director, Operations
rtraut@jackalopes.org
• Eric Pike, Athletic Trainer
Home Ice:
Ector County Coliseum

SHREVEPORT MUDBUGS
3207 PERSHING BLVD
SHREVEPORT, LA 71101
318-636-7094
www.mudbugshockey.com
• Tommy Scott, President/Managing Partner
• Scott Muscutt, General Manager

SPRINGFIELD JR. BLUES
FRANKLIN P. NELSON CENTER
1601 NORTH FIFTH STREET
SPRINGFIELD, IL 62702
217-525-2589
Fax: 217-525-6528
info@jrblues.com
www.jrblues.com
• Dan Ferguson, Owner
• Tyler Rennette, Head Coach/General Manager
trennette@jrblues.com
• Patrick Schafer, Assistant Coach
• Devin Spears, Head Athletic Trainer
• Amanda Wilson, Athletic Trainer
Home Ice:
Franklin P. Nelson Center

ST CLOUD NORSEMEN
500 VETERANS DR
ST CLOUD, MN 56303
www.stcloudnorsemen.com
• Tom Chorske, Director, Operations
• Corey Millen, Head Coach/General Manager

WICHITA FALLS WARRIORS
1000 FIFTH STREET
WICHITA FALLS, TX 76301
940-337-6570
Fax: 940-716-5544
wfhockey@nahl.com
wichitafallswarriors.com
• Jason Rent, President
• Chelsea Huss, Chief Financial Officer
• Garrett Roth, Head Coach/General Manager
• Josh Nelson, Assistant Coach
jnelson@wfwildcatshockey.com
• Debi Fleetwood, Ice Programs Coordinator
dfleetwood@wfwildcatshockey.com
Home Ice:
Kay Yeager Coliseum

ONTARIO HOCKEY LEAGUE
305 MILNER AVE
SUITE 200
SCARBOROUGH, ON, CANADA M1B 3V4
416-299-8700
Fax: 416-299-8787
ontariohockeyleague.com
• David E. Branch, Commissioner
dbranch@chl.ca
• Ted Baker, Vice President
tbaker@chl.ca
• Joe Birch, Vice President, Development
jbirch@chl.ca
Year Founded:
1896

Teams:

BARRIE COLTS
555 BAYVIEW DR
BARRIE, ON, CANADA L4N 8Y2
705-722-6587
Fax: 705-737-6898
operations@barriecolts.com
www.barriecolts.com
• Howie Campbell, President & Owner
hcampbell@barriecolts.com
• Jim Payetta, Co-Owner/VP, Business Development & Marketing
jpayetta@barriecolts.com
• Rob Stewart, General Manager
• Vacant, Head Coach
Home Arena:
Barrie Molson Centre. Seating capacity 4,195.

ERIE OTTERS
201 EAST 8TH STREET
ERIE, PA 16503
814-455-7779
Fax: 814-455-0911
puck@ottershockey.com
www.ottershockey.com
• Jim Waters, Chair, Owner, President & Governor
• Jaime Cieszynski, Director, Business Operations
• Dave Brown, General Manager
• Chris Hartsburg, Head Coach
• B.J. Adams, Associate Coach
• Shane Clifford, Goaltending Coach
Home Ice:
Erie Insurance Arena. Seating capacity 6,716.

FLINT FIREBIRDS
3501 LAPEER ROAD
FLINT, MI 48503
810-742-2004
Fax: 810-744-2906
info@flintfirebirds.com
www.flintfirebirds.com

• Rolf Nilsen, Governor
rolf@flintfirebirds.com
• Jeremy Torrey, President
• Monika Kronenberger, Director, Business Operations
monika@flintfirebirds.com
• Susana Wright, Director, Community Relations & Marketing
susana@flintfirebirds.com
• Dominic Hennig, Director, Broadcasting & Communications
dominic@flintfirebirds.com
• Branch Barclay, General Manager/VP, Hockey Operations
• Eric Wellwood, Head Coach
• Dave Karpa, Assistant Coach
• Petr Jonak, Assistant Coach
Home Ice:
Dort Federal Credit Union Event Center. Seating capacity 4,021.

GUELPH STORM
55 WYNDHAM ST N
2ND FLOOR
GUELPH, ON, CANADA N1H 7T8
519-837-9690
Fax: 519-837-9692
info@guelphstorm.com
guelphstorm.com
• Rick Hoyle, President
• Rick Gaetz, Governor
• George Burnett, General Manager & Head Coach
Home Arena:
Sleeman Centre. Seating capacity 4,715.

HAMILTON BULLDOGS
FIRSTONTARIO CENTRE
101 YORK BLVD
HAMILTON, ON L8R 3L4
905-529-8500
Fax: 905-777-2360
info@hamiltonbulldogs.com
hamiltonbulldogs.com
• Michael Andlauer, Owner
• Steve Staios, President & General Manager
• Dave Matos, Head Coach
Home Arena:
FirstOntario Centre. Seating capacity 17,383.

KINGSTON FRONTENACS
1 THE TRAGICALLY HIP WAY
KINGSTON, ON, CANADA K7K 0B4
613-542-4042
Fax: 613-542-2834
info@kingstonfrontenacs.com
kingstonfrontenacs.com
• Doug Springer, President
• Paul McFarland, General Manager/Head Coach
Home Ice:
Leon's Centre. Seating capacity 5,614.

KITCHENER RANGERS
KITCHENER MEMORIAL AUDITORIUM COMPLEX
1963 EUGENE GEORGE WAY
KITCHENER, ON, CANADA N2H 0B8
519-576-3700
Fax: 519-576-7571
admin@kitchenerrangers.com
kitchenerrangers.com
• Joe Birch, Chief Operating Officer & Governor
• Mike McKenzie, General Manager/Interim Head Coach
Home Arena:
Kitchener Memorial Auditorium. Seating capacity 7,777.

LONDON KNIGHTS
BUDWEISER GARDENS
99 DUNDAS ST
LONDON, ON, CANADA N6A 6K1
519-681-0800
Fax: 519-668-7291
info@londonknights.com
londonknights.com

- Dale Hunter, Owner, President & Head Coach
- Mark Hunter, Owner, Vice President & General Manager
- Basil McRae, Owner
Home Arena:
Budweiser Gardens. Seating capacity 9,036.

MISSISSAUGA STEELHEADS
PARAMOUNT FINE FOODS CENTRE
5500 ROSE CHERRY PLACE
MISSISSAUGA, ON, CANADA L4Z 4B6
905-502-7788
Fax: 905-502-0169
info@mississaugasteelheads.com
www.mississaugasteelheads.com
- Elliott Kerr, President
jekerr@landmarksport.com
- Brandon Reischl, Vice President, Director of Business Operations
- James Richmond, Head Coach & General Manager
jrichmond@mississaugasteelheads.com
Home Ice:
Paramount Fine Foods Centre. Seating capacity 5,612.

NIAGARA ICEDOGS
ONE DAVID S HOWES WAY
ST. CATHARINES, ON, CANADA L2R 0B3
905-687-3641
Fax: 905-682-9129
info@niagaraicedogs.net
niagaraicedogs.net
- Joey Burke, General Manager & Governor
j.burke@niagaraicedogs.net
- Billy Burke, Head Coach
billy.burke@niagaraicedogs.net
Home Ice:
Meridian Centre. Seating capacity 5,300.

NORTH BAY BATTALION
NORTH BAY MEMORIAL GARDENS
100 CHIPPEWA ST W
2ND FLOOR
NORTH BAY, ON, CANADA P1B 6G2
705-495-8603
Fax: 705-475-1673
info@battalionhockey.com
battalionhockey.com
- C. Scott Abbott, Owner/Governor
- Mike Griffin, President
mgriffin@battalionhockey.com
- Ryan Oulahen, Head Coach
Home Arena:
North Bay Memorial Gardens. Seating capacity 4,246.

OSHAWA GENERALS
99 ATHOL ST E
OSHAWA, ON, CANADA L1H IJ8
905-433-0900
admin@oshawagenerals.com
oshawagenerals.com
- Rocco Tullio, President & Governor
- Roger Hunt, Vice President & General Manager
rhunt@oshawagenerals.com
- Mike Kelly, Director of Hockey Operations
- Greg Walters, Head Coach
Home Ice:
General Motors Centre. Seating capacity 6,125.

OTTAWA 67'S
TD PLACE
1015 BANK STREET
OTTAWA, ON, CANADA K1S 3W7
613-232-6767
Fax: 613-690-0468
info@ottawa67s.com
ottawa67s.com
- James Boyd, General Manager
jboyd@ottawa67s.com
- Andre Tourigny, Head Coach & VP, Hockey Operations
atourigny@ottawa67s.com
Home Ice:
TD Place Arena. Seating capacity 10,000.

OWEN SOUND ATTACK
1900 3RD AVENUE E
OWEN SOUND, ON, CANADA N4K 6T5
519-371-7452
866-528-8225
loleary@attackhockey.com
attackhockey.com
- Severs Bob, President
- Dale DeGray, General Manager
ddegray@attackhockey.com
- Alan Letang, Head Coach
Home Ice:
J.D. McArthur Arena, Harry Lumley Bayshore Community Centre. Seating capacity 4,300.

PETERBOROUGH PETES
151 LANDSDOWNE ST WEST
PETERBOROUGH, ON, CANADA K9J 1Y4
705-743-3681
Fax: 705-743-5497
info@gopetesgo.com
gopetesgo.com
- Burton Lee, Executive Director, Business Operations
- Michael Oke, General Manager
- Rob Wilson, Head Coach
Home Ice:
Peterborough Memorial Centre. Seating capacity 4,329.

SAGINAW SPIRIT
PO BOX 6157
SAGINAW, MI 48608
989-497-7747
Fax: 989-799-9261
www.saginawspirit.com
- Richard J. Garber, Owner
- Craig Goslin, President & Managing Partner
- Pat Hengesbach, Chief Financial Officer
- Kae Pankow, Vice President, Sales
- Dave Drinkill, General Manager
- Chris Lazary, Head Coach
Home Ice:
Dow Event Center. Seating capacity 5,527.

SARNIA STING
1455 LONDON RD
SARNIA, ON, CANADA N7S 6K4
519-541-1717
info@sarniasting.com
sarniasting.com
- Derian Hatcher, Owner/Governor
- Bill Abercrombie, President
- David Legwand, President, Hockey Operations
- Dylan Seca, General Manager
- Derian Hatcher, Head Coach
Home Ice:
Progressive Auto Sales Arena. Seating capacity, 5,500.

SAULT STE. MARIE GREYHOUNDS
269 QUEEN STREET EAST
SAULT STE. MARIE, ON, CANADA P6A 1Y9
705-253-5976
Fax: 705-945-9458
info@soogreyhounds.com
soogreyhounds.com
- Tim Lukenda, President
- Kyle Raftis, General Manager
- John Dean, Head Coach
- Jordan Smith, Associate Coach
Home Ice:
GFL Memorial Gardens. Seating capacity 4,928.

SUDBURY WOLVES
240 ELGIN ST
SUDBURY, ON, CANADA P3E 3N6
705-675-3941
Fax: 705-675-3944
office@sudburywolves.com
sudburywolves.com
- Dario Zulich, Owner
- Rob Papineau, Vice President & General Manager

Home Ice:
Sudbury Community Arena. Seating capacity 5,100.

WINDSOR SPITFIRES
8787 MCHUGH STREET
WINDSOR, ON, CANADA N8S 0A1
519-254-9256
Fax: 519-254-9257
frontoffice@windsorspitfires.com
windsorspitfires.com
- John Savage, Owner & President
- Bill Bowler, GM & VP, Hockey Operations
- Trevor Letowski, Head Coach
Home Ice:
WFCU Centre. Seating capacity 6,450.

QUEBEC MAJOR JUNIOR HOCKEY LEAGUE
1205 AMPERE STREET
OFFICE #101
BOUCHERVILLE, QC, CANADA J4B 7M6
450-650-0500
Fax: 450-650-0510
hockey@lhjmq.qc.ca
theqmjhl.ca
- Gilles Courteau, Commissioner
ggonthier@lhjmq.qc.ca
- Pierre Daoust, Vice President, Administration
pdaoust@lhjmq.qc.ca
- Pierre Leduc, Director, Hockey Operations
pleduc@lhjmq.qc.ca
- Maxime Blouin, Director, Communications
mblouin@lhjmq.qc.ca
- Richard Trottier, Director, Officiating
rtrottier@lhjmq.qc.ca
Description:
Member of Canadian Hockey League.

Teams:

ACADIE-BATHURST TITAN
14 SEAN COUTURIER AVE
BATHURST, NB, CANADA E2A 6X2
506-549-3300
Fax: 506-549-3311
info@letitan.com
en.letitan.com
- Gilles Cormier, Executive Director
gilles.cormier@letitan.com
- Sylvain Couturier, General Manager
- Mario Durocher, Head Coach
Home Ice:
K.C. Irving Regional Centre. Seating capacity 3,162.

BAIE-COMEAU DRAKKAR
70, AVENUE MICHEL-HEMON
BAIE-COMEAU, QC, CANADA G4Z 2A5
418-296-2522
Fax: 418-296-0011
le-drakkar.com
- Âtienne Fortier, Administrative Director
etiennefortier@le-drakkar.com
- Pierre Rioux, General Manager
- Gregoire Jean-Francois, Head Coach
Home Ice:
Henry Leonard Center. Seating capacity 3,042.

BLAINVILLE-BOISBRIAND ARMADA
3600, BOUL. GRANDE-ALLEE
CP 9
BOISBRIAND, QC, CANADA J7H 1M9
450-276-2328
855-276-2328
Fax: 450-276-2327
info@armadahockey.ca
armadahockey.ca
- Mario Marois, President
mmarois@armadahockey.ca
- Pierre Cloutier, General Manager
- Dany Gauthier, Deputy General Manager &

Chief Recruiter
• Bruce Richardson, Head Coach
Home Ice:
Centre d'Excellence Sports Rousseau. Seating capacity 3,100.

CAPE BRETON SCREAMING EAGLES
PO BOX 8
481 GEORGE ST
SYDNEY, NS, CANADA B1P 6G9
902-567-6378
Fax: 902-567-6303
admin@capebretoneagles.com
capebretoneagles.com
• Gerard Shaw, President & Governor
• Jacques Carriere, General Manager
• Jake Grimes, Head Coach
Home Ice:
Centre 200. Seating capacity 5,000.

CHARLOTTETOWN ISLANDERS
46 KENSINGTON RD
2ND FLOOR
CHARLOTTETOWN, PE, CANADA C1A 5H7
902-892-7349
Fax: 902-892-7350
admin@charlottetownislanders.com
charlottetownislanders.com
• Craig Foster, President, Operations
craig@charlottetownislanders.com
• Jim Hulton, General Manager & Head Coach
Home Arena:
Eastlink Centre. Seating capacity 3,717.

CHICOUTIMI SAGUENEENS
643 RUE BEGIN
CHICOUTIMI, QC, CANADA G7H 4N7
418-549-9489
Fax: 418-698-3853
administration@sagueneens.com
sagueneens.com
• Renald Nepton, Director, Hockey Operations
• Yanick Jean, Head Coach & General Manager
Home Ice:
George-Vezina Centre. Seating capacity 4,724.

DRUMMONDVILLE VOLTIGEURS
300 RUE COCKBURN
DRUMMONDVILLE, QC, CANADA J2C 4L6
819-477-9400
Fax: 819-477-0561
info@voltigeurs.ca
voltigeurs.ca
• David Boies, Director, Operations
dboies@voltigeurs.ca
• Philippe Boucher, General Manager
• Steve Hartley, Head Coach
Home Ice:
Centre Marcel Dionne. Seating capacity 3,038.

GATINEAU OLYMPIQUES
125 RUE DE CARILLON
GATINEAU, QC, CANADA J8X 2P8
819-777-0661
hockey@olympiquesdegatineau.ca
olympiquesdegatineau.ca
• Francois Beaudry, President
• Marc Saumier, Interim Director, Hockey Operations
• Louis Robitaille, Head Coach/General Manager
Home Ice:
Robert Guertin Centre. Seating capacity 3,196.

HALIFAX MOOSEHEADS
1741 BRUNSWICK ST
SUITE 120
HALIFAX, NS, CANADA B3J 3X8
902-429-3267
Fax: 902-423-6413
mooseheads@halifaxmooseheads.ca
halifaxmooseheads.ca
• Bobby Smith, Majority Owner
• Brian Urquhart, President
• Travis Kennedy, Sr. Vice President, Business Operations

• Cam Russell, General Manager
• J.J. Daigneault, Head Coach
Home Ice:
Scotiabank Centre. Seating capacity 10,595.

MONCTON WILDCATS
AVENIR CENTRE
150 CANADA ST
MONCTON, NB, CANADA E1C 0V2
506-382-5555
Fax: 506-858-2222
info@moncton-wildcats.com
moncton-wildcats.com
• Jean Brousseau, Governor
• Ritchie Thibeau, Assistant Director, Hockey Operations
• Daniel Lacroix, Head Coach
Home Ice:
Avenir Centre. Seating capacity 8,800.

QUEBEC REMPARTS
CENTRE VIDEOTRON
250G, BOUL. WILFRID-HAMEL
QUEBEC, QC, CANADA G1L 5A7
418-525-1212
888-299-9595
Fax: 418-525-2242
info@remparts.ca
remparts.ca
• Jacques Tanguay, President
• Louis Painchaud, Vice President, Operations
louis.painchaud@remparts.ca
• Patrick Roy, Head Coach & General Manager
Home Ice:
Centre Videotron. Seating capacity 18,259.

RIMOUSKI OCEANIC
111, 2E RUE OUEST
CP 816
RIMOUSKI, QC, CANADA G5L 7C9
418-723-4444
800-463-4450
Fax: 418-725-0944
hockey@oceanic.qc.ca
oceanic.qc.ca
• Eric Boucher, President
• Serge Beausoleil, General Manager & Head Coach
Home Ice:
Colisee de Rimouski. Seating capacity 5,062.

ROUYN-NORANDA HUSKIES
ARENA IAMGOLD
218 AVE MURDOCH
ROUYN-NORANDA, QC, CANADA J9X 1E6
819-797-3022
Fax: 819-797-4311
admin@huskies.qc.ca
huskies.qc.ca
• Gilles Berube, Operational Director
• Mario Pouliot, Head Coach & General Manager
Home Ice:
Arena Iamgold. Seating capacity 3,500.

SAINT JOHN SEA DOGS
99 STATION STREET
SUITE 200
SAINT JOHN, NB, CANADA E2L 4X4
506-657-3647
Fax: 506-696-0611
info@saintjohnseadogs.com
sjseadogs.com
• Scott McCain, CEO
• Trevor Georgie, President/General Manager
• Greg Gilbert, Head Coach
Home Ice:
TD Station. Seating capacity 6,300.

SHAWINIGAN CATARACTES
CENTRE GERVAIS AUTO
1, RUE JACQUES-PLANTE
SHAWINIGAN, QC, CANADA G9N 0B7
819-537-6327
cats@cataractes.qc.ca
cataractes.qc.ca

• Roger Lavergne, President
• Martin Mondou, General Manager
• Ron Choules, Head Coach
Home Ice:
Centre Gervais Auto. Seating capacity 5,195.

SHERBROOKE PHOENIX
360 RUE DU CEGEP
2E ETAGE
SHERBROOKE, QC, CANADA J1E 2J9
819-560-8842
info@hockeyphoenix.ca
en.hockeypheonix.ca
• Charline Durand, Director of Operations
• Jocelyn Thibault, VP, Hockey Operations
• Stephane Julien, Head Coach/General Manager
Home Ice:
Palais des Sports Leopold-Drolet. Seating capacity 3,646.

VAL D'OR FOREURS
810, 6TH AVENUE
VAL-D'OR, QC, CANADA J9P 1B4
819-824-0093
Fax: 819-824-7602
admin@foreurs.qc.ca
foreurs.qc.ca
• Dany Marchand, President
• Pascal Daoust, General Manager
• Daniel Renaud, Head Coach
Home Ice:
Centre Air Creebec. Seating capacity 3,504.

VICTORIAVILLE TIGERS
COLISEE DESJARDINS
400 BOULEVARD JUTRAS EST
VICTORIAVILLE, QC, CANADA G6P 7W7
819-752-6353
Fax: 819-758-2846
info@tigresvictoriaville.com
tigresvictoriaville.com
• Martin Paquet, Director, Operations
• Kevin Cloutier, General Manager
• Carl Mallette, Head Coach
Home Ice:
Desjardins Coliseum. Seating capacity 3,420.

SOUTHERN PROFESSIONAL HOCKEY LEAGUE
11330 VANSTORY DRIVE
HUNTERSVILLE, NC 28078
704-897-0545
www.thesphl.com
• Doug Price, Commissioner
• Andy McElman, Vice President, Hockey Operations

Teams:

BIRMINGHAM BULLS
500 AMPHITHEATER RD
PELHAM, AL 35124
205-620-6870
www.bullshockey.net
• Joe Stroud, President
• Craig Simchuk, Head Coach

EVANSVILLE THUNDERBOLTS
FORD CENTER
1 SE MARTIN LUTHER KING JR BLVD
EVANSVILLE, IN 47708
www.evenasvillethunderbolts.com
• Patrick Kelly, General Manager
pkelly@evansvillethunderbolts.com
• Jeff Bes, Head Coach

FAYETTEVILLE MARKSMEN
1960 COLISEUM DRIVE
FAYETTEVILLE, NC 28306
910-321-0123
Fax: 910-321-0200
www.marksmenhockey.com

- Charles Norris, Chief Executive Officer
- Lanai Norris, Chief Financial Officer
- Cory Melkert, Head Coach/Director, Hockey Operations
Home Ice:
Crown Coliseum

HUNTSVILLE HAVOC
700 MONROE STREET
HUNTSVILLE, AL 35801
256-518-6160
Fax: 256-518-6164
info@huntsvillehavoc.com
www.huntsvillehavoc.com
- Keith Jeffries, Owner
- Ashley Balch, President
- Clay Coleman, Vice President
- Cline Thompson, Director, Ticket Sales
- Glenn Detulleo, Head Coach/General Manager
gdetulleo@hsvsports.com
- Jesse Kallechy, Assistant Coach/Director, Hockey Operations
jkallechy@hsvsports.com
Home Ice:
Von Braun Center

KNOXVILLE ICE BEARS
500 HOWARD BAKER JR. DRIVE
KNOXVILLE, TN 37915
865-525-7825
Fax: 865-521-9725
www.knoxvilleicebears.com
- Mike Murray, President/General Manager
mmurray@knoxvilleicebears.com
- Dave Feather, Executive VP
- Jeff Carr, Head Coach
- Jimmy Woodward, Controller
jwoodward@knoxvilleicebears.com
- Dave Feather, Assistant General Manager
dfeather@knoxvilleicebears.com
- Jamie Ronayne, Assistant Coach
- Andy Clark, Head Athletic Trainer
Home Ice:
Knoxville Civic Auditorium and Coliseum

MACON MAYHEM
200 COLISEUM DRIVE
MACON, GA 31217
478-803-1592
www.maconmayhem.com
- Blair Floyd, General Manager
- Kevin Kerr, Director, Hockey Operations/Head Coach
- Aaron Herndon, Athletic Trainer
Home Ice:
Macon Centreplex

PENSACOLA ICE FLYERS
201 EAST GREGORY STREET
PENSACOLA, FL 35202
850-466-3111
Fax: 850-886-5641
info@pensacolaiceflyers.com
www.pensacolaiceflyers.com
- Greg Harris, Majority Team Owner/Governor
greg@pensacolaiceflyers.com
- Brittany Tindell, Vice President of Corporate Fulfillment
brittany@pensacolaiceflyers.com
- Tom Reading, Vice President of Ticketing
tom@pensacolaiceflyers.com
- Geoff Nichols, Communications Manager
geoff@pensacolaiceflyers.com
- Rod Aldoff, Head Coach
rod@pensacolaiceflyers.com
Home Ice:
Pensacola Civic Center

PEORIA RIVERMEN
201 SOUTHWEST JEFFERSON STREET
PEORIA, IL 61602
309-676-1040
info@rivermen.net
www.rivermen.net
- Bill Yuill, Chair/Chief Executive Officer
- Bart Rogers, Chief Operatng Officer/Owner

- Jean-Guy Trudel, General Manager/Head Coach
- Mickey Gray, Assistant General Manager - Corporate Partnerships
(309) 680-3721
mgray@rivermen.net
- Katie Pogeman, Assistant General Manager - Tickets
(309) 680-3791
kpogeman@rivermen.net
- Michelle Novak, Athletic Trainer
mnovak@rivermen.net
Home Ice:
Peoria Civic Center

ROANOKE RAIL YARD DAWGS
710 WILLIAMSON ROAD
ROANOKE, VA 24016
540-344-3294
Fax: 540-344-3294
www.railyarddawgs.com
- Mickey Gray, President
- Dan Bremner, Head Coach/General Manager
- Dan Bremner, Head Coach/General Manager
Home Ice:
Berglund Center. Seating capacity 8,642.

VERMILION COUNTY BOBCATS
PALMER ARENA
DANVILLE, IL

UNITED STATES HOCKEY LEAGUE
850 W. JACKSON BLVD.
UNIT 703
CHICAGO, IL 60607
312-546-7300
Fax: 312-546-7330
ushl-contact@ushl.com
www.ushl.com
- Tom Garrity, President & Commissioner
- Joe MacDonell, Vice President, Business Operations
macdonell@ushl.com
- Doug Christiansen, Director, Player Development & Recruitment
christiansen@ushl.com
- Brian Werger, Director of Communications & Public Relations
werger@ushl.com
- Evan Rand, Director, Hockey Operations
- Dave Siciliano, Senior Advisor of Hockey Operations
- Aaron Westendorf, Manager, Media & Digital Communications
westendorf@ushl.com
- Skip Prince, Senior Advisor
Members Teams:
Cedar Rapids Roughriders, Chicago Steel, Des Moines Buccaneers, Dubuque Fighting Saints, Fargo Force, Green Bay Gamblers, Indiana Ice, Lincoln Stars, Muskegon Lumberjacks, Omaha Lancers, Sioux City Muskateers, Sioux Falls Stampede, Tri-City Storm, USA U-17, USA U-18, Waterloo Blackhawks, Youngstown Phantoms
Member Requirements:
Tier 1 USA Hockey Jr. Hockey League
Publications:
USHL Media Guide

Teams:

CEDAR RAPIDS ROUGHRIDERS
1100 ROCKFORD ROAD SOUTHWEST
CEDAR RAPIDS, IA 52404
319-247-0340
crhockey@roughridershockey.com
www.roughridershockey.com
- Jeff Jauch, Chief Executive Officer
- Mark Meyer, Corporate Partnership Director
mmeyer@roughridershockey.com

- Mark Carlson, President/Head Coach/General Manager
- Jason Shaner, Director, Social Media/Corporate Sales Executive
jshaner@roughridershockey.com
- Shane Connelly, Assistant Coach
- Doug Leaverton, Assistant Coach
- Chris Ipson, MA, ATC, LAT, Certified Athletic Trainer/Equipment Manager
Home Ice:
Cedar Rapids Ice Arena

CHICAGO STEEL
735 EAST JEFFERSON STREET
BENSENVILLE, IL 60106
630-594-1162
Fax: 630-594-1112
www.chicagosteelhockeyteam.com
- Dan Lehv, President
dlehv@chicagosteelhockeyteam.com
- Mark Lotito, President of Hockey Operations
- Dave Campione, Director, Ticket Sales
dcampione@chicagosteelhockeyteam.com
- Katie Sack, Director, Community Relations
ksack@chicagosteelhockeyteam.com
- Ryan Hardy, General Manager
- Brock Sheahan, Head Coach
- Dallas Steward, Associate Head Coach
- Peter Mannino, Assistant Coach
- Virgil Strzelecki, Strength & Conditioning Coach
- Patrick Chun, Head Athletic Trainer
Description:
Edge Ice Arena

DES MOINES BUCCANEERS
7201 HICKMAN ROAD
URBANDALE, IA 50322
515-278-2827
info@bucshockey.com
www.bucshockey.com
- Nate Teut, President
- Scott Owens, Senior Advisor & General Manager
- Kris Klein, Vice President of Marketing & Sales
- Mike Guske, Manager, Ticket Sales
mike@bucshockey.com
- Peter Mannino, Head Coach
- Nate Weossner, Assistant Coach
- Nick Rouse, Head Strength & Conditioning Coach
- Colin Whitte, ATC, Team Trainer
Home Ice:
Buccaneer Arena

DUBUQUE FIGHTING SAINTS
1800 ADMIRAL SHEEHY DRIVE
MYSTIQUE COMMUNITY ICE CENTER
DUBUQUE, IA 52001
563-583-6880
Fax: 563-583-6257
info@dubuquefightingsaints.com
www.dubuquefightingsaints.com
- Casey Weitz, VP, Corporate Partnerships
- Nick Shane, President of Business Operations
nshane@dubuquefightingsaints.com
- Kalle Larsson, General Manager
- Oliver David, Head Coach
Home Ice:
Mystique Community Ice Center

FARGO FORCE
5225 31ST AVENUE SOUTH
FARGO, ND 58104
701-356-7656
Fax: 701-356-7655
fans@fargoforce.com
www.fargoforce.com
- Jon Kram, President
- Cary Eades, General Manager/President, Hockey Operations
- Pierre-Paul Lamoureux, Head Coach
- Byron Pool, Associate Head Coach
- Brad Lutsch, Assistant Coach/Head Scout
- Eli Rosendahl, Goaltender Coach
- Steve Baumgartner, Equipment Manager

• Phil Faught, FAKTR, ATC, Athletic
Trainer/Strength Coach
Home Ice:
Scheels Arena

GREEN BAY GAMBLERS
1901 SOUTH ONEIDA STREET
GREEN BAY, WI 54304
920-405-1237
www.gamblershockey.com
• Jeff Mitchell, President
• Jesse Mertens, Director, Finance
• Pat Mikesch, Head Coach/General Manager
• Terry Charles, Manager, Public Relations
• Paula Testin, Manager, Marketing
• Cody Chupp, Assistant Coach
Home Ice:
The Resch Center

LINCOLN STARS
1880 TRANSFORMATION DRIVE
LINCOLN, NE 68508
402-474-7827
admin@lincolnstars.com
www.lincolnstars.com
• Lori Crocker, President
ext 20
• Chris Michael, General Manager/Head Coach
• Tanner Baker, Rink Manager
tanner@lincolnstars.com
• Mick Berge, Assistant Coach
mick@lincolnstars.com
• Corey Courtney, ATC, L.A.T., Athletic
Trainer/Equipment Manager/Strength Coach
ccourtney@ortholinc.com
Home Ice:
The Ice Box

MADISON CAPITOLS
1880 VETERANS DRIVE
MADISON, WI 53713
608-257-2277
info@madcapshockey.com
www.madcapshockey.com
• Andrew Joudrey, President
• Diane Suter Hyames, Director, Hockey
Operations
• Tom Upton, Head Coach/General Manager
• Jon Marquardt, Group Sales Manager
jon@madcapshockey.com
• Keith Paulsen, Assistant General
Manager/Associate Head Coach
• Ryan Petersen, Assistant Coach
• Brent DuBois, Athletic Trainer
Home Ice:
Veterans Memorial Coliseum

MUSKEGON LUMBERJACKS
470 WEST WESTERN AVENUE
MUSKEGON, MI 49440
231-724-5225
www.muskegonlumberjacks.com
• Andrea Rose, President of Business
Operations
ext 235
• Steve Lowe, Director, Hockey Operations
ext 256
• Jim McGroarty, General Manager
ext 236
• Cara Mendelson, Sales & Marketing
Coordinator
ext 224
• Katie Murphy, Sales & Event Coordinator
ext 255
• Mike Hamilton, Head Coach
ext 286
• Todd Robinson, Assistant Coach
ext 291
• Josh Shields, Assistant Coach
ext 233
Home Ice:
L.C. Walker Arena

OMAHA LANCERS
7300 Q STREET
RALSTON, NE 68127

402-344-7825
Fax: 402-934-4613
www.lancers.com
• David DeLuca, President
• Rob Lippolis, Director, Broadcasting & Media
Relations
rlippolis@lancers.com
• Diana Fisher, Director, Group Sales &
Community Relations
dfisher@lancers.com
• Kelsey Ostendorf, Director, Ticket Operations
kostendorf@lancers.com
• Terri Phillips, Director, Business & Game Night
Operations
tphillips@lancers.com
• Gavin Utesch, Director, Promotions & Fan
Development
gutesch@lancers.com
• David Wilkie, General Manager/Head Coach
• Rick Comley, Jr., Director, Scouting/Assistant
General Manager
rcomley@lancers.com
• Chris Michael, Associate Head Coach
cmichael@lancers.com
• John Faulkner, Assistant Coach
jfaulkner@lancers.com
• Bill Nervig, ATC, Head Athletic
Trainer/Equipment Manager
bnervig@lancers.com
Home Ice:
Ralston Arena

SIOUX CITY MUSKETEERS
401 GORDON DRIVE
SIOUX CITY, IA 51101
712-252-2116
Fax: 712-252-2117
info@musketeershockey.com
www.musketeershockey.com
• Lloyd Ney, Owner/Managing Partner
• Rich Zaber, President
ext 12
• Travis Morgan, Chief Executive Officer
ext 12
• Luke Strand, Head Coach
• Mark LeRose, General Manager
• Tim Artz, Event/Ticketing/Media Manager
ext 11
• Heather Campbell, Community
Relations/Merchandise/Accounting
ext 18
• Mark Abalan, Associate Head Coach
• Jamie Huffman, Assistant General
Manager/Director, Scouting
(612) 275-6325
• Ethan Goldberg, Assistant Coach
• Rob Frost, Athletic Trainer/Equipment
Manager
• Shane Clifford, Goalie Coach
Home Ice:
Tyson Events Center Gateway Arena

SIOUX FALLS STAMPEDE
1001 NORTH WEST AVENUE
SIOUX FALLS, SD 57104
605-336-6060
Fax: 605-333-0139
info@sfstampede.com
www.sfstampede.com
• Jim Olander, President
• Rico Velazquez, Vice President of Sales
rico@sfstampede.com
• Anthony Hegstrom, Sr. Director, Game Night
Operations & Merchandise
• Brian Olthoff, Director, Sales
bolthoff@sfstampede.com
• Marty Murray, General Manager/Head Coach
• Christian Bragnalo, Associate Head Coach
• Nick Oliver, Assistant Coach
• Zach Sikich, Goalie Coach
• Matt Hunter, Athletic Trainer
Home Ice:
Sioux Falls Arena

TRI-CITY STORM
609 PLATTE ROAD
KEARNEY, NE 68845

308-338-8809
Fax: 308-338-8148
www.stormhockey.com
• Dave Vennetti, Majority Owner
• Mark Jalcovik, President, Business
Operations/Owner
• Steve Lowe, President of Hockey Operations
• Mike Lucas, Vice President of Business
Operations
• Andy Ogdahl, Vice President of Sales
• David Fine, Director, Media Relations &
Broadcasting
david@stormhockey.com
• Jason Koehler, General Manager
• Anthony Noreen, President, Hockey
Operation/Head Coach
• Leland Skeen, Corporate Sales
Representative
• Ben Gordon, Assistant Coach
• Dan Bouska, Equipment Manager
d.bouska@stormhockey.com
• Colt Graf, Athletic Trainer
c.graf@stormhockey.com
Home Ice:
Viaero Event Center

US NATIONAL TEAM DEVELOPMENT PROGRAM (USNTDP)
14900 BECK ROAD
PLYMOUTH, MI 48170
734-453-6400
Fax: 734-327-9256
www.usahockeyntdp.com
• Scott Monaghan, Assistant Executive Director
• Dan Muse, Under-18 Team Head Coach
• Adam Nightinglae, Under-17 Team Head
Coach
• Chris Luongo, Under-18 Team Assistant
Coach
chris.luongo@usahockey.org
• Brock Bradley, Head Equipment Manager
brockb@usahockey.org
• Rebecca Northway, Team Physician
rnorthwa@med.umich.edu
• Dennis MacDonald, Athletic Trainer
dcmacdon@med.umich.edu
• Ryan Hardy, Director, Player Personnel
ryanh@usahockey.org
Home Ice:
Ann Arbor Ice Cube

WATERLOO BLACKHAWKS
125 COMMERICAL STREET
WATERLOO, IA 50704
319-232-3444
www.waterlooblackhawks.com
• PK O'Handley, President/Head Coach
• Joe Greene, President, Business Operations
• Tim Harwood, Director, Broadcasting & Media
Relations
radio@waterlooblackhawks.com
• Allison Longnecker, Manager, Retail
Merchandising
allison@waterlooblackhawks.com
• Shane Fukushima, General
Manager/Associate Head Coach
• Steve Howard, Assistant Coach
showard@waterlooblackhawks.com
• Chris Economou, Goalie Coach
• Spenser Popinga, Strength & Conditioning
Coach
Home Ice:
Young Arena

YOUNGSTOWN PHANTOMS
229 EAST FRONT STREET
YOUNGSTOWN, OH 44503
330-747-7825
Fax: 330-746-5175
info@youngstownphantoms.com
www.youngstownphantoms.com
• Bruce J. Zoldan, Co-Owner
• Murry Gunty, Co-Owner/Governor
• Andrew Goldman, President & Alternate
Governor
• Keith Primeau, President, Hockey Operations
• Katie Seminara, Director, Game Day
Operations/Community Relations

kseminara@youngstownphantoms.com
• Brad Patterson, Head Coach/General Manager
• Brad Patterson, Assistant Coach
• Shane Clifford, Goaltending Coach
• Jim Schroeder, Athletic Trainer
• Joshua Famularo, Equipment Manager
Home Ice:
Covelli Center

WESTERN HOCKEY LEAGUE
FATHER DAVID BAUER ARENA
2424 UNIVERSITY DRIVE NW
CALGARY, AB, CANADA T2N 3Y9
403-693-3030
Fax: 403-693-3031
info@whl.ca
whl.ca
• Ron Robison, Commissioner
• Richard Doerksen, VP, Hockey
• Yvonne Bergmann, VP, Business Development
Description:
Member of the Canadian Hockey League.

Teams:

BRANDON WHEAT KINGS
2-1175 18TH STREET
BRANDON, MB, CANADA R7A 7C5
204-726-3535
Fax: 204-726-3540
office@wheatkings.com
wheatkings.com
• Jared Jacobson, Owner/Governor
• Darren Ritchie, General Manager
• Don MacGillivray, Head Coach
Home Ice:
Westman Communications Group Place at Keystone Centre. Seating capacity 5,102.

CALGARY HITMEN
SCOTIABANK SADDLEDOME
555 SADDLEDOME RISE SE
CALGARY, AB, CANADA T2G 2W1
403-777-4646
Fax: 403-571-2211
hitmenhockey.com
• John Bean, President & CEO
• Jeff Chynoweth, General Manager
• Steve Hamilton, Head Coach
Home Ice:
Scotiabank Saddledome. Seating capacity 19,289.

EDMONTON OIL KINGS
FORD HALL, ROGERS PLACE
10214 104 AVENUE NW
EDMONTON, AB, CANADA T5J 0H6
oilkings.ca
• Kirt Hill, President, Hockey Operations/General Manager
• Brad Lauer, Head Coach
Home Arena:
Rogers Place. Seating capacity 18,641.

EVERETT SILVERTIPS
2000 HEWITT AVENUE
SUITE 100
EVERETT, WA 98201
425-252-5100
Fax: 425-257-0700
www.everettsilvertips.com
• Bill Yuill, President
• Zoran Rajcic, Chief Operating Officer/Governor
• Zoran Rajcic, Executive Vice President/Assistant General Manager
zoranr@everettsilvertips.com
• Garry Davidson, General Manager
• Dennis Williams, Head Coach
• Mitch Love, Assistant Coach
• Shane Clifford, Goaltending Coach
• Wayne Duncan, ATC/L, Athletic Trainer

Home Ice:
Xfinity Arena. Seating capacity 8,149.

KAMLOOPS BLAZERS
300 LORNE STREET
KAMLOOPS, BC, CANADA V2C 1W3
250-828-1144
Fax: 250-828-7822
info@blazerhockey.com
blazerhockey.com
• Don Moores, President/COO
• Matt Bardsley, VP/General Manager
• Shaun Clouston, Head Coach
Home Ice:
Sandman Centre. Seating capacity 5,464.

KELOWNA ROCKETS
101-1223 WATER STREET
KELOWNA, BC, CANADA V1Y 9V1
250-860-7825
Fax: 250-860-7880
info@kelownarockets.com
kelownarockets.com
• Bruce Hamilton, Owner/President/General Manager
• Kris Mallette, Head Coach
Home Ice:
Prospera Place. Seating capacity 6,886.

LETHBRIDGE HURRICANES
ENMAX CENTRE
2-2510 SCENIC DRIVE SOUTH
LETHBRIDGE, AB, CANADA T1K 7V7
403-328-1986
Fax: 403-329-1622
admin@lethbridgehurricanes.com
lethbridgehurricanes.com
• Doug Paisley, President/Governor
• Peter Anholt, General Manager
• Brent Kisio, Head Coach
Home Ice:
ENMAX Centre. Seating capacity 5,479.

MEDICINE HAT TIGERS
2802 BOX SPRINGS WAY NW
MEDICINE HAT, AB, CANADA T1C 0H3
403-526-2666
Fax: 403-526-3072
admin@tigershockey.com
tigershockey.com
• Willie Desjardins, General Manager/Head Coach
Home Ice:
Canalta Centre. Seating capacity 5,500.

MOOSE JAW WARRIORS
110 1ST AVENUE NW
MOOSE JAW, SK, CANADA S6H 3L9
306-694-5711
Fax: 306-692-7833
mjwarriors.ca
• Chad Taylor, President/Governor
• Alan Millar, General Manager
• Mark O'Leary, Head Coach
Home Ice:
Mosaic Place. Seating capacity 4,465.

PORTLAND WINTERHAWKS
300 NORTH WINNING WAY
PORTLAND, OR 97227
503-238-6366
Fax: 503-238-7629
hockey@winterhawks.com
www.winterhawks.com
• Bill Gallacher, Owner
• Doug Piper, President & Governor
• Kelley Robinett, Sr. Vice President, Operating & Marketing
• Rich Franklin, Vice President, Sponsorship Sales & Service
• Vicky Talmadge, Director, Finance
• Graham Kendrick, Director, Media & Public Relations
• Mike Johnston, General Manager & Head Coach

• Kyle Gustafson, Assistant Coach
• Matt Bardsley, Assistant General Manager
Home Ice:
Veterans Memorial Coliseum. Seating capacity 10,095. Moda Center. Seating capacity 19,980.

PRINCE ALBERT RAIDERS
690 32ND STREET E
PRINCE ALBERT, SK, CANADA S6V 2W8
306-764-5348
raiderhockey.com
• Gord Broda, President/Governor
• Curtis Hunt, General Manager
• Marc Habscheid, Head Coach
Home Ice:
Art Hauser Centre. Seating capacity 2,591.

PRINCE GEORGE COUGARS
102-2187 OSPIKA BOULEVARD S
PRINCE GEORGE, BC, CANADA V2N 6Z1
250-561-0783
Fax: 250-561-0743
info@pgcougars.com
pgcougars.com
• Greg Pocock, Governor
• Mark Lamb, General Manager/Head Coach
mark.lamb@pgcougars.com
Home Ice:
CN Centre. Seating capacity 5,967.

RED DEER REBELS
4847C 19TH STREET
RED DEER, AB, CANADA T4R 2N7
403-341-6000
Fax: 403-341-6009
info@reddeerrebels.com
www.reddeerrebels.com
• Brent Sutter, Owner/General Manager/Head Coach
Home Ice:
ENMAX Centrium. Seating capacity 6,706.

REGINA PATS
1463 ALBERT STREET
REGINA, SK, CANADA S4R 2R8
306-522-7287
pats@reginapats.com
reginapats.com
• John Paddock, VP, Hockey Operations/General Manager
• Dave Struch, Assistant General Manager/Head Coach
Home Ice:
Brandt Centre. Seating capacity 6,136.

SASKATOON BLADES
SASKTEL CENTRE
201-3515 THATCHER AVENUE
SASKATOON, SK, CANADA S7R 1C4
306-975-8844
info@saskatoonblades.com
saskatoonblades.com
• Mike Priestner, Owner/Governor
• Colin Priestner, President/General Manager
• Colin Priestner, General Manager/President
• Mitch Love, Head Coach
Home Ice:
SaskTel Centre. Seating capacity 15,100.

SEATTLE THUNDERBIRDS
625 WEST JAMES STREET
KENT, WA 98032
253-239-7825
Fax: 253-856-6848
stbirds@seattlethunderbirds.com
www.seattlethunderbirds.com
• Russ Farwell, Vice President, Hockey Operations
• Rick Ronish, Director, Operations
• Ian Henry, Director, Public & Media Relations
• Jason Thomsen, Director, Corporate Partnerships
• Bil La Forge, General Manager
• Matt O'Dette, Head Coach
• Matt O'Dette, Assistant Coach
• Tyler Alos, Assistant Coach

• Ian Gordon, Goaltender Coach
• Phil Varney, Athletic Trainer
Home Ice:
ShoWare Centre. Seating capacity 6,500.

SPOKANE CHIEFS
700 WEST MALLON AVENUE
SPOKANE, WA 99201
509-328-0450
Fax: 509-328-7608
fanmail@spokanechiefs.com
www.spokanechiefs.com
• Bobby Brett, President & Owner
• Mark Miles, Vice President of Business
Operations/Sales
mmiles@spokanechiefs.com
• Dave Pier, Vice President of Marketing
dpier@spokanechiefs.com
• Greg Sloan, Chief Financial Officer
gsloan@spokanechiefs.com
• Scott Carter, General Manager
• Adam Maglio, Head Coach
• Scott Burt, Assistant Coach
Home Ice:
Spokane Veterans Memorial Arena. Seating
capacity 9,916.

SWIFT CURRENT BRONCOS
PO BOX 2345
2001 CHAPLIN STREET E
SWIFT CURRENT, SK, CANADA S9H 4X6
306-773-1509
Fax: 306-773-5406
communications@scbroncos.com
scbroncos.com
• Nathan MacDonald, Director, Business
Operations
• Dean Brockman, Director, Hockey
Operations/Head Coach
Home Ice:
Credit Union iPlex. Seating capacity 3,239.

TRI-CITY AMERICANS
TOYOTA CENTER
7000 WEST GRANDRIDGE BOULEVARD
KENNEWICK, WA 99336
509-736-0606
Fax: 509-783-4591
info@amshockey.com
www.amshockey.com
• Olaf Kolzig, Ownership Partner
• Stu Barnes, Ownership Partner
• Bob Tory, Governor/General
Manager/Ownership Partner
• Dennis Loman, Ownership Partner/Alternate
Governor
• Dan Mulhausen, VP, Business Operations &
Marketing Communications
(509) 737-3769
dmulhausen@amshockey.com
• Craig West, VP, Sponsorship Sales &
Broadcasting
(509) 737-3762
cwest@amshockey.com
• Kelly Buchberger, Head Coach
• Brian Pellerin, Associate Coach
• Zachary Fournier, Athletic Therapist
Home Ice:
Toyota Center. Seating capacity 5,734.

VANCOUVER GIANTS
220-7888 200TH STREET
LANGLEY, BC, CANADA V2Y 3J4
604-444-2687
info@vancouvergiants.com
vancouvergiants.com
• Barclay Parneta, General Manager
• Michael Dyck, Head Coach
Home Ice:
Langley Events Centre. Seating capacity 5,276.

VICTORIA ROYALS
1925 BLANSHARD STREET
VICTORIA, BC, CANADA V8T 4J2
250-220-2600
info@victoriaroyals.com
victoriaroyals.com

• Graham Lee, Owner
• Dan Price, Head Coach/General Manager
Home Ice:
Save-On-Foods Memorial Centre. Seating
capacity 7,006.

WINNIPEG ICE
57 SOUTH LANDING DRIVE
OAK BLUFF, MB, CANADA R4G 0C4
204-489-7465
info@50below.ca
winnipegice.ca
• Greg Fettes, Chair & Governor
• Matt Cockell, President/General
Manager/Alternate Governor
• James Patrick, Head Coach
Home Ice:
Western Financial Place. Seating capacity
4,654.

Hockey, Roller Hockey Organizations

USA ROLLER SPORTS
4730 SOUTH STREET
LINCOLN, NE 68506
402-483-7551
Fax: 402-483-1465
www.teamusa.org/USA-Roller-Sports

Horse Shoe Organizations

**NATIONAL HORSESHOE PITCHERS
ASSOCIATION**
100 BLUESTERN WAY
WENTZVILLE, MO 63385
262-835-9108
info@horseshoepitching.com
www.horseshoepitching.com
• Casey Sluys, President
• Joe Faron, Vice President
• Phyllis Quist, Secretary
• Gary Buehler, Treasurer
Member Services:
Rules available free on request.
Publications:
NEWSLINE, six times annually.
Membership Requirements:
Pay dues of $12.00 annually.
Description:
Founded 1909. The NHPA is a federation of
60 charters in the United States and
Canada, each with numerous clubs and
affiliates. The association strives to promote
and organize the sport of horseshoes, and
to standardize the rules, equipment and
playing procedures.

Inline Skating Organizations

AGGRESSIVE SKATERS ASSOCIATION
201 N RIVERSIDE DR
SUITE C
INDIALANTIC, FL 32903
321-722-9300
Fax: 321-722-9391
media@asaent.com
www.asaentertainment.com
• Rick Bratman, CEO
(321) 722-9300
• Todd Shays, Senior Vice President
• Mark Shays, Senior Vice President
• Valerie Belardinelli, Media/Public Relations

Member Services:
Hat, T-shirt, card, newsletter, insurance at
all ASA-sanctioned events, discounted
events.
Publications:
Newsletter.
Membership Requirements:
Professional members: $195 annual dues.
Amateur members: Pay dues of $40 per
year.
Description:
Founded 1994. Governing body of
aggressive in-line skating. ASA Events is
the largest action sports event and television
production company in the US.

**INTERNATIONAL INLINE SKATING
ASSOCIATION & INLINE SKATING
RESOURCE CENTER**
C/O ZEPHYR ADVENTURES
P O BOX 16
RED LODGE, MT 59068
406-445-0802
1-888-758-8687
www.iisa.org
Description:
The Inline Skating Resource Center (ISRC)
is the website originally operated by the
International Inline Skating Association. The
International Inline Skating Association
(IISA) was founded in 1991 by a group of
manufacturers, retailers, and skaters who
chose to be proactive about enhancing the
future of the sport of inline skating. For 14
years the IISA developed educational
programs, promoted safe skating, and
protected and expanded access to public
skate ways across the country. Areas of
emphasis of the IISA included the Instructor
Certification Program, the National Skate
Patrol, the Gear Up! Program, and the
Government Relations Program.

USA ROLLER SPORTS
4730 SOUTH STREET
LINCOLN, NE 68506
402-483-7551
Fax: 402-483-1465
www.teamusa.org/USA-Roller-Sports

Jai-Lai Organizations

NATIONAL JAI-ALAI ASSOCIATION
5701 LESS STREET NE
ST PETERSBURG, FL 33073
www.national-jai-alai.com
• Paul Kubala, President
Paul@National-Jai-Alai.com
• Tom DeMint, Vice President
TJD1@aol.com
Description:
To introduce the game of Jai-alai to a new
generation of all ages and assist in getting
amateur courts built in the USA for them to
play on. Through a structured format like
Little League baseball, we wil focus on
getting members to understand the true
integrity and sport of the game.

Kayaking Organizations

PADDLE ASSOCIATION OF CANADA
PO BOX 126
STATION MAIN
KINGSTON, ON, CANADA K7L 4V6
613-547-3196
Fax: 613-547-4880
info@paddlecanada.com
www.paddlingcanada.com
• Graham Ketcheson, Executive Director
• Dawn Callan, Events, National Paddling Week & PaddleSmart
• Adrian Camara, Media & Marketing Manager

PADDLE CANADA
613-547-3196 EXT 10
888-252-6292
Fax: 613-547-4880
info@paddlecanada.com
www.paddlecanada.com
• Graham Ketcheson, Executive Director
(613) 547-3196

PROFESSIONAL PADDLESPORTS ASSOCIATION
7432 ALBAN STATION BLVD
P O Box 10847
Knoxville, TN 37939
865-558-3595
office@americaoutdoors.com
www.propaddle.com
• Don Roberts, Chairman
• David Brown, Executive Director
• David Brown, Executive Director
• Cheryl Saam, Treasurer/Director at Large
Nature of Service:
Provides the public with the safest, best quality, on-water outdoor recreational experience available commercially, protecting our nation's waterways and the right of the people to use them.
Year Founded:
1977
Number of Members:
450 Organizations.
Publications:
Paddler. Paddlesports Pro Online: Bi-weekly newsletter.

TRADE ASSOCIATION OF PADDLESPORTS
PO BOX 243
MILNER, BRITISH COLUMBIA, CANADA
V0X 1T0
604-514-5011
800-755-5228
Fax: 604-530-5901
www.gopaddle.org
• Michael Pardy, Executive Director
michael@gopaddle.org
• Nikki Rekman, Events & Administration Director
nikki@gopaddle.org
Notes:
Formerly Trade Association of Sea Kayaking/TASK. Merged with North American Paddle Sports Association.
Number of members:
400
Member Services:
Risk management programs, North America wide promotions for paddle sports, liability insurance benefits, special credit card rates. Trade shows; sponsors a national symposium, and co-sponsors two other symposia.
Publications:
TAPS Journal, bimonthly newsletter for members.
Membership Requirements:
Business involved in paddle sports. Membership fee based upon total gross income of the business derived from paddle sport ($100 and up). Adherence to T.A.S.K. bylaws; payment of dues.
Description:
Established in 1998 (merger). Promotes the sport of sea kayaking in a safe and environmentally sound manner.

USA CANOE/KAYAK
503 SOPHIA ST
SUITE 100
FREDERICKSBURG, VA 22401
540-907-4460
membership@usack.org
http://www.teamusa.org/USA-Canoe-Kayak

Kiting Organizations

AMERICAN KITEFLIERS ASSOCIATION
PO BOX 22365
PORTLAND, OR 97269
609-755-5483
800-252-2550
Fax: 800-252-2550
www.aka.kite.org
• John Lutter, President
(321) 412-1368
• Maria Miller, First VP
(253) 752-7051
Description:
The American Kitefliers Association was founded in 1964 by the late Robert M. Ingraham of New Mexico. Now, with over 4,000 members, in 35 countries, we are the largest association of kiters in the world. Our purpose is to educate the public in the art, history, technology, and practice of building and flying kites - to advance the joys and values of kiting in all nations.
Publications:
KITING quarterly magazine.
Member Services:
Liability Insurance, Discounts at Member Merchants, Website, publications, Kite Event Assistance, National Kite Month.
Number of Members:
3,000

KITE TRADE ASSOCIATION INTERNATIONAL
PO Box 6898
Bend, OR 97708
541-994-9647
800-243-8548
Fax: 503-419-4369
www.kitetrade.org
• Elaine Leitner, President
• Billy Jones, Vice President
• Lolly Hadszicki-Ryno, Secretary/Treasurer
• James Daniel, Director
Number of members:
300
Date Founded and Purpose:
Founded 1983. Serves to advance the cause of kiting and sport kiting in the U.S. and internationally.
Membership Requirements:
Please see www.kitetrade.org.
Publications:
Tradewinds: quarterly newsletter.
Member Services:
Please convention and trade show held every January. Please see www.kitetrader.com.

Lacrosse Organizations

CANADIAN LACROSSE ASSOCIATION
18 LOUISA ST
OTTAWA, CANADA K1R 6Y6
613-260-2028
Fax: 613-260-2029
info1@lacrosse.ca
www.lacrosse.ca
• Joey Harris, President
• Britany Gordon, Events and communications coordinator
britany@lacrosse.ca
• Jane Clapham, Office Administrator
jane@lacrosse.ca
• Joanne Thomson, Executive Director
joanne@lacrosse.ca
Number of members:
150,000
Member Services:
Seven national championships hosted in various Canadian cities each year.
Publications:
CANADIAN LACROSSE NEWS, semi-annually; various technical manuals and programs.
Membership Requirements:
Limited to the governing organizations in the ten provinces and two territories and to the Can Am and Iroquois League. All lacrosse players in Canada (150,000) are members by affiliation.
Description:
Founded 1867. Promotes and develops all forms of lacrosse, the National Summer Sport of Canada - Box (Indoor), Men's Field, Women's Field and Inter-Lacrosse.

INTERCOLLEGIATE WOMEN'S LACROSSE COACHES ASSOCIATION
PO BOX 1124
GRAND LAKE, CO 80447
443-951-9611
Fax: 970-432-7058
www.iwlca.org
• Elizabeth Robertshaw, President
earobert@bu.edu
• Liz Grote, Vice President
egrote@bowdoin.edu
• Julie Young, Treasurer
j.young@villanova.edu
Member Services:
Job openings reported, newsletter, Coach of the Year, All-American selections, team ranking, coaches clinics; Academic Squad, North-South Senior All-Star Games.
Publications:
Membership booklet; newsletter.
Description:
Founded 1982. Develops a deep sense of responsibility in teaching, promoting and maintaining the growth of women's lacrosse in accordance with the highest of ideals of fair play.

US LACROSSE
113 W. UNIVERSITY PKWY
BALTIMORE, MD 21210-3300
410-235-6882
Fax: 410-366-6735
info@uslacrosse.org
www.uslacrosse.org
• Rich Morgan, Chair
  ext 101
• Kristen Murray, Incoming Vice Chair
  ext 178
• George Graffy, Treasurer
  ext 120
• Geroge Hugdahl, Secretary
  ext 128
• Carter Abbott, WG Committee Chair
  ext 111
• Jim Carboneau, MG Committee Chair
• Larry Quinnon, Co-Counsel
  ext 149
Number of Members:
345,000.
Publications:
Lacrosse Magazine; Lacrosse Magazine
Online(www.laxmagazine.com)
Description:
US Lacrosse is the national governing body
of lacrosse. Through responsive and
effective leadership, we provide programs
and services to inspire participation while
protecting the integrity of the sport.
Teams:
U.S. Men's and Women's National Teams

Lacrosse, Leagues/Teams

MAJOR LEAGUE LACROSSE
20 GUEST STREET
SUITE 125
BOSTON, MA 02135
617-746-2233
Fax: 617-746-9988
info@majorleaguelacrosse.com
www.majorleaguelacrosse.com
• David Gross, Commissioner
• Christopher Day, Broadcasting and Digital
Media Manager
• Colin Keane, Lacrosse Operations
Manager
• Kevin Murphy, Marketing and Brand
Manager
• Keith Burkinshaw, Special Events
Manager
Description:
A national league made up of over 350
players; season consists of 60 regular
season games.

Teams:

ATLANTA BLAZE
3200 GEORGE BUSBEE PARKWAY
NORTHWEST
KENNESAW, GA 30144
• Peter Trematerra, Team Owner
• John Tucker, Head Coach & General Manager
• Christopher Meegan, Director of Marketing &
Communications
Stadium:
Fifth Third Bank Stadium. Seating capacity,
8,318.

BOSTON CANNONS
214 LINCOLN STREET
SUITE 320
ALLSTON, MA 02134

617-746-9933
info@bostoncannons.com
www.bostoncannons.com
• Kevin Barney, Vice President & General
Manager
• Sara Berry, Director of Partnerships and
Marketing
• Joe Shannon, Director of Ticket Sales
• Matthew Ryan, Marketing Operations Manager
• Sean Quirk, Head Coach
Stadium:
Harvard Stadium. Seating capacity, 30,323.

CHARLOTTE HOUNDS
210 EAST TRADE STREET
E-482
CHARLOTTE, NC 28202
704-206-1515
charlottehounds@gmail.com
• Jim McPhilliamy, President
• Wade Leaphart, Vice President
• Kristy Boyles, Operations and Community
Relations
• Corbin Nyeste, Ticket Operations
• Jillian Fay, Communications Manager
• Patrick O'Leary, Ticket Sales Manager
Stadium:
American Legion Memorial Stadium. Seating
capacity, 21,000.

CHESAPEAKE BAYHAWKS
1997 ANNAPOLIS EXCHANGE PARKWAY
SUITE 470
ANNAPOLIS, MD 21401
443-482-6094 EXT 1812
www.thebayhawks.com
• Brendan Kelly, Owner
• Dave Cottle, President
• Jon Kemezis, Vice President of Finance
jkemezis@thebayhawks.com
Stadium:
Navy-Marine Corps Memorial Stadium. Seating
capacity, 34,000.

DENVER OUTLAWS
INVESCO FIELD AT MILE HIGH
1701 BRYANT STREET
SUITE 700
DENVER, CO 80204
303-688-5297
Fax: 702-258-3050
www.denveroutlaws.com
• Mac Freeman, President
• Chuck Olney, Director of Business
Development
• Tid Tseng, Director of Sales and Marketing
• Elizabeth Goodman, Ticket Sales Manager
• Tony Seaman, General Manager
Stadium:
Sports Authority Field at Mile High. Seating
capacity, 76,125.

FLORIDA LAUNCH
777 GLADES ROAD
BOCA RATON, FL 33431
www.floridalaunchlacrosse.com
• Brian Clinton, President
• Michael Zeff, Director of Sales and
Sponsorship
Stadium:
FAU Stadium. Seating capacity, 29,419.

NEW YORK LIZARDS
900 FULTON AVENUE
HEMPSTEAD, NY 11549
516-463-8499
www.NYlizards.com
• Jeffrey Rudnick, CEO
• Tom Dissette, VP, Corporate Sales and
Services
• Jason Velez, VP, Ticket Sales and Operations
Description:
Shuart Stadium. Seating capacity, 11,929.

OHIO MACHINE
3811 ATTUCKS DRIVE
POWELL, OH 43065
614-754-1973
www.theohiomachine.com
• Gregg Klein, VP, Business Operations
• Bear Davis, VP, Head Coach
• Dave Brewer, Manager, Operations
Stadium:
Selby Field. Seating capacity, 9,100.

ROCHESTER RATTLERS
EMPIRE PROFESSIONAL LACROSSE
1100 UNIVERSITY AVE
SUITE 120
ROCHESTER, NY 14607
585-454-5425
Fax: 585-454-5453
www.rochesterrattlers.com
• Soudan Tim, General Manager
Stadium:
Eunice Kennedy Shriver Stadium. Seating
capacity, 10,000.

NATIONAL LACROSSE LEAGUE
CONSHOHOCKEN, PA
www.nll.com
• Nick Sakiewicz, Commissioner
• Brian Lemon, VP, Lacrosse Operations
• Justin Rubino, VP, Business Operations
Description:
Founded 1997. Professional Indoor
Lacrosse League.

Teams:

BUFFALO BANDITS
First Niagara Centre
ONE SEYMOUR H. KNOX, III PLAZA
BUFFALO, NY 14203-3096
716-855-4100
888-223-6000
Fax: 716-855-4122
www.bandits.com
• Terry Pegula, Owner
• Steve Dietrich, General Manager
• Troy Cordingley, Head Coach
Home Arena:
First Niagara Center.

CALGARY ROUGHNECKS
SCOTIABANK SADDLEDOME
555 SADDLEDOME RIDE SE
CALGARY, AB, CANADA T2G 2W1
403-777-4646
Fax: 403-777-3695
info@calgaryroughnecks.com
calgaryroughnecks.com
• John Bean, President/CEO
• John Bean, Governor and President
• Mike Board, General Manager
• Curt Malawsky, Assistant General
Manager/Head Coach
Home Arena:
Scotiabank Saddledome. Seating capacity
19,289.

COLORADO MAMMOTH
1000 CHOPPER CIRCLE
DENVER, CO 80204
303-405-1100
Fax: 303-893-8022
mammoth@pepsicenter.com
www.coloradomammoth.com
• Steve Govett, President/General Manager
• Josh Gross, VP, Business Operations and
Alternate Governor
• Pat Coyle, Coach
• Chris Gill, Coach
• Ken Szarka, Performance Coach
• Joel Raether, Head of Sports Performance
Home Arena:
Pepsi Center

GEORGIA SWARM
6340 SUGARLOAF PARKWAY
SUITE 140
DULUTH, GA 30097
844-427-9276
info@georgiaswarm.com
www.georgiaswarm.com
• John J. Arlotta, Owner & Governor
• Andy Arlotta, Co-Owner & President
• Ed Comeau, Head Coach
Home Arena:
Infinite Energy Arena. Seating capacity 11,355.

HALIFAX
SCOTIABANK CENTRE
1800 ARGYLE ST
HALIFAX, NS, CANADA B3J 2V9
902-451-1221
halifaxnll.com

NEW ENGLAND BLACK WOLVES
MOHEGAN SUN ARENA
ONE MOHEGAN SUN BOULEVARD
UNCASVILLE, CT 06382-1355
860-862-4073
info@blackwolves.com
www.blackwolves.com
• Bill Tavares, Media Relations Manager
• Jen Hildebrand, Publicist
Home Arena:
Mohegan Sun Arena. Seating capacity, 7,700.

ROCHESTER KNIGHTHAWKS
BLUE CROSS ARENA
144 EXCHANGE BLVD
SUITE 102
ROCHESTER, NY 14614
585-454-4295
Fax: 585-454-6614
www.knighthawks.com
• Lewis Staats, President
• Curt Styres, Owner/General Manager
• Mike Hasen, Head Coach
• Ted Nolan, Special Advisor to President
• Bob Hathway, Director of Strategic
Development
• Jody Gage, VP of Player Personnel
• John Catalano, VP of Sales
Home Arena:
Blue Cross Arena.

SASKATCHEWAN RUSH
3100 IDYLWYLD DRIVE N
SASKATOON, SK, CANADA S7L 5Y6
306-978-7874
info@saskrush.com
www.saskrush.com
• Bruce Urban, Owner/Governor
• Myrna Januario, Director of Operations
myrna@saskrush.com
• Derek Keenan, Head Coach/General Manager
Home Arena:
SaskTel Centre. Seating capacity 15,195.

TORONTO ROCK
1132 INVICTA DRIVE
2ND FLOOR
OAKVILLE, ON, CANADA L6H 6G1
416-596-3075
Fax: 905-339-3473
info@torontorock.com
torontorock.com
• Jamie Dawick, Owner/President/General
Manager
• Matt Sawyer, Head Coach
Home Arena:
Scotiabank Arena. Seating capacity 18,819.

VANCOUVER WARRIORS
VANCOUVER, BC, CANADA
604-899-4625
ticket.info@vancouverwarriors.com
vancouverwarriors.com
• Chris Gill, Head Coach
• Dan Richardson, General Manager/Lacrosse
Operations

Home Arena:
Langley Events Centre. Seating capacity 5,500.

Luge Organizations

U.S. LUGE ASSOCIATION
57 CHURCH STREET
LAKE PLACID, NY 12946-1805
518-523-2071
Fax: 518-523-4106
info@usaluge.org
www.usaluge.org
• Dwight Bell, President

Martial Arts Organizations

AMATEUR ATHLETIC UNION KARATE PROGRAM
THE WALT DISNEY WORLD RESORT
PO BOX 10,000
LAKE BUENA VISTA, FL 32830
407-934-7200
Fax: 407-934-7242
WWW.AAUKARATE.ORG
• Bobby Dodd, President
• William Tooke, 1st Vice President
• Louis Stout, 2nd Vice President
• Roger Goudy, Secretary
• Ron Crawford, Treasurer
Year Founded:
1988
Description:
To provide amateur programs through a
volunteer base for all people to have the
physical, mental, and moral development of
amateur athletes and to promote good
sportsmanship and good citizenship in
Traditional and freestyle karate programs.
Membership Requirements:
Open to all.

AMERICAN AMATEUR KARATE FEDERATION
1801 Century Park
24th Floor
LOS ANGELES, CA 90067
888-939-8882
Fax: 888-939-8555
office@aakf.org
www.aakf.org
• Alex Tong, President
• Robert Fusaro, VP
• Albert Chea, Secretary
• Mahmoud Tabassi, Treasurer
• Richard Kageyama, Executive Director
Member Services:
Ranking and examination guide; Ranking
recognition system; visiting instructorships;
annual national summer training camp;
Regional seminars; Regional Instructor
Training and Certification Program; Regional
and national karate championships.
Publications:
AAKF TIMES, quarterly; AAKF
DIRECTORY, annually; COMPETITION
RULES, Spanish and English editions.
Membership Requirements:
Open to all. Athletes, instructors, coaches,
judges and administrators must satisfy
AAKF amateur karate qualifications.
Description:
Founded 1961. Serves as national
traditional karate governing body in the U.S.
Organized as a public benefit, non-profit
corporation whose purpose is to improve the
physical and mental health of the U. S.
public through traditional karate. Serves as
U.S. representative within Pan American
Karate Confederation and International
Traditional Karate Federation.

AMERICAN TAEKWONDO ASSOCIATION
6210 BASELINE RD
P O Box 193010
LITTLE ROCK, AR 72209
501-568-2821
Fax: 501-568-2497
welcome@ataonline.com
www.ataonline.com
• In Ho Lee, Grand Master
Membership Requirements:
Must be student of ATA certified instructor.
Description:
Largest centrally administered martial arts
organization in the world. Administers
teaching of taekwondo. International division
is Songahm Taekwondo Federation,
founded in 1985, under same administration
for ATA instructors residing in other
countries.
Number of Members:
350,000
Publications:
THE WAY Magazine.

GEORGIA TAEKWONDO FOUNDATION
PO BOX 2043
KENNESAW, GA 30156
770-528-3580
Fax: 770-528-3590
gtf@georgiagames.org
www.georgiagames.org
• David Wilch, President
david.wilch@gmail.com
• Jenny Matsuoka, Vice President
jenmat123@aol.com
• Eric Pfeifer, Agent
(770) 528-3580
exdirector@georgiagames.org
Year Founded:
2011
Nature of Services:
The governing body for the sport of
Taekwondo in State of Georgia.

INTERNATIONAL SPORT KARATE ASSOCIATION
333 SW 140TH TERRACE
JONESVILLE, FL 32669
352-331-0260
Fax: 352-331-2119
steve.repsold@iskaworldhq.com
www.iskaworldhq.com
• Cory Schafer, President
• Robert Mason, Commissioner
Description:
Maintains a continued commitment to
training and certifying officials and updating
rules and regulations while recognizing both
worthy champions and world rated
contenders in more than twenty different
types of martial arts and combat sports.

JUDO CANADA
212-1725 STREET LAURENT
OTTAWA, ONTARIO, CANADA K1G 3V4
613-738-1200
Fax: 613-738-1299
info@judocanada.org
www.judocanada.org

- Mike Tamura, President
- Roger Deschamps, Vice President
- Daniel Deangelis, General Secretary
- Allan Sattin, General Treasurer

Number of members:
22,000

Member Services:
Conducts official seminars and examinations; conducts grading; provides coaching seminars. Responsible for National Team Programs, including competitions and training camps. Hosts Senior National, Junior National, Juvenile National Tournaments annually.

Publications:
YUDANSHA JOURNAL, three times annually.

Membership Requirements:
Must be a minimum black belt. Associate members through provincial associations.

Description:
Founded 1956. Serves to produce world-caliber athletes while developing the sport of Judo in Canada.

U.S. JUDO, INC/USA JUDO
3625 NW 82 AV
SUITE 100-D
DORAL, FL 33166
786-332-4338
Fax: 719-866-4733
usjiadmin@aol.com
www.usjudo.org
- Lance Nading, President

U.S. TAEKWONDO UNION
ONE OLYMPIC PLAZA
SUITE 104C
COLORADO SPRINGS, CO 80909
719-632-5551
Fax: 719-866-4642
communications@usoc.org
www.usa-taekwondo.us
- Harris Bruce, CEO
Bruce.Harris@usa-taekwondo.us
- Patrick Wentland, Director of High Performance
patrick.wentland@usa-taekwondo.us
- Steve McNally, Director of Marketing and Communications
steve.mcnally@usa-taekwondo.us
- Gary Urie, Director of Finance
gary.urie@usa-taekwondo.us
- Stacy Miller-Andrews, High Performance Manager
stacy.andrews@usa-taekwondo.us
- Casey Miller, Membership Manager
tickets@usataekwondo.uservoice.com
- Jeanna Mendoza, Director of Events
jeanna.mendoza@usa-taekwondo.us
- Michelle George, Dan Certification Manager
michelle.george@usa-taekwondo.us

Number of members:
40,000

Member Services:
Insurance, school relocation listings, certification Black Belt), developmental camps, merchandising, information dissemination, Junior Olympic Taekwondo program.

Publications:
U.S. TAEKWONDO JOURNAL, quarterly.

Membership Requirements:
$35.00 dues for competitors, $12.00 non-competitors, $75.00 for Club, $500.00 for life and $1,000.00 for corporation.

Description:
Founded 1974. Objectives are the development of Taekwondo in the United States; to include grass roots, Pan Am and Olympic as well as public relations and media.

ULTIMATE FIGHTING CHAMPIONSHIP (UFC)
2960 WEST SAHARA AVENUE
LAS VEGAS, NV 89102
702-221-4780
www.ufc.com
- Lorenzo Fertitta, Chairman & CEO
- Dana White, President
- Marc Ratner, VP Regulatory Affairs
- Joe Silva, VP Talent Relations

Description:
The UFC is the world's largest Mixed Martial Arts (MMA) sports association, formed in 2001 by Zuffa LLC. MMA is a combat sports using interdisciplinary forms of fighting, including jiu-jitsu, judo, karate, boxing, and more.

UNITED STATES OF AMERICA NATIONAL KARATE-DO FEDERATION
1631 MESA AVE
SUITE A1
COLORADO SPRINGS, CO 80906
719-477-6925
Fax: 206-839-4148
natoffice@usankf.org
www.usankf.org
- John DiPasquale, President
- Phil Hampel, CEO
- Jessica Luna, Program Manager
- Brody Burns, Director of Operations and Events

Member Services:
National governing body for karate in the United States.

Membership Requirements:
$50 dues for athletes, $75 for coaches, $100 for club, $1,000 for life.

UNITED STATES SOO BAHK DO FEDERATION
20 MILLBURN AVENUE
SUITE 2
SPRINGFIELD TOWNSHIP, NJ 07081
973-467-3971
888-766-2245
Fax: 973-467-5716
headquarters@soobahkdo.com
www.soobahkdo.com
- Kwan Jang Nim HC Hwang, President
- Phil Hampel, Independent Director
- Tokey Hill, Coach Director
- Alex Miladi, Refree Director
- Clay Morton, Athlete Director
- Keith Wildonger, Board Chairman

Description:
Founded 1945. Sponsors competition and training in a special martial arts program, characterized by strict discipline, high kicks and traditional demonstrations.

USA KARATE FEDERATION
1300 KENMORE BOULEVARD
AKRON, OH 44314
330-753-3114
Fax: 330-753-6888
usakarate@usakarate.us
www.usakarate.us
- Patrick M. Hickey, President
- John Linebarger, Vice President

- Roger Jarrett, General Secretary
- Robert Burns, Esq., Treasurer
- Carol Hofer, Assistant Treasurer
- Brian Pendleton, Executive Director
- David G. Lang, CPA

Publications:
KARATE PROFILES, bimonthly magazine.

Description:
Founded 1981.

WORLD KARATE FEDERATION
GALERIA DE VALLEHERMOSO 4
3RD FLOOR
MADRID, SPAIN 28003
34-91-5359632
Fax: 34-91-5359633
www.wkf.net
- Antonio Espinos, President
- William Millerson, 1st Vice President
- Mike Dinsdale, Treasurer
- George Yerolimpos, General Secretary
secretariat@wkf.net

WORLD TAEKWONDO FEDERATION (WTF)
5TH FL, KOLON BLDG
15 HYOJA-RO, JONGNO-GU
SEOUL, KOREA 110-040
www.worldtaekwondofederation.net
- Chungwon Choue, President
- Jean-Marie Ayer, Secretary General
- Tae Eun Lee, Treasurer
- Phillip Walter Coles, Vice President

Description:
International governing body for the sport of taekwondo.

Motorcycle Organizations

AMERICAN MOTORCYCLIST ASSOCIATION
13515 YARMOUTH DRIVE
PICKERINGTON, OH 43147
614-856-1900
800-262-5646
Fax: 614-856-1920
ama@ama-cycle.org
www.americanmotorcyclist.com
- Maggie McNally, Chair
- Perry King, Vice Chair
- Ken Ford, Assistant Treasurer
- Paul Puma, Executive Committee
- Jeff Skeen, Executive Committee Member

Description:
Founded 1924. Member/service organization providing recreational and competition activities for motorcyclists at the amateur and professional levels. Maintains government relations staff to track state, federal and local legislation pertaining to motorcycling enjoyment. AMA Professional Racing Events are run ten months of the year and include events from coast to coast in three major championship series.

Membership Requirements:
Annual dues of $39, $750 for life membership.

Publications:
AMERICAN MOTORCYCLIST, monthly.

Member Services:
Sanctioning of amateur and professional racing and social events. Tracking legislation, monthly magazine, discounts on insurance, car rentals, etc.

Number of members:
265,000

INTERNATIONAL COUNCIL OF MOTORSPORT SCIENCES
9305 CRESTVIEW DRIVE
DENTON, TX 76207
940-262-3481
Fax: 940-262-3482
www.icmsmotorsportsafety.org
• Tom Weisenbach, Executive Director
Year Founded:
1988
Membership Requirements:
Includes physicians, psychologists, physiologists, race drivers and paramedic personnel.
Description:
An association of medical professionals, scientific, allied health and other interested persons with the improvement in performance and safety in motorsport.

MOTORCYCLE SAFETY FOUNDATION
2 JENNER STREET
SUITE 150
IRVINE, CA 92618-3806
949-727-3227
800-446-9227
Fax: 949-727-4217
msf@msf-usa.org
www.msf-usa.org
• Time Buche, President and CEO
• Robert Gladden, Vice President
Publications:
Catalog of publications available.
Membership Requirements:
Must be motorcycle manufacturer.
Description:
Founded 1973. The Motorcycle Safety Foundation is the internationally recognized developer of the comprehensive, research-based, Rider Education and Training System (MSF RETS). RETS curricula promotes lifelong-learning for motorcyclists and continuous professional development for certified RiderCoaches and other trainers. MSF also actively participates in government relations, safety research, public awareness campaigns and the provision of technical assistance to state training and licensing programs.

MOTORCYCLISTE, FEDERATION INTERNATIONALE
11, ROUTE DE SUISSE
MIES, SWITZERLAN CH-1295
41-0-22-950-95-00
Fax: 41-0-22-950-95-01
www.fim-live.com
• Vito Ippolito, President
• Nasser Khalilfa, Deputy President
• Juan Moreta, First Vice President
Description:
International governing body for the sport of motorcycling.

RACING ENTERPRISES MOTOCROSS
13223 BLACK MOUNTAIN ROAD
SUITE 1-176
SAN DIEGO, CA 92129
951-200-0699
Fax: 858-484-7056
remsatmx@gmail.com
www.remsatmx.com

WERA MOTORCYCLE ROADRACING
2555 MARIETTA HWY #104
Suite 104
CANTON, GA 30114
770-720-5010
Fax: 770-720-5015
wera@wera.com
www.wera.com
• Evelyne Clarke, President
Member Services:
Sanctions, promotes and oversees motorcycle; road racing in Amateur and Pro Levels across the U.S.
Membership Requirements:
Must have race school or previous raodracing experience. $100 race license good for one year.
Number of members:
2,850
Publications:
FASTLINE NEWSLETTER and yearly rulebook.

WOMEN ON WHEELS MOTORCYCLE ASSOCIATION
PO BOX 83076
LINCOLN, NE 68501
402-477-1280
800-322-1969
Fax: 360-653-1855
WowOffice@womenonwheels.org
www.womenonwheels.org
• Deana Foster, President
Member Services:
Sponsors annual international rally.
Publications:
WOMEN ON WHEELS, bimonthly magazine.
Membership Requirements:
$30 for one year membership.
Description:
Organization for female motorcycle enthusiasts.

Mountainboard Organizations

MBS MOUNTAINBOARDS
212 Sutton Lane
COLORADO SPRINGS, CO 80907
719-884-1000
877-627-4100
Fax: 719-884-1003
customerservice@mbs.com
www.mbs.com
• Jason Lee, Founder
• Patrick McConnell, Founder
Year Founded:
1992

Netball Organizations

NETBALL ASSOCIATIONS, INTERNATIONAL FEDERATION OF
19 Albion Street
ALBION WHARF
MANCHESTER, ENGLAND M1 5LN
441-(0) 161-234-6515
www.netball.org
• Sue Taylor, VP
• Ann Tod, Finance Director
• Realene Castle, Director
• Sarah Pickford, Global Development

Manager
• Maggie Ross, Administration Manager
• Molly Rhone, President
• Urvasi Naidoo, CEO
Description:
International governing body for the sport of netball.

Orienteering Organizations

CANADIAN ORIENTEERING FEDERATION
1239 COLGROVE AVENUE NE
CALGARY, ALBERTA, CANADA T2E 5C3
403-283-0807
Fax: 403-451-1681
info@orienteering.ca
www.orienteering.ca
• Anne Teutsch, President

ORIENTEERING FEDERATION, INTERNATIONAL
DROTTNINGGATAN 47 31 1/2 TR
KARLSTAD, SWEDEN SE-65225
840-558-1817
Fax: 893-481-3113
iof@orienteering.org
www.orienteering.org
• Tom Hollowell, Secretary General/CEO
tomhollowell@orienteering.org

ORIENTEERING USA
824 SCOTIA ROAD
PHILADELPHIA, PA 19128
215-482-9479
contact@orienteeringusa.org
orienteeringusa.org
• Clare Durand, President
(215) 482-9479
contact@orienteeringusa.org

Pentathlon Organizations

UNION INTERNATIONALE DE PENTATHLON MODERNE (UIPM)
STADE LOUIS II, ENTREE E
13 AV. DES CASTELANS
MONTE CARLO, 98000
377-9777 8555
Fax: 377-9777 8550
uipm@pentathlon.org
www.uipmworld.org
• Shiny Fang, Secretary-General

USA PENTATHLON
1 OLYMPIC PLAZA
COLORADO SPRINGS, CO 80909
www.teamusa.org/USA-Modern-Pentathlon
• Rob Stull, Managing Director
robstull@aol.com

Petanque Organizations

FEDERATION OF PETANQUE USA
PO BOX 34
COPALIS BEACH, WA 98535
253-237-4735
secretary@usapetanque.org
usapetanque.org
• Frank Pipal, President
(707) 833-2020

president@usapetanque.org
• Christine Cragg, Vice President
(415) 302-5069
vicepresident@usapetanque.org
• Joe Martin, Treasurer
treasurer@usapetanque.org
• Dan Feaster, Secretary
(253) 237-4735
secretary@usapetanque.org
• Gilles Canesse, National Sport Director
(941) 724-1845
nsd@usapetanque.org
Member Services:
Communications, participation in
international, national and
FPUSA-sanctioned competitions.
Publications:
Newsletter, quarterly.
Membership Requirements:
Club membership - active operation as local
petanque club with minimum of 10
members; Individual - subscribe to purposes
and objectives of FPUSA, payment of dues,
member of club or independent (if too
distant).
Description:
Founded 1974. Purpose is to build a body of
federation-affiliated clubs and individuals
dedicated to spreading, practicing and
enjoying Petanque, a world wide outdoor
bowling game of modern French derivation
via ancient Greece and Rome. Primary
objective is to foster local, regional and
national competitions, as well as U.S.
participation in international tournaments
and championships.

Platform Tennis Organizations

**AMERICAN PLATFORM TENNIS
ASSOCIATION**
109 WESPORT DRIVE
PITTSBURGH, PA 15238
888-744-9490
apta@platformtennis.org
www.platformtennis.org
• Ann Sheedy, Executive Director
ann.sheedy@platformtennis.org
• Scott Bondurant, President
bondo59@gmail.com
• Bill O'Brien, Vice-President
bill.obrien@att.net
Member Services:
Information bureau, providing
information/assistance to the media.
Publications:
PLATFORM TENNIS NEWS, Newsletter;
PTN UPDATE, three times annually; Rules
Book; Sportsmanship Pamphlet; HOW TO
CONDUCT A TOURNAMENT DRAW.
Membership Requirements:
Annual dues - eight categories of
membership.
Description:
Founded 1934. Provides information and
publications about the game. Coordinates
the scheduling of tournaments and assures
uniformity in specifications of courts and
equipment and establishes official rules.
Serves as non-profit organization chartered
to promote the orderly growth of the game.

Polo Organizations

U.S. POLO ASSOCIATION
9011 LAKE WORTH ROAD
LAKE WORTH, FL 33467
800-232-8772
uspa@uspolo.org
www.uspolo.org
• Duncan Huyler, Chief Executive Officer
dhuyler@uspolo.org
• Susan Present, Chief Financial Officer
spresent@uspolo.org
• Kris Bowman, Executive Director
kbowman@uspolo.org
• Justin Powers, Director of Club
Development
jpowers@uspolo.org
Number of members:
3,488
Member Services:
USPA Yearbook with name listing and
handicap, access to movies of techniques of
polo and on various games; identification
stickers and opportunity to play in all USPA
tournaments within given handicap.
Publications:
Polo Players' Edition
Membership Requirements:
Club - must have regulation field; and
accommodations for horses and tack. Must
have three registered USPA-playing
members as members of the club. $200 per
year. Player - must belong to a registered
USPA club and must follow rules and
regulations stated by USPA. $135 per year.
Description:
Founded 1890. Serves as regulatory body of
polo events played in the U.S. and Canada.
Overseas tournaments, assigns handicaps,
promotes intercollegiate and interscholastic
polo. The Polo Training Foundation,
conducts polo schools across the country.

Racquetball Organizations

**INTERNATIONAL RACQUETBALL
FEDERATION (IRF)**
1631 MESA AVENUE
COLORADO SPRINGS, CO 80906
719-433-2017
lstonge@internationalracquetball.com
www.internationalracquetball.com
• Osvaldo Maggi, President
• Marcelo Gomez, Executive Vice President
• Carlos Ruiz, Treasurer
• Cheryl Kirk, Secretary
Description:
Founded 1979 as the International Amateur
Racquetball Federation. International
governing body for the sport of racquetball,
recognized by the IOC.

**LADIES PROFESSIONAL RACQUETBALL
TOUR**
GEARBOX SPORTS
9375 CUSTOMHOUSE PLAZA
SUITE J
SAN DIEGO, CA 92154
877-443-2726
Fax: 619-474-8523
www.lprtour.com
• TJ Baumbaugh, President
tj@lprtour.com
Description:
The LPRT is a governing body representing

top-tier professional women from the
Americas and elsewhere.

USA RACQUETBALL
2812 W COLORADO AVENUE
Suite 200
COLORADO SPRINGS, CO 80904-2906
719-635-5396
Fax: 719-635-0685
www.teamusa.org/usa-racquetball
• Jason Thoerner, Executive Director
(719) 635-5396
jthoerner@usaracquetball.com
• Nick Irvine, Programming Manager
(209) 817-9984
nirvine@usaracquetball.com
• Renee Gundolff, Membership Manager
(719) 635-5396
rgundolff@usaracquetball.com
Member Services:
Sanctions 1,300 events annually, hosts 30+
regional and five national championships
annually, supports adult and junior U.S.
National Racquetball teams.
Publications:
RACQUETBALL, bimonthly; USRA
Rulebook, Media Guide/Tournament
Program, Program Brochures, released
annually.
Membership Requirements:
$30 annual fee for competitive license, plus
club recreational program membership
available.
Description:
Founded 1968 as International Racquetball
Association. National governing body for the
sport of racquetball. Promotes sport of
racquetball for the amateur, grass roots
player.
Online Magazine:
www.racqmag.com

Ringette Organizations

RINGETTE CANADA
5510 CANOTEK ROAD
SUITE 201
OTTAWA, ON, CANADA K1J 9J4
613-748-5655
Fax: 613-748-5860
ringette@ringette.ca
www.ringette.ca
• Daniel Dussault, President
• Natasha Johnston, Executive Director
(613) 748-5655
natasha@ringette.ca
Description:
Founded 1975. Non-profit, volunteer-based
organization. Promotes, develops and
administrates the sport of Ringette in
Canada. Team sport played on ice, using
straight stick and rubber ring, and using ice
skates. Develops and operates annual
Canadian Ringette Championships
Membership Requirements:
Members are provincial or territorial Ringette
associations.
Publications:
Official rules (English/French), National
Officials Certification Program, Managers
Certification Program, National Coaching
Certification Program, brochures, posters,
gym ringette and various others.
Member Services:
Bilingual publications; audio-visuals:
equipment; promotional videos; goaltending

video.
Number of members:
27,000

Rodeo Organizations

INTERNATIONAL PROFESSIONAL RODEO ASSOCIATION (IPRA)
405-235-6540
Fax: 405-235-6577
www.ipra-rodeo.com
• Dale Yerigan, General Manager
(405) 235-6540
dale@iprarodeo.com
Number of members:
4,000
Description:
1999 International Rodeo Finals Jan 14-16.
Membership Requirements:
Must purchase membership and uphold rules and regulations of association. Publications: PRO RODEO WORLD, monthly.
Description:
Founded 1957. Promotes rodeo as a sport and profession.
Publications:
Pro Rodeo World monthly magazine

NATIONAL HIGH SCHOOL RODEO ASSOCIATION (NHSRA)
12011 TEJON STREET
SUITE 900
DENVER, CO 80234
303-452-0820
Fax: 303-452-0912
www.nhsra.org
• James Higginbotham, Executive Director
Nature of Service:
Annually holds worlds largest rodeo, competitions for national championships, team championships and scholarships.
Year Founded:
1949
Member Services:
College scholarship assistance, crisis fund, knowledge bowl, talent and art contests, safety clinics and training, sports medicine program, insurance.
Membership Requirements:
Grades 9 through 12. Meet minimum grade point average and meet conduct requirements.
Number of members:
13,038
Publications:
NHSRA TIMES, monthly magazine. NHSFR Souviner Program -annual rodeo program.

NATIONAL INTERCOLLEGIATE RODEO ASSOCIATION (NIRA)
2033 WALLA WALLA AVE
WALLA WALLA, WA 99362
509-529-4402
Fax: 509-525-1090
info@collegerodeo.com
www.collegerodeo.com
• Roger Walters, Commissioner
rogerwalters@collegerodeo.com
• Sarah Neely, Director of Public Relations & Administration
sarah@collegerodeo.com
• Claudia Kelly, Membership Director
claudia@collegerodeo.com
• Samantha Vandenberg, National Rodeo

Secretary
samantha@collegerodeo.com
Description:
Founded 1949. Preserves the western heritage through the sport of college rodeo. Education is primary goal.
Membership Requirements:
Eligible according to educational standards.
Number of members:
3,500

NATIONAL LITTLE BRITCHES RODEO ASSOCIATION
5050 EDISON AVE
SUITE 105
COLORADO SPRINGS, CO 80915
719-389-0333
800-763-3694
Fax: 719-578-1367
info@nlbra.com
www.nlbra.com
• Jodi Stoddard, President
(605) 685-8003
jodistoddard7@gmail.com
• Scott Honeycutt, Vice President
(719) 588-7911
slhtophand@gmail.com
Nature of Service:
Promotes and organizes youth rodeo in the U.S.
Year Founded:
1952
Membership Requirements:
Pay dues of $75 per year - open to all ages 5-18.
Number of members:
5,000
Publications:
Monthly newspaper, NLBRA NEWS, distributed to membership and associates.

PROFESSIONAL BULL RIDERS (PBR)
101 W Riverwalk
Pueblo, CO 81003
719-242-2800
Fax: 719-242-2855
admin@pbr.com
www.pbr.com
• Jim Haworth, Chairman
• Sean Gleason, Chief Executive Officer
Sports Service Founded:
1992
Nature of Sports Service:
Organization was founded by 20 accomplished bull riders who joined together to make bull riding the most popular event in traditional rodeo. Since that time, the PBR, unlike any other rodeo or bull riding organization in North America, has been owned and operated by its athletes. Today more than 700 bull riders from the U. S., Canada, Brazil and Australia hold PBR memberships.

PROFESSIONAL RODEO COWBOYS ASSOCIATION (PRCA)
101 PRO RODEO DR
COLORADO SPRINGS, CO 80919
719-593-8840
Fax: 719-548-4876
prorodeo@prorodeo.com
www.prorodeo.org
• Karl Stressman, Commissioner
Publications:
ProRodeo Sports News; bi-weekly, PRCA Media Guide; annually, PRORODEO Souvenir Program distributed at more than

350 rodeo annually.
Membership Requirements:
Must win 1,000 on a PRCA permit allowing individual to gain full membership status. Annual dues: $350.
Description:
Founded 1975. Previously Cowboy Turtle Assn, (1936-1944); Rodeo Cowboys Assn (1945-1974). Serves the professional rodeo industry of the USA for their mutual protection and benefit. Approves and sanctions over 700 rodeos annually. Solicits and services sponsorships in rodeo.
Frequency:
Biweekly.
Number of Pages:
48-80
Price:
$2,540.00

Roller Skating Organizations

FEDERATION INTERNATIONALE ROLLER SPORTS (FIRS)
AV DE RHODANIE, 54
LAUSANNE, 1007
info@rollersports.org
www.rollersports.org
• Sabatino Aracu, President

ROLLER SKATING ASSOCIATION INTERNATIONAL
6905 CORPORATE DR
INDIANAPOLIS, IN 46278
317-347-2626
Fax: 317-347-2636
rsa@rollerskating.com
www.rollerskating.com
• Jim McMahon, Executive Director
Description:
Founded 1937. Non-Profit Trade association for rink operators and coaches.
Membership Requirements:
Must be roller skating rink operator.
Publications:
RSA TODAY COACHES' EDITION monthly newsletter, RSA TODAY biweekly newsletter, ROLLER SKATING BUSINESS bimonthly magazine, RSM NEWS, bimonthly newsletter.
Number of members:
1,000 rinks; 1,000 coaches; 1,000 judges.
Publications:
Roller Skating Business Magazine; RSA Today Newsletter

USA ROLLER SPORTS
4730 SOUTH STREET
LINCOLN, NE 68506
402-483-7551
Fax: 402-483-1465
www.teamusa.org/USA-Roller-Sports
• Richard Hawkins, Executive Director

Rowing/Crew Organizations

DAD VAIL REGATTA
SCHUYLKILL RIVER
2200 KELLY DRIVE
PHILADELPHIA, PA 19130

610-246-5902
levins51@verizon.net
dadvail.org
• Ed Levin, Publicity Director
(610) 246-5902
• John R Galloway, Chairman
Description:
Largest collegiate regatta in the United
States.

EASTERN ASSOCIATION OF ROWING COLLEGES
www.ecac.org
• Phil Buttafuoco, Commissioner
• Mark Corino, President elect, 1st VP
• Mark Griffin, 2nd VP
• Mike Hardisky, Treasurer
• Gene Doris, President
Description:
Eighteen colleges and universities with
men's rowing crews, mostly in the Northeast
and Mid-Atlantic states, affiliated with the
Eastern College Athletic Conference.

NATIONAL ROWING FOUNDATION
67 MYSTIC RD
N STONINGTON, CT 06359
860-535-0634
Fax: 860-535-0637
info@natrowing.org
natrowing.org
• Charles B Hamlin, Executive Director
(203) 434-5180
charlie@natrowing.org
Description:
Supports athletes who pursue excellence in
the sport of rowing with the primary goal of
promoting the United States' participation in
international rowing competition, provide for
the preservation of rowing history and
manage the Rowing Hall of Fame.

PITTSBURGH THREE RIVERS REGATTA
PITTSBURGH, PA
Description:
Founded 1977. Major inland regatta in the
U.S. Event includes powerboat races, drag
boat races, national concert series,
children's village, hot air balloon races, air
shows, laser shows, fireworks show,
champion lumberjack shows, 5 mile run and
walk, rubber ducky race, senior citizen's
day, night-lighted boat parade and many
other events.

SCHOLASTIC ROWING ASSOCIATION OF AMERICA
contact@sraa.net
www.sraa.net
Member Services:
Annual regatta for boys' and girls' crews
from throughout the world.
Membership Requirements:
Payment of dues.
Description:
Founded 1935. Promotes the advancement
of rowing.

USROWING
2 Wall Street
PRINCETON, NJ 08540
609-751-0700
800-314-4769
Fax: 609-924-1578
members@usrowing.org
www.usrowing.org

• Glenn Merry, Chief Executive Officer
(609) 751-0701
glenn@usrowing.org
• Brian Klausner, Chief Financial Officer
(609) 751-0702
brian@usrowing.org
• Beth Kohl, Chief Marketing Officer
(203) 761-8643
beth@usrowing.org
• Brett Johnson, Director of Operations
(609) 751-0707
brett@usrowing.org
Nature of Service:
USRowing is a nonprofit membership
organization recognized by the United
States Olympic Committee as the national
governing body for the sport of rowing in the
United States. USRowing selects, trains and
manages the teams that represent the U.S.
in international competition including the
world championships, Pam American
Games and Olympics. USRowing serves
and promotes the sport on all levels of
competition. USRowing membership reflects
the spectrum of American rowers - juniors,
collegians, masters and those who row for
recreation, competition of fitness.
Year Founded:
Founded in 1872 as the National
Association of Amateur Oarsmen.
Membership:
$65/year (27 and over); $45/year (26 and
under); $75/year (international)
Number of members:
1,050 organizations; 14,000 individuals

WORLD ROWING FEDERATION
MAISON DU SPORT INTERNATIONAL
AV. DE RHODANIE 54
LAUSANNE, 1007
info@fisa.org
www.worldrowing.com
• Matt Smith, Executive Director
matt.smith@fisa.org

Rugby Organizations

CAPE FEAR RUGBY FOOTBALL CLUB
fearrugby.com
• Nate Nemec, President
nrnemec@gmail.com
• Drew Gonzalez, Vice President
drew.gonzalez10@yahoo.com
• Harrison Hargett, Treasurer
hargetth@ymail.com
Publications:
PROGRAM, annual; Newsletter, quarterly.
Membership Requirements:
Entry fee; past successful participation;
member in good standing of U.S. Rugby
Football Union and its affiliates.
Description:
Founded 1975. Fosters growth of amateur
Rugby Union Football by hosting a major
seven-a-side international tournament.

MIDWEST RUGBY FOOTBALL UNION
www.midwestrugbyunion.org
• Jeremiah Johnson, President
jeremiahkjohnson@yahoo.com
• Adrian Gannon, Vice President -
Competitions
rugbyteacher@sbcglobal.net
• Tom Rooney, Vice President - Collegiate &
Youth

tomrooney@aol.com
• Stefan Palches, Secretary
spalches@gmail.com
• Tim Harn, Treasurer
tharn71@yahoo.com
Member Services:
Films, coaching clinics.
Publications:
IN TOUCH, eight times annually.
Membership Requirements:
Clubs that have full playing schedules and
have been in existence for at least one year.
Description:
Founded 1964. Organizes and coordinates
the activities of its member clubs.

USA RUGBY
2655 CRESCENT DR
UNIT A
LAFAYETTE, CO 80026
303-539-0300
Fax: 303-539-0311
www.usarugby.org
• Dan Payne, Chief Executive Officer
dpayne@usarugby.org
• Jen Gray, Director of Operations
jgray@usarugby.org
Description:
Founded 1975. Promotes the development
and expansion of Rugby Union football in
the U.S. Improves standards of play,
coaching and refereeing. Encourages
international competition.
Membership Requirements:
Regional associations within the continental
U.S. that have local associations as
members.
Publications:
Magazine - to full membership
Member Services:
Address lists; coaching and refereeing
clinics; annual meeting - held 2nd weekend
in November; International Games, World
Cup Competition; local, regional, national
sponsorships. Car rental discounts and
Master Card discounts.
Number of Members:
50,000

WESTERN RUGBY FOOTBALL UNION
1409 E. MEADOW LANE
KIRKSVILLE, MO 63501
660-665-6505
www.wrfu.org
• William Sexton, President
(660) 665-6505
• Alan Sharpley, Vice President
(512) 288-3384
• David McPhail, Treasurer
Number of members:
5,500
Member Services:
Coordinates business of WRFU; oversees
operation of championships and all-star
teams; provides communications link with
USARFU and other Unions; represents
WRFU constituency to USARFU.
Publications:
Announcements; periodic newsletters.
Membership Requirements:
Composed of rugby organizations. Limited
to those local area rugby football unions
within jurisdiction of the Union.
Description:
Founded 1975. Coordinates the activities of
seven local area rugby unions throughout
the south central U.S.

WESTERN SUBURBS RUGBY FOOTBALL CLUB
P.O BOX 441
FAIRFAX, VA 22038
www.rugbyfootball.com
• Patrick Robinson, President
• Ben Allen, Vice President
• Danta Moore, Match Secretary
• Mark Bevilacqua, Director of Youth Rugby
• Jeff Carrington, Head Coach
• Erich Weiss, Treasurer
• Jorge Arias, Secretary
Description:
Div II team in the PRU.

WORLD RUGBY
WORLD RUGBY HOUSE
8-10 PEMBROKE STREET LOWER
Dublin, D2
info@worldrugby.org
www.worldrugby.org
• Brett Gosper, Chief Executive Officer
Description:
International governing body of rugby union.
Formerly International Rugby Board (IRB).
Year Founded:
1886

Running Organizations

AMERICAN RUNNING ASSOCIATION
4405 EAST-WEST HWY
SUITE 405
BETHESDA, MD 20814
800-776-2732
Fax: 301-913-9520
• Dave Watt, Executive Director
• Barbara Baldwin, Projects Consultant
Year Founded:
1968
Description:
The American Running Association (ARA) is a nonprofit membership and advocacy organization committed to increasing the physical activity levels of all Americans from youths to adults through vigorous walking and running. ARA has a division or sister association, the American Medical Athletic Association (AMAA) that is comprised of physicians and other health professionals who provide information and overnight a for endurance sports events and the public.
Number of Members:
10,000
Publications:
AMAA Journal; e-Running & Fitness and the American Medical Athletic Association Journal.

AMERICAN TRAIL RUNNING ASSOCIATION
PO BOX 9454
COLORADO SPRINGS, CO 80932
719-573-4133
Fax: 719-573-4408
nancyhobbs@trailrunner.com
www.trailrunner.com
• Adam Chase, President
• Nancy Hobbs, Executive Director
Description:
Founded in 1996, ATRA's mission is to promote trail running, mountain running, ultrarunning on trails, and to provide resources for race directors and participants in the sport.

Publications:
TRAIL TIMES (quarterly); monthly e-newsletter; monthly race director e-newsletter
Membership Requirements:
$25 annual dues for individual membership; $50 for race/club membership.

ASSOCIATION OF INTERNATIONAL MARATHONS AND DISTANCE RACES
OLYMPIC ATHLETIC CENTER OF ATHENS
SPYROS LOUIS AVE
MAROUSI
ATHENS, 15123
aimshq@aims-worldrunning.org
www.aims-worldrunning.org
• Paco Borao, President
borao@correcaminos.org
• Morales Martha, Vice President
maratontangamanga@gmail.com
• Dave Cundy, Vice President
cundysm@ozemail.com.au
Year Founded:
1982

BIG SUR INTERNATIONAL MARATHON
3618 THE BARNYARD
CARMEL, CA 93923
831-625-6226
Fax: 831-625-2119
info@bsim.org
www.bsim.org

BOSTON ATHLETIC ASSOCIATION
185 DARTMOUTH STREET
6TH FLOOR
BOSTON, MA 02116
617-236-1652
Fax: 617-236-4505
info@baa.org
www.baa.org
• Joann E Flaminio, President
• Thomas S Grilk, Chief Executive Officer
• David McGillivray, Race Director
Description:
Founded 1887. Owns and organizes Boston Marathon.

COLUMBUS MARATHON
c/o THE ATHLETIC CLUB OF COLUMBUS
136 E BROAD STREET
COLUMBUS, OH 43215
614-421-7866
Fax: 614-263-3518
info@columbusmarathon.com
www.columbusmarathon.com
• Darris Blackford, Race Director
Description:
Founded 1980. Organizes the tenth largest marathon in the U.S., in Columbus Ohio, with 5,000 runners.

GASPARILLA DISTANCE CLASSIC
215 Verne St
Suite C
TAMPA, FL 33606
813-254-7866
Fax: 813-254-9307
information@tampabayrun.com
www.tampabayrun.com
Description:
Founded 1978. Not-for-profit association sponsoring the annual I5K and 5K races with a wheelchair division. Purpose is to raise funds for local youth charities.

LOS ANGELES MARATHON
871 FIGUEROA TERRACE
LOS ANGELES, CA 90012
213-542-3000
Fax: 213-542-3020
info@goconqur.com
www.lamarathon.com
Description:
6-month training program of the Honda LA Marathon.

NEW YORK ROAD RUNNERS
156 W 56TH STREET
3RD FLOOR
NEW YORK, NY 10019
www.nyrr.org
• Michael Capiraso, President & CEO
• Peter Ciaccia, Race Director
Description:
NYRR is dedicated to promoting the sport of distance running, enhancing health and fitness for all, and responding to community needs. The road races and other fitness programs draw upwards of 300,000 runners annually, and together with the magazine and web site, support and promote professional and recreational running.

ROAD RUNNERS CLUB OF AMERICA
1501 LEE HWY
SUITE 140
ARLINGTON, VA 22209
703-525-3890
office@rrca.org
www.rrca.org
• Mitchell Garner, President
president@rrca.org
• Jean Arthur, Vice President
vicepresident@rrca.org
• Jean Knaack, Executive Director
execdir@rrca.org
Description:
The RRCA is dedicated to supporting the growth of grassroots running clubs, training programs, and running events while promoting the common interests of runners throughout the United States.
Services:
The RRCA oofers a variety of service designed to support and promote the efforts of local running clubs and events. Through their services, RRCA provides a proven national infrastructure for the development of running clubs, training programs, and events.
Programs:
The RRCA strives to provide quality programming that can be replicated throughout the country by member clubs from small towns to large cities. The programs promote and support running and runners at all stages in life.
Membership:
The RRCA is the oldest and largest organization in the US dedicated to distance running. With over 1000 member clubs and events representing over 200,000 running club members, why run with anyone else?

SACRAMENTO RUNNING ASSOCIATION
4181 POWER INN RD
SUITE A
Saramento, CA 95826
916-737-2627
Fax: 916-737-7684
info@runsra.org
runsra.org

• Scott Abbott, Executive Director
Mission:
Since the SRA Board believes strongly in the myriad of health benefits gained from running, the SRA's expanded mission is to find ways to encourage people of all ages and abilities to run.
Events:
California International Marathon; Super Bowl Sunday 10K Run; Sactown 10-Miler; Lake Natoma Four Bridges Half Marathon; Youth Fitness Programs

Sailing Organizations

SAIL AMERICA
50 WATER ST
WARREN, RI 02885
401-289-2540
Fax: 401-247-0074
www.sailamerica.com
• Katie Kelly, Association Manager
kkelly@sailamerica.com
Sports Service Founded:
1988
Event Management Services:
Nonprofit organization, promoting SAIL EXPO & Strictly Sail, sailboat shows.

US SAILING
15 MARITIME DRIVE
PORTSMOUTH, RI 02871
401-683-0800
800-877-2451
Fax: 401-683-0840
info@ussailing.org
www.ussailing.org
• Jack Gierhart, Chief Executive Officer
  ext 631
Number of members:
30,000+
Publications:
AMERICAN SAILOR, monthly.
Membership Requirements:
Open to interested individuals, clubs, sailing associations, corporations.
Description:
Founded in 1897 as the North American Yacht Racing Union. The National Governing Body for the sport of sailing, the mission is to provide leadership for the sport of sailing in the United States and works to achieve this mission through a wide range of programs and events, geared towards providing an equal level playing field for all sailors.

Scuba Organizations

PROFESSIONAL ASSOCIATION OF DIVING INSTRUCTORS (PADI)
30151 TOMAS
RANCHO SANTA MARGARITA, CA 92688
949-858-7234
800-729-7234
Fax: 949-267-1267
customerservice@padi.com
www.padi.com
• Drew Richardson, President & CEO
Number of members:
35,000
Member Services:
PAD - Professional Association of Diving Instructors - as the largest diver certification

organization in the world, with offices in seven countries, accommodates scuba diving needs world-wide. Visit http://www.padi.com/english/common/cours es/pro/ for professional membership. Individual member and professional member levels available. Dive Centers are members of the International Retailers and Resort Association which provides product, training, and business support through all facets of the dive industry business.
Publications:
THE UNDERSEA JOURNAL, quarterly.
DIVE TRAVELER; Dive Travel Directory, semi-annually.
Membership Requirements:
Retail stores, diving resorts; Individuals - must become a PADI Divemaster or PADI instructor at a sanctioned training course. Individual, professional, retail and resort memberships.
Description:
Founded 1966. Serves to promote safe scuba diving as a recreational activity worldwide.

SCUBA SCHOOLS INTERNATIONAL (SSI)
902 CLINT MOORE RD
SUITE 210
BOCA RATON, FL 33487
800-821-4319
usa@divessi.com
www.divessi.com
Member Services:
Education and business support for SSI dealers and instructors.
Publications:
DIVE BUSINESS INTERNATIONAL, bimonthly.
Description:
Founded 1970. Professional SCUBA diving certification agency.

Shooting/Hunting Organizations

AMATEUR TRAPSHOOTING ASSOCIATION
1105 EAST BROADWAY
SPARTA, IL 62286
618-449-2224
Fax: 866-454-5198
info@shootata.com
www.shootata.com
• John Burke, President
jtburke@bbcwb.net
• Lynn Gipson, Executive Director
lgipson@shootata.com
Number of members:
102,686
Member Services:
Retains shooting records, classifies and handicaps shooters according to their ability, hosts regional national championships, governs the rules promotes National Trapshooting Day, conducts youth programs, consults shooting facilities and gun clubs.
Publications:
TRAP & FIELD Magazine, monthly.
Membership Requirements:
$18 for annual and $500 for life memberships.
Description:
Founded: 1900. Serves as the governing

body for the sport of American-style trapshooting. The ATA's mission is to promote and govern the sport throughout the world. The ATA provides trophies, financial Assistance and event management support to the state and provincial associations. The ATA hosts the Grand American World Trap Championships in Vandalia, OH with nearly 6,000 competitors annually.

INTERNATIONAL HANDGUN METALLIC SILHOUETTE ASSOCIATION
3061 SAND HILL RD
BISMARCK, ND 58503
801-733-8423
Fax: 801-733-8424
ihmsaheadquarters@gmail.com
www.ihmsa.org
• Steve Martens, President
smartensj@charter.net
• Bruce Barrett, Vice-President
bruce0162@att.net
Nature of Service:
Sanctioning body for all handgun silhouette matches held throughout the America and the rest of the world. IHMSA rules provide for four categories of competition: production single-shot guns, production revolvers and Unlimited guns, all shot freestyle. The fourth category is for production guns in the standing position. Targets include metallic chickens, pigs, turkeys and rams.
Year Founded:
1975
Member Services:
Rule book, patch, set of scale templates for making full size official silhouette targets.
Number of members:
2,500
Publications:
THE IHMSA NEWS, 10/year

INTERNATIONAL SHOOTING SPORT FEDERATION (ISSF)
BAVARIARING 21
MUNICH, 80336
munich@issf-sports.org
www.issf-sports.org
• Olegario Vazquez Rana, President

NATIONAL RIFLE ASSOCIATION OF AMERICA
11250 WAPLES MILL RD
FAIRFAX, VA 22030
800-672-3888
www.nra.org
• Wayne LaPierre Jr, Executive Vice President
Number of members:
2.6 million.
Member Services:
Hunter safety courses, gun safety and training courses for home and self-defense, law enforcement training, lobbying activities on behalf of its membership regarding gun and gun-related issues, clubs and association activities and range development services. Also serves as governing body for all sanctioned competition in the United States. Endowment, Patron and Benefactor members are also recognized at NRA events, able to vote in NRA elections, and receive certified credentials fit for framing.
Membership Requirements:

$35 for 1 year, $60 for 2 years, $85 for 3 years, $125 for 5 years, $1000 for life membership, $1000 EPL (easy pay for life = 40 $25 payments); JUNIOR MEMBERSHIPS, Dues and Requirements-Age 15+: $15 1 year Junior, $550 Junior Life, $550 EPL Junior Life (22 payments of $25); DISTINGUISHED MEMBERSHIPS, Dues and Requirements-Age 65+ or Disabled Veteran: $30 1 year Distinguished, $375 Distinguished life, $375 EPL Ditinguished life (15 payments of $25); $10 1 year Magazine subscription. CONTRIBUTORY LIFE MEMBERSHIPS (Available to Fully Paid Life Members) Endowment Member $2000, Patron Member $3500, Benefactor $5000

Publications:
AMERICAN HUNTER, monthly; AMERICAN RIFLEMAN, monthly; SHOOTING SPORTS USA and SHOOTING ILLUSTRATED; INSIGHTS, written for junior members; AMERICA's 1st FREEDOM, monthly.

Description:
Founded 1871. Primary purpose is to protect and defend the Second Amendment rights of all law-abiding citizens, to promote proper gun safety and training, to foster and promote the shooting sports, to promote hunter safety and to promote and defend hunting as a shooting sport and as a viable and necessary method of fostering the conservation of our wildlife resources.

NATIONAL SHOOTING SPORTS FOUNDATION
FLINTLOCK RIDGE OFFICE CENTER
11 MILE HILL RD
NEWTOWN, CT 06470
203-426-1320
Fax: 203-426-1087
info@nssf.org
www.nssf.org
• Robert L Scott, Chairman

Description:
Founded 1961. NSSF is the trade association for firearms and ammunition industries, chartered to promote a better understanding of and a more active participation in the shooting sports. Conducts shooting-sport related special events and programs; SHOT Show.

Number of members:
5,600

Publicatios:
Range Report

NATIONAL SKEET SHOOTING ASSOCIATION (NSSA)
5931 ROFT RD
SAN ANTONIO, TX 78253
210-688-3371
800-877-5338
Fax: 210-688-3014
nssa-nsca.org
• Michael Hampton, Jr, Executive Director
(210) 688-3371
mhampton@nssa-nsca.com
• Gary Burley, NSSA Director
(210) 688-3371
gburley@nssa-nsca.com

Member Services:
Reports tournament winners in Skeet Shooting Review and records all scores shot by members for permanent record.

Number of Members:
20,000

Membership Requirements:
Interest in Skeet Shooting and payment of dues.

Description:
Founded 1946. Promotes and advances the interest, welfare and development of skeet shooting and related sports.

Publications:
NSSA SKEET SHOOTING REVIEW MAGAZINE, monthly. NSSA RECORDS ANNUAL.

NATIONAL SPORTING CLAYS ASSOCIATION (NSCA)
5931 ROFT RD
SAN ANTONIO, TX 78253
210-688-3371
800-877-5338
Fax: 210-688-3014
nssa-nsca.org
• Michael Hampton, Jr, Executive Director
(210) 688-3371
mhampton@nssa-nsca.com
• Brett Moyes, NSCA Director
(210) 688-3371
bmoyes@nssa-nsca.com

Member Services:
Subscription to SPORTING CLAYS magazine; national championships, tournaments, state and zone shoots; records of registered shoots; instructor certification courses; NSCA 5-stand sporting demonstration units; All American Teams selected for the Open, and the Ladies, Senior, Veteran, Junior and Sub Junior competitions; official rule book; fun shoots; discounts on rental cars.

Publications:
SPORTING CLAYS MAGAZINE, monthly.

Membership Requirements:
Shooting must be at registered tournaments. Memberships include monthly magazine. Life Membership: $350; One Year Regular Membership: $30; One Year Associate Membership: $20; Canadian and Foreign Membership: $20.

Description:
Founded 1989. Dedicated to the development of the sport of clay shooting at all levels of participation, and to the creation of an atmosphere of safe, healthy competition within the membership. NSCA is operated, directed, and advised by clay target shooters, range owners, and shooting industry representatives.

SHOOTING FEDERATION OF CANADA
45 SHIRLEY BLVD
NEPEAN, ON, CANADA K2K 2W6
613-727-7483
Fax: 613-727-7487
sfc-ftc.ca
• Pat Boulay, President
president@sfc-ftc.ca

Description:
Founded 1932, under the name of the Canadian Small Bore Rifle Association. Responsible for promotion, development and governing of organized recreational and competitive target shooting in and for Canada. Maintains communication with members and affiliates and other organizations with mutual interests; develops information programs for recreational shooters and for clubs, as well as training programs for competitive

shooters, coaches and officials; promotes organized recreational and competitive target shooting as a lifelong sporting activity; conducts international competitions, selecting teams, developing and sanctioning competitions at all

Membership Requirements:
General member $30/year.

Publications:
AIM Magazine, two times per year.

Member Services:
AIM, RTS Program, Insurance, Classifications participation in Registered Tournaments and National Championships/Team Trials to make National Team.

Number of members:
20,000

US PRACTICAL SHOOTING ASSOCIATION (USPSA)
1639 LINDAMOOD LN
BURLINGTON, WA 98233
800-995-5646
office@uspsa.org
www.uspsa.org
• Mike Foley, President

Description:
Non-profit amateur sports association dedicated to the promotion of practical shooting.

Sports Service Founded:
1984

Number of Members:
15,000

Publications:
Front Sight Magazine.

Member Services:
May visit web site (www.uspsa.org) or call the office (360) -855-2245 for more information.

USA SHOOTING
1 OLYMPIC PLAZA
COLORADO SPRINGS, CO 80909
719-866-4670
Fax: 719-866-4884
www.usashooting.org
• David Johnson, Interim CEO

Shuffleboard Organizations

INTERNATIONAL SHUFFLEBOARD ASSOCIATION
info@world-shuffleboard.org
world-shuffleboard.org

Number of members/players:
90,000 participating players; six member countries.

Member Services:
Organizes and promotes an International Tournament each year. Singles World Tournament 2017 to be held in Niteroi, Rio de Janeiro, Brazil.

Publications:
ISA Program Preview, annually with tournament

Membership Requirements:
Must be National Shuffleboard Association for the Country they represent. Fee of $500 to join.

Description:
Founded 1979. Organizes and promotes shuffleboard throughout the world. At

present six countries are involved - USA, Brazil, Canada, Japan, Australia, Zimbabwe.

Skateboard Organizations

FEDERATION INTERNATIONALE ROLLER SPORTS (FIRS)
AV DE RHODANIE, 54
LAUSANNE, 1007
www.rollersports.org

INTERNATIONAL ASSOCIATION OF SKATEBOARD COMPANIES
315 S COAST HWY 101
SUITE U-253
ENCINITAS, CA 92024
949-455-1112
Fax: 949-455-1712
theiasc.org
• Don Brown, Chairman
• Glenn Brumage, Vice President
Nature of Sports Service:
Founded 1995. Dedicated to promoting the sport of skateboarding. Acts as a central voice and information center for media, legislators and others, IASC represents the skateboard industry as it fosters sound business practices and promotes high standards of conduct within the industry. Works with municipalities in the development of designated skateboarding venues, and with sanctioning guidelines for professional and amateur competitions.
Publications:
THE FIVE FIFTEEN, weekly newsletter, THE GRAPEVINE, quarterly report.
Member Services:
Communications resource, reference resource, collections, insurance product liability, sanctions and guidelines, public skate park development, legislative lobbying.
Membership Requirements:
Yearly dues vary based on company's annual revenue.

Skiing Organizations

ALPINE CANADA
CANADA OLYMPIC PARK
151 CANADA OLYMPIC ROAD SW
SUITE 302
CALGARY, AB, CANADA T3B 6B7
403-777-3200
Fax: 403-777-3213
info@alpinecanada.org
alpinecanada.org
• Mark Rubinstein, President & CEO
(403) 777-4246
mrubinstein@alpinecanada.org
• Nicholas Bass, Chief Operating Officer
(403) 777-3218
nbass@alpinecanada.org
Nature of Service:
Develops programs, events, and sponsorship for the Canadian Alpine Ski Team and National Junior team for elite male and female skiers. Membership includes competitive skiers and recreational coaches, medical staff.
Number of members:
45,000+.
Publications:
Newsletter, biweekly, Magazine, quarterly

AMERICAN BIRKEBEINER SKI FOUNDATION (ABSF)
10527 MAIN ST
HAYWARD, WI 54843
715-634-5025
Fax: 715-634-5663
birkie@birkie.com
www.birkie.com
• Ben Popp, Executive Director
• Paul Eckerline, President - 2018
Description:
Membership organization dedicated to hosting cross country ski events, maintaining trails and promoting healthy lifestyles.

AMERICAN SKI RACING ALLIANCE
570-344-2772
Fax: 570-348-2055
asra@skiracer.com
www.skiracer.com
Membership Requirements:
$35 annual dues for individual, $55 for family.

CANADIAN SKI PATROL
4531 SOUTHCLARK PLACE
OTTAWA, ON, CANADA K1T 3V2
613-822-2245
Fax: 613-822-1088
info@skipatrol.ca
www.skipatrol.ca
• Colin Saravanamuttoo, President & CEo
Number of members:
5,000
Member Services:
Central purchasing, training content and materials, communications.
Membership Requirements:
Must be 18 years of age, intermediate skier, complete CSPS training program.
Description:
Founded 1941. Charitable organization promoting skiing safety and offering first-aid services to injured skiers.

CANADIAN SNOWSPORTS ASSOCIATION
1451 WEST BROADWAY
SUITE 202
VANCOUVER, BC, CANADA V6H 1H6
604-734-6800
Fax: 604-669-7954
www.canadiansnowsports.com
• David Pym, Managing Director
dpym@isrm.com
• Lillian Alderton, Administrator
lillianalderton@hotmail.com
Number of members:
Over 85,000
Publications:
ALPINE GUIDE annually, FREESTYLE GUIDE annually, CROSS COUNTRY Annual Media Guide and Competition Guide, JUMPING/NORDIC COMBINED GUIDE annually, CROSS COUNTRY GUIDE annually, brochures, newsletters.
Membership Requirements:
Pay general fee.
Snowsports Represented:
Alpine Canadian Alpin, Canadian Association for Disabled Skiing, Canadian Freestyle Association, Canadian Speed Skating Association, Cross Country Canada, Nordic Combined Ski Canada, Ski Jumping Canada, Telemark Ski Canada Telemark,

Canadian Snowboard Federation, Canadian Ski Coaches Federation.

CROSS COUNTRY CANADA
BILL WARREN TRAINING CENTRE
1995 OLYMPIC WAY
SUITE 100
CANMORE, AB, CANADA T1W 2T6
403-678-6791
877-609-3215
Fax: 403-678-3885
info@cccski.com
www.cccski.com
• Shane Pearsall, Chief Executive Officer
(403) 678-6791
spearsall@cccski.com
• Jamie Coatsworth, Chair
(416) 486-0825
jamie.coatsworth@gmail.com
• Chris Dornan, Media Relations
(403) 620-8731
hpprchris@shaw.ca
• Thomas Holland, Director of High Performance
(403) 678-6791
tholland@cccski.com
Description:
Serves as national sport governing body for Cross Country Skiing in Canada.
Publications:
Monthly Cross Connections Newsletter
Membership Requirements:
Must belong to club affiliated with provincial cross country association.
Member Services:
Jackrabbit program - for youth instruction; School/Ski program - physical activity program at elementary school level; Coaching program - in conjunction with Coaching Association of Canada, Information Service - provides information on any CCC program, National Ski Team results, and other cross country news.
Number of members:
Over 50,000

CROSS COUNTRY SKI AREAS ASSOCIATION
603-239-4341
ccsaa@xcski.org
xcski.org
Number of members:
300
Membership Requirements:
Regular - must own or operate a cross country ski facility in North America. Associate - companies selling goods to the cross country industry. Supporting - guides and outfitters, ski school.
Description:
Founded 1977. Deals with and represents interests of cross country ski operators in North America including promotion and support activities.

EASTERN WINTER SPORTS REPS ASSOCIATION
570-443-7180
Fax: 570-300-2715
info@ewsra.org
www.ewsra.org
• Kerry O'Flaherty, President
ofie@maine.rr.com
• Dave Kleeschulte, Vice President
dkleeschulte@nordicausa.com
Description:
Promotes general welfare of and improves

business conditions for persons engaged in the business related to snow-skiing industry.

Membership Requirements:
Open to anyone who gains his livelihood primarily as a sales rep for firms substantially engaged in manufacturing of goods associated with snow-ski industry and located in ESRA territory (NY, NJ, PA). $750 initiation fee, $300 annual dues.

Publications:
Buyer's Guide, Retail List.

Number of members:
253

FEDERATION INTERNATIONALE DE SKI (FIS)
MARC HODLER HOUSE
BLOCHSTRASSE 2
OBERHOFEN/THUNERSEE, CH-3653
mail@fisski.ch
www.fis-ski.com
• Sarah Lewis, Secretary General

NATIONAL SKI & SNOWBOARD RETAILERS ASSOCIATION
1601 FEEHANVILLE DRIVE
SUITE 300
MOUNT PROSPECT, IL 60056
888-257-1168
Fax: 847-391-9827
info@nssra.com
www.nssra.com
• Teddy Schiavoni, Chairman
teddy@summitskishop.com
• Larry Weindruch, President
lweindruch@nssra.com

Nature of Service:
Develops, improves and promotes the business of retailers, shops, areas and other members of the ski and snowboard industry; furthers the business interests of and promotes friendly relationships with its members; promotes the sports of skiing and snowboarding.

Year Founded:
1987

Number of Members:
250

Publications:
NSSRA NEWSLETTER, 6 time(s) per year

NATIONAL SKI AREAS ASSOCIATION
133 S VAN GORDON ST
SUITE 300
LAKEWOOD, CO 80228
303-987-1111
Fax: 303-986-2345
nsaa@nsaa.org
www.nsaa.org
• Michael Berry, President
(303) 987-1111

Description:
Founded 1962. National trade association for ski resorts and areas in North America. Purpose is to stimulate and promote skiing, snowboarding and safety and to meet the needs of the ski area industry.

Membership Requirements:
Must be a ski area in operation or a supplier of services to the ski and snowboard industry.

Member Services:
Holds two regional winter shows and an annual convention and trade show exclusively for members.

Number of members:

The association represents 313 alpine resorts and has 414 supplier members.

NATIONAL SKI PATROL
133 S VAN GORDON ST
SUITE 100
LAKEWOOD, CO 80228
303-988-1111
Fax: 303-988-3005
nsp@nsp.org
www.nsp.org
• John McMahon, Executive Director
• Bill Finley, Director of Finance

Number of members:
29,000

Publications:
SKI PATROL MAGAZINE, quarterly.

Membership Requirements:
An individual or unit (composed of one or more individuals) who, whether volunteering or receiving pay for services, has met or exceeded the National Qualification Requirements for Ski Patrollers established by the National Ski Patrol System, Inc. and who has registered with the National Ski Patrol System, Inc. as a member of one of its Ski Patrols, and who has remitted the required registration fee. Must be a Winter Emergency Care Technician, and tested (after training) in patroller skills.

Description:
Founded 1938. Promotes the safety of those engaged in winter sports and gives emergency care to those who have suffered injuries.

NEW ENGLAND SPORTS REPRESENTATIVES
21 SOUTH STREET
UNIT 3
WESTBOROUGH, MA 01581
508-898-9559
Fax: 508-772-0013
• Maureen Bliss, Executive Director
• Will Masson, President
(802) 985-4089
will.masson@rossignol.com

Nature of Service:
Organizes two trade shows for retailers in the spring of each year, as well as an On-Snow Demo during winter.

Year Founded:
1968

Membership Requirements:
Must represent a company or companies that sell snow ski equipment, clothing or accessories. $750 initiation fee, $450 annual dues.

Number of members:
325

Publications:
BUYER'S GUIDE, sent to ski shops that have attended previous shows.

PACIFIC NORTHWEST SKI ASSOCIATION
2671 FLOWERY TAIL ROAD
Usk, WA 99180
509-445-4454
Fax: 866-542-8664
pnsa@pnsa.org
www.pnsa.org
• Bill Brooks, President
• Curt Hammond, Vice President
cjhammond@msn.com

Nature of Service:
Division of the U.S. Skiing. Provides skiers with an organized voice. Administers

competition ski programs.

Year Founded:
1931

Member Services:
Administration of competition programs.

Membership Requirements:
Interest in skiing. Dues.

Number of members:
2,200

PROFESSIONAL SNOWSPORTS INSTRUCTORS OF AMERICA - EASTERN
1-A LINCOLN AVE
ALBANY, NY 12205-4907
518-452-6095
Fax: 518-452-6099
psia-e@psia-e.org
www.psia-e.org
• Michael Mendrick, Executive Director
mmendrick@psia-e.org

Number of Members:
Over 11,000

Member Services:
Committee functions involving marketing, certification, education, equipment trends, sports research and information.

Membership Requirements:
Successfully complete an instructor registration clinic and certification exam. Pay annual dues and upgrade every two years.

Description:
Founded 1973. Serves as a non-profit organization whose purpose is the education and certification of Nordic ski instructors.

PROFESSIONAL SNOWSPORTS INSTRUCTORS OF AMERICA - NORTHWEST
338 N WENATCHEE AVENUE
WENATCHEE, WA 98801
206-244-8541
Fax: 206-241-2885
info@psia-nw.org
www.psia-nw.org
• Kirsten Huotte, Executive Director
kirsten@psia-nw.org

Number of members:
27,500

Publications:
Educational manuals; Ski school surveys; Member surveys; THE PROFESSIONAL SKIER, quarterly educational journal.

Membership Requirements:
Must be certified, associate or registered member of one of nine PSIA divisions. Division requirements vary, but basically all require a certain number of hours teaching experience, a classroom test knowledge, and an on-snow test of skill. $30 annual dues for division certified registered member, $70 for non-certified member.

Description:
Founded 1961. Promotes professional ski instruction to both the general public and the ski industry through its education foundation and PSIA marketing programs for its divisions, its member ski schools and its member instructors.

SKI FOR LIGHT
1455 W LAKE ST
MINNEAPOLIS, MN 55408
612-827-3232
www.sfl.org
• Scott McCall, President
• Robert Civiak, Vice President

Member Services:
Sponsors one international x-country ski event annually for visually and mobility impaired persons. Regional programs. Summer programs entitled Sports For Health, for visually and mobility impaired individuals.
Publications:
Ski for Light bulletin, three times a year.
Membership Requirements:
Interest in working with disabled and able-bodied persons on one-on-one basis. Dues are $15 annual, $25 sustaining, $100 Corporate, $250 individual life.
Description:
Founded 1975. Advances and promotes athletic education and participation of blind and other disabled persons in outdoor activities and exposes blind and other disabled persons to the outdoors under supervised physical training.

SNOWSPORTS INDUSTRIES AMERICA
1918 PROSPECTOR AVE
PARK CITY, UT 84060
435-657-5140
Fax: 435-659-3434
info@snowsports.org
www.snowsports.org
• Nick Sargent, President
nick.sargent@snowsports.org
• Maria McNulty, Chief Operating Officer
mmcnulty@snowsports.org
• Mike Adams, Treasurer
• David Currier, Secretary
• Julie Garry, First Vice Chair
• David Ingemie, President
• Leslie L. Groves, Director Marketing/Communications
lgroves@snowsports.org
Nature of Service:
National non-profit trade association of ski, snowboard, on-snow, and outdoor action sports product manufacturers and distributors.
Year Founded:
1954
Membership Requirements:
Provided on written request.
Number of members:
Over 750
Publications:
SIA NEWSLETTERS, SIA SNOWSPORTS DIRECTORY, SIA INDUSTRY PLANNER, variety of research, public relations and educational information and materials.

U.S. DEAF SKI & SNOWBOARD ASSOCIATION
76 KINGS GATE NORTH
ROCHESTER, NY 14617
585-286-2780
info@usdssa.org
usdssa.org
• Ellen Roth, President
• Sean Esson, Vice President
Publications:
Newsletter, three times per year.
Membership Requirements:
Deaf with 55 db loss in hearing eligible to be competitors. Membership dues for individuals are $20 for two years, $30 for families.
Description:
Founded 1968. Promotes skiing for deaf people. Training for Olympics.

U.S. SKI AND SNOWBOARD ASSOCIATION (USSA)
1 VICTORY LANE
PARK CITY, UT 84060
435-649-9090
Fax: 435-649-3613
ussa.org
• Tiger Shaw, President & CEO
• Brooke McAffee, Vice President & Chief Financial Officer
• Trisha Worthington, EVP & Chief Development Officer
Description:
Provides opportunities for athletes in the most exciting Olympic action sports. USSA's programs provide education, development and competition opportunities for young athletes, with from grassroots USSA club programs up through national teams and the Olympic Winter Games.
Membership Requirements:
Anyone can join on an individual, family or club basis.
Publications:
Discipline competition guides (alpine, cross-country, freestyle, jumping/Nordic combined, Snowboard), American Ski Coach, periodically.
Year Founded:
1905

Sled Dog Organizations

IDITAROD
2100 S KNIK GOOSE BAY RD
WASILLA, AK 99654
907-376-5155
Fax: 907-373-6998
iditarod@iditarod.com
www.iditarod.com
• Stan Hooley, Chief Executive Officer
• Mark Nordman, Race Director
Description:
Founded 1973. Known as The Last Great Race On Earth, covers 1,049 miles. Begins first Saturday in March and ends approximately 10 days later.

INTERNATIONAL SLED DOG RACING ASSOCIATION
22702 REBEL RD
MERRIFIELD, MN 56465
218-765-4297
dsteele@brainerd.net
www.isdra.org
Number of members:
1,000+.
Membership Requirements:
$35 membership fee.
Publications:
Dog and Driver Magazine, six times a year.
Description:
Founded 1966.

JOHN BEARGREASE SLED DOG MARATHON
218-722-7631
info@beargrease.com
www.beargrease.com
• Jean Vincent, President
Description:
Founded 1980. Longest sled dog race in the lower 48 states.
Membership Requirements:
$30 trail membership, $100 mile marker

membership, $250 mid-distance membership, $500 marathon membership, $1,000 VIP membership.

Snowboarding Organizations

AMERICAN ASSOCIATION OF SNOWBOARD INSTRUCTORS
133 S VAN GORDON ST
SUITE 200
LAKEWOOD, CO 80228
844-340-7669
www.thesnowpros.org
• Nick Herrin, Chief Executive Officer
nherrin@thesnowpros.org
• Tom Spiess, Chief Financial Officer
tspiess@thesnowpros.org
Description:
World's largest organization dedicated to skiing and snowboarding instruction.
Founded:
1961
Members:
32,000
Member Services:
Professional Development Education Programs, Subaru Incentive Purchase Program, Certification, and Special Purchase Opportunities.
Publications:
THE PRO RIDER magazine, THE PROFESSIONAL SKIER magazine.

U.S. SKI AND SNOWBOARD ASSOCIATION (USSA)
1 VICTORY LANE
PARK CITY, UT 84060
435-649-9090
Fax: 435-649-3613
www.ussa.org
• Tiger Shaw, President & CEO
• Brooke McAffee, Vice President & Chief Financial Officer
• Trisha Worthington, EVP & Chief Development Officer

Snowmobile Organizations

AMERICAN COUNCIL OF SNOWMOBILE ASSOCIATIONS
271 WOODLAND PASS
SUITE 216
EAST LANSING, MI 48823
517-351-4362
Fax: 517-351-1363
info@snowmobilers.org
www.snowmobilers.org
• Bob Kirchner, President
whynotbobk@yahoo.com
Sports Service Founded:
1995
Membership Requirements:
$10 fee for individual, $15 for family, $25 for club.
Publication:
ACSA Newsletter 27 Trails.
Description:
American Council of Snowmobile Associations (ACSA) is a non-profit national association dedicated to providing leadership and advancing the efforts of all snowmobile-affiliated organizations to

promote the expansion and education of responsible snowmobiling in the United States. Acts as national coordinator and spokesperson for state volunteer snowmobile associations and snowmobile clubs.

CANADIAN COUNCIL OF SNOWMOBILE ORGANIZATIONS
807-345-5299
ccso.ccom@tbaytel.net
www.ccso-ccom.ca
• Dale Hickox, President
• Dennis Burns, Executive Director
Year Founded:
1974
Description:
Not-for-profit organization dedicated to providing leadership and support to organized snowmobiling in Canada.

INTERNATIONAL SNOWMOBILE MANUFACTURERS ASSOCIATION
1640 HASLETT ROAD
SUITE 170
HASLETT, MI 48840
517-339-7788
Fax: 517-339-7798
ismasue@aol.com
www.snowmobile.org
Nature of Service:
Organization representing the four snowmobile manufacturers. Coordinates committees within the industry to handle concerns such as snowmobile safety, the promotion of the life-style activity of snowmobiling, keeping accurate statistics, reporting the growth of the industry and the positive economic impact the life-style activity has throughout the world.
Member Services:
Communications, Good Relations.
Membership Requirements:
Manufacturer of Snowmobiles.
Number of Members:
4.

NEW HAMPSHIRE SNOWMOBILE ASSOCIATION
614 LACONIA ROAD
UNIT 4
TILTON, NH 03276
603-273-0220
Fax: 603-273-0218
nhsaoffice@nhsa.com
www.nhsa.com
• Roger Wright, President
(543) 3669
rogr.wright@comcast.net
• Bob Dohetry, Vice President
(899) 9878
• Marie Hixson, Treasurer
(968) 9038
doo-n@metrocast.net
Description:
An association made up of clubs, distributors and dealers working together to promote the sport of snowmobiling.
Year Founded:
1969

ONTARIO FEDERATION OF SNOWMOBILE CLUBS
501 WELHAM ROAD
UNIT 9
BARRIE, ON, CANADA L4N 8Z6

705-739-7669
Fax: 705-739-5005
info@ofsc.on.ca
www.ofsc.on.ca
Sports Service Founded:
1967
Description:
Dedicated to providing strong leadership and support to member clubs, establishing and maintaining quality snowmobile trails, and furthering the enjoyment of organized snowmobiling.

Soccer (Futsal) Organizations

U.S. FUTSAL
510-836-8733
Fax: 650-242-1036
info@futsal.com
www.futsal.com
• Alexander J C Para, President & CEO
Nature of Sports Service:
The national governing body for the sport of Futsal, in the United States. A rapidly growing derivative of soccer played with five-man teams on a basketball style court, with no walls and a low bouncing ball. The term FUTSAL is the international term used for the game. It is derived from the Spanish or Portuguese word for soccer, FUTbol or FUTebol, and the French or Spanish word for indoor, SALon or SALa.
Sports Service Founded:
1981

Soccer Organizations

AMERICAN YOUTH SOCCER ORGANIZATION
19750 S VERMONT AVENUE
SUITE 200
TORRANCE, CA 90502
800-872-2976
Fax: 310-525-1155
www.ayso.org
• Michael Karon, National President
MKreferee@gmail.com
Number of members:
50,000 teams and 650,000 players
Publications:
Whistle Stop, weekly newsletter for referees and referee related positions. Hey Coach!, weekly newsletter for coaches and other coaching positions
Description:
A nationwide non-profit organization that develops and delivers quality youth soccer programs in a fun, family environment.
Year Founded:
1964

CANADA SOCCER
237 MECALFE STREET
OTTAWA, ON, CANADA K2P 1R2
613-237-7678
Fax: 613-237-1516
www.canadasoccer.com
• Peter Montopoli, General Secretary
Number of members:
871,893
Publications:
Canada Soccer Yearbook

Description:
Founded 1912. Strives to lead Canada to victory and encourages Canadians towards a life-long passion for soccer.

GEORGIA SOCCER
2323 PERIMETER PARK DRIVE
SUITE 200
ATLANTA, GA 30341-0505
770-452-0505
www.georgiasoccer.org
• Laura Halfpenny, Executive Director
• Russel Rankenburg, President
Year Founded:
1967
Description:
GSSA is the operational governing body authorized and recognized by US Soccer, US Youth Soccer and US Amateur Soccer. Promotes the sport of soccer statewide and provides educational programs for coaches, referees and administrators. Helps coordinate the development of soccer programs for all levels of play from recreational up through Olympic Development and fosters statewide, national and international competitions and tournaments. Membership is projected to be 75,000 soccer athletes, 5,000 coaches and 2,500 referees.

MY SOCCER LEAGUE.COM
www.mysoccerleague.com
Nature of Sports Service:
Organization provides youth leagues - soccer, baseball, football, etc. - with state-of-the-art, web-based league scheduling, game results, standings, referee and field assignments, plus league-wide communications capabilities in an easy-to-use and affordable online service.

NATIONAL INTERCOLLEGIATE SOCCER OFFICIALS ASSOCIATION
nisoa.com
• Marc Lawrence, President
• Ben Trevino, VP
Description:
Founded 1964. Promotes the improvement of intercollegiate and high school soccer refereeing in the U.S.
Membership Requirements:
All applicants must apply through a local chapter.
Publications:
Newsletters, Camp Brochure, Be Informed Brochure, Diagonal System of Control, Dualsystem of Control, Double Dualsystem of Control, Pre-game Guide for Each System, Alternate Official Manual, Assistant Referee Manual, Information National Referee Program Directory, Lesson Plans on all Topics, Critical Incident Tape, Rules Change Tape
Member Services:
Referee Training Camps, National Referee Clinics, Regional Clinics, Local Clinics.
Number of Members:
5,500

NATIONAL SOCCER HALL OF FAME
9200 WORLD CUP WAY
SUITE 600
FRISCO, TX 75033
469-365-0043
info@nationalsoccerhof.com
www.nationalsoccerhof.com

Description:
Celebrates the history, honors the heroes and preserves the legacy of the sport of soccer in the United States.
Year Founded:
1950

OHIO SOUTH YOUTH SOCCER ASSOCIATION
7228 COLUMBIA ROAD
SUITE 900
MAINEVILLE, OH 45039
513-576-9555
800-267-9721
Fax: 513-576-1666
office@ohio-soccer.org
www.osysa.com
• Gordon Henderson, Executive Director
Publications:
Newsletter

PRO-AM BEACH SOCCER
3032 FULTON STREET
SUITE 2
SAN FRANCISCO, CA 94118
415-308-0603
info@proambeachsoccer.net
proambeachsoccer.net
• Tighe O'Sullivan, CEO
• Luis Palafox, Assistant Director
Founded:
2009
Nature of Service:
Beach soccer tournaments

QUICKFOOT
16330 SCENIC CIRCLE
FORNEY, TX 75126
469-728-7700
Fax: 609-301-9749
info@quickfoot.com
www.quickfoot.com
Description:
Premier small-sided soccer tournament organizers.

SOCCER ASSOCIATION FOR YOUTH USA
11490 SPRINGFIELD PIKE
CINCINNATI, OH 45241
800-233-7291
www.saysoccer.org
• Doug Wood, Executive Director
(800) 233-7291
dwood@saysoccer.org
Number of Members:
150,000
Member Services:
Organization of Recreational Soccer Administration on a National level.
Publications:
Ref News, The Tunnel, SAY Coaching Manual, SAY Rulebook, SAY Coaches Club, The Touchline
Membership Requirements:
Youth Recreational Soccer Player between the ages of 4-18
Description:
Founded 1967; provides guidance and instruction for new participants, an organization structure to form soccer 'leagues and schedule games, andrules and regulations which will ensure safe, enjoyable and fair competition forchildren 4-18 years of age.

SOCCER, FEDERATION INTERNATIONALE DE FOOTBALL ASSOCIATION (FIFA)
FIFA-STRASSE 20
PO BOX 8044
ZURICH
www.fifa.com
• Gianni Infantino, President
Description:
International association for the development of football.
Year Founded:
1904
Member Associations:
211
Publications:
The FIFA Weekly

TENNESSEE STATE SOCCER ASSOCIATION
2630 ELM HILL PIKE
SUITE 100
NASHVILLE, TN 37214
615-590-2200
Fax: 615-590-2205
www.tnsoccer.org
• John Snyder, President
president@tnsoccer.org
• Hans Hobson, Executive Director
(615) 590-2200
hhobson@tnsoccer.org
Year Founded:
1978
Nature of Sports Service:
Advances and promotes soccer at all levels in a state well known for football and baseball.
Number of Members:
41,000 registered players; 5,000 active coaches, referees, and administrators; 105 local member organizations.

U.S. SOCCER FEDERATION
1801 S PRAIRIE AVENUE
CHICAGO, IL 60616
312-808-1300
Fax: 312-808-1301
communications@ussoccer.org
www.ussoccer.com
• Cindy Parlow Cone, President
• Will Wilson, Chief Executive Offcer
Description:
Affiliated with International Soccer Body, FIFA. Governing body for soccer in the U.S. under the 1978 Sports Amateur Act. Promotes soccer in U.S. including national and international games and tournaments. Administers all U.S. national teams. Responsible for marketing the U.S. National Teams' programs as well as marketing programs for the Youth and Amateur Divisions. Resolves questions and controversies not adjustable under rules of state associations concerned. Manages U.S. Cup Tournament, National Challenge Cup, National Amateur Challenge Cup, National Women's Amateur Cup, National Youth Cup competitions, promotes goodwill through physical
Year Founded:
1913
Number of members:
3,000,000
Membership Requirements:
Must be association, league, approved by National Council.
Notes:

1998 - Awarded marketing, licensing and television rights to a partnership between International Management Group and Nike. The 12 year agreement is expected to generate $500 million for U.S. Soccer. In 1997 Nike and US Soccer agreed on a 10 year $120 million apparel agreement.

UNITED SOCCER COACHES
30 W PERSHING ROAD
SUITE 350
KANSAS CITY, MO 64108-2463
816-471-1941
Fax: 816-474-7408
membership@unitedsoccercoaches.org
unitedsoccercoaches.org
• Beth Sullivan, CFO
• Ian Barker, Director, Coaching Education
• Geoff VanDeusen, Director, Operations & Events
Description:
Since its founding in 1941, United Soccer Coaches (formerly known as the National Soccer Coaches Association of America) has grown to include more than 30,000 members who coach both genders at all levels of the sport. In addition to a national rankings program for colleges and high schools, NSCAA offers an extensive recognition program that presents nearly 10,000 individual awards every year. The NSCAA fulfills its mission of coaching education through a nationwide program of clinics and week-long courses, teaching more than 6,000 soccer coaches each year.
Year Founded:
1941
Publications:
184 SOCCER JOURNAL, bi-monthly
Membership Requirements:
Individual meeting the requirements and qualifications provided by the by-laws.
Member Services:
Publications, awards, clinics, soccer academy, liability insurance, All America and Coach of the Year selection, national rankings for colleges and high schools, conventions, and discounts.
Number of members:
30,000

UNITED STATES ADULT SOCCER ASSOCIATION
7000 S HARLEM AVENUE
BRIDGEVIEW, IL 60455
708-496-6870
Fax: 780-496-6879
www.usadultsoccer.com
• Duncan Riddle, Executive Director
• John Motta, President
Description:
A member if the United States Soccer Federation, and is currently the only adult soccer member organization of USSF. Promotes the game of soccer for men and women, in an atmosphere of fun, fair play and friendship.
Membership Requirements:
Must be a member of a state soccer association.
Member Services:
Supervises inter-state All-Star games and interstate cup competitions.
Number of Members:
275,000

single sports

US SOCCER FOUNDATION
1140 CONNECTICUT AVENUE NW
SUITE 1200
WASHINGTON, DC 20036
202-872-9277
Fax: 202-872-6655
info@ussoccerfoundation.org
ussoccerfoundation.org
• Ed Foster-Simeon, President/CEO
Description:
National soccer-based youth development
program.

US YOUTH SOCCER
9220 WORLD CUP WAY
FRISCO, TX 75033
www.usyouthsoccer.org
• Skip Gilbert, CEO
Number of members:
55 State Associations, 3 million players.
Member Services:
Coaching program; young player
development program; referee program;
codes of conduct; Olympic Development
Program; American Cup; Soccer Start
program; Coach of the Year; Snickers U.S.
Youth Soccer National Championship, Youth
Referee of the Year. TOP Soccer (Outreach
program for players with disabilities.
Publications:
U.S. YOUTH SOCCER MAGAZINE, young
player coaching video; U.S. YOUTH
SOCCER NEWS, state soccer publications;
U.S. Youth Soccer National Workshop;
various fee and low cost brochures and
books.
Description:
A non-profit and educational organization
whose mission is to foster the physical,
mental and emotional growth and
development of America's youth through the
sport of soccer at al levels of age and
competition.

Soccer, Leagues/Teams

CANADIAN PREMIER LEAGUE
canpl.ca
• David Clanachan, Commissioner
• Scott Mitchell, CEO
• James Easton, Vice President, Football
Operations

Teams:

ATLÂ□TICO OTTAWA
OTTAWA, ON, CANADA
atleticoottawa.canpl.ca
• Jeff Hunt, Strategic Partner/Owner
• Ferrer Martinez, Head Coach
• Miguel Angel, Head Coach

CAVALRY FC
18011 SPRUCE MEADOWS
WAY SW
CALGARY, AB, CANADA T2X 4B7
403-974-4567
tickets@cavalryfootball.club
cavalryfc.canpl.ca
• Linda A. Southern-Heathcott, Owner, Chair &
CEO
• Ian Allison, Chief Operating Officer
• Tommy Wheeldon, Jr., General Manager/Head
Coach

FC EDMONTON
CLARKE STADIUM
11000 STADIUM ROAD NW
EDMONTON, AB, CANADA T5H 4E2
780-700-2600
fcedmonton.canpl.ca
• Tom Fath, Co-Owner
• Eric Newendorp, President & General
Manager
• Alan Koch, Head Coach

FORGE FC
TIM HORTONS FIELD
64 MELROSE AVE N
HAMILTON, ON, CANADA L8L 8C1
905-527-3674
info@forgefootball.club
forgefc.canpl.ca
• Bobby Smyrniotis, Head Coach/Technical
Director

HFX WANDERERS
HALIFAX, NS, CANADA
902-407-5621
info@hfxwanderersfc.ca
hfxwanderersfc.canpl.ca
• Derek Martin, President
• Stephen Hart, Head Coach

PACIFIC FC
WESTHILLS STADIUM
1089 LANGFORD PARKWAY
VICTORIA, BC, CANADA V9B 0A5
778-584-6732
memberservices@pacificfc.ca
pacificfc.canpl.ca
• Josh Simpson, President
• Rob Friend, CEO
• Dean Shillington, Chairman
• Pa-Modou Kah, Head Coach

VALOUR FC
INVESTORS GROUP FIELD
315 CHANCELLOR MATHESON ROAD
WINNIPEG, MB, CANADA R3T 1Z2
valourfc.canpl.ca
• Wade Miller, President/CEO
• Rob Gale, Head Coach & General Manager

YORK UNITED FC
ALUMNI FIELD
YORK UNIVERSITY
TORONTO, ON, CANADA L8S 4L8
yorkunitedfc.ca
• Angus McNab, CEO/President/General
Manager
• Jimmy Brennan, Head Coach/Technical
Director

CANADIAN SOCCER LEAGUE
75 INTERNATIONAL BOULEVARD
SUITE 203
TORONTO, ON, CANADA M9W 6L9
416-675-5256
info@canadiansoccerleague.ca
canadiansoccerleague.ca
• Pino Jazbec, League Administrator
pjazbec@canadiansoccerleague.ca
Description:
Semi-professional soccer league in
Southern Ontario.

Teams:

BRANTFORD GALAXY SC
HERITAGE SPORT PARK
355 FIRST ROAD W
STONEY CREEK, ON, CANADA L8J 1X5
brantfordgalaxysc@gmail.com
brantfordrleague.ca/brantford-galaxy-sc
• Bosko Borjan, Manager/President
• Sasa Vidovic, Head Coach

Home Field:
Heritage Field

CSC MISSISSAUGA
386 WATLINE AVENUE
MISSISSAUGA, ON, CANADA L4Z 1X2
647-879-6453
cscmississauga@gmail.com
www.cscmississauga.com
• Mile Milkovic, Manager
• Dalibor Vranjic, Head Coach

FC UKRAINE UNITED
CENTENNIAL STADIUM
56 CENTENNIAL PARK ROAD
TORONTO, ON, CANADA M9C 3T3
admin@fcukraineunited.com
www.fcukraineunited.com
• Mykhailo Gurka, Head Coach
• Andrei Malychenkov, Manager

FC VORKUTA
505-1000 FINCH AVENUE W
TORONTO, ON, CANADA M3J 2V5
416-917-2304
fcvorkuta@gmail.com
fcvorkuta.ca
• Igor Demitchev, Founder/Chairman
• Samad Kadirov, Manager
• Denys Yanchuk, Head Coach
Home Field:
Kalar Sports Park

HAMILTON CITY 1
905-921-5838
canadiansoccerleague.ca/hamilton-city
• Sasa Vukovic, Coach

REAL MISSISSAUGA SC
MISSISSAUGA, ON, CANADA L5A 3T2
647-336-3789
www.screalmississauga.ca
• Ross Chonga, Manager
• Krum Bibishkov, Head Coach

SC WATERLOO
WARRIOR FIELD
UNIVERSITY OF WATERLOO
WATERLOO, ON, CANADA
519-465-4050
canadiansocceleague.ca/sc-waterloo
• Tony Kocis, President
• Vojislav Brisevac, Manager
• Radivoj Panic, Head Coach
Home Field:
Warrior Field

SCARBOROUGH SC
BIRCHMOUNT STADIUM
75 BIRCHMOUNT ROAD
TORONTO, ON, CANADA M1N 3J7
canadiansoccerleague.ca/scarborough-sc
• Kiril Dimitrov, Manager
• Mirko Medic, Coach
Home Field:
Birchmount Stadium

SERBIAN WHITE EAGLES FC
30 TITAN ROAD
UNIT 15
TORONTO, ON, CANADA M8Z 5Y2
416-252-4752
info@serbianwhiteeagles.ca
serbianwhiteeagles.ca
• Dragan Bakoc, President
dragan@serbianwhiteeagles.ca
• Uros Stamatovic, Head Coach
Home Field:
Centennial Park Stadium

CAPITAL AREA SOCCER LEAGUE
6025 CURRY LANE
LANSING, MI 48911

517-580-4241
Fax: 517-580-4921
caslsoccer.org
• Oscar Castaneda, President
president@caslsoccer.org
Description:
Provides instructional and competitive youth
soccer opportunities that enhance character,
community and loveof the game of soccer.
Also home toover 20,000 players, coaches,
officials, parents, volunteers and supporters.
Year Founded:
1974

MAJOR LEAGUE SOCCER
420 FIFTH AVENUE
7TH FLOOR
NEW YORK, NY 10018
212-450-1200
feedback@mlssoccer.com
www.mlssoccer.com
• Don Garber, Commissioner
• Mark Abbott, President/Deputy
Commissioner
• Gary Stevenson, Deputy Commissioner

Teams:

ATLANTA UNITED FC
MERCEDES-BENZ STADIUM
409 NELSON ST SW
ATLANTA, GA 30313
470-341-1500
info@atlutd.com
www.atlutd.com
• Arthur Blank, Owner
• Darren Eales, President
• Gabriel Heinze, Head Coach

AUSTIN FC
Q2 STASIUM
AUSTIN, TX
austinfc.com
• Anthony Precourt, Majority Owner/CEO
• Andy Loughnane, President
• Josh Wolff, Head Coach

CF MONTREAL
STADE SAPUTO
4750, RUE SHERBROOKE EST
MONTREAL, QC, CANADA H1V 3S8
514-328-3668
Fax: 514-328-1287
cfmontreal.com
• Joey Saputo, Owner
• Kevin Gilmore, President/CEO
• Nancy Wilfried, Head Coach
Home Field:
Stade Saputo. Seating capacity 20,801.

CHICAGO FIRE FC
1 NORTH DEARBORN ST
SUITE 1300
CHICAGO, IL 60602
888-657-3473
www.chicagofirefc.com
• Joe Mansueto, Owner/Chairman
• Nelson RodrÃ¡guez, President/General
Manager
• RaphaÃ€°l Wicky, Head Coach

COLORADO RAPIDS
DICK'S SPORTING GOODS PARK
6000 VICTORY WAY
COMMERCE CITY, CO 80022
303-727-3500
Fax: 303-727-3536
customerservice@dsgpark.com
www.coloradorapids.com
• E. Stanley Kroenke, Owner
• PÃ draig Smith, Executive VP/General

Manager
• Robin Fraser, Head Coach

COLUMBUS CREW SC
MAPFRE STADIUM
1 BLACK & GOLD BOULEVARD
COLUMBUS, OH 43211
614-447-2739
Fax: 614-447-4109
www.columbuscrewsc.com
• Tim Bezbatchenko, President/General
Manager
• Caleb Porter, Head Coach
Description:
Plays at Columbus Crew Stadium.

D.C. UNITED
AUDI FIELD
100 PTOMAC AVENUE SW
WASHINGTON, DC 20024
202-587-5000
www.dcunited.com
• Jason M. Levien, Chief Executive Officer
• Danita Johnson, President, Business
Operations
• Dave Kasper, General Manager/VP, Soccer
Operations
• Hernan Losada, Head Coach

FC CINCINNATI
14 E 4TH STREET
CINCINNATI, OH 45202
www.fccincinnati.com
• Carl H. Linder, III, CEO/Owner
• Jeff Berding, President
• Gerard Nijkamp, General Manager
• Jaap Stam, Head Coach

FC DALLAS
9200 WORLD CUP WAY
SUITE 202
FRISCO, TX 75033
214-705-6700
customerservice@fcdallas.com
www.fcdallas.com
• Clark Hunt, Chairman/CEO
• Dan Hunt, President
• Luichi Gonzalez, Head Coach
Home Field:
FC Dallas Stadium

HOUSTON DYNAMO
1001 AVENIDA DE LAS AMERICAS
SUITE 200
HOUSTON, TX 77010
713-276-7500
Fax: 713-276-7572
info@houstondynamo.com
www.houstondynamo.com
• Gabriel Brener, Controlling Owner
• John Waker, President, Business Operations
• Matt Jordan, Senior VP/General Manager
• Tab Ramos, Head Coach

INTER MIAMI CF
1350 NW 55TH ST
FORT LAUDERDALE, FL
www.intermiamicf.com
• Jorge Mas, Managing Owner
• David Beckham, Owner/President
• Phil Neville, Head Coach

LA GALAXY
DIGNITY HEALTH SPORTS PARK
18400 AVALON BOULEVARD
SUITE 200
CARSON, CA 90746
310-630-2200
877-342-5299
Fax: 310-630-2250
customerservice@lagalaxy.com
www.lagalaxy.com
• Dan Beckerman, President & CEO
• Chris Klein, President

• Dennis te Kloese, General Manager
• Greg Vanney, Head Coach
Description:
Stadium: The Home Depot Center

LAFC
818 W 7TH STREET
SUITE 1200
LOS ANGELES, CA 90017
213-519-9900
club@lafc.com
www.lafc.com
• Larry Freedman, Co-President/Chief Business
Officer
• John Thorrington, Co-President/General
Manager
• Bob Bradley, Head Coach

MINNESOTA UNITED FC
4150 OLSON MEMORIAL HIGHWAY
SUITE 300
GOLDEN VALLEY, MN 55422
763-476-2237
Fax: 763-331-8788
info@mnufc.com
www.mnufc.com
• Chris Wright, CEO
• Bill McGuire, Managing Director
• Adrian Heath, Head Coach

NASHVILLE SC
NASHVILLE SC STADIUM
NASHVILLE, TN
615-750-8800
info@nashvillesc.com
www.nashvillesc.com
• Ian Ayre, CEO
• Mike Jacobs, General Manager
• Gary Smith, Head Coach

NEW ENGLAND REVOLUTION
GILLETTE STADIUM
ONE PATRIOT PLACE
FOXBOROUGH, MA 02035
508-543-8200
www.revolutionsoccer.net
• Brian Bilello, President
• Bruce Arena, Sporting Director & Head Coach

NEW YORK CITY FC
600 THIRD AVENUE
30TH FLOOR
NEW YORK, NY 10016
212-738-5900
nycfc@nycfc.com
www.nycfc.com
• Brad Sims, CEO
• Matt Pellegrino, Senior Director, Operations
• Ronny Deila, Head Coach
Operated by:
Anschutz Entertainment Group (AEG).

NEW YORK RED BULLS
RED BULL ARENA
600 CAPE MAY STREET
HARRISON, NJ 07029
877-727-6223
www.newyorkredbulls.com
• Kevin Thelwell, Head of Sport
• Gerhard Struber, Head Coach

ORLANDO CITY
655 W CHURCH STREET
ORLANDO, FL 32805
855-675-2489
Fax: 407-745-5376
www.orlandocitysc.com
• Luiz Muzzi, Executive VP, Soccer Operations
• Alex LeitÃ†o, CEO
• Oscar Pareja, Head Coach

PHILADELPHIA UNION
2501 SEAPORT DRIVE
BH SUITE 100
CHESTER, PA 19013
610-497-1657
Fax: 610-497-3309
www.philadelphiaunion.com
• Jay Sugarman, Chairman/Owner
• Tim McDermott, President
• Ernst Tanner, Sporting Director
• Jim Curtin, Head Coach

PORTLAND TIMBERS
1844 SW MORRISON
PORTLAND, OR 97205
503-553-5400
Fax: 503-553-5405
info@timbers.com
www.timbers.com
• Merritt Paulson, CEO
• Gavin Wilkinson, General Manager
• Giovanni Savarese, Head Coach

REAL SALT LAKE
9256 SOUTH STATE STREET
SANDY, UT 84070
801-727-2700
Fax: 801-727-1469
www.rsl.com
• Dell Loy Hansen, Owner
• Elliot Fall, General Manager
• Freddy Juarez, Head Coach

SAN JOSE EARTHQUAKES
EARTHQUAKES STADIUM
1123 COLEMAN AVENUE
SAN JOSE, CA 95110
408-556-7700
Fax: 408-796-5242
www.sjearthquakes.com
• John Fisher, Managing Partner/Board Member
• Jesse Fioranelli, General Manager
• Matias Almeyda, Head Coach

SEATTLE SOUNDERS FC
159 S JACKSON STREET
SUITE 200
SEATTLE, WA 98104
877-657-4625
customerservice@soundersfc.com
www.soundersfc.com
• Garth Lagerwey, General Manager/President
• Brian Schmetzer, Head Coach

SPORTING KANSAS CITY
2020 BALTIMORE AVENUE
KANSAS CITY, MO 64108
913-387-3400
888-452-4625
clientservices@sportingkc.com
www.sportingkc.com
• Peter Vermes, Manager/Sporting Director

TORONTO FC
BMO FIELD
170 PRINCES' BOULEVARD
TORONTO, ON, CANADA M6K 3C3
416-360-4625
www.torontofc.ca
• Bill Manning, President
• Ali Curtis, General Manager
• Chris Armas, Head Coach
Home Field:
BMO Field. Seating capacity 22,453.

VANCOUVER WHITECAPS FC
SUITE 550
THE LANDING
375 WATER STREET
VANCOUVER, BC, CANADA V6B 5C6
604-669-9283
Fax: 604-684-5173
info@whitecapsfc.com
www.whitecapsfc.com

• Axel Schuster, CEO/Sporting Director
• Greg Anderson, VP, Soccer Operations
• Marc Dos Santos, Head Coach
Home Field:
BC Place. Seating capacity 21,000.

NATIONAL WOMEN'S SOCCER LEAGUE
1556 S MICHIGAN AVENUE
FLOOR 2
CHICAGO, IL 60605
312-549-8900
info@nwslsoccer.com
www.nwslsoccer.com
• Lisa Baird, Commissioner
• Amanda Duffy, President
Year Founded:
2007
Decsription:
The highest level of women's professional soccer league in North America. The mission is to be the premier women's soccer league in the world, and the global standard by which women's professional sports are measured.

Teams:

CHICAGO RED STARS
SEATGEEK STADIUM
CHICAGO, IL
info@chicagoredstars.com
chicagoredstars.com
• Arnim Whisler, Owner/CEO
• Lindsay Goldner, Director, Communications & Marketing
• Rory Dames, Head Coach

FC KANSAS CITY
5366 W 95TH STREET
PRAIRIE VILLAGE, KS 66207
855-452-4625
Fax: 913-742-7056
www.fkcwoso.com
• Huw Williams, Head Coach
hwilliams@kcprosoccer.com

HOUSTON DASH
1001 AVENIDA DE LAS AMERICAS
SUITE 200
HOUSTON, TX 77010
713-276-7500
Fax: 713-276-7572
info@houstondynamo.com
www.houstondynamo.com/houstondash
• James Clarkson, Head Coach

NORTH CAROLINA COURAGE
WAKEMED SOCCER PARK
101 SOCCER PARK DRIVE
CARY, NC 27511
919-459-8144
www.nccourage.com
• Curt Johnson, President/General Manager
• Curt Johnson, President/General Manager
• Paul Riley, Head Coach

OL REIGN
CHENEY STADIUM
TACOMA, WA
info@olreign.com
www.olreign.com
• Farid Benstiti, Head Coach

ORLANDO PRIDE
EXPLORIA STADIUM
ORLANDO, FL
orlandocitysc.com/pride
• Alex Leitao, Chief Executive Officer
• Marc Skinner, Head Coach

PORTLAND THORNS FC
1844 SW MORRISON
PORTLAND, OR 97205
503-553-5400
Fax: 503-553-5405
www.timbers.com/thornsfc
• Merritt Paulson, CEO
• Mark Parsons, Head Coach

RACING LOUISVILLE FC
LYNN FAMILY STADIUM
110 W MAIN ST
2ND FL
LOUISVILLE, KY 40202
502-568-2489
info@loucity.com
racingloufc.com
• John Neace, Chair & CEO
• Brad Estes, President
• Christy Holly, Head Coach

SKY BLUE FC
4547 ROUTE 9 N
SUITE Q
HOWELL, NJ 07731
888-723-2849
www.skybluefc.com
• Alyse LaHue, General Manager
• Freya Coome, Head Coach

WASHINGTON SPIRIT
44050 ASHBURN SHOPPING PLAZA
SUITE 195-620
ASHBURN, VA 20147
301-591-0927
washingtonspirit.com
• Larry Best, Chief Executive Officer/Director, Sporting Ops
• Lindsay Barenz, Director, Business Operations
• Richie Burke, Head Coach

USL CHAMPIONSHIP
1715 N WESTSHORE BOULEVARD
SUITE 825
TAMPA, FL 33607
www.uslchampionship.com
• Robert Hoskins, Chairman
• Alec Papadakis, CEO
• Jake Edwards, President

Teams:

ATLANTA UNITED 2
ATLANTA, GA
470-341-1500
atlutd.com
• Stephen Glass, Head Coach

AUSTIN BOLD FC
9201 CIRCUIT OF THE AMERICAS BOULEVARD
AUSTIN, TX 78617
512-872-8700
info@austinboldfc.com
www.austinboldfc.com
• Bobby Epstein, Chairman
• Rick Abbott, Acting General Manager
• Marcelo Serrano, Head Coach

BIRMINGHAM LEGION FC
2213 1ST AVENUE S
BIRMINGHAM, AL 35233
205-791-7145
info@bhmlegion.com
www.bhmlegion.com
• Jay Heaps, President/General Manager
• Tommy Soehn, Head Coach

CHARLESTON BATTERY
1990 DANIEL ISLAND DRIVE
CHARLESTON, SC 29492

843-971-4625
info@charlestonbattery.com
charlestonbattery.com
• Mike Anhaeuser, Head Coach/General Manager

CHARLOTTE INDEPENDENCE
QUEEN CITY SOCCER CLUB
1523 ELIXABETH AVENUE
SUITE 120
CHARLOTTE, NC 28204
704-206-1515
charlotteindependence@gmail.com
www.charlotteindependence.com
• Jim McPhilliamy, CEO & Managing Partner
• Tim Schuldt, COO & President
• Mike Jeffires, Head Coach

COLORADO SPRINGS SWITCHBACKS FC
234 N TEJON STREET
COLORADO SPRINGS, CO 80903
719-368-8480
info@switchbacksfc.com
switchbacksfc.com
• Martin Ragain, Owner
• Nick Ragain, President
• Brian Crookham, General Manager
• Brendan Burke, Head Coach

EL PASO LOCOMOTIVE FC
SOUTHWEST UNIVERSITY PARK
1 BALLPARK PLAZA
EL PASO, TX 79901
915-235-4625
info@eplocomotivefc.com
www.eplocomotivefc.com
• Alan Ledford, President
• Andrew Forrest, General Manager, Business Operations
• Mark Lowry, Head Coach/Technical Director

FC TULSA
TULSA, OK
info@fctulsa.com
www.fctulsa.com
• James Cannon, President
• Michael Nsien, Head Coach

HARTFORD ATHLETIC
DILLON STADIUM
250 HUYSHOPE AVENUE
HARTFORD, CT 06106
860-216-0816
info@hartfordathletic.com
www.hartfordathletic.com
• Bruce Mandell, Chairman
• Jim Burda, Chief Executive Officer
• Harry Watling, Head Coach

INDY ELEVEN
47 S PENNSYLVANIA STREET
SUITE 611
INDIANAPOLIS, IN 46204
317-685-1100
Fax: 317-635-1100
www.indyeleven.com
• Ersal Ozdemir, Owner/Chairman
• Greg Stremlaw, President/CEO
• Martin Renne, Head Coach

LA GALAXY II
DIGNITY HEALTH SPORTS PARK
18400 AVALON BOULEVARD
SUITE 200
CARSON, CA 90746
310-630-2000
www.lagalaxy.com/2
• Dennis te Kloese, General Manager
• Junior Gonzalez, Head Coach

LAS VEGAS LIGHTS FC
850 N LAS VEGAS BOULEVARD
LAS VEGAS, NV 89101

702-728-4625
www.lasvegaslightsfc.com
• Brett Lashbrook, Owner/CEO
• Steve Cherundolo, Head Coach

LOUDOUN UNITED FC
202-655-2842
info@loudoununitedfc.com
www.loudoununitedfc.com
• Ryan Martin, Head Coach

LOUISVILLE CITY FC
110 W MAIN STREET
2ND FLOOR
LOUISVILLE, KY 40202
502-384-8799
www.loucity.com
• Brad Estes, President
• John Hackworth, Head Coach/Sporting Director

MEMPHIS 901 FC
AUTOZONE PARK
198 UNION AVENUE
MEMPHIS, TN 38103
901-721-6000
Fax: 901-328-1102
www.memphis901fc.com
• Craig Unger, President/Owner
• Tim Howard, Sporting Director/Head Coach

MIAMI FC
MIAMI, FL
www.miamifc.com
• Michael Williamson, Chief Executive Officer
• Paul Dalglish, Technical Director/Head Coach

MONTERY BAY FC
www.montereybayfc.com
• Ray Beshoff, Owner/Chair
• Mike DiGiulio, President
• Frank Yallop, Sporting Director

NEW MEXICO UNITED
3500 CENTRAL AVENUE SE
SUITE 2
ALBUQUERQUE, NM 87106
505-209-7529
info@newmexicoutd.com
www.newmexicoutd.com
• Peter Trevisani, Owner/President
• Troy Lesesne, Head Coach/Technical Director

NEW YORK RED BULLS II
RED BULL ARENA
600 CAPE MAY STREET
HARRISON, NJ 07029
877-727-6223
www.newyorkredbulls.com/2
• John Wolyniec, Head Coach

OAKLAND ROOTS SC
OAKLAND
oaklandrootssc.com
• Dario Pot, Head Coach

OKC ENERGY FC
1001 N BROADWAY AVENUE
OKLAHOMA CITY, OK 73102
405-235-5425
www.energyfc.com
• Jason Hawkins, General Manager
• John Pascarella, Head Coach

ORANGE COUNTY SC
CHAMPIONSHIP SOCCER STADIUM
ORANGE COUNTY GREAT PARK
8272 GREAT PARK BOULEVARD
IRVINE, CA 92618
949-647-4625
www.orangecountysoccer.com
• James Keston, Owner/CEO
• Oliver Wyss, General Manager/President,

Soccer Operations
• Braeden Cloutier, Head Coach

PHOENIX RISING FC
8010 E MCDOWELL ROAD
SUITE 103
SCOTTSDALE, AZ 85257
623-594-9606
info@phxrisingfc.com
www.phxrisingfc.com
• Bobby Dulle, General Manager
• Rick Schantz, Head Coach

PITTSBURGH RIVERHOUNDS SC
510 W STATION SQUARE DRIVE
PITTSBURGH, PA 15219
412-224-4900
www.riverhounds.com
• Tuffy Shallenberger, Owner/Interim President
• John Rotz, Director, Operations
• Bob Lilley, Head Coach

QUEENSBORO FC
queensborofc.com
• Josep Gombau, Head Coach & Sporting Director

REAL MONARCHS SLC
9256 S STATE STREET
SANDY, UT 84070
801-727-2700
Fax: 801-727-1469
www.rsl.com/monarchs
• Dell Loy Hansen, Owner
• John Kimball, Interim President
• Elliot Fall, General Manager
• Freddy Juarez, Head Coach

RIO GRANDE VALLEY FC
fernando@rgvfc.com
www.rgvfc.com
• Ron Patel, President
• Wilmer Cabrera, Head Coach

SACRAMENTO REPUBLIC FC
1050 20TH STREET
SUITE 200
SACRAMENTO, CA 95811
916-307-6100
goal@sacrepublicfc.com
www.sacrepublicfc.com
• Todd Dunivant, President & General Manager
• Mark Briggs, Head Coach

SAN ANTONIO FC
5106 DAVID EDWARDS DRIVE
SAN ANTONIO, TX 78233
www.sanantoniofc.com
• Tim Holt, Managing Director & VP
• Alen Marcina, Head Coach

SAN DIEGO LOYAL SC
858-465-4625
info@sdloyal.com
www.sdloyal.com
• Warren Smith, President/CEO
• Landon Donovan, Executive VP, Soccer Operations/Manager

SPORTING KC CITY II
2020 BALTIMORE AVENUE
KANSAS CITY, MO 64108
913-387-3400
888-452-4625
clientservices@sportingkc.com
www.sportingkc.com/sportingkcii
• Peter Vermes, General Manager/Sporting Director
• Paulo Nagamura, Head Coach

TACOMA DEFIANCE
2502 S TYLER STREET
TACOMA, WA 98405

253-752-7707
Tickets@WeRTacoma.com
www.tacdefiance.com
• Wade Weber, Head Coach

TAMPA BAY ROWDIES
230 1ST STREET SE
ST. PETERSBURG, FL 33701
727-222-2000
Fax: 813-282-3800
info@rowdiessoccer.com
www.rowdiessoccer.com
• Lee Cohen, President
• Neill Collins, Head Coach

USL LEAGUE ONE
1715 N WESTSHORE BOULEVARD
SUITE 825
TAMPA, FL 33607
www.uslleagueone.com
• Robert Hoskins, Chairman
• Alec Papadakis, CEO
• jake Edwards, President

Teams:

CHATTANOOGA RED WOLVES SC
6739 RINGGOLD RD
SUITE B, C, D
CHATTANOOGA, TN
chattanoogeredwolves-sc.com
• Sean McDaniel, President & General Manager
• Jimmy Obleda, Head Coach

FORT LAUDERDALE CF
intermiamicf.com
• Chris Henderson, Chief Soccer Officer/Sporting Director
• Jason Kreis, Head Coach

FORWARD MADISON FC
forwardmadisonfc.com
• Vern Stenman, President
• Carl Craig, Technical Director/Head Coach

GREENVILLE TRIUMPH
greenvilletriumph.com
• Chris Lewis, President
• John Harkes, Head Coach/Sporting Director

NEW ENGLAND REVOLUTION II
revolutionsoccer.net/revolutionii
• Clint Peay, Head Coach

NORTH CAROLINA FC
northcarolinafc.com
• John Bradford, Head Coach

NORTH TEXAS FC
fcdallas.com/northtexassc
• Matt Denny, General Manager
• Eric Quill, Head Coach

RICHMOND KICKERS
2001 MAYWILL ST
SUITE 205
RICHMOND, VA 23230
richmondkickers.com
• Rob Ukrop, President
• Darren Sawatzky, Chief Sporting Officer/Head Coach

SOUTH GEORGIA TORMENTA FC
tormentafc.com
• Darin Van Tassell, President
• Ian Cameron, Head Coach

TORONTO FC II
BMO FIELD
170 PRINCES' BOULEVARD
TORONTO, ON, CANADA M6K 3C3
416-360-4625
www.torontofc.ca/tfcii
• Bill Manning, President
• Ali Curtis, General Manager
• Mike Munoz, Head Coach

TUCSON FC
fctucson.com
• Amanda Powers, President
• John Galas, Head Coach

UNION OMAHA
unionomaha.com
• Martie Cordaro, President
• Jay Mims, Head Coch/Technical Director

USL LEAGUE TWO
1715 N WESTSHORE BOULEVARD
SUITE 825
TAMPA, FL 33607
www.uslleaguetwo.com
• Robert Hoskins, Chairman
• Alec Papadakis, CEO
• Jake Edwards, President
Description:
A development league in the U.S. soccer league system.
Founded:
1995
Member Clubs:
74

Teams:

AC CONNECTICUT
153 S MAIN STREET
NEWTOWN, CT 06470
203-270-3522
acconnecticut.com
• Peter D'Amico, President
• Robin Schuppert, General Manager
• Antony Howard, Director, Coaching

AFC ANN ARBOR
3676 S STATE STREET
ANN ARBOR, MI 48108
info@afcannarbor.com
www.afcannarbor.com
• Eric Rudland, Head Coach/Sporting Director

AHFC ROYALS
sgreen@albionhurricanes.org
www.ahfcroyals.com

ALBUQUERQUE SOL FC
3636 MENAUL BOULEVARD NE
SUITE 321
ALBUQUERQUE, NM 87110
505-510-2555
www.abqsolfc.com
• Ron Patel, President
• Matt Gordon, Head Coach

ASHEVILLE CITY SC
management@ashevillecitysc.com
ashevillecitysc.com

BALTIMORE BOHEMIANS
BONVEGNA FIELD
3100 BOSTON STREET
BALTIMORE, MD 21224
info@baltimorebohemians.com
www.baltimorebohemians.com
• Louis Angelos, Managing Partner
• James Tirabassi, General Manager
• Santino Quaranta, Head Coach

BLACK ROCK FC
www.blackrockfc.org
• Jon Moodey, CEO

BOSTON BOLTS
UMASS MOUNT IDA CAMPUS
777 DEDHAM STREET
NEWTON, MA 02459
USL2@BostonBolts.com
www.bostonbolts.com/programs/usl2
• Aidan Byrne, Head Coach

BRAZOS VALLEY CAVALRY FC
252 W CARSON STREET
BRYAN, TX 77801
207-228-1138
www.bvcavalryfc.com
• Uri Geva, Founder/Co-Owner
• Brian Nelson, Director, Soccer Operations
• Gareth Glick, Head Coach

BYU COUGARS
SMITH FIELDHOUSE
SOUTH FIELD
PROVO, UT 84602
801-422-2096
soccer.byu.edu
• Chris Watkins, Head Coach

CALGARY FOOTHILLS FC
MOUNT ROYAL COLLEGE
CALGARY, AB, CANADA
www.foothillsfc.ca
• Leon Hapgood, Head Coach

CEDAR STARS RUSH
3 EMPIRE BOULEVARD
CARLSTADT, NJ 27429
201-939-0651
info@cedarstarsrush.com
www.cedarstarsrush.com
• Justin Miller, General Manager
• Anthony Nixon, Head Coach

CHARLOTTE EAGLES
8510 MCALPINE PARK DRIVE
SUITE 109
CHARLOTTE, NC 28211
704-841-8644
info@charlotteeagles.com
www.charlotteeagles.com
• Mary Toohey, General Manager
mtoohey@charlotteeagles.com
• Garrett Bireline, Head Coach
gbireline@charlotteeagles.com
• David Dixon, Head Coach
ddixon@charlotteeagles.com

CHARLOTTE INDEPENDENCE 2
11148 TREYNORTH DRIVE
SUITE A
CORNELIUS, NC 28031
704-899-4680
info@independencesoccer.club
www.independencesoccer.club
• Thomas Finlay, CEO
• Dave Carton, Technical Director

CHICAGO FC UNITED
3090 N LAKE TERRACE
GLENVIEW, IL 60026
847-386-6579
Fax: 847-410-3926
www.chicagofcunited.com
• Larry Sunderland, Technical Director

CINCINNATI DUTCH LIONS
859-746-5250
info@cdlfc.com
cdlfc.com
• Robert Rack, President
• Brandon Ponchak, General Manager
b.ponchak@cdlfc.com

• Paul Nicholson, Head Coach
p.nicholson@cdlfc.com

COLORADO RUSH
LITTLETON, CO
720-624-9000
www.coloradorush.com/coloradorushsc

CORPUS CHRISTI FC
10201 S PADRE ISLAND DRIVE
SUITE 205
CORPUS CHRISTI, TX 78418
361-214-3236
mediaccfc@gmail.com
corpuscfc.com
• Kingsley Okonkwo, President
• Sebastian Giraldo, Head Coach

D.C. UNITED U-23
2400 E CAPITOL STREET SE
WASHINGTON, DC 20003
202-587-5000
www.dcunited.com/academy

DALTON RED WOLVES SC
411 BROAD STREET
SUITE 101
CHATTANOOGA, TN 37402
423-541-1660
www.chattanoogaredwolves-sc.com
• Sean McDaniel, President/General Manager

DAYTON DUTCH LIONS
1190 W SPRING VALLEY PIKE
CENTERVILLE, OH 45458
937-331-8444
ddlfc.com
• Corey Whisenhunt, General Manager
c.whisenhunt@ddlfc.com
• Dan Griest, Head Coach
d.griest@ddlfc.com
• Sid van Druenen, Director of Soccer & Head
Coach
s.vandruenen@ddlfc.com

DAYTONA SC
206 BEACH STREET
SUITE 204
DAYTONA BEACH, FL 32114
386-238-9639
t.eason@ta-sportsgroup.com
daytonasoccerclub.com

DERBY CITY ROVERS
PO BOX 6066
LOUISVILLE, KY 40206
www.roverssoccer.com
• Nathan Pitcock, President
• Lee Chalmers, Head Coach

DES MOINES MENACE
1459 GRAND AVENUE
DES MOINES, IA 50309
515-226-9890
www.menacesoccer.com
• Tiley Nunnink, General Manager
• Mark McKeever, Head Coach

EAST ATLANTA FC
admin@eastatlantafc.com
www.eastatlantafc.com
• Kelly Shirah, Executive Director
• Sam Walker, Head Coach

EVERGREEN FC
VIRGINIA ALLIANCE
4317 RAVENSWORTH ROAD
ANNANDALE, VA 22003
703-828-8149
royalsgm@novafc.org
vaalliance.soccer

FA EURO NEW YORK
7707 17TH AVENUE
BROOKLYN, NY 11214
718-331-6308
management@faeuro.com
faeuro.com
• Joe Balsamo, President
• Benjamin Marcu, Football Operations
• Kai Haaskivi, Director, Coaching

FC BASCOME BERMUDA
info@fcbascomebermuda.com
www.fcbascomebermuda.com
• Richard Pitcher, Manager, Operations
rpitcher@fcbascomebermuda.com
• Richard Calderon, General Manager
(441) 536-1608
richard@fcbascomebermuda.com

FC MANITOBA

FC MIAMI CITY
CENTRAL BROWARD REGIONAL PARK
3700 NW 11TH PLACE
LAUDERHILL, FL 33311
contact@fcmiamicity.com
www.fcmiamicity.com
• Ravy Truchot, President
• Julian Pedraza, Head Coach

FC TUCSON
3600 SOUTH COUNTRY CLUB
TUCSON, AZ
520-334-1115
www.fctucson.com
• Jon Pearlman, General Manager
• Rick Schantz, Head Coach

FLINT CITY BUCKS
ATWOOD STADIUM AT KETTERING
UNIVERSITY
701 UNIVERSITY AVENUE
FLINT, MI 48503
810-666-2515
www.flintcitybucks.com
• Dan Duggan, Chairman/CEO
• Andy Wagstaff, Technical Director/Head
Coach

FLORIDA ELITE SA
www.floridaeliteusl.com
• Sean Bubb, Executive Director/Head Coach

FLORIDIANS FC
• Franck Gotsman, Chairman
• Fernando Valenzuela, Head Coach

FRESNO FUEGO
1800 TULARE STREET
FRESNO, CA 93721
559-320-2543
www.fresnofuego.com
• Jeremy Schultz, General Manager
• Scott Alcorn, Head Coach

GOLDEN STATE FORCE FC
fcgoldenstateforce.com
• Alex Lujan, Director, Football
• Robert Friedland, Head Coach

GPS PORTLAND PHOENIX
512 WARREN AVENUE
PORTLAND, ME 04103
207-887-9176
Fax: 207-887-9177
jmckenna@globalpremiersoccer.com
www.gps-maine.com

GRAND RAPIDS FC
162 HOUSEMAN AVENUE NE
GRAND RAPIDS, MI 49503

hello@grandrapidsfc.com
grandrapidsfc.com
• Louis Stephens, General Manager
• James Gilpin, Head Coach

GREEN BAY VOYAGEURS
2231 HOLMGREN WAY
GREEN BAY, WI 54304
920-497-7225
grandrapidsfc.com
• Brian Kamler, Head Coach

HOUSTON DUTCH LIONS
14562 I-45 SOUTH
CONROE, TX 77384
713-498-4499
www.houstondutchlionsfc.com
• Martin Kroeze, President
• Marco Pruis, Head Coach

HOUSTON FC
info@hfcpdl.com
www.hfcpdl.com
• Bruce Talbot, Head Coach

IMG ACADEMY BRADENTON
5500 34TH STREET W
BRADENTON, FL 34210
941-755-1000
Fax: 941-752-2630
info@imgacademy.com
www.imgacademy.com
• Tom Durkin, Head Coach

JERSEY EXPRESS S.C.
140 MOUNTAIN AVENUE
SUITE 303
SPRINGFIELD, NJ 07081
917-907-4092
Fax: 718-451-1915
www.jerseyexpresssoccer.org
• Joe Branco, Owner & Chairman
• Gali Maimon, General Manager

KAW VALLEY
www.kawvalleyfc.com
• Marcus Dudley, President/General Manager
• Istvan Urbanyi, Head Coach

KITSAP PUMAS
4020 WHEATON WAY
SUITE P
BREMERTON, WA 98310
360-377-6008
Fax: 360-377-2967
kitsapsoccerclub.com
• Robin Waite, Owner
• Cameron MacDonald, Head Coach

KOKOMO PDL
KOKOMO, IN
www.kokomosoccer.com

LANE UNITED FC
www.laneunitedfc.com
• Dave Galas, Managing Director
• Conner Cappelletti, Head Coach

LAREDO HEAT
7220 BOB BULLOCK LOOP
LAREDO, TX 78041
www.laredoheatsc.com
• Shashi Vaswani, President
• Daniel Galvan, Head Coach

LAS VEGAS MOBSTERS
9555 HILLWOOD DRIVE
SUITE 150
LAS VEGAS, NV 89134
702-318-8802
Fax: 702-318-8801

info@lvmobsters.com
lvmobsters.com
• Martin Melendrez, President
• Phillip Garcia, General Manager
• Paul Barron, Head Coach

LEHIGH VALLEY UNITED
1344 N SHERMAN STREET
ALLENTOWN, PA 18109
610-841-0080
info@lehighvalleyunited.com
www.lehighvalleyunited.com

LIONSBRIDGE FC
www.lionsbridgefc.com
• Chris Whalley, Head Coach

LONG ISLAND ROUGH RIDERS
1425 OLD COUNTRY ROAD
BUILDING A
PLAINVIEW, NY 11803
516-622-3900
Fax: 516-622-3901
info@liroughriders.com
liroughriders.com
• Peter Zaratin, President
• Flavio Ferri, Chief Operating Officer
• David Price, Head Coach

LOUISVILLE CITY FC U23
110 W MAIN STREET
SECOND FLOOR
LOUISVILLE, KY 40202
502-384-8799
info@loucity.com
www.loucity.com
• John Neace, Chairman
• John Hackworth, Head Coach/Sporting Director

MANHATTAN SC
www.manhattanscusl2.org
• Colin Hodge, Head Coach

MIDLAND/ODESSA SOCKERS
5514 CHAMPIONS DRIVE
MIDLAND, TX 79706
sockersfc.org
• Monty Hoppel, General Manager
• Jeff VonHolle, Assistant GM & Director of Soccer Operations
• Matt Barnes, Head Coach

MISSISSIPPI BRILLA FC
PO BOX 281
CLINTON, MS 39060
601-924-3475
Fax: 601-488-0226
info@msbrillafc.org
brillasoccer.org
• Rusty Bryant, Executive Director & General Manager

NEW MEXICO UNITED U23
3500 CENTRAL AVENUE SE
SUITE 2
ALBUQUERQUE, NM 87106
505-209-7529
info@newmexicoutd.com
www.newmexicoutd.com
• Peter Trevisani, Owner/President
• Troy Lesesne, Head Coach

NEW YORK RED BULLS U23
RED BULL AREANA
600 CAPE MAY STREET
HARRISON, NJ 07029
www.redbullsacademy.com/academy
• Sean McCafferty, Academy Director
• Rob Elliott, Coach

NORTH CAROLINA FC U23
1121 SITUS COURT
SUITE 350
RALEIGH, NC 27606
919-459-8144
www.northcarolinafc.com
• Curt Johnson, President/General Manager

NORTH CAROLINA FUSION U23
112 S CHERRY STREET
SUITE B
KERNERSVILLE, NC 17284
336-669-0841
u23.ncfusion.org
• Scott Zapko, General Manager
• Chris Williams, Head Coach

OAKLAND COUNTY FC
935 N CUSTER AVENUE
CLAWSON, MI 48017
248-629-0251
info@oaklandcountyfc.com
www.oaklandcountyfc.com
• Vinnie Vasilevski, Head Coach

OCALA STAMPEDE
109 SE 1ST AVENUE
OCALA, FL 34471
352-804-0132
Fax: 352-867-8864
• Bill Reed, President
• Cheyne Roberts, Executive Director & Head Coach

OCEAN CITY NOR'EASTERS
200 6TH STREET
OCEAN CITY, NJ 08226
609-432-8271
Fax: 609-399-4784
info@oceancityfc.com
www.oceancityfc.com
• Giancarlo Granese, President
• Giancarlo Granese, Jr., General Manager
• Tim Oswald, Head Coach

OGDEN CITY SC
9159 S STATE STREET
SANDY, UT 84070
801-307-5150
Fax: 801-998-8421
www.utahyouthsoccer.net/ogden_city_sc
• Andrew Hiatt, President/CEO
• Bryan Attridge, General Manager
• Eric Landon, Head Coach

ORANGE COUNTY BLUES U-23
16 TECHNOLOGY DRIVE
SUITE 156
IRVINE, CA 92618
• Ali Mansouri, Owner

ORLANDO CITY U-23
618 E SOUTH STREET
SUITE 510
ORLANDO, FL 32801
855-675-2489
www.orlandocitysc.com/topics/u23s

PALM BEACH SUNS FC
5550 GLADES ROAD
SUITE 500
BOCA RATON, FL 33431
www.palmbeachsunsfc.com
• Ronald Da Silva, President
• Eduardo De Souza, Head Coach

PARK CITY RED WOLVES SC
411 BROAD STREET
SUITE 101
CHATTANOOGA, TN 37402
423-541-1660
www.chattanoogaredwolves-sc.com/parkcity

PEACHTREE CITY MOBA
1000 MOBA DRIVE
PEACHTREE CITY, GA 30269
678-817-1374
www.mobasoccer.com
• Jim Robbins, Director, Coaching

PEORIA CITY

PHILADELPHIA LONE STAR
6333 KINGSESSING AVENUE
PHILADELPHIA, PA 19142
484-862-2595
info@philadelphialonestarfc.com
www.philadelphialonestarfc.com
• Fatoma Turay, Head Coach

PITTSBURGH RIVERHOUNDS U-23
510 W STATION SQUARE DRIVE
PITTSBURGH, PA 15219
412-224-4900
www.riverhounds.com
• John Rotz, Operations Manager
jrotz@riverhounds.com
• Josh Rife, Head Coach

PORTLAND TIMBERS U23
PORTLAND, OR
503-553-5400
Fax: 503-553-5405
info@timbersu23.com
www.timbersu23.com
• Collin Box, Executive Director
• Matt Broadhead, Head Coach

PUGET SOUND GUNNERS FC
206-898-6183
Fax: 425-814-7323
• Alex Silva, Assistant Coach/Director

READING UNITED AC
EXT 230
www.readingunitedac.com
• Troy Snyder, President
• Denise Strohmayr, Executive Director
denise@readingunitedac.com
• Alan McCann, Head Coach

REAL BOSTON RAMS
300 MAIN STREET
EASTON, MA 02356
• Mike Madden, President
mmadden@bostonrams.com
• Hobie Hare, Head Coach & General Manager

REAL COLORADO FOXES
SHEA STADIUM
3270 REDSTONE PARK CIRCLE
LITTLETON, CO 80129
720-348-0283
www.rcfoxes.com

SAN FRANSISCO CITY FC
cityfootball@sfcityfc.com
sfcityfc.com
• Jacques Pelham, CEO
• Eddie Soto, Head Coach

SAN FRANSISCO GLENS SC
2521 JUDAH STREET
SAN FRANSISCO, CA 94122
415-349-8333
info@sfglens.com
www.sfglens.com
• Mike McNeill, President/Executive Director, Football

SANTA CRUZ BREAKERS FC
SANTA CRUZ, CA
www.breakersacademy.org
• Mike Runeare, Head Coach

SARASOTA METROPOLIS FC
1620 MAIN STREET
SUITE 5
SARASOTA, FL 34236
941-330-8978
soccer@sarasotametropolisfc.com
www.sarasotametropolisfc.com
• Bill Unzicker, Head Coach

SC UNITED BANTAMS
PO BOX 2082
COLUMBIA, SC 29201
877-457-2832
Fax: 888-675-2704
www.southcarolinaunitedfc.com
• Ron Tryon, Chairman & General Manager
rontryon@southcarolinaunitedfc.com
• David Kenga, Head Coach
davidkenga@southcarolinaunitedfc.com

SEACOAST UNITED PHANTOMS
PO BOX 779
HAMPTON, NH 03843
603-926-8444
Fax: 603-926-8555
www.seacoastunited.com
• Paul Willis, President/CEO
• Alex Ryan, General Manager
aryan@seacoastunited.com

SOUND FC
206-445-2097
www.soundersu23.com
• Jason Prenovost, General Manager/Head Coach
• Lane Smith, Owner/CEO
• Jason Prenovost, General Manager/Head Coach

SOUTH BEND LIONS
SOUTH BEND, IN
www.southbendlions.com
• Thiago Pinto, Head Coach

SOUTHERN CALIFORNIA SEAHORSES
PO BOX 855
LA MIRADA, CA 90637
714-739-8375
info@seahorsesoccer.com
www.seahorsesoccer.com
• Mark Schrock, General Manager
• Todd Elkins, Head Coach

SOUTHERN SOCCER ACADEMY
40 WHITLOCK PLACE
SUITE 200
MARIETTA, GA 30064
678-594-5041
sharon@ssaelite.com
clubs.bluesombrero.com
• Simon Davey, Executive Director/General Manager
• Kelham O'Hanlon, Head Coach

SOUTHERN WEST VIRGINIA KING'S WARRIORS
PO BOX 126
FOREST HILL, WV 24935
304-466-9080
wvkingswarriors@yahoo.com
• James Blume, Jr., President
• Tim Donelli, General Manager
• John Miglarese, Head Coach

SPRINGFIELD SYNERGY FC

ST. LOUIS LIONS
TONY GLAVIN SOCCER COMPLEX
2 WOODLANDS PARKWAY
COTTLEVILLE, MO 63376
636-939-5151
www.stllions.com

• Tony Glavin, Owner/President/Head Coach
• Kevin Hecht, General Manager

SW FLORIDA ADRENALINE
4100 EVANS AVENUE
SUITE 5
FORT MYERS, FL 33901
239-218-5673
swfladrenaline.com
• Jeff Butzke, Owner
• John Robinson, Head Coach

TAMPA BAY ROWDIES U23
230 1ST STEET SE
ST. PETERSBURG, FL 33701
727-222-2000
Fax: 313-282-3800
www.rowdiessoccer.com
• Lee Cohen, President
• Neill Collins, Head Coach

TEXAS UNITED
info@txunitedfc.com
txunitedfc.com
• Arez Ardalani, Head Coach

TFA WILLAMETTE
PO BOX 1354
ALBANY, OR 97321
541-230-7029
info@txunitedfc.com
txunitedfc.com
• Logan Hoffman, Director, Coaching

THE VILLAGES SC
17690 S US HIGHWAY 301
SUMMERFIELD, FL 34491
352-561-8239
info@thevillagessc.com
www.thevillagessc.com
• Anderson DaSilva, Head Coach

THUNDER BAY CHILL
CHAPPLES SOCCER PARK
535 CHAPPLES PARK DRIVE
THUNDER BAY, ON, CANADA P7E 2P2
807-623-5911
giovannipetragliatbc@gmail.com
www.thunderbaychill.com
• John Marrello, General Manager
• Giovanni Petraglia, Head Coach

TOBACCO ROAD FC
DURHAM, NC
678-594-5041
www.tobaccoroadfc.com
• Cedric Burke, Head Coach

TORMENTA FC
STATESBORO, GA
www.tormentafc.com

TORMENTA FC 2
2704 OLD REGISTER ROAD
STATESBORO, GA 30458
news@tormentafc.com
www.tormentafc.com
• Darin Van Tassell, Owner/President
• John Miglarese, Head Coach

TREASURE COAST TRITONS
www.tritonsusl.com
• Ryan Strickland, General Manager
• Thomas Durkin, Head Coach
(781) 708-3271
tdurkin.tctritons@gmail.com

TRI-CITIES OTTERS
423-930-9500
lucas@ottersoccer.com
ottersoccer.com

• Lucas Christiansen, General Manager
• David Strickland, Head Caoch

TSS ROVERS
TSS SOCCER CENTRE
115-1751 SAVAGE ROAD
RICHMOND, BC, CANADA V6V 1R1
soccer@tss.ca
www.tss.ca
• Will Cromack, General Manager
• Colin Elmes, Head Coach

VENTURA COUNTY FUSION
701 E SANTA CLARA STREET
SUITE 21
VENTURA, CA 93001
805-830-8027
Fax: 805-277-9743
info@vcfusion.com
www.vcfusion.com
• Ranbir Shergill, General Manager
• Rudy Ybarra, Head Coach

VICTORIA HIGHLANDERS FC
VICTORIA, BC, CANADA
www.highlandersfc.ca
• Jeremy Dillon, Director, Operations
• Thomas Niendorf, Head Coach

VIRGINIA BEACH UNITED
2044 LANDSTOWN CENTRE WAY
VIRGINIA BEACH, VA 23456
757-427-2990
vbuops@beachsportsplex.com
www.vabeachunited.com
• Matt Mittelstaedt, General Manager
• Matt Ellinger, Head Coach

WAKE FC
PO BOX 1211
HOLLY SPRINGS, NC 27540
919-249-5119
info@wakefc.com
www.wakefcusl.com
• Gary Heale, Head Coach

WASHINGTON CROSSFIRE
12312 134TH COURT NE
REDMOND, WA 98052
www.crossfiresoccer.org
• Peter Chung, President
• Bernie James, Coaching Director

WEST CHESTER UNITED SC
901 S BOLMAR STREET
SUITE P
WEST CHESTER, PA 19382
610-399-5277
www.wcusc.org
• Mark Thomas, Executive Director/General Manager

WEST VIRGINIA ALLIANCE FC
SHAWNEE PARK MULTI SPORTS COMPLEX
1 SALANGO WAY
DUNBAR, WV 25064
www.wvalliancefc.com
• Dan Rollins, General Manager
drollin2@csc.com
• Daniel Smee, Head Coach

WESTCHESTER FLAMES
FLOWERS PARK
491 5TH AVENUE
NEW ROCHELLE, NY 10801
www.westchesterflames.com
• Dan Elias, General Manager
• Edson Buddle, Head Coach

WESTERN MASS PIONEERS
PO BOX 457
LUDLOW, MA 01056

413-583-4814
Fax: 413-547-6225
info@wmpioneers.com
www.wmpioneers.com
• Celso Correia, President
• Greg Kolodziey, General Manager
• Federico Molinari, Head Coach

WESTON FC
4181 WESTON ROAD
SUITE 264
WESTON, FL 33331
954-349-7261
Fax: 877-349-4076
westonfc.org
• Luis Mendoza, Head Coach
luis.mendoza@westonfc.org

WSA WINNIPEG
WINNIPEG, MB, CANADA
204-477-0763
Fax: 204-477-0763
eduardo@world-soccer-academy.com
wsawinnipegpdl.com
• Eduardo Badescu, Head Coach

WOMEN'S PREMIER SOCCER LEAGUE
4041 AMERICAN RIVER DRIVE
SACRAMENTO, CA 95864
916-487-3512
800-854-0913
www.wpslsoccer.com
• Rich Sparling, League Commissioner
Description:
Second tier of women's soccer in the U.S.
with teams in the United States and Mexico.
Founded:
1997
Member Clubs:
86

Teams:

ALABAMA FC
3576 EAST STREET
BIRMINGHAM, AL 35243
205-977-9038
Fax: 205-977-9099
www.birminghamunited.com
• Andrew Brower, Executive Director

ASA CHARGE FC
PO BOX 242
GAMBRILLS, MD 21054
• John Hamrick, President
• Patrick Crawford, General Manager
• Tim Wittman, Co-Head Coach
• Tarik Walker, Co-Head Coach

AUSTIN
401 WEST PECAN STREET
SUITE A
PFLUGERVILLE, TX 78660
832-721-6509

BEACH FUTBOL CLUB
63 SAVONA WALK
LONG BEACH, CA 90803
562-889-8806
• Dalton Kaufman, General Manager & Coach
• Mauricio Ingrassia, Coach

BLUES FC
60 HANOVER AVENUE
SUITE B2
MORRIS PLAINS, NJ 07950
908-285-3358
• Shaun Donnelly, General Manager
• Tom Worthington, Head Coach

BOSTON AZTEC
PO BOX 81
BEVERLY, MA 01915
www.bostonaztec.com
• Brandon Nelson, General Manager
• Costas Flessas, Head Coach

BOSTON BREAKERS COLLEGE ACADEMY
645 WASHINGTON STREET
SUITE A
HANOVER, MA 02339
617-945-1704
Fax: 617-945-1721
info@bostonbreakers.com
www.bostonbreakerssoccer.com
• Stephanie Schafer, Head Coach

BOSTON BREAKERS RESERVES
645 WASHINGTON STREET
SUITE A
HANOVER, MA 02339
617-945-1704
Fax: 617-945-1721
www.bostonbreakerssoccer.com
• Lee Billiard, General Manager
• Frankie D'Agostino, Head Coach

BUXMONT TORCH FC
627 SPRUCE HILL ROAD
OTTSVILLE, PA 18942
215-795-9751
• Rich Sparling, President
• Brittney Ruggierii, Head Coach

CALIFORNIA STORM
4041 AMERICAN RIVER DRIVE
SACRAMENTO, CA 95864
916-718-1925
www.calstormsoccer.com
• Jerry Zanelli, Owner & Head Coach
jerryzanelliwpsl@gmail.com

CHATTANOOGA FC
818 SUNSET MOUNTAIN DRIVE
CHATTANOOGA, TN 37421
423-509-4166 EXT 115
• Moises Drumond, Head Coach

CHESTERFIELD UNITED
6144 BRAD MCNEER PARKWAY
MIDLOTHIAN, VA 23112
804-271-2714
Fax: 804-271-7747
www.chesterfieldunited.com
• Pat McStay, General Manager
• Eric Dutt, Head Coach

CHICAGO RED STAR RESERVES
710 W BELDEN AVENUE
CHICAGO, IL 60614
773-697-8699
Fax: 312-546-3670
chicagoredstars.com
• Neha Shah, Operations Manager

CINCINNATI LADY SAINTS
4222 EILEEN DRIVE
CINCINNATI, OH 45209
513-646-3767

COLUMBUS EAGLES
1312 EPWORTH AVENUE
REYNOLDSBURG, OH 43068
614-868-5033
www.columbuseaglesfc.com
• Mark Wise, Owner & Chief Executive Officer

DALLAS CITY FC
11615 FOREST CENTRAL DRIVE
SUITE 305
DALLAS, TX 75243

972-646-2727 EXT 115
Fax: 972-646-2729

DES MOINES MENACE
6400 WESTOWN PARKWAY
WEST DES MOINES, IA 50266
515-457-6365
www.menacesoccer.com
• Matt Homonoff, General Manager
• Justin Vorster, Head Coach

EMPIRE REVS WNY
18 CAROLILLY COURT
EAST AMHERST, NY 14051
716-480-4033
• Kathleen DiPasquale, General Manager
• Chris Hershey, Head Coach

EUGENE TIMBERS FC AZUL
1200 HIGH STREET
SUITE 130
EUGENE, OR 97401
541-343-5100
info@eugenetimbers.org
eugenetimbers.org
• Jurgen Ruckaberle, Head Coach

FC BUCKS
PO BOX 839
RICHBORO, PA 18954
267-247-6038
www.crusa.net
• Ed Leigh, Head Coach

FC INDIANA
PO BOX 111
INDIANAPOLIS, IN 46527-0310
574-536-0997
• Shek Borkowski, General Manager & Head Coach

FC NASHVILLE WOLVES
781 BELL ROAD
ANTIOCH, TN 37013
615-478-3947
Fax: 615-731-9799
www.nashvillewolves.com
• Daniel Gordon, Director of Coaching

FC PRIDE
9220 HARRISON PARK COURT
INDIANAPOLIS, IN 46216
317-809-0036
www.fcpride.org
• Jamie Gilbert, Head Coach

FC SURGE
8501 SW 68TH STREET ROAD
MIAMI, FL 33143
954-649-5521
www.fcsurgesoccer.com
• Marge Perry, General Manager

FC TACOMA 253
114 ALASKAN WAY S
SUITE 101
SEATTLE, WA 98104
206-790-5971
• Filippo Milano, Coach

FC TUCSON WOMEN
3600 SOUTH COUNTRY ROAD
TUCSON, AZ 85713
520-334-1115
fctucson.com
• Charlie MacCabe, General Manager
• Amy Garelick, Head Coach

FC TULSA SPIRIT
4135 S SHERIDAN
TULSA, OK 74145
918-269-5155

- Brandon Stone, Manager
- Ali Adibi, Coach

FC WESTCHESTER
106 CORPORATE PARK DRIVE
WHITE PLAINS, NY 10606
914-330-9153
- Michael Orth, Executive Director
- Carlos Mejia, Director of Coaching

FEDERAL CITY FC

FIRE & ICE SOCCER CLUB
2346 MASCOUTAH AVENUE
BELLEVILLE, IN 62220
618-910-7076
www.fireandicesc.com
- Lindsay Kennedy-Eversmeyer, Owner & Head Coach

FLORIDA KRUSH
PO BOX 620159
OVIEDO, FL 32765
512-633-0140
Fax: 850-254-7227
www.flkrushwpsl.com
- Kurt Oettl, Manager
- Hue Menzies, Coach

FLORIDA SOL FC
2100 PARK FOREST COURT
FLEMING ISLAND, FL 32003
904-910-5389
www.floridasolsoccer.com
- Luis Torres, General Manager & Head Coach

FORT WORTH PANTHERS
3625 DOMINY LANE
APT 625
FORT WORTH, TX 76179
817-368-0206
Fax: 817-236-9641
- Tarik Guendouzi, Head Coach

FREDERICKSBURG FC
3411 SHANNON PARK DRIVE
FREDERICKSBURG, VA 22408
540-368-5425
www.fredericksburgfc.org
- Grover Gibson, III, President & Head Coach
executivedirector@fredericksburgfc.org
- Ryan Zinkhan, General Manager

FRESNO FREEZE FC
1800 TULARE STREET
FRESNO, CA 93721
559-320-2543
- Alex Ott, Owner
- Jeremy Schultz, General Manager
- Tim Carroll, Head Coach

FUERZA FC
2901 BELLMONTE LANE
EVERETT, WA 98201
425-530-2849
www.fuerzafc.com
- Becky Alvarado, Club Administrator

HERSHEY FC
PO BOX 66
HERSHEY, PA 17033
www.hersheysoccer.com
- Adam Clay, Director of Coaching

HOUSTON ACES
17403 MASONRIDGE ROAD
HOUSTON, TX 77095
713-419-1980
www.thehoustonaces.com
- Aguinaldo Ferreira, Head Coach

HOUSTON ACES SOUTH SELECT
17403 MASONRIDGE ROAD
HOUSTON, TX 77095
713-419-1980
www.thehoustonaces.com/about-south-select

ISC GUNNERS FC
PO BOX 501
ISSAQUAH, WA 98027
425-272-2699
www.iscgunners.org
- Joe Yellig, Executive Director
- Gareth Vaughan, Coach

KC COURAGE
OLATHE, KS 66062
913-220-8771
www.kccourage.com
- Wendy Louque, Director

KNOXVILLE LADY FORCE
1718 N CENTRAL STREET
KNOXVILLE, TN 37917
865-724-5971
www.emeraldyouthsports.org/Default.aspx?tabid=735880

LA PREMIER FC
1434 FOOTHILL BOULEVARD
UNIT B
LA CANADA, CA 91011
626-685-9503
Fax: 818-864-6951
lapremierfc@gmail.com
www.lapremierfc.com
- Louis Hunt, Head Coach

LA VILLA FC
2160 MORENO DRIVE
LOS ANGELES, CA 90039
818-281-4964
lavillafc.managers@gmail.com
www.lavillasoccer.com
- Catherine Davila, Head Coach

LANCASTER INFERNO
559 FRUITVILLE PIKE
MANHEIM, PA 17545
www.lancasterinferno.com
- Francisco Cleaves, Head Coach

LEGENDS FC
13851 ROSWELL AVENUE
SUITE E
CHINO, CA 91710
909-465-1177
Fax: 909-614-7052
www.legendsfc.net
- Angela Wright, Director of Operations
- Josh Hodges, Executive Director of Coaching

LONG ISLAND FURY
PO BOX 0863
BALDWIN, NY 11510
718-869-9749
- Tom DeBonis, General Manager
- Paul Riley, Head Coach

MADISON 56ERS SC
437 S YELLOWSTONE DRIVE
SUITE 220
MADISON, WI 53719
608-273-1956
Fax: 608-273-1959
www.madison56ers.org
- John Reddan, Coach

MICHIGAN LIONS
6757 CASCADE ROAD SE
SUITE 56
GRAND RAPIDS, MN 49546
- Abrahm Shearer, Head Coach

MINNESOTA TWINSTARS FC
11222 86TH AVENUE N
SUITE 101
MAPLE GROVE, MN 55369
minnesotatwinstars.com
- Bulut Ozturk, Head Coach

MOTOR CITY FC
26510 BURG ROAD
WARREN, MI 48089
586-942-9412
mc-fc.com
- Skipper Mukhtar, Jr., Head Coach & General Manager

NEW ENGLAND MUTINY
1 AMES HILL DRIVE
SPRINGFIELD, MA 01105
newenglandmutiny@aol.com
www.mutinysoccer.com
- Joseph Ferrara, Jr., President & General Manager

NEW JERSEY WILDCATS
16 DOREEN DRIVE
OCEANPORT, NJ 07757
732-720-9163
Fax: 732-298-7619
njwildcatskevin@aol.com
www.njwildcats.com
- Kevin McDermott, President

NEW YORK ATHLETIC CLUB
180 CENTRAL PARK S
NEW YORK, NY 10019
212-767-7000
www.nyac.org/soccer
- Andrew Cullen, General Manager
- Kim Wyant, Coach

NORTH BAY FC WAVE
PO BOX 2997
SAN ANSELMO, CA 94979
415-302-6779
www.northbayfc.com
- Birgit Byers, President
- Grahame Reid, General Manager
- Luis Quezada, Head Coach

NORTHWEST FLORIDA UNITED

NTC RUSH
7635 ASHLEY PARK COURT DRIVE
SUITE 503B
ORLANDO, FL 32835
407-948-7642
- Richie Gray, Executive Director
- Erick Garcia, Head Coach

OKLAHOMA CITY FC
414 NW 4TH STREET
SUITE 120
OKLAHOMA CITY, OK 73102
405-232-7223
Fax: 405-232-7230
www.oklahomacityfc.com
- Sean Jones, Owner
- Stephen Phillips, Co-Head Coach
- Yolanda Thomas, Co-Head Coach

OLYMPIC FORCE
1199 UNION AVENUE W
BREMERTON, WA 98312
www.olympicforce.com
- Micah McMonagle, General Manager
- Kate Green, Head Coach

PALM CITY FC
FORT MYERS, FL 33965
- Jeff Varner, General Manager
- Kurt Albrecht, Head Coach

PATEADORES
151 KALMUS DRIVE
SUITE F-5
COSTA MESA, CA 92626
www.pateadores.org
• David Barry, President
• Lisa Brosnan, Operations Manager

PHOENIX DEL SOL
18777 N 32ND STREET
SUITE 100
PHOENIX, AZ 85050
602-867-2302
Fax: 602-493-3165
• Chris Diana, President
• Mark Lowe, Executive Director

PINELLAS COUNTY UNITED SC
PO BOX 40343
ST. PETERSBURG, FL 33743
www.pinellascountysoccerclub.com
• Jeff Kirkwood, President
• Kai Velmer, Director of Soccer Operations
• Don Tobin, Director of Coaching

PORTLAND SPARTANS FC
PORTLAND, OR
www.spartansfutbolclub.com

PRIMERO DE MAYO
2116 STACIA WAY
SACRAMENTO, CA 95822
916-825-0402

QUAD CITY EAGLES FC
20535 240TH STREET
ELDRIDGE, IA 52748
563-343-1612

REAL SALT LAKE WOMEN
9256 S STATE STREET
SANDY, UT 84070
801-556-6941
realsaltlakewomen.com
• Jeff Ginn, Head Coach

RHODE ISLAND REDS FC
PO BOX 9425
PROVIDENCE, RI 02940
888-508-3113
Fax: 866-685-8273
info@riredsfc.com
www.riredsfc.com
• Kabba Joof, Owner
• Jonathan Fonseca, President
• Alex Rozkov, Head Coach

SAN DIEGO WFC SEALIONS
6023 GAINES STREET
SAN DIEGO, CA 92110
760-521-6626
www.sealionsoccer.com
• Lu Snyder, President
• Jen Lalor-Nielsen, Head Coach

SAN FRANCISCO NIGHTHAWKS
85 CARL STREET
SUITE 7
SAN FRANCISCO, CA 94117
www.sfnighthawks.com
• Jill Lounsbury, General Manager

SEACOAST UNITED MARINERS
772 STEVENS AVENUE
PORTLAND, ME 04103
207-729-8444
Fax: 207-729-8999
www.seacoastunitedmaine.org
• Josh Needle, Head Coach

SEACOAST UNITED PHANTOMS
PO BOX 779
HAMPTON, NH 03843
603-758-7114
Fax: 603-926-8555
www.seacoastunited.com
• David Burgess, Head Coach

SOCAL FC
26650 THE OLD ROAD
SUITE 300
VALENCIA, CA 91381
888-501-0533
socalfc.com
• Kristen Arnone, Chief Executive Officer
• Guy Arnone, President
• Dido Tshimanga, Head Coach

SPURS EAST BAY LADIES
SAN FRANCISCO, CA
www.eastbayladies.com

STEEL CITY FC
649 NORTH AVENUE
MILLVALE, PA 15209
724-504-6904
www.steelcityfc.com
• Stephanie Harrison, General Manager
• Anita Rodriguez, Co-Head Coach
• Betsy Warren, Co-Head Coach

SYRACUSE LADY KNIGHTS
7662 WARRIORS PATH
BALDWINSVILLE, NY 13027
• Mike Paolini, Head Coach

TAMPA BAY HELLENIC
7543 LAND O' LAKES BOULEVARD
LAND O' LAKES, FL 34638
813-966-7911
Fax: 813-996-4533
• Maryann Bishop, General Manager
• George Fotopoulos, Head Coach

TEAM BOCA BLAST
7491 N FEDERAL HIGHWAY
SUITE C5-288
BOCA RATON, FL 33487
561-237-8006
Fax: 561-431-7610
info@teamboca.com
www.teamboca.com
• Bill D'Addio, Club Director
bill@teamboca.com

TEXAS SPURS FC
DALLAS, TX

TEXAS TITANS
CYPRESS, TX 77433
281-685-8072
• Courtney Murdoch, Owner & Manager

TIJUANA XOLOS USA
TIJUANA, BC, MEXICO
xolos.com.mx
• Andrea Rodebaugh, Coach

TKARONTO JUSTICE
NEW YORK, NY

TREASURE COAST DYNAMITES
5475 NW ST. JAMES DRIVE
SUITE 144
PORT ST-LUCIE, FL 34983
772-206-0695
treasurecoastdynamites.com
• Gaspard Dalexis, General Manager & Head Coach

VIRGINIA BEACH CITY FC
www.vbcityfc.com
• Steven Wagoner, Owner
• Karen Wagoner, Operations Manager
• Brian Hinkey, Head Coach

WEST COAST WILDKATZ
320 W LARCH ROAD
SUITE 11
TRACY, CA 95304
209-229-1095
Fax: 209-833-0382
westcoastsoccerclub.com
• Troy Dayak, Head Coach

YANKEE LADY FC
69 MARLEY DRIVE
MIDDLEBURY, CT 06762
yankeeunited.com
• Jack Noguiera, Head Coach

Softball Organizations

AMATEUR SOFTBALL ASSOCIATION OF AMERICA (ASA)
2801 NE 50TH STREET
OKLAHOMA CITY, OK 73111
405-424-5266
www.teamusa.org
• Craig Cress, Executive Director
• Mark Loehrs, Chief Financial Officer
• Steve Walker, Director of Operations
• Kevin Ryan, Director of Umpires
Description:
Established in 1933, the ASA is the national governing body of softball in the U.S. and oversees aspects of the grassroots programs and national team programs. ASA has more than 100 championships ranging from 10-under fast pitch to 75-over slow pitch, with more than 40,000 players every year. There is a local association for each state. USA Softball is a brand of the ASA related specifically to the USA National Teams that compete internationally for the United States.
Publications:
Official publication, BALLS & STRIKES SOFTBALL MAGAZINE, published five times annually; OFFICIAL RULE BOOK and SCOREBOOK, both annual.

DIXIE SOFTBALL INC
1101 SKELTON DRIVE
BIRMINGHAM, AL 35224
205-785-2255
obeidsi@aol.com
• James E. Evans, President
• Leonard Preston, Vice President
• Sharon Lafitte, Secretary
Description:
A primarily youth centered softball program for girls 18 years of age and younger, playing on a scaled-down diamond to meet the physical development of the growing child. The main purpose is to provide a recreation outlet for as many as possible with emphasis on local league play rather than tournament play.

INTERNATIONAL SOFTBALL CONGRESS
PO BOX 1083
FINDLAY, OH 45839
801-447-8807
iscken@comcast.net
www.iscfastpitch.com

• Larry Fisher, Executive Director
(419) 722-7448
lfisher838@ameritech.net
• Dean Oscar, President
• Blair Setford, VP, Operations
(416) 625-1757
Publications:
ISC WORLD CHAMPIONSHIP GUIDE,
annually.
Membership Requirements:
Application to commissioners and
participation in area tournaments and/or
affiliated travel leagues.
Description:
A non-profit association for the promotion
and administration of mens and boys
fastpitch softball throughout North America
with athletes coming from literally all over
the world.

INTERNATIONAL SOFTBALL FEDERATION
1900 SOUTH PARK ROAD
PLANT CITY, FL 33563
813-864-0100
Fax: 813-864-0105
info@ISFsoftball.org
www.isfsoftball.org
• Dale McMann, President
dmcmann@isfsoftball.org
• Ron Radigonda, Executive Director
rradigonda@isfsoftball.org
• Laurie Gouthro, Assistant Executive
Director
lgouthro@isfsoftball.org
Description:
The International Softball Federation is a
member of the World Baseball Softball
Confederation. The ISF is in charge of
managing the world championship
competition in various softball events.

NATIONAL FASTPITCH COACHES ASSOCIATION/NFCA
4641 GRINSTEAD DRIVE
LOUISVILLE, KY 40206
502-409-4600
Fax: 502-409-4622
nfca@nfca.org
nfca.org
• Rhonda Revelle, President
rrevelle@huskers.com
• Pat Conlan, 1st VP
pjc72@georgetown.edu
• Kate Drohan, 2nd VP
k-drohan@northwestern.edu
• Lacy Lee Baker, Executive Director
llb@nfca.org
Nature of Sports Service:
Professional organization for all levels of
softball coaches, including two & four year
colleges and universities, highschools and
travel teams.
Membership Requirements:
Annual fees for softball coaches, umpires
and affiliate members.
Member Services:
Subscription to membership newsletter,
annual directory, access to member only
content on web site, discounts on
convention and merchandise.
Publications:
FASTPITCH DELIVERY (monthly);
FASTPITCH CONNECTED (weekly); TOP
RECRUIT-ANNUAL; Directory of Information
(Membership directory)

Number of members:
4,700

NATIONAL SLO-PITCH ATHLETICS ENTERPRISES OF CANADA
BAY 9
1925 - 39TH AVENUE NE
CALGARY, AB, CANADA T2E 6W7
403-250-9655
Fax: 403-769-9055
info@nsacanada.ca
nsacanada.ca
• Terry Sibbick, CEO/President
• Ewan Webster, Executive Vice President
• Wanda Sibbick, Vice President
• Jeremy Thiemann, National Director

NATIONAL SOFTBALL ASSOCIATION
PO BOX 7
NICHOLASVILLE, KY 40340
859-887-4114
Fax: 859-887-4874
nsahdqtrs@playnsa.com
www.playnsa.com
• Hugh Cantrell, CEO
hcantrell@playnsa.com
• Ray Cantrell, President
ecantrell@playnsa.com
• Faye Cantrell, National Office Manager
fcantrell@playnsa.com
Year Founded:
1982
Nature of Sport Services:
A full service organization that offers a
division of play and a level of competition
that youth and adults can enjoy.

NATIONAL WHEELCHAIR SOFTBALL ASSOCIATION
13414 PAUL STREET
OMAHA, NE 68154
402-305-5020
bfroendt@cox.net
www.wheelchairsoftball.org
• Brian Chavez, President
(612) 388-0874
brianchavez1972@msn.com
• Bruce Froendt, Commissioner
(402) 305-5020
bfroendt@cox.net
• Juan Ortiz, 1st Vice President
juor3rd@gmail.com
• John Hamre, 2nd Vice President
jthamre@gmail.com
Publications:
National Wheelchair Softball Association
Newsletter, periodically.
Membership Requirements:
Membership made up of competing teams
of the Association and of the Associate
members.
Description:
Founded in 1976 and serves as the
governing body for wheelchair softball in the
United States. Played under the official rules
of the 16-inch slow pitch softball as
approved by the Amateur Softball
Association of America with some
expectations geared toward the wheelchair
user.

OVER-THE-LINE PLAYERS ASSOCIATION
3890 CARSON STREET
SAN DIEGO, CA 92117
otlpanews@aol.com

• Faustino Medina, President
• Brian McGiveron, Vice President
• Fred Elliott, Secretary
• Gregg Williams, Treasurer
Description:
Founded in 1976. Promotes the sport of
over-the-line by sponsoring tournaments,
overseeing others' tournaments, putting on
clinics and publishing a monthly newsletter
that gives tournament results and supplies
tournament applications.

SENIOR SOFTBALL-USA
2701 K STREET
SUITE 101A
SACRAMENTO, CA 95816
916-326-5303
Fax: 916-326-5304
info@seniorsoftball.com
www.seniorsoftball.com
• Terry Hennessy, CEO
terryh@seniorsoftball.com
• Fran Dowell, Executive Director
• Ross McCulligan, Executives Assistant,
Umpires and Bookkeeping
Number of Members:
1.5 million men and women over 40
Member Services:
Softball tournaments, national and
international; softball newspapers; and
softball ID cards.
Publications:
Senior Softball-USA News
Membership Requirements:
Over 50 years old
Description:
Dedicated to informing and uniting the
Senior Softball Players of America and the
World. Sanctions tournaments and
championships, registers players, writes the
rulebook, hosts International Softball Tours
and promotes Senior Softball throughout the
world.

SOFTBALL CANADA
223 COLONNADE ROAD
SUITE 212
OTTAWA, ON, CANADA K2E 7K3
613-523-3386
Fax: 613-523-5761
info@softball.ca
www.softball.ca
• Kevin Quinn, President
• Hugh Mitchener, Chief Executive Officer
(613) 523-3386
• Mike Branchaud, Manager - National
Teams/Canadian Championships
(613) 523-3386
Member Services:
Publications, clinics, program development.
Publications:
RULES, COACHING, UMPIRING,
CASEBOOK, DRILLS.
Membership Requirements:
Ten provinces, two territories; each
provincial or territorial member has its own
membership structure.
Description:
Founded in 1965. Fosters, develops, and
regulates playing of amateur softball in
Canada.

SOFTBALL FACTORY
9212 BERGER ROAD
SUITE 200
COLUMBIA, MD 21046

855-822-5115
Fax: 410-715-1975
info@softballfactory.com
www.softballfactory.com
Description:
Provides nationwide instruction, college
planning and guidance to softball players.

**UNITED STATES SPECIALTY SPORTS
ASSOCATION**
611 LINE DRIVE
KISSIMMEE, FL 34744
321-697-3636
Fax: 321-697-3647
don.dedonatis@usssa.com
www.usssa.com
• Don DeDonatis, Chairman, Executive
Directionr & CEO
• Jim Swint, Assistant Executive Director
• Robert Boudreaux, Executive Vice
President
Description:
The USSSA is a non-profit, sports governing
body residing in Kissimmee, Florida.

**WORLD BASEBALL SOFTBALL
CONFEDERATION**
MAISON DU SPORT INTERNATIONAL
54, AVE DE RHODAINE
LAUSANNE, SWITZERLAN 1007
+41-2131-88240
Fax: +41-2131-88241
office@wbsc.org
Description:
Comprised of the International Softball
Federation (ISF) and the International
Baseball Federation (IBAF), the WBSC
serves as the global authority for baseball
and softball.

Softball, Leagues/Teams

MAJOR LEAGUE SOFTBALL
621 EAST WALNUT AVENUE
BURBANK, CA 91501
818-559-8787 EXT 3
www.mlsoftball.com

NATIONAL PRO FASTPITCH
3350 HOBSON PIKE
HERMITAGE, TN 37076
615-324-7861
info@profastpitch.com
www.profastpitch.com
• Cheri Kempf, President/Commissioner
cherik@profastpitch.com
• Gaye Lynn Wilson, Vice President
gayelynnw@profastpitch.com
• Mike Raynor, Supervisor of Officials
• Erin Collins, Play By Play
• Barbara Jordan, Color Analyst
Nature of Sports Service:
Formerly the Women's Pro Softball League.
NPF is intended to provide family
entertainment for people of all ages and to
showcase the top talent in softball today. It
is the goal of the league to entertain and
provide positive role models for young
people. NPF demonstrates that a good work
ethic, dedication, and love for what one
does, will allow everyone to achieve their
life's goals. NPF athletes demonstrate this
by their actions, both on-and-off the field.
They are prominent people within their
communities and avail themselves to their

fans, particularly the young ones.
Sports Service Founded:
1989

Teams:

AKRON RACERS
1575 FIRESTONE PARKWAY
AKRON, OH 44301
330-376-8188
Fax: 330-376-8348
www.akronracers.org
• Stout Craig, Owner/CFO
• Joey Arrietta, Co-Owner/GM
(330) 376-8188
joeyarrietta@akronracers.us
• Brian Levin, Field Manager
Stadium:
Firestone Stadium. Seating capacity, 4,576.

CHICAGO BANDITS
27 JENNIE FINCH WAY
ROSEMONT, IL 60018
877-722-6348
Fax: 630-396-3095
banditsinfo@chicagobandits.com
www.chicagobandits.com
• Bill Sokolis, President/CEO
• Aaron M. M Moore, General Manager
aaron.moore@chicagobandits.com
• Jacquie Boatman, Director of Community &
Media Relations
jacquie.boatman@chicagobandits.com
• Johnny Sole, Director of Ticket Sales
Stadium:
Rosemont Stadium.

DALLAS CHARGE
6151 ALMA ROAD
MCKINNEY, TX 75070
724-242-7431
• Kevin Shelton, General Manager
• Laura Villa, Assistant General Manager
• Caitlin Hall, Athletic Trainer
• Richard Levy, Team Doctor
Stadium:
Gate Nesbitt Stadium. Seating capacity, 1,000.

PENNSYLVANIA REBELLION
ONE WASHINGTON FEDERAL WAY
WASHINGTON, PA 15301
724-250-9555
Fax: 724-250-2333
fwwilliams@washingtonwildthings.com
• Francine Williams, Managing Partner
• Steve Zavacky, General Manager
• Christine Blaine, Director of Marketing &
Communications
• Tony Buccilli, Director of Team Operations
• Elana D. Williams, Director of Operations
Stadium:
Consol Energy Park. Seating capacity, 3,200.

SCRAPYARD DAWGS
29607 ROBINSON ROAD
CONROE, TX 77385
855-793-2947
• Kevin Shelton, General Manager
• Whitney Cloer, Assistant General Manager
Stadium:
Scrapyard Softball Complex.

USSSA FLORIDA PRIDE
611 LINE DRIVE
KISSIMMEE, FL 34744
321-697-3635
info@usssapride.com
• Don DeDonatis, General Manager
• Gordon Glennie, Assistant General Manager
• Wendi Brockwell, Director of Accounting Ticket
Operations
• Bernie Guenther, Director of Broadcast
Operations
• Mike Davenport, Head Coach

Stadium:
Champion Stadium. Seating capacity, 9,500.

SLO-PITCH NATIONAL SOFTBALL
63 GALAXY BOULEVARD
UNIT 4
ETOBICOKE, ON, CANADA M9W5R7
416-674-1802
Fax: 416-674-8233
www.slo-pitch.com

Speedskating Organizations

**FEDERATION INTERNATIONALE
ROLLER SPORTS (FIRS)**
AV DE RHODANIE, 54
LAUSANNE, 1007
www.rollersports.org

**INTERNATIONAL SKATING UNION (ISU)
(ICE SKATING)**
AVENUE JUSTE-OLIVIER 17
LAUSANNE, SWITZERLAN 1006
info@isu.ch
isu.org
• Fredi Schmid, Director General
Description:
Founded in 1892, the ISU is the
International Governing Body for ice skating
athletics.

U.S. SPEEDSKATING
5662 S. COUGAR LANE
KEARNS, UT 84118
801-417-5360
Fax: 801-417-5361
media@usspeedskating.org
www.usspeedskating.org
• Ted Morris, Executive Director
tmorris@usspeedskating.org

USA ROLLER SPORTS
4730 SOUTH STREET
LINCOLN, NE 68506
402-483-7551
Fax: 402-483-1465
www.teamusa.org/USA-Roller-Sports

Squash Organizations

**COLLEGE SQUASH ASSOCIATION/MENS
& WOMEN'S INTERCOLLEGIATE
COMPETITION**
HATFIELD, MA
csa@collegesquashassociation.com
collegesquashassociation.com
• Wendy Lawrence, President/Women's
• Hansi Wiens, Vice President/Women's
• Martin Heath, President/Treasurer/Men's
• Tomas Fortson, Vice President/Men's
Membership Requirements:
Membership dues. Intercollegiate schedule
pursued. Competition in the National
Intercollegiate athletics.

PROFESSIONAL SQUASH ASSOCIATION
46 THE CALLS
LEEDS, ENGLAND LS2 7EY
office@psaworldtour.com
psaworldtour.com
• Alex Gough, CEO
alex@psaworldtour.com

• Lee Beachill, COO
lee@psaworldtour.com
• Hannah Ridgard-Mason, Tour Director
Number of members:
750+ Members
Membership Requirements:
Be a squash professional or squash manufacturer.
Description:
The official sanctioning and membership body for men's and women's squash World Rankings.

SQUASH CANADA
20 JAMIE AVENUE
2ND FLOOR
NEPEAN, ON, CANADA K2E 6T6
613-228-7724
Fax: 613-228-7232
info@squash.ca
www.squash.ca
• Lolly Gillen, President
lollygillen@rogers.com
• Shaun Thorson, Vice President, Finance
shaunthor@me.com
• Steve Wren, Vice President Technical
swrenkiwi@gmail.com
• Dan Wolfenden, Executive Director
(613) 228-7724
dan.wolfenden@squash.ca
• Cheryl McEvoy, Operations Manager
(613) 228-7724
cheryl.mcevoy@squash.ca
Member Services:
Coaching and officiating instruction, promotion, junior development, national rankings, national championships, education resource materials.
Description:
Provides a high performance system for athletes, coaches and officials, and sets standards for squash in Canada.

U.S. SQUASH
555 EIGHTH AVENUE
SUITE 1102
NEW YORK, NY 10018-4311
212-268-4090
Fax: 212-268-4091
office@ussquash.com
www.ussquash.com
• Marshall W. Pagon, Chairman of the Board
• Kevin Klipstein, President/Chief Executive Officer
(212) 268-4090
kevin.klipstein@ussquash.com
• Dent Wilkens, Senior Vice President Operations
(212) 269-4090
dent.wilkens@ussquash.com
• Graham Bassett, Director of Doubles and Professional Squash
(212) 268-4090
graham.bassett@ussquash.com
• Bill Buckingham, Director Of Member Services
bill.buckingham@ussquash.com
• Kim Clearkin, Director of National Championships
(212) 268-4090
kim.clearkin@ussquash.com
Number of members:
17,000+
Publications:
Squash Magazine.
Description:

Founded 1904. The national governing body of squash in the United States. Manages 14 national championships and sanctions over 400 tournaments across the USA each year. Pan American member of the United States Olympic Committee. Promotes and governs the game of squash.
Membership Services:
Provides tournaments, leagues and other member services to promote the game of squash for adults and juniors. It Supports singles and doubles as well as softball and hardball. The USSRA selects the teams to represent the United States in Pan American and World Competitions.

WORLD SQUASH FEDERATION/WSF
25 RUSSELL STREET
HASTINGS
EAST SUSSEX, ENGLAND TN34 1QU
www.worldsquash.org
• Jahangir Khan, Emeritus President
tunku_imran@antah.com.my
• Jacques Fontaine, President
• Sarah Fitz-Gerald, Vice President
• Andrew Shelley, Chief Executive
• Lorraine Harding, Operations Manager
• Jasmine Pascoe, Operations Assistant
Description:
International governing body for the sport of squash.
Membership Requirements:
National Federation for Squash

Surfing Organizations

EASTERN SURFING ASSOCIATION
PO BOX 4736
OCEAN CITY, MD 21843
302-988-1953
Fax: 302-258-0735
info@surfesa.org
www.surfesa.org
• Michelle B. Sommers, Executive Director
Year Founded:
1967
Description:
The world's largest amateur surfing association. The ESA is made up of districts from Maine to Alabama. The organization holds competitions and advocates for the preservation of shoreline environments.
Membership Requirements:
Open to all — visit www.surfesa.org to join.

INTERNATIONAL SURFING ASSOCIATION
5580 LA JOLLA BLVD
#145
LA JOLLA, CA 92037
858-551-8580
Fax: 858-551-8563
surf@isasurf.org
www.isasurf.org
• Karin Sierralta, Vice President
• Marcos Bukao, Contest Director
marcosbukao@isasurf.org
• Harrison Robbs, Manager of Event Operations
• Fernando Aguerre, President
president@isasurf.org
• Barbara Kendall, Vice President
• Casper Steinfath, Vice President
• Kirsty Coventry, Vice President

Publications:
Monthly ISA Newsletter(members only), Monthly ISA Press Release (goes to International Media). All sent by email.
Description:
Dedicated to the development of these sports worldwide. Provides guidance and advice to its members around the world on matters such as competition, judging, surf education, adapted surfing, anti doping and other areas of development of the sport.

NATIONAL SCHOLASTIC SURFING ASSOCIATION
PO BOX 495
HUNTINGTON BEACH, CA 92648
714-906-7423
jaragon@nssa.org
www.nssa.org
• Janice Aragon, Executive Director
Member Services:
Provides organized surfing competition and Scholarships for student surfers nationwide.
Membership Requirements:
Must be full time student in either elementary, high school or college or a non-student surfer.
Description:
Founded in 1978, the National Scholastic Surfing Foundation develops fundamental surfing skills and competition skills for young people through participation in events.

SURF INDUSTRY MANUFACTURERS ASSOCIATION/SIMA
27831 LA PAZ ROAD
LAGUNA NIGUEL, CA 92677
949-366-1164
Fax: 949-454-1406
info1@sima.com
www.sima.com
• Kelly Gibson, President
• John Wilson, Vice President
• Johnny Gehris, Treasurer
• Shannon Park Zseleczky, Managing Director
• Sean Smith, Executive Director
Membership Requirements:
Primarily active sportswear and equipment manufacturers serving beach/lifestyle specialty stores.
Description:
An association representing the interests of surfing industry product suppliers.
Year Founded:
1989

SURFLINE.COM
300 PACIFIC COAST HWY
SUITE 300
HUNTINGTON BEACH, CA 92648
714-374-0556
Fax: 714-374-0562
support@surfline.com
www.surfline.com
• Sean Collins, Founder/President
• Jeff Berg, Chariman and Chief Executive Officer
• Mark Willis, Chief Meteorologist
Sports Service Founded:
1985
Nature of Sports Service:
Provider of surf report, forecast and editorial content to consumers, businesses and government agencies worldwide.

WORLD SURF LEAGUE
147 BAY ST
SANTA MONICA, CA 90405
310-450-1212
www.worldsurfleague.com
• Dirk Ziff, Chief Executive Officer
• Meg Bernardo, ASP North America
General Manager
(714) 322-6149
mbernardo@worldsurfleague.com
Description:
Governing body of professional surfing.
Established 1976.
Members:
1000+
Member Services:
World rankings/surfers; event promotion;
judging ranking; coordination of the World
Tour.

Swimming Organizations

AMERICAN SWIMMING COACHES ASSOCIATION
5101 NW 21ST AVENUE, SUITE# 200
FORT LAUDERDALE, FL 33309
954-563-4930
800-356-2722
Fax: 954-563-9813
asca@swimmingcoach.org
www.swimmingcoach.org
• John Leonard, Executive Director
jleonard@swimmingcoach.org
• Guy Edson, Technology Director
gedson@swimmingcoach.org
• Kimberly Aranalde, Certification and
Marketing Coordinator
certification@swimmingcoach.org
Publications:
AMERICAN SWIMMING Magazine; ASCA
Newsletter; ASCA E-news; JOURNAL OF
SWIMMING RESEARCH.
Membership Requirements:
Open to all swimming coaches and
swimming enthusiasts.

COLLEGE SWIMMING COACHES ASSOCIATION OF AMERICA
5101 NW 21ST AVENUE
SUITE 530
FORT LAUDERDALE, FL 33309
954-563-4930
cscaa@swimmingcoach.org
www.cscaa.org
• Susan Teeter, President
• Joel Shinofield, Executive Director
(540) 460-6563
joel@cscaa.org
Number of members:
2,000 member coaches.
Member Services:
Support for intercollegiate athletic issues;
All-American and All-Academic awards;
distinguished service awards.
Description:
The oldest organization of college coaches
in America - is a professional organization of
college swimming and diving coaches
dedicated to serving and providing
leadership for the advancement of the sport
of swimming at the collegiate level.
Year Founded:
1922

LIFE SAVING/UTILITARIAN SPORTS, FEDERATION INTERNATIONALE DE
GEMEENTEPLEIN 26
LEUVEN, Belgium 3010
32-16-89-60-60
Fax: 32-16-89-70-70
info@ilsf.org
www.ilsf.org
• Graham Ford, President
• Dr. Harald Vervaecke PhD, Secretary
General
Description:
The world authority for drowning prevention
and lifesaving sport. ILS leads, supports and
collaborates with national and international
organisations engaged in drowning
prevention, water safety, water rescue,
lifesaving, lifeguarding and lifesaving sport.

SWIMMING/NATATION CANADA
307 GILMOUR STREET
OTTAWA, ON, CANADA K2P 0P7
613-260-1348
Fax: 613-260-0804
natloffice@swimming.ca
www.swimming.ca
• Ahmed El-Awadi, Chief Executive Officer
(613) 260-1348
aelawadi@swimming.ca
• John Atkinson, Director, High Performance
(613) 260-1348
jatkinson@swimming.ca
• Chris Wilson, Director, Marketing
(905) 691-2975
cwilson@swimming.ca
Sports Service Founded:
1909
Member Services:
Canadian non-profit sport organization
provides services to registered amateur
Competitive swimmers through programs
and activities that range across a broad
spectrum including coaching, officiating,
swimming education, sport science, event
coordination, promotion and
communications. The organization's focus is
on the development of world class
competitive swimmers.
Membership Requirements:
Registration as required by the international
governing body, LA Federation
Internationale de Natation, The Aquatic
Federation of Canada and
Swimming/Natation Canada.

SYNCHRO CANADA
700 INDUSTRIAL AVE
SUITE 401
OTTAWA, CANADA K1G 0Y9
613-748-5674
Fax: 613-748-5724
info@synchro.ca
www.synchro.ca
• Jackie Buckingham, Chief Executive
Officer
(613) 748-5674
jackie@synchro.ca
• Jadine Cleary, Domestic Technical
Director
jadine@synchro.ca
• Stephane Cote, Events and
Communications Director
(418) 420-2125
stephane@synchro.ca
• Audrey Frey, Finance & Administration
Manager
(613) 748-5674
audrey@synchro.ca

• Isabelle Lecompte, High performance
Manager
isabelle@synchro.ca
Nature of Service:
Fosters the pursuit of excellence while
developing athletes, citizens and
ambassadors of the sport of synchronized
swimming at all levels.
Year Founded:
1969
Member Services:
Membership card; merchandise discounts.
Annual meetings always in October. Events:
National championships for senior and junior
held once a year, Divisional Championships,
Master National Championships, National
Team Training.
Number of members:
7,000 +

U.S. LIFESAVING ASSOCIATION
www.usla.org
• Peter Davis, President
president@usla.org
• Rob Williams, Vice President
vicepresident@usla.org
• Nikki Bowie, Secretary
secretary@usla.org
• Michael Bradley, Treasurer
treasurer@usla.org
Publications:
American Lifeguard Magazine published
three times a year, Lifeguard News
Membership Requirements:
Five membership categories. Professional,
Alumnus Member, Associate Member,
Associate Junior Lifeguard Member, Junior
Lifeguard Member, Corporate Membership

U.S. SYNCHRONIZED SWIMMING, INC.
1 OLYMPIC PLAZA
COLORADO SPRINGS, CO 80909
719-866-2219
www.usasynchro.org
• Myriam Glez, Chief Executive Officer/High
Performance Director
myriam@usasynchro.org
Description:
USSS acts as the National Governing Body
for synchronized swimming competition.

USA SWIMMING
1 OLYMPIC PLAZA
COLORADO SPRINGS, CO 80909
719-866-4578
Fax: 719-866-4669
info@usaswimming.org
www.usaswimming.org
• Chuck Wielgus, President/Chief Executive
Officer
• Jim Sheehan, Chair of the Board
Description:
USA Swimming acts as the National
Governing Body for the sport, organizaing
competitions and promoting participation.

Table Tennis Organizations

ITTF NORTH AMERICA
18 LOUISA STREET
OTTAWA, ON, CANADA K1R 6Y6
613-733-6272 EXT 223
ittfnorthamerica.com
• Mireille Tallon, Program Coordinator

single sports

TABLE TENNIS CANADA
18 LOUISA STREET
OTTAWA, ON, CANADA K1R 6Y6
613-733-6272
Fax: 613-733-7279
ttcan@ttcan.ca
www.ttcan.ca
• Tony Kiesenhofer, Chief Executive Officer
(613) 733-6272
tonyk@ttcan.ca
• David Jackson, President
davidj@ttcan.ca
Nature of Sports Service:
Founded 1929. Incorporated in 1974.
Develops and promotes table tennis at the highest level across Canada.
Membership Requirements:
Through each provincial organization.
Publications:
20/20, newsletter four times annually.
Member Services:
Support system for provinces; certification of coaches, officials; trains national team; promotes the sport; opportunity for members to obtain videos, manuals.

USA TABLE TENNIS
4065 SINTON RD
SUITE 120
COLORADO SPRINGS, CO 80907
719-866-4583
Fax: 719-632-6071
admin@usatt.org
www.teamusa.org/usa-table-tennis
• Gordon Kaye, CEO
(719) 866-4583
Gordon.Kaye@usatt.org
• Andy Horn, Director of Operations
(719) 866-4583
Andrew.Horn@usatt.org
Description:
National governing body for table tennis in the United States. It oversees a wide variety of membership services, the national teams, and other areas such as the rules of the game, the Hall of Fame, and numerous online instructional and historical articles.
Sports Service Founded:
1933
Description:
Oversees a wide variety of membership services, the national teams, and other areas such as the rules of the game, and numerous online instructional and historical articles.

Tennis Organizations

AMERICAN MEDICAL TENNIS ASSOCIATION
2414 43RD AVENUE E
SUITE B-1
SEATTLE, WA 98112
800-326-2682
www.mdtennis.org
• Bruce Dalkin, MD, President
• Dr. John & Cori Kirkpatrick, Executive Directors
Description:
Founded 1967, a non-profit educational organization whose purpose is to provide Continuing Medical Education programs for physicians.
Membership Requirements:
Doctor of Medicine degree.
Publications:

Newsletter, quarterly. Membership Directory, biannually.

ATP WORLD TOUR
201 ATP TOUR BLVD
PONTE VEDRA BEACH, FL 32082
904-285-8000
Fax: 904-285-5966
www.atptour.com
• Chris Kermode, Executive Chairman/President
• Mark Young, Vice Chairman and Chief Legal and Media Officer
• Flip Galloway, Chief Operating Officer
• Gayle David Bradshaw, Executive Vice President, Rules & Competition
• Ross Hutchins, Chief Player Officer
• Alison Lee, Executive Vice President, International Group
• Gavin Forbes, Tournament Representative
• Mark Webster, Tournament Representative
• Charles Humphrey Smith, Tournament Representative
• David Egdes, Player Representative
• Justin Gimelstob, Player Representative
• Giorgio di Palermo, Player Representative
Additional Offices:
ATP Tour Europe, Monte Carlo Sun, 74 Blvd D'Italie, 98000 Monaco. +377-97-97-04-04; FAX: +377-97-97-04-00. ATP International Group, PO Box N662, Sydney, NSW 1220 Australia. +61-2-92502300; FAX: 61-2-92502333. ATP Executive Offices, IG House Palliser Road, London W14 9EB, United Kingdom, +44-20-7381-7890; FAX: +44-20-7381-7895.
Description:
Founded 1972. Partnership between men's professional tennis players and member tournaments which promote and protect the mutual interests of all men playing professional tennis with over 70 international tennis tournaments in 34 countries on six continents.
Membership Requirements:
Division I player: positioned in top 200 in South African Airways ATP Rankings (singles), or top 100 in ATP Doubles Rankings, and pay ATP dues. Division II player: any player who does not qualify for Division I membership and will be positioned among the top 500 players in the South African Airways ATP Rankings (singles), or top 250 in ATP Doubles Rankings, at the time of application.
Publications:
INTERNATIONAL TENNIS, official magazine; ATP Tour singles and doubles computer rankings.
Member Services:
ATP Tour University - provides information and training for players; ATP Tour Tennis, is seen in more than 180 countries.

INTERCOLLEGIATE TENNIS ASSOCIATION
1130 E UNIVERSITY DRIVE
SUITE 115
TEMPE, AZ 85281
609-497-6920
www.itatennis.com
• Jon Vegosen, Chairman Of The Board
• Timothy Russell, Chief Executive Director
(602) 687-6375
• Cory Brooks, Director Of Events & Championships
(602) 687-6383

cbrooks@itatennis.com
• Laura Schuessler, New Media & Marketing Coordinator
(602) 687-6378
lschuessler@itatennis.com
Description:
The governing body of college tennis at all division levels.
Membership Options:
Corporate and Auxiliary Memberships incl. member categories: alumni, associate, association, collegiate parents, corporation, federation, junior players.
Member Services: (Dependent on Membership type)
Online Membership Directory access; news and ITA ranking updates; ITA Convention membership rates; discounted subscription to the ITA Online Tradeshow; discounted fee for booth at annual ITA Coaches Convention; potential to post video clips online; Junior Players may participate in summer circuit; exposure opportunities; travel dscounts when participating in ITA National & Regional Championship Events; ability to purchase mailing labels & lists of member Coaches; invitation to ITA General Membership Meeting at the ITA Convention.

INTERNATIONAL TENNIS FEDERATION
BANK LANE
ROEHAMPTON
LONDON, ENGLAND SW15 5XZ
communications@itftennis.com
www.itftennis.com
• David Haggerty, President
• Katrina Adams, Vice President
• Luca Santilli, Executive Director Tennis Development
• Mat Pemble, Head of Information And Communications Technology
Description:
The international governing body of tennis.

PETER BURWASH INTERNATIONAL
8909 WEST LANE
MAGNOLIA, TX 77354
281-764-8626
800-324-5494
pbihq@pbitennis.com
www.pbitennis.com
• Peter Burwash, Chief Executive Officer
• Rene Zondag, President
Description:
Founded 1975 by Canadian Davis Cup player, Peter Burwash. Contracts with tennis clubs, resorts and hotels worldwide to direct tennis operations, including instruction, marketing, promotion and management expertise. Provides coaching services and junior development programs to national tennis teams in different countries, as well as on an individual basis to tournament players. Also manages and designs tennis facilities.
Clients include:
Four Seasons, Jumeirah International, Rosewood Hotels & Resorts, Marriott, Hyatt, The American Club
Nature of service:
Tennis program operations, management and direction.
Publications:
PBI Magazine

PROFESSIONAL TENNIS REGISTRY
4 OFFICE WAY
SUITE 200
HILTON HEAD ISLAND, SC 29928
843-785-7244
800-421-6289
Fax: 843-686-2033
ptr@ptrtennis.org
• Dennis Van Der Meer, Chairman / President Emritus
• Dan Santorum, Chief Executive Officer
dan@ptrtennis.org
• Julie Jilly, Vice President of Marketing and Special Event
julie@ptrtennis.org
• Inaki Balzola, International Director
• Peggy Edwards, Director of Communications & Editor TennisPro
• Brian Parkkonen, Director of Development
Nature of Service:
Educates and certifies tennis teachers and coaches internationally.
Year Founded:
1976
Member Services:
Benefits to all aspects of tennis teaching profession.
Publications:
TennisPro Magazine

TENNIS CANADA
AVIVA CENTRE
1 SHOREHAM DRIVE
SUITE 100
TORONTO, ON, CANADA M3N 3A6
416-665-9777
877-283-6647
Fax: 416-665-9017
info@tenniscanada.com
www.tenniscanada.com
• John LeBoutillier, Chair
• Kelly D Murumets, President & Chief Executive Officer
Description:
Shall lead the growth, promotion and showcasing of the sport of tennis in Canada, build a system that helps produce world class players, and foster the pursuit of excellence for all. Owns and operates the men's and women's Rogers Cup events.
Founded:
1890

TENNIS INDUSTRY ASSOCIATION
5 NEW ORLEANS ROAD
SUITE 200
HILTON HEAD ISLAND, SC 29928
843-686-3036
866-686-3036
Fax: 843-686-3078
info@tennisindustry.org
www.tennisindustry.org
• Jolyn DeBoer, Executive Director
Year Founded:
1974
Description:
A not-for-profit trade association representing the interest of its member cmopanies by keeping a pulse on the industry and its needs. Dedicated to maintaining the integrity of the sport and pursuing the growth and vitality of tennis.
Membership Levels:
Industry, Associate, TennisConnect, Supporting, Affiliate, Participating Partners
Publications:
USTA/TIA Participations Study, State of the Industry, market research and consumer reports.
Member Services:
Monthly racquet census, credit interchange, product liability and counterfeiting information, Washington lobbyist, trade show assistance. Participation research project. Meetings held during Sporting Goods Industry Association/SGMA meetings.

U.S. PROFESSIONAL TENNIS ASSOCIATION
3535 BRIARPARK DRIVE
SUITE 202
HOUSTON, TX 77042
713-978-7782
800-877-8248
Fax: 713-978-7780
uspta@uspta.org
www.uspta.com
• Chuck Gill, President
• John Embree, Chief Executive Officer
(713) 358-7782
john.embree@uspta.org
• Fred Viancos, Director Of Professional Development
(713) 358-7782
fred.viancos@uspta.org
• Kathy Buchanan, Director Of Computer Services
(713) 978-7780
kathy.buchanan@uspta.org
• Julie Myers, Director of Communications
(713) 978-7782
julie.myers@uspta.org
• Kimberly Forrester, Publications Manager/Managing Editor
(713) 978-7782
kim.forrester@uspta.org
Nature of Service:
The oldest and largest professional association of tennis-teaching professionals. Offers more than 60 professional benefits to its members, including certification and extensive educational opportunities.
Year Founded:
1927
Membership Requirements:
To be eligible for active membership status, a person must derive or intend to derive a major part of their income from teaching tennis. Persons who derive or intend to derive a major part of their income from prize money in professional tennis tournaments and exhibitions are also eligible. Corporate membership status is available to those persons who have some full-time connection with tennis, either in an executive, administrative or commercial capacity but who are not teachers. All certified members are offered a free, personalized site on the Internet.
Number of members:
15,000
Publications:
Annual Membership Directory; ADDvantage, monthly magazine; World Conference Program, annual.

U.S. RACQUET STRINGERS ASSOCIATION
310 RICHARD ARRINGTON JR/ BLVD N #400
BIRMINGHAM, AL 35203
760-536-1177
Fax: 760-536-1171
usrsa@racquettech.com
www.racquettech.com
• Bob Patterson, MRT, Exective Director
(760) 536-1177
bob@racquettech.com
• Greg Raven, Technical Support &Webmaster
(760) 536-1177
greg@usrsa.com
• John Hanna, Ad Sales
(770) 650-1102
hanna@knowatlanta.com
• Dianne Pray, Membership Director/Office Manager
(760) 536-1177
dianne@racquettech.com
Number of members:
Over 7,000 worldwide.
Publications:
The Stringers Digest; RacquetTECH.com; Racquet Sports Industry Magazine; Racquet TECH Magazine; Racquet Service Video (4 volume set); Racquet Service Interactive CD-ROM workshops, certification, education and testing.
Description:
An organization of racquet technicians, teaching professionals, racquet sports retailers, manufacturers and sales organizations, and tennis, racquetball, squash and badminton players focusing on the servicing of racquets, strings, balls, courts, shoes, and stringing machines.
Year Founded:
1975

UNITED STATES TENNIS ASSOCIATION (USTA)
70 WEST RED OAK LANE
WHITE PLAINS, NY 10604
914-696-7000
www.usta.com
• Gordon Smith, Executive Director & Chief Operating Officer
• Andrea Hirsch, Chief Administrative Officer & General Counsel

Other locations:

USTA CARIBBEAN
PO BOX 190740
SAN JUAN, PUERTO RIC 00919-0740
787-726-8782
Fax: 787-982-7783
www.caribbean.usta.com
• Lydia de la Rosa, Executive Director
delarosa@cta.usta.com
Description:
Embraces the concept that growth in tennis is best achieved by strategic alliances with other organizations, both inside and outside of tennis.

USTA EASTERN
70 WEST RED OAK LANE
WHITE PLAINS, NY 10604
914-697-2300
Fax: 914-694-2402
www.eastern.usta.com
• Jenny Schnitzer, Executive Director & Chief Operating Officer
Description:
One of the 17 geographic sections of the United States Tennis Association which is also the governing body of tennis in the United States. The Eastern Section has over 48,000 members throughout New York, Northern New Jersey and Greenwich, Connecticut. This section promotes and develops the growth of tennis as well as establishes and maintains rules of fair play, high standards of sportsmanship and represents in it

jurisdiction, the programs and policies of the USTA.

USTA FLORIDA
1 DEUCE COURT
SUITE 100
DAYTONA BEACH, FL 32124
386-671-8949
www.ustaflorida.com
• Nancy Horowitz, President -Elect
• Bob Pfaender, President
• Barbara Manzo, Vice president
• Terri Florio, Secretary
• Karen McFarland, Treasurer
• Sherry Beckman, Volunteer Committee,Chair
• Donn Davis, Director At Large
• Robert Hollis, Vice President
Year Founded:
1949
Description:
A not-for-profit tennis association that relies on membership, sponsorships and fundraising to reach its mission-to promote and develop tennis in Florida. Offers tennis programs for all ages and ability levels, including League, Competitive, Recreational and Adaptive services, plus more
Members:
1,000+ member organizations; 50,000 individual members

USTA HAWAII PACIFIC
932 WARD AVENUE
SUITE 490
HONOLULU, HI 96814
808-585-9503
Fax: 808-585-9512
www.hawaii.usta.com
• Ron Romano, Executive Director
(808) 585-9526
romano@hawaii.usta.com
Description:
The USTA/Hawaii Pacific Section is one of 17 sections of the United States Tennis Association. The Hawaii Pacific Section is a not-for-profit volunteer organization. Our mission statement is to promote and develop the growth of tennis. The Hawaii Pacific Section has over 7,000 members and 100 organizations in Hawaii, American Samoa and Guam.

USTA INTERMOUNTAIN
9145 E KENYON AVENUE
SUITE 201
DENVER, CO 80237
303-695-4117
866-695-4117
Fax: 303-695-6518
wanderson@ita.usta.com
www.intermountain.usta.com
• Rob Scott, Executive Director
rscott@ita.usta.com
Description:
Committed to growing the game of tennis by offering quality recreational and competitive programs for people of all ages and abilities. Intermountain has more than 34,000 individual and over 230 organizational members in its six districts: Colorado, Idaho, Montana, Nevada, Utah and Wyoming.

USTA MID-ATLANTIC
11410 ISAAC NEWTON SQUARE NORTH
SUITE 270
RESTON, VA 20190
703-556-6120
Fax: 571-291-4432
www.midatlantic.usta.com
• Lynn Coddington, President
• Tara Fitzpatrick-Navarro, Executive Director
Sports Services Founded:
1923
Description:
The USTA/MAS, one of 17 sections of the United States Tennis Association, is a not-for-profit organization committed to promoting tennis by offering quality recreational and competitive programs for people of all ages

and abilities. We serve 39,000 members in the District of Columbia, Virginia and eastern and southern West Virginia.
Number of Members:
39,000

USTA MIDDLE STATES
1288 VALLEY FORGE ROAD
SUITE 74
PO BOX 987
VALLEY FORGE, PA 19482-0987
610-935-5000
Fax: 610-935-5484
www.middlestates.usta.com
• Christian Sockel, President
• Marlynn Orlando, Executive Director
(484) 302-4404
Description:
The USTA/Middle States section encompasses Pennsylvania, Delaware, New Jersey (exclusive of a 35-mile radius around New york City) and northwestern West Virginia. Also dedicated to carrying out the goals of the national association within its region, particularly with respect to promoting tennis oppotunities for juniors and adults of all abilities and cultural backgrounds.

USTA MIDWEST
1310 EAST 96TH STREET
SUITE 100
INDIANAPOLIS, IN 46240
317-577-5130
Fax: 317-577-5131
feedback@midwest.usta.com
www.midwest.usta.com
• Mark Saunders, Executive Director
(317) 669-0441
• Chad Docktor, Director, Junior Tennis
(317) 669-0445
• Diane Ansay, Director, Adult Tennis
(317) 669-0451
Description:
The mission of the USTA/Midwest section is to promote, develop and service the game of tennis, focusing on the establishment of competitive, developmental, educationl and recreational programs for individuals of all ages and skill levels without regard to race, cree, color or national origin. Also promotes health, character, fair play, sportsmanship and social responsibility through tennis.

USTA MISSOURI VALLEY
6400 WEST 95TH STREET
SUITE 102
OVERLAND PARK, KS 66212
913-322-4800
888-368-8612
Fax: 913-322-4801
www.missourivalley.usta.com
• Stuart Dusenberry, President
sddins62@yahoo.com
• Mary Buschmann, Executive Director
(913) 322-4824
mbuschmann@movalley.usta.com
Description:
Not for profit organization covering a five state region of Iowa, Missouri, Nebraska, Oklahoma and parts of Illinois. This section has more than 22,500 individual members and more than 450 organization members. Also offers recreational and competitive tennis for all ages and abilities.

USTA NEW ENGLAND
110 TURNPIKE ROAD
WESTBOROUGH, MA 01581
508-366-3450
Fax: 508-366-5805
info@newengland.usta.com
www.newengland.usta.com
• Scott Steinberg, President
• Matt Olson, Executive Director & Chief Operating Officer
ext 29
Sports Services Founded:
1927
Description:

A non-profit organization, USTA New England uses its funds to promote and develop the growth of tennis at all levels, offering grants and resources to foster the implementation of programming for players from beginner to veteran; from recreational to competitive and from all ages and backgrounds.

USTA NORTHERN
1001 WEST 98TH STREET
SUITE 101
BLOOMINGTON, MN 55431
952-887-5001
800-536-6982
Fax: 952-887-5061
www.northern.usta.com
• Kathleen Lundberg, President
kathylundberg@comcast.net
• Mike Goldammer, Executive Director
(952) 358-3284
goldammer@northern.usta.com
Sports Services Founded:
1953
Description:
A not-for-profit volunteer-based organization with approximately 35,000 adult members, 9,000 junior members and almost 700 organization members.

USTA NORTHERN CALIFORNIA
1920 NORTH LOOP ROAD
ALAMEDA, CA 94502-8018
510-748-7373
Fax: 510-748-7377
www.norcal.usta.com
• Margie Campbell, President
• Steve Leube, Executive Director
(510) 748-7362
leube@norcal.usta.com
Description:
Non profit volunteer based organization with 34,626 adult members, 7,816 junior members and 503 organization members. THe 8th largest geographic section, USTA Northern California Section has been promoting, servicing, and administering USTA programs for over 49 years. USTA NorCal is devoted to promoting and developing the growth of tennis in Northern California.

USTA PACIFIC NORTHWEST
9746 SW NIMBUS AVENUE
BEAVERTON, OR 97008
503-520-1877
info@pnw.usta.com
www.pnw.usta.com
• Allen Clendaniel, President
• Matthew Warren, Executive Director
ext 19
Description:
A not-for-profit organization comprised of over 24,000 individual and organizational members committed to promoting and developing recreational and competitive tennis. Over 200 volunteers and 300 tournaments make up the backbone for grassroots tennis in the Pacific Northwest.

USTA SOUTHERN
5685 SPALDING DRIVE
NORCROSS, GA 30092
770-368-8200
Fax: 770-368-9091
info@sta.usta.com
www.southern.usta.com
• Paula Hale, President & CEO
• John Callen, Executive Director & Chief Operating Officer
(770) 368-8200
Description:
The 181,000+ members living in Alabama, Arkansas, Georgia, Kentucky, Louisianna, Mississippi, North Carolina, South Carolina, and Tennessee comprise the USTA Southern Section, and account for approximately 25% of the total USAT membership.

single sports

Year Founded:
1881

USTA SOUTHERN CALIFORNIA
420 CHARLES E. YOUNG DRIVE WEST
LOS ANGELES, CA 90024
310-208-3838
Fax: 310-824-7691
www.scta.usta.com
• William Kellogg, President
• Bruce Hunt, Executive Director
(310) 208-3838
bhunt@scta.usta.com
Sports Services Founded:
1887
Description:
Committed to promoting the game of tennis by offering quality recreational and competitive programs for people of all ages and abilities. Comprimising Imperial, Kern, Los Angeles, Orange, Riverside, San Bernardino, San Luis Obispo, Santa barbara and Ventura Counties.

USTA SOUTHWEST
7010 E ACOMA DRIVE
SUITE 201
SCOTTSDALE, AZ 85254
480-289-2351
Fax: 480-289-2701
info@southwest.usta.com
www.southwest.usta.com
• Paul Burns, President
• Eric Mitchell, Executive Director
(480) 289-2351
mitchell@southwest.usta.com
Description:
To promote and develop tennis in the Southwest, the USTA Southwest Section services the needs of the playing public and encourages the growth of tennis by administering tennis programming, providing overall support and guidance to its eight Chatered USTA Community Tennis Associations and serving as a source for comprehensive information on tennis.

USTA TEXAS
8105 EXCHANGE DRIVE
AUSTIN, TX 78754
512-443-1334
Fax: 512-443-4748
www.texas.usta.com
• Frank Kelly, President
• Van Barry, Executive Director
(512) 443-1334
vbarry@texas.usta.com
Sports Services Founded:
1985.
Description:
Not for profit volunteer organization with 47,000 individual members and 421 organizational members. The USTA Texas Section is the fastest growing of the 17 sections and features a Pathway of tennis programs for beginning, recreational and competitive juniors, adults and seniors.

WOMEN'S TENNIS ASSOCIATION TOUR
100 SECOND AVENUE SOUTH
SUITE 1100-S
ST. PETERSBURG, FL 33701
727-895-5000
Fax: 727-894-1982
www.wtatour.com
• Micky Lawler, President
• Steve Simon, Chairman/CEO
• Matthew Cenedella, Chief Operating Officer
• Melissa Pine, Vice President, Tournament Director
• Joan Pennello, Senior Vice President, Operations
• Jean Nachand, Vice President, Competition
• Heather Bowler, Senior Vice President, Communications
• Wendy Jang, Commercial VP, Asia Pacific
Nature of Sport Service:
Leading professional sport for women with over 2,500 players from over 100 nations, the WTA holds competitions comprising of 55 events and 4 grand slams annually.
WTA Tour European Headquarters:
Palliser House, Palliser Road London W14 9EB United Kingdom Phone: +44 20 7386 4100, Fax: +44 20 7386 4102

Tennis, Leagues/Teams

MYLAN WORLD TEAM TENNIS
1776 BROADWAY
SUITE 600
NEW YORK, NY 10019
212-586-3444
Fax: 212-586-6277
customerservice@wtt.com
www.wtt.com
• Billie Jean King, Co-Founder
• Ilana Kloss, Chief Executive Officer & Commissioner
Description:
Founded 1981. Nation's only professional co-ed team sport. Each team consists of four players; two men and two women. Nationwide recreational program following the same format as the professional league.
Publications:
SUPERTIEBREAKER, annual magazine.
Teams:
Boston Lobsters, Philadelphia Freedoms, Washington Kastles, Newport Beach Breakers, plus teams listed below.

Teams:

BOSTON LOBSTERS
BOSTON LOBSTERS TENNIS CENTER
8 ATWATER AVENUE
MANCHESTER BY THE SEA, MA 01944
877-617-5627
• Colleen Hopkins, General Manager

CALIFORNIA DREAM
SUNRISE MALL
5912 SUNRISE MALL ROAD
CITRUS HEIGHTS, CA 95610
916-967-6000
• Jeff Launius, General Manager

ORANGE CITY BREAKERS
2549 EASTBLUFF DRIVE
SUITE 810
NEWPORT BEACH, CA 92660
949-434-4560
www.breakerstennis.com
• Allen Hardison, General Manager

PHILADELPHIA FREEDOMS
PO BOX 268
GWYNEDD, PA 19436
215-667-8132
www.philadelphiafreedoms.com
• Barbara Perry, General Manager

SAN DIEGO AVIATORS
2658 DEL MAR HEIGHTS ROAD
SUITE 199
DEL MAR, CA 92014
888-774-0110
www.sandiegoaviators.com
• Fred Luddy, Owner

SPRINGFIELD LASERS
1923 NORTH WELLER
SPRINGFIELD, MO 65803
417-864-1339
www.springfieldlasers.com
• Paul Nahon, General Manager

WASHINGTON KASTLES
509 7TH STREET NW
WASHINGTON, DC 20004
202-483-6647
www.washingtonkastles.com

USTA LEAGUE
70 WEST RED OAK LANE
WHITE PLAINS, NY 10604
914-696-7000
tennislink.usta.com
Description:
Largest recreational tennis league in the United States with four divisions: Adult, Senior, Super Senior and Mixed Doubles.
Members:
330,000+
Publications:
TENNIS magazine; Tennis Tuesday, weekly digital magazine; Bounce magazine (i)

Track & Field Organizations

ATHLETICS CANADA
2445 ST LAURENT BOULEVARD
SUITE B1-110
OTTAWA, ON, CANADA K1G 6C3
613-260-5580
Fax: 613-260-0341
www.athletics.ca
• Gordon Orlikow, Chairman Board of Directors
gordon.orlikow@kornferry.com
• Rob Guy, CEO
(613) 260-5580
rguy@athletics.ca
• Andrew Cameron, IT, Membership & static Service
(613) 260-5580
acameron@athletics.ca
• Sylvie King, Chief Financial Officer
(613) 260-5580
sylvie.king@athletics.ca
• Judy McCallum, Assistant, Finance
• Andrew Page, Manager, Coach Development
(613) 260-5580
andrew.page@athletics.ca
Member Services:
Coaching Certification Program. Officials Grading Program. National Team, Annual General Meeting each spring, Run Canada Division, Awards program, National Technical Assembly, each fall. Wide range of grassroots and nationally televised sponsorship programs available.
Membership Requirements:
Open to all interested in track and field athletics who pay annual membership fee. Membership categories include affiliated, individual, athletic, associate sustaining, life.
Description:
The national sport governing body for track and field, including cross-country running and road running, Athletics Canada supports high performance athletics excellence at the world level and provides leadership in developmental athletics.

INTERCOLLEGIATE ASSOCIATION OF AMATEUR ATHLETES OF AMERICA/IC4A
39 OLD RIDGEBURY ROAD
SUITE 22
DANBURY, CT 06810
203-745-0434
Fax: 203-745-0440
www.ecac.org
• Steve Bartold, IC4A Administrator
(203) 245-5862
Stevebartold@sbcglobal.net
• Dylan Clark, ECAC Assistant For Championships, Leagues
(203) 745-2786
DClark@ecac.org
Description:
The Intercollegiate Association of Amateur Athletes of America is a men's division I indoor and outdoor track and field competition under the responsibility of the Eastern College Athletic Conference.

INTERNATIONAL ASSOCIATION OF ATHLETICS FEDERATIONS (IAAF)
6-8 QUAI ANTOINE
BP 359
MONTE CARLO, MONACO 98007
info@iaaf.org
www.iaaf.org
• Sebastian Coe, President
Description:
The International Amateur Athletic Federation is the international governing body for track and field sport.

U.S. TRACK & FIELD AND CROSS COUNTRY COACHES ASSOCIATION
1100 POYDRAS STREET
SUITE 1750
NEW ORLEANS, LA 70163
504-599-8900
Fax: 504-599-8909
www.ustfccca.org
• Sam Seemes, CEO
sam@ustfccca.org
• Mike Corn, Assistant Director
(504) 599-8903
mike@ustfccca.org
• Curtis Akey, Communications Manager
(504) 599-8905
curtis@ustfccca.org
• Tyler Mayforth, Communications assistant
(504) 599-8904
tyler@ustfccca.org
• Kristina Taylor, Membership Services And Operations
(504) 599-8901
kristina@ustfccca.org
Membership Requirements:
Collegiate cross country coach.
Description:
A non-profit lobbying for the interests of track and field coaches at all three divisional levels; membership consists of over 6,000.

USA TRACK & FIELD
132 EAST WASHINGTON STREET
SUITE 800
INDIANAPOLIS, IN 46204
317-261-0500
Fax: 317-261-0481
www.usatf.org
• Max Siegel, Chief Executive Officer
ceo@usatf.org
• Terry Crawford, Director Of Coaching
(317) 713-4671
Terry.Crawford@usatf.org

Description:
USA Track & Field acts as the National Governing Body for track and field athletics.

USA TRACK & FIELD - NEW YORK
1365 NORTH RAILROAD AVENUE
#116
STATEN ISLAND, NY 10306
609-915-3039
lauren.primerano@newyork.usatf.org
www.newyork.usatf.org
• Lauren Primerano, President
(609) 915-3039
lauren.primerano@newyork.usatf.org
• John Padula, First Vice President
(718) 809-4915
john.padula@newyork.usatf.org
Year Founded:
1980
Description:
Formerly The Metropolitan Athletics Congress, the regional association of the USA Track and Field (USATF), and sanctions track and field events throughout New York City and the metropolitan area year-round.

Triathlon Organizations

BRITISH TRIATHLON ASSOCIATION
SIR JOHN BECKWITH BUILDING
LOUGHBOROUGH
PO Box 25
LOUGHBOROUGH, ENGLAND LE11 3WX
info@britishtriathlon.org
www.britishtriathlon.org
• Ian Howard, TD, President
• Jack Buckner, CEO
• Bill James, Director Triathlon England
• Andy Salmon, Director Triathlon Scotland
• Nicky Dick, Director Age-Group Team
• Jon Ridgeon, Director major & National Events
• Craig Stewart, Independent Non-Executive Director Finance
• Mike Battersby, Director Welsh Trialthon
Organization activities:
The British Triathlon Federation is a govering organization made up of English, Scotish, and Welsh triathlon associations.

INTERNATIONAL TRIATHLON UNION
998 HARBOURSIDE DRIVE
#220
NORTH VANCOUVER, BC, CANADA V7P 3T2
604-904-9248
Fax: 604-904-3195
ituhdq@triathlon.org
www.triathlon.org
• Marisol Casado, President
• Loreen Barnett, First Vice President

IRONMAN PROPERTIES
2701 NORTH ROCKY POINT DRIVE
SUITE 1250
TAMPA, FL 33607
813-868-5940
Fax: 813-868-5930
• Steve Johnston, President
Sports Service Founded:
1989
Event Management Services:
Producer of the Ironman Triathlon World Championship.

Triathlon Sponsor:
Title Sponsor: Ironman Triathlon World Championship.

TRIATHLON CANADA
1925 BIANSHARD STREET
SUITE 121
VICTORIA, BC, CANADA V8T 4J2
250-412-1795
Fax: 250-412-1794
info@triathloncanada.com
www.triathloncanada.com
• Les Pereira, President
• Kim Van Bruggen, CEO
kim.vanbruggen@triathloncanada.com
• Eugene Liang, High Performance Director
eugene.liang@triathloncanada.com
• Chris Dornan, Communications Manager
(403) 620-8731
hpprchris@shaw.ca
• Tenille Hoogland, Age Group Teams Manager
tenille.hoogland@triathloncanada.com
Description:
Triathlon Canada is a national sanctioning orgnaization which selects national team members, organizes competitions, and advoactes for the promotion and growth of the sport in Canada.

USA TRIATHLON
5825 DELMONICO DRIVE
SUITE 200
COLORADO SPRINGS, CO 80919
719-955-2807
info@usatriathlon.org
www.teamusa.org/usa-triathlon
• Rob Urbach, Chief Executive Officer
• Tim Yount, Chief Operating Officer
(719) 955-2831
tim.yount@usatriathlon.org
Nature of Service:
USA Triathlon is the National Governing Body for triathlon, duathlon, aquathlon and winter triathlon in the United States.
Year Founded:
1982
Member Services:
USAT offers annual memberships which, in addition to many other benefits, cover members at all USAT sanctioned events for 12 full months. One-day licenses which cover one event and annual elite memberships are also available.

Tug of War Organizations

TUG OF WAR FEDERATION
4742 STATE HIGHWAY 213
PO BOX 77
ORFORDVILLE, WI 53576-0077
608-879-2869
Fax: 608-879-2103
twif@t6b.com
www.tugofwar-twif.org
• Anton Rabe, President
anton@hortgro.co.za
• Glen Johnson, Secretary General
(608) 879-2869
twif@t6b.com
• Dariusz Bajkowski, Senior VP
dariusz.bajkowski@tugofwar.pl
• Peter Dyer, Treasurer
pete.dyer@talktalk.net

Volleyball Organizations

AMERICAN VOLLEYBALL COACHES ASSOCIATION
2365 HARRODSBURG ROAD
SUITE A325
LEXINGTON, KY 40504
859-226-4315
866-544-2822
Fax: 859-226-4315
members@avca.org
www.avca.org
• Christy Johnson-Lynch, President
(515) 294-3395
christyj@iastate.edu
• Mark Rosen, President elect
(734) 647-3035
rosenma@umich.edu
• Kirsten Bernthal Booth, Division I rep
(402) 280-5794
kbooth@creighton.edu
• Chuck Waddington, Division II rep
(325) 486-6068
cwaddington@angelo.edu
• Tammy Swearingen, Division III rep
(724) 946-7320
swearitl@westminster.edu
• David Weitl, Club Representative
(360) 779-3802
dw@wvba.org
• William Ebel, III, Assistant Coaches Representative
(615) 491-2560
billy.ebel@lipscomb.edu
Publications:
Coaching Volleyball Magazine, print and digital editions.
Description:
To advance the sport of volleyball and its coaches.
Member Services:
Annual Convention; Awards Program; Weekly Polls; Educational Opportunities.
Number of members:
Over 7,000.

ASSOCIATION OF VOLLEYBALL PROFESSIONALS/AVP
6100 CENTER DR
9TH FLOOR
LOS ANGELES, CA 90045
949-678-3599
contact@avp.com
www.avp.com
• Tony Giarla, Director
tonyg@avp.com
• Marty Suan, Director Of Programs
marty@avp.com
Member Services:
Opportunity to compete in Professional Beach Volleyball tournaments; publicity; health and accident insurance.

FEDERATION INTERNATIONALE DE VOLLEYBALL (FIVB)
CHATEAU LES TOURELLAS
EDOUARD-SANDOZ 2-4
LAUSANNE, SWITZERLAN 1006
info@fivb.org
www.fivb.org
• Ary S. Filho, Dr.
president.office.sec@fivb.org
Purpose of organization:
Acts as international governing body for the sport of volleyball.

LONE STAR CLASSIC NATIONAL VOLLEYBALL QUALIFIER
425 WOODWARD STREET
AUSTIN, TX 78704
512-479-8776
Fax: 512-479-0080
www.austinsportscenter.com
• Glen Lietzke, Executive Director
(512) 433-5110
glen@austinsportscenter.com
• Jonathan Paris, Director of Events
(512) 433-5114
jparis@austinsportscenter.com
• Scott Clouse, Communications/video speacialist
(512) 433-5120
scott@austinsportscenter.com
• Lindsay Dunn, Controller
(512) 433-5104
LDunn@austinsportscenter.com
Event Management & Consulting Services:
Owns and operates the Lone Star Classic National Qualifier and 3rd Coast Volleyball Championships. Creates and manages sports events, focusing on volleyball.

UNITED STATES YOUTH VOLLEYBALL LEAGUE
2771 PLAZA DEL AMO
SUITE 808
TORRANCE, CA 90503
310-212-7008
888-988-7985
Fax: 310-212-7182
info@usyvl.org
www.usyvl.org
• Allen Adams, President
• Jon Bitler, Vice President
• Randy Sapoznik, Secretary
• Bill Martinez, Treasurer
Membership Requirements:
Open registration for boys and girls ages 7-15.
Description:
The United States Youth Volleyball League is a non-profit instructional volley ball organization for children between the ages of 7 and 15.

USA VOLLEYBALL
4065 SINTON ROAD
SUITE 200
COLORADO SPRINGS, CO 80907
719-228-6800
Fax: 719-228-6899
postmaster@usav.org
www.usavolleyball.org
• Lori Okimura, Board Chair
loriokimura@hotmail.com
Organization purpose:
Acting as the national governing body for volleyball in the United States, USA Volleyball promotes growth of the sport and increased success in competition.

VOLLEYBALL CANADA
1A-1084 KENASTON STREET
OTTAWA, ON, CANADA K1B 3P5
613-748-5681
Fax: 613-748-5727
info@volleyball.ca
www.volleyball.ca
• Mark Eckert, President & CEO
(613) 748-5681
meckert@volleyball.ca
• Ian Halliday, High Performance Director
(403) 880-9845
ihalliday@volleyball.ca
• Jackie Skender, Communication Director
(613) 748-5681
jskender@volleyball.ca
• Caitlin Devlin, Domestic Events Coordinator
(613) 748-5681
caitlin@volleyball.ca
• Linden Leung, Finance & Operations Director
(613) 748-5681
linden@volleyball.ca
Description:
Founded 1953. Promotes the sport of volleyball in Canada.
Membership Requirements:
Provincial affiliation.
Publications:
Many technical publications (books, manuals and VHS videos) as well as yearly Indoor and Outdoor Rulebooks.
Member Services:
Organization of national championships; Publications; Elite development programs for coaches and officials; National team programs and events, Labatt Pro Beach Volleyball Tour.

Water Polo Organizations

AMERICAN WATER POLO COACHES ASSOCIATION
2124 MAIN STREET
SUITE 240
HUNTINGTON BEACH, CA 92648
714-500-5445
Fax: 714-960-2431
www.usawaterpolo.com
• Christopher Ramsey, Chief Executive Officer
(714) 500-8506
ceo@usawaterpolo.org
• Greg Mescall, Director Of Communications
(714) 500-5455
gmescall@usawaterpolo.org
• John Adbou, Chief High Performance Director
(714) 500-5445
jabdou@usawaterpolo.org
Description:
Organized to serve as the national governing body for the sport of water polo in the United States under the auspices of the United States olympic Committe.

WATER POLO CANADA
1084 KENASTON STREET
UNIT 1A
OTTAWA, CANADA K1B 3P5
613-748-5682
Fax: 613-748-5777
database@waterpolo.ca
www.waterpolo.ca
• Conrad Hadubiak, President
chadubiak@gmail.com
• Josee Lanouette, Vice President
j.lanouette@johnabbott.qc.ca
• Martin Goulet, Executive Director
(613) 748-5777
mgoulet@waterpolo.ca
• Mylene Turcotte-Fitzgerald, Communication And Domestic Operations Coodinator
(613) 748-5682
mfitzgerald@waterpolo.ca

Member Services:
Insurance-liability and accident; Discounts on publications and merchandise; newsletter; national championships; player development programs, coaching development and officials development. Annual meeting in the month of October
Publications:
Wide range of coaching and refereeing materials; International Rules of Water Polo.
Membership Requirements:
Should be fully registered with both the provincial association as well as the national association.

Water Skiing Organizations

INTERNATIONAL WATER SKI & WAKEBOARD FEDERATION
POST BOX 564
UNTERAEGERI, SWITZERLAN 6314
iwwf@iwwfed.com
www.iwsf.com
• Kuno Ritschard, President
president@iwwfed.com
• Gillian Hill, Secreatry General
gill@mywaterskiemail.com
• David Skillen, Treasurer
daskillen@yahoo.com
Membership Requirements:
International governing body for towed watersports.

USA WATER SKI
1251 HOLY COW ROAD
POLK CITY, FL 33868
863-324-4341
Fax: 863-325-8259
usawaterski@usawaterski.org
www.usawaterski.org
• Jim Grew, President
(971) 871-5500
jimhgrewjr@cs.com
• Dale R. Stevens, Vice President
(561) 596-8710
stevensdalel@gmail.com
• Bob Crowley, Executive Director
(406) 599-1570
bcrowley@usawaterski.org
• Doug Robbins, Chair
(724) 935-5333
drobbins@teleplexinc.com
• Robert R. Rhyne, III, Treasurer
(704) 906-7779
robrhyne@hotmail.com
Nature of Service:
The national governing body of organized water skiing in the United States. A member of the International Water Ski Federation (world governing body), the Pan American Sports Organization and the United States Olympic Committee.
Year Founded:
1939
Member Services:
Sanction competition. Skier's rating system; instructor certification; summer camp program.
Membership Requirements:
Open - dues of $25 for Supporting and $80 for Competitive.
Number of members:
15,000
Publications:
THE WATER SKIER, 6 time(s) annually; how-to booklet series.

WATER SKI & WAKEBOARD CANADA
2420 BANK STREET
OTTAWA, ON, CANADA K1V 8S1
613-526-0685
Fax: 613-701-0385
info@wswc.ca
• Glenn Bowie, Chair
• Jasmine Northcott, Chief Executive Officer
(613) 526-0685
jasmine@wswc.ca
• Steve Jarrett, Director
• Karen McClintock, Director
• Jo-Anne Moore, Director
• Kevin Neveu, Director
Nature of Service:
The sole national sport governing body and recognized water skiing/wakeboard authority in Canada. Mission is to develop and promote organized water skiing, wakeboarding and other towed water sports from beginner to pro.
Year Founded:
1971
Member Services:
Coaching development programs; athlete development programs; publications; officials development program.
Publications:
What's Up In Water Sports (monthly newsletter)

WORLD SPORTS & MARKETING
460 N. ORLANDO AVE
SUITE 200
WINTER PARK, FL 32789
www.bonniercorp.com/other-brands
• Ben Greenwood, Sponsorship Sales
(407) 571-4518
Ben.Greenwood@bonniercorp.com
• Evily Giannopoulos, Associate Director Of Public Relations
(407) 571-4587
Evily.Giannopoulos@bonniercorp.com
• Priscilla Scollin, Marketing Manager & Registration
(407) 405-0121
Priscilla.Scollin@bonniercorp.com
Sports Service Founded:
1988
Services:
Sports: Clearinghouse for the Pro Wakeboard Tour including the coordination of the scheduling, television, global sponsorships, public relations, venue evaluation and event selection.
Event Management Services:
Managed all aspects of the US Pro Water Ski Tour, US Pro Wakeboard Tour, VANS Triple Crown of Wakeboarding, Malibu Just Ride Series, Malibu Open, Water Ski Magazine's America's Cup.

Weightlifting Organizations

INTERNATIONAL POWERLIFTING FEDERATION
1 RUE PASTEUR
DIFFERDANGE, 4642
info@powerlifting-ipf.com
www.powerlifting-ipf.com
• Gaston Parage, President
Gaston.Parage@powerlifting-ipf.com
• Sigurjon Petursson, Vice-President
sigurjonp@gmail.com
• Robert Keller, Secretary General
rhk@verizon.net

• Dietmar Wolf, Treasurer
Dietmar.Wolf@powerlifting-ipf.com
Description:
International governing body for the sport of powerlifting.

INTERNATIONAL WEIGHTLIFTING FEDERATION (IWF)
H-1146
BUDAPEST, ISTVANMEZEI ut 1-3, HUNGARY
iwf@iwf.net
www.iwf.net
• Tamas Ajan, President
• Ma Wenguang, General Secretary
Description:
International governing body for the sport of weightlifting.

U.S. POWERLIFTING ASSOCIATION
3921 E LA PALMER AVE B
ANAHEIM, CA 92807
661-333-9800
steve@uspa.net
uspa.net
• Steve Denison, President
steve@uspa.net
• Shelley Denison, Secretary/Treasurer
shelsters10@yahoo.com
Member Services:
Sanction meets, register clubs, select U.S. teams for international (including world) powerlifting meets, supervise sanctioned events, provide liability insurance.
Membership Requirements:
Minimum age 14, payment of annual dues.
Description:
Founded 1964. Serves to promote powerlifting.

Windsurfing Organizations

U.S. WINDSURFING
8211 SUN SPRING CIR.
UNIT 73
ORLANDO, FL 32825
877-386-8708
info@uswindsurfing.org
www.uswindsurfing.org
• Jerome Samson, President
samson_jerome@yahoo.com
• Jim McGrath, Acting Secretary
(510) 848-8071
macmcgrath@comcast.net
• Bryan McDonald, National Director
(408) 425-3782
dude1@apple.com
• Bill Keitel, VP
(507) 372-7175
bill.keitel@gmail.com
Membership Requirements:
Payment of dues.
Description:
Dedicated to making the whole windsurfing experience more positive for windsurfers in the USA, and to encourage participation and promote excellence in recreational windsurfing and racing in the United States.

Wrestling Organizations

EASTERN INTERCOLLEGIATE WRESTLING ASSOCIATION
641 TAYLOR STREET
BETHLEHEM, PA 18015
eiwawrestling.org
• Dan Wirnsberger, President - EIWA Coaches Association
djw020@bucknell.edu
• Mark Letcher, President - EWIOA Officials Association
mletcher@twcny.rr.com
• Greg Strobel, Executive Director
gos2@lehigh.edu
Description:
Member schools include: Brown, Columbia, Cornell, Franklin & Marshall, Harvard, Lehigh, Pennsylvania, Princeton, Syracuse, U.S. Military Academy, U.S. Naval Academy.

NATIONAL WRESTLING COACHES ASSOCIATION
1976 AUCTION ROAD
PO BOX 254
MANHEIM, PA 17545
717-653-8009
Fax: 717-665-35737
www.nwcaonline.com
• Mike Moyer, Executive Director
(717) 653-8009
mmoyer@nwca.cc
• Pat Tocci, Senior Director
(717) 653-8009
ptocci@nwca.cc
• Amy Dicato, Office Manager
(717) 653-8009
adicato@nwca.cc
• Don Shelly, Finance Manager
(717) 653-8009
dshelly@nwca.cc
Member Services:
Selects Coach of the Year. Provides All-American certificates to top eight places in each weight class at nationals. Provides award for outstanding NCAA Division 1 Wrestler. Provides award for most falls. Provides 25 year service awards. Sponsors NWCA All Star Classic, NWCA National Dual Meet Tournament, National Wrestling Scholastic Showcase, NWCA Annual Convention. Serves as a clearing house for information to both scholastic and collegiate wrestling coaches and fans. Recognizes the National high school coach and assistant coach of the year and the outstanding high school wrestler of the year.
Description:
A professional organization dedicated to serve and provide leadership for the advancement of all levels of the sport of wrestling with primary emphasis on scholastic and collegiate wrestling programs.
Year Founded:
1928

UNITED WORLD WRESTLING
6 RUE DU CHATEAU
CORSIER-SUR-VEVEY, SWITZERLAN
1804
info@unitedworldwrestling.org
unitedworldwrestling.org
• Nenad Lalovic, President
lalovic@unitedworldwrestling.org

• Stan Dziedzic, Vice-President
dziedzic@united-world-wrestling.org
Founded:
1921
Description:
International governing body for amateur olympic wrestling.

USA WRESTLING
6155 LEHMAN DR
COLORADO SPRINGS, CO 80918
719-598-8181
Fax: 719-598-9440
www.usawrestling.org
• Bruce Baumgartner, President
• Rich Bender, Executive Director
rbender@usawrestling.org
Membership:
226,000 members
Organization mission:
As part of the United States Olympic Committe, USA Wrestling oversees and promotes amateur wrestling competition at the national level.

WORLD WRESTLING ENTERTAINMENT
1241 E MAIN STREET
STAMFORD, CT 6902
203-352-8600
Fax: 203-359-5109
www.wwe.com
• Vincent K. McMahon, Chairman/CEO
• George Barrios, CFO
• Kevin Dunn, Executive VP, Television Production
• Paul Levesque, Executive VP, Talent, Live Events & Creative
• Michael Luisi, President, WWE Studios
• Stephanie McMahon, Chief Brand Officer
• Michelle D Wilson, Chief Marketing Officer
Description:
An integrated media organization and recognized leader in global entertainment. The company consists of a portfolio of businesses that create and deliver original content 52 weeks a year to a global audience. WWE is committed to family-friendly, PG content across all of its platforms including television programming, pay-per-view, digital media and publishing. WWE programming is broadcast in more than 180 countries.

WRESTLING CANADA
7-5370 CANOTEK RD
OTTAWA, ON, CANADA K1J 9E6
613-748-5686
Fax: 613-748-5756
info@wrestling.ca
• Don Ryan, President
• Tamara Medwidsky, Executive Director
tamara@wrestling.ca
• Leigh Vierling, High performance Director
lvierling@wrestling.ca
• Tonya Verbeek, International Coach
tverbeek@wrestling.ca
• Eric Smith, Finance and administrative coordinator
ericsmith@wrestling.ca
• Patrick Kenny, Communications Officer
media@wrestling.ca
Description:
The national sport governing body for Olympic style wrestling in Canada. The association's role is to encourage and develop the widest participation and highest proficiency in Olympic wrestling in Canada.

Membership Requirements:
Membership through provincial associations, National Team, Board of Directors.

Yachting Organizations

AMERICAN BOAT & YACHT COUNCIL
613 THIRD STREET
SUITE 10
ANNAPOLIS, MD 21403
410-990-4460
Fax: 410-990-4466
www.abycinc.org
• John Adey, President
(410) 990-4460
jadey@abycinc.org
• Kevin Scullen, Membership Manager
(410) 990-4460
kscullen@abycinc.org
• Kenneth Weinbrecht, Chairman of the Board
• Brian Goodwin, Technical Director
(410) 990-4460
bgoodwin@abycinc.org
Nature of Service:
To develop quality technical practices and engineering standards for the design, construction, maintenance and repair of small crafts with refernce to their safety.

SAIL CANADA
PORTSMOUTH OLYMPIC HARBOUR
53 YONGE STREET
KINGSTON, ON, CANADA K7M 6G4
613-545-3044
Fax: 613-545-3045
sailcanada@sailing.ca
www.sailing.ca
• Todd Irving, President
president@sailing.ca
• Don Adams, Chief Executive Officer
(613) 545-3944
don@sailing.ca
• Ken Dool, Canadian Sailing Team Head coach
(613) 545-3044
ken@sailing.ca
• Sarah Case, Business Development Manager
(613) 545-3044
• Colleen Coderre, High Performance Coordinator
(613) 545-3044
colleen@sailing.ca
Newsletter:
Canadian Sailing Review
Year Founded:
1931
Description:
The national governing body for the sport of sailing. Promotes sailing and power boating through collaboration with partners, the Provincial Sailing Associations, member clubs, schools, and many individual stakeholders.

WORLD SAILING
ARIADNE HOUSE
TOWN QUAY
SOUTHAMPTON, HAMPSHIRE, ENGLAND
SO14 2AQ
secretariat@isaf.co.uk
www.sailing.org
• Kim Andersen, President

Organization Description:
World Sailing acts as the international governing body for the sport of sailing, a responsibility which includes the international promotion of sailing, training of judges and administrators, and the development of rules and regulations for sailing competitions.

YACHTWORLD.COM
150 GRANBY STREEET
NORFOLK, VA 23510

877-354-4069
www.yachtworld.com
• Sam Fulton, President/Chief Executive Officer
Sports Service Founded:
1995
Nature of Sports Service:
Site uses the Internet to establish relationships between yacht brokers and boat dealers, and prospective buyers from around the world. More than 2,402 participating brokers, more than 108,403 current boat listings valued over $41,075,849,605 billion, and the largest photo database of boats for sale on the Internet.

2

multi sports

multi sports

multi sports

multi sports

Athletic Foundations

A.C. GREEN YOUTH FOUNDATION
904 SILVER SPUR ROAD
SUITE 416
ROLLING HILLS, CA 90274
310-465-1470
800-229-6884
Fax: 310-465-1471
info@acgreen.com
www.acgreen.com
• A.C. Green, Jr, Founder/President
Nature of Sports Service:
Provides youth leadership program focused on basketball; promotes abstinence and education on social issues effecting youth.

ANDRE AGASSI FOUNDATION FOR EDUCATION
1120 NORTH TOWN CENTER DRIVE
SUITE 160
LAS VEGAS, NV 89144
702-227-5700
Fax: 702-866-2928
info@agassi.net
www.agassifoundation.org
• Andre Agassi, Chairman/Founder
• Steve Miller, CEO
• Evy Nickell, Executive Assistant
• Julie Pippenger, COO
• Shawn Cable, Chief Financial Officer
• Francisco Aguilar, General Counsel
Year Founded:
1994
Description:
Created to provide recreational and educational oppotunities for at-risk children in Southern Nevada. Athlete: Andre Agassi - Professional Tennis player.

ARTHUR ASHE LEARNING CENTER
67 WEST STREET
SUITE 401
BROOKLYN, NY 11222
646-352-1774
www.arthurashe.org
Description:
A non-profit organization devoted to using the life and legacy of tennis player Arthur Ashe for the promotion of education.

BOOMER ESIASON FOUNDATION
483 10TH AVENUE
SUITE 300
NEW YORK, NY 10018
646-292-7930
Fax: 646-292-7945
www.esiason.org
• Boomer Esiason, Co-Chairman
• David B. B Rimington, President
• Etsuko Murase, Chief Financial Officer/Chief Operations Officer
• Michaela Johnson, President, Team Boomer
• Natalie Stout, Program Director
• Tami Amaker, Special Program Director
• Rich Hahn, Operations Director
• Katie Dougherty, Program Coordinator
Sports Service Founded:
1993
Description:
A foundation comprised of medical and business professionals providing support, education, and financial contributions for research aimed at curing cystic fibrosis.

BRIAN MITCHELL FOUNDATION, THE
PO BOX 230055
CENTREVILLE, VA 20120
866-968-8426
Fax: 866-968-8426

DAN MARINO FOUNDATION
400 NORTH AMERICAN AVENUE
FORT LAUDEDALE, FL 33301
954-368-6000
info@danmarinofoundation.org
www.danmarinofoundation.org
• Dan Marino, Co-Founder/Chairman
• Claire Marino, Co-Founder/Treasurer
• Mary Partin, Chief Executive Officer
mpartin@danmarinofoundation.org
• Charinus Johnson, Chief Operating Officer
cjohnson@danmarinofoundation.org
• Alice Moore, Director of Human Resources
amoore@danmarinofoundation.org
• Tammy Bresnahan, Director Of Academic Programs
tbresnahan@danmarinofoundation.org
• Betsy Christy, Director Of Accounting
bchristy@danmarinofoundation.org
• Mark Pfefer, Director Of Business Development
mpfefer@danmarinofoundation.org
Nature of Sports Service:
Non-profit supports independence for children with special needs, teenagers transitioning from foster care and young adults with disabilities.
Sports Service Founded:
1992

DETLEF SCHREMPF FOUNDATION
1904 THIRD AVENUE
SUITE 339
SEATTLE, WA 98101
206-464-0826
Fax: 206-464-8020
info@detlef.com
www.detlef.com
• Detlef Schrempf, President
• Mari Schrempf, Vice President
• Chris Levitt, Vice President
• Nicole P Morrison, Executive Director
NicoleM@detlef.com
Nature of Sports Service:
Committed to supporting organizations that provide hope, care and assistance to Northwest children and their families. Also fosters relationships with corporate partners that share their vision of serving commuity as a walk of life.
Sports Service Founded:
1996

DOUG FLUTIE, JR. FOUNDATION FOR AUTISM
PO BOX 2157
FRAMINGHAM, MA 01703
www.flutiefoundation.org
• Douglas Flutie, Jr, President/Co-Founder
• Laurie Flutie, Vice President/Co-Founder
• Lisa Borges, Executive Director
• Nicole Guglielmucci, Director of Marketing/Events
• Keith D'Entremont, Director of Development
Sports Service Founded:
1998
Nature of Service:
To promote awareness and support families affected by autism spectrum disorders. Committed to funding organizations that provide direct services, family support grants, education, advocacy and recreational opportunities with the purpose of improvine the quality of life for individuals with autism and their families.

FOREVER YOUNG FOUNDATION
1424 S STAPLEY DRIVE
MESA, AZ 85204
480-507-0416
800-994-3837
www.foreveryoung.org
• Steve Young, Founder/Co-Chair
• Barb Young, Founder/Co-Chair
• Sterling Tanner, President/Executive Director
sterling@foreveryoung.org
• Michelle Knox, Public Relations/Media Director
michelle@foreveryoung.org
• Tina Kempken, Events/Programs Director
tina@foreveryoung.org
Sports Service Founded:
1993
Description:
A non-profit organization that serves children facing significant physical, emotional and financial challenges.

HUNTER'S HOPE FOUNDATION
6368 W QUAKER STREET
PO BOX 643
ORCHARD PARK, NY 14127
716-667-1200
info@huntershope.org
www.huntershope.org
• Chris Billman, Treasurer/Board Member
• Jim Kelly, Co-Founder
• Jill Kelly, Co-Founder
• Jacque Waggoner, CEO
jacque@huntershope.org
Sports Service Founded:
1997
Description:
Established to address the need for information and research with respect to Krabb Disease and realted Leukodystrophies.

JACKIE ROBINSON FOUNDATION
ONE HUDSON SQUARE
75 VARICK STREET, 2ND FLOOR
NEW YORK, NY 10013-1917
212-290-8600
Fax: 212-290-8081
www.jackierobinson.org
• Rachel Robinson, Founder
• Gregg A Gonsalves, Chairman
• Martin Edelman, Secretary
• Jose Rivera, Treasurer
• Della Britton-Baeza, President/CEO
• Danielle F Cornwall, Assistant Director Of Educational Programs
• La'Tonya Johnson, Vice President/Chief Operations Officer
• Ruth Moseley, Events Manager
Sports Service Founded:
1973
Nature of Sports Service:
A not-for-profit, organization founded as a vehicle to continue the legacy of Jackie Robinson through the advancement of higher education among underserved populations.

multi sports

JEFF GORDON FOUNDATION
1310 S. TYRON STREET
SUITE 105
CHARLOTTE, NC 28027
980-999-5145
info@jgcf.org
www.jeffgordonchildrensfoundation.org
• Jeff Gordon, Founder
• Trish Kriger, Executive Director
tkriger@jgcf.org
• Susan Johnston, Director Of
Communications
sjohnston@jgcf.org
Sports Service Founded:
1999
Description:
Supports children battling cancer by funding
programs that improve a patients' quality of
life, treatment programs that increase
survivorship and pediatric medical research
dedicated to finding a cure.

JOHN LYNCH FOUNDATION
PO BOX 172247
TAMPA, FL 33672
866-553-4747
Fax: 813-831-4441
maggie@johnlynchfoundation.org
www.johnlynchfoundation.org
• John Lynch, President
• Lynda Lynch, VP
• Maggie Robinson, Executive Director
maggie@johnlynchfoundation.org
Sports Service Founded:
2000
Description:
Provides encouragement and support
programs for young people todevelop values
and leadership through education, sport,
and community involvement.

JUNIOR SEAU FOUNDATION
5275 MARKET DRIVE
SAN DIEGO, CA 92114
619-264-5555
info@juniorseau.org
www.juniorseau.org
Sports Service Founded:
1992
Description:
Educates and empowers underprivileged
young people in San Diegothrough the
support of child abuse prevention efforts,
drug and alcohol awareness, recreational
opportunites, anti-juvenile delinquency
efforts and complimentary educational
programs.

KURT WARNER FIRST THING'S FIRST FOUNDATION
ONE N FIRST ST.
SUITE 735
PHOENIX, AZ 85004
602-385-0840
www.kurtwarner.org
• Kurt Warner, President/Founder
• Brenda Warner, Co-Founder
Nature of Sports Service:
Founded in 1999 to promote Christian
values by providing opportunities and
encourgagement with those in need.

LANCE ARMSTRONG FOUNDATION
2201 E SIXTH STREET
AUSTIN, TX 78072
877-236-8820
www.livestrong.org
• Lance Armstrong, Founde/Board Emeritus
• Greg Lee, CPA, President
• Kelly Corley, Vice President Finance
• Lori O'Brien, Vice President National
Development
• Candice Aaron, Chair
• Blaine P. Rollins, Secretary
Sports Service Founded:
1997
Nature of Sports Service:
Empowers the cancer community to address
the unmet needs of cancer survivors.
Encourages collaborations,
knowledge-sharing and partnership.
advocates for action in fighting the disease.

MAGIC JOHNSON FOUNDATION
9100 WILSHIRE BOULEVARD
SUITE 700 EAST
BEVERLY HILLS, CA 90212
310-246-4400
888-624-4205
• Earvin Johnson, Chairman
• Shane Jenkins, Vice President
• Jeanella Blair, Director Of Community
Empowerment Centers
Sports Service Founded:
1991

MALIVAI WASHINGTON KIDS FOUNDATION
1096 W 6TH STREET
JACKSONVILLE, FL 32209
904-359-5437
Fax: 904-301-3789
info@malwashington.com
www.malwashington.com
• MaliVi Washington, Founder
• Terri Florio, Executive Director
terri@malwashington.com
• Michael G. Gulley, Jr., Associate Director
michael@malwashington.com
• Marc Atkinson, Head Tennis Professional
marc@malwashington.com
• Tiffany Atkinson, Senior Program
Coordinator
tiffany@malwashington.com
Sports Service Founded:
1994
Member Services:
Tennis and Tutoring (TnT); After school
tennis and recreational program for
elemnetary, middle school youth Homework
assistance and life skills programs also
provided.
Description:
Uses the sport of tennis to support the
academic achievement and leadership skills
of youth in the Jacksonville area.

MARIO LEMIEUX FOUNDATION
TWO CHATHAM CENTER
SUITE 1661
112 WASHINGTON PLACE
PITTSBURGH, PA 15219
412-281-3466
Fax: 412-281-3066
www.mariolemieux.org
• Mario Lemieux, Chairman
• Tom Grealish, President
• Chuck Greenberg, Secretary
• Robert Hofman, Treasurer
• Nancy Angus, Executive Director
nangus@mlf66.org
• Andrew Parish, Marketing Manager
dparish@mlf66.org
Sports Service Founded:
1993
Nature of Sports Service:
The foundation raises funds for cancer and
neonatal research, in addition to supporting
an endowment for pediatric oncology
research and an initiative to create family
playrooms for children in medical care.

MARSHALL FAULK FOUNDATION
7222 OPPORTUNITY ROAD
SAN DIEGO, CA 92111
858-277-2828
Fax: 585-277-2814
info@marshallfaulk.com
www.marshallfaulk.com
• Marshall Faulk, Founder
• Brandi Greenleaf, Executive Director
brandi@marshallfaulk.com
Nature of Sports Service:
Dedicated to improving the quality of life for
San Diego youth by sport and education.
Sports Service Founded:
1994

MIA HAMM FOUNDATION
5315 HIGHGATE DRIVE
SUITE 204
DURHAM, NC 27713
919-544-9848
www.miafoundation.org
• Mia Hamm, Founder
Description:
A non-profit, national organizatio raising
funds and awareness for families in need of
a marrow or cord blood transplant and the
development of more opportunities for
young women to participate in sport.

NATIONAL FOOTBALL LEAGUE ALUMNI
8000 MIDATLANTIC DRIVE
SUITE 130 SOUTH
MOUNT LAUREL, NJ 08054
877-258-6635
Fax: 862-772-0277
memberservice@nflalumni.org
www.nflalumni.org
• Joe Pisarcik, President/CEO
Joe.pisarcik@nflalumni.org
Description:
A non-profit retired players organization for
former National Football League athletes
and associates.

NOBIS WORKS CENTER
1480 BELLS FERRY ROAD
MARIETTA, GA 30066-6014
770-427-9000
Fax: 770-499-9191
www.tommynobiscenter.org
• Dave Ward, President/CEO
• Alan Moak, Board Chairman
• Lisa Hughes, Vice President, Human
Resources & Administration
• Mike Hancock, Vice President, Business
Development
• Cole Chase, Vice President, Vocational
Rehabilitation
• Greg Weigle, Chief Financial Officer
Sports Service Founded:
1975
Description:
To develop and provide job training,
employment and vocational support for
youth and adults with disabilities and other
barriers to employment.

TIGER WOODS FOUNDATION
121 INNOVATION
SUITE 150
IRVINE, CA 92617
Fax: 949-725-3002
help@tigerwoodsfoundation.org
www.tigerwoodsfoundation.org
• Tiger Woods, Founder
• Rick T Singer, President/CEO
• Michelle Bemis, Vice President Events &
Business Development
• Katherine Bihr, Vice President,
Programs/Education
• Jin Thatcher, Vice President, Operations &
Administration
• Marci Gentzkow, Senior Director,
Communications & Marketing
• Kelly Cheng, Finance Director
Sports Service Founded:
1996
Nature of Sports Service:
Organization empowers young people by
initiating and supporting community-based
programs that promote the health, education
and welfare of American children. Athlete:
Tiger Woods - Professional Golfer

TONY HAWK FOUNDATION
1611-A SOUTH MELROSE DRIVE
#360
VISTA, CA 92081
www.tonyhawkfoundation.org
• Tony Hawk, President
• Miki Vuckovich, Executive Director
Description:
The foundation empowers youth through
recreational programs and the creation of
public skateparks.

WALTER AND CONNIE PAYTON
FOUNDATION
1905 MARKETVIEW DRIVE
SUITE 234
YORKVILLE, IL 60560
630-885-4980
Fax: 630-552-7618
information@payton34.com
www.payton34.com
• Kelly Woods, Director
(630) 699-2202
kwoods03@aol.com
• Nancy Hewlett, Office Manager/Events
Coordinator
(630) 885-4980
nancy@payton34.com

Disabled Sports

BLIND GOLF CANADA
451 HIGHWAY 336
UPPER MUSQUODOBIT, NS, CANADA
B0N 2M0
www.blindgolf.ca
• Gerry Nelson, President
• Doug Stoutley, Handicap Secretary
• Boyde Stewart, Vice President Finance

CANADIAN BLIND SPORTS
ASSOCIATION
#325-5055 RUE JOYCE STREET
VANCOUVER BC, CANADA V5R 6B2
604-419-0480
877-604-0480
Fax: 604-419-0481
www.canadianblindsports.ca

• Jane D Blaine, Executive Director
jane@canadianblindsports.ca
• Bob Fenton, President
• Terry Parsons, Vice President
• Donna Jodhan, Communications Director
Membership Requirements:
Provincial associations, pay dues.
Number of members:
9 Provinces, reaching 1,000 - 2,000
Individuals
Description:
The recognized national sport organization
for the Paralympic Sport of Golfball, and
advocates within the sport system for
Canadians who are visually impaired or
blind.
Year Founded:
1976

CANADIAN PARALYMPIC COMMITTEE
225 METCALFE STREET
SUITE 310
OTTAWA ON, CANADA K2P 1P9
613-569-4333
Fax: 604-569-2777
www.paralympic.ca
• Henry Storgaard, CEO/Secretary General
(613) 569-4333
hstorgaard@paralympic.ca
• Eric Paterson, Executive Assistant
epaterson@paralympic.ca
• Alison Korn, Manager, Media Relations &
Communications
(61) -569-433
akorn@paralympic.ca
• Kalie Sinclair, Coordinator, Digital & Social
Media
(613) 569-4333
ksinclair@paralympic.ca
• Laurie Cairns, Director of Finance
(613) 569-4333
lcairns@paralympic.ca
Sports Service Founded:
1981
Membership Requirements:
National sport governing bodies for
Paralympic sports.
Member Services:
Organization of Canada's involvement in the
Paralympic Games; fundraising to support
Canadian Winter and Summer Paralympic
teams.
Description:
The mission of the Foundation is to develop
and grow the Paralympic Movement in
Canada. Recognized by the International
Paralympic Committee (IPC) as the National
Paralympic Committe of Canada. CPC is
responsible for all aspects of Canada's
involvement including the country's
participation in the Summer and Winter
Paralympic Games.

DISABLED SPORTS USA
451 HUNGERFORD DRIVE
SUITE 100
ROCKVILLE, MD 20850
301-217-0960
Fax: 301-217-0968
information@dsusa.org
• Kirk Bauer, Executive Director
kbauer@dsusa.org
• Robert Meserve, President
• Steven D Goodwin, 2nd Vice President
• Todd Sajauskas, Treasurer and Secretary
Sports Services Founded:
1967

Membership Requirements:
Open membership offered through more
than 80 community-based chapters, as well
as through a national at-large membership
program, to all people and organizations
with an interest in sports and recreation for
the disabled; currently serving more than
60,000 people, ages 5 to 85, with
information and programs.
Publications:
CHALLENGE Magazine, FITNESS
PROGRAMMING & PHYSICAL
DISABILITIES book.
Member Services:
Travel discounts; access to information on
disabled sports and recreational activities;
more than 80 community-based chapters in
the U.S.; regional teaching clinics for several
sports; nationally sanctioned regional and
national competition for disabled athletes.
Description:
Established by disabled Vietnam veterans to
serve the war injured. DS/USA now offers
nationwide sports rehabilitation programs to
anyone with a permanent disability.
Activities include winter skiing, water sports,
summer and winter competitions, fitness
and special sports events. Participants
include those with visual impairments,
amputations, spinal cord injury, dwarfism,
multiple sclerosis, head injury, cerebal
palsy, and other neuromuscular and
orthopedic conditions.

INTERNATIONAL COMMITTEE OF
SPORTS FOR THE DEAF
54 AV. DE RHODANIE
LAUSANNE, SWITZERLAN CH-1007
Fax: +41-78-733-35-67
office@ciss.org
www.ciss.org
• Valery N. Rukhledev, President
Sports Service Founded:
1924
Description:
Governing body for the summer and winter
Deaflympics, which promotes the
development of athletics and international
competition.

SPECIAL OLYMPICS INTERNATIONAL
1133 19TH STREET NW
WASHINGTON, DC 2036-3604
202-628-3630
800-700-8585
Fax: 202-824-0200
media@specialolympics.org
www.specialolympics.org
• Timothy Shriver, Chairman of the Board
info@specialolympics.org
• Mary Davis, CEO
• Caroline Chevat, Manager, Brand Content
& Communications
(202) 824-0211
Number of members:
5.7 million athletes and more than a million
coaches and volunteers in 172 countries.
Membership Requirements:
People who have intellectual disabilities.
Sports Services Founded:
The first International Special Olympics
Games were held in Chicago, Illinois, USA
in July 1968.
Description:
The mission of Special Olympics is to
provide year-round sports training and
athletic competition in a variety of

Olympic-type sports for children and adults with intellectual disabilities. This gives them continuing opportunities to develop physical fitness, demonstrate courage, experience joy and participate in a sharing of gifts, skills and friendship with their families, other Special Olympics athletes and the community.

Other locations:

SPECIAL OLYMPICS ALABAMA
880 SOUTH COURT STREET
MONTGOMERY, AL 36104
334-242-3383
800-239-3898
Fax: 334-262-9794
soaloffice@aol.com
specialolympicsalabama.com
• Robert Bushong, Executive Director
soaled@bellsouth.net
• Finlay Randolph, Training Manager
soaltraining@bellsouth.net
• Marilyn Tell, Office Manager
soaltell@bellsouth.net
• Jane Cameron, Staff Assistant

SPECIAL OLYMPICS ALASKA
3200 MOUNTAIN VIEW DRIVE
ANCHORAGE, AK 99501
907-222-7625
888-499-7625
Fax: 907-222-6200
info@specialolympicsalaska.org
www.specialolympicsalaska.org
• Carmela Warfield, Chairman
• James Balamaci, President/CEO
jim@specialolympicsalaska.com

SPECIAL OLYMPICS AMERICAN SAMOA
PO BOX 6172
PAGO PAGO, AMERICAN S 96799
684-733-2351
specialolympicas@gmail.com
www.specialolympics.org
• Tulafono Solaita, Board Chair
tafaimamao@gmail.com
• Nyrese Pato, National Coordinator
n.pato@amsamoa.edu

SPECIAL OLYMPICS ARIZONA
2100 S 75TH AVENUE
PHOENIX, AZ 85043
602-230-1200
800-289-4946
Fax: 602-230-1110
www.specialolympicsarizona.org
• Tim Martin, President/CEO
(602) 230-1200
tim@specialolympicsarizona.org
• Douglas Steele, Chairperson

SPECIAL OLYMPICS ARKANSAS
2115 MAIN STREET
NORTH LITTLE ROCk, AR 72114
501-771-0222
800-722-9063
Fax: 501-771-1020
www.specialolympicsarkansas.org
• Terri Weir, Executive Director
terri@specialolympicsarkansas.org
• Irvin Humphrey, Director of Sports, Training, And Competition
irvin@specialolympicsarkansas.org

SPECIAL OLYMPICS CANADA
21 ST. CLAIR AVENUE EAST
SUITE 600
TORONTO, ON, CANADA M4T 1L9
416-927-9050
888-888-0608
Fax: 416-927-8475

info@specialolympics.ca
www.specialolympics.ca
• Mike Lamontagne, President and Chair
• Sharon Bollenbach, Chief Executive Officer
(416) 927-9050
sbollenbach@specialolympics.ca
• Lisa Dunbar, Director, Marketing & Communications
(416) 927-9050
ldunbar@specialolympics.ca
Description:
As part of the international Special Olympic movement, the organization works to enrich the lives of people with intellectual disabilities through sport/

SPECIAL OLYMPICS COLORADO
384 IVERNESS PARKWAY
SUITE 100
ENGLEWOOD, CO 80112
720-359-3100
800-777-5767
Fax: 303-592-1364
www.specialolympicsco.org
• Mindy Watrous, President/CEO
(720) 359-3111
• Becky Kennedy, Chief Financial Officer
• Chaka Sutton, VP Programs

SPECIAL OLYMPICS CONNECTICUT
2666 STATE STREET
SUITE 1
HAMDEN, CT 06517
203-230-1201
800-443-6105
Fax: 203-230-1202
specialolympicsct@soct.org
www.soct.org
• Robert Doherty, President
• Kelli Bigelow, Executive Assistant, President
kellib@soct.org
• Mike Mason, Senior Vice President/Chief Financial Officer
mimichaelm@soct.org
Description:
SOCT is a non-profit, charitable organization, which contributes to the lifelong physical, social and personal development of people with intellectual disabilities in the state of Connecticut. The SOCT program is one of the most innovative and dynamic in the world, involving thousands of people throughout the state in exciting and rewarding competition, training and events.

SPECIAL OLYMPICS DC
900 2ND STREET NE
SUITE 6
WASHINGTON, DC 20002
202-408-2640
www.specialolympicsdc.org
• Nicole J Preston, President/Chief Operating Officer
npreston@specialolympicsdc.org
• Maria-Nelly Johnson, Director of Finance/Administration
mjohnson@specialolympicsdc.org
• Tom Kling, Senior Director of Sports and Programs
tkling@specialolympicsdc.org
• Anthony Sokenu, Assosiate Director of Sports
asokenu@specialolympicsdc.org
• Rodney Williams, Assistant Director of Sports
rwilliams@specialolympicsdc.org

SPECIAL OLYMPICS DELAWARE
619 S COLLEGE AVENUE
NEWARK, DE 19716
302-831-4653
Fax: 302-831-3483
info@sode.org
www.sode.org
• Michael T. Nash, President
• Dick Huber, Vice-President
• Jeffrey Mitchell, Treasurer
• Ann Grunert, Executive Director
(302) 831-3480

agrunert@udel.edu
• Jon Buzby, Media Relations and Program Innovations Director
(302) 831-3484
jbuzby@udel.edu
• Gary Cimaglia, Senior Director Sports
(302) 831-3481
gcimag@udel.edu

SPECIAL OLYMPICS FLORIDA
1915 DON WICKMAN DRIVE
CLERMONT, FL 34711
352-243-9536
Fax: 352-243-9568
specialolympicsflorida.org
• Sherry Wheelock, President/CEO
(352) 243-9536
sherrywheelock@sofl.org
• Micheal Petramalo, Vice Chair
• Rick Beddow, Chief Operating Officer
(352) 243-9536
rickbeddow@sofl.org
• Pam Bondi, Secretary
• Joe Dzaluk, Treasurer

SPECIAL OLYMPICS GEORGIA
4000 DEKALB TECHNOLOGY PARKWAY
BUILDING 400, SUITE 400
ATLANTA, GA 30340
770-414-9390
www.specialolympicsga.org
• Georgia Milton-Sheats, CEO
(770) 414-9390
georgia.milton-sheats@specialolympicsga.org
• Mike Twiner, Chairperson
• Lee Nunnally, Vice Chair
• Michael Knight, Treasurer
• Chris Turner, Secretatry
Description:
Provides year-round training and competition for people with intellectual disabilities to enrich their lives through sport.

SPECIAL OLYMPICS HAWAII
1833 KALAKAUA AVENUE
SUITE 100
HONOLULU, HI 96815
808-943-8808
888-531-1888
Fax: 808-943-8814
www.specialolympicshawaii.org
• Nancy Bottelo, President/CEO
(808) 695-3522
ceo@sohawaii.org
• Tom Weber, Chairperson
• Tim Brauer, Vice-Chairperson
• Nina Nakaahiki, Secretary
• Dan Epstein, VP Sports & Sports Marketing
(808) 695-3523
sports@sohawaii.org
Description:
The organization missions is to provide year-round training and competition for people with intellectual disabilities to enrich their lives through sport.

SPECIAL OLYMPICS IDAHO
199 E 52ND STREET
GARDEN CITY, ID 83714
800-915-6510
Fax: 208-323-0486
idso.org
www.idso.org
• Laurie La Follette, Chief Executive Officer
(208) 323-0482
llafollette@idso.org
• Shannon Reece, COMMUNITY STATE COORDINATOR
(800) 915-6510
shannon@idso.org
• Bryan Jackson, Finance Director
(208) 629-6989
bryan@idso.org
• Dallas Leatham, VP Operations
(208) 915-6510
operations@idso.org

Description:
A non-profit organization that provides training and athletic competition in 15 Olympic-type sports, year-round and free of charge to over 2,500 children and adults with intellectual disabilities throughout the state of Idaho.

SPECIAL OLYMPICS ILLINOIS
605 EAST WILLOW STREET
NORMAL, IL 61761
309-888-2551
800-394-0562
Fax: 309-888-2570
website@soill.org
www.soill.org
• Jenny Fortner, Chair
• Karen Atwood, Vice-Chair
• Dave Breen, President/CEO
• Jeremy Davidson, Manager Marketing/Communications
jdavidson@soill.org
• Tracy S Hilliard, VP Sports Training/Competition
thilliard@soill.org
Description:
Organization mission is to provide year-round training and competition for people with intellectual disabilities to enrich their lives through sport.

SPECIAL OLYMPICS INDIANA
6200 TECHNOLOGY CENTER DRIVE
SUITE 105
INDIANAPOLIS, IN 46278
317-328-2000
800-742-6012
Fax: 317-328-2018
information@soindiana.org
www.soindiana.org
• Michael Furnish, President/CEO
mfurnish@soindiana.org
• Deb Easterday, Chairperson
• Ron Stiver, Vice-Chair
• Phil Bounsall, Treasurer
• Dana Teasley, Secretary
Description:
Organization mission is to provide year-round training and competition for people with intellectual disabilities to enrich their lives through sport.

SPECIAL OLYMPICS IOWA
551 SE DOVETAIL ROAD
PO BOX 620
GRIMES, IA 50111-0620
515-986-5520
Fax: 515-986-5530
www.soiowa.org
• Rich Fellingham, President/CEO
(515) 986-5520
rfellingham@soiowa.org
• Steve Palmer, Chair
Description:
Organization mission is to provide year-round training and competition for people with intellectual disabilities to enrich their lives through sport.

SPECIAL OLYMPICS KANSAS
5280 FOXRIDGE DRIVE
MISSION, KS 66202
913-236-9290
Fax: 913-236-9771
kso@ksso.org
www.ksso.org
• Chris Hahn, President/CEO
(913) 236-9290
hahnc@ksso.org
• Mark Malick, Chairperson
• Dale Chaffin, Treasurer
• Tim Rehder, Senior VP Program Operations
(913) 236-9290
rehdert@ksso.org
• Michele Johnson, Program Operations Manager
(913) 236-9290
johnsonm@ksso.org

Sports Services Founded:
1970

SPECIAL OLYMPICS KENTUCKY
105 LAKEVIEW COURT
FRANKFORT, KY 40601
502-695-8222
800-633-7403
Fax: 502-695-0496
soky@soky.org
www.soky.org
• Trish Mazzoni, President/CEO
tmazzoni@soky.org
• Teresa Capps-McGill, VP Finance
tacpps-mcgill@soky.org
• Taylor Ballinger, Special Events Director
• Mark Buerger, Communications Director
mbuerger@soky.org
Description:
Organization mission is to provide year-round training and competition for people with intellectual disabilities to enrich their lives through sport.

SPECIAL OLYMPICS LOUISIANA
1000 EAST MORRIS AVENUE
HAMMOND, LA 70403
985-345-6644
800-345-6644
Fax: 985-345-6649
www.laso.org
• John Saye, Chairperson
• Emily Jeffcott, Vice-Chairperson
• Pat Carpenter Bourgeois, President/CEO
• Rhonda Blanford-Green, Secretary
• Sylvia Alaniz, Vice President of Finance
Sports Services Founded:
1968

SPECIAL OLYMPICS MAINE
125 JOHN ROBERTS ROAD
SUITE 5
SOUTH PORTLAND, ME 4106
207-879-0489
Fax: 888-490-0672
www.specialolympicsmaine.org
• Phil Geelhoed, President & CEO
(207) 879-0489
philg@somaine.org
• Lisa Bird, Public Relations & Torch Run
(207) 879-0489
lisab@somaine.org
• Ian Frank, Training/Camp Tall Pines
(207) 879-0489
ianf@somaine.org
Member Services:
Year round program of athletic training and opportunity for competition in sixteen different Olympic Style Sports.
Membership Requirements:
Program serves children and adults with intellectual disabilities in the state of Maine.

SPECIAL OLYMPICS MARYLAND
3071 COMMERCE DRIVE
SUITE 103
BALTIMORE, MD 21227
410-242-1515
800-541-7544
Fax: 410-242-5162
info@somd.org
www.somd.org
• Frank Andracchi, Chairman
• Jennifer Rapacki, Treasurer
• Wayne Luoma, Secretary
• Donny Boyd, At-Large director
• Jim Schmutz, President/CEO
(410) 242-1515
jschmutz@somd.org

SPECIAL OLYMPICS MASSACHUSETTS
THE YAWKEY SPORTS TRAINING CENTER
512 FOREST ST
MARLBOROUGH, MA 1752

508-485-0986
Fax: 508-481-0786
www.specialolympicsma.org
• Mary Beth McMahon, President & CEO
marybeth.mcmahon@specialolympicsma.org
• Gayle Fehlmann, CFO
gayle.fehlmann@specialolympicsma.org
• Matt Ruxton, VP of Sports
matt.ruxton@specialolympicsma.org
• Steve Huftalen, AVP of Corporate Development & Special Events
steve.huftalen@specialolympicsma.org

SPECIAL OLYMPICS MICHIGAN
CENTRAL MICHIGAN UNIVERSITY
MOUNT PLEASANT, MI 48859
989-774-3911
800-644-6404
Fax: 989-774-3034
somi@somi.org
www.somi.org
• Lois Arnold, President/CEO
lois.arnold@cmich.edu
• Alison Miller, Chief Development Officer
mille1as@cmich.edu
• Ann Guzdzial, Chief Program Officer
anna.guzdzial@cmich.edu
• Rick Brady, Sports & Training Coordinator
brady1rp@cmich.edu
Year Founded:
1968 by Eunice Kennedy Shriver. State incorporated in 1972 (Special Olympics Michigan).
Membership Requirements:
Persons aged 8+,identified as a person with an intellectual disability.

SPECIAL OLYMPICS MINNESOTA
900 2ND AVENUE S.
SUITE 300
MINNEAPOLIS, MN 55402
612-333-0999
800-783-7732
Fax: 612-333-8782
info@somn.org
www.specialolympicsminnesota.org
• David Dorn, President/CEO
(763) 270-7130
david.dorn@somn.org
• Chad Trench, Operations Director
(763) 270-7127
chad.trench@somn.org
• Melissa Holmes, Director of Finance
(763) 270-7129
melissa.holmes@somn.org

SPECIAL OLYMPICS MISSISSIPPI
15 OLYMPIC WAY
MADISON, MS 39110
601-856-7748
Fax: 601-856-8132
www.specialolympicsms.org
• Kenny Williamson, Chairman
• Rick Webster, Vice Chairman
• Paul Rogers, Treasurer
Description:
Organization mission is to provide year-round training and competition for people with intellectual disabilities to enrich their lives through sport.

SPECIAL OLYMPICS MISSOURI
1001 DIAMOND RIDGE
SUITE 800
JEFFERSON CITY, MO 65109
573-635-1660
Fax: 573-635-8233
schatsiek@somo.org
www.somo.org
• Mark Musso, President/CEO
musso@somo.org
• Trish Lutz, Senior Director of Programs
lutz@somo.org
Description:
Organization mission is to provide year-round training and competition for people with

multi sports

intellectual disabilities to enrich their lives through sport.

SPECIAL OLYMPICS MONTANA
710 1ST AVENUE NORTH
GREAT FALLS, MT 59401
800-242-6876
info@somt.org
www.somt.org
• Bob Norbie, President/CEO
bnorbie@somt.org
• Rhonda McCarty, Chief Operating Officer
rmccarty@somt.org
Description:
Organization mission is to provide year-round training and competition for people with intellectual disabilities to enrich their lives through sport.

SPECIAL OLYMPICS NEBRASKA
9427 F STREET
OMAHA, NE 68127
402-331-5545
800-247-0105
Fax: 402-331-5964
www.sone.org
• Carolyn Chamberlin, President/CEO
(402) 331-5545
cchamberlin@sone.org
• David Demyan, Director of Sports & Competition
(402) 331-5545
ddemyan@sone.org
Description:
Organization mission is to provide year-round training and competition for people with intellectual disabilities to enrich their lives through sport.

SPECIAL OLYMPICS NEVADA
5670 WYNN ROAD
SUITE H
LAS VEGAS, NV 89118
877-417-2742
Fax: 702-474-0694
www.sonv.org
• Littler Mendelson, P.C, Chair
• Joyce Whitney-Silva, Vice Chair
• David Solo, President/CEO
(925) 944-8801
davids@sonc.org
• Kevin Reeds, Chief Dvelopment Officer
(925) 944-8801
kevinr@sonc.org
• Harry Mong, Regional Sports Director
(702) 474-0690
harrym@sonv.org
Description:
Special Olympics Nevada offers free sports training and competition opportunities to people with intellectual disabilities in several different sports.

SPECIAL OLYMPICS NEW HAMPSHIRE
650 ELM STREET
MANCHESTER, NH 3101
603-624-1250
Fax: 603-624-4911
www.sonh.org
• Mike Dennehy, Chairperson
• Mary Conroy, President
(603) 624-1250
MaryC@sonh.org
• Doug Basnett, Secretary
• Butch Beers, Program Coordinator
ButchB@sonh.org
• Chelsea Gill, Director of Development
(603) 624-1250
ChelseaG@sonh.org
Description:
Special Olympics of New Hampshire (SONH) is a non profit organization providing sports training and athletic competition for children and adults with intellectual disabilities. Currently 2,994 participants and thousands of volunteers, friends and family members take part in SONH activities.

SPECIAL OLYMPICS NEW JERSEY
1 EUNICE KENNEDY SHRIVER WAY
LAWRENCEVILLE, NJ 8648-2301
609-896-8000
Fax: 609-896-8040
info@sonj.org
www.sonj.org
• Heather B. Andersen, President/Chief Executive Officer
HBA@sonj.org
• Richard Gelfond, Director of Operations
RSG@sonj.org
• Jeff Baldino, Competition Director
JJB@sonj.org
Description:
Organization mission is to provide year-round training and competition for people with intellectual disabilities to enrich their lives through sport.

SPECIAL OLYMPICS NEW MEXICO
6600 PALOMAS NE
SUITE 207
ALBUQUERQUE, NM 87109
505-856-0342
Fax: 505-856-0346
www.sonm.org
• Jack Eichorn, Chairman
• Karen Hudson, Vice Chairman
• Randy Mascorella, Executive Director
randymascorella@sonm.org
• Christine Hidalgo, Director Of Development & Special Event
christine@sonm.org
Year Founded:
1968
Description:
Organization mission is to provide year-round training and competition for people with intellectual disabilities to enrich their lives through sport.

SPECIAL OLYMPICS NEW YORK
504 BALLTOWN ROAD
SCHENECTADY, NY 12304
518-388-0790
800-836-6976
Fax: 518-388-0791
specialolympics-ny.org
• Shelly Nangle, Executive VP & COO
mnangle@nyso.org
• Neal J. Johnson, President/CEO
johnsonn@nyso.org
• Steve Fuller, VP Program & Competition
sfuller@nyso.org
• Bill Collins, Director of Training
bcollins@nyso.org
• Lauren Maneri, Program Specialist
lmaneri@nyso.org
• Stacy Eder, Director of Volunteer Management
seder@nyso.org
Sports Services Founded:
1969
Description:
Organization mission is to provide year-round training and competition for people with intellectual disabilities to enrich their lives through sport.

SPECIAL OLYMPICS NORTH CAROLINA
2200 GATEWAY CENTRE BOULVEARD
SUITE 201
MORRISVILLE, NC 27560
919-719-7662
800-843-6276
Fax: 919-719-7663
www.sonc.net
• Keith L. Fishburne, President/CEO
(919) 719-7662
kfishburne@sonc.net
• Kelly Vaughn, Senior Vice President
(919) 719-7662
kvaughn@sonc.net
• Rachel McQuiston, VP Communications
rmcquiston@sonc.net
• Andrea Stamm, Vice President of Sports

(919) 719-7662
astamm@sonc.net
Membership Requirements:
Special Olympics North Carolina is not a membership organization. Volunteers serve as coaches, event committee organizers, fund raisers, and other roles. Registration criteria exists for athletes and volunteers.
Description:
Organization mission is to provide year-round training and competition for people with intellectual disabilities to enrich their lives through sport.

SPECIAL OLYMPICS NORTH DAKOTA
21616 SOUTH 26TH STREET
GRAND FORKS, ND 58201
701-746-0331
Fax: 701-772-1265
info@specialolympicsnd.org
www.specialolympicsnorthdakota.org
• John Erickson, Chairman
• Dr. Julie Blehm, Vice Chair
• Jon Godfread, Secretary
• John Schumacher, Treasurer/Vice Secretary
• Kathy Meagher, President & CEO
president@specialolympicsnd.org
Description:
Organization mission is to provide year-round training and competition for people with intellectual disabilities to enrich their lives through sport.

SPECIAL OLYMPICS NORTHERN CALIFORNIA
3480 BUSKIRK AVENUE
SUITE 340
PLEASANT HILL, CA 94523
925-944-8801
Fax: 925-944-8803
info@sonc.org
www.sonc.org
• Richard Rahm, Chair
• Gretchen Pearson, Secretary
• David Solo, President/CEO
(925) 944-8801
DavidS@sonc.org
• Mike Mayo, CFO
(925) 944-8801
Mike@sonc.org
Description:
Special Olympics Northern California serves over 14,000 individuals with developmental disabilities. From the Oregon border to Monterey and Tulare counties, athletes have the opportunity to participate in a wide variety of sports trainings and competitions that take place throughout the year.

SPECIAL OLYMPICS OHIO
3303 WINCHESTER PIKE
COLUMBUS, OH 43232
614-239-7050
Fax: 614-239-1873
www.sooh.org
• Kraig Makohus, Chief Executive Officer
kmakohus@sooh.org
• Marty Allen, Program Director
mallen@sooh.org
• Tim Etienne, Field Director
tetienne@sooh.org
Sports Services Founded:
Incorporated in 1975.
Description:
Provides year round training and competition opportunities for children and adults with intellectual disabilities.

SPECIAL OLYMPICS OKLAHOMA
6835 SOUTH CANTON AVENUE
TULSA, OK 74136
918-481-1234
800-722-9004
Fax: 918-496-1515
info@sook.org
www.sook.org

- Linda McKown, Chairman
- Adrian DeWendt, President/CEO
- Donna Ham, Marketing Director
- Teri Hockett, Vice President of Programs
- John Seals, Sports Director

Description:
Organization mission is to provide year-round training and competition for people with intellectual disabilities to enrich their lives through sport.

Additional Information:
3701 SE 15th Street, #B-1, Del City, OK 73115; (P) 405-670-3456 (F) 405-670-5678

SPECIAL OLYMPICS OREGON
5901 SW MACADAM AVENUE
SUITE 200
PORTLAND, OR 97239
503-248-0600
Fax: 503-248-0603
info@soor.org
www.soor.org
- Margaret Hunt, CEO
(543) 248-0600
- Chad Carter, Senior Director of Marketing
- Jenelle Clinton, Director of Development
- Joann Stoller, Senior Director of Sports

Sports Services Founded:
1972

Description:
Organization mission is to provide year-round training and competition for people with intellectual disabilities to enrich their lives through sport.

SPECIAL OLYMPICS PENNSYLVANIA
2570 BOULEVARD OF THE GENERALS
SUITE 124
NORRISTOWN, PA 19403
610-630-9450
800-235-9058
www.specialolympicspa.org
- Matthew B Aaron, President & CEO
maaron@specialolympicspa.org
- Michelle Boone, Senior Sport Director
mboone@specialolympicspa.org
- Eric Cushing, VP Development/Marketing
ecushing@specialolympicspa.org
- Susan Wyland, VP Finance/Administration
swyland@specialolympicspa.org

Description:
Organization provides year-round training and competition for 20,000 people with intellectual disabilites in Pennsylvania.

SPECIAL OLYMPICS RHODE ISLAND
370 GEORGE WASHINGTON HIGHWAY
UNIT 1
SMITHFIELD, RI 2917
401-349-4900
info@specialolympicsri.org
specialolympicsri.org
- Thoams Maggiacomo, Chairman
- Lawrence LaSala, Vice Chair
- Michael Sarli, Secretary
- Dennis DeJesus, CEO
dennis@specialolympicsri.org
- Chris Hopkins, Programs Director
chris@specialolympicsri.org
- Gerri Walter, Marketing & Communications Director
gerri@specialolympicsri.org

Description:
Provides over 1,600 year-round sports training and athletic competitions for more than 3,200 athletes with intellectual disabilities.

SPECIAL OLYMPICS SOUTH CAROLINA
109 OAK PARK DRIVE
IRMO, SC 29063
803-772-1555
www.so-sc.org
- Barry Coats, President/CEO
(803) 772-1555
bcoats@so-sc.org
- Edwena Lassiter, Director of Volunteer &

Family Services
(803) 772-1555
elassiter@so-sc.org
- Sue Maner, Executive Vice President
(803) 772-1555
smaner@so-sc.org
- Kelly Garrick, Director of Sports and Competition
(803) 772-1555
kgarrick@so-sc.org
- Barbara Oswald, Senior Director of Programs
(803) 772-1555
boswald@so-sc.org
- Sandye Williams, Director of Marketing and Development
(843) 367-2358
swilliams@so-sc.org

Description:
Organization mission is to provide year-round training and competition for people with intellectual disabilities to enrich their lives through sport.

SPECIAL OLYMPICS SOUTH DAKOTA
800 E, I-90 LANE
SIOUX FALLS, SD 57104
605-331-4117
800-585-2114
Fax: 605-331-4328
www.sosd.org
- Darryl Nordquist, CEO/Executive Director
dnordquist@sosd.org
- Melanie Frosch, Vice President, Sports and Competition
mfrosch@sosd.org
- Johna Thum, Vice President, Field Services
jthum@sosd.org
- Twila Nicholson Hansen, Office Manager
thansen@sosd.org
- Todd Bradwisch, Torch Run Liaison

Description:
Organization mission is to provide year-round training and competition for people with intellectual disabilities to enrich their lives through sport.

SPECIAL OLYMPICS SOUTHERN CALIFORNIA
1600 FORBES WAY
SUITE 200
LONG BEACH, CA 90810
562-502-1100
Fax: 562-502-1119
info@sosc.org
www.sosc.org
- Bill Shumard, President/CEO
- Kelly Johnson, Vice Chair/Treasurer
- Mary Ann Powell, Secretary

Description:
Organization mission is to provide year-round training and competition for people with intellectual disabilities to enrich their lives through sport.

Teams:
Aquatics, Basketball, Bocce, Bowling, Floor Hockey, Golf, Gymnastics, Soccer, Softball, Tennis and Volleyball

SPECIAL OLYMPICS TENNESSEE
461 CRAIGHEAD STREET
NASHVILLE, TN 37204
615-329-1375
800-383-8502
Fax: 615-327-1465
www.specialolympicstn.org
- Alan L Bolick, President
(615) 329-1375
abolick@specialolympicstn.org
- Sean Stake, Vice President Sports
(615) 329-1375
sstake@specialolympicstn.org
- Stacey Blackmore, Director of Finance
(615) 329-1375
sblackmore@specialolympicstn.org

Description:
Organization mission is to provide year-round training and competition for people with

intellectual disabilities to enrich their lives through sport.

SPECIAL OLYMPICS TEXAS
1804 RUTHERFORD LANE
AUSTIN, TX 78754
512-835-9873
800-876-5646
info@sotx.org
www.sotx.org
- Margaret M. Larsen, President/CEO
(512) 835-9873
mlarsen@sotx.org
- Tela Mange, Vice President Communications
(512) 835-9873
tmange@sotx.org

Description:
Organization mission is to provide year-round training and competition for people with intellectual disabilities to enrich their lives through sport.

SPECIAL OLYMPICS UTAH
1400 S. FOOTHILL DRIVE
SUITE 238
SALT LAKE CITY, UT 84108
801-363-1111
information@sout.org
www.sout.org
- D'Arcy Dixon Pignanelli, President/Chief Executive Officer
dixon@sout.org
- Jonathan Embler, Vice President, Sports Programs
embler@sout.org
- Wendy Kelly, Dirsctor of Community Outreach and Partnerships
kelly@sout.org

Description:
Provides year round sports training and competition in a variety of Olympic type sports for children and adults with intellectual disabilities.

SPECIAL OLYMPICS VERMONT
16 GREGORY DRIVE
SUITE 2
SOUTH BURLINGTON, VT 05403
802-863-5222
800-639-1603
Fax: 802-863-3911
info@vtso.org
specialolympicsvermont.org
- Lisa DeNatale, President/CEO
(802) 861-0272
ldenatale@vtso.org

Description:
Organization mission is to provide year-round training and competition for people with intellectual disabilities to enrich their lives through sport.

SPECIAL OLYMPICS VIRGINIA
3212 SKIPWITH ROAD
SUITE 100
RICHMOND, VA 23294
804-346-5544
800-932-4653
Fax: 804-346-9633
info@specialolympicsva.org
www.specialolympicsva.org
- Rick Jeffrey, President
(804) 726-3028
- Roy Zeidman, Senior VP Marketing & Development
(804) 726-3022
rzeidman@specialolympicsva.org

Description:
Organization mission is to provide year-round training and competition for people with intellectual disabilities to enrich their lives through sport.

SPECIAL OLYMPICS WASHINGTON
1809 7TH AVENUE
SUITE 1509
SEATTLE, WA 98101

multi sports

206-362-4949
800-752-7559
Fax: 206-362-8158
info@sowa.org
specialolympicswashington.org
• Dave Lennox, President/CEO
dlenox@sowa.org
• Joe Hampson, VP Sports & Community
Outreach
jhampson@sowa.org
Description:
Organization mission is to provide year-round
training and competition for people with
intellectual disabilities to enrich their lives
through sport.

SPECIAL OLYMPICS WEST VIRGINIA
1206 VIRGINIA STREET
SUITE 100
CHARLESTON, WV 25301
304-345-9310
800-926-1616
Fax: 304-345-9338
info@sowa.org
www.sowv.org
• John Corbett, Chief Executive Officer
john@sowv.org
• Kendra Wallace, Director of Sports and
Training
kendra@sowv.org
Description:
Organization mission is to provide year-round
training and competition for people with
intellectual disabilities to enrich their lives
through sport.

SPECIAL OLYMPICS WISCONSIN
2310 CROSSROADS DRIVE
SUITE 1000
MADISON, WI 53718
608-222-1324
www.specialolympicswisconsin.org
• Kathleen H Roach, President/CEO
(608) 442-5660
kroach@specialolympicswisconsin.org
Description:
A statewide organization providing persons with
cognitive disabilities year-round sports training
and competition. Individuals who are at least
eight years old and are identified as having a
cognitive disability are eligible for participation.

SPECIAL OLYMPICS WYOMING
239 W 1ST STREET
CASPER, WY 82601
307-235-3062
800-735-8345
Fax: 307-235-3063
www.sowy.org
• Priscilla Dowse, President/CEO
pdowse@specialolympicswy.org
• Debbie Huber, Chairperson
• Mark Holland, Vice Chairperson
• Brian Cetak, Treasurer
• Mike Burnett, Secretary
Description:
Organization mission is to provide year-round
training and competition for people with
intellectual disabilities to enrich their lives
through sport.

U.S. ASSOCIATION OF BLIND ATHLETES
1 OLYMPIC PLAZA
COLORADO SPRINGS, CO 80909
719-866-3224
Fax: 719-866-34
• Mark Lucas, Executive Director
mlucas@usaba.org
• Ryan Ortiz, Assistant Executive Director
rortiz@usaba.org
• John Potts, Goalball High-Performance
Director
jpotts@usaba.org
Member Services:
Special literature; clinics; seminars; panel

discussions; group meetings; conventions.
Sports Services Founded:
1976
Description:
Enhances the lives of blind and visually
impaired people by providing the opportunity
for participation in sports and physical
activity.

U.S. PARALYMPICS
ONE OLYMPIC PLAZA
COLORADO SPRINGS, CO 80909
719-632-5551
usparalympics.org
• Scott Blackmun, Chief Executive Officer
• Lisa Baird, Chief Marketing Officer
Sports Services Founded:
2001
Description:
A division of the U.S. Olympic Committee,
dedicated to becoming the world leader in
the paralympic sports movement, and
promoting excellence in the lives of persons
with physical disabilities.

**UNITED FOUNDATION FOR DISABLED
ARCHERS**
20 NE 9TH AVENUE
PO BOX 251
GLENWOOD, MN 56334
320-634-3660
info@uffdaclub.com
www.uffdaclub.com
Description:
Promotes archery for persons with physical
disabilties.
Year Founded:
1994

USA DEAF SPORTS FEDERATION
PO BOX 22011
SANTA FE, NM 87502
support@usdeafsports.org
• Jack C Lamberton, President
lamberton@usdeafsports.org
• Jeffrey L. Salit, Vice President
salit@usdeafsports.org
• Brianne Burger, Secretary
burger@usdeafsports.org
• Mark Apodaca, Chief Financial Officer
apodaca@usdeafsports.org
Member Services:
Club sports on recreational level;
international competition for elite athletes;
CISS deaflympics; national tournaments for
the deaf.
Membership Requirements:
All deaf and hard of hearing individuals with
a hearing loss of 55 db or greater in the
better ear are eligible.
Description:
Founded in 1945, USADSF acts as the
national governing body for deaf sports
organizations, producing annual
competitions and serving as a social
community for the deaf.

USBGA GOLF ASSOCIATION
125 GILBERTS HILL ROAD
LEHIGHTON, PA 18235
info@usblindgolf.com
usblindgolf.com
• Dick Pomo, President
(520) 648-1088
pomodick@Q.com

WHEELCHAIR & AMBULATORY SPORTS
PO BOX 621023
LITTLETON, CO 80162
720-412-7979
Fax: 866-204-8018
www.wasusa.org
• Gregg Baumgarten, Chairperson
chairman@wasusa.org
• Denise Hutchins, Vice Chair
• Mike Burns, Treasurer
• Cory Grant, Secretary
Description:
Founded in 1956, Wheelchair And
Ambulatory Sports USA acts as an outreach
program and competition administrator,
promoting participation in sport for people
with disabilities.

High School Sports

GLOBAL SPORTS & ENTERTAINMENT
300 N CONTINENTAL BLVD
SUITE 140
EL SEGUNDO, CA 90245
310-414-2690
Fax: 310-414-2693
info@globalsports-ent.com
www.globalsports-ent.com
• Nick Zaccagnino, Founder/President
• Evan Levy, Senior Event Manager/Talent
Producer
• Ben Weiss, Senior Talent Booker/Director
Of Digital Marketing
Year Founded:
1996
Description:
Global Sports & Entertainment is a talent
booking and event management firm
specializing in securing celebrity athletes for
mass media programming and events.

**NATIONAL FEDERATION OF STATE
HIGH SCHOOL ASSOCIATIONS**
PO BOX 690
INDIANAPOLIS, IN 46206
317-972-6900
Fax: 317-822-5700
www.nfhs.org
• Gary Musselman, President
• Bob Gardner, Executive Director
• JoAnne Bennett, Chief Financial Officer
• Davis Whitfield, Chief Operating Officer
Member Services:
Scorebooks and rule books for
interscholastic sports. Sports videos used in
the training of coaches, athletes, officials
and spectators. Selection of the National
High School Debate Topic, and other
services in the fields of debate, speech and
music. Athletics Participation Surveys.
Publications:
National High School Rules Books and
related publications in 17 sports. National
High School Sports Record Book. NFHS
Handbook. NHFS NEWS,
INTERSCHOLASTIC ATHLETIC
ADMINISTRATION MAGAZINE. NATIONAL
FEDERATION COACHES' QUARTERLY.
NATIONAL FEDERATION OFFICIALS'
QUARTERLY.
Membership Requirements:
State associations responsible for
administering interscholastic activities.
Description:
Founded 1920. Represents state high
school associations with more than 18,500

high schools, coaches and sponsors and officials and judges throughout the U.S. Provides sanctioning services for interstate and international events. Writes the playing rules for high school athletics. Analyzes equipment for licensing purposes.

Other locations:

ALABAMA HIGH SCHOOL ATHLETIC ASSOCIATION
7325 HALCYON SUMMIT DRIVE
MONTGOMERY, AL 36117
334-263-6994
Fax: 334-387-0075
www.ahsaa.com
• Steve Savarese, Executive Director
ssavarese@ahsaa.com
• Tony Stallworth, Associate Executive Director
tstallworth@ahsaa.com
Sports Service Founded:
1921
Publications:
AHSAA Sports Books; AHSAA eligibility by-laws; Coaches Directory.
Description:
AHSAA is a priavet agency which regulates, coordinates and promotes interscholastic athletic programs among its member public and private schools. Over 75,000 students involved.

ALASKA SCHOOL ACTIVITIES ASSOCIATION
4048 LAUREL STREET
#203
ANCHORAGE, AK 99508
907-563-3723
Fax: 907-563-3739
contactus@asaa.org
www.asaa.org
• Billy Strickland, Executive Director
billy@asaa.org
• Deanna Montagna, Director Of Office Operations & Students Services
deanna@asaa.org
• Doug Stewart, Director of Development & Marketing
Sports Services Founded:
1956
Description:
To advocate participation in cocurricular activities; to regulate sanctioned interscholastic activities, contests and programs; and to promote the academic and social development of students.

ALBERTA SCHOOLS' ATHLETIC ASSOCIATION
11759 GROAT ROAD
EDMONTON, AB, CANADA T5M 3K6
780-427-8182
Fax: 780-415-1833
info@asaa.ca
www.asaa.ca
• Tom Christensen, President
(403) 556-3391
tchristensen@chinooksedge.ab.ca
• Rick Gilson, Vice-Presdient
(403) 653-4991
rick.gilson@westwind.ab.ca
• John Paton, Executive Director
(780) 427-8182
john@asaa.ca
• Tyler Callaghan, Assistant Director
(888) 618-4530
tyler@asaa.ca
• Morgan Munroe, Compliance Officer
(780) 415-1833
morgan@asaa.ca
Description:
A voluntary, non profit organization established to coordinate athletic programs for young people in Alberta schools.

ARIZONA INTERSCHOLASTIC ASSOCIATION
7007 N 18TH STREET
PHOENIX, AZ 85020-5552
602-385-3810
Fax: 602-385-3779
www.aiaonline.org
• Jacob Holiday, President
(928) 697-2172
jacob.holiday@kayenta.k12.az.us
• Harold Slemmer Ed.D, Executive Director
(602) 385-3811
hslemmer@aiaonline.org
Year Founded:
1925

ARKANSAS ACTIVITIES ASSOCIATION
3920 RICHARDS ROAD
NORTH LITTLE ROCK, AR 72117
501-955-2500
Fax: 501-955-2600
www.ahsaa.org
• Lance Taylor, Executive Director
(501) 955-2500
lance@ahsaa.org
• Joey Walters, Deputy Executive Director
(501) 955-2500
joey@ahsaa.org

BC SCHOOL SPORTS
2003A - 3713 KENSINGTON AVENUE
BURNABY, BC, CANADA V5B 0A7
604-477-1488
info@bcschoolsports.ca
www.bcschoolsports.ca
• Mike Allina, President
(604) 713-8215
mallina@vsb.bc.ca
• Rob Colombo, 1st Vice President
(604) 941-6053
rcolombo@sd43.bc.ca
• Mykola Misiak, 2nd Vice President
(604) 531-8354
misiak_m@surreyschools.ca
• Jordan Abney, Executive Director
(604) 477-1488
jabney@bcschoolsports.ca
• Merirlla Thorp, Financial Officer
(604) 477-1488
mthorp@bcschoolsports.ca
Description:
BC School Sports is an assocation of public and private schools governing school sport in the province.
Description:
BC School Sports is an assocation of public and private schools governing school sport in the province.

CALIFORNIA INTERSCHOLASTIC FEDERATION
4658 DUCKHORN DRIVE
SACRAMENTO, CA 95834
916-239-4477
Fax: 916-239-4478
www.cifstate.org
• Roger Blake, Executive Director
rblake@cifstate.org
• Ron Nocetti, Associate Director
rnocetti@cifstate.org
• Brian Seymour, Senior Director
bseymour@cifstate.org
• Chris Fahey, Director Of Corporate Sponsorships
cfahey@cifstate.org

COLORADO HS ACTIVITIES ASSOCIATION
14855 E 2ND AVENUE
AURORA, CO 80011
303-344-5050
www2.chsaa.org
• Eddie Hartnett, President
• Paul Angelico, Secretary-Treasurer
Description:
The association works for the advancement of,

and the student's participation in, interscholastic activities.

CONNECTICUT INTERSCHOLASTIC ATHLETIC CONFERENCE
30 REALTY DRIVE
CHESHIRE, CT 06410
203-250-1111
Fax: 203-250-1345
ciacsports.com/site
• Paul Newton, CSAC Chair
• Richard Dellinger, Middle Level Vice President
• Karissa Niehoff, PhD, Executive Director
(203) 250-1111
kniehoff@casciac.org
• Stephanie Ford, Marketing Director
(203) 250-1111
sford@casciac.org
Sports Services Founded:
1921
Membership:
Any public, private or parochial elementary, middle or senior high school which is approved by the State Board of Education.
Description:
Works to develop, maintain and enforce rules of eligibility and conduct that insure equitable athletic competition among Connecticut's secondary schools. The CIAC serves as the sole governing body for inter-scholastic athletic activities in Connecticut.

DELAWARE INTERSCHOLASTIC ATHLETIC ASSOCIATION
35 COMMERCE WAY
SUITE 1
DOVER, DE 19904
302-857-3365
www.doe.k12.de.us
• Thomas Neubauer, Executive Director
thomas.neubauer@doe.k12.de.us
Description:
Advocates for and promotes and the value of interscholastic athletics, and ensures fair competitions during competition. Promotes healthy lifestyles for youth.

FLORIDA HIGH SCHOOL ATHLETIC ASSOCIATION
1801 NW 80TH BOULEVARD
GAINESVILLE, FL 32606
352-372-9551
800-461-7895
Fax: 352-373-1528
www.fhsaa.org
• Frank Beasley, Director of Athletics
(352) 372-9551
fbeasley@fhsaa.org
• Roger Dearing, Executive Director
(352) 372-9551
rdearing@fhsaa.org
Description:
To promote, direct, supervise and regulate interscholastic athletic programs in which member high schools compete.
Year Founded:
1920

GEORGIA HS ASSOCIATION
151 S BETHEL STREET
PO BOX 271
THOMASTON, GA 30286-0004
706-647-7473
Fax: 706-647-2638
ghsa@ghsa.net
www.ghsa.net
• Gary Phillips, Executive Director
(706) 647-7473
garyphillips@ghsa.net
• Lisa Moore Williams, Vice President
• Steve Figueroa, Director Media Relations
(706) 647-7473
stevefig@ghsa.net
Sports Service Founded:
1904
Description:
Promotes sports education in Georgia.

Standardizes and encourages participation in athletics, and to promote sportsmanship and an appreciation for and study of music, speech , and other fine arts through Region and State competitions.

HAWAII HS ATHLETIC ASSOCIATION
PO BOX 62029
HONOLULU, HI 96839
808-800-4092
info@hhsaa.org
www.sportshigh.com
• Christopher Chun, Executive Director
• Russell Aoki, Associate Director
• Natalie Iwamoto, Director Of Information And Marketing
Sports Services Founded:
1956
Description:
The HHSAA serves public and private high schools by promoting atlhetics in the context of educational programming. As part of this work, the organization holds state championships, and leadership training seminars for coaches, officials and athletic directors.

IDAHO HS ACTIVITIES ASSOCIATION
8011 USTICK ROAD
BOISE, ID 83704
208-375-7027
Fax: 208-322-5505
admin@idhsaa.org
www.idhsaa.org
• Ty Jones, Executive Director
jonest@idhsaa.org

ILLINOIS HS ASSOCIATION
2715 MCGRAW DRIVE
BLOOMINGTON, IL 61704-6011
309-663-6377
Fax: 309-663-7479
general@ihsa.org
www.ihsa.org
• Craig Anderson, Executive Director
canderson@ihsa.org
• Kurt Gibson, Assistant Executive Director
kgibson@ihsa.org
Sports Service Founded:
1900
Description:
The IHSA serves member schools by providing leadership for equitable participation in interscholastic athletics and activities that enrich the educational experience.

INDIANA HS ATHLETIC ASSOCIATION
9150 MERIDIAN STREET
PO BOX 40650
INDIANAPOLIS, IN 46240
317-846-6601
Fax: 317-575-4244
www.ihsaa.org
• Debb Stevens, Chairperson
• Jim Brown, Vice-Chairperson
• Bobby Cox, Commissioner
bcox@ihsaa.org
• Jason Wille, Sports Information Director
jwille@ihsaa.org
Sports Services Founded:
1903
Description:
A not-for-profit organization which encourages and directs amateur athletics in the high schools of Indiana.

IOWA HS ATHLETIC ASSOCIATION
1605 SOUTH STORY STREET
PO BOX 10
BOONE, IA 50036
515-432-2011
Fax: 515-432-2961
www.iahsaa.org
• Alan Beste, Executive Director
abeste@iahsaa.org
• Brett Nanninga, Associate Director
bnanninga@iahsaa.org

• Todd Tharp, Assistant Director
ttharp@iahsaa.org
• Sandra Anderson, Finance Director
sanderson@iahsaa.org
• Lewie Curtis, Officials Director
lcurtis@iahsaa.org
• Bud Legg, Information Director
blegg@iahsaa.org
• Kylie Swanson, Communications Director
kswanson@iahsaa.org
• Laura Brooker, Asst Director of Officials
officials@iahsaa.org
• Chelsea Clark, Administrative Assistant
cclark@iahsaa.org
• Elisa Kahler, Office Manager
ekahler@iahsaa.org
• Amy McNace, Administrative Assistant
amcnace@iahsaa.org
• Kim Mechura, Administrative Assistant
kmechura@iahsaa.org
Description:
Founded in 1903. the association is a non-for-profit organization which officates cross country, fall golf, football, basketball, bowling, swimming, wrestling, soccer, spring golf, tennis, track & field and baseball for itsmember schools.

KANSAS STATE HS ACTIVITIES ASSOCIATION
PO BOX 495
TOPEKA, KS 66601
785-273-5329
Fax: 785-271-0236
kshsaa@kshsaa.org
www.kshsaa.org
• Juan Perez, President
(620) 356-3025
jperez@ulysses.org
• Rod Wittmer, Vice-President
(785) 364-2181
r.wittmer@holtonks.net
• Britton Hart, Secretary-Treasurer
(620) 341-2365
britton.hart@usd253.net
• Gary Musselman, Executive Director
• Cheryl Gleason, Assistant Executive Director
cegleason@kshsaa.org
Description:
Provides guidance for the administration education based sport and other interscholastic activites in the state of Kansas.

KENTUCKY HS ATHLETIC ASSOCIATION
2280 EXECUTIVE DRIVE
LEXINGTON, KY 40505
859-299-5472
Fax: 859-293-5999
general@khsaa.org
www.khsaa.org
• Julian Tackett, Commissioner
(859) 299-5472
• Mike Barren, Assistant Commissioner
(859) 299-5472

LOUISIANA HS ATHLETIC ASSOCIATION
12720 OLD HAMMOND HIGHWAY
BATON ROUGE, LA 70816
225-296-5882
Fax: 225-296-5919
www.lhsaa.org
• Eddie Bonine, Executive Director
ebonine@lhsaa.org
• Keith Alexander, Assistant Executive Director
kalexander@lhsaa.org
• Rhonda Blanford-Green, Assistant Executive Director
rblanfordgreen@lhsaa.org
• BJ Guzzardo, Assistant Executive Director
bguzzardo@lhsaa.org
• Mitch Small, Director of Maeketing
msmall@lhsaa.org

MAINE PRINCIPAL'S ASSOCIATION
50 INDUSTRIAL DRIVE
AUGUSTA, ME 04330

207-622-0217
Fax: 207-622-1513
mpa@mpa.cc
www.mpa.cc
• Dan Welch, President
dwelch@csd3-brhs.org
• Maggie Allen, President Elect
magallen@svrsu.org
• Richard A. A Durost, Executive Director
• Michael Burnham, Assistant Executive Director
mburnham@mpa.cc
• Holly D. Couturier, Assistant Executive Director
• Tammy McNear, Secretary
tmcnear@mpa.cc
Description:
This non-profit organization is conprised of the Division of Professional Activities and Division of Interscholastic Activities.

MANITOBA HS ATHLETIC ASSOCIATION
145 PACIFIC AVENUE
WINNIPEG, MB, CANADA R3B 2Z6
204-925-5640
Fax: 204-925-5624
info@mhsaa.ca
www.mhsaa.ca
• Chris Gudziunas, President
(204) 326-6471
cgudziunas@hsd.ca
• JJ Ross, Urban Representative
jross@sjsd.net
• Chad Falk, Executive Director
chad@mhsaa.ca
• Greg Jarvis, Assistant Executive Director
(204) 925-5642
greg@mhsaa.ca
• Jo-Ann Waskul, Admin. Assistant:
(204) 925-5640
jo-ann@mhsaa.ca
Sports Service Founded:
1962
Description:
Encourages particiaption in high school sport as an essential component of education and personal development.

MARYLAND PUBLIC SECONDARY SCHOOLS ATHLETIC ASSOCIATION
200 WEST BALTIMORE STREET
BALTIMORE, MD 21201
410-767-0555
Fax: 410-333-3111
www.mpssaa.org
• R. Andrew Warner, Executive Director
• Jason Bursick, Assistant Director
Sports Services Founded:
1946
Description:
Promotes and directs public high school interscholastic activities to assure their contribution in the entire educational program of the state of Maryland.

MASSACHUSETTS INTERSCHOLASTIC ATHLETIC ASSOCIATION
33 FORGE PARKWAY
FRANKLIN, MA 02038
508-541-7997
Fax: 508-541-9888
miaa@miaa.net
www.miaa.net
• David King, President
• Marilyn Slattery, Vice President
Description:
Organization sponsors athletic activities in high school sport.

MICHIGAN HS ATHLETIC ASSOCIATION
1661 RAMBLEWOOD DRIVE
EAST LANSING, MI 48823
517-332-5046
Fax: 517-332-4071
info@mhsaa.com
www.mhsaa.com

- John E Roberts, Executive Director
- Nate Hampton, Assistant Director
- Dan Hutcheson, Assistant Director
- Jordan Cobb, Director of Information Systems
- John R Johnson, Communications Director
- Jeremy Sampson, Ticketing, Promotions & Marketing Coordinator

MINNESOTA STATE HS LEAGUE
2100 FREEWAY BOULEVARD
BROOKLYN CENTER, MN 55430-1735
763-560-2262
www.mshsl.org
- David Stead, Executive Director
(763) 560-2262
dstead@mshsl.org
- Lynne Johnson, Executive Assistant
ljohnson@mshsl.org
- Jody Redman, Associate Director
jredman@mshsl.org
- Ellen Rajkowski, Information Specialist
erajkowski@mshsl.org
- Nancy Myers, Ticket Assistant
(763) 560-2262
nmeyers@mshsl.org
Description:
Founded in 1916, this voluntary non-profit association of public and private schools serves area high schools with athletic and fine arts competicion and programming.

MISSISSIPPI HS ACTIVITIES ASSOCIATION
1201 CLINTON/RAYMOND ROAD
CLINTON, MS 39056
601-924-6400
Fax: 601-924-1725
www.misshsaa.com
- Don Hinton, Executive Director
- Lonnie Tillman, Associate Director
- Diane Bruser, Assistant Director
dbruser@misshsaa.com
- Joyce Franklin, Financial Officer
jfranklin@misshsaa.com

MISSOURI STATE HS ACTIVITIES ASSOCIATION
1 N KEENE STREET
COLUMBIA, MO 65201-6645
573-875-4880
Fax: 573-875-1450
email@mshsaa.org
www.mshsaa.org

MONTANA HS ASSOCIATION
1 SOUTH DAKOTA AVENUE
HELENA, MT 59601
406-442-6010
Fax: 406-442-8250
www.mhsa.org
- Mark Beckman, Executive Director
mbeckman@mhsa.org
- Joanne Austin, Associate Director
jpaustin@mhsa.org
- Janie Holmes, Business Office Manger
jholmes@mhsa.org
- Brian Michelotti, Assistant Director
smcdonald@mhsa.org
Sports Services Founded:
1921.

NEBRASKA SCHOOL ACTIVITIES ASSOCIATION
500 CHARLESTON STREET
SUITE 1
LINCOLN, NE 68508-1119
402-489-0386
Fax: 402-489-0934
nsaa@nsaahome.org
www.nsaahome.org
- Jim Tenopir, Executive Director
jtenopir@nsaahome.org
- Debra Velder, Associate Director
dvelder@nsaahome.org
- Jennifer Schwartz, Assistant Director
jschwartz@nsaahome.org

- Megan Huber, Business Manager
mhuber@nsaahome.org
Description:
Developes and regulates policies of competition and sportsmanship for activities of member high schools in interscholastic programs.

NEVADA INTERSCHOLASTIC ACTIVITIES ASSOCIATION
549 COURT STREET
RENO, NV 89501
775-453-1012
Fax: 775-453-1016
www.niaa.com
- Bart Thompson, Executive Director
bthompson@niaa.com
- Jay Bessemyer, Assistant Director
jayb@niaa.com
- Donnie Nelson, Assistant Director
donnien@niaa.com
Year founded:
1922

NEW BRUNSWICK INTERSCHOLASTIC ATHLETIC ASSOCIATION
20 MCGLOIN ST
FREDERICTON, NB, CANADA E3A 5T8
506-457-4843
nbiaa@gnb.ca
www.nbiaa-asinb.org
- Allyson Ouellette, Executive Director
(506) 457-4843
Vision:
NBIAA will promote quality experiences by enriching education and enhancing personal development through high school sports.
Mission:
To be the governing body of high school sports, where we create, promote, and facilitate positive sporting experiences in an educational environment in the province of New Brunswick.
Founded:
1926
Members:
75 member schools
Publications:
NBIAA Handbook; NBIAA Coaches Course

NEW HAMPSHIRE INTERSCHOLASTIC ATHLETIC ASSOCIATION
251 CLINTON STREET
CONCORD, NH 3301
603-228-8671
Fax: 603-225-7978
info@nhiaa.org
www.nhiaa.org
Description:
A voluntary organization operated by a continually changing committee structure and an athletic council. Committee membership is voluntary.

NEW JERSEY STATE INTERSCHOLASTIC ATHLETIC ASSOCIATION
1161 ROUTE 130
PO BOX 487
ROBBINSVILLE, NJ 8691
609-259-2776
Fax: 609-259-3047
www.njsiaa.org
- Steven J Timko, Executive Director
- Kim DeGraw Cole, Assistant Director
- Michele Perez, Accounting
Sports Services Founded:
1918

NEW MEXICO ACTIVITIES ASSOCIATION
6600 PALOMAS AVENUE NE
ALBUQUERQUE, NM 87109
505-923-3110
888-820-6622
Fax: 505-923-3114
feedback@nmact.org
www.nmact.org

- Sally Marquez, Executive Director
(505) 923-3267
sally@nmact.org
- Dusty Young, Associate Director
(505) 923-3268
dusty@nmact.org
Sports Service Founded:
1921

NEW YORK STATE PUBLIC HS ATHLETIC ASSOCIATION
8 AIRPORT PARK BOULEVARD
LATHAM, NY 12110
518-690-0771
Fax: 518-690-0775
www.nysphsaa.org
- Robert Zayas, Executive Director
(518) 690-0771
rzayas@nysphsaa.org
- Todd Nelson, Assistant Director
(518) 690-0771
tnelson@nysphsaa.org
- Joe Altieri, Assistant Director
(518) 690-0771
altieri@nysphsaa.org
- Chris Joyce, Director of Sales & Marketing
cjoyce@nysphsaa.org
- Lisa Arnold, Treasurer
larnold@nysphsaa.org

NORTH CAROLINA HS ATHLETIC ASSOCIATION
222 FINLEY GOLF COURSE
CHAPEL HILL, NC 27517
919-240-7401
Fax: 919-240-7399
info@nchsaa.org
www.nchsaa.org
- Que Tucker, Commissioner
(919) 240-7375
que@nchsaa.org
- Whitney Frye, Associate Commissioner
(919) 240-7379
whitney@nchsaa.org
Description:
Voluntary, non profit corporation which administers the state's interscholastic athletic program. Any North Carolina or non boarding parochial school is eligible for membership, provided it is accredited by the State Department of Public Instruction and that the school adopts and maintains a prescribed code to guarantee fair competition.

NORTH DAKOTA HS ACTIVITIES ASSOCIATION
350 2ND STREET NW
PO BOX 817
VALLEY CITY, ND 58072
701-845-3953
Fax: 701-845-4935
ndhsaa@ndhsaa.org
www.ndhsaa.com
- Matthew Fetsch, Executive Director
matt.fetsch@ndhsaa.org
- Brian Bubach, Associate Director
brian.bubach@ndhsaa.org
Descrition:
A non-profit organization, which exists to contribute to the education of North Dakota High school students by administering programs, promoting citizenship and good sportsmanship, and providing fine arts and athletic programs to supplement general education.

OHIO HS ATHLETIC ASSOCIATION
4080 ROSELEA PLACE
COLUMBUS, OH 43214
614-267-2502
Fax: 614-267-1677
webmaster@ohsaa.org
www.ohsaa.org
- Andy Bixler, Board President
- Jeffrey Snyder, Board Vice President
- Todd Boehm, Comptroller
- Molly Downard, Executive Administrative

Assistant
• Jason Fleming, Assistant Comptroller
Description:
Regulates and administers interscholastic athletic competition in a fair and equitable manner while promoting the values of participation in interscholastic athletics.

OKLAHOMA SECONDARY SCHOOL ACTIVITIES ASSOCIATION
7300 NORTH BROADWAY EXTENSION
PO BOX 14590
OKLAHOMA CITY, OK 73113-0590
405-840-1116
Fax: 405-840-9559
www.ossaa.com
• Mark Hudson, President
• Rick Pool, Vice President
Sports Service Founded:
1911

ONTARIO FED OF SCHOOL ATHLETIC ASSOCIATIONS
3 CONCORDE GATE
SUITE 204
TORONTO, ON, CANADA M3C 3N7
416-426-7391
Fax: 416-426-7317
www.ofsaa.on.ca
Description:
A provincial federation of Associations encompassing volunteer coaschs, students, and administrators. Dedicated to the promotion and enhancement of the educational value and leadership in advancing the educational benefits of participation through its services, resources and the conduct of secondary school sport Championships.

OREGON SCHOOL ACTIVITIES ASSOCIATION
25200 SW PARKWAY AVENUE
SUITE 1
WILSONVILLE, OR 97070
503-682-6722
Fax: 503-682-0960
info@osaa.org
www.osaa.org
• Tony Guevara, President
(503) 391-2639
tonyguevara@blanchetcatholicschool.com
• Peter Weber, Executive Director
(503) 682-6722
peterw@osaa.org
• Cindy Simmons, Assistant Executive Director
(503) 682-6722
cindys@osaa.org
• Brad Garrett, Assistant Executive Director
(503) 682-6722
bradg@osaa.org
• Steve Walker, Sports Information Director
(503) 682-6722
stevew@osaa.org
Sports Services Founded:
1918

PENNSYLVANIA INTERSCHOLASTIC ATHLETIC ASSOCIATION
550 GETTYSBURG ROAD
PO BOX 2008
MECHANICSBURG, PA 17055-0708
717-697-0374
800-382-1392
Fax: 717-697-7721
website@piaa.org
www.piaa.org
• Robert A. R Lombardi, Execuitve Director
• Mark E. A Byers, COO
• Melissa N. N Mertz, Associate Executive Director
• Patrick B. L Gebhart, Esq, Assistant Executive Director
Member Services:
Establishes eligibility, sets contest rules for specific sports, provides registration and training for officials and organizes competitions for member schools.

RHODE ISLAND INTERSCHOLASTIC LEAGUE, INC.
RHODE ISLAND COLLEGE
600 MOUNT PLEASANT AVENUE
BUILDING 6
PROVIDENCE, RI 02908-1991
401-272-9844
Fax: 401-272-9838
info@riil.org
www.riil.org
• Thomas Mezzanotte, Executive Director
• Michael P Lunney, Assistant Director
Description:
The association is conprised of high school principals representing 60 institutions. The league sets rules and regulations for competition and carries out athletic programs in Rhode Island.
Year Founded:
1932

SOUTH CAROLINA HIGH SCHOOL LEAGUE
121 WESTPARK BLVD.
COLUMBIA, SC 29210
803-798-0120
schsl@schsl.org
www.schsl.org
• Mickey Pringle, President
mpringle@bellsouth.net
• Dan Matthews, Vice President
daniel.matthews@kcsdschools.net
• Jerome P Singleton, Commissioner
jsingle@schsl.org
• Nessie Harris, Associate Commissioner
nharris@schsl.org
• Skip Lax, Assistant Commissioner

SOUTH DAKOTA HS ACTIVITIES ASSOCIATION
804 NORTH EUCLID AVENUE
SUITE 102
PO BOX 1217
PIERRE, SD 57501
605-224-9261
Fax: 605-224-9262
www.sdhsaa.com
• Wayne Carney, Executive Director
wayne.carney@sdhsaa.com
• Jo Auch, Assistant Executive Director
jo.auch@sdhsaa.com

TENNESSEE SECONDARY SCHOOL ATHLETIC ASSOCIATION
3333 LEBANON ROAD
PO BOX 319
HERMITAGE, TN 37076
615-889-6740
Fax: 615-889-0544
tssaa@tssaa.org
www.tssaa.org
• Bernard Childress, Executive Director
bchildress@tssaa.org
• Matthew Gillespie, Assistant Executive Director
mgillespie@tssaa.org
• Stephen Bargatze, Student Services Director
sbargatze@tssaa.org
• Courtney Brunetz, Marketing Director
cbrunetz@tssaa.org
Sports Services Founded:
1925

TEXAS UNIVERSITY INTERSCHOLASTIC LEAGUE
1701 MANOR ROAD
AUSTIN, TX 78722
512-471-5883
Fax: 512-471-5908
www.uiltexas.org
• Charles Breithaupt, Executive Director
director@uiltexas.org
• Jamey Harrison, Deputy Director/Marketing
• Kim Carmichael, Chief Of Staff
cos@uiltexas.org
• Susan Doherty, Executive Assistant
director@uiltexas.org

• Caroline Walls, Event Coordinator
info@uiltexas.org
Sports Services Founded:
1909
Description:
Organizes and supervises competition at the high school level. It promotes healthy lifestyles, character building, and educational activities.

UTAH HIGH SCHOOL ACTIVITIES ASSOCIATION
199 EAST 7200 SOUTH
MIDVALE, UT 84047
801-566-0681
Fax: 801-566-0633
Submit@uhsaa.org
www.uhsaa.org
• Rob Cuff, Executive Director
cuff@uhsaa.org
• Kim Monkres, Assistant Director
monkres@uhsaa.org
• Ryan Bishop, Assistant Director
bishop@uhsaa.org
Description:
The UHSAA leads athletic and fine arts programming for high schools in Utah, and promotes involvement in these activities as part of education and citizenship.
Number of Members:
150 member scools
Publications:
UHSAA HANDBOOK: Annually, UHSAA YEARBOOK: Annually.

VERMONT PRINCIPALS' ASSOCIATION
2 PROSPECT STREET
SUITE 3
MONTPELIER, VT 5602
802-229-0547
Fax: 802-229-4801
www.vpaonline.org
• Patrick Burke, VPA President
pburke@sbschools.net
• Linda Wheatley, Development Coordinator
lwheatley@vpaonline.org
• Ken Page, Executive Director
kpage@vpaonline.org
• Bob Johnson, Associate Executive Director
bjohnson@vpaonline.org
Description:
A nonprofit groupn of education leaders collaborating on mentoring, professional development and networking while overseeing Vermont's co-curricular activities.

VIRGINIA HS LEAGUE
1642 STATE FARM BOULEVARD
CHARLOTTESVILLE, VA 22911
434-977-8475
info@vhsl.org
www.vhsl.org
• Jim Stemple, Chair
(540) 658-6840
• John W. Haun, Ed.D., Executive Director
bhaun@vhsl.org
• Shawn Knight, Assistant Director For Athletics
sknight@vhsl.org
• Kelley Haney, Assistant Director Of Athletics
khaney@vhsl.org
• Lisa Giles, Assistant Director of Activities
lgiles@vhsl.org
• David Hopkins, Director of Finance
dhopkins@vhsl.org
Description:
Virginia's public high schools, through their alliance as the Virginia High School League, serve their youth by establishing and maintaining standards for student activities and competitions that promote education, personal growth, sportsmanship, leadership and citizenship.

WASHINGTON INTERSCHOLASTIC ACTIVITIES ASSOCIATION
435 MAIN AVENUE SOUTH
RENTON, WA 98057

425-687-8585
Fax: 425-687-9476
www.wiaa.com
• Eric McCurdy, President
• Mike Colbrese, Executive Director
colbrese@wiaa.com
• Cindy Adsit, Assistant Executive Director
(425) 282-5232
cadsit@wiaa.com
• Leah Francis, Finance/Operations Director
(425) 282-5238
lfrancis@wiaa.com
Sports Services Founded:
1905
Description:
Exists to assist member schools in operating student programs that foster achievement, respect, equity, enthusiasm and excellence in a safe and organized environment. This Association shall plan, supervise and administer the interscholastic activities approved and delegated by the school districts boards of directors.

WEST VIRGINIA SECONDARY SCHOOL ACTIVITIES COMMISSION
2875 STAUNTON TURNPIKE
PARKERSBURG, WV 26104-7219
304-485-5494
Fax: 304-428-5431
wvssac@wvssac.org
www.wvssac.org
• Bernie Dolan, Executive Director
• Kelly Geddis, Assistant Executive Director
• Wayne Ryan, Assistant Executive Director

WYOMING HS ACTIVITIES ASSOCIATION
6571 EAST 2ND STREET
CASPER, WY 82609
307-577-0614
Fax: 307-577-0637
www.whsaa.org
• Ron Laird, Commissioner
rlaird@whsaa.org
• Trevor Wilson, Associate Commissioner
twilson@whsaa.org
Sports Services Founded:
1920

NATIONAL HIGH SCHOOL ATHLETIC COACHES ASSOCIATION
PO BOX 10277
FARGO, ND 58106
701-570-1008
www.hscoaches.org
• Dave Dougherty, Executive Director
Sports Services Founded:
1965
Publications:
www.hscoaches.org source for all NHSACA information.
Description:
The NHSACA is the only high school coaches association created by and governed by coaches. Also provides high school coaches across America with a voice in current national issues. Also provides high school coaches with the first recognition program available in America.

NATIONAL INTERSCHOLASTIC ATHLETIC ADMINISTRATORS ASSOCIATION/NIAAA
9100 KEYSTONE CROSSING
SUITE 650
INDIANAPOLIS, IN 46240
317-587-1450
Fax: 317-587-1451
www.niaaa.org
• Richard Barton, President
• Michael Blackburn, CMAA,Executive

Director
• Josh Scott, Secretary
jscott@waynesville.k12.mo.us
Description:
The National Interscholastic Athletic Administration Association preserves, enhances and promotes the educational values of interscholastic athletics through the professional development of its members in the areas of education. leadership and service. The NIAAA's commitment to leadership programs, resources and services support the athletic administratior's efforts in providing quality athletic participation opportunities for students.
Year Founded:
1977
Publications:
Interscholastic Athletic Administration, Hazing Education, Risk Management.

Other locations:

RESEAU DU SPORTETUDIANT DU QUEBEC
4545, AVENUE PIERRE-DE COUBERTIN
CP 1000, BRANCH M
MONTREAL, QB, CANADA H1V 3R2
514-252-3300
Fax: 514-254-3292
info@rseq.ca
www.rseq.ca
• Gustave Roel, President/Executive Director
groel@rseq.ca
• Pierre Boulerice, Vice President
• Jacques Desrochers, Secretary-Treasurer

STUDENT SPORTS
23954 MADISON STREET
TORRANCE, CA 90505
310-791-1142
800-660-1334
Fax: 310-791-4809
info@studentsports.com
www.studentsports.com
• Andy Bark, CEO/Founder
andy@studentsports.com
• Patrick Bark, Director Of Media
patrick@studentsports.com
Sports Service Founded:
1979

U.S. ARMY ALL-AMERICAN BOWL
100 FORGE WAY
SUITE 1
ROCKAWAY, NJ 07866
973-366-8448
www.allamericangames.com
• Doug Berman, Chairman
• Ed D'Ambola, Manager, Creative Media Services
• Nate Seamon, Vice President, Operations
College Bowl Game:
US Army All-American Bowl.

Other locations:

WISCONSIN INTERSCHOLASTIC ATHLETIC ASSOCIATION
5516 VERN HOLMES DRIVE
STEVENS POINT, WI 54482
715-344-8580
info@wiaawi.org
www.wiaawi.org
• Dave Anderson, Executive Director
danderson@wiaawi.org
• Deb Hauser, Associate Director
dhauser@wiaawi.org

• Todd Clark, Communicators Director
tclark@wiaawi.org

Military Sports

INTERNATIONAL MILITARY SPORTS COUNCIL
RUE JACQUES JORDAENS 26
1000 BRUXELLES, BELGIUM
www.milsport.one
• Dorah Mamby Koita, Secretary General
• Olivier Verhelle, Director Administration and Human Resources

U.S. ARMED FORCES SPORTS
2455 REYNOLDD ROAD
FORT SAM HOUSTON
SAN ANTONIO, TX 78234
210-466-1335
kenneth.j.polk@us.army.mil
www.armedforcessports.com
• Steven Dinote, Armed Forces Sports Secretariat
• Kenneth Polk, Deputy Secretary
kenneth.j.polk@us.army.mil
Description:
Founded 1947. Conducts championships for men and women in basketball, volleyball, marathon, cross country, slow-pitch softball, golf, bowling, triathlon, track, soccer, and for men rugby, wrestling, and boxing. Sponsors international World Military Championships in basketball, cross country, volleyball, parachuting, track and field, shooting, naval pentathlon, modern pentathlon, taekwondo, wrestling and boxing, skiing, fencing, soccer and cycling.

Olympic, International Federations

BADMINTON WORLD FEDERATION
UNIT 17.05, LEVEL 17
AMODA BUILDING
22 JALAN IMBI
KUALA LUMPUR, 55100
bwf@bwfbadminton.org
bwfbadminton.com
• Thomas Lund, Secretary General
t.lund@bwfbadminton.org
Description:
To deliver quality services, world class events and innovative development initiatives which showcase the sport at the highest levels and increase the active participation in badminton at all levels worldwide.

FEDERATION EQUESTRE INTERNATIONALE (FEI)
HM KING HUSSEIN I BUILDING
CHEMIN DE LA JOLIETTE 8
LAUSANNE, SWITZERLAN 1006
www.fei.org
• Ingmar De Vos, President
• Sabrina Ibanez, Secretary General
Nature of Service:
International governing body for equestrian sports.
Number of Members:
132 affiliated national federations.

multi sports

FEDERATION INTERNATIONALE DE SKI (FIS)
MARC HODLER HOUSE
BLOCHSTRASSE 2
OBERHOFEN/THUNERSEE, CH-3653
mail@fisski.ch
www.fis-ski.com
• Jolanda Bruelisauer, Assistant To President
bruelisauer@fisski.com
• Riikka Rakic, Communications manager
• Marcel Looze, Marketing Manager
looze@fisski.com
• Richard Bunn, TV Consultant
rb@rbinetwork.ch
• Francesco Cattaneo, IT Manager
it@fisski.com
• Christian Pirzer, CEO Marketing AG
• Sarah Lewis, Secretary General
lewis@fisski.com
• Sibylle Gafner, Finance & HR Manager
gafner@fisski.com
Sports Services Founded:
February 2, 1924
Description:
The organisation was founded during the first Olympic Games in Chamoix, France with 14 member nations. Today 107 National Ski Associations compise the membership of the FIS.

FEDERATION INTERNATIONALE DE LUGE DE COURSE (FIL)
RATHAUSPLATZ 9
BERCHTESGADEN, 83471
office@fil-luge.org
www.fil-luge.org
Description:
Founded 1957. Responsible for worldwide organization of the sport of luge. Sanctions international luge competitions including the Winter Olympic Games, World Championships, an annual eight race World Cup tour plus other numerous international events.
Membership Requirements:
Limited to national luge federations recognized by their nation's National Olympic Committee.
Publications:
FIL NEWS, twice annually.
Member Services:
Schedules races, sanctions international competitions, certifies international officials, oversees regulations.

FEDERATION INTERNATIONALE D'ESCRIME (FIE)
MAISON DU SPORT INTERNATIONAL
AVENUE DE RHODANIE 54
LAUSANNE, CH 1007
info@fie.ch
www.fie.org
• Nathalie Rodriguez, Chief Executive Officer
nr@fie.ch
Description:
The organization which governs all over the world the sport of fencing. Based in Lausanne, Olympic Capital.
Members:
121 Member Federations

FEDERATION INTERNATIONALE DE FOOTBALL ASSOCIATION (FIFA)
FIFA-STRASSE 20
ZURICH, 8044
www.fifa.com
• Gianni Infantino, President
Description:
International association for the development of football.
Year Founded:
1904
Member Associations:
211
Publications:
The FIFA Weekly

FEDERATION INTERNATIONALE DE NATATION (FINA)
CHEMIN DE BELLEVUE 24a/24b
LAUSANNE, 1005
www.fina.org
• Julio C Maglione, President
• Husain Al Musallam, Vice President
• Cornel Marculescu, Executive Director
Year Founded:
1908
Publications:
FINA newsletter, FINA Handbook, FINA Aquatics World Magazine
Description:
Comprised of 207 national member federations, FINA holds competitions in swimming, open water swimming, diving, water polo, synchronised swimming, high diving and masters.

FEDERATION INTERNATIONALE DE VOLLEYBALL (FIVB)
CHATEAU LES TOURELLES
CH. EDOUARD-SANDOZ 2-4
LAUSANNE, 1006
info@fivb.org
www.fivb.org
• Ari S Graca Filho, President
• Fernando Lima, Secretary General
Description:
The governing body responsible for all forms of Volleyball on a global level. Working closely with national federations and private enterprises the FIVB aims to develop Volleyball as a major world media and entertainment sport through world-class planning and organization of competitions, marketing and development activities.
Publications:
Volley World Magazine, X-Press

INTERNATIONAL ASSOCIATION OF ATHLETICS FEDERATIONS (IAAF)
6-8, QUAI ANTOINE 1ER
BP 359
MONTE CARLO, MONACO 98007
www.iaaf.org
• Sebastian Coe, President
Sports Service Founded:
1912
Publications:
See publication list on www.iaaf.org.
Member Services:
Worldwide governing body of track & field athletics. Assistance at competitions (finance).
Membership Requirements:
Constitution in accord with IAAF's, stage National Championships annually, participation in at least one IAAF competition annually, have an office with technical infrastructure, pay annual fee and complete annual report form.

INTERNATIONAL BASKETBALL FEDERATION (FIBA)
ROUTE SUISSE 5
PO BOX 29
MIES, 1295
info@fiba.com
www.fiba.com
• Baumann Patrick, Secretary General
• Horacio Muratore, President

INTERNATIONAL BIATHLON UNION (IBU)
PEREGRINSTRAÃ¡E 14
SALZBURG, A-5020
biathlon@ibu.at
www.biathlonworld.com
• Anders Besseberg, President
anders.besseberg@ibu.at
• Olle Dahlin, Vice President, Development
olle.dahlin@ibu.at
• James E Carrabre, Vice President, Medical Issues
jim.carrabre@ibu.at
• Nami Kim, Vice President, Special Issues
• Ivor Lehotan, Vice President, Information
• Klaus Leistner, Vice President, Finance
klaus.leistner@ibu.at
• Victor Maygurov, First Vice President
victor.maygurov@ibu.at
• Thomas Pfuller, Vice President, Marketing
thomas.pfueller@ibu.at
• Nicole Resch, Secretary General
nicole.resch@ibu.at
• Max Cobb, Vice President, Sport
max.cobb@ibu.at
Description:
The IBU serves as the international governing body for the sport of biathlon, sanctioning competitions and promoting the sport.
Number of Members:
57
Publications:
Biathlon Calander (annual), BiathlonWorld Magazine.

INTERNATIONAL BOBSLEIGH & SKELETON FEDERATION
MAISON DU SPORT
AVENUE DE RHODANIE 54
LAUSANNE, CH 1007
office@ibsf.org
www.ibsf.org
• Ivo Ferriani, President
ivo.ferriani@ibsf.com
• Heike Groesswang, Secretary General
heike.groesswang@ibsf.org
Nature of Service:
The IBSF is the international organization governing the sports of bobsledding and skeleton tobogganing.
Year Founded:
1923

INTERNATIONAL BOXING ASSOCIATION (AIBA)
MAISON DU SPORT INTERNATIONAL
AVENUE DE RHODANIE 54
LAUSANNE, 1007
www.aiba.org
• Ching-Kuo Wu, President
• William Louis-Marie, Executive Director
william.louis-marie@aiba.org

INTERNATIONAL CANOE FEDERATION (ICF)
AVENUE DE RHODANIE 54
LAUSANNE, CH 1007

info@canoeicf.com
www.canoeicf.com
• Jose Perurena, President
• Simon Toulson, Secretary General
Nature of Service:
To promote & foster foreign touring through production of appropriate river guides, & through the provision of programs about the possibilities of finding accommodation and places of interest.
Publications:
E-Canoeing Express, Canoeing International

INTERNATIONAL HANDBALL FEDERATION
PETER MERIAN-STRASSE 23
BASEL, CH-4052
ihf.office@ihf.info
www.ihf.info
• Hassan Moustafa, President

INTERNATIONAL HOCKEY FEDERATION (FIH)
RUE DU VALENTIN 61
LAUSANNE, 1004
info@fih.ch
• Narinder D Batra, President
• Jason McCracken, Chief Executive Officer

INTERNATIONAL ICE HOCKEY FEDERATION (IIHF)
BRANDSCHENKESTRASSE 50
POSTFACH 1817
ZURICH, 8027
office@iihf.com
www.iihf.com
• Rene Fasel, President
• Horst Lichtner, General Secretary
Year Founded:
1908
Description:
A federation of member national hockey associations governing the sport of ice hockey and in-line hockey for both men and women.

INTERNATIONAL JUDO FEDERATION
NO.24 RESIDENCES
OUCHY-NAVIGATION
AVENUE DE LA HARPE 49
LAUSANNE, 1007
admin@ijf.org
www.ijf.org
• Jean Luc Rouge, General Secretary
• Marius I Vizer, President
Description:
International governing body of the Olympic sport of Judo recognized by the International Olympic Committee and consisting of 187 member National Federations grouped into 5 Continental Unions (Africa, Asis, Europe, Oceania and Panamerica)

INTERNATIONAL ORIENTEERING FEDERATION
DROTTNINGGATAN 47, 3Â« tr.
KARLSTAD, SE-65225
iof@orienteering.org
orienteering.org
• Tom Hollowell, Secretary General & CEO
tom.hollowell@orienteering.org
Description:
International governing body for the sport of orienteering. 72 member countries.

Year Founded:
1977

INTERNATIONAL SHOOTING SPORT FEDERATION (ISSF)
BAVARIARING 21
MUNICH, 80336
www.issf-sports.org
• Olegario Vazquez Rana, President
• Franz Schreiber, Secretary General
Description:
International governing body for the sport of shooting.

INTERNATIONAL SKATING UNION (ISU)
AVENUE JUSTE-OLIVIER 17
LAUSANNE, 1006
www.isu.org
• Jan Dijkema, President
• Fredi Schmid, Director General
Sports Service Founded:
1892
Description:
The oldest governing international winter sport federation.

INTERNATIONAL TABLE TENNIS FEDERATION (ITTF)
CHEMIN DE LA ROCHE 11
RENENS, 1020
ittf@ittfmail.com
www.ittf.com
• Judit Farago, Chief Executive Officer
jfarago@ittfmail.com
• Thomas Welkert, President
tw@ittfmail.com
Publications:
Table Tennis Illustrated

INTERNATIONAL TENNIS FEDERATION
BANK LANE
ROEHAMPTON
LONDON, SW15 5XZ
communications@itftennis.com
www.itftennis.com
• David Haggerty, President

INTERNATIONAL TRIATHLON UNION
MAISON DU SPORT INTERNATIONAL
AV DE RHODANIE 54
LAUSANNE, CH 1007
www.triathlon.org
• Antonio Arimany, Secretary General
Description:
The ITU is the world governing body for the Olympic sport of Triathlon and all related MultiSport disciplines: Duathalon, Aquathon and Winter Triathalon. ITU was founded in 1989 at the first ITU Congress in Avignon, France and has maintained its headquarters in Vancouver, Canada since then. It now has over 120 affiliated National Federations around the world and is the youngest International Federation in the Olympics. Triathalon was awarded Olympic status in 1994. ITU is proudly committed to supporting the development of the sport worldwide through the strong relationships with contintenal and national federations, working with its partners

INTERNATIONAL WEIGHTLIFTING FEDERATION (IWF)
MAISON DU SPORT INTERNATIONAL
AV DE RHODANIE 54
LAUSANNE, CH 1007

iwf@iwf.net
www.iwf.net
• Tamas Ajan, President
• Ma Wenguang, General Secretary

UNION CYCLISTE INTERNATIONALE (UCI)
CH DE LA MELEE 12
AIGLE, 1860
admin@uci.ch
www.uci.ch
• Brian Cookson, President
• Mohamed Wagih Azzam, Vice President
• Tracey Gaudry, Vice President
• David Lappartient, Vice President
Nature of Service:
Founded with the means to develop and promote all aspects of cycling. This is because cycling is more than just a competitive sport. It is a also a leisure activity and environmentally friendly means of transport.
Year Founded:
1900

UNION INTERNATIONALE DE PENTATHLON MODERNE (UIPM)
STADE LOUIS II, ENTREE E
13 AVENUE DES CASTELANS
MONTE CARLO, 98000
uipm@pentathlon.org
www.pentathlon.org
• Shiny Fang, Secretary
• Juan Antonio, 1st Vice President
• John Helmick, Treasurer
Description:
International governing body for the sport of modern pentathlon.

UNITED WORLD WRESTLING
RUE DU CHATEAU 6
CORSIER-SUR-VEVEY, 1804
info@unitedworldwrestling.org
unitedworldwrestling.org
• Nenad Lalovic, President
• Michel Dusson, General Secretary
Description:
International governing body for the sport of wrestling.
Number of Members:
145

WORLD BASEBALL SOFTBALL CONFEDERATION
MAISON DU SPORT INTERNATIONAL
AVENUE DE RHODANIE 54
LAUSANNE, CH-1007
office@wbsc.org
www.wbsc.org
• Riccardo Fraccari, President
• Beng Choo Low, Secretary General
Description:
World governing body for baseball and softball.

WORLD CURLING FEDERATION
3 ATHOLL CRESCENT
PERTH, PH1 5NG
info@worldcurling.org
www.worldcurling.org
• Kate Caithness, President
Description:
International governing body for the sport of curling.
Number of Members:
45

multi sports

WORLD ROWING FEDERATION (FISA)
MAISON DU SPORT INTERNATIONAL
AVENUE DE RHODANIE 54
LAUSANNE, CH 1007
info@fisa.org
www.worldrowing.com
• Matt Smith, Executive Director
matt.smith@fisa.org
Year Founded:
1892
Publications:
FISA Guide, World Rowing Magazine, World Rowing E-Newsletter.
Description:
To make rowing a universally practised and globally relevant sport.

WORLD SAILING
ARIADNE HOUSE
TOWN QUAY
SOUTHAMPTON, HAMPSHIRE, ENGLAND
SO14 2AQ
www.sailing.org
• Helen Fry, Business Operations Director
Description:
World governing body for sailing, responsible for promoting the sport internationally.

Olympic, Organizations

AUSTRALIAN OLYMPIC COMMITTEE
LEVEL 4, 140 GEORGE ST
MUSEUM OF CONTEMPORARY ART
SYDNEY, NSW, AUSTRALIA 2000
corporate.olympics.com.au
• John D Coates, President
Description:
Commited to Australia's athletes and encourages the development of high performance sport through athlete support and funding initiatives. Aims to spread the Olympic spirit and ideals throughout Australia, even in the years between Olympic Games.

CANADIAN OLYMPIC COMMITTEE
21 ST. CLAIR AVE E
SUITE 900
TORONTO, ON, CANADA M4T 1L9
416-962-0262
Fax: 416-967-4902
olympic.ca
• Tricia Smith, President
Nature of Sports Service:
Founded 1904. Recognized by IOC as Canada's National Olympic Committee in 1907. Jurisdiction over all aspects of Canada's participation in the Olympic, Olympic Winter and Pan American Games, including selecting Canadian teams and providing an extensive range of support services before and during Games. Promotes and protects the Olympic Movement in Canada. Conducting and/or financing programs to assist in the development of amateur sport in Canada.
Membership Requirements:
Nine types of membership: (A) The 30 National Sport Federations with jurisdiction over Olympic and Pan Am Sports appoint five members each, (B) Members at large elected by other members from all segments of Canadian society, (C) IOC members in Canada, (D) Honorary members (no voting

power), (E) NSF's with jurisdiction over sports recognized by the IOC but whose sports are not included in the Olympics or Pan Am Games appoint 1 member each, (F) Representatives of each NSF on the COA's Athletes' Council, (G) Representatives of other agencies related to sport, (H) Coaches representative.
Publications:
ANNUAL REPORT, yearly; PODIUM, online monthly newsletter
Member Services:
Extensive range of support services for Canadian Olympic, Olympic Winter & Pan Am teams (including selection, transporting, insuring, housing, feeding, providing administrative and medical services, clothing, security, publicity); financial grants to National Sport Federations; youth and education programs; Olympic Academy of Canada; Canadian participation in International Olympic Academy; Olympic Athlete Career Centers; Olympic Club Canada; Canadian Amateur Sports Hall of Fame; Information Centre.
Number of members:
300

INTERNATIONAL OLYMPIC COMMITTEE (IOC)
OLYMPIC HOUSE
LAUSANNE
www.olympic.org
• Jacques Rogge, President
• Christophe De Kepper, Chief of Staff
• Gilbert Felli, Executive Director, Olympic Games
Description:
International non-governmental, non-profit organisation and the creater of the Olympic Movement. The IOC exists to serve as an umbrella organisation of the Olympic Movement. It owns all rights to the Olympic symbols, flag, motto, anthem and Olympic Games. Its primary responsibility is to supervise the organisation of the summer and winter Olympic Games.

ORIENTEERING CANADA
1239 COLGROVE AVE NE
CALGARY, AB, CANADA T2E 5C3
403-283-0807
Fax: 403-451-1681
www.orienteering.ca
• Anne Teutsch, President
• Tracy Bradley, Executive Director
Description:
Founded 1967.
Publications:
O-zine Newsletter published 3 times a year; Orienteering Today, magazine; Orienteering North America, magazine

ORIENTEERING USA
824 SCOTIA RD
PHILADELPHIA, PA 19128
215-482-9479
contact@orienteeringusa.org
orienteeringusa.org
• Clare Durand, President
(215) 482-9479
contact@orienteeringusa.org
Member Services:
Subscription to ONA; discount on class A meet fees; national rankings; promotional materials and other assistance; some financial assistance for mapping projects;

educational materials; membership in IOF indirectly; voting privileges.
Publications:
ORIENTEERING NORTH AMERICA, 10 times per year (official publication).
Membership Requirements:
Must be U.S. citizen or permanent resident, pay annual membership fee. Most members are indirect members, through member clubs (about 55 nationwide).
Sports Services Founded:
1971.
Description:
Recognized by the International Orienteering Federation and the US Olympic Committee as the National Governing Body for Orienteering in the United States. USOF is a non profit organization with 55 current member clubs and approximately 1,400 family and individual memberships. The Federation's programs are suppported by membership dues and tax-deductible contributions.

U.S. BIATHLON ASSOCIATION
49 PINELAND DRIVE
301A NEW GLOUCESTER HALL
NEW GLOUCESTER, ME 04260
207-688-6500
800-242-8456
Fax: 207-688-6505
info@usbiathlon.org
www.teamusa.org/us-biathlon
• Max Cobb, President & CEO
(207) 688-6500
• Per Nilsson, National Team Head Coach
per.coach@gmail.com
Year Founded:
1980
Description:
The USBA promotes the development of biathlon in the United States by organizing training and competition around the country.
Membership Requirements:
Annual dues

U.S. OLYMPIC AND PARALYMPIC FOUNDATION
ATTN: USOC DEVELOPMENT
1 OLYMPIC PLAZA
COLORADO SPRINGS, CO 80909
800-775-8762
Fax: 719-866-4188
foundation@usoc.org
www.teamusa.org/us-olympic-and-paralympic-foundation
• Jon Denney, President & Chief Development Officer
• Scott Blackmun, CEO

U.S. OLYMPIC TRAINING SITE
1401 PRESQUE ISLE AVE
NORTHERN MICHIGAN UNIVERSITY
MARQUETTE, MI 49855
906-227-2105
Fax: 906-227-2492
usoec@nmu.edu
www.nmu.edu
• Forrest Karr, Athletic Director
fkarr@nmu.edu
• Mike Kaurala, Operations Manager
mkaurala@nmu.edu
• Cora Ohnstad, Head Athletic Trainer
cora.ohnstad@mghs.org
Description:
Founded 1985. Provides a training and

education environment for aspiring Olympic athletes.

UNITED STATES OLYMPIC COMMITTEE
ONE OLYMPIC PLAZA
COLORADO SPRINGS, CO 80909
888-222-2313
www.teamusa.org
• Scott Blackmun, Chief Executive Officer
Description:
To support U.S. Olypic and Paralympic athletes in achieveing sustained competitive excellence and preserve the Olmpic ideals, and thereby inspore all Americans.
Publications:
Official U.S. Olympic Book every four years; press guides; U.S. Olympic Newsletter; Historical Booklets and Annual Report.
Membership Requirements:
National Amateur sports organizations affiliated with an international body. Multi-sport national organization and Disabled in Sport Organizations.

USA DIVING
1060 N CAPITOL AVE
SUITE E-310
INDIANAPOLIS, IN 46204
317-237-5252
Fax: 317-237-5257
www.teamusa.org/usa-diving
• Linda Paul, President & CEO
linda.paul@usadiving.org

USA FENCING
4065 SINTON RD
SUITE 140
COLORADO SPRINGS, CO 80907
719-866-4511
Fax: 719-632-5737
information@usfencing.org
www.usfencing.org
• Kris Ekeren, Executive Director
k.ekeren@usfencing.org
Publications:
AMERICAN FENCING, quarterly; rule book and supplements; USFA National Newsletter, quarterly.
Membership Requirements:
Pay dues.
Description:
To develop fencers to achieve international success and to administer and promote the sport in the USA.
Year Founded:
1891

USA PENTATHLON
1 OLYMPIC PLAZA
COLORADO SPRINGS, CO 80909
www.teamusa.org/USA-Modern-Pentathlon
• Rob Stull, Managing Director
robstull@aol.com
Number of members:
600
Publications:
THE PENTATHLETE, quarterly newsletter for athletes and members.
Membership Requirements:
Individual and organization memberships, annual dues.
Sports Services Founded:
1948
Description:
USA Pentathlon's mission is to prepare American athletes to win medals in the Olympic and Pan American Games and at the World Championships. With National Training Centers in San Antonio, Texas and Colorado Springs, CO, USAPentathlon and its coaches work with elite athletes as well as developing Olympians and juniors to prepare them for the 2004 Athens Olympic Games and beyond.

Olympic, United States Major Governing Bodies

U.S. SKI AND SNOWBOARD ASSOCIATION (USSA)
1 VICTORY LANE
PARK CITY, UT 84060
435-649-9090
Fax: 435-649-3613
ussa.org
• Tiger Shaw, President & CEO
• Brooke McAffee, Vice President & Chief Financial Officer
• Trisha Worthington, EVP & Chief Development Officer
Description:
Provides opportunities for athletes in the most exciting Olympic action sports. USSA's programs provide education, development and competition opportunities for young athletes, with from grassroots USSA club programs up through national teams and the Olympic Winter Games.
Membership Requirements:
Anyone can join on an individual, family or club basis.
Publications:
Discipline competition guides (alpine, cross-country, freestyle, jumping/Nordic combined, Snowboard), American Ski Coach, periodically.
Year Founded:
1905

U.S. SOCCER
1801 S PRAIRIE AVE
CHICAGO, IL 60616
312-808-1300
Fax: 312-808-1301
www.ussoccer.com
• Cindy Parlow Cone, President
• Will Wilson, Chief Executive Offcer
Description:
Affiliated with International Soccer Body, FIFA. Governing body for soccer in the U.S. under the 1978 Sports Amateur Act. Promotes soccer in U.S. including national and international games and tournaments. Administers all U.S. national teams. Responsible for marketing the U.S. National Teams' programs as well as marketing programs for the Youth and Amateur Divisions. Resolves questions and controversies not adjustable under rules of state associations concerned. Manages U.S. Cup Tournament, National Challenge Cup, National Amateur Challenge Cup, National Women's Amateur Cup, National Youth Cup competitions, promotes goodwill through physical
Year Founded:
1913
Number of members:
3,000,000
Membership Requirements:
Must be association, league, approved by National Council.

Notes:
1998 - Awarded marketing, licensing and television rights to a partnership between International Management Group and Nike. The 12 year agreement is expected to generate $500 million for U.S. Soccer. In 1997 Nike and US Soccer agreed on a 10 year $120 million apparel agreement.

US EQUESTRIAN FEDERATION
1040 POTTERSVILLE ROAD
GLADSTONE, NJ 07934-2053
908-234-0848
www.uset.org
• Murray S Kessler, President
mkessler@usef.org
• William J Moroney, Chief Executive Officer
bmoroney@usef.org
• Will Connell, Director of Sport
wconnell@usef.org

US FIGURE SKATING
20 FIRST STREET
COLORADO SPRINGS, CO 80906
719-635-5200
Fax: 719-635-9548
info@usfigureskating.org
www.usfsa.org
• Samuel Auxier, President
• David Raith, Executive Director

US SAILING
15 MARITIME DRIVE
PORTSMOUTH, RI 02871
401-683-0800
800-877-2451
Fax: 401-683-0840
info@ussailing.org
www.ussailing.org
• Jack Gierhart, Chief Executive Officer
jackgierhart@ussailing.org
• Lauren Cotta, Director of Operations
laurencotta@ussailing.org

US SPEEDSKATING
5662 S COUGAR LANE
KEARNS, UT 84118
801-417-5360
Fax: 801-417-5361
www.teamusa.org/us-speedskating
• Ted Morris, Executive Director
Sports Services Founded:
1966
Membership Requirements:
Fee of $50.
Publications:
ICE CHIPS, 8-10 times a year. RACING BLADE, 4 issues per year.
Description:
Mission is to be the premier speedskating organization in the world through excellence in leadership, development and performance.

USA ARCHERY
4065 SINTON RD
SUITE 110
COLORADO SPRINGS, CO 80907
719-866-4576
Fax: 719-632-4733
info@usarchery.org
www.teamusa.org/usa-archery
• Rod Menzer, Chair
Number of members:
6,000
Membership Requirements:

Payment of dues based on various categories

Year Founded:
1879

Description:
National governing body for the olympic sport of archery. dedicated to selecting and training male/female archers for Olympic and Pan american games and world level competitions.

USA BADMINTON
2099 S STATE COLLEGE BLVD
SUITE 600
ANAHEIM, CA 92806
714-765-2952
www.teamusa.org/usa-badminton
• Jeff Dyrek, Chief Executive Officer
(714) 765-2951
jeff.dyrek@usabadminton.org

Description:
USA Badminton oversees sanctioned tournaments nationwide, develops grassroots initiatives to foster increased participation in the sport, certifies and educates coaches and prepares the best players in the nation to excel in international competition, including the Olympic Games.

Membership:
Regular Dues/$30 a year.

Member Services:
Provides memberships cards allowing for play in USA Badminton events; subscription to CrossCourt newsletter; Exclusive member discounts on USA Badminton merchandise; Games locator; special offers; and voting rights on leadership of USA Badminton governing body.

Number of members:
4,000

USA BASEBALL
1030 SWABIA COURT
SUITE 201
DURHAM, NC 27703
919-474-8721
Fax: 855-420-5910
info@usabaseball.com
web.usabaseball.com
• Paul Seiler, Executive Director & CEO

Description:
USA Baseball serves as the national governing body for the sport, and represents American baseball as a member of the United States Olympic Committee and the International Baseball Federation.

Publications:
USA Baseball National Team Yearbook, annual.

Member Services:
Selects official U.S.A. Baseball Teams, Sr. National Team, Jr (18-under), National Team, Youth National Team (16-under) for international competition.

Year Founded:
1978

Official Partners:
Baseball America, Franklin Sports, International Baseball Federation, Majestic Athletic, Major League Baseball, Major League Baseball Advanced Media, New Era, Palm Beach County Sports Council, Rawlings, Reebok, United States Olympic Committee, Upper Deck, Wilson Sporting Goods

USA BASKETBALL
5465 MARK DABLING BLVD
COLORADO SPRINGS, CO 80918-3842
719-590-4800
Fax: 719-590-4811
www.usab.com
• Jim Tooley, CEO
• Craig Miller, Chief Communications Officer
• Brent Baumberger, Chief Financial Officer

Description:
USA Basketball was organized in 1974 and known as the Amateur Basketball Association of the United States of America (ABAUSA). The name change from ABAUSA to USA Basketball occurred October 12, 1989, shortly after FIBA modified its rules to allow professional basketball players to participate in international competitions.

Membership Requirements:
This membership shall be open to all national sports organizations which actively conduct a national program in Basketball as a competitive sport. Active memberships may also be open to other organizations which actively conduct national programs in basketball as a competitive sport. In addition, national basketball coaches associations for men and women shall be included, as approved by the Board of Directors of USA Basketball. Such members shall have voting representation through their chosen officers, or other representatives, at meetings of the Congress membership.

USA BOBSLED & SKELETON
1631 MESA AVE
COPPER BUILDING
SUITE A
COLORADO SPRINGS, CO 80906
Fax: 719-520-3212
www.teamusa.org/USA-Bobsled-Skeleton-Federation
• Darrin Steele, Chief Executive Officer
darrin.steele@usabs.com
• Lisa Carlock, Finance & Operations Director
lisa.carlock@usabs.com
• Lenny Kasten, National Team Manager

Description:
This Federation was formed to advance, encourage, improve and promote amateur bobsledding and skeleton competition in the United States. It is also the National Governing Body of hte sports of bobsled and skeleton and recognized as such by the United States Olympic Committee and the Federation Internationale De Bob Sleigh De and Tobogganing Federation.

Member Services:
Passenger Rider / Sports / Supporting Memberships

Number of members:
525

Publications:
Quarterly newsletter

USA BOXING
1 OLYMPIC PLAZA
COLORADO SPRINGS, CO 80909
719-866-2300
Fax: 719-866-2132
www.teamusa.org/USA-Boxing
• Mike McAtee, Interim Executive Director
mmcatee@usaboxing.org

Nature of Service:
A non-profit organization that is responsible for the administration, development and promotion of Olympic-style boxing in the United States.

Year Founded:
1888

Member Services:
Support and guidance in all facets of amateur boxing.

Membership Requirements:
Must register in the Local Boxing Committee that oversees their locality. Boxers must be eligible for competition in amateur boxing.

Number of members:
30,000

Publications:
USA Boxing Technical & Competition Rules

USA CANOE/KAYAK
503 SOPHIA STREET
SUITE 100
FREDERICKSBURG, VA 22401
504-907-4460 EXT 108
info@usack.org
• Wade Blackwood, CEO
(504) 907-4460
wade@usack.org
• Chris Stec, Chief Operating Officer
(540) 907-4460
chris@usack.org
• Chris Barlow, Sprint High Performance Manager
cbarlow.usack@gmail.com
• Aaron Mann, Communications and Media
(540) 907-4460
aaron@usack.org
• Silvan Poberaj, Head Coach, Whitewater Slalom
(301) 706-2680
spoberaj@usack.org
• Rafal Smolen, Slalom National Team Coach
(828) 301-4805
rafal@usack.org
• Claudiu Ciur, Sprint Nationalteam Coach
claudiuciur.usack@gmail.com

USA CURLING
5525 CLEM'S WAY
STEVENS POINT, WI 54482
715-344-1199
888-287-5377
Fax: 715-344-2279
info@usacurl.org
www.teamusa.org/usa-curling
• Rick Patzke, Secretary General

Description:
As the national governing body for the sport of curling, the USA Curling strives to grow the sport and to win medals in world championships and Olympic Games.

Membership Requirements:
Membership is through membership in a USA Curling member club.

Number of members:
13,000

Publications:
U.S. Curling News

USA CYCLING
210 USA CYCLING POINT
SUITE 100
COLORADO SPRINGS, CO 80919-2215
719-434-4200
help@usacycling.org
www.usacycling.org

- Derek Bouchard-Hall, President/Chief Operating Officer
- Bob Stapleton, Chairman
- Chuck Hodge, Vice President of Operations
chodge@usacycling.org
- Kevin Dessart, Coaching Education/Athlete Development Director
coaches@usacycling.org
- Emily Palmer, Interscholastic/Club Development Director
epalmer@usacycling.org
- Kelly Feilke, Executive Director
kfeilke@usacycling.org

Nature of Service:
Serves as governing body for bicycle racing and amateur cycling in America and, as such, is responsible for selecting Olympic, Pan-Am and World Championship teams. Promotes events and programs, television production.
Year Founded:
1921

USA DIVING
1060 N. CAPITAL AVENUE
SUITE E-310
INDIANAPOLIS, IN 46204
317-237-5252
Fax: 317-237-5257
usadiving@usadiving.org
www.usadiving.org
- Linda Paul, President/Chief Operating Officer
linda.paul@usadiving.org
- Terry Powers, Vice President
terry.powers@usadiving.org
- Joe Clarke, Communications Coordinator
joe.clarke@usadiving.org
- Sean McCarthy, Interim High Performance Director
sean.mccarthy@usadiving.org
- Aurelie Gibson, Director of Education
aurelie.gibson@usadiving.org
Member Services:
Official rule book; annual directory; free admission to national championships, liability insurance.
Sports Services Founded:
1981
Description:
National governing body for the olympic sport of diving in the United States.

USA FIELD HOCKEY
5540 NORTH ACADEMY BLVD
SUITE 100
COLORADO SPRINGS, CO 80918
719-866-4567
Fax: 719-632-0979
information@usafieldhockey.com
www.teamusa.org/usa-field-hockey
- Bree Gillespie, Chair
breegillespie1@gmail.com
Description:
USA Field Hockey is the national governing body for the sport of field hockey in the United States and is a member of the United States Olympic Committee (USOC), the Federation Internationale de Hockey (FIH), and the Pan American Hockey Federation (PAFH)
Member Services:
Quarterly Newsletter, Insurance, Events, Camps, National and International Competitions, Olympic Team Pipeline
Number of Members:

16,000
Publications:
Field Hockey News

USA GYMNASTICS
132 E WASHINGTON ST
SUITE 700
INDIANAPOLIS, IN 46204
317-237-5050
Fax: 317-237-5069
www.usa-gymnastics.org
- Ron Gailmore, Chief Operating Officer
(317) 829-5631
rgalimore@usagym.org
- Paul Parilla, Chairman of the Board
- Leslie King, VP Communications
(317) 826-5656
lking@usagym.org
- Lee Johnson, VP Marketing
(317) 829-5647
ljohnson@usagym.org
Description:
Founded in 1963. The sole national governing body for the sport of gymnastics in the United States. USA Gymnastics is responsibile for selection and training of the Olympic and World Championship teams, and the promotion of gymnastics.
Membership Requirements:
National organization, associations and individual as involved in gymnastics.
Member Services:
Athlete registration; club membership; professional memberships; general memberships, subscriptions; merchandise.

USA HOCKEY
1775 BOB JOHNSON DRIVE
COLORADO SPRINGS, CO 80906-4090
719-576-8724
Fax: 719-538-1160
usah@usahockey.org
www.usahockey.com
- Dave Ogrean, Executive Director
daveo@usahockey.org
- Jim Smith, President
- Ron DeGregorio, Chair
- Bill Hall, Secretary
- Kim Folsom, Executive Assistant
- John Beadle, Vice President
- Donna Guarglia, Treasurer
Description:
The National Governing Body for the sport of ice hockey in the United States. Its mission is to promote the growth of hockey in America and provide the best possible experience for all participants by encouraging, developing, advancing and administering the sport.
Year Founded:
1937

USA JUDO
ONE OLYMPIC PLAZA
COLORADO SPRINGS, CO 80909
719-866-4730
Fax: 719-866-4733
www.teamusa.org/usa-judo
- Keith Bryant, Chief Executive Officer
keith.bryant@usajudo.us
- Ed Liddie, Director of Athlete Performance
eddie.liddie@usajudo.us
Member Services:
Meetings held in conjunction with international invitational championship.
Description:
A non profit organization which is governed

by a Board of Directors with representation from all areas of the judo family, including athletes, coaches, and referees.

USA LUGE
57 CHURCH STREET
LAKE PLACID, NY 12946-1805
518-523-2071
Fax: 518-523-4106
info@usaluge.org
www.teamusa.org/usa-luge
- Dwight Bell, President
- Jim Leahy, CEO & Executive Director
Sports Services Founded:
1978
Member Services:
Provide coaching, equipment for luge athletes. Coordination, organization, and funding of summer and winter training programs for National teams. Train, test, certify officials for luge competitions. Organizes and promotes World Luge Cup Race and numerous national competitions yearly. Selects Olympic and National Teams.
Number of members:
1,000
Description:
An Olympic class member organization of the United States Olympic Committee (USOC) and is the National Governing Body (NGB) for the sport of luge in the United States. To provide for the achievement of athletic excellence in the sport of luge, with the highest degree of sportsmanship, honor, dedication and vicorty as the standard.

USA ROLLER SPORTS
4730 SOUTH STREET
PO BOX 6579
LINCOLN, NE 68506
402-483-7551
Fax: 402-483-1465
www.usarollersports.org
- Trace Hansen, Chairman
- Bill Spooner, President
- Renee Hildebrand, Vice President
- Peggy Young, Secretary
pyoung@usarollersports.org
Description:
USA Roller Sports is the national governing body of competitive roller sports in the United States and is recognized by the United States Olympic Committee.
Sports Services Founded:
1937

USA SHOOTING
1 OLYMPIC PLAZA
COLORADO SPRINGS, CO 80909
719-866-4670
media@usashooting.org
www.usashooting.com
- Jeff Prince, Chair
- David Johnson, Interim Chief Executive Officer
dave.johnson@usashooting.org
Description:
Founded in 1995, prepares American athletes to win Olympic and Paralympic medals, promote the shooting sports throughout the US, and govern the conduct of international shooting in the country.
Membership Requirements:
Open to non-competitive shooting enthusiasts as well as competing shooters. Annual, life, junior and club memberships

available.

Publications:
USA SHOOTING NEWS, 5 times yearly.

Member Services:
Eligible to qualify to compete at USA Shooting-sanctioned events, discounts on U.S. Shooting Team merchandise, additional benefits for life members and clubs, and magazine subscription.

USA SOFTBALL
2801 NE 50TH ST
OKLAHOMA CITY, OK 73111
405-424-5266
Fax: 405-424-3855
info@usasoftball.com
www.teamusa.org/usa-softball
• Craig Cress, Executive Director

Number of Members:
4,500,000 - 5,000,000.

Membership Requirements:
Registration with an ASA commissioner in a state/metro association.

Description:
Founded in 1933, a volunteer driven, not-for-profit organization that has evolved into the strongest softball organization in the country, that is the National Governing Body of Softball.3

USA SWIMMING
ONE OLYMPIC PLAZA
COLORADO SPRINGS, CO 80909
719-866-4578
info@usaswimming.org
www.usaswimming.org
• Chuck Wielgus, President/Chief Operating Officer
• Kathy Parker, Executive Coordinator
• Matt Farrell, Chief Marketing Officer

Description:
The National Governing Body for the sport of swimming in the United States that promotes participation in swimming and the development of the sport.

Membership Requirements:
Offers various types of membership: athletes (400,000 current), coaches, officials, administrators, clubs etc.

Members:
400,000

USA SYNCHRO
1 OLYMPIC PLAZA
COLORADO SPRINGS, CO 80909
719-866-2219
www.teamusa.org/USA-Synchronized-Swimming
• Myriam Glez, High Performance Director & CEO
myriam@usasynchro.org

Number of members:
5,700 +

Publications:
Synchro Swimming USA Magazine, USA Synchro E-Newsletter

Membership Requirements:
Membership Fees, which vary based on membership category.

Description:
Serves as the National Governing Body for the sport of synchronized swimming, appointed as such by the Unted States Olympic Committee. Provides leadership and resources for the promotion and growth of synchronized swimming, to achieve competitive excellence at all levels and to develop broad based participation.

Year Founded:
1977

USA TABLE TENNIS
1 OLYMPIC PLAZA
COLORADO SPRINGS, CO 80909-5769
719-866-4583
Fax: 719-632-6071
www.usatt.org
• Gordon Kaye, CEO
(719) 866-4583
Gordon.Kaye@usatt.org
• Andy Horn, Director of Operations
(719) 866-4583
Andrew.Horn@usatt.org

Description:
National governing body for table tennis in the United States. It oversees a wide variety of membership services, the national teams, and other areas such as the rules of the game, the Hall of Fame, and numerous online instructional and historical articles.

Sports Service Founded:
1933

Description:
Oversees a wide variety of membership services, the national teams, and other areas such as the rules of the game, and numerous online instructional and historical articles.

USA TEAM HANDBALL
801-463-2000
info@usateamhandball.org
www.usateamhandball.org
• Harvey W. Schiller, President
• Michael D. Cavanaugh, CEO
vh@usatemdc@usateamhandball.org
• Javier Garcia Cuesta, Head Coach
jgarciacusta@yahoo.com
• Scott Cronk, Media Specialist/Webmaster
scott@usateamhandball.org
• Dave Gascon, Director of High Performance

Description:
The national governing body for handball in the United States, which works to promote and develop the sport at all levels of competition.

Membership Requirements:
Payment of annual dues. Membership categories include Regular, 3-Year Adult, Junior, Special Event, Associate, Life, Group B.

Year Founded:
2008

USA TRACK & FIELD
132 EAST WASHINGTON STREET
SUITE 800
INDIANAPOLIS, IN 46204
317-261-0500
Fax: 317-261-0481
www.usatf.org
• Max Siegel, Chief Executive Officer
(317) 261-0500
ceo@usatf.org
• Renee Chube Washington, Chief Operating Officer
(317) 713-4657
Renee.Washington@usatf.org
• Jill Geer, Chief Marketing Officer
(317) 713-4654
Jill.Geer@usatf.org
• Duffy Mahoney, Chief of Sport Performance

Description:
The National Governing Body for track and field, long-distance running and race walking in the United States.

Membership Requirements:
Classifications: Associations, Amateur Sports Organizations, National Organizations, Affiliate, Sustaining and Life; registers athletes, and accepts Club Members, through Associations.

Member Services:
Training, development and competition for men and women in five classifications — Junior Olympics (10-under to 18), Youth Athletics (10-under to 18), Junior (14-19), Senior (14-up), Masters (40-80+). Committees: Sports - Men's Track and Field, Women's Track and Field, Men's Long Distance Running, Women's Long Distance Running, Men's and Women's Race Walking, Masters Track and Field, Masters Long Distance Running, Youth Athletics. Administrative: Associations, Athletes Advisory, Athletics for the Disabled, Budget and Audit, Men's Development, Women's Development, Law and Legislation, Membership, Officials and Coaching Education.

USA TRIATHLON
5825 DELMONICO DRIVE
SUITE 200
COLORADO SPRINGS, CO 80919
719-597-9090
Fax: 719-597-2121
info@usatriathlon.org
www.usatriathlon.org
• Rob Urbach, Chief Executive Officer
• Tim Yount, Chief Operating Officer
(719) 955-2831
tim.yount@usatriathlon.org

Nature of Service:
USA Triathlon is the National Governing Body for triathlon, duathlon, aquathlon and winter triathlon in the United States.

Year Founded:
1982

Member Services:
USAT offers annual memberships which, in addition to many other benefits, cover members at all USAT sanctioned events for 12 full months. One-day licenses which cover one event and annual elite memberships are also available.

USA VOLLEYBALL
4065 SINTON ROAD
SUITE 200
COLORADO SPRINGS, CO 80907
719-228-6800
Fax: 719-228-6899
postmaster@usav.org
www.usavolleyball.org
• Jamie Davis, CEO
jamie.davis@usav.org
• Kerry Klostermann, Secretary General
kerry.klostermann@usav.org
• Sarah Young, Finance Manager
Sarah.Young@usav.org
• June Sander, Finance/Corprate Operations Manager
june.sander@usav.org

Nature of Service:
The National Governing Body for the sport of volleyball in the United States and is recognized as such by the Federation International de Volleyball (FIB) and the

United States Olympic Committee (USOC).
Year Founded:
1928
Member Services:
Clinics conducted for coaches, players and officials, competition conducted through regions; conducts elite and international volleyball programs. Member of USOC& FIVB.
Membership Requirements:
Organizations affiliated with volleyball.

Other locations:

ALASKA JUNIOR VOLLEYBALL (MIDNIGHT SUN VOLLEYBALL)
9650 BIRCH ROAD
ANCHORAGE, AK 99507
www.midnightsunvolleyball.com
• Virgil Hooe, Director

ALOHA REGIONAL COMMISSIONER/USA VOLLEYBALL
45-795 PO'OKELA STREET
KANE'OHE, HI 96744
www.aloharegion.com
• Kent Ma, Commissioner

ARIZONA REGIONAL COMMISSIONER/USA VOLLEYBALL
9100 S MCKEMY STREET
TEMPE, AZ 85284
480-626-6740
Fax: 480-626-6743
www.azregionvolleyball.org
• Harold Cranswick, Commissioner
(480) 626-6740
office@azregionvolleyball.org
• Becky Hudson, Secretary/Treasurer
(480) 626-6740
office@azregionvolleyball.org
Sports Services Founded:
1989
Description:
Formerly known as Cactus Region, promotes, governs, oversees, plans and coordinates amateur indoor and outdoor volleyball in the Arizona Region, in order to provide a variety of opportunities for all interested parties to participate in a safe, positive and apporpriately competitive environment.

BADGER REGIONAL VOLLEYBALL ASSOCIATION/USA VOLLEYBALL
2831 NORTH GRANDVIEW BOULEVARD
PEWAUKEE, WI 53072
414-507-1124
Fax: 262-349-9971
badgervolleyball.org
• Terry Paulson, Region Tournament Director
(414) 588-2665
badgerregiontd@wi.rr.com
• BJ Bryant, Secretary
(920) 277-0706
wivbacademy@gmail.com
• Anne Slattery, Treasurer
(414) 659-2663
arslatts@gmail.com
• Jennifer Armson-Dyer, Director of Operations
jarmsondyer@badgervolleyball.org

CAROLINA REGIONAL VOLLEYBALL ASSOCIATION/USA VOLLEYBALL
3770 CLEMMONS ROAD
SUITE C
PO BOX 1757
CLEMMONS, NC 27012-1757
336-766-3581
Fax: 336-766-3501
office@carolinaregionvb.org
www.carolinaregionvb.org
• Mike Spillman, President
(336) 993-8292
• Dan Colleran, Treasurer

(704) 799-7448
• Jim Ross, Secretary
(910) 233-8580
• Kevin Wendelboe, CEO/Executive Director
(336) 766-3581
ceo@carolinaregionvb.org
• Marilyn Thompson, Officials Program Director
Publications:
Carolina Volleyball Review Newsletter
Description:
The Carolina Regional Volleyball Association organizes competition and promotes the sport of volleyball at the State level as one the regional association within USA Volleyball.

CHESAPEAKE REGIONAL COMMISSIONER/USA VOLLEYBALL
42893 APPALOOSA TRAIL COURT
CHANTILLY, VA 20152
703-754-6185
www.chrva.org
• Rebecca Ruis-Johannes, President
(202) 409-7006
Rebecca.Johannes@chrva.org
• Lisa DiGiacinto, Commissioner
(410) 768-4746
lisa.digiacinto@chrva.org
• Tia Storey, Treasurer
(703) 957-4247
tia.storey@chrva.org
Description:
The Chesapeake Region Volleyball Association (CHRVA) is one of 40 Regional Volleyball Associations (RVAs) of USA Volleyball. The Region encompasses the States of Delaware and Maryland, the District of Columbia, and the northern counties of the Commonwealth of Virginia.

COLORADO REGIONAL COMMISSIONER/USA VOLLEYBALL
4155 E. JEWELL AVENUE
SUITE 909
DENVER, CO 80005
303-584-0376
www.rmrvolleyball.org
• Glenn Sapp, Commissioner/Pres
(720) 289-5797
commissioner@rmrvolleyball.org
• Wendy Sapp, Office Manager
(303) 584-0376
wendy@rmrvolleyball.org

COLUMBIA EMPIRE REGIONAL COMMISSIONER/USA VOLLEYBALL
4840 SW WESTERN AVENUE
SUITE 450
BEAVERTON, OR 97005
503-644-7468
region@columbiaempirevolleyball.com
www.columbiaempirevolleyball.com
• Jeff Mozzochi, Executive Director
• Cody March, Director of Operations
• Jen Bolger, Membership & Comm Manager
Description:
CEVA represents Oregon and SW Washington for Junior Girls, Junior Boys, Adults and Outdoor Volleyball.

EVERGREEN REGIONAL COMMISSIONER/USA VOLLEYBALL
7 S. HOWARD STREET
SUITE 418
SPOKANE, WA 99201
509-290-5552
Fax: 509-290-5318
office@evergreenregion.org
www.evergreenregion.org
• Meredith Coupland, Commissioner
mc2coupland@gmail.com
• Kevin Twohig, Assistant Commissioner
(509) 939-4029
• Margie Ray, Treasurer
(509) 484-7467
margieray.ref@gmail.com

FLORIDA REGIONAL COMMISSIONER/USA VOLLEYBALL
15014 US HIGHWAY 441
EUSTIS, FL 32726
352-742-0080
Fax: 352-414-5304
www.floridavolleyball.org
• Steve Bishop, Executive Director/President
(352) 742-0080
steve@floridavolleyball.org
• Mary Andrew, Chair/Commissioner
(904) 242-6935
mary@floridavolleyball.org
• Michele Moriarty, Registrar/Office Manager
Description:
As one of the regional associations within USA Volleyball, the organization pormotes the sport and organizes competition at the State level.

GARDEN EMPIRE VOLLEYBALL ASSOCIATION
PO BOX 554
WESTFIELD, NJ 07091-0554
914-930-6368
Fax: 908-360-1033
www.geva.org
• Bob Baker, Commissioner
(908) 524-0064
• Marianne Lepore, Office Administrator

GATEWAY REGIONAL COMMISSIONER/USA VOLLEYBALL
10075 BAUER ROAD
ST. LOUIS, MO 63128
314-849-1221
Fax: 314-849-7865
mayer@gatewayvb.org
www.gatewayvb.org
• Tim Neels, Commissioner
neels@gatewayvb.org
Description:
As one of the 40 regional associations within USA Volleyball, Gateway represents eastern Missouri and southern Illinois, organizing competition and promoting the sport at the State level for over 7000 members.
Year Founded:
1994

GREAT LAKES REGION/USA VOLLEYBALL
745 MCCLINTOCK DRIVE
SUITE 314
BURR RIDGE, IL 60527-0857
630-986-9000
Fax: 630-828-2663
greatlakesvolleyball@glrvb.com
www.greatlakesvolleyball.org
• Sandy Abbinanti, Commissioner/CEO

GREAT PLAINS REGIONAL VOLLEYBALL ASSOCIATION
7515 MAIN STREET
RALSTON, NE 68127
402-593-9670
866-953-9670
info@gpvb.org
www.gpvb.org
• Sue Mailhot, Regional Commissioner
(402) 598-4782
sue@gpvb.org
• Bill Hamilton, Office Administrator

GULF COAST REGIONAL COMMISSIONER/USA VOLLEYBALL
PO BOX 1985
ORANGE BEACH, AL 36561
251-979-4287
www.gulfcoastvolleyball.org
• Philip Bryant, Commissioner

HEART OF AMERICA REGIONAL COMMISSIONER/USA VOLLEYBALL
548 SOUTH COY STREET
KANSAS CITY, KS 66105

913-233-0445
Fax: 913-233-0085
info@hoavb.org
www.hoavb.org
• Lisa Madsen, Commissioner
ha-commish@hoavb.org

HOOSIER REGION
COMMISSIONER/USA VOLLEYBALL
52428 WINDING WATERS LANE
ELKHART, IN 46514
574-262-9211
www.hoosiervolleyball.org
• Mitchell Stemm,
President/Commissioner/Junior Program
Coordin
(574) 370-9627
dallict@aol.com
• Charles Stemm, Vice President/Treasurer
hoosiervba@comcast.net
• Joan L. Stemm, Registrar
hoosiervba@comcast.net

INTERMOUNTAIN VOLLEYBALL
ASSOCIATION
72 DORMAN AVENUE
SAN FRANCISCO, CA 94124
801-618-8380
info@imvolleyball.org
imvolleyball.org
• Jason Badell, CFO/Commissioner
jasonbadell@imvolleyball.org
• Mike Deaver, Executive Vice President
mikedeaver@imvolleyball.com

IOWA REGION USA VOLLEYBALL
8170 HICKMAN ROAD
SUITE 5
CLIVE, IA 50325
515-727-1860
Fax: 515-727-1861
www.iavbreg.org
• Lynne Updegraff, Commisioner
lynne@iavbreg.org
• Martin Miller, Vice President & Northwest
District
(515) 292-7113
mgmiller@iastate.edu
• Tina Carter, Secretary & Southwest District
(515) 210-4353
tinacarter22@hotmail.com
Description:
IRV is one of the 40 regional associations within
USA Volleyball, promoting and organzing
competition at the State level.

KEYSTONE REGIONAL
COMMISSIONER/USA VOLLEYBALL
1013 BROOKSIDE ROADAD
SUITE 203
WESCOSVILLE, PA 18106
610-401-3362
Fax: 888-391-5782
registration@krva.org
www.krva.org
• Michelle Carlton, Commissioner
commissioner@krva.org
• Deborah Fajerski, Secretary
secretary@krva.org
• Jeff Stubblefield, Treasurer
treasurer@krva.org
Description:
KRVA is one of the 40 regional associations
within the National Governing Body USA
Volleyball, promoting the sport at the State level.

LONE STAR REGIONAL
COMMISSIONER/USA VOLLEYBALL
1608 CANYON OAK
SCHERTZ, TX 78154
210-945-4365
Fax: 210-945-8630
www.lsvolleyball.org
• Will Vick, Commissioner
willvick@satx.rr.com

• Karen Tarmon, Registrar
(830) 358-7714
Publications:
Newsletter-Quarterly

MOKU O KEAWE REGIONAL
COMMISSIONER/USA VOLLEYBALL
178 POHAI STREET
HILO, HI 96720
808-292-5916
mokuregion@yahoo.com
www.leaguelineup.com/mokuokeawe
• Elroy Osorio, Vice President
• Angie Andrade-Morioka, President/Regional
Commissioner
(808) 292-5916

NEW ENGLAND REGIONAL
COMMISSIONER/USA VOLLEYBALL
38983 ACUSHNET AVENUE
NEW BEDFORD, MA 02745
508-922-0803
commissioner@nevolleyball.org
www.nevolleyball.org
• Dave Peixoto, Commissioner

NORTH COUNTRY REGION/USA
VOLLEYBALL
4445 WEST 77TH STREET D
SUITE 109
EDINN, MN 55435
952-831-9150
800-657-6967
Fax: 952-942-5584
www.ncrusav.org
• Judy Praska, Executive Director
(952) 831-9150
judy@ncrusav.org
• Brad Aaberg, Officials Coordinator
(952) 831-9150
brad@ncrusav.org

NORTH TEXAS REGIONAL
COMMISSIONER/USA VOLLEYBALL
PO BOX 941
PLANO, TX 75094
469-326-1873
Fax: 469-326-1875
ntrdonise@gmail.com
ntrvolleyball.net
• Andy Reitinger, Commissioner/President
andysummit@yahoo.com
• Donise King, Executive Director
ntrdonise@gmail.com
• Steve Hargrave, Junior Coordinator
Description:
As one of the 40 regional associations within
USA Volleyball, NTR sactions events and
promotes the sport at the State level.

NORTHERN CALIFORNIA REGIONAL
COMMISSIONER/USA VOLLEYBALL
72 DORMAN AVENUE
SAN FRANCISCO, CA 94124
415-550-7582
Fax: 415-550-7762
vball@ncva.com
www.ncva.com
• Diane Mazzei, Board Chair
• Donna Donaghy, Chief Executive Officer
donna@ncva.com
• Shannon Christie, Region Services
Administrator

NORTHWEST VOLLEYBALL INC.
15801 NE 8TH STREET
REDMOND, WA 98052
425-497-1051
Fax: 425-671-5020
info@volleyballnw.com
nwjuniors.org
• Tony Miranda, Executive Director
(206) 550
tony@volleyballnw.com

OHIO VALLEY REGIONAL
COMMISSIONER/USA VOLLEYBALL
315 JOHNSON ROAD
KENT, OH 44240
330-354-5332
wyzynski@ovr.org
www.ovr.org
• Bob Price, Commissioner/President
(614) 882-2468
Rwprice23@att.net
• Ronald J. Wyzynski, Executive Director/CEO
(614) 402-9445
wyzynski@ovr.org
Description:
As one of the 40 regional associations within
USA Volleyball, OVR promotes and organizes
the sport at the State level. As of 2017,
membership is at 22,557.

OKLAHOMA REGIONAL
COMMISSIONER/USA VOLLEYBALL
18605 ALBERTO PLACE
EDMOND, OK 73013
405-285-6622
Fax: 405-285-0607
www.okrva.com
• Bill Hamiter, President
(405) 789-6939
president@okrva.com
• Shawn McCarty, Commissioner
(405) 285-6622

OLD DOMINION REGIONAL
COMMISSIONER/USA VOLLEYBALL
PO BOX 6828
RICHMOND, VA 23230
804-400-9758
info@odrvb.org
www.odrvb.com
• Skipp Weston, Commissioner
(804) 400-9758
commissioner@odrvb.org

PALMETTO REGIONAL
COMMISSIONER/USA VOLLEYBALL
137 GARDENIA DRIVE
NINETY SIX, SC 29666
864-809-8222
office@palmettovb.com
www.palmettovb.com
• Jimmy Peden, Commissioner
• Kirsten Boessneck, Coordinator
Description:
The Palmetto Volleyball Region is a member of
the USA Volleyball Organization. The Palmetto
Region is a grassroots organization which
sanction events for Club volleyball teams in the
state of South Carolina. Teams include Adult
and Junior teams for boys, girls, men and
women.

PIONEER REGIONAL
COMMISSIONER/USA VOLLEYBALL
OHIO VALLEY VOLLEYBALL CENTER
1820 TAYLOR AVENUE
LOUISVILLE, KY 40213
502-473-1200 EXT 21
www.pioneervb.com
• Ron Kordes, President
(502) 473-1200
ronkordes@ovvc.com
• Nancy Funk, Assistant Commissioner
(502) 239-1818
nfunk@twc.com

PUGET SOUND REGIONAL
COMMISSIONER/USA VOLLEYBALL
22617 76TH AVENUE
SUITE 201
EDMONDS, WA 98026
425-673-4103
Fax: 425-673-4293
office@psrvb.org
www.psrvb.org

- Bil Caillier, Chairperson
- Jim Amsbary, Treasurer
- Elise Quinn, Board Secretary
- John Bryant, Commissioner

Description:
PSR is a not-for-profit organization serving a geographic area in Washington State bound on the north by the Canadian border, on the west by the Pacific Ocean, on the east by the crest of the Cascade Mountains, and on the south by Lewis County. The purpose of PSR is to develop and promote the sport of volleyball through adult, junior, and youth programs at a local, regional, and national level.

ROCKY MOUNTAIN REGIONAL COMMISSIONER/USA VOLLEYBALL
4155 JEWELL AVENUE
SUITE 909
DENVER, CO 80222
303-584-0376
800-503-0969
Fax: 303-782-5577
www.rmrvolleyball.org
- Glenn Sapp, Commissioner
(303) 422-4209
commisioner@rmrvolleyball.org
- Wendy Sapp, Office Manager
wendy@rmrvolleyball.org

SOUTHERN CALIFORNIA REGIONAL COMMISSIONER/USA VOLLEYBALL
1500 SOUTH ANAHEIM BOULEVARD
SUITE 280
ANAHEIM, CA 92805
714-917-3595
Fax: 714-917-3596
info@scvavolleyball.org
www.scvavolleyball.org
- Ann Davenport, Regional Commissioner
ann@scvavolleyball.org
- Shannon Davenport, Office Manager
shannon@scvavolleyball.org
- Ken Taylor, Official's Chair

Description:
SCVA is one of the 40 non-profit associations within USA Volleyball, promoting and organzing the sport at the State level.

SOUTHERN REGIONAL COMMISSIONER/USA VOLLEYBALL
105 ROUNSAVILLE COURT
ROSWELL, GA 30076
844-219-2976
Fax: 770-649-9117
kencain23@gmail.com
www.srva.org

SUN COUNTRY REGIONAL COMMISSIONER/USA VOLLEYBALL
4233 W FARMERS
AMARILLO, TX 79110
806-681-5458
commissioner@suncountryvb.org
www.suncountryvb.org
- Mark Noble, Commissioner
(806) 681-5458
mnoble1822@gmail.com
- Steve Franco, Secretary
(505) 220-8873
secretary@suncountryvb.org
- Jake Bordenave, Treasurer
(505) 823-1344
treasurer@suncountryvb.org

Description:
SURVA is one of the 40 independant associations within USa Volleyball, promoting and organiazing competition for the sport at the State level.

WESTERN EMPIRE
58 MEADOWLARK DRIVE
PENFIELD, NY 14526
585-259-6557
www.wevavolleyball.org

- John W Hughes, Commissioner/Executive Director
wevajohn@gmail.com
- Rocco W Lucci, Jr, President
rocolucci@gmail.com
- Cindy D Errico, Junior Coordinator /Junior Program Director
(585) 548-2598
wevacindy@hotmail.com

Sports Services Founded:
1989

Description:
The purpose of WEVA is the promotion of volleyball and playing the game in all of its forms. In addition to developing players, WEVA has committed resources to train coaches, officials, scorekeepers, and parent volunteers. This is one of 40 USA Volleyball regions representing the sport of volleyball in the 15 western most counties of New York State.

USA WATER POLO, INC.
2124 MAIN STREET
SUITE 240
HUNTINGTON BEACH, CA 92648
714-500-5445
Fax: 714-960-2431
www.usawaterpolo.org
- Christopher Ramsey, CEO
- Jonie Walbring, Human Resources Director
(714) 500-5448
jwalbring@usawaterpolo.org
- Annalece Montgomery, Marketing Coordinator
(714) 500-5434
amontgomery@usawaterpolo.org
- Stephanie London Krogius, Director of Advancement
(714) 500-5427
skrogius@usawaterpolo.org

Sports Services Founded:
1978

Description:
A not-for-profit corporation that serves as the national governing body for the sport of water polo in the United States under authority of the United States Olympic Committee.

USA WEIGHTLIFTING
1 OLYMPIC PLAZA
COLORADO SPRINGS, CO 80909
719-866-4508
Fax: 719-866-4741
usaw@usaweightlifting.org
www.usaweightlifting.org
- Phil Andrews, Chief Executive Officer/General Secretary
(719) 866-3386
Phil.Andrews@usaweightlifting.org
- Brad Suchorski, Membership Manager
(719) 866-3227

Membership Requirements:
No requirements - there are memberships of all kinds and dues related to each membership type.

Description:
USA Weightlifing is the national governing body for olympic weightlifting in the United States. USAW is a member of the US Olympic Committee and of the International Weightlifting Federation.

USA WRESTLING
6155 LEHMAN DR
COLORADO SPRINGS, CO 80918
719-598-8181
Fax: 719-598-9440
www.teamusa.org/usa-wrestling

- Rich Bender, Executive Director
(719) 598-8181
rbender@usawrestling.org
- Bruce Baungartner, President
- Greg Strobel, 1st Vice president
- Mark Reiland, 2nd Vice President
- Duane Morgan, Treasurer
- Tony Black, State Services Manager
(719) 598-8181
tblack@usawrestling.org
- Dwaine Cooper, Assoc Executive Director Finance/Administration
dcooper@usawrestling.org
- Gary Abbott, Special Projects/Communications Director
(719) 598-8181
gabbott@usawrestling.org
- Meredith Wilson, Information Technology Director
(719) 598-8181
mwilson@usawrestling.org

Description:
The national governing body for the sport of wrestling in the United States and, as such, is its representative to the United States Olympic Committee. The central organization that coordinates amateur wrestling programs in the nation and works to create interest and participation in these programs.

Professional Organizations

AMATEUR ATHLETIC UNION OF THE UNITED STATES, INC./AAU
PO BOX 22409
1910 HOTEL PLAZA BOULEVARD
LAKE BUENA VISTA, FL 32830
407-934-7200
800-228-4872
Fax: 407-934-7242
www.aausports.org
- Roger Goudy, President
roger@aausports.org
- Cynthia Diaz, Finance Director
(407) 828-3740
cynthia@aausports.org

Sports Services Founded:
1888

Membership Requirements:
Athlete membership is for anyone involved in an activity. One membership card allows participation in any and all of the AAU sports. Volunteers may participate in annual, sustaining, and lifetime membership programs.

Programs Include:
AAU Junior Olympic Games - The largest national multi-sport event for the youth of America. Encompasses the US territories and American children on military bases.

Other Programs include:
Presidential Sports Award, Presidential Challenge National Youth Physical Fitness Program.

Publications:
Official AAU Handbook, for each sport.

Description:
One of the largest non profit, volunteer, sports organizations in the United States. A multi sport organization, the AAU is dedicated exclusively to the promotion and development of amateur sports and physical fitness programs.

multi sports

Other locations:

ADIRONDACK AAU ASSOCIATION
7 WATERMAN COURT
UNIT 4
DELMAR, NY 12054
518-475-9480
jmallery@aol.com
www.adirondackaau.org
• Mike Friello, Governor
officialaautaekwondo@gmail.com
• Jerry Mallery, Registrar
Sports Services Founded:
Organized January 31, 1920
Description:
Organizes competitions and over 35 sports for
youths. Serves New York State East and North
of Broome, Cortland, Dutchess, Onondaga,
Orange, Oswego and Sullivan Counties.
Neighboring Districts include Connecticut,
Middle Atlantic, New England, New York
Metropolitan and Niagara.

ALASKA AAU ASSOCIATION
THE WALT DISNEY WORLD RESORT
PO BOX 10,000
LAKE BUENA VISTA, FL 32830-1000
407-943-7200
www.aausports.org
Description:
Covers the State of Alaska.

ARIZONA AAU ASSOCIATION
602-228-3209
• Thomas Rogers, Governor
corogers@cox.net
Sports Services Founded:
Organized March 10, 1956

ARKANSAS AAU ASSOCIATION
40 LILES ROAD
BEEBE, AR 72012
501-303-8389
terrie@aamsco.net
www.arkansasaau.org
• Larry Bryant, Governor
(501) 388-1937
bryantlarry5@aol.com
• Farrin Cain, 1ST Lt Governor
aquatics.hfc@gmail.com
• Charlie Wood, 2nd Lt. Governor
(501) 351-1314
wood_charlie@hotmail.com
• Jane Nichols, Secretary
(501) 525-0441
sportsj43@att.net
• Lottie Keaton, Treasurer
(501) 244-5404
lkeatonbrooks@sbcglobal.net
Sports Services Founded:
Organized February 16, 1936
Description:
State of Arkansas and Bowie County, Texas.
Neighboring Districts include Southeastern,
Southern, Southwestern, Oklahoma, Missouri
Valley and Ozark.

CENTRAL AAU ASSOCIATION
7291 CLEM DRIVE
GURNEE, IL 60031
847-456-2617
www.aaucentral.org; www.centralillinoisaau.org
• JB Mirza, Governor
jbmtko@aol.com
Sports Services Founded:
Organized in 1890
Description:
Illinois, except Calhoun, Greene, Jersey,
Madison, Monroe and St. Clair counties.

**CENTRAL CALIFORNIA AAU
ASSOCIATION**
1255 NORTH CHERRY AVENUE
524
TULARE, CA 93274

209-845-9868
centralcalaau@aol.com
www.centralcalaau.com
• Guy Fowler, Governor
• Karen Fowler, Registrar
oakdalegal@yahoo.com
• Dave Schlick, LT.Governor
Sports Services Foudned:
Organized in 1952.
Description:
Counties of Fresno, Inyo, Kern, Kings, Madera,
Mariposa, Merced, Mona and Tulare in the State
of California. Territory re-aligned December
1963.

CONNECTICUT AAU ASSOCIATION
525 BURNSIDE AVENUE
EAST HARTFORD, CT 6108
860-291-8241
866-341-8241
http://www.connecticutaau.org/
• Dan Dembinski, District Registrar
• Jack Bethke, District Govenor
jackbethke@yahoo.com
• George Keurtyka, Lieutenant Governor
kurtyka@sbcglobal.net
• Cindy D Hetu, District Treasurer
clhetu@yahoo.com
Sports Services Founded:
Organized September 17, 1929
Description:
State of Connecticut. Neighboring Districts
include Adirondack, New England and New York
Metropolitan.

FLORIDA AAU ASSOCIATION
4400 N HIGHWAY 19A
UNIT 6
MOUNT DORA, FL 32757
352-357-0477
Fax: 352-357-0474
www.aauflorida.org;
www.eteamz.com/floridaaau
• Chet Lemon, Director
gigi@sunshinesports.net
Sports Services Founded:
Organized in January 1925.
Description:
Florida, execept Miami-Dade Broward, that part
of Hendry County West of Route 833, and Palm
Beach Counties. Territory re-aligned, December
1958, 1959, 1963, 1972, 1999.

**FLORIDA GOLD COAST AAU
ASSOCIATION**
www.aausports.org
Description:
Counties of Broward, Miami Dade, that part of
Hendry County East of Route 833, and Palm
Beach counties. Neighboring District is Florida.

GEORGIA AAU ASSOCIATION
770-380-9749
gaaau@comcast.net
www.gaaau.net
• James Henry, Governor
(770) 846-2009
• Wendy Miller, Registrar
(404) 401-4996
wendmill227@yahoo.com
• Jane Williamson, Secretary and Hospitality
(770) 646-5157
mjanewill2@aol.com
• Peg Adams, Treasurer
(706) 517-7947
pegaau@msn.com
Description:
Territory realigned September 1989. State of
Georgia. Neighboring Districts include Florida,
North Carolina, Southeastern and South
Carolina.

GULF AAU ASSOCIATION
PO BOX 38913
HOUSTON, TX 77238

877-872-7481
info@texasgulfaau.com
www.texasgulfaau.com
• Lola Wesley, Governor
ola.wesley@att.net
Sports Services Founded:
Organized on March 6, 1931
Description:
Texas bounded on the North, including counties
of Angelina, Houston, Leon, Nacogdoches,
Robertson and Shelby, and including the
counties of Austin, Brazos, Colorado, Fort Bend,
Grimes, Matagorda, Robertson, Waller,
Washington and Wharton. Territory re-aligned
September 1992.

HAWAIIAN AAU ASSOCIATION
808-395-2422
www.aausports.org
• Grant K. Kidani, Governor
grant@kidani.com
Sports Services Founded:
Organized November 1910
Description:
State of Hawaii

INDIANA AAU ASSOCIATION
4150 KIDEER DR. SUITE 2A
INDIANAPOLIS, IN 46237
317-362-0615
Fax: 317-362-0763
www.aausports.org
• Lewis Owens, Governor
lewisfowens@hotmail.com
Sports Services Founded:
Organized August 22, 1919
Description:
The State of Indiana except Clark, Dearborn and
Floyd Counties.

INLAND EMPIRE AAU ASSOCIATION
PO BOX 9603
YAKIMA, WA 98909
509-453-2696
Fax: 509-457-0931
aau@ieaau.org
www.ieaau.org
• Paul Campbell, Governor
paul@yvn.com
Sports Services Founded:
Organized April 25, 1937
Description:
State of Washington, counties of Adams, Asotin,
Benton, Chelan, Columbia, Douglas, Ferry,
Franklin, Garfield, Grant, Kittias, Lincoln,
Okanogan, Spokane, Stevens, Walla Walla,
Whitman and Yakima County. State of Idaho,
counties of Benewah, Bonner, Boundary,
Clearwater, Idaho, Kootenai, Latah, Lewis, Nez
Perce, Pend Oreille and Shoshone.

IOWA AAU ASSOCIATION
3021 38TH STREET
DES MOINES, IA 50310-4616
515-255-4058
Fax: 515-279-4971
parmentert@gmail.com
www.aauiowa.org
• Teresa Parmenter, Governor
parmentert13@gmail.com
Sports Services Founded:
Organized January 15, 1939.
Description:
State of Iowa. Neighboring Districts include
Minnesota, South Dakota, Wisconsin, Missouri
Valley, Nebraska, Ozark and Central.

KENTUCKY AAU ASSOCIATION
5609 BRUNS DRIVE
LOUISVILLE, KY 40216
502-449-0101
Fax: 502-449-0101
www.aaukentucky.org
• Jared Prickett, Governor
jared@playkba.com

Sports Services Founded:
Organized February 27, 1939
Description:
The State of Kentucky and Clark and Floyd County in the State of Indiana (except for the sports of wrestling and boys and girls basketball). Neighboring Districts include Central, Indiana, Ohio, Ozark, Southeastern, Virginia and West Virginia.

LAKE ERIE AAU ASSOCIATION
4843 MAYFIELD ROAD
LYNDHURST, OH 44124-2506
www.aausports.org
• Joe Gura, Governor
(440) 452-4481
jegura@roadrunner.com
• Lewis Fellinger, Registrar
(216) 288-3483
Sports Services Founded:
Organized January 5, 1931
Description:
Counties of Ashland, Ashtabula, Belmont Columbiana, Crawford, Cuyahoga, Erie, Geagua, Huron, Jefferson, Lake, Lorain, Mahoning, Medina, Portage, Richland, Seneca, Stark, Summit, Trumball, Tuscarawus and Wayne. Neighboring Districts include Ohio and Western Pennsylvania.

MARYLAND AAU ASSOCIATION
1304 PENTRIDGE ROAD
BALTIMORE, MD 21239
443-794-8967
www.marylandaau.org
• Antoinette Dubose, 1st Lt. Governor/Office Manager
(443) 794-8967
ndubose1744@aol.com
Sports Service Founded:
Organized 1981.
Description:
State of Maryland (except the counties of Montgomery and Prince Georges).

MICHIGAN AAU ASSOCIATION
18516 SNOW
FRASER, MI 48026
586-273-7910
www.michiganaau.org
• Cynthia Trombly-Martin, Governor
cinditrombly@aol.com
Sports Services Founded:
Organized November 1923
Description:
State of Michigan. Neighboring Districts include Indiana and Ohio.

MIDDLE ATLANTIC AAU ASSOCIATION
PO BOX 631
ARDMORE, PA 19003
215-327-9181
www.aausports.org
• Alison Eachus, Director
coacheaby@aol.com
Sports Services Founded:
Organized 1906
Description:
New Jersey, South of Mercer and Monmouth County, all of the state of Delaware and the Commonwealth of Pennsylvania, East of and including Bedford, Centre, Clinton, and Potter Counties. Neighboring Districts include Adirondack, New Jersey, New York Metropolitan, Niagara, Western Pennsylvania and Maryland.

MINNESOTA AAU ASSOCIATION
3610 E. MINNEHAHA PARKWAY
MINNEAPOLIS, MN 55406
651-955-9725
www.minnesotaaau.org
• Willie Braziel, Governor
wbraziel@aol.com

Description:
State of Minnesota. Neighboring Districts Iowa, North Dakota, South Dakota and Wisconsin.

MISSOURI VALLEY AAU ASSOCIATION
1815 N YORK STREET
INDEPENDENCE, MO 64058
816-935-2106
www.aaumissourivalley.org
• Kim Lassley, Governor
mvaaugovernor@aol.com
Sports Services Founded:
Organized February 14, 1931
Description:
All of Kansas and that portion of the western part of the state of Missouri including and bounded by Adair, Audrain, Benton, Callaway, Christian, Cole, Greene, Hickory, Macon, Montineau, Morgan, Polk, Randolph, Schuyler and Taney. Neighboring Districts include Iowa, Nebraska, Colorado, Oklahoma, Arkansas and Ozark.

MONTANA AAU ASSOCIATION
SIDNEY, MT
406-488-7330
mtaau.reg@gmail.com
www.aausports.org
• Jim Scollard, Governor
j_scollard@aol.com
Sports Services Founded:
Organized Febrary 15, 1936
Description:
State of Montana. Neighboring Districts include Inland Empire, North Dakota, South Dakota and Wyoming.

NEW ENGLAND AAU ASSOCIATION
37 THURBER BLVD
SUITE 106
SMITHFIELD, RI 2917
401-349-4304
800-228-4872
www.neaau.org
• Jackie White, Director
oldpro77@msn.com
Sports Services Founded:
Organized 1890.
Description:
New Hampshire, Maine, Massachusetts, Rhode Island and Vermont. Neighboring Districts include Adirondack and Connecticut.

NEW JERSEY AAU ASSOCIATION
29 BROOKSIDE ROAD
LEONARDO, NJ 7737
732-291-2120
njaau@verizon.net
www.aaunewjersey.org
• Diane McGowan, Director
njaau@verizon.net
Sports Services Founded:
Organized April 21, 1930
Description:
New Jersey North of and including Hudson, Mercer and Monmouth Counties. Neighboring Districts include Middle Atlantic and New York Metropolitan.

NEW MEXICO AAU ASSOCIATION
2409 MILLER
CLOVIS, NM 88101
575-763-4572
www.aausports.org
• Pat Miner, Governor
janepatminer@msn.com
• Cathy Mills, Lt. Governor
cmills@plateautel.net
Sports Services Founded:
Organized May 29, 1947.
Description:
State of New Mexico, (except that area en-compassed by the Four Corners District), and the counties of Brewster, Culberton, Crockett, El Paso, Hudspeth, Jeff Davis, Presidio and Terrell in the State of Texas.

Neighboring Districts include, Colorado, Utah, Arizona, West Texas, South Texas and Oklahoma.

NIAGARA AAU ASSOCIATION
4000 HARLEM ROAD
SNYDER, NY 14226
315-759-9457
humphrey@guardian.com
www.aausports.org
• Richard Hill, Governor
rhill75068@aol.comr
Sports Services Founded:
Organized September 27, 1919.
Description:
State of New York West of and including Broome, Cortland, Onondaga and Oswego Counties. Neighboring Districts include Adirondack, Middle Atlantic, and Western Pennsylvania.

NORTH CAROLINA AAU ASSOCIATION
128-A NORTH MCDOWELL STREET
CHARLOTTE, NC 28204
704-786-4754
800-228-4872
Fax: 704-795-1392
www.ncaau.org
• Jane Kilmartin, Director
rmssek@aol.com
Sports Services Founded:
Organized December 5, 1965
Description:
State of North Caolina. Neighboring Districts include Georgia, South Carolina, Southeastern and Virginia.

NORTH DAKOTA AAU ASSOCIATION
AAU HEADQUARTERS
PO BOX 10,000
LAKE BUENA VISTA, ND 32830-1000
407-934-7200
www.aausports.org
Sports Service Founded:
Organized December 1, 1962.
Description:
Neighboring Districts include Minnesota, Montana, and South Dakota.

OHIO AAU ASSOCIATION
7429 KILKENNY DRIVE
WEST CHESTER, OH 45069
www.ohioaau.org
• Mark Hecquet, Governor
ohioaau@gmail.com
Sports Services Founded:
Organized May 1, 1923
Description:
State of Ohio except the counties of Ashland, Ashtabula, Belmont, Crawford, Cuyahoga, Erie, Geauga, Huron, Jefferson, Lake, Lawrence, Lorain, Mahoning, Medina, Portage, Richland, Seneca, Stark, Summit, Trumbull, Tuscarawus, Washington and Wayne; and the Dearborn County in the State of Indiana. Neighboring Districts include Indiana, Lake Erie, Michigan, Kentucky, West Virginia, and Western Pennsylvania.

OKLAHOMA AAU ASSOCIATION
5000 NW 61ST STREET
OKLAHOMA CITY, OK 73122
www.aausports.org
• Bill Meek, Governor
bmeek2004@aol.com
Sports Services Founded:
Organized Feburary 23, 1936
Description:
State of Oklahoma. Neighboring Districts include Missouri Valley, Colorado, New Mexico, West Texas, Southwestern and Arkansas.

OREGON AAU ASSOCIATION
1535 HARBECK ROAD
GRANTS PASS, OR 97527

Multiple Sports: Professional Organizations

541-485-5474
oregonaau@comcast.net
www.oregonaau.org; www.aauoregon.org
• Chuck Wenger, Governor
wenger3826@comcast.net
• Diane Wenger, Secretary
wenger3826@aol.com
• Rosemary Honl, Registrar
jrhonl@msn.com
Sports Services Founded:
Organized September 23, 1935
Description:
State of Oregon and the following counties of Washington: Clark, Cowlitz and Skamania. Neighboring Districts include Inland Empire, Pacific and Pacific Northwest.

OZARK AAU ASSOCIATION
900 WEIDMANN ROAD
TOWN & COUNTRY, MO 63017
hwcrawf@sbcglobal.net
www.aausports.org
• Jack Crider, Governor
jcrider01@sbcglobal.net
Sports Services Founded:
Organized 1935.
Description:
Missouri East and including the following counties, Camden, Dallas, Douglas, Knox, Miller, Monroe, Montgomery, Osage, Ozark, Pike, Scotland, Shelby, including the city of St. Louis and Webster. Counties of Calhoun, Greene, Jersey, Madison, Monroe and St. Clair in Illinois with reservation that all judo therein be controlled by Central District. Neighboring Districts include Arkansas, Central, Kentucky, Iowa, Missouri Valley and Southeastern.

PACIFIC AAU ASSOCIATION
PO BOX 52049
SPARKS, NV 89435
775-530-5446
Fax: 775-358-5598
www.aaupacific.com
• Matt Wiliams, Director
Sports Services Founded:
Organized 1890
Description:
The State of California, North of but not including the counties of Fresno, Madera, Mariposa, Merced, Mono and San Luis Obispo and the Counites of Churchill, Douglas, Humboldt, Lander, Lyon, Mineral, Ormsby, Pershing, Storey and Washoe in the State of Nevada. Neighboring Districts Central California, Inland Empire, Oregon, Southern Nevada and Southern Pacific.

PACIFIC NORTHWEST AAU ASSOCIATION
PO BOX 33305
SHORLINE, WA 98133
206-546-9405
nwsports@gte.net
www.pnaau.org; www.aaupacificnorthwest.org
• Mike Connors, Director
nwsports@pnaau.org
Sports Services Founded:
Organized June 1905
Description:
Washington, West of but not including Chelan, Kittitas, Okanogan and Yakima Counties and North of but not including Cowlitz, Klickitat and Skamania Counties. Neighboring Districts include Inland Empire and Oregon.

PACIFIC SOUTHWEST ASSOCIATION
6731 TOWNVIEW TERRACE
SAN DIEGO, CA 92120-1742
619-265-7675
info@aaupacificsouthwest.org
• Michael Brunker, Governor
michael.brunker@aaupacificsouthwest.org
• Maria Brunker, Registrar/Treasurer
maria.brunker@aaupacificsouthwest.org
Sports Service Founded:
Organized December 10, 1949

Description:
Original name was Southwest Pacific Border District. Name changed at 1956 Convention. Imperial and San Diego Counties.

POTOMAC VALLEY AAU ASSOCIATION
11705 CAPSTAN DRIVE
UPPER MARLBORO, MD 20772
301-374-9189
Fax: 301-324-4123
pksportss@yahoo.com
• Preston Martin, Governor
pksports@yahoo.com
• Jamie Bennett, Registrar
(240) 381-4557
braiyonna@yahoo.com
Sports Services Founded:
Organized October 15, 1929
Description:
All territory within the District of Columbia, counties of Montgomery and Prince Georges in the State of Maryland, and counties of Arlington anf Fairfax and cities of Alexandria and Falls Church in the Commonwealth of Virginia. Neighboring Districts Maryland and Virginia.

PUERTO RICO AAU ASSOCIATION
WALT DISNEY WORLD RESORT
PO BOX 10,000
LAKE BUENA VISTA, FL 32830-1000
407-934-7200
www.aaupuertorico.org
Sports Service Founded:
Organized September, 8, 1984.
Description:
Puerto Rico and U.S. Virgin Islands

SOUTH CAROLINA AAU ASSOCIATION
2428 DUNCAN STREET
COLUMBIA, SC 29205
803-799-6332
bettiq@bellsouth.net
www.scaau.org; www.aausouthcarolina.org
• Frank Pollock, Governor
(803) 957-8692
fspollock@gmail.com
• Betty Quave, Secretary
(803) 799-6332
bettiq@bellsouth.net
Sports Services Founded:
Organized December 5, 1965
Description:
State of Carolina. Neighboring Districts include Georgia and North Carolina.

SOUTH DAKOTA AAU ASSOCIATION
PO BOX 702
EAGLE BUTTE, SD 57625
wohlebera@hotmail.com
• Bob Johnson, Governor
bobj@aaumail.com
Sports Services Founded:
Organized December 4, 1964
Description:
State of South Dakota. Neighboring Districts include Iowa, Minnesota, Montana, Nebraska, North Dakota and Wyoming.

SOUTH TEXAS AAU ASSOCIATION
7314 S TRIPLE ELM
CHINA GROVE, TX 78263
210-656-7670
Fax: 210-656-7670
yayadebra@gmail.com
www.southtexasaau.org
• Augustus Labruce Bray, Governor
braylabruce@yahoo.com
Sports Services Founded:
Organized Novemeber 12, 1945
Description:
That part of the State of Texas bounded on the East by and including the counties of Burleson, Fayette, Jackson, Lavaca, Milam and on the South by the Gulf of Mexico and the Republic of Mexico; on the West by and including the counties of Schleicher, Sutton and Val Verde,

and on the North by and including the counties of Bell, Burnett, Coryell, Falls, Lampasas, Llano, Mason and Menard. Neighboring Districts include Gulf, Southwest, South Texas, New Mexico and West Texas.

SOUTHEASTERN AAU ASSOCIATION
3885 S. PERKINS RD
STE 9
MEMPHIS, TN 38118
901-362-9550
Fax: 901-362-9716
leora@aausports.org
www.seaausports.com
• Darrel Lauderdale, Governor
darrelllauderdale@sevier.org
Sports Services Founded:
Organized August 13, 1951
Description:
The State of Alabama and the State of Tennessee. Neighboring Districts include Kentucky, Virginia, North Carolina, Georgia, Southern, Arkansas and Ozark.

SOUTHERN AAU ASSOCIATION
3244 MASSACHUSETTS STREET
KENNER, LA 70065
504-464-0306
normasaau@aol.com
www.aausports.org
• Charles Domino, Governor
dominosaau@aol.com
Sports Services Founded:
Organized 1892
Description:
The State of Louisiana and the State of Mississippi. Neighboring Districts include Southeastern, Arkansas, Gulf and Southwestern.

SOUTHERN NEVADA AAU ASSOCIATION
2730 S. RANCHO DRIVE
LAS VEGAS, NV 89102
702-807-5404
www.aaulasvegas.com
• Ennis Wesley, Director
coachwesley@tarkbball.com
Sports Services Founded:
Organized January 15, 1959
Description:
Counties of Clark, Esmeralda, Lincoln, Nyle, all within the State of Nevada. Neighboring Districts include Inland Empire, Utah, Arizona, Central California, Pacific and Southern Pacific.

SOUTHERN PACIFIC AAU ASSOCIATION
PO BOX 100
LAKE BUENA VISTA, FL 32830-1000
407-93407200
www.aausouthernpacific.org; www.spa-aau.org
• Eric Elizdale, Governor
eric@socalaaubaseball.com
Sports Services Founded:
Organized November 1909
Description:
Including the counties of Los Angeles, Orange, Riverside, San Bernardino, San Luis Obispo, Santa Barbara and Ventura all within the State of California. Neighboring Districts include Arizona, Central California, Pacific, Pacific Southwest and Southern Nevada.

SOUTHWESTERN AAU ASSOCIATION
3610 S COOPER ST.
SUITE 124
ARLINGTON, TX 76010
s-lewis-mccann@sbcglobal.net
www.aausports.com
• Ivan Lewis, Governor
bushokaiusa@sbcglobal.net
Sports Services Founded:
Organized May 8, 1936
Description:
That part of the State of Texas bounded on the

South but not including the counteis of Angelina, Brown, Callahan, Coryell, Falls, Houston, Lampasas, Leon, Milam, Mills, Nacogdoches, Robertson and Shelby; on the East by the State of Louisiana, State of Arkansas and the county of Bowie, Texas; on the North by the State of Oklahoma and the county of Bowie, Texas and on the West by the counties of, but not including Foard, Hardeman, Haskell, Jones and Knox in the State of Texas. Neighboring Districts include Oklahoma, Arkansas, Southern, Gulf, South Texas and West Texas.

UTAH AAU ASSOCIATION
3731 W. SOUTH JORDAN PARKWAY #411
SOUTH JORDAN, UT 84095
801-381-0326
• Michael Killpack, Governor
killerpup@comcast.net
Sports Services Founded:
Organized November 1910
Description:
State of Utah. Neighboring Districts include Inland Empire, Wyomoing, Colorado, New Mexico, Arizona and Southern Nevada.

VIRGINIA AAU ASSOCIATION
405 LORRAINE AVENUE
FREDERICKSBURG, VA 22408
540-710-1228
Fax: 540-710-7007
aauvirginia.com
• Jeremy Bullock, Governor
(540) 408-3789
jeremy@aauvirginia.com
Sports Services Founded:
Organized December 9, 1934
Description:
State of Virginia except the Counties of Arlington and Fairfax and the cities of Alexandria and Falls Church. Neighboring Districts include Potomac Valley, West Virginia, Kentucky, Southeastern and North Carolina.

WEST TEXAS AAU ASSOCIATION
THE WALT DISNEY WORLD RESORT
PO BOX 10,000
LAKE BUENA VISTA, FL 32830-1000
407-937-7200
www.aauwesttexas.org
• Shanny Rios, Compliance Service Coordinator
(407) 828-3785
shanny@aausports.org
Sports Services Founded:
Organized 1952
Description:
All that part of the State of Texas bounded on the South side and including the counteis of Concho, Irion, McCulloch, Pecos, Reeves, Regan, San Saba, Tom Green and Upton; on the West by the State of New Mexico; on the North by the State of Oklahoma; on the East by the State of Oklahoma and by including the counties of Brown, Callahan, Foard, Hardeman, Haskell, Jones, Knox, Mills and San Saba in the State of Texas. Neighboring Districts include Oklahoma, New Mexico, South Texas and Southwestern.

WESTERN PENNSYLVANIA ASSOCIATION
jonroux@comcast.net
• Jon Roux, Director
jonroux@comcast.net
Sports Services Founded:
Organized November 16, 1917
Description:
All counties in Pennsylvania West of Bedford, Centre, Clinton, Huntingdon and Potter, and the Counties of Brooke, Hancock, Marshall and Ohio in West Virginia. Neighboring Districts include Middle Atlantic, Niagara, Maryland, West Virginia, Ohio and Lake Erie.

WISCONSIN AAU DISTRICT
2409 STOUT ROAD
SUITE ONE
MENOMONIE, WI 54751
715-231-4000
wiaau@wwt.net
• Keith Noll, Governor
slapshot@wwt.net
• Chuck Morning, Registrar
sportsref@wwt.net
Sports Services Founded:
Organized June 6, 1935
Description:
Sanctions AAU Wisconsin sporting events.
Membership Requirements:
AAU Membership

WYOMING ASSOCIATION
THE WALT DISNEY WORLD RESORT
PO BOX 10,000
LAKE BUENA VISTA, FL 32830-1000
407-934-7200
www.aausports.org
Sports Services Founded:
Organized December 9, 1968
Description:
State of Wyoming. Neighboring Districts include Montana, South Dakota, Nebraska, Colorado, Utah and Inland Empire.

AMERICA OUTDOORS/AO
P.O. BOX 10847
KNOXVILLE, TN 37939
865-558-3595
800-524-4814
Fax: 865-558-3598
www.adventurevacation.com;
www.americaoutdoors.org
• Julie Kahlfeldt, Executive Director
• Robin Brown, Communications Director
Nature of Service:
A national association representing adventure travel outfitters, tour companies and outdoor educators, the mission of America Outdoors is supporting and developing outfitting businesses in the United States.

AMERICAN HIKING SOCIETY
8605 SECOND AVENUE
SILVER SPRING, MD 20910
301-565-6704
800-972-8608
info@americanhiking.org
www.americanhiking.org
• Jack Hess, Chair
• Peter Olsen, Interim Executive Director/VP Programs
• Kim Lyons, Director of Development/Marketing
• Libby Wile, Director of Volunteer Stewardship
• Eric Albitz, Finance & Office Manager
Description:
Founded 1976. Promotes hiking and establishes, protects and maintains Foot trails. Promote and enhances interest in hiking activities.
Membership Requirements:
Pay dues.

AMERICAN LIFEGUARD ASSOCIATION
8300 BOONE BOULEVARD
5TH FLOOR
Vienna, VA 22182
703-761-6750
www.americanlifeguard.com
Sports Service Founded:
1990
Description:

Association that is currently one of the largest sponsors of Health and Safety training programs in the United States. Since our establishment in 1990 we have issued over 100,000 certifications in health and safety areas.

AMERICAN RECREATION COALITION
1200 G STREET NW
SUITE 650
WASHINGTON, DC 20005-3832
202-682-9530
Fax: 202-682-9529
bnasta@funoutdoors.com
www.funoutdoors.com/arc
• Derrick Crandall, President
dcrandall@funoutdoors.com
• Catherine Ahern, Vice President Member Services
cahern@funoutdoors.com
Member Services:
Recreation Forums - Quarterly discussions on recreation policy. Recreation Exchange - monthly meetings with key government officials. Member Letter - Periodic updates on recreation related issues and activities.
Membership Requirements:
Interest in outdoor recreation (organizations only).
Description:
Founded 1979. Works to enhance and protect outdoor recreation opportunities and resources.

AMERICAN RED CROSS NATIONAL HEADQUARTERS
431 18TH STREET NW
WASHINGTON, DC 20006
202-303-4498
800-733-2767
www.redcross.org
• Bonnie McElveen-Hunter, Chairman
• Gail McGovern, President/CEO
Description:
Sport Safety training, developed with the United States Olympic Committee, designed to meet the needs of coaches and others who work with athletes for sports-specific injury prevention and first aid (including CPR) training. Other training, safety training for swim coaches, life guarding, swimming and diving, oxygen administration, automated external defibrillation and small craft safety and basic water rescue.
Description:
Provides health and safety training nationwide. Trains organizations, staffs, instructors in sport safety training, first aid and CPR. Also delivers courses on-site to employees, students or members.

AMERICAN SPORT EDUCATION PROGRAM/ASEP
1607 NORTH MARKET STREET
PO BOX 5076
CHAMPAIGN, IL 61825-5076
217-351-5076
800-747-5698
Fax: 217-351-2674
asep@hkusa.com
www.humankinetics.com
• Rainer Martens, President
(217) 351-5076
rainer@hkusa.com
• James Schmutz, Executive Director
Description:
Since 1981, ASEP has been committed to

improving amateur sports by encouraging coaches, officials, administrators, parents, and athlets to embrace the 'Athletes first, winning second' philosophy and by providing the education to put the philosophy to work. ASEP coaching education courses and resources are used and recognized by hundreds of local, state, and national youth sport organizations; state high school associations; individual school districts; national governing bodies of Olympic sports; and colleges and universities in certifying coaches.

AMERICAN SPORTS INSTITUTE
PO BOX 1837
MILL VALLEY, CA 94942
415-383-5750
info@americansportsinstitute.org
americansportsinstitute.org
Sports Services Founded:
1985
Description:
The institute promotes the value of sport culture to society at the personal, social and international level.

AMERICAN SPORTSCASTERS ASSOCIATION, INC.
225 BROADWAY
SUITE 2030
NEW YORK, NY 10007
212-227-8080
Fax: 212-571-0556
inquiry@americansportscastersonline.com
www.americansportscastersonline.com
• Louis O. Schwartz, President/Founder
lschwa8918@aol.com
• Patrick Turturro, Associate Editor
patrickturturro@americansportscastersonline.com
Member Services:
Blog, Job Bank, Library.
Sports Services Founded:
1979
Description:
Dedicated to promoting, supporting and enhancing the work sportscasters. Acts as a resource of information and guidance for those interested in becoming sportscasters, and encourages the highest standards of ethics, integrity and professional conduct.

AMERICAN VOLKSSPORT ASSOCIATION/AVA
1001 PAT BOOKER ROAD
SUITE 101
UNIVERSAL CITY, TX 78148
210-659-2112
Fax: 210-659-1212
AVAWebmaster@ava.org
www.ava.org
• Dennis A. Michele, President
(828) 628-4343
president@ava.org
• Henry Rosales, Executive Director
execdir@ava.org
• Erin Grosso, Finance Manager
Erin@ava.org

ASSOCIATION FOR APPLIED SPORT PSYCHOLOGY/AAASP
8365 KEYSTONE CROSSING
SUITE 107
INDIANAPOLIS, IN 46240
317-205-9225
Fax: 317-205-9481

info@appliedsportpsych.org
www.appliedsportpsych.org
• Angus Mugford, President
angusmugford@gmail.com
• Amy Baltzell, President-Elect
baltzell@bu.edu
• Todd Gilson, Ph.D, Secretary/Treasurer
tgilson@niu.edu
• Natalie Durand-Bush, Publications/Information
Number of members:
2,400
Member Services:
Will certify consultants in applied sport psychology and conduct continuing education programs.
Publications:
AAASP Newsletter-3x ayear; Membership Directory Online and Directory of Graduate Programs; Journal of Applied Sport Psychology; Supervision Brochure
Sports Services Founded:
1986
Description:
Estblished to promote the science and practice of sport psychology, while providing an opportunity for individuals to share information related to theory development, research, and the provisions of psychological services to consumers.

ASSOCIATION FOR WOMEN IN SPORTS MEDIA/AWSM
7742 SPALDING DRIVE
SUITE 337
NORCROSS, GA 30092
717-703-3086
www.awsmonline.org
• Jenny Dial Creech, President
Description:
Founded 1987. Professional organization for women in sports media promoting and helping women pursue careers in sports related media.
Membership Requirements:
Annual dues.
Member Services:
Offers job bank for members; scholarship program for female journalism students. Annual convention, job fair. Also offers a mentoring program for media related occupations.

ASSOCIATION OF LUXURY SUITE DIRECTORS
10017 MCKELVEY ROAD
CINCINNATI, OH 45231
513-674-0555
Fax: 513-674-0577
feedback@alsd.com
www.alsd.com
• Bill Dorsey, Chairman
bill@alsd.com
• Greg C. Hanrahan, President
• Brain Bucciarelli, Vice President
Description:
Founded 1990. Represents more than 500 facilities and affiliates, covers the premium seat marketplace and all its facets. This includes suites, club seats, stadium clubs, stadium and arena financing, and all that comprises the corporate hospitality market.
Publications:
SEAT, quarterly. Targeted to members of the premium-seat industry.
Member Services:
Annual Conference, Quarterly Newsletter,

Suite Reference Manuals, Reference Library, Proprietary Suiteholder Studies.

ATHLETES IN ACTION
651 TAYLOR DRIVE
XENIA, OH 45385
937-352-1000
1-888-278-7233
Fax: 937-352-1001
communications@athletesinaction.org
www.athletesinaction.org
• Mark Householder, President
Sports Services Founded:
1966
Description:
Athletes in Action is uses sport as a platform for spiritual activity and growth.

ATHLETIC EQUIPMENT MANAGERS ASSOCIATION
207 E. BODMAN
BREMENT, IL 61813
217-678-1004
Fax: 217-678-1005
equipmentmanagers.org
• Mike Royster, Executive Director
(423) 755-4567
mike-royster@utc.edu
• Dan Siermine, President
(719) 333-6762
Membership Requirements:
Persons need to be actively engaged in athletic equipment management and have to take a certification exam in order to become certified.
Description:
Founded 1974. Promotes improvements in the field of athletic equipment management, and the safety of athletic equipment.

AWARDS AND PERSONALIZATION ASSOCIATION
8735 W . HIGGINGS ROAD
SUITE 300
CHICAGO, IL 60631
847-375-4800
Fax: 847-375-6480
info@awardspersonalization.org
awardspersonalization.org
• Richard Korbyl, President
(780) 438-3266
rkorbyl@columbia-awards.com
• Cody Stewart, President Elect
sales@eternitycreations.com
• Louise Ristau, Executive Director
(847) 375-4875
lristau@AwardsPersonalization.org
Description:
The association is comprised of reatilers and suppliers of awards, personalized and customized items.

BLACK ENTERTAINMENT & SPORTS LAWYERS ASSOCIATION INC
PO BOX 230794
NEWYORK, NY 10003
301-248-1818
Fax: 301-248-0700
info@besla.org
www.besla.org
• Elke F. Suber, Esq., Chairperson
• Khadijah Sharif-Drinkard, Esq., Vice President
• Emily M Dickens, Esq., Secretary
• Lawrence C. Hinkle II, Esq., President
• Chiquita Woolfolk Banks, Esq.

Description:
Founded in 1980, the organization fosters a diversity in the entertainment and sports legal profession. An annual conference held in October, up to 15 CLE credits each year.
Membership Requirements:
General lawyer (licensed), Associate member practicing in a professional capacity such as financial, producer, etc., law student interested in the area of sports and entertainment.

BLACK SPORTS AGENTS ASSOCIATION
6100 CENTER DR
SUITE 1200
LOS ANGELES, CA 90045
310-858-6565
Fax: 310-858-1520
info@sportsagentsassociation.com
www.blacksportsagents.com
• Andre Farr, Chairman/CEO
Sports Service Founded:
1996
Member Services:
Develops conferences and workshops to update members on trends in the industry with the objective of providing industry data members on trends in the industry. Organization pursues endorsement trends, careers in sports, economic development and business partnerships, and youth development.
Description:
Organization mission is to develop and strengthen the involvment, credibility the involvement, credibility, representation, image and cohesiveness of African Americans in the Sports Industry.

BLACK WOMEN IN SPORT FOUNDATION
4300 MONUMENT ROAD
PHILADELPHIA, PA 19131
215-877-1925 EXT 320
Fax: 215-877-1942
info@blackwomeninsport.org
www.blackwomeninsport.org
• Paulette Branson, Executive Director
Sports Service Founded:
1992
History
The Black Women in Sport Foundation was founded by Tina Sloan Green, Alpha Alexander, Nikki Franke, and Linda Greene as a nonprofit organization dedicated to increasing the involvement of black women and girls in all aspects of sport, including athletics, coaching and administration. The Foundation is resolute in facilitating the involvement of women of color in every aspect of sport in the United States and around the world, through the hands-on development and management of grass roots level outreach programs.
Description:
Dedicated to facilitating the involvement of Black women in sports in the United States through outreach and grassroots intitiatives.

CANADIAN SOCIETY FOR PSYCHOMOTOR LEARNING & SPORT PSYCHOLOGY
360-125 UNIVERISTY PRIVATE
OTTAWA, ON, CANADA K1N 6N5
gvangyn@uvic.ca
www.scapps.org
• Chris Shields, President
• Tony Carlsen, Secretary/Treasurer
• Melanie Gregg, Secretary Communications
• Kelly Arbour, Director Sports& Exercise Psycology
• Nicola Hodges, Director, Motor Learning & Motor Control
Member Services:
Young Scientist Awards.
Publications:
Journal of Exercise, Movement, and Sport (annual)
Membership Requirements:
Membership fee.
Description:
Founded 1969. Disseminates information in areas of sport psychology and psychomotor learning, primarily through annual conference.

CANADIAN SPORTING GOODS ASSOCIATION
10-225 EAST MALL
UNIT 1272
TORONTO, ON, CANADA M9B 0A9
866-496-6805
info@csga.ca
www.csga.ca
• Julian Savory, President/Chief Operating Officer
• Kelly Falls, Director of Sales & Marketing
• Eric Keeping, Social Media Coordinator
Sports Services Founded:
Incorporated in 1945.
Description:
A professional organization for the Canadian sporting goods industry. It was founded to support and promote the growth of the Canadian sporting goods industry and to serve the interests of its memebers. The objective is to conduct quality trade shows and to provide an Industry forum responsive to the professional needs of its members and to initiate programs designed to stimulate sports activity participation.

CENTER FOR THE STUDY OF SPORT IN SOCIETY
360 HUNTINGTON AVENUE
42 BELVIDERE
BOSTON, MA 2115
617-373-4025
Fax: 617-373-8574
www.sportinsociety.org
• Dan Lebowitz, Executive Director
da.lebowitz@northeastern.edu
• Deb Jencunas, Senior Associate Director
• Lisa Markland, Assistant Director of Training
l.markland@northeastern.edu
• Richard E. Lapchick, Founder/Director Emeritus
(407) 823-4887
Sports Services Founded:
1984
Description:
The Center for the Study of Sport in Society, utilizing the power and appeal of sport; works locally, nationally and globally to identify and address social problems in sport and in society. They conduct research, develop programs that offer solutions, and educate and advocate on the emerging issues.

CHALLENGE ASPEN
PO BOX 6639
SNOWMASS VILLAGE, CO 81615
970-923-0578
Fax: 970-923-7338
info@challengeaspen.org
www.challengeaspen.com
• Jeff Hauser, Chief Executive Officer
(970) 923-0578
jhauser@challengeaspen.org
Description:
Founded 1995. Challenge Aspen is dedicated to impacting lives by presenting meaningful recreational and cultural experiences to individuals faced with mental or physical challenges. Committed to creating a community of like-minded individuals, fostering confidence and self-esteem among their participants in an effort to advance the quality of life of those with physical and mental disabilities. Their aim is to carefully orchestrate life changing recreational adventures, giving participants the courage to learn something new, trust their own abilities and carry that ideal forward, reaching toward goals in other areas of their lives.

CLUB MANAGERS ASSOCIATION OF AMERICA
1733 KING STREET
ALEXANDRIA, VA 22314
703-739-9500
cmaa@cmaa.org
www.cmaa.org
• Jeff Morgan, Chief Executive Officer
jeff.morgan@cmaa.org
• Margaret Meleney, Chief Financial Officer
margaret.meleney@cmaa.org
Member Services:
Executive career services; managerial openings lists; mid-management job opportunities listing; interim management and consultant service; outplacement service; certification program; continuing education services; group insurance programs; governmental affairs, bookmart and publications.
Membership Requirements:
General Manager, Manager, Assistant Manager, executive of private membership club.
Sports Services Founded:
1927
Description:
CMAA is a professional association for managers of membership clubs, such as country, city, athletic, faculty, yacht, town and military clubs.

COACHING ASSOCIATION OF CANADA
1155 LOLA STREET
SUITE 201
OTTAWA, ON, CANADA K1K 4C1
613-235-5000
Fax: 613-235-9500
coach@coach.ca
www.coach.ca
• Lorraine Lafraniere, Chief Executive Officer
(613) 235-5000
llafreniere@coach.ca
Sports Services Founded:
1970
Description:
An amateur sport organization with the mandate to improve the effectiveness of coaching across all levels of the sport system. Also to enhance the experiences of

all Canadian athletes through quality coaching.

DESTINATION MARKETING ASSOCIATION INTERNATIONAL
2025 M STREET NW
SUITE 500
WASHINGTON, DC 20036
202-296-7888
Fax: 202-296-7889
info@destinationmarketing.org
www.destinationmarketing.org
• Joseph Marinelli, Chair
mgehrisch@destinationmarketing.org
• Jack Johnson, Chief Advocacy Officer
(202) 835-4217
jjohnson@destinationmarketing.org
Number of members:
4,100 professionals
Member Services:
Data base of meetings, conventions and trade shows.
Description:
Founded 1914 as the International Association of Convention Bureaus. Seeks to foster professionalism and education, to serve as a forum for communication in the industry, advocate on matters of concern to the industry. and encourage recognition and growth of tourism destinations.

DWARF ATHLETIC ASSOCIATION OF AMERICA
300 CENTER DRIVE
SUITE G #150
SUPERIOR, CO 80027
415-915-9572
www.daaa.org
• Lucy Woika, President
(415) 244-9756
• Ted Hannes, Vice President/Fundraising Chair
• Megan Schimmel, Treasurer
• Jeremy Harrison, Sports technical director
jeremy.harrison@daaa.org
Sports Services Founded:
1985
Description:
Formed to develop, promote and provide quality amateur level athletic opportunities for athletes with dwarfism in the United States. The DAAA mission is to encourage people with dwarfism to participate in sports regardless of their level of skills.

EUROPEAN ASSOCIATION FOR SPORT MANAGEMENT, THE
INSTITUTE FOR SPORTS STUDIES
ZERNIKEPLEIN 17
AS GROUNINGEN, HOLLAND 9747
31-612-189505
www.easm.net
• Per-Gâ€ran Fahlstrâ€m, President
• Ruth Crabtree, Vice President
• Gerco Van Dalfsen, Secretary General
• Claas Christian Germelmann, Treasurer
• Bo Carlsson, Scientific Committee
Editors Note:
The phone number listed is from the Portugal office.
Description:
An independent association for individuals or members representing associations, involved or interested in sport management. The association aims to promote, stimulate and encourage studies, research, scholarly writing and professional developments in the field of sport management.

EVENT SERVICE PROFESSIONALS ASSOCIATION
191 CLARKSVILLE ROAD
PRINCETON JUNCTION, NJ 8550
609-799-3712
Fax: 609-799-7032
info@espaonline.org
www.espaonline.org
• Paul Ruby, CMP, President
paul.ruby@sheraton.com
• Lynn McCullough, Executive Director
lmccullough@espaonline.org
• Nicole Lauzon, Membership Coordinator
nlauzon@espaonline.org
• Vikki Hurley-Schubert, Public Relations Manager
vschubert@cmasolutions.com
Description:
Organization comprised of convention Managers and Directors of Convention Centers, Hotels and Convention Bureaus.

FELLOWSHIP OF CHRISTIAN ATHLETES
8701 LEEDS ROAD
KANSAS CITY, MO 64129
816-921-0909
800-289-0909
Fax: 816-921-8755
fca@fca.org
www.fca.org
• Shane Williams, President/Chief Executive Officer
• Ken Williams, Executive Director - National Support Center
• Dan Britton, Executive Vice President - International Ministry
• Jeff Martin, Executive VP Ministry Programs
Description:
Organization promotes Christian faith through platform of athletics. FCA Huddle groups meet regularly on junior high, senior high and college campuses for Bible study, prayer and other faith-based activities.
Year Founded:
1954
Publications:
FCA In Action magazine

INDUSTRIAL FABRICS ASSOCIATION INTERNATIONAL
1801 COUNTY ROAD B WEST
ROSEVILLE, MN 55113
651-222-2508
800-225-4324
Fax: 651-631-9334
generalinfo@ifai.com
www.ifai.com
• Mary C Hennesy, President and CEO
(651) 255-6986
mjhennessy@ifai.com
• Katie Bradford, MFC, IFM, Chairman
• Steve L. Ellington, 1st Vice President
Member Services:
Provides information for technical, promotional, governmental and marketing assistance to its members.
Publications:
Advanced Textiles Source, online; Marine Fabricator; In Tents; Geosynthetics; Fabric Architecture; InTents, bi-monthly; Specialty Fabrics Review.
Membership Requirements:
Members are firms who manufacture industrial fabric products and firms who supply these manufacturers.
Sports Services Founded:
1912
Description:
Trade association with more than 2,000 member companies that represent the international specialty fabrics marketplace.

INSTITUTE FOR INTERNATIONAL SPORT
UNIVERSITY OF RHODE ISLAND
3045 KINGSTOWN ROAD
PO BOX 1710
KINGSTON, RI 02881-1710
401-874-2375
800-447-9889
Fax: 401-874-2375
info@internationalsport.org
www.internationalsport.org
• Daniel E Doyle, Jr, Founder/Executive Director
ddoyle@internationalsport.com
Description:
Founded 1986. Administers programs in international sports such as Sportscorps, National Sportsmanship Day, the World Scholar-Athlete Games, and the International Scholar-Athlete Hall of Fame.

INTERNATIONAL ASSOCIATION FOR SPORTS AND LEISURE FACILITIES
EUPEWER STR 70
KOLN, GERMANY 50933
info@iaks.org
• Klaus Meinel, Secretary General
meinel@iaks.org
• Silke Bardenheuer, Director of Operations
bardenheuer@iaks.org
• Thomas Kick, Marketing and Event Management
kick@iaks.org
Sports Services Founded:
1965
Description:
A non profit organization operating in the field of sports and leisure activities. The IAKS's task is to collect, evaluate and disseminiate information on the design, construction, equipping and maintenance of facilities for sport, games and recreation.
Publications:
sb Magazine: architecture of sports and leisure facilites, bi-monthly.

INTERNATIONAL ASSOCIATION FOR SPORTS INFORMATION
UNIVERSITY OF CALGARY LAW LIBRARY
2500 UNIVERSITY DRIVE NW
CALGARY ALBERTA, CANADA T2N 1N4
403-220-6097
gghent@ucalgary.ca
www.iasi.org
• Gretchen Ghent, President
Publications:
Newsletter annually, providing list of information means. Also publishes directory of international sports governing bodies.
Membership Requirements:
Corporate: $75. Personal: $50.
Description:
Founded 1960. A unique international association that brings together a worldwide network of information experts, librarians, sports sceintists and managers of sport libraries, information and documentation centres. THe primary purpose is to stimulate and support activities in the field of

international documentation, and promote the dissemination of information to physical educators, sports scientists, documentalists and sport researchers.

INTERNATIONAL ASSOCIATION OF VENUE MANAGERS/IAVM
635 FRITZ DRIVE
COPPELL, TX 75019-4442
972-906-7441
Fax: 972-906-7418
www.iavm.org
• Brad Mayne, President and CEO
(972) 538-1021
brad.mayne@iavm.org
• Ronald Melton, Chief Financial Officer/Chief Operations Officer
(972) 538-1034
ronald.melton@iavm.org
• Doug Booher, CFE, 1st Vice Chair
Sports Services Founded:
1924
IAVM History Task Force:
The History Task Force is an IAVM committee whose objective is to emphasize the importance of collecting historical materials served in the IAVM archives at the University of Texas- Austin.
IAAM Foundation:
A non-profit educational organization devoted to providing education and information services to the public assembly facility management profession and to exploring issues relevant to the profession.
Description:
Comprises leaders who represent a diverse industry such as entertainment, sports, conventions, trade, hospitality and tourism. These leaders manage, or provide products and services to public assembly facilities like arenas, ampitheaters, auditoriums, convention centers/exhibit halls, performing arts venues, stadiums and university complexes.

INTERNATIONAL LIVE EVENTS ASSOCIATION
330 N. WABASH AVENUE
SUITE 2000
CHICAGO, IL 60611-4267
312-321-6853
800-688-4737
Fax: 317-673-6953
info@ileahub.com
www.ileahub.com
• Christie Pruyn, Executive Director
cpruyn@ileahub.com
Member Services:
Awards program; professional accreditation; ISES, bulletin board service; annual Conference for Professional Development.
Membership Requirements:
Pay dues. Be involved directly or indirectly in the special events business.
Description:
Founded 1987. Serves to educate, advance, and promote the creative events industry and its network of professionals along with related industries. Strives to uphold the integrity of the creative events profession to the general public throughout Principles of Professional Conduct and Ethics; acquires and disseminates useful business information; fosters spirit of cooperation among members and other special events professionals; Cultivates high standards of business practices.

KROENKE SPORTS ENTERPRISES
1000 CHOPPER CIRCLE
DENVER, CO 80204
303-405-1100
GuestRelations@pepsicenter.com
www.pepsicenter.com
• E Stanley Kroenke, Owner/Govenor
• Mark Waggoner, Sr VP Finance
Nature of Sports Service:
Organization owns NHL's Colorado Avalanche, NBA'S Denver Nuggets, NLL's Colorado Mammoth, AFL's Colorado Rapids.

LA84 FOUNDATION
2141 WEST ADAMS BOULEVARD
LOS ANGELES, CA 90018
323-730-4600
Fax: 323-730-9637
info@la84.org
la84.org
• Renata Simril, President/CEO
renata@la84.org
• Frank M. Sanchez, Chairman
• Wayne Wilson, VP Education Services
wwilson@la84.org
• Anna-Marie Jones, VP Grants/Programs
anne-marie@la84.org
Description:
The Foundation was established to manage Southern California's share of the surplus from the highly successful 1984 Olympic Games in Los Angeles. The Foundation received $93 million at its inception. Since it began operations in 1985, it has invested more than $200 million in sports programs serving more than two and a half million youth in the eight Southern California counties of Los Angeles, Imperial, Orange, Riverside, San Bernardino, San Diego, Santa Barbara and Ventura. Its headquarters is located in the historic Britt House near downtown Los Angeles where it houses the world's premier sports library and meeting facilities. The Foundati

LICENSING INDUSTRY MERCHANDISERS' ASSOCIATION/LIMA
350 FIFTH AVENUE
SUITE 4019
NEW YORK, NY 10118
212-244-1944 EXT 113
info@licensing.org
www.licensing.org
• Charles Riotto, President
(212) 244-1944
info@licensing.org
• Maura Regan, Executive Vice President
(212) 244-1944
mregan@licensing.org
Description:
Founded 1985. Devoted to promoting professionalism in licensing through seminars, exhibits, research, regional and International meetings and publishing.
Membership Requirements:
Four categories of membership: manufacturers, licensers, support groups, retailers. Annual dues for calendar year.
Member Services:
Reference library, seminars; insurance; discount programs; mail rosters, Directories, sample agreements, annual survey on the size of the Licensing Industry.

MACCABI USA/SPORTS FOR ISRAEL
1511 WALNUT STREET
SUITE 401
PHILADELPHIA, PA 19102
215-561-6900
Fax: 215-561-5470
maccabi@maccabiusa.com
www.maccabiusa.com
• Robert Spivak, Chairman
• Sara Feinstein, Marketing Director
sfeinstein@maccabiusa.com
• Julie Churylo, Office Manager
jchurylo@maccabiusa.com
Sports Services Founded:
1948
Description:
The volunteer organization seeks to enrich the lives of Jewish youth in the United States, Israel and the Dispora through athletic, cultural and educational programs. We develop, promote and support international, national and regional athletic based activities and facilities.

MACCABI WORLD UNION
KFAR HAMACCABIAH
RAMAT GAN, Israel 52105
www.maccabi.org
• Eyal Tiberger, Executive Director
eyalt@maccabi.org
• Tzachi Eshkenazi, Controller
tzachi@maccabi.org
• Ilana Ben Namer Kevehazi, Assistnat to the ED
ilana@maccabi.org
Description:
A global Jewish organization spanning five continents and more than 50 countries, with clubs serving as community centers, providing a diversity of educational, cultural, social and sports activities. The Maccabi World Union comprises of six confederations. They are: Maccabi Israel, European Maccabi confederation, confederation Maccabi North America, confederation Maccabi Latin America, Maccabi South Africa and Maccabi Australia.
Membership:
400,000

MIDWESTERN REPRESENTATIVES ASSOCIATION
9450 TREETOP DRIVE
GALESBURG, MI 49053
269-200-3322
MRA@midwestreps.org
www.midwestreps.org
• Bonnie Rathbun, Executive Director
• Tim Simonson, President
Number of members:
115+
Publications:
Newsletter, quarterly; Store Directory, annually; Buyers Guide, annually.
Membership Requirements:
Open to manufacturers representatives who have been in the region for at least one year and/or upon approval of application by membership committee. Initiation fee and annual dues required.
Sports Services Founded:
1965
Description:
A Snow/Outdoor Sports organization representing states from as far east as New York and as far west as Minnesota. The

multi sports

members of the MRA represent products such as ski/snowboard equipment and apparel, outdoor camping/climbing and water sports products. MRA members serve retailers from Illinois, Wisconsin, Indiana, lower/upper Michigan, Ohio and Kentucky

NATIONAL ALLIANCE OF AFRICAN AMERICAN ATHLETES
PO BOX 60743
HARRISBURG, PA 17106-0743
717-312-8162
Fax: 717-260-3877
info@naaaa.com
www.naaaa.com
• J. Everette Pearsall, Executive Director
everette@naaaa.com
• Kevin Clark, Chair
kevin@naaaa.com
Sports Services Founded:
1989
Description:
The goal is to empower young African American males through athletics, education and public programs.

NATIONAL ASSOCIATION FOR GIRLS AND WOMEN IN SPORT
1900 ASSOCIATION DRIVE
RESTON, VA 20191-1599
703-476-3453
800-213-7193
Fax: 703-476-4566
www.aahperd.org/nagwa
• Lynda Randsell, President
• Karen Appleby, VP Marketing
• Charity Bryan, VP Research
Number of members:
4,000
Member Services:
Annual convention; leadership clinics; newsletters; informationpackets, and educational programs.
Publications:
Catalog of publications.
Description:
Founded 1899. Nonprofit, educational organization designed to serve the needs of administrators, teachers, coaches, leaders, and participants of sports programs for girls and women. Its goals include: (1) recruiting, developing, and promoting women for leadership programs, (2) serving as an advocate and promoting women's full participation in physical activity and sport leadership, (3) serving as an advocate for the initiation and enhancement of quality programs of sport and physical activity designed to accommodate females of all ages, races, creeds, ethnic origins, economic levels, abilities, and interests, and (4) promulgating the professi

NATIONAL ASSOCIATION OF POLICE ATHLETIC/ACTIVITES LEAGUES (NATL PAL)
1662 N US HIGHWAY 1
SUITE C
JUPITER, FL 33469
561-745-5535
Fax: 561-745-3147
www.nationalpal.org
• Mike Dillhyon, Executive Director
mdillhyon@nationalpal.org
• Christopher Hill, President
Sports Services Founded:
1914

Description:
As a membership organization, National PAL provides Chapters with resources and opportunities to grow their own programs and enhance the quality of individual programming. These resources include funding opportunities through various grants, general liability protection programs, programming opportunities through affiliate organizations, and goods and services provided by corporate partners and supporting organizations. In addition, National PAL provides Chapter members opportunities to bring their young athletes together to compete in a championship environment in several sports.
Member Services:
Training seminars, produces public service announcements, accident and liability insurance, group purchasing programs, fund-raising programs. Sponsors competition on national level for many sports.
Number of members:
360 (chapters).

NATIONAL ASSOCIATION OF SPORTS OFFICIALS
2017 LATHROP AVENUE
RACINE, WI 53405
262-632-5448
Fax: 262-632-5460
www.naso.org
• Barry Mano, President
• Bill Carollo, Treasurer
Sports Services Founded:
1980
Membership Requirements:
Regular - sports officials; sponsorship - companies; associate - anyone with an interest in sports. Fees are: $94 United States citizens; $121 Canada/Mexico; and $153 for any other.
Description:
The only national organization solely dedicated to officiating with membership at all levels of sport. From the National Football League to Pop Warner, from Major League Baseball to Little League of America, from the National Basketball Association to youth and recreational programs across America, NASO is there.
Publications:
REFEREE Magazine, monthly; IT'S OFFICIAL, monthly newsletter. Manuals. Cyberspace - The NASO Locker room.
Member Services:
Cassettes, videos and books; travel; discounts; $3 million liability insurance protection. Public service ads.
Number of members:
16,000

NATIONAL ASSOCIATION OF UNDERWATER INSTRUCTORS
9030 CAMDEN FIELD PKWY
RIVERVIEW, FL 33578
813-628-6284
800-553-6284
Fax: 813-628-8253
nauihq@naui.org
www.naui.org
• Jim Bram, President
• Jed Livingstone, VP Training & Development
• James R Yaufman II, Chief Information Officer

• Kathy Brownlow, Manager of Operations
• Randy Shaw, Manager Training Department
Member Services:
Certification, educational support material, instructor/training courses, leadership training courses, international conference on underwater education, retail store support program.
Publications:
SOURCES, THE JOURNAL OF; UNDERWATER EDUCATION, quarterly.
Membership Requirements:
Must be certified NAUI scuba instructor, pass the applicable leadership exam by 75% score or better, meet all course administrative requirements, CPR and First Aid sertified, meet all course prerequisites, and complete all portions of the course.
Description:
Founded 1959. Works to promote certification of scuba diving instructors and provides certification credentials to qualified NAUI scuba divers.

NATIONAL CLUB ASSOCIATION
1201 15TH STREET NW
SUITE 450
WASHINGTON, DC 20005
202-822-9822
800-625-6221
Fax: 202-822-9808
info@nationalclub.org
www.nationalclub.org
• Susanne R. Wegrzyn, President & Chief Executive Officer
wegrzyn@nationalclub.org
• Thomas Gaston, Vice Chairman
• Samuel P. Bell, Treasurer
• Kirk O. Reese, Secretary
• Thomas E Gaston Jr. CCM, Chairman
Description:
Since 1961, The National Club Association (NCA) has served as the primary advocate for private clubs, representing their business, legal and legislative interests, while providing a wealth of invaluable resources to address educational needs of clubs related to operations, model club practices and effective leadership.
Membership Requirements:
Regular membership limited to private social, athletic and recreational membership clubs or organizations.
Publications:
CLUB DIRECTOR, quarterly magazine; NCAConnect, monthly newsletter; The National Club Association Smartbrief, weekly news digest; Washington Weekly Update, weekly newsletter.
Number of members:
7,000

NATIONAL CONGRESS OF STATE GAMES
1631 MESA AVENUE
SUITE E
COLORADO SPRINGS, CO 80906
719-634-7333
Fax: 719-634-5198
stori@thesportscorp.org
www.stategames.org
• Marc Riker, Board President
• Kevin Cummings, Vice President
Sports Services Founded:
1986
Membership Requirements:

To conduct or develop a Summer or Winter state game in your state join the National Congress of State Games yearly. NCSG has a yearly symposium and 2 board meetings a year.
Publications:
State of the Games Newsletter, quarterly.
Description:
A membership organization that has 37 Summer State Games and 14 Winter State Games organization and a community based membership of the United States Olympic Committee.

NATIONAL FEDERATION OF PROFESSIONAL TRAINERS
PO BOX 4579
LAFAYETTE, IN 479053
800-729-6378
Fax: 765-471-7369
info@nfpt.com
www.nfpt.com
• Ron Clark, CEO and Founder
• Angie Pattengale, Director of Certification
• Ryan Farrell, Marketing Coordinator
• April Pattee, Director of Customer Service
• Jason Pattee, Distribution Manager
• Charles DeFrancesco, Director of Continuing Education
Description:
Personal fitness trainer certification, credibility and support. Internationally recognized Personal Fitness Trainer Certification. Over 200 professional examination sites around the world. Professional support magazine
Publications:
OnFitness Magazine, quarterly publication that circulates to over 75,000 people.
Member Services:
Personal fitness trainer certification.
Membership Requirements:
No formal education pre-requisites.

NATIONAL GYM ASSOCIATION INC./NGA, THE
PO BOX 970579
COCONUT CREEK, FL 33097
954-344-8410
Fax: 954-344-8412
info@nationalgym.com
www.nationalgym.com
• Richard Yaldizian, Medical Director
• Caryn Nistico, Nutrician Director
Description:
Provides the public and Fitness Professionals with the most advanced update fitness training program and principals in the industry. These fitness principals are our guiding light, which provides you with the best in personal fitness training certification, heatlh, nutrition, continuing education programs, along with being one of the only natural bodybuilding organizations.

NATIONAL INTRAMURAL RECREATIONAL SPORTS ASSOCIATION/NIRSA
4185 SW RESEARCH WAY
CORVALLIS, OR 97333-1067
541-766-8211
Fax: 541-766-8284
nirsa@nirsa.org
www.nirsa.org
• Pat Watts, Interim Executive Director
(541) 766-8211

• Cheri Christenson, Director of Professional Development
(541) 766-8211
karen@nirsa.org
Description:
Founded 1950. Offers the recreational sports administrator a variety of resources through individuals and information resource centers to understand all aspects of recreational sports programming.
Membership Requirements:
Institutional - College/University, Military or park/recreation departments; Professional - must be associated with administration of recreational sports programming field. Student - graduate/undergraduate in sport management field. Associate business with an active interest and market segment applicable to recreational sports.
Publications:
Recreational Sports Directory, published annual; Recreational Sports Journal; NIRSA Know Newsletter

NATIONAL RECREATION & PARK ASSOCIATION
22377 BELMONT RIDGE ROAD
ASHBURN, VA 20148
703-858-0784
800-626-6772
Fax: 703-858-0794
info@nrpa.org
www.nrpa.org
• Barbara Tulipane, President and CEO
• M. Lauren Yost, VP Operations
• Ted Mattingly, Director of Facilities and Admin
Description:
Founded 1965. Promotes the value of recreation and parks in the lives of individuals. Advocates the development and improvement of parks and recreational areas. Advances and improves recreation and park leadership. Educates the public on recreation and park matters beneficial to the communities and to the nation, thereby improving social, moral and industrial conditions.
Membership Requirements:
Annual dues for agencies - based on population of each jurisdiction; annual dues for individuals, based on salary.
Publications:
P&R Magazine; NRPA Cybrary; Journal of Leisure Research; Journal of Park & Recreation Administration; Schole; Therapeutic Recreation Journal; LRS Abstracts
Number of members:
19,000

NATIONAL SENIOR GAMES ASSOCIATION
PO BOX 82059
BATON ROUGE, LA 70884
225-766-6800
nsga@nsga.com
www.nsga.com
• Marc T. Riker, CEO
• Becky Wesley, Vice President of Association Relations
• Collen Keith, Senior Director of Business Affairs
• Jay B. Hall, Senior Director of Business Affairs
• Stephen Rodriguez, Chairman

• Kate Amack, Vice Chair
• Monica Paul, Treasurer
Description:
The National Senior Games Association (NSGA) is a not-for-profit organization founded in 1987 that is dedicated to promoting health and wellness for adults 50 and over through education, fitness and sport. The Organization governs the National Senior Games, the largest multi-sport championship in the world for seniors, and other national senior athletic events. NSGA is an umbrella for 54 Member State Organizations across the United States, Canada, and Mexico that host Senior Games or Senior Olympics.

NATIONAL SPORTS FOUNDATION/NATIONAL SPORTS MUSEUM
415 BARLOW COURT
JOHNS CREEK, GA 30022-6636
678-417-0041
Fax: 678-417-0043
www.natlsportsfoundation.com
• Ed Harris, President/Executive Director
(678) 417-0041
Description:
Founded 1993 with the mission of preserving America's sports heritage. Enhances and supports amateur and professional sports organizations in America, annually honors athletes and sports journalists for lifetime achievement, maintains National Sports Library and produces educational programs and exhibitions.
Publications:
Legend - Quarterly magazine

NATIONAL SPORTS MARKETING NETWORK
BOX 1994
BROOKLINE, MA 2445
617-713-2600
www.sportsmarketingnetwork.com
• Jennifer L Karpf, Founder/President
jenkarpf@sportsmarketingnetwork.com
Member Services:
Individual Membership, $100 per person/per year; Individual Plus, $150 per person/per year; Corporate Membership, $500 per package/per year, Corporate Plus Membership, $1,000 per company/per year
Description:
Founded 1998. The National Sports Marketing Network is the professional trade organization established to serve the needs of sports business professionals across the country. With active membership chapters across the country, NSMN organizes monthly networking events, educational programming; offers industry discounts on publication and conferences; and assists with job placement/career services. Membership is open for sports marketing professionals only.
Membership Requirements:
To qualify for NSMN membership, the applicant must have current or prior work experience in sports or a related discipline. NSMN doesn't accept entry-level applicants who have no prior sports business, marketing or public relations experience.
Number of Members:
6,000+ individual and corporate members

NORTH AMERICAN SOCIETY FOR SPORT MANAGEMENT
C/O DR. ROBIN AMMON JR.
NASSM BUSINESS OFFICE
135 WINTERWOOD DR
BUTLER, PA 16001
724-482-6277
businessoffice@nassm.com
www.nassm.com
• Robin Ammon, President
(724) 482-6277
• Robert Ammon, NASSM Business Office Manager
Nature of Sports Service:
Serves to promote, stimulate and encourage study, research, scholarly writing and professional development in the area of sport management. Members are concerned about theoretical and applied aspects of management theory and practice specifically related to sport, exercise, dance and play throughout all sectors of the population.
Publications:
JOURNAL OF SPORT MANAGEMENT, four times annually.

NORTH AMERICAN SOCIETY FOR THE SOCIOLOGY OF SPORT
BOWLING GREEN UNIVERSITY
BOWLING GREEN, OH 43403
419-372-2217
Fax: 419-372-8306
lv3@umail.umd.edu
www.nasss.org
• Genevieve Rail, President
• Brenda Riemem, Treasurer
Publications:
NASSS NEWSLETTER, quarterly; SPORT SOCIOLOGY JOURNAL, quarterly.
Membership Requirements:
Pay membership dues.
Description:
Founded 1977. Provides forum for communication and exchange of ideas and research and generally promotes benefits of study of sociology as it relates to sport in the U.S., and throughout the world.

NORTH AMERICAN SPORTS FEDERATION
1081 PEBBLE COURT
MECHANICSBURG, PA 17050
717-737-5800
Fax: 717-737-5800
joanna@specialmarkets.com
www.nasf.net
• Andy Loechner, President
aloechner@verizon.net
Description:
Governing body for amateur sports for adults and youth in the sports of softball, volleyball, flag and touch football, soccer, basketball and baseball, body building, and iron sports.

NORTH COUNTRY TRAIL ASSOCIATION
229 EAST MAIN STREET
LOWELL, MI 49331
616-897-5987
866-445-3628
HQ@northcountrytrail.org
www.northcountrytrail.org
Sports Services Founded:
1981
Description:
Develops, maintains, preserves and promotes the North Country National Scenic Trail through a national network of volunteers, chapters, partner organizations and governmental agencies.

ORCA BAY SPORTS & ENTERTAINMENT
800 GRIFFITH WAY
VANCOUVER, BC, CANADA V6B 6G1
604-899-7400
888-GO-CANUKS
Fax: 604-899-7401
www.canucks.com
• John E. McCaw, Jr., Chairman/Governor, NHL
• Victor De Bonis, COO
• Harvey Jones, VP/Genral Manager
• Mike P. Gills, President/General Manager Canucks
Nature of Sports Service:
Parent company of the Vancouver Canucks (NHL) and General Motors Place.

OUTDOOR INDUSTRY ASSOCIATION
4909 PEARL EAST CIRCLE
SUITE 300
BOULDER, CO 80301
303-444-3353
Fax: 303-444-3284
info@outdoorindustry.org
www.outdoorindustry.org
• Frank Hugelmeyer, President
(303) 327-3507
fhugelmeyer@outdoorindustry.org
• Lori Herrera, Executive Vice President/COO
(303) 327-3521
lherrera@outdoorindustry.org
Number of Members:
1,200.
Sports Services Founded:
1989
Description:
Provides trade services for over 4,000 manufacturers, distributors, suppliers, sales representatives and retailers in the Outdoor Industry. Members include brands like Black Diamond, Columbia Sportswear, Eagle Creek, JanSport, Johnson Outdoors, Kelty, Malden Mills, Merrell, Mountain Hardwear, Patagonia, Timberland, The North Face, Perception, Pearl Izumi, Salomon, Swiss Army Brands, W.L.Ã†Gore, Yakima, and numerous others.

PALACE SPORTS & ENTERTAINMENT, INC.
5 CHAMPIONSHIP DRIVE
AUBURN HILLS, MI 48326
248-377-0100
Fax: 248-377-2154
www.palacenet.com
• Tom Gore, Owner
• Dennis Mannion, President
• Jeffrey Ajluni, Vice President
Description:
Owns and operates the NBA's Detroit Pistons, the WNBA's Detroit Shock, and the NHL's Tampa Bay Lightning.

PRO ATHLETES OUTREACH
PO BOX 801
PALO ALTO, CA 94302
650-206-2962
Fax: 650-206-2959
office@pao.org
www.pao.org
• Norm Evans, CEO
• Steve Stenstrom, President
• Mike Outlaw, Managing Director
Member Services:
Four annual Christian leadership training conferences, information available on request.
Publications:
Changing Athletes & Coaches From The Inside Out, quarterly
Sports Services Founded:
1971
Description:
A leadership and life skills development organization committed solely to meeting the unique needs of pro athletes, coaches and their families. Also has helped thousands of active and retired athletes and their spouses find lasting solutions for hte intense pressures of a career in professional sports.

PROFESSIONAL PADDLESPORTS ASSOCIATION
7432 ALBAN STATION BLVD
STE B-232
SPRINGFIELD, VA 22150
703-451-3864
www.propaddle.com

SCHOOL SPORT FEDERATION, INTERNATIONAL
59 RUE ARCHIMEDE
BRUSSELS, BELGIUM 1000
www.isfsports.org
• Laurent Petrynka, President
• Hrvoje Custonja, CEO & Secretary General
Description:
Founded: 1965. International governing body for school sports.

SHAPE AMERICA SOCIETY OF HEALTH AND PHYSICAL EDUCATORS
1900 ASSOCIATION DRIVE
RESTON, VA 20191-1598
703-476-3400
800-213-7193
Fax: 703-476-9527
www.shapeamerica.org
• Dolly Lambdin, President
• Gale Wiedow, Past President
• E. Paul Roetert, CEO
Publications:
Journal of Physical education, Recreation & Dance (JOPERD); Research Quarterly for Exercise & Sport (RQES); STRATEGIES; Women in Sport & Physical Activity Journal; International Journal of Health Education; The Pulse Online Newsletter; American Journal of Health Education; UPDATE
Description:
Founded 1938. Promotes school, community and national programs of leisure services and recreation education.

SPORTING GOODS AGENTS ASSOCIATION
1601 FREEHANVILLE DRIVE
SUITE 300
MOUNT PROSPECT, IL 60056
800-815-5422
Fax: 847-391-9627
www.nsga.org
• Jeff Brusati, Director
• Matt Carlson, President & CEO

Number of members:
1,300
Member Services:
Procurement of product lines for members through manufacturers using the Direct Mail service. Placement service for people seeking sales jobs with established rep agencies. Brochures aimed at start-up manufactures as well as the role of agents within the industry.
Publications:
Membership Roster and diskette, at cost of $275. Q&A Booklet for agents and manufacturers ($10)
Membership Requirements:
One year as an agent in the sporting goods field, with two or more established lines.
Description:
Founded 1934. Keeps members informed of industry functions and pertinent legislation

SPORTING GOODS MANUFACTURERS ASSOCIATION
8505 FENTON STREET
SUITE 211
SILVER SPRINGS, MD 20910
301-495-6321
Fax: 307-495-6322
info@sgma.com
• Tom Cove, President/CEO
(301) 495-6321
• Chip Baldwin, CFO
• Ron Rosenbaum, SVP of Marketing & Business Management
• Bill Sells, VP Of Government Relations
• Jan Ciambor, Office Manager
• V J Mayor, Director, Marketing & Communications
• Mike May, Director of Communications & DTMBA
(561) 784-7325
Sports Services Founded:
1906
Description:
Our purpose is to support our member companies and promote healthy environment for the sporting goods industry by providing access to insight, information, influence and industry connections. SGMA also enhances industry vitality and fosters, sports, fitness and active lifestyle participation.

SPORTS LAW PROGRAM AND NATIONAL SPORTS LAW INSTITUTE
ECKSTEIN HALL, ROOM 138A
1215 WEST MICHIGAN STREET
MILWAUKEE, WI 53233
414-288-5815
Fax: 414-288-5818
munsli@mu.edu
law.marquette.edu/national-sports-law-institute/welcome
• Paul Anderson, Professor & Director
(414) 288-5816
paul.anderson@mu.edu
• Matt Mitten, Professor & Executive Director
(414) 288-7494
Description:
Supports Sports Law Program training law students at Marquette University Law School. Annual Conferences and Seminars; Internships and Externships for Marquette Law Students
Founded:
1989

Publications:
Marquette Sports Law Review; Sports Facility Reports; Recent Developments in Sports Law
Member Services:
Conferences, CLE Programs.
Membership Requirements:
Students $50 annual; Gold $120 annual; Blue $50 annual

SPORTS LAWYERS ASSOCIATION
12100 SUNSET HILLS ROAD
SUITE 130
RESTON, VA 20190
703-437-4377
Fax: 703-435-4390
www.sportslaw.org
• Anthony J Agnone, President
• Peter Roisman, Secretary
• Ash Narayan, Treasurer
Number of members:
1100
Member Services:
Yearly national law conference, annual membership directory, annual journal and special offers from Sports Business Daily and Sports Business Journal.
Publications:
The Sports Lawyer, electronic newsletter; The Sports Lawyers Journal, annual law journal.
Membership Requirements:
Regular - licensed attorneys; Associates - professional with interest in sports law; law educator - full/part time at accredited college of law. Student - full-time law student enrolled at an accredited school of law.
Description:
Founded 1976. Provides educational opportunities in the areas of sports law; provides a forum for sports law professionals to exchange a variety of perspectives and positions; promotes and, where necessary, establishes rules of ethics for its members.

SPORTS TURF MANAGERS ASSOCIATION
805 NEW HAMPSHIRE
SUITE E
LAWRENCE, KS 66044-6875
800-323-3875
Fax: 785-843-2977
www.stma.org
• James Michael Goatley, PhD, President
• Kim Heck, CEO
(800) 323-3875
kheck@stma.org
Number of Members:
2,500 National, 30 Chapters
Publications:
SportsTurf Magazine is the official publication; STMA website; ATMA Membership Roster; STMA E-Digest
Member Services:
Members Only Website section, Job Openings Contact Turf Information Files, Networking Annual Conference & Exhibition, Discount on books & clothing.
Membership Requirements:
Be in the sports turf industry and pay dues.

SPORTSACCORD
4 BD.JU JARDIN EXOTIQUE
MONACO, MONACO 98000
www.agfisonline.com

• Hein Verbruggen, President
• Tamas Ajan, VP
Membership Requirements:
Must be an International Sports Federation. Includes 99 members.
Description:
Founded 1967. GAISF is an association of International Sports Federations and other international organizations which contributes to the development of sport on an educational, scientific and technical level, and whose aim is to serve as a working tool and a center of cooperation, coordination and exchange of information.
Member Services:
Online calandar and directory. Annual convention held as a forum for exchange of ideas and discussion of common problems in sport.
Publications:
AGFIS/GAISF Magazine.

SPORTSPLEX OPERATORS AND DEVELOPERS ASSOCIATION/SODA
NEW YORK REGIONAL OFFICE
PO BOX 24263
WESTGATE STATION
ROCHESTER, NY 14624-0263
525-426-2215
Fax: 525-247-3112
info@SportsplexOperators.com
www.sportsplexoperators.com
• Diane Aselin, EVP
• Kelly Tharp, Secretary
• Norm Rice, Treasurer
• Don Aselin, Executive Director
• John Fitzgerald, President
Description:
Founded 1981. Provides sports complex operators and developers with educational programs and benefits which will make them successful.
Membership Requirements:
Sustained Membership - $995; Professional Membership - $295; Associate Membership - $295; Social Member - $125; Affiliate Member - $100.
Publications:
SODA SITE, bimonthly newsletter.

SSLASPA DBA SPORT & RECREATION LAW ASSOCIATION
C/O MARY MYERS
1608 N REDBARN
1845 Fairmont
Wichita, KS 67212-5855
316-978-3340
Fax: 316-978-5451
lori.miller@wichita.edu
• Colleen McGlone, President
• Mary Myers, Assistant Executive Director
Number of members:
183
Publications:
JOURNAL OF LEGAL ASPECTS OF SPORT, tri-annually; SSLASPA Newsletter, 2-3 times a year.
Description:
Founded 1990. Serves to further the study and dissemination of information regarding legal aspects of sport and physical activity. Addresses legal aspects of sport and physical activity within both public and private sectors. Objectives: (1) to serve as a medium for academic growth, (2) to provide service functions for members, (3) to assist in the development of curricula content, and

multi sports

223

(4) to cooperate closely with allied national and international organizations in related areas.

STADIUM MANAGERS ASSOCIATION
525 SW 5TH STREET
SUITE A
DES MOINES, IA 50309-4501
515-282-8192
Fax: 515-282-9117
sma@assoc-mgmt.com
www.stadiummanagers.org
• David Scott, President
• Mark Burk, Vice President
• Mike Grindle, Corporate Director
Publications:
Membership Directory.
Sports Services Founded:
1974.
Description:
Promotes the professional, efficient and state of the art management of stadiums around the world. Our members are administrators, operators, and marketing personnel from teams, government entities, colleges and universities, and suppliers to the industry.

UNDERWATER SOCIETY OF AMERICA
53 C APPIAN WAY
SOUTH SAN FRANCISCO, CA 94080
650-583-8492
408-286-8840
Fax: 408-294-3496
usafin@aol.com
www.underwater-society.org
• Carol Rose, President
croseusoa@aol.com
• Michael Gower, Secretary
usafin@aol.com
Number of members:
1,500
Member Services:
Life insurance; educational services.
Publications:
VISIBILITY, quarterly newsletter; HOW-TO MANUAL ON HOW TO FORM A DIVE CLUB; Underwater Hockey Referee Manual and Rule Books-free
Membership Requirements:
Active skin or scuba diver, payment of $20 annual dues.
Description:
Founded 1959. Works to make diving safer; active in areas of underwater sports, marine ecology, legislation, catch records.

UNGERBOECK SYSTEMS, INC.
100 UNGERBOEK PARK
O'FALLON, MO 63368-8694
636-300-5606
800-400-4052
Fax: 636-300-5607
marketing@ungerboeck.com
www.ungerboeck.com
• Dieter K K Ungerboeck, President
dieteru@ungerboeck.com
• Doug Archibald, COO
• Ryan Ungerboeck, Treasurer & Lead Developer, Financials
• Chris Bell, Vice President, Software Engineering
• Bruce Higgins, Vice President, Sales - The Americas
• Matt Harris, Vice President - Global Marketing
• Krister D Ungerboeck, Executive Vice President
kristeru@ungerboeck.com
• Krister Underboeck, CEO
Description:
Organization's Event Business Management System (EBMS) is designed to serve the needs of all sectors of the events industries. Exhibition and conference organizers, venues, event contractors and destination managers. Indeed, many of the leading participants operate with EBMS and give us a wealth of ideas for ongoing advancements, particularly regarding the electronic data interchange among each other.

UNITED STATES CORPORATE ATHLETICS ASSOCIATION
PO BOX 208
WEST SIMSBURY, CT 06092-0208
860-651-9453
Fax: 860-226-5670
www.uscaa.org
• Kevin Holtzclaw, President
• Lou Putnam, Vice President
• Sandra Berkner, Treasurer
sandra.berkner@cigna.com
• Cindy Richardson, Secretary
Sports Service Founded:
1985
Description:
A nationwide non profit organization that promotes health and fitness among corporate employees by sponsoring corporate athletic events.

UNITED STATES OLYMPIC EDUCATION CENTER
C/O NORTHERN MICHIGAN UNIVERSITY
SUPERIOR DOME
MARQUETTE, MI 49855
906-227-2888
Fax: 906-227-2848
usoec@nmu.edu
http://nmu.edu
• Brian Gaudreau, Interim Director
(906) 227-2888
bgaudrea@nmu.edu
• Michael Fields, Assistant Director
(906) 227-2896
mfields@nmu.edu
• Michael Kaurala, Operations Manager
(906) 227-2888
mkaurala@nmu.edu
Description:
Founded 1985. Provides a training and education environment for aspiring Olympic athletes.

UNITED STATES SPECIALTY SPORTS ASSOCATION
611 LINE DRIVE
KISSIMMEE, FL 34744
321-697-3636
Fax: 321-697-3647
www.usssa.com
• Beth Torina, Head Coach

WATER SPORTS INDUSTRY ASSOCIATION
PO BOX 568512
ORLANDO, FL 32856-8512
407-251-9039
Fax: 407-251-9039
www.watersportsindustry.com
• Larry Meddock, Executive Director

Description:
Founded 1978. Purpose is to expand interest and participation in water sports.
Number of members:
200

WESTERN WINTER SPORTS REPRESENTATIVES ASSOCIATION
726 TENACITY DR.
UNIT B
LONGMONT, CO 80504
305-532-4002
Fax: 866-929-4572
info@wwsra.com
www.wwsra.com
• Carri Garrison, Association Director
ext 1
• Rachael Mahoney, Territory Manager
ext 3
Number of members:
1,000+
Membership Requirements:
Must reside in the western U.S. and actively travel a territory in a sales capacity in the winter sports business. Trade shows not open to the public.
Sports Services Founded:
1949
Description:
Trade association for the purpose of sponsoring regional trade events for winter sports sales reps. Also to produce timely, cost effective regional events that benefit the membership, and to encourage growth and stability in the Winter and Active Sports Industry through service to membership.

WOMEN'S SPORTS FOUNDATION
1899 HEMPSTEAD TURNPIKE
SUITE 400
EAST MEADOW, NY 11554
516-542-4700
800-227-3988
Fax: 516-542-0095
info@womenssportsfoundation.org
www.womenssportsfoundation.org
• Kathryn Olson, CEO
• Laila Ali, President
• Lisa Cregan, Vice President, Treasurer
Description:
Founded 1974, the Women's Sports FOundation is a national charitable education organization. Mission is to advance the lives of girls and women through sports and physical activity.
Membership Requirements:
Donor membership $30 or more.
Publications:
WOMEN'S SPORTS EXPERIENCE, newsletter 4 times annually; SPORTSTALK, newsletter 4 times annually.
Member Services:
Resource Center, a clearinghouse for information on women's sports; Toll-free (800 227-3988) for information on women's sports; speakers bureau; library; Sportswoman of the Year awards; media awards; internships; Women's Sports Hall of Fame; films; lists; travel and training grants; leadership development grants.
Number of members:
10,000

WORLD FEDERATION OF THE SPORTING GOODS INDUSTRY
OBERE ZOLLGASSE 75
PO BOX 1664

3072 OSTERMUNDIGEN/BERN
BERN
info@wfsgi.org
www.wfsgi.org
• Motoi Oyama, President
• Tom Cove, Vice President, USA
Publications:
International Handbook for the Sporting Goods Industry, annual; WFSGI NEWS ALERT, weekly.
Membership Requirements:
Regular Members: Must be a national organization representing sports equipment manufacturers only. SGMA (North Palm Beach) is the official U.S. delegate and founding member. Member organizations include Argentina, Australia, Austria, Brazil, Canada, Finland, France, Germany, Great Britain, Greece, Italy, Japan, Korea, Malaysia, Netherlands, Pakistan, Spain, Sweden, Switzerland, Taiwan, USA. Also has sustaining and associate memberships.
Description:
The World Federation of the Sporting Goods Industry (WFSGI) is the world authoritative body for the sports industry officially recognized by the IOC as the industry representative within the Olympic family. WFSGI is an independent association with no objective of economic character for its own gains and formed by sports brands, manufacturers, suppliers, retailers, national federations and all sporting goods industry related businesses.

WORLD T.E.A.M. SPORTS
4250 VETERANS MEMORIAL HIGHWAY
SUITE 420E
HOLBROOK, NY 11741-4020
855-987-8326
Fax: 855-288-3377
info@worldteamsports.org
www.worldteamsports.org
• Van Brinson, President & CEO
vanbrinson@worldteamsports.org
• Richard Rhinehart, Director of Communications
richardrhinehart@worldteamsports.org
Description:
Founded 1993. World T.E.A.M. Sports changes lives through sports. For more than 20 years, we have used athletics to challenge disabled men, women and children to accomplish goals they never thought possible. In all our events - whether mountain climbing, biking, white water rafting or many other sports - we include both disabled and able-bodied participants.
Publications:
Newsletter.

Sports Commissions/Convention Visitors Bureau

AKRON SUMMIT CONVENTION & VISITORS BUREAU
77 EAST MILL ST
AKRON, OH 44308-1401
330-374-7560
800-245-4254
Fax: 330-374-7626
www.visitakron-summit.org

• Gregg Mervis, VP/COO
• James E Mahon, II, Director Marketing/Communications

ALABAMA GULF COAST CONVENTION & VISITORS BUREAU
3150 GULF SHORES PARKWAY
GULF SHORES, AL 36542
251-968-7511
800-745-7263
info@gulfshores.com
www.gulfshores.com
• Beth Gendler, VP Sales
• Mary Statkewicz, Sales Manager
Description:
Founded in 1993 and the primary responsibility is to market the Alabama Gulf Coast as a premier year-round destination.

ALABAMA SPORTS FOUNDATION
100 GRANDVIEW PLACE
SUITE 110
BIRMINGHAM, AL 35243
205-967-4745
Fax: 205-967-9940
www.brunoeventteam.com
• Gene Hallman, President/CEO
(205) 967-4745
• John Bochnak, Senior VP, Finance & Administration
(205) 967-4745
• Doug Habgood, Senior VP Golf division
• Amanda Hammac, Director Of Finance
• Lauren Addie, Creative Manager
• Will Borland, Tickets & Ops Coordinator
• Will Coleman, senior Event Manager-Zoom Motorsports
• Anna Lacy McMains, Sales Director
Year Founded:
1996
Description:
Committed to providing patrons and participants with world-class sporting events, presented with the highest standards of professionalism, that offer a return on the investment of our sponsors and vendors while giving back to, and elevating the image of, the community that plays host to the events.

ALBUQUERQUE SPORTS COUNCIL
PO BOX 26866
ALBUQUERQUE, NM 87125-6866
505-842-9918
800-733-9918
Fax: 505-247-9101
www.abqcvb.org
• Dale Lockett, President/CEO
• Jim Walther, Chair
Description:
Stimulates economic growth by marketing Albuquerque as a convention and visitor destination

ALPHARETTA CONVENTION & VISITORS BUREAU
178 SOUTH MAIN STREET
SUITE 200
ALPHARETTA, GA 30009
678-297-2811
877-202-5961
Fax: 678-297-9197
www.awesomealpharetta.com
• Janet Rodgers, President/CEO
janet@awesomealpharetta.com
• Beth Brown, Vice President of Sales
beth@awesomealpharetta.com

• Adam Bernos, Sports Sales Manager
adam@awesomealpharetta.com
Description:
Offers complimentary planning services including, securing group rates for hotels, welcome bags, site visits, vendor information and maps.

AMARILLO CONVENTION & VISITOR COUNCIL
1000 SOUTH POLK STREET
AMARILLO, TX 79101
806-374-1497
800-692-1338
Fax: 806-373-3909
rick@visitamarillotx.com
www.visitamarillotx.com
• Jerry Holt, Vice President
jerry@amarillo-cvb.org
• Dan Quandt, Executive Director
• Jutta Matalka, Director of Tourism & Amarillo Film Commissio
• Tina Brohlin, Director of Convention Sales Agriculture, Spo
• Emilea White, Convention Sales Manager SMERF Markets
• Lindsey Arbeiter, Convention Sales Manager Associations
• Mary Ramirez, Executive Assistant
• Eric Miller, Communications Director
eric@amarillo-cvb.org

AMES AREA SPORTS COMMISSION
1601 GOLDEN ASPEN DRIVE
SUITE 110
AMES, IA 50010
515-232-4032
800-288-7470
www.visitames.com
• Julie Weeks, Director
(515) 956-4600
juliew@amescvb.com
• Seann Demaris, Sports Sales & Services
(515) 956-4604
seannd@amescvb.com
• Sandy Larson, Administrative Services
(515) 956-4603
Sports Services Founded:
Founded 1995.
Facilities:
Hilton Coliseum: Basketball, Wrestling, Volleyball, Gymnastics, Iowa State Cross Country Course; Lied Recreation Center: Track and Field, Martial Arts, Volleyball, Racquet Ball; Ames/ISU Ice Arena: Hockey, Curling, Broomball, Figure Skating; Furman Aquatics Center: Swimming, Water Polo, Synchronized Swimming
Description:
works to build economic activity in the Ames area by promoting convention and visitors activities. The Bureau is a members-based organization supporting businesses and groups, and exists to support member business growth.

ANAHEIM/ORANGE COUNTY VISITOR & CONVENTION BUREAU
800 WEST KATELLA AVENUE
ANAHEIM, CA 92802
855-405-5020
Fax: 714-991-8963
• Charles Ahlers, President
(714) 765-8840
• Charles Ahlers, President
• Jay Burress CTA, President and CEO
(714) 765-8840

multi sports

225

jburress@anaheimoc.org
• Byna Sipos, Executive Assistant
(714) 765-8898
bsipos@anaheimoc.org

ARIZONA DEPARTMENT OF RACING
1110 W WASHINGTON
SUITE 260
PHOENIX, AZ 85007
602-364-1700
Fax: 602-364-1703
ador@racing.state.az.us
www.azracing.gov
• Wlilliam J. Walsh, Director

ARKANSAS DEPARTMENT OF FINANCE & ADMINISTRATION
1509 W 7TH STREET
SUITE 505
LITTLE ROCK, AR 72201
501-682-1467
Fax: 501-682-5273
www.dfa.arkansas.gov
• Cecil Alexander, Chairman
• Thomas Akin, Commissioner

ARLINGTON CONVENTION & VISITORS BUREAU
1905 EAST RANDOL MILL ROAD
ARLINGTON, TX 76011
817-461-3888
800-433-5374
Fax: 817-461-6689
www.experiencearlington.org
• Jay Burress, President/CEO
• Joel McLelland, VP Finance/Administration
joel@arlington.org
Description:
Founded in 1992. It is a private, non-profit, non-membership organization, and is the official destination marketing organization for the City of Arlington, Texas.

ASHEVILLE CHAMBER OF COMMERCE
36 MONTFORD AVENUE
ASHEVILLE, NC 28801
828-258-6114
Fax: 828-251-0926
contactus@ashevillechamber.org
www.ashevillechamber.org
• Kit Cramer, President/CEO
(828) 258-6123
• Rojeanous Rush, VP Finance/Operations
(828) 258-6119
Publications:
Relocation Packet; Employment Resource Package (in print and CD ROM); Asheville Area Phone Book; Asheville Area Map; Asheville Fact Book; Major Employers Directory (in prin and CD ROM); Western North Carolina Industrial Directory (in print and CD ROM)

ASHEVILLE CONVENTION & VISITORS BUREAU
36 MONTFORD AVENUE
ASHEVILLE, NC 28801
828-258-6101
Fax: 828-254-6054
www.exploreasheville.com
• Marla Tambellini, Interim Executive Director
(828) 258-6138
• Jonna Reiff, Executive Director

ATLANTA SPORTS COUNCIL
235 ANDREW YOUNG INTERNATIONAL BOULEVARD NW
ATLANTA, GA 30303
404-880-9000
www.atlantasportscouncil.com
• Richard A Anderson, Chairman
• Sam A Williams, President
• Eric Oberman, Vice President, Business Properties
(404) 586-8506
eoberman@macoc.com
• Bari Love, VP Marketing & Communications
• Ken Chin, Vice President, Events
(404) 586-8492
kchin@macoc.com
• Patti Young, Executive Assistant
(404) 586-8500
pyoung@macoc.com
• Courtenay Carruthers, Member Services Coordinator
(404) 586-8510
Number of Members:
500+.
Publications:
Quarterly Newsletter, Annual Report.
Member Services:
Volunteer opportunities for local sporting events, Committee involvement, Access to tickets to local sporting events. Access to all luncheon, events & complimentary access to power house. Access to all ASC Golf Tournament. Membership fees: Individual $250; Corporate $500; Advisor $2,500.
Description:
Promotes the value of sports growth in Atlanta and Georgia by acting as an authority on the economic impact, viasbility and quality of life issues associated with the goal of building Atlanta's reputation as the Sports Capital of the World.

ATLANTA'S DEKALB CONVENTION & VISITORS BUREAU
1957 LAKESIDE PARKWAY
SUITE 510
TUCKER, GA 30084
770-492-5017
800-999-6055
Fax: 770-492-5033
www.dcvb.org
• James Tsismanakis, Executive Director & CEO
(770) 492-5011
Publications:
Sports DeKalb Facilities Guide; SPORTS DEKALB LEADER, SPORTS DEKALB LATEST LINE, newsletters.
Description:
Founded 1989. Private, not-for-profit sports council for DeKalb County in Metro Atlanta, dedicated to economic development. Represents athletic facilities and the hospitality industry to attract sporting events/visitors.

AUBURN/OPELIKA CONVENTION & VISITORS BUREAU
714 EAST GLENN AVENUE
AUBURN, AL 36830
334-887-8747
866-880-8747
Fax: 334-821-5500
info@aotourism.com
www.auburn-opelika.com

• John C Wild, CHA, President
johnwild@aotourism.com
• Robyn L Bridges, CRDE, Communication Director
rlbridges@aotourism.com
Description:
Am economic enhancement tool for the communities of Auburn, Opelika and Lee County. We promote and develop our area through the travel and tourism industry and introduce the unique spirit of Auburn-Opelika to visitors from around the world.

AUGUSTA SPORTS COUNCIL, GREATER
1450 GREENE STREET
SUITE 110
PO BOX 1331
AUGUSTA, GA 30901
706-722-8326
Fax: 706-823-6609
www.augustasportscouncil.org
• Brinsley Thigpen, CEO
• Randy DuTeau, Event Manager
Description:
Founded 1991. Mission includes bidding for, supporting, and developing quality sports activities in the Greater Augusta area as well as recognizing sports achievements of areas outstanding youth and coaches in sports. Home of Ray Guy Award which recognizes the nation's top college punter.

BAKERSFIELD CONVENTION & VISITORS BUREAU, GREATER
515 TRUXTUN AVENUE
BAKERSFIELD, CA 93301
661-852-7282
866-425-7353
• David Lyman, Manager
(661) 852-7282
• Misty Glasco, Marketing & Events Specialist
(661) 852-7237

BATON ROUGE AREA SPORTS FOUNDATION
359 3RD STREET
BATON ROUGE, LA 7801
225-382-3596
Fax: 225-346-1253
• Jerry Stovall, President
(225) 382-3588
sports@brasf.com
• Eric Engemann, Indoor Sports Coordinator
(225) 382-3571
eric@brasf.com
• Kristen Chighizola, Outdoor Sports Coordinator
(225) 382-3596
Sports Services Founded:
1994
Decription:
To assist in the identification and promotion of athletic activities (competitions and meetings) in the community.
Facilities:
More than 40

BATTLE CREEK SPORTS PROMOTION
KELLOGG ARENA
1 MCCAMLY SQUARE
BATTLE CREEK, MI 49017
269-963-4000
Fax: 269-968-8840
www.kelloggarena.com

• Kevin Scheibler, General Manager
kscheibler@kelloggarena.com
• Ben Randels, Operations Manager
brandels@kelloggarena.com
• Bob Bengttson, Finance Director
(269) 963-4800
bbengtsson@kelloggarena.com
Description:
Serves to attract sports events and
meetings to the greater Battle Creek area.

BEAUMONT CONVENTION & VISITORS BUREAU
505 WILLOW STREET
BEAUMONT, TX 77701
409-880-3749
800-392-4401
Fax: 409-880-3750
www.Beaumontcvb.com
• Dean Conwell, Executive Director
(409) 880-3165
dconwell@ci.beaumont.tx.us
• Rebecca Woodland, Convention Sales
Manager
(409) 880-3169
rwoodland@ci.beaumont.tx.us
• Samantha Moye, Tourism Specialist
(409) 880-3749
smoye@ci.beaumont.tx.us
• Stephanie Dollar Molina, Director
Marketing
(409) 880-3170
smolina@ci.beaumont.tx.us
• Freddie Willard, Director of Sales
(409) 880-3160
Publications:
Beaumont Official Visitors Packet; Annual
Calender of Events; Beaumont Visitor Map;
School Project Information Packet; E-mail
Updates

BELLINGHAM/WHATCOM CHAMBER OF COMMERCE
119 N COMMERCIAL STREET
SUITE 110
BELLINGHAM, WA 98225
360-734-1330
www.bellingham.com
• Ken Oplinger, President/CEO
• Troy Wills, Secretary
• Peter Cutbill, Treasurer
• Jim Darling, Chair

BIRMINGHAM, GREATER CONVENTION & VISITORS BUREAU
2200 9TH AVENUE NORTH
BIRMINGHAM, AL 35203-1100
205-458-8000
800-458-8085
Fax: 205-458-8086
info@birminghamal.org
www.birminghamal.org
• Karen Dobnikar, Human Resource
Manager
(205) 214-9220
kdobnikar@birminghamal.org
• Dilcy Hilley, VP Marketing
(205) 214-9229
dhilley@birminghamal.org
• Michael Gunn, Vice President Sales
(205) 214-9213
mgunn@birminghamal.org
Description:
Established for the purpose of marketing
and promoting the greater Birmingham area
as a destination for conventions, meetings,
and tour and travel. The mission is to
broaden and expand promotional efforts on
behalf of the city and its business
constituency through advertising and
marketing programs designed to sell guest
rooms in area lodging facilities.

BISMARCK-MANDAN CONVENTION & VISITORS BUREAU
1600 BURNT BOAT DRIVE
BISMARCK, ND 58503
701-222-4308
800-767-3555
Fax: 701-222-0647
www.discoverbismarckmandan.com
• Terry Harzinski, Executive Director
• LaRae Nelson, Destination Sales
Specialist
• Lori Yantzer, Destination Sales Specialist
• Camie Lies, Communications Manager
• Barb Balzer, Travel Counselor
• Sheri Grossman, Director Sales
sheri@discoverbismarckmandan.com
Description:
The mission of the Bismarck-Mandan CVB,
in collaboration with our partners is to
entake visitors from around the world to eat,
meet, sleep and play in Bismarck-Mandan.
Facilities:
Bismarck Aquatics Center, Bismarck Civic
Center, Bismarck Community Bowl, All
Seasons Arena, Nishu Archery Arena, 30
Softball fields, 26 outdoor soccer fields, 10
outdoor and 4 indoor tennis courts.

BLOOMINGTON CONVENTION & VISITORS BUREAU
2855 NORTH WALNUT STREET
BLOOMINGTON, IN 47404
812-334-8900
800-800-0037
Fax: 812-334-2344
cvb@visitbloomington.com
www.visitbloomington.com
• Mike McAfee, Executive Director
(812) 355-7720
• Ryan Irvin, Graphic Designer
• Laura Newton, Assistant Director, COO
(812) 355-7721

BLOOMINGTON CONVENTION & VISITORS BUREAU
7900 INTERNATIONAL DRIVE
SUITE 990
BLOOMINGTON, MN 55425
952-858-8500
866-435-7425
800-346-4289
Fax: 952-858-8854
info@bloomingtonmn.org
www.bloomingtonmn.org
• Jennifer Schak, Marketing/Special Events
Coordinator
Publications:
Sports Venue Guide 2005.
Member Services:
Site Inspections, Bid Booklets, Welcome
Packets, Meet & Greet, Intineraries.

BLOOMINGTON-NORMAL AREA SPORTS COMMISSION
3201 CIRA DRIVE
SUITE 201
BLOOMINGTON, IL 61704
309-665-0033
800-433-8226
Fax: 309-661-0743
matt@visitbn.org
www.bloomingtonnormalcvb.org
• Amanda Borden, Convention & Tourism
Marketing Manager
• Danny Harms, Graphic Design & Web
Manager
• Matt Hawkins, Sports Marketing Manager
matt@visitbn.org
• Alesha Stevenson, Convention & Tourism
Marketing Manager
• Crystal Howard, Director
Description:
Mission is to enhance the econoy of McLean
County through promotion, attraction and
retention of events, conventions and
tourism.

BOISE CONVENTION & VISITORS BUREAU
250 S 5th STREET
SUITE 300
BOISE, ID 83702
208-344-7777
800-635-5240
Fax: 208-344-6236
www.boise.org
• John Cohen, Executive Director
(208) 472-5209
jcohen@boisecvb.org
• Terry Kopp, Director of Sales
(208) 472-5208
tkopp@boisecvb.org
• Lisa Edens, Senior Sales Manager
(208) 472-5207
ledens@boisecvb.org
Description:
Soccer, baseball, softball, basketball, biking,
bowling, boxing, climbing, cricket, curling,
disc golf, equestrian, football, golf, hockey,
ice skating and mountain biking

BOSTON CONVENTION & VISITORS BUREAU/SPORTS MARKETING DIVISION, GREATER
TWO COPLEY PLACE
SUITE 105
BOSTON, MA 02116-6501
617-536-4100
888-SEEBOSTON
Fax: 617-424-7664
www.bostonusa.com
• Patrick Moscaritolo, Presdient & CEO
• David Gilbin, Chair
Description:
Founded 1993. Draws upon community
individuals and resources to attract
sport-related meetings and conventions to
Boston.
Publications:
Official Visitor Information Kit; Official
Guidebook to Boston; Boston & Cambridge
Dining, Shopping and Nightlife Guide;
BostonUSA Specials! Card; Travel Planner;
Kids Love Boston; City Pass; Go Boston
Card; Get Ready for Boston; We're Here;
CD Images of Boston; CD Boston History;
CD Boston Festivals & Holidays; CD Boston
Seasons; CD Boston Sports; The Complete
Guide; Boston Flip Flops - Men's; Boston
Flip Flop - Women's

BUFFALO NIAGARA SPORTS COMMISSION
617 MAIN STREET
SUITE 200
BUFFALO, NY 14203-1496

716-852-0511
800-283-3256
Fax: 716-852-0131
info@buffalocvb.org
www.buffaloniagarasports.com
• Pete Harvey, Director of Sport
Development
(716) 218-2929
harvey@buffalocvb.org
• Jay Josker, Sport Services Manager
(716) 218-2932
josker@buffalocvb.org
• Charles Giglia, Director of Sport Sales
(716) 218-2928
giglia@buffalocvb.org
Description:
The Buffalo Niagara Sports Commission
promotes Buffalo & Erie County as a
premier amateur sports destination. From
empire state games to NCAA frozen four
buffalo has the experience & facilities to
host the event.

CANTON/STARK COUNTY CONVENTION & VISITORS BUREAU
THE MILLENNIUM CENTRE
222 MARKET AVENUE NORTH
CANTON, OH 44702
330-454-1439
800-552-6051
Fax: 330-456-3600
www.cantonstarkcvb.com
• John Kiste, Executive Director
johnk@cantonstarkcvb.com
• Allyson Bussey, Tourism Marketing
Manager
Description:
To attract, orient and serve visitors, to
educated local residents, and initiate
projects and programs, which promote and
grow tourism.

CEDAR RAPIDS TOURISM OFFICE
370 FIRST AVENUE NE
CEDAR RAPIDS, IA 52401
319-398-5211
sales@tourismcedarrapids.com
www.tourismcedarrapids.com
• Mary Lee Malmberg, Director of Sports
Tourism
• Mark Meyer, Director of Business
Development
General Description:
Cedar Rapids offers a wide variety of sports
venues, including large arenas, sports
complexes and stadiums.
Publications:
Cedar Rapids Area Visitors Guide, Cedar
Rapids Area Sports Facilities Guide, Cedar
Rapids Area Meeting Planners Guide.
Member Services:
Listing on website and in area visitors guide,
business leads and networking
opportunities.
Membership Requirements:
Must be located within 100 mile radius of
Cedar Rapids.
Facilities Available for Sporting Events:
30,000 sq. ft. arena with seating for 8,000
(wrestling, volleyball, basketball, &
cheerleading); Ice arena with NHL ice sheet
with 3850 seats and an Olympic rink with
viewing for 400; State-of-the-art minor leage
baseball stadium seats 5300; Soccer
complex with 20 fields and parking for
1,000.

CENTRAL FLORIDA SPORTS COMMISSION
400 W. CHURCH STREET
SUITE 205
ORLANDO, FL 32801
407-648-4900
Fax: 407-649-2072
www.centralfloridasports.org
• Brent Nelson, Interim President/CEO
bnelson@centralfloridasports.org
• Jennifer Lastik, Events Director
• Eileen Babich, Operations Assistant
• John Bisignano, President/CEO
(407) 648-0033
jbisignano@centralfloridasports.org
Sports Services Founded:
1992
Description:
Supports activities, events and sports
related businesses that stimulate the Central
Florida economy, construct and utilize
sports facilities, enhance the area's image
worldwide, provide outstanding
entertainment and participatory
opportunities, and contribute to Central
Florida's quality of life.

CENTRAL PENNSYLVANIA/PENN STATE COUNTRY CVB
800 E. PARK AVE
STATE COLLEGE, PA 16803
814-231-1400
800-358-5466
Fax: 814-231-8123
www.centralpacvb.org
• Shirley Smith, Director of Sales
(814) 231-1401
• Betsey Howell, Executive Director
Nature of Sports Service:
Organization offers Site Selection/RFP
Assistance, Housing Bureau Services,
Hospitality Ambassadors, Team of
Volunteers and Community Leaders, Family
Welcome packets/coupons and other
transporation and support services.

CHAMPAIGN COUNTY CONVENTION & VISITORS BUREAU
108 SOUTH NEIL STREET
CHAMPAIGN, IL 61820-7269
217-351-4133
800-369-6151
Fax: 217-351-0906
www.visitchampaigncounty.org
• Sorita Wilson, Chair
• Dennis Robertson, Vice Chair
• Teri Legner, Treasurer
• Jay DeLuce, Secretary
General Description:
The Champaign County Convention and
Visitors Bureau (CVB) and the CVB Board
of Directors would like to welcome you to
their community. Whatever the occasion, the
staff at CVB are there to answer questions,
provide materials and ensure that you feel
welcome. Planning a sporting event?
Champaign County and the University of
Illinois feature state-of-the-art sports
complexes, indoor and outdoor recreational
facilities, and parks that will accommodate
just about any kind of youth, amateur or
adult sporting event.

CHARLESTON METRO SPORTS COUNCIL
423 KING STREET
CHARLESTON, SC 29403

843-805-3030
www.sportscouncil.org
• Kathleen Cartland, Executive Director
kcartland@charlestoncvb.com
Sports Services Founded:
1999
Description:
To lead and support the local sports and
recreational community in collaborative
efforts to maximize the potential of area
sports and sporting events. In adittion, to
promote the Charleston metropolitan area
as a destination for amateur sports and
sporting events.
Number of Members:
100+
Publications:
Sports Scene Magazine.
Member Services:
Sports Business Conference, Sports
Celebration Dinner, Golf Classic, Monthly
membership program.

CHARLOTTE REGIONAL SPORTS COMMISSION
6337 MORRISON BOULEVARD
CHARLOTTE, NC 28211
704-644-4047
www.charlottesports.org
• Will Web, Executive Dierctor
(704) 644-4048
• Will Pitts, Operations Director
(704) 644-4046
Sports Services Founded:
1994
Description:
To bring sporting events to Charlotte which
benefit the region in two major areas,
economic impact and quality of life. In
adittion, we also help attract conferences,
sports organizations and teamd to our
market.

CHATTANOOGA SPORTS & EVENTS COMMITTEE, GREATER
736 MARKET STREET
18TH FLOOR
CHATTANOOGA, TN 37402
855-345-0127
Fax: 423-265-1630
www.chattanoogasports.org
• Scott Smith, Chair
merrill@chattanoogasports.org
• Jeff Sikes, Vice Chairman
Description:
Founded 1992. Serves as the city's
representative in bidding for/recruiting
regional, national and international sports
teams, events and meetings for the
Chattanooga area; creates and stages
sporting events in Chattanooga that have
the potential to lure participants and/or
spectators to the area; acts as catalyst for
improving recreational facilities in area.

CHICAGO SOUTHLAND CONVENTION & VISITORS BUREAU
2304 173RD STREET
LANSING, IL 60438-6006
708-895-8200
888-895-8233
Fax: 708-895-8288
sports@visitchicagosouthland.com
www.playchicagosouthland.com
• Jim Garrett, President
• Sally Schlesinger, Executive Vice
President

Decription:
The Chicago Southland is compromised of 62 south and southwest suburbs of Chicago. Only 25 minutes from Chicago and easily accessible via two airports and several interstates, the Southland is Chicago's most affordable region.
Publications:
Chicago Southland Visitors Guide, annually; Meeting Planner's Guide, as needed; Group Tour Guide, as needed; Sports Venue Guide, as needed; Traveler's Guide, annually; Festivals & Events, annually; Chicago Southland Coupon Book, bi-annually.

CINCINNATI SPORTS CORPORATION, GREATER
9514 KENWOOD ROAD
CINCINNATI, OH 45242
513-686-7782
Fax: 513-322-0139
www.cincyusa.com
• Leslie Spencer, Executive Director
LSpencer@CincyUSA.com
Description:
Founded 1989. Serves to promote sports development and attract sports events to the greater Cincinnati, Ohio area.

CITY OF GREENVILLE - SPECIAL EVENTS
206 S MAIN STREET, 6TH FLOOR
GREENVILLE, SC 29602
864-232-2273
aprosser@greenvillesc.gov
www.greenvillesc.gov
• Angie Prosser, Director Special Events
aprosser@greenvillesc.gov
• Beth Rusch, Permits & Event Coordination
(864) 467-6667
brusch@greenvillesc.gov

CITY OF HUNTSVILLE SPORTS COMMISSION
PO BOX 19064
HUNTSVILLE, AL 35804
256-427-6749
www.huntsvillesports.org
• Ralph Stone, Executive Director
Description:
A not-for profit advocacy organization that promotes an enhanced quality of life in the Huntsville area by identifying, recruiting, and promoting amateur events and meetings.

CLARKSVILLE MONTGOMERY COUNTY CONVENTION & VISITORS BUREAU
25 JEFFERSON ST.
SUITE 300
CLARKSVILLE, TN 37040
931-647-2331
800-530-2487
Fax: 931-645-1574
www.clarksville.tn.us
• Theresa Harrington, Executive Director
• James Chavez, President & CEO
• Sahron Green, Vice President, Finance & Administration of t
(931) 245-4335
sgreen@clarksville.tn.us
• Robin Burton, Vice President of Marketing and Communication
(931) 245-4337
rburton@clarksville.tn.us
• Lisa Knight, Human Resources Manager of the Economic Devel

(931) 245-4336
lisak@clarksville.tn.us
• Wendy Welch, Media Design Specialist of the Economic Devel
(93) -245-433
graphics@clarksville.tn.us
• Cortney Willamson, Accounting & Development Assistant of the Eco
(931) 245-4331
cwilliamson@clarksville.tn.us
Description:
A private, non-profit economic development umbrella that provides staffing and management.

CLEVELAND SPORTS COMMISSION, GREATER
50 PUBLIC SQUARE
SUITE 950
CLEVELAND, OH 44113
216-621-0600
Fax: 216-621-2773
www.clevelandsports.org
• David E. Gilbert, President & CEO
Description:
Founded 1993, the Great Cleveland Sports Commission is responsible for attracting sports events to Northeast Ohio. The GCSC supports the local economy and serves to bring major sports events to Northeast Ohio, creating various sporting opportunities for athletes of all ages.
Nature of Service:
Event attraction, management, marketing, communications, volunteer services and operations.

CLINTON CONVENTION & VISITORS BUREAU
721 SOUTH SECOND STREET
CLINTON, IA 52732
563-242-5702
cvb@clintonia.com
www.clintoniowatourism.com
• Marsha Smith, Director Convention and Visitiors Bureau
• Mary Jo Kinkaid, Administrative Assistant
• Marsha Smith, Director
• Sue Raaymakers, Chair

COBB TRAVEL & TOURISM
ONE GALLERIA PARKWAY
SUITE 1A2A
ATLANTA, GA 30339
678-303-2622
800-451-3480
Fax: 678-303-2625
www.travelcobb.org
• Holly Bass, Chief Executive Officer
• Holly A. Bass, CEO
(678) 303-2641
hbass@travelcobb.org
Sports Service Founded:
1984
Nature of Sports Service:
The bureau markets Cobb County as a sports tourism destination for right holders and meeting planners to host there next event in our community. Our services are free to assist with hotel guest room packaging, bid proposals, venue research, media support, and convention services.
Publications:
Visitor's Guide
Number of Members:
Nine (9)

COLORADO SPRINGS SPORTS CORPORATION
1631 MESA AVENUE
SUITE E
COLORADO SPRINGS, CO 80906
719-634-7333
Fax: 719-634-5198
info@thesportscorp.org
www.thesportscorp.org
• Tom Osborne, President/CEO
(719) 634-7333
tom@thesportscorp.org
• Stori Peterson, Sports Director
• Doug Martin, COO
(719) 634-7333
doug@thesportscorp.org
• Mike Moran, Senior Media Consultant
(719) 634-7333
mike@thesportscorp.org
Description:
Founded 1978. Provides support to the USOC and National governing bodies, active with economic development and youth sports development. Host of the 2005 & 2007 State Games of America.

COLUMBIA REGIONAL SPORTS COUNCIL
1010 LINCOLN STREET
COLUMBIA, SC 29201
803-545-0000
800-264-4884
Fax: 803-545-0013
info@columbiasportscouncil.com
www.columbiasportscouncil.com
• Rick Luber, Executive Director
hubers@columbiasportscouncil.com
• Katie Rankin, Sales Manager
(803) 545-0016
kwilmesherr@columbiasportscouncil.com
Description:
The mission of the Columbia Regional Sports Council is to strengthen the area's economy by marketing and selling the Columbia Riverbanks Region as a premier destination for sporting events, partnering with local sports organizations to grow and develop existing events, and by recruiting new events which provide an economic benefit to the region by generating room nights, food and beverage sales, and associated tax revenues.

COLUMBUS, GA SPORTS & EVENTS COUNCIL
400 4TH STREET
PO BOX 1519
COLUMBUS, GA 31901
706-660-1996
Fax: 706-225-4533
msherman@columbusga.org
www.columbusgasports.com
• Herbert Greene, Executive Director
hgreene@columbusga.org
• Scott Ressmeyer, President
• Scott Ressmeyer, President
• David Boyd, Event Manager
Sports Services Founded:
1995
Description:
Strives to promote tourism through sporting events, creating a positive economic impact on the greater Columbus region.

multi sports

CORPUS CHRISTI CONVENTION & VISTORS BUREAU
101 N SHORELINE BLVD
SUITE 430
CORPUS CHRISTI, TX 78401
800-678-6232
Fax: 361-887-9023
www.corpuschristi.tx.org
• Keith Arnold, CEO
(361) 881-1888
karnold@visitcorpuschristitx.org
• Timothy J Carpenter, VP of Technology &
Interactive Marketing
(361) 881-1861
tcarpenter@visitcorpuschristitx.org
Description:
Provides the community with marketing
support for the tourism and convention
industries.

DALLAS CONVENTION & VISITORS BUREAU
325 NORTH ST. PAUL STREET
SUITE 700
DALLAS, TX 75201
214-571-1000
800-232-5527
Fax: 214-571-1008
• Philip Jones, President & CEO
• Monica Paul, VP, Sports Marketing
• Phyllis Hammond, VP Public Relations
(214) 571-1077
Description:
Promotes Dallas as the ideal business and
pleasure destination to the regional,
national, and international marketplace, and
to favorably impact the Dallas economy
through conventions and tourism.

DALLAS CONVENTION CENTER
650 SOUTH GRIFFIN STREET
DALLAS, TX 75202
214-939-2750
877-850-2100
Fax: 214-939-2795
www.dallasconventioncenter.com
• Ron King, Director
(214) 939-2794
• Al Rojas, Asst Finance/Admin Director
(214) 939-2755
alberto.rojas@dallascityhall.com
• Charlotte Allen, Marketing/Public Relations
Man
(214) 939-2738
charlotte.allen@dallascityhall.com
Description:
Founded 1988, as a non-profit public
charity. Serves as the focal point of sports
support and development activities within
the greater Dallas region. Project
Management: Manage sports programs,
events and projects.
Publications:
DISC NEWS, quarterly newsletter, VIP
invitations.

DANVILLE AREA CONVENTION & VISITOR BUREAU
100 WEST MAIN STREET
#146
DANVILLE, IL 61832
217-442-2096
800-383-4386
Fax: 217-442-2137
info@danvilleareainfo.com
www.danvilleareainfo.com

• Jeanie Cooke, Executive Director
(217) 442-2096
• Barbara Bein, Finance Administrator
BarbaraBein@danvilleareainfo.com
Facilities:
Danville Stadium (Baseball), Winter Park
(Soccer), YMCA (Swimming), Harrison Park
(Golf), Turtle Run (Golf), Wolfe Creek (Golf),
Palmer Arena (Ice Skating/Hockey).

DAYTON/MONTGOMERY COUNTY CONVENTION & VISITORS BUREAU
1 CHAMBER PLAZA
SUITE A
DAYTON, OH 45402
937-226-8211
800-221-8235
Fax: 937-226-8294
reifert@daytoncvb.net
www.daytoncvb.com
• Jacquelyn Powell, Chief Executive Officer
jypowell@daytoncvb.net
• Ron Eifert, Senior Sales Manager
(937) 226-8284
reifert@daytoncvb.net
Nature of Services:
The Dayton/Montgomery County Convention
& Visitors Bureau is a destination marketing
organization which provides numerous
complimentary services to sports groups
and organizations looking to host an event
in the Dayton and Montgomery County area.

DC SPORTS & ENTERTAINMENT COMMISSION
2400 E CAPITOL STREET SE
WASHINGTON, DC 20003
202-608-1100
Fax: 202-547-7460
www.dcsec.com
• Erik A Moses, Senior VP & Managing
Director
emoses@dcsec.com
• Troy Scott, Event Operations
• Teri Washington, Director,
Communications
• Adelle Chenier, Event Manager
• Gregory A. O'Dell, President and Chief
Executive Officer
• Samuel R. Thomas, Senior Vice President
and General Manager Con
(202) 249-3000
sthomas@eventsdc.com
• Erik A. Moses, Senior Vice President and
Managing Director S
(202) 608-1100
emoses@eventsdc.com
• Henry W. Mosley, Chief Financial Officer
(202) 249-3000
hmosley@eventsdc.com
• Chinyere Hubbard, Vice President,
Communications and Marketing
(202) 249-3217
chubbard@eventsdc.com
Venues:
Washington Convention Center, RFK
Stadium, DC Armory, Nationals Park,
Carnegie Library
Summary of Services:
The suite of services is designed to
accommodate events of all sizes and the
commitment to superior service to clients
and patrons is second to none. From start to
finish, the dedicated team of sales, event
management and communications staff
work together to make the event execution
process a homerun every time.

DECATUR AREA CONVENTION & VISITORS BUREAU
202 EAST NORTH STREET
DECATUR, IL 62523
800-331-4479
Fax: 217-423-7455
www.decaturcvb.com
• Mark Avery, Treasurer
• Jeff Hendricks, Executive Director DACVB
• Teri Hammel, Director of Sales & Finance
• Bryce Swanson, Sports and Competitive
Events Manager
• Katrina Wilkerson, Office and Services
Manager
• Sandy Denton, President
• Carol Barnes, Vice-President

DENVER METRO CONVENTION & VISITORS BUREAU
1555 CALIFORNIA STREET
SUITE 300
DENVER, CO 80202-4262
303-892-1112
800-223-6837
Fax: 303-892-1636
www.denver.org
• Richard Scharf, President/CEO
• Jeff Ruffe, VP Finanace/Adminstration
Description:
Promotes Denver and the surrounding areas
as a sight for sporting and entertainment
events.

DES MOINES AREA SPORTS COMMISSION
400 LOCUST STREET
SUITE 265
DES MOINES, IA 50309
515-699-4960
800-451-2625
Fax: 515-244-9757
info@desmoinescvb.com
www.seedesmoines.com
• Chris Coleman, Chair
• Paul Rottenberg, Chair
• Rick Messerschmidt, Secretary/Treasurer
Description:
The Des Moines Area Sports Commission
(DMASC) became an official supporting
organization of the Greater Des Moines
CVB in 2008. The DMASC, previously
known as the Greater Des Moines Sports
Authority, was established as an
organization in 1992 and was known as the
Sports Authority until 2002 when it entered
into a support agreement and came under
the umbrella of the Greater Des Moines
CVB. Today the DMASC's mission is to
establish Greater Des Moines as the
premier Midwest community for recreational
and competitive sport participation and
competition.
Facilities:
Iowa Events Center: HyVee Hall, Wells
Fargo Arena, Veterans Memorial Auditorium
(various sports), Drake Stadium (Track &
Field), James W. Cownie Soccer Complex
(soccer), Richard O. Jacobson Exhibit
Center (various sports)

DES MOINES CONVENTION & VISITORS BUREAU, GREATER
400 LOCUST STREET
SUITE 265
DES MOINES, IA 50309
800-451-2625
Fax: 515-244-9757

info@desmoinescvb.com
www.seedesmoines.com
• Nancy Goode, Vice President ofFinance & Administration
(515) 699-3441
nancy@catchdesmoines.com
• Greg Edwards, President & Chief Executive Officer
(515) 699-3438
gedwards@desmoinescvb.com
• Vicki Comegys, Vice President, Sales & Service
(515) 699-3435
vcomegys@desmoinescvb.com
• Tiffany Tauscheck, Vice President, Marketing
(515) 699-3433
ttauscheck@desmoinescvb.com
Description:
Formed in 1908, the Greater Des Moines Convention and Visitors Bureau is one of the oldest bureaus in the United States. The mission of the Greater Des Moines Convention and Visitors Bureau is to promote Greater Des Moines as an attractive, vibrant and affordable destination statewide, nationally and internationally. Their focus increases visitors to the community through meetings, conventions, events, sports, leisure, travel and group tours, thereby contributing to the local economy.

DETROIT METRO SPORTS COMMISSION
211 WEST FORT STREET
SUITE 1000
DETROIT, MI 48226
313-202-1979
Fax: 313-202-1964
info@detroitsports.org
www.detroitsports.org
• David Beachnau, Executive Director
(313) 202-1979
dbeachnau@visitdetroit.com
• Dave Beachnau, Executive Director
• Sean Krabach, Director of Event Operations
• Andrew Green, Manager, Event Services
• Marty Dobek, Marketing and Communication
• Kris Smith, Sales Manager, Event Development
• Dave Beachnau, Executive Director
(313) 202-1982
dbeachnau@detroitsports.org
Description:
Markets and sells metro Detriot as a premier destination for regional, national and international amateur sporting events.

DICKINSON CONVENTION & VISITORS BUREAU
72 EAST MUSEUM DRIVE
DICKINSON, ND 58601
701-483-4988
800-279-7391
Fax: 701-483-9261
info@visitdickinson.com
www.visitdickinson.com
• Terri Thiel, Executive Director
Description:
Serves to attract sports events and meetings to the greater North Dakota geographic area.

DISCOVER LYNCHBURG
2015 MEMORIAL AVENUE
LYNCHBURG, VA 24501
434-845-5966
800-732-5821
Fax: 434-522-9592
djackson@lynchburgchamber.org
• Denise Jackson, Sales Manager
djackson@lynchburgchamber.org
Description:
Mission is to bring major sports and special events to Lynchburg and surrounding areas.
Sporting Events Held at Facilities:
Soccer; Baseball; Basketball; Paintball; Wrestling; Lacrosse; Golf; Fishing; Canoeing; Boating; Field Hockey; Equestrian; Softball; Tennis; and Track & Field

DIVISION OF BUSINESS & COMMUNITY DEVELOPMENT/SOUTH CAROLINA
1205 PENDLETON ST, STE 110
COLUMBIA, SC 29201
803-734-1700
866-224-9393
Fax: 803-734-1163
www.discoversouthcarolina.com
• Marion Edmonds, Director of Communications
• Amy Duffy, Chief of Staff
Description:
Promotes South Carolina as a sight for sports, entertainment and film.

DOTHAN AREA CONVENTION & VISITORS BUREAU
3311 ROSS CLARK CIRCLE
DOTHAN, AL 36303
334-794-6622
888-449-0212
Fax: 334-712-2731
www.dothanalcvb.com
• Robert Hendrix, Executive Director
• Carmen Bishop, Communications Director
Description:
Serves to attract sports events and meetings to the Dothan geographic area.

DUBLIN CONVENTION & VISITOR BUREAU
9 SOUTH HIGH STREET
DUBLIN, OH 43017
614-792-7666
800-245-8387
info@irishisanattitude.com
www.irishisanattitude.com
• Scott Dring, Executive Director
• Mary Szymkoiwak, Communications/Group Tour Specialist
• Josh Bricker, Sports & Events Sales Manager
Sports Services Founded:
1988
Description:
Mission is to identify and pursue opportunities to attract, service and retain overnight visitors.

DUPAGE CONVENTION & VISITORS BUREAU
915 HARGER ROAD
SUITE 240
OAK BROOK, IL 60523-1476
630-575-8070
800-232-0502
Fax: 630-575-8070
www.dupagecvb.com

• Skip Strittmatter, Executive Director
ext 210
• Beth Marchetti, Director of Development

DURHAM CONVENTION & VISITORS BUREAU
101 EAST MORGAN STREET
DURHAM, NC 27701
919-687-0288
800-446-8604
Fax: 919-683-9555
www.durham-nc.com
• Reyn Bowman, President
reyn@durham-cvb.com
• Corey Bizzell, Director of Sales
corey@durham-cvb.com
Description:
A local tourism development authority chartered by state and local government in cooperation with the private sector to attract and serve visitors to the City and County of Durham by reinvesting a portion of the visitor paid room occupancy and tourism development tax in promotion and marketing.

ELGIN AREA CONVENTION & VISITORS BUREAU
77 RIVERSIDE DRIVE
ELGIN, IL 60120
847-695-7540
800-217-5362
Fax: 847-695-7668
• Pete Garlock, Director Of Sales
pgarlock@northernfoxrivervalley.com
Description:
Regional convention and visitors bureau representing Chicagolands northern Fox River Valley.
Facilities Available for Sporting Events:
Elgin Sports Complex: Softball, Soccer, Baseball, BMX, Football, Rugby, Volleyball; The Centre of Elgin: Basketball, Cheerleading, Dance, Gymnastics, Martial Arts, Swimming, Volleyball, Team Handball, Wrestling; Elgin Community College: Baseball, Basketball, Cheer/Dance, Football, Rugby, Gymnastics, Martial Arts, Soccer, Softball, Volleyball, Wrestling, Team Handball; Judson University: Baseball, Basketball, Cheer/Dance, Gymnastics, Martial Arts, Soccer, Softball, Volleyball, Wrestling, Team Handball

EXPLORE FAIRBANKS
101 DUNKEL STREET
SUITE 111
FAIRBANKS, AK 99701-4806
907-457-3282
800-327-5774
Fax: 907-459-3757
info@explorefairbanks.com
www.explorefairbanks.com
• Deb Hickok, President & Chief Executive Officer
• Deb Hickok, President And CEO
(907) 459-3770
dhickok@explorefairbanks.com
• Dawn Murphy, Finance and Administrative Director
(907) 459-3774
dmurphy@explorefairbanks.com
• Michelle Middleton, Administrative and Finance Coordinator
(907) 459-3772
mmiddleton@explorefairbanks.com
• Amy Geiger, Director of Communications

(907) 459-3775
ageiger@explorefairbanks.com
• Bill Wright, Public Relations Manager
(90-) 59-3776
bwright@explorefairbanks.com
• Deb Hickok, President and CEO
(907) 459-3770
dhickok@explorefairbanks.com
• Michelle Middleton, Administrative and Finance
(907) 459-3772
Description:
The Fairbanks Convention and Visitors Bureau has served as the regional visitor center for fairbanks and interior Alaska for the past 28 years. The mission of the organiation is to enhance and contribute to the economic well-being of the Fairbanks area by marketing to potential visitors. Departments include: Administration, Visitor Services, Membership, Meetings & Conventions, Tourism & Advertising, and Public Relations.
Membership:
Over 400 members (also including non-profits & rural outreach). Categories of membership include: activities, events, shopping, dining, accomodations, convention facilities and services, transportation, visitor planning, services. Any membership questions call direct to: Karen Lane (907) 451-1734, or klane@explorefairbanks.com
Member Services:
Benefits of member services include: vacancy listings, membership, luncheons, evening exchanges, membership mailouts, educational seminars, members-only website, website listings, open houses, membership orientation, prospect seminars, Golden Heart Greeter Program.
Publications:
Visitor Guide, Winter Guide, Meeting Planner Guide, Group tour Manual, Self-Guided Downtown Walking Tour, Membership Directory

FAIRFIELD COUNTY SPORTS COMMISSION
1 UNIVERSITY PLACE
STAMFORD, CT 6901
203-251-8481
Fax: 203-251-8482
• Harry E Peden, IV, President
• Jon Lese, Treasurer
Description:
A non-profit organization dedicated to promoting fitness and personel development through sports and an active healthy lifestyle.

FARGO-MOORHEAD CONVENTION & VISITOR BUREAU
2001 44TH STREET SW
FARGO, ND 58103
701-282-3653
800-235-7654
Fax: 701-282-4366
info@fargomoorhead.org
www.fargomoorhead.org
• Cole Carley, President/CEO
cole@fargomoorhead.org
• Charley Johnson, President and CEO
• Renee M Sander, Director of Operations
Description:
Exists to promote Fargo, North Dakota and Moorehead, Minnesota as a destination for visitors, tour groups, business travel,

conventions, sporting events and trade shows.

FARMINGTON CONVENTION & VISITORS BUREAU
3041 EAST MAIN STREET
FARMINGTON, NM 87402
505-326-7602
800-448-1240
www.farmingtonnm.org
• Debbie Dusenbery, Executive Director
• Tonya Stinson, Executive Director
• Shawna Graham, Administrative & Membership Coordinator
• Ingrid Gilbert, Online Marketing Coordinator

FLORIDA SPORTS FOUNDATION
2930 KERRY FOREST PARKWAY
TALLAHASSEE, FL 32309
850-488-8347
Fax: 850-922-0482
www.flasports.com
• Larry Pendleton, President
lpendleton@flasports.com
• Steven V. Rodriguez, Vice President
svrodriguez@flasports.com
• Nick Gandy, Communications Director
ngandy@flasports.com
• Charlotte Cowen, Finance & Human Resources
ccowen@flasports.com
Description:
Founded 1992. Official sports office for the state of Florida. Promotion and development of the state's sports industry.

FLORIDA'S SPACE COAST OFFICE OF TOURISM
430 BREVARD AVENUE
SUITE 150
COCOA VILLAGE, FL 32922
321-433-4470
877-572-3224
Fax: 321-433-4476
kalina.person@visitspacecoast.com
www.visitspacecoast.com
• Kalina Person, Promotions/Sports Manager
ksubido@aol.com
• Rusty Buchanan
(321) 783-9283
• Connie Alden
(321) 783-9283

FORT SMITH CONVENTION & VISITORS BUREAU
2 NORTH B STREET
FORT SMITH, AR 72901
479-783-8888
800-637-1477
Fax: 479-784-2421
info@FortSmithSports.com
www.FortSmithSports.com
• Amy Jones, Convention & Event Sales Manager
(479) 783-8888
amy@FortSmithSports.com
• Russ Jester, Marketing Communications & Events Services Manager
Description:
Fort Smith CVB (1990) is the official destination marketing organization of Fort Smith, Arkansas. Fort Smith CVB promotes Fort Smith's unique assets that make it ideal for business and leisure tourism, as well as

for large conventions, meetings and events, assisting sporting event planners.

FORT WORTH CONVENTION & VISITORS BUREAU
111 WEST 4TH STREET
SUITE 200
FORT WORTH, TX 76102-3951
817-336-8791
800-433-5747
www.fortworth.com
• David DuBois, CMP, CAE, President/CEO
(817) 698-7822
• Linda G De Jesus, MBA, CPA, CFP, Vice President Finance & Administration
(817) 698-7839
lindadejesus@fortworth.com
• Merianne Roth, Vice President Marketing & Communications
(817) 698-7841
Description:
The mission is to improve the area economy by attracting visitors to Fort Worth.

FOX CITIES CONVENTION AND VISITORS BUREAU
3433 WEST COLLEGE AVENUE
APPLETON, WI 54914
920-734-3358
800-236-6673
Fax: 920-734-1080
mtenhaken@foxcities.org
www.foxcities.org
• Adam Schanke, Sports Marketing Manager
aschanke@foxcities.org
• Matt Ten Haken, Director of Sports Marketing
mtenhaken@foxcities.org
Description:
The Fox Cities Convention and Visitors Bureau helps attract and organize sporting events in the Fox Cities of Wisconsin. Some of the services provided include: touring, evaluating venues and hotels, securing proposals, managing hotel arrangements, coordinating media information, recruiting volunteers, and providing visitor information.
Founded:
1988

FRESNO CONVENTION & VISITORS BUREAU
848 M STREET
3RD FLOOR
FRESNO, CA 93721
559-445-8300
800-788-0836
Fax: 559-445-0122
www.fresnocvb.org
• Wayne Bennett, Executive Director
wayne@fresnocvb.org
• Billie Kerstetter, Director Convention Sales/Marketing
billie@fresnocvb.org
Year Founded:
1966
Nature of Service:
We host Conventions, Religious, Athletic, Commerical events at our Fresno Convention Center.

GAINESVILLE SPORTS COMMISSION
300 EAST UNIVERSITY AVENUE
SUITE 100
GAINESVILLE, FL 32601

352-338-9300
Fax: 352-338-0600
www.gainesvillesportscommission.com
• Jack Hughes, Executive Director
• James Di Virgilio, VP
• Bruce Cribbs, Treasurer
• Esther Yoder, Secretary
• Frank Saier, Legal Counsel
• Lynda Reinhart, President
Sports Services Founded:
1988
Description:
Strives to promote tourism through sports while creating a positive economic impact on Gainesville and Alachula County

GRAND FORKS CONVENTION & VISITORS BUREAU, GREATER
4251 GATEWAY DRIVE
GRAND FORKS, ND 58203
701-746-0444
800-866-4566
info@visitgrandforks.com
www.visitgrandforks.com
• Julie Rygg, Executive Director
julie@visitgrandforks.com
• Deb Stewart, Sales Manager
(Sal) s Manage

GREATER AUSTIN SPORTS ASSOCIATION
PO BOX 28222
AUSTIN, TX 78767
512-239-8830
• Doris Mueller, Chairman
Description:
Founded 1986. Promotes Austin as a site for local, state, national, and international sports events and meetings.

GREATER CLEVELAND SPORTS COMMISSION
334 EUCLID AVENUE
CLEVELAND, OH 44114
216-621-0600
Fax: 216-621-2773
info@clevelandsports.org
www.clevelandsports.org
• David E. Gilbert, President & CEO
Description:
Founded 1993, the Great Cleveland Sports Commission is responsible for attracting sports events to Northeast Ohio. The GCSC supports the local economy and serves to bring major sports events to Northeast Ohio, creating various sporting opportunities for athletes of all ages.
Nature of Service:
Event attraction, management, marketing, communications, volunteer services and operations.

GREATER COLUMBUS SPORTS COMMISSION
45 VINE STREET
COLUMBUS, OH 43215
614-221-6060
800-331-0092
Fax: 614-224-7301
www.ColumbusSports.org
• Linda Logan, Executive Director
LLogan@ColumbusSports.org
• Brain Ellis, Chair
• Paul Astleford, Experience Columbus
• Gregg DiPaolo, Time Warner Cable
• Butch Moore, The Dispatch Printing Company

• Linda Shetina Logan, Executive Director
• Brenda Carter, Executive Assistant , Office Manager
Description:
Mission is to provide leadership, guidance and marketing expertise in attracting regional, national and international sporting events and activities to benefit Greater Columbus economically and socially.

GREATER DENTON SPORTS COMMISSION
2436 S I-35E
SUITE 376-256
DENTON, TX 76205
888-598-1508
www.dentonsports.com
• Jason Piter, Chair
• Frank Kudlac, Treasurer
Description:
To attract, stimulate, and promote sports entertainment events and activities in the greater denton area

GREATER FORT LAUDERDALE CONVENTION & VISITORS BUREAU
1850 ELLER DRIVE
SUITE 303
FORT LAUDERDALE, FL 33316
954-765-4466
800-22-SUNNY
Fax: 954-765-4467
gflcvb@broward.org
www.sunny.org
• Nicki E Grossman, President & CEO
ngrossman@broward.org
• Francine Mason, Vice President Communications
(954) 765-4466
fmason@broward.org
Sports Service Founded:
1987
Description:
Funded by a portion of the five percent tax on hotel rooms. Promotes the Greater Fort Lauderdale area as a premier year-round leisure and marketing destination.
College Bowl Game:
2004 FedEx Orange Bowl.

GREATER LANSING CONVENTION & VISITORS BUREAU
500 EAST MICHIGAN AVENUE
SUITE 180
LANSING, MI 48912
517-487-0077
888-252-6746
Fax: 517-487-5151
www.lansing.org
• Linda Sims, Sr. Advisor on Multi-Cultural Diversity & Com
(517) 372-6892
ssserve@usa.net
• Deborah Bough, Computer & Information Systems Manager
(517) 377-1426
dbough@lansing.org
• Jack Schripsema, President
(517) 377-1404
jschripsema@lansing.org
• Michael B Zumbaugh, CDME, Vice President Finance and Administration
(517) 377-1403
mzumbaugh@lansing.org

GREATER LOUISVILLE CONVENTION & VISITORS BUREAU
401 WEST MAIN STREET
SUITE 2300
LOUISVILLE, KY 40202
502-584-2121
888-568-4784
Fax: 502-584-6697
info@gotolouisville.com
www.gotolouisville.com
• James Wood, President/CEO
jwood@gotolouisville.com
• Karen Williams, Executive Vice President
• Stacy Yates, VP Marketing/Communications
syates@gotolouisville.com
Description:
Since 1968, the primary goal has been to enhance the city's economy through tourism development. The Bureau enhances Greater Louisville's economy through tourism by positioning and selling Greater Louisville worldwide, in partnership with the public and private sector, as a premier destination for convention, tradeshows, corporate meetings, group tours and individual leisure travel.

GREATER OMAHA SPORTS COMMITTEE
7015 SPRING STREET
OMAHA, NE 68106-3518
402-346-8003
800-475-SHOW
Fax: 402-346-5412
info@showofficeonline.com
www.showofficeonline.com
• Bob Mancuso, Chairman
(402) 346-8003
info@showofficeonline.com
Number of Members:
200
Member Services:
Be active in bringing sporting events to city and metro area by working on various committees.
Membership Requirements:
Attend monthly meeting and take part in helping various sporting events in metro Omaha.
Description:
Founded 1971

GREENSBORO SPORTS COMMISSION
2200 PINECROFT ROAD
SUITE 200
GREENSBORO, NC 27407
336-378-4499
Fax: 336-378-1998
admin@greensborosports.org
www.greensborosports.org
• Karah Jennings, Operations Manager
• Mo Milani, Treasurer
• Michael F. Bumpass, Secretary
• Kim Strable, President
• Demp Bradford, VP of Operations
Description:
Founded 1989. Established to recruit, promote and host all types of sports events, sports conferences, and sports meetings. 23,000 seat coliseum adjacent to special events center comprised of 120,000 square feet of exhibit space and a 5,000 seat mini-arena with meeting facilities. Also offers excellent golf, tennis, soccer, cross country and event facilities.

GREENVILLE CONVENTION & VISITORS BUREAU
631 SOUTH MAIN STREET
SUITE 301
GREENVILLE, SC 29601
864-421-0000
800-351-7180
Fax: 864-421-0005
www.greenvillecvb.com
• Chris Stone, President
(864) 421-0000
cstone@greenvillecvb.com
• Chris Stone, President
• Jennifer Stilwel, Chief Marketing Officer
• Michelle Stoudemire, Senior Sales Manager
• Todd Bertka, Vice President, Sales

GWINNETT SPORTS COMMISSION
6500 SUGARLOAF PARKWAY
SUITE 200
DULUTH, GA 30097
770-623-1667
888-494-6638
Fax: 770-623-1667
www.gwinnettsportscommission.org
• Preston Williams, CEO
• Lisa Anders, Executive Director
Publications:
Meeting Planners Guide; Gwinnett Magazine; Facilities Guide

GWINNETT SPORTS COUNCIL
6500 SUGARLOAF PARKWAY
SUITE 200
DULUTH, GA 30097
888-494-6638
Fax: 770-623-1667
lb@vba2000.com
www.gcvb.org
• Lee Baker, Executive Director
lb@vba2000.com
Membership:
Annual membership fee is $125 per member.
Description:
Mission is to promote sports in Gwinnett area; promote local events to have a greater impact; bring new events to the area; publish a magazine dedicated to the sports in the area.

HAGERSTOWN-WASHINGTON COUNTY CONVENTION & VISITORS BUREAU
16 PUBLIC SQUARE
HAGERSTOWN, MD 21740
301-791-3246
888-257-2600
Fax: 301-791-2601
www.marylandmemories.org
• Tom Riford, President/CEO

HAMPTON ROADS CHAMBER OF COMMERCE
PO BOX 327
NORFOLK, VA 23501
757-622-2312
Fax: 757-622-5563
www.hamptonroadschamber.com
• John A Hornbeck, Jr, CCE, President/CEO
• John A Hornbeck, President/CEO
(757) 664-2500
• Sarah Bernick, Administrative Coordinator
(757) 622-2312
• Joel Pearce, Communications Manager
• Sarah Martin, Vice President, Development/Marketing

Description:
To create economic opportunity and prosperity for all of Hampton Roads

HAMPTON ROADS SPORTS COMMISSION
500 E MAIN STREET
SUITE 700
NORFOLK, VA 23510
757-664-2573
Fax: 757-622-5563
info@hamptonroadssports.org
www.hamptonroadssports.org
• Morgan Lang, Hampton Roads Sports Commission
• John Wilson, Chair
• Jack Hornbeck, President
• Sylvia Haines, Secretary-Treasurer
Description:
Attract major amateur athletic events to the area and to emphasize regional collaboration.

HARTFORD SPORTS COMMISSION, GREATER (CONVENTION & VISITORS BUREAU)
31 PRATT STREET
4TH FLOOR
HARTFORD, CT 6103
860-728-6789
800 446-7811
Fax: 860-293-2365
www.enjoyhartford.com
• Michael Van Parys, President
ext 222
• Phyllis Anderson, National Sales Manager
• Keith Voets, Sales/Marketing Manager
(860) 728-6789
Description:
The mission is to enhance the economic fabric and quality of life of Hartford.

HAWAII PACIFIC SPORTS
1493 HALEKKOA DRIVE
HONOLULU, HI 96821
808-732-8805
www.alohastategames.com
• Mark E. Zeug, President/Chief Executive Officer
Description:
Founded 1988. Owns and organizes Aloha State Games; promotes the attraction and development of sports events in the state of Hawaii. Also owns and operates Hawaii Senior Olympics.

HERITAGE CORRIDOR CONVENTION & VISITORS BUREAU
15701 INDEPENDENCE BLVD
ROMEOVILLE, IL 60446
815-727-2323
800-926-2262
Fax: 815-727-2324
info@hccvbil.com
www.heritagecorridorcvb.com
• Robert L Navarro, PhD, President/CEO
(630) 226-1753
• Mary Beth DeGrush, Vice President
(815) 727-4635
maryde@hccvbil.com
Description:
HCCVB was established in 1985. We service communities along the Illinois and Michigan Canal. Mission is to ignite, influence and impact the visitor's experience through tourism partnership.
Publications:

Sun & Fun Spring & Summer Events Guide, Heritage Corridor CVB Visitors Guide, Will/Grundy Visitors Guide, LaSalle County Visitor's Guide

HOT SPRINGS CONVENTION & VISTORS BUREAU
134 CONVENTION BLVD
HOT SPRINGS, AR 71901
501-321-2277
800-543-2284
Fax: 501-321-2136
hscvb@hotsprings.org
www.hotsprings.org
• Steve Arrison, CEO
Description:
Tourists and Arkansas residents alike will find lots of fun things to do in Hot Springs Arkansas.

HOUSTON SPORTS DIVISION/GREATER HOUSTON CONVENTION & VISITORS BUREAU
1331 LAMAR STREET
SUITE 700
HOUSTON, TX 77002
713-437-5200
800-446-8786
Fax: 713-227-6336
www.visithoustontexas.com
• Sara McPhillips, Executive Director
• Ramona Crayton, Convention Services Manager
• Judi Taliaferro, Convention Services/National Accounts
Description:
Serves to attract sports events and sports teams to Greater Houston, TX.

HUNTSVILLE/MADISON COUNTY CONVENTION & VISITORS BUREAU
500 CHURCH STREET
SUITE 1
HUNTSVILLE, AL 35801
256-551-2230
800-843-0468
Fax: 256-551-2324
info@huntsville.org
www.huntsville.org
• Judy Ryals, President and CEO
(256) 551-2230
jryals@huntsville.org
Description:
Serves to attract sports events and sports teams to the Huntsville area.
Member Services:
Provides complimentary brochures and maps of the area as well as other services based on the number of overnight sleeping rooms used.

ILLINOIS BUREAU OF TOURISM & FILM
100 W. RANDOLPH, STE 3-400
CHICAGO, IL 60601
312-814-7179
Fax: 312-814-6175
www.enjoyillinois.com
• Cathy Ritter, Deputy Director, Bureau of Tourism
• Desi Harris, Marketing Director
• Lourdes Ortiz, Assistant Director

INDIANA SPORTS CORPORATION
PAN AMERICAN PLAZA
201 SOUTH CAPITOL AVE

SUITE 1200
INDIANAPOLIS, IN 46225-1069
317-237-5000
800-HI-FIVES
Fax: 317-237-5041
info@indianasportscorp.com
• Susan Williams, President
• Allison Melangton, President
Member Services:
Membership fees: MVP $50, All-Star $100, All-American $250, Champion $500, and Hall of Fame $1000. Included in membership when available: Event VIP Hospitality passes; member receptions, including functions with world-class athletes in attendance; priority seating at select national and international sports events; preferred volunteer opportunities at selected spoting events; thank you gift; advance ticket purchasing opportunities for many events; one year subscription to ISC's Play-by-Play e-newsletter and Events Calender; recognition on ISC's website; and invitation to attend ISC's Holiday Open House.
Publications:
PLAY BY PLAY, newsletter quarterly; President's Letter, quarterly.
Membership Requirements:
Available for tax-deductible donation.
Description:
Founded 1979. Represents Indianapolis in the national and international sports marketplace. Attracts sporting organizations and events to the city and assists in staging. Private, not-for-profit company relying on individual and corporate memberships, contributions and grants as chief funding sources.

IRVING CONVENTION & VISITORS BUREAU
500 WEST LAS COLINAS BOULEVARD
IRVING, TX 75039
972-252-7476
800-2-IRVING
Fax: 972-401-7729
info@irvingtexas.com
www.irvingtexas.com
• Maura Gast, Executive Director
(972) 252-7476
mgast@ci.irving.tx.us
• Maura Gast, Executive Director
• Lori Fojtasek, Assistant Executive Director/Sales
• Jane Kilburn, Assistant Executive Director/Administration
• Mark D Thompson, Assistant Executive Director/Marketing
• Monty White, Marketing Manager
• Karla Prine, Secretary, Marketing and Communications
• Maura Gast, Executive Director
Year Founded:
1972

JACKSON CONVENTION & VISITORS BUREAU
111 EAST CAPITOL STREET
SUITE 102
JACKSON, MS 39201
601-960-1891
800-354-7695
Fax: 601-960-1827
www.visitjackson.com
• Wanda Wilson, President/CEO
• Robert Gibbs, Chairman

• Juanita S Doty, Secretary
• Ken Crowtell, Treasurer
• Wanda Wilson, JCVB President/CEO
• Jennifer Chance, VP of Finance & Administration
• Robert Gibbs, Chairman
Sports Service Founded:
1983
Description:
The Bureau's three departments which are Administration, Marketing and Sales and Services, provides services to visitors, conventions, group tour operators, local hotels, resturants, shops, special events, and attractions, and help to bring millions of dollars to local economy annually.

JACKSONVILLE AND THE BEACHES CONVENTION AND VISITORS BUREAU
208 N LAURA STREET
SUITE 102
JACKSONVILLE, FL 32202
904-798-9111
800-733-2668
Fax: 904-798-9103
www.jaxcvb.com
• Janice Lowe, Chair
• Janice Lowe, Chair
• Bill Prescott, ViceChair
• Shane Frisbee, Marketing Committee Chair
• Barry Sondern, Sales Committee Chair
• Scott Wellington, Treasurer
Nature of Service:
Promotes Jacksonville and its surroundings. Setup and organize presentations. Publishes literature and maps. Assists with all customer needs.
College Sports Sponsor:
Gator Bowl Association - Chairman's Club Member.
Football Sponsor:
River City Showdown.
Golf Sponsor:
The Players Championship.
Baseball Sponsor:
ACC Baseball Championship.

JACKSONVILLE-ONSLOW COUNTY SPORTS COMMISSION
1099 GUM BRANCH ROAD
PO BOX 207
JACKSONVILLE, NC 28540
910-347-3141
800-835-9496
Fax: 910-347-4705
www.jacksonvilleonslowsports.org
• Jesse Newsom, Executive Director
• Julie Keoho, Program Specialist
Description:
Focuses on events, activities, and facilitation that puts people in the motels of our community, people in our restaurants, and shoppers in the stores from out of town. Our target is to encourage activities that bring in teams and people from out of the area who would likely spend the night.

JEDC SPORTS AND ENTERTAINMENT DIVISION/JACKSONVILLE FLORIDA
1 WEST ADAMS STREET
SUITE 200
JACKSONVILLE, FL 32202
904-630-3600
Fax: 904-630-3606
• Michael Bouda, Manager

Nature of Sports Service:
JEDC Sports and Entertainment exists to attract sporting events and activities in Jacksonville that appeal to a large cross-section of citizens; to provide financial and promotional assistance to major events; to provide a full array of fee-paid marketing services to help promoters maximize attendance; and to help bring national and international publicity to the City of Jacksonville.
Facilities Available for Sporting Events:
The Baseball Grounds of Jacksonville (Baseball); Jacksonville Municipal Stadium (variety); Veterans Memorial Arena (variety); Equestrian Center (Equestrian); Prime Osborn Convention Center (Cheerleading); Times Union Center for Performing Arts (variety)

JOHNSON CITY CONVENTION & VISITORS BUREAU
603 EAST MARKET STREET
PO BOX 180
JOHNSON CITY, TN 37061
423-461-8000
800-852-3392
Fax: 423-461-8047
www.johnsoncitytnchamber.com
• Brenda Whitson, Executive Director
(423) 461-8010
• Gary Mabrey, President / CEO
(423) 461-8008
mabrey@johnsoncitytnchamber.com
• Glenda Britt, Director of Finance
(423) 461-8005
glenda@johnsoncitytnchamber.com
• Barbara Mentgen, Director of Operations
(423) 461-8011
mentgen@johnsoncitytnchamber.com
• Elisa Britt, Executive Secretary
(423) 461-8006
britt@johnsoncitytnchamber.com
• Cindy Foster, Executive Assistant CVB
(432) 461-8002
foster@johnsoncitytnchamber.com

JOPLIN CONVENTION & VISITORS BUREAU AND SPORTS AUTHORITY
602 SOUTH MAIN STREET
JOPLIN, MO 64801
417-625-4789
800-657-2534
Fax: 417-624-7948
cvb@joplinmo.com
• Mike Greninger, Executive Director/Sports Authority
• Mike McAffe, Director Joplin Convention/Visotrs Bureau
Description:
Promotes Joplin and surrounding areas as a location for sporting events.

JUNEAU CONVENTION & VISITORS BUREAU
800 GLACIER AVENUE
SUITE 201
JUNEAU, AK 99801
907-586-2201
800-587-2201
Fax: 907-586-1449
info@traveljuneau.com
www.traveljuneau.com
• Lorene Palmer, President
Sports Services Founded:
1985.
Description:

multi sports

Organization dedicated to economic developmetn in Juneau, Alaksa through promoting and marketing Juneau as a year round visitor destination. The primary goal is to increase the overnight stay of business and pleasure travelers who support local businesses through consumer spending, and the city through payment of bed tax.

KANKAKEE COUNTY CONVENTION & VISITORS BUREAU
1 DEARBORN SQUARE
SUITE 1
KANKAKEE, IL 60901
815-935-7390
800-747-4937
Fax: 815-935-5169
info@visitkankakeecounty.com
www.visitkankakeecounty.com
• Larry Williams, Executive Director
• Vicki Layhew, Sales/Marketing Manager
• Nancy Fregeau,
Operations/Communications
• Larry Williams, Executive Director
• Vicki Layhew, Sales & Marketing Manager
• Marilyn McAdoo, General Office Support
General Description:
Kankakee County is home to the Chicago Bears summer training camp, eight golf courses, spacious parks, 57 miles of winding river waters and numerous sports complexes. Located just an hour south of Chicago along Interstate 57 the county offers convenience and accessibility. Sports facilities are conveniently located close to dining, shopping, attractions, and lodging accomodations. Founded in 1983.
Facilities Available for Sporting Events:
Hidden Cove Sportsplex: Basketball, Mini Golf, Gymnastics, Wrestling, Paintball, Soccer, Volleyball; Diamond Sports Complex: Baseball, Softball; National City's River Road Softball Complex - Softball, Youth Baseball; OAK Orthopedic Sports Arena: Hockey, Figure Skating, Curling; Kankakee County Speedway: Stock Car Racing; Kankakee River: Boat Racing, Canoeing, Kayaking; Manteno Lake: Swimming, Triathlons
Publications:
Kankakee County Visitors Guide; Kankakee County Outdoor Guide; Sports Event Planner Kit

KANSAS CITY SPORTS COMMISSION AND FOUNDATION
2600 GRAND BLVD
SUITE 100
KANSAS CITY, MO 64108
816-474-4652
Fax: 816-474-7979
info@sportkc.org
www.sportkc.org
• Kathy Nelson, President/CEO
(816) 474-4652
knelson@sportkc.org
• Jacob Robertson, Executive Coordinator
(816) 389-4193
jrobertson@sportkc.org
• Dave Borchardt, Director, Corporate & Community Relationships
(816) 389-4191
dborchardt@sportkc.org
Member Services:
Sporting Events, volunteer opportunities, networking opportunities.
Publications:
THE SPORTS PAGE.

Membership Requirements:
Annual fees.
Sports Services Founded:
1969
Number of Members:
600
Description:
Goals A) Aims to enhance the quality of life and economic success of Greater Kansas City by taking the lead in maintaining and selectively acquiring a diversity of amateur and professional sporting events. B) To collaborate with area economic development agencies to attract and retain amateur and professional sports organizations. C) To promote the lifetime benefits of sports for the youth of Greater Kansas City.

KINGSPORT CONVENTION & VISITORS BUREAU
400 CLINCHFIELD STREET
SUITE 100
KINGSPORT, TN 37660
423-392-8820
800-743-5282
Fax: 423-392-8803
kcvb@kcvb.org
www.kcvb.org
• Jud Teague, Executive Director
(423) 392-8832
jteague@kcvb.org
• Jud Teague, Executive Director
• Frank Lett, Associate Executive Director/Sports
(423) 392-8831
flett@kcvb.org

KISSIMMEE-ST. CLOUD CONVENTION & VISITORS BUREAU
1925 EAST IRLO BRONSON MEMORIAL HIGHWAY
KISSIMMEE, FL 34744
407-742-8200
800-327-9159
media@floridakiss.com
http://www.experiencekissimmee.com
• Tim Hemphill, Executive Director
Description:
Staff develops and impliments programs and activities that produce solid results through reliable relationships with marketing.

KNOXVILLE TOURISM & SPORTS CORPORATION
• Kim Bumpas, President
• Chad Culver, Senior Director, Sports Commission
• Kristen Combs, Director, Communications
• Parker Medley, Director, Sports Sales
• Kelli Ryman, Director, Event Services
• Erin Simcox, Housing Manager
Description:
The Visit Knoxville Sports Commission promotes the Knoxville/Knox County as a destination for sports-related events. This includes youth events, collegiate events and professional events. The Commission works with local organizers, as well as National Governing Bodies.

LACKAWANNA COUNTY CONVENTION & VISITORS BUREAU
99 GLENMAURA NATIONAL BLVD
MOOSIC, PA 18507

570-496-1701
800-229-3526
Fax: 570-963-6369
info@visitnepa.org
www.visitnepa.org
• Morgan Christopher, Director of Sales
• Carl Puscavage, Marketing Sales Manager

LAFAYETTE CONVENTION & VISITORS BUREAU
1400 NW EVANGELINE TRWY
LAFAYETTE, LA 70501-2829
337-232-3737
800-346-1958
Fax: 337-232-0161
www.lafayettetravel.com
• Gerald Breaux, Executive Director
gerald@lafayettetravel.com
• Felicia Duhon, Controller
felicia@lafayettetravel.com
• Kelly Strenge, PR/Special Projects Manager
Sports Services Founded:
1974
Description:
Created to serves as a tourism promotion and marketing coordinator for all of Lafayette Parish.

LAFAYETTE-WEST LAFAYETTE CONVENTION & VISITORS BUREAU
301 FRONTAGE RD
LAFAYETTE, IN 47905-4564
765-447-9999
800-872-6648
Fax: 765-447-5062
agordon@homeofpurdue.com
www.homeofpurdue.com
• Ashley Gregory, Group Tours & Meeting Manager
• Amanda Gordon, Sports Marketing & CommunicationsManager
• Judy Ryan, Customer Services Coordinator
• Sara Erickson, PR & Social Media Specialist
• Jo Wilson Wade, President/CEO
• Lisa Morrow, Vice President
Description:
Purdue University-Swimming & Diving/Golf/Fencing/Rugby/Soccer etc. Golf-two 4 1/2 star rated courses equipt for tournaments of any size, indoor and outdoor softball and volleyball, outdoor soccer and more.

LAKE COUNTY, ILLINOIS - CONVENTION & VISITORS BUREAU
5465 WEST GRAND AVENUE
SUITE 100
GURNEE, IL 60031
847-662-2700
800-LAKE NOW
Fax: 847-662-2702
tourism@lakecounty.org
www.lakecounty.org
• Maureen Riedy, President
• Maureen Riedy, President
• Peggy Altman, Visitor & Partner Services Coordinator
• Kimberly Ghys, Senior Sales Manager
• Hassan El Neklawy, Chair, Lincolnshire Marriott Resort
• Mike Allison, Treasurer
• Anthony Haag, Marketing Manager
• Theresa Lewis, Sales Manager

Description:
Mission is to increase awareness of Lake County, IL as a premier tourism destination through a collective sales and marketing approach that stimulates overnight stays and enhances visitor spending and ultimately generates a substanitial economic impact for Lake County communities.

LAKE LANIER CVB
2875 BROWNS BRIDGE ROAD
GAINESVILLE, GA 30507
678-696-2491
Fax: 770-503-1349
jennifer@lakelaniercvb.com
www.lakelaniercvb.com
• Stacey Dickson, President
• Jennifer Miller, Vice President
Description:
Founded 1992. Serves to increase sports tourism in the greater Gainesville/Hall County area, to work with existing sports facilities and groups, and to foster new facilities and groups where the community recognizes a need for them.
Number of Members:
100
Members Services:
Co-op advertising; market facility in the facilities guide; trade show representation; CVB member website link.

LAS CRUCES CONVENTION & VISITORS BUREAU
211 NORTH WATER STREET
LAS CRUCES, NM 88001
575-541-2444
Fax: 575-541-2164
cvb@lascrucescvb.org
www.lascrucescvb.org
• Jennifer Bales, Director Of Sales
(575) 541-2258
• Phillip San Filippo, Executive Director
(505) 541-2444
psfilippo@las-cruces.org
• Chris Faivre, Director of Marketing and Communications
(575) 541-2258
cfaivre@las-cruces.org
• Edward S Carnathan, Sports Sales
(505) 541-2216
ecarnathan@las-cruces.org

LAS VEGAS CONVENTION & VISITORS AUTHORITY
3150 PARADISE ROAD
LAS VEGAS, NV 89109
702-892-0711
877-847-4858
www.visitlasvegas.com
• Tom Collins, Chairman
• Tom Jenkins, Treasurer
• Nancy Murphy, Vice President Sales
Nature of Service:
Promotes sports and economic development in Las Vegas and surrounding areas.
Auto Sports Sponsor:
NASCAR Sprint Cup Series: UAW-Dodge 400.
Rodeo Sponsor:
Clark County Fair & Rodeo; Bill Pickett Invitational Rodeo; Wrangler National Finals Rodeo.
Equestrian Sponsor:
Arabian Breeders World Cup.
Supercross/Motocross Sponsor:

Amp'D Mobile Supercross Series.
Wrestling Sponsor:
USA Wrestling World Team Trials.
Martial Arts Sponsor:
Tuff N' Uff Amateur Mixed Martial Arts.

LAS VEGAS EVENTS
770 EAST WARM SPRINGS ROAD
SUITE 140
LAS VEGAS, NV 89119
702-260-8605
Fax: 702-260-8622
www.lasvegasevents.com
• Pat Christenson, President
• Dale Eeles, VP Event Development
Description:
We produce, present, and support premier events that drive tourism and increase awareness of the Las Vegas area as the Entertainment Capital of the World. Events held are: Monster Jam World Finals 2006; 2006 NHRA SummitRacing.co Nationals; LPGA Takefuji Classic; Laughlin River Run; THQ World Superscross GP/THQ AMA Supercross Series Finals; NIRA West Coast Regional Finals Rodeo; AFL Arena Bowl Championships; Vegas Summer League; Las Vegas Prep Basketball Showcase; SCORE Las Vegas Terrible's Cup II; Prim 300 Score; Las Vegas 350(NASCAR Craftsman Truck Series); ACDelco Las Vegas NHRA Nationals; Aviation Nation; Senior Softball Winter Worlds; NF

LAWRENCE SPORTS CORPORATION
734 VERMONT STREET
SUITE 101
LAWRENCE, KS 66044-0586
785-865-4499
888-529-5267
Fax: 785-865-4400
admin@visitlawrence.com
www.visitlawrence.com/sports
• Bob Sanner, Director Sports Conventions
• Judy Billings, Director
(785) 865-4494
Sports Services Founded:
1988
Description:
Markets and promotes Lawrence as the preferred destination for athletic events that benefit the community both economically and socially. The LSC supports these events with assistance in hte areas of funding, management, marketing and organization to help make them as successful as possible.

LEE ISLAND COAST VISITOR & CONVENTION BUREAU
12800 UNIVERSITY DRIVE
SUITE 550
FT. MYERS, FL 33907
239-338-3550
800-237-6444
Fax: 239-334-1106
VCB@leegov.com
www.leeislandcoast.com
• Suya T. Davenport, Executive Director
• Pamela Johnson, CDME, Sales Director
• Lee Rose, APR, Communications Manager
Description:
To increase tourism in the off season and to increase awareness about Lee County as a vacation destination. Serves to promote sports development and attract events and

sport related meetings to the Lee County area which includes Fort Myers Beach, Lehigh Acres, Bonita Springs, Pine Island, Boca Grande and Sanibel/Captiva Islands, Cape Coral in the off peak tourist season, May through December.

LEHIGH VALLEY SPORTS COMMISSION
840 HAMILTON STREET
SUITE 200
ALLENTOWN, PA 18101
610-882-9200
800-747-0561
Fax: 610-882-0343
• Michael Kusinuk, Sports Marketing Director
mkuzy@lehighvalleypa.org
• Kim Lilly, VP
kim@lehighvalleypa.org
Description:
Goal is to promote Lehigh Valley as a sports destination by attracting and retaining sporting events and tournaments, thereby ersulting in economic benefits for the region. Also supports the efforts of local sporting events and facilities.
Facilities Available
10 colleges and universities for multiple sports county parks & fields, Raach Field House, soccer fields, IAX, bowling, golf, basketball, baseball, softball, disc golf.

LEXINGTON AREA SPORTS AUTHORITY
301 EAST VINE STREET
LEXINGTON, KY 40507
859-244-7710
800-848-1224
Fax: 859-389-7225
• Rick Hatcher, President/Executive Director
rhatcher@visitlex.com
Description:
The primary purpose of the Lexington Area Sports Authority (LASA) is to promote amateur sports in the Lexington area by bringing in, and supporting, quality amateur athletic events. These events, which utilize local public and private facilities and resources, have a tremendous social and economic impact on the community.

LINCOLN SPORTS COMMISSION
1135 M ST, STE 200
LINCOLN, NE 68501
402-434-5335
800-423-8212
Fax: 402-434-2360
www.lincoln.org
• Jeff Maul, Executive Director
• Derek Feyerheim, Director Of Sales
Description:
Founded 1988. Develops and implements programs to attract sports events and sports meetings to Lincoln and Lancaster County Nebraska.

LISLE CONVENTION & VISITOR BUREAU
925 BURLINGTON AVENUE
LISLE, IL 60532
630-769-1000
800-733-9811
Fax: 630-769-1006
lislevisitor@stayinlisle.com
www.lislecvb.com
• Hilton Lisle, General Manager
Description:
A full service CVB that will be a valuable resource in making any event, meeting,

multi sports

reunion, retreat or vacation as enjoyable and successful as possible.

LONG ISLAND CVB & SPORTS COMMISSION
330 MOTOR PKWY
SUITE 203
HAUPPAUGE, NY 11788
631-951-3900
877-FUN-ON-LI
jrothman@discoverlongisland.com
www.discoverlongisland.com/sports
• Jennifer Rothman, Sales Manager
(631) 951-3900
jrothman@discoverlongisland.com
• R Moke McGowan, President
(631) 951-3900
mmcgowan@discoverlongisland.com
Description:
Founded 1992. Dedicated to attracting professional and amateur sporting events, championships and related industry conferences to Long Island for the purpose of economic development. Also provides assistance to organizations interested in hosting sporting events or functions on Long Island. Works directly with national governing bodies and sport event planners.
Member Services:
A division of the Long Island Convention & Visitors Bureau. Represents Long Island in the national and international sports marketplace.

LOS ANGELES SPORTS & ENTERTAINMENT COMMISSION
333 SOUTH HOPE STREET
18TH FLOOR
LOS ANGELES, CA 90071
213-236-2381
Fax: 213-326-2368
www.lasec.net
• Kathryn S Schloessman, President
(213) 236-2381
• Cindy Hanson, Sports Manager
(213) 236-2361
Sports Services Founded:
1995
Description:
The official organization for the City of Los Angeles to seek, host, promote and retain major sporting and entertainment events that postively impact the local economy. These events attract visitors to the city, give them a reason to stay longerand return more frequently and reinforce Los Angeles as an event destination for national and international visitors.

LOS ANGELES SPORTS COUNCIL
350 SOUTH BIXEL STREET
SUITE 250
LOS ANGELES, CA 90017
213-482-6333
Fax: 213-482-6340
www.lasports.org
• Karen Brodkin, Chair
• Richard W. Cook, Vice Chair
• Sheldon I Ausman, Treasurer
Description:
A non-profit civic organization which works to attract major events to the area.

LOUISVILLE CONVENTION & VISITORS BUREAU
401 WEST MAIN STREET
SUITE 2300
LOUISVILLE, KY 40202
502-584-2121
888-568-4784
Fax: 502-584-6697
info@gotolouisville.com
www.gotolouisville.com
• Cleo Battle, Executive Vice President
cbattle@gotolouisville.com
• Jennifer Barnett, Vice President of Convention Development
jbarnett@gotolouisville.com
• Stacey Yates, Vice President of Marketing Communications
syates@gotolouisville.com
• James Wood, President/CEO
jwood@gotolouisville.com
• Karen Wiliams, Executive VP
kwilliams@gotolouisville.com
• Stacey Yates, Vice President Communications/Marketing
syates@gotolouisville.com
• Doris Sims, Director of Bureau Services
dsims@gotolouisville.com
Description:
Promotes Louisville and Jefferson County as a potential host sight for sporting events and meetings.

LUBBOCK SPORTS AUTHORITY
1500 BROADWAY
6TH FLOOR
LUBBOCK, TX 79401
806-747-5232
800-692-4035
Fax: 806-747-1419
www.visitlubbock.org
• John Osborne, CEO
• Amy Zientec, Director of Sales
Description:
Serves to attract sports events and meetings to the Lubbock, Texas area.

MACOMB AREA CONVENTION AND VISITORS BUREAU
201 SOUTH LAFAYETTE STREET
MACOMB, IL 61455
309-833-1315
Fax: 309-833-3575
www.makeitmacomb.com
• Tamara Parker, Interim Executive Director
• Katy Vizdai, Special Projects Coordinator
Description:
A non-profit organization began in July of 1998. The CVB is responsible for bringing in and assisting with conferences and conventions while also organizing local events.

MACON-BIBB COUNTY CONVENTION AND VISITORS BUREAU
450 MARTIN LUTHER KING JR BLVD
MACON, GA 31201
478-743-3401
800-768-3401
www.maconga.org
• Monica W Smith, President/CEO
(478) 743-1074
• Valerie Bradley, Communications Manager
(478) 743-1074
vbradley@maconga.org
• Monica Smith CMP CASE CDME, President and CEO
(478) 743-1074

Description:
Founded 1980. Serves to attract sports events and meetings to the greater Macon area.

MANHATTAN AREA SPORTS COMMISSION (CONVENTION AND VISITORS BUREAU)
501 POYNTZ AVENUE
MANHATTAN, KS 66502
785-776-8829
sports@manhattan.org
www.manhattancvb.org
• Marcia Rozell, Tourism Sales Manager
• Karen Hibbard, Director
• Christy Chase, Convention Sales Manager
• Kendra Dekat, Service Coordinator
• Autumn Shoemaker, Marketing Coordinator

MARICOPA COUNTY SPORTS COMMISSION
ARIZONA CENTER
400 EAST VAN BUREN STREET
SUITE 600
PHOENIX, AZ 85004
602-258-6272
• John Schmieder, President
• Ed Durkin, Sales/Marketing Manager
Sports Services Founded:
1988
Description:
Mission is to represent the citizens of Maricopa County in the quest to establish Maricopa County as a premier national and international sports destination; to assist in the promotion of local events and teams; to develop programs that positively affect our community's youth and to provide Maricopa County residents the widest variety of great sports experiences possible.

MARYLAND SPORTS
WAREHOUSE AT CAMDEN YARDS
333 W CAMDEN ST
4TH FLOOR
BALTIMORE, MD 21201
410-223-4158
Fax: 410-333-1888
info@marylandsports.us
www.marylandsports.us
• Ashley Harper Cottrell, Project Manager
(410) 767-1416
acottrell@marylandsports.us
• Terry Hasseltine, Executive Director
(410) 223-4158
thasseltine@marylandsports.us
• Kelli Gerding, Project Coordinator
(410) 223-4671
kgerding@marylandsports.us
Description:
Founded in 2008. Mission: Enhance Maryland's economy, image and quality of life through attraction, promotion, retention and development of regional, national and international sporting events.
Teams:
TEAM Maryland - a statewide initiative designed to collectively market Maryland to the entire sports industry by creating a synergistic approach to the way Maryland is marketed as a sports destination. Currently, fourteen counties have joined the program.

MASHANTUCKET PEQUOT TRIBAL NATION'S ATHLETIC COMMISSION
PO BOX 3378
MASHANTUCKET, CT 06339-3378
860-396-6727
Fax: 860-396-6723
www.boxrec.com
• Joe Letellier, Executive Director
• Richard Butler, Vice Chairman

MASON CITY CONVENTION & VISITOR BUREAU
9 NORTH FEDERAL AVENUE
MASON CITY, IA 50401
641-423-5724
Fax: 641-423-5725
www.masoncityia.com
• Robin Anderson, Executive Director
• Kara Ruge, Program Director
kruge@masoncityia.com
• Debra Derr, President
• Bob Klocke, Treasurer
• David Laundner, Government Affairs DVP
• Troy Swanson, DVP Workforce

MASSACHUSETTS SPORTS & ENTERTAINMENT COMMISSION
PO BOX 170427
BOSTON, MA 2117
617-614-1203
Fax: 617-507-8491
• Sam Weisman, Chairman
• Jonathan H Paris, Executive Director
Description:
Founded in 1992. A private, non-for-profit corporation established to attract and stage major sporting events and sports related meetings throughout Massachusetts. Its principal purposes are to increase economic impact through events, travel and tourism; to enhance the quality of life for all residents by the presence of exciting sporting events; and to improve opportunities for youth in sports.
Publications:
SportsMatters, quarterly newsletter.

MEMPHIS & SHELBY COUNTY SPORTS AUTHORITY
160 N MAIN STREET
MEMPHIS, TN 38103
901-222-2300
www.shelbycountytn.gov
• Bill McGaughey, Chairman
Sports Services Founded:
1997
Description:
To promote the Mid-South region by supporting and developing economic impact and quality of life through sporting events. Our main focus is to attract sporting events to the area, as well as supporting our professional, college and high school athletics.

MESA CONVENTION & VISITORS BUREAU
120 NORTH CENTER
MESA, AZ 85201
480-827-4700
800-283-6372
Fax: 480-827-4704
www.visitmesa.com
• Josh Todd, Sports Sales Manager
• Rick Elder, Communcations Manager
• Milt Ford, Sales/Marketing Director

Description:
Mesa Convention & Visitors Bureau; Mesa Sports & Tourism Development

METRO DENVER SPORTS COMMISSION
444 SHERMAN STREET
SUITE 300
DENVER, CO 80203
303-744-6372
Fax: 303-648-4408
• Sue Baldwin, Interim President
• Debora Hurley, Director Coroprate Membership
(303) 534-5517
Sports Service Founded:
2001
Description:
Founded to attract economically beneficial sporting events to the Denver market. The purpose of the Metro Denver Sports Commission is to create a legacy of economic and social vitality through sports.

METROPOLITAN RICHMOND SPORTS BACKERS
100 AVENUE OF CHAMPIONS
SUITE 300
RICHMOND, VA 23230
804-285-9495
Fax: 804-285-3132
info@sportsbackers.org
www.sportsbackers.org
• Jon Lugbill, Executive Director
jon@sportsbackers.org
• Scott Schricker, Marketing Director
scott@sportsbackers.com
Sports Services Founded:
1991
Description:
A 501(c) (3) charitable non-profit organization whose vision is to transform greater Richmond into the most physically active community in the nation by leading the area in embracing and celebrating an active lifestyle.
Publications:
Sports Backers Quarterly; e-Newsletters

METROPOLITAN SPORTS FACILITIES COMMISSION
900 S. 5TH ST
MINNEAPOLIS, MN 55415
612-332-0386
Fax: 612-332-8334
www.msfc.com
• William Lester, Executive Director
(612) 332-0386
• Steve Maki, PE, Director of Facilities & Engineering
• Mary Fox-Stroman, CPA, Director of Finance
Description:
In addition to being the bome of the Minnesota Vikings, the Metrodome serves the state of Minnesota by hosting amateur events, cultural events, and family-focused activities.

METROPOLITAN TUCSON CONVENTION & VISITORS BUREAU
100 SOUTH CHURCH AVENUE
TUCSON, AZ 85701
520-624-1817
800-638-8350
Fax: 520-884-7804
info@visittucson.org
www.visittucson.org

• Jonathan Walker, President/CEO
(800) 638-8350
• Vince Trinidad, Director Sports Development
(800) 638-8350
• Allison Cooper, Director of Marketing

MIDLAND CHAMBER CONVENTION & VISITORS BUREAU
109 NORTH MAIN
MIDLAND, TX 79701
432-683-3381
800-624-6435
Fax: 432-686-3556
www.visitmidlandtx.com
• Bobby Burns, President & CEO, Midland Chamber of Commerce
bobby@midlandtxchamber.com
• Gaylia Olivas, Vice President, Convention & Visitors Bureau
golivas@visitmidlandtexas.com
• Norma Chavez, Administrative Assistant to CVB
• Brenda Kissko, Tourism & Public Relations Manager
brenda@visitmidlandtexas.com
• Katie Sangl, Sports Sales Manager
ksangl@visitmidlandtexas.com
• Brenda Kissko, Travel &â€™™Tourism Manager
• Gaylia Olivas, Director, Convention & Visitors Bureau
Description:
Promotes the Midland Texas and surrounding areas as an ideal location for sporting events.

MINNEAPOLIS CONVENTION & VISITORS ASSOCIATION, GREATER
1301 SECOND AVENUE SOUTH
MINNEAPOLIS, MN 55401
612-335-6000
Fax: 612-335-6757
www.minneapolis.org
• Jeff D. Johnson, Executive Director
• Mark Zirbel, Director of Events
• Christine Hunjas, Director Business Admistration
Description:
Actively solicits amateur and professional sporting events that result in a direct dollar benefit to Minneapolis and the Twin Cities area. Capable of coordinating all aspects of the bidding process.

MINNEAPOLIS METRO NORTH CONVENTION & VISITORS BUREAU
7100 NORTHLAND CIRCLE NORTH
SUITE 102
MINNEAPOLIS, MN 55428
763-566-7722
800-541-4364
Fax: 763-566-6526
info@visitminneapolisnorth.com
www.minneapolisnorthwest.com
• Dave Looby, Executive Director
(763) 252-1415
• Danielle Moon, Sales & Marketing Coordinator
(763) 252-1410
• Lindsay Spiros, Sales & Marketing Manager
(763) 252-1413
• Tim Zunker, Senior Sports & Marketing Manager
(763) 252-1412
• Katie Blake, Creative Marketing & Project

Coordinator
(763) 252-1416
• Brooke Stoeckel-Whaylen,
Director/Meetings & Events
(763) 252-1420
brooke@visitminneapolisnorth.com
Member Services:
Site visits, bid presentations, team discounts from area businesses, lodgingproperties, welcome packets, itinerary planning assistance, familiarization tours.
Description:
A destination marketing organization representing 11 cities in the north and west suburbs of Minneapolis and Saint Paul. These cities include Anoka, Arden Hills, Blaine, Brooklyn Center, Coon Rapids, Fridley, Ham Lake, maple Grove, Mounds View & Shoreview.

MOBILE BAY CONVENTION & VISITORS BUREAU
PO BOX 204
MOBILE, AL 36601-0204
251-208-2000
800-566-2453
Fax: 251-208-2060
visitmobile@mobile.org
www.mobile.org
• David Buzzard, President
• Jay Garraway, Finance/Administration Director
jay-garraway@mobile.org
• Stacy Hamilton, Vice President Marketing/Commmunications
Description:
Founded 1986. Serves to promote sports development and attract sports events and conventions to the Mobile, Alabama area.

MONROE COUNTY SPORTS COMMISSION
400 ANDRES STREET
SUITE 100
ROCHESTER, NY 14604
585-262-3832
Fax: 585-232-3453
www.monroecountysports.org
• Steve Hausmann, President
• Tim Elie, Vice President
• Gary Mervis, Secretary
• Dan Manson, Treasurer
• Jim Lebeau, Managing Director
(585) 262-2009
jimlebeau@hotmail.com
• Rich Mackey, Marketing/Sales
(585) 262-3832
scottb@monroecountysports.org
• Jacob Linderberry, Sales & Operations
(585) 262-3832
Description:
Serves to promote sports development and attract sports events and conventions to the Rochester, New York Sports Area.

MUNCIE SPORTS COMMISSION INC
3700 SOUTH MADISON STREET
MUNCIE, IN 47302
765-284-2700
800-369-0082
Fax: 765-284-3002
www.visitmuncie.org
• Jim Mansfield, Executive Director
jim@visitmuncie.org
• Julie Ashton, Business Manager
Year Founded:
1993

Description:
Founded to advance economic development and to enhance the quality of life in Delaware County through the development of sports and hobby acticities. 11 Soccer fields with restroom and small concession building. 5 ball diamonds with restroom and concession
Facilities:
Muncie Sportsplex-soccer, softball/fastpitch/little league baseball

NASHVILLE SPORTS COUNCIL
414 UNION STREET
SUITE 800
NASHVILLE, TN 37201
615-743-3120
Fax: 615-244-3540
generalinfo@nashvillesports.com
www.nashvillesports.com
• Scott Ramsey, President and CEO
(615) 743-3122
SRamsey@NashvilleSports.com
• Gary Karl Alexander, Sr. VP and COO
(615) 743-3123
GAlexander@NashvilleSports.com
Description:
Founded 1992. The mission is to postively impact the economy and quality of life of the Greater Nashville Area by attracting and promoting professional and amateur sports.

NASSAU COUNTY SPORTS COMMISSION
1055 STEWART AVENUE
BETHPAGE, NY 11714
516-918-3799
Fax: 516-365-3632
www.nassausports.org
• Gary I. Wadler, Chairman/President
• Bryan Revello, Executive Director
• Edward Mangano, Ex Officio
Description:
Founded 1992. Promotes the advancement of sports in Nassau County from every perspective - amateur, professional, youth and master sports, and activities for the differently-abled. Works cooperatively with the public and private sectors in identifying, coordinating, and developing sports programs, facilities, and events for the benefit of the economy and the enjoyment of the community.

NEBRASKA DIVISION OF TRAVEL AND TOURISM
1135 M STREET
SUITE 300
LINCOLN, NE 68501
402-434-5335
800-423-8212
Fax: 402-436-2360
www.lincoln.org
• Derek Feyerherm, Director of Sales & Operations
(402) 436-2354
• Melanie Maynard, Social, Military, Education, Religious, Frate
(402) 436-2310
• Jeff Maul, Executive Director
• Tracie Simpson, Service Coordinator
Publications:
Nebraska Travel Guide

NEW ORLEANS METROPOLITAN CONVENTION & VISITORS BUREAU
2020 ST CHARLES AVENUE
NEW ORLEANS, LA 70130
504-566-5011
800-672-6124
Fax: 504-566-5046
internet@neworleanscvb.com
www.neworleanscvb.com
• Kelly Schulz, Vice President
(504) 566-5019
• Sarah Forman, Community Coordinator
(504) 566-5021
Description:
Serves to attract sports-related meetings, conventions and shows to the greater New Orleans area. Provides assistance with hotel, meeting facility and venue selection, convention services and visitor information.

NEW ORLEANS SPORTS FOUNDATION, GREATER
2020 ST CHARLES AVENUE
4TH FLOOR
NEW ORLEANS, LA 70130
504-525-5678
Fax: 504-529-1622
media@gnosports.com
www.gnosports.com
• Jay Cicero, President/Chief Executive Officer
jcicero@gnosf.org
• Billy Ferrante, Vice President/Marketing/Events
bferrante@gnosf.org
• Sam Joffray, Vice President/Communications
administration@gnosf.org
• Alison Comeaux, Events/Operations
acomeaux@gnosf.org
Description:
Founded 1988.The Greater New Orleans Sports Foundation (GNOSF) was formed with a vision to enhance the city's ability to attract, promote and manage major sporting events that have a positive economic impact on the Greater New Orleans area. The GNOSF has been involved in attracting or promoting nearly 75 events including Super Bowl XXX1 (1997) and Super Bowl XXXVI (2002), The NCAA Final Four (1993) and the Olympic Track & Field Trials (1992). The GNOSF was selected as the Sports Commission of the Year in 1996 by the International Sports Summit.

NORFOLK CONVENTION & VISITORS BUREAU
232 EAST MAIN STREET
NORFOLK, VA 23510
757-664-6620
800-368-3097
Fax: 757-622-3663
rsteven@norfolkcvb.com
www.norfolkcvb.com
• Anthony J. DiFilippo, President & CEO
• Erin Filarecki, Media Relations Manager
• Sarah Caroll, Executive Assistant
• Jennifer Mullin, Marketing & Public Relations Assistant
• Mary Garrett, Director Marketing/Communications
mgarrett@norfolkcvb.com
• Donna Allen, Vice President of Sales & Marketing
dallen@norfolkcvb.com

NORMAN CONVENTION & VISITORS BUREAU
2424 SPRINGER DRIVE
SUITE 107
NORMAN, OK 73069
405-366-8095
800-767-7260
stephen@visitnorman.com
www.visitnorman.com
• Stephen Koranda, Executive Director
stephen@visitnorman.com
• Susan Bash, Sales Manager
• Stefanie Brickman, Communications
Manager
• Michelle Samp, Group Sales Manager
• Taylor Mauldin, Visitor Services Specialist

NORTH CAROLINA AMATEUR SPORTS
406 BLACKWELL STREET
SUITE 120
DURHAM, NC 27701
919-361-1133
Fax: 919-361-2559
ncas@ncsports.org
www.ncsports.org
• Chuck Hobgood, President
ext 5
• Ragan Williams, Event Director/State
Games
ext 3
Description:
Founded 1983. Develops and promotes
amateur athletics and the Olympic
movement in North Carolina. Hosts such
activities as State Games of North Carolina.
Sponsorship packages available for all
events and forming a bicycle tour across
North Carolina.

NORTH CAROLINA SPORTS DEVELOPMENT OFFICE
301 NORTH WILMINGTON ST
RALEIGH, NC 27601-1058
919-733-4151
800-VISIT NC
Fax: 919-733-8582
mmcglohon@nccommerce.com
www.nccommerce.com/sports
• Kristi Driver, Sports Manager
ext 5
kdriver@nccommerce.com
Nature of Sports Service:
Founded 1990. Promotes North Carolina as
a premier sports destination for amateur,
collegiate and professional sports teams
and organizations.
Publications:
North Carolina Sports Events Directory,
annually with mid-year update. North
Carolina Sports Facility Guide, annually.

NORTH LITTLE ROCK VISITORS BUREAU
PO BOX 5511
NORTH LITTLE ROCK, AR 72119
501-758-1424
800-643-4690
Fax: 501-758-5752
www.northlittlerock.org
• Shannon Harris, Sports & Special Events
Coordinator
• Summer Toyne, VIC Coordinator
stoyne@northlittlerock.org
Description:
Founded 1975. Serves to promote sports
development and attract sports events to the

North Little Rock, and the Central Arkansas
area.

NYC & COMPANY
810 SEVENTH AVENUE
3RD FLOOR
NEW YORK, NY 10019
212-484-1200
www.nycgo.com/sports
• Jeff Mohl, Vice President, Sports
Marketing
• Evan Ely, Manager, Sports Marketing
Description:
The Sports Marketing Department at NYC &
Company is responsible for attracting,
creating and promoting sporting events
throughout New York City's five boroughs.
The department facilitates the production of
a diverse line-up of high-profile professional
and amateur events that excite area sports
fans, generates revenue for the region and
garners positive exposure for New York City.

OKLAHOMA CITY ALL SPORTS ASSOCIATION
211 NORTH ROBINSON
SUITE 250
OKLAHOMA CITY, OK 73102
405-236-5000
800-434-5000
Fax: 405-236-5008
• Tim Brassfield, Executive Director
tbrassfield@okcallsports.org
• David Forester, Director of Event
Operations
• Sean Maguire, Director of communications
and marketing
• Claire Oliver, Events manager
• Tris Thomas, Controller
• Tim Brassfield, Executive Director
(405) 236-5000
tim@okcallsports.org
Other Events Sponsored/Co-Sponsored:
All Sports Pro/Am golf Invitational Sportsfest
(winter games of our state games). Big XII
Baseball Tournament, NCAA Women's
College World Series, Sooner State Games
(State Games of Oklahoma).
Member Services:
Priority on ticket purchasing for events, plus
two reserved seats for the All-College
tournament with many other benefits
depending on amount of sponsor
participation.
Publications:
Souvenir programs for events.
Membership Requirements:
$200 VIP membership; $350 ELITE
membership.
Description:
Founded 1957 as a non-profit Corporation.
Promotes sponsor and finances the
All-College Basketball Tournament and
other sporting events in the Oklahoma City
area.

OREGON SPORTS AUTHORITY
1888 SW MADISON STREET
2ND FLOOR
PORTLAND, OR 97205-1717
503-234-4500
Fax: 503-234-3853
info@oregonsports.org
• Drew Mahalic, Chief Executive Officer
drew@oregonsports.org

Description:
Local sponsorhip opportunities for major
Oregon sports events

OVERLAND PARK CONVENTION & VISITORS BUREAU
CORPORATE WOODS BUILDING 29
9001 W. 110TH STREET
SUITE 100
OVERLAND PARK, KS 66210
913-491-0123
800-262-7275
Fax: 913-491-0015
info@opcvb.org
• Jerry Cook, President
jcook@opcvb.org
• Judy Shellhorn, Information Services
(913) 491-0123
jshell@visitoverlandpark.com
• Libby Shilpey, Director of Finance
(913) 491-0123
libbysply@visitoverlandpark.com
• Brad Plumb, Sales Manager
(913) 491-0123
bplumb@visitoverlandpark.com
• Justin Stine, Director
(913) 491-0123
jstine@overlandparksportsalliance.com
• Liron BenDor, Vice President of Marketing
(913) 491-0123
lbendor@visitoverlandpark.com
• Kelly Peetoom, Vice President Sales
kpeetoom@opcvb.org
Description:
Serves to promote Overland Park and the
surrounding areas as a location for sports
events, conventions, meetings etc.

PALM BEACH COUNTY SPORTS COMMISSION, INC.
1555 PALM BEACH LAKES BOULEVARD
SUITE 930
WEST PALM BEACH, FL 33401
561-233-3180
Fax: 561-233-3125
info@palmbeachsports.com
www.palmbeachsports.com
• Stephanie Lanza, Secretary/Treasurer
• George Linely, Executive Director
(561) 233-3123
glinley@palmbeachsports.com
• Kris Pursell, Director or Event Operations
(561) 233-3124
kpursell@palmbeachsports.com
Member Services:
Discounts to luncheons and special events;
other discounts; lapel pin; certificate;
membership card.
Publications:
Annual Report; SCOREBOARD, monthly
newsletter; Membership Directory.
Membership Requirements:
Pay dues of $50, $100, $500
Description:
Founded 1985. Serves to promote Palm
Beach County as a location for sports
entertainment. Also develops programs to
improve the quality of life for the youth of
Palm Beach County through sports.

PANAMA CITY BEACH CHAMBER OF COMMERCE
309 RICHARD JACKSON BOULEVARD
SUITE 101
PANAMA CITY BEACH, FL 32407
850-235-1159
Fax: 850-235-2301

multi sports

chamber@pcbeach.org
www.pcbeach.org
• Beth Oltman, CEO, President
• Marta Rose, Vice President of
Communications
• Derrick Bennett, Chairman
(850) 588-8909
derrick@derrickbennett.com
• Mike Burke, Secretary
(850) 236-4444
mburke@Burkeblue.com
• Jayna Leach, Treasurer
(850) 230-6110
jleach@sterlingresorts.com
Description:
Founded 1987.

PANAMA CITY BEACH CONVENTION & VISITORS BUREAU, INC.
17001 PANAMA CITY BEACH PARKWAY
PANAMA CITY BEACH, FL 32413
850-233-5070
800-327-8352
Fax: 850-233-5072
www.playpanamacitybeach.com
• Richard Sanders, VP of Sports Marketing
(850) 233-5070
rsanders@visitpanamacitybeach.com
• Richard Sanders, VP of Sports Marketing
& Special Events

PENSACOLA SPORTS ASSOCIATION
P.O. BOX 12463
PENSACOLA, FL 32591
850-434-2800
Fax: 850-432-4237
events@pensacolasports.com
www.pensacolasports.com
• James Currie, Event Specialist
• Jason Libbert, Events
(850) 748-0197
• Liz Hamrick, Event Coordinator
(850) 291-1787
• Ray Palmer, Executive Director
rpalmer@pensacolasports.com
• Sally Garst, Special Events
(850) 434-2800
sgarst@pensacolasports.com
Description:
Promotes Pensacola and the surrounding
areas as a location for sports events,
meetings, conventions etc.
Year Founded:
1955

PEORIA AREA CONVENTION & VISITORS BUREAU
456 FULTON STREET
SUITE 300
PEORIA, IL 61602
309-676-0303
800-747-0302
info@peoria.org
www.peoria.org
• Don Welch, President/CEO
(309) 282-3273
dwelch@peoria.org
• Sue Altherton, Vice President of Sales and
Marketing
(309) 282-3281
satherton@peoria.org
• Gail Erti, Vice Presidentof Finance and
Administration
(309) 282-3275
gertl@peoria.org
• Lelonie Luff, Partnership/Tourism Sales
Manager

(309) 282-3282
lluff@peoria.org
Description:
Founded in 1980. Promotes Peoria and the
surrounding areas as a location for sports
events, meetings, conventions, and leisure
and group travel to increase overnight
visitors to the Peoria area.
Number of Members:
480
Member Services:
Members are promoted by PACVB and its
staff. Members are listed in visitors guide,
area maps and on PACVB website.
Members are on PACVB mailing list to
receive notices, updates of information and
PACVB sponsored events
Member Requirements:
Annual Dues.
Publications:
Peoria Area Visitor Guide, Calendar of
Events, Peoria area ePromoter newsletter,
Website, Facilities and Destination Guide
CD-Rom, Driving Maps, Illinois River
Country, Online Business Directory.

PHILADELPHIA SPORTS CONGRESS
1700 MARKET STREET
SUITE 3000
PHILADELPHIA, PA 19103
215-636-3300
Fax: 215-636-3327
sportscongress@pcvb.org
• Dan Miller, Executive Director, Hotel Sales
(215) 636-3479
danm@pcvb.org
• Pat Kraft, Executive Director, Citywide
Sales
(215) 636-3305
pkraft@pcvb.org
Publications:
E-Newsletter: Quarterly
Description:
Founded 1987. Promotes the Philadelphia
region as a major sports capital, both
nationally and internationally, by attracting,
developing and supporting professional and
amateur athletic events, meetings,
conventions and clinics which will contribute
to the economic development and quality of
life throughout the region.

PHOENIX CONVENTION & VISITORS BUREAU, GREATER
400 EAST VAN BURENT
SUITE 60
PHOENIX, AZ 85004
602-254-6500
877-CALLPHX
Fax: 602-253-4415
visitors@visitphoenix.com
www.phoenixcvb.com
• Maria Lane, National Sales Manager
Online:
BLOG:
www.thehotsheetblog.com/visitphoenix;
FACEBOOK: visit phoenix; TWITTER:
visitphoenix

PLANO CONVENTION & VISITORS BUREAU
2000 EAST SPRING CREEK PARKWAY
PLANO, TX 75074
972-941-5843
800-81-PLANO
Fax: 972-424-0002

• Melanie Copeland, Administration
Assistant
(972) 941-5843
• Anastasia Hoosman, Convention Service
Coordinator
(972) 941-5842
• Milleran Jockel, Marketing Manager
(972) 941-5825
• Cissy Aberg, Sports Marketing Manager
(972) 941-5849
• Karen Fogle, Association & Corporate
Sales Manager
(972) 941-5848
• Mark Thompson, CVB Director
(972) 422-6805
markth@plano.gov
Description:
Serves to recruit and promote amateur and
professional sports events to the greater
Plano and surrounding areas.

POLK COUNTY SPORTS MARKETING
2701 LAKE MYRTLE PARK ROAD
AUBURNDALE, FL 33823
863-551-4750
Fax: 863-551-4740
zimm@centralfloridasports.com
www.centralfloridasports.com
• Marc Zimmerman, Sales & Event Manager
mzimmerman@centralfloridasports.com
• Mark Jackson, Director Tourism/Sports
Marketing
mark@centralfloridasports.com
• Kris Keprios, Marketing Manager
kris@centralfloridasports.com
• Neal Duncan, Sponsorship Sales Manager
neal@centralfloridasports.com
Description:
Serves to recruit and promote amateur and
professional sports events to Polk County
and the surrounding areas.

PRINCE GEORGE'S COUNTY CONFERENCE & VISITORS BUREAU, INC.
9200 BASIL COURT
SUITE 101
LARGO, MD 20774
301-925-8300
Fax: 301-925-2053
visitorinfo@co.pg.md.us
www.visitprincegeorges.com
• J. Matthew Neitzey, Executive Director
mneitzey@co.pg.md.us
• Danny M. Brown, Administration Manager
dmbrown@co.pg.md.us
• Carl Smith, Jr., Marketing Manager
csmith@co.pg.md.us

PRINCE WILLIAM COUNTY/MANASSAS CONVENTION & VISITORS BUREAU
10611 BALLS FORD ROAD
SUITE 110
MANASSAS, VA 20109
703-396-7130
800-432-1792
Fax: 703-396-7160
info@visitpwc.com
www.visitpwc.com
• Tabatha Mullins, Executive Director
(703) 396-7130
tmullins@visitpwc.com
Description:
The destination marketing organization for
Prince William County and Manassas.
Through targeted marketing efforts the CVB
promotes the region to potential leisure

visitors, tour groups, and media representatives for the purpose of increasing tourism and economic growth. The CVB is an independent, non-profit organization funded by Prince William County.

QUAD CITIES SPORTS COMMISSION
1601 RIVER DRIVE
SUITE 110
MOLINE, IL 61265
800-747-7800
Fax: 309-764-9443
lhunt@visitquadcities.com
www.quadcitiessports.com
• Joe Taylor, Chair/President/CEO
• Lynn Hunt, Vice President Tourism
(309) 277-0937
lhunt@visitquadcities.com
Sports Service Founded:
1996
Description:
Quad Cities Sports Commission is a not-for-profit (non-profit) organization dedicated to developing the quality of life in the Quad Cities by attracting and hosting sporting events that bring a economic impact to our communities. The QCSC is a full-service sports commission that takes a turn-key approach to attracting and hosting each event it bring to the Quad Cities.
Description:
Promotes Moline and the surrounding Illinois area for sports competitions, games, conventions and meetings. The Quad Cities is a cluster of communities located on the Mississippi River, connecting eastern Iowa and western Illinois. The sports commission promotes tournaments, competitions, meets, meeting & convention.

RALEIGH CONVENTION & VISITORS BUREAU (GREATER)
421 FAYETTEVILLE ST SUITE 1505
RALEIGH, NC 27601-2995
919-834-5900
800-849-8499
info@raleighsports.org
www.raleighsports.org
• Scott Dupree, VP Sports Marketing
(919) 645-2657
sdupree@raleighsports.org
• Tori Collins, Assistant Director of Sports Marketing
(919) 645-2664
tori@raleighsports.org
• Jason Philbeck, Sports Marketing Manager
(919) 645-2660
jphilbeck@raleighsports.org
Publications:
Maps, Visitors Guide.

RENO-SPARKS CONVENTION AUTHORITY
PO BOX 837
RENO, NV 89504-0837
775-827-7600
800-367-7366
www.visitrenotahoe.com
• Christopher Baum, President/Chief Executive Officer
(775) 827-7618
• Christopher Baum, President/CEO
• Joe Kelly, Vice President of Facilities
• John Leinen, Vice President of Convention & Tour

• Jennifer Cinningham, Executive Director of Marketing
• Brain Rivers, Director of Finance
• Charlotte Andreson, ASSISTANT TO THE PRESIDENT AND CEO
• Brian River, Vice President Sales/Marketing
(775) 827-7626
Description:
Promotes Reno-Sparks and the surrounding area for sports competitions, games, conventions and meetings.

ROANOKE VALLEY CONVENTION & VISITORS BUREAU
101 SHENANDOAH AVENUE NE
ROANOKE, VA 24016
540-342-6025
1-800-635-5535
Fax: 540-342-7119
info@visitroanokeva.com
www.visitroanokeva.com
• Landon C Howard, Executive Director
dlkjolhede@aol.com
• Kelly Burd-Adams, Director Convention Sales
kburdadams@visitroanokeva.com
Publications:
MEETING PLANNERS GUIDE
Member Services:
Site Inspection Arrangements, Facility, Rate and Contact Information, Local Support Contacts, Family Activity Coordination, Slides and Digital Photography.

ROCHESTER AMATEUR SPORTS COMMISSION
30 CIVIC CENTER DRIVE SE
ROCHESTER, MN 55904
507-280-4701
Fax: 507-280-4703
www.rochsports.com
• Zac Carlson, Operations Coordinator
• Jay Fanta, Operations Assistant
• Ed Hruska, Executive Director
ehruska@rochsports.com
• Ben Boldt, Event Operations Manager
• Shelley Boettcher, Operations Manager
Description:
The Rochester Sports Commission (RASC) was formed by a group of business and sports visionaries. The vision was to bring to Rochester, major national and international events, and along with them, the recognition of Rochester as a hub for amateur sports.

ROCK HILL/YORK COUNTY CONVENTION & VISITORS BUREAU
452 SOUTH ANDERSON RD
PO BOX 11377
ROCK HILL, SC 29730
803-329-5200
888-702-1320
Fax: 803-329-0145
www.visityorkcounty.com
• Bennish Brown, Executive Director
• Lisa Meadows, Executive Director
(803) 329-5200
lmeadows@visityorkcounty.com
• Mikki rentschler, Director of Finance & Administration
(803) 329-5200
• Sonja R Burris, Communications Manager
(803) 329-5200
sburris@visityorkcounty.com

ROCKFORD AREA CONVENTION & VISITORS BUREAU
102 NORTH MAIN STREET
ROCKFORD, IL 61101-1102
815-963-8111
800-521-0849
Fax: 815-963-4298
www.gorockford.com
• Lindsey Arellano, Sports Sales Manager
(815) 489-1653
• John Groh, CEO, President
• Linda Heckert, Chairman
(815) 847-5014
• Darrel Snorek, Vice-Chairman
(815) 282-3535
• Patrick okeefe, Secretary
(815) 637-7269
• Solomon Foley, Treasurer
(815) 397-3377
• Beverly Broyles, Executive Director
(815) 964-9713
• Robert Bob Burden, City of Loves Park Liaison
(815) 654-5034
Description:
Serves to promote sports development and attract sports events to the Rockford Illinois area.

ROSEVILLE PARKS AND RECREATION
2660 CIVIC CENTER DRIVE
ROSEVILLE, MN 55113
651-792-7000
Fax: 651-792-7100
www.ci.roseville.mn.us
• Lonnie Brokke, Director
• Jill Anfang, Assistant Director

ROSEVILLE VISITORS ASSOCIATION
1700 WEST HIGHWAY 36
SUITE 600
ROSEVILLE, MN 55113
651-633-3002
877-980-3002
Fax: 651-636-0475
info@visitroseville.com
www.visitroseville.com
• Julie Wearn, Executive Director
• Shannon Hirstein, Sales Manager
(651) 633-3002
shirstein@visitroseville.com
Description:
Roseville is located outside of Minneapolis and Saint Paul. Home to the Guidant John Rose Oval, and minutes from the University of Minnesota, Bethel University, Hamline University, and the University of Saint Thomas and National Sports Center.

SACRAMENTO SPORTS COMMISSION
1606 I STREET
SACRAMENTO, CA 95814
916-808-7777
Fax: 916-566-6566
fan@sacsports.com
www.sacsports.com
• Brad M. Hillard, Director of sports development
Description:
Founded 1988. Formed to attract major professional and amateur sports events to the city and county of Sacramento.

SAINT JOHN DESTINATION MANAGEMENT INC
CITY HALL
15 MARKET SQUARE

11TH FLOOR
SAINT JOHN, NB, CANADA E2K 1E8
506-658-2990
1-866-GO FUNDY
Fax: 506-632-6118
visitsj@saintjohn.ca
www.tourismsaintjohn.com
• Kevin Carson, Manager
(506) 658-4731
• Marcy Loeman, Administrative coordinator
• Shawnna Garnhum, Sales
• Jen Tupper, Manager of visitors
• Ross Jefferson, Executive director
Nature of Sports Service::
Destination management organization to increase visitation to Saint John NB.

SALT LAKE CONVENTION & VISITORS BUREAU
90 SOUTH WEST TEMPLE
SALT LAKE CITY, UT 84101
801-534-4900
800-541-4955
Fax: 801-534-4926
www.visitsaltlake.com
• Scott Beck, President/CEO
(801) 534-4911
sbeck@saltlake.org
• Eric Thompson, Director Marketing
(801) 534-4912
ethompson@saltlake.org
• Shawn Stinson, Director Communications
(801) 534-4913
sstinson@saltlake.org
Description:
A private non-profit community organization promoting Salt Lake as a travel destination. The SLCVB and its members provide assistance to convention & meeting planners, tourism professionals, media and visitors.

SAN ANTONIO SPORTS
PO BOX 830386
SAN ANTONIO, TX 78283
210-820-2100
Fax: 210-820-2199
www.sanantoniosports.org
• Susan Blackwood, Executive Director
(210) 820-2110
• David Blank, Volunteer Coordinator
(210) 820-2191
dblank@sanantoniosports.org
• Russ Bookbinder, President/CEO
(210) 820-2120
rbookbinder@sanantoniosports.org
• Jenny Carnes, Associate Executive Director, Business Develo
(210) 820-2104
jcarnes@sanantoniosports.org
• Gina Castro, Youth Program Director
(210) 820-2102
• Karl Chapman, Finance Manager
(210) 820-2107
• Bill Hanson, Associate Executive Director Operations
(210) 820-2111
• Mary Ullmann Japhet, Associate Executive Director/External Affairs
(210) 820-2123
mjaphet@sanantoniosports.org
Description:
Founded 1984. A not-for-profit organization dedicated to creating sports opportunities for our community and its youth. We hold major athletic events to generate money. Our DREAMS FOR YOUTH program provides training in six Olympic sports, and our

DIAMOND SHAMROCK GO!KIDS CHALLENGE is designed to combat childhood obesity through routine activity and education.

SAN BERNARDINO AREA CONVENTION & VISITORS BUREAU
1955 HUNTS LANE
SUITE 102
SAN BERNARDINO, CA 92401
909-889-3980
800-867-8366
Fax: 909-888-5998
• Wayne Austin, President/Chief Executive Officer
• Barbara Daugherty, Director of Business Operations
Description:
The San Bernardino Convention & Visitors Bureau (SBCVB) shall attract conventions, conferences, group tours and business meetings while coordinationg attractions, resteraunts and services to meet each organization's specific needs. The SBCVB shall also provide aggressive marketing strategies; develop and impliment special events to generate additional visitor days for the city of San Bernardino.

SAN JOSE SPORTS AUTHORITY
345 PARK AVENUE
MS E6-500
SAN JOSE, CA 95110
408-288-2930
Fax: 408-278-1868
info@sjsa.org
www.sjsa.org
• Patricia Ernstrom, Executive Director
patricia@sjsa.org
• Carrie Benjamin, Event Manager
carrie@sjsa.org
• Greg Jamison, Chair
Description:
Formed to attract major sports events to the city of San Jose and surrounding areas.

SAN MATEO COUNTY/SILICON VALLEY CONVENTION & VISITORS BUREAU
111 ANZA BLVD, STE 410
BURLINGAME, CA 94010
650-348-7600
800-288-4748
Fax: 650-348-7687
www.sanmateocountycvb.com
• Anne LeClair, President/Chief Executive Officer
annel@smccvb.com
• Michelle Adle, Sports Marketing Manager
• Gina Allhands, Vice President, Chief Financial Officer
gina@smccvb.com

SAVANNAH SPORTS COUNCIL
101 E. BAY ST
SAVANNAH, GA 31401
912-644-6414
info@savcvb.com
• Benjamin Wilder, Director
Description:
Founded 1992.The Savannah Sports Council markets Savannah as a site for major sports events in pre-Olympic training, as well as enhancing participation in area athletic programs and serves as a catalyst to develop sports infrastructure in the community.

SIOUX FALLS CONVENTION & VISITORS BUREAU
200 N. PHILLIPS AVENUE
SUITE 102
SIOUX FALLS, SD 57104
605-336-1620
800-333-2072
Fax: 605-336-6499
www.siouxfallscvb.com
• Teri Ellis Schmidt, CVB Executive Director
• Krista Orsack, Sales/Marketing Director

SIOUXLAND SPORTS & CULTURAL EVENTS CONGRESS
801 4TH STREET
SIOUX CITY, IA 51101
712-279-4800
800-593-2228
Fax: 712-279-4800
www.siouxcitytourism.com
• Dennis Gann, Executive Director
(800) 593-2228
• Angie Watson, Marketing Director
Description:
Founded 1992. Serves to attract sporting and cultural events to the greater Sioux City area.

SOUTH CAROLINA PARKS, RECREATION & TOURISM
1205 PENDLETON STREET
SUITE 110
COLUMBIA, SC 29201
803-734-1700
866-224-9339
Fax: 803-734-1741
tnance@scprt.com
www.discoversouthcarolina.com
• Amy Duffy, Chief of Staff
• Marion Edmunds, Director of Communications
Description:
Promotes South Carolina as a good location for professional and amateur sporting events. Assists local communities in their sports development initiatives.

SOUTH PADRE ISLAND CONVENTION & VISITORS BUREAU
7355 PADRE BLVD
SOUTH PADRE ISLAND, TX 78597
956-761-3000
800-657-2373
Fax: 956-761-3024
www.sopadre.com
• Lacey Ekberg, Director of CVB
(956) 761-8308
• Dinora Garcia, Administrative Assistant to CVB Director
(956) 761-8308
• Lori Moore, Accounting Coordinator
• Celia Sally Garza, Services Manager
(956) 761-3000
• Dinora Garcia, Executive Assistant

TEAM SPARTANBURG
111 IDLE WYLDE COURT
SPARTANBURG, SC 29301
864-597-4180
Fax: 864-316-1326
www.teamspartanburgsc.org
• Laura Corbin, Chairwoman, Publicity Manager
Member Services:
Team Spartanburg, The Sports Council of the Spartanburg Convention & Visitors

Bureau, Assists event holders with their events to make them successful.

SPOKANE REGIONAL SPORTS COMMISSION
714 N IRON BRIDGE WAY
SUITE 202
SPOKANE, WA 99202
509-456-5812
800-900-5837
Fax: 509-456-5837
chrisf@spokanesports.org
www.spokanesports.org
• Eric Sawyer, President/CEO
(509) 742-9371
erics@spokanesports.org
• Jodi Kyler, Ph.D., VP of Marketing and Communications
(509) 742-9389
chrisf@spokanesports.org
• Paul Christiarnsen, Director of Event Services
(509) 363-2682
Description:
Since 1988, the Spokane Regional Sports Commission has provided leadership in economic and community development through sports to the Spokane Region.

SPORTS AND EVENTS COUNCIL OF SEATTLE/KING COUNTY
701 PIKE STREET
SUITE 800
SEATTLE, WA 98101-2611
206-461-5800
Fax: 206-461-5855
www.seattlesports.org
• Ralph R. Morton, Executive Director
• Kirk Nelson, Vice Chair
• Greg Root, Secretary/Treasurer
Description:
Founded 1989. Mission is to bring major sports and special events to the region; create sports and special events for the region; support the existing sports franchises; and ensure modern, state-of-the-art facilities.

SPORTS PROMOTION - BATTLE CREEK, MICHIGAN
KELLOGG ARENA
1 MCCAMLY SQUARE
BATTLE CREEK, MI 49017
269-963-4800
Fax: 269-968-8840
www.kelloggarena.com
• Kevin M. Scheibler, General Manager
kscheibler@kelloggarena.com
• Kevin Scheibler, GM
(269) 963-4800
• Lindsay Lerette, Sales and Marketing Manager
(269) 963-4800
• Jimmy Biggs, Food and Beverage Manager
(269) 963-4800
jbiggs@kelloggarena.com
• Bob Benqtsson, Interim Director of Finance
(269) 963-4800
bbengtsson@kelloggarena.com
• Ben Randels, Operations Manager, Treasurer
• Sylvester Trease, Director of Finance
tsylvester@kelloggarena.com
Description:
Identify and bring existing major sporting

events to Battle Creek Michigan and the surrounding area.

SPORTS VIRGINIA INC.
405 LORRAINE AVE
FREDERICKSBURG, VA 22408
540-710-1228
Fax: 540-710-7007
Member Services:
Liaison between national governing bodies and Virginia member clubs; processes registrations; sanctions athlete's cards; collects fees for clubs.
Publications:
Virginia State Games Annual Program; annual reports; individual newsletters for each sport.
Description:
Founded 1989. Serves and promotes amateur sports groups in Virginia including the Amateur Athletic Union (AAU), USA Track & Field, the U.S. Diving Federation, U.S. Weightlifting Federation, and produces the Virginia State Games.

SPRINGFIELD AREA SPORTS COMMISSION
815 E ST. LOUIS STREET
SPRINGFIELD, MO 65806
417-881-5300
800-678-8767
Fax: 417-881-7201
lkettering@springfieldmo.org
www.springfieldmosports.org
• Bill Hobbs, Chair
• Tracy Kimberlin, Secretary
• Mary Decker, Treasurer
• Lance Kettering, Executive Director
• Shiela Fish, Assistant Director
Description:
Mission is to enhance the quality of life and stimulate positive economic growth for the community by promoting and developing the greater Springfield area as a sports venue for quality amateur and professional sporting events.

SPRINGFIELD, MO CONVENTION & VISITORS BUREAU
815 E SAINT LOUIS STREET
SUITE 100
SPRINGFIELD, MO 65806
417-881-5300
800-678-8767
Fax: 417-881-2231
cvb@springfieldmo.org
www.springfieldmo.org
• Tracy Kimberlin, Executive Director

ST. AUGUSTINE, PONTE VEDRA & THE BEACHES VISITORS & CONVENTION BUREAU
29 OLD MISSION AVENUE
ST. AUGUSTINE, FL 32084
904-829-1711 EXT 310
800-653-2489
Fax: 904-829-6149
www.getaway4florida.com
• Ron Goldman, Executive Director
(904) 829-1711
• Rick Hensler, Promotions Director
• Eris Masters, Database manager
• Richard Goldman, Executive Director
ext 311
RGoldman@FloridasHistoricCoast.com
• Carey Cramer, Office Manager

(904) 829-1711
CCramer@FloridasHistoricCoast.com
Year Founded:
1994
Description:
Serves to attract sports meetings and events to the St. John's county area.

ST. CHARLES CONVENTION & VISITORS BUREAU, GREATER
230 SOUTH MAIN STREET
ST. CHARLES, MO 63301
636-366-2427
800-366-2427
Fax: 636-949-3217
gsccvb@historicstcharles.com
www.historicstcharles.com
• David A Leezer, CEO, Director

ST. CLOUD AREA CONVENTION VISITORS BUREAU
525 HIGHWAY 10 SOUTH
SUITE 1
ST. CLOUD, MN 56304
320-251-4170
800-264-2940
Fax: 320-656-0401
info@visitstcloudmn.com
www.granitecountry.com
• Julie Lunning, Executive Director
(320) 202-6711
julie@granitecountry.com
• Judy Okerstrom, Director of Sales & Marketing
(320) 202-6712
judy@granitecountry.com

ST. JOSEPH CONVENTION & VISITORS BUREAU/ REGIONAL SPORTS COMMISSION
109 SOUTH 4TH STREET
ST. JOSEPH, MO 64501
816-233-6688
800-785-0360
Fax: 816-233-9120
cvb@stjomo.com
www.stjomo.com
• Marci Bennett, Executive Director
mbennett@stjomo.com
• Mary Supple, Director Sales
msupple@stjomo.com
Description:
Serves to attract sports meetings and events to the St. Joseph Missouri Area.

ST. LOUIS SPORTS COMMISSION
308 NORTH 21ST STREET
SUITE 500
ST. LOUIS, MO 63101
314-345-5100
Fax: 314-621-1391
ncohan@stlouissports.org
• Frank Viverito, President
fviverito@stlouissports.org
• Chris Roseman, Vice President of Events
croseman@stlouissports.org
Description:
Founded 1989. Generate economic benefit and enhanced quality of life in the St. Louis region through sports events, national promotion, local awareness, amateur sports development, and youth programs.
Membership Requirements:
$250 for individuals; $500 for companies/organizations.
Publications:
Newsletter, quarterly.

245

Member Services:
Meetings, board meetings and frequent special events and activities.

ST. PETERSBURG/CLEARWATER SPORTS COMMISSION
13805 58TH ST
STE 2-200
CLEARWATER, FL 33760-3733
727-464-7200
877-352-2473
info@floridasbeachsports.com
www.floridasbeachsports.com
• Kevin Smith, Director Of Sports Commission
• Angel Natal, Senior Sales Manager
• Kit Dunbar, Sales manager of sports commission
• Robin Gwaltney-Harris, Administrative Assistant
Description:
Founded 1999. Serves to attract professional, collegiate, amateur and youth sports training and tournaments to the St. Petersburg/Clearwater area.

STOCKTON CONVENTION & VISITORS BUREAU
125 BRIDGE PLACE
STOCKTON, CA 95202
209-938-1555
877-778-6258
Fax: 209-938-1554
www.visitstockton.org
• Tim Pasisz, Sports Development Director
(209) 938-1556
Description;
Full service visitors bureau to assist in recruiting sporting events to Stockton. Site selection, logistic support & sponsorships available.

SYRACUSE CONVENTION + VISITORS BUREAU
115 WEST FAYETTE STREET
SYRACUSE, NY 13202-3320
315-470-1910
800-234-4797
Fax: 315-471-8545
www.visitsyracuse.org
• David C. Holder, President
(315) 470-1911
dholder@visitsyracuse.org
• Carol M. Eaton, Director of Market Development
(315) 470-1904
ceaton@visitsyracuse.org
Description:
Founded 1985. Serves to attract, organize and stage amateur sports events in the Syracuse area as well as coordinate the resources and efforts within the community in working toward that end.

TACOMA/PIERCE COUNTY SPORTS COMMISSION
1119 PACIFIC AVENUE
SUITE 500
TACOMA, WA 98402
253-327-1866
800-272-2662
Fax: 253-627-8783
www.tacomasports.com
• Tim Waer, TPCSC, Executive Director
timw@tacomasports.com
Description:
Founded 1992. A non-profit organization that promotes the region of Tacoma/Pierce County as a destination for state, regional, national and international amateur sports events.

TALLAHASSEE SPORTS COUNCIL
106 EAST JEFFERSON STREET
TALLAHASSEE, FL 32301
850-606-2305
800-628-2866
Fax: 850-487-4621
• Lee Daniel, Executive Director
• Colleen Dwyer, Visitor Services Director
Description:
Fosters, encourages and promotes athletic events in the Tallahassee area for the economic benefits, visibility and civic pride these activities may bring to the community. Events include international, national, regional and state events and span a wide spectrum of sports and performance levels.

TAMPA BAY SPORTS COMMISSION
401 EAST JACKSON STREET
SUITE 2100
TAMPA, FL 33602
813-218-3892
info@tampabaysports.org
www.tampabaysports.org
• Rob Higgins, Executive Director
rhiggins@visittampabay.com
• Jason Aughey, Senior Director
• Tony Diaz, Sales and Events Coordinator
• Claire Lessinger, Sales/Events Manager
• Rob Higgins, Executive Director
RHiggins@VisitTampaBay.com
Description:
The Tampa Bay Sports Commission works to unite all interests in the Bay Area under one full-service approach that provides leadership and guidance for the benefit of all parties involved with amateur and youth sports. The Sports Commission works with area convention and visitors bureaus to provide a wealth of services to potential events and their governing bodies.

TAMPA CONVENTION & VISITORS BUREAU
401 EAST JACKSON STREET
STE 2100
TAMPA, FL 33602
813-223-1111
800-44tampa
Fax: 813-229-6616
www.visittampabay.com
• JoLynn Lokey, VP of Administration
(813) 342-4089
JLokey@VisitTampaBay.com
• Lisa Urban, Human Resources Coordinator
(813) 342-4064
LUrban@VisitTampaBay.com
• Gregory Orchard, Chief Financial Officer
(813) 342-4082
GOrchard@VisitTampaBay.com
• Jennifer Finnegan, Accounting Coordinator
(813) 342-4059
JFinnegan@VisitTampaBay.com
• Alex Kaptzan, Vice President of Convention Sales and Servic
(81) -218-383
AKaptzan@VisitTampaBay.com
• Santiago Corrada, President/Chief Executive Officer
(813) 223-1111
SCorrada@VisitTampaBay.com

• JoLynn Lokey SPHR, VP of Administration
(813) 342-4089
JLokey@VisitTampaBay.com

TAMPA SPORTS AUTHORITY
4201 NORTH DALE MABRY HIGHWAY
TAMPA, FL 33607
813-350-6500
Fax: 813-350-6565
www.tampasportsauthority.com
• Janice Hosey, Executive assistant
• Eric Hart, President, CEO
(813) 350-6516
• Mickey Farrell, Director of Operations
(813) 350-6507
mfarrell@tampasportsauthority.com
• Jeanette Baker, VP of finance and administration
• Sue Maciejewski, HRM
Description:
Created 1965. Owns and operates Houlihan's Stadium, owns Yankees training complex and NHL Lightning Ice Palace and manages 3 city-owned golf courses. Currently building a 65,000 seat open air, natural turf stadium adjacent to Houlihan's Stadium.

SPORTS CLUB OF TAMPA BAY
P.O. BOX 10753
TAMPA, FL 33609
813-282-3400
Fax: 813-287-8369
• Mitch Shriber, President
• Gill Swalls, First Vice President
Description:
Promotes various functions to raise funds for charitable donations. Hosts annual Sports Award Banquet, Golf Tournament, etc.

TEXAS DEPT. OF ECO. DEVELOPMENT, TOURISM DIV.
P.O. BOX 12428
AUSTIN, TX 78711
512-936-0101
www.traveltex.com
Description:
Looks to develop and attract events to the Austin Texas region.

THUNDERBIRDS, THE
7226 NORTH 16TH STREET
SUITE 100
PHOENIX, AZ 85020
602-870-0163
Fax: 602-870-4162
www.phoenixopen.com
• John Bridger, Executive Director
Nature of Sports Service:
Special Events Committee of the Phoenix Chamber of Commerce, whose sole purpose is to promote Phoenix and its neighboring communities through sporting events, such as the FBR Open golf tournament, formerly the Phoenix Open.

TOURISM BUREAU ILLINOISOUTH
4387 NORTH ILLINOIS STREET
SUITE 200
SWANSEA, IL 62226
618-257-1488
800-442-1488
Fax: 618-257-3403
www.thetourismbureau.org

• Jo Kathmann, President/CEO
jkathmann@thetourismbureau.org
Publications:
Annual Free Visitors Guide, Bi-Monthly News from the Road Magazine.
Member Services:
Web Link, Hospitality Training, AD Credit in Visitors Guide, Marketing Consultation, AD Placement, Levereged Buying. Housing and group services.
Membership Requirements:
Membership levels range form $225.00 up.

TOURISM VANCOUVER, THE GREATER VANCOUVER CONVENTION & VISITORS BUREAU
STE 210-200 BURRARD ST
VANCOUVER, BC, CANADA V6C 3L6
604-682-2222
Fax: 604-682-1717
www.tourismvancouver.com
• Ted Lee, Chief Financial Officer & VP Visitor Services
(604) 631-2807
• Stephen Pearce, Vice President
(604) 631-2808
• Patti Smolen, Director
(640) 631-2801
• Rick Antonson, President/Chief Executive Officer
(604) 631-2888
ricka@tourismvancouver.com
• Paul Vallee, Executive Vice President
(604) 631-2815
pvallee@tourismvancouver.com
• Walt Judas, Vice President
(604) 631-2882
wjudas@tourismvancouver.com
Description:
Tourism Vancouver's focus is on building exceptional relationships. Our primary customers are meeting planners, travel influencers, travel media, and independent tourists. Our efforts generate demand for the destination, thereby creating value for members and stakeholders innovation, partnership, research and accountability guide our approach.

TRI-CITIES SPORTS COUNCIL
7130 W GRANDRIDGE BLVD
KENNEWICK, WA 99336
509-735-8486
800-254-5824
hector@visittri-cities.com
www.VisitTri-Cities.com
• Kris Watkins, President/CEO
kris@VisitTri-Cities.com
• Kim Shugart, SeniorVice President
• Jordan Youngs, Marketing & Public Relations Director
• Michelle Chunn, Community Relations Director
• Holly Siler, Director ofConvention Sales
Publications:
Tri-Cities Sports Facilities Guide.
Member Services:
Acts as a liaison with our hotel properties to gather rates and availability information. The Council can assist in locating sports venues and playing fields to meet the needs of the tournament as well as providing contact information for local tournament directors and officials. We can also provide an assortment of informational brochures and maps featuring the Tri-Cities to assis visitors.

TULSA SPORTS COMMISSION
1 WEST 3RD STREET
SUITE 100
TULSA, OK 74103
918-560-0215
Fax: 918-592-6244
www.tulsasports.org
• Vince Trinidad, Executive Director
• Ray Hoyt, Sr. VP
Member Services:
Newsletter; preferred invitations; tickets.
Membership Requirements:
Financial contribution.
Description:
Founded 1993. Serves as a catalyst for the solicitation and development of major regional and national amateur sporting events in the Tulsa metro area, while fostering the development of improved facilities and growth of local associations, teams, and organizing committees necessary to accommodate these events.

TUPELO CONVENTION & VISITORS BUREAU
399 EAST MAIN STREET
PO BOX 47
TUPELO, MS 38801
662-841-6521
800-533-0611
Fax: 662-841-6558
visittupelo@tupelo.net
www.tupelo.net
• Neal McCoy, Director Sports Development
• Linda Elliff, Director of Sales
• Linda Butler-Johnson, Executive Director

TUSCALOOSA CONVENTION & VISITORS BUREAU
1900 JACK WARNER PARKWAY
TUSCALOOSA
TUSCALOOSA, AL 35401
205-391-9200
800-538-8696
Fax: 250-759-2002
www.visittuscaloosa.com
• Robert Ratliff, Executive Director
• Susan West, CEO
swest@visittuscaloosa.com
• Don Staley, Executive Director of Sports
dstaley@visittuscaloosa.com
• Tina Jones, Director of Corporate & Group Tourism
tjones@visittuscaloosa.com
• Shaunee Lynch, AssistantDirector of Corporate & Group Touri
• Kelsey Colglazier, Director of Sports Marketing and Public Relat
kcolglazier@visittuscaloosa.com
• Jessika White, Multimedia Communication & Public Relations M

UTAH SPORTS COMMISSION
201 SOUTH MAIN
SUITE 2125
SALT LAKE CITY, UT 84111
801-328-2372
Fax: 801-328-2372
www.utahsportscommission.com
• Jeff Robbins, President/Chief Executive Officer
jlrobbins@utah.gov
• Laura Shaw, Marketing Director
(801) 323-4254
lshaw@utah.gov
• Steve Rich, VP Operations
(801) 328-2361

Description:
The mission of the Utah Sports Commission is to enhance Utah's economy, image, and quality of life through the attraction, promotion, and development of regional, national, and international sports.

UTAH VALLEY CONVENTION & VISITORS BUREAU
220 WEST CENTER STREET
SUITE 100
PROVO, UT 84601
801-851-2100
Fax: 801-851-2109
www.utahvalley.org
• Joel Racker, President/CEO
(801) 851-2101
joelr@utahvalley.org
• Candace Winmill, Executive Administrative Assistant
• Courtney Brown, Marketing Assistant
• Andrella Cross, Visitor Information Specialist
• Julia Currey, Senior Sales Manager
(801) 851-2106
juliac@utahvalley.org
• Charlene Christensen, Director of Services
(801) 851-2102
charlene@utahvalley.org
Description:
Utah Valley Convention & Visitors Bureau staff are ready to assist tourists, business travelers, meeting planners, event organizers, film companies, tour operators, reunion planners, and conferences. Our staff members are professional, friendly, and knowledgeable. Our desire is to make your planning easy and to make certain your time in Utah Valley is successful, memorable and hassel-free.

VALDOSTA-LOWNDES COUNTY CONFERENCE CENTER & TOURISM AUTHORITY/CVB
1 MEETING PLACE
VALDOSTA, GA 31601
229-245-0513
800-569-8687
Fax: 229-245-5240
www.valdostatourism.com
• Joel Racker, President, Chief Executive Officer
• Charlene Christensen, Director of Services
Description:
Founded 1996. The Sports Commission is an affiliate of the Valdosta-Lowndes County Convention & Visitors Bureau, whose mission is to market Valdosta and Lowndes County as a destination for athletic competition; To enhance and stimulate positive economic growth through youth and adult sporting events.
Publications:
Sports Facilities Guide.

VENTURA VISITORS & CONVENTION BUREAU
101 S CALIFORNIA STREET
VENTURA, CA 93001
800-333-2989
Fax: 805-648-2150
www.ventura-usa.com
• Jim Luttjohann, Executive Director
• Marlyss Auster, Executive Director
Description:
Serves to attract and promote sporting events to Ventura California. Sports include:

auto racing, baseball, basketball, beach volleyball, boating, equestrian, golf, junior Olympics, roller hockey, senior Olympics, soccer, softball, track and field, tennis, water polo.
Publications:
Ventura Official Visitors Guide; Meeting Planner Guide

VERMONT SPORTS & EVENTS COUNCIL
60 MAIN STREET
SUITE 100
BURLINGTON, VT 5401
877-686-5253
877-264-3503
www.vermontmeetings.org
• Dave Hakins, Executive Director
(802) 863-3489
Description:
The Vermont State Sports Council serves to attract and initiate local, national, and international sporting events in Vermont.

VIRGINIA AMATEUR SPORTS, INC.
711 C FIFTH STREET NE
ROANOKE, VA 24016
540-343-0987
Fax: 540-343-7407
www.commonwealthgames.org
• Peter R. Lampman, President
pete@commonwealthgames.org
• Diane Williams, Marketing Director
dwilliams@commonwealthgames.org
Description:
Founded 1989. Established to promote the development of amateur athletics in the state. Sports event planner and organizer of the Coventry Commonwealth Games of Virginia.

VIRGINIA BEACH CONVENTION AND VISITOR BUREAU/SPORTS MARKETING
2101 PARKS AVE
STE 500
VIRGINIA BEACH, VA 23451
757-385-4700
800-700-7702
Fax: 757-437-4747
bwheeler@vbgov.com
• James B. Ricketts, Director
jrickett@VisitVirginiaBeach.com
• Brande Rumpf, Executive Assistant
brumpf@VisitVirginiaBeach.com
• Tiffany Twine, Media and Communications Coordinator
ttwine@VisitVirginiaBeach.com
• Chuck Applebach, Marketing and Strategic Partnerships
cappleba@vbgov.com
• Teresa Diaz, InteractiveCommunications
tdiaz@VisitVirginiaBeach.com
• Buddy Wheeler, Sports Marketing Coordinator
(757) 437-4795
bwheeler@vbgov.com
• Nancy Helman, Sales Marketing Representative
Description:
Serves to increase sport tourism to Virginia Beach. Assists sports event planners in all phases of the event, including facility acquisition, lodging, transportation coordination, visitor relations, and volunteer recruitment.

VISIT ANCHORAGE
524 W FOURTH AVENUE
ANCHORAGE, AK 99501-2212
907-276-4118
Fax: 907-278-5559
info@anchorage.net
www.anchorage.net
• R.J. (Jim) Henderson, VP Convention Sales
• Julie Dodds, Director of Convention Sales
Description:
Promotes Anchorage Alaska as a destination for tourism, events and meetings.

VISIT BINGHAMTON
5 SOUTH COLLEGE DR.
SUITE 102
BINGHAMTON, NY 13905
607-772-8860
800-836-6740
www.visitbinghamton.org
• Cassie Green, Sales & Social Media Manager
(607) 296-2103
cassandra@visitbinghamton.org
• Judi Hess, Director
judi@visitbinghamton.org
Description:
Greater Binghamton - a sports friendly community waiting to welcome new groups. CVB offers free services to event planners. Offering first class venues, plentiful & affordable hotel rooms and over 250 restaurants... Come and be part of our story.
Publications:
Travel Guide, Summer Calendar of Events, Map Brochure, Sports Venue Guide, Meeting Planners Guide, Group Tour Planner, Treasures Brochure, Golf Brochure

VISIT EAU CLAIRE
4319 JEFFERS ROAD
SUITE 201
EAU CLAIRE, WI 54703
715-831-2345
888-523-3866
Fax: 715-831-2340
info@chippewavalley.net
www.visiteauclaire.com
• Linda John, Executive Director
• Michael Strubel, Sports Sales
michael@chippewavalley.net
Description:
Promotes Eau Claire WI and surrounding areas as a host site for sports meetings and events.

VISIT FORT WAYNE
927 SOUTH HARRISON ST
FORT WAYNE, IN 46802
260-424-3700
800-767-7752
Fax: 260-424-3914
josie@visitfortwayne.com
www.visitfortwayne.com
• Dan O'Connell, CAE, President/CEO
dan@visitfortwayne.com
• Josie O'Connell, Sports Sales Manager
josie@visitfortwayne.com
Description:
Founded 1949. Acts as an agent for the city of Fort Wayne in attracting conventions, tourists, trade shows, and sporting events for the economic and social benefits of a prosperous visitor industry.
Facilities:

Extensive facilities for groups including basketball, soccer, ice sports and field sports.
Fort Wayne Professional Teams:
Fort Wayne Komet Hockey, Fort Wayne TinCaps, Fort Wayne Mad Ants

VISIT KNOXVILLE SPORTS COMMISSION
301 SOUTH GAY STREET
KNOXVILLE, TN 37902
865-523-7263
800-727-8045
Fax: 865-522-3974
cculver@knoxville.org
sports.visitknoxville.com
• Kim Bumpas, President
• Chad Culver, Senior Director, Sports Commission
• Kristen Combs, Director, Communications
• Parker Medley, Director, Sports Sales
• Kelli Ryman, Director, Event Services
• Erin Simcox, Housing Manager
Description:
The Visit Knoxville Sports Commission promotes the Knoxville/Knox County as a destination for sports-related events. This includes youth events, collegiate events and professional events. The Commission works with local organizers, as well as National Governing Bodies.

VISIT NEW HAVEN
127 WASHINGTON AVENUE
NEW HAVEN, CT 6473
203-777-8550
800-332-STAY
www.visitnewhaven.com
• Sarah Washburn, Tourism Sales Representative
(203) 777-8550
sarahw@rexdevelopment.org
• Virginia Kozlowski, Director
• Ginny Kozlowski, Executive Director
(203) 777-8550
ginnyk@visitnewhaven.com
Description:
Serves to promote New Haven and the surrounding area to attract sporting events and attractions.
Member Services:
Bid, market and host sporting events that generate positive economic impact on the community.

VISIT WINSTON-SALEM
200 BROOKSTOWN AVENUE
WINSTON-SALEM, NC 27101
336-728-4200
866-728-4200
Fax: 336-721-2202
info@visitwinstonsalem.com
www.visitwinstonsalem.com
• Bonny Bernat, Sports/Event Sales Manager
(336) 728-4215
bonny@visitwinstonsalem.com
• Richard Geiger, President
richard@visitwinstonsalem.com

WATERLOO CONVENTION & VISITORS BUREAU
5 W JEFFERSON STREET
WATERLOO, IA 50703
319-233-8350
800-728-8431
Fax: 319-233-4580
www.waterloocvb.org

- Aaron Buzza, Executive Director
- Lornnie Elmore, Director of Group Sales
- Susan Lewis, Director of Visitor Services
- Beth Kenny, Marketing & Communications

WAYNE COUNTY CONVENTION & VISITORS BUREAU

5701 NATIONAL ROAD EAST
RICHMOND, IN 47374
765-935-8687
800-828-8414
Fax: 765-935-0440
grouprequest@visitrichmond.org
www.visitrichmond.org
- Mary Walker, General Manager
Facilities:
Basketball, bowling, golf, baseball, gymnastics, martial arts, skating, water sports, fishing, swimming.

WENATCHEE VALLEY SPORTS COUNCIL

5 SOUTH WENATCHEE AVENUE
SUITE C-100
WENATCHEE, WA 98801
509-663-3723
800-572-7753
Fax: 509-663-3983
www.wenatcheevalleysports.com
- Trina Elmes, Secreatry
- Caryl Morrell, President
- Sally Brawley, Vice President
Description:
Formed to promote, market and sell the Wenatchee Valley as a destination for businesses and leisure travel including conventions, trade shows, corporate meetings, and tourist travel to maximize additional overnight visitors. visotor expenditures, state and local tax revenues, and job opportunities.

WICHITA AREA SPORTS COMMISSION, GREATER

515 S MAIN STREET
SUITE 515
WICHITA, KS 67202
316-265-6236
800-526-9424
Fax: 316-265-0162
bob@wichitasports.com
www.wichitasports.com
- Byron Crawford, Director of Marketing & Promotions
(316) 518-0482
byron@wichitasports.com
- Jared Simon, Event Manager
jared@wichitasports.com
- Robert E Hanson, President/CEO
(316) 461-7767
bob@wichitasports.com
- Brian Hargrove, Events Director
(316) 990-7689
brian@wichitasports.com
- Tonya Atta, Director of Operations & Communications
tonya@wichitasports.com
Year Founded:
1997
Description:
Promotes Whicita and the surrounding area as a location for sporting events. Manages annual events such as Wichita Corporate Challenge and Prairie Fire Marathon.
Facilities:
INTRUST Bank Arena, Hartman Arena, Lawrence-Dumont Stadium, Charles Koch Arena, Cessna Stadium

WISCONSIN CONVENTION & VISITORS BUREAU

648 NORTH PLANKINTON AVENUE
SUITE 425
MILWAUKEE, WI 53203
414-273-3950
800-554-1448
Fax: 414-273-5596
www.visitmilwaukee.org
- Paul Upchurch, President/Chief Executive Officer
- Dana Jones, Director of finance and administration
- Margaret Casey, Executive Assistant
- Daron Fine, Technology Manager
- Paul Upchurch, President and CEO
Publications:
Visitors Guide
Description:
Founded 1990. Packages, promotes the entire sports product of Wisconsin. Includes attracting new events to the state and promoting the current organizations, events, teams, and facilities. Promotes value of sports in Wisconsin by acting as authority on economic impact, visibility and quality of life issues with sports.

WISCONSIN SPORTS DEVELOPMENT CORPORATION

313 WEST BELTLINE HIGHWAY
SUITE 161
MADISON, WI 53713
608-226-4780
www.sportsinwisconsin.com
- Darien Schaefer, Executive Director
- Richard Barrett, Director of Sales
- Tracy Baltz, Director Marketing

WOODFIELD CHICAGO NORTHWEST CONVENTION BUREAU

1375 E WOODFIELD RD
SUITE 120
SCHAUMBURG, IL 60173
847-490-1010
800-847-4849
Fax: 847-490-1212
info@chicagonorthwest.com
www.chicagonorthwest.com
- Dave Parulo, President
Description:
Woodfield Chicago Northwest is a dynamic destination for all types of sporting events. The area is centrally located at the crossroads of major interstate highways, is minutes from O'Hare Airport, offers plenty of free parking, and affords easy access to downtown Chicago. Facilities include the 10,000 sq. ft. Renaissance Schaumberg Hotel & Convention Center, soccer fields, baseball/softball fields, college facilities, and indoor complexes. We offer unique attractions, an unparalleled choice of restaurants, and lodging properties from world-class to economy. You will find warm Mid-Western hospitality and service throughout the area.
Attractions:
LEGOLAND Discovery Center, the only one in the U.S.; Medieval Times Dinner and Tournament; Arlington Park Racecourse; IKEA; Cabela's World Foremost Outfitters; Dave & Buster's; Gameworks; TopGolf

Publication:
Woodfield Chicago Northwest Visitor Guide

YAKIMA VALLEY VISITORS & CONVENTION BUREAU

10 NORTH 8TH STREET
YAKIMA, WA 98901-2515
509-575-3010
800-221-0751
Fax: 509-575-6252
www.visityakima.com
- John Cooper, CEO, President
- Wendi Bixler, Controller and HR Manager

YPSILANTI AREA CONVENTION AND VISITORS BUREAU

106 WEST MICHIGAN AVENUE
YPSILANTI, MI 48197
734-483-4444
- Debbie Locke-Daniel, Executive Director
dlocke@ypsilanti.org
- Mary Zucchero, Director of Sales
- Taryn Sulkes, Sales Coordinator
- Christine Laughren, Manager of Marketing & Communications
- Cory Hamlin, Marketing and Communications Assistant
- Mitzi McMahon, Office Manager
Mmcmahon@ypsilanti.org
Description:
Promotes sporting events and meetings to the local area which includes attracting new events to the state and promoting the current organizations, events, teams, and facilities.

YUMA CONVENTION & VISITORS BUREAU

201 NORTH FOURTH STREET
YUMA, AZ 85364
928-783-0071
800-293-0071
Fax: 928-783-1897
info@visityuma.com
www.visityuma.com
- Linda Jordan, Executive Director
- Linda Morgan, Executive Director
Publications:
GUIDE TO YUMA, NATIONAL HERITAGE AREA WALKING MAP, GERMAN BROCHURE.
Member Services:
We can help you book your group from 20-800 people.

Sports Halls of Fame, Libraries, Museums

AMERICAN SPORT ART MUSEUM AND ARCHIVES (ASAMA)

ONE ACADEMY DRIVE
DAPHNE, AL 36526
251-626-3303
800-223-2668
Fax: 251-626-3874
asama@ussa.edu
www.asama.org
- Robert Zemmit, Curator
- Thomas Rosandich, President United States Sports Academy
- Jack B. Scharr, Chairman International Advisory Board
Description:
Founded 1984. ASAMA contains a unique

multi sports

collection of classic and contemporary art featuring works of the Academy's Sports Artists of the Year. Over 1,000 pieces in all media.
Membership:
Gold $1,000; Silver $500; Bronze $250; Coach $100; Other anything under $100. With a membership you will receive invitations to the opening receptions of the exhibits and a 10% discount on all purchases in the gift shop.

AMERICAN WATER SKI EDUCATIONAL FOUNDATION/WATER SKI HALL OF FAME/MUSEUM
1251 HOLY COW ROAD
POLK CITY, FL 33868-8200
863-324-2472
Fax: 863-342-3996
info@waterskihalloffame.com
www.waterskihalloffame.com
• Paul Chaplin, President
• kim Laskoff, Secretary
• Mark Harvet, Treasurer
• Carole Lowe, Director
• J.D Morgan, Board Of Trustee
• Jim Grew, Chairman of the Board
• Robert Reich, Vice President
Description:
Founded 1968. Dedicated to the preservation of the traditions of water skiing, and to the encouragement of and education in the safe enjoyment of the challenges of water skiing. To these ends, the Foundation administers the Water Ski Museum/Hall of Fame, supervises scholarship programs to further the education of deserving water skiers, and provides financing for other activities which are consistent with the spirit in which the Foundation was formed.
Publications:
The Water Skier Magazine published nine times a year.
Membership:
Prices range from Free to $60. There are over 37,500 members.

BABE RUTH BIRTHPLACE AND SPORTS LEGENDS MUSEUM
216 EMORY ST
BALTIMORE, MD 21230
410-727-1539
Fax: 410-727-1652
info@baberuthmuseum.com
baberuthmuseum.org
• Shawn M. Herne, Executive Director
  ext 3040
• Michael L. Gibbons, Director Emeritus & Historian
  ext 3040
• Cathy Zaorski, Communications & Media Director
  ext 3040

BARCELONA MUSEUM AND SPORTS STUDY CENTER
BUENOS AIRES ST 56-58 (TORRE)
BARCELONA, SPAIN 8036

• Ricardo Sanchez, Coordinator
Description:
Founded 1986. Promotes cultural aspects of sport, preserve the history of sports in Catalonia - an autonomous community - and projects the values of the Olympic movement.

BRITISH COLUMBIA SPORTS HALL OF FAME MUSEUM
777 PACIFIC BOULEVARD
VANCOUVER, BC, CANADA V6B 4Y8
604-687-5520
Fax: 604-687-5510
www.bcsportshalloffame.com
• Sue Griffin, Executive Director
• Gareth Rees, Chairman
• Alan Tynan, Vice-Chair
• John Ormiston, Secretary/Treasurer
• Allison Mailer, Executive Director
allison.mailer@bcsportshalloffame.com
Publications:
FOR THE RECORD, twice annually.
Description:
Founded 1966. Serves to honor British Columbia athletes, builders and coaches; provides research facilities for the media and the public. Also has 18,000 square feet of exhibit space, including hands-on participation gallery. Non-profit Organization.

BRYANT MUSEUM, PAUL W.
300 PAUL W. BRYANT DRIVE
UNIVERSITY OF ALABAMA
BOX 870385
TUSCALOOSA, AL 35487
205-348-4668
866-772-BEAR (2327)
Fax: 205-348-8883
bryant-info@ua.edu
bryantmuseum.com
• Kenneth Gaddy, Director
kgaddy@bama.ua.edu
Description:
Founded in 1988. Named in honor of the legendary coach Paul 'Bear' Bryant the Museum exhibit gallery displays over 100 years of Alabama football history using memorabilia, photographs, art, audio and visual material from its exstensive collection. The Museum collects, preserves and researches material relating to the sports history of the University of Alabama and is a Must See attraction for all fans of college sports. The media, public and researchers rely on the BRyant Museum as areliable source for images and information. The collection facility continually acquires historic artifacts, library and archival materials which are interprete
Membership Requirements:
Bryant Gold Club, $1,000 and over; William Little Club, $500-$999; Director's Club, $250-499; Press Box Club, $100-$249; Locker Room Club, $30 fam/$20 ind; Sideline Club (Students) $15.
Publications:
Newsletter, three times annually.
Member Services:
Membership meetings, Complimentary admission and discounts on museum merchandise.

CANADA'S SPORTS HALL OF FAME
169 CANADA OLYMPIC ROAD SW
CALGARY, ALBERTA, CANADA T3B 5R5
403-776-1040
Fax: 416-260-9347
info@cshof.ca
www.sportshall.ca
• Jake G. Gaudaur, Chairman of the Board
• Mario W. Sicilliano, President and CEO
msiciliano@cshof.ca
• Marnie Krell, Marketing & Communications

Coordinator
mkrell@cshof.ca
• Sam Shefsky, Governor
• Robert Bundy, Governor
• Emerson Mascoll, Governor
• Dennis Flynn, Governor
Member Services:
Collects and displays sports memorabilia. Disseminates sports information and photographs. Maintains theater, library and archives.
Publications:
CANADIAN SPORTS ACHIEVERS; newsletter, two times annually; brochures.
Membership Requirements:
Decision of National Selection Committee.
Description:
Founded 1955. Works to preserve and promote Canada's sporting heritage by recognizing through selections of Honored Members important achievements by Canadians in the sports field. Maintains large display facility open throughout the year.

CATSKILL FLY FISHING CENTER & MUSEUM
1031 OLD ROUTE 17
PO BOX 1295
LIVINGSTON MANOR, NY 12758-1295
845-439-4810
Fax: 845-439-3387
office@cffcm.com
www.cffcm.com
• Jim Krul, Executive Director
Publications:
Newsletter Catskill Angler, Monthly Calendar of Events April and October.
Member Services:
Members receive free admission to the Museum, 10% off in our Museum Gift Shop and notices of all events held at the Center.
Membership Requirements:
Individual membership $35.00, Family membership $50.00, Student membership $15.00, Contributing membership $75.00, Sustaining membership $100.00, Patron membership $250.00, Sponsor membership $500.00, Benefactor membership $1000.00.
Description:
Is a nonprofit, educational organization dedicated to: preserving America's flyfishing heritage; teaching its future generations of flyfishers; and protecting its flyfishing environment.

COLLEGE FOOTBALL HALL OF FAME
433 E LAS COLINAS BLVD
SUITE 1130
SOUTH BEND, IN 75039
972-556-1000
800-440-3263
Fax: 972-556-9032
www.collegefootball.org
• Lisa Malin Klunder, Executive Director
• Archie Manning, Chair
• Steven J. Hatchell, President and CEO
  ext 5706
• Clayton I. Bennett, Vice Chair
  ext 5715
• Richard Allen, Multimedia & IT Manager
• Bill Donoghue, Volunteer Coordinator

DELAWARE SPORTS MUSEUM AND HALL OF FAME
801 SHIPYARD DRIVE
WILMINGTON, DE 19801-5121

302-425-3263
Fax: 302-425-3713
www.desports.org
• Bob Tattersall, President
• Beth Brown, Secretary
• Bill Hayes, Treasurer
• Tom Fort, President
• Ben Sirman, 1st Vice President
• Jack A. Holloway, CPA, 2nd
Vice-President

Description:
Since 1976 the Delaware Hall of Fame has honored and promoted Delaware's outstanding athletic performers including those who have brought recognition to the First State through their coaching, officiating administrative and journalism contributions. Additionally, the museum shall preserve the performances of Delaware inductees and other athletes through the display of memorabilia, artifacts and photos and videos.

DON GARLITS MUSEUM OF DRAG RACING AND INTERNATIONAL DRAG RACING HALL OF FAME
13700 SW 16TH AVENUE
I-75, EXIT 341
OCALA, FL 34473
352-245-8661
877-271-3278
Fax: 352-245-6895
don@garlits.com
www.garlits.com
• Don Garlits, Chief Executive Officer
(352) 245-8661
don@garlits.com
• Charles "Chuck" Keppel, Controller and General Manager
(352) 245-8661
chuck@garlits.com
• Lisa Crigar, Personal Assistant and PR Manager
(352) 547-9160
lcrigar65@gmail.com

Description:
Founded in 1976. A drag racing and antique car museum.

FIGURE SKATING HALL OF FAME AND MUSEUM, THE WORLD
20 FIRST ST
COLORADO SPRINGS, CO 80906-3697
719-635-5200
Fax: 719-635-9548
info@worldskatingmuseum.org
www.worldskatingmuseum.org
• Jim Fox, Assistant to the Executive Director
jfox@usfsa.org
• Karen Cover, Museum Archivist
(719) 228-3450
kcover@worldskatingmuseum.org

Description:
Founded 1956. The Hall of Fame contains two separate halls of fame - World and U.S. There presently are 33 World inductees and 23 U.S. inductees, with induction taking place yearly. All memorabilia relating to figure skating over the past 100 years are displayed in the museum, including international and U.S. medals for the past 100 years. There is an extensive art collection from the seventeenth century to the present, costumes of skaters from the World War I period to the present, and a skaters gallery with ice skates from 1200 years ago to the present. The museum is

the official world repository of U.S., World and Olympic records. It also

GEORGIA SPORTS HALL OF FAME
301 CHERRY STREET
PO BOX 4644
MACON, GA 31208
478-752-1585
Fax: 478-752-1587
www.gshf.org
• Benjamin Baughman, Curator
benjaminb@gshf.org
• Ben Sapp, Managing Director
(478) 752-1585
bens@gshf.org
• Eric Thomas, Rental Coordinator
ext 107

Description:
Founded 1989. Promotes the health and physical fitness of the citizens of Georgia; promotes participation in amateur sports by citizens of all ages and skill levels; promotes statewide program of amateur athletic competition, culminating with the Georgia Games Championships; promotes state, national and international amateur sports through the establishment of Olympic training facilities within the state.

GREEN BAY PACKER HALL OF FAME
LAMBEAU FIELD ATRIUM
1265 LOMBARDI AVENUE
GREEN BAY, WI 54304
920-569-7512 EXT 1
888-442-7225
Fax: 920-569-7144
www.lambeaufield.com
• Krissy Zegers, Hall of Fame & Stadium Tour Manager

GREYHOUND HALL OF FAME
407 SOUTH BUCKEYE
ABILENE, KS 67410
785-263-3000
800-932-7881
Fax: 785-263-2604
www.greyhoundhalloffame.com
• Edward Scheele, Director

HARNESS RACING MUSEUM & HALL OF FAME, THE
240 MAIN STREET
GOSHEN, NY 10924
845-294-6330
Fax: 845-294-3463
hrm@frontiernet.net
www.harnessmuseum.com
• Gail C. Cunard, Executive Director
• E. T. Gerry, Jr., President

Year Founded:
1951

HOCKEY HALL OF FAME AND MUSEUM
BCE PLACE
30 YONGE STREET
TORONTO, ON, CANADA M5E 1X8
416-360-7735
Fax: 416-360-1501
info@hhof.com
www.hhof.com
• Bill Hay, Chairman/Chief Executive Officer
bhay@hhof.com
• Darren Bouko, Manager Business Development
• Jackie Schwartz, Manager marketing & Promotions

• Wendy Cramer, Co-Ordinator, group Booking
• Jeff Denomme, President/Chief Operating Officer/Treasurer
jdenomme@hhof.com
• Craig Baines, Vice President, Operations
cbaines@hhof.com
• Peter Jagla, Vice President, Marketing
pjagla@hhof.com
• Phil Pritchard, Vice President, Resource Centre and Curator
ppritchard@hhof.com
• Ron Ellis, Director, Public Affairs/Assistant to Preside
rellis@hhof.com

Publications:
LEGENDS-The Official Program of the Hockey Hall of Fame.

Description:
Founded 1943, the Hockey Hall of Fame exists in order to honour and preserve the history of the game of ice hockey, and in particular, those who have made outstanding contributions and achievements in the development of the game. Home of the Stanley Cup, the world's most exstensive collection of hockey memorabilia, and the state-of-the-art interactive games, the Hockey Hall of Fame offers guests of all ages and levels of interest a vibrant and innovative look at the game of hockey. The Hockey Hall of Fam

INDIANA BASKETBALL HALL OF FAME
ONE HALL OF FAME COURT
NEW CASTLE, IN 47362
765-529-1891
Fax: 765-529-0273
www.hoopshall.com
• Marvin Tudor, President
• Jim Callane, Executive Vice President

Description:
Founded 1966. Devoted to the history of Indiana high school basketball. Honors contributors to the game; explores what basketball means to the state's culture and personality. Celebrates Indian's basketball history with videos and artifacts of the greatest basketball players to come out of Indiana, Also includes great moments and interactive exhibits.

Publications:
INDIANA BASKETBALL HISTORY, quarterly magazine $15 year subscription.

Member Services:
$100 Annual fee includes unlimited free admission, free subscription to magazine, invitation to all events and activities given to hall of famers.

INDIANA FOOTBALL HALL OF FAME
815 NORTH A STREET
BOX 1035
RICHMOND, IN 47375
765-966-2235
contact@indiana-football.org
www.indiana-football.org
• Richard Bryant, President
• Ken Jorden, VP
• Fred Goss, Secretary
joyce@indiana-football.org

Description:
Establishes endowments and scholarships for excellence in football in Indiana. Candidates for induction include coaches, players, officials, sport media and Indiana citizens who have made prominent contributions in the advancement of football

excellence.
Year Founded:
1973

INDIANAPOLIS MOTOR SPEEDWAY HALL OF FAME MUSEUM
4790 WEST 16TH STREET
INDIANAPOLIS, IN 46222
317-492-8500
www.indyracingmuseum.org
• Ellen Bireley, Director
Publications:
OFFICIAL 500 PROGRAM, annually; INDY REVIEW, after each year's race, usually by November 15.
Description:
Founded 1956. Located on the grounds of the Indianapolis Motor Speedway. Displayed are more than 75 racing cars, including Indianapolis winners as well as race cars from international renowned motorsports events world wide. Also displayed are several examples of early antique and classic passenger cars. Surrounding the restored cars are numerous displays of engines, trophies, helmets, historic photographs, and other priceless memorabilia.

INTERNATIONAL BOWLING MUSEUM AND HALL OF FAME
612 SIX FLAGS DRIVE
ARLINGTON, TX 76011
817-385-8215
Fax: 314-231-4054
hofm@bowlingmuseum.com
www.bowlingmuseum.com
• Keith Hamilton, Chairman, President
• John Walker, VP
• Terry Brenneman, Treasurer
• Bob Gudorf, Secretary
Description:
Opened in June, 1984. Visitors will enjoy computerized exhibits, movie, art and sculpture, museum shop, and bowling on computerized or hand-set lanes. The museum is also home to the St. Louis Cardinals Hall of Fame Museum. Receptions, catered events and meeting space available.
Publications:
Hall of Fame newsletter, three times annually.

INTERNATIONAL BOXING HALL OF FAME
1 HALL OF FAME DRIVE
CANASTOTA, NY 13032
315-697-7095
Fax: 315-697-5356
www.ibhof.com
• Edward P. Brophy, Executive Director
Description:
Mission is to honor and preserve boxing's rich heritage, chronicle the achievements of those who excelled and provide an educational for our many visitors.

INTERNATIONAL GYMNASTICS HALL OF FAME & MUSEUM
120 NORTH ROBINSON
EAST CONCOURSE
OKLAHOMA CITY, OK 73102
405-235-5600
Fax: 405-235-5678
contact@ighof.com
www.ighof.com

• Whitney Anson, President
• Paul Ziert, Chief Executive Officer
Description:
Founded 1987. Serves to recognize the sport of Gymnastics and the personalities involved in all aspects.
Membership Requirements:
Donations.
Publications:
International Gymnastics HALL OF FAME Newsletter, random; INTERNATIONAL GYMNAST Magazine, 10 times annually.

INTERNATIONAL INSTITUTE FOR SPORT HISTORY
PO BOX 175
STATE COLLEGE, PA 16804
814-321-4018
habrams@iisoh.org
www.sportlibrary.org
• Harvey Abrams, President
(814) 321-4018
habrams@iisoh.org
Year founded:
2001
Description:
Specialized research library and museum for the history of sport, physical education, recreation, dance, sport in art and the Olympic Games.
Online resources:
National Olympic Committee Directory, Sport in Pennsylvania, Sport in Austria, Sport in Art Poster Series at www.sportlibrary.org
Nature of Service:
Comprehensive Library & Museum for the History of Sport, Physical Education, Recreation, Dance, Sport in Art and the Olympic Games.

INTERNATIONAL JEWISH SPORTS HALL OF FAME
7922 TURNCREST DR
POTOMAC, MD 20854-2773
jsportslegends@aol.com
www.jewishsports.net
• Efraim Yaacobi, Executive Secretary
• Alan Sherman, Chairman
• R. Stephen Rubin, Honorary Chairman
• Joseph Siegman, Chairman Selection Committee Member Services
Address in Israel:
Wingate Institute, Wingate Post Office, Netanya, Israel
Description:
Honors Jewish men and women worldwide, elected annually in December, who have accomplished extraordinary achievements in sports, and recognizes other Jewish men and women who have made significant contributions to society through sports. Actual location of Hall of Fame is Wingate Institute for Physical Education, Netanya 42902 Israel.
Publications:
International Jewish Sports Hall of Fame and Jewish Sports Legends vol. 4. June 2005
Member Services:
Lifetime Achievement Award, awarded annually for outstanding contributions to the State of Israel, and society through sports.
Number of Members:
Over 420 inductees as of 2018.

INTERNATIONAL MOTOR SPORTS HALL OF FAME
PO BOX 1018
TALLADEGA, AL 35160
256-362-5002
Fax: 256-315-4565
www.motorsportshalloffame.com
• Grant Lynch, Executive Director
• Cindy Bradford, Office Manager
• Bruce Ramey, Hall of Fame Manager
Description:
Founded 1983. Serves to preserve the history of motorsports on a worldwide basis, and to enshrine forever the people that have been responsible for it's growth. Home of the Official International Motorsports Hall of Fame where the Inductees are permanently enshrined. Also features a collection of racing cars, memorabilia, race car simulator, gift shop and research library.

INTERNATIONAL SNOWMOBILE HALL OF FAME & MUSEUM
8481 HIGHWAY 70 WEST
PO BOX 720
ST. GERMAIN, WI 54558
715-542-4463
Fax: 715-542-4260
info@snowmobilehalloffame.com
www.snowmobilehalloffame.com
• Loren R. Anderson, President
Description:
Founded 1983. Honors snowmobile racing greats and club volunteers; serves as museum of historic sleds from both trail and track.
Publications:
THE FINISH LINE, Newsletter, periodic.
Number of members:
53 Inductees.

INTERNATIONAL SPORTS HALL OF FAME AND OLYMPIC MUSEUM
110 NE HIGHWAY 101
DEPOE BAY, OR 97341
541-765-2923
Fax: 541-765-3231
• Eric Nash, Executive Director
enash327@yahoo.com
Description:
Founded 1992. Museum will display international Olympic memorabilia from 1896 to the present. Specializes in the 1984 Olympics, with one of the largest collections in the U.S. The collection includes: medals, banners, flags, posters, pins, programs, books, and reports.

INTERNATIONAL SPORTS HERITAGE ASSOCIATION
PO BOX 2384
FLORENCE, OR 32004-3093
541-991-7315
Fax: 904-997-3871
info@sportsheritage.org
www.sportsheritage.org
• Michael Gibbons, President
• Rick Walls, Vice President
Publications:
Newsletter, bimonthly 'Honoring Our Heroes'
Description:
Founded 1971. Serves as a forum for directors/curators of halls of fame and museums to exchange ideas and information and generally strengthen and promote their respective organizations.

INTERNATIONAL SWIMMING HALL OF FAME
ONE HALL OF FAME DRIVE
FT. LAUDERDALE, FL 33316
954-462-6536
Fax: 954-
ishof@ishof.org
www.ishof.org
• Bruce Wigo, President/CEO
brucewigo@yahoo.com
• Bob Duenkel, Executive Director
• Meg Keller Marvin, Assistant to CEO
• Ivonne Schmid, Assistant to Executive Director
• Laurie Marchwinski, Director of Basketball Operations
• Marcia Meiners, Assistant To The President
• Jarret Streiner, Webmaster
• Bob Duenkel, Executive Director/Curator
bduenkel@ishof.org
Description:
Founded 1965. Swimming, diving, pools, synchronized swimming, and water polo, past and present. Olympic gold medals and uniforms, trophies, short movies and Henning Library. Memorabilia from Johnny (Tarzan) Weissmuller, Esther Williams, Mark Spitz, Greg Louganis and many more.
Publications:
Newsletter, quarterly.
Member Services:
Site of College Coaches Swim Forum and national and international events each year. Annual meetings held in conjunction with Honor Ceremonies.

INTERNATIONAL TENNIS HALL OF FAME AND MUSEUM
194 BELLEVUE AVE
NEWPORT, RI 2840
401-849-3990
800-457-1144
Fax: 401-849-8780
newport@tennisfame.com
www.tennisfame.com
• Mark Stenning, Chief Executive Officer
• Amelia Ahlborg, Assistant To CEO
• Nancy Cardoza, Vice president
• Baebara Klassner, Accounting Manager
• Sarah Rivard, Accountant
• Jane Sherman, Office manager
• Mary Health, Chief Marketing Officer
New York Office:
100 Park Ave, 10th Floor, New York, NY 10017. 212 880-4179.
Description:
Founded 1954. Non-profit organization dedicated to preserving the history of the game and maintaining a museum in Newport, Rhode Island. The organization also promotes junior tennis and professional tennis tournaments. The Hall of Fame inducts outstanding players, officials and administrators. Since 1954, 175 enshrinees have been elected.
Publications:
Tennis Hall of Fame Newsletter.

JAPANESE BASEBALL HALL OF FAME AND MUSEUM
1-3-61, KORAKU
BUNKYO-KU
TOKYO, JAPAN 112-0004

• Yasuchika Negoro, Chairman
• Ryozo Kato, Chairman of the Board of Directors
• Hideo Okabe, Director
• Hajime Toyokura, Executive Director
Description:
Founded 1959, its purpose is to contribute to the development of baseball in Japan through a dedication of baseball greats-players, executives, and umpires, as Hall of Famers and the exhibition and collection of as many memorable baseball materials as possible, including various kinds of baseball literature.

JOYCE SPORTS RESEARCH COLLECTION, UNIVERSITY OF NOTRE DAME
221 HESBURGH LIBRARY
UNIVERSITY OF NOTRE DAME
NOTRE DAME, IN 46556-5629
574-631-6258
Fax: 574-631-6772
rarebook@nd.edu
• George Rugg, Curator
george.k.rugg.1@nd.edu
Description:
Comprises all of the University Librarie's sports related materials. These include a circulating collection of close to 10,000 volumes, and a non circulating collection.

KENTUCKY DERBY MUSEUM
704 CENTRAL AVENUE
LOUISVILLE, KY 40208
502-637-7097
Fax: 502-637-1111
info@derbymuseum.org
www.derbymuseum.org
• Lynn Ashton, Executive Director
lashton@derbymuseum.org
• Sherry Crose, Chief Operating Officer
scrose@derbymuseum.org
• Wendy Treinen, Public Relations Manager
cmangeot@derbymuseum.org
Description:
Founded 1985. Promotes sport of Thoroughbred racing, preserves the history and heritage of the Kentucky Derby and Churchill Downs, and serves as a forum for the equine industry.
Membership Requirements:
Completion of membership application to be returned with membership fee. Corporate farm and individual memberships available.
Publications:
THE INSIDE TRACK, quarterly newsletter.
Official Sponsor:
2002 - American Airlines.

LA84 FOUNDATION
2141 WEST ADAMS BOULEVARD
LOS ANGELES, CA 90018
323-730-4600
Fax: 323-730-9637
info@la84foundation.org
www.la84foundation.org
• Anita L. Defrantz, President
• Wayne Wilson, Vice President Education Services
• Conrad Freund, Chief Operating Officer
Description:
The LA84 Foundation is endowed with surplus funds from the 1984 Los Angeles Olympic Games. Their mission is to serve youth through sport and to increase knowledge of sport and its impact on people's lives. The LA84 Foundation supports a wide array of youth sports programming. They award grants to youth sports organizations within the eight southernmost counties of California. They also conduct their own youth sports and coaching education programs, a number of which have become models for similar programs nationwide.
Publications:
Biennial publications
Member Services:
Open to students, athletes, coaches, journalists, researchers and public. Copy capabilities; meeting and conference rooms; video and audio-visual equipment; computerized catalog system; on-line database.

LACROSSE MUSEUM AND NATIONAL HALL OF FAME MUSEUM
113 WEST UNIVERSITY PARKWAY
BALTIMORE, MD 21210
410-235-6882
Fax: 410-366-6735
info@uslacrosse.org
www.uslacrosse.org
• Bill Schoonmaker, Chief Operating Officer
• Steven Stenersen, President and CEO
Description:
Founded 1959. Displays and chronicles the history of the sport of lacrosse, from its native American origin to the present day. Museum includes photographs, lithographs, trophies, equipment, uniforms, statues, books, videos and rare memorabilia for men's and women's lacrosse.

LITTLE LEAGUE BASEBALL MUSEUM
525 ROUTE 15 HIGHWAY
PO BOX 3485
WILLIAMSPORT, PA 17701-0485
570-326-1921
Fax: 570-326-1074
museum@littleleague.org
www.littleleague.org
• John Littner, Director
Description:
Founded 1982. Purpose is to chart history and growth of Little League Baseball and Softball movement from founding in Williamsport to its worldwide growth by means of visual and audio displays, exhibits and memorabilia that are both educational and entertaining.

MANITOBA SPORTS HALL OF FAME & MUSEUM INC.
SPORTS FOR LIFE CENTRE
145 PACIFIC AVENUE
WINNIPEG, MB, CANADA R3B 2Z6
204-925-5736
Fax: 204-925-5916
halloffame@sport.mb.ca
• Rick D. Brownlee, Executive Director
• Don Pincock, President
• Lois Howard, Secretary
Description:
Founded 1980. Preserves Manitoba's sport heritage; honors athletes, builders, teams with induction to the Hall of Fame.
Publications:
Newsletter, quarterly; Annual Induction Program.

MISSOURI SPORTS HALL OF FAME
3861 E. STAN MUSIAL DR
SPRINGFIELD, MO 65809

417-889-3100
800-498-5678
Fax: 417-889-2761
www.mosportshalloffame.com
• Jerald Andrews, President/Executive Director
• Marty Willadsen, Vp/Operations And Administration
• Jerry Vickery, Historian
Description:
Founded 1993, by John Q. Hammons. Serves to preserve sports history of Missouri; honor individuals and teams that have made significant contributions to sports, and to promote sports throughout the state of Missouri.

MOTORSPORTS MUSEUM AND HALL OF FAME OF AMERICA
43700 EXPO CENTER DRIVE
NOVI, MI 48375
248-349-RACE
800-250-7223
Fax: 248-349-2113
info@mshf.com
www.mshf.com
• Ronald A. Watson, President
• Tom Gravalos, Vice-Chairman
• John Doonan, Chairman
• Denny Darnell, Secretary
• Ross Hotz, Treasurer
Member Services:
Hall of Fame Induction held in August during NASCAR at the Michigan International Speedway. Membership package includes yearbook, poster, decal, Novi Race Car Pin, free admission to museum, discounts on gift items and subscription to HORSEPOWER Newsletter.
Publications:
Annual Hall of Fame Souvenir Yearbook
Description:
Serves as the Hall of Fame of America for Motorsports and as a museum. Over 70 racing vehicles in the following seven categories are displayed: Open Wheel, Stock Car, Sports Car, Drag Racing, Motorcycle, Air Racing and Power Boat.
Museum Location:
Novi Expo Center, S.W. Corner of I-96 and Novi Road

MUSEUM OF POLO AND HALL OF FAME
9011 LAKE WORTH ROAD
LAKE WORTH, FL 33467
561-969-3210
Fax: 561-964-8299
polomuseum@att.net
www.polomuseum.com
• George J Dupont Sr, Jr., Executive Director, Vice President
• Brenda Lynn, Director of Development
Publications:
Newsletter, annually.
Description:
Founded 1984. Museum houses polo's records, art, memorabilia, honors heroes of polo through Polo Hall of Fame, offers education and knowledge about polo and provides history of the sport.

MUSEUM OF YACHTING
FORT ADAMS STATE PARK
NEWPORT, RI 2840
401-847-1018
Fax: 401-847-8320

museum@moy.org
www.museumofyachting.org
• Terry Nathan, President
• Rhonda Landers, Chief Financial Officer
Description:
Founded 1980. Promotes yachting history and hosts annual classic yacht regatta.
Membership Requirements:
Interest in Yachting, past and present.
Publications:
Newsletter, quarterly.
Member Services:
Free admission to Museum; use of library, discounts on Museum programs, and events and merchandise.

NAISMITH MEMORIAL BASKETBALL HALL OF FAME
1000 WEST COLUMBUS AVENUE
SPRINGFIELD, MA 1105
413-781-6500
877-446-6752
www.hoophall.com
• John Doleva, President/Chief Executive Officer
doleva@hoophall.com
• Donald R. Senecal, Vice President/Finance/Operations
senecal@hoophall.com
Member Services:
Hall of Fame induction, Hall of Fame Tip-Off Classic, Frances Pomeroy Naismith Award, Ed Steitz Award, John W. Bunn Award, Bob Cousy Collegiate Point-Guard Award, Curt Gowdy Media Award, Chip Hilton Award, Clare Bee Award, High School Excellence Award, Museum.
Publications:
Magazine, Yearbook.
Membership Requirements:
To be eligible to be inducted, candidate must first be nominated; players must be retired five years, coaches with 25 years of serve are eligible. Candidate must have made significant contributions to the game in many distinct areas.
Description:
Founded 1949. Preserves and promotes basketball at all levels, including the professional, collegiate, scholastic, international game and pays tribute to both men and women, trainers, referees, contributors.

NATIONAL ART MUSEUM OF SPORT
UNIVERSITY PLACE - IUPUI
850 WEST MICHIGAN ST
INDIANAPOLIS, IN 46202-5198
317-274-3627
Fax: 317-274-3878
• Elizabeth C. Varner, President
• Ann M. Rein, Executive Director
(317) 274-3627
Description:
Founded 1959. Brings to the public a comprehensive collection of Sport Art (over 50 different sports). Educates the public on the close relationship over the ages between art and sport.
Publications:
SCORE BOARD NEWSLETTER 3 issues per year. Exhibit check list.

NATIONAL AUTOMOBILE MUSEUM
10 SOUTH LAKE STREET
RENO, NV 89501-1558

775-333-9300
Fax: 775-333-9309
info@automuseum.org
www.automuseum.org
• Jackie Frady, President and ED
• Barbara Bolenbaker, Retail manager
• Barbara Clark, Sr Support services manager
• Becky Contos, Sales and marketing manager
Description:
Founded 1989. General automobile museum with collection of racing and speed record autos. Automotive research library available through mail service.

NATIONAL BASEBALL HALL OF FAME AND MUSEUM
25 MAIN STREET
COOPERSTOWN, NY 13326
607-547-7200
888-425-5633
Fax: 607-547-2044
info@baseballhalloffame.org
www.baseballhall.org
• William E. Haase, Senior Vice President (607) 547-7200
• Joe Morgan, Vice Chairman
• Jeff Idelson, President
• Craig Muder, Directoro of Communications
Publications:
Annual Hall of Fame Yearbook, Memories and Dreams Quarterly Magazine
Membership Requirements:
Must have played at least 10 years in Major Leagues or Negro Leagues or can have been executive, manager or umpire.
Description:
Museum/Educational Facility

NATIONAL FOOTBALL FOUNDATION AND COLLEGE HALL OF FAME, INC., THE
433 LAS COLINAS BLVD
SUITE 1130
IRVING, TX 75039
972-556-1000
Fax: 972-556-9032
membership@footballfoundation.com
www.footballfoundation.com
• Archie Manning, Chairman
• Steven J. Hatchell, President and CEO
• Clayton I. Bennett, Vice Chair
• Matthew Sigo, Chief Operating Officer
Description:
Established: 1947. Our mission is to promote and develop the power of amateur football in developing the qualities of leadership, sportsmanship, competitive zeal and the drive for academic excellence in America's young people.
Number of Members:
13,000.
Publications:
Footballletter 4 times per year.
Member Services:
120 Chapters, Footballletter Magazine, Free Admission to the Hall of Fame, Grants, Programs, Scholorships.
Membership Requirements:
$40.00 year.

NATIONAL FRESH WATER FISHING HALL OF FAME
10360 ONE HALL OF FAME DR
HAYWARD, WI 54843

715-634-4440
www.freshwater-fishing.org
• Emmett A Brown, Executive Director
Description:
Museum displaying fishing artifacts, including 300 antique outboard motors, thousands of lures, rods, reels, mounted fish, tackle boxes and all other memorabilia involved in the sport of fresh water fishing.
Number of members:
6,500
Publications:
Quarterly Newsletter with record updates; Fish Record Book, early April; Annual Calendar.
Member Services:
Unlimited admission pass to members and family members under 18 to museum. Receipt of all publications.
Membership Requirements:
$30.00 Annual membership, $250.00 Lifetime membership, $50.00 Club and Business memberships.

NATIONAL HIGH SCHOOL SPORTS HALL OF FAME
PO BOX 690
1802 ALONZO WATFORD SR. DRIVE
INDIANAPOLIS, IN 46206
317-972-6900
Fax: 317-822-5700
www.nfhs.org
• Bruce L. Howard, Director of Publications and Communications
(816) 464-5400
Description:
Founded 1982. Currently housed in an auditorium area of the National Federation of State High School Associations. Induction into the Hall of Fame is conducted annually on the basis of special achievement in four categories - athlete, coach, official and administrator.

NATIONAL ITALIAN-AMERICAN SPORTS HALL OF FAME
1431 W. TAYLOR ST
CHICAGO, IL 60607
312-226-5566
Fax: 312-226-5678
www.niashf.org
• George Randazzo, Founder/Chairman
george@niashf.org
• Wayne Randazzo, Editor Red White & Green Magazine
Publications:
NIASHF Newsletter; Red White and Green Magazine
Description:
Founded 1977. Preservation of achievements of professional and amateur Italian-American athletes who have contributed to international sports.

NATIONAL MISSISSIPPI RIVER MUSEUM & AQUARIUM
350 EAST 3RD STREET HARBOR
PORT OF DUBUQUE
DUBUQUE, IA 52001
563-557-9545
800-226-3369
Fax: 563-583-1241
info@rivermuseum.com
www.mississippirivermuseum.com
• Jerry Enzler, Executive Director
• Cristin Waterbury, Curator

Member Services:
Annual meeting held in May in Dubuque, IA.
Publications:
Newsletter, quarterly.
Membership Requirements:
Pay annual dues.
Description:
Founded 1985. Serves to preserve the history of men and women of the inland waters of America - explorers, builders, inventors, river people and artists, writers and musicians; part of the Mississippi River Museum.

NATIONAL MOTORSPORTS PRESS ASSOCIATION
PO BOX 500
DARLINGTON, SC 29540
843-395-8900
Fax: 843-393-3911
www.nmpaonline.com
• Rea White, President
• Kenny Bruce, President
• Brian Nelson, VP
• Bob Pockrass, Secretary/Treasurer
Description:
Comprised of individuals in news media and other individuals in the automotive/racing field. Promotes better news coverage of motorsports news events. Maintains Stock Car Hall of Fame and Joe Weatherly Museum at Darlington Raceway. Sponsors competitions; bestows awards.
Publications:
NMPA NEWSLETTER, twice a year.

NATIONAL MUSEUM OF RACING HALL OF FAME
191 UNION AVENUE
SARATOGA SPRINGS, NY 12866-3566
518-584-0400
800-JOCKEY4
Fax: 518-584-4574
nmrmedia@racingmuseum.net
www.racingmuseum.org
• Christopher Dragone, Director
(518) 584-0400
• Christopher Dragone, Director
• Victoria Tokarowski, Membership and business manager
• Brien Bouyea, Communications coordinator
• Allan Carter, Historian
Membership Requirements:
Contributor, Donor, Associate, Patron, Benefactor, Gold Cup
Description:
Founded 1950. Interprets the history and conveys the excitement of Thoroughbred racing in America. Fosters education and understanding of Thoroughbred racing by providing public access to equine art, artifacts, memorabilia, film, video, books and historical archives. Collects, preserves, researches, interprets and exhibits the entire spectrum of Thoroughbred racing enhanced by interactive displays.

NATIONAL SOCCER HALL OF FAME
18 STADIUM CIRCLE
ONEONTA, NY 13820
607-432-3351
Fax: 607-432-8429
www.soccerhall.org
Description:
Celebrates the history, honors the heroes and preserves the legacy of the sport of

soccer in the United States.
Year Founded:
1950

NATIONAL SOFTBALL HALL OF FAME & MUSEUM & STADIUM COMPLEX
2801 NE 50TH STREET
OKLAHOMA CITY, OK 73111
405-424-5266
Fax: 405-424-3855
www.asasoftball.org
• Ron Radigonda, Executive Director
(405) 424-5266
• Bill Plummer, Museum Curator
(405) 425-3433
• Kelly McKeown, Director Marketing
(405) 424-5266
Number of members
180
Description:
Founded 1957. Honors former outstanding players and traces evolution and history of softball with various displays and exhibits. Holds induction ceremonies annually.

NATIONAL SPORTING LIBRARY, THE
102 THE PLAINS ROAD
MIDDLEBURG, VA 20118
540-687-6542
Fax: 540-687-8540
www.nsl.org
• Rick Stoutamyer, Executive Director
• Melanie Leigh Mathews, Executive Director
• Diana Kingsbury Smith, Development Coordinator
• Judy Sheehan, Event & Office Manager
• Charles T Akre jr, Treasurer
• Manuel H Johnson, Chairman Of The Board
• Jacqueline B Mars, Vice Chairman
• Lisa Campbell, Secretary
Description:
Founded 1954. Contains more than 15,000 volumes on horse and field sports dating back to 1523, including horsemanship, racing, breeding, foxhunting, veterinary care and sporting art.
Publications:
Newsletter, quarterly.

NATIONAL SPRINT CAR HALL OF FAME AND MUSEUM FOUNDATION, INC.
ONE SPRINT CAPITAL PLACE
KNOXVILLE, IA 50138
641-842-6176
800-874-4488
Fax: 641-842-6177
sprintcarhof@sprintcarhof.com
www.sprintcarhof.com
• Bob Baker, Executive Director
bbaker@sprintcarhof.com
Description:
Founded 1986. Historical preservation of the sport of sprint car racing. Exhibition of sprint cars from 1900 to the present and memorabilia.
Publications:
National Sprint Car Hall of Fame induction Program; HALLMARKS, quarterly newsletter.

NEGRO LEAGUES BASEBALL MUSEUM
1616 EAST 18TH STREET
KANSAS CITY, MO 64108
816-221-1920
888-221-6526

Fax: 816-221-8424
www.nlbm.com
• Bob Kenrick, President
• Betty Brown, Chairman
• Margo Weatherby, Treasuerer
• Monte Irvin, NATIONAL ADVISORY BOARD
• Don B. Motley, Executive Director Emeritus
• Michael R. Kanaley, Vice Chairman/Secretary
Description:
Founded 1991. Dedicated to researching, preserving and disseminating the history of Negro Leagues Baseball.

NEW BRUNSWICK SPORTS HALL OF FAME
PO BOX 6000
503 RUE QUEEN STREET
FREDERICTON, CANADA E3B SH1
506-453-3747
nbsportshalloffame@gnb.ca
www.nbsportshalloffame.nb.ca
• Jamie Wolverton, Executive Director (506) 453-8930
Publications:
Newsletter twice a year.

NEWPORT SPORTS MUSEUM
100 NEWPORT CENTER DRIVE
SUITE 100
NEWPORT BEACH, CA 92660
949-721-9333
Fax: 949-721-9399
www.newportsportsmuseum.org
• John W. Hamilton, Founder
• Stephen H Andreson, President, S.H.A. Enterprises
• Pat Bolter, Vice President/ General Manager, Mercedes Ben
Member Services:
Educational programs involved professional athletes speaking with youth concerning drug abuse, gang involvement and the importance of an education.
Description:
Non-profit organization dedicated to mentoring children and preserving the history of sport. Using the collection as a vehicle to mentor at-risk children about the virtues of athletics and academics and the dangers of drugs and gangs.

OLYMPIC HALL OF FAME AND MUSEUM
88 CANADA OLYMPIC ROAD SW
CALGARY, AB, CANADA T3B 5R5
403-247-5452
Fax: 403-286-7213
• Bob Nicolay, President/CEO
Description:
Founded 1988. Preserves the material heritage of the XV Olympic Winter Games; provides a tribute to the achievements of Canada's Olympians.

OLYMPIC MUSEUM, LIBRARY AND STUDIES CENTRE
1 QUAI D'OUCHY
PO BOX CH-1001
LAUSANNE, SWITZERLAN 1001
www.olympic.org
• Jacques Rogge, President
Description:
The world's largest repository of information on the Olympic Movement. A living tribute to the association of sport, art and culture, it retraces the history of the Olympics from Ancient Greece to the modern day. It is a new type of museum based on high technology-computer and audiovisual technology have generated a new art of the image.

OREGON SPORTS HALL OF FAME
4840 SOUTH WEST WESTERN AVENUE
SUITE 600
BEAVERTON, OR 97005
503-227-7466
Fax: 503-227-6925
info@oregonsportshall.org
www.oregonsportshall.org
• Donna Smoot, Administrative Assistant & Collection Manager
• Jack Elder, Executive Director
Description:
Serves to recognize and appreciate Oregon's rich athletic history. Our goal is for this legacy to inspire participation in sport and foster awareness of the values and life-long rewards gained from this participation.

PENNSYLVANIA SPORTS HALL OF FAME
PO BOX 7152
LANCASTER, PA 17601
717-684-2714
Fax: 717-684-2714
www.pashof.org
• Dr. Stephen J. George, Jr., President
• Edward L Ludwig, Executive Vice President
• Jeffery Fortna, State Treasurer
Description:
Founded 1962. Serves to perpetuate the memory of individuals who have brought lasting fame and recognition to the Commonwealth of Pennsylvania and its people through their achievements in athletics and sports.

PGA WORLD GOLF HALL OF FAME
1 WORLD GOLF PLACE
ST. AUGUSTINE, FL 32092
904-940-4000
www.worldgolfhalloffame.org
• Bruce Laht, General Manager
Description:
Founded 1974. Museum and hall of fame dedicated to the game of golf.

PIKES PEAK INTERNATIONAL RACEWAY
1631 MESA AVENUE
SUITE B-1
COLORADO SPRINGS, CO 80906
719-685-4400
Fax: 719-634-5198
info@ppihc.com
www.ppihc.com
• Megan Leatham, Director Operations
• Lincoln Floyd, Director of development
• Tom Osborn, Chairman, Board of Directors
• Megan Leatham, Executive director of operations
laytonpc123@msn.com
Description:
Founded 1989. Houses a collection of race vehicles from the Chevrolet Pikes Peak International Hill Climb, racing apparel and memorabilia. Organizes and runs the annual July 4 Pikes Peak International Hill climb.

The second oldest continually run motorsporting event in the United States.

PRO FOOTBALL HALL OF FAME
2121 GEORGE HALAS DRIVE NW
CANTON, OH 44708
330-456-8207
Fax: 330-456-9080
www.profootballhof.com
• Stephen A Perry, President/Executive Director
• Steve Strawbridge, Vice President Merchadise Sales/Licensing
• Joe Horrigan, Vice President and Chief Financial Officer
• Bill Allen, Vice President/CFO
• Dave Motts, Vice President/Marketing/Operations
Description:
The mission of the Pro Football Hall of Fame is to honor, preserve, educate and promote. To honor individuals who have made outstanding contributions to professstional football. To preserve professional football's historic documents and artifacts. To educate the public regarding the origin, development and growth of professional football as an important part of American culture. To promote the positive values of the sport.
Year Founded:
1963

PROFESSIONAL GOLFERS' ASSOCIATION HALL OF FAME
100 AVENUE OF THE CHAMPIONS
PALM BEACH GARDENS, FL 33410
561-624-8400
www.pga.com
• Allen Wrukowski, President
• Ted Bishop, Vice President
Description:
The ultimate destination for the celebration and recognition of golf's greatest players and contributors and serves as an inspiration to golfers and golf fans throughout the world.

ROME SPORTS HALL OF FAME & MUSEUM
5790 LONDON ROAD
ROME, NY 13440
315-339-9038
www.when-in-rome.com
• Ruth M. Demers, Executive Director
• Bill Fleet, Co-Chairman
Membership Requirements:
Open membership, annual dues.
Description:
Founded 1977. Offers recognition and display of Rome sports personalities. Continued excellence inductees, etc. for City of Rome residents.

ROSE BOWL HALL OF FAME
391 S. ORANGE GROVE BLVD
PASADENA, CA 91184
626-449-4100
Fax: 626-449-9066
rosepr@rosemail.org
www.tournamentofroses.com
• Jeffery J Allen, COO and CFO
• Richard L Chinen, President
Description:
Founded 1989. The Rose Bowl Hall of Fame honors outstanding individuals whose achievements have contributed to the

success of the Rose Bowl Game.
Membership Requirements:
Idividuals inducted into the Rose Bowl Hall of Fame include players, coaches, school administrators, athletic directors, conference officials and others who have made special contributions to the Rose Bowl Game.
Number of Inductees:
87
Publications:
ROSE BOWL GAME PROGRAM

SAN DIEGO HALL OF CHAMPIONS SPORTS MUSEUM, THE
2131 PAN AMERICAN PLAZA - BALBOA PARK
SAN DIEGO, CA 92101
619-234-2544
Fax: 619-234-4543
info@sdhoc.com
www.sdhoc.com
• Angela LaChica, Vice President
• Denise Cooper, President
Description:
The nations largest multi-sport museum, boasting three levels of memorabilia and 68,000 square feet. The museum offers a state-of-the-art theatre, an interactive media center and fascinating displays on the nation's favorite sports.

SPORT INFORMATION RESOURCE CENTER/SIRC
180 ELGIN STREET
SUITE 1400
OTTAWA, ON, CANADA K2P 2K3
613-231-7472
800-665-6413
Fax: 613-231-3739
webmaster@sirc.ca
www.sirc.ca
• Debra Gassewitz, President/CEO
• David Roberts, CEO
• Kim Sparling, Communications Manager
• Nancy Rebel, Director of Content Development
Description:
Founded in 1973, SIRC identifies, collects and organizes information about sports, fitness and other related fields. Every month, SIRC scans over 1,200 magazines and journals from around the world as well as monographs and theses covering practical and research material. From this information, SIRC produces the online SPORT Database and its equivalent on CD-ROM, the SPORT Discus. Also provides Sport Information Service on World Wide Web, www.SPORTQuest.com, which provides links to a wide range of sports web sites for Olympic Sports, Winter Sports, Water Sports, Professional Sports, Coaching, Statistics and Results, Sports Medicine and Individ

SPORTS IMMORTALS
6830 NORTH FEDERAL HWY
BOCA RATON, FL 33487
561-997-2575
Fax: 561-997-6949
legends@sportsimmortals.com
www.sportsimmortals.com
• Jim Platt, Vice President
(561) 997-2575
legends@sportsimmortals.com
• Joel Platt, Chairman
• John Murpy, Manager/Curator

(561) 997-2575
football@sportsimmortals.com
Year Founded:
1992.
Nature of Service:
Sports Immortals Museum and Memorabilia Mart Museum features over one million mementos, the largest collection on all sports in the world. The Memorabilia Mart offers a selection of over 20,000 items to purchase.

SPORTS MUSEUM OF NEW ENGLAND, THE
100 LEGENDS WAY
BOSTON, MA 2134
617-624-1234
Fax: 617-787-8152
www.sportsmuseum.org
• Rusty Sullivan, Executive Director
(617) 624-1237
rsullivan@dncboston.com
• Brian Codangnone, Associate Curator
(617) 624-1235
bcodagnone@dncboston.com
Number of members:
1,207
Membership Requirements:
$50 for individuals; $100 for family; $1,500 for corporate membership.
Description:
Founded 1977. Preserves and showcases the unique sports heritage of New England through creative and interactive exhibits. Amateur, professional, Olympic, scholastic. Provides educational and community outreach programs that encourage achievement, establish friendships, and build leadership skills, especially in our youth.

ST. LOUIS CARDINALS HALL OF FAME MUSEUM
ST. LOUIS CARDINALS L.P.
700 CLARK AVENUE
ST. LOUIS, MO 63102
314-345-9600
Fax: 314-231-4054
• Jeff Boje, Co-Owner
Notes:
The St. Louis Cardinals Hall of Fame and Museum and the International Bowling Museum and Hall of Fame became partners. Dedicated to exhibit, educate and preserve. The two Museums can now be found under one roof.

STATE OF KANSAS SPORTS HALL OF FAME
515 SOUTH WICHITA ST
Wichita, KS 67202
316-262-2038
Fax: 316-263-2539
info@kshof.org
www.kshof.org
• Ted Hayes, Chief Executive Officer, President
• Laura Hartley, BoatHouse Event Manager
lhartley@kshof.org
• Jordan Poland, Marketing Manager
jpoland@kshof.org
• Tim Daniel, Chairman
Description:
Founded 1961. Serves to preserve the Kansas tradition of producing world class teams and athletes. 90 of Kansas' most famous sports figures are presently

enshrined in the Hall of Fame, including Jim Ryun, Gale Sayers, Walter Johnson, Adolph Rupp, Dean Smith, Barry Sanders, John Riggins and Lynette Woodard.

TEXAS SPORTS HALL OF FAME & MUSEUM
1108 SOUTH UNIVERSITY PARKS DRIVE
WACO, TX 76706
254-756-1633
800-567-9561
Fax: 254-756-2384
info@tshof.org
• Steve Fallon, Executive Director
• Betsy Edwards, Marketing & Sales Director
(757) 393-8031
• Jay Black, Curator
• Paige Davis, Collections Manager
Description:
The official sports hall of fame for the Commonwealth of Virginia. From memorabilia to interactives, it's fun for the whole family.

TRAPSHOOTING HALL OF FAME AND MUSEUM
601 W. NATIONAL RD
VANDALIA, OH 45377
937-898-4638 EXT 528
Fax: 937-898-5541
hof@shootata.com
www.traphof.org
• Gene Anastasio, President
• Tami Daniel, Office Coordinator
Description:
Founded 1968. Devoted solely to the history of Trapshooting. Extensive exhibits, large research library. Annual induction to Hall of Fame ceremonies.

U.S. BICYCLING HALL OF FAME
303 3RD STREET
DAVIS, CA 95616
530-341-3263
www.usbhof.org
• Joe Herget, Executive Director
• Anthony Costello, President
Description:
Founded 1986. Honors competitors and contributors to the sport and recreational activity of cycling. Establishes a permanent institution devoted to the past, present and future of bicycling in America.
Membership Requirements:
Annual memberships from $25 (individual) to $500 (corporate).
Publications:
Newsletter
Member Services:
Membership - newsletter, discount on merchandise. Annual Hall of Fame Memorial Day Weekend includes Super Saturday - road race - criterium events - Sunday annual induction ceremonies. Other events during the year; 4th of July and Labor Day Cycling Classic.

U.S. HOCKEY HALL OF FAME
801 HAT TRICK AVE
PO BOX 679
EVELETH, MN 55734-0657
218-744-5167
800-443-7825
Fax: 218-744-2590
www.ushockeyhall.com

- Doug Palazzari, Executive Director
- Tom Sersha, Curator
- David Tomassoni, Chairman Of The board
- Calvin Cossalter, President
- Bob Pazzelli, Vice President
- Mitch Brunfelt, Secretary
- Mike Lenich, Treasurer
- Michelle Putzel, Administrative Assistant,Coordinator

Annual event:
Enshrinement ceremonies each October.

Publications:
ENSHRINEE BIOGRAPHIES 1973-1983, with updated enshrinee listings.

Membership Requirements:
Enshrinees must be retired from the sport for five years, American birth and training and have made a significant contribution to hockey.

Description:
The United States Hockey Hall of Fame was dedicated in 1973 as the 'National Shrine of American Hockey,' to be America's hockey showplace to honor the legends of the gamewith the Great Wall of Fame of Enshrinees, and to preserve the precious memories of ice hocky in the United States. To date the Hall has honored 130 outstanding coaches, players,builders, administrators and 2 Olympic teams who have contributed to the success and promotion of American hockey. In 2007, USA Hockey reached an agreement with the hall to continue being the exclusive enshrinement museum of American hockey.

U.S. NATIONAL SKI HALL OF FAME & MUSEUM
610 PALMS AVENUE
PO BOX 191
ISHPEMING, MI 49849
906-485-6323
Fax: 906-486-4570
www.skihall.com
- Thomas J West, President/CEO
- Bernard Wenchsel, Chairman
- Tom Anderson, Executive Committee
- David Brule, Executive Committee
- Phillip Camp, Executive committee
- Rudy Maki, Executive Committee

Description:
Founded 1954. Honors persons who have contributed much to the sport of skiing. Preserves and protects artifacts and historically valuable lore of skiing, conducts research and dispenses information to those requesting it related to the sport of skiing.

Hall of Fame Induction Requirements:
Must be nominated and elected according to the U.S. Skiing Rules of Governance. U.S. Skiing administers the nomination and election of honored individuals. Annual memberships.

Membership:
Individual $40; Family $50; Supporting $100; Corporate $500; Patron $1,000; Benefactor $ 5,000; Olympic Circle $ 10,000

USGA MUSEUM AND LIBRARY
77 LIBERTY CORNER ROAD
PO BOX 708
FAR HILLS, NJ 7931
908-234-2300
Fax: 908-234-0319
www.usga.org
- Robert M. Williams, Director
(908) 234-2300

- Susan Wasser, Coordinator of Special Projects
(908) 234-2300

Year Founded:
1936

Description:
The USGA Museum and Arnold Palmer Center for Golf History showcases the nation's largest and most significant collection of golf artifacts and documents. The interactive multimedia exhibits tell the story of the game;s development in the United States, highlighting the greatest moments in the game's hisotry, with a particular focus on USGA champions and championships.

Facilities Available for Sporting Events:
Pynes Putting Course

VIRGINIA SPORTS HALL OF FAME & MUSEUM
206 HIGH STREET
PO BOX 370
PORTSMOUTH, VA 23704
757-393-8031
Fax: 757-393-8288
www.vshof.com
- Eddie Webb, President
webbe@vshfm.com
- Betsy Edwards, Director of Marketing/Sales
(757) 393-8031
- Elizabeth Goodwin, Museum Services Director
(757) 393-8031
goodwine@vshfm.com

Description:
The official sports hall of fame for the Commonwealth of Virginia. From memorabilia to interactive, it's fun for the whole family.

Membership Requirements:
Fans and visitors are invited to become members and then nominate virginians for the hall. Inductees must meet residential requirements and should have achieved a level at success or had a mjaor impact on his record, school or community.

Publications:
Newsletter, quarterly; annual program, website (www.vshfm.com)

VOLLEYBALL HALL OF FAME INC.
444 Dwight Street
HOLYOKE, MA 1040
413-536-0926
Fax: 413-539-6673
info@volleyhall.org
www.volleyhall.org
- Jerry Fitzsimons, Executive Director
jerry.fitzsimons@volleyhall.org

Description:
The Volleyball Hall of Fame opened to the public on June 6 1987. A two day volleyball tournament was hosted by the Volleyball hall of Fame to celebrate the grand opening.

WOMEN'S BASKETBALL HALL OF FAME
700 HALL OF FAME DRIVE
KNOXVILLE, TN 37915
865-633-9000
Fax: 865-633-9294
dhart@wbhof.com
www.wbhof.com
- Dana Hart, President
- Josh Sullivan, Director of Basketball

Operations and Technology
jsullivan@wbhof.com

Description:
Founded 1999. National and international hall of fame dedicated to honoring the past, celebreating the present and promoting the future of women's basketball.

WRESTLING HALL OF FAME, NATIONAL
405 WEST HALL OF FAME AVENUE
STILLWATER, OK 74075
405-377-5243
Fax: 405-377-5244
www.wrestlinghalloffame.org
- Lee Roy Smith, Executive Director
lsmith@wrestlinghalloffame.org
- Jim keen, Chairman
- Stan Zeamer, Vice Chairman
- Terry Shockley, Secretary
- Rusty Shaw, Treasurer
- David Barry, Member

Description:
Founded 1976. Perpetuates the history of wrestling in the U.S. through national museum featuring displays of memorabilia, uniforms, awards, photographs along with a library, theater and Honors Court of Distinguished Members.

State Games Organizations

ALABAMA SPORTS FESTIVAL
2530 E. SOUTH BOULEVARD
MONTGOMERY, AL 36120
334-280-0065
800-467-0422
Fax: 334-280-0988
info@alagames.com
www.alagames.com
- Ronald J. Creel, Founder, President, CEO
- Tommy Kennedy, Director of Administration
tommy.kennedy@alagames.com
- Chris Wilkins, Communications Director
eric.engelbarts@alagames.com

Description:
The Alabama Sports Festival was organized in 1982 at the request of the United States Olympic Committee to develop grassroots Olympic-style competitions and expose athletes, volunteers and spectators of all ages and abilities, espacially our youth, to Olympic sports and the overall Olympic experience with all of its tradition and ceremony.

Publications:
Official Registration Book.

Member Services:
Assists in promoting leadership, academics, good citizenship, sportsmanship and competitive values through Alabama amateur athletics.

ALASKA STATE FAIR
2075 GLEN HWY
PALMER, AK 99645
907-745-4827
800-850-3247
Fax: 907-746-2699
info@alaskastatefair.org
www.alaskastatefair.org
- Ray Ritari, General Manager
ritari@alaskastatefair.org
- John Harkey, President
- John Tracy, Vice-Presdeint

- Caroline Kenley, Secretary
- Danny Consenstein, Treasurer
- Richard Stryken, Director
- Kristy Bernier, Director
- Dean Phipps, Dir. Marketing Development & Corp. Partnershi
(907) 746-7153
dean@alaskastatefair.org
Description:
The Alaska State Fair is the gathering place to showcase the best of our great state as we kick off a celebration of Alaska's 50th Anniversary of Statehood on August 21, 2008.

AUSTRALIAN SPORTS COMMISSION
61-02-6214-1111
Fax: 61-02-6214-1836
asc@ausport.gov.au
www.ausport.gov.au
- Matthew Favier, Director
- Simon Hollingsworth, Chief Executive Officer
Description:
The ASC is the Australian Government body that managers, develops and invests in sport at all levels. It works closely with a range of national sporting organizations, state and local governments, schools and community organizations to ensure sport is well run and accessible.

BADGER STATE GAMES
219 JEFFERSON STREET
WAUSAU, WI 54403
715-355-8788
badger@badgerstategames.org
www.badgerstategames.org
- Darien Schaefer, Executive Director
- Richard Barrett, Sales Director
- Tracy Baltz, Marketing Director
Description:
Founded 1984. Provides opportunity for Olympic-style amateur sports competition for the citizens of the State of Wisconsin. Winter games held each February in Wausau and North Central Wisconsin; summer games every June in Madison.

BAY STATE GAMES
55 SIXTH ROAD
SUITE 200
WOBURN, MA 1801
781-932-6555
Fax: 781-932-3441
info@baystategames.org
www.baystategames.org
- Jeff Baker, Assistant Director
- Kevin Cummings, Executive Director
Description:
Founded 1982. Statewide amateur sports festival involving 12,000 athletes in 25 sports of the Olympic family. Promotes the development of opportunity through participation and advancement in amateur sports. Member National Congress of State Games. U.S. Olympic Committee games recognition. Provides $12,000 in scholarships for recognition in academics, athletics and community involvement.
Member Services:
Produces Bay State Games and Bay State Winter Games, statewide multi-sports festivals.
Publications:
THE TORCH, newsletter; annual yearbook, coaches manual

Membership Requirements:
Massachusetts amateur athlete.

BIG SKY STATE GAMES
490 NORTH 31ST STREET
SUITE 304
BILLINGS, MT 59101
406-254-7426
Fax: 406-254-7439
info@bigskygames.org
www.bigskygames.org
- Karen Sanford Gall, Executive Director
- Liana Susott, Sports Director
- Kelly Elletson, Operations Director
Description:
The Big Sky Games is a privately funded, not-for-profit organization founded in 1986, that has responsibility of organizing an Olympic-style festival for the citizens of Montana. Big Sky State Games stands as the largest State Games per capita in the nation. During the summer of 2007 the games hosted over 10,500 athletes from over 250 communities in 36 different sporting events. The Big Sky State Games organizes a variety of other healthy lifestyle events and programs.
Nature of Service:
Providing quality competitions and programs to promote healthy and active lifestyles.

BIRMINGHAM, GREATER CONVENTION & VISITORS BUREAU
2200 9TH AVENUE NORTH
BIRMINGHAM, AL 35203-1100
205-458-8000
800-458-8085
Fax: 205-458-8086
info@birminghamal.org
www.birminghamal.org
- Karen Dobnikar, Human Resource Manager
(205) 214-9220
kdobnikar@birminghamal.org
- Dilcy Hilley, VP Marketing
(205) 214-9229
dhilley@birminghamal.org
- Michael Gunn, Vice President Sales
(205) 214-9213
mgunn@birminghamal.org
Description:
Established for the purpose of marketing and promoting the greater Birmingham area as a destination for conventions, meetings, and tour and travel. The mission is to broaden and expand promotional efforts on behalf of the city and its business constituency through advertising and marketing programs designed to sell guest rooms in area lodging facilities.

BLUEGRASS STATE GAMES
200 EAST MAIN STREET
LEXINGTON, KY 40507
859-255-0336
800-722-2474
Fax: 859-258-3022
info@bgsg.org
www.bgsg.org
- Amy Ratcliff, Operations Manager
- Terry Johnson, Executive Director
(859) 258-3040
tjohnson@bluegrasssports.org
Membership (Participation)
Requirements:
Must be amateur Kentucky resident.
Description:

Founded 1985. Produces state games in state of Kentucky for amateur athletes. Various competitions for all ages and levels with many events for the handicapped. Based on festival concept. Also holds clinics, symposiums and state-wide tournament.

BRYAN-COLLEGE STATION CONVENTION & VISITORS BUREAU, SPORTS DEPT
715 UNIVERSITY DRIVE EAST
COLLEGE STATION, TX 77840
979-260-9898
800-777-8292
Fax: 979-260-9800
www.visitaggieland.com
- Kindra Fry, Director of Sales-Sports & Conventions
kindra@bcscvb.org
- Pattie Sears, Destination Sales & Servicing Executive
Description:
A Department of the Bryan-College Station Convention & Visitors Bureau, the Sports Department prides itself on attracting quality sports events to the community with state-of-the-art facilities and services.

CALIFORNIA STATE GAMES
3260 ROSECRANS STREET
SAN DIEGO, CA 92110
619-223-2033 EXT 2127
Fax: 619-233-2242
info@calstategames.org
www.calstategames.org
- Sandi Hill, Executive Director
calgames@sosinet.net
- Joe Rubendall, Sport manager
Description:
Mission is to promote and nurture the health, education, and competitive spirit of residents of California by managing a quality amateur sports event that encourages participation and provides an Olympic experience.

CANTON/STARK COUNTY CONVENTION & VISITORS BUREAU
THE MILLENNIUM CENTRE
222 MARKET AVENUE NORTH
CANTON, OH 44702
330-454-1439
800-552-6051
Fax: 330-456-3600
www.visitcanton.com
- John Kiste, Executive Director
johnk@cantonstarkcvb.com
- Tonja Marshall, Sports Program Manager

CENTRAL FLORIDA SPORTS COMMISSION
400 W CHURCH STREET
SUITE 205
ORLANDO, FL 32801
407-648-4900
Fax: 407-649-2072
www.centralfloridasports.org
- Brent Nelson, President/CEO
- John Bisignano, President/CEO
jbisignano@centralfloridasports.org
- Jennifer Lastik, Director of Events
jlastik@centralfloridasports.org
- Dave Zsembik, Seminole County Marketing & EventsManager
dzsembik@centralfloridasports.org
- Miranda Smith, Volusia County Marketing

& EventsManager
msmith@centralfloridasports.org
• Georgiana Brown, Marketing &
Communications Manager
gbrown@centralfloridasports.org
• Kevin Coulthart, Vice President
(407) 648-0465
Description:
Created to attract international, national and
regional events and sports-related business
and activities to Central Florida.

COMMONWEALTH GAMES FEDERATION
138 PICADILLY
LONDON, ENGLAND W1J 7NR
info@commonwealthgames.ca
www.thecgf.com
• Michael Hooper, Chief Executive Officer
Publications:
Directory.
Membership Requirements:
Each sport has a member and there are
members-at-large. Officers are elected for a
four-year term.
Description:
Founded 1930. Organizes and finances
Canada's participation in the
Commonwealth Games every four years.

COMMONWEALTH GAMES OF VIRGINIA
711 C FIFTH STREET NE
ROANOKE, VA 24016
540-343-0987
800-333-8274
Fax: 540-343-7407
www.commonwealthgames.org
• Peter R. Lampman, President
pete@commonwealthgames.org
• Diane Williams, Marketing/Fundraising
Director
dwilliams@commonwealthgames.org
• Owen Grogan, Games Director
ogrogan@commonwealthgames.org
Description:
Virginia's Olympics for the citizens of the
Commonwealth. A multi sport festival
including opening ceremonies and 45
sports.

COWBOY STATE GAMES
WYOMING FINANCIAL BUILDING
400 EAST FIRST STREET
SUITE 315
CASPER, WY 85602
307-577-1125
Fax: 307-577-8111
www.cowboystategames.com
• Eileen Ford, Executive Director
Description:
Founded 1986. Provides Olympic style
amateur sports festivals for athletes of all
ages and abilities, enables all citizens the
opportunity to utilize quality sports facilities,
and creates an amateur sports network
throughout Wyoming.
Member Services:
Participants receive CSG Tee-shirts and
participant packets including passes to the
Opening Ceremony, coupons, and
mementos.
Publications:
Registration Handbook for each event.
Membership Requirements:
Summer Games - must be a Wyoming
resident; Winter Sports Festival - open to
residents of any state that does not conduct
Winter Games.

EMPIRE STATE GAMES
1 EMPIRE STATE PLAZA
ALBANY, NY 12238
518-474-8889
Fax: 518-474-7944
esgstaff@global2000.net
www.empirestategames.org
• Frederick Smith, Executive Director
Description:
Founded 1978. Yearly amateur sports
festival consisting of 28 summer sports and
10 winter sports for New York state athletes.
Scholastic, open and masters divisions. Also
conducts senior games and games for the
physically challenged.

ESPN X GAMES
6033 WEST CENTURY BOULEVARD
SUITE 601
LOS ANGELES, CA 90045
310-642-1500
Fax: 310-568-8577
www.expn.com
• Jack Wienert, Executive Director
• Chris Stiepock, Vice President
• Deane Swanson, Senior Director of
Operations
Editors Note:
The Xgames frequently change locations. In
order to completely keep up please contact
ESPN, or go to the website espn.com and
look for Xgames.
Description:
Creation and implementation of annual
sporting events focusing on adventure-type
sports.

FLAGSTAFF CONVENTION AND
VISITORS BUREAU
ONE EAST ROUTE 66
FLAGSTAFF, AZ 86001
928-213-2951
800-379-0065
visitorcenter@flagstaffaz.gov
www.flagstaffarizona.org
• Heldi Hansen, CVB Director
(800) 213-2921
hhansen@flagstaffaz.gov
• Heather Ainardi, Marketing and Public
Relations Manager/Film
(800) 217-2367
hainardi@flagstaffaz.gov
• Carrie Nelson, Administrative Specialist
(928) 213-2919
cnelson@flagstaffaz.gov
• Gail Jackson, Meeting and Events
Specialist
(928) 213-2920
gjackson@flagstaffaz.gov
• Heather Ainardi, Director, Film
Commissioner
(928) 779-7645
• Carrie Nelson, Administrative Specialist
(928) 779-7636
Description:
Founded 1983. Honors snowmobile racing
greats and club volunteers, serves as
museum of historic sleds from both trail and
track.
Publications:
THE FINISH LINE, Newsletter, periodic.
Number of Members:
67 Inductees as of 2005.

GARDEN STATE GAMES
44 FARRINGTON STREET
PO BOX 271
CALDWELL, NJ 7006
973-618-1111
Fax: 973-618-1112
mjg129@aol.com
comp.entryeeze.com/Home.aspx?cid=299
• Michael Garamella, Executive Director
(973) 575-8817

GEORGETOWN COLLEGE SPORTS
COUNCIL
400 E. COLLEGE STREET
GEORGETOWN, KY 40324
502-863-8115
Fax: 502-868-8892
www.georgetowncollegeathletics.com
• Brian Evans, Director of Athletics
(502) 863-8040
• Austin Sparks, Associate AD/Compliance
Director
• Jenny Elder, SID/Senior Women's
Administrator
(502) 863-7972
• Randy McGuire, Head Athletic Trainer
(502) 863-7032
• Mary Brooks, Assistant Athletic Trainer
• Ricker Adkins, Athletic Trainer
• Ray Valentine, Head JV Men's Basketball
Coach
(502) 681-3529
Description:
Goal is to promote sporting events in the
surrounding Kentucky area.

GEORGIA STATE GAMES COMMISSION
PO BOX 2043
KENNESAW, GA 30156-9100
770-528-3580
Fax: 770-528-3590
www.georgiagames.org
• Eric Pfeifer, Executive Director
Description:
Founded 1989. Mission is to promote
grassroots amateur sports and development
of active lifestyles among Georgia residents.
Offers 42 sports during Championships in
Atlanta in mid July and 160 events during
eight District Sports Festivals throughout the
state in May and June. Other activities
include statewide Torch Run, Opening
Ceremonies, World of Sports Expo, Art
Exhibition, Environmental Expo, sports
clinics, spring sports and other events
throughout the year.

GRAND CANYON STATE GAMES
2120 EAST 6TH STREET
SUITE 4
TEMPE, AZ 85281
480-517-9700
Fax: 480-517-9739
• Erik Widmark, Executive Director
wid@gcsg.org
• Alan Young, Executive Director
• Maark R. Keith, Senior Director of
Development
Description:
The Grand Canyon State Games is a
multi-sport Olympic Festival for Arizona
amatur athletes of all ages and abilites. The
Games is organized by the Arizona Sports
Council and is affiliated with 47 other state
games throughout the United States. It is
sanctioned by the U.S. Olympic Committee
through the National Congress of State

Games. The Games seeks to provide Arizonans with an avenue for personal development through sports.

HERMES SPORTS & EVENTS, INC.
1624 ST. CLAIR AVENUE
CLEVELAND, OH 44114
216-623-9933
Fax: 216-363-0698
jneroni@hermescleveland.com
www.hermescleveland.com
• Joe Neroni, Director of Sales & Marketing
jneroni@hermescleveland.com
• Neal Neroni, President/Principal
(216) 623-9933
nneroni@hermescleveland.com
• Nick Swingos, Principal
(216) 623-9933
nswingos@hermescleveland.com
• Katherine Gessner, Director of Race Operations
(216) 623-9933
kgessner@hermescleveland.com
Description:
hermes was founded in 1981 and has built a reputation as Northeast Ohio's premier sport and race management company. Hermes Road Racing manages and operates over 140 local and national races during the year. From course set up and event logistics, to marketing and promotional opportunities, to database management and services, Hermes offers full service management tools. The Cleveland Corporate Challenge is a health and wellness, business networking, team building, and charitable initiative promoting camaraderie, pride and fitness among employees and organizations in Northeast Ohio. And Hermes Sport & Social provides the highest quality sport

HOT SPRINGS CONVENTION & VISTORS BUREAU
134 CONVENTION BLVD
HOT SPRINGS, AR 71901
501-321-2277
800-543-2284
Fax: 501-321-2136
hscvb@hotsprings.org
www.hotsprings.org
• Steve Arrison, CEO
Description:
Tourists and Arkansas residents alike will find lots of fun things to do in Hot Springs Arkansas.

ILLINOIS HEALTH & SPORTS FOUNDATION
RICHLAND EXECUTIVE PLAZA
525 WEST MAIN STREET
SUITE 110
BELLEVILLE, IL 62220
618-233-8665
Fax: 618-233-8690
• Maureen Moore, President
Description:
The Illinois Health and Sports Foundation, through the Prairie State Games, provides Illinois citizens a wholesome avenue for personal development through organized sports competition and physical activity. Additionally, the Foundation seeks to further amateur athletics at the grassroots level through regional competition, training and education in sport.

INTERNATIONAL MASTERS GAMES ASSOCIATION
MAISON DU SPORT INTERNATIONAL
AVENUE DE RHODAINE
1007
LAUSANNE, SWITZERLAN
41-216 018 171
Fax: 42-216 018 173
imga@dif.dk
www.imga.ch
• Borge Kaas-Andersen, Secretary General
• Kai Holm, President
Description:
Constituted 1995. Governing body for the World Masters Games (25 different sports), held every four years.

INTERNATIONAL WORLD GAMES ASSOCIATION/IWGA
10 LAKE CIRCLE
COLORADO SPRINGS, CO 80906
719-471-8096
Fax: 719-471-8105
www.theworldgames.org
• Ron Froehlich, President
• Joachim Gossow, Chief Executive Officer
Description:
Founded 1981. Oversees World Games, which have been set up as a sporting events for non-Olympic sports, and is regarded as complementary to the Olympics. Sports in the World Games include: bowling, casting, cycling, faustball, korfball, netball, roller-skating, softball, tug of war, body building, powerlifting, sombo, racquetball, lifesaving, sport acrobatic, taekwondo, karate, trampoline, tumbling, field archery, fin swimming, water ski, and sport boule.

IOWA GAMES
1421 SOUTH BELL AVENUE
104
AMES, IA 50010
515-292-3251
888-777-8881
Fax: 515-292-3254
info@iowagames.org
www.iowagames.org
• Clarence Hudson, Executive Director
• Kevin Bourke, Chief Creations Officer
kevin@iowagames.org
• Lori Judge, Assistant Director Of Sports & Operations
lori@iowagames.org
Member Services:
Iowa Games Summer Sports Festival is held annually in Ames in Mid-July, also sponsors Winter Sports Festival in Dubuque the first weekend in February.
Membership Requirements:
Entry fees vary by sport. $15 per individual per sport.
Description:
Founded 1987. Provides Iowa citizens with a wholesome avenue for positive personal development through sports and physical activity. Also, Iowa games give Iowans the Olympic experience on a grassroots level.

KEYSTONE STATE GAMES, INC.
31 S. HANCOCK ST
PO BOX 1166
WILKES-BARRE, PA 18702
570-823-3164
888-445-4559
Fax: 570-822-6558

• Owen Costello, President/Chief Executive Officer
• James Costello, Director of Events
• David H. Farrand, Executive Director
keystones@aol.com
Description:
Founded 1981. Serves to develop a state-wide amateur athletic program to promote physical fitness.
Membership Requirements:
Must be a resident of Pennsylvania.
Member Services:
Conducts annual Summer Games in August, annual Winter Sports Festival in February, annual Pennsylvania Senior Games in July.

KISSIMMEE-ST. CLOUD CONVENTION & VISITORS BUREAU
1925 EAST IRLO BRONSON MEMORIAL HIGHWAY
KISSIMMEE, FL 34744
407-742-8200
800-327-9159
www.floridakiss.com www.visitstcloud.com
• Tim Hemphill, Executive Director
Description:
Staff develops and impliments programs and activities that produce solid results through reliable relationships with marketing.

MASSACHUSETTS AMATEUR SPORTS FOUNDATION
55 SIXTH ROAD
WOBURN, MA 1801
781-932-6555
Fax: 781-932-3441
www.baystategames.org
• Arthur Pappas, Chairman
Description:
Founded 1982. Creates and develops events and programs for the development of opportunities through amateur sports in Massachusetts.
Member Services:
Bay State Games, Bay State Winter Games, Lead By Example Scholarship, Bay State Games Sports Medicine Clinic. Assists in the development and management of amateur sports events and fundraising activities for local and national sports associations.

MICHIGAN FITNESS FOUNDATION
1213 CENTER STREET
SUITE D
LANSING, MI 48864
517-347-7891
877-4MI-EPEC
Fax: 517-347-8145
www.michiganfitness.org
• Marilyn Lieber, Preisdent/Chief Executive Officer
mlieber@michiganfitness.org
Description:
Represents the Governor's Council on Physical Fitness, Health and Sports, the Regional Fitness Council promote healthy lifestyles and physical activity at the local level.

MISSISSIPPI, STATE GAMES OF
5201 14TH STREET
PO BOX 5866
MERIDIAN, MS 39307

601-482-0209
800-482-0205
Fax: 601-483-0650
info@stategamesofms.org
www.stategamesofms.org
• Missye Dozier, Sports Director
• Carolyn Smith, Executive Director
Description:
Created in 1992, the State Games of Mississippi offers an opportunity for athletes of all ages and skill levels to compete in a variety of competitions. Games consist of 29 different, olympic-style sports.

NEBRASKA SPORTS COUNCIL
4903 NORTH 57TH
LINCOLN, NE 68507
402-471-2544
800-304-2637
Fax: 402-471-9712
info@cornhuskerstategames.com
www.cornhuskerstategames.com
• Dave Mlnarik, Executive Director
dmlnarik@nebraskasportscouncil.com
• Jeff Maul, Secretary/Treasurer
• Dave Mlnarik, Executive director
• Brian Larrington, President
• Roger Lempke, VP
Description:
Founded 1985. Amateur multi-sport festival for Nebraskans of all ages and skill levels. Involves 57 competitive activities.

NEW MEXICO GAMES
1205 CONSTITUTION NE
PO BOX 30627
ALBUQUERQUE, NM 87110
505-764-1510
Fax: 505-764-1719
• Fred Hultberg, Executive Director

NUTMEG STATE GAMES
975 MIDDLE STREET
UNIT G
MIDDLETOWN, CT 06457
860-788-7041
Fax: 860-894-2654
nutmeg@csmg.org
www.nutmegstategames.org
• Patrick Fisher, Executive Director
Description:
Founded in 1989, the Nutmeg State Games is a multi-sport festival of Olympic-style competition offering 24 different sports for Connecticut's amateur athletes. The Games are endorsed by the Governor's Committee on Physical Fitness & Health, governed by the National Congress of State Games and recognized by the United States Olympic Committee as the Official State Games of Connecticut.

OREGON, STATE GAMES OF
4840 SW WESTERN AVENUE
SUITE 900
BEAVERTON, OR 97005-3430
503-520-1319
Fax: 503-520-9747
• Kerry Duffy, President/Chief Executive Officer
• Dan Duffy, Executive Director
Publications:
Athlete entry handbooks, quarterly newsletters, annual; souvenir programs. Also presents Winter Games of Oregon and Learn to shoot Hoop Clinics.
Membership Requirements:

Must be a 30-day resident of Oregon.
Description:
Founded 1986. Oregon's largest Olympic-style amateur sports festival. For all ages and abilities. 40 different summer sports. Includes Oregon Senior Games for age 50+.

OVERLAND PARK CONVENTION & VISITORS BUREAU
CORPORATE WOODS BUILDING 29
9001 W. 110TH STREET
SUITE 100
OVERLAND PARK, KS 66210
913-491-0123
800-262-7275
Fax: 913-491-0015
info@opcvb.org
• Jerry Cook, President
jcook@opcvb.org
• Judy Shellhorn, Information Services
(913) 491-0123
jshell@visitoverlandpark.com
• Libby Shilpey, Director of Finance
(913) 491-0123
libbysply@visitoverlandpark.com
• Brad Plumb, Sales Manager
(913) 491-0123
bplumb@visitoverlandpark.com
• Justin Stine, Director
(913) 491-0123
jstine@overlandparksportsalliance.com
• Liron BenDor, Vice President of Marketing
(913) 491-0123
lbendor@visitoverlandpark.com
• Kelly Peetoom, Vice President Sales
kpeetoom@opcvb.org
Description:
Serves to promote Overland Park and the surrounding areas as a location for sports events, conventions, meetings etc.

PRAIRIE ROSE STATE GAMES
400 EAST FRONT AVENUE
BISMARCK, ND 58504
701-223-4263
bisparks@bisparks.org
• Robert King, President
• Melanie Carvell, VP
• Arik Spencer, Secretary/Treasurer
Description:
Founded 1987. Promotes physical fitness and an active lifestyle through offering an annual sports festival. The program is designed for maximum participation and involvement.

PRAIRIE STATE GAMES
RICHLAND EXECUTIVE PLAZA
525 WEST MAIN STREET
SUITE 110
BELLEVILLE, IL 62220
618-233-8665
Fax: 618-233-8690
• Maureen Moore, President
maureen@prairiestategames.org
Description:
Founded 1984. Provides Illinois amateur athletes with Olympic-style competition in over 25 sporting events throughout various venues in Southwestern Illinois. Program of the Illinois Health & Sports Foundation. A member of the national congress of state games. Recognized as the official sports festival for the state of Illinois.

QUAD CITIES SPORTS COMMISSION
1601 RIVER DRIVE
SUITE 110
MOLINE, IL 61265
800-747-7800
Fax: 309-764-9443
lhunt@visitquadcities.com
• Joe Taylor, Chair/President/CEO
• Lynn Hunt, Vice President Tourism
(309) 277-0937
lhunt@visitquadcities.com
Sports Service Founded:
1996
Description:
Quad Cities Sports Commission is a not-for-profit (non-profit) organization dedicated to developing the quality of life in the Quad Cities by attracting and hosting sporting events that bring a economic impact to our communities. The QCSC is a full-service sports commission that takes a turn-key approach to attracting and hosting each event it bring to the Quad Cities.
Description:
Promotes Moline and the surrounding Illinois area for sports competitions, games, conventions and meetings. The Quad Cities is a cluster of communities located on the Mississippi River, connecting eastern Iowa and western Illinois. The sports commission promotes tournaments, competitions, meets, meeting & convention.

SHOW ME STATE GAMES
UNIVERSITY OF MISSOURI
1105 CARRIE FRANCKE DRIVE
ROOM 1
COLUMBIA, MO 65211
573-882-2101
Fax: 573-884-4004
smsg@missouri.edu
www.smsg.org
• Ken Ash, Executive Director
(573) 882-2102
• Emily Lorenz, Marketing Coordinator
• Karen Harms, Mr., Administrative Assistant
(573) 882-2101
Description:
The Show-Me State Games is an olympic-style sports festival with more than 40 sports for all ages and ability levels. Now the largest state games in the nation. The SMSG is hosted by the University of Missouri, and is a non-profit program of the Governor's Council of Physical Fitness and Health. The SMSG hosts events year-round to promote health, fitness, family and fun.

SOONER STATE GAMES
211 NORTH ROBINSON
SUITE 250
OKLAHOMA CITY, OK 73102
405-236-5000
Fax: 405-236-5008
www.soonerstategames.org
• Tim L. Brassfield, Executive Director
Member Services:
The games are held the last two weekends in June every year. The Games also hosts Sportsfest, the winter version, which is held the first weekend in February.
Description:
Founded 1983. The Sooner State Games is Oklahoma's amateur sports festival and is the largest multi -sport event in the state. Based on the Olympic format and endorsed

by the USOC, The games are open to every athlete in the state.

SOUTH BEND/MISHAWAKA CONVENTION & VISITORS BUREAU
401 EAST COLFAX AVENUE
SUITE 310
SOUTH BEND, IN 46617
574-400-4009
800-519-0577
Fax: 574-289-0358
www.visitsouthbend.com
• Rob DeCleene, Executive Director
(574) 400-4022
rdecleene@visitsouthbend.com
• Ben Murray, Creative Specialist
(574) 400-4031
bmurray@visitsouthbend.com
• Megan Huff, Sports Sales Manager
(574) 400-4021
mhuff@visitsouthbend.com
• Lindsey Talboom, Communications & Public Relations Coordinator
(574) 400-4025
ltalboom@visitsouthbend.com
• Nicole Lawler, Director of TourismMarketing & Development
(574) 400-4020
nlawler@visitsouthbend.com
• Carolyne Wallace, Director Of Sales
(574) 400-4023
Description:
Promotes South Bend and Mishawaka as a host site for sports events, meetings etc.

SOUTH CAROLINA PARKS, RECREATION & TOURISM
1205 PENDLETON STREET
SUITE 110
COLUMBIA, SC 29201
803-734-1700
866-224-9339
Fax: 803-734-1741
tnance@scprt.com
www.discoversouthcarolina.com
• Amy Duffy, Chief of Staff
• Marion Edmunds, Director of Communications
Description:
Promotes South Carolina as a good location for professional and amateur sporting events. Assists local communities in their sports development initiatives.

STAR OF THE NORTH STATE GAMES
ROCHESTER UNIVERSITY CENTER FIELDHOUSE
ROCHESTER COMMUNITY & TECHNICAL COLLEGE
851-30TH AVENUE SE
ROCHESTER, MN 55904
763-785-5603
800-756-STAR
Fax: 763-785-5699
sgames@mnsports.org
www.starofthenorthgames.org
• Barclay Kruse, Executive Director
bkruse@citilink.com
Membership Requirements:
Must be Minnesota resident to participate, with limited exceptions for some sports.
Description:
Founded 1987. Series of events (winter and summer) providing all Minnesota citizens an opportunity to experience amateur sports in a friendly atmosphere of fun and open

participation that promotes health, fitness, and good sportsmanship.

STATE GAMES OF AMERICA
COLORADO SPRINGS SPORT CORPORATION
1631 MESA AVENUE
SUITE E (COPPER BUILDING)
COLORADO SPRINGS, CO 80906
719-634-7333 EXT 1000
Fax: 719-634-5198
info@thesportscorp.org
www.thesportscorp.org
• Tom Osborne, President/CEO
• Dave Palenchar, Chairman Emeritus
• Carolyn Kruse, Vice Chairman
• Walt Glower, Treasurer
• Stan Kensinger, Secretary
• Mike Moran, Director Of Communications
• Theo Gregory, Assistant to the CEO
(719) 577-7081
theo@thesportscorp.org
Description:
The State Games of America (SGA) is the premier, national multi-sport event for athletes of all ages and abilities held every biennium. Medal winners from 49 State Games nationwide earn the right to compete against other winners and match their skills and competitive desire in a national arena.

SUNFLOWER STATE GAMES
820 S KANSAS AVENUE
TOPEKA, KS 66612
785-235-2295
888-774-7721
Fax: 785-235-1308
www.sunflowergames.com
• Mitch Gross, Executive Director
• Susie Coleman, President
• Rick Bryant, VP
• Doug Vance, Secretary
• Brad Rhoden, Treasurer
Description:
The Sunflower State Games is an Olympic style sports festival for Kansans of all ages and skill levels. The event takes place over three weekends each July in Topeka, Kansas, through sports and physical activity, to recognize their dedication and achievement, and to provide an opportunity to participate in an Olympic-style event.

SUNSHINE STATE GAMES
FLORIDA SPORTS FOUNDATION
2930 KERRY FOREST PARKWAY
SUITE 101
TALLAHASSEE, FL 32309
850-488-8347
Fax: 850-922-0482
www.flasports.com
• Larry Pendleton, President/CEO
lpendleton@flasports.com
• Nick Gandy, Director of Communications
ngandy@flasports.com
• Stephen V. Rodriguez, Vice President
svrodriguez@flasports.com
Participation Requirements:
Must reside in the state of Florida or attend a university or college in Florida or military branch in Florida, and must have resided in Florida for at least 3 months.
Description:
Founded 1980. Serves as direct support non-profit organization of Florida Governor's Council on Physical Fitness & Sports, and actively holds amateur events throughout

Florida to promote physical fitness and sports to Floridians. Events are multi-sport Olympic styled sports festivals for athletes of all ages.

TEXAS AMATEUR ATHLETIC FEDERATION
421 NORTH IH 35
GEORGETOWN, TX 78628
512-863-9400
Fax: 512-869-2393
www.taaf.com
• Michael Anne Lord, Executive Director
Description:
Founded 1925. State governing body for Texas amateur athletic programs conducted by local parks and recreation departments. Organizes and conducts 61 state championships and the Games of Texas (State Games for Texas) every year.

UTAH SUMMER GAMES
351 WEST UNIVERSITY BOULEVARD
CEDAR CITY, UT 84720
435-865-8421
Fax: 435-865-8548
usg@suu.edu
www.utahsummergames.org
• Casey McClellan, Director
mcclellan@suu.edu
• Jeannine Davis, Office Manager
• Bob Tate, Sports Director
• Steve Ahlgreen, Marketing/Operations Coordinator
(435) 865-8423
ahlgreen@suu.edu
Description:
Founded 1986. Games are comprised of 10,000 athletes competing in 50 sports (from Olympic to Action sports) Archery, Baseball, Basketball, Soccer, Track & Field.

UTAH WINTER GAMES
PO BOX 718
PARK CITY, UT 84060
435-513-0207
Fax: 801-406-0108
• Matthew Terwillegar, Director
Description:
Founded 1987. Organizes and promotes Winter Sports Festival and competition to develop physical fitness and lifetime winter sports participation and grass roots developmental sports programs. Competitive events in all winter sports, from ski jumping and telemark to figure and speed skating. Sponsors over 30 free instructional clinics in every winter sport.

WINTER GAMES OF IDAHO
PO BOX 9047
BOISE, ID 83707
208-342-2722
800-442-3794
Fax: 208-343-6725
• Heather Price, Executive Director
Number of Members:
Over 3,500 athletes, sponsors and volunteers.
Publications:
Four color brochure
Member Services:
The Winter Games of Idaho is a non-profit sports festival created for Idaho's amateur athletes and is recognized as the state's official winter sports competition. This 16 year tradition brings fun winter competitions

multi sports

all acros Idaho in January and February each year.

Youth Organizations

ALL-AMERICAN SOAP BOX DERBY
789 DERBY DOWNS DRIVE
PO BOX 7225
AKRON, OH 44306
330-733-8723
Fax: 330-733-1370
soapbox@aasbd.org
www.aasbd.org
• William Ginter, Chairman of the Board
(330) 733-8723
Year Founded:
1934
Description:
A youth racing organization that consists of three divisions: Stock Division, ages 8 through 13. Super Stock Division, ages 10 through 17, and Masters Division, ages 10 through 17.

AMERICAN YOUTH FOOTBALL
1000 SOUTH POINTE DRIVE
TH-A9
MIAMI, FL 33139
800-622-7370
jlaufer@americanyouthfootball.com
www.americanyouthfootball.com

AMERICAN YOUTH SOCCER ORGANIZATION
19750 SOUTH VERMONT AVENUE
SUITE 200
TORRANCE, CA 90502
310-525-1155
800 872-2976
webmaster@ayso.org
www.ayso.org
• Paula Berriz, President
• Dave Oram, Vice President
• Jeff Sterm, Treasurer
• Mark Stewart, National Vice President
• Bill Hummbell, National Secretary
Description:
AYSO has been the leader in establishing groundbreaking youth soccer programs in the United States. The organization is proud to have paved the road for youth soccer and looks forward to meeting the challenges of the 21st centruy.

BOYS & GIRLS CLUBS OF AMERICA
1275 PEACHTREE STREET NE
ATLANTA, GA 30309-3506
404-487-5700
Fax: 404-487-5789
info@bgca.org
www.bgca.org
• Emil J Brouck, Chairman
• Ronald J. Gidwitz, Chairman of the Board
• Emil J. Brolick, Chairman Emeritus
• Robert J. Bach, Chairman Emeritus
• Thomas J. Falk, Vice Chairman
• Gary C. Wendt, Treasurer
• Jean C. Crystal, Secretary
• James Clark, President, CEO
Description:
The mission of the Boys & Girls Clubs of America is to enable all young people especially those who need us most, to reach their fullest potential as productive, caring, responsible citizens.

CALIFORNIA POLICE ACTIVITIES LEAGUE
2000 EAST 14TH STREET
SAN LEANDRO, CA 94577
510-544-4300
800-622-5725
Fax: 510-544-4350
info@calpal.org
www.californiapal.org
• Gregg Wilson, Executive Director
• Barbara Robertson, Director of Finance
Description:
(CAL PAL) provides directly and indirectly through its 110 local pals, educational, recreational and athletic programs to the youth of California with an emphasis on 'disadvantaged or at risk youth. Support comes from individuals, business leaders, corporations and foundations.

CATHOLIC YOUTH ORGANIZATION (CYO)
1011 FIRST AVENUE
FLOOR 17
NEW YORK, NY 10022
212-371-1011 EXT 2972
Fax: 212-319-8265
karl.adler@archny.org
www.ny-archdiocese.org
• Fran Davies, Director of Communications & Marketing
(212) 371-1000
Fran.Davies@archny.org
• Pierette Imbriano, Director of Communications and Marketing
(646) 794-2477
Pierette.Imbriano@archny.org
Description:
CYO promotes the total spiritual and personal development of youth and young adults through various ministry centers, community centers, scouting programs, summer camps, athletic leagues, art and essay contests, leadership training programs and other religous, social and education activities in parishes.

DIXIE BOYS & MAJORS BASEBALL
PO BOX 8263
DOTHAN, AL 36304
334-793-3331
Fax: 334-793-3331
dixieoffice@gmail.com
www.dixie.org/boys
• J Sandy Jones, Commissioner/CEO
jjones29@se.rr.com
Description:
Primarily a youth baseball program for YOUTH (ages 12 & under playing on a 60'-70' diamond) and BOYS (ages 13-14 playing on a 80' diamond) to meet the physical development of growing boys. The main purpose of these programs is to provide a recreational outlet for as many boys as possible, with emphasis being on local league play rather than tournament play.

DIXIE SOFTBALL INC
110 SKELTON DRIVE
BIRMINGHAM, AL 35224
205-785-2255
obeidsi@aol.com
softball.dixie.org
• James Obie E. Evans, President

DIXIE YOUTH BASEBALL
C/O WES SKELTON
PO BOX 877
MARSHALL, TX 75671
903-927-2255
Fax: 903-927-1846
dyb@dixie.org
youth.dixie.org
• Wes Skelton, Commissioner
Description:
Promoting the development of strong character, a right attitude and a sense of responsibility and citizenship among youngsters since 1955. Visit on Facebook and Twitter.

LITTLE LEAGUE BASEBALL
539 US ROUTE 15 HWY
PO BOX 3485
WILLIAMSPORT, PA 17701-0485
570-326-1921
Fax: 570-326-1074
eastregion@littleleague.org
www.littleleague.org
• Don B. Soucy, Eastern Region Director
dsoucy@littleleague.org
• Corey D. Wright, Assistant Eastern Region Director
cwright@littleleague.org
• Patrick Holden, Assistant Eastern Region Director
pholden@littleleague.org
Description:
A non-profit organization whose mission is to promote, develop, supervise, and voluntarily assist in all lawful ways, the interest of those who will participate in Little League Baseball and Softball.
Membership Requirements:
Must be baseball or softball league - players ages 5-18
Publications:
Little League Magazine, Little Leaguer Newsletter, World Series Programs (8 Divisions).
Member Services:
Official Playing and Tournament Rules. Safety Program. Annual meeting each November.
Number of Members:
3.7 million.
Sponsors:
ACE Hardware®, Active Network®, Allstate, Bank of America®, Choice Hotels International™, Dick's Sporting Goods®, Easton, Honda, Kellogg's Frosted Flakes®, Musco Lighting®, New Era™, Pledgeplay®, Powerade®, Russell Athletic®, M&M/Mars® Snickers®, Subway®, Sunkist®

MY SOCCER LEAGUE.COM
6114 LASALLE AVENUE
SUITE 502
OAKLAND, CA 94619
510-836-8733
Fax: 510-654-2253
sales@mysoccerleague.com
www.mysoccerleague.com
Nature of Sports Service:
Organization provides youth leagues - soccer, baseball, football, etc. - with state-of-the-art, web-based league scheduling, game results, standings, referee and field assignments, plus league-wide communications capabilities in an easy-to-use and affordable online service.

NATIONAL ALLIANCE FOR YOUTH SPORTS
2050 VISTA PARKWAY
WEST PALM BEACH, FL 33411
561-684-1141
800-729-2057
Fax: 561-684-2546
nays@nays.org
www.nays.org
• Fred C. Engh, President/CEO
fengh@nays.org
• John Engh, COO
• Yolanda Williams, CFO
• Emmy Martinez, VP Memberhip Programs
The National Alliance for Youth Sports'
Youth Deve
Hook a Kid on Golf, SMART START, Kids
on Target.
Parents Association for Youth Sports:
Features innovative materials and
information for youth leagues to utilize to
help make parents aware of their roles and
responsibilities in youth sports. The program
includes the Youth Sport Parent video which
is ideal for preseason parent meetings and
outlines the importance of positive
parent-volunteer coach relationships to a
child's well-being.
National Clearinghouse for Youth Sports
Informati
Provides the public with access to a wide
variety of resource information and materials
pertaining to youth sports. Materials include
academic research, publications,
instructional videos and other general
information relative to youth sports.
National Youth Sports Officials
Association:
Trains youth sports officials through a
certification program that covers basic skills,
fundamentals and common problem areas.
The program, which enhances the abilities
of both beginning and veteran officials, also
covers the eight characteristics every good
official must possess. NYSOA officials also
receive a variety of member benefits.
National Institute for Youth Sports
Administration
Provides training, education and resource
materials to assist administrators of youth
sports programming in public, private and
military organizations. Its Child Abuse and
Youth Sports: A Comprehensive Risk
Management Program features important
information on the screening, training and
evaluation of volunteers; policies and
procedures on responding to abuse; how to
safeguard organizations and participants,
parental education and more. The NIYSA
also provides administrators with the
opportunity to become a Certified Youth
Sports Administrator through the Academy
for Youth Sports Administrators program
which is held at various sites nationwide
National Youth Sports Coaches
Association:
More than 2 million volunteer coaches have
been trained on how to work with children in
all aspects of sports through NYSCA's
certification clinics. The clinics provide
information on the psychology of coaching
children, maximizing athletic performance,
first aid, safety, organizing fun and
interesting practices, tips on teaching proper
sports techniques, as well as many other
important areas. NYSCA coaches receive a
variety of benefits. There are 3,300 NYSCA
chapters that exist nationwide.

Other locations:

HOOK A KID ON GOLF
2050 VISTA PARKWAY
WEST PALM BEACH, FL 33411
561-684-1141
800-729-2057
Fax: 561-684-2546
www.nays.org/hook_a_kid_on_golf
• John Engh, President
• Fred Engh, CEO, President
Number of members:
20,000+ have participated.
Membership Requirements:
Youngsters ages 8-14.
Description:
Founded 1990. Provides neighborhood
youngsters the opportunity to be introduced to
golf and to continue playing. Includes
introductory clinics for first time golfers.
Follow-up programs include skills challenge
competitions and challenge leagues.

NATIONAL CLEARINGHOUSE FOR YOUTH SPORTS INFORMATION
2050 VISTA PARKWAY
WEST PALM BEACH, FL 33411
561-684-1141
800-729-2057
Fax: 561-684-2546
nays@nays.org
www.nays.org
• Fred Engh, Founder/CEO
fengh@nays.org
• John Engh, COO
• Yolanda Williams, CFO
• Greg Bach, VP Communications
Description:
Founded 1993. Provides the public with access
to a wide variety of resource information and
materials pertaining to youth sports. Materials
include academic research, publications,
instructional videos and other general
information relative to youth sports.

NATIONAL YOUTH SPORTS COACHES ASSOCIATION
2050 VISTA PARKWAY
WEST PALM BEACH, FL 33411
561-684-1141
800-668-5437
Fax: 561-684-2546
nays@nays.org
www.nays.org
• Fred Engh, Founder/CEO
fengh@nays.org
• John Engh, COO
• Yolanda Williams, CFO
• Greg Bach, VP Communications
Member Services:
$500,000 liability insurance for coaches,
membership card, membership patch, education
materials and eligibility for National Youth Sport
Coach of the Year program.
Publications:
Youth Fitness Guide; Head Injuries Fact Sheet,
Eating Disorders Fact Sheet, Coaching
Education Fact Sheet, Individual Risk Factors
Fact Sheet, In-Line Skating Injuries Fact Sheet,
Eye Injuries Fact Sheet, Youth Sports Injuries,
Yearbook of Youth Sports Safety.
Membership Requirements:
Volunteer coaches must successfully complete
the NYSCA three-level training program, sign a
Coaches' Code of Ethics pledge and remit a $15
annual membership fee.
Description:
Founded 1981. Provides parent and coach
education programs for volunteers working with
children in out-of-school youth sports. NYSCA
focuses on the implementation of the Coaches'
Code of Ethics which stresses the importance of
coaches providing for the physical, emotional
and psychological needs of children as their
primary objective.

NATIONAL YOUTH SPORTS OFFICIALS ASSOCIATION
2050 VISTA PARKWAY
WEST PALM BEACH, FL 33411
561-684-1141
800-729-2057
Fax: 561-684-2546
nays@nays.org
www.nays.org
• Fred C. Engh, President/Chief Executive
Officer
fengh@nays.org
• John Engh, COO
• Yolanda Williams, CFO
• Greg Bach, VP Communications
Member Services:
Membership card, benefits, training course.
Insurance; educational materials including
books, videos, audiocassettes; officiating
equipment, apparel and accessories.
Description:
Founded 1995. Provides youth leagues and
programs in training quality sports officials.

YOUTH DEVELOPMENT/A DIVISION OF THE NATIONAL ALLIANCE FOR YOUTH SPORTS
2050 VISTA PARKWAY
WEST PALM BEACH, FL 33411
561-684-1141
800-688-5437
Fax: 561-684-2546
nays@nays.org
www.nays.org
• Fred Engh, Founder/CEO
fengh@nays.org
• John Engh, COO
• Yolanda Williams, CFO
• Greg Bach, VP Communications
Description:
Founded 1993. Develops programs that build
the proficiency and confidence youngsters need
to participate and remain active in sports.
Involves youngsters in programs that teach the
basic motor skills necessary for meaningful
sports participation. Programs include the Start
Smart sports development program and Hook A
Kid on Golf, and the Kids on Target archery
program.

NATIONAL CENTER FOR SPORTS SAFETY
2316 FIRST AVENUE SOUTH
BIRMINGHAM, AL 35203
205-329-7535
866-508-6277
Fax: 205-329-7526
info@SportsSafety.org
www.sportssafety.org
• Matthew Lemak, Chairman
• Kathryn Gwaltney, Executive Director,
Operations
• Beth Kates, Athletic Trainer/Outreach
Coordinator
• Jennifer Byrd, Director, Athletic Training
• Pat Lynch, Coach

NATIONAL COUNCIL OF YOUTH SPORTS
7185 SE SEAGATE LANE
STUART, FL 34997
772-781-1452
Fax: 772-781-7298
youthsports@ncys.org
www.ncys.org
• Sally S. Johnson, Executive Director
• Wanda Rutledge, President
• Jon Butler, Vice President
Publications:
WIN OR LOSE-A guide to Sports Parenting
Member Services:
Member organizations of the National
Council of Youth Sports (NCYS) comprise
the youth sport industry representing more

multi sports

than 52,000,000 boys and girls in organized youth sports programs across the United States. Some of its members are Little League Baseball, Pop Warner Football, American Youth Soccer Organization, Boys & Girls Clubs of America, AAU-Amateur Athletic Union, Parks & Recreation Departments.

NATIONAL HIGH SCHOOL BASEBALL COACHES ASSOCIATION
PO BOX 12843
TEMPE, AZ 85284
602-615-0571
Fax: 480-838-7133
rdavini@cox.net
www.baseballcoaches.org

NATIONAL LITTLE BRITCHES RODEO ASSOCIATION
5050 EDISON AVENUE
SUITE 105
COLORADO SPRINGS, CO 80915
719-389-0333
800-763-3694
Fax: 719-578-1367
info@nlbra.com
www.nlbra.com
• John Freeman, Vice President
• Rob Lay, President
Description:
One of the oldest, continuing junior rodeo associations in the nation. The aims and purposes of the organization are directed towards the interests of the western-minded youth of the nation. It is a non-profit venture to build sound, health minds and bodies-to develop character, self-reliance and good sportsmanship through competition in the great sport of rodeo.

NATIONAL VENTURING DIVISION, BOY SCOUTS OF AMERICA
1325 WEST WALNUT HILL LANE
IRVING, TX 75038
972-580-2000
Fax: 972-580-2502
www.scouting.org
• Dustin M. Readenour, President
• Sarah Mittrucken, Vice President
Description:
Helps advance Venturing as well as promote the idea that the venturing program for YOUNG ADULTS who want a broader experience in leadership, vocations, and hobbies.

NAVY RUN JUMP N' THROW
5248 N VALENTINE AVENUE
FRESNO, CA 93711
559-841-8400
navyrjt@yahoo.com
• Jim Santos, President/Founder
Year Founded:
2000
Nature of Sports Service:
The Navy Run Jump n'Throw program is supported by the United States Navy to enhance physical fitness, health and physical development for students grades 1-12 in the United States. The Navy RJT program is an excellent opportunity for kids in school or recreation programs to enjoy sports activities that are designed to meet their needs in sports.

OHIO SOUTH YOUTH SOCCER ASSOCIATION, INC.
25 WHITNEY DRIVE
SUITE 104
MILFORD, OH 45150
513-576-9555
Fax: 513-576-1666
office@osysa.com
www.osysa.com
• Gordon Henderson, Executive Director
Publications:
Newsletter

POSITIVE COACHING ALLIANCE
1001 N RENGSTORFF AVENUE
SUITE 100
MOUNTAIN VIEW, CA 94303
703-888-3983
866-725-0024
Fax: 650-969-1650
pca@positivecoach.org
www.positivecoach.org
• Jim Thompson, Chief Executive Officer, Founder
(650) 354-0909
jim@positivecoach.org
• Heana Simpson, Deputy Director
(650) 354-0908
heana@positivecoach.org
• David Jacobson, Marketing Communications Manager
(650) 354-0903
david_jacobson@positivecoach.org
• Tina Syer, Associate Director
(415) 202-0905
tina@positivecoach.org
• Silvia Rivas, Partnership Administrator
(408) 846-9619
silvia@positivecoach.org
Nature of Sports Service:
A Stanford University-based non-profit organization, works with coaches, organizational leaders and parents to teach young athletes not only how to win, but also how to learn about teamwork, discipline, respect and goal-setting through their sports experience.

Other locations:

POSITIVE COACHING ALLIANCE (CHICAGO)
4611 N RAVENSWOOD AVENUE
SUITE 207
CHICAGO, IL 60640
866-725-0024
• Jason Sacks, Executive Director
Description:
A non-profit organization, works with coaches, organizational leaders and parents to teach young athletes not only how to win, but also how to learn about teamwork, discipline, respect and a goal-setting through their sports experience.

POSITIVE COACHING ALLIANCE (HAWAII)
C/O UNIVERSITY OF HAWAII
DEPARTMENT OF KINESIOLOGY
1337 LOWER CAMPUS DRIVE
HONOLULU, HI 96822
866-725-0024
www.positivecoach.org
• Stacy Matsuda, Local Coordinator
Description:
Non-profit organization, works with coaches, organizational leaders and parents to teach young athletes not only how to win, but also how to learn about teamwork, discipline, respect and goal-setting through their sports experience.

POSITIVE COACHING ALLIANCE (WASHINGTON, DC)
1001 N RENGSTORFF AVENUE
SUITE 100
MOUNTAIN VIEW, CA 94303
703-888-3983
866-725-0024
Fax: 650-969-1650
www.positivecoach.org
• Clint Sanchez, Senior Partner Development Association
• Scott Chapman, Founder/CEO
• Karen Francis, Chairman & CEO
• Doug Galen, Chief RevenueOfficer

SOCCER ASSOCIATION FOR YOUTH
2812 EAST KEMPER ROAD
CINCINNATI, OH 45241
513-769-3800
800-233-7291
Fax: 513-769-0500
sayusa@saysoccer.org
www.saysoccer.org
• Shiela Shay-Mole, National Executive Director
• Doug Wood, National Marketing/Business Operations Direct
dwood@saysoccer.org
• Neil Bradford, National Director of Coaching
nbradford@saysoccer.org
• Jamie Blanton, National Administrative Coordinator
jblanton@saysoccer.org
• Amanda Weiss, National Media Specialist/Graphic Designer
aweiss@saysoccer.org
• Brain Begly, National Resource Manager
bbegley@saysoccer.org
Description:
Formed to provide an organization within which children could learn and play soccer, the worlds most popular sport.

U.S. YOUTH SOCCER ASSOCIATION
9220 WORLD CUP WAY
FRISCO, TX 75034
972-235-4499
800-476-2237
Fax: 972-334-9960
www.youthsoccer.org
• Jim Cosgrove, Executive Director
• Rob Martella, Director of Operations
• John Sutter, President
jsutter@usyouthsoccer.org
• Evelyn Gill, Vice-President
egill@usyouthsoccer.org
• Alan Blinzler, Secretary
ablinzler@usyouthsoccer.org
• Dennis Brumfield, Treasurer
Description:
US youth soccer is a non-profit and educational organization whose misson is to foster the physical, mental and emotional growth and development of America's youth through the sport of soccer at all levels of age and competition.

UNITED STATES YOUTH VOLLEYBALL LEAGUE
2771 PLAZA DEL AMO
SUITE 808
TORRANCE, CA 90503
310-212-7008
888-988-7985
Fax: 310-212-7182
questions@usyvl.org
www.usyvl.org

3

college sports

3

college sports

college sports

college sports

college sports

college sports

college sports

college sports

College Associations

CANADIAN COLLEGIATE ATHLETIC ASSOCIATION
ST LAWRENCE COLLEGE
2 ST LAWRENCE DRIVE
CORNWALL, ON, CANADA K6H 4Z1
613-937-1508
Fax: 613-937-1530
www.ccaa.ca
• Leigh Goldie, President
(416) 780-539-29
lgoldie@gprc.ab.ca
• Alan Rogan, VP Eligibiity
(780) 853-8711
alan.rogan@lakelandcollege.ca
• Rogan Alan, VP Finance and Administration
(250) 489-8201
alan.rogan@lakelandcollege.ca
• Michelle McConney, Governance
(902) 7057221577
Michelle.McConney@GeorgianCollege.ca
• Sandra Murray-MacDonell, Executive Director
sandra@ccaa.ca
Description:
Founded 1973 to provide leadership, programs and services for student-athletes involved in intercollegiate sport. Conducts 10 national championships annually.
Membership Requirements:
Post-secondary school institution.
Number of Members:
92 collegiate institutions across Canada.

CANADIAN INTERUNIVERSITY SPORT
801 KING EDWARD, STE N205
OTTAWA, ON, CANADA KIN 6N5
613-562-5670
Fax: 613-562-5669
http://cis-sic.ca/splash/index
• Debbie Villeneuve, Director Finance & Administration
 ext 24
Villeneuve@universitysport.ca
• Sheila Ann Newton, Manager Events & Programs
 ext 23
snewton@universitysport.ca
• Tom Huisman, Director Operations & Development
Description:
Founded 1961. Coordinates and administers university sports in Canada. Membership includes 48 universities coast to coast. Conducts 17 national championships in 11 sports and holds the Canadian franchise in the World University Games.
Membership Requirements:
Canadian post-secondary degree-granting institution with concurrent membership in one of six recognized regional associations.
Publications:
Championship Programs, annually; Almanac, annually; Membership Directory; Drug Education Handbook, annually.
Member Services:
Coordinating television schedules, corporate sponsorship, national promotional and publicity programs.

COLLEGE ATHLETIC BUSINESS MANAGEMENT ASSOCIATION/CABMA
24651 DETROIT ROAD
WESTLAKE, OH 44145

440-892-4000
Fax: 440-892-4007
www.nacda.com
• Chris Lacoi, President
(303) 310-206-68
ciacoi@athletics.ucla.edu
• Pat Manak, Senior Associate Executive Director
pmanak@nacda.com
• Bubba Cunningham, Director of Athletics
(919) 962-8200
bubbac@unc.edu
• Andy Platt, 1st Vice President
(310) 7065421306
aplatt@sports.uga.edu
• Omar Banks, 2nd Vice President
(301) 513-556-06
omar.banks@uc.edu
• Michael Boele, 3rd Vice President
(573) 951-827-54
• Katie Newman, Secretary
(417) 440-788-74
knewman@nacda.com
Membership Requirements:
Must be college athletic business manager or assistant or ticket manager or associate director of athletics or assistant systems manager, fund raisers, facility managers, and individuals performing similar duties but under different titles connected with colleges or universities.
Description:
Founded 1949. Promotes, establishes and maintains highest standards of integrity and efficiency in scope, policy and procedures of the management and administration of business in the athletics department of colleges and universities.

COLLEGE SPORTS INFORMATION DIRECTORS OF AMERICA/COSIDA
TEMPLE UNIVERSITY
1700 N BROAD STREET, 4TH FLOOR
PHILADELPHIA, PA 19122-0842
Fax: 740-368-3332
kafcn00@tamuk.edu
www.cosida.com
• Doug Vance, Executive Director
(785) 691-7708
dougvance@cosida.com
• Barb Kowel, Director Of Professional Development
(785) 739-2905
barbkowal@cosida.com
• Will Roleson, Director of Internal Operations / Treasurer
(317) 490-2905
willroleson@cosida.com
Nature of Sports Service:
Founded 1957. Provides for the exchange of ideas among members of sports information profession.
Membership Requirements:
Active in the sports information field in the U.S. or Canada.
Publications:
COSIDA DIGEST, monthly newsletter. DIRECTORY OF SPORTS INFORMATION DIRECTORS, annually.
Member Services:
Job opportunity and placement service. Annual workshops, contests for brochures and programs. Academic All-America teams in football, men's and women's basketball, women's volleyball, baseball, women's softball, and men's and women's at large. COSIDA Scholarship Program.

COLLEGIATE COMMISSIONER'S ASSOCIATION
C/O MID-CONTINENT CONFERENCE
340 BUTTERFIELD 3-D
ELMHURST, IL 60126
630-516-0661
Fax: 630-516-0673
• Val Ackerman, Commissioner
• Rick Gentile, Senior Associate Commissioner (Men's Basketball)
• Katie Willett, Associate Commissioner (Compliance & Governance)
• Tracy Ellis-Ward, Associate Commissioner (Women's Basketball)
• Stu Jackson, Associate Commissioner
Description:
Founded 1939. Encourages and promotes intercollegiate athletics and high standards of sportsmanship as desirable incidents of higher education. Develops and adopts policies beneficial to intercollegiate athletics. Sponsors and develops uniformly high standards for all sports in intercollegiate athletics. Encourages discussion, consideration and promotion of the views and policies of members in relation to intercollegiate and other amateur athletics.
Publications:
Officiating Mechanics Manuals.
Member Services:
Administers National Letter of Intent Program.

COLLEGIATE SPORTS OF AMERICA
22900 VENTURA BLVD, SUITE 100
WOODLAND HILLS, CA 91364
818-844-Prepstar 844-773-7782
Fax: 818-225-1098
info@csaprepstar.com
csaprepstar.com
• Jeff Duva, Founder/President
Year Founded: 1981
Provides services for high school athletes assisting them in locating colleges, receiving financial aid, and getting admitted.
CSA Publication:
PrepSTAR Magazine - college football recruiting publication. www.PrepStar.com

FLORIDA COLLEGE SYSTEM ACTIVITIES ASSOCIATION
113 E. COLLEGE AVENUE
TALLAHASSEE, FL 32301
850-222-2949
Fax: 850-222-2327
www.flccaa.org
• Kelly Warren, Executive Director
(850) 222-2949
KellyWarren@thefcsaa.com
• John Schultz, President
Description:
A statewide non-profit corporation regulating, coordinating, and promoting intercollegiate activities in: Athletics, Brain Bowl, Forensics, Music, Student Government, Student Publications, and Theatre.

INTERCOLLEGIATE OFFICIATING ASSOCIATION
P.O. BOX 16679
CLEVELAND, OH 44116
440-871-8100
Fax: 440-871-4221
ioa@northcoast.org
• Amy Williams, President
• Keri Luchowski, Executive Director

(734) 913-6078
ioa@northcoast.org
• Roger Ingles, Director Of Athletics
(317) 254-0714
• Joe Haklin, Director Of Athletics
(216) 269-3538
Description:
Oversees all aspects of officiating in the sports of men's and women's basketball and football for the North Coast Athletic Conference and other subscribers.
Year Founded:
1992

INTERNATIONAL COLLEGIATE LICENSING ASSOCIATION/ICLA

24651 DETROIT RD
WESTLAKE, OH 44145
440-892-4000
Fax: 440-892-4007
www.nacda.com
• Brett Eden, President
(801) 581-8298
brett.eden@aux.utah.edu
• Robin Cooper, 1st Vice President
(812) 855-8830
cooperrL@iu.edu
• Rachael Bickerton, 2nd Vice President
(208) 426-1358
rachaelbickerton@boisestate.edu
• Tami Breymeyer, 3rd Vice President and Secretary
(785) 532-6269
Tbreymeyer@Kstatesports.com
• Don Tencher, Secretary
(401) 456-8007
dtencher@ric.edu
Description:
The purpose of ICLA is to foster the highest possible professional and ethical standards, while providing collegiate licensing practitioners a broad range of professional advancement opportunities. Further, it is ICLA's mission to improve the overall understanding and effectiveness of institutional trademarks/tradenames and licensing, while upholding the ideals of higher education.
Membership Requirements:
Open to all individuals whose responsibilities include the regular implementation of campus policies regarding trademark and licensing administration. There are five levels of membership — College/University, Affiliate/Conference, Student, Bowl/Conference and Emeritus.
Year Founded:
2002
Publications:
Athletics Administration published bi-monthly.

MID-STATES FOOTBALL ASSOCIATION

UNIVERSITY OF FINDLAY
1000 N. MAIN STREET
FINDLAY, OH 45840
419-434-4551
Fax: 419-423-2895
houdeshell@findlay.edu
www.mid-statesfootball.org
• Dave Laketa, Chairman
(815) 740-3842
• Gary Newsome, Commissioner
(815) 939-5120
gnewsome@olivet.edu
• Larry Alter, Information Director

(419) 427-8407
LAlter@woh.rr.com
Year Founded:
1993
Affiliations:
Collegiate NAIA Conference
Member Schools:
Concordia College, Grand View College, Iowa Wesleyan College, Malone College, Marain College, McKendree College, Olivet Nazarene University, Quincy University, Siena Hts. College, St. Xavier University, St. Ambrose University, Taylor University, Trinity Int. University, University of Saint Francis-Indiana, University of Saint Francis-Illinois, Waldorf College, Walsh University, William Penn University.

NATIONAL ASSOCIATION OF ACADEMIC ADVISORS FOR ATHLETICS/N4A

240 JETER DRIVE
300 CASE ACADEMIC CENTER, NC STATE UNIV.
RALEIGH, NC 27695
919-513-1007
Fax: 919-513-0541
N4A@athletics.tamu.edu
www.nacda.com
• Jim Phillips, PhD, President
(847) 491-8880
j-phillips@northwestern.edu
• Tim Selgo, 1st Vice President
(616) 331-8800
selgot@gvsu.edu
• Chris Plonsky, 2nd Vice President
(512) 471-4787
cp@utexas.edu
• Don Tencher, Secretary
(401) 456-8007
dtencher@ric.edu
Year Founded:
1975
Description:
A diverse educational, service and professional nonprofit organization. N4A members are academic support and student services personnel who are committed to enhancing the opportunities for academic, athletic, and personal success for collegiate student-athletes. These objectives are achieved primarily by providing informed, competent advising and by serving as a liaison between the academic and athletic communities on college campuses across the country.
Publications:
THE ACADEMIC-ATHLETIC JOURNAL, biannually; THE N4A NEWS, three times annually.
Membership Requirements:
Regular; Affiliate; Student; Alumni.

NATIONAL ASSOCIATION OF ATHLETIC DEVELOPMENT DIRECTORS/NAADD

24651 DETROIT RD
WESTLAKE, OH 44145
440-892-4000
Fax: 440-892-4007
www.nacda.com
• Bob Vecchione, Executive Director
(208) 426-3557
• Pat Manak, Sr. Associate Executive Director
• Julie Work, Assistant Executive Director
(440) 788-7468
• Jason Galaska, Assistant Executive Director

(440) 788-7470
jgalaska@nacda.com
• Virtue Ryan, Manager-Affiliate Associations
(440) 788-7473
Year Founded:
1993
Member Services:
Reduced rates for the annual workshop; complimentary subscription to the bi-monthly magazine ATHLETICS ADMINISTRATION.
Membership Requirements:
Individuals employed by the athletics department or the development arm for the department of a college or university that is responsible for the development activities of the department.
Number of members:
520
Description:
A professional organization created by intercollegiate athletic development directors for intercollegiate athletic development directors. This professional organization provides for the exchange of current trends in intercollegiate fund raising and development.

NATIONAL ASSOCIATION OF COLLEGIATE DIRECTORS OF ATHLETICS/NACDA

24561 DETROIT RD
WESTLAKE, OH 44145
440-892-4000
Fax: 440-892-4007
www.nacda.com
• Bob J. Vecchione, Executive Director
(440) 788-7466
• Pat J. Manak, Senior Associate Executive Director
(440) 788-7467
• Julie Work, Assistant Executive Director
(440) 788-7485
• Jason Galaska, Assistant Executive Director
(440) 788-7470
jgalaska@nacda.com
Description:
Establishes educational standards and objectives among individuals responsible for administering college athletic programs.
Year Founded:
1965
Membership Requirements:
Athletics directors of two or four-year colleges in the U.S., Mexico or Canada. Associate Membership open to associate and assistant athletics directors, conference commissioners and their assistants.
Publications:
ATHLETICS ADMINISTRATION, bimonthly magazine.
Member Services:
Reduced fee for the NACDA convention and all meetings; NACDA's bi-monthly publication of ATHLETICS ADMINISTRATION.
Number of Members:
6,100 individuals; 1,600 institutions

NATIONAL ASSOCIATION OF COLLEGIATE MARKETING ADMINISTRATORS/

24651 DETROIT RD
WESTLAKE, OH 44145

440-892-4000
Fax: 440-892-4007
www.nacma.com
• Bob Vecchione, Executive Director
(440) 788-788-74
• Pat Manak, Sr. Associate Executive
Director
(440) 788-7467
• Chris Green, Ass. Executive
Director-Communications
(440) 788-7485
Year Founded:
1990
Description:
Serves to foster the highest possible
professional and ethical standards in
collegiate marketing, while providing
athletics marketing and promotions
practitioners a broad range of professional
advancement opportunities.
Membership Requirements:
Individuals employed by athletics
departments and engaged in administering
sports marketing, public relations or
promotion activities.
Publications:
NACMA IDEAS, quarterly newsletter.
Number of members:
500
Member Services:
Reduced rates to the NACMA convention,
free copies of ATHETICS
ADMINISTRATION magazine, access to the
Member Only section of the website and
access to the membership directory.

**NATIONAL ASSOCIATION OF
INTERCOLLEGIATE ATHLETICS/NAIA**
1200 GRAND BLVD.
KANSAS CITY, MO 64106
816-595-8000
Fax: 816-595-8200
thasseltine@naia.org
www.naia.org
• Jim Carr, Interim President/CEO
(816) 595-8105
jcarr@naia.org
• Dan Wood, Executive Director
(913) 791-0044
dwood@thenccaa.org
• John Leavens, COO
(816) 595-8111
jleavens@naia.org
Year Founded:
1937
Nature of Sports Service:
Organizes and administers all areas of
intercollegiate athletics. Conducts 23
national championships.
Membership Requirements:
Fully accredited four year colleges and
universities that subscribe to NAIA policies
and tenets.
Publications:
NAIA OFFICIAL HANDBOOK. NAIA Daily.
NAIA Coaches/Events Manual. NAIA
Championship Host Manual. National
championship events programs.
Number of Members:
300 colleges and universities.

**NATIONAL CHRISTIAN COLLEGE
ATHLETIC ASSOCIATION/NCCAA**
302 W. WASHINGTON ST
GREENVILLE, SC 29601
864-250-1199
Fax: 864-250-1141

info@thenccaa.org
www.thenccaa.org
• Dan Wood, Executive Director
• Ben Belleman, Director Of Member
Services & Compliance
• Brandon Gilmore, Media &
Communications Coordinator
Year Founded:
1966
Description:
Non-profit intercollegiate athletic association
management serving 100 Christian
colleges/universities through championship
competition, sports outreach and program
governance.
Publications:
The Pursuit
Number of Members:
101

**NATIONAL COLLEGIATE ATHLETIC
ASSOCIATION/NCAA**
700 W WASHINGTON ST
PO BOX 6222
INDIANAPOLIS, IN 46206-6222
317-917-6222
Fax: 317-917-6888
www.ncaa.org
• Joni Comstock, Sr. VP President For
Championships
• Bernard Franklin, Executive VP Of
Education & Community Engagement
• Dan Gavitt, Sr. VP Of Basketball
• Brian Hanline, Sr. VP Anf Chief Medical
Officer
• David Berst, Chief of Staff Division I
• Mike L. Racy, Chief of Staff Division II
• David Price, Enforcement/Reinstatement
VP
• James L. Isch, Senor VP
Administration/CFO
• Judy Sweet, Championships Vice
President
• Ronald J. Stratten, Education Services
Vice President
• Daniel Boggan, Chief Operations Officer
• Thomas W. Jernstedt, Executive Vice
President
• Mark Emmert, President
• Phillip Austin, Chairman/Board of Directors
Div. I
Year Founded:
1906
Description:
Promotes the sound administration of
intercollegiate athletics for men and women
among its more than 1,000 voluntary
member institutions, conferences and
affiliated organizations.
Membership Requirements:
Accredited colleges or universities that
maintain a minimum of four intercollegiate
sports, with one sport in each of the
traditional seasons of the academic year.
Compliance with all NCAA legislation
dealing with financial aid, recruiting, playing
and practice sessions, post-season
competition and other areas of athletic
administration.
Publications:
NCAA NEWS, weekly; rule books; records
books; and general publications.
Member Services:
Statistics forms. Guides and rule books.
Number of Members:
1,250

**NATIONAL JUNIOR COLLEGE ATHLETIC
ASSOCIATION/NJCAA**
1631 MESA AVENUE
SUITE B
COLORADO SPRINGS, CO 80906
719-590-9788
Fax: 719-590-7324
meleicht@njcaa.org
www.njcaa.org
• Mary Ellen Leicht, Executive Director
• Mark Krug, Assistant Executive Director;
Sports Informat
mkrug@njcaa.org
• Brain Beck, Assistant Executive Director;
Compliance
• Sarah Horrmann, Compliance Assistant
shoormann@njcaa.org
• Wanda Bodey, Associate Director of
Compliance
wbodey@njcaa.org
• Lorna Brizzle, Bookkeeper/Membership
Services
lbrizzie@njcaa.org
Description:
Our propose is to promote and foster junior
college athletics on intersectional and
national levels to that results will be
consistent with the total educational
program of its members.
Membership Requirements:
Accredited two-year college and comparable
institutions that have been approved by their
respective NJCAA regions.
Number of Members:
530 institutions; 50 national championship
tournaments hosted, and 9 football bowl
games.
Publications:
JUCO REVIEW
Frequency:
1 time(s) per month
Member Services:
Weekly polls and statistical information.

**NATIONAL SPORTING GOODS
ASSOCIATION**
1601 FEEHANVILLE DR, STE 300
MT. PROSPECT, IL 60056
800-815-5422
Fax: 847-391-9827
info@nsga.org
• Matt Carlson, President/Chief Executive
Officer
(800) 815-5422
• Meghan Beach, Director Of Membership
ext 1280
• Dan Wiersma, CFO
ext 1040
• Marty Maciaszek, Communications
Director
ext 1260
• Dustin Dorbin, Director of Research &
Information
ext 1170
Description:
Our mission is to help its members profit in a
competitive marketplace. It does so by
providing cost-saving services, information
and education. In addition, NSGA serves as
the voice of the retailer/dealer, speaking out
on issues that affect sporting goods
retailers/dealers.
Year Founded:
1929
Publications:
NSGA RETAIL FOCUS magazine;
SPORTING GOODS ALERT newsletter;
NSGA BUYING GUIDE; INTERNATIONAL

college sports

DIRECTORY OF RETAIL SPORTING
GOODS ASSOCIATIONS & BUYING
ORGANIZATIONS

NATIONAL SPORTING GOODS CORPORATION
376 HOLLYWOOD AVE
SUITE 202
FAIRFIELD, NJ 7004
973-779-2323
800-242-7476
Fax: 973-779-0084
skater@chicagoskates.com
www.chicagoskates.com
• Joel Aranson, VP
• Greg Adelsheimer, President
Manufacturer, Distributor:
Bowling - Shoes; Ice Skating - Skate Bags;
In-Line Skating - Accessories, Skates; Roller
Skating - Skates; Skateboards,
Snowboards.
Brands:
Chicago Skates

NEW ENGLAND INTERCOLLEGIATE AMATEUR ATHLETIC ASSOCIATION
C/O JACK MCDONALD, PRESIDENT
QUINNIPIAC UNIVERSITY
275 MOUNT CARMEL AVENUE
HADEN, CT 6518
203-582-8200
NEICAAA@aol.com
• Irwin Cohen, Commissioner
• John L Lahey, President
(203) 582-8700
• Patricia Nicol, 1st Vice President
• Branwen Smith-King, 2nd Vice President
Year Founded:
1886
Description:
This Association is the second oldest
collegiate group in the country; only the
IC4A is older, having been formed in 1876.
Its purpose was the promotion and
protection of intercollegiate competition in
track and field among the colleges which
were members of the Association.
Member Schools:
Amherst, Bates, Bentley, Boston Col.,
Boston U., Bowdoin, Brandeis U., Brown U.,
Bryant, Central Connecticut State U., U. of
Connecticut, Colby, Dartmouth, Holy Cross,
Lowell Tech, U. of Maine, U. of
Maine-Portland/Gorham, Massachusetts
Inst. of Tech., U. of Massachusetts, U. of
New Hampshire, Nichols, Northeastern U.,
Norwich U., Providence Col., U. of Rhode
Island, Southern Connecticut State U.,
Springfield Col., St. Anselm's, Trinity, Tufts,
U. of Vermont, U.S. Coast Guard Academy,
Wesleyan U., Westfield State, Worcester
Poly.
Membership Requirements:
Membership is open to any recognized
college in New England which sponsors
cross country and or track and field and it is
one of the last remaining championships
that offers competition across all three levels
of NCAA membership.

NJCAA 1ST VICE PRESIDENT
SINCLAIR COMMUNITY COLLEGE
444 W. THIRD ST
DAYTON, OH 45402
937-512-2353
800-315-3000
Fax: 937-512-3056

info@sinclair.edu
www.sinclair.edu
• Norma Dycus, Athletic Director
Enrollment:
12000
Mascot:
Tartans.
Description:
National governing body for 2 year collegiate
athletics.

NJCAA REGION I MEN'S
C/O GREG SILOX
PARADISE VALLEY COMMUNITY
COLLEGE
18401 N 32ND STREET
PHOENIX, AZ 85032
602-787-7173
Fax: 602-787-6715
www.njcaa.org
• Paul Dale, President
(602) 787-6610
• Mary Lou Mosley, VP Academic Affairs
(602) 787-6607
marylou.mosley@pvmail.maricopa.edu
• Anthony Asti, Interim VP Administrative
Services
(608) 787-6601
• Shirley Green, Interim VP Student Affairs
(608) 787-6604
shirley.green@pvmail.maricopa.edu
• Paul Golisch, Dean of Information
Technology
(608) 787-7789
paul.golisch@pvmail.maricopa.edu
• Denise Digianfilippo, Dean of Academic
Affairs
(608) 787-6602
denise.digianfilippo@pvmail.maricopa.edu
• Julia Devous, Director of Development &
Community Relations
(608) 787-6684
julia.devous@pvmail.maricopa.edu
Number of Championships:
9
Championship Years:
1982, 1983, 1988, 1989, 1993, 1994, 1998,
2001, 2002
Mascot:
The Fighting Artichokes.
Enrollment:
6450

NJCAA REGION I WOMEN'S
SOUTH MOUNTAIN COMMUNITY
COLLEGE
7050 S 24TH STREET
PHOENIX, AZ 85040
602-243-8236
Fax: 602-243-8116
chris.haines@smcmail.maricopa.edu
• Todd Eastin, Interim Athletic
Director/Baseball Coach
(602) 243-8245
todd.eastin@smcmail.maricopa.edu
• Shai Olsen, President
• Danelle Dykstra-Wade, Athletic Trainer
(602) 243-8232
danelle.dykstra@smcmail.maricopa.edu
• Sophie Rodriguez, Office Coordinator
(602) 243-8236
sophie.rodriguez@smcmail.maricopa.edu
• Christa Pfeninger, Women's Softball Head
Coach
(602) 243-8242
christa.pfeninger@southmountaincc.edu
• Andy Walker, Men's Golf Head Coach

andres.walker@smcmail.maricopa.edu
• Andy Walker, Women's Golf Head Coach
andres.walker@smcmail.maricopa.edu
• Pat Mooney, Volleyball Head Coach
(602) 243-8239
pat.mooney@smcmail.maricopa.edu
• Daven Vo, Men's Basketball Head Coach
• Justin Bogus, Men's & Women's Soccer
Head Coach
(602) 243-8247
justin.bogus@smcmail.maricopa.edu
• Terry Robinson, Women's Basketball
Head Coach
(602) 243-8244
Number of Championships:
1
Championship Years:
1994
Enrollment:
11104
Mascot:
Gauchos

NJCAA REGION II MEN'S
CONNORS STATE COLLEGE
ROUTE 1, BOX 1000
700 COLLEGE RD.
WARNER, OK 74469
918-463-2931
Fax: 918-463-2233
• Cameron Hendreson, Mens Basketball
Assistant Coach
• Eddie Kite
• Jamie Fisher, Womens Basketball
Assistant Coach
• Perry Keith, Baseball Head Coach
• Bobby Foreman, Baseball Assistant Coach
• Bill Muse, Athletic Director/Men's
Basketball Head Coach
(918) 463-6231
• Donnie Nero, President
(918) 463-6214
Number of Championships:
1
Championship Years:
1990
Enrollment:
1616

NJCAA REGION II WOMEN'S
CONNORS STATE COLLEGE
700 COLLEGE ROAD
WARNER, OK 74469
918-463-2931
Fax: 918-463-2233
• Cameron Hendreson, Mens Basketball
Assistant Coach
• Rusty Laverentz, Womens Basketball
Head Coach
• Jamie Fisher, Womens Basketball
Assistant Coach
• Perry Keith, Baseball Head Coach
• Bobby Foreman, Baseball Assistant Coach
• Bill Muse, Athletic Director
(918) 463-6231
wmuse@connorsstate.edu
• Donnie Nero, President
(918) 463-6214
Number of Championships:
1
Championship Years:
1985

NJCAA REGION III MEN'S
JAMESTOWN COMMUNITY COLLEGE
525 FALCONER ST

PO BOX 20
JAMESTOWN, NY 14702-0020
716-338-1000
800-388-8557
www.sunyjcc.edu
• Keith Martin, Athletic Director
• Barry Andreson, Maintenance Mechanic II
• Laura Anderson, Assistant Professor
Spanish
• Curt Anderson, Small Business Advisor
• Mary Augustine, Assistant Director,
Campus Store
• Dawn Babbage, Associate Professor
• Aimee Brunelle, Athletic Trainer
• Gregory DeCinque, President
Number of Championships:
1
Championship Years:
2000
Mascot:
Jayhawks.
Enrollment:
2600
Year Founded:
1950

NJCAA REGION III WOMEN'S
ALFRED STATE COLLEGE
10 UPPER COLLEGE DR
ALFRED, NY 14802
607-587-4361
800-425-3733
Fax: 607-587-4331
www.alfredstate.edu
• John M Anderson, President
• Kelly Higgins, Athletic Director
(607) 587-4361
• Sandy Kinnerney, Department Secretary
(607) 587-4361
kinnersa@alfredstate.edu
• Paul Welker, Sports Information Director
(607) 587-4563
welkerpm@alfredstate.edu
• Gerard Gingras, Athletic Trainer
(607) 587-4388
gingrag@alfredstate.edu
• Alexe Paske, Assistant Athletic Trainer
(607) 587-4568
paskak@alfredstate.edu
Number of Championships:
1
Championship Years:
2003
Mascot:
Pioneers.
Enrollment:
2900

NJCAA REGION IV MEN'S
OAKTON COMMUNITY COLLEGE
1600 E. GOLF RD
DES PLAINES, IL 60016
847-635-1600
Fax: 847-635-1606
mreuter@oakton.edu
www.oakton.edu
• Lisa Bolinder, Athletic Trainer/Women's
Golf Head Coach
(847) 635-1729
lbolinde@oakton.edu
• Peg Lee, President
(847) 635-1801
plee@oakton.edu
Enrollment:
5354
Mascot:
Raiders.

NJCAA REGION IV WOMEN'S
SOUTH SUBURBAN COLLEGE
15800 S STATE STREET
S HOLLAND, IL 60473
708-596-2000 EXT 5718
Fax: 708-210-5733
• Steve Ruzich, Athletic Director
(708) 596-2000
• Don Manhing, President
Enrollment:
8063
Mascot:
Bulldogs.

NJCAA REGION IX MEN'S
SHERIDAN COLLEGE
BOX 1500
SHERIDAN, WY 82801
307-674-4664
800-913-9139
Fax: 307-674-4293
www.sheridan.edu
• Matt Hammer, Athletic Director/Men's
Basketball Coach
• Annette Murray, Public Information
Director
• Kati Sherwood, Chair
• R.Scott Ludwig, Vice-Chair
• Norleen Healy, Secretary
Enrollment:
1867
Mascot:
Generals/Lady Generals.

NJCAA REGION IX WOMEN'S
EASTERN WYOMING COLLEGE
3200 W. C ST
TORRINGTON, WY 82240
307-532-8248
Fax: 307-532-8215
• Tom Anderson, Director Of Athletics
(307) 532-8321
• Jordan Rice, Athletic Trainer
(307) 532-8249
Enrollment:
985
Mascot:
Lancers.
Year Founded:
1948

NJCAA REGION V MEN'S
SOUTH PLAINS COLLEGE
1401 S. COLLEGE AVE
LEVELLAND, TX 79336
806-894-9611 EXT 220
Fax: 806-897-0139
www.spc.cc.tx.us
• Joe Tubb, Athletic Director
• Mike Box, Chairman
• Bobby Neal, Vice-Chairman
Number of Championships:
6
Championship Years:
1986, 1991, 1993, 1995, 1996, 1997
Enrollment:
4230
Mascot:
Texans.

NJCAA REGION V WOMEN'S
MCLENNAN COMMUNITY COLLEGE
1400 COLLEGE DR
WACO, TX 76708
254-299-8811
Fax: 254-299-8814

strochim@mclennan.edu
www.mclennan.edu
• Johnette McKown, President
• Shawn Trochim, Athletic Director
• Teresa Lopez, Athletic Secretary
• Candice Kelm, Sports Information
Specialist
(254) 299-8833
Number of Championships:
3
Championship Years:
1997, 1998, 2002
Enrollment:
9,500
Mascot:
Highlanders.
Year Founded:
1965

NJCAA REGION VI MEN'S
GARDEN CITY COMMUNITY COLLEGE
801 CAMPUS DR
GARDEN CITY, KS 67846
620-276-7611
800-658-1696
Fax: 620-276-9646
www.gccks.edu
• Vi Trilli, Athletic Director
• Ryan Ruda, Athletic Director
• Dan Delgado, SID/Promotions
(620) 276-9620
• Jacob Ripple, Assistant Athletic Director
for Student Succe
(620) 276-9610
• Dennis Harp, Director Of Athletic
Advancement
(620) 276-9595
• Bob Larson, Coordinator of Athletic
Activities
(620) 276-0352
Number of Championships:
3
Championship Years:
1992, 1994, 1995
Enrollment:
1364
Mastcot:
Broncbusters.

NJCAA REGION VI WOMEN'S
HIGHLAND COMMUNITY COLLEGE -
KANAS
606 W MAIN
HIGHLAND, KS 66035
785-442-6000
Fax: 785-442-6104
Gdelzeit@highlandcc.edu
www.highlandcc.edu
• Greg Delzeit, Athletic Director
• Arnold Aaron, Assistant Football Coach
(784) 442-6014
• Kyle Montgomery, Head Athletic Trainer
(785) 442-6049
• David Reist, President
(785) 442-6010
• Eberly Rick, Baseball Head Coach
(785) 442-6043
Enrollment:
659
Mascot:
Scotties.

NJCAA REGION VII MEN'S
VOLUNTEER STATE COMMUNITY
COLLEGE
1480 NASHVILLE PK
GALLATIN, TN 37066

615-452-8600
Fax: 615-355-8722
Bobby.Hudson@volstate.edu
www.volstate.edu
• Tyler Nordman, Athletic Director
tnordman@highlandcc.edu
• Melissa Humphres, Athletic Trainer
melissa.humphres@volstate.edu
• Warren Nichols, President
Enrollment:
4,568
Mascot:
Pioneers.

NJCAA REGION VII WOMEN'S
CHATTANOOGA STATE TECHNICAL
COMMUNITY COLLEGE
4501 AMNICOLA HWY
CHATTANOOGA, TN 37406
423-697-4400
866-547-3733
Fax: 423-697-2405
www.chattanoogastate.edu
• Steve Jaecks, Athletic Director
• James Catanzaro, President
Enrollment:
4909
Mascot:
Tiger.

NJCAA REGION VIII WOMEN'S
OKALOOSA-WALTON COLLEGE
100 COLLEGE BLVD
NICEVILLE, FL 32578
850-729-5379
Fax: 850-729-5200
• Mickey Englett, Athletic Director
• Mike Holmes, Athletic Trainer
• James Richburg, President
Enrollment:
3739
Mascot:
Raiders.

NJCAA REGION X MEN'S
SPARTANBURG METHODIST COLLEGE
1000 POWELL MILL RD
SPARTANBURG, SC 29301
864-587-4000
800-772-7286
Fax: 864-587-4355
perduem@smcsc.edu
www.smcsc.edu
• Mark Perdue, Athletic Director
(864) 587-4237
perduem@smcsc.edu
• John Gramling, Chairman
• Bill Painter, Vice-Chairman
Number of Championships:
1
Championship Years:
1994
Enrollment:
740
Mascot:
Pioneers.

NJCAA REGION X WOMEN'S
LOUISBURG COLLEGE
501 N. MAIN ST
LOUISBURG, NC 27549
919-497-3249
Fax: 919-496-7330
mholloman@louisburg.edu
www.louisburg.edu
• Mike Holloman, Athletic Director
(919) 497-3249

mholloman@louisburg.edu
• Mandy Kiger, Athletic Trainer
(919) 497-3435
• Alyssa Rabert, Assistant Athletic Trainer
(919) 497-3435
arabert@louisburg.edu
Number of Championships:
2
Championship Years:
1981, 1992
Enrollment:
764
Mascot:
Hurricanes.

NJCAA REGION XI MEN'S
IOWA CENTRAL COMMUNITY COLLEGE
330 AVENUE M
FORT DODGE, IA 50501
515-576-7201
Fax: 515-576-7724
www.iowacentral.com
• Rick Sandquist, Athletic Director
(515) 574-1354
sandquist@iowacentral.edu
• Andrew Newell, Athletic Trainer
(515) 574-1349
• Dan Kinney, President
(515) 574-1150
kinney@iowacentral.edu
Number of Championships:
3
Championship Years:
1978, 1981, 2002
Enrollment:
3392
Mascot:
Tritons.

NJCAA REGION XI WOMEN'S
SOUTHWESTERN COMMUNITY
COLLEGE
1501 W. TOWNLINE ST
CRESTON, IA 50801
641-782-7081 EXT 459
Fax: 641-782-3312
• Bill Krejci, Athletic Director
(641) 782-7081
krejci@swcciowa.edu
• Bill Kejci, Athletic Director
• Barbara Crittenden, President
(641) 782-7081
crittenden@swcciowa.edu
Enrollment:
891
Mascot:
Spartans.

NJCAA REGION XII MEN'S
LAKELAND COMMUNITY COLLEGE
7700 CLOCKTOWER DR
KIRTLAND, OH 44094
440-525-7000
800-589-8520
Fax: 440-525-7636
sbarlow@lakelandcc.edu
www.lakelandcc.edu
• Scott Barlow, Athletic Director
sbarlow@lakelandcc.edu
• Julie Phillips, Athletic Trainer
• Morris Beverage, President
(440) 525-7177
mbeverage@lakelandcc.edu
Number of Championships:
2
Championship Years:
1978, 1980

Enrollment:
4874
Mascot:
Lakers.

NJCAA REGION XIII MEN'S
NORTHLAND COMMUNITY & TECHNICAL
COLLEGE
1101 HIGHWAY 1 EAST
THIEF RIVER FALLS, MN 56701
218-683-8800
800-959-6282
Fax: 218-681-6604
www.northlandcollege.edu
• Paul Peterson, Athletic Coordinator
(218) 683-8556
• Anita Lizakowski, Athletic Trainer
• Anne Temte, President
Enrollment:
2600
Mascot:
Pioneers.

NJCAA REGION XIII WOMEN'S
ROCHESTER COMMUNITY & TECHNICAL
COLLEGE
851 30TH AVENUE SE
ROCHESTER, MN 55904
507-285-7210
800-247-1296
Fax: 507-280-5577
www.rctc.edu/athletics
• Jean Musgjerd, Women's Athletic Director
• Jim Williams, Athletic Trainer
• Don Supalla, President
Enrollment:
4250
Mascot:
Yellowjackets.

NJCAA REGION XIV MEN'S
BLINN COLLEGE
902 COLLEGE AVE
BRENHAM, TX 77833
979-830-4170
Fax: 979-830-4032
greg.hinze@blinn.edu
www.blinn.edu
• Greg Hinze, Athletic Director
• Rob Redding, Athletic Trainer
• Becky Krebs, President
(979) 830-4112
bkrebs@blinn.edu
• Dan Holt, President
(979) 830-4112
Number of Championships:
22
Championship Years:
1987-1996
Enrollment:
2470
Mascot:
Buccaneers.

NJCAA REGION XIV WOMEN'S
ALVIN COMMUNITY COLLEGE
3110 MUSTANG RD
ALVIN, TX 77511-4898
281-756-3500
Fax: 281-756-3878
jhightower@alvincollege.edu
www.alvincollege.edu
• Jennifer Hightower, Athletic Director
• Rooney Allbright, President
(281) 756-3598
Number of Championships:
1

Championship Years:
1974
Enrollment:
1358
Mascot:
Dolphins.

NJCAA REGION XIX MEN'S
MIDDLESEX COUNTY COLLEGE
2600 WOODBRIDGE AVE
EDISON, NJ 08818-3050
732-548-6000
Fax: 732-906-4179
www.middlesexcc.edu
• Robert Wisniewski, Athletic Director
• Robert Edmonds, Athletic Trainer
• Joann La Perla-Morales, President
(732) 906-2517
jlaperla@middlesexcc.edu
Enrollment:
9554
Mascot:
Colts.

NJCAA REGION XIX WOMEN'S
OCEAN COUNTY COLLEGE
1 COLLEGE DR
TOMS RIVER, NJ 08754-2001
732-255-0400
Fax: 732-255-0408
icohen@ocean.edu
www.ocean.edu
• Ilene Cohen, Athletic Director
• Michael Klecan, Athletic Trainer
• Jon Larson, President
Number of Championships:
2
Championship Years:
1985, 1989
Enrollment:
5700
Mascot:
Vikings.

NJCAA REGION XV MEN'S
NASSAU COMMUNITY COLLEGE
1 EDUCATION DR
GARDEN CITY, NY 11530-6793
516-572-7501
Fax: 516-228-3531
pellicm@sunynassau.edu
www.ncc.edu
• Michael Pelliccia, Athletics Physical
Education Director
(516) 572-7537
michael.pelliccia@ncc.edu
• Tim Prohinsie, Athletic Trainer
• Kenneth P Saunders, President
(516) 572-7205
Kenneth.Saunders@ncc.edu
Number of Championships:
33
Championship Years:
1966, 1970-1976, 1978, 1980, 1982-1986,
1990, 1991, 1994, 1995, 1997-2004
Enrollment:
14000
Mascot:
Lions.

NJCAA REGION XV WOMEN'S
ORANGE COUNTY COMMUNITY
COLLEGE
115 SOUTH ST
MIDDLETOWN, NY 10940

845-344-6222
Fax: 845-341-4216
wsmith@sunyorange.edu
www.orange.cc.ny.us
• Wayne Smith, Athletic Director
• William Richards, President
• Carol Murray, Executive Assistant to the
President
Enrollment:
2100
Mascot:
Colts.

NJCAA REGION XVI MEN'S
1000 VIKING DRIVE
HILLSBORO, MO 63050
636-789-3000 EXT 386
Fax: 636-789-2419
dmaples@jeffco.edu
www.jeffco.edu
• Jo Ellen Stringer, Athletic Director
• Bill McKenna, President
Enrollment:
2839
Mascot:
Vikings.
Year Founded:
1991

NJCAA REGION XVI WOMEN'S
ST. LOUIS COMMUNITY COLLEGE -
FLORISSANT VALLEY
3400 PERSHALL RD
ST. LOUIS, MO 63135-1408
314-513-4200
Fax: 314-513-4732
jkinney@stlcc.edu
www.stlcc.edu
• Johnna Kinney, Athletic Director
• Craig H. Larson, Chair
• Doris Graham, Vice Chair
Number of Championships:
3
Championship Years:
1976, 1988, 1990
Enrollment:
6242
Mascot:
Norsemen/Norsewomen.

NJCAA REGION XVII MEN'S
ANDREW COLLEGE
501 COLLEGE ST
CUTHBERT, GA 39840-5550
912-732-5953
Fax: 229-732-2176
www.andrewcollege.edu
• Mike Riffe, Athletic Director
• Andy Brubaker, Director of Development
(229) 732-5935
andybrubaker@andrewcollege.edu
• Jonathan Lodge, Development
Communications and Alumni Coordin
(229) 732-5941
• Hilliari Flippo, Development & Public
Relations Assistant
(229) 732-5990
hilliariflippo@andrewcollege.edu
• Beth Saunders, Director of Athletic
Training
(229) 209-5380
• David Seyle, President
Enrollment:
400
Mascot:
Fighting Tigers.

NJCAA REGION XVII WOMEN'S
GEORGIA PERIMETER COLLEGE
3251 PANTHERSVILLE RD
DECATUR, GA 30034-3832
678-891-2300
Fax: 770-604-3798
• Alfred Barney, Athletic Director
(678) 891-2360
• Anthony Tricoli, President
(678) 891-2700
Number of Championships:
1
Championship Years:
2000
Enrollment:
18986
Mascot:
Jaguars.

NJCAA REGION XVIII MEN'S
UTAH VALLEY STATE COLLEGE
800 W. UNIVERSITY PKWY
OREM, UT 84058
801-222-8998
Fax: 801-222-8813
www.uvu.edu
• Nathan B Mathis, Athletic Director
nate.mathis@uvu.edu
• Clint T Burgi, Athletic Director-Sports
Information
clint.burgi@uvu.edu
• Matthew Holland, President

NJCAA REGION XVIII WOMEN'S
SALT LAKE COMMUNITY COLLEGE
4600 S. REDWOOD RD
SALT LAKE CITY, UT 84123
801-957-7522
Fax: 801-957-4957
www.slcc.edu
• Norma Carr, Athletic Director
• Steven Earl, Athletic Trainer
• Cynthia Bioteau, President
Enrollment:
12000
Mascot:
Bears.

NJCAA REGION XX MEN'S
PRINCE GEORGE'S COMMUNITY
COLLEGE
301 LARGO RD
UPPER MARLBORO, MD 20774-2199
301-322-0066
Fax: 301-350-7868
jtodaro@pgcc.edu
www.pgcc.edu
• Jo Ann Todaro, Athletic Director
• Charlene M Dukes, President
(301) 336-6000
Enrollment:
6914
Mascot:
Owls.

NJCAA REGION XX WOMEN'S
GARRETT COLLEGE
687 MOSSER RD
MCHENRY, MD 21541
301-387-3000
Fax: 301-387-3055
www.garrettcollege.edu
• Ann Welham, Athletic Director
• Eric Hallenbeck, Head Baseball Coach
(301) 387-3331
eric.hallenbeck@garrettcollege.edu

college sports

• Angela Sincell, Head Cross Country
Coach
(301) 387-3717
angela.sincell@garrettcollege.edu
• Dennis Gibson, Athletic Director
(301) 387-3051
dennis.gibson@garrettcollege.edu
Enrollment:
562
Mascot:
Lakers.

NJCAA REGION XXI MEN'S
C/O DOUGLAS YARNALL
MITCHELL COLLEGE 437 PEQUOT AVE
437 PEQUOT AVE
NEW LONDON, CT 6320
860-701-5047
Fax: 860-701-5085
• Mo White, Athletic Director
(860) 701-5049
white_m@mitchell.edu
• Jim muren, Chairman
• Lucy Leske, Vice-Chairman
• Paul Nunes, Secretary
• Scott Gibson, Treasurer
• Nick Van Vught, Athletic Trainer
(860) 629-6144
athletictrainer@mitchell.edu
• Mary Ellen Jukoski, EdD, President

NJCAA REGION XXI WOMEN'S
DEAN COLLEGE
99 MAIN ST
FRANKLIN, MA 2038
508-541-1814
Fax: 508-541-1817
www.dean.edu
• John Jackson, Athletic Director
• Sandra Cain, Executive Assistant to the
President
• Cindy Kozil, Vice President
• J. Darrell Kulesza, Vice-President
• John F. Marcus, Vice President
• Peter Martel, Vice President
• Brian Stefanik, Athletic Trainer
• Paula Rooney, President
Enrollment:
925
Mascot:
Bulldogs.

NJCAA REGION XXII WOMEN'S
JEFFERSON DAVIS COMMUNITY
COLLEGE
220 ALCO DR
BREWTON, AL 36426
251-867-4832
Fax: 334-867-7399
www.jdcc.edu
• Daniel Head, Athletic Director
• Susan McBride, President
Enrollment:
844
Mascot:
Warhawks.

NJCAA REGION XXIII MEN'S
MISSISSIPPI GULF COAST COMMUNITY
COLLEGE
PO BOX 548
PERKINSTON, MS 39573
601-928-5211
Fax: 601-928-6299
chris.calcote@mgccc.edu
www.mgccc.edu

• Robin Jeffries, Athletic Director
robin.jeffries@mgccc.edu
• Don Hammack, Sports Information
Director
Number of Championships:
2
Championship Years:
1971, 1984
Enrollment:
9510
Mascot:
Bulldogs.

NJCAA REGION XXIII WOMEN'S
JONES COUNTY JUNIOR COLLEGE
900 S. COURT ST
ELLISVILLE, MS 39437
601-477-4000
Fax: 601-477-4250
www.jcjc.edu
• Katie Herrington, Athletic Director
• David Garner, Chairman
• William Boone, Vice-President
• Danielle M. Ready, Secretary
Enrollment:
5002
Mascot:
Bobcats.

NJCAA REGION XXIV MEN'S
SOUTHWESTERN ILLINOIS COLLEGE
2500 CARLYLE RD
BELLEVILLE, IL 62221
618-235-2700
Fax: 618-235-1578
jay.harrington@swic.edu
www.swic.edu
• Mike Juenger, Athletic Director
• Kathy Bernal, Asst. Athletic Director
• Neil Fiala, Athletic Program Coordinator
• Vicki Channer, Administrative Assistant
Enrollment:
6860
Mascot:
Blue Storm.

NJCAA REGION XXIV WOMEN'S
JOHN A. LOGAN COLLEGE
700 LOGAN COLLEGE RD
CARTERVILLE, IL 62918
618-985-3741
Fax: 618-985-6610
• Jerry Halstead, Athletic Director
(618) 985-3741
jerryhalstead@jalc.edu
• Robert Mees, President
Enrollment:
5301
Mascot:
Volunteers.

SPORTING GOODS AGENTS
ASSOCIATION (SGAA)
PO BOX 998
GROVE, IL 60053
847-296-3670
Fax: 847-827-0196
sgaa998@aol.com
• Lois Hamilton, Chief Operating Officer
• Skip Nipper, President
• Tracy Paoletti, Vice President
• James Riebandt, Legal Counsel
Manufacturers:
Associations
Year Founded:
1934

Membership Requirements:
An applicant must be the principal of his or
her agency for at least one year and act as
an independent agent or independent
contractor, representing one or more lines in
the sporting goods business.
Number of Members:
500

U.S. COLLEGIATE SPORTS COUNCIL
C/O NICHOLAS RODIS, EXECUTIVE
DIRECTOR
BRANDEIS UNIVERSITY
415 SOUTH ST
WALTHAM, MA 2454-9110
781-736-3657
Fax: 781-736-3656
• Fred Lawrence, President
(781) 736-3001
• Michael Doonan, PhD, Executive Director
Description:
Founded 1967. Selects teams for the World
University Games.
Membership Requirements:
National collegiate sports bodies. National
Collegiate Coaches Associations. National
governing bodies for those sports included
on World University Games calendar.

UNITED STATES COLLEGIATE ATHLETIC
ASSOCIATION/USCAA
739 THIMBLE SHOALS BLVD
SUITE 1011 E
NEWPORT NEWS, VA 23606
757-706-3756
Fax: 757-706-3758
info@theuscaa.com
www.theuscaa.com
• Bill Casto, Executive Director
billcasto@cox.net
• Matthew Simms, COO
(757) 534-9229
matthew.simms@theuscaa.com
Description:
Provides a national organization to hold
national championships, name
all-americans, scholar-athletes and promote
USCAA member schools. The USCAA was
incorporated to provide an opportunity for
smaller college members to compete on an
equal level of competition with schools of
like size and athletic programs.
Year Founded:
2001

College Athletic Conferences

AMERICA EAST CONFERENCE
215 FIRST STREET
SUITE 140
CAMBRIDGE, MA 02110-1605
617-695-6369
Fax: 617-695-6380
americaeast@americaeast.com
www.americaeast.com
• Patrick Nero, Commissioner
(617) 695-6369
nero@americaeast.com
• Frank Sullivan, Assoc Commissioner
Men's Basketball
(617) 695-6369
sullivan@americaeast.com
• Chad Dwyer, Director of
Championships/Sports Administrator

(617) 695-6369
dwyer@americaeast.com
Members:
University at Albany, Binghamton University, Boston University, University of Hartford, University of Maine, University of New Hampshire, Baltimore County (UMBC), Stony Brook University, University of Vermont.
Year Founded:
1979
Description:
America East has evolved into one of the most comprehensive NCAA Division I conferences with a commitment to broad-based, competitive athletics programs, complementing the academic integrity and missions of the member institutions.

AMERICAN SOUTHWEST CONFERENCE
1221 W CAMPBELL RD
SUITE 171
RICHARDSON, TX 75080
972-234-0033
Fax: 972-234-4110
info@americansouthwestconf.org
www.americansouthwestconf.org
• R Morgan, President
• Tom Cedel, Vice President
Year Founded:
1996
Description:
A group of institutions with similar educational and athletic philosophies. The ASC was founded to provide a structure for intercollegiate athletics among the member institutions.
Member Schools:
Austin College, Concordia University at Austin, East Texas Baptist University, Hardin-Simmons University, Howard Payne University, LeTourneau university, Louisiana College, Mississippi College, McMurry University, Sul Ross State University, Schreiner University, Texas Lutheran University, University of the Ozarks, University of Texas at Tyler

APPALACHIAN ATHLETIC CONFERENCE
PO BOX 19371
ASHEVILLE, NC 28815
828-669-8011
sid@aacsports.com
www.aacsports.com
• John Sullivan, Commissioner
(828) 298-8822
commissioner@aacsports.com
• Bill Popp, Vice President
(770) 720-5568
WCP@reinhardt.edu
• Jay Stancil, Sports Information Director
(606) 546-1292
sid@aacsports.com
• Barb Robinson, Assistant to the Commissioner
(828) 230-3150
robinson.barb13@gmail.com
• Larry Inkster, Faculty Athletic Representative
linkster@unionky.edu
• Bill Greer, NAIA COP Representative
bgreer@milligan.edu
Member Schools:
Bluefield College, Bryan College, Milligan College, Montreat College, Point University, St. Andrews University, SCAD Atlanta,

Reinhardt University, Tennessee Wesleyan College, and Union College.
Description:
The mission of the Conference is to promote the education and development of students and to provide athletic competition among its member institutions for the purpose of designating champions in sponsored sports, to increase visibility of its members to their publics, and to promote the highest ethical standards of character, conduct, sportsmanship, and fair play.

ATLANTIC 10 CONFERENCE
11827 CANON BLVD.
SUITE 200
NEWPORT NEWS, VA 23606
757-706-3042
Fax: 757-706-3042
http://www.atlantic10.com/
• Bernadette V McGlade, Commissioner
BMcGlade@atlantic10.org
• Jay DeFruscio, Associate Commissioner
JDeFruscio@atlantic10.org
• Mitchell Kendall, Associate Commissioner/Finance
• Jill Redmond, Assistant Commissioner/Compliance & Governance
• Caitlin Bonner, Director of Advanced Media
CBonner@atlantic10.org
• Lucas Feller, Assistant Commissioner/Administration & Operations
lFeller@atlantic10.org
Year Founded:
1976
Publications:
Media press guides, post season tournament guides, annually. Weekly press releases throughout academic year. Men's Basketball Fan Guide.
Description:
The idea of what is now the Atlantic 10 Conference was conceived. What started as an eight-school, men's basketball-only affiliation has grown into a 14-university, 21-sport league that is universally hailed as one of the best conferences in the country.
Member Schools:
University of Delaware, University of North Carolina at Charlotte, University of Dayton, Hofstra University, Duquesne University, James Madison University, Fordham University, University of Maine, University of Massachusetts, George Washington University, University of New Hampshire, LaSalle University, Northeastern University, University of Rhode Island, University of Richmond, Towson University, St. Bonaventure University, Villanova University, Saint Joseph's University, Saint Louis University, College of William & Mary, Temple University, Xavier University.

ATLANTIC COAST CONFERENCE
4512 WEYBRIDGE LANE
GREENSBORO, NC 27407
336-854-8787
Fax: 336-854-8797
feedback@theacc.org
www.theacc.com
• John D Swofford, Commissioner
• Mike Finn, Associate Commissioner/Football Communications
• W. Scott McBurney, Assoc. Commissioner of Advanced Media
• Nora Lynn Finch, Assoc Commissioner Women's Basketball/SWA

• Mike Burgemeister, Assoc. Commissioner Compliance/Governance
• Amy Yakola, Assoc Commissioner Public Realtions/Marketing
• Heather Hirschman, Website Coordinator
Year Founded:
1953
Description:
Provides athletic competition for baseball, men's and women's basketball, men's and women's cross country, women's field hockey, football, men's and women's golf, men's and women's indoor track, men's and women's outdoor track, men's and women's Lacrosse, men's and women's rowing, men's and women's soccer, women's softball, men's and women's swimming, men's and women's tennis, women's volleyball and wrestling.
Membership Requirements:
Must be voted upon by existing members.
Number of Members:
12
Members:
Boston College, Clemson University, Duke University, Florida State University, Georgia Institute of Technology, University of Louisville, University of Miami, University of North Carolina at Chapel Hill, North Carolina State University, University of Notre Dame, University of Pittsburgh, Syracuse University, University of Virginia, Virginia Tech, Wake Forest University
Corporate Sponsors:
RBC Centura, Alltel, Pepsi, Aquafina, Geico, Progress Energy, Chick-fil-A, Jeep, Chrysler, Food Lion.

ATLANTIC SUN CONFERENCE
3370 VINEVILLE AVE, STE 108-B
MACON, GA 31204-0790
478-474-3394
Fax: 478-474-4272
www.atlanticsun.org
• Ted Gumbart, Commissioner
(478) 474-3394
tgumbart@atlanticsun.org
• Meredith Eaker, Associate Commissioner/Sports Administration
(478) 474-3394
meaker@atlanticsun.org
• Mike Hagen, Asst. Commissioner for Compliance
(478) 474-3394
mhagen@atlanticsun.org
• Patrick McCoy, Assistant Director of Media Relations
• Keith Hendrix, Director for Championships
(478) 474-3394
khendrix@atlanticsun.org
• Melody Battle, Executive Assistant/Office Manager
(478) 474-3394
mbattle@atlanticsun.org
• Olivia Walter, Director of Broadcast Services
(478) 474-3394
owalter@atlanticsun.org
Year Founded:
1978
Publications:
Men's BASKETBALL MEDIA GUIDE, annual; Women's BASKETBALL MEDIA GUIDE, annual; Men's RECORD BOOK, annual; Women's RECORD BOOK, annual; Officials Directory, annual; Prospectus for each conference sport, annually; Phone Directory, annually.

Membership Requirements:
NCAA Div I.
Description:
Organizes and promotes conference championships in baseball, basketball, cross country, golf, soccer, softball, tennis, volleyball.
Members:
Belmont Bruins, Campbell Camels, East Tennessee State Bucs, Florida Atlantic Owls, Gardner-Webb Bulldogs, Jacksonville Dolphins, Kennesaw State Owls, Lipscomb Bisons, Mercer Bears, North Florida Ospreys, Stetson Hatters.

BIG 12 CONFERENCE
2201 STEMMONS FREEWAY
28TH FL
DALLAS, TX 75207-2805
214-742-1212
Fax: 214-753-0145
www.big12sports.com
• Bob Bowlsby, Commissioner
• Tim Weiser, Deputy Commissioner
• Tim Allen, Sr. Associate Commissioner

BIG EAST CONFERENCE
655 THIRD AVENUE
NEW YORK, NY 10017
646-663-3444
Fax: 646-838-8304
www.bigeast.com
• Val Ackerman, Commissioner
vackerman@bigeast.com
• Lisa Zanecchia, Assistant to Commissioner
• Nicholas Carparelli, Senior Associate Commissioner
• James Greene, Director of Championships
• Tom Odjakjian, Associate Commissioner
• Donna DeMarco, Associate Commissioner
• Sara Naggar, Communications Director
• John Paquette, Associate Commissioner, Sports Media Relations
jpaquette@bigeast.com
• Susan Eaton, Business Affairs Director
• Briana Weiss, Director of Conference Operations
bweiss@bigeast.com
• Jackie Finn, Manager, Social Media and Marketing Operations
jfinn@bigeast.com
• Brad Zakn, Manager, Digital Media
bzak@bigeast.com
Description:
Conducts championships, oversees activities of the member schools. Men's sports include baseball, football, cross country, indoor track, outdoor track, golf, tennis, soccer, swimming, basketball. Women's sports include basketball, cross country, field hockey, lacrosse, indoor track, outdoor track, softball, swimming, tennis, volleyball.
Membership Requirements:
Must be voted and approved by existing membership. Must be 4-year school.
Publications:
BIGEAST newsletter.
Year Founded:
1979
Member Schools:
Butler University, Creighton University, DePaul University, Georgetown University, Marquette University, Providence College, St. John's University, Seton Hall University, Villanova University, Xavier University.

Corporate Sponsors:
OppenheimerFunds, Turn Heads, Aeropostale, Comcast, Amtrak, Gatorade, 7-UP, Cooper Tires, MBNA.

BIG SKY CONFERENCE
2491 WASHINGTON BLVD, STE 201
OGDEN, UT 84401
801-392-1978
Fax: 801-392-5568
jkasper@bigskyconf.com
www.bigskyconf.com
• Ron Loghry, Senior Associate, Deputy Commissioner
(801) 392-1978
rloghry@bigskyconference.org
• Doug Toole, Football Officials Coordinator
• Marla Denham, Coordinator of Basketball, Volleyball Officials
• Jaynee Nadolski, Asst. Commissioner/Championships Info
• Jon Kasper, Asst. Commissioner of Media Relations
(801) 392-1978
jkasper@bigskyconf.com
• Doug Fullerton, Commissioner
(801) 392-1978
• Janet Carpenter, Administrative Assistant
(801) 392-1978
jcarpenter@bigskyconference.org
• Natanee Spencer, Business Manager
(801) 392-1978
nspencer@bigskyconference.org
• Jason Ashcraft, Media Relations Director
(801) 392-1978
jashcraft@bigskyconference.org
• Dave Champlin, Director of Corporate Partnerships
(801) 660-7066
dchamplin@bigskyconference.org
Description:
Conducts championships in cross country, basketball, golf, women's soccer, tennis, indoor and outdoor track and volleyball.
Number of Members:
8
Year Founded:
1963
Affiliation:
NCAA, Division I-AA in football, Division I in all other sports.
Member Schools:
Eastern Washington University, Idaho State, University of Montana, Montana State University-Bozeman, Northern Arizona University, Portland State University, California State University-Sacramento, Weber State University.
Sponsors:
Hampton Inn Spokane, Red Lion Hotels, Holiday Inn Spokane Airport, Spokane Airport Ramada Inn, Hilton Garden Inn Missoula, Best Western Grain Tree Inn, Holiday Inn Flagstaff, Ramada Limited, Fairfield Inn-Marriot, Days Inn in Flagstaff, Hilton Sacramento Arden West, Double Tree Sacramento, Sacramento Marriot Rancho Cordova, Hampton Inn Layton, Hampton Inn & Suites-Ogden, Holiday Inn Express-Layton, Ogden Marriot, BestRest Inn, Fairfield Inn by Marriott, TownPlace Suites by Marriott, Courtyard by Marriott-Layton, Hilton Garden Inn-Layton, Sterling Savings Bank, Baden Sports, Wilson Sporting Goods.

BIG SOUTH CONFERENCE
7233 PINEVILLE-MATTHEWS ROAD
SUITE 100
CHARLOTTE, NC 28226
704-341-7990
Fax: 704-341-7991
bigsouth@bigsouth.org
www.bigsouthsports.com
• Kyle Kallander, Commissioner
(704) 341-7990
• Jeff Jackson, Deputy Commissioner
• Mark Simpson, Assistant Commissioner Public Relations
(704) 341-7990
• Chad Cook, Associate Commissioner Marketing
(704) 341-7990
• Mark Bryant, Director of Multimedia Development
(704) 341-7990
• Matt VanSandt, Director of Championships
(704) 341-7990
• Stephanie Roe, Director of Administration
(704) 341-7990
Year Founded:
1983
Number of Members:
11
Description:
Developing leadership through athletics.
Member Schools:
Campbell, Charleston Southern, Coastal Carolina, Gardner-Webb, High Point, Liberty, Presbtierian College, Radford, UNC Asheville, VMC, Winthrop.
Publications:
Football Media Guide, Fan Guide, Basketball Media Guide.

BIG TEN ATHLETIC CONFERENCE
1500 W. HIGGINS RD
PARK RIDGE, IL 60068-6300
847-696-1010
Fax: 847-696-1150
www.bigten.org
• James E Delany, Commissioner
• Wendy Fallen, Associate Commissioner, Championships
• Chad Hawley, Associate Commissioner, Compliance
• Mark Rudner, Senior Associate Commissioner, Television Admin.
• Wayne Baskerville, Associate Commissioner
• Brad Traviolia, Deputy Commissioner/COO/CFO
• Teri Lenth, Corporate Sponsorships Director
• Josh Munk, Associate Director of Football Operations
• Bill Carollo, Football Officials Coordinator
• Patty Broderick, Women's Basketball Officials Coord.
• Rick Boyages, Associate Commissioner, Men's Basketball
• Jade Burroughs, Director, Branding
• Jessica Palermo, Director, Championships
• Kerry Kenny, Director, Compliance
• Scott Bailey, General Manager
Description:
An association of 11 world-class universities who member institutes share a common mission of research, graduate, professional and undergraduate teaching and public service.
Corporate Sponsors:
Cooper Tires, U.S. Bank, Liberty Mutual, Gatorade, Ramada Worldwide, Under

Armour, 7-UP, Xbox Live.
Publications:
GAMETRACKER newsletter, SCORE, Big Ten Records Book.
Year Founded:
1896
Member Schools:
University of Illinois, Indiana University, University of Iowa, University of Michigan, Michigan State University, University of Minnesota, Northwestern University, Ohio State University, Penn State University, Purdue University, University of Wisconsin.

BIG WEST CONFERENCE
2 CORPORATE PARK, STE 206
IRVINE, CA 92606
949-261-2525
Fax: 949-261-2528
dfarrell@bigwest.org
www.bigwest.org
• Dennis Farrell, Commissioner
dfarrell@bigwest.org
• Rob Halvaks, Deputy Associate Commissioner
rhalvaks@bigwest.org
• Jody McRoberts, Sr. Associate Commissioner
jmcroberts@bigwest.org
• Mike Daniels, Assistant Commissioner Marketing
• Mike Villamor, Assistant Commissioner
• Erica Satterfield, Assistant Commissioner Compliance
• Christopher Hargraves, Assistant Information Director
chargraves@bigwest.org
• Julie St. Cyr, Director of Communications
jstcyr@bigwest.org
• Steve Chen, Director of New Media
schen@bigwest.org
Year Founded:
1969
Membership Requirements:
Must be voted/approved by the existing membership. Must be a 4-year school.
Publications:
Big West Conference Baseball, Men's & Women's Basketball, Softball, Volleyball Media Guides, annual.
Number of Members:
8
Description:
Providing a competitive athletic conference for institutions in the great state of California. It is also the home to prestigious California institutions that are at the forefront of academic success.

CALIFORNIA COLLEGIATE ATHLETIC ASSOCIATION
1350 TREAT BOULEVARD
SUITE 285
WALNUT CREEK, CA 94597
925-472-8299
Fax: 925-472-8887
www.goccaa.org
• Nathan Salant, Esq., Commissioner
(205) 999-8375
nsalant@goccaa.org
• Rebecca Bennett, Director of Communications
(925) 472-8299
rbennett@goccaa.org
• Bill Fusco, President
• Al Barba, Asst. Commissioner/Media Relations

(925) 472-8299
• Bill White, Officiating Coordinator
• Christine Halsey, Sr. Woman Administrator Coordinator
• Carol Rivera, Assistant Commissioner/Compliance and Internal Ops
(925) 472-8299
• John McCasey, Director of Championships and Marketing
(925) 472-8299
Year Founded:
1938
Description:
CCAA has been one of the nation's most successful intercollegiate athletic conferences since its establishment. The institutions compete in seven women's and six men's CCAA-sponsored sports. Fall sports include men's and women's cross country, men's and women's soccer and women's volleyball. Men's and women's basketball are contested in the winter, and women's tennis, men's golf, men's and women's outdoor track & field, softball and baseball comprise spring competition.
Member Schools:
Cal Poly Pomona, Cal State Bakersfield, Cal State Dominguez Hills, Cal State L.A., Cal State San Bernardino, Cal State Stanislaus, Chico State, UC San Diego, San Francisco State and Sonoma State, California State University-Monterey Bay.
Number of Members:
12
Corporate Sponsors:
Apple Computer, Wilson Sporting Goods, Brine, Molten USA, Enterprise Rent-A-Car.

CAROLINAS-VIRGINIA ATHLETICS CONFERENCE
26 CUB DR
THOMASVILLE, NC 27360
336-884-0482
Fax: 336-884-0315
• Angela Tressel, Assistant Commissioner
(336) 884-0482
• Brook Patterson, Associate Commissioner
(336) 884-0482
Year Founded:
1938
Description:
Sponsors intercollegiate athletics in baseball, basketball, cross country, golf, soccer, softball, tennis, volleyball.
Member Schools:
Anderson University, Barton College, Belmont Abbey College, Coker College, Erskine College, Lees-McRae College, Limestone College, Mount Olive College, Pfeiffer University, Queens University of Charlotte, St. Andrews Presbyterian College, Converse College.
Number of Members:
12

CASCADE COLLEGIATE CONFERENCE
C/O SOUTHERN OREGON UNIVERSITY
1250 SISKIYOU BLVD
ASHLAND, OR 97520
541-552-7672
Fax: 541-552-6543
www.cascadeconference.org
• Robert Cashell, Commissioner
(541) 605-0137
ccccommish@gmail.com
• Mickie Bush, Eligibility Coordinator
(503) 494-1277

mickiebush@gmail.com
• Sam Ghrist, Conference Statistician
(541) 962-3929
sam.ghrist1@frontier.com
Description:
Intercollegiate athletics men's and women's conference Sports include baseball, men's and women's basketball, men's and women's cross country, softball, track & field, women's volleyball.
Member Schools:
Albertson College, Cascade College, Concordia University, Corban College (formerly Western Baptist College), Eastern Oregon University, Evergreen State College, Northwest University, Oregon Institute of Technology, Southern Oregon University, Warner Pacific College.
Affiliation:
National Association of Intercollegiate Athletics.

CENTENNIAL CONFERENCE
563 COLLEGE AVE, STE B-101
LANCASTER, PA 17603
717-358-4463
Fax: 717-358-4480
steve.ulrich@centennial.org
www.centennial.org
• Kimberly Wenger, Associate Director
(717) 358-4463
kimberly.wenger@centennial.org
Year Founded:
1981
Description:
The Centennial Conference encourages athletic competition among national liberal arts colleges and universities that share similar academic aspirations and a commitment to the importance of the total educational experience of students engaged in sports. Intercollegiate athletics programs are an integral part of the life of the member institutions and flow from their educational objectives. Each institution provides a comprehensive, broad-based athletics program. All varsity sports are treated equitably, and every sport is important.
Member Schools:
Bryn Mawr College, Dickinson College, Franklin & Marshall College, Gettysburg College, Haverford College, Johns Hopkins University, McDaniel College, Muhlenberg College, Swarthmore College, Ursinus College, Washington College.
Publications:
THE CENTENNIAL CONFERENCE MANUAL.

CENTRAL ATLANTIC COLLEGIATE CONFERENCE
111 WATER ST
PO BOX 35751
NEW HAVEN, CT 06525
203-298-4806
Fax: 203-773-6450
www.caccathletics.org
• Dan Mara, Internal Operations
(203) 298-4809
• Ellen O'Brien, Associate Commissioner/SWA
(203) 298-4807
eobrien@caccathletics.org
• Doug DeBaise, Assistant Commissioner for Strategic Communic
(203) 298-4806

• Allison McDonald, Internal Operations
(203) 298-4809
Member Schools:
Bloomfield College, Caldwell College, Dominican College, Felician College, Georgian Court College, Goldey-Beacom College, Holy Family College, NJIT College, Nyack College, Philadelphia University, Teikyo Post College, University of the Sciences in Philadelphia, Wilmington College.
Description:
Intercollegiate athletics conference.

CENTRAL INTERCOLLEGIATE ATHLETIC ASSOCIATION
22 ENTERPRISE PARKWAY
SUITE 210
HAMPTON, VA 23666
757-865-0071
Fax: 757-865-8436
TheCIAA@aol.com
www.theciaa.com
• Jacqie McWilliams, Commisioner
(757) 865-0071
• Jessica Incorminias, Assistant To The Commissioner
(757) 865-0071
jincorminias@ciaa.com
• Eddie Weatherington, Associate Commissioner of Governance/Complian
(757) 865-0071
eweatherington@theciaa.com
• Sherry Shaw, Associate Commissioner of Business Operations
(757) 865-0071
sshaw@theciaa.com
• Suzette McQueen, Assistant Commissioner of External Operations
(757) 865-0071
smcqueen@theciaa.com
Year Founded:
1912
Description:
An athletic conference consisting of historically African-American institutions of higher education.
Number of Members:
13
Member Schools:
Bowie State University, Elizabeth City State University, Fayetteville State University, Johnson C. Smith University, Livingstone College, North Carolina Central University, St. Augustine's College, St. Paul's College, Shaw University, Virginia State University, Virginia Union University, Winston-Salem State University.
Membership Requirements:
Historically black colleges and universities.

CENTRAL STATES FOOTBALL LEAGUE
709 OKLAHOMA BLVD
ALVA, OK 73717
580-327-8653
Fax: 508-772-3159
rshintergardt@nwosu.edu
• Andy Carter, Director of Athletics
(580) 327-8632
• Ryan Kaiser, Associate Director of Athletics for Internal
(580) 327-8578
• Wendy McManus, Associate Director of Athletics for Complianc
(580) 327-8632
Description:
Intercollegiate football league which

represents five schools within the National Association of Intercollegiate Athletics.
Member Schools:
Bacone College, Northwestern Oklahoma State University, Peru State College, Southern Nazarene University, Texas College.
Year Founded:
2000

CHICAGOLAND COLLEGIATE ATHLETIC CONFERENCE
500 WILCOX STREET
JOLIET, IL 60435
815-740-3842
Fax: 815-740-3841
dlaketa@stfrancis.edu
www.ccacsports.com
• Dave Laketa, Interim Commissioner
dlaketa@stfrancis.edu
• Peter Haring, Vice Commissioner/Treasurer
(219) 473-4327
pharing@ccsj.edu
• Jeff Schimmelpfenning, Commissioner
(815) 592-5303
ccacjeff@gmail.com
• Tony Grimm, FAR/Eligibility Chairperson
(815) 939-5108
tgrimm@olivet.edu
Description:
An affiliated conference of the National Association of Intercollegiate Athletics. The CCAC sanctions play in five mens sports which are soccer, cross country, basketball division I, basketball division II, and baseball. There are six sanctioned womens sports which are soccer, volleyball, cross country, basketball division I, basketball division II, and softball. In all sports, it sanctions regular season league play as well as a post-season tourney. It is the only conference in the NAIA nationally to be affiliated in both divisions of mens and womens basketball.
Year Founded:
1949
Member Schools:
Calumet St. Joseph, Cardinal Stritch, Holy Cross, Illinois Tech, Indiana, South Bend, Judson, Olivet Nazarene, Purdue Calumet, Purdue North Central, Robert Morris, Roosevelt, Saint Xavier, St. Francis, Trinity Christian, Trinity International
Number of Members:
15 Schools

CITY UNIVERSITY OF NEW YORK/CUNY ATHLETIC CONFERENCE
LEHMAN COLLEGE
250 BEDFORD PARK BOULEVARD W
BRONX, NY 10468
718-960-8000
Fax: 718-960-7194
dgansell@yahoo.com
www.lehman.edu
• Martin Zwiren, Athletics Director
martin.zwiren@lehman.cuny.edu
• Andrew Pearson, Sports Information Director/Intramurals Coord
andrew.pearson@lehman.cuny.edu
• Nichole Kieltyka, Athletic Trainer
nichole.kieltyka@lehman.cuny.edu
Year Founded:
1987
Description:
Sponsored sports include baseball,

basketball (M & W), cross-country (M & W), soccer, softball, tennis (M & W), swimming & diving (M&W), track & field (indoor and outdoor/M & W), volleyball (M & W), Member schools include Bernard M. Baruch Col., Bronx CC, Brooklyn Col., City Col. of NY, Herbert H. Lehman Col., Hostos CC, Hunter Col., John Jay Col., Kingsborough Com. Col., New York City Technical College, Borough of Manhattan Community Col., Medgar Evers Col., New York City Tech. Col., Queensborough Community Col., Col. of Staten Island, York Col. (NY).
Member Schools:
Baruch College, Brooklyn College, The City College of New York, Hunter College, John Jay College, Lehman College, Medgar Evers College, New York City College of Technology, The College of Staten Island, York College.
Publications:
CUNY SPORTS newsletter.

COLLEGE CONFERENCE OF ILLINOIS AND WISCONSIN
C/O CHRIS MARTIN, COMMISSIONER
30 N. BRAINARD ST #402
NAPERVILLE, IL 60540
630-637-56934
Fax: 630-637-5694
cmartin@cciw.org
www.cciw.org
• Chris Martin, Commissioner
(630) 637-5693
cmartin@cciw.org
• Bill Carollo, Coordinator of Football Officials
carollo@bigten.org
• Justin Basovsky, Coordinator of Volleyball Officials
(847) 553-5297
footin86@hotmail.com
• Steve Siomos, Coordinator of Men's & Women's Soccer Officia
(630) 258-0883
siomos@aol.com
• Al Raya, Coordinator of Women's Basketball Officials
(773) 539-7938
arref_bb@yahoo.com
• Mike Krizman, Asst. Commissioner/Sports Info Dir.
(630) 637-5719
mkrizman@cciw.org
Year Founded:
1969
Description:
The CCIW exists to serve a select group of private colleges and universities of similar size and heritage, which share a deep commitment to superior undergraduate education and a common perspective on the role of intercollegiate athletics in that education.
Number of Members:
8
Member Schools:
Augustana College, Carthage College, Elmhurst College, Illinois Wesleyan University, Millikin University, North Central College, North Park University, Wheaton College.
Corporate Sponsors:
Select Sport America, Wilson Sporting Goods, Molten USA, Diamond Sports, Choice Hotels, La Quinta Inns & Suites, National Car Rental.

COLONIAL ATHLETIC ASSOCIATION
8625 PATTERSON AVE
RICHMOND, VA 23229
804-754-1616
Fax: 804-754-1973
rwashburn@caasports.com
www.caasports.com
• Jerry Stone, Senior Associate
Commissioner
• Kathleen Batterson, Sr Assoc
Commissioner/Internal Operations/SWA
• Robert Goodman, Sr Associate
Commissioner, Marketing/Developm
• Rob Washburn, Asst. Commissioner of
Communications
• Melissa Conti, Asst. Commissioner of
Championships
• Brad Gregg, Operations Director
• Pamela Stone, Officiating Administrator
Description:
The CAA conducts championships in 21
sports. Male athletes compete for
championships in baseball, basketball, cross
country, golf, lacrosse, soccer, swimming &
diving, tennis, track & field and wrestling.
Female athletes battle for conference titles
in basketball, cross country, field hockey,
golf, lacrosse, soccer, softball, swimming &
diving, tennis, track & field and volleyball.
The CAA will also begin sponsorship of a
12-team Division I-AA football league in the
fall of 2007.
Member Schools:
University of Delaware, Drexel University,
George Mason University, Hofstra
University, James Madison University,
Northeastern University, Old Dominion
University, Towson University, University of
North Carolina-Wilmington, Virginia
Commonwealth University, College of
William & Mary, Georgia State University.
Year Founded:
1986
Number of Members:
12

CONFERENCE USA
5201 N. O'CONNOR BLVD
STE 300
IRVING, TX 75039
214-774-1300
www.conferenceusa.com
• Judy MacLeod, Commissioner
• Catrina Gibson, Assistant Commissioner
for Business Affairs
• Courtney Morrison-Archer, Assistant
Commissioner of Media Relations
Year Founded:
1995
Description:
We embrace a new era with fresh faces and
a renewed commitment to excellence and
leadership in athletics, academics and
community involvement. All C-USA
institutions sponsor Division I-A football,
along with several other men's and women's
athletic programs, many of which compete
regularly for NCAA Championships. C-USA
sponsors competition in 19 sports - nine for
men (baseball, basketball, cross country,
football, golf, soccer, tennis and indoor and
outdoor track and field) and 10 for women
(basketball, cross country, golf, softball,
soccer, swimming and diving, tennis, indoor
and outdoor track and field and volleyball).
Member Schools:
East Carolina University, University of
Houston, Marshall University, University of

Memphis, Rice University, Southern
Methodist University, University of Southern
Mississippi, Tulane University, University of
Tulsa, University of Alabama at Birmingham.
Corporate Sponsors:
Aeropostale.

DAKOTA-10 ATHLETIC CONFERENCE
C/O LAVERN JESSEN, COMMISSIONER
DICKINSON STATE - MAIL BOX 9
DICKINSON, ND 58601
605-336-1095
Fax: 605-336-8976
jimdahl@pop.ctctel.com
• LaVern Jessen, Commissioner
• Thomas Flickema, President
• Jim Dahl, Sports Information Director
• Allen Dockter, Football Officials Supervisor
• Ben Franson, Basketball Officials
Supervisor
Year Founded:
1921
Description:
The DAC is a member of the NAIA and
promotes sportsmanship and well-rounded
athletic programs that contribute to the total
education process of each athlete.
Member Schools:
Black Hills State, Dakota State, Dickinson
State, Jamestown College, Mayville State,
Minot State, South Dakota Tech, Valley City
State.

EASTERN COLLEGE ATHLETIC CONFERENCE/ECAC
1311 CRAIGVILLE BEACH RD
CENTERVILLE, MA 2632
508-771-5060
Fax: 508-771-9486
kroberts@ecac.org
www.ecac.org
• Dan Coonan, President/CEO
(508) 771-5060
dcoonan@ecac.org
• John Rollins, VP Administration/CFO
(508) 771-5060
jrollins@ecac.org
• Meghan O'Brien, Director Of Marketing
And Communications
(508) 771-5060
mobrien@ecac.org
Description:
The mission is to initiate, stimulate and
improve intercollegiate athletics programs
for student-athletes and to promote and
develop educational leadership, athletic
excellence and athletics participation.
Publications:
ECAC newsletter.

EASTERN INTERCOLLEGIATE ATHLETIC CONFERENCE
1463 GRANTLAND PL
GREENSBORO, NC 27410
336-855-0391
Fax: 336-855-0391
• Kenneth Free, Commissioner
• Willie Jefferson, President
• Henry Smith, Vice President
• David Eikerenkotter, Secretary
• Dorothy Patterson, Treasurer/Staff
Secretary
• Rodney Johnson, Sports Information
Director
• John Russell, Basketball Officials
Supervisor

Year Founded:
1983
Description:
Originating from the Southeastern Athletic
Conference, the SEAC was founded by
Bethune-Cookman College, Claflin College,
Florida Memorial College, and Morris
College. In 1968, Voorhees College joined
the SEAC along with Edward Waters
College. Florida Memorial College relocated
its campus to Miami, Florida and dropped
out of the SEAC.
Member Schools:
Allen University, Barber-Scotia College,
Clafin University, Edward Waters College,
Morris College, Voorhees College.
Number of Members:
6

EMPIRE 8
104 YORKTOWN DR
ROCHESTER, NY 14616
585-581-0834
Fax: 585-581-1127
cmitrano@empire8.com
www.empire8.com
• Mark Zupan, President
zupan@elmira.edu
• Chuck Mitrano, Commissioner
cmitrano@empire8.com
• Janelle Zera, Associate Commissioner
jzera@empire8.com
• Timothy Farrell, Assistant Commissioner
(216) 751-8836
tfarrell@empire8.com
Year Founded:
1964
Description:
Intercollegiate conference holding
competition (men) in sports of baseball,
basketball, cross country, golf, indoor and
outdoor track, lacrosse, soccer, swimming,
tennis. Women's competition offered in
basketball, cross country, outdoor track,
soccer, swimming, tennis and volleyball.
Publications:
EMPIRE8 NEWS BULLETIN.
Member Schools:
Alfred University, Elmira College, Hartwick
College, Ithaca College, Nazareth College,
Rochester Institute of Technology, St. John
Fisher College, Utica College.
Membership Requirements:
Academic achievement as well athletic
prowess and sportsmanship on the playing
fields.

FLORIDA SUN CONFERENCE
FLAGLER COLLEGE
74 KING ST
ST. AUGUSTINE, FL 32084
904-829-6481
Fax: 904-810-2253
jamie.joss@erau.edu
www.thesunconference.com
• Mark Pope, Commissioner
(904) 819-6252
sinconference@aol.com
• Jennifer Rinnert, Athletic Trainer
(904) 819-6402
jrinnert@flagler.edu
• John Jordan, Sports Information Director
(904) 819-6465
jjordan@flagler.edu
Year Founded:
1990
Description:

The institutions in the conference believe in strong educational commitment combined with balanced athletic competition. Originally formed in March 1990 as the Florida Intercollegiate Athletic Conference (FIAC), the FSC was established as a conference for small independent institutions within the NAIA. The name Florida Sun Conference was adopted in 1992.
Member Schools:
Embry-Riddle University, Flagler College, Florida Memorial College, Northwood University, St. Thomas University, Savannah College of Art and Design, Warner Southern College, Webber International University.
Number of Members:
8

FRONTIER CONFERENCE
966 COLORADO AVENUE
WHITEFISH, MT
fronconf@in-tch.com
www.frontierconference.com
• Charlie Gross, Athletic Director
(406) 447-5479
• Reagan Rossi, Athletic Director
(208) 459-5850
• Thomas Evans, President
(406) 657-1015
Year Founded:
1935
Description:
Sponsors athletic competition in men's and women's basketball, men's football, golf and women's volleyball. Montana State University-Northern and University of Great Falls are participants in wrestling.
Member Schools:
Carroll College, Eastern Oregon University, Montana State University-Northern, Rocky Mountain College-Montana, Westminster College-Utah, University of Great Falls, University of Montana-Western, Montana Tech of the University of Montana, Lewis-Clark State College.

GOLDEN STATE ATHLETIC CONFERENCE
AZUSA PACIFIC UNIVERSITY
901 E. ALOSTA AVE
AZUSA, CA 91702
626-812-3097
Fax: 626-812-3068
chamlow@apu.edu
www.gsacsports.org
• Brian Gleason, Administrative Assistant
(626) 815-4538
• Sheri Pine, Sports Information Director
(909) 392-9225
Year Founded:
1986
Description:
The members are all church-related Christian colleges. They are purposely aligned to be similar in enrollment, academics, athletics and student life.
Number of Members:
11
Member Schools:
Azusa Pacific University, Biola University, California Baptist University, Concordia University, Fresno Pacific University, Hope International University, The Master's College, Point Loma Nazarene University, San Diego Christian College, Vanguard University, Westmont College.

GREAT LAKES INTERCOLLEGIATE ATHLETIC CONFERENCE
1110 WASHINGTON AVE
BAY CITY, MI 48708
989-894-2529
Fax: 989-894-2825
www.gliac.org
• Jeff Ligney, Commissioner
jligney@gliac.org
Year Founded:
1972
Description:
Championships in 21 sports, 11 for men and 10 for women.
Member Schools:
Ashland University, Ferris State University, University of Findlay, Gannon University, Grand Valley State University, Hillsdale College, Lake Superior State University, Mercyhurst College, Michigan Tech University, Northern Michigan University, Northwood University, Saginaw Valley State University, Wayne State University.
Corporate Sponsors:
Bastian Brothers & Co., HoopMatch.com, Enterprises Rent-A-Car, Rawlings, Molten USA, Schelde, Wilson.
Number of Members:
13

GREAT LAKES VALLEY CONFERENCE
PAN AM PLAZA
201 S. CAPITOL AVE, STE 560
INDIANAPOLIS, IN 46225
317-237-2105
Fax: 317-237-5632
Jim@glvc-sports.org
www.glvcsports.com
• Jim Naumovich, Commissioner
(317) 237-5633
jim@glvc-sports.org
• Tonya Charland, Assistant Commissioner, Compliance/Senior Wom
(317) 237-5636
tonya@glvc-sports.org
• Jeff Smith, Assistant Commissioner, Communications
(317) 237-2106
jeff@glvc-sports.org
• Jennifer DeMotte, Public Information Assistant
(317) 237-2106
glvcsports@gmail.com
• Wispeny Ellis, Assistant Commissioner
• John Meisel, President
• Erin Merz, Sports Information Director
Year Founded:
1972
Description:
Men's sports include baseball, basketball, cross country, golf, soccer and tennis; women's include basketball, cross country, softball, tennis, volleyball.
Member Schools:
Bellarmine College, Indiana Purdue/Fort Wayne, University of Indianapolis, Kentucky Wesleyan College, Lewis University, Quincy University, St. Joseph College, Southern Illinois University at Edwardsville, University of Southern Indiana, University of Wisconsin-Parkside.

GREAT PLAINS ATHLETIC CONFERENCE
4728 BIRCH WAY
SIOUX CITY, IA 51106

712-226-4722
Fax: 303-374-5868
corey.westra@gpacsports.com
www.gpacsports.com
• Corey Westra, Commissioner
• Lucas Mohrman, Assistant Commissioner
lucas.mohrman@gpacsports.com
Year Founded:
1969
Description:
An affiliated conference of the National Association of Intercollegiate Athletics (NAIA), consisting of 13 private, faith-based colleges and universities in Nebraska, Iowa and South Dakota.
Member Schools:
Briar Cliff University, Concordia University, Dakota Wesleyan University, Dana College, Doane College, Dordt College, Hastings College, Midland Lutheran College, Morningside College, Mount Marty College, Nebraska Wesleyan University, Northwestern College, University of Sioux Falls.

GULF COAST ATHLETIC CONFERENCE
LOUISIANA COLLEGE
1140 COLLEGE DR
PINEVILLE, LA 71360
318-487-7102
Fax: 318-487-7288
howell@lacollege.edu
www.gcaconf.com
• Steve Martin, Commissioner
(504) 382-7694
steveb22@msn.com
• Kiki Barnes, President
(504) 816-4752
kbarnes@dillard.edu
• Dennis Cousin, Vice President
(504) 520-7330
• Grace Flickinger, Faculty Athletic Representative
(504) 520-7526
gflickin@xula.edu
• Robin Bunting, Secretary/Treasurer
(318) 229-3791
albunting4@gmail.com
Number of Members:
10
Member Schools:
Belhaven College, Dillard University, Loyola University New Orleans, Louisiana State University-Shreveport, University of Mobile-Alabama, Spring Hill College, Southern University at New Orleans, Tougaloo College, William Carey College, Xavier University of Louisiana.
Membership Requirements:
NAIA Division I, a minimum of one men's and one women's sport in fall, winter, and spring seasons.
Member Services:
Provides championship competition in 12 men's and women's sports for member schools.

GULF SOUTH CONFERENCE
2101 PROVIDENCE PARK
STE 200
BIRMINGHAM, AL 35242
205-991-9880
Fax: 205-437-0505
gulfsout@ix.netcom.com
www.gscsports.org
• Jim Cavale, Director of Broadcasting
jimcavale@mac.com

• A.A. Moore, Assistant Sports Information Director
(205) 991-9880
aamoore@gscsports.org
• Michael Stagno, Assistant Sports Information Director
(205) 991-9880
gsccompliance@gmail.com
• Matt Wilson, Commissioner
• Michael Anderson, Assistant Commissioner
(205) 991-9880
mikeanderson@gscsports.org
• Andrea Anderson, Assistant Commissioner for Complaince
(205) 991-9880
gsccompliance@gmail.com
Year Founded:
1970
Description:
GSC members feature comprehensive athletic programs that compete for 14 official conference championships: football, men's and women's cross country, men's and women's soccer, women's volleyball, men's and women's basketball, baseball, softball, men's and women's tennis and men's and women's golf.
Number of Members:
17
Member Schools:
Alabama-Huntsville; Christian Brothers; Delta State; New Orleans; North Alabama; Valdosta State; West Alabama; West Florida; West Georgia
Publications:
Media Guides, Tournament, Championship Programs.

HEART OF AMERICA ATHLETIC CONFERENCE
15221 MIDLAND DR
SHAWNEE, KS 66217
913-631-5579
Fax: 913-631-5579
splack@comcast.net
• Larry Lady, Commissioner
(913) 631-5579
• Steven Minnis, President
(913) 360-7400
president@benedictine.edu
• Charlie Gertenmayer, Board of Governors Chair
(913) 360-7583
cgartenmayer@benedictine.edu
• Eric Montgomery, Director of Sports info. / Marketing
(520) 954-4098
ericmontgomery@haacsports.com
Year Founded:
1970
Description:
A college athletic conference affiliated with the NAIA. Member institutions are located in Iowa, Kansas, and Missouri in the United States.
Member Schools:
Avila University, Baker University, Benedictine College, Central Methodist University, Culver-Stockton College, Evangel University, Graceland University, Lindenwood University, MidAmerica Nazarene University, Missouri Valley College, William Jewell College.

HORIZON LEAGUE
201 S. CAPITOL ST
STE 500
INDIANAPOLIS, IN 46225
317-237-5622
Fax: 317-237-5620
www.horizonleague.org
• Jonathan LeCrone, Commissioner
• Cindy French, Senior Executive Associate
• Alfreeda Goff, Sr. Assoc. Commissioner/Chief Staff
• Beth Opell, Finance Director
• Wayne Burrow, Asst Commissioner, Championships/Sports Admin
• Bill Potter, Communications Director
Year Founded:
1979
Description:
Originally founded as the Midwestern City Conference, the League was a men's-only sports conference until the 1986-87 academic year when it added women's athletics. The Horizon League offers 19 championships (nine men's sports and 10 women's sports). The League enjoys NCAA automatic qualification in baseball, men's basketball, women's basketball, men's golf, men's soccer, women's soccer, softball, men's tennis, women's tennis and women's volleyball.
Member Schools:
Butler University, Cleveland State University, University of Detroit Mercy, University of Illinois at Chicago, Loyola University Chicago, University of Wisconsin-Green Bay, University of Wisconsin-Milwaukee, Wright State University, Youngstown State University.
Corporate Sponsors:
American Family Insurance, Sprint, Bill Estes Chevrolet, Nike, Merrill Lynch, Sirius Satellite Radio, Wilson Sporting Goods.
Publications:
GAMETRACKER newsletter.

ILLINIBADGER FOOTBALL CONFERENCE
CONCORDIA UNIVERSITY
12800 N. LAKE SHORE DR
MEQUON, WI 53097
262-243-4544
Fax: 262-243-4475
james.saleska@cuw.edu
www.cuw.edu
• Robert Barnhill, Athletic Director
(262) 243-4404
• Rick Riehl, Sports Information Director
(262) 243-4544
Year Founded:
1881

IOWA INTERCOLLEGIATE ATHLETIC CONFERENCE
222 THIRD ST SE
STE 423
CEDAR RAPIDS, IA 52401
319-366-4845
Fax: 319-366-4911
www.iowaconference.com
• Chuck Yrigoyen, Commissioner
• Dan Hammes, Deputy Commissioner
• Paula Carlson, Chair, Presidents Council
Year Founded:
1922
Description:
The IIAC consists of independent, regionally accredited, residential four-year, liberal arts colleges that share common academic philosophies and goals and that place primary emphasis on the academic progress of students. To that end the athletic programs of IIAC member institutions facilitate the intellectual, spiritual and physical development of all students, whether as participants or spectators.
Member Schools:
Buena Vista University, Central College, Coe College, Cornell College, University of Dubuque, Loras College, Luther College, Simpson College, Wartburg College.
Publications:
IIAC Yearbook & Directory.

IVY LEAGUE GROUP
228 ALEXANDER ST
PRINCETON, NJ 8544
609-258-6426
Fax: 609-258-1690
info@ivyleaguesports.com
www.ivyleaguesports.com
• Robin Harris, Executive Director
robinharris@ivyleaguesports.com
• Carolyn Campbell-McGovern, Deputy Executive Director
carolyn@ivyleaguesports.com
Year Founded:
1954
Description:
Sponsoring conference championships in 33 men's and women's sports, and averaging more than 35 varsity teams at each school. The Ivy League provides intercollegiate athletic opportunities for more men and women than any other conference in the country.
Number of Members:
8
Member Schools:
Brown University, Columbia University, Cornell University, Dartmouth University, Harvard University, Penn State University, Princeton University, Yale University.
Membership Requirements:
Must be voted on by existing members.

KANSAS COLLEGIATE ATHLETIC CONFERENCE
BETHANY COLLEGE
335 E SWENSSON STREET
LINDSBORG, KS 67456
785-227-3380 EXT 8456
Fax: 785-227-2021
www.kcacsports.com
• Scott Crawford, Commissioner
(316) 337-5999
scott.crawford@kcacsports.com
• Robert Brennecke, Assistant Commissioner
(316) 337-5999
• Heidi Hoskinson, Conference Registrar
(316) 295-5861
heidi_hoskinson@friends.edu
• Joyce Pigge, Eligibility Chairm
Year Founded:
1902
Description:
A prominent intercollegiate athletics conference comprised of outstanding independent or private institutions of higher education in the state.
Number of Members:
10
Member Schools:
Bethany Colllege, Bethel College, Friends

University, Kansas Wesleyan University, McPherson College, Ottawa University, Southwestern College, Sterling College, Tabor College, University of Saint Mary.

KENTUCKY INTERCOLLEGIATE ATHLETIC CONFERENCE
C/O BILLY C. MELTON, COMMISSIONER
313 BOCOTE DRIVE
BEREA, KY 40403
859-200-3510
www.kiacsports.com
• Joe Glover, President Elect/Secretary
• Ken Pickerill, Eligibility Chair/FAR
• Bill Melton, Commissioner
Year Founded:
1918
Description:
An association organized to promote and enhance the competitive experience of intercollegiate athletics.
Member Schools:
Alice Lloyd College, Asbury College, Berea College, Bethel College, Brescia University, Indian University Southeast, Mid-Continent College, Midway College, Spalding University, St. Louis College of Pharmacy.

LITTLE EAST CONFERENCE
C/O JONATHAN G HARPER, COMMISSIONER
285 OLD WESTPORT ROAD
NORTH DARTMOUTH, MA 2747
860-677-1269
Fax: 860-674-8363
www.LittleEast.com
• Jack Holleran, Assistant Commissioner
(508) 910-6287
• Ian Day, Treasurer
(508) 999-8722
iday@umassd.edu
• John P. Clark, Executive Committee Chair
(603) 535-2770
• Jonathan Harper, Commissioner
(508) 910-6299
• Donald Tencher, Secretary/Treasurer
• Mike Christie, Communications Director
Year Founded:
1986
Description:
Sports sponsored include baseball, basketball, men's and women's cross country, men's and women's soccer, field hockey (women), lacrosse (men and women), softball, swimming (women) and tennis (men and women), track & field indoor/outdoor (men and women), volleyball (women).
Number of Members:
8
Member Schools:
Eastern Connecticut State University, Keene State College, Plymouth State College, Rhode Island College, University of Massachusetts-Boston, University of Massachusetts-Dartmouth, University of Southern Maine, Western Connecticut State University.

LONE STAR CONFERENCE
1221 W. CAMPBELL ROAD
SUITE 171
RICHARDSON, TX 75080
972-234-0033
Fax: 972-234-4110
lscinfo2003@yahoo.com
www.lonestarconference.org

• Jay Poerner, Commissioner
(972) 234-0033
jay@lonestarconference.org
• Melanie Robotham, Assistant Commissioner
(972) 234-0033
melanie@lonestarconference.org
• Danielle Anderson, Assistant Commissioner
(972) 234-0033
danielle@lonestarconference.org
• Cheryl Scott, Business Manager
(972) 234-0033
cheryl@lonestarconference.org
Year Founded:
1931
Description:
Conducts conference championships in 15 sports (seven men and eight women). Men's championships include football, cross country, basketball, baseball, track and field, tennis and golf. Women's titles are determined in volleyball, soccer, cross country, basketball, softball, track and field, tennis and golf.
Member Schools:
Abilene Christian University, Angelo State University, Cameron University, University of Central Oklahoma, East Central State University, Eastern New Mexico University, Midwest State University, Northeastern State University, Southeastern Oklahoma State University, Southwestern Oklahoma State University, Tarleton State, Texas A&M University-Commerce, Texas A&M University-Kingsville, Texas Woman's University, West Texas A&M University.
Membership Requirements:
Approval by faculty representatives of member universities.

MASSACHUSETTS STATE COLLEGE ATHLETIC CONFERENCE
BRIDGEWATER STATE COLLEGE
131 SUMMER STREET
TINSLEY CENTER
BRIDGEWATER, MA 02325
508-531-1000
Fax: 508-531-1356
www.bridgew.edu
• Michele Wakin, Executive Assistant to the President
(508) 531-1793
mwakin@bridgew.edu
• Sue Chapman, Assistant Commissioner
• Tim Shea, Vice President
• Carey Williams-Eggen, Media Relations/Web Site Director
Year Founded:
1971
Description:
Sponsors intercollegiate athletic competition in baseball, basketball, cross country, football, ice hockey, soccer, track (men) and basketball, cross country, field hockey, soccer, softball, track, volleyball (women).
Member Schools:
Bridgewater State, Fitchburg State, Framingham State, Massachusetts College, Massachusetts Maritime, Salem State, Westfield State, Worcester State.
Member Services:
Rules interpretation and establishment; conference championships; post-season tournaments.

METRO ATLANTIC ATHLETIC CONFERENCE
712 AMBOY AVENUE
EDISON, NJ 8837
732-738-5455
Fax: 732-738-8310
www.maacsports.com
• Richard J Ensor, Commissioner
(732) 738-5455
• Rob DeVita, Assistant Commissioner for New Media
(721) 738-5455
• Jessica Hegmann, Senior Associate Commissioner
• Jordan Confessore, Asst. Commissioner of Championships
Year Founded:
1980
Description:
Sports include men's basketball, women's basketball, baseball, men's and women's crew, men's and women's golf plus men's and women's cross country, men's and women's indoor & outdoor track, men's and women's lacrosse, men's and women's soccer, softball, men's and women's tennis, men's and women's swimming, women's volleyball.
Member Schools:
Canisius College, Fairfield University, Iona College, Loyola College, Manhattan College, Marist College, Niagara University, Rider University, Saint Peter's College, Siena College, Duquesne University, La Salle University, Le Moyne College, Mount St. Mary's University, Providence College, Saint Joseph's University, Virginia Military Institute, Wagner College, St. Francis College, Villanova University.
Membership Requirements:
NCAA Division I.
Corporate Sponsors:
Pepsi, Verizon Wireless, Fye, Fidelis Care, Anaconda Sports, I Love NY Tourism, New York State Lottery, JetBlue Airways, Verizon Yellow Pages, Aeropostale, Coach USA, Fox 40, Gatorade, Sirius Satellite Radio, Broadway Marketing Ltd.

MICHIGAN INTERCOLLEGIATE ATHLETIC ASSOCIATION
29488 WOODWARD AVE
SUITE 308
ROYAL OAK, MI 48073
248-336-1677
Fax: 248-547-3445
miaacommish@ameritech.net
www.miaa.org
• David Neilson, Commissioner
(248) 336-1677
• Greg Chandler, Publicist
(616) 392-8434
Year Founded:
1888
Description:
NCAA DIII Athletic Conference- The Nation's Oldest Collegiate Athletic Conference.
Member Schools:
Adrian College, Albion College, Alma College, Calvin College, Hope College, Kalamazoo College, Olivet College, Saint Mary's (IN) College, Trine University (IN)
Membership Requirements:
NCAA Division III affiliation, endorsement of the NCAA Division III mission statement and adherence to NCAA Division III rules and regulations.

Publications:
MIAA FACT FINDER.

MID-AMERICA INTERCOLLEGIATE ATHLETICS ASSOCIATION
114 W 11TH STREET
SUITE 105
KANSAS CITY, MO 64105
816-421-6422
www.themiaa.com/athletics
• Mike Racy, Commissioner
mracy@themiaa.com
• Larry House, Asst Commissioner
Championships/Business Dev
(816) 421-6422
lhouse@themiaa.com
• Josh Slaughter, Communications Director
(816) 421-6422
jslaughter@themiaa.com
Year Founded:
1912
Description:
Conducts conference championships in eight men's and eight women's sports. Men's championships include football, cross country, basketball, indoor and outdoor track and field, baseball, tennis, and golf. Women's champions are determined in volleyball, soccer, cross country, basketball, indoor and outdoor track and field, softball and tennis.
Member Schools:
Central Missouri State University, Emporia State University, Missouri Southern State University, Missouri Western State University, Northwest Missouri State University, Pittsburg State University, Southwest Baptist University, Truman State University, Washburn University.

MID-AMERICAN ATHLETIC CONFERENCE
24 PUBLIC SQUARE
15TH FLOOR
CLEVELAND, OH 44113-2213
216-566-4622
Fax: 216-696-2622
www.mac-sports.com
• Jon Steinbrecher, Commissioner
• Bob Gennarelli, Senior Associate Commissioner/COO
(216) 566-4622
• Korinth Patterson, Director of Compliance/Championships
(216) 566-4622
• Betty Sislak, Finance Director
(216) 566-4622
• Erin Dugan, Assoc Director Media Relations & External Aff
(216) 566-4622
• Jeremy Guy, Communications Director
(216) 566-4622
Year Founded:
1946
Nature of Sports Service:
For men, championships are sponsored in football, basketball, baseball, cross country, soccer, swimming and diving, indoor track and field, outdoor track and field, wrestling, golf and tennis. For women, championships are sponsored in basketball, softball, volleyball, cross country, field hockey, golf, soccer, swimming and diving, gymnastics, indoor track and field, outdoor track and tennis.
Member Schools:
University of Akron, Ball State University,

Bowling Green State University, Central Michigan University, University at Buffalo, Kent State University, Miami University, Ohio University
Membership Requirements:
Invitation only.
Publications:
Annual football, basketball, volleyball, baseball and softball media guides and annual records book for all other sports.

MID-CENTRAL COLLEGE CONFERENCE
INDIANA WESLEYAN UNIVERSITY
4201 S. WASHINGTON STREET
MARION, IN 46953
765-677-2318
Fax: 765-677-2328
mfratzke@indwes.edu
www.mid-centralconf.org
• Kyle Schmidt, Sports Information
(765) 677-1938
• J.D. Collins, Commissioner
(765) 748-1776
• Eric Smith, Sports Information Director
(765) 998-4569
• Karen Roorbach, Registar
• Gabriel Wallis, Sports Information Director/Webmaster
stats@thenccaa.org
Nature of Sports Service:
The purpose and function is to promote intercollegiate athletics in a well-rounded athletic program, maintain high ideas and promote sportsmanship. The members are encouraged to stress the supporting role of athletics in the total education process and keep athletics in proper prospective.
Member Schools:
Bethel College, Goshen College, Grace College, Huntington University, Indiana Wesleyan University, Marian College, Spring Arbor University, Taylor University, University of St. Francis.

MID-EASTERN ATHLETIC CONFERENCE
2730 ELLSMERE AVENUE
PO BOX 10247
NORFOLK, VA 23513
757-951-2055
Fax: 757-951-2076
www.meacsports.com
• Dennis Thomas, Commissioner
thomasd@themeac.com
• Raynoid Dedeaux, Assistant Commissioner of Championships
dedeauxr@themeac.com
• Sonja O. Stills, Associate Commissioner for Administration
stillss@themeac.com
• Ryan McGuinty, Assistant Commissioner for Media Relations
mcgintyr@themeac.com
Year Founded:
1970
Description:
Made up of 11 outstanding historically black institutions across Atlanta Coastline.
Member Schools:
Bethune-Cookman College, Coppin State University, Delaware State University, Florida A&M University, Hampton University, Howard University, University of Maryland-Eastern Shore, Morgan State University, Norfolk State University, North Carolina A&T State University, South Carolina State University.
Member Services:

Weekly statistics, results, standings and releases; newsletter.
Corporate Sponsors:
Coke, Delta, Nike, Russell Athletic, State Farm.

MID-SOUTH CONFERENCE
401 W. MAIN STREET
SUITE 2200
LOUISVILLE, KY 40202
502-587-7767
Fax: 502-587-6767
www.mid-southconference.org
• Steve Baker, Commissioner
(502) 587-7767
• Chris Wells, Sports Information Director
(270) 384-8071
wellsc@lindsey.edu
• Mark Mulloy, Sports Information/Media Relations
• Gene Lovel, Eligibility Chair
Year Founded:
1995
Description:
The conference is unique in its broad based athletic competition for men and women, offering championships in 15 sports. The presidents of each school serves on the Board of Directors which directly oversees the conference and the office of the commissioner. This administrative hands on role of each school's president is unique among athletic conferences and ensures a proper balance in the academic pursuits of student athletes.
Number of Members:
13
Member Schools:
Campbellsville University, University of the Cumberlands, Georgetown College, Lindsey Wilson College, Pikeville College, University of Rio Grande, St. Catharine College, Shawnee State University, University of Virginia at Wise, West Virginia University Institute of Technology. Affiliate Member Schools- Belhaven College, Bethel University, Cumberland University, Faulkner University, Kentucky Christian University, Shorter College, and Union College.

MIDDLE ATLANTIC STATES COLLEGIATE ATHLETIC CORPORATION
LEBANON VALLEY COLLEGE
101 N. COLLEGE AVENUE
ANNVILLE, PA 17003-0501
717-867-6395
Fax: 717-867-5008
andrews@lvc.edu
www.gomacsports.com
• Ken Andrews, Executive Director
(717) 645-9809
andrews@lvc.edu
• Marie Stroman, Coordinator of MAC 100
(717) 645-9786
stroman@lvc.edu
• Patrick Ross, Director of Media Relations
(570) 854-1137
ross@lvc.edu
• Tim Flynn, Sports Information Director
(717) 867-6033
flynn@lvc.edu
• Erin Kolacek, Athletic Trainer
(717) 867-6269
kolacek@lvc.edu
Year Founded:
1912
Description:

Formerly called the Middle Atlantic States Collegiate Athletic Conference, it was originated 1912 as a loose confederation of colleges. It was unified into an actual all-sports playing conference in 1952, and is the largest Division III Conference holding NCAA associate membership.
Member Schools:
Albright College, Delaware Valley College, Drew University, Elizabethtown College, Fairleigh-Dickinson College at Fordham, Juniata College, King's College, Lebanon Valley College, Lycoming College, Messiah College, Moravian College, University of Scranton, Susquehanna University, Widener University, Wilkes University.
Publications:
FACT BOOK, annual.

MIDLANDS COLLEGIATE ATHLETIC CONFERENCE
C/O AL WALLER, COMMISSIONER
COLLEGE OF THE OZARKS
PO BOX 17
POINT LOOKOUT, MO 65726-0017
417-334-6411 EXT 4568
• Steve Eckman, President
• Al Waller,
Commissioner/Secretary/Treasurer
(417) 690-2568
• Jerod Dahlgren, Information Director
(716) 775-6747
• Hal Hoxie, President
(620) 241-0723
• Joyce Pigge, Eligibility Chair
(785) 227-3380
Description:
The main objective is to promote the development of athletic programs as an integral part of the educational offerings of member institutions by means of democratic participation at the conference level.
Member Schools:
Bellevue University, Central Christian College of Saint Mary, College of the Ozarks, Haskell University, Newman University, Oklahoma Wesleyan University, Park University, Peru State College, York College.
Membership Requirements:
Colleges in the states of Kansas, Missouri, Nebraska and Oklahoma which offers a minimum of four years of academic work, awards the bachelor's degree, are active members of the National Association of Intercollegiate Athletics and are accredited by the North Central Association of Colleges and Secondary Schools. Members have compatible purposes and histories as private, liberal arts institution of high learning.

MIDWEST CONFERENCE
C/O CHRIS GRAHAM, COMMISSIONER
RIPON COLLEGE
300 SEWARD STREET
RIPON, WI 54971
920-748-8157
Fax: 920-748-8158
www.midwestconference.org
• Chris Graham, Commissioner
• Cory Weibel, Sports Information Director
Year Founded:
1921
Description:
Sponsors intercollegiate athletics in baseball, basketball, cross country, football, golf, soccer, swimming, tennis, indoor and outdoor track, wrestling for men; basketball, cross country, indoor and outdoor track, soccer, softball, swimming, tennis, volleyball for women.
Number of Members;
10
Member Schools:
Beloit College, Carroll College, Grinnell College, Illinois College, Knox College, Lake Forest College, Lawrence University, Monmouth College, Ripon College, St. Norbert College.

MINNESOTA INTERCOLLEGIATE ATHLETIC CONFERENCE
475 CLEVELAND AVENUE NORTH
SUITE 307
SAINT PAUL, MN 55104
651-644-3965
Fax: 651-647-6422
dpmckane@miacathletics.com
www.miacathletics.com
• Dan McKane, Executive Director
(651) 644-3964
dpmckane@miacathletics.com
• Matt Higgins, Assistant to the Executive Director
(651) 644-3965
Year Founded:
1920
Description:
Sponsors championships in 22 sports; 11 for men and 11 for women. Conference teams are all affiliated with the NCAA Division III and the MIAC is recognized as one of the toughest NCAA Division III intercollegiate athletic conferences in the country.
Number of Members:
13
Member Schools:
Augsburg College, Bethel University, Carleton College, Concordia Moorhead College, Gustavus Adolphus College, Hamline University, Macalester College, College of St. Benedict, College of St. Catherine, St. John's University, St. Mary's University, St. Olaf College, University of St. Thomas.

MISSOURI VALLEY CONFERENCE
1818 CHOUTEAU AVENUE
ST. LOUIS, MO 63103
314-444-4300
Fax: 314-421-3505
kern@mvc.org
www.mvc.org
• Doug Elgin, Commissioner
(314) 444-4324
elgin@mvc.org
• Patty Viverito, Senior Associate Commissioner
(314) 444-4343
pattyv@mvc.org
• Jack R. Watkins, Associate Commissioner
• Greg Walter, Assistant Commissioner for Institutional Serv
• Mike Kern, Associate Commissioner Communications
(314) 444-4356
kern@mvc.org
Year Founded:
1907
Description:
Promotes the proper role of intercollegiate athletics in education. Encourages high standards of competitive performance and promotes good sportsmanship among individuals and institutions.
Member Schools:
Bradley University, Creighton University, Drake University, University of Evansville, Indiana State University, Illinois State University, Missouri State University, University of Northern Iowa, Southern Illinois University, Wichita State University.
Membership Requirements:
Division I in all sports. Institutions with complete faculty control of athletics.
Publications:
CENTENNIAL BOOK, SOFTBALL MEDIA GUIDE, BASEBALL MEDIA GUIDE, SOCCER MEDIA GUIDE, VOLLEYBALL MEDIA GUIDE, WOMEN'S BASKETBALL GUIDE, MEN'S BASKETBALL GUIDE, MVC TOURNAMENT PROGRAM.

MISSOURI VALLEY FOOTBALL CONFERENCE
1818 CHOUTEAU AVENUE
ST. LOUIS, MO 63103
314-444-4360
Fax: 314-444-4361
pattyv@mvc.org
www.valley-football.org

MOUNTAIN WEST CONFERENCE
15455 GLENEAGLE DRIVE
SUITE 200
COLORADO SPRINGS, CO 80921-2591
719-488—4040
Fax: 719-487-7240
www.themwc.com
• Craig Thompson, Commissioner
(719) 488-4047
• Bret Gilliland, Deputy Commissioner
(719) 488-4045
bgilliland@themwc.com
• Jaime Hixson, Assistant Commisioner
(719) 488-4049
jhixson@themwc.com
• Jim Andrus, Assoc. Commissioner Business/Finance
(719) 488-4020
jandrus@themwc.com
Year Founded:
1999
Description:
Committed to excellence in intercollegiate athletics, while promoting the academic missions of its member institutions. Progressive in its approach, the MWC continues to cultivate opportunities for student-athletes to compete at the highest level, while fostering academic achievement and sportsmanship. Now in its seventh year, the MWC has been assertive in its involvement with the NCAA governance structure and has taken a leadership role in the overall administration of intercollegiate athletics.
Member Schools:
U.S. Air Force Academy, Brigham Young University, Colorado State University, University of New Mexico, University of Nevada-Las Vegas, San Diego State University, University of Utah, University of Wyoming, Texas Christian University.

NEW ENGLAND FOOTBALL CONFERENCE
C/O SUE LAUDER, COMMISSIONER
FITCHBURG STATE COLLEGE

160 PEARL STREET
FITCHBURG, MA 01420
• John Harper, Commissioner
(508) 954-0621
thenefc8@gmail.com
• Roger Crosley, Publicity Director
(603) 606-1134
nefc_14@hotmail.com
Year Founded:
1965
Description:
Sponsors intercollegiate football competition.
Number of Members:
16
Member Schools:
Bridgewater State College, Curry College, Endicott College, Fitchburg State College, Framingham State College, Maine Maritime Academy, Massachusetts Maritime Academy, MIT, Nichols College, Plymouth State University, UMass Dartmouth, United States Coast Guard Academy, Salve Regina University, Western New England College, Westfield State College, Worcester State College.

NEW JERSEY ATHLETIC CONFERENCE
528 ALCYON BOULEVARD
PITMAN, NJ 08071
856-582-3679
Fax: 856-582-5877
www.njacsports.com
• Terry Small, Commissioner
(856) 582-3679
tsmall@njacsports.com
• Michelle Serabian, Assistant Commissioner
(609) 709-4291
mserabian@njacsports.com
Year Founded:
1985
Description:
Championships were originally offered in twelve sports: men's and women's basketball, baseball, softball, women's volleyball, men's golf, men's and women's tennis, men's and women's swimming and diving, wrestling and football. Today, the NJAC hosts seventeen championships: nine for women (cross country, basketball, field hockey, soccer, softball, tennis, indoor track and field, outdoor track and field, volleyball) and seven for men (cross country, baseball, basketball, football, soccer, indoor track and field, outdoor track and field).
Member Schools:
Kean University, Montclair State University, New Jersey City University, Ramapo College, Richard Stockton College, Rowan University, Rutgers-Camden, Rutgers-Newark, College of New Jersey, William Patterson University, SUNY Cortland, Western Connecticut State University.

NEW YORK COLLEGIATE ATHLETIC CONFERENCE
733 THIRD AVENUE
SUITE 1910
NEW YORK, NY 10017
212-682-6318
Fax: 212-286-1243
gonycac@nycac.net
www.nycac.net
• Edward Manetta, Commissioner
• Billi Godsey, Assoc. Commissioner of

Operations
• Bob Hartwell, President
• Jerry Milani, Assoc. Commissioner Media Relations
• Gerry Oswald, Treasurer
Description:
Commited to the highest standards of scholarship, sportsmanship, teamwork, and citizenship. Its mission is to promote the total person concept in its student-athletes which stresses the abilities to excel in academic achievement, athletic competition, and positive character traits.
Member Schools:
Adelphi University, Concordia College, Dowling College, Mercy College, Molloy College, L.I.U.-CW Post College, Queens College, University of Bridgeport, University of New Haven, St. Thomas Aquinas, New York Institute of Technology.

NORTH CENTRAL INTERCOLLEGIATE ATHLETIC CONFERENCE
RAMKOTA INN
3200 W. MAPLE
SIOUX FALLS, SD 57107
605-338-0907
Fax: 605-338-1889
• Roger Thomas, Commissioner
• Melanie Nelson, Interim Commissioner
melanie@northcentralconference.org
• Jon Martin, Assistant Commissioner
info@northcentralconference.org
• Colin Kapitan, Officials Coordinator
Year Founded:
1921
Description:
Promotes intercollegiate athletics and conducts men's championships in football, basketball, baseball, outdoor track, indoor track, cross country, wrestling, swimming, golf, tennis. Conducts women's championships in basketball, cross country, golf, indoor track, outdoor track, softball, swimming, tennis and volleyball.
Number of Members:
7
Member Schools:
Augustana College, University of Minnesota-Duluth, Minnesota State University-Mankato, University of Nebraska-Omaha, University of South Dakota, St. Cloud State University, University of North Dakota.

NORTH COAST ATHLETIC CONFERENCE
815 CROCKER ROAD
BUILDING B, SUITE 5
WESTLAKE, OH 44145
440-871-8100
Fax: 440-871-4221
www.northcoast.org
• Marvin Krislov, President
(330) 569-5120
marvin.krislov@hiram.edu
• Rock Jones, Vice President
(440) 871-8100
Year Founded:
1983
Description:
Dedicated to fostering a complementary relationship between intercollegiate athletics and the pursuit of academic excellence. Consisting of 10 academically selective colleges and universities in Ohio, Indiana and Pennsylvania.
Member Schools:

Allegheny College, Denison University, Earlham College, Hiram College, Kenyon College, Oberlin College, Ohio Wesleyan University, Wabash College, Wittenberg University, College of Wooster.

NORTHEAST CONFERENCE
399 CAMPUS DRIVE
SOMERSET, NJ 8873
732-469-0440
Fax: 732-469-0744
rbalut@northeastconference.org
www.northeastconference.org
• Noreen Morris, Commissioner
nmorris@northeastconference.org
• Ralph Ventre, Assistant Director of Communications
rventre@northeastconference.org
• Benjamin Shove, Sports Services Director
bshove@northeastconference.org
• Michelle Boone, Assistant Commissioner
mboone@northeastconference.org
• Rachelle Held, Assistant Commissioner of Compliance
rheld@northeastconference.org
Year Founded:
1981
Description:
A 21 sport conference committed to enhancing the experience of its student-athletes, while strengthening its competitive position both regionally and nationally.
Number of Members:
11
Member Schools:
Central Connecticut State Univ., Fairleigh Dickinson Univ., Long Island Univ., UMBC, Monmouth Univ., Mount St. Mary's College, Quinnipiac Univ., Robert Morris Univ., Sacred Heart Univ., St. Francis (NY) College, St. Francis (PA) Univ., Wagner College.

NORTHEAST-10 CONFERENCE
792 SOUTH MAIN STREET
SUITE 104
MANSFIELD, MA 02048
508-230-9845
www.northeast10.org
• Julie Ruppert, Commissioner
(508) 230-9844
jruppert@northeast10.org
• Kerri Fagan, Assoc. Commissioner For Sports Admin
(508) 230-9844
kfagan@northeast10.org
• Molly Belden, Associate Commissioner For Compliance
(508) 230-9844
mmyers@northeast10.org
Year Founded:
1979
Description:
Men's basketball & baseball, soccer, cross country, football, golf, lacrosse, tennis. Women's basketball, field hockey, volleyball, cross country, softball, tennis, soccer. Men's and Women's indoor & outdoor track & field.
Member Schools:
American International College, Assumption College, Bentley University, Bryant University, Franklin Pierce College, Le Moyne College, Merrimack College, Pace University, Saint Anselm College, College of Saint Rose, Saint Michaels's College, Southern Connecticut State University,

Southern New Hampshire University, Stonehill College, UMass Lowell University
Publications:
Basketball tournament program; conference record book and directory; weekly statistical release.

NORTHERN ILLINOIS-IOWA CONFERENCE
C/O CHRIS COOK
EUREKA COLLEGE
300 E. COLLEGE AVENUE
EUREKA, IL 61530
309-467-6377
www.eureka.edu/athletics/directory
• Steve Thompson, Director Of Athletics
• Cory McCain, Asst. To The Athletics Director
(309) 467-6456
Year Founded:
1969
Description:
Offers conference competition in soccer, cross country, basketball, baseball, golf, tennis for men, and volleyball, tennis, basketball and softball for women. Selects annual all-scholastic team for athletes who excel in the classroom and on the field.
Number of Members:
6
Member Schools:
Aurora University, Benedictine University, Clarke College, Concordia University, Eureka College, Rockford College.

NORTHERN SUN INTERCOLLEGIATE CONFERENCE
2999 COUNTY ROAD 42 W
SUITE 136
BURNSVILLE, MN 55306
952-500-8052
Fax: 952-378-1694
media@northernsun.org
www.northernsun.org
• Erin Lind, Commissioner
lind@northernsun.org
• Michelle Beck, Asst. Commissioner For External Relations
beck@northernsun.org
• Nick Kornder, Asst. Commissioner For Media Relations
kornder@northernsun.org
• Melissa Sewick, Asst. Commissioner For Compliance
sewick@northernsun.org
Year Founded:
1932
Description:
Sponsors intercollegiate competition in baseball, basketball, cross country, tennis, football, golf, indoor and outdoor track, wrestling.
Number of Members:
8
Member Schools:
Bemidji State University, Concordia University-St. Paul, University of Minnesota-Crookston, Minnesota State University-Moorhead, Northern State University, Southwest Minnesota State, Wayne State College, Winona State.

NORTHWEST CONFERENCE
9594 1ST AVENUE NE
SUITE 332
SEATTLE, WA 98115
206-432-9531
Fax: 541-388-1943
information@nwcsports.com
www.nwcsports.com
• Wendy Guthrie, Interim Commissioner
(206) 432-9531
guthrie@nwcsports.com
• Kimberly Wenger, Commissioner
(503) 352-2173
wenger@nwcsports.com
• Christopher Brown, Assistant Commissioner
(208) 861-9465
Year Founded:
1926
Nature of Sports Service:
Organization is a collegiate athletic conference. Sports include baseball, basketball, cross country, golf, soccer, softball, swimming, tennis, track, volleyball.
Number of Members:
9
Member Schools:
George Fox University, Lewis & Clark College, Linfield College, Pacific University, Pacific Lutheran University, University of Puget Sound, Whitman College, Whitworth College, Willamette University.
Membership Requirements:
Private colleges in the Northwest with comprehensive athletic programs.

OHIO ATHLETIC CONFERENCE
4990 MAHONING AVE
SUITE C
PO BOX 4656
AUSTINTOWN, OH 44515
330-259-9090
Fax: 330-259-9091
www.oac.org
• Tim Gleason, Commissioner
• Larry Shank, President of OAC Athletic Council
• Tom Simmons, VP Of OAC Athletic Council
Year Founded:
1902
Description:
Regulates men's and women's intercollegiate athletics, establishes and enforces rules and regulations to maintain the proper balance between athletics and academics, sponsors championship competitions.
Number of Members:
10
Member Schools:
Baldwin-Wallace College, Capital University, Heidelberg College, John Carroll University, Marietta College, Mount Union College, Muskingum College, Ohio Northern University, Otterbein College, Wilmington College.
Membership Requirements:
Invitation only. Must be approved by existing membership, two-thirds vote.

OHIO VALLEY CONFERENCE
215 CENTERVIEW DRIVE
SUITE 115
BRENTWOOD, TN 37027
615-371-1698
Fax: 615-371-1788
information@ovc.org
www.ovcsports.com
• DeBauche Beth, Commissioner
(Ext) 6682

• Kate Barnett, Asst. Commissioner For Championships
(Ext) 6692
kbarnett@ovc.org
• Kyle Schwartz, Assistant Commissioner for Strategic Communication
• Brian Pulley, Assistant Commissioner for External Affairs
Year Founded:
1948
Description:
Sponsors the following sports: baseball, basketball, cross country, football, golf, tennis and track for men, and basketball, cross country, golf, soccer, softball, tennis, track and volleyball for women. In addition, the OVC also sponsors the combined men's and women's sport of rifle.
Number of Members:
11
Member Schools:
Austin Peay State University, Eastern Illinois University, Eastern Kentucky University, Jacksonville State University, Morehead State University, Murray State University, Samford University, Southeast Missouri State University, University of Tennessee-Martin, Tennessee State University, Tennessee Technological University.
Publications:
OVC HANDBOOK; Football, Basketball and Volleyball Media Guides; Weekly press releases (Aug-May).
Corporate Sponsors:
O'Reilly Auto Parts, HCA's TriStar Family of Hospitals, Aeropostale, Sirius Radio, Tachikara, Brine, Holiday Inn Brentwood, Schutt Sports, Big Idea.

OLD DOMINION ATHLETIC CONFERENCE
402-B IDAHO STREET
SALEM, VA 24153
540-387-9073
Fax: 540-389-6196
brad@odaconline.com
www.odaconline.com
• JJ Nekoloff, Commissioner
(540) 389-7373
jnekoloff@odaconline.com
• Chris Kilcoyne, Sports Information Director
• R. Carey Harveycutter, Civic Facilities Director
• Curt Kendall, President
ckendall@bridgewater.edu
• Molly Robertson, Assistant to Commissioner/Championships Direc
(540) 389-7373
mollie@odaconline.com
Year Founded:
1975
Description:
Entering its 30th year, the Old Dominion Athletic Conference (ODAC) is one of the nation's largest Division III conferences. The 14-member ODAC, including Catholic's associate status, stands as the second-largest multi-sport NCAA Division III conference in the country behind the 15-member American Southwest Conference in Texas.
Number of Members:
14
Member Schools:
Bridgewater College, Catholic University, Eastern Mennonite University, Emory & Henry College, Guilford College,

Hampden-Sydney College, Hollins University, Lynchburg College, Randolph-Macon College, Randolph-Macon Woman's College, Roanoke College, Sweet Briar College, Virginia Wesleyan College, Washington and Lee University.
Membership Requirements:
NCAA Div III, Private institutions.
Publications:
Weekly statistical reports. Annual information guide and directory, sport media guide.

PACIFIC WEST CONFERENCE
1777 ALA MOANA BLVD
SUITE 223
HONOLULU, HI 96815
808-285-5537
Fax: 808-922-4225
www.thepacwest.com
• Bob Hogue, Commissioner
• Jane Teixeria, Assistant Commissioner, Compliance
janeteixeira@thepacwest.com
• Jimmy Knodel, Director Of Strategic Positioning
(480) 983-6605
jimmyknodel@thepacwest.com
• Wayne Coito, Multimedia Specialist
waynecoito@thepacwest.com
Description:
An intercollegiate college athletic conference affiliated with NCAA Division II. Formed in 1992 when the Great Northwest Conference (a men's conference) merged with the Continental Divide Conference (a women's conference containing some of the same members, in response to several member-departures and new NCA legislation requiring conferences to have at least six members.
Number of Members:
4
Member Schools:
Brigham Young University, Chaminade University, University of Hawaii, Hawaii Pacific University.

PACIFIC-10 CONFERENCE
800 S. BROADWAY
SUITE 400
WALNUT CREEK, CA 94596
925-932-4411
Fax: 925-932-4601
www.pac-10.org
• Thomas Hansen, Commissioner
• Christine Hoyles, Asst. Commissioner Championships/Admin.
• James Muldoon, Asst. Commissioner of Public Relations
• Duane Lindberg, Asst. Commissioner Electronic Commun.
• Mike Matthews, Asst. Commissioner Compliance
• Ben Jay, Asst. Commissioner Business/Finance
• Tammy Newman, Governance/Enforcement Asst. Director
• David Hirsh, Public Relations Assistant Director
• Kevin Anderson, Championships Assistant Director
Year Founded:
1916
Nature of Sports Service:
Sponsors 11 men's sports and 11 women's sports. Additionally, the Conference is a

member of the Mountain Pacific Sports Federation (MPSF) in four other men's sports and two other women's sports.
Number of Members:
10
Member Schools:
Arizona State University, University of Arizona, University of Cal-Berkeley, UCLA, University of Oregon, Oregon State University, University of Southern California, Stanford University, University of Washington, Washington State University.
Corporate Sponsors:
Satellite Radio, Pontiac, Cooper Tires, 7-UP, US Bank, Pacific Life, Gatorade, State Farm Insurance.

PATRIOT LEAGUE
3773 CORPORATE PARKWAY
SUITE 190
CENTER VALLEY, PA 18034
610-289-1950
Fax: 610-289-1951
www.patriotleague.com
• Jennifer Heppel, Commissioner
(610) 289-1950
• Deb Herman, Executive Assistant And Business Manager
• Richard Wanniger, Sr. Assoc. Commissioner For External Relations
• Ginger Fulton, Sr. Assoc. Commissioner
Year Founded:
1986
Description:
A unique collection of highly selective colleges and universities linked by a number of common values. Our institutions are relatively small in size and are focused on providing the highest quality education to our undergraduate students.
Number of Members:
9
Member Schools:
American University, Bucknell University, Colgate University, Lafayette College, Lehigh College, U.S. Military Academy, U.S. Naval Academy, Fordham University, Georgetown University.

PEACH BELT ATHLETIC CONFERENCE
503 BLACKBURN DRIVE
MARTINEZ, GA 30907
706-860-8499
Fax: 706-650-8113
www.peachbelt.com
• David Brunk, Commissioner
• Diana Kling, Assistant Commissioner for Internal Operation
• Ken Gerlinger, Assistant Commissioner for Communications
• Carl Segura, Director of External Operations
Year Founded:
1991
Description:
Committed to providing through its dependent collegiate members, a forum for student participation in athletic, academic and co-curricular events under the auspices of the National Collegiate Athletic Association, Division II. Sponsors men's baseball, basketball, cross country, golf, soccer, tennis, women's basketball, cross country, soccer, tennis and volleyball.
Member Schools:
Armstrong Atlantic State University, Augusta State University, Clayton State University,

Columbus State University, Francis Marion University, Georgia College & State University, University of North Carolina-Pembroke, North Georgia College & State University, University of South Carolina-Aiken, University of South Carolina-Upstate.

PENNSYLVANIA STATE ATHLETIC CONFERENCE
LOCK HAVEN UNIVERSITY
206 ANNEX BUILDING
LOCK HAVEN, PA 17745
570-893-2780
Fax: 570-893-2206
wadair@lhup.edu
www.psacsports.org
• Carley McCool, Director of Strategic Communication & New Med
(570) 484-2884
• Steve Murray, Commissioner
(570) 893-2512
• Will Adair, Associate Commissioner
(570) 484-2780
• Carlin Chesick, Associate Commissioner
(570) 484-2512
cchesick@psacsports.org
Year Founded:
1951
Description:
Sponsors intercollegiate competition in baseball, basketball, cross country, field hockey, football, men's golf, women's lacrosse, soccer, softball, swimming, tennis, track, women's volleyball, wrestling.
Number of Members:
14
Member Schools:
Bloomburg University of Pennsylvania, California University of Pennsylvania, Cheyney University of Pennsylvania, Clarion University, East Stroudsburg University of Pennsylvania, Edinboro University of Pennsylvania, Indiana University of Pennsylvania, Kutztown University, Lock Haven University, Mansfield University, Millersville University, Shippensburg University, Slippery Rock University, West Chester University.
Publications:
PSAC Handbook.

PRESIDENTS' ATHLETIC CONFERENCE
8500 BROOKTREE ROAD
SUITE 130
WEXFORD, PA 15090
724-933-4630
Fax: 724-933-4635
www.pacathletics.org
• Joe Onderko, Commissioner
• Kevin Fenstermacher, Assistant Commissioner / Director of Communic
(724) 456-7897
fenstermacher@pacathletics.org
Year Founded:
1955
Description:
Schools are located in Western Pennsylvania, West Virginia and Kentucky. Members in scheduling outside the conference will seek schools which most nearly follow the principles of the Presidents' Athletic Conference.
Number of Members:
7
Member Schools:
Bethany College, Grove City College, Thiel

college sports

College, Thomas More College, Washington & Jefferson College, Waynesburg College, Westminster College.

RED RIVER ATHLETIC CONFERENCE
100 N. 6TH STREET
SUITE 201
WACO, TX 76701
254-755-8170
www.redriverconference.com
• Tony Stigliano, Commissioner
(254) 744-8542
tonystig@aol.com
• Ann Stigliano, Secretary
(254) 755-8170
stigann@aol.com
• Larry Earvin, President
(512) 505-3001
llearvin@htu.edu
Description:
Sponsored sports include; Men's basketball, baseball, cross country, track & field, soccer, women's cross country, track & field, softball and volleyball.
Number of Members:
13
Member Schools:
Bacone College, College of the Southwest-New Mexico, Houston Baptist University, Houston-Tillotson University, Jarvis Christian College, Northwood University, Paul Quinn College, SW Assemblies of God University, Texas College, Texas A&M International University, Texas Wesleyan University, University of Texas of the Permian Basin, Wiley College.

ROCKY MOUNTAIN ATHLETIC CONFERENCE
1867 AUSTIN BLUFFS PARKWAY
SUITE 101
COLORADO SPRINGS, CO 80918
719-471-0066
Fax: 719-471-0088
www.rmacsports.org
• Chris Graham, Commissioner
cgraham@rmacsports.org
• Kirsten Ford, Assistant Commissioner
Year Founded:
1909
Description:
A premier NCAA Division II conference located in the states of Colorado, Kansas, Nebraska and New Mexico. The RMAC currently competes in 19 NCAA Division II sports and has earned 30 NCAA Division II national championships and 19 national runner-ups since 1992
Number of Members:
15
Member Schools:
Adams State Col., Chadron State Col., Colorado Christian, Colorado School of Mines, UC-Colorado Springs, Fort Hays State U., Fort Lewis Col., Metropolitan State College of Denver, Mesa State Col., U. of Nebraska-Kearney, New Mexico Highlands U., U. of Southern Colorado, Regis U., Western State Col.

SOONER ATHLETIC CONFERENCE
16200 SONOMA PARK DRIVE
EDMOND, OK 73013
405-848-1581
Fax: 405-840-4671

jhud@ionet.net
www.soonerathletic.org
• Stan Wagnon, Commissioner
stan.wagnon@gmail.com
• Justin Tinder, Information Director
(405) 878-2109
sacsportsinfo@gmail.com
Nature of Sports Service:
Intercollegiate athletic conference.
Number of Members:
10
Member Schools:
John Brown University (Ark), Lubbock Christian University, Northwestern Oklahoma State University, Oklahoma Baptist University, Oklahoma Christian University, Oklahoma City University, University of Science & Arts of Oklahoma, Southern Nazarene University, St. Gregory's University, Wayland Baptist University.

SOUTH ATLANTIC CONFERENCE
226 N. PARK DRIVE
GATEWAY PLAZA, SUITE 130
ROCK HILL, SC 29730
803-981-5240
Fax: 803-981-9444
www.thesac.com
• James T. Burch, Coordinator of Men's Basketball Officials
(919) 661-2751
jimtburch@aol.com
• Betsy Kidd, Coordinator of Softball Officials
(404) 786-0361
betsykidd@att.net
• Patrick Britz, Commissioner
(803) 981-5240
• Amanda Osburne, Asst. to Commissioner Internal Ops.
(803) 981-5240
• Eric Wieberg, Assistant Commissioner For Strategic Communic
(803) 981-5240
Year Founded:
1975
Description:
NCAA Div II conference, administers programs for basketball, baseball, cross country, football, golf, soccer, softball, tennis, volleyball.
Number of Members:
8
Member Schools:
Carson-Newman College, Catawba College, Lenoir-Rhyne College, Mars Hill College, Newberry College, Presbyterian College, Tusculum College, Wingate University.
Membership Requirements:
Must be approved by current members.
Publications:
Media Guides, Fall, Winter, Spring Annually.

SOUTHEASTERN CONFERENCE/SEC
2201 RICHARD ARRINGTON BOULEVARD
N. BIRMINGHAM, AL 35203
205-458-3000
Fax: 205-458-3031
www.secsports.com
• Greg Sankey, Commissioner
• Mark Womack, Executive Associate Commissioner
• Charlie Hussey, Associate Commissioner Sports Admin.
• Leslie Claybrook, Assistant Commissioner Championships

Year Founded:
1933
Description:
Administers intercollegiate athletics and encompasses athletics within the academic system.
Number of Members:
12
Member Schools:
University of Alabama, University of Arkansas, Auburn University, University of Florida, University of Georgia, University of Kentucky, Louisiana State University, University of Mississippi, Mississippi State University, University of South Carolina, University of Tennessee, Vanderbilt University.
Membership Requirements:
Must be accepted by the presidents of 3/4 of membership.
Publications:
Annual data books on baseball, basketball, football, gymnastics, soccer, volleyball. Weekly news releases on each sport (during the season).

SOUTHERN COLLEGIATE ATHLETIC CONFERENCE
2935 HORIZON PARK DR
SUWANEE, GA 30024-7229
678-546-3470
Fax: 770-495-9363
www.scacsports.com
• Stephen Argo, Commissioner
• Dwayne Hanberry, Sports Information Director
Year Founded:
1962
Description:
Sponsors conference championships in 19 sports, including nine for men and 10 for women. The SCAC currently hosts conference championships in baseball, men's basketball, women's basketball, men's cross country, women's cross country, field hockey, football, men's golf, women's golf, men's soccer, women's soccer, softball, men's swimming and diving, women's swimming and diving, men's tennis, women's tennis, men's outdoor track, women's outdoor track, and women's volleyball.
Number of Members:
10
Member Schools:
Centre College of Danville, DePauw University, Hendrix College of Conway, Millsaps College of Jackson, Oglethorpe University of Atlanta, Rhodes College of Memphis, Rose-Hulman Institute of Technology of Terre Haute, The University of the South of Sewanee, Southwestern University of Georgetown, Trinity University of San Antonio.

SOUTHERN CONFERENCE, THE
702 N. PINE STREET
SPARTANBURG, SC 29303
864-591-5100
Fax: 864-591-3448
www.soconsports.com
• John Iamarino, Commissioner
jiamarino@socon.org
• Jason Yaman, Assistant Commissioner for Media Relations
Year Founded:
1921

Description:
The Conference currently consists of members in four states throughout the Southeast and sponsors 19 varsity sports and championships that produce participants for NCAA Division I Championships.
Number of Members:
11
Member Schools:
Appalachian State University, College of Charleston, The Citadel, Davidson College, Elon University, Furman University, Georgia Southern University, University of North Carolina at Greensboro, University of Tennessee at Chattanooga, Western Carolina University, Wofford College.
Publications:
Football, basketball press guides; basketball tournament programs; women's basketball press guide.
Membership Requirements:
Must be active NCAA Division I member with acceptable admissions requirements and academic standards.

SOUTHERN INTERCOLLEGIATE ATHLETIC CONFERENCE
PEACHTREE CENTER-SOUTH TOWER
225 PEACHTREE STREET NE
SUITE 1975
ATLANTA, GA 30303
404-221-1041
Fax: 404-221-1042
www.thesiac.com
• Gregory Moore, Commissioner
(404) 221-1041
gmoore@thesiac.com
• Kelly Elliott, Asst. Commissioner For Compliance
(404) 221-1041
elliott@thesiac.com
• Britney R Reddick, Asst. Commissioner For New Media
(404) 221-1041
reddick@thesiac.com
Year Founded:
1913
Description:
The SIAC is a member of the National Collegiate Athletic Association (NCAA) and participates at the Division II level. On an annual basis, the SIAC sponsors six men's championships (baseball, basketball, cross country, football, outdoor track & field and tennis) and six women's championships (basketball, cross country, outdoor track & field, softball, tennis and volleyball).
Number of Members:
11
Member Schools:
Albany State University, Benedict College, Clark Atlanta University, Fort Valley State University, Kentucky State University, Lane College, LeMoyne-Owen College, Miles College, Morehouse College, Paine College, Tuskegee University.

SOUTHERN STATES ATHLETIC CONFERENCE
1364 BIRCH RIVER DR
DAHLONEGA, GA 30533
706-864-7060
Fax: 706-864-9342
www.ssacsports.com
• Kurt Patberg, Conference Consultant
(404) 434-5146

• Jonathan Wojciechowski, Interim/Assistant Commissioner
(770) 880-7839
jwojo411@yahoo.com
• Mike Hall, Commissioner
(864) 266-3621
mhall.ssac@gmail.com
• Sally Shouppe, Treasurer
(251) 442-2278
sshouppe@umobile.edu
• Katie Bright, Assistant Commissioner
(334) 300-8520
kbright.ssac@gmail.com
• Ron Melton, Eligibility Chairman
(912) 583-3238
rmelton@bpc.edu
Description:
NAIA Division I conference with schools and universities in Georgia, Alabama, South Carolina and Tennessee.
Member Schools:
Auburn University-Montgomery, Berry College, Brenau University, Brewton-Parker College, Columbia College, Emmanuel College, Faulkner University, Georgia Southwestern State University, Lee University, Reinhardt College, Shorter College, Southern Polytechnic State University, Southern Wesleyan University.

SOUTHLAND CONFERENCE
2600 NETWORK BLVD
SUITE 150
FRISCO, TX 75034
972-422-9500
Fax: 972-422-9225
tburnett@southland.org
www.southland.org
• Tom Burnett, Commissioner
tburnett@southland.org
• Bruce Ludlow, Assoc. Commissioner, Operations
• Jenny McGhee, Assoc. Commissioner, External Relations
(214) 350-7522
Year Founded:
1963
Description:
NCAA Division I Athletics
Number of Members:
12
Member Schools:
University of Central Arkansas, Lamar University, McNeese State University, Nicholls State University, Northwestern State University, Sam Houston State University, Southeastern Louisiana University, Stephen F. Austin State University, University of Texas at Arlington, University of Texas at San Antonio, Texas A&M University-Corpus Christi, Texas State University-San Marcos
Corporate Sponsors:
O'Reilly Auto Parts, State Farm Insurance, Hibernia Bank, Advantage Rent-a-Car, Aeropostale, BellSouth, American Airlines, Best Western, Sign-a-Rama, Jostens, Wilson Sporting Goods, Rawlings, Brine, Team Tachikara USA.
Publications:
ALL-SPORT RECORD BOOK.

SOUTHWESTERN ATHLETIC CONFERENCE
2101 6TH AVENUE N
SUITE 700
BIRMINGHAM, AL 35203

205-521-7573
Fax: 205-297-9820
www.swac.org
• Duer Sharp, Commissioner
• Edgar Gantt, Associate Commissioner
ext 3466
Year Founded:
1920
Description:
Organized exclusively for the purpose of encouraging, promoting, advancing, and conducting intercollegiate sports activities and other recreational and not-for-profit activities among the members of the Conference.
Number of Members:
10
Member Schools:
Alabama A&M University, Alabama State University, Alcorn State University, Grambling State University, Jackson State University, Mississippi Valley State University, Prairie View A&M University, Southern University and A&M University, Texas Southern University, University of Arkansas at Pine Bluff.
Corporate Sponsors:
Aeropostale, Burger King, Russell Athletic, Jostens, Alabama Power, Golden Flake, ESPN, Coca-Cola, City of Birmingham, Alabama, State Farm Insurance.

STATE UNIVERSITY OF NEW YORK ATHLETIC CONFERENCE
SUNY CORTLAND
PO BOX 2000
CORTLAND, NY 13045
607-753-2278
Fax: 607-753-2280
sunyac@fredonia.edu
• Tom Di Camillo, Commissioner
(607) 753-2279
sunyacsports@gmail.com
• Megan Cross, Assistant Commissioner
(607) 753-2277
info@sunyac.com
Year Founded:
1958
Description:
The conference members compete in 20 sports: nine for men and eleven for women.
Number of Members:
10
Member Schools:
SUNY Brockport, Buffalo State, SUNY Cortland, SUNY Fredonia, Geneseo, New Paltz, Oneonta, Oswego, Plattsburgh, Potsdam.
Membership Requirements:
Four year colleges and universities in the State University of New York system.

SUN BELT CONFERENCE
1500 SUGAR BOWL DRIVE
NEW ORLEANS, LA 70122
504-299-9066
Fax: 504-299-9067
www.sunbeltsports.org
• Bert Carter, Associate Commissioner/CFO
(504) 299-9066
• Karl Benson, Commissioner
(504) 556-0888
benson@sunbeltsports.org
• Kathy Keene, Sr. Associate Commissioner / COO
(504) 556-0887
keene@sunbeltsports.org

• Keith Nunez, Assistant Director of Communicaions
(504) 299-9066
nunez@sunbeltsports.org

Year Founded:
1976

Description:
Sponsors 19 sports; 9 for men and 10 for women. The men's sports include baseball, basketball, cross country, football, golf, tennis, indoor track and field, outdoor track and field and swimming and diving. The women's sports include basketball, cross country, golf, soccer, softball, swimming and diving, tennis, indoor and outdoor track and field, and volleyball.

Number of Members:
13

Member Schools:
Arkansas State University, Florida Atlantic University, Florida International University, University of Louisiana-Monroe, Middle Tennessee State, New Mexico State, University of Arkansas at Little Rock, University of Denver, University of New Orleans, University of North Texas, University of South Alabama, University of Louisiana - Lafayette, Western Kentucky University, and University of Denver.

Publications:
MEDIA GUIDES.

SUNSHINE STATE CONFERENCE
400 PARK AVENUE SOUTH
WINTER PARK, FL 32789
321-972-1803
Fax: 321-972-1805
www.sunshinestateconference.com
• Ed Pasque, Commissioner
• Maryanne Simkulak, Assistant Commissioner
• Robert Brennecke, Assistant Commissioner

Year Founded:
1975

Description:
Offers league championships in 14 intercollegiate sports. SSC institutions have won 4 NCAA titles in 2004-2005 and a total of 61 national championships in baseball, men's basketball

Number of Members:
9

Member Schools:
Barry University, Eckerd College, Florida Southern College, Florida Tech, Lynn University, Nova Southeastern University, Rollins College, Saint Leo University, University of Tampa.

THE MIDWEST COLLEGIATE CONFERENCE
C/O RAY SHOVLAIN
518 W. LOCUST STREET
DAVENPORT, IA 52803
563-333-6229
Fax: 563-333-6239
• Rick Sanders, Commissioner
(888) 430-7705
rick@midwest-classic.com
• Ray Shovlain, President
(563) 333-6229
shovlainraymondj@sau.edu
• Kent Henning, President
• Adam Glatczak, Sports Information Director

Year Founded:
1988

Description:
The MCC links eight private universities and colleges in an athletic affiliation featuring 13 varsity level sports for men and women. MCC sports compete in the National Association of Intercollegiate Athletics (NAIA), and routinely send qualifying teams and individuals to NAIA national tournaments.

Member Schools:
Ashford University, Grand View College, Iowa Wesleyan College, Mount Mercy College, St. Ambrose University, Viterbo University, Waldorf College, William Penn University.

TRANSOUTH ATHLETIC CONFERENCE
C/O E.L. HUTTON, COMMISSION
506 MELODY LANE
MEMPHIS, TN 38120
901-767-6194
gruff@trevecca.edu
• E.L. Hutton, Commissioner
• Tommy Sadler, President
(731) 661-5218
tsadler@uu.edu
• Mike McCutchen, Vice President
(731) 989-6901
mmccutchen@fhu.edu
• Nancy Bennett, Secretary
(731) 989-6913
nbennett@fhu.edu
• Gregory Ruff, Sports Information Director
(615) 248-1606
gruff@trevecca.edu

Year Founded:
1996

Nature of Sports Service:
The conference changed its name to TranSouth Athletic Conference prior to the 1996-97 school year. Conference members have fielded NAIA national champions in women's basketball, men's basketball, baseball, and wrestling.

Number of Members:
8

Member Schools:
Blue Mountain College, Crichton College, Cumberland University, Freed-Hardeman University, Lyon College, Martin Methodist College, Trevecca Nazarene University, Union University.

UNIVERSITY ATHLETIC ASSOCIATION
30 CORPORATE WOODS
SUITE 280
ROCHESTER, NY 14623
585-784-8442
Fax: 585-784-8309
www.uaasports.info
• Joel Seligman, President
• John Sexton, President
• Russ J Hamberger, Assistant Provost

Year Founded:
1986

Description:
Sponsors competition in 22 sports, twelve sports for men and ten sports for women - including football, soccer, cross country, volleyball, basketball, fencing, wrestling, swimming and diving, indoor track and field, baseball, softball, outdoor track and field, tennis, and golf.

Number of Members:
9

Member Schools:
Brandeis University, Carnegie Mellon University, Case Western Reserve University, Emory University, Johns Hopkins University, New York University, University of Chicago, University of Rochester, Washington University-St. Louis.

USA SOUTH CONFERENCE
C/O RITA WIGGS, COMMISSIONER
5400 RAMSEY STREET
FAYETTEVILLE, NC 28311
910-630-7326
Fax: 910-630-7622
admin@USASouth.net
www.usasouth.net
• Rita Wiggs, Commissioner
commish@usasouth.net
• Kendall Schram, President
• Mike Christie, Assistant Commissioner
(910) 630-7326
sid@usasouth.net

Year Founded:
1963

Nature of Sports Service:
The Conference is comprised of eight full member institutions located in the North Carolina and Virginia area. Sports include women's basketball, cross country, lacrosse, soccer, tennis, volleyball, men's baseball, basketball, cross country, football, golf, soccer and tennis.

Member Schools:
Averett University, Christopher Newport University, Ferrum College, Greensboro College, Maryville College, Methodist College, North Carolina Wesleyan College, Peace College, Shenandoah University.

Corporate Sponsors:
Bank of America, Wells Trophy Sportswear & Specialties, Molten USA, The Rock.

WEST COAST CONFERENCE
1111 BAYHILL DRIVE
SUITE 405
SAN BRUNO, CA 94066
650-873-8622
Fax: 650-873-7846
www.wccsports.com
• Lynn Holzman, Commiosner
lholzman@westcoast.org
• Connie Hurlbut, Senior Associate Commissioner,Governance & Ad
(650) 873-1960
churlbut@westcoast.org
• Aaron Woliczko, Assistant Commissioner,Championships & Admini
(650) 873-3053
awoliczko@westcoast.org

Year Founded:
1952

Description:
The current members of the WCC span the western coast of the United States from Canada to Mexico. The WCC crowns champions in 13 sports: baseball, men's and women's basketball, men's and women's cross country, men's and women's golf, women's rowing, men's and women's soccer, men's and women's tennis and women's volleyball.

Number of Members:
8

Member Schools:
Gonzaga University, Loyola Marymount, Pepperdine University, University of Portland, Saint Mary's College, University of

San Diego, University of San Francisco, Santa Clara University.
Publications:
Weekly press releases on NCAA Division I athletics.
Membership Requirements:
Requires approval of WCC Executive Committee.

WEST VIRGINIA INTERCOLLEGIATE ATHLETIC CONFERENCE
1422 MAIN STREET
PRINCETON, WV 24740
304-487-6298
Fax: 304-487-6299
• Barry Blizzard, Commissioner
• Ben Bronlee, Associate Commissioner for Internal Affairs
brownlee.wviac@gmail.com
• Brent Hager, Associate Commissioner for External Operation
wviacsid@gmail.com
• John Holt, Supervisor of Basketball Officials
jholt4golf@aol.com
• Joe Merendino, Supervisor of Baseball Officials
• Will Prewitt, Associate Commissioner
• Karen Mandeville, Administrative Assistant
Year Founded:
1925
Description:
The Conference sponsors and conducts 18 championships for men and women in baseball, basketball, cross country, football, golf, soccer, swimming, tennis.
Number of Members:
15
Member Schools:
Alderson-Broaddus College, Bluefield State College, Concord University, University of Charleston, Davis & Elkins College, Fairmont State University, Glenville State College, Ohio Valley University, Salem International University, Shepherd University, West Liberty State College, West Virginia State University, West Virginia University-Tech, West Virginia Wesleyan College, Wheeling Jesuit University.
Corporate Sponsors:
First Community Bank, Charleston Town Center Marriott, Embassy Suites Charleston, Hampton Inn-Downtown Charleston, Holiday Inn Express Civic Center, Rotary Clubs International, City of Vienna, Lion Clubs International.

WESTERN ATHLETIC CONFERENCE
9250 E. COSTILLA AVENUE
SUITE 300
ENGLEWOOD, CO 80112
303-799-9221
Fax: 303-799-3888
wac@wac.org
www.wacsports.com
• Jeff Hurd, Commissioner
• Mollie Lehman, Senior Associate Commissioner, CFO
(303) 962-4205
• Vicky Eggleston, Director of Graphic Design & Publications
(303) 962-4207
• David Chaffin, Asst. Commissioner for Technology & Conference
(303) 962-4212
dchaffin@wac.org
• Marlon Edge, Asst. Commissioner

Compliance
(303) 962-4211
Year Founded:
1962
Description:
The WAC crowns team and individual champions in 19 sports - eight men's and 11 women's. For the men there are championships in baseball, basketball, cross country, football, golf, tennis, indoor track and field and outdoor track and field. Championships for women are held in basketball, cross country, golf, gymnastics, soccer, softball, swimming and diving, tennis, indoor track and field, outdoor track and field and volleyball.
Number of Members:
8
Member Schools:
Fresno State University, University of Hawaii, University of Idaho, Louisiana Tech University, University of Nevada, New Mexico State University, San Jose State University, Utah State University.
Corporate Sponsors:
XBOX Live, Gatorade, Molten, Sirius Satellite Radio, Wells Fargo.
Publications:
WAC MEDIA GUIDES, annual for football, basketball, volleyball, winter and spring sports. Weekly releases on conference sports.

WISCONSIN INTERCOLLEGIATE ATHLETIC CONFERENCE
780 REGENT ST
MADISON, WI 53715
608-263-4402
Fax: 608-265-3176
gkarner@uwsa.edu
www.wiacsports.com
• Gary Karner, Commissioner
(608) 263-7683
gkarner@uwsa.edu
• Matt Stanek, Assistant Commissioner For Media Relations
(608) 225-8662
mstanek@uwsa.edu
• Becky Blank, Coordinator of Women's Basketball Officials
(262) 375-3849
beckyblank@hotmail.com
• Jim Doden, Coordinator of Baseball Umpires
(920) 731-1556
jdoden@sbcglobal.net
Publications:
WIAC Records Book, annual; news release, weekly.
Number of Members:
9
Description:
Founded 1913. Sponsors intercollegiate competition in cross country, gymnastics (women's), soccer (women's), football, basketball, hockey, swimming, wrestling, baseball, tennis (women's), golf (women's), volleyball (women's), softball, indoor/outdoor track & field. Member schools include the University of Wisconsin at the following locations: Eau Claire, La Crosse, Oshkosh, Platteville, River Falls, Stevens Point, Stout, Superior, Whitewater.

WOLVERINE-HOOSIER ATHLETIC CONFERENCE
43747 CRANFORD
CANTON, MI 48187
734-981-9509
www.whac.net
• Rob Miller, Commissioner
• Mike Dean, Statistician
(913) 449-3356
• Dawn Harmon, Media Director
(913) 991-0878

NAIA I Colleges

ALBERTA ATHLETICS, UNIVERSITY OF
116 STREET & 85 AVENUE
EDMONTON, AB, CANADA T6G 2R3
780-492-2327
Fax: 780-492-7307
uascores@ualberta.ca
athletics.ualberta.ca
• Ian Reade, Director of Athletics
(780) 492-3365
ian.reade@ualberta.ca
• Vang Ioannides, Associates Athletic Director
(780) 492-5603
• Katie Spriggs, Associate Athletic Director
• Tawana McLeod, Associate Athletic Director

ALBERTSON COLLEGE OF IDAHO ATHLETICS
2112 CLEVELAND BOULEVARD
CALDWELL, ID 83605
208-459-5011
Fax: 208-459-5175
yoteathletics.com
• Reagan Rossi, Director of Athletics
• Marty Holly, Associate Athletic Director
• Mark Owen, Compliance Officer

ALICE LLOYD COLLEGE ATHLETICS
100 PURPOSE ROAD
PIPPA PASSES, KY 41844
606-368-6000
888-280-4252
www.alc.edu/athletics
• Joe Stepp, President
• Gary Stepp, Athletic Director

ALLEN UNIVERSITY ATHLETICS
1530 HARDEN STREET
COLUMBIA, SC 29204
803-376-5700
Fax: 803-376-5733
www.allenuniversity.edu/campus-life/athletics
• Lady June Cole, President
• Chad Washington, Athletic Director
cwashington@allenuniversity.edu

AQUINAS COLLEGE ATHLETICS
1607 ROBINSON ROAD SE
GRAND RAPIDS, MI 49506-1799
616-632-8900
Fax: 616-732-4548
athletics@aquinas.edu
www.aquinas.edu/athletics
• Nick Davidson, Athletic Director
(616) 632-2475
nws001@aquinas.edu
• Linda Nash, Assistant Athletic Director
(616) 632-2473
nashlin@aquinas.edu

• Dave Wood, Associate Athletic Director
(616) 632-2474
• Mike Wojciakowski, Sports Information
Director
(616) 632-2482
wojcimic@aquinas.edu

ASBURY COLLEGE ATHLETICS
ONE MACKLEM DRIVE
WILMORE, KY 40390
859-858-3511
athletics@asbury.edu
www.asbury.edu/athletics
• Mark Perdue, Athletic Director
(859) 858-3511
• Ron Anderson, Director of Financial Aid
(859) 858-3511
• Josh Stewart, Sports Information Director
(859) 858-3511
• Andrew Bolt, Head Athletic Trainer
(859) 858-3511

ASHFORD UNIVERSITY
400 NORTH BLUFF BOULEVARD
CLINTON, IA 52732
800-242-4153
• Andy Eberhart, Director of Athletics
andy.eberhart@ashford.edu
• Michelle Burton, Administrative Assistant
michelle.burton@ashford.edu
• Kelsay McCausland, Sports Information
Director
(563) 242-4023
kelsay.mccausland@ashford.edu
Description:
Formerly The Franciscan University
Athletics.

ATHENS STATE COLLEGE ATHLETICS
300 NORTH BEATY STREET
ATHENS, AL 35611
256-233-8100
www.athens.edu
• Bob Glenn, President
• Mike McCoy, Vice President for Financial
Affairs

**AUBURN UNIVERSITY AT
MONTGOMERY ATHLETICS**
PO BOX 244023
MONTGOMERY, AL 36124-4023
334-244-3000
800-227-2649
www.aum.edu; www.aumathletics.com
• Jessie Rosa, Director of Athletics
(334) 244-3541
jrosa@aum.edu
• Andree Houston, Assistant AD For
Compliance
(334) 244-3712
ahousto4@aum.edu
• Michelle Crompton, Athletic Program
Specialist
(334) 244-3541
mcrompto@aum.edu
• Tim Lutz, Sports Information Director
(334) 244-3832
tlutz1@aum.edu

AVILA UNIVERSITY ATHLETICS
11901 WORNALL ROAD
KANSAS CITY, MO 64145
816-501-3634
Fax: 816-941-4503
athletics@avila.edu
www.avilaathletics.com

• Cristina Cowan, Director Of Athletics
(816) 501-3778
christina.cowan@avila.edu
• Brandon Droge, Sports Information
Director
(816) 501-2936
brandon.droge@avila.edu

AZUSA PACIFIC UNIVERSITY ATHLETICS
901 EAST ALOSTA AVENUE
PO BOX 7000
AZUSA, CA 91702-7000
626-815-5081
Fax: 626-815-5084
www.apu.edu/athletics
• Gary Pine, Director of Athletics
(626) 815-5081
gpine@apu.edu
• April Hoy, Associate Athletics Director
(626) 815-6000
areed@apu.edu
• Peter Bond, Director of Athletic
Development
(626) 815-6000
pbond@apu.edu
Teams:
Acrobatics & Tumbling, Baseball, Basketball
(M/W), Cross Country (M/W), Football,
Soccer (M/W), Softball, Tennis (M/W), Track
& Field (M/W), Volleyball, Water Polo (W).

BACONE COLLEGE ATHLETICS
2299 OLD BACONE ROAD
MUSKOGEE, OK 74403
918-683-4581
888-682-5514
info@bacone.edu
athletics.bacone.edu
• Alan Foster, Athletics Director
(918) 685-0450
fostera@bacone.edu
• John Pickens, Assistant Athletic Director
(918) 685-0450
pickensj@bacone.edu

BAKER UNIVERSITY ATHLETICS
618 EIGHTH STREET
BALDWIN CITY, KS 66006
785-594-6451
www.bakeru.edu/athletics
• Theresa Yetmar, Director of Athletics
(785) 594-8316
theresa.yetmar@bakeru.edu
• Tyler Price, Assistant Director of Athletics,
Communications
(785) 594-8495

BARBER-SCOTIA COLLEGE
145 CABARRUS AVENUE WEST
CONCORD, NC 28025
704-789-2900
Fax: 704-789-2901
ecummings@b-sc.edu
www.b-sc.edu
• Brenda Simms, Executive Administrator
• Sophia Woodward, Vice President for
Academic Affairs
• Jonathan Sisk, Athletic Director
bsimms@b-sc.edu

BELHAVEN COLLEGE ATHLETICS
1500 PEACHTREE STREET
BOX 171
JACKSON, MS 39202
601-968-5956
800-960-5940

Fax: 601-510-2789
jbrower@belhaven.edu
blazers.belhaven.edu
• Scott Little, Director of Athletics
(601) 968-5956
slittle@belhaven.edu
• Candace Dailey, Associate Director of
Athletics
(601) 968-8952
cdailey@belhaven.edu
• Layton Jackson, Director of Athletics
Communication
(601) 968-8765

BELLEVUE UNIVERSITY ATHLETICS
1000 GALVIN ROAD SOUTH
BELLEVUE, NE 68005
402-557-7058
Fax: 402-557-5407
onestop@bellevue.edu
www.bubruins.com
• Ed Lehotak, Athletic Director
(402) 557-7050
ed.lehotak@bellevue.edu

BENEDICTINE COLLEGE ATHLETICS
1020 NORTH 2ND STREET
ATCHINSON, KS 66002
913-367-5340
800-467-5340
Fax: 913-367-2564
www.ravenathletics.com
• Charles Gartenmayer, Athletic Director
cgartenmayer@benedictine.edu
• Michael Faucett, Assistant Athletic Director
• Josh Pound, Sports Information Director

BEREA COLLEGE ATHLETICS
290 CAMPUS DRIVE
BEREA, KY 40404
859-985-3000
beverly_harkleroad@berea.edu
www.bereaathletics.com
• Mark Cartmill, Director of Athletics
(859) 985-3922
mark_cartmill@berea.edu
• Ryan Hess, Assistant Director of Athletics
(859) 985-3426
ryan_hess@berea.edu
• Shawn Jakubowski, Sports Information
Director
(859) 985-3406
shawn_jakubowski@berea.edu

BERRY COLLEGE ATHLETICS
2277 MARTHA BERRY HIGHWAY NW
MOUNT BERRY, GA 30149
706-290-2146
Fax: 706-236-5497
www.berry.edu/athletics
• Todd Brooks, Director of Athletics
(706) 236-1721
tbrooks@berry.edu
• David Beasley, Assistand Athletics
Director
(706) 290-2146
dbeasley@berry.edu

BETHANY COLLEGE ATHLETICS (KS)
335 EAST SWENSSON STREET
LINDSBORG, KS 67456
785-227-3380
Fax: 785-227-2021
www.bethanyswedes.com
• Dane Pavlovich, Dean of Athletics
(785) 227-3380

pavlovichd@bethanylb.edu
• Sara Blackburn, Sports Information Director
(785) 227-3380
blackburnsk@bethanylb.edu
• M.J Cerenio, Assistant Sports Information Director
(785) 227-3380
cerenio-jordanmr@bethanylb.edu

BETHEL COLLEGE (TN) ATHLETICS
325 CHERRY AVENUE
MCKENZIE, TN 38201
731-352-4231
Fax: 731-352-4238
www.bethelathletics.com
• Dale Kelley, Director of Athletics
(731) 352-6428
kelleyd@bethelu.edu
• Rick Vaughn, Associate Athletics Director
(731) 352-4201
• Kristy Dunn, Athletic Operations Coordinator
(731) 352-6428
dunnk@bethelu.edu
• Dave McCulley, Sports Information Director
(731) 352-4231
mcculleyd@bethelu.edu

BIOLA UNIVERSITY ATHLETICS
13800 BIOLA AVENUE
LA MIRADA, CA 90639
562-903-6000
www.biola.edu/undergrad/athletics
• Bethany Miller, Director of Athletics
(562) 777-4082
bethany.miller@biola.edu
• Dave Holmquist, Senior Associate Athletic Director
(562) 906-4519
terri.pixler@biola.edu
• Terri Pixler, Assistant to Athletic Director
terri.pixler@biola.edu
• Karen Stare, Athlete Department Secretary
(562) 903-4887

BLACK HILLS UNIVERSITY ATHLETICS
1200 UNIVERSITY STREET
UNIT 9424
SPEARFISH, SD 57799-9424
605-642-6096
www.bhsuathletics.com
• Jhett Albers, Director of Athletics
(605) 642-6885
jhett.albers@bhsu.edu
• Jade Temple, Assistant Athletic Director/Compliance
(606) 642-6630
Jade.temple@bhsu.edu
• Ryan Hilgemann, Sports Information Director
(605) 642-6832
ryan.hilgemann@bhsu.edu
• Aaron Siekmann, Athletic Performance Director
aaron.siekmann@bhsu.edu

BLUE MOUNTAIN COLLEGE ATHLETICS
PO BOX 160
BLUE MOUNTAIN, MS 38610
662-685-4771
Fax: 662-685-4776
webmaster@bmc.edu
www.bmcsports.com
• Lavon Driskell, Athletic Director
ldriskell@bmc.edu

BLUEFIELD COLLEGE ATHLETICS
3000 COLLEGE AVENUE
BLUEFIELD, VA 24605
276-326-4316
www.bcrams.com
• Mike White, Interim Athletic Director
(276) 326-4316
mwhite@bluefield.edu
• Tom Price, Assistant Athletic Director
• Chase Neidig, Director of Athletic Broadcasting
cneidig@bluefield.edu
• Dee Odom, Division Manager for Athletics
• Bob Redd, Sports Information Director
rredd@bluefield.edu

BRENAU UNIVERSITY ATHLETICS
500 WASHINGTON STREET SE
GAINESVILLE, GA 30501
770-534-6231
www.brenautigers.com
• Mike Lochstampfor, Director of Athletics
(770) 534-6231
mlochstampfor@brenau.edu
• Pat Felt, Financial Assistnat
(770) 538-4443
pfelt@brenau.edu
• Kris Stewart, Sports Information Director
(770) 531-2048
kstewart@brenau.edu

BRESCIA COLLEGE ATHLETICS
717 FREDERICA STREET
OWENSBORO, KY 42301
270-686-6416
www.bresciabearcats.com
• Brian Skortz, Athletic Director
(270) 686-6416
brian.skortz@brescia.edu
• Andrew Dickson, Assistant Athletic Director
(270) 686-4292
andrew.dickson@brescia.edu
• Jerry Forbes, Sports Information Director
jerry.forbes@brescia.edu

BREVARD COLLEGE ATHLETICS
ONE BREVARD COLLEGE DRIVE
BREVARD, NC 28712
828-884-8276
Fax: 828-884-8274
bctornados.com
• Juan Mascaro, Athletic Director
(828) 884-8108
• Jamie Atkinson, Assistant Athletic Director
(828) 884-8365
• Joseph Swanson, Athletic Media Relations Director
(828) 884-8288
• Raychel Diver, Director of Internal Operations
(828) 884-8280
• Matt Bummer, Head Athletic Trainer
(828) 884-8316

BREWTON PARKER COLLEGE ATHLETICS
201 DAVID ELIZA FOUNTAIN CIRCLE
MOUNT VERNON, GA 30445
912-583-2241
Fax: 912-583-4352
www.gobaronsgo.com
• Steven Echols, President
sechols@bpc.edu
• Ronald Melton, Faculty Athletics Representative
rmelton@bpc.edu

• Nate Tompkins, Sports Information Director
ntompkins@bpc.edu
• Katelynn Staley, Athletic Trainer
athtrainer@bpc.edu

BRIAR CLIFF UNIVERSITY ATHLETICS
3303 REBECCA STREET
SIOUX CITY, IA 51104
712-279-5200
Fax: 712-279-1632
admissions@briarcliff.edu
www.bcuchargers.com
• Stephen Gast, Director of Athletics
(712) 279-1707
• Jared Bodammer, Associate Athletic Director
(712) 279-1653

BRITISH COLUMBIA ATHLETICS, UNIVERSITY OF
272-6081 UNIVERSITY BOULEVARD
WAR MEMORIAL GYMNASIUM
VANCOUVER, BC, CANADA V6T 1Z1
604-827-0707
www.gothunderbirds.ca
• Gilles Lepine, Director, Performance and Team Support
(604) 827-0707
gilles.lepine@ubc.ca
• Gord Hopper, Director, Performance And Team Support
gord.hopper@ubc.ca
• James Brotherhood, Senior Manager, Sports Science & Sport Medicine
(604) 822-4176
james.brotherhood@ubc.ca

BRYAN COLLEGE ATHLETICS
721 BRYAN HILL
PO BOX 7000
DAYTON, TN 37321
423-775-7568
info@bryan.edu
www.bryanlions.com
• Taylor Hasty, Athletic Director
(423) 775-7568
taylor.hasty@bryan.edu
• Will Tholken, Coordinator of Athletic Operations
(423) 775-7193
will.tholken@bryan.edu
• Wesley Sanders, Sports Information Director
(423) 775-2041
wesley.sanders@bryan.edu
• T.J. Zinke, Interim Head Athletic Trainer
(423) 775-7240
tj.zinke@bryan.edu
• David Jenkinson, Medical Director & Team Physician
(423) 285-1691
dmj@polyclinics.net

CALGARY ATHLETICS, UNIVERSITY OF
FACULTY OF KINESIOLOGY
2500 UNIVERSITY DRIVE NW
CALGARY, AB, CANADA T2N 1N4
403-220-8143
Fax: 403-210-8187
christine.stapleton@ucalgary.ca
www.godinos.com
• Christine Stapleton, Director of Athletics
(403) 220-3409
christine.stapleton@ucalgary.ca
• Mike Boyles, Associate Director
(403) 220-4413

mboyles@ucalgary.ca
• Ben Matchett, Assistant Athletic Director
(403) 220-8143
ben.matchett@ucalgary.ca

CALIFORNIA - SANTA CRUZ ATHLETICS, UNIVERSITY OF
1156 HIGH STREET
SANTA CRUZ, CA 95064
831-459-2531
Fax: 831-459-4070
www.goslugs.com
• Cliff Dochterman, Director of Athletics
(831) 459-4524
bananaslugdoc@ucsc.edu
• Collin Pregliasco, Associate Athletics Director
(831) 459-4964
• Marcus Wirth, Assistant Athletics Director
(831) 459-4159
Description of Sport Organization:
Division III, Part of the Independent Conference.
Teams:
Men/Women's Tennis, Men/Women's Soccer, Men/Women's Volleyball, Men/Women's Basketball, Men/Women's Swimming/Diving, Women's Golf, and Women's Cross Country.

CALIFORNIA BAPTIST UNIVERSITY ATHLETICS
8432 MAGNOLIA AVENUE
RIVERSIDE, CA 92504
951-343-4318
Fax: 951-689-4754
miparker@calbaptist.edu
www.cbulancers.com
• Micah Parker, Director of Athletics
(951) 343-4318
miparker@calbaptist.edu
• Michael Scarano, Associate Athletic Director
(951) 343-4839
mscarano@calbaptist.edu
• Bryan Engle, Assistant Athletic Director
(951) 343-5021
bengle@calbaptist.edu
• Sammi Wellman, Director of Sports Information
(951) 343-4297
ssheppard@calbaptist.edu
• Amy Leonard, Director of Development for Athletics
(951) 343-4689
aleonard@calbaptist.edu

CALIFORNIA MARITIME ACADEMY ATHLETICS
200 MARITIME ACADEMY DRIVE
VALLEJO, CA 94590
707-654-1050
Fax: 707-654-1051
www.cmakeelhaulers.com
• Marv Christopher, Athletic Director
mchristopher@csum.edu
• Patrick Hollister, Associate Athletic Director
(707) 654-1052
phollister@csum.edu
• Tony Lewis, Faculty Representative to Athletics
tlewis@csum.edu
• Jeff Ward, Head Trainer
(707) 654-1055
jward@csum.edu

CALIFORNIA STATE UNIVERSITY - SAN MARCOS ATHLETICS
M. GORDON CLARKE FIELD HOUSE, SUITE 106
CALIFORNIA STATE UNIVERSITY SAN MARCOS
333 SOUTH TWIN OAKS VALLEY ROAD
SAN MARCOS, CA 92096-0001
760-750-7100
Fax: 760-750-3660
www.csusmcougars.com
• Jennifer Milo, Director of Athletics
(760) 750-7100
jmilo@csusm.edu
• Todd Snedden, Associate Director of Athletics
(760) 750-7109
tsnedden@csusm.edu
• Michelle Hamilton, Assistant Director of Athletics
(760) 750-7111
mhamilto@csusm.edu
• Sean Briner, Director of Athletic Development
(760) 750-4404
sbriner@csusm.edu
• Fernando Brown, Equipment Manager

CALUMET COLLEGE OF ST. JOSEPH ATHLETICS
2400 NEW YORK AVENUE
WHITING, IN 46394
219-473-4276
www.ccsjathletics.com
• Rick Torres, Athletic Director
(219) 473-4323
etorres6@ccsj.edu
• Ashley Lake, Asst. Athletic Director
(219) 473-43275
• Rebecca Leevey, Coordinator for Student-Athletes
(219) 644-7207
rleevey@ccsj.edu

CAMPBELLSVILLE UNIVERSITY ATHLETICS
1 UNIVERSITY DRIVE
CAMPBELLSVILLE, KY 42718
270-789-5257
Fax: 270-789-5048
athletics@campbellsville.edu
www.campbellsvilletigers.com
• Rusty Hollingsworth, Director of Athletics
(270) 789-5257
rhollingsworth@campbellsville.edu
• Jim Hardy, Assistant Athletics Director
(270) 789-5528
jhardy@campbellsville.edu
• Karen Fawcett, Athletics Secretary
• Jordan Alves, Sports Information Director
(270) 789-5276
jtalves@campbellsville.edu
• Richard RoBards, Sports Information Assistant
(270) 403-3905
rbrobards@gmail.com

CARDINAL STRITCH UNIVERSITY ATHLETICS
6801 NORTH YATES ROAD
MILWAUKEE, WI 53217
800-347-8822
Fax: 414-410-4127
www.stritch.edu
• Tim Van Alstine, Director of Athletics
(414) 410-4839
tvanalstine@stritch.edu

• John Pfaffl, Assistant Director of Athletics
(414) 410-1423
jppfaffl@stritch.edu
• Dan Kuklinski, Director of Athletic Communications
(414) 410-4043
dpkuklinski@stritch.edu
• Melissa Wenig, Head Athletic Trainer
(414) 410-4129
mawenig@stritch.edu

CARLOW COLLEGE ATHLETICS
3333 FIFTH AVENUE
PITTSBURGH, PA 15213
412-578-8826
Fax: 412-578-8704
athletics@carlow.edu
www.carlow.edu/athletics
• George Sliman, Director of Athletics
(412) 578-8826
gssliman@carlow.edu
• Maria Yeater, Athletic Trainers
(412) 578-6332
masunday@carlow.edu

CARROLL UNIVERSITY ATHLETICS
1601 NORTH BENTON AVENUE
HELENA, MT 59625
406-447-4300
800-992-3648
Fax: 406-447-4955
www.carrollathletics.com
• Joe Baker, Director Of Athletics
(406) 447-5480
• Michael Schulist, Associate Athletic Director
(406) 447-4374

CEDARVILLE UNIVERSITY ATHLETICS
251 NORTH MAIN STREET
CEDARVILLE, OH 45314
937-766-7768
Fax: 937-766-7742
yellowjackets.cedarville.edu
• Alan Geist, Athletic Director
(937) 766-7768
geista@cedarville.edu
• Chris Reese, Associate Athletic Director
(937) 766-7790
chrisreese@cedarville.edu
• Christopher Cross, Assistant Athletic Director
(937) 766-6222
ccross@cedarville.edu
• Wes Stephens, Head Athletic Trainer
(937) 766-7622
wrstephens@cedarville.edu

CENTRAL CHRISTIAN COLLEGE
1200 SOUTH MAIN STREET
PO BOX 1403
MCPHERSON, KS 67460
620-241-0723
800-835-0078
Fax: 620-241-6032
athletics@centralchristian.edu
www.ccctigers.com
• Twiggs Reed, Athletic Director
(620) 241-0723
steve.reed@centralchristian.edu
• Jeremy Nelson, Sports Information Director
(620) 241-0723
jeremy.nelson@centralchristian.edu
• Maggie Burnette, Head Athletic Trainer
(620) 241-0723
maggie.burnette@centralchristian.edu

CENTRAL METHODIST COLLEGE ATHLETICS
411 CENTRAL METHODIST SQUARE
FAYETTE, MO 65248
660-248-6225
Fax: 660-248-6266
www.cmueagles.com
• Ken Oliver, Vice President for Institutional Growth
(660) 248-6225
koliver@centralmethodist.edu
• Brian Spielbauer, Athletics Director
(660) 248-6390
bspielba@centralmethodist.edu
• Sally Hackman, Faculty Athletics Representative
(660) 248-6633
shackman@centralmethodist.edu

CENTRAL STATE UNIVERSITY ATHLETICS
1400 BRUSH ROW ROAD
PO BOX 1004
WILBERFORCE, OH 45384
937-376-6011
1-800-388-2781
Fax: 937-376-6291
www.maraudersports.com
• Jahan Culbreath, Vice President of Institutional Advancement
(937) 376-6289
jculbreath@centralstate.edu
• Harry Stinson, III, Associate Athletic Director
(937) 376-6295
hstinson@centralstate.edu
• Nick Novy, Sports Information Director
(937) 376-6345
nnovy@centralstate.edu
• LaShaunta Jones, Sports Information Director
(937) 376-6345
ljones@centralstate.edu

CLARKE UNIVERSITY ATHLETICS
1550 CLARKE DRIVE
DUBUQUE, IA 52001
563-588-6657
800-383-2345
Fax: 563-588-6666
• Curt Long, Director of Athletics
(563) 588-6462
curt.long@clarke.edu
• Casey Tauber, Assistant Athletic Director
(563) 588-6397
casey.tauber@clarke.edu
• Jerry Hanson, Sports Information Director
(563) 588-6360
jerry.hanson@clarke.edu
• Marissa Stewart, Athletic Trainer
marissa.stewart@clarke.edu

COLUMBIA COLLEGE OF MISSOURI ATHLETICS
1001 ROGERS STREET
COLUMBIA, MO 65216
573-875-7433
Fax: 573-875-7415
www.columbiacougars.com
• Bob Burchard, Director of Athletics
(573) 875-7410
rpburchard@ccis.edu
• Cindy Potter, Associate Director of Athletics
(573) 875-7454
cnpotter@ccis.edu
• Drew Grzella, Assistant Director of

Athletics
(573) 875-7419
• Kim Kliegel, Coordinator of Athletic Services
(573) 875-7433
kakliegel1@ccis.edu
• Jon Barfknecht, Head Athletic Trainer
(573) 875-7407
jbarfknecht@ccis.edu

COLUMBIA COLLEGE OF S. CAROLINA ATHLETICS
1301 COLUMBIA COLLEGE DRIVE
COLUMBIA, SC 29203
803-786-3778
800-277-1301
Fax: 803-786-3868
www.columbiasc.edu
• Kellyann Stubblefield, Director of Athletics
(803) 786-3723
kstubblefield@columbiasc.edu
• Lindsey Hughes, Assistant Athletic Director
(803) 786-3802
lhughes@columbiasc.edu
• Greyson Deal, Head Athletic Trainer
(803) 786-3089
gdeal@columbiasc.edu

CONCORDIA UNIVERSITY (MI) ATHLETICS
4090 GEDDES ROAD
ANN ARBOR, MI 48105
734-995-7300
1-877-995-7520
Fax: 734-995-4883
lonnie.priest@cuaa.edu
www.concordiacardinals.com
• Lonnie Pries, Director of Athletics
(734) 904-4685
lonnie.pries@cuaa.edu
• Karen Graves, Assistant Athletic Director
(734) 995-7342
karen.graves@cuaa.edu
• Zachary Johnston, Sports Information Director
(616) 902-3563
zachary.johnston@cuaa.edu

CONCORDIA UNIVERSITY (NE) ATHLETICS
800 NORTH COLUMBIA AVENUE
SEWARD, NE 68434
402-643-7328
800-535-5494
info@cune.edu
www.cune.edu/athletics
• Devin Smith, Athletic Director
(402) 643-7424
Devin.Smith@cune.edu
• Angela Muller, Associate Director Of Athletics
(402) 643-7424
angela.muller@cune.edu

CORBAN UNIVERSITY ATHLETICS
5000 DEER PARK DRIVE SE
SALEM, OR 97317-9392
503-375-7021
800-845-3005
Fax: 503-315-2947
athletics@corban.edu
www.corbanwarriors.com
• Greg Eide, Director of Athletics
(503) 589-8119
geide@corban.edu
• Bryce Bernard, Faculty Athletics

Representative
(503) 375-7034
bbernard@corban.edu
• Danny Day, Sports Information Director
(503) 589-8121
dday@corban.edu

CORNERSTONE COLLEGE ATHLETICS
1001 EAST BELTLINE AVENUE NE
GRAND RAPIDS, MI 49525
616-949-5300
info@cornerstone.edu
www.cugoldeneagles.com
• Chip Huber, Director of Athletics
(616) 222-1425
chip.huber@cornerstone.edu
• Aaron Sagraves, Assistant Athletics Director
(616) 977-5415
aaron.sagraves@Cornerstone.edu
• Phil Keith, Athletic Trainer
(616) 222-1425
phil.keith@cornerstone.edu

CROWN COLLEGE ATHLETICS
8700 COLLEGE VIEW DRIVE
SAINT BONIFACIUS, MN 55375
952-446-4100
800-68-CROWN
athletics.crown.edu
• Jamie Ross, Interim Director of Athletics
(952) 446-4106
rossj@crown.edu
• Luke Herbert, Assistant Athletic Director for Communication
(952) 446-4146
herbertl@crown.edu
• Danielle Hall, Assistant Athletics Director for Operations
(952) 446-4243
halld@crown.edu
• Patty Pitts, Faculty Athletics Representative
(952) 446-4211
pittspa@crown.edu
• Karen Moberg, Haed Athletic Trainer
(952) 446-4429
rothk@crown.edu

CULVER-STOCKTON COLLEGE ATHLETICS
ONE COLLEGE HILL
CANTON, MO 63435
573-288-6000
www.cswildcats.com
• Pat Atwell, Director of Athletics
(573) 288-6424
patwell@culver.edu
• John Schild, Assistant Athletic Director
(573) 288-6532
jschild@culver.edu
• Dan Mahoney, Faculty Athletic Representative
(573) 288-6358
dmahoney@culver.edu
• Rob Carmichael, Head Athletic Trainer
(573) 288-6304
rcarmichael@culver.edu

CUMBERLAND COLLEGE ATHLETICS
7526 COLLEGE STATION DRIVE
WILLIAMSBURG, KY 40769
606-539-4389
Fax: 606-539-4467
www.cumberlandspatriots.com
• Chris Kraftick, Athletic Director
(606) 539-4540

• Lana West, Athletics Administrative
Assistant
(606) 539-4389
lana.west@ucumberlands.edu
• Tommmy Chasanoff, Sports Information
Director
(606) 539-4479
thomas.chasanoff@ucumberlands.edu

CUMBERLAND UNIVERSITY ATHLETICS
ONE CUMBERLAND SQUARE
LEBANON, TN 37087
615-547-1348
800-467-0562
Fax: 615-443-8422
www.gocumberlandathletics.com
• Ron Pavan, Director of Athletics
(615) 547-1348
rpavan@cumberland.edu
• Mitch Walters, Assistant Athletics Director
(615) 547-1288
mwalters@cumberland.edu
• Jo Jo Freeman, Sports Information
Director
(615) 547-1350
jfreeman@cumberland.edu

DAKOTA STATE UNIVERSITY
ATHLETICS
820 NORTH WASHINGTON AVENUE
MADISON, SD 57042
605-256-5229
888-378-9988
Fax: 605-256-5138
www.dsu.edu
• Jeff Dittman, Athletic Director
(605) 256-5229
jeff.dittman@dsu.edu
• Jared Indahl, Assistant Athletic Director
(605) 256-5229
jared.indahl@dsu.edu
• Nick Huntimer, Sports Information Director
(605) 256-5229
nick.huntimer@dsu.edu
• Brad Gilbert, Athletic Trainer
(605) 480-2608
brad.gilbert@dsu.edu
Teams:
Baseball, Basketball (M & W), Cross
Country (M & W), Football, Indoor Track (M
& W), Outdoor Track (M & W), Softball.

DAKOTA WESLEYAN UNIVERSITY
ATHLETICS
1200 WEST UNIVERSITY AVENUE
MITCHELL, SD 57301
605-995-2112
800-333-8506
Fax: 605-995-2150
www.dwuathletics.com
• Curt Hart, Assistant Athletics Director
cuhart@dwu.edu
• Jon Hart, Athletic Director
(605) 995-2898
johart1@dwu.edu
• Marlene Warnke, Athletic Business
Manager
(605) 995-2112
mawarnke@dwu.edu
• Nick McCutcheon, Sports Information
Director
(605) 995-2854
nimccutc@dwu.edu
• Jarod Guthmiller, Head Athletic Trainer
(605) 995-2144
jaguthmi@dwu.edu

DAVENPORT UNIVERSITY ATHLETICS
415 FULTON STREET EAST
GRAND RAPIDS, MI 49503-5926
616-451-3511
800-686-1600
Fax: 616-233-3410
www.davenport.edu
• Paul Lowden, Director of Athletics
(616) 554-5050
plowden@davenport.edu
• Ronda Varnesdeel, Associate Director of
Athletics
(616) 871-6183
rvarnesdeel@davenport.edu
• Lauren Ferullo, Assistant Director of
Athletics
(616) 871-6197
lferullo@davenport.edu
• Nicole Chase, Manager of Athletic
Facilities
(616) 554-5126
nchase2@davenport.edu
• Ryan Thompson, Assistant Director of
Athletics
(616) 554-5045
rthompson62@davenport.edu
• Nicole Chase, Manager of Athletic
Facilities

DICKINSON STATE UNIVERSITY
ATHLETICS
291 CAMPUS DRIVE
DICKINSON, ND 58601
701-483-2507
800 279-HAWK
Fax: 701-483-0501
dsu.hawk@dickinsonstate.edu
www.dsubluehawks.com
• Tim Daniel, Director of Athletics
(701) 483-2100
tim.daniel@dickinsonstate.edu
• Kristen Fleury, Assistant Athletic Director
(701) 483-2567
kristen.fleury@dickinsonstate.edu
• Jason Watson, Sports Information Director
(701) 483-2716
jason.p.watson@dickinsonstate.edu
• Tim Kreidt, Head Athletic Trainer
(701) 483-2184
timothy.kreidt@dickinsonstate.edu

DILLARD UNIVERSITY ATHLETICS
2601 GENTILLY BOULEVARD
NEW ORLEANS, LA 70122
504-283-8822
Fax: 504-816-4365
www.dillardbleudevils.com
• Kiki Baker Barnes, Athletic Director
(504) 816-4752
kbarnes@dillard.edu
• Habtom Keleta, Sports Information
Director
(504) 816-4953
hkeleta@dillard.edu
• Britt Vallot, Athletic Trainer
(504) 816-4070
bvallot@ochsner.org

DOANE COLLEGE ATHLETICS
1014 BOSWELL AVENUE
CRETE, NE 68333
800-333-6263
Fax: 402-826-8600
athletics@doane.edu
www.doaneathletics.com
• Jill McCartney, Athletic Director
(402) 826-8583

jill.mccartney@doane.edu
• Cody Vance, Assistant Athletic Director
(402) 826-8549
cody.vance@doane.edu
• Rick Schmuecker, Sports Information
Director
(402) 826-8248
rick.schmuecker@doane.edu
• Greg Seier, Athletic Trainer
(402) 826-8500
greg.seier@doane.edu

DORDT COLLEGE ATHLETICS
498 4TH AVENUE NE
SIOUX CENTER, IA 51250-1606
712-722-6000
800-343-6738
Fax: 712-722-6303
www.dordt.edu/athletics
• Glenn Bouma, Athletics Director
(712) 722-6305
• Mike Byker, Sports Information Director
(712) 722-6301
mike.byker@dordt.edu

EASTERN OREGON UNIVERSITY
ATHLETICS
ONE UNIVERSITY BLVD
LA GRANDE, OR 97850-2807
541-962-3497
Fax: 541-962-3577
www.eousports.com
• Anji Weissenfluh, Director of Athletics
(541) 962-3236
aweissen@eou.edu
• Stephanie Upshaw, Assistant Athletic
Director
(541) 962-3518
upshaws@eou.edu
• Seth Dahle, Sports Information Director
(541) 962-3946
sdahle@eou.edu
• Sam Ghrist, Business Coordinator
(541) 962-3929
sam.ghrist@eou.edu

EDWARD WATERS COLLEGE
ATHLETICS
1658 KINGS ROAD
JACKSONVILLE, FL 32209-6199
904-470-8000
888-898-3191
• Stanley Cromartie, Assistant Director of
Athletics
(904) 470-8278
• Henry Smith, Sports Information Director
(904) 470-8045
hsmith@ewc.edu

EMBRY-RIDDLE AERONAUTICAL
UNIVERSITY ATHLETICS - (AZ)
3700 WILLOW CREEK ROAD
PRESCOTT, AZ 86301
928-777-3728
blakeba3@erau.edu
erauathletics.com
• John Phillips, Director of Athletics
(928) 777-3791
john.phillips@erau.edu
• John Adkison, Associate Director of
Athletics
(928) 777-3737
john.adkison@erau.edu
• Sonja Taylor, Executive Director Of
Student Support
(928) 777-6930
taylorso@erau.edu

EVANGEL UNIVERSITY ATHLETICS
1111 NORTH GLENSTONE
SPRINGFIELD, MO 65802
417-865-2815
Fax: 417-865-9599
www.evangelathletics.com
• Dennis McDonald, Director of Athletics
(417) 865-2815
mcdonaldd@evangel.edu
• Sara Underwood, Athletics Administrative
Assistant
(417) 865-2815
• Marisa Foltz, Head Athletic Trainer

**EVERGREEN STATE UNIVERSITY
ATHLETICS**
2700 EVERGREEN PARKWAY NW
OLYMPIA, WA 98505
360-867-6000
Fax: 360-867-6783
www.gogeoducks.com
• Andrew Beattie, Director Of Recreation &
Athletics
(360) 867-6549
beattiea@evergreen.edu
• Monica Heuer, Interim Assistant Director
of Athletics
(360) 867-6858
heuerm@evergreen.edu
• Brian Meade, Business Operations
Manager
(360) 867-6607
meadeb@evergreen.edu
• Nick Dawson, Sports Information Director
(360) 867-6525
dawsonn@evergreen.edu

FAULKNER UNIVERSITY ATHLETICS
5345 ATLANTA HIGHWAY
MONTGOMERY, AL 36109
800-879-9816 EXT 7148
www.faulknereagles.com
• Hal Wynn, Acting Athletic Director
(334) 386-7285
• Ryan Bartels, Sports Information
(334) 386-7525
• Cindy Walker, Faculty Athletic
Representative
(334) 386-7402
cwalker@faulkner.edu

FISHER COLLEGE ATHLETICS
1 ARLINGTON STREET
LOWER LEVEL
BOSTON, MA 02116
617-236-8877
www.fisherfalcons.com
• Robert Melaragni, Director of Athletics
(617) 670-4524
rmelaragni@fisher.edu

**FLORIDA MEMORIAL UNIVERSITY
ATHLETICS**
15800 NW 42ND AVENUE
MIAMI GARDENS, FL 33054
305-626-3600
Fax: 305-626-3169
www.fmuathletics.com
• Robert Smith, Athletic Director
(305) 626-3168
robert.smith@fmuniv.edu
• Artis Maddox, Assistant Athletic Director
(305) 626-3165
artis.maddox@fmuniv.edu
• Damian Alexander, Sports Information
Director

(305) 626-3194
damian.alexander@fmuniv.edu

**FREED-HARDEMAN UNIVERSITY
ATHLETICS**
158 EAST MAIN STREET
HENDERSON, TN 38340
731-989-6000
800-FHU-FHU-1
Fax: 731-989-6910
mbarker@fhu.edu
www.gofhulions.com
• Mike McCutchen, Athletic Director
(731) 989-6901
mmccutchen@fhu.edu
• Matt Barker, Sports Information Director
(731) 989-6356
mbarker@fhu.edu
Year founded:
1869.

FRIENDS UNIVERSITY ATHLETICS
2100 WEST UNIVERSITY AVENUE
WICHITA, KS 67213
316-295-5000
800-794-6945
Fax: 316-295-5030
www.friends.edu/athletics
• Carole Obermeyer, Athletic Director
(316) 295-5779
obermeyer@friends.edu
• Luke Dechant, Sports Information Director
(316) 295-5116
sports_information@friends.edu

GENEVA COLLEGE ATHLETICS
3200 COLLEGE AVENUE
BEAVER FALLS, PA 15010
724-847-6650
855-979-5563
• Van Zanic, Athletic Director
(724) 847-6886
vgzanic@geneva.edu
• Alan Summer, Assistant Athletic Director
• Christy Lear, Sports Information Director

GEORGETOWN COLLEGE ATHLETICS
400 EAST COLLEGE STREET
GEORGETOWN, KY 40324
502-863-8115
Fax: 502-863-8892
www.georgetowncollegeathletics.com
• Brian Evans, Director of Athletics
(502) 863-8223
brian_evans@georgetowncollege.edu
• Austin Sparks, Associate Director of
Athletics
(502) 863-8222
• Jenny Elder, Sports Information Director
(502) 863-7972
• Randy McGuire, Head Athletic Trainer
(502) 863-7032

GOSHEN COLLEGE ATHLETICS
1700 SOUTH MAIN STREET
GOSHEN, IN 46526
574-535-7496
Fax: 574-535-7531
info@goshen.edu
www.goleafs.net
• Josh Gleason, Athletic Director
(574) 535-7491
joshag@goshen.edu
• Josh Keister, Associate Athletic Director
(574) 535-7475
joshdk@goshen.edu

• Erica Albertin, Head Athletic Trainer
(574) 535-7417
ealbertin@goshen.edu

GRACE COLLEGE ATHLETICS
200 SEMINARY DRIVE
WINONA LAKE, IN 46580
574-372-5100 EXT 6266
Fax: 574-372-5137
www.gclancers.com
• Chad Briscoe, Director of Athletics
(574) 372-5100
chad.briscoe@grace.edu
• Kelly Sharp, Athletic Office Manager
(574) 372-5100
• Abby Sroufe, Head Athletic Trainer
(574) 372-5100
sroufea@grace.edu

GRACELAND UNIVERSITY ATHLETICS
1 UNIVERSITY PLACE
LAMONI, IA 50140
641-784-5000
www.gujackets.com
• Joe Worlund, Athletic Director
(641) 784-5341
joew1@graceland.edu
• Stew McDole, Associate Athletic Director
(641) 784-5346
mcdole@graceland.edu
• Erin Lundy, Head Athletic Trainer
(641) 784-5037

GRAND VIEW COLLEGE ATHLETICS
1200 GRANDVIEW AVENUE
DES MOINES, IA 50316
515-263-2800
800-444-6083
Fax: 515-263-2882
www.gvvikings.com
• Troy Plummer, Director of Athletics
(515) 263-6050
tplummer@grandview.edu
• Britt Erps, Assistant to the Athletic Director
(515) 263-6050
berps@grandview.edu
• Michelle Prange, Athletic Success
Coordinator
(515) 263-6196
mprange@grandview.edu
• Luke Steele, Director of Athletic Training
Services
(515) 263-6045
lsteele@grandview.edu
• Travis Dibbet, Athletic Trainer
(515) 263-6045
tdibbet@grandview.edu

**GREAT FALLS ATHLETICS, UNIVERSITY
OF**
1301 20TH STREET SOUTH
GREAT FALLS, MT 59405
406-791-5925
800-856-9544
Fax: 406-791-5994
www.ugfargos.com
• Brad Beffert, Head Athletic Trainer
(406) 791-5222
• Dave Gantt, Vice President Of Athletics
(406) 791-5922
dave.gantt@ugf.edu

**HANNIBAL-LA GRANGE COLLEGE
ATHLETICS**
2800 PALMYRA ROAD
HANNIBAL, MO 63401

573-221-3675
www.hlgtrojans.com
• Jason Nichols, Athletic Director
(573) 629-3211
jnichols@hlg.edu
• Michelle Mundle, Athletic Department Secretary
(573) 629-3210
mmundle@hlg.edu
• Jason Farr, Director of Sports Information
(573) 629-3227
jason.farr@hlg.edu
• Josh Miley, Head Athletic Trainer
(573) 629-3219
josh.miley@hlg.edu

HARRIS-STOWE STATE COLLEGE ATHLETICS
3026 LACLEDE AVENUE
ST. LOUIS, MO 63103
314-340-3530
Fax: 314-340-3322
www.hornetsathletics.com
• Jamaal Mayo, Director of Athletics
(314) 340-3534
mayoj@hssu.edu
• Tim Fuller, Sports Advisor
(314) 340-5721
fullert@hssu.edu

HASKELL INDIAN NATIONS UNIVERSITY ATHLETICS
155 INDIAN AVENUE
BOX 5011
LAWRENCE, KS 66046
785-749-8459
Fax: 785-832-6632
www.haskellathletics.com
• Venida Chenault, University President
(785) 749-8497
venida.chenault@bie.edu
• Todd Davis, Athletic Director
(785) 749-8459
• Denise Cesare, Program Assistant
(785) 749-8459
• Tim Kriley, Athletic Trainer
(785) 830-2759
tkriley@haskell.edu

HASTINGS COLLEGE ATHLETICS
710 NORTH TURNER AVENUE
HASTINGS, NE 68901
402-461-7395
psitorius@hastings.edu
www.hastingsbroncos.com
• Patty Sitorius, Athletic Director
(402) 461-7331
psitorius@hastings.edu
• Chris Kranjc, Assistant Athletic Director
(402) 461-7707
• Adam Maser, Sports Information Director
(402) 461-7798
amaser@hastings.edu

HOPE INTERNATIONAL UNIVERSITY ATHLETICS
2500 EAST NUTWOOD AVENUE
FULLERTON, CA 92831
714-879-3901
Fax: 714-681-7224
www.hiuroyals.com
• John Turek, Athletic Director
(714) 879-3901
jgturek@hiu.edu
• Midge Madden, Administrative Assistant
mfmadden@hiu.edu
• Joe Lurker, Assistant Athletic Director

(714) 879-3901
jdlurker@hiu.edu
• Seth Preuss, Sports Information Director
(714) 879-3901
swpreuss@hiu.edu
• Jon Clasen, Compliance Director
(714) 879-3901
jaclasen@hiu.edu
• Kim Jaramillo, Head Athletic Trainer
(714) 879-3901
kajaramillo@hiu.edu

HOUSTON BAPTIST UNIVERSITY ATHLETICS
7502 FONDREN ROAD
HOUSTON, TX 77074
281-649-3096
Fax: 281-649-3040
www.hbuhuskies.com
• Steve Moniaci, Director of Athletics
(281) 649-3096
smoniaci@hbu.edu
• Ron Cottrell, Associate Athletic Director
(281) 649-3250
rcottrell@hbu.edu
• Tom Payne, Director of Business and Operations
(281) 649-3743
tpayne@hbu.edu
• Ted Seilheimer, Assistant Athletic Director
(281) 649-3046
tseilheimer@hbu.edu

HUNTINGTON UNIVERSITY ATHLETICS
2303 COLLEGE AVENUE
HUNTINGTON, IN 46750
260-359-4212
Fax: 260-359-4295
lculler@huntington.edu
• Lori Culler, Director of Athletics
(260) 359-4213
lculler@huntington.edu
• Mike Frame, Assistant for Auxiliary Athletic Services
(260) 359-4082
mframe@huntington.edu
• Joanne Green, Sports Information Director
(260) 359-4284
jgreen@huntington.edu
• Lori Ingle, Athletics Secretary
(260) 359-4212
lingle@huntington.edu

HUSTON-TILLOTSON COLLEGE ATHLETICS
900 CHICON STREET
AUSTIN, TX 78702-2795
512-505-3000
Fax: 512-505-3190
htu.edu/athletics
• Charles H. Dubra, Interim Director of Athletics
(512) 505-3050
chdubra@htu.edu

INDIANA INSTITUTE OF TECHNOLOGY ATHLETICS
1600 EAST WASHINGTON BOULEVARD
FORT WAYNE, IN 46803
260-422-5561
dpwarren@indianatech.edu
www.indianatechwarriors.com
• Debbie Warren, Director of Athletics
(260) 422-5561
• Jessie Biggs, Assistant Athletic Director
(260) 422-5561
• Tyler Stevenson, Sports Information

Director
(260) 422-5561
• Rich Riles, Head Athletic Trainer
(260) 422-5561
rlriles@indianatech.edu

INDIANA UNIVERSITY NORTHWEST ATHLETICS
3400 BROADWAY
GARY, IN 46408
219-980-6793
www.iunredhawkathletics.com
• Kristofer Schnatz, Athletic Director
(219) 980-6793
• Anne Villanueva, Director of Operations
(219) 980-6944
avillanu@iun.edu
• Scott Fulk, Director of Student Activities
(219) 980-6792
sfulk@iun.edu
• Stephanie Smith, Head Athletic Trainer
(219) 981-5636
ss85@iun.edu

INDIANA UNIVERSITY SOUTH BEND ATHLETICS
1700 MISHAWAKA AVENUE
SOUTH BEND, IN 46615
574-520-4100
Fax: 574-239-5041
stbruce@iusb.edu
www.iusbtitans.com
• Steve Bruce, Director of Athletics
(574) 520-5084
stbruce@iusb.edu
• Tom Norris, Assistant Director of Athletics
(574) 520-4827
tomnorr@iusb.edu
• Scott Strittmatter, Director of Student Life
(574) 520-5533
sstrittm@iusb.edu
• Rachel Weitzel, Head Athletic Trainer
(574) 520-4283

INDIANA UNIVERSITY SOUTHEAST ATHLETICS
4201 GRANT LINE ROAD
NEW ALBANY, IN 47150-6405
812-941-2432
Fax: 812-941-2434
athletics@ius.edu
www.iusathletics.com
• Joe Glover, Director of Athletics
(812) 941-2433
joglover@indiana.edu
• Denny Williams, Deputy Director of Athletics
(812) 941-2482
dennwill@ius.edu
• Eric Brian, Athletic Academic Coordinator
(812) 941-2172
erbrian@ius.edu
• Stephen Utz, Sports Information Director
(812) 941-2001
sutz@ius.edu
• Tiffany Hammond, Head Athletic Trainer
(812) 941-2099
tsettle@ius.edu

INDIANA WESLEYAN UNIVERSITY ATHLETICS
4201 SOUTH WASHINGTON STREET
MARION, IN 46953
765-677-2318
mark.demichael@indwes.edu
www.iwuwildcats.com

• Mark DeMichael, Athletic Director
(765) 677-2317
mark.demichael@indwes.edu
• Kyle Schmidt, Sports Information Director
(765) 677-1938
kyle.schmidt@indwes.edu
• Adam Thompson, Director of Athletic
Training Education
(765) 677-3482
adam.thompson@indwes.edu
• Mary Jacobs, Head Athletic Trainer
(765) 677-3484
mary.jacobs@indwes.edu

JARVIS CHRISTIAN COLLEGE ATHLETICS
PO BOX 1470
HAWKINS, TX 75765
404-679-4500
Fax: 404-679-4558

JOHN BROWN UNIVERSITY ATHLETICS
2000 WEST UNIVERSITY STREET
SILOAM SPRINGS, AR 72761
479-524-9500
Fax: 501-524-7412
jbuinfo@jbu.edu
www.jbu.edu/athletics
• Robyn Daugherty, Director of Athletics
(479) 524-7301
rdaugherty@jbu.edu
• Jeff Soderquist, Assistant Director of
Athletics
(479) 524-7306
jsoderqu@jbu.edu
• Nicholas Robinson, Director of Sports
Information
(479) 524-7304
nrobinson@jbu.edu
• Todd Bowden, Director of Athletic Training
(479) 524-7313
tbowden@jbu.edu

JUDSON UNIVERSITY
1151 NORTH STATE STREET
ELGIN, IL 60123
847-628-2500
www.judsoneagles.com
• Chad Gassman, Athletic Director
(847) 628-1579
chad.gassman@judsonu.edu
• Darrell Cosden, Academics/Athletics
Liaison
(847) 628-1055
dcosden@judsonu.edu
• Joel Cotton, Associate Athletic Director
(847) 628-1551
jcotton@judsonu.edu
• Brandon Fowkes, Sports Information
Director
(847) 628-1580
brandon.fowkes@judsonu.edu
• Andrew Carlson, Head Athletic Trainer
(847) 628-1592

KANSAS WESLEYAN UNIVERSITY ATHLETICS
100 EAST CHAFLIN AVENUE
SALINA, KS 67401-6196
785-833-4400
www.kwucoyotes.com
• Mike Hermann, Director of Athletics
(785) 833-4410
mike.hermann@kwu.edu
• Hannah Martin, Athletics Administrative
Assistant
(785) 833-4400

• David Toelle, Sports Information Director
(785) 833-4402
sports.info@kwu.edu
• Dan O'Connell, Head Athletic Trainer
(785) 833-4430

LA SIERRA UNIVERSITY ATHLETICS
4500 RIVERWALK PARKWAY
RIVERSIDE, CA 92515
951-785-2084
Fax: 951-785-2291
athletics@lasierra.edu
www.lsugoldeneagles.com
• Javier Krumm, Athletic Director
(951) 785-2295
jkrumm@lasierra.edu
• Robert Castillo, Sports Information
Director
(951) 785-2603
rcastill@lasierra.edu
• Brian Murphy, Head Athletic Trainer
(951) 785-2534
bmurphy@lasierra.edu
• Brianne Carroll, Clubs and Leagues
Director
(951) 785-2608
bcarroll@lasierra.edu

LANGSTON UNIVERSITY ATHLETICS
PO BOX 1500
LANGSTON, OK 73050
405-466-3262
Fax: 405-466-3461
jhilliard@lunet.edu
www.langstonsports.com

LEWIS-CLARK STATE COLLEGE ATHLETICS
500 8TH AVENUE
LEWISTON, ID 83501
208-792-5272
Fax: 208-792-2731
www.lcwarriors.com
• Gary Picone, Athletic Director
(208) 792-2863
gapicone@lcsc.edu
• Brooke Cushman, Associate Athletic
Director
(208) 792-2675
blcushman@lcsc.edu
• Zachary Shore, Sports Information Director
(208) 792-2289
zrshore@lcsc.edu
• Allie Canfield, Athletic Operations
(208) 792-2492
djshirley@lcsc.edu
• Michael Benke, Director of Facilities &
Operations
(208) 792-2366
mbbenke@lcsc.edu

LINDSEY WILSON COLLEGE ATHLETICS
210 LINDSEY WILSON STREET
COLUMBIA, KY 42728
270-384-8070
Fax: 270-384-8078
poolerw@lindsey.edu
www.lindseyathletics.com
• Willis Pooler, Athletic Director
(270) 384-8186
poolerw@lindsey.edu
• Chris Wells, Assistant Athletic Director
(270) 384-8071
wellsc@lindsey.edu
• Mike Talley, Facilities and Event
Management
(270) 384-8074

talleym@lindsey.edu
• Chris Miller, Head Athletic Trainer
(270) 384-8167
millerc@lindsey.edu

LOUISIANA STATE UNIVERSITY (SHREVEPORT) ATHLETICS
ONE UNIVERSITY PLACE
SHREVEPORT, LA 71115
318-797-5000
chad.mcdowell@lsus.edu
www.lsusathletics.com
• Chad McDowell, Athletic Director
(318) 798-4107
chad.mcdowell@lsus.edu
• David Gustavson, Associate Athletic
Director
(318) 797-5030
david.gustavson@lsus.edu
• Mark Cantrell, Sports Information Director
(318) 795-2475
mark.cantrell@lsus.edu
• Lance Champagne, Head Athletic Trainer
(318) 795-2446
lance.champagne@lsus.edu

LOYOLA UNIVERSITY (NEW ORLEANS) ATHLETICS
6363 ST. CHARLES AVENUE
CAMPUS BOX 21
NEW ORLEANS, LA 70118-6143
504-864-7539
Fax: 504-864-7380
www.loyolaramblers.com
• Steve Watson, Director Of Athletics
(504) 864-7539
swatson@luc.edu
• Jermaine Truax, Deputy Director Of
Athletics
(504) 864-7396
jtruax@luc.edu
• Tom Sorboro, Senior Associate Athletics
Director
(504) 864-7577
tsorboro@luc.edu

LUBBOCK CHRISTIAN UNIVERSITY ATHLETICS
5601 19TH STREET
LUBBOCK, TX 79407-2099
800-933-7601
www.lcuchaps.com
• Paul Hise, Director of Athletics
(806) 720-7279
paul.hise@lcu.edu
• Scott Larson, Associate Athletics Director
(806) 720-7266
scott.larson@lcu.edu
• Chris Due, Director of Athletic
Communication
(806) 720-7283
chris.due@lcu.edu
• Zack Chavez, Sports Information
Coordinator
(806) 283-2502
chavez_zack11@yahoo.com
• Dustin Driskill, Director of Sports Medicine
(806) 720-7284
dustin.driskill@lcu.edu

LYON COLLEGE ATHLETICS
2300 HIGHLAND ROAD
BATESVILLE, AR 72501
870-793-1764
Fax: 870-793-1763
athletics@lyon.edu
www.lyonscots.com

college sports

• Kevin Jenkins, Director of Athletics
(870) 307-7220
kevin.jenkins@lyon.edu
• John Krueger, Director of Sports
Information
(870) 307-7516
john.krueger@lyon.edu
• Shawn Tackett, Head Athletic Trainer
(870) 307-7330
shaw.tackett@lyon.edu

MADONNA UNIVERSITY ATHLETICS
36600 SCHOOLCRAFT
LIVONIA, MI 48150-1176
734-432-5608
Fax: 734-432-5611
sportsinfo@madonna.edu
www.madonnacrusaders.com
• Scott Kennell, Athletic Director
(734) 432-5604
skennell@madonna.edu
• Noel Emenhiser, Assistant Athletic
Director
(734) 432-5610
nemenhiser@madonna.edu
• Zachary Shore, Director of Sports
Information
(734) 432-5834
zshore@madonna.edu
• Peter Benjamin, Athletic Trainer
(734) 432-5605
pbenjamin@madonna.edu

**MAINE AT FORT KENT ATHLETICS,
UNIVERSITY OF**
23 UNIVERSITY DRIVE
FORT KENT, ME 04743
207-834-7500
athletics.umfk.edu
• Kyle Fisher, Athletic Trainer
(207) 834-7572
kyle.fisher@maine.edu
• Bill Ashby, Athletics Director
(207) 834-7571
bill.ashby@maine.edu
• Lucas Levesque, Assistant Director of
Athletics
(207) 834-7876
lucas.levesque@maine.edu
• Tom Bird, Sports Information Director
(207) 834-7828
thomas.bird@maine.edu
• James Harvey, Team Manager
jamesd_harveyjr@yahoo.com

**MAINE AT MACHIAS ATHLETICS,
UNIVERSITY OF**
116 O'BRIEN AVENUE
MACHIAS, ME 04654
207-255-1200
www.ummclippers.com
• Nicholas Cowell, Athletic Director
(207) 255-1290
nicholas.cowell@maine.edu
• Travis Cargnan, Athletic Director
(207) 255-1290
travis.carignan@maine.edu

MALONE COLLEGE ATHLETICS
2600 CLEVELAND AVENUE NW
CANTON, OH 44709
330-471-8300
Fax: 330-471-8298
www.malonepioneers.com
• Charlie Grimes, Director of Athletics
(330) 471-8438
cgrimes@malone.edu

• John Russell, Associate Athletic Director
(330) 471-8389
jcrussell@malone.edu
• Caleb Norrick, Assistant Athletic Director
(330) 471-8412
cnorrick@malone.edu
• Mike Leggett, Sports Information Director
(330) 471-8253
mleggett@malone.edu
• Chris Watson, Director of Sports Medicine
(330) 471-8297
cwatson@malone.edu

MARTIN LUTHER COLLEGE ATHLETICS
1995 LUTHER COURT
NEW ULM, MN 56073
507-354-8221 EXT 232
Fax: 507-354-8225
www.mlcknights.com
• Jim Unke, Athletic Director
(507) 354-8221
unkejm@mlc-wels.edu
• Randy Cox, Assistant Athletic Director
(507) 354-8221
coxra@mlc-wels.edu
• Sheree Danell, Administrative Assistant to
Athletics
(608) 354-8221
danellsj@mlc-wels.edu

**MARTIN METHODIST COLLEGE
ATHLETICS**
433 WEST MADISON STREET
PULASKI, TN 38478
931-363-9868
800-467-1273
Fax: 931-363-9873
www.goredhawks.com
• Robby Shelton, Interim President
(931) 363-9876
rshelton@martinmethodist.edu
• Jeff Bain, Executive Director of Athletics
(931) 363-9872
jbain@martinmethodist.edu
• Kelly Bratton, Associate Athletic Director
(931) 363-9827
kbratton@martinmethodist.edu
• Wade Neely, Assistant Athletic Director
(921) 363-9883
wneely@martinmethodist.edu
• Grant Fairchild, Director of Athletic
Training
(921) 363-9874
gfairchild@martinmethodist.edu

MASTER'S COLLEGE ATHLETICS, THE
21726 PLACERITA CANYON ROAD
SANTA CLARITA, CA 91321
661-362-2761
800-568-6248
Fax: 661-362-2697
www.masters.edu/athletics
• Steve Waldeck, Director of Athletics
(661) 362-2767
swaldeck@masters.edu
• Mike Crawford, Sports Information Director
(661) 362-2775
mcrawford@masters.edu
• Holly Gnuse, Administrative Assistant
(661) 362-2761
hgnuse@masters.edu
• Don Gilmore, Assistant Director, Sports
Information
(661) 362-2811
dgilmore@masters.edu

**MAYVILLE STATE UNIVERSITY
ATHLETICS**
330 THIRD STREET NE
MAYVILLE, ND 58257
800-437-4104
Fax: 701-788-4748
www.msucomets.com
• Mike Moore, Athletic Director
(701) 788-4706
mike.moore@mayvillestate.edu
• Scott Berry, Assistant Athletic Director
(701) 788-4771
scott.berry.2@mayvillestate.edu
• John Murphy, Assistant Sports Information
Director
j.thiessenmurphy@gmail.com
• Tim O'Brien, Head Athletic Trainer
(107) 788-4844
tim.obrien@mayvillestate.edu

MCPHERSON COLLEGE ATHLETICS
1600 EAST EUCLID
PO BOX 1402
MCPHERSON, KS 67460
646-737-2725
Fax: 620-245-9706
sportsinfo@mcpherson.edu
www.macbulldogs.com
• Andrew Ehling, Director of Athletics
(620) 242-0578
ehlinga@mcpherson.edu
• Joshua Schroeder, Director Of Athletic
Communications
(646) 737-2725
schroedj@mcpherson.edu
• Phil Schoenwetter, Head Athletic Trainer
(620) 242-0584
schoenwp@mcpherson.edu

MENLO COLLEGE ATHLETICS
1000 EL CAMINO REAL
ATHERTON, CA 94027
800-556-3656
Fax: 800-556-3769
www.menloathletics.com
• Keith Spataro, Director of Athletics
(650) 543-3853
kspataro@menlo.edu
• Mark Fowler, Assistant Athletic Director
(650) 543-3852
mfowler@menlo.edu
• Aaron Gillespie, Sports Information
Director
(650) 543-3912
aaron.gillespie@menlo.edu
• Lucas Armstrong, Director of Events and
Game Ops
(650) 543-3729
lucas.armstrong@menlo.edu
• Ashley Vogds, Head Athletic Trainer
(650) 543-3931
ashley.vogds@menlo.edu

**MICHIGAN-DEARBORN ATHLETICS,
UNIVERSITY OF**
4901 EVERGREEN ROAD
DEARBORN, MI 48128
313-593-3534
umdearbornathletics@gmail.com
athletics.umdearborn.edu
• Matt Beaudry, Director of Athletics &
Recreation
(313) 593-3534
mdbeau@umich.edu
• Byan Earl, Assistant Director of Athletics
(313) 593-5671
earlb@umich.edu

MIDAMERICA NAZARENE UNIVERSITY ATHLETICS
2030 EAST COLLEGE WAY
OLATHE, KS 66062-1899
913-973-3760
Fax: 913-971-3456
www.mnusports.com
• Todd Garrett, Director of Athletics
(913) 971-3760
tgarrett@mnu.edu
• Chad Jenkins, Sports Information Director
(913) 973-3457
cwjenkins@mnu.edu
• Kristine Farrell, Director of Sports Medicine
(913) 973-3388
brpowers@mnu.edu

MIDLAND UNIVERSITY
900 NORTH CLARKSON STREET
FREMONT, NE 68025
402-941-6360
800-642-8382
Fax: 401-721-9406
info@midlandu.edu
www.midlandathletics.com
• Dave Gillespie, Director of Athletics
(402) 941-6545
gillespie@midlandu.edu
• Keith Kramme, Director of Retention
(402) 941-6059
kkramme@midlandu.edu
• Theo Bland, Assistant Athletic Director
(402) 941-6062
bland@midlandu.edu

MIDWAY UNIVERSITY ATHLETICS
512 STEPHENS STREET
MIDWAY, KY 40347
859-354-8221
Fax: 859-354-5754
www.gomidwayeagles.com
• Rusty Kennedy, Athletic Director
(859) 846-5456
wkennedy@midway.edu
• John Kenger, Assistant Athletic Director
(859) 846-5726
jkenger@midway.edu
• Dylan Brown, Sports Information Director
(859) 846-5394
dpbrown@midway.edu

MILLIGAN COLLEGE ATHLETICS
1 BLOWERS BOULEVARD
MILLIGAN COLLEGE, TN 37682
423-461-8700
www.milliganbuffs.com
• Mark Fox, Vice President for Athletics
(423) 461-8784
mpfox@milligan.edu
• Ray Smith, Associate Athletic Director for Facilities
(426) 461-8990
resmith@milligan.edu
• Daniel Manget, Sports Information Director
(423) 461-8980
sportsinfo@milligan.edu
• Zach Allen, Head Athletic Trainer
(423) 461-8991
zlallen@milligan.edu

MISSOURI BAPTIST COLLEGE ATHLETICS
ONE COLLEGE PARK DRIVE
SAINT LOUIS, MO 63141-8698
314-434-1115
877-434-1115

Fax: 314-434-7596
www.mbuspartans.com
• Thomas Smith, Associate VP, Director of Athletics
(314) 392-2264
smitht@mobap.edu
• Pitzer Lowell, Faculty Athletics Representative
(314) 392-2279
pitzer@mobap.edu
• Meredith Dill, Head Athletic Trainer
(314) 392-2399
dillm@mobap.edu

MISSOURI VALLEY COLLEGE ATHLETICS
500 EAST COLLEGE
MARSHALL, MO 65340
660-831-4000
Fax: 831-831-4003
www.moval.edu/athletics
• Tom Fifer, Director of Athletics
(660) 831-4219
fifert@moval.edu
• Mike Maccholz, Associate Athletic Director
(660) 831-4158
machholzm@moval.edu
• Colin Smith, Assistant Athletic Director
(660) 831-4230
smithc@moval.edu

MOBILE ATHLETICS, UNIVERSITY OF
5735 COLLEGE PARKWAY
MOBILE, AL 36613
251-675-5990
www.umobilerams.com
• Joe Niland, Athletic Director
(251) 442-2288
jniland@umobile.edu
• Jacob Lewis, Head Athletic Trainer
(251) 442-2561
jlewis@umobile.edu

MONTANA STATE UNIVERSITY-NORTHERN ATHLETICS
300 WEST 13TH STREET
HAVRE, MT 59501-7751
406-265-3761
Fax: 406-265-4129
www.msun.edu/athletics
• Christian Oberquell, Athletic Director
(406) 265-4109
coberquell@msun.edu
• Nichole Borst, Head Athletic Trainer
(406) 265-3593
nichole.borst@msun.edu
• Nichole Yazzie, Sports Information Director
(406) 265-3779

MONTANA TECH ATHLETICS
1300 WEST PARK STREET
BUTTE, MT 59701
406-496-4105
1-800-445-8324
Fax: 406-496-4711
www.godiggers.com
• Chuck Morrell, Head Coach/Athletic Director
(406) 496-4325
CMorrell@mtech.edu
• Nick Bowsher, Associate Athletic Director
(406) 496-4737
NBowsher@mtech.edu
• Chris Heard, Head Athletic Trainer
(406) 496-4296
cheard@mtech.edu

MONTANA WESTERN ATHLETICS, THE UNIVERSITY OF
710 SOUTH ATLANTIC STREET
DILLON, MT 59725
406-683-7220
www.umwbulldogs.com
• Russ Richardson, Director of Athletics
(409) 683-7220
ryan.nourse@umwestern.edu
• Megan Woolley, Administrative Assistant
(406) 683-7220
megan.woolley@umwestern.edu

MONTREAT COLLEGE ATHLETICS
310 GAITHER CIRCLE
PO BOX 1267
MONTREAT, NC 28757
828-669-8012
Fax: 828-669-8014
www.montreatcavaliers.com
• Jose Larios, Athletic Director
(828) 669-8011
jlarios14@montreat.edu
• Jason Lewkowicz, Sports Information Director
(573) 795-5807
jlewkowicz@montreat.edu
• Mark Neely, Head Athletic Trainer
(216) 401-8850
mneely@montreat.edu

MORNINGSIDE COLLEGE ATHLETICS
1501 MORNINGSIDE AVENUE
SIOUX CITY, IA 51106
712-274-5000
800-831-0806
Fax: 712-274-5101
www.morningside.edu
• Tim Jager, Athletic Director
(712) 274-5313
jager@morningside.edu
• Dave Rebstock, Sports Information Director
(712) 274-5127
rebstock@morningside.edu
• Katy Burford, Head Athletic Trainer
(712) 274-5314
burfordk@morningside.edu

MORRIS COLLEGE ATHLETICS
100 WEST COLLEGE STREET
SUMTER, SC 29150-3599
803-934-3200
Fax: 803-773-3687
chouck@morris.edu
www.morris.edu/athletics
• Clarence Houck, Athletic Director
(803) 934-3235
chouck@morris.edu

MOUNT MARTY COLLEGE ATHLETICS
1105 WEST 8TH STREET
YANKTON, SD 57078-3725
605-668-1545
Fax: 605-668-1508
www.mmclancers.com
• Chuck Iverson, Athletic Director
(605) 668-1529
civerson@mtmc.edu
• Andy Bernatow, Sports Information Director
(605) 668-1601
abernatow@mtmc.edu
• Sara Bortscheller, Athletic Trainer
(605) 668-1397
sara.bortscheller@mtmc.edu

MOUNT MERCY COLLEGE ATHLETICS
1330 ELMHURST DRIVE
CEDAR RAPIDS, IA 52402-4797
319-363-1323 EXT 1376
Fax: 319-363-6341
pgavin@mtmercy.edu
www.mountmercymustangs.com
• Paul Gavin, Director of Athletics
(319) 363-1323
pgavin@mtmercy.edu
• Rhonda Martin, Athletics Office Manager
(319) 363-1323
rmartin@mtmercy.edu
• Jason Furler, Sports Information Director
(319) 363-1323
furler@mtmercy.edu
• Lydia LaMere, Associate Head Athletic
Trainer
(319) 363-1323
llamere@mtmercy.edu

**MOUNT VERNON NAZARENE
UNIVERSITY ATHLETICS**
800 MARTINSBURG ROAD
MOUNT VERNON, OH 43050
740-392-6868
keith.veale@mvnu.edu
www.mvnucougars.com
• Keith Veale, Director of Athletics
(740) 393-6868
keith.veale@mvnu.edu
• Jeana Howald, Assistant Director of
Athletics
(740) 393-6868
jeana.howald@mvnu.edu
• Hannah Miller, Sports Information Director
(740) 392-6868
kirk.mcdonnell@mvnu.edu
• Brian Humphrey, Athletic Trainer
(740) 392-6868
brian.humphrey@mvnu.edu

NORTHWEST COLLEGE ATHLETICS
231 WEST 6TH STREET
POWELL, WY 82435
800-560-4692
www.nwc.edu
• Lourra Barthuly, Athletic Director
(307) 754-6441
lourra.barthuly@nwc.edu
• Leslie Kenney, Head Athletic Trainer
(307) 754-6053
leslie.kenney@nwc.edu
• Janis Beal, Women's Basketball Coach
(307) 754-6026
janis.beal@nwc.edu

**NORTHWESTERN COLLEGE (IA)
ATHLETICS**
101 7TH STREET SW
ORANGE CITY, IA 51041
712-707-7292
earl@nwciowa.edu
nwcraiders.com
• Earl Woudstra, Athletic Director
(712) 707-7292
earl@nwciowa.edu
• Alison Cahill, Athletic Facilities Director
(712) 707-7270
allison.fredin@nwciowa.edu
• Matt Bos, Sports Information Director
(712) 707-7289
matt.bos@nwciowa.edu

**NORTHWESTERN COLLEGE (MN)
ATHLETICS**
3003 SNELLING AVENUE NORTH
ST. PAUL, MN 55113-1598
651-631-5219
Fax: 651-628-3350
unweagles.com
• Matt Hill, Vice President for Student Life &
Athletics
(651) 631-5362
mbhill@unwsp.edu
• Tim Grosz, Associate Director of Athletics
(651) 631-5238
tsgrosz@unwsp.edu
• Bell Wilmeth, Assistant Director of
Athletics
(651) 286-7486
bkwilmeth@unwsp.edu
• Dave Hieb, Head Mens Athletic Trainer
(651) 631-5345
dhieb@unwsp.edu
• Melissa Vavra, Head Womens Athletic
Trainer
(651) 628-3499
mmvavra@unwsp.edu

**OHIO DOMINICAN UNIVERSITY
ATHLETICS**
1216 SUNBURY ROAD
COLUMBUS, OH 43219
614-251-4577
Fax: 614-252-2556
athleticsdepartment@ohiodominican.edu
www.ohiodominicanpanthers.com
• Jeff Blair, Athletic Director
(614) 251-4735
blairj@ohiodominican.edu
• Sandy Rowley, Assistant Athletic Director
(614) 251-4538
rowleys@ohiodominican.edu
• Cindy Hahn, Director of Compliance
(614) 251-4642
hahnc@ohiodominican.edu
• Jamison French, Head Athletic Trainer
(614) 253-4851
frenchj@ohiodominican.edu

**OKLAHOMA ATHLETICS, UNIVERSITY
OF SCIENCE & ARTS OF**
1727 WEST ALABAMA AVENUE
CHICKASHA, OK 73018
405-224-3140
800-933-8726
facmcphersonb@usao.edu
www.usao.edu
• Brisco McPherson, Athletic Director
(405) 574-1249
• Leslie Beaty, Athletic Trainer
(405) 574-1398
lbeaty@usao.edu
• Justin Tinder, Sports Information Director
(405) 574-1210
jtinder@usao.edu

**OKLAHOMA CITY UNIVERSITY
ATHLETICS**
2501 NORTH BLACKWELDER AVENUE
OKLAHOMA CITY, OK 73106
405-208-5000
800-633-7242
Fax: 405-208-5305
www.ocusports.com
• Jim Abbott, Director of Athletics
(405) 208-5301
jabbott@okcu.edu
• Greg Kersgieter, Associate Athletic
Director

(405) 208-5317
gkersgieter@okcu.edu
• Kelly Perry, Assistant Athletic Director
(405) 208-5660
kperry@okcu.edu
• Joe Fidelie, Athletic Trainer
(405) 208-6500
jifidele@okcu.edu
• Rich Tortorelli, Assistant Athletic Director
for Communications
(405) 208-5304
rtortorelli@okcu.edu

**OKLAHOMA WESLEYAN UNIVERSITY
ATHLETICS**
2201 SILVER LAKE ROAD
BARTLESVILLE, OK 74006
918-335-6219
800 468-6292
info@okwu.edu
www.okwu.edu/athletics
• Mark Molder, Director of Athletics
mmolder@okwu.edu
• Matt Parker, Assistant Director of Athletics
mparker@okwu.edu
• Nick Morris, Sports Information Director
(918) 327-4373
nmorris@okwu.edu

**OLIVET NAZARENE UNIVERSITY
ATHLETICS**
ONE UNIVERSITY AVE
BOURBONNAIS, IL 60914-2345
815-939-5011
800-648-1463
www.onutigers.com
• Gary Newsome, Director of Athletics
(815) 939-5372
gnewsome@olivet.edu
• Brian Hyma, Athletic Training Program
Director
(819) 939-5115
bhyma@olivet.edu
• Scott Armstrong, Associate Director of
Athletics
(815) 939-5372
sarmstr2@olivet.edu
• Wendy Reid, Sports Information Director
(815) 953-8908
wkreid@olivet.edu
• Nick Birkey, Assistant Sports Information
(815) 928-5565
nbirkey@olivet.edu

**OREGON INSTITUTE OF TECHNOLOGY
ATHLETICS**
3201 CAMPUS DRIVE
KLAMATH FALLS, OR 97601
541-885-1000
800-422-2017
www.oit.edu
• Greg Stewart, Director of Athletics
(541) 885-1452
• Paul Poetsch, Associate Athletic Director
(541) 885-1632
• Michael Garrard, Sports Information
(541) 885-1851

OTTAWA UNIVERSITY ATHLETICS
1001 SOUTH CEDAR STREET
OTTAWA, KS 66067
785-242-5200 EXT 5420
Fax: 785-229-1015
www.ottawabraves.com
• Arabie Conner, Director of Athletics
(785) 248-2600
arabie.conner@ottawa.edu

• Bruce Tate, Associate Director of Athletics
(785) 248-2603
bruce.tate@ottawa.edu
• Kathy Hinderliter, Athletic Department
Coordinator
(785) 248-2601
katherine.hinderliter@ottawa.edu
• Jennifer Raybern, Head Athletic Trainer
(785) 248-2627
jennifer.raybern@ottawa.edu

OZARKS ATHLETICS, COLLEGE OF THE
100 OPPORTUNITY AVENUE
POINT LOOKOUT, MO 65726
800-222-0525
bobcats.cofo.edu
• Steve Shepherd, Athletic Director
shepherd@cofo.edu
• Dori Rapinchuk, Sports Information
Director
drapinchuk@cofo.edu
• Gary Turbak, Athletic Trainer
turbak@cofo.edu

PACIFIC UNION COLLEGE ATHLETICS
ONE ANGWIN AVENUE
ANGWIN, CA 94508
707-965-6346
Fax: 707-965-6780
www.puc.edu/pioneers
• Brittany Brown, Athletics Director
(707) 965-6349
bjbrown@puc.edu
• Brandon Lucas, Assistant Athletic Director
(707) 965-6652
blucas@puc.edu
• Michael Hellie, Faculty Athletic
Representative
(707) 965-6346
mlhellie@puc.edu

PARK UNIVERSITY PIRATE ATHLETICS
8700 NORTHWEST RIVER PARK DRIVE
PMB 66
PARKVILLE, MO 64152
816-584-6425
Fax: 816-505-5448
www.parkathletics.com
• Claude English, Director of Athletics
(816) 584-6492
• Steve Wilson, Assistant Athletic Director
(816) 584-6490
• Nadine Leishman, Sports Communications
Coordinator
(816) 584-6751
• Jamal James, Lead Athletic Trainer
(816) 584-6353

PATTEN UNIVERSITY ATHLETICS
2433 COOLIDGE AVENUE
OAKLAND, CA 94601
415-813-6147
Fax: 415-299-6339
patten.edu

PAUL QUINN COLLEGE ATHLETICS
3837 SIMPSON STUART
DALLAS, TX 75241
214-379-5551
Fax: 214-302-3559
www.pqc.edu/athletics
• Kelsel Thompson, Athletic Director
(214) 379-5551
kthompson@pqc.edu
• Archie Cooley, Football Coach
• Keith McKinnon, Men's Basketball Coach

• Tina Wagoner, Women's Basketball
Coach

PERU STATE COLLEGE ATHLETICS
600 HOYT STREET
PERU, NE 68421
800-742-4412
www.pscbobcats.com
• Steve Schneider, Athletic Director
(402) 872-2393
sschneider@peru.edu
• Ted L. Harshbarger, Associate Athletic
Director
(402) 872-2380
tharshbarger@peru.edu
• Brenda Lutz, Project Coordinator
(402) 872-2350
blutz@peru.edu

**PHILANDER SMITH COLLEGE
ATHLETICS**
900 WEST DAISY L. GATSON BATES
DRIVE
LITTLE ROCK, AR 72202
501-375-9845
Fax: 501-370-5260
www.philanderathletics.com
• Nathan Cochran, Athletic Director
(501) 370-5317
ncochran@philander.edu
• Roderick Smothers, President
(501) 370-5224
• Daniel Egbe, Faculty Athletic
Representative
(501) 370-5232
degbe@philander.edu

POINT PARK UNIVERSITY ATHLETICS
DEPARTMENT OF ATHLETICS
POINT PARK UNIVERSITY
201 WOOD STREET
PITTSBURGH, PA 15222-1984
412-392-3844
Fax: 412-392-4780
www.pointpark.edu/athletics
• Dan Swalga, Director of Athletics
(412) 392-3911
dswalga@pointpark.edu
• Kevin Taylor, Director of Athletic
Communications
(412) 392-3997
ktaylor@pointpark.edu

POINT UNIVERSITY ATHLETICS
507 WEST 10TH STREET
WEST POINT, GA 31833
706-385-1000
www.pointskyhawks.com
• Alan Wilson, Interim Athletic Director
(706) 385-1059
alan.wilson@point.edu
• Monroe Bell, Asst. Sports Information
Director
(706) 385-1414
monroe.bell@point.edu
• Steve Schwepker, Sports Information
Director
(706) 385-1093
steve.schwepker@point.edu

PRESENTATION COLLEGE ATHLETICS
1500 NORTH MAIN STREET
ABERDEEN, SD 57401
605-229-8587
800-437-6060

Fax: 605-229-8548
www.pcsaints.com
• Greg Heier, Director of Athletics
(605) 229-8587
greg.heier@presentation.edu
• Robb Garofalo, Sports Information Director
(605) 229-8310
robb.garofalo@presentation.edu
• Blake Spindler, Director of Athletic
Training Services
(605) 229-8321
blake.spindler@presentation.edu

**PURDUE UNIVERSITY CALUMET
ATHLETICS**
2200 169TH STREET
HAMMOND, IN 46323
219-989-2400
Fax: 219-989-2766
www.purduecalsports.com
• Rick Costello, Director of Athletics
(219) 989-2540
rick.costello@purduecal.edu
• Jennifer Madgiak, Associate Athletic
Director
(219) 989-2728
jennifer.madgiak@purduecal.edu
• Nicole Watkins, Assistant Athletic Director
(219) 989-2506
nicole.watkins@purduecal.edu
• John Friend, Athletics Consultant
(219) 989-2540
john.friend@purduecal.edu

**PURDUE UNIVERSITY NORTH CENTRAL
ATHLETICS**
1401 SOUTH U.S. 421
WESTVILLE, IN 46391
219-785-5200
www.pncathletics.com
• Tom Albano, Athletic Director
(219) 785-5273
talbano@pnc.edu
• Shane Prance, Athletic Coordinator
(219) 785-5660
spranc00@pnc.edu
• Doug Cassell, Athletic Trainer
(219) 785-5562
dmcassel@pnc.edu

REINHARDT UNIVERSITY ATHLETICS
7300 REINHARDT CIRCLE
WALESKA, GA 30183-2981
770-720-5600
Fax: 770-720-5622
www.reinhardteagles.com
• Bill Popp, Director of Athletics
(770) 720-5568
wcp@reinhardt.edu
• Devante Wynn, Coordinator of Athletic
Operations
(770) 720-5825
ddw1@reinhardt.edu
• Jason Hanes, Sports Information Director
(770) 720-9129
jah@reinhardt.edu
• Jeffrey Pourchier, Assistant Athletic
Director
(770) 720-5824
jmp@reinhardt.edu
• Ashley Wolary, Head Athletic Trainer
(770) 720-5821
alw@reinhardt.edu

college sports

RIO GRANDE ATHLETICS, UNIVERSITY OF
218 NORTH COLLEGE AVENUE
RIO GRANDE, OH 45674
740-245-7295
800-282-7201
Fax: 740-245-7555
www.rioredstorm.com
• Jeff Lanham, Athletic Director
(740) 245-7485
jlanham@rio.edu
• Randy Payton, Sports Information Director
(740) 245-7213
rpayton@rio.edu
• Tara Gerlach, Head Athletic Trainer
(740) 245-7299
tgerlach@rio.edu

ROBERT MORRIS COLLEGE (IL) ATHLETICS
401 SOUTH STATE STREET
CHICAGO, IL 60605
312-935-6801
www.rmueagles.com
• Megan Smith Eggert, Director of Athletics
(312) 935-4141
msmith@robertmorris.edu
• Jared Williamson, Associate Athletic Director - Chicago
(312) 935-4110
jwilliamson@robertmorris.edu
• Tom Czop, Director of Sports Information
(312) 935-4047
tczop@robertmorris.edu

ROBERTS WESLEYAN COLLEGE ATHLETICS
2301 WESTSIDE DRIVE
ROCHESTER, NY 14624
585-594-6100
800-777-4RWC
Fax: 585-594-6580
www.roberts.edu/athletics
• Micah Chapman, Sports Information Director
(585) 594-6168
chapman_micah@roberts.edu

ROCKY MOUNTAIN COLLEGE ATHLETICS
1511 POLY DRIVE
BILLINGS, MT 59102
406-657-1000
800-877-6259
Fax: 406-259-9751
www.rocky.edu/athletics
• Bruce Parker, Director of Athletics
(406) 657-1124
bruce.parker@rocky.edu
• Jeff Malby, Sports Information Director

SAINT MARY ATHLETICS, COLLEGE OF
7000 MERCY ROAD
OMAHA, NE 68106-2377
402-399-2400
800-926-5534
Fax: 402-399-2381
www.csmflames.com
• Peter Haze Haring, Athletic Director
(402) 399-2332
pharing@csm.edu
• Emilee Powell, Assistant Athletic Director
(402) 399-2607
epowell@csm.edu
• Carolyn Todd Bray, Sports Information Director

(402) 399-6287
cbray@csm.edu

SAINT MARY ATHLETICS, UNIVERSITY OF
4100 SOUTH 4TH STREET
LEAVENWORTH, KS 66048
913-682-5151
Fax: 913-758-6140
www.gospires.com
• Rob Miller, Athletic Director
(913) 758-6160
millerro@stmary.edu
• Tony Hurla, Sports Information Director
(913) 758-4337
hurla333@stmary.edu
• Raeann Bromert, Head Athletic Trainer
(913) 758-4334
taylor02@stmary.edu
• Erin Koch, Assistant Athletic Trainer
(913) 758-4380
erin.koch@stmary.edu

SAINT MARY'S UNIVERSITY (TX) ATHLETICS
ONE CAMINO SANTA MARIA
SAN ANTONIO, TX 78228
210-436-3528
Fax: 210-436-3040
www.rattlerathletics.com
• Elizabeth Dalton, Athletics Director
(210) 436-3605
edalton@stmarytx.edu
• Brian Martinek, Associate Athletics Director
(210) 436-3434
bmartinek@stmarytx.edu
• Chris Thompson, Assistant Athletics Director
(210) 436-3528
cthompson@stmarytx.edu
• Nathan Byerley, Head Athletic Trainer
(210) 436-3342
nbyerley@stmarytx.edu
• Brittany Davis, Assistant Athletic Trainer
(210) 436-5043
bdavis23@mail.stmarytx.edu

SAINT XAVIER UNIVERSITY ATHLETICS
3700 WEST 103RD STREET
CHICAGO, IL 60655
773-298-3000
Fax: 773-298-3111
www.sxucougars.com
• Bob Hallberg, Athletics Director
(773) 298-3109
hallberg@sxu.edu
• Rob Huizenga, Assistant Athletics Director
(773) 298-3100
huizenga@sxu.edu
• Chris Gbur, Assistant Sports Information
(773) 298-3146
gbur@sxu.edu
• Katherine DeGaetano, Head Athletic Trainer
(773) 298-3128
degaetano@sxu.edu

SAN DIEGO CHRISTIAN COLLEGE ATHLETICS
200 RIVERVIEW PARKWAY
SANTEE, CA 92071
619-201-8700
Fax: 619-201-8797
www.sdcchawks.com
• Carolyn Peters, Director of Athletics
(619) 201-8746

cpeters@sdcc.edu
• Nick Fortini, Director of Sports Information
(619) 540-9185
nfortini@sdcc.edu
• Jon DePriest, Compliance and Eligibility Officer
(619) 201-8746
jon.depriest@sdcc.edu
• Carolyn Peters, Head Athletic Trainer
(619) 201-8734
cpeters@sdcc.edu

SCHREINER UNIVERSITY ATHLETICS
2100 MEMORIAL BOULEVARD
KERRVILLE, TX 78028-5697
830-896-5411
800-343-4919
Fax: 800-436-5435
athletics.schreiner.edu
• Ron Masosko, Director of Athletics
(830) 792-7482
rpmacosko@schreiner.edu
• Ryan Brisbin, Sports Information Director
(830) 792-7292
rsbrisbin@schreiner.edu
• Carlile Janel, Head Athletic Trainer
(830) 792-7299
jacarlile@schreiner.edu

SCIENCE AND ARTS OF OKLAHOMA ATHLETICS, UNIVERSITY OF
1727 WEST ALABAMA AVENUE
CHICKASHA, OK 73018
405-224-3140
Fax: 405-574-1220
www.usao.edu/sports
• Brisco McPherson, Athletic Director
(405) 574-1249
facmcphersonb@usao.edu
• Leslie Beaty, Athletic Trainer
(405) 574-1398
lbeaty@usao.edu
• Justin Tinder, Sports Information Director
(405) 574-1210
jtinder@usao.edu

SEATTLE UNIVERSITY ATHLETICS
SEATTLE UNIVERSITY ATHLETICS
901 12TH AVENUE
PO BOX 222000
SEATTLE, WA 98122
206-296-2154
Fax: 206-296-2154
www.goseattleu.com
• Shaney Fink, Director of Athletics
(206) 296-5451
hoganw@seattleu.edu
• Eric Guerra, Associate Athletic Director
(206) 296-6027
guerrae@seattleu.edu
• Erin Engelhardt, Assistant Athletic Director
(206) 296-5603
engelhardte@seattleu.edu
• Suzy Barcomb, Women's Basketball Head Coach
(206) 296-6406
• Sarah Finney, Athletics Communications Director
(206) 296-5915
finneysa@seattleu.edu

SETON HILL UNIVERSITY ATHLETICS
ONE SETON HILL DRIVE
GREENSBURG, PA 15601
724-834-2200
800-826-6234

Fax: 724-830-1127
athletics.setonhill.edu
• Chris Snyder, Executive Director of
Athletics
(724) 830-1895
csnyder@setonhill.edu
• Bruce Ivory, Associate Athletic Director
(724) 552-1714
ivory@setonhill.edu
• Jason Greene, Director of Athletic
Communication
(724) 830-1132
greene@setonhill.edu

**SHAWNEE STATE UNIVERSITY
ATHLETICS**
940 SECOND STREET
PORTSMOUTH, OH 45662-4344
740-351-3205
jhamilton@shawnee.edu
www.ssubears.com
• Jeff Hamilton, Athletic Director
(740) 351-3393
jhamilton@shawnee.edu
• Jonathon Loughridge, Sports Information
Director
(740) 351-3313
jloughridge@shawnee.edu
• Jeff Nickel, Women's Basketball Head
Coach
(740) 351-3271
jnickel@shawnee.edu

**SIENA HEIGHTS UNIVERSITY
ATHLETICS**
1247 EAST SIENA HEIGHTS DRIVE
ADRIAN, MI 49221
517-264-7876
800-521-0009
Fax: 517-264-7737
shusaints.com
• Fred Smith, Athletic Director
(517) 264-7876
fsmith@sienaheights.edu
• Sue Syljebeck, Assistant Athletic Director
(517) 264-7871
ssyljebe@sienaheights.edu
• Crystal Wilcoxen, Sports Information
Director
(517) 264-7843

**SOUTHERN OREGON UNIVERSITY
ATHLETICS**
1250 SISKIYOU BOULEVARD
ASHLAND, OR 97520
541-552-7672
Fax: 541-552-6543
souraiders.com
• Matt Sayre, Director of Athletics
(541) 552-6273
sayrem@sou.edu
• Bobby Heiken, Associate Athletic Director
(541) 552-6824
heikenb@sou.edu
• Josh McDermott, Sports Information
Director
(541) 552-6801
mcdermotj@sou.edu
• Kristy Johnson, Head Athletic Trainer
(541) 552-6830
johnsok10@sou.edu

**SOUTHERN UNIVERSITY (NEW
ORLEANS) ATHLETICS**
6400 PRESS DRIVE
NEW ORLEANS, LA 70126

504-286-5000
Fax: 504-284-5520
www.suno.edu/athletics
• Yhann Plummer, Interim Athletic Director
(504) 286-5191
yplummer@suno.edu

SOUTHWEST ADVENTIST UNIVERSITY
100 WEST HILLCREST
KEENE, TX 76059
817-645-3921
800-433-2240
Fax: 817-556-4744
• James The, Vice President for Student
Services
(817) 202-6719
jthe@swau.edu

**SOUTHWEST ATHLETICS, COLLEGE OF
THE**
6610 NORTH LOVINGTON HIGHWAY
HOBBS, NM 88240
505-392-6561
800-530-4400
Fax: 505-392-6006
• William J. Weidner, Director of Athletics
(575) 492-2187
wweidner@usw.edu
• Betty Casey, Student-Athlete Academic
Support Liaison
(575) 492-2143
bcasey@usw.edu
• Dana Lambert, Sports Information Liaison
(575) 492-2144
dlambert@usw.edu
• Steve Burback, Head Athletic Trainer
(575) 492-2150
sburback@usw.edu

**SOUTHWESTERN ASSEMBLIES OF GOD
UNIVERSITY ATHLETICS**
1200 SYCAMORE STREET
WAXAHACHIE, TX 75165
972-937-4010
888-YES-SAGU
info@sagu.edu
www.sagu.edu/athletics/athletics-home
• Jesse Godding, Athletic Director
(975) 825-4811
jgodding@sagu.edu
• Stuart Dunn, Athletic Trainer
(972) 825-4671
sdunn@sagu.edu
• Natalie Tristan, Sports Information Director
ntristan@sagu.edu

SOUTHWESTERN COLLEGE ATHLETICS
100 COLLEGE STREET
WINFIELD, KS 67156-2499
620-229-6359
800-846-1543
Fax: 620-229-6124
www.buildersports.com
• Matt Shelton, Associate Athletic Director
(620) 229-6359
matt.shelton@sckans.edu
• Scott Nuss, Assistant Athletic Director
(620) 229-6299
scott.nuss@sckans.edu
• Jeanice Lowry, Athletic Administrative
Assistant
(620) 229-6218
jeanice.lowry@sckans.edu
• Lock Schnelle, Head Athletic Trainer
(620) 229-6375
lock.schnelle@sckans.edu

SPALDING UNIVERSITY ATHLETICS
845 SOUTH THIRD STREET
LOUISVILLE, KY 40203
502-585-9911
800-896-8941
Fax: 502-585-7117
www.spaldingathletics.com
• Roger Burkman, Director of Athletics
(502) 873-7141
rburkman@spalding.edu
• Brian Clinard, Sports Information Director
(502) 873-4206
bclinard@spalding.edu

SPRING ARBOR COLLEGE ATHLETICS
106 EAST MAIN STREET
SPRING ARBOR, MI 49283
517-750-6503
800-968-0011
Fax: 517-750-2745
www.saucougars.com
• Ryan Cottingham, Athletic Director
(517) 750-6505
ryan.cottingham@arbor.edu
• Ryan Frost, Assistant Athletic Director
(517) 750-6568
ryan.frost@arbor.edu
• Betsy Martinez, Assistant Athletic Director
(517) 750-6523
elizabeth.martinez2@arbor.edu
• Chris Bauman, Sports Information Director
(517) 750-6504
christopher.bauman@arbor.edu

SPRING HILL COLLEGE ATHLETICS
4000 DAUPHIN STREET
MOBILE, AL 36608
251-380-3485
800-742-6704
Fax: 251-460-2196
www.shcbadgers.com
• Jim Hall, Director of Athletics & Recreation
(251) 380-3491
jhall@shc.edu
• Chad LeBlanc, Assistant Athletic Director
(251) 380-4077
cleblanc@shc.edu
• Jim Stennett, Sports Information Director
(251) 380-4468
jstennett@shc.edu

**ST. ANDREWS PRESBYTERIAN
ATHLETICS**
1700 DOGWOOD MILE
LAURINBURG, NC 28352
910-277-5555
800-763-0198
Fax: 910-277-5020
battengt@sa.edu
www.sauknights.com
• Glenn Batten, Athletic Director
(910) 277-5556
battengt@sa.edu
• Elizabeth Burris, Director of Compliance
(910) 277-5480
burrises@sa.edu
• Troy Baranik, Sports Information Director
(910) 277-5751
baraniktn@sa.edu
• Brianne Morith, Head Athletic Trainer
(910) 277-3977
morithb@sa.edu

**ST. FRANCIS ATHLETICS, UNIVERSITY
OF**
500 WILCOX STREET
JOLIET, IL 60435

815-740-3464
800-735-7500
Fax: 815-740-3841
dlaketa@stfrancis.edu
www.gofightingsaints.com
• Dave Laketa, Director of Athletics
(815) 740-3842
dlaketa@stfrancis.edu
• Cara Currier, Assistant Director of
Athletics
(815) 740-3407
ccurrier@stfrancis.edu
• Art Campos, Head Certified Athletic
Trainer
(815) 740-3845
acampos@stfrancis.edu
• Dave Hilbert, Sports Information Director
(815) 740-3614
dhilbert@stfrancis.edu

ST. JOSEPH ATHLETICS, COLLEGE OF
71 CLEMENT ROAD
RUTLAND, VT 05701
802-773-5900
802-773-5900
www.csj.edu/athletics
• Jeffrey Brown, Athletic Director
(802) 776-5278
jeffrey.brown@csj.edu
• Jack Boymer, Sports Information Director
(802) 776-5278
jack.boymer@csj.edu

**ST. LOUIS COLLEGE OF PHARMACY
ATHLETICS**
4588 PARKVIEW PLACE
ST. LOUIS, MO 63110
314-367-8700
800-2STLCOP
jill.harter@stlcop.edu
www.eutecticsports.com
• Jill Harter, Director of Athletics
(314) 446-8346
jill.harter@stlcop.edu
• Katie Payne, Athletic Department
Assistant
(314) 446-8343
katie.e.payne@stlcop.edu
• Briana Hepfinger, Sports Information
Director
(314) 446-8348
briana.hepfinger@stlcop.edu

**STATE UNIVERSITY OF NEW YORK AT
DELHI ATHLETICS**
2 MAIN ST
DELHI, NY 13753
607-746-4675
Fax: 607-746-4119
delhibroncos.com
• Bob Backus, Director of Athletics
(607) 746-4677
backusrh@delhi.edu
• Lynn Oles, Athletics Department Secretary
(607) 746-4794
olesmg@delhi.edu

STERLING COLLEGE ATHLETICS
125 WEST COOPER
STERLING, KS 67579
620-278-4335
800-346-1017
Fax: 620-278-4319
www.scwarriors.com
• Gary Kempf, Athletic Director
(620) 278-4469
gkempf@sterling.edu

• Justin Morris, Assistant Athletic Director
(620) 278-4324
jmorris@sterling.edu
• Caden Ford, Sports Information Director
(858) 204-4762
caden.ford@sterling.edu
• Joe Streckfus, Certified Athletic Trainer
(620) 278-4338
jstreckfus@sterling.edu

TABOR COLLEGE ATHLETICS
400 SOUTH JEFFERSON
HILLSBORO, KS 67063
620-947-3121
Fax: 620-947-6276
www.taborbluejays.com
• Rusty Allen, Vice President of Athletics
(620) 947-3121
rustya@tabor.edu
• Karol Hunt, Associate Athletic Director
(620) 947-3121
karolh@tabor.edu
• John Ruder, Assistant Athletic Director
(620) 947-3121
johnr@tabor.edu

TALLADEGA COLLEGE ATHLETICS
627 WEST BATTLE STREET
TALLADEGA, AL 35160
256-326-0206
www.talladegatornadoes.com
• Kevin Herod, Athletic Director
(256) 761-8757
• Demond Walker, Associate Athletic
Director
(256) 589-2001
dwalker@talladega.edu
• Demond Walker, Sports Information
Director
(256) 761-6411
dlwalker@talladega.edu

TAYLOR UNIVERSITY ATHLETICS
236 WEST READE AVENUE
UPLAND, IN 46989
765-998-5311
Fax: 765-998-4920
amstucky@taylor.edu
athletics.taylor.edu
• Kyle Gould, Athletics Director
(765) 998-5314
kygould@taylor.edu
• Amy Stucky, Associate Athletic Director
(765) 998-4635
amstucky@taylor.edu
• Seth Mikel, Assitant Athletics Director for
Communications
(765) 998-4569
stmikel@taylor.edu

**TENNESSEE WESLEYAN COLLEGE
ATHLETICS**
204 EAST COLLEGE STREET
ATHENS, TN 37303
423-745-7504
800-742-5892
Fax: 423-744-9968
www.twcbulldogs.com
• Donny Mayfield, Athletic Director
(423) 746-5253
dmayfield@twcnet.edu
• Jennifer Harrison, Director of Sports
Information
(423) 252-1365
jharrison@twcnet.edu
• Kelley Seekins, Head Athletic Trainer

(423) 252-1104
mneffendorf@twcnet.edu

**TEXAS AT TYLER ATHLETICS,
UNIVERSITY OF**
3900 UNIVERSITY BOULEVARD
TYLER, TX 75799
903-566-7105
Fax: 903-566-7078
www.uttylerpatriots.com

TEXAS COLLEGE ATHLETICS
2404 NORTH GRAND AVENUE
TYLER, TX 75702
903-593-8311 EXT 67
800-306-6299
Fax: 903-593-0588
www.texascollege.edu/pages/athletics
• Elissia Burwell, Athletic Director
(903) 593-8311
eburwell@texascollege.edu
• Angela Lawson, Athletic Coordinator
(903) 593-8311
alawson@texascollege.edu

**TEXAS WESLEYAN UNIVERSITY
ATHLETICS**
1201 WESLEYAN STREET
FORT WORTH, TX 76105
817-531-4857
Fax: 817-531-4208
www.ramsports.net
• Steven Trachier, Director of Athletics
(817) 531-4874
satrachier@txwes.edu
• Kevin Millikan, Associate Athletic Director
(817) 531-7518
kmillikan@txwes.edu

**TEXAS-PERMIAN BASIN ATHLETICS,
UNIVERSITY OF**
4901 EAST UNIVERSITY
ODESSA, TX 79762
432-552-2675
Fax: 432-552-3675
www.utpbfalcons.com
• Steve Aicinena, Athletics Director
(432) 552-2675
aicinena_s@utpb.edu
• Erin Brohn, Director of Compliance
(432) 552-3676
bohn_e@utpb.edu

THOMAS UNIVERSITY ATHLETICS
1501 MILLPOND ROAD
THOMASVILLE, GA 31792
229-226-1621
800-538-9784
Fax: 229-226-1653
www.tunighthawks.com
• Mike Lee, Athletic Director
(229) 584-2432
mlee@thomasu.edu
• Ricky Zambrano, Associate Athletic
Director
(229) 584-2437
rzambrano@thomasu.edu

TOUGALOO COLLEGE ATHLETICS
500 WEST COUNTY LINE ROAD
TOUGALOO, MS 39174
601-977-7700
Fax: 601-977-7866
www.tougaloo.edu/athletics

• Yolanda Brown, Assistant Athletic Director
(601) 977-6171
ybrown@tougaloo.edu

TRINE UNIVERSITY ATHLETICS
HERSHEY HALL
1 UNIVERSITY AVE
ANGOLA, IN 46703
260-665-4142
Fax: 260-665-4839
trinethunder.com
• Matt Land, Athletic Director
(260) 665-4142
landm@trine.edu
• Brooks Miller, Assistant Athletic Director
(260) 665-4843
millerb@trine.edu
• Matt Vader, Sports Information Director
(260) 665-4446
vaderm@trine.edu

**TRINITY CHRISTIAN COLLEGE
ATHLETICS**
6601 WEST COLLEGE DRIVE
PALOS HEIGHTS, IL 60463
708-239-4779
Fax: 708-396-7460
athletics@trnty.edu
athletics.trnty.edu
• Bill Schepel, Athletics Director
(708) 239-4805
bill.schepel@trnty.edu
• Josh Lenarz, Assistant Athletics Director
(708) 239-4824
josh.lenarz@trnty.edu
• Melanie Monroe, Head Athletic Trainer
(708) 239-4774
melanie.monroe@trnty.edu

UNION COLLEGE (KY) ATHLETICS
310 COLLEGE STREET
BARBOURVILLE, KY 40906
606-546-1236
800-489-8646
Fax: 606-546-1286
www.ucbulldogs.com
• Tim Curry, Director of Athletics
(606) 546-1682
tcurry@unionky.edu
• Jay Stancil, Director of Strategic Sports
Communications
(606) 546-1292
jstancil@unionky.edu
• Jon North, Director of Sports Broadcasting
(606) 546-1546
jnorth@unionky.edu
• Clay Butler, Director of Sports Medicine
(606) 546-1303
cbutler@unionky.edu

UNITY COLLEGE ATHLETICS
90 QUAKER HILL ROAD
UNITY, ME 04988
207-509-7100
Fax: 207-948-5626
info@unity.edu
athletics.unity.edu
• Chris Kein, Athletic Director
(207) 509-7283
ckein@unity.edu

**UNIVERSITY OF JAMESTOWN
ATHLETICS**
6000 COLLEGE LANE
JAMESTOWN, ND 58405

701-252-3467
800-336-2554
Fax: 701-253-4318
www.jimmieathletics.com
• Sean Johnson, Director of Athletics
sean.johnson@uj.edu
• Tom Hager, Associate Athletics Director
thager@uj.edu
• Kelsey Titus, Assistant Athletics Director
ktitus@uj.edu
• Ryan Mikkelson, Sports Information
Director
rmikkels@uj.edu
• Mitch Lang, Head Athletic Trainer
lang@uj.edu

UNIVERSITY OF PIKEVILLE ATHLETICS
147 SYCAMORE STREET
PIKEVILLE, KY 41501
606-218-5250
Fax: 606-218-5269
athletics@pc.edu
upikebears.com
• Robert Staggs, Athletic Director
(606) 218-5357
robertstaggs@upike.edu
• Dan White, Assistant Athletic Director
(606) 218-5350
danielwhite@upike.edu
• Meg Wright Sidle, Athletics Compliance
Officer
(606) 218-5290
margaretsidle@upike.edu
• Erica Pitt, Head Athletic Trainer
(606) 218-5359
ericapitt@upike.edu

URBANA UNIVERSITY ATHLETICS
579 COLLEGE WAY
URBANA, OH 43078
937-484-1325
Fax: 937-772-9238
athletics@urbana.edu
www.uublueknights.com
• Larry Cox, Director of Athletics
(937) 772-9238
larry.cox@urbana.edu
• Nikki Pluger, Associate Athletic Director of
Compliance
(937) 772-9305
nicole.pluger@urbana.edu
• Derrick Blyberg, Sports Information
Director
(937) 772-9211
derrick.blyberg@urbana.edu
• Jassen Dobyns, Head Athletic Trainer
(937) 772-9304
jassen.dobyns@urbana.edu

**VANGUARD UNIVERSITY OF SOUTHERN
CALIFORNIA ATHLETICS**
55 FAIR DRIVE
COSTA MESA, CA 92626
714-556-3610
athletics@vanguard.edu
www.vanguardlions.com
• Rhett Soliday, Athletic Director
(714) 619-6601
rhett.soliday@vanguard.edu
• Jeff Bussell, Associate Athletic Director
(714) 619-6602
jeffrey.bussell@vanguard.edu
• Mike Teague, Coordinator of Compliance
(714) 619-6605
michael.teague@vanguard.edu
• Darin Voigt, Head Athletic Trainer

(714) 619-6617
dvoigt@vanguard.edu

VITERBO ATHLETICS UNIVERSITY
400 VITERBO DRIVE
LA CROSSE, WI 54601
608-796-3811
Fax: 608-796-3818
athletics@viterbo.edu
www.viterboathletics.com
• Barry Fried, Director of Athletics
(608) 796-3812
bjfried@viterbo.edu
• Wayne Wagner, Assistant Athletics
Director
(608) 796-3814
wrwagner@viterbo.edu
• Jo Ann Marson, Faculty Athletics
Representative
(608) 796-3363
jmmarson@viterbo.edu
• Nicole Ross, Athletic Trainer
(608) 796-3815
nrross@gundersenhealth.org

VOORHEES COLLEGE ATHLETICS
213 WIGGINS DRIVE
PO BOX 678
DENMARK, SC 29042
803-780-1234
866-685-9904
Fax: 803-793-4584
www.voorhees.edu/athletics
• Willie Jefferson, Director of Athletics
(803) 780-1049

WALDORF COLLEGE ATHLETICS
106 SOUTH 6TH STREET
FOREST CITY, IA 50436
641-585-8182
Fax: 641-585-8184
www.waldorfwarriors.com
• Denny Jerome, Director of Athletics
(641) 585-8163
jeromed@waldorf.edu
• Kristi Osheim, Manager of Athletic
Operations
(641) 585-8782
osheimk@waldorf.edu
• Joe Squires, Director of Athletic Events
(641) 585-1655
joe.squires@waldorf.edu
• Heidi Laube, Head Athletic Trainer
(641) 585-8394
whiteh@waldorf.edu

WALSH UNIVERSITY ATHLETICS
2020 EAST MAPLE STREET
NORTH CANTON, OH 44720
330-490-7090
800-362-9846
Fax: 330-490-7038
athletics.walsh.edu
• Dale Howard, Director of Athletics
(330) 490-7303
dhoward@walsh.edu
• Jason Fautas, Assistant Athletic Director
(330) 490-7437
jfautas@walsh.edu
• Logan Smith, Sports Information Director
(330) 490-7254
lsmith@walsh.edu

WARNER PACIFIC COLLEGE ATHLETICS
2219 SE 68TH AVENUE
PORTLAND, OR 97215

college sports

503-517-1261
Fax: 503-517-1352
www.wpcknights.com
• Frank Johnson, Interim Athletic Director
(503) 734-6463
fjjohnson@warnerpacific.edu
• Matt Gregg, Assistant Athletic Director
(503) 517-1370
mgregg@warnerpacific.edu
• Amy Engilis, Head Athletic Trainer
(503) 517-1063
aengilis@warnerpacific.edu

WARNER UNIVERSITY ATHLETICS
13895 HIGHWAY 27
LAKE WALES, FL 33859
863-638-1426
800-309-9563
Fax: 863-638-3776
www.warnerroyals.com
• Kevin Jones, Athletic Director
(863) 638-7297
kevin.jones@warner.edu
• John Dunlap, Assistant Athletic Director
(863) 638-7135
john.dunlap@warner.edu

**WAYLAND BAPTIST UNIVERSITY
ATHLETICS**
1900 WEST 7TH STREET
PLAINVIEW, TX 79072
806-291-1000
800-588-1928
Fax: 806-291-1962
rick.cooper@wbu.edu
www.wbuathletics.com
• Rick Cooper, Athletics Director
(806) 291-3801
rick.cooper@wbu.edu
• Landon Schumacher, Head Athletic
Trainer
(806) 291-3803
schumacherl@wbu.edu

**WEBBER INTERNATIONAL UNIVERSITY
ATHLETICS**
1201 NORTH SCENIC HIGHWAY
BABSON PARK, FL 33827
863-638-2980
1-800-741-1844
Fax: 863-638-2979
www.webberathletics.com
• Richie Darren, Director of Athletics
(863) 638-2953
richieda@webber.edu
• Tim Desmarteau, Assistant Athletic
Director
(863) 638-2989
desmarteautj@webber.edu
• Kyle Blue, Sports Information Director
(863) 638-2980
bluekyler@webber.edu
• Jen Hamil, Game Day Operations
Coordinator
(863) 899-1431
hamilje@webber.edu

**WEST VIRGINIA UNIVERSITY INSTITUTE
OF TECHNOLOGY ATHLETICS**
405 FAYETTE PIKE
MONTGOMERY, WV 25136
304-442-3121
Fax: 304-442-3499
tech-athletics@mail.wvu.edu
goldenbearathletics.com
• Kenneth Howell, Director of Athletics
(304) 442-3380

kenneth.howell@mail.wvu.edu
• Jenna Everhart, Senior Woman
Administrator
(304) 981-6216
jenna.lehmann@mail.wvu.edu
• Becky Brouse, Sports Information Director
(304) 981-6211
rsbrouse@mail.wvu.edu
• Carrie Williams, Athletic Trainer
(304) 442-3181
cwilliam@mail.wvu.edu

WESTMONT COLLEGE ATHLETICS
955 LA PAZ ROAD
SANTA BARBARA, CA 93108
805-565-6000
Fax: 805-565-6221
athletics.westmont.edu
• Dave Odell, Director of Athletics
(805) 565-6010
dodell@westmont.edu
• John Moore, Associate Athletic Director
(805) 565-6013
moore@westmont.edu
• Kirsten Moore, Associate Athletic Director
(805) 565-6836
kirstenmoore@westmont.edu

WILEY COLLEGE ATHLETICS
711 WILEY AVENUE
MARSHALL, TX 75670
903-927-3300
Fax: 903-938-8100
www.wileyathletics.com
• Joseph Morale, Acting Director of Athletics
(903) 927-3233
jmorale@wileyc.edu
• Andrew Glover, Sports Information
Director
(903) 927-3399
adglover@wileyc.edu
• Jameus Hartsfield, Assistant Sports
Information Director
(903) 927-2486
jlhartsfield@wileyc.edu
• LaKyva Bason, Assistant Athletic Director
(903) 927-3294
lwalton-bason@wileyc.edu

WILLIAM CAREY COLLEGE ATHLETICS
498 TUSCAN AVENUE
HATTIESBURG, MS 39401
601-318-6051
Fax: 601-318-6454
www.wmcarey.edu
• Steve Knight, Athletic Director
(601) 318-6415
sknight@wmcarey.edu
• Kevin Rosiere, Graduate Asst Sports
Informations Golf Head C
(601) 466-6380

WILLIAM PENN UNIVERSITY ATHLETICS
201 TRUEBLOOD AVENUE
OSKALOOSA, IA 52577
641-673-1018
Fax: 641-673-1373
www.statesmenathletics.com
• Greg Hafner, Athletics Director
(641) 673-2168
hafnerg@wmpenn.edu
• Mike Christner, Assistant Athletic Director
(641) 673-1707
• Wade Steinlage, Sports Information
Director
(641) 673-1025
steinlagew@wmpenn.edu

**WILLIAM WOODS UNIVERSITY
ATHLETICS**
ONE UNIVERSITY AVE
FULTON, MO 65251
573-642-2251
Fax: 573-592-1146
wwuowls.com
• Jason Vittone, Director of Intercollegiate
Athletics
(573) 592-1642
jason.vittone@williamwoods.edu
• Tracy Gastineau, Associate Director of
Intercollegiate Athletics
(573) 592-4326
tracy.gastineau@williamwoods.edu

**WILLIAMS BAPTIST COLLEGE
ATHLETICS**
60 WEST FULBRIGHT AVE
WALNUT RIDGE, AR 72476
870-886-6741
Fax: 870-886-3924
www.wbceagles.com
• Jeff Rider, Director of Athletics
(870) 759-4194
jrider@wbcoll.edu
• Shane Stolz, Sports Information Director
(870) 759-4156
sstolz@wbcoll.edu
• Misty Colvey, Head Athletic Trainer
(870) 759-4196
mcolvey@wbcoll.edu

WINDSOR ATHLETICS, UNIVERSITY OF
401 SUNSET AVENUE
WINDSOR, ON, CANADA N9B 3P4
519-253-3000 EXT 2437
lancers@uwindsor.ca
golancers.ca
• Mike Harvey, Athletic Director
havey@uwindsor.ca
• Eric Vandenbroucke, Associate Athletic
Director
evander@uwindsor.ca
• Elisa Mitton, Sports Information
Coordinator

**XAVIER UNIVERSITY OF LOUISIANA
ATHLETICS**
1 DREXEL DR
CAMPUS BOX 92
NEW ORLEANS, LA 70125
504-520-7329
www.xulagold.com
• Jason Horn, Director of Athletics and
Recreation
(504) 520-7329
jhorn1@xula.edu

YORK COLLEGE (NE) ATHLETICS
1125 EAST 8TH STREET
YORK, NE 68467
402-363-5635
800-950-9675
Fax: 402-363-5738
www.ycpanthers.com
• Jared Stark, Director of Athletics
(402) 363-5635
jastark@york.edu
• Trent Hinton, Sports Information Director
(402) 363-5698
thinton@york.edu
• Chad Karcher, Athletic Trainer
(402) 363-5734
cekarcher@york.edu

NCAA Division I Colleges

AKRON ATHLETICS, UNIVERSITY OF
DEPT. OF INTERCOLLEGIATE
ATHLETICS
JAMES A. RHODES ARENA
373 CARROLL ST
AKRON, OH 44325
330-972-7080
888-992-5766
Fax: 330-972-5473
gozips.com
• Larry Williams, Director of Athletics
(330) 972-7080
krex@uakron.edu
• Brock Cline, Assoc. Athletics Director
(330) 972-7117
bmc35@uakron.edu
• George Van Horne, Sr. Assoc. AD, Devel.
& Marketing
(330) 972-8255
ghvanhorne@uakron.edu

ALABAMA ATHLETICS, UNIVERSITY OF
DEPT. OF INTERCOLLEGIATE
ATHLETICS
UNIV. OF ALABAMA
PO BOX 870323
TUSCALOOSA, AL 35487
205-348-3600
www.rolltide.com
• Kevin Almond, Executive Associate
Athletic Director
(205) 348-3638
kalmond@ia.ua.edu
• Finus Gaston, Executive Associate Athletic
Director/CFO
(205) 348-5231
fgaston@ia.ua.edu

ALABAMA BIRMINGHAM ATHLETICS, UNIVERSITY OF
1720 2ND AVENUE S
BARTOW ARENA
BIRMINGHAM, AL 35294-1160
www.uabsports.com
• Mark Ingram, Director of Athletics
(205) 934-0766
ingramad@uab.edu

ALABAMA STATE UNIVERSITY ATHLETICS
ALABAMA STATE UNIVERSITY
915 S JACKSON STREET
MONTGOMERY, AL 36106
334-229-4507
asuathletics@alasu.edu
www.bamastatesports.com
• Jennifer Williams, Director of Athletics
(334) 229-4507
jenniferwilliams@alasu.edu
• Terrance Jones, Deputy Director of
Athletics
(334) 207-1756
tjones@alasu.edu

ALCORN STATE UNIVERSITY ATHLETICS
1000 ASU DRIVE
SUITE 510
LORMAN, MS 39096
601-877-6500
Fax: 601-877-3821
www.alcornsports.com
• Derek Horne, Director of Intercollegiate
Athletics

djhorne@alcorn.edu
• Danielle Ferguson, Assoc. Athletic
Director/Sr. Women's Administrator
(601) 877-6509
dferguson@alcorn.edu
• Larry Smith, Director of Athletic
Development
(601) 877-2470
lsmith@alcorn.edu
• Tim Smith, Asst. Athletic Director for
Internal Operations
(601) 877-6504
tcsmith@alcorn.edu

AMERICAN UNIVERSITY ATHLETICS
AMERICAN UNIVERSITY ATHLETICS
BENDER ARENA
4400 MASSACHUSETTS AVENUE NW
WASHINGTON, DC 20016-8005
202-885-3000
athcom@american.edu
www.aueagles.com
• Billy Walker, Director of Athletics &
Recreation
(202) 885-3001
walker@american.edu
• Josephine Harrington, Deputy Director of
Athletics
(202) 885-3006
finamore@american.edu
• Brian Chepulis, Assoc. AD, Facilities &
Operations
(202) 885-3074
chepulis@american.edu

APPALACHIAN STATE UNIVERSITY ATHLETICS
ATHLETICS CENTER
ASU BOX 32025
BOONE, NC 28608
828-262-7825
Fax: 828-262-2556
www.appstatesports.com
• Doug Gillin, Director of Athletics
(828) 262-7825
gillindp@appstate.edu
• Jonathan Reeder, Exec. Assoc. AD, CFO
(828) 406-5992
reederjb@appstate.edu
• Rene Salinas, Faculty Athletics
Representative
(828) 262-2866
salinasra@appstate.edu
• Makini Thompson, Sr. Assoc. AD
(828) 262-8580
thompsonm2@appstate.edu

ARIZONA ATHLETICS, UNIVERSITY OF
MCKALE CENTER
1 NATIONAL CHAMPIONSHIP DRIVE
PO BOX 210096
TUCSON, AZ 85721-0096
520-621-2200
arizonawildcats.com
• Dave Heeke, Vice President, Director of
Athletics
(520) 621-4622
uofaad@arizona.edu

ARIZONA STATE UNIVERSITY ATHLETICS
CARSON CENTER
PO BOX 872505
TEMPE, AZ 85287-2505
480-965-3482
sparkycares@asu.edu
thesundevils.com

• Ray Anderson, Vice President for
University Athletics
(480) 965-0983
ray.anderson@asu.edu
• Jean Boyd, Deputy Athletics Director
(480) 965-8054
jean.boyd@asu.edu

ARKANSAS LITTLE ROCK ATHLETICS, UNIVERSITY OF
2801 S UNIVERSITY AVENUE
JACK STEPHENS CENTER
LITTLE ROCK, AR 72204
lrtrojans.com
• George Lee, Director of Athletics
(501) 916-5347
gllee@ualr.edu
• Tyson Baldwin, Assoc. AD for External
Operations
(501) 350-4653
twbaldwin@ualr.edu
• Darius Maize, Deputy AD for Internal
Operations
(501) 907-5861
damaize@ualr.edu
• Maggie Strange, Sr. Assoc. AD,
Compliance
(501) 569-3448
mestrange@ualr.edu

ARKANSAS PINE BLUFF ATHLETICS, UNIVERSITY OF
1200 NORTH UNIVERSITY DRIVE
MAIL SLOT 4891
PINE BLUFF, AR 71601
www.uapblionsroar.com
• Chris Robinson, Interim Director of
Athletics
• Temeka Samuels, Sr. Woman
Administrator
(870) 575-8273
samuelst@uapb.edu
• Roger Totten, Senior Associate Athletic
Director
(870) 575-8544
tottenr@uapb.edu

ARKANSAS STATE UNIVERSITY ATHLETICS
ARKANSAS STATE ATHLETIC DEPT.
217 OLYMPIC DRIVE
JONESBORO, AR 72401
870-972-3880
www.astateredwolves.com
• Tom Bowen, Vice Chancellor for
Intercollegiate Athletics
(870) 972-3115
athleticsdirector@astate.edu
• Rich Zvosec, Deputy Director of Athletics
(870) 972-3005
rzvosec@astate.edu
• Amy Holt, Associate Athletics
Director/SWA
(870) 680-4163
aholt@astate.edu

AUBURN UNIVERSITY ATHLETICS
AUBURN ATHLETICS COMPLEX
392 S DONAHUE DRIVE
AUBURN, AL 36849
855-282-2010
athletics@auburn.edu
www.auburntigers.com
• Allen Greene, Director of Athletics
(334) 844-9891
athletic_director@auburn.edu

AUSTIN PEAY STATE UNIVERSITY ATHLETICS
WINFIELD DUNN CENTER
CORNER OF MARION STREET & ROBB ABENUE
ROOM 227
CLARKSVILLE, TN 37040
931-221-7904
letsgopeay.com
• Gerald Harrison, Director of Athletics
(931) 221-7904
• Sara A Robson, Sr. Assoc. AD, Internal Operations
(931) 221-7008
robsons@apsu.edu
• Lisa Varytimidis, Deputy Director of Athletics/SWA
(931) 221-7904
varytimidisa@apsu.edu

BALL STATE UNIVERSITY ATHLETICS
BALL STATE ATHLETICS
HP 260
MUNCIE, IN 47306-0929
www.ballstatesports.com
• Beth Goetz, Director of Athletics
(765) 285-5131
• Haven Fields, Deputy AD
(765) 285-8907
hcfields@bsu.edu
• Karin Lee, Senior Associate AD/Senior Woman Administrator
(765) 285-5127
kalee2@bsu.edu

BAYLOR UNIVERSITY ATHLETICS
1500 S UNIVERSITY PARKS DRIVE
WACO, TX 76706
254-710-1234
www.baylorbears.com
• Mack Rhoades, VP & Director of Intercollegiate Athletics
(254) 710-1222
lauren_phillips@baylor.edu
• Dawn Rogers, Deputy Athletics Director
(254) 710-3040
dawn_rogers@baylor.edu

BELMONT UNIVERSITY ATHLETICS
1900 BELMONT BOULEVARD
NASHVILLE, TN 37212-3757
615-460-6420
Fax: 615-460-5584
www.belmontbruins.com
• Scott Corley, Director of Athletics
(615) 460-5547
scott.corley@belmont.edu
• Steve Barrick, Associate AD/Director of Facilities
(615) 460-6857
steve.barrick@belmont.edu
• Renee Schultz, Associate AD, Student Services/SWA
(615) 460-6015
renee.schultz@belmont.edu
• Josh Wardltz, Associate AD, Marketing & Sales
(615) 460-6205
josh.ward@belmont.edu

BETHUNE-COOKMAN UNIVERSITY ATHLETICS
640 DR. MARY MCLEOD BETHUNE BOULEVARD
DAYTONA BEACH, FL 32114
386-481-2000
www.bcuathletics.com

• Lynn W. Thompson, Vice President for Intercollegiate Athletics
(386) 481-2215
• Sandra Booker, Sr. Assoc. AD, Internal Operations/SWA
(386) 481-2212
bookers@cookman.edu
• Carla A. Lester, Faculty Athletics Representative
(386) 481-2717
lesterc@cookman.edu
• Reginald L. Thomas, Sr. Assoc. AD, Student Athlete Services
(386) 481-2763
thomasre@cookman.edu

BINGHAMTON UNIVERSITY
PO BOX 6000
BINGHAMTON, NY 13902-6000
607-777-2043
www.bubearcats.com
• Patrick Elliott, PhD, Director of Athletics
(607) 777-2043
elliott@binghamton.edu
• Dennis Kalina, Deputy Director of Athletics
(607) 777-6730
dkalina@binghamton.edu
• Leigh Ann Savidge-Morris, Sr. Assoc. Dir. of Athletics, Internal Ops./SWA
(607) 777-3323
lsavidge@binghamton.edu

BIRMINGHAM-SOUTHERN COLLEGE ATHLETICS
900 ARKADELPHIA ROAD
BIRMINGHAM, AL 35254
www.bscsports.net
• Kyndall Waters, Athletics Director
(205) 226-4935
kwaters@bsc.edu
• Sheri S. Salmon, Assistant AD/SWA
(205) 226-4692
ssalmon@bsc.edu
• Jan Weisberg, Associate AD, Internal Relations
(205) 226-4797
jweiber@bsc.edu

BOISE STATE UNIVERSITY ATHLETICS
1910 UNIVERSITY DRIVE
MAIL STOP 1020
BOISE, ID 83725-1020
www.broncosports.com
• Jeramiah Dickey, Director of Athletics
(208) 426-1826
athleticdirector@boisestate.edu
• Christina Van Tol, Deputy Athletic Director/SWA
(208) 426-1655
cvantol@boisestate.edu
• Da'Vell Winters, Chief of Staff
• Bob Carney, Sr. Associate AD/Strategic Planning
(208) 426-1826

BOSTON COLLEGE ATHLETICS
CONTE FORUM
140 COMMONWEALTH AVENUE
CHESTNUT HILL, MA 02467
617-552-3000
bceagles.com
• Parick Kraft, Director of Athletics
(617) 552-4681
ad@bc.edu

BOSTON UNIVERSITY ATHLETICS
285 BABCOCK STREET
BOSTON, MA 02215
617-353-4630
Fax: 617-353-5286
gobu@bu.edu
goterriers.com
• Drew Marrochello, Director of Athletics
(617) 353-4631
bmkane@bu.edu
• Kirstie Bowers, Senior Associate Director of Athletics/SWA
(617) 353-4683
kbowers@bu.edu
• Brittany Kane, Senior Associate Director of Athletics
(617) 353-4631
bmkane@bu.edu
• Brendan Sullivan, Sr. Assoc. Director of Athletics
(617) 353-1905
bjsulliv@bu.edu

BOWLING GREEN STATE UNIVERSITY ATHLETICS
SEBO ATHLETIC CENTER
1610 STADIUM DRIVE
BOWLING GREEN, OH 43403
419-372-2401
bgsufalcons.com
• Bob Moosbrugger, Director of Athletics
(419) 372-7052
athleticdirector@bgsu.edu
• Kit Hughes, Senior Associate AD
(419) 372-7675
cchughe@bgsu.edu
• Jim Elsasser, Associate AD, Internal Affairs
(419) 372-7054
jelsass@bgsu.edu
• Dan Meyer, Associate AD, Development
(419) 372-7057
dbmeyer@bgsu.edu

BRADLEY UNIVERSITY ATHLETICS
BRADLEY UNIVERSITY ATHLETICS DEPT.
1501 W BRADLEY AVENUE
PEORIA, IL 61625
309-677-2666
Fax: 309-677-3626
www.bradleybraves.com
• Chris Reynolds, Director of Athletics
(309) 677-2670
• J Locklier, Sr. Associate AD for Development
(309) 677-4856
jlocklier@fsmail.bradley.edu
• Craig Dahlquist, Sr. Associate AD, Finance & Administration
(309) 677-2673
cad@bradley.edu
• Jennifer Jones, Sr. Associate AD, Academics & Student Dev./SWA
(309) 677-2846
jenjones@bradley.edu

BRIGHAM YOUNG UNIVERSITY ATHLETICS
331 STUDENT ATHLETE BUILDING
PROVO, UT 84602
801-422-2096
byucougars.com
• Tom Holmoe, Director of Athletics
(801) 422-7649
• Brian Santiago, Deputy AD
(801) 422-9059

• Liz Darger, Sr. Associate AD/SWA
(801) 422-7306
• Bob Schirmer, Associate AD, Finance
(801) 422-2098
• Duff Tittle, Associate AD, Communications
(801) 422-4910
• Chad Lewis, Associate AD, Development
(801) 422-4858

BROWN UNIVERSITY ATHLETICS
235 HOPE STREET
PO BOX 1932
PROVIDENCE, RI 02912
www.brownbears.com
• Colin Sullivan, Deputy Director of Athletics
(401) 863-2272
colin_sullivan@brown.edu

BRYANT UNIVERSITY ATHLETICS
1150 DOUGLAS PIKE
SMITHFIELD, RI 02917
401-232-6070
Fax: 401-232-6361
bryantbulldogs.com
• Bill Smith, Director of Athletics
(401) 232-6078
bsmith8@bryant.edu
• John Ruppert, Deputy Director of Athletics
(401) 232-6737
jruppert@bryant.edu
• Beth Wandyes, Sr. Assoc. AD,
Compliance/SWA
(401) 232-6277
bwandyes@bryant.edu

BUCKNELL UNIVERSITY ATHLETICS
KENNETH LANGONE ATHLETICS &
RECREATION CENTER
ONE DENT DRIVE
LEWISBURG, PA 17837
www.bucknellbison.com
• Jermaine Truax, Director of Athletics
(570) 577-3054
jmt027@bucknell.edu
• Tim Pavlechko, Deputy Director of
Athletics
(570) 577-3588
tpaclech@bucknell.edu

BUTLER UNIVERSITY ATHLETICS
510 W 49TH STREET
INDIANAPOLIS, IN 46208
317-940-9375
butlersports.com
• Barry Collier, Director of Athletics
(317) 940-6803
athleticdirector@butler.edu
• Alex Perry, Assoc. AD, Internal Operations
(317) 940-9523
aperry2@butler.edu
• Mike Freeman, Sr. Associate AD, External
Operations
(317) 940-6452
msfreema@butler.edu
• Ralph Reiff, MEd, ATC, LAT, Sr. Associate
AD, Student-Athlete Health
(317) 940-9379
rreiff@butler.edu

CAL STATE FULLERTON ATHLETICS
800 NORTH STATE COLLEGE
BOULEVARD
PO BOX 6810
FULLERTON, CA 92834
657-278-2777
www.fullertontitans.com

• Jim Donovan, Director of Athletics
(657) 278-2777
jdonovan@fullerton.edu
• Steve DiTolla, Senior Associate Athletic
Director
(657) 278-7791
sditolla@fullerton.edu
• Greg Paules, Associate Athletic Director,
Development
(657) 278-4516
gpaules@fullerton.edu
• Meredith Basil, Associate Athletics
Director/SWA
(657) 278-2648
mbasil@fullerton.edu

CAL STATE NORTHRIDGE ATHLETICS
18111 NORDHOFF STREET
NORTHRIDGE, CA 91330-8276
818-677-3208
Fax: 818-677-4762
www.gomatadors.com
• Michael Izzi, Director of Athletics
• Valerie Richardson, Executive Senior
Associate AD/SWA
valerie.richardson@csun.edu
• Julius Hicks, Senior Associate AD,
External Relations
(818) 677-4837
julius.hicks@csun.edu
• Bob Alejo, Senior Associate AD,
Performance & Student Welfare
robert.alejo@csun.edu

CAMPBELL UNIVERSITY ATHLETICS
78 DR. MCKOY ROAD
BUIES CREEK, NC 27506
www.gocamels.com
• Omar Banks, Director of Athletics
(910) 893-1327
campbellAD@campbell.edu
• Ricky Ray, Deputiy Director of Athletics
(910) 814-4392
ray@campbell.edu
• Wanda Watkins, Associate AD/SWA
(910) 893-1330
watkins@campbell.edu
• Kendra Hancock, Director for
Student-Athlete Support
(910) 814-4386
hancock@campbell.edu
• Stan Cole, Assoc. AD, Communications
(910) 893-1331
cole@campbell.edu
• Tony Delp, Assoc. AD, Advancement
(910) 893-1329
delp@campbell.edu
• Christian Pope, Assoc. AD, Compliance
(910) 893-1323
popec@campbell.edu
• Andrew Carter, Assoc. AD, Health &
Nutrition
(910) 814-4366
cartera@campbell.edu

CANISIUS COLLEGE ATHLETICS
2001 MAIN STREET
BUFFALO, NY 14208
Fax: 716-888-3174
gogriffs.com
• Bill Maher, Director of Athletics
(716) 888-2972
maherw@canisius.edu
• Lisa Liotta, Associate AD/SWA
(716) 888-2959
liottal@canisius.edu

CENTRAL CONNECTICUT STATE ATHLETICS
CCSU DEPT. OF ATHLETICS
1615 STANLEY STREET
NEW BRITAIN, CT 06050
860-832-2583
www.ccsubluedevils.com
• Thomas Pincince, Interim Director of
Athletics
pincincet@ccsu.edu
• Michael Ansarra, Senior Associate
Athletics Director
(860) 832-3072
ansarra@ccsu.edu
• Stephen Villanti, Associate AD, External
Services
(860) 832-3078
villantis@ccsu.edu
• Molly McCarthy, Associate AD,
Compliance & Student Services/SWA
(860) 832-3048
McCarthyM@ccsu.edu
• Mike Ericksen, Associate AD, Sports
Performance
(860) 832-3085
ericksenm@ccsu.edu

CENTRAL FLORIDA ATHLETICS
UCF ATHLETICS
ROTH ATHLETICS CENTER
4192 NORTH ORION BOULEVARD
ORLANDO, FL 32816
407-823-1000
ucfknights.com
• Terry J. Mohajir, VP & Director of Athletics
adoffice@athletics.ucf.edu
• Chris McFarlane, Deputy AD, Competitive
Excellence
cmcfarlane@athletics.ucf.edu
• Scott Carr, Deputy AD, Brand Activation
scarr@athletics.ucf.edu
• Mark Wright, Deputy AD
(407) 823-2001
mwright@athletics.ucf.edu

CENTRAL MICHIGAN UNIVERSITY ATHLETICS
100 ROSE CENTER
MOUNT PLEASANT, MI 48859
989-774-3041
www.cmuchippewas.com
• Amy Folan, Director of Athletics
(989) 774-3043
athleticdirector@cmich.edu
• Craig Willey, Deputy Athletic Director,
External Operations
(989) 774-6192
wille1cl@cmich.edu
• Rob Peterson, Deputy Athletic Director,
Internal Operations
(989) 774-3473
peter1r@cmich.edu

CHARLESTON SOUTHERN UNIVERSITY ATHLETICS
9200 UNIVERSITY BOULEVARD
CHARLESTON, SC 29423
www.csusports.com
• Jeff Barber, Director of Athletics
(843) 863-7678
jbarber@csuniv.edu
• Courtney Hall, Associate AD, Business
Administration
(843) 863-7670
chall@csuniv.edu
• Seth Montgomery, Asst. AD,
Communications/Public Relations

college sports

(843) 863-7853
smontgomery@csuniv.edu
• Cliff Miller, Asst. AD, Development
(843) 863-7523
clmiller@csuniv.edu
• Alex Redding, Assoc. AD, Facilities
(843) 863-7677
aredding@csuniv.edu
• Betty Palmer, Assoc. AD, Academics
(843) 863-7629
epalmer@csuniv.edu

CHICAGO STATE UNIVERSITY ATHLETICS
JCC 1502
9501 S KING DRIVE
CHICAGO, IL 60628
773-995-2295
Fax: 773-995-3656
www.gocsucougars.com
• Elliott Charles, Director of Athletics
(773) 995-2295
athleticdirector@csu.edu
• Ahmad Boyd, Associate AD, Academics/Student Services
aboyd30@csu.edu
• Jamie Johnson, Associate AD, Compliance
jjohnt41@csu.edu
• Jessica Poole, Senior Associate AD, External Operations/SWA
jpoole23@csu.edu

CINCINNATI ATHLETICS, UNIVERSITY OF
RICHARD E. LINDNER CENTER
2751 O'VARSITY WAY
CINCINNATI, OH 45221-0021
513-556-4603
Fax: 513-556-0405
gobearcats.com
• John Cunningham, Director of Athletics
(513) 556-0626
bearcat.ad@uc.edu
• Karen Hatcher, Exec. Sr. Assoc. AD, External Relations
(513) 556-2539
karen.hatcher@uc.edu
• Maggie McKinley, Exec. Sr. Assoc. AD/SWA
(513) 556-3559
maggie.mckinley@uc.edu

CITADEL ATHLETICS, THE
171 MOULTRIE STREET
CHARLESTON, SC 29409
843-953-5070
www.citadelsports.com
• Mike Capaccio, Athletic Director
(843) 953-4806
mcapaccio@citadel.edu
• Kathy Kroupa, Sr. Assoc. AD, Internal Operations/SWA
(843) 953-6604
kkroupa@citadel.edu
• Geoff Von Dollen, Sr. Assoc. AD, Finance/Operations
(843) 953-5352
vondolleng1@citadel.edu

CLEMSON UNIVERSITY ATHLETICS
JERVEY ATHLETIC CENTER
300 PERIMETER ROAD
CLEMSON, SC 29634-0031
800-253-6766
www.clemsontigers.com

• Dan Radakovich, Director of Athletics
(864) 656-1935
danrad1@clemson.edu
• Graham Neff, Deputy Director of Athletics
(864) 656-0128
neffg@clemson.edu
• Steve Duzan, Sr. Assoc. AD, Student-Athlete Services
(864) 656-0945
sduzan@clemson.edu
• Stephanie Ellison, Sr. Assoc. AD, Sports Administrator/SWA
(864) 656-7163
saellis@clemson.edu

CLEVELAND STATE UNIVERSITY ATHLETICS
PE BUILDING - WOODLING GYM
2451 EUCLID AVENUE
ROOM 337
CLEVELAND, OH 44115
www.csuvikings.com
• Scott Garrett, Director of Athletics
(216) 687-4539
csudirectorofathletics@csuohio.edu
• Tyler Jones, Deputy AD, External Operations
(216) 687-5235
t.r.jones43@csuohio.edu
• Kelsie Gory Harkey, Deputy AD, Student-Athlete Experience
(216) 687-4756
k.gory@csuohio.edu
• Danielle Cohea, Associate AD, Compliance
(216) 523-7491
d.cohea@csuohio.edu
• Jamar Ross, Associate AD, Business Affairs
(216) 687-2378
j.s.ross13@csuohio.edu

COASTAL CAROLINA UNIVERSITY ATHLETICS
132 CHANTICLEER DRIVE WEST
CONWAY, SC 29526
Fax: 843-349-2231
www.goccusports.com
• Matt Hogue, Director of Athletics
(843) 349-2231
dhogue@coastal.edu
• Cari Rosiek, Associate AD, Student-Athlete Enhancement/SWA
(843) 349-4126
cari@coastal.edu
• Dwayne Beam, Deputy Athletic Director
(843) 349-2825
dbeam@coastal.edu
• Jess Dannelly, Associate AD, Community Outreach
(843) 349-6699
jess@coastal.edu

COLGATE UNIVERSITY ATHLETICS
13 OAK DRIVE
HAMILTON, NY 13346
gocolgateraiders.com
• Nicki Moore, Director of Athletics
(315) 228-7783
colgateAD@colgate.edu
• Juliana Smith, Deputy AD/SWA
(315) 228-7852
jbsmith@colgate.edu
• Yariv Amir, Senior Associate AD
(315) 228-6547
yamir@colgate.edu
• Laura Sgrecci, Senior Associate AD,

External Affairs
(315) 228-7783
lsgrecci@colgate.edu

COLLEGE OF CHARLESTON ATHLETICS
301 MEETING STREET
CHARLESTON, SC 29401
843-953-5556
www.cofcsports.com
• Matt Roberts, Director of Athletics
(843) 953-8254
robertsmj1@cofc.edu
• Laura Lageman, Senior Associate AD/SWA
(843) 953-5467
lagemanl@cofc.edu
• J.B. Weber, Associstant AD, Compliance
(843) 953-9562
jbweber@cofc.edu
• Jamaal Walton, Associate AD, External Operations
(843) 953-5498
waltonjo@cofc.edu
• Kate Tiller, Assistant AD, Student-Athlete Services
(843) 953-3660
tillerk@cofc.edu

COLORADO ATHLETICS, UNIVERSITY OF
2150 STADIUM DRIVE
CHAMPIONS CENTER
FIFTH FLOOR
BOULDER, CO 80309
303-492-9675
Fax: 303-492-7753
cubuffs.com
• Rick George, Athletic Director
(303) 492-6843
rick.george@colorado.edu
• Lance Carl, Associate AD
lance.s.carl@colorado.edu
• Lance Gerlach, Sr. Associate AD
lance.gerlach@colorado.edu

COLORADO STATE UNIVERSITY ATHLETICS
MCGRAW ATHLETIC CENTER
FORT COLLINS, CO 80523-0120
970-491-7217
Fax: 970-491-1348
csurams.com
• Joe Parker, Director of Athletics
(970) 491-7217
ath_athletic_director@mail.colostate.edu
• Steve Cottingham, Deputy Director of Athletics
(970) 491-7075
steve.cottingham@colostate.edu
• Shalini Shanker, Sr. Assoc. AD, Compliance/SWA
(970) 491-6170
shalini.shanker@colostate.edu
• Albert Bimper, Jr., Assistant VP of Student Affairs
(970) 491-1859
albert.bimper@colostate.edu
• David Crum, Sr. Assoc. AD, Development
(970) 491-1665
david.crum@colostate.edu
• Terry DeZeeuw, Sr. Assoc. AD, Health & Performance
(970) 491-6756
terry.dezeeuw@colostate.edu
• Chris Ferris, Sr. Assoc. AD, Sales, Marketing & Communications
(970) 491-0438

chris.ferris@colostate.edu
• Mark Paquette, Sr. Assoc. AD, Facilities & Stadium Manager
(970) 491-7414
mark.paquette@colostate.edu

COLUMBIA UNIVERSITY ATHLETICS
DODGE PHYSICAL FITNESS CENTER
3030 BROADWAY
NEW YORK, NY 10027
www.gocolumbialions.com
• Peter Pilling, Director of Intercollegiate Athletics
(212) 854-4774
ppilling@columbia.edu
• Katie Day Benvenuto, Sr. Exec. AD, Development
(212) 854-4025
kad575@columbia.edu
• Jacqueline Blackett, Sr. Assoc. AD, Athletics/SWA
(212) 854-2544
jpb3@columbia.edu
• Joe Quinlan, Sr. Assoc. AD, Internal Operations
(212) 854-4805
jq2246@columbia.edu

CONNECTICUT ATHLETICS, UNIVERSITY OF
OFFICE OF ATHLETIC DIRECTOR
2095 HILLSIDE ROAD
UNIT 1173
STORRS, CT 06269
860-486-2725
Fax: 860-486-3300
www.uconnhuskies.com
• David Benedict, Director of Athletics
athleticdirector@uconn.edu
• Rachel Rubin, Deputy Director of Athletics/Chief of Staff
rachel.rubin@uconn.edu
• Neal Eskin, Executive Associate AD
neal.eskin@uconn.edu
• Adrianne Swinney, Chief Operating Officer/SWA
adrianne.swinney@uconn.edu

COPPIN STATE UNIVERSITY ATHLETICS
COPPIN STATE DEPT. OF ATHLETICS
2523 GWYNNS FALLS PARKWAY
BALTIMORE, MD 21216-3698
410-951-3737
Fax: 410-951-3717
www.coppinstatesports.com
• Derek Carter, Director of Athletics
(410) 951-3743
decarter@coppin.edu
• Nichole Person, Associate AD/SWA
(410) 951-3732
nperson@coppin.edu

CORNELL UNIVERSITY ATHLETICS
TEAGLE HALL
CAMPUS ROAD
ITHACA, NY 14853
cornellbigred.com
• Andy Noel, Director of Athletics
(607) 254-8921
jan16@cornell.edu
• Anita Brenner, Deputy Director of Athletics/SWA
(607) 255-8283
amb42@cornell.edu
• Larry Quant, Deputy Director of Athletics, Finance & Admin.

(607) 255-1317
lwq2@cornell.edu

CREIGHTON UNIVERSITY ATHLETICS
CREIGHTON ATHLETIC DEVELOPMENT OFFICE
RYAN ATHLETIC CENTER
2500 CALIFORNIA PLAZA
OMAHA, NE 68178
402-280-4483
gocreighton.com
• Bruce Rasmussen, Athletic Director
(402) 280-1795
bdrass@creighton.edu
• Mark Burgers, Associate Athletic Director
(402) 280-5561
butch@creighton.edu
• Kevin Sarver, Associate Athletic Director
(402) 280-5810
ksarver@creighton.edu
• Steve Brace, Associate Athletic Director
(402) 280-2484
scbrace@creighton.edu

DARTMOUTH COLLEGE ATHLETICS
DARTMOUTH ATHLETICS
6083 ALUMNI GYM
HANOVER, NH 03755
sportspub@dartmouth.edu
www.dartmouthsports.com
• Peter Roby, Interim Director of Athletics & Recreation
(603) 646-2465
dartmouth.athletics@dartmouth.edu
• Richard Whitmore, Executive Associate Athletics Director
(603) 646-2673
richard.l.whitmore@dartmouth.edu

DAVIDSON COLLEGE ATHLETICS
PO BOX 7158
DAVIDSON, NC 28035
www.davidsonwildcats.com
• Chris Clunie, Director of Athletics
(704) 894-2373
chclunie@davidson.edu
• Scott Applegate, Senior Associate AD
(704) 894-2914
scapplegate@davidson.edu
• Katy McNay, Associate AD/SWA
(704) 894-2637
kamcnay@davidson.edu
• Dick Cooke, Associate AD
(704) 894-2368
dicooke@davidson.edu

DAYTON ATHLETICS, UNIVERSITY OF
300 COLLEGE PARK
DAYTON, OH 45469
Fax: 937-229-4969
daytonflyers.com
• Neil Sullivan, Director of Athletics
(937) 229-2165
ad@udayton.edu
• Mike Kelly, Assistant Vice President for Athletics
(937) 229-4404
mkelly1@udayton.edu
• Scott DeBolt, Assistant to the AD
(937) 229-4613
sdebolt1@udayton.edu
• Joe Owens, Senior Associate AD, Performance Enhancement
(937) 229-2663
jowens1@udayton.edu
• Angie Petrovic, Sr. Associate AD, Compliance & Bus. Services/SWA

(937) 229-1285
apetrovic1@udayton.edu
• Robby Poteat, Senior Associate AD, External Affairs/Development
(937) 229-5207
rpoteat1@udayton.edu
• Adam Tschuor, Senior Associate AD, Administration
(937) 229-5473
atschuor1@udayton.edu

DELAWARE ATHLETICS, UNIVERSITY OF
631 S COLLEGE AVE
BOB CARPENTER CENTER
NEWARK, DE 19716
302-831-8600
www.bluehens.com
• Chrissi Rawak, Director of Athletics
(302) 831-4006
athletics-dir@udel.edu
• Jordan Skolnick, Deputy AD, External Relations
(302) 831-1075
jsko@udel.edu
• Dan Watson, Senior Associate AD, Sport Performance
(302) 831-7228
dwatson@udel.edu
• Nicole Jones, Senior Associate AD, External Relations
(302) 831-4988
nmjones@udel.edu
• Jake Schrum, Senior Associate AD, Facilities/Operations
(302) 831-4125
jschrum@udel.edu
• Jenn Judy, Senior Associate AD, Student Services
(302) 831-8610
jjudy@udel.edu

DELAWARE STATE UNIVERSITY ATHLETICS
1200 N DUPONT HWY
DOVER, DE 19901
www.dsuhornets.com
• Scott Gines, Director of Athletics
(302) 857-6030
• Dennis Hawkins, Associate AD, Finance & Administration
(302) 857-7633
dahawkins@desu.edu
• Matt Fortune, Associate AD, Facilities
(302) 857-7258
mfortune@desu.edu
• Alecia Shields-Gadson, Senior Associate AD, Compliance/SWA
(302) 857-7087
agadson@desu.edu

DENVER ATHLETICS, UNIVERSITY OF
ATHLETICS DEPARTMENT
2201 EAST ASBURY AVE
DENVER, CO 80210
www.denverpioneers.com
• Karlton Creech, Vice Chancellor for Athletics
(303) 871-3399
lisa.bridges@du.edu
• Josh Boone, Deputy AD/CFO
(303) 871-4224
joshua.boone@du.edu
• Lynn Coutts, Deputy AD, Student-Athlete Excellence
(303) 871-3892
lynn.coutts@du.edu

college sports

• Stu Halsall, Deputy AD/COO
(303) 871-3058
shalsall@du.edu
• Brandon MacNeill, Deputy AD/Chief
Revenue Officer
(303) 871-2785
brandon.macneill@du.edu
• Bob Willis, Deputy AD, Community &
Diversity
(303) 871-4966
robert.willis@du.edu

DEPAUL UNIVERSITY ATHLETICS
SULLIVAN ATHLETICS CENTER
2323 N SHEFFIELD AVENUE
CHICAGO, IL 60614
773-325-7526
www.depaulbluedemons.com
• DeWayne Peevy, Director of Athletics
(773) 325-7504
athleticsdirector@depaul.edu
• Jill Hollembeak, Senior Associate AD/SWA
(773) 325-4034
jhollemb@depaul.edu
• Peter Tombasco, Senior Associate AD,
External Affairs
(773) 325-7245
ptombasc@depaul.edu

**DETROIT MERCY ATHLETICS,
UNIVERSITY OF**
4001 W MCNICHOLS ROAD
DETROIT, MI 48221
313-993-1700
Fax: 313-993-2449
www.detroittitans.com
• Robert C. Vowels, Jr., Director of Athletics
(313) 993-1700
vowelsrc@udmercy.edu
• Teri Kromrei, Associate AD/SWA
(313) 993-1700
teri.kromrei@udmercy.edu
• Mike Miller, Associate AD
(313) 993-1700
millerma@udmercy.edu
• Holly Kerstner, Associate AD,
Student-Athlete Services
(248) 563-9892
kerstnhl@udmercy.edu

DRAKE UNIVERSITY ATHLETICS
2507 UNIVERSITY AVENUE
DES MOINES, IA 50311-4505
515-271-2889
Fax: 515-271-4189
www.godrakebulldogs.com
• Brian Hardin, Director of Athletics
(515) 271-2889
drakead@drake.edu
• Blake Boldon, Senior Associate AD
(515) 271-3007
blake.boldton@drake.edu
• Megan Franklin, PhD, Senior Associate
AD/SWA
(515) 271-2809
megan.franklin@drake.edu
• Patrick Tomka, Senior Associate AD,
Fiance & Operation
(515) 271-2138
patrick.tomka@drake.edu
• Matt Lyons, Senior Associate AD, External
Affairs
(515) 271-4628
matt.lyons@drake.edu

DREXEL UNIVERSITY ATHLETICS
DASKALAKIS ATHLETIC CENTER
3141 CHESTNUT STREET
PHILADELPHIA, PA 19104
www.drexeldragons.com
• Eric Zillmer, Director of Athletics
(215) 895-1977
sports@drexel.edu
• Nick Gannon, Deputy AD
(215) 895-1589
njg24@drexel.edu
• Laura White, Senior Associate AD/SWA
(215) 895-1417
ludwicle@drexel.edu
• Kathy O'Brien, Assoc. AD, Academic
Services
(215) 895-2031
ko33@drexel.edu

DUKE UNIVERSITY ATHLETICS
SCOTT FAMILY ATHLETICS
PERFORMANCE CENTER
ROOM 364
110 WHITFORD DRIVE
DURHAM, NC 27708
919-681-2583
www.goduke.com
• Kevin White, Director of Athletics
(919) 684-2431
kevin.white@duke.edu
• Chris Kennedy, Senior Deputy AD
(919) 668-5702
ckennedy@duke.edu
• Nina King, Senior Deputy AD,
Administration
(919) 613-6225
nina.king@duke.edu
• Tom Coffman, Deputy AD, Development
(919) 613-7553
tom.coffman@duke.edu
• Jon Jackson, Deputy AD, External Affairs
(919) 684-2624
jon.jackson@duke.edu
• Mitch Moser, Deputy AD, Resource
Development
(919) 668-5705
mmoser@duke.edu

DUQUESNE UNIVERSITY ATHLETICS
A.J. PALUMBO CENTER
600 FORBES AVENUE
PITTSBURGH, PA 15282
www.goduquesne.com
• Dave Harper, Director of Athletics
(412) 396-6565
harperd1@duq.edu
• Sherene Brantley, Associate AD,
Academic & Student Services/SWA
(412) 396-5243
lemoniass@duq.edu
• Bryan Colonna, Associaate AD,
Development
(412) 396-5927
colonna770@duq.edu
• Rick Christensen, Associate AD, Admin. &
Compliance
(412) 396-4917
christensen@duq.edu
• Megan Jahrling, Associate AD, External
Relations
(412) 396-5333
jahrlingm@duq.edu
• Dave Saba, Associate AD, Media
Relations
(412) 396-5861
saba@duq.edu
• Michael Scerbo, Associate AD, Sports &
Facilities Operations

(412) 396-5244
scerbom@duq.edu
• Joseph Setting, Associate AD, Business
(412) 396-1359
settingj@duq.edu

**EAST CAROLINA UNIVERSITY
ATHLETICS**
WARD SPORTS MEDICINE BUILDING
1 FICKLEN DR
MAIL STOP 158
GREENVILLE, NC 27858-4353
252-737-4600
www.ecupirates.com
• Jon Gilbert, Director of Athletics
(252) 737-4502
athletic_director@ecu.edu
• Ryan Robinson, Executive Associate AD,
External Operations
(252) 737-4945
robinsonry18@ecu.edu
• Alex Keddie, Senior Associate AD,
Compliance
(252) 737-4533
keddiea19@ecu.edu
• Caroline Bevillard, Senior Associate AD,
Administration/SWA
(252) 737-4531
bevillardc18@ecu.edu

**EAST TENNESSEE STATE UNIVERSITY
ATHLETICS**
PO BOX 70707
JOHNSON CITY, TN 37614
www.etsubucs.com
• Scott Carter, Director of Athletics
(423) 439-4343
athleticsdirector@etsu.edu
• Mac Hart, Senior Associate AD/CFO
(423) 439-6140
hartpm@etsu.edu
• Lauren Aksionoff, Senior Associate
AD/SWA
(423) 439-4809
aksionoff@mail.etsu.edu
• Matt McGahey, Senior Associate AD,
External Operations
(423) 439-5925
mcgaheym@etsu.edu
• Jo Anne Paty, Associate AD, Development
(423) 439-4738
paty@mail.etsu.edu

**EASTERN ILLINOIS UNIVERSITY
ATHLETICS**
EASTERN ILLINOIS ATHLETIC DEPT.
600 LINCOLN AVENUE
CHARLESTON, IL 61920
217-581-6014
www.eiupanthers.com
• Tom Michael, Athletic Director
(217) 581-6014
trmichael@eiu.edu
• Mark Bonnstetter, Deputy AD
(217) 581-7614
mdbonnstetter@eiu.edu
• Rich Moser, Associate AD, Media & Public
Relations
(217) 581-7480
rlmoser@eiu.edu

**EASTERN KENTUCKY UNIVERSITY
ATHLETICS**
521 LANCASTER AVENUE
RICHMOND, KY 40475
www.ekusports.com

• Matt Roan, Director of Athletics
matt.roan@eku.edu
• Mark Howard, Sr. Associate AD,
Operations
(859) 622-8422
mark.howard@eku.edu

**EASTERN MICHIGAN UNIVERSITY
ATHLETICS**
CONVOCATION CENTER
799 N HEWITT ROAD
YPSILANTI, MI 48197
734-487-1050
www.emueagles.com
• Scott Wetherbee, Director of Athletics
(734) 487-1050
scott.wetherbee@emich.edu
• Erin Kido, Senior Associate AD/SWA
(734) 487-8172
ekido@mich.edu
• Gretchen Buskirk, Assoc. AD, Sports
Medicine
(734) 487-5183
gbuskirk@emich.edu
• Dan McLean, Senior Associate AD,
Development
(734) 487-1050
dmclean4@emich.edu
• Andy Rowdon, Senior Associate AD,
External Affairs
(734) 487-1050
arowdon@emich.edu

**EASTERN WASHINGTON UNIVERSITY
ATHLETICS**
EWU ATHLETICS DEPARTMENT
207 PHYSICAL EDUCATION BUILDING
CHENEY, WA 99004
509-359-2463
Fax: 509-359-2828
www.goeags.com
• Lynn Hickey, Director of Athletics
(509) 359-2347
lhickey@ewu.edu
• Devon Thomas, Deputy AD, External
Affairs
(509) 359-2079
dthomas28@ewu.edu
• Sarah Adams, Deputy AD/SWA
(509) 359-2511
sadams39@ewu.edu

ELON UNIVERSITY ATHLETICS
2500 CAMPUS BOX
100 CAMPUS DRIVE
ELON, NC 27244
elonphoenix.com
• Dave Blank, Director of Athletics
(336) 278-6800
• Mike Ward, Deputy Director of Athletics
(336) 278-6897
mward31@elon.edu

**EVANSVILLE ATHLETICS, UNIVERSITY
OF**
UE ATHLETICS
1800 LINCOLN AVENUE
EVANSVILLE, IN 47722
812-488-2237
Fax: 812-488-2199
gopurpleaces.com
• Mark Spencer, Director of Athletics
(812) 488-2569
athletics@evansville.edu
• Sarah Solinsky, Senion Associitate AD,
Internal Operations/SWA
(812) 488-2759

ss78@evansville.edu
• Bob Pristash, Associate AD, Media
Relations
(812) 488-2285
rp113@evansville.edu
• Terry Collins, Associate AD, Sports
Medicine
(812) 488-2091
tc7@evansville.edu

FAIRFIELD UNIVERSITY ATHLETICS
WALSH ATHLETIC CENTER
1073 NORTH BENSON ROAD
FAIRFIELD, CT 06824
Fax: 203-254-4130
fairfieldstags.com
• Paul Schlickmann, Director of Athletics
(203) 254-4000
kgeiling@fairfield.edu
• Zach Dayton, Deputy AD
(203) 254-4000
zdayton@fairfield.edu
• Alison Sexton, Senior Associate AD,
Internal Affairs/SWA
(203) 254-4000
asexton@fairfield.edu

**FAIRLEIGH DICKINSON UNIVERSITY
ATHLETICS**
1000 RIVER ROAD
H-AT1-01
TEANECK, NJ 07666
201-692-2208
Fax: 201-692-9361
fduknights.com
• Bradford Hurlbut, Director of Athletics
(201) 692-9867
hurlbut@fdu.edu
• Cathy Liggett, Associate AD, Facilites
(201) 692-2172
liggett@fdu.edu
• Jennifer Quirk, Associate AD, Compliance
(201) 692-9892
quirk@fdu.edu
• Jason Young, Associate AD, External
Affairs
(201) 692-9552
jryoung@fdu.edu
• Bryan Jackson, Associate AD,
Communications
(201) 692-2149
bjackson@fdu.edu

FLORIDA A&M UNIVERSITY ATHLETICS
1835 WAHNISH WAY
TALLAHASSEE, FL 32307
850-599-3868
Fax: 850-599-3810
www.famuathletics.com
• Kortne Gosha, Director of Athletics
(850) 599-3868
• Keith McCluney, Deputy Director of
Athletics
(850) 561-2165
keith.mccluney@famu.edu
• Karai Lockley, Senio Associat AD,
Business & Finance/SWA
(850) 599-3868
karai.lockley@famu.edu

FLORIDA ATHLETICS, UNIVERSITY OF
UNIVERSITY ATHLETICS ASSN.
PO BOX 14485
GAINESVILLE, FL 32604
352-375-4683
floridagators.com

• Scott Stricklin, Director of Athletics
(352) 375-4683
administration@gators.ufl.edu
• Jay Jacobs, Executive Associate AD,
External Affairs
(352) 375-4683
JayJ@gators.ufl.edu
• Chip Howard, Executive Associate AD,
Internal Affairs
(352) 375-4683
chiph@gators.ufl.edu
• Lynda Tealer, Executive Associate AD,
Administration
(352) 375-4683
lyndat@gators.ufl.edu

**FLORIDA ATLANTIC UNIVERSITY
ATHLETICS**
DEPARTMENT OF ATHLETICS
777 GLADES ROAD
BOCA RATON, FL 33431
Fax: 561-297-3963
www.fausports.com
• Brian White, Director of Athletics
(561) 297-3199
• Eric Coleman, Senior Associate AD,
Academics/Student Development
(561) 297-6957
colemane@fau.edu
• Mary Giardina, Sr. Assoc. AD,
Administration/SWA/Chief of Staff
(561) 297-3199
mgiardina@fau.edu
• Andy Seeley, Senior Associate AD,
External Relations
aseeley@fau.edu

**FLORIDA INTERNATIONAL UNIVERSITY
ATHLETICS**
FIU ATHLETICS
11200 SW 8TH STREET
MIAMI, FL 33199
305-348-8392
www.fiusports.com
• Pete Garcia, Executive Director of Sports
& Entertainment
• Julie Berg, Senior Association AD/SWA
bergj@fiu.edu
• Heath Glick, Senior Associate AD/COO
(305) 348-6711
glickh@fiu.edu
• Alex Kelley, Associate AD, External
Relations
(305) 348-2971
ajkelley@fiu.edu
• Kevin D Kendrick, Associate AD,
Compliance
(305) 348-2843
kkendric@fiu.edu

**FLORIDA STATE UNIVERSITY
ATHLETICS**
FSU ATHLETICS DEPARTMENT
403 STADIUM DRIVE W
ROOM D0107
TALLAHASSEE, FL 32306
850-645-2527
Fax: 850-644-7293
seminoles.com
• David Coburn, Director of Athletics
(850) 644-1079
vcupp@fsu.edu
• Cindy Hartmann, Deputy AD,
Administration
(850) 645-2368
cmhartmann@fsu.edu
• Ross Cobb, Senior Associate AD/CFO

college sports

(850) 644-8091
ross.cobb@fsu.edu
• Jim Curry, Senior Associate AD
(850) 644-7926
jmcurrry@fsu.edu
• Vanessa Fuchs, Senior Associate
AD/SWA
(850) 644-4933
vfuchs@fsu.edu
• Michele Osborne, Senior Associate AD,
Governance & Compliance
(850) 644-1890
mosborne@fsu.edu

FORDHAM UNIVERSITY ATHLETICS
ROSE HILL CAMPUS
441 E FORDHAM ROAD
BRONX, NY 10458
www.fordhamsports.com
• Ed Kull, Director of Intercollegiate Athletics
(212) 636-6565
ekull@fordham.edu
• Charlie Elwood, Deputy Director of
Athletics
(718) 817-4308
celwood@fordham.edu
• John Barrett, Senior Associate AD,
Business Affairs
(718) 817-4307
jbarrett14@fordham.edu
• Djenane Paul, Senior Associate AD/SWA
(718) 817-4304
dpaul2@fordham.edu

FRESNO STATE ATHLETICS
FRESNO STATE ATHLETICS DEPT.
1620 E BULLDOG LANE, OF 87
FRESNO, CA 93740
559-278-2643
www.gobulldogs.com
• Terry Tumey, Director of Athletics
• Meredith Jenkins, Deputy AD
(559) 278-4905
meredithjenkins@csufresno.edu
• Carrie Coll, Senior Associate AD, Sport
Services/SWA
(559) 278-8262
ccoll@csufresno.edu
• Tim Collins, Senior Associate AD,
Development
(559) 278-8256
tcollins@csufresno.edu
• Frank Pucher, Senior Associate AD,
External Relations
(559) 278-8006
fpucher@csufresno.edu
• David Hall, Senior Associate AD,
Compliance
(559) 278-1825
dhall@csufresno.edu

FURMAN UNIVERSITY ATHLETICS
FURMAN ATHLETICS
3300 POINSETT HIGHWAY
GREENVILLE, SC 29613
864-294-2000
www.furmanpaladins.com
• Jason Donnelly, Athletics Director
athletics.director@furman.edu
• Erin Wissing, Sr. Assoc. AD/Director of
Athletics Development
(864) 294-3732
erin.wissing@furman.edu

GARDNER-WEBB UNIVERSITY ATHLETICS
110 S MAIN STREET
BOILING SPRINGS, NC 28017
www.gwusports.com
• Chuck Burch, Vice President for Athletics
(704) 406-4342
cburch@gardner-webb.edu
• Pam Scruggs, Associate Athletic
Director/SWA
(704) 406-4341
pscruggs@gardner-webb.edu
• Tyler Rosenberger, Assistant AD,
Compliance
(704) 406-3329
trosenberger@gardner-webb.edu
• Kevin Jones, Assistant AD, Athletic
Training
(704) 406-3926
kjones@gardner-webb.edu
• Marc Rabb, Assistant AD, Media Relations
(704) 406-4355
mrabb@gardner-webb.edu

GEORGE MASON UNIVERSITY ATHLETICS
GEORGE MASON ATHLETICS
MS 3A5
4400 UNIVERSITY DRIVE
FAIRFAX, VA 22030
www.gomason.com
• Brad Edwards, Director of Athletics
(703) 993-3256
bedwards@gmu.edu
• Kevin McNamee, Deputy AD
(703) 993-3209
kmcnamee@gmu.edu
• Zack Bolno, Deputy AD, External
Operations
(703) 993-3217
zbolno@gmu.edu
• Deborah Cobatto, Deputy AD, Internal
Operations
(703) 993-9536
dcorbatt@gmu.edu
• Kristi Giddings, Deputy AD, Compliance
(703) 993-5420
kgidding@gmu.edu

GEORGE WASHINGTON UNIVERSITY ATHLETICS
GW DEPT. OF ATHLETICS AND REC.
CHARLES E. SMITH CENTER
600 22ND STREET NW
WASHINGTON, DC 20052
www.gwsports.com
• Tanya Vogel, Director of Athletics
(202) 994-5558
gwad@gwu.edu
• Chandra Bierwirth, Associate AD,
Compliance
(202) 994-6282
cbwirth@gwu.edu
• Brian Sereno, Associate AD,
Communications
(202) 994-6654
bsereno@gwu.edu
• Chris Hennelly, Associate AD,
Student-Athlete Health
(202) 994-3557
henz@gwu.edu
• John Square, Associate AD, Internal
Operations
(202) 994-0363
johnsquare@gwu.edu

GEORGETOWN UNIVERSITY ATHLETICS
ATHLETIC DEPARTMENT
MCDONOUGH ARENA
WASHINGTON, DC 20057
202-687-2435
www.guhoyas.com
• Lee Reed, Director of Athletics
(202) 687-6513
athleticdirector@georgetown.edu
• Dan O'Neil, Senior Associate AD, External
Affairs
(202) 687-6708
djo23@georgetown.edu
• Dan Trump, Senior Associate AD, Internal
Operations
(202) 687-6573
dan.trump@georgetown.edu
• Sharon Brummell, Senior Associate AD,
Business & Finance/SWA
(202) 687-2669
sdb46@georgetown.edu

GEORGIA ATHLETICS, UNIVERSITY OF
1 SELIG CIRCLE
ATHENS, GA 30602
706-542-9036
georgiadogs.com
• Josh Brooks, Director of Athletics
(705) 542-9037
athdir@uga.edu
• Darrice Griffin, Senior Deputy AD
(706) 542-9103
dgriffin@sports.uga.edu
• Matthew Borman, Deputy AD,
Development
(706) 452-9239
mborman@sports.uga.edu
• Will Lawler, Deputy AD, Compliance
(706) 542-9103
wlawler@sports.uga.edu
• Stephanie Ransom, Deputy AD, Finance
(706) 542-1306
sransom@sports.uga.edu
• Magdi El Shahawy, Deputy AD,
Academics
(706) 542-8388
magdi@sports.uga.edu

GEORGIA SOUTHERN UNIVERSITY ATHLETICS
DAN J. PARRISH SR. BUILDING
651 FAIR ROAD
STATESBORO, GA 30458
912-478-2845
Fax: 912-478-0095
gsathletics@georgiasouthern.edu
www.gseagles.com
• Jared Benko, Director of Athletics
(912) 478-2845
gsathletics@georgiasouthern.edu
• Brandy Clouse, Senior Associate AD,
Administration/SWA
(912) 478-7581
bpetty@georgiasouthern.edu
• Tracy Ham, Senior Associate AD,
Administration
(912) 478-5366
tham@georgiasouthern.edu
• Gleen Hart, Senior Associate AD,
Student-Athlete Development
(912) 478-5817
ghart@georgiasouthern.edu
• Larry Mays, Senior Associate AD, External
Affairs
(912) 478-1230
lmays@georgiasouthern.edu
• Keith Roughton, Senior Associate AD,
Compliance

(912) 478-0747
kroughton@georgiasouthern.edu
• Reggie Simpkins, Senior Associate AD, Student-Athlete Services
(912) 478-8467
rsimpkins@georgiasouthern.edu

GEORGIA STATE UNIVERSITY ATHLETICS
GEORGIA STATE STADIUM
755 HANK AARON DRIVE
ATLANTA, GA 30315
404-413-4000
www.georgiastatesports.com
• Charlie Cobb, Director of Athletics
(404) 413-4004
ccobb13@gsu.edu
• Doug Justice, Senior Associate AD
(404) 413-4013
djustice@gsu.edu
• Brian Kelly, Senior Associate AD, External Affairs
(404) 413-4152
bkelly@gsu.edu
• Kelcey Roegiers, Senior Associate AD/SWA
(404) 413-4005
kroegiers@gsu.edu
• Brad Horton, Senior Associate AD, Student-Athlete Development
(404) 413-4045
bhorton6@gsu.edu
• Elisha Howell-Williams, Senior Associate AD, Business & Human Resources
(404) 413-4016
ehowell@gsu.edu

GEORGIA TECH ATHLETICS
GEORGIA TECH ATHLETIC ASSOCIATION
150 BOBBY DODD WAY NW
ATLANTA, GA 30332
404-894-5411
www.ramblinwreck.com
• Todd Stansbury, Director of Athletics
(404) 894-5411
athleticdirector@athletics.gatech.edu
• Mark Rountree, Deputy Director of Athletics
(404) 894-5411
mrountree@athletics.gatech.edu

GONZAGA UNIVERSITY ATHLETICS
502 E BOONE
SPOKANE, WA 99258-0066
509-313-4202
Fax: 509-313-5787
www.gozags.com
• Mike Roth, Director of Athletics
(509) 313-4204
roth@gonzaga.edu
• Chris Standiford, Deputy Director of Athletics/COO
(509) 313-4210
standiford@gonzaga.edu
• Shannon Strahl, Senior Associate AD, Compliance/SWA
(509) 313-5700
strahl@gonzaga.edu
• Jared Hertz, Sr. Assoc. AD, Major Gifts
(509) 313-4203
hertzj@gonzaga.edu

GRAMBLING STATE UNIVERSITY ATHLETICS
HOBDY ASSEMBLY CENTER
100 NORTH STADIUM DRIVE
GRAMBLING, LA 71245
318-274-2374
www.gsutigers.com
• David Ponton, Director of Athletics
(318) 274-2374
pontond@gram.edu
• Wanda Currie, Associate AD, Internal Operations
(318) 274-6540
curriew@gram.edu

GRAND CANYON UNIVERSITY ATHLETICS
GCU ATHLETICS
3300 W CAMELBACK ROAD
PHOENIX, AZ 85017
www.gculopes.com
• Jamie Boggs, Interim Vice President of Athletics
(602) 639-6053
jamie.boggs@gcu.edu
• Nick Ojea, Executive Senior Associate AD, Admin.
(602) 639-7455
nicholas.ojea@gcu.edu
• Jason Frank, Senior Associate AD, Student-Athlete Development
(602) 639-7403
jason.frank@gcu.edu

HAMPTON UNIVERSITY ATHLETICS
100 E QUEEN STREET
121 HOLLAND HALL
HAMPTON, VA 23668
757-727-5641
Fax: 757-728-6995
hamptonpirates.com
• Eugene Marshall, Jr., Director of Athletics
• Paula Jackson, Senior Woman Administrator
(757) 727-2122
paula.jackson@haptonu.edu

HARTFORD ATHLETICS, UNIVERSITY OF
DEPT. OF ATHLETICS
SPORTS CENTER
200 BLOOMFIELD AVE
WEST HARTFORD, CT 06117
860-768-4653
Fax: 860-768-5047
www.hartfordhawks.com
• Maria Feeley, Interim Director of Athletics
• Jarrett Kratzer, Associate AD, Operations
(860) 768-7915
jkratzer@hartford.edu
• Ted Stavropoulos, Sr. Assoc. AD, Facilities & Events
(860) 768-4650
tstavropo@hartford.edu
• Matthew Raidbard, Sr. Assoc. AD, Student-Athlete Welfare Services
(860) 768-4657
raidbard@hartford.edu

HARVARD UNIVERSITY ATHLETICS
MURR CENTER
65 N HARVARD STREET
BOSTON, MA 02163
617-495-3454
www.gocrimson.com
• Erin McDermott, Director of Athletics
(617) 495-3633
emcdermott@fas.harvard.edu

• Gerrie Mahoney, Senior Associate AD
(617) 495-2781
gamahon@fas.harvard.edu
• Tim Troville, Senior Associate AD
(617) 384-8426
ttroville@fas.harvard.edu
• Nathan Fry, Senior Associate AD
(617) 495-4992
nfry@fas.harvard.edu

HAWAII ATHLETICS, UNIVERSITY OF
OFFICE OF INTERCOLLEGIATE ATHLETICS
1337 LOWER CAMPUS RD
HONOLULU, HI 96822
Fax: 808-956-4637
hawaiiathletics.com
• David AK Matlin, Athletics Director
(808) 956-7301
athdir@hawaii.edu
• Carl Clapp, Associate AD, Administrative Services
(808) 956-6523
cclapp@hawaii.edu

HIGH POINT UNIVERSITY ATHLETICS
ONE UNIVERSITY PARKWAY
HIGH POINT, NC 27268
Fax: 336-841-9182
www.highpointpanthers.com
• Dan Hauser, Athletic Director
(336) 841-9281
dhauser@highpoint.edu
• Drew Sanchez, Associate AD, Internal Operations
(336) 841-4652
dsanchez@highpoint.edu
• April Wines, Associate AD/SWA
(336) 841-4645
awines@highpoint.edu
• Kim Grissett, Senior Associate AD, Business & Tickets
(336) 841-9276
kgrisset@highpoint.edu

HOFSTRA UNIVERSITY ATHLETICS
JAMES C. METZGER HALL
147 HOFSTRA UNIVERSITY
HEMPSTEAD, NY 11549
516-463-5315
gohofstra.com
• Rick Cole, Jr., Director of Athletics
(516) 463-6750
rick.coleJr@hofstra.edu
• Jay Artinian, Deputy Director of Athletics/Chief Revenue Officer
(516) 463-7931
jay.m.artinian@hofstra.edu
• Cindy Lewis, Senior Associate AD/SWA
(516) 463-6748
cindy.lewis@hofstra.edu

HOLY CROSS ATHLETICS, COLLEGE OF THE
DEPARTMENT OF ATHLETICS
ONE COLLEGE STREET
WORCESTER, MA 01610
www.goholycross.com
• Marcus Blossom, Director of Athletics
(508) 793-2571
• Rosemary Shea, Senior Associate AD/SWA
(508) 793-2318
rshea@holycross.edu
• Nick Smith, Senior Associate AD, External Operations

college sports

(508) 793-3583
nasmith@holycross.edu

HOUSTON ATHLETICS, UNIVERSITY OF
3204 CULLEN BOULEVARD
HOUSTON, TX 77204-6002
www.uhcougars.com
• Chris Pezman, Vice President for Athletics
directorofathletics@uh.edu
• David Tagliarino, Deputy Athletics
Director/Chief Revenue Officer
dtagliar@central.uh.edu
• Monty Porter, Deputy Athletics
Director/COO
mmporte2@central.uh.edu

HOWARD UNIVERSITY ATHLETICS
BURR GYMNASIUM
6TH & GIRARD STREETS NW
SUITE 1013
WASHINGTON, DC 20059
202-806-7141
Fax: 202-806-9090
www.hubison.com
• Kery Davis, Director of Athletics
(202) 806-7141
kery.davis@howard.edu
• Amy Olson, Associate AD,
Administration/SWA
(202) 806-6697
amy.olson@howard.edu
• Nicholas Latham, Associate AD,
Operations
(202) 806-7144
nicholas.latham@howard.edu
• Paul Bowden, Associate AD,
Student-Athlete Support Services
(202) 806-5165
paul.bowden@howard.edu

IDAHO ATHLETICS, UNIVERSITY OF
KIBBIE-ASUI ACTIVITY CENTER
875 PERIMETER DRIVE
MS 2302
MOSCOW, ID 83844-2302
Fax: 208-885-2862
govandals.com
• Terry Gawlik, Director of Athletics
(208) 885-0243
ath-director@uidaho.edu
• Tim Mooney, Associate AD
(208) 885-0258
tmooney@uidaho.edu
• Heath Senour, Associate AD, Compliance
(208) 885-0214
heathsenour@uidaho.edu
• Mahmood Sheikh, Associate AD,
Development
(208) 885-4566
msheikh@uidaho.edu

IDAHO STATE UNIVERSITY ATHLETICS
IDAHO STATE ATHLETICS
921 S 8TH
STOP 8173
POCATELLO, ID 83209-8173
www.isubengals.com
• Pauline Thiros, Director of Athletics
thirpaul@isu.edu
• Steve Schaack, Senior Associate AD,
External Operations
(208) 282-2621
schaste4@isu.edu
• Joel Moersch, Associate AD, Development
(208) 282-4503
moerjoel@isu.edu

ILLINOIS AT CHICAGO ATHLETICS, UNIVERSITY OF
FLAMES ATHLETIC CENTER
839 W ROOSEVELT ROAD
CHICAGO, IL 60608
Fax: 312-996-8349
uicflames.com
• Michael Lipitz, Director of Athletics
(312) 996-4639
uicad@uic.edu
• Farrah Manthei, Deputy AD/SWA
(312) 996-5633
fmanthei@uic.edu
• Mike Bamonti, Senior Associate AD,
Advancement
(312) 996-2042
mbamonti@uic.edu
• Bill Thomas, Senior Associate AD,
Business Operations
(312) 996-8523
wthomas9@uic.edu
• Dan Yopchick, Senior Associate AD,
External Operations
(312) 413-9340
yopchick@uic.edu

ILLINOIS ATHLETICS, UNIVERSITY OF
BIELFELDT ATHLETIC ADMIN. BLDG.
1700 S FOURTH STREET
CHAMPAIGN, IL 61820
217-333-3631
fightingillini.com
• Josh Whitman, Director of Athletics
(217) 333-3631
illiniad@illinois.edu
• Warren Hood, Deputy Director of Athletics
(217) 244-0764
whood1@illinois.edu
• Sara Burton, Executive Senior Associate
AD/SWA
(217) 300-8112
sarab4@illinois.edu
• Susan Young, Executive Senior Associate
AD/CFO
(217) 244-4286
sly2362@illinois.edu

ILLINOIS STATE UNIVERSITY ATHLETICS
CAMPUS BOX 2660
NORMAL, IL 61790-2660
309-438-2000
www.goredbirds.com
• Kyle Brennan, Director of Athletics
(309) 438-3636
ksbren1@ilstu.edu
• Leanna Bordner, Deputy Director of
Athletics/SWA
(309) 438-7143
lkbordn@ilstu.edu
• Dwight Merilatt, Executove Associate AD,
External Affairs
(309) 438-0643
dameril@ilstu.edu

INDIANA STATE UNIVERSITY ATHLETICS
401 NORTH 4TH STREET
ISU ARENA
SUITE 110
TERRE HAUTE, IN 47809
Fax: 812-237-4041
gosycamores.com
• Sherard Clinkscales, Director of Athletics
(812) 237-4092
• Angie Lansing, Senior Associate AD/SWA
(812) 237-4091
angie.lansing@indstate.edu

• John Sherman, Senior Asssistant AD
(812) 237-3047
john.sherman@indstate.edu
• Joel McMullen, Asst. AD, Compliance
(812) 237-8025
joel.mcmullen@indstate.edu
• Dennis Darke, Asst. AD, Facilities &
Operations
(812) 237-4158
dennis.darke@indstate.edu

INDIANA UNIVERSITY ATHLETICS
SIMON SKJODT ASSEMBLY HALL
1001 E 17TH STREET
BLOOMINGTON, IN 47408-1590
812-855-2794
iuhoosiers.com
• Scott Dolson, Director of Athletics
(812) 855-1966
athldir@indiana.edu

INDIANA UNIVERSITY-PURDUE UNIVERSITY FORT WAYNE
DEPT. OF INTERCOLLEGIATE
ATHLETICS
2101 E COLISEUM BOULEVARD
FORT WAYNE, IN 46805-1499
www.gomastodons.com
• Kelley Hartley Hutton, Athletic Director
(260) 481-5445
• Christine Kuznar, Senior Associate AD,
Academics/SWA
(260) 481-6192
kuznarc@pfw.edu
• Rachel Holycross, Associate AD,
Compliance
(260) 481-0281
newstedr@pfw.edu

INDIANA UNIVERSITY-PURDUE UNIVERSITY INDIANAPOLIS
IUPUI ATHLETICS
250 UNIVERSITY BOULEVARD
INDIANAPOLIS, IN 46202
317-278-5247
Fax: 317-278-2683
www.iupuijags.com
• Roderick Perry, Director of Athletics
(317) 278-5247
perryrd@iupui.edu
• Jaunelle White, Senior Associate AD,
Internal Operations/SWA
(317) 274-4549
jahwhite@iupui.edu
• John Rasmussen, Senior Associate AD,
External Affairs
(317) 274-5453
jrrasmus@iupui.edu
• Laura Hue, Associate AD, Compliance
(317) 278-4281
lhue@iupui.edu
• Denise O'Grady, Associate AD,
Academics
(317) 278-1648
dogrady@iupui.edu

IONA COLLEGE ATHLETICS
HYNES CENTER
715 NORTH AVENUE
NEW ROCHELLE, NY 10801
914-633-2654
www.icgaels.com
• Matt Glovaski, Director of Athletics
(914) 633-2311
mglovaski@iona.edu
• Jamie Fogarty, Senior Associate AD/SWA
(914) 633-2320

jfogarty@iona.edu
• Brian Beyrer, Senior Associate AD, Communications
(914) 637-2726
bbeyrer@iona.edu
• Sam De Rosa, Senior Associate AD, Sports Medicine
(914) 633-2333
sderosa@iona.edu
• Tom Moran, Senior Associate AD, External Affairs
(914) 633-2627
tmoran@iona.edu

IOWA ATHLETICS, UNIVERSITY OF
N411 CARVER-HAWKEYE ARENA
IOWA CITY, IA 52242-1020
319-335-9320
800-424-2957
Fax: 319-335-9726
hawkeyesports.com
• Gary Barta, Director of Athletics
(319) 335-9435
gary-barta@uiowa.edu
• Barbara Burkey, Deputy AD/SWA
(319) 335-4557
barbara-burke@uiowa.edu
• Matt Henderson, Senior Associate AD, Revenue & External Operations
(319) 335-6487
matt-henderson@uiowa.edu
• Marcus Wilson, Senior Associate AD, Internal Operations
(319) 335-9247
marcus-m-wilson@uiowa.edu

IOWA STATE UNIVERSITY ATHLETICS
JACOBSON ATHLETIC BUILDING
1800 S FOURTH STREET
AMES, IA 50011
cyclones.com
• Jamie Pollard, Director of Athletics
jbp@iastate.edu
• Chris Jorgensen, Senior Associate AD, Operations
cjorg@iastate.edu
• Steve Malchow, Senior Associate AD, Communications
sdm@iastate.edu
• Frank Nogel, Senior Associate AD, External Relations
fnogel@iastate.edu
• Calli Sanders, Senior Associate AD, Sports Administration
csanders@iastate.edu
• Small Charles, Senior Associate AD, Student Services
csmall@iastate.edu

JACKSON STATE UNIVERSITY ATHLETICS
1400 JOHN R. LYNCH STREET
JACKSON, MS 39217
www.gojsutigers.com
• Ashley Robinson, Vice President & Director of Athletics
• Derek Scott, Associate AD, Internal Operations
(601) 979-7821
derek.l.scott@jsums.edu
• Hakim McClellan, Associate AD, Compliance
(601) 979-3410
hakim.r.mcclellan@jsums.edu
• Dennis Driscoll, Associate AD, Sports Media

(601) 979-0857
dennis.r.driscoll@jsums.edu

JACKSONVILLE STATE UNIVERSITY ATHLETICS
JSU ATHLETIC DEPT.
700 PELHAM ROAD N
JACKSONVILLE, AL 36265
jsugamecocksports.com
• Greg Seitz, Athletic Director
(256) 782-5368
gseitz@jsu.edu
• Greg Bonds, Senior Associate AD
(256) 782-5988
gbonds@jsu.edu

JACKSONVILLE UNIVERSITY ATHLETICS
2800 UNIVERSITY BOULEBARD N
JACKSONVILLE, FL 32211
904-256-7400
www.judolphins.com
• Alex Ricker-Gilbert, Athletic Director
(904) 256-7400
• Lauren Cevis, Deputy Athletic Director/SWA
(904) 256-7794
lcevis@ju.edu
• David Farraday, Senior Associate AD, Internal Operations
(904) 256-7403
dfarrad@ju.edu

JAMES MADISON UNIVERSITY ATHLETICS
800 SOUTH MAIN STREET
HARRISONBURG, VA 22807
540-568-6164
jmusports.com
• Jeff Bourne, Director of Athletics
(540) 568-6164
cainml@jmu.edu
• Geoff Polglase, Deputy Director of Athletics
(540) 568-6164
polglagh@jmu.edu
• Jennifer Phillips, Associate AD, Compliance/SWA
(540) 568-7834
phill2jr@jmu.edu
• Kevin White, Associate AD, Sports Programs
(540) 568-6104
whitekj@jmu.edu
• Tom Kuster, Associate AD, Sports Performance
(540) 568-3893
kusterj@jmu.edu

KANSAS STATE UNIVERSITY ATHLETICS
BRAMLAGE COLISEUM
1800 COLLEGE AVENUE
MANHATTAN, KS 66502
800-221-2287
www.kstatesports.com
• Gene Taylor, Director of Athletics
(785) 532-6910
gtaylor@kstatesports.com
• Jill Shields, Deputy AD/SWA
(785) 532-6620
jshields@kstatesports.com
• Jim Bach, Associate AD, Business Operations
(785) 532-6020
jbach@kstatesports.com
• Casey Scott, Executive Associate AD,

Internal Operations
(785) 532-5263
cscott@kstatesports.com
• Kenny Lannou, Executive Associate AD, Communications
(785) 532-7977
klannou@kstatesports.com
• Kristin Waller, Associate AD of Student-Athlete Services
(785) 532-5409
kwaller@kstatesports.com

KANSAS UNIVERSITY ATHLETICS
ALLEN FIELDHOUSE
1651 NAISMITH DRIVE
LAWRENCE, KS 66045
785-864-8200
kuathletics@ku.edu
kuathletics.com
• Kurt Watson, Interim Athletics Director
(875) 864-3143
kuathletics@ku.edu
• Chris Freet, Deputy AD, External Engagement
(785) 864-6670
freet@ku.edu
• Sean Lester, Deputy AD, Administration
(785) 864-3470
slester@ku.edu
• Nicole Corcoran, Executive Associate AD/SWA
(785) 864-5999
ncorcoran@ku.edu

KENNESAW STATE UNIVERSITY ATHLETICS
590 COBB AVENUE
MAILBOX 0201
KENNESAW, GA 30144
470-578-6284
Fax: 470-578-9029
www.ksuowls.com
• Milton Overton, Director of Athletics
(470) 578-6284
moverton@kennesaw.edu
• Matt Griffin, Deputy AD
(470) 578-6284
mgriff82@kennesaw.edu
• Travis Glasgow, Senior Associate AD
(470) 578-7793
tglasgo2@kennesaw.edu
• Donovan Charles, Assistant AD, Development
(470) 578-7985
dcharle6@kennesaw.edu
• Kendra Jenkins, Senior Associate AD, Finance
(470) 578-2582
kjenki55@kennesaw.edu

KENT STATE UNIVERSITY ATHLETICS
MAC CENTER
PO BOX 5190
KENT, OH 44242
330-672-5974
kentstatesports.com
• Joel Nielsen, Director of Athletics
(330) 672-3120
nielsen@kent.edu
• Casey Cegles, Deputy AD, External Operations
(330) 672-2175
ccegles@kent.edu
• Amy Densevich, Associate AD/SWA
(330) 672-2961
adensevi@kent.edu
• Angie Hull, Associate AD, Academic

Service
(330) 672-4733
hull@kent.edu
• Stephanie Rosinski, Associate AD,
Compliance
(330) 672-2243
srosinsk@kent.edu
• Trent Stratton, Associate AD, Sports
Medicine
(330) 672-8426
tstratto@kent.edu

KENTUCKY ATHLETICS, UNIVERSITY OF
UK ATHLETICS
JOE CRAFT CENTER
338 LEXINGTON AVENUE
LEXINGTON, KY 40506-0604
859-257-8000
ukathletics.com
• Mitch Barnhart, Athletics Director
(859) 257-8015
mbarn@uky.edu
• Marc Hill, Deputy AD
(859) 257-1423
mhill@uky.edu

LA SALLE UNIVERSITY ATHLETICS
TRUMARK FINANCIAL CENTER
1900 WEST OLNEY AVENUE
PHILADELPHIA, PA 19141
215-951-1425
Fax: 215-951-1694
www.goexplorers.com
• Brian Baptise, Director of Athletics
(215) 951-1425
athletics@lasalle.edu
• Brian Quinn, Senior AD, Development
(215) 951-1543
quinng@lasalle.edu
• Christine Pereira, Associate AD,
Compliance
pereira@lasalle.edu
• Phil Snead, Associate AD, Business
(215) 951-1678
snead@lasalle.edu
• Dan Lobacz, Associate AD, External
Relations
(215) 951-1932
lobacz@lasalle.edu

LAFAYETTE COLLEGE ATHLETICS
KIRBY SPORTS CENTER
700 W PIERCE STREET
EASTON, PA 18042
610-330-5470
www.goleopards.com
• Sherryta Freeman, Director of Athletics
(610) 330-5470
athleticdirector@lafayette.edu
• Kaitlyn McKittrick, Deputy AD/SWA
(610) 330-5474
mckittrk@lafayette.edu
• Andrew Foster, Associate AD, Operations
& Facilities
(610) 330-5472
fostera@lafayette.edu
• Michael Chamberlain, Associate AD,
Compliance
(610) 330-4421
chambemi@lafayette.edu

LAMAR UNIVERSITY ATHLETICS
211 REDBIRD LANE
BEAUMONT, TX 77710
Fax: 409-880-1814
luathletics@lamar.edu
www.lamarcardinals.com

• Marco Born, Director of Athletics
mborn@lamar.edu
• Conner Moreno, Senior AD,
Administration/CFO
(409) 880-2249
cmoreno13@lamar.edu
• Moses Dupree, Assistant Athletic Director,
Compliance
(409) 880-8323
moses.dupre@lamar.edu
• Helene Thill, Associate AD/SWA
(409) 880-8333
helene.thill@lamar.edu

LEHIGH UNIVERSITY ATHLETICS
641 TAYLOR STREET
BETHLEHEM, PA 18015
610-758-4300
Fax: 610-758-6629
www.lehighsports.com
• Joe Sterrett, Dean of Athletics
(610) 758-4320
jds7@lehigh.edu
• Taryn Gall, Associate AD, Compliance
(610) 758-4607
taf6@lehigh.edu
• Stacy Shiffert, Associate AD, Business &
Budget
(610) 758-6332
stsa@lehigh.edu
• Chris Wakely, Associate AD, Recruitment
(610) 758-6553
cjw5@lehigh.edu

LIBERTY UNIVERSITY ATHLETICS
1971 UNIVERSITY BOULEVARD
LYNCHBURG, VA 24515
434-582-2100
Fax: 434-582-2205
www.liberty.edu/flames
• Ian McCaw, Director of Athletics
athletics@liberty.edu
• Mickey Guridy, Senior Associate AD,
Internal Operations
maguridy@liberty.edu
• Tim East, Senior Associate AD, External
Operations
tmeast@liberty.edu
• Todd Patulski, Senior Associate AD/CFO
tpatulski@liberty.edu
• Chris Casola, Assoc. AD, Student-Athlete
Welfare & Performance
ccasola@liberty.edu
• Erin Hagen, Assoc. AD, Admin. &
Strategic Inits./SWA
ehagen1@liberty.edu

LIPSCOMB UNIVERSITY ATHLETICS
ONE UNIVERSITY PARK DRIVE
NASHVILLE, TN 37204
www.lipscombsports.com
• Philip Hutcheson, Athletic Director
(615) 966-5850
• Brent McMillian, Associate AD, External
Affairs
(615) 966-5850
brent.mcmillian@lipscomb.edu
• John Ezell, Associate AD, Compliance &
Budgets
(615) 966-5911
john.ezell@lipscomb.edu
• Grace A Miller, Associate AD,
Academics/SWA
(615) 966-5999
graceann.miller@lipscomb.edu

LONG BEACH STATE ATHLETICS
BARRETT ATHLETIC ADMIN. CENTER
1250 BELLFLOWER BOULEVARD
LONG BEACH, CA 90840
562-985-4655
Fax: 562-985-8197
www.longbeachstate.com
• Andy Fee, Athletic Director
(562) 985-7976
andy.fee@csulb.edu
• Ashlie Kite, Senior Associate AD/SWA
(562) 985-8527
ashlie.kite@csulb.edu
• Mark Edrington, Senior Associate AD,
Capital Enhancement
(562) 985-5661
mark.edrington@csulb.edu
• Tiffany Edlin, Senior Associate AD,
Business
(562) 985-1626
tiffany.edlin@csulb.edu

**LONG ISLAND UNIVERSITY BROOKLYN
ATHLETICS**
1 UNIVERISITY PLAZA
BROOKLYN, NY 11201
718-780-4591
www.liuathletics.com
• William Martinov, Director of Athletics
(516) 299-2289
• Lloyd Ribner, III, Deputy AD
(718) 488-1530
lloyd.ribner@liu.edu
• Carla Pennolino, Associate AD,
Operations
(516) 299-3987
carla.pennolino@liu.edu
• Stephen Clacherty, Associate AD,
Compliance
(516) 299-3819
stephen.clacherty@liu.edu
• Deirdre Moore, Associate AD/SWA
(516) 299-3853
deirdre.moore@liu.edu
• Casey Snedecor, Assistant AD
(718) 488-1307
catherine.snedecor@liu.edu

LONGWOOD UNIVERSITY ATHLETICS
201 HIGH STREET
TABB BUILDING
FARMVILLE, VA 23909
434-395-2057
Fax: 434-395-2568
www.longwoodlancers.com
• Michelle Meadows, Athletics Director
(434) 395-2057
• Laura Snead, Senior Associate AD,
Administration
(434) 395-4855
sneadlm@longwood.edu
• Katie Pate, Associate AD, External
Operations
(434) 395-2058
patekj@longwood.edu

**LOUISIANA AT LAFAYETTE ATHLETICS,
UNIVERSITY OF**
COX COMMUNICATIONS BUILDING
201 REINHARDT DRIVE
LAFAYETTE, LA 70506
337-482-5393
Fax: 337-482-1041
ragincajuns.com
• Bryan Maggard, Ph.D., Director of
Athletics
(337) 482-5393

• Jessica Leger, Ph.D., Deputy AD/SWA
(337) 482-5393
jessica@louisiana.edu
• Nico Yantko, Deputy AD, External
Operations
(337) 482-1836
nico.yantko@louisiana.edu
• Duane Bailey, Deputy AD/CFO
(337) 482-1362
duane.bailey@louisiana.edu
• Lee De Leon, Deputy AD
(337) 482-2904
lee.deleon@louisiana.edu

**LOUISIANA AT MONROE ATHLETICS,
UNIVERSITY OF**
ULM ATHLETICS
308 WARHAWK WAY
MONROE, LA 71209
318-342-5360
www.ulmwarhawks.com
• Scott McDonald, Director of Athletics
(318) 342-5361
mcdonald@ulm.edu
• Benji Buffington, Executive AD, Business
Operations
(318) 342-5363
buffington@ulm.edu
• John Lewandowski, Senior Associate AD,
Communications
(318) 342-5378
lewandowski@ulm.edu
• Ashleigh Simmons, Assistant AD,
Compliance/SWA
(318) 342-5380
asimmons@ulm.edu

**LOUISIANA STATE UNIVERSITY
ATHLETICS**
LSU ATHLETICS ADMIN. BLDG.
BATON ROUGE, LA 70803
225-578-8001
www.lsusports.net
• Scott Woodward, Director of Athletics
(225) 578-8001
• Verge Ausberry, Executive Deputy AD,
External Relations
(225) 578-6603
vausbe1@lsu.edu
• Stephanie Rempe, Executive Deputy
Ad/COO
(225) 578-8001
srempe@lsu.edu
• Miriam Segar, Sr. Assoc. AD/SWA
(225) 578-5785
msegar@lsu.edu

**LOUISIANA TECH UNIVERSITY
ATHLETICS**
THOMAS ASSEMBLY CENTER
1650 W ALABAMA
PO BOX 3046
RUSTON, LA 71272
www.latechsports.com
• Wood A Eric, Athletics Director
athleticdirector@latech.edu
• Mary Kay Hungate, Deputy Athletics
Director/SWA
(318) 257-5654
mhungate@latech.edu
• Paul Kabbes, Senior Associate AD,
External Operations
(318) 257-2933
paul@latech.edu

**LOUISVILLE ATHLETICS, UNIVERSITY
OF**
ATHLETIC DEPT., SAC BUILDING
2100 S FLOYD STREET
LOUISVILLE, KY 40208
502-852-5735
gocards.com
• Vince Tyra, Director of Athletics
vince@gocards.com
• Josh Heird, Deputy AD
heird@gocards.com
• John Carns, Senior Associate AD,
Compliance
(502) 852-7728
john@gocards.com
• Kenny Klein, Senior Associate AD
(502) 852-0112
kenny@gocards.com
• Marvin Mitchell, Senior Associate AD,
Student Services
(502) 852-7100
marvin@gocards.com
• Amy Calabrese, Associate AD/SWA
(502) 852-4939
amyc@GoCards.com

LOYOLA MARYMOUNT UNIVERSITY
1 LMU DRIVE
MS 8505
LOS ANGELES, CA 90045
310-338-5915
www.lmulions.com
• Craig Pintens, Athletics Director
(310) 338-3047
craig.pintens@lmu.edu
• Ashley Armstrong, Deputy AD/SWA
(310) 258-7246
ashley.armstrong@lmu.edu
• Maria Behm, Senior Associate AD,
Business Affairs
(310) 338-7645
mbehm@lmu.edu
• James Batley, Senior Associate AD,
Development
(310) 338-7880
james.batley@lmu.edu

**LOYOLA UNIVERSITY CHICAGO
ATHLETICS**
THE NORVILLE CENTER
6526 N WINTHROP AVENUE
CHICAGO, IL 60626
773-508-2747
Fax: 773-508-3884
www.loyolaramblers.com
• Steve Watson, Director of Athletics
(773) 508-2747
swatson4@luc.edu
• Holly Strauss-O'Brien, Deputy Director of
Athletics
(773) 508-2655
hstaussobrien@luc.edu
• Tom Sorboro, Senior Associate AD,
External Operations
(773) 508-2731
tsorboro@luc.edu
• Tom Hitcho, Senior Associate AD,
Operations
(773) 508-2567
thitch@luc.edu

**LOYOLA UNIVERSITY MARYLAND
ATHLETICS**
4501 N CHARLES STREET
BALTIMORE, MD 21210

410-617-5013
Fax: 410-617-2008
www.loyolagreyhounds.com
• Donna M. Woodruff, Director of Athletics
(410) 617-5013
• Teddi Burns, Associate AD, Facils. &
Ops./SWA
(410) 617-2643
tburns@loyola.edu
• Dave Gerrity, Associate AD
(410) 617-2547
dgerrity@loyola.edu
• Bill Wnek, Associate AD, Compliance
(410) 617-2172
bwnek@loyola.edu
• Chris Archacki, Associate AD, Business &
Internal Operations
(410) 617-2718
carchacki@loyola.edu
• Ryan Eigenbrode, Associate AD,
Communications
(410) 617-2337
rceigenbrode@loyola.edu

MAINE ATHLETICS, UNIVERSITY OF
5747 MEMORIAL GYMNASIUM
ORONO, ME 04469-5747
207-581-1865
goblackbears.com
• Ken Ralph, Director of Athletics
• Brian Faison, Deputy Director of Athletics
brian.faison@maine.edu
• Seth Woodcock, Senior Associate AD,
Development
seth.woodcock@maine.edu
• Tyson McHatten, Senior Associate AD,
External Operations
(207) 581-3596
tysone.mchatten@maine.edu
• Matt Curtis, Associate AD, Business
(207) 581-1544
matthew.curtis@maine.edu
• Samantha Hegmann, Associate AD,
Compliance/SWA
(207) 581-1845
samantha.hegmann@maine.edu

MANHATTAN COLLEGE ATHLETICS
4513 MANHATTAN COLLEGE PARKWAY
RIVERDALE, NY 10471
Fax: 718-862-7219
www.gojaspers.com
• Marianne Reilly, Director of Athletics
(718) 862-7891
ad@manhattan.edu
• Tony Vecchione, Deputy Athletic Director
(718) 862-7230
avecchione01@manhattan.edu

MARIST COLLEGE ATHLETICS
MCCANN CENTER
3399 NORTH ROAD
POUGHKEEPSIE, NY 12601
845-575-3000
www.goredfoxes.com
• Tim Murray, Director of Athletics
(845) 575-3000
athletics@marist.edu
• Elizabeth Donohue, Associate AD,
Compliance/SWA
(845) 575-3000
elizabeth.donohue@marist.edu
• Darren McCormack, Associate AD,
Facilities & Operations
(845) 575-3000
darren.mccormack1@marist.edu
• Harrison Baker, Associate AD, External

Affairs
(845) 575-3000
harrison.baker@marist.edu

MARQUETTE UNIVERSITY ATHLETICS
770 N 12TH STREET
MILWAUKEE, WI 53233
414-288-6303
www.gomarquette.com
• Bill Scholl, Director of Athletics
(414) 288-6303
athleticdirector@marquette.edu
• Mike Broeker, Deputy Athletic Director
(414) 288-5287
michael.broeker@marquette.edu
• Danielle Josetti, Executive Associate AD,
Compliance
(414) 288-3983
danielle.josetti@marquette.edu
• Adrienne Ridgeway, Executive Associate
AD, Academic Services
(414) 288-0266
adrienne.ridgeway@marquette.edu
• Sarah Bobert, Executive Associate AD,
Internal Operations/SWA
(414) 288-5253
sarah.bobert@marquette.edu

MARSHALL UNIVERSITY ATHLETICS
MARSHALL ATHLETIC DEPT.
PO BOX 1360
HUNTINGTON, WV 25715
www.herdzone.com
• Mike Hamrick, Director of Athletics
(304) 696-5408
• Jeff O'Malley, Associate AD/Chief of Staff
(304) 696-4310
omalley@marshall.edu
• David Steele, Associate AD,
Administration & Business
(304) 696-2483
steele@marshall.edu
• Beatrice Crane Banford, Associate
AD/SWA
(304) 696-5225
craneb@marshall.edu
• John Sutherland, Associate AD,
Development
(304) 696-3402
sutherland@marshall.edu
• Scott Morehouse, Associate AD, Facilities
Operations
(304) 696-6022
morehou1@marshall.edu

MARY ATHLETICS, UNIVERSITY OF
UM ATHLETICS
7500 UNIVERSITY DRIVE
BISMARCK, ND 58504
701-335-8200
Fax: 701-335-8302
www.goumary.com
• Dale Lennon, Director of Athletics
(701) 355-8315
dclennon@umary.edu
• Daniel Huntley, Associate AD
(701) 355-8337
djhuntley@umary.edu

MARYGROVE COLLEGE ATHLETICS
8100 CURTIS STREET
DETROIT, MI 48221
313-928-1487
athletics@marygrove.edu
www.marygrovemustangs.com
• Jonathan T. Bradbury, Director of Athletics
(313) 928-1487

sbloomfi@marygrove.edu
• Andrew D. Thompson, Assistant AD
(313) 927-1484
wpugh@marygrove.edu

MARYLAND ATHLETICS, UNIVERSITY OF
DEPT. OF INTERCOLLEGIATE
ATHLETICS
XFINITY CENTER
8500 PAINT BRANCH DRIVE
COLLEGE PARK, MD 20742
www.umterps.com
• Damon Evans, Director of Athletics
(301) 314-0013
devans16@umd.edu
• Colleen Sorem, Deputy AD
(301) 314-7046
csorem@umd.edu
• Brian Ullmann, Executive Associate
AD/CSO
(301) 314-1482
ullmann@umd.edu

**MARYLAND EASTERN SHORE
ATHLETICS, UNIVERSITY OF**
WILLIAM P. HYTCHE ATHLETIC CENTER
BACKBONE ROAD RM. 1133
PRINCESS ANNE, MD 21853
www.easternshorehawks.com
• Keith Davidson, Director of Athletics
(410) 651-7814
kdavidson@umes.edu
• Kristen Drummond, Associate AD,
Compliance/SWA
(410) 651-8150
kddrummond@umes.edu

**MARYLAND-BALTIMORE COUNTY
ATHLETICS, UNIVERSITY OF**
UMBC RETRIEVER ACTIVITIES CENTER
1000 HILLTOP CIRCLE
BALTIMORE, MD 21250
www.umbcretrievers.com
• Brian Barrio, Director of Athletics
(410) 455-2207
bbarrio@umbc.edu
• Jessica Hammond-Graf, Deputy AD/SWA
(410) 455-2290
hammond@umbc.edu
• Gary Wohlstetter, Senior Associate AD,
P.E. & Recreation
(410) 455-2638
wohlstet@umbc.edu

**MCNEESE STATE UNIVERSITY
ATHLETICS**
700 E MCNEESE STREET
LAKE CHARLES, LA 70609
337-562-4678
Fax: 337-475-5220
www.mcneesesports.com
• Heath Schroyer, Director of Athletics
(337) 475-5480
hschroyer@mcneese.edu
• Bridget Martin, Senior Associate AD,
Compliance/SWA
(337) 475-5296
bmartin@mcneese.edu

MEMPHIS ATHLETICS, UNIVERSITY OF
570 NORMAL
MEMPHIS, TN 38152
901-678-2335
gotigersgo.com
• Laird Veatch, Athletic Director
(901) 678-5395

athleticdirector@memphis.edu
• Jeff Crane, Deputy Athletic Director
(901) 678-5395
jeff.c@memphis.edu
• Adam Walker, Senior Associate AD,
Administration
(901) 678-1720
awalker9@memphis.edu
• Blair DeBord, Associate AD, Development
(901) 678-1369
bdebord@memphis.edu
• Andrew Roberts, Senior Associate AD,
Finance
(901) 678-4142
andrew.roberts@memphis.edu

MERCER UNIVERSITY ATHLETICS
MERCER ATHLETICS
1501 MERCER UNIVERSITY DRIVE
MACON, GA 31207
478-301-2994
mercerbears.com
• Jim Cole, Director of Athletics
(478) 301-2737
cole_jm@mercer.edu
• Sybil Blalock, Deputy AD, Acad.
Affairs/SWA
(478) 301-2301
blalock_sa@mercer.edu
• Brian Gerrity, Senior Associate AD
(478) 301-4003
gerrity_bt@mercer.edu

MIAMI ATHLETICS, UNIVERSITY OF
5821 SAN AMARO DRIVE
CORAL GABLES, FL 33146
305-284-3822
miamihurricanes.com
• Blake James, Director of Athletics
(305) 284-2689
• Jennifer Strawley, Deputy Director of
Athletics/COO
(305) 284-2651
jennstrawley@miami.edu
• Jason Layton, Deputy Director of
Athletics/CFO
(305) 284-3231
jlayton@miami.edu

MIAMI UNIVERSITY ATHLETICS
230 MILLETT HALL
OXFORD, OH 45056
513-529-3113
Fax: 513-529-0407
wellspl@miamioh.edu
www.miamiredhawks.com
• David Sayler, Director of Athletics
(513) 529-7286
• Jude Killy, Deputy Director of Athletics
(513) 529-3113
killyja@miamioh.edu
• Steve Cady, Senior Associate AD
(513) 529-8174
cadysd@miamioh.edu
• Jennifer Gilbert, Senior Associate
AD/SWA
(513) 529-8285
gilberj2@miamioh.edu

MICHIGAN ATHLETICS, UNIVERSITY OF
ATHLETIC DEPARTMENT
1000 S STATE STREET
ANN ARBOR, MI 48109-2201
734-647-2583
Fax: 734-764-3221
mgoblue.com

• Warde Manuel, Director of Athletics
(734) 764-9416
• Rob Rademacher, Executive Senior
Associate AD/COO
(734) 647-9763
• Katie Fraumann, Executive Associate AD,
Development
(734) 647-9895
• Doug Gnodtke, Executive Associate
AD/Chief of Staff
(734) 936-1992

MICHIGAN STATE UNIVERSITY ATHLETICS
ATHLETICS ADMIN.
1855 PLACE
550 S HARRISON RD
EAST LANSING, MI 48823
517-355-1630
www.msuspartans.com
• Bill Beekman, Athletics Director
(507) 355-1623
ad@ath.mus.edu
• Alan Haller, Deputy Athletic Director
(517) 355-1630
haller@ath.msu.edu
• Jennifer Smith, Deputy Athletic
Director/SWA
(517) 432-2606
smith170@ath.msu.edu

MIDDLE TENNESSEE ATHLETICS
1500 GREENLAND DRIVE
MURFREESBORO, TN 37132
615-898-2450
Fax: 615-898-2777
goblueraiders.com
• Chris Massaro, Director of Athletics
(615) 898-2452
chris.massaro@mtsu.edu
• David Blackburn, Senior Associate AD,
External Affairs
(615) 898-2210
david.blackburn@mtsu.edu
• Diane Turnham, Senior Associate
AD/SWA
(615) 898-2938
diane.turnham@mtsu.edu

MINNESOTA ATHLETICS, UNIVERSITY OF
516 15TH AVENUE SE
MINNEAPOLIS, MN 55455
gophers@umn.edu
www.gophersports.com
• Mark Coyle, Director of Athletics
icaadmin@umn.edu
• Tim McCleary, Deputy Athletics
Director/CFO
• Julie Manning, Deputy Athletics
Director/SWA
jmanning@umn.edu

MISSISSIPPI ATHLETICS, UNIVERSITY OF
OLE MISS ATHLETICS
908 ALL-AMERICAN DRIVE
UNIVERSITY, MS 38677
www.olemisssports.com
• Keith Carter, Athletics Director
(662) 915-7546
jkcarter@olemiss.edu
• Lynnette Johnson, Deputy AD, Sports
Administration
(662) 915-7303
lys@olemiss.edu
• Tom Kleinlein, Deputy AD, External

(662) 915-8803
tmkleinl@olemiss.edu

MISSISSIPPI STATE UNIVERSITY ATHLETICS
MISSISSIPPI STATE, MS 39762
hailstate.com
• John Cohen, Director of Athletics
(662) 325-0863
johncohen@athletics.msstate.edu
• Eric George, Deputy AD/CFO
(662) 325-8670
egeorge@athletics.msstate.edu
• Bo Hemphill, Deputy AD, Development
(662) 325-1533
bhemphill@athletics.msstate.edu

MISSISSIPPI VALLEY STATE UNIVERSITY ATHLETICS
DEPT. OF ATHLETICS
14000 HIGHWAY 82 WEST
BOX 7246
ITTA BENA, MS 38941
662-254-3550
Fax: 662-254-3639
www.mvsusports.com
• Dianthia Ford-Kee, Director of Athletics
(662) 254-3550
• K. Renia Edwards, Senior Associate AD,
Compliance/SWA
(662) 254-3024
kredwards@mvsu.edu
• Lee Smith, Associate AD
(662) 254-3721
lcsmith@mvsu.edu

MISSOURI ATHLETICS, UNIVERSITY OF
MIZZOU ATHLETICS
1 CHAMPIONS DRIVE
SUITE 200
COLUMBIA, MO 65211
573-884-7297
Fax: 573-882-6501
mutigers.com
• Jim Sterk, Athletic Director
(573) 882-2055
muathmizzouad@missouri.edu
• Sarah Reesman, Senior Deputy AD/SWA
(573) 884-6428
reesman@missouri.edu
• Tim Hickman, Deputy AD/CFO
(573) 884-6428
hickmantl@missouri.edu
• Nick Joos, Deputy AD/COO
joosn@missouri.edu

MISSOURI STATE ATHLETICS
901 S NATIONAL AVENUE
SPRINGFIELD, MO 65897
www.missouristatebears.com
• Kyle Moats, Director of Athletics
(417) 836-5244
athletics@missouristate.edu
• Casey Hunt, Senior Associate AD/SWA
(417) 836-5244
caseyhunt@missouristate.edu
• Keith Boaz, Sr. Assoc. AD, Athletics &
Entertainment
(417) 836-5240
keithboaz@missouristate.edu

MISSOURI-KANSAS CITY ATHLETICS, UNIVERSITY OF
5030 HOLMES
KANSAS CITY, MO 64110
www.umkckangaroos.com

• Brandon Martin, Director of Athletics
(816) 235-1020
• Ursula Gurney, Deputy Director of
Athletics/SWA
(816) 235-5093
gurneyu@umkc.edu
• Curt Jacey, Deputy AD, External Relations
(816) 235-1039
jaceyc@umkc.edu

MONMOUTH UNIVERSITY ATHLETICS
400 CEDAR AVENUE
WEST LONG BRANCH, NJ 07764
732-571-3415
Fax: 732-571-3535
monmouthhawks.com
• Marilyn McNeil, Director of Athletics
(732) 571-3414
mmcneil@monmouth.edu
• Jeff Stapleton, Deputy Director of
Athletics, Internal Affairs
(732) 571-3673
jstaplet@monmouth.edu
• Jon Roos, Senior Associate AD, Internal
Affairs
(732) 263-5189
jroos@monmouth.edu
• Jennifer Lawler, Senior Associate
AD/SWA
(732) 571-3604
jlawlor@monmouth.edu

MONTANA ATHLETICS, UNIVERSITY OF
MONTANA ATHLETICS
ADAMS CENTER
32 CAMPUS DRIVE
MISSOULA, MT 59812
gogriz.com
• Kent Haslam, Director of Athletics
(406) 243-5348
kent.haslam@mso.umt.edu
• Jean Gee, Senior Associate AD/SWA
(406) 243-5370
jean.gee@mso.umt.edu
• Greg Sundberg, Senior Associate AD,
External Operations
(406) 243-6481
sundbergg@mso.umt.edu
• Chuck Maes, Senior Associate AD,
Facilities & Events
(406) 243-2213
maescf@mso.umt.edu
• Ryan Martin, Senior Associate AD/CFO
(406) 243-6926
ryan.martin@mso.umt.edu

MONTANA STATE UNIVERSITY ATHLETICS
MONTANA STATE UNIVERSITY
1 BOBCAT CIRCLE
PO BOX 173380
BOZEMAN, MT 59717-3380
406-994-4221
Fax: 406-994-2278
msubobcats.com
• Leon Costello, Director of Athletics
(406) 994-3499
lcostello@msubobcats.com
• Dan Davies, Senior Associate AD, Internal
Operations
(406) 994-2301
ddavies@msubobcats.com
• Camie Bechtold, Senior Associate AD,
Administration
(406) 994-3947
cbechtold@msubobcats.com
• Casey Fox, Senior Associate AD, External

Operations
(406) 994-5707
casey.fox2@msubobcats.com
• Thijs Goossens, Senior Associate AD,
Business Operations/CFO
(406) 994-3742
thijs.goossens@msubobcats.com
• Bethany Cordell, Senior Associate AD,
Annual Giving
(406) 994-6267
bcordell@msubobcats.com

MOREHEAD STATE UNIVERSITY ATHLETICS
195 ACADEMIC-ATHLETIC CENTER
MOREHEAD, KY 40351
606-783-2088
Fax: 606-783-5035
www.msueagles.com
• Jaime Gordon, Director of Athletics
(606) 783-2089
j.gordon@moreheadstate.edu
• Richard Fletcher, Deputy Director of
Athletics
(606) 783-5136
r.fletcher@moreheadstate.edu
• Jamey Carver, Assistant AD, Compliance
(606) 783-2086
j.carver@moreheadstate.edu
• Sara Hacker, Assistant AD , External
Affairs/SWA
(606) 783-9018
skhacker@moreheadstate.edu

MORGAN STATE UNIVERSITY ATHLETICS
1700 E COLD SPRING LANE
BALTIMORE, MD 21251
443-885-3333
www.morganstatebears.com
• Edward Scott, Director of Athletics
(443) 885-3050
edward.scott@morgan.edu

MOUNT ST. MARY'S UNIVERSITY ATHLETICS
16300 OLD EMMITSBURG ROAD
EMMITSBURG, MD 21727
301-447-5384
www.mountathletics.com
• Lynne Robinson, Director of Athletics
(301) 447-3808
lrobinso@msmary.edu
• Doug White, Assistant AD, Operations
(301) 447-5385
dwhite@msmary.edu
• Mark Vandergrift, Assistant AD, Athletic
Communications
(301) 447-5384
vandergrift@msmary.edu
• Justine Miller, Asst. AD, Acads. & Student
Athlete Support Srvcs.
(301) 447-6782
justine_miller@msmary.edu

MURRAY STATE UNIVERSITY ATHLETICS
RACER ATHLETICS
217 STEWART STADIUM
MURRAY, KY 42071
270-809-6800
goracers.com
• Kevin Saal, Director of Athletics
(270) 809-3164
msu.athletics@murraystate.edu
• Matt Kelly, Senior Associate AD
(270) 809-4424

mkelly@murraystate.edu
• Scott Barnhart, Associate AD, Business &
Resources Operations
(270) 809-3430
sbarnhart2@murraystate.edu
• Dave Winder, Associate AD,
Communication & Public Relations
(270) 809-4271
dwinder@murraystate.edu

NEBRASKA ATHLETICS, UNIVERSITY OF
ONE MEMORIAL STADIUM
800 STADIUM DRIVE
LINCOLN, NE 68588
402-472-4224
www.huskers.com
• Bill Moos, Director of Athletics
(402) 472-3011
ad@huskers.com
• John Johnson, Senior Deputy AD/Chief of
Staff
(402) 472-3011
jwjohnson@huskers.com
• Garrett Klassy, Senior Deputy AD
(402) 472-3011
gklassy@huskers.com
• Bob Burton, Deputy AD, Facilities
(402) 472-3011
bburton@huskers.com
• John Jentz, Deputy AD/CFO
(402) 472-2273
jjentz@huskers.com
• Pat Logsdon, Deputy AD/SWA
(402) 472-3011
plogsdon@huskers.com

NEVADA AT LAS VEGAS ATHLETICS, UNIVERSITY OF
UNLV ATHLETICS DEPARTMENT
4505 MARYLAND PARKWAY
LAS VEGAS, NV 89154
www.unlvrebels.com
• Desiree Reed-Francois, Director of
Athletics
(702) 895-4729
unlvad@unlv.edu
• Megan Caligiuri, Senior Associate AD,
External Operations
(702) 895-0294
megan.caligiuri@unlv.edu
• John Gladchuk, Senior Associate AD,
External Affairs
(702) 895-4729
john.gladchuk@unlv.edu
• Erick Harper, Senior Associate AD,
Development
(702) 895-1712
erick.harper@unlv.edu
• Eric Nepomuceno, Senior Associate AD,
Compliance
(702) 895-1314
eric.nepomuceno@unlv.edu

NEVADA ATHLETICS, UNIVERSITY OF
UNIV. OF NEVADA ATHETICS
1664 N VIRGINIA STREET
LEGACY HALL/MS 232
RENO, NV 89557-0232
Fax: 775-784-4497
nevadawolfpack.com
• Doug Knuth, Director of Athletics
(775) 682-6969
dknuth@unr.edu
• Kent Hegenauer, Senior Associate AD
(775) 682-6975
khegenauer@unr.edu
• Rhonda Lundin Bennett, Senior Associate

AD/SWA
(775) 682-6981
rlundin@unr.edu
• Ann Larson, Senior Associate AD, Event &
Facility Management
(775) 682-7657
amlarson@unr.edu

NEW HAMPSHIRE ATHLETICS, UNIVERSITY OF
UNH FIELD HOUSE
145 MAIN STREET
DURHAM, NH 03824
www.unhwildcats.com
• Marty Scarano, Director of Athletics
(603) 862-2013
marty.scarano@unh.edu
• Michelle Bronner, Deputy Director of
Athletics/SWA
(603) 319-7491
michelle.bronner@unh.edu
• Jon Danos, Exec. Director of Athletics
(603) 862-4677
jon.danos@unh.edu

NEW MEXICO STATE UNIVERSITY ATHLETICS
NEW MEXICO STATE UNIVERSITY
FULTON CENTER
1815 WELLS STREET
LAS CRUCES, NM 88003-8001
575-646-1658
nmstatesports.com
• Mario Moccia, Director of Athletics
(575) 646-7630
moccia@nmsu.edu
• Braun Cartwright, Deputy AD/COO
(575) 646-5713
braunc@nmsu.edu
• Chet Savage, Deputy AD
(575) 646-2569
savagec@nmsu.edu

NEW MEXICO, UNIVERSITY OF
UNIVERSITY OF NEW MEXICO
ATHLETICS
1414 UNIVERSITY DRIVE
ALBUQUERQUE, NM 87106
golobos.com
• Eddie Nuñez, Director of Athletics
(505) 925-5510
eddienunez@unm.edu
• Janice Ruggiero, Deputy AD, Internal
Operations/SWA
(505) 277-5067
ruggiero@unm.edu
• David Williams, Deputy AD, External
Affairs
(505) 925-5500
davidwilliams@unm.edu

NEW ORLEANS ATHLETICS, UNIVERSITY OF
THE HUMAN PERFORMANCE CENTER
2000 LAKESHORE DRIVE
NEW ORLEANS, LA 70148
504-280-6102
Fax: 504-280-3977
www.unoprivateers.com
• Tim Duncan, Director of Athletics
(504) 280-6102
athleticdirector@uno.edu
• Steve Stroud, Deputy AD
(504) 280-7403
sstroud1@uno.edu
• Dena Freeman-Patton, Deputy AD/COO
(504) 280-3874

dfreema1@uno.edu
• Kirsten Elleby, Associate Deputy AD/SWA
(504) 280-6392
kcelleby@uno.edu

NEWMAN UNIVERSITY ATHLETICS
3100 MCCORMICK AVENUE
WICHITA, KS 67213
316-942-4291
Fax: 316-942-4483
www.newmanjets.com
• Joanna Pryor, Athletic Director
(316) 942-4291
pryorj@newmanu.edu
• Maureen Rohleder, Associate AD,
Compliance/SWA
(316) 942-4291
rohlederm@newman.edu
• Zane Ehling, Associate AD, External
Operations
(316) 942-4291
ehlingz@newmanu.edu

NIAGARA UNIVERSITY ATHLETICS
UPPER LEVEL GALLAGHER CENTER
PO BOX 2009
NIAGARA UNIVERSITY, NY 14109
716-286-8600
purpleeagles.com
• Simon Gray, Director of Athletics
(716) 286-8600
sgray@niagara.edu
• Stephen Butler, Deputy DA/COO
(716) 286-8602
sbutler@niagara.edu
• Dedra Palmer, Associate AD/SWA
(716) 286-8781
dpalmer@niagara.edu

**NICHOLLS STATE UNIVERSITY
ATHLETICS**
PO BOX 2032
THIBODAUX, LA 70310
www.geauxcolonels.com
• Jonathan Terrell, Athletics Director
jonathan.terrell@nicholls.edu
• Andrew Kearney, Associate AD,
Compliance & Admin.
(985) 448-4812
andrew.kearney@nicholls.edu

**NORTH CAROLINA A&T STATE
UNIVERSITY ATHLETICS**
DEPT. OF ATHLETICS
1601 E MARKET STREET
GREENSBORO, NC 27411
www.ncataggies.com
• Earl Hilton, III, Director of Intercollegiate
Athletics
(336) 334-7686
hiltone@ncat.edu
• Shamika Pyfrom, Associate AD
(336) 285-3063
spyfrom@ncat.edu
• Carl Hairston, Associate AD, External
Affairs
(336) 285-3606
gchairst@ncat.edu
• Cory Lima, Associate AD, Compliance
(336) 285-3620
cmlima@ncat.edu
• Brian Holloway, Associate AD,
Communications
(336) 285-3608
bmhollow@ncat.edu
• Billy Edringston, Associate AD, Facilities

(336) 398-8673
edringst@ncat.edu

**NORTH CAROLINA ASHEVILLE
ATHLETICS, UNIVERSITY OF**
ATHLETICS DEPT.
JUSTICE CENTER, CPO#2600
ONE UNIVERSITY HEIGHTS
ASHEVILLE, NC 28804
828-251-6459
Fax: 828-251-6386
www.uncabulldogs.com
• Janet R. Cone, Director of Athletics
(828) 251-6922
jcone@unca.edu
• Terri Brne, Senior Associate AD/SWA
(828) 251-6930
tbrne@unca.edu

**NORTH CAROLINA AT CHAPEL HILL
ATHLETICS, UNIVERSITY OF**
UNC ATHLETIC DEPT.
PO BOX 2126
CHAPEL HILL, NC 27515
919-962-6000
goheels.com
• Bubba Cunningham, Athletic Director
bubba.cunningham@unc.edu
• Larry Gallo, Executive Associate AD
(919) 962-8200
athgallo@unc.edu
• Dwight Hollier, Senior Associate AD,
Student-Athlete Health
dhollier@unc.edu
• Vince Ille, Senior Associate AD
ille@unc.edu

**NORTH CAROLINA ATHLETICS,
UNIVERSITY OF**
UNC ATHLETIC DEPT.
PO BOX 2126
CHAPEL HILL, NC 27515
919-962-6000
goheels.com
• Bubba Cunningham, Athletic Director
(919) 962-6000
bubba.cunningham@unc.edu
• Larry Gallo, Exec. Assoc. AD
(919) 962-6000
athgallo@uncaa.unc.edu

**NORTH CAROLINA CENTRAL
UNIVERSITY ATHLETICS**
DEPT. OF ATHLETICS
MCDOUGALD-MCLENDON ARENA
1801 FAYETTEVILLE STREET
DURHAM, NC 27707
919-530-7057
Fax: 919-530-5426
nccueaglepride.com
• Ingrid Wicker McCree, Director of Athletics
(919) 530-7057
• Derrick Magee, Deputy AD/CFO
(919) 530-6868
dmagee@nccu.edu
• Kyle Serba, Executive Senior Assoc. AD,
Strategic Comms.
(919) 530-7054
kserba@nccu.edu

**NORTH CAROLINA CHARLOTTE
ATHLETICS, UNIVERSITY OF**
CHARLOTTE 49ERS ATHLETICS
9201 UNIVERSITY CITY BOULEVARD
CHARLOTTE, NC 28223

704-687-1054
www.charlotte49ers.com
• Mike Hill, Director of Athletics
(704) 687-1054
athleticdirector@uncc.edu
• Darin Spease, Deputy AD
(704) 687-0400
dspease@uncc.edu
• Chris Fuller, Deputy AD, External Affairs
(704) 687-1419
cfulle21@uncc.edu

**NORTH CAROLINA GREENSBORO
ATHLETICS, UNIVERSITY OF**
UNCG ATHLETIC DEPT.
PO BOX 26168
GREENSBORO, NC 27402
www.uncgspartans.com
• Kim Record, Director of Athletics
(336) 944-6206
ksrecord@uncg.edu
• Tim George, Senior Associate AD,
External Operations
(336) 683-1875
tbgeorge@uncg.edu
• Jody Smith, Senior Associate AD/SWA
(336) 334-4076
jody.smith@uncg.edu

**NORTH CAROLINA STATE UNIVERSITY
ATHLETICS**
WEISIGER BROWN BLDG.
2500 WARREN CARROLL DRIVE
CAMPUS BOX 8502
RALEIGH, NC 27695
919-515-2101
gopack.com
• Boo Corrigan, Director of Athletics
(919) 515-2109
wolfpackad@ncsu.edu
• Staphanie Menio, Deputy AD
(919) 515-4778
samenio@ncsu.edu

**NORTH CAROLINA WILMINGTON
ATHLETICS, UNIVERSITY OF**
601 SOUTH COLLEGE ROAD
WILMINGTON, NC 28403
uncwsports.com
• Jimmy Bass, Director of Athletics
(910) 962-3571
• Tiffany Tucker, Senior Associate AD/SWA
(910) 962-3767
tuckert@uncw.edu
• Mark Wagner, Senior Associate AD,
Internal Operations
(910) 962-3580
wagnerm@uncw.edu
• Joe Browning, Senior Associate AD,
Communications
(910) 962-3236
browningj@uncw.edu

**NORTH TEXAS ATHLETICS, UNIVERSITY
OF**
1301 S BONNIE BRAE STREET
DENTON, TX 76207
940-565-2789
www.meangreensports.com
• Baker Wren, Director of Athletics
(940) 565-2789
• Ryan Peck, Deputy AD, External
Operations
(940) 369-7630
ryan.peck@unt.edu

college sports

NORTHEASTERN STATE UNIVERSITY ATHLETICS
600 N GRAND AVENUE
TAHLEQUAH, OK 74464
www.goriverhawksgo.com
• Matt Cochran, Director of Athletics
(918) 444-3901
cochranm@nsuok.edu
• Scott Pettus, Assistant AD, External
Operations
(918) 444-3955
pettusr@msuok.edu
• Don Vieth, Assistant AD, Strategic
Communications
(918) 444-3930
veith@msuok.edu
• Jamie Hall, Assistant AD, Academic
Services
(918) 444-3940
westjl@msuok.edu

NORTHEASTERN UNIVERSITY ATHLETICS
360 HUNTINGTON AVENUE
219 CABOT CENTER
BOSTON, MA 02115
617-373-2672
Fax: 617-373-8988
www.gonu.com
• Jeff Konya, Athletic Director
• Regina Sullivan, Executive Senior
Associate AD/SWA
re.sullivan@northeastern.edu
• Marshall Foley, Executive Sr. Associate
AD, Operations
ma.foley@northeastern.edu
• Scott MacDonald, Associate AD,
Communications
(617) 373-4154
s.macdonald@northeastern.edu

NORTHERN ARIZONA UNIVERSITY ATHLETICS
PO BOX 15400
1705 S SAN FRANCISCO STREET
FLAGSTAFF, AZ 86011
928-523-5353
Fax: 928-523-6035
www.nauathletics.com
• Mike Marlow, Vice President for
Intercollegiate Athletics
(928) 523-5353
lumberjackad@nau.edu
• Uri Farkas, Deputy AD
(928) 523-3095
uri.farkas@nau.edu
• Beth Vechinski, Senior Associate AD,
Internal Operations/SWA
(928) 523-3326
beth.vechinksi@nau.edu
• Matt Howdeshell, Senior Associate AD,
Administration
(928) 523-0293
matt.howdshell@nau.edu
• Syed Moinuddin, Senior Associate AD,
Compliance
(928) 523-6763
syed.moinuddin@nau.edu

NORTHERN ILLINOIS UNIVERSITY ATHLETICS
INTERCOLLEGIATE ATHLETICS
CONVOCATION CENTER
DEKALB, IL 60115
815-753-7225
Fax: 815-753-7700
www.niuhuskies.com

• Sean T. Frazier, Director of Athletics
(815) 753-9473
athleticdirector@niu.edu
• John Cheney, Executive Associate AD
(815) 753-1801
jcheney2@niu.edu

NORTHERN IOWA ATHLETICS, UNIVERSITY OF
203 MCLEOD CENTER
CEDAR FALLS, IA 50614-0312
unipanthers.com
• David Harris, Director of Athletics
(319) 273-2470
uniad@uni.edu
• Justin Schemmel, Deputy AD, Internal
Operations
(319) 273-2410
justin.schemmel@uni.edu
• Beth West, Senior Associate AD, Business
(319) 273-7855
beth.west@uni.edu

NORTHERN KENTUCKY UNIVERSITY ATHLETICS
133 BB&T ARENA
500 NUNN DRIVE
HIGHLAND HEIGHTS, KY 41099
859-572-6639
www.nkunorse.com
• Ken Bothof, Director of Athletics
(859) 572-6539
bothofk1@nku.edu
• Dan McIver, Deputy AD
(859) 572-7744
mciverd1@nku.edu
• Chris Hafling, Associate AD, Operations
(859) 572-7665
haflingc1@nku.edu
• Debbie Kirch, Associate AD,
Compliance/SWA
(859) 572-5140
kirchd1@nku.edu

NORTHWESTERN OKLAHOMA STATE UNIVERSITY ATHLETICS
709 OKLAHOMA BOULEVARD
ALVA, OK 73717
580-327-8639
Fax: 580-327-8669
www.riderangersride.com
• Brad Franz, Director of Athletics
(580) 327-8632
bmfranz@nwosu.edu
• Tim Lauderdale, Associate AD, Internal
Operations
(580) 327-8578
tjlauderdale@nwosu.edu
• Sadiaa Jones, Associate AD,
Compliance/Student Services
(580) 327-8635
syjones@nwosu.edu

NORTHWESTERN STATE UNIVERSITY OF LOUISIANA ATHLETICS
ATHLETIC FIELDHOUSE
468 CASPARI DRIVE
NATCHITOCHES, LA 71497
athleticsinfo@nsula.edu
www.nsudemons.com
• Greg Burke, Director of Athletics
(318) 357-5251
burkeg@nsula.edu
• Taitano Haley, Associate AD, External
Relations/SWA
(318) 357-4278
blounth@nsula.edu

• Dustin Eubanks, Associate AD,
Compliance
(318) 357-4210
eubanksd@nsula.edu

NORTHWESTERN UNIVERSITY ATHLETICS
WALTER ATHLETICS CENTER
2255 CAMPUS DRIVE
EVANSTON, IL 60208
847-491-3205
nusports.com
• Denee Barracato, Deputy AD, Operations
(847) 491-4646
denee.barracato@northwestern.edu
• Janna Blais, Deputy AD, Admin./SWA
(847) 491-7893
j-blais@northwestern.edu
• Travis Goff, Deputy AD, Development
(847) 467-3575
travis.goff@northwestern.edu
• Mike Polisky, Deputy AD, External Affairs
(847) 491-7880
polisky@northwestern.edu
• Kevin White, Deputy AD/CFO
kevin.white@northwestern.edu

NOTRE DAME ATHLETICS, UNIVERSITY OF
C113 JOYCE CENTER
NOTRE DAME, IN 46556
www.und.com
• Jack Swarbrick, Director of Athletics
(574) 631-6107
• Missy Conboy, Senior Deputy AD, Sports
Operations
(574) 631-1602
• Jim Fraleigh, Deputy AD, Corporate
Relations
(574) 631-8801
• Jody Sadler, Deputy AD, Competitive
Excellence
(574) 631-8801
• Mario Morris, Deputy AD, Business
Operations
(574) 631-8942

OHIO STATE UNIVERSITY ATHLETICS
2400 OLENTANGY RIVER ROAD
COLUMBUS, OH 43210
614-292-7572
www.ohiostatebuckeyes.com
• Gene Smith, Athletics Director
(614) 292-2477
athletic_director@osu.edu
• Dan Cloran, Executive Associate AD,
Development
(614) 292-7744
cloran.10@osu.edu
• Joe Odoguardi, Executive Associate
AD/CFo
(614) 292-5263
odoguardi.1@osu.edu
• Mike Penner, Executive Associate AD,
Internal Operations
(614) 292-1848
penner.2@osu.edu

OHIO UNIVERSITY ATHLETICS
OHIO UNIVERSITY
INTERCOLLEGE ATHLETICS
CONVOCATION CENTER
ATHENS, OH 45701
740-593-1173
www.ohiobobcats.com
• Julie Cromer, Director of Athletics
(740) 593-0983

athleticsdir@ohio.edu
• Amy Dean, Deputy AD/SWA
(740) 593-1171
deana@ohio.edu
• Ken Winstead, Senior Associate AD,
Development
(740) 593-1197
winstead@ohio.edu
• Michael Stephens, Senior Associate AD,
External Operations
(740) 597-1375
stephem1@ohio.edu
• Randee Duffy, Senior Associate AD,
NCAA Eligibility
(740) 593-1172
duffyr1@ohio.edu
• Mary Ann Boyle, Associate AD, Business
Operations/CFO
boylem1@ohio.edu

**OKLAHOMA ATHLETICS, UNIVERSITY
OF**
MCCLENDON CENTER FOR
INTERCOLLEGIATE ATHLETICS
180 W BROOKS
NORMAN, OK 73019
405-325-8200
www.soonersports.com
• Joe Castiglione, Director for Athletics
(405) 325-8208
• Larry Naifeh, Executive Associate AD
(405) 325-8241
lnaifeh@ou.edu
• Kenny Mossman, Sr. Assoc. AD, External
Operations
(405) 325-8228
kmossman@ou.edu
• Zac Selmon, Sr. Assoc. AD, Devel. &
Admin.
(405) 325-3396
zacselmon@ou.edu

**OKLAHOMA STATE UNIVERSITY
ATHLETICS**
ATHLETICS CENTER
OKLAHOMA STATE UNIV.
STILLWATER, OK 74078
405-744-7714
Fax: 405-744-7754
okstate.com
• Mike Holder, Director of Athletics
(405) 744-7263
mike.holder@okstate.edu
• Jason Lewis, Executive Senior Associate
AD
(405) 744-7132
jason.lewis@okstate.edu

OLD DOMINION UNIVERSITY ATHLETICS
INTERCOLLEGIATE ATHLETICS
JIM JARRETT ATHLETIC ADMIN. BLDG.
NORFOLK, VA 23529-0201
757-683-3369
www.odusports.com
• Camden Wood Selig, Athletic Director
(757) 683-3369
wselig@odu.edu
• Kevin Brown, Deputy AD
(757) 683-5224
klbrown@odu.edu

OREGON ATHLETICS, UNIVERSITY OF
2727 LEO HARRIS PARKWAY
EUGENE, OR 97401
541-346-4481
Fax: 541-346-5031
goducks.com

• Rob Mullens, Athletic Director
(541) 346-5455
athleticdirector@uoregon.edu
• Eric Roedl, Deputy Athletic Director
(541) 346-5942
roedl@uoregon.edu
• Lisa Peterson, Deputy Athletic
Director/SWA
(541) 346-5329
lpete@uoregon.edu

**OREGON STATE UNIVERSITY
ATHLETICS**
104 GILL COLISEUM
CORVALLIS, OR 97331
541-737-3969
wecare@oregonstate.edu
osubeavers.com
• Scott Barnes, Director of Intercollegiate
Athletics
(541) 737-3969
k.bjornstad@oregonstate.edu

**PACIFIC ATHLETICS, UNIVERSITY OF
THE**
3601 PACIFIC AVE
STOCKTON, CA 95204
www.pacifictigers.com
• Janet Lucas, Director of Athletics
(209) 946-3208
athleticdirector@pacific.edu
• Tim Dickson, Executive Associate AD,
Development
(209) 946-3177
tdickson@pacific.edu
• Holly Trexler, Senior Associate AD,
Compliance/SWA
(209) 946-2307
htrexler@pacific.edu
• Wes Yourth, Senior Associate AD, Internal
Affairs
(209) 946-7408
wyourth@pacific.edu

PENN STATE UNIVERSITY ATHLETICS
201 OLD MAIN, UNIVERSITY PARK
UNIVERSITY PARK, PA 16802
www.gopsusports.com
• Sandy Barbour, Director of Athletics
(814) 865-1086
athletic_director@athletics.psu.edu
• Lynn Holleran, Deputy AD, Administration
(814) 867-6352
lkh5222@psu.edu
• Scott Sidwell, Deputy AD, External
(814) 867-6115
sas7431@psu.edu
• Joe Foley, Senior Associate AD,
Advancement
(814) 867-1598
foley@psu.edu
• Vacant, Senior Associate AD,
Student-Athlete Perf./SWA
• Carl Heck, Senior Associate AD,
Administration & Events
ckh5446@psu.edu
• Rick Kaluza, Senior Associate AD,
Finance & Business Operations
(814) 865-7780
rck11@psu.edu

**PENNSYLVANIA ATHLETICS,
UNIVERSITY OF**
WEIGHTMAN HALL
235 S 33RD STREET
PHILADELPHIA, PA 19104
www.pennathletics.com

• M. Grace Calhoun, PhD, Director of
Athletics
(215) 898-1096
athdir@upenn.edu
• Joy De JesÂ£S, Senior Associate AD/CFO
(215) 898-4430
joydejesus@upenn.edu
• Tim Folan, Senior Associate AD,
Development
(215) 573-0315
tfolan@upenn.edu
• Rudy Fuller, Senior Associate AD,
Intercollegiate Programs
(215) 746-7125
bfuller@upenn.edu
• Scott Ward, Senior Associate AD/COO
(215) 898-6153
sward2@upenn.edu
• Kevin Bonner, Senior Associate AD,
Administration
(215) 898-9192
bonnerke@upenn.edu

PEPPERDINE UNIVERSITY ATHLETICS
24255 PACIFIC COAST HIGHWAY
MALIBU, CA 90263
310-506-4150
www.pepperdinewaves.com
• Steve Potts, Director of Athletics
(310) 506-4749
steven.potts@pepperdine.edu
• Amanda Kurtz, Senior Associate AD/SWA
(310) 506-6813
amanda.kurtz@pepperdine.edu

**PITTSBURGH ATHLETICS, UNIVERSITY
OF**
PETERSEN EVENTS CENTER
3719 TERRACE STREET
PITTSBURGH, PA 15261
412-648-8230
Fax: 412-648-8306
pittsburghpanthers.com
• Heather Lyke, Director of Athletics
(412) 648-8230
athleticdirector@athletics.pitt.edu
• Christian Spears, Deputy Athletic
Director/COO
(412) 648-8280
cspears@athletics.pitt.edu

PORTLAND ATHLETICS, UNIVERSITY OF
DEPT. OF ATHLETICS
5000 N WILLAMETTE BOULEVARD
PORTLAND, OR 97203-5798
www.portlandpilots.com
• Scott Leykam, Vice President for Athletics
(503) 943-8420
leykam@up.edu
• Karen Peters, Senior Associate AD/SWA
(503) 943-8110
peters@up.edu
• Jason Brough, Senior Associate AD
(503) 943-8439
brough@up.edu
• Karina Handerland, Senior Associate AD
(503) 943-7808
handelan@up.edu

**PORTLAND STATE UNIVERSITY
ATHLETICS**
PETER W. STOTT CENTER
930 SW HALL STREET
PORTLAND, OR 97201
503-725-4000
goviks.com

• Valerie Cleary, Director of Athletics
vcleary@pdx.edu
• Mike Lund, Associate AD, Media &
Communication
(503) 725-5602
lundm@pdx.edu
• Dana Cappelucci, Associate AD,
Compliance/SWA
(503) 725-5621
dlc2@pdx.edu
• Trinity Gibbons, Associate AD, External
Operations
(503) 725-5667
tjg@pdx.edu
• Josh Keller, Associate AD, Development
(503) 725-5607
kellerj@pdx.edu

**PRAIRIE VIEW A&M UNIVERSITY
ATHLETICS**
PVAMU ATHLETICS DEPT.
PO BOX 519 - MAIL STOP 1500
PRAIRIE VIEW, TX 77446
936-261-9100
Fax: 936-261-9159
pvpanthers.com
• Donald Reed, Athletic Director
(936) 261-9100
• Alicia Pete, Assoc. AD, Internal
Operations/SWA
(936) 261-9100
alpete@pvamu.edu
• Brittney Johnson, Associate AD,
Compliance
(936) 261-9108
bnjohnson@pvamu.edu

PRINCETON UNIVERSITY ATHLETICS
PRINCETON UNIVERSITY
JADWIN GYM
PRINCETON, NJ 08544
609-258-3534
goprincetontigers.com
• Mollie Marcoux Samaan, Director of
Athletics
(609) 258-3535
athdirector@princeton.edu
• Anthony Archbald, Executive Assocociate
AD
(609) 258-4948
archbald@princeton.edu
• Chris Brock, Executive Associate AD,
Finance & Admin.
(609) 258-5073
cbrock@princeton.edu

PROVIDENCE COLLEGE ATHLETICS
ONE CUNNINGHAM SQUARE
PROVIDENCE COLLEGE
PROVIDENCE, RI 02918
www.friars.com
• Robert G. Driscoll, Jr., Athletic Director
(401) 865-2265
rdriscol@providence.edu
• Jill LaPoint, Deputy Athletic Director/SWA
(401) 865-2588
jlapoint@providence.edu
• Steve Napolillo, Senior Executive
Associate AD, External Relations
(401) 865-2677
snapolil@providence.edu

PURDUE UNIVERSITY ATHLETICS
MACKEY ARENA, ROOM 2315
900 JOHN R WOODEN DRIVE
WEST LAFAYETTE, IN 47907

Fax: 765-494-1178
www.purduesports.com
• Mike Bobinski, Director of Intercollegiate
Athletics
(765) 494-3189
mbobinski@purdue.edu

QUINNIPIAC UNIVERSITY ATHLETICS
275 MOUNT CARMEL AVENUE
HAMDEN, CT 06518
203-582-8200
quinnipiacbobcats.com
• Greg Amodio, Director of Athletics
(203) 582-8621
greg.amodio@qu.edu
• Sarah Fraser, Deputy Director of Athletics
(203) 582-8090
sarah.fraser@qu.edu
• Bill Mecca, Senior Associate AD
(203) 582-8624
mecca@quinnipiac.edu
• Shanna Kornachuk, Senior Associate AD,
Compliance & Student Dev.
(203) 582-7332
shanna.kornachuk@qu.edu

RADFORD UNIVERSITY ATHLETICS
PO BOX 6913
RADFORD, VA 24142
540-831-5228
Fax: 540-831-6095
www.radfordathletics.com
• Robert Lineburg, Director of Athletics
(540) 831-6194
rlineburg@radford.edu
• Cory Durand, Deputy AD
(540) 831-6423
cdurand@radford.edu

**RHODE ISLAND ATHLETICS,
UNIVERSITY OF**
THREE KEANEY ROAD
SUITE ONE
KINGSTON, RI 02881
Fax: 401-874-4935
www.gorhody.com
• Thorr Bjorn, Director of Athletics
(401) 874-5245
tbjorn@uri.edu

RICE UNIVERSITY ATHLETICS
MS 548
6100 MAIN STREET
HOUSTON, TX 77005
713-348-6957
www.riceowls.com
• Joe Karlgaard, Director of Athletics
(713) 348-4077
athleticdirector@rice.edu
• Rick Mello, Deputy Athletics Director
(713) 348-8872
rmello@rice.edu
• Tanner Gardner, Senior Associate
AD/COO
(713) s48-8258
tgardner@rice.edu
• Stacy Mosely, Senior Associate AD/SWA
(713) 348-5829
mosely@rice.edu
• Mike Melendez, Senior Associate
AD/Chief Development Officer
(713) 348-6970
mike.melendz@rice.edu

RICHMOND ATHLETICS, UNIVERSITY OF
ROBINS CENTER
365 COLLEGE ROAD
RICHMOND, VA 23173
804-289-8363
Fax: 804-287-1919
richmondspiders.com
• John Hardt, Director of Athletics
(804) 289-8694
athleticdirector@richmond.edu
• David Walsh, Deputy Athletic
Director/COO
(804) 289-8009
dwalsh@richmond.edu
• LaRee Sugg, Deputy Athletic
Director/SWA
(804) 289-6371
lsugg@richmond.edu

RIDER UNIVERSITY ATHLETICS
2083 LAWRENCEVILLE ROAD
LAWRENCEVILLE, NJ 08648-3001
www.gobroncs.com
• Don Harnum, Athletic Director
(609) 896-5054
• Karin Torchia, Sr. Associate AD, External
Operations/SWA
(609) 896-5249
ktorchia@rider.edu
• Greg Busch, Senior Associate AD,
Compliance
(609) 895-5642
gbusch@rider.edu

**ROBERT MORRIS UNIVERSITY
ATHLETICS**
DEPT. OF ATHLETICS
6001 UNIVERSITY BLVD
MOON TOWNSHIP, PA 15108-1189
Fax: 412-397-4943
rmucolonials.com
• Chris King, Director of Athletics
(412) 397-4913
kingc@rmu.edu
• Marty Galosi, Senior Associate AD/Chief
of Staff
(412) 397-4920
galosi@rmu.edu
• Chlesea Blakely, Deputy AD/SWA/Chief
Marketing Officer
(412) 397-4964
blakely@rmu.edu
• Kim Graham, Deputy AD/COO
(412) 397-4928
grahamk@rmu.edu

ROLLINS COLLEGE ATHLETICS
1000 HOLT AVENUE
WINTER PARK, FL 32789
407-646-2366
www.rollinssports.com
• Pennie Parker, Director of Athletics
(407) 646-2636
pparker@rollins.edu
• Margie Sullivan, Assistant AD,
Compliance/SWA
(407) 646-2531
msullivan@rollins.edu
• Paul Giannotti, Assistant AD, Sports
Medicine
(407) 646-2361
pgiannotti@rollins.edu

RUTGERS UNIVERSITY ATHLETICS
RUTGERS ATHLETIC CENTER
83 ROCKAFELLER ROAD
PISCATAWAY, NJ 08854

scarletknights.com
• Patrick Hobbs, Director of Intercollegiate Athletics
(732) 445-8610
ad@scarletknights.com
• Sarah Baumgartner, Deputy Director of Athletics
(732) 445-8610
sbaumgartner@scarletknights.com

SACRED HEART UNIVERSITY ATHLETICS
DEPT. OF ATHLETICS
5151 PARK AVENUE
FAIRFIELD, CT 06825
203-371-7917
Fax: 203-365-7696
www.sacredheartpioneers.com
• Bobby Valentine, Executive Director of Athletics
(203) 396-8444
valentiner@sacredheart.edu
• Charlie Dowd, Deputy AD, External Operations
(203) 396-8181
dowdc@sacredheart.edu

SAINT FRANCIS UNIVERSITY ATHLETICS
DEPT. OF ATHLETICS
140 LAKEVIEW DRIVE
LORETTO, PA 15940
Fax: 814-472-3209
sfuathletics.com
• James Downer, Director of Athletics
(814) 472-3280
jdowner@francis.edu
• Erika Renwick, Deputy Director of Athletics/SWA
(814) 472-3286
erenwick@francis.edu
• Jim Brazill, Senior Associate AD
(814) 472-2774
jbrazill@francis.edu

SAINT LOUIS UNIVERSITY ATHLETICS
DEPT. OF ATHLETICS
CHAIFETZ ARENA
3330 LACLEDE AVENUE
ST. LOUIS, MO 63103
314-977-3177
Fax: 314-977-3178
www.slubillikens.com
• Chris May, Director of Athletics
(314) 977-3167
sluadmay@slu.edu
• Janet Oberle, Senior Assocociate AD/SWA
(314) 977-3265
janet.oberle@slu.edu

SAINT PETER'S UNIVERSITY ATHLETICS
2641 JOHN F. KENNEDY BOULEVARD
JERSEY CITY, NJ 07306
Fax: 201-761-7301
saintpeterspeacocks.com
• Rachelle Paul, Director of Athletics
(201) 761-7302
rpaul2@saintpeters.edu
• Debbie Gregory, Senior Associate AD, Business Affairs
(201) 761-7304
dgregory@saintpeters.edu

SAM HOUSTON STATE UNIVERSITY ATHLETICS
SAM HOUSTON ATHLETICS
PO BOX 2268
HUNTSVILLE, TX 77341
www.gobearkats.com
• Bobby Williams, Athletic Director
(936) 294-3286
bwilliams@shsu.edu
• Chris Thompson, Senior Associate AD, Student Services
(936) 294-3542
cthompson@shsu.edu
• Greg Hinze, Senior Associate AD, Operations
(936) 294-1725
ghinze@shsu.edu

SAMFORD UNIVERSITY ATHLETICS
800 LAKESHORE DRIVE
BIRMINGHAM, AL 35229
205-726-2966
samfordsports.com
• Martin Newton, Director of Athletics
(205) 726-2966
cnewton@samford.edu
• Michelle Durban, Deputy AD, Student-Athlete Well-Being/SWA
(205) 726-4562
mldurban@samford.edu
• Bo Kerr, Deputy AD, Development & Corp. Affairs
(205) 726-2139
jkerr@samford.edu

SAN DIEGO ATHLETICS, UNIVERSITY OF
5998 ALCALA PARK
SAN DIEGO, CA 92110
619-260-4803
www.usdtoreros.com
• Bill McGillis, Exec. Director of Athletics
(619) 260-2982
athleticdirector@sandiego.edu
• Marcy Lanoue, Senior Associate AD/SWA
(619) 260-4755
mlanoue@sandiego.edu
• Dan Yourg, Senior Associate AD, Administration
(619) 260-4803
yourg@sandiego.edu

SAN DIEGO STATE UNIVERSITY ATHLETICS
DEPT. OF ATHLETICS
5500 CAMPANILE DRIVE
SAN DIEGO, CA 92182-4313
619-594-3019
www.goaztecs.com
• John David Wicker, Director of Intercollegiate Athletics
(619) 594-6357
adsdsu@sdsu.edu
• Jenny Bramer, Executive Associate AD/SWA
(619) 594-0394
jbramer@sdsu.edu
• Steve Schnall, Executive Associate AD, External Relations
(619) 594-3210
sschnall@sdsu.edu
• Tim Rice, Executive Associate AD, Development
(619) 594-7924
tjrice@sdsu.edu

SAN FRANCISCO ATHLETICS, UNIVERSITY OF
2130 FULTON STREET
SAN FRANCISCO, CA 94117
415-422-2873
www.usfdons.com
• Joan McDermott, Director of Athletics
jmcdermott2@usfca.edu
• Frank Allocco, Executive Sr. Associate AD, External Relations
(415) 422-6561
fallocco@usfca.edu
• Linda Lappe, Senior Associate AD/SWA
llappe@usfca.edu

SAN JOSE STATE UNIVERSITY ATHLETICS
ONE WASHINGTON SQUARE
SAN JOSE, CA 95192-0062
408-924-1200
www.sjsuspartans.com
• Marie Tuite, Athletics Director
(408) 924-1200
marie.tuite@sjsu.edu
• Bob Clark, Deputy AD, Development
(408) 924-1175
rob.clark@sjsu.edu

SANTA CLARA UNIVERSITY ATHLETICS
500 EL CAMINO REAL
SANTA CLARA, CA 95053
408-554-4063
Fax: 408-554-6969
www.santaclarabroncos.com
• Renee Baumgartner, Director of Athletics
(408) 554-5344
rbaumgartner@scu.edu
• Staci Gustafson, Deputy AD
(408) 554-6982
sgustafson@scu.edu
• Bob De Carolis, Deputy AD
(408) 551-1782
rdecarolis@scu.edu
• Peter Fields, Senior Associate AD, Development
(408) 551-7040
pfields@scu.edu

SETON HALL UNIVERSITY ATHLETICS
400 SOUTH ORANGE AVENUE
RICHIE REGAN REC. & ATHLS. CENTER
SOUTH ORANGE, NJ 07079
shupirates.com
• Bryan Felt, Director of Athletics
(973) 761-9498
mary.walch@shu.edu
• Tatum Colitz, Senior Associate AD, Compliance/SWA
(973) 761-9494
tatum.colitz@shu.edu
• Jay Judge, Sr. Assoc. AD, Development & External Operations
(973) 275-2202
jay.judge@shu.edu
• Kathy Matta, Senior Associate AD, Recreational Services
(973) 761-9723
kathleen.matta@shu.edu
• Jimmy O'Donnell, Senior Associate AD, Team Operations
(973) 761-9725
jimmy.odonnell@shu.edu
• Jim Semerad, Senior Associate AD, Internal Operations
(973) 761-9724
james.semerad@shu.edu
• Kevin Sponzo, Senior Associate AD,

Facilities & Operations
(973) 761-2949
kevin.sponzo@shu.edu

SIENA COLLEGE ATHLETICS
515 LOUDON ROAD
LOUDONVILLE, NY 12211-1462
518-783-2551
Fax: 518-783-2449
www.sienasaints.com
• John D'Argenio, Director of Athletics
(518) 783-2450
dargenio@siena.edu
• Andrew Santandera, Associate AD,
Operations
(518) 782-6454
asantandera@siena.edu
• Dennis Bates, Assoc. AD, Finance
(518) 782-6454
dbates@siena.edu

SILVER LAKE COLLEGE ATHLETICS
2406 SOUTH ALVERNO
MANITOWOC, WI 54220
EXT 175
800-236-4752
www.slclakers.com
• Brandt Danals, Athletics Director
(920) 686-6135
brandt.danals@holyfamilycollege.edu

**SOUTH ALABAMA ATHLETICS,
UNIVERSITY OF**
6001 USA DRIVE S
SUITE 35
MOBILE, AL 36688
Fax: 251-460-6505
www.usajaguars.com
• Joel Erdmann, PhD, Director of Athletics
(251) 460-7121
jerdmann@southalabama.edu
• Daniel McCarthy, Ed D, Deputy AD
(251) 460-6057
dmccarthy@southalabama.edu
• Jinni Frisbey, Senior Associate AD/SWA
(251) 445-9551
jfrisbey@southalabama.edu
• Travis Toth, Senior Associate AD, External
Affairs
(251) 414-8274
toth@southalabama.edu

**SOUTH CAROLINA ATHLETICS,
UNIVERSITY OF**
RICE ATHLETICS CENTER
1304 HEYWARD STREET
COLUMBIA, SC 29208
803-777-4202
Fax: 803-777-8226
www.gamecocksonline.com
• Ray Tanner, Athletics Director
addirect@mailbox.sc.edu
• Chance Miller, Senior Deputy AD
ccmiller@mailbox.sc.edu
• Judy Van Horn, Deputy AD
vanhorn@mailbox.sc.edu

**SOUTH CAROLINA STATE UNIVERSITY
ATHLETICS**
300 COLLEGE STREET NE
ORANGEBURG, SC 29117
803-533-3743
Fax: 803-533-3634
www.scsuathletics.com
• Stacy Danley, Director of Athletics
(803) 533-3743

sdanley@scsu.edu
• Monique Carroll, Deputy AD, Internal
Ops./SWA
(803) 536-7200
mcarroll@scsu.edu
• Kemberly Greene, Assistant AD,
Community Relations
(803) 516-4562
kgreen29@scsu.edu

**SOUTH DAKOTA SCHOOL OF MINES &
TECHNOLOGY ATHLETICS**
501 EAST SAINT JOSEPH STREET
RAPID CITY, SD 57701
gorockers.com
• Joel Lueken, Athletic Director
(605) 394-2352
joel.lueken@sdsmt.edu
• Cassie Kosiba, Associate AD, Internal
Ops./SWA
(605) 394-2643
cassie.kosiba@sdsmt.edu
• Kevin Price, Sr. Assoc. AD
(605) 394-2601
kevin.price@sdsmt.edu

**SOUTH FLORIDA ATHLETICS,
UNIVERSITY OF**
USF ATHLETICS DEPT.
4202 E FOWLER AVENUE, ATH 100
TAMPA, FL 33620
813-974-2125
gousfbulls.com
• Michael Kelly, Vice President of Athletics
(813) 974-1442
• Barry Clements, Deputy AD/CFO
(813) 974-0469
clements@usf.edu
• Lelo Prado, Deputy AD, Development &
Sports Admin.
(813) 974-5045
leloprado@usf.edu

**SOUTHEAST MISSOURI STATE
UNIVERSITY ATHLETICS**
ONE UNIVERSITY PLAZA
MS0200
CAPE GIRARDEAU, MO 63701
gosoutheast.com
• Brady Barke, Director of Athletics
(573) 651-2227
bbarke@semo.edu
• Shannon Yates, Associate AD/SWA
(573) 651-2997
syates@semo.edu
• Nate Saverino, Associate AD, External
Affairs
(573) 651-2962
nsaverino@semo.edu
• Robert Greim, Associate AD, Compliance
& Student Service
(573) 986-6844
rgreim@semo.edu

**SOUTHEASTERN LOUISIANA
UNIVERSITY ATHLETICS**
DUGAS CENTER FOR SOUTHEASTERN
ATHLETICS
800 GALLOWAY DRIVE
HAMMOND, LA 70402
985-549-2253
Fax: 985-549-3495
www.lionsports.net
• Jay Artigues, Director of Athletics
(985) 549-2395
jartigues@southeastern.edu
• Andrew Bechac, Senior Associate AD,

Internal Ops.
(985) 549-3419
andrew.bechac@southeastern.edu
• Ola Adegboye, Executive Associate AD,
Business
(985) 549-5100
ola.adegboye@southeastern.edu

**SOUTHERN CALIFORNIA ATHLETICS,
UNIVERSITY OF**
LOS ANGELES, CA
213-740-3843
usctrojans.com
• Lynn Swann, Director of Athletics
• Ron Orr, Senior Associate AD
(213) 740-4161
rorr@usc.edu
• Donna C. Heinel, Sr. Assoc. AD/SWA
(213) 740-1636
dheinel@usc.edu

**SOUTHERN ILLINOIS UNIVERSITY
ATHLETICS**
SIU ATHLETICS
MAILCODE 6620, LINGLE HALL 118
1490 DOUGLAS DRIVE
CARBONDALE, IL 62901
618-453-5311
siusalukis.com
• Liz Jarnigan, Director of Athletics
(618) 453-5279
elizabeth.jarnigan@siu.edu
• Jeff Jones, Executive Senior Associate
AD, Internal Ops.
(618) 453-5481
jeffrey.jones@siu.edu
• Jimmy Karayiannis, Senior Associate AD,
External Operations
(618) 453-7250
james.karayiannis@siu.edu

**SOUTHERN METHODIST UNIVERSITY
ATHLETICS**
PO BOX 750315
5800 OWNBY DRIVE
DALLAS, TX 75275
214-768-4301
smumustangs.com
• Rick Hart, Director of Athletics
(214) 768-4301
rlhart@smu.edu
• Kurt Pottkotter, Deputy Director of Athletics
(214) 768-3639
kpottkotter@smu.edu
• Lauren Adee, Senior Associate AD,
Executive Affairs
(214) 768-1650
ladee@smu.edu
• Kyle Conder, Senior Associate AD,
Compliance
(214) 768-4051
kconder@smu.edu
• Brad Sutton, Senior Associate AD,
External Affairs
(214) 768-1651
bsutton@smu.edu
• Matt Peters, Senior Associate AD,
Development
(214) 768-7009
mjpeters@smu.edu

SOUTHERN MISS ATHLETICS
118 COLLEGE DRIVE
#5017
HATTIESBURG, MS 39406-0001

601-266-5017
Fax: 601-266-6595
www.southernmiss.com
• Jeremy McClain, Director of Athletics
athleticdirector@usm.edu
• Jeff Mitchell, Deputy AD
jeff.mitchell@usm.edu
• E.K. Franks, Executive Senior Associate AD
ek.franks@usm.edu

SOUTHERN NEW HAMPSHIRE UNIVERSITY
2500 N RIVER ROAD
MANCHESTER, NH 03106
603-645-9604
Fax: 603-645-9686
www.snhupenmen.com
• Anthony Fallacaro, Director of Athletics
(603) 645-9604
a.fallacaro@snhu.edu
• Tom Wilkins, Associate AD
(603) 645-9786
t.wilkins@snhu.edu
• Tricia Cote, Associate AD, Business Manager/SWA
(603) 645-9699
p.cote1@snhu.edu
• James Gassman, Associate AD, Operations
(603) 645-9788
j.gassman@snhu.edu
Year Founded:
1992
Description:
Offers B.S. Sport Managment, B.S. Business Studies with concentration in Sport Managment, M.B.A. with certificate in Sport Administration, M.S. Sport Managment.

SOUTHERN UNIVERSITY ATHLETICS
SU ATHLETICS DEPT.
A.W. MUMFORD FIELDHOUSE
1 SWAN ST
BATON ROUGE, LA 70813
225-771-3171
www.gojagsports.com
• Roman Banks, Director Of Athletics
(225) 771-5609
Roman_banks@subr.edu
• Trayvean Scott, Deputy AD
(225) 771-5930
trayvean_scott@subr.edu
• Rodney Kirschner, Senior Associate AD
(225) 771-5609
rodney_kirschner@subr.edu

SOUTHERN UTAH UNIVERSITY ATHLETICS
351 W UNIVERSITY BOULEVARD
CEDAR CITY, UT 84720
435-865-8355
Fax: 435-586-8078
www.suutbirds.com
• Debbie Corum, Athletic Director
• Todd Brown, Deputy Director of Athletics
brownt@suu.edu
• Dan Moye, Executive Senior Associate AD, Internal Ops.
(435) 865-8355
danmoye@suu.edu
• Shon Spevak, Executive Senior Associate AD
(435) 586-7872
spevak@suu.edu

ST. BONAVENTURE UNIVERSITY ATHLETICS
DEPT. OF ATHLETICS
3261 W STATE ROAD
ST. BONAVENTURE, NY 14778
716-375-2282
Fax: 716-375-2280
gobonnies.sbu.edu
• Tim Kenney, Director of Athletics
(716) 375-2282
• Barb Questa, Deputy Director of Athletics
(716) 375-2290
bquesta@sbu.edu

ST. JOHN'S UNIVERSITY ATHLETICS
DEPT. OF ATHLETICS
8000 UTOPIA PARKWAY
QUEENS, NY 11439
718-990-6138
www.redstormsports.com
• Mike Cragg, Director of Athletics
(718) 990-6138
craggm@stjohns.edu
• Kathleen Meehan, Senior Deputy AD/SWA
(718) 990-6173
meehank@stjohns.edu
• John Diffley, Deputy AD/COO
(718) 990-6836
diffleyj@stjohns.edu

ST. JOSEPH'S UNIVERSITY ATHLETICS
ATHLETIC DEPT.
5600 CITY AVENUE
PHILADELPHIA, PA 19131
610-660-1707
www.sjuhawks.com
• Jill Bodensteiner, Athletic Director
(610) 660-1707
athleticdirector@sju.edu
• Renie Shields, Senior Associate AD, Student Experience/SWA
(610) 660-2584
shields@sju.edu
• Katie Shields, Senior Associate AD, Development
(610) 660-1231
kshields@sju.edu
• Rob Sullivan, Senior Associate AD, External Affairs
(610) 660-1768
robert.sullivan@sju.edu
• Eric Laudano, Senior Associate AD, High Performance
(610) 660-1753
elaudano@sju.edu

ST. MARY'S COLLEGE ATHLETICS
DEPT. OF ATHLETICS
PMB 5100
MORAGA, CA 94575
www.smcgaels.com
• Mike Matoso, Director of Athletics
(925) 631-4399
snittler@stmarys-ca.edu
• Kami Gray, Deputy AD, Internal Operations/SWA
(925) 631-4521
kgray@stmarys-ca.edu
• Ryan Reggiani, Deputy AD, External Operations
(925) 631-4402
rmr9@stmarys-ca.edu

STANFORD UNIVERSITY ATHLETICS
ARRILLAGA FAMILY SPORTS CENTER
641 EAST CAMPUS DRIVE
STANFORD, CA 94305-6201

650-723-4591
Fax: 650-725-8642
gostanford.com
• Bernard Muir, Director of Athletics
(650) 723-4596
athleticdirector@stanford.edu
• Patrick Dunkley, Deputy AD
(650) 725-7655
pdunkley@stanford.edu
• Ray Purpur, Deputy AD
(650) 723-1820
ray.purpur@stanford.edu

STEPHEN F. AUSTIN STATE UNIVERSITY ATHLETICS
SFA ATHLETICS
PO BOX 13010
SFA STATION
NACOGDOCHES, TX 75962
936-468-3501
sfajacks.com
• Ryan Ivey, Director of Athletics
(936) 468-4540
iveyrm@sfasu.edu
• Rob Meyers, Associate AD, Business
(936) 468-4080
rmeyers@sfasu.edu
• Brandi Bryant, Associate AD, Student-Athlete Services
(936) 468-5800
brandi.bryant@sfasu.edu
• Loree McCary, Associate AD, Administration/SWA
(936) 468-3751
lmccary@sfasu.edu

STETSON UNIVERSITY ATHLETICS
421 N WOODLAND BOULEVARD
UNIT 8359
DELAND, FL 32723
Fax: 386-822-7486
www.gohatters.com
• Jeff Altier, Director of Athletics
(386) 822-7157
ad@stetson.edu
• Alicia Queally, Deputy AD/SWA
(386) 738-6676
aqueally@stetson.edu

SUNY BUFFALO
102 ALUMNI ARENA
BUFFALO, NY 14260
716-645-3142
Fax: 716-645-3756
www.ubbulls.com
• Mark Alnutt, Athletic Director
(716) 645-3142
athleticdirector@buffalo.edu
• Eric Gross, Deputy AD, External Operations
(716) 645-6761
etgross@buffalo.edu
• Nate Wills, Deputy AD/COO
(716) 645-5548
ntwills@buffalo.edu
• Donald Reed, Ph.D., Senior Associate AD, Performance
(716) 645-3338
drreed@buffalo.edu
• D'Ann Keller, Senior Associate AD, Administration/SWA
(716) 645-6866
dannkell@buffalo.edu

college sports

345

SYRACUSE UNIVERSITY ATHLETICS
MANLEY FIELD HOUSE
1301 E COLVIN STREET
SYRACUSE, NY 13244
315-443-2385
cuse.com
• John Wildhack, Director of Athletics
(315) 443-8705
jwildhac@syr.edu
• Herman Frazier, Senior Deputy AD
(315) 443-8705
hrfrazie@syr.edu

TEMPLE UNIVERSITY ATHLETICS
TEMPLE ATHLETICS
STAR COMPLEX
1816 N 15TH STREET, 3RD FLOOR
PHILADELPHIA, PA 19121
215-204-7759
athletics@temple.edu
owlsports.com
• Patrick Kraft, Director of Athletics
(215) 204-7759
athletics@temple.edu
• Craig Angelos, Deputy Director of Athletics
(215) 204-8555
cangelos@temple.edu
• Jessica Reo, Executive Senior Associate
AD/SWA
(215) 204-7871
jessica.reo@temple.edu

**TENNESSEE CHATTANOOGA
ATHLETICS, UNIVERSITY OF**
615 MCCALLIE AVENUE
DEPT. 3503
CHATTANOOGA, TN 37403
gomocs.com
• Mark Wharton, Director of Athletics
• Scott Altizer, Deputy Athletics Director
(423) 425-5739
scott-altizer@utc.edu
• Laura Herron, Executive Associate
AD/SWA
(423) 425-4583
laura-herron@utc.edu

**TENNESSEE KNOXVILLE ATHLETICS,
UNIVERSITY OF**
PO BOX 15016
KNOXVILLE, TN 37901-5016
865-974-1224
utsports.com
• Phillip Fulmer, Director of Athletics
athleticdirector@utk.edu
• Reid Sigmon, Deputy AD/COO
(865) 974-1224
rsigmon@utk.edu

**TENNESSEE MARTIN ATHLETICS,
UNIVERSITY OF**
UT MARTIN
1022 ELAM CENTER
15 MT PELIA ROAD
MARTIN, TN 38238
731-881-7661
www.utmsports.com
• Kurt McGuffin, Athletic Director
(731) 881-7661
kmcguffi@utm.edu
• Danelle Fabianich, Senior Associate AD,
Aministration/SWA
(731) 881-3688
danellef@utm.edu

**TENNESSEE STATE UNIVERSITY
ATHLETICS**
CAMPUS BOX 9633
3500 JOHN A. MERRITT BOULEVARD
NASHVILLE, TN 37209
615-963-5000
Fax: 615-963-7589
www.tsutigers.com
• Teresa Phillips, Director of Athletics
(615) 963-5034
tphillips@tnstate.edu
• Valencia Jordan, Associate AD/SWA
(615) 963-5754
vjordan@tnstate.edu
• Jennifer Bell, Associate AD, Compliance
(615) 963-5887
jbell@tnstate.edu

**TENNESSEE TECH UNIVERSITY
ATHLETICS**
1100 MCGEE BOULEVARD
TTU BOX 5057
COOKEVILLE, TN 38505
931-372-3940
800-825-3948
www.ttusports.com
• Mark Wilson, Director of Athletics
(931) 372-6306
mwilson@tntech.edu
• Frank Harrell, Associate AD, Sports &
Compliance
(931) 372-3939
fharrell@tntech.edu
• Tammie McMillan, Associate AD/SWA
(931) 372-3944
tmcmillan@tntech.edu
• Lesley Loftis, Associate AD, Development
(931) 372-3997
lloftis@tntech.edu

TEXAS A&M UNIVERSITY ATHLETICS
TEXAS A&M ATHLETICS
1228 TAMU
COLLEGE STATION, TX 77843-1228
979-845-5129
12thman.com
• Ross Bjork, Director of Athletics
• Michael Thompson, Jr., Deputy Director of
Athletics

**TEXAS AT ARLINGTON ATHLETICS,
UNIVERSITY OF**
1309 W MITCHELL STREET
ARLINGTON, TX 76019-0079
817-272-2261
Fax: 817-272-5037
www.utamavs.com
• Jim Baker, Director of Athletics
(817) 272-7170
jimbaker@uta.edu
• Russell Warren, Deputy Director of
Athletics
(817) 272-5706
rwarren@uta.edu
• Debbie Garcia, Executive Senior
Associate AD/SWA
(817) 272-2047
ranee@uta.edu

**TEXAS AT AUSTIN ATHLETICS,
UNIVERSITY OF**
403 DELOSS DODDS WAY
AUSTIN, TX 78712
512-471-5757
texassports.com
• Chris Del Conte, Athletic Director
(512) 471-5757

• Shawn Eichorst, Deputy A/COO
(512) 232-2144
• Chris Plonsky, Executive Senior Associate
AD
(512) 471-4787
• Arthur Johnson, Executive Senior
Associate AD
(512) 232-4248
• Amy Folan, Executive Senior Associate
AD
(512) 471-1257
• Drew Martin, Executive Senior Associate
AD, External Affairs
(512) 471-8689

**TEXAS AT EL PASO ATHLETICS,
UNIVERSITY OF**
500 W UNIVERSITY AVE
BRUMBELOW BUILDING
EL PASO, TX 79968-0579
915-747-5347
utepathletics.com
• Jim Senter, Director of Athletics
(915) 747-6822
jsenter@utep.edu
• Jeff Darby, Senior Associate AD,
Communications
(915) 747-6652
jdarby@utep.edu
• Julie Levesque, Senior Associate AD/SWA
(915) 747-6806
jmlevesque@utep.edu
• Nick Popplewell, Senior Associate AD,
Development
(915) 747-6141
nlpopplewell@utep.edu

**TEXAS AT SAN ANTONIO ATHLETICS,
UNIVERSITY OF**
UTSA DEPT. OF INTERCOLLEGIATE
ATHLETICS
ONE UTSA CIRCLE
SAN ANTONIO, TX 78249-0691
210-458-8149
Fax: 210-458-4813
www.goutsa.com
• Lisa Campos, Athletics Director
(210) 458-4444
roadrunnerad@utsa.edu
• Katie Douglass, Executive Senior
Associate AD
(210) 458-4168
katie.douglass@utsa.edu
• Mike Bazemore, Executive Senior
Associate AD
(210) 458-4666
miachael.bazemore@utsa.edu

**TEXAS CHRISTIAN UNIVERSITY
ATHLETICS**
TCU ATHLETICS DEPT.
TCU BOX 297600
FORT WORTH, TX 76129
817-257-5658
Fax: 817-257-7656
www.gofrogs.com
• Jeremiah Donati, JD, Director of
Intercollegiate Athletics
athleticsdirector@tcu.edu
• Mike Sinquefield, Deputy AD
m.sinquefield@tcu.edu

**TEXAS RIO GRANDE VALLEY
ATHLETICS, UNIVERSITY OF**
UTRGV DEPT. OF INTERCOLLEGIATE
ATHLETICS

1201 W UNIVERSITY DRIVE
EDINBURG, TX 78539
956-665-2221
Fax: 956-665-2261
goutrgv.com
• Chasse Conque, Director of Athletics
(956) 665-2221
chasse.conque@utrgv.edu
• Vince Volpe, Deputy Director of Athletics
(956) 665-3897
vince.volpe@utrgv.edu
• Molly Castner, Deputy Director of
Athletics/SWA
(956) 665-2205
molly.castner@utrgv.edu

TEXAS SOUTHERN UNIVERSITY ATHLETICS
3100 CLEBURNE STREET
HOUSTON, TX 77004
713-313-6830
www.tsusports.com
• Kevin Granger, Vice President of
Intercollegiate Athletics
(713) 313-4378
kevin.granger@tsu.edu
• Michael Moleta, Senior Associate AD
(713) 313-7629
michael.moleta@tsu.edu

TEXAS STATE UNIVERSITY ATHLETICS
TSU DEPT. OF ATHLETICS
DARREN B. CASEY ATHLETIC ADMIN.
COMPLEX
601 UNIVERSITY DRIVE
SAN MARCOS, TX 78666
Fax: 512-245-8387
athletics@txstate.edu
txstatebobcats.com
• Larry Teis, Director of Athletics
(512) 245-2963
lt10@txstate.edu
• Don Coryell, Executive Senior Associate
AD, External Ops.
(512) 245-2220
dc32@txstate.edu
• Tracy Shoemake, Executive Senior Assoc.
AD, Internal Ops./SWA
(512) 245-2114
ts23@txstate.edu
• Travis Comer, Executive Senior Associate
AD, Development
(512) 245-2247
tc26@txstate.edu
• Lacy Needham, Assoc. AD, Business Ops.
(512) 245-2203
ln19@txstate.edu

TEXAS TECH UNIVERSITY ATHLETICS
JONES AT&T STADIUM
2526 6TH STREET
LUBBOCK, TX 79409
806-742-3355
texastech.com
• Kirby Hocutt, Director of Athletics
• Tony Hernandez, Deputy Director of
Athletics
(806) 834-6167
tony.hernandez@ttu.edu
• Judi Henry, Executive Senior Associate
AD/SWA
(806) 834-0976
judi.henry@ttu.edu

TOLEDO ATHLETICS, UNIVERSITY OF
ATHLETIC DEPT. - MS302
SAVAGE ARENA

2801 W BANCROFT STREET
TOLEDO, OH 43606
Fax: 419-530-4428
utrockets.com
• Mike O'Brien, Director of Athletics
(419) 530-4987
michael.obrien6@utoledo.edu
• Dave Nottke, Deputy Director of Athletics
(419) 530-2510
david.nottke@utoledo.edu
• Kelly Adnrews, Senior Associate AD/SWA
(419) 530-2810
kelly.andrews@utoledo.edu

TOWSON STATE UNIVERSITY ATHLETICS
DEPT. OF ATHLETICS
8000 YORK RD
TOWSON, MD 21252-0001
410-704-2759
towsontigers.com
• Tim Leonard, Director of Athletics
(410) 704-2759
tleonard@towson.edu
• Tricia Turley Brandenburg, Deputy Director
of Athletics/SWA
(410) 704-4177
tbrandenburg@towson.edu
• Will Huff, Deputy Director of Athletics,
Operations
(410) 704-5564
whuff@towson.edu

TROY UNIVERSITY ATHLETICS
TINE DAVIS FIELDHOUSE
5000 VETERANS STADIUM DRIVE
TROY, AL 36082
334-670-3482
Fax: 334-670-3278
www.troytrojans.com
• Brent Jones, Director of Athletics
(334) 670-3682
brentjones@troy.edu
• Sandy Atkins, Deputy AD,
Administration/SWA
(334) 670-5745
satkins@troy.edu
• Kyle George, Executive Associate AD,
External Ops.
(334) 670-5650
kylegeorge@troy.edu

TULANE UNIVERSITY ATHLETICS
JAMES W. WILSON JR.
INTERCOLLEGIATE ATHLETICS CENTER
333 BEN WEINER DRIVE
NEW ORLEANS, LA 70118
504-865-5017
Fax: 504-862-8569
tulanegreenwave.com
• Troy Dannen, Director of Athletics
(504) 865-5569
tdannen@tulane.edu
• Monica Lebron, Deputy AD/COO
(504) 865-5512
monical@tulane.edu
• Chris Maitre, Executive Associate AD,
Business
(504) 314-2261
cmaitre@tulane.edu

TULSA ATHLETICS, UNIVERSITY OF
800 S TUCKER DRIVE
TULSA, OK 74104
918-631-3112
tulsahurricane.com

• Derrick Gragg, Director of Athletics
(918) 631-3112
derrick-gragg@utulsa.edu
• Brian Scislo, Senior Associate AD,
Administration
(918) 631-2703
brain-scislo@utulsa.edu

U.S. AIR FORCE ACADEMY ATHLETICS
ATHLETIC DEPT.
2169 FIELD HOUSE DRIVE
Colorado Springs, CO 80840-9500
719-333-4008
www.goairforcefalcons.com
• Nathan Pine, Director of Athletics
(719) 333-4008
ad@usafa.edu
• Jen Block, Executive AD
(719) 333-4008
ad@usafa.edu
• Nancy Hixon, Deputy AD, External Affairs
(719) 333-3501
nancy.hixon@airforceathletics.org

U.S. MILITARY ACADEMY ATHLETICS
ARMY WEST POINT ATHLETICS
639 HOWARD ROAD
WEST POINT, NY 10996
845-938-3701
goarmywestpoint.com
• Mike Buddie, Director of Athletics
(845) 938-3701
• Dan McCarthy, Deputy AD
(845) 938-9699
dan.mccarthy@westpoint.edu

U.S. NAVAL ACADEMY ATHLETICS
RICKETTS HALL
566 BROWNSON ROAD
ANNAPOLIS, MD 21402
Fax: 410-293-8954
www.navysports.com
• Chet Gladchuk, Director of Athletics
(410) 293-8910
gladchuk@usna.edu
• Eric Ruden, Deputy Director of Athletics
(410) 293-8748
ruden@usna.edu
• Robb Dunn, Deputy Director of Athletics,
Administration
(410) 293-8776
rdunn@usna.edu

UC BERKELEY ATHLETICS
HAAS PAVILION #4422
BERKELEY, CA 94720-4422
510-642-0580
Fax: 510-642-3399
calbears.com
• Jim Knowlton, Director of Athletics
• Jennifer Simon-O'Neill, Executive Senior
Associate AD/SWA
jenny.simon@berkeley.edu
• Joe Mulford, Senior Associate AD
joemulford@berkeley.edu
• Brian Mann, Senior Associate AD
bmann@berkeley.edu
• Ryan Cobb, Senior Assoc. AD,
Performance, Health & Welfare
ryancobb@berkeley.edu
• Jay Larson, Senior Associate AD,
Administration
jlarson@berkeley.edu
• Josh Hummel, Senior Associate AD,
Facilities
johummel@berkeley.edu

• Tom Lowry, Senior Associate AD/CFO
thomaslowry@berkeley.edu

UC IRVINE ATHLETICS
INTERCOLLEGIATE ATHLETICS
BUILDING
IRVINE, CA 92697-4500
949-824-6931
athleticsdirector@uci.edu
ucirvinesports.com
• Paula Smith, Director of Intercollegiate
Athletics
(949) 824-6932
paula.smith@uci.edu
• Phil Wang, Senior Associate AD, External
Affairs
(949) 824-7591
philw@uci.edu
• Paul Hope, Senior Associate AD, Facilites
(949) 824-5941
phope@uci.edu
• Darrin Nelson, Senior Associate AD,
Sports
(949) 824-8286
nelsondm@uci.edu
• John Hauscarriague, Senior Associate AD,
Finance
(949) 824-6979
jhauscar@uci.edu

UC LOS ANGELES ATHLETICS
J.D. MORGAN CENTER
325 WESTWOOD PLAZA
LOS ANGELES, CA 90095
310-825-8699
Fax: 310-206-7047
uclabruins.com
• Dan Guerrero, Director of Athletics
ad@athletics.ucla.edu
• Matt Elliott, Senior Associate AD, Internal
Operations
melliott@athletics.ucla.edu
• Christopher Iacoi, Senior Associate AD,
CFO
ciacoi@athletics.ucla.edu
• Josh Rebholz, Senior Associate AD,
External Relations
jrebholz@athletics.ucla.edu
• Christina Rivera, Senior Associate
AD/SWA
crivera@athletics.ucla.edu
• Shana Wilson, Senior Associate AD,
Communications
swilson@athletics.ucla.edu

UC SANTA BARBARA ATHLETICS
INTERCOLLEGIATE ATHLETICS
DEPARTMENT
ICA BUILDING
SANTA BARBARA, CA 93106-5200
805-893-8272
Fax: 802-893-8640
www.ucsbgauchos.com
• John McCutcheon, Director of
Intercollegiate Athletics
(805) 893-8320
jmccutch@athletics.ucsb.edu
• Kelly Barsky, Deputy Athletics
Director/SWA
(805) 893-2247
kelly.barsky@athletics.ucsb.edu
• Tom Hastings, Deputy Athletics Director
(805) 893-6019
tom.hastings@athletics.ucsb.edu

UMASS AMHERST ATHLETICS
200 COMMONWEALTH AVENUE
3RD FLOOR
AMHERST, MA 01003
413-545-9652
www.umassathletics.com
• Ryan Bamford, Director of Athletics
(413) 545-9652
kdisanto@umass.edu
• Kirsten Britton, Senior Associate AD,
Administration/SWA
(413) 545-1086
britton@umass.edu
• David Biancamano, Senior Associate AD,
Development
(413) 545-4290
dbiancamano@umass.edu
• Jeff Smith, Senior Associate AD, Internal
Operations
(413) 545-2866
jbsmith@umass.edu

UTAH ATHLETICS, UNIVERSITY OF
ATHLETICS DEPT.
1825 E SOUTH CAMPUS DRIVE
SALT LAKE CITY, UT 84112-0900
801-581-8171
utahutes.com
• Mark Harlan, Athletics Director
athleticsdirector@utah.edu
• Kyle Brennan, Deputy AD, Internal
Operations
(801) 587-7629
kbrennan@huntsman.utah.edu
• Scott Kull, Deputy AD, External Operations
(801) 201-5724
skull@huntsman.utah.edu

UTAH STATE UNIVERSITY ATHLETICS
7400 OLD MAIN HILL
LOGAN, UT 84322
435-797-1850
www.utahstateaggies.com
• John Hartwell, Athletics Director
(435) 797-2060
john.hartwell@usu.edu
• Jerry Bovee, Deputy AD, External Affairs
(435) 797-1880
jerry.bovee@usu.edu
• Amy Crosbie, Executive Associate AD,
Internal Affairs/SWA
(435) 797-0612
amy.crosbie@usu.edu

VALPARAISO UNIVERSITY ATHLETICS
ATHLETICS RECREATION CENTER
1009 UNION STREET
VALPARAISO, IN 46383
www.valpoathletics.com
• Mark LaBarbera, Director of Athletics
(219) 464-6894
valpoad@valpo.edu

VANDERBILT UNIVERSITY ATHLETICS
2601 JESS NEELY DRIVE
NASHVILLE, TN 37212
615-322-4653
Fax: 615-343-7064
www.vucommodores.com
• Candice Storey Lee, Interim Athletics
Director
• Lori Alexander, Senior Associate AD,
Internal Operations
(615) 322-4118
lori.alexander@vanderbilt.edu
• Martin Salamone, Senior Associate AD,
Sales & Marketing

(615) 343-2580
martin.salamone@vanderbilt.edu

VERMONT ATHLETICS, UNIVERSITY OF
PATRICK GYMNASIUM
97 SPEAR STREET
BURLINGTON, VT 05405
802-656-3074
www.uvmathletics.com
• Jeff Schulman, Director of Athletics
(802) 656-7417
jeffrey.schulman@uvm.edu

VILLANOVA UNIVERSITY ATHLETICS
800 EAST LANCASTER AVENUE
JAKE NEVIN FIELD HOUSE
VILLANOVA, PA 19085
610-519-4090
www.villanova.com
• Mark Jackson, Director of Athletics
(610) 519-4110
athleticsdirector@villanova.edu
• Lynn Tighe, Senior Associate AD/SWA
(610) 519-4121
lynn.tighe@villanova.edu
• Ashwin Puri, Senior Associate AD/COO
(610) 519-6721
ashwin.puri@villanova.edu
• Rob Hagan, Senior Associate AD,
Student-Athlete Welfare
(610) 519-6485
robert.hagan@villanova.edu
• Dean Kenefick, Senior Associate AD,
Communications
(610) 519-6514
dean.kenefick@villanova.edu

VIRGINIA ATHLETICS, UNIVERSITY OF
MCCUE CENTER
PO BOX 400846
CHARLOTTESVILLE, VA 22904
434-982-5100
Fax: 434-982-5012
www.virginiasports.com
• Carla Williams, Director of Athletics
(434) 982-5100
cgw4j@virginia.edu
• Jim Booz, Deputy AD
(434) 982-5100
jwb8q@virginia.edu
• Ted White, Deputy AD
(434) 982-3474
tedwhite@virginia.edu

VIRGINIA COMMONWEALTH
UNIVERSITY ATHLETICS
VCU ATHLETICS
SIEGEL CENTER, 1200 W BROAD ST
PO BOX 843013
RICHMOND, VA 23284-3013
Fax: 804-828-9428
www.vcuathletics.com
• Ed McLaughlin, Director of Athletics
(804) 828-6692
athleticsdir@vcu.edu
• Mak Afework, Deputy Director of Athletics
(804) 827-0805
mafework@vcu.edu

VIRGINIA MILITARY INSTITUTE
ATHLETICS
LEXINGTON, VA 24450
www.vmikeydets.com
• Dave Diles, Athletic Director
(540) 464-7251
dilesdl@vmi.edu

• Wade Branner, Associate AD, Communications
(540) 464-7515
brannerwh@vmi.edu
• Lance Fujiwara, Associate AD, Sports Medicine
(540) 464-7310
fujiwaralm@vmi.edu
• Daniel Whitehead, Associate AD, Communications
(540) 464-7514
whiteheaddk@vmi.edu

VIRGINIA TECH ATHLETICS
25 BEAMER WAY
BLACKSBURG, VA 24061
540-231-9984
Fax: 540-231-3060
www.hokiesports.com
• Whit Babcock, Director of Athletics
(540) 231-3977
hokiead@vt.edu
• John Ballein, Executive Associate AD
(540) 231-3357
jballein@vt.edu
• Omar Banks, Exec. Assoc. AD
(540) 231-6553
omar17@vt.edu

WAGNER COLLEGE ATHLETICS
ONE CAMPUS ROAD
STATEN ISLAND, NY 10301-4495
718-390-3433
Fax: 718-390-3347
www.wagnerathletics.com
• Walt Hameline, Director of Athletics
(718) 390-3488
whamelin@wagner.edu
• Brendan Fahey, Deputy AD
(718) 390-3210
brendan.fahey@wagner.edu

WAKE FOREST UNIVERSITY ATHLETICS
519 DEACON BOULEVARD
WINSTON-SALEM, NC 27109
336-758-5616
www.wakeforestsports.com
• John Currie, Director of Athletics
(336) 758-3140
wfuad@wfu.edu
• Barbara Walker, Deputy AD/SWA
(336) 758-5753
walkerbg@wfu.edu

WASHINGTON ATHLETICS, UNIVERSITY OF
DEPT. OF INTERCOLLEGIATE ATHLETICS
BOX 354070
GRAVES BUILDING
SEATTLE, WA 98195
206-543-2210
gohuskies.com
• Jennifer Cohen, Director of Athletics
• Shondell Reed, Senior Associate AD
sdreed3@uw.edu
• Erin O'Connell, Senior Associate AD
oconnell@uw.edu
• Kim Durand, Senior Associate AD, Student Development
(206) 221-3551
durand@uw.edu
• Carter Henderson, Senior Associate AD, External Relations
(206) 685-8879
chender2@uw.edu

WASHINGTON STATE UNIVERSITY ATHLETICS
WSU ATHLETICS
BOHLER ATHLETIC COMPLEX
COUGAR WAY
PULLMAN, WA 99164-1602
509-335-0320
Fax: 509-335-0328
wsucougars.com
• Patrick Chun, Director of Athletics
(509) 335-0200
athleticdirector@wsu.edu
• Anne McCoy, Deputy AD/SWA
(509) 335-7149
amccoy@wsu.edu

WEBER STATE UNIVERSITY ATHLETICS
3870 STADIUM WAY
DEPT. 2701
OGDEN, UT 84408
801-626-6817
weberstatesports.com
• Tim Crompton, Director of Athletics
(801) 626-7738
tcrompton@weber.edu
• Will Pridemore, Associate AD, Student Athlete Services
(801) 626-8552
williampridemore@weber.edu
• Jerry Graybeal, Assoc. AD, Development
(801) 626-8114
jgraybeal@weber.edu
• Ron Goch, Assoc. AD, External Ops.
(801) 626-6731
rongoch@weber.edu
• Jerry Graybeal, Associate AD, Development
(801) 626-8114
jgraybeal@weber.edu
• Ron Goch, Associate AD, Internal Operations
(801) 626-6731
rongoch@weber.edu
• Derek Dawes, Associate AD, External Operations
(801) 626-6564
derekdawes@weber.edu

WEST VIRGINIA UNIVERSITY ATHLETICS
PO BOX 0877
MORGANTOWN, WV 26507-0877
304-293-9873
Fax: 304-293-4904
wvusports.com
• Shane Lyons, Director of Athletics
(304) 293-5621
• Keli Zinn, Deputy Athletic Director
(304) 293-6758
keli.zinn@mail.wvu.edu
• Steve Uryasz, Executive Senior Associate AD
(304) 293-5682
steven.uryasz@mail.wvu.edu

WESTERN CAROLINA UNIVERSITY ATHLETICS
92 CATAMOUNT ROAD
RAMSEY CENTER
CULLOWHEE, NC 28723
828-227-7338
Fax: 828-227-7688
www.catamountsports.com
• Randy Eaton, Director of Athletics
(828) 227-7338
jreaton@email.wcu.edu
• Stacey Miller, Associate AD, Student Success/SWA

(828) 227-2541
srmiller@email.wcu.edu
• Larry Arbaugh, Associate AD, Administration
(828) 227-2015
lgarbaugh@email.wcu.edu
• Rick Fulton, Associate AD, Business
(828) 227-2105
rwfulton@email.wcu.edu
• Chad Gerrety, Associate AD, External Affairs
(828) 227-2767
cgerrety@email.wcu.edu

WESTERN ILLINOIS UNIVERSITY ATHLETICS
1 UNIVERSITY CIRCLE
MACOMB, IL 61455
www.goleathernecks.com
• Danielle Surprenant, Director of Athletics
(309) 298-1190
DE-Surprenant@wiu.edu
• Danielle Surprenant, Sr. Assoc. AD, Internal Ops./SWA
(309) 298-1190
de-surprenant@wiu.edu

WESTERN KENTUCKY UNIVERSITY ATHLETICS
E.A. DIDDLE ARENA
1605 AVENUE OF CHAMPIONS
BOWLING GREEN, KY 42101-6412
270-745-3542
wkusports.com
• Todd Stewart, Director of Athletics
(270) 745-5276

WESTERN MICHIGAN UNIVERSITY ATHLETICS
WMU BRONCO ATHLETICS
READ FIELDHOUSE
1903 W MICHIGAN AVENUE
KALAMAZOO, MI 49008
269-387-3120
Fax: 269-387-3668
wmubroncos.com
• Kathy Beauregard, Director of Athletics
(269) 387-3061
kathy.beauregard@wmich.edu
• Jeff Stone, Senior Associate AD, Compliance
(269) 387-3082
jeffrey.stone@wmich.edu
• Keanah Smith, Senior Associate AD/SWA
(269) 387-3090
keanah.smith@wmich.edu

WICHITA STATE UNIVERSITY ATHLETICS
WSU DEPT. OF INTERCOLLEGIATE ATHLETICS
1845 FAIRMOUNT STREET
WICHITA, KS 67260-0018
316-978-3251
goshockers.com
• Darron Boatright, Director of Athletics
(316) 978-5498
dboatright@goshockers.com
• Becky Endicott, Senior Associate AD/SWA
(316) 978-3250
rendicott@goshockers.com
• Rege Klitzke, Senior Associate AD, Business Ops.
(316) 978-3251
rklitzke@goshockers.com
• Brad Pittman, Senior Associate AD, Facilities

(316) 978-5556
bpittman@goshockers.com

WILLIAM & MARY ATHLETICS, COLLEGE OF
PO BOX 399
WILLIAMSBURG, VA 23187
757-221-3400
Fax: 757-221-2048
www.tribeathletics.com
• Samantha K. Huge, Athletics Director
(757) 221-3332
athleticdir@wm.edu
• Chelsey Burk, Deputy AD
(757) 221-3373
cpburk@wm.edu
• Tiffany Christian, Senior Associate AD,
Student Services/SWA
(757) 221-7601
ttchristian@wm.edu
• Kevin Dwan, Senior Associate AD,
External Operations
(757) 221-7557
kdwan@wm.edu
• Anthony D. Henderson, Sr., Senior
Associate AD
(757) 221-2059
adhenderson@wm.edu
• Erik Korem, PhD, Senior Associate AD,
Student-Athlete Performance
(757) 221-3078
ekorem@wm.edu

WILLIAM JEWELL COLLEGE ATHLETICS
500 COLLEGE HILL STREET
LIBERTY, MO 64068
816-781-7700
www.jewellcardinals.com
• Tom Eisenhauer, Director of Athletics
(816) 415-5292
eisenhauer@william.jewell.edu

WINTHROP UNIVERSITY ATHLETICS
WINTHROP COLISEUM
1162 EDEN TERRACE
ROCK HILL, SC 29733
803-323-2129
Fax: 803-323-2433
winthropeagles.com
• Ken Halpin, PhD, Director of Athletics
(803) 323-2129
ad@winthrop.edu
• Hank Harrawood, Deputy AD
(803) 323-2129
harrawoodh@winthrop.edu
• Kelley Kish, Senior Associate AD,
Business/SWA
(803) 323-2129
kishk@winthrop.edu

WISCONSIN ATHLETICS, UNIVERSITY OF
INTERCOLLEGIATE ATHLETICS
KELLNER HALL
1440 MONROE STREET
MADISON, WI 53711
608-262-1866
Fax: 608-265-8051
contactus@uwbadgers.com
uwbadgers.com
• Barry Alvarez, Director of Athletics
bla@athletics.wisc.edu
• Christopher McIntosh, Deputy Athletic
Director
(608) 265-0769
cpm@athletics.wisc.edu

WISCONSIN GREEN BAY ATHLETICS, UNIVERSITY OF
2420 NICOLET DRIVE
GREEN BAY, WI 54311-7001
920-465-2145
Fax: 920-465-2652
www.greenbayphoenix.com
• Charles Guthrie, Director of Athletics
(920) 465-2145
• Kassie Batchelor, Senior Associate AD,
Compliance/SWA
(920) 465-2837
batchelk@uwgb.edu
• Molly Vandervest, Senior Associate AD,
Development
vandermo@uwgb.edu

WISCONSIN MILWAUKEE ATHLETICS, UNIVERSITY OF
MILWAUKEE ATHLETICS
PO BOX 413
THE PAVILION - ROOM 150
MILWAUKEE, WI 53201
414-229-5151
Fax: 414-229-5749
mkepanthers.com
• Amanda Braun, Director of Athletics
(414) 229-5151
uwm-ad@uwm.edu
• Cathy Rossi, Deputy Athletics Director
(414) 229-2655
rossic@uwm.edu
• Kathy Litzau, Senior Associate AD/SWA
(414) 750-4510
kclitzau@uwm.edu
• Adam Schemm, Senior Associate AD,
External Relations
(414) 229-1105
schemm@uwm.edu

WRIGHT STATE UNIVERSITY ATHLETICS
ERVIN J. NUTTER CENTER
3640 COLONEL GLENN HIGHWAY
DAYTON, OH 45435
937-775-2771
Fax: 937-775-2368
www.wsuraiders.com
• Bob Grant, Director of Athletics
(937) 775-2771
bob.grant@wright.edu
• Joylynn Brown, Senior Associate AD/SWA
(937) 775-2721
joylynn.brown@wright.edu
Description:
NCAA, Division I Department, Horizon
League, 16 sports.

WYOMING ATHLETICS, UNIVERSITY OF
DEPT. OF INTERCOLLEGIATE
ATHLETICS
DEPT. 3414
1000 E UNIVERSITY AVENUE
LARAMIE, WY 82071
307-766-2929
gowyo.com
• Tom Burman, Director of Athletics
(307) 766-2292
uwad@uwyo.edu
• Matt Whisenant, Deputy Director of
Athletics
(307) 766-5551
mwhise@uwyo.edu

XAVIER UNIVERSITY ATHLETICS
ATHLETICS DEPT.
3800 VICTORY PARKWAY
CINCINNATI, OH 45207-7530

goxavier.com
• Greg Christopher, Director of Athletics
(513) 745-3417
athleticdirector@xavier.edu
• Susan Cross Lipnickey, Associate AD,
Student-Athlete Services/SWA
(513) 745-2855
lipnickeys@xavier.edu
• Brian Hicks, Associate AD, External
Relations
(513) 745-3604
hicksb@xavier.edu
• Tom Eiser, Associate AD,
Communications
(513) 745-3124
eiser@xavier.edu
• Mario Mercurio, Associate AD
(513) 745-3417
mercuriom@xavier.edu

YALE UNIVERSITY ATHLETICS
PO BOX 208216
NEW HAVEN, CT 06520-8216
203-432-4747
Fax: 203-432-7772
www.yalebulldogs.com
• Victoria Chun, Director of Athletics
(203) 432-1414
• Wayne Dean, Deputy AD
(203) 432-1462
wayne.dean@yale.edu
• Mary Berdo, Deputy AD
mary.berdo@yale.edu
• Ann-Marie Guglieri, Deputy AD
(203) 432-1414
ann-marie.guglieri@yale.edu

YOUNGSTOWN STATE UNIVERSITY ATHLETICS
ATHLETIC DEPT.
ONE UNIVERSITY PLAZA
YOUNGSTOWN, OH 44555
330-941-1910
Fax: 330-941-2733
ysusports.com
• Ron Strollo, Exec. Director of
Intercollegiate Athletics
(330) 941-1910
• Elaine Jacobs, Associate AD/SWA
(330) 941-2282
eajacobs@ysu.edu
• Rick Love, Associate AD
(330) 941-7227
rwlove@ysu.edu
• Emily Wollet, Associate AD
(330) 941-7208
eewollet@ysu.edu

NCAA Division II Colleges

ABILENE CHRISTIAN UNIVERSITY ATHLETICS
ACU BOX 27916
ABILENE, TX 79699-7916
325-674-2287
800-766-0228
Fax: 325-674-6798
athleticdirector@acu.edu
www.acusports.com
• Lee De Leon, Director of Athletics
(325) 674-2353
athleticdirector@acu.edu
• Dave Kinard, Senior Associate Director of
Athletics
(325) 674-6483
dlk15a@acu.edu

ADAMS STATE UNIVERSITY ATHLETICS
208 EDGEMONT BOULEVARD
ALAMOSA, CO 81101
719-587-7401
Fax: 719-587-7276
www.asugrizzlies.com
• Larry Mortensen, Athletic Director
(719) 587-7402
lsmorten@adams.edu
• Dianne Lee, Associate Athletic Director
(719) 587-7401
diannelee@adams.edu
• Michael Skinner, Sports Information
Director
(719) 587-7825
mdskinner@adams.edu
• Josh Dreher, Head Athletic Trainer
(719) 587-8233
joshdreher@adams.edu

ADELPHI UNIVERSITY ATHLETICS
1 SOUTH AVENUE
GARDEN CITY, NY 11530
516-877-4179
Fax: 516-877-4237
www.aupanthers.com
• Danny McCabe, Director of Athletics
(516) 877-4231
dmccabe@adelphi.edu
• Kate Whalen, Senior Associate Athletic
Director
(516) 877-4235
kwhalen@adelphi.edu
• Emily Dorko, Associate Athletic Director
(516) 877-4293
edorko@adelphi.edu

ALABAMA A&M ATHLETICS
4900 MERIDIAN STREET
NORMAL, AL 35762
256-372-8057
Fax: 256-372-5372
www.aamusports.com
• Bryan Hicks, Director of Athletics
(256) 372-4001
bryan.hicks@aamu.edu
• Cara Wright, Assoc. Director Of
Athletics/SWA
(256) 372-4759
cara.wright@aamu.edu
• Bud McLaughlin, Director of Sports
Information
(256) 372-4005
aamusportsinfo@yahoo.com

**UNVIERSITY OF ALASKA ANCHORAGE
ATHLETICS**
3550 PROVIDENCE DRIVE
ANCHORAGE, AK 99508
907-786-1250
Fax: 907-786-1142
athletics@uaa.alaska.edu
www.goseawolves.com
• Keith Hackett, Director of Athletics
(907) 786-7800
khackett2@uaa.alaska.edu
• Tim McDiffett, Senior Associate Director of
Athletics
(907) 786-1307
tim@uaa.alaska.edu

ALBANY STATE COLLEGE ATHLETICS
504 COLLEGE DRIVE
ALBANY, GA 31705
229-430-4754
Fax: 229-430-1774
www.asugoldenrams.com

• Arthur N. Dunning, University President
(229) 430-4605
art.dunning@asurams.edu
• Richard H. Williams, Director of Athletics
(229) 430-4763
richard.williams@asurams.edu
• Stephanie Harrison-Dyer, Assistant
Athletic Director
(229) 460-1394
stephanie.harrison@asurams.edu
• Stan McCormick, Sports Information
Director
(229) 420-7013
stanley.mccormick@asurams.edu

**ALDERSON-BROADDUS UNIVERSITY
ATHLETICS**
101 COLLEGE HILL DRIVE
PHILIPPI, WV 26416
304-457-6262
Fax: 304-457-6291
www.gobattlers.com
• Dennis Creeham, Athletic Director
(304) 457-6404
creehandw@ab.edu
• Carrie Bodkins, Senior Associate Athletic
Director
(304) 457-6347
bodkinscl@ab.edu
• Luke Harrigan, Assistant Athletic Director
(304) 457-6265
harriganlw@ab.edu
• Craig Butler, Sports Information Director
(304) 457-6445
butlercj@ab.edu

**AMERICAN INTERNATIONAL COLLEGE
ATHLETICS**
1000 STATE STREET
BOX 4B
SPRINGFIELD, MA 01109
413-205-3916
800 242-3142
Fax: 413-205-3916
richard.bedard@aic.edu
www.aicyellowjackets.com
• Matt Johnson, Director of Athletics
(413) 205-3539
matthew.johnson@aic.edu
• Benjamin Rosenfeld, Associate Athletic
Director
(413) 654-1738
benjamin.rosenfeld@aic.edu
• Art Wilkins, Assistant Athletic Director
(413) 205-3545
art.wilkins@aic.edu
• John Culp, Head Athletic Trainer
(413) 205-3541
john.culp@aic.edu

ANDERSON UNIVERSITY ATHLETICS
316 BOULEVARD
ANDERSON, SC 29621
864-231-2029
Fax: 864-231-5601
autrojans.com
• Bill D'Andrea, Athletic Director
(864) 231-2023
bdandrea@andersonuniversity.edu
• Jennifer Bell, Associate Athletic Director
(864) 231-5679
jbell@andersonuniversity.edu
• Randy Jones, Sports Information Director
(864) 231-2097
rjones@andersonuniversity.edu
• Ed Duvall, Head Athletic Trainer

(864) 231-2144
wduvall@andersonuniversity.edu

**ANGELO STATE UNIVERSITY
ATHLETICS**
2601 WEST AVENUE NORTH
SAN ANGELO, TX 76909
324-942-2091
800-946-8627
Fax: 325-942-2277
www.angelosports.com
• James Reid, Interim Director of Athletics
(325) 942-2267
james.reid@angelo.edu
• Christina Whetsel, Assistant Athletics
Director
(325) 486-6072
christina.whetsel@angelo.edu
• Steve Mahaffey, Associate Athletics
Director
(325) 486-6584
steven.mahaffey@angelo.edu
• Joe'l Sefcik, Director of Athletic Academic
Services
(325) 486-6048

**ARKANSAS TECH UNIVERSITY
ATHLETICS**
TUCKER COLISEUM
1604 COLISEUM DRIVE
RUSSELLVILLE, AR 72801
479-968-0245
Fax: 479-964-0829
arkansastechsports.com
• Steve Mullins, Director of Athletics
(479) 968-0345
smullins@atu.edu
• Paul Smith, Director of Athletic
Communications
(479) 968-0645
psmith6@atu.edu
• Brett Waldon, Head Athletic Trainer
(479) 968-0642
bwaldon@atu.edu

**ARKANSAS-MONTICELLO ATHLETICS,
UNIVERSITY OF**
663 UNIVERSITY DRIVE
MONTICELLO, AR 71656
870-460-1058
Fax: 870-460-1458
www.uamsports.com
• Chris Ratcliff, Director of Athletics
(870) 460-1058
ratcliff@uamont.edu
• Matt Whiting, Associate Athletic Director
(870) 460-1758
whitingpm@uamont.edu
• Seth Dutton, Assistant Athletic Director
(870) 460-1756
dutton@uamont.edu
• Mike Newell, Men's Basketball Head
Coach
(870) 460-1258
• Bob Boldon, Women's Basketball Head
Coach
(870) 460-1357
• Kevin Downing, Baseball Head Coach
(870) 460-1257

**ARMSTRONG ATLANTIC STATE
UNIVERSITY ATHLETICS**
11935 ABERCORN STREET
SAVANNAH, GA 31419-1997
912-344-2813
800-633-2349

Fax: 912-344-3422
armstrongpirates.com
• Lisa Sweany, Director of Athletics
(912) 344-2813
lisa.sweany@armstrong.edu
• Jennifer Rushton, Associate Director of
Athletics
(912) 344-3368
jennifer.rushton@armstrong.edu
• Chad Juckson, Director of Sports
Communications
(912) 344-3114
chad.jackson@armstrong.edu
• Ken Tessier, Head Athletic Trainer
(912) 344-2866
ken.tessier@armstrong.edu

ASHLAND UNIVERSITY ATHLETICS
ATHLETIC DEPARTMENT
KATES GYMNASIUM
401 COLLEGE AVENUE
ASHLAND, OH 44805
419-289-4142
800-882-1548
Fax: 419-289-5468
goashlandeagles.com
• Al King, Director of Athletics
(419) 289-5959
aking@ashland.edu
• Adam Bracken, Assistant Athletic Director
(419) 289-5297
abracken@ashland.edu
• Dusty Sloan, Sports Information Director
(419) 289-5954
dsloan2@ashland.edu
• Jeremy Hancock, Head Athletic Trainer
(419) 207-6195
jhancock@ashland.edu

ASSUMPTION COLLEGE ATHLETICS
500 SALISBURY STREET
WORCESTER, MA 01609
508-767-7279
Fax: 508-798-2568
www.assumptiongreyhounds.com
• Nick Smith, Director of Athletics
(508) 767-7297
na.smith@assumption.edu
• Peter Gardula, Senior Associate Director
of Athletics
(508) 767-7427
pgardula@assumption.edu
• Christine Lowthert, Associate Director of
Athletics
(508) 767-7086
c.lowthert@assumption.edu
• Jim Mullen, Assistant Director of Athletics
(508) 767-7288
jmullen@assumption.edu

**AUGUSTA STATE UNIVERSITY
ATHLETICS**
3109 WRIGHTSBORO ROAD
AUGUSTA, GA 30909
706-737-1626
Fax: 706-729-2445
www.jaguarsroar.com
• Clint Bryant, Director of Athletics
(706) 737-1626
cbryant1@gru.edu
• John Sullivan, Assistant Athletic Director
(706) 731-7908
jsullivan1@gru.edu
• Taylor Lamb, Director of Athletic Media
Relations
(706) 731-7925
talamb@gru.edu

• Dip Metress, Men's Basketball Head
Coach
(706) 731-4765
• Josh Gregory, Mens's Golf Head Coach
(706) 731-7992

BAPTIST BIBLE COLLEGE
628 EAST KEARNEY STREET
SPRINGFIELD, MO 65803
417-268-6000
Fax: 800-819-8330
gobbc.edu
• Daniel Blakeslee, President

BARCLAY COLLEGE ATHLETICS
607 NORTH KINGMAN
HAVILAND, KS 67059
620-862-5252
800-862-0226
Fax: 620-862-5403
www.barclaycollege.edu
• Royce Bryan, Athletic Director
royce.bryan@barclaycollege.edu
• Ray Anderson, Assistant Athletic Director
ray.anderson@barclaycollege.edu

BARRY UNIVERSITY ATHLETICS
11300 NE SECOND AVENUE
MIAMI SHORES, FL 33161-6695
305-899-3000
800-756-6000 ext. 3550
dkluka@barry.edu
gobarrybucs.com
• Michael L. Covone, Director of Athletics
mcovone@barry.edu
• Jamie Carrig, Associate Director of
Athletics
jcarrig@barry.edu
• Cesar Odio, Assistant Director of Athletics
codio@barry.edu

BARTON COLLEGE ATHLETICS
PO BOX 5000
WILSON, NC 27893
252-399-6317
800-345-4973
Fax: 252-399-6572
www.barton.edu
• Todd Wilkinson, Director of Athletics
(259) 399-6552
twilkinson@barton.edu
• Matt Atkins, Assistant Athletic Director
(252) 399-6609
mgakins@barton.edu
• Benny Benton, Sports Information Director
(252) 399-6515
bbenton@barton.edu
• Ricardo Oliveira, Athletic Operations
Coordinator
(252) 399-6610
roliveira@barton.edu
• Nathan Pickel, Head Athletic Trainer
(252) 399-6568
nspickel@barton.edu
• Tim Dornemann, Director of Sports
Performance
(252) 399-6534
tdornemann@barton.edu

BELLARMINE UNIVERSITY ATHLETICS
2001 NEWBURG ROAD
LOUISVILLE, KY 40205
502-272-8380
800-274-4723
athletics.bellarmine.edu

• Scott Wiegandt, Director of Athletics
swiegandt@bellarmine.edu
• Pam Stackhouse, Associate Director of
Athletics
pstackhouse@bellarmine.edu
• John Spugnardi, Sports Information
Director
jspugnardi@bellarmine.edu
• Melanie Brunsdon, Assistant Director of
Athletics
mbrunsdon@bellarmine.edu

BEMIDJI STATE UNIVERSITY ATHLETICS
1500 BIRCHMONT DRIVE NE
BEMIDJI, MN 56601-2699
218-755-2001
800 475-2001
Fax: 218-755-4048
www.bsubeavers.com
• Tracy Dill, Director of Athletics
(218) 755-4022
tdill@bemidjistate.edu
• Sarah Levesque, Associate Athletic
Director
(218) 755-2142
slevesque@bemidjistate.edu
• Wayne Chadwick, Assistant Athletic
Director
(218) 755-3784
wchadwick@bemidjistate.edu
• Debbie Slough, Athletics Secretary
(218) 755-2941
dslough@bemidjistate.edu
• Bill Crews, Head Athletic Trainer
(218) 755-2769
wcrews@bemidjistate.edu

BENEDICT COLLEGE ATHLETICS
1600 HARDEN STREET
COLUMBIA, SC 29204
803-705-4910
Fax: 803-705-4840
washingtonw@benedict.edu
www.benedicttigers.com
• Willie Washington, Athletic Director
(803) 705-4734
washingtonw@benedict.edu
• Fred Watson, Associate Athletic Director
(803) 705-4735
watsonf@benedict.edu
• Margaret Jones, Athletics Compliance
Coordinator
(803) 705-4437
jonesm@benedict.edu
• Loraine Dunbar, Athletics Operations
Coordinator
(803) 705-4426
dunbarl@benedict.edu

BENTLEY UNIVERSITY ATHLETICS
175 FOREST STREET
WALTHAM, MA 02452-4705
781-891-2000
Fax: 781-891-2648
www.bentleyfalcons.com
• Bob DeFelice, Director of Athletics
(781) 891-2256
rdefelice@bentley.edu
• Kevin Loftus, Associate Athletics Director
(781) 891-2196
kloftus@bentley.edu
• Cindy Scott, Assistant Athletic Director
(781) 891-2218
cscott@bentley.edu
• Courtney Finn, Athletic Operations
Assistant

(781) 891-2368
cfinn1@bentley.edu

BLOOMFIELD COLLEGE ATHLETICS
467 FRANKLIN STREET
BLOOMFIELD, NJ 7003
973-748-9000 EXT 363
Fax: 973-259-1085
www.bcbearsathletics.com
• Sheila Wooten, Athletic Director
(973) 748-9000
sheila_wooten@bloomfield.edu
• Gerald Holmes, Assistant Director of
Athletics
(973) 748-9000
• Gladstone Harris, Sports Information
Director
(973) 748-9000
gladstone_harris@bloomfield.edu
• Lauren Mastrobuoni, Head Athletic Trainer
(973) 748-9000
lauren_mastrobuoni@bloomfield.edu
• Jackie Cividanes, Associate Athletic
Trainer
(973) 748-9000
jacqueline_cividanes@bloomfield.edu

BLOOMSBURG UNIVERSITY ATHLETICS
400 EAST SECOND STREET
BLOOMSBURG, PA 17815-1301
570-389-4000
Fax: 570-389-4724
www.buhuskies.com
• Michael McFarland, Director of Athletics
(570) 389-4050
mcfarland@bloomu.edu
• Kathy Heitzman, Associate Director of
Athletics
(570) 389-4555
kheitzma@bloomu.edu
• James Updike, Director of Athletic
Operations
(570) 389-4371
jupdike@bloomu.edu
• David Leisering, Interim Director of Sports
Information
(570) 389-4413
dleisering@bloomu.edu
• Allen Larsen, Head Athletic Trainer
(570) 389-4369
alarsen@bloomu.edu

BLUEFIELD COLLEGE ATHLETICS
3000 COLLEGE DRIVE
BLUEFIELD, VA 24605
276-326-4253
800-872-0175
Fax: 276-326-4386
mwhite@bluefield.edu
www.bcrams.com
• Mike White, Interim Athletic Director
(276) 326-4316
mwhite@bluefield.edu
• Tom Price, Assistant Athletic Director
(276) 326-4254
tprice1@bluefield.edu
• Chase Neidig, Director of Athletic
Broadcasting
cneidig@bluefield.edu
• Bob Redd, Sports Information Director
(276) 326-4342
rredd@bluefield.edu

BOWIE STATE UNIVERSITY ATHLETICS
14000 JERICHO PARK ROAD
BOWIE, MD 20715-9465

301-860-3570
Fax: 301-860-3585
bsubulldogs.com
• Clyde Doughty, Jr., Athletic Director
(301) 860-3559
cdoughty@bowiestate.edu
• Arlene Creek, Associate Athletic Director
(301) 860-3588
acreek@bowiestate.edu
• Gregory Goings, Sports Information
Director
(301) 860-3574
ggoings@bowiestate.edu
• Teresa Gruchacz, Head Athletic Trainer
(301) 860-3581
tgruchacz@bowiestate.edu

BRIGHAM YOUNG UNIVERSITY-HAWAII ATHLETICS
55-220 KULANUI STREET
LAIE, HI 96762
808-675-3211
Fax: 808-675-3763
byuhawaiisports.com
• Brad Jones, Athletic Director
(808) 675-3760
bjones@byuh.edu
• Dawn Akana, Assistant Athletic Director
(808) 675-3318
kuriharC@byuh.edu
• Spencer Shamo, Sports Information
Director
(808) 675-3397
spencer.shamo@byuh.edu

CALDWELL UNIVERSITY ATHLETICS
120 BLOOMFIELD AVENUE
CALDWELL, NJ 07006
973-618-3260
Fax: 973-618-3370
admissions@caldwell.edu
www.caldwellathletics.com
• Mark A. Corino, Director of Athletics
(973) 618-3260
mcorino@caldwell.edu
• Dean Johnson, Associate Director of
Athletics
(973) 618-3321
djohnson@caldwell.edu
• Megan Bratkovich, Assistant Director of
Athletics
(973) 618-3591
mbratkovich@caldwell.edu
• John Tagliaferri, Director of Athletic Media
Relations
(973) 618-3567
jtagliaferri@caldwell.edu
• Mike Molinaro, Athletic Trainer
(973) 618-3574
mmolinaro@caldwell.edu

CALIFORNIA POLY STATE UNIVERSITY ATHLETICS
MOTT ATHLETICS CENTER
1 GRAND AVENUE
SAN LUIS OBISPO, CA 93407-0388
805-756-2924
Fax: 805-756-2699
www.gopoly.com
• Don Oberhelman, Director of Athletics
(805) 756-2924
obe@calpoly.edu
• Nick Pettit, Deputy Director of Athletics
(805) 756-2882
ndpettit@calpoly.edu
• Chris Baker, Associate Athletic Director
(805) 756-7188

baker@calpoly.edu
• Ashley Offerman, Associate Athletic
Director, Development
(805) 756-0280
aofferma@calpoly.edu

CALIFORNIA STATE POLY UNIVERSITY ATHLETICS
KELLOGG GYM, BUILDING 43 ROOM 116
3801 WEST TEMPLE AVENUE
POMONA, CA 91768
909-869-2810
Fax: 909-869-2814
www.broncoathletics.com
• Brian Swanson, Director of Intercollegiate
Athletics
(909) 869-2810
bswanson@cpp.edu
• Stephanie Duke, Associate Athletic
Director
(909) 869-3778
sduke@cpp.edu
• Ruem Malasarn, Assistant Athletics
Director
(909) 869-2834
rmalasarn@cpp.edu

CALIFORNIA STATE UNIVERSITY-CHICO ATHLETICS
DEPARTMENT OF INTERCOLLEGIATE
ATHLETICS
ACKER GYM 131
CHICO, CA 95929-0300
530-898-6470
Fax: 530-898-6582
abarker@csuchico.edu
www.chicowildcats.com
• Anita Barker, Athletic Director
(530) 898-6470
abarker@csuchico.edu
• Scott Barker, Head Athletic Trainer
(530) 898-5873
sbarker@csuchico.edu
• Mitch Cox, Associate Director of Athletics
(530) 898-6470
mscox@csuchico.edu

CALIFORNIA STATE UNIVERSITY-DOMINGUEZ HILLS ATHLETICS
DEPARTMENT OF ATHLETICS
1000 EAST VICTORIA STREET
CARSON, CA 90747
310-243-3893
Fax: 310-217-6975
www.gotoros.com
• Jeff Falkner, Athletics Director
(310) 243-3893
jfalkner@csudh.edu
• Jamie Purnell, Associate Director of
Athletics/SWA
(310) 243-2224
jbouyer@csudh.edu
• Mel Miranda, Assistant Athletics Director
(310) 243-3135
mmiranda@csudh.edu
• Ashley Musick, Head Athletic Trainer
(310) 243-2492
amusick@csudh.edu

CALIFORNIA STATE UNIVERSITY-EAST BAY ATHLETICS
25800 CARLOS BEE BOULEVARD
HAYWARD, CA 94542
510-885-3038
Fax: 510-885-2282
www.eastbaypioneers.com

college sports

• Jason Carmichael, Director of Athletics
(510) 885-3039
jason.carmichael@csueastbay.edu
• Darrell Bailey, Jr., Assistant Athletics
Director
(510) 885-3585
• Steve Connolly, Director of Athletic
Communications
(510) 885-4509
steve.connolly@csueastbay.edu
• Patrick Lazaro, Interim Head Athletic
Trainer
(510) 885-3055
patrick.lazaro@csueastbay.edu

CALIFORNIA STATE UNIVERSITY-LOS ANGELES ATHLETICS
5151 STATE UNIVERSITY DRIVE
LOS ANGELES, CA 90032
323-343-3080
Fax: 323-343-6535
calstatelaathletics.com
• Daryl Gross, Executive Director of
Intercollegiate Athletics
(323) 343-3080
daryl.gross@calstatela.edu
• Daniel Garrett, Assistant Director of
Intercollegiate Athletics
(323) 343-5466
dgarret4@calstatela.edu
• Lori Rudd, Athletic Head Trainer
(323) 343-3097
lrudd@calstatela.edu

CALIFORNIA STATE UNIVERSITY-SAN BERNARDINO ATHLETICS
5500 UNIVERSITY PARKWAY
SAN BERNARDINO, CA 92407-2318
909-537-5011
Fax: 909-537-5984
csusbathletics.com
• Morgan Walker, Interim Director Of
Athletics
(909) 537-5011
mwalker@csusb.edu

CALIFORNIA STATE UNIVERSITY-STANISLAUS ATHLETICS
ONE UNIVERSITY CIRCLE
TURLOCK, CA 95382
209-667-3016
Fax: 209-667-3084
mmatoso@csustan.edu
www.warriorathletics.com
• Michael Matoso, Director of Athletics
(209) 667-3016
mmatoso@csustan.edu
• Kim Duyst, Associate Athletics Director
(209) 667-3312
kduyst@csustan.edu
• Hung P. Tsai, Assistant Athletics Director
(209) 667-3168
htsai@csustan.edu
• Dake Walden, Head Athletic Trainer
(209) 664-6838
dwalden@csustan.edu

CALIFORNIA UNIVERSITY OF PENNSYLVANIA ATHLETICS
250 UNIVERSITY AVE
BOX 34
CALIFORNIA, PA 15419
724-938-4000
Fax: 724-938-5849
www.calvulcans.com
• Karen Hjerpe, Athletic Director
(724) 938-4167

hjerpe@calu.edu
• Ron McGrew, Director of Athletic Facilities
(724) 938-4524
sealy_r@calu.edu
• Jenni Morrison, Assistant to the Athletic
Director
(724) 938-5790
morrison@calu.edu
• Jamie Weary, Head Athletic Trainer
(724) 938-4562
weary@calu.edu

CAMERON UNIVERSITY ATHLETICS
2800 WEST GORE BOULEVARD
LAWTON, OK 73505
580-581-2460
Fax: 580-581-5537
jjackson@cameron.edu
www.cameronaggies.com
• Jim Jackson, Athletic Director
(580) 581-2306
jjackson@cameron.edu
Affiliations:
Members of the Lone Star Conference -
NCAA Division II
Teams:
Baseball, Basketball (M/W), Cheerleading,
Cross Country (M), Golf (M/W), Softball,
Tennis, Volleyball.
Description:
Athletics have played a large role in campus
life since Cameron's inception in 1908. Over
the years, the Aggies have won numerous
conference (42), regional (44), and national
(9) titles - including a women's tennis
regional championship in 2011, baseball
and men's tennis conference championships
in 2009 and a men's tennis regional
championship in 2008. To further celebrate
these milestones, the CU Athletic
Department, in 2007, established an Athletic
Hall of Fame to highlight CU's athletic
history and feature numerous Aggie greats.
The CU Athletic Department offers 11
intercollegiate athletic programs and is a
proud member of both the NCAA Di

CARSON-NEWMAN COLLEGE ATHLETICS
HOLT FIELDHOUSE
2130 SOUTH BRANNER AVENUE
JEFFERSON CITY, TN 37760
865-471-3360
Fax: 865-471-3514
amorgan@cn.edu
www.cneagles.com
• Allen Morgan, Athletics Director
(865) 471-3372
amorgan@cn.edu
• Eddie Carter, Assistant Athletic Director
(865) 471-3365
ecarter@cn.edu
• Mikeee Van Bruggen, Director of Sports
Medicine
(865) 471-3368
mvanbruggen@cn.edu

CATAWBA COLLEGE ATHLETICS
2300 WEST INNES STREET
SALISBURY, NC 28144
704-637-4474
Fax: 704-645-4887
www.gocatawbaindians.com
• Larry Leckonby, Athletic Director
(704) 637-4474
lleckonb14@catawba.edu
• Craig Turnbull, Associate Athletics Director

(704) 637-4475
• Peter Bourque, Assistant Athletic Director
(704) 637-4485
• Bob Casmus, Head Athletic Trianer
(704) 637-4350

UNIVERSITY OF CENTRAL ARKANSAS ATHLETICS
201 DONAGHEY AVENUE
CONWAY, AR 72035
501-450-3150
Fax: 501-450-3151
bteague@uca.edu
ucasports.com
• Brad Teague, Athletic Director
(501) 450-3150
bteague@uca.edu
• Darrell Walsh, Associate Athletic Director
(501) 450-3255
darrellw@uca.edu
• Natalie Shock, Assistant Athletic Director
(501) 450-3212
natalies@uca.edu
• Kai Caddy, Video Marketing Coordinator
(501) 450-3219
kcaddy@uca.edu

CENTRAL MISSOURI STATE UNIVERSITY ATHLETICS
203 MULTIPURPOSE BUILDING
500 SOUTH WASHINGTON STREET
WARRENSBURG, MO 64093
660-543-4250
Fax: 660-543-8034
ucmathletics.com
• Jerry Hughes, Athletics Director
(660) 543-4250
hughes@ucmo.edu
• Kathy Anderson, Senior Associate Athletic
Director
(660) 543-4310
klanderson@ucmo.edu
• Mike Knipper, Assistant Athletic Director
(660) 543-4312
knipper@ucmo.edu
• Bob Jackson, Marketing & Promotions
Director
(660) 543-8194
jackson@ucmo.edu

CENTRAL OKLAHOMA ATHLETICS, UNIVERSITY OF
100 NORTH UNIVERSITY DRIVE
EDMOND, OK 73034
405-974-2142
Fax: 405-974-3820
www.bronchosports.com
• Joe Muller, Athletic Director
(405) 974-2500
jmuller2@uco.edu
• Gunnar Poff, Assistant Athletic Director
(405) 974-2176
gpoff@uco.edu
• Britni Brannon, Assistant Athletic Director
(405) 974-2168
bbrannon@uco.edu
• Ed Kabrick, Head Athletic Trainer
(405) 974-2188
ekabrick@uco.edu

CENTRAL WASHINGTON UNIVERSITY ATHLETICS
NICHOLSON PAVILION
400 EAST UNIVERSITY WAY
ELLENSBURG, WA 98926-7570

509-963-1914
Fax: 509-963-2390
www.wildcatsports.com
• Dennis Francois, Director of Athletics
(509) 963-1945
francoisd@cwu.edu
• Gary Hyatt, Associate Athletic Director
(509) 963-1681
hyattg@cwu.edu
• Tyler Unsicker, Assistant Athletic Director
(509) 963-3290
unsickert@cwu.edu
• Chris Thew, Head Athletic Trainer
(509) 963-3238
christopher.thew@cwu.edu

CHADRON STATE COLLEGE ATHLETICS
ARMSTRONG BUILDING
1000 MAIN STREET
CHADRON, NE 69337
308-432-6345
Fax: 308-432-6493
rrhine@csc.edu
chadroneagles.com
• Randy Rhine, President
(308) 432-6201
rrhine@csc.edu
• Joel R. Smith, Athletic Director
(308) 432-6253
jsmith@csc.edu
• Kaleb Center, Interim Sports Information
Director
(308) 432-7082
kcenter@csc.edu
• Don Watt, Head Athletic Trainer
(308) 432-6340
dwatt@csc.edu
• Chris Green, Associate Athletic Director
(308) 432-6344
cgreen@csc.edu

CHAMINADE UNIVERSITY ATHLETICS
3140 WAIALAE AVENUE
HONOLULU, HI 96816
808-735-4790
Fax: 808-739-4695
www.goswords.com
• Bill Villa, Director of Athletics
(808) 739-8578
william.villa@chaminade.edu
• Bonnie Bedoya, Assistant to the Athletic
Director
(808) 735-4790
bonnie.bedoya@chaminade.edu
• Kevin Hashiro, Sports Information Director
(808) 739-8579
athletics-sid@chaminade.edu

CHARLESTON ATHLETICS, UNIVERSITY OF
2300 MACCORKLE AVENUE SE
CHARLESTON, WV 25304
304-357-4820
Fax: 304-357-4989
www.ucwv.edu
• Bren Stevens, Director of Athletics
(304) 357-4911
brenstevens@ucwv.edu
• Todd Diuguid, Associate Athletic Director
(304) 357-4827
todddiuguid@ucwv.edu
• Travis Chandler, Assistant Athletic Director
(304) 357-4751
travischandler@ucwv.edu
• Raymond Loeser, Sports Information
Director
(304) 357-4976

rayloeser@ucwv.edu
• Michael Nyquist, Head Athletic Trainer
(304) 357-4395
michaelnyquist@ucwv.edu

CHESTNUT HILL COLLEGE ATHLETICS
9601 GERMANTOWN AVENUE
PHILADELPHIA, PA 19118
215-248-7060
Fax: 215-248-7047
athletics@chc.edu
www.griffinathletics.com
• Lynn Tubman, Director of Athletics
(215) 248-7046
tubmanl@chc.edu
• Jesse Balcer, Associate Director of
Athletics
(215) 753-3790
balcerj@chc.edu
• Jessica Day, Assistant Director of Athletics
(215) 242-7729
dayj@chc.edu
• Gregory Gornick, Athletic Communications
Coordinator
(215) 248-7060
gornickg@chc.edu
• Erin Fidler, Head Athletic Trainer
(215) 248-7191
fidlere@chc.edu

CHEYNEY UNIVERSITY ATHLETICS
1837 UNIVERSITY CIRCLE
PO BOX 200
CHEYNEY, PA 19319
610-399-2441
Fax: 610-399-2291
www.cheyneywolves.com
• Suzanne Kilian, Interim Athletic Director
(610) 399-2110
skilian@cheyney.edu
• Conrad DeJoy, Interim Sports Information
Director
(305) 586-9530
• Andrew Dunn, Athletic Trainer
(610) 399-2310
adunn@cheyney.edu

CHOWAN COLLEGE ATHLETICS
HELMS CENTER
ONE UNIVERSITY PLACE
MURFREESBORO, NC 27855
252-398-6378
Fax: 252-398-6532
akolezynski0814@chowan.edu
gocuhawks.com
• Ozzie McFarland, Director of Athletics
(252) 398-6244
mcfarf@chowan.edu
• Meredith Long, Deputy Athletics Director
(252) 398-6468
longm@chowan.edu
• Alexis Avery, Assistant Athletic Director,
Compliance
(252) 398-6243
averya@chowan.edu
• Lisa Bland, Director of Sports Medicine
(252) 398-6458
blandl@chowan.edu
• Eric Gustafson, Head Athletic Trainer
(252) 398-6442
gustae@chowan.edu

CIRCLEVILLE BIBLE COLLEGE
1476 LANCASTER PIKE
CIRCLEVILLE, OH 43113
740-474-8896
877-762-8669

Fax: 740-477-7755
www.ocutrailblazers.com
• David Bireline, Athletic Director
(740) 477-7769
dbireline@ohiochristian.edu
• Ryan Wall, Sports Information Director
(740) 477-7769
sportsinformation@ohiochristian.edu

CLAFLIN UNIVERSITY ATHLETICS
400 MAGNOLIA STREET
ORANGEBURG, SC 29115-9970
803-535-5362
Fax: 803-535-5610
athletics.claflin.edu
• Jerome Fitch, Athletic Director
(803) 535-5549
jfitch@claflin.edu
• Marilynn Stacey-Suggs, Assistant Athletics
Director
(803) 535-5365
mstacey-suggs@claflin.edu
• Romanda Noble-Watson, Sports
Information Director
(803) 535-5548
rnoble-watson@claflin.edu
• Akeem Boneparte, Athletic Academic
Advisor
(803) 535-5022
akeem.bonepart@claflin.edu
• Tiffany Davis, Head Athletic Trainer
(803) 535-5726
tidavis@claflin.edu

CLARION UNIVERSITY OF PENNSYLVANIA ATHLETICS
112 TIPPIN GYM
CLARION, PA 16214
814-393-1997
Fax: 814-393-2430
www.clariongoldeneagles.com
• Wendy Snodgrass, Interim Athletic
Director
(814) 393-1997
wsnodgrass@clarion.edu
• D.J. Bevevino, Interim Associate Athletic
Director
(814) 393-1989
dbevevino@clarion.edu
• Scott Courtney, Athletics
Event/Promotions Coordinator
(814) 393-2057
scourtney@clarion.edu
• Jim Thornton, Head Athletic Trainer
(814) 393-2456
jthornton@clarion.edu

CLARK ATLANTA UNIVERSITY ATHLETICS
223 JAMES P. BRAWLEY DRIVE SW
ATLANTA, GA 30314
404-880-8123
Fax: 404-880-8397
clarkatlantasports.com
• Lin Dawson, Athletics Director
(404) 880-8123
jldawson@cau.edu
• Cliff Huff, Senior Associate Athletics
Director
(404) 880-8798
chuff@cau.edu
• James Vallone, Sports Information
(404) 880-6685
jvallone@cau.edu
• Rick Flateau, Head Athletic Trainer
(404) 880-8943
rflateau@cau.edu

CLAYTON COLLEGE & STATE UNIVERSITY ATHLETICS
2000 CLAYTON STATE BOULEVARD
MORROW, GA 30260
678-466-4692
Fax: 678-466-4699
timothyduncan@clayton.edu
www.claytonstatesports.com
• Tim Duncan, Director of Athletics
(678) 466-4692
timothyduncan@clayton.edu
• Echols Sherry, Athletics Business Manager
(678) 466-4692
sherryduncan@clayton.edu
• Mike Mead, Assistant Athletic Director
(678) 466-4679
mikemead@clayton.edu
• Alicia M. Roane, Head Athletic Trainer
(678) 466-4685
aliciaroane@clayton.edu
• Joshua J. Darling, Sports Information Director
(678) 466-4681
joshuadarling@clayton.edu

COKER COLLEGE ATHLETICS
300 EAST COLLEGE AVENUE
HARTSVILLE, SC 29550
843-383-8073
Fax: 843-383-8167
www.cokercobras.com
• Lynn Griffin, Vice President of Athletics
(843) 383-8071
lgriffin@coker.edu
• Mary Buchner, Assistant To The VP For Athletics
(843) 383-8262
mbuchner@coker.edu
• Chris Jeppson, Head Athletic Trainer
(843) 383-8390
cjeppson@coker.edu

COLORADO ATHLETICS, UNIVERSITY OF (COLORADO SPRINGS)
1420 AUSTIN BLUFFS PARKWAY
UNIVERSITY CENTER
COLORADO SPRINGS, CO 80918
719-255-3029
Fax: 719-255-3131
gomountainlions.com
• Nathan Gibson, Executive Athletic Director
• Sandee Mott, Senior Associate Athletic Director/SWA
(719) 255-3601
smott@uccs.edu
• Heather Sanders, Assistant Athletic Director
(719) 255-3004
hsander2@uccs.edu

COLORADO CHRISTIAN UNIVERSITY ATHLETICS
8787 WEST ALAMEDA AVENUE
LAKEWOOD, CO 80226
303-963-3026
Fax: 303-963-3187
cougars@ccu.edu
www.ccucougars.com
• Brian Wall, Athletic Director
(303) 963-3187
bwall@ccu.edu
• Christy Hinch, Assistant Athletic Director/SWA
(303) 963-3185
chinch@ccu.edu
• Heidi Tebrink, Head Athletic Trainer

(303) 963-3199
htebrink@ccu.edu
• Brooke Carbajal, Director of Sports Information
(303) 963-3026
bcarbajal@ccu.edu

COLORADO SCHOOL OF MINES ATHLETICS
1500 ILLINOIS STREET
GOLDEN, CO 80401
303-273-3360
Fax: 303-273-3362
www.csmorediggers.com
• David Hansburg, Director of Athletics
(303) 273-3300
hansburg@mines.edu
• Dixie Cirillo, Associate Athletics Director
(303) 273-3206
dcirillo@mines.edu
• Tim Flynn, Assistant Athletics Director
(303) 273-3095
flynn@mines.edu

COLUMBUS STATE UNIVERSITY ATHLETICS
4225 UNIVERSITY AVENUE
COLUMBUS, GA 31907
706-507-8800
866-264-2035
Fax: 706-569-3435
www.csucougars.com
• Todd Reeser, Director of Athletics
(706) 565-3669
treeser@columbusstate.edu
• Jimbo Davis, Assistant Athletic Director
(706) 568-2317
davis_james@columbusstate.edu
• Julio Llanos, Associate Athletic Director
(706) 507-8297
llanos_julio@columbusstate.edu
• Stephen Williams, Sports Information Director
(706) 569-3434
swilliams@columbusstate.edu

CONCORD UNIVERSITY ATHLETICS
VERMILLION STREET
PO BOX 1000
ATHENS, WV 24712-1000
304-384-5340
Fax: 304-384-5117
www.cumountainlions.com
• Kevin Garrett, Director of Athletics
(304) 384-5340
coachgarrett@concord.edu
• Tracy Gill, Assistant Athletic Director
(304) 384-5954
tmccallister@concord.edu
• Kenny Osborne, Associate Athletic Director
(304) 384-5344
coachosborne@concord.edu
• Wes McKinney, Sports Information Director
(304) 384-6259
sportsinformation@concord.edu

CONCORDIA COLLEGE (NY) ATHLETICS
171 WHITE PLAINS ROAD
BRONXVILLE, NY 10708
914-337-9300
Fax: 914-395-4515
www.concordiaclippers.com
• Kathy Laoutaris, Director of Athletics/SWA
(914) 337-9300
kathy.laoutaris@concordia-ny.edu

• Kathy Laoutaris, Associate Athletic Director
(914) 337-9300
kathy.laoutaris@concordia-ny.edu
• Jillian Ayson, Head Athletic Trainer
(914) 337-9300
jillian.ayson@concordia-ny.edu

CONCORDIA UNIVERSITY (OR) ATHLETICS
2811 NORTHEAST HOLMAN STREET
PORTLAND, OR 97211
503-280-8582
Fax: 503-280-8591
www.gocugo.com
• Brian Jamros, Director of Athletics
(503) 280-8554
bjamros@cu-portland.edu
• Lauren Eads, Associate Athletics Director-Busines Mgmt
(503) 280-8516
laeds@cu-portland.edu
• Amy Dames Smith, Assistant Athletics Director
(503) 280-8581
adames@cu-portland.edu
• Cisco Reyes, Director of Athletic Performance
greyes@cu-portland.edu
• Kyle Nelson, Head Athletic Trainer
(503) 280-8695
kynelson@cu-portland.edu
• Joe Danahey, Assistant AD For Sports Information
(503) 280-8506
jdanahey@cu-portland.edu

CONCORDIA UNIVERSITY IRVINE ATHLETICS
1530 CONCORDIA WEST
IRVINE, CA 92612-3203
949-854-8002 EXT 1423
Fax: 949-854-6771
www.cuieagles.com
• Mo Roberson, Interim Director of Athletics
(949) 214-3210
mo.roberson@cui.edu
• Brittany Brasington, Assistant Athletic Director
(949) 514-3212
brittany.brasington@cui.edu
• Crystal Rosenthal, Senior Woman Administrator
(949) 214-3223
crystal.rosenthal@cui.edu
• Brian Gaul, Director of Athletic Communications
(949) 214-3211
brian.gaul@cui.edu
• Terilyn Jackson, Director of Equity and Inclusion
(949) 214-3039
terilyn.jackson@cui.edu
• Glory Fung, Head Athletic Trainer
(949) 214-3245
glory.fung@cui.edu

DAEMEN COLLEGE ATHLETICS
4380 MAIN STREET
AMHERST, NY 14226
716-839-8346
800-462-7652
Fax: 716-566-7858
www.daemen.edu
• Bridget Niland, Director of Athletics
• Mike MacDonald, Associate Athletics Director

• Tom McDermott, Sports Information
Consultant
• Stephen Beatty, Athletics Operations
Assistant
(716) 566-7698
sbeatty@daemen.edu

**DALLAS BAPTIST UNIVERSITY
ATHLETICS**
3000 MOUNTAIN CREEK PARKWAY
DALLAS, TX 75211
214-333-5324
Fax: 214-333-5306
sports@dbu.edu
dbupatriots.com
• Connor Smith, Director of Athletics
(214) 333-5324
connors@dbu.edu
• Tyler Knox, Associate Director of Athletics
(214) 333-5349
tyler@dbu.edu
• Chris Weatherly, Director of Athletic
Operations
(214) 333-5436
chriswe@dbu.edu
• Josh Freeze, Director of Athletic Facilities
(214) 333-5350
joshf@dbu.edu

DELTA STATE UNIVERSITY ATHLETICS
C/O CHADWICK-DICKSON ATHLETIC
FIELD HOUSE
DSU BOX A3
CLEVELAND, MS 38733
662-846-4300
800.GO.TO.DSU
athletics@deltastate.edu
www.gostatesmen.com
• Ronnie Mayers, Director of Athletics
(662) 846-4730
rmayers@deltastate.edu
• David Pryor, Assistant Athletic Director,
Sports Medicine
(662) 846-4280
dpryor@deltastate.edu

**DISTRICT OF COLUMBIA ATHLETICS,
UNIVERSITY OF**
4200 CONNECTICUT AVENUE NW
BUILDING 47, ROOM A02
WASHINGTON, DC 20008
202-274-5024
Fax: 202-274-5065
www.udcfirebirds.com
• Patricia Thomas, Director of Intercollegiate
Athletics
(202) 274-7257
pthomas@udc.edu
• Joseph Lang, Senior Associate Director of
Athletics
(202) 274-6314
jlang@udc.edu
• Andre Myers, Aquatics Director
(202) 274-5343
andrew.myers@udc.edu
• Alison Hammer, Assistant Director of
Athletics, Sports Medicine
(202) 274-6269
alison.hammer@udc.edu

DOMINICAN COLLEGE ATHLETICS
470 WESTERN HIGHWAY
ORANGEBURG, NY 10962
845-848-7702
Fax: 845-398-3042
www.chargerathletics.com

• Joseph Clinton, Director of Athletics
(845) 848-7700
joe.clinton@dc.edu
• Kelly-Ann Di Giulio, Director of Sports
Information
(845) 848-7706
kellyann.digiulio@dc.edu
• Rick Giannetti, Assistant Director of
Athletics
(845) 848-7707
rick.giannetti@dc.edu
• Samantha James, Head Athletic Trainer
(845) 848-7709
samantha.james@dc.edu

**DOMINICAN UNIVERSITY OF
CALIFORNIA ATHLETICS**
1475 GRAND AVENUE
SAN RAFAEL, CA 94901
415-482-3500
Fax: 415-485-9746
amy.henkelman@dominican.edu
www.dominicanathletics.com
• Amy Henkelman, Acting Director of
Athletics
amy.henkelman@dominican.edu
• Cassandra Urroz, Associate Director of
Athletics and Compliance
(415) 482-3503
cassandra.urroz@dominican.edu
• Patrick Huser, Assistant Director of
Athletics
(415) 485-3219
patrick.huser@dominican.edu

DOWLING COLLEGE ATHLETICS
RUDOLPH-OAKDALE CAMPUS
150 IDLE HOUR BOULEVARD
OAKDALE, NY 11769
631-244-3030
800-369-5464
Fax: 631-244-3317
• Melody Cope, Vice President for Athletics
(631) 244-3023
copem@dowling.edu
• Jason Trufant, Senior Associate Athletic
Director
(631) 244-1113
trufantj@dowling.edu
• Kevin DesLauriers, Assistant Athletics
Director
(631) 244-1075
deslaurk@dowling.edu
• Jackie Rogers, Director of Athletic
Communications
(631) 244-1095
rogersj@dowling.edu

DRURY UNIVERSITY ATHLETICS
900 NORTH BENTON AVENUE
SPRINGFIELD, MO 65802
417-873-7879
800-922-2274
Fax: 417-873-7510
drury@drury.edu
www.drury.edu
• Mark Fisher, Athletic Director
(417) 873-7294
• Eric Pannell, Assistant Director of Sports
Information
(417) 873-7374
• Barbara Cowherd, Associate Director of
Athletics
(417) 873-7363
• Bryan Beatty, Assistant Athletic Director,
Compliance
(417) 873-6382

**EAST CENTRAL UNIVERSITY
ATHLETICS**
1100 EAST 14TH STREET
ADA, OK 74820
580-332-8000
jwillims@ecok.edu
ecutigers.com
• Jeff Williams, Director of Athletics
(580) 559-5261
jwillims@ecok.edu
• Justin Graham, Assistant Athletic Director
(580) 559-5653
juspgra@ecok.edu
• Teri LaJeunesse, Sports Information
Director
(580) 559-5258
tlajeune@ecok.edu

**EAST STROUDSBURG UNIVERSITY OF
PENNSYLVANIA ATHLETICS**
KOEHLER FIELDHOUSE
200 PROSPECT STREET
EAST STROUDSBURG, PA 18301
570-422-3211
Fax: 570-422-3306
www.esuwarriors.com
• Josh Looney, Director of Athletics
(570) 422-3642
• Carey Snyder, Associate Athletic Director
(570) 422-3034
csnyder@esu.edu
• Philip Miller, Assistant to the Athletic
Director
(570) 422-3578
pmiller17@esu.edu
• Greg Knowlden, Sports Information
Director
(570) 422-3312
gknowlden@esu.edu
• Wendy Dietrich, Athletic Trainer
(570) 422-3166
wwheeler@esu.edu

**EASTERN NEW MEXICO UNIVERSITY
ATHLETICS**
ENMU STATION 17
1500 SOUTH AVENUE K
PORTALES, NM 88130
575-562-1011
Fax: 505-562-2822
athletics@enmu.edu
www.goeasternathletics.com
• Greg Waggoner, Athletic Director
(575) 562-2153
greg.waggoner@enmu.edu
• Lora Ferguson, Head Athletic Trainer
(575) 562-2273
lora.ferguson@enmu.edu
• Kimberley Sites, Athletic Office
Coordinator
(575) 562-2153
• Adam Pitterman, Director of Athletic
Communications
(575) 562-4309
adam.pitterman@enmu.edu

ECKERD COLLEGE ATHLETICS
4200 54TH AVENUE SOUTH
ST. PETERSBURG, FL 33711
727-867-1166
800-456-9009
Fax: 727-864-8968
www.eckerdtritons.com
• Bob Fortosis, Director of Athletics
(727) 864-8252
fortoscr@eckerd.edu
• Tom Ryan, Associate Director of Athletics

(727) 864-8305
ryantj@eckerd.edu
• Bill Matthews, Assistant Director of
Athletics
(727) 864-8253
mathewwj@eckerd.edu
• Jeff Bromley, Director of Athletics
Development
(727) 864-8403
bromlejm@eckerd.edu

**EDINBORO UNIVERSITY OF
PENNSYLVANIA ATHLETICS**
MCCOMB FIELDHOUSE
455 SCOTLAND ROAD
EDINBORO, PA 16444-0001
814-732-1834
Fax: 814-732-2190
www.gofightingscots.com
• Bruce Baumgartner, Director of Athletics
(814) 732-1823
bbaumgartner@edinboro.edu
• Todd Jay, Associate Athletic Director
(814) 732-1835
jay@edinboro.edu
• Dave Higham, Athletic Administrative
Coordinator
(814) 732-1825
dhigham@edinboro.edu
• Gary Hanna, Head Athletic Trainer
(814) 732-1860
ghanna@edinboro.edu
• Bob Shreve, Sports Information Director
(814) 732-1834
rshreve@edinboro.edu

**ELIZABETH CITY STATE UNIVERSITY
ATHLETICS**
1704 WEEKSVILLE ROAD
CAMPUS BOX 900
ELIZABETH CITY, NC 27909
252-335-3388
Fax: 252-335-3627
www.ecsuvikings.com
• Derrick Johnson, Athletic Director
(252) 335-3396
dajohnson2@ecsu.edu
• Alico Dunk, Assistant Athletic Director -
Academics
(252) 335-3461
ajdunk@ecsu.edu
• John Westbrook, Sports Information
Director
(252) 335-3278
jwwestbrookjr@ecsu.edu

**EMBRY-RIDDLE AERONAUTICAL
UNIVERSITY ATHLETICS - (FL)**
600 SOUTH CLYDE MORRIS BOULEVARD
DAYTONA BEACH, FL 32114
386-226-6100
erauathletics.com
• John Phillips, Director of Athletics
(386) 323-5020
john.phillips@erau.edu
• John Mark Adkison, Associate Director of
Athletics
(386) 323-5033
john.adkison@erau.edu
• Maryellen Wynn, Director of Finance -
Athletics
(386) 323-5004
maryellen.wynn@erau.edu
• Jenni Craig, Director of Sports Marketing
and Promotions
(386) 323-5037
craig10@erau.edu

• Alison Smalling, Director of Sports
Information
(386) 323-5001
alison.smalling@erau.edu

EMMANUEL COLLEGE (EC) ATHLETICS
181 SPRINGS STREET
PO BOX 129
FRANKLIN SPRINGS, GA 30639
706-245-2917
800-860-8800
Fax: 706-245-4424
www.goeclions.com
• Nate Moorman, Athletic Director
(706) 245-2884
nmoorman@ec.edu
• JaVonte Ashford, Assistant Athletic
Director
(706) 988-0103
jashford@ec.edu
• Richard Reiselt, Faculty Athletics
Representative
(706) 245-7226
rreiselt@ec.edu
• Sandy Campbell, Director for Sports
Medicine
(706) 245-2889
scampbell@ec.edu
• Kethan Darbar, Sports Information
Coordinator
(731) 444-4737
kdarbar@ec.edu

**EMPORIA STATE UNIVERSITY
ATHLETICS**
1 KELLOGG CIRCLE
HPER 113
CAMPUS BOX 4020
EMPORIA, KS 66801
620-341-5354
Fax: 620-341-5603
www.esuhornets.com
• Kent Weiser, Athletic Director
(620) 341-5350
kweiser@emporia.edu
• Shane Shivley, Senior Associate Athletic
Director
(620) 341-6988
sshivley@emporia.edu
• Don Weast, Assistant Athletic Director
(620) 341-5526
dweast@emporia.edu
• Tess Shepherd, Athletic Business
Manager
(620) 341-5925
tshepher@emporia.edu
• Dustin Enslinger, Head Athletic Trainer
(620) 341-5021
densling@emporia.edu

ERSKINE COLLEGE ATHLETICS
PO BOX 338
2 WASHINGTON STREET
DUE WEST, SC 29639
864-379-8859
888-359-4358
Fax: 864-379-2197
erskinesports.com
• Mark Peeler, Vice President for
Intercollegiate Athletics
(864) 379-8850
mlp@erskine.edu
• Kevin Nichols, Associate Director of
Athletics
(864) 379-8890
nichols@erskine.edu
• Thomas Holland, Co-Sports Information

Director
(864) 379-6782
tholland@erskine.edu

**FAIRMONT STATE UNIVERSITY
ATHLETICS**
1201 LOCUST AVENUE
FAIRMONT, WV 26554
304-367-4220
Fax: 304-333-3597
www.fightingfalcons.com
• Tim McNeely, Director of Athletics
(304) 367-4220
tim.mcneely@fairmontstate.edu
• Bob Cable, Associate Athletic Director
(304) 367-4273
rcable@fairmontstate.edu
• Chad Fowler, Assistant Athletic Director
for Development
(304) 333-3650
chad.fowler@fairmontstate.edu
• Chris Thomas, Sports Information Director
(304) 367-4264
christopher.thomas@fairmontstate.edu

**FAYETTEVILLE STATE UNIVERSITY
ATHLETICS**
FELTON J. CAPEL ARENA
1200 MURCHISON ROAD
FAYETTEVILLE, NC 28301
910-672-1314
Fax: 910-672-1241
www.fsubroncos.com
• Anthony Todd Bennett, Director of
Athletics
(910) 672-1314
abennett@uncfsu.edu
• LaWanda Miller, Assistant Athletics
Director
(910) 672-1420
lmiller@uncfsu.edu
• Carlitta Moore, Director of Sports Medicine
(910) 672-1065
cmmoore02@uncfsu.edu

FELICIAN COLLEGE ATHLETICS
ONE FELICIAN WAY
RUTHERFORD, NJ 07070
201-559-3333
Fax: 201-559-3601
felicianathletics.com
• Ben DiNallo, Jr., Director of Athletics
(201) 559-3507
Dinallob@felician.edu
• Lori McGuinness, Assistant Director of
Athletics, Compliance
(201) 559-3996
kwiatkowskil@felician.edu
• Mark Mentone, Sports Information Director
(201) 559-3257
mentonem@felician.edu
• Dan Trinh, Head Athletic Trainer
(201) 559-3502
trinhd@felician.edu

FERRIS STATE UNIVERSITY ATHLETICS
1201 SOUTH STATE STREET
BIG RAPIDS, MI 49307
231-591-2860
Fax: 231-591-2869
www.ferrisstatebulldogs.com
• Perk Weisenburger, Athletics Director
(231) 591-2862
weisenj1@ferris.edu
• Jon Coles, Associate Athletic Director
(231) 591-2864
coelsj@ferris.edu

• Rob Bentley, Assistant Athletic Director,
Communications
(231) 591-3821
bentleyr@ferris.edu
• Dave Lucey, Head Athletic Trainer
(231) 250-7931
luceyd@ferris.edu

FINDLAY ATHLETICS, UNIVERSITY OF
1000 NORTH MAIN STREET
FINDLAY, OH 45840
419-434-4663
800-472-9502
Fax: 419-434-4618
athletics.findlay.edu
• Brandi Laurita, Director of Athletics
(419) 434-4663
laurita@findlay.edu
• Jim Givens, Associate Athletic Director
(419) 434-4793
givens@findlay.edu
• David Buck, Assistant Athletic Director
(419) 434-4727
buckd@findlay.edu
• Fiona Hanks, Head Athletic Trainer
(419) 434-6785
hanks@findlay.edu

FLAGLER COLLEGE ATHLETICS
74 KING STREET
ST. AUGUSTINE, FL 32084
904-829-6481
athletics.flagler.edu
• Jud Damon, Director of Athletics
(904) 819-6252
jdamon@flagler.edu
• Ryan Erlacher, Associate Director of
Athletics
(904) 819-6488
rerlacher@flagler.edu
• John Jordan, Sports Information Director
(904) 819-6465
jjordan@flagler.edu
• Cade Smith, Athletics Operations
Coordinator
(904) 826-8632
ksmith@flagler.edu
• Aerial Tirado, Head Athletic Trainer
(904) 819-6361
atirado@flagler.edu

FLORIDA GULF COAST UNIVERSITY
ATHLETICS
10501 FGCU BOULEVARD SOUTH
FORT MYERS, FL 33965
239-590-7012
Fax: 239-590-7014
pblankenship@fgcu.edu
www.fgcuathletics.com
• Ken Kavanagh, Director of Athletics
kavanagh@fgcu.edu
• Trish Blankenship, Administrative
Assistant
pblankenship@fgcu.edu
• Mike Estes, Senior Associate AD,
Administration
(239) 590-7006
mestes@fgcu.edu
• Kathy Peterson, Assoc. AD,
Student-Athlete Svcs./Snr. Woman Admin.
(239) 590-7018
kpeterson@fgcu.edu
Team Nickname:
Eagles
Conference:
NCAA Division I
Founded:

1997
Enrollment:
15,000

FLORIDA INSTITUTE OF TECHNOLOGY
ATHLETICS
150 WEST UNIVERSITY BOULEVARD
MELBOURNE, FL 32901
321-674-8032
Fax: 321-984-8529
bjurgens@fit.edu
www.floridatechsports.com
• Bill Jurgens, Jr., Athletic Director
(321) 674-8032
bjurgens@fit.edu
• Frank M. Webbe, Faculty Athletics
Representative
(321) 674-8104
• Michael Craig, Assistant Athletic Director,
Communications
(321) 674-8250
• Jay Johnson, Head Athletic Trainer
(321) 674-8438
jayjohnson@fit.edu

FLORIDA SOUTHERN COLLEGE
ATHLETICS
111 LAKE HOLLINGSWORTH DRIVE
LAKELAND, FL 33801-5698
863-680-4246
Fax: 863-680-4122
fscmocs.com
• Pete Meyer, Director of Athletics
(863) 680-4264
pmeyer@flsouthern.edu
• Al Green, Head Athletic Trainer
(863) 680-4267
agreen@flsouthern.edu
• Drew Howard, Associate Athletic Director
(863) 680-4266
ahoward@flsouthern.edu
• Brink Schoonmaker, Manager of Athletic
Facilities
(750) 919-3054
bschoonmaker@flsouthern.edu

FORT HAYS STATE UNIVERSITY
ATHLETICS
600 PARK STREET
HAYS, KS 67601-4099
785-628-3478
Fax: 785-625-4881
fhsuathletics.com
• Curtis Hammeke, Athletic Director
(785) 628-4050
chammeke@fhsu.edu
• Brad Haynes, Assistant Athletic Director
(785) 628-5288
behaynes@fhsu.edu
• Ryan Prickett, Sports Information Director
(785) 628-5903
rpricket@fhsu.edu

FORT LEWIS COLLEGE ATHLETICS
1000 RIM DRIVE
DURANGO, CO 81301
970-247-7171
Fax: 970-247-7655
www.goskyhawks.com
• Gary Hunter, Director of Athletics
(970) 247-7224
ghunter@fortlewis.edu
• Steve Stovall, Faculty Athletics
Representative
• Wayne Barger, Director of Sports Medicine
(970) 247-7576
barger_w@fortlewis.edu

• Adam Ruetschie, Athletic Operations
Coordinator
(970) 247-7171

FORT VALLEY STATE UNIVERSITY
ATHLETICS
1005 STATE UNIVERSITY DRIVE
FORT VALLEY, GA 31030
478-825-3054
Fax: 478-825-6889
www.fvsusports.com
• Darryl Pope, Director of Athletics
(478) 825-6238
• LuWanna Williams, Associate Director of
Athletics
(478) 825-6179
williamsl@fvsu.edu
• Jerry Haywood, Faculty Athletic
Representative
(478) 825-6710
• Willie K. Patterson, Jr., Director of Sports
Information
(478) 825-6437
pattersonw@fvsu.edu

FRANCIS MARION UNIVERSITY
ATHLETICS
PO BOX 100547
FLORENCE, SC 29502-0547
843-661-1240
Fax: 843-661-4645
www.fmupatriots.com
• Murray Hartzler, Athletics Director
(843) 661-1237
mhartzler@fmarion.edu
• Dean Blackburn, Director of Smith
University Center
(843) 661-1189
dblackburn@fmarion.edu
• Reghan Boehmke, Head Athletic Trainer
(843) 661-1358
rboehmke@fmarion.edu

FRANKLIN PIERCE UNIVERSITY
ATHLETICS
40 UNIVERSITY DRIVE
RINDGE, NH 03461
603-899-4087
Fax: 603-899-4328
• Bruce Kirsh, Director of Athletics
(603) 899-4080
kirshb@franklinpierce.edu
• Dan Blair, Associate Director of Athletics
(603) 899-4367
blaird@franklinpierce.edu
• Stephanie Dragan, Assistant Athletics
Director
(603) 899-4084
dragans@franklinpierce.edu
• Matthew Janik, Director of Athletic
Communication
(603) 899-4223
janikm@franklinpierce.edu
• Cynthia Arman, Head Athletic Trainer
(603) 899-4083
armanca@franklinpierce.edu

FRESNO PACIFIC UNIVERSITY
ATHLETICS
DEPARTMENT OF ATHLETICS
1717 SOUTH CHESTNUT AVENUE
FRESNO, CA 93702
559-453-2009
Fax: 559-453-2005
fpuathletics.com
• Aaron Henderson, Director of Athletics
(559) 453-2009

aaron.henderson@fresno.edu
• Jeremiah Wood, Assistant Athletics
Director for Communications
(559) 453-4646
jeremiah.wood@fresno.edu
• Jessi Wallace, Assistant Director for
External Relations
(559) 453-5694
jessi.wallace@fresno.edu

GANNON UNIVERSITY ATHLETICS
109 UNIVERSITY SQUARE
ERIE, PA 16541
814-871-7000
Fax: 814-871-7794
www.gannonsports.com
• Lisa Goddard McGuirk, Director of
Athletics
(814) 871-7664
mcguirk001@gannon.edu
• Don Sherman, Associate Director of
Athletics
(814) 871-7763
sherman001@gannon.edu
• Dan Teliski, Assistant Director of Athletics,
Media Relations
(814) 871-7418
teliski002@gannon.edu
• Todd Matlak, Head Athletic Trainer
(814) 871-7420
matlak003@gannon.edu

**GEORGIA COLLEGE & STATE
UNIVERSITY ATHLETICS**
231 WEST HANCOCK STREET
MILLEDGEVILLE, GA 31061
478-445-1779
800-342-0471
Fax: 478-445-1790
gsu.sid@gcsu.edu
www.gcsu.edu/athletics
• Wendell Staton, Athletic Director
(478) 445-6341
wendell.staton@gcsu.edu
• Jimmy Wilson, Associate Athletic Director
(478) 445-2082
jimmy.wilson@gcsu.edu
• Steve Barsby, Assistant Athletic Director
(478) 445-1778
steve.barsby@gcsu.edu
• Paul Higgs, Head Athletic Trainer
(478) 445-1787
paul.higgs@gcsu.edu

**GEORGIA SOUTHWESTERN STATE
UNIVERSITY ATHLETICS**
800 GSW UNIVERSITY DRIVE
AMERICUS, GA 31709
229-931-2222
800-388-0082
Fax: 229-931-2143
www.gswcanes.com
• Mike Leeder, Athletic Director
(229) 931-2225
mike.leeder@gsw.edu
• Christie Ward, Associate Athletic Director
for Compliance
(229) 931-7012
christie.ward@gsw.edu
• Keith Michlig, Assistant Athletic Director
for Sports Information
(229) 931-2217
keith.michlig@gsw.edu

**GEORGIAN COURT COLLEGE
ATHLETICS**
900 LAKEWOOD AVENUE
LAKEWOOD, NJ 08701
732-987-2683
Fax: 732-987-2002
www.gculions.com
• Laura Liesman, Director of Athletics &
Recreation
(732) 987-2683
liesmanl@georgian.edu
• Christopher McKibben, Associate Director
of Athletics
(732) 987-2690
mckibbenc@georgian.edu
• Joe Friedrich, Coordinator of Sports
Medicine
(732) 987-2676
friedrichj@georgian.edu

**GLENVILLE STATE COLLEGE
ATHLETICS**
200 HIGH STREET
GLENVILLE, WV 26351
304-462-4102
Fax: 304-462-8619
www.glenville.edu
• Marcel Lazenby, Athletic
Director/Compliance Coordinator
(304) 462-7361
marcel.lazenby@glenville.edu
• Jonathan Griffin, Sports Information
Director
(304) 462-6238

**GOLDEY BEACOM COLLEGE
ATHLETICS**
4701 LIMESTONE ROAD
WILMINGTON, DE 19808
302-225-6352
Fax: 302-998-6823
hammond@gbc.edu
www.gbcathletics.com
• Tom Brennan, Director of Athletics
(302) 225-6352
brennan@gbc.edu
• Bethann Burke, Assistant Director of
Athletics
(302) 225-6334
burkeb@gbc.edu
• Derek Crudele, Sports Information &
Communications Specialist
(302) 225-6330
crudele@gbc.edu
• Brandon Sonson, Certified Athletic Trainer
(302) 225-6217
atc@gbc.edu

**GRAND VALLEY STATE UNIVERSITY
ATHLETICS**
92 FIELDHOUSE, 1 CAMPUS DRIVE
ALLENDALE, MI 49401
616-331-5000
www.gvsulakers.com
• Keri Becker, Athletic Director
(616) 331-8800
keri_becker@gvsu.edu

HARDING UNIVERSITY ATHLETICS
915 EAST MARKET AVENUE
SEARCY, AR 72149-5615
501-279-4305
Fax: 501-279-4138
gharnden@harding.edu
www.hardingsports.com
• Greg Harnden, Athletic Director
(501) 279-4305

gharnden@harding.edu
• Brenda Seawel, Assistant Athletic Director
(501) 279-4770
bseawel@harding.edu
• Scott Goode, Assistant Athletic Director,
Sports Information
(501) 279-4760
sgoode@harding.edu
• Nathan Looney, Assistant Sports
Information Director
(501) 279-4760
nclooney@harding.edu

**HAWAII PACIFIC UNIVERSITY
ATHLETICS**
1060 BISHOP STREET
SUITE 400
HONOLULU, HI 96813
808-356-5214
Fax: 808-566-2405
athletics@hpu.edu
www.hpusharks.com
• Vince Baldemor, Executive Director of
Athletics
(808) 544-0209
vbaldemor@hpu.edu
• Natasa Revere, Associate Athletics
Director
(808) 356-5278
nsubotic@hpu.edu
• Bill Powers, Sports Information Director
(808) 544-0220
bpowers@hpu.edu
• Chelsea Patton, Athletics Business
Manager
(808) 687-7046
cpatton@hpu.edu

**HAWAII-HILO ATHLETICS, UNIVERSITY
OF**
200 WEST KAWILI STREET
HILO, HI 96720-4091
808-932-7170
Fax: 808-974-7711
hiloathletics.com
• Patrick Guillen, Director of Athletics
(808) 932-7170
pguillen@hawaii.edu
• Diane Wissing, Assistant Compliance
Officer
(808) 932-7801
dwissing@hawaii.edu

**HENDERSON STATE UNIVERSITY
ATHLETICS**
1100 HENDERSON STREET
BOX 7630
ARKADELPHIA, AR 71999
870-230-5161
Fax: 870-230-5408
jonessh@hsu.edu
www.hsusports.com
• Shawn Jones, Director of Athletics
(870) 230-5072
jonessh@hsu.edu
• Lenette Jones, Assistnat Athletic Director
(870) 230-5881
joneslc@hsu.edu
• Troy Mitchell, Sports Information Director
(870) 230-5197
mitchet@hsu.edu
• Rob Redding, Director for Sports Medicine
(870) 230-5069
reddinr@hsu.edu

HILLSDALE COLLEGE ATHLETICS
33 EAST COLLEGE STREET
HILLSDALE, MI 49242
517-437-7341
Fax: 517-437-3923
www.hillsdalechargers.com
• Don Brubacher, Director of Athletics
(517) 437-7364
dbrubacher@hillsdale.edu
• Jeff Lantis, Director of External Relations
(517) 607-3182
jlantis@hillsdale.edu
• Anita Gordon, Aid To Athletic Director
(517) 607-3140
agordon@hillsdale.edu
• Brad Monastiere, Assistant Athletic
Director
(517) 607-3172
bmonastiere@hillsdale.edu
• Lynne Neukom, Head Athletic Trainer
(517) 607-3157
lneukom@hillsdale.edu

HOLY FAMILY COLLEGE ATHLETICS
9801 FRANKFORD AVENUE
PHILADELPHIA, PA 19114
215-637-6675
Fax: 215-827-0137
athletics@holyfamily.edu
athletics.holyfamily.edu
• Sandra Michael, Assistant Vice President
of Athletics
(267) 341-3368
smichael@holyfamily.edu
• Robin Arnold, Associate Athletic Director
(267) 341-3675
rarnold1@holyfamily.edu
• Jermaine Rolle, Assistant Athletic Director
(267) 341-3663
jrolle@holyfamily.edu
• Jami Hughes, Assistant Athletic
Director-Daily Operations
(267) 341-3514
jhughes2@holyfamily.edu

HOLY NAMES COLLEGE ATHLETICS
3500 MOUNTAIN BOULEVARD
OAKLAND, CA 94619
510-436-1047
Fax: 510-436-1553
www.hnuhawks.com
• Debbie Snell, Director of Athletics
(510) 436-1049
snell@hnu.edu
• Marcie Haduca, Associate Director of
Athletics
(510) 436-1428
haduca@hnu.edu

**HUMBOLDT STATE UNIVERSITY
ATHLETICS**
ATHLETIC DEPARTMENT
1 HARPST STREET
ARCATA, CA 95521-8299
707-826-3666
Fax: 707-826-5446
www.hsujacks.com
• Tom Trepiak, Interim Athletic Director
(707) 826-3666
trt2@humboldt.edu
• Kelly Kime, Interim Associate Athletic
Director/SWA
(707) 826-5959
kjk42@humboldt.edu
• Laurie Sheppard, Assistant Athletic
Director, Business Operations

(707) 826-4530
sheppard@humboldt.edu

**ILLINOIS AT SPRINGFIELD ATHLETICS,
UNIVERSITY OF**
2171 UNIVERSITY DRIVE
SPRINGFIELD, IL 62703
217-206-6674
Fax: 217-206-7706
kpate80@uis.edu
www.uisprairiestars.com
• Jim Sarra, Director of Athletics
(217) 206-7592
kpate80@uis.edu
• Hayley Ross Treadway, Associate Athletic
Director/SWA
(217) 206-8547
hross3@uis.edu
• Ashlyn Beasley, Director for Game
Operations
(217) 206-7017
jdors2@uis.edu
• Katie Bowers, Head Athletic Trainer
(217) 206-7597
kbowe6@uis.edu

**INCARNATE WORD ATHLETICS,
UNIVERSITY OF THE**
4301 BROADWAY
SAN ANTONIO, TX 78209
210-829-6052
Fax: 210-805-3574
witt@uiwtx.edu
www.cardinalathletics.com
• Mark Papichs, Director of Athletics
(210) 829-6053
papich@uiwtx.edu
• Dustin York, Deputy Athletic Director
(210) 283-6968
dyork@uiwtx.edu
• Lydia Andrade, Faculty Athletic
Representative
(210) 829-3877
andrade@uiwtx.edu

**INDIANA UNIVERSITY OF
PENNSYLVANIA ATHLETICS**
711 PRATT DRIVE
SUITE 204
INDIANA, PA 15705
724-357-4295
Fax: 724-357-2754
www.iupathletics.com
• Steve Roach, Athletic Director
(724) 357-4295
sroach@iup.edu
• Samantha Traver, Assistant Athletic
Director
(724) 357-6948
traver@iup.edu
• Ryan Rebholz, Sports Information Director
(724) 357-2747
rrebholz@iup.edu

**INDIANAPOLIS ATHLETICS, UNIVERSITY
OF**
1400 EAST HANNA AVENUE
INDIANAPOLIS, IN 46227
317-788-3412
Fax: 317-788-3472
athletics@uindy.edu
athletics.uindy.edu
• Sue Willey, Vice President for
Intercollegiate Athletics
(317) 788-3412
swilley@uindy.edu
• Jackie Paquette, Associate Athletics

Director
(317) 788-5008
paquettej@uindy.edu
• Matt Donovan, Sr. Associate AD For
Development
(317) 788-6122
mdonovan@uindy.edu
• Kyle Piercy, Sports Information Director
(317) 788-3494
thomasrf@uindy.edu
• Ned Shannon, Head Athletic Trainer
(317) 788-6112
nshannon@uindy.edu

**JOHNSON C. SMITH UNIVERSITY
ATHLETICS**
100 BEATTIES FORD ROAD
CHARLOTTE, NC 28216
704-378-1205
Fax: 704-378-1170
www.goldenbullsports.com
• Stephen Joyner, Athletic Director
(704) 378-3522
• K.C. Culler, Sports Information Director
(704) 378-1118
• Katie Hanes-Romano, Head Athletic
Trainer
(704) 378-1222

**KENTUCKY STATE UNIVERSITY
ATHLETICS**
400 EAST MAIN STREET
FRANKFORT, KY 40601
502-597-6000
Fax: 502-597-6466
william.head@kysu.edu
www.ksuthorobreds.com
• William K. Graham, Director of Athletics
(502) 597-6922
william.graham@kysu.edu
• Kim Harriford, Assistant to the Athletic
Director
(502) 597-6011
kim.harriford@kysu.edu
• Anthony Passarette, Head Athletic Trainer
(502) 597-5558
anthony.passarette@kysu.edu

**KENTUCKY WESLEYAN COLLEGE
ATHLETICS**
3000 FREDERICA STREET
OWENSBORO, KY 42301
270-852-3330
Fax: 270-852-3356
rmallory@kwc.edu
www.kwcpanthers.com
• Rob Mallory, Director of Athletics
(270) 852-3331
rmallory@kwc.edu
• Tom DeVinney, Assistant Athletic Director
(270) 852-3349
tdevinney@kwc.edu
• Roy Pickerill, Sports Information Director
(270) 852-3347
pickerill@kwc.edu
• Martin Daniel, Director of Athletic Training
(270) 852-3333
billhu@kwc.edu

KING UNIVERSITY ATHLETICS
1350 KING COLLEGE ROAD
BRISTOL, TN 37620
423-652-4779
jdhicks@king.edu
kingtornado.com
• David Hicks, Athletic Director
(423) 652-4779

jdhicks@king.edu
• Sheila Crockett, Head Athletic Trainer
(423) 652-4762
sccrocke@king.edu
• George Pitts, Head Coach
(423) 652-4781
gspitts@king.edu
• Nancye Rahn, Assistant Athletic Director
(423) 652-6469
nrahn@king.edu

KUTZTOWN UNIVERSITY ATHLETICS
15200 KUTZTOWN ROAD
KUTZTOWN, PA 19530
610-683-4094
Fax: 610-683-1379
www.kubears.com
• Greg Bamberger, Director of Athletics
(610) 683-4094
gbamberg@kutztown.edu
• Michelle Gober, Associate Director of
Athletics
(610) 683-4096
gober@kutztown.edu
• Alta Hart, Assistant to the Director of
Athletics
(610) 683-4681
• Jason Lanter, Faculty Athletics
Representative
(610) 683-4458
lanter@kutztown.edu
• Bryan Salvadore, Sports Information
Director
(610) 683-4182
salvadore@kutztown.edu
• Rennie Sacco, Director of Sports Medicine
(610) 683-4085
sacco@kutztown.edu

LAKE SUPERIOR STATE UNIVERSITY
ATHLETICS
650 WEST EASTERDAY AVENUE
NORRIS CENTER
SAULT STE. MARIE, MI 49783
906-632-6841
Fax: 906-635-2753
foundation@lssu.edu
www.lssu.edu
• Kris Dunbar, Athletic Director
(906) 635-2625
kdunbar@lssu.edu
• Eddie Bishop, Sports Information Director
(906) 635-2807
ebishop@lssu.edu
• Jennifer Constantino, NCAA Compliance
Officer
(906) 635-2809
jconstantino@lssu.edu

LANDER UNIVERSITY ATHLETICS
320 STANLEY AVENUE
GREENWOOD, SC 29649
864-388-8000
Fax: 864-388-8898
www.landerbearcats.com
• Jeff May, Director of Athletics
(864) 388-8314
jmay@lander.edu
• Kent Atkins, Sports Medicine Director
(864) 388-8818
katkins@lander.edu
• Sophia Bonadies, Athletic Trainer
(864) 388-8281
sbonadies@lander.edu
• Bob Stoner, Assistant Athletic Director,
Media

(864) 388-8962
bstoner@lander.edu

LE MOYNE COLLEGE ATHLETICS
1419 SALT SPRINGS ROAD
SYRACUSE, NY 13214
315-445-4450
Fax: 315-445-4678
www.lemoynedolphins.com
• Matthew Bassett, Director of Athletics
(315) 445-4450
bassetmd@lemoyne.edu
• Steve Evans, Associate Athletics Director
(315) 445-4416
evanssw@lemoyne.edu
• Scott Peterson, Head Athletic Trainer
(315) 445-4686
peterssm@lemoyne.edu

LE MOYNE-OWEN COLLEGE ATHLETICS
(LOC)
807 WALKER AVENUE
MEMPHIS, TN 38126
901-435-1235
Fax: 901-435-1244
athletics.loc.edu
• Clint Jackson, Athletic Director
(901) 435-1238
clint_jackson@loc.edu
• Angela Littlejohn, Sports Information
Director
(901) 435-1226
• Kristal Coleman, Athletic Business
Coordinator
(901) 435-1235
kristal_coleman1@loc.edu

LEE UNIVERSITY ATHLETICS
1120 NORTH OCOEE STREET
PO BOX 3450
CLEVELAND, TN 37320-3450
423-614-8440
www.goleeflames.com
• Larry Carpenter, Athletic Director
(423) 614-8440
lcarpenter@leeuniversity.edu
• Andrea Hudson, Assistant Athletic Director
(423) 614-8453
ahudson@leeuniversity.edu
• Jessica McIntyre, Director of Internal
Affairs
(423) 473-1191
jmcintyre@leeuniversity.edu
• Andrea Hudson, Volleyball Head Coach
(423) 614-8453
ahudson@leeuniversity.edu
• George Star, Sports Information Director
(423) 614-8442
gstarr@leeuniversity.edu

LEES-MCRAE COLLEGE ATHLETICS
191 MAIN STREET
PO BOX 128
BANNER ELK, NC 28604
828-898-5241
800-280-4562
Fax: 828-898-8742
lmcbobcats.com
• Craig McPhail, Vice President of Athletics
(828) 898-2483
mcphail@lmc.edu
• Chris Parker, Director of Sports
Information
(828) 898-8725
parkerc@lmc.edu
• Jeff Merrill, Director of Compliance
(828) 898-8793

merrillj@lmc.edu
• Rita Smith, Director of Athletic Training
(828) 898-8768
smithr@lmc.edu
• Zsachlayne Roguska, Head Athletc Trainer
(828) 898-8868
roguskaz@lmc.edu

LENOIR-RHYNE UNIVERSITY ATHLETICS
625 7TH AVENUE NE
PO BOX 7356
HICKORY, NC 28603
828-328-7116
Fax: 828-267-3445
www.lrbears.com
• Kim Pate, Executive Director of
Intercollegiate Athletics
(828) 328-7128
kim.pate@lr.edu
• Shena Hollar, Associate Athletics
Director/SWA
(828) 328-7114
hollars@lr.edu
• John Karrs, Sports Information Director
(828) 328-7174
karrsjd@lr.edu
• Michael McGee, Athletic Training Program
Director
(828) 328-7127
mcgee@lr.edu
• Michael Flicker, Director of Athletic
Training
(828) 328-7054

LEWIS UNIVERSITY ATHLETICS
ONE UNIVERSITY PARKWAY
ROMEOVILLE, IL 60446-2200
815-838-0500
800-897-9000
Fax: 815-836-5002
www.lewisu.edu
• Jill Siegfried, Director of Student
Recreation
(815) 836-5277
siegfrji@lewisu.edu
• Adam Burkhart, Assistant Director of
Student Recreation
(815) 836-5835
burkhaad@lewisu.edu

LIFE PACIFIC COLLEGE ATHLETICS
1100 WEST COVINA BOULEVARD
SAN DIMAS, CA 91773
909-599-5433
877-886-5433
Fax: 909-706-3070
athletics@lifepacific.edu
www.lpcwarriors.org
• Tim Cook, Athletics Director
(909) 599-5433
tcook@lifepacific.edu
• Micah Mulock, Sports Information Director
(909) 599-5433
mmulock15@lifepacific.edu
• Dana Haines, Head Athletic Trainer
(909) 599-5433
dhaines@lifepacific.edu

LIMESTONE COLLEGE ATHLETICS
1115 COLLEGE DRIVE
GAFFNEY, SC 29340
864-488-8370
Fax: 864-488-8249
www.limestone.edu
• Michael H. Cerino, Vice President for
Intercollegiate Athletics
(864) 488-4564

mcerino@limestone.edu
• Amber Anthony, Assistant Athletic Director
(864) 488-8289
aanthony@limestone.edu
• Curt Lamb, Assistant Athletic Director
(864) 488-8354
clamb@limestone.edu
• Adam Ranns, Head Athletic Trainer
(864) 488-8361
aranns@limestone.edu

LINCOLN MEMORIAL UNIVERSITY ATHLETICS
6965 CUMBERLAND GAP PARKWAY
HARROGATE, TN 37752
423-869-6285
800-325-0900
Fax: 423-869-6382
www.lmurailsplitters.com
• Matt Green, Athletic Director
(423) 869-6241
matthew.green@lmunet.edu
• Mike Smith, Associate Athletic Director
(423) 869-6239
mike.smith@lmunet.edu
• Cameron Whicker, Assistant Athletic Director
(423) 869-6346
cameron.whicker@lmunet.edu
• Bill Porter, Director of Athletic Statistics
(423) 869-6376
bill.porter@lmunet.edu
• Scott Erland, Director of Athletic Communications
(423) 869-6236
scott.erland@lmunet.edu

LINCOLN UNIVERSITY (MISSOURI) ATHLETICS
820 CHESTNUT STREET
JEFFERSON CITY, MO 65101
573-681-5342
Fax: 573-681-5998
athletics@lincolnu.edu
www.lubluetigers.com
• John Moseley, Interim Director of Athletics
(573) 681-5333
moseleyj@lincolnu.edu
• Betty Kemna, Assistant Athletic Director
(573) 681-5953
kemnab@lincolnu.edu
• Dan Carr, Assistant Athletic Director, Media
(573) 681-5343
carrd@lincolnu.edu
• Austin Matlock, Head Athletic Trainer
(573) 681-5331
matlocka@lincolnu.edu

LINCOLN UNIVERSITY ATHLETICS
1570 BALTIMORE PIKES
PO BOX 179
LINCOLN UNIVERSITY, PA 19532-0999
484-365-7391
Fax: 484-365-8120
www.lulions.com
• Anthony Pla, Interim Director of Athletics\Facilities Director
(484) 365-7391
apla@lincoln.edu
• Kisha Middleton, Athletic Business Manager
(484) 365-7632
kmiddleton@lincoln.edu
• Dana Flint, Faculty Athletics Representative
(484) 365-7299

flint@lincoln.edu
• Chris Vigneault, Director of Sports Medicine
(484) 365-7343
cvigneault@lincoln.edu

LINDENWOOD UNIVERSITY ATHLETICS
209 SOUTH KINGSHIGHWAY
ST. CHARLES, MO 63301
636-949-4600
Fax: 636-949-4636
www.lindenwoodlions.com
• Brad Wachler, Vice President For Intercollegiate Athletics
(636) 949-4777
bwachler@lindenwood.edu
• Tom Wagganer, Associate Athletics Director
(636) 949-4533
twagganer@lindenwood.edu
• Anna Girdwood, Director of Compliance
(636) 949-4654
agirdwood@lindenwood.edu
• Carl Hutter, Assistant Athletics Director
(636) 949-4813
chutter@lindenwood.edu
• Kathy Kinkeade, Athletics Business Manager
(636) 949-4339
kkinkeade@lindenwood.edu
• Randy Biggerstaff, Director of Athletic Training
(636) 949-4683
rbiggerstaff@lindenwood.edu

LIVINGSTONE COLLEGE ATHLETICS
701 WEST MONROE STREET
SALISBURY, NC 28144
704-216-6012
Fax: 704-216-6278
bluebearathletics.com
• Jimmy R. Jenkins, Sr., President
(704) 216-6098
jjenkins@livingstone.edu
• Andre Springs, Director of Athletics
(704) 216-6012
asprings@livingstone.edu
• Charles Pinckney, Faculty Athletic Representative
(704) 216-6053
cpinckney@livingstone.edu
• Jaime Kent, Head Certified Athletic Trainer
(704) 216-6011
jkent@livingstone.edu

LOCK HAVEN UNIVERSITY ATHLETICS (LHU)
THOMAS FIELDHOUSE
401 NORTH FAIRVIEW STREET
LOCK HAVEN, PA 17745
570-484-2102
Fax: 570-484-2414
www.golhu.com
• Tom Gioglio, Director of Athletics
(570) 484-2102
tmg252@lhup.edu
• Danielle Barney, Associate Director of Athletics
(570) 484-2871
dbarney@lhup.edu
• Cheryl Gardner, Athletic Department Secretary
(570) 484-2102
cgardne1@lhup.edu
• Doug Spatafore, Director of Sports Information

(570) 484-2350
dspatafo@lhup.edu

LONG ISLAND UNIVERSITY, C.W. POST ATHLETICS
C.W. POST CAMPUS
720 NORTHERN BOULEVARD
BROOKVILLE, NY 11548
516-299-2000
Fax: 516-299-3829
www.liuathletics.com
• Brad Cohen, Director of Athletics
(718) 488-1030
brad.cohen@liu.edu
• Margaret Alaimo, Deputy Director of Athletics
(718) 488-1524
margaret.alaimo@liu.edu
• Casey Snedecor, Director of Media Relations
(718) 488-1420
catherine.snedecor@liu.edu

LYNN UNIVERSITY ATHLETICS
3601 NORTH MILITARY TRAIL
BOCA RATON, FL 33431
561-237-7279
800-888-5966
Fax: 561-237-7268
www.lynnfightingknights.com
• Devin Crosby, Director of Athletics
(561) 237-7213
dcrosby@lynn.edu
• Sara Quatrocky, Associate Athletics Director
(561) 237-7765
squatrocky@lynn.edu
• Jon Lobbe, Assistant Athletics Director
(561) 237-4403
jlobbe@lynn.edu
• Chad Beattie, Director of Athletic Communications
(561) 237-7341
cbeattie@lynn.edu
• Sarah Holton, Head Athletic Trainer
(561) 537-7058
sholton@lynn.edu

MANSFIELD UNIVERSITY ATHLETICS
DECKER GYMNASIUM
70 SOUTH STADIUM DRIVE
MANSFIELD, PA 16933
570-662-4860
Fax: 570-662-4116
www.gomounties.com
• Ryan Ehrie, Director of Athletics
(570) 662-4636
rehrie@mansfield.edu
• Diane Monkiewicz, Interim Assistant Director of Athletics
(570) 662-4632
dmonkiew@mansfield.edu
• Laurie Zaparzynski, Head Athletic Trainer
(570) 662-4467
lzaparzy@mansfield.edu

MARS HILL UNIVERSITY ATHLETICS
100 ATHLETIC STREET
MARS HILL, NC 28754
828-689-1373
866-642-4968
Fax: 828-689-1440
www.marshilllions.com
• David Riggins, Athletic Director
(828) 689-1215
driggins@mhu.edu
• Rick Baker, Sports Information Director

college sports

(828) 689-1373
rbaker@mhu.edu
• Chelsea Lawing, Assistant Athletic Trainer
(828) 689-1108
clawing@mhu.edu
• Allen Shelley, Head Athletic Trainer
(828) 689-1176
ashelley@mhu.edu

MARYVILLE UNIVERSITY ATHLETICS
650 MARYVILLE UNIVERSITY DRIVE
ST. LOUIS, MO 63141
314-529-9300
www.maryvillesaints.com
• Marcus Manning, Director of Athletics
(314) 529-9288
mmanning@maryville.edu
• Austin DeBoer, Assistant Athletic Director
(314) 529-6886
adeboer@maryville.edu
• Alden Craddock, Faculty Athletics
Representative
(314) 529-6687
acraddock@maryville.edu
• Scott Harley, Head Athletic Trainer
(314) 529-9314
sharley@maryville.edu
• Chuck Yahng, Director for
Communications
(314) 529-9312
cyahng@maryville.edu

UMASS-LOWELL ATHLETICS
1 UNIVERSITY AVENUE
LOWELL, MA 01854
978-934-2310
athletics@uml.edu
goriverhawks.com
• Dana Skinner, Director of Athletics
(978) 934-2301
Dana_Skinner@uml.edu
• Peter Casey, Deputy Director of Athletics
(978) 934-2310
peter_casey@uml.edu
• Artie Poitras, Head Certified Athletic
Trainer
(978) 934-2321
j_poitras@uml.edu

MCKENDREE UNIVERSITY ATHLETICS
701 COLLEGE ROAD
LEBANON, IL 62254
618-537-6513
Fax: 618-537-8316
mckbearcats.com
• Chuck Brueggemann, Athletic Director
cebrueggemann@mckendree.edu
• Brad Oster, Athletics Equipment Manager
(618) 537-6918
bjoster@mckendree.edu
• Lance Ringhausen, Head Athletic Trainer
(618) 537-6929
llringhausen@mckendree.edu
• Danny Jackson, Head Baseball Coach
(618) 537-6906
dbjackson@mckendree.edu

MERCY COLLEGE ATHLETICS
555 BROADWAY
DOBBS FERRY, NY 10522
914-674-7220
Fax: 914-674-7561
athletics@mercy.edu
www.mercyathletics.com
• Matt Kilcullen, Jr., Director of Athletics
(914) 674-3065
mkilcullen@mercy.edu

• Bill Sullivan, Senior Associate Director of
Athletics
(914) 674-7566
wsullivan@mercy.edu
• Jordan Levine, Associate Director of
Athletics
(914) 674-7343
jlevine@mercy.edu
• Danielle Minerva, Head Athletic Trainer
(914) 674-7281
dminerva@mercy.edu

MERCYHURST UNIVERSITY ATHLETICS
501 EAST 38TH STREET
ERIE, PA 16546
814-824-2228
Fax: 814-824-2591
hurstathletics.com
• Joe Kimball, Director of Athletics
(814) 824-2559
jkimball@mercyhurst.edu
• Lauren Packer, Associate Director of
Athletics
(814) 824-3101
lwebster@mercyhurst.edu
• Stacey Gaudette, Assistant Athletic
Director
(814) 824-2079
sgaudette@mercyhurst.edu
• Josh Reilly, Director of Athletic
Communications
(814) 824-2525
jreilly@mercyhurst.edu
• Andy Simon-Wambach, Head Athletic
Trainer
(814) 824-2259
asimonwambach@mercyhurst.edu

MERRIMACK COLLEGE ATHLETICS
315 TURNPIKE STREET
NORTH ANDOVER, MA 01845
978-837-5341
Fax: 978-837-5032
www.merrimackathletics.com
• Jeremy Gibson, Director of Athletics
(978) 837-3555
gibsonj@merrimack.edu
• Brad Davis, Associate Athletic Director
(978) 837-5364
davisb@merrimack.edu
• Birgid Hopkins, Director of Sports
Medicine
(978) 837-5332
hopkinsb@merrimack.edu
• Chris Aliano, Director of Athletic
Communications
(978) 837-3472
alianoc@merrimack.edu

MESA STATE COLLEGE ATHLETICS
1100 NORTH AVENUE
GRAND JUNCTION, CO 81501
970-248-1503
Fax: 970-248-1980
cmumavericks.com
• Tom Spicer, Director of Athletics
(970) 248-1669
tspicer@coloradomesa.edu
• Kristin Mort, Senior Assciate Director Of
Athletics For Finance
(970) 248-1714
kmort@coloradomesa.edu
• Bryan Rooks, Associate Athletic Director
(970) 248-1252
brooks@coloradomesa.edu
• Ian Marks, Sports Information Director

(970) 248-1143
imarks@coloradomesa.edu

METROPOLITAN STATE UNIVERSITY OF DENVER ATHLETICS
CAMPUS BOX 9
PO BOX 173362
DENVER, CO 80217-3362
303-556-2158
Fax: 303-556-2720
roadrunnersathletics.com
• Anthony Grant, Director of Athletics
• Shawn Worthy, Faculty Athletics
Representative
(303) 556-2158
worthys@msudenver.edu
• Jim Gillen, Associate Athletic Director
(303) 556-4062
jgillen7@msudenver.edu
• Stephanie Begley, Head Athletic Trainer
(303) 556-3871
sbegley@msudenver.edu

MICHIGAN TECHNOLOGICAL UNIVERSITY ATHLETICS
1400 TOWNSEND DRIVE
HOUGHTON, MI 49931
906-487-3070
Fax: 906-487-3062
srsanreg@mtu.edu
www.michigantechhuskies.com
• Suzanne Sanregret, Athletic Director
(906) 487-3070
srsanreg@mtu.edu
• Joel Isaacson, Associate Athletic Director
(906) 487-1915
jdisaacs@mtu.edu
• Dave Nordstrom, Associate Athletic
Director, Operations
(906) 487-2578
dpnordst@mtu.edu

MIDWESTERN STATE UNIVERSITY ATHLETICS
DEPARTMENT OF ATHLETICS
MIDWESTERN STATE UNIVERSITY
3410 TAFT BOULEVARD
WICHITA FALLS, TX 76308
904-397-4044
888-MSU-9977
Fax: 940-397-4892
msumustangs.com
• Suzanna Shipley, President
(940) 397-4211
suzanne.shipley@mwsu.edu
• Charlie Carr, Athletic Director
charlie.carr@mwsu.edu
• Kurt Portman, Executive Associate Athletic
Director
• Blake Barington, Sports Information
Director

MILES COLLEGE ATHLETICS
5500 MYRON MASSEY BOULEVARD
FAIRFIELD, AL 35064
205-929-1615
Fax: 205-929-1616
www.miles.edu
• Phillip Wallace, Jr., Athletic Director
(205) 929-1063
pwallace@miles.edu
• Deleon Fancher, Jr., Faculty Athletic Rep.
(205) 929-1816
dfancher@miles.edu
• Deborah Jones, Assistant Athletic Director
(205) 929-1109

MILLERSVILLE UNIVERSITY ATHLETICS
ONE SOUTH GEORGE STREET
PO BOX 1002
MILLERSVILLE, PA 17551
717-872-3011
Fax: 717-871-2125
mgallagher@millersville.edu
www.millersvilleathletics.com
• Miles Gallagher, Director of Athletics
(718) 871-7694
mgallagher@millersville.edu
• Peg Kauffman, Associate Director of
Athletics
(717) 871-7693
pkauffman@millersville.edu
• Ethan Hulsey, Director of Athletic
Communications
(717) 871-4154
ehulsey@millersville.edu
• Donna Eshleman, Athletic Operations
(717) 871-4230
deshleman@millersville.edu

**MINNESOTA STATE UNIVERSITY -
MOORHEAD ATHLETICS**
1104 7TH AVENUE SOUTH
MOORHEAD, MN 56563
218-477-2622
Fax: 218-477-2324
president@mnstate.edu
www.msumdragons.com
• Anne Blackhurst, President
(218) 477-2243
president@mnstate.edu
• Doug Peters, Director of Athletics
(218) 477-2306
petersd@mnstate.edu
• Chad Markuson, Deputy Athletic Director
(218) 477-2401
chad.markuson@mnstate.edu
• Andrea Scott, Head Athletic Trainer
(218) 477-2626
scotta@mnstate.edu

**MINNESOTA STATE UNVERSITY -
MANKATO ATHLETICS**
135 MYERS FIELD HOUSE
MANKATO, MN 56001
507-389-6111
Fax: 507-389-2904
www.msumavericks.com
• Kevin Buisman, Director of Athletics
(507) 389-6111
kevin.buisman@mnsu.edu
• Paul Allan, Associate Athletic Director
(507) 389-2625
paul.allan@mnsu.edu
• Jeffrey Chambers, Assistant Athletic
Director
(507) 389-3229
jeffrey.chambers@mnsu.edu
• Jeffrey Pribyl, Faculty Athletic
Representative
(507) 389-6024
jeffrey.pribyl@mnsu.edu

**MINNESOTA-CROOKSTON ATHLETICS,
UNIVERSITY OF**
139 SPORTS CENTER
2900 UNIVERSITY AVE
CROOKSTON, MN 56716
218-281-8506
Fax: 218-281-8430
helgeson@umn.edu
www.goldeneaglesports.com
• Stephanie Helgeson, Director of Athletics
(218) 281-8422

helgeson@umn.edu
• Jason Tangquist, Assistant Athletic
Director
(218) 281-8424
jtangqui@umn.edu
• Shawn Smith, Sports Information Director
(218) 281-8414
smithsd@umn.edu
• Don Stopa, Assistant Sports Information
Director
(218) 281-8435
djstopa@umn.edu

**MINNESOTA-DULUTH ATHLETICS,
UNIVERSITY OF**
170 SPORTS & HEALTH CENTER
1216 ORDEAN COURT
DULUTH, MN 55812
218-726-8168
Fax: 218-726-6529
www.umdbulldogs.com
• Josh Berlo, Athletic Director
(218) 726-8718
jpberlon@d.umn.edu
• Karen Stromme, Associate Athletic
Director
(218) 726-7143
kstromme@d.umn.edu
• Bob Nygaard, Assistant Athletic Director
(218) 726-8191
bnygaard@d.umn.edu
• Bob Nygaard, Athletic Communications
(218) 726-8514
bnygaard@d.umn.edu

MINOT STATE UNIVERSITY ATHLETICS
500 UNIVERSITY AVENUE WEST
MINOT, ND 58701
701-858-3041
Fax: 701-858-3136
rick.hedberg@minotstateu.edu
www.msubeavers.com
• Andy Carter, Athletic Director
(701) 858-3042
andrew.carter@minotstateu.edu
• Wendy McManus, Associate Athletic
Director/SWA
(701) 858-4451
wendy.mcmanus@minotstateu.edu
• Michael Linnell, Assistant Athletic Director
(701) 858-3681
michael.linnell@minotstateu.edu
• Josh Sandy, Director of Athletic Marketing
& Promotions
(701) 858-4094
joshua.sandy@minotstateu.edu

MISSISSIPPI COLLEGE ATHLETICS
200 SOUTH CAPITOL STREET
CLINTON, MS 39056
601-925-3000
Fax: 601-925-7294
www.gochoctaws.com
• Mike Jones, Athletic Director
(601) 925-3819
jones01@mc.edu
• Susan Musselwhite, Assistant Athletic
Director
(601) 925-3362
musselwh@mc.edu
• Kyle Lewis, Sports Information Director
(601) 925-7890
klewis1@mc.edu

**MISSOURI SOUTHERN STATE
UNIVERSITY ATHLETICS**
3950 EAST NEWMAN ROAD
JOPLIN, MO 64801
417-625-3075
800-606-6772
Fax: 417-625-9601
info@mssu.edu
mssulions.com
• Jared Bruggeman, Director of Athletics
(417) 625-9317
• Rachel Burleson, Associate Athletics
Director
(417) 625-9712
burleson-r@mssu.edu
• Darin Moore, Head Athletic Trainer
(417) 625-9337
moore-da@mssu.edu
• Randon Coffey, Director of Marketing
(417) 625-3075
coffey-r@mssu.edu

**MISSOURI WESTERN STATE COLLEGE
ATHLETICS**
4525 DOWNS DRIVE
ST. JOSEPH, MO 64507
816-271-4481
Fax: 816-271-5901
gogriffons.com
• Kurt McGuffin, Director of Athletics
(816) 271-5623
kmcguffin@missouriwestern.edu
• Brett Esely, Associate Director of Athletics
(816) 271-5904
esely@missouriwestern.edu
• Mike Halloran, Director of Athletic Facilities
(816) 271-4556
mhalloran@missouriwestern.edu
• Nick McCutcheon, Director of Athletic
Media Relations
(816) 271-4257
nmccutcheon@missouriwestern.edu

**MISSOURI-ROLLA ATHLETICS,
UNIVERSITY OF**
705 WEST 10TH STREET
ROLLA, MO 65409
573-341-4175
Fax: 573-341-4880
minerathletics.com
• Mark Mullin, Director of Athletics
(573) 341-4175
memullin@mst.edu
• Ron Henderson, Assistant Director of
Athletics
(573) 341-4673
hendersonro@mst.edu
• Josh Lind, Assistant Athletics Compliance
Director
(573) 341-7598
lindja@mst.edu

MOLLOY COLLEGE ATHLETICS
1000 HEMPSTEAD AVENUE
ROCKVILLE CENTER, NY 11571
516-323-3608
Fax: 516-323-3622
www.molloylions.com
• Susan Cassidy-Lyke, Director of Athletics
(516) 323-3608
scassidy@molloy.edu
• Michael Grasso, Associate Director of
Athletics
(516) 323-3602
mgrasso@molloy.edu
• Kevin DesLauriers, Assistant Director of
Athletics, Operations

college sports

(516) 323-3603
kdleslauriers@molloy.edu
• Kelly Thompson, Director of Athletic Communications
(516) 323-3605
kthompson3@molloy.edu

MONTANA STATE UNIVERSITY BILLINGS ATHLETICS
1500 UNIVERSITY DRIVE
BILLINGS, MT 59101-0298
406-657-2369
Fax: 406-657-2919
sports@msubillings.edu
www.msubsports.com
• Krista L. Montague, Athletic Director
(406) 657-2061
kmontague@msubillings.edu
• Evan O'Kelly, Director of Communications
(406) 657-2130
evan.okelly@msubillings.edu
• Thomas Ebel, Head Athletic Trainer
(406) 657-2375
tebel@msubillings.edu

MONTEVALLO ATHLETICS, UNIVERSITY OF
75 COLLEGE DRIVE
MONTEVALLO, AL 35115
205-665-6600
Fax: 205-665-6587
www.montevallofalcons.com
• Mark Richard, Director of Athletics
(205) 665-6612
mrichard11@montevallo.edu
• Dawn Makofski, Assistant Athletic Director
(205) 665-6633
makofskidb@montevallo.edu
• Marcelo Takejame Galafassi, Head Athletic Trainer
(205) 665-6602
mgalafassi@montevallo.edu
• Wesley Hallman, Sports Information Director
(205) 665-6197
whallman@montevallo.edu

MOREHOUSE COLLEGE ATHLETICS
830 WESTVIEW DRIVE SW
ATLANTA, GA 30314
404-681-2800
Fax: 404-521-9073
athletics.morehouse.edu
• Andre Pattillo, Director of Athletics
(404) 215-2669
apattillo@morehouse.edu
• Yusuf Davis, Sports Information Director
(404) 222-2575
yusuf.davis@morehouse.edu
• Craig Boyd, Head Athletic Trainer
cboyd@morehouse.edu

MOUNT OLIVE COLLEGE ATHLETICS
586 HENDERSON STREET
MOUNT OLIVE, NC 28365
919-658-7759
Fax: 919-658-7180
www.umotrojans.com
• Jeff Eisen, Vice President of Athletics
(919) 658-7759
jeisen@umo.edu
• LaToya Greene, Associate Director of Athletics
(919) 658-4928
llindsey@umo.edu
• Kristen Gibson, Director of Sports Medicine

(919) 658-7810
kgibson@umo.edu
• Ryan Smith, Director of Athletics Communications
(919) 658-7802
rjsmith@umo.edu

NEBRASKA AT OMAHA ATHLETICS, UNIVERSITY OF
SAPP FIELDHOUSE
6001 DODGE STREET
OMAHA, NE 68182
Fax: 402-554-2555
• Trev Alberts, Vice Chancellor, Athletics
(402) 554-2305
trevalberts@unomaha.edu
• Ann Oatman, Senior Associate Athletic Director
(402) 554-3270
aoatman@unomaha.edu
• Connie Claussen, Athletic Director Emeritus
• Dave Ahlers, Assistant Athletic Director, Communications
(402) 554-3387
dahlers@unomaha.edu

NEBRASKA-KEARNEY ATHLETICS, UNIVERSITY OF
DEPT OF INTERCOLLEGIATE ATHLETICS
2501 15TH AVENUE
KEARNEY, NE 68849
308-865-8514
Fax: 308-865-8187
www.lopers.com
• Paul Plinske, Athletic Director
(308) 865-8514
plinksep@unk.edu
• Josh Jorgensen, Senior Associate Athletic Director
(308) 865-8069
jorgensenjm@unk.edu
• Peter Yazvac, Assistant Athletic Director, Media Relations
(308) 865-8334
yazvacpa@unk.edu

NEW HAVEN ATHLETICS, UNIVERSITY OF
CHARGER GYM
300 BOSTON POST ROAD
WEST HAVEN, CT 06516
203-932-7016
Fax: 203-932-7470
newhavenchargers@newhaven.edu
www.newhavenchargers.com
• Jim McCoy, Interim Director of Athletics
(203) 932-7020
jmccoy@newhaven.edu
• Robin Salters, Associate Director of Athletics, Facilities
(203) 932-7022
rsalters@newhaven.edu
• Janet Dinihanian, Athletics Administrative Specialist
(203) 932-7016
jdinihanian@newhaven.edu
• Dan Ruede, Director of Athletic Communications
(203) 932-7025
druede@newhaven.edu

NEW HOPE CHRISTIAN COLLEGE
2155 BAILEY HILL ROAD
EUGENE, OR 97405
541-485-1780
800-322-2638

Fax: 541-343-5801
www.godeacons.com
• Matt Binkerd, Athletic Director
mattbinkerd@newhope.edu

NEW MEXICO HIGHLANDS UNIVERSITY ATHLETICS
PO BOX 9000
LAS VEGAS, NM 87701
877-850-9064
Fax: 505-426-2014
nmhucowboys.com
• Bob Clifford, Athletic Director
bclifford@nmhu.edu
• Jim Deisler, Assistant Athletic Director
(505) 426-2017
jedeisler@nmhu.edu
• Cwynnci Lobaugh, Sports Information Director
(505) 454-3361
cwynnci@nmhu.edu
• Yvette Pomponi, Head Athletic Trainer
(505) 454-3355
ypomponi@nmhu.edu

NEW YORK INSTITUTE OF TECHNOLOGY ATHLETICS
PO BOX 8000
NORTHERN BOULEVARD
OLD WESTBURY, NY 11568-8000
516-686-1216
Fax: 516-686-1168
athletics@nyit.edu
www.nyitbears.com
• Dan Velez, Director of Intercollegiate Athletics
(516) 686-1216

NEWBERRY COLLEGE ATHLETICS
2100 COLLEGE STREET
NEWBERRY, SC 29108
803-321-5127
Fax: 803-321-5632
www.newberrywolves.com
• Ralph Patterson, Director of Athletics
(803) 947-2064
ralph.patterson@newberry.edu
• Mike Hold, Director of External Operations
(803) 321-5247
mike.hold@newberry.edu
• Randall Stewart, Director of Athletic Communications
(803) 321-5667
randall.stewart@newberry.edu
• John Lopez, Director of Sports Medicine
(803) 321-3327
john.lopez@newberry.edu

NORFOLK STATE UNIVERSITY ATHLETICS
700 PARK AVENUE
NORFOLK, VA 23504
757-823-8152
Fax: 757-823-2566
mlmiller@nsu.edu
www.nsuspartans.com
• Marty L. Miller, Athletics Director
(757) 823-8152
mlmiller@nsu.edu
• Carray Banks, Faculty Athletics Representative
(757) 823-2421
cbanks@nsu.edu
• Alisha Tucker, Director of Student Services
(757) 823-2337
amtucker@nsu.edu

• Matt Michalec, Director of Sports
Communications
(757) 823-2628
mmichalec@nsu.edu

**NORTH ALABAMA ATHLETICS,
UNIVERSITY OF**
UNA BOX 5071
FLORENCE, AL 35632
256-765-4397
Fax: 256-765-4685
www.roarlions.com
• Mark Linder, Director of Athletics
(256) 765-4397
mdlinder@una.edu
• Todd Vardaman, Assistant Athletic
Director of Compliance
(256) 765-4618
tdvardaman@una.edu
• Jeff Dodges, Director of Communications
(256) 765-4595
sportsinformation@una.edu
• Josh Penny, Head Athletic Trainer
(256) 765-4563
jdpenny@una.edu

**NORTH CAROLINA, PEMBROKE
ATHLETICS, UNIVERSITY OF**
ONE UNIVERSITY DRIVE
PO BOX 1510
PEMBROKE, NC 28372-1510
910-521-6227
Fax: 910-521-6540
athletics@uncp.edu
www.uncpbraves.com
• Andrea Branch, Executive Assistant
(910) 521-6227
andrea.branch@uncp.edu
• Dick Christy, Athletics Director
(910) 521-6227
dick.christy@uncp.edu
• Todd Anderson, Director of
Communications
(910) 521-6371
todd.anderson@uncp.edu
• Michael Blackburn, Director of Sports
Medicine
(910) 522-5727
michael.blackburn@uncp.edu

**NORTH DAKOTA ATHLETICS,
UNIVERSITY OF**
UND ATHLETICS
HYSLOP SPORTS CENTER ROOM 120
2751 2ND AVENUE NORTH
GRAND FORKS, ND 58202
701-777-2234
Fax: 701-777-2285
www.undsports.com
• Brian Faison, Athletics Director
brian.faison@athletics.und.edu
• Daniella Irle, Deputy Director of Athletics
daniella.irle@athletics.und.edu
• Steve Brekke, Associate Athletic Director,
Development
steveb@undfoundation.org
• Jayson Hajdu, Director of Media Relations
jayson.hajdu@athletics.und.edu
• Amanda Hajdu, Director of Academic
Services
amanda.hajdu@athletics.und.edu

**NORTH DAKOTA STATE UNIVERSITY
ATHLETICS**
1340 ADMINISTRATION AVENUE
FARGO, ND 58102

701-231-8981
Fax: 701-231-6246
www.gobison.com
• Matt Larsen, Director of Athletics
(701) 231-8985
matthew.larsen@ndsu.edu
• Todd Phelps, Deputy Director of Athletics
(701) 231-7807
todd.phelps@ndsu.edu
• Ryan Perreault, Director of Athletic
Communications
(701) 231-8331
ryan.perreault@ndsu.edu

**NORTH GEORGIA COLLEGE & STATE
UNIVERSITY ATHLETICS**
130 GEORGIA CIRCLE
DAHLONEGA, GA 30597
706-864-1758
Fax: 706-897-2850
ungathletics.com
• Lindsay Reeves, Director of Athletics
(706) 867-3212
lindsay.reeves@ung.edu
• Derek Suraine, Associate Director of
Athletics
(706) 867-2770
derek.suranie@ung.edu
• Lee Glenn, Assistant Director of Athletics
(706) 867-3250
lee.glenn@ung.edu
• Matt Daniel, Head Athletic Trainer
(706) 864-1669
matt.daniel@ung.edu

**NORTHERN COLORADO ATHLETICS,
UNIVERSITY OF**
270D BUTLER COLORADO ATHLETICS
GREELEY, CO 80639
970-351-1890
Fax: 970-351-2018
events@unco.edu
uncbears.com
• Darren Dunn, Director of Athletics
(970) 351-2362
• Kobee Stalder, Director of Athletic
Communications
(970) 351-1065
kobee.stalder@unco.edu
• Bob Heiny, Faculty Athletics
Representative
(970) 351-2049
robert.heiny@unco.edu

**NORTHERN MICHIGAN UNIVERSITY
ATHLETICS**
1401 PRESQUE ISLE AVENUE
MARQUETTE, MI 49855
906-227-2105
Fax: 906-227-2492
www.nmuwildcats.com
• Forrest Karr, Director of Athletics
(906) 227-1826
fkarr@nmu.edu
• Carl Bammert, Assistant Athletic Director
(906) 227-2465
cbammert@nmu.edu
• Alex Tieso, Director of Compliance
(906) 227-1780
altiseo@nmu.edu

**NORTHERN STATE UNIVERSITY
ATHLETICS**
1200 SOUTH JAY STREET
ABERDEEN, SD 57401
605-626-7748
Fax: 605-626-2238

ashley.n.gabler@northern.edu
nsuwolves.com
• Josh Moon, Director of Athletics
(605) 626-3336
joshua.moon@northern.edu
• Zach Flakus, Deputy Director of Athletics
(605) 626-7741
flakusz@northern.edu
• Terri Holmes, Assistant Director of
Athletics
(605) 626-2578
terri.holmes@northern.edu
• Ashley Gauer, Director of Athletic
Communications
(605) 626-7748
ashley.gauer@northern.edu
• Sara Christensen Blair, Faculty Athletic
Representative
(605) 626-2515
sara.blair@northern.edu

**NORTHWEST MISSOURI STATE
UNIVERSITY ATHLETICS**
800 UNIVERSITY DRIVE
MARYVILLE, MO 64468
660-562-1212
Fax: 660-562-1493
coacht@nwmissouri.edu
www.bearcatsports.com
• Mel Tjeerdsma, Director of Athletics
(660) 562-1306
coacht@nwmissouri.edu
• Lori Hopkins, Associate Athletic Director
(660) 562-1142
lorih@nwmissouri.edu
• Mark Clements, Director for Internal
Operations
(660) 532-1308
mclem@nwmissouri.edu
• Kelly Quinlin, Head Athletic Trainer
(660) 562-1313
kellyq@nwmissouri.edu

**NORTHWOOD UNIVERSITY (MI)
ATHLETICS**
4000 WHITING DRIVE
MIDLAND, MI 48640
989-837-5244
800-622-9000
Fax: 989-837-4484
career@northwood.edu
www.northwood.edu
• Dave Marsh, Athletic Director
(989) 837-4389
dmarsh@northwood.edu
• Krista Plummer, Assistant Athletic Director
(989) 837-4817
plummek@northwood.edu
• Kate Dornbos, Head Athletic Trainer
(989) 837-4387
dornbosk@northwood.edu
• Travis McCurdy, Sports Information
Director
(989) 837-4239
mccurdyt@northwood.edu

NOTRE DAME COLLEGE ATHLETICS
4545 COLLEGE ROAD
SOUTH EUCLID, OH 44121
216-373-5138
877-632-6446
Fax: 216-373-5400
www.notredamefalcons.com
• Scott Swain, Director of Athletics
(216) 373-6365
sswain@ndc.edu
• John Van Benschoten, Assistant Athletic

Director
(216) 373-6362
jvanben@ndc.edu
• Isaac Hunt, Manager of Sports Information
(216) 373-6342
ihunt@ndc.edu
• Matt Murphy, Manager of Athletic
Operations
(216) 373-5171
mmurphy@ndc.edu
• Jay Garfield, Head Athletic Trainer
(216) 373-5354
jgarfield@ndc.edu

NOTRE DAME DE NAMUR UNIVERSITY ATHLETICS
1500 RALSTON AVENUE
BELMONT, CA 94002
650-508-3500
Fax: 650-508-3691
www.ndnuargos.com
• Joshua Doody, Director of Athletics
(650) 508-3638
jdoody@ndnu.edu
• George Puou, Assistant Athletics Director
(650) 508-3655
gpuou@ndnu.edu
• Scott Kimmelman, Sports Information
Director
(650) 508-3690
skimmelman@ndnu.edu
• Christian Stamates, Athletic Trainer
(650) 508-3448
cstamates@ndnu.edu

NYACK COLLEGE ATHLETICS
1 SOUTH BOULEVARD
NYACK, NY 10960
845-675-4776 EXT 181
Fax: 845-353-2147
athletics.nyack.edu
• Keith Davie, Athletic Director
(845) 675-4770
keith.davie@nyack.edu
• Amanda Aikens, Assistant Athletic Director
(845) 675-4772
mandy.aikens@nyack.edu
• Matt Cornacchione, Director of Athletic
Facilities
(845) 675-4787
matthew.cornacchione@nyack.edu
• Penny Foland, Head Athletic Trainer
(845) 675-4780
penny.foland@nyack.edu

OAKLAND UNIVERSITY ATHLETICS
ATHLETICS DEPARTMENT
201 ATHLETICS CENTER
ROCHESTER, MI 48309
248-370-3190
Fax: 248-370-4056
www.goldengrizzlies.com
• George W. Hynd, President
(248) 370-3500
hynd@oakland.edu
• Jeff Konya, Director of Athletics
(248) 370-2669
konya@oakland.edu
• Marshall Foley, Associate Athletic Director
(248) 370-4004
mfoley@oakland.edu
• Evan Dermidoff, Athletics Academic
Adviser
(248) 370-3224
dermido2@oakland.edu

OKLAHOMA BAPTIST UNIVERSITY ATHLETICS
500 WEST UNIVERSITY
SHAWNEE, OK 74804
405-275-2850
www.obubison.com
• Robert Davenport, Director of Athletics
(405) 585-5300
robert.davenport@okbu.edu
• Steve Fluke, Associate Athletics Director
for Compliance
(405) 585-5305
robert.davenport@okbu.edu
• Anna Howle, Assistant Athletics Director
(405) 585-5355
anna.howle@okbu.edu
• Ray Fink, Director of Athletic Media
Relations
(405) 585-5304
ray.fink@okbu.edu

OKLAHOMA CHRISTIAN UNVERSITY ATHLETICS
2501 EAST MEMORIAL ROAD
EDMOND, OK 73013
405-425-5350
800-877-5010
Fax: 405-425-5351
athletics@oc.edu
www.oceagles.com
• David Lynn, Director of Athletics
(405) 425-5358
david.lynn@oc.edu
• Curtis McAuliff, Director of Athletic
Training
(405) 425-1960
curtis.mcauliff@oc.edu
• Sydney Ringer, Head Athletic Trainer
(405) 425-1961
sydney.ringer@oc.edu

OUACHITA BAPTIST UNIVERSITY ATHLETICS
410 OUACHITA STREET
OBU BOX 378
ARKADELPHIA, AR 71998-0001
870-245-5181
Fax: 870-245-5598
www.obutigers.com
• David Sharp, Director of Athletics
(870) 245-5182
sharpd@obu.edu
• Margaret McGraw, Assistant Athletic
Director
(870) 245-5397
mcgrawma@obu.edu
• Kyle Parris, Sports Information Director
(870) 245-5186
parrisk@obu.edu
• Terry DeWitt, Coordinator of Athletic
Training
(870) 245-5264
dewitt@obu.edu

PACE UNIVERSITY ATHLETICS
ATHLETICS DEPARTMENT
861 BEDFORD ROAD
PLEASANTVILLE, NY 10570
914-773-3411
Fax: 914-773-3491
mbrown@pace.edu
www.paceathletics.com
• Mark R. Brown, Director of Athletics
(914) 773-3285
mbrownn@pace.edu
• Mike Winn, Associate Athletic Director
(914) 773-3272

mwinn@pace.edu
• David Spiegel, Director of Athletic
Communications
(914) 773-3888
dspiegel@pace.edu

PAINE COLLEGE
1235 FIFTEENTH STREET
AUGUSTA, GA 30901
706-821-8200
Fax: 706-396-8154
www.paineathletics.com
• Selina B. Kohn, Director of Athletics
(706) 821-8428
skohn@paine.edu
• J.C. Gafford, Sports Information Director
(706) 821-8438
jgafford@paine.edu
• Lisa Branon, Athletic Trianer
(706) 396-7567
lbranon@paine.edu

PALM BEACH ATLANTIC UNIVERSITY ATHLETICS
901 SOUTH FLAGLER DRIVE
WEST PALM BEACH, FL 33401
561-803-2333
Fax: 561-803-2532
pbasailfish.com
• Carolyn Stone, Director of Athletics
(561) 803-2333
carolyn_stone@pba.edu
• Michael Brown, Senior Associate Athletic
Director
(561) 803-2529
michael_brown@pba.edu
• Goeun Lee, Assistant Athletic Director for
Compliance
(561) 803-2399
goeun_lee@pba.edu
• Chi Ly, Student-Athlete Development
Coordinator
(561) 803-2520
chi_ly@pba.edu
• TJ Budd, Sports Information Director
(561) 803-2525
tj_budd@pba.edu
• Sam Eisen, Head Athletic Trainer
(561) 803-2338
sam_eisen@pba.edu

PANHANDLE STATE UNIVERSITY ATHLETICS
PO BOX 430
GOODWELL, OK 73939
580-349-2611
800-664-6778
Fax: 580-349-2302
www.opsuaggies.com
• Wayne Stewart, Athletic Director
(580) 349-1408
rwstewart@opsu.edu
• Justine Gaskamp, Sports Information
Director
(580) 349-1354
jgaskamp@opsu.edu
• Brian Lankford, Head Athletic Trainer
(580) 349-1338
brian@opsu.edu

PFEIFFER UNIVERSITY ATHLETICS
48380 US HIGHWAY 52
MISENHEIMER, NC 28109
704-521-9116
Fax: 704-463-5051
gofalconsports.com

• Bob Reasso, Vice President for Athletics
(704) 463-3203
bob.reasso@pfeiffer.edu
• Tony Faticoni, Deputy Director of Athletics
(704) 463-3214
tony.faticoni@pfeiffer.edu
• Jeremy Zalacca, Director for Athletic
Communications
(704) 463-3192
jeremy.zalacca@pfeiffer.edu
• Robyn Horner, Assistant Athletic Director
(704) 463-3227
robyn.horner@pfeiffer.edu

PHILADELPHIA UNIVERSITY ATHLETICS
4201 HENRY AVENUE
PHILADELPHIA, PA 19144
215-951-2720
Fax: 215-951-2775
www.philaurams.com
• Tom Shirley, Director of Athletics
(215) 951-2720
shirleyt@philau.edu
• Rose Kelly, Assistant Director of Athletics
(215) 951-5638
kellyr@philau.edu
• Chris O'Brien, Assistant Director of
Athletics
(215) 951-5943
obrienc@philau.edu

PITTSBURG STATE UNIVERSITY
ATHLETICS
1701 BROADWAY STREET
PITTSBURG, KS 66762
620-231-7000
Fax: 620-235-4661
www.pittstategorillas.com
• Jim Johnson, Athletic Director
(620) 235-4389
jjohnson@pittstate.edu
• Russ Jewett, Senior Associate Athletic
Director
(620) 235-4659
rjewett@pittstate.edu
• Phil Carr, Head Athletic Trainer
(620) 249-4401
pcarr@pittstate.edu
• Dan Wilkes, Associate Director Of
Communications
(620) 235-4138
dwilkes@pittstate.edu

PITTSBURGH-JOHNSTOWN ATHLETICS,
UNIVERSITY OF
450 SCHOOLHOUSE ROAD
JOHNSTOWN, PA 15904
814-269-7000
Fax: 814-269-2026
pittjohnstownathletics.com
• Pat Pecora, Athletic Director
(814) 269-2001
ppecora@pitt.edu
• Chris Caputo, Sports Information Director
(814) 269-2031
ccaputo@pitt.edu
• Elissa Till, Head Athletic Trainer
(814) 269-1935
till@pitt.edu

POINT LOMA NAZARENE UNIVERSITY
ATHLETICS
3900 LOMALAND DRIVE
SAN DIEGO, CA 92106
619-849-2265
Fax: 619-849-2553
www.plnusealions.com

• Ethan Hamilton, Athletic Director
(619) 849-2265
ethanhamilton@pointloma.edu
• Brian Thornton, Senior Associate Athletic
Director
(619) 849-2944
brianthornton@pointloma.edu
• Steven Riddle, Assistant Athletic Director
(619) 849-2268
steveriddle@pointloma.edu
• Shawna Baker, Head Athletic Trainer
(619) 849-2914
shawnabaker@pointloma.edu

PRESBYTERIAN COLLEGE ATHLETICS
PRESBYTERIAN COLLEGE ATHLETICS
105 ASHLAND AVENUE
CLINTON, SC 29325
864-833-8240
Fax: 864-833-8323
www.gobluehose.com
• Ed Steers, Interim Athletic Director
(864) 833-8242
• James Downer, Senior Associate Athletic
Director
(864) 833-8253
jmdowner@presby.edu
• Simon Whitaker, Director of Sports
Information
(864) 833-8252
swhitaker@presby.edu

QUEENS COLLEGE (NEW YORK)
ATHLETICS
65-30 KISSENA BOULEVARD
QUEENS, NY 11367
718-997-2795
Fax: 718-997-5745
athleticsinfo@qc.cuny.edu
www.queensknights.com
• China Jude, Assistant Vice President,
Athletics
(718) 997-2795
• Rob Twible, Associate Athletics Director,
Facilities
(718) 997-2754
robert.twible@qc.cuny.edu

QUEENS UNIVERSITY OF CHARLOTTE
1900 SELWYN AVENUE
CHARLOTTE, NC 28274
704-337-2509
800-849-8400
Fax: 704-337-2237
www.queensathletics.com
• Cherie Swarthout, Interim Director of
Athletics
(704) 688-2809
swarthoutc@queens.edu
• Robbie Garriett, Coordinator of
Administrative Services
(704) 337-2509
garriettr@queens.edu
• Tim Burke, Assistant Athletic Director
(704) 688-2818
burket@queens.edu

QUINCY UNIVERSITY ATHLETICS
1800 COLLEGE AVENUE
QUINCY, IL 62301
217-222-8020
Fax: 217-228-5034
quhawks.com
• Marty Bell, Vice President of
Intercollegiate Athletics
(217) 228-5432
bellma@quincy.edu

• Danielle Surprenant, Associate Athletic
Director
(217) 228-5432
• Mike Davis, Assistant Athletic Director
(217) 228-5432
davismi@quincy.edu
• Stephanie Killday, Athletic Trainer
(217) 228-5432
taylost@quincy.edu

REGIS UNIVERSITY ATHLETICS
3333 REGIS BOULEVARD
DENVER, CO 80221-1099
303-458-4070
800-388-2366
Fax: 303-964-5499
dspafford@regis.edu
www.regisrangers.com
• David Spafford, Interim Director of
Athletics
(303) 964-6648
dspafford@regis.edu
• Kelly McLaughlin, Associate Athletic
Director
(303) 458-4071
kmclaughlin001@regis.edu
• Whitney Lawler, Sports Information
Director
(303) 458-4052
wfranker@regis.edu

ROCKHURST UNIVERSITY ATHLETICS
1100 ROCKHURST ROAD
KANSAS CITY, MO 64110
816-501-4000
Fax: 816-501-4241
gary.burns@rockhurst.edu
www.rockhursthawks.com
• Gary Burns, Director of Athletics
(816) 501-4854
• Kathy Strecker, Assistant Director of
Athletics
(816) 501-4857
kathleen.strecker@rockhurst.edu
• John Dodderidge, Sports Information
Director
(816) 501-4850
john.dodderidge@rockhurst.edu
• Jaime Rojas, Head Athletic Trainer
(720) 778-6490
jaime.rojas@rockhurst.edu

ROLLINS COLLEGE ATHLETICS
1000 HOLT AVENUE
WINTER PARK, FL 32789
407-646-2000
Fax: 407-646-1562
pparker@rollins.edu
www.rollinssports.com
• Pennie Parker, Director of Athletics
(407) 646-2636
pparker@rollins.edu
• Margie Sullivan, Assistant Athletics
Director
(407) 646-2531
msullivan@rollins.edu
• Paul Giannotti, Director of Sports Medicine
(407) 646-2361
pgiannotti@rollins.edu
• Clay Starrett, Director for Athletic
Communications
(407) 646-2661
cstarrett@rollins.edu

SAGINAW VALLEY STATE UNIVERSITY ATHLETICS
7400 BAY ROAD
UNIVERSITY CENTER, MI 48710-0001
989-964-4000
Fax: 989-964-7389
sid@svsu.edu
www.svsucardinals.com
• Mike Watson, Athletic Director
(989) 964-7306
mewatson@svsu.edu
• Angela Pohl, Associate Athletic Director
(989) 964-7311
aspohl@svsu.edu
• Eric Brookhouse, Director of Athletic Media Relations
(989) 964-4053
embrookh@svsu.edu

SAINT ANSELM COLLEGE ATHLETICS
100 SAINT ANSELM DRIVE
PO BOX 1727
MANCHESTER, NH 03102
603-641-7800
Fax: 603-641-7172
athletics@anselm.edu
www.saintanselmhawks.com
• Daron Montgomery, Director of Athletics
(603) 641-7800
dmontgomery@anselm.edu
• Neil Duval, Associate Director of Athletics
(603) 641-7802
nduval@anselm.edu
• Chris Barroso, Director of Athletic Communications
(603) 641-7810
cbarroso@anselm.edu
• Michael Sirois, Head Athletic Trainer
(603) 641-7807
msirois@anselm.edu

SAINT JOSEPH'S COLLEGE ATHLETICS
PO BOX 870
RENSSELAER, IN 47978
219-866-6000
Fax: 219-866-6276
athletics.saintjoe.edu
• Bill Massoels, Athletic Director
billm@saintjoe.edu
• Linda Deno, Associate Director of Athletics
(219) 866-6275
lindad@saintjoe.edu
• Ken Badylak, Sports Information Director
(219) 866-6141
kbadylak@saintjoe.edu

SAINT LEO UNIVERSITY
33701 STATE ROAD 52
PO BOX 6665
SAINT LEO, FL 33574
800-334-5532
800-334-5532
Fax: 912-353-9937
fran.reidy@saintleo.edu
www.saintleolions.com
• William J. Lennox, University President
(352) 588-8242
• Francis X. Reidy, Director of Athletics
fran.reidy@saintleo.edu
• Michelle Edwards, Associate Athletic Director
(352) 588-7314
michelle.edwards05@saintleo.edu
• Barbara Wilson, Director of Sports Medicine
(352) 588-8222
barbara.wilson@saintleo.edu

SAINT MARTIN'S COLLEGE ATHLETICS
5300 PACIFIC AVENUE SE
LACEY, WA 98503
360-438-4305
Fax: 360-412-6191
bgrisham@stmartin.edu
www.smusaints.com
• Bob Grisham, Athletic Director
(360) 438-4368
bgrisham@stmartin.edu
• Chris Gregor, Associate Athletic Director
(360) 438-4510
cgregor@stmartin.edu
• Austin Byrnes, Sports Information Director
(360) 438-4328
aloebsack@stmartin.edu
• Ramzy Assaf, Assistant Athletic Trainer
(360) 438-4536
rassaf@stmartin.edu

SAINT ROSE ATHLETICS, COLLEGE OF
432 WESTERN AVENUE
ALBANY, NY 12203
518-454-5158
Fax: 518-458-5457
gogoldenknights.com
• Catherine Cummings Haker, Director of Athletics
(518) 454-5282
hakerc@strose.edu
• David Alexander, Director for Communications
(518) 458-5491
alexandd@strose.edu
• Lisa Geiger, Director for Athletic Training
(518) 454-2009
geigerl@strose.edu

SALEM INTERNATIONAL UNIVERSITY ATHLETICS
223 WEST MAIN STREET
SALEM, WV 26426
304-782-6143
800-283-4562
Fax: 304-782-5246
www.siutigerpride.com
• Florin Marton, Athletic Director
(304) 326-1540
fmarton@salemu.edu
• Steve Potts, Assistant Athletic Director
(304) 326-1394
spotts@salemu.edu
• Douglas Page, Sports Information Director
(304) 326-1299
douglas.page@salemu.edu
• Tera Fetty, Head Athletic Trainer
(304) 326-1561
tfetty@salemu.edu

SAN FRANCISCO STATE UNIVERSITY ATHLETICS
1600 HOLLOWAY AVENUE
SAN FRANCISCO, CA 94132
415-338-2218
Fax: 415-338-1967
charlesg@sfsu.edu
www.sfstategators.com
• Charles Guthrie, Director Of Athletics
(415) 338-1579
charles@sfsu.edu
• Joey Logan, Associate Athletic Director For Compliance
(415) 338-2485
jologan@sfsu.edu
• Cathy McDermott, Assistant Director of Athletics for Developme
(415) 338-1193

cathym@sfsu.edu
• Trevor Getz, Faculty Athletic Representative
(415) 338-2716
tgetz@sfsu.edu

SCIENCES IN PHILADELPHIA ATHLETICS, UNIVERSITY OF THE
600 SOUTH 43RD STREET
PHILADELPHIA, PA 19104-4495
215-895-3133
athletics@usciences.edu
www.devilsathletics.com
• Marc Caserio, Athletic Director
(215) 596-7432
m.caseri@usciences.edu
• Scott Sisson, Associate Athletic Director
(215) 895-1109
s.sisson@usciences.edu
• Nicole Shipos, Head Athletic Trainer
(215) 596-7430
n.shipos@usciences.edu

SHAW UNIVERSITY ATHLETICS
118 EAST SOUTH STREET
RALEIGH, NC 27601
919-546-8200
Fax: 919-546-8444
alcarter@shawu.edu
www.shawbears.com
• Alfonza Carter, Director of Athletics
(919) 546-8527
alcarter@shawu.edu
• Jacques Curtis, Associate Athletic Director
(919) 546-8597
jcurtis@shawu.edu
• Jolisa Williams, Sports Information Director
(919) 546-8311
jamesm@shawu.edu
• David Mills, Director of Sports Medicine
(919) 546-8582
dmills@shawu.edu

SHIPPENSBURG UNIVERSITY OF PENNSYLVANIA ATHLETICS
1871 OLD MAIN DRIVE
SHIPPENSBURG, PA 17257
717-477-1711
Fax: 717-477-4090
www.ship.edu
• Jeff Michaels, Director of Athletics
(717) 477-1711
• Carrie Michaels, Associate Director of Athletics
(717) 477-1711
camichaels@ship.edu
• Ashley Grimm, Assistant Director of Athletics
(717) 477-1711
ajgrimm@ship.edu
• Wes Mallicone, Director of Sports Medicine
(717) 477-1749
wrmall@ship.edu
• Bill Morgal, Sports Information Director
(717) 477-1206
wjmorgal@ship.edu

SHORTER UNIVERSITY ATHLETICS
315 SHORTER AVENUE
ROME, GA 30165
706-233-7347
Fax: 706-233-7575
goshorterhawks.com
• Aaron Kelton, Interim Athletic Director
(706) 233-7469

akelton@shorter.edu
• Amber Lee, Senior Woman Administrator
(706) 233-7348
alee@shorter.edu
• Karen Allen, Assistant Athletic Director
(706) 233-7966
kallen@shorter.edu
• Andre Roach, Associate Athletic Director
(706) 233-7468
aroach@shorter.edu

SIMON FRASER UNIVERSITY ATHLETICS
8888 UNIVERSITY DRIVE
BURNABY, BC, CANADA V5A 1S6
778-782-3111
athletics.sfu.ca
• Theresa Hanson, Senior Director of
Athletics
theresa_hanson@sfu.ca
• Shelley Howieson, Manager of Facilities
(778) 782-3931
howieson@sfu.ca
• Kelly Weber, Manager of Compliance
(778) 782-3314
weber@sfu.ca
• Steve Frost, Sports Information
Coordinator
(778) 782-4057
sfrost@sfu.ca

SIOUX FALLS ATHLETICS, UNIVERSITY OF
1101 WEST 22ND STREET
SIOUX FALLS, SD 57105
605-331-6791
Fax: 605-331-6792
athletics.web@usiouxfalls.edu
www.usfcougars.com
• Josh Snyder, Athletic Director
(605) 331-6895
• Pam Gohl, Associate Athletic Director
(605) 331-6652
• Ben Krush, Assistant Athletic Director
(605) 575-2032
• Dan Genzler, Sports Information Director
(605) 331-6774
• Zach Mathers, Head Athletic Trainer
(605) 575-2035

SLIPPERY ROCK UNIVERSITY ATHLETICS
1 MORROW WAY
SLIPPERY ROCK, PA 16057
724-738-2027
Fax: 724-738-4797
www.rockathletics.com
• Paul Lueken, Director of Athletics
(724) 738-2767
paul.lueken@sru.edu
• Torry Rollins, Associate Athletic Director
(724) 738-4491
torry.rollins@sru.edu
• Jon Holtz, Director of Athletic
Communication
(724) 738-4925
jonathan.holtz@sru.edu

SOUTH CAROLINA-SPARTANBURG ATHLETICS, UNIVERSITY OF
800 UNIVERSITY WAY
SPARTANBURG, SC 29303
864-503-5141
Fax: 864-503-5130
info@uscupstate.edu
www.upstatespartans.com
• Julio Freire, Athletic Director
(864) 503-5140

jfreire@uscupstate.edu
• Michael Sandago, Director of Sports
Medicine
(864) 503-5104
ssandago@uscupstate.edu
• Kanett Haynes, Athletics Business
Manager
(864) 503-5173
khaynes@uscupstate.edu

SOUTH DAKOTA STATE UNIVERSITY ATHLETICS
2820 STANLEY J. MARSHALL CENTER
BROOKINGS, SD 57007
605-688-5625
Fax: 605-688-5999
Justin.Sell@sdstate.edu
www.gojacks.com
• Justin Sell, Director of Athletics
(605) 688-6388
justin.sell@sdstate.edu
• Jennifer Sell, Director of Academics
(605) 688-4094
jennifer.sell@sdstate.edu
• Jonathan Treiber, Director of Athletic
Marketing
(605) 688-6747
jonathan.treiber@sdstate.edu

SOUTHEASTERN OKLAHOMA STATE UNIVERSITY ATHLETICS
1405 NORTH 4TH
DURANT, OK 74701
580-745-2000
800-435-1327
Fax: 580-745-7493
www.se.edu
• Keith Baxter, Director of Athletics
(580) 745-2250
kbaxter@se.edu
• Cherrie Wilmoth, Associate Athletics
Director
(580) 745-2690
cwilmoth@se.edu
• Blake Allen, Assistant Athletics Director
(580) 745-3386
ballen@se.edu
• Matt Thomas, Sports Information Director
(580) 745-2646
mthomas@se.edu
• Scott Willman, Head Athletic Trainer
(580) 745-2026

SOUTHERN COLORADO ATHLETICS, UNIVERSITY OF
MASSARI ARENA
2200 BONFORTE BOULEVARD
PUEBLO, CO 81001
719-549-2711
Fax: 719-549-2570
www.gothunderwolves.com
• Joe Folda, Director of Athletics
(719) 549-2730
joe.folda@csupueblo.edu
• Jackie Wallgren, Associate Athletic
Director
(719) 549-2021
jackie.wallgren@csupueblo.edu
• Racheal Morris, Associate Athletic Director
(719) 549-2013
racheal.morris@csupueblo.edu
• Dax Larson, Athletic Media Relations
Director
(719) 549-2022
dax.larson@csupueblo.edu
• Roger Clark, Director of Athletic Training

(719) 549-2530
roger.clark@csupueblo.edu

SOUTHERN CONNECTICUT STATE UNIVERSITY ATHLETICS
MOORE FIELDHOUSE
125 WINTERGREEN AVENUE
NEW HAVEN, CT 06515
203-392-6045
Fax: 203-392-6006
www.southernctowls.com
• Jay Moran, Director of Athletics
(203) 392-6045
moranj15@southernct.edu
• Michael Kobylanski, Associate Director of
Athletics Communications
(203) 392-6005
kobylanskim1@southernct.edu
• Joe Hines, Interim Coordinator of Athletic
Facilities
(203) 392-6016
hinesj1@southernct.edu
• Carol Nelson, Head Athletic Trainer
(203) 392-6007
nelsonc4@southernct.edu

SOUTHERN INDIANA ATHLETICS, UNIVERSITY OF
8600 UNIVERSITY BOULEVARD
EVANSVILLE, IN 47712
812-464-1846
Fax: 812-465-1129
www.gousieagles.com
• Jon Mark Hall, Director of Athletics
(812) 464-1846
jmhall@usi.edu
• Alex Eaton, Associate Director of Athletics
(812) 464-1841
aceaton1@usi.edu
• Mandi Fulton, Assistant Director of
Athletics
(812) 465-1022
mfulton@usi.edu
• Scott Hooker, Head Athletic Trainer
(812) 465-1298
sjhooker@usi.edu
• Ray Simmons, Director of Athletic
Communications
(812) 465-1622
rsimmons@usi.edu

SOUTHERN NAZARENE UNIVERSITY ATHLETICS
6729 NORTHWEST 39TH EXPRESSWAY
BETHANY, OK 73008
405-789-6400
Fax: 405-491-6387
www.snuathletics.com
• Bobby Martin, Director of Athletics
(405) 491-6339
bgmartin@snu.edu
• Paul McGrady, Associate Director of
Athletics
(405) 491-6338
pmcgrady@snu.edu
• Kathy League, Assistant Athletics Director
(405) 717-6280
kleague@snu.edu
• David Noblett, Director of Athletics
Communications
(405) 491-6619
dnoblett@snu.edu
• Mike Mathis, Head Athletic Trainer
(405) 717-6236
mmathis@snu.edu

SOUTHERN NEW HAMPSHIRE UNIVERSITY ATHLETICS
2500 NORTH RIVER ROAD
MANCHESTER, NH 03106
603-645-9604
Fax: 603-645-9686
info@snhu.edu
www.snhupenmen.com
• Anthony Fallacaro, Director of Athletics
(603) 645-9604
a.fallacaro@snhu.edu
• Tom Wilkins, Associate Director of Athletics
(603) 645-9786
t.wilkins@snhu.edu
• Shawn Green, Assistant Director of Athletics
(603) 645-9783
s.green@snhu.edu
• Eric Coplin, Director of Athletics Communications
(603) 645-9638
e.coplin@snhu.edu

SOUTHERN WESLEYAN UNIVERSITY ATHLETICS
907 WESLEYAN DRIVE
CENTRAL, SC 29630
864-644-5000
877-644-5556
swuathletics.com
• Chris Williams, Director of Athletics
(864) 644-5303
cwilliams@swu.edu
• Becky Bowman, Director of Compliance
(864) 644-5307
bbowman@swu.edu
• Grace Eckert, Sports Information Director
(864) 644-5308
geckert@swu.edu

SOUTHWEST BAPTIST UNIVERSITY ATHLETICS
1600 UNIVERSITY AVENUE
BOLIVAR, MO 65613
417-328-1948
Fax: 417-328-2009
mpitts@sbuniv.edu
sbubearcats.com
• Mike Pitts, Director of Athletics
(417) 328-1412
mpitts@sbuniv.edu
• Chris Martin, Assistant Athletics Director
(417) 328-1784
ccmartin@sbuniv.edu
• Jeff Weseloh, Director of Athletics Media Relations
(417) 328-1799
jweseloh@sbuniv.edu
• Mike Wolhoy, Head Athletic Trainer
(417) 328-3296
mwolhoy@sbuniv.edu

SOUTHWEST STATE UNIVERSITY ATHLETICS
1501 STATE STREET
MARSHALL, MN 56258
507-537-7271
Fax: 507-537-6578
smsumustangs.com
• Rick Hart, Director of Athletics
(507) 537-7984
• Kelly Loft, Athletic Communications Director
(507) 537-7177
kelly.loft@smsu.edu
• Tim Steinbach, Athletic Development

Director
(507) 537-7204
tim.steinbach@smsu.edu
• Jenn Graven, Director of Marketing and Promotions
(507) 537-6233
jennifer.graven@smsu.edu
• Laura Crowell, Head Athletic Trainer
(507) 537-7165
laura.crowell@smsu.edu

SOUTHWESTERN OKLAHOMA STATE UNIVERSITY ATHLETICS
100 CAMPUS DRIVE
WEATHERFORD, OK 73096
580-774-3068
Fax: 580-774-7106
todd.thurman@swosu.edu
www.swosuathletics.com
• Todd Thurman, Director of Athletics
(580) 774-3701
todd.thurman@swosu.edu
• Doug Self, Sports Information Director
(580) 774-7162
doug.self@swosu.edu
• Edwin Detweiler, Head Athletic Trainer
(580) 774-3073
edwin.detweiler@swosu.edu

SPRINGFIELD COLLEGE ATHLETICS
263 ALDEN STREET
SPRINGFIELD, MA 01109
413-748-3692
Fax: 413-748-3022
athleticdirector@springfieldcollege.edu
www.springfieldcollegepride.com
• Craig Poisson, Director of Athletics
(413) 748-3333
athleticdirector@springfieldcollege.edu
• Kiki Jacobs, Associate Director of Athletics
(413) 748-3334
kjacobs@springfieldcollege.edu
• Barclay Dugger, Coordinator of Athletic Training Services
(413) 748-3650
rdugger@springfieldcollege.edu
• Brian Magoffin, Director of Sports Communications
(413) 748-3341
bmagoffin@springfieldcollege.edu

ST. AUGUSTINE'S UNIVERSITY ATHLETICS
1315 OAKWOOD AVENUE
RALEIGH, NC 24610
919-516-4250
Fax: 919-516-4639
saintaugfalcons.com
• Everett B. Ward, President
(919) 516-4200
• George Williams, Athletic Director
(919) 516-4236
gdwilliams@st-aug.edu
• Anthony Jeffries, Sports Information Director
(919) 516-4517
awjeffries@st-aug.edu
• LaKida Whetstone, Head Athletic Trainer
(919) 516-4219
lmwhetstone@st-aug.edu

ST. CLOUD STATE UNIVERSITY ATHLETICS
720 FOURTH AVENUE SOUTH
ST. CLOUD, MN 56301-4498
320-308-0121
Fax: 320-308-6164

hlweems@stcloudstate.edu
www.scsuhuskies.com
• Heather Weems, Director of Athletics
(320) 308-3102
hlweems@stcloudstate.edu
• Chad Sheetz, Associate Athletics Director of Operations
(320) 308-4910
chsheetz@stcloudstate.edu
• Nate Swenson, Assistant AD Of Marketing & Promotions
(320) 308-2137
nsswenson@stcloudstate.edu
• Thomas Nelson, Director of Athletic Media Relations
(320) 308-5400
tcnelson@stcloudstate.edu

ST. EDWARDS UNIVERSITY ATHLETICS
3001 SOUTH CONGRESS AVENUE
AUSTIN, TX 78704
512-448-8448
Fax: 512-416-5834
athl@stedwards.edu
athletics.stedwards.edu
• Debbie Taylor, Athletic Director
(512) 448-8744
deboraw@stedwards.edu
• Melinda Terry, Associate Athletic Director
(512) 233-1637
melindat@stedwards.edu
• Jameson Adams, Associate Athletic Director
(512) 233-1495
jadams7@stedwards.edu
• Lisa Lowe, Assistant Athletic Director
(512) 448-8498
lisalo@stedwards.edu

ST. FRANCIS COLLEGE ATHLETICS
180 REMSEN STREET
BROOKLYN HEIGHTS, NY 11201
718-489-5490
Fax: 718-797-2140
www.sfcathletics.com
• Irma Garcia, Director of Athletics
igarcia@sfc.edu
• Anthony Kurtin, Associate Director of Athletics
akurtin@sfc.edu
• Carl Quigley, Assistant Athletic Director
cquigley@sfc.edu
• Jim Hoffman, Director of Compliance
jhoffman@sfc.edu
• Meghan O'Brien, Director of Athletic Marketing/Senior Woman A
mobrien@sfc.edu

ST. MICHAEL'S COLLEGE ATHLETICS
ONE WINOOSKI PARK
COLCHESTER, VT 05439
802-654-2450
802-654-2000
Fax: 802-654-2497
www.smcathletics.com
• Chris Kenny, Director of Athletics
(802) 654-2200
ckenny@smcvt.edu
• Meggan Dulude, Associate Director of Athletics
(802) 654-2506
mdulude@smcvt.edu
• Tacy Lincoln, Associate Director of Athletics
(802) 654-2507
tlincoln@smcvt.edu
• Josh Kessler, Director of Athletic

Communications
(802) 654-2537
jkessler@smcvt.edu
• Renee Breault, Head Athletic Trainer
(802) 654-2496
rbreault2@smcvt.edu

ST. THOMAS AQUINAS COLLEGE ATHLETICS
125 ROUTE 340
SPARKILL, NY 10976
845-398-4000
Fax: 914-359-8136
www.stacathletics.com
• Gerry Oswald, Athletics Director
(845) 398-4186
goswald@stac.edu
• Nicole Ryan, Associate Athletic Director/SWA
(845) 398-4163
goswald@stac.edu
• Kim Lusk, Assistant Athletic Director
(845) 398-4026
klusk@stac.edu
• Lori Rahaim, Head Athletic Trainer
(845) 398-4057
lrahaim@stac.edu

STATE UNIVERSITY OF WEST GEORGIA ATHLETICS
1601 MAPLE STREET
CARROLLTON, GA 30118
678-839-6533
Fax: 678-839-6538
www.uwgsports.com
• Daryl Dickey, Athletic Director
(678) 839-6539
ddickey@westga.edu
• Laura Clayton, Assistant Athletic Director
(678) 839-3964
lclayton@westga.edu
• Skip Fite, Head Baseball Coach
(678) 839-3956
• Michael Cooney, Men's Basketball Coach
(678) 839-3974
mcooney@westga.edu
• Scott Groninger, Women's Basketball Coach
(678) 839-3967
sgroning@westga.edu

STILLMAN COLLEGE ATHLETICS
BATCHELOR HALL
3601 STILLMAN BOULEVARD
TUSCALOOSA, AL 35403
205-366-8980
Fax: 205-366-8865
• Donte Jackson, Director of Athletics
(205) 366-8980
djackson@stillman.edu
• Daphne Hood, Assistant Athletic Director
(205) 247-8184
dhood@stillman.edu
• Joel Worthington, Sports Information Director
(205) 247-8101
jworthington@stillman.edu
• Pam Phillips, Senior Women's Administrator
(205) 247-8041
pphillips@stillman.edu

STONEHILL COLLEGE ATHLETICS
320 WASHINGTON STREET
NORTH EASTON, MA 02357

508-565-1384
Fax: 508-565-1460
www.stonehillskyhawks.com
• Dean O'Keefe, Director of Athletics
(508) 565-1384
dokeefe@stonehill.edu
• MacDonald Cindy, Sr. Associate Director of Athletics
(508) 565-1064
cmacdonald@stonehill.edu
• Doug Monson, Director of Athletic Communications
(508) 565-1352
dmonson@stonehill.edu
• Pete Krysko, Head Athletic Trainer
(508) 565-1514
pkrysko@stonehill.edu

TAMPA ATHLETICS, UNIVERSITY OF
401 WEST KENNEDY BOULEVARD
BOX 1
TAMPA, FL 33606
813-253-6240
Fax: 813-253-6288
tampaspartans.com
• Larry Marfise, Athletic Director
(813) 257-3100
lmarfise@ut.edu
• Tom Kolbe, Assistant Athletic Director, Communications
(813) 257-3473
tkolbe@ut.edu
• Scott Brickett, Assistant Athletic Director, Sports Medicine
(813) 257-3264
wbrickett@ut.edu

TARLETON STATE UNIVERSITY ATHLETICS
BOX T-0080
DEPARTMENT OF ATHLETICS
STEPHENVILLE, TX 76402
254-968-9178
Fax: 254-968-9674
www.tarletonsports.com
• Lonn Reisman, Athletics Director
reisman@tarleton.edu
• Troy Jones, Assistant Athletics Director, Operations
(254) 968-9546
tjones01@tarleton.edu
• Nathan Bural, Director of Athletic Communications
(254) 968-1802
bural@tarleton.edu
• Rod Cole, Director for Athletic Performance
(254) 968-9671
rcole@tarleton.edu
• Adam Deimling, Head Athletic Trainer
(254) 968-1809
deimling@tarleton.edu

TEXAS A&M INTERNATIONAL UNIVERSITY ATHLETICS
5201 UNIVERSITY BOULEVARD
LAREDO, TX 78041-1900
956-326-3000
Fax: 956-326-2889
www.godustdevils.com
• Pablo Arenaz, President
(956) 326-2320
pablo.arenaz@tamiu.edu
• Griz Zimmermann, Director of Athletics
(956) 326-2890
griz@tamiu.edu
• Daniel Lathey, Associate Athletic Director

(956) 326-2892
dlathey@tamiu.edu
• Amanda Ruthman, Sports Information Director
(956) 326-3007

TEXAS A&M UNIVERSITY-COMMERCE ATHLETICS
PO BOX 3011
COMMERCE, TX 75429
903-886-5558
Fax: 903-468-3033
timm@tamuc.edu
www.lionathletics.com
• Tim McMurray, Director of Athletics
(903) 886-5568
timm@tamuc.edu
• Conner Moreno, Assistant AD For International Operations
(903) 468-8760
conner.moreno@tamuc.edu
• Dustan Thrift, Director of Sports Medicine
(903) 468-3035
dustan.thrift@tamuc.edu
• Josh Manck, Assistant AD For Communications
(903) 886-5131
josh.manck@tamuc.edu
• Chase Stoltenberg, Assistant Athletics Trainer
(903) 468-3193
chase.stoltenberg@tamuc.edu

TEXAS A&M UNIVERSITY-KINGSVILLE ATHLETICS
700 UNIVERSITY BOULEVARD
MSC 202
KINGSVILLE, TX 78363
361-593-2800
Fax: 361-593-3587
www.javelinaathletics.com
• D. Scott Gines, Vice President of Intercollegiate Athletics
(361) 593-2800
• Ruben Cantu, Head Athletic Trainer
(361) 593-2493
karjc00@tamuk.edu
• Kelvin Queliz, Director of Sports Information
(361) 593-2870
kelvin.queliz@tamuk.edu

TIFFIN UNIVERSITY ATHLETICS
155 MIAMI STREET
TIFFIN, OH 44883
419-448-3359
www.gotiffindragons.com
• Lonny Allen, Athletic Director
(419) 448-3359
lallen@tiffin.edu
• Darby Roggow, Assistant Athletic Director
(419) 448-3425
droggow@tiffin.edu
• Shane O'Donnell, Sports Information Director
(419) 448-3288
sodonnel@tiffin.edu

TOCCOA FALLS COLLEGE ATHLETICS
107 KINCAID DRIVE
TOCCOA FALLS, GA 30598
706-886-6831
athletic@tfc.edu
www.tfc.edu
• Kevin Hall, Athletic Director
khall@tfc.edu
• Jeff Mullikin, Assistant Athletic Director

jmullikin@tfc.edu
• Kaelyn Watson, Sports Information Director
kwatson@tfc.edu

TREVECCA NAZARENE UNIVERSITY ATHLETICS
333 MURFREESBORO ROAD
NASHVILLE, TN 37210-2877
615-248-1606
Fax: 615-248-1565
www.tnutrojans.com
• Mark Elliott, Director of Athletics
(615) 248-1275
melliott@trevecca.edu
• Larry Knight, Compliance Coordinator
(615) 248-1639
lknight@trevecca.edu
• Gregory Ruff, Communications/Broadcasting
(615) 248-1606
gruff@trevecca.edu

TRUMAN STATE UNIVERSITY ATHLETICS
PERSHING BUILDING #212
100 EAST NORMAL
KIRKSVILLE, MO 63501
660-785-4236
Fax: 660-785-4189
athletics@truman.edu
www.trumanbulldogs.com
• Jerry Wollmering, Director of Athletics
(660) 785-4236
jerryw@truman.edu
• Liz Jorn, Faculty Athletic Representative
(660) 785-7747
ljorn@truman.edu
• Kevin White, Director of Athletic Communications
(660) 785-4276
kwhite@truman.edu
• Michelle Boyd, Head Athletic Trainer
(660) 785-7364
mboyd@truman.edu

TUSKEGEE UNIVERSITY ATHLETICS
DEPARTMENT OF ATHLETICS
1200 WEST MONTGOMERY ROAD
TUSKEGEE, AL 36088
334-724-4545
Fax: 334-724-4233
www.goldentigersports.com
• Curtis Campbell, Director of Athletics
(334) 724-4545
ccampbell@mytu.tuskegee.edu
• Joe Jimmeh, Faculty Athletic Representative
(334) 724-4495
kaija@mytu.tuskegee.edu
• Deana Person, Director of Compliance
(334) 727-8926
dperson@mytu.tuskegee.edu
• Travis Jarome, Director of Athletic Communications
(334) 727-8150
tjarome@mytu.tuskegee.edu

UC RIVERSIDE ATHLETICS
900 UNIVERSITY AVENUE
RIVERSIDE, CA 92521
951-827-5432
Fax: 951-827-3569
www.gohighlanders.com
• Tamica Smith Jones, Director of Intercollegiate Athletics
(951) 827-5432

athleticsdirector@ucr.edu
• Michael Boele, Senior Associate Athletics Director
(951) 827-5446
michael.boele@ucr.edu
• Tony Ontiveros, Director of Sports Medicine
(951) 827-3813
tony.ontiveros@ucr.edu
• Walter Clark, Faculty Athletics Representative
(951) 827-2114
walter.clark@ucr.edu

UNION UNIVERSITY ATHLETICS
1050 UNION UNIVERSITY DRIVE
JACKSON, TN 38305
731-661-5130
Fax: 731-661-5182
tsadler@uu.edu
uuathletics.com
• Tommy Sadler, Director of Athletics
(731) 661-5218
tsadler@uu.edu
• Teresa Thomas, Athletics Secretary
(731) 661-5325
tthomas@uu.edu
• Rebekah McFarland, Head Athletic Trainer
(731) 661-5221
rmcfarland@uu.edu
• Steven Aldridge, Sports Information Director
(731) 661-5027
saldridge@uu.edu

UNIVERSITY OF ALABAMA IN HUNTSVILLE ATHLETICS
205 SPRAGINS HALL
HUNTSVILLE, AL 35899
256-824-6100
Fax: 256-824-7306
www.uah.edu/Athletics
• E. J. Brophy, Director of Athletics
(256) 824-2677
william.brophy@uah.edu
• Sam Baldwin, Sports Information Coordinator
(256) 824-2201
samuel.baldwin@uah.edu
• Taylor Flatt, Sports Information Director
(256) 824-6008
taylor.flatt@uah.edu

UNIVESRITY OF ALASKA FAIRBANKS ATHLETICS
ATHLETICS AND RECREATION DEPARTMENT
211 PATTY CENTER
PO BOX 757440
FAIRBANKS, AK 99775-7440
907-474-7205
Fax: 907-474-5162
• Gary Gray, Director of Athletics
(907) 474-6812
grgray@alaska.edu
• Kelly Wien, Assistant Athletic Director
(907) 474-6870
kelly.wien@alaska.edu
• Nona Letuligasenoa, Assistant Athletic Director, Communications
(907) 474-6805
nona.l@alaska.edu

UNIVERSITY OF BRIDGEPORT ATHLETICS
126 PARK AVENUE
BRIDGEPORT, CT 06604

203-576-4000
Fax: 203-576-4057
anthonyv@bridgeport.edu
www.ubknights.com
• Anthony Vitti, Director of Athletics
(203) 576-4733
anthonyv@bridgeport.edu
• Kate Smullen, Assistant Athletic Director
(203) 576-4725
kbackman@bridgeport.edu
• Chuck Sadowski, Sports Information Director
(203) 576-4726
csadowsk@bridgeport.edu
• Scott Baird, Associate Athletic Trainer
(203) 576-4798
sbaird@bridgeport.edu

UNIVERSITY OF CALIFORNIA, DAVIS - ATHLETICS
HICKEY GYM 264
ONE SHIELDS AVENUE
DAVIS, CA 95616
530-752-1111
Fax: 530-752-6681
www.ucdavisaggies.com
• Kevin Blue, Athletic Director
(530) 752-4557
athleticsdirector@ucdavis.edu
• Rocko DeLuca, Deputy Director Of Athletics
(530) 752-5096
• Scott Carrell, Faculty Athletics Representative
(530) 752-5858

UNIVERSITY OF MISSOURI-ST. LOUIS ATHLETICS
225 MARK TWAIN BUILDING
ONE UNIVERSITY BOULEVARD
ST. LOUIS, MO 63121
314-516-5661
Fax: 314-516-5503
www.umsltritons.com
• Lori Flanagan, Director of Athletics
(314) 516-5661
• Mary Ann Mitchell, Assistant Director of Athletics
(314) 516-5660
tierneym@umsl.edu
• Mike Berry, Director of Sports Medicine
(314) 516-5686
berrymp@umsl.edu
• Josh McMillian, Head of Sports Performance
(314) 516-5663
mcmillianj@umsl.edu

UPPER IOWA UNIVERSITY ATHLETICS(UIU)
ATHLETICS DEPARTMENT
605 WASHINGTON STREET
PO BOX 1857
FAYETTE, IA 52142
563-425-5700
Fax: 563-425-5334
info@uiu.edu
www.upperiowaathletics.com
• David Miller, Director of Athletics
(563) 425-5293
millerds@uiu.edu
• Kent McElvania, Associate Athletic Director
(563) 425-5285
mcelvaniak@uiu.edu
• Brock Wissmiller, Assistant Athletic Director

(563) 425-5700
wissmillerb@uiu.edu
• Angie Leete, Program Director
(563) 425-5782
leetea@uiu.edu
• Matt Rueckert, Head Athletic Trainer
(563) 425-5364
rueckertm@uiu.edu

URSULINE COLLEGE ATHLETICS
2550 LANDER ROAD
PEPPER PIKE, OH 44124
440-684-6102
Fax: 440-684-6097
info@ursuline.edu
www.ursulinearrows.com
• Cindy McKnight, Athletic Director
(440) 684-6102
cmcknight@ursuline.edu
• Cathy Rook, Athletic Trainer
(440) 684-6100
crook@ursuline.edu
• Brandon Stewart, Sports Information Director
(440) 684-6062
brandon.stewart@ursuline.edu

VALDOSTA STATE UNIVERSITY ATHLETICS
DEPARTMENT OF ATHLETICS
1500 NORTH PATTERSON STREET
VALDOSTA, GA 31698
229-333-5890
Fax: 229-333-5972
www.vstateblazers.com
• Herb Reinhard, Director of Athletics
(229) 333-5462
hreinhar@valdosta.edu
• Mason Barfield, Director of Internal Operations
(229) 293-6069
• Whit Chappell, Director of Athletic Development
(229) 249-2631
wchappel@valdosta.edu
• Matt Malone, Sports Information Director
(229) 333-5903
mwmalone@valdosta.edu

VIRGINIA STATE UNIVERSITY ATHLETICS
20720 FOURTH AVENUE
PETERSBURG, VA 23806
804-524-5030
Fax: 804-524-5763
govsutrojans.com
• Peggy Davis, Director of Athletics
(804) 524-5030
pdavis@vsu.edu
• Deborah C. Mallory, Associate Athletic Director, Compliance
(804) 524-5571
dmallory@vsu.edu
• John E. Wilson, Jr., Assistant Athletic Director, Logistics
(804) 524-5020
jwilson@vsu.edu
• Roland T. Lovelace, Head Athletic Trainer
(804) 524-6798
rlovelace@vsu.edu

VIRGINIA UNION UNIVERSITY ATHLETICS
1500 NORTH LOMBARDY STREET
RICHMOND, VA 23220
804-257-5600
800-368-3227

Fax: 804-342-3511
visitus@vuu.edu
vuusports.com
• Joe Taylor, Director of Athletics
(804) 342-1484
jdtaylor@vuu.edu
• Felicia Johnson, Associate Athletic Director
(804) 342-5933
fmjohnson@vuu.edu
• Jim Junot, Sports Information Director
(804) 342-1493
jjunot@vuu.edu
• Valerie Allen, Head Athletic Trainer
(804) 359-9408
vpallen@vuu.edu

WASHBURN UNIVERSITY OF TOPEKA ATHLETICS
1700 SW COLLEGE AVENUE
TOPEKA, KS 66621
785-670-1134
Fax: 785-670-1091
www.wusports.com
• Loren Ferre, Director of Athletics
(785) 670-1794
• Brittany Simmerman, Assistant Athletic Director
(785) 670-1790
• Gene Cassell, Sports Information Director
(785) 670-1791
gene.cassell@washburn.edu
• Brent Hogan, Marketing and Special Events Coordinator
(785) 670-1333
• Steve Ice, Head Athletic Trainer
(785) 670-1753
steve.ice@washburn.edu

WAYNE STATE COLLEGE
1111 MAIN STREET
WAYNE, NE 68787
402-375-7000
Fax: 402-375-7271
www.wscwildcats.com
• Mike Powicki, Athletic Director
(402) 375-7520
mipowic1@wsc.edu
• Mike Barry, Associate Director of Athletics
(402) 375-7521
mibarry1@wsc.edu
• Linda Anderson, Assistant Athletic Director, Internal Affairs
(402) 375-7308
liander1@wsc.edu
• Muffin Morris, Head Athletic Trainer
(402) 375-7700
mumorri1@wsc.edu

WAYNE STATE UNIVERSITY ATHLETICS
5101 JOHN C. LODGE
101 MATTHAEI BUILDING
DETROIT, MI 48202
313-577-4280
Fax: 313-577-5996
www.wsuathletics.com
• Rob Fournier, Director of Athletics
ai5611@wayne.edu
• Jason Clark, Executive Senior Associate Athletics Director
jason.clark@wayne.edu
• Theresa Arist, Chief of Staff
theresa.arist@wayne.edu
• Michael Chan, Head Athletic Trainer
michaelchan@wayne.edu

WEST ALABAMA ATHLETICS, UNIVERSITY OF
UWA STATION 5
LIVINGSTON, AL 35470
205-652-3784
Fax: 205-652-3600
www.uwaathletics.com
• Stan Williamson, Director of Athletics
(205) 652-3784
swilliamson@uwa.edu
• Janet Montgomery, Associate Athletic Director
(205) 652-3630
jlm@uwa.edu
• R.T. Floyd, Director of Athletic Training & Sports Medicine
(205) 652-3714
rtf@uwa.edu
• Kent Partridge, Director for Athletic Communications
(205) 652-3719
kpartridge@uwa.edu

WEST CHESTER UNIVERSITY ATHLETICS
700 SOUTH HIGH STREET
WEST CHESTER, PA 19383
610-436-1000
Fax: 610-436-1020
www.wcupagoldenrams.com
• Edward Matejkovic, Director of Athletics
(610) 436-3555
ematejkovic@wcupa.edu
• Terry Beattie, Associate Athletic Director
(610) 436-3317
tbeattie@wcupa.edu
• James Zuhlke, Sports Information Director
(610) 436-3316
jzuhlke@wcupa.edu
• Craig Stevens, Faculty Athletic Representative
(610) 436-2386
cstevens@wcupa.edu

WEST FLORIDA ATHLETICS, UNIVERSITY OF
11000 UNIVERSITY PARKWAY
BUILDING 54
PENSACOLA, FL 32514
850-474-3003
Fax: 850-474-3342
dscott@uwf.edu
goargos.com
• Dave Scott, Director of Athletics
(850) 474-3003
dscott@uwf.edu
• Meghan Barter, Associate Athletic Director
(850) 474-3055
mbarter@uwf.edu
• Jake Marg, Assistant Athletic Director
(850) 474-3057
jmarg2@uwf.edu
• Brian Henry, Director of Athletic Communications
(850) 474-2140
bhenry@uwf.edu
• Arnold Gamber, Head Athletic Trainer
(850) 474-2985
jgamber@uwf.edu

WEST LIBERTY UNIVERSITY ATHLETICS
101 FACULTY DRIVE
WEST LIBERTY, WV 26074-0295
304-336-5000
Fax: 304-336-8304
hilltoppersports.com

college sports

• Aaron Huffman, Athletic Director
(304) 336-8046
ahuffman@westliberty.edu
• Lynn Ullom, Associate Athletic Director
(304) 336-8320
ullomlyn@westliberty.edu
• Heather Gallagher, Assistant Director of
Athletics
(304) 336-8225
hgallagher@westliberty.edu
• Herb Minch, Head Athletic Trainer
(304) 336-8476
minchhp@westliberty.edu

**WEST TEXAS A&M UNIVERSITY
ATHLETICS**
2403 RUSSELL LONG BOULEVARD
CANYON, TX 79015
806-651-0000
Fax: 806-651-2213
www.gobuffsgo.com
• Michael McBroom, Director of
Intercollegiate Athletics
(806) 651-4400
mmcbroom@wtamu.edu
• David Rausch, Faculty Athletic
Representative
(806) 651-2423
drausch@wtamu.edu
• Paul Sweetgall, Director for Compliance
(806) 651-4437
psweetgall@wtamu.edu
• Chris Dane, Head Athletic Trainer
(806) 651-3640
cdane@wtamu.edu
• Sarah Ramey, Head Strength &
Conditioning Coach
(806) 651-4433
sramey@wtamu.edu

**WEST VIRGINIA STATE COLLEGE
ATHLETICS**
PO BOX 1000
INSTITUTE, WV 25112-1000
304-766-3165
800-987-2112
Fax: 304-766-4126
www.wvsuyellowjackets.com
• Sandy Kessell, Athletic Department
Secretary
(304) 766-3165
skessel1@wvstateu.edu
• Nate Burton, Interim Athletic Director
(304) 766-3165
nburton2@wvstateu.edu
• Shannon Gerencir, Assistant Athletic
Director
(304) 766-5750
• John Simms, Sports Information Director
(304) 766-5760
simmsj@wvstateu.edu

WEST VIRGINIA WESLEYAN ATHLETICS
59 COLLEGE AVENUE
BUCKHANNON, WV 26201
304-473-8000
Fax: 304-472-2571
www.wesleyanbobcats.com
• Randy Tenney, Athletic Director
(304) 473-8098
tenney_r@wvwc.edu
• Rae Emrick, Head Athletic Trainer
(304) 473-8002
emrick_r@wvwc.edu
• Patrick Holguin, Assistant Athletic Director
(304) 473-8101
holguin_p@wvwc.edu

• Allison Hull, Faculty Athletic
Representative
(304) 473-8061
hull_a@wvwc.edu
• Duane Carpenter, Sports Information
Director
(304) 473-8102
carpenter_d@wvwc.edu

**WESTERN OREGON UNIVERSITY
ATHLETICS**
345 MONMOUTH AVENUE NORTH
MONMOUTH, OR 97361
503-838-9030
Fax: 503-838-8370
www.wouwolves.com
• Barbara Dearing, Executive Director of
Intercollegiate Athletics
(503) 838-8094
dearingb@wou.edu
• Randi Lydum, Director of Compliance
(503) 838-8121
lydumr@wou.edu
• John Bartlett, Director of Athletic Facilities
(503) 838-8531
bartlej@wou.edu
• John Potter, Director of Media Relations
(503) 838-8051
potterj@wou.edu
• Kurtis Kidd, Head Athletic Trainer
(503) 838-8343
kiddk@wou.edu

**WESTERN STATE COLLEGE ATHLETICS
(WSC)**
210 PAUL WRIGHT GYM
600 NORTH ADAMS
GUNNISON, CO 81231
970-943-2079
Fax: 970-943-2754
www.gomountaineers.com
• Miles Van Hee, Director of Athletics
mvanhee@western.edu
• Kim Miller, Associate Athletic Director
(970) 943-2021
kdmiller@western.edu
• Shaun Wicen, Assistant Sports Information
Director
(970) 943-2223
swicen@western.edu
• Don Mundell, Head Athletic Trainer
(970) 943-2080
dmundell@western.edu

**WESTERN WASHINGTON UNIVERSITY
ATHLETICS**
516 HIGH STREET
BELLINGHAM, WA 98225
360-650-3000
Fax: 360-650-3495
www.vu.wwu.edu
• Steven Card, Director of Athletics
steven.card@wwu.edu
• Steve Brummel, Associate Athletic
Director Facilities
steve.brummel@wwu.edu
• Jeff Evans, Director of Sports Info
jeff.evans@wwu.edu
• Lonnie Lyon, Head Athletic Trainer
lonnie.lyon@wwu.edu

**WESTMINSTER COLLEGE (UT)
ATHLETICS**
1840 SOUTH 1300 EAST
SALT LAKE CITY, UT 84105

801-832-2344
Fax: 801-474-2511
www.westminstergriffins.com
• Shay Wyatt, Director of Athletics
(801) 832-2344
swyatt@westminstercollege.edu
• Susan Heath, Associate Athletic Director
(801) 832-2283
sheath@westminstercollege.edu
• Rick Hackford, Head Athletic Trainer
(801) 832-2355
rhackford@westminstercollege.edu

**WHEELING JESUIT UNIVERSITY
ATHLETICS**
316 WASHINGTON AVENUE
WHEELING, WV 26003
304-243-2365
Fax: 304-243-2243
www.wju.edu/athletics
• Kevin Forde, Director of Athletics
(304) 243-2291
kforde@wju.edu
• Dan Sancomb, Director of Athletic
Fundraising
(304) 243-2053
dsancomb@wju.edu
• Chris Myers, Sports Information Director
(304) 243-2012
mmcdonald@wju.edu

**WILMINGTON UNIVERSITY ATHLETICS
(DELAWARE)**
320 NORTH DUPONT HIGHWAY
NEW CASTLE, DE 19720
877-967-5464
infocenter@wilmu.edu
athletics.wilmu.edu
• Linda Van Drie-Andrzjewski, Director of
Athletics
linda.m.andrzjewski@wilmu.edu
• Brian August, Associate Athletic Director
(302) 356-6753
brian.m.august@wilmu.edu
• Erin Harvey, Assistant Athletic Director
(302) 356-2023
erin.t.harvey@wilmu.edu

WINGATE UNIVERSITY ATHLETICS
230 NORTH CAMDEN ROAD
WINGATE, NC 28174
704-233-8193
Fax: 704-233-8170
www.wingatebulldogs.com
• Steve Poston, Director of Athletics
(704) 233-8194
poston@wingate.edu
• Michelle Caddigan, Associate Athletic
Director, Internal Operations
(704) 233-8174
caddigan@wingate.edu
• David Sherwood, Director for Sports
Information
(704) 233-8186
dsherwood@wingate.edu
• Robby Wise, Director of Sports Medicine
(704) 233-6706
r.wise@wingate.edu

**WINONA STATE UNIVERSITY
ATHLETICS**
PO BOX 5838
WINONA, MN 55987
507-457-5210
Fax: 507-457-5479
www.winonastatewarriors.com

• Eric Schoh, Director of Athletics
(507) 457-5212
eschoh@winona.edu
• Myranda Nash, Associate Athletics
Director
(507) 457-2250
mnash@winona.edu
• Stacey Czaplewski, Head Athletic Trainer
(507) 457-2333
sczaplewski@winona.edu

WINSTON-SALEM STATE UNIVERSITY ATHLETICS
ATHLETICS DEPARTMENT
200 C.E. GAINES CENTER
WINSTON-SALEM, NC 27110
336-750-2141
Fax: 336-750-8880
www.wssurams.com
• Tonia Walker, Director of Athletics
(336) 750-2141
• George Knox, Associate Director for
Compliance
(336) 750-2146
knoxge@wssu.edu
• Kevin Manns, Director of Athletics for
Media Relations
(336) 750-2152
mannskj@wssu.edu
• Ian Mushinski, Head Athletic Trainer
(336) 750-2597
mushinskiia@wssu.edu

WISCONSIN-PARKSIDE ATHLETICS, UNIVERSITY OF
900 WOOD ROAD
PO BOX 2000
KENOSHA, WI 53141-2000
262-595-2345
Fax: 262-595-2225
www.parksiderangers.com
• Tamie Falk-Day, Director of Athletics
(262) 595-2485
tamie.falk-day@uwp.edu
• Roger McAfee, Director for Sports Media
Relations
(262) 595-2045
mcafee@uwp.edu
• Kenny Wilka, Director of Sports Medicine
(262) 595-2164
wilka@uwp.edu
• Tyler Martin, Athletic Trainer
(262) 595-2164
tylerm@uwp.edu

WOFFORD COLLEGE ATHLETICS
429 NORTH CHURCH STREET
SPARTANBURG, SC 29303
864-597-4090
Fax: 864-597-4129
athletics@wofford.edu
athletics.wofford.edu
• Richard Johnson, Director of Athletics
(864) 597-4090
athletics@wofford.edu
• Jameica Hill, Faculty Athletic
Representative
(864) 597-4635
• Andy Kiah, Director of Athletic Facilities
(864) 597-4157
kiahal@wofford.edu
• Will Christman, Head Athletic Trainer
(864) 597-4114
christmanwl@wofford.edu

NCAA Division III Colleges

ADRIAN COLLEGE ATHLETICS
110 SOUTH MADISON STREET
ADRIAN, MI 49221
517-265-5161
800-877-2246
Fax: 517-264-3802
adrianbulldogs.com
• Michael Duffy, Athletic Director
(517) 264-3997
mduffy@adrian.edu
• Patrick Stewart, Sports Information
Director
(517) 264-3280
pstewart@adrian.edu
• Jamie Fetter, Head Athletic Trainer
(517) 264-3969
jfetter@adrian.edu

ALBERTUS MAGNUS COLLEGE ATHLETICS
700 PROSPECT STREET
NEW HAVEN, CT 06511
203-773-8596
Fax: 203-776-7533
athletics.albertus.edu
• Jim Abromaitis, Director of Athletics
(203) 773-8578
jabromaitis@albertus.edu
• Nicholas Wajnowski, Associate Director of
Athletics
(203) 773-8579
nwajnowski@albertus.edu
• Samantha Masayda, Sports Information
Director
(203) 773-8586
smasayda@albertus.edu

ALBION COLLEGE ATHLETICS
611 EAST PORTER STREET
ALBION, MI 49224
517-629-1000
Fax: 517-629-0495
marend@albion.edu
gobrits.com
• Matt Arend, Athletic Director
(517) 629-0583
marend@albion.edu
• Greg Polnasek, Associate Athletic Director
(517) 629-0288
gpolnasek@albion.edu
• Andy Lawrence, Head Athletic Trainer
(517) 629-0522
alawrence@albion.edu
• Bobby Lee, Director of Sports Information
(517) 629-0434
blee@albion.edu

ALBRIGHT COLLEGE ATHLETICS
13TH & BERN STREETS
PO BOX 15234
READING, PA 19612-5234
610-921-7535
Fax: 610-921-7566
athletics@alb.edu
www.albrightathletics.com
• Rick Ferry, Co-Director of Athletics
(610) 921-7825
rferry@albright.edu
• Janice Luck, Co-Director of Athletics
(610) 921-7824
jluck@albright.edu
• Jeff Feiler, Assistant Director of Athletics
(610) 921-7678
jfeiler@albright.edu

• Rick Partsch, Head Athletic Trainer
(610) 921-7827
rpartsch@albright.edu

ALFRED UNIVERSITY ATHLETICS
ONE SAXON DRIVE
ALFRED, NY 14802
607-871-2193
Fax: 607-871-2712
gosaxons.com
• Paul Vecchio, Athletic Director
(607) 871-2030
vecchio@alfred.edu
• Mark Whitehouse, Sport Information
Director
(607) 871-2904
whitehouse@alfred.edu
• Jessica Hurlbut, Head Athletic Trainer
(607) 871-2916
dunster@alfred.edu

ALLEGHENY COLLEGE ATHLETICS
520 NORTH MAIN STREET
MEADVILLE, PA 16335
814-332-3350
Fax: 814-337-1217
alleghenysports.com
• Portia Hoeg, Director of Athletics
(814) 332-3350
phoeg@allegheny.edu
• Samantha Avery, Manager of Athletic
Operations
(814) 332-3350
savery@allegheny.edu
• Jim Berger, Director of Athletic
Communications
(814) 332-5952
• Jamie Plunkett, Head Athletic Trainer
(814) 332-2817
james.plunkett@allegheny.edu

ALMA COLLEGE ATHLETICS
614 WEST SUPERIOR STREET
ALMA, MI 48801
989-463.7279
Fax: 989-463-7018
www.goalmascots.com
• Steven Rackley, Athletic Director
rackleysp@alma.edu
• Paul Thomas, Sports Information Director
(989) 463-7114
thomaspw@alma.edu
• Brett Knight, Head Athletic Trainer
(989) 463-7288
knightbd@alma.edu

ALVERNIA UNIVERSITY ATHLETICS
400 SAINT BERNARDINE STREET
READING, PA 19607
610-796-8276
Fax: 610-796-8349
bill.stiles@alvernia.edu
athletics.alvernia.edu
• Bill Stiles, Director of Athletics
(610) 796-3015
bill.stiles@alvernia.edu
• Laura Gingrich, Associate Athletic Director
(610) 796-8273
laura.gingrich@alvernia.edu
• Mike Miller, Assistant Athletic Director
(610) 796-8471
mike.miller@alvernia.edu
• Tom Porrazzo, Head Athletic Trainer
(484) 256-6194
tom.porrazzo@alvernia.edu

AMHERST COLLEGE ATHLETICS
ALUMNI GYMNASIUM
PO BOX 5000
AMHERST, MA 01002-5000
413-542-2000
Fax: 413-542-2026
athletics@amherst.edu
athletics.amherst.edu
• Don Faulstick, Director of Athletics
(413) 542-8266
drfaulstick@amherst.edu
• David Hixon, Senior Associate Athletics
Director
(413) 542-2069
• Gregg DiNardo, Assistant Athletic Director
(413) 542-5630
gdinardo@amherst.edu
• Chris Attwood, Director of Athletic
Communications
(413) 542-2390
cattwood@amherst.edu
• Stan Zieja, Director of Sports Medicine
(413) 542-8188
smzieja@amherst.edu

ANDERSON UNIVERSITY ATHLETICS
1100 EAST FIFTH STREET
ANDERSON, IN 46012
765-641-4479
800-428-6414
Fax: 765-641-3857
mjtaylor@anderson.edu
athletics.anderson.edu
• Marcie Taylor, Athletic Director
(765) 641-4495
mjtaylor@anderson.edu
• Steve Heath, Sports Information Director
(765) 641-4479
sjheath@anderson.edu
• Adam Crosby, Head Athletic Trainer
(765) 641-4491
ajcrosby@anderson.edu

ANNA MARIA COLLEGE ATHLETICS
50 SUNSET LANE
PAXTON, MA 01612
508-849-3447
800-344-4586
Fax: 508-849-3449
lhabacker@annamaria.edu
goamcats.com
• Serge DeBari, Interim Athletic Director
(508) 849-3447
sdebari@annamaria.edu
• Shawn Conrad, Assistant Athletic Director
(508) 849-3310
sconrad@annamaria.edu
• Ray LeBoeuf, Jr., Head Athletic Trainer
(508) 849-3448
rleboeuf@annamaria.edu
• Sammi Chickering, Sports Information
Director
(508) 849-3252
schickering@annamaria.edu

ARCADIA UNIVERSITY ATHLETICS
450 SOUTH EASTON ROAD
GLENSIDE, PA 19038
215-572-2955
877-272-2342
Fax: 215-572-2159
granatab@arcadia.edu
athletics.arcadia.edu
• Brian Granata, Director of Athletics
(215) 572-2955
granatab@arcadia.edu
• Rick Brownell, Associate Director of

Athletics
(215) 572-4066
brownelr@arcadia.edu
• Justin Scott, Assistant Athletic Director
(215) 572-2976
scottj@arcadia.edu
• Darryl Konicki, Sports Information Director
(215) 572-4048
konickid@arcadia.edu
• Danielle Duffy, Head Athletic Trainer
(215) 572-2848
duffyd@arcadia.edu

AUGSBURG COLLEGE ATHLETICS
2211 RIVERSIDE AVENUE SOUTH
MINNEAPOLIS, MN 55454
612-330-1000
Fax: 612-330-1372
athletics.augsburg.edu
• Jeff Swenson, Athletic Director
(612) 330-1241
swensonj@augsburg.edu
• Kelly Anderson Diercks, Associate Athletic
Director
(612) 330-1245
diercks@augsburg.edu
• Don Stoner, Sports Information Director
(612) 330-1677
stoner@augsburg.edu
• Missy Strauch, Head Athletic Trainer
(612) 330-1310
strauch@augsburg.edu

AUGUSTANA COLLEGE ATHLETICS
639 38TH STREET
ROCK ISLAND, IL 61201-2296
309-794-7000
athletics.augustana.edu
• Mike Zapolski, Director of Athletics
(309) 794-7223
mikezapolski@augustana.edu
• Dave Wrath, Associate Director of
Athletics
(309) 794-7265
davewrath@augustana.edu

AURORA UNIVERSITY ATHLETICS
347 SOUTH GLADSTONE AVENUE
AURORA, IL 60506-4892
630-892-6431
Fax: 630-844-7809
athletics.aurora.edu
• Jim Hamad, Director of Athletics
(630) 844-6181
jhamad@aurora.edu
• Nicki Pieart, Assistant Director of Athletics
(630) 844-6174
npieart@aurora.edu
• Brian Kipley, Director of Sports Information
(630) 844-7575
bkipley@aurora.edu

AVERETT UNIVERSITY ATHLETICS
707 MOUNT CROSS ROAD
DANVILLE, VA 24540
434-791-5700
Fax: 434-791-5740
www.averettcougars.com
• Meg Stevens, Director of Athletics
(434) 791-5700
mstevens@averett.edu
• Danny Miller, Associate Director of
Athletics
(434) 791-5737
dmiller@averett.edu
• Drew Wilson, Sports Information Director
(434) 791-5621

drew.wilson@averett.edu
• Thomas Underwood, Head Athletic Trainer
(434) 791-7270
tunderwood@averett.edu

BABSON COLLEGE ATHLETICS
231 FOREST STREET
BABSON PARK, MA 02457-0310
781-239-4250
Fax: 781-239-5218
www.babsonathletics.com
• Mike Lynch, Interim Director of Athletics
(781) 239-4250
mlynch4@babson.edu
• Judy Blinstrub, Associate Athletics Director
(781) 239-4418
blinstrub@babson.edu
• Andy Dutton, Assistant Athletics Director
(781) 239-5650
dutton@babson.edu
• Rick Burr, Director of Athletics
Performance
(781) 239-5690
rburr@babson.edu

BALDWIN-WALLACE COLLEGE
ATHLETICS
275 EASTLAND ROAD
BEREA, OH 44017
440-826-2900
Fax: 440-826-2192
info@bw.edu
www.bwyellowjackets.com
• Kris A. Diaz, Director of Athletics
(440) 826-2309
kdiaz@bw.edu
• Duane Smith, Stadium Operations Director
(440) 826-2195
djsmith@bw.edu
• Cindy Zilko, Interim Head Athletic Trainer
(440) 826-2186
czilko@bw.edu
• Garry Miller, Assistant Athletic Trainer
(440) 826-8570
gmiller@bw.edu

BARD COLLEGE ATHLETICS
PO BOX 5000
ANNANDALE-ON-HUDSON, NY
12504-5000
845-758-7531
Fax: 845-758-7647
athletics@bard.edu
www.bardathletics.com
• Kristen Hall, Director of Athletics
(845) 758-7528
hall@bard.edu
• Jim Sheahan, Director of Athletic
Communications
(845) 752-4929
jsheahan@bard.edu
• Sarah Cartmill, Assistant Director of
Athletics
(845) 758-6822
scartmil@bard.edu
• Sam McMullen, Head Athletic Trainer
(845) 758-7694
smcmulle@bard.edu

BARUCH COLLEGE ATHLETICS
ATHLETIC DEPARTMENT
BOX B1-110
55 LEXINGTON AVENUE
NEW YORK, NY 10010
646-312-5049
Fax: 646-312-5041
athletics.baruch.cuny.edu

• Carrie Thomas, Administrator in Chargector
(646) 312-5053
carrie.thomas@baruch.cuny.edu
• Machli Joseph, Deputy Director of Athletics
(646) 312-5044
machli.joseph@baruch.cuny.edu
• John Neves, Director of Sports Information
(646) 312-5048
john.neves@baruch.cuny.edu
• Naomi Chang, Athletic Trainer
(646) 312-5059
naomi.chung@baruch.cuny.edu
• John Alesi, Athletic Coordinator
(646) 312-5064
john.alesi@baruch.cuny.edu

BATES COLLEGE ATHLETICS
130 CENTRAL AVENUE
LEWISTON, ME 04240
207-786-6255
Fax: 207-786-8232
athletics.bates.edu
• Kevin McHugh, Director of Athletics
(207) 786-6341
kmchugh@bates.edu
• Sue Harriman, Assistant Athletic Director
(207) 786-6238
sharrima@bates.edu
• Mike Verville, Director of Sports Medicine
(207) 786-6359
mvervill@bates.edu

BECKER COLLEGE
964 MAIN STREET
LEICESTER, MA 01524
508-791-9241
Fax: 508-892-8131
info@becker.edu
www.beckerhawks.com
• Frank Millerick, Director of Athletics
(774) 354-0481
frank.millerick@becker.edu
• Gene Alley, Associate Athletic Director
(774) 354-0484
gene.alley@becker.edu
• Steve Hoar, Assistant Athletic Director
(774) 354-0483
steve.hoar@becker.edu
• Matt Tittle, Director of Sports Information
(774) 354-0485
matt.tittle@becker.edu
• Brenda LaRow, Head Athletic Trainer
(774) 354-0490
brenda.larow@becker.edu

BELOIT COLLEGE ATHLETICS
700 COLLEGE STREET
BELOIT, WI 53511-5509
608-363-2229
Fax: 608-363-2044
www.beloit.edu/athletics
• Tim Schmiechen, Director of Athletics
(608) 363-2259
schmiech@beloit.edu
• Dave DeGeorge, Assistant Director of Athletics
(608) 363-2039
degeorge@beloit.edu
• Terry Owens, Director of Sports Information
(608) 363-2229
owenst@beloit.edu
• Peggy Steffen, Business Operations Manager

(608) 363-2296
steffenp@beloit.edu

BENEDICTINE UNIVERSITY ATHLETICS
5700 COLLEGE ROAD
LISLE, IL 60532
630-829-6140
Fax: 630-960-0899
benueagles.com
• Mark McHorney, Director of Athletics
(630) 829-6150
mmchorney@ben.edu
• Paul Nelson, Associate Director of Athletics
(603) 829-6144
pnelson@ben.edu
• Matthew Jones, Assistant Director of Athletics
(630) 829-6135
mjones@ben.edu
• Jessica Steadman Jelinek, Director of Athletic Marketing
(630) 829-6143
jjelinek@ben.edu
• Tarah Ellington Geve, Head Athletic Trainer
(630) 829-6154
tgeye@ben.edu

BETHEL COLLEGE ATHLETICS
1001 BETHEL CIRCLE
MISHAWAKA, IN 46545
574-807-7000
Fax: 574-807-7426
www.bethelcollegepilots.com
• Tom Visker, Athletics Director
(574) 807-7259
viskert@bethelcollege.edu
• Christopher Hess, Assistant Athletics Director
(574) 807-7236
hessc@bethelcollege.edu
• Natalie Young, Sports Information Director
(574) 807-7031
natalie.young@bethelcollege.edu

BLACKBURN COLLEGE ATHLETICS
700 COLLEGE AVE
CARLINVILLE, IL 62626
217-854-3231
800-233-3550
Fax: 217-854-5520
john.malin@blackburn.edu
www.blackburnbeavers.com
• John Malin, Athletic Director
(217) 854-5572
john.malin@blackburn.edu
• Michael Neal, Sports Information Director
(217) 854-5699
michael.neal@blackburn.edu
• Malia Murphy, Head Athletic Trainer
(217) 854-5610
malia.murphy@blackburn.edu

BLUFFTON COLLEGE ATHLETICS
1 UNIVERSITY DRIVE
BLUFFTON, OH 45817-2104
419-358-3227
800-488-3257
Fax: 419-358-3070
sportsinfo@bluffton.edu
www.bluffton.edu/athletics
• Phil Talavinia, Athletics Director
(419) 358-3227
talaviniap@bluffton.edu
• Bill Hanefeld, Jr., Sports Information Director

(419) 358-3241
sportsinfo@bluffton.edu
• Kim Schimmoeller, Associate Athletics Director
(419) 358-3221
schimmoellerk@bluffton.edu

BOWDOIN COLLEGE ATHLETICS
9000 COLLEGE STATION
BRUNSWICK, ME 04011
207-725-3326
Fax: 207-725-3019
tryan@bowdoin.edu
athletics.bowdoin.edu
• Tim Ryan, Ashmead White Director of Athletics
(207) 725-3247
tryan@bowdoin.edu
• Alice Wiercinski, Associate Director of Athletics
(207) 798-4342
awiercin@bowdoin.edu
• James Caton, Director for Communications
(207) 725-3254
jcaton@bowdoin.edu
• Dan Davis, Director of Athletic Training
(207) 725-3018
ddavies@bowdoin.edu
• Liz Grote, NCAA Compliance Coordinator
(207) 798-4148
egrote@bowdoin.edu

BRANDEIS UNIVERSITY ATHLETICS
GOSMAN SPORTS CENTER
MS 007
WALTHAM, MA 02254-9110
781-736-3668
Fax: 781-736-3656
www.brandeisjudges.com
• Lynne Dempsey, Acting Director of Athletics
(781) 736-3635
dempsey@brandeis.edu
• Tom Rand, Associate Director of Athletics
(781) 736-3632
rand@brandeis.edu
• Jim Zotz, Assistant Director of Athletics
(781) 736-3649
zotz@brandeis.edu
• Adam Levin, Sports Information Director
(781) 736-3631
aslevin@brandeis.edu
• Lisa Denicola, Head Athletic Trainer
(781) 736-3666
denicola@brandeis.edu

BRIDGEWATER COLLEGE ATHLETICS
402 EAST COLLEGE STREET
BRIDGEWATER, VA 22812
540-828-8000
800-759-8328
Fax: 540-828-5484
bridgewatereagles.com
• Curt Kendall, Director of Athletics
(540) 828-5407
ckendall@bridgewater.edu
• Jean Willi, Associate Director of Athletics
(540) 828-5400
jwilli@bridgewater.edu
• Jimmy McCumber, Director of Athletic Media Relations
(540) 828-5615
jmccumber@bridgewater.edu
• Heather Grant, Director of Clinical Athletic Training
(540) 828-5368

hgrant@bridgewater.edu
• Brandon Beach, Director of Strength and Conditioning
(540) 828-5783
bbeach@bridgewater.edu

BRIDGEWATER STATE COLLEGE ATHLETICS
131 SUMMER STREET
335 PLYMOUTH STREET
BRIDGEWATER, MA 02325
508-531-1352
Fax: 508-531-1356
bsubears.com
• Marybeth Lamb, Director of Athletics
(508) 531-1353
marybeth.lamb@bridgew.edu
• Mike Storey, Associate Director of Athletics
(508) 531-2350
mstorey@bridgew.edu
• Michael Holbrook, Director of Sports Information
(508) 531-2656
mholbrook@bridgew.edu
• Dan Rezendes, Director of Fitness
(508) 531-2976
drezendes@bridgew.edu
• Jeanne O'Brien, Director for Sports Medicine
(508) 531-1765
j5obrien@bridgew.edu

BUENA VISTA UNIVERSITY ATHLETICS
SIEBENS FIELDHOUSE
610 WEST FOURTH STREET
STORM LAKE, IA 50588
712-749-2253
Fax: 712-749-1460
phelpss@bvu.edu
bvuathletics.com
• Jack Denholm, Director of Athletics
(712) 749-2016
denholmj@bvu.edu
• Amy Santucci, Assistant Director of Athletics
(712) 749-2254
santuccia@bvu.edu
• Dominic Worrell, Head Athletic Trainer
(712) 749-2258
worrelld@bvu.edu
• Steven Phelps, Director of Sports Information
(712) 749-2633
phelpss@bvu.edu
• Ryder Weischedel, Director of Athletic Performance
(712) 749-2291
weischedelr@bvu.edu

BUFFALO STATE COLLEGE ATHLETICS
1300 ELMWOOD AVENUE
HOUSTON GYM 248
BUFFALO, NY 14222
716-878-6533
Fax: 716-878-3401
www.buffalostateathletics.com
• Jerry Boyes, Director of Athletics
(716) 878-6534
boyesjs@buffalostate.edu
• Jeff Ventura, Sports Information Director
(716) 878-6030
venturjm@buffalostate.edu
• Jim Fowler, Athletics Budget Manager
(716) 878-6516
fowlerjc@buffalostate.edu
• Sean Roberts, Head Atheltic Trainer

(716) 878-5328
robertsm@buffalostate.edu

CABRINI COLLEGE ATHLETICS
610 KING OF PRUSSIA ROAD
RADNOR, PA 19087
610-902-8387
Fax: 610-902-8385
brk39@cabrini.edu
www.cabriniathletics.com
• Brad Koch, Director of Athletics
(610) 902-8571
brk39@cabrini.edu
• Orlin Jespersen, Associate Director of Athletics
(610) 225-3909
ojj722@cabrini.edu
• Jess Huda, Assistant Director of Athletics
(610) 902-8318
jess.huda@cabrini.edu
• David Howell, Sports Information Director
(610) 902-8529

CALIFORNIA - SANTA CRUZ ATHLETICS, UNIVERSITY OF
1156 HIGH STREET
SANTA CRUZ, CA 95064
831-459-2531
Fax: 831-459-4070
admissions@ucsc.edu
www.goslugs.com
• Cliff Dochterman, Director of Athletics
(831) 459-4524
bananaslugdoc@ucsc.edu
• Collin Pregliasco, Associate Athletics Director
(831) 459-4964
• Marcus Wirth, Assistant Athletics Director
(831) 459-4159
Description of Sport Organization:
Division III, Part of the Independent Conference.
Teams:
Men/Women's Tennis, Men/Women's Soccer, Men/Women's Volleyball, Men/Women's Basketball, Men/Women's Swimming/Diving, Women's Golf, and Women's Cross Country.

CALIFORNIA INSTITUTE OF TECHNOLOGY ATHLETICS
1200 EAST CALIFORNIA BOULEVARD
MC 1-2
PASADENA, CA 91125
626-395-3253
Fax: 626-584-0589
wjack@caltech.edu
gocaltech.com
• Betsy Mitchell, Director of Athletics
(626) 395-6148
betsy.mitchell@caltech.edu
• John Carter, Associate Director of Athletics
(626) 395-3252
john.carter@caltech.edu
• Heather Semelmacher, Assistant Director, Intercollegiate Teams
(626) 395-4695
heather.semelmacher@caltech.edu
• Mark Becker, Director of Sports Information
(626) 395-3262
mbecker@caltech.edu
• Sally Alway, Head Athletic Trainer
(626) 395-1205
salway@caltech.edu

CALIFORNIA LUTHERAN UNIVERSITY ATHLETICS
60 WEST OLSEN ROAD
THOUSAND OAKS, CA 91360
805-493-3400
Fax: 805-493-3860
tmaple@callutheran.edu
www.clusports.com
• Daniel Kuntz, Athletic Director
(805) 493-3400
kuntz@callutheran.edu
• Debby Day, Assistant Athletic Director
(805) 493-3408
dday@callutheran.edu
• Kecia Davis, Head Athletic Trainer
(805) 493-3406
kgdavis@callutheran.edu
• Tracy L. Olson, Sports Information Director
(805) 493-3153
tmaple@callutheran.edu
• Thomas Dodd, Director of Aquatics
(805) 493-3530
dodd@callutheran.edu

CALVIN COLLEGE ATHLETICS
3201 BURTON STREET SE
GRAND RAPIDS, MI 49546
616-526-6000
Fax: 616-526-6060
meyn@calvin.edu
www.calvinknights.com
• Nancy Meyer, Director of Athletics, Internal Operations
(616) 526-6224
meyn@calvin.edu
• James Timmer, Director of Athletics, External Relations
(616) 526-6037
jrt3@calvin.edu
• Jeff Febus, Sports Information Coordinator
(616) 526-6169
jfebus@calvin.edu
• Joe Dykstra, Head Athletic Trainer
(616) 526-7630
jhd7@calvin.edu
• Justin TeBrake, Facilities Manager
(616) 526-7741
jtebra33@calvin.edu

CAPITAL UNIVERSITY ATHLETICS
1 COLLEGE AND MAIN
COLUMBUS, OH 43209
614-236-6209
Fax: 614-236-6178
sbruning@capital.edu
athletics.capital.edu
• Steve Bruning, Director of Athletics
(614) 236-6528
sbruning@capital.edu
• Dixie Jeffers, Associate Director of Athletics
(614) 236-6551
djeffers@capital.edu
• Alex Borchers, Director of Intramurals
(614) 236-6979
aborchers2@capital.edu
• Ryan Gasser, Sports Information Director
(614) 236-6174
rgasser@capital.edu

CARLETON COLLEGE ATHLETICS
ONE NORTH COLLEGE STREET
NORTHFIELD, MN 55057
507-222-4057
Fax: 507-646-5550
llunder@carleton.edu
apps.carleton.edu/athletics

• Gerald Young, Athletic Director
(507) 222-4057
gyoung@carleton.edu
• Heidi Jaynes, Associate Athletic Director
(507) 222-4447
hjaynes@carleton.edu
• Jenny Bourne, Faculty Athletic
Representative
(507) 222-4007
jbourne@carleton.edu
• David Pape, Sports Information Director
(507) 222-4185
dpape@carleton.edu
• Chad Alladin, Head Athletic Trainer
(507) 222-7371
calladin@carleton.edu

CARNEGIE MELLON UNIVERSITY ATHLETICS
SKIBO GYMNASIUM TECH AND FREW STREETS
PITTSBURGH, PA 15213
412-268-8551
Fax: 412-268-3099
jcentor@andrew.cmu.edu
athletics.cmu.edu
• Josh Centor, Director of Athletics
(412) 268-8054
jcentor@andrew.cmu.edu
• Patrick Sterk, Associate Director of Athletics
(412) 268-6042
psterk@andrew.cmu.edu
• Sara Gauntner, Assistant Director of Athletics
(412) 268-7030
sarap@andrew.cmu.edu
• Mark Fisher, Sports Information Director
(412) 268-3087
mwfisher@andrew.cmu.edu
• Adam Hindes, Head Athletic Trainer
(412) 268-2222
ahindes@andrew.cmu.edu

CARTHAGE COLLEGE ATHLETICS
2001 ALFORD PARK DRIVE
KENOSHA, WI 53140
262-551-5942
Fax: 262-551-5995
athletics.carthage.edu
• Robert Bonn, Director of Athletics
(262) 551-5931
rbonn@carthage.edu
• Chris Barker, Director of Athletic Operations
(262) 551-6177
cbarker1@carthage.edu
• Phil Burwell, Director of Athletic Communications
(262) 551-5740
pburwell@carthage.edu
• Jake Dinauer, Head Athletic Trainer
(262) 551-6107
jdinauer@carthage.edu

CASE WESTERN RESERVE UNIVERSITY ATHLETICS
10900 EUCLID AVENUE
CLEVELAND, OH 44106
216-368-2420
Fax: 216-368-5475
athletics@case.edu
athletics.case.edu
• Amy Backus, Director of Athletics
(216) 368-0848
amy.backus@case.edu
• Pat Kennedy, Associate Athletic Director

(216) 368-3874
patrick.kennedy@case.edu
• Jon Schwartz, Sports Information Director
(216) 368-6517
jon.schwartz@case.edu
• Jessica White, Head Athletic Trainer
(216) 368-2863
jessica.m.white2@case.edu

CASTLETON STATE UNIVERSITY ATHLETICS
190 COLLEGE STREET
CASTLETON, VT 05735
802-468-6275
Fax: 802-468-2189
www.castletonsports.com
• Deanna Tyson, Associate Dean of Athletics and Recreation
(802) 468-1365
deanna.tyson@castleton.edu
• Tim Barrett, Senior Associate Director of Athletics
(802) 468-1468
tim.barrett@castleton.edu
• Brittany Higgins, Assistant Director of Compliance
(802) 468-6422
brittany.higgings@castleton.edu
• Steve Austin, Head Athletic Trainer
stephen.austin@castleton.edu
• Benjamin Stockwell, Director of Athletic Communications
(802) 468-6172
ben.stockwell@castleton.edu

CATHOLIC UNIVERSITY OF AMERICA ATHLETICS
DUFOUR ATHLETIC CENTER
3606 JOHN MCCORMACK DRIVE NE
WASHINGTON, DC 20064
202-319-5286
Fax: 202-319-6199
www.cuacardinals.com
• Sean Sullivan, Director of Athletics
(202) 319-5286
sullivansm@cua.edu
• Dan Ambrose, Assistant Athletic Director
(202) 319-6043
• Mike Gambardella, Director for Communications
(202) 319-5610
gambardella@cua.edu

CAZENOVIA COLLEGE ATHLETICS
22 SULLIVAN STREET
CAZENOVIA, NY 13035
315-655-7266
Fax: 315-655-1099
athletics@cazenovia.edu
www.cazenoviawildcats.com
• Michael Brooks, Director of Intercollegiate Athletics
(315) 655-7141
mdbrooks@cazenovia.edu
• Pete Way, Senior Associate Director of Athletics
(315) 655-7142
pmway@cazenovia.edu
• Bryon McAllister, Director for Sports Medicine
(315) 655-7321
mcallister@cazenovia.edu
• Chris Comino, Sports Information Contact
(315) 655-7184
ccomino@cazenovia.edu
• Bryon McAllister, Sports Information Contact

(315) 655-7321
bmcallister@cazenovia.edu

CENTRAL COLLEGE ATHLETICS
812 UNIVERSITY STREET
PELLA, IA 50219
641-628-5226
Fax: 641-628-5356
www.central.edu/athletics
• Eric Van Kley, Athletic Director
(641) 628-5422
vankleye@central.edu
• Alicia O'Brien, Associate Athletics Director
(641) 628-5434
obriena@central.edu
• Jeffy Schuring, Athletics Office Manager
(641) 628-5226
schuringj@central.edu
• Frank Neu, Head Athletic Trainer
(641) 628-5451
neuf@central.edu

CENTRE COLLEGE ATHLETICS
600 WEST WALNUT STREET
DANVILLE, KY 40422
859-238-5491
Fax: 859-236-6081
centrecolonels.com
• Brad Fields, Director of Athletics and Recreation
(859) 238-5485
brad.fields@centre.edu
• Gina Nicoletti, Associate Athletic Director
(859) 238-5493
gina.nicoletti@centre.edu
• Sonny Evans, Director of Athletic Facilities
(859) 238-8734
sonny.evans@centre.edu
• Jamey Gay, Head Athletic Trainer
(859) 238-5497
jamey.gay@centre.edu
• Liam Halferty, Director of Athletics Communications
(859) 238-6158
liam.halferty@centre.edu

CHAPMAN UNIVERSITY ATHLETICS
ONE UNIVERSITY DRIVE
ORANGE, CA 92866
714-997-6691
Fax: 714-532-6010
www.chapman.edu
• Terry Boesel, Director of Athletics
(714) 997-6818
boesel@chapman.edu
• Doug Aiken, Associate Director of Athletics
(714) 997-6900
daiken@chapman.edu
• Mike Bokosky, Assistant Athletics Director
(714) 532-6083
bokosky@chapman.edu
• Steven Olveda, Sports Information Director
(714) 744-7889
olveda@chapman.edu
• Pam Gibbons, Director of Athletic Training
(303) 997-6640
gibbons@chapman.edu

CHICAGO ATHLETICS, UNIVERSITY OF
5530 SOUTH ELLIS AVENUE
CHICAGO, IL 60637
773-702-7684
Fax: 773-702-6517
athletics.uchicago.edu
• Erin McDermott, Director of Athletics
(773) 702-7684

erinmcd@uchicago.edu
• Rosalie Resch, Associate Athletic Director, Compliance
(773) 702-4659
rresch@uchicago.edu
• Nathan Lindquist, Director of Sports Information
(773) 702-4638
nlindquist@uchicago.edu
• Jennifer Coleman, Associate Athletic Director, Facilities
(773) 834-1664
colemanj@uchicago.edu

CHRISTOPHER NEWPORT UNIVERSITY ATHLETICS
1 UNIVERSITY PLACE
NEWPORT NEWS, VA 23606
757-594-7025
Fax: 757-594-7839
cnusports.com
• Carrie Gardner, Associate Director of Athletics
(757) 594-7462
carrie.gardner@cnu.edu
• Francis Tommasino, Director of Athletic Communications
(757) 594-7884
ftommasi@cnu.edu
• Shanika Ellis, Athletics Finance Manager
(757) 594-7288
sellis@cnu.edu
• Rob Silsbee, Sports Information Director
(757) 594-7382
rob.silsbee@cnu.edu

CITY COLLEGE OF NEW YORK ATHLETICS
160 CONVENT AVENUE
NEW YORK, NY 10031
212-650-8228
Fax: 212-650-8230
www.ccnyathletics.com
• Kevin H. Abdur-Rahman, Director of Athletics
(212) 650-7556
krahman@ccny.cuny.edu
• Karina Jorge, Assistant Director of Athletics
(212) 650-7524
kjorge@ccny.cuny.edu
• Roberto Ignaccolo, Head Coach
(212) 650-5448
rignacocolo@ccny.cuny.edu
• Catherine Prince, Sports Information Director
(212) 650-6925
cprince@ccny.cuny.edu

CLAREMONT-MUDD-SCRIPPS COLLEGES ATHLETICS
500 EAST NINTH STREET
CLAREMONT, CA 91711
909-607-2904
Fax: 909-621-8848
www.cmsathletics.org
• Michael Sutton, Director of Athletics
(909) 607-3562
michael.sutton@cms.claremont.edu
• Adam Pruett, Director of Recreational Sports
(909) 607-8331
adam.pruett@cms.claremont.edu
• Emily Nordhoff, Sports Information Director
(909) 607-1123
emily.nordhoff@cms.claremont.edu
• Steve Graves, Head Athletic Trainer

(909) 607-3248
steve.graves@cms.claremont.edu

CLARK UNIVERSITY ATHLETICS
950 MAIN STREET
WORCESTER, MA 01610
508-793-7161
Fax: 508-793-7627
www.clarku.edu/athletics
• Patricia Cronin, Director of Athletics
(508) 793-7305
tcronin@clarku.edu
• Joe Brady, Associate Athletic Director
(508) 421-3796
jbrady@clarku.edu
• Paul E. Phillips, Assistant Athletic Director
(508) 793-7170
pephillips@clarku.edu
• Kevin D. Anderson, Sports Information Director
(508) 793-7164
keanderson@clarku.edu

CLARKSON UNIVERSITY ATHLETICS
8 CLARKSON AVENUE
BOX 5830
POTSDAM, NY 13699
315-268-6622
Fax: 315-268-7613
www.clarksonathletics.com
• Steve Yianoukos, Athletic Director
(315) 268-7021
stevey@clarkson.edu
• Laurel Kane, Associate Athletic Director
(315) 268-6594
lkane@clarkson.edu
• Mick Maquire, Assistant Athletic Director
(315) 268-3745
• Kelly Norman, Fitness Center Director
(315) 268-3768
normankl@clarkson.edu
• Mike Pitts, Head Athletic Trainer
(315) 268-2123
mpitts@clarkson.edu

COE COLLEGE ATHLETICS
1220 FIRST AVENUE NORTHEAST
CEDAR RAPIDS, IA 52402
319-399-8500
800-332-8404
Fax: 319-399-8816
www.coeathletics.com
• John Chandler, Athletic Director
(319) 399-8622
jchandle@coe.edu
• Ryan Workman, Sports Information Director
(319) 399-8570
sid@coe.edu
• Steve Cook, Assistant Athletic Director
(319) 399-8849
scook@coe.edu
• Nick Bender, Director of Athletic Training Services
(319) 399-8653
nbender@coe.edu

COLBY COLLEGE ATHLETICS
4900 MAYFLOWER HILL
WATERVILLE, ME 04901-8849
207-859-4900
athletics@colby.edu
www.colby-sawyerathletics.com
• Tim Wheaton, Director of Athletics
(207) 859-4904
tim.wheaton@colby.edu
• Tom Burton, Associate Director of

Athletics
(207) 859-4922
tom.burton@colby.edu
• Bill Sodoma, Sports Information Director
(207) 859-4940
wcsodoma@colby.edu
• Tim Weston, Head Athletic Trainer
(207) 859-4970
tsweston@colby.edu
• Dawn Strout, Strength & Conditioning Coordinator
(207) 859-4944
dawn.strout@colby.edu

COLBY-SAWYER COLLEGE ATHLETICS
541 MAIN STREET
NEW LONDON, NH 03257
603-526-3610
Fax: 603-526-3435
www.colby-sawyerathletics.com
• Bill Foti, Director of Athletics
(603) 526-3613
wfoti@colby-sawyer.edu
• Ryan Emerson, Director of Athletics for Sports Information
(603) 526-3783
remerson@colby-sawyer.edu
• Ruth Clark, Athletic Program Manager
(603) 526-3610
rclark@colby-sawyer.edu
• Scott Roy, Head Athletic Trainer
(603) 526-3607

COLLEGE OF NEW JERSEY ATHLETICS (TCNJ)
2000 PENNINGTON ROAD
PO BOX 7718
EWING, NJ 08628-0718
609-771-2230
Fax: 609-637-5133
www.tcnjathletics.com
• Sharon Beverly, Executive Director of Athletics
(609) 771-2231
beverlys@tcnj.edu
• LaKitha Murray, Senior Associate Director of Athletics
(609) 771-3037
murrayl@tcnj.edu
• Dawn Henderson, Associate Director of Athletics
(609) 771-3030
dhenders@tcnj.edu
• Megan Guicheteau, Head Athletic Trainer
(609) 771-2387
quichete@tcnj.edu
• Aaron Becker, Athletics Facilities Coordinator
(609) 771-2288
beckera@tcnj.edu

COLORADO COLLEGE ATHLETICS
14 EAST CACHE LA POUDRE
COLORADO SPRINGS, CO 80903
719-389-6476
Fax: 719-389-6873
cctigers.com
• Ken Ralph, Director of Athletics
(719) 389-6475
ken.ralph@coloradocollege.edu
• Greg Capell, Senior Associate Director of Athletics
(719) 389-6493
greg.capell@coloradocollege.edu
• Andy Obringer, Assistant Athletics Director
(719) 389-6107
andy.obringer@coloradocollege.edu

• Jerry Cross, Director of Athletics
Communications
(719) 389-6755
jerry.cross@coloradocollege.edu
• Ian Wood, Coordinator of Sports Medicine
(719) 389-6813
ian.wood@coloradocollege.edu

CONCORDIA COLLEGE (MN) ATHLETICS
901 8TH STREET SOUTH
MOORHEAD, MN 56562
218-299-4000
Fax: 218-299-4189
concordiamn.prestosports.com
• Rich Glas, Athletic Director
(218) 299-4231
glas@cord.edu
• Rachel Bergeson, Associate Athletic
Director
(218) 299-4728
bergeson@cord.edu
• Jim Cella, Sports Information Director
(218) 299-3194
cella@cord.edu
• Don Bruenjes, Head Athletic Trainer
(218) 299-4208
bruenjes@cord.edu

**CONCORDIA UNIVERSITY (WI)
ATHLETICS**
12800 NORTH LAKE SHORE DRIVE
MEQUON, WI 53097
262-243-4385
Fax: 262-243-4475
www.cuwfalcons.com
• Rob Barnhill, Director of Athletics
(262) 243-4404
rob.barnhill@cuw.edu
• Steve Crook, Associate Director of
Athletics
(262) 243-4419
steve.crook@cuw.edu
• Erik Halling, Director of Athletic Relations
(262) 243-4549
erik.halling@cuw.edu
• Steven Schauer, Director of Athletic
Communications
(262) 243-2664
steven.schauer@cuw.edu
• Angela Steffen, Director of Sports
Medicine
(262) 243-4537
angela.steffen@cuw.edu

**CONCORDIA UNIVERSITY AT AUSTIN
ATHLETICS**
11400 CONCORDIA UNIVERSITY DRIVE
AUSTIN, TX 78726
512-313-4524
Fax: 512-313-4599
athletics.concordia.edu
• Ronda Seagraves, Director of Athletics
(512) 313-4501
ronda.seagraves@concordia.edu
• Stan Bonewitz, Assistant Athletics Director
(512) 313-4504
stan.bonewitz@concordia.edu
• Martha Baldwin, Head Athletic Trainer
(512) 313-4506
martha.baldwin@concordia.edu

**CONCORDIA UNIVERSITY CHICAGO
ATHLETICS**
7400 AUGUSTA STREET
RIVER FOREST, IL 60305-1402
708-209-3116
Fax: 708-209-3154

crfathletics@cuchicago.edu
www.cucougars.com
• Jeff Hynes, Vice President for Student
Services
(708) 209-3444
jeff.hynes@cuchicago.edu
• Pete Gnan, Director of Athletics
(708) 209-3192
pete.gnan@cuchicago.edu
• Mandy Semenik, Assistant Director of
Athletics
(708) 209-3735
• Jim Egan, Sports Information Director
(708) 209-3541
james.egan@cuchicago.edu
• Terri Woods, Head Athletic Trainer
(708) 209-3120

CONNECTICUT COLLEGE ATHLETICS
270 MOHEGAN AVENUE
NEW LONDON, CT 06320
860-439-2541
Fax: 860-439-2516
camelathletics.com
• Crocker Cooker, Director of Athletics
(860) 439-2570
bscro@conncoll.edu
• Eva Kovach, Athletic Department
Coordinator
(860) 439-2541
edkov@conncoll.edu
• John Heck, Interim Head Athletic Trainer
(860) 439-5155
jphec@conncoll.edu

CORNELL COLLEGE ATHLETICS
600 FIRST STREET SOUTHWEST
MOUNT VERNON, IA 52314
319-895-4483
Fax: 319-895-5682
www.cornellrams.com
• John Cochrane, Director of Athletics
(319) 895-4230
jcochrane@cornellcollege.edu
• Dick R. Simmons, Associate Director of
Athletics
(319) 895-4270
dsimmons@cornellcollege.edu
• Shanda Ness, Asssitant Director of
Athletics
(319) 895-4411
sness@cornellcollege.edu
• Kerry Kahl, Sports Information Director
(319) 895-4483
kkahl@cornellcollege.edu
• Eric Dybvig, Head Athletic Trainer
(319) 895-4009
edybvig@cornellcollege.edu

COVENANT COLLEGE ATHLETICS
14049 SCENIC HIGHWAY
LOOKOUT MOUNTAIN, GA 30750
706-419-1525
Fax: 706-419-1660
sid@covenant.edu
athletics.covenant.edu
• Derek Halvorson, President
(706) 419-1117
president@covenant.edu
• Brad Voyles, VP for Student Development
(706) 419-1107
brad.voyles@covenant.edu
• Kyle Taylor, Director of Athletics
(706) 419-1516
• Andrew Mindeman, Sports Information
Director
(706) 419-1514

andrew.mindeman@covenant.edu
• Meredith Atwood, Head Athletic Trainer
(706) 419-1523
meredith.atwood@covenant.edu

CURRY COLLEGE ATHLETICS
1071 BLUE HILL AVENUE
MILTON, MA 02186
617-333-0500
Fax: 617-333-2027
www.curryathletics.com
• Vinnie Eruzione, Athletic Director
(617) 333-2202
veruzion@curry.edu
• Ken Golner, Director for Communications
(617) 333-2324
kgolner@curry.edu
• Caitlin Roberts, Sports Information
Director
(617) 333-2324
kgolner@curry.edu
• Kelly Melville, Head Athletic Trainer
(617) 333-2203
kmorriso0612@curry.edu

D'YOUVILLE COLLEGE ATHLETICS
320 PORTER AVENUE
BUFFALO, NY 14201
716-829-8000
800-777-3921
athletics.dyc.edu
• Brian Cavanaugh, Director of Athletics
(716) 829-7878
• Rob Kennuth, Head Athletic Trainer
(716) 829-8309
• Stephen McCarthy, Sports Information
Director
(716) 829-8131
• Earl Schunk, Assistant Athletic Director
(716) 829-8300

DALLAS ATHLETICS, UNIVERSITY OF
1845 EAST NORTHGATE DRIVE
IRVING, TX 75062-4376
972-721-5009
Fax: 972-721-5208
www.udallasathletics.com
• Dick Strockbine, Athletics Director
(972) 721-5207
dick@udallas.edu
• Robb Leibold, Lead Athletics Trainer
(972) 721-5010
rleibold@udallas.edu
• Nathan Yacovissi, Sports Information
Manager
(972) 721-5378
nyacovissi@udallas.edu

**DANIEL WEBSTER COLLEGE
ATHLETICS**
20 UNIVERSITY DRIVE
NASHUA, NH 03063
603-577-6381
Fax: 603-577-6597
• Chris Gilmore, Director of Athletics
(603) 577-6381
cgilmore@dwc.edu
• Ken Belbin, Sports Information Director
(603) 577-6648
belbin_ken@dwc.edu
• Andrea Woodbury, Assistant Athletic
Director
(603) 577-6495
awoodbury@dwc.edu
• Charles Barfelz, Head Trainer
(603) 577-6492
barfelz@dwc.edu

DE PAUW UNIVERSITY ATHLETICS
702 SOUTH COLLEGE AVENUE
PO BOX 37
GREENCASTLE, IN 46135-0037
765-658-4800
800-446-5295
Fax: 765-658-4964
depauwtigers.com
• Stevie Baker-Watson, Director of Athletics
(765) 658-6075
steviebaker-watson@depauw.edu
• Kellen Wells-Mangold, Assistant Athletics
Director, Internal Operations
(765) 658-4934
kwells-mangold@depauw.edu
• Kris Huffman, Assistant Athletics Director
(765) 658-4960
khuffman@depauw.edu

DE SALES UNIVERSITY ATHLETICS
BILLERA HALL
2755 STATION AVENUE
CENTER VALLEY, PA 18034
610-282-1100
Fax: 610-282-2279
athletics.desales.edu
• Scott Coval, Director of Athletics
(610) 282-1100
scott.coval@desales.edu
• Gracia Perilli, Assistant Director of
Athletics
(610) 282-1100
gracia.perilli@desales.edu
• BJ Spigelmyer, Sports Information Director
(610) 282-1100
william.spigelmyer@desales.edu

DEFIANCE COLLEGE ATHLETICS
701 NORTH CLINTON STREET
DEFIANCE, OH 43512
419-783-2342
Fax: 419-783-2369
www.defianceathletics.com
• Jodie Holava, Interim Director of Athletics
(419) 783-2379
rholava@defiance.edu
• Kathleen Westfall, Asst. Athletics
Director/SWA
(419) 783-2345
kwestfall@defiance.edu
• Derek Woodley, Interim Asst. Athletics
Director
(419) 783-2341
dwoodley@defiance.edu

**DELAWARE VALLEY COLLEGE
ATHLETICS**
700 E. BUTLER AVENUE
DOYLESTOWN, PA 18901
215-489-2268
Fax: 215-230-2963
athletics.delval.edu
• Steve Cantrell, Director of Athletics
(215) 489-2268
steve.cantrell@delval.edu
• Matt Levy, Director of Sports Information
(215) 489-2937
matthew.levy@delval.edu
• Carol Di Girolamo, Assistant Athletic
Director
(215) 489-2300
carol.digirolamo@delval.edu
• Valerie Rice-Smith, Head Athletic Trainer
(215) 489-2353
valerie.rice@delval.edu

DENISON UNIVERSITY ATHLETICS
200 LIVINGSTON DRIVE
GRANVILLE, OH 43023
740-587-6580
Fax: 740-587-6362
carneydebord@denison.edu
denisonbigred.com
• Nan Carney-DeBoard, Director of Athletics
(740) 587-6428
carneydebord@denison.edu
• Lynn Schweizer, Senior Associate Director
of Athletics
(740) 587-6657
schweizer@denison.edu
• Larry Schneiderer, Director of Athletic
Operations
(740) 587-5560
schneiderer@denison.edu
• Craig Hicks, Sports Information Director
(740) 587-6546
hiscksc@denison.edu

DICKINSON COLLEGE ATHLETICS
20 SOUTH COLLEGE STREET
CARLISLE, PA 17013
717-245-1320
Fax: 717-245-1441
www.dickinsonathletics.com
• Joe Giunta, Director of Athletics
(717) 245-1320
giuntaj@dickinson.edu
• Joel Quattrone, Senior Associate Athletics
Director
(717) 245-1364
quattron@dickinson.edu
• Charlie McGuire, Director of Sports
Information
(717) 245-1652
mcguire@dickinson.edu
• Janelle Nolt, Head Athletic Trainer
(717) 245-1651
noltj@dickinson.edu
• Bob Penner, Equipment Manager
(717) 245-1265
penner@dickinson.edu

DOMINICAN UNIVERSITY ATHLETICS
7900 WEST DIVISION STREET
RIVER FOREST, IL 60305
708-524-6232
Fax: 708-488-5095
athletics@dom.edu
www.dustars.com
• Erick Baumann, Director of Athletics
(708) 488-5054
ebauman@dom.edu
• Mark White, Associate Director of Athletics
(708) 524-6518
mkwhite@dom.edu
• Jeff Halsema, Assistant Director of
Athletics
(708) 524-6552
jhalsema@dom.edu
• Ken Trendel, Director of Sports Information
(708) 524-6232
ktrendel@dom.edu
• Erica Albertin, Head Athletic Trainer
(708) 524-6226
ehedges@dom.edu

DREW UNIVERSITY ATHLETICS
36 MADISON AVENUE
MADISON, NJ 7940
973-408-3441
Fax: 973-408-3014
www.drewrangers.com

• Jason Fein, Director of Athletics
(973) 408-3441
jfein@drew.edu
• Vincent Masco, Associate Director of
Athletics
(973) 408-3443
vmasco@drew.edu
• Matt Choquette, Director of Athletic
Communications
(973) 408-3574
mchoquette@drew.edu

DUBUQUE ATHLETICS, UNIVERSITY OF
2000 UNIVERSITY AVENUE
DUBUQUE, IA 52001
563-589-3000
Fax: 563-589-3425
www.dbq.edu/athletics
• Dan Runkle, Director of Athletics
(563) 589-3599
drunkle@dbq.edu
• Jason Berna, Assistant Athletic Director
(563) 589-3786
jberna@dbq.edu
• Debra R. Runkle, Head Athletic Trainer
(563) 589-3244
drrunkle@dbq.edu

EARLHAM COLLEGE ATHLETICS
801 NATIONAL ROAD WEST
RICHMOND, IN 47374-4095
765-983-1414
Fax: 765-983-1446
www.goearlham.com
• Mike Bergum, Director of Athletics
(765) 983-1624
bergumi@earlham.edu
• Kaitlin Leach, Associate Director of
Athletics
(765) 983-1481
leachka@earlham.edu
• Mitch Blankespoor, Director of Sports
Marketing
(765) 983-1795
blankmi@earlham.edu
• Bill Kinsey, Head Athletic Trainer
(765) 983-1312
kinsebi@earlham.edu
• Catheryn Dickman, Director of Wellness
Programs
(765) 983-1899
cathrynd@earlham.edu

**EASTERN CONNECTICUT STATE
UNIVERSITY ATHLETICS**
ATHLETIC DEPARTMENT
83 WINDHAM STREET
WILLIMANTIC, CT 06226
860-465-5172
Fax: 860-465-4696
molta@easternct.edu
gowarriorathletics.com
• Lori Runksmeier, Director of Athletics
(860) 465-5091
runksmeierl@easternct.edu
• Cynthia Washburne, Associate Director of
Athletics
(860) 465-4347
washburnec@easternct.edu
• Bob Molta, Sports Information Director
(860) 465-5172
molta@easternct.edu
• Julie Alexander, Athletic Trainer
(860) 465-5506
alexanderju@easternct.edu

EASTERN MENNONITE UNIVERSITY ATHLETICS
1200 PARK ROAD
HARRISONBURG, VA 22802-2462
540-432-4440
Fax: 540-432-4443
www.emuroyals.com
• Dave King, Director of Athletics
(540) 432-4646
david.king@emu.edu
• Mike Downey, Head Athletic Trainer
(540) 432-4336
mike.downey@emu.edu
• James De Boer, Sports Information Director
(540) 432-4441
james.deboer@emu.edu

EASTERN NAZARENE COLLEGE ATHLETICS
23 EAST ELM AVENUE
QUINCY, MA 02170
617-745-7000
Fax: 617-745-3938
athletics.enc.edu
• Brad Zarges, Director of Athletics
brad.zarges@enc.edu
• Jim Aller, Assistant Athletic Director
(617) 745-3637
james.aller@enc.edu
• Rob Rossi, Sports Information Director
(617) 745-3641
robert.rossi@enc.edu

EASTERN UNIVERSITY ATHLETICS
1300 EAGLE ROAD
ST. DAVIDS, PA 19087
610-341-1736
Fax: 610-341-1317
www.goeasterneagles.com
• Nate Stewart, Director of Athletics
(610) 225-5032
• Heidi Birtwistle, Associate Athletic Director
(610) 341-1738
hbirtwis@eastern.edu
• Dan Mouw, Assistant Athlteic Director for Promotions
(215) 888-4422
dmouw@eastern.edu
• Justin Farrell, Sports Information Director
(610) 608-0233
jfarrel1@eastern.edu
• John Post, Director for Sports Medicine
(610) 341-1316
jpost@eastern.edu

EDGEWOOD COLLEGE ATHLETICS
1000 EDGEWOOD COLLEGE DRIVE
MADISON, WI 53711
608-663-4861
Fax: 608-663-2391
www.edgewoodcollegeeagles.com
• Al Brisack, Director of Athletics
(608) 663-3289
abrisack@edgewood.edu
• Susann Saltzberry, Assistant Director of Athletics
(608) 663-3249
ssaltzberry@edgewood.edu
• David Petroff, Director of Athletics Communications
(608) 663-6734
deptroff@edgewood.edu
• Adam Krueger, Head Athletic Trainer
(608) 663-3326
adamkrueger@edgewood.edu

ELIZABETHTOWN COLLEGE ATHLETICS
ONE ALPHA DRIVE
ELIZABETHTOWN, PA 17022
717-361-1137
Fax: 717-361-1488
www.etownbluejays.com
• Chris Morgan, Director of Athletics
(717) 361-1407
morganc@etown.edu
• Cliff Smith, Assistant Director of Athletics
(717) 361-1463
smithhc@etown.edu
• Bob Schlosser, Associate Director of Athletics
(717) 361-1141
schlosra@etown.edu
• Yvonne Kauffman, Director of Atletic Advancement
(717) 361-1138
kauffmye@etown.edu
• Bridget Spooner, Head Athletic Trainer
(717) 361-1591
spoonerb@etown.edu
• Matt Heffelfinger, Director of Athletic Communications
(717) 361-1311
heffelfingerm@etown.edu

ELMHURST COLLEGE ATHLETICS
190 PROSPECT AVENUE
ELMHURST, IL 60126-3296
630-617-3140
Fax: 630-617-3726
athletic@elmhurst.edu
www.elmhurstbluejays.com
• Paul Krohn, Director of Athletics
(630) 617-3142
paulk@elmhurst.edu
• Julie Hall, Assistant Athletic Director
(630) 617-3145
julieh@elmhurst.edu
• Kevin Juday, Director of Sports Information
(630) 617-3380
kevinj@elmhurst.edu
• Anne Hutchins, Head Athletic Trainer
(630) 617-3174
anneh@elmhurst.edu

ELMIRA COLLEGE ATHLETICS
ONE PARK PLACE
ELMIRA, NY 14901
607-735-1730
Fax: 607-735-1717
athletics@elmira.edu
athletics.elmira.edu
• Pat Thompson, Vice President of Athletics
(607) 735-1730
pthompson@elmira.edu
• Jen Bozek, Senior Associate Director of Athletics
(607) 735-1748
jbozek@elmira.edu
• Jerry Fisk, Assistant Athletic Director of Event
(607) 735-1110
gfisk@elmira.edu
• Don Sherman, Director of Sports Information
(607) 735-1131
dsherman@elmira.edu
• Dave Tomkalski, Head Athletics Trainer
(607) 735-1752
dtomkalski@elmira.edu

EMERSON COLLEGE ATHLETICS
120 BOYLSTON STREET
BOSTON, MA 02116-4624

617-824-8500
Fax: 617-824-8529
athletics@emerson.edu
www.emersonlions.com
• Patricia Nicol, Director of Athletics
(617) 824-8969
patricia_nicol@emerson.edu
• Stanford Nance, Senior Associate Director of Athletics
(617) 824-8930
stanford_nance@emerson.edu
• Matt Ulrich, Director of Media Relations
(617) 824-8458
matthew_ulrich@emerson.edu
• Mandy Nicoles, Head Athletic Trainer
(617) 824-3232
amanda_nicoles@emerson.edu

EMORY & HENRY COLLEGE ATHLETICS
12228 ITTA BENA ROAD
PO BOX 947
EMORY, VA 24327
276-944-6233
Fax: 276-944-6738
www.gowasps.com
• Myra Sims, Director of Athletics
(276) 944-6236
msims@ehc.edu
• Dave Griffore, Associate Director of Athletics
(276) 944-6747
• Trey McCall, Assistant Director of Athletics
(276) 944-6860
tmccall@ehc.edu
• Melissa Davis, Head Athletic Trainer
(276) 944-6786
mdavis@ehc.edu
• Joe Matthews, Director of Sports Information
(276) 944-6830
jmatthews@ehc.edu

EMORY UNIVERSITY ATHLETICS
26 EAGLE ROW
ATLANTA, GA 30322
404-727-6547
Fax: 404-727-4989
www.emoryathletics.com
• Michael Vienna, Director of Athletics
(404) 727-6532
mvienna@emory.edu
• Timber Hines, Director of Athletic Facilities
(404) 712-2435
thines@emory.edu
• Blair Vickery, Athletics Business Manager
(404) 727-1771
bvicker@emory.edu
• John Farina, Sports Information Director
(404) 727-6553
jfarina@emory.edu

ENDICOTT COLLEGE ATHLETICS
376 HALE STREET
BEVERLY, MA 01915
978-232-2312
Fax: 978-232-2600
www.ecgulls.com
• Brian Wylie, Director of Athletics
(978) 232-2440
bwylie@endicott.edu
• Jodi Kenyon, Associate Athletic Director
(978) 232-2234
jkenyon@endicott.edu
• Jodi Cipolla, Marketing & Promotions
(978) 232-2303
jcipolla@endicott.edu
• Jay Lilly, Director of Arena Operations

(978) 998-7731
jlilly@endicott.edu

EUREKA COLLEGE ATHLETICS
300 EAST COLLEGE AVENUE
EUREKA, IL 61530
309-467-6370
Fax: 309-467-6402
www.eurekareddevils.com
• Steve Thompson, Director of Athletics
(309) 467-6370
sthompson@eureka.edu
• Kurt Barth, Assistant Athletic Director
(309) 467-6369
kbarth@eureka.edu
• Alex Hess, Sports Information Director
(309) 467-6456
ahess@eureka.edu
• Chris Sharkey, Head Athletic Trainer
(309) 467-6370
csharkey@eureka.edu

FAIRLEIGH DICKINSON UNIVERSITY/FLORHAM
285 MADISON AVENUE
MADISON, NJ 07940
973-443-8500
fdudevils.com
• Bill Klika, Director of Athletics
(973) 443-8972
klikaad@fdu.edu
• Roger Kindel, Associate Director of Athletics
(973) 443-8964
kindel@fdu.edu
• Bryan Jackson, Director of Sports Information
(973) 443-8965
bjackson@fdu.edu
• Jay Ashby, Equipment Manager
(973) 443-8966
• Tom Wilkinson, Head Athletic Trainer
(973) 443-8967
tgwsr@fdu.edu

FARMINGDALE STATE UNIVERSITY (FSU) ATHLETICS
2350 BROADHOLLOW ROAD
FARMINGDALE, NY 11735
631-420-2482
Fax: 631-420-2994
www.farmingdalesports.com
• Michael Harrington, Director of Athletics
(631) 420-2482
harrinm@farmingdale.edu
• Tom Azzara, Associate Athletic Director
(631) 420-2599
azzaratf@farmingdale.edu
• Deana Ward, Assistant Athletic Director
(631) 420-2178
warddt@farmingdale.edu
• Don Haworth, Director of Sports Medicine
(631) 794-6282
hawortde@farmingdale.edu

FERRUM COLLEGE ATHLETICS
590 FERRUM MOUNTAIN ROAD
FERRUM, VA 24088
540-365-4493
Fax: 540-365-4540
anaff@ferrum.edu
ferrumpanthers.com
• Abe Naff, Director of Athletics
(540) 365-4488
anaff@ferrum.edu
• Gary Holden, Sports Information Director
(540) 365-4306

gholden@ferrum.edu
• Gail Holley, Athletics Office Manager
(540) 365-4493
gholley@ferrum.edu
• John Zubal, Head Athletic Trainer
(540) 365-4528
jzubal@ferrum.edu

FINLANDIA UNIVERSITY (FU) ATHLETICS
601 QUINCY STREET
HANCOCK, MI 49930
906-482-5300
800-682-7604
Fax: 906-487-7383
www.fulions.com
• Chris Salani, Director of Athletics
(906) 487-7378
chris.salani@finlandia.edu
• Curtis Wittenberg, Assistant Athletic Director for Operations
(906) 487-7214
curtis.wittenberg@finlandia.edu
• Nate Larson, Certified Athletic Trainer
(906) 487-7532
nlarson@portagehealth.org

FISK UNIVERSITY ATHLETICS
1000 SEVENTEENTH AVENUE NORTH
NASHVILLE, TN 37208-3051
615-329-8826
Fax: 615-329-8686
www.fisk.edu
• Larry E. Glover, Athletics Director
lglover@fisk.edu
• Sarah Grams, Assistant Athletics Director
sgrams@fisk.edu
• Russell Acklin, Sport Information Director
racklin@fisk.edu
• Bradford Sims, Director of Operations

FITCHBURG STATE COLLEGE ATHLETICS
160 PEARL STREET
FITCHBURG, MA 01420-2697
978-665-3314
Fax: 978-665-3710
www.fitchburgfalcons.com
• Sue Lauder, Director of Athletics
(978) 665-3314
slauder@fitchburgstate.edu
• Bettiann Michalik, Sports Information Director
(978) 665-3343
bmichali@fitchburgstate.edu
• Merry MacDonald, Assistant Director of Athletics
(978) 665-4681
mmacdo22@fitchburgstate.edu
• Todd Souliere, Head Athletic Trainer
(978) 665-3774
tsouliere@fitchburgstate.edu

FONTBONNE UNIVERSITY ATHLETICS
6800 WYDOWN BOULEVARD
ST. LOUIS, MO 63105
314-889-1444
Fax: 314-889-4507
athletics@fontbonne.edu
fontbonnegriffins.com
• Maria Eftink, Director of Athletics
• Maureen Sias, Compliance Director
(314) 719-4356
msias@fontbonne.edu
• Ann Schmerbauch, Head Athletic Trainer
(314) 719-3510
aschmerbauch@fontbonne.edu
• Danielle Donze, Sports Information

Director
(314) 719-8032
ddonze@fontbonne.edu

FRAMINGHAM STATE UNIVERSITY ATHLETICS
100 STATE STREET
PO BOX 9101
FRAMINGHAM, MA 01701-9101
508-626-4614
Fax: 508-626-4069
tkelley@framingham.edu
www.fsurams.com
• Thomas Kelley, Director of Athletics
(508) 626-4614
tkelley@framingham.edu
• Carey Eggen, Associate Director of Athletics
(508) 626-4565
ceggen@framingham.edu
• Kathy Lynch, Sports Information Director
(508) 626-4612
klynch@framingham.edu
• Laura Rusk, Head Athletic Trainer
(508) 626-4564
lrusk@framingham.edu

FRANKLIN & MARSHALL COLLEGE ATHLETICS
PO BOX 3003
LANCASTER, PA 17604-3003
717-358-4477
Fax: 717-358-4440
www.godiplomats.com
• Daniel R. Porterfield, President
(717) 358-3971
president@fandm.edu
• Patricia Epps, Director of Athletics
(717) 358-3819
patty.epps@fandm.edu
• Mickey Blymier, Director of Athletic Communications
(717) 358-4857
• Matt Keller, Director of Sports Medicine
(717) 358-4111
matthew.keller@fandm.edu

FRANKLIN COLLEGE ATHLETICS
101 BRANIGIN BOULEVARD
FRANKLIN, IN 46131
317-738-8123
Fax: 317-738-8175
kprather@franklincollege.edu
franklingrizzlies.com
• Kerry Prather, Director of Athletics
(317) 738-8121
kprather@franklincollege.edu
• Lance Marshall, Assistant Director of Athletics
(317) 738-8136
lmarshall@franklincollege.edu
• Mary Johnston, Assistant Director of Athletics
(317) 738-8130
mjohnston@franklincollege.edu
• Dale Long, Sports Information Director
(317) 738-8184
dlong@franklincollege.edu

FROSTBURG STATE UNIVERSITY ATHLETICS
HAROLD J CORDTS PHYSICAL EDUCATION CENTER
101 BRADDOCK ROAD
FROSTBURG, MD 21532

301-687-4371
Fax: 301-687-4780
www.frostburgsports.com
• Troy Dell, Director of Athletics
(301) 687-4455
tadell@frostburg.edu
• Rubin Stevenson, Associate Athletic
Director
(301) 687-4086
rstevenson@frostburg.edu
• Crystal Satterfield, Assistant Athletic
Director
(301) 687-4455
cgsatterfield@frostburg.edu
• Karla Schoenly, Head Athletic Trainer
(301) 687-3027
kschoenly@frostburg.edu
• Noah Becker, Director of Athletic
Communications
(301) 687-4371
nzbecker@frostburg.edu

**GALLAUDET UNIVERSITY ATHLETICS
DEPARTMENT**
800 FLORIDA AVENUE NE
WASHINGTON, DC 20002
202-651-5603
Fax: 202-651-5274
sam.atkinson@gallaudet.edu
www.gallaudetathletics.com
• Michael Weinstock, Athletic Director
(202) 250-2685
michael.weinstock@gallaudet.edu
• Lynn Ray Boren, Assistant Athletic
Director
(202) 250-2461
lynn.boren@gallaudet.edu
• Sam Atkinson, Sports Information Director
(202) 448-7081
sam.atkinson@gallaudet.edu
• Mariko Kobanawa, Head Athletic Trainer
(202) 651-5265
mariko.kobanawa@gallaudet.edu

GEORGE FOX UNIVERSITY ATHLETICS
414 NORTH MERIDIAN STREET
NEWBERG, OR 97132
503-538-8383
Fax: 503-554-3864
ctaylor@georgefox.edu
athletics.georgefox.edu
• Craig Taylor, Director of Athletics
(503) 554-2911
ctaylor@georgefox.edu
• Elise Trask, Associate Director of Athletics
(503) 554-2934
etrask@georgefox.edu
• Sarah Reid, Director of Sports Marketing
(503) 554-2105
sreid@georgefox.edu
• Danny Cross, Sports Information Director
(503) 554-2926
dcross@georgefox.edu

GETTYSBURG COLLEGE ATHLETICS
300 NORTH WASHINGTON STREET
BOX 400
GETTYSBURG, PA 17325
717-337-6300
Fax: 717-337-6528
www.gettysburgsports.com
• David Wright, Assistant Vice President for
Athletics
(717) 337-6400
dwright@gettysburg.edu
• Susan Furmagalli, Associate Director of
Athletics

(717) 337-6401
sfumagal@gettysburg.edu
• Carol Cantele, Assistant Director of
Athletics
(717) 337-6404
ccantele@gettysburg.edu
• Mike Cantele, Head Athletic Trainer
(717) 337-6429
mcantele@gettysburg.edu

GORDON COLLEGE ATHLETICS
255 GRAPEVINE ROAD
WENHAM, MA 01984
978-927-2300
Fax: 978-867-4682
info@gordon.edu
athletics.gordon.edu
• Jonathan Tymann, Director of Athletics
(978) 867-4039
jon.tymann@gordon.edu
• Cory Ward, Assistant Athletic Director for
Operations
(978) 867-4334
cory.ward@gordon.edu
• Bess Watson, Director of Athletic
Communications
(978) 867-4330
bess.watson@gordon.edu
• Josh Cornwall, Sports Information Director
(978) 867-4516
joshua.cornwall@gordon.edu

GOUCHER COLLEGE ATHLETICS
1021 DULANEY VALLEY ROAD
TOWSON, MD 21204
410-337-6383
Fax: 410-337-6576
athletics.goucher.edu
• Geoffrey Miller, Director of Athletics
(410) 337-6385
gmiller@goucher.edu
• Sally Baum, Associate Athletic Director
(410) 337-6389
sbaum@goucher.edu
• Tati Korba, Assistant Athletic Director
(410) 337-6577
korba@goucher.edu
• Mike Sanders, Sports Information Director
(410) 337-6474
msanders@goucher.edu
• Jean Perez, Director of Sports Medicine
(410) 337-6286
jean.perez@goucher.edu

**GREEN MOUNTAIN COLLEGE
ATHLETICS**
ONE BRENNAN CIRCLE
POULTNEY, VT 05764
802-287-8238
800-776-6675
Fax: 802-287-8099
• Kip Shipley, Athletic Director
(802) 287-8244
kip.shipley@greenmtn.edu
• James Thivierge, Associate Athletic
Director
(802) 287-8244
thiviegej@greenmtn.edu

GREENSBORO COLLEGE ATHLETICS
815 WEST MARKET STREET
GREENSBORO, NC 27401
336-272-7102 EXT 5250
Fax: 336-217-7237
greensboro.sidearmsports.com
• Bryan Galuski, Director of Athletics
(336) 272-7102

bgaluski@greensboro.edu
• Randy Tuggle, Assistant Director of
Athletics
(336) 272-7102
randy.tuggle@greensboro.edu
• Wes Gullett, Director of Sports Information
(336) 272-7102
wgullett@greensboro.edu
• Ray Babnik, Head Athletic Trainer
(336) 272-7102
ray.babnik@greensboro.edu

GREENVILLE COLLEGE ATHLETICS
315 EAST COLLEGE AVENUE
GREENVILLE, IL 62246-1145
618-664-6622
800-345-4440
Fax: 618-664-1060
www.greenville.edu/athletics
• Kent Krober, Athletic Director
(618) 664-6622
kent.krober@greenville.edu
• Tracy Cromer, Senior Women's
Administrator
(618) 664-6835
tracy.cromer@greenville.edu
• B.J. Schneck, Sports Information Director
(618) 664-6621
william.schneck@greenville.edu
• Mike Peppler, Head Athletic Trainer
(618) 664-6731
mike.peppler@greenville.edu

GRINNELL COLLEGE ATHLETICS
1201 10TH AVENUE
GRINNELL, IA 50112
641-269-4000
Fax: 641-269-3818
pioneers.grinnell.edu
• Greg Wallace, Director of Athletics
(641) 269-4219
wallaceg@grinnell.edu
• Erin Hurley, Senior Women's Administrator
(641) 269-4848
hurley@grinnell.edu
• Ted Schultz, Sports Information Director
(641) 269-3675
schultzt@grinnell.edu

GROVE CITY COLLEGE ATHLETICS
100 CAMPUS DRIVE
GROVE CITY, PA 16127
724-458-2000
Fax: 724-458-3855
www.gcc.edu/sports
• Todd Gibson, Director of Athletics
(724) 458-2147
tdgibson@gcc.edu
• Mike Dreves, Interim Department Chair
(724) 458-2151
mfdreves@gcc.edu
• Kay Mitchell Emigh, Head Athletic Trainer
(724) 458-2108
kmemigh@gcc.edu
• Ryan Briggs, Sports Information Director
(724) 458-3365
rabriggs@gcc.edu

GUILFORD COLLEGE ATHLETICS
5800 WEST FRIENDLY AVENUE
GREENSBORO, NC 27410
336-316-2107
Fax: 336-316-2953
athletics@guilford.edu
www.guilfordquakers.com
• Tom Palombo, Director of Athletics
(336) 316-2190

tpalombo@guilford.edu
• Stephanie Flamini, Assistant Athletics Director
(336) 316-2344
sflamini@guilford.edu
• Dave Walters, Sports Inforamtion Director
(336) 316-2107
dwalters@guilford.edu
• Gary Rizza, Head Athletic Trainer
(336) 316-2513
rizzagn@guilford.edu

GUSTAVUS ADOLPHUS COLLEGE ATHLETICS
800 WEST COLLEGE AVENUE
SAINT PETER, MN 56082
507-933-7617
Fax: 507-933-8412
web@gustavus.edu
www.gustavus.edu/athletics
• Tom Brown, Athletics Director
(507) 933-7005
brownie@gustavus.edu
• Jared Phillips, Assistant Athletic Director
(507) 933-8493
jphilli2@gustavus.edu
• Troy Banse, Head Athletic Trainer
(507) 933-6463
tbanse@gustavus.edu
• CJ Siewert, Sports Information Director
(507) 933-7647
siewert@gustavus.edu

GWYNEDD MERCY COLLEGE ATHLETICS
1325 SUMNEYTOWN PIKE
PO BOX 901
GWYNEDD VALLEY, PA 19437
215-646-7300 EXT 2152
Fax: 215-542-4683
gwyneddathletics.com
• Keith Mondillo, Director of Athletics
(215) 641-5574
mondillo.k@gmercyu.edu
• Paul Murphy, Associate Director of Athletics
(215) 641-5533
murphy.p@gmercyu.edu
• Laura-Ann Lane, Senior Women's Administrator
(215) 646-7300
lane.l@gmercyu.edu
• Chris Panter, Sports Information Director
(215) 646-7300
panter.c@gmercyu.edu
• Jenna Allonardo, Head Athletic Trainer
(215) 646-7300
allonardo.j@gmercyu.edu

HAMILTON COLLEGE ATHLETICS
198 COLLEGE HILL ROAD
CLINTON, NY 13323
315-859-4751
Fax: 315-859-4117
jhind@hamilton.edu
athletics.hamilton.edu
• Joe Hind, Director of Athletics
(315) 859-4116
jhind@hamilton.edu
• Miriam Merrill, Associate Director of Athletics
(315) 859-4753
mmerrill@hamilton.edu
• Todd Rayne, Faculty Athletics Representative
(315) 859-4698
trayne@hamilton.edu

• Scott Siddon, Director of Sports Medicine
(315) 859-4766
ssiddon@hamilton.edu
• Jim Taylor, Sports Information Director
(315) 859-4685
jtaylor@hamilton.edu

HAMLINE UNIVERSITY ATHLETICS
1536 HEWITT AVENUE
SAINT PAUL, MN 55104
651-523-2800
Fax: 651-523-2390
jverdugo@hamline.edu
www.hamlineathletics.com
• Jason Verdugo, Athletic Director
(651) 523-2035
jverdugo@hamline.edu
• Beth Rittler, Associate Director for Athletics
(651) 523-2838
bbjork@hamline.edu
• Chris Hartman, Assistant Athletic Director
(651) 526-2716
chartman01@hamline.edu
• Dave Wright, Sports Information Director
(651) 523-2786
dwright08@hamline.edu
• Tara Dooley, Head Athletic Trainer
(651) 523-3094
tdooley01@hamline.edu

HAMPDEN-SYDNEY COLLEGE ATHLETICS
PO BOX 698
HAMPDEN-SYDNEY, VA 23943
434-223-6151
Fax: 434-223-6348
info@hsc.edu
hscathletics.com
• Richard Epperson, Athletic Director
(434) 223-6153
repperson@hsc.edu
• Davis Yake, Director for Media Relations
(434) 223-6156
dyake@hsc.edu
• Scott Harris, Assistant Sports Information Director
(434) 223-6168
sharris@hsc.edu
• Brandon Davis, Head Athletic Trainer
(434) 223-6237
bdavis@hsc.edu

HANOVER COLLEGE ATHLETICS
484 BALL DRIVE
PO BOX 108
HANOVER, IN 47243
812-866-6800
Fax: 812-866-6818
info@hanover.edu
www.hanover.edu/athletics
• Lynn Hall, Athletic Director
(812) 866-7385
hall@hanover.edu
• John Jones, Associate Athletic Directors
(812) 866-7382
jjones@hanover.edu
• M. Tony Carlton, Head Athletic Trainer
(812) 866-7378
carlton@hanover.edu

HARDIN-SIMMONS UNIVERSITY ATHLETICS
2200 HICKORY
ABILENE, TX 79698
325-670-1435
Fax: 325-670-1572

jneese@hsutx.edu
hsuathletics.com
• John Neese, Director of Athletics
(325) 670-1273
jneese@hsutx.edu
• Chad Grubbs, Director of Athletic Communication
(325) 670-1473
cgrubbs@hsutx.edu
• Bert De Ka Garza, Assistant Athletic Trainerach
(325) 670-1358
bgarza@hsutx.edu
• Wade Green, Head Athletic Trainer
(325) 670-1188
wade.a.green@hsutx.edu

HARTWICK COLLEGE ATHLETICS
ONE HARTWICK DRIVE
PO BOX 4020
ONEONTA, NY 13820
607-431-4700
Fax: 607-431-4018
fierkek@hartwick.edu
www.hartwickhawks.com
• Kim Fierke, Director of Athletics
(607) 431-4702
fierkek@hartwick.edu
• Betty Powell, Associate Director of Athletics
(607) 431-4701
powellb@hartwick.edu
• Chris Gondek, Director of Athletic Communications
(607) 431-4703
gondekc@hartwick.edu
• Matt Pohren, Assistant Athletic Director
(607) 431-4711
pohrenm@hartwick.edu
• Heidi Hofbauer-Buzzy, Head Athletic Trainer
(607) 431-4694
hofbauerh@hartwick.edu

HAVERFORD COLLEGE ATHLETICS
370 LANCASTER AVENUE
HAVERFORD, PA 19041
610-896-1117
Fax: 610-896-4220
www.haverfordathletics.com
• Wendy Smith, Director of Smith
(610) 896-1120
w1smith@haverford.edu
• Casey Londergan, Faculty Athletic Representative
(610) 896-1217
clonderg@haverford.edu
• Jim Kenyon, Facilities Manager
(610) 896-1125
jkenyon@haverford.edu
• Cory Walts, Fitness Center Director
(610) 795-7014
cwalts@haverford.edu
• Curt Mauger, Head Athletic Trainer
(610) 896-1425
cmauger@haverford.edu
• Justin Grube, Director of Sports Information
(610) 896-1042
jgrube@haverford.edu

HEIDELBERG UNIVERSITY ATHLETICS
310 EAST MARKET STREET
TIFFIN, OH 44883-2462
419-448-2019
1-800-434-3352
www.heidelberg.edu

• Matt Palm, Athletic Director
(419) 448-2009
mpalm@heidelberg.edu
• Jeff Garvin, Director of Athletic Marketing
& Information
(413) 448-2140
jgarvin@heidelberg.edu

HENDRIX COLLEGE ATHLETICS
1600 WASHINGTON AVENUE
CONWAY, AR 72032
501-505-2966
Fax: 501-450-3805
www.hendrixwarriors.com
• Amy Weaver, Director of Athletics
(501) 450-3899
weaver@hendrix.edu
• Rebecca Beagley, Senior Woman
Administrator
(501) 450-1382
begley@hendrix.edu

HILBERT COLLEGE ATHLETICS
5200 SOUTH PARK AVENUE
HAMBURG, NY 14075
716-926-8794
Fax: 716-649-6429
info@hilbert.edu
www.hilberthawks.com
• John Czarnecki, Director of Athletics
(716) 926-8800
jczarnecki@hilbert.edu
• Kara Rehbaum, Assistant Athletics
Director
(716) 926-8805
krehbaum@hilbert.edu
• Matt Diegelman, Athletic Facilities
Coordinator
(716) 926-8796
mdiegelman@hilbert.edu
• Greg Peri, Head Athletic Trainer
(716) 926-8806
gperi@hilbert.edu

HIRAM COLLEGE ATHLETICS
11715 GARFIELD ROAD
PO BOX 1777
HIRAM, OH 44234
330-569-5340
Fax: 330-569-5392
athletics@hiram.edu
www.hiramterriers.com
• Ellen Dempsey, Director of Athletics
(330) 569-5340
dempseyee@hiram.edu
• Jim Schweickert, Director of Facilities and
Operations
(330) 569-5365
schweickertjm@hiram.edu
• Jim Johnston, Head Athletic Trainer
(330) 569-5351
johnstonjw@hiram.edu
• Andrew Korba, Director of Sports
Information
(330) 569-5495
korbaam@hiram.edu

STATESMEN
HOBART ATHLETICS
BRISTOL GYMNASIUM
300 PULTENEY STREET
GENEVA, NY 14456
315-781-3565
Fax: 315-781-3570
www.hwsathletics.com
• Mike Hanna, Director of Athletics
(315) 781-3574

hanna@hws.edu
• Ken DeBolt, Director of Athletic
Communications
(315) 781-3146
debolt@hws.edu
• Brian Miller, Assistant Athletics Director for
Compliance
(315) 781-3548
bmiller@hws.edu
• Nick Cooke, Coordinator of Sports
Medicine
(315) 781-3568
cooke@hws.edu
Year Founded:
1822

HOOD COLLEGE ATHLETICS
401 ROSEMONT AVENUE
FREDERICK, MD 21701
301-696-3499
Fax: 301-696-3488
www.hoodathletics.com
• Tom Dickman, Director of Athletics
(301) 696-3494
dickman@hood.edu
• Staci Brennan, Associate Director of
Athletics
(301) 696-3785
brennans@hood.edu
• Geoff Goyne, Sports Information Director
(301) 696-3978
goyne@hood.edu
• Jennie Bowker, Head Athletic Trainer
(301) 696-3836
bowker@hood.edu

HOPE COLLEGE ATHLETICS
DEVOS FIELDHOUSE
222 FAIRBANKS AVENUE
HOLLAND, MI 49423
616-395-7070
Fax: 616-395-7175
schoonveld@hope.edu
athletics.hope.edu
• Tim Schoonveld, Co-Athletic Director
(616) 395-7698
schoonveld@hope.edu
• Melinda Larson, Co-Athletic Director
(616) 395-7694
larson@hope.edu
• Lindsey Engelsman, Athletics Brand
Manager
(616) 395-7688
engelsman@hope.edu
• Alan Babbitt, Sports Information Director
(616) 395-7856
babbitt@hope.edu
• Tim Koberna, Head Athletic Trainer
(616) 395-7705
koberna@hope.edu
• Meg Frens, Athletic Training Program
Director
(616) 395-7450
frens@hope.edu

HOUGHTON COLLEGE ATHLETICS
1 WILLARD AVENUE
HOUGHTON, NY 14744
585-567-9645
Fax: 585-567-9365
harold.lord@houghton.edu
athletics.houghton.edu
• H. Skip Lord, Executive Director of
Athletics
(585) 567-9645
harold.lord@houghton.edu
• Deanna Hand, Associate Director of

Athletics
(585) 567-9563
deanna.hand@houghton.edu
• Jason Mucher, Director of Compliance and
Communications
(585) 567-9276
jason.mucher@houghton.edu
• Eden Palmer, Athletic Trainer
(585) 567-9563
eden.palmer@houghton.edu

HUNTER COLLEGE ATHLETICS
695 PARK AVENUE
NEW YORK, NY 10065
212-772-4783
Fax: 212-650-3161
athletic@hunter.cuny.edu
www.huntercollegeathletics.com
• Terry Wansart, Director of Athletics
(212) 722-4783
terry.wansart@hunter.cuny.edu
• Stephanie Thorburn, Associate Athletic
Director
(212) 650-3123
stephanie.thorburn@hunter.cuny.edu
• Kelsey Campbell, Sports Information
Director
(212) 396-6773

HUNTINGDON COLLEGE ATHLETICS
1500 EAST FAIRVIEW AVENUE
MONTGOMERY, AL 36106
334-833-4565
Fax: 334-833-4486
www.huntingdonhawks.com
• Mike Turk, Director of Athletics
(334) 833-4322
mturk@hawks.huntingdon.edu
• Buzz Phillips, Director of Athletics
Emeritus
(334) 833-4581
bphillips@hawks.huntingdon.edu
• Eric Levanda, Associate Athletic Director
(334) 833-4335
elevanda@hawks.huntingdon.edu
• Wesley Lyle, Sports Information Director
(334) 833-4579
sid@hawks.huntingdon.edu
• Kyle Huff, Head Athletic Trainer
(334) 833-4025
khuff@hawks.huntingdon.edu

HUSSON UNIVERSITY ATHLETICS
ONE COLLEGE CIRCLE
BANGOR, ME 04401-2929
207-941-7026
Fax: 207-973-1015
athletics@husson.edu
• Frank Pergolizzi, Director of Athletics
(207) 973-1069
pergolizzif@husson.edu
• Janine Gmitter, Senior Woman
Administrator
(207) 941-7021
gmitterj@husson.edu
• Janine Gmitter, Head Athletic Trainer
(207) 941-7021
gmitterj@husson.edu

ILLINOIS COLLEGE ATHLETICS
1101 WEST COLLEGE AVENUE
JACKSONVILLE, IL 62650
217-245-3400
Fax: 217-245-3398
www.illinoiscollegeathletics.com
• Mike Snyder, Director of Athletics
(217) 245-3000

college sports

mike.snyder@mail.ic.edu
• Meghan Roman, Senior Woman Administrator
(217) 245-3197
meghan.roman@mail.ic.edu
• Alex Keil, Sports Information Director
(217) 245-3894
alex.keil@mail.ic.edu
• Terry Geirnaeirt, Head Athletic Trainer
(217) 245-3397
tlgeirna@mail.ic.edu

ILLINOIS WESLEYAN UNIVERSITY ATHLETICS
1312 PARK STREET
BLOOMINGTON, IL 61701
309-556-1000
Fax: 309-556-3484
iwusports.com
• Mike Wagner, Athletic Director
(309) 556-3341
mwagner@iwu.edu
• Norm Eash, Associate Athletic Director
(309) 556-3344
neash@iwu.edu
• Kim Nelson-Brown, Senior Women Administrator
(309) 556-3349
knbrown@iwu.edu
• Tony Bankston, Assistant Athletic Director
bankston@iwu.edu
• Bill Kauth, Head Athletic Trainer
(309) 556-3601
bkauth@iwu.edu
• Stew Salowitz, Sports Information Director
(309) 556-3206
salowitz@iwu.edu

IOWA WESLEYAN COLLEGE ATHLETICS
601 NORTH MAIN STREET
MOUNT PLEASANT, IA 52641
319-385-6332
Fax: 319-385-6384
swilliam@iw.edu
www.iwtigers.com
• Steve Williamson, Athletic Director
(319) 385-6332
swilliam@iw.edu
• B.J. Wagy, Assistant Athletic Director
(319) 385-6305
bj.wagy@iw.edu
• Derek Zander, NCAA Compliance Officer
(319) 385-6349
derek.zander@iw.edu
• Andy Niemann, Athletic Trainer
(319) 385-6417
andrew.niemann@iw.edu
• Dave Stecker, Assistant Athletic Trainer
(319) 385-6417

ITHACA COLLEGE ATHLETICS
953 DANBY ROAD
ITHACA, NY 14850-7198
607-274-3209
Fax: 607-274-1667
ithacan@ithaca.edu
athletics.ithaca.edu
• Susan Bassett, Director of Intercollegiate Athletics
(607) 274-3209
scassett@ithaca.edu
• Will Rothermel, Associate Athletic Director
(607) 274-3199
jrothermel@ithaca.edu
• Michelle Manning, Senior Woman Administrator
(607) 274-5708

mmanning@ithaca.edu
• Sean Fitzmaurice, Coordinator of Facilities
(607) 274-1972
sfitzmaurice@ithaca.edu

JOHN CARROLL UNIVERSITY ATHLETICS
ONE JOHN CARROLL BOULEVARD
UNIVERSITY HEIGHTS, OH 44118
216-397-1886
Fax: 216-397-3043
www.jcusports.com
• Laurie Massa, Director of Athletics
(216) 397-1525
lmassa@jcu.edu
• Gretchen Weitbrecht, Associate Athletic Director
(216) 397-4194
gweitbrecht@jcu.edu
• Christopher Wenzler, Sports Information Director
(216) 397-4676
cwenzler@jcu.edu

JOHN JAY COLLEGE OF CRIMINAL JUSTICE ATHLETICS
525 WEST 59TH STREET
NEW YORK, NY 10019
212-237-8371
Fax: 212-237-8474
ckashow@jjay.cuny.edu
www.johnjayathletics.com
• Carol Kashow, Director of Athletics
(212) 393-6329
ckashow@jjay.cuny.edu
• Catherine Alves, Senior Associate Athletic Director
(212) 237-8395
calves@jjay.cuny.edu
• Corey Berg, Assistant Athletic Director
(212) 237-8396
cberg@jjay.cuny.edu
• Brandon Fieland, Sports Information Director
(212) 237-8322
bfieland@jjay.cuny.edu
• Lindsay Roderick, Head Athletic Trainer
(212) 237-8324
lroderick@jjay.cuny.edu

JOHNS HOPKINS UNIVERSITY ATHLETICS
3400 NORTH CHARLES STREET
BALTIMORE, MD 21218
410-516-7490
Fax: 410-516-7482
tcalder@jhu.edu
www.hopkinssports.com
• Alanna Shanahan, Director of Athletics
(410) 516-7490
alanna.shanahan@jhu.edu
• Bill Harrington, Senior Associate Director of Athletics
(410) 516-5279
aggie@jhu.edu
• Grant Kelly, Director of Development
(410) 516-4096
gkelly@jhu.edu
• Ernie Larossa, Director of Athletic Communications
(410) 516-0552
elarossa@jhu.edu

JOHNSON STATE COLLEGE ATHLETICS
337 COLLEGE HILL
JOHNSON, VT 05656

802-635-1485
800-635-2356
Fax: 802-635-1497
athletics.jsc.edu
• Jamey Ventura, Director of Athletics and Recreation
(802) 635-1285
jamey.ventura@jsc.edu
• Miles Smith, Assistant Athletics Director
(802) 635-1470
miles.smith@jsc.edu
• Elaine Harvey, Assistant Athletics Director for Communications
(802) 635-1384
elaine.harvey@jsc.edu
• James Nichols, Head Athletic Trainer
(802) 635-1487
james.nichols@jsc.edu

JUNIATA COLLEGE ATHLETICS
1700 MOORE STREET
HUNTINGDON, PA 16652
814-641-3512
Fax: 814-641-3508
info@juniata.edu
www.juniatasports.net
• Greg Curley, Athletic Director
(814) 641-3521
curleyg@juniata.edu
• Danny Young-Uhrich, Senior Woman Administrator
(814) 641-3518
youngd@juniata.edu
• Scott McKenzie, Director for Athletic Communications
(814) 641-3503
mckenzs@juniata.edu
• David Heberger, Sports Information Director
(814) 641-3134
hebergd@juniata.edu
• Jeff Leydig, Head Athletic Trainer
(814) 641-3516
leydigj@juniata.edu

KALAMAZOO COLLEGE ATHLETICS
1200 ACADEMY STREET
KALAMAZOO, MI 49006
269-337-7082
Fax: 269-337-7401
sports@kzoo.edu
hornets.kzoo.edu
• Kristen Smith, Director of Athletics
(269) 337-7090
kristens@kzoo.edu
• Kathy Milliken, Senior Woman Administrator
(269) 337-7091
milliken@kzoo.edu
• Steve Wideen, Sports Information Director
(269) 337-7287
swideen@kzoo.edu
• Kathleen White, Interim Head Athletic Trainer
(269) 337-7093
ofarrell@kzoo.edu

KEAN UNIVERSITY ATHLETICS
1000 MORRIS AVENUE
UNION, NJ 07083
908-737-0600
Fax: 908-737-0605
www.keanathletics.com
• Jack McKiernan, Director of Athletics
(908) 737-0604
jmckiern@kean.edu
• Denise Wujciak, Head Athletic Trainer

(908) 737-5454
wujciakd@kean.edu
• Kimberly DeRitter, Director of Sports Information
(908) 737-0615
kderitte@kean.edu

KEENE STATE COLLEGE ATHLETICS
229 MAIN STREET
KEENE, NH 03435
603-358-2813
Fax: 603-358-2888
keeneowls.com
• Kemal Atkins, Director of Athletics
(603) 358-2108
kemal.atkins@keene.edu
• Abe Osheyack, Sports Information Director
(603) 358-2630
abe.osheyack@keene.edu
• Bob Merrow, Head Athletic Trainer
(603) 358-2824
rmerrow@keene.edu

KENYON COLLEGE ATHLETICS
221 DUFF STREET
KENYON ATHLETIC CENTER
GAMBIER, OH 43022
740-427-5456
Fax: 740-427-5402
athletics.kenyon.edu
• Peter Smith, Director of Athletics
(740) 427-5811
smithp@kenyon.edu
• Justin Newell, Assistant Athletic Director
(740) 427-5460
newellj@kenyon.edu
• Andy Wheeler, Head Athletic Trainer
(740) 427-5553
• Marty Fuller, Sports Information Director
(740) 427-5471
fullerm@kenyon.edu

KEUKA COLLEGE ATHLETICS
141 CENTRAL AVENUE
KEUKA PARK, NY 14478
315-279-5249
Fax: 315-279-5325
dsweet@keuka.edu
www.kcwolfpack.com
• David Sweet, Director of Athletics
(315) 279-5682
dsweet@keuka.edu
• Jeff Bray, Associate Athletics Director
(315) 279-5656
jbray@keuka.edu
• Jonathan Accardi, Assistant Athletics Director
(315) 279-5690
jaccardi@keuka.edu
• Jimmy Habecker, Sports Information Director
(315) 279-5241
jhabecker@keuka.edu

KING'S COLLEGE ATHLETICS
133 NORTH RIVER STREET
WILKES-BARRE, PA 18711
570-208-5934
Fax: 570-208-5937
www.kingscollegeathletics.com
• Cheryl Ish, Director of Intercollegiate Athletics
(570) 208-5900
cherylish@kings.edu
• J.P. Andrejko, Assistant Director of Intercollegiate Athletics
(570) 208-5900

johnandrejko@kings.edu
• Megan Mundy, Athletic Business and Operations Coordinator
(570) 208-5855
meganmundy@kings.edu
• Bob Ziadie, Director of Sports Information
(570) 208-5934
robertziadie@kings.edu

KNOX COLLEGE ATHLETICS
2 EAST SOUTH STREET
GALESBURG, IL 61401-4999
309-341-7000
Fax: 309-341-7806
athletics@knox.edu
• Chad Eisele, Director of Athletics
(309) 341-7280
ceisele@knox.edu
• Scott Sunderland, Assistant Athletic Director
(309) 341-7378
ssunderl@knox.edu
• James Clark, Sports Information Director
(309) 341-7714
jrclark@knox.edu
• Andy Gibbons, Fitness Center Director
(309) 341-7379
agibbons@knox.edu

KNOXVILLE COLLEGE ATHLETICS
901 KNOXVILLE COLLEGE DRIVE
KNOXVILLE, TN 37921
865-524-6511
Fax: 865-524-6603
www.knoxvillecollege.edu
• Geoffery Mallory, Men's Basketball Head Coach
• Will Dorsey, Men's Basketball Assistant Coach

LA GRANGE COLLEGE ATHLETICS
601 BROAD STREET
LA GRANGE, GA 30240
706-880-8330
Fax: 706-880-8350
www.lagrangepanthers.com
• Jennifer Claybrook, Athletic Director
(706) 880-8262
jclaybrook@lagrange.edu
• Kendal Wallace, Assistant Athletic Director
(706) 880-8328
kwallace@lagrange.edu
• Jenna Jones, Athletics Program Coordinator
(706) 880-8330
jjones@lagrange.edu
• John Hughes, Sports Information Director
(706) 880-8318
jhughes@lagrange.edu
• Rob Dicks, Director of Athletic Training
(706) 880-8099
rdicks@lagrange.edu

LA ROCHE COLLEGE ATHLETICS
9000 BABCOCK BOULEVARD
PITTSBURGH, PA 15237
412-536-1041
Fax: 412-536-1012
www.larochesports.com
• Jim Tinkey, Director of Athletics
(412) 536-1011
jim.tinkey@laroche.edu
• Katherine Golebie, Assistant Director of Athletics
(412) 536-1019
katherine.golebie@laroche.edu
• Chase Rowe, Manager of Athletic

Facilities
(412) 536-1046
chase.rowe@laroche.edu
• Jimmy Finley, Sports Information Director
(412) 536-1041
james.finley@laroche.edu

LA VERNE ATHLETICS, UNIVERSITY OF
1950 THIRD STREET
LA VERNE, CA 91750
909-593-3511 EXT 4261
Fax: 909-392-2760
jkline@laverne.edu
www.leopardathletics.com
• Julie Kline, Director of Athletics
(909) 448-4345
jkline@laverne.edu
• Julie Smith, Assistant Athletics Director
(909) 448-4343
jsmith2@laverne.edu
• Joanna Engel, Director of Athletic Training Services
(909) 448-4986
jengel@laverne.edu
• Sean Lee, Athletics Communication Director
(909) 448-4639
slee5@laverne.edu

LAKE FOREST COLLEGE ATHLETICS
555 NORTH SHERIDAN ROAD
LAKE FOREST, IL 60045
847-735-6054
Fax: 847-735-6299
wajerski@lakeforest.edu
www.goforesters.com
• Jackie Slaats, Director of Athletics
(847) 735-5290
slaats@lakeforest.edu
• Cheryl Brazil, Assistant Director of Athletics
(847) 735-6134
cbrazil@lakeforest.edu
• Chris Pier, Operations Director for Compliance
(847) 735-5288
cpier@lakeforest.edu
• Blake Theisen, Director of Athletic Programming
(847) 735-6155
theisen@lakeforest.edu
• Mike Gilboe, Head Athletic Trainer
(847) 735-5296
gilboe@lakeforest.edu
• Brian Bruha, Director of Athletic Facilities
(847) 735-5293
bruha@lakeforest.edu

LAKELAND COLLEGE ATHLETICS
PO BOX 359
SHEBOYGAN, WI 53082-0359
920-565-1024
Fax: 920-565-1069
lakelandmuskies.com
• April Arvan, Director of Athletics
(920) 565-1024
arvanaa@lakeland.edu
• Aaron Aanonsen, Senior Associate Director of Athletics
(920) 565-1024
aanonsenaa@lakeland.edu
• Dona Richardson, Head Athletic Trainer
(920) 565-1024
richardsonda@lakeland.edu
• Adam Glatczak, Sports Information Director

(920) 565-1028
glatczakaj@lakeland.edu

LASELL COLLEGE ATHLETICS
1844 COMMONWEALTH AVENUE
NEWTON, MA 02466
617-243-2000
Fax: 617-243-2037
kwalter@lasell.edu
laserpride.lasell.edu
• Kristy Walter, Director of Athletics
(617) 243-2147
kwalter@lasell.edu
• Aaron Galletta, Facilities Coordinator
(617) 243-2188
agalletta@lasell.edu
• Todd Montana, Assistant Director of
Athletics
(617) 243-2232
tmontana@lasell.edu
• Emily Machado, Director of Sports
Information
(617) 243-2035
emachado@lasell.edu
• Christopher Noyes, Head Athletic Trainer
(617) 243-2297
cnoyes@lasell.edu

LAWRENCE UNIVERSITY ATHLETICS
711 EAST BOLDT WAY
APPLETON, WI 54911
920-832-7000
Fax: 920-832-7349
www.lawrence.edu
• Christyn Abaray, Director of Athletics
(920) 832-6888
christyn.abaray@lawrence.edu
• Kim Tatro, Associate Director of Athletics
(920) 832-6975
kimberly.n.tatro@lawrence.edu
• Joel DePagter, Assistant Director of
Athletics
(920) 993-6281
joel.t.depagter@lawrence.edu
• Joe Vanden Acker, Director of Athletic
Media Relations
(920) 832-6878
joseph.m.vandenacker@lawrence.edu
• Jami Rogers, Head Athletic Trainer
(920) 832-6762
jami.l.rogers@lawrence.edu

LEBANON VALLEY COLLEGE
ATHLETICS
101 NORTH COLLEGE AVENUE
ANNVILLE, PA 17003-1400
717-867-6260
Fax: 717-867-6990
godutchmen.com
• Rick Beard, Director of Athletics
(717) 867-6363
rbeard@lvc.edu
• Stacey Hollinger, Assistant Athletic
Director
(717) 867-6891
sholling@lvc.edu
• Thomas Klemick, Director of Athletic
Communications
(717) 867-6580
klemick@lvc.edu
• Erin Ulrich, Head Athletic Trainer
(717) 867-6269
ulrich@lvc.edu
• Kevin Yeiser, Director of Grounds
(717) 867-6342
yeiser@lvc.edu

LEHMAN COLLEGE ATHLETICS
250 BEDFORD PARK BOULEVARD WEST
BRONX, NY 10468
718-960-8101
Fax: 718-960-8815
lehmanathletics.com
• Martin L. Zwiren, Director of Athletics
(718) 960-1117
martin.zwiren@lehman.cuny.edu
• Robert Harris, Fitness Center Director
(718) 960-1133
robert.harris@lehman.cuny.edu
• Durval Morgan, Head Athletic Trainer
(718) 960-7175
eric.harrison@lehman.cuny.edu
• Lenn Margolis, Director of Sports
Information
(718) 960-1130
lenn.margolis@lehman.cuny.edu
• David Gonzalez, Director of Sports
Medicine
(718) 960-1171
dgonzale@montefiore.org

LEWIS & CLARK COLLEGE ATHLETICS
0615 SW PALATINE HILL ROAD
PORTLAND, OR 97219-7889
503-768-7545
Fax: 503-768-7058
www.lcpioneers.com
• Shana Levine, Director of Athletics
(503) 768-7548
slevine@lclark.edu
• Sharon Sexton, Associate Director of
Physical Education
(503) 768-7073
sextons@lclark.edu
• Mark Pietrok, Head Athletic Trainer
(503) 768-7065
pietrok@lclark.edu
• Ryan Goff, Interim Sports Information
Director
(503) 768-7067
rgoff@lclark.edu

LINFIELD COLLEGE ATHLETICS
900 SE BAKER STREET
MCMINNVILLE, OR 97128
503-883-2200
Fax: 503-434-2453
www.linfield.edu/sports
• Scott Carnahan, Athletic Director
(503) 883-2229
scarnah@linfield.edu
• Lisa Macy-Baker, Compliance Officer
(503) 883-2710
lmacybak@linfield.edu
• Doug Hire, Assistant Athletic Director
(503) 883-2419
dhire@linfield.edu
• Kelly Bird, Sports Information Director
(503) 883-2439
kbird@linfield.edu
• Duane Duey, Certified Athletic Trainer
(503) 883-2415
dduey@linfield.edu

LOUISIANA COLLEGE ATHLETICS
1140 COLLEGE DRIVE
PINEVILLE, LA 71360
318-487-7559
Fax: 318-487-7174
athletics@lacollege.edu
www.lcwildcats.net
• Dennis Dunn, Athletics Director
(318) 487-7725
dunn@lacollege.edu

• Jonathan Small, Associate Athletics
Director
(318) 487-7965
jonathan.small@lacollege.edu
• Paula Hunter, Assistant Athletics Director
(318) 487-7559
paula.hunter@lacollege.edu
• Jon Hay, Head Athletic Trainer
(318) 487-7792
jon.hay@lacollege.edu

LUTHER COLLEGE ATHLETICS
700 COLLEGE DRIVE
DECORAH, IA 52101
563-387-1575
Fax: 563-387-1228
www.sports.luther.edu
• Renae Hartl, Athletic Director
(563) 387-1575
hartre01@luther.edu
• Alex Smith, Associate Athletic Director for
Operations
(563) 387-1382
smithale@luther.edu
• Bryan Nikkel, Director of Facilities
(563) 387-1590
nikkbr01@luther.edu
• Dave Blanchard, Sports Information
Director
(563) 387-1586
blanchda@luther.edu

LYCOMING COLLEGE ATHLETICS
700 COLLEGE PLACE
WILLIAMSPORT, PA 17701
570-321-4110
Fax: 570-321-4158
clarkm@lycoming.edu
athletics.lycoming.edu
• Mike Clark, Director of Athletics
(570) 321-4110
clarkm@lycoming.edu
• Joe Guistina, Associate Athletic Director of
Communications
(570) 321-4028
guistina@lycoming.edu
• Christen Ditzler, Assistant Athletic Director
(570) 321-4261
ditzler@lycoming.edu
• Andrea Lucas, Head Athletic Trainer
(570) 321-4271
lucasa@lycoming.edu
• Christen Ditzler, SWA/Head Women's
Basketball Coach
(570) 321-4261
ditzler@lycoming.edu
• Jamie Spencer, Head Golf Coach

LYNCHBURG COLLEGE ATHLETICS
TURNER GYM, 1501 LAKESIDE DRIVE
LYNCHBURG, VA 24501-3199
434-544-8100
Fax: 434-544-8365
www.lynchburg.edu
• Jon Waters, Athletic Director
(434) 544-8498
waters.j@lynchburg.edu
• Steve Koudelka, Assistant Athletic Director
(434) 544-8494
koudelka@lynchburg.edu
• Kelley Gunter, Coordinator of Athletic
Operations
(434) 544-8286
gunter@lynchburg.edu
• Mike Carpenter, Sports Information
Director
(434) 544-8495

carpenter@lynchburg.edu
• Chris Casola, Director of Athletic Training Services
(434) 544-8180
casola.c@lynchburg.edu

LYNDON STATE COLLEGE ATHLETICS
1001 COLLEGE ROAD
PO BOX 919
LYNDONVILLE, VT 05851
802-626-6200
800-225-1998
www.lyndonstate.edu/athletics
• Chris Ummer, Director of Athletics
(802) 626-6224
christopher.ummer@lyndonstate.edu
• Kate Roy, Associate Director of Athletics
(802) 626-6439
katherine.roy@lyndonstate.edu
• Zac Harrison, Sports Information Coordinator
(802) 626-6341
zachary.harrison@lyndonstate.edu
• Evita Sandoval, Head Athletic Trainer
(802) 626-6477
evita.sandoval@lyndonstate.edu

MACALESTER COLLEGE ATHLETICS
1600 GRAND AVENUE
SAINT PAUL, MN 55105
651-696-6000
Fax: 651-696-6328
athletics.macalester.edu
• Kim Chandler, Director of Athletics
(651) 696-6366
kchandle@macalester.edu
• Vanessa Seljeskog, Associate Director of Athletics
(651) 696-6736
seljeskog@macalester.edu
• Ron Osterman, Assistant Athletic Director
(651) 696-6607
osterman@macalester.edu
• Matt McLagan, Director of Sports Information
(651) 696-6563
mmclagan@macalester.edu
• Paula Natvig, Head Athletic Trainer
(651) 696-6162
natvig@macalester.edu

MACMURRAY COLLEGE ATHLETICS
447 EAST COLLEGE AVENUE
JACKSONVILLE, IL 62650
217-479-7142
Fax: 217-479-7147
athletics@mac.edu
www.mac.edu/athletics
• Justin Fuhler, Athletic Director
(217) 479-7142
• Randi Armstrong, Sports Information Director
(217) 479-7157
• Bryan Langan, Athletic Trainer
(217) 479-7193

MAINE AT FARMINGTON ATHLETICS, UNIVERSITY OF
111 SOUTH STREET
FARMINGTON, ME 04938
207-778-7535
Fax: 207-778-8177
athletics.umf.maine.edu
• Julie Davis, Director of Athletics
(207) 778-7264
jadavis@maine.edu
• Jamie Beaudoin, Associate Athletics

Director
(207) 778-8168
jbeaudoin@maine.edu
• Dustin Parker, Director of Athletics Communications
(207) 778-7535
dustin.parker@maine.edu

MAINE AT PRESQUE ISLE ATHLETICS, UNIVERSITY OF
181 MAIN STREET
PRESQUE ISLE, ME 04769
207-768-9400
Fax: 207-768-9777
owls.umpi.edu/athletics
• Mike Holmes, Athletic Director
michael.s.holmes@umpi.edu
• Doug Carter, Assistant Athletic Director
(207) 768-9523
douglas.carter@umpi.edu
• Mike Pankow, Sports Information Director
(207) 768-9792
michael.pankow@maine.edu
• Patrick Baker, Head Athletic Trainer
(207) 968-9474
lucas.bartlett@maine.edu

MAINE MARITIME ACADEMY ATHLETICS(MMA)
ONE PLEASANT STREET
CASTINE, ME 04420
207-326-0299
Fax: 207-326-2513
marinersports.org
• Steve Peed, Director of Athletics
(207) 326-2451
steve.peed@mma.edu
• Tricia Carver-Watson, Associate Athletic Director
(207) 326-0253
tricia.carverwatson@mma.edu
• Riana Sidelinger, Athletic Communications Coordinator
(207) 326-0113
riana.sidelinger@mma.edu
• Richard Osheim, Certified Athletic Trainer
(207) 326-0238
richard.osheim@mma.edu

MANCHESTER UNIVERSITY ATHLETICS
604 EAST COLLEGE AVENUE
NORTH MANCHESTER, IN 46962
260-982-5390
800-852-3648
Fax: 260-982-5032
sportsinfo@manchester.edu
www.muspartans.com
• Rick Espeset, Director of Athletics
(260) 982-5390
rbespeset@manchester.edu
• Josh Dzurick, Assistant Director of Athletics
(260) 982-5379
jndzurick@manchester.edu
• Tami Hoagland, Athletic Department Office Manager
(260) 982-5390
tlhoagland@manchester.edu
• Mark Adkins, Sports Information Director
(260) 982-5035
mtadkins@manchester.edu

MANHATTANVILLE COLLEGE ATHLETICS
2900 PURCHASE STREET
PURCHASE, NY 10577

914-323-5280
Fax: 914-323-5130
athletics@govaliants.com
www.govaliants.com
• Keith Levinthal, Director of Athletics
(914) 323-7270
levinthal@govaliants.com
• Julene Fisher, Assistant Director of Athletics
(914) 323-7285
fisher@govaliants.com
• Steve Sheridan, Director of Athletics for Communications
(914) 323-7280
sheridan@govaliants.com
• Casey Schermick, Sports Information Director
(914) 323-7280
schermick@govaliants.com
• Scott McIver, Head Athletic Trainer
(914) 323-7276
mciver@govaliants.com

MARANATHA BAPTIST UNIVERSITY
745 WEST MAIN STREET
WATERTOWN, WI 53094
920-206-2376
Fax: 920-261-9109
www.mbu.edu
• Rob Thompson, Athletic Director
(920) 206-2377
rob.thompson@mbu.edu
• Ann Bolton, Assistant Athletic Director
(920) 206-2379
ann.bolton@mbu.edu
• Taylor Pill, Sports Information Director
(920) 206-2379
taylor.pill@mbu.edu
• Zachary Sweatman, Certified Athletic Trainer
(920) 206-3476
zachary.sweatman@mbu.edu

MARIAN COLLEGE OF FOND DU LAC ATHLETICS
45 SOUTH NATIONAL AVENUE
FOND DU LAC, WI 54935-4699
920-923-8156
Fax: 920-923-8134
www.sabreathletics.com
• Jason Bartelt, Director of Athletics
(920) 923-8090
jbartelt@marianuniversity.edu
• Kerri Huebel, Assistant Athletic Director
(920) 923-8516
kahuebel@marianuniversity.edu
• Dennis Driscoll, Director of Athletic Communications
(920) 923-8155
drdriscoll83@marianuniversity.edu
• Kim Sorensen, Head Athletic Trainer
(920) 923-8754
kasorensen61@marianuniversity.edu

MARIETTA COLLEGE ATHLETICS
215 FIFTH STREET
MARIETTA, OH 45750
740-376-4665
Fax: 740-376-4674
pioneers.marietta.edu
• Larry Hiser, Athletics Director
(740) 376-4667
larry.hiser@marietta.edu
• John Tynan, Faculty Athletic Representative
(740) 376-4873
john.tynan@marietta.edu

• Jeanne Arbuckle, Associate Athletics Director
(740) 376-4668
arbucklj@marietta.edu
• Sam Crowther, Director of Athletic Training Program
(740) 376-4774
crowthes@marietta.edu
• Jaclyn Schwieterman, Head Athletic Trainer
(740) 376-4773
sj004@marietta.edu

MARY HARDIN-BAYLOR ATHLETICS, UNIVERSITY OF
900 COLLEGE STREET
UMHB BOX 8010
BELTON, TX 76513
254-295-8642
Fax: 254-295-4614
jwallin@umhb.edu
www.cruathletics.com
• Randy Mann, Vice President for Athletics
(254) 295-4618
rmann@umhb.edu
• Darla Kirby, Associate Athletic Director
(254) 295-5046
dkirby@umhb.edu
• Jon Wallin, Sports Information Director
(254) 295-4611
jwallin@umhb.edu
• Jake Fralicks, Office and Ticket Coordinator
(254) 295-5593
jfralicks@umhb.edu

MARY WASHINGTON UNIVERSITY ATHLETICS
1301 COLLEGE AVENUE
FREDERICKSBURG, VA 22401
540-654-1039
Fax: 540-654-1892
umweagles.com
• Ken Tyler, Director of Athletics
(540) 654-1876
ktyler2@umw.edu
• Dana Hall, Senior Associate Director of Athletics
(540) 654-1890
dhall@umw.edu
• Clint Often, Director of Communications
(540) 654-1743
coften@umw.edu
• Philip Pierce, Director of Athletic Development
(540) 654-1153
ppierce@umw.edu
• Ian Rogol, Head Athletic Trainer
(540) 654-1872
irogol@umw.edu

MARYMOUNT UNIVERSITY
2807 NORTH GLEBE ROAD
ARLINGTON, VA 22207
703-284-1619
Fax: 703-527-3684
www.marymount.edu/athletics
• Jamie Reynolds, Director of Athletics
(703) 908-7619
jamie.reynolds@marymount.edu
• Sarah Gustin, Associate Athletics Director for Compliance
(703) 284-3334
sgustin@marymount.edu
• Kyle Gurganious, Director of Athletic Communications
(703) 284-3332

kgurgani@marymount.edu
• Ryan Wildenhain, Head of Sports Medicine
(703) 284-1672
rwildeha@marymount.edu

MARYWOOD UNIVERSITY ATHLETICS
2300 ADAMS AVENUE
SCRANTON, PA 18509-1598
570-961-4724
Fax: 570-961-4730
marywoodpacers.com
• Mary Jo Gunning, Director of Athletics and Recreation
(570) 961-4724
gunning@marywood.edu
• Eric Grundman, Assistant Director of Athletics
(570) 961-4724
grundman@marywood.edu
• Andrew Smith, Director of Athletics for Communications
(570) 961-4724
aesmith@marywood.edu
• Nicole Malloy, Director of Athletics for Internal Operations
(570) 961-4724
malloy@marywood.edu
• Scott Summers, Head Athletic Trainer
(570) 961-4724
srsummers@marywood.edu

MASSACHUSETTS BOSTON ATHLETICS, UNIVERSITY OF
100 MORRISSEY BOULEVARD
BOSTON, MA 02125-3393
617-287-7801
Fax: 617-287-7840
www.umb.edu
• Charlie Titus, Director of Athletics
(617) 287-7810
charlie.titus@umb.edu
• Chris Collins, Interim Associate Director of Athletics
(617) 287-7861
chris.collins@umb.edu
• Paula Ayers, Director of Finance
(617) 287-7808
paula.ayers@umb.edu
• Terry Condon, Senior Associate Director of Athletics
(617) 287-7832
terry.condon@umb.edu

MASSACHUSETTS COLLEGE OF LIBERAL ARTS ATHLETICS
375 CHURCH STREET
NORTH ADAMS, MA 01247
413-662-5411
Fax: 413-662-5357
athletics.mcla.edu
• Laura Mooney, Director of Athletics
(413) 662-5411
laura.mooney@mcla.edu
• Dot Houston, Associate Athletic Director for Administration
(413) 662-5437
d.houston@mcla.edu
• Jeff Puleri, Assistant Athletic Director for Communications
(413) 662-5403
j.puleri@mcla.edu
• Matthew Boillat, Head Athletic Trainer
(413) 662-5414
matthew.boillat@mcla.edu

MASSACHUSETTS DARTMOUTH ATHLETICS, UNIVERSITY OF
TRIPP ATHLETIC CENTER
285 OLD WESTPORT ROAD
DARTMOUTH, MA 02747-2300
508-999-8720
Fax: 508-999-8867
www.corsairathletics.com
• Amanda Van Voorhis, Director of Athletics
(508) 999-9114
avanvoorhis@umassd.edu
• Jack Holleran, Associate Director of Athletics
(508) 990-9651
jholleran@umassd.edu
• Jim Mullins, Assistant Director of Athletics
(508) 910-6930
jmullins@umassd.edu
• Megan Erbes, Sports Information Director
(508) 910-9528
merbes@umassd.edu

MASSACHUSETTS INSTITUTE OF TECHNOLOGY (MIT) ATHLETICS
120 VASSAR STREET
CAMBRIDGE, MA 02139-7404
617-253-4498
Fax: 617-258-7343
athletics@mit.edu
mitathletics.com
• Julie Soriero, Director of Athletics
(617) 253-4499
jsoriero@mit.edu
• Dan Martin, Director of Facilities and Operations
(617) 253-5003
djmartin@mit.edu
• John Benedick, Associate Director of Athletics
(617) 253-9892
h20coach@mit.edu
• Tom Cronan, Director of Sports Medicine
(617) 253-3473
cronan@mit.edu
• Carrie Sampson Moore, Director of Physical Education
(617) 253-5004
clsmoore@mit.edu
• Tim Mertz, Director of Recreational Sports
(617) 452-4364
tmertz@mit.edu

MASSACHUSETTS MARITIME ACADEMY ATHLETICS
101 ACADEMY DRIVE
BUZZARDS BAY, MA 02532
508-830-5054
Fax: 508-830-5224
mmabucs.com
• Garin Veris, Director of Athletics
(508) 830-5055
gveris@maritime.edu
• Patricia O'Brien, Assistant Director of Athletics
(508) 830-5076
• Jim Seavey, Director of Sports Information
(508) 830-5054
jseavey@maritime.edu
• Chris Barry, Head Athletic Trainer
(508) 830-5000
cbarry@maritime.edu

MCDANIEL COLLEGE ATHLETICS
2 COLLEGE HILL
WESTMINSTER, MD 21157

410-857-2580
Fax: 410-857-2586
www.mcdanielathletics.com
• Paul Moyer, Director of Athletics
(410) 386-4043
pmoyer@mcdaniel.edu
• Becky Martin, Assistant Director of
Athletics
(410) 857-2577
rmartin@mcdaniel.edu
• Luke Stillson, Director of Sports
Information
(410) 857-2291
sid@mcdaniel.edu
• Phil Smith, Director of Athletics Facilities
(410) 857-2568
pdsmith@mcdaniel.edu
• Kim Easterday, Director of Athletics
Operations
(410) 857-2717
keasterd@mcdaniel.edu
• Gregg Nibbelink, Head Athletic Trainer
(410) 857-2584
gnibbeli@mcdaniel.edu

MCMURRY UNIVERSITY ATHLETICS
1400 SAYLES BOULEVARD
MCM STATION BOX 188
ABILENE, TX 79697
325-793-4633
Fax: 915-793-4659
www.mcmurrysports.com
• Sam Ferguson, Director of Athletics
(325) 793-4647
ferguson.sam@mcm.edu
• Robert Wallace, Faculty Athletics
Representative
(325) 793-3895
rwallace@mcm.edu
• Shusaku Hayashi, Head Athletic Trainer
(325) 793-4648
hayashi.shusaku@mcm.edu
• Dave Beyer, Sports Information Director
(325) 793-4612
beyer.dave@mcm.edu

MEDGAR EVERS COLLEGE ATHLETICS
1150 CARROLL STREET
BROOKLYN, NY 11225
718-270-6072
Fax: 718-804-8204
rbostic@mec.cuny.edu
www.mecathletics.com
• Renee Bostic, Director of Athletics
(718) 270-6071
rbostic@mec.cuny.edu
• Chetara M. Murphy, Assistant Director of
Athletics
(718) 270-6067
cmurphy@mec.cuny.edu
• Videl Price, Director of Compliance
(718) 270-6494
vprice@mec.cuny.edu
• Christopher Ryan, Sports Information
Director
crryanchris@gmail.com

MESSIAH COLLEGE ATHLETICS
ONE COLLEGE AVENUE
SUITE 4501
MECHANICSBURG, PA 17055
717-691-6018
Fax: 717-691-2310
www.gomessiah.com
• Jack Cole, Director of Athletics
(717) 796-1800
jcole@messiah.edu

• Brad McCarty, Associate Athletics Director
for Facilities
(717) 796-1800
bmccarty@messiah.edu
• Amy Weaver, Associate Athletics Director
for Operations
(717) 796-1800
aweaver@messiah.edu
• Steve King, Associate Athletics Director for
Communications
(717) 796-1800
sking@messiah.edu

METHODIST COLLEGE ATHLETICS
5400 RAMSEY STREET
FAYETTEVILLE, NC 28311
910-630-7175
Fax: 910-630-7676
www.mumonarchs.com
• Bob McEvoy, Director of Athletics
(910) 630-7182
mcevoy@methodist.edu
• DeeDee Jarman, Senior Associate Athletic
Director
(910) 630-7283
djarman@methodist.edu
• Dave Eavenson, Assistant Director of
Athletics
(910) 630-7396
deavenson@methodist.edu
• Nate Jervey, Sports Information Director
(910) 630-7172
sportsinfo@methodist.edu
• Brandon Reynolds, Head Athletic Trainer
(910) 630-7177
brandonr@methodist.edu

MIDDLEBURY COLLEGE ATHLETICS
219 SOUTH MAIN STREET
MIDDLEBURY, VT 05753
802-443-5250
Fax: 802-443-2124
athletics.middlebury.edu
• Erin Quinn, Director of Athletics
(802) 443-5253
quinn@middlebury.edu
• Katharine DeLorenzo, Assistant Athletic
Director
(802) 443-5422
kdeloren@middlebury.edu
• Kelly Bevere, Director of Compliance
(802) 443-5386
kbevere@middlebury.edu
• Brad Nadeau, Director of Athletic
Communications
(802) 443-5193
nadeau@middlebury.edu
• Kelly Cray, Acting Director of Sports
Medicine
(802) 443-5259
cray@middlebury.edu

MILLIKIN UNIVERSITY ATHLETICS
1184 WEST MAIN STREET
DECATUR, IL 62522
217-362-6429
Fax: 217-362-6414
ccwhite@millikin.edu
athletics.millikin.edu
• Craig White, Director of Athletics
(217) 424-6344
ccwhite@millikin.edu
• Patrick Allgeier, Assistant Athletic Director
(217) 424-3605
pallgeier@millikin.edu
• Bryan Marshall, Director for Sports
Information

(217) 362-6429
bmarshall@millikin.edu
• Travis Wilcoxen, Faculty Athletics
Representative
(217) 424-6236
twilcoxen@millikin.edu

MILLS COLLEGE ATHLETICS
5000 MACARTHUR BOULEVARD
OAKLAND, CA 94613
510-430-2255
millscyclones.com
• Themy Adachi, Director of Athletics
(510) 430-3285
themy@mills.edu
• Allie Fox, Communications and
Compliance Coordinator
(510) 430-2232
afox@mills.edu
• Natalie Sprangler, Head Athletic Trainer
(510) 430-3323
nspangle@mills.edu
• Hilary Worthen, Assistant Athletic Trainer
(510) 430-3323
hworthen@mills.edu

MILLSAPS COLLEGE ATHLETICS
1701 NORTH STATE STREET
JACKSON, MS 39210
601-974-1190
Fax: 601-974-1209
gomajors.com
• Tim Wise, Associate Athletic Director
(601) 974-1188
wiseta@millsaps.edu
• Will Purcell, Sports Information Director
(601) 974-1394
purcews@millsaps.edu

**MILWAUKEE SCHOOL OF ENGINEERING
ATHLETICS**
1025 NORTH BROADWAY
MILWAUKEE, WI 53202-3109
414-277-6497
800-332-6763
millerbj@msoe.edu
go-raiders.com
• Brian Miller, Athletic Director
(414) 277-6947
millerbj@msoe.edu
• Jessica Ott, Assistant Athletic Director
(414) 277-2411
ott@msoe.edu
• Jimmy Banks, Director of Intramurals
(414) 277-7493
banks@msoe.edu
• Kevin Conway, Sports Information Director
(414) 277-2412
conway@msoe.edu
• Dave Bugalski, Head Athletic Trainer
(414) 277-2812
bugalski@msoe.edu

**MINNESOTA-MORRIS ATHLETICS,
UNIVERSITY OF**
600 EAST FOURTH STREET
MORRIS, MN 56267
320-589-6035
Fax: 320-589-6428
ummcougars.org
• Jason Herbers, Director of Intercollegiate
Athletics
(320) 589-6406
jherbers@morris.umn.edu
• Paul Grove, Assistant Athletic Director
(320) 589-6433
grovep@morris.umn.edu

• Stephen Batcher, Sports Information Director
(320) 589-6423
sabatche@morris.umn.edu
• Raymond Bowman, Head Athletic Trainer
(320) 589-6438
bowmanr@morris.umn.edu

MISERICORDIA UNIVERSITY ATHLETICS
301 LAKE STREET
DALLAS, PA 18612
570-674-6374
Fax: 570-674-3024
athletics.misericordia.edu
• Chuck Edkins, Athletic Director
(570) 674-6397
cedkins@misericordia.edu
• Scott Crispell, Sports Information Director
(570) 674-6398
scrispel@misericordia.edu

MITCHELL COLLEGE ATHLETICS
437 PEQUOT AVENUE
NEW LONDON, CT 06320
860-701-5049
Fax: 860-701-5085
athletics@mitchell.edu
mitchellathletics.com
• Dana Fulmer Garfield, Director of Athletics
(860) 701-5050
fulmer_d@mitchell.edu
• David Longolucco, Sports Information Director
(860) 701-5078
longolucco_d@mitchell.edu
• Aimee Sevigny Krenicki, Head Athletic Trainer
(860) 629-6156
krenicki_a@mitchell.edu

MONMOUTH COLLEGE ATHLETICS
700 EAST BROADWAY
MONMOUTH, IL 61462-1998
309-457-2311
Fax: 309-457-2168
rogerh@monmouthcollege.edu
www.monmouthscots.com
• Roger Haynes, Director of Athletics
(309) 457-2177
rogerh@monmouthcollege.edu
• Tom Burek, Director of Aquatics
(309) 457-2265
tburek@monmouthcollege.edu
• Bob Foster, Head Athletic Trainer
(309) 457-2180
jfoster@monmouthcollege.edu
• Dan Nolan, Sports Information Director
(309) 457-2322
dnolan@monmouthcollege.edu

MONTCLAIR STATE UNIVERSITY ATHLETICS
MONTCLAIR, NJ 7043
973-655-5234
Fax: 973-655-5390
www.montclairathletics.com
• Holly Gera, Director of Athletics
(973) 655-5234
• Rob Chesney, Associate Director of Athletics
(973) 655-6804
chesneyr@mail.montclair.edu
• Anita Kubicka, Assistant Director of Athletics
(973) 655-6790
kubickaa@mail.montclair.edu
• Michael Scala, Director of Sports Publicity

(973) 655-6787
scalam@mail.montclair.edu

MORAVIAN COLLEGE ATHLETICS
1200 MAIN STREET
BETHLEHEM, PA 18018
610-861-1534
Fax: 610-625-7954
dapps@moravian.edu
moraviansports.com
• Scott Dapp, Interim Director of Athletics
dapps@moravian.edu
• John Byrne, Associate Athletics Director
(610) 861-1321
byrnej@moravian.edu
• Sara Steinman, Assistant Athletic Director
(610) 861-1531
steinmans@moravian.edu
• Bob Ward, Head Athletics Trainer
(610) 861-1537
bward@moravian.edu

MOUNT ST. JOSEPH ATHLETICS, COLLEGE OF
5701 DELHI ROAD
CINCINNATI, OH 45233-1670
513-244-4311
Fax: 513-244-4928
www.msjsports.com
• Steve Radcliffe, Director of Athletics
(513) 244-4381
steve.radcliffe@msj.edu
• Melanee Wagener, Associate Director of Athletics
(513) 244-8585
• Ryan Lengerich, Director of Sports Information
(513) 244-4319
ryan.lengerich@msj.edu
• Brian Lewton, Head Athletic Trainer
(513) 244-8588
brian.lewton@msj.edu

MOUNT ST. MARY COLLEGE ATHLETICS
330 POWELL AVENUE
NEWBURGH, NY 12550
845-569-3594
Fax: 845-569-3589
athletics@msmc.edu
www.msmcknights.com
• Dan Twomey, Director of Athletics
(845) 569-3591
dan.twomey@msmc.edu
• Jessica Mushel, Assistant Director of Athletics
(845) 569-3684
jessica.mushel@msmc.edu
• Michele Dreistadt, Director of Intramurals
(845) 569-3583
michele.dreistadt@msmc.edu
• Mike Doughty, Sports Information Director
(845) 569-3341
michael.doughty@msmc.edu
• Steven Iorio, Director of Sports Medicine
(845) 569-3342
steven.iorio@msmc.edu

MOUNT ST. VINCENT ATHLETICS, COLLEGE OF
6301 RIVERDALE AVENUE
RIVERDALE, NY 10471
718-405-3267
Fax: 718-405-3765
www.cmsvathletics.com
• Laura Pruitt, Director of Athletics
(718) 405-3789
laura.pruitt@mountsaintvincent.edu

• Brian Nigro, Associate Director of Athletics
(718) 405-3415
brian.nigro@mountsaintvincent.edu
• Nathan Rauscher, Assistant Director of Athletics
(718) 405-3410
• Brendan Kennedy, Director of Sports Information
(718) 405-3413
brendan.kennedy@mountsaintvincent.edu

MUHLENBERG COLLEGE ATHLETICS
ATHLETIC DEPARTMENT
2400 CHEW STREET
ALLENTOWN, PA 18104-5586
484-664-3100
Fax: 484-664-3035
muhlenbergsports.com
• Corey Goff, Director of Athletics
(484) 664-3380
cgoff@muhlenberg.edu
• Megan Patruno, Assistant Athletic Director
(484) 664-3785
mpatruno@muhlenberg.edu
• Steve Nemes, Head Athletic Trainer
(484) 664-3391
snemes@muhlenberg.edu
• Dawud Abdur-Rahkman, Coordinator of Diversity
(484) 664-4085
dabdur-rahkman@muhlenberg.edu

MUSKINGUM UNIVERSITY ATHLETICS
163 STORMONT STREET
NEW CONCORD, OH 43762
740-826-8211
Fax: 740-826-8300
www.fightingmuskies.com
• Larry Shank, Athletic Director
(740) 826-6109
lshank@muskingum.edu
• Tom Caudill, Sports Information Director
(740) 826-8022
tcaudill@muskingum.edu
• Ken Blood, Head Athletic Trainer
(740) 826-8327
kblood@muskingum.edu

NEBRASKA WESLEYAN UNIVERSITY ATHLETICS
5000 SAINT PAUL AVENUE
LINCOLN, NE 68504-2794
402-465-2360
Fax: 402-465-2170
www.nwusports.com
• Ira Zeff, Director of Athletics
(402) 465-2360
izeff@nebrwesleyan.edu
• Jo Bunstock, Assistant Athletic Director
(402) 465-2355
jeb@nebrwesleyan.edu
• Alex Linden, Sports Information Director
(402) 465-2151
alinden@nebrwesleyan.edu
• Jason Ensrud, Head Athletic Trainer
(402) 465-7508
jensrud@nebrwesleyan.edu

NEUMANN UNIVERSITY ATHLETICS
ONE NEUMANN DRIVE
ASTON, PA 19014-1298
610-459-0905
Fax: 484-840-4798
neumann@neumann.edu
www.neumannathletics.com
• Chuck Sack, Director of Athletics
(484) 840-4711

sackc@neumann.edu
• Len Schuler, Associate Athletic Director
(484) 840-4712
lschuler@neumann.edu
• Jill Weigel, Director of Sports Information
(484) 840-4715
weigelj@neumann.edu
• Mike Cox, Head Athletic Trainer
(484) 840-4719
coxm@neumann.edu

NEW ENGLAND ATHLETICS, UNIVERSITY OF
11 HILLS BEACH ROAD
BIDDEFORD, ME 04005
207-602-2499
Fax: 207-602-5963
athletics.une.edu
• Jack McDonald, Director of Athletics
(207) 602-2499
jmcdonald10@une.edu
• Curt Smyth, Sports Information Director
(207) 602-2562
smyth@une.edu
• Dennis Leighton, Faculty Athletics Representative
(207) 221-4594
dleighton@une.edu
• Brian Razak, Head Athletic Trainer
(207) 602-2496
brazak@une.edu

NEW ENGLAND COLLEGE ATHLETICS
98 BRIDGE STREET
HENNIKER, NH 03242
603-428-2335
Fax: 603-428-6023
athletics.nec.edu
• Lou Izzi, Director of Athletics
(603) 428-2292
lizzi@nec.edu
• Renee Hellert, Associate Athletic Director
(603) 428-2335
rhellert@nec.edu
• Heather Jones, Head Athletic Trainer
(603) 428-2260
hjones@nec.edu

NEW JERSEY CITY UNIVERSITY ATHLETICS
2039 KENNEDY BOULEVARD
JERSEY CITY, NJ 07305
201-200-3317
Fax: 201-200-2365
www.njcugothicknights.com
• Alice De Fazio, Director of Athletics
(201) 200-2243
adefazio@njcu.edu
• George Deaver, Assistant Director of Athletics
(201) 200-2155
gdeaver@njcu.edu
• Juan E. Arroyo, Faculty Athletics Representative
(201) 200-3570
jarroyo@njcu.edu
• Ira Thor, Director of Sports Information
(201) 200-3301
ithor@njcu.edu
• Ann Marie Stoebling, Head Athletic Trainer
(201) 200-3163
astoebling@njcu.edu

NEW JERSEY INSTITUTE OF TECHNOLOGY ATHLETICS
80 LOCK STREET
NEWARK, NJ 07103-

973-596-3623
Fax: 973-642-7333
kaplan@njit.edu
www.njithighlanders.com
• Lenny Kaplan, Director of Athletics
(973) 596-3638
kaplan@njit.edu
• Andrew Schwartz, Senior Associate Director of Athletics
(973) 642-7224
aschwart@njit.edu
• Stephanie Pillari, Assistant Sports Information Director
(973) 596-8324
pillari@njit.edu
• Tim Camp, Director for Sports Information
(973) 596-8461
• Matt Koscs, Head Athletic Trainer
(973) 596-3661
mkoscs@njit.edu

NEW YORK UNIVERSITY ATHLETICS
181 MERCER STREET
NEW YORK, NY 10012
212-998-2021
Fax: 212-995-4591
christopher.bledsoe@nyu.edu
www.gonyuathletics.com
• Christopher Bledsoe, Director of Athletics
(212) 998-2040
christopher.bledsoe@nyu.edu
• Janice Quinn, Senior Associate Director of Athletics
(212) 998-2033
jq1@nyu.edu
• Jeffrey Bernstein, Athletic Director of Sports Information
(212) 998-2031
jeffrey.bernstein@nyu.edu
• Nikki Webb, Coordinator of Athletic Training
(212) 998-2083
nikki.webb@nyu.edu

NICHOLS COLLEGE ATHLETICS
129 CENTER ROAD
DUDLEY, MA 01571
508-213-1560
800-470-3379
Fax: 508-213-2490
reference@nichols.edu
www.nicholsathletics.com
• Chris Colvin, Director of Athletics
(508) 213-2281
chris.colvin@nichols.edu
• Eric Gobiel, Associate Director of Athletics
(508) 213-2351
eric.gobiel@nichols.edu
• Kristan Mallet, Assistant Director of Athletics
(508) 213-2369
kristan.mallet@nichols.edu
• Pete DiVito, Sports Informatino Director
(508) 213-2352
pete.divito@nichols.edu
• Tim Bennett, Head Athletic Trainer
(508) 213-2183
timothy.bennett@nichols.edu

NORTH CAROLINA WESLEYAN COLLEGE ATHLETICS
3400 NORTH WESLEYAN BOULEVARD
ROCKY MOUNT, NC 27804
252-985-5213
Fax: 252-985-5252
jthompson@ncwc.edu
www.ncwcsports.com

• John Thompson, Director of Athletics
(252) 985-5218
jthompson@ncwc.edu
• Martha Proctor, Coordinator of Internal Operations
(252) 985-5213
mproctor@ncwc.edu
• Rikki C. Rich, Assistant Athletic Director of Communications
(252) 985-5271
rcrich@ncwc.edu
• Carol Carson, Head Athletic Trainer
(252) 985-5221
ccarson@ncwc.edu

NORTH CENTRAL COLLEGE ATHLETICS
30 NORTH BRAINARD STREET
NAPERVILLE, IL 60540
630-637-5500
Fax: 630-637-5521
northcentralcardinals.com
• Troy Hammond, President
• James Miller, Athletic Director
(630) 637-5513
jlmiller@noctrl.edu
• Susan Kane, Assistant Athletic Director
(630) 637-5501
smkane@noctrl.edu
• Sara Furlette-Koski, Head Athletic Trainer
(630) 637-5534
sakoski@noctrl.edu
• Clark Teuscher, Sports Information Director
(630) 637-5302
ccteuscher@noctrl.edu
• James Kluckhohn, Athletic Facilities and Recreation Manager
(630) 637-5581
jckluckhohn@noctrl.edu

NORTH PARK UNIVERSITY ATHLETICS
3225 WEST FOSTER AVENUE
CHICAGO, IL 60625
773-244-5685
Fax: 773-244-4952
athletics.northpark.edu
• Jack Surridge, Director of Athletics
(773) 244-5685
jsurridge@northpark.edu
• Susan Zimmer, Associate Director of Athletics
(773) 244-5673
szimmer@northpark.edu
• Kevin Shepke, Director of Sports Information
(773) 244-5594
kshepke@northpark.edu
• Eric McQuaid, Head Athletic Trainer
(773) 244-5701
emcquaid@northpark.edu

NORTHLAND COLLEGE ATHLETICS
1411 ELLIS AVENUE
ASHLAND, WI 54806-3999
715-682-1699
kfalkenhagen@northland.edu
www.northlandcollegesports.com
• Kim Falkenhagen, Director of Athletics
(715) 682-1868
kfalkenhagen@northland.edu
• Seamus Gregory, Assistant Athletic Director
(715) 682-1395
sgregory@northland.edu
• Chas Johnson, Sports Information Director
(715) 682-1985
cjohnson@northland.edu

• Abby Kaufman, Athletic Trainer
(715) 682-1245
akaufman@northland.edu

NORWICH UNIVERSITY ATHLETICS
158 HARMON DRIVE
NORTHFIELD, VT 05663
802-485-2230
Fax: 802-485-2234
www.norwichathletics.com
• Anthony Mariano, Director of Athletics
(802) 485-2232
tmariano@norwich.edu
• Derek Dunning, Director of Athletic
Communications
(802) 485-2902
ddunning@norwich.edu
• Jeff Dobbin, Assistant Director of Athletic
Communications
(802) 485-2241
jdobbin@norwich.edu
• Dave Botelho, Head Athletic Trainer
(802) 485-2236
dbotelho@norwich.edu

OBERLIN COLLEGE ATHLETICS
200 WOODLAND AVENUE
OBERLIN, OH 44074
440-775-8500
Fax: 440-775-8957
www.goyeo.com
• Natalie Winkelfoos, Director of Athletics
(440) 775-6463
natalie.winkelfoos@oberlin.edu
• Creg Jantz, Senior Associate Director of
Athletics
(440) 775-6401
creg.jantz@oberlin.edu
• Eric Lahetta, Director of Athletics for
Intercollegiate Sports
(440) 775-8534
eric.lahetta@oberlin.edu
• Mike Mancini, Director of Athletics for
Communications
(440) 775-8503
mike.mancini@oberlin.edu
• Tim Carver, Director of Sports Medicine
(440) 775-8589
tim.carver@oberlin.edu

OCCIDENTAL COLLEGE ATHLETICS
1600 CAMPUS RD
DEPARTMENT OF ATHLETICS M-19
LOS ANGELES, CA 90041
323-259-2608
800-765-8002
Fax: 323-341-4993
jhoffman@oxy.edu
www.oxyathletics.com
• Jaime Hoffman, Athletic Director
(323) 259-2699
dfarmer@oxy.edu
• Andy Holmes, Sports Information Director
(323) 259-2724
holmesa@oxy.edu
• Dale Widolff, Football Coach
(323) 259-2708
dwidolff@oxy.edu
• Brian Newhall, Men's Basketball Coach
(323) 259-2608
bnewhall@oxy.edu
• Kevin Hall, Women's Basketball Coach
(323) 259-2682
khall@oxy.edu

OGLETHORPE UNIVERSITY ATHLETICS
4484 PEACHTREE ROAD NE
ATLANTA, GA 30319
404-364-8419
Fax: 404-364-8445
athletics@oglethorpe.edu
gopetrels.com
• Becky Hall, Director of Athletics
• Iona Wynter Parks, Faculty Athletics
Representative
iwynterparks@oglethorpe.edu
• Mike Rulison, Faculty Athletics
Representative
mrulison@oglethorpe.edu

**OHIO NORTHERN UNIVERSITY
ATHLETICS**
KING HORN CENTER
525 SOUTH MAIN STREET
ADA, OH 45810
419-772-2440
Fax: 419-772-2470
www.onusports.com
• Tom Simmons, Athletic Director
(419) 772-2450
t-simmons@onu.edu
• Kate Witte, Senior Woman Administrator
(419) 772-2446
k-witte@onu.edu
• Brian Hofman, Assistant Athletic Director
(419) 772-1878
b-hofman@onu.edu
• Tim Glon, Sports Information Director
(419) 772-2046
t-glon@onu.edu
• Kurt Wilson, Head Athletic Trainer
(419) 772-2559
k-wilson.1@onu.edu

**OHIO WESLEYAN UNIVERSITY
ATHLETICS**
61 SOUTH SANDUSKY STREET
DELAWARE, OH 43015
740-368-3725
Fax: 740-368-3751
www.battlingbishops.com
• Roger Ingles, Athletics Director
(740) 368-3738
rdingles@owu.edu
• Mike DeWitt, Associate Athletics Director
(740) 368-3744
mddewitt@owu.edu
• Kris Boey, Associate Athletics Director
(740) 368-3731
kwboey@owu.edu
• Todd Miller, Athletic Trainer
(740) 368-3747
tcmiller@owu.edu

OLIVET COLLEGE ATHLETICS
320 SOUTH MAIN STREET
OLIVET, MI 49076
269-749-7601
Fax: 269-749-7229
www.olivetcomets.com
• Ryan Shockey, Athletic Director
(269) 749-7189
rshockey@olivetcollege.edu
• Megan Merchant, Senior Woman
Administrator
(269) 749-6677
mjmiller@olivetcollege.edu
• Charlie Wilson, Coordinator of Eligibility
and Compliance
(269) 749-6649
chwilson@olivetcollege.edu
• Geoff Henson, Sports Information Director

(269) 749-7602
ghenson@olivetcollege.edu

OTTERBEIN UNIVERSITY ATHLETICS
ONE SOUTH GROVE STREET
WESTERVILLE, OH 43081
614-823-3546
Fax: 614-823-1966
dstewart@otterbein.edu
www.otterbeincardinals.com
• Dawn Stewart, Director of Athletics
(614) 823-3518
dstewart@otterbein.edu
• Connie Richardson, Associate Athletic
Director
(614) 823-3517
crichardson@otterbein.edu
• Tim Doup, Assistant Athletic Director
(614) 823-3527
tdoup@otterbein.edu
• Adam Prescott, Sports Information
Director
(614) 823-1951
aprescott@otterbein.edu
• Charles Goodwin, Head Athletic Trainer
(614) 823-1634
cgoodwin@otterbein.edu

**OZARKS ATHLETICS, UNIVERSITY OF
THE**
415 NORTH COLLEGE AVENUE
CLARKSVILLE, AR 72830
479-979-1465
Fax: 479-979-1330
• Jimmy Clark, Athletic Director
(479) 979-1484
jclark@ozarks.edu
• Matt Torok, Assistant Athletic Director
(479) 979-1210
• Josh Peppas, Sports Information Director
(479) 979-1483
jpeppas@ozarks.edu
• Chad Floyd, Head Athletic Trainer
(479) 979-1472
cfloyd@ozarks.edu

**PACIFIC LUTHERAN UNIVERSITY
ATHLETICS**
1010 122ND STREET SOUTH
TACOMA, WA 98447
253-535-7350
Fax: 253-535-7584
athletic@plu.edu
golutes.com
• Laurie Turner, Director of Athletics
(253) 535-7361
turnerll@plu.edu
• Jennifer Thomas, Associate Director of
Athletics
(253) 535-8109
thomasjl@plu.edu
• Jessica Roswell, Assistant Athletic
Director for Marketing
(253) 535-8504
roswellj@plu.edu
• Aaron Gunther, Head Athletic Trainer
(253) 535-7366
guntheam@plu.edu
• Tyler Scott, Director of Athletics
Communications
(253) 535-7356

PACIFIC UNIVERSITY ATHLETICS
2043 COLLEGE WAY
FOREST GROVE, OR 97116

503-352-2767
Fax: 503-352-2209
www.goboxers.com
• Ken Schumann, Director of Athletics
(503) 352-2180
schumank@pacificu.edu
• Lauren Esbensen, Associate Director of
Athletics
(503) 352-2186
• Scott Cowan, Assistant Facilities Manager
(503) 352-2284
scowan@pacificu.edu
• Angela Moberg, Director of Intramurals
(503) 352-2138
• Russ Blunck, Sports Information Director
(503) 352-2161
• Eric Pitkanen, Head Athletic Trainer
(503) 352-2896

PENN STATE BEHREND ATHLETICS
5103 STATION ROAD
ERIE, PA 16563-0400
814-898-6163
Fax: 814-898-6013
www.psblions.com
• Brian Streeter, Director of Athletics
(814) 898-6379
• Torie Craven, Assistant Athletic Director
(814) 898-6240
• Jill Yamma, Sports Information Director
(814) 898-6322
jey117@psu.edu
• Jeff Webster, Head Athletic Trainer
(814) 898-6340

PIEDMONT COLLEGE ATHLETICS
1021 CENTRAL AVENUE
DEMOREST, GA 30535
706-778-3000 EXT 1358
Fax: 706-776-0145
piedmontlions.com
• Jim Peeples, Director of Athletics
(706) 778-3000
jpeeples@piedmont.edu
• Liz Butikofer, Director of Daily Operations
(706) 778-3000
lbutikofer@piedmont.edu
• Jamie Purdy, Assistant Director of
Athletics
(706) 778-3000
jpurdy@piedmont.edu
• Debra Dooley, Faculty Athletic
Representative
(706) 778-3000
ddooley@piedmont.edu
• Timmy McCormack, Assistant Director of
Athletics
(706) 778-3000
tmccormack@piedmont.edu

PITTSBURGH AT BRADFORD
ATHLETICS, U. OF
300 CAMPUS DRIVE
BRADFORD, PA 16701
814-362-7521
800-872-1787
Fax: 814-362-7503
athletics.pittbradford.org
• Bret Butler, Athletic Director
(814) 362-5093
bab15@pitt.edu
• Tina Phillips, Assistant Athletic Director
(814) 362-5086
tmp14@pitt.edu
• Tim Sneeringer, Director of Recreation
(814) 362-7526
sneering@pitt.edu

• Josh Horton, Director of Sports Information
(814) 362-7564
jhorton@pitt.edu
• Jeff Timlin, Interim Athletic Trainer
(814) 362-7516
jtimlin@pitt.edu

PLYMOUTH STATE UNIVERSITY
ATHLETICS
P.E. CENTER
MSC #32
PLYMOUTH, NH 03264
603-535-2770
Fax: 603-535-2777
athletics.plymouth.edu
• Kim Bownes, Interim Athletic Director
(603) 535-2771
kbownes@plymouth.edu
• Courtney O'Clair, Associate Athletic
Director
(603) 535-2750
c_oclair@plymouth.edu
• Lauren Lavigne, Assistant Athletic Director
(603) 535-2763
l_lavign@plymouth.edu
• Mark Legacy, Head Athletic Trainer
(603) 535-2757
mdlegacy@plymouth.edu
• Kent Cherrington, Sports Information
Director
(603) 535-2477
kcherrington@plymouth.edu

POMONA-PITZER COLLEGES
ATHLETICS
333 NORTH COLLEGE WAY
CLAREMONT, CA 91711
909-621-8423
Fax: 909-621-8547
www.pe.pomona.edu
• Lesley Irvine, Director of Athletics
(909) 621-8016
lesley.irvine@pomona.edu
• Lisa Beckett, Associate Director of
Athletics
(909) 621-8428
lbeckett@pomona.edu
• Brandon Johnson, Director of Intramurals
(909) 621-8420
brandon.johnson@pomona.edu
• Kirk Jones, Head Athletic Trainer
(909) 607-2473
kjones@pomona.edu
• Sam Porter, Sports Information Director
(909) 607-3737
samuel.porter@pomona.edu

PRATT INSTITUTE ATHLETICS
200 WILLOUGHBY AVENUE
BROOKLYN, NY 11205
718-636-3600
Fax: 718-636-3772
www.goprattgo.com
• Walter Rickard, Director of Athletics
(718) 636-3771
wrickard@pratt.edu
• Ryan McCarthy, Associate Director for
Intercollegiate Athletics
(718) 399-4530
rmccar12@pratt.edu

PRINCIPIA COLLEGE ATHLETICS
1 MAYBECK PLACE
ELSAH, IL 62028
618-374-5024
800-277-4648

Fax: 618-374-5221
www.principiaathletics.com
• Lee Ellis, Athletic Director
(618) 374-5030
lee.ellis@principia.edu
• Mary Ann Sprague, Associate Athletic
Director
(618) 374-5038
maryann.sprague@principia.edu
• Heather Fairbanks, Sports Information
Director
(618) 374-5456
heather.fairbanks@principia.edu

PUGET SOUND ATHLETICS, UNIVERSITY
OF
1500 NORTH WARNER STREET
CMB 1044
TACOMA, WA 98416-1044
253-879-3140
Fax: 253-879-3634
ahackett@pugetsound.edu
www.loggerathletics.com
• Amy Hackett, Director of Athletics
(253) 879-3426
ahackett@pugetsound.edu
• Robin Hamilton, Associate Athletic
Director
(253) 879-3141
rhamilton@pugetsound.edu
• Gregor Walz, Director of Athletic
Communications
(253) 879-3974
gwalz@pugetsound.edu
• Paige McFeeley, Assistant Director of
Athletic Communications
(253) 879-3458
pmcfeeley@pugetsound.edu
• Craig Bennett, Director of Sports Medicine
(253) 879-3441
cabennett@pugetsound.edu

RAMAPO COLLEGE OF NEW JERSEY
ATHLETICS
505 RAMAPO VALLEY ROAD
MAHWAH, NJ 07430
201-684-7674
Fax: 201-684-7958
hcrocker@ramapo.edu
www.ramapoathletics.com
• Harold Crocker, Director of Athletics
(201) 684-7091
hcrocker@ramapo.edu
• Kathleen Finnegan, Associate Director of
Athletics
(201) 684-7683
kfinnega@ramapo.edu
• Megan Bageorgos, Head Athletic Trainer
(201) 684-7913
mpriddy@ramapo.edu
• Rachel L. Pinton, Director of Sports
Information
(201) 684-7679
rpinton@ramapo.edu

RANDOLPH-MACON COLLEGE
ATHLETICS
103 EAST PATRICK STREET
ASHLAND, VA 23005
804-752-7223
jburns@rmc.edu
rmcathletics.com
• Jeff Burns, Director of Athletics
(804) 752-7367
jburns@rmc.edu
• MK Geratowski, Director of Compliance
(804) 752-7366

mkgeratowski@rmc.edu
• Phil Stanton, Sports Information Director
(804) 752-7387
philipstanton@rmc.edu
• Heather Bauby, Head Athletic Trainer
(804) 752-3215
hbauby@rmc.edu

REDLANDS ATHLETICS, UNIVERSITY OF
1200 EAST COLTON AVE
REDLANDS, CA 92373-0999
909-748-8400
866-946-3294
Fax: 909-335-4088
jill_joiner@redlands.edu
www.goredlands.com
• Jeff Martinez, Director of Athletics
(909) 748-8400
jeff_martinez@redlands.edu
• Rachel Roche, Sports Information Director
(909) 748-8418
rachel_roche@redlands.edu
• Janelle Kratz, Head Athletic Trainer
(909) 748-8399
janelle_kratz@redlands.edu

RENSSELAER POLYTECHNIC INSTITUTE ATHLETICS
110 8TH STREET
TROY, NY 12180
518-276-2187
Fax: 518-276-8997
mcelrl@rpi.edu
www.rpiathletics.com
• Lee McElroy, Athletic Director
(518) 276-6685
mcelrl@rpi.edu
• Karen Hansen, Associate Athletic Director for Business
(518) 276-6264
hansek2@rpi.edu
• Kevin Beattie, Associate Athletic Director for Communications
(518) 276-2187
beattk@rpi.edu
• Sachi Vines, Director of Marketing
(518) 276-4855
enas@rpi.edu
• Chris Thompson, Head Athletic Trainer
(518) 276-6186
thompc@rpi.edu

RHODE ISLAND COLLEGE ATHLETICS
600 MOUNT PLEASANT AVENUE
PROVIDENCE, RI 2908
401-456-8007
Fax: 401-456-8514
dtencher@ric.edu
www.goanchormen.com
• Donald Tencher, Director of Athletics and Recreation
(401) 456-8007
dtencher@ric.edu
• Jo-Ann D'Alessandro, Associate Athletic Director
(401) 456-9882
jdalessandro@ric.edu
• Scott Roy, Assistant Athletic Director
(401) 465-8515
sroy@ric.edu
• Carlo Cantarella, Head Athletic Trainer
(401) 456-4686
ccantarella@ric.edu

RHODES COLLEGE ATHLETICS
2000 NORTH PARKWAY
MEMPHIS, TN 38112

901-843-3063
Fax: 901-843-3749
rhodeslynx.com
• Mike Clary, Director of Athletics
(901) 843-3939
clary@rhodes.edu
• Jeff Cleanthes, Assistant Athletic Director
(901) 843-3456
cleanthesj@rhodes.edu
• Janes Wells, Senior Womens Administrator
(901) 843-3013
wellsj@rhodes.edu
• James Hill, Coordinator of Sports Information
(901) 843-3063
hillj2@rhodes.edu
• Drew Gibson, Head Athletic Trainer
(901) 843-3465
gibsona@rhodes.edu

RICHARD STOCKTON COLLEGE OF NJ ATHLETICS
101 VERA KING FARRIS DRIVE
GALLOWAY, NJ 08205
609-652-4874
Fax: 609-748-5510
folksl@stockton.edu
www.stocktonathletics.com
• Lonnie Folks, Director of Athletics and Recreation
(609) 652-4877
folksl@stockton.edu
• Jon Heck, Director of Athletic Operations
(609) 652-4952
heckj@stockton.edu
• Linda Yost, Associate Director of Intercollegiate Athletics
(609) 652-4875
yostl@stockton.edu
• Brooke Rollman, Assistant Director of Athletics - Finance
(609) 652-4517
rollmanb@stockton.edu
• Chris Rollman, Sports Information Director
(609) 626-6011
rollmanc@stockton.edu

RIPON COLLEGE ATHLETICS
300 SEWARD STREET
PO BOX 248
RIPON, WI 54971-0248
800-947-4766
Fax: 920-748-7386
johnsonj@ripon.edu
redhawks.ripon.edu
• Julie Johnson, Athletic Director
(920) 748-8772
johnsonj@ripon.edu
• Ron Ernst, Assistant Athlteic Director
(920) 748-8708
ernstr@ripon.edu
• Brian Azinger, Head Athletic Trainer
(920) 748-8775
azingerb@ripon.edu

RIVIER UNIVERSITY ATHLETICS
420 SOUTH MAIN STREET
NASHUA, NH 03060
603-888-1311
Fax: 603-897-8616
jmerrill@rivier.edu
www.rivierathletics.com
• Joanne Merrill, Athletic Director
(603) 897-8257
jmerrill@rivier.edu
• Craig Kolek, Associate Athletic Director

(603) 897-8467
ckolek@rivier.edu
• Anthony Perry, Sports Informatino Director
(603) 897-8760
aperry@rivier.edu
• Laura Ray, Senior Women Administrator
(603) 897-8763
lray@rivier.edu
• Keith Rupp, Head Athletic Trainer
(603) 897-8616
krupp@rivier.edu

ROCHESTER ATHLETICS, UNIVERSITY OF
GOERGEN ATHLETIC CENTER
LIBRARY ROAD
BOX 270296
ROCHESTER, NY 14627
585-275-4301
Fax: 585-461-5081
uofrathletics.com
• George VanderZwaag, Executive Director of Athletics
(585) 275-4301
zwaag@sports.rochester.edu
• Jane Possee, Associate Director of Recreation
(585) 275-6914
jane@sports.rochester.edu
• Terry Gurnett, Associate Director of Advancement
(585) 275-6698
tgurnett@sports.rochester.edu
• Eric Rozen, Head Athletic Trainer
(585) 275-9540
erozen@sports.rochester.edu
• Dennis O'Donnell, Director of Athletic Communications
(585) 275-5955
dennis.odonnell@rochester.edu

ROCHESTER INSTITUTE OF TECHNOLOGY ATHLETICS
CLARK GYMNASIUM
51 LOMB MEMORIAL DRIVE
ROCHESTER, NY 14623-5603
585-475-2614
Fax: 716-475-2617
ammgla@rit.edu
www.ritathletics.com
• Lou Spiotti, Jr., Executive Director of Athletics
(585) 475-2615
lxs4798@rit.edu
• Scott McVean, Senior Associate Director of Athletics
(585) 475-7448
rsmatl@rit.edu
• Lex Sleeman, Associate Director of Intercollegiate Athletics
(585) 475-7372
atsped@rit.edu
• Joanne Bagley, Senior Staff Specialist
(585) 475-5814
jpbatl@rit.edu
• Ben Emke, Head Athletic Trainer
(585) 475-4513
bweatl@rit.edu

ROCKFORD COLLEGE ATHLETICS
5050 EAST STATE STREET
ROCKFORD, IL 61108
815-226-4000
Fax: 815-226-4166
kking@rockford.edu
www.goregents.com

• Kristyn King, Director of Athletics
(815) 394-5061
kking@rockford.edu
• Bob Koopmann, Assistant Athletic Director
(815) 394-5062
rkoopmann@rockford.edu
• Jessica Stanek, Senior Women Administrator
(815) 394-5065
jstanek@rockford.edu
• Brian Vanden Acker, Sports Information Director
(815) 394-5060
bvandenacker@rockford.edu
• Holli Newcomer, Head Athletic Trainer
(815) 394-5075
hnewcomer@rockford.edu

ROGER WILLIAMS UNIVERSITY ATHLETICS
ONE OLD FERRY ROAD
BRISTOL, RI 02809
401-254-3050
Fax: 401-254-3535
nwilliams@rwu.edu
rwuhawks.com
• Mark J. Andreozzi, Fitness Coordinator, Club Sports Director
(401) 254-3069
mandreozzi@rwu.edu
• Amanda Callahan, Assistant Athletic Director
(401) 254-5325
acallahan@rwu.edu
• Jon Egan, Athletic Operations Coordinator
(401) 286-2086
jegan@rwu.edu
• David Kemmy, Director of Athletics
(401) 254-3428
dkemmy@rwu.edu
• Joshua King, Head Athletic Trainer
(401) 254-3287
jnking@rwu.edu
• Nicholas Williams, Athletics Communications Director
(401) 254-3852
nwilliams@rwu.edu

ROSE-HULMAN INST. OF TECH ATHLETICS
5500 WABASH AVENUE
TERRE HAUTE, IN 47803
812-877-1511
Fax: 812-877-8407
athletics.rose-hulman.edu
• Jeff Jenkins, Athletic Director
(812) 877-8209
jenkins@rose-hulman.edu
• Jon Prevo, Associate Athletic Director
(812) 877-8932
prevo@rose-hulman.edu
• Kevin Lanke, Director for Sports Information
(812) 877-8180
lanke@rose-hulman.edu
• Scott Keller, Head Athletic Trainer
(812) 877-8270
scott.keller@rose-hulman.edu

ROWAN UNIVERSITY ATHLETICS
201 MULLICA HILL ROAD
GLASSBORO, NJ 08028
856-256-4000
Fax: 856-256-4916
www.rowanathletics.com
• Dan Gilmore, Athletic Director
(856) 256-4686
gilmore@rowan.edu
• Penny Kempf, Associate Athletic Director
(856) 256-4679
kempf@rowan.edu
• Gabby Lisella, Assistant Athletic Director
(856) 256-4681
lisella@rowan.edu
• Sheila Stevenson, Director of Athletic Communications
(856) 256-4253
stevenson@rowan.edu
• Colleen Grugan, Head Athletic Trainer
(856) 256-4699
grugan@rowan.edu

RUST COLLEGE ATHLETICS
150 RUST AVENUE
HOLLY SPRINGS, MS 38635
662-252-8000
Fax: 662-252-8862
www.rustcollegesports.com
• Ishmell Edwards, Athletics Director
(662) 252-8000
iedwards@rustcollege.edu
• Aurby Burdine, Student Activities Coach
(662) 252-8000
aburdine@rustcollege.edu

RUTGERS UNIVERSITY-CAMDEN ATHLETICS
301 LINDEN STREET
CAMDEN, NJ 08102
856-225-6198
Fax: 856-225-6024
mballard@camden.rutgers.edu
scarletraptors.com
• Jeff Dean, Director of Athletics
(856) 225-2747
jldean@camden.rutgers.edu
• Tom Thomasson, Associate Director of Athletics
(856) 225-2746
tthomass@camden.rutgers.edu
• Karen Freed, Assistant Director of Athletics
(856) 225-6200
karen.freed@camden.rutgers.edu
• Michael Ballard, Sports Information Director
(856) 225-6198
mballard@camden.rutgers.edu

RUTGERS UNIVERSITY-NEWARK ATHLETICS
GOLDEN DOME ATHLETIC CENTER
42 WARREN STREET
NEWARK, NJ 07102
973-353-5474
Fax: 973-353-1431
markg@newark.rutgers.edu
www.rutgersnewarkathletics.com
• Mark Griffin, Director of Athletics
(973) 353-1458
markg@newark.rutgers.edu
• Mary Stadelmann, Senior Woman Administrator
(973) 353-1460
mary.stad@rutgers.edu
• Mike Alvarez, Assistant Athletic Director
(973) 353-3716
mjalvare@newark.rutgers.edu
• Rob Kulish, Director of Athletic Communications
(973) 353-1466
robert.kulish@rutgers.edu

SAINT MARY'S UNIVERSITY (MN) ATHLETICS
700 TERRACE HEIGHTS
WINONA, MN 55987
507-457-1579
Fax: 507-457-6640
www.saintmaryssports.com
• Nikki Fennern, Athletic Director
(507) 457-1638
nfennern@smumn.edu
• Mike Lester, Director of Compliance
(507) 457-6954
mlester@smumn.edu
• Donny Nadeau, Sports Information Director
(507) 457-1634
dnadeau@smumn.edu
• Jill Collum, Head Athletic Trainer
(507) 457-1759
jcollum@smumn.edu

SAINT NORBERT COLLEGE ATHLETICS
100 GRANT STREET
DE PERE, WI 54115-2099
920-337-3181
Fax: 920-403-3128
www.snc.edu
• Tim Bald, Athletic Director
(920) 403-3986
tim.bald@snc.edu
• Jim Purtill, Football Coach
(920) 403-3172
• Paul DeNoble, Men's Basketball Coach
(920) 403-3137
• Connie Tilley, Women's Basketball Coach
(920) 403-3033
connie.tilley@snc.edu
• Joann Krueger, Softball Coach
(920) 403-4080
joann.krueger@snc.edu
• Thomas Winske, Baseball Coach
(920) 403-3545
thomas.winske@snc.edu

SAINT SCHOLASTICA ATHLETICS, COLLEGE OF
1200 KENWOOD AVENUE
DULUTH, MN 55811
218-723-6000
Fax: 218-723-5958
www.csssaints.com
• Don Olson, Athletics Director
(218) 723-5934
dolson4@css.edu
• Merissa Edwards, Director of Compliance
(218) 723-6551
medwards@css.edu
• Jesse Robinson, Director of Athletics Communications
(218) 723-6643
jrobinso@css.edu
• Tom Rheaume, Head Athletic Trainer
(218) 723-5918
trheaume@css.edu

SAINT VINCENT COLLEGE ATHLETICS
300 FRASER PURCHASE ROAD
LATROBE, PA 15650-2690
724-532-6600
sports@stvincent.edu
athletics.stvincent.edu
• Myron Kirsch, Athletic Director
(724) 805-2111
myron.kirsch@email.stvincent.edu
• Sue Hozak, Associate Athletic Director
(724) 805-2112
sue.hozak@stvincent.edu

college sports

• Jeff Zidek, Sports Information Director
(724) 805-2476
jeff.zidek@stvincent.edu
• Aaron Thompson, Assistant Sports
Information Director
(724) 805-2741
aaron.thompson@stvincent.edu
• Becky Pizer, Head Athletic Trainer
(724) 805-2400
becky.pizer@stvincent.edu

SALEM STATE COLLEGE ATHLETICS
O'KEEFE SPORTS COMPLEX
225 CANAL STREET
SALEM, MA 1970
978-542-7260
Fax: 978-542-2926
www.salemstatevikings.com
• Peggy Carl, Director of Athletics &
Recreation
(978) 542-7260
pcarl@salemstate.edu
• Jason Doviak, Senior Associate Director of
Athletics
(978) 542-6569
jdoviak@salemstate.edu
• Kelly Janos, Associate Director of Athletics
(978) 542-4442
kjason@salemstate.edu
• Joseph Beitz, Sports Information Director
(978) 542-6544
jbeitz@salemstate.edu
• Carey MacDonald, Head Athletic Trainer
(978) 542-7195
cmacdonald@salemstate.edu

SALISBURY UNIVERSITY ATHLETICS
1101 CAMDEN AVENUE
SALISBURY, MD 21801
410-548-3503
Fax: 410-546-2639
www.suseagulls.com
• Gerry DiBartolo, Athletic Director
(410) 548-3503
grdibartolo@salisbury.edu
• Dawn Chamberlin, Associate Athletic
Director
(410) 548-2588
drchamberlin@salisbury.edu
• Tim Brennan, Sports Information Director
(410) 543-6016
tmbrennan@salisbury.edu
• Pat Lamboni, Head Athletic Trainer
(410) 543-6355
pmlamboni@salisbury.edu

SALVE REGINA UNIVERSITY ATHLETICS
100 OCHRE POINT AVENUE
NEWPORT, RI 02840-4192
401-341-2268
Fax: 401-341-2960
www.salveathletics.com
• Jody Mooradian, Director of Athletics
(401) 341-2268
jody.mooradian@salve.edu
• Kelly Scafariello, Associate Director of
Athletics
(401) 341-2247
kelly.scafariello@salve.edu
• Ed Habershaw, Sports Information Director
(401) 341-2271
habershe@salve.edu
• David Cox, Head Athletic Trainer
(401) 341-3221
david.cox@salve.edu
• Tom Blaney, Fitness Center Manager

(401) 341-2606
tom.blaney@salve.edu

**SAVANNAH COLLEGE OF ART & DESIGN
ATHLETICS**
115 EAST YORK STREET
SAVANNAH, GA 31401
912-525-4800
Fax: 912-525-4814
savannah.scadathletics.com
• Doug Wollenburg, Athletics Director
(912) 525-4781
dwollenbu@scad.edu
• Darrell Naylor-Johnson, Faculty Athletics
Representative
(912) 525-5723
dnaylorj@scad.edu
• Tommy Chasanoff, Sports Information
Director
(912) 525-4815
tchasano@scad.edu
• Eddie Concepcion, Director of Intramurals
and Recreation
(912) 525-6958
egconcep@scad.edu

SCRANTON ATHLETICS, UNIVERSITY OF
THE UNIVERSITY OF SCRANTON
800 LINDEN STREET
SCRANTON, PA 18510
570-941-7440
Fax: 570-941-4223
athletics@scranton.edu
athletics.scranton.edu
• Dave Martin, Director of Athletics
(570) 941-7440
david.martin2@scranton.edu
• Toby Lovecchio, Associate Director of
Athletics
(570) 941-7441
francis.lovecchio@scranton.edu
• Colleen Pivirotto, Senior Woman
Administrator
(570) 941-6191
colleen.pivirotto@scranton.edu
• Erin Maguire, Athletics Operations
Manager
(570) 941-7440
erin.maguire@scranton.edu
• Randy Shemanski, Athletics
Communications Manager
(570) 941-7029
randall.shemanski@scranton.edu
• Kristin Littzi, Sports Medicine Manager
(570) 941-7473
kristin.littzi@scranton.edu

**SEWANEE, UNIVERSITY OF THE SOUTH
ATHLETICS**
735 UNIVERSITY AVENUE
SEWANEE, TN 37383
931-598-1284
Fax: 931-598-1673
sewaneetigers.com
• Mark Webb, Director of Athletics
(931) 598-1388
mwebb@sewanee.edu
• Nancy Ladd, Assistant Director of Athletics
(931) 598-1320
nladd@sewanee.edu
• Dickie McCarthy, Director of Internal
Operations
(931) 598-1323
dmccarth@sewanee.edu
• Clayton Felts, Director of Athletic
Communication
(931) 598-1136

cafelts@sewanee.edu
• Ray Knight, Head Athletic Trainer
(931) 598-1293
rknight@sewanee.edu

SHENANDOAH UNIVERSITY ATHLETICS
1460 UNIVERSITY DRIVE
WINCHESTER, VA 22601
540-665-4566
Fax: 540-665-4934
www.suhornets.com
• Doug Zipp, Athletic Director
(540) 665-4566
dzipp@su.edu
• Sarah Pelster, Associate Athletic Director
(540) 545-7366
spelster@su.edu
• Kevin Anderson, Assistant Athletic Director
(540) 665-4531
kanders2@su.edu
• Scott Musa, Athletic Communications
Director
(540) 655-5417
smusa@su.edu

SIMPSON COLLEGE ATHLETICS
701 NORTH C. STREET
INDIANOLA, IA 50125
515-961-6251
simpsonathletics.com
• Brian Niemuth, Director of Athletics
(515) 961-1670
brian.niemuth@simpson.edu
• Lana Smith, Assistant Athletic Director
(515) 961-1641
lana.smith@simpson.edu
• Bryan Geelan, Athletics Communication
Director
(515) 961-1577
bryan.geelan@simpson.edu

SKIDMORE COLLEGE ATHLETICS
815 NORTH BROADWAY
SARATOGA SPRINGS, NY 12866
518-580-5370
Fax: 518-580-5395
info@skidmore.edu
skidmoreathletics.com
• Gail Cummings-Danson, Athletics Director
(518) 580-5370
gcumming@skidmore.edu
• Megan Buchanan, Associate Athletic
Director
(518) 580-5351
mbuchana@skidmore.edu
• Nekisha Quinney, Assistant Athletic
Director
(518) 580-5456
nquinney@skidmore.edu
• Bill Jones, Athletic Marketing Manager
(518) 580-5364
bjones@skidmore.edu
• Meghan Nicchi, Head Athletic Trainer
(518) 580-5390
mnicchi@skidmore.edu

**SOUTHERN MAINE ATHLETICS,
UNIVERSITY OF**
37 COLLEGE AVENUE
GORHAM, ME 04038
207-780-5430
Fax: 207-780-5994
sid@usm.maine.edu
www.southernmainehuskies.com
• Al Bean, Director of Athletics
(207) 780-5588
albean@maine.edu

- Meredith Bickford, Associate Director of Athletics
(207) 780-5997
meredith.bickford@maine.edu
- B. L. Elfring, Director of Athletics for Compliance
(207) 780-5434
elfring@maine.edu
- Robert Kuech, Faculty Athletics Representative
(207) 780-5089
robert.kuech@maine.edu
- Matthew Gerken, Head Athletic Trainer
(207) 780-5140
matthew.gerken@maine.edu

SOUTHERN VERMONT COLLEGE ATHLETICS
982 MANSION DRIVE
BENNINGTON, VT 05201-6002
802-447-4000
Fax: 802-447-4652
shashim@svc.edu
www.svcathletics.com
- Sharief Hashim, Interim Director of Athletics
(802) 447-4606
shashim@svc.edu
- Ashley Hodges, Assistant Athletics Director/Senior Womens Admin
(802) 447-4670
ahodges@svc.edu
- Michael Nosek, Sports Information Director
(802) 447-4672
mknosek@svc.edu
- Bob Kurtzner, Strength & Conditioning Coordinator
rkurtzner@svc.edu

SOUTHERN VIRGINIA UNIVERSITY ATHLETICS
ONE UNIVERSITY HILL DRIVE
BUENA VISTA, VA 24416
540-261-8507
800-229-8420
Fax: 540-266-3866
athletics@svu.edu
athletics.svu.edu
- Jason Lamb, Director of Athletics
(540) 261-8525
jason.lamb@svu.edu
- Deidra Dryden, Associate Athletic Director
(540) 261-8516
deidra.dryden@svu.edu
- Tony Caputo, Assistant Athletic Director
(540) 261-8526
tony.caputo@svu.edu
- Scott Winterton, Athletic Relations
(540) 261-8524
scott.winterton@svu.edu

SOUTHWESTERN UNIVERSITY ATHLETICS
1001 EAST UNIVERSITY AVENUE
GEORGETOWN, TX 78626
512-863-1381
Fax: 512-863-1393
athletics@southwestern.edu
southwesternpirates.com
- Glada Munt, Director of Intercollegiate Athletics
(512) 863-1381
muntg@southwestern.edu
- Glenn Schwab, Director of Athletic Training Services
(512) 863-1697

schwabg@southwestern.edu
- Bill Raleigh, Chair of Exercise & Sports Science
(512) 863-1611
raleighb@southwestern.edu
- Megan Hardin, Sports Information Director
(512) 863-1254
hardinm@southwestern.edu

ST. JOHN FISHER COLLEGE ATHLETICS
3690 EAST AVENUE
ROCHESTER, NY 14618
585-385-8309
Fax: 585-385-7308
athletics.sjfc.edu
- Bob Ward, Athletics Director
(585) 385-8310
bward@sjfc.edu
- Jill McCabe, Associate Athletics Director
(585) 385-8312
jmccabe@sjfc.edu
- Norm Kieffer, Sports Information Director
(585) 385-8421
nkieffer@sjfc.edu
- Jennifer Granger, Assistant Athletics Director
(585) 385-8315
jgranger@sjfc.edu
- Jim Grant, Head Athletic Trainer
(585) 899-3744
jgrant@sjfc.edu

ST. JOSEPH'S COLLEGE (NY) ATHLETICS
212 VANDERBILT AVENUE
BROOKLYN, NY 11205
718-940-5833
Fax: 718-940-5328
www.sjcbears.com
- Alex Winnicker, Interim Director of Athletics
(718) 940-5348
awinnicker@sjcny.edu
- Hope Mitchell, Director for Sport Programs
(718) 940-5835
hmitchell@sjcny.edu
- Maciej Siekierski, Director of Recreational Sports
(718) 940-5325
msiekierski@sjcny.edu
- Anthony Macapugay, Manager of Athletic Communications
(718) 940-5834
amacapugay@sjcny.edu
- Oscar Melendez, Head Athletic Trainer
(718) 940-5806
omelendez@sjcny.edu

ST. LAWRENCE UNIVERSITY ATHLETICS
23 ROMODA DRIVE
CANTON, NY 13617
315-229-5421
Fax: 315-229-5589
ckennedy@stlawu.edu
www.saintsathletics.com
- Bob Durocher, Director of Athletics
(315) 229-5870
ckennedy@stlawu.edu
- Randy LaBrake, Associate Director of Athletics
(315) 229-5466
rlabrake@stlawu.edu
- Fran Grembowicz, Assistant Director of Athletics
(315) 229-5780
fgrembowicz@stlawu.edu
- Wally Johnson, Director of Athletic Media

Relations
(315) 229-5588
wjohnson@stlawu.edu
- Brian Atkins, Head Athletic Trainer
(315) 229-5835
batkins@stlawu.edu

ST. MARY'S COLLEGE OF MARYLAND ATHLETICS
18952 EAST FISHER ROAD
ST. MARY'S CITY, MD 20686-3001
240-895-4295
Fax: 240-895-4480
swdevine@smcm.edu
www.smcmathletics.com
- Scott Devine, Director of Athletics
(240) 895-4295
swdevine@smcm.edu
- Jim Cranmer, Athletic Director for Operations
(240) 895-2167
wjcranmer@smcm.edu
- Crystal Gibson, Senior Woman Administrator
(240) 895-4323
clgibson@smcm.edu
- Nairem Moran, Sports Information Director
(240) 895-4482
nmoran@smcm.edu
- Jen Robertson, Head Athletic Trainer
(240) 895-2102
jarobertson@smcm.edu

ST. OLAF COLLEGE ATHLETICS
1520 ST. OLAF AVENUE
NORTHFIELD, MN 55057
507-646-3638
Fax: 507-646-3572
athletics.stolaf.edu
- Ryan Bowles, Athletic Director
(507) 786-3965
bowles@stolaf.edu
- Mike Ludwig, Sports Information Director
(507) 786-3834
ludwigm@stolaf.edu
- Natalie Walseth, Assistant Athletic Director for New Media
(507) 786-3834
walset1@stolaf.edu
- Dan Hagen, Head Athletic Trainer
(507) 786-3261
dhagen@stolaf.edu

ST. THOMAS UNIVERSITY ATHLETICS
2115 SUMMIT AVENUE
ST. PAUL, MN 55105
651-962-5903
Fax: 651-962-5910
www.tommiesports.com
- Steve Fritz, Athletic Director
(651) 962-5901
sjfritz@stthomas.edu
- Michelle Morgan, Associate Athletic Director
(651) 962-6186
morg7978@stthomas.edu
- Tyler Grey, Assistant Athletic Director
(651) 962-5976
grey0003@stthomas.edu
- Gene McGivern, Sports Information Director
(651) 962-5903
ejmcgivern@stthomas.edu
- Jim Rakow, Head Athletic Trainer
(651) 962-5973
rako0006@stthomas.edu

SUNY AT NEW PALTZ ATHLETICS
1 HAWK DRIVE
NEW PALTZ, NY 12561
845-257-3910
Fax: 845-257-3920
www.nphawks.com
• Stuart Robinson, Director of Athletics
(845) 257-3908
robinsos@newpaltz.edu
• Brian Williams, Associate Director of
Athletics
(845) 257-3912
williamb@newpaltz.edu
• Keith Kenney, Director of Wellness &
Recreation
(845) 257-6956
kenneyk@newpaltz.edu
• Shanna Vitale, Senior Woman
Administrator
(845) 257-3929
vitales@newpaltz.edu
• Ryan Novitsky, Athletic Operations
Manager
(845) 257-2341
novitskr@newpaltz.edu
• Bryan Lurie, Head Athletic Trainer
(845) 257-3913
lurieb@newpaltz.edu

**STATE UNIVERSITY OF NEW YORK
COLLEGE AT BROCKPORT ATHLETICS
(SUNY)**
350 NEW CAMPUS DRIVE
BROCKPORT, NY 14420
585-395-5328
Fax: 585-395-2160
athletics@brockport.edu
www.gobrockport.com
• Erick Hart, Director of Athletics
(585) 395-2579
ehart@brockport.edu
• Susan Hoffman, Associate Director of
Athletics
(585) 395-5327
shoffman@brockport.edu
• Liam Welsh, Assistant Director of Athletics
(585) 395-5329
• Lynda Cochran, Faculty Athletics
Representative
(585) 395-5490
lcochran@brockport.edu
• Stacey Corry, Director of Athletic
Communications
(585) 395-2218
scorry@brockport.edu

**SUNY COLLEGE AT GENESEO
ATHLETICS**
1 COLLEGE CIRCLE
GENESEO, NY 14454
585-245-5000
Fax: 585-245-5347
mooney@geneseo.edu
geneseoknights.com
• Mike Mooney, Director of Athletics
(585) 245-5343
mooney@geneseo.edu
• George Gagnier, Assistant Director of
Athletics
(585) 245-5208
gagnier@geneseo.edu
• Jim Lyons, Assistant Director of Athletics
(585) 245-5450
lyons@geneseo.edu
• Tim Volkmann, Director of Athletic
Communications
(585) 245-5346
volkmann@geneseo.edu

• Angelo Zegarelli, Head Athletic Trainer
(585) 245-5341
zegarelli@geneseo.edu

**SUNY COLLEGE AT OLD WESTBURY
ATHLETICS**
223 STORE HILL ROAD
PO BOX 210
OLD WESTBURY, NY 11568
516-876-3241
Fax: 516-876-3230
athletics@oldwestbury.edu
www.oldwestburypanthers.com
• Lenore Walsh, Director of Athletics
(516) 876-3241
walshle@oldwestbury.edu
• Harris Rappel, Sports Information Director
(516) 876-3032
harrisrappel@oldwestbury.edu
• Brittany Villalta, Athletics Facility Manager
(516) 876-3238
ranaldob@oldwestbury.edu
• Zsolt Hajdu, Head Athletics Trainer
(516) 876-3468
hajduz@oldwestbury.edu

**SUNY COLLEGE AT ONEONTA
ATHLETICS**
ALUMNI FIELD HOUSE
RAVINE PARKWAY
ONEONTA, NY 13820
607-436-3494
Fax: 607-436-3581
www.oneontaathletics.com
• Tracey Ranieri, Director of Athletics
(607) 436-2446
tracey.ranieri@oneonta.edu
• Ryan Hooper, Associate Director of
Athletics
(607) 436-2317
ryan.hooper@oneonta.edu
• Geoffrey Hassard, Sports Information
Director
(607) 436-2106
geoff.hassard@oneonta.edu
• Nate Jones, Associate Sports Information
Director
(607) 436-2106
geoff.hassard@oneonta.edu
• Alicia Simmonds, Head Athletic Trainer
(607) 436-3580
alicia.simmonds@oneonta.edu

**SUNY COLLEGE AT OSWEGO
ATHLETICS**
SUNY OSWEGO
LAKER HALL
OSWEGO, NY 13126
315-312-2488
Fax: 315-312-6397
oswegolakers.com
• Susan Viscomi, Director of Athletics
(315) 312-3056
susan.viscomi@oswego.edu
• Eric Summers, Associate Director of
Athletics
(315) 312-3303
eric.summers@oswego.edu
• Malcolm Huggins, Assistant Director of
Athletics
(315) 312-3360
malcolm.huggins@oswego.edu
• Michael Bielak, Director of Athletic
Communications
(315) 312-2488
michael.bielak@oswego.edu

**SUNY COLLEGE AT PLATTSBURGH
ATHLETICS**
101 BROAD STREET
PLATTSBURGH, NY 12901-2681
518-564-3140
Fax: 518-564-4155
dutt1167@plattsburgh.edu
gocardinalsports.com
• Stephanie Dutton, Interim Athletic Director
(518) 564-4536
dutt1167@plattsburgh.edu
• Cheryl Cole, Senior Woman Administrator
(518) 564-4147
coleca@plattsburgh.edu
• Tom Curle, Assistant Athletic Director
(518) 564-4143
curleto@plattsburgh.edu
• Allan Leavy, Interim Sports Information
Director
(518) 564-4148
aleav001@plattsburgh.edu
• Merritt Spear, Director of Sports Medicine
(518) 564-3089
spearmf@plattsburgh.edu
• Jason Pachter, Head Athletic Trainer
(518) 564-3089
pachteja@plattsburgh.edu

**SUNY INSTITUTE OF TECHNOLOGY
ATHLETICS**
100 SEYMOUR ROAD
UTICA, NY 13502
315-792-7520
Fax: 315-792-7536
• Kevin Grimmer, Athletic Director
(315) 792-7520
kevin.grimmer@sunyit.edu
• Kevin Edick, Assistant Athletic Director
(315) 792-7520
kevin.edick@sunyit.edu
• Kelly Colbert, Assistant Athletic Director
(315) 792-7519
kelly.colbert@sunyit.edu
• Patrick Baker, Sports Information Director
(315) 792-7515
patrick.baker@sunyit.edu
• Matthew Madia, Head Athletic Trainer
(315) 792-7520
matthew.madia@sunyit.edu

**STATEN ISLAND ATHLETICS, COLLEGE
OF**
2800 VICTORY BOULEVARD
1R-204
STATEN ISLAND, NY 10314
718-982-3160
Fax: 718-982-3138
www.csidolphins.com
• Charles Gomes, Director of Athletics
(718) 982-3160
charles.gomes@csi.cuny.edu
• David Pizzuto, Sports Information Director
(718) 982-3169
david.pizzuto@csi.cuny.edu
• Fran Mitilieri, Assistant Athletic Director
(718) 982-3167
fran.mitilieri@csi.cuny.edu
• Joe Abruzzo, Head Athletic Trainer
(718) 982-3135
joe.abruzzo@csi.cuny.edu

**STEVENS INSTITUTE OF TECHNOLOGY
ATHLETICS**
CASTLE POINT ON HUDSON
HOBOKEN, NJ 7030
201-216-5693
Fax: 201-216-8244

rrogers@stevens.edu
www.stevensducks.com
• Russell Rogers, Director of Athletics
(201) 216-5688
rrogers@stevens.edu
• Michael Lippencott, Senior Associate
Director of Athletics
(201) 216-8038
mlippenc@stevens.edu
• Celine Cunningham, Senior Woman
Administrator
(201) 216-8056
ccunning@stevens.edu
• Emily Kaczmarek, Assistant Athletic
Director for Administration
(201) 216-5078
ekaczmar@stevens.edu
• Danny Vohden, Athletic Director for
Communications and Events
(201) 216-8740
dvohden@stevens.edu

STEVENSON UNIVERSITY
11001 OWINGS MILLS BOULEVARD
OWINGS MILLS, MD 21117
443-394-9379
Fax: 443-352-4278
ffidler@stevenson.edu
gomustangsports.com
• Brett Adams, Director of Athletics
(443) 352-4250
bcadams@stevenson.edu
• Kathy Railey, Associate Athletics Director
(443) 352-4255
krailey@stevenson.edu
• Jackie Boswell, Assistant Athletics Director
(443) 352-4048
jboswell@stevenson.edu
• Scott Zema, Head Athletic Trainer
(443) 352-4263
mzema@stevenson.edu
• Matthew Grimm, Director of Campus
Recreation
(443) 352-4280
mgrimm@stevenson.edu

SUFFOLK UNIVERSITY ATHLETICS
73 TREMONT STREET
BOSTON, MA 02108
617-573-8379
Fax: 617-227-4935
www.gosuffolkrams.com
• Cary McConnell, Director of Athletics
(617) 573-8575
cmcconnell@suffolk.edu
• Anthony Del Prete, Associate Director of
Athletics
(617) 994-6459
ajdelprete@suffolk.edu
• Jaclyn Davis, Senior Women's
Administrator
(617) 994-6457
jmdavis@suffolk.edu
• Jeff Stone, Head Athletic Trainer
(617) 573-8772
jstone@suffolk.com
• Amy Barry, Sports Information Director
(617) 305-1756
abarry7@suffolk.edu

SUL ROSS STATE UNIVERSITY
ATHLETICS
EAST HIGHWAY 90
ALPINE, TX 79832
432-837-8226
Fax: 432-837-8234
www.srlobos.com

• Bobby Mesker, Director of Athletics
(432) 837-8231
bmesker@sulross.edu
• Sandra Chambers, Assistant Athletic
Director
(432) 837-8277
schambers@sulross.edu
• Sierra White, Head Athletics Trainer
(432) 837-8241
sierra.white@sulross.edu
• Travis Hendryx, Sports Information
Coordinator
(432) 837-8673
travis.hendryx@sulross.edu

SUSQUEHANNA UNIVERSITY
ATHLETICS
514 UNIVERSITY AVENUE
SELINSGROVE, PA 17870
570-372-4270
Fax: 570-372-2758
gallese@susqu.edu
www.gosusqu.com
• Pamela S. Samuelson, Director of
Athletics
(570) 372-4273
samuelson@susqu.edu
• Frank Marcinek, Assistant Director of
Athletics
(570) 372-4230
marcinek@susqu.edu
• Katie Meier, Director of Athletic
Communications
(570) 372-4587
robertsmc@susqu.edu
• Mike Keeney, Head Athletic Trainer
(570) 372-4278
keeney@susqu.edu

SWARTHMORE COLLEGE ATHLETICS
500 COLLEGE AVENUE
SWARTHMORE, PA 19081
610-328-8218
Fax: 610-328-7798
athletics@swarthmore.edu
www.swarthmoreathletics.com
• Adam Hertz, Director of Athletics
(610) 328-8325
ahertz1@swarthmore.edu
• Nnenna Akotaobi, Associate Athletics
Director
(610) 328-8222
nakotao2@swarthmore.edu
• Renee Clarke, Facilities Operations
Coordinator
(610) 690-6883
rclarke1@swarthmore.edu
• Brandon Hodnett, Director of Athletic
Communications
(610) 328-8206
bhodnet1@swarthmore.edu
• Marie Mancini, Head Athletic Trainer
(610) 328-8223
mmancin1@swarthmore.edu

TEXAS AT DALLAS ATHLETICS,
UNIVERSITY OF
800 WEST CAMPBELL ROAD
RICHARDSON, TX 75080-3021
972-883-4490
Fax: 972-883-4496
cometsports.utdallas.edu
• Bill Petitt, Director of Intercollegiate
Athletics
(972) 883-2055
bpetitt@utdallas.edu
• Bruce Unrue, Associate Athletic Director

(972) 883-6308
bruceunrue@utdallas.edu
• Angela Marin, Assistant Athletic Director
(972) 883-4498
angela.marin@utdallas.edu
• Tom Monagan, Head Athletic Trainer
(972) 883-4066
tomm@utdallas.edu

TEXAS LUTHERAN UNIVERSITY
ATHLETICS
1000 WEST COURT STREET
SEGUIN, TX 78155
830-372-8000
Fax: 830-372-8135
sports@tlu.edu
www.tlubulldogs.com
• Bill Miller, Director of Athletics
(830) 372-8124
bmiller@tlu.edu
• Tiffany Davis, Senior Woman
Administrator
(830) 372-8130
tdavis@tlu.edu
• Tim Kent, Head Athletic Trainer
(830) 372-8133
tkent@tlu.edu

THIEL COLLEGE ATHLETICS
ATHLETICS DEPARTMENT
75 COLLEGE AVENUE
GREENVILLE, PA 16125
724-589-2138
Fax: 724-589-2880
aschafer@thiel.edu
thielathletics.com
• Amy Schafer, Director of Athletics
(724) 589-2212
aschafer@thiel.edu
• Joe Schaly, Assistant Director of Athletics
(724) 589-2138
jschaly@thiel.edu
• Lori Schimmel, Director of Compliance
(724) 589-2164
lschimmel@thiel.edu
• Ed Topoleski, Director of Sports
Information
(724) 589-2180
etopoleski@thiel.edu

THOMAS COLLEGE ATHLETICS
180 WEST RIVER ROAD
WATERVILLE, ME 04901
207-859-1111
Fax: 207-859-1114
info@thomas.edu
www.thomas.edu
• David Roussel, Director of Athletics
(207) 859-1404
rousseld@thomas.edu
• Deb Biche-Labbe, Associate Athletic
Director
(207) 859-1406
biched@thomas.edu
• Andrea Thebarge, Senior Assistant
Director of Athletics
(207) 859-1314
thebargea@thomas.edu
• Joshua Schroeder, Director of Athletic
Communications
(207) 859-1408
athsi@thomas.edu

THOMAS MORE COLLEGE ATHLETICS
333 THOMAS MORE PARKWAY
CRESTVIEW HILLS, KY 41017

college sports

859-344-3536
Fax: 859-344-3536
athletics@thomasmore.edu
www.tmcsaints.com
• Terry Connor, Director of Athletics
(859) 344-3308
terry.connor@thomasmore.edu
• Jeff Hetzer, Associate Athletic Director
(859) 344-3532
jeff.hetzer@thomasmore.edu
• Cory Blackson, Director of Athletic
Communications
(859) 344-3672
cory.blackson@thomasmore.edu
• Theresa Behan, Head Athletic Trainer
(859) 344-4060
theresa.behan@thomasmore.edu

TRANSYLVANIA UNIVERSITY ATHLETICS
300 NORTH BROADWAY
LEXINGTON, KY 40508
859-233-8300
Fax: 859-233-8797
www.transysports.com
• Holly Sheilley, Vice President of Athletics
(859) 233-8270
hsheilley@transy.edu
• Keith Cecil, Assistant Athletic Director
(859) 281-3690
kcecil@transy.edu
• Justin Sweeney, Sports Information
Director
(859) 233-8284
jsweeney@transy.edu
• Alaina White, Head Athletic Trainer
(859) 233-8850

TRINITY COLLEGE ATHLETICS
300 SUMMIT STREET
HARTFORD, CT 06106
860-297-2057
Fax: 860-297-2492
www.trincoll.edu
• Michael Renwick, Director of Athletics &
Recreation
(860) 297-2055
michael.renwick@trincoll.edu
• JoAnn Acquarulo, Assistant Athletic
Director for Operations
(860) 297-4262
joann.acquarulo@trincoll.edu
• David Kingsley, Director of Sports
Communications
(860) 297-2137
david.kingsley@trincoll.edu
• Justin LeDuc, Head Athletic Trainer
(860) 297-2575
justin.leduc@trincoll.edu

TRINITY UNIVERSITY ATHLETICS
ONE TRINITY PLACE
SAN ANTONIO, TX 78212-7200
210-999-8237
Fax: 210-999-8292
athletics@trinity.edu
trinitytigers.com
• Bob King, Director of Athletics
(210) 999-8237
rking2@trinity.edu
• Julie Jenkins, Associate Director of
Athletics
(210) 999-8274
jjenkins@trinity.edu
• Sylvia Finch, Athletics Business Manager
(210) 999-8224
sfinch@trinity.edu

• Justin Parker, Sports Information Director
(210) 999-8447
jparker@trinity.edu
• Marc Powell, Head Athletic Trainer
(210) 999-8293
mpowell@trinity.edu

UNION COLLEGE (NY) ATHLETICS
807 UNION STREET
ALUMNI GYMNASIUM
SCHENECTADY, NY 12308
518-388-6284
Fax: 518-388-6695
www.unionathletics.com
• Jim McLaughlin, Director of Athletics
(518) 388-6284
mclaughj@union.edu
• Joanne Little, Senior Associate Director of
Athletics
(518) 388-6433
littlej@union.edu
• Beth Tiffany, Associate Athletics Director
(518) 388-6286
tiffanye@union.edu
• Eric McDowell, Sports Information Director
(518) 388-6170
mcdowele@union.edu
• Adam Brinker, Assistant Athletics Director,
Facilities
(518) 388-8365
brinkera@union.edu

UNITED STATES COAST GUARD ACADEMY ATHLETICS
33 MOHEGAN AVENUE
NEW LONDON, CT 06320-8104
860-444-8600
Fax: 860-444-8607
www.uscgasports.com
• Tim Fitzpatrick, Director of Athletics
(860) 444-8600
timothy.m.fitzpatrick@uscga.edu
• Dan Rose, Director of Physical Education
(860) 701-6798
dan.c.rose@uscga.edu
• Tim Opstrup, Associate Athletic Director
for Finance
(860) 444-8602
timothy.j.opstrup@uscga.edu
• Jason Southard, Director of Media
Relations
(860) 701-6800
jason.s.southard@uscga.edu
• Ken Niedzwiecki, Head Athletic Trainer
(860) 444-8619
ken.j.niedzwiecki@uscga.edu

UNITED STATES MERCHANT MARINE ACADEMY ATHLETICS
300 STEAMBOAT ROAD
KINGS POINT, NY 11024
516-726-5800
Fax: 516-773-5469
www.usmmasports.com
• Mo White, Director of Athletics
(516) 726-5632
whitem@usmma.edu
• Mike Toop, Associate Athletic Director
(516) 726-5262
toopm@usmma.edu
• Michael Notebaert, Assistant Athletic
Director
(516) 726-5259
notebaertm@usmma.edu
• Joe Guster, Sports Information Director
(516) 726-5609
gusterj@usmma.edu

UNIVERSITY OF MOUNT UNION ATHLETICS
1972 CLARK AVENUE
ALLIANCE, OH 44601
330-823-4880
athletics.mountunion.edu
• Larry Kehres, Director of Athletics
(330) 823-4880
kehreslt@mountunion.edu
• Leonard Reich, Assistant to the Athletic
Director
(330) 823-6093
reichl@mountunion.edu
• Melanie Patterson, Assistant Sports
Information Director
(330) 823-4780
patterme@mountunion.edu

URSINUS COLLEGE ATHLETICS
601 EAST MAIN STREET
PO BOX 1000
COLLEGEVILLE, PA 19426-1000
610-409-3000
Fax: 610-409-3620
www.ursinusathletics.com
• Laura Moliken, Director of Athletics
(610) 409-3606
lmoliken@ursinus.edu
• Erin Stroble, Associate Athletic Director
(610) 409-3761
estroble@ursinus.edu
• Kevin Small, Assistant Director of Athletics
(610) 409-3350
ksmall@ursinus.edu
• Pam Chlad, Head Athletic Trainer
(610) 409-3104
pchlad@ursinus.edu
• Andy Edwards, Director of Athletic
Communications
(610) 409-3612

UTICA COLLEGE ATHLETICS
1600 BURRSTONE ROAD
UTICA, NY 13502
315-792-3051
Fax: 315-792-3211
www.ucpioneers.com
• David Fontaine, Director of Athletics
(315) 792-3050
dsfontai@utica.edu
• Jim Murnane, Associate Athletic Director
(315) 792-3281
jmurnan@utica.edu
• Gil Burgmaster, Sports Information
Director
(315) 792-3772
gburgma@utica.edu
• Chris Warner, Head Athletic Trainer
(315) 792-3461
cwarner@utica.edu

VASSAR COLLEGE ATHLETICS
124 RAYMOND AVENUE
BOX 750
POUGHKEEPSIE, NY 12604
845-437-7450
Fax: 845-437-7033
athletics@vassar.edu
www.vassarathletics.com
• Michelle Walsh, Director of Athletics
(845) 437-7452
michwalsh@vassar.edu
• Kim Culligan, Associate Director of
Athletics
(845) 437-7453
kiculligan@vassar.edu
• Kathy Campbell, Director of Physical

Education
(845) 437-7460
kacampbell@vassar.edu
• Marc Graham, Director of Athletics
Operations
(845) 437-7456
magraham@vassar.edu
• Jamie Chagnon, Athletic Communications
Director
(845) 437-7469
jachagnon@vassar.edu

**VIRGINIA WESLEYAN COLLEGE
ATHLETICS**
1584 WESLEYAN DRIVE
NORFOLK, VA 23502
757-455-3303
Fax: 757-461-2262
vwcathletics.com
• Joanne Renn, Executive Director of
Athletics
(757) 455-5723
jrenn@vwc.edu
• Jeff Bowers, Associate Director of
Athletics
(757) 455-3285
jbowers@vwc.edu
• Stephany Dunmyer, Assistant Director of
Athletics
(757) 455-2122
sdunmyer@vwc.edu
• Cody Clifton, Sports Information Director
(757) 455-3393
cclifton@vwc.edu
• Corey Wingen, Head Athletic Trainer
(757) 455-3417
cjwingen@vwc.edu

WABASH COLLEGE ATHLETICS
301 WEST WABASH AVENUE
CRAWFORDSVILLE, IN 47933
765-361-6220
Fax: 765-361-6447
webmaster@wabash.edu
sports.wabash.edu
• Joseph Haklin, Director of Athletics
(765) 361-6233
haklinj@wabash.edu
• Brent Harris, Director of Sports Information
(765) 361-6165
harrisb@wabash.edu
• Mark Elizondo, Head Athletics Trainer
(765) 361-6235
elizondm@wabash.edu

WARTBURG COLLEGE ATHLETICS
100 WARTBURG BOULEVARD
WAVERLY, IA 50677
319-352-8447
Fax: 319-352-8213
www.go-knights.net
• Rick Willis, Athletic Director
(319) 352-8470
rick.willis@wartburg.edu
• Marcus Newsom, Assistant Athletic
Director
(319) 352-8356
marcus.newsom@wartburg.edu
• Monica Severson, Senior Woman
Administrator
(319) 352-8469
monica.severson@wartburg.edu
• Katie Jo Kuhens, Sports Information
Director
(319) 352-8208
katiejo.kuhens@wartburg.edu
• Ryan Callahan, Head Athletic Trainer

(319) 352-8534
ryan.callahan@wartburg.edu

**WASHINGTON & JEFFERSON COLLEGE
ATHLETICS**
HENRY MEMORIAL CENTER
60 SOUTH LINCOLN STREET
WASHINGTON, PA 15301
724-223-6054
Fax: 724-250-3329
gopresidents.com
• Scott McGuinness, Director of Athletics
(724) 250-3308
smcguinness@washjeff.edu
• Mark Lesako, Head Athletic Trainer
(724) 503-1001
mlesako1@washjeff.edu
• Jeff Mountain, Assistant Director of
Athletics
(724) 250-3306
jmountain@washjeff.edu
• Sean King, Sports Information Director
(724) 223-6080
sking@washjeff.edu

**WASHINGTON AND LEE UNIVERSITY
ATHLETICS**
WARNER CENTER
204 WEST WASHINGTON STREET
LEXINGTON, VA 24450
540-458-8670
Fax: 540-458-8173
www.generalssports.com
• Jan Hathorn, Athletic Director
(540) 458-8671
hathornj@wlu.edu
• Elizabeth Igo LeRose, Associate Athletic
Director
(540) 458-8687
lerosee@wlu.edu
• Neil Cunningham, Assistant Athletic
Director
(540) 458-8056
cunninghamn@wlu.edu
• Brian Laubscher, Sports Information
Director
(540) 458-8676
blaubsch@wlu.edu

WASHINGTON COLLEGE ATHLETICS
300 WASHINGTON AVENUE
CHESTERTOWN, MD 21620
410-778-2800
800-422-1782
Fax: 410-778-7741
washingtoncollegesports.com
• Bryan Matthews, Director of Athletics
(410) 778-7232
bmatthews2@washcoll.edu
• Thad Moore, Deputy Athletic Director
(410) 778-7243
tmoore2@washcoll.edu
• Jeff Shirk, Assistant Athletic Director
(410) 778-7248
jshirk2@washcoll.edu

WASHINGTON UNIVERSITY ATHLETICS
ONE BOOKINGS DRIVE
CAMPUS BOX 1067
ST. LOUIS, MO 63130-4899
314-935-5220
Fax: 314-935-5545
bearsports.wustl.edu
• Josh Whitman, Director of Athletics
(314) 935-5534
• Chris Peacock, Deputy Director of
Athletics

(314) 935-7015
cpeacock@wustl.edu
• Chris Mitchell, Athletic Director for
Communications
(314) 935-5077
mitchell@wustl.edu
• Kelcey Buck, Sports Information Director
(314) 935-4709
• Andrew Koch, Director of Facilities
(314) 935-4703
ajkoch@wustl.edu

WAYNESBURG COLLEGE ATHLETICS
51 WEST COLLEGE STREET
WAYNESBURG, PA 15370
724-852-3230
Fax: 724-852-4122
www.waynesburgsports.com
• Larry Marshall, Director of Athletics
(724) 852-3477
• Bobby Fox, Sports Information Director
(724) 852-3334
• Andy Palko, Head Athletic Trainer
(724) 852-3306

WEBSTER UNIVERSITY ATHLETICS
470 EAST LOCKWOOD AVENUE
ST. LOUIS, MO 63119-3914
314-968-6984
Fax: 314-963-6092
www.websterathletics.com
• Scott Kilgallon, Director of Athletics
(314) 246-7576
• Chris Bunch, Assistant Athletics Director
(314) 246-7529
bunch@webster.edu
• Niel DeVasto, Sports Information Director
(314) 246-6989
devastnd@webster.edu

**WENTWORTH INSTITUTE OF
TECHNOLOGY ATHLETICS**
550 HUNTINGTON AVENUE
BOSTON, MA 02115
617-989-4590
Fax: 617-989-4150
athletics@wit.edu
www.wentworthathletics.com
• Cheryl Aaron, Director of Athletics
(617) 989-4159
aaronc@wit.edu
• Bill Gorman, Associate Director of
Athletics
(617) 989-4147
gormanb@wit.edu
• Danielle Ferrara, Senior Woman
Administrator
(617) 989-4432
ferrarad@wit.edu
• Ben Butterfield, Director of Sport
Performance
(617) 989-4103
butterfieldb@wit.edu

WESLEY COLLEGE ATHLETICS
120 NORTH STATE STREET
DOVER, DE 19901
302-736-2435
Fax: 302-730-3894
www.gowesleyathletics.com
• Mike Drass, Executive Director of Athletics
(302) 736-2363
michael.drass@wesley.edu
• Tracey Short, Associate Director for
Compliance
(302) 736-2541
tracey.short@wesley.edu

• Brett Ford, Sports Information Director
(302) 736-2450
brett.ford@wesley.edu
• Brandon Sonson, Head Athletic Trainer
(302) 736-2553

WESLEYAN UNIVERSITY ATHLETICS
FREEMAN ATHLETIC CENTER
161 CROSS STREET
MIDDLETOWN, CT 6459
860-685-2690
Fax: 860-685-2691
www.wesleyan.edu/athletics
• Mike Whalen, Director of Athletics
(860) 685-2908
mwhalen@wesleyan.edu
• Rachel Ludwig, Associate Director of
Athletics
(860) 685-3555
rludwig@wesleyan.edu
• Mike O'Brien, Director of Athletic
Communication
(860) 685-2887
mobrien03@wesleyan.edu

**WESTERN CONNECTICUT STATE
UNIVERSITY ATHLETICS**
181 WHITE STREET
DANBURY, CT 06810
203-837-9015
Fax: 203-837-9050
www.wcsuathletics.com
• Scott Ames, Interim Athletic Director
(203) 837-9014
amess@wcsu.edu
• Jill Cook, Senior Woman Administrator
(203) 837-8624
cookj@wcsu.edu
• Mark Allen, Head Athletic Trainer
(203) 837-9016
allenm@wcsu.edu

**WESTERN NEW ENGLAND COLLEGE
ATHLETICS**
1215 WILBRAHAM ROAD
SPRINGFIELD, MA 01119
413-782-1202
Fax: 413-796-1508
www.wnegoldenbears.com
• Mike Theulen, Director of Athletics
(413) 782-1503
mtheulen@wne.edu
• Joe Sassi, Senior Associate Director of
Athletics
(413) 782-1208
jsassi@wne.edu
• Lori Mayhew, Assistant Athletic Director
(413) 796-2230
lmayhew@wne.edu
• Wes Poplizio, Director of Athletic
Communications
(413) 782-1227
wes.popolizio@wne.edu
• Mike Vallee, Head Athletic Trainer
(413) 782-1599
mvallee@wne.edu

**WESTFIELD STATE COLLEGE
ATHLETICS**
577 WESTERN AVENUE
WESTFIELD, MA 01086-1630
413-572-5405
Fax: 413-572-5477
www.westfieldstateowls.com
• Richard Lenfest, Athletics Director
(413) 572-8229
rlenfest@westfield.ma.edu

• Nancy Bals, Associate Athletics Director
(413) 572-5515
nbals@westfield.ma.edu
• Nathan Bashaw, Sports Information
Director
(413) 572-8155
nbashaw@westfield.ma.edu
• Cheryl Lee, Head Athletic Trainer
(413) 572-5418
clee@westfield.ma.edu

**WESTMINSTER COLLEGE (MO)
ATHLETICS**
501 WESTMINSTER AVENUE
FULTON, MO 65251
573-592-5200
Fax: 800-475-3361
www.wcbluejays.com
• Matt Mitchell, Athletics Director
(573) 592-5301
matt.mitchell@westminster-mo.edu
• Julie Moses, Athletic Department Manager
(573) 592-5200
julie.moses@westminster-mo.edu
• Tracey Braden, Senior Women's
Administrator
(573) 592-5345
bradent@westminster-mo.edu
• Alysha Hodge, Sports Information Director
(573) 592-5302
alysha.hodge@westminster-mo.edu
• Josh Thompson, Head of Athletic Training
(573) 592-5332
josh.thompson@westminster-mo.edu

**WESTMINSTER COLLEGE (PA)
ATHLETICS**
319 SOUTH MARKET STREET
NEW WILMINGTON, PA 16172-0001
724-946-7307
Fax: 724-946-7187
athletics.westminster.edu
• Jim Dafler, Director of Athletics
(724) 946-7313
daflerje@westminster.edu
• Tammy Swearingen, Senior Women's
Administrator
(724) 946-7320
swearitl@westminster.edu
• Shaun Toomey, Head Athletic Trainer
(724) 946-7314
toomeysj@westminster.edu
• Nathan LaRiccia, Sports Information
Director
(724) 946-6357
lariccnj@westminster.edu

WHEATON COLLEGE (IL) ATHLETICS
501 COLLEGE AVENUE
WHEATON, IL 60187-5593
630-752-5000
Fax: 630-752-7007
webmaster@wheaton.edu
athletics.wheaton.edu
• Julie Davis, Director of Athletics
(630) 752-5079
julie.davis@wheaton.edu
• Bill Stukes, Associate Athletics Director
(630) 752-5734
william.stukes@wheaton.edu
• Kent Madsen, Assistant Athletic Director
(630) 752-7057
kent.madsen@wheaton.edu
• Brett Marhanka, Athletics Communications
Director
(630) 752-5747
brett.marhanka@wheaton.edu

WHEATON COLLEGE (MA) ATHLETICS
26 EAST MAIN STREET
NORTON, MA 2766
508-286-8200
Fax: 508-286-8249
info@wheatoncollege.edu
wheatoncollege.edu
• John Sutyak, Director of Athletics
(508) 286-8216
sutyak_john@wheatoncollege.edu
• Lisa Yenush, Associate Director of
Athletics
(508) 286-3982
yenush_lisa@wheatoncollege.edu
• Gregory J. Steele, Head Athletic Trainer
(508) 286-3986
gsteele@wheatoncollege.edu

WHEELOCK COLLEGE ATHLETICS
200 THE RIVERWAY
BOSTON, MA 02215
617-879-2022
Fax: 617-879-2277
• Dwight Datcher, Director of Athletics
(617) 879-2238
ddatcher@wheelock.edu
• Stephanie Smyrl, Senior Women's
Administrator
(617) 879-2189
ssmyrl@wheelock.edu
• Amanda Cuiffo, Associate Director of
Athletics
(617) 879-2171
acuiffo@wheelock.edu
• Meghan Griffin, Director of Sports
Information
(617) 879-2022
mgriffin@wheelock.edu
• Jayson Hill, Head Athletic Trainer
(617) 879-2305
jhill@wheelock.edu

WHITMAN COLLEGE ATHLETICS
345 BOYER AVENUE
WALLA WALLA, WA 99362
509-527-5111
Fax: 509-527-5960
athletics.whitman.edu
• Dean Snider, Athletics Director
(509) 527-5288
sniderdc@whitman.edu
• Michelle Ferenz, Associate Athletic
Director
(509) 527-5261
ferenzmk@whitman.edu
• Gregg Petcoff, Sports Communications
Director
(509) 527-5902
petcofgr@whitman.edu
• John Eckel, Head Athletic Trainer
(509) 527-5590
eckeljw@whitman.edu

WHITTIER COLLEGE ATHLETICS
GRAHAM ATHLETICS CENTER
13847 EARLHAM DRIVE
WHITTIER, CA 90602
562-907-4271
Fax: 562-945-8024
www.wcpoets.com
• Robert Coleman, Executive Director of
Athletics
(562) 907-4268
rcoleman@whittier.edu
• Rock Carter, Associate Director of
Athletics
(562) 907-4972

rcarter@whittier.edu
• Mike Rizzo, Assistant Director of Athletics
(562) 907-4967
mrizzo@whittier.edu
• Lance Franey, Director of Communications
(562) 907-4852
lfraney@whittier.edu
• Keith Candelaria, Head Athletic Trainer
(562) 907-4965
kcandele@whittier.edu

WHITWORTH COLLEGE ATHLETICS
300 WEST HAWTHORNE ROADD
SPOKANE, WA 99251
509-777-1000
Fax: 509-777-3720
sflegel@whitworth.edu
www.whitworthpirates.com
• Tim Demant, Director of Athletics
(509) 777-3600
tdemant@whitworth.edu
• Jo Ann Wagstaff, Senior Women's
Administrator
(509) 777-4311
jwagstaff@whitworth.edu
• Steve Flegel, Sports Information Director
(509) 777-3239
sflegel@whitworth.edu
• Jon Bosh, Head Athletics Trainer
(509) 777-3728
jbosh@whitworth.edu

WIDENER UNIVERSITY ATHLETICS
ONE UNIVERSITY PLACE
CHESTER, PA 19013
610-499-4442
Fax: 610-499-4481
widenerpride.com
• Jack Shafer, Director of Athletics
(610) 499-4437
jlshafer@widener.edu
• Larissa Gillespie, Associate Director of
Athletics
(610) 499-4434
lagillespie@widener.edu
• Chris Carideo, Assistant Athletic Director
(610) 499-4454
cjcarideo@widener.edu
• A.J. Duffy, III, Head Athletic Trainer
(610) 499-4445
aduffy@widener.edu
• Matt Chmura, Sports Information Director
(610) 499-4436
machmura@widener.edu

WILLAMETTE UNIVERSITY ATHLETICS
900 STATE STREET
SALEM, OR 97301
503-370-6420
Fax: 503-370-6379
athletics@willamette.edu
www.wubearcats.com
• Valerie Cleary, Athletics Director
(503) 370-6262
vcleary@willamette.edu
• Judy Gordon, Senior Woman Administrator
(503) 370-6506
jgordon@willamette.edu
• Ken Smith, Head Athletic Trainer
(503) 370-6672
kosmith@willamette.edu
• Robert McKinney, Athletics
Communications Director
(503) 370-6110
rmckinne@willamette.edu

WILLIAM PATERSON UNIVERSITY OF NEW JERSEY ATHLETICS
300 POMPTON ROAD
WAYNE, NJ 07470
973-720-2356
Fax: 973-720-3017
wpupioneers.com
• Sabrina Grant, Director of Athletics
(973) 720-2754
grantsa@wpunj.edu
• Cindy Cohen, Associate Athletic Director
(973) 720-3861
cohenc@wpunj.edu
• Alison Moquin, Head Athletic Trainer
(973) 720-2358
moquina@wpunj.edu
• Heather Brocious, Sports Information
Director
(973) 720-2705
brocioush@wpunj.edu

WILLIAMS COLLEGE ATHLETICS
22 SPRING STREET
WILLIAMSTOWN, MA 01267
413-597-2366
Fax: 413-597-4272
athletics.williams.edu
• Lisa Melendy, Director of Athletics
(413) 597-3511
lmelendy@williams.edu
• Gary Guerin, Associate Director for
Operations
(413) 597-3321
gguerin@williams.edu
• Judy Fraser, Assistant Director of Athletics
(413) 597-3006
jfraser@williams.edu
• Dick Quinn, Sports Information Director
(413) 597-4982
dquinn@williams.edu

WILMINGTON COLLEGE ATHLETICS
1870 QUAKER WAY
WILMINGTON, OH 45177
937-382-6661
800-341-9318
Fax: 937-383-8557
wilmingtonquakers.com
• Terry Rupert, Director of Athletics
(937) 481-2255
terry_rupert@wilmington.edu
• Stacey Conley, Athletics Business
Manager
(937) 481-2467
stacey_conley@wilmington.edu
• Jayson Ameer Rasheed, Director of
Athletic Communications
(937) 481-2347
ameer_rasheed@wilmington.edu
• Brian Dykhuizen, Head Athletic Trainer
(937) 481-2252
brian_dykhuizen@wilmington.edu

WISCONSIN - EAU CLAIRE ATHLETICS, UNIVERSITY OF
131 GARFIELD AVENUE
EAU CLAIRE, WI 54701
715-836-3062
Fax: 715-836-4074
sportsinfo@uwec.edu
www.blugolds.com
• Dan Schumacher, Director of Athletics
(715) 836-5858
schumadj@uwec.edu
• Robin Baker, Associate Athletic Director
(715) 836-5529
bakerrk@uwec.edu

• Amanda Hopkins, Assistant Athletic
Director
(715) 836-3939
hopkinak@uwec.edu
• Jill Millis, Sports Information Director
(715) 836-4184
millisjl@uwec.edu
• Garry Grant, Head Athletic Trainer
(715) 836-3877
grantga@uwec.edu

WISCONSIN - OSHKOSH ATHLETICS, UNIVERSITY OF
785 HIGH AVENUE
OSHKOSH, WI 54901
920-424-1034
Fax: 920-424-1035
www.uwoshkoshtitans.com
• Darryl Sims, Director of Athletics
(920) 424-1034
sims@uwosh.edu
• Vicci Stimac, Senior Woman Administrator
(920) 424-1384
stimacv@uwosh.edu
• Kennan Timm, Sports Information Director
(920) 424-0365
timmk@uwosh.edu
• Wade Peitersen, Head Athletic Trainer
(920) 424-7138

WISCONSIN LUTHERAN COLLEGE ATHLETICS
8800 WEST BLUEMOUND ROAD
MILWAUKEE, WI 53226
414-443-8800
Fax: 414-443-8514
sports.info@wlc.edu
wlcsports.com
• Skip Noon, Director of Athletics
(414) 443-8871
skip.noon@wlc.edu
• Pam Tullberg, Senior Woman
Administrator
(414) 443-8876
pamela.tullberg@wlc.edu
• Dave Reinemann, Assistant Athletics
Director
(414) 443-8990
dave.reinemann@wlc.edu
• Bill Curtis, Director of Athletic
Development
(414) 443-8546
william.curtis@wlc.edu
• Adam Heinzen, Director of Athletic
Communications
(414) 443-8746
sports.info@wlc.edu

WISCONSIN - LA CROSSE ATHLETICS, UNIVERSITY OF
126 MITCHELL HALL
1725 STATE STREET
LA CROSSE, WI 54601
608-785-8616
Fax: 608-785-8674
athletics@uwlax.edu
www.uwlathletics.com
• Kim Blum, Director of Athletics
(608) 785-8194
• David Johnson, Assistant Athletic Director
for Media Relations
(608) 785-8493
djohnson@uwlax.edu
• Jason Murphy, Facilities Director
(608) 785-5175
jmurphy@uwlax.edu
• Joel Luedke, Director of Athletic Training

Services
(608) 785-6542
jluedke@uwlax.edu

WISCONSIN - PLATTEVILLE ATHLETICS, UNIVERSITY OF
1 UNIVERSITY PLAZA
PLATTEVILLE, WI 53818
608-342-1567
Fax: 608-342-1576
athletics@uwplatt.edu
• Mike Emendorfer, Interim Athletic Director
(608) 342-1801
emendorm@uwplatt.edu
• Deb Schulman, Associate Athletic Director
(608) 342-1255
schulman@uwplatt.edu
• Megan Wilson, Sports Information Coordinator
(608) 342-1488
wilsonmeg@uwplatt.edu
• Ryanne Breckenridge, Head Athletic Trainer
(608) 342-1575
breckenridgr@uwplatt.edu

WISCONSIN - RIVER FALLS ATHLETICS, UNIVERSITY OF
410 SOUTH THIRD STREET
RIVER FALLS, WI 54022
715-425-3911
Fax: 715-425-3257
sportsinformation@uwrf.edu
www.uwrfsports.com
• Roger Ternes, Director of Athletics
(715) 425-3246
roger.ternes@uwrf.edu
• Amber Dohlman, Co-Sports Information Director
(715) 425-3846
amber.dohlman@uwrf.edu
• Jake Wissing, Co-Sports Information Director
(715) 425-3846
jacob.wissing@uwrf.edu
• Andrew Baker, Head Athletic Trainer
(715) 425-3130
andrew.baker@uwrf.edu

WISCONSIN - STEVENS POINT ATHLETICS, UNIVERSITY OF
2050 FOURTH AVENUE
STEVENS POINT, WI 54481
715-346-4494
Fax: 715-346-4655
athletics.uwsp.edu
• Frank O'Brien, Interim Director of Athletics
(715) 346-3888
fobrien@uwsp.edu
• Shirley Egner, Senior Woman Administrator
(715) 346-3397
segner@uwsp.edu
• Kris Ficken, Director of Sports Medicine
(715) 346-3931
kris.ficken@uwsp.edu
• Holly Schmies, Director of Athletic Training Education
(715) 346-2922
hschmies@uwsp.edu

WISCONSIN - STOUT ATHLETICS, UNIVERSITY OF
712 SOUTH BROADWAY STREET
MENOMONIE, WI 54751
715-232-1122
Fax: 715-232-1684

naatzd@uwstout.edu
athletics.uwstout.edu
• Duey Naatz, Athletic Director
(715) 232-2758
naatzd@uwstout.edu
• Susan Lew, Head Athletic Trainer
(715) 232-2213
lews@uwstout.edu
• Layne Pitt, Sports Information Director
(715) 232-2275
pittl@uwstout.edu

WISCONSIN - WHITEWATER ATHLETICS, UNIVERSITY OF
800 WEST MAIN STREET
WHITEWATER, WI 53190-1790
262-472-4661
Fax: 262-472-2791
www.uwwsports.com
• Amy Edmonds, Director of Intercollegiate Athletics
(262) 472-4661
edmondsa@uww.edu
• Bob Lanza, Associate Athletic Director
(262) 472-3190
lanzar@uww.edu
• Keri Carollo, Senior Woman Administrator
(262) 472-5782
carollok@uww.edu
• Chris Lindeke, Director of Athletic Communications
(262) 472-1147
lindekec@uww.edu
• Steve Hillmer, Director of Athletic Training
(262) 472-1150
hillmers@uww.edu

WITTENBERG UNIVERSITY ATHLETICS
PO BOX 720
SPRINGFIELD, OH 45501
937-327-6415
Fax: 937-327-6428
www.wittenbergtigers.com
• Gary Williams, Director of Athletics & Recreation
(937) 327-6458
williamsg1@wittenberg.edu
• Sarah Jurewicz, Senior Woman Director
(937) 327-6457
sjurewicz@wittenberg.edu
• Joe Fincham, Associate Director of Athletics
(937) 327-6498
wfincham@wittenberg.edu
• Matt Croci, Assistant Director of Athletics
(937) 327-6469
crocim@wittenberg.edu
• Ryan Maurer, Director of Atheltics Communications
(937) 327-6114
rmaurer@wittenberg.edu

WOOSTER ATHLETICS, THE COLLEGE OF
1189 BEALL AVENUE
WOOSTER, OH 44691
330-263-2000
Fax: 330-263-2537
kbeckett@wooster.edu
www.woosterathletics.com
• Keith Beckett, Director of Athletics
(330) 263-2189
kbeckett@wooster.edu
• Russell Houser, Assistant Director of Athletics
(330) 263-2183
rhouser@wooster.edu

• Ashley Reid, Assistant Athletic Director for Inclusion
(330) 263-2181
• Tom Love, Head Athletic Trainer
(330) 263-2184
tlove@wooster.edu
• Hugh Howard, Director of Sports Information
(330) 263-2374
hhoward@wooster.edu

WORCESTER POLYTECHNIC INSTITUTE ATHLETICS
100 INSTITUTE ROAD
WORCESTER, MA 01609-2280
508-831-5243
Fax: 508-831-5775
athletics@wpi.edu
athletics.wpi.edu
• Dana L. Harmon, Director of Athletics
(508) 831-5243
dharmon@wpi.edu
• Cherie Galasso, Associate Athletic Director
(508) 831-5063
cgalasso@wpi.edu
• Wendy Walsh, Assistant Athletic Director
(508) 831-5327
wlwc@wpi.edu
• Rusty Eggen, Sports Information Director
(508) 831-5328
rusty@wpi.edu

WORCESTER STATE UNIVERSITY ATHLETICS
486 CHANDLER STREET
WORCESTER, MA 01602
508-929-8034
Fax: 508-929-8184
schapman@worcester.edu
www.wsulancers.com
• Michael Mudd, Director of Athletics
(508) 929-8034
mmudd@worcester.edu
• John Meany, Deputy Director of Athletics
(508) 929-8746
jmeany@worcester.edu
• Karen Tessmer, Associate Athletic Director
(508) 929-8769
ktessmer@worcester.edu
• Dave Lindberg, Assistant Athletic Director
(508) 929-8593
dlindberg@worcester.edu
• Jessica Meany, Head Athletic Trainer
(508) 929-8024
jessica.meany@worcester.edu

YESHIVA UNIVERSITY ATHLETICS
500 WEST 185TH STREET
NEW YORK, NY 10033
212-960-5211
Fax: 212-960-0088
jbednrsh@yu.edu
www.yumacs.com
• Joe Bednarsh, Athletic Director
(212) 960-0015
jbednrsh@yu.edu
• Shelley Whitaker, Associate Athletics Director
(212) 960-0042
shelley.whitaker@yu.edu
• Erica Lemm, Senior Woman Administrator
(212) 340-7727
erica.lemm@yu.edu
• A.J. O'Hagan, Sports Information Director
(212) 960-5291

anthony.ohagan@yu.edu
• Aaronn Baker, Women's Athletic Trainer
(347) 758-2266
aaron.baker@yu.edu
• Xavier Alzate, Men's Athletic Trainer
(212) 960-5486
xavier.alzate@yu.edu

YORK COLLEGE (CUNY) ATHLETICS
94-20 GUY R. BREWER BOULEVARD
JAMAICA, NY 11451
718-262-5101
Fax: 718-262-5216
stjohn@york.cuny.edu
www.yorkathletics.com
• Ronald St. John, Director of Athletics
(718) 262-5114
stjohn@york.cuny.edu
• Jessica Cherry, Senior Women
Administrator
(718) 262-5115
jcherry@york.cuny.edu
• John Scarinci, Sports Information Director
(718) 262-5104
jscarinci@york.cuny.edu
• Dan Matte, Head Athletic Trainer
(718) 262-5212
matte@york.cuny.edu

YORK COLLEGE (PENNSYLVANIA) ATHLETICS
441 COUNTRY CLUB ROAD
YORK, PA 17405-7199
717-846-7788
Fax: 717-849-1626
www.ycpspartans.com
• Paul Saikia, Assistant Dean for Athletics
(717) 815-1245
psaikia@ycp.edu
• Matt Day, Associate Director for Athletics
(717) 815-6604
gday@ycp.edu
• Jen Muston, Assistant Director of Athletics
(717) 815-1516
jmuston@ycp.edu
• Scott Guise, Director of Athletic
Communications
(717) 815-1394
sguise@ycp.edu
• Nate Cooke, Head Athletic Trainer
(717) 815-1962
ncooke@ycp.edu

Sport Management Degree Programs

ADAMS STATE COLLEGE
208 EDGEMONT BLVD.
ALAMOSA, CO 81101
719-587-7011
800-824-6494
Fax: 719-587-7522
www.adams.edu/athletics
• Eric Carpio, Assistant Vice President for
Enrollment Management
ecarpio@adams.edu
• Karie Velleses, Administrative Assistant
(719) 587-8152
• David Svaldi, President
• Larry Mortensen, Athletic Director
Description:
Founded in 1921 as a teachers' college,
Adams State is now a comprehensive liberal
arts college offering 16 undergraduate
majors with 28 minors and emphases, as

well as 8 master's degree programs- most
offered online. Offering sport management
programs in Bachelor's and Master's
degree.
Mission:
Adams State College dedicates its
resources to provide opportunity and access
for all students. The College is an innovative
leader that recognizes the inherent
educational value of diversity. It is a catalyst
for the educational, cultural, and economic
interests of rural Colorado, the surrounding
region, and the global community.
About Sport Management Program:
The online MA in Sport Management at
Adams College is a 36-credit program that
offers a wide range of courses and practical
experiences in order to prepare students for
employment in sport management related
careers. All courses are offered online which
allows for greater flexibility and optimum
convenience for students who hold full-time
careers or cannot relocate. Students can
complete the program in two years which
includes all coursework and two short
on-campus residencies. The MA in Sport
Management at Adams State is the least
expensive of any other fully online master's
degree in the US. Applications are due May
1st and cohorts begin ea

ADELPHI UNIVERSITY - RUTH S. AMMON SCHOOL OF EDUCATION
ADELPHI UNIVERSITY
1 SOUTH AVE
P.O BOX 701
GARDEN CITY, NY 11530-0701
516-877-4100
800-233-5744
Fax: 516-877-4258
letter@adelphi.edu
www.adelphi.edu
• Robert A. Scott, Adelphi University
President
• Audrey Blumberg, Sr. Associate Provost
Academic Affairs
(516) 877-3159
blumberg@adelphi.edu
Description:
M.S. in Sport Management; The Sport
Management program prepares students for
management roles in academic or
professional sports. With the assistance of
an advisor, graduate students tailor the
sport management and business electives
to target their desirable career goals.

ALCORN STATE UNIVERSITY
DEPARTMENT OF HPER
1000 ASU DRIVE
ALCORN STATE, MS 39096
601-877-6100
Fax: 601-877-3821
www.alcorn.edu
• David Gomez, HPER Instructor
(601) 877-4083
dgomez@alcorn.edu
• Garry Lewis, HPER Assistant Professor
(601) 877-6278
glewis1@alcorn.edu
• Willie McGowan, Jr., HPER Instructor
(601) 877-6465
w_mcgowan@alcorn.edu
• Richard Myles, Sr., HPER Instructor
(601) 877-6505
rmyles@alcorn.edu
• Kevin Montgomery, HPER Instructor

(601) 877-6275
kevinm@alcorn.edu
Description:
Undergrad Degree: B.S. Recreation. Grad
Degree: M.E.D. Areas of Specialization:
Undergrad: Recreation. Grad: Athletic
Administration and Coaching.

ALFRED STATE COLLEGE- SUNY COLLEGE OF TECHNOLOGY
10 UPPER COLLEGE DRIVE
ALFRED, NY 14802
607-587-4215
800-425-3733
www.alfredstate.edu/athletics
Description:
Alfred State College is a public,
coeducational, two- and four- year,
nonsectarian college of approximately 3,700
undergraduates. The College was founded
in 1908 and joined the newly organized
State University of New York (SUNY)
system in 1948.
**Information on Sport Management
Program:**
The goal of the sports management
program is to provide students with a
concentration of courses aimed at preparing
them for a career in the management and
administration of the sport and fitness
industry. A laptop computer is
recommended, but not required, for students
entering the sports management program.
**Entrance Requirements &
Recommendations:**
Required: Algebra, Geometry (Math A)
Recommended: Algebra 2/Trigonometry
(Math B)

ALVERNIA COLLEGE
400 SAINT BERNARDINE STREET
2ND FLOOR STUDENT CENTER
READING, PA 19607
610-796-8269
888-253-7642
Fax: 610-790-2873
admissions@alvernia.edu
**Description of Sport Management
Program:**
Alvernia College's interdiciplinary and
comprehensive program provides students
with specific competencies in management,
marketing, communication, law, finance and
accounting, economics, ethics, and
computer literacy as they relate to sport. In
addition, the program provides critical
thinking, writing, and problem solving skills
that are essential ingredients to success in
today's workplaces. Internships are an
integral part of the Alvernia Sport
Management program.

AMERICAN MILITARY UNIVERSITY
10110 BATTLEVIEW PARKWAY
SUITE 114
MANASSAS, VA 20109
877-777-9081
info@apus.edu
• Wallace E Boston, President & Chief
Executive Officer
• Harry T. Wilkins, CPA, Executive Vice
President, Chief Financial Officer
• Sharon van Wyk, Executive Vice
President, Chief Operations Officer
• Carol Gilbert, Executive Vice President,
Programs & Marketing
• Karan Powell, Executive Vice President,

Provost
• Peter W Gibbons, Senior Vice President, Chief Administrative Office
• Gwen Hall, Sr Vice President, Academic Operations Officer
• W. Dale Young, Sr Vice President, Chief Information Officer

Description of Sports Management Program:
This degree is designed for those who are interested in sports management, coaching, and administration. The core curriculum includes the social contexts of sport in historical and modern society, fundamentals of the sports industry, and specifically focuses on sports law, marketing, promotion, public relations, finance, and economics. Students are provided with and opportunity to concentrate in an area of specific interest, to include sports administration for the aspiring collegiate, community, or high school athletic official; coaching theory and strategy for those interested in leading and coaching teams; management for those interested i

APPALACHIAN STATE UNIVERSITY
DEPARTMENT OF HEALTH, LEISURE AND EXERCISE SCIENCE
PO BOX 32071
BOONE, NC 28608
828-262-2120 EXT 2120
Fax: 828-262-3138
admissions@appstate.edu
www.hles.appstate.edu
• Michael W. Kernodle, Professor
(828) 262-3138
kernodlemw@appstate.edu
• Magdalena Anoufriev, Staff
(036) 262-3141
anoufrievm@appstate.edu
• Gregory Anoufriev, Clinical Assistant Professor
(082) 262-7466
anoufrievg@appstate.edu
• Debbie Arnette, Women's Equipment Supervisor
arnetteda@appstate.edu
• Melanie Austin, Practitioner in Residence
(828) 262-3142
austinm@appstate.edu
• Rebecca A Battista, Associate Professor
(828) 262-3047
battistara@appstate.edu
• Mary Ann Bo Bolick, Lecturer
(828) 262-2935
bolickma@appstate.edu
• Jeffrey T. Soukup, Asst Professor
(828) 262-3138
soukupjt@appstate.edu

Description:
Grad Degree: M.A. in Sport Management; Exercise Science, Spec in Sports Management; M.S. in Exercise Science. Areas of Specialization: Athletic Administration and Sport Management; Exercise Science. The mission of the Department of Health, Leisure, and Exercise Science (HLES) is to deliver student-centered education that is accentuated by quality teachin, scholarly activity, and service.

AQUINAS COLLEGE SPORTS MANAGEMENT PROGRAM
1607 ROBINSON ROAD S.E.
GRAND RAPIDS, MI 49506-1799
616-632-8900
admissions@aquinas.edu
www.aquinas.edu/athletics
• Juan Olivarez, Ph.D, President
(616) 632-2881
• Charles D. Gunnoe, Jr., Ph.D., Provost & Dean of Faculty
(616) 632-2151
• Gregory W. McAleenan, J.D., VP for Institutional Advancement
(616) 632-2809
odonndeb@aquinas.edu
• Paula T. Meehan, B.A., VP For Enrollment Management
(616) 632-2852
meehapau@aquinas.edu
• Nathalie Meyer, Secretary
• Michael Lown, Treasurer

Description of Sport Management Program:
Aquinas developed the Business Administration/Sport Management major in 1996 with Ernie Romine as the founder. This major provides students with the knowledge and background of a business degree and the field specific knowledge needed for success in the careers tracks of sport, athletics, and fitness. In addition, students can gain hands on experience through internships and the Sport Management Club. One of the top ten largest majors on campus, sport management is a growing field with great potential for any student interested in sports and business.

ARIZONA STATE UNIVERSITY
TEMPE CAMPUS
UNIVERSITY DRIVE & MILL AVENUE
TEMPE, AZ 85287
480-965-9011
www.thesundevils.com
• Ray Artigue, Executive Director Sports Business Program

Degree Offered
B.S. concentration in Tourism Development & Management, from College of Public Programs; B.S. concentration in Parks & Recreation Management, from college of public programs; B.A. concentration in Business (Tourism) from W.P. Carey School of Business

ARKANSAS STATE UNIVERSITY - DEPT OF HEALTH, PE & SPORT SCIENCES
State University, AR 72467
870-972-3066
Fax: 870-972-3096
www.astateredwolves.com
• David LaVetter, Director, Sport Management Program

Degree:
B.S. Sport Management, College of Education Department of Health, PE, and Sport Sciences. The BS degree in Sport Management is designed to provide students the needed background, knowledge, and experiences to be prepared for careers in intercollegiate and professional athletics organizations.

ARKANSAS, UNIVERSITY OF
232 SILAS H. HUNT HALL
1 UNIVERSITY OF ARKANSAS
FAYETTEVILLE, AR 72701
479-575-5346
800-377-8632
Fax: 479-575-7515
uofa@uark.edu
www.uark.edu
• David G. Gearhart, Chancellor

Degrees Offered:
Bachelor of Science in Education with major in recreation and sport management.

ASHLAND UNIVERSITY
401 COLLEGE AVENUE
ASHLAND, OH 44805
419-289-4142
800-882-1548
www.goashlandeagles.com
• Frederick J Finks, President

Description of Sport Management Program:
Majors in athletic training, exercise science, physical education and sport management train well-rounded students for professional careers in all areas of wellness and sport. Students are prepared in and out of the classroom with relevant course content, professional development days with people already working for major sport organizations, and plenty of field experience leading up to a full-time internship.

AUBURN UNIVERSITY SPORT MANAGEMENT PROGRAM
AUBURN, AL 36849
334-844-4000
www.education.auburn.edu/kinesiology

Description of Sport Management Program:
The Higher Education program with a minor in Sport Management is structured in conformity with the curriculum requirements of the North American Society for Sport management (NASSM). The 18 hours of sport courses are distributed among sport management, sociology of sport, sport finance and marketing, sport ethics and public relations, and practicum in athletic administration.

AVERETT COLLEGE SPORT MANAGEMENT PROGRAM
420 WEST MAIN ST
DANVILLE, VA 24541
434-791-5600
800-AVERETT (283-7388)
www.averettcougars.com

Sport Management Program:
Averett offers a bachelor's degree in physical education in a number of concentrations including: physical education (non-teaching), physical education: PK-12, sport management, wellness/ sports medicine, & coaching. Physical education majors are encouraged to develop in-depth competency in at least one performance area or one sport. Students have the opportunity to participate in a variety of internships.

BALDWIN-WALLACE COLLEGE
DEPT OF HEALTH AND PHYSICAL EDUCATION
275 EASTLAND ROAD
BEREA, OH 44017-2088
440-826-2900
Fax: 440-826-6980
www.bw.edu
• Gregory Flanik, CIO
(440) 826-2700
gflanik@bw.edu
• Donna Gutschmidt, Technical Writer

(440) 826-2705
dgutschm@bw.edu
• Verlyn Mol, Manager of Administrative
Information Systems
(440) 826-2316
vmol@bw.edu
• Mardele Hawley, Administrative Support
Coordinator
(440) 826-2318
mhawley@bw.edu
• Randy Lingenfelter, ERP Systems
Administrator
(440) 826-2701
rlingenf@bw.edu
• Lorrie Morehouse, Institutional
ResearchAnalyst
(440) 826-2315
lmorehou@bw.edu
• Scott Armstrong, Dept. Chairperson
scarmstr@bw.edu
Description:
Undergrad Degree: B.A. in HPE, with
concentration in sport management or
fitness management combined with second
major or minor in business administration.
Areas of Specialization: General within
guidelines of program.

BALL STATE UNIVERSITY
PHYSICAL EDUCATION, SPORT AND
EXERCISE SCIENCE
2000 W. UNIVERSITY AVENUE
MUNCIE, IN 47306
765-289-1241
800-382-8540
mwhaley@bsu.edu
www.bsu.edu
• Mitchel Whaley, Dept. Chairperson
(765) 285-3206
mwhaley@bsu.edu
• Ronald Davis, Dept. Associate
Chairperson
(765) 285-1462
rdavis@bsu.edu
• Gina Pauline, Sport Administration/Mgmt
Instructor
(765) 285-4211
gbonante@bsu.edu
Description:
This area of specialization is designed to
prepare individuals to administer
intercollegiate athletic programs and
professional sport organizations. This
program is open to graduate physical
education majors and to graduates with
majors in fields other than physical
education.
Requirements:
A minimum of twelve hours in this area of
specialization must be taken in the College
of Business. The capstone course is a sport
management internship with a
college/university or a professional sports
organization.

BARRY UNIVERSITY
SCHOOL OF HUMAN PERFORMANCE &
LEISURE SCIENCES PROGRAM
11300 NE 2ND AVENUE
MIAMI SHORES, FL 33161-6695
305-899-3490
800-756-6000, ext 3490
Fax: 305-899-3556
sportsciences@mail.barry.edu
www.barry.edu
• Kathryn Ludwig, Associate Professor,
Chair, Sport and Exercis

• Tal Amasay, Assistant Professor,
Coordinator, Physical Ed
• Carl Cramer, Associate Dean HPLS
• Claire Egret, Assistant Professor,
Coordinator, Biomechanic
• Annie Clement, Sport Management
Coordinator/Professor
Description:
Barry University's program is designed to
give students the skills and experience to
excel in supervisory positions, and, at Barry,
students have the option of enhancing their
sport management degree with an MBA.
The sport management masters from Barry
University can also prepare students for
entry into a top-rated doctoral program.

BARTON COLLEGE
DEPARTMENT OF PHYSICAL
EDUCATION AND SPORT STUDIES
PO BOX 5000
WILSON, NC 27893
252-399-6300
800-345-4973
Fax: 252-399-6516
www.barton.edu/athletics
• Claudia Duncan, Dept. Chairperson
cduncan@barton.edu
Description:
B.S. sport management; The Sport
Management curriculum provides for a
variety of opportunities for students. They
can focus only on sport management or very
easily add another major or minor in the
business area as most students do.
Students complete internships in either a
sport setting or a business setting,
whichever will provide them with the best
experience for their future employment.

BAYLOR UNIVERSITY
DEPARTMENT OF HEALTH, HUMAN
PERFORMANCE & RECREATION
ONE BEAR PLACE
#97313
WACO, TX 76798-7313
254-710-3505
Fax: 254-710-3527
www.baylor.edu
• Andy Pittman, Ph.D., Graduate Program
Coordinator
andy_pittman@baylor.edu
• Brain Leutholtz, Graduate Program
Director
• Andrew Gallucci, Undergraduate Program
Directors
• Ted Poers, Administrative Coordinators
• Andrew Gallucci, Laboratory Directors
• Eva Rhodes, Staff
• Janet Green, Administrative Associate
• John Faribault, Program Coordinator
Description:
Prepare students for careers as Health
Educators, Exercise Physiologists, Sport
Management Specialists, Physical
Education Specialists, or Coaches. A six
hour core curriculum is required for each
major. Students then specialize in one of the
following areas; Exercise Physiology, Health
Education, Sport Management, Sport
Pedagogy.
Degrees Offered:
M.S. Ed., Sport Management.

BELLEVUE UNIVERSITY
1000 GALVIN ROAD SOUTH
BELLEVUE, NE 68005

402-293-2000
www.bubruins.com
• Keith B. Edquist, Treasurer
• Robert S. Howard, Secretary
Sports Management Program:
The Sports Management major prepares
students to enter sports management
careers with the knowledge and skills,
including critical thinking, communication,
management, problem solving, and
leadership, required to be successful in
today's sports industry. Students are
encouraged to pursue a Business
Administration minor, which enhances the
knowledge and skills of the Sports
Management major.

BELMONT UNIVERSITY SPORT
MANAGEMENT PROGRAM
1900 BELMONT BLVD
NASHVILLE, TN 37212
615-460-6000
www.belmont.edu/athletics
Sport Administration:
The Master Sport Administration (MSA) is
designed to prepare graduate students for
work in the sport industry.

BEMIDJI STATE UNIVERSITY
DEPARTMENT OF HUMAN
PERFORMANCE, SPORT & HEALTH
SPORT MANAGEMENT PROGRAM
1500 BIRCHMONT DRIVE NE #29
BEMIDJI, MN 56601-2699
218-755-2940
Fax: 218-755-3898
www.bemidjistate.edu
• Donna Palivec, Department Chair
dpalivec@bemidjistate.edu
Description:
Sport Management offers specialized
training and education for individuals
seeking careers in the sport business
industry. The Sport Management curriculum
is designed to meet the NASPE/NASSM
accreditation requirements: sociocultural
dimensions, management and leadership,
ethics, marketing, communications, budget
and finance, legal aspects, economics, and
governance.
Degrees Offered:
BA; Sport Management, Minor; Sport
Management.

BOWLING GREEN STATE UNIVERSITY
SPORT MANAGEMENT DIVISION
112 EPPLER CENTER
BOWLING GREEN, OH 43403-0248
419-372-2876
Fax: 419-372-6015
mebobb@bgsu.edu
www.bgsu.edu/
• Jacquelyn Cuneen, Chair/Professor
(419) 372-7231
jcuneen@bgsu.edu
Description:
Undergrad Degree: B.S. Grad Degree:
M.Ed. Areas of Specialization: Undergrad:
Athletic Training and Clinic Management;
Sport Marketing; Sports Information; Sport
Enterprise. Grad: Sport Administration.

BROOKLYN COLLEGE OF THE CITY
UNIVERSITY OF NEW YORK
2900 BEDFORD AVENUE
BROOKLYN, NY 11210

718-951-5000
Fax: 718-951-4882
www.brooklyncollegeathletics.com
• Bruce Filos, Director of Recreation, Intramurals and Inter
(718) 951-5366
bfilosa@brooklyn.edu
Degrees Offered:
M.S. Sports Management, Physical Education

BUCKS COUNTY COMMUNITY COLLEGE - DEPT OF HEALTH, PE & NURSING
275 SWAMP ROAD
GYMNASIUM 102
NEWTON, PA 18940
215-968-8451
admissions@bucks.edu
www.bucks.edu/athletics
• Priscilla Rice, Director
ricep@bucks.edu
Degrees/Majors Offered:
A.A.; The Sport Management major prepares the undergraduate student for a career in sport management, athletics, marketing, campus recreation, intramurals, student activities, as well as other related areas.

CAL STATE UNIVERSITY - BAKERSFIELD, SCHOOL OF BUSINESS AND PUBLIC ADMINISTRATION
9001 STOCKDALE HWY.
BAKERSFIELD, CA 93311-1022
661-654-CSUB (2782)
excellence@csub.edu
www.gorunners.com
• John Emery, Ph.D., Dean and Professor of Finance
(661) 654-2023
jemery@csub.edu
• Mark Evans, Associate Dean & Professor of Economics
(661) 654-2023
mevans@csub.edu
• Margaret Moorhead, Administrative Analyst/Specialist
(661) 654-2234
mmoorhead@csub.edu
• Isabel Gonzalez, Administrative Coordinator
(661) 654-2023
igonzalez4@csub.edu
Sport Management Program:
Courses include; Introduction to Sports Management, Sports Marketing, Sport in Court, Professional Sport Selling and Sport Sponsorship, Special Topics in Sports Management, & Internship in Sports Management.

CALIFORNIA BAPTIST UNIVERSITY
8432 MAGNOLIA AVENUE
RIVERSIDE, CA 92504
951-689-5771
800-782-3382
Fax: 951-351-1808
www.cbulancers.com
• Micah Parker, Director of Athletics
(951) 343-4318
miparker@calbaptist.edu
Degree Offered:
M.S. Kinesiology with a concentration in sport management.

CALIFORNIA POLYTECHNIC STATE UNIVERSITY - RECREATION, PARKS, &TOURISM DEPT.
SAN LUIS OBISPO, CA 93407
805-756-1111
www.gopoly.com

CALIFORNIA STATE UNIVERSITY- FRESNO- CRAIG SCHOOL OF BUSINESS
PETERS BUSINESS BUILDING, #388
5245 N. BACKER AVE, M/S PB 7
FRESNO, CA 93740-8001
559-278-7830
Fax: 559-278-8577
kathyu@csufresno.edu
www.craig.csufresno.edu
Sports Management Program offered:
Graduate master's in sports management

CALIFORNIA STATE UNIVERSITY- LONG BEACH- DEPARTMENT OF KINESIOLOGY
COLLEGE OF HEALTH AND HUMAN SERVICES
1250 BELLFLOWER BLVD
LONG BEACH, CA 90840-8306
562-985-2044
Fax: 562-985-7581
gpsm.ga@gmail.com
www.csulb.edu/athletics
Description:
The Master of Arts in Kinesiology, Option: Sport Management program is offered by the Department of Kinesiology in partnership with College of Continuing and Professional Education (CCPE), at California State University, Long Beach. This accelerated 36-unit program allows students to earn a master's degree in 18 months and is designed to prepare students for a career in the management and administration of sport.

CALIFORNIA STATE UNIVERSITY-FULLERTON
DEPARTMENT OF KINESIOLOGY
800 N. STATE COLLEGE BOULEVARD
ROOM KHS-121
FULLERTON, CA 92634
714-278-3316
Fax: 714-278-5317
• Kathy Koser, Department Chairperson
(714) 278-3316
kkoser@fullerton.edu
• Debra Rose, Kinesiology Graduate Coordinator
(714) 278-5846
drose@fullerton.edu
• Patti Laguna, Kinesiology Undergraduate Coordinator
(714) 278-3783
plaguna@fullerton.edu
Description:
Grad Degree: M.S. in Phys Ed, with emphasis on Sport and Exercise Management. Areas of Specialization: Grad: Corporate Fitness Management, Professional Sports Management, etc.

CALIFORNIA UNIVERSITY OF PENNSYLVANIA
DEPARTMENT OF HEALTH AND SPORT STUDIES
250 UNIVERSITY AVENUE
CALIFORNIA, PA 15419
724-938-4356
Fax: 724-938-4454

yarbrough@calu.edu
www.calvulcans.com
• Roy Yarbrough, Ed.D, Professor
(724) 938-4356
yarbrough@calu.edu
• Brian Wood, Assistant Professor
(724) 938-5033
wood_b@calu.edu
Description:
The sport management studies program is one of the largest programs at California University of Pennsylvania. In sports business, the term 'player' takes on a new meaning. From the executive boardroom to the playing field, to creating the balance sheets, and even at the scoreboard, sport management majors are doing it all. Three distinct sport management tracks are offered: Sport Management; Professional Golf Management; and Wellness and Fitness (online).

CAMPBELL UNIVERSITY - COLLEGE OF ARTS & SCIENCES
DEPARTMENT OF EXERCISE SCIENCE
PO BOX 567
BUIES CREEK, NC 27506
910-893-1360
800-334-4111
Fax: 910-893-1424
www.campbell.edu
• William Freeman, Chairman/Professor
(910) 893-1362
• Brian Bergemann, Exercise Science Professor
(910) 893-1352
bergemannb@campbell.edu
Description:
B.S. athletic training, fitness wellness management, kinesiology, exercise and sport science, pysical education, sport management.

CANISIUS COLLEGE - SCHOOL OF EDUCATION & HUMAN SERVICES
SCHOOL OF EDUCATION & HUMAN SERVICES
BAGEN HALL 201
2001 MAIN STREET
BUFFALO, NY 14208-1098
716-888-3294
800-843-1517
Fax: 716-888-3164
www.canisius.edu
• Don Sheldon, Director of Athletic Communications
(716) 888-8265
reitnoum@canisius.edu
• Shawn O'Rourke, Associate Dean for Undergraduate & Graduate P
orourke1@canisius.edu
• Yann Abdourazakou, Assistant Professor
• Nicholas Lorgnier, Assistant Professor
lorgnien@canisius.edu
• Matt Reitnour, Director of Athletic Communications
reitnoum@canisius.edu
• Traci Murphy, Associate Athletic Director
murphy30@canisius.edu
• Bill Maher, Director of Athletics
maherw@canisius.edu
Description:
M.S. in Sports Administration. This bachelor's degree program provides students with the skills and training to effectively manage in a wide variety of sports related fields. Graduates of this program are prepared to work in fields such

as intercollegiate athletics, amateur and professional sports, sport-marketing firms, special event management as well as facility management. Students gain practical experience through an internship opportunity in a wide variety of settings in the sport industry.

CAPITAL UNIVERSITY
DEPARTMENT OF HEALTH & SCIENCE
1 COLLEGE AND MAIN
COLUMBUS, OH 43209
614-236-6911
Fax: 614-236-6178
lreich@capital.edu
www.capital.edu
• Leonard Reich, Sports Information Director
(614) 236-6174
Description:
Undergrad Degree: B.A. Areas of Specialization: Sport Management.

CARDINAL STRITCH UNIVERSITY-SPORT MANAGEMENT PROGRAM
6801 N. YATES ROAD
MILWAUKEE, WI 53217
414-410-4000
800-347-8822
www.stritch.edu/mssm/
Master's program sport management-
Program is designed for working adults seeking to become leaders in the sports industry in a variety of settings, including professional and collegiate sports, health and fitness clubs, recreation departments, sport organizations, and retail sporting goods stores.

CASTLETON STATE COLLEGE
86 Seminary Street
Castleton, VT 5735
802-468-5611
Fax: 802-468-5237
www.castleton.edu/athletics
• John Feenick, Director
john.feenick@castleton.edu
Degrees/Majors Offered:
B.S. sports medicine, athletic training, exercise science, physical education, and teaching license. The sports administration concentration trains and develops students for employment in the sport industry. The goal is to prepare students for administrative positions in professional and amateur athletics, recreation, stadium, arena and convention facilities, college and university athletic departments, health and fitness centers, management companies, sports marketing and other programs that require a sports and business background.

CAZENOVIA COLLEGE
7 NICKERSON STREET
CAZENOVIA, NY 13035
315-655-7992
800-654-3210
Fax: 315-655-2157
mjbrimecombe@cazenovia.edu
www.cazenovia.edu
• Michelle Brimecombe, Assistant Professor & Program Director, Sport
(315) 655-7992
mjbrimecombe@cazenovia.edu
Bachelor of Professional Studies:
The Sport Management program at Cazenovia College prepares students for a number of interesting and exciting career

opportunities in the sport industry - from youth to scholastic to collegiate to professional sport management and marketing, from event and facility management to sport sport agency. The Sport Management curriculum combines both classroom learning and internship experiences that help broaden the students' understanding as well as experiential and networking opportunities.

CEDARVILLE UNIVERSITY-DEPARTMENT OF KINESIOLOGY AND ALLIED HEALTH
251 N. MAIN STREET
CEDARVILLE, OH 45314
937-766-7755
www.cedarville.edu
Sport Management Program:
Students can major in; Allied Health, Athletic Training, Exercise Science- Bachelor of Arts, Exercise Science - Bachelor of Science, Multi-Age Physical Education, Sport and Exercise Studies, and Sport Management.

CENTENARY COLLEGE- SPORTS MANAGEMENT BUSINESS PROGRAM
400 JEFFERSON STREET
HACKETTSTOWN, NJ 7840
908-852-1400
800-236-8679
Description:
Major in business administration with a concentration in Sports Management.

CENTRAL FLORIDA, UNIVERSITY OF
COLLEGE OF BUSINESS ADMINISTRATION
4000 CENTRAL FLORIDA BLVD
PO BOX 161991
ORLANDO, FL 32816-1991
407-823-2766
Fax: 407-823-6442
business.ucf.edu
• Richard Lapchick, Director, DeVos Sport Business Management Pro
Degree Offered:
MSBM Sport Business Management

CENTRAL MICHIGAN UNIVERSITY
DEPARTMENT OF PHYSICAL EDUCATION AND SPORT
2240 HEALTH PROFESSIONS BUILDING
MT. PLEASANT, MI 48859
989-774-1040
Fax: 989-774-5391
globalsportleadership@cmich.edu
www.chp.cmich.edu
• James Hornak, Dept. Chairman
(517) 774-6659
horna1je@cmich.edu
• Scott Smith, Sport Management Division Co-Director
(517) 774-2859
Scott.J.Smith@cmich.edu
• Marcia Mackey, Sport Management Program Director
(989) 774-2377
Marcia.J.Mackey@cmich.edu
Description:
Undergrad Degree: B.A. with major in Sport Studies and Minor in Business Management. Grad Degree: M.A. in Sport Administration; M.A. in Phys Ed/Athletic Administration. Areas of Specialization:

Grad: Sport Administration, Athletic Administration.

CENTRAL MISSOURI STATE UNIVERSITY
DEPARTMENT OF HEALTH & HUMAN PERFORMANCE
PO BOX 800
WARRENSBURG, MO 64093
660-543-4256
877-729-8266
Fax: 660-543-4167
admit@ucmo.edu
• Dan Gerdes, Health Human Performance Professor
(660) 543-4732
Description:
Undergrad Degree: B.S. Grad Degree: M.S. Areas of Specialization: Undergrad: Coaching. Grad: Exercise and Sport Science; Athletic Training; Athletic & Business Administration.

CENTRAL WASHINGTON UNIVERSITY
DEPARTMENT OF HEALTH, HUMAN PERFORMANCE & RECREATION
400 E. UNIVERSITY WAY
ELLENSBURG, WA 98926
509-963-1111
Fax: 509-963-1848
buschr@cwu.edu
www.cwu.edu
• Bob McGowan, Chairman/Professor
(509) 963-1051
mcgowanr@cwu.edu
• Kirk Mathias, Physical Education Director
(509) 963-1051
mathiask@cwu.edu
Description:
Undergrad Degree: B.S., Fitness and Sport Management. Grad Degree: M.S. in PEHLS. Areas of Specialization: Undergrad: Athletic Training, Coaching. Grad: Health Ed; Leisure Services; Athletic Adm; Exercise Science; Pedagogy/Coaching.

CHOWAN UNIVERSITY
SCHOOL OF ARTS & SCIENCES; SPORTS STUDIES & PE
200 JONES DRIVE
MURFREESBORO, NC 27855
252-398-6243
Fax: 252-398-1390
www.chowan.edu
Description:
B.S. in Sport Management; Sports Science Major - Directed for Personal Trainers, Fitness, Cardiac Evaluations; Physical Education Teacher Education; Athletic Training. Internships offered in a variety of areas.

CHRISTIAN BROTHERS UNIVERSITY
SCHOOL OF BUSINESS
650 EAST PARKWAY SOUTH
MEMPHIS, TN 38104
901-321-3000
877-321-4228
www.cbu.edu
Program Description:
Bachelor's in Sport Management from CBU School of Business.

CITADEL, THE
DEPT OF HEALTH, EXERCISE AND SPORT SCIENCE
DEAS HALL

college sports

171 MOULTRIE STREET
CHARLESTON, SC 29409
843-953-5060
Fax: 843-953-6798
garnerd1@citadel.edu
www.citadel.edu
• Harry Davakos, Director
harry.davakos@citadel.edu
• Terry Giguiere, Dept. Coordinator
terry.giguiere@citadel.edu
Description:
B.S. health, exercise and sport science,
concentration in sport management.

CLAFLIN UNIVERSITY
400 MAGNOLIA STREET
ORANGEBURG, SC 29115
803-535-5000
800-922-1276
www.claflin.edu/athletics
• Marta N Mack, Chair/Director
Description:
B.A. sport management: Courses in the core
program are interdisciplinary with the Sport
Management program and the Business
Administration program. The Sport
Management program prepares students to
become highly-trained managers who find
success in complex and varied sport
settings.

CLEVELAND STATE UNIVERSITY
HPERD BUILDING
2121 EUCLID AVENUE
CLEVELAND, OH 44115-2214
216-687-2000
Fax: 216-687-5410
www.csuohio.edu
• Nancy Carlucci Smith, Communication
Account Representative
(216) 687-2290
pr@csuohio.edu
• Eddie Lam, Sport Management Program
Coordinator
(216) 687-5051
t.lam@csuohio.edu
Description:
Undergrad Degree Major Sport
Management; Minor Sport Management.
Grad Degree M.Ed Sport Management;
M.Ed Exercise Science.

**COASTAL CAROLINA UNIVERSIY-
COLLEGE OF SCIENCE**
843-349-2026
800-277-7000
Fax: 843-349-6436
www.coastal.edu/rsm/
Sport Management Program:
The Department of Kinesiology, Recreation,
and Sport Studies at Coastal Carolina
University is a dynamic unit of high quality
faculty and academic programs that study
and promote human movement as applied
to current and emerging physical activity,
sport, therapeutic, and recreation settings.

COLBY-SAWYER COLLEGE
DEPARTMENT OF EXERCISE AND
SPORT SCIENCES
541 MAIN STREET
NEW LONDON, NH 3257
603-526-3000
rmedbery@colby-sawyer.edu
www.colby-sawyerathletics.com
• Russell Medbery, Ph.D, Associate
Professor and Chair

(603) 526-3870
rmedbery@colby-sawyer.edu
• Gregory R Austin, Ph.D., Associate
Professor
(603) 526-3615
Degree Offered:
The Exercise and Sport Sciences
Department offers B.S. degrees in Athletic
Training, Exercise Science and Sport
Management. All three majors integrate the
liberal arts and sciences with professional
preparation.
Description:
An expanding field that integrates the study
of sport and business to provide a thorough
background in the sport industry. You will
develop skills necessary to assume
leadership in the implementation,
development, management and marketing
of sport programs. As opportunities and
interest in sport continue to develop, career
options have expanded. These include, but
are not limited to, marketing directors,
athletics administrators, sport facilities
managers, youth sport and recreation
directors, corporate sponsor coordinators,
event managers and coaches.
Requirements:
In addition to requirements for all exercise
and sport sciences majors, the following
courses are required for the sport
management program; Exercise and Sport
Science, Business, Economics, Sociology.

COLLEGE OF IDAHO
2112 CLEVELAND BOULEVARD
CALDWELL, ID 83605
208-459-5011
Fax: 208-459-5175
• James R. Fennell, Director
Degree:
B.S. exercise science, B.A. physical
education (teaching), B.A. physical
education (non-teaching),B.A. sport and
fitness center management.

**COLLEGE OF MOUNT ST. JOSEPH-
SPORT MANAGEMENT DEPARTMENT**
5701 DELHI ROAD
CINCINNATI, OH 45233-1670
513-244-4200
800-654-9314
Fax: 513-244-4601
www.msj.edu
**Bachelor's Program for Sport
Management:**
This degree is designed to develop skills
related to planning, organizing, directing,
controlling, budgeting, leading and
evaluating an organization or department
whose primary product or service is related
to sport and/or recreation. Career
possibilities related to this field include work
in a variety of sport or sport-related settings
such as: professional athletics/franchise
management, college athletics, corporation
fitness/health club management, facility
operations, corporate sport marketing/public
relations, event marketing and
management, journalism/communications,
media relations and sports equipment sales,
specialized sports managem

**COLLEGE OF SAINT ROSE, ALBANY-
SCHOOL OF BUSINESS**
432 WESTERN AVENUE
ALBANY, NY 12203

518-454-5158
800-637-8556
Fax: 518-458-5457
www.strose.edu
Concentration Sports Management:
Sport Management is a broad area of study
that introduces students to the concepts and
techniques needed to successfully work
within a host of organizations in a
sport-related context. Courses provide
students with a firm foundation in the human
relations, marketing and ethical and legal
aspects that influence and shape the people
and organizations in the business of sport.

**COLORADO MESA UNIVERSITY -
DEPARTMENT OF KINESIOLOGY**
1100 NORTH AVENUE
GRAND JUNCTION, CO 81501-3122
970-248-1020
800-982-6372
www.coloradomesa.edu/kinesiology
Program Description:
Bachelor of Science in Sport Management:
MBA Sport Management

**COLUMBIA COLLEGE CHICAGO- ARTS,
ENTERTAINMENT AND MEDIA
MANAGEMENT**
600 S. MICHIGAN AVENUE
CHICAGO, IL 60605
312-369-7652
mmaye@colum.edu
www.colum.edu/academics
Description:
The Sports Management Concentration
leads to professions in the Sports Industry in
the fields of audience building, box office
management, special events, facilities
management, career and talent
development, broadcasting and media
management, and merchandising. This
unique to Chicago region concentration
offers a comprehensive curriculum that
emphasizes specifics of Sports
Entertainment Management while providing
knowledge and skills applicable to other
areas of entertainment management.

COLUMBIA UNIVERSITY
SCHOOL OF CONTINUING EDUCATION
203 LEWISOHN HALL
2970 BROADWAY, MC 4119
NEW YORK, NY 10027
212-854-1754
www.ce.columbia.edu/Sports-Management
• Lucas Robin, Director of Sports
Management Program
Degree Offered:
MS Sport Management

**COLUMBUS STATE COMMUNITY
COLLEGE**
UNION HALL
550 E. SPRING STREET
PO BOX 1609
COLUMBUS, OH 43215
614-287-5353 EXT 5422
Fax: 614-287-5144
information@cscc.edu
www.cscc.edu/athletics
• Amy Hart, Associate Professor, Sports &
Exercise Studies
(614) 287-2581
ahart@cscc.edu
• Antoinette Perkins, Associate Professor

(614) 287-5744
aperki01@cscc.edu
Degrees Offered:
Associate Degrees in Exercise Science; Physical Education; and Sport Management
Description:
The Sport and Exercise Studies program prepares students to work in sport, recreation, health and/or fitness centers. From private clubs to public facilities, trained managers, instructors, and programmers are needed to develop, train, staff, and implement programming to address the wellness needs of the general public or specific clients/populations, in compliance with local, state, and federal guidelines. Exercise science, strength and resistance training, risk management, human nutrition, anatomy, physiology, sport business/marketing, and health and physical education courses blends with the college's General Education course work.

COLUMBUS STATE UNIVERSITY
DEPARTMENT OF COUNSELING EDUCATION & PROFESSIONAL STUDIES
103 JORDAN HALL
4225 UNIVERSITY AVENUE
COLUMBUS, GA 31907-5645
706-568-2301
Fax: 706-568-5088
• Tom Ford, Dept. Chairperson
• Patty Jamieson, Dept. Coordinator
Description:
Undergrad Degree: B.S. Areas of Specialization: Undergrad: Sport Fitness Management. Associate Degree - Exercise Science Major, Associate Degree- Physical Education Major, Associate Degree- Sport Management Major, Exercise Specialist Certificate.

CONCORDIA UNIVERSITY OF CHICAGO
7400 AUGUSTA STREET
RIVER FOREST, IL 60305
708-771-8300
• Lynn Lashbrook, Professor, Program Coordinator
Degrees:
Online Programs: Ed.D. Sports Leadership & Management; Ph.D. Sports Leadership & Management; MASL (M.A. in Sports Leadership); The bachelor of science in sports management includes an in-depth business curriculum covering classes focusing on business and sports.

CONNECTICUT, UNIVERSITY OF
NEAG SCHOOL OF EDUCATION, DEPARTMENT OF KINESIOLOGY
249 GLENBROOK ROAD
UNIT 1110
STORRS, CT 06269-1110
860-486-3623
Fax: 860-486-1123
• Carl Maresh, Department Head/Professor
(860) 486-5322
carl.maresh@uconn.edu
• Laura Burton, Sport Management Assistant Professor
(860) 486-3095
laura.burton@uconn.edu
Description:
The Sport Management program offers two undergraduate degrees and two graduate degrees. The Coaching and Administration Concentration prepares students to coach

teams at amateur, collegiate, and professional levels. The undergraduate program in Sport Management is designed to prepare students to enter careers in the sport industry. The M.A. and Ph.D. degrees in Sport Management prepare students in the theoretical, research-oriented, and applied dimensions of the sport industry.

COPPIN STATE UNIVERSITY
DEPARTMENT OF HEALTH, PHYSICAL EDUCATION, RECREATION & DANCE
2500 W. NORTH AVENUE
BALTIMORE, MD 21216
410-951-3384
800-635-3674
Fax: 410-951-3376
health@coppin.edu
www.coppin.edu/athletics
• Edna Simmons, Ph.D, Dept. Chairperson/Professor
(410) 951-3384
• Beahta Davis, Ph.D, Sports Management Adjunct Instructor
(410) 951-3377
Description:
Sports Management program at Coppin State University prepares undergraduate students for professional careers in Sports Management, including both the private and public sectors. The program is designed to assist students in acquiring organizational and managerial expertise in the health, fitness and sports management fields as well as to assist students in gaining an understanding of personnel management and supervision.
Courses:
B.S. sports management, concentrations in sport business, sport marketing, sport journalism and sports medicine.

CORBAN UNIVERSITY- HUMAN PERFORMANCE, SPORT MANAGEMENT
5000 DEER PARK DRIVE SE
SALEM, OR 97317
503-581-8600
admissions@corban.edu
www.corban.edu
Program Description:
The foundational basis of the program lies in its focus on biblical principles through which individual understanding and development prepare one for a life of service to others. A primary function of the program is to provide the student with activity-oriented knowledge and problem solving skills to meet the demands of a life of ministry in the human performance fields. The Human Performance major may select one of three emphases: Exercise Science, Sports Management or Physical Education. The Exercise Science option has a research project requirement with an option for majors to add an internship experience. The Sports Management option has

DAEMEN COLLEGE- DIVISION OF HEALTH & HUMAN SERVICES
4380 MAIN STREET
AMHERST, NY 14226
800-462-7652
www.daemen.edu
Program Description:
Division of Health & Human Services: Undergraduate program of Bachelor of

Science in Business Administration, Specialization; Sport Management.

DAKOTA WESLEYAN UNIVERSITY
1200 W. UNIVERSITY AVENUE
MITCHELL, SD 57301
605-995-2600
800-333-8506
www.dwu.edu/athletics
• Scott Gines, Director
scgines@dwu.edu
Degree:
DWU offers three emphases within the sports management program: Marketing and Sports Information, Human Resource Management, and Finance.

DALLAS BAPTIST UNIVERSITY
3000 MOUNTAIN CREEK PARKWAY
DALLAS, TX 75211
214-333-5329
800-460-1328
Fax: 214-333-5306
sports@dbu.edu
www.dbupatriots.com
Teams:
NCAA Sports: Men's Baseball, Men's Basketball, Women's Soccer, Women's Volleyball, Men and Women's Tennis, Men and Women's Golf, Men and Women's Cross Country, Men and Women's Indoor Track, Men and Women's Outdoor Track
Club Sports: Bass Fishing, Ice Hockey, Drill Team, Cheerleading

DANIEL WEBSTER COLLEGE
20 UNIVERSITY DRIVE
NASHUA, NH 3063
603-577-6000
800325-6876
• Robin Seidman, Director of Athletics
(603) 577-6381
rseidman@dwc.edu
Description:
One of very few such programs offered by the business and management division at an American college. You'll be prepared for work in professional and recreational sports in areas such as public relations, marketing and sales; sports facilities management; athletic administration at secondary school, collegiate and professional levels; sports information; or recreational sport management in a private or public setting.
Degrees Offered:
BS; Sport Management.

DAVENPORT UNIVERSITY- BUSINESS ADMINISTRATION DEPARTMENT
45 OTTAWA NW
GRAND RAPIDS, MI 49503
616-698-7111 EXT 1361
800-686-1600
info@davenport.edu
www.davenport.edu
Program Description:
Bachelor of Business Administration, Sport Management. Students gain skills in business fundamentals and specific sport management disciplines in a learning environment that balances textbook theory with real-world business application. Through varied learning methodologies including an internship, students are exposed to the legal, regulatory, marketing and operational aspects of sport venue management. Graduates earn a Bachelor of

Business Administration degree with a major in Sport Management.

DAVIS & ELKINS COLLEGE
DEPARTMENT OF HEALTH, SPORT & MOVEMENT SCIENCE
100 CAMPUS DRIVE
ELKINS, WV 26241-3996
304-637-1348
Fax: 304-637-1414
• Mary Ann DeLuca, Dept. Chairperson
• Jeffrey Goodman, Associate Professor
Description:
Undergrad Degree: B.S. Areas of Specialization: Physical Education, Exercise Science; Athletic Training, Sport Management, Health.

DAYTON, UNIVERSITY OF
DEPARTMENT OF HEALTH AND SPORT SCIENCE
300 COLLEGE PARK
DAYTON, OH 45469-2925
937-229-5600
Fax: 937-229-5601
• Paul Vanderburgh, Dept. Chairperson
(937) 229-4213
vanderburgh@udayton.edu
• George DeMarco, Associate Professor/Coordinator
(937) 229-4210
George.DeMarco@notes.udayton.edu
Description:
Undergrad Degree: B.S. in Education. Areas of Specialization: 2 core areas: Sports Business, Sports Marketing. Through studies in sport management, students gain an understanding of facilities, finance, human resource management, law, marketing, media and sales - and how they relate to sports.

DE SALES UNIVERSITY
2755 STATION AVE
CENTER VALLEY, PA 18034
610-282-1100 EXT 1894
Fax: 610-282-2279
www.desales.edu
• Brian Turner, Director
• Jay C Lacke, Chair/Director
Degree Offered:
Undergrad Degree: B.S. Sports Administration/Management. Areas of Specialization: Sport and Fitness Management; Athletic Administration. The Sport Management major at DeSales University provides a curriculum that combines theory and practice with the wide world of sport and business.

DEFIANCE COLLEGE- BUSINESS & ALLIED HEALTH DIVISION
701 N. CLINTON ST.
DEFIANCE, OH 43512
800-520-4632
www.defiance.edu/pages/bus_majors_sports_management.html
Sport Management Program:
The program is designed to prepare students to either obtain an entry-level position upon graduation or to continue studies in graduate school. Sport management lets students participate in the exciting world of sports from a business standpoint. In this major, students learn about various sports, the psychological principles at work behind them, and how

sports fit into society. Also gain a strong knowledge foundation in business, examining how the worlds of business and sports interact and how they can make those interactions more profitable and beneficial for every person and interest involved. At Defiance College, sport management professo

DELAWARE STATE UNIVERSITY
DEPARTMENT OF SPORT SCIENCES
1200 N. DUPONT HIGHWAY
MEMORIAL HALL ROOM 163
DOVER, DE 19901
302-857-6600
Fax: 302-857-6601
www.desu.edu/student-life/athletics
• Li Chen, Dept. Chairperson
• Jan Blade, Sports Administration Director
(302) 857-6602
jblade@desu.edu
Degree/Majors Offered:
BS; Sport Management. Master of Science in Sport Administration offered by Department of Sport management within College of Health and Public Policy, Delaware State University that professionally prepares ethical leaders for advanced responsibilities within sport organizations and/or to design and implement new sport or sport-relatec to changing economic, legal, political, and social influences.

DELTA STATE UNIVERSITY
DEPARTMENT OF HEALTH, PHYSICAL EDUCATION AND RECREATION
HIGHWAY 8 WEST
CLEVELAND, MS 38733
662-846-4555
800-468-6378
Fax: 662-846-4680
www.deltastate.edu
• Darvin Barnes, Dept. Chairperson
(662) 846-4561
dbarnes@deltastate.edu
Description:
Undergrad Degree: B.S. in Phys Ed. Grad Degree: M.E.D. Areas of Specialization: Undergrad: Health, Recreation, Sport Management, Sports Information. Grad: Phys Ed.

DENVER, UNIVERSITY OF
DANIELS COLLEGE OF BUSINESS
2050 E. EVANS AVENUE, SUITE 30
DENVER, CO 80208
303-871-2150
800-622-4723
Fax: 303-871-4466
career@du.edu
www.daniels.du.edu
• Wayne Murdy, Chair
• Micheal John, Vice Chair
• Scott Lowery, Vice Chair
• Stewart Glendinning, CEO
• George Spentzos, Executive Advisory Board
• Peg Bradlet-Doppes, Vice Chancellor for Athletics and Recreation
(303) 871-3399
Description:
M.S., and M.B.A. in sport management concentration.

DESALES UNIVERSITY- DIVISION OF BUSINESS
2755 STATION AVENUE
CENTER VALLEY, PA 18034
610-282-1100
web1.desales.edu/default.aspx?pageid=304
Program Description:
The Bachelor of Science degree in Sport Management provides you with career and professional training in sport management within the context of a liberal arts education. The program is one of only 20 approved by the Sport Management Program Review Council (SMPRC) at the undergraduate level in the United States. The Sport Management program is also endorsed by The National Association for Sport and Physical Education (NASPE) and The North American Society for Sport Management (NASSM). The major focuses on the conceptual, managerial, and practical skills that prepare you to become a visionary leader in various areas of the sport industry.

DOWLING COLLEGE
150 IDLE HOUR BOULEVARD
Oakdale, NY 11769
631-244-3000
800-DOWLING
• Marilyn Mather, Director
matherm@dowling.edu
• Christopher Celano, Sports Information Director
Degrees/Major Offered:
B.S. sport management. A combine degree that integrates the qualities and expertise of two of the most dynamic departments at Dowling College: The Department of Physical Education and the Department of Management.

DREXEL UNIVERSITY
3141 CHESTNUT STREET
Philadelphia, PA 19104
215-895-2000
• Dave O'Brian, Director of Sport Management
Degrees/Majors Offered:
M.S. in sport management through Goodwin College. Four areas of focus are sports marketing, sports business, sports media and sports law. Online program is also available.

DUQUESNE UNIVERSITY
600 FORBES AVENUE
PITTSBURGH, PA 15282
412-396-6000
admissions@duq.edu
www.duq.edu/athletics
• Keith M Gorse, EdD, ATC, Clinical Coordinator
(412) 396-5959
gorse@duq.edu
• Paula Sammarone Turocy, EdD, ATC, Department Chair
(412) 396-5695
turocyp@duq.edu
Degrees Offered:
B.S. in Athletic Training; B.S., M.H.M.S. in Health Management Systems; M.S. in Health Sciences Master of Science; M.S. in Occupational Therapy; D.P.T. in Physical Therapy; M.P.A.S. in Physician Assistant Studies; M.S. in Speech-Language Pathology; Ph.D. in Rehabilitation Science; M.S. in Leadership, Concentration in Sports

Leadership
Description:
Students in the Rangos School are challenged with contemporary curricula, clinically-skilled, nationally-known faculty, master their clinical skills in state-of-the-industry laboratories, and have varied and excellent internship/clinical placements.

DeVOS SPORT BUSINESS MANAGEMENT
4000 CENTRAL FLORIDA BOULEVARD
COLLEGE OF BUSINESS
ADMINISTRATION
ORLANDO, FL 32816
407-823-4887
Fax: 407-823-4771
rlapchick@bus.ucf.edu
www.bus.ucf.edu/athletics
• Richard Lapchick, Director Chair
rlapchick@bus.ucf.edu
• C. Keith Harrison, Associate Professor
• William A Sutton, Associate Director
wsutton@bus.ucf.edu
Description:
The DeVos Program has been named one of the nation's top five programs by the Wall Street Journal, ESPN The Magazine and the New York Times. In 2009 it was named the number 1 MBA program in the nation for volunteer service.

EAST CAROLINA UNIVERSITY - DEPARTMENT OF KINESIOLOGY
A-20 MINGES COLISEUM
GREENVILLE, NC 27858
252-328-4643
sartorem@ecu.edu
www.ecu.edu/athletics
• Melanie Sartore-Baldwin, Assistant Professor
(252) 328-4643
sartorem@ecu.edu
Description:
M.A. exercise and sport science, concentration in sport management.

EAST CENTRAL UNIVERSITY- SCHOOL OF BUSINESS
1100 E. 14TH STREET
ADA, OK 74820
580-332-8000
www.ecok.edu/
Sports Administration:
Master of Education in Secondary Education - Sports Administration.

EAST STROUDSBURG UNIVERSITY OF
DEPARTMENT OF SPORTS STUDIES
SPORT MANAGEMENT PROGRAM
200 PROSPECT STREET
EAST STROUDSBURG, PA 18301-2999
570-422-3211
Fax: 570-422-3423
www.esu.edu
• Paula M Parker, Associate Professor
• Robert P. Fleischman, Professor/Sport Management Program Coordinator
(570) 422-3316
• Frank M Pullo, Chair/Director
(570) 422-3265
fpullo@po-box.esu.edu
Degrees Offered:
B.S. sport management, M.S. sport management, M.S. management and

leadership studies, concentration in sport management.

EAST TENNESSEE STATE UNIVERSITY-KINESIOLOGY DEPT
DEPT OF KINESIOLOGY, LEISURE, & SPORT SCIENCES
BOX 70654
JOHNSON CITY, TN 37614-1701
423-439-4362
Fax: 423-439-5383
KLSS@etsu.edu
www.etsu.edu
Program Description:
The ETSU undergraduate Sport Management Concentration introduces students to the sport industry and provides them with the opportunity to study a wide variety of fulfilling sport-related careers. Program emphasizes a unique mix of academic preparation along with required real-world practical field experiences. The curriculum examines three main segments of the sport industry (performance, production, promotion), and it encompasses all levels of sport: youth, high school, collegiate, professional, amateur, competitive, non-competitive, recreational, private, and nonprofit/profit organizations.

EASTERN STATE UNIVERSITY
DEPARTMENT OF HEALTH & PHYSICAL EDUCATION
SPORTS CENTER
83 WINDHAM STREET
Willimantic, CT 6226
860-465-5371
Fax: 860-465-0186
horrocks@easternct.edu
gowarriorathletics.com
• Neil Williams, Professor/Chair
(860) 465-5170
williamsn@easternct.edu
Degrees/Majors Offered:
B.S. sport leisure management.

EASTERN ILLINOIS UNIVERSITY
BUZZARD HALL, ROOM 1420
600 LINCOLN AVENUE
CHARLESTON, IL 61920
217-581-5000
Fax: 217-581-2518
ceps@eiu.edu
www.eiu.edu
• Nancy Crone, Academic Advisor
(217) 581-8582
• Phyllis Croisant, Professor
(217) 581-7596
ptcroisant@eiu.edu
• Larry Ankenbrand, Professor
(217) 581-2215
Description:
Undergrad Degree: B.S. Grad Degree: M.S. Areas of Specialization: Undergrad: Corporate Fitness and Club Management; Grad: Specialization: Sport Management in the Education Sector - designed to prepare athletic directors at the high school and college levels; Sport Management in the Private Sector - may include entrepreneurial approach or professional sports management approach depending on type of internship experience chosen by the student.

EASTERN KENTUCKY UNIVERSITY
521 LANCASTER AVENUE
MOBERLY 231
RICHMOND, KY 40475-3134
859-622-1887
Fax: 859-622-1254
www.ess.eku.edu
• Doug Whitlock, President
Description:
Undergrad Degree: B.S. Degree, M.S. Degree. Areas of Specialization; Undergrad; Athletic Training, Sports Administration; Wellness. K-12 Teaching, Adult fitness, Sports Administration, Generalist.

EASTERN MICHIGAN UNIVERSITY-COLLEGE OF HEALTH & HUMAN SERVICES
SCHOOL OF HEALTH PROMOTION AND HUMAN PERFORMANCE
318 PORTER BUILDING
YPSILANTI, MI 48197
734-487-0090
www.emich.edu
Program Description:
Graduate studies in Sport Management MS Degree. The Sport Management program at Eastern Michigan University is designed for students who are interested in athletic administration (high school sports) and sport management in elite level sports (such as collegiate sport). Although there is a program of study for students, it remains flexible so that they can receive the education that is best suited for their future careers.

ELMS COLLEGE- BUSINESS AND LAW DIVISION
291 SPRINGFIELD STREET
CHICOPEE, MA 01013-2839
413-594-2761
www.elms.edu
Program Description:
Bachelor of Arts Degree, Major in Sport Management.

ELON UNIVERSITY
DEPARTMENT OF LEISURE AND SPORT MANAGEMENT
100 CAMPUS DRIVE
ELON, NC 27244-2010
336-278-2000
Fax: 336-278-5918
drummond@elon.edu
www.elon.edu
Description:
The Sport and Event Management major prepares students to plan, manage and sustain effective, sport and recreation experiences in private, public and commercial settings. Through classroom and real world experiences students develop an understanding of service and skills applicable to the sport, event and recreation professions.

ENDICOTT COLLEGE
376 HALE ST
BEVERLY, MA 1915
978-927-0585
800-325-1114
Fax: 978-232-2600
dswanton@endicott.edu
www.endicott.edu

• Deborah Swanton, Dean of Sport Science & Fitness Studies
dswanton@endicott.edu
Description:
Within the School of Sport Science and Fitness Studies, students select innovative programs in Athletic Training, Sport Management, Physical Education Teacher Licensure, Physical Education Exercise Science, and Exercise Science minor.

ERSKINE COLLEGE- DEPT OF HEALTH, PE, SPORTS MANAGEMENT
2 WASHINGTON ST.
DUE WEST, SC 29639
864-379-8840
888-359-4358
Fax: 864-379-2197
alston@erskine.edu
www.erskine.edu
• Scott DeCiantis, Athletic Training Ed. Program Director
(864) 379-8899
deciantis@erskine.edu
• Adam Hayes Weyer, Head Athletic Trainer
(864) 379-8890
weyer@erskine.edu
Degrees Offered:
B.S. Sport Management. Physical education, Sports Management-Fitness Concentration; Athletic Training.

EVANSVILLE, UNIVERSITY OF
DEPARTMENT OF EXERCISE AND SPORT SCIENCE
1800 LINCOLN AVENUE
EVANSVILLE, IN 47722
812-479-2848
Fax: 812-479-2717
exss.evansville.edu
• Pam Young, EXSS Administrative Assistant
(812) 488-2848
py2@evansville.edu
• Terry Collins, Instructor
(812) 488-2091
tc7@evansville.edu
• Gregg Wilson, Department Chair/Exercise & SportsScience
(812) 488-2847
gw3@evansville.edu
• Kathy Liu, Assistant Professor/Exercise & Sports Science
(812) 488-2284
kl154@evansville.edu
• Laura McDonald, Assistant Professor/Exercise & SportsScience
(812) 488-2358
lm179@evansville.edu
• Michael Newhouse Bailey, Assistant Professor/Exercise & SportsScience
(812) 488-2288
mn41@evansville.edu
• Payal Patel Dovlatabadi, Assistant Professor/Exercise & SportsScience
(812) 488-2210
pp42@evansville.edu
• Donald Rodd, Professor Exercise SportScience/Physical The
(812) 488-1026
dr24@evansville.edu
• Troy Coppus, Instructor
(812) 488-2202
tc88@evansville.edu
Degrees Offered:
Undergrad Degree: B.S. Grad Degree: M.S. Areas of Specialization: Undergrad: Sports Administration; Athletic Training; Sports

Communications; Sports Studies. Grad: Physical Therapy.

FINGER LAKES COMMUNITY COLLEGE
3325 MARVIN SANDS DRIVE
Canandaigua, NY 14424
585-394-FLCC
www.flccathletics.com
• Barbara Risser, President/ Chief Executive Officer
• Charles P. McCausland, Chair
Degrees/Majors Offered:
A.S. sports and tourism studies.

FLAGLER COLLEGE
74 KING STREET
ST. AUGUSTINE, FL 32084
904-819-6481
800-304-4208
admissions@flagler.edu
www.flagler.edu
• Bernadette Twardy, Professor, Department Chair
• Danielle Stanley, Adjunct Sports Management
• Allan Bohl, Adjunct Sports Management
• Anne DeMartini, Assistant Professor
• Calvin Hunter, Professor, Sport Management
Degree Offered:
B.A. Sport Management

FLORIDA A&M UNIVERSITY- DEPARTMENT OF HEALTH & PHYSICAL EDUCATION
1800 WAHNISH WAY
LAWSON MULTIPURPOSE CTR/TEACHING
GYM SUITE 433
TALLAHASSEE, FL 32307
850-599-3135
Fax: 850-599-8365
www.famu.edu/athletics
• Janet M. Sermon, Chair & Assistant Professor
(850) 599-3135
janet.sermon@famu.edu
Degree/Majors Offered:
M.S. physical education.

FLORIDA ATLANTIC UNIVERSITY COLLEGE OF BUSINESS
777 GLADES ROAD
FLEMING HALL WEST 116
BOCA RATON, FL 33431
561-297-3000
Fax: 561-297-4054
jriordan@fau.edu
www.fau.edu/mbasport
• Dr Jim Riordan, MBA Sport Management Program Director
jriordan@fau.edu
• David Abrams, Executive Director/Sports Financing
Description:
Florida's Original AACSB-Accredited MBA in Sports Management Program. Admission to, and retention in program is highly competitive and rigorous. MBA Sports students may not work outside the sports industry while enrolled in the program. Transfer students are not accepted into the program. MBA Sport is not designed for those aspiring to be coaches, fitness trainers, athletic trainers, or other sport medicine professions.
Curriculum

The MBASport curriculum consists of the core courses required of all FAU MBA students, plus a 12 credit specialization in Sport Management. Full-time course load is considered to be nine hours for the fall and spring semesters and six hours in the summer semester. Part-time study or a certificate program is not offered.

FLORIDA INTERNATIONAL UNIVERSITY
DEPARTMENT OF LEADERSHIP & PROFESSIONAL SERVICES
BS & MS IN RECREATION AND SPORT MANAGEMENT
MIAMI, FL 33199
305-348-2114
Fax: 305-348-1515
robert.wolff@fiu.edu
• Robert Wolff, Professor/Program Director
(305) 348-2114
wolffr@fiu.edu
• Richard Lopez, Assoc. Professor/Program Coordinator
(305) 348-2075
lopezr@fiu.edu
• Charmaine DeFrancesco, Associate Professor
(305) 348-3163
defrance@fiu.edu
Description:
BS and MS degrees in Recreation and Sport Management.

FLORIDA SOUTHERN COLLEGE- BARNEY BARNETT SCHOOL OF BUSINESS & FREE ENTERPRISE
CARLISLE ROGERS BUILDING
MCDONALD STREET
111 LAKE HOLLINGSWORTH DRIVE
LAKELAND, FL 33801-5698
863-680-4280
Fax: 863-680-4355
www.flsouthern.edu//athletics
• Anne B. Kerr, President of Florida Southern College
Degree/Majors Offered:
Business degree, concentration in sport management.

FLORIDA STATE UNIVERSITY
THE COLLEGE OF EDUCATION,FLORIDA STATE UNIVERSITY
P.O BOX 3064450, 1114 W. CALL STREET
SUITE 1100 STB
TALLAHASSEE, FL 32306-4450
850-644-6885
Fax: 850-644-2725
www.coe.fsu.edu
• Jordan Bass, Coordinator, Lifetime Activities Program
(850) 644-7903
jbass@fsu.edu
• Karen L White, Executive Support Assistant
(850) 644-0371
klwhite@fsu.edu
• Janice Reed, Executive Support Assistant
(850) 644-1141
jreed@fsu.edu
• Shannon Barksdale, Departmental Accounting Associate
(850) 644-4854
sbarksdale@fsu.edu
• Kerry Behnke, Administrative Support Asstistant
(850) 645-8382
kbehnke@fsu.edu

• Michaela Densmore, Research and Information Coordinator
(850) 644-8823
mdensmore@admin.fsu.edu
• Derek Taylor, Human Resources Administrator
(850) 644-4944
det02@admin.fsu.edu
• Erika Bettilyon, Office Manager
(850) 644-7197
ebettilyon@fsu.edu
Description:
Undergrad Degree: B.S. Grad Degree: M.S., Ph.D., Ed.D. Areas of Specialization: Undergrad: Degree in Physical Education with Major in Sport Management. Grad: Degree in Physical Education with Major in Sport Administration. Non-Degree Specialization: Coaching.

FLORIDA, UNIVERSITY OF
PO BOX 118205
GAINESVILLE, FL 32611
352-392-3261
Fax: 352-392-5262
www.ufl.edu
• Charles E. Young, President of the University
• Bernie Macheen, President
• David R. Colburn, Provost & Vice President Academic Affairs
• Winfred M. Phillips, VP for Research & Dean of the Graduate School
• Ed Poppell, Vice President Academic Affairs
Description:
B.S. in Sport Management; M.S. in Sport Management, PH.D. with a majow in sport management.

FONTBONNE UNIVERSITY- ECKELKAMP COLLEGE OF GLOBAL BUSINESS & PROFESSIONAL STUDY
6800 WYDOWN BOULEVARD
ST. LOUIS, MO 63105
314-862-3456
800-205-5862
fbyou@fontbonne.edu
www.fontbonne.edu
Sports Management Major:
Fontbonne's sports management program is unique because of its emphasis on business, science, nutrition and health. Plus, with Fontbonne's student-centered approach to teaching and small student-to-teacher ratio, student's always receive individual attention.

FRANKLIN PIERCE UNIVERSITY
40 UNIVERSITY DRIVE
Rindge, NH 03461-0060
603-899-4000
800-437-0048
• Rodney Blackman, Assistant Professor, Business Administration
blackmanr@franklinpierce.edu
Degrees/Majors Offered:
B.S. within Division of Business Administration in sports and recreation management, marketing, arts management, accounting/finance.

FRESNO PACIFIC UNIVERSITY-
1717 S. CHESTNUT AVENUE
FRESNO, CA 93702-4709
559-453-2000
www.fresno.edu

GARDNER-WEBB UNIVERSITY
110 SOUTH MAIN STREET
PO BOX 997
BOILING SPRINGS, NC 28017
704-406-4000
800-253-6472
admissions@gardner-webb.edu
www.gardner-webb.edu/athletics
• A Frank Bonner, President
Description:
Sport management

GARRETT COLLEGE
ADVENTURESPORT INSTITUTE
687 MOSSER ROAD
MCHENRY, MD 21541
301-387-3000
Fax: 301-387-3325
adventuresports@garrettcollege.edu
www.garrettcollege.edu/athletics
• Michael Logsdon, Chair/Director
avs@garrettcollege.edu
Description:
A.A.S. adventure sports, certificate in adventure sports

GEORGE MASON UNIVERSITY- SCHOOL OF RECREATION, HEALTH, AND TOURISM
4400 UNIVERSITY DRIVE MS4F3
FAIRFAX, VA 22030
www.csm.gmu.edu
Sports Management Program
Description:
Mission at the Center for Sport Management is to advance the study and practice of sport management in all of its dimensions. The Center will support substantive research initiatives and provide service to stakeholders in sport for the purpose of enhancing sport industry practice. The Center for Sport Management was founded in the Spring of 2008 under a George Mason University Charter prepared by Dr. Robert E. Baker. The Center is housed within the College of Education and Human Development.

GEORGE WASHINGTON UNIVERSITY - THE GW SCHOOL OF BUSINESS
2201 G STREET NW
DUQUES HALL
WASHINGTON, DC 20052
202-994-6380
Fax: 202-994-2286
delpy@gwu.edu
www.business.gwu.edu
• Edard Barrientos, President & CEO
• Mitchell Blaser, CFO & COO
• James T. Blumenthal, Executive Vice President & CFO
• Burlie Brunson, President and Chief Operating Officer Defense
• Doug Guthrie, Professor/ Dean GS School of Business
(202) 994-6623
delpy@gwu.edu
• Cassandra Howard, Administrative Director
(202) 994-4530
• Laura Ortiz-Calder, Associate Director
(202) 994-9326
Description:
Graduate degrees, fields of concentration: sport management, event and meeting management, individualized studes; M.B.A. and online programs.

GEORGETOWN UNIVERSITY
SCHOOL OF CONTINUING STUDIES
3307 M ST, NW
SUITE 202
WASHINGTON, DC 20007
202-687-8700
• Matt Winkler, Associate Dean of MPS Sports Industry Management
(202) 687-7149
mvw4@georgetown.edu
• Kristen Consolo, MPS Sports Industry Management Program Manage
(202) 687-0924
kac225@georgetown.edu
Degrees Offered:
MPS Sports Industry Management

GEORGIA SOUTHERN UNIVERSITY-DEPT OF HOSPITALITY, TOURISM, & FAMILY CONSUMER SCI
PO BOX 8034
STATESBORO, GA 30460
912-478-5345
Fax: 912-681-0386
www.georgiasouthern.edu
• Henry Eisenhart, Chair/Director
(912) 681-5462
henry_e@georgiasouthern.edu
• Tony Lachowetz, Professor
burdenw@gsaixz.cc.gasou.edu
• Willie Burden, Associate Professor
(912) 681-5922
Description:
Undergrad Degree: B.S. Health Science, with Major in Sport Management. Grad Degree: M.S. in Sport Management. Areas of Specialization: Athletic Administration; Sport Promotion; Sport Communications.

GEORGIA STATE UNIVERSITY
125 DECATUR STREET
ATLANTA, GA 30303
404-651-2536
Fax: 404-651-4814
www.georgiastatesports.com
• Jeffrey Rupp, Exercise Science Associate Professor
(404) 651-3978
jrupp@gsu.edu
• Cheryl Levick, Director of Athletics
(404) 413-4005
• James Greenwell, Executive Senior Associate Athletics Director
(404) 413-4007
jgreenwell@gsu.edu
• Jamie Boggs, Senior Associate Athletics Director, Compliance
(404) 413-4008
jboggs@gsu.edu
• Tiffany Daniels, Senior Associate Athletics Director, External
(404) 413-4018
tdaniels8@gsu.edu
• John Portland, Senior Associate Athletics Director, Internal
(404) 413-4006
jportland@gsu.edu
• Mark Nagel, Recreation Associate Professor
(404) 651-4680
mnagel@gsu.edu
• Sekeia Smith, Administrative Coordinator
(404) 651-2536
ssmith@gsu.edu
Description:
Grad Degree: M.S. Areas of Specialization: College and University; Sports Club Management; Facilities Management;

Sports Information; Sports Marketing & Promotion; Coaching.

GEORGIA, UNIVERSITY OF
DEPARTMENT OF KINESIOLOGY
115 RAMSEY
ATHENS, GA 30602
706-542-4378
Fax: 706-542-3148
www.coe.uga.edu
• Priscilla Carter, Academic Advisor II
• David Avin, Senior Accounatant
(706) 542-4384
• Thomas Baker, Assistant Professor - Sport Management Progra
• Ted Baumgartner, Professor - Exercise Science Program
• Kevin Byon, Assistant Professor - Sport Management Progra
• Billy Hawkins, Sport Studies Program Coordinator
(706) 542-4427
bhawk@uga.edu
• Ted Baumgartner, Graduate Program Coordinator/Prof.
(706) 542-4424
Description:
Grad Degree: M.Ed. Areas of Specialization: Intercollegiate and Pofessional Sport Management; Facility and Event Management; Management of Sports Agencies and/or Organizations. M.Ed., M.S. and PhD. in sport studies

GLENVILLE STATE COLLEGE-
200 HIGH STREET
GLENVILLE, WV 26351
304-462-7361
800-924-2010
www.glenville.edu
Sport Management Program:
Offers bachelor's undergraduate studies in sport management.

GRACELAND UNIVERSITY-COLLEGE OF LIBERAL ARTS AND SCIENCES
DIVISION OF HEALTH & MOVEMENT SCIENCES
1 UNIVERSITY PLACE
LAMONI, IA 50140
641-784-5000
800-833-0524
www.graceland.edu
Programs:
B.A. in Sport Management

GRAMBLING STATE UNIVERSITY
SCHOOL OF GRADUATE STUDIES
GSU BOX 4244
ASSEMBLY CENTER ROOM 148
GRAMBLING, LA 71245
318-274-2294
Fax: 318-274-6053
www.gram.edu
• Willie Daniel, Director
(318) 274-2294
• Robert Lyons, Coordinator
• Darlene Kluka
Description:
Grad Degree: M.S. Areas of Specialization: Sport Administration.

GREENSBORO COLLEGE
815 WEST MARKET STREET
GREENSBORO, NC 27401

800-346-8226
www.greensborocollegesports.com
• Randy Hunt, Chair/Director
Description:
B.S. athletic training, B.S. physical education, B.S. exercise and sport studies. Concentrations in exercise science, sport administration, sport behavior, sport coaching.

GREENVILLE COLLEGE
DEPARTMENT OF HEALTH, PHYSICAL EDUCATION & RECREATION
315 E. COLLEGE AVENUE
GREENVILLE, IL 62246-1145
618-664-2800
800-345-4440
Fax: 618-664-1060
www.greenville.edu
• Roy Molholland, Department Chair/Associate Professor
(618) 664-6625
roy.molholland@greenville.edu
• Eugene Dunkley, Biology Department Chair and Associate Profes
(618) 664-6543
eugene.dunkley@greenville.edu
• Doug Faulkner, Athletic Director; Associate Professor of Hea
(618) 664-6620
doug.faulkner@greenville.edu
• Norm Hall, Vice President and Dean of Student Developmen
(618) 664-7119
norm.hall@greenville.edu
• Steven Heilmer, Art Department Chair and Associate Professor
(618) 664-6811
susan.hughey-rasler@greenville.edu
• Richard Huston, History and Political Science Department Chai
(618) 664-6824
richard.huston@greenville.edu
• Darell Ller, Chemistry Department Chair, Professor of Chem
(618) 664-6540
darrell.iler@greenville.edu
• Robert Johnson, Professor/Department Head
(618) 664-6626
robert.johnnson@greenville.edu
Description:
Undergrad Degree: B.S. in Recreation. Areas of Specialization: Adult Fitness, Sports Administration, Recreation Leadership.

GUILFORD COLLEGE
DEPARTMENT OF SPORT STUDIES
5800 W. FRIENDLY AVENUE
GREENSBORO, NC 27410
336-316-2000
Fax: 336-316-2956
www.guilford.edu
• Robert Malekoff, Sport Studies Coordinator
(336) 316-2329
• Lavon Williams, Chairman/Associate Professor
(336) 316-2495
Description:
Undergrad Degree: B.S., Sport Management. Areas of Specialization: Sport Management, Physical Education Teaching/Coaching, Sports Medicine.

HAMPTON UNIVERSITY
130 HOLLAND HALL, ROOM 130
HAMPTON, VA 23668
757-727-5000
Fax: 757-727-5813
www.hamptonu.edu
• William R. Harvey, President of Hampton University
Description:
B.S. in Sport Management.

HARDIN-SIMMONS UNIVERSITY
2200 HICKORY
ABILENE, TX 79698-6210
325-670-1000
877-GO-HSUTX
Fax: 325-670-1572
www.hsuathletics.com
• Bob Moore, Director for Kinesiology, Sport And Recreatio
(325) 670-1265
bemoore@hsutx.edu
Degrees Offered:
M.Ed. Sports and Recreation Management; M.Ed. Advanced Physical Education, Physical Therapy.

HARDING UNIVERSITY
915 E. MARKET AVENUE
SEARCY, AR 72143
501-279-4761
Fax: 501-279-4138
Kinesiology@harding.edu
www.harding.edu
• Stephen Burks, Department Chairman
(501) 279-4761
Description:
College recreational setting.
Affiliations:
Member of NCAA Division II

HENDERSON STATE UNIVERSITY
1100 Henderson Street
ARKADELPHIA, AR 71999-0001
870-230-5000
hsusports.com
• Ron Dewlen, Director
Degree:
B.S.E. physical education, B.S. recreation, B.S. athletics training, M.S. sport administration, M.S.E. crriculum instruction/physical education.

HIGH POINT UNIVERSITY - EARL N. PHILLIPS SCHOOL OF BUSINESS
833 MONTIEU AVENUE
HIGH POINT, NC 27262
800-345-6993
www.highpoint.edu/sport-management
• Jim Wehrley, Dean of the School of Business
(336) 841-4560
jwehrley@highpoint.edu
Description:
B.S. sport management, M.S. sports studies

HOLY FAMILY UNIVERSITY
9801 Frankford Avenue
Philadelphia, PA 19114
215-637-7700
Fax: 215-637-6675
• Tony DiPrimio, Director
• Sandra Michael, Athletics Director
(215) 637-7700
smichael@holyfamily.edu

Degree/majors offered:
B.A. sports marketing management.

HOUSTON, UNIVERSITY OF
104 GARRISON GYMNASIUM
HOUSTON, TX 77204-6321
713-743-9849
Fax: 713-743-9860
www.hhp.uh.edu
• Norma Olvera, Director
• James J. Zhang, Associate Professor
(713) 743-9869
• Demetrius Pearson, Associate Professor and Program Coordinator
• Warren Whisenant, Director
wwhisenant@uh.edu
Description:
B.S. in Kinesiology with concentration in Sports Administration/M.Ed, in Sports and Fitness Administration.

HOWARD PAYNE UNIVERSITY
1000 Fisk Street
Brownwood, TX 76801
325-649-8020
800-880-4HPU
Fax: 325-649-8901
enroll@hputx.edu
www.hputx.edu
• Rick Beelby, Director
rbeelby@hputx.edu
Degree:
B.S. exercise and sport science with the following specialization: physical education, exercise and sport management, athletics training.

IDAHO STATE UNIVERSITY-DEPARTMENT OF SPORT SCIENCE AND PHYSICAL EDUCATION
921 S 8TH AVE, STOP 8105
POCATELLO, ID 83209-8089
208-282-2783
www.ed.isu.edu
Sport Management Program:
Offering Sport Management as a minor course of study in the undergraduate program.

IDAHO, UNIVERSITY OF
RECREATION DEPARTMENT
875 PERIMETER DR.
MS 2302
MOSCOW, ID 83844-2302
208-885-7921
Fax: 208-885-2862
www.govandals.com
• Kathy Browder, Interim Dept. Chairperson
(208) 885-7921
hperd@uidaho.edu
• Rob Spear, Director of Athletics
(208) 885-0243
• Matt Kleffner, Associate AD for Administration
(208) 885-0214
• Tim Mooney, Associate AD for External Operations
(208) 885-0258
• John Wallace, Associate AD for Compliance and Eligibility
(208) 885-0219
• Mario Reyes, Faculty Athletic Representative
(208) 885-6478
• Emily Adams, Administrative Assistant Sr.
(208) 885-0259

Description:
Undergrad Degree: B. S. Recreation. Grad Degree: M.S. Recreation. Areas of Specialization: Sport & Recreation Management; Sports Science; Athletic Training.

ILLINOIS AT CHICAGO, UNIVERSITY OF
DEPT OF KINESIOLOGY
901 W. ROOSEVELT RD
CHICAGO, IL 60608
312-996-9685
Fax: 312-413-3699
www.uc.edu
Description:
Grad Degree: M.S. Areas of Specialization: Sport Management, Adult Fitness, Exercise Physiology, Curriculum and Instruction.

ILLINOIS AT URBANA-CHAMPAIGN, UNIVERSITY OF
DEPARTMENT OF RECREATION, SPORT AND TOURISM
104 HUFF HALL
1206 S. 4TH STREET
CHAMPAGNE, IL 61820
217-333-4410
Fax: 217-244-1935
www.rst.uiuc.edu
• Cary McDonald, Dept. Head
• Bill McKinney, Ph.D, Dept. Associate Professor
• Jim Hefferman, Wrestling Head Coach
(217) 333-5853
Description:
B.S. in Leisure Studies with a concentration in Sport Management/M.S., PhD in Sport Management.

ILLINOIS STATE UNIVERSITY
SCHOOL OF KINESIOLOGY AND RECREATION
CAMPUS BOX 5120
NORMAL, IL 61790-5120
309-438-8661
Fax: 309-438-5559
kinrec@ilstu.edu
www.kinrec.ilstu.edu
• Babara Arboqast, Office Support Specialist
(304) 438-5952
barbogas@ilstu.edu
• Terri Jordan, Chief Clerk
(309) 438-5782
tljorda@ilstu.edu
• Miranda D. Kinney, Academic Advisor
(309) 438-5782
mdkinn2@ilstu.edu
• Alan Lacy, Professor & Director
(309) 438-3054
aclacy@ilstu.edu
• Alan Lacy, Professor/Director
(309) 438-8661
aclacy@ilstu.edu
• Robert Rossman, Ph.D, Professor/Dean
(309) 438-7602
jrrossm@ilstu.edu
• Steve McCaw, Professor
Description:
Grad Degree: M.S. in Health & Physical Education, with concentration in Sports Administration. Areas of Specialization: Sport Management, Recreational Sport Management, Recreational Park Administration.

INCARNATE WORD, UNIVERSITY OF THE
SPORT MANAGEMENT
4301 BROADWAY
SAN ANTONIO, TX 78209
210-829-6000
800-749-WORD
Fax: 210-805-3574
www.uiw.edu/athletics

INDIANA STATE UNIVERSITY
200 NORTH SEVENTH STREET
TERRE HAUTE, IN 47809-1902
812-237-2183
Fax: 812-237-2493
www.indstate.edu
• Dan McLean, Chairperson
• Linda Swift, Office Manager
(812) 237-2183
l-swift@indstate.edu
Description:
Grad Degree: M.S./M.A. Areas of Specialization: Sports Management, On-line Degree.

INDIANA UNIVERSITY
KELLEY SCHOOL OF BUSINESS
INDIANA UNIVERSITY
1309 E. 10TH STREET
BLOOMINGTON, IN 47405-1701
812-855-0221
Fax: 812-855-8679
kelleyse@indiana.edu
• Thomas Bowers, Co-Director
bowers@indiana.edu
• Timothy Baldwin, Co-Director
Degrees Offered:
M.B.A. with majors in marketing, strategic management, consulting, finance, e-business.

INDIANA UNIVERSITY OF PENNSYLVANIA
1011 South Drive
Indiana, PA 15705
724-357-2100
iupathletics.com
• Elaine Blair, Director
bkostel@iup.edu
Degree/Majors Offered:
Bachelor's in physical education and sport, sport administration track, master's in sport science, sport management track.

INDIANA UNIVERSITY, BOOMINGTON-DEPARTMENT OF KINESIOLOGY
1025 E.7TH STREET
HPER 112
BLOOMINGTON, IN 47405
812-855-5523
www.indiana.edu
Sport Management Program:
Graduate sport management program offers course work providing an interdisciplinary approach to the study of sport management intended to provide a thorough foundation in business and sport while allowing flexibility for students to explore a wide variety of opportunities within the field.

INDIANA UNIVERSITY-PURDUE UNIVERSITY INDIANAPOLIS
SCHOOL OF PHYSICAL EDUCATION & TOURISM MANAGEMENT
420 UNIVERSITY BLVD.
INDIANAPOLIS, IN 46202

317-274-5555
www.iupui.edu
Program Description:
The curriculum for Bachelor of Science in Physical Education includes classes from a variety of disciplines, a minor or certificate in business, and culminates with an internship program designed to give the student hands-on experience in the field. Students must pursue the business minor or business certificate in conjunction with sport management courses to earn their degree.

IOWA STATE UNIVERSITY
DEPARTMENT OF HEALTH AND HUMAN PERFORMANCE
FORKER BUILDING
AMES, IA 50011
515-294-8009
Fax: 515-294-8740
hhp@iastate.edu
www.facsen.iastate.edu
• Rick Sharp, Professor/Graduate Coordinator
(515) 294-8650
rlsharp@iastate.edu
• Suzzane Hendrich, President
• Jerry Thomas, Dept. Chairperson
Degrees Offered:
Undergrad Degree: B.S. Emphasis - Sports Management. Grad Degree: Ph.D. Emphasis - Sports Management, M.S. Emphasis - Sports Management, M.Ed. Emphasis - Sports Management.

IOWA, UNIVERSITY OF
DEPARTMENT OF HSS
E115 FIELD HOUSE
IOWA CITY, IA 52242-1111
319-335-9335
Fax: 319-335-6669
joyce-murphy@uiowa.edu
www.uiowa.edu
• Susan Birrell, Dept. Chairperson
(319) 335-9335
susan-birrell@uiowa.edu
• Katie Dougherty, Womens Tennis Head Coach
(319) 335-9259
katherine-dougherty@uiowa.edu
• Christine Grant, Athletic Administration
(319) 335-9186
christine-grant@uiowa.edu
• Larry Wieczorek, Track And Field Head Coach
(319) 335-3257
larry-wieczorek@uiowa.edu
• Sharon Dingman, Volleyball Head Coach
(319) 335-8181
sharon-dingman@uiowa.edu
Degrees Offered:
M.A. Sport and Leisure Management Ph.D. Athletic Administration

ITHACA COLLEGE
DEPARTMENT OF SPORT MANAGEMENT & MEDIA
12 HILL CENTER
ITHACA, NY 14850-7193
607-274-3192
Fax: 607-274-1943
jwocohan@ithaca.edu
www.ithaca.edu
• Annemarie Farrel, Associate Professor and Chair
• Criag Paiement, Assistant Professor and Chair Graduate Progra

• Wayne Blann, Professor
• Beth Cavalier, Lecturer
• Heather Dicter, Assistant Professor
• Lana Walsh, Administrative Assistant
• John Wolohan, Department Chair, Sports Management/Media
Degrees Offered:
Offfers both undergraduate and graduate sports management programs. Undergraduate focus is on sports media and sports studies; graduate focus is on sports management.

JACKSONVILLE UNIVERSITY- SCHOOL OF EDUCATION
2800 UNIVERSITY BLVD N
JACKSONVILLE, FL 32211
800-255-2027
www.ju.edu
Sport Management Program:
The School of Education offers a Masters of Education with three concentrations: Instructional Leadership and Organizational Development, Sport Management and Leadership, and Educational Leadership (Aspiring Principals).

JERSEY CITY STATE COLLEGE
ATHL RECREATIONAL FITNESS CENTER
324-338 W. SIDE AVE
JERSEY CITY, NJ 7305
201-547-3315
www.njcu.edu
• Eugene E. Bacha, Chairman Sport & Leisure Studies
Description:
Undergrad Degree: B.S. in Business, with concentration in Sport Management. Also offer minors in Fitness Specialist and Movement Training.

JOHNSON & WALES UNIVERSITY SPORTS ENT. / EVENT MANAGEMENT
THE HOSPITALITY COLLEGE
8 ABBOTT PARK PLACE
PROVIDENCE, RI 2903
401-598-1475
Fax: 401-598-1125
www.jwu.edu
• Richard Brush, Dean
(401) 598-4621
richard.brush@jwu.edu
• Katie Davin, Dept. Chairperson/Associate Professor
(401) 598-4623
kdavin@jwu.edu
• Jennifer Adams-Gailpeau, Associate Professor
(401) 598-1813
jennifer.galipeau@jwu.edu
Description:
Undergrad Degree: B.S. Sports/Facilities. Grad Degree: Hospitality Administration. Areas of Specialization: Skills necessary to manage sports/entertainment venues, public assembly facilities and event operations.

JUDSON UNIVERSITY- COLLEGE OF LIBERAL ARTS & SCIENCES
1151 N. STATE STREET
ELGIN, IL 60123
847-628-2500
www.judsonu.edu/
Sport Management Program:
Sport Administration is a cross-divisional concentration (sport, physical education,

business administration and communication arts).

KANSAS UNIVERSITY
DEPARTMENT OF HEALTH, SPORT AND EXERCISE SCIENCES
ROBINSON CENTER, ROOM 161
1301 SUNNYSIDE DRIVE
LAWRENCE, KS 66045-7567
785-864-5552
Fax: 785-864-3343
hsesinfo@ku.edu
www.soe.ku.edu
• James LaPoint, Graduate Coordinator
• Keith Tennant, Dept. Chairman
• Leon Greene, Undergraduate Coordinator
(785) 864-0775
jlg@ku.edu
Description:
Undergrad Degree: B.S. in Ed. Grad Degree: M.S., Ph.D., Ed.D. Areas of Specialization: Undergrad: Sport Sciences; Sport Administration (in Physical Education); Grad: Sport Administration (Specialization in Physical Education) at Master's, Doctorate level.

KENNESAW STATE UNIVERSITY
DEPARTMENT OF EXERCISE SCIENCE AND SPORT MANAGEMENT
1000 CHASTAIN ROAD
KENNESAW, GA 30144
470-578-6000
tdonovan@kennesaw.edu
www.kennesaw.edu
Description:
Undergrad Degree: B.S. in Sport Management.

KENT STATE UNIVERSITY
SCHOOL OF FOUNDATION, LEADERSHIP AND ADMIN. -SPORT ADM.
264 MEMORIAL ANNEX
KENT, OH 44242
330-672-2015
Fax: 330-672-4106
www.kent.edu
• Mark Lyberger, Sports Coordinator/Professor
mlyberge@kent.edu

KENTUCKY, UNIVERSITY OF
UK ATHLETICS
JOE CRAFT CENTER
338 LEXINGTON AVE.
LEXINGTON, KY 40506-0219
859-257-8000
www.ukathletics.com
• Mitch Barnhart, Director of Athletics
(859) 257-8015
mbarn@uky.edu
• Gary Henderson, Baseball Head Coach
(859) 257-2880
Description:
M.S. in Sport Management; Ed.D with emphasis in Sport Management.

KEUKA COLLEGE
141 CENTRAL AVENUE
KEUKA PARK, NY 14478
315-279-5000
800-33-KEUKA
keukaathletics.com
• Ann M Tuttle, Director
atuttle@mail.keuka.edu
• David Sweet, Athletics Director

(315) 279-5682
dsweet@mail.keuka.edu
• Seth Fikes, Sports Information Director
(315) 279-5241
Degrees/Majors Offered:
Management major, concentration in sports management.

KEYSTONE COLLEGE- SPORT AND RECREATION MANAGEMENT
ONE COLLEGE GREEN
PO BOX 50
LA PLUME, PA 18440-0200
570-945-8000
877-426-5549
www.keystone.edu/
Program:
Bachelor's Degree in Sport and Recreation Management.

KUTZTOWN UNIVERSITY- DEPARTMENT OF SPORT MANAGEMENT
15200 KUTZTOWN ROAD
KUTZTOWN, PA 19530
610-683-4499
www2.kutztown.edu
Description:
Leisure & sport studies, Kutztown University's leisure & sport studies program allows students to become prepared for a variety of opportunities ranging from community recreation program and health club management to the world of professional athletics operations.

LAKE ERIE COLLEGE-
391 WEST WASHINGTON STREET
PAINESVILLE, OH 44077
440-296-1856
800-533-4996
www.lec.edu
Description:
Offers undergraduate Bachelor's degree in Sport Management.

LANCASTER BIBLE COLLEGE-
901 EDEN ROAD
LANCASTER, PA 17601
717-569-7071
800-544-7335
www.lbc.edu
Sports Management & Ministry:
The Sports Management & Ministry major prepares men and women to serve Christ in the fields of sports management, sports ministry, and coaching. Students learn how to use biblical principles as they work in secular organizations, churches, or parachurch ministries. Field internships are key to the students' education because it is where they put into practice what they have learned in the classroom.

LASELL COLLEGE- SPORT MANAGEMENT DEPARTMENT
1844 COMMONWEALTH AVENUE
NEWTON, MA 2466
617-243-2000
Fax: 617-243-2380
www.lasell.edu
Program Description:
B.S. in Sport Management

LAURENTIAN UNIVERSITY
SCHOOL OF SPORTS ADMINISTRATION
935 RAMSEY LAKE ROAD
SUDBURY, ON, CANADA P3E 2C6
705-675-1151 EXT 4834
705-675-4834
Fax: 705-675-4836
www.laurentian.ca
• Ann Pegoraro, Director and Associate Professor
(705) 675-1151
• Lynn Levac, Administrative Assistant
(705) 675-4834
llevac@laurentian.ca
• Anthony Church, Associate Professor/ Internship Coordinator
(705) 675-1151
• Claude Vincent, Assistant Professor
(705) 675-1151
• Xiaoyan Xing, Assistant Professor
(705) 675-1151
Year Founded:
1972
Description:
Undergrad Degree: School of Sports Administration - Hon. B. Comm. (Sports Administration). Areas of Specialization: Undergrad: Sport Business Management.
Number of Members:
5 (4 faculty and 1 staff)

LE TOURNEAU UNIVERSITY
2100 S. MOBBERLY
LONGVIEW, TX 75602
903-753-0231
800-759-8811
Fax: 903-233-3495
www.letu.edu
• Melba Burry, Director Physical Education
Description:
Undergrad Degree: B.S. w/option in Sport Management.

LEES-MCRAE COLLEGE- WILLIAMS PHYSICAL EDUCATION CENTER
191 MAIN STREET
BANNER ELK, NC 28604
828-898-2484
Fax: 828-898-8742
www.lmc.edu
Sports Management Program:
The BS in Sport Management program is designed for those students with a career interest in athletic administration, coaching, recreational management, facilities management, and sport marketing.

LEHIGH CARBON COMMUNITY COLLEGE
4525 EDUCATION PARK DRIVE
SCHNECKSVILLE, PA 18078
610-799-2121
gocougarsports.com
• Joseph M Flaherty, Director
jflaherty@lccc.edu
Degree/Majors Offered:
A.S. sport management.

LENOIR-RHYNE COLLEGE
625 7TH AVENUE NE
HICKORY, NC 28601
828-328-7300
800-277-5721
Fax: 828-267-3445
• Michael McGee, Professor, Program Chair
(828) 328-7127
mcgee@lr.edu

• Katherine Pasour, Professor, Dean College of Health Sciences
(828) 328-7126
pasourk@lr.edu
Description:
Several quality programs are offered to students interested in athletic training, physical education, health and exercise science, and sports management. The programs are designed to provide optimum development of both physical and mental abilities in these areas.

LEWIS UNIVERSITY
ONE UNIVERSITY PARKWAY
ROMEOVILLE, IL 60446-2200
815-838-0500
800-897-9000
www.lewisu.edu/academics/sportsmanage/
Sport Management Program:
BA in Sport Management.

LIBERTY UNIVERSITY
SPORT MANAGEMENT DEPARTMENT
1971 UNIVERSITY BOULEVARD
LYNCHBURG, VA 24506
434-582-2445
Fax: 434-582-2468
www.liberty.edu/academics/education/sport
• Christoper Amos, Assistant Professor
• Philip Blosser, Associate Professor
• Andrew Coleman, Assistant Professor
• Jordan Davies, Adjunct Professor
• Scott Hawkins, Chairperson/Assistant Professor
(434) 582-2155
• Vicky Martin, Associate Professor,Chair
(434) 582-2445
Description:
The mission is to help students develop skills to organize, administer, and facilitate sport programs at the corporate, agency, professional, and amateur levels. Opportunities are provided to develop knowledge and skills relevant to the performance of these functions.
Degrees:
Undergrad Degree: B.S. Sport Management.

LIMESTONE COLLEGE- SPORT MANAGEMENT
1115 COLLEGE DR.
GAFFNEY, SC 29340-3799
864-489-7151
www.limestone.edu
Sport Management Major:
The Sport Management major is designed to provide students with an introductory understanding and preparation necessary to become successful managers in academic institutions or the sports industry. The program combines cor courses from the business administration and physical education disciplines that emphasize management skills, human resource skills, sound accounting practices, facilities management and wellness.

LINCOLN COLLEGE- SPORT MANAGEMENT PROGRAM
715 W. RAAB ROAD
NORMAL, IL 61761
309-452-0500
800-569-0558
www.lincolncollege.edu

Sport Management Program:
offers a bachelors degree program in sports management.

LINDENWOOD UNIVERSITY- SCHOOL OF BUSINESS & ENTREPRENEURSHIP
209 S. KINGSHIGHWAY
ST. CHARLES, MO 63301
636-949-4840
www.lindenwood.edu/business/index.html
Sports Management Program:
The MA in Sport Management is designed to prepare students for a career within the expanding sport industry. The MA curriculum is a unique blend of formal coursework and opportunities designed for practical experience.

LIPSCOMB UNIVERSITY- GRADUATE SCHOOL OF BUSINESS
ONE UNIVERSITY PARK DRIVE
NASHVILLE, TN 37204-3951
615-966-1000
800-333-4358
www.lipscomb.edu/gsb
Sport Management Program:
Offers A masters in business administration with concentration in sport management.

LIVINGSTONE COLLEGE
701 W. MONROE STREET
SALISBURY, NC 28144
704-216-6012
Fax: 704-216-6278
www.bluebearathletics.com
• Jimmy R. Jenkins Sr., President
(704) 216-6098
jjenkins@livingstone.edu
• Andre Springs, Men's Golf Coach
(704) 216-6933
asprings@livingstone.edu
• Blanche Ford, Administrative Assisstant
(704) 216-6012
bford@livingstone.edu
• Jamie Kent, Senior Womens Admin
(704) 216-6011
jkent@livingstone.edu
• Justin Davis, Track Head Coach
(704) 216-6317
jdavis@livingstone.edu
• James Stinson, Head Coach Men's Basketbal
(704) 216-6016
jstinson@livingstone.edu
• John Daniels, Athletic Photographer
(704) 216-6934
Description:
B.S. physical education, B.S. sport management

LOCK HAVEN UNIVERSITY OF PENNSYLVANIA
401 N. FAIRVIEW STREET
LOCK HAVEN, PA 17745
570-484-2011
www.lhup.edu/catalog/sport_administration/
Program Description:
B.S. Sport Administration. This well-reputed LHU degree is approved by the North American Society for Sport Management (NASSM). It emphasizes the administration of athletic programs and activities as well as sport business, marketing, media, and communications.

LONG BEACH STATE UNIVERSITY
DEPARTMENT OF KINSIOLOGY
HHS2 BUILDING, 1ST FLOOR
1250 BELLFLOWER BOULEVARD
LONG BEACH, CA 90840
562-985-4051
Fax: 562-985-8067
www.csulb.edu/programs/sportmanagement
• Sharon Guthrie, Ph.D, Dept. Chairperson
• Stephem Buchan, Associate Program Director / Adjunct Professo
• Diane Higgs, Manager of Student Affairs
• Ketra Armstrong, Ph.D, Graduate Program Director
• Chris Tsangaris, Managing Director/Internship Coord.
Description:
Undergrad Degree: B.A. Phys Ed. Grad Degree: M.A., Phys Ed, Sports Management specialization.

LORAS COLLEGE
1450 ALTA VISTA
PO BOX 178
CENTER GROVE, IA 52001
563-588-7053
Fax: 563-588-4975
www.loras.edu
• Susie Wehring, Physical Ed. Chair/Sports Program Dir.
Susie.Wehring@loras.edu
• William Joensen, Dean of Campus Spiritual Life
(563) 588-7463
william.joensen@loras.edu
• Collen Kuhl, Director of Campus Ministry
(563) 588-7924
colleen.kuhl@loras.edu
• Robert Gross, Associate Chaplain
(563) 588-7108
robert.gross@loras.edu
• Heather Jungblut, Executive Assistant to the Dean of Campus Spi
(563) 588-7104
heather.jungblut@loras.edu
• Debbie Gross, Campus Minister
(563) 588-7934
debbie.gross@loras.edu
• Matt Garrett, Sport Management Coordinator
(319) 588-7165
matthew.garrett@loras.edu
• Lori Behnke, Academic Secretary
lori.behnke@loras.edu
Degrees Offered:
B.A. Sport Management, M.A. Sport Administration.

LOUISIANA STATE UNIVERSITY
DEPARTMENT OF KINESIOLOGY
112 LONG FIELDHOUSE
BATON ROUGE, LA 70803-2401
225-578-2036
Fax: 225-578-3680
www.lsu.edu/athletics
• Amelia Lee, Dept. Chairperson/Professor
(225) 578-3551
amlee@lsu.edu
• Roy Hill, Sport Studies Instructor Coordinator
(225) 578-2926
rhill@lsu.edu

LOUISVILLE, UNIVERSITY OF
DEPARTMENT OF HEALTH AND SPORT SCIENCE
CRAWFORD GYM

ROOM 211
LOUISVILLE, KY 40292
502-852-6645
Fax: 502-852-4534
• Adelson Jill, Assistant Profesor
(502) 852-4877
jladel01@louisville.edu
• Meera Alagaraja, Assistant Professor
(502) 852-0617
m0alag01@louisville.edu
• Tammy Albers, Academic Advisor
(502) 852-3204
tammy.albers@louisville.edu
• Oscar A Aliaga, ProgramDirector
(502) 852-0585
oaalia01@louisville.edu
• Micheal ball, AdministrativeAssistant
(502) 852-6645
jmball01@louisville.edu
• Anita Moorman, Associate Professor/Asst. Dept. Chair
amm@louisville.edu
• Mary Hums, Sport Administration Professor
mhums@louisville.edu
Description:
Undergrad Degree: B.S. in Sport Administration, Graduate Degree: M.S. in Sport Administration. Minors in Business, Marketing, Communications, Exercise Science and Health Promotion.
Requirements:
Need 123 Hours in order to graduate with a degree in Health and Human Performance or Sport Administration, must apply for a degree check after completing 80-90 hours, apply for a degree during the first three weeks that you are going to graduate, must have 50 hours of 300 level or above courses in order to graduate, must have a 2.25 GPA in order to graduate, the normal load is 15 hours - maximum load is 17 hours; students wishing to take more than 17 hours must make application to seek permission.

LOYOLA UNIVERSITY CHICAGO
WATER TOWER CAMPUS
820 NORTH MICHIGAN AVENUE
CHICAGO, IL 60611
312-915-6000
www.luc.edu/athletics
• Keith Lambrecht, Director, Sport Management Program
(312) 915-6514
klambre@luc.edu

LUTHER COLLEGE
DEPARTMENT OF PHYSICAL EDUCATION AND HEALTH
700 COLLEGE DRIVE
DECORAH, IA 52101
563-387-2000
800-458-8437
Fax: 563-387-1458
thompsjo@luther.edu
www.luther.edu
• Joe Thompson, Dept. Chairperson/Associate Professor
(563) 387-1583
thompsjo@luther.edu
• Brian Solberg, Associate Prof. of HPE and Prog. Director Ath
(563) 387-1246
solberbr@luther.edu
• Gregory Lonning, Director of the Nena Amundson Lifetime Wellne
(563) 387-2075
lonningr@luther.edu

• Ellen Stoen, Assistant Professor of Health and Physical Ed
(563) 387-1587
drewesel@luther.edu
• Joe Thompson, Director of Intercollegiate Athletics
(563) 387-1575
thompsjo@luther.edu
• Jeffery Wettach, Assistant Professor of Health and Physical Ed
(563) 387-1577
wettacje@luther.edu
• Jacquelyn Wright, Associate Professor of Health and Physical Ed
(563) 387-1581
wrightja@luther.edu
• Mary Moen, HPE Secretary
(563) 387-1245
Description:
Undergrad Degree: B.A. Areas of Specialization: Phys Ed and Management programs.

LYNCHBURG COLLEGE- SPORT MANAGEMENT
1501 LAKESIDE DRIVE
LYNCHBURG, VA 24501
434-544-8100
www.lynchburg.edu/academics/majors-and-minors/sport-management
Sport Management Program:
offers bachelor's programs in sports management.

LYNN UNIVERSITY
3601 N. MILITARY TRAIL
BOCA RATON, FL 33431
561-237-7279
Fax: 561-237-7268
www.lynnfightingknights.com
• Kristen Migliano, Director of Athletics
(561) 237-7765
gmalfitano@lynn.edu
• Rudy Garbalosa, Baseball Head Coach
(561) 237-7242
rgarbolosa@lynn.edu
• Scott McMillin, Men's Basketball Head Coach
(561) 237-7053
smcmillin@lynn.edu
• Niki Washington, Women's Basketball Head Coach
(561) 237-7282
nwashington@lynn.edu
• Niki Alvarez, Women's Swimming/Women's Cross Country Head C
nalvarez@lynn.edu
Description:
Undergraduate degree in sports management that includes The Final Four, taking students into the field from Baseball Winter Meetings to the PGA Golf Tour.

MACMURRAY COLLEGE- SPORT MANAGEMENT
447 EAST COLLEGE AVENUE
JACKSONVILLE, IL 62650
217-479-7000
800-252-7485
publicinformation@mac.edu
www.mac.edu/
Sports management:
Offers a bachelor's program in sport management.

MADONNA UNIVERSITY- SPORT MANAGEMENT
36600 SCHOOLCRAFT ROAD
LIVONIA, MI 48150
800-852-4951
Fax: 734-432-5393
www.madonna.edu
Program Description:
The Sport Management program offers several educational opportunities.

MARIAN COLLEGE
DEPARTMENT OF SPORT STUDIES
3200 COLD SPRING ROAD
INDIANAPOLIS, IN 46222
317-955-6124
800-772-7264
morrell@marian.edu
• Lynn Morrell, Dept. Chairperson
morrell@marian.edu
• Leigh Ann Bussell, Sport Studies Professor
drbussell@marian.edu
Description:
The operation side of the sport industry. Sport management professionals, found both in amateur and professional realms, may be found performing a variety of tasks which include marketing, management, advertising, ticket sales, directing facilities and events, public relations, working in conjunction with sport agents, directing recreation programs, operating fitness systems, and working as a coach both in and outside school systems.
Requirements:
Major for Bachelor Degree (B.A. or B.S.) Sport Management: 37 to 40 hours, including HPE 128, 139, 230, 310, 354, 360, 410, ACC 210, BUS 101, 240, 250, ECN 200 or 201 or 202, MIS 102, 103, 104, PSY 101 or 220. Sport management majors desiring to minor in business must consult with the business department chair.

MARIAN UNIVERSITY-FOND DU LAC, SPORT MANAGEMENT PROGRAM
45 S. NATIONAL AVENUE
FOND DU LAC, WI 54935-4699
800-262-7426
Program:
Offering undergraduate programs in sports management.

MARQUETTE UNIVERSITY
1250 W. WISCONSIN AVENUE
MILWAUKEE, WI 53233
414-288-7250
800-222-6544
Fax: 414-288-5818
www.marquette.edu
• William E Cullinan, Ph.D., Dean, College of Health Science
(414) 288-5053
william.cullinan@marquette.edu
• Kim L Halula, R.D.H., Ph.D., Associate Dean
(414) 288-0656
kim.halula@marquette.edu
Description:
Departments within the College of Health Sciences include: Athletic Training; Biomedical Sciences; Clinical Laboratory Science; Exercise Science; Physical Therapy; Physician Assistant; and Speech Pathology and Audiology

MARSHALL UNIVERSITY
DIV OF ESSR
COLLEGE OF EDUCATION
ONE JOHN MARSHALL DR
HUNTINGTON, WV 25755
304-696-5408
800-642-3463
Fax: 304-696-6448
www.marshall.edu
• T. Jeff Chandler, Chairman
Description:
Undergrad Degree: B.S. Sport Management & Marketing. Grad Degree: M.S. in Phys Ed with concentration in Athletic Administration and Sport Management. Areas of Specialization: Undergrad: Interdisciplinary comprehensive program in Sport Management and Marketing. Arena Management, Athletic Administration. Grad: Athletic Administration.

MARTIN METHODIST COLLEGE
SPORT MANAGEMENT
433 W. MADISON STREET
PULASKI, TN 38478
931-363-9804
800-467-1273
Fax: 931-363-9868
info@martinmethodist.edu
www.martinmethodist.edu
• Tim Wilson, Assistant Professor of Sport Management
(931) 363-9847
twilson@martinmethodist.edu
• Jeff Bain, Director of Athletics
Degree Offered:
B.S. Sport Management

MARYLAND, UNIVERSITY OF
DEPARTMENT OF KINESIOLOGY
HHP BUILDING, ROOM 2351
COLLEGE PARK, MD 20742-2611
301-405-2450
Fax: 301-405-5578
www.hhp.umd.edu/KNES/
• Jane Clark, Ph.D, Dept. Chairperson
jeclark@umd.edu
• Steve McDaniel, Pro General Manager Coordinator
• Wallace D. Loh, President
• Yunjoo Koo, HHP Coordinator
(301) 405-2497
ykoo@umd.edu
Description:
Grad Degree: M.A. Areas of Specialization: Professional sport, educational sport, club management, executive fitness programs.

MARYMOUNT UNIVERSITY- SPORT MANAGEMENT
2807 NORTH GLEBE ROAD
ARLINGTON, VA 22207
703-522-5600
www.marymount.edu
Program Description:
The Sport Management specialty focuses on marketing, law, economics, and promotions within a sports context. In addition, the required internship provides students with an opportunity to gain a real-world experience with sports-related organizations and professional, semiprofessional, and collegiate teams in the DC area. Graduates with a Sport Management specialty are prepared for a variety of positions in the sports industry,

college sports

427

including marketing specialist, consultant, agent, and more.

MARYVILLE UNIVERSITY - JOHN E. SIMON SCHOOL OF BUSINESS
650 MARYVILLE UNIVERSITY DRIVE
ST. LOUIS, MO 63141
314-529-9300
800-627-9855
www.maryville.edu/academics-bu-sportsmanagement.htm
Sport Business Management Program:
The Maryville Sport Business Management program focuses on the general business disciplines of management, finance, marketing, operations management and communications and teaches students how to apply them to the sports industry.

MASSACHUSETTS AMHERST, UNIVERSITY OF
104 SKINNER HALL
AMHERST, MA 1003
413-545-0441
Fax: 413-577-0642
umsmdb@sportstudy.umass.edu
www.umassathletics.com
• Tracy Schoenadel, Director, Center for Sports Research
• Lisa Pike Masteralexis, Chair/Director
swl@sportmgt.umass.edu
• Ed Matz, Women's Soccer Head Coach
(413) 545-4343
edmatz@admin.umass.edu
• Elaine Sortino, Softball Head Coach
(413) 545-4099
elaine@admin.umass.edu
• Russ Yarworth, Men's Swimming & Diving Head Coach
(413) 545-0093
yarworth@admin.umass.edu
• Bob Newcomb, Women's Swimming & Diving Head Coach
(413) 545-4342
rnewc@admin.umass.edu
Degree Offered:
Ranking as the second oldest sports management department in the country, UMASS Amherst offers a B.S., M.S.,P.M.B.A./M.S., & Ph.D. in Sport Management. It has one of the few programs with a stand alone department in the business school.

MASSACHUSETTS COLLEGE OF LIBERAL ARTS- SPORT MANAGEMENT PROGRAM
375 CHURCH STREET
NORTH ADAMS, MA 1247
413-662-5000
Description:
B.A. with concentration in sport management

MCDANIEL COLLEGE - EXERCISE SCIENCE & PHYSICAL EDUCATION DEPARTMENT
2 COLLEGE HILL
WESTMINSTER, MD 21157
410-848-7000
www.mcdaniel.edu
Description:
B.A. & M.S. in Sport Management

MEDAILLE COLLEGE
SPORT MANAGEMENT
18 AGASSIZ CIRCLE
BUFFALO, NY 14214
716-880-2000
Fax: 800-292-1582
rjacob@medaille.edu
www.medaille.edu
• Richard Jacob, Sport Management Program Coordinator
rfacob@medaille.edu
• Douglas Hoard, Vice-President
• Judith Horoitz, Associate Professor, Associate Vice President
• Norman Muir, Associate Professor, and Dean, Undergraduate
• Illana Lane, Dean, School of Education, Associate Professo
• Brad Hollingshead, Associate Professor and Associate Dean for Fo
Description:
Undergrad Degree: B.S. Areas of Specialization: Sport Management, Recreation, Sports Communication.

MEMPHIS, UNIVERSITY OF
UNIVERSITY OF MEMPHIS
101 ILDER TOWER
MEMPHIS, TN 38152-3520
901-678-3480
Fax: 901-678-3591
• Mike Hamrick, Dept. Chairperson
(901) 678-4165
mhamrick@memphis.edu
• Richard Irwin, Director
(901) 678-3476
rirwin@memphis.edu
• Ryan Luttrell, National Sports Forum (NSF) Competition
Description:
Grad Degree: M.S. in Sport and Leisure Commerce. Areas of Specialization: Professional and Commercial Sport and Leisure, With Emphasis in Marketing. B.S. Ed. in Sport and Leisure Studies.

MENLO COLLEGE - SPORTS MANAGEMENT PROGRAM
1000 EL CAMINO REAL
ATHERTON, CA 94027-4301
650-543-3936
Fax: 650-543-4003
academics@menlo.edu
www.menlo.edu/academics/degrees/sports-management-degree
Description:
Sports Management Option in Management Major, B.S. in Business; The Sports Management program exposes students to all facets of the business of sports, including sports sponsorship relationships, team and league equity issues, labor and personnel management, and a wide variety of ethical and social issues facing business professionals in both professional and amateur athletics.

MERCY COLLEGE - SCHOOL OF HEALTH & NATURAL SCIENCES
555 BROADWAY
DOBBS FERRY, NY 10522
877-637-2946
www.mercy.edu
Sport Management Program Description:
B.S. in Exercise Science; The B.S. in Exercise Science is also valuable to help prepare students moving into graduate

programs for careers in physical therapy, occupational therapy, sports psychology, and physicians assistants, and kinesiology.

MERCYHURST COLLEGE
501 E. 38TH STREET
ERIE, PA 16546-0001
814-824-2000
Fax: 814-824-2172
www.mercyhurst.edu
• David Rubino, Ph.D., Interim Dean of Walker School
(814) 824-3034
• Amy Doolan, MBA, DBA, Associate Professor & Associate Dean
(814) 824-3604
Degree Offered:
B.A. Sport Business Management
Description:
The business of sport is one of the largest industries in the United States. Today's sport business managers need to have skills in the areas of planning, budgeting, managing, marketing, and leading organizations whose focus is on the sport industry. The curriculum of the sport business management major will prepare students for leadership roles in professional and amateur sports, school and college sports programs, the sporting goods industry, the sports news media, resorts, military and social agency sports programs, health and fitness clubs, and sport marketing and consulting firms.

MEREDITH COLLEGE
DEPARTMENT OF HEALTH, EXERCISE & SPORTS SCIENCE
3800 HILLSBOROUGH STREET
101 WEATHERSPOON ANNEX
RALEIGH, NC 27607
919-760-8309
Fax: 919-760-2828
campbellm@meredith.edu
www.meredith.edu
• Melinda Campbell, Dept. Head/Professor
Description:
B.S. exercise and sports science; B.S. exercise and sports science, concentration in physical education; B.S. exercise and sports science, concentration in fitness and sports management.

MERRIMACK COLLEGE - SPORT MANAGEMENT PROGRAM
315 TURNPIKE STREET
NORTH ANDOVER, MA 1845
978-837-5000
www.merrimack.edu/academics/business/sport-management/
Program Description:
B.S. in Sport Management: The sport management concentration is ideal for anyone who desires a career in sport marketing, events management, athletic administration, or facilities management, but also seeks the general business preparation for other career opportunities.

MESSIAH COLLEGE
One College Avenue
Grantham, PA 17027
717-766-2511
800-233-4220
www.messiah.edu/athletics
• Jack Cole, Director
jcole@messiah.edu

Degree/Majors Offered:
B.A. sport and exercise science, sport management concentration.

METHODIST COLLEGE
5400 RAMSEY STREET
FAYETTEVILLE, NC 28311
910-630-7000
800-488-7110
webmaster@methodist.edu
www.mumonarchs.com
• Greg Combs, Sports Management Coordinator
gcombs@methodist.edu
Description:
Graduates with a concentration in Sports Management (SMA) will have the skills and knowledge necessary to become effective entry-level managers and administrators in the business of sport. Students who choose a concentration in Sports Management are qualified for entry level management positions within professional sports teams and businesses affiliated with sport, sporting goods manufacturers, recreation facilities, and health and fitness clubs.
Degrees Offered:
B.A. major in sports management, sports administration concentration; B.A. major in sports management, well/fitness concentration; B.S. major in sports management, sports administration concentration; B.S. major in sports management, wellness/fitness concentraton.
Requirements:
Writing-Enrichment Course: BUS 352, Computer Intensive Course: BUS 225, Ethics Course: BUS 315. Requirements for the concentration in Sports Management: 21 s.h. _ SMA 321, SMA 322, SMA 421, SMA 422, BUS 354, BUS 375, and a 3 s.h. internship.

METROPOLITAN STATE COLLEGE OF DENVER - SPORT MANAGEMENT PROGRAM
CAMPUS BOX 25
PO BOX 17336
DENVER, CO 80217-3362
Program Description:
Human Performance and Sports Major with the Sports Industry Operations concentration. Students can get up to 16 hours of real world experiences for credit with two field experiences and an optional 10-credit hour internships are vital to the development of skills for individuals seeking a career in Sport Industry Operations. From player relations and media to day-of-game operations or facility management, the courses are designed to inspire and equip students with the knowledge they need to get the ball rolling.

MIAMI, UNIVERSITY OF
DEPARTMENT OF EXERCISE & SPORTS SCIENCES
SCHOOL OF EDUCATION
PO BOX 248065
CORAL GABLES, FL 33124-2040
305-284-3024
Fax: 305-284-5168
www.cehd.umn.edu
• Arlette Perry, Phd., Chairman
aperry@miami.edu
• Andy Gillentine, Chair/Director
soe@miami.edu

Description:
Undergrad Degree: Fifteen (15) credit undergraduate minors in Sports Management, Exercise Physiology and Sports Medicine. B.S.C.D. Sports Administration and B.S. Biology/Exercise Physiology; Grad Degree: M.S. Ed., Sports Administration, Sports Medicine and Exercise Physiology. Areas of Specialization: Intercollegiate and Professional Sports Management, Exercise & Sports Sciences, Human Performance and Wellness, Sports Medicine.

MICHIGAN STATE UNIVERSITY - DEPARTMENT OF KINESIOLOGY
102 IM SPORTS CIRCLE
MICHIGAN STATE UNIVERISTY
EAST LANSING, MI 48824-1049
517-432-1514
Fax: 517-432-2426
McNeilR@msu.edu
www.msu.edu
Program Description:
M.S. Concentration in Sport Administration: The master's degree concentration in sports administration is designed for individuals who are preparing for careers in administration of intercollegiate and interscholastic sport and recreation programs. Internships are available at local high schools, college/university settings, and other sports-related organizations and agencies.

MIDAMERICA NAZARENE UNIVERSITY - HEALTH AND EXERCISE SCIENCE
2030 E. COLLEGE WAY
OLATHE, KS 66062-1899
913-782-3750
800-800-8887
www.mnu.edu
Description:
B.A. in Sports Management

MIDDLE TENNESSEE STATE UNIVERSITY - HPERS DEPARTMENT
1301 EAST MAIN STREET
MURFREESBORO, TN 37132-0001
615-898-2300
Program Description:
M.S. in Sport Management; The graduate sport management concentration offers a cross discipline curriculum, focusing on professional preparation for the sports industry. Students will complete a degree program that includes courses in management, legal issues and facility design. Sport management courses will focus on the business aspects of sport in culture, interscholastic/intercollegiate and professional sports, facility management, sport ethics, sport marketing, sport law and sport finance.

MIDWAY COLLEGE - BUSINESS DEPARTMENT
512 E. STEPHENS ST.
MIDWAY, KY 40347
859-846-4421
800-755-0031
www.midway.edu/majors-programs/schools/business
Description:
B.A. in Sport Management

MILLERVILLE UNIVERSITY
OFFICE OF GRADUATE STUDIES
104 DILWORTH HALL
PO BOX 1002
MILLERVILLE, PA 17551-0302
717-872-3490
Fax: 717-871-2393
www.millersvilleathletics.com
• Stanley Kabacinski, Dept. Chairperson
• Rebecca Mowrey, Graduate Program Coordinator
• Esther Hernandez-Montano, Dept. Secretary
• Kyle Almoney, Women's Swimming Head Coach
(717) 872-3872
kalmoney@millersville.edu
• Shari Bucklin-Webber, Men's and Women's Tennis Head Coach
(717) 872-3946
swebber@millersville.edu
• Brian Smith, Women's Volleyball Head Coach
(717) 872-3946
bsmith1@millersville.edu
Degree Offered
M.Ed. Sport Management

MILLIKIN UNIVERSITY - COLLEGE OF PROFESSIONAL STUDIES
1184 WEST MAIN STREET
DECATUR, IL 62522
800-373-7733
www.millikin.edu/ess
Description:
B.S. in Sport Management; Students will learn the business of sports through a combination of coursework from the Department of Exercise Science & Sport and the Tabor School of Business. The business core provides a broad spectum of courses in specialized areas of the sport business community. The Sport Management curriculum follows the recommendations of the North American Society for Sport Management (NASSM).

MINNESOTA STATE UNIVERSITY-MANKATO
DEPARTMENT OF HUMAN PERFORMANCE
228 WIECKING CENTER
MANKATO, MN 56002-8400
507-389-6313
Fax: 507-389-5618
www.mnsu.edu
• Kent Kalm, Dept. Acting Chairperson
kent.kalm@mnsu.edu
• Jill Binstock, Dept. Secretary
(507) 389-6313
jilane.binstock@mnsu.edu
• Gary Rushing, Graduate Coordinator Sports Administration
(507) 389-2217
garold.rushing@mnsu.edu
Description:
Undergrad Degree: B. S. Grad Degree: M.A., M.S. Areas of Specialization: Sports Administration, Psycho-Social Aspects of Sports.

MINNESOTA, UNIVERSITY OF
DEPARTMENT OF KINESIOLOGY
111 COOKE HALL
1900 UNIVERSITY AVENUE SE
MINNEAPOLIS, MN 55455

612-625-5300
Fax: 612-626-7700
kin@umn.edu
• Mary Jo Kane, Director/Professor
maryjo@umn.edu
• Jo Ann Buysse, Sport Studies Program
Coordinator
(612) 625-5331
buyss003@umn.edu
Description:
Grad Degree: M.A. and Ph.D. in Kinesiology
or Recreation & Leisure Studies. Areas of
Specialization: Multi-Disciplinary Program
including Business, Communications,
Education and Sociology, in addition to
Kinesiology and Leisure Studies courses.

MISERICORDIA UNIVERSITY
301 Lake Street
Dallas, PA 18612
570-674-6400
info@misericordia.edu
www.misericordia.edu/athletics
• Deron G Grabel, Director
dgrabel@misericordia.edu
• David Martin, Athletics Director
(570) 674-6294
dmartin@misericordia.edu
Degrees/Majors Offered:
B.S. sport management.

MISSISSIPPI STATE UNIVERSITY
ATHLETIC DEPARTMENT
P.O. BOX 5327
MISSISSIPPI STATE, MS 39762
662-325-2066
Fax: 662-325-0589
www.hailstate.com
• Scott Stricklin, Director of Athletics
(662) 325-0863
scottstricklin@athletics.msstate.edu
Degree Offered:
M.S. Sport Administration

MISSISSIPPI, UNIVERSITY OF
DEPARTMENT OF HEALTH, EXERCISE
SCIENCE & RECREATION MGMT
215 TURNER CENTER
PO BOX 1848
UNIVERSITY, MS 38677
662-915-5521
Fax: 662-915-5525
jlmcbrid@olemiss.edu
www.olemiss.edu
• David Scott Hargrove, Dept. Interim
Chairperson
jlmcbrid@olemiss.edu
• Scott G Owens, Interim Chair of Health,
Exercise Science and
(662) 915-5527
sgowens@olemiss.edu
• Martha Bass, Associate Professor of
Health and Exercise Sc
(662) 915-5563
mabass1@olemiss.edu
• Christi Brewer, Instructor in Exercise
Science Health, Exerci
(662) 915-5528
• Christoper Black, Assistant Professor of
Health, Exercise Scien
(662) 915-5521
vblackcd@olemiss.edu
• Kim Beason, Professor of Park &
Recreation Management and
(662) 915-5555
hpbeason@olemiss.edu
• Dale Bramlett, HESRM Senior Secretary

(662) 915-5844
dbramlet@olemiss.edu
• Michael Dupper, HESRM Assistant
Professor
(662) 915-5564
mad@olemiss.edu
Description:
Undergrad Degree: B.S. Areas of
Specialization: Sports Management.

MISSOURI BAPTIST UNIVERSITY
One College Park Drive
St. Louis, MO 63141-8698
314-434-1115
877-434-1115
Fax: 314-434-7596
• P. Greg Comfort, Director
comfort@mobap.edu
Degrees/Majors Offered:
B.S., B.A. sport management, B.S. sport
medicine, B.S.E., B.S., B.A. kinesiology,
B.S.E., B.S., B.A. health; graduate
certificate in sport management.

MISSOURI WESTERN STATE COLLEGE
DEPARTMENT OF HEALTH, PHYSICAL
EDUCATION & RECREATION
214 LOONEY COMPLEX
ST. JOSEPH, MO 64507
816-271-4491
Fax: 816-271-5940
blessing@missouriwestern.edu
www.missouriwestern.edu/HPER
• Brenda Blessing, Professor of
Recreation/Chairperson
(816) 271-4208
blessing@missouriwestern.edu
• Paul Choi, Assistant Professor of
Recreation
(816) 271-4246
hchoi@missouriwestern.edu
• Regan Dodd, Assistant Professor of
Health
(816) 271-4474
rdodd@missouriwestern.edu
• Rick Hardy, Assistant Professor of
Recreation
(816) 271-5931
• Britton Johnson, Assistant Professor of
Physical Education
• Justin Kraft, Assistant Professor of
Physical Education
(816) 271-4290
jkraft@missouriwestern.edu
• Nannette Wolford, Physical Education
Asst. Professor
(816) 271-4487
wolford@missouriwestern.edu
Description:
Undergrad Degree: B.S. Areas of
Specialization: Sports
Marketing/Management.

MISSOURI, UNIVERSITY OF
HEALTH AND EXERCISE SCIENCES
102 ROTHWELL GYMNASIUM
COLUMBIA, MO 65211
573-882-6501
Fax: 573-882-4720
www.missouri.edu
• Linda Schoonmaker, Coordinator
Description:
Grad Degree: M.Ed. Areas of Specialization:
Sport Management, Human Performance.

**MONTANA STATE
UNIVERSITY-BOZEMAN**
DEPARTMENT OF HEALTH & HUMAN
DEVELOPMENT
218 HERRICK HALL
PO BOX 173540
BOZEMAN, MT 59717-3360
406-994-3242
Fax: 406-994-6314
hhd@montana.edu
www.montana.edu
• Craig Stewart, Dept.
Chairperson/Professor
cstewart@montana.edu
• Lynn Owens, Dept. Coordinator
lowens@montana.edu

MOUNT SAINT MARY'S UNIVERSITY
16300 OLD EMMITSBURG ROAD
EMITTSBURG, MD 21727
301-447-6122
www.msmary.edu/athletics
• Karl W Einolf, Chair/Director
einolf@msmary.edu
Description:
B.S. busines, concentration in sports
management

NATIONAL-LOUIS UNIVERSITY
2840 SHERIDAN RD
EVANSTON, IL 60201
847-475-1100
Fax: 847-256-1057
www.nl.edu
• Curtis McCray, President
(847) 475-1100
Description:
Undergrad Degree: B.A. Grad Degree: M.S.
Areas of Specialization: Exercise
Physiology, specializing in preventive and
rehabilitative cardiovascular health.

NEBRASKA WESLEYAN UNIVERSITY
DEPARTMENT OF HEALTH AND HUMAN
PERFORMANCE
5000 ST. PAUL AVENUE
LINCOLN, NE 68504
402-465-2366
800-541-3818
Fax: 402-465-2179
bmj@nebrwesleyan.edu
nwusports.com
• Berniece Jones, Dept.
Chairperson/Associate Professor
(402) 465-2364
bmj@nebrwesleyan.edu
• Patricia Dotson, Dept. Professor
(402) 465-2361
pdp@nebrwesleyan.edu

NEUMANN COLLEGE
ONE NEUMANN DR
ASTON, PA 19014
610-459-0905
800-9-NEUMANN
Fax: 484-840-4798
slabiks@neumann.edu
www.neumann.edu/athletics
Degrees Offered:
B.S. Sport Management; M.S. Sport
Management.
Description:
The Sport and Entertainment Management
major offers career-minded students the
opportunity to gain a broad based
understanding of the major areas of Sport
and Entertainment Management. Graduates

move on to challenging and exciting careers in academic settings, professional sports, sports and recreation facilities, as well as health, fitness, and sport clubs.

NEVADA, LAS VEGAS, UNIVERSITY OF
DEPARTMENT OF KINESILOGY
4505 S. MARYLAND PARKWAY
PO BOX 453034
LAS VEGAS, NV 89154-3035
702-895-0996
Fax: 702-895-1500
www.unlvrebels.com
• John Mercer, Ph.D, Dept. Chairperson
(702) 895-4672
jmercer@unlv.nevada.edu
• John Massengale, Sports Studies Director
(702) 895-4096
• Cindy Fredrick, Volleyball Head Coach
(702) 895-1898
cindy.fredrick@unlv.edu

NEW ENGLAND COLLEGE
24 Bridge Street
Henniker, NH 3242
603-428-2211
www.nec.edu/athletics
• John O'Connor, Director
joconnor@nec.edu
• Lori Runksmeier, Athletics Director
(603) 428-2292
lrunksmei@nec.edu
Degrees/Majors Offered:
B.A. sport and recereation management.

NEW HAMPSHIRE, UNIVERSITY OF
HEIIT HALL
105 MAIN STREET
THE UNIVERSITY OF NE HAMPSHIRE
DURHAM, NH 3824
603-862-1234
800-735-2964
Fax: 603-862-0154
www.unh.edu/sport-studies
• Karen Collins, Option Coordinator
• Heather Barber, Associate Professor
• Tim Ashwell, Sr. Lecturer
Description:
B.S. Kinesiology: sport studies, M.S. kinesiology: sport studies.

NEW HAVEN, UNIVERSITY OF
DEPT OF SPORT MANAGEMENT
300 Boston Post Road
W. HAVEN, CT 6516
203-932-7016
800-225-5864
Fax: 203-932-7470
asack@newhaven.edu
www.newhavenchargers.com
• Deborah Chin, Associate Vice President, Director of Athleti
(203) 932-7020
dchin@newhaven.edu
• Sue Zawacki, Senior Associate Director of Athletics
(203) 932-7357
• Robin Salters, Associate Director of Athletics for Facilitie
(203) 932-7022
rsalters@newhaven.edu
• Bryan Graff, Associate Director of Athletics for External
(203) 932-7017
bgraff@newhaven.edu
• lou Scala, Director of Sports Medicine
(203) 479-4890

• Allen L. Sack, Coordinator Sports Management
asack@newhaven.edu
• Gil Fried, Professor/Chair
gfried@newhaven.edu
Description:
B.S. management of sports industries, B.S. business administration with a concentration in sports management, M.S. management of sports industries, M.S. management of sports industries with a concentration in facility management, M.B.A. with a concentration in sports management.
Number of Members:
Three full time faculty.

NEW YORK UNIVERSITY
PRESTON ROBERT TISCH CENTER
7 EAST 12TH STREET
NEW YORK, NY 10003
212-998-9104
Fax: 212-995-4676
tish.center@nyu.edu
www.scps.nyu.edu/tischcenter
• Jennifer Burns, Director of Industry Relations and Administration
Degrees Offered:
B.S. in sport management and leisure studies.

NEWBERRY COLLEGE
DEPARTMENT OF PHYSICAL EDUCATION
2100 COLLEGE STREET
NEWBERRY, SC 29108
803-321-5161
800-845-4955
www.newberrywolves.com
• Peggy Barnes, Dept. Chair/PE Associate Professor
pbarnes@newberry.edu
• Cody McMurtry, Physical Education Asst. Professor
(803) 321-5163
• Jason Valek, Wrestling Head Coach
(803) 321-5659
jason.valek@newberry.edu
• Emily Bikowski, Women's Lacrosse Head Coach
(803) 321-5199
emily.bikowski@newberry.edu
• Amber Morrell, Cheerleading Head Coach
amber.morrell@newberry.edu

NHTI, CONCORD COMMUNITY COLLEGE
31 COLLEGE DRIVE
CONCORD, NH 3301
603-271-6426
Fax: 603-271-6431
www.nhti.edu
• Paul Hogan, Director of Athletics/Men's Basketball Head C
(603) 271-6426
nhtiathletics@ccsnh.edu
Teams:
Baseball, Basketball (M/W), Bowling, Cross Country (M/W), Dance, Golf, Soccer (M/W), Softball, Spirit.

NICHOLS COLLEGE
SPORT MANAGEMENT PROGRAM
124 CENTER ROAD
PO BOX 5000
DUDLEY, MA 1571
508-213-1560
800-470-3379

Fax: 508-213-2225
www.nichols.edu/athletics
• Timothy Liptrap, Sport Management Assistant Professor
• Colleen Colles, Chairperson/Assistant Professor
(508) 213-2254
Colleen.Colles@nichols.edu
Description:
The sport management program provides the academic and practical experiences needed to gain successful employment in the field. The specialization provides the skills necessary for success in a variety of areas including: sport facility management, event management, high school and collegiate athletics, sporting goods manufacturers, and amateur and professional sports organizations.
Requirements:
A Bachelors of Science in Business Administration requires the successful completion of 121 academic credit hours (approximately 40 courses). To specialize in Sport Management, students are required to complete 30 credit hours (7 classes and one-9 credit internship) in this area of expertise.
Degree Offered:
B.S. business administration with emphasis in sport management, M.B.A. with emphasis in sport management.

NORTH CAROLINA STATE UNIVERSITY
COLLEGE OF NATURAL RESOURCES
2820 FAUCETTE DRIVE
BILTMORE HALL
RALEIGH, NC 27695-8001
919-515-2883
Fax: 919-515-7231
naturalresources@ncsu.edu
www.cfr.ncsu.edu
• Michael A. Kanters, Chair/Director
mkanters@ncsu.edu
• Mary Atzin, Dean
(919) 513-5723
mary_watzin@@ncsu.edu
• Julia Brooks, Executive Assistant to the Dean
(919) 513.0152
julia_brooks@ncsu.edu
• Robert Bardon, Associate Dean for Extension and Engagement
(919) 515-5575
Robert_Bardon@ncsu.edu
• David Ashcraft, Director of External Relations & Development
(919) 515.5723
David_Ashcraft@ncsu.edu
• Jennifer Viets, Assistant Director of External Relations
(919) 513.7734
Jennifer_Viets@ncsu.edu
• Jennifer Piercy, Director of the Pulp and Paper Foundation
(919) 515.7709
Jennifer_Piercy@ncsu.edu
Description:
B.S. parks, recreation and tourism management, concentration in sport management; B.S. sport management.

NORTH CAROLINA, UNIVERSITY OF
DEPARTMENT OF EXERCISE AND SPORT SCIENCE
FETZER GYM
CAMPUS BOX 8700
CHAPEL HILL, NC 27599-8700

college sports

919-962-0017
Fax: 919-962-0489
atkins@email.unc.edu
www.unc.edu/depts
• Cindy Atkins, Dept. Administrative
Assistant
atkins@email.unc.edu
• Frederick Mueller, Sport Administration
Professor
mueller@email.unc.edu
• Barbara Osborne, Sport Admin.
Specialization Coordinator
(919) 962-5173
sportlaw@unc.edu
Description:
B.A. exercise and sport science, sport
administration; M.S. sport administration,
M.A./J.D. sport administration and law dual
degree.

NORTH FLORIDA UNIVERSITY OF
4567 ST JOHN'S BLUFF ROAD
JACKSONVILLE,, FL 32224
904-628-1000
www.unfospreys.com
• Jennifer Kane, Chair/Director
Description:
B.A.E. sport leadership

NORTHEASTERN UNIVERSITY
360 HUNTINGTON AVE
BOSTON, MA 2115
617-373-2672
Fax: 617-373-8988
www.northeastern.edu
• Robert Curtin, Chairman Sport & Leisure
Studies
• Richard Lapchick, Executive Director
Description:
Undergrad Degree: B.S. Grad Degree: M.S.
Areas of Specialization: Undergrad:
Cardiovascular Health and Exercise; Athletic
Training; Physical Education; Health
Education; Recreation Management. Grad:
Clinical Exercise Physiology;
Recreation/Sport/Fitness Management.

**NORTHERN COLORADO, UNIVERSITY
OF**
SCHOOL OF SPORT AND EXERCISE
SCIENCE
GUNTER 2590
PO BOX 39
GREELEY, CO 80639
970-351-2535
Fax: 970-351-1762
www.unco.edu/nhs/ses
• Shannon Courtney, Athletic Training
• Jim Turk, Athletic Training
• Gary Heise, Biomechanics
• Scott Douglas, Teacher Education
• Melissa Parker, Teacher Education
• David Stotlar, Director
david.stotlar@unco.edu
• Linda Sharp, Professor
linda.sharp@unco.edu
Description:
M.A., and Ph.D. in sport and exercise
science,with an emphasis in sport
administration.

NORTHERN ILLINOIS UNIVERSITY
228 AN
DEKALB, IL 60115
815-753-3907
Fax: 815-753-1413
rcaughron@niu.edu

• Rod Caughron, Director of Graduate
Studies in Sport Managem
Description:
MS in Sport Management: Program is a
sport business program with an emphasis
on leadership, communications
(oral/written), and sound business and sales
practices.

NORTHERN KENTUCKY UNIVERSITY
DEPARTMENT OF MANAGEMENT &
MARKETING
BEP 475
NUNN DRIVE
HIGHLAND HEIGHTS, KY 41099-7500
859-572-6559
Fax: 859-572-5150
• Matthew Shank, Dept.
Chairperson/Professor
(859) 572-6642
shank@nku.edu
• Tom Gamble, Sports Business Program
Inaugural Dir.
(859) 572-5906
Description:
Sports Business is the multidisciplinary
study of business principles and processes
applied to the sports industry. The sports
business certificate is for individuals that
seek a solid foundation in the principles and
practices of the sports industry. Students
enrolled in this certificate program must
meet all course pre-requisites except class
standing and certification.
Required Courses:
SPB 305 Sports Marketing, SPB 308 Sports
Promotion Tools, SPB 330 Sports Legal
Environment, SPB 480 Sports Business
Strategies and Policies.

**NORTHWESTERN STATE UNIVERSITY
OF LOUISIANA**
DEPARTMENT OF HEALTH & HUMAN
PERFORMANCE
143 HEALTH AND HUMAN
PERFORMANCE BUILDING
NATCHITOCHES, LA 71497
318-357-5126
Fax: 318-357-5904
health@nsula.edu
www.nsula.edu
• Vickie Gentry, Dept. Chairperson
gentryv@nsula.edu
• Susan Molstad, Professor
molstad@nsula.edu
• Newton C. Wilkes, Professor
wilkes@nsula.edu
Description:
Grad Degree: M.Ed. in Phys Ed. Areas of
Specialization: Sport Administration, Health
Promotion, Physical Education.

NORTHWESTERN UNIVERSITY
SPORTS
ADMINISTRATION/MANAGEMENT
339 E. CHICAGO AVENUE
CHICAGO, IL 60611-3008
312-503-6951
Fax: 312-503-4942
scsadmissions@northwestern.edu
www.nusports.com
• Maureen Harty, Athletic Director
Description:
The School of Continuing Studies has
developed a master's program to prepare
students to take on leadership positions in
all segments of the sports industry. Students

who are serious about the business of
sports will gain an understanding of
theoretical concepts and the ability to apply
those concepts in a 10-course curriculum
encompassing the diverse aspects of the
sports profession.
Degree Offered:
MSA in Sports Administration

**NORTHWOOD UNIVERSITY FLORIDA
CAMPUS**
2600 MILITARY TRAIL
WEST PALM BEACH, FL 33409
561-478-5500
Fax: 561-697-9495
www.northwood.edu/athletics
• Dennis Bechtol, Chair/Director
bechtold@northwood.edu
Description:
Bachelor's in business administration, major
in sport and entertainment management.

OHIO NORTHERN UNIVERSITY
SPORTS CENTER
525 S. MAIN ST
ADA, OH 45810
419-772-2000
Fax: 419-772-2470
r-beaschler@onu.edu
www.onu.edu
• Ron Beaschler, Coordinator
Description:
Undergrad Degree: B.S. Grad Degree:
M.Ed. in Sports Management. Areas of
Specialization: Sports Management.

OHIO STATE UNIVERSITY
395 DREESE LABORATIES
2015 NEIL AVE.
COLUMBUS, OH 43210-1277
614-292-5813
Fax: 614-292-2911
sportmanagement@osu.edu
www.cse.ohio-state.edu
• Catrena Collins, Human Resources Officer
• Tamera Cramer, Annual Report, Faculty
Search Secretary, Depa
• Donald Havard, Fiscal Officer
• Janet Fink, Sport Management Program
Coord/Prof.
(614) 292-0867
fink.26@osu.edu
• Packianathan Chelladurai, Professor
(614) 692-0816
chelladurai.1@osu.edu
• David Brown, Associate Athletic Director
• Justin Doyle, Director of Business
Development
Description:
A specialization of the Sport and Exercise
Sciences program in the School of Physical
Activity and Educational Services, provides
programs of study that will lead to Master's
and doctoral degrees. Established in 1978,
more than 500 alumni of the Sport
Management program now hold prestigious
positions in all segments of the industry and
serve as athletic directors for universities,
general managers of professional sport
franchises, and executive directors of public
and private sport, leisure, and fitness
organizations.
Degrees:
Grad Degree: M.A., Ph.D. Areas of
Specialization: Collegiate Athletic
Administration; Professional Sport
Management; Recreation and Intramural

Sport Management; Arena and Facility Management.

OHIO UNIVERSITY
DEPARTMENT OF RECREATION AND SPORT SCIENCES
GROVER CENTER E-160
ATHENS, OH 45701
740-593-4656
Fax: 740-593-0284
rsps@ohio.edu
www.hhs.ohiou.edu/
• James Kahler, Sports Administration Exec. Director
(740) 593-4666
kahler@ohio.edu
• Ming Li, Dept. Dir./Sports Admin. Assoc. Prof.
mingli@ohio.edu
• Andrew Kreutzer, Sports Administration Assoc. Professor
(740) 593-9495
kreutzer@ohio.edu
• Andrew Agro, National Sports Forum (NSF) Competition
• AJ Andrassy, National Sports Forum (NSF) Competition
• David Bamford, National Sports Forum (NSF) Competition
Description:
One of the few undergraduate programs in the United State that have received program approval from the Sport Management Program Review Council. The curriculum provides the student with academic preparation and practical training required for success in such career fields as professional sport, college athletics, youth sports, or corporate positions with a sport-related component. Related areas to the sport industry include facility management, sport promotion and marketing, sport media, customer or community relations, sport sponsorship, licensing, sport information and sport law.
Degrees:
Grad Degree: Master in Sports Administration. Areas of Specialization: Sports Administration, Facility Management. Dual Degree of M.B.A./M.S.A. Joint Degree with The Capital University Law Center; M.S.A/J.D.
Requirements:
See web site for list.

OKLAHOMA STATE UNIVERSITY
DEPARTMENT OF MANAGEMENT
320 SPEARS SCHOOL OF BUSINESS
STILLWATER, OK 74078-5070
405-744-5201
Fax: 405-744-5180
mgmt@okstate.edu
www.spears.okstate.edu/management
• Ken Eastman, Dept. Head/Associate Professor
(405) 744-5201
ken.eastman@okstate.edu
Description:
Undergrad Degree: B.S. Health, Phys Ed & Leisure. Grad Degree: M.S., Ed.D. Health, Phys Ed & Leisure. Areas of Specialization: Undergrad: Sport Science. Grad: Sport Administration, Exercise Science, Adapted Phys Ed, Pedagogy.

OKLAHOMA, UNIVERSITY OF
DEPARTMENT OF HEALTH AND EXERCISE SCIENCE
633 ELM AVENUE
NORMAN, OK 73019-3118
405-325-2077
Fax: 405-325-7709
cas@ou.edu
• Laurette Taylor, Dept. Chairperson
etaylor@ou.edu
• Paul Bell, Dean and Vice Provost for Instruction
(405) 325-2077
pbell@ou.edu
• Sharron Oelke, Assistant to the Dean
(405) 325-4303
soelke@ou.edu
• Edward Sankowski, Associate Dean
(405) 325-0321
esankowski@ou.edu
• Kelly Damphousse, Associate Dean
(405) 325-2529
kdamp@ou.edu
• Gail Brown, Administrative Assistant
(405) 325-2077
gtbrown@ou.edu
• David Quirk, Director of Development
(405) 325-3724
dquirk@ou.edu
Description:
An interdisciplinary program integrating the study of legal aspects within sport, marketing, management and promotion of sport as a business, and the study of the behavioral aspects of management and leadership.
Degrees:
Undergrad Degree: (1) Sports Sciences, (2) Health Promotion. Grad Degree: M.S. Areas of Specialization: Sport Management; Sport Marketing; Sport Psychology; Exercise Physiology, Health Promotion.

OLD DOMINION UNIVERSITY
STUDENT RECREATION CENTER
ROOM 2025
NORFOLK, VA 23529
757-683-5962
Fax: 757-683-4270
rcase@odu.edu
www.odu.edu/sprtmgt
• Robert Case, Graduate Program Director
(757) 683-5962
rcase@odu.edu
• Lynn Ridinger, Undergraduate Program Coordinator
(757) 683-4353
lridinge@odu.edu
Degrees Offered:
Undergrad Degree: B.S. Grad Degree: M.S. in Physical Education with emphasis on Sport Management.

OREGON, UNIVERSITY OF/ WARSAW SPORTS MARKETING CENTER
LUNDQUIST COLLEGE OF BUSINESS
1208 UNIVERSITY OF OREGON
EUGENE, OR 97403-1208
541-346-3495
Fax: 541-346-3341
www.warsawcenter.com
• Paul Swangard, Director
• Dennis Howard, Professor
Degrees/Majors offered:
B.A., M.B.A., and Ph.D. business administration with a sports business concentration.

PACIFIC CHRISTIAN
PHYS ED DEPT
2500 E. NUTWOOD AVE
FULLERTON, CA 92631
909-879-3901
Fax: 909-526-0231

PACIFIC, UNIVERSITY OF THE
SPORT MANAGEMENT PROGRAM
C/O SPORT SCIENCES DEPT
3601 PACIFIC AVE
STOCKTON, CA 95211
209-946-2531
Fax: 209-946-3225
lkoehler@uop.edu
• Linda S. Koehler, Coordinator Sports Management
(209) 946-2531
lkoehler@uop.edu
• Linda Lyman, Director
(209) 946-2531
llyman@pacific.edu
Degrees/Majors offered:
B.A. sport sciences concentrations: sport management, pedagogy, athletics training, sports medicine.

PALM BEACH ATLANTIC UNIVERSITY
SPORT MANAGEMENT
901 S. FLAGER DRIVE
PO BOX 24708
WEST PALM BEACH, FL 33416
561-803-2450
Fax: 561-803-2455
www.pba.edu/athletics
• Robert Myers, Dept. Dean
Robert_Myers@pba.edu
• Ed Langlois, MBA Program Director
Ed_Langlois@pba.edu
• Susan Williams, Secretary
Susan_Williams@pba.edu
Description:
Sport Management involves applying the management principles of planning, organizing, leading, and directing to the unique industry of sport. Emphasis is placed on the production, facilitation, promotion, and organization of sport products.

PENN STATE UNIVERSITY/PGA SANCTIONED GOLF MANAGEMENT PROGRAM
201 MATEER BUILDING
UNIVERSITY PARK, PA 16802
814-863-7000
Fax: 814-863-4257
www.psu.edu
Year Founded:
1991
Description:
Prepares undergraduate students for a career in professional golf management. Entrance Requirements: Meet university requirements plus have golf handicap of eight (8) or lower

PFEIFFER UNIVERSITY
48380 US HIGHWAY 52 NORTH
MISENHEIMER, NC 28109
704-463-1360
800-338-2060
Fax: 704-463-1363
gofalconsports.com
• Jack Ingram, Chair/Director
Description:
B.A. sports management.

POINT PARK UNIVERSITY
201 Wood Street
Pittsburgh, PA 15222
412-391-4100
800-321-0129
www.pointpark.edu/athletics
• Robert D. Bunnell, Director
rbunnell@pointpark.edu
Degree/Majors Offered:
B.S. sport, arts and entertainment
management.

PRINCIPIA COLLEGE
SPORT MANAGEMENT
1 MAYBECK PLACE
ELSAH, IL 62028
618-374-2131
Fax: 618-374-5221
www.principia.edu
• Lee Ellis, Atletic Director
(618) 374-5030
lee.ellis@principia.edu
Degree Offered:
BA in Sports Management.

QUINCY UNIVERSITY
1800 COLLEGE AVE
QUINCY, IL 62301-2699
217-228-8020
Fax: 217-228-5034
• Ivan Paul, Sport Management Program
Director
Description:
This four-year undergraduate program leads
to the Bachelor of Science degree in Sport
Management. The sports management
curriculum is designed to prepare students
for a variety of exciting careers. Growth in
professional sports, intercollegiate athletics,
recreation, corporate fitness, private health
clubs, sports broadcasting and writing, and
a constant media exposure combine to
make sports management a diverse and
dynamic field.

RADFORD UNIVERSTIY
PHYSICAL AND HEALTH EDUCATION
PO BOX 6957
RADFORD, VA 24142
540-831-6650
Fax: 540-831-6650
www.ruhighlanders.com
• Bev Zeakes, Dept. Chairperson
(540) 831-5305
• April Hunt, Dept. Administrator
• Brent Chumbley, Men's & Women's Cross
Country/Track & Field C
schumbley@radford.edu
• Marci Jenkins, Women's Volleyball Head
Coach
(540) 831-5879
mtjenkins@radford.edu
Degrees Offered:
M.S. Research Areas: Sports Science
Sports Administration Coaching Education
Physical Education Pedagogy

RICE UNIVERSITY
DEPARTMENT OF HP & HS
6100 MAIN ST
HOUSTON, TX 77005-1892
713-527-4077
Fax: 713-527-6019
www.sport.rice.edu
• Harmon Gallant, Sport Management
Director
• Clark Haptonstall, Director

Description:
B.A. in sport management.

ROBERT MORRIS UNIVERSITY
DEPARTMENT OF SPORT
ADMINISTRATION
6001 UNIVERSITY BOULEVARD
MOON TOWNSHIP, PA 15108-1189
412-262-8416
800-762-0097
Fax: 412-262-8494
synowka@rmu.edu
www.rmu.edu
• David Synowka, Chairman/Program Head
Sports Management
synowka@rmu.edu
Degrees Offered:
B.S. business administration; M.S. sport
management; M.B.A., concentration in sport
management.

RUTGERS
70 Lipman Drive
New Brunswick, NJ 08901-8525
848-932-9525
Fax: 732-932-9151
www.exsci.rutgers.edu
• Jan Houtman, Administrative Assistant
Degrees/Majors Offered:
B.S. exercise science and sports studies,
sport management option.

SACRED HEART UNIVERSITY
JOHN F. WELCH COLLEGE OF BUSINESS
5151 PARK AVE
FAIRFIELD, CT 06825-1000
203-371-7999
Fax: 203-365-7538
santomierj@sacredheart.edu
www.sacredheart.edu
• Joshua Shuart, Ph.D., Chair, Department
of Marketing & Sport Manage
(203) 416-3601
sportmanagement@sacredheart.edu
Degree Offered
B.S. Sport Management
Curriculum:
The Sport Management curriculum provides
a theoretical and skill-based framework in
core business disciplines, functional
business skills and in specific sport
management areas. Focus is on the
financial, marketing, media, legal and ethical
dimensions of sport management. The
program provides students with dynamic
internship opportunities.

SALEM STATE COLLEGE
352 Lafayette Street
Salem, MA 1970
978-542-6000
www.salemstate.edu/athletics
• Stuart G McMahon, Director
smcmahon@salemstate.edu
Degrees/Majors Offered:
B.S. sport, fitness and leisure studies with a
concentration in sport management.

SAN FRANCISCO, UNIVERSITY OF
WAR MEMORIAL GYMNASIUM
2130 FULTON STREET
SAN FRANCISCO, CA 94117-1080
415-422-6891
Fax: 415-422-2510
sfm@usfca.edu
www.usfdons.com

• Scott Sidwell, Director of Athletics
(415) 422-6893
sasidwell@usfca.edu
• Nino Giarrantano, Baseball Head Coach
(415) 422-2934
giarrantano@usfca.edu
• Rex Walters, Men's Baskebtall Head
Coach
Degrees/Majors offered:
M.A. sport management.

SAN JOSE STATE UNIVERSITY
DEPARTMENT OF HUMAN
PERFORMANCE
1 WASHINGTON SQUARE
SAN JOSE, CA 95192-0054
408-924-3019
Fax: 408-924-3053
www2.sjsu.edu/depts/hup/SM/
• Mark Nagel, Chairman
(408) 924-3019
• Tracy Spencer, Athletic Ticket Manager
• Sonja Lilienthal, Director
Description:
B.S., and M.A. in kinesiology, and emphasis
in sport management.

SEATTLE PACIFIC UNIVERSITY
DEPARTMENT OF PHYSICAL
EDUCATION & EXERCISE SCIENCE
3307-3RD AVENUE W.
SEATTLE, WA 98119
206-281-2081
Fax: 206-281-2784
wndnh2o@spu.edu
www.spu.edu/depts/pe
• Dan Tripps, Dept. Chairperson
dtripps@spu.edu
Description:
Undergrad Degree: B.A. Physical Education,
B.S. Exercise Science; Grad Degree: M.A.
Sport and Exercise Leadership.

SETON HALL UNIVERSITY
SETON HALL ATHLETICS
400 SOUTH ORANGE AVENUE
REGAN ATHLETICS CENTER
SOUTH ORANGE, NJ 07079-2692
973-761-9498
Fax: 973-761-9675
www.shupirates.com
Degrees Offered:
B.S., B.A. with a concentration in sport
management; M.B.A. with a concentration in
sport management; joint M.B.A./J.D. sport
management/sport and entertainment law;
postgraduate certificate sport management.

SHAWNEE STATE UNIVERSITY
ATHLETICS DEPARTMENT
940 SECOND STREET
PORTSMOUTH, OH 45662
740-351-4778
srader@shawnee.edu
www.ssubears.com

SHEPHERD UNIVERSITY
PO BOX 3210
SHEPHERDSTOWN, WV 25443
304-876-5000
800-344-5231
Fax: 304-876-3101
www.shepherd.edu/athletics
• Matthew McIntosh, Chair/Director
mmcintos@shepherd.edu

Description:
Recreation and leisure studies, sport and event management, commercial recreation and tourism, sport communication, therapeutic recreation, fitness/exercise science, health and physical education teacher education.

SIENA HEIGHTS UNIVERSITY
BUSINESS AND MANAGEMENT DIVISION
1247 E. SIENA HEIGHTS DRIVE
ADRIAN, MI 49221
517-264-7624
• Mary Beth Leibold, Sport Management Program Coordinator
Description:
The field of sport has experienced phenomenal growth; thus, this is an excellent time for students to pursue an academic degree that will allow them to specialize in the area of sport management. Through a curriculum that includes both theoretical foundations of sport and practical experience opportunities, Siena Heights University's Sport Management Program is designed to provide students with this specialization which will provide them an opportunity to compete for a highly competitive and exciting careers in sport.

SLIPPERY ROCK UNIVERSITY
WEST GYM, #224
C/O SPORT MANAGEMENT COORDINATOR
SLIPPERY ROCK, PA 16057
724-738-2967
Fax: 724-738-4858
www.rockathletics.com
• Robin Ammon, Jr., Director
(724) 738-2967
robert.ammon@sru.edu
• Robertha A. Abney, Associate Professor
robertha.abney@sru.edu
• Catriana Higgs, Professor
catriana.higgs@sru.edu
• Jeff Messer, Assistant Professor
jeffrey.messer@sru.edu
• Brian Crow, Assistant Professor
brian.crowe@sru.edu
Degrees Offered:
Undergrad Degree: B.S. in Sport Management; Grad Degree: M.S. in Sport Management.

SOUTH CAROLINA, UNIVERSITY OF
DEPARTMENT OF SPORT & ENTERTAINMENT MANAGEMENT
COLLEGE OF HOSPITALITY, RETAIL AND SPORTS MANAGEMENT
CAROLINA COLISEUM, ROOM 2012
COLUMBIA, SC 29208
803-777-4690
Fax: 803-777-8788
www.hrsm.sc.edu
• Thomas Regan, Dept. Chairperson
(803) 777-4690
regan@gwm.sc.edu
• Matthew Bernthal, Dept. Associate Professor
bernthal@gwm.sc.edu
• Peter Graham, Dept. Professor
Description:
Master's in sport and entertainment management, with an emphasis in public assembly facility management and live entertainment; B.S. sport and entertainment management.

SOUTHEAST MISSOURI STATE UNIVERSITY
DEPARTMENT OF HEALTH, HUMAN PERFORMANCE & RECREATION
1 UNIVERSITY PLAZA
Cape Girardeau, MO 63701
573-651-2197
Fax: 573-651-5150
www.semo.edu/athletics
• Beth Easter, Sport Management Program Director
(573) 986-6744
baeaster@semo.edu
• Joseph Pujol, Dept. Chairperson
(573) 651-2664
jpujol@semo.edu
Description:
The Sport Management program at Southeast Missouri State University is the only sport management of its kind in Missouri. Sport Management is a field of study preparing students to work in the sport industry. Our program combines sport specific courses with a business administration minor. The curriculum is designed to meet the curricular guidelines for sport management established by professional organizations
Degree/Majors Offered:
B.S. sport management with a minor in business administration, M.A. higher education with option in athletics administration.

SOUTHEASTERN LOUISIANA UNIVERSITY
DEPARTMENT OF KINESIOLOGY AND HEALTH STUDIES
TENNESSEE AVENUE
SLU 10845
HAMMOND, LA 70402
985-549-2130
800-222-7358
Fax: 985-549-5119
www.selu.edu
• Eddie Hebert, Dept. Head/Associate Professor
(985) 549-2130
ehebert@selu.edu
• Linda Synovitz, Graduate Coordinator
(985) 549-3867
lsynovitz@selu.edu
Description:
Undergrad Degree: B.A. Grad Degree: M.A. Areas of Specialization: Undergrad: Non-teaching Phys Ed degree in which students can choose alternate career options in Sport Management, Health/Fitness Promotion. Grad: Health Promotion, Exercise Science.

SOUTHERN ILLINOIS UNIVERSITY AT EDWARDSVILLE
KINESIOLOGY AND HEALTH EDUCATION SPORT MANAGEMENT
VADALABENE CENTER 1126
EDWARDSVILLE, IL 62026-1126
618-650-3252
Fax: 618-650-3369
dbruegg@siue.edu
www.siusalukis.com
• Bill Vogler, Dept. Chairperson
(618) 650-2984
wvogler@siue.edu
• John Baker, Sport Management Program Coordinator
(618) 650-3028
jobaker@siue.edu

• David Ray, Wrestling Head Coach
(618) 650-2949
daray@siue.edu
Description:
Prepares students with management skills for careers as administrators in athletics programs, physical education departments, community recreation programs, and for management positions in the burgeoning sport industry.
Degrees Offered:
M.S.Ed. Kinesiology; Research Areas: Exercise, Sport, Health and Rehabilitation Psychology, Exercise Physiology, Sport Administration/Management

SOUTHERN MISSISSIPPI, UNIVERSITY OF
DEPARTMENT HUMAN PERFORMANCE AND RECREATION
118 COLLEGE DRIVE
HATTIESBURG, MS 39406-5142
601-266-6085
Fax: 601-266-4445
www.usm.edu/hpr
• Lou Marciani, Dept. School Director
lou.marciani@usm.edu
• Matthew Wilson, Sport Management Assistant Professor
matthew.j.wilson@usm.edu
• Benito Velasquez, Dept. Assistant Director
benito.velasquez@usm.edu
Description:
Undergrad Degree: B.S. Grad Degree: M.S. Areas of Specialization: Undergrad: Coaching; Sports Administration; Fitness Management; Strength Training & Conditioning. Grad: Sports Administration, Fitness Management; Strength Training and Conditioning Coach, and Coaching Education options.
Marketing Partner
International Sports Properties Inc.

SOUTHERN NEW HAMPSHIRE UNIVERSITY
SCHOOL OF BUSINESS
2500 N. RIVER RD
MANCHESTER, NH 03106-1045
603-644-3145
Fax: 603-629-4693
d.blais@snhu.edu
www.snhu.edu/athletics
• Doug Blais, Ph.d., Professor & Chair, Sport Management Department
(603) 644-3145
d.blais@snhu.edu
• Deb Robitaille, Softball Head Coach
(603) 645-9776
d.robitaille@snhu.edu
• Greg Coache, Men's & Women's Tennis Head Coach
(603) 645-9741
g.coache@snhu.edu
• Peter Viteritti, Volleyball Head Coach
(603) 645-9764
p.viteritti@snhu.edu
Degrees Offered:
B.S. Sport Management, B.S. Business Studies with a concentration in Sport Managament; M.B.A. with a certificate in Sport Administration, M.S. Sport Management.

SOUTHWEST MISSOURI STATE UNIVERSITY
901 South National
Springfield, MO 65804
417-836-5000
• Philip Rothschild, Director
pcr259f@smsu.edu
Degree/Majors Offered:
B.S. entertainment management.

SPRING ARBOR COLLEGE
DEPT OF EXER & SPORT SCIENCE
106 E. MAIN ST
SPRING ARBOR, MI 49283
517-750-6508
800-968-0011
Fax: 517-750-2745
www.arbor.edu
• Ted Comden, Chairman
Description:
Undergrad Degree: B.A. Areas of Specialization: Sports Administration, Fitness Management.

SPRINGFIELD COLLEGE
263 ALDEN ST
SPRINGFIELD, MA 01109-3797
413-748-3332
Fax: 413-748-3855
• Ronald Ziemba, Director Marketing
• Matthew J. Pantera, Chair/Director
• Dana M. Riefer, Assistant Director Athletics
• Charles Redmond
(413) 748-3231
• Susan Langlois
(413) 748-3809
Description:
Undergrad Degree: B.S., concentration in Phys Ed or Sport Management. Grad Degree: M.Ed., M.P.E., or M.S. Areas of Specialization: Sport Management/Athlete Administration.

ST. CLOUD STATE UNIVERSITY
329 HALENBECK HALL
720 FOURTH AVENUE S.
ST. CLOUD, MN 56301-4498
320-308-3102
Fax: 320-308-6146
hperss@stcloudstate.edu
Degree Offered:
M.S. Sports Management

ST. EDWARDS UNIVERSITY
SCHOOL OF MANAGEMENT AND BUSINESS
3001 S. CONGRESS AVENUE
TRUSTEE HALL 1049
AUSTIN, TX 78704
512-448-8400
Fax: 512-448-1975
www.stedwards.edu/athletics
• Marsha Kelliher, Dean of School Management & Business
• Donna Goodner, Administrative Coordinator
(512) 448-8593
Description:
The Sports Management Concentration provides students who are interested in sport related organizations with the opportunity to learn the skills necessary to manage in either the private or public sector. This concentration is made up of four courses that familiarize students with the theoretical and practical implications of the management, marketing, legal, and ethical aspects of sports. The scope of sports management in this context includes small public schools' athletic departments, startup entrepreneurial ventures, professional sports, and the larger sports industry.

ST. JOHN FISHER COLLEGE
3690 EAST AVE
ROCHESTER, NY 14618
585-385-8441
Fax: 585-385-7311
tharrison@sjfc.edu
• Todd Harrison, Program Chair, Sport Management Dept.
(585) 385-8441
tharrison@sjfc.edu
Degree Offered:
B.S. in Sport Management
Curriculum:
The Sport Studies Department seeks to develop in students the knowledge, skills and experience that will enable them to obtain leadership positions in the sport management field. Serving students directly and the sport management industry indirectly, the department provides a broad-based curriculum that is grounded in the liberal arts and encourages critical analysis of the cultural and social significance of sport, the need for ethical and moral decision-making and the role of sport as a business.

ST. JOHN'S UNIVERSITY
SPORT MANAGEMENT PROGRAM
201 BRENT HALL
8000 UTOPIA PARKWAY
JAMAICA, NY 11439
718-390-4449
misserea@stjohns.edu
www.stjohns.edu
• Anthony Missere, Chairperson/Sport Mgmt. Program Dir.
(718) 990-7391
misserea@stjohns.edu
• Carol Fletcher, Sports Management Assistant Professor
Description:
The program in sport management at St. John's University leads to a Bachelor of Science degree and is available on both the Queens and Staten Island campuses. Sport management also offers a certificate program which is open to individuals who have completed a bachelor's degree in an unrelated area.
Degrees Offered:
B.S. sport management.

ST. LEO UNIVERSITY
DIV OF PROFESSIONAL STUDIES/MC 2067
33701 STATE ROAD 52
ST. LEO, FL 33574
352-588-8304
Fax: 352-588-8289
tphillip@saintleo.edu
www.saintleo.edu
• Stewart Gillman, Program Chair
stewart.gillman@saintleo.edu
• Susan Brown Foster, Chair/Director
susan.foster@saintleo.edu
Degrees Offered:
Undergrad Degree: B.A. Areas of Specialization: Sports Management,
Physical Education-Teaching and B.S. sport management.

ST. THOMAS UNIVERSITY
16401 NW 37TH AVE
MIAMI GARDENS, FL 33054
305-628-6634
800-367-9010
800 367-9006
Fax: 305-628-6790
spo-ad@stu.edu
www.stu.edu
• Jan Bell, Director
(305) 628-6634
jbell@stu.edu
• Ted Abernethy, Undergraduate Program Coordinator
(305) 628-6630
tabernet@stu.edu
• Seok-Ho Song, Assistant Professor
(305) 474-6909
ssong@stu.edu
Description:
St. Thomas University offers an academic major in sports administration that prepares students to work in the business aspects of sports.

STETSON UNIVESITY
421 NORTH WOODLAND BOULEVARD
DELAND, FL 32723
386-822-7100
800-688-0101
admissions@stetson.edu
www.stetson.edu/athletics
• Michele Skelton, Chair/Director
Description:
B.A. sport management

SUNY, STATE UNIVERSITY OF NEW YORK-BROCKPORT
DEPARTMENT OF PHYSICAL EDUCATION & SPORT
TUTTLE N. 212
350 NEW CAMPUS DRIVE
BROCKPORT, NY 14420
585-395-5332
Fax: 585-395-2771
• William Stier, Director: Athletic Admin/Sport Mgmt & Coaching Edu
(585) 395-5331
• Susan Peterson, Department Chair
(585) 395-5332
Departments:
Kinesiology, Sports Studies, and Physical Education
Description:
Degrees in: Sports, Sports Management, Aports Health, Physical Education, Athletic Administration; BS in Sports Management, Ed.M. Physical Education/Athletic Administration; online degree options.

SUNY, STATE UNIVERSITY OF NEW YORK-CORTLAND
PO BOX 2000-PARK P.E.R. CENTER
CORTLAND, NY 13045
607-753-4953
Fax: 607-753-4929
www.cortland.edu
• Suzanne Wingate, Coordinator
• Ted Fay, Chair/Director
fayt@cortland.edu
Description:
B.S., B.A. sport management.

TAMPA, UNIVERSITY OF
DEPARTMENT OF EXERCISE SCIENCE
AND SPORT STUDIES
401 W. KENNEDY BOULEVARD
TAMPA, FL 33606
813-253-3333
Fax: 813-253-6288
www.ut.edu
• Robert Birrenkott, Dept. Associate
Professor
(813) 253-3333
rbirrenkott@ut.edu
• Eric Vlahov, Dept. Chairperson
(813) 253-3333
evlahov@ut.edu
• Jay Jisha, Sports Management Assistant
Professor
(813) 253-3333
jjisha@ut.edu
Description:
Sport management trains new professionals
in a variety of sport business fields. This is
the choice for those who crave the
excitement of front office positions with
professional sports teams or the busy world
of stadium and arena management.
Degrees Offered:
Undergrad Degree: B.A. sports
management.

TEMPLE UNIVERSITY
SPORT AND RECREATION
MANAGEMENT
1700 N. BROAD STREET
PHILADELPHIA, PA 19122
215-204-8701
Fax: 215-204-8705
jeffrey.montague@temple.edu
• Ira Shapiro, Dept. Chairperson
(215) 204-6295
• Jeff Montague, Undergraduate
Coordinator/Asst. Dean
(215) 204-8701
jeffrey.montague@temple.edu
• Michael Jackson, Graduate Program Dir.
in Sport Admin.
Degrees Offered:
BS, Sport and Recreation Management;
M.Ed, Sport and Recreation Administration.

TENNESSEE STATE UNIVERSITY
DEPARTMENT OF HUMAN
PERFORMANCE & SPORT SCIENCES
3500 JOHN A MERRITT BLVD
NASHVILLE, TN 37209-1561
615-963-5000
Fax: 615-963-5594
www.tnstate.edu
• Catana Starks, Dept. Acting
Chairperson/Professor
cstarks@tnstate.edu
• James Bass, Assistant Professor
jbass@tnstate.edu

TENNESSEE, KNOXVILLE, UNIVERSITY OF
DEPARTMENT OF EXERCISE, SPORT
AND LEISURE STUDIES
1914 ANDY HOLT AVENUE
KNOXVILLE, TN 37996-2700
865-974-1282
Fax: 865-974-8981
desensi@utk.edu
www.coe.utk.edu
• Joy DeSensi, Dept. Head/Professor
desensi@utk.edu
• David Bassett, Professor

(865) 974-8766
dbassett@utk.edu
• Frankie Stroud, Dept. Receptionist/Senior
Secretary
fstroud@utk.edu

TENNESSEE-CHATTANOOGA, UNIVERSITY OF
CHATTANOOGA ATHLETICS
615 MCCALLIE AVE., DEPT3505
CHATTANOOGA, TN 37403-2598
423-425-4323
Fax: 423-425-4457
www.gomocs.com
• Rick Hart, Director of Intercollegiate
Athletics
(423) 425-2270
Rick-Hart@utc.edu
Description:
B.S. Sport Management.

TEXAS A&M UNIVERSITY
DEPARTMENT OF HEALTH &
KINESIOLOGY
TAMU 4243
COLLEGE STATION, TX 77845
979-845-3109
Fax: 979-847-8987
info@hlkn.tamu.edu
• Stephen Crouse, Dept.
Head/Chairperson/Professor
s-crouse@tamu.edu
• Michael Sagas, Sports Management
Assistant Professor
msagas@hlkn.tamu.edu
Description:
This specialization prepares students for
teaching and research careers in sport
management. Graduates are trained for
post-doctoral appointments and positions in
universities, industry, and research
institutions. The program prepares students
to conduct research in applied and basic
areas of sport management.
Degrees Offered:
Undergrad Degree: B. S. in Kinesiolgy with
specialization in Sport Management. Grad
Degree: M.S., and Ph.D. in Kinesiology with
specialization in Sport Management.

TEXAS AT AUSTIN, UNIVERSITY OF
DEPARTMENT OF KINESIOLOGY AND
HEALTH EDUCATION
SPORT MANAGEMENT
BELLMONT 222
AUSTIN, TX 78712
512-471-1273
Fax: 512-471-8914
education.utexas.edu/departments/kinesiolo
gy-health-education
• John Ivy, Dept. Chairperson
(512) 471-1273
johnivy@mail.utexas.edu
• Laurence Chalip, Ph.D, Sport
Management Program Coordinator
(512) 232-2373
• Phillip Salazar, Graduate Program
Coordinator
(512) 232-6015
• Richard Hogeda, Graduate Program
Coordinator
(512) 471-1273
rhogeda1@mail.utexas.edu
Description:
An outstanding faculty and curriculum
prepare graduates for work in the growing
sport industry. Many graduates from the

Sport Management program at The
University of Texas at Austin have enjoyed
prosperous careers in all levels of sport,
both in the United States and internationally.
These alumni, along with several other
experienced sport administrators connected
to the program, serve as a valuable network
for both graduate and undergraduate
students studying Sport Management.
Degrees Offered:
BS, MA, M.Ed, Ph.D. in kinesiology with a
major in sport management.

TEXAS WESLEYAN UNIVERSITY
DEPARTMENT OF EXERCISE AND
SPORTS STUDIES
1201 WESLEYAN STREET
FT. WORTH, TX 76105
817-531-4964
Fax: 817-531-4208
• Karen Denny Wallace, Dept. Assistant
Professor
kwallace@txwes.edu
• Albert Peters, Exercise Sports Studies
Professor
apeters@txwes.edu
Description:
Undergrad Degree: B.S. Areas of
Specialization: Sports Management
Teaching.

THE COLLEGE AT BROCKPORT STATE UNIVERSITY OF NEW YORK
SCHOOL OF HEALTH AND HUMAN
PERFORMANCE
350 NEW CAMPUS DRIVE
BROCKPORT, NY 14420-2989
585-395-5332
Fax: 585-395-2771
www.brockport.edu/athletics
• Susan C Peterson, Ed.D., Associate
Professor & Chair
(585) 395-5341
speterse@brockport.edu
• Cathy Houston-Wilson, Associate
Department Chairperson
(585) 395-5352
chouston@brockport.edu
Degree Offered:
The Kinesiology, Sport Studies and Physical
Education Department supports five majors:
Athletic Training, Exercise Physiology,
Kinesiology, Physical Education Teacher
Education and Sport Management. Two
concentrations include: Adapted Physical
Education and Sport Management -
Coaching

TIFFIN UNIVERSITY
SCHOOL OF BUSINESS DEPARTMENT
155 MIAMI STREET
TIFFIN, OH 44883
419-448-3423
800-YOU-OHIO
Fax: 419-443-5007
www.tiffin.edu
• Debra Gatton, Dept. Chairperson
(419) 488-3307
• Paul Marion, President
• Lillian Drimmer, Associate Professor of
Management
(419) 488-5688
• Bonnie Tiell, Sports Management
Instructor
(419) 488-3261
btiell@tiffin.edu

Description:
Undergrad Degree: B.S. in Bus Adm. Grad Degree: MBA. Areas of Specialization: Sport Management.

TOMPKINS CORTLAND COMMUNITY COLLEGE
SPORT MANAGEMENT PROGRAM
170 N. STREET
PO BOX 139
DRYDEN, NY 13053
607-844-8211
888-567-8211
Fax: 607-844-9665
• Kevin Haverlock, Business Dept. Chairperson
• Larry Chase, Sport Management Program Coordinator
Description:
The A.S. degree in Sport Management provides an overview of the sports industry, with emphasis on business and the liberal arts, sports information, and media relations. The program includes a two-credit practicum involving supervised work experiences in game and event administration. Course work also includes a foundation in accounting, finance, management, marketing, and economics and general education course work in the arts, communication, computer applications, history, humanities, mathematics, natural sciences, and the social sciences.
Degrees/Majors Offered:
A.S. sport management.

TOWSON STATE UNIVERSITY
DEPARTMENT OF KINESIOLOGY
8000 YORK ROAD
TOWSON, MD 2000
410-704-2384
Fax: 410-830-4322
• Vince Angotti, Sports Management Program Coordinator
(410) 704-2384
• Gaul Parr, Associate Professor
gparr@towson.edu
Description:
Undergrad Degree: B.S. Areas of Specialization: Sport Studies; Sport Management; Sports Communications.

TULANE LAW SCHOOL
SPORTS LAW PROGRAM
6329 FERET STREET
NEW ORLEANS, LA 70118-6231
504-862-8826
Fax: 504-865-6748
www.law.tulane.edu
• Gary Roberts, Law Program Director
groberts@law.tulane.edu
Degree Offered
JD with a certificate in Sports Law

UNITED STATES SPORTS ACADEMY
ONE ACADEMY DRIVE
DAPHNE, AL 36526-7055
251-626-3303
800-223-2668
Fax: 251-625-1035
admissions@ussa.edu
www.ussa.edu
• Thomas Rosandich, President
(251) 626-3303
president@ussa.edu
• Andrea Jordan, Assistant Dean of Administration and Finance

(261) 626-3303
ajordan@ussa.edu
• Annita Alldredge, Finance Director
(261) 626-3303
aalldredge@ussa.edu
Description:
An independent, non-profit, special mission school offering sport-specific residential and online distance learning programs to students, teachers and administrators around the world.
Description:
Provides a wide range of services including: facility consulting to marketing equipment packages domestically and internationally; fitness-related programs including cardio risk assessment, nutritional analysis and other types of health-related programs.
Year Founded:
1972

UNIVERSITY OF ALABAMA - COLLEGE OF EDUCATION/ HUMAN ENVIRONMENTAL SCIENCES
DEPARTMENT OF HUMAN STUDIES
901 13TH STREET SOUTH
BIRMINGHAM, AL 35294-1250
205-934-4642
Fax: 205-975-8040
act@uab.edu
www.uab.edu
• David Macrina, Human Studies Professor
dmacrina@uab.edu
• Retta Evens, Health Education
• larry Tyson, Counceler Education
• Loucrecia Collins, Educational Leadership
• Andre McKnight, Educational Foundations
• Maxie Kohler, Educational Psychology and Research
• Donna Hester, Physical Education Program Coordinator
(205) 934-8336
dhester@uab.edu
Description:
College of Education- Master of Arts in Human Performance, emphasis in Sport Management; College of Human Environmental Sciences- Master of Science, General Studies in HES, Sport Management

UNIVERSITY OF DALLAS
GRADUATE SCHOOL OF MANAGEMENT
1845 E. NORTHGATE DRIVE
IRVING, TX 75062
972-721-5007
www.udallas.edu/gsm
• Scott Wysong, Ph.D., Department Chair
(972) 721-5007
Description:
Our unique program combines the managerial knowledge to work in both the sports and entertainment industries by using a combination of full-time faculty with academic expertise and part-time faculty with industry experience. Our program liberates students from the idea that work is never fun.
Degrees Offered:
MBA, MS-MBA, MM and a Graduate Certificate Program in Sports and Entertainment Management.

UNIVERSITY OF DELAWARE
Newark, DE 19716
302-831-2000
www.udel.edu/athletics

• Matthew J Robinson, Director
mjrobins@udel.edu
Degree/Majors Offered:
Undergraduates degree in health behavior management, with a concentration in sport management.

UNIVERSITY OF MOUNT UNION
ATHLETICS
1972 CLARK AVENUE
ALLIANCE, OH 44601
330-823-4880
www.mountunion.edu
• Ronald Mendel, Chair of Human Performance/Sport Business Dept.
(330) 823-4765
mendelrw@mountunion.edu

UNIVERSITY OF NEBRASKA KEARNEY
DEPARTMENT OF HEALTH, PE, RECREATION & LEISURE STUDIES
905 W. 25TH STREET
KEARNEY, NE 68849
308-865-8331
Fax: 308-865-8073
unruhnc@unk.edu
www.unk.edu/acad/hperls
• Nita Unruh, Department Chair
Description:
The Sports Administration major is a business oriented program designed for individuals who desires a career in the business side of sports. Students complete a set of comprehensive courses including sport psychology and sociology, sport law, sport marketing, organization and administration of sport and financing sport, as well as an array of business courses. We strongly encourage the majors to complete an additional six business courses which would qualify them for a business administration major to compliment their Sports Administration Major.
Degree/Majors Offered:
B.S. sport administration, B.S. sports administration comprehensive, master's in general physical education.

UNIVERSITY OF NEW ENGLAND
DEPARTMENT OF EXERCISE AND SPORT PERFORMANCE
11 HILLS BEACH ROAD
BIDDEFORD, ME 4005
207-283-0171
Fax: 207-602-5900
• Richard LaRue, Dept. Chairperson/Sport Mgmt. Coord.
(207) 602-2605
rlarule@une.edu
• Wayne Lamarre, Assistant Professor
(207) 602-2412
wlanarre@une.edu
Degrees/Majors Offered:
B.S. sport management, athletics training education, and exercise and health promotion.

UNIVERSITY OF WEST GEORGIA
DEPARTMENT OF PHYSICAL EDUCATION & RECREATION
1600 MAPLE STREET
CARROLLTON, GA 30118
678-839-6530
Fax: 678-839-6195
• Frank Butts, Department Chair, Associate Professor
fbutts@westga.edu

• Leigh Ann Bussell, Assistant Professor
• Courtney Flowers, Assistant Professor
Description:
This course provides an overview of basic knowledge areas for the successful sport manager. Fundamental sports management principles and key skills as well as information on current issues are emphasized.

VALPARAISO UNIVERSITY
DEPARTMENT OF PHYSICAL EDUCATION
252 ATH-REC CENTER
VALPARAISO, IN 46383
219-464-5235
Fax: 219-464-5154
www.valpo.edu
• Jerry Stieger, Ph.D, Sports Management Program Coordinator
(219) 464-5235
jerry.stieger@valpo.edu
• Mark LaBarbera, Director of Athletics
(219) 464-6894
Mark.LaBarbera@valpo.edu
• Stephen Anthony, Associate Director of Athletics for Business
(219) 464-5242
Stephen.Anthony@valpo.edu
• Anne VanKeppel, Associate Director of Athletics for Marketing
(219) 464-6130
Anne.VanKeppel@valpo.edu
• Homer Drew, Associate Director of Athletics
(219) 464-5231
Homer.Drew@valpo.edu
• john kuka, Associate Director of Athletics
(219) 464-5967
John.Kuka@valpo.edu
• Adam Klos, Assistant Director of Athletics for Event Man
(219) 464-6125
Adam.Klos@valpo.edu
• Marba Paskash, Department Administrative Assistant
(219) 464-5235
Description:
Undergrad Degree: B.S. Sports Management. Areas of Specialization: Athletic Administration, Facilities Management, Fitness Management, Sports Information, Sports Promotion, Sports Business Management.

VIRGINIA COMMONWEALTH UNIVERSITY
SPORTS MEDICINE BUILDING
1300 W. BROAD STREET
RICHMOND, VA 23284-3013
804-827-7821
Fax: 804-828-4938
sportscenter@vcu.edu
www.vcu.edu/sportscenter
• Richard Sander, Asst. to President & Athletics Dir.
• Gary Ness, Sport Management Adjunct Professor
Degree Offered:
M.S. sport leadership.

WARNER SOUTHERN COLLEGE
13895 HIGHWAY 27
LAKE WALES, FL 33859
863-638-1426
800-949-7248

Fax: 863-638-1472
www.warnerroyals.com
• Dennis Obermeyer, Chair/Director
Description:
B.A. sports management, B.A. exercise science

WASHBURN UNIVERSITY OF TOPEKA
DEPARTMENT OF HEALTH, PHYSICAL EDUCATION, EXERCISE SCIENCE
PETRO 201
1700 SW COLLEGE AVENUE
TOPEKA, KS 66621
785-670-1010
Fax: 785-231-1059
www.washburn.edu
• Bill Sparks, Chairman/Professor
• Susan Miller, Associate Professor
Susan.miller@washburn.edu
• Nancy Province, Department Secretary
nancy.province@washburn.edu
Description:
Undergrad Degree: B.Ed., B.A. Areas of Specialization: Physical Education K-12 Teaching, Athletic Training, Sports Facilities Management, Exercise Physiology.

WASHINGTON STATE UNIVERSITY
SPORT MANAGEMENT PROGRAM
COLLEGE OF EDUCATION
PO BOX 642114
PULLMAN, WA 99164-2136
509-335-1738
Fax: 509-335-0328
mc@wsu.edu
www.wsu.edu
• Jo Washburn, Program Coordinator
(509) 335-6363
jwashbur@mail.wsu.edu
• Cathryn Claussen, Associate Professor
(509) 335-7232
claussen@wsu.edu
• Judy Schultz, Instructor & Advisor
(509) 335-5672
jaschultz@wsu.edu
Description:
A sport management education provides students with the planning and administrative skills needed for the success of organizations that focus on sport activities, sport products, or sport services.
Degrees:
Under Grad, BA in Sports Management. Grad Degree: M.A., Ed.M. Areas of Athletic Administration. Areas of specialization: Business, Communications, Leadership Studies.

WAYNE STATE COLLEGE
1111 Main Street
Wayne, NE 68787
800-228-9972
www.wsc.edu/athletics
• Tammy Evetovich, Director
Degrees:
Sport management, M.S. education in sport management.

WAYNE STATE UNIVERSITY
DEPARTMENT OF ATHLETICS
5101 JOHN C. LODGE 101 MATTHAEI
DETROIT, MI 48202
313-577-4280
Fax: 313-577-0208
www.wsuathletics.com
• Jason Clark, Senior Assoc. Athletics Director

jason.clark@wayne.edu
• Mary Beth Buchan, Assoc. Athletics Director/Fiscal Operations
ay3203@wayne.edu
• Lisa Seymour, Assistant Athletics Director
aw6975@wayne.edu
• Nicole Blaszczyk, Asst. Athletics Director for Marketing & Prom
aw4970@wayne.edu
• Jim Campbell, Supervisor, Multipurpose Indoor Facility
soupy@wayne.edu
• Robert M. Ackerman, Faculty Athletics Representative
ackerman@wayne.edu
• Fournier Rob, Director of Athletics
(313) 577-5996
ai5611@wayne.edu
Degrees Offered:
Grad Degree: M.A. Sports Administration. Areas of Specialization: Interscholastic Athletic Administration; Intercollegiate Athletic Administration; Professional Sports Administration; Commercial Sports Program Administration.

WEBBER INTERNATIONAL UNIVERSITY
1201 NORTH SCENIC HIGHWAY
BABSON, FL 33827
863-638-2929
800-741-1844
Fax: 863-638-1317
registrar@webber.edu
• Thomas C Aaron, Chair/Director
tomaaron@msn.com
Description:
B.S. busness administration, concentration in sport management;M.B.A., concentration in sport management.

WEST CHESTER UNIVERSITY
DEPARTMENT OF KINESIOLOGY
206 STURZEBECKER HEALTH SCIENCES CENTER
WEST CHESTER, PA 19383
610-436-2610
Fax: 610-436-2860
rzetts@wcupa.edu
• Raymond Zetts, Chairperson
(610) 436-2610
rzetts@wcupa.edu
• Diane Riley, Department Secretary
• Kendall Walkes, Mens Soccer Head Coach
(610) 436-2221
• Bett Ann Kempf Townsley, Womens Soccer Head Coach
(610) 436-6903
ekempf@wcupa.edu
• Diane Lokey, Softball Head Coach
(610) 436-2170
dlokey@wcupa.edu
• Jamie Ruddisill, Swimming and Diving Head Coach
(610) 436-2127
Description:
Grad Degree: M.S. Areas of Specialization: Physical Education; Sport and Athletic Administration; Exercise and Sport Physiology.

WEST VIRGINIA UNIVERSITY
COLLEGE OF PHYSICAL ACTIVITY AND SPORT SCIENCES
PO BOX 6116
MORGANTOWN, WV 26506-6116

304-293-0861 EXT 5265
Fax: 304-293-4641
dbranch@wvu.edu
www.wvu.edu
• Dallas Branch, Jr., Sport Management
Program Coordinator
(304) 293-0861
dbranch@mail.wvu.edu
• Floyd Jones, Sport Mgmt. Undergraduate
Coordinator
(304) 293-3295
Floyd.Jones@mail.wvu.edu
• Tina Samara, Women's Tennis Head
Coach
(304) 293-9882
tina.samara@mail.wvu.edu
• Sean Cleary, Women's Track and Cross
Country
(304) 293-9875
sean.cleary@mail.wvu.edu
• Jill Kramer, Women's Volleyball Head
Coach
(304) 293-4234
jillian.kramer@mail.wvu.edu
Description:
Undergrad Degree: B.S. Grad Degree: M.S.
Areas of Specialization: Undergrad: Sport
Management. Grad: Sport
Management/Administration.

WESTERN CAROLINA UNIVERSITY
WESTERN CAROLINA UNIVERSITY
RAMSEY CENTER-ATHLETICS
CULLOWHEE, NC 28723
828-227-7338
Fax: 828-227-7688
www.catamountsports.com
• Randy Eaton, Director of Athletics
(828) 227-7338
jreaton@email.wcu.edu
• Bobby Moranda, Baseball Head Coach
(828) 227-7338
• Larry Hunter, Men's Basketball Head
Coach
(828) 227-7338
hunter@email.wcu.edu
Description:
B.S. sport management. Concentrations:
athletic administration, exercise science and
fitness management, event and facility
management and marketing, professional
sports management sales, sports
information.

WESTERN ILLINOIS UNIVERSITY
DEPARTMENT OF KINESIOLOGY
BROPHY HALL 212
1 UNIVERSITY CIRCLE
MACOMB, IL 61455
309-298-1981
Fax: 309-298-2981
kinesiology@wiu.edu
www.wiu.edu/kinesiology
• Janet Wigglesworth, Professor/Department
Chairperson
(309) 298-1981
• Darlene Young, Sports Management
Coordinator
(309) 298-1225
DS-Young@wiu.edu
• April Hall, Volleyball Head Coach
(309) 298-1855
ak-hall2@wiu.edu
Degree Offered:
The Master of Science degree in Sport
Management was established in 1972 and is
one of the oldest Sport Management
programs in the United States. The mission

of the degree program is to develop
students' conceptual skills, theoretical
comprehension, and practical knowledge in
order that they are prepared to become the
next generation of leaders in the sports
industry. Students finish the program ready
to embark on careers as practioners,
managers, admnistrators and
researchers/scholars. In addition, the
program at WIU provides current students
with an active and comprehensive network
of alumni working in all aspects of the sports
industry.

WESTERN MICHIGAN UNIVERSITY
DEPARTMENT OF HEALTH, PHYSICAL
EDUCATION & RECREATION
1903 W. MICHIGAN AVENUE
4024 STUDENT RECREATION CENTER
KALAMAZOO, MI 49008
269-387-2710
Fax: 269-387-2704
• Debra Berkey, Dept. Chairperson
debra.berkey@wmich.edu
• Ronald Winter, Dept. Associate Professor
(269) 387-2694
ronald.winter@wmich.edu
• Jody Brylinsky, Ph.D, Dept. Professor
(269) 387-2677
jody.brylinsky@wmich.edu

WESTERN NEW ENGLAND COLLEGE
DEPARTMENT OF MANAGEMENT
1215 WILBRAHAM ROAD
SPRINGFIELD, MA 01119-2684
413-782-1389
Fax: 413-782-1746
www.wnegoldenbears.com
• Sharianne Walker, Dept. Chair/Sport Mgmt
Asst. Prof.
(413) 782-1389
• Daniel Covell, Associate Professor
(413) 782-1689
• Jennifer Kolins, Men's Tennis Head Coach
(413) 796-2230
jkolins@wne.edu
• Lori Mayhew, Softball Head Coach
(413) 796-2230
lmayhew@wne.edu
• Andrea Daley, Women's Swimming Head
Coach
(413) 796-2228
daleyandrea@hotmail.com
• Bret Stothart, Women's Volleyball Head
Coach
(413) 782-1550
bstothart@wne.edu
Description:
Unlike some colleges where sport
management is aligned with physical
education, the Sport Management Program
at Western New England College
emphasizes the business side of the field. In
our leading edge program, you'll take a
common core of business and liberal arts
classes including accounting, business law,
marketing and more. The sport
management curriculum includes such
courses as the Economic of Sports, Sport
Facility Planning and Management, and the
Structure of Sport Industry.
Degrees Offered:
B.S, .B.A. in Sport Management.

WICHITA STATE UNIVERSITY
DEPT. of SPORT MANAGEMENT
109 HESKETT CENTER
WICHITA, KS 67260-0127
316-978-5445
Fax: 316-978-5451
www.goshockers.com
• Eric Sexton, Director of Athletics
(316) 978-3250

WIDENER UNIVERSITY
1 UNIVERSITY PL
CHESTER, PA 19013
610-499-4300
www.widener.edu/athletics
• Joe DiAngelo
• Brian Larson, Director
Degree Offered
Degree in Sports Management.

WILLIAM WOODS UNIVERSITY
One University Avenue
Fulton, MO 65257
800-995-3159
www.williamwoods.edu/athletics
• Marshall Robb, Director
smrobb@williamwoods.edu
Degree/Majors Offered:
Athletics training, exercise science, physical
education, sport management.

WILMINGTON COLLEGE
SPORT MANAGEMENT
320 N. DUPONT HIGHWAY
NEW CASTLE, DE 19720-6491
877-967-5464
• Janice Wardle, Sports Management
Program Coordinator
• Robert Edelson, Business Division
Chairperson
Description:
Students receive a broad-based,
personalized education in sports
management. The program, which
integrates theory with practical internship
requirements, develops students for the
opportunities available in sports
management. In addition to the sports
management curriculum, the program
includes a strong business management
component, providing students with the
skills necessary to succeed in the corporate
areas of this field.
Degree/Majors Offered:
B.S. sport management.

WINDSOR, UNIVERSITY OF
HUMAN KINETICS BUILDING
401 SUNSET AVENUE
WINDSOR, ON, CANADA
519-253-3000 EXT 2432
hk@uwindsor.ca
www.uwindsor.ca/athletics
• Robert Boucher, Dean of Human Kinetics
(519) 253-3000
bouche4@uwindsor.ca
• Wayne Marino, Head of Human Kinetics
(519) 253-3000
wmarino@uwindsor.ca
Degree Offered
Bachelor's and Master's of Human Kinetics
(Sport Management)

WINGATE UNIVERSITY
DEPARTMENT OF SPORT SCIENCES
220 N. CAMDEN ST.

PO BOX 159
WINGATE, NC 28174
704-233-8000
800-755-5550
Fax: 704-233-8170
wingatebulldogs.com
• Dennis Johnson, Sport Sciences Assoc.
Prof./Asst. Dean
(704) 233-8182
• Lauren Merkle, Sport Sciences Assistant
Professor
(704) 233-8297
Description:
Sport Management combines courses in
Sport Sciences with courses in Business
Administration to provide today's student
with the skills necessary for success in the
new millennium. In addition to the general
education requirements (GER) of the
university, the student will take courses in
facility management, sport law, sport history,
and sport leadership from the Department of
Sport Sciences as well as courses in
economics, accounting, marketing, and
business management from the School of
Business and Economics.
Description:
B.S. sport management.

WINSTON-SALEM STATE UNIVERSITY
WSSU DEPT.OF ATHLETICS
200 C.E. GAINES CENTER
WINSTON-SALEM, NC 27110
336-750-2141
Fax: 336-750-8880
www.wssurams.com
• William Hayes, Director of Athletics
(336) 750-2142
hayeswl@wssu.edu
Description:
B.S. sport management major.
Requirements:
Completion of the general studies program,
a minimum of 2.5 grade point average prior
to entry, volunteer experiences in sport
management or related areas and a
commitment toward full participation in the
Major's Club.

WINTHROP UNIVERSITY
DEPARTMENT OF HEALTH & PHYSICAL
EDUCATION
114 TILLMAN HALL
ROCK HILL, SC 29733
803-323-2225
Fax: 803-323-3001
www.winthrop.edu
• Linda Schoonmaker, Associate Professor
schoonmakerl@winthrop.edu
• Curt Laird, Assistant Professor
lairdc@winthrop.edu
Degree Offered
BS in Sport Management

WISCONSIN, LA CROSSE, UNIVERSITY OF
EXERCISE AND SPORT SCIENCE
147 MITCHELL HALL
1725 STATE STREET
LA CROSSE, WI 54601
608-785-8683
Fax: 608-785-8686
www.uwlax.edu
• Patrick DiRocco, Assoc. Professor/Dept.
Chairman
(608) 785-8173
dirocco.patr@uwlax.edu

• John Porcari, Professor/Executive Director
(608) 785-8684
porcari.john@uwlax.edu
• Chris Heilixon, Softball Head Coach
(608) 785-6536
chelixon@uwlax.edu
• Sara Burton, Soccer Head Coach
(608) 785-6534
sburton@uwlax.edu
• Lily Hallock, Volleyball Head Coach
(608) 785-8191
Description:
Undergrad Degree: B.S. Grad Degree: M.S.
Cardiac Rehab/Human Performance; M.S.
Sport Administration. Areas of
Specialization: Undergrad: Athletic
Administration; Sport Management; Fitness
Management. Grad: Exercise Physiology,
Adult Fitness, Sport Administration.

WISCONSIN-PARKSIDE, UNIVERSITY OF
DEPARTMENT OF HEALTH, EXERCISE
SCIENCE AND SPORT MANAGEMENT
900 WOOD ROAD
PO BOX 2000
KENOSHA, WI 53141-2000
262-595-2345
Fax: 262-595-2225
lyter@uwp.edu
• Penny Lyter, Dept. Chairperson
(262) 595-2494
lyter@uwp.edu
• William Miller, Sport Management Advisor
(262) 595-3359
Description:
The Sport and Fitness Industry has
experienced dramatic growth over the past
twenty years. The need for expertise in sport
and fitness management has grown into a
discipline where specialization exists in a
multidimensional sense in the various areas
of business, communications, and
health-related areas. Professional positions
in this exciting area require that persons are
trained and qualified in many areas such as
programming, marketing, management,
communications, facility development,
finance, economics, politics, and legal
aspects.

WITTENBERG UNIVERSITY
DEPARTMENT OF HEALTH/SPORT
SCIENCE
BOX 720
SPRINGFIELD, OH 45501
937-327-6452
Fax: 937-327-6340
www.wittenberg.edu
• Thomas Martin, Professor
(937) 327-6470
tmartin@wittenberg.edu
• Linda Arena, Professor/Chairperson
(937) 327-6452
• Steven Dawson, Associate Professor
(937) 327-6456
sdawson@wittenberg.edu
• Natalie Koukis, Men's and Women's
Swimming/Diving Head Coach
(937) 327-6446
• Justin Stuckey, Men's and Women's Head
Coach
(937) 327-6453
• Paco Labrador, Volleyball Head Coach
(937) 327-6492
flabrador@wittenberg.edu
Description:
Undergrad Degree: B.A. Areas of
Specialization: Sports Medicine; Corporate

Fitness; Sport Management; Sport
Psychology; Exercise Physiology;
Recreation.

XAVIER UNIVERSITY
3800 VICTORY PARKWAY
CINCINNATI, OH 45207-7530
513-745-3417
Fax: 513-745-4930
www.goxavier.com
• Mike Bobinski, Director of Athletics
(513) 745-3417
athleticdirector@xavier.edu
• Scott Googins, Baseball Head Coach
(513) 745-2891
googins@xavier.edu
Description:
Sport management includes any
combination of skills related to planning,
organizing, directing, controlling, budgeting,
leading and evaluating in an organization or
department whose primary product or
service is related to sport and/or physical
activity.
Degrees:
Undergrad Degree: B.S. in Sport
Management or Sport Marketing. Grad
Degree: M.S. in Sports Administration.
Areas of Specialization: Undergrad: Sport
Management or Sport Marketing. Grad:
Sports Administration.
Requirements:
Beyond the core curriculum, sport
management students must successfully
complete 71 semester hours of required
courses.

YORK COLLEGE OF PENNSYLVANIA
SPORT MANAGEMENT
YORK, PA 17405-7199
717-815-1366
Fax: 717-849-1642
pmassa@ycp.edu
www.ycp.edu/athletics
• Patrick Massa, Dept.
Chairperson/Professor
(717) 815-1366
pmassa@ycp.edu
• Tim Newman, Program
Coordinator/Professor
(717) 815-1794
tjnewman@ycp.edu
Description:
The mission of the Sport Management
program encompasses the following: to
provide an environment rich in academics
and in the field experiences oriented toward
developing broad-based leadership skills in
the many areas of the sport industry, not
limited to but including, management, sport
media, and entrepreneurship.
Requirements:
Sport Management majors are required to
complete an elective sequence in another
academic discipline. An elective sequence
consists of between 15 and 18 credits of
coursework in one of the following areas:
accounting, aquatic facility management,
asset protection, athletic administration,
entrepreneurial Studies human resource
management, information Systems,
management, marketing, Operations
Management, organizational development,
public relations, retailing, Speech
Communication, Student Initiated
Degree Offered:
BS in Sport Management

college sports

4
media

A

ABC SPORTS, INC., 681
ABERDEEN AMERICAN NEWS, 461
ABILENE REPORTER NEWS, 461
ACADEMIC-ATHLETIC JOURNAL/N4A NATIONAL OFFICE, 553
ACTION PURSUIT GAMES, 553
ACTION SPORTS ADVENTURE, 603
THE ACTIVE NETWORK, INC., 723
ADA EVENING NEWS, 461
THE ADAM GOLD SHOW, 613
ADIRONDACK DAILY ENTERPRISE, 461
ADIRONDACK SPORTS & FITNESS, 553
ADVENTURE CYCLIST, 554
ADVENTURE SPORTS OUTDOORS, 554
THE ADVERTISER, 543
ADVERTISER-TRIBUNE, 461
ADVOCATE, 461
ADVOCATE-MESSENGER, 461
AEGIS, THE, 543
AIKEN STANDARD, 461
AIKIDO TODAY MAGAZINE, 554
AKRON BEACON JOURNAL, 461
ALAMEDA JOURNAL, 461
ALASKA HORSE JOURNAL, 554
ALBANY DEMOCRAT-HERALD, 461
ALBANY HERALD, 461
ALBERT LEA TRIBUNE, 461
ALBUQUERQUE JOURNAL, 461
ALEXANDRIA DAILY TOWN TALK, 461
ALICE ECHO NEWS, 462
ALLIANCE REVIEW, 462
ALLIANCE TIMES-HERALD, 462
ALPHARETTA NEIGHBOR, 462
ALTOONA MIRROR, 462
ALTUS TIMES, 462
AM 620 WZON THE SPORTS ZONE, 618
AM 850 THE BUZZ SPORTS RADIO, 618
AM 950 THE FAN, 618
AM NEW YORK, 462
AMARILLO GLOBE-NEWS, 462
AMERICA OGGI, 462
AMERICAN BOWLER, 554
AMERICAN CHEERLEADER, 554
AMERICAN FARRIERS JOURNAL, 554
AMERICAN FOOTBALL MONTHLY, 554
AMERICAN PRESS, 462
AMERICAN QUARTER HORSE RACING JOURNAL, 554
AMERICAN SAILOR, 554
AMERICAN SNOWMOBILER, 554
AMERICAN SPORTS, 554
AMERICAN TURF MONTHLY, 555
AMERICAN URBAN RADIO NETWORKS, 610
AMERICAN WINDSURFER, 555
AMERICUS TIMES-RECORDER, 462
AMI NEWS, SAN FRANCISCO/NEW YORK, 618
ANCHORAGE DAILY NEWS, 462
ANDALUSIA STAR NEWS, 462
ANDERSON INDEPENDENT-MAIL, 462
ANN ARBOR NEWS, 462
ANN LIGUORI PRODUCTIONS, INC., 681
ANNISTON STAR, 462
ANTELOPE VALLEY PRESS, 463
ANTIGO DAILY JOURNAL, 463
ANVIL'S RING, 555
AOL SPORTS, 604
APPALOOSA JOURNAL, 555
APPEAL-DEMOCRAT, 463
ARABIAN HORSE WORLD, 555
AREA AUTO RACING NEWS, 555
THE ARGUS, 543
ARGUS LEADER, 463
ARGUS-PRESS, 463
ARIZONA DAILY STAR, 463
ARIZONA DAILY SUN, 463
ARIZONA REPUBLIC, 463
ARIZONA, THE STATE OF GOLF, 555
ARKANSAS CITY TRAVELER, 463
ARKANSAS DEMOCRAT-GAZETTE, 463
ARKANSAS OUTDOORS, 686
AROUND THE HORN, 690
AROUND THE RINGS, 610
ARTESIA DAILY PRESS, 463
ASA PRODUCTIONS, 604
ASBURY PARK PRESS, 463
ASHEVILLE CITIZEN-TIMES, 463
ASHLAND TIMES-GAZETTE, 464
ASPEN TIMES, 464

ASSOCIATED PRESS, 464
ATCHISON DAILY GLOBE, 464
ATHENS BANNER-HERALD, 464
ATHENS DAILY REVIEW, 464
ATHENS MESSENGER, 464
ATHENS NEWS COURIER, 464
ATHLETIC BUSINESS, 555
ATHLETIC DIRECTORY, 600
ATHLETIC GUIDE PUBLISHING, 600
ATHLETIC MANAGEMENT, 555
ATHLETICS ADMINISTRATION, 555
ATHLON SPORTS COMMUNICATIONS, 555
ATHOL DAILY NEWS, 464
ATLANTA JOURNAL-CONSTITUTION, 464
ATLANTA SPORTS AND FITNESS MAGAZINE, 556
ATLANTIC NEWS-TELEGRAPH, 464
ATLANTIC RACQUET PRESS, 556
AUBURN JOURNAL, 464
AUGUSTA CHRONICLE, 464
AUGUSTA DAILY GAZETTE, 464
AUSTIN AMERICAN-STATESMAN, 464
AUSTIN DAILY HERALD, 464
AUTOTRADER.COM, INC, 681
AUTOZONE, 618
AVID GOLFER MAGAZINE, 556
AZTEC SPORTS WEEKLY, 690
AZTECA NEWS, 465

B

BACK COUNTRY MAGAZINE, 556
BACKPACKER MAGAZINE, 556
BAKER CITY HERALD, 465
BAKERSFIELD CALIFORNIAN, 465
BALLOON LIFE, 556
BALLS AND STRIKES SOFTBALL MAGAZINE, 556
BALTIMORE SUN, 465
BANGOR DAILY NEWS, 465
BANNER-GRAPHIC, 465
BANNER-NEWS, 465
BARABOO NEWS REPUBLIC, 465
BARREL HORSE NEWS, 556
BASEBALL AMERICA, 556
BASEBALL BLUEBOOK, LLC, 600
BASEBALL DIGEST, 556
BASEBALL TONIGHT, 690
BASEBALLVIDEOS.COM, 604
BASKETBALL TIMES, 556
BASSMASTERS, THE, 604
BASTROP DAILY ENTERPRISE, 465
BATESVILLE GUARD, 465
BATTLE CREEK ENQUIRER, 465
BAXTER BULLETIN, 465
BAY & DELTA YACHTSMAN, 556
BAY CITY TIMES, 465
BAY CITY TRIBUNE, 465
BAYTOWN SUN, 466
BEACH REPORTER, 466
BEACON-NEWS, 466
BEARS KICK OFF LIVE, 686
BEATRICE DAILY SUN, 466
BEAUMONT ENTERPRISE, 466
BEAVER COUNTY TIMES, 466
BEAVERCREEK NEWS CURRENT, 466
BEDTIME STORIES FOR YOUNG ATHLETES, 557
BEHIND THE WHEEL, 557
BELLEFONTAINE EXAMINER, 466
BELLEVILLE NEWS-DEMOCRAT, 466
BELLEVUE GAZETTE, 466
BELLINGHAM HERALD, 466
BENICIA HERALD, 466
BENNINGTON BANNER, 466
BENTON COUNTY DAILY RECORD, 466
BENTON EVENING NEWS, 466
BERKELEY HEIGHTS/NEW PROVIDENCE INDEPENDENT PRESS, 467
BERKSHIRE EAGLE, 467
BERWYN-CICERO-STICKNEY-FOREST VIEW LIFE, 467
BETWEEN THE TOUCHLINES, 557
BICYCLE RETAILER AND INDUSTRY NEWS, 557
BICYCLING, 557
BIG BOARD SPORTS, 686
BIG SPORTS X-TRA, 686
BIKE, 557
BILLIARDS DIGEST, 557

BILLINGS GAZETTE, 467
BIRMINGHAM NEWS, 467
BISBEE DAILY REVIEW, 467
BISMARCK TRIBUNE, 467
BLACK ATHLETE SPORTS NETWORK, 557
BLACK BELT, 557
BLACK ENTERTAINMENT TELEVISION, 681
BLACK HILLS PIONEER, 467
BLACK TENNIS MAGAZINE, 557
BLACKWELL JOURNAL-TRIBUNE, 467
BLADE, 467
BLADE-EMPIRE, 467
BLADES ON ICE, 557
BLEACHER REPORT, 721
BLOOD-HORSE, 557
BLUE BOOK OF COLLEGE ATHLETICS, 600
BLUE WATER SAILING, 557
BLUEFIELD DAILY TELEGRAPH, 467
BMX PLUS, 558
BO GANZ PRODUCTIONS, 604
BOAT & MOTOR DEALER, 558
BOAT BROKER OUTDOOR, 558
BOAT U.S. MAGAZINE, 558
BOATING, 558
BOATING INDUSTRY, 558
BOATING LIFE, 558
BOATING WORLD, 558
BOB COSTAS NOW, 690
BOLIVAR COMMERCIAL, 467
BOMBO SPORTS & ENTERTAINMENT, 604
BONNER COUNTY DAILY BEE, 467
BONNEVILLE RACING NEWS, 558
BOONVILLE DAILY NEWS, 467
BORGER NEWS-HERALD, 468
BOSTON GLOBE, 468
BOSTON HANNAH INTERNATIONAL, 558
BOSTON HERALD, 468
BOURNE ENTERPRISE, 468
BOWIE BLADE-NEWS, 468
BOWLERS JOURNAL INTERNATIONAL, 558
BOWLING CENTER MANAGEMENT, 558
BOWLING WORLD, 559
BOXEO TELEMUNDO, 690
BOXING USA, 559
BOZEMAN DAILY CHRONICLE, 468
BRADENTON HERALD, 468
BRADFORD ERA, 468
BRAINERD DAILY DISPATCH, 468
BRANSON TRI-LAKES DAILY NEWS, 468
BRAZIL TIMES, 468
BRENHAM BANNER-PRESS, 468
BRIDGETON NEWS, 468
BRISTOL HERALD COURIER, 469
BRISTOL PRESS, 469
BROOKINGS REGISTER, 469
BROWNSVILLE HERALD, 469
BROWNWOOD BULLETIN, 469
BRUNSWICK NEWS, 469
BRYAN TIMES, 469
BRYAN-COLLEGE STATION EAGLE, 469
BSKYB, 617
BUCKS COUNTY COURIER TIMES, 469
BUCS ZONE, 686
BUFFALO NEWS, 469
BULLETIN, 469
BULLPEN, 559
BURBANK LEADER, 469
BURLINGTON COUNTY TIMES, 469
BURLINGTON FREE PRESS, 470
BUSCH NORTH SCENE, 559
BUTLER EAGLE, 470

C

CABLE NEWS NETWORK/CNN, 681
CAL-HI SPORTS, 559
CALAMARI VIDEO, 604
CALEDONIAN RECORD, 470
CALGARY HERALD, 470
CALIFORNIA BOWLING NEWS, 559
CALIFORNIA DIVING NEWS, 559
CALIFORNIA HOCKEY & SKATING, 559
CALIFORNIA THOROUGHBRED, 559
CALIFORNIA TRACK AND RUNNING NEWS, 559
CALL, 470
CALL-LEADER, 470
CAMDEN NEWS, 470
CANADIAN BROADCASTING CORPORATION/CBC, 681
CANOE & KAYAK MAGAZINE, 559

media

media

Media Alphabetical Index

WCBS-TV, 708
WCBT-AM, 647
WCCB-TV, 708
WCCO, 647
WCCO-TV, 708
WCCP, 647
WCCW-AM, 647
WCDK-FM, 647
WCDO-AM, 647
WCEM-AM, 648
WCFM-FM, 648
WCFN-TV, 708
WCFW-FM, 648
WCGQ-FM, 648
WCHC-FM, 648
WCHO-AM, 648
WCHO-FM, 648
WCHS-TV, 708
WCIA-TV, 708
WCIV-TV, 709
WCJB-TV, 709
WCJW-AM, 648
WCKY-AM, 648
WCLG-FM, 648
WCLH-FM, 648
WCLN-AM, 648
WCLO-AM, 648
WCLT-AM, 648
WCNC - NBC6, 709
WCNC-AM, 648
WCNC-AM / WZBO-AM, 648
WCNC-TV, 709
WCOS, 648
WCPO-TV, 709
WCSC-TV, 709
WCSH-TV, 709
WCSL, 649
WCSL-AM, 649
WCST-AM, 649
WCTA-AM, 649
WCTK-FM, 649
WCUM-AM, 649
WCVB-TV, 709
WCVM-FM, 649
WCWT-FM, 649
WCYJ-FM, 649
WDAE-AM 620, 649
WDAF-TV, 709
WDAM-TV, 709
WDAS-AM, 649
WDAZ-TV, 709
WDBJ-TV, 709
WDBO-AM, 649
WDBQ-AM, 649
WDDD-AM, 649
WDDD-FM, 649
WDDK-FM, 649
WDEF, 709
WDEF-TV, 709
WDEL-AM, 649
WDFN, 649
WDFN - 1130 AM THE FAN, 650
WDHC-FM, 650
WDIV-TV, 709
WDJT-TV, 709
WDKD-AM, 650
WDKX-FM, 650
WDLB, 650
WDLZ-FM, 650
WDNE-FM, 650
WDOE-AM/FM, 650
WDOG-FM, 650
WDOR-FM, 650
WDOW-AM, 650
WDPN-AM, 650
WDSL-AM, 650
WDSM SPORTS RADIO 710, 650
WDSM-AM, 650
WDUN-AM, 651
WDUX-AM/FM, 651
WDUX-FM, 651
WDZN-FM, 651
WE ARE THERE SATURDAY, 617
WEAI-FM, 651
WEAQ-AM, 651
WEAR-TV, 710
WEAS-FM, 651
WEATHERFORD DEMOCRAT, 551
WEAU-TV, 710
WEBB ELECTRONICS, 610

WECT-TV, 710
WEDM-FM, 651
WEDO-AM, 651
WEEB-AM, 651
WEEI SPORTS RADIO, 651
WEEK-TV, 710
WEEKDAY SPORTSBEAT, 614
WEEKEND, 551
WEEKEND GAMENIGHT, 617
WEEO-AM, 651
WEEU-AM, 651
WEEX-AM, 651
WEHT-TV, 710
WEIDER PUBLICATIONS, 598
WEIU-FM, 651
WEJL-AM, 651
WEKS-FM, 651
WEKT-AM, 651
WEKX-FM, 651
WELLINGTON DAILY NEWS, 551
WELLSVILLE DAILY REPORTER, 551
WELM-AM, 652
WELW-AM, 652
WEMJ-AM, 652
WENATCHEE WORLD, 551
WENE, 652
WENG, 652
WENK-AM, 652
WENY-TV, 710
WEPG-AM, 652
WERQ-FM, 652
WESH-TV, 710
WEST BEND DAILY NEWS, 551
WEST CENTRAL TRIBUNE, 551
WEST COUNTY TIMES, 551
WEST GLEN COMMUNICATIONS, INC., 610
WEST HAWAII TODAY, 551
WEST PLAINS DAILY QUILL, 551
WEST VALLEY VIEW, 551
WEST-AM, 652
WESTERN GUIDE TO SNOWMOBILING, 598
WESTERN HORSEMAN, 598
WESTERN OUTDOOR NEWS, 598
WESTERN OUTDOORS, 598
WESTERN SPORTS GUIDE, 603
WESTWOODONE, 611
WETM-TV, 710
WEVR-AM, 652
WEVR-FM, 652
WEWS-TV, 710
WFAA-TV, 710
WFAN SPORTS RADIO, 652
WFAT-FM, 652
WFDF 910AM RADIO, 652
WFEB, 652
WFEB-AM, 652
WFFC-FM, 653
WFFF-AM, 653
WFGN-AM, 653
WFHR, 653
WFIE-TV, 710
WFIN RADIO, 653
WFIS-AM, 653
WFLA-TV, 710
WFLD TV CHANNEL 32 CHICAGO/FOX, 710
WFLD-TV, 710
WFLF-AM, 653
WFMB-AM SPORTS RADIO 1450, 653
WFMJ-TV, 710
WFMQ-FM, 653
WFMY-TV, 710
WFMZ-TV, 710
WFNR, 653
WFNR-AM, 653
WFNZ-AM 610 SPORTS RADIO, 653
WFPR-AM, 653
WFRD-FM, 653
WFRM-AM, 653
WFRV-TV, 711
WFRX-AM, 653
WFSB-TV, 711
WFSE-FM, 653
WFTG-AM, 654
WFTS-TV, 711
WFTV-TV, 711
WFUV-FM, 654
WFXE-FM, 654
WFYY-FM, 654
WGAB, 654
WGAD, 654

WGAD-AM, 654
WGAI-AM, 654
WGAL-TV, 711
WGAN, 654
WGAN-AM, 654
WGAP-AM, 654
WGAW-AM, 654
WGBA-TV, 711
WGBK-FM, 654
WGCL-TV, 711
WGCM-AM, 654
WGCY-FM, 654
WGET, 654
WGFR-FM, 654
WGGA-AM, 654
WGGB-TV, 711
WGH-AM THE SCORE, 655
WGHB-AM, 655
WGHT-AM, 655
WGL-AM, 655
WGLU-FM, 655
WGLV-FM, 655
WGMA-AM, 655
WGME-TV, 711
WGMN-AM, 655
WGN-9 CHICAGO'S CW, 711
WGN-AM, 655
WGNC, 655
WGOM-AM, 655
WGOW-AM, 655
WGR 55 SPORTS RADIO, 655
WGRE-FM, 655
WGRM-AM, 655
WGRM-FM, 655
WGXA-TV, 711
WHAI-FM/WPVQ, 655
WHAM-TV, 711
WHAN-AM, 655
WHB-AM, 656
WHBC-FM, 656
WHBG-AM, 656
WHBN-AM, 656
WHBQ SPORTS 56, 656
WHBQ-TV, 711
WHBU 1240, 656
WHBU-AM, 656
WHBY-AM, 656
WHCC-FM, 656
WHCY-FM, 656
WHDH-TV, 712
WHDL-AM, 656
WHEELIN' SPORTSMAN, 598
WHEELING NEWS-REGISTER, 551
WHEELSTV, 685
WHEN, 656
WHHB-FM, 656
WHHS-FM, 656
WHIO-TV, 712
WHIP-AM, 656
WHIT, 656
WHIZ-TV, 712
WHKS-AM, 657
WHKY-TV, 712
WHLA-TV, 712
WHMB-TV, 712
WHME-TV, 712
WHNT-TV, 712
WHO-TV, 712
WHOC-AM, 657
WHOI-TV, 712
WHOL-AM, 657
WHRM-TV, 712
WHTC-AM, 657
WHTG-AM, 657
WHTG-FM, 657
WHTK, 657
WHTK-AM, 657
WHTL-FM, 657
WHTM-TV, 712
WHTQ-FM, 657
WHWC-TV, 712
WHYN-AM, 657
WIAT - CBS 42, 712
WIBC, 657
WIBM-AM, 657
WIBN-FM, 657
WIBR, 657
WIBW AM 580 RADIO, 657
WICHITA EAGLE, 551

media

Newspapers

ABERDEEN AMERICAN NEWS
124 SOUTH 2ND STREET
PO BOX 4430
ABERDEEN, SD 57402
605-229-5555
800-925-4100
news@aberdeennews.com
http://www.aberdeennews.com
• John Papendick, Sports Editor
• Ryan Deal, Sports Reporter
Frequency:
7 time(s) per week

ABILENE REPORTER NEWS
101 CYPRESS STREET
PO BOX 30
ABILENE, TX 79601-5816
325-673-4271
Fax: 325-670-5270
http://www.reporternews.com
• Trish Choate, Sports Editor
• Nellie Doneva, Sports Writer
• Rick Myers, Sports Columnist
Frequency:
7 time(s) per week

ADA EVENING NEWS
116 NORTH BROADWAY
ADA, OK 74820
580-332-4433
800-259-8489
Fax: 580-332-8734
http://www.adaevingnews.com
• Jeff Cali, Sports Editor
(580) 310-7526
adanewssports@cableone.net
• Maurisa Nelson, Advertising Director
(580) 310-7502
mnelson@adaeveningnews.com
Frequency:
6 time(s) per week

ADIRONDACK DAILY ENTERPRISE
54 BROADWAY
SARANAC LAKE, NY 12983-1703
518-891-2600
Fax: 518-891-2756
adenews@adirondackguide.com
http://adirondackguide.com
• Morgan Ryan, Sports Editor
Frequency:
6 time(s) per week

ADVERTISER-TRIBUNE
320 NELSON STREET
TIFFIN, OH 44883-9359
419-448-3200
800-448-3235
Fax: 419-447-3274
rweaver@advertiser-tribune.com
http://www.advertiser-tribune.com
• Zach Baker, Sports Reporter
(419) 448-3256
zbaker@advertiser-tribune.com
• Tony Maluso, Sports
(419) 448-3256
tmaluso@advertiser-tribune.com
Frequency:
7 time(s) per week

ADVOCATE
7290 BLUEBONNET BLVD.
BATON ROUGE, LA 70810

225-383-1111
Fax: 225-388-0371
http://www.2theadvocate.com/
• Joseph Schierfelbein, Executive Sports Editor
(225) 388-0321
jschiefelbein@theadvocate.com
• Les East, Sports Reporter
(225) 388-0325
least@theadvocate.com
Frequency:
7 time(s) per week

ADVOCATE-MESSENGER
330 SOUTH 4TH STREET
DANVILLE, KY 40422-2033
859-236-2551
800-428-0409
Fax: 859-236-9566
advocate@amnews.com
http://www.amnews.com
• Larry Vaught, Sports Editor
(859) 236-2551
• Mike Marsee, Sports Writer
(859) 236-2551
Frequency:
6 time(s) per week

AIKEN STANDARD
P.O. BOX 456
AIKEN, SC 29801-4083
803-648-2311
Fax: 803-648-6052
editorial@aikenstandard.com
http://www.aikenstandard.com
• Noah Feit, Sports Editor
(803) 644-2389
• Jeremy Timmerman, Sports Reporter
(803) 644-2339
Frequency:
7 time(s) per week

AKRON BEACON JOURNAL
44 EAST EXCHANGE STREET
AKRON, OH 44308
330-996-3000
800-777-7232
Fax: 330-376-9235
http://www.ohio.com
• Scott Fagerstrom, Sports Editor
(330) 996-3828
sfagerstrom@thebeaconjournal.com
• Marla Ridenour, Sports Columnist
mridenour@thebeaconjournal.com
Frequency:
7 time(s) per week

ALAMEDA JOURNAL
1516 OAK STREET
ALAMEDA, CA 94501
510-748-1666
888-978-2760
http://www.insidebayarea.com/alameda
• Dave Belli, Assistant Sports Editor
(925) 977-8592
• Joe Deloach, Sports Copy Editor
(925) 943-8122
• Jimmy Durkin, Sports Reporter
(510) 208-6457
• Ron Ellis, Sports Copy Editor
(925) 943-8244
• Ben Enos, Sports Reporter
(925) 943-8108
• Don Peterson, Sports Copy Editor
(925) 943-8194
Frequency:
7 time(s) per week

ALBANY DEMOCRAT-HERALD
600 LYON STREET, S.W.
PO BOX 130
ALBANY, OR 97321-0041
541-926-2211
Fax: 541-926-5298
news@dhonline.com
www.democratherald.com
• Les Gehrett, Sports Editor
(541) 812-6092
les.gehret@lee.net
• Jesse Sowa, Assistant Sports Editor
(541) 812-6091
jesse.sowa@lee.net
Frequency:
7 time(s) per week

ALBANY HERALD
126 N WASHINGTON ST
ALBANY, GA 31701
229-888-9300
800-234-3725
Fax: 229-888-9312
news@albanyherald.com
http://www.albanyherald.com
• John Millikan, Sports Reporter
(229) 888-9307
• Tim Morse, Sports Reporter
(229) 888-9306
tim.morse@albanyherald.com
Frequency:
7 time(s) per week

ALBERT LEA TRIBUNE
808 WEST FRONT STREET
ALBERT LEA, MN 56007-1947
507-373-1411
800-657-4996
Fax: 507-373-0333
news@albertleatribune.com
http://www.albertleatribune.com
• Micah Bader, Sports Editor
(507) 379-3434
micah.bader@albertleatribune.com
• Drew Claussen, Sports Reporter
(507) 402-6610
Frequency:
6 time(s) per week

ALBUQUERQUE JOURNAL
7777 JEFFERSON STREET, NE
ALBUQUERQUE, NM 87109-4343
505-823-3800
800-990-5765
Fax: 505-823-3994
journal@abqjournal.com
http://www.abqjournal.com/
• Ed Johnson, Assistant Sports Editor
(505) 823-3933
• Mark Smith, Assistant Sports Editor
(505) 823-3935
• Randy Harrison, Sports Editor
(505) 823-3907
rharrison@abqjournal.com
Frequency:
7 time(s) per week

ALEXANDRIA DAILY TOWN TALK
PO BOX 7558
ALEXANDRIA, LA 71306
318-487-6397
800-523-8391
Fax: 318-487-6488
sports@thetowntalk.com
http://www.thetowntalk.com
• Randy Benson, Sports Editor
(318) 487-6431

media

Frequency:
7 time(s) per week

ALICE ECHO NEWS
405 EAST MAIN STREET
PO BOX 1610
ALICE, TX 78333
361-664-6588
Fax: 361-668-1030
http://www.aliceechonews.com
• Stephen Garcia, Sports Reporter
(361) 664-6588
Frequency:
6 time(s) per week

ALLIANCE REVIEW
40 SOUTH LINDEN AVENUE
ALLIANCE, OH 44601-2447
330-821-1300
Fax: 330-821-8258
reviewedit@the-review.com
http://www.the-review.com
• Michael Brown, Sports Editor
mjbrown@the-review.com
• Jeffrey Zupanic, Sports Reporter
jzupanic@the-review.com
Frequency:
6 time(s) per week

ALLIANCE TIMES-HERALD
114 EAST FOURTH STREET
PO BOX G
ALLIANCE, NE 69301
308-762-3060
Fax: 308-762-3063
http://www.alliancetimes.com
• Kristi Hulsey, Sports Editor
(308) 762-3060
Frequency:
6 time(s) per week

ALPHARETTA NEIGHBOR
10930 CRABAPPLE ROAD
SUITE 9
ROSWELL, GA 30075
770-993-7400
Fax: 770-518-6062
nfulton@neighbornewspapers.com
http://www.neighbornewspapers.com
Frequency:
1 time(s) per week

ALTOONA MIRROR
P.O. BOX 2008
301 CAYUGA AVE.
ALTOONA, PA 16602-4323
814-946-7411
800-222-1962
Fax: 814-946-7547
news@altoonamirror.com
http://www.altoonamirror.com
• Buck Frank, Sports Editor
(814) 946-7461
bfrank@altoonamirror.com
• Philip Cmor, Assistant Sports Director
(814) 946-7440
pcmor@altoonamirror.com
Frequency:
7 time(s) per week

ALTUS TIMES
PO BOX 578
218 W. COMMERCE
ALTUS, OK 73521
580-482-1221
800-303-1221

Fax: 580-482-5709
editor@altustimes.com
http://www.altustimes.com
• Mark Glenn, Sports Editor
(580) 482-1221
mglenn@civitasmedia.com
Frequency:
6 time(s) per week

AM NEW YORK
240 W. 35TH STREET
9TH FLOOR
NEW YORK, NY 10001
646-293-9499
Fax: 212-239-2828
am-letters@am-ny.com
www.amny.com
• Scott Fontana, Sports Writer
Frequency:
5 time(s) per week

AMARILLO GLOBE-NEWS
P.O. BOX 2091
900 S. HARRISON
AMARILLO, TX 79101
806-376-4488
800-692-4052
Fax: 806-373-0810
http://www.amarillo.com
• Lance Lahnert, Sports Editor
(806) 345-3312
lance.lahnert@amarillo.com
• Terrence Hunley, Sports Reporter
(806) 345-3307
terrence.hunley@amarillo.com
• Lee Passmore, Sports Reporter
(806) 345-3313
lee.passmore@amarillo.com
Frequency:
7 time(s) per week

AMERICA OGGI
475 WALNUT STREET
NORWOOD, NJ 07648-1318
201-358-6692
Fax: 201-258-0250
americoggi@aol.com
http://www.americaoggi.info
• Antonio Cirino, Sports Editor
(201) 358-6692
americoggi@aol.com
Frequency:
7 time(s) per week

AMERICAN PRESS
PO BOX 2893
LAKE CHARLES, LA 70602
337-494-4080
800-531-4080
Fax: 337-494-4070
news@americanpress.com
http://www.americanpress.com
• Alex Hickey, Sports Writer
(337) 494-4071
ahickey@americanpress.com
• Scooter Hobbs, Sports Editor
(337) 494-4075
shobbs@americanpress.com
Frequency:
7 time(s) per week

AMERICUS TIMES-RECORDER
101 HIGHWAY 27 EAST
PO BOX 1247
AMERICUS, GA 31709

229-924-2751
Fax: 229-928-6344
http://www.AmericusTimesRecorder.com
• Scott Phillips, Sports Editor
(229) 924-2751
Frequency:
Daily

ANCHORAGE DAILY NEWS
P.O. BOX 149001
ANCHORAGE, AK 99514-9001
907-257-4200
800-478-4200
Fax: 907-258-2157
newsroom@adn.com
http://www.adn.com
• Beth Bragg, Sports Editor
(907) 257-4335
bbragg@adn.com
Frequency
Daily

ANDALUSIA STAR NEWS
207 DUNSON STREET
ANDALUSIA, AL 36420-3705
334-222-2402
Fax: 334-222-6597
http://www.andalusiastarnews.com
• Andrew Garner, Sports Editor
sports@andalusiastarnews.com
Frequency:
Daily

ANDERSON INDEPENDENT-MAIL
1000 WILLIAMSTON RD
ANDERSON, SC 29621-6508
864-224-4321
888-789-0820
Fax: 864-260-1276
http://www.independentmail.com
• Scott Adamson, Executive Sports Editor
(864) 260-12367
Frequency:
7 time(s) per week

ANN ARBOR NEWS
301 E LIBERTY STREET
SUITE 700
ANN ARBOR, MI 48104
734-623-2500
800-589-6397
Fax: 734-222-0298
sports@annarbor.com
http://www.annarbor.com
• Peter Cunningham, Sports Director
petercunningham@mlive.com
• Kyle Austin, Sports Reporter
kyleaustin2@mlive.com
Frequency:
Thursday and Sunday.

ANNISTON STAR
4305 MCCLELLAN BOULEVARD
PO BOX 189
ANNISTON, AL 36202
256-236-1551
866-814-9253
Fax: 256-241-1991
bdavis@annistonstar.com
http://www.annistonstar.com
• Al Muskewitz, Golf and JSU Teams Writer
(256) 235-3577
amuskewitz@annistonstar.com
• Joe Medley, Sports Columnist
(256) 235-3576
jmedley@annistonstar.com

Frequency:
7 time(s) per week

ANTELOPE VALLEY PRESS
37404 SIEERA HIGHWAY
PO BOX 4050
PALMDALE, CA 93590-4050
661-273-2700
Fax: 661-947-4870
editor@avpress.com
http://www.avpress.com
• Brian Golden, Sports Writer
(661) 267-5344
bgolden@avpress.com
• Alan Hendry, Sports Writer
(661) 267-4170
ahendry@avpress.com
• Merisa Jensen, Sports Writer
(661) 267-4158
mjensen@avpress.com
Frequency:
7 time(s) per week

ANTIGO DAILY JOURNAL
612 SUPERIOR STREET
ANTIGO, WI 54409-2049
715-623-4191
Fax: 715-623-4193
ADJ@dwave.net
http://antigodailyjournal.com
• Fred Berner, Publisher
(715) 623-4191
adj@dwave.net
Frequency:
7 time(s) per week
Teams:
Antigo High School, Elcho High School,
White Lake High School,
Wittenberg-Birnamwood High School.
Sports:
Football, volleyball, boys & girls soccer,
boys & girls tennis, boys & girls track, boys
& girls hockey, boys & girls crosscountry,
boys & girls basketball, softball, wrestling,
gymnastics, and boys golf.

APPEAL-DEMOCRAT
1530 ELLIS LAKE DRIVE
MARYSVILLE, CA 95901-4258
530-749-4700
800-831-2345
Fax: 530-741-1195
http://www.appeal-democrat.com
• Jimmy Graben, Sports Editor
(530) 749-4791
jgraben@appealdemocrat.com
• Andy Arrenquin, Sports Reporter
(530) 749-4790
aarrenquin@appealdemocrat.com
Frequency:
7 time(s) per week

ARGUS LEADER
200 S MINNESOTA AVENUE
PO BOX 5034
SIOUX FALLS, SD 57117
605-331-2200
800-952-0127
Fax: 605-331-2294
argusnews@argusleader.com
http://www.argusleader.com
• Matt Zimmer, Sports Editor
(605) 331-2213
• Michael Klinski, Assistant Sports Editor;
News Reporter
(605) 331-2213

Frequency:
7 time(s) per week

ARGUS-PRESS
201 EAST EXCHANGE STREET
OWOSSO, MI 48867
989-725-5136
Fax: 989-725-6376
http://www.argus-press.com
• Jason Barczy, Sports Editor
• Jerome Murphy, Sports Reporter
jmurphy@argus-press.com
Frequency:
7 time(s) per week

ARIZONA DAILY STAR
4850 SOUTH PARK AVENUE
TUCSON, AZ 85714-1637
520-573-4220
800-695-4111
Fax: 520-573-4141
support@azstarnet.com
http://www.azstarnet.com
• Ryan Finley, Sports Editor
(520) 4312
rfinley@azstarnet.com
• Paul Brown, Sports News Assistant
(520) 573-4145
• Charles Constantino, Sports News
Assistant
(520) 573-4145
Frequency:
7 time(s) per week

ARIZONA DAILY SUN
1751 SOUTH THOMPSON
FLAGSTAFF, AZ 86001
928-774-4545
Fax: 928-773-1934
azdsnews@azdailysun.com
http://www.azdailysun.com
• Cody Bashore, Sports Editor
(928) 556-2251
cbashore@azdailysun.com
Frequency:
7 time(s) per week

ARIZONA REPUBLIC
200 EAST VAN BUREN STREET
PHOENIX, AZ 85004-2238
602-444-8000
800-331-9303
Fax: 602-444-8044
newstips@arizonarepublic.com
http://www.azcentral.com
• Dan Bickley, Sports Columnist
(602) 444-8253
dan.bickley@arizonarepublic.com
• Paul Coro, Sports/NBA Reporter
(602) 444-2470
paul.coro@arizonarepublic.com
• Mark Faller, Sports Editor/Director of
Sports Center
(602) 444-4937
Mark.Faller@arizonarepublic.com
• Richard Obert, High School Sports
Reporter
(602) 444-4894
richard.obert@arizonarepublic.com
• Kent Somers, Sports/Cardinals Reporter
(602) 444-8335
kent.somers@arizonarepublic.com
Frequency:
7 time(s) per week

ARKANSAS CITY TRAVELER
200 EAST 5TH AVENUE
PO BOX 988
ARKANSAS CITY, KS 67005-2606
620-442-4200
Fax: 620-442-7483
http://www.arkcity.com
• Joey Sprinkle, Sports Editor
sports@arkcity.net
Frequency:
6 time(s) per week

ARKANSAS DEMOCRAT-GAZETTE
121 EAST CAPITOL AVENUE
LITTLE ROCK, AR 72201-3819
501-378-3400
800-345-2395
Fax: 501-372-4765
news@ardemgaz.com
http://www.arkansasonline.com
• Jim Bailey, Contributing Sports Columnist
(501) 378-3539
jbailey@arkansasonline.com
• Tim Cooper, Sports Reporter
(501) 378-3576
tcooper@arkansasonline.com
• Bob Holt, Razorbacks Beat Reporter
(479) 770-8464
bholt@arkansasonline.com
• Jeff Krupsaw, Deputy Sports Editor
(501) 399-3637
jkrupsaw@arkansasonline.com
• Robert Yates, Horse Racing/High School
Football Sports Reporter
(501) 378-3579
ryates@arkansasonline.com
Frequency:
7 time(s) per week

ARTESIA DAILY PRESS
PO BOX 190
ARTESIA, NM 88211-0190
575-746-3524
Fax: 575-746-8795
sports@artesianews.com
www.artesianews.com
• Brienne Green, Sports Editor
Frequency:
5 time(s) per week

ASBURY PARK PRESS
3601 HIGHWAY 66
PO BOX 1550
NEPTUNE, NJ 07754
732-922-6000
800-822-9770
Fax: 732-922-4818
sports@app.com
http://www.app.com
• Steve Feitl, Sports Editor
Frequency:
7 time(s) per week

ASHEVILLE CITIZEN-TIMES
14 O. HENRY AVENUE
ASHEVILLE, NC 28801-2604
828-232-5866
800-800-4204
Fax: 828-251-0585
news@citizen-times.com
www.citizen-times.com
• Andrew Pearson, High School Sports
Reporter & Blogger
(828) 232-5863
apearson@citizen-times.com
Frequency:
7 time(s) per week

media

ASHLAND TIMES-GAZETTE
40 EAST SECOND STREET
ASHLAND, OH 44805-2304
419-281-0581
888-463-9711
Fax: 419-281-5591
newsroom@times-gazette.com
http://www.times-gazette.com
• Doug Haidet, Sports Editor
(419) 281-0581
dhaidet@times-gazette.com
• Becky Tener, Sports Writer
(419) 281-0581
btener@times-gazette.com
Frequency:
6 time(s) per week

ASPEN TIMES
310 EAST MAIN STREET
ASPEN, CO 81611
970-925-3414
Fax: 970-925-6240
mail@aspentimes.com
http://www.aspentimes.com
• Dale Strode, Sports Editor
(970) 925-3414
Frequency:
6 time(s) per week

ASSOCIATED PRESS
50 ROCKEFELLER PLAZA
NEW YORK, NY 10020
212-621-1500
Fax: 212-621-5447
info@ap.org
www.ap.org
• Rick Haas, SNTV North America Editor
(212) 621-7417
Frequency
All day, every day

ATCHISON DAILY GLOBE
308 COMMERCIAL STREET
PO BOX 247
ATCHISON, KS 66002
913-367-0583
800-748-7615
Fax: 913-367-7531
globe@npgco.com
http://www.atchisondailyglobe.com
• Logan Jackson, Sports Editor
• Christy McKibben, Advertising Manager
christym@npgco.com
Frequency:
7 time(s) per week

ATHENS BANNER-HERALD
1 PRESS PLACE
ATHENS, GA 30601-2605
706-208-2200
800-553-4252
Fax: 706-543-5234
news@onlineathens.com
http://www.onlineathens.com
• Marc Weiszer, UGA Beat Writer
(706) 208-2238
marc.weiszer@onlineathens.com
• Nicole Saavedra, Sports Reporter
nicole.saavedra@onlineathens.com
• Rachel G. Bowers, Sports Editor
(706) 208-2237
rachel.bowers@onlineathens.com
Frequency:
7 time(s) per week

ATHENS DAILY REVIEW
PO BOX 32
201 S. PRAIRIEVILLE ST.
ATHENS, TX 75751-2541
903-675-5626
Fax: 903-675-9450
editor@athensreview.com
http://www.athensreview.com
• Jayson Larson, Sports Editor
(903) 675-5626
sportseditor@athensreview.com
Frequency:
6 time(s) per week

ATHENS MESSENGER
P.O. BOX 4210
9300 JOHNSON HOLLOW ROAD
ATHENS, OH 45701
740-592-6612
800-233-6611
Fax: 740-592-4647
info@athensmessenger.com
www.athensohiotoday.com
• Jason Arkley, Ohio University Sports
(740) 592-6612
jarkley@athensmessenger.com
• Kevin Wiseman, Sports Editor
(740) 592-6612
kwiseman@athensmessenger.com
Frequency:
6 time(s) per week

ATHENS NEWS COURIER
410 W. GREEN ST
ATHENS, AL 35611
256-232-2720
Fax: 256-233-7753
ann@athensnews-courier.com
http://enewscourier.com
• Jonathan Deal, Sports Writer
jonathan@athensnews-courier.com
Frequency
6x weekly

ATHOL DAILY NEWS
225 EXCHANGE STREET
PO BOX 1000
ATHOL, MA 01331
978-249-3535
Fax: 978-249-9630
http://www.atholdailynews.com
• Josh Talbot, Sports Editor
(978) 249-3535
sports@atholdailynews.com
Frequency:
6 time(s) per week

ATLANTA JOURNAL-CONSTITUTION
223 PERIMETER CENTER PKWY
ATLANTA, GA 30346
404-526-5151
800-846-6672
Fax: 404-526-5746
listen@ajc.com
http://www.ajc.com
• Ray Cox, Sports Content Editor
Frequency:
7 time(s) per week

ATLANTIC NEWS-TELEGRAPH
PO BOX 230 STREET
ATLANTIC, IA 50022-1365
712-243-2624
800-926-6397
Fax: 712-243-4988

news@ant-news.com
www.swiowanewssource.com
• Drew Herron, Sports Editor
sports@ant-news.com
Frequency:
6 time(s) per week

AUBURN JOURNAL
1030 HIGH STREET
AUBURN, CA 95603-4707
530-885-5656
Fax: 530-885-7235
http://www.auburnjournal.com
• Matthew Kimel, Sports Editor
(530) 852-0240
Frequency:
6 time(s) per week

AUGUSTA CHRONICLE
725 BROAD STREET
AUGUSTA, GA 30901-1305
706-724-0851
866-249-0851
Fax: 706-823-3408
newsroom@augustachronicle.com
http://www.chronicle.augusta.com
• John Boyette, Sports Editor
• Chris Gay, Sports Reporter
• Wayne Staats, Sports Writer
• Scott Michaux, Sports Columnist
• David Lee, Sports Writer
Frequency:
7 time(s) per week

AUGUSTA DAILY GAZETTE
204 EAST 5TH STREET
PO BOX 9
AUGUSTA, KS 67010
316-775-2218
Fax: 316-775-3220
http://www.augustagazette.com
• Jeremy Costello, Sports Editor
jcostello@augustagazette.com
Frequency:
5 time(s) per week

AUSTIN AMERICAN-STATESMAN
PO BOX 670
AUSTIN, TX 78767-1200
512-445-3500
800-445-9898
Fax: 512-445-3679
news@statesman.com
http://www.statesman.com/
• James Wangemann, Assistant Sports Editor
(512) 445-3659
• Richard Tijerina, Deputy Sports Editor
(512) 445-3627
• Kevin Lyttle, Sports Writer
(512) 445-3615
• Danny Davis, H.S. Sports Reporter
(512) 445-3952
Frequency:
7 time(s) per week

AUSTIN DAILY HERALD
310 2ND STREET NE
AUSTIN, MN 55912-3436
507-433-8851
Fax: 507-437-8644
http://www.austindailyherald.com/
• Rocky Hulne, Sports Editor
(507) 434-2234
rocky.hulne@austindailyherald.com

Frequency:
6 time(s) per week

AZTECA NEWS
810 N BROADWAY
SANTA ANA, CA 92701-3424
714-972-9912
Fax: 714-973-8117
http://www.aztecanews.com
Frequency:
1 time(s) per week

BAKER CITY HERALD
1915 1ST STREET
PO BOX 807
BAKER CITY, OR 97814-3338
541-523-3673
888-318-7508
Fax: 541-523-6426
news@bakercityherald.com
http://www.bakercityherald.com
• Kathy Orr, Sports Photographer
korr@bakercityherald.com
• Gerry Steele, Sports Editor
gsteele@bakercityherald.com
Frequency:
5 time(s) per week

BAKERSFIELD CALIFORNIAN
P.O. BIN 440
1707 EYE STREET
BAKERSFIELD, CA 93302-0440
661-395-7500
800-540-0646
Fax: 661-395-7285
opinion@bakersfield.com
http://www.bakersfield.com
• Ron Stapp, Sports Copy Editor
(661) 395-7388
rstapp@bakersfield.com
• Zach Ewing, H.S. Sports Reporter
(661) 395-7324
• Tony Lacava, Sports Editor
(661) 395-7393
• Jeff Evans, College Sports Reporter
(661) 395-7389
jevans@bakerfield.com
• Mike Griffith, Condors/Racing Reporter
(661) 395-7390
Frequency:
7 time(s) per week

BALTIMORE SUN
501 N CALVERT STREET
BALTIMORE, MD 21278
410-332-6000
800-829-8000
Fax: 410-783-2518
customersatisfaction@baltsun.com
www.baltimoresun.com
• Andrew Knobel, Deputy Sports Editor
(410) 332-6659
andy.knobel@baltsun.com
• Dan Connolly, Orioles and National
Baseball Reporter
(410) 332-6200
dan.connolly@baltsun.com
• Ron Fritz, Head of Sports
(410) 332-6421
ron.fritz@baltsun.com
Frequency:
7 time(s) per week
Baseball Sponsor:
MLB Baltimore Orioles.

BANGOR DAILY NEWS
491 MAIN STREET
PO BOX 1329
BANGOR, ME 04402-1329
207-990-8000
800-432-7964
Fax: 207-941-9476
http://www.bangornews.com/
• Joseph McLaughlin, Sports Editor
(207) 990-8229
Frequency:
5 time(s) per week

BANNER-GRAPHIC
100 NORTH JACKSON STREET
PO BOX 509
GREENCASTLE, IN 46135
765-653-5151
800-778-8877
Fax: 765-653-2063
news@bannergraphic.com
http://www.bannergraphic.com
• Grant Wieman, Sports Editor
gwieman@bannergraphic.com
Frequency:
6 time(s) per week

BANNER-NEWS
130 SOUTH WASHINGTON
MAGNOLIA, AR 71753-3523
870-234-5130
Fax: 870-234-2551
http://www.bannernews.net
• William Korff, Sports Reporter
• Chris Gilliam, Sports Editor
cgilliam@bannernews.net
Frequency:
6 time(s) per week

BARABOO NEWS REPUBLIC
714 MATT'S FERRY ROAD
PO BOX 9
BARABOO, WI 53913
608-356-4808
Fax: 608-356-0344
bnr-sports@capitalnewspapers.com
http://www.wiscnews.com/baraboonewsrepublic/
• Pete Watson, Sports Editor
(608) 356-4808
Frequency:
6 time(s) per week

BASTROP DAILY ENTERPRISE
119 EAST HICKORY
PO BOX 311
BASTROP, LA 71220-
318-281-4421
Fax: 318-283-1699
news@bastropenterprise.com
http://www.bastropenterprise.com
• Marq Mitcham, Sports Editor
(318) 281-2691
mmitcham@bastropenterprise.com
Frequency:
5 time(s) per week

BATESVILLE GUARD
258 WEST MAIN STREET
PO BOX 236
BATESVILLE, AR 72503
870-793-2383
870-559-2383
Fax: 870-793-9268
news@guardonline.com
http://www.guardonline.com

• Paul Glover, Sports Editor
(870) 793-2383
paulg@guardonline.com
• John David Sonnier, Sports Writer
(870) 793-2383
Frequency:
5 time(s) per week

BATTLE CREEK ENQUIRER
77 EAST MICHIGAN AVENUE
SUITE 101
BATTLE CREEK, MI 49017-3002
269-964-7161
Fax: 269-964-0299
amorin@battlecr.gannett.com
http://www.battlecreekenquirer.com
• Nick Buckley, General Sports
(269) 966-0679
• Bill Broderick, Sports Editor
(269) 966-0678
bbroderi@battlecr.gannett.com
• Will Kowalski, Golf, Bowling, General
Sports
(269) 966-0657
Frequency:
7 time(s) per week

BAXTER BULLETIN
16 W. 6TH STREET
PO BOX 1750
MOUNTAIN HOME, AR 72653-3508
870-508-8000
Fax: 870-508-8020
newsroom@baxterbulletin.com
http://www.baxterbulletin.com/
• Sonny Elliott, Sports Editor
(870) 508-8060
sonnye@baxterbulletin.com
• Scott McDonald, Sports Writer
• Neal Denton, Sports Reporter
(870) 508-8061
ndenton@baxterbulletin.com
Frequency:
6 time(s) per week

BAY CITY TIMES
311 5TH STREET
BAY CITY, MI 48708-5806
989-894-9641
800-219-9919
Fax: 989-893-0649
bcsports@mlive.com
www.mlivemediagroup.com
• Lee Thompson, Sports Reporter
(989) 895-3542
lthomps2@mlive.com
• Cory Butzin, Sports Reporter
cbutzin@mlive.com
Frequency:
7 time(s) per week

BAY CITY TRIBUNE
2901 CAREY SMITH BOULEVARD
BAY CITY, TX 77414
979-245-5555
Fax: 979-244-5908
support@baycitytribune.com
http://www.baycitytribune.com
• Barry Halvoson, Sports Editor
sports@baycitytribune.com
Frequency:
5 time(s) per week

media

BAYTOWN SUN
1301 MEMORIAL DRIVE
PO BOX 90
BAYTOWN, TX 77520-2401
281-422-8302
Fax: 281-427-6283
sunnews@baytownsun.com
http://www.baytownsun.com
• Todd Hveem, Assistant Editor/Sports Editor
(281) 425-8031
Frequency:
5 time(s) per week. Tues-Sat
Circulation:
10,000

BEACH REPORTER
2615 PACIFIC COAST HIGHWAY
SUITE 329
HERMOSA BEACH, CA 90254
310-372-0388
Fax: 310-372-6113
http://www.tbrnews.com
• Erin Michael Stitt, Sports Editor
(310) 372-0388
estitt@tbrnews.com
Frequency:
1 time(s) per week

BEACON-NEWS
495 N COMMONS DRIVE
SUITE 200
AURORA, IL 60504
630-978-8880
800-244-5844
Fax: 630-978-8509
http://www.beaconnews.suntimes.com
• Jason Bauman, Assistant Sports Editor
(630) 978-8412
• R.J. Gerber, Sports Editor
(630) 978-8175
Frequency:
7 time(s) per week

BEATRICE DAILY SUN
200 NORTH 7TH STREET
BEATRICE, NE 68310
402-223-5233
800-666-5233
Fax: 402-228-3571
news@beatricedailysun.com
http://www.beatricedailysun.com
• Janet Harms, Advertising Manager
Frequency:
6 time(s) per week

BEAUMONT ENTERPRISE
380 MAIN STREET
BEAUMONT, TX 77701-2331
409-838-2815
Fax: 409-838-2869
localnews@beaumontenterprise.com
http://www.beaumontenterprise.com
• David Berry, Sports Reporter
(409) 880-0747
• Avi Zaleon, Sports Reporter
(409) 838-2839
• Jared Ainsworth, Sports Reporter
(409) 880-0723
• Christopher Dabe, Sports Editor
(409) 880-0746
Frequency:
7 time(s) per week

BEAVER COUNTY TIMES
400 FAIR AVENUE
BEAVER, PA 15009-1907
724-775-3200
800-899-6397
Fax: 724-775-4180
timesnews@timesonline.com
http://www.timesonline.com
• Mike Bires, Sports Reporter
(724) 775-3200
mbires@timesonline.com
• Ed Rose, Sports Editor
(724) 266-3330
Frequency:
6 time(s) per week

BEAVERCREEK NEWS CURRENT
1836 WEST PARK SQUARE
XENIA, OH 45385
937-372-4444
Fax: 937-372-1951
www.beavercreeknewscurrent.com
• Shawn Bauman, Sports
(937) 372-4444
• Wayne Baker, Sports
(937) 372-4444
wbaker@civitasmedia.com
Frequency:
6 time(s) per week

BELLEFONTAINE EXAMINER
127 EAST CHILLICOTHE AVENUE
PO BOX 40
BELLEFONTAINE, OH 43311-1957
937-592-3060
Fax: 937-592-4463
news@examiner.org
http://www.examiner.org/
• Matt Hammond, Sports Editor
(937) 592-3060
mhammond@examiner.org
Frequency:
6 time(s) per week

BELLEVILLE NEWS-DEMOCRAT
120 SOUTH ILLINOIS
PO BOX 427
BELLEVILLE, IL 62222-2130
618-239-2552
800-642-3878
Fax: 618-345-4223
newsroom@bnd.com
http://www.belleville.com
• Dean Criddle, Sports Reporter
(618) 239-2665
dcriddle@bnd.com
• Steve Korte, Sports Reporter
(618) 239-2522
• Pat Kuhl, Sports Editor
(618) 239-2537
• Norm Sanders, Sports Writer
(618) 239-2454
nsanders@bnd.com
• Dave Wilhelm, Sports Reporter
(618) 239-2661
dwilhelm@bnd.com
Frequency:
7 time(s) per week

BELLEVUE GAZETTE
10990 WILSHIRE BLVD
LOS ANGELES, CA 90024
310-966-4101
Fax: 905-949-4984
admin@landmarksport.com
www.landmarksport.com
• Elliott Kerr, President

Founded:
1987
Frequency:
Daily newspaper (Tuesday - Saturday)
Teams Covered:
Bellevue, Ohio, Redman, & Lady Red

BELLINGHAM HERALD
1155 NORTH STATE STREET
SUITE 200
BELLINGHAM, WA 98225-5037
360-676-2660
Fax: 360-756-2826
http://www.bellinghamherald.com
• Colin Howser, Sports Copy Editor
(360) 715-2268
colin.howser@bellinghamherald.com
• David Rasbach, Sports Editor
(360) 715-2271
david.rasbach@bellinghamherald.com
• Andrew Lang, Sports Reporter
(360) 715-2862
Frequency:
7 time(s) per week

BENICIA HERALD
820 1ST STREET
BENICIA, CA 94510
707-745-0733
Fax: 707-745-8583
beniciaherald@gmail.com
http://beniciaherald.wordpress.com
• Donna Beth Weilenman, Staff Reporter
• Steve Guertin, Sports Editor
Frequency:
5 time(s) per week

BENNINGTON BANNER
425 MAIN STREET
BENNINGTON, VT 05201-2141
802-447-7567
800-245-0254
Fax: 802-442-3413
news@benningtonbanner.com
http://www.benningtonbanner.com
• Austin Danforth, Sports Reporter
(802) 447-7567
• Adam Samrov, Sports Editor
(802) 447-7567
asamrov@benningtonbanner.com
Frequency:
6 time(s) per week

BENTON COUNTY DAILY RECORD
104 SOUTHWEST A STREET
BENTONVILLE, AR 72712-5867
479-271-3700
Fax: 479-271-3744
newsroom@nwanews.com
http://www.nwanews.com
• Paul Gatling, Sports Editor
(479) 271-3792
sports@nwanews.com
• Carolyn Kirkland, Advertising Manager
(479) 770-8414
carolynk@nwanews.com
• Diane Williams, Classified Manager
(479) 571-6421
dwilliams@nwanews.com
Frequency:
7 time(s) per week

BENTON EVENING NEWS
111 EAST CHURCH STREET
BENTON, IL 62812

618-438-5611
Fax: 618-435-2413
http://www.bentoneveningnews.com
• Allen Parker, Sports Editor
sports@bentoneveningnews.com
Frequency:
6 time(s) per week

BERKELEY HEIGHTS/NEW PROVIDENCE INDEPENDENT PRESS
80 SOUTH STREET
NEW PROVIDENCE, NJ 07974-1941
908-464-1025
Fax: 908-464-9085
ipeditors@njnpublishing.com
www.nj.com/independentpress
• Art Polakowski, Sports Editor
Frequency:
1 time(s) per week

BERKSHIRE EAGLE
75 SOUTH CHURCH STREET
PO BOX 1171
PITTSFIELD, MA 01202-6132
413-447-7311
800-245-0254
Fax: 413-499-3419
news@berkshireeagle.com
http://www.berkshireeagle.com
• Matt Sprague, Sports Editor
(413) 496-6254
msprague@berkshireeagle.com
• Howard Herman, Sports Columnist
(413) 496-6253
hherman@berkshireeagle.com
Frequency:
7 time(s) per week

BERWYN-CICERO-STICKNEY-FOREST VIEW LIFE
1101 W. 31ST STREET
SUITE260
DOWNERS GROVE, IL 60515-5581
708-447-9810
Fax: 708-447-9871
http://www.mysuburbanlife.com
• David Good, Sports Editor
(630) 427-6270
dgood@shawmedia.com
Frequency:
3 time(s) per week

BILLINGS GAZETTE
P.O. BOX 36300
BILLINGS, MT 59101-1243
406-657-1200
800-543-2505
Fax: 406-657-1208
news@billingsgazette.com
http://www.billingsgazette.com
• Mike Zimmer, Sports Editor
(406) 657-1291
• Mike Scherting, Assistant Sports Editor
(406) 657-1302
mscherting@billingsgazette.com
Frequency:
7 time(s) per week

BIRMINGHAM NEWS
P.O. BOX 2553
BIRMINGHAM, AL 35203-3802
205-325-2444
800-283-4048
Fax: 205-325-2283
epage@bhamnews.com
http://www.bhamnews.com

• Tom Arenberg, Sports Editor
(205) 325-2433
tarenberg@bhamnews.com
• Charles Hollis, Assistant Editor
(205) 325-2161
chollis@bhamnews.com
Frequency:
7 time(s) per week

BISBEE DAILY REVIEW
12 MAIN STREET
BISBEE, AZ 85603
520-432-2231
Fax: 520-432-2356
http://www.svherald.com
• Matt Hickman, Sports Editor
(515) 520-4612
sports@svherald.com
• Shar Porier, Bisbee Reporter
(520) 515-4692
Frequency:
6 time(s) per week

BISMARCK TRIBUNE
P.O. BOX 5516
BISMARCK, ND 58506
701-223-2500
800-472-2273
Fax: 701-223-2063
http://www.bismarcktribune.com/
• Lou Babiarz, Sports Editor
(701) 250-8243
• Steve Thomas, Sports Reporter
(701) 250-8244
steve.thomas@bismarcktribune.com
• Mike Weber, Sports Reporter
(701) 355-8839
mike.weber@bismarcktribune.com
• Eric Hammond, Sports Copy Editor
(701) 250-8246
• Cindy Peterson, Sports Reporter
(701) 250-8245
Frequency:
7 time(s) per week

BLACK HILLS PIONEER
315 SEATON CIRCLE
PO BOX 7
SPEARFISH, SD 57783-3212
605-642-2761
800-676-2761
Fax: 605-642-9060
news@bhpioneer.com
http://www.bhpioneer.com
• Dennis Knuckles, Sports Editor
sports@bhpioneer.com
Frequency:
6 time(s) per week

BLACKWELL JOURNAL-TRIBUNE
113 EAST BLACKWELL AVENUE
PO BOX 760
BLACKWELL, OK 74631-0760
580-363-3370
Fax: 580-363-4415
http://www.blackwelljournaltribune.net
• Belinda Ramsey, Publisher/Editor
(580) 363-3370
Frequency:
5 time(s) per week

BLADE
541 NORTH SUPERIOR STREET
TOLEDO, OH 43660-1000
419-724-6000
800-245-3317

Fax: 419-724-6391
letters@theblade.com
http://www.toledoblade.com
• Frank Corsoe, Sports Editor
(419) 724-6115
fcorsoe@theblade.com
• Donald Emmons, Sports Writer
(419) 724-6110
• Dave Hackenberg, Sports Reporter
(419) 724-6110
• Dan Firestone, Assistant Sports Editor
(419) 724-6110
• Matt Markey, Outdoors Editor
(419) 724-6110
mmarkey@theblade.com
• Mark Monroe, Sports Writer
(419) 724-6110
mmonroe@theblade.com
Frequency:
7 time(s) per week

BLADE-EMPIRE
510 WASHINGTON STREET
CONCORDIA, KS 66901-2117
785-243-2424
Fax: 785-243-4407
http://www.bladeempire.com
• Jim Lowell, Sports Editor
jimlowell@nckcn.com
Frequency:
5 time(s) per week

BLUEFIELD DAILY TELEGRAPH
P.O. BOX 1599
BLUEFIELD, WV 24701-2744
304-327-2800
800-763-2459
Fax: 304-327-6179
sports@bdtonline.com
http://www.bdtonline.com
• Terri Hale, Advertising Director
(304) 327-2816
thale@bdtonline.com
Frequency:
7 time(s) per week

BOLIVAR COMMERCIAL
821 NORTH CHRISMAN AVENUE
PO BOX 1050
CLEVELAND, MS 38732-1050
662-843-4241
Fax: 662-843-1830
news@bolivarcommercial.com
• Andy Collier, Sports Editor
(662) 843-4241
Frequency:
5 time(s) per week

BONNER COUNTY DAILY BEE
310 CHURCH STREET
PO BOX 159
SANDPOINT, ID 83864
208-263-9534
Fax: 208-263-9091
http://www.bonnercountydailybee.com
• Eric Plummer, Sports Editor
eplummer@bonnercountydailybee.com
Frequency:
6 time(s) per week

BOONVILLE DAILY NEWS
412 HIGH STREET
BOONVILLE, MO 65233-1242
660-882-5335
Fax: 660-882-2256

news@boonvilledailynews.com
http://www.boonvilledailynews.com
• Chris Bowie, Sports Editor
(660) 882-5335
cbowie@boonvilledailynews.com
Frequency:
5 time(s) per week

BORGER NEWS-HERALD
PO BOX 5130
BORGER, TX 79008
806-273-5611
Fax: 806-273-2552
editor@borgernewsherald.com
http://www.borgernewsherald.com
• Mikala Reiswig, Sports Editor
sports@borgernewsherald.com
Frequency:
6 time(s) per week

BOSTON GLOBE
135 WILLIAM MORRISSEY BOULEVARD
BOSTON, MA 02125-3310
617-929-2000
Fax: 617-929-3186
localnews@globe.com
http://www.boston.com
• Gregory Lang, Assistant Sports Editor
(617) 929-2531
glang@globe.com
• Pete Goodwin, Copy Editor
(617) 929-2847
p_goodwin@globe.com
• Nicholas Cafardo, Sports Reporter
(617) 929-2878
cafardo@globe.com
• Chad Finn, Sports Media Columnist
(617) 929-3080
finn@globe.com
• Bob Hohler, Sports Reporter
(617) 929-2860
hohler@globe.com
• Robert Holmes, Sports Assistant Editor
(617) 929-2876
r_holmes@globe.com
• Nancy Marrapese-Burrell, Sports Reporter
(617) 929-3014
marrapese@globe.com
• Shira Springer, Sports Reporter
(617) 929-2835
springer@globe.com
Frequency:
7 time(s) per week

BOSTON HERALD
ONE HERALD SQUARE
BOSTON, MA 02205
617-426-3000
800-882-2024
Fax: 617-619-6450
sports@bostonherald.com
http://www.bostonherald.com
• Steve Buckley, Sports Columnist
(617) 426-3000
sbuckley@bostonherald.com
• Steve Bulpett, Basketball Reporter
(617) 426-3000
sports@bostonherald.com
• Jim Clark, High School Sports Reporter
(617) 426-3000
sports@bostonherald.com
• John Connolly, Sports Reporter
(617) 426-3000
sports@bostonherald.com
• Mark Torpey, Sports Executive Editor
(617) 426-3000
sports@bostonherald.com

• Mark Murphy, Deputy Sports Editor
(617) 426-3000
mjmurphy@bostonherald.com
• Michael Silverman, Sports Reporter
(617) 426-3000
sports@bostonherald.com
• Rich Thompson, Sports Reporter
(617) 426-3000
sports@bostonherald.com
Frequency:
7 time(s) per week

BOURNE ENTERPRISE
50 DEPOT AVENUE
FALMOUTH, MA 02540-2302
508-548-4700
800-286-7744
Fax: 508-540-8407
http://www.capenews.net
• Dan Crowley, Sports Editor
(508) 548-4700
crowley@capenews.net
Frequency:
1 time(s) per week

BOWIE BLADE-NEWS
2000 CAPITAL DRIVE
ANNAPOLIS, MD 21401
410-268-5000
Fax: 410-280-5953
tips@capgaznews.com
http://www.hometownbowie.com
• Gerry Jackson, Sports Editor
(410) 280-5926
• Dave Broughton, Sports Writer
(410) 280-5940
• John McNamara, Sports Writer/Maryland
(410) 280-5925
• Mike Peters, High School Sports Editor
(410) 280-5923
• Bill Wagner, Sports Writer/Navy
(410) 280-5952
Frequency:
1 time(s) per week

BOZEMAN DAILY CHRONICLE
2820 WEST COLLEGE
PO BOX 1190
BOZEMAN, MT 59718-3925
406-587-4491
800-275-0401
Fax: 406-587-7995
citydesk@dailychronicle.com
http://www.bozemandailychronicle.com
• Jon Maletz, Sports Editor
(406) 582-2690
jmaletz@dailychronicle.com
Frequency:
7 time(s) per week

BRADENTON HERALD
102 MANATEE AVENUE WEST
BRADENTON, FL 34205-8810
941-748-0411
Fax: 941-745-7097
http://www.bradenton.com
• Alan Dell, Sports Reporter
(941) 745-7080
• Tim Wolfrum, Sports Editor
(941) 748-0411
• Jason Dill, Sports Reporter
(941) 748-0411
jdill@bradenton.com
Frequency:
7 time(s) per week

BRADFORD ERA
43 MAIN STREET
BRADFORD, PA 16701-2019
814-368-3173
800-346-7353
Fax: 814-362-6510
http://www.bradfordera.com
• Joe Vinelli, Sports Editor
(814) 362-6531
joev@bradfordera.com
Frequency:
6 time(s) per week

BRAINERD DAILY DISPATCH
506 JAMES STREET
BRAINERD, MN 56401-2942
218-829-4705
800-432-3703
Fax: 218-829-7735
http://www.brainerddispatch.com
• Mike Bialka, Sports Editor
(218) 855-5861
mike.bialka@brainerddispatch.com
• Jeremy Millsop, Sports Writer
(218) 855-5856
jeremy.millsop@brainerddispatch.com
Frequency:
6 time(s) per week

BRANSON TRI-LAKES DAILY NEWS
200 INDUSTRIAL PARK DRIVE
PO BOX 1900
HOLLISTER, MO 65672-5327
417-334-3161
Fax: 417-334-1460
http://www.bransondailynews.com
• Pat Dailey, Sports Editor
pdailey@bransontrilakesnews.com
Frequency:
2 time(s) per week

BRAZIL TIMES
100 NORTH MERIDIAN STREET
PO BOX 429
BRAZIL, IN 47834-2172
812-446-2216
800-489-5090
Fax: 812-446-0938
http://www.thebraziltimes.com
• Carey Fox, Sports Editor
(812) 446-2216
redwood17257@yahoo.com
Frequency:
6 time(s) per week

BRENHAM BANNER-PRESS
PO BOX 585
BRENHAM, TX 77834
979-836-7956
Fax: 979-830-8577
sports@brenhambanner.com
http://www.brenhambanner.com
• Matt Keyser, Sports Editor
(979) 836-7956
sports@brenhambanner.com
Frequency:
6 time(s) per week

BRIDGETON NEWS
100 EAST COMMERCE STREET
BRIDGETON, NJ 08302-2602
856-451-1000
Fax: 856-455-2633
http://www.nj.com/bridgeton

• Eric Goldstein, Sports Editor
(856) 451-1000
egoldstein@sjnewsco.com
Frequency:
6 time(s) per week

BRISTOL HERALD COURIER
320 BOB MORRISON BOULEVARD
BRISTOL, VA 24201
276-669-2181
Fax: 276-669-3696
sports@bristolnews.com
http://www.tricities.com
• Jim Sacco, Sports Editor
(276) 645-2569
jsacco@bristolnews.com
Frequency
7x/week

BRISTOL PRESS
188 MAIN STREET
BRISTOL, CT 06010
860-584-0501
800-220-6229
Fax: 860-584-2192
editor@bristolpress.com
http://www.bristolpress.com
• Brad Carroll, Executive Sports Editor
(860) 225-4601
bcarroll@newbritainherald.com
• Paul Angilly, Sports Editor
(860) 584-0501
pangilly@centralctcommunications.com
Frequency:
7 time(s) per week

BROOKINGS REGISTER
312 5TH STREET
BROOKINGS, SD 57006
605-692-6271
Fax: 605-692-2979
register@brookings.net
http://www.brookingsregister.com/
• Troy Maroney, Sports Editor
(605) 692-6271
sports@brookingsregister.com
Frequency:
6 time(s) per week

BROWNSVILLE HERALD
1135 EAST VAN BUREN STREET
BROWNSVILLE, TX 78520
956-542-4301
800-488-4301
Fax: 956-542-0840
http://www.brownsvilleherald.com
• Bryan Read, Sports Director
(956) 542-4301
bread@brownsvilleherald.com
Frequency:
7 time(s) per week

BROWNWOOD BULLETIN
700 CARNEGIE STREET
BROWNWOOD, TX 76801-7040
325-646-2541
Fax: 325-646-6835
news@brownwoodbulletin.com
http://www.brownwoodbulletin.com/
• Derrick Stuckly, Sports Editor
(325) 646-2541
news@brownwoodbulletin.com
Frequency:
6 time(s) per week

BRUNSWICK NEWS
3011 ALTAMA AVENUE
BRUNSWICK, GA 31520-4608
912-265-8320
Fax: 912-264-4973
editor@thebrunswicknews.com
http://www.thebrunswicknews.com
• Dave Jordan, Sports Editor
(912) 265-8320
djordan@thebrunswicknews.com
Frequency:
6 time(s) per week

BRYAN TIMES
127 SOUTH WALNUT STREET
BRYAN, OH 43506
419-636-1111
Fax: 419-636-8937
http://www.bryantimes.com
• Nate Parsons, Sports Editor
• Amy Thompson, Classified Manager
amy@bryantimes.com
• Tom Voigt, Advertising Manager
Frequency:
6 time(s) per week
Description:
Daily Newspaper

BRYAN-COLLEGE STATION EAGLE
1729 BRIARCREST
BRYAN, TX 77802-2712
979-776-4444
Fax: 979-774-0053
news@theeagle.com
http://www.theeagle.com
• Robert Cessna, Sports Editor
(979) 731-4638
robert.cessna@theeagle.com
• Tammye Mineo, Advertising Manager
(979) 776-4444
tammye.mineo@theeagle.com
Frequency:
7 time(s) per week

BUCKS COUNTY COURIER TIMES
8400 NORTH BRISTOL PIKE
LEVITTOWN, PA 19057
215-949-4000
Fax: 215-949-4177
feedback@phillyburbs.com
http://www.phillyburbs.com
• Timothy J. Birch, Advertising Director
(215) 949-4120
tbirch@phillyburbs.com
• Kate Rochelle, Classified Manager
(215) 949-4107
krochelle@phillyburbs.com
• Gary Silvers, Sports Editor
(215) 949-4212
gsilvers@phillyburbs.com
• Kevin Cooney, Sports Writer
(215) 949-4209
kcooney@phillyBurbs.com
Frequency:
6 time(s) per week

BUFFALO NEWS
1 NEWS PLAZA
BUFFALO, NY 14240
800-777-8610
Fax: 716-856-5150
sports@buffnews.com
http://www.buffnews.com
• Steve Jones, Sports Editor
• Tom Borrelli, Sports Writer
tborrelli@buffnews.com
• Greg Connors, Sports Reporter

gconnors@buffnews.com
• Greg Connors, Sports Writer
gconnors@buffnews.com
• Dennis Danheiser, Sports Assistant Editor
(716) 849-4461
• Bob Dicesare, Sports Columnist
(716) 849-4463
• Mark Gaughan, Sports Writer
(716) 849-4461
• Bucky Gleason, Sports Writer
(716) 849-4461
• Tim Graham, Sports Writer
(716) 849-4461
• Mike Harrington, Sports Writer
mharrington@buffnews.com
• Scott Johnston, Sports Assistant Editor
(716) 849-4461
• Steve Jones, Sports Deputy Editor
sjones@buffnews.com
• Rodney McKissic, Sports Reporter
rmckissic@buffnews.com
• Keith McShea, Sports Writer
kmcshea@buffnews.com
• Mary Jo Monnin, Sports Writer
(716) 849-4461
• Amy Moritz, Sports Writer
(716) 849-4002
• Milt Northrop, Sports Writer
mnorthrop@buffnews.com
• Howard Smith, Sports Executive Editor
• Jerry Sullivan, Sports Columnist
(716) 849-4461
• Bob Summers, Sports Writer
(716) 849-4461
• John Vogl, Sports Writer
jvogl@buffnews.com
• Allen Wilson, Sports Writer
(716) 849-4461
Frequency:
7 time(s) per week

BULLETIN
P.O. BOX 6020
BEND, OR 97702
541-382-1811
Fax: 541-385-5804
news@bendbulletin.com
http://www.bendbulletin.com
• Bill Bigelow, Sports Editor
(541) 383-0359
• Zack Hall, Sports Reporter
(541) 617-7868
Frequency:
7 time(s) per week

BURBANK LEADER
221 N BRAND BLVD, 2ND FLOOR
GLENDALE, CA 91203
818-637-3200
Fax: 818-241-1975
burbankleader@latimes.com
http://www.burbankleader.com
• Jeff Tully, Sports Editor
(818) 637-3245
jeff.tully@latimes.com
Frequency:
2 time(s) per week

BURLINGTON COUNTY TIMES
4284 ROUTE 130
WILLINGBORO, NJ 08046-2027
609-871-8000
Fax: 609-871-0490
bct.letters@phillyburbs.com
http://www.phillyburbs.com
• Wayne Richardson, Sports Editor
(609) 871-8000

wrichardson@phillyburbs.com
• Reuben Frank, Sports Reporter
(609) 871-8054
rfrank@phillyburbs.com
Frequency:
6 time(s) per week

BURLINGTON FREE PRESS
191 COLLEGE STREET
BURLINGTON, VT 05402-0494
802-863-3441
Fax: 802-660-1802
metro@burlingtonfreepress.com
http://www.burlingtonfreepress.com
• John Fantino, Sports Editor
(802) 651-4851
jfantino@burlingtonfreepress.com
• Kevin Commo, Sports Reporter
(802) 660-1855
Frequency:
7 time(s) per week

BUTLER EAGLE
P.O. BOX 271
BUTLER, PA 16001
724-282-8000
Fax: 724-282-4180
news@butlereagle.com
http://www.butlereagle.com
• John Enrietto, Sports Editor
(724) 282-8000
jenrietto@butlereagle.com
• Mace Pavelek, Advertising Director
(724) 282-8000
macepavelek@hotmail.com
Frequency:
6 time(s) per week

CALEDONIAN RECORD
190 FEDERAL STREET
SAINT JOHNSBURY, VT 05819-2636
802-748-8121
800-523-6397
Fax: 802-748-1613
http://www.caledonianrecord.com
• Craig Beck, Sports Writer
• Michael Beniash, Sports Editor
beniashm@caledonian-record.com
Frequency:
6 time(s) per week

CALGARY HERALD
PO BOX 2400, STATION M
CALGARY, AB, CANADA T2P0W8
403-235-7100
800-372-9219
Fax: 403-235-7379
letters@calgaryherald.com
www.calgaryherald.com
• Keith Bradford, Sports Editor
(403) 235-7578
kbradford@calgaryherald.com

CALL
75 MAIN STREET
WOONSOCKET, RI 02895-4312
401-762-3000
800-934-3142
Fax: 401-765-0303
news@woonsocketcall.com
http://www.woonsocketcall.com
• Terry Nau, Sports Editor
(401) 727-9292
sports@woonsocketcall.com
Frequency:
7 time(s) per week

CALL-LEADER
317 SOUTH ANDERSON STREET
ELWOOD, IN 46036-2018
765-552-3355
Fax: 765-552-3358
http://www.elwoodpublishing.com
• Ed Hamilton, Sports Editor
Frequency:
6 time(s) per week

CAMDEN NEWS
113 MADISON AVENUE
CAMDEN, AR 71701
870-836-8192
Fax: 870-837-1414
http://www.camdenarknews.com
• Kelly Blair, Sports Editor
(870) 836-8192
sports@camdenarknews.com
Frequency:
5 time(s) per week

CANTON LIFE
106 SOUTH STREET
WEST HARTFORD, CT 06110
860-953-0444
Fax: 860-953-0455
http://www.ctlife.net
• Steve Frank, Sports Editor
(860) 953-0444
sfrank@ctlife.net
Frequency:
1 time(s) per month

CAPE COD TIMES
319 MAIN STREET
HYANNIS, MA 02601-4037
508-775-1200
800-451-7887
Fax: 508-771-3292
news@capecodonline.com
http://www.capecodonline.com
• Bill Higgins, Sports Editor/Columnist
(508) 862-1151
• Walter Bingham, Sports Writer
(508) 775-1200
Frequency:
7 time(s) per week

CAPE CORAL DAILY BREEZE
2510 DEL PRADO BOULEVARD
CAPE CORAL, FL 33904-5750
239-574-1110
Fax: 239-574-5693
news@breezenewspapers.com
http://www.flguide.com
• Jim Linette, Sports Editor
(941) 574-1110
jlinette@breezenewspapers.com
Frequency:
6 time(s) per week

CAPITAL
2000 CAPITAL DRIVE
ANNAPOLIS, MD 21401
410-268-5000
Fax: 410-268-4643
capstaff@capitalgazette.com
http://www.hometownannapolis.com
• Dave Broughton, Sports Writer
(410) 280-5940
dbroughton@capitalgazette.com
• Gerry Jackson, Sports Editor
(410) 280-5926
gjackson@capitalgazette.com
• John McNamara, Sports Writer

(410) 280-5925
jmcnamara@capitalgazette.com
• Bill Wagner, Sports Writer
(410) 280-5952
bwagner@capitalgazette.com
• Mike Peters, Sports Reporter
(410) 280-5923
mpeters@capitalgazette.com
Frequency:
7 time(s) per week

CAPITAL JOURNAL
333 WEST DAKOTA AVENUE
PIERRE, SD 57501
605-224-7301
800-658-3063
Fax: 605-224-9210
news@capjournal.com
http://www.capjournal.com
• April Pullman, Advertising Manager
(605) 224-7301
• Chris Mangan, Sports Editor
Frequency:
5 time(s) per week

CAPITAL TIMES
P.O. BOX 8060
MADISON, WI 53713-1248
608-252-6400
800-362-8333
Fax: 608-252-6445
http://www.madison.com
• Brent Engh, Sports Reporter
(608) 252-6471
• Todd Finkelmeyer, Sports Reporter
(608) 252-6465
• Joe Hart, Sports Columnist
(608) 252-6479
• Mike Lucas, Sports Columnist
(608) 252-6470
• Adam Mertz, Sports Editor
(608) 252-6474
• Jim Polzin, Sports Reporter
(608) 252-6473
polzin@madison.com
• Rob Schultz, Sports Reporter
(608) 252-6487
rschultz@madison.com
• Dennis Semrau, Sports Reporter
(608) 252-6490
• Tamira Surprenant, Sports Reporter
(608) 252-6472
Frequency:
6 time(s) per week

CARMI TIMES
323 EAST MAIN STREET
CARMI, IL 62821-1810
618-382-4176
800-245-4488
Fax: 618-384-2163
http://www.carmitimes.com
• Toby Brown, Sports Editor
(618) 382-4176
• Linda Prince, Advertising Manager
Frequency:
5 time(s) per week

CARROLL COUNTY TIMES
201 RAILROAD AVENUE
WESTMINSTER, MD 21158
410-848-4400
Fax: 410-857-8749
cctnews@carrollcountytimes.com
http://www.carrollcounty.com
• Bob Blubaugh, Sports Editor
(410) 857-7895

bob.blubaugh@carrollcountytimes.com
• Pat Stoetzer, Sports Reporter
(410) 751-7894
pstoetzer@lcniofmd.com
• Aaron Wilson, Sports Writer
(410) 857-7896
sports@lcniofmd.com
Frequency:
7 time(s) per week

CASA GRANDE DISPATCH
200 WEST 2ND
CASA GRANDE, AZ 85230
520-836-7461
Fax: 520-836-0343
dkramerjr@trivalleycentral.com
http://www.trivalleycentral.com
• Ed Petruska, Sports Editor
Frequency:
6 time(s) per week

CECIL WHIG
601 BRIDGE STREET
ELKTON, MD 21921
410-398-3311
800-220-3311
Fax: 410-398-4044
http://www.cecilwhig.com
• Mike Curry, Sports Editor
• John Davis, Sports Reporter
• Robert DeAngelo, Sports Editor
(410) 398-3311
Frequency:
5 time(s) per week

CENTRAL KITSAP REPORTER
9989 SILVERDALE WAY, N.W. SUITE 109
SILVERDALE, WA 98383
360-308-9161
Fax: 360-308-9363
editor@centralkitsapreporter.com
http://www.centralkitsapreporter.com
• Mike Baldwin, Sports Writer
Frequency:
2 time(s) per week

CENTRAL MICHIGAN LIFE
436 MOORE HALL
MT. PLEASANT, MI 48859
989-774-5433
Fax: 989-774-3040
www.cm-life.com
• Andrew Stover, Sports Reporter
stove1aj@cmich.edu
• Matt Thompson, Sports Writer
thomp3mj@cmich.edu

CENTRAL NEWS/JOURNAL/STAR WAVE
4201 WILSHIRE BOULEVARD SUITE 600
LOS ANGELES, CA 90010-3601
323-556-5720
800-404-9283
Fax: 323-556-5704
http://www.wavenewspapers.com
• Ron Guild, Sports Writer
(323) 556-5720
rguild@wavenewspapers.com
Frequency:
2 time(s) per week

CENTRALIA SENTINEL
232 EAST BROADWAY
CENTRALIA, IL 62801-3251
618-532-5604
800-371-9892
Fax: 618-532-1212

news@morningsentinel.com
http://www.morningsentinel.com
• Mike McManus, Sports Reporter
sports@morningsentinel.com
Frequency:
7 time(s) per week

CENTRE DAILY TIMES
3400 EAST COLLEGE AVENUE
STATE COLLEGE, PA 16801
814-238-5000
800-327-5500
Fax: 814-238-1811
http://www.centredaily.com
• Walt Moody, Sports Editor
(814) 231-4630
• Jeff Rice, Sports Reporter
(814) 231-4609
Frequency:
7 time(s) per week

CENTRE VIEW
1606 KING STREET
ALEXANDRIA, VA 22314
703-917-6444
Fax: 703-917-0991
centreview@connectionnewspapers.com
http://www.connectionnewspapers.com
• Jeff Graham, Sports Editor
(703) 917-6445
Frequency:
1 time(s) per week

CHANUTE TRIBUNE
15 NORTH EVERGREEN
CHANUTE, KS 66720-1831
620-431-4100
Fax: 620-431-2635
news@chanute.com
http://www.chanute.com
• Nancy Isaac, Advertising Manager
tribune@chanute.com
• Jason Peake, Sports Editor
sports@chanute.com
Frequency:
6 time(s) per week

CHAPEL HILL NEWS
505 WEST FRANKLIN STREET
CHAPEL HILL, NC 27516-2315
919-932-2003
Fax: 919-968-4953
http://www.chapelhillnews.com
• Elliott Warnock, Sports Editor
(919) 932-8743
chnsports@nando.com
Frequency:
3 time(s) per week

CHARLES CITY PRESS
801 RIVERSIDE DRIVE
CHARLES CITY, IA 50616-2248
641-228-3211
Fax: 641-228-2641
editor@charlescitypress.com
http://www.charlescitypress.com
• Ryan Kronberg, Sports Editor
sports@charlescitypress.com
• Joel Gray, Advertising Manager
joelg@charlescitypress.com
Frequency:
5 time(s) per week

CHARLESTON GAZETTE
1001 VIRGINIA STREET, EAST
CHARLESTON, WV 25301-2835

304-348-5100
800-982-6397
Fax: 304-348-1233
gazette@wvgazette.com
http://www.wvgazette.com
• Larry Levak, Advertising Manager
(304) 348-4895
• Renae Roberts, Classified Manager
(304) 348-1221
• Mitch Vingle, Sports Editor
(304) 348-4827
mitchv@wvgazette.com
Frequency:
7 time(s) per week

CHARLOTTE OBSERVER
600 S TRYON STREET
CHARLOTTE, NC 28202
704-358-5000
800-332-0686
Fax: 704-358-5036
http://www.charlotte.com
• Rick Bonnell, Sports Reporter
(704) 358-5129
rbonnell@charlotteobserver.com
• Scott Fowler, Sports Columnist
(704) 358-5140
sfowler@charlotteobserver.com
• Ron Green, Jr., Sports Writer
(704) 358-5118
• Harry Pickett, Sports Deputy Editor
(704) 358-5127
hpickett@charlotteobserver.com
• David Scott, Sports Columnist
(704) 358-5889
dscott@charlotteobserver.com
• Tom Sorensen, Sports Columnist
(704) 358-5119
• Jim Utter, Sports Reporter
(704) 358-5113
• Langston Wertz, Reporter
(704) 358-5133
lwertz@charlotteobserver.com
• Gary Schwab
(704) 358-5120
gschwab@charlotteobserver.com
Frequency:
7 time(s) per week

CHARLOTTE SUN HERALD
23170 HARBORVIEW ROAD
PORT CHARLOTTE, FL 33980
941-206-1000
800-830-7861
Fax: 941-629-2085
http://www.sun-herald.com
• Gary Brown, Sports Writer
(941) 206-1140
• Debbie Dunn-Rankin, Advertising Manager
(941) 206-1500
debbie@sun-herald.com
• John Fineran, Sports Columnist
(941) 206-1122
jfineran@sun-herald.com
• John Fineran, Sports Editor
(941) 206-1122
Frequency:
7 time(s) per week

CHATTANOOGA TIMES FREE PRESS
400 EAST 11TH STREET
CHATTANOOGA, TN 37402
423-757-6322
Fax: 423-668-5052
news@timesfreepress.com
http://www.timesfreepress.com

• Jay Greeson, Sports Editor
(423) 757-6273
jgreeson@timesfreepress.com
Frequency:
7 time(s) per week

CHEBOYGAN DAILY TRIBUNE
308 NORTH MAIN STREET
CHEBOYGAN, MI 49721-1545
231-627-7144
Fax: 231-627-5331
http://www.cheboygannews.com/
• Jared Greenleaf, Sports Editor
sports@cheboygantribune.com
Frequency:
5 time(s) per week

CHESTERTON TRIBUNE
193 SOUTH CALUMET ROAD
CHESTERTON, IN 46304-2433
219-926-1131
Fax: 219-926-6389
chestertontrib@earthlink.net
http://www.chestertontribune.com
• T.R Harlen, Sports Editor
• Harry Lewis, Advertising Manager
Frequency:
5 time(s) per week

CHICAGO CHINESE NEWS
424 FORT HILL, BLDG. 100
NAPERVILLE, IL 60540
630-717-4567
Fax: 630-717-7999
http://www.chicagochinesenews.com
• Judy Lee, Advertising Manager
• Danny Lee, Sports Editor
(312) 388-8011
ccn@chicagochinesenews.com
Frequency:
6 time(s) per week

CHICAGO SUN-TIMES
350 NORTH ORLEANS STREET, 10TH
FLOOR
CHICAGO, IL 60654
312-321-3000
Fax: 312-321-3027
metro@suntimes.com
http://www.suntimes.com
• Lacy Banks, Sports Reporter
(312) 321-2632
lbanks@sun-times.com
• Dale Bowman, Sports Writer (Outdoors)
dbowman@suntimes.com
• Greg Couch, Sports Columnist
(312) 321-2604
• Chris De Luca, Sports Editor
(312) 321-3000
• Brian Hanley, Sports Writer (Hockey)
(312) 321-2664
• Roman Modrowski, Assistant Sports Editor
(312) 321-2619
• Mike Mulligan, Sports Columnist
(312) 321-2651
• Jim O'Donnell, Sports Columnist/Reporter
(312) 321-2605
• Mark Potash, Sports Reporter
(312) 321-2634
mpotash@suntimes.com
• Ron Rapoport, Sports Columnist
(312) 321-2613
• Carol Slezak, Sports Columnist
(312) 321-2636
• Steve Tucker, High School Sports Editor
(312) 321-2247
• Len Ziehm, Sports Writer

(312) 321-2664
• Tina Akouris, High School Sports Reporter
(312) 321-2663
Frequency:
7 time(s) per week

CHICAGO TRIBUNE
435 NORTH MICHIGAN AVENUE
CHICAGO, IL 60611-4066
312-222-4440
Fax: 312-222-4674
http://www.chicagotribune.com
• Tim Bannon, Sports Editor
(312) 222-2434
• Mark Gonzales, Sports Reporter
• Lee Gordon, Associate Sports Editor
(312) 222-3478
• Teddy Greenstein, Sports Reporter
• Jim Harding, Assistant Editor
• Brian Hamilton, Sports Reporter
(312) 222-4204
• Steven Huang, Sports Copy Editor
• K.C. Johnson, Sports Writer
• Fred Mitchell, Sports Columnist
(312) 222-5428
kick3485@aol.com
• Avani Patel, Sports Reporter
(312) 222-4440
• Ken Paxson, Sports Associate Editor
(312) 222-4171
• Phil Rogers, Sports Writer
• Steve Rosenbloom, Sports Columnist
(312) 222-3038
• Mike Sansone, Sports Associate Editor
(312) 222-5018
• Benjamin Trecroci, Sports Assistant Editor
Frequency:
7 time(s) per week

CHICO ENTERPRISE-RECORD
400 EAST PARK AVENUE
CHICO, CA 95928-7127
530-891-1234
Fax: 530-342-3617
localnews@chicoer.com
http://www.chicoer.com
• Fred Crosthwaite, Advertising Director
(530) 896-7751
fcrosthwaite@chicoer.com
• Dave Davies, Sports Editor
(530) 896-7779
ddavies@chicoer.com
Frequency:
7 time(s) per week

CHILLICOTHE CONSTITUTION-TRIBUNE
818 WASHINGTON STREET
CHILLICOTHE, MO 64601-2232
660-646-2411
800-373-0256
Fax: 660-646-2028
ctribune@greenhills.net
http://www.chillicothenews.com
• Andrea Graves, Advertising Manager
• Paul Sturm, Sports Editor
ctsports@chillicothenews.com
Frequency:
5 time(s) per week

CHRISTIAN SCIENCE MONITOR
210 MASSACHUSETTS
BOSTON, MA 02115-3195
617-450-2000
800-288-7090
Fax: 617-450-2031
www.csmonitor.com

• Mark Sappenfield, Editor
sappenfieldm@csps.com
Frequency:
5 time(s) per week

CHRONICLE (CT)
1 CHRONICLE ROAD
WILLIMANTIC, CT 06226
860-423-8466
Fax: 860-423-7641
chron@thechronicle.com
http://www.thechronicle.com
• Jean Beckley, Advertising Manager
(860) 423-8466
sales@thechronicle.com
• Mike Sypher, Sports Editor
(860) 423-8466
msypher@thechronicle.com
Frequency:
6 time(s) per week

CHRONICLE (WA)
321 NORTH PEARL STREET
CENTRALIA, WA 98531-0351
360-736-3311
800-562-6084
Fax: 360-736-4796
news@chronline.com
http://www.chronline.com
• Aaron Van Tuyl, Sports Editor
(360) 807-8229
avantuyl@chronline.com
• Tom May, Advertising Manager
(360) 736-3311
Frequency:
6 time(s) per week

CHRONICLE-TELEGRAM
225 EAST AVENUE
ELYRIA, OH 44035-5634
440-329-7000
800-848-6397
Fax: 440-329-7282
http://www.chronicletelegram.com
• Kevin Aprile, Sports Editor
(440) 329-7135
• Linda Cudlin, Sports Reporter
(440) 329-7130
lcudlin@chroniclet.com
• Scott Petrak, Sports Reporter
(440) 329-7254
spetrak@chroniclet.com
Frequency:
7 time(s) per week

CHRONICLE-TRIBUNE
610 SOUTH ADAMS STREET
MARION, IN 46953-2041
765-664-5111
800-955-7888
Fax: 765-668-4256
reporter@comteck.com
http://www.chronicle-tribune.com/
• Kristine Dowell, Advertising Manager
• Chuck Landis, Sports Reporter
(765) 664-5111
clandis@marion.gannett.com
• Adam Wire, Sports Editor
(765) 671-1264
Frequency:
7 time(s) per week

CINCINNATI ENQUIRER
312 ELM STREET
CINCINNATI, OH 45202-2724

513-721-2700
Fax: 513-768-8340
news@enquirer.com
http://www.enquirer.com
• Barry Forbis, Sports Editor
(513) 768-8301
• Paul Daugherty, Sports Columnist
(513) 768-8454
pdaugherty@enquirer.com
• Joe Reedy, Sports Reporter
(513) 768-8684
jreedy@enquirer.com
• John Fay, Sports Reporter
Frequency:
7 time(s) per week

CINCINNATI POST
125 EAST COURT STREET
CINCINNATI, OH 45202-1214
513-352-2000
Fax: 513-621-3962
http://www.cincypost.com
• Mike Gleason, Advertising Manager
(513) 768-6965
mgleason@enquirer.com
• Keith Herrell, Sports Editor
Frequency:
6 time(s) per week

CIRCLEVILLE HERALD
210 NORTH COURT STREET
CIRCLEVILLE, OH 43113-1608
740-474-3131
Fax: 740-474-9525
http://www.circlevilleherald.com/
• Brad Morris, Sports Editor
bmorris@circlevilleherald.com
• Jerry Shasteen, Advertising Manager
news@circlevilleherald.com
Frequency:
6 time(s) per week

CITIZEN
25 DILL STREET
AUBURN, NY 13021-3632
315-253-5311
800-878-5311
Fax: 315-253-6031
http://www.auburnpub.com
• Tom Kirkwood, Advertising Manager
(315) 282-2224
tom.kirkwood@lee.net
• Ryan Day, Sports Editor
(315) 282-2258
Frequency:
7 time(s) per week

CITIZEN TRIBUNE
1609 WEST 1ST NORTH STREET
MORRISTOWN, TN 37814-3724
423-581-5630
Fax: 423-581-8863
ctmaned@lcs.net
http://www.citizentribune.com
• Lee Huguenard, Classified Manager
• Brian Trent, Sports Editor
(423) 581-5630
• Mike Walker, Advertising Manager
(423) 581-5630
• Chris Ayers, Sports Reporter
(423) 581-5630
Frequency:
6 time(s) per week

CITIZENS' VOICE
75 N. WASHINGTON ST
WILKES-BARRE, PA 18711-0502
570-821-2000
Fax: 570-821-2247
www.citizensvoice.com
• Neil Corbett, Sports Editor
sports@citizensvoice.com

CITRUS COUNTY CHRONICLE
1624 NORTH MEADOWCREST
BOULEVARD
CRYSTAL RIVER, FL 34429-5760
352-563-6363
Fax: 352-563-3280
newsdesk@chronicleonline.com
http://www.chronicleonline.com
• Andy Marks, Sports Editor
• Khuong Phan, Sports Writer
(352) 563-3261
Frequency:
7 time(s) per week

CLAREMORE DAILY PROGRESS
315 WEST WILL ROGERS BOULEVARD
CLAREMORE, OK 74017-7021
918-341-1101
Fax: 918-341-1131
maned@swbell.net
http://www.claremoreprogress.com
• Tom Ritter, Sports Editor
tritter@claremoreprogress.com
• Cindy Vaughan, Advertising Director
Frequency:
5 time(s) per week

CLARION HERALD
P.O. BOX 53247
NEW ORLEANS, LA 70153
504-596-3030
Fax: 504-596-3020
clarionherald@clarionherald.org
http://www.clarionherald.org
• Ron Brocato, Sports Editor
(504) 596-3030
rbrocato@clarionherald.org
Frequency:
2 time(s) per month

CLARION-LEDGER
P.O. BOX 40
JACKSON, MS 39201-4202
601-961-7000
800-367-3384
Fax: 601-961-7211
http://www.clarionledger.com
• Rick Cleveland, Sports Columnist
(601) 961-7210
rcleveland@clarionledger.com
• Rusty Hampton, Sports Editor
(601) 961-7293
rhampton@clarionledger.com
• Roland Weeks, Advertising Director
(601) 961-7143
rweeks@jackson.gannett.com
Frequency:
7 time(s) per week

CLARKSDALE PRESS REGISTER
128 EAST SECOND STREET
CLARKSDALE, MS 38614
662-627-2201
Fax: 662-624-5125
http://www.pressregister.com
• Josh Troy, Sports Writer
sports@pressregister.com

Frequency:
6 time(s) per week

CLAY CENTER DISPATCH
805 5TH STREET
CLAY CENTER, KS 67432-2502
785-632-2127
Fax: 785-632-6526
dispatch@claycenter.com
http://www.claycenter.com
• David Berggren, Sports Editor
• Kathy Pippenger, Advertising Manager
Frequency:
5 time(s) per week

CLEAR-RIDGE REPORTER
6225 SOUTH KEDZIE AVENUE
CHICAGO, IL 60629-3304
773-476-4800
Fax: 773-476-7811
http://www.swnewsherald.com
• Tom Danz, Sports Editor
(773) 476-4800
Frequency:
1 time(s) per week

CLEBURNE TIMES-REVIEW
P.O. BOX 1569
CLEBURNE, TX 76031-5602
817-645-2441
Fax: 817-645-4020
http://www.cleburnetimesreview.com
• Zack Cunningham, Sports Editor
(817) 645-2441
sports@trcle.com
• Kay Helms, Publisher
(817) 645-2441
kpace@trcle.com
Frequency:
6 time(s) per week

CLEVELAND DAILY BANNER
P.O. BOX 3600
CLEVELAND, TN 37320-3600
423-472-5041
Fax: 423-476-1046
lifestyles@clevelandbanner.com
http://www.clevelandbanner.com
• Jack Bennett, Advertising Manager
(423) 472-5041
advertising@clevelandbanner.com
• Richard Melvin, Sports Editor
(423) 472-5041
Frequency:
6 time(s) per week

CLINTON DAILY NEWS
522 AVANT AVENUE
CLINTON, OK 73601-3436
580-323-5151
Fax: 580-323-5154
cdnews@swbell.net
http://www.clintondailynews.com
• Reba Donley, Advertising Manager
cdnads@swbell.net
• Sean Stephens, Sports Editor
Frequency:
6 time(s) per week

CLINTON HERALD
221 6TH AVENUE SOUTH
CLINTON, IA 52733-2961
563-242-7101
800-729-7101
Fax: 563-242-3854

news@clintonherald.com
http://www.clintonherald.com
• Sherri Enwright, Classified Manager
(563) 242-7101
senwright@clintonherald.com
• Jon Gremmels, Sports Editor
(563) 242-7142
jongremmels@clintonherald.com
• Wayne Larkey, Advertising Manager
(563) 242-7101
• Kurt Ritzman, Assistant Sports Editor
(563) 242-7101
Frequency:
6 time(s) per week

CLINTON JOURNAL
11 S MONROE
PO BOX 615
CLINTON, IL 61727
217-935-3171
Fax: 217-935-6086
www.theclintonjournal.com
• Luke Smucker, Sports Editor
• Byron Painter, Sports Editor
(217) 935-3171
sports@clintondailyjournal.com
Frequency:
5 time(s) per week

COEUR D'ALENE PRESS
201 NORTH 2ND STREET
COEUR D ALENE, ID 83814
208-664-8176
Fax: 208-664-0212
editor@cdapress.com
http://www.cdapress.com
• Paul Burke, Advertising Director
pburke@cda.com
• Mark Nelke, Sports Editor
(208) 664-8176
mnelke@cdapress.com
Frequency:
7 time(s) per week

COFFEYVILLE JOURNAL
8TH & ELM STREETS
COFFEYVILLE, KS 67337
620-251-3300
Fax: 620-251-1905
• Tina Alvidrez, Advertising Director
• Kevin Krier, Sports Reporter
Frequency:
5 time(s) per week

COLORADOAN
1300 RIVERSIDE AVENUE
FORT COLLINS, CO 80524
970-493-6397
Fax: 970-224-7899
news@coloradoan.com
http://www.coloradoan.com
• Sean Duff, Sports Editor
(970) 224-7750
Frequency:
7 time(s) per week

COLUMBIA DAILY TRIBUNE
P.O. BOX 798
COLUMBIA, MO 65201-4416
573-815-1700
800-333-6799
Fax: 573-815-1701
editor@tribmail.com
http://www.columbiatribune.com

• Joe Walljasper, Sports Editor
(573) 815-1783
jwalljasper@tribmail.com
Frequency:
7 time(s) per week

COLUMBIA MISSOURIAN
221 S EIGHTH ST
COLUMBIA, MO 65201
573-882-5700
Fax: 573-882-5702
editor@columbiamissourian.com
www.columbiamissourian.com
• Michael Knisley, Sports Editor
Frequency:
6 time(s) per week

COLUMBIAN
P.O. BOX 180
VANCOUVER, WA 98660-0180
360-699-6006
800-743-3391
Fax: 360-699-6033
metrodesk@columbian.com
http://www.columbian.com
• Paul Danzer, Sports Writer
(360) 759-8020
• Nick Daschel, Sports Columnist
(360) 759-8056
• Greg Jayne, Sports Editor
(360) 759-8059
greg.jayne@columbian.com
• Tim Martinez, Assistant Sports Editor
(360) 759-8057
tim.martinez@columbian.com
• Tim Pyle, Sports Reporter
(360) 759-8070
• Andy Seligman, Sports Reporter
(360) 759-8051
• Al Thomas, Sports Reporter
(360) 759-8054
al.thomas@columbian.com
• Dan Trujillo, Sports Reporter
(360) 759-8051
• Paul Valencia, Sports Reporter
(360) 759-8055
paul.valencia@columbian.com
Frequency:
7 time(s) per week

COLUMBUS DISPATCH
34 SOUTH 3RD STREET
COLUMBUS, OH 43215-4201
614-461-5200
Fax: 614-461-7580
letters@dispatch.com
http://www.dispatch.com
• Michael Arace, Sports Reporter
(614) 461-5000
marace@dispatch.com
• Bob Baptist, Sports Reporter
• Ray Stein, Sports Editor
rstein@dispatch.com
• Steve Blackledge, Sports Reporter
(614) 461-5000
sblackle@dispatch.com
• Scott Davis, Assistant Sports Editor
(614) 461-5000
sdavis@dispatch.com
• Ken Gordon, Sports Reporter
(614) 461-5000
kgordon@dispatch.com
• Brian Hofmann, Assistant Sports Editor
(614) 461-5200
bhofmann@dispatch.com
• Bob Hunter, Sports Columnist
(614) 461-5148

bhunter@dispatch.com
• Todd Jones, Sports Columnist
(614) 461-8756
tjones@dispatch.com
• Jim Massie, Sports Reporter
(614) 461-5000
jmassie@dispatch.com
• Tim May, Sports Reporter
(614) 461-5000
tmay@dispatch.com
• Gary Merrell, Advertising Vice President
• Rob Oller, Sports Reporter
(641) 461-5234
roller@dispatch.com
• Aaron Portzline, Sports Reporter
(614) 461-5000
aportzli@dispatch.com
• Bill Rabinowitz, Sports Reporter
(614) 461-5000
brabinow@dispatch.com
• Barnet D. Wolf, Advertising Reporter
• Mark Znidar, Sports Reporter
(614) 461-5000
mznidar@dispatch.com
Frequency:
7 time(s) per week

COLUMBUS LEDGER-ENQUIRER
17 WEST 12TH STREET
COLUMBUS, GA 31901-2413
706-324-5526
800-282-7859
Fax: 706-576-6290
hwilliams@ledger-enquirer.com
http://www.ledger-enquirer.com
• Kevin Price, Sports Editor
(706) 571-8590
kprice@ledger-enquirer.com
• Chris White, Sports Writer
Frequency:
7 time(s) per week

COLUMBUS TELEGRAM
P.O. BOX 648
COLUMBUS, NE 68601-5656
402-564-2741
800-279-1123
Fax: 402-563-7500
telegram@megavision.com
http://www.columbustelegram.com
• Don Strecker, Sports Editor
(402) 564-2741
don.strecker@lee.net
• Lincoln Arneal, Sports Editor
(402) 564-2741
lincoln.arneal@lee.net
Frequency:
6 time(s) per week

COMMERCIAL APPEAL
P.O. BOX 334
MEMPHIS, TN 38103-3217
901-529-2345
800-444-6397
Fax: 901-529-2787
appeal@gomemphis.com
http://www.commercialappeal.com
• Randy Bruce, Sports Assistant Editor
(901) 529-2822
bruce@commercialappeal.com
• Geoff Calkins, Sports Columnist
(901) 529-2364
calkins@commercialappeal.com
• Ron Higgins, Sports Writer
(901) 529-2525
higgins@commercialappeal.com
• Linda Moore, Business Columnist

(901) 529-2702
lmoore@commercialappeal.com
• Marlon Morgan, Sports Writer
(901) 529-2792
morgan@commercialappeal.com
• Gary Robinson, Executive Sports Editor
(901) 529-2352
robinson@commercialappeal.com
• Jason Smith, Sports Writer
(901) 529-5804
SmithJas@commercialappeal.com
• Mike Stanley, Classified Manager
(901) 529-2221
• Phil Stukenborg, Sports Writer
(901) 529-2543
stukenborg@commercialappeal.com
• Ronald Tillery, Sports Writer
(901) 529-2353
tillery@commercialappeal.com
• David Williams, Sports Content Editor
(901) 529-2310
 williams@commercialappeal.com
Frequency:
7 time(s) per week

COMMERCIAL DISPATCH
516 MAIN STREET
COLUMBUS, MS 39701
662-328-2424
Fax: 662-796-9016
voice@cdispatch.com
http://www.cdispatch.com
• Beth Proffitt, Advertising Director
(662) 328-2427
• Adam Minichino, Sports Editor
aminichino@cdispatch.com
Frequency:
6 time(s) per week

COMMERCIAL NEWS
17 WEST NORTH STREET
DANVILLE, IL 61832-5765
217-446-1000
800-729-2992
Fax: 217-446-9625
admin@dancomnews.com
http://www.dancomnews.com
• Marvin Hollman, Sports Reporter
(217) 477-5210
mholman@dancomnews.com
• Chad Dare, Sports Editor
(217) 477-5151
cdare@dancomnews.com
Frequency:
7 time(s) per week

COMMONWEALTH-JOURNAL
110-112 EAST MOUNT VERNON STREET
SOMERSET, KY 42501-1411
606-678-8191
Fax: 606-679-9225
jneal@somerset-kentucky.com
http://www.somerset-kentucky.com
• Steve Cornelius, Sports Editor
(606) 678-8191
scornelius@somerset-kentucky.com
Frequency:
6 time(s) per week

COMMUNICATOR NEWS
90 WEST CAMPUS VIEW BOULEVARD
COLUMBUS, OH 43235
614-781-1160
Fax: 614-781-1176
tcneditor@aol.com
http://www.communicatornews.com

• Ron Rall, Assistant Sports Editor
• Charlene Rall, Sports Editor
Frequency:
1 time(s) per week

COMMUNITY JOURNAL-CLERMONT
394 WARDS CORNER ROAD SUITE 170
LOVELAND, OH 45140-8300
513-248-8600
Fax: 513-248-1938
http://www.communitypress.com
• Anthony Amorini, Sports Reporter
(513) 248-7570
aamorini@communitypress.com
• Mark Chalifoux, Sports Reporter
(513) 576-8255
Frequency:
1 time(s) per week

COMMUNITY NEWS
5748 HELEN AVENUE
JENNINGS, MO 63136-3615
314-261-5555
Fax: 314-261-2776
• Jerry Baute, Sports Editor
Frequency:
1 time(s) per week

CONCORD CALL
9977 LIN FERRY DRIVE
SAINT LOUIS, MO 63123
314-843-0102
Fax: 314-843-0508
news@callnewspapers.com
http://www.callnewspapers.com
• Mike Anthony, Sports Editor
news1@callnewspapers.com
Frequency:
1 time(s) per week

CONCORD MONITOR
1 MONITOR DRIVE
CONCORD, NH 03301-1834
603-224-5301
800-464-3415
Fax: 603-224-5301
news@cmonitor.com
http://www.concordmonitor.com
• Ray Duckler, Sports Columnist
(603) 224-5301
rduckler@cmonitor.com
• Jefferey Novotny, Sports Assistant Editor
(603) 224-5301
• Sandra Smith, Sports Editor
(603) 224-5301
Frequency:
7 time(s) per week

CONNECTICUT POST
410 STATE STREET
BRIDGEPORT, CT 06604-4501
203-333-0161
800-423-8058
Fax: 203-366-3373
grogo@ctpost.com
www.ctpost.com
• Chris Casavant, Sports Writer
(203) 330-6210
• Rich Elliott, Sports Reporter
• Chris Elsberry, Sports Columnist
celsberry@ctpost.com
• Michael Fornabaio, Sports Reporter
mfornabaio@ctpost.com
• Brenda MacDonald, Advertising Sales Director
(203) 330-6460

• Neill Ostrout, Sports Reporter
(203) 330-6210
nostrout@ctpost.com
• Dirk Perrefort, Sports Writer
(203) 878-2130
dperrefort@ctpost.com
• Gary Rogo, Sports Editor
(203) 330-6223
grogo@ctpost.com
Frequency:
7 time(s) per week

CONNERSVILLE NEWS-EXAMINER
406 CENTRAL AVENUE
CONNERSVILLE, IN 47331-1926
765-825-0581
Fax: 765-825-4599
newsexaminer@newsexaminer.com
http://www.newsexaminer.com
• Grady Tate, Sports Editor
Frequency:
6 time(s) per week
Description:
Daily newspaper

CONROE COURIER
100 AVENUE A
CONROE, TX 77301-2946
936-756-6671
800-659-8313
Fax: 936-756-6676
http://www.thecourier-online.com
• Mike Jones, Sports Editor
(936) 756-6671
careersports@hcnonline.com
• Karen Mauermann, Advertising Director
(936) 442-3439
kmauermann@hcnonline.com
Frequency:
7 time(s) per week

CONTINENTAL
212 48TH STREET
UNION CITY, NJ 07087
201-864-9505
Fax: 201-864-9456
continews@aol.com
• Mario Ciria, Sports Editor
Frequency:
1 time(s) per week

CONTRA COSTA TIMES
2640 SHADELANDS DRIVE
WALNUT CREEK, CA 94598
925-935-2525
Fax: 925-943-8362
http://www.contracostatimes.com
• Mike Lefkow, Sports Editor
(925) 943-8149
mlefkow@bayareanewsgroup.com
• Steve Corkran, Sports Reporter (NFL)
(925) 943-8122
• Rick Hurd, Sports Reporter
(925) 977-8589
• Cam Inman, Sports Columnist
(925) 977-8493
• Phil Jensen, Sports Reporter
(925) 943-8243
pjensen@cctimes.com
• Jonathan Okanes, Sports Reporter
(925) 943-8194
• Gary Peterson, Sports Columnist
(925) 943-8338
• Joe Stiglich, Sports Staff Writer
(925) 943-8108
• Marcus Thompson, Sports Reporter
(925) 847-2196

media

• Mike Wood, Assistant Sports Editor
(925) 977-8493
Frequency:
7 time(s) per week

CORAL SPRINGS-PARKLAND FORUM
4611 JOHNSON ROAD SUITE 4
COCONUT CREEK, FL 33073
954-420-0955
Fax: 954-420-0415
• Rick Menning, Sports Editor
Frequency:
1 time(s) per week

CORPUS CHRISTI CALLER-TIMES
PO BOX 9136
CORPUS CHRISTI, TX 78401
361-884-2011
800-827-2011
Fax: 361-886-3732
metrodesk@caller.com
http://www.caller.com
• Gaylon Krizak, Sports Editor
(361) 886-3663
• Lee Goddard, Sports Reporter
(361) 886-3613

CORSICANA DAILY SUN
405 EAST COLLIN
CORSICANA, TX 75110-5325
903-872-3931
Fax: 903-872-6878
http://www.corsicanadailysun.com
• Joe Zigtema, Sports Editor
joe@corsicanadailysun.com
Frequency:
7 time(s) per week

CORTLAND STANDARD
PO BOX 5548
CORTLAND, NY 13045
607-756-5665
Fax: 607-756-5665
office@cortlandstandard.net
www.cortlandstandard.net
• Michael Anderson, Advertising Manager
(607) 756-5665
addesign@cortlandstandard.net
• Al Butler, Sports Editor
(607) 756-5665
sports@cortlandstandard.net
Frequency:
6 time(s) per week

CORVALLIS GAZETTE-TIMES
P.O. BOX 368
CORVALLIS, OR 97333
541-753-2641
800-653-3755
Fax: 541-758-9505
news@gtconnect.com
http://www.gazettetimes.com
• Steve Greff, Sports Editor
(541) 758-9544
• Gary Tackett, Advertising Director
(541) 812-6074
Frequency:
7 time(s) per week

COSHOCTON TRIBUNE
550 MAIN STREET
COSHOCTON, OH 43812-1612
740-622-1122
800-589-8689
Fax: 740-622-7341
http://www.coshoctontribune.com

• Jim Barstow, Sports Editor
(740) 622-1122
jbarstow@nncogannett.com
Frequency:
7 time(s) per week

COURIER
P.O. BOX 887
RUSSELLVILLE, AR 72811-0887
479-968-4037
800-369-5252
Fax: 479-968-4037
http://www.couriernews.com
• Kevin Hill, Assistant Sports Editor
sports@couriernews.com
• Michelle Harris, Advertising Director
michelle@couriernews.com
• Sean Ingram, Sports Editor
sportseditor@couriernews.com
Frequency:
7 time(s) per week

COURIER NEWS
92 EAST MAIN STREET, SUITE 202
SOMERVILLE, NJ 08876
908-707-3111
Fax: 732-565-7209
cnbusiness@c-n.com
http://www.c-n.com
• Steve Feiti, Sports Editor
(732) 643-4232
hntsports@mycentraljersey.com
Frequency:
7 time(s) per week

COURIER-EXPRESS
P.O. BOX 407
DU BOIS, PA 15801-2430
814-371-4200
800-442-4217
Fax: 814-371-3241
newsroom@thecourierexpress.com
http://www.thecourierexpress.com
• Scott Shindledecker, Sports Editor
(814) 371-4200
sports@thecourierexpress.com
• Don Harris, Sports Reporter
(814) 371-4200
Frequency:
6 time(s) per week

COURIER-JOURNAL
P.O. BOX 740031
LOUISVILLE, KY 40202-2206
502-582-4691
800-765-4011
Fax: 502-582-4200
neighborhoods@courier-journal.com
http://www.courier-journal.com
• C.L. Brown, Sports Reporter
(502) 582-4044
cbrown@courier-journal.com
• Richard Bozich, Sports Columnist
(502) 582-4650
• Glenn Brownstein, Sports Assistant Editor
(502) 582-4362
gbrownstein@courier-journal.com
• Harry Bryan, Sports Editor
(502) 582-4060
hbryan@courier-journal.com
• Eric Crawford, Sports Writer
(502) 582-4372
ecrawford@courier-journal.com
• Jody Demling, Sports Reporter
(502) 582-7176
jdemling@courier-journal.com
• Creig Ewing, Assistant Sports Editor

(502) 582-4043
cewing@courier-journal.com
• Nick Lazaroff, Advertising Director
(Display)
(502) 582-4011
• Jennie Rees, Sports Writer
(502) 582-4042
jrees@courier-journal.com
• Michael Smith, Sports Reporter
(859) 254-7888
mssmith@courier-journal.com
Frequency:
7 time(s) per week

COURIER-NEWS
495 COMMONS DRIVE
AURORA, IL 60504
630-978-8880
http://couriernews.suntimes.com
• R. J. Gerber, Sports Editor
(630) 978-8175
• Jason Bauman, Assistant Sports Editor
(630) 978-8412
jbauman@stmedianetwork.com
Frequency:
7 time(s) per week

COURIER-OBSERVER
5 BEAL STREET
POTSDAM, NY 13676-1746
315-661-2512
Fax: 315-386-2855
http://www.mpcourier.com
• Al St. Pierre, Sports Editor
(315) 393-1000
astpierre@ogd.com
Frequency:
5 time(s) per week

COURIER-POST
301 CUTHBERT BOULEVARD
CHERRY HILL, NJ 08002
856-486-2600
Fax: 856-663-2831
http://www.courierpostonline.com
• Gary Silvers, Sports Editor
(856) 486-2420
gsilvers@courierpostonline.com
• Don Benevento, Sports Reporter
(856) 486-2424
dbenevento@courierpostonline.com
• Kevin Callahan, Sports Reporter
(865) 486-2424
kcallahan@courierpostonline.com
• Chuck Gormley, Sports Reporter
(856) 486-2424
cgormley@courierpostonline.com
• Ray Ventura, Sports Reporter
• Bob Viggiano, Sports Reporter
bviggiano@courierpostonline.com
• Celeste Whittaker, Sports Reporter
(856) 486-2424
cwhittaker@courierpostonline.com
Frequency:
7 time(s) per week

COURIER-TIMES
201 SOUTH 14TH STREET
NEW CASTLE, IN 47362-3328
765-529-1111
800-489-2472
Fax: 765-529-1731
http://www.thecouriertimes.com
• Jeremy Hines, Sports Editor
(765) 529-1111
Frequency:
6 time(s) per week

CRAIG DAILY PRESS
466 YAMPA AVENUE
CRAIG, CO 81625
970-824-7031
Fax: 970-824-6810
http://www.craigdailypress.com
• David Pressgrove, Sports Writer
(970) 824-7031
Frequency:
5 time(s) per week

CRESCENT-NEWS
624 WEST 2ND STREET
DEFIANCE, OH 43512-2161
419-784-5441
Fax: 419-784-1492
crescent@crescent-news.com
http://www.crescent-news.com
• Bruce Hefflinger, Sports Editor
(419) 784-5441
hefflinger@crescent-news.com
• Mark Ryan, Advertising Manager
(419) 784-5441
Frequency:
6 time(s) per week

CRESTON NEWS-ADVERTISER
503 WEST ADAMS STREET
CRESTON, IA 50801-3112
641-782-2141
Fax: 641-782-6628
office@crestonnews.com
http://www.crestonnewsadvertiser.com
• Matt Pfiffner, Sports Editor
(641) 782-2141
mfiffner@crestonnews.com
• Craig Mittag, Advertising Manager
(641) 782-2141
cmittag@crestonnews.com
Frequency:
5 time(s) per week

CROOKSTON DAILY TIMES
124 SOUTH BROADWAY
CROOKSTON, MN 56716-1955
218-281-2730
Fax: 218-281-7234
editor@crookstontimes.com
http://www.crookstontimes.com
• Calvin Anderson, Advertising Manager
calvin@crookstontimes.com
• Derek Martin, Sports Editor
sports@crookstontimes.com
Frequency:
5 time(s) per week

CROWLEY POST-SIGNAL
602 NORTH PARKERSON AVENUE
CROWLEY, LA 70526-4354
337-783-3450
Fax: 337-788-0949
crowleyps@aol.com
http://www.crowleypostsignal.com
• Chris Quebedeaux, Sports Editor
chris.quebedeaux@crowleytoday.com
Frequency:
5 time(s) per week

CULLMAN TIMES
300 4TH AVENUE, S.E.
CULLMAN, AL 35055
256-734-2131
Fax: 256-737-1006
http://www.cullmantimes.com
• Justin Graves, Sports Editor
(256) 734-2131

jgraves@cullmantimes.com
• Stan Veitch, Sports Writer
(256) 734-2131
stanv@cullmantimes.com
• Kathy McLeroy, Advertising Director
(256) 734-2131
Frequency:
6 time(s) per week

CULPEPER STAR-EXPONENT
471 JAMES MADISON HIGHWAY, SUITE 201
CULPEPER, VA 22701
540-825-0771
Fax: 540-825-0778
http://www.starexponent.com
• Ron Counts, Sports Reporter
(540) 825-0771
rcounts@starexponent.com
• Gloria Williams, Advertising Manager
(540) 825-0771
gwilliams@starexponent.com
Frequency:
7 time(s) per week

CUMBERLAND TIMES-NEWS
19 BALTIMORE STREET
CUMBERLAND, MD 21502-3023
301-722-4600
Fax: 301-722-5270
ctn@times-news.com
http://www.times-news.com
• Mike Burke, Sports Editor
(301) 722-4600
mburke@times-news.com
Frequency:
7 time(s) per week

CUSHING DAILY CITIZEN
202 N HARRISON
CUSHING, OK 74023
918-285-5555
http://www.cushingcitizen.com
• Amy Grissom, Advertising Manager
(918) 225-3333
ads@cushingdaily.com
• Luke Boyd, Sports Reporter
Frequency:
5 time(s) per week

CUYAHOGA FALLS NEWS-PRESS
1619 COMMERCE DRIVE
STOW, OH 44224
330-688-0088
800-966-6565
Fax: 330-688-1588
http://www.recordpub.com
• Tom Nader, Sports Editor
(330) 296-9657
Frequency:
1 time(s) per week

DAILY ADVANCE
P.O. BOX 588
ELIZABETH CITY, NC 27909
252-335-8076
Fax: 252-335-4415
http://www.dailyadvance.com
• Chic Riebel, Sports Editor
(252) 335-8123
criebel@dailyadvance.com
• Will Harris, Sports Writer
(252) 335-8124
waharris@dailyadvance.com
Frequency:
7 time(s) per week

DAILY ADVOCATE
P.O. BOX 220
GREENVILLE, OH 45331-1926
937-548-3151
Fax: 937-548-3913
editor@dailyadvocate.com
http://www.dailyadvocate.com/
• Kyle Shaner, Sports Editor
(937) 548-3151
Frequency:
7 time(s) per week

DAILY AMERICAN
334 WEST MAIN STREET
SOMERSET, PA 15501-1508
814-445-5900
800-452-0823
Fax: 814-445-2935
news@dailyamerican.com
http://www.dailyamerican.com
• Ron Pritts, Sports Editor
(814) 444-5926
ronp@dailyamerican.com
Frequency:
6 time(s) per week

DAILY AMERICAN REPUBLIC
208 POPLAR STREET
POPLAR BLUFF, MO 63901-5842
573-785-1414
888-276-2242
Fax: 573-785-2706
http://info.darnews.com
• Christy Pierce, Advertising Manager
(573) 785-1414
ads@darnews.com
• Brian Rosener, Sports Editor
(573) 785-1414
sports@darnews.com
Frequency:
6 time(s) per week

DAILY ARDMOREITE
117 WEST BROADWAY
ARDMORE, OK 73401-6226
580-223-2200
800-873-0211
Fax: 580-226-0050
http://www.ardmoreite.com
• James Jordan, Sports Writer
(580) 221-6527
• Erik Horne, Sports Editor
(580) 221-6522
• Lisa Wilkinson, Advertising Manager
(580) 221-6513
Frequency:
6 time(s) per week

DAILY ASTORIAN
949 EXCHANGE STREET
ASTORIA, OR 97103-4605
503-325-3211
800-781-3211
Fax: 503-458-6000
daily.astorian@dailyastorian.com
www.dailyastorian.com
• Gary Henley, Sports Writer
ghenley@dailyastorian.com
Frequency:
5 time(s) per week

DAILY BREEZE
21250 HAWTHORNE BLVD
TORRANCE, CA 90503
310-540-5511
Fax: 310-540-6272

newsroom@dailybreeze.com
http://www.dailybreeze.com
• Todd Bailey, Sports Editor
(310) 540-5511
• Tony Ciniglio, Sports Columnist
(310) 540-5511
tony.ciniglio@dailybreeze.com
• Bill Cizek, Sports Reporter
(310) 540-5511
• Phil Collin, Sports Reporter
(310) 540-5511
phil.collin@dailybreeze.com
• Bob Holtzman, Sports Columnist
(310) 540-5511
• Eric Mandel, Sports Reporter
(310) 540-5511
• Jim Thomas, Sports Reporter
(310) 540-5511
• Mike Waldner, Sports Reporter
(310) 540-5511
• Woody Woodburn, Sports Columnist
Frequency:
7 time(s) per week

DAILY CAMERA
PO BOX 591
BOULDER, CO 80306
303-442-1202
Fax: 303-449-9358
http://www.dailycamera.com
• Jennifer Osieczanek, Sports Editor
(303) 473-1316
• Mark Kranjcec, Retail Advertising Director
• Kyle Ringo, Sports Reporter
(303) 442-1202
• Mike Sandrock, Sports Reporter
(303) 442-1202
• Chris Shelton, Sports Editor
(303) 442-1202
• Ryan Thorburn, Sports Reporter
thorburnr@thedailycamera.com
Frequency:
7 time(s) per week

DAILY CAPITAL NEWS
210 MONROE STREET
JEFFERSON CITY, MO 65101-3210
573-636-3131
Fax: 573-636-7035
news@newstribune.com
http://www.newstribune.com
• Debbie Kiser, Advertising Manager
(573) 761-0226
display@newstribune.com
• Tom Rackers, Sports Editor
sports@newstribune.com
Frequency:
7 time(s) per week

DAILY CHRONICLE
1586 BARBAR GREENE RD
DEKALB, IL 60115
815-756-4841
Fax: 815-758-5059
www.daily-chronicle.com
• John Sahly, Sports Editor
jsahly@shawsuburban.com
• Karen Pletsch, Advertising Director

DAILY CITIZEN
3000 EAST RACE
SEARCY, AR 72143
501-268-8621
800-400-3142
Fax: 501-268-6277
http://www.thedailycitizen.com

• Craig Woodson, Sports Editor
(513) 763-5500
cwoodson@thedailycitizen.com
• Terasa Harvey, Advertising Director
(800) 400-3142
tharvey@thedailycitizen.com
Frequency:
6 time(s) per week

**DAILY CLAY COUNTY
ADVOCATE-PRESS**
105 WEST NORTH AVENUE
FLORA, IL 62839
618-662-2108
Fax: 618-662-2939
editor@advocatepress.com
http://www.advocatepress.com
• Mike Linville, Sports Editor
sports@advocatepress.com
Frequency:
5 time(s) per week

DAILY COMET
104 HICKORY STREET
THIBODAUX, LA 70301
985-448-7600
800-256-1305
Fax: 985-448-7606
http://www.dailycomet.com
• Marion Long, Advertising Director
• Brent St. Germain, Sports Editor
(985) 448-7616
brent.st.germain@dailycomet.com
Frequency:
5 time(s) per week

DAILY COMMERCIAL
212 EAST MAIN STREET
LEESBURG, FL 34748
352-365-8200
Fax: 352-365-1951
news@dailycommercial.com
http://www.dailycommercial.com
• Frank Jolley, Sports Editor
(352) 365-8283
frankjolley@dailycommercial.com
Frequency:
7 time(s) per week

DAILY CORINTHIAN
1607 SOUTH HARPER ROAD
CORINTH, MS 38834
662-287-6111
Fax: 662-287-3525
news@dailycorinthian.com
http://www.dailycorinthian.com
• Lee Smith, Sports Editor
(662) 287-6111
Frequency:
6 time(s) per week

DAILY COURIER (AZ)
1958 COMMERCE CENTER CIRCLE
PRESCOTT, AZ 86301
928-445-3333
Fax: 928-445-2062
http://www.prescottaz.com
• Keith Jiron, Sports Editor
• Dick Larson, Advertising Director
• Tom Regnier, Advertising Manager
Frequency:
6 time(s) per week

DAILY COURIER (PA)
127 WEST APPLE STREET
CONNELLSVILLE, PA 15425-3132

724-628-2000
800-801-9000
Fax: 724-626-3567
• Jason Black, Sports Editor
(724) 626-3534
jblack@tribweb.com
Frequency:
6 time(s) per week

DAILY DEMOCRAT
711 MAIN STREET
WOODLAND, CA 95695-3406
530-662-5421
Fax: 530-406-6262
http://www.dailydemocrat.com
• Bruce Burton, Sports Editor
(530) 406-6236
Frequency:
7 time(s) per week

DAILY DISPATCH
530 E 11TH STREET
DOUGLAS, AZ 85607-2014
520-364-3424
Fax: 520-364-6750
editor@douglasdispatch.com
http://www.douglasdispatch.com
• Bruce Whetten, Sports Reporter
(520) 364-3424
Frequency:
5 time(s) per week

DAILY DUNKLIN DEMOCRAT
203 1ST STREET
KENNETT, MO 63857-2052
573-888-4505
Fax: 573-888-5114
http://www.dddnews.com
• Dustin Ward, Sports Editor
dward@dddnews.com
• Terri Coleman, Advertising Manager
tcoleman@dddnews.com
Frequency:
5 time(s) per week

DAILY FREEMAN
79 HURLEY AVENUE
KINGSTON, NY 12401
845-331-5000
Fax: 845-331-3557
news@freemanonline.com
http://www.midhudsoncentral.com
• Gregory Appel, Advertising Director
• Babara Norton, Retail Advertising
Manager
(845) 331-5000
bnorton@freemanonline.com
• Ron Rosner, Sports Editor
(845) 331-5000
rrosner@freemanonline.com
Frequency:
7 time(s) per week

DAILY FREEMAN-JOURNAL
720 2ND STREET
WEBSTER CITY, IA 50595-1437
515-832-4350
Fax: 515-832-2314
editor@freemanjournal.net
http://www.freemanjournal.net
• Troy Banning, Sports Editor
(515) 832-4350
sports@freemanjournal.net
Frequency:
5 time(s) per week

DAILY GATE CITY
1016 MAIN STREET
KEOKUK, IA 52632
319-524-8300
800-779-8819
Fax: 319-524-4363
http://www.dailygate.com
• Brad Cameron, Editor
(319) 524-8300
sports@dailygate.com
• Doug Shipman, Advertising Manager
(319) 524-8300
advertising@dailygate.com
Frequency:
5 time(s) per week

DAILY GAZETTE (IL)
3200 EAST LINCOLN WAY
STERLING, IL 61081
815-625-3600
800-798-4085
Fax: 815-625-9390
news@svnmail.com
http://www.saukvalley.com
• Dan Goetz, Advertising Director
(815) 625-3600
jbaratta@svnmail.com
• Brian Weidman, Sports Editor
bweidman@svnmail.com
Frequency:
7 time(s) per week

DAILY GAZETTE (NY)
2345 MAXON RD (12308)
PO BOX 1090
SCHENECTADY, NY 12301-1090
518-374-4141
800-262-2211
Fax: 518-395-3072
www.dailygazette.com
• Butch Walker, Sports Editor
(518) 395-3160
• Tom Boggie, Assistant Sports Editor
(518) 395-3153

DAILY GLOBE (MI)
P.O. BOX 548
IRONWOOD, MI 49938-2120
906-932-2211
800-236-2887
Fax: 906-932-5358
http://www.ironwoodglobe.com/
• Jason Juno, Sports Editor
(906) 932-2211
• Cathy Syreini, Advertising Manager
(906) 932-2211
Frequency:
6 time(s) per week

DAILY GLOBE (OH)
37 WEST MAIN STREET
SHELBY, OH 44875-1238
419-342-4276
Fax: 419-342-4246
globe@sdgnewsgroup.com
http://www.sdgnewsgroup.com
• Chuck Ridenour, Sports Editor
(419) 342-3261
Frequency:
6 time(s) per week

DAILY GUIDE
108 HOLLY DRIVE
SAINT ROBERT, MO 65584

573-336-3711
Fax: 573-336-4640
http://www.waynesvilledailyguide.com
• Brent Foster, Sports Editor
sports@waynesvilledailyguide.com
Frequency:
5 time(s) per week

DAILY HAMPSHIRE GAZETTE
115 CONZ STREET
NORTHAMPTON, MA 01061
413-584-5000
Fax: 413-585-5299
newsroom@gazettenet.com
http://www.gazettenet.com
• Mark Elliott, Advertising Manager
(413) 584-5000
• Stanley Moulton, Sports Editor
(413) 584-5000
sports@gazettenet.com
Frequency:
6 time(s) per week

DAILY HERALD (IL)
155 EAST ALGONQUIN ROAD
ARLINGTON HEIGHTS, IL 60005-4617
847-427-4300
Fax: 847-427-4608
news@dailyherald.com
http://www.dailyherald.com
• Robert Frisk, Assistant Managing
Editor/Sports
(847) 427-4441
bfrisk@dailyherald.com
• Aaron Gabriel, Sports Editor
(847) 427-4439
agabriel@dailyherald.com
• Mike Imrem, Sports Columnist
(847) 427-4456
mimrem@dailyherald.com
• Tom Quinlan, Sports Editor
(847) 427-4455
tquinlan@dailyherald.com
Frequency:
7 time(s) per week

DAILY HERALD (UT)
P.O. BOX 717
PROVO, UT 84603-0717
801-373-5050
800-880-8075
Fax: 801-344-2985
http://www.heraldextra.com
• Darnell Dickson, Sports Editor
(801) 344-2555
ddickson@heraldextra.com
Frequency:
7 time(s) per week

DAILY IBERIAN
926 EAST MAIN STREET
NEW IBERIA, LA 70560-3866
337-365-6773
Fax: 337-367-9640
dailyiberian@bellsouth.net
http://www.iberianet.com
• Chris Landry, Sports Editor
(337) 365-6773
chris.landry@daily-iberian.com
• Alan Rini, Advertising Manager
(337) 365-6773
iberianadmgr@bellsouth.net
Frequency:
7 time(s) per week

DAILY INDEPENDENT
P.O. BOX 311
ASHLAND, KY 41101-7606
606-326-2600
800-955-5860
Fax: 606-326-2678
letters@dailyindependent.com
http://www.dailyindependent.com
• Nikki Clay, Advertising Director
(606) 326-2611
nclay@dailyindependent.com
• Adam Vankirk, Sports Editor
(606) 326-2664
avankirk@dailyindependent.com
• Rocky Stanley, Sports Writer
(606) 326-2671
rstanley@dailyindependent.com
Frequency:
7 time(s) per week

DAILY INTER LAKE
P.O. BOX 7610
KALISPELL, MT 59901-3202
406-755-7000
Fax: 406-752-6114
edit@dailyinterlake.com
http://www.dailyinterlake.com
• Cindy Cece, Advertising Director
• David Lesnick, Sports Editor
(406) 758-4426
dlesnick@dailyinterlake.com
Frequency:
7 time(s) per week

DAILY IOWEGIAN
105 N MAIN ST
CENTERVILLE, IA 52544-1732
641-856-6336
Fax: 641-856-8118
http://www.dailyiowegian.com
• Becky Maxwell, Advertising Manager
• Jason McGrann, Sports Editor
(641) 856-6336
Frequency:
5 time(s) per week

DAILY ITEM (MA)
38 EXCHANGE STREET
LYNN, MA 01901
781-593-7700
Fax: 781-581-3178
http://www.itemlive.com
• B. J. Frazier, Advertising Director
(781) 593-7700
• Steve Krause, Sports Editor
(781) 593-7700
Frequency:
6 time(s) per week

DAILY ITEM (PA)
200 MARKET STREET
SUNBURY, PA 17801-3402
570-286-5671
Fax: 570-988-5348
news@dailyitem.com
http://www.dailyitem.com
• Will Strout, Advertising Manager
• Bill Bowman, Sports Editor
(570) 286-5671
bbowman@dailyitem.com
Frequency:
7 time(s) per week

DAILY JEFFERSON COUNTY UNION
28 MILWAUKEE AVENUE WEST
FORT ATKINSON, WI 53538-2018

920-563-5553
Fax: 920-563-2329
http://www.dailyunion.com
• Diane Niemeyer, Advertising Manager
(920) 563-5553
dneimeyer@dailyunion.com
• Sam Rodriguez, Sports Editor
(920) 563-5553
srodriguez@dailyunion.com
• Jeff Seisser, Sports Editor
(920) 563-5553
jseisser@dailyunion.com
Frequency:
5 time(s) per week

DAILY JEFFERSONIAN
P.O. BOX 10
CAMBRIDGE, OH 43725
740-439-3531
800-897-2262
Fax: 740-432-6219
newsroom@daily-jeff.com
http://www.daily-jeff.com
• Ed Archibald, Advertising Manager
(740) 439-3531
• Jeff Harrison, Sports Editor
(740) 439-3531
sports@daily-jeff.com
Frequency:
6 time(s) per week

DAILY JOURNAL (IL)
8 DEARBORN SQUARE
KANKAKEE, IL 60901
815-937-3300
800-892-1861
Fax: 815-937-3301
http://www.daily-journal.com
• Dave Surico, Sports Editor
(815) 937-3391
cbenoit@daily-journal.com
• Ken Munjoy, Advertising Director
(815) 937-3303
nshannon@daily-journal.com
Frequency:
6 time(s) per week

DAILY JOURNAL (MO)
1513 SAINT JOE DRIVE
PARK HILLS, MO 63601-2402
573-431-2010
800-660-8166
Fax: 573-431-7640
mbelken@pulitzer.net
• Donn Adamson, Sports Editor
(573) 431-2010
Frequency:
7 time(s) per week

DAILY LEADER (IL)
318 NORTH MAIN STREET
PONTIAC, IL 61764-1930
815-842-1153
Fax: 815-842-4388
http://www.pontiacdailyleader.com
• Judy Sweitzer, Advertising Manager
(815) 842-1153
jsweitzer@pontiacdailyleader.com
• Erich Murphy, Sports Editor
(815) 842-1153
Frequency:
6 time(s) per week

DAILY LEADER (MS)
P.O. BOX 551
BROOKHAVEN, MS 39601

601-833-6961
800-833-6961
Fax: 601-833-6714
news@dailyleader.com
http://www.dailyleader.com
• Tom Goetz, Sports Editor
(601) 833-6961
sports@dailyleader.com
• David Culpepper, Advertising Director
Frequency:
6 time(s) per week

DAILY LEDGER
53 WEST ELM STREET
CANTON, IL 61520-2511
309-647-5100
Fax: 309-647-4665
editor@cantondailyledger.com
http://www.cantondailyledger.com
• Stephen Shank, Sports Editor
sports@cantondailyledger.com
Frequency:
6 time(s) per week

DAILY LOCAL NEWS
250 NORTH BRADFORD AVENUE
WEST CHESTER, PA 19382-2800
610-696-1775
800-456-6397
Fax: 610-430-1194
news@dailylocal.com
http://www.dailylocal.com
• Bryan Davis, Sports Editor
(610) 430-1179
news@dailylocal.com
Frequency:
7 time(s) per week

DAILY MAIL
100 SUMMIT AVENUE
HAGERSTOWN, MD 21740
301-733-5131
Fax: 301-714-0245
news@herald-mail.com
http://www.herald-mail.com
• Mark Keller, Sports Editor
(301) 733-5131
Frequency:
7 time(s) per week

DAILY MESSENGER
73 BUFFALO STREET
CANANDAIGUA, NY 14424-1001
585-394-0770
Fax: 585-394-1675
http://www.mpnnow.com/
• Paul Gangarossa, Sports Editor
(585) 394-0770
• Ron Wilson, Sports Reporter
(585) 394-0770
Frequency:
6 time(s) per week

DAILY MINING GAZETTE
P.O. BOX 368
HOUGHTON, MI 49931-2134
906-482-1500
800-682-7607
Fax: 906-482-2726
http://www.mininggazette.com
• Brandon Veale, Sports Editor
(906) 483-2216
• Yvonne Robillard, Advertising Manager
(906) 483-2220
yrobillard@mininggazette.com

Frequency:
6 time(s) per week

DAILY MOUNTAIN EAGLE
1301 VIKING DRIVE
JASPER, AL 35501-4983
205-221-2840
800-518-6397
Fax: 205-221-6203
jasper@mountaineagle.com
http://www.mountaineagle.com
• Jonathan Bentley, Sports Editor
(205) 221-2840
jonathan.bentley@mountaineagle.com
• Jerry Geddings, Advertising Director
ads@mountaineagle.com
Frequency:
7 time(s) per week

DAILY NEWS (CA)
21860 BURBANK BOULEVARD
SUITE 200
WOODLAND HILLS, CA 91367
818-713-3000
Fax: 818-713-0058
http://www.dailynews.com
• Jon Clifford, Sports Editor
(818) 713-3628
• Steve Dilbeck, Sports Columnist
• Rick Hazeltine, Sports Assistant Editor
(818) 713-3632
• Tom Hoffarth, Sports Columnist
(Television)
• Kevin Modesti, Sports Columnist
(818) 713-3617
kevin.modesti@dailynews.com
Frequency:
7 time(s) per week

DAILY NEWS (KY)
813 COLLEGE STREET
BOWLING GREEN, KY 42101
270-781-1700
800-599-NEWS
Fax: 270-783-3237
editor@bgdailynews.com
http://www.bgdailynews.com
• Malcolm Knox, Sports Editor
(270) 783-3271
• Michael Compton, Sports Reporter
(270) 783-3247
• Mark Mahagan, Advertising Director

DAILY NEWS (WA)
770 11TH AVENUE
LONGVIEW, WA 98632-2412
360-577-2500
Fax: 360-577-2536
http://www.tdn.com
• Zack Buchanan, Sports Editor
(360) 577-2527
zbuchanan@tdn.com
• Rick McCorkle, Sports Reporter
(360) 577-2529
rmccorkle@tdn.com
• Steve Quaife, Advertising Manager
(360) 577-2559
squaife@tdn.com
• Ben Zimmerman, Sports Editor
(360) 577-2541
czimmerman@tdn.com
Frequency:
7 time(s) per week

DAILY NEWS JOURNAL
P.O. BOX 68
MURFREESBORO, TN 37130-3622
615-893-5860
Fax: 615-896-8702
online@dnj.com
http://www.dnj.com
• Jolene McKenzie, Advertising Director
(615) 893-5860
jmckenzie@dnj.com
• Greg Pogue, Executive Sports Editor
(615) 893-5860
Frequency:
7 time(s) per week

DAILY NEWS OF NEWBURYPORT
23 LIBERTY STREET
NEWBURYPORT, MA 01950
978-462-6666
Fax: 978-465-8505
http://www.newburyportnews.com
• Bill Trefethen, Advertising Manager
btrefethen@newburyportnews.com
• Dan Guttenplan, Sports Editor
(978) 462-6666
Frequency:
6 time(s) per week

DAILY NEWS SUN
10102 SANTE FE DRIVE
SUN CITY, AZ 85351
623-977-8351
Fax: 623-876-3698
http://www.northwestvalleynewspapers.com
• Rich Bolas, Sports Editor
(623) 876-2523
Frequency:
6 time(s) per week

DAILY NEWS TRANSCRIPT
254 2ND AVENUE
NEEDHAM, MA 02494
781-433-6700
Fax: 781-433-8375
neponset@cnc.com
http://www.townonline.com
• Tom Fargo, Sports Editor
tfargo@cnc.com
• Adam Kurkjian, Sports Writer
(781) 433-8371
akurkjin@cnc.com
Frequency:
5 time(s) per week

DAILY NEWS TRIBUNE
738A MAIN STREET
WALTHAM, MA 02451
781-647-7898
Fax: 781-398-8010
newstribune@cnc.com
http://www.dailynewstribune.com
• Cris Warren, Advertising Manager
(781) 433-8313
cwarren@cnc.com
• Scott Souza, Sports Editor
(781) 398-8006
ssouza@cnc.com
Frequency:
5 time(s) per week

DAILY NEWS-RECORD
231 SOUTH LIBERTY STREET
HARRISONBURG, VA 22803
540-574-6200
Fax: 540-433-9112

letters@dnronline.com
http://www.dnronline.com
• Chris Simmons, Sports Editor
(540) 574-6291
• Steve Turner, Advertising Director
(540) 574-6229
sturner@dnronline.com
Frequency:
6 time(s) per week

DAILY NONPAREIL
535 WEST BROADWAY SUITE 300
COUNCIL BLUFFS, IA 51503
712-328-1811
Fax: 712-325-5776
editorial@nonpareilonline.com
http://www.nonpareilonline.com
• Tony Boone, Sports Writer
(712) 325-5756
• Evan Bland, Sports Writer
(712) 325-5758
• Kevin White, Sports Editor
(712) 325-5718
Frequency:
7 time(s) per week

DAILY POST-ATHENIAN
320 SOUTH JACKSON STREET
ATHENS, TN 37303-4715
423-745-5664
Fax: 423-745-8295
http://www.dpa.xtn.net
• Sarah Jane Locke, Advertising Manager
sjlocke@xtn.net
• Sarah Jane Locke, Classified Manager
sjlocke@xtn.net
• Jack Slayton, Sports Editor
jacks@xtn.net
Frequency:
5 time(s) per week

DAILY PRESS (VA)
7505 WARWICK BOULEVARD
NEWPORT NEWS, VA 23607-1517
757-247-4730
800-543-8908
Fax: 757-245-8618
news@dailypress.com
http://www.dailypress.com
• Dave Fairbank, College Sports Reporter
(757) 247-4637
dfairbank@dailypress.com
• Warner Hessler, Sports Reporter
(757) 247-4648
whessler@dailypress.com
• Dave Johnson, College Sports Reporter
(757) 247-4649
djohnson@dailypress.com
• David Nicholson, Advertising Reporter
(757) 247-4794
dnicholson@dailypress.com
• Marty O'Brien, Sports Reporter
(757) 247-4963
mobrien@dailypress.com
• Ed Richards, Sports Reporter
(757) 247-4645
erichards@dailypress.com
• Doug Roberson, Sports Editor
(757) 247-4638
droberson@dailypress.com
• David Teel, Sports Columnist
(757) 247-4636
dteel@dailypress.com
• Jennifer Williams, College Sports Reporter
(757) 247-4644
jwilliams@dailypress.com
• Norm Wood, College Sports Reporter

(757) 247-4642
nwood@dailypress.com
Frequency:
7 time(s) per week

DAILY PRESS (WI)
122 WEST 3RD STREET
ASHLAND, WI 54806-1620
715-682-2313
Fax: 715-682-4699
ashpress@cheqnet.net
http://www.ashlandwi.com
• Larry Servinsky, Sports Editor
(715) 682-2313
• Jeff Swiston, Advertising Manager
Frequency:
6 time(s) per week

DAILY PROGRESS
P.O. BOX 9030
CHARLOTTESVILLE, VA 22901-1413
434-978-7200
Fax: 434-978-7223
http://www.dailyprogress.com
• John Kimbel, Advertising Manager
(434) 975-7112
jkimbel@dailyprogress.com
• Jerry Ratcliffe, Sports Editor
(434) 978-7251
jratcliffe@dailyprogress.com
• Todd Merchant, Sports Writer
(434) 978-7250
jjenkins@dailyprogress.com
Frequency:
7 time(s) per week

DAILY RACING FORM
708 THIRD AVENUE, 12TH FLOOR
NEW YORK, NY 10017
212-366-7600
800-306-3676
editor@drf.com
http://www.drf.com
• Steven Crist, Editor
(212) 366-7700
scrist@drf.com
• Steven Crist, Publisher
(212) 366-7700
scrist@drf.com
• Duke Dosik, Managing Editor
(212) 366-7623
ddosik@drf.com
• Rich Rosenbush, Executive Editor
(212) 366-7651
rrosenbush@drf.com
Frequency:
7 time(s) per week

DAILY RECORD (OH)
P.O. BOX 918
WOOSTER, OH 44691-4348
330-264-1125
800-686-2958
Fax: 330-264-3756
news@the-daily-record.com
http://www.the-daily-record.com
• Aaron Dorksen, Sports Editor
(330) 264-1125
• Rhonda Geer, Advertising Director
(330) 287-1653
• Art Holden, Sports Writer
(330) 264-1125
aholden@the-daily-record.com
• Bruce Polen, Classified Manager
(330) 264-1125
• Kevin Lynch, Sports Writer
(330) 674-5676

klynch@the-daily-record.com
• Mike Plant, Sports Writer
(330) 264-1125
mplant@the-daily-record.com
Frequency:
7 time(s) per week

DAILY RECORD (WA)
401 NORTH MAIN STREET
ELLENSBURG, WA 98926-3107
509-925-1414
Fax: 509-925-5696
dailyrecord@kvnews.com
http://www.kvnews.com
• Tyler Miller, Advertising Director
tmiller@kvnews.com
• Colter Nuanez, Sports Writer
(509) 925-1414
cnuanez@kvnews.com
Frequency:
6 time(s) per week

DAILY REFLECTOR
P.O. BOX 1967
GREENVILLE, NC 27834
252-752-6166
800-849-6166
Fax: 252-754-8140
http://www.reflector.com
• Jim Gentry, Sports Editor
(252) 329-9594
jgentry@reflector.com
• Nate Summers, Sports Writer
(252) 329-9595
nsummers@reflector.com
• Betty Williams, Advertising Director
(252) 329-9511
• Tony Castleberry, Sports Writer
(252) 329-9591
tcastleberry@reflector.com
Frequency:
7 time(s) per week

DAILY REGISTER
35 SOUTH VINE STREET
HARRISBURG, IL 62946
618-253-7146
800-283-8117
Fax: 618-252-0863
http://www.dailyregister.com
• Michael Dann, Sports Editor
(618) 253-7146
hbgsports@yourclearwave.com
• Doris Wilson, Advertising Manager
(618) 253-7416
Frequency:
6 time(s) per week

DAILY REPUBLIC
1250 TEXAS STREET
FAIRFIELD, CA 94533
707-425-4646
Fax: 707-425-5924
http://www.dailyrepublic.com
• Mike Corpos, Sports Writer
(707) 427-6979
• Sharon Guy, Advertising Director
(707) 425-4646
• Paul Farmer, Sports Editor
(707) 425-4646
pfarmer@dailyrepublic.net
Frequency:
7 time(s) per week

DAILY REPUBLICAN REGISTER
115 EAST 4TH STREET
MOUNT CARMEL, IL 62863-0550
618-262-5144
Fax: 618-263-4437
http://www.tristate-media.com
• Robert Livingston, Sports Editor
(618) 262-5144
• Brenna Crooks, Advertising Manager
Frequency:
5 time(s) per week

DAILY REVIEW (CA)
22533 FOOT HILL BOULEVARD
HAYWARD, CA 94541-
510-783-6111
800-595-9595
Fax: 510-293-2490
http://www.dailyreviewonline.com
• Jon Becker, Sports Editor
(925) 416-4803
• Dave Newhouse, Sports Reporter
(510) 208-6466
• Monte Poole, Sports Columnist
• Mark Saxon, Sports Reporter
• Ken Silman, Sports Reporter
(510) 293-2455
• Art Spander, Sports Reporter
(510) 531-8068
typoes@aol.com
• Carl Steward, Sports Reporter
(510) 293-2451
• Josh Suchon, Sports Reporter
Frequency:
7 time(s) per week

DAILY REVIEW (PA)
116 MAIN STREET
TOWANDA, PA 18848-1832
570-265-2151
800-253-3662
Fax: 570-265-6130
rhosie@epix.net
http://www.thedailyreview.com
• Brian Fees, Sports Editor
(570) 265-1631
reviewsports@thedailyreview.com
• Beverly Kline, Advertising Director
(570) 265-1624
bkline@epix.net
Frequency:
7 time(s) per week

DAILY REVIEW ATLAS
400 SOUTH MAIN STREET
MONMOUTH, IL 61462
309-734-3176
Fax: 309-734-7649
http://www.reviewatlas.com
• Jeff Holt, Sports Editor
• Wendy Todd, Advertising Manager
Frequency:
5 time(s) per week

DAILY SENTINEL (CO)
P.O. BOX 668
GRAND JUNCTION, CO 81501-7737
970-242-5050
800-332-5832
Fax: 970-241-6860
http://www.gjsentinel.com
• Patti Arnold, Sports Editor
(970) 242-5050
patti.arnold@gjsentinel.com
Frequency:
7 time(s) per week

DAILY SENTINEL (NY)
333 WEST DOMINICK STREET
ROME, NY 13440-5701
315-337-4000
Fax: 315-337-4704
sentinel@rny.com
http://www.rny.com
• Linda Carlson, Classified Manager
• Joe Entelisano, Advertising Manager
(315) 337-4000
joesano@rny.com
• Joseph Silkowski, Sports Editor
(315) 337-4000
release@rny.com
Frequency:
7 time(s) per week

DAILY SENTINEL STAR
50 CORPORATE ROW
GRENADA, MS 38901
662-226-4321
Fax: 662-226-8310
editor@grenadastar.com
http://www.grenadastar.com
• Chuck Hathcock, Sports Editor
(662) 226-4321
sports@grenadastar.com
Frequency:
5 time(s) per week

DAILY SITKA SENTINEL
112 BARRACKS STREET
SITKA, AK 99835
907-747-3219
Fax: 907-747-8898
news@sitkasentinel.com
www.sitkasentinel.com
• Susan McFadden, Advertising Manager
(907) 747-3219
susan@sitkasentinel.com
• Cyndi Cassedy, Classified Manager
• Garland Kennedy, Sports Editor
(907) 747-3219
garland@sitkasentinel.com
• Craig Giammona, Sports Editor
(907) 747-3219
craig@sitkasentinel.com
Frequency:
5 time(s) per week

Sports page- Daily newspaper

DAILY SOUTHERNER
504 WEST WILSON STREET
TARBORO, NC 27886-4239
252-823-3106
Fax: 252-823-4599
http://www.dailysoutherner.com
• Calvin Adkins, Sports Editor
(252) 823-3106
• Gene Hudson, Advertising Manager
(252) 823-3106
dailysoutherner@gmail.com
Frequency:
5 time(s) per week

DAILY SPARKS TRIBUNE
1002 C STREET
SPARKS, NV 89431
775-358-8061
800-669-1338
Fax: 775-359-3837
http://www.sparkstribune.net
• Dan Eckles, Sports Editor
(775) 358-8061
Frequency:
6 time(s) per week

DAILY STANDARD
123 EAST MARKET STREET
CELINA, OH 45822-1730
419-586-2371
Fax: 419-586-6271
sports@dailystandard.com
http://www.dailystandard.com
• Ryan Hines, Sports Editor
(419) 586-2371
sports@dailystandard.com
• John Lake, Advertising Manager
jlake@dailystandard.com
Frequency:
6 time(s) per week

DAILY STAR
725 SOUTH MORRISON BOULEVARD
HAMMOND, LA 70403-5401
985-254-7827
800-844-2333
Fax: 985-543-0006
http://www.hammondstar.com
• Fred Batiste, Sports Reporter
(985) 254-7822
sports2@hammondstar.com
• Al Guidry, Sports Reporter
• John Lenz, Sports Editor
(985) 254-7821
sports@hammondstar.com
Frequency:
6 time(s) per week

DAILY TIDINGS
1661 SISKIYOU BOULEVARD
ASHLAND, OR 97520
541-482-3456
Fax: 541-482-3688
http://www.dailytidings.com
• Joe Zavala, Sports Editor
(541) 482-3456
joe.zavala@dailytidings.com
Frequency:
6 time(s) per week

DAILY TIMES (NM)
201 NORTH ALLEN AVENUE
FARMINGTON, NM 87499
505-325-4545
800-395-6397
Fax: 505-564-4630
jelchert@daily-times.com
http://www.daily-times.com
• John Livingston, Sports Reporter
• Renee Lucero, Sports Reporter
• Yvonne Gomez, Advertising Director
ygomez@daily-times.com
Frequency:
7 time(s) per week

DAILY TIMES (OK)
105 SOUTH ADAIR
PRYOR, OK 74361-3625
918-825-3292
Fax: 918-825-1965
prynews@swbell.net
http://www.pryordailytimes.com
• Kerrll Lester, Sports Editor
Frequency:
5 time(s) per week

DAILY TIMES CHRONICLE
1 ARROW DRIVE
WOBURN, MA 01801-2039
781-933-3700
Fax: 781-932-3321

news@woburnonline.com
http://www.woburnonline.com
• Steve Algeri, Sports Editor
(781) 933-3700
woburnnews@rcn.com
• Thomas R. Kirk, Advertising Director
(781) 933-3700
Frequency:
5 time(s) per week

DAILY TIMES LEADER
221 EAST MAIN STREET
WEST POINT, MS 39773
662-494-1422
Fax: 662-494-1414
http://www.dailytimesleader.com
• Brian Davis, Sports Editor
Frequency:
5 time(s) per week

DAILY TRIBUNE (IA)
317 5TH STREET
AMES, IA 50010-6101
515-232-2160
800-234-8742
Fax: 515-232-2364
news@amestrib.com
http://www.amestrib.com
• Mark Sharpe, Advertising Manager
(515) 663-6968
msharpe@amestrib.com
• Bobby LaGesse, Sports Editor
(515) 663-6929
Frequency:
6 time(s) per week

DAILY TRIBUNE (WI)
220 1ST AVENUE SOUTH
WISCONSIN RAPIDS, WI 54495-4154
715-423-7200
800-362-8315
Fax: 715-421-1545
editor@wisconsinrapidstribune.com
http://www.wisconsinrapidstribune.com
• Mark Massoglia, Sports Editor
(715) 422-6736
mark.massoglia@cwnews.net
Frequency:
6 time(s) per week

DAILY TRIBUNE NEWS
P.O. BOX 70
CARTERSVILLE, GA 30120
770-382-4545
Fax: 770-382-2711
news@daily-tribune.com
http://www.daily-tribune.com
• David Royal, Sports Writer
(770) 382-4545
• Chike Nwakamma, Associate Sports Editor
(770) 382-4545
Frequency:
6 time(s) per week

DAILY WORLD
315 MICHIGAN STREET
ABERDEEN, WA 98520-6037
360-532-4000
Fax: 360-533-6039
press_releases@thedailyworld.com
http://www.thedailyworld.com
• Rob Burns, Sports Editor
(360) 537-3926
rburns@thedailyworld.com

Frequency:
7 time(s) per week

DALLAS MORNING NEWS
508 YOUNG STREET
DALLAS, TX 75202
214-977-8222
800-431-0010
Fax: 214-977-8319
feedback@dallasnews.com
http://www.dallasnews.com
• Kevin B. Blackistone, Sports Columnist
(214) 977-8780
• Terry Blount, Sports Reporter
(214) 977-7661
• Chip Brown, Sports Writer
(214) 977-8444
• Chuck Carlton, Sports Reporter
(214) 977-8444
ccarlton@dallasnews.com
• Rachel Cohen, Sports Reporter
(214) 977-8444
• Tim Cowlishaw, Sports Columnist
(214) 977-8446
wtcowlishaw@dallasnews.com
• Sylvia Curiel, Sports Group Leader
(214) 977-8075
• Brian Davis, Sports Reporter
(214) 977-8869
• Jason Dugger, Sports Copy Editor
(214) 977-7665
• Gerry Fraley, Sports Columnist
(214) 977-8377
gfraley@dallasnews.com
• Brandon George, Sports Reporter
(817) 695-3319
bgeorge@dallasnews.com
• Rick Gosselin, Sports Columnist
(214) 977-8033
• Evan Grant, Sports Reporter (Baseball)
(214) 977-8184
egrant@dallasnews.com
• Kate Hairopoulos, Sports Reporter
(214) 977-8032
khairopoulos@dallasnews.com
• Dennis Hall, Sports Assistant Editor
(214) 977-8972
dhall@dallasnews.com
• Cathy Harasta, Sports Reporter
(214) 977-8759
• Mike Heika, Sports Reporter
(214) 977-8034
mheika@dallasnews.com
• Gary Jacobson, Sports Editor
(214) 977-2791
• Randy Jennings, Sports Reporter
(817) 695-3323
• Mark Konradi, Sports Assistant Editor
(214) 977-8983
Mkonradi@dallasnews.com
• Tim MacMahon, Sports Reporter
(214) 977-7632
• Jeff Miller, Sports Reporter
(214) 977-8174
• Bill Nichols, Sports Reporter
(214) 977-8455
• Dan Noxon, Sports Copy Editor
(214) 977-8444
dnoxon@dallasnews.com
• Roxanna Pellin-Scott, (214) 977-8961
Sports Assistant Editor
• Dave Renbarger, Sports Assistant Editor
(214) 977-8961
drenbarger@dallasnews.com
• Ray Sasser, Sports Writer (Outdoors)
(214) 977-8380
rsasser@dallasnews.com
• Damon L. Sayles, Sports Reporter

(817) 695-3321
• Shawna Seed, Sports Deputy Editor
(214) 977-8385
• Eddie Sefko, Sports Writer (NBA)
(214) 997-8451
esefko@dallasnews.com
Frequency:
7 time(s) per week

DALLES DAILY CHRONICLE
315 FEDERAL STREET
THE DALLES, OR 97058
541-296-2141
Fax: 541-298-1365
http://www.thedalleschronicle.com
• Jodi Nofziger, Sports Editor
(541) 506-4618
• Skip Tschanz, Advertising Manager
(541) 506-4609
Frequency:
6 time(s) per week

DANVILLE NEWS
14 EAST MAHONING STREET
DANVILLE, PA 17821-1934
570-275-3235
Fax: 570-275-7624
http://www.thedanvillenews.com
• William Bowman, Sports Editor
(570) 275-3235
Frequency:
6 time(s) per week

DANVILLE REGISTER AND BEE
700 MONUMENT STREET
DANVILLE, VA 24541-1512
434-791-7971
Fax: 434-797-2299
news@registerbee.com
http://www.registerbee.com
• Damien Sordelett, Sports Editor
(434) 791-7998
dsordelett@registerbee.com
Frequency:
7 time(s) per week

DAVIS COUNTY CLIPPER
P.O. BOX 267
BOUNTIFUL, UT 84011
801-295-2251
Fax: 801-295-3044
http://www.clippertoday.com
• Russ Riggs, Sports Editor
(801) 295-2251
• Ben De Voe, Sports Editor
(801) 295-2251
Frequency:
2 time(s) per week

DAVIS ENTERPRISE
315 G STREET
DAVIS, CA 95616-4119
530-756-0800
Fax: 530-756-6707
newsroom@davisenterprise.net
http://www.davisenterprise.com
• C. Colton, Sports Writer
(530) 747-8059
• Nancy Hannell, Advertising Director
ads@davisenterprise.net
• Matt O'Donnell, Sports Editor
(530) 747-8049
Frequency:
6 time(s) per week

DAY
P.O. BOX 1231
NEW LONDON, CT 06320
860-442-2200
800-542-3354
Fax: 860-442-5599
http://www.theday.com
• Chuck Banning, Sports Editor
(860) 701-4441
c.banning@theday.com
• Dave Davis, Sports Wire Editor
(860) 701-4443
d.davis@theday.com
Frequency:
7 time(s) per week

DAYTON DAILY NEWS
1611 SOUTH MAIN STREET
DAYTON, OH 45402
937-225-2275
800-686-6397
Fax: 937-225-2489
localnews@coxohio.com
http://www.daytondailynews.com/
• Bucky Albers, Sports Writer
(937) 225-2412
balbers@daytondailynews.com
• Tom Archdeacon, Sports Columnist
(937) 225-2156
tarchdeacon@daytondailynews.com
• Greg Billing, Motorsports Reporter
(937) 225-2250
gbilling@daytondailynews.com
• Doug Harris, College Sports Reporter
(937) 324-0376
dharris@DaytonDailyNews.com
• Marc Katz, Sports Reporter
(937) 225-2157
mkatz@daytondailynews.com
• Brian Kollars, Sports Section Editor
(937) 225-2163
bkollars@daytondailynews.com
• Dave Long, Sports Reporter
(937) 225-2251
dlong@daytondailynews.com
• Chick Ludwig, Sports Reporter
(937) 225-2253
cludwig@daytondailynews.com
• Sean McClelland, Sports Writer
(937) 225-2408
smcclelland@DaytonDailyNews.com
• Hal McCoy, Sports Columnist
(937) 225-2250
hmccoy@daytondailynews.com
Frequency:
7 time(s) per week

DAYTONA BEACH NEWS-JOURNAL
P.O. BOX 2831
DAYTONA BEACH, FL 32117
386-252-1511 EXT 2281
Fax: 386-258-8465
http://www.news-journalonline.com
• Burke Noel, Sports Columnist
(386) 681-2416
• Jordan Kahn, Outdoors Writer
(386) 681-2798
• Godwin Kelly, Sports Editor (Motor Sports)
godwin.kelly@news-jrnl.com
• Ken Willis, Sports Columnist
(386) 681-2549
ken.willis@news-jrnl.com
Frequency:
7 time(s) per week

DE SOTO TIMES TODAY
2445 HWY 51
HERNANDO, MS 38632
662-429-6397
Fax: 662-429-5229
editor@desototimes.com
http://www.desototimes.com
• Ron Caldwell, Sports Editor
sports@desototimes.com
Frequency:
5 time(s) per week

DECATUR DAILY
201 1ST AVENUE, S.E.
DECATUR, AL 35609
256-353-4612
888-353-4612
Fax: 256-340-2366
news@decaturdaily.com
http://www.decaturdaily.com
• Mark Edwards, Sports Editor
(256) 340-3461
medwards@decaturdaily.com
• Scott Brown, Advertising Manager
(256) 340-2381
scott.brown@decaturdaily.com
Frequency:
7 time(s) per week

DECATUR DAILY DEMOCRAT
141 SOUTH 2ND STREET
DECATUR, IN 46733-1664
260-724-2121
Fax: 260-724-7981
comp@decaturdailydemocrat.com
http://www.decaturdailydemocrat.com
• Ron Platt, Advertising Manager
(260) 724-2121
advertising@decaturdailydemocrat.com
• Joe Spaulding, Sports Editor
(260) 724-2121
Frequency:
6 time(s) per week

DELAWARE COUNTY DAILY TIMES
500 MILDRED AVENUE
PRIMOS, PA 19018-2914
610-622-8800
Fax: 610-622-8887
newsroom@delcotimes.com
http://www.delcotimes.com
• Rob Parent, Sports Editor
(610) 622-8884
rparent@delcotimes.com
• Dennis Deitch, Sports Reporter
(610) 622-8800
sports@delcotimes.com
Frequency:
7 time(s) per week

DELAWARE GAZETTE
18 EAST WILLIAM STREET
DELAWARE, OH 43015-2332
740-363-1161
Fax: 740-363-6262
http://www.delgazette.com
• Ryan Oswald, Advertising Manager
(740) 363-1161
roswald@delgazette.com
• Ben Stroup, Sports Editor
bstroup@delgazette.com
Frequency:
6 time(s) per week

DELAWARE STATE NEWS
WEBBS LANE & NEW BURTON ROAD
DOVER, DE 19901
302-674-3600
800-282-8586
Fax: 302-741-8252
newsroom@newszap.com
http://www.newszap.com
• Diane Cahall, Advertising Manager
• Andy Walter, Sports Editor
(302) 674-3600
Frequency:
7 time(s) per week

DELTA DEMOCRAT-TIMES
988 NORTH BROADWAY
GREENVILLE, MS 38701-2349
662-335-1155
800-844-1618
Fax: 662-335-2860
http://www.ddtonline.com
• Kenneth Mister, Sports Editor
(662) 378-0722
Frequency:
6 time(s) per week

DEMOCRAT AND CHRONICLE
55 EXCHANGE BOULEVARD
ROCHESTER, NY 14614-2001
585-232-7100
800-767-7539
Fax: 585-258-2237
editor@DemocratandChronicle.com
http://www.democratandchronicle.com/
• Thomas Batzold, Sports Editor
(585) 258-2262
sports@democratandchronicle.com
• Steve Bradley, Sports Assistant Editor
(585) 258-2569
sbradley@democratandchronicle.com
• James Castor, Assistant Sports Editor
(585) 258-2352
• James Johnson, Sports Reporter
(585) 258-2754
• James Mandelaro, Sports Writer
(585) 258-2761
jmand@democratandchronicle.com
• Robert Matthews, Sports Columnist
(585) 258-2325
matthews@democratandchronicle.com
• Kevin Oklobzija, Sports Writer
(585) 258-2277
kevino@democratandchronicle.com
• Scott Pitoniak, Sports Writer
(585) 258-2455
spitoniak@democratandchronicle.com
• Leo Roth, Sports Columnist
(585) 258-2764
lroth@democratandchronicle.com
Frequency:
7 time(s) per week

DENTON RECORD-CHRONICLE
P.O. BOX 369
DENTON, TX 76202
940-387-3811
800-275-1722
Fax: 940-566-6888
drc@dentonrc.com
http://www.dentonrc.com
• Todd Jorgenson, Sports Editor
(940) 566-6871
• Adam Boedeker, Sports Reporter
(940) 566-6872
Frequency:
7 time(s) per week

DENVER POST
101 WEST COLFAX AVENUE
DENVER, CO 80202
303-954-1201
800-336-7678
Fax: 303-954-1369
sports@denverpost.com
http://www.denverpost.com
• Jim Armstrong, Sports Writer
(303) 954-1294
• Jason Blevins, Sports Reporter
(303) 820-1374
jblevins@denverpost.com
• Patrick Saunders, Online Sports Editor
(303) 954-1720
psaunders@denverpost.com
• Bill Briggs, Sports Writer
(303) 820-1720
• Mike Chambers, Sports Writer
(303) 954-1357
mchambers@denverpost.com
• Anthony Cotton, Sports Writer
(303) 820-1292
• Kevin Dale, Assistant Managing Editor
(303) 954-1294
smonserud@denverpost.com
• Adrian Dater, Sports Writer
(303) 954-1201
• Neil Devlin, Sports Editor (High School)
(303) 820-1714
• Nick Groke, Sports Writer
(303) 954-1015
ngroke@denverpost.com
• Thomas George, Sports Columnist
(303) 820-1994
• Mark Kiszla, Sports Writer
(303) 954-1053
mkiszla@denverpost.com
• Nancy Lofholm, Skiing Reporter
(970) 256-1957
• John Meyer, Sports Writer
(303) 954-1010
jmeyer@denverpost.com
• Charlie Meyers, Outdoors Editor
(303) 954-1294
• Woody Paige, Sports Columnist
(303) 820-1398
• Joseph Sanchez, Sports Reporter
(303) 820-1294
• Patrick Saunders, Sports Writer
(303) 954-1201
psaunders@denverpost.com
• Adam Thompson, Sports Writer
(303) 820-5447
Frequency:
7 time(s) per week

DERRICK
1510 WEST 1ST STREET
OIL CITY, PA 16301-3211
814-676-7444
800-352-1002
Fax: 814-677-8351
newsroom@usachoice.net
http://www.thederrick.com
• Ed Brannon, Sports Editor
(814) 676-7444
sports.thederrick@gmail.com
• Ned Cowart, Advertising Director
(814) 676-7444
info@thederrick.com
• Ed Finck, Sports Writer
(814) 676-7056
• Carla Sheatz, Classified Manager
(814) 676-7444
info@thederrick.com
Frequency:
6 time(s) per week

DES MOINES NEWS AND HIGHLINE TIMES
133 SW 153RD STREET
BURIEN, WA 98166-2311
206-444-4873
Fax: 206-444-4877
hteditor@robinsonnews.com
http://www.robinsonnews.com
• Tim Clinton, Sports Editor
(253) 838-7622
sports@robinsonnews.com
Frequency:
1 time(s) per week

DES MOINES REGISTER
P.O. BOX 957
DES MOINES, IA 50306
515-284-8000
Fax: 515-286-2504
metroiowa@dmreg.com
http://www.dmregister.com/
• Nancy Clark, Sports Reporter
(515) 286-2517
nclark@dmreg.com
• Rob Gray, Sports Writer (High School)
(515) 284-8194
rgray@dmreg.com
• Marc Hansen, Media Columnist
(515) 284-8534
mhansen@dmreg.com
• Dan Johnson, Sports Reporter
(515) 284-8375
dansjohn@dmreg.com
• Gary Lake, Sports Assistant Editor
(515) 284-8573
• Andrew Logue, High School Sports Writer
(515) 284-8368
alogue@dmreg.com
• Bryce Miller, Executive Sports Editor
(515) 284-8130
brmiller@dmreg.com
• John Naughton, High School/Prep Sports Chief
(515) 284-8000
jnaughto@dmreg.com
• Randy Peterson, Sports Reporter
(515) 284-8000
rapeters@dmreg.com
• Brad Robertson, Advertising Vice President
(515) 284-8384
brobertson@dmreg.com
• Dave Stockdale, Sports Copy Editor
(515) 284-8284
dstockdale@dmreg.com
• Tom Witosky, Sports Writer (Football)
(515) 284-8522
twitosky@dmreg.com
Frequency:
7 time(s) per week

DESERET MORNING NEWS
55 NORTH 300 WEST
SALT LAKE CITY, UT 84101
801-236-6000
800-662-9076
Fax: 801-237-2121
http://www.deseretnews.com
• Tim Buckley, Sports Writer
(801) 237-2161
• Jeff Call, Sports Writer
(801) 437-7605
jeffc@desnews.com
• Kent Condon, Sports Editor
(801) 236-6075
kcondon@desnews.com
• Rich Evans, Sports Writer
(801) 236-6075

• Dirk Facer, Sports Writer
(801) 236-6073
dirk@desnews.com
• Linda A. Hamilton, Sports Writer
(801) 237-2161
• Jay Hinton, Sports Writer
(801) 237-2114
jhinton@desnews.com
• Loren D. Jorgensen, Sports Writer
(801) 236-6056
lojo@desnews.com
• Jon Ringwood, Sports Writer
(801) 236-6035
• Brad Rock, Sports Columnist
(801) 333-7454
rock@desnews.com
• David Schneider, Sports Editor
(801) 237-2158
 daves@desnews.com
• Mike Sorensen, Sports Writer
(801) 236-6055
sor@desnews.com
• Scott Taylor, Sports Editor
(801) 437-7601
taylor@desnews.com
Frequency:
7 time(s) per week

DESERT DISPATCH
130 COOLWATER LANE
BARSTOW, CA 92311-3222
760-256-2257
Fax: 760-256-0685
http://www.desertdispatch.com
• Bea Lint, Advertising Director
(760) 256-4140
• David Heldreth, Sports Editor
(760) 256-4124
Frequency:
7 time(s) per week

DESERT SUN
PO BOX 2734
PALM SPRINGS, CA 92263
760-322-8889
800-834-6052
Fax: 760-778-4659
http://www.mydesert.com
• Larry Bohannan, Sports Reporter
larry.bohannan@thedesertsun.com
• Jeff Hendrickson, Sports Editor
(760) 778-4632
jeff.hendrickson@thedesertsun.com
• Michelle Rico, Classified Manager
(760) 778-4517
michelle.rico@thedesertsun.com
• Matt Solinsky, Sports Editor
(760) 778-4629
matt.solinsky@thedesertsun.com
• Leighton Ginn, Sports Reporter
(760) 778-4631
Leighton.ginn@thedesertsun.com
Frequency:
7 time(s) per week

DETROIT FREE PRESS
600 WEST FORT STREET
DETROIT, MI 48226-3138
313-222-6400
Fax: 313-222-5981
letters@freepress.com
http://www.freep.com
• Mitch Albom, Sports Columnist
(313) 223-4581
malbom@freepress.com
• Joann Barnas-Taylor, Sports Reporter
(313) 222-2037

barnas@freepress.com
• Paul Barrett, Sports Editor
• Brad Betker, Sports Copy Editor
betker@freepress.com
• Mike Brudenell, Sports Staff Writer
(313) 222-2115
mbrudenell@freepress.com
• Bill Collison, Sports Copy Editor
bcollison@freepress.com
• Nicholas J. Cotsonika, Sports Reporter
• Bernie Czarniecki, Sports Editor
czarni@freepress.com
• David Darby, Sports Editor
darby@freepress.com
• Owen Davis, Sports Deputy Managing
Editor
davis@freepress.com
• Jim Dwight, Sports Editor
 dwight@freepress.com
• Bob Ellis, Sports Copy Editor
ellis@freepress.com
• Perry A. Farrell, Sports Reporter
(313) 222-2555
farrell@freepress.com
• Matt Fiorito, Sports Writer (Bowling)
(313) 222-6721
fiorit@freepress.com
• Maureen Ground, Sports Copy Editor
ground@freepress.com
• Gene Guidi, Sports Reporter
(313) 222-6665
guidi@freepress.com
• Krista Ann Latham, Sports Reporter
• John Lowe, Sports Reporter
(313) 223-4053
• Tim Marcinkoski, Sports Copy Editor
(313) 223-4427
marcinkoski@freepress.com
• Mick McCabe, Sports Reporter (Prep)
(313) 223-4744
mccabe@freepress.com
• Carlos Monarrez, Sports Copy Editor
(313) 222-6697
monarrez@freepress.com
• Carlos Monarrez, Sports Writer
(313) 222-6697
monarrez@freepress.com
• Gene Myers, Sports Editor
(313) 222-6400
gmyers@freepress.com
• Gene Myers, Sports Editor
(313) 222-6736
myers@freepress.com
• Tom Panzenhagen, (313) 222-6730
Sports Assistant Editor
• Dave Robinson, Sports Deputy Managing
Editor
(313) 222-6736
• Michael Rosenberg, Sports Columnist
(313) 222-6052
mrosenberg@freepress.com
• Steve Schrader, Sports Assistant Editor
• Drew Sharp, Sports Columnist
(313) 223-4055
dsharp@freepress.com
• Shannon Shelton, Sports Reporter
(313) 222-6400
slshelton@freepress.com
Frequency:
7 time(s) per week

DETROIT NEWS
615 WEST LAFAYETTE BOULEVARD
DETROIT, MI 48226-3124
313-222-2300
800-678-4115
Fax: 313-222-2451

letters@detnews.com
http://www.detnews.com
• Robert Allstetter, Sports Deputy Editor
(313) 222-1486
rallstetter@detnews.com
• Rod Beard, Sports Producer
rbeard@detnews.com
• Dave Dye, Sports Reporter
(313) 222-2260
ddye@detnews.com
• Ron French, Sports Reporter
rfrench@detnews.com
• Tom Gage, Sports Reporter
(313) 222-1495
tgage@detnews.com
• Joanne Gerstner, Sports Reporter
(313) 223-4644
jgerstner@detnews.com
• Dave Goricki, Sports Reporter
dgoricki@detnews.com
• Brian Handley, Sports Assistant Editor
• Lynn Henning, Sports Reporter
lhenning@detnews.com
• Ted Kulfan, Sports Reporter
(313) 222-2260
tkulfan@detnews.com
• Phil Laciura, Sports Editor
 placiura@detnews.com
• Ruben Luna, Sports Editor
(313) 222-4642
rluna@detnews.com
• Tom Markowski, Sports Reporter
(313) 222-4633
tmarkowski@detnews.com
• Chris McCosky, Sports Reporter
(313) 222-2300
cmccosky@detnews.com
• William McMillan, Sports Ass't Managing
Editor
(313) 222-4643
wmcmillan@detnews.com
• Tenisha Mercer, Advertising Reporter
tmercer@detnews.com
• Michael O'Hara, Sports Writer (Pro
Football)
(313) 222-1488
mohara@detnews.com
• Rob Parker, Sports Columnist
(313) 222-2260
rparker@detnews.com
• James Russ, Sports Assistant Editor
jruss@detnews.com
• Jim Spadafore, Sports Reporter
(313) 222-4638
jspadafore@detnews.com
Frequency:
7 time(s) per week

DEVILS LAKE DAILY JOURNAL
516 4TH STREET
DEVILS LAKE, ND 58301
701-662-2127
Fax: 701-662-3115
news@devilslakejournal.com
http://www.devilslakejournal.com
• Ray Maloney, Sports Editor
(701) 662-2127
• Paula Ramsey, Advertising Manager
(701) 662-2127
advertising@devilslakejournal.com
Frequency:
5 time(s) per week

DIARIO LAS AMERICAS
P.O. BOX 593177
MIAMI, FL 33142-5149
305-633-3341
Fax: 305-635-7668

cartas@diariolasamericas.com
http://www.diariolasamericas.com
• Marino Martinez, Sports Editor
• Jose A. Yuste, Classified Manager
(305) 633-3341
Frequency:
6 time(s) per week

DICKINSON PRESS
1815 1ST STREET WEST
DICKINSON, ND 58602
701-225-8111
Fax: 701-225-6653
newsroom@thedickinsonpress.com
http://www.thedickinsonpress.com/
• Dustin Monke, Sports Editor
• Justin Nutter, Sports Writer
Frequency:
6 time(s) per week

DISPATCH (CA)
6400 MONTEREY ROAD
GILROY, CA 95020-6628
408-842-6400
Fax: 408-842-7105
editor@gilroydispatch.com
http://www.gilroydispatch.com
• Anna Patejdl, Sports Reporter
(408) 842-6400
apatejdl@gilroydispatch.com
• Josh Weaver, Sports Editor
(408) 842-1694
sports@gilroydispatch.com
Frequency:
5 time(s) per week

DISPATCH (IL)
1720 5TH AVE
MOLINE, IL 61265
309-764-4344
Fax: 309-797-0321
www.qconline.com
• Bill Allee, Sports Editor
• Tom Johnston, Sports Reporter
• Steve Tappa, Sports Reporter

DODGE CITY DAILY GLOBE
705 2ND AVENUE
DODGE CITY, KS 67801
620-225-4151
800-279-8795
Fax: 620-225-4154
dcnews@dodgeglobe.com
http://dodgeglobe.com
• Nicole Dirks, Advertising Director
(620) 408-9919
• Ryan Buchan, Sports Editor
(620) 408-9913
Frequency:
6 time(s) per week

DOMINION-POST
1251 EARL CORE ROAD
MORGANTOWN, WV 26505-5881
304-292-6301
800-654-4676
Fax: 304-291-2326
http://www.dominionpost.com
• Drew Rubenstein, Sports Editor
(304) 291-9431
drubenstein@dominionpost.com
Frequency:
7 time(s) per week

DOTHAN EAGLE
227 NORTH OATES STREET
DOTHAN, AL 36303-4555
334-792-3141
Fax: 334-712-7992
http://www.dothaneagle.com
• Jon Johnson, Sports Editor
(334) 712-7965
jjohnson@dothaneagle.com
Frequency:
7 time(s) per week

DOUGLAS COUNTY SENTINEL
8501 BOWDEN STREET
DOUGLASVILLE, GA 30134
770-942-6571
Fax: 770-949-7556
news@douglascountysentinel.com
http://www.douglascountysentinel.com
• Bill Evans, Sports Reporter
(770) 942-6571
evans@douglascountysentinel.com
Frequency:
6 time(s) per week

DOWAGIAC DAILY NEWS
205 SPAULDING STREET
DOWAGIAC, MI 49047-1451
269-782-2101
888-725-0108
Fax: 269-782-5290
http://www.leaderpub.com
• Diana Kingsley, Advertising Director
• Scott Novak, Sports Editor
scott.novak@leaderpub.com
• Hal Shue, Classified Manager
(269) 782-2101
Frequency:
5 time(s) per week

DU QUOIN EVENING CALL
9 NORTH DIVISION STREET
DU QUOIN, IL 62832
618-542-2133
800-455-2133
Fax: 618-542-2726
http://www.duquoin.com
• Terri Fisher, Advertising Manager
(618) 542-2133
admanager@frontier.com
• Doug Daniels, Sports Editor
(618) 542-2133
dqsports@frontier.com
• John Croessman, Publisher
(618) 542-2133
jcroessman@frontier.com
Frequency:
6 time(s) per week

DULUTH NEWS-TRIBUNE
424 WEST 1ST STREET
DULUTH, MN 55802-1516
218-723-5303
800-456-8181
Fax: 218-720-4120
sports@duluthnews.com
http://www.duluthnewstribune.com
• Rick Weegman, Sports Reporter
(218) 720-4138
rweegman@duluthnews.com
• Rick Lubbers, Sports Editor
(218) 723-5307
rlubbers@duluthnews.com
• Kevin Pates, Sports Reporter
• John Nowacki, Sports Reporter
jnowacki@duluthnews.com

Frequency:
7 time(s) per week

DUNCAN BANNER
1001 ELM STREET
DUNCAN, OK 73533-4746
580-255-5354
Fax: 580-255-8889
news@duncanbanner.com
http://www.duncanbanner.com
• Paula Blair, Classified Manager
(580) 255-5354
paula.blair@duncanbanner.com
• Ron Booth, Sports Editor
• Dana Boyles, Advertising Manager
(580) 255-5354
Frequency:
6 time(s) per week

DUNDALK EAGLE
4 NORTH CENTER PLACE
DUNDALK, MD 21222-4300
410-288-6060
Fax: 410-288-6963
info@dundalkeagle.com
http://www.dundalkeagle.com
• William Gates, Sports Editor
sports@dundalkeagle.com
Frequency:
1 time(s) per week

DURANGO HERALD
1275 MAIN AVENUE
DURANGO, CO 81301
970-247-3504
800-530-8318
Fax: 970-259-5011
herald@durangoherald.com
http://www.durangoherald.com
• Dominick McCullough, Advertising
Manager
(970) 375-4519
• Aaron Unterreiner, Sports Editor
(970) 375-4557
Frequency:
7 time(s) per week

DURANT DAILY DEMOCRAT
200 WEST BEECH STREET
DURANT, OK 74701
580-924-4388
800-729-4388
Fax: 580-924-0962
http://www.durantdemocrat.com
• Karl Oakley, Advertising Manager
koakley@durantdemocrat.com
• Beau Simmons, Sports Editor
ddsports@durantdemocrat.com
Frequency:
6 time(s) per week

EAGLE HERALD
1809 DUNLAP AVENUE
MARINETTE, WI 54143-1706
715-735-6611
800-777-0345
Fax: 715-735-0229
news@eagleherald.com
http://www.eagleherald.com
• Jim Hofer, Advertising Manager
(715) 735-6611
• Jody Korch, Sports Editor
(715) 735-6611
jkorch@eagleherald.com
• Tom Kaeser, Assistant Sports Editor
(715) 735-6611

Frequency:
7 time(s) per week

EAGLE-TIMES
401 RIVER ROAD
CLAREMONT, NH 03743
603-543-3100
Fax: 603-542-9705
news@eagletimes.com
http://www.eagletimes.com/
• Jeff Miller, Sports Editor
(603) 543-3100
• Clyde Pinson, Advertising Director
(603) 543-3100
dfraser@tsvmedia.net
Frequency:
6 time(s) per week

EAGLE-TRIBUNE
100 TURNPIKE STREET
NORTH ANDOVER, MA 01845
978-946-2000
Fax: 978-685-1588
news@eagletribune.com
http://www.eagletribune.com
• Bill Burt, Sports Executive Editor
(978) 946-2227
bburt@eagletribune.com
• Dave Dyer, Sports Writer
ddyer@eagletribune.com
• Hector Longo, Sports Reporter
• Mike Muldoon, Sports Writer
mmuldoon@eagletribune.com
• Joe Murphy, Sports Writer
Frequency:
7 time(s) per week

EAST OREGONIAN
211 SOUTHEAST BYERS STREET
PENDLETON, OR 97801
541-276-2211
800-522-0255
Fax: 541-278-2688
http://www.eastoregonian.info
• Bill Marcum, Advertising Manager
(541) 278-2669
• Matt Entrup, Sports Editor
(541) 966-0838
mentrup@eastoregonian.com
Frequency:
7 time(s) per week

EAST VALLEY TRIBUNE
120 WEST FIRST AVENUE
MESA, AZ 85210-1312
480-898-6500
800-541-8016
Fax: 480-898-6362
newstips@aztrib.com
http://www.eastvalleytribune.com
• Scott Bordow, Sports Columnist
(480) 898-6598
• Bob Romantic, Sports Editor
(480) 898-6538
bromantic@aztrib.com
• Matt Simpson, Sports Reporter
(480) 898-6497
msimpson@aztrib.com
• Dan Zeiger, Sports Writer
(480) 898-6525
dzeiger@aztrib.com
Frequency:
7 time(s) per week

LOUDOUN TIMES-MIRROR
9 EAST MARKET STREET
LEESBURG, VA 20176
703-771-0036
Fax: 703-771-0036
http://www.loudountimes.com
• Carl Lulat, Sports Editor
(703) 209-5148
clukat@timespapers.com
Frequency:
1 time(s) per week

EASTSIDER
13650 11 MILE ROAD
WARREN, MI 48089-1422
586-756-8800
Fax: 586-498-9627
http://www.candgnews.com
• Susan Shanley, Sports Editor
(586) 498-1048
sshanley@candgnews.com

EDWARDSVILLE INTELLIGENCER
117 NORTH 2ND STREET
EDWARDSVILLE, IL 62025
618-656-4700
Fax: 618-656-7618
http://www.theintelligencer.com
• Christopher Templeton, Sports Reporter
(618) 656-4700
• Bill Yarbrough, Sports Editor
Frequency:
6 time(s) per week

EFFINGHAM DAILY NEWS
201 NORTH BANKER STREET
EFFINGHAM, IL 62401
217-347-7151
Fax: 217-342-9315
http://www.effinghamdailynews.com
• Seth Whitehead, Sports Editor
(217) 347-7151
• Scott Richey, Sports Reporter
(217) 347-7151
Frequency:
7 time(s) per week, Monday-Sunday

EL BOHEMIO NEWS
4178 MISSION STREET
SAN FRANCISCO, CA 94112
415-469-9579
Fax: 415-469-9481
bohemio@ix.netcom.com
http://www.bohemionews.com
• Santiago Hernandez, News Director
(415) 469-9579
bohemio@ix.netcom.com
Frequency:
1 time(s) per week

EL DIARIO LA PRENSA
345 HUDSON STREET 13TH FLOOR
NEW YORK, NY 10014
212-807-4600
Fax: 212-807-4705
editorial@eldiariony.com
http://www.eldiariony.com
• Mario Concha, Sports Editor
(212) 807-4779
mconcha@eldiariolaprensa.com
• Ricardo Vasconcellos, Sports Editor
(212) 807-4789
Frequency:
7 time(s) per week

EL DORADO NEWS-TIMES
P.O. BOX 912
EL DORADO, AR 71730-6124
870-862-6611
Fax: 870-862-5226
editorial@eldoradonews.com
http://epaper.wehco.com/Daily/Skins/ElDorado/index.asp
• Tony Burns, Sports Editor
(870) 862-6611
sports@eldoradonews.com
Frequency:
7 time(s) per week

EL DORADO TIMES
114 NORTH VINE
EL DORADO, KS 67042-2028
316-321-1120
Fax: 316-321-7722
http://www.eldoradotimes.com
• Diane Lacy-Trostle, Advertising Manager
• John Curtis, Sports Editor
Frequency:
6 time(s) per week

EL HISPANO NEWS
2102 EMPIRE CENTRAL
DALLAS, TX 75235-4302
214-357-2186
Fax: 214-357-2195
http://www.elhispanonews.com
• Gustavo Burgadt, Sports Editor
(214) 357-2186
Frequency:
1 time(s) per week

EL INFORMADOR HISPANO
2235 NORTH MAIN STREET
FORT WORTH, TX 76106
817-626-8624
888-269-8353
Fax: 817-626-1855
http://www.elinformadorhispano.com
• Jose Tiscareno, Sports Editor
Frequency:
1 time(s) per week

EL MUNDO
750 N. EASTERN
LAS VEGAS, NV 89101
702-649-8553
Fax: 702-649-7429
editorial@elmundo.net
http://www.elmundo.net
• Francisco Alexander, Sports Editor
(702) 649-8553
• Antonio Carranza, Sports Writer
(702) 649-8553
editorial@elmundo.net
Frequency:
1 time(s) per week

EL NUEVO HERALD
ONE HERALD PLAZA
MIAMI, FL 33132-1609
305-376-3535
Fax: 305-376-2378
perspectiva@elnuevoherald.com
http://www.elherald.com
• Jorge Ebro, Deportero de Deportes
(305) 376-3535
jebro@elnuevoherald.com
• Manolo Hernandez, Sports Editor
(305) 376-2055
• Luis Sanchez, Sports Reporter (Soccer)
(305) 376-3535

perspectiva@elnuevoherald.com
• Luis Sanchez, Sports Editor
Frequency:
7 time(s) per week

EL NUEVO HERALDO BROWNSVILLE
1135 EAST VAN BUREN
BROWNSVILLE, TX 78520
956-542-4301
http://www.elnuevoheraldo.com
• Juan Sanchez, Sports Editor
(956) 982-6623
Frequency:
52 time(s) per week

EL NUEVO PATRIA
P.O. BOX 2
MIAMI, FL 33014
305-530-8787
Fax: 305-376-2378
patrianews@aol.com
http://www.miami.com/mld/elnuevo
• Sarvelio Delvalle, Sports Editor
(305) 530-8787
patrianews@aol.com
• Sarvelio DelValle, Sports Editor
(305) 530-8787
patrianews@aol.com
Frequency:
1 time(s) per week

EL PASO TIMES
300 NORTH CAMPBELL STREET
EL PASO, TX 79901-1402
915-546-6300
Fax: 915-546-6415
elpasonews@elpasotimes.com
http://www.elpasotimes.com
• Margaret Gallardo, Sports Editor
(915) 546-6166
mgallardo@elpasotimes.com
• Mike Price, Advertising Director
(915) 546-6250
mprice@elpasotimes.com
• Robert Rios, Advertising Manager
(915) 546-6231
rrios@elpasotimes.com
Frequency:
7 time(s) per week

EL TIEMPO DE NUEVA YORK
37 37 88TH STREET SUITE A 8
JACKSON HEIGHTS, NY 11372
718-507-0832
Fax: 718-507-2105
http://www.tiempo.com/nueva-york.htm
• Armando Dalebera, Sports Editor
Frequency:
1 time(s) per week

EL TIEMPO LATINO
1150 15TH STREET NW
WASHINGTON, DC 22201-2909
202-334-9100
Fax: 202-496-3599
ramon@eltiempolatino.com
http://www.eltiempolatino.com/
• Miguel Guilarte, Sports Editor
(202) 334-9142
miguel@eltiempolatino.com
Frequency:
1 time(s) per week

ELIZABETHTON STAR
P.O. BOX 1960
ELIZABETHTON, TN 37643

423-928-4151
Fax: 423-542-2004
http://www.starhq.com
• Ivan Sanders, Sports Editor
(423) 542-4141
• Tim Chambers, Sports Writer
(423) 297-9061
Frequency:
6 time(s) per week

ELKHART TRUTH
COMMUNICANA BLDG
PO BOX 487
ELKHART, IN 46515-0487
574-294-1661
Fax: 574-294-3895
• Mary Alexander, Advertising Director
• Ben Ford, Sports Writer
• Bill Beck, Sports Editor
bbeck@etruth.com

ELKO DAILY FREE PRESS
3720 IDAHO STREET
ELKO, NV 89801
775-738-3118
Fax: 775-778-3131
editor@elkodaily.com
http://www.elkodaily.com/
• Mike Christianson, Sports Editor
(775) 738-3118
sports@elkodaily.com
• Ashley Wilson, Advertising Manager
(775) 748-2706
Frequency:
6 time(s) per week

ELLWOOD CITY LEDGER
P.O. BOX 471
ELLWOOD CITY, PA 16117-5908
724-568-7529
Fax: 724-758-2410
eclnews@ellwoodcityledger.com
http://www.ellwoodcityledger.com
• Randy Senior, Sports Editor
(724) 758-7529
• Don Vaccari, Advertising Manager
Frequency:
6 time(s) per week

EMPORIA GAZETTE
517 MERCHANT STREET
EMPORIA, KS 66801-7206
620-342-4800
Fax: 620-342-8108
newsroom@emporiagazette.com
http://www.emporiagazette.com
• Stuart Goldman, Sports Editor
(620) 342-4805
sports@emporiagazette.com
• Carolyn Hatting, Advertising Manager
(620) 342-4800
Frequency:
6 time(s) per week

ENID NEWS AND EAGLE
227 WEST BROADWAY
ENID, OK 73701-4017
580-233-6600
800-299-6397
Fax: 580-548-8147
http://www.enidnews.com
• Mark Rountree, Sports Editor
(580) 548-8153
• Bruce Campbell, Sports Columnist
(580) 548-8144
bcampbell@enidnews.com

Frequency:
7 time(s) per week

ENNIS DAILY NEWS
213 NORTH DALLAS STREET
ENNIS, TX 75119-4011
972-875-3801
Fax: 972-875-9747
http://www.ennisdailynews.com/
• Tye Chandler, Sports Editor
(972) 875-3801
sports@ennisdailynews.com
Frequency:
6 time(s) per week

ENQUIRER-JOURNAL
500 WEST JEFFERSON STREET
MONROE, NC 28111
704-289-1541
Fax: 704-289-2929
news@theej.com
http://www.enquirerjournal.com
• Jerry Snow, Sports Editor
(704) 261-2225
jsnow@theej.com
• Justin Murdock, Sports Writer
(704) 261-2224
Frequency:
6 time(s) per week

ENTERPRISE
1324 BELMONT STREET
SUITE 10
BROCKTON, MA 02301
508-586-6200
Fax: 508-586-6506
newsroom@enterprisenews.com
http://enterprisenews.com
• Bill Abramson, Sports Editor
(508) 427-4049
newsroom@enterprisenews.com
• Win Bates, Sports Writer
(508) 427-4052
• Mark Ducharme, Sports Reporter
(508) 427-4051
• Ron Dziergowski, Sports Writer
(508) 427-4051
• Jim Fenton, Sports Writer
(508) 427-4048
jfenton@enterprisenews.com
• Michael Harwood, Advertising Director
(508) 427-4009
• Mark Mahoney, Advertising Services
Manager
(508) 427-4089
mmahoney@enterprisenews.com
• Linda Siemers, Classified Manager
(508) 427-4070
Frequency:
7 time(s) per week

ENTERPRISE LEDGER
106 NORTH EDWARDS STREET
ENTERPRISE, AL 36330-2524
334-347-9533
Fax: 334-347-0825
http://www.eprisenow.com/
• Brandon Patterson, Sports Editor
(334) 347-9533
spatterson@eprisenow.com
Frequency:
5 time(s) per week

ENTERPRISE-JOURNAL
112 OLIVER EMMERICH DRIVE
MCCOMB, MS 39648-6330

media

601-684-2421
800-748-9845
Fax: 601-684-0836
news@enterprise-journal.com
http://www.enterprise-journal.com
• Lauren Devereaux, Advertising Manager
advertising@enterprise-journal.com
• Dale Constance, Sports Editor
(601) 684-2421
sports@enterprise-journal.com
Frequency:
6 time(s) per week

ESTHERVILLE DAILY NEWS
10 NORTH 7TH STREET
ESTHERVILLE, IA 51334
712-362-2622
Fax: 712-362-2624
http://esthervilledailynews.com/
• David Swartz, Sports Editor
(712) 362-2622
dswartz@esthervilledailynews.com
Frequency:
6 time(s) per week

EVANSVILLE COURIER & PRESS
300 EAST WALNUT STREET
EVANSVILLE, IN 47713-1945
812-424-7711
800-288-3200
Fax: 812-422-8196
courier@courierpress.com
http://www.courierpress.com
• Tim Etheridge, Sports Editor
(812) 464-7416
• Steve Ford, Sports Reporter
(812) 464-7511
Frequency:
7 time(s) per week

EVENING NEWS
109 ARLINGTON STREET
SAULT SAINTE MARIE, MI 49783-1901
906-632-2235
Fax: 906-632-1222
http://www.sooeveningnews.com
• Cathy Kaiser, Classified Manager
enclass@sooeveningnews.com
• Rob Roos, Sports Editor
(906) 632-2235
sports@sooeveningnews.com
Frequency:
6 time(s) per week

EVENING SUN (NY)
29 LACKAWANNA AVENUE
NORWICH, NY 13815-1404
607-334-3276
800-836-6780
Fax: 607-334-8273
news@evesun.com
http://www.evesun.com
• Russell Foote, Advertising Manager
• Patrick Newell, Sports Editor
pnewell@evesun.com
Frequency:
6 time(s) per week

EVENING SUN (PA)
135 BALTIMORE STREET
HANOVER, PA 17331-3111
717-637-3736
800-877-3786
Fax: 717-637-7730
news@eveningsun.com
http://www.eveningsun.com

• Chuck Curley, Sports Editor
(717) 637-3736
ccurley@eveningsun.com
• Travis Johnson, Sports Reporter
(717) 637-3736
Frequency:
7 time(s) per week

EVENING TELEGRAM
111 GREEN STREET
HERKIMER, NY 13350
315-866-2220
Fax: 315-866-5913
trends@herkimertelegram.com
http://www.herkimertelegram.com
• Gary Urich, Sports Editor
sports@herkimertelegram.com
Frequency:
6 time(s) per week

EVENING TIMES (NY)
347 SOUTH 2ND STREET
LITTLE FALLS, NY 13365-1411
315-823-3680
Fax: 315-823-4086
news@littlefallstimes.com
http://www.littlefallstimes.com
• Jon Rathbun, Sports Editor
(315) 823-3682
• Peggy Vespi, Advertising Manager
(315) 823-3680
• Beth Brewer, Publisher
(315) 866-2222
Frequency:
6 time(s) per week

EVENING TIMES (PA)
201 NORTH LEHIGH AVENUE
SAYRE, PA 18840-2220
570-888-9643
800-459-6397
Fax: 570-888-6463
news@morning-times.com
http://www.morningtimes.com
• Vickee Mike, Advertising Manager
• Dave Post, Sports Editor
dpost@morning-times.com
Frequency:
6 time(s) per week

EXAMINER
410 S. LIBERTY
INDEPENDENCE, MO 64050
816-254-8600
Fax: 816-254-0211
http://examiner.net
• Bill Althaus, Sports Writer
(816) 350-6333
bill.althaus@examiner.net
• Charlie Slenker, Assistant Sports Editor

EXAMINER-ENTERPRISE
4125 NOWATA ROAD
BARTLESVILLE, OK 74006-5120
918-335-8200
Fax: 918-335-3111
• Tom Bradley, Advertising Director
• Mike Tupa, Sports Editor
(918) 335-8239
mtupa@examiner-enterprise.com
Frequency:
6 time(s) per week

EXCELSIOR
523 N GRAND AVE
SANTA ANA, CA 92701

714-796-4300
Fax: 714-796-4319
http://www.ocexcelsior.com
• Francisco Valverde, Sports Editor
(714) 796-4300
Frequency:
1 time(s) per week

EXPONENT TELEGRAM
324 HEWES AVENUE
CLARKSBURG, WV 26302
304-626-1400
Fax: 304-624-4188
http://www.cpubco.com
• Danny Carpenter, Sports Editor
(304) 626-1444
sports@exponent-telegram.com
• Sara Shingleton, Classified Manager
(304) 626-1415
Frequency:
7 time(s) per week

EXPRESS-TIMES
P.O. BOX 391
EASTON, PA 18042-3528
610-258-7171
800-360-3601
Fax: 610-258-1434
news@express-times.com
http://www.lehighvalleylive.com
• Edward Laubach, Sports Editor
(610) 258-7171
sports@express-times.com
• David Yanoshik, Advertising Vice
President
dyanoshik@express-times.com
Frequency:
7 time(s) per week

FACTS
720 SOUTH MAIN STREET
CLUTE, TX 77531-5411
979-265-7411
800-864-8340
Fax: 979-265-9052
news@thefacts.com
http://www.thefacts.com
• Chris Greene, Sports Editor
(979) 265-7411
news@thefacts.com
Frequency:
7 time(s) per week

FAIRBANKS DAILY NEWS-MINER
P.O. BOX 70710
FAIRBANKS, AK 99701
907-456-6661
Fax: 907-452-7917
newsroom@newsminer.com
http://www.newsminer.com
• Bob Eley, Sports Editor
(907) 459-7581
beley@newsminer.com
• Paula Kothe, Advertising Director
(907) 459-7525
pkothe@newsminer.com
Frequency:
7 time(s) per week

FAIRBORN DAILY HERALD
30 SOUTH DETROIT STREET
XENIA, OH 45385
937-372-4444
Fax: 937-372-1951
wbaker@xeniagazette.com
http://www.xeniagazette.com

• Wayne Baker, Sports Editor
(937) 372-4444
wbaker@xeniagazette.com
• Tammy Tootle, Classified Manager
(937) 372-9609
Frequency:
6 time(s) per week

FAIRFAX JOURNAL
6408 ESALL
ALEXANDRIA, VA 22312
703-560-4000
Fax: 703-846-8366
www.jrnl.com
• Michelle Gates, Marketing/Promotions
Manager
• Kevin Dunleavy, Sports Editor

FARIBAULT DAILY NEWS
P.O. BOX 249
FARIBAULT, MN 55021
507-333-3131
Fax: 507-333-3102
http://www.faribault.com
• Corey Voegele, Sports Editor
(507) 333-3129
• Sean Lafavor, Sports Writer
(507) 333-3131
Frequency:
6 time(s) per week

FARMINGTON PRESS
218 NORTH WASHINGTON STREET
FARMINGTON, MO 63640-3169
573-756-8927
Fax: 573-756-9160
dsmith@pulitzer.net
http://www.dailypress.com
• Matt King, Sports Editor
(573) 431-2010
Frequency:
7 time(s) per week

FAYETTEVILLE OBSERVER
458 WHITFIELD STREET
FAYETTEVILLE, NC 28306-1698
910-486-3500
800-682-3476
Fax: 910-486-3545
sports@fayobserver.com
www.fayobserver.com
• Michael Arnholt, Executive Editor
(910) 486-3558
arnholtm@fayobserver.com
• Larry Graham, Sports Editor
(910) 486-3530
• Thomas Pope, Assistnat Sports Editor
(910) 486-3520
Frequency:
7 time(s) per week

FINE PRINT NEWS
806 FILLMORE AVENUE
BUFFALO, NY 14212-1356
716-855-3810
Fax: 716-855-3810
• Vincent Cook, Sports Editor
(716) 855-3810
Frequency:
1 time(s) per week

FINGER LAKES TIMES
218 GENESESE STREET
GENEVA, NY 14456-2323
315-789-3333
800-388-4346

Fax: 315-789-4077
http://www.fltimes.com
• Alan Brignall, Sports Editor
(315) 789-3333
abrignall@fltimes.com
• Diane Lahr-Smith, Advertising Manager
(315) 789-3333
fltimes@fltimes.com
Frequency:
6 time(s) per week

FLINT JOURNAL
200 EAST FIRST STREET
FLINT, MI 48502-1925
810-766-6200
Fax: 810-767-7518
www.mlive.com/flintjournal
• Tom Eason, Advertising Director
(810) 766-6381
• Dave Graham, Sports Writer
(810) 766-6306
• Rickey Hampton, Sports Columnist
(810) 766-6396
• Dean Howe, Sports Columnist
(810) 766-6392
• Len Hoyes, Sports Reporter
(810) 766-6184
• Bill Khan, Assistant Sports Editor
(810) 766-6184
• Dan Nilsen, Sports Reporter
(810) 766-6394
• Jody O'Hara, Sports Reporter
(810) 766-6184
• Tammy Reaves, Classified Manager
(810) 766-6155
• Brendan Savage, Sports Reporter
(810) 766-6388
• Mark Csapo, Sports Writer
(810) 766-6184
Frequency:
7 time(s) per week

FLORIDA TIMES-UNION
1 RIVERSIDE AVENUE
JACKSONVILLE, FL 32202
904-359-4111
800-472-6397
Fax: 904-359-4478
http://www.jacksonville.com
• Michael Dirocco, Sports Writer
(904) 705-3878
michael.dirocco@jacksonville.com
• Jeffrey Elliott, Sports Writer
(904) 359-4292
jeff.elliott@jacksonville.com
• Chet Fussman, Sports Editor
(904) 359-4574
chet.fussman@jacksonville.com
• Scott Kendrick, Assistant Sports Editor
(904) 359-4646
scott.kendrick@jacksonville.com
• Francine King, Sports Writer
(904) 359-4372
francine.king@jacksonville.com
• Bobby Smith, Sports Copy Editor
(904) 359-4246
robert.smith@jacksonville.com
• Garry Smits, Sports Reporter
(904) 359-4362
garry.smits@jacksonville.com
• Kevin Upright, Sports Copy Editor
(904) 359-4354
kevin.upright@jacksonville.com
Frequency:
7 time(s) per week

FLORIDA TODAY
P. O. BOX 419000
MELBOURNE, FL 32940
321-242-3500
800-633-8449
Fax: 321-242-6620
communities@floridatoday.com
http://www.floridatoday.com
• Michael Parsons, Sports Editor
(321) 242-3576
Frequency:
7 time(s) per week

**FORT BEND HERALD & TEAXS
COASTER**
1902 SOUTH 4TH STREET
ROSENBERG, TX 77471
281-342-4474
Fax: 281-342-3219
http://www.fbherald.com
• Lee Hartman, Advertising Manager
• Gary Martin, Sports Editor
(281) 342-4474
gmartin@fbherald.com
Frequency:
6 time(s) per week

FORT MORGAN TIMES
329 MAIN STREET
FORT MORGAN, CO 80701
970-867-5651
Fax: 970-867-7448
http://www.fmtimes.com
• Veronica Ivey, Sports Reporter
(970) 867-5651
sports@fmtimes.com
• John LaPorte, Sports Editor
(970) 867-5651
news@fmtimes.com
Frequency:
6 time(s) per week

FORT SCOTT TRIBUNE
12 E WALL STREET
FORT SCOTT, KS 66701
620-223-1460
Fax: 620-223-1469
snuzum@fstribune.com
• Scott Nuzum, Sports Editor
(620) 223-1462
snuzum@fstribune.com
Frequency:
6 time(s) per week
Publications:
Fort Scott Tribune (Tu-F); Weekend
Herald-Tribune (Sat.)

FORT WORTH STAR-TELEGRAM
P.O. BOX 1870
FORT WORTH, TX 76101
817-390-7761
800-776-7827
Fax: 817-390-7789
newsroom@star-telegram.com
http://www.star-telegram.com
• Joe Garza, Sports Managing Editor
(817) 390-7241
• Wendell Barnhouse, Senior Reporter
(817) 390-7760
• Don Bowman, Sports Reporter
(817) 390-7760
• Ray Buck, Sports Columnist
(817) 390-7760
• Jimmy Burch, Staff Writer
(817) 390-7475
jburch@star-telegram.com
• Andy Clay, Sports Copy Editor

(817) 390-7374
• Mac Engel, Sports Reporter (Rangers)
(817) 390-7400
tengel@star-telegram.com
• Jennifer Floyd Engel, Sports Reporter
(817) 390-7760
• Bryan French, Sports Copy Editor
(817) 390-7191
• Andy Friedlander, Sports Reporter
(817) 390-7760
• Randy Galloway, Sports Columnist
(817) 390-7760
• Arthur Garcia, Sports Writer (College)
(817) 390-7400
• Clarence Hill, Sports Reporter (High School)
(817) 390-7760
• Brett Hoffman, Sports Reporter
(817) 390-7707
• Bob Hood, Sports Reporter (Outdoors)
(817) 390-7735
• David Humphrey, Sports Deputy Editor
(817) 390-7162
dchumphrey@star-telegram.com
• Tom Johanningmeier, Sports Deputy Editor
(817) 390-7383
tjohanningmeier@star-telegram.com
• Mike Jones, Sports Writer (College)
(817) 390-7760
thejonz@email.com
• Vince Langford, Sports Copy Editor
vlangford@star-telegram.com
• Gil LeBreton, Sports Columnist
(817) 390-7760
glebreton@star-telegram.com
• Mercedes Mayer, Sports Reporter
(817) 390-7760
• Carlos Mendez, Sports Reporter
(817) 548-5413
cmendez@star-telegram.com
• Randall Perry, Sports Copy Editor
• Troy Phillips, Sports Writer
• Roger Pinckney, (817) 390-7760
Sports Copy Editor
rpinckney@star-telegram.com
• Charles Polansky, Sports Writer
(817) 390-7760
• Tim Price, Sports Reporter (Horse Racing)
(972) 237-4845
• Dwain Price, Sports Reporter
(817) 390-7760
dprice@star-telegram.com
• Jim Reeves, Sports Columnist
(817) 390-7760
• John Sturbin, Auto Racing Staff Writer
(817) 390-7408
Frequency:
7 time(s) per week

FORUM
101 5TH STREET NORTH
FARGO, ND 58102
701-235-7311
Fax: 701-241-5406
news@forumcomm.com
http://www.inforum.com
• James Boberg, Advertising Manager
(701) 241-5410
• Kevin Schnepf, Sports Editor
(701) 241-5549
kschnepf@forumcomm.com
• Tom Mix, Sports Writer
Frequency:
7 time(s) per week

FREDERICK NEWS-POST
351 BALLENGER CENTER DRIVE
FREDERICK, MD 21703
301-662-1177
800-486-1177
Fax: 301-662-8299
http://www.fredericknewspost.com
• Stan Goldberg, Sports Editor
(301) 662-1177
sgoldberg@fredericknewspost.com
Frequency:
7 time(s) per week

FREE LANCE
350 6TH STREET
HOLLISTER, CA 95023
831-637-5566
Fax: 831-637-4104
http://www.freelancenews.com
• Cindy Courter, Advertising Manager
(408) 842-1922
cindyc@freelancenews.com
• Andrew Matheson, Sports Editor
(831) 637-5566
sports@freelancenews.com
Frequency:
5 time(s) per week

FREE LANCE-STAR
616 AMELIA STREET
FREDERICKSBURG, VA 22401
540-374-5000
800-877-0500
Fax: 540-373-8455
newsroom@freelancestar.com
http://www.fredericksburg.com/
• Steve DeShazo, Sports Editor
(540) 374-5433
sdeshazo@freelancestar.com
Frequency:
7 time(s) per week

FREE PRESS
418 SOUTH 2ND STREET
MANKATO, MN 56001-3727
507-625-4451
800-657-4662
Fax: 507-388-4355
editor@mankatofreepress.com
http://mankatofreepress.com
• Chad Courrier, Sports Reporter
(507) 344-6353
ccourrier@mankatofreepress.com
• Brian Ojanpa, Sports Reporter
(507) 344-6316
Frequency:
6 time(s) per week

FREEMAN
801 NORTH BARSTOW STREET
WAUKESHA, WI 53186
262-542-2501
Fax: 262-542-6082
thaffemann@conleynet.com
http://www.gmtoday.com
• Jim Baumgart, Advertising Director
(262) 513-2621
jbaumgart@conleynet.com
• Lee Fensin, Sports Editor
(262) 513-2667
Frequency:
6 time(s) per week

FREMONT TRIBUNE
P.O. BOX 9
FREMONT, NE 68025-5673

402-721-5000
800-927-7598
Fax: 402-721-8047
newsroom@fremonttribune.com
http://www.fremontneb.com
• Brent Wasenius, Managing Editor
(402) 721-5000
bwasenius@hotmail.com
• Brent Wasenius, Sports Editor
(402) 941-1430
brent.wasenius@lee.net
Frequency:
6 time(s) per week

FRESNO BEE
1626 E-STREET
FRESNO, CA 93706-2006
559-441-6111
800-877-7300
Fax: 559-441-6436
http://www.fresnobee.com
• Matt Lloyd, Sports Reporter
(559) 441-6340
mlloyd@fresnobee.com
• Jeff Davis, Sports Reporter
(559) 441-6401
• David Cooper, Assistant Sports Editor
(559) 441-6623
dcooper@fresnobee.com
Frequency:
7 time(s) per week

FULTON SUN
115 EAST 5TH STREET
FULTON, MO 65251-1714
573-642-7272
Fax: 573-642-0656
news@fultonsun.com
http://www.fultonsun.com
• Ryan Boland, Sports Editor
• Rachel Reed, Display Advertising Manager
display@fultonsun.com
Frequency:
5 time(s) per week

GADSDEN TIMES
P.O. BOX 188
GADSDEN, AL 35901-3737
800-762-2464
Fax: 256-549-2105
http://www.gadsdentimes.com
• Glenn Porter, Advertising Director
(256) 549-2000
• Kim Craft, Sports Editor
(256) 549-2051
• Nick Johnston, Sports Writer
(256) 549-2052
Frequency:
7 time(s) per week

GAINESVILLE DAILY REGISTER
306 EAST CALIFORNIA STREET
GAINESVILLE, TX 76240
940-665-5511
Fax: 940-665-0920
http://www.gainesvilleregister.com
• Darin Allred, Sports Editor
(940) 665-5511
dallredgdr@ntin.net
Frequency:
6 time(s) per week

GAINESVILLE SUN
P.O. BOX 147147
GAINESVILLE, FL 32608

352-374-5000
800-443-4245
Fax: 352-338-3128
sun@atlantic.net
http://www.gainesvillesun.com
• Arnold Feliciano, Sports Editor
(352) 374-5055
Frequency:
7 time(s) per week

GALION INQUIRER
378 NORTH MARKET STREET
GALION, OH 44833-1924
419-468-1117
Fax: 419-468-7255
http://www.galioninquirer.com
• Jon Kleinknecht, Sports Editor
sports@galioninquirer.com
Frequency:
6 time(s) per week

GALLUP INDEPENDENT
500 NORTH 9TH STREET
GALLUP, NM 87301-5379
505-863-6811
800-545-3817
Fax: 505-722-5750
http://www.gallupindependent.com
• Alan Arthur, Sports Editor
(505) 863-6811
• Mike Peretti, Sports Writer
(505) 863-6811
Frequency:
6 time(s) per week

GALVESTON COUNTY DAILY NEWS
8522 TEICHMAN ROAD
GALVESTON, TX 77554-9119
409-683-5200
800-561-3611
Fax: 409-744-7679
news@galvnews.com
www.galvnews.com
• Leonard Woolsey, Publisher
(409) 683-5207
leonard.woolsey@galvnews.com
• Michael Smith, Editor
(409) 683-5206
michael.smith@galvnews.com
Frequency:
7 time(s) per week

GARDEN ISLAND
P.O. BOX 231
LIHUE, HI 96766
808-245-3681
800-296-2880
Fax: 808-245-5286
http://www.thegardenisland.com
• David Simon, Sports Writer
(808) 245-3681
dsimon@thegardenisland.com
• Casey Quel, Advertising Director
Frequency:
7 time(s) per week

GARDNER NEWS
309 CENTRAL STREET
GARDNER, MA 01440
978-632-8000
Fax: 978-630-2231
http://www.thegardnernews.com
• Tom Trainque, Sports Editor
(978) 632-8000
sports@thegardnernews.com
• John Ballou, Sports Writer

(978) 632-8000
jballou@thegardnernews.com
Frequency:
6 time(s) per week

GASTON GAZETTE
1893 REMOUNT ROAD
GASTONIA, NC 28054
704-864-3291
Fax: 704-884-3031
http://www.gastongazette.com/
• Gabe Whisnant, Sports Editor
(704) 869-1841
gwhisnant@gastongazette.com
• Jamey Jenkins, Advertising Manager
(704) 869-1741
jamey_jenkins@link.freedom.com
Frequency:
7 time(s) per week

GAZETTE
500 3RD AVE, SE
CEDAR RAPIDS, IA 52401
319-398-8211
800-397-8211
Fax: 319-398-5861
www.thegazette.com
• Steve Gravelle, Sports Editor
(319) 398-5819

GAZETTE COLORADO SPRINGS
30 S. PROSPECT STREET
COLORADO SPRINGS, CO 80903
719-636-0250
Fax: 719-636-0163
www.gazette.com
• Jim O'Connell, Sports Editor
(719) 636-0263
jim.oconnell@gazette.com
• Nathan Van Dyne, Deputy Sports Editor
(719) 636-0195
nathan.vandyne@gazette.com
Frequency:
7 time(s) per week

GETTYSBURG TIMES
1570 FAIRFIELD ROAD
GETTYSBURG, PA 17325
717-334-1131
Fax: 717-334-4243
info@gburgtimes.com
http://www.gettysburgtimes.com
• Josh Martin, Sports Editor
(717) 334-1131
sports@gburgtimes.com
Frequency:
6 time(s) per week

GLEANER
P.O. BOX 4
HENDERSON, KY 42419
270-827-2000
Fax: 270-827-2765
news@thegleaner.com
http://www.thegleaner.com
• Tim Ethridge, Sports Editor
(812) 464-7416
tethridge@thegleaner.com
Frequency:
6 time(s) per week

GLENDALE NEWS-PRESS
221 N BRAND BLVD
GLENDALE, CA 91203
818-637-3247
Fax: 818-241-1975

gnp@latimes.com
http://www.glendalenewspress.com
• Grant Gordon, Sports Editor
(818) 637-3225
grant.gordon@latimes.com
• Charles Rich, Sports Reporter
(818) 637-3225
charles.rich@latimes.com
Frequency:
6 time(s) per week

GLENWOOD SPRINGS POST INDEPENDENT
2014 GRAND AVENUE
GLENWOOD SPRINGS, CO 81601-4162
970-945-8515
Fax: 970-945-4487
news@postindependent.com
http://www.postindependent.com
• Jeff Caspersen, Sports Editor
(970) 384-9123
• Gunilla Asher, Advertising Manager
(970) 949-9170
Frequency:
6 time(s) per week

GLOBE-GAZETTE
300 NORTH WASHINGTON AVENUE
MASON CITY, IA 50401
641-421-0500
800-421-0546
Fax: 641-421-0516
news@globegazette.com
http://www.globegazette.com
• Jared Patterson, Sports Editor
Frequency:
7 time(s) per week

GLOUCESTER COUNTY TIMES
309 SOUTH BROAD STREET
WOODBURY, NJ 08096
856-845-3300
Fax: 856-845-5480
http://www.nj.com/gloucester/
• Shawn Leary, Sports Editor
(856) 686-3633
sleary@sjnewsco.com
• Marie Vito, Classified Manager
(856) 686-3637
mvito@sjnewsco.com
• Kevin Minnick, Sports Reporter
(856) 845-7484
kminnick@sjnewsco.com
Frequency:
6 time(s) per week

GRAND FORKS HERALD
P.O. BOX 6008
GRAND FORKS, ND 58206
701-780-1100
800-477-6572
Fax: 701-795-4604
http://www.gfherald.com
• Zack Ahrens, Advertising Manager
• Wayne Nelson, Sports Editor
wnelson@gfherald.com
• Jeff New, Assistant Sports Editor
Frequency:
7 time(s) per week

GRAND HAVEN TRIBUNE
101 N 3RD ST
GRAND HAVEN, MI 49417-1209
616-842-6400
800-874-7180
Fax: 616-842-9584

bvargo@grandhaventribune.com
http://www.grandhaventribune.com
• Matt DeYoung, Sports Editor
(616) 842-6400
mdeyoung@grandhaventribune.com
• Matt Tjapkes, Sports Writer
(616) 842-6400
• Mike Kohon, Sports Writer
(616) 842-6400
Frequency:
6 time(s) per week

GRAND RAPIDS PRESS
155 MICHIGAN STREET, N.W.
GRAND RAPIDS, MI 49503-2353
616-222-5400
800-878-1411
Fax: 616-222-5269
http://www.mlive.com/grpress/
• Robert Becker, Sports Editor
(616) 222-5674
• Dave Mayo, Sports Writer
(616) 222-5670
Frequency:
7 time(s) per week

GRANTS PASS DAILY COURIER
409 S.E. 7TH STREET
GRANTS PASS, OR 97526-3003
541-474-3700
800-228-0457
Fax: 541-474-3824
news@thedailycourier.com
http://www.thedailycourier.com/
• Lance Ogden, Sports Editor
(541) 474-3729
• Zack Urness, Sports Reporter
(541) 474-3825
Frequency:
6 time(s) per week

GREAT FALLS TRIBUNE
P.O. BOX 5468
GREAT FALLS, MT 59405-1854
406-791-1444
800-438-6600
Fax: 406-791-1431
tribcity@greatfallstribune.com
http://www.greatfallstribune.com
• George Geise, Sports Editor
(406) 791-1470
ggeise@greatfal.gannett.com
Frequency:
7 time(s) per week

GREELEY TRIBUNE
501 8TH AVENUE
GREELEY, CO 80631-3913
800-275-0321
800-275-0321
Fax: 970-356-5780
http://www.greeleytribune.com
• Mike Distelhorst, Advertising Director
(970) 392-4406
• Scott Rosenberg, Sports Editor
(970) 392-4441
srosenberg@greeleytribune.com
Frequency:
7 time(s) per week

GREEN BAY PRESS-GAZETTE
435 EAST WALNUT STREET
GREEN BAY, WI 54301-5001
920-431-8400
800-444-0007
Fax: 920-431-8379

businessnews@greenbaypressgazette.com
http://www.greenbaypressgazette.com
• Mike Vandermause, Sports Editor
(920) 431-8413
mvandermause@greenbaypressgazette.com
• Jeff Ash, Assistant Sports Editor
(920) 431-8336
jash@greenbaypressgazette.com
Frequency:
7 time(s) per week

GREENEVILLE SUN
P.O. BOX 1630
GREENEVILLE, TN 37743-4923
423-638-4181
Fax: 423-638-3645
info@greenevillesun.com
http://www.greenevillesun.com
• Wayne Phillips, Sports Editor
(423) 359-3137
wayne.phillips@greenevillesun.com
• Artie Wehenkel, Advertising Director
(423) 359-3160
artie.wehenkel@greenevillesun.com
• Joe Byrd, Assistant Sports Editor
(423) 359-3140
joe.byrd@greenevillesun.com
Frequency:
6 time(s) per week

GREENSBORO NEWS & RECORD
200 EAST MARKET STREET
GREENSBORO, NC 27401
336-373-7000
800-553-6880
Fax: 336-373-7067
http://www.news-record.com
• Jeff Carlton, Sports Reporter
jcarlton@news-record.com
• Rob Daniels, Sports Reporter
rdaniels@news-record.com
• Ed Hardin, Sports Columnist
ehardin@news-record.com
• Charles Hardin, Sports Writer
chardin@news-record.com
• Bill Hass, Sports Writer
bhass@news-record.com
• Dustin Long, Sports Writer
(704) 987-0624
dlong@news-record.com
• John Newsom, Sports Assistant Editor
(336) 373-7312
jnewsom@news-record.com
• Joe Sirera, Sports Editor
jsirera@news-record.com
Frequency:
7 time(s) per week

GREENSBURG DAILY NEWS
135 SOUTH FRANKLIN STREET
GREENSBURG, IN 47240-2023
812-663-3111
Fax: 812-663-2985
http://www.greenburgdailynews.com
• Nick Gonnella, Sports Editor
(812) 663-3111
• Laura Welborn, Advertising Manager
(812) 663-3111
Frequency:
6 time(s) per week

GREENVILLE HERALD BANNER
2305 KING STREET
GREENVILLE, TX 75401-3257

903-455-4220
Fax: 903-455-6281
http://www.heraldbanner.com/
• David Claybourn, Sports Editor
(903) 455-4220
• Latarah Edmond, Advertising Manager
(903) 455-4220
ledmond@heraldbanner.com
Frequency:
7 time(s) per week

GREENVILLE NEWS
P.O. BOX 1688
GREENVILLE, SC 29601
864-298-4100
800-736-7136
Fax: 864-298-4395
http://www.greenvillenews.com
• Bart Wright, Sports Editor
(864) 298-4239
rbwright@greenvillenews.com
• Jim Rice, Sports News Editor
(864) 298-4268
jdrice@greenvillenews.com
• Willie Smith, III, Sports Reporter
(864) 298-4038
wtsmith@greenvillenews.com
Frequency:
7 time(s) per week
Number of Members:
13 full time
Teams:
Clemson University, Furman University,
Carolina Panthers, Atlanta Falcons, Univ. of
South Carolina, Greenville Drive (MILB),
Greenville Road Warriors (ECHL)
Publications:
The Greenville News, Greenvilleonline.com,
TigersNow.com, The Tribune-Times,
Greater GreenNews and Pickens County
News.

GREENWICH POST
10 CORBIN DRIVE, FLOOR 3
DARIEN, CT 06820
203-861-9191
Fax: 203-861-0023
post@acorn-online.com
http://www.greenwich-post.com
• Paul Silverfarb, Sports Editor
(203) 861-9191
Frequency:
1 time(s) per week

GREENWICH TIME
1455 EAST PUTNAM AVENUE
GREENWICH, CT 06870
203-625-4400
Fax: 203-964-2345
letters.greenwichtime@scni.com
http://www.greenwichtime.com
• Chris McNamee, Sports Editor
(203) 330-6324
chris.mcnamee@scni.com
Frequency:
7 time(s) per week

GREENWOOD COMMONWEALTH
PO BOX 8050
GREENWOOD, MS 38935
662-453-5312
Fax: 662-453-2908
commonwealth@gwcommonwealth.com
http://www.gwcommonwealth.com
• Larry Alderman, Advertising Manager
(662) 453-5312
lalderman@gwcommonwealth.com

• Bill Burrus, Sports Editor
(662) 453-5312
bburrus@gwcommonwealth.com
Frequency:
6 time(s) per week

GRIFFIN DAILY NEWS
323 EAST SOLOMON
GRIFFIN, GA 30224
770-227-3276
Fax: 770-412-1678
http://www.griffindailynews.com
• John Sullivan, Sports Editor
jsullivan@griffindailynews.com
Frequency:
7 time(s) per week

GWINNETT DAILY POST
P.O. BOX 603
LAWRENCEVILLE, GA 30046
770-963-9205
Fax: 770-339-8081
news@gwinnettdailypost.com
http://www.gwinnettdailypost.com/
• Will Hammock, Sports Editor
(770) 963-9205
will.hammock@gwinnettdailypost.com
• Ben Beitzel, Sports Reporter
(770) 963-9205
ben.beitzel@gwinnettdailypost.com
Frequency:
6 time(s) per week

HANFORD SENTINEL
300 WEST 6TH STREET
HANFORD, CA 93230-4518
559-582-0471
Fax: 559-582-8631
http://www.hanfordsentinel.com
• Rich De Give, Sports Editor
(559) 583-2430
Frequency:
7 time(s) per week

HARRISON DAILY TIMES
PO BOX 40
HARRISON, AR 72602
870-741-2325
Fax: 870-741-5632
http://www.harrisondailytimes.com
• Jason Overman, Advertising Manager
jasono@harrisondaily.com
• Jeff Brasel, Sports Editor
(870) 741-2325
jeffb@harrisondaily.com
Frequency:
6 time(s) per week

HARTFORD COURANT
285 BROAD STREET
HARTFORD, CT 06115-2510
860-241-6200
800-524-4242
Fax: 860-241-3865
letters@courant.com
http://www.ctnow.com
• Dom Amore, Sports Reporter (Baseball)
(860) 241-3988
damore@courant.com
• Woody Anderson, Sports Reporter
(College)
(860) 241-6441
wanderson@courant.com
• William Armstrong, Sports Assistant Editor
(860) 241-3145
• Bruce Berlet, Sports Writer (Golf)

(860) 241-3732
• Desmond Conner, Sports
Reporter/Columnist
(860) 241-3871
dconner@courant.com
• Shawn Courchesne, Sports Reporter
(860) 241-6200
• Paul Doyle, Sports Reporter (Baseball)
(860) 241-6699
pdoyle@courant.com
• Jeff Goldberg, Sports Columnist/Reporter
(860) 241-6435
• David Heuschkel, Sports Reporter
(Baseball)
(860) 241-6707
dheuschkel@courant.com
• Jeff Jacobs, Sports Columnist
(860) 241-3983
jjacobs@courant.com
• Jack O'Connell, Sports Reporter
(Baseball)
(860) 241-6435
• Jeffrey Otterbein, Sports Editor
(860) 241-6434
jotterbein@courant.com
• Terry Price, Sports Reporter (Boxing)
(860) 241-6437
• Paul Rosano, Assistant Sports Editor
(860) 241-3978
prosano@courant.com
• Jeff Smith, Sports Deputy Editor
(860) 241-3820
jsmith@courant.com
• Tom Yantz, Sports Reporter (College)
(860) 241-3985
tyantz@courant.com
Frequency:
7 time(s) per week

HASTINGS TRIBUNE
908 WEST 2ND STREET
HASTINGS, NE 68902
402-462-2131
800-742-6397
Fax: 402-461-4657
tribune@hastingstribune.com
http://www.hastingstribune.com
• Vince Kuppig, Sports Editor
(402) 461-1270
vkuppig@hastingstribune.com
• Kathy Avis, Advertising Manager
(402) 461-1234
kavis@hastingstribune.com
Frequency:
6 time(s) per week

HATTIESBURG AMERICAN
PO BOX 1111
HATTIESBURG, MS 39401
601-582-4321
800-844-2637
Fax: 601-584-3130
http://www.hattiesburgamerican.com
• Alan Hinton, Sports Editor
(601) 584-3136
Frequency:
7 time(s) per week

HAWAII TRIBUNE-HERALD
PO BOX 767
HILO, HI 96721
808-935-6621
Fax: 808-969-9100
http://www.hawaiitribune-herald.com
• Bill O'Rear, Sports Editor
(808) 935-6621

• Alice Sledge, Advertising Director
asledge@hawaiitribune-herald.com
Frequency:
6 time(s) per week

HAWK EYE
800 SOUTH MAIN STREET
BURLINGTON, IA 52601-5850
319-754-8461
Fax: 319-754-6824
news@thehawkeye.com
http://www.thehawkeye.com
• Susan Denk, Sports Reporter
(319) 758-8146
• Matt Levins, Sports Reporter
(319) 758-8147
mlevins@thehawkeye.com
• Laurie Trautner, Classified Manager
(319) 758-8128
• John Bohnenkamp, Sports Editor
(319) 758-8133
jbohnenkamp@thehawkeye.com
Frequency:
7 time(s) per week

HAYS DAILY NEWS
507 MAIN STREET
HAYS, KS 67601-4228
785-628-1081
800-657-6017
Fax: 785-628-8186
newsroom@dailynews.net
www.hdnews.net
• Nick McQueen, Sports Editor
nmcqueen@dailynews.net
Frequency:
6 time(s) per week

HELENA INDEPENDENT RECORD
317 CRUSE AVE
HELENA, MT 59601
406-447-4000
Fax: 406-447-4052
irads@helenair.com
www.helenair.com
• Jeff Windmueller, Sports Editor
(406) 447-4065
jeff.windmueller@lee.net
• Randy Rickman, Publisher
(406) 447-4002

HENDERSON DAILY DISPATCH
304 SOUTH CHESTNUT STREET
HENDERSON, NC 27536-4225
252-436-2700
800-326-3894
Fax: 252-430-0125
news@hendersondispatch.com
http://www.hendersondispatch.com
• Eric Robinson, Sports Editor
(252) 436-2840
• Deborah Tuck, Advertising Manager
(252) 436-2821
Frequency:
6 time(s) per week

HENDERSON DAILY NEWS
PO BOX 30
HENDERSON, TX 75653
903-657-2501
Fax: 903-657-0056
http://www.hendersondailynews.com
• J.D. Issac, Sports Editor
(903) 657-2501
sports@hendersondailynews.com

Frequency:
6 time(s) per week

HERALD & REVIEW
601 EAST WILLIAM STREET
DECATUR, IL 62523-1142
217-429-5151
800-437-2533
Fax: 217-421-7965
http://www.herald-review.com
• Mike Albright, Sports Editor
(217) 421-7909
mike.albright@lee.net
• Mark Tupper, Executive Sports Editor
(217) 421-7983
mark.tupper@lee.net
Frequency:
7 time(s) per week

HERALD (CT)
ONE HERALD SQUARE
NEW BRITAIN, CT 06050
860-225-4601
800-327-3237
Fax: 860-223-8171
www.newbritainherald.com.
• Matt Straub, Sports Editor
(860) 225-4601
mstraub@newbritainherald.com
• Brad Carroll, Executive Sports Editor
(860) 225-4601
bcarroll@newbritainherald.com

HERALD (WA)
1213 CALIFORNIA AVENUE
EVERETT, WA 98201
425-339-3000
Fax: 425-339-3049
sports@heraldnet.com
http://www.heraldnet.com
• Kirby Arnold, Sports Reporter
(425) 339-3478
• Kevin Brown, Sports Editor
(425) 339-3474
kbrown@heraldnet.com
• Aaron Coe, Sports Reporter
(425) 339-3471
• Steve Hawes, Advertising Manager
(425) 339-3051
• Sally Kortekaas, Classified Manager
(425) 339-3070
• Bob Mortenson, Sports Reporter
(425) 339-3489
• Rich Myhre, Sports Reporter
(425) 339-3478
myhre@heraldnet.com
• John Sleeper, Sports Reporter
(425) 339-3478
Frequency:
7 time(s) per week

HERALD AND NEWS
2703 FOOTHILLS BOULEVARD
KLAMATH FALLS, OR 97603
541-885-4411
800-275-0982
Fax: 541-885-4456
sports@heraldandnews.com
http://www.heraldandnews.com
• Steve Matthies, Sports Editor
(541) 885-4411
smatthies@heraldandnews.com
Frequency:
6 time(s) per week

HERALD DEMOCRAT
P.O. BOX 1128
SHERMAN, TX 75090-7258
903-893-8181
Fax: 903-868-2106
news@heralddemocrat.com
http://www.heralddemocrat.com
• Todd Hutchinson, Sports Editor
sports@heralddemocrat.com
• Jason Dellarosa, Sports Writer
(903) 893-8181
Frequency:
6 time(s) per week

HERALD JOURNAL
75 WEST 300 NORTH
LOGAN, UT 84321
435-752-2121
800-275-0423
Fax: 435-753-6642
http://www.hjnews.com
• Shawn Harrison, Sports Editor
(435) 752-2121
sharrison@hjnews.com
• Rick G. Wallace, Advertising Director
(435) 792-7275
Frequency:
7 time(s) per week

HERALD NEWS
1 GARRET MOUNTAIN PLAZA
WEST PATERSON, NJ 07424
973-569-7000
Fax: 973-569-7129
hncitydesk@northjersey.com
• Ives Galarcep, Sports Reporter
(973) 586-8180
galarcep@northjersey.com
• Kerry Rubin, Classified Manager
Frequency:
7 time(s) per week

HERALD TIMES-REPORTER
902 FRANKLIN STREET
MANITOWOC, WI 54221-4514
920-684-4433
800-783-7323
Fax: 920-684-4416
htrnews@htrnews.com
http://www.htrnews.com
• Pete Barth, Sports Editor
(920) 453-5156
pbarth@sheboyganpress.com
• James Maurer, Advertising Manager
(920) 686-2124
jmaurer2@htrnews.com
Frequency:
7 time(s) per week

HERALD-BULLETIN
1133 JACKSON STREET
ANDERSON, IN 46015
765-622-1212
800-750-5049
Fax: 765-640-4815
newsroom@heraldbulletin.com
http://www.theheraldbulletin.com
• Rick Teverbaugh, Sports Writer
(765) 622-1212
rick.teverbaugh@heraldbulletin.com
Frequency:
7 time(s) per week

HERALD-CITIZEN
P.O. BOX 2729
COOKEVILLE, TN 38502

931-526-9715
Fax: 931-526-1209
editor@herald-citizen.com
http://www.herald-citizen.com
• Buddy Pearson, Sports Editor
(931) 526-9715
sports@herald-citizen.com
• Albert Thompson, Advertising Manager
(931) 526-9715
ads@herald-citizen.com
• Thomas Corhern, Sports Writer
(931) 526-9715
sports@herald-citizen.com
Frequency:
6 time(s) per week

HERALD-DISPATCH
P.O. BOX 2017
HUNTINGTON, WV 25701
304-526-4000
800-955-6110
Fax: 304-526-2857
news@heralddispatch.com
http://www.hdonline.com
• Rick McCann, Sports Editor
(304) 526-2759
rmccann@heralddispatch.com
• Amy Howat, Advertising Director
(304) 526-2820

HERALD-JOURNAL
PO BOX 1657
SPARTANBURG, SC 29304
864-582-4511
800-922-4158
Fax: 864-594-6350
online@shj.com
www.goupstate.com
• Robert Dalton, Sports Editor
(864) 562-7293
bob.dalton@shj.com
• Mark Egan, Sports Copy Editor
(864) 562-7244

HERALD-NEWS
300 CATERPILLAR DRIVE
JOLIET, IL 60436
815-729-6031
800-397-9397
Fax: 815-729-6059
http://www.suburbanchicagonews.com
• Dick Goss, Sports Editor
(815) 729-6040
• Ron Kremer, Sports Writer
(815) 729-6040
• Bill Scheibe, Sports Writer
(815) 729-6040
• Steve Vanisko, Advertising Manager
(815) 729-6120
Frequency:
7 time(s) per week

HERALD-PALLADIUM
3450 HOLLYWOOD ROAD
SAINT JOSEPH, MI 49085-9581
269-429-2400
800-356-4262
Fax: 269-429-4398
http://www.heraldpalladium.com
• Jason Mitchell, Sports Editor
(269) 429-1294
jmitchell@heraldpalladium.com
Frequency:
7 time(s) per week

HERALD-STANDARD
8-18 CHURCH STREET
UNIONTOWN, PA 15401-3563
724-439-7565
800-342-8254
Fax: 724-439-7559
http://www.heraldstandard.com
• Rob Burchianti, Assistant Sports Editor
(724) 439-7565
• Mike Ciarochi, Sports Editor
(724) 439-7576
mciarochi@heraldstandard.com
• Maureen Zorichak, Advertising Manager
mzorichak@heraldstandard.com
Frequency:
6 time(s) per week

HERALD-STAR
401 HERALD SQUARE
STEUBENVILLE, OH 43952-2059
740-283-4711
800-526-7987
Fax: 740-284-7355
http://www.hsconnect.com
• Judy Gelestor, Advertising Manager
• Mike Mathison, Sports Editor
(740) 283-4711
mmathison@heraldstaronline.com
Frequency:
7 time(s) per week

HERALD-SUN
2828 PICKETT ROAD
DURHAM, NC 27705-5613
919-419-6500
800-672-0061
Fax: 919-419-6889
http://www.heraldsun.com
• Jimmy Dupree, Sports Editor
(919) 419-6674
• Brian Gorman, Sports Reporter
(919) 419-6664
bgorman@heraldsun.com
• Bryan Strickland, Sports Reporter
(919) 419-6671
bstrickland@heraldsun.com
Frequency:
7 time(s) per week

HERALD-TIMES
P.O. BOX 909
BLOOMINGTON, IN 47401-7720
812-332-4401
800-422-0070
Fax: 812-331-4285
http://www.heraldtimesonline.com
• Pat Beane, Sports Editor
(812) 331-4340
pbeane@heraldt.com
Frequency:
7 time(s) per week

HERNANDO TODAY
15299 CORTEZ BLVD
BROOKSVILLE, FL 34613-6005
352-544-5280
Fax: 352-544-5246
jcason@hernandotoday.com
http://www.hernandotoday.com
• Antonio Castro, Sports Editor
(352) 544-5278
acastro@hernandotoday.com
Frequency:
7 time(s) per week

HIBBING DAILY TRIBUNE
2142 1ST AVENUE
HIBBING, MN 55746-1805
218-262-1011
Fax: 218-262-4318
http://www.hibbingmn.com
• Gary Giombetti, Sports Editor
(218) 262-1011
ggiombetti@hibbingdailytribune.net
• Brian Palokangas, Advertising Director
Frequency:
7 time(s) per week

HICKORY DAILY RECORD
1100 PARK PLACE 11TH BOULEVARD S.E.
HICKORY, NC 28603
828-322-4510
800-849-8586
Fax: 828-328-9378
http://www.hickoryrecord.com
• Peter Cook, Advertising Director
pcook@hickoryrecord.com
• Chris Hobbs, Sports Editor
(828) 322-4510
chobbs@hickoryrecord.com
Frequency:
7 time(s) per week

HIGH POINT ENTERPRISE
210 CHURCH AVENUE
HIGH POINT, NC 27262-4806
336-888-3500
800-933-5760
Fax: 336-841-5582
http://www.hpe.com
• Lynn Wagner, Advertising Director
(336) 888-3545
• Benny Phillips, Sports Editor
(336) 888-3520
• Tom Berry, Sports Columnist
(336) 888-3500
Frequency:
7 time(s) per week

HIGHLANDS TODAY
231 US 27 NORTH
SEBRING, FL 33870
863-382-4947
Fax: 863-382-2509
highlandstoday@highlandstoday.com
http://www.highlandstoday.com
• Mark Pinson, Sports Editor
(863) 382-4947
mpinson@highlandstoday.com
Frequency:
7 time(s) per week

HIGHLINE TIMES
133 SOUTHWEST 153RD STREET
BURIEN, WA 98166-2311
206-444-4873
Fax: 206-444-4877
hteditor@robinsonnews.com
http://www.robinsonnews.com
• Tim Clinton, Sports Editor
(253) 838-7622
hteditor@highlinetimes.com
Frequency:
1 time(s) per week

HOBBS DAILY NEWS-SUN
201 NORTH THORP
HOBBS, NM 88240-6058
575-393-2123
800-993-2123

Fax: 575-393-5724
http://www.hobbsnews.com
• Jason Watkins, Sports Editor
(505) 391-5430
Frequency:
6 time(s) per week

HOLDREGE DAILY CITIZEN
PO BOX 344
HOLDREGE, NE 68949-2219
308-995-4441
Fax: 308-995-5992
holdredgecitizen@aol.com
• Richard Headley, Sports Editor
• Barbara Penrod, Advertising Manager
• Jack Donoghue, Sports Editor
(308) 995-4441
Frequency:
5 time(s) per week

HOLLAND SENTINEL
54 WEST 8TH STREET
HOLLAND, MI 49423-3104
616-392-2311
800-968-3497
Fax: 616-392-3526
newsroom@hollandsentinel.com
www.hollandsentinel.com
• Alan Babbitt, Sports Editor
(616) 546-4271
alan.babbitt@hollandsentinel.com
• Janet Johnson, Advertising Manager
(616) 546-4227
Frequency:
7 time(s) per week

HOME NEWS TRIBUNE
35 KENNEDY BOULEVARD
EAST BRUNSWICK, NJ 08816
732-246-5500
800-627-4663
Fax: 732-565-7208
metro@thnt.com
http://www.thnt.com
• Brenda Cumomo, Advertising Manager
(732) 565-7420
apads@adtransit.injersey.com
• Jack Genung, Sports Editor
(732) 565-7231
jgenung@thnt.com
• Keith Sargeant, Sports Writer
(732) 246-5500
• Paul Franklin, Sports Writer
(732) 246-5500
Frequency:
7 time(s) per week

HONOLULU ADVERTISER
500 ALA MOANA BOULEVARD
#7-500
HONOLULU, HI 96813-4920
808-529-4700
877-233-1133
Fax: 808-529-4898
citydesk@staradvertiser.com
http://www.staradvertiser.com
• Stacy Kaneshiro, Sports Reporter
(808) 525-8042
• Ferd Lewis, Sports Reporter
(808) 525-8044
• Paul Arnett, Sports Editor
(808) 529-4786
• Wes Nakama, High School Sports Reporter
(808) 535-2456
• Kyle Sakamoto, High School Sports
(808) 525-8041

• Stephen Tsai, Sports Reporter
(808) 525-8051
Frequency:
7 time(s) per week

HOPE STAR
522 W THIRD STREET
HOPE, AR 71802
870-777-8841
Fax: 870-777-3311
http://www.hopestar.com
• Richard Haycox, Advertising Manager
(870) 777-8841
• Garren Smith, Sports Editor
(870) 777-8841
Frequency:
5 time(s) per week

HOUR
1 SELLECK STREET
NORWALK, CT 06855
203-846-3281
Fax: 203-840-1802
features@thehour.com
http://www.thehour.com
• Matthew Doran, Sports Editor
(203) 354-1058
• Steve Geoghegan, Sports Writer
(203) 354-1119
Frequency:
7 time(s) per week

HOUSTON CHRONICLE
P.O. BOX 4260
HOUSTON, TX 77210
713-362-7171
800-735-3820
Fax: 713-362-6677
news@chron.com
http://www.chron.com
• David Barron, Sports Reporter
(713) 362-6922
david.barron@chron.com
• Charlie Crixell, Assistant Sports Editor
(713) 362-7171
• Fred M. Faour, Sports Editor
(713) 362-6931
• Terrance Harris, Sports Writer
(713) 362-2167
• Neil Hohlfeld, Sports Writer
• Richard Justice, Sports Columnist
(713) 362-7171
• John Lopez, Columnist
(713) 362-6968
• Brian McTaggart, Sports Columnist
(713) 362-2950
• Jesus Ortiz, Sports Reporter
(713) 362-7891
jesus.ortiz@chron.com
• Doug Pike, Sports Writer
(713) 362-6095
• Dale Robertson, Sports Columnist
(713) 362-7891
dale.robertson@chron.com
• Jeff Rosen, Sports Sunday Editor
(713) 362-4293
• William H. Stickney, Sports Reporter
(713) 362-7891
• Carlton Thompson, Sports Editor
(713) 362-6926
• Shannon R. Tompkins, Sports Columnist
shannon.tompkins@chron.com
Frequency:
7 time(s) per week

HOUSTON DEFENDER
12401 SOUTH POST OAK #233
HOUSTON, TX 77288
713-663-6996
Fax: 713-663-7116
http://www.defendernetwork.com
• Darrel Ardison, Sports Editor
(713) 663-6996
Frequency:
1 time(s) per week

HOY-NEW YORK
330 WEST 34TH STREET
NEW YORK, NY 10001
917-339-0800
Fax: 212-971-4412
http://www.holahoy.com
• Juan Aya, Sports Reporter
(917) 339-0800
• Sadiel Lebron, Sports Reporter
(917) 339-0800
Frequency:
6 time(s) per week

HUGO DAILY NEWS
128 EAST JACKSON STREET
HUGO, OK 74743-4035
580-326-3311
800-900-3311
Fax: 580-326-6397
http://www.hugonews.com
• Maddie Kuhn, Sports Reporter
(580) 326-3311
hdnsports@sbcglobal.net
Frequency:
5 time(s) per week

HUNTINGTON HERALD-PRESS
7 NORTH JEFFERSON STREET
HUNTINGTON, IN 46750-2839
260-356-6700
Fax: 260-356-9026
hpnews@h-ponline.com
http://www.h-ponline.com
• Marty Alexander, Advertising Manager
(260) 356-6700
• Brenda Ross, Classified Manager
• Paul Siegfried, Sports Editor
(260) 356-6700
Frequency:
6 time(s) per week

HUNTSVILLE ITEM
1409 10TH STREET
HUNTSVILLE, TX 77320
936-295-5407
Fax: 936-435-0135
www.itemonline.com
• Tom Waddilld, Sports Editor
(936) 295-5407
• Cody Smith, Assistant Sports Editor
(936) 295-5407
• Gene Schullenberg, Sports Writer
(936) 295-5407
Frequency:
7 time(s) per week

HUNTSVILLE TIMES
P.O. BOX 1487
HUNTSVILLE, AL 35801
256-532-4000
800-239-5271
Fax: 256-532-4420
http://www.htimes.com
• Billy Bryant, Sports Executive Editor
(256) 532-4407

bill.bryant@htimes.com
• Mark McCarter, Sports Columnist
(256) 532-4234
mark.mccarter@htimes.com
• Steve Wilson, Retail Advertising Manager
(256) 532-4269
steve.wilson@htimes.com
Frequency:
7 time(s) per week

HURON DAILY TRIBUNE
211 NORTH HEISTERMAN STREET
BAD AXE, MI 48413
989-269-6461
800-322-1184
Fax: 989-269-9435
http://www.michigansthumb.com
• Mike Bogan, Sports Editor
(989) 269-6461
• Vicki Yaroch, Advertising Manager
vyaroch@hearstnp.com
Frequency:
6 time(s) per week

HUTCHINSON NEWS
300 WEST 2ND STREET
HUTCHINSON, KS 67501-5211
620-694-5700
800-766-3311
Fax: 620-662-4186
jgreen@hutchnews.com
http://www.hutchnews.com
• Pat Sangimino, Sports Editor
(620) 694-5742
Frequency:
7 time(s) per week

IDAHO PRESS-TRIBUNE
P.O. BOX 9399
NAMPA, ID 83652
208-467-9251
Fax: 208-467-9562
newsroom@idahopress.com
http://www.idahopress.com
• Matt Davidson, Advertising Manager
• Colin Howser, Sports Editor
(208) 465-8111
sports@idahopress.com
Frequency:
7 time(s) per week

IDAHO STATE JOURNAL
305 SOUTH ARTHUR AVENUE
POCATELLO, ID 83204-1510
208-232-4161
800-275-0774
Fax: 208-233-8007
newsclerk@journalnet.com
http://www.journalnet.com/
• Brady Slater, Sports Editor
(208) 232-4161
Frequency:
7 time(s) per week

IDAHO STATESMAN
P.O. BOX 40
BOISE, ID 83706-1239
208-377-6400
800-635-8934
Fax: 208-377-6449
newsroom@idahostatesman.com
http://www.idahostatesman.com
• Chadd Cripe, Sports Reporter
(208) 377-6398
ccripe@idahostatesman.com
• Johnna Espinoza, Sports Reporter

(208) 377-6430
• Nick Jezierny, Sports Reporter
(208) 377-6420
• Mike Prater, Sports Editor
(208) 377-6421
mprater@idahostatesman.com
Frequency:
7 time(s) per week

IMPERIAL VALLEY PRESS
205 8TH STREET, N.
EL CENTRO, CA 92243-2902
760-337-3400
Fax: 760-353-3003
http://www.ivpressonline.com
• Mario Renteria, Sports Editor
(760) 337-3434
mrenteria@ivpressonline.com
• John Yanni, Advertising Manager
(760) 337-3430
advertising@ivpressonline.com
• Chris Grant, Sports Editor
(760) 337-3400
Frequency:
6 time(s) per week

INDEPENDENCE DAILY REPORTER
320 NORTH 6TH STREET
INDEPENDENCE, KS 67301-3129
620-331-3550
Fax: 620-331-3550
• Steve McBride, Advertising Manager
• Brian Thomas, Sports Editor
(620) 331-3550
Frequency:
6 time(s) per week

INDEPENDENT (NE)
422 WEST 1ST STREET
GRAND ISLAND, NE 68801
308-382-1000
800-658-3160
Fax: 308-382-8129
editor@theindependent.com
http://www.theindependent.com
• Terry Douglass, Sports Editor
(308) 381-9414
terry.douglass@theindependent.com
Frequency:
7 time(s) per week

INDEPENDENT (OH)
50 NORTH AVENUE, N.W.
MASSILLON, OH 44647-5444
330-833-2633
Fax: 330-833-2635
http://www.indeonline.com
• Joe Shaheen, Managing Editor
• Chris Easterling, Sports Editor
(330) 775-1128
chris.easterling@indeonline.com
Frequency:
7 time(s) per week

INDEPENDENT RECORD
317 CRUSE AVENUE
HELENA, MT 59601-5003
406-447-4000
800-523-2272
Fax: 406-447-4052
irstaff@helenair.com
http://www.helenair.com
• Jeff Windmueller, Sports Editor
(406) 447-4065
• Tonda Meyer, Advertising Manager
(406) 447-4015

Frequency:
7 time(s) per week

INDEPENDENT TRIBUNE
363 CHURCH STREET N STE. 140
CONCORD, NC 28025
704-789-9147
Fax: 704-786-0645
news@independenttribune.com
http://www.independenttribune.com
• Steve Winzenread, Sports Editor
(704) 789-9147
swinzenread@independenttribune.com
• Lynn Wagner, Advertising Manager
(704) 786-9102
lwagner@independenttribune.com
Frequency:
7 time(s) per week

INDEX-JOURNAL
610 PHOENIX STREET
GREENWOOD, SC 29646
864-223-1411
Fax: 864-223-7331
http://www.indexjournal.com
• Paul Still, Advertising Manager
(864) 943-2509
• Scott Chancey, Sports Editor
(864) 223-1813
Frequency:
7 time(s) per week

INDIANA GAZETTE
899 WATER STREET
INDIANA, PA 15701
724-465-5555
Fax: 724-465-0402
http://www.sportsindianagazette.net
• Tony Coccagna, Sports Editor
tonyc@indianagazette.net
• Bob Yaselonis, Advertising Manager
• Robert Yesilonis, Advertising Director
Frequency:
7 time(s) per week

INDIANA HERALD
2170 NORTH ILLINOIS STREET
INDIANAPOLIS, IN 46202
317-923-8291
Fax: 317-923-8292
http://www.indianaherald.com
• Leroy Bryant, Sports Editor
(317) 923-8291
herald1@earthlink.net
Frequency:
1 time(s) per week

INDIANAPOLIS STAR
P.O. BOX 145
INDIANAPOLIS, IN 46204
317-444-6246
800-669-7827
Fax: 317-444-6200
indystarnewsroom@indystar.com
http://www.indystar.com
• Steve Ballard, Sports Reporter
(317) 444-6184
steve.ballard@indystar.com
• Curt Cavin, Sports Reporter
(317) 444-6409
curt.cavin@indystar.com
• Mike Chappell, Sports Reporter
(317) 444-6830
mike.chappell@indystar.com
• Howard Hewitt, Sports Reporter
(317) 444-2703

howard.hewitt@indystar.com
• Terry Hutchens, Sports Reporter
(317) 444-6469
terry.hutchens@indystar.com
• Bob Kravitz, Sports Columnist
(317) 444-6643
bob.kravitz@indystar.com
• Jim Lefko, Sports Editor
(317) 444-6352
jim.lefko@indystar.com
• Jim Lefko, Sports Desk Editor
(317) 444-6352
jim.lefko@indystar.com
• Jim Lefko, Sports Editor
(317) 444-6352
jim.lefko@indystar.com
• Nat Newell, Sports Reporter
(317) 444-6649
nat.newell@indystar.com
• Michael Pointer, Sports Reporter
(317) 444-2709
 michael.pointer@indystar.com
• Jeff Rabjohns, Sports Reporter
(317) 444-6183
jeff.rabjohns@indystar.com
• Phil Richards, Sports Reporter
(317) 444-6408
phil.richards@indystar.com
• Phillip Wilson, Sports Reporter
(317) 444-6642
phillip.wilson@indystar.com
• David Woods, Sports Reporter
(317) 444-6195
david.woods@indystar.com
Frequency:
7 time(s) per week

INLAND VALLEY DAILY BULLETIN
P.O. BOX 4000
ONTARIO, CA 91764
909-987-6397
Fax: 909-948-9038
http://www.dailybulletin.com
• Louis Brewster, Sports Editor
(909) 483-9363
• Jim Gazzolo, Sports Editor
(909) 483-9374
Frequency:
7 time(s) per week

INTELLIGENCER
1500 MAIN STREET
WHEELING, WV 26003-2826
304-233-0100
800-852-5475
Fax: 304-232-1399
mccabe@thein.net
http://www.theintelligencer.net
• Shawn Rine, Sports Editor
(304) 233-0100
rine@theintelligencer.net
• Mike Myer, Executive Editor
(304) 233-0100
myer@news-register.net
Frequency:
6 time(s) per week

INTELLIGENCER JOURNAL
P.O. BOX 1328
LANCASTER, PA 17603-3824
717-291-8811
800-809-4666
Fax: 717-399-6507
intellnews@lnpnews.com
http://lancasteronline.com
• Russell C. Gillespie, Classified Director
(717) 291-8722

media

rgillespie@lnpnews.com
• Jeff Young, Sports Editor
jyoung@lnpnews.com
• Kevin Freeman, Sports Writer
(717) 291-8666
kfreeman@lnpnews.com
Frequency:
6 time(s) per week

INTERMOUNTAIN JEWISH NEWS
1177 GRANT STRET
DENVER, CO 80203
303-861-2234
Fax: 303-832-6942
email@ijn.com
http://www.ijn.com
• Gerald Mellman, Sports Editor
(303) 823-6625
carol@ijn.com
Frequency:
1 time(s) per week

INTERNATIONAL HERALD TRIBUNE
229 WEST 43RD STREET
NEW YORK, NY 10036
212-556-7714
800-882-2884
Fax: 212-556-7706
http://www.iht.com
• Peter Berlin, Sports Editor
• Rob Hughes, Sports Reporter
• Huw Richards, Sports Reporter
Frequency:
6 time(s) per week

IOLA REGISTER
302 SOUTH WASHINGTON STREET
IOLA, KS 66749-3255
620-365-2111
800-365-1901
Fax: 620-365-6289
editorial@iolaregister.com
http://www.iolaregister.com
• Mark Hastings, Advertising Manager
registerdisplay@gmail.com
• Jocelyn Sheets, Sports Editor
sports@iolaregister.com
Frequency:
6 time(s) per week

IOWA CITY GAZETTE
201 SOUTH CLINTON STREET SUITE 200
IOWA CITY, IA 52240
319-339-3155
Fax: 319-354-1266
http://www.gazetteonline.com
• Steve Gravelle, Sports Editor
(319) 338-5819
Frequency:
7 time(s) per week

IOWA CITY PRESS-CITIZEN
P.O. BOX 2480
IOWA CITY, IA 52245
319-337-3181
Fax: 319-834-1083
newsroom@press-citizen.com
http://www.press-citizen.com
• Susan Harman, Sports Reporter
(319) 337-3181
sharman@press-citizen.com
• Andy Hamilton, Sports Writer
(319) 337-3181
Frequency:
7 time(s) per week

IRONTON TRIBUNE
2903 SOUTH 5TH STREET
IRONTON, OH 45638-2866
740-532-1441
Fax: 740-532-1506
publisher@irontontribune.com
http://www.irontontribune.com
• Jim Walker, Sports Editor
jim.walker@irontontribune.com
Frequency:
6 time(s) per week

ISLAND PACKET
10 BUCK ISLAND ROAD
BLUFFTON, SC 29910
843-706-8100
877-706-8100
Fax: 843-706-3070
newsroom@islandpacket.com
http://www.islandpacket.com
• Sandra Gillis, Advertising Director
(843) 706-8160
sgillis@islandpacket.com
• Justin Jarrett, Sports Editor
(843) 706-8120
Frequency:
7 time(s) per week

ITEM
P.O. BOX 1677
SUMTER, SC 29150
803-774-1226
Fax: 803-774-1210
http://www.theitem.com
• Dennis Brunson, Sports Editor
(803) 774-1241
dennisb@theitem.com
• Jack Osteen, Advertising Director
(803) 774-1238
jack@theitem.com
• Bobby Touchberry, Classified Manager
(803) 774-1252
bobbyt@item.com
• Justin Driggers, Sports Writer
(803) 774-1235
jdriggers@theitem.com
Frequency:
7 time(s) per week

ITHACA JOURNAL
123 WEST STATE STREET
ITHACA, NY 14850-5427
607-272-2321
800-328-2860
Fax: 607-272-4335
ithjournal@clarityconnect.com
http://www.theithacajournal.com
• Carol Becker, Advertising Director
• Chris Feaver, Sports Editor
(607) 274-9214
cfeaver@ithaca.gannett.com
Frequency:
6 time(s) per week

JACKSON CITIZEN PATRIOT
214 SOUTH JACKSON STREET
JACKSON, MI 49201-2282
517-789-1250
800-878-6397
Fax: 517-787-9711
sports@citpat.com
www.mlive.com
• Jeff Bleiler, Night Editor
(517) 768-4984
• Mike Pryson, Sports Reporter
(517) 768-4963

• Gary Kalahar, Sports Reporter
(517) 768-4966
Description:
Newspaper

JACKSON COUNTY FLORIDAN
4403 CONSTITUTION LANE
MARIANNA, FL 32448
850-526-3614
Fax: 850-482-4478
editorial@jcfloridan.com
http://www.jcfloridan.com
• Valeria Roberts, Advertising Manager
(850) 526-3614
vroberts@jcfloridan.com
• Amy Fuller, Sports Editor
(850) 526-3614
Frequency:
5 time(s) per week

JACKSON SUN
245 WEST LAFAYETTE AVENUE
JACKSON, TN 38301-6126
731-427-3333
800-372-3922
Fax: 731-425-9604
contactus@jacksonsun.com
http://www.jacksonsun.com
• Brandon Shields, Sports Editor
(731) 425-9751
bjshields@jacksntn.gannett.com
Frequency:
7 time(s) per week

JACKSONVILLE DAILY PROGRESS
525 EAST COMMERCE STREET
JACKSONVILLE, TX 75766-4909
903-586-2236
Fax: 903-586-0987
http://www.jacksonvilleprogress.com
• Jay Neal, Sports Editor
sports@jacksonvilleprogress.com
• Toni Johnson, Advertising Director
addirector@jacksonvilleprogress.com
Frequency:
6 time(s) per week

JACKSONVILLE FREE PRESS
903 EDGEWOOD AVENUE WEST
JACKSONVILLE, FL 32208-3279
904-634-1993
Fax: 904-765-8611
jfreepress@aol.com
http://www.jacksonvillefreepress.com
• Charles Griggs, Sports Editor
(904) 634-1993
jfreepress@aol.com
Frequency:
1 time(s) per week

JACKSONVILLE JOURNAL-COURIER
235 WEST STATE STREET
JACKSONVILLE, IL 62651-1048
217-245-6121
Fax: 217-245-1226
http://www.myjournalcourier.com
• Tom Linstromberg, Advertising Manager
• Dennis Mathes, Sports Editor
(217) 245-6121
dennis_mathes@journal-courier.net
• Jeanne Strubbe, Classified Manager
(217) 245-6121
Frequency:
7 time(s) per week

JACKSONVILLE PATRIOT
PO BOX 5329
CABOT, AR 72023-1058
501-982-6506
Fax: 501-370-8391
http://www.jacksonvillepatriot.com/
• Susie Magie, Advertising Manager
• Jeff Reed, Sports Editor
(501) 370-8317
Frequency:
4 time(s) per week

JANESVILLE GAZETTE
P.O. BOX 5001
JANESVILLE, WI 53545-3928
608-754-3311
Fax: 608-755-8349
newsroom@gazetteextra.com
http://www.gazeteextra.com
• Dave Wedeward, Sports Editor
(608) 755-8249
dwedeward@gazetteextra.com
• Dan White, Advertising Vice President
(608) 755-8216
dwhite@gazetteextra.com
• John Barry, Sports Writer
(608) 755-8247
jbarry@gazetteextra.com
Frequency:
7 time(s) per week

JEFFERSON COUNTY JOURNAL
1405 NORTH TRUMAN
FESTUS, MO 63028
636-931-6636
800-931-6636
Fax: 636-931-2638
http://www.yourjournal.com
• Dennis Barnidge, Sports Editor
Frequency:
2 time(s) per week

JERSEY JOURNAL
30 JOURNAL SQUARE
JERSEY CITY, NJ 07306
201-653-1000
Fax: 201-653-2243
jjletters@jjournal.com
http://www.nj.com/jjournal/
• Ron Zeitlinger, Deputy Managing Editor
(201) 217-2429
rzeitlinger@jjournal.com
Frequency:
6 time(s) per week

JOHNSON CITY PRESS
P.O. BOX 1717
JOHNSON CITY, TN 37604-6212
423-929-3111
Fax: 423-929-7484
newsroom@johnsoncitypress.com
http://www.johnsoncitypress.com
• Robbie Carson, Classified Manager
• Tom Harris, Advertising Manager
(423) 929-3111
• Kelly Hodge, Managing Sports Editor
(423) 929-3111
• Joe Avento, Sports Reporter
(423) 929-3111
javento@johnsoncitypress.com
Frequency:
7 time(s) per week

JONESBORO SUN
PO BOX 1249
JONESBORO, AR 72401-3128

870-935-5525
800-237-5341
Fax: 870-935-5823
newsroom@jonesborosun.com
http://www.jonesborosun.com
• Kevin Turbeville, Sports Editor
(870) 935-5525
kturbeville@jonesborosun.com
Frequency:
7 time(s) per week

JOPLIN GLOBE
117 EAST 4TH STREET
JOPLIN, MO 64802
417-623-3480
800-444-8514
Fax: 417-623-8450
http://www.joplinglobe.com
• Jim Henry, Sports Editor
(417) 627-7268
jhenry@joplinglobe.com
Frequency:
7 time(s) per week

JOURNAL
13650 11 MILE ROAD
WARREN, MI 48089-1422
586-756-8800
Fax: 586-498-9627
http://www.candgnews.com
• Susan Shanley, Sports Editor
(586) 498-8000
sshanley@candgnews.com

JOURNAL AND COURIER
217 NORTH 6TH STREET
LAFAYETTE, IN 47901-1420
765-423-5511
800-407-5813
Fax: 765-742-5633
editor@journalandcourier.com
http://www.jconline.com
• Jim Holm, Advertising Manager
(765) 423-5511
• Jim Stafford, Sports Editor
(765) 420-5235
jstafford@journalandcourier.com
Frequency:
7 time(s) per week

JOURNAL GAZETTE
600 W MAIN STREET
FORT WAYNE, IN 46802
260-461-8333
Fax: 260-461-8648
jgnews@jg.net
www.journalgazette.net
• Justin Cohn, Sports Reporter
(260) 461-8333
jgnews@jg.net
• Mark Jaworski, Sports Editor
(260) 461-8260
mjaworski@jg.net
• Michael Rothstein, Sports Writer
(260) 461-8223
Frequency:
Daily - 7 time(s) per week

JOURNAL INQUIRER
P.O. BOX 510
MANCHESTER, CT 06040
860-646-0500
800-237-3606
Fax: 860-646-9867
cpowell@journalinquirer.com
http://www.journalinquirer.com

• Brian Coyne, Sports Editor
(860) 646-0500
bcoyne@journalinquirer.com
• Bill Cybert, Advertising Manager
• Phil Chardis, Sports Reporter
(860) 646-0500
Frequency:
6 time(s) per week

JOURNAL NEWS
1 GANNETT DRIVE
WHITE PLAINS, NY 10604-3402
914-694-9300
Fax: 914-696-8396
letters@lohud.com
http://www.lohud.com/
• Sean Mayer, Sports Editor
(914) 696-8527
Frequency:
7 time(s) per week

JOURNAL STAR
1 NEWS PLAZA
PEORIA, IL 61643
309-686-3000
800-225-5757
Fax: 309-686-3296
news@pjstar.com
http://www.pjstar.com
• Joe Bates, Sports Reporter
(309) 686-3000
• Scott Blicharz, Sports Editor
(309) 686-3211
• Dave Eminian, Sports Reporter
(309) 686-3206
deminian@pjstar.com
• Jeff Lampe, Sports Reporter
(309) 686-3212
• Andy Latora, Sports Copy Editor
(309) 686-3215
alatora@pjstar.com
• Bill Liesse, Sports Editor
(309) 686-3213
• Jane Miller, Sports Reporter
(309) 686-3207
• Ryan Ori, Sports Reporter
(309) 686-3208
• Dave Reynolds, Sports Reporter
(309) 686-3210
dreynolds@pjstar.com
• Nick Vlahos, Sports Copy Editor
(309) 686-3203
nvlahos@pjstar.com
• Kirk Wessler, Executive Sports Editor
(309) 686-3216
kwessler@pjstar.com
Frequency:
7 time(s) per week

JOURNAL TIMES
212 4TH STREET
RACINE, WI 53403
262-634-3322
Fax: 262-631-1702
http://www.journaltimesonline.com
• Steve Lovejoy, Editor
(262) 631-1722
• Susan Shemanske, Sports Editor
(262) 631-1708
susan.shemanske@lee.net
• Heidi Ward, Retail Advertising Manager
(262) 631-1742
heidi.ward@lee.net
Frequency:
7 time(s) per week

JOURNAL TRIBUNE
457 ALFRED STREET
BIDDEFORD, ME 04005-9447
207-282-1535
Fax: 207-282-3138
http://www.journaltribune.com
• Al Edwards, Sports Editor
(207) 282-1535
Frequency:
6 time(s) per week
Sports:
New England pro, minor league, York
County High School and York County
non-high school affiliated

JOURNAL-ADVOCATE
504 NORTH 3RD STREET
STERLING, CO 80751
970-522-1990
Fax: 970-522-2320
http://www.journal-advocate.com
• Brent Arnold, Advertising Manager
• Jonathan Seib, Sports Reporter
(970) 526-9285
Frequency:
6 time(s) per week

JOURNAL-REVIEW
119 NORTH GREEN STREET
CRAWFORDSVILLE, IN 47933-1708
765-362-1200
800-488-4414
Fax: 765-364-5424
http://www.journalreview.com
• Jeff Arenz, Sports Editor
(765) 362-1200
• Mark Deacon, Advertising Manager
Frequency:
6 time(s) per week

JOURNAL-WORLD
609 NEW HAMPSHIRE
LAWRENCE, KS 66044-2243
785-843-1000
800-578-8748
Fax: 785-843-4512
news@ljworld.com
http://www.ljworld.com
• Gary Bedore, Sports Assistant Editor
(785) 832-7186
• Chuck Woodling, Sports Editor
(785) 832-7148
Frequency:
7 time(s) per week

JUNEAU EMPIRE
3100 CHANNEL DRIVE
JUNEAU, AK 99801-7814
907-586-3740
888-458-6328
Fax: 907-586-3028
editor@juneauempire.com
http://www.juneauempire.com
• Paul Hay, Vice President of Advertising
(907) 523-2274
pail.hay@juneauempire.com
• Lee Leschper, Advertising Manager
(907) 523-2246
lee.leschper@juneauempire.com
• Matthew Tynan, Sports Reporter
(907) 523-2267
matthew.tynan@juneauempire.com
Frequency:
6 time(s) per week

KALAMAZOO GAZETTE
401 SOUTH BURDICK STREET
KALAMAZOO, MI 49007-5217
269-345-3511
800-466-2472
Fax: 269-388-8447
news@kalamazoogazette.com
http://www.kalamazoogazette.com
• Linda Depta, Advertising Director
(269) 388-8460
• Howard Thomas, Sports Editor
(269) 345-3511
Frequency:
7 time(s) per week

KANE COUNTY CHRONICLE
333 N. RANDALL ROAD
SUITE 2
ST. CHARLES, IL 60174
630-232-9222
Fax: 630-444-1641
kcchronicle@aol.com
http://www.kcchronicle.com
• Terri Landa, Advertising Manager
(630) 845-5236
tlanda@kcchronicle.com
• Jay Schwab, Sports Editor
(630) 232-9222
jschwab@shawsuburban.com
Frequency:
6 time(s) per week

KANSAS CITY KANSAN
P.O. BOX 122800
KANSAS CITY, KS 66112
913-371-4300
Fax: 913-342-8620
http://www.kansascitykansan.com
• Jeremy Banks, Editor
(913) 371-4300
jbanks@kansascitykansan.com
• Ken Yarnevich, Advertising Manager
(913) 371-4300
keny@kansascitykansan.com
Frequency:
5 time(s) per week

KANSAS CITY STAR
1729 GRAND BOULEVARD
KANSAS CITY, MO 64108-1413
816-234-4141
Fax: 816-234-4926
http://www.kcstar.com
• David Boyce, Sports Reporter
(816) 234-4745
• Randy Covitz, Sports Reporter
(816) 234-4796
rcovitz@kcstar.com
• Mike DeArmond, Sports Writer
(816) 234-4355
• Bob Dutton, Sports Reporter
(816) 234-4352
• Mike Fannin, Managing Editor/Sports and
Features
(816) 234-4355
mfannin@kcstar.com
• Jeffrey Flanagan, Sports Reporter
(816) 234-4355
• Tom Ibarra, Sports Assistant Editor
(816) 234-4882
• Blair Kerkhoff, Reporter
(816) 234-4730
bkerkhoff@kcstar.com
• Jason King, Sports Reporter
(816) 234-4141
• Holly Lawton, Deputy Sports Editor
(816) 234-4350

• Bob Luder, Sports Reporter
(816) 234-4877
• Jennifer Mann, Reporter -Advertising,
Marketing, Public
(816) 234-4453
• Sam Mellinger, Sports Writer
(816) 234-4389
smellinger@kcstar.com
• Jim Pedley, Sports Writer
(816) 234-4860
• Joe Posnanski, Sports Columnist
(816) 234-4355
• Howard Richman, Sports Reporter
(816) 234-4701
• Mechelle Voepel, Sports Reporter
(816) 234-4351
• Jason Whitlock, Sports Reporter
(816) 234-4869
• Mark Zeligman, Assistant Sports Editor
(816) 234-4339
Frequency:
7 time(s) per week

KEARNEY HUB
13 EAST 22ND STREET
KEARNEY, NE 68847
308-237-2152
800-950-6113
Fax: 308-233-9736
news@kearneyhub.com
http://www.kearneyhub.com
• Seth Blank, Sports Reporter
(308) 233-9729
seth.blank@kearneyhub.com
• Buck Mahoney, Sports Editor
(308) 233-9750
buck.mahoney@kearneyhub.com
Frequency:
6 time(s) per week

KEENE SENTINEL
60 WEST STREET
KEENE, NH 03431-3373
603-352-1234
Fax: 603-352-0437
news@keenesentinel.com
http://www.sentinelsource.com
• Lorraine Ellis, Classified Manager
lellis@keenesentinel.com
• David Lanier, Sports Editor
(603) 352-1234
Frequency:
7 time(s) per week

KENNEBEC JOURNAL
274 WESTERN AVENUE
AUGUSTA, ME 04330-4976
207-623-3811
800-537-5508
Fax: 207-623-2220
http://www.kjonline.com
• Scott Martin, Sports Editor
(207) 621-5618
smartin@centralmaine.com
• Gary Hawkins, Deputy Sports Editor &
Columnist
(207) 621-5638
ghawkins@centralmain.com
Frequency:
7 time(s) per week

KENOSHA NEWS
5800 7TH AVENUE
KENOSHA, WI 53140
262-657-1800
Fax: 262-657-8455

newsroom@kenoshanews.com
http://www.kenoshacounty.com
• Dave Marran, Sports Editor
(262) 656-6290
dmarran@kenoshanews.com
• Lani Renneau, Advertising Director
(262) 656-6243
Frequency:
7 time(s) per week

KENTON TIMES
201 EAST COLUMBUS STREET
KENTON, OH 43326-1544
419-674-4066
Fax: 419-673-1125
kteditor@kentontimes.com
http://www.kentontimes.com
• Lesa Heacock, Advertising Manager
(419) 674-4066
lheacock@kentontimes.com
• Kendrick Jesionowski, Sports Editor
(419) 674-4066
ktsports@kentontimes.com
Frequency:
6 time(s) per week

KENTUCKY NEW ERA
P.O. BOX 729
HOPKINSVILLE, KY 42240-4430
270-886-4444
877-463-9372
Fax: 270-887-3222
editor@kentuckynewera.com
http://www.kentuckynewera.com
• Joe Wilson, Sports Editor
(270) 887-3230
• Alex Byington, Sports Writer/Columnist
(270) 887-3230
Frequency:
6 time(s) per week

KERRVILLE DAILY TIMES
429 JEFFERSON STREET
KERRVILLE, TX 78028
830-896-7000
800-898-7000
Fax: 830-896-1150
http://www.dailytimes.com
• Joe Harrington, Sports Editor
(830) 257-0318
sports@dailytimes.com
Frequency:
6 time(s) per week

KETCHIKAN DAILY NEWS
501 DOCK STREET
KETCHIKAN, AK 99901
907-225-3157
Fax: 907-225-1096
news@ketchikandailynews.com
http://www.ketchikandailynews.com
• Lyle Goulding, Sports Editor
lyle@ketchikandailynews.com
Frequency:
6 time(s) per week

KING COUNTY JOURNAL
600 WASHINGTON AVENUE SOUTH
KENT, WA 98032-5708
253-872-6600
Fax: 253-854-1006
http://www.kingcountyjournal.com
• Jim Cnockaert, Sports Editor
(253) 872-6678
• Michael Stevens, Advertising Manager
(253) 872-6729

Frequency:
7 time(s) per week

KINGMAN DAILY MINER
3015 STOCKTON HILL ROAD
KINGMAN, AZ 86401 3909
928-753-6397
Fax: 928-753-5661
kingmannewspapers@mcimail.com
http://www.kingmandailyminer.com
• Brent Hinckley, Sports Editor
(928) 753-6397
bhinckley@kingmandailyminer.com
• Colleen Machado, Advertising Manager
(928) 753-6397
jlyman@kingmandailyminer.com
Frequency:
6 time(s) per week

KINGSPORT TIMES-NEWS
701 LYNN GARDEN DRIVE
KINGSPORT, TN 37660
423-246-8121 EXT 323
800-251-0328
Fax: 423-392-1385
retail@timesnews.net
www.timesnews.net
• Andy Barnes, Creative Services Director
• Pat Kenney, Sports Editor
(423) 723-1434
pkenney@timesnews.net
Frequency:
7 time(s) per week

KIRKSVILLE DAILY EXPRESS & NEWS
110 EAST MCPHERSON STREET
KIRKSVILLE, MO 63501-3506
660-665-2808
Fax: 660-665-2608
• Bud Schrader, Sports Reporter
dailyexpress_sports@yahoo.com
• George Wriedt, Advertising Manager
kvdaily@sbcglobal.net
Frequency:
6 time(s) per week

KNOXVILLE NEWS-SENTINEL
2332 NEWS SENTINEL DR
KNOXVILLE, TN 37921-5766
865-523-3131
800-237-5821
Fax: 865-342-6400
gvpolitics@hotmail.com
www.knoxnews.com
• John Adams, Sports Editor
Frequency:
7 time(s) per week

KOKOMO TRIBUNE
300 NORTH UNION STREET
KOKOMO, IN 46901-4612
765-454-8584
800-382-0696
Fax: 765-456-3815
ktnews@kokomotribune.com
http://www.komotribune.com
• Bryan Gaskins, Sports Editor
(765) 459-3121
bryan.gaskins@kokomotribune.com
Frequency:
7 time(s) per week

KOREAN CENTRAL DAILY
690 WILSHIRE PLACE
LOS ANGELES, CA 90005-3980

213-368-2500
Fax: 213-389-6196
http://www.koreadaily.com
• Ja G Ku, Sports Editor
• Thomas Yang, Sports Editor
(213) 368-2696
Frequency:
6 time(s) per week

LA CROSSE TRIBUNE
401 3RD ST N
LA CROSSE, WI 54601-3281
608-782-9710
800-262-0420
Fax: 608-782-9723
news@lacrossetribune.com
http://www.lacrossetribune.com
• Joel Badzinski, Sports Reporter
(608) 791-8402
• Jeff Brown, Sports Editor
(608) 791-8202
jbrown@lacrossetribune.com
• Jared Heintz, Assistant Sports Editor
(608) 791-8877
Frequency:
7 time(s) per week

LA GRANGE DAILY NEWS
105 ASHTON STREET
LAGRANGE, GA 30241-3111
706-884-7311
Fax: 706-884-8712
http://www.lagrangenews.com
• Kevin Eckleberry, Sports Editor
(706) 884-7311
keckleberry@lagrangenews.com
• Karen Brown, Advertising Director
(706) 884-7311
kbrown@heartlandpublications.com
• Natalie Trout, Sports Writer
ntrout@lagrangenews.com
Frequency:
7 time(s) per week

LA OFERTA NEWSPAPER
1376 NORTH 4TH STREET
SAN JOSE, CA 95112-4713
408-436-7850
Fax: 408-436-7861
http://www.laoferta.com
• Patty Canz, Sports Writer
• Frank Andrade, Publisher
Frequency:
1 time(s) per week
Circulation:
20,000
Description:
Tab size newspaper whose primary
audience is the spanish citizens.

LA OPINION
P.O. BOX 15093
LOS ANGELES, CA 90013-1000
213-622-8332
Fax: 213-896-2171
editorial@laopinion.com
http://www.laopinion.com
• Rafael Ramos, Sports Editor
(213) 622-8332
Frequency:
7 time(s) per week

LA PORTE HERALD-ARGUS
701 STATE STREET
LA PORTE, IN 46350-3328

media

219-362-2161
Fax: 219-362-2166
http://www.heraldargus.com
• Adam Parkhouse, Sports Editor
(219) 362-3869
sports@heraldargus.com
• Donna Maglio, Advertising Manager
(219) 326-3881
breisig@heraldargus.com
Frequency:
6 time(s) per week

LA PRENSA DE SAN ANTONIO
318 SOUTH FLORES STREET
SAN ANTONIO, TX 78204-1106
210-242-7900
Fax: 210-242-7901
http://www.laprensa.com
• Jose Franco, Sports Editor
(210) 242-7900
ads@laprensa.com
Frequency:
2 time(s) per week

LA PRENSA SAN DIEGO
651 3RD AVENUE, SUITE C
CHULA VISTA, CA 91910
619-425-7400
Fax: 619-336-0372
http://www.laprensa-sandiego.org
• Daniel Munoz, Editor
• Paco Zavala, Sports Writer
• Fred Sidhu, Sports Editor
Frequency:
1 time(s) per week

LA TRIBUNA DE NORTH JERSEY
300 36TH STREET
UNION CITY, NJ 07087-4724
201-617-1360
Fax: 201-617-0042
rumolenaar@aol.com
http://www.latribuna.com
• Pablo Laserna, Sports Editor
Frequency:
2 time(s) per month

LAKE CHARLES AMERICAN PRESS
4900 HWY 90 E.
LAKE CHARLES, LA 70615
337-433-3000
Fax: 337-494-4070
news@americanpress.com
www.americanpress.com
• Scooter Hobbs, Sports Editor
(337) 494-4069
shobbs@americanpress.com
• Brett Downer, Editor

LAKE CITY REPORTER
P.O. BOX 1709
LAKE CITY, FL 32056-1709
386-752-1297
Fax: 386-752-9400
news@lakecityreporter.com
http://www.lakecityreporter.com
• Tim Kirby, Sports Editor
(386) 754-0421
tkirby@lakecityreporter.com
Frequency:
6 time(s) per week

LAKE COUNTY RECORD-BEE
2150 SOUTH MAIN
LAKEPORT, CA 95453-5620

707-263-5636
Fax: 707-263-0600
http://www.record-bee.com
• Brian Sumpter, Sports Editor
(707) 263-5636
RBSports@aol.com
Frequency:
5 time(s) per week

LAMAR DAILY NEWS
310 SOUTH 5TH STREET
LAMAR, CO 81052-2712
719-336-2266
Fax: 719-336-2526
editor@lamardaily.com
http://www.lamardaily.com
• John Contreras, Editor
Frequency:
2 time(s) per week
Circulation:
2,800
Sports:
Area High School, Some National - AP

LANCASTER EAGLE-GAZETTE
P.O. BOX 848
LANCASTER, OH 43130-4308
740-654-1321
Fax: 740-681-4456
lancaster@nncogannett.com
http://www.lancastereaglegazette.com/
• Joe Arnold, Sports Editor
(740) 681-4358
jarnold@nncogannett.com
Frequency:
7 time(s) per week

LANCASTER NEW ERA
8 WEST KING STREET
LANCASTER, PA 17608-3824
717-291-8733
800-809-4666
Fax: 717-399-6506
neweranews@lnpnews.com
http://www.lancasteronline.com
• Dennis Fisher, Sports Editor
(717) 291-8779
dfisher@lnpnews.com
• Jeffrey Reinhart, Sports Writer
(717) 291-8778
jreinhart@lnpnews.com
• Keith Schweigert, Sports Writer
(717) 291-8777
kschweigert@lnpnews.com
• Harold Zeigler, Sports Writer
(717) 291-8778
hzeigler@lnpnews.com
Frequency:
6 time(s) per week

LANSING STATE JOURNAL
120 EAST LENAWEE STREET
LANSING, MI 48919
517-702-4257
Fax: 517-377-1298
http://www.lansingstatejournal.com
• Mark Meyer, Sports Editor
(517) 377-1073
• Barry Kiel, Sports Assistant Editor
(517) 267-1393
bkiel@lsj.com
• Neil Koepke, Sports Reporter
(517) 377-1070
Frequency:
7 time(s) per week

LARAMIE DAILY BOOMERANG
320 EAST GRAND AVENUE
LARAMIE, WY 82070-3712
307-742-2176
Fax: 307-742-2046
http://www.laramieboomerang.com
• Robert Hammond, Sports Editor
(307) 742-2176
• Matt Petrie, Advertising Manager
Frequency:
6 time(s) per week

LAREDO MORNING TIMES
111 ESPERANZA DRIVE
LAREDO, TX 78041
956-728-2500
Fax: 956-723-1227
http://www.lmtonline.com
• Dennis Silva, Sports Editor
(956) 728-2579
• Salo Otero, Assistant Sports Editor
(956) 728-2578
• Kenny Ryan, Sports Reporter
(956) 728-2576
Frequency:
7 time(s) per week

LAS CRUCES SUN-NEWS
256 WEST LAS CRUCES AVENUE
LAS CRUCES, NM 88005
505-541-5400
800-745-5851
Fax: 505-541-5499
http://www.lcsun-news.com
• Teddy Feinberg, Sports Editor
(505) 541-5455
tfeinberg@lcsun-news.com
• Heidi Melendrez, Advertising Director
Frequency:
7 time(s) per week

LAS VEGAS DAILY OPTIC
614 LINCOLN AVENUE
LAS VEGAS, NM 87701
505-425-6796
800-767-6796
Fax: 505-425-1005
composing@lasvegasoptic.com
http://www.lasvegasoptic.com
• Sherry An Clancy, Advertising Manager
adv@lasvegasoptic.com
• Dave Wesner, Sports Editor
dwesner@lasvegasoptic.com
Frequency:
5 time(s) per week

LAS VEGAS REVIEW-JOURNAL
1111 WEST BONANZA ROAD
LAS VEGAS, NV 89106
702-383-0211
Fax: 702-383-4676
letters@reviewjournal.com
http://www.reviewjournal.com
• Mark Anderson, Sports Reporter
(702) 387-2914
manderson@reviewjournal.com
• Steve Carp, Reporter
(702) 387-2913
SCarp@reviewjournal.com
• Jim Fossum, Sports Editor
(702) 383-4618
• Karen Grover, National Advertising
Manager
• Joe Hawk, Sports Editor
(702) 387-2912
jhawk@reviewjournal.com
• Kevin Iole, Sports Reporter

(702) 387-2916
• Allen Leiker, Sports Assistant Editor
(702) 383-0297
ALeiker@reviewjournal.com
• Damon Seiters, Sports Editor (High School)
(702) 380-4587
DSeiters@reviewjournal.com
• Jeff Wolf, Sports Reporter & Columnist
(702) 383-0247
• Steve Addy, Sports Copy Editor
(702) 383-0442
SAddy@reviewjournal.com
Frequency:
7 time(s) per week

LAS VEGAS SUN
2275 CORPORATE CIRCLE DRIVE SUITE 300
HENDERSON, NV 89074
702-385-3111
Fax: 702-383-7264
http://www.lasvegassun.com
• Adam Candee, Sports Reporter
(702) 259-2312
candee@lasvegassun.com
• Steve Guiremand, Sports Reporter
steveg@lasvegassun.com
• Brian Hilderbrand, Motorsports Reporter
(702) 259-4089
bh@lasvegassun.com
• Ron Kantowski, Sports Columnist
(702) 259-4088
ron@lasvegassun.com
• Rob Miech, Sports Reporter
miech@lasvegassun.com
• Jeff Haney, Sports Columnist
(702) 259-4041
jeff.haney@lasvegassun.com
Frequency:
7 time(s) per week

LATINO INTERNATIONAL-ORLANDO
672 NORTH SEMORAN BOULEVARD SUITE 304
ORLANDO, FL 32807
407-381-9119
Fax: 407-381-3197
latinointl@aol.com
http://www.latinointlnews.com
• Zulay Perez, Sports Editor
Frequency:
1 time(s) per week

LATROBE BULLETIN
P.O. BOX 111
LATROBE, PA 15650-1921
724-537-3351
Fax: 724-537-0489
lb.news@verizon.net
• Randy Skubek, Sports Editor
Frequency:
6 time(s) per week

LAUREL LEADER-CALL
130 BEACON STREET
LAUREL, MS 39440
601-428-0551
Fax: 601-426-3550
editor@laurelleadercall.com
http://www.leadercall.com
• Randy Hammons, Sports Editor
(601) 428-0551
sports@laurelleadercall.com
• John Blackledge, Sports Reporter
(601) 428-0551
llcsportswriter@gmail.com

Frequency:
7 time(s) per week

LAWTON CONSTITUTION
102 SOUTHWEST 3RD STREET
LAWTON, OK 73502-4031
580-353-0620
Fax: 580-585-5103
http://www.swoknews.com
• Jim Garrett, Advertising Manager
(580) 585-5107
• Joey Goodman, Sports Editor
(580) 585-5124
Frequency:
7 time(s) per week

LE MARS DAILY SENTINEL
41 1ST AVENUE, N.E.
LE MARS, IA 51031-0930
712-546-7031
Fax: 712-546-7035
http://www.lemarssentinel.com
• Jesse Geleynse, Sports Editor
(712) 546-7031
• Monte Jost, Advertising Manager
(712) 546-7031
Frequency:
5 time(s) per week

LEADER
34 WEST PULTENEY STREET
CORNING, NY 14830-2211
607-936-4651
Fax: 607-936-9939
http://www.the-leader.com
• Kurt Bartenstein, Advertising Manager
(607) 936-4651
• Shawn Vargo, Sports Editor
(607) 936-4651
svargo@the-leader.com
Frequency:
7 time(s) per week

LEADER-TELEGRAM
701 S. FARWELL ST
EAU CLAIRE, WI 54701
715-833-9200
800-236-8808
Fax: 715-833-9244
• Joe Ziemer, Sports Reporter
(715) 833-9212
• John Casper, Sports Editor
(715) 833-9212

LEADER-TIMES
115-121 NORTH GRANT AVENUE
KITTANNING, PA 16201-1401
724-543-1303
Fax: 724-545-6768
• Gavin Jenkins, Sports Editor
(724) 543-1303
gjenkins@tribweb.com
• Kathy Master, Advertising Coordinator
(724) 543-1303
kmaster@tribweb.com
Frequency:
6 time(s) per week

LEAF-CHRONICLE
P.O. BOX 31029
CLARKSVILLE, TN 37040
931-552-1808
Fax: 931-648-8001
news@theleafchronicle.com
http://www.theleafchronicle.com

• Robb Scott, Advertising Manager
(931) 552-1808
• Jimmy Trodglen, Sports Editor
(931) 245-0261
jimmytrodglen@theleafchronicle.com
• George Robinson, Sports Reporter
(931) 245-6747
georgerobinson@theleafchronicle.com
Frequency:
7 time(s) per week

LEAVENWORTH TIMES
422 SENECA STREET
LEAVENWORTH, KS 66048-1910
913-682-0305
Fax: 913-682-1114
http://www.leavenworthtimes.com
• Sara Mettlen, Sports Editor
Frequency:
6 time(s) per week

LEBANON DEMOCRAT
402 NORTH CUMBERLAND STREET
LEBANON, TN 37087-2306
615-444-3952
Fax: 615-444-1358
http://www.lebanondemocrat.com
• Andy Reed, Sports Editor
(615) 444-3952
andy.reed@lebanondemocrat.com
Frequency:
5 time(s) per week

LEDGER
P.O. BOX 408
LAKELAND, FL 33802
863-802-7000
Fax: 863-802-7810
features@theledger.com
http://www.theledger.com
• Ray Beasock, Sports Copy Editor
(863) 802-7537
ray.beasock@theledger.com
• Lisa Coffey, Sports Reporter
(863) 401-6971
• Del Milligan, Outdoors Editor
(863) 802-7555
del.milligan@theledger.com
Frequency:
7 time(s) per week

LEDGER INDEPENDENT
P.O. BOX 518
MAYSVILLE, KY 41056-1101
606-564-9091
800-264-9091
Fax: 606-564-6893
http://www.maysville-online.com
• Patty Moore, Advertising Manager
patty.moore@lee.net
• Chuck Hamilton, Sports Editor
(606) 564-9091
Frequency:
6 time(s) per week

LEWISTON MORNING TRIBUNE
505 CAPITAL STREET
LEWISTON, ID 83501-1843
208-743-9411
800-745-9411
Fax: 208-746-7341
city@lmtribune.com
http://www.lmtribune.com
• Matt Baney, Sports Editor
mbaney@lmtribune.com

• Dana Strong, Sports Writer
dstrong@lmtribune.com
Frequency:
7 time(s) per week

LEXINGTON HERALD-LEADER
100 MIDLAND AVENUE
LEXINGTON, KY 40508-1943
859-231-3200
800-274-7355
Fax: (85- 231-3332
hleditorial@herald-leader.com
http://www.kentucky.com
• Gene Abell, Sports Editor
(859) 231-3237
gabell@herald-leader.com
• John Clay, Sports Columnist
(859) 231-3226
jclay@herald-leader.com
• Chip Cosby, Sports Reporter
(859) 231-3440
• Mike Fields, High School Sports Reporter
(859) 231-3337
• Mat Graf, Assistant Sports Editor
(859) 231-3529
mgraf@herald-leader.com
• Rob Kandt, News Editor
(859) 231-3513
• Mark Maloney, Sports Reporter
(859) 231-3229
• Mark Story, Sports Columnist
(859) 231-3230
mstory@herald-leader.com
• Jerry Tipton, Sports Reporter
(859) 231-3227
jtipton@herald-leader.com
Frequency:
7 time(s) per week

LINCOLN COURIER
P.O. BOX 740
LINCOLN, IL 62656-2825
217-732-2101
800-747-5462
Fax: 217-732-7039
courier@lincolncourier.com
http://www.lincolncourier.com
• Dylan Polk, Sports Editor
(217) 732-2101
Frequency:
6 time(s) per week

LINCOLN JOURNAL STAR
926 P STREET
LINCOLN, NE 68508
402-475-4200
800-742-7315
Fax: 402-473-7291
newsroom@journalstar.com
http://www.journalstar.com
• Ken Hambleton, Sports Reporter
(402) 473-7331
khambleton@journalstar.com
• John Mabry, Sports Editor
(402) 473-7331
sports@journalstar.com
• Curt McKeever, Sports Columnist
(402) 473-7431
Frequency:
7 time(s) per week

LINTON DAILY CITIZEN
79 SOUTH MAIN STREET
LINTON, IN 47441-1818
812-847-4487
Fax: 812-847-9513
http://www.dailycitizen.com

• BJ Hargis, Sports Editor
(812) 847-4487
hargisbj@gmail.com
Frequency:
6 time(s) per week

LIVINGSTON COUNTY DAILY PRESS & ARGUS
323 EAST GRAND RIVER
HOWELL, MI 48843
517-548-2000
Fax: 517-548-3005
http://www.hometownlife.com
• Tim Robinson, Sports Editor
(517) 552-2863
Frequency:
7 time(s) per week

LOCKPORT UNION-SUN & JOURNAL
170 EAST AVENUE
LOCKPORT, NY 14094
716-439-9222
Fax: 716-439-9239
http://www.lockportjournal.com
• Diane Crowe, Advertising Manager
(716) 439-9222
• John D'Onofrio, Sports Editor
Frequency:
7 time(s) per week

LODI NEWS-SENTINEL
125 NORTH CHURCH STREET
LODI, CA 95240-2102
209-369-7035
Fax: 209-369-6706
news@lodinews.com
http://www.lodinews.com
• Kimberly Anger, Advertising Director
(209) 369-2761
• Scott Howell, Sports Editor
(209) 369-7035
scotth@lodinews.com
• Joelle Milholm, Sports Reporter
Frequency:
6 time(s) per week

LOG CABIN DEMOCRAT
1058 FRONT STREET
CONWAY, AR 72032-4356
501-327-6621
800-678-4523
Fax: 501-327-6787
http://www.thecabin.net
• Fran Plymale, Classified Manager
(501) 505-1242
fran.plymale@thecabin.net
• Mark Burke, Sports Editor
(501) 505-1237
mark.burke@thecabin.net
• Rhonda Overbey, Advertising Manager
rhonda.overbey@thecabin.net
Frequency:
6 time(s) per week

LOGAN BANNER
PO BOX 720
LOGAN, WV 25601
304-752-6950
Fax: 304-752-1239
http://www.loganbanner.com
• Paul Adkins, Sports Editor
(304) 752-6950
padkins@loganbanner.com
• Kathy Chafin, Advertising Manager
(304) 752-6950
kchafin@loganbanner.com

• Dottie Hatfield, Classified Manager
lbclassifieds@loganbanner.com
Frequency:
6 time(s) per week

LOGAN DAILY NEWS
72 EAST MAIN STREET
LOGAN, OH 43138-1221
740-385-2107
Fax: 740-385-4514
info@logandaily.com
www.logandaily.com
• Craig Dunn, Sports Editor
• James Shine, Publisher
(740) 385-2107
publisher@logandaily.com
Frequency:
5 time(s) per week

LONGMONT DAILY TIMES-CALL
350 TERRY STREET
LONGMONT, CO 80501
303-776-2244
800-796-8201
Fax: 303-678-8615
opinion@times-call.com
http://www.longmontfyi.com
• Penny Dille, Advertising Director
(303) 776-2244
• Karen Lambert, Classified Manager
(303) 635-3603
klambert@times-call.com
• Brian Howell, Sports Editor
(303) 684-5298
Frequency:
7 time(s) per week

LONGVIEW NEWS-JOURNAL
P.O. BOX 1792
LONGVIEW, TX 75601-7323
903-757-3311
Fax: 903-757-3742
info@news-journal.com
http://www.news-journal.com
• Gabriel Brooks, Sports Reporter
(903) 237-7745
gbrooks@news-journal.com
• Jack Stallard, Sports Editor
(903) 237-7760
jstallard@news-journal.com
Frequency:
7 time(s) per week

LOS ALAMOS MONITOR
256 D.P. ROAD
LOS ALAMOS, NM 87544
505-662-4185
Fax: 505-662-4334
lamonitor@lamonitor.com
http://www.lamonitor.com
• Matt Hietala, Sports Editor
(505) 662-4185
lasports@lamonitor.com
Frequency:
5 time(s) per week

LOS ANGELES SENTINEL
3800 CRENSHAW BOULEVARD
LOS ANGELES, CA 90008-1813
323-299-3800
Fax: 323-299-3896
sentinelrd@aol.com
http://www.losangelessentinel.com/index.html
• Frank Reneau, Sports Editor
(323) 299-3800

Frequency:
1 time(s) per week

LOS ANGELES TIMES
202 WEST 1ST STREET
LOS ANGELES, CA 90012-4105
213-237-5000
800-528-4637
Fax: 213-237-4712
www.latimes.com
• J.A. Adande, Sports Columnist
(213) 237-7145
j.a.adande@latimes.com
• Dan Arritt, High School Sports Staff Writer
(213) 237-6471
dan.arritt@latimes.com
• Athan Atsales, Assistant Sports Editor
(213) 237-3615
athan.atsales@latimes.com
• Ben Bolch, College Sports Staff Writer
(213) 237-6479
ben.bolch@latimes.com
• Thomas Bonk, Sports Reporter
(213) 237-7145
thomas.bonk@latimes.com
• Mike Bresnahan, Professional Basketball
Staff Writer
(213) 237-6482
mike.bresnahan@latimes.com
• Tim Brown, Sports Reporter (Baseball)
tim.brown@latimes.com
• Todd Brownrout, Advertising Senior VP
• Bill Christine, Sports Writer (Horse Racing)
(310) 376-9989
bill.christine@latimes.com
• John Cherwa, Deputy Editor
(213) 237-7617
john.cherwa@latimes.com
• Jerry Crowe, Sports Reporter (Clippers)
(213) 237-3653
 jerry.crowe@latimes.com
• Mike DiGiovanna, Sports Reporter
(Baseball)
mike.digiovanna@latimes.com
• Lisa Dillman, Sports Reporter (Tennis)
(213) 237-7145
lisa.dillman@latimes.com
• Chris Dufresne, Sports Reporter
(213) 237-7145
chris.dufresne@latimes.com
• Bill Dwyre, Executive Sports Editor
(213) 237-3569
bill.dwyre@latimes.com
• Helene Elliott, Sports Columnist
(213) 237-2508
helene.elliott@latimes.com
• Sam Farmer, Sports Reporter (National)
(213) 237-7145
sam.farmer@latimes.com
• Chris Foster, Sports Reporter (Kings)
(213) 237-7145
chris.foster@latimes.com
• Shav Glick, Sports Writer (Motor Sports)
shav.glick@latimes.com
• Paul Gutierrez, Sports Writer (Soccer)
paul.gutierrez@latimes.com
• Mark Heisler, Sports Reporter (Basketball)
(213) 237-7145
mark.heisler@latimes.com
• Martin Henderson, Sports Writer
martin.henderson@latimes.com
• Steve Henson, Sports Writer
(213) 237-5000
stephen.hench@latimes.com
• Mike Hiserman, Sports Senior Assistant
Editor
(213) 237-3633
mike.hiserman@latimes.com

• Greg Johnson, (213) 237-5000
Sports Writer
greg.johnson@latimes.com
• Grahame Jones, Sports Reporter (Soccer)
(213) 237-7145
grahame.jones@latimes.com
• Mike Kennedy, Sports Reporter (Local)
mike.kennedy@latimes.com
• Alex Kimball, Assistant Sports Editor
(213) 237-7145
alex.kimball@latimes.com
• Gary Klein, Sports Reporter (USC)
(213) 237-7145
gary.klein@latimes.com
• Mike Kupper, Senior Assistant Sports
Editor
(213) 237-7145
mike.kupper@latimes.com
Frequency:
7 time(s) per week

LOVELAND DAILY REPORTER-HERALD
201 EAST 5TH STREET
LOVELAND, CO 80537-
970-669-5050
Fax: 970-667-1111
news@reporter-herald.com
http://www.lovelandfyi.com
• Mike Brohard, Sports Editor
(970) 635-3633
• Linda Story, Advertising Manager
(970) 635-3614
Frequency:
7 time(s) per week

LUBBOCK AVALANCHE-JOURNAL
710 AVENUE J
LUBBOCK, TX 79401
806-762-8844
800-692-4021
Fax: 806-744-9603
http://www.lubbockonline.com
• Courtney Linehan, Sports Editor
(806) 766-8735
courtney.linehan@lubbockonline.com
• George Watson, Assistant Sports Editor
(806) 766-2166
george.watson@lubbockonline.com

LUDINGTON DAILY NEWS
202 NORTH RATH AVENUE
LUDINGTON, MI 49431-1663
231-845-5181
800-748-0407
Fax: 231-843-4011
ldn@ludingtondailynews.com
http://www.ludingtondailynews.com
• John Walker, Advertising Manager
jwalker@ludingtondailynews.com
• Lloyd Wallace, Sports Editor
(231) 845-5182
lwallace@ludingtondailynews.com
Frequency:
6 time(s) per week

LUSO AMERICANO
66 UNION STREET
NEWARK, NJ 07105
973-344-3200
Fax: 973-344-4201
http://www.lusoamericano.com
• Ilidio Martins, Sports Editor
(973) 344-3200
imartins@lusoamericano.com
Frequency:
2 time(s) per week

MACOMB DAILY
100 MACOMB DAILY DRIVE
MOUNT CLEMENS, MI 48043-5802
586-469-4510
Fax: 586-469-2892
ken.kish@macombdaily.com
http://www.macombdaily.com
• Roger Hages, Retail Advertising Manager
(586) 783-0234
• Bruce MacLeod, Sports Columnist
(586) 783-0358
• George Pohly, Sports Editor
(586) 783-0270
george.pohly@macombdaily.com
Frequency:
7 time(s) per week

MACOMB JOURNAL
203 NORTH RANDOLPH STREET
MACOMB, IL 61455
309-833-2114
800-237-6858
Fax: 309-833-2346
http://www.macombjournal.com
• Shelby Burget, Sports Editor
(309) 833-2345
sports@macombjournal.com
• Lynne Campbell, Advertising Manager
lynne@macombjournal.com
Frequency:
6 time(s) per week

MACON CHRONICLE-HERALD
204 WEST BOURKE STREET
MACON, MO 63552-1504
660-385-3121
Fax: 660-385-3082
http://www.maconch.com
• Chuck Kindle, Advertising Manager
• Jim Brown, Sports Editor
(660) 385-3121
Frequency:
4 time(s) per week

MACON TELEGRAPH
120 BROADWAY
MACON, GA 31201-3444
478-744-4411
800-342-5845
Fax: 478-744-4385
http://www.macontelegraph.com
• Rick Nolte, Sports Editor
(478) 744-4401
rnolte@macontel.com
Frequency:
7 time(s) per week

MADERA TRIBUNE
100 EAST 7TH STREET
MADERA, CA 93638-3742
559-674-2424
Fax: 559-673-6526
cdoud@maderatribune.net
http://www.maderatribune.net
• Paul Stanford, Sports Writer
(559) 674-8134
• Corrie Valdez, Advertising Manager
Frequency:
6 time(s) per week

MADISON COURIER
310 COURIER SQUARE
MADISON, IN 47250
812-265-3641
800-333-2885
Fax: 812-273-6903

news@madisoncourier.com
http://www.madisoncourier.com
• Mark Campbell, Sports Editor
mcampbell@madisoncourier.com
• Curt Jacobs, Advertising Manager
(812) 265-3641
cjacobs@madisoncourier.com
Frequency:
6 time(s) per week

MADISON DAILY LEADER
214 SOUTH EGAN AVENUE
MADISON, SD 57042
605-256-4555
Fax: 605-256-6190
news@madisondailyleader.com
http://www.madisondailyleader.com
• Dan Holsworth, Sports Editor
sports@madisondailyleader.com
• Karen Maxwell, Classified Manager
Frequency:
5 time(s) per week

MADISON INDEPENDENT PRESS
80 SOUTH STREET
NEW PROVIDENCE, NJ 07974
908-464-1025
Fax: 908-464-9085
ipeditors@njnpublishing.com
http://www.nj.com/independentpress/
• Art Polakowski, Sports Editor
Frequency:
1 time(s) per week

MADISON PRESS
55 WEST HIGH STREET
LONDON, OH 43140-1066
740-852-1616
800-282-3838
Fax: 740-852-1620
http://www.madison-press.com
• David Biddle, Sports Editor
publisher@madison-press.com
• Linda Marx, Classified Manager
(740) 852-1616
classads@madison-press.com
Frequency:
5 time(s) per week

MALONE TELEGRAM
469 EAST MAIN STREET
MALONE, NY 12953
518-483-2000
Fax: 518-483-8579
news@mtelegram.com
• Karen Carre, Advertising Manager
(518) 483-2000
ads@mtelegram.com
• Eric Meachen, Sports Editor
(518) 483-2000
sports@mtelegram.com
Frequency:
6 time(s) per week

MALVERN DAILY RECORD
219 LOCUST STREET
MALVERN, AR 72104
501-337-7523
800-582-5794
Fax: 501-337-1226
http://www.malvern-online.com
• Sean Rock, Sports Writer
sports@malvern-online.com
Frequency:
6 time(s) per week

MANASSAS JOURNAL MESSENGER
P.O. BOX 431
MANASSAS, VA 20110
703-368-3101
Fax: 703-368-9017
http://www.manassasjm.com
• Dave Fawcett, Sports Editor
(703) 530-3911
dfawcett@insidenova.com
• Brent Morris, Advertising Director
(703) 530-3930
• Robert Daski, Sports Reporter
(703) 530-3913
rdaski@insidenova.com
Frequency:
7 time(s) per week

MANHATTAN MERCURY
318 NORTH 5TH STREET
MANHATTAN, KS 66502-5910
785-776-2200
Fax: 785-776-8807
news@themercury.com
http://www.themercury.com
• Mark Janssen, Sports Editor
(785) 776-2200
• Steve Stallwitz, Advertising Manager
(785) 776-2200
adv@themercury.com
Frequency:
6 time(s) per week

MANTECA BULLETIN
531 EAST YOSEMITE AVENUE
MANTECA, CA 95336-5806
209-249-3500
Fax: 209-249-3551
news@mantecabulletin.com
http://www.mantecabulletin.com/
• Jonamar Jacinto, Sports Editor
(209) 249-3538
jjacinto@mantecabulletin.com
Frequency:
7 time(s) per week

MARIETTA DAILY JOURNAL
P.O. BOX 449
MARIETTA, GA 30060
770-428-9411
Fax: 770-422-9533
lifestyle@mdjonline.com
http://www.mdjonline.com
• John Bednarowski, Sports Editor
(770) 428-9411
sportseditor@mdjonline.com
Frequency:
7 time(s) per week

MARIETTA TIMES
700 CHANNEL LANE
MARIETTA, OH 45750-2342
740-373-2121
800-531-1215
Fax: 740-376-5475
mariettatimes@ee.net
http://www.mariettatimes.com
• Ron Johnston, Sports Editor
(740) 376-5441
rjohnston@mariettatimes.com
Frequency:
6 time(s) per week

MARIN INDEPENDENT JOURNAL
P.O. BOX 6150
NOVATO, CA 94949-6665

415-883-8600
Fax: 415-382-7209
http://www.marinij.com
• Dave Allen, Sports Editor
(415) 382-7206
dallen@marinij.com
Frequency:
7 time(s) per week

MARSHALL INDEPENDENT
PO BOX 411
MARSHALL, MN 56258-1317
507-537-1551
Fax: 507-537-1557
news@marshallindependent.com
http://www.marshallindependent.com
• Joe Brown, Sports Editor
(507) 537-1551
• Tara Brandl, Advertising Manager
(507) 537-1551
tbrandl@marshallindependent.com
Frequency:
6 time(s) per week

MARSHALL NEWS MESSENGER
P.O. BOX 730
MARSHALL, TX 75670-3475
903-935-7914
Fax: 903-935-6242
http://www.marshallnewsmessenger.com
• Edward Carifo, Sports Editor
(903) 935-7914
ecarifo@coxnews.com
• Deb Green, Advertising Manager
(903) 927-5984
dgreen@marshallnewsmessenger.com
Frequency:
7 time(s) per week

MARSHFIELD NEWS-HERALD
111 WEST 3RD STREET
MARSHFIELD, WI 54449-2811
715-384-3131
Fax: 715-387-4175
http://www.marshfieldnewsherald.com
• Chris Schulte, Sports Editor
cschulte@wdhprint.com
• Tara Marcoux, Advertising Manager
tmarcoux@marshfieldnewsherald.com
Frequency:
7 time(s) per week

MARYLAND GAZETTE
306 CRAIN HIGHWAY SOUTH WEST
GLEN BURNIE, MD 21061
410-766-3700
Fax: 410-280-5953
gazletters@mdgazette.com
http://www.hometownglenburnie.com
• Sean Burns, Sports Editor
(410) 766-3700
sburns@mdgazette.com
Frequency:
2 time(s) per week

MARYLAND INDEPENDENT
7 INDUSTRIAL PARK DRIVE
WALDORF, MD 20602-2700
301-645-9480
Fax: 301-645-2175
http://www.maryland-independent.com
• Jason Jay, Sports Editor
(301) 645-9480
Frequency:
2 time(s) per week

MARYSVILLE JOURNAL-TRIBUNE
207 NORTH MAIN STREET
MARYSVILLE, OH 43040-1161
937-644-9111
Fax: 937-644-9211
http://www.marysvllejt.com
• Tim Miller, Sports Editor
tim@marysvillejt.com
• Marie Woodford, Advertising Manager
(937) 644-9111
mariew@marysvillejt.com
Frequency:
6 time(s) per week

MARYVILLE DAILY FORUM
111 EAST JENKINS STREET
MARYVILLE, MO 64468-2318
660-562-2424
888-660-2424
Fax: 660-562-2823
newsroom@asde.net
http://www.maryvilledailyforum.com
• Charlie Slenker, Sports Editor
Frequency:
5 time(s) per week

MATTOON JOURNAL GAZETTE
100 BROADWAY
MATTOON, IL 61938-4512
217-235-5656
800-627-0151
Fax: 217-235-1925
editorial@jg-tc.com
http://www.jg-tc.com
• Brian Nielsen, Sports Editor
(217) 238-6856
Frequency:
6 time(s) per week

MAUI NEWS
100 MAHALANI STREET
WAILUKU, HI 96793-2529
808-244-3981
800-827-0347
Fax: 808-242-9087
http://www.mauinews.com
• Dana McBratney, Sports Editor
sports@mauinews.com
• Dawne Miguel-Minford, Advertising
Manager
(808) 242-6319
advmgr@mauinews.com
Frequency:
7 time(s) per week

MCALESTER NEWS-CAPITAL
500 SOUTH 2ND STREET
MCALESTER, OK 74502-5812
918-423-1700
Fax: 918-426-3081
editor@mcalesternews.com
http://www.mcalesternewscapital.com
• Jay Knight, Sports Writer
(918) 421-2025
• Charlotte Klutts, Advertising Manager
(918) 421-2006
Frequency:
6 time(s) per week

MCCOOK DAILY GAZETTE
P.O. BOX 1268
MCCOOK, NE 69001
308-345-4500
Fax: 308-345-7881
regionalnews@mccookgazette.com
http://www.mccookgazette.com

• Karry Coburn, Advertising Manager
(308) 345-4500
• Steve Kodad, Sports Editor
(308) 345-4500
sports@mccookgazette.com
Frequency:
6 time(s) per week

MCCURTAIN DAILY GAZETTE
107 SOUTH CENTRAL AVENUE
IDABEL, OK 74745-4847
580-286-3321
Fax: 580-286-2208
paper@mccurtain.com
http://www.mccurtain.com
• Marge Jones, Advertising Manager
• Brad Reesing, Sports Editor
(580) 286-3321
paper@mccurtain.com
Frequency:
5 time(s) per week

MCDOWELL NEWS
26 NORTH LOGAN STREET
MARION, NC 28752-3944
828-652-3313
Fax: 828-652-4769
news@mcdowellnews.com
http://www.mcdowellnews.com
• Keith Austin, Advertising Manager
(828) 652-3313
maustin@mcdowellnews.com
• Marty Queen, Sports Editor
sports@mcdowellnews.com
Frequency:
5 time(s) per week

MCKINNEY COURIER-GAZETTE
624 KRONA DRIVE
SUITE 170
PLANO, TX 75074
972-398-4200
Fax: 972-398-4470
http://www.courier-gazette.com
• Andrew May, Sports Editor
(972) 398-4246
Frequency:
6 time(s) per week

MCPHERSON SENTINEL
301 SOUTH MAIN STREET
MCPHERSON, KS 67460-4831
620-241-2422
Fax: 620-241-2425
http://www.mcphersonsentinel.com
• Chris Swick, Sports Editor
Frequency:
6 time(s) per week

MEADVILLE TRIBUNE
947 FEDERAL COURT
MEADVILLE, PA 16335-3234
814-724-6370
800-879-0006
Fax: 814-724-8755
tribune@meadvilletribune.com
http://www.meadvilletribune.com
• Dominick Dinardo, Sports Editor
(814) 724-6370
• Lon Wilson, Advertising Director
(814) 724-6370
Frequency:
7 time(s) per week

MEDFORD MAIL TRIBUNE
111 NORTH FIR STREET
MEDFORD, OR 97501-2772
541-776-4411
Fax: 541-776-4376
news@mailtribune.com
http://www.mailtribune.com
• Tim Trower, Sports Editor
(541) 776-4479
ttrower@mailtribune.com
• Dena DeRose, Advertising Manager
(541) 776-4425
dderose@mailtribune.com
Frequency:
7 time(s) per week

MERCED SUN-STAR
P.O. BOX 739
MERCED, CA 95340-2108
209-722-1511
800-310-8080
Fax: 209-385-2460
http://www.mercedsun-star.com
• Samantha Yniguez, Advertising Director
(209) 385-2498
• James Tennapel, Sports Editor
(209) 385-2417
sports@mercedsun-star.com
Frequency:
7 time(s) per week

MERCURY
24 NORTH HANOVER STREET
POTTSTOWN, PA 19464-5410
610-323-3000
Fax: 610-323-0682
mercury@pottsmerc.com
http://www.pottsmerc.com
• Maryann Edlemann, Classified Manager
• Don Seeley, Sports Editor
(610) 323-3000
Frequency:
7 time(s) per week

MERIDIAN STAR
P.O. BOX 1591
MERIDIAN, MS 39301
601-693-1551
800-232-2525
Fax: 601-485-1275
publisher@themeridianstar.com
http://www.meridianstar.com
• Ricky Higginbotham, Sports Editor
(601) 693-1551
Frequency:
7 time(s) per week

MESQUITE NEWS
303 NORTH GALLOWAY STREET
MESQUITE, TX 75149
972-285-6301
Fax: 972-288-9383
http://www.mesquitenews.com
• Devin Hasson, Sports Editor
(972) 285-6301
Frequency:
1 time(s) per week

MESSENGER
PO BOX 659
FORT DODGE, IA 50501
800-622-6613
800-622-6613
Fax: 515-574-4529
editor@frontiernet.net
http://www.messengernews.net

media

• Eric Pratt, Sports Editor
(515) 574-4435
sports@messengernews.net
Frequency:
6 time(s) per week

METRO
30 SOUTH 15TH STREET 9TH FLOOR
PHILADELPHIA, PA 19102
215-717-2600
Fax: 215-717-2626
http://www.metropoint.com
• Christopher Baud, Sports Editor
Frequency:
5 time(s) per week

METROWEST DAILY NEWS
33 NEW YORK AVENUE
FRAMINGHAM, MA 01701-8805
508-626-3800
800-397-5852
Fax: 508-626-3900
metrowest@cnc.com
http://www.metrowestdailynews.com
• Art Davidson, Sports Editor
(508) 626-4403
artd@wickedlocal.com
• Mark Olivieri, Advertising Director
(508) 626-3925
molivier@cnc.com
Frequency:
7 time(s) per week

MEXICO LEDGER
300 NORTH WASHINGTON
MEXICO, MO 65265-2756
573-581-1111
Fax: 573-581-2029
news@mexicoledger.com
http://www.mexicoledger.com
• Jim Stanley, Sports Editor
ledgersports@socket.net
Frequency:
5 time(s) per week
Circulation:
6,125

MIAMI HERALD
1 HERALD PLAZA
MIAMI, FL 33132-1693
305-350-2111
800-437-2535
Fax: 305-376-5287
heralded@miamiherald.com
http://www.herald.com
• Kevin Baxter, Sports Reporter
(305) 376-3655
• Jason Cole, Sports Writer
(305) 376-3675
• Greg Cote, Sports Columnist
(305) 376-3492
gcote@herald.com
• Andre Fernandez, High School Sports
Writer
(305) 350-2111
a1fernandez@miamiherald.com
• Dan Lebatard, Sports Columnist
(305) 376-3498
• Jorge Rojas, Sports Editor
jrojas@miamiherald.com
• Manny Navarro, Sports Writer
(305) 350-2111
mnavarro@miamiherald.com
• David Neal, Sports Reporter (Hockey)
(305) 376-3559
dneal@herald.com
• Santos Perez, Sports Writer

(305) 350-2111
• Mike Phillips, Sports Reporter
(305) 350-2111
• Edwin Pope, Sports Columnist
(305) 376-3483
• Linda Robertson, Sports Columnist
lrobertson@herald.com
• Gorge Rojas, Sports Editor
• Armando Salguero, Sports Reporter
(305) 376-3675
asalguero@miamiherald.com
• Jeff Shain, Sports Writer
(305) 376-3500
• Clark Spencer, Sports Reporter
(305) 376-3603
cspencer@miamiherald.com
• Judy Stapleton, Sports News Assistant
Frequency:
7 time(s) per week

MICHIGAN CHRONICLE
479 LEDYARD STREET
DETROIT, MI 48201
313-963-5522
800-203-2229
Fax: 313-963-8788
chronicle4@aol.com
http://www.michronicleonline.com
• Terry Cabell, Sports Writer
(313) 963-5522
Frequency:
1 time(s) per week

MIDDLEBORO GAZETTE
148 WEST GROVE STREET
MIDDLEBORO, MA 02346-1457
508-947-1760
Fax: 508-947-9426
editor@gazettenewsonline.com
• Jon Haglof, Sports Editor
(508) 947-1760
sports@gazettenewsonline.com
Frequency:
1 time(s) per week

MIDDLESBORO DAILY NEWS
P.O. BOX 579
MIDDLESBORO, KY 40965-1024
606-248-1010
Fax: 606-248-7614
http://www.middlesborodailynews.com
• Patricia Cheek, Advertising Manager
advertising@middlesborodailynews.com
• Jay Compton, Sports Editor
(606) 248-1010
sports@middlesborodailynews.com
Frequency:
6 time(s) per week

MIDDLETOWN JOURNAL
PO BOX 490
MIDDLETOWN, OH 45044-4031
513-705-2525
Fax: 513-423-6940
http://www.middletown.com
• John Bombatch, Sports Writer
(512) 705-2851
jbombatch@coxohio.com
• Jake Trotter, Sports Editor
(513) 705-2837
jtrotter@coxohio.com
Frequency:
7 time(s) per week

MIDDLETOWN PRESS
2 MAIN ST
MIDDLETOWN, CT 06457
860-347-3331
Fax: 860-347-3380
editor@middletown.com
www.middletownpress.com
• Erika Heyer, Assistant Sports Editor
(860) 347-3331
• Robert Briere, Advertising Director
(860) 347-3331

MIDLAND REPORTER-TELEGRAM
201 EAST ILLINOIS AVENUE
MIDLAND, TX 79701-4852
432-682-5311
800-542-3952
Fax: 432-682-3793
http://www.mywesttexas.com
• Chuck Evers, Advertising Director
(432) 682-5311
• Len Hayward, Sports Editor
(432) 682-5311
Frequency:
7 time(s) per week

MILFORD DAILY NEWS
COMMUNITY NEWSPAPER COMPANY
MILFORD, MA 01757-3255
508-473-1111
Fax: 508-634-7514
http://www.milforddailynews.com/
• Art Davidson, Sports Editor
(508) 626-4403
Frequency:
7 time(s) per week

MILWAUKEE JOURNAL SENTINEL
P.O. BOX 661
MILWAUKEE, WI 53203-1309
414-224-2000
800-456-5943
Fax: 414-224-2047
jsbiz@journalsentinel.com
http://www.jsonline.com
• Lori Nickel, Sports Writer
(414) 224-2310
lnickel@journalsentinel.com
• Louisa Rosenau, Sports Assistant Editor
lrosenau@journalsentinel.com
• Tom Silverstein, Sports Reporter
tsilverstein@journalsentinel.com
• Don Walker, Sports Reporter
dwalker@journalsentinel.com
• Bill Windler, Senior Sports Editor
(414) 224-2173
bwindler@journalsentinel.com
• Bob Wolfley, Sports Columnist
(414) 223-5531
bwolfley@journalsentinel.com
• Dennis Black, Assistant Sports Editor
(414) 224-2342
Frequency:
7 time(s) per week

MINDEN PRESS-HERALD
P.O. BOX 1339
MINDEN, LA 71055-3455
318-377-1866
Fax: 318-377-1895
http://www.press-herald.com
• Gregg Parks, Sports Editor
(318) 377-1866
gparks@press-herald.com
Frequency:
5 time(s) per week

MINERAL WELLS INDEX
P.O. BOX 370
MINERAL WELLS, TX 76067-5331
940-325-4465
Fax: 940-325-2020
editor@mineralwellsindex.com
http://www.mineralwellsindex.com
• Craig Holamon, Sports Editor
• Ric Holly, Advertising Director
Frequency:
5 time(s) per week

MINIONDAS
2025 S. MAIN STREET
SANTA ANA, CA 92707-1836
714-668-1010
Fax: 714-668-1013
miniondas@miniondas.com
http://www.miniondas.com
• Patricia Garcia, Sports Editor
(714) 668-1010
miniondas@miniondas.com
Frequency:
1 time(s) per week

MINNEAPOLIS STAR TRIBUNE
425 PORTLAND AVENUE S
MINNEAPOLIS, MN 55488
612-673-4000
800-827-8742
Fax: 612-673-7774
www.startribune.com
• Dennis Anderson, Sports Editor
(612) 673-4424
danderson@startribune.com

MINOT DAILY NEWS
301 4TH STREET, S.E.
MINOT, ND 58702
701-857-1900
800-735-3119
Fax: 701-857-1907
news@minotdailynews.com
http://www.minotdailynews.com
• Chris Bieri, Sports Editor
(701) 857-1935
Frequency:
7 time(s) per week

MINUTEMAN-WESTPORT
877 POST ROAD EAST
WESTPORT, CT 06880-5224
203-752-2711
Fax: 203-789-5309
http://www.westportminuteman.com
• Eric Montgomery, Sports Editor
(203) 789-5761
sports@westportminuteman.com
Frequency:
1 time(s) per week

MISSISSIPPI PRESS
P.O. BOX 849
PASCAGOULA, MS 39567-4136
228-762-1111
800-655-6597
Fax: 228-934-1454
http://www.gulflive.com/mississippipress/
• J.R. Wittner, Sports Editor
(228) 934-1426
Frequency:
7 time(s) per week

MISSOULIAN
500 SOUTH HIGGINS AVENUE
MISSOULA, MT 59801-2736

406-523-5200
800-366-7102
Fax: 406-523-5294
newsdesk@missoulian.com
http://www.missoulian.com
• Bob Meseroll, Sports Editor
(406) 523-5265
Frequency:
7 time(s) per week

MOBERLY MONITOR-INDEX & DEMOCRAT
218 NORTH WILLIAMS
MOBERLY, MO 65270-1534
660-263-4123
Fax: 660-263-3626
http://www.moberlymonitor.com
• Chuck Embree, Sports Editor
• Marsha Hargus, Advertising Manager
advertising@moberlymonitor.com
Frequency:
6 time(s) per week

MODESTO BEE
1325 H STREET
MODESTO, CA 95354
209-578-2330
Fax: 209-578-2207
http://www.modbee.com
• Ron Agostini, Sports Columnist
(209) 578-2300
ragostini@modbee.com
• Will Deboard, Sports Columnist
(209) 578-2300
• Joel Hood, Sports Columnist
(209) 238-4574
• Kelly Jones, Sports Writer
(209) 578-2330
• Joe Silva, Sports Columnist
(209) 578-2301
jsilva@modbee.com
• Noel Harris, Assistant Sports Editor
(209) 578-2330
Frequency:
7 time(s) per week

MOHAVE VALLEY DAILY NEWS
2435 MIRACLE MILE
BULLHEAD CITY, AZ 86442
928-763-2505
Fax: 928-763-7820
http://www.mohavedailynews.com
• Paul Click, Sports Editor
(928) 763-2505
• Jackie Walker, Advertising Manager
(928) 763-2505
Frequency:
6 time(s) per week

MONETT TIMES
505 EAST BROADWAY
MONETT, MO 65708-2333
417-235-3135
Fax: 417-235-8852
http://www.monett-times.com
• Charles Brady, Sports Editor
sports@monett-times.com
• Robyn Blankenship, Advertising/Marketing Manager
Frequency:
5 time(s) per week

MONITOR
P.O. BOX 3267
MCALLEN, TX 78502

956-683-4000
800-366-4343
Fax: 956-683-4401
news@themonitor.com
http://www.themonitor.com
• Oscar Gonzalez, Sports Editor
(956) 683-4443
• Brian Sales, Advertising Director
(956) 683-4141
Frequency:
7 time(s) per week

MONROE EVENING NEWS
20 WEST 1ST STREET
MONROE, MI 48161-2333
734-242-1100
Fax: 734-242-3175
http://www.monroenews.com
• Niles Kruger, Sports Editor
• Jeff Meade, Sports Editor
(734) 240-5783
sports@monroenews.com
• Ron Montri, Sports Editor
(734) 240-5780
Frequency:
7 time(s) per week

MONROE TIMES
1065 4TH AVENUE WEST
MONROE, WI 53566-1318
608-328-4202
800-236-2240
Fax: 608-328-4217
newsclerk@themonroetimes.com
www.themonroetimes.com
• Matt Johnson, Publisher
(608) 328-4202
mpj46@yahoo.com
• Mark Newbitt, Sports Writer
(608) 328-4202
mnesbitt@themonroetimes.com
Frequency:
6 time(s) per week

MONTANA STANDARD
25 WEST GRANITE STREET
BUTTE, MT 59701-9213
406-496-5500
800-877-1074
Fax: 406-496-5551
editor@mtstandard.com
http://www.mtstandard.com
• Bruce Sayler, Sports Editor
(406) 496-5544
• Pat Ryan, Sports Reporter
(406) 496-5544
pat.ryan@lee.net
Frequency:
7 time(s) per week

MONTGOMERY ADVERTISER
425 MOLTON STREET
MONTGOMERY, AL 36104-4250
334-262-1611
Fax: 334-261-1520
http://www.montgomeryadvertiser.com
• Ron Davidson, Advertising Director
(334) 261-1571
• Brad Zimanek, Sports Editor
(334) 261-1586
bzimanek@gannett.com
Frequency:
7 time(s) per week

media

MORNING CALL
101 NORTH 6TH STREET
ALLENTOWN, PA 18101
610-820-6500
Fax: 610-820-6693
news@mcall.com
http://www.mcall.com
• Keith Groller, Senior Sports Reporter
(610) 820-6740
keith.groller@mcall.com
• Ernie Long, Sports Editor
(610) 820-6772
ernest.long@mcall.com
• Stephen Miller, Sports Reporter
(610) 820-6750
• Jeff Schuler, Sports Reporter
(610) 820-6781
jeffrey.schuler@mcall.com
• Andre Williams, Sports Reporter
(610) 820-6529
• Mark Wogenrich, Sports Reporter
(610) 820-6588
mark.wogenrich@mcall.com
Frequency:
7 time(s) per week

MORNING HERALD
100 SUMMIT AVENUE
HAGERSTOWN, MD 21740
301-733-5131
Fax: 301-714-0245
news@herald-mail.com
http://www.herald-mail.com
• Mark Keller, Sports Editor
mkeller@herald-mail.com
Frequency:
7 time(s) per week

MORNING JOURNAL
1657 BROADWAY
LORAIN, OH 44052-3439
440-245-6901
800-765-6901
Fax: 440-245-6912
news@morningjournal.com
http://www.morningjournal.com
• Ron Beal, Advertising Manager
(440) 245-6901
advertising@morningjournal.com
• Colin Wilson, Sports Editor
(440) 245-6901
Frequency:
7 time(s) per week

MORNING NEWS (ID)
34 NORTH ASH STREET
BLACKFOOT, ID 83221
208-785-1100
Fax: 208-785-4239
http://www.am-news.com
• Mark High, Sports Editor
(208) 785-1100
sports@cableone.net
Frequency:
6 time(s) per week

MORNING NEWS (SC)
P.O. BOX 100528
FLORENCE, SC 29501
843-317-6397
Fax: 843-317-7292
http://www.morningnewsonline.com
• Sam Bundy, Sports Editor
(843) 317-7274
• Charlie Price, Advertising Manager
(843) 317-7232
• Justin Driggers, Sports Writer

(843) 317-7262
jdriggers@florencenews.com
Frequency:
7 time(s) per week

MORNING STAR
1003 S. 17TH ST
WILMINGTON, NC 28401
910-343-2000
Fax: 910-343-2227
www.wilmingtonstar.com
• Dan Spears, Sports Editor
dan.spears@starnewsonline.com

MORNING SUN (KS)
P.O. BOX H
PITTSBURG, KS 66762-4038
620-231-2600
800-794-6536
Fax: 620-231-0645
http://www.morningsun.net
• Cindy Clingan, Advertising Manager
(620) 231-2600
• Brock Sisney, Sports Editor
(620) 231-2600
• Jim Henry, Sports Reporter
(260) 231-2600
Frequency:
7 time(s) per week

MORNING SUN (MI)
711 W PICKARD STREET
MOUNT PLEASANT, MI 48858-1585
989-779-6000
800-616-6397
Fax: 989-779-6051
news@michigannewspapers.com
http://www.themorningsun.com/
• Jim Lahde, Sports Editor
(989) 779-6061
jlahde@michigannewspapers.com
Frequency:
6 time(s) per week

MORRIS DAILY HERALD
1804 NORTH DIVISION STREET
MORRIS, IL 60450-0749
815-942-3221
Fax: 815-942-0988
news@morrisdailyherald.com
http://www.morrisdailyherald.com/
• Richard Ponulak, Advertising Manager
(815) 942-3221
• Tim Smith, Sports Editor
(815) 942-3221
tsmith@morrisdailyherald.com
Frequency:
5 time(s) per week
Description:
Community Newspaper

MOSCOW-PULLMAN DAILY NEWS
409 SOUTH JACKSON STREET
MOSCOW, ID 83843
208-882-5561
800-776-4137
Fax: 208-883-8205
briefs@dnews.com
http://www.dnews.com
• Sandra Kelly, Sports Editor
(208) 882-5561
skelly@dnews.com
• Craig Staszkow, Advertising Manager
(208) 882-5561
cstaszkow@dnews.com
• Andrew Nemec, Sports Editor

(208) 882-5561
anemec@dnews.com
Frequency:
6 time(s) per week

MOULTRIE OBSERVER
25 NORTH MAIN STREET
MOULTRIE, GA 31768-3861
229-985-4545
Fax: 229-985-3569
southga.online@gaflnews.com
http://www.moultrieobserver.com
• Wayne Grandy, Sports Editor
(229) 985-4545
Frequency:
6 time(s) per week

MOUNT AIRY NEWS
319 N RENFRO STREET
MOUNT AIRY, NC 27030
336-786-4141
Fax: 336-789-2816
http://www.mtairynews.com
• Thomas Smith, Sports Editor
(336) 719-1920
tsmith@mtairynews.com
• Beth Mechum, Sports Editor
(336) 719-1921
bmechum@mtairynews.com
Frequency:
7 time(s) per week
Primary Audience:
Mount Airy, Surry County

MOUNT PLEASANT DAILY TRIBUNE
P.O. BOX 1177
MOUNT PLEASANT, TX 75456
903-572-1705
Fax: 903-572-6026
http://www.dailytribune.net
• Amy Hinton, Advertising Manager
(903) 572-1705
advertise@dailytribune.net
• John Whitten, Sports Editor
(903) 572-1705
sports@dailytribune.net
Frequency:
6 time(s) per week

MOUNT PLEASANT NEWS
215 WEST MONROE STREET
MOUNT PLEASANT, IA 52641
319-986-5186
Fax: 319-385-8048
pub@mpnews.net
http://www.mpnews.net
• Billie Allender, Advertising Manager
adv@mpnews.net
• Joe Birkestrand, Sports Editor
Frequency:
5 time(s) per week

MOUNTAIN DEMOCRAT
P.O. BOX 1088
PLACERVILLE, CA 95667-5902
530-622-1255
Fax: 530-622-7894
mtdemo@mtdemocrat.net
http://www.mtdemocrat.com
• Jerry Heinzer, Sports Writer
jheinzer@mtdemocrat.net
• Liz Kane, Sports Editor
(530) 344-5079
• Ian Balentine, Advertising Manager
(530) 344-5048
ibalentine@mtdemocrat.net

Frequency:
4 time(s) per week

MOUNTAIN MAIL
P.O. BOX 189
SALIDA, CO 81201
830-539-6691
888-539-1880
Fax: 719-539-6630
mtnmail@chaffe.net
http://www.themountainmail.com
• Randa Bess, Classified Manager
(719) 539-6691
• Denise Ronald, Sports Writer
(830) 539-6691
• Vickie Vigil, Advertising Director
Frequency:
5 time(s) per week

MOUNTAIN PRESS
P.O. BOX 4810
SEVIERVILLE, TN 37876-1943
865-428-0746
Fax: 865-453-4913
editor@themountainpress.com
http://www.themountainpress.com
• Jason Davis, Sports Editor
(865) 428-0748
Frequency:
7 time(s) per week

MUNDO HISPANICO
1927 PIEDMONT CIRCLE SUITE B
ATLANTA, GA 30324-4820
404-881-0441
Fax: 404-881-6085
editorial@mundohispanico.com
http://www.mundohispanico.com
• Marta Garcia, Sports Editor
(404) 881-0441
mgarcia@mundohispanico.com
Frequency:
1 time(s) per week

MURRAY LEDGER AND TIMES
1001 WHITNELL STREET
MURRAY, KY 42071
270-753-1916
Fax: 270-753-1927
mlt@murrayledger.com
http://www.murrayledger.com
• Tommy Dillard, Sports Editor
(270) 753-1916
sports@murrayledger.com
Frequency:
6 time(s) per week

MUSKEGON CHRONICLE
981 3RD STREET
MUSKEGON, MI 49443
231-722-3161
Fax: 231-728-3330
http://www.muskegonchronicle.com
• Tom Kendra, Sports Editor
(231) 725-6363
• Kevin Newton, Advertising Director
(231) 725-6311
Frequency:
7 time(s) per week

NAPA VALLEY REGISTER
1615 SECOND STREET
NAPA, CA 94559
707-226-3711
Fax: 707-224-3963
http://www.napanews.com

• Marty James, Sports Editor
(707) 256-2223
napasports@napanews.com
• Norma Kostecka, Advertising Director
(707) 226-3711
nkostecka@napanews.com
Frequency:
7 time(s) per week

NAPERVILLE SUN
495 N COMMONS DRIVE
SUITE 200
AURORA, IL 60504
630-978-8880
Fax: 630-416-5163
http://www.napersun.com
• Joni Blackman, Sports Writer
(630) 416-6728
jonihb@aol.com
• R.J. Gerber, Sports Editor
(630) 978-8175
rjgerber@stmedianetwork.com
Frequency:
3 time(s) per week

NAPLES DAILY NEWS
1075 CENTRAL AVENUE
NAPLES, FL 34102
239-263-3161
888-262-3161
Fax: 239-263-4816
http://www.naplesnews.com
• Sis Berube, Classified Manager
(239) 263-4718
• Greg Hardwig, Sports Editor
(239) 263-4767
gshardwig@naplesnews.com
• Bob Sandy, Advertising Sales Director
(239) 435-3433
rhsandy@naplesnews.com
Frequency:
7 time(s) per week

NATCHEZ DEMOCRAT
503 NORTH CANAL STREET
NATCHEZ, MS 39120-2902
601-442-9101
Fax: 601-442-7315
newsroom@natchezdemocrat.com
http://www.natchezdemocrat.com
• Adam Daigle, Sports Editor
(601) 445-3632
Frequency:
7 time(s) per week

NATCHITOCHES TIMES
PO BOX 448
NATCHITOCHES, LA 71458
318-352-3618
Fax: 318-352-7842
http://www.natchitochestimes.com
• Al Guidry, Sports Editor
(318) 352-3618
sportseditor@natchitochestimes.com
• Charles Norman, Advertising Manager
(318) 352-3618
advertising@natchitochestimes.com
Frequency:
5 time(s) per week

NEBRASKA CITY NEWS-PRESS
823 CENTRAL AVENUE
NEBRASKA CITY, NE 68410-2409
402-873-3334
Fax: 402-873-5436
http://www.ncnewspress.com

• Kathy Kaufman, Advertising Manager
(402) 873-3334
• Kirt Manion, Sports Editor
(402) 873-3334
kmanion@ncnewspress.com
Frequency:
5 time(s) per week

NEIGHBORS
1405 BROADWAY
SCOTTSBLUFF, NE 69361-3151
308-632-9000
800-846-6102
Fax: 308-632-9001
news@starherald.com
http://www.starherald.com
• Jeff Fielder, Sports Editor
(308) 632-9050
sports@starherald.com
Frequency:
1 time(s) per week

NEVADA APPEAL
PO BOX 2288
CARSON CITY, NV 89701
775-882-2111
800-221-8013
Fax: 775-887-2420
editor@nevadaappeal.com
http://www.nevadaappeal.com/
• Darrell Moody, Sports Reporter
(775) 881-1281
dmoody@nevadaappeal.com
• Gloria Thomas, Advertising Director
(775) 881-1262
Frequency:
7 time(s) per week

NEVADA DAILY MAIL AND SUNDAY HERALD
131 SOUTH CEDAR STREET
NEVADA, MO 64772-3309
417-667-3344
Fax: 417-667-7475
editorial@nevadadailymail.com
http://www.nevadadailymail.com
• Kari Vincent, Advertising Manager
composing@nevadadailymail.com
• Eric Wade, Sports Writer
ewade@nevadadailymail.com
Frequency:
5 time(s) per week

NEW CASTLE NEWS
27 MERCER STREET
NEW CASTLE, PA 16101
724-654-6651
Fax: 724-654-5976
http://www.ncnewsonline.com
• Kayleen Cubbal, Sports Editor
(724) 654-6651
kcubbal@ncnewsonline.com
• Ed Gaydos, Advertising Manager
(724) 654-6651
advertising@ncnewsonline.com
• Ron Poniewasz, Sports Writer
(724) 654-6651
rponiewasz@ncnewsonline.com
Frequency:
6 time(s) per week

NEW HAVEN REGISTER
40 SARGENT DRIVE
NEW HAVEN, CT 06511-6111
203-789-5200
800-925-2472

Fax: 203-865-7894
business@nhregister.com
http://www.newhavenregister.com
• Sean Barker, Sports Editor
(203) 789-5700
sbarker@nhregister.com
Frequency:
7 time(s) per week

NEW JERSEY HERALD
P.O. BOX 10
NEWTON, NJ 07860
973-383-1500
Fax: 973-383-8477
newsroom@njherald.com
http://www.njherald.com
• Jim Dente, Sports Editor
(973) 383-1253
jdente@mjherald.com
• Mitch Mayer, Advertising Manager
(973) 383-1010
mmayer@njherald.com
• James Conrad, Sports Writer
(973) 383-1250
jconrad@njherald.com
Frequency:
6 time(s) per week

NEW MEXICAN
202 EAST MARCY STREET
SANTA FE, NM 87501-2021
505-983-3303
800-873-3362
Fax: 505-986-9147
newsroom@sfnewmexican.com
http://www.santafenewmexican.com
• Laura Harding, Classified Manager
(505) 986-3009
lharding@sfnewmexican.com
• Pancho Morris, Sports Writer
(505) 986-3045
panchom@sfnewmexican.com
• Virginia Sohn, Advertising Director
(505) 986-3006
ginny@sfnewmexican.com
• Tommy Trujillo, Sports Editor
(505) 986-3060
ttrujillo@sfnewmexican.com
Frequency:
7 time(s) per week

NEW YORK DAILY CHALLENGE
1195 ATLANTIC AVENUE
BROOKLYN, NY 11216-2600
718-636-9500
Fax: 718-857-9115
challengegroup@yahoo.com
http://www.challenge-group.com
• Kyle Bostic, Sports Editor
Frequency:
5 time(s) per week

NEW YORK DAILY NEWS
450 WEST 33RD STREET
NEW YORK, NY 10001
212-210-2100
Fax: 212-643-7831
news@edit.nydailynews.com
http://www.nydailynews.com
• Leon Carter, Sports Editor
(212) 210-2348

NEW YORK POST
1211 AVENUE OF THE AMERICAS
NEW YORK, NY 10036-8790

212-930-8271
Fax: 212-930-8540
letters@nypost.com
http://www.nypost.com
• Larry Brooks, Sports Writer
(212) 930-8000
larry.brooks@nypost.com
• Mark Cannizzaro, Sports Reporter
mcannizzaro@nypost.com
• Dave Curtis, Sports Reporter
(212) 930-8280
• Mark Everson, Sports Writer
(212) 930-8000
• Ed Fountaine, Sports Reporter
• Greg Gallo, Sports Executive Editor
(212) 930-8700
sports@nypost.com
• Jay Greenberg, Sports Reporter
jgreenberg@nypost.com
• Mark Hale, Sports Reporter
mark.hale@nypost.com
• Fred Kerber, Sports Writer
(212) 930-8700
Fred.Kerber@nypost.com
• Kevin Kernan, Sports Reporter
kevin.kernan@nypost.com
• George King, Sports Reporter
(212) 930-8700
george.king@nypost.com
• Brian Lewis, Sports Reporter
(212) 930-8700
brian.lewis@nypost.com
• Dan Martin, Sports Reporter
(212) 930-8700
dan.martin@nypost.com
• Ken Moran, Sports Columnist
(212) 930-8700
sports@nypost.com
• Phil Mushnick, Sports Columnist
(212) 930-8271
phil.mushnick@nypost.com
• Paul Schwartz, Sports Reporter
(212) 930-8700
paul.schwartz@nypost.com
• Joel Sherman, Sports Writer
(212) 930-8700
sports@nypost.com
• Andy Soltis, Sports Reporter
• Anthony Stabile, Sports Reporter
• Mike Vaccaro, Sports Columnist
(212) 930-8700
sports@nypost.com
• Peter Vecsey, Sports Columnist
• George Willis, Sports Columnist
(212) 930-8700
sports@nypost.com
Frequency:
7 time(s) per week

NEW YORK SUN
105 CHAMBERS STREET
NEW YORK, NY 10007-1093
212-406-2000
Fax: 212-608-7348
newsdesk@nysun.com
http://www.nysun.com
• Jonathan Mahler, Sports Columnist
• Wallace Matthews, Sports Writer
(212) 901-2681
• Paul Gardner, Sports Reporter
(212) 406-2000
Frequency:
5 time(s) per week

NEW YORK TIMES
620 EIGHTH AVENUE
NEW YORK, NY 10036-3959

212-556-1234
Fax: 212-556-3815
letters@nytimes.com
http://www.nytimes.com
• Dave Anderson, Sports Columnist
(212) 556-7371
sports@nytimes.com
• Judy Battista, Sports Reporter
sports@nytimes.com
• Howard Beck, Sports Reporter
• John Branch, Sports Columnist
• Clifton Brown, Sports Reporter
(212) 556-7371
sports@nytimes.com
• Dave Caldwell, Sports Reporter
(212) 556-7371
• Murray Chass, Sports Columnist
(212) 556-7371
• Christopher Clarey, Sports Reporter
• Karen Crouse, Sports Reporter
sports@nytimes.com
• Larry Dorman, Sports Reporter
sports@nytimes.com
• Joe Drape, Sports Reporter
(212) 556-7371
drape@nytimes.com
• Stuart Elliott, Advertising Columnist
(212) 556-1234
• Gerald Eskenazi, Sports Reporter
(212) 556-7450
• Ray Glier, Sports Writer
(212) 556-7371
sports@nytimes.com
• Damon Hack, Sports Reporter
(212) 556-7371
• Tyler Kepner, Sports Writer
(212) 556-7371
kepner@nytimes.com
• Jeff Klein, Sports Reporter
• Tom Jolly, Sports Editor
sports@nytimes.com
• Sandy Keenan, Deputy Sports Editor
• Brandon Lilly, Sports Writer
(212) 556-7371
sports@nytimes.com
• Frank Litsky, Sports Reporter
(212) 556-7371
• Jere Longman, Sports Reporter
(212) 556-7371
sports@nytimes.com
• Juliet Macur, Sports Reporter
(212) 556-7371
macur@nytimes.com
• Carl Nelson
(212) 556-3647
• Bill Pennington, (212) 556-7371
Sports Reporter
sports@nytimes.com
• Steve Popper, Sports Writer
(212) 556-7371
sports@nytimes.com
• William C. Rhoden, Sports Columnist
• Liz Robbins, Sports Writer
(212) 556-7371
sports@nytimes.com
• Ben Shpigel, Yankees Reporter
• Richard Sandomir, Sports Reporter
sandomir@nytimes.com
Frequency:
7 time(s) per week

NEWNAN TIMES-HERALD
16 JEFFERSON STREET
NEWNAN, GA 30263
770-253-1576
news@newnan.com
times-herald.com

• Doug Gorman, Sports Editor
(770) 683-1781
dgorman@newnan.com
• Jeff Armstrong, Sports Writer
jarmstrong@newnan.com
• Katie Atwood, Multimedia Sales Specialist
(770) 683-1747
katwood@newnan.com
Frequency:
7 time(s) per week

NEWPORT BEACH COSTA MESA DAILY PILOT
330 WEST BAY STREET
COSTA MESA, CA 92627
714-966-4600
Fax: 714-966-4667
dailypilot@latimes.com
http://www.dailypilot.com
• Barry Faulkner, Sports Writer
barry.faulkner@latimes.com
• James Lee, Sports Editor
(714) 966-4616
james.lee@latimes.com
Frequency:
6 time(s) per week

NEWPORT DAILY EXPRESS
P.O. BOX 347
NEWPORT, VT 05855
802-334-6568
Fax: 802-334-6891
http://www.newportvermontdailyexpress.com
• Ken Wells, Sports Editor
(802) 334-6568
kwells@newportdailyadv.com
• Ellen Howell, Advertising Manager
advertising@newportdailyadv.com
Frequency:
5 time(s) per week

NEWPORT DAILY NEWS
101 MALBONE ROAD
NEWPORT, RI 02840-1340
401-849-3300
Fax: 401-849-3306
editor@newportri.com
http://www.newportdailynews.com
• Scott Barrett, Sports Editor
(401) 849-3300
sports@newportri.com
• Rick McGowan, Sports Reporter
(401) 849-3300
Frequency:
6 time(s) per week

NEWPORT INDEPENDENT
2408 HIGHWAY 67 NORTH
NEWPORT, AR 72112-2324
870-523-5855
800-439-8466
Fax: 870-523-6540
news@newportindependent.com
http://www.newportindependent.com
• Ken Duvall, Sports Editor
sports@newportindependent.com
Frequency:
5 time(s) per week

NEWPORT PLAIN TALK
145 EAST BROADWAY
NEWPORT, TN 37822
423-623-6171
Fax: 423-625-1995

info@newportplaintalk.com
http://www.newportplaintalk.com
• Paul Meador, Sports Editor
(423) 623-6171
sports@newportplaintalk.com
Frequency:
5 time(s) per week

NEWS & ADVANCE
101 WYNDALE DRIVE
LYNCHBURG, VA 24501
434-385-5555
800-275-8831
Fax: 434-385-5538
http://www.newsadvance.com
• Chris Morris, Sports Editor
(434) 385-5528
cmorris@newsadvance.com
• Joy Monopli, Advertising Director

NEWS & OBSERVER
P.O. BOX 191
RALEIGH, NC 27601-1331
919-829-4500
800-365-6115
Fax: 919-836-2840
forum@newsobserver.com
http://www.newsobserver.com
• Gary Schwab, Senior Sports Editor
(919) 829-4552
• Lorenzo Perez, Assistant Sports Editor
(919) 829-4643
• Tim Stevens, Sports Reporter
(919) 829-8910
• Caulton Tudor, Sports Columnist
(919) 829-8946
Frequency:
7 time(s) per week

NEWS & RECORD
P.O. BOX 20848
GREENSBORO, NC 27420
336-373-7000
800-553-6880
Fax: 336-373-7382
http://www.news-record.com
• Tony Martinette, Advertising Director

NEWS CHIEF
300 WEST LIME STREET
PO BOX 408
LAKELAND, FL 33802
863-802-7508
Fax: 863-802-7577
news@newschief.com
http://www.newschief.com
• Eroca Filmore, Advertising Director
(863) 421-5504
• Matt Cote, Sports Reporter
Frequency:
7 time(s) per week

NEWS DAILY
P.O. BOX 368
JONESBORO, GA 30236-3514
770-478-5753
Fax: 770-954-0282
cfuller@news-daily.com
http://www.news-daily.com
• Doug Gorman, Sports Editor
(770) 478-5753
dgorman@news-daily.com
Frequency:
7 time(s) per week

NEWS DEMOCRAT JOURNAL
1405 NORTH TRUMAN
FESTUS, MO 63028
636-931-6636
800-931-6636
Fax: 636-931-2638
sitehelp@stltoday.com
http://www.stltoday.com
• Don Reed, Sports Editor
dreed@post-dispatch.com
Frequency:
2 time(s) per week

NEWS HERALD
P.O. BOX 1940
PANAMA CITY, FL 32401-2330
850-747-5000
Fax: 850-747-5097
news@pcnh.com
http://www.newsherald.com
• Pat McCann, Sports Executive Editor
(850) 747-5068
pmccann@pcnh.com
Frequency:
7 time(s) per week

NEWS JOURNAL (DE)
950 WEST BASIN ROAD
NEW CASTLE, DE 19720
302-324-2500
800-235-9100
Fax: 302-324-5509
http://www.delawareonline.com
• Betty An Dobek, Classified Manager
(302) 324-2932
bdobek@delewareonline.com
• Martin Frank, Sports Reporter
(302) 324-2500
mfrank@delawareonline.com
• Ron Fritz, Sports Editor
(302) 324-2919
rfritz@delawareonline.com
• Buddy Hurlock, Sports Reporter
• Jack Ireland, Sports Reporter
(302) 324-2808
jireland@delawareonline.com
• Doug Lesmerises, Sports Reporter
(302) 324-2500
• Kristian Pope, Sports Writer
(302) 734-7946
• Kevin Tresolini, Sports Reporter
(302) 324-2807
ktresolini@delawareonline.com
Frequency:
7 time(s) per week

NEWS JOURNAL (OH)
70 WEST 4TH STREET
MANSFIELD, OH 44903-1676
419-522-3311
800-472-5547
Fax: 419-521-7415
http://www.mansfieldnewsjournal.com
• Rob McCurdy, Sports Reporter
(419) 521-7241
rmccurdy@gannett.com
• Scott Miller, Advertising Manager
(419) 521-7329
• Jon Spencer, Sports Columnist
(419) 521-7239
jspencer@gannett.com
Frequency:
7 time(s) per week

NEWS LEADER
P. O. BOX 59
STAUNTON, VA 24402

540-885-7281
800-793-2459
Fax: 540-885-1904
news@newsleader.com
http://www.newsleader.com
• Hubert Grim, III, Sports Editor
(540) 213-9131
hgrimiii@newsleader.com
• Jim McCloskey, Advertising Manager
(540) 213-9144
Frequency:
7 time(s) per week

NEWS PRESS
211 W. 9TH ST
STILLWATER, OK 74074
405-372-5000 EXT 201
800-364-5000
Fax: 405-372-3112
editor@stwnewspress.com
www.stwnewspress.com
• Roger Moore, Sports Editor
sports@stwnewspress.com

NEWS SUN
2383 NORTH DELANY ROAD
WAUKEGAN, IL 60087
847-336-7000
Fax: 847-249-7202
http://www.suburbanchicagonews.com
• Jeff Bonato, Sports Editor
(847) 249-7231
• Darren Day, Sports Writer
(847) 249-7244
• Bob Ulmer, Advertising Director
(847) 249-7210
Frequency:
6 time(s) per week

NEWS TRIBUNE
1950 SOUTH STATE STREET
TACOMA, WA 98405-2817
253-597-8742
800-388-8742
Fax: 253-597-8274
newstips@thenewstribune.com
http://www.thenewstribune.com
• Darrin Beene, Sports Writer
(253) 597-8656
darrin.beene@thenewstribune.com
• Dave Boling, Sports Columnist
(253) 597-8440
dave.boling@thenewstribune.com
• Larry LaRue, Sports Reporter
(253) 597-7000
• John McGrath, Sports Columnist
(253) 552-7000
john.mcgrath@thenewstribune.com
• Todd Milles, Sports Reporter
(253) 597-8442
todd.milles@thenewstribune.com
• Don Ruiz, Sports Columnist
(253) 597-8808
Frequency:
7 time(s) per week

NEWS-BANNER
125 NORTH JOHNSON STREET
BLUFFTON, IN 46714-1907
260-824-0224
Fax: 260-824-0700
email@news-banner.com
http://www.news-banner.com
• Paul Beitler, Sports Editor
(260) 824-0224
sports@news-banner.com
• Jean Bordner, Advertising Manager

Frequency:
6 time(s) per week

NEWS-COURIER
P.O. BOX 670
ATHENS, AL 35612
256-232-2720
800-844-5480
Fax: 256-233-7753
ann@athensnews-courier.com
http://www.enewscourier.com
• Ashley Hargrove, Sports Editor
(256) 232-2720
Frequency:
5 time(s) per week

NEWS-DISPATCH
121 WEST MICHIGAN BOULEVARD
MICHIGAN CITY, IN 46360-3274
219-874-7211
800-489-9292
Fax: 219-872-8511
news@thenewsdispatch.com
http://www.thenewsdispatch.com/
• Isis Cains, Advertising Manager
(219) 874-7211
icains@thenewsdispatch.com
• Adam Parkhouse, Sports Editor
(219) 874-7211
aparkhouse@thenewsdispatch.com
• Drew White, Sports Writer
(219) 874-7211
Frequency:
7 time(s) per week

NEWS-ENTERPRISE
408 WEST DIXIE AVENUE
ELIZABETHTOWN, KY 42701-2433
270-769-1200
Fax: 270-765-7318
ne@thenewsenterprise.com
http://www.thenewsenterprise.com
• Chuck Jones, Sports Editor
(270) 769-1200
cjones@thenewsenterprise.com
• Josh Claywell, Sports Writer
(270) 769-1200
Frequency:
6 time(s) per week

NEWS-GAZETTE
15 MAIN STREET
CHAMPAIGN, IL 61820-3625
217-351-5252
Fax: 217-351-5291
http://www.news-gazette.com
• Jim Rossow, Sports Editor
Frequency:
7 time(s) per week

NEWS-HERALD (PORT CLINTON)
PO BOX 550
PORT CLINTON, OH 43452-1012
419-734-3141
800-636-6906
Fax: 419-734-1850
http://www.portclintonnewsherald.com/apps/
pbcs.dll/frontpage
• David Barth, Advertising Manager
(419) 734-7501
• Josh Chapin, Sports Editor
jchapin@fremont.gannett.com
• Aaron Smith, Sports Editor
(419) 734-3141
Frequency:
6 time(s) per week

NEWS-HERALD (WILLOUGHBY)
7085 MENTOR AVENUE
WILLOUGHBY, OH 44094-7932
440-951-0000
800-947-2737
Fax: 440-975-2836
editor@news-herald.com
http://www.news-herald.com
• Scott Kendrick, Sports Editor
(440) 951-0000
sports@news-herald.com
Frequency:
7 time(s) per week

NEWS-ITEM
707 NORTH ROCK STREET
SHAMOKIN, PA 17872-4930
570-644-6397
Fax: 570-648-7581
nieditor@ptd.net
http://www.newsitem.com
• Jennifer Crone, Classified Manager
(570) 644-6397
• Chris Nagy, Sports Editor
(570) 644-6397
Frequency:
6 time(s) per week

NEWS-PRESS (FL)
2442 DR MARTIN LUTHER KING JR. BLVD
FORT MYERS, FL 33901-3987
941-335-0200
Fax: 941-957-5276
www.news-press.com
• Ed Reed, Sports Editor
(239) 335-0357
ereed@fortmyer.gannett.com
• Bob Carlson, Advertising Director
bcarlson@fortmyer.gannett.com

NEWS-PRESS (OK)
211 WEST 9TH STREET
STILLWATER, OK 74074-4406
405-372-5000
800-364-5000
Fax: 405-372-3112
news@stwnewspress.com
http://www.stwnewspress.com
• Roger Moore, Sports Editor
(405) 372-5000
sports@stwnewspress.com
Frequency:
7 time(s) per week

NEWS-RECORD
P.O. BOX 3006
GILLETTE, WY 82716-3301
307-682-9306
800-447-4539
Fax: 307-686-9306
news@gillettenewsrecord.com
http://www.gillettenewsrecord.com
• Kathy Brown, Sports Editor
(307) 682-9306
sports@gillettenewsrecord.com
• Cher Rhoades, Advertising Manager
(307) 682-9306
newsad@vcn.com
Frequency:
6 time(s) per week

NEWS-REVIEW
P.O. BOX 1248
ROSEBURG, OR 97470

541-672-3321
Fax: 541-673-5994
http://www.oregonnews.com
• John McDermott, Sports Reporter
(541) 957-4219
• Rob McCallum, Sports Reporter
(541) 957-4221
• Tom Eggers, Sports Editor
(541) 957-4220
teggers@nrtoday.com
• Pat Bridges, Advertising Director
(541) 957-4250
Frequency:
6 time(s) per week

NEWS-SENTINEL
600 WEST MAIN STREET
FORT WAYNE, IN 46802-1408
260-461-8222
800-444-3303
Fax: 260-461-8817
http://www.news-sentinel.com\ns
• Tom Davis, Sports Editor
(260) 461-8240
tdavis@news-sentinel.com
• Blake Sebring, Assistant Sports Editor
(260) 461-8497
bsebring@news-sentinel.com
• Don Converset, Assistant Sports Editor
(260) 461-8346
dconverset@news-sentinel.com
Frequency:
6 time(s) per week

NEWS-STAR
411 NORTH 4TH STREET
MONROE, LA 71201
318-362-0289
800-259-7788
Fax: 318-362-0273
news@thenewsstar.com
http://www.thenewsstar.com
• Jerit Roser, Sports Writer
(318) 362-0234
• Christina Pierce, Advertising Director
(318) 362-0214
christina.pierce@monroe.gannett.com
Frequency:
7 time(s) per week

NEWS-TIMES
333 MAIN STREET
DANBURY, CT 06810-5818
203-744-5100
Fax: 203-792-8730
http://www.newstimes.com
• Brian Koonz, Sports Reporter
(203) 731-3379
sports@newstimes.com
• Bob Reigeluth, Sports Reporter
(203) 731-3379
sports@newstimes.com
• Jason Sonski, Sports Editor
(203) 731-3377
sports@newstimes.com
• James Stout, Sports Reporter
(203) 731-3377
sports@newstimes.com
• Edward Flink, Sports Writer
(203) 731-3379
sports@newstimes.com
Frequency:
7 time(s) per week

NEWSDAY
235 PINELAWN ROAD
MELVILLE, NY 11747-4226

631-843-2020
Fax: 631-843-2953
bizeditor@newsday.com
http://www.newsday.com
• Barbara Barker, Contributing Sports Columnist
(631) 843-2020
barbara.barker@newsday.com
• Neil Best, Sports Reporter
(631) 843-3891
neil.best@newsday.com
• Bill Bleyer, Boating Reporter
• Margaret Corvini, Sports Editor
(631) 843-3435
margaret.corvini@newsday.com
• Ken Davidoff, Sports Writer
(631) 843-2020
• Michael Dobie, Sports Reporter
(631) 843-4839
Michael.Dobie@newsday.com
• Bill Eichenberger, Sports Deputy Editor
(631) 843-4842
• Joe Gergen, Sports Columnist
(631) 843-2020
• Bob Glauber, Sports Columnist (NFL)
(631) 843-3890
bglaubs2@aol.com
• Mark Herrmann, Sports Columnist
(631) 843-2826
• Jon Heyman, Sports Columnist (Baseball)
(631) 843-2810
jonhheyman@aol.com
• Johnette Howard, Sports Columnist
(631) 843-2810
• Aileen Jacobson, Advertising Writer
(631) 843-2960
• John Jeansonne, Sports Reporter
(631) 843-4836
• Mark LaMonica, Sports Writer
(631) 843-2020
mark.lamonica@newsday.com
• Dave Lennon, Sports Reporter (Yankees)
(631) 843-2810
• Greg Logan, Sports Correspondent
(631) 843-2823
• Steven Marcus, Sports Reporter
steve.marcus@newsday.com
• Raymond J. McCutcheon, Advertising Vice President
• Jason Molinet, Sports Reporter (High School)
(631) 843-4830
• Paul Moran, Sports Reporter (Horse Racing)
(631) 843-2810
pmoran1686@aol.com
• Marty Noble, Sports Reporter (Baseball Mets)
(631) 843-2810
dw5254@aol.com
• Monty Phan, Advertising Reporter
(631) 843-2436
• Shaun Powell, Sports Columnist
(631) 843-3892
• Gregg Sarra, (631) 843-2810 Assistant Sports Editor
gregg.sarra@newsday.com
• Elaine Sung, Sports Assistant Editor
(718) 575-2554
• Dave Whitehorn, Deputy News Sports Editor
(631) 843-4820
• Steve Zipay, Sports Media Columnist
(631) 251-6657
steve.zipay@newsday.com
Frequency:
7 time(s) per week

NEWTON DAILY NEWS
200 1ST AVENUE EAST
NEWTON, IA 50208-3716
641-792-3121
Fax: 641-791-7104
newsroom@newtondailynews.com
http://www.newtondailynews.com
• Jeff Holschuh, Advertising Manager
(641) 792-3121
jholschuh@newtondailynews.com
• Andrew Potter, Sports Editor
(641) 792-3121
ndnsports@newtondailynews.com
Frequency:
6 time(s) per week

NEWTON KANSAN
P.O. BOX 268
NEWTON, KS 67114-2117
316-283-1500
Fax: 316-283-2471
news@thekansan.com
http://www.thekansan.com
• Joni Regnier, Advertising Manager
(316) 283-1500
• Mark Schnabel, Sports Editor
(316) 283-1500
mark.schnabel@thekansan.com
Frequency:
6 time(s) per week

NIAGARA GAZETTE
PO BOX 549
NIAGARA FALLS, NY 14303-1141
716-282-2311
Fax: 716-286-3895
http://niagara-gazette.com/
• Jonah Bronstein, Sports Writer
(716) 282-2311
Frequency:
7 time(s) per week

NORFOLK DAILY NEWS
525 NORFOLK AVENUE
NORFOLK, NE 68701
402-371-1020
800-672-8351
Fax: 402-371-5802
http://www.norfolkdailynews.com
• Larry Bartscher, Advertising Director
(402) 371-1020
• Jay Prauner, Sports Editor
(402) 371-1020
jprauner@norfolkdailynews.com
Frequency:
6 time(s) per week

NORMAN TRANSCRIPT
215 E. COMANCHE ST
PO DRAWER 1058
NORMAN, OK 73070-1058
405-366-3530
Fax: 405-366-3516
www.normantranscript.com
• Andy Rieger, Managing Editor
(405) 366-3543
editor@normantranscript.com
• Justin Harper, Sports Editor

NORTH COUNTY JOURNAL
7751 NORTH LINDBERGH BOULEVARD
HAZELWOOD, MO 63042
314-972-1111
Fax: 314-831-7643
http://www.stltoday.com

• Mike Elder, Sports Editor
(314) 972-1111
Frequency:
2 time(s) per week

NORTH COUNTY TIMES
207 EAST PENNSYLVANIA AVENUE
ESCONDIDO, CA 92025-2808
760-745-6611
Fax: 760-745-3769
editor@nctimes.com
http://www.nctimes.com
• Eric Breier, Assistant Sports Editor
(760) 740-3548
ebreier@nctimes.com
• Rick Hoff, Sports Writer
(760) 740-3545
hoff@nctimes.com
• Howard Wahl, Retail Advertising Manager
(760) 740-5435
hwahl@nctimes.com
• Bill Williamson, Advertising Director
(760) 740-3506
bwilliamson@nctimes.com
Frequency:
7 time(s) per week

NORTHEAST MISSISSIPPI DAILY JOURNAL
1242 SOUTH GREEN STREET
TUPELO, MS 38804
662-842-2611
800-264-6397
Fax: 662-842-2233
http://www.djournal.com
• Gene Phelps, Sports Editor
(662) 678-1593
gene.phelps@djournal.com
• Parrish Alford, Collegiate Sports Reporter
(662) 678-1600
parrish.alford@djournal.com
Frequency:
7 time(s) per week

NORTHEAST TIMES
2512 METROPOLITAN DRIVE
TREVOSE, PA 19053-6738
215-355-9009
Fax: 215-355-4857
http://www.northeasttimes.com
• Sheil Kapadia, Sports Editor
(215) 854-2455
Frequency:
1 time(s) per week

NORTHERN VIRGINIA DAILY
152 NORTH HOLLIDAY STREET
STRASBURG, VA 22657-2143
540-465-5137
800-296-5137
Fax: 540-465-6155
http://www.nvdaily.com
• Brian French, Sports Editor
(800) 465-5137
Frequency:
6 time(s) per week

NORTHERN WYOMING DAILY NEWS
201 NORTH 8TH STREET
WORLAND, WY 82401-2614
307-347-3241
Fax: 307-347-4267
http://www.wyodaily.com
• Dustin Fuller, Advertising Manager
ext a
ads@wyodaily.com

• Judy Lockhart, Sports Editor
sports@wyodaily.com
Frequency:
5 time(s) per week

NORTHWEST ARKANSAS TIMES
212 NORTH EAST AVENUE
FAYETTEVILLE, AR 72701-5225
479-442-1700
800-803-8144
Fax: 479-442-1714
http://www.nwaonline.com
• Heath Allen, Sports Reporter
(479) 571-6419
• Kay Hunton, Classified Manager
(479) 571-6435
• Joe West, Sports Reporter
• Terry Wood, Sports Editor
(479) 442-1700
sports@nwaonline.com
Frequency:
7 time(s) per week

NORTHWEST FLORIDA DAILY NEWS
P.O. BOX 2949
FORT WALTON BEACH, FL 32547
850-863-1111
800-755-1185
Fax: 850-863-7834
news@nwfdailynews.com
http://www.nwfdailynews.com
• Travis Downey, Sports Editor
(850) 863-1111
• Patrick Flynn, Sports Writer
• Adam Rosenburg, Sports Reporter
• John Whitehead, Advertising Manager
Frequency:
7 time(s) per week

NORTHWEST HERALD
7717 SOUTH ROUTE 31
CRYSTAL LAKE, IL 60014-8196
815-459-4122
800-589-8910
Fax: 815-459-5640
http://www.nwherald.com
• Eric Olson, Sports Editor
eolson@nwherald.com
Frequency:
7 time(s) per week

NORTHWEST-SIGNAL
595 EAST RIVERVIEW AVENUE
NAPOLEON, OH 43545-1865
419-592-5055
Fax: 419-592-9778
http://www.northwestsignal.net
• Sally Heaston, Advertising Manager
ads@northwestsignal.net
• Jeff Ratcliff, Sports Editor
jeffr@northwestsignal.net
Frequency:
5 time(s) per week

NORWALK REFLECTOR
61 EAST MONROE STREET
NORWALK, OH 44857-1532
419-668-3771
Fax: 419-668-2424
http://www.goreflector.com
• Michael Greco, Sports Editor
(419) 668-3771
• Don Hohler, Sports Writer
• John Ringenberg, Advertising Manager
(419) 668-3771

Frequency:
6 time(s) per week

NOVOYE RUSSKOYE SLOVO
861 BAY RIDGE AVENUE
BROOKLYN, NY 11220
718-648-3511
Fax: 718-648-3047
http://www.inforeklama.com
• Alex Orlov, Sports Editor
• Leena Varskay, Advertising Manager
(646) 218-6900
Frequency:
6 time(s) per week

NOWY DZIENNIK/POLISH DAILY NEWS
333 WEST 38TH STREET
2ND FLOOR
NEW YORK, NY 10018-2914
212-594-2266
Fax: 212-594-2383
http://www.dziennik.com
• Jerry Gierusvczak, Sports Editor
(212) 594-2266
Frequency:
7 time(s) per week, Daily

O.C. WEEKLY
1666 NORTH MAIN STREET SUITE 500
SANTA ANA, CA 92701
714-550-5900
Fax: 714-550-5903
letters@ocweekly.com
http://www.ocweekly.com
• Steve Lowery, Sports Editor
Frequency:
1 time(s) per week

OAK RIDGER
P.O. BOX 3446
OAK RIDGE, TN 37830-7076
865-482-1021
Fax: 865-220-5460
http://www.oakridger.com
• Tank Johnson, Sports Editor
(865) 220-5508
Frequency:
5 time(s) per week

OAKLAND PRESS
48 WEST HURON STREET
PONTIAC, MI 48342-2101
248-332-8181
Fax: 248-332-8885
http://www.theoaklandpress.com
• Pat Caputo, Sports Columnist
(248) 745-4682
pat.caputo@oakpress.com
• Dana Gauruder, Sports Columnist
(248) 745-4673
• Paula Pasche, Sports Writer
(248) 745-4682
paula.pasche@oakpress.com
• Jeff Kuehn, Sports Editor
(248) 745-4682
jeff.kuehn@oakpress.com
• Keith Dunlap, Sports Reporter
(248) 745-4674
keith.dunlap@oakpress.com
Frequency:
7 time(s) per week

OAKLAND TRIBUNE
7677 OAKPORT STREET
OAKLAND, CA 94607

510-208-6300
800-488-2070
Fax: 510-208-6477
http://www.oaklandtribune.com
• Mario Dianda, News Editor
• Steve Herendeen, Sports Editor
(510) 208-6462

OBSERVER (NY)
10 EAST 2ND STREET
DUNKIRK, NY 14048-0391
716-366-3000
Fax: 716-366-2389
editorial@observertoday.com
http://www.observertoday.com
• Craig Harvey, Sports Editor
(716) 366-3000
sports@observertoday.com
Frequency:
7 time(s) per week

OBSERVER (OR)
1406 5TH STREET
LA GRANDE, OR 97850
541-963-3161
800-422-3110
Fax: 541-963-7804
news@lagrandeobserver.com
http://www.lagrandeobserver.com
• Paul Harder, Sports Editor
(541) 963-3161
sports@lagrandeobserver.com
• Ted Kramer, Publisher
• Casey Kellas, Sports Writer
(541) 963-3161
• Joe Sova, Sports Reporter
(541) 963-3161
Frequency:
5 time(s) per week
Primary Audience:
Union and Wallowa Counties

OBSERVER-DISPATCH
221 ORISKANY PLAZA
UTICA, NY 13501
315-792-5000
Fax: 315-792-5033
http://www.uticaod.com
• Anne Delaney, Sports Writer
(315) 792-4963
• Ronald Moshier, Sports Reporter
(315) 792-5031
rmoshier@uticaod.com
• Francis Perritano, Sports Editor
(315) 792-5007
fperrita@uticaod.com
• John Pitarresi, Sports Writer
(315) 792-5032
jpitarresi@uticaod.com
Frequency:
7 time(s) per week

OBSERVER-REPORTER
122 SOUTH MAIN STREET
WASHINGTON, PA 15301-4904
724-222-2200
800-222-6397
Fax: 724-225-2077
newsroom@observer-reporter.com
http://www.observer-reporter.com
• Chris Dugan, Assistant Sports Editor
(724) 222-2200
dugan@observer-reporter.com
• Mike Kovak, Sports Reporter
(724) 222-2200
mkovak@observer-reporter.com
• Dale Lolley, Sports Reporter

(724) 222-2200
dlolley@observer-reporter.com
• Matt Miller, Advertising Manager
(724) 222-2200
mtmiller@observer-reporter.com
• Chris Dugan, Sports Editor
(724) 222-2200
dugan@observer-reporter.com
• Joe Tuscano, Assistant Editor
(724) 222-2200
jtuscano@observer-reporter.com
Frequency:
7 time(s) per week

OCEAN COUNTY OBSERVER
8 ROBBINS STREET
TOMS RIVER, NJ 08753-7629
732-349-3000
Fax: 732-557-5758
observer@app.com
http://www.injersey.com/observer
• Matt Underwood, Sports Editor
(732) 349-3000
munderwood@app.com
Frequency:
6 time(s) per week

ODESSA AMERICAN
222 EAST 4TH STREET
ODESSA, TX 79761-5122
432-337-6262
800-375-4661
Fax: 432-333-7742
http://www.oaoa.com
• Chris Gove, Sports Assistant Editor
(432) 333-7791
Frequency:
7 time(s) per week

OKLAHOMAN
9000 NORTH BROADWAY
OKLAHOMA CITY, OK 73114-3708
405-475-3311
Fax: 405-475-3183
http://www.newsok.com
• Mike Baldwin, Sports Writer
(405) 475-3314
• Jenni Carlson, Sports Columnist
(405) 475-4125
jcarlson@opubco.com
• Ed Godfrey, Sports Writer
(405) 475-3159
egodfrey@opubco.com
• John Helsley, Sports Writer
(405) 475-3313
jhelsley@opubco.com
• Joe Hite, Classified Manager
• Scott Munn, Sports Assistant Editor
(405) 475-3313
smunn@opubco.com
• John Rohde, Sports Writer
• Todd Schoenthaler, Sports News Assistant
tschoenthaler@opubco.com
• Mike Sherman, Sports Editor
• Darla Smith, Sports Coordinator (Day)
dsmith@oklahoman.com
• Berry Tramel, Sports Columnist
btramel@oklahoman.com
• John White, Display Advertising Manager
(405) 475-3392
Frequency:
7 time(s) per week

OLATHE NEWS
514 SOUTH KANSAS AVENUE
OLATHE, KS 66061

913-764-2211
800-467-2720
Fax: 913-764-2251
http://www.theolathenews.com
• Tod Palmer, Sports Editor
(913) 764-2211
todpalmer@theolathenews.com
Frequency:
6 time(s) per week

OLEAN TIMES HERALD
639 NORTON DRIVE
OLEAN, NY 14760-1402
716-372-3121
800-722-8812
Fax: 716-373-6397
news@oleantimesherald.com
http://www.oleantimesherald.com
• Jim Melaro, Sports Editor
(716) 372-3121
jmelaro@oleantimesherald.com
• Charles Pollock, Sports Managing Editor
(716) 372-3121
cpollock@oleantimesherald.com
Frequency:
7 time(s) per week

OLNEY DAILY MAIL
206 WHITTLE AVENUE
OLNEY, IL 62450
618-393-2931
Fax: 618-392-2953
editor@olneydailymail.com
http://www.olneydailymail.com
• Ray McGrew, Advertising Manager
advertising@olneydailymail.com
• Justin Hatten, Sports Editor
(618) 393-2931
sports@olneydailymail.com
Frequency:
6 time(s) per week

OLYMPIAN
P.O. BOX 407
OLYMPIA, WA 98507
360-754-5420
800-869-7080
Fax: 360-357-0202
news@theolympian.com
http://www.theolympian.com/
• Frank Bauer, Advertising Manager
(360) 754-5461
• Cindy Broome, Classified Manager
(360) 754-5447
• Adam Thaler, Sports Assistant Editor
(360) 704-6868
athaler@theolympian.com
• Gail Wood, Sports Reporter
(360) 754-5432
• Megan Wochnick, Sports Reporter
(360) 754-5473
Frequency:
7 time(s) per week

OMAHA WORLD-HERALD
1334 DODGE STREET
OMAHA, NE 68102-1138
402-444-1000
800-284-6397
Fax: 402-345-4547
news@owh.com
http://www.omaha.com
• Lee Barfknecht, College Sports Reporter
(402) 444-1024
lee.barfknecht@owh.com
• Marjie Ducey, State College Sports Writer
(402) 444-1000

marjie.ducey@owh.com
• Rich Kaipust, College Sports Reporter
(402) 444-1000
rich.kaipust@owh.com
• Mike Kelly, Sports Columnist
mike.kelly@owh.com
• Elizabeth Merrill, Sports Reporter
(402) 444-1000
liz.merrill@owh.com
• Mike Patterson, High School Sports
Reporter
(402) 444-1000
mike.patterson@owh.com
• Steve Pivovar, College Sports Reporter
(402) 444-1026
steve.pivovar@owh.com
• Larry Porter, Sports Writer
(402) 476-3132
larry.porter@owh.com
• Stu Pospisil, High School Sports Writer
(402) 444-1000
stu.pospisil@owh.com
• Craig Sesker, Sports Reporter
(402) 444-1000
craig.sesker@owh.com
• Tom Shatel, Sports Columnist
(402) 444-1000
 tom.shatel@owh.com
• Mitch Sherman, College Sports Writer
(402) 444-1000
mitch.sherman@owh.com
• Steve Sinclair, Sports Editor
(402) 444-1000
steve.sinclair@owh.com
• Kevin White, High School Sports Reporter
(402) 444-1000
kevin.white@owh.com
• Dave Winegarden, Advertising Director
(402) 444-1406
dave.winegarden@owh.com
Frequency:
7 time(s) per week

ORANGE COUNTY REGISTER
625 NORTH GRAND AVENUE
SANTA ANA, CA 92701-4347
714-796-7000
Fax: 714-796-3681
http://www.ocregister.com
• Carlos Arias, Sports Reporter
(949) 606-3602
• Janis Carr, Sports Reporter
• Kevin Ding, Sports Reporter
• Damian Dottore, Sports Reporter
(714) 796-5050
ddottore@ocregister.com
• Steve Fryer, Sports Reporter
(714) 796-2245
sfryer@ocregister.com
• Ryan Hammill, Sports Reporter
• Lee Jenkins, Sports Reporter
• Robert Kuwada, Sports Reporter (UCLA)
• Eric La Pack, Sports Editor
(949) 454-7391
• Michael Lev, Sports Reporter
(714) 796-7804
• Bill Plunkett, Sports Reporter
(714) 796-5050
 bplunkett@ocregister.com
• Scott Reid, Sports Reporter
(714) 932-1809
sreid@ocregister.com
• Marcia Smith, Sports Reporter
(714) 796-2259
• Mark Whicker, Sports Reporter
• Randy Youngman, Sports Columnist
(714) 796-5050

• Curtis Zupke, Sports Reporter
czupre@ocregister.com
Frequency:
7 time(s) per week

ORANGE LEADER
200 FRONT STREET
ORANGE, TX 77630
409-883-3571
Fax: 409-883-6342
editorial@orangeleader.com
http://www.orangeleader.com
• Kim Dwyer, Advertising Manager
• Van Wade, Sports Editor
(409) 721-2817
sports@orangeleader.com
Frequency:
7 time(s) per week

OREGONIAN
1320 SOUTHWEST BROADWAY
PORTLAND, OR 97201-3499
503-221-8100
800-826-0376
Fax: 503-227-5306
http://www.oregonlive.com/oregonian
• Geoffrey Arnold, Sports Reporter
(503) 221-8556
garnold@oregonian.com
• Rachel Bachman, Sports Reporter
(503) 221-4373
rbachman@oregonian.com
• Jim Beseda, Sports Reporter
(503) 221-8380
jbeseda@oregonian.com
• Molly Blue, Sports Writer
(503) 294-7608
mblue@oregonian.com
• Paul Buker, Sports Reporter
(503) 221-8167
• John Canzano, Sports Columnist
(503) 294-5065
• Aaron Fentress, Sports Writer
(503) 221-8211
afentress@oregonian.com
• Joe Freeman, Sports Writer
(503) 294-5183
joefreeman@oregonian.com
• Ken Goe, Sports Reporter
(503) 221-8040
kgoe@oregonian.com
• Mark Hester, Sports Editor
(503) 221-8548
mhester@oregonian.com
• John Hunt, Sports Writer
(503) 294-7643
 jhunt@oregonian.com
• John Killen, Sports Editor
(503) 221-8538
jkillen@oregonian.com
• Jeff Manning, Advertising Reporter
(503) 294-7606
jmanning@oregonian.com
• Dennis Peck, Sports Editor
(503) 221-8164
dpeck@oregonian.com
• Jason Quick, Sports Reporter
(503) 221-4372
jquick@oregonian.com
• Mike Tokito, Sports Reporter
(503) 294-7603
mtokito@oregonian.com
• Jerry Ulmer, Sports Reporter
(503) 221-8161
julmer@oregonian.com
• Ryan White, Sports Writer
(503) 412-7024
rwhite@oregonian.com

• Michael Wilson, Sports Copy Editor
(503) 412-7065
mlwilson@oregonian.com
Frequency:
7 time(s) per week

ORLANDO SENTINEL
633 NORTH ORANGE AVENUE
ORLANDO, FL 32801-1300
407-420-5000
800-347-6868
Fax: 407-420-5350
http://www.orlandosentinel.com
• Mike Bianchi, Sports Senior Columnist
(407) 420-5395
mbianchi@orlandosentinel.com
• Todd Adams, Sports Editor
(407) 420-5355
tmadams@orlandosentinel.com
• George Diaz, Sports Columnist
(407) 420-5533
gdiaz@orlandosentinel.com
• Chris Hayes, Production Editor
(407) 420-6178
chays@orlandosentinel.com
• Matt Humphrey, Manager,
Production/Online Sports
(407) 420-5078
mhumphrey@orlandosentinel.com
• Josh Robbins, Sports Reporter
jrobbins@orlandosentinel.com
• Brian Schmitz, Sports Columnist
(407) 420-5063
bschmitz@orlandosentinel.com
• Joe Williams, Sports Reporter
(352) 742-5921
jwilliams@orlandosentinel.com
Frequency:
7 time(s) per week

OSHKOSH NORTHWESTERN
224 STATE STREET
OSHKOSH, WI 54901-4839
920-235-7700
Fax: 920-235-1527
http://www.oshkoshonline.com
• Rob Ebert, Senior Sports Reporter
(920) 426-6679
• Steve Clark, Sports Editor
(920) 426-6659
sclark@thenorthwestern.com
Frequency:
7 time(s) per week

OSKALOOSA HERALD
1901-A AVENUE WEST
OSKALOOSA, IA 52577-1962
641-672-2581
888-672-2581
Fax: 641-672-2294
http://www.oskaloosaherald.com
• Jim Gries, Sports Editor
(641) 672-2581
sports@oskyherald.com
• Deb Van Engelenhoven, Advertising
Manager
(641) 672-2581
Frequency:
6 time(s) per week

OTTAWA HERALD
104 SOUTH CEDAR STREET
OTTAWA, KS 66067-2318
785-242-4700
800-467-8383
Fax: 785-242-9420

news@ottawaherald.com
http://www.ottawaherald.com
• Greg Mast, Sports Editor
sports@ottawaherald.com
Frequency:
6 time(s) per week

OTTUMWA COURIER
213 EAST SECOND STREET
OTTUMWA, IA 52501-2902
641-684-4611
800-532-1504
Fax: 641-684-7326
news@ottumwacourier.com
http://www.ottumwacourier.com
• James Grob, Sports Editor
(641) 684-4611
sports@ottumwacourier.com
Frequency:
6 time(s) per week

OWATONNA PEOPLE'S PRESS
135 WEST PEARL STREET
OWATONNA, MN 55060
507-451-2840
Fax: 507-451-6020
http://www.owatonna.com
• Debbie Ensley, Advertising Manager
densley@owatonna.com
• Chad Urdahl, Sports Editor
(507) 444-2374
• Derek Sullivan, Sports Editor
(507) 444-2374
Frequency:
6 time(s) per week

OWENSBORO MESSENGER-INQUIRER
1401 FREDERICA STREET
OWENSBORO, KY 42301-4804
270-926-0123
800-633-2008
Fax: 270-685-3446
news@messenger-inquirer.com
http://www.messenger-inquirer.com
• Jake Jennings, Sports Reporter
(270) 691-7312
• Mark Mathis, Sports Reporter
(270) 691-7313
mmathis@messenger-inquirer.com
• Saye Murry, Advertising Manager
(270) 691-7240
fmurry@messenger-inquirer.com
• Scott Hagerman, Sports Editor
(270) 691-7314
shagerman@messenger-inquirer.com
• Harold Martin, Sports Copy Editor
(270) 691-7153
Frequency:
7 time(s) per week

OXFORD EAGLE
916 JACKSON AVENUE
OXFORD, MS 38655-
662-234-4331
Fax: 662-234-4351
news@oxfordeagle.com
http://www.oxfordeagle.com
• John Davis, Sports Editor
• Anna Zemek, Advertising Manager
Frequency:
5 time(s) per week

PADUCAH SUN
P.O. BOX 2300
PADUCAH, KY 42003-1550

270-575-8600
800-599-1771
Fax: 270-442-8188
http://www.paducahsun.com
• Steve Millizer, Sports Editor
(270) 575-8663
smillizer@paducahsun.com
• Joey Fosko, Sports Reporter
(270) 575-8600
jfosko@paducahsun.com
Frequency:
7 time(s) per week

PALISADIAN
626 MCCARTHY DRIVE
NEW MILFORD, NJ 07646
201-385-2000
• Dave Nay, Sports Editor
• Robert Nesoff, Sports Columnist
bobmetnews@aol.com
Frequency:
1 time(s) per week

PALLADIUM-ITEM
1175 NORTH A STREET
RICHMOND, IN 47374-3226
765-962-1575
800-686-1330
Fax: 765-973-4570
palitem@richmond.gannett.com
http://www.pal-item.com
• Josh Chapin, Sports Editor
(765) 973-4463
Frequency:
7 time(s) per week

PALLADIUM-TIMES
140 WEST FIRST STREET
OSWEGO, NY 13126-1514
315-343-3800
Fax: 315-343-0273
editorial@palltimes.com
http://www.palltimes.com/
• Mike LeBoeuf, Sports Editor
(315) 343-3800
mleboeuf@palltimes.com
Frequency:
6 time(s) per week

PALM BEACH DAILY NEWS
265 ROYAL POINCIANA WAY
PALM BEACH, FL 33480-4041
561-820-3800
800-432-7595
Fax: 561-655-4594
http://www.palmbeachdailynews.com
• Linda Goings, Advertising Director
lgoings@pbdailynews.com
• Michael Strauss, Sports Editor
Frequency:
7 time(s) per week

PALM BEACH POST
2751 SOUTH DIXIE HIGHWAY
WEST PALM BEACH, FL 33405-1233
561-820-4100
800-432-7595
Fax: 561-831-4340
pb_metro@pbpost.com
http://www.palmbeachpost.com
• Brian Biggane, Sports Reporter
(561) 820-4440
brian_biggane@pbpost.com
• Joe Capozzi, Sports Reporter
(561) 820-4814
joe_capozzi@pbpost.com

• Tom D'Angelo, Sports Reporter
(561) 820-4714
tom_dangelo@pbpost.com
• Craig Dolch, Sports Reporter
(561) 820-4467
craig_dolch@pbpost.com
• Steve Dorsey, Sports Writer
(561) 820-4738
steve_dorsey@pbpost.com
• Charles Elmore, Sports Columnist
(561) 820-4811
charles_elmore@pbpost.com
• Dave George, Sports Columnist
(561) 820-4468
dave_george@pbpost.com
• Melanie Gerik-Fordyce, Sports Assistant
Editor
(561) 820-4444
melanie_gerik@pbpost.com
• Willie Howard, Sports Reporter
(561) 820-4715
willie_howard@pbpost.com
• Jorge Milian, Sports Reporter
(954) 327-3506
jorge_milian@pbpost.com
• Robb Olsen, Advertising Vice President
(561) 820-4265
 robb_olsen@pbpost.com
• Greg Stoda, Sports Columnist
(561) 820-4717
greg_stoda@pbpost.com
• Alan Tays, Sports Reporter
(561) 820-4813
al_tays@pbpost.com
• Dave Tepps, Sports Deputy Editor
(561) 820-4742
• Edgar Thompson, Sports Reporter
(561) 820-4440
edgar_thompson@pbpost.com
Frequency:
7 time(s) per week

PALO ALTO WEEKLY
450 CAMBRIDGE AVE.
PALO ALTO, CA 94306
650-326-8210
Fax: 650-326-3928
editor@paweekly.com
http://www.paloaltoonline.com
• Rick Eymer, Sports Assistant Editor
reymer@paweekly.com
• Keith Peters, Sports Editor
(650) 223-6516
Frequency:
Weekly print; daily online

PAMPA NEWS
403 WEST ATCHISON
PAMPA, TX 79065-6303
806-669-2525
800-687-3348
Fax: 806-669-2520
pamnews1@pan-tex.net
http://www.thepampanews.com
• Michael J. Stevens, Sports Editor
(806) 669-2525
• Beverly Taylor, Classified Manager
• Redonn Woods, Advertising Manager
(806) 669-2525
Frequency:
6 time(s) per week

PANTAGRAPH
P.O. BOX 2907
BLOOMINGTON, IL 61702-2907
309-829-9411
800-747-7323

media

521

Fax: 309-829-7000
newsroom@pantagraph.com
http://www.pantagraph.com
• Jim Benson, Sports Writer
jbenson@pantagraph.com
• Mike Egenes, Sports Editor
(309) 820-3246
• Randy Kindred, Assistant Sports Editor
(309) 829-9411
rkindred@pantagraph.com
• Randy Reinhardt, Sports Writer
(309) 829-9411
rreinhardt@pantagraph.com
• Randy Sharer, Sports Writer
(309) 829-9411
rsharer@pantagraph.com
Frequency:
7 time(s) per week

PARAGOULD DAILY PRESS
1401 WEST HUNT STREET
PARAGOULD, AR 72450
870-239-8562
Fax: 870-239-8565
http://www.paragoulddailypress.com
• Mike McKinney, Sports Editor
sports@paragoulddailypress.com
• Angie Spencer, Classified Manager
Frequency:
6 time(s) per week

PARIS DAILY BEACON NEWS
218 NORTH MAIN STREET
PARIS, IL 61944
217-465-6424
800-587-5955
Fax: 217-463-1232
http://www.parisbeacon.com
• Angie Bierly, Advertising Manager
• Andrew Majors, Sports Editor
(217) 465-6424
Frequency:
6 time(s) per week

PARIS NEWS
P.O. BOX 1078
PARIS, TX 75460
903-785-8744
Fax: 903-785-1263
editor@theparisnews.com
http://www.theparisnews.com
• Tommy Culkin, Sports Editor
(903) 785-6972
tommy.culkin@theparisnews.com
• Klark Byrd, Managing Editor
(903) 785-6960
klark.byrd@theparisnews.com
Frequency:
6 time(s) per week

PARIS POST-INTELLIGENCER
208 EAST WOOD
PARIS, TN 38242-4139
731-642-1162
Fax: 731-642-1165
parispi@parispi.net
http://www.parispi.net
• Laura Dougherty, Advertising Manager
advertising@parispi.net
• Tommy Priddy, Sports Editor
sports@parispi.net
Frequency:
5 time(s) per week

PARKERSBURG NEWS
519 JULIANA STREET
PARKERSBURG, WV 26101
304-485-1891
800-642-1997
Fax: 304-485-2061
editorial@newsandsentinel.com
http://www.newsandsentinel.com
• Jay W. Bennett, Sports Reporter
(304) 485-1891
jbennett@newsandsentinel.com
• Jim Butta, Sports Reporter
jbutta@newsandsentinel.com
• Steve Hemmelgarn, Sports Reporter
(304) 485-1891
shemmelgarn@newsandsentinel.com
• David Poe, Sports Editor
(304) 485-1891
dpoe@newsandsentinel.com
Frequency:
7 time(s) per week

PARSONS SUN
P.O. BOX 836
PARSONS, KS 67357
620-421-2000
800-530-5723
Fax: 620-421-2217
news@parsonssun.com
http://www.parsonssun.com
• Anthony Cook, Sports Editor
acook@parsonssun.com
• Tisha Mitchell, Advertising Manager
tmitchell@parsonssun.com
Frequency:
6 time(s) per week

PASADENA CITIZEN
102 SOUTH SHAVER STREET
PASADENA, TX 77506
713-477-0221
Fax: 713-477-9090
pasadenacitizen@hcnonline.com
www.yourhoustonnews.com/pasadena
• Rob Avery, Sports Editor
(713) 477-0221
ravery@hcnonline.com
Frequency:
5 time(s) per week

**PASADENA/SAN GABRIEL VALLEY
JOURNAL-NEWS**
1541 NORTH LAKE AVENUE
PASADENA, CA 91104-2374
626-798-3972
Fax: 626-798-3282
pasjour@pacbell.net
http://www.pasadenajournal.com
• John Rando Rodgers, Sports Editor
Frequency:
1 time(s) per week

PATRIOT LEDGER
400 CROWN COLONY DRIVE
QUINCY, MA 02269-9159
617-786-7333
800-972-5070
Fax: 617-786-7193
http://www.patriotledger.com/
• Earl Lachance, Sports Editor
(617) 786-7057
sports@ledger.com
• Eric McHugh, Sports Writer
(617) 786-7057
emchugh@ledger.com
• Rick Seto, Sports Writer
(617) 786-7058

• Mike Fine, Sports Reporter
(617) 786-7058
Frequency:
6 time(s) per week

PATRIOT-NEWS
P.O. BOX 2265
HARRISBURG, PA 17105-2808
717-255-8100
800-692-7207
Fax: 717-705-3699
citydesk@patriot-news.com
http://www.pennlive.com
• Nick Horvath, Sports Editor
(717) 255-8404
nhorvath@patriot-news.com
• Michael Bullock, Sports Reporter
(717) 255-8124
mbullock@patriot-news.com
Frequency:
7 time(s) per week

PAULS VALLEY DAILY DEMOCRAT
108 SOUTH WILLOW STREET
PAULS VALLEY, OK 73075
405-238-6464
Fax: 405-238-3042
pvpub@swbell.net
http://www.paulsvalleydailydemocrat.com
• Mike Arie, Sports Editor
(405) 238-6464
marie@pvdemocrat.com
• Sara Fisher, Advertising Manager
sfisher@pvdemocrat.com
Frequency:
5 time(s) per week

PEKIN DAILY TIMES
20 SOUTH 4TH STREET
PEKIN, IL 61554
309-346-1111
800-888-6397
Fax: 309-346-1446
http://www.pekintimes.com/
Frequency:
6 time(s) per week

PENINSULA DAILY NEWS
P.O. BOX 1330
PORT ANGELES, WA 98362-2205
360-452-2345
800-826-7714
Fax: 360-417-3521
news@peninsuladailynews.com
http://www.peninsuladailynews.com
• Brad LaBrie, Sports Editor
(360) 417-3525
Frequency:
6 time(s) per week

PENINSULA GATEWAY/GATEWAY PLUS
3555 ERICKSON STREET
GIG HARBOR, WA 98335-1268
253-851-9921
Fax: 253-851-3939
http://www.gateline.com
• Neil Pierson, Sports Editor
(253) 853-9246
Frequency:
2 time(s) per week

PENSACOLA NEWS JOURNAL
P.O. BOX 12710
PENSACOLA, FL 32502
850-435-8500
800-288-2021

Fax: 850-435-8633
afail@pnj.com
http://www.pensacolanewsjournal.com
• Bob Heist, Sports Editor
(850) 435-8546
Frequency:
7 time(s) per week

PERRY DAILY JOURNAL
714 DELAWARE
PERRY, OK 73077-6425
580-336-2222
Fax: 580-336-3222
• Scott Barber, Sports Editor
Frequency:
5 time(s) per week

PHAROS-TRIBUNE
PO BOX 210
LOGANSPORT, IN 46947-3154
574-722-5000
800-676-4125
Fax: 574-732-5070
ptnews@pharostribune.com
http://www.pharostribune.com
• Beau Wicker, Sports Editor
beau.wicker@pharostribune.com
Frequency:
7 time(s) per week

PHILADELPHIA DAILY NEWS
P.O. BOX 7788
PHILADELPHIA, PA 19130-4015
215-854-5900
800-222-2765
Fax: 215-854-5910
http://www.philly.com/dailynews/
• Josh Barnett, Sports Editor
(215) 854-5212
• Les Bowen, Professional Football Reporter
(215) 854-4133
bowenl@phillynews.com
• Bill Conlin, Sports Columnist
(215) 854-5700
bill1chair@aol.com
• Bob Cooney, Sports Reporter
(215) 854-5900
cooneyb@phillynews.com
• Sam Donnellon, Sports Columnist
(215) 854-4550
donnels@phillynews.com
• Bernard Fernandez, Sports Writer
(215) 854-5700
• Bill Fleischman, Assistant Sports Editor
(215) 854-5705
fleiscb@phillynews.com
• Paul Hagen, National Baseball Reporter
(215) 854-4550
• Marcus Hayes, Sports Writer
(215) 854-5700
hayesm@phillynews.com
• Rich Hofmann, Sports Columnist
(215) 854-5130
hofmanr@phillynews.com
• Phil Jasner, Basketball Reporter
(215) 854-5700
• Dick Jerardi, Sports Reporter/Columnist
(215) 854-5700
jerardd@phillynews.com
• Pat McLoone, Sports Executive Editor
(215) 854-5700
mcloonp@phillynews.com
• Ed Moran, Sports Business Writer
(215) 854-5940
• Ted Silary, High School Sports Reporter
(215) 854-5900
• John Smallwood, Sports Columnist

(215) 854-5847
smallwj@phillynews.com
• Paul Vigna, Sports Reporter
(215) 854-5900
Frequency:
6 time(s) per week

PHILADELPHIA INQUIRER
400 NORTH BROAD STREET
PHILADELPHIA, PA 19130-4015
215-854-2000
Fax: 215-854-5099
http://www.philly.com
• Don Beideman, Sports Reporter
(610) 701-7613
• Bob Brookover, Professional Football Reporter
(215) 854-2577
bbrookover@phillynews.com
• Sam Carchidi, Sports Reporter
(215) 854-5181
scarchidi@phillynews.com
• Deirdre Childress, Sports Deputy Editor
• Frank Fitzpatrick, Sports Reporter
(215) 854-5068
ffitzpatrick@phillynews.com
• Bob Ford, Sports Reporter
(215) 854-5842
bford@phillynews.com
• Mel Greenberg, Sports Reporter
(215) 854-5725
• Bill Iezzi, Sports Writer
• Jim Jenks, Sports Editor
• Mike Jensen, Sports Writer
(215) 854-4489
mjensen@phillynews.com
• Joe Juliano, Sports Writer
(215) 854-4494
jjuliano@phillynews.com
• Joe Logan, Sports Writer
(215) 854-5604
• Bill Lyon, Sports Columnist
(215) 854-5508
• Sheil Kapadia, Sports Editor
(215) 854-2455
• Ashley McGeachy Fox, Sports Writer
• Tom McGurk, Sports Reporter
(215) 854-5721
• Gary Miles, Sports Deputy Editor
(215) 854-4487
gmiles@phillynews.com
• Marc Narducci, Sports Reporter
(856) 779-3325
mnarducci@phillynews.com
• Rick O'Brien, Sports Reporter
(215) 854-4550
robrien@phillynews.com
• Tim Panaccio, Sports Writer
(215) 854-2847
• Rob Parent, Sports Writer
(610) 313-8025
• Ray Parrillo, Sports Writer
(215) 854-2743
• John Quinn, Sports Deputy Editor
jquinn@phillynews.com
• Shannon Ryan, Sports Reporter
(610) 701-7607
• James T. Salisbury, (215) 854-4983
Sports Writer
• Don Sapatkin, Sports Writer
(610) 313-8246
dsapatkin@phillynews.com
• Michael Cu Schaeffer, Sports Assistant Editor
(215) 854-2537
• Mike Schaffer, Sports Assistant Editor
(215) 854-2537
mschaffer@phillynews.com

• Pete Schnatz, Sports Writer
(215) 854-5817
• Phil Sheridan, Sports Columnist
(215) 854-2844
Frequency:
7 time(s) per week

PHILADELPHIA NEW OBSERVER
1520 LOCUST STREET SUITE 700
PHILADELPHIA, PA 19102
215-545-7500
Fax: 215-545-5548
http://www.pnonews.com
• Walter Davis, Sports Editor
bblessed1983@yahoo.com
Frequency:
1 time(s) per week

PHILADELPHIA TRIBUNE
526 SOUTH 16TH STREET
PHILADELPHIA, PA 19146-1565
215-893-4050
Fax: 215-735-3612
info@phillytrib.com
http://www.phillytrib.com
• Chris Murray, Sports Editor
(215) 893-5790
editorial@phila-tribune.com
Frequency:
3 time(s) per week

PHOENIX
POTTSTOWN, PA 19464
610-933-8926
Fax: 610-933-1187
editor@phoenixvillenews.com
http://www.phoenixvillenews.com
• Barry Sankey, Sports Writer
bsankey@phoenixvillenews.com
• Jason Wolf, Sports Editor
Frequency:
6 time(s) per week

PILOT NEWS
PO BOX 220
PLYMOUTH, IN 46563-2135
574-936-3101
800-933-0356
Fax: 574-936-3844
http://www.thepilotnews.com/
• James Costello, Sports Editor
sports@thepilotnews.com
Frequency:
6 time(s) per week

PIONEER
PO BOX 455
BEMIDJI, MN 56619
218-333-9200
Fax: 218-333-9819
news@bemidjipioneer.com
http://www.bemidjipioneer.com
• Mary Default, Classified Manager
classifieds@bemidjipioneer.com
• Jim Carrington, Sports Editor
(218) 751-3740
sports@bemidjipioneer.com
• Pat Miller, Sports Reporter
(218) 751-3740
sports@bemidjipioneer.com
• Jaclyn King, Advertising Manager
jking@bemidji.com
Frequency:
6 time(s) per week

PIQUA DAILY CALL
310 SPRING STREET
PIQUA, OH 45356-2334
937-773-2721
Fax: 937-773-2782
editorial@dailycall.com
http://www.dailycall.com
• Rob Kiser, Sports Editor
(937) 773-2721
rkiser@dailycall.com
• Leiann Stewart, Advertising Manager
(937) 440-5252
lstewart@brownpublishing.com
Frequency:
6 time(s) per week

PITTSBURGH POST-GAZETTE
34 BOULEVARD OF THE ALLIES
PITTSBURGH, PA 15222-1204
412-263-1100
800-228-6397
Fax: 412-263-1313
editors@post-gazette.com
http://www.post-gazette.com
• Shelly Anderson, Reporter
(412) 263-1721
shanderson@post-gazette.com
• Gene Collier, Sports Columnist
(412) 263-1283
gcollier@post-gazette.com
• Ron Cook, Sports Columnist
(412) 263-1525
rcook@post-gazette.com
• Chuck Finder, Sports Columnist
(412) 263-1724
cfinder@post-gazette.com
• Teresa Lindeman, Retail Reporter
(412) 263-2018
tlindeman@post-gazette.com
• Paul Meyer, Sports Writer
(412) 263-1144
pmeyer@post-gazette.com
• Jerry Micco, Assistant Managing
Editor/Sports
(412) 263-3052
jmicco@post-gazette.com
• Carl Remensky, Sports Associate Editor
(412) 263-1607
cremensky@post-gazette.com
• Terry Shields, Assistant Sports Editor
(412) 263-1989
tshields@post-gazette.com
• Bob Smizik, Sports Columnist
(412) 263-1468
bsmizik@post-gazette.com
• Larry Walsh, Snowsports Reporter
(412) 263-1488
lwalsh@post-gazette.com
• Steve Ziants, Sports Writer
(412) 263-1474
sziants@post-gazette.com
Frequency:
7 time(s) per week

PITTSBURGH TRIBUNE-REVIEW
503 MARTINDALE STREET
PITTSBURGH, PA 15212-5705
412-321-6460
800-433-3045
Fax: 412-320-7965
release@tribweb.com
http://www.pittsburghlive.com
• Rob Biertempfel, Sports Writer
(412) 320-7811
rbiertempfel@tribweb.com
• Jerry DiPaola, Sports Reporter
(412) 320-7997
jdipaola@tribweb.com

• Dave Mackall, Sports Reporter
(412) 380-5617
dmackall@tribweb.com
• Kevin Smith, Executive Sports Editor
(412) 320-7848
ksmith@tribweb.com
• Joe Starkey, Sports Reporter
(412) 320-7810
jstarkey@tribweb.com
Frequency:
7 time(s) per week

PLAIN DEALER
1801 SUPERIOR AVENUE
CLEVELAND, OH 44114
216-999-4800
800-688-4802
Fax: 216-999-6354
http://www.plaindealer.com
• Elton Alexander, Sports Reporter (College)
(216) 999-4370
ealexander@plaind.com
• Roger Brown, Sports Writer
rbrown@plaind.com
• Mary Kay Cabot, Sports Reporter
(Football)
(216) 999-4370
mcabot@plaind.com
• Dave Campbell, Metro Sports Editor
(216) 999-4335
dcampbell@plaind.com
• Bob Dolgan, Sports Writer
(216) 999-3540
bdolgan@plaind.com
• Eddie Dwyer, Sports Writer
(216) 999-4677
edwyer@plaind.com
• Bob Fortuna, High School Sports Writer
(216) 999-4665
bfortuna@plaind.com
• Pat Galbincea, Sports Writer
pgalbincea@plaind.com
• Tony Grossi, Sports Reporter
(216) 999-4670
tgrossi@plaind.com
• Roy Hewitt, Sports Editor
(216) 999-4101
rhewitt@plaind.com
• Bruce Hooley, Sports Writer
bhooley@plaind.com
• Paul Hoynes, Sports Reporter
(216) 999-5158
phoynes@plaind.com
• Bill Livingston, Sports Columnist
(216) 999-4672
blivingston@plaind.com
• Dennis Manoloff, Sports Writer
(216) 999-4664
dmanoloff@plaind.com
• Joe Maxse, Sports Writer
(216) 999-5168
jmaxse@plaind.com
• Jack McDermott, Sports Writer
jmcdermott@plaind.com
• Rich Medeiros, Advertising Director
(216) 999-4350
rmedeiros@plaind.com
• Bob Migra, Sports Writer
(440) 324-3793
bmigra@plaind.com
• Mike Peticca, Sports Writer
(215) 999-6177
mpeticca@plaind.com
• Marcia Pledger, Business Columnist
(216) 999-4813
mpledger@plaind.com
• Bob Roberts, Sports Reporter
(216) 999-5754

broberts@plaind.com
• Tim Rogers, Reporter
(330) 376-7309
trogers@plaind.com
• Mary Schmitt Boyer, Sports Reporter
(216) 999-4668
mschmitt@plaind.com
• Bud Shaw, Sports Columnist
bshaw@plaind.com
• George Sweda, (216) 999-5809
Sports Reporter
gsweda@plaind.com
• Branson Wright, Sports Writer
(216) 999-4671
bwright@plaind.com
Frequency:
7 time(s) per week

PLAINSMAN
49 3RD STREET, S.E.
HURON, SD 57350-2015
605-352-6401
800-859-3045
Fax: 605-352-7754
editor.plainsman@midconetwork.com
http://www.plainsman.com
• Mike Carroll, Sports Writer
(605) 353-7435
mcarroll.plainsman@midconetwork.com
• Darian Dudrick, Sports Editor
(605) 353-7425
Frequency:
6 time(s) per week

PLANO STAR COURIER
P.O. BOX 860248
PLANO, TX 75074
972-398-4200
http://www.planostar.com
• Geoff Blaine, Sports Editor
geoff.blaine@scntx.com
• Brian Porter, Sports Editor
(972) 398-4200
brian.porter@scntx.com
• Derek Price, Media News Editor
derek.price@scntx.com
Frequency:
5 time(s) per week

POCONO RECORD
511 LENOX STREET
STROUDSBURG, PA 18360-1516
570-421-3000
800-756-4237
Fax: 570-424-2625
newsroom@poconorecord.com
http://www.poconorecord.com
• Peter L. Berry, Advertising Director
(570) 420-4372
• Mike Kuhns, Sports Editor
(570) 420-4389
mkuhns@poconorecord.com
Frequency:
7 time(s) per week

PONCA CITY NEWS
300 NORTH 3RD STREET
PONCA CITY, OK 74601
580-765-3311
Fax: 580-762-6397
news@poncacitynews.com
http://www.poncacitynews.com
• Fred Hilton, Sports Writer
(580) 765-3311
sports@poncacitynews.com
• Everett Lockwood, Advertising Manager

(580) 765-3311
ads@poncacitynews.com
Frequency:
6 time(s) per week

PORTAGE DAILY REGISTER
P.O. BOX 470
PORTAGE, WI 53901-2113
608-742-2111
Fax: 608-742-8346
pdr-news@capitalnewspapers.com
http://www.wiscnews.com/portagedailyregister/
• Dan Larson, Sports Reporter
(608) 745-3512
dlarson@capitalnewspapers.com
• Travis Houslet, Sports Editor
(608) 745-3518
thouslet@capitalnewspapers.com
Frequency:
6 time(s) per week

PORTERVILLE RECORDER
115 EAST OAK AVENUE
PORTERVILLE, CA 93257-3807
559-784-5000
Fax: 559-784-1172
recorder@portervillerecorder.com
http://www.portervillerecorder.com
• Doug Moore, Advertising Manager
(559) 784-5000
• Jan Parnell, Classified Manager
(559) 784-5000
jparnell@link.freedom.com
• Charles Whisnand, Sports Editor
(559) 784-5000
Frequency:
6 time(s) per week

PORTLAND PRESS HERALD, MAINE SUNDAY TELEGRAM
390 CONGRESS STREET
PORTLAND, ME 04101-3514
207-791-6650
Fax: 207-791-6920
communitynews@pressherald.com
http://www.pressherald.com
• Paul Betit, Sports Reporter
• Sue Burtchell, Advertising Manager
(207) 791-6213
sburtchell@pressherald.com
• Glenn Jordan, Sports Reporter
(207) 791-6425
gjordan@mainetoday.com
• Joe Grant, Sports Editor
(207) 791-6480
jgrant@mainetoday.com
• Kevin Thomas, Sports Writer
(207) 791-6411
kthomas@mainetoday.com
Frequency:
7 time(s) per week

PORTLAND TRIBUNE
6605 S.E. LAKE ROAD
PORTLAND, OR 97222
503-226-6397
Fax: 503-226-7023
tribnews@portlandtribune.com
http://www.portlandtribune.com
• Steve Brandon, Sports Editor
(503) 546-5144
stevebrandon@portlandtribune.com
Frequency:
2 time(s) per week

PORTSMOUTH HERALD
111 MAPLEWOOD AVENUE
PORTSMOUTH, NH 03801-3715
603-436-1800
800-439-0303
Fax: 603-433-5760
news@seacoastonline.com
http://www.seacoastonline.com/news/index.htm
• Frank Coppola, Sports Editor
(603) 436-1800
fcoppola@seacoastonline.com
• Mike Zhe, Sports Writer
(603) 436-1800
mzhe@seacoastonline.com
Frequency:
7 time(s) per week

POST AND COURIER
134 COLUMBUS STREET
CHARLESTON, SC 29403
843-577-7111
Fax: 843-937-5579
www.postandcourier.com
• Phil Bowman, High School Sports Reporter
(843) 577-7111
• Tommy Braswell, Outdoors Writer
(843) 937-5580
• David Caraviello, Sports Reporter
• Jeff Hartsell, Sports Reporter
(843) 577-7111
• Mike Mooneyham, Sports Columnist
(843) 577-7111
• Keith Namm, Sports Reporter
Frequency:
7 time(s) per week

POST REGISTER
333 NORTHGATE MILE
IDAHO FALLS, ID 83401-2529
208-522-1800
Fax: 208-529-9683
http://www.postregister.com
• Ken Clements, Retail Advertising Manager
(208) 522-1800
• Jeff Pinkham, Sports Editor
(208) 542-6772
prsports@postregister.com
• Paul Lambert, Sports Reporter
(208) 542-6770
plambert@postregister.com
• Ron Lee, Advertising Director
(208) 522-1800
• Robyn Steins, Sports Reporter
(208) 522-1800
Frequency:
7 time(s) per week

POST-BULLETIN
18 1ST AVENUE, S.E.
ROCHESTER, MN 55904-3722
507-285-7600
Fax: 507-285-7666
news@postbulletin.com
http://www.postbulletin.com
• Craig Swalboski, Sports Editor
(507) 285-7721
swal@postbulletin.com
Frequency:
6 time(s) per week

POST-CRESCENT
P.O. BOX 59
APPLETON, WI 54911
920-933-1000
800-236-6397

Fax: 920-733-1945
pcnews@postcrescent.com
http://www.wisinfo.com/postcrescent/index.shtml
• Mike Sherry, Sports Editor
(920) 993-1000
msherry@postcrescent.com
• Brett Christopherson, Sports Reporter
(920) 993-1000
bchristopherson@postcrescent.com
Frequency:
7 time(s) per week

POST-JOURNAL
15 WEST 2ND STREET
JAMESTOWN, NY 14702-5215
716-487-1111
Fax: 716-664-3119
editorial@post-journal.com
http://www.post-journal.com
• Debbie Brunner, Advertising Manager
(716) 487-1111
dbrunner@post-journal.com
• Scott Kindberg, Sports Assistant Editor
(716) 487-1111
skindberg@post-journal.com
• Jim Riggs, Sports Editor
(716) 487-1111
jriggs@post-journal.com
Frequency:
7 time(s) per week

POST-STANDARD, SYRACUSE HERALD-JOURNAL, SYRACUSE HERALD AMERICAN
CLINTON SQUARE
BOX 4915
SYRACUSE, NY 13221-4915
315-470-0011
800-765-3231
Fax: 315-470-3187
• Bud Poliquin, Sports Columnist
• Bob Snyder, Sports Columnist

POST-STAR
P.O. BOX 2157
GLENS FALLS, NY 12801
518-792-3131 EXT 3220
800-724-2543
Fax: 518-761-1255
obits@poststar.com
http://www.poststar.com
• Greg Brownell, Sports Editor
(518) 792-3131
brownell@poststar.com
• Warren Alber, Sports Reporter
(518) 792-3131
Frequency:
7 time(s) per week

POST-TRIBUNE (IN)
1433 E. 83RD AVE
GARY, IN 46410-6307
219-648-3000
Fax: 219-648-3236
http://posttrib.suntimes.com/
• Mark Lazerus, Sports Editor
(219) 648-3140
mlazerus@post-trib.com
• Rick Cains, Advertising Director
(219) 648-3189
rcains@post-trib.com

POST-TRIBUNE (MO)
210 MONROE STREET
JEFFERSON CITY, MO 65101-3210

573-636-3131
Fax: 573-636-7035
news@newstribune.com
http://www.newstribune.com
• Debbie Kiser, Advertising Manager
(573) 761-0226
dkiser@newstribune.com
• Tom Rackers, Sports Editor
(573) 636-3131
sports@newstribune.com
Frequency:
7 time(s) per week

POTEAU DAILY NEWS
804 NORTH BROADWAY
SUITE C
POTEAU, OK 74953-3503
918-647-3188
800-495-6397
Fax: 918-647-8198
http://www.poteaudailynews.com
• Samantha Hess, Advertising Director
(918) 647-3188
addept@poteaudailynews.com
• David Seeley, Sports Editor
sports@poteaudailynews.com
Frequency:
5 time(s) per week

POTOMAC NEWS
PO BOX 351
MANASSAS, VA 20108
571-333-1538
http://www.insidenova.com/
• Dave Fawcett, Sports Editor
(703) 530-3911
dfawcett@insidenova.com
• Robert Daski, Sports Reporter
(703) 530-3913
• Dave Utnik, Sports Reporter
(703) 530-3914
dutnik@insidenova.com
Frequency:
7 time(s) per week

POUGHKEEPSIE JOURNAL
P.O. BOX 1231
POUGHKEEPSIE, NY 12602
845-437-4800
Fax: 845-437-4921
newsroom@poughkee.gannett.com
http://www.poughkeepsiejournal.com
• Jan Dewey, Advertising Director
(845) 437-4975
jdewey@poughkee.gannett.com
• Dan Pietrafesa, Sports Editor
(845) 437-4849
Frequency:
7 time(s) per week

PRENSA GRAFICA
121 NW 38 COURT
MIAMI, FL 33126
305-649-6267
Fax: 305-649-6300
• Orestes Llana, Sports Editor
Frequency:
1 time(s) per week

PRESS & SUN-BULLETIN
33 LEWIS ROAD
BINGHAMTON, NY 13905
607-798-1234
800-365-0077
Fax: 607-798-1113
http://www.pressconnects.com

• Charlie Jaworski, Sports Executive Editor
(607) 798-1191
bgmsports@gannett.com
• Jodie Riesbeck, Advertising Director
(607) 798-1100
JRIESBEC@binghamt.gannett.com
• Dave Schultz, Sports Assistant Editor
(607) 798-1191
Frequency:
7 time(s) per week

PRESS DEMOCRAT
427 MENDOCINO AVENUE
SANTA ROSA, CA 95401
707-546-2020
Fax: 707-521-5330
http://www.pressdemocrat.com
• Phil Barber, Sports Reporter
(707) 526-8672
pbarber@pressdemocrat.com
• Lowell Cohn, Sports Reporter
(707) 521-5486
lcohn@pressdemocrat.com
• Jeff Fletcher, Sports Reporter
jeff_fletcher@pacbell.net
• Bruce Meadows, Sports Reporter
(707) 521-5263
bmeadows@pressdemocrat.com
• Bob Padecky, Sports Reporter
(707) 521-5490
bpadecky@pressdemocrat.com
• Bill Pinella, Sports Assistant Editor
(707) 526-8500
bpinella@pressdemocrat.com
• Robert Rubino, Sports Reporter
rrubino@pressdemocrat.com
Frequency:
7 time(s) per week

PRESS DISPATCH-TRIBUNE
P.O. BOX 28100
GLADSTONE, MO 64188
816-454-9660
Fax: 816-414-3331
http://www.kccommunitynews.com
• Kevin Goodwin, Sports Editor
(816) 454-9660
Frequency:
2 time(s) per week

PRESS JOURNAL
14522 SOUTH OUTER FORTY ROAD
TOWN AND COUNTRY, MO 63017
314-821-1110
Fax: 314-821-0843
http://www.stltoday.com
• Greg Uptain, Sports Editor
(314) 821-1110
guptain@yourjournal.com
Frequency:
2 time(s) per week

PRESS OF ATLANTIC CITY
11 DEVINS LANE
PLEASANTVILLE, NJ 08232
609-272-7000
Fax: 609-272-7224
newstips@pressofac.com
http://www.pressofac.com
• John Celestino, Advertising Director
(609) 272-7047
jcelestino@pressofac.com
• Michael McGarry, Sports Writer
(609) 272-7185
mmcgarry@pressofac.com
• Mark Melhorn, Sports Assistant Editor
(609) 272-7179

mmelhorn@pressofac.com
• Michael Shepherd, Sports Editor
(609) 272-7180
mshepherd@pressofac.com
• Kathy Waldron, Classified Manager
(609) 272-7002
kwaldron@pressofac.com
Frequency:
7 time(s) per week

PRESS REPUBLICAN
170 MARGARET STREET
PLATTSBURGH, NY 12901
518-561-2300
800-288-7323
Fax: 518-561-3362
http://www.pressrepublican.com
• Robert Goetz, Sports Editor
(518) 565-4124
bgoetz@pressrepublican.com
• George Rock, Advertising Manager
grock@pressrepublican.com
Frequency:
7 time(s) per week

PRESS-ENTERPRISE (CA)
3512 14TH STREET
RIVERSIDE, CA 92501
951-684-1200
Fax: 951-368-9024
news@pe.com
http://www.pe.com
• Jim Alexander, Sports Reporter
(951) 368-9543
jalexander@pe.com
• David Ammenheuser, Sports Editor
(951) 368-9520
• Sue Barry, Advertising Vice President
(951) 368-9201
• Luis Bueno, Sports Columnist
• Joe Hamelin, Sports Writer
(909) 368-9527
• Eric Johnson, Sports Columnist
(951) 368-9530
ejohnson@pe.com
• Eric Johnson, Sports Writer
(951) 368-9530
ejohnson@pe.com
• Jeff Parenti, Sports Assistant Editor
(951) 368-9523
jparenti@pe.com
• Jeff Parenti, Sports Assistant Editor
(909) 368-9523
jparenti@pe.com
• Gregg Patton, Sports Columnist
(951) 368-9597
• Kevin Pearson, Sports Reporter
(951) 368-9525
• Broderick Turner, Sports Writer
(951) 368-9542
Frequency:
7 time(s) per week

PRESS-ENTERPRISE (PA)
3185 LACKAWANNA AVENUE
BLOOMSBURG, PA 17815-3329
570-784-2121
800-228-3483
Fax: 570-784-9226
http://www.pressenterpriseonline.com
• Sandra Sterner, Advertising Manager
(570) 387-1234
news@pressenterprise.net
• John Medeiros, Sports Editor
(570) 784-2121
sports@pressenterprise.net

Frequency:
7 time(s) per week

PRESS-REGISTER
401 NORTH WATER STREET
MOBILE, AL 36602-2600
251-219-5400
800-239-1340
Fax: 251-219-5799
http://www.al.com
• Steve Hall, Classified Manager
(251) 219-5503
• Randy Kennedy, Sports Editor
(251) 219-5689
Frequency:
7 time(s) per week

PRESS-TELEGRAM
300 OCEANGATE
LONG BEACH, CA 90802-1329
562-435-1161
800-436-3676
Fax: 562-437-7892
ptnews@presstelegram.com
http://www.presstelegram.com
• Jennifer Lemon, Advertising Director
(562) 499-1378
• Bob Keisser, Sports Columnist
(562) 435-1161
• Doug Kirkorian, Sports Columnist
(562) 499-1338
Frequency:
7 time(s) per week

PRINCETON DAILY CLARION
100 NORTH GIBSON
PRINCETON, IN 47670-1855
812-385-2525
Fax: 812-386-6199
news@pdclarion.com
http://www.pdclarion.com
• Tom Guest, Advertising Manager
• Pete Swanson, Sports Editor
(812) 385-2525
Frequency:
5 time(s) per week

PROGRESS-INDEX
15 FRANKLIN STREET
PETERSBURG, VA 23803-4514
804-732-3456
Fax: 804-861-9452
newsroom@progress-index.com
http://www.progress-index.com
• Tom Dozier, Sports Editor
(804) 722-5151
• Mike Gochenour, Advertising Manager
(804) 722-5137
Frequency:
7 time(s) per week

PROVIDENCE JOURNAL
75 FOUNTAIN STREET
PROVIDENCE, RI 02902
401-277-7000
888-697-7656
breakingnews@providencejournal.com
www.providencejournal.com
• Bill Corey, Sports Editor
(401) 277-7125
bcorey@providencejournal.com
Frequency:
7 time(s) per week

PUBLIC OPINION
77 NORTH 3RD STREET
CHAMBERSBURG, PA 17201
717-264-6161
800-782-0661
Fax: 717-264-0377
business@publicopinionnews.com
http://www.publicopiniononline.com
• Ginny Harriger, Advertising Director
(717) 262-4710
• Ed Gotwals, Sports Editor
(717) 262-4755
egotwals@publicopinionnews.com
Frequency:
6 time(s) per week

PUEBLO CHIEFTAIN
825 WEST SIXTH STREET
PUEBLO, CO 81003-2313
719-544-3520
800-279-6397
Fax: 719-544-5897
newsroom@chieftain.com
http://www.chieftain.com
• Bernie Schutz, Advertising Director
(719) 546-2277
• Judy Hildner, Sports Editor
(719) 404-2765
jhildner@chieftain.com
• Joe Cervi, Sports Writer
(719) 404-2769
jcervi@chieftain.com
Frequency:
7 time(s) per week

QUAD-CITY TIMES
500 EAST 3RD STREET
DAVENPORT, IA 52801-1708
563-383-2244
800-437-4640
Fax: 563-383-2370
http://www.qctimes.com
• Don Doxsie, Sports Editor
(563) 383-2280
ddoxsie@qctimes.com
Frequency:
7 time(s) per week

QUINCY HERALD-WHIG
130 SOUTH 5TH STREET
QUINCY, IL 62301-3916
217-223-5100
800-373-9444
Fax: 217-223-9757
http://www.whig.com
• Don O'Brien, Sports Editor
(217) 221-3365
dobrien@whig.com
Frequency:
7 time(s) per week

RAPID CITY JOURNAL
507 MAIN STREET
RAPID CITY, SD 57701
605-394-8300
800-843-2300
Fax: 605-394-8462
news@rapidcityjournal.com
http://www.rapidcityjournal.com
• Andrew Cutler, Sports Editor
(605) 394-8291
• Brad Slater, Advertising Director
(605) 394-8331
Frequency:
7 time(s) per week

RAVALLI REPUBLIC
232 WEST MAIN STREET
HAMILTON, MT 59840
406-363-3300
800-640-2010
Fax: 406-363-1767
editor@ravallirepublic.com
http://www.ravallirepublic.com
• Erin Hollern, Sports Editor
(406) 363-3300
Frequency:
5 time(s) per week

READING EAGLE
P.O. BOX 582
READING, PA 19601-4029
610-371-5000
800-633-7222
Fax: 610-371-5098
news@readingeagle.com
http://www.readingeagle.com
• Terry Bickhart, Sports Editor
(610) 371-5061
tbickhart@readingeagle.com
• Darryl Grumling, Sports Reporter
(610) 371-5072
• Steve Patton, Sports Reporter
(610) 371-5097
spatton@readingeagle.com
• Mike Berres, Sports Writer
(610) 371-5000
Frequency:
7 time(s) per week

RECORD (CA)
P.O. BOX 900
STOCKTON, CA 95201
209-943-6397
800-606-9741
Fax: 209-547-8186
newsroom@recordnet.com
http://www.recordnet.com/
• Tony Acosta, Sports Copy Editor
(209) 546-8290
tacosta@recordnet.com
• Jason Anderson, Sports Reporter
(209) 546-8283
janderson@recordnet.com
• Patsy Prato, Classified Manager
(209) 546-8213
• Jagdip Dhillon, Sports Reporter
(209) 546-8292
jdhillon@recordnet.com
• Lori Gilbert, Sports Columnist
(209) 546-8284
lgilbert@recordnet.com
• Scott Linesburgh, Sports Reporter
(209) 546-8281
• Pete Ottesen, Sports Reporter
(209) 546-8269
pottesen@recordnet.com
• Sam Smith, Assistant Sports Editor
(209) 546-8289
sports@recordnet.com
Frequency:
7 time(s) per week

RECORD (NJ)
150 RIVER ST
HACKENSACK, NJ 07601
201-646-4000
Fax: 201-646-4428
www.bergen.com
• mitch Krugel, Sports Editor
• Rhona Bronson, Director Marketing
Services

media

RECORD (NY)
501 BROADWAY
TROY, NY 12181
518-270-1295
Fax: 518-270-1202
www.troyrecord.com
• Kevin Moran, Sports Editor
• Joan Marro Harris, Advertising Director

RECORD SEARCHLIGHT
1101 TWIN VIEW BOULEVARD
REDDING, CA 96003-1531
530-225-8210
800-666-2772
Fax: 530-225-8236
editor@redding.com
http://www.redding.com
• Nathan Zeliff, Sports Editor
(530) 474-3267
Frequency:
7 time(s) per week

RECORD-ARGUS
10 PENN AVENUE
GREENVILLE, PA 16125
724-588-5000
800-542-3100
Fax: 724-588-4691
argusnews@rrbiznet.com
• Whendy Kozminski, Sports Editor
(724) 588-5000
argussports@rrbiznet.com
• Jim Rust, Advertising Manager
(724) 588-5000
argusads@rrbiznet.com
Frequency:
6 time(s) per week

RECORD-COURIER
P.O. BOX 1201
RAVENNA, OH 44266-2254
330-296-9657
800-560-9657
Fax: 330-296-2698
editor@recordpub.com
http://www.recordpub.com
• Tom Nader, Sports Editor
(330) 296-9657
tnader@recordpub.com
Frequency:
7 time(s) per week

RECORD-HERALD
30 WALNUT STREET
WAYNESBORO, PA 17268-1644
717-762-2151
Fax: 717-762-3824
news@therecordherald.com
http://www.therecordherald.com
• Dennis Shockey, Advertising Manager
(717) 762-2151
• Lee Goodwin, Sports Editor
(717) 762-2151
sports@therecordherald.com
Frequency:
6 time(s) per week

RECORD-JOURNAL
11 CROWN STREET
MERIDEN, CT 06450-5713
203-235-1661
Fax: 203-639-0210
newsroom@record-journal.com
http://www.record-journal.com
• Bryant Carpenter, Sports Editor
(203) 317-2208

bcarpenter@record-journal.com
• John Pettit, Sports Writer
(203) 317-2238
• Kimberley Boath, Director Advertising
(203) 317-2300
Frequency:
7 time(s) per week

RECORDER
ONE VENNER ROAD
AMSTERDAM, NY 12010-5617
518-843-1100
800-453-6397
Fax: 518-843-1338
news@recordernews.com
http://www.recordernews.com
• Paul Antonelli, Sports Editor
paul.antonelli@recordernews.com
• Kevin McClary, Advertising Manager
sales@recordernews.com
Frequency:
7 time(s) per week

REDLANDS DAILY FACTS
700 BROOKSIDE AVENUE
REDLANDS, CA 92373
909-793-3221
Fax: 909-793-9588
http://www.redlandsdailyfacts.com
• Fred Board, Advertising Director
(909) 793-3221
• Kevin Trudgeon, Sports Editor
(909) 793-3221
Frequency:
6 time(s) per week

REGISTER NEWS
911 BROADWAY
MOUNT VERNON, IL 62864-4008
618-242-0113
Fax: 618-242-8286
mtv@intrnet.net
http://register-news.com
• Todd Adams, Sports Editor
• Janie Daniels, Classified Manager
(618) 242-0113
Frequency:
6 time(s) per week

REGISTER-GUARD
P.O. BOX 10188
EUGENE, OR 97408
541-485-1234
Fax: 541-683-7631
http://www.registerguard.com
• Ron Bellamy, Sports Editor
(541) 485-1234
ron.bellamy@registerguard.com
• Michael Raz, Advertising Director

REGISTER-HERALD
P.O. BOX 2398
BECKLEY, WV 25801-3822
304-255-4400
800-950-0250
Fax: 304-256-5625
http://www.register-herald.com
• Gary Fauber, Sports Assistant Editor
(304) 255-4400
gfauber@register-herald.com
• Charles Jessup, Advertising Manager
(304) 255-4425
• Dave Morrison, Sports Editor
(304) 255-4475
Frequency:
7 time(s) per week

REGISTER-MAIL
140 SOUTH PRAIRIE STREET
GALESBURG, IL 61401-4605
309-343-7181
800-747-7181
Fax: 309-342-5171
tmartin@register-mail.com
http://www.register-mail.com
• Doris Medhurst, Advertising Manager
(309) 343-7181
• Mike Trueblood, Sports Editor
(309) 343-7181
mtrueblood@register-mail.com
Frequency:
7 time(s) per week

REIDSVILLE REVIEW
1921 VANCE STREET
REIDSVILLE, NC 27320-3254
336-349-4331
Fax: 336-342-2513
news@reidsvillereview.com
http://www.reidsvillereview.com
• Steve Canulli, Sports Editor
scanulli@reidsvillereview.com
Frequency:
5 time(s) per week

RENO GAZETTE-JOURNAL
P.O. BOX 22000
RENO, NV 89502
775-788-6200
800-648-5048
Fax: 775-788-6458
http://www.rgj.com
• Charle Carlson, Sports Editor
(775) 788-6345
ccarlson@rgj.com
• Dan Hinxman, Sports Reporter
(775) 327-6346
dhinxman@rgj.com
Frequency:
7 time(s) per week

RENSSELAER REPUBLICAN
117 NORTH VAN RENSSELAER STREET
RENSSELAER, IN 47978-2651
219-866-5111
888-729-2454
Fax: 219-866-3775
daily@rensselaerrepublican.com
http://www.rensselaerrepublican.com
• Don Hurd, President
• Harley Tomlinson, Sports Editor
daily@rensselaerrepublican.com
Frequency:
6 time(s) per week

REPORTER
916 COTTING LANE
VACAVILLE, CA 95688-9338
707-448-2200
Fax: 707-447-7405
http://thereporter.com
• Eliav Applebaum, Sports Reporter
(707) 453-8157
sports@thereporter.com
• Matt Miller, Sports Production Editor
(707) 453-8156
sports@thereporter.com
• Tim Roe, Sports Editor
(707) 453-8158
sports@thereporter.com
• Derek Wilson, Sports Reporter
(707) 453-8141
sports@thereporter.com

Frequency:
7 time(s) per week

REPORTER-TIMES
50 SOUTH JEFFERSON STREET
MARTINSVILLE, IN 46151
765-342-3311
Fax: 765-342-1446
http://www.reporter-times.com
• Steve Page, Sports Editor
(765) 342-3311
spage@reportert.com
• Matthew Swanson, Advertising Director
(765) 342-3311
mswanson@reportert.com
Frequency:
7 time(s) per week

REPOSITORY
500 MARKET AVENUE SOUTH
CANTON, OH 44702-2112
330-580-8544
Fax: 330-454-5745
letters@cantonrep.com
http://www.cantonrep.com
• Andy Call, Sports Reporter
(330) 580-8346
• Donald J. Detore, Sports Editor
(330) 580-8344
• Todd Porter, Sports Reporter
(330) 580-8340
todd.porter@cantonrep.com
Frequency:
7 time(s) per week

REPUBLIC
333 2ND STREET
COLUMBUS, IN 47201-6709
812-372-7811
800-435-5601
Fax: 812-379-5711
editorial@therepublic.com
http://www.therepublic.com
• Kirk Johannesen, Sports Editor
(812) 379-5632
kjohannesen@therepublic.com
• Bret Kroger, Advertising Director
(812) 379-5764
bkroger@therepublic.com
Frequency:
7 time(s) per week

REPUBLICAN & HERALD
122 MAHANTONGO STREET
POTTSVILLE, PA 17901-3008
570-622-3456
Fax: 570-628-6092
http://www.schuylkill.com
• Leroy Boyer, Sports Editor
lboyer@republicanherald.com
• Michael A. Joyce, Advertising Manager
• James Riotto, Classified Manager
Frequency:
6 time(s) per week

REPUBLICAN AND REPUBLICAN SUNDAY
1860 MAIN STREET
SPRINGFIELD, MA 01103-1000
413-788-1000
Fax: 413-788-1301
news@repub.com
http://www.masslive.com
• Joe Deburro, Sports Editor
(413) 788-1117
jdeburro@repub.com

• Maureen Thorpe, Classified Manager
(413) 788-1000
mthorpe@repub.com
Frequency:
7 time(s) per week

REPUBLICAN-AMERICAN
389 MEADOW STREET
WATERBURY, CT 06702-1808
203-574-3636
800-992-3232
Fax: 203-596-9277
http://www.rep-am.com
• Lee Lewis, Sports Editor
llewis@rep-am.com
• Andrew Pape, Classified Manager
(203) 574-3636
apape@rep-am.com
Frequency:
7 time(s) per week

REVIEW TIMES
113 EAST CENTER STREET
FOSTORIA, OH 44830-2905
419-435-6641
Fax: 419-435-9073
rtnews@reviewtimes.com
http://www.reviewtimes.com
• Scott Cottos, Sports Editor
(419) 435-6641
scottcottos@reviewtimes.com
Frequency:
6 time(s) per week

RICHMOND TIMES-DISPATCH
P.O. BOX 85333
RICHMOND, VA 23219
804-649-6000
Fax: 804-819-1216
news@timesdispatch.com
http://www.timesdispatch.com
• Jack Berninger, Sports Editor
(804) 649-6445
• Vic Dorr, Reporter
(804) 649-6442
vdorr@timesdispatch.com
• David Hamlin, Section Editor
(804) 649-6109
dhamlin@timesdispatch.com
• Mike Harris, College Sports Writer
(804) 649-6839
mharris@timesdispatch.com
• Jerry Lindquist, Sports Reporter
(804) 649-6323
jlindquist@timesdispatch.com
• Bob Lipper, Sports Columnist
(804) 649-6555
blipper@timesdispatch.com
• John O'Connor, College Sports Writer
(804) 649-6233
joconnor@timesdispatch.com
• John Packett, Sports Reporter
(804) 649-6313
jpackett@timesdispatch.com
• Tim Pearrell, Sports Reporter
(804) 649-6965
tpearrell@timesdispatch.com
• Nate Ryan, Sports Reporter
(804) 649-6851
nryan@timesdispatch.com
• Heather Tucker, Sports Assistant Editor
(804) 649-6456
htucker@timesdispatch.com
• Arthur Utley, Sports/Golf Writer
(804) 649-6559
autley@timesdispatch.com
• Jeff White, College Sports Writer

(804) 649-6838
jwhite@timesdispatch.com
• Paul Woody, Sports Columnist
(804) 649-6444
pwoody@timesdispatch.com
Frequency:
7 time(s) per week

RIDGWAY RECORD
20 MAIN STREET
RIDGWAY, PA 15853
814-773-3161
Fax: 814-776-1086
record@shop-right.com
http://www.ridgewayrecord.com
• Darlene Coder, Advertising Manager
• Jim Peterson, Sports Editor
richwayrecord@shop-right.com
Frequency:
6 time(s) per week

ROANOKE TIMES
P.O. BOX 2491
ROANOKE, VA 24010-2491
540-981-3100
800-346-1234
Fax: 540-981-3346
http://www.roanoke.com
• Mark Berman, Sports Reporter
(540) 981-3125
mark.berman@roanoke.com
• Ray Cox, Sports Reporter
(540) 381-1672
ray.cox@roanoke.com
• Doug Doughty, Sports Reporter
(540) 981-3129
doug.doughty@roanoke.com
• Laurence Hammack, Public Integrity Reporter
(540) 981-3100
laurence.hammack@roanoke.com
• Randy King, Sports Reporter
(540) 981-3100
randy.king@roanoke.com
• Aaron McFarling, Sports Columnist
(540) 981-3222
aaron.mcfarling@roanoke.com
• Jim Reedy, Local News Reporter
(540) 981-3100
jim.reedy@roanoke.com
• Michael Stowe, Managing Editor
(540) 981-3100
michael.stowe@roanoke.com
• Belinda Harris, Librarian
Frequency:
7 time(s) per week

ROBESONIAN
P.O. BOX 1028
LUMBERTON, NC 28358-5538
910-739-4322
Fax: 910-739-6553
http://www.robesonian.com
• Curt Vincent, Sports Editor
(910) 739-4322
• Willis Jacobson, Sports Writer
(910) 739-4322
Frequency:
7 time(s) per week

ROCHESTER SENTINEL
118 EAST 8TH STREET
ROCHESTER, IN 46975-1508
574-223-2111
800-686-2112
Fax: 574-223-5782

news@rochsent.com
http://www.rochsent.com
• Val Tsoutsouris, Sports Editor
(574) 224-5326
valsports@rochsent.com
• Karen Vojtasek, Advertising Manager
(574) 223-2111
karenv@rochsent.com
Frequency:
6 time(s) per week

ROCKDALE CITIZEN
969 SOUTH MAIN STREET
CONYERS, GA 30012
770-483-7108
Fax: 770-483-5797
http://www.rockdalecitizen.com
• Jeff Gillespie, Sports Editor
(770) 483-7108
jeff.gillespie@rockdalecitizen.com
Frequency:
7 time(s) per week

ROCKFORD REGISTER STAR
99 EAST STATE STREET
ROCKFORD, IL 61104-1009
815-987-1350
800-383-7827
Fax: 815-987-1365
http://www.rrstar.com
• Greg Newell, Sports Assistant Editor
(815) 987-1203
• Lani Renneau, Advertising Director
(815) 987-1320
• Randy Ruef, Sports Editor
(815) 987-1203
sports@rrstar.com
• Mike DeDoncker, Sports Reporter
(815) 987-1382
Frequency:
7 time(s) per week

ROCKLAND JOURNAL-NEWS
200 NORTH ROUTE 303
WEST NYACK, NY 10994
845-578-2402
Fax: 845-578-2477
74514.3620@compuserve.com
http://www.nynews.com
• John Humenn, Sports Editor
(845) 578-2464
jhumenn@thejournalnews.com
• Enedina Vega, Advertising Director
(845) 578-2320
Frequency:
7 time(s) per week

ROCKY MOUNT TELEGRAM
800 TIFFANY BOULEVARD
ROCKY MOUNT, NC 27804-5713
252-407-9966
Fax: 252-446-4057
http://www.rockymounttelegram.com
• Jennifer Brown, Classified Manager
(252) 407-9926
• Mike Schuttinga, Advertising Manager
(252) 407-9922
• Ben Jones, Sports Editor
(252) 407-9959
Frequency:
7 time(s) per week

ROCKY MOUNTAIN NEWS
101 WEST COLFAX AVENUE
DENVER, CO 80218

303-954-5000
800-345-7461
Fax: 303-954-2841
http://www.insidedenver.com
• Sam Adams, Sports Columnist
(303) 954-2623
adamss@rockymountainnews.com
• Michael Bialas, Assistant Sports Editor
(303) 954-5281
bialasm@rockymountainnews.com
• B.G. Brooks, College Sports Reporter
(303) 954-5466
brooksb@rockymountainnews.com
• Lynn DeBruin, Sports Reporter
sports@rockymountainnews.com
• Jack Etkin, Sports Reporter
(303) 892-2921
sports@rockymountainnews.com
• Barry Forbis, Sports Editor
(303) 954-5100
forbis@rockymountainnews.com
• Randy Holtz, Sports Reporter
(303) 892-5439
sports@rockymountainnews.com
• Kevin Huhn, Deputy Sports Editor
(303) 954-5100
huhnk@rockymountainnews.com
• Dave Krieger, Sports Columnist
(303) 954-5000
kriegerd@rockymountainnews.com
• Clay Latimer, Sports Reporter
(303) 892-2596
latimerc@rockymountainnews.com
• Bernie Lincicome, Sports Columnist
(303) 954-2411
lincicomeb@rockymountainnews.com
• Aaron Lopez, Sports Reporter
(303) 892-5388
lopezaa@rockymountainnews.com
• Lee Rasizer, Sports Reporter
(303) 892-5100
sports@rockymountainnews.com
• Tracy Ringolsby, Sports Reporter
(303) 892-2843
ringolsbyt@rockymountainnews.com
• Rick Sadowski, Sports Reporter
(303) 892-2587
sports@rockymountainnews.com
• Scott Stocker, Sports Reporter
(303) 954-5275
stockers@rockymountainnews.com
• Chris Tomasson, Sports Reporter
(303) 892-5100
tomassonc@rockymountainnews.com
• Gerry Valerio, Sports Editor (High School)
(303) 892-2848
sports@rockymountainnews.com
• Bob Willis, Assistant Sports Editor
(303) 892-5100
willisb@rockymountainnews.com
Frequency:
7 time(s) per week

ROLLA DAILY NEWS
P.O. BOX 808
ROLLA, MO 65401-3243
573-364-2468
Fax: 573-341-5847
http://www.therolladailynews.com/
• Seth Sowers, Sports Editor
(573) 364-2468
• Lonna Stephenson, Advertising Manager
(573) 364-2468
Frequency:
6 time(s) per week

ROME NEWS-TRIBUNE
305 EAST 6TH AVENUE
ROME, GA 30162-6007
706-291-6397
Fax: 706-234-6478
http://www.romenews-tribune.com
• Trip Hatley, Advertising Manager
(706) 290-5217
• Jim O'Hara, Sports Editor
(706) 290-5258
• David Dawson, Sports Writer
(706) 291-6397
Frequency:
7 time(s) per week

ROSWELL NEIGHBOR
10930 CRABAPPLE ROAD SUITE 9
ROSWELL, GA 30075
770-993-7400
Fax: 770-518-6062
http://www.neighbornewspapers.com
• Carten Cordell, Sports Editor
nfulton@neighbornewspapers.com
Frequency:
1 time(s) per week

RUSHVILLE REPUBLICAN
219 NORTH PERKINS STREET
RUSHVILLE, IN 46173-1851
765-932-2222
Fax: 765-932-4358
http://www.rushvillerepublican.com
• Aaron Kirchoff, Sports Editor
(765) 932-2222
• Marilyn Land, Advertising Manager
Frequency:
6 time(s) per week

RUSTON DAILY LEADER
212 WEST PARK AVENUE
RUSTON, LA 71270-
318-255-4353
Fax: 318-255-4006
http://www.rustonleader.com
• O. K. Davis, Sports Editor
• Jeanie McCartney, Advertising Manager
jeanie@rustonleader.com
Frequency:
6 time(s) per week

RUTLAND HERALD
P.O. BOX 668
RUTLAND, VT 05701-4027
802-747-6133
800-498-4296
Fax: 802-773-0311
pressrelease@rutlandherald.com
http://www.rutlandherald.com
• Chuck Clarino, Sports Writer
(802) 747-6121
chuck.clarino@rutlandherald.com
• Bob Fredette, Sports Editor
(802) 747-6121
bob.fredette@rutlandherald.com
• Glenda Hawley, Advertising Director
(802) 747-6121
Frequency:
7 time(s) per week

SACRAMENTO BEE
P. O. BOX 15779
SACRAMENTO, CA 95816-6816
916-321-1000
800-284-3233
Fax: 916-321-1109
http://www.sacbee.com

• Debbie Arrington, Sports Reporter
(916) 326-5514
darrington@sacbee.com
• Gregg Bell, Sports Senior Writer
• Marcos Breton, Sports Senior Writer
(916) 321-1096
mbreton@sacbee.com
• Victor Contreras, Assistant Sports Editor
(916) 321-1000
vcontreras@sacbee.com
• Joe Davidson, Sports Senior Writer
(916) 321-1280
jdavidson@sacbee.com
• Larry Hicks, Sports Assistant Editor
(916) 321-5519
• Scott Howard-Cooper, Sports Senior
Writer
(916) 321-1210
• Mark Kreidler, Sports Columnist
(916) 321-1149
• Mark McDermott, Sports Writer
(916) 326-5525
• Martin McNeal, Sports Senior Writer
(916) 326-5516
• Tom Negrete, Assistant Managing Ed.,
Sports and Busin
(916) 321-1171
• Nick Peters, Sports Senior Writer
• John Schumacher, Sports Senior Editor
(916) 326-5523
• Quwan Spears, Sports Reporter
(916) 326-5517
• Ailene Voisin, Sports Senior Writer
(916) 321-1208
avoisin@sacbee.com
• Barbara Zumwalt, Sports Deputy Editor
(916) 321-1190
Frequency:
7 time(s) per week

SAGINAW NEWS
100 SOUTH MICHIGAN AVENUE
SUITE 3
SAGINAW, MI 48602
989-752-7171
800-875-6397
Fax: 989-752-3115
metro@thesaginawnews.com
http://www.mlive.com/saginaw
• Paul Neumeyer, Sports Topic Editor
(989) 372-2503
• Hugh Bernreuter, Assistant Sports Editor
(989) 752-7171
Frequency:
7 time(s) per week

SAINT CLOUD TIMES
3000 NORTH 7TH STREET
SAINT CLOUD, MN 56303-3108
320-255-8700
800-759-7653
Fax: 320-255-8775
sctimes@cloudnet.com
http://www.sctimes.com
• Dave DeLand, Sports Editor
(320) 255-8771
Frequency:
7 time(s) per week

SAINT LOUIS AMERICAN
4242 LINDELL BOULEVARD
SAINT LOUIS, MO 63108-2927
314-533-8000
Fax: 314-533-0038
stlamer@mvp.net
http://www.stlamerican.com

• Earl Austin, Sports Editor
eaustin@stlamerican.com
Frequency:
1 time(s) per week

SAINT LOUIS ARGUS
4595 MARTIN LUTHER KING DRIVE
SAINT LOUIS, MO 63113
314-531-1323
Fax: 314-531-1324
http://www.stlouisargus.com
• Charles Edwards, Sports Editor
media@stlouisargus.com
Frequency:
1 time(s) per week

SAINT LOUIS POST-DISPATCH
900 NORTH TUCKER BOULEVARD
SAINT LOUIS, MO 63101-1069
314-340-8000
800-365-0820
Fax: 314-340-3050
metro@post-dispatch.com
http://www.stltoday.com
• Bryan Burwell, Sports Columnist
(314) 340-8185
• William Coats, Sports Reporter
(314) 340-8189
• Stu Durando, Sports Reporter
(314) 340-8232
sdurando@post-dispatch.com
• Derrick Goold, Sports Reporter
(314) 340-8170
dgoold@post-dispatch.com
• Roger Hensley, Sports Deputy Editor
(314) 340-8301
rhensley@post-dispatch.com
• Rick Hummel, Sports Reporter
(314) 340-8199
rhummel@post-dispatch.com
• Joe Lyons, Sports Reporter
(314) 946-3903
jlyons@post-dispatch.com
• Bernie Miklasz, Sports Columnist
(314) 340-8192
• Kathleen Nelson, Sports Reporter
(314) 340-8233
• Dan O'Neill, Sports Columnist
(314) 340-8186
• Donald Reed, Sports Deputy Editor
(314) 340-8313
 dreed@post-dispatch.com
• Kenneth Roberts, Sports Reporter
(618) 257-0745
• Joe Strauss, Sports Reporter
(314) 340-8170
• James Thomas, Sports Reporter
(314) 340-8197
jthomas@post-dispatch.com
• Tom Timmermann, Sports Reporter
(314) 340-8190
ttimmermann@post-dispatch.com
• James Woodworth, Sports Copy Editor
(314) 340-8165
Frequency:
7 time(s) per week

SAINT PAUL PIONEER PRESS
345 CEDAR STREET
SAINT PAUL, MN 55101-1014
651-222-1111
Fax: 651-228-5500
http://www.twincities.com
• Thom Fladung, Editor/Vice President
tfladung@pioneerpress.com
• Rick Alonzo, Sports Reporter
(Timberwolves)

(651) 222-5539
• Mike Bass, Sports Editor
(651) 228-5108
• Bruce Brothers, Sports Reporter/Running
Columnist
(651) 228-5518
• Kevin Cusick, Sports Deputy Editor
(651) 228-5471
kcusick@pioneerpress.com
• Tim Leighton, Sports Reporter (High
School)
(651) 228-5598
tleighton@pioneerpress.com
• Jeff Hruza, Sports Clerk
(651) 228-5155
• John Pluym, High School Sports Editor
(651) 228-5239
Frequency:
7 time(s) per week

SALAMANCA PRESS
36 RIVER STREET
SALAMANCA, NY 14779-1474
716-945-1644
Fax: 716-945-4285
salpressnews@verizon.net
http://www.salamancapress.com
• Darren Riethmiller, Sports Editor
• Casey Stockman, Advertising Manager
salpressads@verizon.net
• Brian Jewell, Sports Editor
(716) 945-1644
salpressnews@verizon.net
Frequency:
5 time(s) per week

SALEM NEWS
161 NORTH LINCOLN AVENUE
SALEM, OH 44460-2903
330-332-4601
Fax: 330-332-1441
http://www.salemnews.net
• B.J Lisko, Sports Editor
(330) 332-4601
Frequency:
7 time(s) per week

SALINA JOURNAL
333 SOUTH 4TH STREET
SALINA, KS 67402
785-823-6363
800-827-6363
Fax: 785-827-6363
http://www.saljournal.com
• Bob Davidson, Sports Editor
(785) 822-1404
Frequency:
7 time(s) per week

SALINAS CALIFORNIAN
123 WEST ALISAL STREET
SALINAS, CA 93901
831-424-2221
800-300-6397
Fax: 831-754-4104
http://www.salinascalifornian.com
• Joey Delgado, Sports Editor
(831) 754-4265
jdelgado@salinas.gannett.com
• Janine Perkingson, Advertising Director
• Dave Nordstrand, Sports Columnist
(831) 754-4268
dnordstrand@thecalifornian.com
Frequency:
6 time(s) per week

SALISBURY POST
131 WEST INNES STREET
SALISBURY, NC 28144-4338
704-633-8950
800-633-8957
Fax: 704-639-0003
news@salisburypost.com
http://www.salisburypost.com
• Mark Bee, Advertising Director
(704) 633-8950
• Ronnie Gallagher, Sports Editor
(704) 797-4287
sports@salisburypost.com
Frequency:
7 time(s) per week

SALT LAKE TRIBUNE
90 SOUTH 400 WEST, SUITE 700
SALT LAKE CITY, UT 84111-1924
801-257-8742
Fax: 801-257-8525
letters@sltrib.com
http://www.sltrib.com
• Michael Anastasi, Sports Managing Editor
(801) 257-8905
• Jay Drew, Sports Reporter
(801) 257-8906
drew@sltrib.com
• Kurt Kragthorpe, Sports Writer
(801) 257-8916
kkragthorpe@sltrib.com
• Michael Lewis, Sports Reporter
(801) 257-8903
• Steve Luhm, Sports Reporter
(801) 257-8913
• Gordon Monson, Sports Columnist
(801) 257-8923
gmonson@sltrib.com
• Martin Renzhofer, Sports Reporter
(801) 257-8908
• Lya Wodraska, Sports Writer
(801) 257-8907
Frequency:
7 time(s) per week

SAMPSON INDEPENDENT
P.O. BOX 110
CLINTON, NC 28328-4426
910-592-8137
Fax: 910-592-8756
http://www.clintonnc.com
• Wanda Buckner, Advertising Manager
(910) 592-8137
ad@interstar.com
• Billy Todd, Sports Editor
(910) 592-8137
Frequency:
6 time(s) per week

SAN ANGELO STANDARD TIMES
P.O. BOX 5111
SAN ANGELO, TX 76903-5838
325-653-1221
Fax: 325-659-8173
http://www.sanangelostandardtimes.com
• Charles Bryce, Sports Editor
(325) 653-1221
Frequency:
7 time(s) per week

SAN ANTONIO EXPRESS-NEWS
P.O. BOX 2171
SAN ANTONIO, TX 78287-2171
210-250-3105
800-555-1551
Fax: 210-250-3121

citydesk@express-news.net
http://www.mysanantonio.com/expressnews
• Jennifer Bellis, Sports Reporter
(210) 250-3391
• Jerry Briggs, Assistant Sports Editor
(210) 250-3000
jbriggs@express-news.net
• Al Carter, Deputy Sports Editor
(210) 250-3000
• Raul Dominguez, Sports Reporter
(210) 250-3362
• Mike Finger, Sports Columnist (College)
(210) 250-3000
mfinger@express-news.net
• David Flores, Sports Columnist
(210) 250-3356
• Tim Griffin, Sports Columnist
• Buck Harvey, Sports Columnist
(210) 250-3372
bharvey@express-news.net
• John Hines, High School/Prep Sports
Reporter
(210) 250-3364
• David King, Sports Reporter (Baseball,
high schools)
(210) 250-3000
• LeAnna Kosub, Assistant Sports Editor
(210) 250-3000
 lkosub@express-news.net
• Johnny Ludden, Sports Reporter (NBA)
(210) 250-3369
jludden@express-news.net
• Dan McCarney, Sports Columnist (Soccer)
(210) 250-3351
dmccarney@express-news.net
• Mike Monroe, NBA Sports Writer
(210) 250-3000
mikemonroe@express-news.net
• Richard Oliver, Sports Columnist
(210) 250-3390
• Tom Orsborn, Sports Reporter
(210) 250-3367
torsborn@express-news.net
• Harry Page, Sports Reporter
(210) 250-3000
• Steve Quintana, Assistant Managing
Editor/Sports, Online
(210) 250-3000
• Lee Scheide, Sports Reporter (Minors)
(210) 250-3000
lscheide@expressnews.net
• Ron Henry Strait, Sports Columnist
(210) 250-3358
• Mark Wangrin, Sports Writer (College)
(210) 250-3000
• John Whisler, Sports Columnist (Boxing,
golf)
(210) 250-3392
jwhisler@express-news.net
• Brent Zwerneman, Sports Writer
(210) 250-3000
bzwerneman@express-news.net
Frequency:
7 time(s) per week

SAN BERNARDINO SUN
399 NORTH D STREET
SAN BERNARDINO, CA 92401
909-889-9666
Fax: 909-885-8741
http://www.sbsun.com
• Louis Brewster, Sports Editor
(909) 386-3865
louis.brewster@sbsun.com
• Paul Oberjuerge, Sports Columnist
(951) 386-3849
paul.oberjuerge@sbsun.com

• Gene Pearlman, Advertising Director
gene.pearlman@sbsun.com
Frequency:
7 time(s) per week

SAN DIEGO UNION-TRIBUNE
350 CAMINO DE LA REINA
SAN DIEGO, CA 92108-0565
619-299-3131
800-244-6397
Fax: 619-293-1896
http://www.signonsandiego.com
• Kevin Acee, Sports Reporter
(619) 293-1857
kevin.acee@uniontrib.com
• Nick Canepa, Sports Columnist
(619) 293-1397
nick.canepa@uniontrib.com
• Bill Center, Boating Reporter
(619) 293-1851
bill.center@uniontrib.com
• Chris Jenkins, Sports Reporter
(619) 293-1267
chris.jenkins@uniontrib.com
• Tod Leonard, Sports Reporter
(619) 293-1858
tod.leonard@uniontrib.com
• Don Norcross, Sports Reporter
(619) 293-1858
don.norcross@uniontrib.com
• Tim Sullivan, Sports Columnist
(619) 293-1033
tim.sullivan@uniontrib.com
• Jay Posner, Sports Editor
(619) 293-1834
jay.posner@uniontrib.com
• Edward Zieralski, Sports Reporter
(619) 293-1225
ed.zieralski@uniontrib.com
Frequency:
7 time(s) per week

SAN FRANCISCO CHRONICLE
901 MISSION STREET
SAN FRANCISCO, CA 94103
415-777-7100
Fax: 415-543-7708
metro@sfchronicle.com
http://www.sfgate.com/chronicle
• John Crumpacker, Sports Reporter
(415) 777-7201
• Thomas Fitzgerald, Sports Reporter
(415) 777-7201
tfitzgerald@sfchronicle.com
• Bruce Jenkins, Sports Columnist
(415) 777-7169
bjenkins@sfchronicle.com
• Allen Johnson, Sports Copy Editor
ajohnson@sfchronicle.com
• Ron Kroichick, Sports Reporter
(415) 777-7201
• Steve Kroner, Sports Columnist
(415) 777-8415
skroner@sfchronicle.com
• Mike Massa, Sports News Editor
mmassa@sfchronicle.com
• Scott Ostler, Sports Columnist
(415) 777-7031
sostler@sfchronicle.com
• Alan Saracevic, Sports Editor
asaracevic@sfchronicle.com
• Henry Schulman, Sports Writer
hschulman@sfchronicle.com
• John Shea, Sports Reporter
 jshea@sfchronicle.com
• Susan Slusser, Sports Reporter
(415) 777-8859
sslusser@sfchronicle.com

• Mark Smoyer, Deputy Sports Editor
• Tom Stienstra, Sports Reporter
tstienstra@sfchronicle.com
Frequency:
7 time(s) per week

SAN FRANCISCO EXAMINER
450 MISSION STREET 5TH FLOOR
SAN FRANCISCO, CA 94105
415-826-1100
866-733-7323
Fax: 415-359-2766
http://www.examiner.com
• Paul Ingegneri, Advertising Vice President
(415) 359-2809
• Chad Morelli, Sports Reporter
(415) 359-2855
• Jason Phillips, Advertising Director
(415) 359-2629
• Eric White, Sports Reporter
(415) 359-2637
• Rick Barry, Sports Columnist
(415) 995-6830
Frequency:
5 time(s) per week

SAN GABRIEL VALLEY DAILY TRIBUNE
1210 NORTH AZUSA CANYON ROAD
WEST COVINA, CA 91790-1003
626-962-8811
800-788-1200
Fax: 626-856-2758
news.tribune@sgvn.com
http://www.sgvtribune.com
• Steve Ramirez, Sports Columnist
(626) 962-8811
steve.ramirez@sgvn.com
• Doug Spoon, Sports Editor
(626) 962-8811
Frequency:
7 time(s) per week

SAN JOSE MERCURY NEWS
750 RIDDER PARK DRIVE
SAN JOSE, CA 95190
408-920-5000
800-870-6397
Fax: 408-288-8060
business@mercurynews.com
http://www.mercurynews.com
• Elliott Almond, Sports Reporter
(408) 920-5865
ealmond@mercurynews.com
• Daniel Brown, Sports Reporter
(408) 920-5000
dbrown@mercurynews.com
• Victor Chi, Sports Reporter
(408) 920-5720
• Dennis Deisenroth, Sports Copy Editor
(408) 920-5354
• David Early, Sports Reporter
(408) 920-5836
• Mark Emmons, Sports Columnist
(408) 920-5745
• Dennis Georgatos, Sports Reporter
(408) 920-5434
• Mark Gomez, Sports Reporter
(408) 920-5354
mgomez@mercurynews.com
• Mike Guersch, Sports Deputy Editor
(408) 920-5648
• Bud Geracie, Sports Executive Editor
(408) 920-5389
sports@mercurynews.com
• Chris Haft, Sports Reporter
• Bruce Hammel, Sports Copy Editor
(408) 920-5354

• Gary Hoh, Sports Copy Editor
(408) 920-5354
• Chris Hutchison, Sports Copy Editor
(408) 920-5354
• Tim Kawakami, Sports Columnist
(408) 920-5442
tkawakami@mercurynews.com
• Greg Keraghosian, Sports Copy Editor
(408) 920-5354
• David Kiefer, Sports Reporter
• Ann Killion, Sports Columnist
(408) 920-5805
• Dennis Knight, High School Sports
Reporter
(408) 920-5899
• Darryl Matsuda, Assistant Sports Editor
(408) 920-5215
dmatsuda@mercurynews.com
• Laurence Miedema, Sports Reporter
lsmiedema@mercurynews.com
• Richard Parrish, Sports Copy Editor
(408) 920-5354
• Eric Pinkela, Sports Copy Editor
(408) 920-2709
• Sal Pizarro, Sports Editor
(408) 920-5473
spizarro@mercurynews.com
• David Pollak, (408) 920-5940
Sports Writer
• Mark Purdy, Sports Columnist
(408) 920-5092
mpurdy@mercurynews.com
• Darren Sabedra, Sports Writer
(408) 920-5815
dsabedra@mercurynews.com
• Ken Stutz, Sports Copy Editor
(408) 920-5354
• Randy Sumimoto, Sports Copy Editor
(408) 920-5354
• Pam Tso, Sports Copy Editor
(408) 920-2704
Frequency:
7 time(s) per week

SAN MATEO COUNTY TIMES
477 NINTH AVENUE
SAN MATEO, CA 94402
650-348-4321
800-843-6397
Fax: 650-348-4446
http://www.sanmateocountytimes.com
• Glenn Reeves, Sports Editor
(650) 348-4345
Frequency:
6 time(s) per week

SANDUSKY REGISTER
314 WEST MARKET STREET
SANDUSKY, OH 44870-2410
419-625-5500
800-466-1243
Fax: 419-625-3007
http://www.sanduskyregister.com
• Dan Angelo, Sports Editor
(419) 625-5500
• Josh DeSonne, Sports Writer
(419) 625-5500
• Nabil Shaheen, Sports Writer
(419) 625-5500
• Mark Yocum, Advertising Director
Frequency:
7 time(s) per week

SANFORD HERALD
P.O. BOX 100
SANFORD, NC 27330-3916

919-708-9000
800-849-5677
Fax: 919-708-9001
obits@sanfordherald.com
http://www.sanfordherald.com
• Alex Poblogar, Sports Editor
(919) 718-1222
alexp@sanfordherald.com
• Doug Rowe, Advertising Director
(919) 718-1259
Frequency:
6 time(s) per week

SANTA BARBARA NEWS-PRESS
P. O. BOX 1359
SANTA BARBARA, CA 93101-2203
805-564-5200
800-654-3292
Fax: 805-966-6258
businessnews@newspress.com
http://www.newspress.com
• Gerry Spratt, Sports Editor
(805) 564-5173
• Mark Patton, Sports Columnist
(805) 564-5117
mpatton@newspress.com
Frequency:
7 time(s) per week

SANTA CRUZ SENTINEL
207 CHURCH STREET
SANTA CRUZ, CA 95060
831-423-4242
Fax: 831-429-9620
editorial@santacruzsentinel.com
http://www.santacruzsentinel.com
• Arlene Hudson, Advertising Manager
(831) 429-2442
• Jess Mitchell, Advertising Director
(831) 429-2432
• Tom Moore, Sports Editor
Frequency:
7 time(s) per week

SANTA FE NEW MEXICAN
202 E. MARCY
SANTE FE, NM 87501
505-995-3885
Fax: 505-986-3067
www.sfnewmexican.com
• Robin McKinney, Chief Exectuive
Officer/Editor & Publisher
• Robert McKinney, Editor & Publisher
• Ty Ransdell, General Manager

SANTA MARIA TIMES
P.O. BOX 400
SANTA MARIA, CA 93455
805-739-2228
Fax: 805-928-5657
http://www.santamariatimes.com
• Elliott Stern, Sports Editor
(805) 739-2235
elliottstern@santamariatimes.com
• Kenny Cress, Sports Reporter
(805) 739-2237
kcress@santamariatimes.com
Frequency:
7 time(s) per week

SARASOTA HERALD-TRIBUNE
1741 MAIN STREET
SARASOTA, FL 34236-7824
941-361-4800
Fax: 941-361-4699
http://www.newscoast.com

media

• John Brockmann, Sports Reporter
(941) 957-5177
• Mark Cardon, Weekend Sports Editor
(941) 957-5176
• Doug Fernandes, Sports Writer
(941) 957-5179
doug.fernandes@heraldtribune.com
• Bill Herald, Sports Columnist
(941) 957-5172
• Mic Huber, Assistant Sports Editor
(941) 957-5170
mic.huber@heraldtribune.com
• Scott Peterson, Sports Editor
(941) 957-5172
scott.peterson@heraldtribune.com
• Jerry Reed, Sports Editor
(941) 957-5184
• Jody Royce, Sports Reporter
(941) 361-4860
Frequency:
7 time(s) per week

SAVANNAH MORNING NEWS
P.O. BOX 1088
SAVANNAH, GA 31405-1108
912-236-9511
800-533-1150
Fax: 912-234-6522
http://www.savannahnow.com
• Noell Barnidge, Sports Reporter
(912) 652-0347
noell.barnidge@savannahnow.com
• Sean Coughlin, Assistant Sports Editor
(912) 652-0348
coughlin@savannahnow.com
• Tim Guidera, Sports Writer
(912) 652-0352
tim.guidera@savannahnow.com
• Don Heath, Sports Writer
(912) 652-0353
dheath@savannahnow.com
• Anthony Stastny, Sports Editor
anthony.stastny@savannahnow.com
• Jim Thomas, Sports Writer
(912) 652-0350
jimt@savannahnow.com
Frequency:
7 time(s) per week

SCOTTSDALE TRIBUNE
6991 EAST CAMELBACK ROAD SUITE
A10
SCOTTSDALE, AZ 85251
480-970-2330
Fax: 480-970-2360
newstips@aztrib.com
http://www.scottsdaletribune.com
• Scott Bordow, Sports Columnist
(480) 898-6598
sbordow@aztrib.com
• Betsy Goreham, Advertising Director
(480) 898-6500
• Bob Romantic, Sports Editor
(480) 898-6538
bromantic@aztrib.com
Frequency:
7 time(s) per week

SEATTLE POST-INTELLIGENCER
2601 ELLIOT AVENUE
SUITE 300A
SEATTLE, WA 98121
206-448-8036
Fax: 206-448-8190
citydesk@seattlepi.com
http://www.seattlepi.com

• Scott Anderson, Sports Copy Editor
(206) 448-8372
• Clare Farnsworth, Sports Reporter
(206) 448-8016
• John Hickey, Sports Reporter
(206) 448-8004
• John Levesque, Sports Columnist
(206) 448-8330
• Michael McLaughlin, Sports Reporter
(206) 448-8187
• Ted Miller, Sports Columnist
(206) 448-8017
• Jim Moore, Sports Columnist
(206) 448-8013
• Keith Olson, Sports Copy Editor
(206) 448-8375
• Dan Raley, Sports Reporter
(206) 448-8008
• Nick Rousso, Sports Editor
(206) 448-8211
• Steve Rudman, Sports News Editor
(206) 448-8379
• Art Thiel, Sports Columnist
(206) 448-8009
• Molly Yanity, Sports Reporter
(206) 448-8295
Frequency:
7 time(s) per week

SEATTLE TIMES
1120 JOHN STREET
SEATTLE, WA 98109-5321
206-464-2111
Fax: 206-464-2261
newstips@seattletimes.com
http://www.seattletimes.com
• Percy Allen, Sports Reporter
(206) 464-2278
pallen@seattletimes.com
• Bob Condotta, Sports Reporter
(206) 515-5699
bcondotta@seattletimes.com
• Jayda Evans, Sports Reporter
(206) 464-2067
jevans@seattletimes.com
• Steve Kelley, Sports Columnist
(206) 464-2176
skelley@seattletimes.com
• Bill Reader, Sports Assistant Editor
(206) 464-2416
breader@seattletimes.com
• Don Shelton, Sports Assistant Editor
(206) 464-8284
dshelton@seattletimes.com
• Larry Stone, Sports Columnist
(206) 464-3146
lstone@seattletimes.com
• Bud Withers, Sports Reporter
(206) 464-8281
bwithers@seattletimes.com
Frequency:
7 time(s) per week

SEDALIA DEMOCRAT
700 S MASSACHUSETTS AVE
SEDALIA, MO 65301-4548
660-826-1000
Fax: 660-826-2413
news@sedaliademocrat.com
www.sedaliademocrat.com
• Zana Meek, Advertising Manager
(660) 826-1000
zanam@sedaliademocrat.com
• Kyle Smith, Sports Editor
(660) 826-1000
kylesmith@sedaliademocrat.com
Founded:
1868

Frequency:
Tuesday - Saturday
Publications:
Sedalia Democrat, Plainsman and
Whiteman Warrior

SEGUIN GAZETTE-ENTERPRISE
1012 SCHRIEWER ROAD
SEGUIN, TX 78155-7473
830-379-5441
Fax: 830-379-8328
http://www.seguingazette.com
• Tucker Stephenson, Sports Editor
(830) 379-5441
sports@seguingazette.com
Frequency:
5 time(s) per week

SELMA TIMES-JOURNAL
1018 WATER AVE
SELMA, AL 36701-4617
334-875-2110
Fax: 334-872-4588
news@selmatimesjournal.com
http://www.selmatimesjournal.com/
• Dale Constance, Sports Editor
(334) 875-2110
• Griffin Pritchard, Sports Writer
(334) 875-2110
Frequency:
6 time(s) per week

SEMINOLE PRODUCER
121 NORTH MAIN STREET
SEMINOLE, OK 74868-4627
405-382-1100
Fax: 405-382-1104
http://www.seminoleproducer.com
• Mike Gifford, Advertising Manager
ads@seminoleproducer.com
• Josh Griffin, Sports Editor
sports@seminoleproducer.com
Frequency:
5 time(s) per week

SENTINEL
64 DOWNTOWN PLAZA
FAIRMONT, MN 56031-
507-235-3303
Fax: 507-235-3718
news@fairmontsentinel.com
• Kathy Ratcliff, Advertising Manager
kathy@fairmontsentinel.com
• Charlie Sorrells, Sports Editor
illinoisroots@yahoo.com
Frequency:
6 time(s) per week

SENTINEL AND ENTERPRISE
808 MAIN STREET
FITCHBURG, MA 01420
978-343-6911
888-842-3633
Fax: 978-342-1158
news@sentinelandenterprise.com
http://www.sentinelandenterprise.com
• Ross Edwards, Sports Reporter
(978) 343-6911
redwards@sentinelandenterprise.com
• Chad Garner, Sports Editor
(978) 343-6911
cgarner@sentinelandenterprise.com
Frequency:
7 time(s) per week

SENTINEL-RECORD
300 SPRING STREET
HOT SPRINGS NATIONAL, AR 71901-4148
501-623-7711
Fax: 501-623-2984
mark@hotsr.com
http://www.hotsr.com
• Penny Thornton, Advertising Director
(501) 623-7711
pthornton@wehco.com
• Bob Wisener, Sports Editor
Frequency:
7 time(s) per week

SENTINEL-TRIBUNE
P.O. BOX 88
BOWLING GREEN, OH 43402-1329
419-352-4611
Fax: 419-354-0314
local_news@sentinel-tribune.com
http://www.sentinel-tribune.com
• Jack Carle, Sports Editor
(419) 352-4611
sports@sentinel-tribune.com
• Rob Davenport, Advertising Manager
(419) 352-4611
ads@sentinel-tribune.com
Frequency:
6 time(s) per week

SF WEEKLY
185 BERRY STREET LOBBY 4, SUITE
3800
SAN FRANCISCO, CA 94107-1701
415-536-8100
Fax: 415-541-9096
http://www.sfweekly.com
• Matthew Smith, Sports Columnist
Frequency:
1 time(s) per week

SHAWANO LEADER
1464 EAST GREEN BAY STREET
SHAWANO, WI 54166-2258
715-526-2121
800-236-2105
Fax: 715-524-3941
editor@shawanoleader.com
http://www.shawanoleader.com
• Cory Dellenbach, Sports Editor
Frequency:
6 time(s) per week

SHAWNEE NEWS-STAR
P.O. BOX 1688
SHAWNEE, OK 74801-6913
405-273-4200
800-332-2305
Fax: 405-273-4207
newsroom@news-star.com
http://www.news-star.com
• Fred Fehr, Sports Editor
(405) 273-4200
• Sherry Lankford, Advertising Manager
(405) 214-3950
Frequency:
6 time(s) per week

SHEBOYGAN PRESS
632 CENTER AVENUE
SHEBOYGAN, WI 53081-4621
920-457-7711
800-686-3900
Fax: 920-457-0178
http://www.sheboygan-press.com

• Pete Barth, Sports Editor
(920) 453-5156
Frequency:
7 time(s) per week

SHELBY STAR
P. O. BOX 48
SHELBY, NC 28150-5452
704-484-7000
Fax: 704-484-0805
http://www.shelbystar.com
• Alan Ford, Sports Editor
(704) 484-7000
alanford@shelbystar.com
Frequency:
7 time(s) per week

SHELBY SUN TIMES
7508 CAPITAL DRIVE
GERMANTOWN, TN 38138-0801
901-755-7386
Fax: 901-755-0827
• Buck Patton, Sports Editor
(901) 755-7386
Frequency:
1 time(s) per week

SHELBY-UTICA NEWS
13650 11 MILE ROAD
WARREN, MI 48089-1422
586-498-8000
Fax: 586-498-9627
http://www.candgnews.com
• Susan Shanley, Sports Editor
(586) 498-1048
sshanley@candgnews.com
Frequency:
1 time(s) per week

SHELBYVILLE NEWS
123 EAST WASHINGTON STREET
SHELBYVILLE, IN 46176-1463
317-398-6631
800-362-0114
Fax: 317-398-0194
shelbynews@shelbynews.com
http://www.shelbynews.com
• Dennis Bonner, Advertising Manager
(317) 398-6631
• Jeff Brown, Sports Editor
(317) 398-6631
jbrown@shelbynews.com
Frequency:
6 time(s) per week

SIDNEY DAILY NEWS
1451 NORTH VANDERMARK ROAD
SIDNEY, OH 45365
937-498-8088
800-688-4820
Fax: 937-498-5991
http://www.sidneydailynews.com
• Ken Barhorst, Sports Editor
(937) 498-5960
Frequency:
6 time(s) per week

SIDNEY SUN TELEGRAPH
1136 ILLINOIS
SIDNEY, NE 69162
308-254-2818
Fax: 308-254-3925
• Doug Law, Sports Reporter
(308) 254-2818
Frequency:
5 time(s) per week

SIERRA VISTA HERALD
102 FAB AVENUE
SIERRA VISTA, AZ 85635-1741
520-458-9440
Fax: 520-459-0120
http://www.svherald.com
• Matt Hickman, Sports Editor
(520) 458-9440
• Paul Manhufe, Advertising Manager
(520) 515-4630
• Bruce Bourquin, Sports Reporter
(520) 458-9440
Frequency:
6 time(s) per week

SIGNAL
24000 CREEKSIDE ROAD
VALENCIA, CA 91355-1726
661-259-1234
Fax: 661-254-8068
letters@the-signal.com
http://www.the-signal.com
• Grant Gordon, Sports Editor
(661) 259-1234
ggordon@the-signal.com
Frequency:
7 time(s) per week

**SILVER CITY DAILY PRESS &
INDEPENDENT**
300 WEST MARKET
SILVER CITY, NM 88061
505-388-1576
Fax: 505-388-1196
http://www.thedailypress.com
• Vince Cong, Sports Editor
• Wanda Sleep, Classified Manager
(505) 388-1576
• Mikey Torrez, Advertising Manager
(505) 388-1576
Frequency:
6 time(s) per week

SIOUX CITY JOURNAL
P.O. BOX 118
SIOUX CITY, IA 51101-
712-293-4250
800-397-9820
Fax: 712-279-5059
http://www.siouxcityjournal.com
• Steven Allspach, Sports Writer / Columnist
(712) 293-4250
• Bob Carruth, Advertising Manager
(712) 293-4320
• Terry Hersom, Sports Editor
(712) 293-4250
Frequency:
7 time(s) per week

SKAGIT VALLEY HERALD
1000 EAST COLLEGE WAY
MOUNT VERNON, WA 98273-5624
360-424-3251
800-683-3300
Fax: 360-428-0400
http://www.skagitvalleyherald.com
• Jeannette Kales, Classified Manager
(360) 424-3251
classified@skagitvalleyherald.com
• Trevor Pyle, Sports Reporter
(360) 416-2156
tpyle@skagitvalleyherald.com
• Dan Ruthemeyer, Sports Editor
(360) 424-3251
druthemeyer@skagitvalleyherald.com
Frequency:
7 time(s) per week

media

SLIDELL SENTRY-NEWS
364 PONTCHARTRAIN DRIVE SUITE B
SLIDELL, LA 70458-4816
985-643-4918
Fax: 985-649-0254
http://www.slidellsentry.com
• Mary Christopher, Retail Advertising Manager
(985) 643-4918
• David Purdum, Sports Editor
(985) 643-4918
Frequency:
6 time(s) per week

SOUTH BEND TRIBUNE
225 WEST COLFAX AVENUE
SOUTH BEND, IN 46626-1001
574-235-6161
Fax: 574-236-1765
sbtnews@sbtinfo.com
http://www.southbendtribune.com
• Bill Bilinski, Sports Editor
(574) 235-6331
bbilinski@sbtinfo.com
• Al Lesar, Assistant Sports Editor
alesar@sbtinfo.com
• Eric Hansen, Notre Dame Beat Writer
ehansen@sbtinfo.com
• Matt Ingle, Sports Writer
mingle@sbtinfo.com
• Jason Kelly, Sports Reporter
(547) 235-6152
jkelly@sbtinfo.com
• Matt Kopsea, Sports Reporter
(574) 235-6161
mkopsea@sbtinfo.com
• Al Lesar, Sports Assistant Editor
(574) 235-6318
alesar@sbtinfo.com
• Steve Lowe, Sports Reporter
(574) 235-6161
stevelowe@sbtinfo.com
• Forrest Miller, Sports Writer
(574) 235-6161
wmiller@sbtinfo.com
• Tom Noie, Sports Writer
(574) 235-6161
tnoie@sbtinfo.com
• Bob Oppenheim, Michigan High School Sports Reporter
(574) 235-6161
roppenheim@sbtinfo.com
• Curt Rallo, Sports Reporter
(574) 235-6161
crallo@sbtinfo.com
• Louie Stout, Sports Correspondent
(574) 235-6332
• Jack Walkden, Sports Reporter
(574) 235-6161
jwalkden@sbtinfo.com
Frequency:
7 time(s) per week
Circulation:
75,000 daily; 100,000 Sunday

SOUTH CITY JOURNAL
4210 CHIPPEWA STREET
SAINT LOUIS, MO 63116
314-664-2700
Fax: 314-664-8533
southnews@yourjournal.com
http://www.stltoday.com
• Scott Fitzgerald, Sports Editor
(314) 664-2700
sfitzgerald@yourjournal.com
Frequency:
1 time(s) per week

SOUTH COUNTY JOURNAL
4210 CHIPPEWA STREET
SAINT LOUIS, MO 63116
314-664-2700
Fax: 314-664-8533
http://www.stltoday.com
• Scott Fitzgerald, Sports Editor
(314) 664-2700
sfitzgerald@yourjournal.com
Frequency:
2 time(s) per week

SOUTH COUNTY NEWS
2045 GRANT STREET
SELMA, CA 93662-3508
559-896-1976
Fax: 559-896-9160
mmiyamoto@pulitzer.net
http://www.selmaenterprise.com
• Will Goldbeck, Sports Reporter
(559) 896-1976
Frequency:
1 time(s) per week

SOUTH FLORIDA SUN-SENTINEL
200 EAST LAS OLAS BOULEVARD
FORT LAUDERDALE, FL 33301-2293
954-356-4000
Fax: 954-356-4680
sfeedback@sun-sentinel.com
http://www.sun-sentinel.com
• Craig Barnes, College Sports Reporter
(954) 356-4000
cbarnes@sun-sentinel.com
• Mike Berardino, College Sports Reporter
(954) 356-4635
mberardino@sun-sentinel.com
• Charles Bricker, Sports Columnist
(954) 356-4000
cbricker@sun-sentinel.com
• Dave Brousseau, Sports Reporter
(954) 356-4649
dbrousseau@sun-sentinel.com
• Christy Cabrera, High School Sports Writer
(954) 356-4000
ccabrera@sun-sentinel.com
• Tom Christensen, Assistant Sports Editor
(954) 356-4682
• Michael Cunningham, Sports Reporter
mcunningham@sun-sentinel.com
• Bonnie DiPacio, Sports Coordinator (Day)
(954) 356-4644
bdipacio@sun-sentinel.com
• Harvey Fialkov, Sports Reporter
(954) 356-4865
hfialkov@sun-sentinel.com
• Dave Heeren, Sports Reporter
(954) 356-4635
dheeren@sun-sentinel.com
• Ted Hutton, Sports Writer
(954) 356-4635
thutton@sun-sentinel.com
• Dave Hyde, Sports Columnist
(954) 356-4650
dhyde@sun-sentinel.com
• Dave Joseph, Sports Columnist
(954) 356-4635
djoseph@sun-sentinel.com
• Omar Kelly, Sports Reporter
(954) 356-4000
• Alex Marvez, Sports Writer
(954) 356-4000
amarvez@sun-sentinel.com
• Randall Mell, Sports Columnist
rmell@sun-sentinel.com
• Randy Mell, Sports Writer (Golf)
rmell@sun-sentinel.com

• Shandel Richardson, Sports Reporter
sdrichardson@sun-sentinel.com
• Sharon Robb, High School Sports Editor
(954) 356-4000
srobb@sun-sentinel.com
• Juan Rodriguez, Sports Writer (Baseball)
(954) 356-4635
jrodriguez@sun-sentinel.com
• Jeff Rusnak, Sports Columnist
(954) 356-4635
• Michael Russo, Sports Columnist
(954) 356-4635
mrusso@sun-sentinel.com
• Ethan Skolnick, Sports Columnist
(954) 356-4000
eskolnick@sun-sentinel.com
• Sarah Talalay, Sports Business Writer
(954) 356-4173
stalalay@sun-sentinel.com
• Steve Waters, (954) 356-4648
Sports Writer (Outdoors)
swaters@sun-sentinel.com
• Brian White, Sports Editor
(954) 356-4653
bwhite@sun-sentinel.com
• Ira Winderman, Sports Writer (Basketball)
iwinderman@sun-sentinel.com
Frequency:
7 time(s) per week

SOUTH SIDE JOURNAL
4210 CHIPPEWA STREET
SAINT LOUIS, MO 63116
314-664-2700
Fax: 314-664-8533
http://www.stltoday.com
• Scott Fitzgerald, Sports Editor
(314) 664-2700
sfitzgerald@yourjournal.com
Frequency:
2 time(s) per week

SOUTHBRIDGE EVENING NEWS
25 ELM STREET
SOUTHBRIDGE, MA 01550-2605
508-764-4325
800-367-9898
Fax: 508-764-8015
http://www.southbridgeeveningnews.com
• Jean Ashton, Advertising Manager
(508) 764-4325
jashton@stonebridgepress.com
• David Forbes, Sports Editor
(508) 764-4325
Frequency:
5 time(s) per week

SOUTHEAST MISSOURIAN
P.O. BOX 699
CAPE GIRARDEAU, MO 63701-7330
573-335-6611
800-877-1210
Fax: 573-334-7288
news@semissourian.com
http://www.semissourian.com
• Jeff Breer, Reporter
(573) 335-6611
jbreer@semissourian.com
• Toby Carrig, Sports Editor
(573) 335-6611
• Donna Denson, Advertising Manager
(573) 335-6611
ddenson@semissourian.com
Frequency:
7 time(s) per week

SOUTHERN ILLINOISAN
P.O. BOX 2108
CARBONDALE, IL 62902-1283
618-351-5000
Fax: 618-529-3774
news@TheSouthern.com
http://www.southernillinoisan.com
• Les Winkeler, Sports Editor
(618) 351-5000
Les.Winkeler@TheSouthern.com
Frequency:
7 time(s) per week

SOUTHSIDE REPORTER
2203 SOUTH HACKBERRY
SAN ANTONIO, TX 78210-4199
210-534-8848
Fax: 210-534-7134
http://www.primetimenewspapers.com
• Gabe Farias, Sports Editor
(210) 534-8848
gfariasssr@postmark.net
Frequency:
1 time(s) per week

SOUTHTOWN STAR
6901 WEST 159TH STREET
TINLEY PARK, IL 60477-1789
708-633-6700
Fax: 708-633-5999
news@southtownstar.com
www.southtownstar.com
• Phil Arvia, Sports Columnist
(708) 633-5949
• John O'Brien, Sports Ass't Managing
Editor
(708) 633-5931
jobrien@dailysouthtown.com
• John O'Brien, Sports Editor
(708) 633-5931
Frequency:
6 time(s) per week

SOUTHWEST CITY JOURNAL
4210 CHIPPEWA STREET
SAINT LOUIS, MO 63116
314-664-2700
Fax: 314-664-8533
http://www.stltoday.com
• Scott Fitzgerald, Sports Editor
(314) 664-2700
sfitzgerald@yourjournal.com
Frequency:
2 time(s) per week

SOUTHWEST COUNTY JOURNAL
4210 CHIPPEWA STREET
SAINT LOUIS, MO 63116
314-664-2700
Fax: 314-664-8533
http://www.stltoday.com
• Scott Fitzgerald, Sports Editor
(314) 664-2700
Frequency:
2 time(s) per week

SOUTHWEST DAILY NEWS
716 EAST NAPOLEON STREET
SULPHUR, LA 70663-3402
337-527-7075
Fax: 337-528-3044
editorial@sulphurdailynews.com
http://www.sulphurdailynews.com
• David Folser, Sports Editor
• Suzanne Peveto, Advertising Director
(337) 527-7075

swtdaily@yahoo.com
• Jonathan Manning, Sports Editor
(337) 527-7075
Frequency:
6 time(s) per week

SOUTHWEST NEWS-HERALD
6225 SOUTH KEDZIE AVENUE
CHICAGO, IL 60629-3304
773-476-4800
Fax: 773-476-7811
http://www.swnewsherald.com
• Tom Danz, Sports Editor
(773) 476-4800
Frequency:
1 time(s) per week

SOUTHWEST TIMES
P.O. BOX 391
PULASKI, VA 24301-4608
540-980-5220
Fax: 540-980-3618
editor@southwesttimes.com
http://www.southwesttimes.com
• Vanessa Young, Advertising Director
• David Bissett, Sports Editor
(540) 980-5220
sports@southwesttimes.com
Frequency:
6 time(s) per week

SOUTHWEST TIMES RECORD
3600 WHEELER AVENUE
FORT SMITH, AR 72901
479-785-7700
888-274-3992
Fax: 479-784-0413
http://www.swtimes.com
• Scott Faldon, Sports Editor
(479) 784-0469
• John Speck, Advertising Director
Frequency:
7 time(s) per week

SPARTANBURG HERALD-JOURNAL
P.O. BOX 1657
SPARTANBURG, SC 29306-2334
864-582-4511
800-922-4158
Fax: 864-594-6350
http://www.goupstate.com
• Burke Noel, Sports Editor
(864) 562-7241
• Kathy Towell, Advertising Manager
(864) 562-7350
Frequency:
7 time(s) per week

SPECTRUM
275 EAST SAINT GEORGE BOULEVARD
SAINT GEORGE, UT 84770-2954
435-674-6200
800-748-5489
Fax: 435-674-6265
aperkins@thespectrum.com
http://www.thespectrum.com
• Bob Hudson, Sports Editor
(435) 674-6250
Frequency:
7 time(s) per week

SPENCER DAILY REPORTER
310 EAST MILWAUKEE STREET
SPENCER, IA 51301-4569

712-262-6610
Fax: 712-262-3044
news@spencerdailyreporter.com
• Nate Shaughnessy, Sports Editor
sports@spencerdailyreporter.com
• Randy Cauthron, Managing Editor
Frequency:
5 time(s) per week

SPIRIT
510 PINE STREET
PUNXSUTAWNEY, PA 15767-1404
814-938-8740
Fax: 814-938-3794
composing@punxsutawneyspirit.com
http://www.punxsutawneyspirit.com
• Adam Pavock, Sports Editor
sports@punxsutawneyspirit.com
Frequency:
6 time(s) per week

SPOKESMAN-REVIEW
P.O. BOX 2160
SPOKANE, WA 99201-1006
509-459-5000
800-789-0029
Fax: 509-459-5482
http://www.spokesmanreview.com
• Steve Bergum, Sports Writer
(509) 927-2177
• John Blanchette, Sports Columnist
(509) 459-5509
• Gil Hulse, Sports Assistant Editor
(509) 459-5510
gilh@spokesman.com
• Joe Palmquist, Sports Editor
(509) 459-5503
joep@spokesman.com
• Nick Eaton, College Sports Writer
(509) 990-9630
Frequency:
7 time(s) per week

SPORTS EYE
18 INDUSTRIAL PARK DRIVE
PORT WASHINGTON, NY 11050-4621
516-484-3300
800-568-7907
Fax: 516-484-6104
• Jack Cohen, Publisher
• Derrick N/A, Editor
• Tina Vitello, Advertising Manager
Frequency:
7 time(s) per week

SPRINGFIELD NEWS-LEADER
651 BOONVILLE
SPRINGFIELD, MO 65806
417-836-1100
800-695-1969
Fax: 417-837-1381
http://directory.ozarksnow.com
• Jeff Majeske, Sports Editor
• Rhonda Barlow, Advertising Director

SPRINGFIELD NEWS-SUN
P.O. BOX 3090
SPRINGFIELD, OH 45503-4202
937-328-0300
Fax: 937-328-0328
newssuneditor@coxohio.com
http://www.springfieldnewssun.com
• Rob Mercer, Advertising Director
(937) 328-0240
rmercer@coxohio.com
• Kermit Rowe, Sports Editor

media

(937) 328-0300
krowe@coxohio.com
Frequency:
7 time(s) per week

ST. ALBANS MESSENGER
P.O. BOX 1250
SAINT ALBANS, VT 05478-2503
802-524-9771
Fax: 802-527-1948
news@samessenger.com
http://www.samessenger.com/
• Jeremy Read, Advertising Manager
jeremy@samessenger.com
• Josh Kaufmann, Sports Editor
(802) 524-9771
josh@samessenger.com
Frequency:
6 time(s) per week

ST. AUGUSTINE RECORD
1 NEWS PLACE
SAINT AUGUSTINE, FL 32086
904-829-6562
Fax: 904-819-3558
http://www.staugustinerecord.com
• Justin Barney, Sports Editor
(904) 819-3492
justin.barney@staugustinerecord.com
• Dawn Ginnane, Advertising Director
(904) 819-3440
dawn.ginnane@staugustinerecord.com
Frequency:
7 time(s) per week

ST. CHARLES JOURNAL
4212 NORTH SERVICE ROAD
SAINT PETERS, MO 63376
636-946-6111
Fax: 314-657-3354
http://www.yourjournal.com
• Russell Korando, Sports Editor
Frequency:
3 time(s) per week

ST. JOSEPH NEWS-PRESS
825 EDMOND STREET
SAINT JOSEPH, MO 64501-2737
816-271-8500
800-779-6397
Fax: 816-271-8692
photo@npgco.com
http://www.stjoenews-press.com/
• Brent Briggemann, Sports Writer
(816) 271-8553
• Scott Dochterman, Sports Editor
(816) 271-8577
• Clark Grell, Sports Assistant Editor
(816) 271-8555
• Tim Weddle, Advertising Director
(816) 271-8510
• Eddie Burns, Sports Reporter
(816) 271-8558
Frequency:
7 time(s) per week

ST. LOUIS POST-DISPATCH
900 N. TUCKER BLVD
ST. LOUIS, MO 63101
314-340-8000
Fax: 314-340-3070
www.post-dispatch.com
• Tom Rees, Vice President/Director of Advertising
• Cameron Hollway, Sports Director/High School

ST. PETERSBURG TIMES
490 FIRST AVENUE SOUTH
ST. PETERSBURG, FL 33701-4204
727-893-8111
800-333-7505
Fax: 727-893-8675
www.tampabay.com
• Damian Cristodero, Sports Writer
(727) 893-8662
cristodero@sptimes.com
• Antonya English, Sports Writer
(727) 893-8123
english@sptimes.com
• Dona Hankins, Sports Night Editor
(727) 893-8401
hankins@sptimes.com
• Bob Harig, Sports Writer
(727) 893-8806
harig@sptimes.com
• Brant James, Sports Writer
(727) 893-8111
• Tom Jones, Sports Writer
(727) 893-8111
sptsnews@sptimes.com
• Roy LeBlanc, Sports Editor
(727) 893-8925
leblanc@sptimes.com
• Rodney Page, Sports Writer
(727) 893-8818
page@sptimes.com
• Frank Pastor, Sports Writer
(727) 893-8123
pastor@sptimes.com
• Scott Purks, Sports Writer
(813) 226-3353
purks@sptimes.com
• Bob Putnam, Sports Writer
(727) 445-4169
putnam@sptimes.com
• Gary Shelton, Sports Columnist
(727) 893-8805
shelton@sptimes.com
• Mike Stephenson, Sports Editor
(727) 893-8201
mstephenson@sptimes.com
• Rick Stroud, Sports Writer
(727) 893-8123
stroud@sptimes.com
• Marc Topkin, Sports Writer
(727) 893-8801
topkin@sptimes.com
• John Cotey, Sports Writer
(727) 893-8123
cotey@sptimes.com
Frequency:
7 time(s) per week

STAMFORD ADVOCATE
75 TRESSER BOULEVARD
STAMFORD, CT 06901-3304
203-964-2200
Fax: 203-964-2345
letters.advocate@scni.com
http://www.stamfordadvocate.com
• Bob Kennedy, Sports Editor
(203) 964-2275
Frequency:
7 time(s) per week

STANDARD DEMOCRAT
205 S NEW MADRID ST
SIKESTON, MO 63801-2953
573-471-1137
800-675-6980
Fax: 573-471-6981
standem@yahoo.com
http://www.standard-democrat.com

• Shawn Crawford, Classified Manager
(573) 471-4141
class@standard-democrat.com
• Derek James, Sports Editor
news@standard-democrat.com
• Deanna Nelson, Advertising Manager
(573) 471-4141
Frequency:
6 time(s) per week

STANDARD-EXAMINER
PO BOX 12790
OGDEN, UT 84404
801-625-4200
Fax: 801-625-4299
cityed@standard.net
http://www.standard.net
• Chris Miller, Executive Sports Editor
(801) 625-4261
sports@standard.net
• Brad Roghaar, Advertising Manager
(801) 625-4310
• Jasen Asay, College Sports Reporter
(801) 625-4260
Frequency:
7 time(s) per week

STANDARD-JOURNAL
21 NORTH ARCH STREET
MILTON, PA 17847
570-742-9671
Fax: 570-742-9876
newsroom@standard-journal.com
http://www.standard-journal.com
• Chris Brady, Staff Writer
(570) 742-9671
sports@standard-journal.com
Frequency:
6 time(s) per week

STANDARD-SPEAKER
21 NORTH WYOMING STREET
HAZLETON, PA 18201-6068
570-455-3636
800-843-6680
Fax: 570-455-4244
editorial@standardspeaker.com
http://www.standardspeaker.com
• Ron Kollar, Sports Editor
(570) 455-3636
sports@standardspeaker.com
• Bruce Leonard, Classified Manager
• Gary Yacubeck, Advertising Director
(570) 455-3636
Frequency:
7 time(s) per week

STANDARD-TIMES
P.O. BOX 5912
NEW BEDFORD, MA 02740-6228
508-979-4440
800-286-9876
Fax: 508-997-7491
newsroom@s-t.com
http://www.southcoasttoday.com
• Jonathan Comey, Sports Editor
(508) 979-4442
Frequency:
7 time(s) per week

STAR NEWS
296 THIRD
CHULA VISTA, CA 91910
619-427-3000
Fax: 619-426-6346

info@thestarnews.com
http://www.thestarnews.com
• Phillip Brents, Sports Editor
(619) 427-3000
Frequency:
1 time(s) per week

STAR PRESS
P.O. BOX 2408
MUNCIE, IN 47305-1620
765-747-5717
800-783-7827
Fax: 765-213-5858
news@thestarpress.com
http://www.thestarpress.com
• Phil Beebe, Sports Editor
(765) 213-5730
pbeebe@muncie.gannett.com
• Brian Saparnis, Sports Assistant Editor
(765) 213-5811
• Rob Sullivan, Sports Reporter
(765) 213-5816
rsullivan@muncie.gannett.com
• Mary Young, Advertising Director
(765) 213-5711
myoung@muncie.gannett.com
• Doug Zaleski, Sports Reporter
(765) 213-5813
dzaleski@muncie.gannett.com
Frequency:
7 time(s) per week

STAR TRIBUNE
425 PORTLAND AVENUE
MINNEAPOLIS, MN 55488-1511
612-673-4000
800-827-8742
Fax: 612-673-4359
http://www.startribune.com
• Rachel Blount, Sports Columnist
(612) 673-4389
rblount@startribune.com
• Dennis Brackin, Sports Team Leader
(612) 673-1740
dbrackin@startribune.com
• Mark Craig, Sports Reporter
(612) 673-7011
mcraig@startribune.com
Frequency:
7 time(s) per week

STAR-BANNER
P.O. BOX 490
OCALA, FL 34474-7052
352-867-4010
800-541-2171
Fax: 352-867-4018
http://www.ocala.com
• Eric Barnes, Sports Editor
(352) 867-4143
• Mike Hodge, Sports Writer
Frequency:
7 time(s) per week

STAR-BEACON
4626 PARK AVENUE
ASHTABULA, OH 44005-2100
440-998-2323
Fax: 440-998-7938
http://www.starbeacon.com
• Karl Pearson, Staff Writer
(440) 998-2323
• Don McCormack, Sports Editor
(440) 998-2323
donmac@suite224.net
• Bob Ettinger, Staff Writer
(440) 998-2323

Frequency:
7 time(s) per week
Circulation:
20,000

STAR-COURIER
105 EAST CENTRAL BOULEVARD
KEWANEE, IL 61443-2245
309-852-2181
800-397-7827
Fax: 309-852-0010
editor@starcourier.com
http://www.starcourier.com
• Brian Murphy, Sports Editor
(309) 852-2181
Frequency:
6 time(s) per week

STAR-DEMOCRAT
29088 AIRPARK DRIVE
EASTON, MD 21601-7000
410-822-1500
Fax: 410-770-4019
stardem@chespub.com
http://www.stardem.com
• Derek Coleman, Sports Reporter
(410) 770-4095
• David Fike, Advertising Manager
(410) 770-4040
dfike@chespub.com
• Kevin George, Sports Assistant Editor
(410) 770-4095
• Bill Haufe, Sports Editor
(410) 770-4095
bhaufe@chespub.com
• Sil Morrison, Classified Manager
(410) 770-4054
Frequency:
6 time(s) per week

STAR-GAZETTE
201 BALDWIN STREET
ELMIRA, NY 14901-3002
607-734-5151
800-836-8970
Fax: 607-733-4408
http://www.stargazette.com
• Roger Neumann, Sports Editor
(607) 271-8242
• Andrew Legare, Sports Editor
(607) 734-5151
alegare@stargazette.com
Frequency:
7 time(s) per week

STAR-HERALD
1405 BROADWAY
SCOTTSBLUFF, NE 69361-3151
308-632-9000
800-846-6102
Fax: 308-632-9001
news@starherald.com
http://www.starherald.com
• Jeff Fielder, Sports Editor
(308) 632-9000
jeff.fielder@starherald.com
Frequency:
6 time(s) per week

STAR-LEDGER
1 STAR-LEDGER PLAZA
NEWARK, NJ 07102-1200
973-392-4040
Fax: 973-392-1886
http://www.nj.com/starledger

• Fred Aun, Outdoors Writer
(973) 392-4040
outdoors@starledger.com
• Richard Chere, Sports Reporter (Hockey)
• Dave D'Alessandro, Basketball Columnist
(973) 392-4203
ddalessandro@starledger.com
• Chris D'Amico, Deputy Managing
Editor/Production
(973) 392-5732
cdamico@starledger.com
• Sid Dorfman, Sports Columnist
(973) 392-4023
sdorfman@starledger.com
• Matthew Futterman, Sports Business
Reporter
(973) 392-1732
mfutterman@starledger.com
• Jim Hague, Sports Reporter
(201) 955-0016
ogsmar@aol.com
• Jerry Izenberg, Sports Columnist
jizenberg@starledger.com
• Kevin Manahan, Sports Reporter
kmanahan@starledger.com
• Steve Politi, Sports Writer
(973) 392-4023
spoliti@starledger.com
Frequency:
7 time(s) per week

STAR-TELEGRAM (FORT WORTH)
400 W. 7TH St
FORT WORTH, TX 76102
817-390-7400
Fax: 817-390-7789
www.star-telegram.com
• Paul Harral, Editorial Director
• Celeste Williams, Sports Editor
(817) 390-7697
cxwilliams@star-telegram.com
Description:
Covers Sports local and national. Rangers
Cowboys High School Football College
Sports Mavericks/NBA Stars/Pro Hockey
Motorsports Horse Racing Rodeo/Horse

STAR-TRIBUNE
170 STAR LANE
CASPER, WY 82604-2883
307-266-0550
Fax: 307-266-0568
http://www.casperstartribune.net
• Ron Gullberg, Sports Editor
(307) 266-0573
Frequency:
7 time(s) per week

STARKVILLE DAILY NEWS
316 UNIVERSITY DRIVE
STARKVILLE, MS 39759
662-323-1642
Fax: 662-323-6586
http://www.starkvilledailynews.com
• Don Foster, Sports Editor
Frequency:
7 time(s) per week

STATE
P.O. BOX 1333
COLUMBIA, SC 29202-4814
803-771-8465
800-288-2727
Fax: 803-771-8430
biznews@thestate.com
http://www.thestate.com

media

• Gerald Davis, Sports Assistant Editor
(803) 771-8442
• Bob Gillespie, Golf Columnist
(803) 771-8304
bgillespie@thestate.com
• Craig McHugh, Sports Editor
(803) 771-8450
• Jim McLaurin, Sports Writer
(803) 771-8542
• Rick Millians, Executive Sports Editor
(803) 771-8450
rmillians@thestate.com
• Ron Morris, Sports Columnist
(803) 771-8432
• David Newton, Sports Senior Writer
(803) 548-3769
• Patrick Obley, Sports Reporter
(803) 771-8465
• Joe Person, Sports Reporter
(803) 771-8496
• Bob Spear, Sports Columnist
bspear@thestate.com
Frequency:
7 time(s) per week

STATE GAZETTE
294 HIGHWAY 51 BYPASS
DYERSBURG, TN 38024
731-285-4091
Fax: 731-285-9747
http://www.stategazette.com
• Mike Smith, Sports Editor
(731) 285-4091
msmith@stategazette.com
Frequency:
6 time(s) per week

STATE JOURNAL-REGISTER
1 COPLEY PLAZA
SPRINGFIELD, IL 62701
217-788-1300
800-397-8757
Fax: 217-788-1372
sjr@sj-r.com
http://www.sj-r.com
• Robert Burns, Sports Writer
(217) 788-1546
• Dave Kane, Sports Writer
dave.kane@sj-r.com
• Marcia Martinez, Sports Writer
marcia.martinez@sj-r.com
• Hal Pilger, Sports Writer
• Jim Ruppert, Sports Editor
• Tim Stacy, Advertising Manager
(217) 788-1300
• John Supinie, Sports Writer
• Tom Tillman, Display Advertising Manager
(217) 788-1359
Frequency:
7 time(s) per week

STATEN ISLAND ADVANCE
950 FINGERBOARD ROAD
STATEN ISLAND, NY 10305-1453
718-981-1234
Fax: 718-981-5679
editor@siadvance.com
http://www.silive.com
• Carmine Angioli, Sports Editor
(718) 816-2803
angioli@siadvance.com
• Tom Flannagan, Sports Columnist
(718) 816-2582
tflannagan@siadvance.com
• Stephen Hart, Sports Columnist
(718) 981-2241
hart@siadvance.com

Frequency:
7 time(s) per week

STATESMAN JOURNAL
P.O. BOX 13009
SALEM, OR 97301-3734
503-399-6611
Fax: 503-399-6706
newsroom@statesmanjournal.com
http://www.statesmanjournal.com/apps/pbcs
.dll/frontpage
• James Day, Sports Editor
(503) 399-6801
jday@statesmanjournal.com
• Teresa Kepplinger, Advertising Director
(503) 399-6648
tkepling@statesmanjournal.com
Frequency:
7 time(s) per week

STATESVILLE RECORD & LANDMARK
222 EAST BROAD STREET
STATESVILLE, NC 28677-5325
704-873-1451
Fax: 704-872-3150
news@statesville.com
http://www.statesville.com
• Jon Dunham, Advertising Director
(704) 873-1451
jdunham@statesville.com
• Bill Kiser, Sports Editor
(704) 873-1451
• Jason Bullard, Sports Editor
(704) 873-1451
Frequency:
7 time(s) per week

STEPHENVILLE EMPIRE-TRIBUNE
590 SOUTH LOOP
STEPHENVILLE, TX 76401-4224
254-965-3124
Fax: 254-965-4269
http://www.empiretribune.com
• John Menzies, Sports Editor
(254) 965-3124
sports@empiretribune.com
Frequency:
6 time(s) per week

STEVENS POINT JOURNAL
P.O. BOX 7
STEVENS POINT, WI 54481-2855
715-344-6100
Fax: 715-344-7229
spj@coredcs.com
http://www.stevenspointjournal.com
• Chris Schulte, Sports Editor
(715) 845-0700
cschulte@gannett.com
• Scott Williams, Sports Reporter
(715) 345-2282
scott.williams@cwnews.net
• Nathan Vine, Sports Reporter
(715) 345-2281
nvine@stevenspoint.gannett.com
Frequency:
7 time(s) per week

STILLWATER GAZETTE
1931 CURVE CREST BOULEVARD
STILLWATER, MN 55082
651-439-3130
Fax: 651-439-4713
http://www.stillwatergazette.com/
• Stuart Groskreutz, Sports Editor
(651) 796-1107

Frequency:
5 time(s) per week

STUTTGART DAILY LEADER
111 WEST 6TH STREET
STUTTGART, AR 72160-4243
870-673-8533
800-244-3966
Fax: 870-673-3671
http://www.stuttgartdailyleader.com
• Patrick Geans, Sports Editor
(870) 673-8533
Frequency:
5 time(s) per week

SUFFOLK NEWS-HERALD
P.O. BOX 1220
SUFFOLK, VA 23434-5323
757-539-3437
Fax: 757-539-3000
http://www.suffolknewsherald.com
• Earl Jones, Advertising Director
(757) 934-9607
• Andrew Giermak, Sports Editor
(757) 934-9614
Frequency:
6 time(s) per week

SULLIVAN DAILY TIMES
115 WEST JACKSON AVENUE
SULLIVAN, IN 47882-1505
812-268-6356
800-264-6356
Fax: 812-268-3110
• Rick Curl, Sports Editor
• Matt Wilson, Sports Editor
(812) 268-6356
Frequency:
5 time(s) per week

SULPHUR SPRINGS NEWS-TELEGRAM
401 CHURCH STREET
SULPHUR SPRINGS, TX 75482-2681
903-885-8663
800-245-2149
Fax: 903-885-8768
cityed@ssecho.com
http://www.ssnewstelegram.com/
• Bobby Burney, Sports Editor
(903) 885-8663
sportsed@ssecho.com
• Johnie Hargrave, Advertising Manager
Frequency:
6 time(s) per week

SUMMIT DAILY NEWS
40 WEST MAIN STREET
FRISCO, CO 80443
970-668-3998
Fax: 970-668-0755
news@summitdaily.com
http://www.summitdaily.com
• Christine Holaday-Schriock, Classified Manager
(970) 668-9937
cschriock@cmnm.org
• Devon O'Neil, Sports Editor
(970) 668-3998
• Adam Boffey, Sports Editor
(970) 668-3998
Frequency:
7 time(s) per week

SUN (CA)
399 N. D ST
SAN BERNARDINO, CA 92401

909-889-9666
Fax: 909-384-0327
www.sbcsun.com
• Paul Oberjuerge, Sports Editor
• Glenn Rabinowitz, Managing Editor

SUN (MD)
501 N. CALVERT ST
BALTIMORE, MD 21278
410-332-6000
Fax: 410-269-4224
www.sunspot.net
• Ron Fritz, Sports Editor
ron.fritz@baltsun.com

SUN (WA)
545 5TH STREET
BREMERTON, WA 98337-1413
360-377-3711
Fax: 360-377-9237
• Annette Griffus, Sports Reporter
(360) 792-9224
agriffus@kitsapsun.com
• Nathan Joyce, Sports Reporter
(360) 792-9209
njoyce@kitsapsun.com
• Chuck Stark, Sports Editor
(360) 792-9231
Frequency:
7 time(s) per week

SUN CHRONICLE
P.O. BOX 600
ATTLEBORO, MA 02703
508-222-7000
Fax: 508-236-0462
http://www.thesunchronicle.com
• Mark Farinella, Sports Reporter
• Dale Ransom, Sports Reporter
Frequency:
7 time(s) per week

SUN JOURNAL
3200 WELLONS BOULEVARD
NEW BERN, NC 28562
252-638-8101
Fax: 252-638-4664
http://www.newbernsj.com
• Randy Jones, Sports Editor
(252) 638-8101
Frequency:
7 time(s) per week

SUN NEWS
P.O. BOX 406
MYRTLE BEACH, SC 29577-6700
843-626-8555
800-568-1800
Fax: 843-626-0356
sneditors@thesunnews.com
http://www.thesunnews.com
• Al Blondin, Sports Reporter Golf
(843) 626-0284
ablondin@thesunnews.com
• Shane Bowen, Sports Editor
(843) 626-0302
• Terry Massey, Columnist
(843) 626-0371
Frequency:
7 time(s) per week

SUN-GAZETTE
6408 EDSALL ROAD
ALEXANDRIA, VA 22312
703-738-2520
Fax: 703-738-2530

news@sungazette.net
http://www.sungazette.net
• David Facinoli, Sports Editor
(703) 738-2533
sports@sungazette.net
Frequency:
1 time(s) per week

SUN-SENTINEL
200 E. LAS OLAS BLVD
FORT LAUDERDALE, FL 33301-2293
954-356-4000
Fax: 954-356-4676
www.sun-sentinel.com
• Fred Turner, Sports Editor

SUNDAY GAZETTE-MAIL
1001 VIRGINIA ST E.
CHARLESTON, WV 25301
304-348-4827
Fax: 304-348-4847
http://wvgazette.com
• Mitch Vingle, Sports Editor

SUNDAY NEWS
P.O. BOX 1328
LANCASTER, PA 17603
717-291-8811
800-809-4666
Fax: 717-291-4950
http://www.lancasteronline.com
• James Hersh, Sports Editor
(717) 291-8699
jhersh@lnpnews.com
• Dave Byrne, Sports Reporter
(717) 291-8699
dbyrne@lnpnews.com
Frequency:
1 time(s) per week

SUPERIOR TELEGRAM
424 W FIRST ST
DULUTH, MN 55802
editorial@superiortelegram.com
www.superiortelegram.com
• Ken Olson, Sports Writer
(715) 395-5023
Frequency:
Tuesday and Friday

SWEETWATER REPORTER
112 WEST THIRD STREET
SWEETWATER, TX 79556
325-236-6677
Fax: 325-235-4967
editor@sweetwaterreporter.com
www.sweetwaterreporter.com
• Ron Howell, Sports Writer
Frequency:
6 time(s) per week
Circulation:
3,400

TAHOE DAILY TRIBUNE
3079 HARRISON AVENUE
SOUTH LAKE TAHOE, CA 96150-7931
530-541-3880
Fax: 530-541-0373
editor@tahoedailytribune.com
http://www.tahoedailytribune.com/
• Steve Yingling, Sports Editor
(530) 542-8010
Frequency:
5 time(s) per week

TALLADEGA DAILY HOME
4 SYLACAUGA HIGHWAY
TALLADEGA, AL 35160
256-362-1000
Fax: 256-299-2192
news@dailyhome.com
http://www.dailyhome.com
• Pam Adamson, Advertising Director
(256) 299-2140
padamson@dailyhome.com
• Alta Bolding, Classified Manager
(256) 299-2150
abolding@dailyhome.com
• Sandy Carden, Retail Advertising Manager
(256) 299-2141
scarden@dailyhome.com
• Will Heath, Sports Editor
wheath@dailyhome.com
• Austin Moore, Sports Assistant Editor
amoore@dailyhome.com
• Bran Strickland, Sports Editor
(256) 299-2132
bstrickland@dailyhome.com
Frequency:
6 time(s) per week

TALLAHASSEE DEMOCRAT
P.O. BOX 990
TALLAHASSEE, FL 32301-2695
850-599-2100
800-777-2154
Fax: 850-599-2295
http://www.tallahassee.com
• Randy Beard, Executive Sports Editor
(850) 599-2160
rbeard@tallahassee.com
• Jack Corcoran, Sports Reporter
(850) 599-2172
• Steve Ellis, Senior College Sports Writer
(850) 599-2100
sellis@tallahassee.com
• Ike Morgan, Sports Editor
(850) 599-2297
• Clair Murraine, Sports Reporter
(850) 599-2317
scmurraine@tallahassee.com
Frequency:
7 time(s) per week

TAMPA TRIBUNE
200 S PARKER STREET
TAMPA, FL 33606
813-259-7655
800-527-2718
Fax: 813-259-8148
sports@tampatrib.com
www.tbo.com
• Kim Pendery, MLB/Rays/Auto
Racing/Colleges
(813) 259-8406
kpendery@tampatrib.com
• Doug Jacobs, Prep
(813) 259-7615
djacobs@tampatrib.com
• Joanne Korth, NFL, Bucs, NHL/Lightning
(813) 259-7998
jkorth@tampatrib.com
• Roy Cummings, Sports Reporter
(813) 259-7859
RCummings@tampatrib.com
• Bob D'Angelo, Sports Copy Editor
rdangelo@tampatrib.com
• Eddie Daniels, Sports Writer / Pasco
County
(813) 259-7600
EDaniels@tampatrib.com
• Eddie Daniels, Sports Reporter
(813) 948-4274

edaniels@tampatrib.com
• Mick Elliott, Columnist
(813) 259-7341
melliott@tampatrib.com
• Erik Erlendsson, Sports Writer
(813) 259-7600
eerlendsson@tampatrib.com
• Tony Fabrizio, Auto Racing Reporter
(813) 259-7655
afabrizio@tampatrib.com
• Martin Fennelly, Sports Columnist
(813) 259-7352
 mfennelly@tampatrib.com
• Carter Gaddis, Sports Reporter
(813) 259-7979
cgaddis@tampatrib.com
• Mike Garbett, Sports Copy Editor
mgarbett@tampatrib.com
• Mike Harris, Team Leader/Local Sports
(813) 259-7302
mharris@tampatrib.com
• Joe Henderson, Sports Writer
(813) 259-7861
JHenderson@tampatrib.com
• Doug Jacobs, Deputy Sports Editor
(813) 259-7600
djacobs@tampatrib.com
• Barb Jiannetti, Sports Copy Editor
BJiannetti@tampatrib.com
• Joey Johnston, Sports Writer
(813) 259-7711
jjohnston@tampatrib.com
• Ira Kaufman, Sports Reporter
(813) 259-7655
ikaufman@tampatrib.com
• Joey Knight, Sports Reporter
(813) 948-4202
jknight@tampatrib.com
• Rozel Lee, Sports Reporter
RLee@tampatrib.com
• Brett McMurphy, Sports Reporter
(813) 259-7928
bmcmurphy@tampatrib.com
• Mike Pennetti, Sports Team Leader
MPennetti@tampatrib.com
• Wes Phillips, Sports Copy Editor
wphillips@tampatrib.com
• Nick Pugliese, (813) 259-7854
Sports Senior Editor
DPugliese@tampatrib.com
• Anwar Richardson, Sports Reporter
arichardson@tampatrib.com
• Matt Severance, Sports Editor
(813) 259-7064
mseverance@tampatrib.com
• Katherine Smith, Sports Writer
(813) 259-7600
ksmith@tampatrib.com
• Alan Snel, Sports Business Writer
(813) 259-7850
ASnel@tampatrib.com
• Andy Staples, Sports Writer
(813) 259-7600
astaples@tampatrib.com
Frequency:
7 time(s) per week

TAYLOR DAILY PRESS
211 WEST 3RD STREET
TAYLOR, TX 76574-3518
512-352-8535
Fax: 512-352-2227
http://www.taylordailypress.net
• Maurine Stutler, Classified Manager
classified@taylordailypress.net
• Jeremy Weber, Sports Editor
• Don Wilson, Advertising Manager

• Brian Smith, Sports Editor
(512) 352-8535
Frequency:
5 time(s) per week

TELEGRAM & GAZETTE
20 FRANKLIN STREET
WORCESTER, MA 01615
508-793-9100
800-678-6680
Fax: 508-793-9281
newstips@telegram.com
http://www.telegram.com
• Bill Ballou, Sports Reporter
(508) 793-9350
sports@telegram.com
• Bud Barth, Sports Reporter
(508) 793-9350
sports@telegram.com
• Rich Garven, Sports Reporter
(508) 793-9350
sports@telegram.com
• Dave Greenslit, Sports Editor
(508) 793-9375
• Nick Manzello, Sports Columnist
sports@telegram.com
• Phil O'Neill, Sports Reporter
(508) 793-9350
sports@telegram.com
• Jennifer Toland, Sports Reporter
(508) 793-9350
sports@telegram.com
Frequency:
7 time(s) per week

TELEGRAPH (IL)
111 EAST BROADWAY
ALTON, IL 65606
618-463-2500
800-477-1447
Fax: 618-463-9829
telegraph_pub@hotmail.com
http://www.thetelegraph.com
• Pete Hayes, Sports Editor
(618) 463-2565
phayes93@hotmail.com
• Greg Shashack, Sports Assistant Editor
gshashack@hotmail.com
Frequency:
7 time(s) per week

TELEGRAPH (NE)
621 NORTH CHESTNUT STREET
NORTH PLATTE, NE 69101-4131
308-532-6000
800-753-7092
Fax: 308-532-9268
editor@nptelegraph.com
http://www.thenptelegraph.com
• Job Vigil, Sports Editor
(308) 532-6000
jvigil@nptelegraph.com
Frequency:
6 time(s) per week

TELEGRAPH (NH)
17 EXECUTIVE DR
HUDSON, NH 03051
603-594-6576
Fax: 603-882-2681
www.nashuatelegraph.com
• Alan Greenwood, Sports Editor
• Steve Daly, Asst Sports Director

TELEGRAPH HERALD
801 BLUFF STREET
DUBUQUE, IA 52001-4661
563-588-5611
800-553-4801
Fax: 563-588-5745
thonline@wcinet.com
http://www.thonline.com
• Clete Campbell, Sports Reporter
(563) 588-5623
• Steve Fisher, Advertising Director
(563) 588-5754
sfisher@wcinet.com
• Troy Johnson, Sports Reporter
(563) 588-5626
• Jim Leitner, Sports Editor
(563) 588-5783
jleitner@wcinet.com
• Bill Speltz, Sports Reporter
(563) 588-5632
Frequency:
7 time(s) per week

TEMPLE DAILY TELEGRAM
10 SOUTH 3RD STREET
TEMPLE, TX 76501-7619
254-778-4444
800-460-6397
Fax: 254-771-3516
tdt@temple-telegram.com
http://www.temple-telegram.com
• Gary Garner, Advertising Manager
(254) 778-4444
advertiz@temple-telegram.com
• Stan Thomas, Classified Manager
(254) 778-4444
tdt@vvm.com
• Greg Willi, Sports Editor
(254) 778-4444
sports@temple-telegram.com
Frequency:
7 time(s) per week

TENNESSEAN
1100 BROADWAY
NASHVILLE, TN 37203
615-259-8000
Fax: 615-259-8093
newstips@tennessean.com
http://www.tennessean.com
• Joe Biddle, Sports Columnist
(615) 259-8255
jbiddle@tennessean.com
• Larry Taft, Sports Editor
(615) 259-8352
• Chip Cirillo, Sports Reporter
(615) 664-2194
ccirillo@tennessean.com
• David Climer, Sports Columnist
(615) 259-8020
dclimer@tennessean.com
• John Glennon, Sports Reporter
(615) 259-8262
jglennon@tennessean.com
• Mike Jones, Deputy Sports Editor
(615) 259-8013
mjones@tennessean.com
• Jeff Lockridge, Sports Reporter
(615) 259-8023
• Bryan Mullen, Sports Writer
(615) 259-8017
• Mike Organ, Sports Reporter
(615) 259-8021
morgan@tennessean.com
• Maurice Patton, Sports Reporter
(615) 259-8018
mpatton@tennessean.com

• Kevin Procter, Sports Reporter
(615) 259-8014
kprocter@tennessean.com
• Jim Wyatt, Sports Reporter
(615) 259-8015
Frequency:
7 time(s) per week

TERRELL TRIBUNE
150 9TH STREET
TERRELL, TX 75160
972-563-6476
Fax: 972-563-0340
ttrib@swbell.net
http://www.terrelltribune.com
• Kent Miller, Sports Editor
• Nicole Petet, Advertising Manager
ttribads@swbell.net
Frequency:
6 time(s) per week

TEXARKANA GAZETTE
PO BOX 621
TEXARKANA, TX 75501-5655
903-794-3311
Fax: 903-794-3315
http://www.texarkanagazette.com
• Louie Avery, Sports Writer
(903) 794-3311
lavery@texarkanagazette.com
• Johnny Green, Sports Editor
(903) 794-3311
• Rick Meredith, Advertising Manager
(903) 794-3311
rmeredith@texarkanagazette.com
• James Williams, Sports Editor
(903) 794-3311
Frequency:
7 time(s) per week

THE ADVERTISER
221 JEFFERSON ST
LAFAYETTE, LA 70501
337-289-6303
Fax: 337-289-6443
www.acadiananow.com
• Brady Aymond, Sports Writer
(337) 289-6357
• Kevin Foote, Sports Editor
(337) 289-6317

AEGIS, THE
139 NORTH MAIN STREET
SUITE 203
BEL AIR, MD 21014
410-838-4400
888-879-1710
Fax: 410-838-7867
news@theaegis.com
www.baltimoresun.com/news/maryland/harford/aegis
• Randy McRoberts, Sports Editor
(410) 332-6718
rmcroberts@theaegis.com
Frequency:
7 time(s) per week

THE ARGUS
37468 FREMONT BLVD
FREMONT, CA 94536
510-353-7027
Fax: 510-353-7029
bangcirc@bayareanewsgroup.com
http://www.insidebayarea.com/argus/

• Mike Lefkow, Sports Editor
(925) 943-8149
mlefkow@bayareanewsgroup.com
Frequency:
7 time(s) per week

THE STAR
118 WEST 9TH STREET
AUBURN, IN 46706-2225
260-925-2611
800-717-4679
Fax: 260-925-2625
dkurtz@kpcnews.net
http://www.kpcnews.com
• Mark Murdock, Sports Editor
(260) 925-2611
markm@kpcnews.net
Frequency:
7 time(s) per week

THE TRIANGLE TRIBUNE
115 MARKET STREET
SUITE 360-G
DURHAM, NC 27701
919-688-9408
Fax: 919-688-2740
editor@triangletribune.com
www.triangletribune.com
• Bonitta Best, Sports Editor/Managing Editor
Frequency:
1 time(s) per week
Description:
Weekly newspaper
Year Founded:
1998

THREE RIVERS COMMERCIAL-NEWS
PO BOX 130
THREE RIVERS, MI 49093
269-279-7488
Fax: 269-279-6007
http://www.threeriversnews.com
• Marnie Apa, Advertising Manager
marnie@threeriversnews.com
• Scott Hassinger, Sports Reporter
(269) 279-7488
scott@threeriversnews.com
Frequency:
6 time(s) per week

TIFTON GAZETTE
211 NORTH TIFT AVENUE
TIFTON, GA 31793
229-382-4321
Fax: 229-387-7322
http://www.tiftongazette.com
• Tom Mark, Sports Editor
(229) 382-4321
• Darrin Wilson, Advertising Manager
Frequency:
6 time(s) per week

TIMES (IN)
601 45TH AVENUE, W.
MUNSTER, IN 46321-2875
219-933-3200
800-589-3331
Fax: 219-933-3249
newstips@nwi.com
http://www.nwi.com
• Mike Clark, Assistant Sports Editor
(219) 933-3200
Frequency:
7 time(s) per week

TIMES (LA)
222 LAKE STREET
SHREVEPORT, LA 71101-3738
318-459-3270
800-551-8892
Fax: 318-459-3301
http://www.shreveporttimes.com
• Scott Ferrell, Sports Editor
(318) 459-3300
sferrell@gannett.com
• Brian Vernellis, Sports Reporter
(318) 459-3300
bvernellis@gannett.com
Frequency:
7 time(s) per week

TIMES AND DEMOCRAT
1010 BROUGHTON STREET, S.E.
ORANGEBURG, SC 29115-5955
803-534-3352
Fax: 803-533-5526
news@timesanddemocrat.com
http://www.timesanddemocrat.com
• Thomas Grant, Sports Senior Reporter
(803) 533-5547
• John Weiss, Advertising Manager
(803) 533-5542
Frequency:
7 time(s) per week

TIMES ARGUS
P.O. BOX 707
BARRE, VT 05641-2504
802-479-0191
Fax: 802-479-4032
news@timesargus.com
http://www.timesargus.com
• Derek Armstrong, Sports Editor
(802) 479-0191
• David Cousins, Advertising Manager
(802) 479-0191
Frequency:
7 time(s) per week

TIMES DAILY
P.O. BOX 797
FLORENCE, AL 35630-5440
256-766-3434
Fax: 256-740-4717
http://www.timesdaily.com
• Gregg Dewalt, Sports Editor
(256) 740-5748
gregg.dewalt@timesdaily.com
• Jeff McIntyre, Assistant Sports Editor
(256) 740-5737
jeff.mcintyre@timesdaily.com
Frequency:
7 time(s) per week

TIMES GAZETTE
209 SOUTH HIGH STREET
HILLSBORO, OH 45133-1444
937-393-3456
Fax: 937-393-2059
http://www.timesgazette.com
• Lori Boatman-Roush, Sports Editor
lboatman@timesgazette.com
• Sharon Kersey, Advertising Manager
Frequency:
6 time(s) per week

TIMES GEORGIAN
901 HAYS MILL ROAD
CARROLLTON, GA 30117-9576
770-834-6631
Fax: 770-834-9991

media

bbrowning@times-georgian.com
http://www.times-georgian.com
• Corey Cusick, Sports Editor
(770) 834-6631
• Tim Holder, Advertising Director
tholder@times-georgian.com
Frequency:
6 time(s) per week

TIMES HERALD (MI)
911 MILITARY STREET
PORT HURON, MI 48061-5009
810-985-7171
800-462-4057
Fax: 810-989-6294
timesherald@gannett.com
http://www.thetimesherald.com
• Lori Driscoll, Advertising Director
(810) 989-6236
ldriscoll@gannett.com
• Jim Wymer, Sports Editor
(810) 989-6267
Frequency:
7 time(s) per week

TIMES HERALD (PA)
410 MARKLEY STREET
NORRISTOWN, PA 19401-4617
610-272-2501
800-887-2501
Fax: 610-272-0660
shuskey@timesherald.com
http://www.timesherald.com
• Tim Fonde, Sports Editor
(610) 272-2500
• Tom Kerrane, Sports Writer
(610) 272-2232
Frequency:
7 time(s) per week

TIMES HERALD RECORD
40 MULBERRY STREET
MIDDLETOWN, NY 10940
845-341-1100
Fax: 845-343-2170
http://www.th-record.com
• Kevin Gleason, Sports Columnist
(845) 346-3193
kgleason@th-record.com
• Douglas Mohart, Sports Editor
(845) 346-3191
dmohart@th-record.com
• Kathleen Passineau, Retail Advertising
Manager
(845) 346-3013
• Justin Rodriguez, Sports Reporter
(845) 346-3192
jrodriguez@th-record.com
Frequency:
7 time(s) per week

TIMES JOURNAL
811 GREENHILL BOULEVARD NW
FORT PAYNE, AL 35967
256-845-2550
800-348-4637
Fax: 256-845-7459
http://www.times-journal.com
• Lew Gilliland, Sports Editor
(256) 304-0053
• Gloria Jackson, Advertising Manager
(256) 304-060
gjackson@times-journal.com
Frequency:
5 time(s) per week

TIMES LEADER
15 N. MAIN ST
WILKES-BARRE, PA 18711
570-829-7101
Fax: 570-831-7319
• Kurt Knapek, Sports Editor
• Paul Graham, Advertising Director

TIMES NEWS
1ST & IRON STREETS
LEHIGHTON, PA 18235
610-377-2051
Fax: 610-826-9608
tnsports@tnonline.com
www.tnonline.com
• Rod Heckman, Sports Reporter
(610) 377-2051
rheckman@tnonline.com
• Ed Hedes, Managing Sports Editor
(610) 377-2051
ehedes@tnonline.com
• Emmett McCall, Sports Reporter
(610) 377-2051
emccall@tnonline.com
• Linda Moyer, Classified Manager
(610) 377-2051
lmoyer@tnonline.com
Frequency:
6 time(s) per week

TIMES OBSERVER
P.O. BOX 188
WARREN, PA 16365-2412
814-723-8200
Fax: 814-723-6922
editorial@timesobserver.com
http://www.timesobserver.com
• Jon Sitler, Sports Editor
(814) 723-8200
jsitler@timesobserver.com
Frequency:
6 time(s) per week

TIMES RECORD
3 BUSINESS PARKWAY
BRUNSWICK, ME 04011-1302
207-729-3311
800-734-6397
Fax: 207-729-5728
news@timesrecord.com
http://www.timesrecord.com/
• George Almasi, Sports Editor
(207) 504-8240
• John Bamford, Advertising Manager
(207) 729-3311
Frequency:
5 time(s) per week

TIMES RECORD NEWS
1301 LAMAR STREET
WICHITA FALLS, TX 76301
940-767-8341
800-627-1646
Fax: 940-767-1741
choatet@wtr.com
http://www.timesrecordnews.com
• Lee Anderson, Sports Reporter
(940) 720-3470
• Nick Gholson, Sports Editor
(940) 720-3470
Frequency:
7 time(s) per week

TIMES RECORDER
34 SOUTH 4TH STREET
ZANESVILLE, OH 43701-3417

740-452-4561
800-866-7326
Fax: 740-450-6780
http://www.zanesvilletimesrecorder.com
• Dave Weidig, Sports Editor
dweidig@nncogannett.com
Frequency:
6 time(s) per week

TIMES UNION
645 ALBANY SHAKER ROAD
ALBANY, NY 12211
518-454-5694
800-724-0775
Fax: 518-454-5628
tusports@timesunion.com
http://www.timesunion.com
• James Alan, Sports Writer
(518) 454-5062
jallen@timesunion.com
• Bill Callen, Executive Sports Editor
(518) 454-5560
• Pete Dougherty, Sports Columnist
(518) 454-5416
pdougherty@timesunion.com
• Kathleen A. Hallion, Advertising Director
(518) 454-5568
khallion@timesunion.com
Frequency:
7 time(s) per week

TIMES-COURIER
2110 WOODFALL DRIVE
CHARLESTON, IL 61920
217-345-7085
Fax: 217-345-7090
editorial@jg-tc.com
http://www.jg-tc.com
• Brian Nielsen, Sports Editor
(217) 238-6865
sports@jg-tc.com
Frequency:
6 time(s) per week

TIMES-HERALD
222 NORTH IZARD STREET
FORREST CITY, AR 72335-3324
870-633-3130
Fax: 870-633-0599
fctimes@thnews.com
http://www.thnews.com
• Fred Conley, Sports Reporter
(870) 633-3130
• Jim Wirski, Advertising Manager
(870) 633-3130
Frequency:
5 time(s) per week

TIMES-LEADER
200 SOUTH 4TH STREET
MARTINS FERRY, OH 43935-1312
740-633-1131
800-244-5671
Fax: 740-633-1122
timesleader@timesleaderonline.com
http://www.timesleaderonline.com/
• Robert Kapral, Sports Editor
(740) 633-1131
bkapral@timesleaderonline.com
• Kevin Kolanski, Advertising Manager
(740) 633-1131
Frequency:
6 time(s) per week

TIMES-MAIL
813 16TH STREET
BEDFORD, IN 47421-3822
812-275-3355
800-782-4405
Fax: 812-275-4191
tmnews@tmnews.com
http://www.tmnews.com
• Jeff Bartlett, Sports Writer
(812) 277-7284
jeff@tmnews.com
• Sean Duncan, Sports Editor
(812) 277-7283
sean@tmnews.com
Frequency:
7 time(s) per week

TIMES-NEWS
132 FAIRFIELD STREET WEST
TWIN FALLS, ID 83301-5842
208-733-0931
Fax: 208-734-5538
http://www.magicvalley.com
• Joe Paisley, Sports Editor
Frequency:
7 time(s) per week

TIMES-PICAYUNE
3800 HOWARD AVENUE
NEW ORLEANS, LA 70125
504-826-3279
Fax: 504-826-3812
living@timespicayune.com
http://www.timespicayune.com
• Peter Barrouquere, Sports Writer
(504) 826-3803
pbarrouquere@timespicayune.com
• John Deshazier, Sports Columnist
(504) 826-3279
jdeshazier@timespicayune.com
• Jeff Duncan, Sports Columnist (NFL)
(504) 826-3405
jduncan@timespicayune.com
• Peter Finney, Sports Columnist
(504) 826-3802
pfinney@timespicayune.com
• Bob Fortus, Sports Columnist (Horse Racing)
(504) 826-3279
rfortus@timespicayune.com
• Joy Hirdes, Sports Writer
(504) 826-3807
jhirdes@timespicayune.com
• Ted Lewis, Sports Reporter
(504) 826-3405
tlewis@timespicayune.com
• Lori Lyons, Sports Reporter
(504) 826-3405
llyons@timespicayune.com
• David Meeks, Sports Editor
(504) 826-3279
dmeeks@timespicayune.com
• Marty Mule, Sports Writer
(504) 826-3279
mmule@timespicayune.com
• John Reid, Sports Columnist
(504) 826-3279
jreid@timespicayune.com
• Fred Robinson, Sports Reporter
(504) 826-3279
frobinson@timespicayune.com
• Larry Simpson, Sports Writer
(504) 826-3279
sports@timespicayune.com
• Jimmy Smith, Sports Writer
(504) 826-3814
jsmith@timespicayune.com

• Mike Strom, Sports Reporter
(504) 826-3787
mstrom@timespicayune.com
• Billy Turner, Sports Editor (High School)
(504) 826-3405
bturner@timespicayune.com
• Brian Allee-Walsh, Sports Writer
(504) 826-3279
ballee-walsh@timespicayune.com
Frequency:
7 time(s) per week

TIMES-REPORTER
629 WABASH AVENUE, N.W.
NEW PHILADELPHIA, OH 44663-4145
330-364-5577
Fax: 330-364-8416
http://www.timesreporter.com
• Jack Clay, Advertising Director
• Hank Keathley, Sports Columnist
(330) 364-8426
sports@timesreporter.com
• David Whitmer, Sports Editor
(330) 364-5577
david.whitmer@timesreporter.com
Frequency:
7 time(s) per week

TIMES-REPUBLICAN
135 WEST MAIN STREET
MARSHALLTOWN, IA 50158-5843
641-753-6611
800-542-7893
Fax: 641-753-7221
http://www.timesrepublican.com
• Ross Thede, Sports Editor
(641) 753-6611
rthede@timesrepublican.com
Frequency:
7 time(s) per week

TIMES-STANDARD
930 6TH STREET
EUREKA, CA 95501
707-441-0500
Fax: 707-441-0501
editor@times-standard.com
http://www.times-standard.com
• Ray Hamill, Sports Editor
(707) 441-0528
• Brad Botkin, Sports Writer
(707) 441-0500
Frequency:
7 time(s) per week

TIMES-TRIBUNE
149 PENN AVENUE
SCRANTON, PA 18503
570-348-9100
800-228-4637
Fax: 570-348-9135
newsroom@timesshamrock.com
http://www.scrantontimes.com
• Ed Christine, Sports Editor
Frequency:
7 time(s) per week

TIMES/NORTHWEST INDIANA
1111 GLENDALE BLVD
VALPARAISO, IN 46383
219-462-5151
Fax: 219-465-7298
www.nwitimes.com
• Greg Smith, Sports Editor
• Debbie Anslm, Advertising Director

TIPTON COUNTY TRIBUNE
116 SOUTH MAIN STREET
SUITE A
TIPTON, IN 46072-1832
765-675-2115
Fax: 765-675-4147
tiptontribune@elwoodpublishing.com
http://www.elwoodpublishing.com
• Michael Brown, Director of Marketing
• Michelle Gormon, Sports Editor
(765) 675-2115
tiptonsports@elwoodpublishing.com
Frequency:
6 time(s) per week

TODAY IN PEACHTREE CITY
210 JEFF DAVIS PLACE
FAYETTEVILLE, GA 30214
770-461-6317
Fax: 770-460-8172
http://www.fayettedailynews.com
• Cindy Morley, Sports Reporter
(770) 461-6317
• Joyce Wojcik, Advertising Director
(770) 461-6317
Frequency:
5 time(s) per week

TODAY'S NEWS HERALD
2225 WEST ACOMA BOULEVARD
LAKE HAVASU CITY, AZ 86403-2907
928-453-4237
Fax: 928-855-2637
news@havasunews.com
http://www.havasunews.com
• Steve Stevens, Advertising Manager
• Ric Swats, Sports Editor
(928) 453-4237
sports@havasunews.com
Frequency:
5 time(s) per week

TONAWANDA NEWS
P.O. BOX 668
NORTH TONAWANDA, NY 14120-6809
716-693-1007
Fax: 716-693-8573
http://www.tonawanda-news.com/
• Jack Karlis, Sports Editor
(716) 693-1000
• Tom Meranto, Advertising Manager
(716) 693-1000
• Ernie Green, Sports Editor
(716) 693-1000
Frequency:
7 time(s) per week

TOPEKA CAPITAL-JOURNAL
616 SOUTHEAST JEFFERSON STREET
TOPEKA, KS 66607-1120
785-295-1111
800-777-7171
Fax: 785-295-1230
news@cjonline.com
http://www.cjonline.com
• Leslie Palace, Advertising Sales Manager
• Kurt Caywood, Sports Columnist
(785) 295-1188
kurt.caywood@cjonline.com
• Roger Brokke, Director of Advertising
• Jennifer Burkhart, New Media/Sports Editor

TRAVERSE CITY RECORD-EAGLE
120 WEST FRONT STREET
TRAVERSE CITY, MI 49684-2202

media

231-946-2000
Fax: 231-946-8273
• Denny Chase, Sports Editor
(231) 933-1494
dchase@record-eagle.com
Frequency:
7 time(s) per week

TRENTON TIMES
500 PERRY ST
TRENTON, NJ 08618
609-989-5454
800-753-3088
Fax: 609-394-2819
www.nj.com/times
• Jim Gauger, Sports Editor
• Diane M. Day, Advertising Director

TRENTONIAN
600 PERRY STREET
TRENTON, NJ 08618-3934
609-989-7800
800-825-7653
Fax: 609-393-6072
editor@trentonian.com
http://www.trentonian.com
• Matt Osborne, Sports Editor
• Lorie German, Advertising Manager
(609) 989-7800
• Joe O'Gorman, Sports Writer
jogorman@trentonian.com
Frequency:
7 time(s) per week

TRI-CITY HERALD
107 NORTH CASCADE STREET
KENNEWICK, WA 99336-3851
509-582-1500
800-874-0445
Fax: 509-582-1510
news@tri-cityherald.com
http://www.tri-cityherald.com
• Jeff Morrow, Sports Editor
(509) 582-1507
• Rene Ferran, Sports Writer
(509) 582-1526
Frequency:
7 time(s) per week

TRI-STATE DEFENDER
203 BEALE STREET, SUITE 200
MEMPHIS, TN 38103
901-523-1818
Fax: 901-578-5037
editorial@tri-statedefender.com
http://www.tri-statedefender.com
• William Little, Sports Editor
Frequency:
1 time(s) per week

TRI-VALLEY HERALD
127 SPRING STREET
PLEASANTON, CA 94588
925-734-8600
Fax: 925-416-4850
http://www.insidebayarea.com/trivalleyherald
• Cecil Conley, Sports Reporter
(925) 734-8600
• Steve Herendeen, Sports Reporter
• Dennis Miller, Sports Editor (Local)
• Billy Ortiz, Sports Reporter
(925) 416-4833
Frequency:
7 time(s) per week

TRIBUNE (CA)
3825 SOUTH HIGUERA STREET
SAN LUIS OBISPO, CA 93406
805-781-7800
800-456-8449
Fax: 805-781-7905
newsroom@thetribunenews.com
http://www.thetribunenews.com
• Melissa Geisler, Sports Editor
(805) 781-7991
Frequency:
7 time(s) per week

TRIBUNE (FL)
600 EDWARDS ROAD
FORT PIERCE, FL 34982-6230
772-461-2050
Fax: 772-461-4447
http://www.tcpalm.com
• Mike Graham, Sports Editor
(772) 692-8987
mike.graham@scripps.com
Frequency:
7 time(s) per week

TRIBUNE CHRONICLE
240 FRANKLIN STREET
WARREN, OH 44482-5711
330-841-1738
888-550-8742
Fax: 330-841-1717
http://www.tribune-chronicle.com
• Dave Burcham, Sports Editor
• Mike McClain, Sports Reporter
(330) 841-1738
sports@tribune-chronicle.com
Frequency:
7 time(s) per week

TRIBUNE, SCRANTON TIMES
149 PENN AVE
SCRANTON, PA 18503
570-348-9100
Fax: 570-348-9135
www.nepanews.com
• Ed Christine, Sports Editor
• Steve Sauder, Advertising Manager

TRIBUNE-DEMOCRAT
425 LOCUST STREET
JOHNSTOWN, PA 15907
814-532-5050
800-473-0998
Fax: 814-539-1409
tribdem@tribune-democrat.com
http://www.tribune-democrat.com
• Mike Elswick, Sports Editor
• Hugh Hudnall, Director of
Marketing/Advertising/Marketing
• Eric Kropsnyder, Sports Editor
(814) 532-5085

TRIBUNE-STAR
222 SOUTH 7TH STREET
TERRE HAUTE, IN 47807-3601
812-231-4200
800-783-8742
Fax: 812-231-4234
community@tribstar.com
http://www.tribstar.com
• Andy Amey, Sports Reporter
(812) 231-4277
andy.amey@tribstar.com
• Todd Golden, Sports Editor
(812) 231-4272
todd.golden@tribstar.com

• David Hughes, Sports Reporter
(812) 231-4224
david.hughes@tribstar.com
• Craig Pearson, Sports Reporter
(812) 231-4276
craig.pearson@tribstar.com
• James Willis, Sports Reporter
(812) 231-4357
james.willis@tribstar.com
Frequency:
7 time(s) per week

TROY DAILY NEWS
224 SOUTH MARKET STREET
TROY, OH 45373-3327
937-335-5634
Fax: 937-335-3552
http://www.tdn-net.com
• David Fong, Sports Editor
(937) 440-5251
fong@tdnpublishing.com
• Leann Stewart, Advertising Manager
elfstewart@dailycall.com
Frequency:
7 time(s) per week

TROY TIMES
13650 11 MILE ROAD
WARREN, MI 48089-1422
586-756-8800
Fax: 586-498-9627
http://www.candgnews.com
• Susan Shanley, Sports Editor
(586) 498-8000
sshanley@candgnews.com
Frequency:
1 time(s) per week

TRUTH
421 SOUTH SECOND STREET
ELKHART, IN 46516-3238
574-296-5904
Fax: 574-293-8324
http://www.etruth.com
• Bill Beck, Sports Editor
(574) 294-1661
bbeck@etruth.com
• Anthony Anderson, Assistant Sports Editor
(574) 296-5904
Frequency:
7 time(s) per week

TRYON DAILY BULLETIN
16 NORTH TRADE STREET
TRYON, NC 28782-3012
828-859-9151
Fax: 828-859-5575
news@tryondailybulletin.com
http://www.tryondailybulletin.com
• Mike Edwards, Advertising Manager
(828) 859-9151
• Joey Millwood, Sports Editor
Frequency:
5 time(s) per week

TUCSON CITIZEN
4850 SOUTH PARK AVENUE
TUCSON, AZ 85714-1637
520-573-4561
800-754-9332
Fax: 520-573-4590
http://www.tucsoncitizen.com
• Dan Adams, Advertising Vice President
(520) 573-4415
danadams@tucson.com
• Ken Brazzle, Sports

(520) 573-4561
• Shelly Lewellen, Sports Reporter
• John Moredich, Sports Reporter
(520) 573-4561
• Dave Petruska, Sports Reporter
(520) 573-4635
Frequency:
6 time(s) per week

TULARE ADVANCE-REGISTER
388 EAST CROSS AVENUE
TULARE, CA 93274-2854
559-688-0521
Fax: 559-688-5580
tularenews@gannett.com
http://www.tulareadvanceregister.com
• Kevin McCusker, Sports Editor
(559) 735-3295
kmccuske@visalia.gannett.com
Frequency:
6 time(s) per week

TULSA WORLD
318 SOUTH MAIN
TULSA, OK 74103-3401
918-583-2161
800-999-6397
Fax: 918-581-8353
http://www.tulsaworld.com
• Mike Brown, College Sports Reporter
(918) 581-8390
mike.brown@tulsaworld.com
• Matt Doyle, Sports Writer
(918) 581-8316
matt.doyle@tulsaworld.com
• John Ferguson, Sports Writer
(918) 581-8358
johnd.ferguson@tulsaworld.com
• Mark Foster, Sports Reporter
(918) 581-8355
mark.foster@tulsaworld.com
• Bill Haisten, Sports Reporter
(918) 581-8397
bill.haisten@tulsaworld.com
• Glenn Hibdon, Reporter
(918) 581-8396
glenn.hibdon@tulsaworld.com
• John Hoover, College Sports Writer
(918) 581-8384
john.hoover@tulsaworld.com
• Lynn Jacobsen, Sports Reporter
(918) 581-8461
lynn.jacobsen@tulsaworld.com
• John Klein, Senior Sports Columnist
(918) 581-8368
john.klein@tulsaworld.com
• Barry Lewis, Sports Writer
(918) 581-8355
barry.lewis@tulsaworld.com
• Tom Morris, Advertising Manager
(918) 581-8512
 tom.morris@tulsaworld.com
• Dan O'Kane, Sports Reporter
(918) 581-8391
dan.okane@tulsaworld.com
• Sam Powell, Sports Writer
(918) 581-8357
sam.powell@tulsaworld.com
• Patrick Prince, Sports Assistant Editor
(918) 581-8355
patrick.prince@tulsaworld.com
• Dave Sittler, Sports Writer
(918) 583-2161
• Mike Strain, Sports Editor
(918) 581-8356
• Nate Allen, Sports Reporter
(918) 583-2161
nate.allen@tulsaworld.com

Frequency:
7 time(s) per week

TUSCALOOSA NEWS
315 28TH AVENUE
TUSCALOOSA, AL 35402
205-722-0220
Fax: 205-722-0187
news@tuscaloosanews.com
http://www.tuscaloosanews.com
• Cecil Hurt, Sports Editor
(205) 722-0225
cecil.hurt@tuscaloosanews.com
• Harold Stout, Sports Editor
(205) 722-0228
Frequency:
7 time(s) per week

TYLER MORNING TELEGRAPH
410 WEST ERWIN STREET
TYLER, TX 75702-7133
903-596-6397
Fax: 903-595-0335
news@tylerpaper.com
http://www.tylerpaper.com/
• Phil Hicks, Sports Editor
(903) 596-6275
sports@tylerpaper.com
• Art McClelland, Advertising Director
• Clint Buckley, Sports Reporter
(903) 596-6292
sports@tylerpaper.com
Frequency:
7 time(s) per week

TYRONE DAILY HERALD
1067 PENNSYLVANIA AVENUE
TYRONE, PA 16686-1514
814-684-4000
Fax: 814-684-4238
dherald@verizon.net
• Kylie Hyde, Advertising Manager
• Bob Miller, Sports Editor
dheraldsports@verizon.net
Frequency:
6 time(s) per week

UNION
464 SUTTON WAY
GRASS VALLEY, CA 95945
530-273-9561
Fax: 530-477-4292
http://www.theunion.com
• Craig Dennis, Advertising Director
(530) 477-4265
craigd@theunion.com
• Brian Hamilton, Sports Editor
(530) 477-4240
brianh@theunion.com
• Stacy Hicklin, Sports Reporter
(530) 477-4244
stacyh@theunion.com
Frequency:
6 time(s) per week

UNION CITY DAILY MESSENGER
613 JACKSON STREET
UNION CITY, TN 38261
731-885-0744
Fax: 731-885-0782
ucdm@ucmessenger.com
http://www.ucmessenger.com
• Gloria Chesteen, Advertising Manager
(731) 885-0744
• Mike Hutchens, Sports Editor
mhutch@ucmessenger.com

• Glenda Lingford, Classified Manager
(731) 885-0744
Frequency:
5 time(s) per week

UNION DAILY TIMES
P.O. BOX 749
UNION, SC 29379-7705
864-427-1234
Fax: 864-427-1237
http://www.uniondailytimes.com
• Brian Whitmore, Sports Editor
(864) 427-1234
bwhitmore@uniondailytimes.com
Frequency:
6 time(s) per week

UNION DEMOCRAT
84 SOUTH WASHINGTON STREET
SONORA, CA 95370
209-532-7151
800-786-6466
Fax: 209-532-6451
newsroom@uniondemocrat.com
http://www.uniondemocrat.com
• Kevin Sauls, Sports Editor
Frequency:
5 time(s) per week

UNION LEADER
100 WILLIAM LOEB DRIVE
MANCHESTER, NH 03109-5309
603-668-4321
Fax: 603-668-0382
http://www.theunionleader.com
• John Hussey, Sports Writer
• Kevin Provencher, Sports Writer
• Vin Sylvia, Sports Editor
(603) 668-4321
Frequency:
7 time(s) per week

UNION-NEWS, SUNDAY REPUBLICAN
1860 MAIN ST
SPRINGFIELD, MA 01101
413-788-1210
Fax: 413-788-1259
• Wayne Phaneuf, Executive Editor
• Joseph Deburro, Sports Editor

UNION-RECORDER
165 GARRETT WAY
MILLEDGEVILLE, GA 31061-2318
478-452-0567
Fax: 478-453-1449
http://www.unionrecord.com
• Ross Couch, Sports Editor
(478) 453-1465
newsroom@unionrecorder.com
Frequency:
5 time(s) per week

URBANA DAILY CITIZEN
220 EAST COURT STREET
URBANA, OH 43078-1805
937-652-1331
Fax: 937-652-1336
http://www.urbanacitizen.com
• Steve Stout, Sports Editor
(937) 652-1337
editor@urbanacitizen.com
Frequency:
6 time(s) per week

media

USA TODAY
7950 JONES BRANCH DRIVE
MCLEAN, VA 22108
703-854-3400
800-872-0001
Fax: 703-854-2079
editor@usatoday.com
http://www.usatoday.com
• Kevin Allen, Ice Hockey Columnist
(703) 854-6519
kmallen@usatoday.com
• Mel Antonen, Sports Reporter
(703) 854-3739
mantonen@usatoday.com
• Deborah Barrington, Senior Sports
Assignment Editor
(703) 854-3400
dbarrington@usatoday.com
• Peter Barzilai, Baseball Assignment Editor
(703) 854-5954
pbarzilai@usatoday.com
• Jarrett Bell, Professional Football Reporter
(703) 854-3738
jbell@usatoday.com
• Hal Bodley, Professional Baseball
Columnist
(302) 378-7766
hbodley@usatoday.com
• Greg Boeck, Sports Reporter
(480) 659-6958
gboeck@usatoday.com
• Erik Brady, Sports Features Reporter
(703) 854-3707
ebrady@usatoday.com
• Mike Brehm, Ice Hockey Assignment
Editor
(703) 854-6519
mbrehm@usatoday.com
• Christine Brennan, Sports Columnist
(703) 854-3400
cbrennan@usatoday.com
• Mary Burn, Sports Editor
(703) 854-3731
mburn@usatoday.com
• Jack Carey, Sports Writer
(703) 854-3687
jcarey@usatoday.com
• Reid Cherner, Sports Senior Editor
(703) 854-3694
rcherner@usatoday.com
• Matt Cimento, Sports Assignment Editor
(703) 854-3746
mcimento@usatoday.com
• Oscar Dixon, Sports Editor
(703) 854-3690
• David DuPree, Sports Reporter
(410) 964-3690
ddupree@usatoday.com
• Andy Gardiner, Sports Writer
(215) 854-8013
agardiner@usatoday.com
• Gary Graves, Sports Reporter
(703) 854-3710
ggraves@usatoday.com
• Michael Hiestand, Sports Reporter
(703) 854-5420
mhiestand@usatoday.com
• Bruce Horovitz, Advertising Reporter
(703) 854-3473
bhorovitz@usatoday.com
• Chris Jenkins, Sports Reporter
• Janice Lloyd, Senior Sports Assignment
Editor
(703) 854-6514
jlloyd@usatoday.com
• Mike Lopresti, Sports Columnist
(765) 962-0989
mjl5853@aol.com

• Monte Lorell, Sports Managing Editor
(703) 854-3743
mlorell@usatoday.com
• Vicki Michaelis, (703) 570-8777
Sports Reporter
vmichaelis@usatoday.com
• Malcolm Moran, Sports Reporter (College)
mmoran@usatoday.com
• Tom O'Toole, Sports Editor (Collegiate)
(703) 854-7629
totoole@usatoday.com
• Dick Patrick, College Sports Reporter
(703) 854-6518
dpatrick@usatoday.com
• Tom Pedulla, Sports Reporter
(703) 854-3400
tpedulla@usatoday.com
• Jerry Potter, Sports Reporter
(703) 854-5317
jpotter@usatoday.com
Frequency:
5 time(s) per week

VAIL DAILY
40780 HIGHWAY 6 & 24
AVON, CO 81620
970-949-0555
Fax: 970-949-7094
newsroom@vaildaily.com
http://www.vaildaily.com
• Chris Freud, Sports Editor
(970) 949-0555
sports@vaildaily.com
• Andrea Palm-Porter, Advertising Director
Frequency:
7 time(s) per week

VALLEJO TIMES-HERALD
440 CURTOLA PARKWAY
VALLEJO, CA 94590
707-644-1141
800-600-1141
Fax: 707-643-0128
http://www.timesheraldonline.com
• Ken Hart, Sports Editor
(707) 553-6837
• Heidi Hoffman, Advertising Director
(707) 553-6811
• J.P. Hoonstra, Sports Writer
• Brad Kvederis, Sports Writer
• Timothy Scott, Sports Writer
Frequency:
7 time(s) per week

VALLEY CITY TIMES-RECORD
146 3RD STREET, N.E.
VALLEY CITY, ND 58072
701-845-0463
Fax: 701-845-0175
vctr@daktel.com
http://www.times-online.com
• Tony Lam, Sports Editor
trsports@daktel.com
Frequency:
5 time(s) per week

VALLEY COURIER
401-407 STATE AVENUE
ALAMOSA, CO 81101-2645
719-589-2553
Fax: 719-589-6573
http://www.alamosanews.com
• Lloyd Engen, Sports Editor
Frequency:
5 time(s) per week

VALLEY INDEPENDENT
EASTGATE 19
MONESSEN, PA 15062
724-684-5200
800-564-9000
Fax: 724-684-2603
http://www.valleyindependent.com
• Brian Herman, Sports Editor
(724) 684-2667
bherman@tribweb.com
• Karen Strickland, Advertising Manager
kstrickland@tribweb.com
Frequency:
6 time(s) per week

VALLEY MORNING STAR
P.O. BOX 511
HARLINGEN, TX 78550-7711
956-430-6200
Fax: 956-430-6231
http://www.valleystar.com
• Mary Lou Davis, Classified Manager
(956) 430-6222
• Buddy Green, Sports Editor
(956) 430-6200
• David Favila, Sports Editor
(956) 430-6200
davidf@valleystar.com
Frequency:
7 time(s) per week

VALLEY NEWS
24 INTERCHANGE DRIVE
WEST LEBANON, NH 03784-2002
603-298-8711
800-874-2226
Fax: 603-298-0212
news@vnews.com
http://www.vnews.com
• Dave Corriveau, Sports Reporter
dcorriveau@vnews.com
• Greg Fennell, Sports Reporter
(603) 298-8711
• Bob Hookway, Sports Reporter
(603) 298-8711
• Don Mahler, Sports Editor
(603) 298-8711
imaginedon@aol.com
• Richard Wallace, Advertising Manager
(603) 298-8711
rwallace@vnews.com
• Bruce Wood, Sports Reporter
(603) 298-8711
bruce.b.wood@valley.net
Frequency:
7 time(s) per week

VALLEY NEWS DISPATCH
4TH AVENUE & WOOD STREET
TARENTUM, PA 15084
724-224-4321
800-698-2553
Fax: 724-226-4677
vndnews@tribweb.com
www.valleynewsdispatch.com
• Kevin Smith, Executive Sports Editor
• Melanie Murray, Advertising Manager
(724) 226-7701
mmurray@tribweb.com
Frequency:
7 time(s) per week

VALLEY NEWS TODAY
702 WEST SHERIDAN
SHENANDOAH, IA 51601
712-246-3097
800-369-3097

Fax: 712-246-3099
editorial@valleynewstoday.com
http://www.valleynewstoday.com
• Kevin Slater, Sports Editor
Frequency:
5 time(s) per week

VALLEY TIMES-NEWS
220 NORTH 12TH STREET
LANETT, AL 36863-6422
334-644-1101
Fax: 334-644-5587
news@valleytimes-news.com
http://www.valleytimes-news.com
• Phillip Jones, Advertising Manager
(334) 644-8110
• Scott Sickler, Sports Editor
(334) 644-8106
sports@valleytimes-news.com
Frequency:
5 time(s) per week

VENTURA COUNTY STAR
P.O. BOX 6711
VENTURA, CA 93003
805-650-2900
800-660-6211
Fax: 805-482-6167
http://www.venturacountystar.com
• Larry Ames, Sports Editor
(805) 655-5818
lames@venturacountystar.com
• Mike Blackwell, Sports Ass't Managing
Editor
(805) 655-5821
• Bob Buttitta, Sports Reporter
(805) 655-5860
bbuttitta@venturacountystar.com
• Jim Carlisle, Sports Writer
(805) 655-1740
jcarlisle@venturacountystar.com
• Joe Curley, Sports Writer
(805) 655-5820
jcurley@venturacountystar.com
• Derry Eads, Sports Reporter
• Ben Kwasney, Sports Copy Editor
(805) 655-5820
• David Lassen, Sports Reporter
• Rhiannon Potkey, Sports Writer
(805) 655-5828
rpotkey@VenturaCountyStar.com
• Rich Romine, Sports Writer
(805) 496-8316
• Jonathan Catalini, Sports Copy Editor
(805) 655-5819
Frequency:
7 time(s) per week

VERNON DAILY RECORD
3214 WILBARGER STREET
VERNON, TX 76384
940-552-5454
800-234-9014
Fax: 940-553-4823
http://www.vernonrecord.com/
• Kathy McClellan, Sports Editor
(940) 552-5454
• Jim Surber, Advertising Manager
advertising@vernonrecord.com
Frequency:
6 time(s) per week

VICKSBURG POST
P.O. BOX 821668
VICKSBURG, MS 39180

601-636-4545
Fax: 601-634-0897
http://www.vicksburgpost.com
• David Gillis, Advertising Director
(601) 636-4545
• Sheila Mantz, Advertising Manager
(601) 636-4545
smantz@vicksburgpost.com
• Sean Murphy, Assistant Managing Editor -
Sports
(601) 636-4545
Frequency:
7 time(s) per week

VICTORIA ADVOCATE
311 EAST CONSTITUTION
VICTORIA, TX 77901-8140
361-575-1451
Fax: 361-574-1220
newsroom@vicad.com
http://www.victoriaadvocate.com
• Coy Slavik, Sports Editor
Frequency:
7 time(s) per week

VIDA NEWSPAPER
130 PALM DR
OXNARD, CA 93030
805-483-1008
Fax: 805-483-6233
vidanews@aol.com
• Ramon Arceo, Sports Editor
(805) 483-1008
Frequency:
1 time(s) per week

VILLAGER
1600 LAKEFRONT CIRCLE
THE WOODLANDS, TX 77380-3633
281-367-5309
800-659-6997
Fax: 281-363-3299
villagereditor@hcnonline.com
http://www.hcnonline.com
• Kim Richardson, Sports Editor
• Corey Turner, Sports Editor
(281) 367-5309
cturner@hcnonline.com
Frequency:
1 time(s) per week

VINCENNES SUN-COMMERCIAL
PO BOX 396
VINCENNES, IN 47591-2910
812-886-9955
800-876-9955
Fax: 812-885-2235
vscnews@suncommercial.com
http://www.suncommercial.com/
• Dave Staver, Sports Editor
(812) 886-9955
dstaver@suncommercial.com
• Tom Graham, Sports Reporter
(812) 886-9955
tgraham@suncommercial.com
Frequency:
6 time(s) per week

VINDICATOR
P.O. BOX 780
YOUNGSTOWN, OH 44503-1136
330-747-1471
Fax: 330-747-6712
news@vindy.com
http://www.vindy.com

• Rob Todor, Sports Editor
(330) 747-1471
sports@vindy.com
• John Bassetti, High School ; Prep Sports
Staff Writer
(330) 747-1471
sports@vindy.com
Frequency:
7 time(s) per week

VIRGINIAN REVIEW
128 NORTH MAPLE AVENUE
COVINGTON, VA 24426-1545
540-962-2121
Fax: 540-962-5072
virginianreview@aol.com
http://www.alleghanyhighlands.com/
• Mark Pifer, Sports Editor
(540) 962-2121
• Donna Via, Classified Manager
vrclassifieds@yahoo.com
Frequency:
6 time(s) per week

VIRGINIAN-PILOT
150 WEST BRAMBLETON AVENUE
NORFOLK, VA 23510-2018
757-446-2000
800-446-2004
Fax: 757-446-2531
elizabeth.simpson@pilotonline.com
http://www.pilotonline.com
• Bryan Black, Sports Team Leader
(757) 446-2376
• Vicki Friedman, Sports Writer
(757) 446-2039
• Michael Keech, Sports Assistant Editor
• James Miller, Sports Writer
(757) 446-2372
ed.miller@pilotonline.com
• Bob Molinaro, Sports Columnist
(757) 446-2373
• Patricia Peterson, Sports Assistant Editor
(757) 446-5434
• Charles Riebel, Sports Editor
(757) 446-2369
• Thomas Robinson, Sports Columnist
(757) 446-2518
• Larry Rubama, Sports Writer
(757) 446-2273
larry.rubama@pilotonline.com
• Tom White, Sports Team Leader
(757) 446-2360
tom.white@pilotonline.com
Frequency:
7 time(s) per week

VISALIA TIMES-DELTA
330 STREET, N.W.
VISALIA, CA 93291-6010
559-735-3200
Fax: 559-735-3399
news@visaliatimesdelta.com
http://www.visaliatimesdelta.com
• Mark Daniels, Classified Manager
• Mark Devaughn, Sports Reporter
(559) 735-3289
visalianews@mindinfo.com
• Konan Hauser, Advertising Director
(559) 735-3235
• Kevin Mcusker, Sports Editor
(559) 735-3200
news@visaliatimesdelta.com
• Andrew Bettencourt, Sports Reporter
(559) 688-0521
abettenc@visalia.gannett.com

media

WABASH PLAIN DEALER
123 WEST CANAL STREET
WABASH, IN 46992-3042
260-563-2131
800-659-6321
Fax: 260-563-0816
http://www.wabashplaindealer.com
• Aaron Turner, Sports Editor
Frequency:
6 time(s) per week

WACO TRIBUNE-HERALD
P .O. BOX 2588
WACO, TX 76701-1906
254-757-5701
Fax: 254-757-0302
letters@wacotrib.com
http://www.wacotrib.com/
• Carla D'Andrea, Advertising Director
(254) 757-5788
cdandrea@wacotrib.com
• Kim Gorum, Sports Editor
(254) 757-5713
kgorum@wacotrib.com
• Ann Marie Penrod, Classified Manager
(254) 757-5867
apenrod@wacotrib.com
• Brice Cherry, Sports Columnist
(254) 757-5714
bcherry@wacotrib.com
Frequency:
7 time(s) per week

WAKEFIELD DAILY ITEM
26 ALBION STREET
WAKEFIELD, MA 01880-2803
781-245-0080
Fax: 781-246-0061
http://www.wakefielditem.com
• Jim Southmayd, Sports Editor
(781) 245-0080
wakefielditem@rcn.com
Frequency:
5 time(s) per week

WALL STREET JOURNAL
1211 AVENUE OF THE AMERICAS
NEW YORK, NY 10036
212-416-2000
800-568-7625
Fax: 212-416-2653
nywireroom@dowjones.com
http://www.wsj.com
• Conor Dougherty, Sports Reporter
(212) 416-3917
conor.dougherty@wsj.com
• Erin Friar, Sports News Editor
(212) 416-3999
erin.friar@wsj.com
• Allen John, Sports Columnist
• Brian Steinberg, Advertising Reporter
(212) 416-3155
brian.steinberg@wsj.com
• Russell Adams, Sports Writer
(212) 416-2000
russell.adams@wsj.com
Frequency:
5 time(s) per week

WALLA WALLA UNION-BULLETIN
112 1ST STREET, S.
WALLA WALLA, WA 99362-0306

509-525-3300
Fax: 509-525-1232
http://www.union-bulletin.com
• Jay Brodt, Advertising Director
j.brodt@ubnet.com
• Jim Buchan, Sports Editor
(509) 525-3300
jbuchan@ubnet.com
Frequency:
6 time(s) per week

WARREN WEEKLY
13650 11 MILE ROAD
WARREN, MI 48089
586-756-8800
Fax: 586-498-9627
jhorn@candgnews.com
http://www.candgnews.com
• Susan Shanley, Sports Editor
(586) 498-8000
sshanley@candgnews.com
Frequency:
1 time(s) per week

WASHINGTON DAILY NEWS
217 NORTH MARKET STREET
WASHINGTON, NC 27889-4949
252-946-2144
Fax: 252-946-9797
news@wdnweb.com
http://www.wdnweb.com
• Brenda Foster, Classified Manager
(252) 946-2144
classified@wdnweb.com
• Ray McKerthan, Sports Editor
• Kevin Travis, Sports Editor
(252) 946-2144
Frequency:
7 time(s) per week

WASHINGTON EXAMINER
6408 EDSALL ROAD
ALEXANDRIA, VA 22312-6410
703-846-8324
Fax: 703-846-8366
http://www.dcexaminer.com
• Dan Rubin, Sports Editor
(703) 846-8335

WASHINGTON POST
1150 15TH STREET, N.W.
WASHINGTON, DC 20071
202-334-6000
800-627-1150
Fax: 202-334-5417
national@washpost.com
http://www.washingtonpost.com
• Mark Asher, Sports Staff Writer/College Sports
• Josh Barr, High School Sports Reporter
(202) 334-7350
• Matt Bonesteel, Editorial Assistant/Sports
(202) 334-6000
bonesteelm@washpost.com

WASHINGTON TIMES
3600 NEW YORK AVENUE, N.E.
WASHINGTON, DC 20002-1947
202-636-3000
Fax: 202-636-8906
http://www.washtimes.com
• Bob Cohn, Sports Writer
(202) 636-3260
• Dan Daly, Sports Columnist
• Barker Davis, College Sports Reporter
(202) 636-8892

• Donna De Marco, Advertising Reporter
(202) 636-4884
• David Elfin, Sports Reporter
(202) 636-3269
• David Fay, Sports Reporter (Hockey)
(202) 636-3260
• Jody Foldesy, Sports Reporter
(202) 636-4932
• Mike Harris, Sports Editor
(202) 636-4865
• John Haydon, Sports Reporter
(202) 636-3093
• Dick Heller, Sports Columnist
(202) 636-3260
• Tom Knott, Sports Columnist
(202) 636-3260
• Thom Loverro, Sports Columnist
(202) 636-3260
• John Mitchell, Sports Reporter (Pro Basketball)
(202) 636-3260
• Rick Snider, Sports Reporter (Pro Football)
(202) 636-3260
• Patrick Stevens, Sports Reporter
(202) 636-3000
• Mark Zuckerman, Sports Reporter
(202) 636-3000
Frequency:
7 time(s) per week

WATERBURY REPUBLICAN-AMERICAN
P.O. BOX 2090
WATERBURY, CT 06722
203-574-3636
Fax: 203-596-9277
releases@rep-am.com
http://www.rep-am.com
• Tom Talarico, Sports Editor
(203) 574-3636
ttalrico@rep-am.com
• Lee Lewis, Executive Sports Editor
(203) 574-3636
llewis@rep-am.com
• Roger Cleaveland, Sports Reporter
(203) 574-3636
rcleaveland@rep-am.com

WATERLOO-CEDAR FALLS COURIER
P.O. BOX 540
WATERLOO, IA 50701
319-291-1400
800-798-1702
Fax: 319-291-2069
http://www.wcfcourier.com
• Kelly Beaton, Sports Writer
(319) 291-1456
• Kevin Evans, Sports Editor
(319) 291-1469
• Sean Hylton, Sports Writer
(319) 291-1428
• Jim Nelson, Sports Writer
(319) 291-1521
• Doug Newhoff, Sports Editor
(319) 291-1467
• David Tansey, Advertising Manager
(319) 291-1403
Frequency:
6 time(s) per week

WATERTOWN DAILY TIMES
P.O. BOX 140
WATERTOWN, WI 53094-7623
920-261-4949
Fax: 920-261-5102
news1@wdtimes.com
http://www.wdtimes.com

• Judy Christian, Advertising Manager
judyk@wdtimes.com
• Kevin Wilson, Sports Editor
(920) 261-4949
news@wdtimes.com
• Adam Burdsall, Sports Reporter
(920) 261-5161
Frequency:
6 time(s) per week

WATERTOWN PUBLIC OPINION
P.O. BOX 10
WATERTOWN, SD 57201-2311
605-886-6901
800-658-5401
Fax: 605-886-4280
news@thepublicopinion.com
http://www.thepublicopinion.com/
• Roger Merriam, Sports Editor
(605) 886-6903
rogerm@thepublicopinion.com
Frequency:
6 time(s) per week

WAUSAU DAILY HERALD
800 SCOTT STREET
WAUSAU, WI 54403-4951
715-842-2101
800-477-4838
Fax: 715-848-9360
http://www.wausaudailyherald.com
• Sandy Falk, Advertising Director
(715) 845-0621
sfalk@smgpo.gannett.com
• Mark Multer, Sports Editor
(715) 845-0701
mmulter@wdhprint.com
Frequency:
7 time(s) per week

WAXAHACHIE DAILY LIGHT
200 WEST MARVIN
WAXAHACHIE, TX 75165-3040
972-937-3310
Fax: 972-937-1139
http://www.thedailylight.com
• John Hicks, Sports Editor
(972) 937-3310
• Jenniffer Kestersen, Advertising Manager
Frequency:
6 time(s) per week

WAYCROSS JOURNAL-HERALD
400 ISABELLA STREET
WAYCROSS, GA 31501-3637
912-283-2244
Fax: 912-285-5255
http://www.wjhnews.com
• Larry Purdom, Sports Editor
(912) 283-2244
sports@wjhnews.com
• Gary Keels, Sports Reporter
(912) 283-2244
Frequency:
6 time(s) per week

WEATHERFORD DEMOCRAT
512 PALO PINTO STREET
WEATHERFORD, TX 76086
817-594-7447
Fax: 817-594-9734
http://www.weatherforddemocrat.com
• Tommy Brown, Sports Editor
(817) 594-7447
sports@weatherforddemocrat.com

Frequency:
6 time(s) per week

WEEKEND
3612 NORTH MARTIN LUTHER KING
DRIVE
MILWAUKEE, WI 53212-4134
414-265-5300
Fax: 414-265-1536
editorial@communityjournal.net
http://www.communityjournal.net
• Tom Mitchell, Sports Editor
(414) 265-5300
Frequency:
1 time(s) per week

WELLINGTON DAILY NEWS
113 WEST HARVEY STREET
WELLINGTON, KS 67152-3840
620-326-3326
Fax: 620-326-3290
http://www.wgtndailynews.com
• Rick Horn, Advertising Manager
• Ryan Metzen, Sports Editor
(620) 326-3326
Frequency:
5 time(s) per week

WELLSVILLE DAILY REPORTER
159 NORTH MAIN STREET
WELLSVILLE, NY 14895-1149
585-593-5300
Fax: 585-593-5303
editor@wellsvilledaily.com
http://www.wellsviledaily.com
• Oak Duke, Advertising Manager
oduke51895@aol.com
• Jim Sweet, Sports Writer
(585) 593-5300
• Heather Matta, Sports
(585) 593-5300
Frequency:
6 time(s) per week

WENATCHEE WORLD
14 NORTH MISSION STREET
WENATCHEE, WA 98801-2250
509-663-5161
800-572-4433
Fax: 509-665-1183
http://www.wenworld.com
• Nick Babcock, Sports Editor
(509) 664-7145
Frequency:
6 time(s) per week

WEST BEND DAILY NEWS
100 SOUTH 6TH AVENUE
WEST BEND, WI 53095-3309
262-306-5000
800-924-3142
Fax: 262-338-1984
http://www.dailynewsol.com
• Lois Evans, Advertising Manager
(262) 306-5070
• Keith Schmidt, Sports Editor
(262) 306-5051
Frequency:
6 time(s) per week

WEST CENTRAL TRIBUNE
2208 TROTT AVENUE, SW
WILLMAR, MN 56201
320-235-1150
Fax: 320-235-6769

kboldan@wctrib.com
http://www.wctrib.com
• Jesse Fuchs, Sports Reporter
• Rand Middleton, Sports Reporter
Frequency:
1 time(s) per week

WEST COUNTY TIMES
4301 LAKESIDE DRIVE
RICHMOND, CA 94806
510-758-8400
Fax: 510-262-2776
http://www.contracostatimes.com
• Phil Jensen, Sports Writer
(510) 262-2739
Frequency:
7 time(s) per week

WEST HAWAII TODAY
75-5580 KUAKINI HIGHWAY
KAILUA KONA, HI 96740
808-329-9311
800-355-3911
Fax: 808-329-3659
wht@aloha.net
http://www.westhawaiitoday.com
• Joe Ferraro, Sports Editor
(808) 329-9311
• Gloria Fleming, Advertising Manager
Frequency:
6 time(s) per week

WEST PLAINS DAILY QUILL
P.O. BOX 110
WEST PLAINS, MO 65775-2753
417-256-9191
Fax: 417-256-9196
http://www.westplainsquill.com
• Carla Bean, Advertising Manager
ads@westplainsquill.com
• Dennis Crider, Sports Editor
(417) 256-9191
wpqnews@centurytel.net
Frequency:
5 time(s) per week

WEST VALLEY VIEW
200 WEST WIGWAM BOULEVARD
LITCHFIELD PARK, AZ 85340-4636
623-535-8439
Fax: 623-935-2103
news1@westvalleyview.com
http://www.westvalleyview.com
• Mike Russo, Sports Editor
(623) 535-8439
• Justin Doom, Sports Writer
(623) 535-8439
Frequency:
1 time(s) per week

WHEELING NEWS-REGISTER
1500 MAIN STREET
WHEELING, WV 26003-2826
304-233-0100
Fax: 304-232-1399
mccabe@theintelligencer.net
http://www.news-register.net
• Nick Bedway, Sports Editor
Frequency:
6 time(s) per week

WICHITA EAGLE
825 EAST DOUGLAS AVENUE
WICHITA, KS 67202-3512
316-268-6000
800-825-6397

media

Fax: 316-268-6627
wenews@wichitaeagle.com
http://www.kansas.com
• Joanna Chadwick, Sports Reporter
(316) 268-6270
• Duane Frazier, Sports Reporter
(316) 268-6296
• Adam Knapp, Sports Reporter
(316) 268-6284
• Dan Loving, Sports Assistant Editor
(316) 269-6706
• Bob Lutz, Sports Columnist
(316) 268-6597
blutz@wichitaeagle.com
• Jeff Parson, Sports Reporter
(316) 268-6398
• Scott Paske, Sports Reporter
(316) 268-6513
• Rick Plumlee, Sports Reporter
(785) 842-4479
• Kirk Seminoff, Sports Editor
(316) 268-6278
kseminoff@wichitaeagle.com
Frequency:
7 time(s) per week

WICHITA FALLS TIMES RECORD NEWS
1301 LAMAR ST
WICHITA FALLS, TX 76307
940-767-8341
800-627-1646
Fax: 940-767-1741
• Nick Gholson, Sports Editor
• Monica Bartling, Advertising Director

WILLIAMSON DAILY NEWS
100 EAST 3RD AVENUE
WILLIAMSON, WV 25661-3620
304-235-4242
Fax: 304-235-0730
editor@williamsondailynews.com
http://www.williamsondailynews.com
• Joshua Ball, Sports Editor
(304) 235-4242
jball@williamsondailynews.com
Frequency:
7 time(s) per week

WILLIAMSPORT SUN-GAZETTE
P.O. BOX 728
WILLIAMSPORT, PA 17701-6102
570-326-1551
Fax: 570-326-0314
news@sungazette.com
http://www.sungazette.com
• Ben Brigandi, Sports Editor
(570) 326-1551
bbrigandi@sungazette.com
Frequency:
7 time(s) per week

WILMINGTON NEWS JOURNAL
47 S. SOUTH STREET
WILMINGTON, OH 45177-2231
937-382-2574
Fax: 937-382-4392
info@wnewsj.com
http://www.wnewsj.com
• Sarah Clark, Sports Editor
(937) 382-2574
sclark@wnewsj.com
Frequency:
6 time(s) per week

WILMINGTON STAR NEWS
1003 SOUTH 17TH STREET
WILMINGTON, NC 28401
910-343-2000
800-222-2385
Fax: 910-343-2227
http://www.starnewsonline.com
• Dan Spears, Sports Editor
dan.spears@starnewsonline.com
Frequency:
7 time(s) per week

WILSON DAILY TIMES
P.O. BOX 2447
WILSON, NC 27893-4611
252-243-5151
Fax: 252-243-7501
editor@wilsondaily.com
http://www.wilsondaily.com
• Tom Ham, Sports Editor
(252) 265-7809
hammer@wilsondaily.com
• Wayne Johnson, Advertising Manager
(252) 265-7858
wjohnson@wilsondaily.com
• Paul Durham, Assistant Sports Editor
(252) 265-7808
paul@wilsondaily.com
Frequency:
6 time(s) per week

WINCHESTER STAR
2 NORTH KENT STREET
WINCHESTER, VA 22601
540-667-3200
800-296-8639
Fax: 540-667-1649
news@winchesterstar.com
http://www.winchesterstar.com
• Ben Brooks, Sports Editor
(540) 667-3200
• John Parkinson, Advertising Manager
(540) 665-4950
Frequency:
6 time(s) per week

WINCHESTER SUN
P.O. BOX 4300
WINCHESTER, KY 40391-1900
859-744-3123
Fax: 859-745-0638
http://www.winchestersun.com
• Kim Hays, Advertising Director
(859) 744-3123
advertising@winchestersun.com
• Keith Taylor, Sports Editor
(859) 744-3123
Frequency:
6 time(s) per week

WINFIELD DAILY COURIER
201 EAST 9TH STREET
WINFIELD, KS 67156-2817
620-221-1050
Fax: 620-221-1101
http://www.winfieldcourier.com
• Tracy McCue, Sports Editor
sports@winfieldcourier.com
• Marsha Wesseler, Advertising Manager
advertising@winfieldcourier.com
Frequency:
6 time(s) per week

WINONA DAILY NEWS
PO BOX 5147
WINONA, MN 55987

507-453-3500
800-328-2182
Fax: 507-453-3517
news@winonadailynews.com
http://www.winonadailynews.com
• Jeff Bersch, Sports Editor
(507) 453-3528
jeff.bersch@lee.net
• Tom Kelly, Advertising Director
Frequency:
7 time(s) per week

WINSTON-SALEM JOURNAL
P.O. BOX 3159
WINSTON-SALEM, NC 27101-2805
336-727-7308
800-642-0925
Fax: 336-727-7315
http://www.journalnow.com
• Tommy Bowman, Sports Reporter
(336) 727-7320
jbowman@wsjournal.com
• Bill Cole, College Sports Reporter
(336) 727-7310
bcole@wsjournal.com
• Dan Collins, Sports Reporter
(336) 727-7323
dcollins@wsjournal.com
• John Dell, Sports Writer
(336) 727-4081
jdell@wsjournal.com
• John Delong, Sports Reporter
(336) 727-7324
jdelong@wsjournal.com
• Phil Hrichak, Sports Editor
(336) 727-4080
phrichak@wsjournal.com
• Dan Kibler, Outdoors Writer
(336) 727-7383
wkibler@wsjournal.com
• Mason Linker, Sports Columnist
(336) 727-7326
mlinker@wsjournal.com
• Terry Oberle, Sports Editor
(336) 727-7321
toberle@wsjournal.com
Frequency:
7 time(s) per week

WISCONSIN STATE JOURNAL
P.O. BOX 8056
MADISON, WI 53713-1248
608-252-6100
800-362-8333
Fax: 608-252-6119
http://www.madison.com/wsj/
• Eric Anderson, Assistant Sports Editor
(608) 252-6177
• Andy Baggot, College Sports Reporter
(608) 252-6175
• Vic Feuerherd, Sports Reporter
(608) 252-6175
• Perry Hibner, Sports Assistant Editor
(608) 252-6190
• Tom Mulhern, Sports Reporter
(608) 252-6169
• John Nolan, Sports Copy Editor
(608) 252-6168
jnolan@madison.com
• Jesse Osborne, Sports Reporter
(608) 252-6176
• Greg Sprout, Sports Senior Editor
(608) 252-6171
gsprout@madison.com
• Jason Wilde, Sports Reporter
(680) 252-6176
• Nick Zizzo, Sports Reporter

(680) 252-6167
nzizzo@madison.com
Frequency:
7 time(s) per week

WOODWARD NEWS
904 OKLAHOMA AVENUE
WOODWARD, OK 73801-4660
580-256-2200
Fax: 580-254-2159
www.woodwardnews.net
• Johnny McMahan, Sports Editor
Frequency:
6 time(s) per week

WORLD
350 COMMERCIAL STREET
COOS BAY, OR 97420
541-269-1222
800-437-6397
Fax: 541-267-0294
theworldnews@theworldlink.com
http://www.theworldlink.com
• John Gunther, Sports Editor
(541) 269-1222
jgunther@theworldlink.com
• Bob Reitz, Advertising Manager
(541) 269-1222
Frequency:
6 time(s) per week

WYOMING TRIBUNE-EAGLE
702 WEST LINCOLN WAY
CHEYENNE, WY 82001-4359
307-634-3361
Fax: 307-633-3189
http://www.wyomingnews.com
• Scott Nulph, Sports Editor
(307) 634-3361
snulph@wyosports.net
Frequency:
7 time(s) per week

XENIA DAILY GAZETTE
30 SOUTH DETROIT STREET
XENIA, OH 45385-0400
937-372-4444
Fax: 937-372-1951
wbaker@xeniagazette.com
http://www.xeniagazette.com
• Josh Brown, Sports Editor
pgirton@xeniagazette.com
• Barbara Vandeventer, Advertising
Manager
bvandeventer@xeniagazette.com
Frequency:
6 time(s) per week

YAKIMA HERALD-REPUBLIC
114 N. FOURTH ST
YANKIMA, WA 98901
509-248-1251
Fax: 509-577-7767
www.yakima-herald.com
• Jamie Stickel, Advertising Director
• Mike Anderson, Sports Editor

YANKTON DAILY PRESS & DAKOTAN
319 WALNUT STREET
YANKTON, SD 57078
605-665-7811
800-743-2968
Fax: 605-665-1721
sports@yankton.net
www.yankton.net

• James Cimburek, Sports Editor
(605) 665-7811
james.cimburek@yankton.net
• Cathy Sudbeck, Advertising Sales
• Jeremy Hoack, Assistant Sports Editor
(605) 665-7811
Frequency:
6 time(s) per week
Teams:
University of South Dakota-NCAA Division I
, and Mount Marty College - NAIA

YORK DAILY RECORD/YORK SUNDAY NEWS
1891 LOUCKS ROAD
YORK, PA 17408-9708
717-771-2000
800-788-9675
Fax: 717-771-2009
news@ydr.com
www.ydr.com
• Chris Otto, Sports Editor
(717) 771-2000
• Frank Bodani, Sports Reporter
(717) 771-2104
fbodani@ydr.com
• Bryan Kelley, Advertising Director
Frequency:
6 time(s) per week

YORK DISPATCH
205 NORTH GEORGE STREET
YORK, PA 17401-1107
717-854-1575
Fax: 717-843-2958
http://www.yorkdispatch.com
• Steve Heiser, Sports Editor
(717) 854-1575
sheiser@yorkdispatch.com
Frequency:
6 time(s) per week

YORK NEWS-TIMES
327 PLATTE AVENUE
YORK, NE 68467
402-362-4478
800-334-4530
Fax: 402-362-6748
news@yorknewstimes.com
http://www.yorknewstimes.com/
• Ken Kush, Sports Editor/Writer
• SJ Munoz, Sports Editor/Writer
• Steve Moseley, Sports Editor/Writer
Frequency:
6 time(s) per week

YUMA DAILY SUN
2055 ARIZONA AVE
PO BOX 271
YUMA, AZ 85364
928-539-6880
Fax: 928-782-7369
www.yumasun.com
• Ross Priest, Sports Editor
• Lisa Miller, Advertising Director

Magazines

3-D TIMES ARCHERY MAGAZINE
5158 MAIN STREET
LUCEDALE, MS 39452
800-891-5558
Fax: 601-766-9626
http://www.3-dtimes.com

• Royce Armstrong, Editor
royce@3-dtimes.com
Frequency:
8 time(s) per year
Description:
Publication is a source for archery news,
competitions, short schedules, interviews,
and profiles of top shoots and tournament
results.

48 DEGREES NORTH
6327 SEAVIEW AVENUE, N.W.
SEATTLE, WA 98107
206-789-7350
Fax: 206-789-6392
http://www.48north.com
• Rich Hazelton, Editor
• Karen Higginson, Associate Editor
karen@48north.com
• Chuck Streatch, Publisher
Frequency:
1 time(s) per month
Description:
Publication includes information for boating
enthusiasts in Washington, Oregon, Idaho,
Alaska, and British Columbia.

ACADEMIC-ATHLETIC JOURNAL/N4A NATIONAL OFFICE
1630 LYNDON FARM COURT
LOUISVILLE, KY 40233
502-992-8000
Fax: 502-992-8001
www.nfoura.org
• Kathi Ley, N4A National Office Director
Description:
Provides professional research and position
papers to the NAAAA (National Association
of Academic Advisors) for Athletics
membership regarding professional
academic-athletic advising.
Circulation:
300
Sports:
General
Primary Audience:
Association membership
Frequency:
Semiannual
Publishing Company:
NAAAA/Athletic Guidance Center.

ACTION PURSUIT GAMES
4201 VANOWEN PLACE
BURBANK, CA 91505
818-845-2656
800-332-3330
Fax: 818-845-7761
http://www.cfwgroup.com
• Dan Reeves, Editor
(573) 674-4040
• Gabe Frimmel, Advertising Director
(818) 845-2656
gabefrimmel@cfwenterprises.com
• Curtis F. Wong, Publisher
(818) 845-2656
Frequency:
1 time(s) per month
Description:
Publication covers the sport of paintball for
players of all levels; contains articles on
technology, safety issues, play techniques,
tournaments, and news.

ADIRONDACK SPORTS & FITNESS
15 COVENTRY DRIVE
CLIFTON PARK, NY 12065-1747

518-877-8788
Fax: 518-877-0619
info@adksports.com
www.AdKSports.com
• Mona Caron, Editor
mona@adksportsfitness.com
• Darryl Caron, Publisher
(518) 877-8788
darryl@adksportsfitness.com
Frequency:
1 time(s) per month
Description:
Regional monthly active lifestyle magazine and producer of summer/winter sports expos in upstate New York.

ADVENTURE CYCLIST
150 EAST PINE
MISSOULA, MT 59802-4515
406-721-1776
800-755-2453
Fax: 406-721-8754
info@adventurecycling.org
http://www.adventurecycling.org
• Mike Deme, Editor
(406) 721-1776
mdeme@adventurecycling.org
Frequency:
9 time(s) per year
Description:
Publication is a bicycle travel magazine with emphasis on destinations.

ADVENTURE SPORTS OUTDOORS
201 GLORIA PARKWAY
WASHIONTON, IL 61571
309-437-2247
877-778-4868
Fax: 309-925-4868
www.asomagazine.com
• Cathy Canterbury, Publisher
(309) 925-7313
• Andy Bugos, Publisher
(309) 437-2247
asoandyb@gmail.com
Frequency:
1 time(s) per month
Description:
Print and online publication geared toward outdoor sporting.
Year Founded:
1996.

AIKIDO TODAY MAGAZINE
1420 NORTH CLAREMONT BOULEVARD
CLAREMONT, CA 91711-3528
909-624-7770
Fax: 909-398-1840
http://www.aiki.com
• Susan Perry, Editor-in-Chief
(909) 624-7770
Frequency:
6 time(s) per year
Description:
Publication is a martial arts magazine.

ALASKA HORSE JOURNAL
4311 EAST CRANE ROAD
WASILLA, AK 99654
907-376-4470
Fax: 907-376-4470
http://www.alaskahorsejournal.printroom.com
• Sandy Shacklett, Editor
• Sandy Shacklett, Advertising Manager
• Sandy Shacklett, Publisher

Frequency:
1 time(s) per month
Description:
Publication provides horse enthusiasts with information on all breeds of horses and all disciplines.

AMERICAN BOWLER
5301 SOUTH 76TH STREET
GREENDALE, WI 53129
414-421-6401
Fax: 414-321-8356
americanbowler@bowl.com
http://www.bowl.com
• Rory Gillespie, Editor
(414) 321-8310
rorygillespie@sleepingdogscommunications.com
Frequency:
4 time(s) per year

AMERICAN CHEERLEADER
110 WILLLIAM STREET
NEW YORK, NY 10038
212-265-8890
Fax: 212-265-8908
editors@americancheerleader.com
http://www.americancheerleader.com
• Marisa Walker, Managing Editor
(212) 265-8890
• Joanna Harp, Publisher
(646) 459-4806
• Sheila Noone, Editorial Director
(212) 265-8890
snoon@lifestyleventures.com
• Jennifer Smith, Senior Editor
(646) 459-4832
• Brittany Geragotelis, Associate Editor
(212) 265-8890
Frequency:
6 time(s) per year
Description:
Publication is written for cheerleaders; features articles on competitions, fitness and exercise, fashion, and footwear.

AMERICAN FARRIERS JOURNAL
16655 W. WISCONSIN AVE
BROOKFIELD, WI 53005
262-782-4480
800-645-8455
Fax: 262-782-1252
info@lessitermedia.com
www.lessitermedia.com
• Jeremy McGovern, Executive Editor/Publisher
• Patrick Sharpe, VP, Audience Development
(262) 777-2406
psharpe@lessitermedia.com
• Mike Lessiter, President
(262) 777-2403
mlessiter@lessitermedia.com
• Frank Lessiter, Editor
Frequency:
8 time(s) per year
Description:
Publication is a hands-on magazine for professional farriers.

AMERICAN FOOTBALL MONTHLY
840 US HIGHWAY 1
NORTH PALM BEACH, FL 33408
561-627-3393
800-537-4271
Fax: 561-627-5275
http://www.americanfootballmonthly.com

• Rex Lardner, Managing Editor
(561) 627-3393
• Travis Davis, Advertising Manager
(561) 627-3393
• Travis Davis, Publisher
(561) 627-3393
• Jeff Case, Associate Editor
(561) 627-3393
Frequency:
1 time(s) per month
Description:
Publication targets football coaches at all levels.

AMERICAN QUARTER HORSE RACING JOURNAL
1600 QUARTER HORSE DRIVE
AMARILLO, TX 79104
806-376-4888
Fax: 806-349-6400
aqhajrnl@aqha.org
http://www.aqharacing.com
• Jennifer Hancock, Editor
(806) 376-4888
• Richard Chamberlain, Senior Staff Writer
(806) 376-4888
richc@aqha.org
• Jim Jennings, Publication Executive Director
• Jim Persinger, Advertising Manager
(806) 378-4386
Frequency:
1 time(s) per month
Description:
Publication focuses on Amercian Quarter Horse racing.

AMERICAN SAILOR
5 DOCK SQUARE
KENNEBUNKPORT, ME 04046
207-967-0866
800-877-2451
Fax: 401-683-0840
http://www.olyc.com/ussailing
Frequency:
10 time(s) per year
Description:
Magazine is the official publication of the U.S. Sailing Association.

AMERICAN SNOWMOBILER
21027 CROSSROADS CIRCLE
WAUKESHA, WI 53187-1612
262-796-8776
Fax: 262-798-6468
http://www.amsnow.com
• Mark Savage, Editor
(262) 796-8776
msavage@kalmbach.com
• Mark Savage, Executive Editor
(262) 796-8776
msavage@kalmbach.com
• Mark Boncher, Associate Editor
(262) 798-6453
mboncher@amsnow.com
Frequency:
6 time(s) per year
Description:
Publication provides complete news updates about snowmobiling, and other articles relevant to the sport.

AMERICAN SPORTS
PO BOX 6100
ROSEMEAD, CA 91770

626-292-2222
Fax: 626-292-2221
am@asntv.com
• Steve Roquet, Editor
Publishing Company:
American Sports Network, Inc.
Frequency:
Monthly
Primary Audience:
Consumer
Sports:
Prep, collegiate, professional
Circulation:
5% non-paid subscr contr, 95% paid subscr.
Description:
General sports, recreational sports magazine.

AMERICAN TURF MONTHLY
299 EASTSHORE ROAD SUITE 204
GREAT NECK, NY 11023
516-773-4075
800-645-2240
Fax: 516-773-2944
editor@americanturf.com
http://www.americanturf.com
• Howard Rowe, Senior Editor
• James Corbett, Editor-in-Chief
• Allen Hakim, Publisher
publisher@americanturf.com
Frequency:
1 time(s) per month

AMERICAN WINDSURFER
10 BAYVIEW BUSINESS PARK
GILFORD, NH 03247
603-293-2727
Fax: 603-293-2723
editor@americanwindsurfer.com
http://www.americanwindsurfer.com
• John Chao, Editor
(603) 293-2721
Frequency:
6 time(s) per year
Description:
Publication is geared toward windsurfers of all degrees of skill.

ANVIL'S RING
6690 WENTWORTH SPRINGS ROAD
GEORGETOWN, CA 95634
530-333-2687
Fax: 530-333-2689
http://www.sebastianpublishing.com
• Rob Edwards, Editor
• Rob Edwards, Publisher
Frequency:
4 time(s) per year
Description:
Publication is directed at professional and hobby blacksmiths in the United States and abroad.

APPALOOSA JOURNAL
2720 WEST PULLMAN ROAD
MOSCOW, ID 83843-4000
208-882-5578
Fax: 208-882-8150
journal@appaloosa.com
http://www.appaloosa.com
• Diane Rice, Editor
(208) 882-5578
drice@appoloosa.com
• Katie Elliott, Advertising Director
(208) 882-5578
advertising@appaloosa.com

• Diane Rice, Associate Editor
(208) 882-5578
drice@appaloosa.com
Frequency:
1 time(s) per month

ARABIAN HORSE WORLD
1316 TAMSON DRIVE SUITE 101
CAMBRIA, CA 93428-3328
805-771-2300
Fax: 805-927-6522
http://www.ahwmagazine.com
• Denise Hearst, Publisher
(805) 771-2302
• Lynn Anderson, Advertising Manager
Frequency:
1 time(s) per month
Description:
Publication focuses on the positive rewards of worldwide involvement with the Arabian bred horse.

AREA AUTO RACING NEWS
PO BOX 8547
TRENTON, NJ 08610-3603
609-888-3618
Fax: 609-888-2538
news@aarn.com
www.aarn.com
• Lenny H. Sammons, Publisher
lhs@aarn.com
• Tim Hogue, Advertising Director
• Earl Krause, Asst Editor
earl@aarn.com
Frequency:
1 time(s) per week
Description:
Publication covers both local and national automobile racing events.

ARIZONA, THE STATE OF GOLF
7226 NORTH 16TH STREET SUITE 200
PHOENIX, AZ 85020-5255
602-944-3035
Fax: 602-944-3228
http://www.azgolf.org
• Peter Wofford, Editor
(843) 856-3290
peterwofford@comcast.net
Frequency:
6 time(s) per year
Description:
Publication deals with regional golf amateurs in the state of Arizona and features stories and profiles of the players.

ATHLETIC BUSINESS
4130 LIEN ROAD
MADISON, WI 53704
608-249-0186
800-722-8764
Fax: 608-249-1153
editors@athleticbusiness.com
http://www.athleticbusiness.com
• Sue Searls, Publisher
(608) 249-0186
• Brad Zaugg, Publisher
(608) 249-0186
editors@athleticbusiness.com
• Marvin Bynum, Assistant Editor
(608) 249-0186
editors@athleticbusiness.com
Frequency:
1 time(s) per month
Description:
Publication is geared toward operators of athletic and fitness programs and facilities.

ATHLETIC MANAGEMENT
31 DUTCH MILL ROAD
ITHACA, NY 14850
607-257-6970
Fax: 607-257-7328
info@momentummedia.com
www.momentummedia.com
• Mark Goldberg, Publisher
(607) 257-6970
mg@momentummedia.com
• Eleanor Frankel, Editor-in-Chief
(607) 257-6970
• Dave Dubin, Circulation Director
(607) 257-6970
• Don Anderson, Production Manager
(607) 257-6970
Publishing Company:
Momentum Media.
Frequency:
6 time(s) a year
Circulation:
30,037.
Nature of Service:
Articles discuss topics in the field including working with coaches, marketing and fundraising strategies, Title IX and other legal issues, starting new sports, understanding today's student-athletes, and much more.
Primary Audience:
Athletic administrations at high school and college levels.
Sports:
Most.

ATHLETICS ADMINISTRATION
24651 DETROIT ROAD
WESTLAKE, OH 44145
440-892-4000
Fax: 440-892-4007
jwork@nacda.com
http://www.nacda.com
• Julie Work, Editor
jwork@nacda.com
• Craig Baroncelli, Publisher
(859) 226-4678
craig.baroncelli@hostcommunications.com
• Michael Cleary, Executive Editor
(440) 892-4000
Frequency:
8 time(s) per year
Description:
Publication features articles on the administration of collegiate athletics.

ATHLON SPORTS COMMUNICATIONS
2451 ATRMWY BUILDING 2
SUITE 320
NASHVILLE, TN 37203
615-327-0747
800-ATHLON-8
Fax: 615-327-1149
www.athlonsports.com
• Charlie Miller, Managing Editor
• Robert T. Doster, III, Senior Editor
• Mitch Light, Editor
• Scott Garrettt, President, Advertising Sales
• Roger Di Silvestro, Chairman/Chief Executive Officer
• Scott Garrett, Advertising Sales Director
• Troy Childers, Director Circulation
Publishes:
Eastern Football, Southeastern Football, The Really Big 12, Southwest Football, Big 12 Football, PAC-10 Football, Western Football, Atlantic Coast Football, Athlon's Pro Football, Athlon's Inside Saturday,

Athlon's Pro Baseball, Athlon's College, Pro Basketball, Golf.

ATLANTA SPORTS AND FITNESS MAGAZINE
3535 PIEDMONT ROAD
ATLANTA, GA 30305
404-843-2257
Fax: 404-843-1339
http://www.atlantasportsmag.com
• Beth Weithzman, Editor
(404) 870-0123
• Scott Thompson, Director
(404) 843-2257
• JoAnn Carroll, Art/Production Manager
(404) 843-2257
Frequency:
1 time(s) per month
Description:
Articles related to amateur sports and health and fitness topics.

ATLANTIC RACQUET PRESS
11 BUXTON
EAST WINDSOR, NJ 08520
609-371-3737
Fax: 609-448-6642
http://www.atlanticracquetpress.com
• Judith F. Arnold, Editor
Frequency:
4 time(s) per year
Description:
Publication contains articles on tennis in the Mid-Atlantic states.

AVID GOLFER MAGAZINE
7200 SOUTH ALTON WAY
SUITE B-180
CENTENNIAL, CO 80112
720-493-1729
Fax: 720-482-0784
info@coloradoavidgolfer.com
http://www.coloradoavidgolfer.com
• Jon Rizzi, Editor
(720) 493-1729
jon@coloradoavidgolfer.com
• Allen J. Walters, Publisher
(720) 493-1729
allen@coloradoavidgolfer.com
Frequency:
2 time(s) per month
Description:
Publication provides information of interest to professional and amateur golfers.

BACK COUNTRY MAGAZINE
P.O. BOX 190
JEFFERSONVILLE, VT 05464
802-644-6606
Fax: 802-644-6328
http://www.backcountrymagazine.com
• Adam Howard, Editor
howie@backcountrymagazine.com
Frequency:
4 time(s) per year

BACKPACKER MAGAZINE
33 E. MINOR ST
RODALE PRESS, PA 18098
610-967-8296
Fax: 610-967-8181
www.backpacker.com or
www.bpbasecamp.com
• Jonathan Dorn, Executive Editor
• Eric Zinczenko, Publisher

Publishing Company:
Rodale Press
Frequency:
Nine times annually
Primary Audience:
Consumer
Sports:
Backpacking, hiking, paddle sports, cross country skiing.
Circulation:
NA.
Description:
Devoted to information and features relating to self-propelled wilderness travel.

BALLOON LIFE
P.O. BOX 7
LITCHFIELD, CT 06759
860-567-2061
Fax: 206-935-3326
blarney007@aol.com
http://www.balloonlife.com
• Michael P Murphy, Editor
• William G Armstrong, Publisher
(203) 629-1241
Frequency:
1 time(s) per month
Description:
Publication covers issues of interest to hot air ballooning enthusiasts.

BALLS AND STRIKES SOFTBALL MAGAZINE
2801 NORTHEAST 50TH STREET
OKLAHOMA CITY, OK 73111-7203
405-424-5266
Fax: 405-424-4734
info@softball.org
http://www.softball.org
• Brian McCall, Editor
(405) 425-3463
bmccall@softball.org
• Julie Eversgerd, Associate Editor
(405) 425-3431
• Brian McCall, Editor-in-Chief
(405) 425-3463
bmccall@softball.org
• Brian McCall, Publisher
(405) 425-3463
Frequency:
2 time(s) per year
Description:
Publication is geared toward amateur softball enthusiasts.

BARREL HORSE NEWS
2112 MONTGOMERY STREET
FORT WORTH, TX 76107
817-731-7867
Fax: 817-737-9266
http://www.barrelhorsenews.com
• Teri Lee, Managing Editor
• Trisha Johnson, Editorial Coordinator
(817) 737-6397
• Glory Ann Kurtz, Executive Editor
(817) 731-7867
gloryann.kurtz@cowboypublishing.com
• Carl Mullins, Publisher
(817) 731-7867
carl.mullins@cowboypublishing.com
• Patty Tiberg, General Manager
(817) 731-7867
patty.tiberg@cowboypublishing.com
Frequency:
1 time(s) per month
Description:
Publication focuses on barrel racing.

BASEBALL AMERICA
4319 SOUTH ALSTON AVENUE
SUITE 103
DURHAM, NC 27713
919-682-9635
800-845-2726
Fax: 919-682-2880
letters@baseballamerica.com
www.baseballamerica.com
• Will Lingo, Co-Editor in Chief
(919) 682-9635
willlingo@baseballamerica.com
• Lee Folger, President
(919) 682-9635
leefolger@baseballamerica.com
• John Manuel, Co-Editor in Chief
(919) 682-9635
johnmanuel@baseballamerica.com
Frequency:
26 times yearly.
Description:
A full-service media division of Source InterLink and Grind Media with in-depth coverage of every level of baseball, including; high school, college, the minor leagues and major league baseball.

BASEBALL DIGEST
990 GROVE STREET
EVANSTON, IL 60201-4370
847-491-6440
Fax: 847-491-0459
http://www.centurysports.net
• Bob Kuenster, Editor
bkuenster@centurysports.net
• Norman Jacobs, Publisher
Frequency:
1 time(s) per month
Description:
Publication focuses on baseball players, managers, rosters, statistics, trades, player profiles, and schedules.

BASKETBALL TIMES
P.O. BOX 1269
PINEHURST, NC 28370
910-295-5559
Fax: 910-295-6566
http://www.basketballtimes.com
• John Akers, Editor
• Nanci Donald, Publisher
Frequency:
1 time(s) per month
Description:
Publication contains information about college, junior college, women's coverage and high school basketball, as well as recruiting and the NBA.

BAY & DELTA YACHTSMAN
4090 SOUTH MCCARRAN BOULEVARD
UNIT-E
RENO, NV 89502
775-353-5100
800-878-7886
Fax: 775-353-5111
http://www.yachtsforsale.com
• Don Abbott, Co-Publisher & Editor
(775) 353-5100
don.abbott@yachtsmanmagazine.com
Frequency:
1 time(s) per month
Description:
Publication contains articles on power and sail boats.

BEDTIME STORIES FOR YOUNG ATHLETES
1060 MAIN STREET
SUITE 307
RIVER EDGE, NJ 07661
201-342-3663
800-580-9663
Fax: 201-342-2258
info@stayinthezone.com
www.stayinthezone.com

BEHIND THE WHEEL
30301 BRIGHT AVENUE
FAYETTEVILLE, TN 37334-1013
931-438-5765
Fax: 931-433-8480
http://www.btwonline.net
• Sam Holbrooks, Publisher & Editor
(931) 438-5765
btwlma@vallnet.com
• Sam Holbrooks, Publisher
Frequency:
34 time(s) per year
Description:
Publication is geared toward racing professionals and enthusiasts.

BETWEEN THE TOUCHLINES
13540 LAKE CITY WAY N.E. SUITE 3
SEATTLE, WA 98125
206-367-2420
Fax: 206-367-2636
http://www.varsitycommunications.com
• Luciano Pastor, Editor
(423) 559-1150
• Luciano Pastor, Publisher
(423) 559-1150
Frequency:
3 time(s) per year

BICYCLE RETAILER AND INDUSTRY NEWS
25431 CABOT ROAD SUITE 204
LAGUNA HILLS, CA 92653
949-206-1677
Fax: 949-206-1675
http://www.bicycleretailer.com
• Megan Tomkins, Editor-in-Chief
• Marc Sani, Publisher
msani@bicycleretailer.com
• Lynette Carpiet, Managing Editor
(949) 206-1677
lcarpiet@bicycleretailer.com
Frequency:
18 time(s) per year
Description:
Publication is a news magazine for the bicycle industry; focuses on trends, finance, management, and new products.

BICYCLING
33 EAST MINOR STREET
EMMAUS, PA 18098-0099
610-967-8722
Fax: 610-967-8960
bicycling@rodale.com
http://www.bicycling.com
• Christine Bucher, Senior Editor
(610) 967-8273
christine.bucher@rodale.com
• Michael Frank, Deputy Editor
michael.frank@rodale.com
• Steve Madden, Editor-in-Chief
(212) 573-0229
steve.madden@rodale.com
• Susan G. Snyder, Advertising Business Manager

(610) 259-4082
susan.snyder@det.amedd.army.mil
• William Strickland, Executive Editor
bill.strickland@rodale.com
Frequency:
11 time(s) per year
Description:
Publication features information of interest to cycling enthusiasts.

BIKE
33046 CALLE AVIADOR
SAN JUAN CAPISTRANO, CA 92675-4704
949-496-5922
Fax: 949-496-7849
http://www.bikemag.com
• Mike Ferrentino, Editor
(949) 661-5158
• Derek DeJonge, Publisher
(949) 661-5153
• Ron Ige, Editor
• Lou Mazzante, Managing Editor
(949) 661-5191
Frequency:
6 time(s) per year
Description:
Publication is geared toward the mountain biking enthusiast.

BILLIARDS DIGEST
122 SOUTH MICHIGAN AVENUE SUITE 1506
CHICAGO, IL 60603
312-341-1110
Fax: 312-341-1469
http://www.billiardsdigest.com
• Mason King, Editor
(312) 341-1110
masonk@billiardsdigest.com
• Mike Panozzo, Publisher
mikep@billiardsdigest.com
• Mike Shamos, Contributing Editor
• Ruth Welte, Assistant Editor
(312) 341-1110
ruthwelte@billardsdigest.com
Frequency:
1 time(s) per month
Description:
Publication contains information on billiards.

BLACK ATHLETE SPORTS NETWORK
421 W. 144TH ST
NEW YORK, NY 10031
212-926-0402
ceo@blackathlete.net
www.blackathlete.net
• Roland Rogers, Chief Executive Officer
Sports Service Founded:
1999
Nature of Sports Service:
E-Zine - Source for information and breaking news stories about Black athletes at all levels from around the globe. Black writers, from across the country, provide sports coverage about the Black athlete, past, present, and future. Site features include daily updates, weekly columns, audio broadcasts, free email, and chat.

BLACK BELT
300 NORTH CONTINENTAL BOULEVARD
SUITE 65
EL SEGUNDO, CA 90245
310-356-4100
800-423-2874
Fax: 661-257-3028
http://www.aimmedia.com

• Robert Young, Executive Editor
(661) 257-4066
• Robert Young, Sports Executive Editor
(661) 257-4066
Frequency:
1 time(s) per month
Description:
Publication focuses on martial arts.

BLACK TENNIS MAGAZINE
PO BOX 210767
DALLAS, TX 75211
214-339-7370
Fax: 214-339-7370
marcus.freeman.tennis@airmail.net
http://www.btmag.com
• Olando Temple, Editor-in-Chief
Frequency:
4 time(s) per year
Description:
A quarterly sports magazine centered around tennis and related activities with subscribers located in major cities of the USA, Europe, Africa, Australia and South America.

BLADES ON ICE
7040 NORTH MONA LISA ROAD
TUCSON, AZ 85741-2633
520-575-1747
888-525-8605
Fax: 520-575-1484
azpublish@aol.com
• Gerri Walbert, Executive Editor
boimag1@aol.com
Frequency:
6 time(s) per year
Description:
National and international figure skating information; events, interviews, photos.
Circulation:
10,000 - 20,000

BLOOD-HORSE
3101 BEAMOUNT CENTER CIRCLE
LEXINGTON, KY 40513
859-278-2361
800-866-2361
Fax: 859-276-6743
admin@bloodhorse.com
http://www.bloodhorse.com
• Dan Liebman, Managing Editor
• Stacy V. Bearse, Publisher
sbearse@bloodhorse.com
• Jim Cox, Advertising Director
(859) 276-6792
jcox@bloodhorse.com
• Ray Paulick, Editor-in-Chief
Frequency:
1 time(s) per week
Description:
Publication offers information on legal, economic, and operational aspects of the Thoroughbred horse industry.

BLUE WATER SAILING
747 AQUIDNECK AVENUE SUITE 201
MIDDLETOWN, RI 02842
401-847-7612
888-800-7245
Fax: 401-845-8580
george@bwsailing.com
http://www.bwsailing.com
• George Day, Editor
• George Day, Publisher
• Greg Jones, Senior Editor
greg@bwsailing.com

• Alice Noble, Managing Editor
alice@bwsailing.com
• Sandy Parks, Advertising Manager
sandy@bwsailing.com
• Jen Brett, Managing Editor
(401) 847-7612
jen@bwsailing.com
Frequency:
10 time(s) per year
Description:
Publication focuses on gear and
seamanship for off-shore sailors.

BMX PLUS
25233 ANZA DRIVE
VALENCIA, CA 91355
661-295-1910
Fax: 661-295-1278
http://www.bmxplusmag.com
• Adam Booth, Editor
• Roland Hinz, Publisher
Frequency:
1 time(s) per month
Description:
Publication features information on bicycling
for a teenage audience.

BOAT & MOTOR DEALER
6600 WEST TOUHY AVENUE
NILES, IL 60714
847-647-2900
Fax: 847-647-1155
webmaster@prestonpub.com
http://www.boatmotordealer.com
• Jerry Koncel, Editor
(847) 647-2900
jkoncel@prestonpub.com
• Janice S. Gordon, Publisher
(847) 647-2900
jgordon@prestonpub.com
• Jerry Koncel, Managing Editor
jkoncel@prestonpub.com
• Adolfo Mendez, Managing Editor
(847) 647-2900
amendez@boatmotordealer.com
Frequency:
11 time(s) per year
Description:
Publication covers information of interest to
boat and motor dealership owners and
marine suppliers; includes coverage of retail
operations.

BOAT BROKER OUTDOOR
1910 ALEX HOLDEN WAY
JUNEAU, AK 99801-9384
907-789-4144
Fax: 907-789-0987
http://www.outdoorsak.com
• Amanda Gragert, Editor
(907) 789-4144
editor@capweek.com
Frequency:
1 time(s) per month
Description:
Publication contains information of interest
to commercial, sport, and recreational
boaters in Alaska, including equipment and
services.

BOAT U.S. MAGAZINE
880 SOUTH PICKETT STREET
ALEXANDRIA, VA 22304-4606
703-461-2864
Fax: 703-461-2845
magazine@boatus.com
http://www.boatus.com

• Bernadette Bernon, Consulting Editor
bbernon@boatus.com
• Elaine Dickinson, Managing Editor
• Michael Vatalaro, Executive Editor
mvatalaro@boatus.com
Frequency:
6 time(s) per year
Description:
Advocate for recretaional boats providing
over half million members with government
representation, programs and money-saving
services.
Circulation:
over 500,000

BOATING
460 NORTH ORLAND AVENUE
WINTER PARK, FL 32789
407-628-4802
Fax: 407-628-7061
http://www.boatingmag.com
• Randy Steele, Editor
• Daniel Long, Technical Editor
(212) 767-4820
• Wade Luce, Publisher
(323) 954-4853
• Nancy Nisselbaum, Executive Editor
(212) 767-4813
• David Seidman, Executive Features Editor
(212) 767-6030
Frequency:
1 time(s) per month
Description:
Publication is geared toward powerboat
enthusiasts.

BOATING INDUSTRY
6420 SYCAMORE LANE SUITE 100
MAPLE GROVE, MN 55369
763-383-4448
Fax: 763-383-4499
http://www.boating-industry.com
• Matt Gruhn, Editor
(763) 383-4402
• Matt Gruhn, Publisher
• Matt Gruhn, Sports Editor
• Liz Walz, Executive Editor
Frequency:
6 time(s) per year
Description:
Publication is geared toward the
international boating industry; contains trend
analysis about manufacturers, sales
merchandising, international legislation.

BOATING LIFE
460 NORTH ORLANDO AVENUE SUITE
200
WINTER PARK, FL 32789
407-628-4802
Fax: 407-628-7061
http://www.boatinglifemag.com
• Randy Vance, Editor
randy.vance@worldpub.net
• John McEver, Jr., Publisher
(407) 571-4682
john.mcever@worldpub.net
• Robert Stephens, Executive Editor
(407) 571-1131
• Chris Tauber, Senior Writer
(407) 571-1164
• Sue Whitney, Managing Editor
(407) 571-1146
Frequency:
7 time(s) per year

BOATING WORLD
11782 COWAN
SUITE A
IRVINE, CA 92614-6045
949-660-6150
Fax: 949-660-6172
www.boatingworld.com
• Kristina Ackermann, Managing Editor
(949) 660-6150
• Alan Jones, Executive Editor
• Jeffrey Fleming, Associate Publisher
(949) 660-6150
• Duncan McIntosh, Publisher
Frequency:
8 time(s) per year
Description:
Publication is written for active families that
own trailerable power boats up to 36 feet in
length; contains articles on new boats and
marine products, safety, navigation, and
maintenance

BONNEVILLE RACING NEWS
6489 WEST STETSON AVENUE
HEMET, CA 92545-9711
951-926-2277
Fax: 951-926-4619
• Wendy Jeffries, Editor
(951) 926-2277
• Wendy Jeffries, Advertising Manager
salt@ivic.net
Frequency:
10 time(s) per year
Description:
Publication is aimed at automobile hot
rodders and land speed racers.

BOSTON HANNAH INTERNATIONAL
274 MADISON AVE
9TH FLOOR
NEW YORK, NY 10016
212-889-8191
Fax: 312-284-5864
www.bostonhannah.com
• Kevin Harrington, Chief Executive
• Charles Ford, Managing Editor
• Phillip Lau, Art Director
Frequency:
Annual

BOWLERS JOURNAL INTERNATIONAL
122 SOUTH MICHIGAN AVENUE SUITE
1506
CHICAGO, IL 60603
312-341-1110
Fax: 312-341-1469
http://www.bowlersjournal.com
• Jim Dressel, Editor
(312) 341-1110
jimd@bowlersjournal.com
• Mike Panozzo, Publisher
mikep@billiardsdigest.com
Frequency:
1 time(s) per month
Description:
Publication covers the bowling industry.

BOWLING CENTER MANAGEMENT
122 SOUTH MICHIGAN AVENUE SUITE
1506
CHICAGO, IL 60603
312-341-1110
Fax: 312-341-1469
http://www.bcmmag.com
• Mike Mazek, Editor
mikem@lubypublishing.com

• Barbara Peltz, Advertising Manager
(312) 341-1110
barbp@lubypublishing.com
• Michael Mazek, Editor
(312) 341-1110
mikem@lubypublishing.com
Frequency:
11 time(s) per year
Description:
Publication contains instructional and
interpretive articles on bowling equipment,
maintenance, management, promotions,
and products.

BOWLING WORLD
900 SOUTH WINCESTER BOULEVARD
SUITE 11
SAN JOSE, CA 95128-2932
925-215-2242
Fax: 408-366-0847
readit@bowlingworld.com
http://www.bowlingworld.com
• Donna Hazel, Managing Editor
• Nicole Martindill, Assistant Editor
Frequency:
1 time(s) per month

BOXING USA
1 OLYMPIC PLAZA
COLORADO SPRINGS, CO 80909-5746
719-866-4506
Fax: 719-635-3246
http://www.usaboxing.org
• Julie Goldsticker, Editor
(719) 866-2304
Frequency:
4 time(s) per year
Description:
Publication focuses on Olympic style boxing
in the United States.

BULLPEN
1770 BRUNSWICK PIKE
TRENTON, NJ 08638
609-695-1434
Fax: 609-695-2505
http://www.baberuthleague.org
• Colleen Higgins, Editor
colleen@baberuthleague.org
• Rosemary Schoellkopf, Editor
(609) 695-1434
rosemary@baberuthleague.org
Frequency:
4 time(s) per year
Description:
Publication focuses on baseball and softball;
contains information on programs, clinic
notes, promotions, and membership.

BUSCH NORTH SCENE
542 PLEASANT POND ROAD
TURNER, ME 04282
207-224-2060
Fax: 207-224-2060
soup@neracing.com
http://www.neracing.com
• George Campbell, Editor
scene@neracing.com
Frequency:
2 time(s) per month
Description:
Publication focus intended for auto racing
enthusiasts in the Northeast area.

CAL-HI SPORTS
2780 SKYPARK DRIVE SUITE 475
TORRANCE, CA 90505
310-791-1142
800-660-1334
Fax: 310-257-4444
http://www.studentsports.com
• Mark Tennis, Editor
(209) 463-9050
mark@studentsupports.com
• Andy Bark, Publisher
andy@studentsupports.com
Frequency:
1 time(s) per week
Description:
Publication covers high school sports.

CALIFORNIA BOWLING NEWS
2606 WEST BURBANK BOULEVARD
BURBANK, CA 91505-2303
562-807-3600
Fax: 818-845-6321
news@californiabowlingnews.com
http://www.californiabowlingnews.com
• Carol Mancini, Publisher
news@californiabowlingnews.net
• Lillian Oak, Advertising Manager
Frequency:
1 time(s) per week
Description:
Publication covers bowling news.

CALIFORNIA DIVING NEWS
P.O. BOX 11231
TORRANCE, CA 90510-1231
310-792-2333
Fax: 310-792-2336
mail@saintbrendan.com
http://www.saintbrendan.com
• Dale Sheckler, Editor
dale@saintbrendan.com
• Mary L. Reed, Associate Editor
• Dale Sheckler, Advertising Sales
dale@saintbrendan.com
• Kim Sheckler, Executive Editor
kim@saintbrendan.com
• Dale Sheckler, Publisher
dale@saintbrendan.com
Frequency:
1 time(s) per month
Description:
Publication is dedicated to California diving;
covers dive sites, diving gear, underwater
photography, and special events.

CALIFORNIA HOCKEY & SKATING
701 DE LONG AVENUE SUITE I
NOVATO, CA 94945-3224
415-898-5414
Fax: 415-892-6484
hockeyskate@aol.com
• Reggie Winner, Editor
hockyskate@aol.com
• Bill Schoen, Publisher
bill@winecountryguide.com
• Reggie Winner, Managing Editor

CALIFORNIA THOROUGHBRED
201 COLORADO PLACE
ARCADIA, CA 91007-2604
626-445-7800
Fax: 626-574-0852
www.ctba.com
• Rudi Groothedde, Managing Editor
(626) 445-7800
Frequency:
1 time(s) per month

Description:
Publication contains information of interest
to Thoroughbred horse breeders, trainers,
and racing in the state of California.

CALIFORNIA TRACK AND RUNNING NEWS
583 D'ONOFRIO DRIVE SUITE 203
MADISON, WI 53719
608-827-0806
Fax: 608-827-0811
ssmedit@aol.com
http://www.caltrack.com
• Christine Jhonson, Editor
• Larry Eder, Group Publisher
(920) 560-8112
stanederjr@aol.com
• Larry Eder, Publisher
(920) 560-8112
Frequency:
1 time(s) per month
Description:
Publication is a complete guide to running
and racing; includes feature articles and
race results.

CANOE & KAYAK MAGAZINE
10526 NORTHEAST 68TH STREET
SUITE 3
KIRKLAND, WA 98033-7004
425-827-6363
800-692-2663
Fax: 425-827-1893
http://www.canoekayak.com
• Jim Marsh, Advertising Manager
(425) 827-6363
• Scott Waidelich, Advertising Operations
(425) 827-6363
Frequency:
6 time(s) per year
Description:
Publication is North America's resource for
canoeing and kayaking.

CASCADE HORSEMAN
1301 ESPLANADE AVENUE
KLAMATH FALLS, OR 97601-5902
541-885-4460
Fax: 530-842-6787
cascade.magazines@heraldandnews.com
http://www.cascadehorseman.com
• Rod Dowse, Editor
• Rod Dowse, General Manager
Frequency:
1 time(s) per month

CHESAPEAKE BAY MAGAZINE
1819 BAY RIDGE AVENUE SUITE 180
ANNAPOLIS, MD 21403-2896
410-974-8870
Fax: 410-267-6924
editor@cbmmag.net
http://www.boatingonline.net
• Tim Sayles, Editor
(410) 974-8870
• Jane Meneely, Managing Editor
(410) 263-2662
• Richard J. Royer, Publisher
(410) 263-2662
Frequency:
1 time(s) per month
Description:
Publication focuses on boating in the
Chesapeake Bay region.

media

CHICAGO DISTRICT GOLFER
11855 ARCHER AVENUE
LEMONT, IL 60439
630-257-2005
Fax: 630-257-2088
info@cdga.org
http://www.cdga.org
• Cathy Miles-Ralston, Editor
cralston@cdga.org
• Robert Markionni, Executive Director
(630) 685-2303
rmarkionni@cdga.org
• Mia Brown, Editor
(630) 685-2324
mbrown@cdga.org
Frequency:
6 time(s) per year

CHICAGO SPORTS PROFILE
4711 GOLF ROAD SUITE 900
SKOKIE, IL 60076-1234
847-673-0592
Fax: 847-673-0633
http://www.sportsprofilesplus.com
• Paula Blaine, Editor
paula@sportsprofilesplus.com
• Paula Blaine, Publisher
• Lisa A. Levine, President
(847) 673-0592
Frequency:
4 time(s) per year
Description:
Publication is written for the general sports fan; includes information about coverage and movie releases.

CHICAGO'S AMATEUR ATHLETE
7840 NORTH LINCOLN AVENUE SUITE 204
SKOKIE, IL 60077
847-675-0200
Fax: 847-675-2903
chicagorun@aol.com
http://www.chicagoaa.com
• Brenda Barrera, Editor
• Eliot Wineberg, Publisher
Frequency:
10 time(s) per year
Description:
Publication contains information on running, cycling, and various other sports.

CHICAGOLAND GOLF
6825 HOBSON VALLEY DRIVE SUITE 204
WOODRIDGE, IL 60517
630-719-1000
Fax: 630-719-1030
chicagolandgolf@aol.com
• Phil Kosin, Editor-in-Chief
• Phil Kosin, Publisher
• Joanne Miller, Assistant Editor
(630) 719-1000
chicagolandgolf2@aol.com
Frequency:
15 time(s) per year
Description:
Publication covers the national and regional golfing scene; includes information on tours, events, vacation spots, health, and golfers.

CHRISTIAN MOTORSPORTS ILLUSTRATED
RR 3, BOX 120A
COLUMBIA CROSS ROADS, PA 16914
570-549-2282
888-548-2282
Fax: 570-549-3366
cpo7@loving-hearts.org
http://www.christianmotorsports.com
• Roland Osborne, Publisher
Frequency:
4 time(s) per year
Description:
Publication focuses on motorsports venues.

CHRONICLE OF THE HORSE
108 THE PLAINS ROAD
MIDDLEBURG, VA 20117
540-687-6341
Fax: 540-687-3937
staff@chronofhorse.com
http://www.chronofhorse.com
• John Strassburger, Editor
(540) 687-6341
• Robert L. Banner, Jr., Publisher
(540) 687-6341
rbanner@chronofhorse.com
• Trisha Booker, Managing Editor
(540) 687-6341
tbooker@chronofhorse.com
• Beth Rasin, Assistant Editor
(540) 687-6341
bethr@chronofhorse.com
Frequency:
1 time(s) per week
Description:
Publication is geared toward the horse lover; covers horse shows, combined training events, steeplechase racing, dressage, fox hunting, and endurance riding.

CIRCLE TRACK & RACING TECHNOLOGY MAGAZINE
9036 BRITTNAY WAY
TAMPA, FL 33619
863-644-0449
Fax: 813-675-3559
http://www.circletrack.com
• Larry Jewett, Editor
(813) 675-3525
• Raquel Jerkins, Managing Editor
(813) 675-3536
Frequency:
1 time(s) per month
Description:
Publication covers circle track auto racing and events, technical articles, personalities, and includes information and entertainment columns.

CITY SPORTS MAGAZINE
444 S. CEDROS AVE, #185
SOLANA BEACH, CA 92075
858-793-2711
Fax: 858-793-2710
bfit@competitor.com
www.citysportsmag.com
• Lois Schwartz, Publisher/Photo Ed/Event Sales
• Bob Babbitt, Publisher
• John Smith, Publisher/Advertising Director
• Diana Babb, Senior Editor
Publishing Company:
National Sports Network
Description:
Provides guides, destination articles and trend pieces with a
Frequency:
11 times annual
Primary Audience:
Consumer
Sports:
Active lifestyle sports such as bicycling, running, skiing, hiking; travel; family activities
Circulation:
75,000 in Northern California. Contr non-paid.

CITYSPORTS MAGAZINE
2220 FILLMORE STREET
SAN FRANCISCO, CA 94115
858-793-2711
Fax: 858-793-2710
http://www.citysportsmag.com
• Diana Babb, Senior Editor
diana@competitor.com
• Diana Babb, Sports Senior Editor
diana@competitor.com
• Bob Babbitt, Publisher
bob@competitor.com
• John Smith, Advertising Director
(858) 793-2711
john@competitor.com
• John Smith, Publisher
(858) 793-2711
john@competitor.com
Frequency:
11 time(s) per year

CLIMBING
0326 HIGHWAY 133 SUITE 190
CARBONDALE, CO 81623-1571
970-963-9449
Fax: 970-963-9442
http://www.climbing.com
• Jeff Achey, Managing Editor
(970) 704-2602
jeff@climbing.com
• Al Crolius, Publisher
(949) 661-5107
al.crolius@primemedia.com
• John Dicuollo, Advertising Director
jld@climbing.com
Frequency:
8 time(s) per year
Description:
Publication is geared toward rock climbers, ice climbers, and mountaineers.

COACHES REPORT
141 LAURIER AVE W.
STE 300
OTTAWA, ON, CANADA K1P 5J3
613-235-5000
Fax: 613-235-9500
www.coach.ca
• Sheila Robertson, Editor
Description:
The official publication of the Canadian Professional Coaches Association. In-depth articles on various injuries, nutrition, strategy, psychology, special topics, physical training (ex. physiology, biomechanics, strength), testing (physical, psychological), and administration. The magazine examines current issues, profiles top Canadian coaches, and provides a unique perspective on the changing world of sport.
Circulation:
3,000
Sports:
General
Primary Audience:
Top level coaches
Frequency:
Four times annually
Publishing Company:
Coaching Association of Canada

COACHING MANAGEMENT
31 DUTCH MILL ROAD
ITHACA, NY 14850
607-257-6970
Fax: 607-257-7328
info@momentummedia.com
http://www.athleticsearch.com
• Eleanor Frankel, Editor-in-Chief
(607) 257-6970
info@momentummedia.com
• Mark Goldberg, Publisher
(607) 257-6970
info@momentummedia.com
• Mark Goldberg, Publisher
(607) 257-6970
mg@momentummedia.com
• Jim Catalano, New Products Editor
(607) 257-6970
info@momentummedia.com
Frequency:
6 time(s) per year
Description:
Publication focuses on maintaining and managing athletic departments and coaching staffs at high schools and colleges.

COLLEGE & PRO FOOTBALL NEWSWEEKLY
150 MAIN STREET SUITE 11
PORT WASHINGTON, NY 11050
516-883-4550
800-368-7907
Fax: 516-484-6104
bobbabowski@aol.com
http://www.cpsn.com
• Vic DeNicola, Editor-in-Chief
• Jack Cohen, Publisher
• Tina Vitello, Advertising Manager
Frequency:
1 time(s) per week
Description:
Publication covers college and professional football.

COLLEGIATE BASEBALL
2515 NORTH STONE AVENUE
TUCSON, AZ 85705-4530
520-623-4530
Fax: 520-624-5501
editor@baseballnews.com
http://www.baseballnews.com
• Lou Pavlovich, Jr., Editor
lou@baseballnews.com
• Diane Pavlovich, Advertising Director
diane@baseballnews.com
Frequency:
14 time(s) per year
Description:
This tabloid-sized newspaper covers college and high school baseball across the nation. Includes National polls, All-Americans, features and news stories on players and coaches and instructional baseball articles. The paper was started in 1958 as a result of an idea by a group of college baseball coaches.

COLORADO GOLF MAGAZINE
559 2ND AVENUE
CASTLE ROCK, CO 80108-9214
303-688-5853
pade@coloradogolf.com
http://www.coloradogolf.com
• Timothy Pade, Publisher & Editor
(303) 688-5853

pade@coloradogolf.com
• Timothy Pade, Publisher
Frequency:
4 time(s) per year
Description:
Publication is written for golfers; contains information on travel, instruction, and tournaments.

COMPETITOR
444 SOUTH CEDROS AVENUE SUITE 185
SOLANA BEACH, CA 92075-1917
858-793-2711
Fax: 858-793-2710
http://www.competitor.com
• Bob Babbitt, Editor
(858) 793-2711
bob@competitor.com
• Diana Babb, Senior Editor
diana@competitor.com
• Bob Babbitt, Publisher
bob@competitor.com
• John Smith, Advertising Manager
(858) 793-2711
john@competitor.com
Frequency:
11 time(s) per year

COMPETITOR MAGAZINE
605 BELVEDERE ROAD SUITE 9
WEST PALM BEACH, FL 33405
561-838-9060
Fax: 561-838-9037
www.competitor.com
• Rebecca Heaton, Editor
rheaton@competitorgroup.com
Frequency:
11 times per year
Description:
Active Sports Magazine for runners, cyclists, swimmer, mountain bikers and active people.
Circulation:
50,000

CONQUISTADOR
PO BOX 1922
SANTA YNEX, CA 93460
805-688-8318
888-882-6446
Fax: 267-821-1043
http://www.conquistador.com
• Charlotte Dickey, Editor
(805) 350-1232
charlotte@conquistador.com
Frequency:
6 time(s) per year
Description:
Publication features information on horse breeding, history, riding, and training.

COULOIR
P.O. BOX 2349
TRUCKEE, CA 96160
530-582-1884
Fax: 530-582-1887
http://www.couloirmag.com
• Craig Dostie, Editor
publisher@coloir.com
Frequency:
3 time(s) per year
Description:
Publication for skiers and snowboarders; includes coverage of backcountry riding.

CRITTENDEN GOLF
3990 OLD TOWN AVENUE
SUITE C-205
SAN DIEGO, CA 92110
800-211-1697
Fax: 619-374-1979
http://www.crittendengolf.com
• Jim Dunlap, Editor-in-Chief
(858) 503-7568
• Jack Crittenden, Publisher
(858) 503-7786
Frequency:
1 time(s) per month
Description:
Publication contains news for owners, developers, and managers of golf courses.

CROSS COUNTRY SKIER
17280 PIONEER ROAD
CABLE, WI 54821-4743
715-798-5500
800-827-0607
Fax: 715-798-3599
info@crosscountryskier.com
http://www.crosscountryskier.com
• Ron Bergin, Publisher & Editor
(715) 798-3599
ron@crosscountryskier.com
• Lou Dzierzak, Executive Editor
Frequency:
4 times per year
Description:
Publication is geared toward the cross-country skiing enthusiast; focuses on touring, travel, technique, lifestyle, and fitness.
Primary Audience:
Nordic ski/lifetyle enthusiast
Circulation:
30,000
Publications:
Nordic Skiing

CRUISING WORLD
55 HAMMARLUND WAY
MIDDLETOWN, RI 02842
401-845-5100
Fax: 401-845-5180
editorial@sailingworld.com
http://www.cruisingworld.com
• John Burnham, Editor
(401) 845-5106
• Sally Helme, Publisher
(401) 845-5105
sally.helme@worldpub.net
• Gary Jobson, Editor-at-Large
(410) 263-4630
jobsonsailing@compuserve.com
• Elaine Lembo, Managing Editor
• Tim Murphy, Executive Editor
• Jason White, Associate Publisher
(401) 845-5155
jason.white@worldpub.net
Frequency:
1 time(s) per month
Description:
Publication focuses on sailing and seamanship.

CUTTING HORSE CHATTER
260 BAILEY AVENUE
FORT WORTH, TX 76107
817-244-6188
Fax: 817-244-2015
http://www.nchacutting.com
• Alan Gold, Editor
(817) 244-6188

• Shawn McCoy, Advertising Manager
(817) 244-6188
Frequency:
1 time(s) per month
Description:
Publication contains articles on horse care, veterinary advice, riding tips, and NCHA event Courage.

DESERT BOWLER
8925 NORTH 43RD AVENUE SUITE 2
PHOENIX, AZ 85051-3642
623-435-0867
800-347-1229
Fax: 623-937-9377
desertbowler@senecapublishing.com
• Herb Grassl, Editor
herb@senecapublishing.com
• Herb Grassl, Advertising Manager
herb@senecapublishing.com
• Herb Grassl, Publisher
herb@senecapublishing.com
Frequency:
1 time(s) per month
Description:
Publication contains bowling industry news.

DIRT RAG
3483 SAXONBURG BOULEVARD
PITTSBURGH, PA 15238-1100
412-767-9910
800-762-7617
Fax: 412-767-9920
dirtrag@dirtragmag.com
http://www.dirtragmag.com
• Michael Browne, Editor
press@dirtragmag.com
• Chris Cosby, Advertising Coordinator
• Chris Cosby, Advertising Manager
• Maurice Tierney, Publisher
publisher@dirtragmag.com
• Karen Brooks, Editor
(412) 767-9910
operations@dirtragmag.com
Frequency:
7 time(s) per year
Description:
Publication targets mountain bike enthusiasts.
Primary Audience:
Cyclists

DOLPHIN DIGEST
8033 NORTHWEST 36TH STREET
MIAMI, FL 33166-6644
305-594-0508
800-334-4005
Fax: 305-594-0518
digest@curtispub.net
http://www.dolphindigest.net
• Andrew Cohen, Editor
acohen@curtispub.net
• Thomas Curtis, Publisher
newtcurtis@curtispub.net
• Alain Poupart, Associate Editor
(305) 594-0508
Frequency:
26 time(s) per year
Description:
Publication features the Miami Dolphins football team and the National Football League.

DRAG RACER MAGAZINE
265 SOUTH ANITA DRIVE SUITE 120
ORANGE, CA 92868-3310

714-939-9991
Fax: 714-939-9909
http://www.dragracermag.com
• Randy Fish, Editor
(714) 939-9991
randy.fish@apg-media.com
Frequency:
6 time(s) per year

DRAG REVIEW
9 1/2 EAST MAIN STREET
NORWALK, OH 44857
419-663-6666
Fax: 419-663-4472
comments@ihra.com
http://www.ihra.com
• Pam Marchyshyn, Managing Editor
(419) 660-4214
• Kimberly Parsons, Production Designer
(419) 660-4215
kparsons@ihra.com
• Tom Roman, Advertising Manager
(860) 489-7516
thomasroman@aol.com
Frequency:
2 time(s) per month
Description:
Publication is the membership magazine of the International Hot Rod Association; covers IHRA national and regional drag races, as well as races run by or on IHRA sanctioned strips.

DRESSAGE TODAY
656 QUINCE ORCHARD ROAD
SUITE 600
GAITHERSBURG, MD 20878-1409
301-977-3900
Fax: 301-990-9015
dtletters@aol.com
http://www.equisearch.com
• Patricia Lasko, Editor
(301) 977-3900
• Susan M Harding, Publisher
(301) 977-3900
Frequency:
1 time(s) per month
Description:
Publication focuses on dressage.

DUSTY TIMES
20761 PLUMER STREET
CHATSWORTH, CA 91311-4408
818-882-0004
Fax: 818-882-0090
http://www.dustytimes.com
• John Calvin, Editor/Publisher
(818) 882-0004
Frequency:
1 time(s) per month
Description:
Publication covers off-road racing and rallying around the world.

EAGLES DIGEST
8033 NORTHWEST 36TH STREET
MIAMI, FL 33166-6644
305-594-0508
800-334-4005
Fax: 305-594-0518
http://www.eagles.com
• Dave Spadaro, Editor
(215) 463-2500
• Thomas Curtis, Publisher
(305) 594-0508
newtcurtis@curtispub.net

• Kenneth Keidel, Advertising Manager
(305) 594-0508
Frequency:
2 time(s) per month
Description:
Publication focuses on the Philadelphia Eagles football team.

EASTERN BASKETBALL
P.O. BOX 1269
PINEHURST, NC 28370
910-295-5559
Fax: 910-295-6566
http://www.basketballtimes.com
• Nanci Donald, Publisher
Frequency:
11 time(s) per year
Description:
Publication contains information of interest to fans of high school and college basketball on the East Coast, including commentary and profiles.

EMPLOYEE SERVICES MANAGEMENT
2211 YORK RD, STE 207
OAK BROOK, IL 60523-2371
630-368-1280
Fax: 630-368-1286
• Patrick B. Stinson, Publisher
• Rene Mulay, Editor
• Alison Bashian, Marketing Manager
Description:
Provides information, trends to persons responsible for administration of employee services and recreation programs - wellness programs, discount programs, pre-retirement planning, fitness facilities, hobby clubs, community service projects, child/elder care, and employee stores.
Circulation:
5,000. 65% association membership, 15% paid subscr, 10% contr non-paid.
Sports:
General
Primary Audience:
Association membership
Frequency:
10 times annually
Publishing Company:
Employee Services Management

ENSIGN
1504 BLUE RIDGE ROAD
RALEIGH, NC 27607-3906
919-821-0892
888-367-8777
Fax: 888-304-0813
ensign@hq.usps.org
http://www.theensign.org
• Yvonne Hill, Editor
(919) 821-0892
ensign@hq.usps.org
• Kelly Anderson, Associate Editor
andersonk@hq.usps.org
Publications:
The Ensign (quarterly print publication); USPS Compass (monthly e-mail newsletter)
Description:
The Ensign is a nonprofit boating safety and education organization. Our members are sailors, powerboaters and paddleboaters. We publishes articles of general interest to recreational boaters, including maintenance articles, product reviews, and safe-boating information.
Primary Audience:
Members of U.S. Power Squadrons

Circulation:
40,000
Sports:
Sailing, Power Boating, Paddle Sports

ENTERTAINMENT LAW REPORTER
2118 WILSHIRE BLVD, #311
SANTA MONICA, CA 90403-5784
310-829-9335
Fax: 310-829-9335
www.entertainmentlawreporter.com
• Lionel Sobel, Editor
Description:
Edits periodical that reports recent developments in sports law.

EPM LICENSING LETTER SOURCEBOOK
19 W 21ST STREET
#303
NEW YORK, NY 10010
212-941-0099
888-852-9467
Fax: 212-941-1622
www.epmcom.com
• Riva Bennett, Chief Operating Officer
• Ira Mayer, Publisher
• Michele Jensen, Vice President of Marketing
• Melissa Trosterman, Marketing Coordinator
mtrosterman@epm.com
• Loretta Netzer, Circulation Manager
• Ben Jurin, Associate Editor, The Licensing Letter
Publishing Company:
EPM Communications, Inc.
Frequency:
Annual
Primary Audience:
Licensing business executives
Sports:
General
Circulation:
NA.
Description:
Directory of licensing agents, products, and manufacturers.

EQUESTRIAN
4047 IRON WORKS PARKWAY
LEXINGTON, KY 40511
859-258-2472
Fax: 859-231-6662
http://www.usef.org
• Brian Sosby, Editor-in-Chief
(859) 225-6923
editor@ahsa.org
• Scott Carling, Advertising Manager
(859) 225-6928
scarling@uses.org
Frequency:
10 time(s) per year
Description:
Publication is an equestrian guide.

EQUIERY
PO BOX 610
LISBON, MD 21765-0610
410-489-7826
Fax: 410-489-7828
info@equiery.com
www.equiery.com
• Tracy McKenna, Associate Publisher
(410) 489-7826
tracy.mckenna@equiery.com
• Katherine Rizzo, Editor
(410) 489-7826

katherine.rizzo@equiery.com
• Carrie Hull, Executive Director, Maryland Horse Council
(410) 489-7826
chull@mdhorsecouncil.org
• Neil Agate, President, Maryland Horse Council
nagate@mdhorsecouncil.org
Frequency:
1 time(s) per month
Description:
Publication features information for horsemen; covers trainers, riding programs, breeding facilities, association news, services, and sales.

EQUINE JOURNAL
103 ROXBURY STREET
KEENE, NH 03431
603-357-4271
800-742-9171
Fax: 603-357-7851
editorial@equinejournal.com
http://www.equinejournal.com
• Kathleen Labonville, Managing Editor
(603) 357-4271
• Lynn Jenkins, Advertising
(603) 357-4271
advertising@equinejournal.com
Frequency:
1 time(s) per month
Description:
Publication contains news and feature articles for people who ride horses competitively or for recreation.

EQUINE TIMES
331 EAST BELL
CAMDEN, MI 49232-9613
517-368-0365
800-222-6336
Fax: 517-368-5131
http://www.equine.com
• Cindy Bealer, General Manager
Frequency:
1 time(s) per month
Description:
Publication is for horse enthusiasts.

EQUUS
656 QUINCE ORCHARD ROAD SUITE 600
GAITHERSBURG, MD 20878-1409
301-977-3900
Fax: 301-990-9015
equuslts@aol.com
http://www.equisearch.com
• Laurie Prinz, Editor
(301) 977-3900
• Bob Kliner, Advertising Manager
(301) 977-3900
• Christine Barakat, Assignments Editor
(301) 977-3900
Frequency:
1 time(s) per month
Description:
Publication focuses on horse health care and training.

ERNIE SAXTON'S MOTORSPORTS SPONSORSHIP MARKETING
1448 HOLLYWOOD AVENUE
LANGHORNE, PA 19047-7417
215-752-7797
Fax: 215-752-1518
esaxton144@aol.com
www.saxtonsponsormarket.com

• Marilyn Saxton, Editor
(215) 752-2392
msaxton188@aol.com
• Joe McHugh, Account Executive
• Ernie Saxton, Publisher
Frequency:
1 time(s) per month
Description:
Publication focuses on sponsorship, marketing, and promotion through motor sports.

ESPN OUTDOORS/B.A.S.S.
5845 CARMICHAEL RD
MONTGOMERY, AL 36117
334-272-9530
Fax: 334-279-7148
www.bassmaster.com
• Dean Kessel, Vice President and General Manager
• Jeff Long, Director of Finance, Operations & Administrat
Publishing Company:
ESPN Productions - B.A.S.S., LLC.
Frequency:
10 times annually with 2 special issues.
Primary Audience:
Consumer
Sports:
Boating, fishing, hunting
Circulation:
550,000+.
Description:
Provides information of interest to outdoor sports participants.

ESPN THE MAGAZINE
19 EAST 34TH STREET
NEW YORK, NY 10016-4303
212-515-1000
Fax: 212-515-1290
http://www.espnmag.com
• Alison Overholt, General Editor
(212) 515-1000
• Shaun Assael, Senior Writer
(212) 515-1000
Shaun.Assael@espnmag.com
• Gary Belsky, Editor
(212) 515-1089
• Jerry Bembry, Senior Writer
(212) 515-1012
• Jeff Bradley, Senior Writer
(212) 515-1000
• Chris Broussard, Senior Writer
• Ric Bucher, Senior Writer
(212) 515-1000
• Chris Collins, Publisher
(212) 515-1136
• Luke Cyphers, Senior Editor-at-Large
(212) 515-1000
• Bruce Feldman, Senior Writer
(212) 515-1000
bruce.feldman@espnmag.com
• Neil Fine, Executive Editor
(212) 515-1006
• David Fleming, Senior Writer
(212) 515-1000
david.fleming@espnmag.com
• Tom Friend, Senior Writer
(212) 515-1000
• Peter Gammons, Senior Writer
(212) 515-1000
• L.Z. Granderson, General Editor
(212) 515-1012
• John Gustafson, Contributing Writer
(212) 515-1000
• John Hassan, Senior Editor

(860) 766-4878
• John Hassan, Sports Senior Editor
(860) 766-4878
• Gary Hoenig, Editor in Chief
(212) 515-1030
• Sue Hovey, Senior Deputy Editor
(212) 515-1031
• E.J. Hradek, Senior Writer
(212) 515-1059
• Roxanne Jones, Senior Editor
(212) 515-1016
• Tim Keown, Senior Writer
(212) 515-1000
tim.keown@espnmag.com
• Ivan Maisel, Sports Senior Writer
• Steve Malley, (212) 515-1000
Sports Editor
• J.B. Morris, Senior Editor
(212) 515-1042
john.b.morris@espn3.com
• Jon Pessah, Deputy Editor
(212) 515-1000
• Perry Van Der Meer, Managing Editor
• Glen Waggoner, Executive Editor
(212) 515-1004
glen.waggoner@espn3.com
• Glen Waggoner, Sports Deputy Editor
Description:
ESPN targets young, active men whose
lifestyles include watching sports, attending
games, and participating in all kinds of
athletics. The editorial focus plays off the
news and includes what will happen in
sports and which match-ups and young
players to watch. Covers sports news.
Focuses on baseball, hockey, basketball
and foot ball, but also features articles on
sports like in-line skating, bicycling and
snowboarding.
Circulation:
1,900,000
Frequency:
Bi-weekly.

EXECUTIVE GOLFER
2171 CAMPUS DRIVE SUITE 330
IRVINE, CA 92612-1422
949-752-6474
Fax: 949-752-0398
http://www.executivegolfermagazine.com
• Joyce Stevens, Managing Editor
joyce@executivegolfermagazine.com
• Shaun Mehr, Advertising Director
• Edward F. Pazdur, Director
edward@executivegolfermagazine.com
• Mark Pazdur, Publisher
mpazdur@aol.com
Frequency:
6 time(s) per year
Description:
Publication focuses on golf resorts and golf
communities; includes annual guides to golf
resorts, golf communities, CEO interviews,
and a private country club guest policy
directory.

**FACILITIES & EVENT MANAGEMENT
MAGAZINE**
152 MADISON AVE
SUITE 802
NEW YORK, NY 10016
646-580-1860
Fax: 212-578-8398
• Michael Caffin, Managing Editor
Description:
Covers the sports facility and event market
place.

Circulation:
31,000. Contr non-paid.
Sports:
General
Primary Audience:
CEO's, General Managers, Executive
Directors, Entertainment, sports and
convention facilities.
Frequency:
Bi-monthly
Publishing Company:
Bedrock Communications, Inc.

FAIRWAYS
77 EAST CENTER STREET
SUITE B
PROVO, UT 84606
801-360-2440
randy@fairwaysmag.com
www.fairwaysmag.com
• Randy Dodson, Publisher
randy@fairwaysmag.com
• Garrit Johnson, Art Director
Garrit@Fairwaysmag.com
Frequency:
4 time(s) per year
Description:
Founded in 1992, Fairways magazine is the
official publication of the Utah Golf
Association.

FANTASY SPORTS
700 E STATE ST
IOLA, WI 54990-0001
715-445-2214
888-457-2873
Fax: 715-445-4087
http://www.krause.com
• Greg Ambrosius, Editor
(715) 445-2214
• Dean Listle, Publisher
Frequency:
6 time(s) per year
Description:
Publication is geared toward fans of fantasy
baseball, football, basketball, golf, and
hockey.

FAR POST
13540 LAKE CITY WAY N.E. SUITE 3
SEATTLE, WA 98125
206-367-2420
Fax: 206-367-2636
http://www.varsitycommunications.com
• Earl Starkoff, Publisher
(800) 643-6061
Frequency:
4 time(s) per year

FIELD & STREAM MAGAZINE
TWO PARK AVE, 10 TH FL
NEW YORK, NY 10016
212-779-5000
Fax: 212-686-6877
www.fieldandstream.com
• Thomas Ott, Group Publisher
• Slaton White, Editor
• Stephen Crow, Advertising Director
Fishing Sponsor:
2003 Co-Title - Wal-Mart FLW Tour; 2004
Field & Stream Big Bass Contest.
Nature of Service:
Lifestyle magazine of the outdoors, focusing
on the fishing/hunting experience and man's
relationship with nature. Editorial covers
conservation and environmental issues as
well as sports current events and ethics. In

addition, magazine has a strong literary
tradition. Editorial also informs enthusiasts
of products, techniques, and locales to
support an outdoor lifestyle.
Publishing Company:
Times Mirror Magazines, Inc.
Frequency:
Monthly.
Primary Audience:
Consumer.
Sports:
Hunting, fishing.
Circulation:
2,007,901. 97% paid subscr, 3% newsstand.

**FITNESS BUSINESS CANADA
MAGAZINE/FITNESS TRAINER CANADA
MAGAZINE**
30 MILL POND DR
RR #3
GEORGETOWN, CANADA L7G 4S6
905-873-0850
888-920-6537
Fax: 905-873-8611
fbc@fitnet.ca
www.fitnet.ca
• Lori Longwell, Advertising Manager
• Graham Longwell, Editor/Publisher
fbc@fitnet.ca
Publishing Company:
Mill Pond Publishing Inc.
Frequency:
Bimonthly.
Primary Audience:
Fitness providers in Canada.
Sports:
Health & Fitness.
Circulation:
Fitness Business 8,000, Fitness Trainer
15,000

FITNESS INFORMATION TECHNOLOGY
1137 VAN VOORHIS RD
CHELSEA SQUARE, STE 32
MORGANTOWN, WV 26505
304-599-3483
800-477-4348
Fax: 304-599-3482
• Andrew Ostrow, FIT President
(304) 599-3483
• Drew Krantz, Marketing Associate
(304) 599-3483
drew@fitinfotech.com
• Julie B. Burrell, Editor
(304) 599-3483
julie@fitinfotech.com
Publishing Company:
Fitness Information Technology, Inc.
Frequency:
4 times a year.
Nature of Service:
Academic publication in sport marketing
worldwide.
Primary Audience:
College.

FLORIDA GOLF NEWS
301 3RD STREET, N.W. SUITE 216
WINTER HAVEN, FL 33881
863-401-9744
Fax: 863-401-9542
http://www.flgolfnews.com
• Ed Travis, Editor
golfscribe@tampabay.rr.com
Frequency:
1 time(s) per month
Description:

Publication contains information of interest to golfing enthusiasts in the state of Florida, including coverage of events and equipment reviews.

FLORIDA GREEN
P.O. BOX 65
JENSEN BEACH, FL 34958
772-334-7515
800-732-6053
Fax: 772-334-6015
flgrn@aol.com
http://www.floridagcsa.com
• Larry Keiffer, Publication Manager
(863) 398-4057
• Marie Roberts, Advertising Manager
Frequency:
4 time(s) per year
Description:
Publication contains information on golf course management.

FLORIDA HORSEMEN
12788 WEST FOREST HILL BOULEVARD
SUITE 1
WELLINGTON, FL 33414
561-793-7606
Fax: 561-793-6090
http://www.horsemenonline.com
• Joshua Manning, Editor
news@gotowncrier.com
Frequency:
9 time(s) per year

FLORIDA SPORTS & FITNESS MAGAZINE
102 DRENNEN ROAD
ORLANDO, FL 32806
407-816-9596
888-352-5484
Fax: 407-816-9373
http://www.floridamagazine.com
• E. Douglas Cifers, Publisher
dcifers@floridamagazine.com
• Elizabeth Ashton, Administrative Coordinator
(407) 816-9596
• Susan Cerulean, Writer
(407) 816-9596
Frequency:
1 time(s) per year

FLORIDA SPORTSMAN
2700 SOUTH KANNER HIGHWAY
STUART, FL 34994
772-219-7400
Fax: 772-219-6900
http://www.floridasportsman.com
• Herb Allen, Department Editor
(772) 219-7400
• Karl Wickstrom, Editor-in-Chief
(772) 219-7400
karl@floridasportsman.com
• Blair Wickstrom, Publisher
(772) 219-7400
• Bob Mitchell, Marketing Director
bob@floridasportsman.com
• Eric Wickstrom, Internet Editor
(772) 219-7400
editor@floridasportsman.com
• Vic Dunaway, Senior Editor
(772) 219-7400
vic@floridasportsman.com
• Jeff Weakley, Editor
(772) 219-7400
jeff@floridasportsman.com

Description:
Edited for more than 48 million visitors and residents of Florida, the Bahamas, and the American tropics. Content is directed to the ardent sportsman who fishes, hunts, boats, camps, swims and creates a vast consumer area. Editorial philosophy is geared to these active devotees and the full enjoyment of the natural resources. Articles prepared by Florida's best known outdoors experts emphasize the how-to and where-to approach.
Circulation:
114,066
Sports:
Outdoor sports
Primary Audience:
Consumer
Frequency:
Monthly.
Publishing Company:
Primedia, Inc.

FLORIDA TENNIS
1760 NORTHWEST 107TH AVENUE
PEMBROKE PINES, FL 33026-2806
954-431-4069
800-779-4069
Fax: 954-438-7330
fltennis@aol.com
• Jim Martz, Editor
• Gary Ferman, Managing Editor
Frequency:
1 time(s) per month
Description:
Publication features tennis news in Florida.

FOOTBALL DIGEST
990 GROVE STREET
EVANSTON, IL 60201-4370
847-491-6440
800-334-4005
Fax: 847-491-0459
http://www.centurysports.net
• William Wagner, Editor
(847) 491-6440
wwagner@centurysports.net
• Norman Jacobs, Publisher
(847) 491-6440
njacobs@centurysports.net
Frequency:
10 time(s) per year
Description:
Publication covers professional football; includes interviews, stats, reports, rosters, and predictions.

FOOTBALL NEWS
8033 NORTHWEST 36TH STREET
SUITE 438
DORAL, FL 33166-6644
305-594-0508
Fax: 305-594-0518
Frequency:
20 time(s) per year
Description:
Publication covers college and professional football.

FOOTWEAR PLUS
8 WEST 38TH STREET
NEW YORK, NY 10120
646-278-1550
Fax: 646-278-1553
http://www.footwearplusonline.com
• Greg Dutter, Editor-in-Chief
(646) 278-1550

• Thomas Hudson, Jr., Publisher
• Caroline Diaco, Publisher
(646) 278-1550
• Petra Guglielmetti, Asociate Fashion Editor
• Kristen Koba, Associate Fashion Editor
• Caletha Crawford, Associate Editor
Publishing Company:
Wickstrom Publishers, Inc.
Frequency:
Monthly except for bi-monthly-April/May; November/December.
Primary Audience:
Trade
Sports:
All Sports.
Description:
The fashion magazine of the footwear industry.

FORE
3740 CAHUENGA BOULEVARD
NORTH HOLLYWOOD, CA 91604-3502
818-980-3630
Fax: 818-980-1808
http://www.scga.org
• Robert D. Thomas, Editor
(818) 980-3630
• Katie Denbo, Assistant Editor
(818) 980-3630
• Robert D. Thomas, Publisher
(818) 980-3630
• Teri Silvi, Communications/Marketing Specialist
(818) 980-3630
• Timmie High, Production Supervisor
(818) 980-3630
timmiehigh@scga.org
Frequency:
6 time(s) per year
Description:
Publication contains golf news and information focusing on California amateur golf; includes features on resorts, tours, and new products.

FREESKIER
1630 30TH STREET SUITE 272
BOULDER, CO 80301
303-449-2165
Fax: 303-449-2427
http://www.freeskier.com
• Patrick Crawford, Editor
(303) 449-8212
• Bradford Fayfield, Publisher
(303) 449-5100
bradford@freeskier.com
• Christopher Jerard, Advertising Manager
(303) 449-2165
Frequency:
4 time(s) per year
Description:
Publication is a lifestyle magazine for skiers between the ages of 18 and 34; showcases today's new, youthful ski movement.

GATER RACING PHOTO NEWS
206 FERNCLIFF AVENUE
LIVERPOOL, NY 13088-6410
315-457-0175
Fax: 315-457-0346
http://www.gaternews.com
• Joseph Patrick, Editor
(315) 457-0175
news@gaternews.com
• Joseph Patrick, Advertising Manager
ads@gaternews.com

media

• Joseph Patrick, Publisher
ads@gaternews.com
Frequency:
37 time(s) per year
Description:
Publication covers oval track auto racing
and is a regional trade newspaper for sports
personnel and fans.

GATOR BAIT
PO BOX 14022
GAINESVILLE, FL 32604
352-372-1215
800-782-3216
Fax: 352-371-9420
www.gatorbait.net
• Marty Cohen, General Manager/Editor
• Guerry Smith, Assistant Editor
• Laura Cohen, Web Editor
• J.L. Kirby, Staff Writer
Description:
Features and information about all sports at
the University of Florida.
Circulation:
21,000
Sports:
All sports at the University of Florida
Primary Audience:
Consumer
Frequency:
32 times annually
Publishing Company:
Florida Sports News, Inc.

GOLD SHEET
4717 VAN NUYS BOULEVARD
SHERMAN OAKS, CA 91403
800-798-4653
Fax: 323-273-5932
www.goldsheet.com
• Mort Olshan, Founder/Chairman
• P. Carl Giordano, Managing Editor
Description:
Analysts and commentators of college and
pro football and basketball handicapping.
Circulation:
102,712.34% paid subscr, 66% newsstand.
Sports:
Football & Basketball
Primary Audience:
Consumer
Frequency:
Weekly Sept-April
Publishing Company:
Olshan Enterprises, Inc.

GOLF BUSINESS
291 SEVEN FARMS DRIVE 2ND FLOOR
CHARLESTON, SC 29492
843-881-9956
Fax: 843-881-9958
http://www.golfbusiness.com
• Rodney Foushee, Editor
(843) 881-9956
• Bill Gurney, Director
(843) 881-9956
• Joe Rice, Publisher
(843) 881-9956
jrice@ngcoa.org
Frequency:
1 time(s) per month
Description:
Publication focuses on golf course
management.

GOLF CONNOISSEUR MAGAZINE
8988-L SOUTH SHERIDAN ROAD SUITE
360
TULSA, OK 74133
918-492-0660
Fax: 918-492-0680
http://www.golfconnoisseur.com
• James A. Frank, Editor-in-Chief
(212) 222-0033
Frequency:
4 time(s) per year

GOLF COURSE MANAGEMENT
1421 RESEARCH PARK DRIVE
LAWRENCE, KS 66049-3858
785-832-4431
800-472-7878
Fax: 785-832-3665
http://www.gcsaa.org
• Bunny Smith, Managing Editor
(785) 832-4490
bsmith@gcsaa.org
• Ed Hiscock, Editor In Chief
(785) 832-4431
• Seth Jones, Senior Associate Editor
(785) 832-3682
• Angela Nitz, Senior Associate Editor
Frequency:
1 time(s) per month
Description:
Publication is geared toward golf course
superintendents; includes news, features,
and research.

GOLF COURSE NEWS
4012 BRIDGE AVENUE
CLEVELAND, OH 44113
216-961-4130
Fax: 216-961-0364
http://www.golfcourse.com
• Kevin Gilbride, Publisher
(330) 657-2889
kgilbride@gie.net
• John Walsh, Managing Editor
(216) 961-4130
jwalsh@gie.net
Frequency:
1 time(s) per month
Description:
Publication focuses on golf course
management for superintendents, owners,
architects, developers, and suppliers.

GOLF DIGEST
20 WESTPORT ROAD
WILTON, CT 06897
203-761-5100
Fax: 203-761-5129
editor@golfdigest.com
http://www.golfdigest.com
• Roger Schiffman, Managing Editor
(203) 761-5237
roger.schiffman@golfdigest.com
• Max Adler, Assistant Editor
(203) 761-5344
max.adler@golfdigest.com
• Tom Bair, Publisher
(212) 286-3856
tom.bair@golfdigest.com
• Mike O'Malley, Executive Editor
(203) 761-5234
mike.omalley@golfdigest.com
• Craig Bestrom, Senior Editor
(203) 761-5224
craig.bestrom@golfdigest.com
Frequency:
1 time(s) per month

Description:
Publication offers instruction and features
for all golfers from beginners to experienced
players.

GOLF FOR WOMEN
20 WESTPORT ROAD 7TH FLOOR
WILTON, CT 06897
212-286-2888
Fax: 212-286-5340
editors@golfforwomen.com
http://www.golfforwomen.com
• Susan K. Reed, Editor
(212) 286-3905
susan.reed@golfforwomen.com
• Samantha Hallock, Assistant Editor
(212) 286-3906
samantha.hallock@golfforwomen.com
• Johnette Howard, Contributing Writer
• Janine Hughes, Managing Editor
(212) 286-3908
janine.hughes@golfforwomen.com
• Sally Jenkins, Contributing Writer
• Argy Koutsothanasis, Contributing Writer
(212) 286-3941
akoutsothanasis@golfforwomen.com
• Kate Meyers, Contributing Writer
• Lee Slattery, Publisher
(212) 286-2498
lee.slattery@golfforwomen.com
• Stina Sternberg, Senior Editor
(212) 286-3934
stina.sternberg@golfforwomen.com
• Stina Sternberg, Sports Senior Editor
(212) 286-3934
stina.sternberg@golfforwomen.com
• Sarah Turcotte, Assistant Editor
(212) 286-3954
sarah.turcotte@golfforwomen.com
• Sarah Turcotte, Sports Assistant Editor
(212) 286-3954
sarah.turcotte@golfforwomen.com
• Dana White, Executive Editor
(212) 286-4360
dana.white@golfforwomen.com
Frequency:
6 time(s) per year
Description:
Publication focuses on golf subjects for
women.

GOLF GEORGIA
121 VILLAGE PARKWAY BUILDING 3
MARIETTA, GA 30067-4061
770-955-4572
800-949-4742
Fax: 770-955-1156
sbower@levelparmedia.com
http://www.gsga.org
• Stan Awtrey, Editor
• Shannon Bower, Publisher
Frequency:
6 time(s) per year
Description:
Publication targets private and public golf
club members; focuses on golf-related news
and activities around the state, including
competitions, new course openings, and
other items of interest.

GOLF ILLUSTRATED
15115 SOUTH 76TH EAST AVENUE
BIXBY, OK 74008
918-366-6191
Fax: 918-366-6512
http://www.golfillustrated.com

• Jason Sowards, Editor
(918) 366-6191
• Gerald W. Pope, Publisher
(918) 366-6191
Frequency:
4 time(s) per year
Description:
Publication is a lifestyle magazine for
advanced golfers.

GOLF MAGAZINE
2 PARK AVENUE 10TH FLOOR
NEW YORK, NY 10016-5675
212-779-5000
Fax: 212-779-5522
http://www.golfonline.com
• Robert Sauerhaft, Managing Editor -
Equipment
(212) 779-5064
robert.sauerhaft@time4.com
• Dave Allen, Senior Associate Editor
(212) 779-5051
dave.allen@time4.com
• Lorin Anderson, Managing Editor
(212) 779-5514
lorin.anderson@time4.com
• Connell Barrett, Senior Editor
connell.barrett@time4.com
• David Clarke, Editor-in-Chief
• David Dusek, Associate Editor
(212) 779-5016
david.dusek@time4.com
• Carl Mehlhope, Associate Publisher
(212) 779-5000
carl.mehlhope@time4.com
• Greg Midland, Associate Editor
(212) 779-5567
greg.midland@time4.com
• Peter Morrice, Executive Editor
peter.morrice@time4.com
• Ron Mulliken, Advertising Director
• Jack Nicklaus, Special Contributor
• Evan Rothman, Executive Editor
evan.rothman@time4.com
• Alan Bastable, Senior Associate Editor
(212) 522-8630
alan_bastable@golf.com
Frequency:
1 time(s) per month
Description:
Publication is written for golf enthusiasts.

GOLF NEWS
10 NORTH NEWNAN STREET
JACKSONVILLE, FL 32202-3322
904-356-2466
Fax: 904-353-2628
admin@baileypub.com
http://www.baileypub.com
• James Bailey, Publisher
jbailey@baileypub.com
• Fred Seely, Editorial Director
(904) 356-2466
fseely@baileypub.com
• Melanie White, Advertising Manager
mwhite@baileypub.com
Frequency:
1 time(s) per month
Description:
Publication features information of interest
to golf enthusiasts.

GOLF ON CAPE COD
143 A UPPER COUNTY ROAD
DENNIS PORT, MA 02639

508-398-6101
Fax: 508-398-4711
http://www.golfoncapecod.com
• Paul Reiss, Editor
(508) 398-6101
• Paul Reiss, Publisher
(508) 398-6101
Frequency:
4 time(s) per year
Description:
Publication covers regional courses,
players, and tournaments.

GOLF PRODUCT NEWS
217 MOUNTAIN BROOK DRIVE SUITE 201
MARIETTA, GA 30064
678-355-1007
http://www.golfproductnews.com
• Jack Bacot, Editor-in-Chief
(843) 437-5473
• Laurie Dee Dovey, Contributing Editor
• Peter W. Finney, Jr., Contributing Editor
pfinney@clarionherald.org
• Dan Gleason, Contributing Editor
• Robert Nitkewicz, Publisher
rnitkewicz@bellsouth.net
• Jack O'Leary, Contributing Editor
• Barbara Sabella, Contributing Editor
• John Torsiello, Contributing Editor
• Bill Varner, Contributing Editor
Frequency:
8 time(s) per year
Description:
Publication focuses on the golf products and
accessories industry.

GOLF RANGE TIMES
2807 NORTH PARHAM ROAD SUITE 107
RICHMOND, VA 23294
804-379-5760
Fax: 804-282-5780
http://www.golfrangetimes.com
• James E. Turner, Editor
jamie@forecastgolf.com
• Betty Jo Bass, Advertising Manager
(804) 360-0158
• Virginia Sowers, Managing Editor
virginia.sowers@douglasmurphy.com
• James E. Turner, Publisher
jamie@forecastgolf.com
Frequency:
7 time(s) per year
Description:
Publication focuses on the golf range
business.

GOLF TIPS
12121 WILSHIRE BOULEVARD SUITE
1200
LOS ANGELES, CA 90025
310-820-1500
Fax: 310-820-2793
http://www.warnerpublishing.com
• Mike Chwasky, Editor
• Steve Werner, Publisher
swerner@wernerpublishing.com
Frequency:
1 time(s) per month
Description:
Publication provides golf instruction.

GOLF TRAVELER
2575 VISTA DEL MAR DRIVE
VENTURA, CA 93001
805-667-4100
800-765-1912
Fax: 805-667-4217

info@golfcard.com
http://www.golfcard.com
• Ken Cohen, Editor
Frequency:
6 time(s) per year
Description:
Publication contains information on affiliated
Golf Card resorts, accommodations, golf
courses, the senior PGA tour, golfing
techniques, and developments in equipment
and sportswear.

GOLF VIEWS
P.O. BOX 620999
LITTLETON, CO 80162
303-797-8700
Fax: 303-797-1119
http://www.golfviews.com
• Karl O'Keefe, Editor
• Karl O'Keefe, Publisher
Frequency:
9 time(s) per year
Description:
Publication is geared toward the golf pro.

GOLF WORLD
20 WESTPORT ROAD
WILTON, CT 06897
203-761-5100
Fax: 203-761-5129
golfworld@golf.com
http://www.golfdigest.com
• Geoff Russell, Features Editor
(203) 761-5253
geoff.russell@golfworld.com
• Mark Furlong, Publisher
(212) 286-4120
mark.furlong@golfdigest.com
• Ron Sirak, Managing Editor
(203) 761-5260
ron.sirak@golfworld.com
• Jerry Tarde, Editor-in-Chief
(203) 761-5225
jerry.tarde@golfdigest.com
• John Antonini, Senior Editor of Tour Talk
(203) 761-5254
john.antonini@golfworld.com
Frequency:
48 time(s) per year
Description:
Publication is geared toward amateur and
professional golfers; reports on PGA and
LPGA tours and tournaments as well as
college golf.

GOLFDOM
7500 OLD OAK BOULEVARD
CLEVELAND, OH 44130-3369
440-243-8100
Fax: 440-891-2675
http://www.golfdom.com
• Frank Andorka, Managing Editor
(440) 891-2708
• Larry Aylward, Editor in Chief
(216) 706-3737
laylward@questex.com
• Patrick Roberts, Publisher
(440) 891-2609
proberts@questex.com
Frequency:
1 time(s) per month
Description:
Publication delivers technical information on
golf course maintenance topics, case
studies, news, columns, and opinions.

media

GOLFER
59 EAST 72ND STREET
NEW YORK, NY 100021
212-867-7070
Fax: 212-867-8550
thegolfer@thegolfermag.com
http://www.thegolfermag.com/
• Cliffard Blodgett, Managing Editor
cliffard@thegolfermag.com
• H. Kevan Pickens, Editor-in-Chief
kevan@thegolfermag.com
• H. Kevan Pickens, Publisher
kevan@thegolfermag.com
• Colin Sheehan, Senior Editor
(212) 867-7070
colin@thegolfermag.com
• John Clarke, Jr., Managing Editor
(212) 867-7070
Frequency:
6 time(s) per year
Description:
Publication is a golf lifestyle magazine with tournament coverage, course selections and country club updates. Also provides new equipment reviews and suggests spas & restaurants for readers.

GOLFWEEK
1500 PARK CENTER DRIVE
ORLANDO, FL 32835
407-563-7000
Fax: 407-563-7077
email@golfweek.com
http://www.golfweek.com
• David Seanor, Editor
dseanor@golfweek.com
• Jeff Babineau, Deputy Editor
(407) 563-7046
jbabineau@golfweek.com
• Beth Ann Baldry, Senior Writer
(407) 563-7041
bbaldry@golfweek.com
• Jay Coffin, Staff Writer
(407) 563-7043
jcoffin@golfweek.com
• Craig Horan, Managing Editor
(407) 563-7030
choran@golfweek.com
• Martin Kaufmann, Assistant Editor
(407) 563-7044
mkaufmann@golfweek.com
• Bradley S Klein, Staff Writer
(860) 243-3296
bklein@golfweek.com
• Jim Nugent, Publisher
(407) 563-7014
jnugent@golfweek.com
• David Seanor, Editorial Director
• James Achenbach, Associate Editor
(760) 863-4377
jachenbach@golfweek.com
Frequency:
1 time(s) per week
Description:
Publication contains information of interest to golf enthusiasts, including pro golf news, commentary, amateur and college news, rankings, business news, and America's best courses.

GOLFWEEK'S SUPERINTENDENT NEWS
1500 PARK CENTER DRIVE
ORLANDO, FL 32835
407-563-7000
Fax: 407-563-7076
esoderstrom@golfweek.com
http://www.golfweek.com

• James E. Nugent, Publisher
jnugent@golfweek.com
Frequency:
2 time(s) per month
Description:
Publication is a golf management magazine.

GOWDY PRINTCRAFT PRESS
22 N. SIERRA MADRE
COLORADO SPRINGS, CO 80903
719-634-1593
Fax: 719-632-0762
• Tex Stuart, Director
Description:
The Fort Carson Mountaineer newspaper since 1942 The Air Force Academy Academy Spirit newspaper since 1959 The Schriever Air Force Base Satellite Flyer newspaper since 1999 The Peterson Air Force Base Space Observer And the P3 Sports Guide series since 1990

GRASSROOTS MOTORSPORTS
P.O. BOX 1568
ORMOND BEACH, FL 32175
386-239-0523
888-676-0573
Fax: 386-239-0573
http://www.grassrootsmotorsports.com
• David Wallens, Editor
• Marjorie Suddard, Editor
(386) 673-4148
marjorie@grassrootsmotorsports.com
• Timothy P. Suddard, Publisher
• Noelle Omer, Editorial Assistant
(386) 673-4148
Frequency:
6 time(s) per year

GRAY'S SPORTING JOURNAL
735 BROAD ST
AUGUSTA, GA 30901
978-462-6335
Fax: 978-462-6445
www.graysportingjournal.com
• William S. Morris, Publisher
• David C. Foster, Editor-in-Chief
• James Babb, Editor
(706) 722-6060
jrbabb@verizon.net
Description:
Explores the sophisticated outdoor adventurer's world of hunting, fishing and conservation through literature, fine sporting photography, art and travel.
Publishing Company:
Morris Communications, Inc.
Circulation:
NA.
Sports:
Flyfishing, fishing, bird hunting, big game hunting
Primary Audience:
Consumer
Frequency:
Six times annually plus Annual Expedition and Guide Books.

GREAT LAKES BOATING MAGAZINE
1032 NORTH LA SALLE
CHICAGO, IL 60610
312-266-8400
Fax: 312-266-8470
http://www.greatlakesboating.com
• Karen Malonis, Managing Editor
glb@greatlakesboating.com

• F. Ned Dikmen, Publisher
• Karen Malonis, Sports Managing Editor
Frequency:
6 time(s) per year
Description:
Publication focuses on recreational boating on the Great Lakes.

GREYHOUND REVIEW
729 OLD HIGHWAY 40
ABILENE, KS 67410
785-263-4660
Fax: 785-263-4689
nga@ngagreyhounds.com
http://www.ngagreyhounds.com
• Tim Horan, Managing Editor
timh@ngagreyhounds.com
• Gary Guccione, Executive Editor
garyg@ngagreyhounds.com
Frequency:
12 time(s) per year
Description:
Publication contains articles from greyhound racetracks and breeding farms throughout the country. Aimed towards the professional greyhound racing.

H.O. ZIMMAN
SEAPORT LANDING
152 THE LYNNWAY
LYNN, MA 01902
781-598-9230
Fax: 781-599-4018
www.hozinc.com
• Joshua A. Zimman, President
• David Zimman, Advertising Director
• Dan Vinton, Director of Business Development
Description:
Publishes over 200 magazines which include: U.S. Open Tennis Magazine, Tennis Championships Magazine, U.S. Soccer, The Olympian.

HACHETTE FILIPACCHI MEDIA
1633 BROADWAY
NEW YORK, NY 10019
212-767-6000
Fax: 212-767-5602
• Nick Matarazzo, Sr. VP/Director Group Publisher Automotive Group
• Nicolas Ricci, Senior Vice President, Sales & Marketing
• Tony Catalano, Vice President National Sales Manager
• Lucilla Sitra, Regional Sales
• Adam Meyerson, Regional Sales Director
• Pete Beckenbach, Regional Sales Director
• Lawrence Peters, Managing Director, Director Response Advertis
Description:
Publishes wide range of consumer magazines.

HAND GLIDING & PARA GLIDING MAGAZINE
P.O. BOX 1330
COLORADO SPRINGS, CO 80901
800-616-6888
Fax: 719-632-6417
http://www.ushga.org
• C. J. Sturtevant, Editor
editor@ushga.org
Frequency:
1 time(s) per month

HEALTH & FITNESS MAGAZINE
5001 WOODWAY
SUITE 1404
HOUSTON, TX 77057
713-552-9991
Fax: 713-552-9997
editorial@healthandfitnessmag.com
www.healthandfitnessmag.com
• Rod Evans, Editor
(713) 552-9991
rod@healthandfitnessmag.com
• Pat Monfrey, Publisher
(713) 552-9991
pat@healthandfitnessmag.com
Frequency:
1 time(s) per month
Description:
Publication contains information on nutrition, exercise, sports, and beauty for the residents of the greater Houston area.

HEARTLAND BOATING
319 NORTH 4TH STREET
SUITE 650
ST LOUIS, MO 63102-1998
314-241-4310
800-366-9630
Fax: 314-241-4207
info@heartlandboating.com
http://www.heartlandboating.com
• Lee C Braff, Editor
(314) 241-4310
lbraff@heartlandboating.com
• Greg Klohr, Advertising Sales Manager
(314) 241-4310
greg@heartlandboating.com
• H. Nelson Spencer, Publisher
(314) 241-4310
Frequency:
8 times per year, March - October
Description:
Publication focuses on freshwater recreational boating.
Circulation:
10,000
Primary Audience:
Recreational boat owners in the South and the Mid-West.

HECKLER MAGAZINE
1915 25TH STREET
SACRAMENTO, CA 95814
916-456-2300
888-897-6247
Fax: 916-444-8972
info@heckler.com
http://www.heckler.com
• Brad Oates, Co-Editor
(916) 456-2300
brad@heckler.com
Frequency:
7 time(s) per year
Description:
Publication contains articles about snowboarding, skateboarding, and music.

HIGH SURF ADVISORY
P.O. BOX 789
HALEIWA, HI 96712
808-551-9397
Fax: 808-637-4701
http://www.highsurfadvisory.com
Frequency:
8 time(s) per year
Description:
Publication is a surfing magazine for enthusiasts in Hawaii.

HOMETOWN GOLF
9933 ALLIANCE ROAD
CINCINNATI, OH 45242
513-794-4100
Fax: 513-794-4140
mmurphy@reachusa.com
http://www.cincygolf.com
• Ed Letsinger, Managing Editor
(513) 794-4177
eletsinger@reachusa.com
Frequency:
6 time(s) per year
Description:
Publication features local golf stories and information in the Greater Cincinnati area.

HOOF BEATS
6130 S SUNBURY ROAD
WESTERVILLE, OH 43081
614-224-2291
877-800-8782
Fax: 614-222-6791
hoofbeats@ustrotting.com
www.hoofbeatsmagazine.com
• Dan Leary, Executive Editor
(614) 224-2291
hoofbeats@ustrotting.com
• Kim French, Editor
(570) 506-9948
hoofbeats@ustrotting.com
• Gena Gallagher, Art Director/Production Manager
ggalla@ustrotting.com
• Paul Ramlow, Copy Editor
pramlow@ustrotting.com
Frequency:
1 time(s) per month
Description:
Publication offers news and practical information for owners, trainers, drivers, and fans of standardbred racing and breeding.

HOOK
209 SOUTH MARSHALL STREET
MARSHFIELD, MO 65706-2142
417-468-7000
Fax: 417-859-6075
editor@hookmagazine.com
http://www.hookmagazine.com
• Dana Marlin, Editor
• Dana Marlin, Advertising Manager
• Dana Marlin, Publisher
Frequency:
6 time(s) per year
Description:
Publication covers all aspects of antique and classic tractor pulling.

HOOP
355 LEXINGTON AVENUE
NEW YORK, NY 10017-6603
212-697-1460
Fax: 212-286-8154
• Tony Gervino, Editor
mwong@pspsports.com
• Ming Wong, Managing Editor
mwong@pspsports.com
Frequency:
8 time(s) per year
Description:
Publication focuses on professional basketball.

HORSE
3101 BEAMOUNT CENTER CIRCLE
LEXINGTON, KY 40513

859-278-2361
800-866-2361
Fax: 859-276-6706
admin@thehorse.com
thehorse.com
• Kim Herbert, Editor
• Michelle Adaway, Advertising Manager
(859) 276-6701
• Stacy V. Bearse, Publisher
(859) 276-6701
• Jim Cox, Advertising Director
(859) 276-6792
Frequency:
1 time(s) per month
Description:
Publication provides practical information on all aspects of horse breeding, training, and related business, with a focus on health/veterinary topics.

HORSE & RIDER
656 QUINCE ORCHARD ROAD
SUITE 600
GAITHERSBURG, MD 20878
301-977-3900
Fax: 301-990-9015
equineeditor@equinetwork.com
http://www.horseandrider.com
• Darrell Dodds, Editor
(940) 479-4600
Frequency:
1 time(s) per month
Description:
Publication focuses on Western style training and horse care for competitive riders, horse owners, and recreational riders.

HORSE ILLUSTRATED
3 BURROUGHS
IRVINE, CA 92618
949-855-8822
Fax: 949-855-3045
http://www.animalnetwork.com
• Moira Harris, Editor
(949) 855-8822
• Liz Moyer, Managing Editor
(949) 855-8822
• Norman Ridker, President
• Pat Trowbridge, Publisher
(213) 385-2222
Frequency:
1 time(s) per month
Description:
Publication is geared toward horse owners.

HORSE NEWS
8 MINNEAKOING
FLEMINGTON, NJ 08822
908-782-4747
Fax: 908-782-6572
http://www.horsenewsonline.com
• Shaneen Kohler, Editor
(908) 782-4747
horsenews@hcdemocrat.com
• Lillian Shupe, Senior Contributing Editor
Frequency:
1 time(s) per month

HORSE OF DELAWARE VALLEY
PO BOX 223
UNIONVILLE, PA 19375-0223
610-793-1425
Fax: 610-793-3119
http://www.horsedelval.com
• Sara Cavanagh, Editor
• H. L. Schwartz, Publisher

thehorse1@erols.com
• Deb Vandenberg, Advertising Manager
Frequency:
1 time(s) per month
Description:
An equine publication.

HORSE WORLD
730 MADISON STREET
SHELBYVILLE, TN 37160-3519
931-684-8123
Fax: 931-684-8196
http://www.horseworld.net
• Bonnie Vannatta, Editor
• Christy Parsons, Editor
cparsons@horseworld.net
• Christy Parsons, Publisher
cparsons@horseworld.net
Frequency:
1 time(s) per month
Description:
Publication reports on horse shows.

HORSEMAN'S JOURNAL
P.O. BOX 202290
AUSTIN, TX 78720-2290
859-259-0451
Fax: 512-249-7446
hj@nationalhbpa.com
http://www.hbpa.org
• Richard Glover, Managing Editor
(512) 246-9100
Frequency:
4 time(s) per year
Description:
Magazine is the official publication of the
Horsemen's Benevolent Protective
Association; provides news and information
helpful to owners, trainers, and breeders of
race horses.

HORSEMAN'S NEWS
34311 DEPORTOLA ROAD
TEMECULA, CA 92592
951-303-3900
Fax: 951-303-3905
horsemannew@aol.com
http://www.horsemansnews.com
• Virginia McClintock, Editor
virginia@horsemansnews.com
• Virginia McClintock, Publisher
virginia@horsemansnews.com
Frequency:
1 time(s) per month
Description:
Publication provides information to
professional horsemen in the western
United States.

HOW TO AVOID CHOKING GET
MENTALLY TOUGH AND STAY IN THE
ZONE
1060 MAIN STREET
SUITE 307
RIVER EDGE, NJ 07661
201-342-3663
800-580-9663
Fax: 201-342-2258
info@stayinthezone.com
www.stayinthezone.com

HOW TO BOWL IN THE ZONE WITH
SPORTS PSYCHOLOGY
1060 MAIN STREET
SUITE 307
RIVER EDGE, NJ 07661

201-342-3663
800-580-9663
Fax: 201-342-2258
info@stayinthezone.com
www.stayinthezone.com

HOW TO GET INTO THE ZONE IN JUST
ONE MINUTE
1060 MAIN STREET
SUITE 307
RIVER EDGE, NJ 07661
201-342-3663
800-580-9663
Fax: 201-342-2258
info@stayinthezone.com
www.stayinthezone.com

HOW TO LOWER YOUR GOLF SCORE
WITH SPORT PSYCHOLOGY AND
SELF-HYPNOSIS
1060 MAIN STREET
SUITE 307
RIVER EDGE, NJ 07661
201-342-3663
800-580-9663
Fax: 201-342-2258
info@stayinthezone.com
www.stayinthezone.com

HUNTER & SPORT HORSE
12204 COVINGTON ROAD
FORT WAYNE, IN 46814
260-625-4030
Fax: 260-625-3480
hshhorse@aol.com
http://www.hunterandsporthorsemag.com
• Laura Allen, Editor
(260) 625-4030
• Lisa Allen, Publisher
• Kerry Scarbrough, Advertising Manager
(260) 625-4030
HSHHorse@aol.com
Frequency:
6 time(s) per year
Description:
Publication covers issues of interest to the
sport horse enthusiast, including dressage,
combined training, and hunter/jumper.

IEG SPONSORSHIP REPORT
350 NORTH ORLEANS
SUITE 1200
CHICAGO, IL 60654
312-944-1727
800-834-4850
Fax: 312-944-1897
ieg@sponsorship.com
www.sponsorship.com
• Lesa Ukman, Executive Editor
• Jim Andrews, Executive Vice President /
Content Strategy
• William Chipps, Senior Editor
• Penny Perrey, Vice President Marketing
Description:
Your online source for news and articles
covering sponsorship of sports, music,
festivals, the arts and causes. Who
sponsors what and why. How companies
evaluate sponsorship. Majority (about 70%)
of editorial deals specifically with sports
sponsorship. Corporate contacts and phone
numbers listed with each article.
Circulation:
100% paid subscription
Sports:
General
Primary Audience:

Corporate sponsors, rightsholders, agencies
and event producers
Frequency:
24/7 online access
Publishing Company:
IEG, Inc.

ILLINOIS RACING NEWS
111 SHORE DRIVE
BURR RIDGE, IL 60527
630-887-7722
Fax: 630-887-1958
info@midwestoutdoors.com
http://www.illinoisracingnews.com
• Joan Colby, Editor/Advertising Manager
(630) 887-7722
• Cheryl Magana, Sales Representative
(630) 887-7722
CherylMagana@aol.com
Frequency:
1 time(s) per month
Description:
Publication features Thoroughbred racing
and breeding news.

INDIANA BASKETBALL HISTORY
1 HALL OF FAME COURT
NEW CASTLE, IN 47362-2941
765-529-1891
Fax: 765-529-0273
info@hoopshall.com
• Roger Dickinson, Publisher
roger@hoopshall.com
Frequency:
4 time(s) per year
Description:
Publication contains historic photos and
articles on Indiana basketball.

INPLAY
12501 SOUTH ISIS AVENUE
HAWTHORNE, CA 90250
310-643-6455
800-872-2976
Fax: 310-643-5310
soccernow@ayso.org
http://www.soccer.org
• David Frickman, Sports Editor
(800) 872-2976
davidfrickman@ayso.org
• David Frickman, Sports Editor
(310) 643-6455
davidfrickman@ayso.org
• Sean Hilferty, Publication Coordinator
(310) 643-6455
seanhilferty@ayso.org
Frequency:
4 time(s) per year
Description:
Publication is geared toward soccer
coaches and referees.

INSIDE INDIANA
3901 EAST HAGAN STREET
BLOOMINGTON, IN 47401
812-334-9722
800-282-4648
Fax: 812-334-9756
http://www.insideiu.com
• Ed Magoni, Editor
(812) 334-9722
ed@insideiu.com
• Ken Bikoff, Editor
(812) 334-9722
kbikoff@insideiu.com

Description:
Publication covers sports at the University of Indiana.

INSIDE KUNG-FU
4201 VANOWEN PLACE
BURBANK, CA 91505
818-845-2656
800-332-3330
Fax: 818-845-7761
http://www.cfwenterprises.com
• Dave Cater, Editor
(818) 845-2656
Frequency:
1 time(s) per month
Description:
Publication covers the world of kung-fu.

INSIDE SPORTING GOODS
770 BROADWAY
NEW YORK, NY 10003-9595
646-654-4997
Fax: 646-654-5005
• Robert E. Carr, Editor
(646) 654-4997
rcarr@sgbmag.com
Publishing Company:
VNU.
Frequency:
48 times a year.
Primary Audience:
Sporting Goods Trade and Investors.
Primary Audience:
Manufacturers, Retailers, Merchandisers
Frequency:
48 times, annually, delivered by fax or e-mail.
Publishing Company:
Bill Communications.

INSIDE TENNIS
2220 MOUNTAIN BOULEVARD
SUITE 200
OAKLAND, CA 94611
510-530-2200
Fax: 510-530-1483
http://www.insidetennis.com
• William G. Simons, Editor
simons@insidetennis.com
• Matt Cronin, Senior Editor
(510) 530-2200
editorial@insidetennis.com
• Richard Osborn, Associate Editor
osborn@insidetennis.com
• William G. Simons, Publisher
simons@insidetennis.com
Frequency:
1 time(s) per month

INSIDE TEXAS RUNNING
2470 GRAY FALLS DRIVE
SUITE 110
HOUSTON, TX 77077-1909
281-759-0555
800-441-9837
Fax: 713-935-0559
marie@runningmags.com
http://www.insidetexasrunning.com
• Lance Phegley, Editor
(281) 759-0555
lance@runningmags.com
• Lee Sheffer, Production Manager
Frequency:
1 time(s) per month
Primary Audience:
Road runners and marathon runners.

Circulation:
10,000
Description:
We are a publisher of a magazine devoted to roadracing and multi-sports (i.e. triathlon).

INSIDE TRIATHLON
1830 NORTH 55TH STREET
BOULDER, CO 80301-2700
303-440-0601
Fax: 303-444-6788
http://www.insidetri.com
Frequency:
1 time(s) per month
Description:
Publication provides complete coverage of the triathlon and duathlon.

INTERNATIONAL AEROBATICS CLUB, INC.
3000 POBERENZY ROAD
OSHKOSH, WI 54902-8939
920-426-4800
800-843-3612
Fax: 920-426-6579
iac@eaa.org
http://www.iac.org
Frequency
12x/year

INTERNATIONAL FIGURE SKATING
420 BOYLSTON STREET 5TH FLOOR
BOSTON, MA 02116
508-756-2595
800-437-5828
Fax: 617-536-0102
http://www.ifsmagazine.com
• Susan Wessling, Editor-in-Chief
swessling@madavor.com
• Susan Fitzgerald, Publisher
(508) 756-2595
sfitzgerald@madavor.com
• Jeff Wolk, Owner
(508) 756-2595
jwolk@madavor.com
• Kathleen Bangs, Staff Writer
(617) 536-0100
Frequency:
6 time(s) per year
Description:
Publication is a international news magazine for the sport of figure skating.

INTERNATIONAL GYMNAST
3214 BART CONNER DRIVE
NORMAN, OK 73072-2406
405-447-9988
Fax: 405-447-5810
http://www.intlgymnast.com
• Dwight Normile, Editor
(405) 447-9988
dnormile@intlgymnast.com
• Ben Fox, Advertising Manager
(405) 364-5344
• Paul Ziert, Publisher
(405) 364-5344
paul@intlgymnast.com
• John Crumlish, Web Site Editor & Staff Writer
(405) 447-9988
jcrumlish@intlgymnast.com
Frequency:
10 time(s) per year
Description:
Publication covers gymnastics for serious competitors, coaches, judges, and enthusiasts; contains information on

international competitions, interviews, training tips, and nutrition.

INTERNATIONAL JOURNAL OF SPORT NUTRITION
1607 NORTH MARKET STREET
CHAMPAIGN, IL 61820
217-351-5076
800-747-4457
Fax: 217-351-2674
journals@hkusa.com
http://www.humankinetics.com
• Ronald Maughan, Co-Editor
r.j.maughan@lboro.ac.uk
• Priscilla Clarkson, Editorial Board Member
• Rainer Martens, Publisher
rainerm@hkusa.com
• Jack Wolowiec, Managing Editor
(217) 351-5076
Frequency:
4 time(s) per year
Description:
Publication focuses on the nutritional aspects of human physical and athletic performance; includes experimental and experiential evidence on all aspects of athletic ability.

INTERNATIONAL JOURNAL OF ATHLETIC THERAPY AND TRAINING
1607 NORTH MARKET STREET
CHAMPAIGN, IL 61820
217-351-5076
800-747-4457
Fax: 217-351-2674
journals@hkusa.com
www.humankinetics.com
• Gary Wilkerson, Editor
(423) 425-5394
gary-wilkerson@utc.edu
• Greg Reed, Journal Director
(423) 757-1733
• Margery Kane, Journal Managing Editor
Frequency:
6 time(s) per year
Description:
Publication is written for sports healthcare providers.

INTERNATIONAL TENNIS WEEKLY
201 ATP BOULEVARD
PONTE VEDRA BEACH, FL 32082-3211
904-285-8000
Fax: 904-285-5966
http://www.atptennis.com
• Alex Kennison, Editor
akennison@atptennis.com
• Alex Kennison, Editor-in-Chief
Frequency:
1 time(s) per week
Description:
Publication features news, information, and statistics concerning ATP Tour players and competitions.

INTERSCHOLASTIC ATHLETIC ADMINISTRATION
PO BOX 690
INDIANAPOLIS, IN 46206
317-972-6900
Fax: 317-822-5700
www.nfhs.org
• Bob Kanaby, Publisher
• Treva Dayton, Editor
• Judy Thomas, Advertising Director
Description:
Professional journal for high school athletic

administrators. Also the official organ for the National Interscholastic Athletic Administrators Association.

Circulation:
6,250. 95% paid subscr, 5% non-paid contr.
Sports:
General
Primary Audience:
High school athletic administrators
Frequency:
Quarterly
Publishing Company:
National Federation of State High School Associations

IRISH SPORTS REPORT
225 WEST COLFAX AVENUE
SOUTH BEND, IN 46626-1000
574-235-6469
Fax: 574-235-6091
isr@irishsportsreport.com
http://www.irishsportsreport.com
• Bill Bilinski, Editor
(574) 235-6331
bbilinski@sbtinfo.com
• Jennifer Gaby, General Manager
(574) 235-6073
• Eric Hansen, Managing Editor
(574) 235-6470
ehansen@sbtinfo.com
• David Ray, Publisher
(574) 235-6241
dray@sbtinfo.com
• Jeff Carroll, Staff Writer
(574) 235-6161
jcarroll@sbtinfo.com
Frequency:
21 time(s) per year
Description:
Publication covers all Notre Dame sports, especially football.

JET SPORTS
27142 BURBANK
FOOTHILL RANCH, CA 92610
714-751-8695
Fax: 631-427-4498
• Rick Lake, Editor
Frequency:
6 time(s) per year
Description:
Publication features news about personal watercraft racing activities sanctioned by the International Jet Sports Boating Association; includes personality profiles of racers, previews of regional clubs, and racing activities.

JOURNAL OF APPLIED SPORT PSYCHOLOGY
DEPARTMENT OF PHYSICAL EDUCATION, HEALTH AND SPORT STUDIES
PHILLIPS HALL
MIAMI UNIVERSITY, OH 45056
513-529-2728
weinber@muohio.edu
www.aaasponline.org/journal.html#eddy
• Robert S. Weinberg, Editor
• Bonnie Berger, Associate Editor of Health Psychology
• Karen Cogan, Associate Editor/Clinical Counseling
• Trent Petrie, Associate Editor/Clinical Counseling
• Robert Eklund, Associate Editor/Performance Psychology

• Thelma Horn, Associate Editor/Social Psychology
Description:
Official journal of the Association for the Advancement of Applied Sport Psychology. Articles and information of interest to sport psychology researchers, practitioners, and coaches.
Circulation:
1,000. Association membership.
Sports:
General
Primary Audience:
Sport psychologists, counselors, coaches, athletes
Frequency:
Twice annually
Publishing Company:
Allen Press

JOURNAL OF ATHLETIC TRAINING
2952 STEMMONS FREEWAY
DALLAS, TX 75247-6103
214-637-6282
800-879-6282
Fax: 214-637-2206
http://www.nata.org/jat/
• Chris Ingersoll, Editor
• Leslie Neistadt, Managing Editor
(706) 494-3322
• Christopher Ingersoll, Editor-in-Chief
(214) 637-6282
ingersoll@virginia.edu
Frequency:
4 time(s) per year
Description:
Publication is geared toward athletic trainers, allied health personnel, students, and physicians participating in sports medicine.

JOURNAL OF LEGAL ASPECTS OF SPORT
WICHITA STATE UNIVERSITY
CAMPUS BOX 16
1845 FAIRMOUNT
WITCHITA, KS 67260-0016
316-978-3340
Fax: 316-798-5451
mary.myers@wichita.edu
www.law.marquette.edu/jw/jlas
• Paul M. Anderson, Editor
• Rebecca Mowrey, Book Review Editor
Description:
Official journal of the Society for the Study of Legal Aspects of Sport & Physical Activity.
Publishing Company:
Scott Printing & Binding.
Frequency:
3 times annually.
Primary Audience:
Association membership.
Sports:
General.
Circulation:
325

JOURNAL OF SPORT BEHAVIOR
JOURNAL OF SPORT BEHAVIOR OFFICE
DEPARTMENT OF PSYCHOLOGY
307 UNIVERSITY BOULEVARD N, UCOM 1000
MOBILE, AL 36608-0002
251-460-6371
Fax: 251-460-6320
chauff@southalabama.edu
www.journalofsportsbehavior.org

• Caitlyn Hauff, Co-Editor
(251) 460-7698
chauff@southalabama.edu
• Benjamin Hill, Co-Editor
(251) 341-3079
bdhill@southalabama.edu
Frequency:
4 time(s) per year
Description:
Publication features original, empirical investigations and theoretical papers dealing with studies of social behavior in the areas of games and sport.

JOURNAL OF SPORT HISTORY
PO BOX 1026
LEMONT, PA 16851-1026
814-238-1288
Fax: 814-238-1288
www.nassh.org
• Ronald A. Smith, Secretary/National
(814) 238-1288
• Melvin Adelman, Editor
(703) 993-2057
Description:
Contains scholarly articles on sport history.
Circulation:
1,000. 100% association membership.
Sports:
General
Primary Audience:
Association membership
Frequency:
Three times annually
Publishing Company:
North American Society for Sport History

JOURNAL OF SPORT MANAGEMENT
1607 NORTH MARKET STREET
CHAMPAIGN, IL 61820
217-351-5076
800-747-4457
Fax: 217-351-2674
humank@hkusa.com
http://www.humankinetics.com
• Jake Jaquet, Journal Director
• Jennifer Davis, Managing Editor
(217) 351-5076
Publishing Company:
Human Kinetics Publishers, Inc.
Frequency:
Quarterly
Primary Audience:
Professionals, scholars and students of sport management
Sports:
General
Circulation:
1062
Description:
Journal for North American Society for Sport Management. Includes theoretical and applied articles pertaining to all areas of sport management including athletic administration, recreation, and leisure.

JOURNAL OF THE PHILOSOPHY OF SPORT
1607 N. MARKET ST
CHAMPAIGN, IL 61820
217-351-5076
800-747-4457
Fax: 217-351-2674
www.kinetics.com
• Greg Reed, Journal Director
• Jeff King, Managing Editor
• J.S. Russell, JPS Editor

Publishing Company:
Human Kinetics Publishers, Inc.
Frequency:
Annual
Primary Audience:
Association membership
Sports:
General
Circulation:
512
Description:
Includes critical reviews of work completed and philosophic discussions about the philosophy of sport. Published annually for the Philosophic Society for the Study of Sport.

JUCO REVIEW
1755 TELSTAR DRIVE
SUITE 103
COLORADO SPRINGS, CO 80920
719-590-9788
Fax: 719-590-7324
www.njcaa.org
• Mary Ellen Leicht, Editor
meleicht@njcaa.org
Publishing Company:
NJCAA
Frequency:
Monthly, Sept-May
Primary Audience:
Association membership
Sports:
General
Circulation:
3,750. 100% association membership.
Description:
Includes articles about college sports, including basketball, baseball, football, volleyball, soccer, tennis. Highlights National Championship events.

JUICE SOUND, SURF SKATE MAGAZINE
2633 LINCOLN BOULEVARD 411
SANTA MONICA, CA 90405
310-399-5336
juicesss@aol.com
http://www.juicemagazine.com
• Jim Murphy, Sports Editor
Frequency:
6 time(s) per year
Description:
Publication features underground music, skateboarding, snowboarding, and surfing; includes lifestyle features, and investigative journalism.

JUNIOR BASEBALL
14 WOODWAY LANE
WILTON, CT 06897
203-210-5726
888-487-2448
Fax: 408-475-3055
editor@juniorbaseball.com
www.juniorbaseball.com
• Jim Beecher, Publisher/Editor
Frequency:
6 time(s) per year
Description:
'America's Youth Baseball Magazine' for players, ages 7-17, their parents, and coaches.
Year Founded:
1996
Publications:
Junior Baseball Magazine and Youth Baseball Star e-zine.

KART MARKETING INTERNATIONAL
PO BOX 101
WHEATON, IL 60189
630-653-7368
Fax: 630-653-2637
karting@msn.com
www.e-kmi.com
• Darrell Sitarz, President/Chief Executive Officer
(630) 653-7368
karting@msn.com
• Craig Ellsworth, Marketing Manager
(630) 653-7368
karting@msn.com
• Len Manley, Sales Director
(859) 983-9234
lenmanley27@aol.com
Nature of Service:
Advertising and Marketing
Publication:
Contains information of interest to people involved with go-karting and go-karting-related businesses.
Frequency:
6 time(s) per year

KEEPING IN TOUCH
13540 LAKE CITY WAY N.E. SUITE 3
SEATTLE, WA 98125
206-367-2420
Fax: 206-367-2636
http://www.varsitycommunications.com
• Earl Starkoff, Publisher
(800) 643-6061
els730@aol.com
Frequency:
3 time(s) per year

KING PANIAGUA
518 5TH AVE
NEW YORK, NY 10036
212-869-7007
Fax: 212-869-7009
• Joseph A. Paniagua, Vice President
• John Mas, Vice President Marketing
Description:
Publishes variety of bilingual magazines in baseball, boxing, and soccer serving the Hispanic market.

LA GOLF MAGAZINE
1451 QUAIL STREET SUITE 208
NEWPORT BEACH, CA 92660-2741
949-833-7601
Fax: 949-833-9895
http://www.churmpublishing.com
• Eric Marson, Editor
(949) 833-7601
emarson@churmpublishing.com
• Steven Churm, Publisher
(949) 833-7601
schurm@churmpublishing.com

LACROSSE MAGAZINE
113 WEST UNIVERSITY PARKWAY
BALTIMORE, MD 21210-3301
410-235-6882
Fax: 410-366-6735
• Paul Krome, Editor
(410) 235-6882
• Kira Muller, Director of Advertising Sales
(410) 235-6882
kmuller@uslacrosse.org
• Bill Tanton, Senior Associate Editor
(410) 235-6882
Frequency:
12 times per year

Description:
Monthly magazine celebrating the lacrosse life style, on and off the field, and delivered to an affluent, acid and active readership.
Primary Audience:
Youth through High School. 91% of audience is age 24 or less.

LATE MODEL DIGEST
P.O. BOX 340
MURPHY, NC 28906
828-837-9539
Fax: 828-837-7718
http://www.latemodeldigest.net
• Jim Carson, Editor
(828) 837-9539
• Brian McLeod, Publisher
Frequency:
24 time(s) per year
Description:
Publication reports on late model stock car racing on pavement.

LATITUDE 38
15 LOCUST AVENUE
MILL VALLEY, CA 94941-2805
415-383-8200
Fax: 415-383-5816
editorial@latitude38.com
http://www.latitude38.com
• John Riise, Managing Editor
(415) 383-8200
• John Arndt, Advertising Sales
(415) 383-8200
john@latitude38.com
• Rob Moore, Senior Editor
(415) 383-8200
rob@latitude38.com
• Richard Spindler, Executive Editor
(415) 383-8200
richard@latitude38.com
• Richard Spindler, Publisher
(415) 383-8200
richard@latitude38.com
• Andy Turpin, Senior Editor
(415) 383-8200
andy@latitude38.com
Description:
Publication is geared toward those with an interest in sailing.

LATITUDES & ATTITUDES
270 PORTFINO WAY SUITE 510
REDONDO BEACH, CA 90277
310-798-3445
888-893-7245
Fax: 310-798-3448
http://www.latsandatts.net
• Sue Morgan, Editor
• Bob Bitchin, Publisher & Co-Editor
(310) 798-3445
bbftw@aol.com
• Mike Sweeney, Advertising Director
(727) 224-2116
Frequency:
6 time(s) per year
Description:
Publication focuses on sailing and long-distance cruising.

LEAGUE OF AMERICAN BICYCLISTS MAGAZINE
1612 K STREET NORTH WEST SUITE 800
WASHINGTON, DC 20006-2802
202-822-1333
Fax: 202-822-1334

media

bikeleague@bikeleague.org
http://www.bikeleague.org
• Elizabeth Preston, Editor
(202) 822-1333
elizabeth@bikeleague.org
Frequency:
4 time(s) per year
Description:
Publication is a membership magazine of the League of American Bicyclists; focuses on bicycle education, advocacy, and recreation.

LETS PLAY HOCKEY
2721 EAST 42ND STREET
MINNEAPOLIS, MN 55406-3061
612-729-0023
Fax: 612-729-0259
letsplay@letsplayhockey.com
http://www.letsplayhockey.com
• Dave McMahon, Editor
editor@letsplaysoftball.com
• Doug Johnson, Publisher
Frequency:
29 time(s) per year
Description:
Publication covers the world of hockey; includes information on the professional sport, equipment, and the media surrounding hockey.

LETS PLAY SOFTBALL
2721 EAST 42ND STREET
MINNEAPOLIS, MN 55406-3061
612-729-0023
Fax: 612-729-0259
http://www.letsplaysoftball.com
• Dave McMahon, Editor-in-Chief
editor@letsplaysoftball.com
• Doug Johnson, Publisher
Frequency:
2 time(s) per month
Description:
Publication is written for softball enthusiasts.

LICENSING BOOK
1501 BROADWAY, STE 500
NEW YORK, NY 10036-5503
212-575-4510
Fax: 212-575-4521
www.licensingbook.com
• Andy Krinner, Publisher
• Jennifer Jaronczak, Advertising Director
• Jim Silver, Group Publisher
Publishing Company:
Adventure Publishing Group, Inc.
Frequency:
Monthly
Primary Audience:
Retailers, Licensors, Licensees, Manufacturers
Sports:
General
Circulation:
22,000. 100% contr non-paid.
Description:
Reports on all aspects of consumer-based licensed properties and licensing activity in the U.S. and abroad. Sports licensing prominently featured.

LIFESTYLE MEDIA
100 WILLIAM STREET
23RD FLOOR
NEW YORK, NY 10038
646-459-4800
Fax: 646-459-4900

• Robe Holmes, Chief Executive Officer / Chairman
• Peter Cipriano, EVP Finance and Operations
Products:
Magazines

LIGHT SPORT AND ULTRALIGHT FLYING MAGAZINE
1085 BAILEY AVENUE
CHATTANOOGA, TN 37404-2802
423-629-5375
Fax: 423-629-5379
www.ultralightflying.com
• Sharon Wilcox, Editor-in-Chief
(423) 629-5375
• Tracy Knauss, Publisher
tracy@ultralightflying.com
• David Prestridge, Advertising Manager
dave@ultralightflying.com
Frequency:
1 time(s) per month
Description:
Publication is written for people who fly ultralight and light sport aircraft.

LINKS MAGAZINE-THE BEST OF GOLF
10 POPE AVENUE EXECUTIVE PARK
SUITE 202
HILTON HEAD ISLAND, SC 29928
843-842-6200
Fax: 843-842-6233
http://www.linksmagazine.com
• Allen Allnoch, Features Editor
(843) 842-6200
• Richard Cerame, Associate Editor
(843) 842-6200
• Andrew Clifford, Marketing Art Director
(203) 977-8600
• David Gould, Editor
(843) 842-6200
• Jack Purcell, Jr., Publisher
(843) 842-6200
jpurcell@linksmagazine.com
• Elaine Yeager, Advertising Coordinator
(843) 842-6200
Frequency:
7 time(s) per year
Description:
Publication contains information of interest to golf enthusiasts, including profiles of new courses.

LIVING ABOARD MAGAZINE
PO BOX 668
3
REDONDO BEACH, CA 90277
888-893-7245
Fax: 310-798-3448
http://www.livingaboard.com
• Judy Behler, Advertising Manager
• Fred C. Walters, Publisher
• Sam Bruce, Assistant Editor
(512) 892-4446
Frequency:
6 time(s) per year
Description:
Publication focuses on how to make the move from land to water and make life on board more enjoyable.

LOG
4918 NORTH HARBOUR DRIVE SUITE
201
SAN DIEGO, CA 92106
619-226-1608
800-841-4377

Fax: 619-226-0573
http://www.thelog.com
• Jane Hascher, Editor
(619) 226-1608
• Duncan McIntosh, Publisher
(619) 226-1608
Frequency:
26 time(s) per year
Description:
Publication focuses on boating news and is published in three separate editions as follows: San Diego Log; Orange County & Los Angeles Log; and the Ventura & San Francisco Log.

LONG BOARD MAGAZINE
110 EAST PALIZADA SUITE 301
SAN CLEMENTE, CA 92672
949-366-8282
Fax: 949-366-8280
lngdmag@aol.com
http://www.longboardmag.com
• Guy Motil, Publisher
lngbdmag@aol.com
Description:
Publication covers surfing.

LONG ISLAND GOLFER MAGAZINE
22 WEST NICHOLAS STREET
HICKSVILLE, NY 11801-3806
516-822-5446
800-564-2445
Fax: 516-822-5446
ligolfer@aol.com
http://www.longislandgolfermagazine.com
• Paul Smith, Managing Editor
• John J. Glozek, Jr., Publisher
Frequency:
6 time(s) per year
Description:
Publication is written for golf enthusiasts; contains instructional articles, human interest stories, and features on destinations for golf vacations.

LOWRIDER BICYCLE
2400 KATELLA AVENUE 11TH FLOOR
ANAHEIM, CA 92806
714-939-2400
Fax: 714-978-6390
info@lowridermagazine.com
http://www.lowridermagazine.com
• Ralph Fuentes, Editor
• John Jarasa, Publisher
Frequency:
4 time(s) per year
Description:
Publication is a custom bicycle magazine.

MAINE BOATS & HARBORS
218 SOUTH MAIN STREET
PO BOX 566
ROCKLAND, ME 04841
207-594-8622
Fax: 207-593-0026
editor@maineboats.com
www.maineboats.com
• John K. Hanson, Publisher
john@maineboats.com
• Polly Saltonstall, Editor
(207) 594-8622
editor@maineboats.com
Frequency:
6 time(s) per year
Description:
Publication focuses on boating in Maine.

MAINE COASTAL NEWS
966 NORTH MAIN STREET
WINTERPORT, ME 04496
207-223-8846
888-333-8379
Fax: 207-223-9004
igmatats@aol.com
http://www.mainescoast.com
• Jon B. Johansen, Editor
• Jon B. Johansen, Publisher
Frequency:
18 time(s) per year
Description:
Publication covers yachting, commercial fishing, and the maritime history of Maine.

MARC TIMES RACING NEWS
5845 MOUNT VERNON AVENUE
PORTAGE, MI 49024
269-345-7086
Fax: 269-345-6397
http://www.marctimes.com
• Dick Beebe, Editor-in-Chief
• Dick Beebe, Publisher
Frequency:
1 time(s) per week
Description:
Publication covers all forms of motorized sports, with emphasis on auto racing and stock car racing, from street stocks to the NASCAR Winston Cup and Indy Cars.

MARINA DOCK AGE
6600 WEST TOUHY AVENUE
NILES, IL 60714-4516
847-647-2900
Fax: 847-647-1155
ppreston@prestonpub.com
http://www.prestonpub.com
• Jerry Koncel, Editor
jkoncel@prestonpub.com
• Janice S. Gordon, Publisher
(847) 647-2900
jgordon@prestonpub.com
Frequency:
8 time(s) per year
Description:
Publication is geared toward owners and operators of marinas; covers marina management, government regulations, and environmental issues.

MARINE BUSINESS JOURNAL
330 NORTH ANDREWS AVENUE
2ND FLOOR
FORT LAUDERDALE, FL 33301-1020
954-522-5515
Fax: 954-522-2260
http://www.marinebusinessjournal.com
• Marilyn Mower, Editor
(954) 522-5515
• Bill Ando, Senior Editor
(954) 522-5515
bill@southernboating.com
• Kellie Mackenroth, Marketing & Circulation Manager
kellie@southernboating.com
Frequency:
Quarterly
Description:
Publication is a resource guide for the marine industry.

MARINER
601 NORTH BRIDGE STREET
ELKTON, MD 21921

410-398-3311
Fax: 410-398-4044
http://www.themariner.net
• Chris Knauss, Editor
(410) 482-7503
• Jeffrey Mezzatesta, Publisher
Frequency:
24 time(s) per year
Description:
Publication contains information on pleasure boating in the Chesapeake Bay area, including coverage of local events.

MARINER'S LOG
17511 EL CAMINO REAL SUITE 148
HOUSTON, TX 77058
281-488-1108
Fax: 281-286-0750
http://www.thecitizenonline.com
• Chuck Hlava, Editor
(281) 488-1108
chlava@hcnonline.com
• Sharon Rickel, Publisher
(281) 488-1108
srickel@hcnonline.com
Frequency:
1 time(s) per month
Description:
Publication is written for boating enthusiasts.

MARYLAND SOCCER NEWS
13540 LAKE CITY WAY N.E. SUITE 3
SEATTLE, WA 98125
206-367-2420
Fax: 206-367-2636
http://www.varsitycommunications.com
• Jay Goldstein, Editor
(410) 987-7898
Frequency:
4 time(s) per year

MATERIAL MATTERS
21-00 STATE ROUTE 208
FAIR LAWN, NJ 07410
800-665-2456
Fax: 201-796-5206
http://golfproductnews.com
• Ruth Rasche, Editor
(352) 332-1252
ruth@naylor.com
• Steve Stramm, Publisher
(352) 332-1252
Frequency:
5 time(s) per year
Description:
Publication features apparel for golf players.

MEDIA SPORTS BUSINESS
126 CLOCK TOWER PLACE
CARMEL, CA 93923-8734
831-624-1536
Fax: 831-625-3225
www.kagan.com
• Robin Flynn, Analyst
• Larry Gerbrandt, Analyst
• Sharon Armbrust, Analyst
• Derek Baine, Analyst
• John Mansell, Analyst
• Ian Olgeirson, Analyst
• Richelle Elberg, Analyst
• Deana Myers, Analyst
Publishing Company:
Paul Kagan Associates, Inc.
Frequency:
Monthly
Primary Audience:
Sports media executives

Sports:
General
Circulation:
100% paid subscr.
Description:
Newsletter dealing with sports media rights fees, cable TV syndication opportunities and developments, regional sports network census, ratings, viewership data, team valuations, etc.

MEN'S JOURNAL
1290 AVE OF THE AMERICAS, 2ND FL
NEW YORK, NY 10104
212-484-1616
Fax: 212-484-3435
www.mensjournal.com
• Jann S. Wenner, Editor-in-Chief
• Bob Wallace, Editor
Description:
Focuses on features covering sports travel, fitness and adventure of interest to the active male. Covers sporting equipment reviews, new products, and other information relating to the market.
Circulation:
225,000. 90% newsstand, 10% paid subscr.
Sports:
Outdoor, recreational sports
Primary Audience:
Consumer
Frequency:
Monthly
Publishing Company:
Straight Arrow Publishers, Inc.

METRO SPORTS NEW YORK
259 WEST 30TH STREET 3RD FLOOR
NEW YORK, NY 10001
212-563-7329
Fax: 212-563-7573
http://www.metrosportsny.com
• Jeremy Shweder, Managing Editor
jshweder@metrosports.com
• Doug Kaplan, Publisher
(312) 421-1551
dkaplan@metrosports.com
• Jeremy Shweder, Editorial Director
jshweder@metrosports.com
Frequency:
1 time(s) per month
Description:
Publication focuses on sports, recreation, and travel.

METRO SPORTS NY
259 W. 30TH STREET
3RD FLOOR
NEW YORK CITY, NY 10001
212-563-7329
Fax: 212-563-7573
www.metrosportsny.com
• Doug Kaplan, President/Publisher
doug@windycitysports.com
• Melanie Stuparyk, Managing Editor
melanie@metrosports.com
• Michelle Mullin, Sales Vice President
michelle@windycitysports.com
Description:
Encourages and inspires readers' commitments to sports and fitness. Offers sound enlightened advice on life in the active mode. Includes leading aerobics and fitness consumer events in the Northeast; Boston fitness events.
Circulation:
130,000 total. New York Metro: 80,000;

Boston: 50,000. 90% contr non-paid, 5% paid subscr, 5% association membership.
Sports:
Skiing, tennis, aerobics, running, cycling, triathlons, in-line skating, fitness
Primary Audience:
Consumer
Frequency:
10 times annually
Publishing Company:
Tate House Enterprises, Inc.
Additional Offices:
164 Brattle St, Cambridge, MA 02138. 617 492-0636; FAX: 617 492-0756. Connecticut Office: 415 Howe Ave, Shelton, CT 06484. 203 924-0141; FAX: 203 924-8434. Washington/Baltimore Office: 2779 N. Wakefield St, Arlington, VA 22207. 703 528-4154; FAX: 703 528-4239

METRO SPORTS WASHINGTON
4405 EAST WEST HIGHWAY SUITE 206B
BETHESDA, MD 20814
202-289-4551
Fax: 301-907-0973
http://metrosportsdc.com
• Jeremy Shweder, Editor
jshweder@metrosports.com
• Doug Kaplan, Publisher
Frequency:
1 time(s) per month
Description:
Publication focuses on sports, recreation, and travel.

MICHIGAN GOLFER
P.O. BOX 7007
GRAND RAPIDS, MI 49510-7007
734-507-0241
http://www.webgolfer.com
• Art McCafferty, Editor
artmccaf@glsp.com
• Art McCafferty, Advertising Manager
Frequency:
6 time(s) per year

MICHIGAN LINKS
24116 RESEARCH DRIVE
FARMINGTON HILLS, MI 48335
248-478-9242
Fax: 248-478-5536
http://www.gam.org
• Tonia Branch, Publisher & Editor
(248) 478-9242
tbranch@gam.org
• Ed Peabody, Publisher
(248) 691-1800
epeabody@hourdetroit.com
Frequency:
6 time(s) per year
Description:
Publication is devoted to the most active golfers in the state of Michigan.

MICHIGAN SNOWMOBILER
P.O. BOX 417
EAST JORDAN, MI 49727-0417
231-536-2371
Fax: 231-536-7691
publisher@michsnowmag.com
http://www.michsnowmag.com
• Lyle Shipe, Editor-in-Chief
• Lyle Shipe, Advertising Manager
• Lyle Shipe, Publisher
Frequency:
6 time(s) per year
Description:

Publication features information about snowmobiles and related activities.

MICHIGAN SOCCER
13540 LAKE CITY WAY N.E. SUITE 3
SEATTLE, WA 98125
206-367-2420
Fax: 206-367-2636
http://www.varsitycommunications.com
• Scott Leader, Editor
Frequency:
4 time(s) per year

MID OHIO GOLFER
5255 SINCLAIR ROAD
COLUMBUS, OH 43229-7513
614-848-4653
Fax: 614-848-3838
• Phil Shie, Editor
• Max Brown, Publisher
Frequency:
18 time(s) per year
Description:
Publication serves golfers throughout central Ohio and the surrounding area.

MID-ATLANTIC THOROUGHBRED
30 EAST PADONIA ROAD SUITE 303
TIMONIUM, MD 21093
410-252-2100
Fax: 410-560-0503
info@marylandthoroughbred.com
www.marylandthoroughbred.com
• Joe Clancy, Editor
(410) 252-2100
editor@marylandthoroughbred.com
Frequency:
Monthly
Description:
Publication contains information of interest to Thoroughbred owners, breeders, and trainers in Maryland, New Jersey, North Carolina, Pennsylvania, Delaware, Virginia, and West Virginia.
Primary Audience:
Thoroughbred breeders, owners, trainers and enthusiasts in the Mid-Atlantic region.

MID-SOUTH HORSE REVIEW
16814 HIGHWAY 64
SOMERVILLE, TN 38068-6156
901-465-4042
800-869-7941
Fax: 901-465-5493
http://www.midsouthhorsereview.com
• Don Dowdle, Publisher
don@gofayette.com
Frequency:
1 time(s) per month

MID-STATES RACING NEWS
719 DES MOINES STREET
WEBSTER CITY, IA 50595-2117
515-832-3713
Fax: 515-832-4531
http://www.mrnol.com
• Howard Mellinger, Publisher
(515) 832-6043
Frequency:
34 time(s) per year
Description:
Publication is an auto racing magazine; publishes weekly April-September and monthly October-March.

MIDWEST RACING NEWS
1001 LISBON AVENUE
MILWAUKEE, WI 53222
262-238-6397
800-432-4212
Fax: 262-242-9450
http://www.mrnol.com
• Brian Gapinski, Editor
• Ken Ubert, Publisher
Frequency:
1 time(s) per week
Description:
Publication contains auto racing news.

MIDWEST SOCCER NEWS
4030 MOUNT CARMEL-TOBASCO SUITE 317
CINCINNATI, OH 45255
800-511-1574
Fax: 513-688-0526
http://hammerhead.net/newpublishing.html
• Beverly Spearman, Staff Writer
Frequency:
4 time(s) per year

MIGALA REPORT
247 W. SCOTT STREET
SUITE 208
CHICAGO, IL 60610
312-932-4002
Fax: 312-932-9177
www.migalareport.com
• Dan Migala, Founder/Publisher
• Katie Migala, Customer Service
Nature of Sports Service:
Electronic newletter which provides sports industry executives with information and trends for ticketing and sponsorship issues.
Sports Service Founded:
2003

MINNESOTA GOLFER
6550 YORK AVENUE, SOUTH SUITE 211
EDINA, MN 55435
952-927-4643
800-642-4405
Fax: 952-927-9642
wp@mngolf.org
http://www.mngolf.org
• W.P. Ryan, Editor
(952) 345-3966
wp@mngolf.org
Frequency:
4 time(s) per year
Description:
Association publication that contains stories, profiles, and features on the Minnesota golf scene, including tournament information, results, and where to play.
Circulation:
80,000

MINNESOTA HOCKEY JOURNAL
6160 SUMMIT DRIVE
MINNEAPOLIS, MN 55422
763-595-0808
Fax: 763-595-0016
info@tpgsports.com
http://www.tpgsports.com
• Greg Anzelc, Editor
(763) 595-0808
greg@tpgsports.com
• Greg Ancelz, Editor
(763) 595-0808
Frequency:
5 time(s) per year

MINNESOTA SOCCER TIMES
12510 NORTH EAST 33RD AVENUE
SUITE 301
SEATTLE, WA 98125
206-367-2420
Fax: 206-367-2636
http://www.varsitycommunications.com
• Charles Beene, Editor
(206) 367-2420
charles@varsitycommunications.com
Frequency:
8 time(s) per year
Description:
Publication contains association news, coaching tips, and tournament updates.

MISSISSIPPY IN TOUCH
13540 LAKE CITY WAY N.E. SUITE 3
SEATTLE, WA 98125
206-367-2420
Fax: 206-367-2636
http://www.varsitycommunications.com
• Earl Starkoff, Publisher
(800) 643-6061
els730@aol.com
Frequency:
4 time(s) per year

MOD-STOCK COMPETITION
360 B STREET
IDAHO FALLS, ID 83402
208-524-7000
800-638-0153
Fax: 208-522-5241
info@snowest.com
www.snowest.com
• Lane Lindstrom, Editor
(208) 542-2234
lindstrm@snowest.com
• Steve Janes, Publisher
(208) 542-2214
stevejanes@snowest.com
• Ryan Harris, Assistant Editor
(208) 542-2243
rharris@snowest.com
Frequency:
1 time(s) per year
Description:
Publication contains technical information on all aspects of performance snowmobiling, as well as new product news for the performance snowmobile community.
Circulation:
36,000

MORGAN HORSE
4066 SHELBURNE ROAD
SUITE 5
SHELBURNE, VT 05482-7521
802-985-4944
Fax: 802-985-8897
magazine@morganhorse.com
http://www.morganhorse.com
• Stephen Kinney, Editorial Director
(802) 985-4944
stephen@morganhorse.com
Frequency:
1 time(s) per month
Description:
Publication aims to promote the Morgan horse and the activities of Morgan owners and AMHA members.

MOTOR BOATING
18 MARSHALL STREET
SUITE 114
NORWALK, CT 06854-2237
203-299-5900
Fax: 203-299-5951
http://www.motorboating.com
• John Wooldridge, Managing Editor
(212) 649-4127
• Jeanne Craig, Executive Editor
(203) 299-5958
jeanne.craig@time4.com
• Dan Fales, Editor-at-Large
(207) 372-8598
danfales@verizon.net
• Brad Kovach, Senior Associate Editor
brad.kovach@time4.com
Frequency:
1 time(s) per month
Description:
Publication is written for boating enthusiasts; includes information on purchasing, maintaining, and enjoying boats.

MOTORACING
P.O. BOX 1203
PLEASANTON, CA 94566-0120
925-846-7728
800-585-3559
76067.1750@compuserve.com
http://www.usmotoracing.com
• John Kelly, Publisher & Editor
(925) 846-7728
• Patricia J. Kelly, Advertising Manager
• John F. Kelly, Jr., Editor-in-Chief
• John F. Kelly, Jr., Publisher
Frequency:
1 time(s) per month
Description:
Publication covers Western United States sports car road races, oval track races; both pavement and dirt surfaces.

MOUNTAIN BIKE
2509 WEST EMPIRE AVENUE SUITE 2
BURBANK, CA 91504-3320
610-967-8722
Fax: 610-967-8960
http://www.mountainbike.com
• Jennifer Sherry, Senior Editor
• Robert Davidowitz, Group Publisher
(212) 573-0354
• Nicholas Freedman, Publisher
(610) 967-7544
mbelectro@earthlink.net
• Matt Phillips, Senior Editor
(818) 953-8732
mbelectro@earthlink.net
• Susan G. Snyder, Advertising Business Manager
(610) 259-4082
Frequency:
1 time(s) per month
Description:
Publication focuses on off-road bicycling adventure, techniques, equipment, and racing.

MOUNTAIN BIKE ACTION
25233 ANZA DRIVE
VALENCIA, CA 91355
661-295-1910
800-767-0345
Fax: 661-295-1178
http://www.mbaction.com
• Jody Weisel, Features Editor
(661) 295-1910
• Ryan Cleek, Assistant Editor
(661) 367-2150
• Richard Cunningham, Editor-at-Large
(661) 295-1910
• Carrie Greer, Executive Assistant
cgreer@hi-torque.com
• Carrie Greer, Office Manager
• Roland Hinz, Publisher
(661) 295-1910
• John Ker, Assistant Editor
(661) 295-1910
• Jimmy Mac, Editor
(661) 295-1910
• Jim McIlvain, Editor
(661) 367-2145
• Robb Mesecher, Advertising Manager
(661) 367-2105
robbm@hi-torque.com
• Mark Thomas, Advertising Executive
(661) 295-1910
Frequency:
1 time(s) per month
Description:
Publication is written for all-terrain bicycle enthusiasts.

MOUNTAIN BIKING
9509 VASSAR AVENUE UNIT A
CHATSWORTH, CA 91311
818-700-6868
Fax: 818-700-6282
http://www.mtbiking.com
• Alan Davis, Editor
(818) 700-6868
adavis@challengeweb.com
Frequency:
1 time(s) per month

MOUNTAIN ZONE
316 OCCIDENTAL AVE S.
STE 400
SEATTLE, WA 98104
206-839-8719
800-644-5236
Fax: 206-625-0271
info@mountainzone.com
www.mountainzone.com
• Tim O'Mara, President
Description:
Online magazine focusing on all mountain sports activities, including cybercasting of all types of mountain sports events.

MOUNTAINEER LAKES & MOUNTAINS
ROUTE 3 FAIRGROUNDS ROAD
PLYMOUTH, NH 03264-9803
603-536-1311
800-491-4612
Fax: 603-536-8940
http://www.record-enterprise.com
• Leigh Sharps, Editor
Frequency:
1 time(s) per week
Description:
Publication focuses on ski tours.

MUSCULAR DEVELOPMENT
690 ROUTE 25A
SETAUKET, NY 11733
631-751-9696
Fax: 631-751-9699
editor@musculardevelopment.com
http://www.musculardevelopment.com
• Steve Blechman, Editor
sblechman@arp-ink.com
• Steve Blechman, Editor-in-Chief
sblechman@arp-ink.com
• Adam Ginsberg, Advertising Manager
(631) 751-9696
Frequency:
1 time(s) per month

Description:
Publication features Sports Nutrition training and performance.

MUSHING MAGAZINE
PO BOX 1195
WILLOW, AK 99688
907-495-2468
Fax: 907-479-3137
editor@mushing.com
http://www.mushing.com
• Mary Haley, Managing Editor
• Amanda Byrd, Managing Editor
(907) 458-0888
editor@mushing.com
Frequency:
6 time(s) per year
Description:
Publication provides information and entertainment content covering the sports of dogsledding, skijoring, carting, dog packing, and weight pulling.

NAIA
23500 W. 105TH ST
OLATHE, KS 66051
913-791-0044
Fax: 816-595-8301
khenry@naia.org
www.naia.org
• Steve Baker, President/Chief Operating Officer
• Jim Carr, Chief Operating Officer
• Mark Chiarucci, Director Corporate Sponsorships Regional Dire
• Natalie Cronkhite, Director of Championships
Circulation:
7,500. 95% association membership, 5% paid subscr.
Sports:
General - collegiate
Primary Audience:
Association membership
Frequency:
Monthly (11 times yearly)
Publishing Company:
NAIA

NASCAR ILLUSTRATED
120 WEST MOREHEAD STREET
SUITE 320
CHARLOTTE, NC 28202-1826
704-973-1300
800-883-7323
Fax: 704-973-1303
• Jon Gunn, Managing Editor
• Steve Waid, Executive Editor
(704) 973-1329
swaid@amcity.com
• Steve Waid, Publisher
(704) 973-1329
• Mark Ashenfelter, Associate Editor
(704) 973-1300
Frequency:
1 time(s) per month
Description:
Publication features Winston Cup racing reports, profiles, interviews, and photo spreads.

NASCAR MAGAZINE
1801 WEST INTERNATIONAL SPEEDWAY BLVD
DAYTONA BEACH, FL 32114

386-253-0611
Fax: 386-239-8615
http://www.nascar.com
• Paul Schaefer, Editor
(386) 947-6788
pschaefer@nascar.com
Frequency:
1 time(s) per month
Description:
Magazine is the official membership publication of the National Association for Stock Car Racing.

NATIONAL CROQUET CALENDAR
718 EAST JACKSON STREET
MONMOUTH, OR 97361-1814
503-838-5697
• Garth Eliassen, Publisher & Editor
(503) 838-5697
eliassen@open.org
• Garth Eliassen, Publisher
Frequency:
6 time(s) per year
Description:
Publication covers the world of championship croquet; includes news, results, schedules of events, and strategy analysis.

NATIONAL DRAGSTER
P.O. BOX 5555
GLENDORA, CA 91740-4694
626-963-8475
Fax: 626-335-4307
http://www.nhra.com
• Phil Burgess, Editor
(626) 963-8475
• Vicky Walker, Managing Editor
(626) 963-7695
vwalker@nhra.com
Frequency:
1 time(s) per week
Description:
Publication serves the drag racing industry.

NATIONAL HAWKEYE RACING NEWS
180 EAST 5TH ST
PO BOX 720
VINTON, IA 52349-2500
319-472-4763
800-472-4006
Fax: 319-472-3117
http://www.hawkeyeracingnews.com
• Jim Morrison, Editor
(319) 472-4763
• Debbie Madorin, Publisher & Editor
(319) 472-4763
• Kathy Root, Publisher
Frequency:
33 time(s) per year
Description:
Hawkeye Racing news is a Midwestern based publication in its 45th year of publication. From Sprints and Midgets to Late Models to Modifieds to Short Tracks to entry-level divisions we cover it all. We offer our readers 33 issues a year and we are weekly from April until October.

NATIONAL PAL COPSNKIDS CRONICLES
618 N. U.S. HWY 1, STE 201
N. PALM BEACH, FL 33408
561-844-1823
Fax: 561-863-6120
copnkid1@aol.com
• Brad Hart, Associate Director/Sports

Description:
Communications from national to locals (PAL). Subjects covered - latest information in the sports world, fundraising programs, events, tournaments, success stories - sport page editorial.
Circulation:
147,756. 80% association memb, 20% contr non-paid.
Sports:
General
Primary Audience:
Association membership, corporate and local community coaches, law enforcement agencies/departments, national associations, media
Frequency:
Quarterly
Publishing Company:
Natl Assn of Police Athletic Leagues

NATIONAL SPEED SPORT NEWS
6509 HUDSPETH ROAD
HARRISBURG, NC 28075
704-455-2531
Fax: 704-455-2605
http://www.nationalspeedsportnews.com
• Mike Kerchner, Managing Editor
(704) 455-8050
mikek@nationalspeedsportnews.com
• Chris Economaki, Editor In Chief
(704) 455-2531
• Mike Kerchner, Associate Editor
(704) 455-2531
mikek@nationalspeedsportnews.com
• Michael Parra, Advertising Director
(704) 455-2531
mparra@nationalspeedsportnews.com
• Jim Savas, Publisher
(704) 455-2531
Frequency:
1 time(s) per week
Description:
Covers all professional motorsports in U.S. plus F-1
Circulation:
35,000
Primary Audience:
Motorsports fans and participants
Sport:
Automobile racing

NBA INSIDE STUFF
355 LEXINGTON AVENUE
NEW YORK, NY 10017-6603
212-697-1460
Fax: 212-286-8154
t.gervino@pspsports.com
http://www.nba.com
Frequency:
6 time(s) per year
Description:
Publication is the official teen magazine of the NBA, providing coverage of the league for fans aged 12 to 19.

NCAA NEWS
700 W. WASHINGTON
INDIANAPOLIS, IN 46206-6222
317-917-6222
Fax: 317-917-6831
news_editorial@ncaa.org
www.ncaa.org
• P. Da Pickle, Editor
• Jack L. Copeland, Managing Editor
Description:
Primary means of communication for NCAA

with its more than 1,000 member institutions, organizations and conferences, as well as the news media and other persons interested in staying abreast of developments in college athletics. Covers hard news of all NCAA activities and includes administrative content important to all athletic administrators and coaches, as well as classified employment advertising for positions in athletics.
Circulation:
25,000. 100% paid.
Sports:
NCAA sponsored sports
Primary Audience:
Association membership
Frequency:
Weekly except biweekly in summer
Publishing Company:
National Collegiate Athletic Association

NET NEWS
450 NORTHRIDGE PARKWAY
SUITE 202
ATLANTA, GA 30350
770-650-1102
800-536-5669
Fax: 770-650-2848
http://www.knowatlanta.com
• Laura Newsome, Editor
(770) 650-1102
laura@knowatlanta.com
• John Hanna, Publisher
• John Hanna, Advertising Manager/Publisher
(770) 650-1102
hanna@knowatlanta.com
Frequency:
6 time(s) per year
Description:
Publication contains information about the Atlanta Lawn Tennis Association and its members; includes articles on new products, tennis camps, tennis resorts, tennis communities, preventive medicine, and nutrition.

NEW ENGLAND SPORTS
11 HASKAL STREET
SUITE 2
BEVERLY, MA 01915
978-236-1001
Fax: 978-236-1061
http://www.metrosportsboston.com
• Rebecca Delaney, Editor
rdelaney@metrosports.com
• Jeff Banowetz, Editorial Director
jeff@twincitiessports.com
• Doug Kaplan, President/Publisher
doug@windycitysports.com
Frequency:
1 time(s) per month

NEW ENGLAND WINDSURFING JOURNAL
P.O. BOX 371
MILFORD, CT 06460-0371
203-876-2001
Fax: 203-876-2868
newjournal@aol.com
http://www.worldwindsurf.com
• Peter Bogucki, Advertising Director
(203) 876-2001
• Peter Bogucki, Advertising Director
• Peter Bogucki, Publisher
Frequency:
9 time(s) per year

Description:
Publication contains windsurfing news.

NEW YORK METS INSIDE PITCH
505 SOUTH DUKE STREET SUITE 504
DURHAM, NC 27701-3153
919-688-0218
800-421-7751
Fax: 919-682-1532
comanpub@comanpub.com
• Bryan Hoch, Managing Editor
(201) 483-3520
metsinsidepitch@aol.com
Frequency:
1 time(s) per month
Description:
Publication includes player features, historical articles, and complete team and individual statistics.

NEW YORK SPORTS & NEWS DIGEST
217 W. FULTON ST
LONG BEACH, NY 11561
516-432-7074
Fax: 516-432-7074
• Robert Elkin, Editor
Description:
Covers all national sports, especially New York and New Jersey; features on players; flashbacks in sports.
Circulation:
50,000+. Newsstand and paid subscription.
Sports:
High School, College, Professional.
Primary Audience:
Consumer.
Frequency:
Monthly.

NEW YORK TIMES SYNDICATION
620 8TH AVENUE
FRNT 5
NEW YORK, NY 10168
212-556-4063
Fax: 212-499-3382
www.nytsyn.com
• Cristian Edwards, President
(212) 499-3300
• Michael Oricchio, Managing Editor
(212) 499-3300
• Tim Hilchey, Deputy Managing Editor
(212) 499-3300
• Lawrence Paul, Executive Editor
(212) 499-3300
Description:
Newspaper syndication of sports stories, graphics and photos from THE NEW YORK TIMES and other U.S. and international sources.

NFHS NEWS
PO BOX 690
INDIANAPOLIS, IN 46206
317-972-6900
Fax: 317-822-5700
www.nfhs.org
• Robert Kanady, Executive Director
• Bruce L. Howard, Director of Pulications and Communications
• Judy Thomas, Director of Marketing
Description:
Details NFS and member state association programs and services; promotes professional growth and image of high school coaches, officials and athletic directors and serves the interests of interscholastic athletic programs of 20,000

member high schools accordingly.
Circulation:
12,000 95% association memb, 5% contr non-paid.
Sports:
General
Primary Audience:
Association membership (State High School Associations; National Federation of Speech and Music Organizations)
Frequency:
Nine issues annually
Publishing Company:
National Federation of State High School Associations

NIRSA JOURNAL
4185 SOUTHWEST RESEARCH WAY
CORVALLIS, OR 97333-1067
541-766-8211
Fax: 541-766-8284
sarah@nirsa.org
http://www.nirsa.org
• Sarah Hubart, Managing Editor
(541) 766-8211
sarah@nirsa.org
Frequency:
2 time(s) per year
Description:
Publication is written for recreational sports administrators.

NORDIC NETWORK
PO BOX 818
WOODSTOCK, VT 05091
802-236-3021
ccsaa@xcski.org
• Reese Brown, Editor
(802) 236-3021
reese@xcski.org
Frequency:
4 time(s) per year

NORTH AMERICAN PYLON
P.O. BOX 1203
PLEASANTON, CA 94566-0120
925-846-7728
800-585-3559
76067.1750@compuserve.com
http://www.napylon.com
• John F. Kelly, Jr., Editor
• Patricia Kelly, Business Manager
(925) 846-7728
• John F. Kelly, Jr., Publisher
Frequency:
1 time(s) per month
Description:
Publication covers sports car autocrossing and automotive time trial events in the United States and Canada.

NORTH CAROLINA YOUTH SOCCER
12510 NORTH EAST 33RD AVENUE
SUITE 300
SEATTLE, WA 98125
206-367-2420
Fax: 206-367-2636
http://www.varsitycommunications.com
• Charles Beene, Editor
(206) 367-2420
charles@varsitycommunications.com
Frequency:
6 time(s) per year

NSGA RETAIL FOCUS
1601 FEEHANVILLE DRIVE
MOUNT PROSPECT, IL 60056
847-296-6742
Fax: 847-391-9827
info@nsga.org
http://www.nsga.org
• Larry Weindruch, Editor
(847) 296-6742
lweindruch@nsga.org
• Paul M. Prince, Advertising Manager
(847) 296-6742
pprince@nsga.org
• Larry Weindruch, Publisher
(847) 296-6742
lweindruch@nsga.org
• Paul M Prince, Editorial
(800) 815-5422
Frequency:
6 time(s) per year
Description:
Publication is geared toward top level
executives of sporting goods retail
companies.

OCEAN NAVIGATOR
58 FORE STREET
PORTLAND, ME 04101-4502
207-772-2466
Fax: 207-772-2879
editors@oceannavigator.com
http://www.oceannavigator.com
• Tim Queeney, Editor
(207) 772-2466
tqueeney@oceannavigator.com
• Alex Agnew, Publisher
(207) 772-2466
aagnew@oceannavigator.com
Frequency:
8 time(s) per year
Description:
Publication focuses on offshore and coastal
voyaging techniques, procedures, and
equipment; also covers meteorology,
astronomy, and oceanography for mariners.

OFFSHORE
500 VICTORY ROAD
QUINCY, MA 02171
617-221-1400
Fax: 617-847-1871
http://www.boatingonline.net
• Gaelen Phyfe, Managing Editor
• Joe Myerson, Senior Editor
• Richard Royer, Publisher
rjroyer@cbmmag.net
• Kendra Sousa, Advertising Director
Frequency:
1 time(s) per month
Description:
Publication contains articles about boats
and boating in the Northeast.

OHIO SOCCER
13540 LAKE CITY WAY N.E. SUITE 3
SEATTLE, WA 98125
206-367-2420
Fax: 206-367-2636
http://www.varsitycommunications.com
• Kay Catlett, Editor
(330) 659-0989
oysan@aol.com
Frequency:
5 time(s) per year

OHIO STANDARDBRED
12555 BENNER ROAD
RITTMAN, OH 44270-9703
330-925-3040
Fax: 330-927-6890
trogdon@apk.net
http://www.tradingpostnewspapers.com
• Mike Trogdon, Managing Editor
(330) 722-6322
mtrogdon@thepostnewspapers.com
• Bruce Trogdon, President/Publisher
(330) 925-3040
btrogdon@thepostnewspapers.com
Frequency:
1 time(s) per week
Description:
Publication covers Ohio harness racing.

OREGON CYCLING MAGAZINE
455 WEST 1ST AVENUE
EUGENE, OR 97401-2276
541-686-9885
Fax: 541-344-1197
ocycling@catoregon.org
http://www.catoregon.org
• Karl Benedek, Editor
Frequency:
10 time(s) per year
Description:
Publication covers information of interest to
bicycling enthusiasts in Oregon, including
touring, racing, commuting, and mountain
biking.

OREGON GOAL LINES
12510 NORTH EAST 33RD AVENUE
SUITE 301
SEATTLE, WA 98125
206-367-2420
Fax: 206-367-2636
http://www.varsitycommunications.com
• Charles Beene, Editor
(206) 367-2420
charles@varsitycommunications.com
Frequency:
7 time(s) per year
Description:
Publication features articles that bring
readers reliable news and information about
soccer.

OUTDOOR AMERICA MAGAZINE
707 CONSERVATION LANE
GAITHERSBURG, MD 20878
301-548-0150
800-453-5463
Fax: 301-548-0146
general@iwla.org
www.iwla.org
• Paul Hansen, Executive Director
• Jason McGarvey, Editor
Publishing Company:
NA
Frequency:
Quarterly
Primary Audience:
Association membership
Sports:
Fishing, hunting, camping, hiking, canoeing,
winter sports
Circulation:
40,000. 95% association memb, 5% other.
Description:
Contains articles on nationwide
conservation issues plus features on
outdoor recreation.

OUTDOOR LIFE
TWO PARK AVE
10TH FL
NEW YORK, NY 10016
212-779-5000
800-227-2224
Fax: 212-779-5366
olmagazine@aol.com
www.outdoorlife.com
• Todd Smith, Editor-in-Chief
(212) 779-5090
• Camille Rankin, Senior Managing Editor
(212) 779-5244
• Colin Moore, Executive Editor
(212) 779-5246
• John Snow, Articles Editor
(212) 779-5258
• Frank Miniter, Senior Editor/New Products
(212) 779-5254
• John Taranto, Associate Editor/Midwest &
West Regions
(212) 779-5101
• Will Snyder, Associate Editor/East & South
Regions
(212) 779-5401
• Joi Harvey, Senior Administrative
Assistant
(212) 779-5090
Publishing Company:
Time, Inc.
Frequency:
9 issues per year.
Circulation:
925,000.
Primary Audience:
Hunters, Fishermen.

OUTSIDE MAGAZINE
400 MARKET ST
SANTA FE, NM 87501
505-989-7100
Fax: 505-989-4700
letters@outsidemag.com
www.outsidemag.com
• Lawrence J. Burke,
Chairman/Editor-In-Chief
• Hal Espen, Editor
Description:
Active outdoor lifestyle magazine dedicated
to inspiring people to enjoy fuller, more
rewarding lives through year-round editorial
coverage of the participatory sports, travel,
adventure, people, politics, art and literature
of the world outside.
Circulation:
NA.
Sports:
Year-round sports
Primary Audience:
Consumer
Frequency:
Monthly
Publishing Company:
Mariah Publications Corp.

OUTSIDE PITCH
722 LIGHT STREET
BALTIMORE, MD 21230-3850
410-234-8888
Fax: 410-234-1029
http://www.outsidepitch.com
• David Hill, Editor
(410) 234-8888
• Robert Peregoy, Advertising Manager
• David Simone, Publisher
(410) 234-8888

Frequency:
9 time(s) per year
Description:
Publication features articles on the Baltimore Orioles baseball team.

PACIFIC NORTHWEST GOLFER
355 118TH AVENUE S.E. SUITE 100
BELLEVUE, WA 98005
206-526-1238
Fax: 206-343-4784
http://www.pngamedia.com
• Paul Ramsdell, Editor
(206) 343-4788
• John Bodenahmer, Publisher & Editor
(206) 526-1238
Frequency:
4 time(s) per year
Description:
Publication focuses on topics of interest to golfers in the northwestern United States.

PACKER REPORT
112 MARKET STREET
SUN PRAIRIE, WI 53590
608-837-2200
Fax: 608-825-3053
packredted@aol.com
http://www.packerreport.com
• Todd Korth, Editor
(920) 497-6500
packrepted@aol.com
• Art Daley, Columnist
(920) 497-7225
packrepted@aol.com
• Johnny Gray, Columnist
gray24@tds.net
• Lee Remmel, Columnist
(920) 497-6500
remmell@packers.com
Frequency:
26 time(s) per year
Description:
Publication contains information of interest to fans of the National Football League in general, and the Green Bay Packers in particular.

PADDLER
735 OAK
STEAMBOAT SPRINGS, CO 80487
970-879-1450
Fax: 970-870-1404
editor@aca-paddler.org
http://www.paddlermagazine.com
• Jeff Moag, Managing Editor
(970) 879-1450
jeff@paddlermagazine.com
• Eugene Buchanan, Editor-in-Chief
(970) 879-1450
eugene@paddlermagazine.com
• Eugene Buchanan, Publisher
(970) 879-1450
eugene@paddlermagazine.com
• Kevin Thompson, Advertising Director
(970) 879-1450
kevin@paddlermagazine.com
Frequency:
6 time(s) per year
Description:
Publication is a resource for paddle sports enthusiasts from beginner to expert; includes advice for those who paddle flat water and white water in canoes, kayaks, rafts, sit-on tops, wave skis, and surf skis.

PAINT HORSE JOURNAL
2800 MEACHAM BOULEVARD
FORT WORTH, TX 76137
817-834-2742
Fax: 817-222-8466
jnice@apha.com
http://www.painthorsejournal.com
• Jessica Smith, Managing Editor
Frequency:
1 time(s) per month
Description:
Publication features articles for horse enthusiasts interested in riding, training, breeding or racing American Paint horses.

PAINTBALL MAGAZINE
4201 VANOWEN PLACE
BURBANK, CA 91505
818-845-2656
Fax: 818-845-7761
http://www.paintball.com
• Jessica Sparks, Editor
(818) 845-2656
• Gabe Frimmel, Advertising Manager
(818) 845-2656
Frequency:
6 time(s) per year
Description:
Publication features news and events for the paintball enthusiast.

PANASTADIA INTERNATIONAL
STADIUM CENTRE II, HALL FARM HOUSE
9 HIGH ST
CASTLE DONINGTON
DERBYSHIRE, ENGLAND DE74 2PP
www.panstadia.com
• Julian A. Radley
• Tony Chakraborty, Editor
• Katie Else, Marketing Director
Description:
Journal covering the international sports facility industry.
Frequency:
4 times a year

PAR EXCELLANCE MAGAZINE
10401 WEST LINCOLN AVENUE SUITE 207
WEST ALLIS, WI 53227-1255
414-327-7707
414-327-4146
Fax: 414-327-4146
http://www.golfparexcellence.com
• Neal Kotlarek, Editor
• Doug Neumann, Publisher
• Doug Newmann, Publisher
Frequency:
5 time(s) per year
Description:
Publication reviews golf courses in the Midwest and other golf related activities or travel.

PARACHUTIST
1440 DUKE STREET
ALEXANDRIA, VA 22314-3403
703-836-3495
Fax: 540-604-9741
uspa@uspa.org
http://www.uspa.org
• Nancy Koreen, Managing Editor
(703) 836-3495
nkoreen@uspa.org
• Chris Needels, Executive Director
• Kevin Gibson, Editor In Chief

(703) 836-3495
kgibson@uspa.org
Frequency:
1 time(s) per month
Description:
Publication includes articles on safety issues, current events, instructional methods, and association business.

PARKS & RECREATION
22377 BELMONT RIDGE RD
ASHBURN, VA 20148-4501
703-858-0784
Fax: 703-858-0794
www.nrpa.org
• Rachel Roberts, Editor
(703) 858-2175
rroberts@nrpa.org
• Tracey Ellis, Advertising Director
(703) 858-2176
tellis@nrpa.org
• Maya Avrasin, Associate Editor
(703) 858-2145
mavrasin@nrpa.org
Publishing Company:
National Recreation & Park Association.
Frequency:
12 times a year.
Circulation:
23,000.
Nature of Service:
A national, non-profit association dedicated to advancing parks, recreation and environmental conservation efforts that enhance the quality of life for all people.
Primary Audience:
Park, Parks and Recreation.
Sports:
Professionals.

PASSAGEMAKER-THE TRAWLER AND OCEAN MOTORBOAT MAG
105 EASTERN AVENUE SUITE 103
ANNAPOLIS, MD 21403
410-990-9086
888-487-2953
Fax: 410-990-9094
onlineorders@passagemaker.com
http://www.passagemaker.com
• Bill Parlatore, Editor
editor@passagemaker.com
• Eileen Nonemaker, Advertising Director
(410) 990-9086
eileen@passagemaker.com
• Candace Orsetti, Associate Editor
(410) 990-9086
candace@passagemaker.com
• Laurene Parlatore, Publisher
(410) 990-9086
Laurene@passagemaker.com
Frequency:
6 time(s) per year
Description:
Publication offers news and information on ocean motorboats and recreational trawlers.

PENNSYLVANIA EQUESTRIAN
40 STREET NORTH LINE STREET
LANCASTER, PA 17602
717-509-9800
Fax: 717-509-0297
debbie@paequestrian.com
http://www.pennsylvaniaequestrian.com
• Stephanie Lawson, Editor
paequest@aol.com
• Debbie Hocke, Advertising Manager

media

• Stephanie Lawson, Publisher
paequest@aol.com
Frequency:
6 time(s) per year
Description:
Publication is written for horse owners and equestrian enthusiasts throughout Pennsylvania and neighboring states.

PERFORMANCE RACING INDUSTRY
31706 SOUTH COAST HIGHWAY
LAGUNA BEACH, CA 92651-0327
949-499-5413
Fax: 949-499-0410
mail@performanceracing.com
http://www.performanceracing.com
• Meredith Kaplan Burns, Managing Editor
(949) 499-5413
meredithk@performanceracing.com
• John Kilroy, Vice President & Editor
(949) 499-5413
johnk@performanceracing.com
• Steve Lewis, Publisher
Frequency:
1 time(s) per month
Description:
Trade magazine focusing on auto racing.

PGA TOUR PARTNERS
12301 WHITEWATER DRIVE SUITE 260
MINNETONKA, MN 55343-4104
952-988-7244
800-688-7611
Fax: 952-936-9169
mail@pgatourpartners.com
http://www.pgatourpartners.com
• Tom Stine, Editor
• Seth Hoyt, Publisher
Frequency:
6 time(s) per year
Description:
Publication contains articles on golf skills for professionals.

PHILADELPHIA GOLFER
290 COMMERCE DRIVE
FORT WASHINGTON, PA 19034-2400
215-542-0200
Fax: 215-643-9475
http://www.montgomerynews.com
• Dave Holloway, Sports Editor
(215) 542-0200
dholloway@montgomerynews.com
• Betsy Wilson, Publisher
(215) 628-8330
Frequency:
1 time(s) per month
Description:
Publication offers regional golf information.

PITCH
13540 LAKE CITY WAY, N.E. SUITE 3
SEATTLE, WA 98125-3665
206-367-2420
Fax: 206-363-9099
http://www.varsitycommunications.com
Frequency:
1 time(s) per month

PLAY ON: WASHINGTON STATE YOUTH SOCCER NEWS
500 SOUTH 336TH STREET SUITE 10
FEDERAL WAY, WA 98003
253-476-2237
Fax: 253-925-1830

playon@wsysa.com
http://www.varsitycommunications.com
• Erin Freehan, Editor
• Leslie Groce, Contact
(253) 476-2237
leslie@wsysa.com
Frequency:
10 time(s) per year
Description:
Publication contains association news, coaching tips, and tournament updates.

POLO PLAYERS EDITION
3500 FAIRLANE FARMS ROAD SUITE 9
WELLINGTON, FL 33414-8746
561-793-9524
Fax: 561-793-9576
info@poloplayersedition.com
http://www.poloplayersedition.com
• Gwen Rizzo, Editor
gwen@poloplayersedition.com
• Judy Doyle, Advertising Manager
• Gwen Rizzo, Publisher
gwen@poloplayersedition.com
Frequency:
1 time(s) per month
Description:
Publication focuses on lifestyle, game coverage, action photos, and how-to-do articles related to polo.

PONTOON & DECK BOAT
360 B STREET
IDAHO FALLS, ID 83402
208-524-7000
Fax: 208-522-5241
info@snowest.com
http://www.pontoon.net
• Brady Kay, Editor
• Mike Harris, Publisher
Frequency:
8 time(s) per year
Description:
Publication is a boating magazine for pontoon and deck boat owners, dealers, and manufacturers.

PONY BASEBALL AND SOFTBALL
1951 PONY PLACE
WASHINGTON, PA 15301
724-225-1060
Fax: 724-225-9852
info@pony.org
www.pony.org

POWDER
33046 CALLE AVIADOR
SAN JUAN CAPISTRANO, CA 92675
949-496-5922
Fax: 949-496-7849
http://www.powdermag.com
• Tom Bie, Editor
(949) 661-5155
Frequency:
7 time(s) per year
Description:
Publication is geared toward advanced skiers.

POWER & MOTORYACHT
260 MADISON AVENUE 8TH FLOOR
NEW YORK, NY 10016
212-726-4300
Fax: 212-726-4310
http://www.primedia.com

• Elizabeth Britten, Associate Editor
(917) 256-2278
• Eileen Mansfield, Managing Editor
(917) 256-2277
• Dennis O'Neil, Publisher
(917) 256-2292
• Richard Thiel, Editor-in-Chief
(917) 256-2267
Frequency:
1 time(s) per month
Description:
Publication covers issues of interest to owners of powerboats.

POWERBOAT
1691 SPINNAKER DRIVE SUITE 206
VENTURA, CA 93001-4378
805-667-4100
800-738-5571
Fax: 805-667-4336
info@powerboatmag.com
• Gregg Mansfield, Editor
gregg@powerboatmag.com
• Jason Johnson, Managing Editor
jason@powerboatmag.com
• Jerry Nordskog, Publisher
(805) 667-4100
Frequency:
11 time(s) per year
Description:
Publication is for the performance-conscious boater; contains technical articles, race coverage, personality profiles, water skiing, recreational boating, and performance evaluations.

PRACTICAL HORSEMAN
656 QUINCH ORCHID ROAD SUITE 600
GAITHERSBURG, MD 20878-1409
301-977-3900
800-829-3340
Fax: 301-990-9015
http://www.equisearch.com
• Sandy Oliynyk, Editor
(301) 977-3900
Frequency:
1 time(s) per month
Description:
Publication focuses on English-style horseback riding.

PRICE MEDIA
10002 AURORA AVENUE N
#36
SEATTLE, WA 98133
206-418-0747
800-935-1083
Fax: 206-418-0746
info@outdoorsnw.com
• Carolyn Price, Publisher/Sales
• Greg Price, Associate Publisher
• Matthew Butler, Sales Associate
• Kristen Carlton, Editor
• Laurie Scholleart, Art Director
Publishing Company:
Price Media, Inc.
Primary Audience:
Consumer
Sports:
Outdoor, non-mainstream
Circulation:
40,000 per Month.
Description:
News and features about outdoor individual pursuits and non-mainstream outdoor sports, including places to go in the Pacific

Northwest. Publishes a calendar of sport events in the Northwest.

PRIMEDIA
3585 ENGINEERING DRIVE
SUITE 100
NORCROSS, GA 30092
678-421-3000
800-216-1423
www.primedia.com
Description:
Publishes wide range of consumer sports and special interest publications.

PRO FOOTBALL WEEKLY
302 SAUNDERS ROAD
RIVERWOODS, IL 60015
847-940-1100
800-331-7529
Fax: 847-940-1108
http://www.profootballweekly.com
• Hub Arkush, Co-Publisher & Editor
(847) 405-7750
• Hub Arkush, Publisher
• Mike Holbrook, Managing Editor
• Keith Schleiden, Managing Editor
(847) 405-7707
• Hub Arkash, Sports Editor
(847) 940-1100
football@pfwa.com
Frequency:
1 time(s) per week
Description:
Publication features previews, reviews, upcoming events, and postgame coverage.

PROFESSIONAL BOATBUILDER
NASKEAG ROAD
BROOKLIN, ME 04616
207-359-4651
Fax: 207-359-8920
proboat@proboat.com
http://www.proboat.com
• Paul Lazarus, Editor
• Carl Cramer, Publisher
(207) 359-4651
carl@woodenboat.com
Frequency:
6 time(s) per year
Description:
Publication covers a wide range of subjects of importance to the boatbuilding industry.

PRORODEO SPORTS NEWS
101 PRO RODEO DRIVE
COLORADO SPRINGS, CO 80919-
719-593-8840
Fax: 719-548-4889
http://www.prorodeo.com
• Sean Daniels, Properties VP
• Neal Reid, Editor
• Kendra Santos, Communications Director
Frequency:
26 time(s) per year
Description:
The PRCA, headquartered in Colorado Springs, Colo, is the largest and oldest professional rodeo-sanctioning body in the world. The recognized leader in ProRodeo, the PRCA is committed to maintaining the highest standards. The PRCA, a membership-based organization, sanctions approximately 600 rodeos annually, and there are nearly 30 million fans in the U.S. The PRCA showcases the world's best cowboys in premier events through the Wrangler Million Dollar Tour presented by

Justin Boots, and its subsequent Justin Boots Playoffs, the PRCA Xtreme Bulls Tour presented by B&W Trailer Hitches; and the world-renowned Wrangler National FInals Rodeo. Act

PROFESSIONAL SPORTS PUBLICATIONS
355 LEXINGTON AVE, 9TH FL
NEW YORK, NY 10017
212-697-1460
Fax: 212-286-8154
www.pspsports.com
• Thom Hering, Chief Operating Officer
• Kevin Hahn, Executive Vice President of Sales/Marketing
• Amy Ehrlich, Vice President/Marketing Services
• Neil A. Farber, Vice President
• Paul Abramson, Vice President of National Accounts
Description:
Publishes game day magazines, including HOOP magazine, the official publications of the NBA. Other properties include Major League Baseball programs, National Hockey League programs, TOUCHDOWN ILLUSTRATED (college football), COLLEGE HOOPS ILLUSTRATED (college basketball), program magazines for 9 major College Bowl games. Licensed custom publisher of the United States Olympic Committee. Also provides sports marketing and professional services.

QUARTER HORSE NEWS
2112 MONTGOMERY STREET
FORT WORTH, TX 76107-4517
817-737-6397
Fax: 817-737-9266
http://www.quarterhorsenews.com
• Glory Ann Kurtz, Editor
(817) 737-6397
gloryann.kurtz@cowboypublishing.com
• Carl Mullins, Publisher
(817) 737-6397
carl.mullins@cowboypublishing.com
• Patty Tiberg, General Manager
(817) 737-6397
patty.tiberg@cowboypublishing.com
Frequency:
2 time(s) per month
Description:
Publication is written for the Quarter horse industry; includes news about reining, cutting, barrel racing, western pleasure shows, sales, and futurities.

RACE PLACE
16888 SAINT ANDREWS DRIVE
POWAY, CA 92064-1135
858-485-9806
Fax: 858-485-9805
http://www.raceplace.com
• Rose Reilly, Editor
Frequency:
6 time(s) per year
Description:
Publication provides participants, event organizers, and businesses with a bimonthly reference schedule of all Southern California and selected regional running, walking, endurance, and recreational events.

RACER
16842 VON KARMAN SUITE 125
IRVINE, CA 92606

714-259-8240
800-999-9718
Fax: 949-417-6750
comments@racer.com
http://www.racer.com
• Dyanne Gilliam, Managing Editor
(949) 417-6700
dgilliam@racer.com
• Andrew Crask, Executive Editor
(949) 417-6700
acrask@racer.com
• Laurence Foster, Editor In Chief
(949) 417-6700
lfoster@racer.com
• Ian Havard, Publisher
(949) 417-6700
Frequency:
1 time(s) per month
Description:
Publication focuses on top level international auto racing.

RACING WHEELS
5212 NORTH EAST SAINT JOHNS ROAD
VANCOUVER, WA 98661
360-892-5590
888-892-2574
Fax: 360-892-8021
http://www.racingwheels.net
• Dale Redinger, Editor
• Dale Redinger, Advertising Manager
Frequency:
40 time(s) per year
Description:
Publication is geared toward oval track auto racers and enthusiasts.

RACQUETBALL MAGAZINE
1685 WEST UINTAH ST
COLORADO SPRINGS, CO 80904-2921
719-635-5396
Fax: 719-635-0685
hizzett@usra.org
www.usaracquetball.com
• Jim Hiser, Publisher
(719) 635-5396
jhiser@usra.org
• Heather Izzett, Editor
(719) 635-5396
hizzett@usra.org
Frequency:
6 time(s) per year

RAIDER FAN MAGAZINE
22888 GRAND STREET
HAYWARD, CA 94541
510-881-1860
Fax: 510-881-7603
http://www.raiderfanmagazine.com
• Tim Del Rosario, Editor
tdr@raiderfans.com
Frequency:
2 time(s) per month
Description:
Publication is for fans of the Oakland Raiders football team.

RECREATION SPORTS & FITNESS
825 OLD COUNTRY ROAD
WESTBURY, NY 11590
516-334-3030
Fax: 516-334-8958
ebmpubs2@aol.com
http://www.ebmpubs.com
• Paul Ragusa, Features Editor
(516) 334-3030
paul@ebmpubs4.com

media

Description:
Publication provides the latest-breaking news about the ever-changing fitness market; includes interviews with people who make it work.

RECREATIONAL SPORTS JOURNAL
4185 SW RESEARCH WAY
CORVALLIS, OR 97333
541-766-8211
Fax: 541-766-8284
nirsa@nirsa.org
www.nirsa.org
• Kent Blumenthal, Executive Director
• Lynn Jamieson, Editor
Publishing Company:
National Intramural Recreational Sports Association
Frequency:
Two times annually
Primary Audience:
Association membership
Sports:
General
Circulation:
3,400. 80% association membership.
Description:
Devoted solely to recreational sports: aquatic programs, extramural sports, fitness programs, informal sports, instructional programs, intramural sports, outdoor recreation, special events, special populations, sport clubs, and facility development and management. Content includes approximately 8 articles, special features, advertising and professional editorials.

REDLEGS WEEKLY
100 MAIN STREET
CINCINNATI, OH 45202
513-765-7000
Fax: 513-765-7027
http://www.cincinnatireds.com
• Ralph Mitchell, Editor
rmitchell@reds.com
Frequency:
1 time(s) per month
Description:
Publication is the official newsletter of the Cincinnati Reds.

REFEREE MAGAZINE
2017 LATHROP AVENUE
RACINE, WI 53405
262-632-8855
Fax: 262-632-5460
referee@referee.com
www.referee.com
• Barry Mano, Publisher
(262) 632-8855
bmano@referee.com
• Patrick Miles, Advertising Manager
pmiles@referee.com
• Bill Topp, Editor-in-Chief
(262) 632-8855
btopp@referee.com
Frequency:
1 time(s) per month
Description:
Publication contains information of interest to officials, fans, athletes, and school administrators involved in amateur sports.

REFEREE MAGAZINE
PO BOX 161
FRANKSVILLE, WI 53126-0012

262-632-8855
Fax: 262-632-5460
www.referee.com
• Barry Mano, Publisher
• Patrick Sharp, VP Marketing & Business Development
• Bill Topp, VP Publishing & Management Services
Publishing Company:
Referee Enterprises, Inc.
Primary Audience:
Referees, sports officials
Sports:
All major sports
Circulation:
35,000. 55% paid association subscr, 45% paid subscr.
Description:
Provides a balanced look at events that involve sports officials; informs officials about their colleagues' activities.

RIDE MAGAZINE
728 CHERRY STREET
CHICO, CA 95928
530-343-9994
Fax: 530-343-4218
editor@ridepublishing.com
http://www.ridemagazine.com
• Diana Bishop, Editor
(530) 343-9994
• Dan Swofford, Publisher
dan@ridepublishing.com
Frequency:
1 time(s) per month
Description:
Publication offers articles and information on horse shows, as well as other equestrian topics.

RING
6198 BUTLER PIKE
SUITE 200
BLUE BELL, PA 19422
215-643-6385
Fax: 215-628-3571
www.kappapublishing.com
• Stuart Saks, Assistant Vice President
• Vincent Bellissima, Advertising Manager
Year Founded:
1922
Description:
The sport of Boxing.
Frequency:
Monthly.

RINKSIDE
60 EAST 42ND STREET SUITE 1405
NEW YORK, NY 10165-0721
212-697-0530
Fax: 212-697-0533
• Keith Loria, Editor
• Alan Adams, Contributing Writer
• Lucas Akroyd, Contributing Writer
• Don Cherry, Senior Contributing Editor
• Jim Connelly, Contributing Writer
• Robert F. Corrao, Publisher
• Stan Fischler, Contributing Editor
• Shirley Fischler, Contributing Writer
• Brett Friedlander, Contributing Writer
• Bruce Garrioch, Contributing Writer
• Jay Greenberg, Contributing Writer
• John Kreisen, Contributing Writer
• Dave Luecking, Contributing Writer
• Joe Starkey, Contributing Writer
• Ralph Vacchiano, Contributing Writer

Frequency:
6 time(s) per year

ROCHESTER GOLF WEEK
2535 BRIGHTON HENRIETTA TOWN LINE ROAD
ROCHESTER, NY 14623-2711
585-427-2468
Fax: 585-427-8521
golfweek@frontiernet.net
http://www.golfweekrochester.com
• Dave Eaton, Editor
• George Morgenstern, Publisher
golfweekrochester@frontiernet.net
Frequency:
1 time(s) per week
Description:
Publication contains news and features about golf and travel related information.

ROCKY MOUNTAIN SPORTS
2525 15TH STREET
SUITE 1-A
DENVER, CO 80211
303-477-9770
Fax: 303-477-9747
• Mary Thorne, Publisher
• Jeff Banowetz, Editorial Director
(303) 477-9770
jeff@windycitysports.com
• Rebecca Heaton, Editor
Publishing Company:
Rocky Mountain Sports Publishing Company, Inc.
Frequency:
Monthly
Primary Audience:
Consumer
Sports:
Individual endurance sports - running, in-line, bicycling, triathlons
Circulation:
80,000. 1% paid subscr, 99% contr non-paid.
Description:
Covers running, Adventure travel, paddling, rock climbing, cycling, in-line skating, triathlons, skiing and health club activities in the Colorado area.

RODALE'S SCUBA DIVING
6600 ABERCORN STREET SUITE 208
SAVANNAH, GA 31405-5800
912-351-0855
Fax: 912-351-0890
edit@scubadiving.com
http://www.scubadiving.com
• Robert S. Butler, Editor
(912) 351-6226
• Dane Farnum, Publisher
(912) 351-6233
Frequency:
11 time(s) per year
Description:
Publication contains information of interest to recreational diving enthusiasts, including advice on equipment and travel.

RSV/REVENUES FROM SPORTS VENUES
PO BOX 240854
MILWAUKEE, WI 53224
414-354-0966
• Jim Grinstead, Editor/Publisher
Publishing Company:
Mediaventures

Frequency:
Weekly.
Primary Audience:
Team and venue owners, marketing management, marketing consultants, architects, contractors, premium service vendors, management companies.
Description:
A weekly news service focusing on issues dealing with stadium and arena revenues.

RUGBY
36 W. 84TH ST.
9-B
NEW YORK, NY 10024
917-538-3567
rugbymag@aol.com
http://www.rugbymag.com
• Edward F. Hagerty, Publisher
(917) 538-3567
rugbymag@aol.com
• Ed Hagerty, Editor
(212) 787-1160
rugbymag@aol.com
Frequency:
1 time(s) per month
Description:
Publication focuses on worldwide rugby events and unions.

SADDLE HORSE REPORT
730 MADISON STREET
SHELBYVILLE, TN 37160-3519
931-684-8123
Fax: 931-684-8196
http://www.horseworld.net
• Diana Davidson, Editor
• Bob Funkhouser, Executive Editor
• Christy Howard Parsons, Publisher
• Richard T. Hudgins, Advertising Manager
Frequency:
1 time(s) per week
Description:
Publication reports on American Saddlebred, Hackney Pony, and Morgan horse shows and association news, as well as personalities, instruction, and horse facilities.

SAIL MAGAZINE
98 NORTH WASHINGTON STREET
BOSTON, MA 02114
617-720-8600
800-745-7245
Fax: 617-723-0911
sailmail@primemedia.com
http://www.sailmag.com
• Peter Nielsen, Editor
(617) 720-8601
• Charles Mason, Executive Editor
(617) 720-8637
cmason@sailmag.com
• Josh Adams, Publisher
(617) 720-8605
jadams@sailmag.com
• Bill Springer, Senior Editor
(617) 720-8607
• Amy Ullrich, Managing Editor
(617) 720-8629
Frequency:
1 time(s) per month
Description:
Publication is written for sailors of all types.

SAILING MAGAZINE
125 EAST MAIN STREET
PORT WASHINGTON, WI 53074-

262-284-3494
800-236-7444
Fax: 262-284-7764
gretas@sailingmagazine.net
www.sailingmagazine.net
• William F Schanen, Publiser/Editor
• Jane Farnham, Production Director
Frequency:
1 time(s) per month
Description:
Publication features information of interest to sailing enthusiasts.

SAILING WORLD
55 HAMMARLUND WAY
MIDDLETOWN, RI 02842
401-845-5100
Fax: 401-845-5180
editorial@sailingworld.com
http://www.sailingworld.com
• David Reed, Editor
dave.reed@sailingworld.com
• John Burnham, Editor-in-Chief
• Gary Jobson, Editor-at-Large
(410) 263-4630
• Michelle Roche, Classified Manager
• Jason White, Associate Publisher
(401) 845-5155
• Tony Bessinger, Associate Editor
(401) 845-5107
Frequency:
10 time(s) per year
Description:
Publication is written for sailing enthusiasts, with an emphasis on sailboat racing and performance cruising.

SAND SPORTS
2950 AIRWAY AVENUE
COSTA MESA, CA 92626-6031
714-979-2560
Fax: 714-979-3998
msommer@hotvws.com
http://www.sandsports.net
• Mike Sommers, Editor
(714) 979-2560
• Linda Dill, Advertising Director
(714) 979-2560
ldill@hotvws.com
• Newell Dunn, Associate Editor
(714) 979-2560
• Skip Coiner, Art Director
(714) 979-2560
Frequency:
5 time(s) per year
Description:
Publication targets recreational, off-road vehicle owners and businesses.

SANTANA
15548 GRAHAM STREET
HUNTINGTON BEACH, CA 92649-1609
714-379-3070
Fax: 714-379-9976
santanarag@aol.com
• Kitty James, Editor
Frequency:
1 time(s) per month
Description:
Publication contains information of interest to boating enthusiasts, including Cruising, Yacht Racing, Learning to Sail, and Boat Maintenance.

SCHOLASTIC COACH & ATHLETIC DIRECTOR MAGAZINE
225 REGENCY COURT
BROOKFIELD, WI 53045
262-782-4480
800-645-8455
Fax: 262-786-5564
www.coachad.com
• Bruce Weber, Publisher
ext 6370
• Herman L. Masin, Editor
ext 6371
• Kevin Newell, Managing Editor
ext 4792
• Michael Wallace, Marketing Manager
ext 6131
Description:
Athletic professionals constantly seek the competitive edge. That's why they demand Coach & A.D. It provides what no other resource offers - in depth coverage of all sports and unbeatable advice from the best coaches around.
Circulation:
52,826. 88% paid subscr, 12% non-paid subscr contr.
Sports:
General.
Primary Audience:
HS/college coaches, athletic directors.
Frequency:
10 times annually.
Publishing Company:
Scholastic Inc.

SEA KAYAKER
6012 SEAVIEW AVENUE NORTH WEST
SEATTLE, WA 98107-2657
206-789-9536
Fax: 206-781-1141
http://www.seakayakermag.com
• Chris Cunningham, Editor
(206) 789-9536
editorial@seakayakermag.com
• Michael Collins, Publisher
(206) 789-9536
michael@seakayakermag.com
• Paul Riek, Advertising Manager
(206) 789-6413
paul@seakayakermag.com
Frequency:
6 time(s) per year
Description:
An invaluable resource for novice and experienced touring kayakers. Every issue covers destinations, navigation of coastal and inland waters, safety, technique, and the latest in kayaks and gear. Focuses on the promotion of kayaking that ensures the safety of the paddler and the preservation of the fragile marine environment.

SEA MAGAZINE
17782 COWAN SUITE A
IRVINE, CA 92614
949-660-6150
Fax: 949-660-6172
http://www.goboatingamerica.com
• Holly Simpson, Managing Editor
(949) 660-6150
• Jeffrey Fleming, Associate Publisher
(949) 660-6150
• Duncan McIntosh, Publisher
duncan@goboatingamerica.com
• Stephanie Porter, Assistant Editor
(949) 660-6150

media

Frequency:
1 time(s) per month
Description:
Publication covers recreational boating in the 13 western states, with emphasis on power boating.

SHARING THE VICTORY
8701 LEEDS ROAD
KANSAS CITY, MO 64129-1680
816-921-0909
Fax: 816-921-8755
stv@fca.org
http://www.gospelcom.net
• Jill Ewert, Managing Editor
(816) 892-1156
jewert@fca.org
• Les Steckel, Publisher
• Dal Shealy, Publisher
(816) 921-0909
dshealy@fca.org
Frequency:
9 time(s) per year
Description:
Publication serves the Fellowship of Christian Athletes.

SHOW CIRCUIT MAGAZINE
1911 FOOTHILL BOULEVARD SUITE 300
LA VERNE, CA 91750-3511
909-392-8089
Fax: 309-365-8879
showcmag@aol.com
http://www.showcircuit.com
• Kitty Bowe Hearty, Editor-in-Chief
Description:
Publication features news and articles concerning equestrian competition in the United States.

SIERRA MAGAZINE
85 SECOND ST, 2ND FL
SAN FRANCISCO, CA 94105-3441
415-977-5500
Fax: 415-977-5799
sierra.letters@sierraclub.org
www.sierraclub.org
• Joan Hamilton, Editor-in-Chief
• Robert Schildgen, Managing Director
• Kristi Rummel, National Advertising Director
Description:
Official magazine of the Sierra Club. Definitive voice of the environmental movement. Color photography, editorial informs readers about environmental issues.
Circulation:
500,000. 97% association membership, 2% newsstand, 1% paid subscr.
Sports:
Hiking, rafting, camping, skiing
Primary Audience:
Consumer
Frequency:
Bimonthly
Publishing Company:
Sierra Club

SILENT SPORTS
717 10TH STREET
WAUPACA, WI 54981-1934
715-258-5546
Fax: 715-258-8162
http://www.silentsports.net
• Joel Patenaude, Editor
(715) 258-5546
silentsports@charterinternet.net

• Scott Turner, Publisher
(715) 258-5546
• Jim Wendt, Advertising Manager
• Greg Marr, Editor-in-Chief
(715) 258-5546
Frequency:
1 time(s) per month
Description:
Publication provides information and features stories on self-propelled recreation such as bicycling, paddlesports, cross country skiing, running, and inline skating.

SKATEBOARDER MAGAZINE
33046 CALLE AVIADOR
SAN JUAN CAPISTRANO, CA 92675-4704
949-661-5141
Fax: 949-496-7849
http://www.skateboardermag.com
• Lauralyn Loynes, Managing Editor
(949) 661-5113
• Roger Harrell, Associate Publisher
(949) 661-5186
• Brian Peech, Editor-in-Chief
Frequency:
6 time(s) per year
Description:
Publication profiles skateboarding culture; includes new moves, features on prominent professionals, and entertaining columns.

SKATING
20 1ST STREET
COLORADO SPRINGS, CO 80906
719-635-5200
Fax: 719-635-9548
memberservices@usfigureskating.org
www.usfigureskating.org
• Laura Fawcett, Editor
lfawcett@usfigureskating.org
• Jenny Driscoll, Assistant Editor
jdriscoll@usfsa.org
Frequency:
10 time(s) per year
Description:
Publication features news and profiles from the world of figure skating.

SKI AREA MANAGEMENT
45 MAIN STREET, N.
WOODBURY, CT 06798-2915
203-263-0888
Fax: 203-266-0452
http://www.saminfo.com
• Jennifer Rowan, Publisher
jenn@saminfo.com
• Olivia Rowan, Associate Publisher
(508) 655-6408
olivia@saminfo.com
• Sharon Walsh, Advertising Manager
(508) 655-6408
sharon@saminfo.com
• Nils Ericksen, Technical Editor
(203) 263-0888
Frequency:
6 time(s) per year
Description:
Publication targets owners and operators of ski resorts; focuses on lift systems, cross-country skiing, trail grooming, risk management, show mailing, marketing, and foodservice.

SKI MAGAZINE
929 PEARL STREET SUITE 200
BOULDER, CO 80302

303-448-7600
Fax: 303-448-7638
editor@skimag.com
http://www.skimag.com/skimag
• Kendall Hamilton, Editor
(303) 448-7615
khamilton@skimag.com
• Kim Beekman, Managing Editor
(303) 448-7683
• Samantha Berman, Senior Editor
(303) 448-7600
• Greg Ditrinco, Executive Editor
(303) 448-7641
greg.ditrinco@time4.com
• Maureen Drummey, Sports Assistant Editor
maureen.drummey@time4.com
• Kate Richardson, Assistant
(303) 448-7610
kate.richardson@time4.com
Frequency:
11 time(s) per year
Description:
Ultimate Insiders Guide to Ski Life focusing on travel, family and gear.

SKI PATROL
133 SOUTH VAN GORDON STREET
SUITE 100
LAKEWOOD, CO 80228
303-988-1111
Fax: 303-988-3005
http://www.nsp.org
• Stephen M. Over, Executive Director
• Jim Schnebly, Assistant Editor
• Wendy Schrupp, Associate Editor
(303) 988-1111
Frequency:
3 time(s) per year

SKI RACING
1830 NORTH 55TH STREET
BOULDER, CO 80301-2700
303-440-0601
800-552-1558
Fax: 303-444-6788
http://www.skiracing.com
• Eric McCollom, Features Editor
emcollom@insideinc.com
• Don Cameron, Editor-in-Chief
dcameron@insideinc.com
• Andy Hawk, Advertising Manager
(303) 440-0601
ahawk@insideinc.com
• Andy Hawk, Associate Publisher
(303) 440-0601
ahawk@insideinc.com
• Alex Pasquariello, Managing Editor
apasquariello@insideinc.com
Frequency:
20 time(s) per year
Description:
Publication is an international journal of ski competition.

SKIER NEWS
P.O. BOX 77327
WEST TRENTON, NJ 08628-6327
609-882-1111
Fax: 609-882-2700
http://www.skiernews.com
• Dave Leonardi, Publisher
Frequency:
4 time(s) per year
Description:
Publication focuses on timely topics for skiers around the country; includes

information on fitness, technical information, and destinations.

SKIING
929 PEARL STREET
BOULDER, CO 80302
303-448-7600
Fax: 303-442-6321
editors@skiingmag.com
http://www.skiingmag.com/skiing
• Marc Peruzzi, Editor-in-Chief
(303) 448-7623
marc.peruzzi@time4.com
• Mike Kessler, Executive Editor
(303) 448-7658
mike.kessler@time4.com
• Jamie Pentz, Publisher
(303) 448-7650
jamie.pentz@time4.com
• Evelyn Spence, Articles Editor
(303) 448-7667
evelyn.spence@time4.com
Frequency:
7 time(s) per year

SKIING HERITAGE
499 TOWN HILL ROAD
NEW HARTFORD, CT 06057-2516
203-263-2176
Fax: 203-266-0452
http://www.skiinghistory.org
• Dick Needhan, Editor
Frequency:
3 time(s) per year
Description:
Publication is the official journal of the International Skiing History Association.

SKIING TRADE NEWS
929 PEARL STREET
BOULDER, CO 80302-5108
303-448-7600
Fax: 303-442-6321
http://www.mountainsportsmedia.com
• Bill Grout, Editor
(303) 448-7663
Bill.Grout@time4.com
• Andy Clurman, Publisher
• Andrew Clurman, Publisher
(303) 448-7600
Frequency:
2 time(s) per year
Description:
Publication covers the retail ski industry, ski specialty shops, mass merchandise sporting goods chains, and manufacturers of consumer ski equipment and fashion.

SKYDIVING
1725 NORTH LEXINGTON AVENUE
DELAND, FL 32724-2148
386-736-4793
editor@skydivingmagazine.com
http://www.skydivingmagazine.com
• Sue Clifton, Editor-in-Chief
sue@skydivingmagazine.com
• Michael Truffer, Publisher
michael@skydivingmagazine.com
Frequency:
1 time(s) per month
Description:
Publication focuses on the equipment, events, people, places, and techniques of sport parachuting.

SLAM
1115 BROADWAY
8TH FLOOR
NEW YORK, NY 10010
212-462-9550
800-333-6411
Fax: 212-620-7787
http://www.slamonline.com
• Susan Price, Managing Editor
(212) 462-9635
• Robert Jackson, Editor-at-Large
(773) 324-7790
• Ryan Jones, Editor-in-Chief
• Dennis Page, Publisher
(212) 462-9550
• Khalid Salaam, Associate Editor
(212) 462-9659
• Russ Bengtson, Editor-in-Chief
(212) 807-7100
Frequency:
6 time(s) per year
Description:
Publication is a consumer magazine devoted to all aspects of basketball; includes pro, college, high school, and playground ball.

SLAP MAGAZINE
1303 UNDERWOOD AVENUE
SAN FRANCISCO, CA 94124-3308
415-822-3083
888-520-9099
Fax: 415-822-8359
http://www.slapmagazine.com
• Mark Whitely, Editor
• Eben Sterling, Advertising Director
eben@thrashermagazine.com
Frequency:
1 time(s) per month
Description:
Publication centers around skateboarding; covers youth culture, music, art, fashion, and fun.

SNOW GOER
3300 FERNBROOK LANE
SUITE 200
PLYMOUTH, MN 55447
763-383-4400
800-848-6247
Fax: 763-383-4499
www.snowgoer.com
• Tim Erickson, Editor
(763) 383-4400
• Andy Swanson, Managing Editor
(763) 383-4400
• Mark Rosacker, Associate Publisher
Snow Goer Magazine
The recognized leader in snowmobiling magazines, Snow Goer procides everything the enthusiast wants to know; from how-to modifications, new product evaluations, snowmobile desintations, events, and standings: this is the magazine for snow power sports.

SNOWBOARDER MAGAZINE
33046 CALLE AVIADOR
SAN JUAN CAPISTRANO, CA 92675-4704
949-496-5922
Fax: 949-496-7849
snwbrdrmag@primemedia.com
http://www.snowboardermag.com
• Pat Bridges, Editor
(949) 661-5197
• Mike Nusenow, Publisher
(949) 661-5110

Frequency:
8 time(s) per year
Description:
Publication covers issues of interest to snowboarding enthusiasts.

SNOWEST
360 B STREET
IDAHO FALLS, ID 83402
208-524-7000
800-657-0135
Fax: 208-522-5241
info@snowest.com
www.snowest.com
• Lane Lindstrom, Editor
(208) 542-2234
lindstrm@snowest.com
• Steve Janes, Publisher
(208) 542-2214
stevejanes@snowest.com
• Ryan Harris, Tech Editor
(208) 542-2243
rharris@snowest.com
Frequency:
6 times per year
Description:
Publication contains information on snowmobiling in the western mountains, including vacation ideas, racing coverage, and other winter activities of interest to snowmobile enthusiasts. Specializes in how-to ride, what-to ride and where-to ride in the west.
Circulation:
36,000

SNOWTECH MAGAZINE
630 HIAWATHA CIRCLE NORTH WEST
ALEXANDRIA, MN 56308-8117
320-763-5411
Fax: 320-763-1775
http://www.snowtechmagazine.com
• Jim Beilke, Editor
jim@snowtechmagazine.com
• Jim Beilke, Publisher
jim@snowtechmagazine.com
• Kevin Beilke, Managing Editor
(320) 763-5411
kevin@snowtechmagazine.com
Frequency:
5 time(s) per year
Description:
Publication provides information on all aspects of snowmobiling.

SOARING
PO BOX 2100
HOBBS, NM 88241-2100
575-392-1177
Fax: 575-392-8154
feedback@ssa.org
http://www.ssa.org
• Denise Layton, Features Editor
(505) 392-1177
denise@ssa.org
• Denise Layton, Managing Editor
(505) 392-1177
denise@ssa.org
Frequency:
1 time(s) per month
Description:
Publication contains general, safety, technical, and recreational material related to the sport of soaring.

SOCCER CALIFORNIA
12510 NORTH EAST 33RD AVENUE
SUITE 300
SEATTLE, WA 98125
206-367-2420
Fax: 206-367-2636
http://www.varsitycommunications.com
• Charles Beene, Editor
(206) 367-2420
charles@varsitycommunications.com
Frequency:
6 time(s) per year
Description:
Publication is aimed at soccer coaches and administrators; includes coaching tips and tournament information.

SOCCER IN NEVADA
13540 LAKE CITY WAY N.E. SUITE 3
SEATTLE, WA 98125
206-367-2420
Fax: 206-367-2636
http://www.varsitycommunications.com
• Andrea Thompson, Editor
(702) 870-3024
usysny@aol.com
Frequency:
4 time(s) per year

SOCCER JR.
557 BROADWAY
NEW YORK, NY 10012 3999
212-343-6830
Fax: 212-343-4808
http://www.soccerjr.com
• Mark Wright, Editor
(212) 343-6199
• Anthony Guido, Managing Editor
• Bill Kelchner, Publisher
(212) 343-6443
Frequency:
6 time(s) per year
Description:
Publication is written for children ages 8-14 who are active athletes.

SOCCER NEW JERSEY
13540 LAKE CITY WAY N.E. SUITE 3
SEATTLE, WA 98125
206-367-2420
Fax: 206-367-2636
http://www.varsitycommunications.com
• Charles Beene, Editor
charles@varsitycommunications.com
Frequency:
4 time(s) per year

SOCCER NOW
12501 SOUTH ISIS AVENUE
HAWTHORNE, CA 90250-4149
310-643-6455
800-872-2976
Fax: 310-643-5310
soccernow@ayso.org
http://www.soccer.org
• Melissa Sterzick, Editor
(310) 643-6455
melissasterzick@ayso.org
Frequency:
4 time(s) per year
Description:
Publication focuses on the players and volunteers of the American Youth Soccer Organization; includes articles on general membership, news, volunteers, players and events in the world of soccer.

SOCCER OHIO SOUTH
4114 198TH STREET SOUTHWEST
SUITE 5
LYNNWOOD, WA 98046-5008
425-412-7070
888-367-6420
Fax: 425-412-7082
stephens@varsitycommunications.com
http://www.varsitycommunications.com
• Scott Leader, Editor
Frequency:
4 time(s) per year

SOCIOLOGY OF SPORT JOURNAL
1607 N. MARKET ST
CHAMPAIGN, IL 61820
217-351-5076
800-747-4457
Fax: 217-351-2674
www.humankinetics.com
• Jake Jaquet, Journal Director
• Chad Hoffman, Advertising Sales Manager
Publishing Company:
Human Kinetics Publishers, Inc.
Frequency:
Quarterly
Primary Audience:
Association membership, sport sociologists
Sports:
General
Circulation:
997
Description:
Journal of the North American Society for the Sociology of Sport, focuses on the understanding of human behavior within the context of sport and physical activity. Includes research articles on sociology of sport, teaching innovations and research notes and book reviews.

SOUNDINGS
10 BOKUM ROAD
ESSEX, CT 06426-1500
860-767-3200
Fax: 860-767-0642
soundings@soundingspub.com
http://www.soundingsonline.com
• William Sisson, Editor
(860) 767-3200
sisson@soundingspub.com
• Mark Hoag, Advertising Manager
• Rich Armstrong, Associate Editor
(860) 767-3200
r.armstrong@soundingspub.com
Frequency:
1 time(s) per month
Description:
Publication focuses on recreational boating.

SOUNDINGS:TRADE ONLY
10 BOKUM ROAD
ESSEX, CT 06426-1152
860-767-3200
Fax: 860-767-0642
editorial@tradeonlytoday.com
http://www.tradeonlytoday.com
• Tom Hubbard, Editor
t.hubbard@tradeonlytoday.com
• Joann Goddard, Staff Writer
j.gaddard@soundingspub.com
• Mark Hoag, Advertising Director
m.hoag@tradeonlytoday.com
• Esther Pope, Editorial Assistant
(860) 767-3200
e.pope@soundingspub.com

• Melanie Winters, Associate Editor
m.winters@tradeonlytoday.com
Frequency:
1 time(s) per month
Description:
Publication contains business news on the boating industry.

SOURCE INTERLINK MEDIA
831 S DOUGLAS STREET
EL SEGUNDO, CA 90245
310-531-5962
Fax: 310-531-9374
www.sourceinterlinkmedia.com
• Rick Stark, Vice President, Sales
(310) 531-5076
• Carol McGovney, Sales Support Manager
(310) 531-5962

SOUTHERN BOATING MAGAZINE
330 NORTH ANDREWS AVENUE
2ND FLOOR
FORT LAUDERDALE, FL 33301
954-522-5515
Fax: 954-522-2260
sboating@southernboating.com
http://www.southernboating.com
• Marilyn Mower, Editor
(954) 522-5515
marilyn@southernboating.com
• Bill Ando, Senior Editor
(954) 522-5515
bill@southernboating.com
• Kellie Mackenroth, Marketing & Circulation Manager
kellie@southernboating.com
Frequency:
1 time(s) per month
Description:
Publication is geared toward yachtsmen in the southern United States and the Caribbean; focuses on sailing, cruising, maintenance, and destinations.
Primary Audience:
Marine and Boating Industry enthusiasts.

SOUTHERN HORSEMAN
3839 OLD HIGHWAY 45 NORTH
MERIDIAN, MS 39301
601-693-6607
Fax: 903-297-2264
http://www.southernhorseman.com
• Thelma Thompson, Editor
• Tracy Thompson, Executive Editor
Frequency:
1 time(s) per month
Description:
Publication is dedicated to the horse showman and breeder.

SOUTHERN MOTORACING
1049 NORTHWEST BOULEVARD
WINSTON-SALEM, NC 27101-1171
336-723-5227
Fax: 336-722-3757
• Hank Schoolfield, Editor
• Hank Schoolfield, Publisher
• Don Wilson, General Manager
Frequency:
25 time(s) per year
Description:
Publication focuses on stock car racing.

SOUTHWEST HORSE TRACK
P.O. BOX 222
MORGAN MILL, TX 76465

254-965-9667
Fax: 254-965-3936
http://www.trackmagazine.com
• Ben Hudson, Editor
ben@trackmagazine.com
• Ben Hudson, Publisher
Frequency:
11 time(s) per year
Description:
Publication focuses on racing news, breeding, and training.

SPECIAL EVENTS MAGAZINE
23805 STUART RANCH RD, STE 235
MALIBU, CA 90265
310-317-4522
800-543-4116
Fax: 310-317-9644
www.specialevents.com
• Lisa Perrin, Publisher
• Lisa Hurley, Editor
• Natasha Garber, Senior Editor
• Cindy Dell'Amico, West/Midwest Sales Manager
• Diane McGee, East Coast Sales Manager
Frequency:
Monthly
Primary Audience:
Individuals and companies involved in producing and/or managing events
Sports:
General
Circulation:
25,675
Description:
Focuses on hospitality activities related to events, including sports events.

SPEEDHORSE-THE RACING REPORT
1903 48TH AVENUE
NORMAN, OK 73072
405-573-1050
Fax: 405-573-1059
speedhorse@coxinet.net
http://www.speedhorsemagazine.com
• Andrew Golden, Editor-in-Chief
• Andrew Golden, Advertising Manager
• Connie Golden, Publisher
Frequency:
1 time(s) per week
Description:
Publication is for Quarter horse racing owners and breeders.

SPONSORSHIP REPORT
PO BOX 378
STATION MAIN
CAMPBELLFORD, CANADA K0L 1L0
705-653-1112
Fax: 705-653-1113
www.sponsorship.ca
• Mark Sabourin, Publisher/Editor
Sports Service Founded:
1988
Primary Audience:
Sponsoring companies, advertising agencies, sports marketers, etc.
Sports:
General.
Description:
The aim of the newsletter is to foster successful partnerships between Canadian corporations and arts groups, sports organizations, charities, government initiatives, events, and festivals.

SPONSORVISION
39 VISTA MIRAGE WAY
RANCHO MIRAGE, CA 92270
253-223-9119
Fax: 253-566-6771
• Michael Jensen, Chief Executive Officer
Sports Service Founded:
1995
Nature of Sports Service:
Publisher of comprehensive sponsorship marketing publications and printed resources to for-profit and nonprofit corporations, organizations, agencies, foundations, events and venues internationally

SPORT HISTORY REVIEW
1607 NORTH MARKET STREET
CHAMPAIGN, IL 61820
217-351-5076
800-747-4457
Fax: 217-351-2674
journals@hkusa.com
http://www.humankinetics.com
• Don Morrow, Editor
(519) 661-4128
donmor@uwo.ca
• Rainer Martens, Publisher
rainerm@hkusa.com
• Rohn Koester, Managing Editor
(217) 351-5076
Frequency:
2 time(s) per year
Description:
Publication is devoted to promoting the study of all facets of sports.

SPORT JOURNAL
ONE ACADEMY DRIVE
DAPHNE, AL 36526
251-626-3303
Fax: 251-626-8829
sportjournal@ussa.edu
www.thesportjournal.org
• Thomas P Rosandich, Publisher
president@ussa.edu
• Kelly E Flanagan, Editor
flanagan@ussa.edu
• Jordan Moon, Associate Editor
jmoon@ussa.edu
Frequency:
4 time(s) per year
Description:
The Sport Journal, is a publication of the United State Sports Academy. It is designed to further the knowledge of sport by allowing professionals in the field to publish articles at this site.

SPORT PSYCHOLOGIST
1607 N. MARKET ST
CHAMPAIGN, IL 61820
217-351-5076
800-747-4457
Fax: 217-351-2674
www.humankinetics.com
• Jake Jaquez, Journal Director
• Chad Hoffman, Advertising Sales Manager
Publishing Company:
Human Kinetics Publishers, Inc.
Frequency:
Quarterly
Primary Audience:
Sport psychologists, coaches, trainers
Sports:
General
Circulation:

1,205
Description:
Journal of the International Society of Sport Psychology. Provides forum for dissemination of applied sport psychology information to practitioners. This journal will focus on issues pertaining to application of this information to coaches and athletes. International in scope and receptive to nontraditional or nonscientific methodologies.

SPORT SCENE:FOCUS ON YOUTH PROGRAMS
PO BOX 140
HUDDLESTON, VA 24104
336-407-2157
800-767-4916
Jack@naysi.com
www.naysi.com
• Jack Hutslar, Publisher/Editor
• Sally Hutslar, Education Consultant
• Roman Perez Villejo, Mexico
Description:
Focus on youth programs. Consulting services. Program development objectives. Training. Management ideas. Leadership & Coaching. Program expansion. Lectures. For leaders and parents who work with tots, children and teens. All sports. Youth development. Latest methods, Do's and Don'ts, Safety, Fitness, Health. Mission is to help make sport, recreation, fitness and youth activities more positive.
Circulation:
1,000-15,000. 70% paid by NAYSI, 10% paid subscr, 20% other.
Sports:
General
Primary Audience:
Youth leaders, coaches, teachers, parents, community leaders involved with tots, children and teens
Frequency:
Quarterly or more frequently as direct mail piece for business and industry
Publishing Company:
North American Youth Sport Institute
Founded:
1979

SPORT SUPPLEMENT
ONE ACADEMY DRIVE
DAPHNE, AL 36526
251-626-3303
Fax: 251-626-8829
aodom@ussa.edu
http://sportsupplement.org/
• Thomas P. Rosandich, Publisher
(251) 626-3303
trosandich@ussa.edu
• Brian Wallace, Assistant Editor
(251) 626-3303
bwallace@ussa.edu
• Enrico Esposito, Editor
(251) 626-3303
esposito@ussa.edu
Frequency:
4 time(s) per year
Description:
The Sport Supplement, an electronic document, is a publication of the United States Sports Academy. It is designed to further knowledge about issues of sport, fitness and health for professionals as well as anyone seeking knowledge and information in this field.

media

SPORTBUSINESS GROUP
ELIZABETH HOUSE
39 YORK RD, 6TH FL
LONDON, ENGLAND SE1 7NQ
copydesk@sportbusiness.com
www.sportbusiness.com
• Ben Cawford, Managing Director
• Kevin Roberts, Managing Editor
• Richard Rusell, Editorial
Director/Broadcast
Description:
International coverage of news about
sponsorship, marketing agencies, sports
facilities, sports events and sanctioning
bodies, sports broadcasting developments,
athletes, sports business personalities, and
sports event sites.
Publishing Company:
Sport Business International

SPORTING GOODS BUSINESS
770 BROADWAY
NEW YORK, NY 10003
800-562-2706
Fax: 646-654-5365
http://www.adweek.com
• Hilary Cassidy, Environmental Reporter
(800) 562-2706
• Mark Sullivan, Group Publisher
(646) 654-4981
msullivan@sgbmag.com
• Robert E. Carr, ISG News Editor
(646) 654-4997
rcarr@sgbmag.com
• Judy Leand, Executive Editor
(800) 562-2706
jleand@sportinggoodsbusiness.com
• Cara Griffin, Managing Editor
(646) 654-5006
cgriffin@sportsonesource.com
• Tom Ryan, Business/Licensing Editor
(646) 654-5384
tryan@sgbmag.com
Publishing Company:
VNU.
Frequency:
Monthly.
Primary Audience:
Sporting Goods Trade.

SPORTING GOODS INTELLIGENCE
442 FEATHERBED LANE
GLEN MILLS, PA 19342
610-459-4040
800-328-6397
Fax: 610-459-4010
editor@sginews.com
www.sginews.com
• Jon Bogert, Editor
Frequency:
Weekly/Daily
Description:
Publication features news and analysis
concerning the international sporting goods
industry.

SPORTING KID MAGAZINE
240 PROSPECT PL
UNIT E1
ALPHARETTA, GA 30005
678-297-3903
Fax: 678-297-0704
• Tina D'Aversa-Williams, Publisher
• Michael J. Pallerino, Editor

SPORTING NEWS
10176 CORPORATE SQUARE DRIVE
SAINT LOUIS, MO 63132-2924
314-997-7111
Fax: 314-997-0765
editors@sportingnews.com
http://www.sportingnews.com
• Steve Greeberg, Managing Editor
• John D. Rawlings, Editorial Director
• Ken Rosenthal, Sports Senior Writer
(410) 602-8193
kenrosenthal@sportingnews.com
• Pete Spina, Publisher
(646) 424-2227
pspina@sportingnews.com
Frequency:
1 time(s) per week
Description:
Publication is a sports weekly focusing on
baseball, football, basketball, and hockey
coverage.

SPORTING NEWS
10176 CORPORATE SQUARE DR
#200
ST. LOUIS, MO 63132-2924
314-997-7111
Fax: 314-997-0765
www.sportingnews.com
• C. Richard Allen, President and Chief
Executive Officer
• John D. Rawlings, Senior Vice
President/Editorial Director
• Peter A. Spina, Vice President/Publisher
Publishing Company:
The Sporting News
Frequency:
Weekly
Primary Audience:
Consumer
Sports:
Major League Baseball, College and Pro
Football, College and Pro Basketball, Pro
Hockey and NASCAR.
Circulation:
600,000. 95% paid subscr, 5% newsstand.
Description:
Features and articles of interest to sports
fans, including statistical summaries,
updates of trades, etc.

SPORTS 'N SPOKES MAGAZINE
2111 E. HIGHLAND, STE 180
PHOENIX, AZ 85016-4702
602-224-0500
888-888-2201
Fax: 602-224-0507
snsmagaz@aol.com
www.sportsnspokes.com
• Cliff Crase, Editor
• Sherri Shea, Marketing Director
Publishing Company:
Paralyzed Veterans of America
Frequency:
8X per year.
Primary Audience:
Consumer
Sports:
Wheelchair sports
Circulation:
10,000
Description:
Covers wheelchair competitive sports and
recreation primarily for the spinal cord
injured, amputee or polio, plus some
congenital defects; cerebral palsy, spina
bifida.

SPORTS AFIELD
15621 CHEMICAL LANE
HUNTINGTON BEACH, CA 92649
714-373-4910
Fax: 714-894-4949
letters@sportsafield.com
www.sportsafield.com
• Diana Rupp, Editor-in-Chief
(714) 373-4910
letters@sportsafield.com
• Sid Evans, Editor
(714) 373-4910
letters@sportsafield.com
• Ludo J. Wurfbain, Chief Eexecutive Officer
Field Sports Publicat
(714) 373-4910
publisher@sportsfield.com
Publishing Company:
Field Sports Publications.
Frequency:
9 times a year.
Circulation:
50,000.
Nature of Service:
Magazine.
Primary AudienceL
Men 35-65.
Sports:
Hunting.

SPORTS ARIZONA MAGAZINE
67 EAST WELDON AVENUE SUITE 240
PHOENIX, AZ 85012
480-970-6999
888-553-7979
Fax: 602-279-8061
http://www.sportsaz.com
• Curt Blakeney, Editor
(602) 279-6375
• Joel Harnett, Publisher
Frequency:
6 time(s) per year
Description:
Publication focuses on professional, college,
and amateur sports of all kinds in Arizona.

SPORTS BUSINESS JOURNAL
1166 AVENUE OF THE AMERICAS
14TH FLOOR
NEW YORK, NY 10036
212-500-0700
Fax: 212-500-0701
• Abraham Madkour, Executive Editor
(704) 973-1511
amadkour@sportsbusinessjournal.com
• Ross Nethery, Managing Editor
(704) 973-1437
methery@sportsbusinessjournal.com
• Rob Knapp, Assistant Managing
Editor/News
(704) 973-1416
rknapp@sportsbusinessjournal.com
• David Bourne, Special Reports Editor
(704) 973-1417
dbourne@sportsbusinessjournal.com
Description:
Sports Business Journal provides coverage
of the deals, trades, contracts, and
boardroom power plays that shape the
rapidly changing sports landscape. Regular
columns cover every aspect of the industry,
from media and marketing to finance,
facilities, and labor.
Founded:
In 1999.

SPORTS COLLECTORS DIGEST
700 EAST STATE STREET
IOLA, WI 54990
715-445-2214
888-457-2873
Fax: 715-445-4087
http://www.krause.com
• Dean Listle, Publisher and Advertising Director
• TS O'Connell, Editor
Publishing Company:
Krause Publications, Inc.
Frequency:
Weekly
Primary Audience:
Consumer/Trade
Sports:
All sports
Circulation:
48,000
Description:
Covers news of the collecting hobby with special focus for the dealer, investor and advanced collector. Marketplace offers widest variety of sports collectibles and baseball cards available. Includes columns, sports card show listings and updated sports card price guide in each issue.

SPORTS EDGE MAGAZINE
240 PROSPECT PL
UNIT E1
ALPHARETTA, GA 30005
678-297-3903
Fax: 678-297-0704
www.sportsedgemag.com
• Tina D'Aversa-Williams, Publisher
• Michael J. Pallerino, Editor
• John Agoglia, Fitness Editor
• Roy Wallack, Outdoor Editor
• Mike Fickes, Retail Editor
• Dinah Ledford, Circulation & Reader Service Manager

SPORTS ILLUSTRATED
TIME-LIFE BUILDING
NEW YORK, NY 10020-1393
212-522-1212
Fax: 212-522-4543
http://www.si.com
• Terry McDonell, Managing Editor
(212) 522-1650
terry_mcdonell@simail.com
• Connie Aitcheson, Reporter
(212) 522-1212
connie_aitcheson@simail.com
• Kelli Anderson, Senior Writer
(212) 522-1212
kelli_anderson@simail.com
• Lars Anderson, Staff Writer
(212) 522-7510
lars_anderson@simail.com
• Chris Ballard, Staff Writer
(212) 522-2665
chris_ballard@simail.com
• Michael Bamberger, Senior Writer
(212) 522-0028
michael_bamberger@simail.com
• Michael Bamberger, Sports Senior Writer
(212) 522-0028
michael_bamberger@simail.com
• David Bauer, Deputy Managing Editor
(212) 522-2210
david_bauer@simail.com
• Mark Bechtel, Senior Editor
(212) 522-1278
mark_bechtel@simail.com

• Michael Bevans, Executive Editor
(212) 522-3334
michael_bevans@simail.com
• Trisha Blackmar, Associate Editor
(212) 522-0073
trisha_lucey@simail.com
• John Ed Bradley, Special Contributor
(212) 522-2747
john_bradley@simail.com
• Sheila Buckley, Publisher
• Larry Burke, Sports Senior Editor
(212) 522-1130
larry_burke@simail.com
• Stephen Cannella, Senior Editor
(212) 522-1212
stephen_cannella@simail.com
• Stephen Cannella, Staff Writer
stephen_cannella@simail.com
• Brian Cazeneuve, Staff Writer
(212) 522-8227
brian_cazeneuve@time-inc.com
• Brian Cazeneuve, Staff Writer
(212) 522-8227
brian_cazeneuve@simail.com
• Jeffri Chadiha, Senior Writer
(212) 522-1212
jeffri_chadiha@simail.com
• Bobby Clay, Senior Editor
(212) 522-1212
bobby_clay@simail.com
• Seth Davis, Staff Writer
(212) 522-6431
seth_davis@simail.com
• Frank Deford, Senior Contributing Editor
(212) 522-1212
frank_deford@simail.com
• Richard Deitsch, Special Projects Editor
(212) 522-2929
richard_deitsch@simail.com
• Richard Demak, Chief of Reporters & Senior Editor
(212) 522-3962
richard_demak@simail.com
• Nunyo Demasio
Staff Writer
nunyo_demasio@simail.com
• George Dohrmann, Staff Writer
(212) 522-1212
george_dohrmann@simail.com
• Michael Farber, Senior Writer
(212) 522-4165
michael_farber@simail.com
• Luis Fernando Llosa, Reporter
(212) 522-0847
luis_llosa@simail.com
• Rob Fleder, Sports Executive Editor
(212) 522-8388
rob_fleder@simail.com
• Dick Friedman, Senior Editor
(212) 522-1212
dick_friedman@time-inc.com
Frequency:
1 time(s) per week
Description:
Publication is devoted to total in depth sports news coverage through articles, interviews, and photography. Also provided is information on recreation and leisure activities for both participants and spectators

SPORTS ILLUSTRATED FOR KIDS
135 WEST 50TH STREET
NEW YORK, NY 10020
212-522-3112
Fax: 212-467-1669
talkback@sikids.com
http://www.sikids.com

• Norman Pearlstine, Editor
• Andre Carter, Chief Reporter
(212) 522-0402
andre_carter@timeinc.com
• Andre Carter, Sports Reporter
andre_carter@sikids.com
• Neil Cohen, Managing Editor
(212) 522-4876
neil_cohen@sikids.com
• Ellen Cosgrove-Labrecque, Sports Associate Editor
(212) 522-8164
ellen_labrecque@sikids.com
• Jerry Craft, Editorial Director
• Erin Egan, Sports Senior Editor
(212) 522-5829
erin_egan@sikids.com
• Gary Gramling, Editorial Assistant
• Scott Hendrickson, Advertising Director
• Bill Hinds, Contributing Writer
(212) 522-3112
bill_hinds@simail.com
• Ted Keith, Sports Reporter
• Peter King, Assistant Managing Editor
• Peter King, Sports Ass't Managing Editor
• Shawn Nicholls, Associate Producer
(212) 522-3112
• Timothy Pitt, Editorial Director
timothy_pitt@sikids.com
• John Rolfe, Senior Editor
(212) 522-1847
john_rolfe@sikids.com
• Sachin Shenolikar, Chief of Reporters
• Justin Tejada, Senior Editor/SI Kids.com
(212) 522-5829
justin_tejada@timeinc.com
• Justin Tejada, Editor
(212) 522-8853
justin_tejada@sikids.com
• David Watt, Publisher
(212) 522-7789
dave_watt@timeinc.com
Frequency:
13 time(s) per year
Description:
Publication is a sports magazine for young people ages 8-14.

SPORTS JOURNAL
UNITED STATES SPORTS ACADEMY
ONE ACADEMY DRIVE
DAPHNE, AL 36526-7055
251-626-3303
Fax: 251-626-3874
• Thomas P. Rosandich, Publisher
(251) 626-3303
• Kelly Flanagan, Assistant Editor
(251) 626-3303
Description:
An electronic journal, is a publication of the United States Sports Academy in cooperation with the International Coaches Association and the International Association of Sports Academies. It is designed to further the knowledge of sport by allowing professionals in the field to publish articles at this site.

SPORTS MARKETING LETTER COMPANY
89 PAUL PL
FARFIELD, CT 06824
203-259-3890
• Brian J. Murphy, Publisher/Editor
Description:
Publishes the daily email briefing Sports Industry Daily, covering all aspects of the sports industry, and allied industries.

Circulation:
NA.
Sports:
All
Primary Audience:
High level executives in sports related industry.
Frequency:
Daily
Publishing Company:
Published by the The Sports Marketing Letter Company.

SPORTS PAGES
THE OAST HOUSE
PARK ROW
FARNHAM, SURREY, ENGLAND GU9 7JH
+44-1252 737333
Fax: +44-1252 737333
info@sportspages.com
www.sportspages.com
• Rich Johnson, Chief Editorial Officer
rj@sportspages.com
• Rick Scott, Chief Executive Officer
rickscott@sportpages.com
Sports Service Founded:
1997
Nature of Sports Service:
Online collection of articles and direct links to the sports sections of the major papers in the U.S. and those in and around cities with major league professional teams.

SPORTS PROFILES
4711 GOLF ROAD
SUITE 900
SKOKIE, IL 60076
800-725-9423
800-725-9423 ext 10
info@sppsports.com
• Lisa Levine, President
• Allen Redman, Chief Financial Officer
• Deborah Levine, Vice President

SPORTS REPORTER
527 THIRD AVE (3RD AVE)
BOX 327
NEW YORK, NY 10016
800-305-9604
Fax: 212-683.-1012
• Joe Lazzaro, Editor
Description:
Provides in-depth analysis of all football and basketball games.
Circulation:
30,000
Sports:
Football, basketball, baseball
Primary Audience:
Consumer
Frequency:
Weekly
Publishing Company:
Sports Reporter

SPORTS TRAVELER
1803 WEST 95TH ST., STE 101
CHICAGO, IL 60643
888-654-7755
Fax: 773-881-0389
www.sportstraveler.net
• Anbritt Stengele, Owner
Primary Audience:
Women interested in outdoor-oriented sports
Frequency:

6 times annually
Publishing Company:
Sports Traveler
Advertising Sales Office:
101 E. 52nd St, 9th Floor, New York, NY 10022. 212 759-1357; FAX: 212 759-1282

SPORTSCAR
16842 VON KARMAN AVENUE SUITE 125
IRVINE, CA 92606
949-417-6700
800-722-7140
Fax: 714-259-1502
sportscar@racer.com
http://www.racer.com
• Richard James, Editor
rjames@racer.com
• Celia Shambaugh, Advertising Manager
(949) 417-6700
cshambaugh@racer.com
Frequency:
1 time(s) per month
Description:
Publication reports on the motor sports activities of the membership, including event reports, results, photos of professional racing, amateur road racing, and road rallies.

SPORTSONE SOURCE
2151 HAWKINS STREET
SUITE 200
CHARLOTTE, NC 28203
704-987-3450
800-950-1314
Fax: 704-987-3455
http://www.sgdealer.com
• Bob Carr, Editor
(646) 654-4997
rcarr@sgbmag.com
Frequency:
1 time(s) per week
Description:
Publication contains marketing and financial news for the sporting goods industry.

SPORTSTRAVEL MAGAZINE
11835 W. OLYMPIC BLVD #1265
LOS ANGELES, CA 90064
310-577-3700
877-577-3700
Fax: 310-577-3715
info@schneiderpublishing.com
www.schneiderpublishing.com
• Timothy Schneider, Publisher
tim.schneider@schneiderpublishing.com
• Lisa Furfine, Associate Publisher
lisa.furfine@schneiderpublishing.com
• Jason Gewirtz, Managing Editor
jason.gewirtz@schneiderpublishing.com
• Rita Burris, Client Services Manager
(877) 577-3700
rita.burris@schneiderpublishing.com
• Martha Romero, Office Manager
(877) 577-3700
martha.romero@schneiderpublishing.com
Year Founded:
1997
Nature of Sports Service:
Publishers of SportsTravel and Association News magazines and producers of the TEAMS Conference & Expo.
Circulation:
16,000+
Frequency:
10 time(s) per year

SQUASH MAGAZINE
6001 1ST AVENUE
SUITE 500
SEATTLE, WA 98104
206-748-0085
Fax: 206-748-0277
www.squashmagazine.com
• Jay D. Prince, Publisher
editor@squashmagazine.com
• Ryan Lewis, Director of Operations
ryan@squashmagazine.com
• Paul Hueregue, Design Director
paul@squashmagazine.com
• James Zug, Senior Writer
zug@squashmagazine.com
Description:
The magazine for the sport of Squash.

STADIA MAGAZINE
THE GRAIN STORE
127 GLOUCESTER RD
BRIGHTON, ENGLAND BN1 4AF
44-(0) 1273 601-900
Fax: 44-(0) 1273 601 973
www.stadia.tv
• Ian Nuttall, Managing Director
• Sam Wibrew, Publications Director
• Tim Sewell, Publications Manager
• Mark Bisson, Deputy Editor
Publishing Company:
Broadcast Publishing Ltd.
Frequency:
Quarterly.

STEELERS DIGEST
3000 SOUTHWEST 148TH AVENUE
SUITE 112
MIRAMAR, FL 33027-4181
305-594-0508
800-334-4005
Fax: 305-594-0518
digest@curtispub.net
http://www.steelersdigestonline.com
• Andrew Cohen, Co-Editor
(412) 481-1846
acohen@curtispub.net
• Thomas Curtis, Publisher
newtcurtis@curtispub.net
• Bob Labriola, Co-Editor
(412) 481-1846
Frequency:
26 time(s) per year
Description:
Publication is a sports magazine devoted to the Pittsburgh Steelers.

STOCK CAR RACING
9036 BRITTANY WAY
TAMPA, FL 33619
863-644-0449
800-333-2633
Fax: 813-675-3559
http://www.primedia.com
• Larry Cothren, Editor
• Jana Huss, Managing Editor
(813) 675-3529
Frequency:
1 time(s) per month
Description:
Publication reports on stock car racing; includes personality profiles, technical articles, and race reports.

STRATEGIES: A JOURNAL FOR PHYSICAL AND SPORT ED
1900 ASSOCIATION DRIVE
RESTON, VA 20191-1599

703-476-3400
800-213-7193
Fax: 703-476-8316
strategies@aahperd.org
http://www.aahperd.org
• Carrie Nygaard, Editor
(703) 476-3451
Frequency:
6 time(s) per year
Description:
Publication provides how-to information for physical and sport educators.

STREET & SMITH'S SPORTSBUSINESS DAILY
120 W MOREHEAD STREET
SUITE 104
CHARLOTTE, NC 28202
704-973-1515
Fax: 704-973-1501
editorial@sportsbusinessdaily.com
www.sportsbusinessdaily.com
• Abraham Madkour, Executive Editor
(704) 973-1511
amadkovr@sportsbusinessdaily.com
• Rick Ellington, Managing Editor
(704) 973-1528
rellington@sportsbusinessdaily.com
• Bill Magrath, Media Relations Manager
(704) 973-1515
billm@sportsbusinessdaily.com
• Beverly Padgett, Director of Circulation
(704) 973-1455
bpadgett@sportsbusinessdaily.com
Publishing Company:
Street & Smith's Sports Group.
Frequency:
Daily
Sports:
Sports Business - all sports.
Circulation:
30,000
Nature of Services:
We provide decision-makers in the sports industry with comprehensive, real-time Sports Business News, summarizes industry news reported by more than 500 media outlets in the U.S. and abroad. We also offer relevant original features of in-depth analysis of the industry's latest trends.
Publications:
Morning Buzz; Closing Bell; Sports Business Daily.

STREET & SMITH'S SPORTS GEAR
120 W. MOREHEAD STREET
CHARLOTTE, NC 28202-1844
704-973-1300
Fax: 704-973-1576
annuals@streetandsmiths.com
www.streetandsmiths.com
• Mike Kallay, Publisher
• Scott Smith, Managing Editor
• Patrick Wood, Advertising Director
• Amy Taylor, Senior Marketing Manager
• Jim Penegar, Circulation General Manager
Description:
Brings you great-looking sport collectibles that you can use at home, at the office or at the tailgate.

STREET & SMITH'S SPORTSBUSINESS JOURNAL
120 W. MOREHEAD STREET
SUITE 310
CHARLOTTE, NC 28202

704-973-1400
800-829-9839
Fax: 704-973-1401
help@sportsbusinessjournal.com
www.sportsbusinessjournal.com
• Richard Weiss, Publisher
(704) 973-1410
rweiss@sportsbusinessjournal.com
• Abraham Madkour, Executive Editor
(704) 973-1511
amadkour@sportsbusinessjournal.com
• Jerry Kavanagh, New York Bureau Chief
(212) 500-0714
jkavanagh@sportsbusinessjournal.com
• Martin Bounds, VP Business Development
(704) 973-1413
mbounds@sportsbusinessjournal.com
• Paige Montgomery, Circulation Director
(212) 500-0710
pmontgomery@sportsbusinessjournal.com
• Tom Stinson, Assistant Managing Editor
(704) 973-1424
tstinson@sportsbusinessjournal.com
• David Broughton, Research Director
(704) 973-1433
dbroughton@sportsbusinessjournal.com
• Mark Mensheha, Assistant Managing Editor
(704) 973-1427
mmensheha@sportsbusinessjournal.com
• Jake Kyler, Copy Editor
(704) 973-1436
jkyler@sportsbusinessjournal.com
• Rob Knapp, Assistant Managing Editor/News
(704) 973-1416
rknapp@sportsbusinessjournal.com
Publishing Company:
Street & Smith Sport Group.
Frequency:
49 times a year; Audience 54,400; Annual subscription $254 USD.
Primary Audience:
Sports industry executives, business executives, team leagues and broadcast media.
Sports:
All.
Nature of Service:
Sports Business Journal provides the critical news and information sports industry leaders need to complete, negotiate and succeed. Every issue features coverage of the deals, trades, contracts and board room power plays that shape the rapidly changing sports industry. Regular columns cover every aspect of the sports industry from media and marketing to finance and facilities.
Circulation:
17,000

STRIKER-WEST
13540 LAKE CITY WAY, N.E. SUITE 3
SEATTLE, WA 98125-3665
607-962-9923
Fax: 206-367-2636
http://www.varsitycommunications.com
• Charles Beene, Editor
(607) 962-9923
charles@varsitycommunications.com
Frequency:
4 time(s) per year
Description:
Publication is the official magazine of the New York State West Youth Soccer Association; contains association news, coaching tips, and tournament updates.

STUDENT SPORTS
2780 SKYPARK DRIVE
TORRANCE, CA 90505
310-791-1142
800-660-1334
Fax: 310-257-4444
http://www.studentsports.com
• Mark Tennis, Editor
(209) 463-9050
brent@studentsport.com
• Andy Bark, Publisher
• Mark Tennis, Editorial Vice President
(209) 463-9050
• Brent Eads, Editor
(310) 791-1142
Frequency:
10 time(s) per year
Description:
Publication covers sports at the high school level.

SURF NEWS
485 EAST 17TH STREET SUITE 202
COSTA MESA, CA 92627
949-548-6740
Fax: 949-548-5572
surfnewsed@aol.com
• Bill Sharp, Editor
• Bill Sharp, Publisher
Frequency:
1 time(s) per month
Description:
Publication focuses on the beach lifestyle in Southern California; geared toward surfers, as well as people who enjoy the beach.

SURFER
33046 CALLE AVIADOR
SAN JUAN CAPISTRANO, CA 92675-4704
949-496-5922
Fax: 949-496-7849
smithch@primemedia.com
http://www.surfermag.com
• Chris Mauro, Editor
(949) 661-5115
• Jake Howard, Associate Editor
(949) 661-5130
• Rick Irons, Publisher
(949) 661-5112
Frequency:
1 time(s) per month
Description:
Publication focuses on information of interest to surfing enthusiasts.

SURFER TRAVEL REPORT
33046 CALLE AVIADOR
SAN JUAN CAPISTRANO, CA 92675-4704
949-496-5922
Fax: 949-496-7849
surfreport@primemedia.com
http://www.surfermag.com
• Luke Seile, Editor
(949) 661-5108
Frequency:
1 time(s) per month
Description:
Publication is a travel guide for surfers.

SURFING
950 CALLE AMANECER SUITE C
SAN CLEMENTE, CA 92673
949-492-7873
Fax: 949-498-6485
http://www.surfingthemag.com

- Don Meek, Publisher
- Hagan Kelley, Associate Editor
- James Lynch, Advertising Manager
Frequency:
1 time(s) per month
Description:
Publication provides information on equipment, destinations, and competitions for surfers.

SWIMMING WORLD & JUNIOR SWIMMER
2744 EAST GLENROSA AVENUE
PHOENIX, AZ 85015
928-284-4005
800-345-7946
Fax: 928-284-2477
swimworld@swiminfo.com
http://www.swiminfo.com
- Bob Ingram, Editor
bobi@swiminfo.com
- Toni Blake, Advertising Manager
(310) 379-2278
- Richard Deal, Publisher
- Phillip Whitten, Editor-in-Chief
(480) 874-9364
philw@swiminfo.com
Frequency:
1 time(s) per month
Description:
Publication contains information of interest to children and young adults involved in competitive swimming.

T & L GOLF
1120 AVENUE OF THE AMERICAS 11TH
FLOOR
NEW YORK, NY 10036-6700
212-642-1965
Fax: 212-642-1960
http://www.tlgolf.com
- Jonathan Lesser, Editor
(212) 642-1934
jonathan.s.lesser@aexp.com
- John Atwood, Editor
- John Atwood, Editor-in-Chief
- Felice Kaplan, Managing Editor
(212) 382-1965
- Jonathan Lesser, Sports Associate Editor
(212) 642-1934
- John P. Newport, Sports Senior Editor
(212) 642-1938
- John Rodenburg, Publisher
(212) 536-2030
Frequency:
6 time(s) per year
Description:
Publication contains information for golfers who also appreciate fine living and elegance.

TEAM MARKETING REPORT
660 WEST GRAND AVENUE
CHICAGO, IL 60611
312-829-7060
Fax: 847-256-2594
http://tmr.nelix.com/Resources.asp
- Dan Migala, Executive Editor
(312) 202-6551
- Michael Lane, Managing Editor
- Kurt Hunzeker, Director of Business Development and Marketin
- Meghann Dunlap, Project Manager
Publishing Company:
Team Marketing Report Inc.
Frequency:
Monthly
Primary Audience:

Sports teams, sports venues, sports TV/radio sales execs, sports marketing agencies, corporate sponsors, auto racing/tennis/golf promoters
Sports:
Professional and Collegiate Sports
Circulation:
NA.
Description:
Monthly newsletter reporting innovative and successful marketing activities of sports marketers, corporate sponsors and sports marketing agencies. Provides in-depth details of new ideas to help marketers, sponsors and agencies increase sales and exposure through sports marketing. Exclusive and original research advertising rates, ticket prices and examining consumer attitudes towards sports and sponsors included in each issue. Other features include columns by prominent sports marketing executives, sponsor news, personnel changes within the sports marketing field.

TENNIS
79 MADISON AVENUE 8TH FLOOR
NEW YORK, NY 10016
212-636-2700
Fax: 212-636-2720
editors@tennis.com
http://www.tennis.com
- Stephen Tignor, Managing Editor
stignor@tennismagazine.com
- Peter Bodo, Senior Editor
(212) 636-2714
- Chris Evert, Publisher
cevert@tennismagazine.com
- Norb Garrett, Editorial Director
ngarrett@tennismagazine.com
- Tony Lance, Associate Editor
(212) 636-2731
- Jon Levey, Senior Editor
(212) 636-2719
jlevey@tennis.com
- James Martin, Senior Editor
(212) 636-2708
jmartin@tennismagazine.com
- Jeff Williams, Publisher
jwilliams@tennismagazine.com
- Mark Woodruff, Editor-at-Large
Frequency:
1 time(s) per month
Description:
Publication features information of interest to tennis enthusiasts.

TEXAS COACH
2553 HIGHWAY 35, S.
SAN MARCOS, TX 78666
512-392-3741
Fax: 512-392-3762
http://www.thsca.com
- Sheryl Honeycutt, Editor
(512) 392-3741
sherylhoneycutt@thsca.com
Frequency:
9 time(s) per year
Description:
Publication is geared toward coaches at educational institutions throughout Texas.

TEXAS COACH MAGAZINE
1011 E. 53 1/2 ST
AUSTIN, TX 78751

512-454-6709
Fax: 512-454-3950
www.thsca.com
- Sheryl Honeycutt, Editor
Publishing Company:
Texas High School Coaches Association
Frequency:
Nine times annually
Primary Audience:
Texas high school coaches and coaches in neighboring states
Sports:
General
Circulation:
16,200. 81% association membership, 19% non-paid contr.
Description:
Concerned with coach's job as a coach in his or her sport as well as to make the coaching profession more professional. Editorial covers all phases of each sport.

TEXAS FOOTBALL
546 E. MAIN STREET
LEXINGTON, KY 40505
859-226-4678
Fax: 859-226-4567
hostpr@hostcommunications.com
- Logan Lawton, Collegiate Sports Director
(859) 226-4342
lawton.logan@hostcommunications.com
- David Nunnery, Print Advertising Director
(859) 226-4678
david.nunnery@hostcommunications.com
- Matt Briggs, Circulation/Fulfillment Specialist
(866) 313-4678
- Adam Hochfelder, Magazine Executive Director
(888) 484-4678
adam.hochfelder@hostcommunications.com
- Jake Shaw, Managing Editor
(972) 392-5849
jake.shaw@hostcommunications.com
Description:
Sports magazine in the State of Texas that covers all levels of football programs in the Lone Star State whether it be High School Level, College Level, Or Professional Level.
Frequency:
Annually.

TEXAS GOLFER MAGAZINE
4920 CENTER STREET
HOUSTON, TX 77027
877-536-1088
Fax: 713-680-0138
http://www.texasgolfermagazine.com
- Wayne Morkovsky, Editor
Frequency:
1 time(s) per month
Description:
Publication provides tournament and competition information about golf in southern Texas.

TEXAS RUNNER & TRIATHLETE
713-935-0555
Fax: 713-935-0559
Loren@runningmags.com
www.texasrunnertriathlete.com
- Lance Phegley, Editor
Frequency:
1 time(s) per month
Primary Audience:
Runners and triathletes

Circulation:
6,000

TEXAS THOROUGHBRED
1016 LA POSADA SUITE 130
AUSTIN, TX 78752
512-458-6133
Fax: 512-453-5919
denisb@texasthoroughbred.com
http://www.texasthoroughbred.com
• Denis Blake, Editor
• David Hooper, Executive Director
davidh@texasthoroughbred.com
• Judy Rosson, Advertising Manager
(512) 458-6133
judyr@texasthoroughbred.com
Frequency:
9 time(s) per year
Description:
Publication contains information of interest to Thoroughbred horse breeders, trainers, and racing in the state of Texas.

THRASHER SKATEBOARD MAGAZINE
1303 UNDERWOOD AVENUE
SAN FRANCISCO, CA 94124-3308
415-822-3083
888-520-9099
Fax: 415-822-8359
mail@thrashermagazine.com
http://www.thrashermagazine.com
• Jake Phelps, Editor
jake@thrashermagazine.com
• Dean Huitrado, Advertising Director
dean@slapmagazine.com
• Edward H. Riggins, Publisher
• Eben Sterling, Advertising Director
eben@thrashermagazine.com
Frequency:
1 time(s) per month
Description:
Publication fuses on the excitement of top-level skateboarding with reader participation, hard edged music, and lots of attitude.

TOUCHLINE-EASTERN PENNSYLVANIA
13540 LAKE CITY WAY N.E. SUITE 3
SEATTLE, WA 98125-3665
206-367-2420
Fax: 206-363-9099
http://www.varsitycommunications.com
• Charles Beene, Editor
(206) 367-2420
charles@varsitycommunications.com
• Peter Paige, Publisher
(215) 321-9822
repete@paige2.com
Frequency:
4 time(s) per year
Description:
Publication features articles that bring readers reliable news and information about soccer.

TRACK & FIELD NEWS
2570 W. EL CAMINO REAL
SUITE 480
MOUNTAIN VIEW, CA 94040-1306
650-948-8188
Fax: 650-948-9445
business@trackandfieldnews.com
http://www.trackandfieldnews.com
• E. Garry Hill, Editor
(650) 948-8188
gh@trackandfieldnews.com
• Ed Fox, Publisher

ef@trackandfieldnews.com
• Jon Hendershott, Associate Editor
jh@trackandfieldnews.com
• Tom Jordan, Advertising Manager
• Sieg Lindstrom, Managing Editor
(650) 948-8188
sl@trackandfieldnews.com
• Janet Vitu, Publisher
Frequency:
1 time(s) per month
Description:
Publication covers all track events from high school to the Olympics; includes news and results of major meets, interviews with leading athletes, profiles, photos, performance lists, records, rankings and opinion columns.

TRACK COACH
2570 EL CAMINO REAL
MOUNTAIN VIEW, CA 94040-1306
650-948-8188
Fax: 650-948-9445
http://www.trackandfieldnews.com
• Russ Ebbets, Editor
(650) 948-8188
spinedoctor229@hotmail.com
• Ed Fox, Publisher
(650) 948-8188
ef@trackandfieldnews.com
Frequency:
4 time(s) per year
Description:
Publication provides technical information on track and field for coaches.

TRAILER BOATS
20700 BELSHAW AVENUE
CARSON, CA 90746-3510
310-537-6322
Fax: 310-537-8735
http://www.trailerboats.com
• Ron Eldridge, Editor
(310) 537-6322
reldridge@ehlertpublishing.com
• Ron Eldridge, Executive Editor
• Jim Hendricks, Associate Publisher
(310) 537-6322
• Wiley Poole, Publisher
• Steve Quinlan, Editor
• Dan Armitage, Field Editor
(310) 537-6322
editors@trailerboats.com
Frequency:
11 time(s) per year
Description:
Publication covers issues of interest to owners and prospective buyers of trailerable power boats.

TRAINING AND CONDITIONING
31 DUTCH MILL ROAD
ITHACA, NY 14850
607-257-6970
Fax: 607-257-7328
info@momentummedia.com
http://www.athleticsearch.com
• Mark Goldberg, Publisher
(607) 257-6970
mg@momentummedia.com
Frequency:
9 time(s) per year
Description:
Publication is written for people who are involved in training and conditioning competitive athletes at all levels.

TRANSWORLD BUSINESS
353 AIRPORT ROAD
OCEANSIDE, CA 92054-1203
760-722-7777
800-788-7020
Fax: 760-722-0653
http://www.twsnow.com
• Sean O'Brien, Editor In Chief
(760) 722-7777
sean@twsnet.com
• Brad McDonald, President
(760) 722-7777
brad.mcdonald@time4.com
• Jamey Stone, Advertising Director
(760) 722-7777
jstone@twsnet.com
• Kristina Ackermann, Associate Editor
(760) 722-7777
Frequency:
6 time(s) per year
Description:
Publication is written for snowboard retailers; includes news, analysis, trends, technical studies, and company profiles.

TRANSWORLD SKATEBOARDING
353 AIRPORT ROAD
OCEANSIDE, CA 92054-1203
760-722-7777
800-334-8152
Fax: 760-722-0653
http://www.skateboarding.com
• Eric Stricker, Editor
(760) 722-7777
estricker@twsnet.com
• Carleton Curtis, Managing Editor
(760) 722-7777
carleton@twsnet.com
• Skin Phillips, Editor-in-Chief
(760) 722-7777
skin@twsnet.com
• Jamey Stone, Advertising Director
(760) 722-7777
jstone@twsnet.com
Frequency:
1 time(s) per month
Description:
Publication contains interviews with pro-skaters, contest coverage, and columns on improving skating skills.

TRIAD GOLF TODAY
P.O. BOX 11784
WINSTON-SALEM, NC 27106
336-924-1619
Fax: 336-922-9449
http://www.triadgolf.com
• Steve Williams, Editor
(336) 349-2739
editor@triadgolf.com
• Jay Allred, Publisher
Frequency:
8 time(s) per year
Description:
Publication offers in-depth news and features about the local golfing community.

TROTTINGBRED
60 GULF ROAD
GOUVERNEUR, NY 13642
315-287-2294
Fax: 315-287-5010
http://www.trottingbred.com
• Kathy Denesha, Editor
Frequency:
6 time(s) per year

TUFF STUFF PUBLICATIONS
700 E. STATE ST
IOLA, WI 54990
715-445-2214
800-345-3168
Fax: 715-445-4087
www.tuffstuff.com
• Dean Listle, Publisher
• Rocky Landsverk, Editorial Director
Description:
Comprehensive information (magazines, books, online) about sports and non-sports/entertainment player trading cards, autographs, and memorabilia, including prices, card evaluations, player interviews and industry trends. Also publishes fantasy guides for participants in football and baseball rotisserie leagues.
Circulation:
130,000
Sports:
Baseball, basketball, football, hockey
Primary Audience:
Trading cards & sports memorabilia.
Frequency:
Monthly
Publishing Company:
Tuff Stuff Publications, Inc.

TV SPORTSFILE
PO BOX 4159
ANNA MARIA, FL 34216
941-778-5960
800-876-6604
Fax: 941-778-2895
www.gouldmedia.com
• Barry Gould, Publisher
• Dantia Gould, Editor
Publishing Company:
Gould Media.
Frequency:
Twice Weekly
Description:
Fax/E-mail newsletter dealing with televised sports events, broadcasting organizations and executives, also publishes netSports tracking activities of organizations involved with sports content and e-commerce on the Internet. Annual research reports include Television Sports Rights and Net Sports, 2000.

TWIN CITIES SPORTS
P.O. BOX 1203
PRIOR LAKE, MN 55372
952-440-4898
Fax: 952-440-3628
http://www.twincitiessports.com
• Jeff Banowetz, Editor
jeff@windycitysportsmag.com
• Doug Kaplan, Publisher
(312) 421-1551
doug@windycitysports.com
Frequency:
11 time(s) per year
Description:
Publication promotes participation in grass-roots and amateur sports in Minnesota and the Midwest; emphasis is on running, cycling, in-line skating, triathlon, volleyball, hiking, canoeing, kayaking, aerobics, skiing, snowboarding, and snowshoeing.

UNDERCURRENT
3020 BRIDGEWAY
SUITE 201
SAUSALITO, CA 94965-1439
415-289-0501
800-326-1896
Fax: 415-289-0137
http://www.undercurrent.org
• Ben Davison, Editor
(415) 289-0501
bendavison@aol.com
• Ben Davison, Publisher
bendavison@aol.com
Frequency:
11 time(s) per year
Description:
Publication is geared toward the recreational scuba diver; includes safety tips, equipment reviews, and reviews of international diving resorts.

UNDERSEA JOURNAL
30151 TOMAS
RANCHO SANTA MARGARI, CA 92688
949-858-7234
800-729-7234
Fax: 949-267-1267
journal@padi.com
http://www.padi.com
• Susan Tate, Editor
(949) 858-7234
Frequency:
4 time(s) per year

UNITED STATES SPORTS ACADEMY
ONE ACADEMY DRIVE
DAPHNE, AL 36526
251-626-3303
Fax: 251-626-8829
academy@ussa.edu
www.ussa.edu
• Thomas Rosandich, President/Chief Executive Officer
• Andrea Jordan, Assistant Dean of Administration and Finance
(251) 626-3303
ajordan@ussa.edu
• Annita Alldredge, Finance Director
(251) 626-3303
aalldredge@ussa.edu
Description:
The United States Sports Academy is an independent, non-profit, accredited, special mission sports university created to serve the nation and the world with programs in instruction, research and service. The role of the Academy is to prepare men and women for careers in the profession of sports.
Year Founded:
1972

USA CYCLING NEWSLETTER
210 USA CYCLING POINT
SUITE 100
COLORADO SPRINGS, CO 80919-2215
719-434-4200
Fax: 719-434-4300
membership@usacycling.org
www.usacycling.org/media/
• Steve Johnson, Chief Executive Officer
• Sean Petty, Chief Operating Officer
• Todd Sowl, Chief Financial Officer
• Susan Diller, Membership Director
Frequency:
Monthly
Description:
Publication focuses on bicycle racing; contains USA Cycling news, race coverage and results, feature articles, and information on training and coaching; includes race schedules.

USA GYMNASTICS
PAN AMERICAN PLAZA
201 SOUTH CAPITOL AVENUE
INDIANAPOLIS, IN 46225-1000
317-237-5050
800-345-4719
Fax: 317-237-5069
http://www.usa-gymnastics.org
• Adrienne Willy, Marketing Coordinator
awilly@usagym.org
• Steven Penny, President
spenny@usa-gymnastics.org
• Luan Peszek, Publisher
(317) 829-5645
lpeszek@usa-gymnastics.org
• Robert Colarossi, Publisher
(317) 237-5050
Frequency:
6 time(s) per year
Description:
Publication is designed to educate readers on fitness, health, safety, technique, trends, and personalities related to the gymnastics and fitness field.

USA HOCKEY MAGAZINE
1775 BOB JOHNSON DRIVE
COLORADO SPRINGS, CO 80906
719-576-8724
Fax: 719-538-1160
usah@usahockey.org
www.usahockeymagazine.com
• Harry Thompson, Editor-in-Chief
(719) 576-8724
harryt@usahockey.org
Frequency:
10 time(s) per year
Description:
Publication is the official magazine of USA Hockey, and is written for registered players, coaches, officials, parents and volunteers; includes human interest stories, instructional pieces, and pages devoted to children.

USA ROLLER SPORTS MAGAZINE
4730 SOUTH STREET
LINCOLN, NE 68506-1256
402-483-7551
Fax: 402-483-1465
http://www.usarollersports.org
• Kellie Habeeb, Editor
(402) 483-7551
Frequency:
6 time(s) per year
Description:
Publication contains articles on roller skating for athletes who compete in this sport.

USA TODAY SPORTS WEEKLY
7950 JONES BRANCH DRIVE
MCLEAN, VA 22108-0605
703-854-3400
800-872-1415
Fax: 703-854-2034
sportsweekly@usatoday.com
http://www.usatoday.com
• Tim McQuay, Managing Editor
(703) 854-6456
tmcquay@usatoday.com
• Lee Ivory, Publisher
(703) 854-5630
livory@usatoday.com

• Lee Ivory, Publisher
(703) 854-8014
livory@usatoday.com
• Bob Nightengale, Columnist
(703) 854-5630
bobnighte@aol.com
• Paul White, Senior Writer
(703) 854-3756
• Chris Colston, Baseball Reporter
(703) 854-3723
ccolston@usatoday.com
Frequency:
1 time(s) per week
Description:
Publication covers major league, minor league, and college baseball.

USA WEIGHTLIFTING
1 OLYMPIC PLAZA
COLORADO SPRINGS, CO 80909-5764
719-866-4508
Fax: 719-866-4741
usaw@usaweightlifting.org
www.usaweightlifting.org
• Phil Andrews, Chief Executive
Officer/General Secretary
(719) 866-3386
Phil.Andrews@usaweightlifting.org
• Brad Suchorski, Membership Manager
(719) 866-3227
Membership Requirements:
No requirements - there are memberships of
all kinds and dues related to each
membership type.
Description:
USA Weightlifing is the national governing
body for olympic weightlifting in the United
States. USAW is a member of the US
Olympic Committee and of the International
Weightlifting Federation.

USDF CONNECTION
220 LEXINGTON GREEN CIRCLE SUITE
510
LEXINGTON, KY 40503
859-971-2277
Fax: 859-971-7722
connection@usdf.org
http://www.usdf.org
• Jennifer Bryant, Editor
(610) 344-0116
jbryant@usdf.org
Frequency:
1 time(s) per month
Description:
Publication is the membership magazine of
the United States Dressage Federation and
is dedicated to education, recognition of
achievement, and promoting the sport of
dressage.

USROWING
201 SOUTH CAPITOL AVENUE
INDIANAPOLIS, IN 46225-1068
317-237-5656
Fax: 317-237-5646
members@usrowing.org
http://www.usrowing.org
• Brett Johnson, Editor
(317) 237-5656
brett@usrowing.org
Description:
Publication covers rowing in the United
States; includes event results, nutrition,
fitness, technique, and instructional articles.

VELO NEWS
1830 NORTH 55TH STREET
BOULDER, CO 80301-2700
303-440-0601
Fax: 303-444-6788
http://www.velonews.com
• Kip Mikler, Editor
kmikler@insightinc.com
• Steve Brawley, Advertising Manager
(303) 440-0601
sbrawley@insideinc.com
• Ted Costantino, Publisher
(303) 440-0601
tcostantino@insideinc.com
Frequency:
20 time(s) per year
Description:
Publication focuses on bicycle racing and
race stories; includes columns on business,
components, European news, off-road
racing, training and physiology, personality
interviews, and a complete calendar and
results of North American events.

VERMONT SOCCER ASSOCIATION NEWS
13540 LAKE CITY WAY N.E. SUITE 3
SEATTLE, WA 98125
206-367-2420
Fax: 206-367-2636
http://www.varsitycommunications.com
• Charles Beene, Editor
(206) 367-2420
Frequency:
4 time(s) per year

VERMONT SPORTS TODAY
35 SOUTH MAIN STREET RIVER ROAD
HOLDINGS
HANOVER, NH 03755
603-643-1441
Fax: 603-643-4644
http://www.vtsports.com
• Kathryn Carter, Managing Editor
(802) 244-5796
• Chris Blau, Publisher
(603) 643-1441
Frequency:
1 time(s) per month
Description:
Publication reports on individual aerobic
sports in Vermont and the surrounding area.

VINTAGE BECKETT SPORTS COLLECTIBLES
15850 DALLAS PKWY
DALLAS, TX 75248
972-991-6657
Fax: 972-991-8930
www.beckett.com
• James Beckett, Owner
• Mark Harwell, President
Description:
Includes action-packed pages featuring
price guides for and articles about:
autographed sports collectibles, game-used
apparel and equipment, sports cereal boxes,
championship tickets and more.
Circulation:
43,494. 85% newsstand, 15% paid subscr.
Sports:
Major and minor league baseball, college
football and basketball cards
Primary Audience:
Consumer
Frequency:
Monthly

Publishing Company:
Beckett Publications, Inc.

VINTAGE MOTORSPORT
5151 SOUTH LAKELAND DRIVE
SUITE 15
LAKELAND, FL 33813-2556
415-898-5776
800-626-9937
Fax: 415-898-3756
drandy@vintagemotorsport.com
http://www.vintagemotorsport.com
• D. Randy Riggs, Editor-in-Chief
drandy@vintagemotorsport.com
• Randy Riggs, Editor in Chief
(863) 607-9701
drriggs@vintagemotorsport.com
Frequency:
6 time(s) per year
Description:
Publication focuses on vintage motor racing
and motor racing history.

VISIBILITY
P.O. BOX 628
DALY CITY, CA 94017-0628
650-583-8492
Fax: 650-583-0614
croseusoac@aol.com
http://www.underwater-society.org
• Carol Rose, Editor
Frequency:
5 time(s) per year
Description:
Publication covers underwater sports;
includes skin and scuba diving, diving
safety, diving education, and marine
ecology.

VOICE OF THE HAWKEYES
P.O. BOX 187
IOWA CITY, IA 52244
319-530-2272
888-474-8669
Fax: 319-665-3699
voiceofthehawkeyes@yahoo.com
http://www.voiceofthehawkeyes.com
• Todd Brommelkamp, Editor
Frequency:
25 time(s) per year
Description:
Publication focuses on sports at the
University of Iowa.

VOICE OF THE TENNESSEE WALKING HORSE MAGAZINE
250 NORTH ELLINGTON PARKWAY
LEWISBURG, TN 37091-2835
931-359-1567
800-467-0232
Fax: 931-270-8743
http://www.twhbea.com
• Dan Butt, Managing Editor
• Sarah Gee, Staff Writer
(931) 359-0590
sgee@twhbea.com
• Richard Hudgins, Advertising Manager
(931) 359-1567
Frequency:
11 time(s) per year
Description:
Publication gives information about events
for the Tennessee Walking Horses.

media

597

VOLLEYBALL MAGAZINE
420 BOYLSTON STREET 5TH FLOOR
BOSTON, MA 02116
617-536-0100
800-876-2509
Fax: 617-536-0102
http://www.volleyballmag.com
• Mike Miazga, Editor
mmiazga@madavor.com
Frequency:
1 time(s) per month
Description:
Publication provides information on the entire indoor and outdoor volleyball sport; includes instruction, how-to articles, training, fitness, court strategies, and coaching.

WAKE BOARDING MAGAZINE
460 NORTH ORLANDO AVENUE SUITE 200
WINTER PARK, FL 32789-3150
407-628-4802
Fax: 407-628-7061
http://www.wakeboardingmag.com
• Luke Woodling, Managing Editor
(407) 628-4802
luke.woodling@worldpub.net
• Jason Bingham, Advertising Manager
(407) 628-4802
• Jim Emmons, Associate Publisher
(407) 628-4802
• John McEver, Jr., Publisher
(407) 571-4682
john.mcever@worldpub.net
• Kevin Michael, Senior Editor
(407) 628-4802
Frequency:
8 time(s) per year
Description:
Publication includes instructional tips and photographs for water sports fans, particularly wake boarders.

WALKING HORSE REPORT
730 MADISON STREET
SHELBYVILLE, TN 37160-3519
931-684-8123
Fax: 931-684-8196
admin@walkinghorsereport.com
www.walkinghorsereport.com/
• Jennifer Styskal, Editorial Director
• Jeffrey Howard, Publisher
jhoward@horseworld.net
Frequency:
1 time(s) per week
Description:
Publication covers walking horse shows and major events.

WATER SKI
460 NORTH ORLANDO AVENUE SUITE 200
WINTER PARK, FL 32789-3150
407-628-4802
800-879-0495
Fax: 407-628-7061
editor@waterskimag.com
http://www.worldpub.net
• Todd Ristorcelli, Editor
• John McEver, Jr., Publisher
(407) 571-4682
john.mcever@worldpub.net
Frequency:
9 time(s) per year

WATER SKIER
1251 COW ROAD
POLK CITY, FL 33868
863-324-4341
800-533-2972
Fax: 863-325-8259
http://www.usawaterski.org
• Scott Atkinson, Editor
(863) 324-4341
satkinson@usawaterski.org
• Steve Utt, Advertising Manager
Frequency:
7 time(s) per year
Description:
Publication features information of interest to water skiing enthusiasts.

WATERCRAFT WORLD
6420 SYCAMORE LANE SUITE 100
MAPLE GROVE, MN 55369
805-667-4100
800-848-6247
Fax: 805-667-4336
• Lee Hetherington, Publisher
• Meghan Orazen, Advertising Sales Manager
morazen@affinitygroup.com
Frequency:
6 time(s) per year
Description:
Publication is geared toward personal watercraft enthusiasts.

WEIDER PUBLICATIONS
21100 ERWIN ST
WOODLAND HILLS, CA 91367
818-884-6800
Fax: 818-884-0371
www.fitnessonline.com
• Eric Weider, President
Description:
Publishes several magazines in the health and fitness field, including FLEX, LIVING FIT, MEN'S FITNESS, MUSCLE & FITNESS, SENIOR GOLFER, and SHAPE.
New York Address:
451 Park Ave South, New York, NY 10016.
212 251-0640; FAX: 212 251-0641

WESTERN GUIDE TO SNOWMOBILING
360 B STREET
IDAHO FALLS, ID 83402
208-524-7000
800-638-0135
Fax: 208-522-5241
http://www.snowest.com
• Lane Lindstrom, Editor
(208) 542-2234
lindstrm@snowest.com
• Ryan Harris, Assistant Editor
(208) 542-2243
rharris@snowest.com
Frequency:
1 time(s) per month
Description:
The exclusive most useful reference guide in print for western snowmobile vacation information. Aimed towards snowmobilers.
Circulation:
26,258

WESTERN HORSEMAN
3850 NORTH NEVADA AVENUE
COLORADO SPRINGS, CO 80907-5339
719-633-5524
Fax: 817-737-9266

edit@westernhorseman.com
http://www.westernhorseman.com
• A. J. Mangum, Editor
aj.mangum@westernhorseman.com
• Fran Smith, Managing Editor
(719) 633-5524
fran.smith@westernhorseman.com
• Randy Witte, Publisher
r.witte@westernhorseman.com
Frequency:
1 time(s) per month
Description:
Publication is a general interest horse magazine with emphasis on the training, care, and use of horses for work and pleasure, particularly in the American West.

WESTERN OUTDOOR NEWS
PO BOX 73370
SAN CLEMENTE, CA 92673
949-366-0030
Fax: 949-366-0804
• Robert Twilegar, President
• Pat McDonell, Editor
• Joe Higgins, Advertising Manager
Description:
Covers fishing and hunting news in California and Arizona, plus Baja.
Circulation:
74,990. 81% paid subscr, 8% newsstand, 11% contr non-paid.
Sports:
Hunting, fishing, related outdoor recreation
Primary Audience:
Consumer
Frequency:
52 times annually
Publishing Company:
Western Outdoor Publications

WESTERN OUTDOORS
PO BOX 2027
NEWPORT BEACH, CA 92659-1027
949-546-4370
Fax: 949-662-3486
• Robert S. Twilegar, President/Chief Executive Officer
• Joe Higgins, Publisher
• Pat McDonnell, Editorial Director
Description:
Features articles on fishing and hunting techniques, where-to-go and current events affecting sportsmen in the 11 western states, Baja, Alaska, Hawaii and Western Canada.
Circulation:
130,000. 95% paid subscr, 5% other.
Sports:
Hunting, fishing, related outdoor recreation
Primary Audience:
Consumer
Frequency:
Nine times annually
Publishing Company:
Western Outdoor Publications

WHEELIN' SPORTSMAN
770 AUGUSTA ROAD
EDGEFIELD, SC 29824-1510
803-637-3106
Fax: 803-637-0034
http://www.nwtf.org
• Karen Lee, Editor
klee@nwtf.net
• Chasiti Kirkland, Managing Editor
(803) 637-3106

Frequency:
4 time(s) per year
Description:
Publication features tips, secrets, and information on sports pertaining to the disabled members of the NWTF.

WINDSURFING
460 NORTH ORLANDO AVENUE SUITE 200
WINTER PARK, FL 32789-3150
407-628-4802
888-259-6753
Fax: 407-628-7061
http://www.worldpub.net
• Eddy Patracelli, Editor
(407) 628-4802
eddy.patricelli@worldpub.net
• David Combe, Publisher
(805) 403-8095
david.combe@worldpub.net
Frequency:
8 time(s) per year
Description:
Publication is geared toward windsurfing enthusiasts.

WINDY CITY SPORTS
1450 WEST RANDOLPH
CHICAGO, IL 60607
312-421-1551
Fax: 312-421-1454
http://www.windycitysports.com
• Doug Kaplan, President/Publisher
• Kate Bongiovanni, Managing Editor & Web Site Editor
(312) 421-1551
kateb@windycitysports.com
Sports Service Founded:
1992
Publication:
Our first issue was printed in 1987. Covers amateur athletics in the Chicago area; focuses primarily on running, cycling, and in-line skating.
Frequency:
1 time(s) per month

WINGFOOT
1303 HIGHTOWER TRAIL SUITE 101
ATLANTA, GA 30350
770-650-1102
Fax: 770-650-2848
http://www.knowatlanta.com
• Riley McDermid, Editor
(770) 650-1102
• Craig Dekshenieks, Publisher
(770) 650-1102
• Michelle Bourg, Co-Editor & Features Writer
(404) 231-9064
Frequency:
9 time(s) per year

WISCONSIN GOLFER
333 BISHOP'S WAY SUITE 104
BROOKFIELD, WI 53005
262-786-4301
Fax: 262-786-4202
info@wsga.org
http://www.wsga.org
• John Hughes, Editor
killer@aol.com
• John Hughes, Publisher
killer@aol.com
• Rick Pledl, Associate Editor

Frequency:
6 time(s) per year
Description:
Publication provides information and resources for golfers in the state of Wisconsin.

WISCONSIN SOCCER POST
13540 LAKE CITY WAY N.E. SUITE 3
SEATTLE, WA 98125
206-367-2420
Fax: 206-367-2636
http://www.varsitycommunications.com
• Kelly Ross, Editor
(414) 545-7227
kross@wysa.org
Frequency:
4 time(s) per year

WOLFPACKER
PO BOX 2331
DURHAM, NC 27702
919-688-0218
Fax: 919-682-1532
www.thewolfpacker.com
• Stuart Coman, Publisher
• Scott Vogelsburg, Editor
• Dave Searcy, Advertising Director/Marketing Director
Publishing Company:
Coman Publishing Company, Inc.
Frequency:
20 times annually
Primary Audience:
NC State sports fans
Sports:
General - North Carolina State sports
Description:
Covers NC State sports exclusively, including features about athletes, coaches, provides coverage of events in which NC State participates, information pertaining to team lineups and player statistics.

WOLVERINE
PO BOX 1304
ANN ARBOR, MI 48106
734-996-9092
Fax: 734-996-8196
www.thewolverine.com
• Stuart Coman, Publisher
• John Borton, Editor
Description:
Covers Michigan sports exclusively, including features about athletes, coaches, coverage of events in which Michigan participates, information pertaining to team lineups and player statistics.
Circulation:
16,000. 95% paid subscr, 5% newsstand.
Sports:
General
Primary Audience:
U. of Michigan sports fans
Frequency:
25 times annually
Publishing Company:
Coman Publishing Company, Inc.

WOMEN'S PRO RODEO NEWS
1235 LAKE PLAZA DRIVE
COLORADO SPRINGS, CO 80906
719-576-0900
Fax: 719-576-1386
http://www.horseworlddata.com

• Tim Gentry, Editor
• Glory Ann Kurtz, Editor
(719) 576-0900
Frequency:
1 time(s) per month

WOODENBOAT
86GREAT COVE
BROOKLIN, ME 04616
207-359-4651
Fax: 207-359-8920
woodenboat@woodenboat.com
http://www.woodenboat.com
• Matthew P. Murphy, Editor
(207) 359-4651
matt@woodenboat.com
• Carl Cramer, Publisher
(207) 359-4651
• Tom Jackson, Associate Editor
tom@woodenboat.com
• Mike O'Brien, Senior Editor
(207) 359-4651
m.obrien@woodenboat.com
• Jonathan A. Wilson, Editor-in-Chief
(207) 359-4651
jon@woodenboat.com
• Sarah Bray, Editorial Assistant
(207) 359-4651
Frequency:
6 time(s) per year
Description:
Publication provides information on the design, building, care, preservation, and use of wooden boats.

WORLD WIDE SPORTS RADIO NETWORK
22 DORFER LANE
NESCONSET, NY 11767
631-965-4990
www.worldwidesportsradio.com
• Errol Marks, CEO/Editor/Host
(631) 965-4990
e.marks@sportsonthego1.com
Frequency:
1 time(s) per month
Description:
All professional sporting events in New York, New Jersey and national major sporting events.

WSS EXECUTIVE SEARCH
7755 CENTER AVENUE
SUITE 1100
HUNTINGTON BEACH, CA 92647
714-848-1201
Fax: 714-848-5111
info@WSSExecutiveSearch.com
www.WSSExecutiveSearch.com
• Becky Heidesch, Founder & Chief Executive Officer
• Mary Lou Youngblood, Chief Operating Officer
Description:
WSS Executive Search, a division of Women Sourcing Soltions, is a WBENC certified, women-owned business specializing in women and minority sourcing solutions. WSS partners with their clients to provide them with sourcing solutions to solve their most challenging diversity hiring efforts. WSS specializes in the sports, financial and technology industry.
Nature of Service:
WSS customizes their recruitment and management process for each client. By offering personalized sourcing solutions,

media

WSS matches qualified professional candidates with top-tier companies who are often challenged in their industry in finding women and minority candidates. WSS has years of experience assisting companies in reaching their diversity goals and empowering candidates to realize their career dreams!

Primary Audience:
Corporate America, specialty companies in the sports, financial and technology sectors. Candidate pool: Mid-management to Executive Level.

Sports
All.

YACHTING
PO BOX 420235
PALM COAST, FL 32142-0235
203-299-5900
800-999-0869
Fax: 401-845-5180
http://www.yachtingnet.com
• John Wooldridge, Managing Editor
(203) 299-5900
• Peter Janssen, Editorial Director
• Don Wallace, Executive Editor
• John Young, Publisher
(212) 779-5263
john.young@time4.com
Frequency:
1 time(s) per month
Description:
Publication is written for the active sailor or powerboater.

YACHTS INTERNATIONAL
1850 SOUTHEAST 17TH STREET SUITE 310
FORT LAUDERDALE, FL 33316
954-761-8777
Fax: 954-761-8890
• Jamie Welch, Editor
• Michel Karsenti, Publisher
Frequency:
6 time(s) per year
Description:
Publication features information on yachts 40 feet and longer.

YOUTH SPORTS JOURNAL
2050 VISTA PKWY
W. PALM BEACH, FL 33411
561-684-1141
800-729-2057
Fax: 561-684-2546
nays@nays.org
www.nays.org
• Fred C. Engh, President/Chief Executive Officer
• Greg Bach, Editor/Communication Director
• Nathan Washer, Director Education
Description:
Official publication of the National Youth Sports Coaches Association. Covers news, programs, tips relating to sports, innovative products, safety and drug awareness programs. Provides product information and advertising geared toward the organized youth sports programs.
Publishing Company:
National Youth Sports Coaches Assn
Frequency:
Quarterly
Primary Audience:
NYSCA membership, coaches, and parents involved in youth sports, recreation

professionals (municipal and military), YMCA, YWCA, CYO, Boys Clubs, etc.
Sports:
Baseball, Softball, Football, Basketball, Soccer, Volleyball, Ice Hockey, Flag Football, Cheerleading, Ringette
Circulation:
140,600+.

ZONE TENNIS
1060 MAIN STREET
SUITE 307
RIVER EDGE, NJ 07661
201-342-3663
800-580-9663
Fax: 201-342-2258
info@stayinthezone.com
www.stayinthezone.com
• Jay Granat, Psychotherapist/Founder
(201) 342-3663

Sports Business Directories

ATHLETIC DIRECTORY
20622 OTTAWA ROAD
APPLE VALLEY, CA 92308
760-247-4717
• Dick Sauers, Publisher/Editor
Description:
Covers information and features about coaching, fitness and other subjects of interest to athletic coaches. Includes listings of coaching books and manuals and also includes interviews with coaches about techniques and methods used in coaching. Also publishes Sports Psychology newsletter on a quarterly basis.
Circulation:
NA.
Sports:
General
Primary Audience:
Coaches
Frequency:
Six times annually
Publishing Company:
Scholastic Resources Unlimited

ATHLETIC GUIDE PUBLISHING
509 SOUTH CENTRAL AVENUE
FLAGLER BEACH, FL 32136-1050
386-439-2050
800-255-1050
flaglernet@gmail.com
www.prepschoolhockeyguide.com
• Tom Keegan, Publisher/Editor
(386) 439-2050
flagernet@gmail.com
• Sharyn Keegan, Production Manager
• Bryan Mitchell, Graphic Design
Description:
Publishes annual guides covering pro hockey, college hockey, prep school hockey, junior hockey.
Publishing Company:
Athletic Guide Publishing.
Circulation:
10,000
Frequency:
Annual.
Sports:
College Hockey.

BASEBALL BLUEBOOK, LLC
8373 N CEDAR HILLS LANE
FAIR GROVE, MO 65648
417-833-6550
Fax: 417-833-9911
dj@baseballbluebook.com
www.baseballbluebook.com
• Jodi Wubbena, Publisher
• Dennis Wubbena, Publisher
Baseball Bluebook - Professional Edition
Annual publication. Lists Major League, Minor League and Independent League personnel, contact information, schedules, and scouts. Available spiral bound or in a 3-ring binder
Baseball Bluebook - College Edition
Annual publication. Lists Division I, II, & III, NAIA, and JUCO personnel, contact information, and schedules; includes conference informationand prospects. Available spiral bound or in a 3-ring binder.

BLUE BOOK OF COLLEGE ATHLETICS
P O BOX 931
MONTGOMERY, AL 36101
334-263-4436
Fax: 334-263-4437
www.athleticpubco.com
• John A. Dees, Jr., Publisher
• Chris Beasley, Marketing Director
Publishing Company:
Athletic Publishing Company
Frequency:
Annually
Primary Audience:
Executives and coaches of educational institutions
Circulation:
13,000 100% paid subscription
Description:
Includes listings for all senior, junior and community colleges in the United States and Canada; male and female colleges. Lists address, phone, fax nambers. Listings include school name, coaches listed by sport, stadium size and school colors.
Sports:
General

CLELL WADE COACHES DIRECTORY, INC.
701 MAIN STREET
CASSVILLE, MO 65625
417-847-2783
Fax: 417-847-5920
www.coachesdirectory.com
• Karan Nickle, Publisher/Editor/Advertising Sales Director
Publishing Company:
Clell Wade Coaches Directory, Inc.
Frequency:
Annually
Primary Audience:
Athletic administrators, coaches, institutions, and team sporting goods companies
Sports:
General
Circulation:
70,000. 69% paid subscr, 31% non-paid contr.
Description:
Provides high school and college enrollment, school colors, nicknames, telephone numbers and names of current coaching personnel in 38 separate directories, covering the U.S. and Canada.

DEGREES IN SPORTS
7010 E CHAUNCEY LANE
PHOENIX, AZ 85054
480-905-8480
Fax: 480-905-7231
info@degreesinsports.com
www.degreesinsports.com
• Randy Just, National Account Manager
(480) 905-8480
Description:
Online directory of Sport Management
Degrees in the United States.

**EPM LICENSING LETTER
SOURCEBOOK, THE**
160 MERCER ST, 3RD FL
NEW YORK, NY 10012-3212
212-941-0099
888-852-9467
Fax: 212-941-1622
www.epmcom.com
• Riva Bennett, Chief Operating Officer
• Ira Mayer, Publisher
• Michele Jensen, Vice President of
Marketing
• Melissa Trosterman, Marketing
Coordinator
mtrosterman@epm.com
• Loretta Netzer, Circulation Manager
• Ben Jurin, Associate Editor, The Licensing
Letter
Publishing Company:
EPM Communications, Inc.
Frequency:
Annual
Primary Audience:
Licensing business executives
Sports:
General
Circulation:
NA.
Description:
Directory of licensing agents, products, and
manufacturers.

FOOTBALL GREEN BOOK
310 W. WALNUT STREET
SPRINGFIELD, MO 65806
417-866-3464
800-909-0010
Fax: 417-866-3469
www.sportdirectories.com
• Michelle Johnson, Editor
• Joe Terry, Associate Editor
• Jeff Schrag, Publisher
Frequency:
Annual Publications.
Description:
The Football Green Book is a
comprehensive directory of every team in
the sport in the US and Canada: college,
pros; administration, coaching; contracts;
conferences,bowl games, and more.
Primary Audience:
Coaches, Scouts, Agents.

**GAISF CALENDAR OF INTERNATIONAL
SPORTS COMPETITIONS**
4, BD DU JARDIN EXOTIQUE
MONTE CARLO, MONACO 98000
www.agfisonline.com
• Jean C. Schupp, Publisher
Description:
Contains long-term calendar for each sport,
the programs of the Olympic and regional
Games, and the May/November calendar in
chronological order.

Circulation:
NA.
Sports:
General.
Primary Audience:
Sports Business Executives, Sports
Organizations, Sports Media
Frequency:
Semi-annually (May 1, Nov 1).
Publishing Company:
General Association of International Sports
Federations.

GLOBAL SPORTS PRODUCTIONS
16810 CRYSTAL DRIVE EAST
ENUMCLAW, WA 98022
310-454-9480
www.sportsbookempire.com/
• Ed Kobak, President
• Bistro Loving, VP Operations
• Barbara Boldtmann, Vice President
• Greg Andrews, VP of Business Operations
Publishing Company:
Global Sports Productions. Publisher of
sport reference books. Publisher of sport
magazines.
Description:
Global Sports Productions; 464 page
reference directory with 7,500+ listings that
includes addresses, telephone & fax
numbers, cable & telex numbers, websites,
e-mail addresses and contact persons from
international and national sports
organizations in addition to federations,
leagues, teams, clubs, and global
publications.
Frequency:
Annually
Primary Audience:
Industry
Sports:
General/International
Publications:
International Sports Directory, Sports Logo
Guide, Sports Hall of Oblvion, The Guide to
a Sports Career, Sports Address Bible, The
Baseball Autograph Collector's Guide, The
Celebrity Address Directory Guide, The
Encyclopedia of Sports Business Contacts,
The NACDA Collegiate Sports Directory and
the Dream Job in Sports Publicity,
Promotions & Marketing.

HOCKEY BLACK BOOK
PO BOX 400
WOODMERE, NY 11598
917-327-9500
Fax: 201-567-4514
HockeyBlackBook@aol.com
www.HockeyBlackBook.com
• David Kolb, Publisher
Hockey Black Book
Annual publication. Includes in-depth
information on professional, amateur,
collegiate, and junior hockey leagues;
associations, media, organizations;
schedules, arenas, staff,and contact
information.

IEG SPONSORSHIP SOURCEBOOK
640 NORTH LA SALLE STREET
SUITE 600
CHICAGO, IL 60610-3777
800-834-4850
Fax: 312-458-7111
ieg@sponsorship.com
www.sponsorship.com

• Jon Ukman, Publisher
• Lesa Ukman, President
• Meg Pound, Advertising Sales Director
• Penny Perrey, Associate Publisher
• Laren Ukman, General Manager
• Maureen Gilroy, Marketing Director
Description:
Lists 3,000 major sports events and
properties available for sponsorship.
Directory listings include contact, address
and phone of each event plus budget,
attendance, prior sponsors. Events indexed
by category, location, date, budget and
attendance. Also includes index of sponsors
and the properties they tie into, industry
yellow pages and event marketing agencies,
sports organizations and industry suppliers.
Frequency:
Annually.
Publishing Company:
IEG, Inc.

ILLINOIS COACHES DIRECTORY
1311 LITTLE JOHN DRIVE
ELGIN, IL 60120
847-742-6262
• Ken Olson, Publisher/Editor
Description:
Contains complete listings for all boys' and
girls' high school, college and junior college
coaches in Illinois, giving name, address,
phone, sports coached, enrollment of
school, school colors, nickname of teams,
conference.
Circulation:
6,000. 100% paid subscr.
Sports:
General
Primary Audience:
Athletic institutional executives/coaches
Publishing Company:
Illinois Coaches Directory

INTERNATIONAL AUDARENA GUIDE
P O BOX 15158
NORTH HOLLYWOOD, CA 91606-5158
818-487-4582
800-562-2706
Fax: 818-487-4550
www.billboard.com/bbcom/index.jsp
• Brian Kennedy, Vice President Integrated
Sales
bkennedy@billboard.com
• Derek Senter, Advertising Director
Digital/Consumer Brands
dsentner@billboard.com
• Arkady Fridman, Inside Sales Manager
afridman@billboard.com
Description:
The International AudArena Guide provides
complete data on over 4,300 venues
worldwide, including Amphitheaters, Arenas,
Stadiums, Sports facilities, Concert Halls
and New Constructions including complete
listings of companies offering services to the
touring industry in the Facility Buyer's Guide.
AudArena International Guide includes:
contact names; phone and fax numbers;
email and Website addresses; market
population; facility capacities and staging
configurations in addition to rental fees and
Ticketing Rights.
Publishing Company:
Billboard Store; 310 pages; published
October 2004; unit price $99.00; Item#
BLBDD35.
Sports:

General
Frequency:
Annually

INTERNATIONAL HANDBOOK FOR THE SPORTING GOODS INDUSTRY
LA MAISON DU SPORT
PO BOX 480
VERBIER, SWITZERLAN CH-196
info@wfsgi.org
www.wfsgi.org
• Anne Gorgemans, Publisher
Description:
Includes, but not limited to, directory of senior WFSGI officials, sports event and trade show calendar, and directory of member organizations.
Circulation:
NA.
Sports:
General
Primary Audience:
Sporting Goods Manufacturers
Frequency:
Annually
Publishing Company:
World Federation of the Sporting Goods Industry

INTERNATIONAL KARTING INDUSTRY BUYER'S GUIDE
PO BOX 101
WHEATON, IL 60189
630-653-7368
Fax: 630-653-2637
karting@msn.com
• Darrell E. Sitarz, Publisher/President/CEO
(630) 653-7368
karting@msn.com
• Jim Logan, Sales Manager
(630) 653-7368
karting@msn.com
Frequency:
Annually
Primary Audience:
Trade
Sport:
Go Karting
Circulation:
10,000 (60% subscriber, 40% newstand)
Description:
A directory of products and services with nearly 350 categories and more than 2,000 company entries. Each entry includes the company name, address, contact name, phone, fax numbers, web site, and email addresses. Included are manufacturers, safety equipment and apparel, insurance carriers, ticketing, track designers and tools.

NATIONAL DIRECTORY OF COLLEGE ATHLETICS ONLINE & APP
PO BOX 450640
CLEVELAND, OH 44145
216-465-2914
info@collegiatedirectories.com
www.collegiatedirectories.com
• Kevin Cleary, General Manager
Publishing Company:
Collegiate Directories, Inc.
Year Founded:
1969 & 1991
Frequency:
Annual
Primary Audience:
Coaches, Athletic Directors
Sports:

All
Description:
Spiral bound directory lists over 2,100 junior and senior colleges that compete in intercollegiate athletics. Contact information available for every college coach and athletic administrator in the U.S. and Canada. Official publication of the National Association of Collegiate Directors of Athletics (NACDA). For men's and women's sports, contains names, addresses and telephone numbers of all college athletic officials including athletic directors, coaches, sports information directors, athletic business managers and athletic trainers, and includes two major editorial features dealing with all aspects of college athletics.

NATIONAL DIRECTORY OF HIGH SCHOOL COACHES
2540 EAST FIFTH STREET
MONTGOMERY, AL 36107
334-263-4436
Fax: 334-263-4437
• John Al Dees, Publisher
• Chris Al Beasley, Jr., Marketing Director
Publishing Company:
Athletic Publishing Co.
Frequency:
Annually
Primary Audience:
Executives and coaches of athletic institutions
Sports:
General
Circulation:
18,000. 100% paid subscr.
Description:
Provides listings for 19,500 schools and over 240,000 coaches throughout the U.S.

NSGA BUYING GUIDE
1601 FEEHANVILLE DRIVE
SUITE 300
MT. PROSPECT, IL 60056-6035
847-296-6742
800-815-5422
Fax: 847-391-9827
info@nsga.org
www.nsga.org
• James Faltinek, President/Chief Executive Officer
• Paul Prince, Vice President/Business Development
• Cyndi Boehm, MIS Manager/Editor
Publishing Company:
National Sporting Goods Association
Frequency:
Annually
Primary Audience:
Retail, manufacturing trade
Sports:
General
Circulation:
3,000 Members only.
Desription:
Buying guide for retailers and dealers.

RECREATIONAL SPORTS DIRECTORY
NIRSA
4185 SOUTHWEST RESEARCH WAY
CORVALLIS, OR 97333-1067
541-766-8211
Fax: 541-766-8284
nirsa@nirsa.org
www.nirsa.org

• Kent Blumenthal, Executive Director
• Sarah Hubert, Editor
• Carole Hobrock, Advertising Manager
Publishing Company:
Natl Intramural-Recreational Sports Association/NIRSA
Frequency:
Annually
Primary Audience:
Association membership
Sports:
General
Circulation:
2,000. 80% association membership, 10% contr non-paid, 10% other.
Description:
Listing of colleges, universities, community-junior colleges, military installations. Includes personnel and areas of responsibility, facility managers, sport clubs, intramurals, fitness, instructional programs, outdoor recreation, informal sports, aquatics, extramural sports, individuals with disabilities, special events, and wellness. Includes buyers guide.

REVENUES FROM SPORTS VENUES
2813 HARBOR LIGHTS DRIVE
NASHVILLE, TN 37217
615-367-4241
• Jim Grimstead, Editor/Publisher
• Linda Mansur, Editor/Publisher
Publishing Company:
Mediaventures
Frequency:
Annually
Primary Audience:
Team and venue owners, marketing management, marketing consultants, architects, contractors, premium service vendors, management companies.
Sports:
General
Description:
A directory listing prices and providing analysis for signage, luxury suites, club seats, advertising placements, ticket prices and naming rights deals in addition to number of concession stands and caterer information.

SALESMAN'S GUIDE
2807 NORTH PARHAM ROAD
SUITE 200
RICHMOND, VA 23294
804-762-9600
Fax: 804-217-8999
www.douglaspublications.com
• Alan Douglas, President
• Frank Finn, VP/Editor-in-Chief
Sports:
General
Primary Audience:
Manufacturing, wholesale trade
Frequency:
Annually
Publishing Company:
Douglas Publishing
Description:
Composed of a diverse array of companies, including manufacturers, retailers, marketing agencies and companies. Over 12,000 firms who purchase premiums and incentives are listed, as well as the 20,000 decision-markers that plan to purchase ad specialties, corporate gifts and awards, sales incentives and safety incentives.

Circulation:
5,000. 100% paid subscr.

SPORT INFORMATION RESOURCE CENTER/SIRC
180 ELGIN STREET
SUITE 1400
OTTAWA, ON, CANADA K2P 3K3
613-231-7472
800-665-6413
Fax: 613-231-3739
webmaster@sirc.ca
www.sirc.ca
• Debra Gassewitz, President/CEO
• David Roberts, COO
• Jean-Michel Johnson, Director of Indexing Services
• Linda Wheeler, Director Product Development
Sports Service Founded:
1973
Nature of Sports Service:
Database producer of sport, fitness and sports medicine information. Organization has been identifying, organizing and communicating sport and fitness information and providing it through a variety of products and services. These include SPORTDiscus, SIRCDetective, SIRCRetriever, SIRCExpress and SIRCUIT.Our subscribers range from universities, libraries and hospitals to coaches, athletes, professors and medical practitioners worldwide.

SPORTING GOODS & ACTIVEWEAR BUYERS DIRECTORY
2807 NORTH PARHAM ROAD
SUITE 200
RICHMOND, VA 23294
804-762-9600
Fax: 804-217-8999
www.douglaspublications.com
• Alan Douglas, President
• Frank Finn, VP/Editor-in-Chief
Sports:
General
Primary Audience:
Manufacturing, wholesale trade
Frequency:
Annually
Publishing Company:
Douglas Publishing
Description:
Includes information about more than 18,400 buyers and executives, including those who purchase sporting goods equipment, accessories, activewear, resortwear, surfwear and swimwear.

SPORTS BUSINESS RESOURCE GUIDE & FACT BOOK
1166 AVENUE OF THE AMERICAS
14TH FLOOR
NEW YORK, NY 10036
212-500-0700
Fax: 212-500-0701
www.sportsbusinessdaily.com/journal
• Derick Moss, Editor
(703) 973-1434
derickmoss@sportsbusinessjournal.com
• Laurie Garrison, Copy Editor, Sports Business Awards Coordinator
(703) 973-1331
lgarrison@sportsbusinessjournal.com
• Ryan Baucom, Associate Editor
(703) 973-1419
rbaucom@sportsbusinessjournal.com

Description:
The Resource Guide & Fact Book is a comprehensive, detailed, reference covering the business of sports. With contacts, addresses, phone numbers, sponsorship information, naming rights, and media rights for more than 8,900 listings, and 60,000 individual contacts, it is a must-have for sports executives.

SPORTS MARKET PLACE DIRECTORY
4919 ROUTE 22
AMENIA, NY 12501
518-789-8700
800-562-2139
Fax: 518-789-0545
www.sportsmarketplace.com
• Richard Gottlieb, President
• Leslie Mackenzie, Publisher
• Laura Mars-Proietti, Editorial Director
Publishing Company:
Grey House Publishing
Frequency:
Annual.
Primary Audience:
Sports executives in advertising, marketing, sales, sponsorships, public relations, events, media, facilities and sports law. Sports management programs and career seekers.
Sports:
General
Circulation:
1,000
Description:
Provides comprehensive listing of organizations and business firms including associations, college athletic conferences, professional sports leagues and teams, sports publications, sports promotion and marketing firms, sports broadcasting firms, sports market and information data services, sports equipment, apparel and footwear manufacturers, colleges and universities with Sports Management Degree Programs. Also available on GOLD online.

THE FOOTBALL GREEN BOOK
310 W WALNUT STREET
SPRINGFIELD, MO 65806
417-866-3464
800-909-0010
Fax: 417-866-3469
www.sportdirectories.com
• Michelle Johnson, Editor
• Joe Terry, Associate Editor
• Jeff Schrag, Publisher
Frequency:
Annual Publications.
Description:
The Football Green Book is a comprehensive directory of every team in the sport in the US and Canada: college, pros; administration, coaching; contracts; conferences,bowl games, and more.
Primary Audience:
Coaches, Scouts, Agents.

THE SPORT SUMMIT SPORTS BUSINESS DIRECTORY
6550 ROCK SPRING DRIVE
SUITE 500
BETHESDA, MD 20817-1126
301-493-5500
800-EJK- EXPO
Fax: 301-493-5705
www.sportsummit.com

• Jim Farlenza, VP/Executive Director Sports Division
• Jamie Attanasia, Managing Editor
Published By:
E.J. Krause & Associates, Inc. 8th Edition, Annual Publication, Topic: Sports Informational.
Description:
A comprehensive annual guide to over 9,000 companies and organizations and 25,000 executives involved in sports marketing, events, media, sponsorship, facilities, manufacturing, teams, finance, law and more. The Sports Business Directory is available in two forms: the traditional Print Version, and Online Version, with a powerful search engine to help you find the decision-makers in the sports industry, and daily updates to ensure the accuracy of the listings included.

WESTERN SPORTS GUIDE
3992 DONIPHAN DRIVE
EL PASO, TX 79922
915-584-7791
Fax: 888-584-7791
• Emily Anderson, Owner
Description:
Publishes high school directories listing sports, coaches, nicknames, addresses, etc. States covered: Texas, California-Nevada-Hawaii, Arizona-New Mexico, Arkansas-Louisiana, Washington-Oregon-Alaska (Pacific Northwest), Idaho-Wyoming-Montana, Colorado-Utah, Mississippi-Alabama, Oklahoma-Kansas, South Carolina.
Circulation:
Texas-5,600; Cal/Nev-1,600; others 300-800 per edition. Total all editions-10,800. 95% paid subscr, 3% contr non-paid, 2% other.
Sports:
General
Primary Audience:
Coaches, officials, trade
Frequency:
Annually
Publishing Company:
Craftsman Publications, Inc.

Media Production

44 BLUE PRODUCTIONS, INC.
4040 VINELAND AVE, STE 105
STUDIO CITY, CA 91604
818-760-4442
Fax: 818-760-1509
reception@44blue.com
www.44blue.com
• Rasha Drachkovitch, Founder
(818) 760-4442
Nature of Sports Service:
National. Syndicated and cable TV programmer. Current properties include Discovery Sport, weekly series; Future Stars in Sport, hosted by Mike Schmidt; The History of College Football, The History of College Basketball, and other programs.

ACTION SPORTS ADVENTURE
322 8TH AVE
NEW YORK, NY 10001
212-375-7622
866-473-5264
Fax: 212-807-9201

AOL SPORTS
1100 AVE OF THE AMERICAS
H11
NEW YORK, NY 10036
212-512-1648
800-937-2212
Fax: 212-512-1751
• Tim Armstrong, Chairman/Chief Executive Officer, AOL
Sports Service Founded:
1990
Marketing & Consulting Services:
Pay-Per-View Programming development and acquisition; purchase of sports properties for marketing and broadcasting.
Description:
Offers sports scores, as well as sports news, including fantasy sports information.

ASA PRODUCTIONS
5210 E. 65TH ST
INDIANAPOLIS, IN 46220
317-579-7777
Fax: 317-579-7774
george@asaproductions.com
www.asaproductions.com
• Scott Kemper, Partner/Creative
• Rich Airis, Partner/Creative

BASEBALLVIDEOS.COM
502 ANCHORAGE LANE
HOUSTON, TX 77079
888-907-0790
Fax: 281-368-1630
www.baseballvideos.com
Nature of Sports Service:
National. Producer and distributor of sports home videocassettes and programming. Current sports video cassettes include: Baseball Skills and Drills; and You and Your Horse.

BASSMASTERS, THE
5845 CARMICHAEL RD
MONTGOMERY, MN 36117
334-272-9530
Fax: 334-279-7148
www.bassmaster.com
• Diehl Unger, Executive Producer
• Dave Precht, Executive Producer
• Mike Harris, Consultant Account Manager
• Don McPherson, Advertising Director
• Ken Woodard, Vice President/Advertising
Nature of Sports Service:
National. TV program producer/packager. Programs feature B.A.S.S. tournament highlights and how-to of bass angling.

BMORE SPORTS
1430 JOH AVENUE
BUILDING M
BALTIMORE, MD 21227
410-247-2345
gandracchio@ptcintl.com
www.bmoresports.com or www.ptcintl.com
Nature of Services:
Bmore Sports is a manufacturer of a variety of game-day promotional products including sports leather binders and jotters, wood ticket boxes, custom coolers and dog tag collectibles.
Year Founded:
1980

BO GANZ PRODUCTIONS
1701 LASHLEY ST
LONGMONT, CO 80504
303-772-9273
Fax: 303-772-9273
boganz@peakpeak.com
• Bo Ganz, Products/Director
Nature of Sports Service:
National. Film and video production company, specializing in sports categories.

BOMBO SPORTS & ENTERTAINMENT
41 MADISON AVE
NEW YORK, NY 10010
212-685-9080
Fax: 212-685-9088
• Bob Potter, Chief Executive Officer/Managing Partner
Sports Service Founded:
1984
Nature of Sports Service:
Develops sports film documentaries on teams and individual athletes.

CALAMARI VIDEO
2973 HOWELL AVE
SANTA CLARA, CA 95051
408-241-1231
• Lon McEachern, Partner
• Amy Smolens, Partner
Nature of Sports Service:
International. TV, video production company. Produces promotional and marketing videotapes, video news releases, and corporate and sports training tapes for events, teams and products.

CAPPY PRODUCTIONS INC.
118 E. 57TH ST, 3RD FL
NEW YORK, NY 10022
212-249-1800
Fax: 212-439-9165
cappyprod@hotmail.com
• Bud Greenspan, President
• Nancy Beffa, Vice President/Executive Vice President
• Bruce Beffa, Senior Producer
• Sydney Thayer, Coordinator Production
Nature of Sports Service:
National. TV film production. Broad production capabilities. Production credits include The Olympiad series; Numero Uno series; Wilma (movie of the week); The Glory of their Times; Olympic Vignettes (4-7 minute documentary spots); Time Capsule: The 1932 Los Angeles Olympics; Time Capsule: The 1932 Los Angeles Olympics; Time Capsule: The 1936 Berlin Olympics. This Day in Sports 16 Days of Glory, The Official Film of the 1984 Los Angeles Olympic Games; The Official Olympics; 16 Days of Glory; The Official Film of the 1988 Seoul Olympics; 16 Days of Glory; The Official Film of the Days of Glory; The Official Film of the 1992 Barcelona Olympics

CBS SPORTS COLLEGE NETWORK
28 EAST 28TH STREET
NEW YORK, NY 10016
• Patricia Power, Senior Vice President of Operations
• Barbara Shulman, Senior Vice President and General Counsel
• Kelly Dunne, Vice President of Creative Services
• Joseph Salerno, Vice President of Midwest Affiliate Sales

Sports Service Founded:
2002
Nature of Sports Service:
Cable network devoted exclusively to college sports, including a significant commitment to women's sports. Network was co-founded by Brian Bedol, Stephen Greenberg and Chris Bevilacqua. Mr. Bedol and Mr. Greenberg were co-founders of Classic Sports Network.

CENTER CITY FILM & VIDEO
1501-1503 WALNUT STREET
PHILADELPHIA, PA 19102
215-568-4134
www.ccfv.com
• Brian Iseley, Vice President/General Manager
• Melanie Macready, Account Executive
Nature of Sports Service:
National. Remote TV production, post production. Capabilities for sports programs, sports production.

CISNEROS MEDIA DISTRIBUTION
305-507-6837
msomoza@cisneros.com
www.cisnerosmediadist.com
• Miguel Somoza, North America/Asia Sales Director
Nature of Sports Service:
International. Program distributor. Program offerings include El Boxeador.

CLEAR CHANNEL BROADCASTING
621 MAINSTREAM DR, STE 230
NASHVILLE, TN 37228
615-742-6100
800-346-9467
Fax: 615-742-6124
www.clearchannel.com
• Bob Pittman, Chief Executive Officer
Nature of Sports Service:
National. Radio program producer/packager, broadcaster, program distribution. Current properties include: U. of Florida football and basketball; Penn State football and basketball; Texas A&M football and basketball; and Iowa State University football and basketball.

CLTV - CABLE CHANNEL
200 YORK RD
OAK BROOK, IL 60521
630-368-4000
Fax: 630-368-4468
http://cltv.trb.com

CNBC
2200 FLETCHER AVE
FT. LEE, NJ 07024
201-585-2622
800-788-CNBC
Fax: 201-585-6244
www.cnbc.com
• Mark Hoffman, President/Chief Executive Officer

COLONY SPORTS
CORNER OLD ROUTE 9 & MIDDLEBUSH RD
WAPPINGERS FALLS, NY 12590
845-297-5645
Fax: 845-297-3262
• Michael McCartney, Executive Producer
• Hugh Taylor, Director

Nature of Sports Service:
Regional. Program producer, broadcaster for Cable TV. Provides package of Marist College men's basketball events.

CORE DIGITAL
330 S. RIVER DR
TEMPE, AZ 85281
480-707-1000
Fax: 480-707-1010
• Jonae Taylor, VP Sales/Marketing
jtaylor@swtv.net
• Stephanie Brooks, Sales
Nature of Sports Service:
Mobile production company. Mobile Unit capable of simultaneous production of both HD and Standard 601 signals.
Sports Service Founded:
1983

COWEN MEDIA
277 FAIRFIELD ROAD
SUITE 304
FAIRFIELD, NJ 07004
973-575-1234
Fax: 973-575-1238
www.cowenmedia.com
• Robert Cowen, President
• Karen Cowen, Vice President
Nature of Service:
A full service media company that provides superior quality television/video production, editing and consulting to the sports industry. Winner of 10 EMMY awards.
Clients:
Cardinal Health, CSTV, ESPN, ESPN Classic, Fazoli's, Hunter Public Relations, LPGA Tour, Maui Invitational, Northern California Golf Association, Octagon Marketing, The Sporting News, United States Golf Association

COX COMMUNICATIONS
1400 LAKE HEARN DR NE
ATLANTA, GA 30319
404-843-5000
Fax: 404-843-5777
www.cox.com
• Patrick J Esser, President
• James O. Robbins, President/Chief Executive Officer/Director
• John F. Dyer, Senior Vice President/Operations
• William Farina, Vice President Advertising Sales
• Ellen M. East, Vice President Communications/Investor Relati
• Joseph Rooney, Vice President Marketing

CTV TELEVISION NETWORK LTD.
9 CHANNEL NINE CT
SCARBORO, ON, CANADA M1S 4B5
416-332-5000
Fax: 416-299-2342
www.ctv.ca
• Lance Brown, Sports Director
• Virginia Gibberd, Director Production Operations
• Rick Brace, Vice President

CWI PRODUCTIONS, INC.
PO BOX 442
UNIONVALE, PA 19375
610-793-0979
Fax: 203-762-0207

info@healthyaging.net
www.healthyaging.net
Nature of Sports Service:
National. Sports film, video producer. Specializes in corporate-sponsored sports programming for television distribution. Full-service production company handling television syndication as well. Have produced programs on professional bicycle racing. Olympic race walking, running Olympic wrestling, equestrian, exercise/fitness, skiing, aging and athletes.

DYNOCOMM SPORTS TV
9675 4TH ST N.
ST. PETERSBURG, FL 33702
949-361-2063
Fax: 949-361-1716
• George E. Orgera, President
• Robert W. Eisenstaedt, Vice President
• Jeffrey Green, Senior Producer
• Connie Vizaro, Operations Manager
Nature of Sports Service:
National. Program producer/packager, distributor for Broadcast and Cable TV. On-site sponsor arrangements since 1982. Event promotion, broadcast production and syndication, airings in syndication and on ESPN and Fox Sports Net. Programs include OP pro Surfing Championship; World Cup of Sailboarding; Super Bowl of Motocross; Hawaiian International Billfish Tournament; Pro Bodyguard Championship; World Jet Ski Finals; Curacao Open Sailboard Championships, Pro Skateboard Championship: Team USA Skydiving Team Tour-Rep of China; Fiji Pro Surfing Championships; Another Classic Summer; ESPN Classic Summer; ESPN's A Day at the Beach; Budweiser Islamo

ESPN REGIONAL TELEVISION
11001 RUSHMORE DR
CHARLOTTE, NC 28277
704-973-5000
Fax: 704-973-5090
www.espn.com
• Arnie Sgalio, Director Big 10 Programs
• Chuck Gerber, Executive VP/General Manager
• Pete Derzes, Senior VP University Marketing/Program
Nature of Sports Service:
National. Regional, Local. Program producer and distributor. Syndicating programming includes: Philadelphia 76ers, IMSA racing and Top Rank boxing for ESPN; coaches show for University of Kansas and Iowa State; NCAA Championship week on ESPN; and college basketball games for various conferences, including Big Eight, Big West, Great Midwest, Sun Belt, Southern Missouri Valley, Midwestern Collegiate, Ohio Valley, Big 10, Big East, also produces various sports specials.

FOX SPORTS NET SOUTHWEST
100 E. ROYAL LANE, STE 200
IRVING, TX 75039
972-868-1800
Fax: 972-868-1678
foxsports.com
• Jon Heidtke, Vice President/General Manager
Nature of Sports Service:
Regional. Cable and satellite TV sports network. Current programs: Houston Astros

home and road games; Texas Rangers home and road games; Dallas Mavericks home a road games; San Antonio Spurs home and road games; Dallas Stars home and road games; Houston Aeros home and road games; Dallas Burn home and road games; Dallas Cowboys weekly programming; Texas high school sports; College football-featuring the Big 12, Conference USA, Pac-10, SEC, Southland Football League; College basketball-featuring the big 12, Pac-10 and WAC; FOX Sports News; Fight Time on FOX; professional boxing; early round PGA coverage; Texas Special Olympics; weekly hunting

FREEDOM SPORTS NETWORK/DELCOM MARKETING GROUP
2055 ANGLO DR, STE 201
COLORADO SPRINGS, CO 80918
719-264-8112
Fax: 719-264-8243
• Ron Delorenzo, President
Nature of Sports Service:
National. Full service packager, syndicator and distributor. Provides television production of events needed separately. Experienced in NFL Football (games & weekly shows), college football, college basketball, hockey, golf, tennis, bowling, rodeo and various anthologies.

GOLF CHANNEL, THE
7580 GOLF CHANNEL DRIVE
ORLANDO, FL 32819
407-363-4653
www.golfchannel.com
• Mike McCarley, President
• Jeff Dilley, Chief Financial Officer
• Robert Greenway, SVP Production/Programming/Ops
• Gene Pizzolato, SVP Advertising Sales
• Kevin Byrnes, Vice President Advertising Sales
• John Houde, Vice President New Media
• R. Andy Murphy, Vice President Network Operations
• Mark Oldham, Vice President Tournament Affairs
• Christine Sullivan, Vice President Marketing
• Tony Tortorici, Vice President Production
Description:
National. Cable Television programmer offering 24-hour, 7 basic service. Live coverage of the PGA Tour, Champions Tour, LPGA, Nationwide, European and Australian Tours. Programming also includes: GOLF TALK LIVE, a call -in interview show with golfers. GOLF CHANNEL ACADEMY LIVE, a call-in instructional show. GOLF CENTRAL, a live news show, PROFILE OF A PRO, PASSAGE TO PARADISE, a golf travel program. THE GOLF CHANNEL ACADEMY, an instructional series

GOLF MARKETING BY BIGGS
120 WEBSTER STREET
SUITE 216
LOUISVILLE, KY 40206
502-585-2299
Fax: 502-585-3574
• Biggs Tabler, President
Nature of Sports Service:
Properties include: The National Horse

media

Show, the Tennessee Walking Horse Show, and Thoroughbreds. Tabler Communications specializes in media buying using Regional Sports Networks.

GOULD ENTERTAINMENT CORPORATION
101 W. 57TH ST
NEW YORK, NY 10019
212-586-5760
• Michael J. Gould, President
Nature of Sports Service:
National. Cable TV programmer. TV syndicator, packager, consultant. Current programs: A Man Named Lombardi.

GRAVITY TELEVISION & SPORTS MARKETING
450 BRYANT STREET
SAN FRANCISCO, CA 94107-1303
415-495-5515
andi@gravity.com
www.gravity.com
• Amit Kapur, Founder/Chief Executive Officer
• Jim Benedetto, Chief Technology Officer

HUNTERDON GROUP, INC.
5 LEXINGTON RD
ANNANDALE, NJ 08801
908-730-0369
• Mark Dau, President
Sports Service Founded:
1998
Nature of Sports Service:
Sports television production company specializing in live-event and taped programs.

IMPACT SPORTS
7322 E. BROADWAY AVE
SPOKANE, WA 99212-1135
509-924-7768
Fax: 509-924-7668
buck@indirect.com
www.tnb.net/impactsports
• Gary Knudson, President
• Murray Walden, Vice President
• Paul Sorensen, Chief Executive Officer
Nature of Sports Service:
Regional/National. TV, radio program producer and broadcaster. Current properties include Washington State U. football, basketball, baseball; Arizona State football, basketball and baseball; Arizona High School football, basketball, baseball championships; AA/AAA Boys/Girls basketball championships; statewide championships; Washington Trust cycling championships; Eastern Washington U. football and basketball; U. of Arizona, signage; USC/UCLA/San Diego State marketing reps; Big 12 Football Show TV - 7 states. Tacoma Raniers AAA baseball; State B broadcasts; Mike Price Coaches Show; Big Sky football/basketball games; Olympic swimming championsh

INTERNATIONAL MANAGEMENT GROUP (IMG)
200 5TH AVENUE
7TH FLOOR
NEW YORK, NY 10010
212-489-8300
Fax: 646-558-8399
www.img.com

• Michael J Dolan, Ph.D., Chairman/Chief Executive Officer
Nature of Sports Service:
National. Program production. Live coverage of sports, special events; institutional films - taped segments and programs; syndicated films; rights representation. TWI is IMG's subsidiary television production company
London Office:
TWI House, 23 Eyot Gardens, London, W6 9TR Great Britain. 44.81.846 8070; FAX: 44.81.746 5334

INTERNATIONAL SPORTS COMMUNICATIONS
230 NEW YORK AVE
HUNTINGTON, NY 11743
631-351-5878
Fax: 631-351-5875
jalbert@jalbertfilm.com
www.jalbertfilm.com
• Joe Jay Jalbert, President
• Carol Randel, Syndication Manager
Year Founded:
1970

INTERSPORT, INC.
20 W KINZIE STREET
SUITE 1600
CHICAGO, IL 60610
312-661-0616
Fax: 312-661-0622
www.intersportnet.com
• Mark Adamle, President, Sales
• David Boblink, Chief Financial Officer
Signature Events:
College Football All-Star Challenge (ESPN) College Slam Dunk and Three-Point Basketball Championships. (ESPN) The ARETE Awards (CBS), Liberty Mutual Coach of the Year Senes (ABC)
Services:
Original sports and entertainment programmins, event marketing and corporate and fan hospitality

ITV SPORT
THE NETWORK CENTER
200 GRAY'S INN RD
LONDON, ENGLAND WC1X 8HF
www.itv.com
• Adrian Chiles, Chief Presenter
Nature of Sports Service:
International. Commercial broadcasting network in the United Kingdom.

JALBERT PRODUCTIONS, INC.
230 NEW YORK AVE
HUNTINGTON, NY 11743
631-351-5878
Fax: 631-351-5875
jalbert@jalbertfilm.com
www.jalbertfilm.com
• Joe Jay Jalbert, President
• Carol Randel, Vice President Syndication Sales
• Jay Jalbert, Vice President Production Services
Nature of Service:
Producer of sports TV programs, commercials, motivational videos, syndicator of summer and winter sports shows.

JFM SPORTS, INC.
20 SEARS DR
LAKE PLACID, NY 12946
518-523-3593
Fax: 518-523-1774
www.bobsleigh.com
• John F. Morgan, President

LEARFIELD SPORTS
2400 DALLAS PARKWAY
SUITE 500
PLANO, TX 75093
469-241-9191
Fax: 469-241-0110
www.learfieldsports.com
• Andy Rawlings, Executive VP/COO
(469) 241-9191
arwalings@learfield.com
• Greg Brown, President-Learfield Sports
(469) 241-9191
gbrown@learfield.com
• Keith Sampson, Executive Producer
Nature of Sports Service:
Regional. Over-the-air radio/TV program producer, broadcaster, program distributor. Produces and distributes collegiate sports in Big 12, Big Ten, ACC and PAC-10. Men's football and basketball for U. of Alabama, Clemson U., U. of Colorado, Indiana U., U. of Iowa, U. 0of Memphis, U. of Missouri, U. of North Carolina, Oklahoma State U., U. of Oklahoma, Oregon State U., Syracuse U., and Villanova U.

LEWIS PRODUCTIONS INC., BUTCH
250 W. 57TH ST, STE 311
NEW YORK, NY 10019
212-582-4344
Fax: 212-582-4346
Services:
Sports Productions and Promotions
Nature of Sports Service:
Program producer/packager. Boxing promotions and client representation.
Sports Service Founded:
1886

LINCOLN FINANCIAL MEDIA
3340 PEACHTREE ROAD NE
SUITE 1430
ATLANTA, GA 30326
404-239-7211
• Edward Hull, President
• Jeff E. Tennant, Vice President/Sales & Marketing
• Powell Kidd, Assistant Vice President/Technology Operation
• Jimmy Rayburn, Vice President/Operations Manager
Nature of Service:
Regional Television produces, syndicates and sells ACC and SEC football and basketball throughout the region. 10 ACC Football Telecasts, 12 SEC Football Telecasts, 32 ACC Basketball Telecasts, 33 SEC Basketbal Telecasts.

MAIN EVENTS
772 UNION BLVD
TOTOWA, NJ 07512
973-200-7050
Fax: 973-200-7061
knewman@mainevents.com
www.mainevents.com
• Jolene Mizzone, Vice President of Operations

MEDIA VISTA PRODUCTIONS
500 Railway Avenue
Campbell, CA 85008
408-282-1960
Fax: 408-549-9870
www.mediavista.com
• Peter Liebengood, Founder
• Cassandra Bellantoni, Owner/Executive
Producer
Nature of Sports Service:
National. Television production. Specializes
in sports news and events.

MEDIALINK WORLDWIDE
6430 SUNSET BLVD, STE 1100
LOS ANGELES, CA 90028
323-465-0111
Fax: 323-465-9230
jshulman@medialink.com
www.medialink.com
• Michael E. Kassan, Founder
Additional Offices:
Atlanta, Chicago, Dallas, London, New York,
Washington, DC

MOFFETT PRODUCTIONS, INC.
16140 KUYKENDAHL ST, STE 126
HOUSTON, TX 77068
281-440-0044
Fax: 281-580-3227
info@moffett.com
www.moffett.com
• Bill Moffett, President
(281) 440-0044
bill@moffett.com
• Layne Belchic, Vice President
(281) 440-0044
• Joe Krath, Vice President/Creative
Director
(281) 440-0044
joe@moffett.com
Nature of Service:
Radio & TV Production Company. Leading
producer for Sporting Events, Sporting
Equipment and Promotional
Advertisements.

MOTOR SPORTS RADIO
C/O SPORTCOM ASSOCIATES
80 ZEVAN RD
JOHNSON CITY, NY 13790
607-770-9165
Fax: 607-770-9165
• Paul Kaminski, General Manager
Nature of Sports Service:
Produces Radio shows dealing with motor
sports.

MOTORSPORTS MEDIA GROUP
3455 PEACHTREE INDUSTRIAL BLVD,
#305
DULUTH, GA 30096-9102
770-662-8334
Fax: 770-458-0276
Nature of Sports Service:
National. Full-service producers of television
and video programming, focusing on racing.
Lineup includes 30-minute magazine shows,
behind-the-scenes coverage, team and
event coverage, corporate and sponsor
promotions, and television broadcast
production services. Current properties
include: Racers, Checkered Past, This
Week at Road Atlanta, Lanier Raceweek,
Vintage and Historical Documentary Series;
and many other series and documentary

concepts. IMAGE Magnification (IMAG) at
races is a specialty.

MOUNTAINEER SPORTS NETWORK
WVU COLISEUM, ROOM 107
MORGANTOWN, WV 26505
304-293-2821
Fax: 304-293-4105
www.msnsportsnet.com
Nature of Sports Service:
Regional. Regional program producer.
Produces West Virginia University football
and basketball games for radio (60 stations)
and television (7 stations). Also produces
Mountaineer Magazine, a weekly football
show (TV) and Mountaineer Jammin, a
weekly television basketball show.

NASCAR COUNTRY
181 N. HARBOR DR
DAVIDSON, NC 28036
704-987-8454
Fax: 704-896-3441
• Sid Morris, President/Chief Executive
Officer
• Mike Helton, Chief Operating Officer
Nature of Sports Service:
Produces shows and news highlighting
NASCAR.

NATIONAL FILM BOARD OF CANADA
350 5TH AVE, STE 4820
NEW YORK, NY 10118
212-629-8890
Fax: 212-629-8502
Nature of Sports Service:
Distributor of award-winning films and
videos. Current properties include Chuvalo
vs Ali, a documentary depicting the Battle of
Toronto boxing match of 1966; King of the
Hill, about black Canadian Hall-of-Famer
Ferguson Jenkins; Baseball Girls, a
documentary on the history of womens
participation in the largely male dominated
worlds of baseball and softball; The Rocket,
a profile of legendary Montreal Canadian
Maurice Richard; The Sweater, an animated
short about boyhood passion for hockey;
Path of the Paddle, series of four films which
give clear-cut, well-illustrated explanations
of paddling techniques.

**NATIONAL MOBILE TELEVISION
PRODUCTIONS, INC.**
2740 CALIFORNIA ST
TORRANCE, CA 90503
310-782-9945
Fax: 310-782-9949
• Dave Cooper, Vice President Saless
• Michael Fillner, Sales
• Frank Coll, National Vice President of
Operations
• Stephanie Hampton, Director of
Operations
Nature of Sports Service:
National and international. Television
productions. Full Service video production
company specializing in remote television
production. Supplies mobile television
production facilities, production personnel,
technical crews and transmission for live
and live-to-tape sporting events. Provides
facilities, producers, directors, graphics,
design and consultation and editing. Current
productions include NBA, NFL, NHL, CFL.
Major League Baseball productions:
Executive producers for Colorado Rockies;

regional, national and international
production services for major sporting
events including auto racing, baseball,
basketball, boxing, bowling, boxing

NCAA
BROADCASTING
PO BOX 6222
INDIANAPOLIS, IN 46206
317-917-6222
Fax: 317-917-6807
jmichiaels@ncaa.org
www.ncaa.com
• Greg Weitekamp, Director of Broadcasting
(317) 917-6265
gweitekamp@ncaa.org
• Chris Fitzpatrick, Associate Director of
Braodcasting
cfitzpatrick@ncaa.org
• Frank Rhodes, Associate Director of
Broadcasting
frhodes@ncaa.org
• Jeramy Michiaels, Associate Director of
Broadcasting
jmichiaels@ncaa.org
Nature of Sports Service:
National. Produce various NCAA
Championship Events for national cable
networks and syndication. Produce NCAA
:30 PSA's for NCAA championship Events.
Sell television rights to local stations that air
NCAA championship events. License and
sell stock NCAA Championship footage.

NFL FILMS
1 NFL PLAZA
MOUNT LAUREL TOWNSHIP, NJ 08054
856-222-3500
• Howard Katz, Chief Operating Officer
• Barry Wolper, Chief Operating Officer
• Hal Lipman, Vice President/Production
Director
• Jim Jorden, Vice President/Producers
Nature of Sports Service:
National. Program producer. Provides
pre-recorded videotapes and full range
production facility and capabilities. Specific
programs include: Football Follies Series;
NFL Crunch Course; The NFL's Greatest
Games; Super Bowl Highlight series; and
individual annual team highlights.

NORTH AMERICAN MEDIA GROUP, INC.
12301 WHITEWATER DR
MINNETONKA, MN 55343
952-988-7117
800-688-7611
Fax: 952-936-9169
• Russell M. Nolan, Vice President/Group
Publisher
• Rich Sundberg, Publisher (North American
Hunter)
• Rich Sundberg, Publisher (North American
Fisherman)
• Seth Hoyt, Publisher (PGA Tour Partners)
Nature of Sports Service:
National. Produces outdoor sports
programming. Current properties: North
American Outdoors, portraying all types of
hunting and fishing, appearing on ESPN.
Also publishes NORTH AMERICAN
HUNTER, NORTH AMERICAN
FISHERMAN, PGA TOUR PARTNERS
magazines. How To and Gardening How To
magazines.

P.A.S.S. SPORTS
550 W. LAFAYETTE BLVD
DETROIT, MI 48231-3040
313-222-7277
Fax: 313-223-2299
• Jeffrey H. Genthner, General Manager
• Karen Kanigowski, Business Manager
• Keith Allo, Executive Producer
• Tom Maclean, General Sales Manager
Nature of Sports Service:
Regional. Cable TV program producer.
Carries Detroit Tigers, Detroit Pistons,
Detroit Red Wings, local Michigan
universities and other selected amateur and
professional events.

PETER ROGERES, INC LTD
1800 N. HIGHLAND AVE, STE 100
LOS ANGELES, CA 90028
323-962-1778
Fax: 323-962-7174
• Stephen M. Rodgers, Chief Executive
Officer
• Tay Dall, Distribution Associate
Nature of Sports Service:
National. Sports TV program syndicator.
Current programs: Championship Wrestling;
White Search, Skiing.

**PLATINUM ENTERTAINMENT PARTNERS
II**
4310 S. CAMERON, STE 4
LAS VEGAS, NV 89103
702-252-3900
Fax: 702-252-4300
• Andrew Fonfa, Chief Executive Officer
• Bill Lastra, President
• Cheryl E Cohen, Vice President/Executive
Producer
• Patrick Mauro, Hospitality/Production

PROMARK TELEVISION
500 S. PALM CANYON DR, #220
PALM SPRINGS, CA 92264
760-322-7776
800-266-6662
Fax: 310-276-3208
www.promarktv.com
• David Levine, President
Nature of Sports Service:
National. Sports TV program syndicator.

**RAI, ITALIAN RADIO & TELEVISION
SYSTEM**
1350 AVE OF THE AMERICAS, 21ST FL
NEW YORK, NY 10019
212-468-2500
Fax: 212-765-1956
• Mario Bona, President
Nature of Sports Service:
International. Program producer,
broadcaster, distributor for cable,
Over-The-Air TV and Over-The-Air Radio.
Italian Radio & TV system. Produces,
broadcasts and distributes sports
programming (originating in Italy). In the
U.S., broadcasts Italian League soccer.
Current properties include: Italian soccer
leagues A & B; Italian basketball league;
Italian rugby league; rugby.

ROBBINS MEDIA
375 GREENWICH ST
NEW YORK, NY 10013
212-661-7670
Fax: 212-656-1997

info@robbinsmedia.com
www.robbinsmedia.com
• Shawn Robbins, Producer/Director
Description:
Robbins Media is an award winning full
service production company specializing in
creative images and ideas for a diverse
range of clients. Collaborates closely with
networks, marketing, public relations, and
advertising agencies by giving them a full
service creative sports production arm
capable of any size project.

ROGERS SPORTSNET, INC.
PO BOX 9, STATION O
TORONTO, ON, CANADA M4A 2M9
877-288-7767
www.sportsnet.ca

RUFFOLO COMMUNICATIONS
9 MIDWAY DR
WILLOWBROOK, IL 60527
630-887-7361
Fax: 630-887-7361
trcomm@aol.com
• Jeff Ruffolo, President
Nature of Sports Service:
National. Programmer, distributor, marketer
of regular season, championship and tour
events of professional and collegiate athletic
programming for radio and television.

SFM ENTERTAINMENT
800 WESTCHESTER AVENUE
SUITE N-345
RYE BROOK, NY 10573
212-790-4496
Fax: 212-398-5738
www.sfment.com
• Stanley Moger,
Co-Founder/President/Chief Executive
Office5r
• Michael Maizes, Senior Vice
President/In-House Counsel

SNTV
5 LONGWALK ROAD
STOCKLEY PARK
LONDON, UB11 1FE
+44-203 314 5770
planning@sntv.com
www.sntv.com
• Andrew Parkinson, Editor
(44-) 0-8233-5
aparkinson@imgworld.com
Description:
Sports news video agency, providing six
bulletins a day of action, highlights and
breaking news, gathered 24 hours a day,
365 days of the year.

SONIFI SOLUTIONS
3900 W. INNOVATION ST
SIOUX FALLS, SD 57107
605-988-1000
888-563-4363
hotelsupport@sonifi.com
www.sonifi.com
• Steven Truckenmiller, Senior VP
Programming & Content Management
Frequency:
Daily.
Primary Audience:
Hotel guests.
Sports:
All available leagues.

Nature of Service:
Distribution of live sports packages into
hotel rooms on a pay-per-view basis.

SPEED CHANNEL NETWORK, INC.
1220 WEST WT HARRIS BOULEVARD
CHARLOTTE, NC 28262-8536
704-501-5700
Fax: 704-731-2197
www.speedtv.com
• Todd Siegel, Senior Vice President of
Advertising Sales
(212) 822-8681
richy@speedtv.com
• Bobby Akin, Vice President Integrated
Sales/Marketing
• Nancy MacDonald, Director, Marketing &
Promotions
(704) 501-5790
nancy.macdonald@speed.com
Description:
Speed Channel, a member of the FOX
Sports Media Group, recognized
experimental marketing as an opportunity to
build awareness of the network and boost
their SPEED Fanatic program, a group of
passionate motorsports fans.

SPORTS BYLINE USA
300 BROADWAY, STE 8
SAN FRANCISCO, CA 94133
415-434-8300
800-783-7529
Fax: 415-391-2569
byline@pacbell.net
www.sportsbyline.com
• Ron Barr, CEO
xhighflyer@aol.com
• Darren Peck, President
dpeck@sportsbyline.com
• Ira Hankin, Production Director
• Jessizo Geich, Traffic Director
• James Homs, Web Developer

**SPORTS ILLUSTRATED
TELEVISION/SITV**
1271 AVE OF THE AMERICAS, 21ST FL
C/O SPORTS ILLUSTRATED
NEW YORK, NY 10020
212-522-2845
Fax: 212-522-0138
Nature of Sports Service:
1994. SITV produces television
programming for distribution in broadcast
network and non-traditional formats.

SPORTSBLAST
94209 RESEDA BLVD
NORTHRIDGE, CA 91324
818-882-7297
Fax: 818-882-7563
• Peter Kjenaas, Producer
Marketing & Consulting Services:
SportsBlast specializes in animation.
Produces The Kelly's an animated series
that evolves around auto sports. SportsBlast
has signed a deal with Turner sports
Interactive for the animated series.
Sports Service Founded:
1994

SPORTVISION
4410 NORTH RAVENSWOOD AVE
CHICAGO, IL 60093
773-293-4300
Fax: 773-293-2155

info@sportvision.com
www.sportvision.com
• Ryan Zander, Baseball, Motorsports
• Hank Adams, Chief Executive Officer
• Stan Honey, President/Chief Technology
Officer
• Rich Magid, Cheif Financial Officer
• Mike Jakob, Chief Operating Officer
• Steve Roberts, EVP/Business
Development
• David Goldberg, EVP, Corporate
Development
• Marv White, EVP, Development and Field
Engineer
• Barry Schliesmann, EVP Interactive
Technology
• Tom Worcester, EVP Sales and Marketing
• Russell Quy, VP Media
Prduction/Executive Producer
Sports Service Founded:
1998
Nature of Sports Service:
Develop products and applications that
enhance the fan's experience on television,
the Internet and convergence platforms.
Organization's fan-centric technology
applications allow broadcasters, sports
leagues, teams and internet sites to enrich
content. Creators of 1st and 10 electronic
first down line for television.

**STEINFELD PRODUCTIONS, INC.,
ROBERT**
18031 ROCK BRANCH DR
DALLAS, TX 75287
972-868-1718
Fax: 972-868-1678
• Robert Steinfeld, President
Nature of Sports Service:
National. Program producer/packager.
Producer and director of live sports events
including NBA basketball, Major League
Baseball, NCAA basketball and other
events. Associated with Home Sports
Entertainment and ESPN Sports Networks.
Also produces, markets and distributes Tom
House instructional baseball videos.

STELLARTV-SPORTS
2327 N. VERDUGO RD
GLENDALE, CA 91208
818-240-9581
Fax: 831-401-2627
www.stellartv.com
• Rinny Manzano, Vice President

**THE PHOENIX COMUNICATIONS GROUP,
INC.**
3 EMPIRE BLVD
S. HACKENSACK, NJ 07606
201-807-0888
Fax: 201-807-0272
• Tom L. Filip, Public Relations/Event
Services
(201) 807-0888
• James E. Holland, President
ext 470
• Geoffrey W. Belinfante, Senior
VP/Executive Producer
ext 460
• Richard Domich, Senior VP
Sales/Marketing
• Jean-Marie Cap, Senior VP
Finance/Administration
• Tim Roberts, VP News Service

**THE SPORTS AND ENTERTAINMENT
COMPANY LLC**
2525 15TH STREET
SUITE 1-B
DENVER, CO 80211
303-427-3200
Fax: 303-427-3201
info@sports-entco.com
www.sports-entco.com
• Jon J. Franklin, JD, President & Chief
Executive Officer
jonf@sports-entco.com
• Briar Sangiuliano, JD, MBA, VP Marketing
(720) 352-3101
briars@sports-entco.com
• Andrew Madigan, MBA, Operations
Director
(303) 427-3200
andrewm@sports-entco.com
• Brian Harris, Events Director
(303) 427-3200
brianh@sports-entco.com
• Nina Kim, Marketing Manager
(303) 427-3200
ninak@sports-entco.com
Description:
On site event activation; video production;
athlete management.
Clients:
Barilla pasta; Rip It Energy Fuel; Golden
Gloves Boxing; World Series of Boxing; Tuff
shed marketing; television rights sales for
extreme sports, skiing & snowboarding.

TIMELINE VIDEO
ONE BRIDGE ST
IRVINGTON, NY 10533
914-591-7360
Fax: 914-591-7461
www.timelinevideo.com
• Diane Cricchio, President/Creative
Director
diane@timelinevideo.com
• Sean LaGamma, Managing Director
sean@timelinevideo.com
Clients Include:
Lucent Technologies, IBM, Minolta.
Nature of Sports Service:
A full service production company. Produces
film and video for special events,
documentaries, new product introductions,
corporate image campaigns, video news
releases, commercials, etc.

TRANSMEDIA GROUP
240 West Palmetto Park Road
Suite 300
Boca Raton, FL 33432
561-750-9800
Fax: 561-750-4660
pr@transmediagroup.com
www.transmediagroup.com
• Thomas Madden, Chairman & Chief
Executive Officer

TRZ COMMUNICATIONS INC.
4682 STATE ROUTE 43
KENT, OH 44240
800-846-4630
Fax: 800-846-4632
staff@trz.cc
www.trz.cc
• Thomas R. Zawistowski, Chief Executive
Officer
• Mike Wilt, Director Team Relations
Nature of Sports Service:
National, Radio program distributor, Live

telephone broadcast systems - play-by-play
of college, NBA, NFL, NHL, Major League
Baseball and auto racing from flagship radio
stations.

**U.S. OLYMPIC COMMITTEE
BROADCASTING DIVISION**
ONE OLYMPIC PLAZA
COLORADO SPRINGS, CO 80909
719-578-4740
Fax: 719-632-0250
www.usoc.org
• Mark Jones, Senior Director of
Communications
(719) 866-2226
• Lindsay Hogan, Senior Director of
Communications
(719) 866-4566
• Beth Bourgeois, Director, Communications
• Patrick Sandusky, Chief Communications
& Public Affairs Officer
Nature of Sports Service:
National. Over-The-Air and cable program
placement for the U.S. Olympic Committee
and National Governing bodies. Involves the
U.S. Olympic Committee and its member
organizations. Programming includes the
U.S. Olympic Festivals, major NGB national
and international events. Offers a
full-service off-line and on-line production
house to service members of the Olympic
Family with all aspects of video and audio
needs, and serves as a clearing house for
vintage Olympic footage and non-Olympic
competitions for 41 sports within the United
States.

VIDEO SPORTS, INC.
PO BOX 10
DELMAR, NY 12054
518-439-1998
800-USA-1996
Fax: 888-872-2024
• Jonathan Fishbein, President
(518) 439-1998
info@skatetape.com
Nature of Service:
World's largest selection of figure skating
videos.
Sports:
Figure skating.

VILCOM
88 VILCOM CENTER
CHAPEL HILL, NC 27514
919-968-4811
800-318-7103
Fax: 919-968-3748
• Jim Heavner, President
• Bob Woodruff, Chief Financial
Officer/Executive Vice Presid
• Dean Linke, Vice
President/Sales/Marketing
• Tim Noonan, Marketing Director Tar Heel
Sports
Nature of Sports Service:
Retains broadcast rights (TV & Radio) to the
University of North Carolina athletic
programs. Programs include men's
basketball and football. Also included is:
coaches shows, ACC Hotline show, game
programs and web site.

WALLACH ENTERTAINMENT
1400 BRAERIDGE DRIVE
BEVERLY HILLS, CA 90210

310-278-4574
Fax: 310-273-0548
wallach1@sbcglobal.net
• George Wallach, President
(310) 278-4574
wallach1@sbcglobal.net
Nature of Sports Service:
National. Cable TV programmer, syndicator.
Produces sports-related shows for national
cable and syndication.

WEBB ELECTRONICS
1410 WESTWAY CIRCLE
CARROLLTON, TX 75005
972-242-5400
Fax: 972-245-4517
www.webbelectronics.com
Sports Service Founded:
1986

WEST GLEN COMMUNICATIONS, INC.
1430 BROADWAY
NEW YORK, NY 10018-3396
212-921-2800
800-325-8677
Fax: 212-944-9055
www.westglen.com
• Stanley S. Zeitlin, President
• Mark Dembo, Senior Vice
President/Marketing
• Annette Minkalis, Senior Vice
President/Broadcast
• John Summerlin, Senior Vice
President/Production
• Cathy Boje, Vice President/Operations
Nature of Sports Service:
National. Specializes in developing targeted
media networks for audio, video and
multi-media program distribution to
television, radio and specialized audiences
such as schools, clubs, and civic
organizations. Services include production
and audience development, VNRs, PSAs,
satellite media tours, B-roll, web casting,
video conferencing, customized feedback
and reporting.

WINNERCOMM, INC.
6120 S. YALE, 2ND FL
TULSA, OK 74136
918-496-1900
Fax: 918-496-8606
www.winnercomm.com
• Tom Bergstrand, Sports Sales
tbergstrand@outdoorchannel.com
• Chris Lincoln, Executive Vice President
• Doug Wren, Executive Vice
President/Programs/Production
• Bill Flesher, Executive Vice President
Description:
Founded 1981. A full service video
production company and one of the largest
independent packagers of programming of
the ESPN networks.
Nature of Sports Service:
National. Program producer. Racing To The
Kentucky Derby, Racing To The Breeders'
Cup; 2Day At The Races; Racehorse
Digest; Wrangler World of Rodeo; America's
Horse; American Championship Harness
Series; Under Wild Skies; Cabela's
Sportsman's Quest; Major League Soccer,
BASS Masters, World Championship
Fishing, In Search of Fly Water.

WORLD WIDE SKI CORPORATION
312 AABC
SUITE I
ASPEN, CO 81611-2568
970-925-7864
Fax: 970-925-7882
Nature of Sports Service:
National, Full service producer/distributor of
Ski television programming. Ski industry
marketing consulting.

iPAYATTENTION LLC
203-329-0707
harvey@ipayattention.com
www.ipayattention.com
• Harvey Rubin, Executive
Sports Service Founded:
1994
Nature of Sports Service:
National. Arranges for sports events to be
produced for network and cable network
programs, including arranging the deal,
complete production, and coordination of all
elements including budgeting and financial
business planning. Events produced
include: PGA Chattanooga Classic; World
Cup Skeleton, Luge and Bobsled; National
Grand Champions of Dog Shows. Also
provides network program development and
consultation services.

Sports Radio Networks

AMERICAN URBAN RADIO NETWORKS
42 PARK AVE SOUTH
14TH FL
NEW YORK, NY 10016
212-883-2100
Fax: 212-297-2571
www.aurn.com
• Jerry . Lopes, President, Program
Operations & Affiliations
• Barry Feldman, Vice President Research
(212) 883-2104
bfeldman@aurn.com
• Shanta Manickam, Manager of Marketing
and Digital Services
(21-) 83-2121
Nature of Sports Service:
National. Radio broadcasting network.

AROUND THE RINGS
1776 PEACHTREE ST, STE 436 N
ATLANTA, GA 30309
404-874-1603
Fax: 404-874-3248
www.AroundTheRings.com
• Ed Hula, Founder
Comment@AroundTheRings.com
• Sheila S. Hula, Publisher
Sheila@AroundTheRings.com
• Brian Baker, Director Of Business
Development
Brian@AroundTheRings.com
• Kathy Kuzcka, Circulation
Kathy@AroundTheRings.com
Description:
Full Service news agency, specializing in
Olympic coverage, Radio production,
specializing in reporting. Publication is the
leading publication focusing on business of
the Olympic movement.

CAPITOL BROADCASTING COMPANY
2619 WESTERN BLVD
PO BOX 12800
RALEIGH, NC 27606
919-890-6000
Fax: 919-890-6095
webmaster@cbc-raleigh.com
www.capitolnet.com
• James F. Goodmon, President/CEO
(919) 821-8504
jgoodmon@cbc-raleigh.com
• James F. Goodmon, Jr., Vice President
CBC New Media Group
(919) 821-8605
jgoodmon@cbcnewmedia.com
• George W Habel, III, Vice President Radio
Networks/Sports/99.9 The Fan
(919) 687-6531
Nature of Sports Service:
Produces play by play broadcasts, and
coaches shows.

CORUS RADIO
CKNW 980AM
700 W. GEORGIA ST, STE 2000
VANCOUVER, BC, CANADA V7Y 1K9
604-331-2711
888-399-9898
Fax: 604-331-2722
www.cknw.com
• Mike Searson, Director of Sales
• Raila Gutman, Marketing Manager
• Tamara Von Dohren, Promotional
Coordinator
Nature of Sports Service:
National (Canadian). 24-hour
regional/national news and sports satellite
service (Canada-Wide). B.C. Lions (CFL);
Vancouver Canucks (NHL).

COX MEDIA GROUP
6205 PEACHTREE DUNWOODY RD
ATLANTA, GA 30328
678-645-0000
Fax: 678-645-5002
www.coxmediagroup.com
• Bill Hoffman, President
• Kim Guthrie, Senior Vice President of
Radio
• Richard J. Reis, Senior Vice President
Radio Operations
• Donna Hall, Senior Vice President
Marketing & Client Solu
• Nick Peluso, Senior Vice President Radio
Operations
Nature of Sports Service:
National. Cox Media Group is an integrated
broadcasting, publishing, direct marketing
and digital media company.

DIALGLOBAL, INC.
CANDLER TOWER
220 W 42ND STREET
NEW YORK, NY 10036
212-967-2888
888-435-7450
www.dialglobal.com
• Spencer Brown, Chief Executive Officer
• Ken Williams, President
• Marty Damin, Vice President Sports Sales
• Ed Quagliariello, Head of New York Sales
Nature of Sports Service:
National. An independent radio network,
offering formats, prep, sports programming,
music, jingles,imaging and advertising.
Current sports programming: NFL, NBC
Sports Radio, NCAA and Golf.

ESPN NETWORK
935 MIDDLE ST
BRISTOL, CT 06010
860-766-2000
Fax: 860-766-2213
www.espn.go.com
• John Skipper, President
Nature of Sports Service:
Worldwide. Covers a wide array of sporting events, shows, interviews and sports talk.

ESPN ON ABC
545 MIDDLE STREET
BRISTOL, CT 06010
860-766-2000
http://espn.go.com/espntv/onair/index
• John Skipper, Executive Vice President Content
• Steve Downs, Senior Vice Presidnt Programming
• Steve Anderson, Vice President Products
Nature of Sports Service:
National. Radio broadcasting network.

MOTOR RACING NETWORK/MRN
555 MRN DRIVE
CONCORD, NC 28027
704-262-6700
Fax: 704-262-6811
www.motorracingnetwork.com
• David Hyatt, President
• Chris D'Aprile, Director
• John Singler, News Director
• Lauren Schweppe, Associate Producer
Nature of Sports Service:
National. Produces radio broadcasts for NASACAR Sprint Cup, NASCAR Nationwide Series, NASCAR Camping World Truck Series, NASCAR K&N Pro Series, NASCAR Whelen Modified Tour and GRAND-AM Road Racing.

PREMIERE RADIO NETWORKS
15260 VENTURA BOULEVARD
SHERMAN OAKS, CA 91403
818-377-5300
Fax: 818-377-5333
http://www.premiereradio.com
• Steve Lehman, Chairman and Chief Executive Officer
• Jennifer Leimgruber, Senior Vice President of Programming
Nature of Sports Service:
National. Radio Network - sports talk programs.

WESTWOODONE
CANDLE TOWER
220 W 42ND ST
NEW YORK, NY 10036
212-641-2888
888-435-7450
www.westwoodone.com
• Paul Caine, Chief Executive Officer and Director
• Chris B Corcoran, Vice President/Affiliate Management
• Marty Damin, Vice President/Sales Sports
Nature of Sports Service:
National. Leader in live play-by-play radio sports. Sports line-up includes NCAA football and basketball, Men's Basketball Tournament and Final Four; regular season NFL football, the Playoffs and the Super Bowl; College World Series; Frozen Four; the Masters and the Olympics.

YAHOO! SPORTS RADIO
5353 W ALABAMA
STE 415
HOUSTON, TX 77056
713-479-5300
www.yahoosportsradio.com
• David Gow, CEO
dgow@yahoosportsradio.com
• Craig Larson, Program Director
(713) 479-5373
clarson@yahoosportsradio.com
• Josh Vexker, Affiliate Relations Director
(713) 479-5358
affiliates@yahoosportsradio.com
• John M Cravens, VP Operations/Stations Operations
jcravens@sportingnews.com
• Matt Nahigian, Sports Director
mnahigian@sportingnews.com
• Ryan Williams, Sports Director
rwilliams@sportingnews.com
• Randy Merkin, Executive Producer
rmerkin@sportingnews.com
• Jennifer Hadden, Executive Producer
jhadden@sportingnews.com
• Kelly Murphy, Host Appearances
kmurphy@sportingnews.com
• Beth Roncke, Marketing Manager
broncke@sportingnews.com
Nature of Sports Service:
National. 24-hour sports radio network with over 430 affiliated stations. Organization also operates Boston's Sporting News Radio 1510, WWZN The Zone, New York's 620 WSNR, Sporting News Radio, Los Angeles KMPC 1540 Sporting News Radio and 820 WCSN, Chicago's Sporting News. Broadcasts are streamed live through www.sportingnews.com.

Sports Radio Programs, Local

1500 ESPN SPORTSTALK
3415 UNIVERSITY AVENUE
MINNEAPOLIS, MN 55414
651-647-1500
877-615-1500
Fax: 651-649-1515
www.1500espn.com
• Brad Lane, Programming
• Ryan Giles, Promotions
• Bernie Laur, Online Sales
Description:
Talk Radio. Sports programming: M-F SportsTalk 3-4pm, Sports center/All Night 12-4pm, Sports Center/AM 4-5am; Saturday SportsTalk 10-12pm and Sunday SportsTalk 10-12pm.

970 WATH
300 COLUMBUS ROAD
PO BOX 210
ATHENS, OH 45701
740-593-6651
Fax: 740-594-3488
www.970wath.com
• Dave W Palmer, President
palmer@wxtq.com
• Thom Williams, Station and General Sales Manager
twilliams@wxtq.com
• Marianne Williams, National Sales Manager/Special Events
mwilliams@wxtq.com

• Bob Beyette, News Director
news@wxtq.com
Description:
Commentary, Sports. Monday, Tuesday, Wednesday, Thursday, Friday at 6:00PM for 1 hour. Program is a sports call-in show.

CBS PHILLY - SPORTSRADIO 94WIP
400 MARKET ST - 9TH FL
PHILADELPHIA, PA 19106
215-625-9460
wippromotions@cbsradio.com
• Andy Bloom, Operations Manager
(215) 625-6570
• Spike Eskin, Program Director
(215) 625-6568
spike@cbsphilly.com
• Ruby Ross, General Sales Manager
(215) 625-6530
suby.ross@cbsradio.com
• Vince Gambino, Local Sales Manager
(215) 625-6579
vince.gambino@cbsradio.com
• Cindy Webster, Marketing Director
(610) 668-5952
cswebster@cbs.com
Description:
News, Sports and Weather. Sports updates include: local, Phillies, Sixers, Flyers, Eagles, Wings, Wing Bowl.

CHARLESTON SPORTS RADIO
60 MARK FIELD DRIVE
SUITE 4
CHARLESTON, SC 29407
843-763-6631
Fax: 843-766-1239
ted@kirkmanbroadcasting.com
www.charlestonsportsradio.com
• Ted Byrne, Operations Manager
Description:
Sports Talk Radio. Call-In, Commentary, Current Events, Entertainment, Information, Interview, Sports, Talk, Traffic.

CHIEFS RADIO NETWORK
5800 FOXRIDGE DRIVE
6TH FL
MISSION, KS 66202
913-514-3000
Fax: 913-514-3004
rich.mcardle@cumulus.com
www.kcchiefsradio.com
• Mark Sullivan, President General Manager
(913) 514-3121
mark.sullivan@cumulus.com
• Rich McArdle, Radio Network Sales Manager
rich.mcardle@cumulus.com
Description:
Sports. Talk. Exclusive radio home of Chiefs Gameday coverage.

GATOR IMG SPORTS NETWORK
3909 W. NEWBERRY ROAD
STE D
GAINESVILLE, FL 32607
352-375-4683
www.gatornetwork.com
• Mick Hubert, Broadcast Announcer
Nature of Sports Service:
Play-by-Play action of Florida Gators Football.

media

HY-VEE RADIO COACHES CORNER
700 MAIN STREET SUITE 211
PELLA, IA 50219
641-842-3161
Fax: 641-842-5606
www.kniakrls.com
Description:
Interview, Play-by-Play, Talk. Monday at
7:00 PM for 1 hour. Program interviews local
high school and college coaches.

IDAHO SPORTS TALK
1419 WEST BANNOCK STREET
BOISE, ID 83702
208-336-3670
Fax: 252-473-1584
www.ktik.com
Description:
Call-In, Commentary, Entertainment,
Interview, Sports, Talk. Monday-Friday at
3:00PM for 2.00 hours. Team coverage:
Idaho Steelheads hHockey and Boise
Hawks baseball.

KGSO 1410 SPORTS RADIO
1632 S MAIZE ROAD
WICHITA, KS 67209
312-721-8484
Fax: 316-721-8276
www.kgso.com
• Harry Finch, General Manager
• Lisa Bryce, Business Manager
lbryce@maanradio.com
• Greg Steckline, Owner
Description:
Wichita's premier 24-hour all-sports radio
station.
Format:
All sports

LET'S TALK RACING
700 MAIN STREET SUITE 211
PELLA, IA 50219
641-842-3161
Fax: 641-842-5606
kniakrls@kniakrls.com
http://www.kniakrls.com
• Derek Cardwell, Host
sportsdude61@hotmail.com
Description:
Interview, Play-by-Play, Talk. Saturday at
11:00AM for 30 minutes. Program features
informative talks with sprint car drivers,
owners, and promoters.

LET'S TALK SPORTS
3755 KARICIO LANE SUITE 2C
PRESCOTT, AZ 86303
928-445-8289
800-264-5449
Fax: 928-442-0448
http://www.kqna.com
• Sanford Cohen, Host
Description:
Call-In, Interview, Play-by-Play, Talk. Friday
at 4:00PM for 2.00 hours. Program focuses
on local and national sports.

LOCKED ON SPORTS
351 ELLIOTT AVENUE WEST SUITE 300
SEATTLE, WA 98119
206-494-2000
800-726-0950
Fax: 206-494-2969
jaykelly@clearchannel.com
http://www.kjram.com

• John Fure, Producer
(206) 494-2000
johnfure@clearchannel.com
• David Locke, Host
davidlocke@clearchannel.com
Description:
Call-In, Commentary, Entertainment,
Interview, Play-by-Play, Sports, Talk.
Monday, Tuesday, Wednesday, Thursday,
Friday at 7:00PM for 4.00 hours.

LONE STAR FISHING
1080 BALLPARK WAY
ARLINGTON, TX 76011-5164
817-543-5400
Fax: 817-543-5572
krldeditor@cbs.com
http://www.krld.com
• Brian Hughes, Host
(817) 543-5455
tofishtx@aol.com
Description:
Call-In, Commentary, Educational,
Information, Interview, News, Sports, Talk,
Traffic, Weather. Sunday, Saturday at
5:00AM for 1 hour. Program focuses on
fishing.

LOOSE CANNONS
9660 GRANITE RIDGE DRIVE
SAN DIEGO, CA 92123-2657
818-559-2252
800-776-1690
Fax: 858-522-5768
http://www.xtrasports690.com
Description:
Call-In, Interview, Sports, Talk. Monday,
Tuesday, Wednesday, Thursday, Friday at
9:00AM for 4.00 hours. Program is a sports
talk show.

MICHIGAN RADIO NETWORK
325 SOUTH WALNUT
LANSING, MI 48933
517-484-4888
Fax: 517-484-1389
• Dennis Mellott, President/General
Manager
(517) 484-4888
dmellott@sagacom.com
• Rob Baykian, News Director
(517) 484-4888
news@mrnradionet.com
Nature of Sports Service:
Covers University of Michigan (Wolverines)
sports; Local Sports, Central Michigan
University Football, Michigan Racing
Network, Michigan State University/MSU
Football.
Football:
NFL - Detroit Lions.

NORTH STAR BROADCASTING
1356 MACKINAW AVENUE
CHEBOYGAN, MI 49721
231-627-2341
Fax: 231-627-7000
mary@nsbroadcasting.com
www.nsbroadcasting.com
• Mary Reynolds, General Manager/VP
Sales & Marketing
mary@nsbroadcasting.com
Description:
Play-by-Play, Sports, Talk.

RACING ROUNDUP
418 NORTH CENTER STREET
CORRY, PA 16407
814-664-8694
800-513-1370
Fax: 814-664-8695
power1370@yahoo.com
http://www.wwcb.com
• Kevin Thomas, Host/Producer/Program
Director
Description:
Interview, Sports, Talk. Saturday at
10:00AM for 30 minutes. Program features
information on regional and NASCAR auto
racing events.

SOUL EXPRESSION
1000 ASU DRIVE BOX 269
ALCORN STATE, MS 39096
601-877-6290
Fax: 601-877-2213
http://www.alcornstateuniversity.com
• Charles Edmond, Sports Director
(601) 877-2480
cedmund@lorman.alcorn.edu
Description:
Call-In, Interview, News, Play-by-Play,
Sports. Sunday, Monday, Tuesday,
Wednesday, Thursday, Friday, Saturday at
6:00AM for 8.00 hours.

SPORTS NIGHT
9660 GRANITE RIDGE DRIVE
SAN DIEGO, CA 92123-2657
818-559-2252
800-776-1690
Fax: 858-522-5768
http://www.xtrasports690.com
• Lee Hamilton, Host
(818) 559-2252
leehamilton@clearchannel.com
Description:
Call-In, Interview, Play-by-Play, Sports, Talk.
Monday, Tuesday, Wednesday, Thursday,
Friday at 4:00PM for 4.00 hours. Program
features sports commentary and interviews.

SPORTS OPEN LINE
1 SOUTH MEMORIAL DRIVE
SAINT LOUIS, MO 63102
314-621-2345
Fax: 314-444-3230
kmox@kmox.com
http://www.kmox.com
• Mike Grimm, Host
(314) 444-1872
mdgrimm@cbs.com
• Ron Jacober, Sports Director
(314) 444-3275
Description:
Call-In, Interview, Sports, Talk. Sunday,
Monday, Tuesday, Wednesday, Thursday,
Friday, Saturday at 6:00PM for 2.00 hours.
Program is a sports talk show with
interviews and listener participation.

SPORTS RADIO KJR
190 QUEEN ANNE AVE N
SEATTLE, WA 98109
206-286-9595
Fax: 206-494-2969
jaykelly@clearchannel.com
www.sportsradiokjr.com
• Dick Fain, Sports Director
Description:
Call-In, Interview, Play-by-Play, Sports, Talk.

SPORTS RAP
24 EAST MEADOW STREET SUITE 1
FAYETTEVILLE, AR 72701-5320
479-521-5566
Fax: 479-521-4968
anita.cowan@cumulus.com
• Chuck Barrett, Executive Producer/Host
(479) 521-5329
Description:
Sports. Monday, Tuesday, Wednesday,
Thursday, Friday at 4:00PM for 2.00 hours.

SPORTS TALK
P.O. BOX 13048 SFA
NACOGDOCHES, TX 75962
936-468-4000
http://www.sfasu.edu/ksau
• Sherry Williford, Executive Producer
(936) 468-4001
Description:
Call-In, Sports, Talk. Tuesday, Thursday at
5:30PM for 30 minutes. Program gives
listeners a chance to call in and express
opinions or make predictions about a wide
range of sporting events.

SPORTS TALK/THE TICKET
20450 NW 2ND AVENUE
MIAMI, FL 33169-2505
305-521-5100
877-790-1015
Fax: 305-521-1416
www.theticketmiami.com
• Larry Most, General Manager
(305) 521-5234
• Scott Prichett, Director Of Marketing
• Donna Mairs, National Sales Manager
• Von Freeman, National Sales Manager
• Eric Stenger, Promotions Director
• Victoria Aguirre, Traffic Director
• Marc Budine, Interactive/Online Sales
Manager
(305) 521-5231
Description:
Call-In, Commentary, Entertainment, Sports.
Team coverage: Miami Marlins, Miami
Dolphins, Miami HEAT, Miamia Hurricanes,
FL Int'l University and Florida Panthers.

SPORTS TO THE MAX
625 2ND AVENUE SOUTH
MINNEAPOLIS, MN 55402
612-370-0611
Fax: 612-370-0159
http://www.wccoradio.com
• Jimmy Erickson, Producer
(612) 370-0665
jerickson@wccoradio.cbs.com
• Mike Max, Host
(612) 375-7264
mmax@wccoradio.cbs.com
Description:
Sports, Talk. Monday, Tuesday,
Wednesday, Thursday, Friday at 6:00PM for
3.00 hours.

SPORTS ZOO
4695 SOUTH MONACO STREET
DENVER, CO 80237-3403
303-713-8415
Fax: 303-713-8424
http://www.850koa.com/
• Scott Hastings, Host
(303) 713-8585
scotthastings@clearchannel.com
• Alan Jackson, Sports Director
(303) 713-8689

alanjackson@clearchannel.com
• Dave Logan, Host
(303) 713-8689
davelogan@clearchannel.com
• Lois Melkonian, Host
(303) 713-8585
loismelkonian@clearchannel.com
Description:
Sports, Talk. Monday, Tuesday,
Wednesday, Thursday, Friday at 3:10PM for
3.00 hours.

SPORTSBEAT
2000 WEST LOOP STREET SUITE 300
HOUSTON, TX 77027-3510
713-212-8000
Fax: 713-212-8958
http://www.ktrh.com
• Carl Dukes, Host
carldukes@clearchannel.com
Description:
Commentary, Play-by-Play, Sports, Talk.
Monday, Tuesday, Wednesday, Thursday,
Friday at 5:00PM for 3.00 hours. Program
focuses on local and national sports.

SPORTSLINE
1749 NORTH 2ND STREET
ABILENE, TX 79603
325-673-1455
Fax: 915-673-3485
http://www.abileneradio.com
• Al Pickett, Producer
Description:
Call-In, Play-by-Play. Monday, Tuesday,
Wednesday, Thursday, Friday at 5:00PM for
1 hour. Program discusses the world of
sports and incorporates listener input.

SPORTSPHONE 68 WITH LARRY KRUEGER
55 HAWTHORNE STREET SUITE 1000
SAN FRANCISCO, CA 94105-3914
415-995-6800
Fax: 415-995-6907
www.knbr.com
• Tony Salvadore, General Manager
Description:
Call-In, Commentary, Current Events,
Information, Interview, News, Sports, Talk.
Monday, Tuesday, Wednesday, Thursday,
Friday at 7:00PM for 3.00 hours. Program
covers the latest sports news and human
interest stories.

SPORTSTALK
2601 NICHOLASVILLE ROAD
LEXINGTON, KY 40503-3307
859-422-1000
Fax: 859-422-1038
• Tom Leach, Host/Producer
(859) 422-1096
tomleach@clearchannel.com
• Jim Tirey, Host/Producer
jimtyree@clearchannel.com
Description:
Play-by-Play. Monday, Tuesday,
Wednesday, Thursday, Friday at 4:00PM for
3.00 hours. Program is a sports show,
featuring local, regional, and national
guests.

SUTER ON SATURDAYS
4404 SOUTHEAST NAPOLEON STREET
IOWA CITY, IA 52240

319-354-1242
Fax: 319-354-1921
kcjjam@aol.com
http://www.1630kcjj.com
• Tom Suter, Host/Producer
suterman7@aol.com
Description:
Call-In, Play-by-Play, Talk. Saturday at
9:00AM for 1 hour. Program discusses the
world of sports and takes listener call-ins.

THE ADAM GOLD SHOW
5000 FALLS OF NEUSE RD STE 308
SUITE 308
RALEIGH, NC 27609-5480
919-875-9100
Fax: 919-875-9080
http://www.850thebuzz.com
• Adam Gold, Host
(919) 875-9100
• Joe Ovies, Producer
Description:
Call-In, Commentary, Entertainment,
Interview, News, Sports, Talk. Monday,
Tuesday, Wednesday, Thursday, Friday at
3:00PM for 3.00 hours.

THE D-103 MORNING SHOW
P.O. BOX 98
DOVER FOXCROFT, ME 04426
207-564-2642
Fax: 207-564-8905
http://www.zoneradio.com
• Toby Nelson, Sports Director
(207) 990-2800
Description:
Call-In, Commentary, Current Events,
Entertainment, Full Service, Information,
Interview, Magazine,. Sunday at 7:00AM for
3.00 hours; Monday, Tuesday, Wednesday,
Thursday, Friday, Saturday at 6:00AM for
3.00 hours. Program is a news,
entertainment, and mu

THE FISHING REPORT WITH BRIAN HOFFMAN
55 HAWTHORNE STREET SUITE 1100
SAN FRANCISCO, CA 94105-3906
415-995-6800
Fax: 415-995-6867
sports@knbr.com
http://www.knbr.com
• Brian Hoffman, Host/Producer
Description:
Call-In, Interview, Sports, Talk. Sunday at
6:00AM for 1 hour. Program features news
and information for sport fishing enthusiasts.

THE FRED HONSBERGER SHOW
1 GATEWAY CENTER
PITTSBURGH, PA 15222
412-575-2200
Fax: 412-575-2424
http://www.kdkaradio.com
• Paul Alexander, Sports Anchor
(412) 575-2328
Description:
Call-In, News, Sports, Talk, Weather.
Monday, Tuesday, Wednesday, Thursday,
Friday at 3:00PM for 3.00 hours. Program
covers current events and news.

THE GARY RADNICH SHOW
55 HAWTHORNE STREET SUITE 1100
SAN FRANCISCO, CA 94105-3906

media

415-995-6800
Fax: 415-995-6867
sports@knbr.com
http://www.knbr.com
• Gary Radnich, Sports Host
gary@knbr.com
• Patrick Connor, Producer
(415) 995-6935
Description:
Call-In, Entertainment, News, Sports, Talk, Weather. Monday, Tuesday, Wednesday, Thursday, Friday at 6:00AM for 3.00 hours. Program features news, entertainment, and sports coverage.

THE GOLF SHOW
1819 PEACHTREE ROAD N.E. SUITE 700
ATLANTA, GA 30309-1849
404-367-0640
800-776-4638
Fax: 404-367-6401
http://www.wgst.com
• Danny McNulty, Host
Description:
Call-In, Sports, Talk. Sunday at 7:00AM for 2.00 hours.

THE INSIDE TRACK
93351 OVERSEAS HIGHWAY
TAVERNIER, FL 33070
305-852-9085
Fax: 305-852-2304
davedonahue@clearchannel.com
http://www.keysradio.com
• Ed McClean, Host
edmcclean@clearchannel.com
Description:
Call-In, Interview, Sports, Talk. Tuesday at 6:30PM for 1 hour. Program features a weekly update on the world of motorsports and interviews with drivers.

THE JAMIE AND GREGG SHOW
27675 HALSTED ROAD
FARMINGTON HILLS, MI 48331
248-324-5800
Fax: 248-848-0272
http://www.wdfn.com
• Jon Klimczuk, Producer
jonklimczuk@clearchannel.com
• Jamie Samuelsen, Host
jamiesamuelsen@clearchannel.com
Description:
Sports, Talk. Monday, Tuesday, Wednesday, Thursday, Friday at 6:00AM for 3.00 hours.

THE JOHN CORBY SHOW
50 EAST RIVERCENTER BLVD. SUITE 1200
COVINGTON, KY 41011
614-486-6101
800-610-9886
Fax: 614-487-2559
stevekonrad@clearchannel.com
http://www.wtvn.com
• Joe Bradley, Producer
(614) 487-2534
joebradley@clearchannel.com
• John Corby, Host
(614) 487-6428
johncorby@clearchannel.com
Description:
Call-In, Sports, Talk. Saturday at 12:30PM for 2.00 hours.

THE MARK MADDEN SHOW
400 ARDMORE BOULEVARD
PITTSBURGH, PA 15221-3019
412-731-1250
Fax: 412-244-4596
http://www.espnradio1250.com
• Mark Madden, Host
mark.madden@abc.com
Description:
Call-In, Commentary, Sports, Talk. Monday, Tuesday, Wednesday, Thursday, Friday at 4:00PM for 4.00 hours.

THE MIKE TRIVISONNO SHOW
6200 OAK TREE BOULEVARD 4TH FLOOR
INDEPENDENCE, OH 44131
216-520-2600
Fax: 216-524-3200
http://www.wtam.com
• Marty Allen, Sports Producer
(216) 520-2600
bigdaddy@wtam.com
• Mike Snyder, Sports Director
(216) 642-4636
mikesnyder@wtam.com
• Mike Trivisonno, Sports Host
(216) 520-2600
trivshow@wtam.com
Description:
Call-In, Current Events, Sports, Talk. Monday, Tuesday, Wednesday, Thursday, Friday at 3:00PM for 4.00 hours.

THE MORNING SHOW
121 SUB BASE
ST THOMAS, U.S. VIRGI 00802
340-774-1340
Fax: 340-776-1316
pottley@wsta.com
http://www.wsta.com
• Bob Wilmer, Sports Host
Description:
Call-In, Commentary, Current Events, Educational, Entertainment, Full Service, Information, Intervie. Sunday at 7:00AM; Monday, Tuesday, Wednesday, Thursday, Friday, Saturday at 7:00AM for 4.00 hours.

THE POWER PLAY
3911 SOUTH 1ST STREET
ABILENE, TX 79605
325-676-7711
800-588-5326
Fax: 325-676-3851
shayhill@clearchannel.com
http://www.keanradio.com
• Rudy Fernandez, Program Director
(325) 676-7711
rudyfernandez@clearchannel.com
• Chaz McGuire, Host
chazmcguire@clearchannel.com
Description:
Call-In, Interview, Play-by-Play. Monday, Tuesday, Wednesday, Thursday, Friday at 5:00PM for 2.00 hours. Program focuses on sports.

THE RAZOR & MR. T
55 HAWTHORNE STREET SUITE 1100
SAN FRANCISCO, CA 94105-3906
415-995-6800
Fax: 415-995-6867
http://www.knbr.com
• Jennifer Violet, Executive Producer
Description:
Call-In, Current Events, Entertainment,

Information, Interview, Sports, Talk, Traffic. Monday, Tuesday, Wednesday, Thursday, Friday at 3:00PM for 4.00 hours. Program is a talk show with emphasis on sports and entertainment; includes news and sports update

THE SPORTS TABLE
134 4TH AVENUE
HUNTINGTON, WV 25701
304-525-7788
Fax: 304-525-3299
billcornwell@clearchannel.com
http://800wvhu.com
• Paul Swann, Host
Description:
Call-In, Play-by-Play, Talk. Sunday, Monday, Tuesday, Wednesday, Thursday, Friday, Saturday at 6:30PM for 30 minutes. Program is a collection of network and local sports talk, plus national, regional, and local team play-by-plays.

UNSPORTSMANLIKE CONDUCT
5011 CAPITOL AVENUE
OMAHA, NE 68132
402-342-2000
Fax: 402-342-7041
• Kevin Kugler, Host/Sports Director
(402) 977-9215
• Neil Nelkin, Program Director
(402) 977-9294
• Mike'l Severe, Host
(402) 977-9217
Description:
Call-In, Sports, Talk. Monday, Tuesday, Wednesday, Thursday, Friday at 3:00PM for 3.00 hours.

WBFH RADIO
4200 ANDOVER ROAD
BLOOMFIELD HILLS, MI 48302-2000
248-341-5690
Fax: 248-341-5679
http://www.wbfh.fm
• Pete Bowers, Station Manager
Description:
Sports talk show "Sportscan" - Call-In, Interview, News, Play-by-Play, Talk. Monday at 8:00PM for 1 hour. Program discusses regional sports.

WEEKDAY SPORTSBEAT
300 WEST JEFFERSON BOULEVARD
SOUTH BEND, IN 46601-1513
574-233-3141
Fax: 574-289-7382
http://www.wsbt.com
• Rick Carter, Host
(574) 472-8254
wsbtnews@wsbt.com
• Darin Pritchett, Host/Producer
(574) 282-2696
pritchett@wsbt.com
Description:
Call-In, Entertainment, Interview, Sports, Talk. Monday, Tuesday, Wednesday, Thursday, Friday at 5:15PM for 1.00 hours. Program focuses on national and local sports.

WILLTIME MOTORSPORTS
1711 EAST WABASH ROAD
PERU, IN 46970

765-473-4448
Fax: 765-473-4449
waru@sbcglobal.net
• Justin Howard, Program Director
waru@sbcglobal.net
Description:
Interview, Sports, Talk. Monday at 7:00PM
for 1 hour. Program focuses on motorsports
news and events.

Sports Radio Programs, National

CHET COPPOCK
190 NORTH STATE STREET 9TH FL
CHICAGO, IL 60601
312-984-0890
800-224-2004
Fax: 312-591-8900
wls.feedback@wlsam.com
www.wlsam.com
• Chet Coppock, Host
• Donna Baker, Vice President/Market
Manager
donna.baker@cumulus.com
• Tracy Slutzkin, Program Director
• Michael Mann, Sales Manager
• Lorraine Lynn, Promotions Director
lorraine.lynn@wlsam.com
Description:
Talk radio; news, weather, sports and traffic
reports.

COLLEGE FOOTBALL CENTER
ESPN PLAZA
935 MIDDLE ST
BRISTOL, CT 06010-1001
860-766-2000
800-999-9985
Fax: 860-589-5523
www.espn.com
• Mo Davenport, SVP and General Manager
• Bob Picozzi, News Anchor
• Matt Murphy, SVP Broadband and
Interactive Sales
• Rob Adamski, ESPN Event Production
Description:
Commentary, Talk. Live play-by-play of
seasonal games, "College GameDay"
football analysis, "ESPNU College Football"
podcast and road trips on "The Herd" and
"SVP & Russillo."

COLLEGE GAMEDAY
ESPN PLAZA
935 MIDDLE ST
BRISTOL, CT 06010-1001
860-766-2000
800-999-9985
Fax: 860-766-2213
collegegameday@espnradio.com
www.espn.com
• Rece Davis, Host
• Jay Bilas, Analyst
• Digger Phelps, Analyst
• Jalen Rose, Analyst
Description:
Commentary, Interview, Talk. Program
features sports news, game analysis,
conversations with sports newsmakers, and
previews of upcoming games. Satuday - first
hr begins at 10AM ET on ESPNU continuing
at 11AM on ESPN with a one-hour edition at
8PM on ESPN.

COUNTDOWN TO KICKOFF
935 MIDDLE STREET
BRISTOL, CT 06010-1001
860-766-2000
Fax: 860-589-5523
http://www.espn.com
• Keith Goralski, Senior Producer
• Stosh Cienki, Associate Producer
countdown@espnradio.com
Description:
Talk. Sunday at 11:00AM for 2.00 hours.
Program features analysis of upcoming NFL
games.

ESPN RADIO - SUNDAY GAMENIGHT
935 MIDDLE STREET
BRISTOL, CT 06010-1001
860-766-2000
800-999-9985
Fax: 860-589-5523
http://www.espn.com
• Sean Tyman, Producer
• Doug Gottlieb, Host
gamenight@espnradio.com
Description:
Call-In, Interview, Talk. Sunday at 7:00PM
for 4.00 hours. Program features sports
scores, interviews with sports figures, and
game analysis.

ESPN THE MAGAZINE
935 MIDDLE STREET
BRISTOL, CT 06010-1001
860-766-2000
Fax: 860-589-5523
http://www.espn.com
• Melissa Jacobs, Producer
• Dan Lebatard, Host
(305) 376-3498
Description:
Call-In, Commentary, Magazine, Sports,
Talk. Sunday at 7:00AM for 4.00 hours.
Program features analysis of the week in
sports and a look at the coming week.

GAMEDAY
935 MIDDLE STREET
BRISTOL, CT 06010-1001
860-766-2000
800-999-9985
Fax: 860-589-5523
gameday@espn.com
http://www.espn.com
• Bill Rodman, Executive Producer
• Jack Arute, Reporter
Description:
Call-In, Commentary, Current Events,
Educational, Entertainment, Information,
Interview, Investigati. Monday at 4:00PM for
3.00 hours; Tuesday at 4:00PM for 3.00
hours; Wednesday at 4:00PM for 3.00
hours; Thursday at 4:00PM for 3.00 hours;
Friday at 4:00P

GAMENIGHT
935 MIDDLE STREET
BRISTOL, CT 06010-1001
860-766-2000
Fax: 860-766-2213
http://www.espn.com
• Louise Cornetta, Senior Producer
gamenight@espnradio.com
• Chuck Wilson, Host
gamenight@espnradio.com
• Doug Gottlieb, Host
gamenight@espnradio.com

Description:
Call-In, Commentary, Interview, Talk.
Monday at 7:00PM for 4.00 hours; Tuesday
at 7:00PM for 4.00 hours; Wednesday at
7:00PM for 4.00 hours; Thursday at 7:00PM
for 4.00 hours; Friday at 7:00PM for 4.00
hours. Program features the latest scores,
news updat

HILL & SCHLERETH
ESPN PLAZA
935 MIDDLE ST
BRISTOL, CT 06010
860-766-2000
800-999-9985
Fax: 860-589-5523
www.espnradio.com
• Mike Hill, Host
• Mark Schlereth, Host
• Steve Anderson, EVP/News, Talent &
Content Operations
• Mo Davenport, SVP and General Manager
• Michelle Lynch, Event Operations
Producer
Description:
Talk. Sports weeknights 7PM - 10PM ET.

INDIANA SPORTS TALK
1 EMMIS PLAZA SUITE 400
INDIANAPOLIS, IN 46204-2902
317-266-9422
800-800-3044
Fax: 317-684-2008
http://www.wibc.com
• Bob Lovell, Host
(317) 684-4179
bob@indianasportstalk.com
Description:
Commentary, News, Talk. Monday at
7:00PM; Tuesday at 7:00PM; Wednesday at
7:00PM; Thursday at 7:00PM; Friday at
7:00PM. Program features local and
national sports news.

LATE GAMENIGHT
935 MIDDLE STREET
BRISTOL, CT 06010-1001
860-766-2000
Fax: 860-766-2213
http://www.espn.com
• Louise Cornetta, Program Director
gamenight@espnradio.com
• Bob Valvano, Host
gamenight@espnradio.com
Description:
Call-In, Commentary, Interview, Talk.
Monday at 11:00PM for 4.00 hours; Tuesday
at 11:00PM for 4.00 hours; Wednesday at
11:00PM for 4.00 hours; Thursday at
11:00PM for 4.00 hours; Friday at 11:00PM
for 4.00 hours. Program features the latest
scores, news

MIKE AND MIKE IN THE MORNING
ESPN PLAZA
935 MIDDLE ST
BRISTOL, CT 06010-1001
860-766-2000
800-999-9985
Fax: 860-589-5523
www.espnradio.com
• Mike Greenberg, Host
• Mike Golic, Host
Description:
Call-In, Commentary, Current Events,
Entertainment, Information, News, Panel
Discussion, Sports, Tal. M-F, 6AM-10AM.

MIKE NORTH
4334 MARTINGALE LN NW
ACWORTH, GA 30101-3873
770-917-8228
www.foxsports.com
• Mike North, Host
Description:
Talk. Sunday 8:00PM-1:00AM. Program
features the latest sports news, as well as
Mike's winning picks for the upcoming
games of the weekend.

**MONDAY MORNING RACING
REFRESHER**
1801 WEST INTERNATIONAL SPEEDWAY
BOULEVA
DAYTONA BEACH, FL 32114-1215
386-947-6400
Fax: 386-947-6716
http://www.mrnradio.com
Description:
Information, News. Monday at 6:45AM.
Program features a recap of the previous
weekend's NASCAR events.

NASCAR LIVE
1801 WEST INTERNATIONAL SPEEDWAY
BOULEVA
DAYTONA BEACH, FL 32114-1215
386-947-6400
Fax: 386-947-6716
http://www.mrnradio.com
• Steve Blevins, Producer
sblevins@mrnradio.com
• Eli Gold, Host
Description:
Talk. Tuesday at 7:00PM for 1 hour.
Program features NASCAR racing news and
features.

NASCAR TODAY
1801 WEST INTERNATIONAL SPEEDWAY
BOULEVA
DAYTONA BEACH, FL 32114-1215
386-947-6400
Fax: 386-947-6716
http://www.mrnradio.com
• Steve Blevins, Producer
sblevins@mrnradio.com
• Joe Moore, Host
Description:
Interview, News. Monday at 4:45PM;
Tuesday at 4:45PM; Wednesday at 4:45PM;
Thursday at 4:45PM; Friday at 4:45PM.
Program features race results, driver
interviews, and news from the NASCAR
circuit.

**NASCAR USA: COUNTRY MUSIC AT THE
SPEED OF SOUND**
1801 WEST INTERNATIONAL SPEEDWAY
BOULEVA
DAYTONA BEACH, FL 32114-1215
386-947-6400
Fax: 386-947-6716
http://www.mrnradio.com
Description:
Entertainment, Interview, Music, Talk.
Sunday at 9:00AM. Program features music,
artist interviews, race previews, and
NASCAR news; airs live on Sunday
mornings.

SPORTS BIZ
1490 DAYTON AVENUE P.O. BOX 4826
GREENWICH, CT 06831-9998

203-422-2800
800-249-8852
Fax: 203-422-2288
mmetter@businesstalkradio.net
http://www.businesstalkradio.net
• Fred Wallin, Host
sportsfred@aol.com
Description:
Talk. Saturday at 7:00PM for 2.00 hours.
Program focuses on the financial aspect of
the sports industry.

SPORTS BYLINE
300 BROADWAY SUITE 8
SAN FRANCISCO, CA 94133
415-434-8300
800-783-7528
Fax: 415-391-2569
byline@pacbell.net
www.sportsbyline.com
• Ron Barr, CEO
xhighflyer@aol.com
• Darren Peck, President
dpeck@sportsbyline.com
Description:
Call-In, Commentary, Information, Interview,
Sports, Talk. Monday at 10:00PM for 3.00
hours; Tuesday at 10:00PM for 3.00 hours;
Wednesday at 10:00PM for 3.00 hours;
Thursday at 10:00PM for 3.00 hours; Friday
at 10:00PM for 3.00 hours. Program
features int

SPORTS BYLINE WEEKEND
300 BROADWAY SUITE 8
SAN FRANCISCO, CA 94133
415-434-8300
800-783-7528
Fax: 415-391-2569
www.sportsbyline.com
• Ron Barr, CEO
xhighflyer@aol.com
• Darren Peck, President
dpeck@sportsbyline.com
Description:
Call-In, Commentary, Interview, Sports,
Talk. Sunday at 10:00PM for 3.00 hours;
Saturday at 10:00PM for 3.00 hours.

SPORTS CALL
125 WEST END AVENUE 6TH FLOOR
NEW YORK, NY 10023-6387
212-456-5185
Fax: 212-456-5150
abcradio@abc.com
http://www.abcradio.com
• Mike Rizzo, Executive Director
(212) 456-5185
michael.rizzo@abc.com
Description:
Interview, Talk. Sunday, Monday, Tuesday,
Wednesday, Thursday, Friday, Saturday
Program is an audio feed to affiliate stations
airing throughout the day.. Program features
sports news, talk, and game highlights.

**SPORTS OVERNIGHT AMERICA
WEEKEND**
300 BROADWAY SUITE 8
SAN FRANCISCO, CA 94133
415-434-8300
800-783-7528
Fax: 415-391-2569
www.sportsbyline.com
• Ron Barr, CEO
xhighflyer@aol.com

• Darren Peck, President
dpeck@sportsbyline.com
Description:
Call-In, Sports, Talk. Sunday at 1:00AM for
5.00 hours; Saturday at 1:00AM for 5.00
hours. Program offers listeners the
opportunity to discuss today's results and
hot sports topics and debate tomorrow's
possibilities, while also presenting the day's
score

SPORTS TALK
3710 LANDMARK DRIVE SUITE 100
COLUMBIA, SC 29204-4062
803-790-4300
800-956-7266
Fax: 803-790-4309
www.sportstalkgolive.com
• Carlton Green, Producer
• Phil Kornblut, Host
(803) 790-4300
• Tom Jackson, General Manager
(803) 790-4307
• Kevin McCrarey, Host
Description:
Call-In, Information, Interview, Sports, Talk.
Monday at 6:00PM for 2.00 hours; Tuesday
at 6:00PM for 2.00 hours; Wednesday at
6:00PM for 2.00 hours; Thursday at 6:00PM
for 2.00 hours; Friday at 6:00PM for 2.00
hours. Program features the latest sports ne

THE DAN PATRICK SHOW
935 MIDDLE STREET
BRISTOL, CT 06010-1001
860-766-2000
Fax: 860-589-5523
http://www.espn.com
• Dan Patrick, Host
danpatrickshow@espnradio.com
Description:
Commentary, Interview, Talk. Monday at
1:00PM for 3.00 hours; Tuesday at 1:00PM
for 3.00 hours; Wednesday at 1:00PM for
3.00 hours; Thursday at 1:00PM for 3.00
hours; Friday at 1:00PM for 3.00 hours.
Program features guest athletes, coaches,
entertainers

THE GOLF SHOW
935 MIDDLE STREET
BRISTOL, CT 06010-1001
860-766-2000
Fax: 860-589-5523
http://www.espn.com
• Dave Zaslowsky, Producer
• Bob Stevens, Host
(860) 766-2000
Description:
Commentary, Talk. Sunday at 6:00AM for 1
hour. Program takes a look at the latest
professional golf news.

THE JIM ROME SHOW
15260 VENTURA BOULEVARD SUITE 500
SHERMAN OAKS, CA 91403-5307
818-377-5300
Fax: 818-995-8079
webmaster@premierradio.com
http://www.premierradio.com
• Travis Rodgers, Producer
(818) 461-5426
trodgers@premiereradio.com
• Jim Rome, Host
(800) 636-8686
Description:
Call-In, Interview, Talk. Monday at 9:00AM

for 3.00 hours; Tuesday at 9:00AM for 3.00 hours; Wednesday at 9:00AM for 3.00 hours; Thursday at 9:00AM for 3.00 hours; Friday at 9:00AM for 3.00 hours. Program presents sports commentary and analysis with an ou

THE KEVIN WHEELER SHOW
1935 TECHNY ROAD SUITE 18
NORTHBROOK, IL 60062
847-509-1661
800-224-2004
Fax: 847-509-1677
http://www.sportingnewsradio.com
• Brad Robinson, Producer
(847) 400-3137
brobinson@sportingnews.com
• Kevin Wheeler, Host
(847) 400-3137
kwheeler@sportingnews.com
Description:
Call-In, Interview, Talk. Sunday at 1:00AM for 4.00 hours; Saturday at 2:00AM for 4.00 hours. Program features game previews from sports personalities and experts.

THE NFL ON ESPN RADIO
935 MIDDLE STREET
BRISTOL, CT 06010-1001
860-766-2000
Fax: 860-589-5523
http://www.espn.go.com/radio
• Mike Urrunaga, Producer
Description:
Sports. Sunday at 1:00PM for 6.00 hours. Program features analysis and discussions of professional football.

THE RICK BALLOU SHOW
1935 TECHNY ROAD SUITE 18
NORTHBROOK, IL 60062
847-509-1661
800-224-2004
Fax: 847-509-1677
http://www.radio.sportingnews.com
• Matt Nahigian, Program Director
(847) 400-3075
mnahigian@sportingnews.com
• Rick Ballou, Host
(847) 400-3132
rballou@sportingnews.com
Description:
Call-In, Interview, Talk. Monday at 10:00PM for 4.00 hours; Tuesday at 10:00PM for 4.00 hours; Wednesday at 10:00PM for 4.00 hours; Thursday at 10:00PM for 4.00 hours; Friday at 10:00PM for 4.00 hours. Program features sports analysis and lively interview

TONY BRUNO SHOW
1935 TECHNY ROAD SUITE 18
NORTHBROOK, IL 60062
800-565-1540
800-224-2004
Fax: 847-509-1677
http://radio.sportingnews.com/shows/tony_bruno
• Tony Bruno, Host
• Mark Willard, Co-Host
Description:
Talk. Monday at 8:00AM for 4.00 hours; Tuesday at 8:00AM for 4.00 hours; Wednesday at 8:00AM for 4.00 hours; Thursday at 8:00AM for 4.00 hours; Friday at 8:00AM for 4.00 hours. Program features the latest sports news.

WE ARE THERE SATURDAY
15260 VENTURA BOULEVARD SUITE 500
SHERMAN OAKS, CA 91403 5339
818-461-8291
Fax: 818-461-8219
http://www.foxsports.com
• Michael Coover, Producer
mcoover@premiereradio.com
Description:
Call-In, Talk. Saturday at 12:00PM for 8.00 hours. Program features sports news and commentary.

WEEKEND GAMENIGHT
935 MIDDLE STREET
BRISTOL, CT 06010-1001
860-766-2000
800-999-9985
Fax: 860-766-2213
http://www.espn.com
• Chuck Wilson, Host
gamenight@espnradio.com
• Louise Cornetta, Senior Coordinating Producer
gamenight@espnradio.com
Description:
Call-In, Commentary, Interview, Talk. Sunday at 7:00PM for 4.00 hours; Saturday at 7:00PM for 6.00 hours. Program features the latest scores, news updates, and lively conversation with sports stars.

WORLD OF RACING
1801 WEST INTERNATIONAL SPEEDWAY BOULEVA
DAYTONA BEACH, FL 32114-1215
386-947-6400
Fax: 386-947-6716
http://www.mrnradio.com
• Amanda Trautman, Producer
• David Hyatt, Director
dhyatt@mrnradio.com
• Ned Jarrett, Host
• Mike Storms, Executive Producer
Description:
Talk. Monday at 7:00AM; Tuesday at 7:00AM; Wednesday at 7:00AM; Thursday at 7:00AM; Friday at 7:00AM. Program focuses on racing personalities.

Sports Satellite Radio

BSKYB
6 CENTAURS BUSINESS PARK
GRANT WAY
ISLEWORTH
MIDDLESEX, ENGLAND TW7 5QD
http://phx.corporate-ir.net/phoenix.zhtml?c=104016&p=irol-corphome
• Tim Mason, Program Manager
• Roger Moody, Deputy Director Sports
Description:
International. Satellite broadcasting services.

PROSTAR ENTERTAINMENT NETWORK
12831 ROYAL DR
STAFFORD, TX 77477
281-240-1399
800-967-7827
Fax: 281-240-1447
• John C. Parks, President
• Scott Hoffman, Vice President
Nature of Sports Service:
National. Ad supported sports service, via

satellite, offering 16 hours of programming focusing on sports videos (Sports Video TV-SVTV), designed for sports bars, night clubs, colleges, military bases, taverns, country clubs and commercial establishments. Programming includes sports highlights, Tribune media's Sports Plus and News Plus service, SportsTicker, and pay-per-view events, sports fantasy and trivia.

SIRIUS XM RADIO INC.
1221 AVENUE OF THE AMERICAS
36TH FLOOR
NEW YORK, NY 10020
212-584-5100
http://www.sirius.com
• Hartenstein Eddy, Chairman
• Meyer James, Director/Chief Executive Officer
• Greenstein Scott, President/Chief Content Officer
Nature of Sports Service:
International. Satellite broadcasting services. Programming includes National Football League (NFL), Major League Baseball (MLB), and college sports games.

Sports Radio Stations

107.9 THE BULL
1011 N LINCOLN STREET
WEST POINT, NE 68788
402-372-5423
800-422-3664
Fax: 402-372-5425
http://www.kticradio.com
• Dwight Lane, Station Manager
dlane@krvn.com
• Tom McMahon, Sports Director
tmcmahon@kticradio.com
Description:
Music, News, Sports.
Frequency:
107.9 fm

1210 THE TICKET
FLINN BRDCASTING
6080 MT. MORIAH
MEMPHIS, TN 38115
901-375-9324
Fax: 901-375-5889
www.flinn.com
• Dan Frazier, Sales/Promotions Sports 56
• Bill Grafeman, Talent Director Sports 56
Nature of Sports Service:
24 Hour Sports.

1320 WAMR
282 N AUBURN RD
VENICE, FL 34292
941-388-3936
Fax: 941-388-3720

1390AM AND 97.1FM THE POINT
P. O. BOX 71
MIDDLEPORT, OH 45760
740-992-6485
866-374-5888
Fax: 740-992-6486
office@wyvk.com
• Rick Ash, Director
(740) 992-6485
office@wyvk.com

• Brenda Merritt, General Manager
(740) 992-6485
Description:
Music, News, Sports. Broadcasting high
school, collegiate and professional sports.

1510 THE ZONE
308 VICTORY ROAD
QUINCY, MA 02171
617-237-1200
Fax: 617-237-1177
www.revolutionboston.com
• Mike Kellogg, General Manager
• Bill Flaherty, Director of Sales
• Anthony Pepe, Director of Marketing
• Tod Rosensweig, Director of
Communications
Nature of Sports Service:
24 Hour Sports.

850 KOA RADIO
4695 S. MONACO ST
DENVER, CO 80237
303-713-8000
Fax: 303-713-8735
www.850koa.com
• Lee Larsen, General Manager
• Larry Zimmer, Sports Director
Nature of Sports Service:
24 Hour Sports Radio.
Baseball:
MLB - Colorado Rockies.
College Sports:
Football - University of Colorado.
Football:
NFL - Denver Broncos.

930 AM THE FOX
11700 CENTRAL PKWY
JACKSONVILLE, FL 32224
904-596-7320
• Jack O'Brien, General Sales Manager
Nature of Sports Service:
24 Hour Sports.
NCAA:
Florida Gators.

96.5 KHMX MIX
3050 POST OAK BOULEVARD
12TH FLOOR
HOUSTON, TX 77056
713-968-1000
Fax: 713-968-1044
• Buddy Scott, Program Director
• Tim Sutherland, Promotion Director

AM 620 WZON THE SPORTS ZONE
861 BROADWAY
BANGOR, ME 04402
207-990-2800
Fax: 207-990-2444
www.zoneradio.com
• Dale Duff, Program Director/WZON
• Clem Labree, Sports Reporter
• Scott Sassone, Sports Reporter

AM 850 THE BUZZ SPORTS RADIO
5000 FALLS OF NEUSE RD
STE 308
RALEIGH, NC 27609
919-875-9100
Fax: 919-875-9080
www.850thebuzz.com
• Brian Maloney, General Manager
• Jarrett Whaley, Sports Sunday/Producer

• Tim Chasteen, Production
Manager/Producer
ESPN:
Affiliate.
NCAA:
Duke University East Carolina University,
North Carolina State University.
NFL:
Carolina Panthers.

AM 950 THE FAN
7800 EAST ORCHARD ROAD
SUITE 400
GREENWOOD VILLAGE, CO 80111
303-321-0950
Fax: 303-676-6294
www.1043thefan.com
Sports Teams Covered:
Colorado Avalanche (NHL), Denver Nuggets
(NBA), Denver Pioneers (University of
Denver NCAA), Air Force Falcons.

AMI NEWS, SAN FRANCISCO/NEW YORK
50 VASHELL WAY, STE 200
ORINDA, CA 94563-3020
925-254-4456
800-736-0370
Fax: 925-254-7923
www.onthesnow.com;
www.mountainsports.com
• Rob Brown, President
• Chad Dyer, Internet Director
Nature of Sports Service:
National. Radio producer/news bureau;
world wide web producer. Regional reports
on participation sports and recreational
activities on a national level. Most reports
have immediacy factor and are updated by
phone. Seasonal services include condition
reports on skiing, fishing, camping, beach
and water sports. Also reports from major
events on behalf of sponsoring companies.

AUTOZONE
123 S. FRONT STREET
MEMPHIS, TN 38103
901-495-6500
800-850-6050
Fax: 901-495-8300
www.autozone.com
• Lynn Campbell, Marketing Director
Media Sponsor:
ESPN Radio Question of the Game brought
to you by AutoZone

CJCL
777 JARVIS ST
TORONTO, ON, CANADA M4Y 3B7
416-935-0590
Fax: 416-935-8288
www.fan590.com
• Scott Metcalfe, Sports Director
• Nelson Millman, Program Director
Auto Sports:
Indy Car Racing, NASCAR.
Baseball:
MLB - Sunday Night Game of the Week;
Playoffs - ALCS, NLCS, World Series.
Basketball:
NBA - Toronto Raptors.

ESPN 1490 THE FAN
3438 N COUNTRY CLUB
TUCSON, AZ 85716
520-795-1490
Fax: 520-327-2260

• Diane Frisch, General Manager
• Darla Thomas, Operations Manager
• LarVin Cassmin, Marketing Director
• Jody Oehler, On-Air Personality
joehler@journalbroadcastgroup.com
Baseball:
MLB - Colorado Rockies.
College Sports:
Basketball - Women's Arizona State
University.
Football:
NFL - San Francisco 49ers.

ESPN RADIO 1000
190 N. STATE ST
CHICAGO, IL 60601
312-980-1000
Fax: 312-332-3776
www.am1000.com
• Bob Snyder, General Manager
• Mitch Rosen, Program Director
Shows:
The ESPN Morning Show, with Mike Golic &
Mike Greenberg; Tony Kornheiser; Dan
Patrick; McNeil, Jurko & Harry; Chicago
Bulls Basketball; ESPN Gamenight; AllNight
With Todd Wright; ESPN Gameday; Bears
NFL Game Day Parlay; Silvy on Sports; The
Point After with Peggy Kusinski; Talking
Baseball, With Bruce Levine; RPM Now;
ESPN Magazine.

ESPN RADIO 1250 PITTSBURGH
400 ARDMORE BOULEVARD
PITTSBURGH, PA 15221
412-731-1250
Fax: 412-244-4596
www.1250espn.com
• Mike Thompson, General Manager
• David Waugaman, National Sales
Manager
(412) 244-4555
Primary Audience:
Men 18-49.

ESPN RADIO 920
8755 W. FLAMINGO
LAS VEGAS, NV 89147
702-876-1460
Fax: 702-876-6685
• John Hanson, Program Director
• Derek Roy, Promotions Director
Nature of Sports Service:
24 Hour Sports.

ESPN990 SPORTS RADIO
PO BOX 608
MASSILLON, OH 44648
330-837-9900
Fax: 330-837-9844
espn@espn990.com
www.espn990.com
• Ray Jeske, Station Contact
ray@espn990.com
• Donovan Resh, II, Media Contact
donresh@gmail.com
Nature of Sports Service:
Radio.
Football:
NFL/CBS Radio.
College Sports:
Basketball, Football.
Primary Audience:
Male.
Sports:
Local and ESPN Cincinnati Reds, Columbus
Blue Jackets.

KAAN-AM
HIGHWAY 69 SOUTH
BETHANY, MO 64424
660-425-6380
800-892-5959
Fax: 660-425-8148
• Stuart Johnson, Program/Sports Director
Description:
Music, News, Sports.

KAAN-FM
HIGHWAY 69 SOUTH
BETHANY, MO 64424
660-425-6380
800-892-5959
Fax: 660-425-8148
• Stuart Johnson, News/Sports Director
• Mike Mattson, Advertising Manager
Description:
Music, News, Sports.

KAAQ-FM
1210 WEST 10TH STREET
ALLIANCE, NE 69301-2804
308-762-1400
800-584-9310
Fax: 308-762-7804
http://www.doubleqcountry.com
• Mike Glesinger, Sports Director
mike.glesinger@eagleradio.net
• Kevin Horn, News Director
kcowstudio@bbc.net
Description:
Music.

KABZ-FM
2400 COTTONDALE LANE
LITTLE ROCK, AR 72202-2020
501-661-1037
800-477-1037
Fax: 501-664-5871
http://www.kabzfm.com/
• Tanya Hatfield, Promotions Director
• Randy Rainwater, Sports Director
(501) 661-1037
randy@1037thebuzz.com
Description:
Music, Talk.

KACC-FM
3110 MUSTANG RD
ALVIN, TX 77511-4807
281-388-4675
Fax: 281-388-4910
• Mark Moss, Program Director
(281) 388-4675
Description:
Music, News, Sports.

KACI-AM
502 WASHINGTON
THE DALLES, OR 97058-2217
541-296-2211
Fax: 541-296-2213
http://www.kaciamfm.com
• Rick Cavagnaro, Advertising Manager
(541) 386-5111
rick@gorgeradio.com
• Greg LeBlanc, News Director
greg@gorgeradio.com
Description:
Music, News, Talk.

KACI-FM
502 WASHINGTON
THE DALLES, OR 97058-2217
541-296-2211
Fax: 541-296-2213
http://www.kaciamfm.com
• Rick Cavagnaro, Advertising Manager
(541) 386-1511
rick@gorgeradio.com
• Greg LeBlanc, News Director
greg@gorgeradio.com
Description:
Music, News.

KACQ-FM
505 NORTH KEY AVENUE
LAMPASAS, TX 76550
512-556-6193
Fax: 512-556-2197
• Ronnie Witcher, General Manager
• Debra Witcher, Owner
Description:
Music, News, Sports.

KADA-AM
1019 NORTH BROADWAY
ADA, OK 74821-0609
580-332-1212
Fax: 580-332-0128
kada@wilnet1.com
• Mike Manos, Program Director
(580) 332-1212
Description:
Music, News, Sports.

KAGJ-FM
150 EAST COLLEGE AVENUE
EPHRAIM, UT 84627
435-283-7000
Fax: 435-283-7424
http://www.snow.edu
• Paul Sorensen, News/Sports Director
(435) 283-7439
jonny_54@hotmail.com
• Leslie Nixon, News and Sports Director
(435) 283-7000

KAIR-AM
P.O. BOX G
ATCHISON, KS 66002-0197
913-367-1470
800-367-9370
Fax: 913-367-7021
kairbri@hotmail.com
• Jim Ervin, Advertising Manager
• Brian Hagen, News Director
kair@mail.lvnworth.com
Description:
Music, News, Sports.

KALE-AM
830 NORTH COLUMBIA CENTER
BOULEVARD SUIT
KENNEWICK, WA 99336
509-783-0783
Fax: 509-735-8627
• Don Morin, General Manager
don.morin@nnbradio.com
• Kris Edwards, Program Director
(509) 783-0783
Description:
Music.

KALV-AM
ROUTE 1, BOX 53
ALVA, OK 73717-9706
580-327-1430
Fax: 580-327-1433

• Craig Killman, News Director
• Todd Miller, Sports Director
tmiller87@sbcglobal.net
Description:
Music, News, Sports.

KAML-FM
2810 SOUTHERN DRIVE
GILLETTE, WY 82716
607-686-2242
Fax: 307-686-7736
theedge@basinsradio.com
http://www.basinsradio.com/KAML/index.ht
ml
• Gina Decker, News Director
ginad@basinsradio.com
Description:
Music, News, Sports.

KANE-AM
2316 EAST MAIN
NEW IBERIA, LA 70560-4032
337-365-3434
Fax: 337-365-9117
kane@kane1240.com
• Jeff Botts, Program Director
jeff@kane1240.com
Description:
Music, News, Sports.

KAPB-FM
520 CHESTER STREET
MARKSVILLE, LA 71351-2844
318-253-9331
Fax: 318-253-5262
kapbfm@yahoo.com
• Pamela Couvillion, General Manager
• Mike Neck, Sports Director

KAQX-FM
1006 WEST MARINE DRIVE
ASTORIA, OR 97103
503-325-2911
Fax: 503-325-5570
• Zetty Mckay, News Director
(503) 325-2911
Description:
Music, News, Sports.

KATA-AM
5640 SOUTH BROADWAY
EUREKA, CA 95503
707-442-2000
Fax: 707-443-6848
kata1340.com
• J.B. Mathers, News & Sports Director
(707) 442-2000
Description:
ESPN sports talk radio
Frequency:
1340 AM
Description:
Sister stations KFMI, KKHB, KRED, KGOE

KAUR-FM
2001 SOUTH SUMMIT AVENUE
SIOUX FALLS, SD 57197
605-274-0770
800-727-2844
Fax: 605-336-5299
• Alex Beck, General Manager
(605) 336-4388
Description:
Music, News, Sports.

KAYS-AM
2300 HALL STREET
HAYS, KS 67601
785-625-2578
Fax: 785-625-3632
http://www.kaysradio.com
• Mike Cooper, Program Director
(785) 625-2578
• Todd Lynd, Advertising Manager
• Gerard Wellbrock, Sports Director
(785) 625-2578
gerard.wellbrock@eagleradio.net
Description:
Music.

KAZA-AM
765 STORY ROAD SUITE 120
SAN JOSE, CA 95122
408-881-1290
Fax: 408-881-1292
• Ruby Carrasco, Promotion Director
Description:
Music, News, Sports.

KBCR-AM
2110 MOUNT WERNER ROAD
STEAMBOAT SPRINGS, CO 80487-9011
970-879-2270
Fax: 970-879-1404
http://www.kbcr.com
• Tom Palmer, Sports Director
kbcrpalmer@nctelecom.net
Description:
Music, News, Sports, Talk.

KBCR-FM
2110 MOUNT WERNER ROAD
STEAMBOAT SPRINGS, CO 80487-9011
970-879-2270
Fax: 970-879-1404
http://www.kbcr.com
• Dave Lancaster, Sports Director
Description:
Music.

KBEE-FM
434 BEARCAT DRIVE
SALT LAKE CITY, UT 84115-2520
801-485-6700
Fax: 801-487-5369
http://www.b987.com
• Ginger Buchanan, Promotions Director
• Tammy Rodgers, News Director
(801) 493-8689
• Bryce Taylor, Advertising Manager
(801) 464-8514
Description:
Music, News, Sports.

KBEL-AM
P.O. BOX 418
IDABEL, OK 74745-0418
580-286-6642
Fax: 580-286-6643
kbel96fm@aol.com
• Paul Box, Program Director
Description:
Educational, Music, News, Sports, Talk.

KBER-FM
434 BEARCAT DRIVE
SALT LAKE CITY, UT 84115-2520
801-485-6700
Fax: 801-487-5369
• Kelly Hammer, Program Director
khammer5@hotmail.com

Description:
Music, News, Sports.

KBFI-AM
327 MARION AVENUE
SANDPOINT, ID 83864-1723
208-263-2179
888-263-2013
Fax: 208-267-5594
• Mike Brown, News Director
mikeb@953kpnd.com
Description:
Music, News, Sports.

KBFS-AM
707 HA ROADING STREET
BELLE FOURCHE, SD 57717-0787
605-892-2571
Fax: 605-892-2573
http://www.kbfs.com
• Karl Grimmelmann, General Manager
Description:
Music, News, Sports.

KBGG-AM
4143 109TH ST
URBANDALE, IA 50322-7925
515-331-9200
Fax: 515-278-4117
www.1700thechamp.com
Description:
Educational, Music, News, Talk.

KBHU-FM
1200 UNIVERSITY P.O. BOX 9665
SPEARFISH, SD 57799-0001
605-642-6265
Fax: 605-642-6272
http://www.bhsu.edu/studentlife/organizations/kbhu
• Scott Holbert, Sports Director
• Cody Oliver, News Director
kbhufm@hotmail.com
Description:
Music, News, Sports.

KBIX-AM
315 STATE STREET SUITE 910
MUSKOGEE, OK 74401-6350
918-682-9700
800-540-5369
Fax: 918-682-6775
http://www.bossjock.com
• Matt Hutson, Sports Director
(918) 492-2660
matt@sportsanimaltulsa.com
• David Stephens, General Manager
(918) 492-2660
stephens@kxoj.com
Description:
Talk.

KBIZ-AM
209 SOUTH MARKET
OTTUMWA, IA 52501-2924
641-682-4535
Fax: 641-684-5892
• Mike Buchanan, News Director
Description:
Music, News, Sports, Talk.

KBLJ-AM
116 DALTON AVENUE
LA JUNTA, CO 81050-1352

719-384-5456
Fax: 719-384-5450
kblj@rural-com.com
• Pat McGee, Sports Director
(719) 384-5456
Description:
Music, News, Talk.

KBLP-FM
204 SOUTH MAIN
LINDSAY, OK 73052-5634
405-756-4438
Fax: 405-756-2040
• Jason Wollenberg, News Director
Description:
Music, News, Sports, Talk.

KBND-AM
711 NORTHEAST BUTLER MARKET ROAD
BEND, OR 97701
541-382-5263
Fax: 541-388-0456
http://www.kbnd.com
• Kenn Brown, Advertising Manager
• Mike Cheney, General Manager
Description:
News, Talk.

KBRX-FM
251 NORTH JEFFERSON STREET
ONEILL, NE 68763
402-336-1612
Fax: 402-336-3585
scott@kbrx.com
http://www.kbrx.com
• Michael Wiiest, Sports Director
(402) 336-1612
sports@kbrx.com
• Scott Poese, General Manager
(402) 336-1612
scott@kbrx.com
Description:
Music, News.

KBSF-AM
P.O. BOX 127
SPRINGHILL, LA 71075-0127
760-322-7890
Fax: 760-322-5493
Description:
Music, News, Sports.

KBST-AM
608 JOHNSON STREET
BIG SPRING, TX 79720-2851
432-267-6391
Fax: 432-267-1579
http://www.kbst.com
• Mike Henery, News Director
(432) 267-6397
news@kbst.com
• Kris Moore, Advertising Manager
kris@kvst.com
• Tom Ruiz, Sports Director
onair@kbst.com
Description:
Music.

KBUN-AM
502 BELTRAMI AVENUE, N.W.
BEMIDJI, MN 56601-1656
218-444-1500
Fax: 218-751-8091
production@pbbroadcasting.com

• Kevin Jackson, Sports Director
kjackson@pbbroadcasting.com
• Mardy Karger, News Director
Description:
Music, News, Sports.

KBUN-AM SPORTS RADIO
502 BELTRAMI AVE
BEMIDJI, MN 56601
218-444-1500
Fax: 218-751-8091
• Lou Buron, General Manager
• Kevin Jackson, Pro General Manager
Director
kjackson@pbbroadcasting.com
• Peggy Hanson, General Sales Manager
Baseball:
MLB - Minnesota Twins.
Football:
NFL - Minnesota Vikings.
College Sports:
Basketball, Football - University of
Minnesota.

KBVU-FM
BUENA VISTA UNIVERSITY
STORM LAKE, IA 50588
712-749-1220
kbvu@bvu.edu
http://www.edgebvu.edu
• Fred Seel, General Manager
seelfre@bvu.edu
Description:
Music, News, Sports.

KBYR - TALK 700
1007 W. 32ND AVE
ANCHORAGE, AK 99503
907-562-3456
Fax: 907-273-3189
• Jerry Beaver, General Manager
• Sam Adams, Sports Director
Nature of Sports Service:
News/Sports/Talk.
College Sports:
University of Alaska Anchorage Hockey.

KCBS-AM
865 BATTERY STREET
SAN FRANCISCO, CA 94111
415-765-4000
Fax: 415-765-4080
http://www.kcbs.com
• Justin Erickson, Advertising Sales Rep
(415) 765-4036
• Hal Ramey, Sports Director
(415) 765-4112
• Steve Bitker, Sports Anchor
(415) 765-4000
kcbsnews@cbs.com
Description:
News.

KCCL-FM
1436 AUBURN BOULEVARD
SACRAMENTO, CA 95815
916-646-4000
Fax: 916-648-6020
http://www.kool1019.fm
• Don Langsford, Promotion Director
(916) 648-6012
dlangford@kool1019.fm
Description:
Music, News, Sports.

KCFS-FM
1101 WEST 22ND STREET
SIOUX FALLS, SD 57105-1600
605-331-6691
Fax: 605-331-6615
http://www.thecoo.edu/misc/kcfs
• Justin Whitcomb, General Manager
kcfs@usiouxfalls.edu
Description:
Music, News, Sports.

KCFV-FM
3400 PERSHALL RD
SAINT LOUIS, MO 63135-1408
314-513-4472
Fax: 314-513-4217
http://www.stlcc.cc.mo.us/fv/kcfv
• Mike Grayson, Sports Director
stew8@hotmail.com
• Ben James, News Director
Description:
Educational, Music, News, Sports.

KCHS-AM
P.O. BOX 351
TRUTH OR CONSEQUENCE, NM 87901
505-894-2400
Fax: 505-894-3998
http://www.gpkmedia.com
• Patrick Kohs, News/Sports Director
pat@gpkmedia.com
• Patrick Kohs, Sports Director
pat@gpkmedia.com
Description:
Music.
Year Founded:
1946

KCII-AM
110 EAST MAIN STREET
WASHINGTON, IA 52353
319-653-2113
Fax: 319-653-3500
kcii@kciiradio.com
http://www.kciiradio.com
• Drew Shradel, Sports Director
Description:
Music.

KCII-FM
110 EAST MAIN STREET
WASHINGTON, IA 52353
319-653-2113
Fax: 319-653-3500
kcii@kciiradio.com
http://www.kciiradio.com
• Jeremy Aitken, News Director
• Matt Veto, Sports Director
Description:
Music.

KCKX-AM
1665 JAMES STREET
WOODBURN, OR 97071-3644
503-769-1460
Fax: 503-981-3561
http://www.cowboy-country.com
• Dorecia Luce, Program Director
Description:
Music.

KCLA-AM
920 COMMERCE ROAD
PINE BLUFF, AR 71601
870-534-8978
Fax: 870-534-8984

• Andy Hodges, General Manager
Description:
Music, News, Sports.

KCLV-AM
2112 THORNTON
CLOVIS, NM 88101-4130
505-763-4401
Fax: 505-769-2564
kclv@hotmail.com
• Roy Norman, Advertising Manager
(505) 763-4401
kclv@allsups.com
• Roy Norman, Program Director
kclvradio@hotmail.com
Description:
Music, News, Sports.

KCMC
PO BOX 6397
TEXARKANA, TX 75505
903-793-1137
Fax: 903-792-4261
• Mike Simpson, General Manager
• Al Hanna, Sports Director
Nature of Sports Service:
Local. 24 Hour sports programming.
Baseball:
MLB - Texas Rangers.
College Sports:
Football - Texas A&M.
Football:
Dallas Cowboys.

KCOB-AM
1801 NORTH 13TH AVENUE EAST
NEWTON, IA 50208
641-792-5262
Fax: 641-792-8403
http://www.kcobradio.com
• Frank Liebl, Advertising Manager
• Randy Van, News Director
• Terry Walter, Sports Director
Description:
Music.

KCOW-AM
1210 WEST 10TH STREET
ALLIANCE, NE 69301
308-762-1400
800-584-9310
Fax: 308-762-7804
http://www.kcowradio.com
• Mike Glesinger, Sports Director
mike.glesinger@eagleradio.net
• Kevin Horn, News Director
• John Jones, Advertising Manager
Description:
Music, News, Sports.

KCRH-FM
25555 HESPERIAN BOULEVARD
HAYWARD, CA 94545-2447
510-723-6954
http://www.kcrh.net
• Ted Guiness, Sports Editor
Description:
Educational, Music, News, Sports.

KCRV-AM
777 HIGHWAY 84 WEST
CARUTHERSVILLE, MO 63830
573-333-1370
800-552-1055
Fax: 573-333-1371

media

Description:
Music, News, Sports.

KCSI-FM
1991 IRONWOOD AVENUE
RED OAK, IA 51566
712-623-2584
800-766-5274
Fax: 712-623-2583
kcsifm@yahoo.com
• Jerry V. Dietz, Program Director
Description:
Music, News, Sports, Talk.

KCTI-AM
615 SAINT PAUL STREET
GONZALES, TX 78629
830-672-3631
800-266-8531
Fax: 830-672-9603
• L. D. Decker, News Director
(830) 672-3631
ld44bigjake@hotmail.com
• Joe Haynes, Advertising Manager
(830) 672-3631
Description:
Music, News, Sports.

KCUB-AM
575 WEST ROGER ROAD
TUCSON, AZ 85705-2616
520-887-1000
Fax: 520-887-7585
http://www.fox1290.com/
• Carole Mendoza, Promotion Manager
Description:
Music, News.

KCUL-AM
200 WEST INTERSTATE 20
MARSHALL, TX 75672-9708
903-935-2500
Fax: 903-938-9730
• Mike Duncan, Program Director
Description:
Music, News, Sports, Talk.

KCUL-FM
200 WEST INTERSTATE 20
MARSHALL, TX 75672
903-935-2500
Fax: 903-938-9730
• Mike Duncan, Program Director
Description:
Music, News, Sports.

KCYL-AM
505 NORTH KEY AVENUE
LAMPASAS, TX 76550
512-556-6193
Fax: 512-556-2197
• Ronald K. Witcher, General Manager
Description:
Music, News, Sports.

KDAK-AM
859 MAIN STREET
CARRINGTON, ND 58421-1257
701-652-3151
Fax: 701-652-2916
• Dave Reed, General Manager
kdakam@daktel.com
Description:
Music, News, Sports.

KDBS-AM
1515 JACKSON STREET
ALEXANDRIA, LA 71301-6934
318-443-7454
Fax: 318-442-2747
• Cindy B Goode, News Director
(318) 443-7454
cindydickey@clearchannel.com
Description:
News, Talk.

KDCR-FM
498 4TH AVENUE, N.E.
SIOUX CENTER, IA 51250-1606
712-722-0885
Fax: 712-722-6244
kdcr@dordt.edu
http://www.kdcr.dordt.edu
• John Slegers, News Director
jslegers@dordt.edu
Description:
Music, News, Sports.

KDDR-AM
412 MAIN AVENUE
OAKES, ND 58474-1637
701-742-2187
Fax: 701-742-2009
• Tim Ost, General Manager
Description:
Music, News, Sports.

KDEX-AM
20487 STATE HIGHWAY 114 EAST
DEXTER, MO 63841
573-624-3545
Fax: 573-624-9926
kdex1@sbcglobal.net
• Joe Bowling, News Director
kdex1@sbcglobal.net
• Jim La Brot, Sports Director
kdex1@sbcglobal.net
Description:
Music, News, Sports.

KDIX-AM
119 2ND AVENUE, WEST
DICKINSON, ND 58601
701-225-5133
800-934-1230
Fax: 701-225-4136
kdix@kdix.net
http://www.kdix.net
• Rod Kleinjan, Sports Director
rod@kdix.net
• Jim Dahl, Associate Sports Director
(701) 225-5134
dahl@kdix.net
• Mike Renner, Rodeo Director
(701) 225-9662
mike@kdix.net
Description:
Music and Sports
Sports Discussed:
Football, Baseball, Basketball, Track,
Volleyball and Golf
Frequency:
1230 AM

KDJS-AM
730 NORTHEAST HIGHWAY 71
WILLMAR, MN 56201
320-231-1600
Fax: 320-235-7010
http://www.k-musicradio.com/index.html

• Bev Ahlquist, News Director
bahlquist@k-musicradio.com
• Doug Hanson, Promotions Manager
csmdrhanson@yahoo.com
• Randy Quitney, Sports Director
Description:
Music, News, Sports.

KDJW-AM
1721 AVONDALE AVENUE
AMARILLO, TX 79106-4516
806-331-2826
Fax: 806-358-9285
kdjw_production@yahoo.com
http://www.kdjw.com
• Ron Slover, General Manager
(806) 358-9280
kdjw-production@yahoo.com
Description:
Music.

KDKB-FM
1167 WEST JAVELINA AVENUE
MESA, AZ 85206-4706
480-897-9300
Fax: 480-491-9482
http://www.kdkb.com
• Matt Spaetzel, Promotions Director
• Todd Walsh, Sports Director
Description:
Music.

KDLR-AM
P.O. BOX 190
DEVILS LAKE, ND 58301-0190
701-662-2161
Fax: 701-662-2222
kdlrkdvl@stellarnet.com
• Mark Beighley, Sports Director
(701) 662-7563
• Curt Teigen, General Manager
kzzyprod@stellarnet.com
Description:
Music.

KDOM-AM
1450 NORTH HIGHWAY 60/71
WINDOM, MN 56101-2018
507-831-3908
800-950-5366
Fax: 507-831-3913
http://www.kdomradio.com
• Dirk Abraham, News/Sports Director
Description:
Music, News, Sports.

KDOM-FM
1450 NORTH HIGHWAY 60/71
WINDOM, MN 56101-2018
507-831-3908
800-950-5366
Fax: 507-831-3913
http://www.kdomradio.com
• Dirk Abraham, News/Sports Director
Description:
Music, News, Sports.

KDSJ-AM
745 MAIN STREET
DEADWOOD, SD 57732-1015
605-578-1826
Fax: 605-578-1827
kdsj@deadwood.com
http://www.kdsj980.com
• Pam Bachs, Advertising Manager
• Ryan Reider, Program Director

Description:
Music, News, Sports.

KDUS-AM 1060 SPORTS
1900 W. CARMEN ST
TEMPE, AZ 85283
602-260-1060
Fax: 480-838-0252
• Chuck Artigue, General Manager
• Henry Lopez, Program Director
• Fred Pandrok, Marketing Director
• Mark Randall, Promotions Director
Nature of Sports Service:
24-hour sports radio programming station part of the Sporting News Radio.
Football:
NFL - Arizona Cardinals
Ice Hockey:
NHL - Phoenix Coyotes

KDUZ-AM
20132 HIGHWAY 15
HUTCHINSON, MN 55350
320-587-2140
Fax: 320-587-5158
kduz@hutchtel.net
http://www.kduz.com
• Joel Niemeyer, Sports Director
(320) 587-2140
• Mark Wodarczyk, News Director
news@kduz.com
Description:
Music, News, Sports, Talk.

KDWA-AM
514 VERMILLION STREET
HASTINGS, MN 55033-1941
651-437-1460
Fax: 651-438-3042
http://www.kdwa.com
• Nick Ridley, News Director
news@kdwa.com
• Nick Tuckner, Sports Director
sports@kdwa.com
Description:
Music, News, Sports.

KDWN
1 MAIN ST
CARE OF : PLAZA HOTEL
LAS VEGAS, NV 89101
702-385-7212
800-338-8255
www.kdwn.com
• Claire Reis, General Manager
• Buzz Jones, Sports Director
Nature of Sports Service
Local. Sports/News/Talk radio programming.
Baseball:
MLB - Los Angeles Dodgers.

KDXL-FM
6425 WEST 33 ROAD STREET
SAINT LOUIS PARK, MN 55426-3403
952-928-6299
Fax: 952-928-6206
• Charlie Fiss, News Director
Description:
Music, News, Sports.

KEES-AM
1001 EAST SOUTH EAST LOOP 323
SUITE 455
TYLER, TX 75701
903-593-2519
Fax: 903-597-8378

• Paul Gleiser, Owner
(903) 593-2519
rogergray@ktbb.com
• Roger Gray, News Director
(903) 593-2519
rogergray@ktbb.com
• David Smoak, Sports Director
(903) 593-2519
smoaky@ktbb.com
Description:
Talk.

KELA
1635 S GOLD
CENTRALIA, WA 98531
360-736-3321
Fax: 360-736-0150
www.kelaam.com
• John Dimeo, General Manager
(360) 736-3321
johndimeo@clearchannel.com
• Ryan Trotter, Sports Director
ryantrotter@clearchannel.com
• Steve Richert, Operations Manager
steverichert@clearchannel.com
• Harland Forrest, General Sales Manager
harlandforrest@clearchannel.com
Nature of Sports Service
News, Talk, Sports.
Baseball:
MLB - Seattle Mariners.
College Sports:
Basketball - University of Washington;
Football - University of Washington,
Washington State University.
Football:
NFL - Seattle Seahawks.
Pro Basketball:
Seattle Sonics

KELO-AM
500 SOUTH PHILLIPS AVENUE
SIOUX FALLS, SD 57104
605-331-5350
Fax: 605-336-0415
http://www.keloam.com
• Greg Belfrage, News Director
(605) 271-5867
greg.belfrage@bybradio.com
Description:
Music, News.

KELY-AM
PO BOX 151465
ELY, NV 89315
775-289-2077
Fax: 775-289-6997
kelynews@gmail.com
www.kely1230.com
• Howard Tenke, Program Director
Description:
News, Sports, Talk
Frequency:
1230 am

KEOL-FM
ONE UNIVERSITY BOULEVARD
LA GRANDE, OR 97850-2899
541-962-3333
keol@eou.edu
http://www.eou.edu/keol
• Steven Kalb, Program Director
Description:
Music, News, Sports.

KEOM-FM
2600 MOTLEY DRIVE
MESQUITE, TX 75150-3840
972-882-7560
Fax: 972-882-7569
http://www.keom.fm
• Steve Glenn, Sports Director
(972) 882-7379
sglenn@mesquiteisd.org
• James Griffin, Station Manager
Description:
Music, News, Sports.

KERN
1400 EASTON DR, STE 144
BAKERSFIELD, CA 93309
661-328-1410
Fax: 661-328-0873
www.liveradio.com
• Roger Fessler, General Manager
• Jon Zimmery, Program Director
Nature of Sports Service:
Local. 24-hour sports radio programming.
College Sports:
Basketball - Cal State University.
Football:
Oakland Raiders.

KERX-FM
1915 CHURCH STREET
BARLING, AR 72923
479-484-7285
800-680-2261
Fax: 479-484-7290
tommy@pearsonbroadcasting.com
• Tommy Craft, Advertising Manager
• Derek Ruscin, Program Director
(479) 484-7285
derek@pearsonbroadcasting.com
Description:
Music, News, Sports.
Sports Discussed:
College Football, NFL, College Basketball
Frequency:
96.3 fm

KESN-FM
2221 LAMAR, E.
ARLINGTON, TX 76006-7419
817-640-3776
Fax: 903-455-3692
http://www.espn1033.com
• Keri Korzeniewski, President
(817) 695-0893
• Scott Masteller, Program Director
(817) 640-3776
Description:
Music.

KETR-FM
2600 SOUTH NEAL
COMMERCE, TX 75429-4504
903-886-5848
800-882-5387
Fax: 903-886-5850
• Kevin Jefferies, News Director
(903) 886-5334
Description:
Music, News, Sports.

KEWI-AM
102 WEST SOUTH
BENTON, AR 72015-3777
501-778-6677
Fax: 501-778-7717
http://www.kewi690.com

media

• Jim Landers, Sports Director
Description:
Music, News, Sports.

KEYG-AM
58053 SPOKANE BOULEVARD
NORTHEAST
GRAND COULEE, WA 99133
509-633-2020
Fax: 509-633-1014
http://www.thedamsite.com
• Mark Wheeler, Advertising/General
Manager
(509) 662-3842
mwheeler@genext.net
Description:
Music, News.

KEZM-AM
208 S HUNTINGTON STREET
SULPHUR, LA 70663
337-527-3611
Fax: 337-527-0213
kezm1310am@structurex.net
• Bruce Merchant, Program/Sports Director
Description:
Sports/Talk Radop
Year Founded:
1955

KFAN SPORTS RADIO
1600 UTICA AVENUE SOUTH
SUITE 400
ST. LOUIS PARK, MN 55416
651-417-3000
Fax: 952-417-3001
www.kfan.com
• Doug Westerman, Program Director
• Greg Swedberg, Operations Manager
• Mick Anselmo, General Manager
Nature of Sports Service:
Local. 24-hour sports radio programming.
Has exclusive rights to broadcast Minnesota
Tiberwolves games.

KFCR-AM
145 MOUNT RUSHMORE ROAD
CUSTER, SD 57730
605-673-5327
Fax: 605-673-3079
• Gary Baker, General Manager
Description:
Music, News, Sports.

KFFX-FM
1420 C OF E DRIVE
EMPORIA, KS 66801-2585
620-342-1400
800-279-1964
Fax: 620-342-0804
kvoe@kvoe.com
• Jeff O'Dell, News Director
• Greg Rahe, Sports Director
raheg@kvoe.com
Description:
Music, News, Sports.

KFGE-FM
4343 O STREET
LINCOLN, NE 68510-1753
402-475-4567
800-444-5546
Fax: 402-479-1411
http://www.FroggY981.com
• Steve Albertsen, Program Director
salbertsen@broadcasthouse.com

• John Bishop, Sports Director
(402) 475-4567
jbishop@broadcasthouse.com
• Mark Halverson, Market Manager
Description:
Music.

KFLD
2621 W. A ST
PASCO, WA 99301
509-547-9791
Fax: 509-547-8509
• Scott Souhrada, General Manager
• Tim O'Rourke, Program Director
Nature of Sports Service:
Local. 24-hour sports radio programming.
Baseball:
Seattle Mariners.
College Sports:
Basketball, Football - Washington State
University.
Ice Hockey:
NHL.

KFLS-AM
1338 OREGON AVENUE
KLAMATH FALLS, OR 97601
541-882-4656
Fax: 541-884-2845
http://www.kflsradio.com
• Jim Estabrook, News Director
(541) 882-4656
jim@klamathradio.com
Description:
Music, News, Sports.

KFLW-FM
P.O. BOX 1131 SRB
WAYNESVILLE, MO 65583
573-336-5359
800-336-5399
Fax: 573-336-5809
http://www.kflw99.com
• Jamie Turner, News Director
Description:
Music, News.

KFML-FM
16405 HEAVEN ROAD
LITTLE FALLS, MN 56345
320-632-5414
800-568-7249
Fax: 320-632-2571
ads@fallsradio.com
http://www.fallsradio.com
• Rod Grams, Program Director
(320) 632-5414
rod@fallsradio.com
Description:
Music, News, Sports.
Year Founded:
1985

KFMO-AM
804 SAINT JOE DRIVE
PARK HILLS, MO 63601
573-431-1000
800-959-5366
Fax: 573-431-0850
news@b104fm.com
• Greg Alan, Sports Director
(573) 431-1000
sports@b104fm.com
• Greg Camp, Promotions Director
(573) 431-1000
greg@b104fm.com

• Gib Collins, News Director
(573) 431-2000
gib@b104fm.com
Description:
Music, News, Sports, Talk.

KFMT-FM
P. O. BOX 669
FREMONT, NE 68026-0669
402-721-5012
Fax: 402-721-5023
http://www.kfmt.com
• Rich Ray, Sports Director
(402) 721-5012
• Barry Reker, Advertising Manager
(402) 721-5012
Description:
Music, News, Sports.

KFNS-AM
8045 BIG BEND BOULEVARD
WEBSTER GROVES, MO 63119
314-962-0590
Fax: 314-962-7576
http://www.kfns.com
• Jason Komito, Marketing/Promotion
Manager
jkomito@kfns.com
• Rob Weingarten, Program Director
rweingarten@kfns.com
Description:
News, Sports, Talk.

KFNS-AM SPORTS RADIO
8045 BIG BEND BLVD, STE 200
ST. LOUIS, MO 63119
314-962-0590
Fax: 314-962-7576
http://kfns.com
• Mike Claiborne, Program Director/Sports
Director
Nature of Sports Service:
Local. 24-hour sports radio programming.
College Sports:
Football - Notre Dame University.
Football:
St.. Louis Rams.

KFNZ
434 BEARCAT DR
SALT LAKE CITY, UT 84115
801-485-6700
Fax: 801-485-6611
• Eric Hauenstein, General Manager
• Jeff Rickard, Program Director
• Eric Ray, Operations Manager
Nature of Sports Service:
Local. 24-hour sports radio programming.
Baseball:
Minor League - Pacific Coast
League/PCL/Salt Lake Buzz.
Basketball:
NBA - Utah Jazz.
Football:
NFL - Denver Broncos.

KFOR-AM
3800 CORNHUSKER HIGHWAY SUITE 11
LINCOLN, NE 68504
402-466-1234
Fax: 402-467-4095
http://www.kfor1240.com
• Dale Johnson, News Director
(402) 466-1234
• Chuck Stevens, Sports Director
(402) 466-1234

Description:
Music, News, Sports.

KFSR-FM
5201 NORTH MAPLE
FRESNO, CA 93740
559-278-2598
Fax: 559-278-6985
kfsrfresno@hotmail.com
http://www.csufresno.edu/MCJ/kfsr-fm.htm
• Guy Haberman, Sports Director
Description:
Music, News, Sports.

KFTM-AM
P.O. BOX 430
FORT MORGAN, CO 80701-4105
970-867-5674
Fax: 970-542-1023
• Wayne Johnson, Owner
wayne@kftm.net
• John Waters, Sports Director
Description:
Music.

KFXN-AM
1600 UTICA AVENUE SOUTH SUITE 400
MINNEAPOLIS, MN 55416
952-417-3000
Fax: 952-417-3001
http://www.thescore690.com/main.html
• Chad Abbott, Program Director
chadabbott@clearchannel.com
• Mick Anselmo, Vice President
(952) 417-3020
mickanselmo@clearchannel.com
Description:
Music, News, Sports.

KFXX SPORTS RADIO 910 THE FAN
0700 SW BANCROFT ST
PORTLAND, OR 97239
503-223-1441
Fax: 503-222-6909
www.kfxx.com
• Suzanne Loseth, Marketing/Promotions
Director
• Meghan Olsen, Marketing/Promotions Mgr
LINEUP:
The Herd, Jim Rome, Dan Patrick Show,
The Big Show, Tee In'it up.

KFYN-AM
P.O. BOX 248
BONHAM, TX 75418-0248
903-583-3151
800-828-5396
Fax: 903-583-2728
• Jeff Davis, News Director
• Laura Kelso, Advertising Manager
(903) 583-4901
Description:
Music, News, Sports.

KGAL-AM
P.O. BOX 749
LEBANON, OR 97355-9642
541-451-5425
888-920-5746
Fax: 541-451-5429
http://www.kgal.com/
• Weldon Greig, News Director
news@kgal.com
• Radio Ray, Sports Director
(541) 926-8683
production@kgal.com

Description:
News, Talk, Sports
Frequency:
1580 AM
Sports Discussed:
All

KGBR-FM
29795 ELLENSBURG AVENUE SUITE-E
GOLD BEACH, OR 97444
541-247-7211
Fax: 541-247-4155
dale@kgbr.com
http://www.kgbr.com
• Bill Bailey, News Director
(541) 247-7418
bill@kgbr.com
• Randy Robbins, Sports Announcer
randy@kgbr.com
• Dale St. Marie, Owner, General Manager
Description:
Music, News, Sports.
Sports Discussed:
Gold Beach High School football.
Frequency:
92.7 fm

KGEO-AM SPORTS RADIO
1400 EASTON DR, STE 144
BAKERSFIELD, CA 93309
661-328-1410
800-840-5376
Fax: 661-328-0873
www.liveradio.com
• Roger Fessler, General Manager
• Jon Zimney, Sports Director
Nature of Sports Service:
Local. 24-hour sports radio programming.
Baseball:
MLB - San Francisco Giants.
Ice Hockey:
NHL - Anaheim Mighty Ducks.

KGFW-AM
2223 CENTRAL AVENUE
KEARNEY, NE 68847-5346
Fax: 308-237-0312
http://www.kgfw.com
• Bill Boyer, Operations Manager
(308) 698-2100
• John McDonald, General Manager
(308) 698-2100
Description:
News, Talk.
Year Founded:
1927

KGGG-FM
106 NORTH MAIN
HUTCHINSON, KS 67501-5219
620-665-5758
800-300-1061
Fax: 620-665-6655
ksku@ourtownusa.net
• Cliff Shank, General Manager
ksku@cis.compuserve.com
• Cliff Shank, Sports Director
Description:
Music, News, Sports.

KGHL-AM
222 NORTH 32ND STREET 10TH FLOOR
BILLINGS, MT 59101
406-238-1000
800-607-5445

Fax: 406-238-1038
http://790kghl.com/
• Jeff Howell, Program Director
(406) 238-1099
Description:
Music, News, Sports.

KGHS-AM
PO BOX 591
INTERNATIONAL FALLS, MN 56649-2317
218-283-3481
Fax: 218-283-3087
kghsksdm@northwind.net
http://www.ksdmradio.com
• Jerry Franzen, News Director
production@ksdmradio.com
• Roger Jerome, Sports Director
(218) 283-3481
Description:
Music, News, Sports, Talk.

KGMM ""THE GAME"" 1280 SPORTS
3911 S. FIRST
ABILENE, TX 79605
915-676-7711
Fax: 915-676-3851
www.keanradio.com
• Dean Minnick, General Manager
(915) 676-7111
• Jay Barry, Sports Director
(915) 676-7711
Auto Sports Sponsor:
Indianapolis 500.
Baseball:
MLB - Texas Rangers; World Series.
Basketball:
NBA - Draft; NBA - Finals.
College Sports:
NCAA Football - Texas A&M; NCAA
Basketball - Men's Tournament.
Equestrian:
Kentucky Derby.
Football:
NFL - Dallas Cowboys; Sunday & Monday
Night Football; Super Bowl.

KGNB-AM
1540 LOOP 337 NORTH
NEW BRAUNFELS, TX 78130
830-625-7311
800-594-2056
Fax: 830-625-7336
http://www.bradio.com
• David Ferguson, News Director
(830) 625-7311
Description:
Music, News, Sports.

KGPQ-FM
279 MIDWAY ROUTE
MONTICELLO, AR 71655
870-367-6854
800-367-8527
Fax: 870-367-9564
• P. Q. Gardner, Owner
Description:
Music.

KGRG-FM
12401 SOUTHEAST 320TH STREET
AUBURN, WA 98092-3622
253-833-9111
Fax: 253-288-3439
http://www.kgrg.com
• Eric Lucz, Program Director

Description:
Music, News, Sports.

KGSP-FM
8700 RIVER PARK DRIVE BOX 2
PARKVILLE, MO 64152-4358
816-741-2000
Fax: 816-741-4911
• Steve Youngblood, General Manager
Description:
Music, News, Sports.

KGVL-AM
1517 WOLFE CITY DRIVE
GREENVILLE, TX 75401-2111
903-455-1400
Fax: 903-455-5485
http://www.kgvlradio.com
• Bubba Knoetzes, News Director
kgblradio@hotmail.com
Description:
Music, News, Sports.

KHBT-FM
2196 MONTANA AVENUE
HUMBOLDT, IA 50548
515-332-4100
Fax: 515-332-2723
http://www.thebolt977.com
• Joe Hassett, Sports Director
• Duren Watts, News Director
Description:
Music, News, Sports.

KHHO-AM
645 ELLIOTT AVENUE WEST SUITE 300
SEATTLE, WA 98119
206-494-2000
richmoore@iheartmedia.com
www.sportsradioKJR.com
• Michelle Grosenick, General Manager
(206) 285-2295

KHKC-FM
P.O. BOX 810
ATOKA, OK 74525-0810
580-889-3392
Fax: 580-889-9308
• Ricky Chase, Program Director
khkc103@yahoo.com
Description:
Music, News, Sports.

KHMX-FM
24 GREENWAY PLAZA
SUITE 1900
HOUSTON, TX 77046
713-881-5100
Fax: 713-212-8965
http://www.khmx.com
• Buddy Scott, Program Director
(713) 830-8035
buddyscott@clearchannel.com
• Tim Sutherland, Marketing Director
(713) 212-8190
timsutherland@clearchannel.com
Description:
Music, News, Sports.

KHOP-FM
1581 CUMMINS DRIVE SUITE 135
MODESTO, CA 95358-6402
209-766-5000
800-548-0951

Fax: 209-522-2061
http://www.khop.com
• Geoff Silvius, Promotions Manager
(209) 523-7756
Description:
Music, News, Sports.

KHTK 1140 SPORTS RADIO
5244 MADISON AVE
SACRAMENTO, CA 95841
916-338-8700
Fax: 916-338-8777
• Mike Remy, Program Director
(916) 338-9226
mremy@infinitysac.com
• Michael Hernandez, General Sales
Manager
(916) 338-8781
mhernandez@infinitysac.com
• Jason Ross, Sports Director
(916) 338-9250
jross@infinitysac.com
Nature of Sports Service:
Local. Sports radio programming.
College Sports:
Basketball - Sacramento State University;
Football - UC Davis.
Football:
NFL - Oakland Raiders.

KHTR-FM
1101 OLD WAWAWAI ROAD
PULLMAN, WA 99163
509-332-6551
Fax: 509-332-5151
khtr@aol.com
http://www.hot104.net
• Evan Ellis, News Director
• Rod Schwartz, Advertising Manager
(509) 595-1244
Description:
Music.

KHUB-AM
P.O. BOX 669
FREMONT, NE 68026-0669
402-721-1340
Fax: 402-721-5023
http://www.kfmt.com
• Jessica Meistrell, News Director
(402) 721-1340
• Rich Ray, Sports Director
(402) 721-1340
• Barry Reker, Advertising Manager
Description:
Educational, News, Sports, Talk.

KHYL-FM
1440 ETHAN WAY SUITE 200
SACRAMENTO, CA 95825-2214
916-929-5325
Fax: 916-925-0118
http://www.v1011fm.com
• Sonia Jackson, Promotions Director
soniajackson@clearchannel.com
Description:
Music, News, Sports, Talk.

KICE-AM
969 SOUTHWEST COLORADO
BEND, OR 97702
541-382-5611
Fax: 541-389-7885
mflanagan@bendradiogroup.com
http://www.kxux.com

• R.L. Garrigus, News Director
(541) 617-5286
rl@bendradiogroup.com
Description:
Music, News.

KICS-AM
500 EAST J STREET
HASTINGS, NE 68901
402-462-5101
Fax: 402-461-3866
www.espnsuperstation.com
• Wayne Specht, General Manager
• Mike Will, Sports Director
(402) 463-1230
• Doug Duda, Sports Director
(308) 236-9900
Description:
News, Talk.

KIFG-AM
406 STEVENS STREET
IOWA FALLS, IA 50126
641-648-4281
Fax: 641-648-4606
• Jay Knoll, News Director
(641) 648-4281
kifg@iafalls.com
• T.J. Norman, Sports Director
kifg@iafalls.com
Description:
Educational, Music, News, Sports, Talk.

KIFG-FM
406 STEVENS STREET
IOWA FALLS, IA 50126
641-648-4281
Fax: 641-648-4606
• Jay Knoll, News Director
(641) 648-4281
kifg@iafalls.com
• T.J. Norman, Advertising/Sports Director
kifg@iafalls.com
Description:
Educational, Music, News, Sports, Talk.

KIGS-AM
6165 LACEY BLVD
HANFORD, CA 93230-8812
559-582-0361
Fax: 559-582-3981
info@kigs.com
http://www.kigs.com
• Tony Vieira, General Manager & News
Director
(559) 582-0361
vieira@kigs.com
• Eduardo Paim, Sports Director
(559) 582-0361
info@kigs.com
Description:
Music, News, Sports.

KIIX-AM
1612 LA PORTE AVENUE
FORT COLLINS, CO 80521
970-482-5991
888-212-9418
Fax: 970-482-5994
jeffersonchase@clearchannel.com
http://www.1410kiix.com
• Rich Bircumshaw, Sports Director
richbircumshaw@clearchannel.com
Description:
Music, News, Sports, Talk.

KIKR-AM
755 SOUTH 11TH STREET SUITE 102
BEAUMONT, TX 77701
409-833-9421
Fax: 409-833-9296
jbernard2@gt.rr.com
• Jay Bernard, Program Director

KILI-FM
P.O. BOX 150
PORCUPINE, SD 57772
605-867-5002
Fax: 605-867-5634
lakotaco@gwtc.net
http://www.lakotamall.com
• Wilson Two Lance, Program Director
(605) 867-5059
Description:
Music, News, Sports.

KILT AM 610 SPORTS RADIO
HOUSTON, TX
713-572-7767
www.sportsradio610.com
Basketball:
NBA - Houston Rockets, WNBA - Houston
Comets.
College Sports:
NCAA - Texas Longhorns.
Football:
NFL - Houston Texans.

KIMX-FM
302 SOUTH 2ND STREET SUITE 202
LARAMIE, WY 82070-3650
307-745-5208
Fax: 307-745-8570
• Jim O'Reilly, Program Director
Description:
Music, News, Sports.

KINI-FM
P. O. BOX 499
SAINT FRANCIS, SD 57572-0419
605-747-2291
Fax: 605-747-5791
kinifm@gwtc.net
http://www.gwtc.net/~kinifm
• Bernard Whiting, Jr., General Manager
knifm@gwtc.net
• Jay Claymore, Sports Anchor
(605) 747-2291
kinifm@gwtc.net
Description:
Music, News, Sports.

KIPA-AM
688 KINOOLE STREET SUITE 112
HILO, HI 96720-3868
808-935-6858
Fax: 808-443-0888
• Chip Begay, Sports Director
chip@lava105.com
Description:
Music, News, Sports.

KIT
4010 SUMMIT VIEW
YAKIMA, WA 98908
509-972-3461
Fax: 509-972-3540
• Dave Aamodt, General Manager
• Brian Teegarden, Sports Director
Office Address:
114 S. 4th St, Yakima, WA 98901.
Nature of Sports Service:

News, Sports, Talk.
Baseball:
MLB - Seattle Mariners.
Basketball:
NBA - Seattle Supersonics.
Football:
NFL - Seattle Seahawks.

KITO-AM
402 NORTH WILSON
VINITA, OK 74301
918-256-2255
Fax: 918-256-2633
kitoamfm@yahoo.com
• Leona Boyd, Advertising Manager
• Dave Boyd, Program Director
Description:
Music, News, Sports.

KITO-FM
402 NORTH WILSON
VINITA, OK 74301
918-256-2255
Fax: 918-256-2633
kitoamfm@yahoo.com
• Dave Boyd, Program Director
Description:
Music.

KJAK-FM
PO BOX 6490
LUBBOCK, TX 79493
806-745-6677
Fax: 806-745-8141
kjak@kjak.com
http://www.kjak.com
• Woody Van Dyke, General Manager
(806) 745-3347
Description:
Provider of live High School games on the
radio in Texas.
Year Founded:
1978

KJBZ-FM
902 EAST CALTON ROAD
LAREDO, TX 78041-6359
956-724-9800
Fax: 956-724-9915
• Carny Guerra, Program Director
Description:
Music, News, Sports.

KJCK-FM
US HIGHWAY 77 AND WEST ASH
JUNCTION CITY, KS 66441
785-762-5525
Fax: 785-762-5387
http://www.kjck.com
• Ed Klimek, Advertising Manager
eklimek@kjck.com
• Dewey Terrill, News/Sports Director
dterrill@kjck.com
Description:
Music, News.

KJFF-AM
1026 PHONEX DRIVE
FESTUS, MO 63028-0368
636-937-7642
Fax: 636-937-3636
http://www.kjff.com
• Ryan Reinheimer, Sports Director
• Matt West, News Director
Description:
Educational, News, Sports, Talk.

KJFM-FM
615 GEORGIA STREET
LOUISIANA, MO 63353-0438
573-754-5102
Fax: 573-754-5544
kjfmradio@yahoo.com
www.kjfmeagle102.net
• Thom Sanders, General Manager
(573) 324-0303
• Marianne Everhart, Operations Manager
(573) 324-0303
kjfmradioeagle102@yahoo.com
Description:
Mainstream country music.
Frequency:
102.1 fm

KJIM-AM
4367 WOODLAWN ROAD
DENISON, TX 75021-8037
903-893-1197
• Bob Allen, Advertising Manager/News
Director
Description:
Music, News.

KJIN-AM
P. O. BOX 2068
HOUMA, LA 70364
985-851-1020
Fax: 985-872-4403
• Glen Gomez, News Director
Description:
Music, News, Sports.

KJJJ-FM
1845 MCCULLOCH BOULEVARD SUITE
A-14
LAKE HAVASU CITY, AZ 86403
928-855-9336
Fax: 928-855-9333
http://www.kjjjfm.com
• Steve Greeley, Owner
Description:
Music, News, Sports.

KJNO-AM
3161 CHANNEL DRIVE SUITE 2
JUNEAU, AK 99801
907-586-3630
Fax: 907-463-3685
http://www.kjno.com
• Roy Paschal, President
Description:
Music.

KJOC-AM SPORTS RADIO
1229 BRADY ST
DAVENPORT, IA 52803
563-326-2541
Fax: 563-326-1819
• Scott Dailey, Program Director/Sports
Director
Nature of Sports Service:
Local. 24-hour sports radio programming.
Baseball:
MLB - Chicago White Sox, Chicago Cubs.
College Sports:
Football - Iowa State University; Basketball -
Iowa State University.
Football:
NFL - Chicago Bears.

KJR/KHHO SPORTS RADIO
351 ELLIOTT
SEATTLE, WA 98119

media

206-286-9595
800-829-0950
Fax: 206-494-2102
www.kjram.com

KJSK-AM
1418, 25 STREET
COLUMBUS, NE 68601-2820
402-564-2891
800-900-3511
Fax: 402-564-1999
http://www.kjsk.com
• Kara Asmus, Advertising Manager
(402) 564-9101
• Dean Johnson, Program Director
dejohnson@kzen.threeeagles.com
• James Nickel, Program Director ; Sports
Director
(402) 564-2891
clearnet@megavision.com
Description:
Educational, News, Sports, Talk.

KKFN
1095 S. MONACO PKWY
DENVER, CO 80224
303-321-0950
Fax: 303-333-5313
www.sportsradio.com/fan
• Bob Call, General Manager
• Tim Spence, Sports Director
Nature of Sports Service:
Local. 24-hour sports radio programming.
College Sports:
Basketball, Football - Colorado State
University.
Ice Hockey:
NHL - Colorado Avalanche.

KKIA-FM
145 OLD CREEK ROAD
STORM LAKE, IA 50588-7525
712-732-9200
877-220-3261
Fax: 712-732-3095
themoose@pionet.net
• Matt Fisher, News/Sports Director
Description:
Music, News, Sports.

KKIN-AM
37208 US HIGHWAY 169
AITKIN, MN 56431
218-927-2100
800-450-5546
Fax: 218-927-4090
kkinradio@embarqmail.com
• Tom Martin, Sports Director
Description:
Music, News, Sports, Talk.
Format:
All sports
Frequency:
94.3 Weekly sports show, 'Sports Call.'

KKLZ-FM
1455 EAST TROPICANA AVENUE SUITE
800
LAS VEGAS, NV 89119-8326
702-739-9600
Fax: 702-736-8447
• Kelly Hawkins, Promotion Director
(702) 730-0345
• Dennis Mitchell, News Director
(702) 739-9600
abbeyrd@cox.net

Description:
Music, News, Sports.

KKML-AM
6805 CORPORATE DRIVE SUITE 130
COLORADO SPRINGS, CO 80919
719-593-2700
Fax: 719-593-2727
• Jim Arthur, Program Director
(719) 593-2706
• Brenda Goodrich, General Manager
(719) 593-2766
• Jim Ryan, News Director
(719) 593-2774
Description:
Music.

KKNN-FM
315 KENNEDY AVENUE
GRAND JUNCTION, CO 81501
970-242-7788
Fax: 970-243-0567
http://www.coloradowest.com
• Tommy Rocker, Program Director
(970) 241-9595
• Kevin Wodlinger, Marketing Manager
(970) 242-7788
• Kim Gordon, PSA Director/Sports
(970) 242-7788
Description:
Music, News, Sports.

KKRC-FM
PO BOX 513
MONTEVIDEO, MN 56265
320-269-8815
Fax: 320-269-8449
• Deanna Hodge, Manager/News Director
(320) 269-8815
deekdma@yahoo.com
• Perry Sachariason, Sports Director

KKRF-FM
204 SOUTH DIVISION STREET
STUART, IA 50250-5021
515-523-1107
Fax: 515-465-3952
http://www.realcountryonline.com
• Ben Keller, News Director
productiontok107@yahoo.com
• Sue Thomsen, Advertising Manager
suetrealcountry@yahoo.com
Description:
Music, News, Sports.

KKSJ-FM
3225 AMBASSADOR CAFFERY PARKWAY
LAFAYETTE, LA 70506-7214
337-993-5500
Fax: 337-993-5510
bdaigle@pittmanbroadcasting.com
Description:
Music, News, Sports.

KKTX-FM
3810 BROOKSIDE DRIVE
TYLER, TX 75701-9420
903-581-0606
Fax: 903-581-2011
• Craig Reininger, General Manager
(903) 581-0606
craigreininger@clearchannel.com
Description:
Music, News, Sports.

KKZN-AM
4695 SOUTH MONACO STREET
DENVER, CO 80237-3403
303-713-8000
Fax: 303-713-8509
http://www.thezone760.com
• Andy Lindahl, Sports Producer
andylindahl@clearchannel.com
Description:
Music, News, Sports, Talk.

KLAC-AM
3400 OLIVE AVENUE, W.
BURBANK, CA 91505-5544
818-559-2252
Fax: 818-260-9335
http://www.am570radio.com
• Kiyo Knight, Office Manager
kiyoknight@clearchannel.com
Description:
Music.

KLAY
10025 LAKEWOOD DR, SW
TACOMA, WA 98499
253-581-0324
Fax: 253-581-0326
klayrad@wol.com
• Clay Huntington, General Manager/Sports
Director
• Bob McCluskey, Sales Manager
• Bruce Bond, Producer
• Walker Mattson, Traffic
• Nick Winter, Engineering Executive
• Evan Brown, Human Resources Manager
Nature of Sports Service:
24-hour sports, talk and news radio
programming station.
College Sports:
Basketball, Football.

KLAY-AM
10025 LAKEWOOD DRIVE SUITE B
TACOMA, WA 98499-3878
253-581-0324
Fax: 253-581-0326
klay1180@blarg.net
http://www.klay1180.com
• Lynn Benson, News Director
radiolynnbenson@aol.com
Description:
Music, News, Sports.

KLBJ-AM
8309 NORTH IH 35
AUSTIN, TX 78753
512-832-4000
877-590-5525
Fax: 512-832-4081
http://www.590klbj.com
• Ed Clements, Sports Director
(512) 832-4028
eclements@emmisaustin.com
• Todd Jeffries, News Director
tjeffries@emmisaustin.com
Description:
News, Talk.

KLCI-FM
32215 124TH STREET
PRINCETON, MN 55371
612-389-1300
800-850-1061
Fax: 763-389-1359
• Troy Edwards, Program Director

Description:
Music, News, Sports, Talk.

KLCK-AM
514 SOUTH COLUMBUS
GOLDENDALE, WA 98620
509-773-3300
Fax: 509-773-3301
• Nettie Cramer, News Director
(541) 296-9102
Description:
Music, News, Sports.

KLEB-AM
11603 HIGHWAY 308
PO BOX 1350
LAROSE, LA 70373
985-798-7792
Fax: 985-798-7793
klrz@cajunnet.com
www.klrzfm.com
• Jerry Gisclair, Owner
klrz@mobiletel.com
• Brennan Matherne, News/Sports Director
bmatherne@klrzfm.com
Description:
Music.

KLGA-FM
P.O. BOX 160
ALGONA, IA 50511-0160
515-295-2475
Fax: 515-295-3851
• Vic Doane, Sports Director
• Chuck Shockley, News Director
Description:
Music.

KLGR-FM
639 WEST BRIDGE STREET
REDWOOD FALLS, MN 56283
507-637-2989
Fax: 507-637-5347
klgr@mchsi.com
www.klgram.com
• Randy Clausen, Sports Director
• Laura Olson, News Director
Description:
Music.

KLIF-FM
1109 HUDSON LANE
MONROE, LA 71201-6003
318-388-2323
Fax: 318-388-0569
la105@bayou.com
http://www.la105.com
• Gene Ponti, Sports Director
gino@bayou.com
• John Reynolds, News Director
jreynolds@bayou.com

KLIK-AM
3605 COUNTRY CLUB DRIVE
JEFFERSON CITY, MO 65109-1070
573-893-5100
800-500-9107
Fax: 573-893-8330
http://www.klik1240.com
• Brian Wilson, Program Director
(573) 893-5100
brian.wilson@cumulus.com
Description:
Music, News, Sports, Talk.

KLIN
4343 O STREET
LINCOLN, NE 68510
402-475-4567
800-444-5546
Fax: 402-479-1411
www.broadcasthouse.com
• Mark Halverson, General Manager
• John Bishop, Sports Director
Nature of Sports Service:
News, Sports, Talk.
College Sports:
Baseball, Basketball, Football - University of Nebraska.

KLLC-FM
865 BATTERY STREET 3RD FLOOR
SAN FRANCISCO, CA 94111-1503
415-765-4097
800-400-3697
Fax: 415-781-3697
studio@radioalice.com
http://www.radioalice.com
• Greg Nemitz, Vice President
• Denise St. Louis, Promotions Director
(415) 765-4137
Description:
Music, News, Sports.

KLOE-AM
3023 WEST 31ST
GOODLAND, KS 67735-0569
785-899-2309
Fax: 785-899-3062
http://www.kloe.com
• Curtis Duncan, News Director
(785) 899-2309
• Andrew Melia, Sports Director
Description:
Music, News, Sports, Talk.

KLOG-AM
506 COWLITZ WAY WEST
KELSO, WA 98626
360-636-0110
Fax: 360-577-6949
news@klog.com
http://www.klog.com
• Kirc Roland, News/Sports Director
Description:
Music.

KLOL-FM
2000 WEST LOOP SOUTH SUITE 300
HOUSTON, TX 77027
713-212-8000
Fax: 713-212-8101
http://mega101houston.com/
• Laurent Fouilloud, News Director
laurentfouilloud@clearchannel.com
Description:
Music, News, Sports.

KLRM-FM
33374 VERNONIA HIGHWAY
SCAPPOOSE, OR 97056
805-922-1041
Fax: 805-928-3069
http://www.air1radio.com
• David Pierce, Program Director
david@klove.com
Description:
Music, News, Sports.

KLSS-FM
402-19TH STREET, SW
MASON CITY, IA 50401-6435
641-423-8634
Fax: 641-423-8206
http://www.klssradio.com
• Bob Fisher, News Director
rfisher@klssradio.com
Description:
Music.

KLSX-FM
3580 WILSHIRE BOULEVARD
LOS ANGELES, CA 90010-2501
213-383-4222
Fax: 213-386-3649
http://www.fmtalki.com
• David Saverino, Advertising Manager
Description:
Music, Talk.

KLTF-AM
16405 HAVEN RD
LITTLE FALLS, MN 56345
320-632-5414
800-568-7249
Fax: 320-632-2571
http://www.fallsradio.com
• Rod Grams, Program Director
rod@fallsradio.com
• Al Windsperger, Sports Director
al@fallsradio.com
Description:
Music, News, Sports.

KLUP-AM
9601 MCALLISTER FREEWAY SUITE 1200
SAN ANTONIO, TX 78216
210-344-8481
877-630-5757
Fax: 210-340-1213
http://www.klup.com
• Milton Glueck, Account Manager
(210) 344-8481
• Baron Wiley, Program Director
(210) 344-8481
Description:
Music, News.

KLVI-AM 560
2885 I-10 EAST
BEAVMONT, TX 77702
409-896-5555
Fax: 409-896-5599
klvi@klvi.com
www.klvi.com
• Harold Mann, News/Sports Director
• Jim Love, Program Director
jimlove@clearchannel.com
Teams:
Houston Texans; Lamar University.
Nature of Sports Service:
24-hour sports radio programming station.

KLXS-FM
106 WEST CAPITOL AVENUE
PIERRE, SD 57501-2018
605-224-1240
Fax: 605-224-0095
• John P. Saboor, President
• Brent Nelson, Vice President
• Kevin Coulthart, Vice President Events
• Jonathan Baran, Lake County Sports Marketing Manager
• Chad Baransky, Osceola County Sports Marketing Manager

media

• Jennifer Lastik, Orange County Sports Marketing Manager
• Jason Maderer, Volusia County Sports Marketing Manager
• Keith Station, Seminole County Sports Marketing Manager
• Bob Deglauries, Sports Director
• Tony Mangan, News Director
Description:
Music.

KLZZ-FM
640 SOUTHEAST LINCOLN AVENUE
SAINT CLOUD, MN 56304
320-251-4422
Fax: 320-251-1855
lee@wjon.com
http://1037theloon.com/
• David Engberg, General Manager
Description:
Music.

KMA-AM
209 NORTH ELM
SHENANDOAH, IA 51601
712-246-5270
800-234-5622
Fax: 712-246-5275
http://www.kmakkbz.com/kma/
• Lee Hughes, Sports Director
(712) 246-5270
• Mike Peterson, News Director
(712) 246-5270
Description:
Music, News, Sports.

KMAV-FM
1000 MAIN STREET SOUTH WEST
PO BOX 216
MAYVILLE, ND 58257
701-786-2335
Fax: 701-786-2268
news@kmav.com
www.kmavradio.com
• Mary Keating, Owner/Sales Manager
mary@kmav.com
• Dan Keating, General Manager/Sports Director
dan@kmav.com
Description:
Music, News, Sports.

KMEM-FM
326 EAST JEFFERSON
MEMPHIS, MO 63555-1100
660-465-7225
800-748-7875
Fax: 660-465-2626
mdenney@kmemfm.com
• Rick Fischer, News Director
(660) 465-2716
rfischer@kmemfm.com
• Donnie Middleton, Sports Director
Description:
Music, News, Sports.

KMFY-FM
507 SOUTHEAST 11TH STREET
GRAND RAPIDS, MN 55744-3950
218-326-3446
Fax: 218-326-3448
• Bill Betz, Sports Director
• Kenn Fideldy, News Director
Description:
Music.

KMHI-AM
1871 CANYON CREEK ROAD
MOUNTAIN HOME, ID 83647-3747
208-587-8424
Fax: 208-587-8425
• Alvin Lee Powers, Sports Director
(208) 537-8424
Description:
Educational, News, Sports, Talk and local sports broadcasts
Sports Discussed:
local high school baseball, softball, football, volleyball, basketball, wrestling and American Legion Baseball
Frequency:
Daily

KMIS-AM
1303 SOUTHWEST DRIVE
KENNETT, MO 63857
573-888-4616
Fax: 573-888-4991
ktmo@i1.net
• Monte Lyons, Program Director
(573) 888-4616
Description:
Music, News.

KMJ
1071 W. SHAW
FRESNO, CA 93711
559-266-5800
www.kmj580.com
• Al Smith, General Manager
• Bill Woodward, Sports Director
Office Address:
1110 E. Olive, Fresno, CA 93744.
Nature of Sports Service:
News, Talk, Sports.

KMLB
1109 HUDSON LANE
MONROE, LA 71201
318-388-2323
800-259-1440
Fax: 318-388-0569
kmlb@bayou.com
• Bob Holladay, General Manager
• Greg Gulyas, Sports Director
Nature of Sports Service:
News, Talk, Sports.
Auto Sports:
NASCAR.
Baseball:
CBS - MLB.
Basketball:
Louisiana State University/LSU; Final Four.
College Sports:
Baseball - Northeast Louisiana University
Football:
Notre Dame University, Louisiana State University/LSU.
Football:
NFL - CBS.

KMMJ
3205 W. NORTH FRONT ST
GRAND ISLAND, NE 68802
308-382-2800
Fax: 308-382-6701
kmmj@aol.com
• Brad Fossberg, Sports Director
Nature of Sports Service:
News, Talk.

KMND-AM
11300 HIGHWAY 191 BUILDING 2
MIDLAND, TX 79707
432-563-9300
Fax: 432-563-3823
• Robie Burns, Program Director
(432) 563-5499
Description:
Music, News, Sports.

KMNS-AM
1113 NEBRASKA STREET
SIOUX CITY, IA 51105-1438
712-258-5595
Fax: 712-252-2430
kmnsnews@clearchannel.com
http://www.620kmns.com
• Curtis Anderson, Sports Director
(712) 224-5487
curtisanderson@clearchannel.com
• Rick Schorg, General Manager
rickschorg@clearchannel.com
Description:
Music.

KMOX
ONE MEMORIAL DR
ST. LOUIS, MO 63102
314-621-2345
Fax: 314-444-3230
kmoxspt@kmox.com
www.kmox.com
• Ron Jacober, Sports Director
(314) 444-+187
rdjacober@cbs.com
• Tom Langmyer, VP/General Manager
(314) 444-3285
telangmyer@cbs.com
• Steve Moore, Program Director
(314) 444-3286
swmoore@cbs.com
Baseball:
MLB - St. Louis Cardinals.
College Sports:
Basketball - St. Louis University; University of Missouri. Football - University of Missouri.
Football:
NFL/CBS.
Nature of Sports Service:
News, talk & sports.
Primary Audience:
Men & women between 35-64 years old.

KMPC-AM
2800 28TH STREET
SUITE 308
SANTA MONICA, CA 90405
213-487-1300
Fax: 310-452-5950
editors@sportingnews.com
• Roger Nadel, VP/General Manager
• Tim Parker, Program Director
(310) 664-2384

KMRS-AM
P.O. BOX 570
MORRIS, MN 56267-0570
320-589-3131
Fax: 320-589-2715
• Paul Schwarz, News Director
Description:
Music, News, Sports.

KMSA-FM
1175 TEXAS AVENUE
GRAND JUNCTION, CO 81501-7605

970-248-1240
Fax: 970-248-1708
http://www.kmsa.com
• Ryan Gruwell, Sports Director
Description:
Music, News, Sports.

KMSR-AM
1000 MAIN STREET WEST
MAYVILLE, ND 58257
701-786-2335
Fax: 701-786-2268
news@kmavradio.com
www.kmavradio.com
• Dan Keating, General Manager/Sports
Director
dan@kmav.com
• Mary Keating, Owner/Sales Manager
mary@kmav.com
Description:
Station carries NBC sports talk, including
the Dan Patrick and Colin Cowherd shows,
NFL football, NCAA football and basketball.

KMUN-FM
COAST COMMUNITY RADIO
PO BOX 269
ASTORIA, OR 97103
503-325-0010
Fax: 503-325-3956
http://www.kmun.org
• David Hammock, General Manager
news1@kmun.org
Description:
Educational, Full Service, Music, News.

KMVP 860 AM SPORTS RADIO
5300 N. CENTRAL AVE
PHOENIX, AZ 85012
602-277-5687
Fax: 602-241-6810
• Chris Gallu, General Manager
• Kevin Ray, Program Director/Sports
Director
• Doug Cannon, Assistant Program Director
Nature of Sports Service:
24-hour sports radio programming station.

KMVP-AM
201 EAST JEFFERSON STREET
PHOENIX, AZ 85004
602-514-8333
Fax: 602-514-8303
newsradio620@ktar.com
http://www.kmvp.com
• Mike Golic, Sports Host
(888) 729-3776
• Mike Greenberg, Sports Host
(888) 729-3776
• Kevin Ray, Sports Director
(602) 514-8333
kray@ktar.com

KNBR 1050
55 HAWTHORNE ST
SUITE 1100
SAN FRANCISCO, CA 94105-3914
415-995-6800
Fax: 415-995-6867
www.knbr.com
• Lee Hammer, Program Director
Football:
NFL - Oakland Raiders.
College Sports:
NCAA - Stanford Cardinal.
Basketball:

NBA - Golden State Warriors.
Baseball:
MLB - Oakland Athletics.
Auto Sports:
NASCAR.

KNBR RADIO
55 HAWTHORNE STREET
SUITE 1000
SAN FRANCISCO, CA 94105-3914
415-995-6800
Fax: 415-995-6907
www.knbr.com
• Tony Salvadore, General Manager
• Lee Hammer, Program Director
(415) 995-6385
Nature of Sports Service:
24-hour sports radio programming station.
Baseball:
MLB - San Francisco Giants, Oakland
Athletics.
Basketball:
NBA - Golden State Warriors.
Football:
NFL - Oakland Raiders. San Francisco
49'ers.
Ice Hockey:
NHL - San Jose Sharks.

KNBU-FM
7TH & DEARBORN STREETS
BALDWIN CITY, KS 66006
785-594-6451
Fax: 785-594-3570
communication@bakeru.edu
• Ann Rosenthal, General Manager
(785) 594-6451
Description:
Music, News, Sports.

KNDK-FM
9453 HIGHWAY 1
LANGDON, ND 58249-9398
701-256-1080
Fax: 701-256-1081
http://www.kndk1080.com
• Jake Kulland, Sports Director
kndk1080@utma.com
• Bob Simmons, News Director
(701) 256-1080
kndk1080@utma.com
Description:
Music.

KNEB RADIO
PO BOX 239
SCOTTSBLUFF, NE 69363
308-632-7121
888-632-5653
Fax: 308-635-1079
www.kneb.com
• Craig Larson, Station Manager
clarson@kneb.com
• Rob Barney, Sports Director
(308) 632-7121
rbarney@kneb.com
Baseball:
MLB - Kansas City Royals.
College Sports:
Baseball, Men's & Women's Basketball,
Football, Volleyball - University of
Nebraska-Lincoln; NCAA.
Football:
NFL - Denver Broncos.
Ice Hockey:
NHL - Colorado Avalanche.

KNEB-FM
1928 EAST PORTAL PLACE
SCOTTSBLUFF, NE 69361
308-632-7121
Fax: 308-635-1079
http://www.kneb.com
• Rob Barney, Sports Director
• Barbara Martinson, Advertising Manager
• Kevin Mooney, News Director
Description:
Music.

KNEI-AM
14 WEST MAIN STREET
WAUKON, IA 52172
563-568-3476
Fax: 563-568-3391
knei@netins.net
• Chuck Bloxham, News Director
Description:
Music.

KNES-FM
627 WEST COMMERCE
FAIRFIELD, TX 75840
903-389-5637
Fax: 903-389-7172
texas99@texas99.com
http://www.knesfm.com
• Buzz Russell, Sports/Program Director
(903) 389-5637
buzzman@texas99.com
Description:
Music, News, Sports, Talk.

KNIM-AM
1618 SOUTH MAIN
MARYVILLE, MO 64468
660-582-2151
800-748-1496
Fax: 660-582-3211
http://www.knimmaryville.com
• Matt Gaarder, News Director
knimnews@knimmaryville.com
Description:
Music, News, Sports.

KNML - ALBUQUERQUE
500 4TH STREET NW
ALBURQUERQUE, NM 87102
505-767-6700
888-922-0610
Fax: 505-767-6767
• Milt McConnell, General Manager
• Ian Martin, Program Director
Nature of Sports Service:
All Sports Station. Broadcasts: Notre Dame
Football (College NCAA I), College
Basketball, New Mexico Scorpions (Western
Professional Hockey League/Minor League
Hockey.

KNOX
OLD BELMONT RD, SOUTH
PO BOX 13638
GRAND FORKS, ND 58208-3638
701-775-4611
Fax: 701-772-0540
• Linn Hodgson, General Manager
• Paul Roberts, Sports Director
Office Address:
Old South Belmont Road, Grand Forks, ND
58208.
Nature of Sports Service:
News, Sports, Talk.
Baseball:

MLB - Minnesota Twins.
College Sports:
Football - Notre Dame; Basketball - University of North Dakota.

KNPT-AM
906 ALDER STREET, S.W.
NEWPORT, OR 97365
541-265-2266
Fax: 541-265-6397
news@ybcradio.com
http://www.knptam.com/
• Kiera Morgan, News Director
• Bob Spangler, Sports Director
(541) 265-2266
bspangler@ybcradio.com
Description:
Music, News, Sports.

KNWD-FM
P.O. BOX 3038
NATCHITOCHES, LA 71497-0010
318-357-4180
Fax: 318-357-4398
knwd9876@aol.com
http://www.nsula.edu/knwd
• Brad Hartley, General Manager
nad9876@aol.com
Description:
Music, News, Sports, Talk.

KNX-AM
5670 WILSHIRE BOULEVARD
LOS ANGELES, CA 90036-5679
323-900-2070
Fax: 323-964-8329
knxnews@cbsradio.com
http://www.knx1070.com
• Steve Grad, Sports Reporter
(323) 900-2070
Description:
News.

KNZR-AM
3651 PEGASUS DRIVE SUITE 107
BAKERSFIELD, CA 93308-6836
661-393-1900
Fax: 661-393-1915
http://www.knzr.com
• Michael Briggs, Promotions Director
mbriggs@klly.com
• Otis Warren, Advertising Manager
owarren@klly.com
Description:
News, Talk.

KOAK-AM
1991 IRONWOOD AVENUE
RED OAK, IA 51566
712-623-2584
800-766-5274
Fax: 712-623-2583
kcsifm@yahoo.com
• Jerry V. Dietz, Program Director
Description:
Music, News, Sports, Talk.

KOFE-AM
201 NORTH 8TH STREET
SAINT MARIES, ID 83861-1869
208-245-1240
Fax: 208-245-6525
http://www.koferadio.com
• Theresa Plank, General Manager
Description:
Music, News, Sports.

KOGT-AM RADIO
PO BOX 1667
ORANGE, TX 77631
409-863-4381
Fax: 409-883-7996
www.kogt.com
• Gary Stelly, General Manager/Sports Director
Nature of Sports Service:
Sports, News, Country Music.
Baseball:
MLB - Texas Rangers.
College Sports:
Basketball, Football - Texas A&M.

KOHI-AM
36200 PITTSBURG ROAD
SUITE C
SAINT HELENS, OR 97051-0398
503-397-1600
877-397-1632
Fax: 503-397-1601
kohi.radio@gmail.com
www.am1600kohi.com
• Marty Rowe, General Manager
• Phil Dietz, Sports Director
Description:
Local sports and Western OR University football and 49er Football
Teams:
St. Helens, Scappoose, WOU, San Francisco 49ers

KOHS-FM
175 SOUTH 400 EAST
OREM, UT 84058-6382
801-224-9236
• Kenneth B. Seastrand, Station Manager
Description:
Music, News, Sports.

KOKB-AM
P.O. BOX 2509
PONCA CITY, OK 74602
580-765-2485
Fax: 580-767-1103
bill@eteamradio.com
http://www.eteamradio.com
• Bill Coleman, Owner/News Director
(580) 765-2485
Description:
Music, News, Sports.

KOKC-AM
400 EAST BRITTON ROAD
OKLAHOMA CITY, OK 73114
405-478-5104
Fax: 405-793-0514
• Ken Johnson, News Director
Description:
Music.

KOMO 1000 AM RADIO
140 FOURTH AVE
NORTH SEATTLE, WA 98109
206-404-4000
Fax: 206-404-4422
• J.shannon Sweatte, Group Head
• Bill Swartz, Sports Director
• Rob Dunlop, General Manager
• Bill Aanenson, General Sales Manager
• Alyson Soma, Promotions Director
• Wanda Hutton, UW Husky Sports Coordinator
• Paul Duckworth, Program/News Director

Nature of Sports Service:
News.
College Sports:
Basketball, Football - University of Washington.

KONA-AM
2823 WEST LOUIS STREET
PASCO, WA 99301
509-547-1618
Fax: 509-546-2678
http://www.konaradio.com
• Michael McDonnal, Sports Director
• Dennis Shannon, News Director
Description:
Music, News, Sports, Talk.

KOOC-FM
608 MOODY LANE
TEMPLE, TX 76504
254-773-5252
Fax: 254-773-0115
• Brian Mack, Program Director
(254) 773-5252
Description:
Music, News, Sports.

KORN-AM
319 NORTH MAIN STREET
MITCHELL, SD 57301-2611
605-996-1073
Fax: 605-996-6680
http://www.sbcradop.com
• J.P. Skelly, News Director
Description:
Music, News, Talk.

KOVC-AM
136 CENTRAL AVENUE, NORTH
VALLEY CITY, ND 58072
701-845-1490
Fax: 701-845-1245
dcountry@daktel.com
• Ryan Cunningham, Sports Director
• Kerry Johnson, Advertising Manager
• Ronnie Lee, Program Director
Description:
Music, News, Sports.

KOVO-AM
26 WEST CENTER SUITE 101
PROVO, UT 84601
801-818-1074
Fax: 801-818-3308
• Randy Rogers, General Manager
(801) 412-6040
Description:
Music.

KOWB-AM
3525 SOLDIER SPRINGS ROAD
LARAMIE, WY 82070
307-745-4888
800-352-5249
Fax: 307-742-4576
www.kowb1290.com
• Dave Geist, Program Director
(307) 745-9242
davegeist@kcgy95country.com
• Keri Eakins, KOWB Sports Assistant
(307) 745-4888
• David Settle, Operations Manager & Sports Director
(307) 745-4888
davidsettle@gapbroadcasting.com

Description:
News/talk.
Sports Discussed:
National, regional and local.
Frequency:
1290 am

KOY-AM
4686 EAST VAN BUREN STREET
SUITE 300
PHOENIX, AZ 85008
602-374-6000
Fax: 480-966-7435
http://www.am1230koy.com
• Joe Puglise, Market Manager
joepuglise@clearchannel.com
Description:
Music.

KOZB-FM
5445 JOHNSON ROAD
BOZEMAN, MT 59718
406-587-9999
Fax: 406-587-5855
• Les Clay, News Director
Description:
Music, News.

KOZN-AM
5011 CAPITOL AVENUE
OMAHA, NE 68132
402-342-2000
Fax: 402-342-7041
• Ken Searnaw, General Manager

KPEL-AM
1749 BERTRAND DRIVE
LAFAYETTE, LA 70506-2054
337-233-6000
Fax: 337-234-7360
• Mike Grimsley, General Manager
(337) 233-6000
• Bernadette Lee, News Director
(337) 233-6000
bernie.lee@regentcomm.com
• Jay Walker, Sports/Program Director
(337) 233-6000
jay.walker@regentcomm.com
Description:
News.

KPEL-FM
1749 BERTRAND DR
LAFAYETTE, LA 70506-2054
337-232-2242
Fax: 337-234-7360
steve.peloquin@regentcomm.com
http://www.espn1420.com
• Bernadette Lee, News Director
(337) 232-2242
bernie.lee@regentcomm.com
• Jay Walker, Sports Director
(337) 232-2242
Description:
News, Talk.

KPLY
255 W. MOANA LANE, STE 208
RENO, NV 89509
775-829-1964
Fax: 775-825-3183
• Mike Bushey, Program Director
Nature of Sports Service:
Local. 24 Hour Sports.
Baseball:
MLB - San Francisco Giants.

Football:
NFL - Oakland Raiders.
Ice Hockey:
NHL - San Jose Sharks.

KPOK-AM
11 1/2 NORTH MAIN STREET
BOWMAN, ND 58623
701-523-3883
Fax: 701-523-3885
www.kpokradio.com
• Tim Trumbal, Advertising Manager
• Tim Norman, News Director
Description:
Music.

KPRB-FM
231 MAIN STREET
FORT MORGAN, CO 80701-2148
970-867-7271
888-556-5747
Fax: 970-867-2676
thesting@b106.com
http://www.b106.com
• John Beltran, Sports Director
(970) 867-7271
john@necolorado.com

KPSI-AM
2100 EAST TAHQUITZ-CANYON WAY
PALM SPRINGS, CA 92262
760-325-2582
Fax: 760-322-3562
• Gregg Aratin, Advertising Manager
(760) 325-2582
• Lisa Giles, Promotion Manager
(760) 325-2582
Description:
News, Talk.

KPTT-AM
2900 SUTRO STREET
RENO, NV 89512-1616
775-329-9261
Fax: 775-323-1450
• Steve Diamond, News Director
(775) 329-9261
steved@lotusradio.com
• Don Morchand, Sports Director
(775) 329-9261
• Raina Weathers, Advertising Sales
Director
rainarocks@aol.com

KPUG-AM
2219 YEW STREET ROAD
BELLINGHAM, WA 98229
360-734-9790
Fax: 360-733-4551
http://www.kpug1170.com
• Doug Lang, Program Director
doug@kpug1170.com
Description:
News, Sports.

KQAD-AM
1140 150TH AVENUE
LUVERNE, MN 56156
507-283-4444
Fax: 507-283-4445
http://www.kqad.net
• Matt Crosby, News Director
• Bruce Thalhuber, Sports Director
Description:
Music, News, Sports.

KQAL-FM
P.O. BOX 5838
WINONA, MN 55987
507-453-2222
Fax: 507-453-5226
http://www.kqal.org/
• Asafsina Yildiz, Program Director
Description:
Music, News, Sports.

KQLL - AM
5801 E. 41ST
TULSA, OK 74135
918-664-2810
Fax: 918-665-0555
• Allen McGlaughlin, General Manager
• Chris Plank, Operations Manager
• Gerry Wilburn, Local Sales Manager
• Bruce Simons, Network Sales Manager
Nature of Sports Service:
Local. 24 Hour Sports.
Baseball:
Minor League - Texas Baseball League/AA -
Tulsa Drillers.
College Sports:
Basketball, Football - Tulsa University.
Football:
NFL - Dallas Cowboys.

KQWC-AM
1020 EAST 2ND STREET
WEBSTER CITY, IA 50595-0550
515-832-1570
800-958-2417
Fax: 515-832-2079
http://www.kqradio.com
• Mary Harris, General Manager/Advertising
Director
(515) 832-1570
• Rhonda Martin, Business Manager
(515) 832-1570
• Pat Powers, News Director
(515) 832-1570
• Chris Lockwood, Program Director
(515) 832-1570
Description:
Music, News, Sports, Talk.

KRAN
514 E. BELLEVUE
ATWATER, CA 95301
209-358-9723
Fax: 209-358-9793
• Kelly Leonard, General Manager
• Yolanda Navarro, Program Director
Baseball:
MLB - San Francisco Giants.
College Sports:
Basketball, Football.
Football:
NFL - Oakland Raiders, San Francisco
49ers.

KRDO SPORTS RADIO 1240AM
3 S. 7TH ST
COLORADO SPRINGS, CO 80905
719-632-1515
Fax: 719-635-8455
• Neil Klockziem, General Manager
• Mike Lewis, Operations/Sports Director
(719) 575-6245
m.lewis@krdotv.com
• Jim Totum, Afternoon Talk Show Host
(719) 575-6248
jitotum@krdotv.com
Nature of Sports Service:
Sports, Talk.

media

Baseball:
MLB - Chicago Cubs; Minor League - Pacific Coast League/AAA - Colorado Springs Sky Sox.

KRDZ-AM
32992 U.S. HIGHWAY 34
WRAY, CO 80758
970-332-4171
Fax: 970-332-4172
robert@medialogicradio.com
www.krdz.com
• Wayne Johnson, Owner
(970) 867-5674
• Robert Lovell, Sports Director KRDZ 1440 AM
(970) 630-8615
robert@medialogicradio.com
Description:
Music, News, Sports.
Sport Broadcasts
We cover Wray High School sports and carry Denver Nuggets and Colorado Avalanche games.

KREI-AM
1401 KREI BOULEVARD
FARMINGTON, MO 63640-0461
573-756-6476
Fax: 573-756-9127
mymoinfo.com
• Scott Kubala, Program Director
(573) 756-6476
• Tim Ryan, Sports Director
(573) 756-6476
Description:
Music, News, Sports.

KRFO-FM
245 18TH STREET SOUTHEAST
OWATONNA, MN 55060
507-451-2250
Fax: 507-451-8837
http://www.krfo.com
• John Connor, Advertising Manager
• Loren Hart, Program Director
Description:
Music, News, Sports.

KRFS-AM
RR 2, BOX 149
SUPERIOR, NE 68978-9802
402-879-3207
Fax: 402-879-4741
• Cory Kopsa, Advertising Manager/News & Sports Director
krfsfm@yahoo.com
Description:
Music, News, Sports.

KRFX-FM
4695 SOUTH MONACO STREET
DENVER, CO 80237-3403
303-713-8000
Fax: 303-713-8743
• Lee Larsen, Senior Vice President
(303) 694-6300
leelarson@clearchannel.com
• Rich Goins, Sports Director
(303) 713-8000
richgoins@clearchannel.com
Description:
Music, News, Sports.

KRHC-AM
5526 HIGHWAY 281 NORTH
MARBLE FALLS, TX 78654-0639
830-693-5551
Fax: 830-693-5107
http://www.khlb.com
• Art D'Lugach, News Director
art@radiohillcountry.com
• Art D'Lugach, Sports Director
art@radiohillcountry.com
Description:
Music.

KRJB-FM
312 WEST MAIN STREET
ADA, MN 56510-1252
218-784-2844
800-569-4171
Fax: 218-784-3749
krjbada@loretel.net
http://krjb.outbackpc.net/
• Jim Birkemeyer, Advertising Manager
krjbkmav@loretel.net
• Dennis Roux, News Director
Description:
Music, News, Sports.

KRKO-AM
2707 COLBY AVENUE #1380
EVERETT, WA 98201-3528
425-304-1381
Fax: 425-304-1382
rkonews@krko.com
www.krko.com
• Ed Ramirez, Advertising Manager
ed.ramirez@northsound1380.com
• Tony Stevens, Program Director
(425) 304-1381
tony.stevens@krko.com
Description:
News, Talk.
Frequency:
1380 am

KRKR-FM
3800 CORNHUSKER HIGHWAY SUITE 11
LINCOLN, NE 68504
402-466-1234
Fax: 402-467-4095
http://www.knetfm.com
• Dale Johnson, News Director
(402) 466-1234
Description:
Music, News, Sports.

KRMD-AM
3109 ALEXANDER STREET
SHREVEPORT, LA 71104-4628
318-865-5173
Fax: 318-865-3657
cumulus.shreveport@cumulus.com
http://www.krmd.com
• C J Jones, General Manager
(318) 865-5173
• Tony King, News Director
(318) 603-4730
Description:
Music.

KRNB-FM
621 NORTHWEST 6TH STREET
GRAND PRAIRIE, TX 75050-5555
972-263-9911
972-558-0007
Fax: 972-558-0010
http://www.broadcast.com/radio/urban/krnb

• Jack Hines, News Director
Description:
Music, News, Sports.

KROD
4150 PINNACLE ST, STE 120
EL PASO, TX 79902
915-544-8864
Fax: 915-532-6342
www.krod.com
• Brad Dubow, General Manager
• Steve Kaplowitz, Sports Director
Nature of Sports Service:
Sports, Talk, News.
Baseball:
Minor League/Texas Baseball League/AA - El Paso Diablos.
College Sports:
Football - University of Texas Longhorns.
Football:
NFL - Dallas Cowboys.
Ice Hockey:
Minor League/Western Professional Hockey League - El Paso Buzzards.

KROF-AM
1749 BERTRAND DRIVE
LAFAYETTE, LA 70506-2054
337-233-6000
Fax: 337-234-7360
• Bernadette Lee, Program Director
(337) 233-6000
bernie.lee@regentcomm.com
Description:
Music, News, Sports.

KROX-AM
208 SOUTH MAIN STREET
CROOKSTON, MN 56716
218-281-1140
Fax: 218-281-5036
kroxam@hotmail.com
http://www.kroxam.com/
• Frank Fee, Advertising Manager/Sports Director
ffee@rrv.net
• Maryann Simmons, News Director
maryann_simmons@hotmail.com
Description:
Music, News, Sports.

KRSC-FM
1701 WEST WILL ROGERS BOULEVARD
CLAREMORE, OK 74017
918-343-7669
Fax: 918-343-7592
http://www.rsu.edu
• Cathy Coomer, General Manager
(918) 343-7571
ccoomer@rsu.edu
Description:
Music, News, Sports.

KRSY-AM
P.O. BOX 2710
ALAMOGORDO, NM 88310
505-437-1505
Fax: 505-437-5566
alamogordo@snmradio.com
http://www.snmradio.com
• Les Henke, Advertising Manager
lhenke@snmradio.com
• Phillip Runnels, General Manager
(505) 437-1505
phil@snmradio.com

Description:
Music.

KRVL-FM
1021 EAST MAIN SUITE 200
KERRVILLE, TX 78028-3553
830-896-1230
Fax: 830-792-4142
http://www.krvl.com
• Monte Spearman, General Manager
Description:
Music, News.

KRYS-FM
501 TUPPER LANE
CORPUS CHRISTI, TX 78417
361-289-0111
Fax: 361-289-5035
frankedwards@clearchannel.com
http://www.krysfm.com
• Frank Edwards, Program
Director/Promotion Manager
(361) 289-0111
frankedward@clearchannel.com
• Mike Lind, Advertising Manager
mikelind@clearchannel.com
Description:
Music, News, Sports.

KSAL
PO BOX 80
SALINA, KS 67402
785-823-1111
Fax: 785-823-2034
• Jerry Hinrikus, General Manager
• Bruce Steinbrock, Sports Director
Nature of Sports Service:
Sports, Talk, News.
Baseball:
MLB - Kansas City Royals.
College Sports:
Basketball, Football - Kansas State
University; CBS.
Football:
NFL.

KSBL-FM
414 EAST COTA STREET
SANTA BARBARA, CA 93101-1624
805-879-8300
Fax: 805-879-8430
peterbie@clearchannel.com
• Lin Aubuchon, Promotion Director
(805) 879-8306
linaubuchon@clearchannel.com
Description:
Music, News, Sports.

KSCU-FM
SANTA CLARA UNIVERSITY
500 EL CAMINO ROAD
SANTA CLARA, CA 95053
408-554-4414
Fax: 408-985-5728
info@kscu.org
http://www.kscu.org
• Jason Magrisso, Sports Director
Description:
Music, News, Sports.

KSDM-FM
519 3RD STREET
INTERNATIONAL FALLS, MN 56649-2317
218-283-2622
888-283-1041
Fax: 218-283-3087

kghsksdm@northwinds.net
http://www.ksdmradio.com/
• Jerry Franzen, News Director
production@ksdmradio.com
• Roger Jerome, Sports Director
production@ksdmradio.com
Description:
Music, News, Sports.

KSDR-AM
3 EAST KEMP AVENUE SUITE 300
WATERTOWN, SD 57201-6480
605-886-5747
800-234-5793
Fax: 605-886-2121
http://www.ksdr.com
• Heather Lentz, Promotions Director
(605) 882-1480
• Shari Wirkus, News Director
(605) 882-1480
Description:
Music, News, Sports.

KSEG-FM
5345 MADISON AVENUE
SACRAMENTO, CA 95841-3141
916-334-7777
Fax: 916-339-4559
http://www.eagle969.com
• Lizann Hunt, Promotion Director
(916) 334-7777
Description:
Music, News, Sports.

KSEI-AM
544 NORTH ARTHUR STREET
POCATELLO, ID 83204-3002
208-233-2121
800-726-5734
Fax: 208-234-7682
http://www.am930ksei.com
• Sean McCoy, News Director
sean@classicrock102.fm
Description:
News, Talk.

KSEK-AM
P.O. BOX 383
PITTSBURG, KS 66762
620-232-9912
800-215-3853
Fax: 620-232-5550
• Mike Snow, Program Director
Description:
Music, News, Talk.

KSFN-AM
6655 WEST SAHARA AVENUE SUITE
D-110
LAS VEGAS, NV 89146-0851
702-889-7300
Fax: 702-889-7373
http://www.spike1140.com/
• Jack Landreth, Program Director
• Derek Sante, Promotions Coordinator
Description:
Educational, News.

KSFT-AM
4104 COUNTRY LANE
SAINT JOSEPH, MO 64506
816-233-8881
Fax: 816-279-8280
Description:
Music.

KSGL-AM
3337 WEST CENTRAL AVENUE
WICHITA, KS 67203
316-942-3231
Fax: 316-942-9314
• Terry Atherton, Program Director
Description:
Educational, Music, News, Talk.

KSHE-FM
800 ST. LOUIS UNION STATION
SAINT LOUIS, MO 63103-2256
314-621-0095
Fax: 314-621-3428
http://www.kshe95.com/
• Tony Busekrus, Promotions Director
(314) 613-7714
tonyb@stl.emmis.com
• John Cooper, News Director
(314) 613-7865
• John Ulett, Sports Director
(314) 621-0095
johnu@stl.emmis.com
Description:
Music, News, Sports.

KSHP-AM
2400 SOUTH JONES BOULEVARD SUITE
3
LAS VEGAS, NV 89146-3127
702-221-1200
Fax: 702-221-2285
mail@kshp.com
http://www.kshp.com
• Brett Grant, General Manager
(702) 221-1200
brettgrant@kshp.com
Description:
Talk.

KSIS-AM
2209 SOUTH LIMIT
SEDALIA, MO 65301
660-826-1050
800-748-8354
Fax: 660-827-5072
http://www.ksdl.com
• Danny Hampton, News Director
(660) 826-1050
dhampton@bickbroadcasting.com
Description:
Music, News, Talk.

KSIX-AM
710 BUFFALO STREET SUITE 608
CORPUS CHRISTI, TX 78401
361-882-5749
800-765-8810
Fax: 361-884-1204
• Bill Doerner, Station Manager
Description:
Music, News.

KSJS-FM
132 HUGH GILLIS HALL
SAN JOSE, CA 95192-0094
408-924-4548
Fax: 408-924-4558
ksjs@ksjs.org
http://www.ksjs.org
• Swen Johnson, Sports Director
Description:
Music.

media

KSJX-AM
501 WOOSTER AVENUE #C
SAN JOSE, CA 95116
408-280-1515
Fax: 408-280-1585
ksjx1500@fbcglobal.net
• Andrea Yamazaki, Advertising Sales
andreay@mrbi.net
Description:
Music, News, Sports.

KSKI-FM
201 SOUTH MAIN STREET
HAILEY, ID 83333
208-726-5324
877-725-5754
Fax: 208-726-5459
kskiprogramming@yahoo.com
http://www.kski.com
• Scott Anderson, General Manager
• Jody Zarkos
(802) 726-7118
Description:
Music.

KSKU-FM
10 EAST 5TH AVENUE
HUTCHINSON, KS 67501
620-665-5758
800-300-1061
Fax: 620-662-5758
• Lucky Kidd, News/Sports Director
• Cliff Shank, Sports Director
(316) 665-5758
Description:
Music, News, Sports.

KSKY-AM
6400 NORTH BELTLINE ROAD SUITE 110
IRVING, TX 75063
214-561-9660
Fax: 214-561-9662
kskyradio@aol.com
http://www.ksky.com
• David Darling, Program Director
Description:
Music, News, Sports.

KSMO-AM
800 SOUTH MAIN STREET
SALEM, MO 65560-1637
573-729-6117
Fax: 573-729-7337
ksmoski@fidnet.com
http://www.ksmoradio.com
• Melba Headrick, Advertising Manager
ksmoradio@ksmoradio.com
• Stan Stevens, News Director
ksmoradio@ksmoradio.com
Description:
Music, News, Sports.

KSSK-AM
650 IWILEI ROAD SUITE 400
HONOLULU, HI 96817-4822
808-550-9200
Fax: 808-550-9510
http://www.ksskradio.com
• Jamie Hartnett, Promotions Director
(808) 550-9200
jamiehartnett@clearchannel.com
Description:
Music, News, Sports.

KSSR-AM
2818 WILL RODGERS DRIVE
SANTA ROSA, NM 88435
505-472-5777
Fax: 505-472-5777
kssrradio@yahoo.com
• Gabe Esquibel, Program Director
kssrradio@hotmail.com
Description:
Music, News, Sports.

KSUE-AM
3015 JOHNSTONVILLE ROAD
SUSANVILLE, CA 96130-8739
530-257-2121
800-366-9162
Fax: 530-257-6955
http://www.theradionetwork.com
• Scott Blackwood, Sports Director
scott@theradionetwork.com
Description:
Music.

KSVP-AM
317 WEST QUAY
ARTESIA, NM 88210-2158
505-746-2751
800-530-4855
Fax: 505-748-3748
http://www.ksvpradio.com
• Jamie Reynolds, News Director
news@ksvpradio.com
Description:
News, Talk.

KSWH-FM
1100 HENDERSON STREET
ARKADELPHIA, AR 71999
870-230-5185
Fax: 870-230-5046
kswh@hsu.edu
• Derrell Young, Sports Director
Description:
Music, News, Sports.

KTBB-AM
1001 EAST SOUTHEAST LOOP 323 SUITE 455
TYLER, TX 75701
903-593-2519
Fax: 903-597-8378
pberry@kdok.com
http://www.ktbb.com
• Jack Benner, Promotions Manager
• Roger Gray, Program Director
(903) 593-2519
rogergray@ktbb.com
• David Smoak, Sports Director
(903) 593-2519
smoaky@ktbb.com
Description:
News, Talk.

KTBK-FM
3500 MAPLE AVENUE SUITE 1300
DALLAS, TX 75219-3931
214-526-7400
Fax: 214-525-2525
http://www.theticket.com
• Jimmy Christopher, News Director
(214) 520-4423

KTCC-FM
1255 SOUTH RANGE
COLBY, KS 67701-4007

785-462-3984
Fax: 785-462-4600
• Corey Sorenson, General Manager
(785) 462-3984
Description:
Music, News, Sports.

KTCK/THE TICKET
3500 MAPLE AVE, STE 1310
DALLAS, TX 75219
214-526-7400
Fax: 214-525-2525
www.theticket.com
• Dan Bennett, General Manager
• Mark Follovill, Sports Director
Nature of Sports Service:
Local. 24-hour sports radio programming.
College Sports:
Basketball - Texas Christian University/TCU;
Football - Texas Tech.

KTCV-FM
5929 WEST METALINE
KENNEWICK, WA 99336-1494
509-734-3621
Fax: 509-734-3609
dailed@ksd.org
http://www.ktcv.net
• Ed Dailey, General Manager
(509) 947-5785
Description:
Music, News, Sports.

KTEM
68 MOODY LANE
TEMPLE, TX 76504
254-773-5252
Fax: 254-773-0115
• Mark McLain, Program Director/Sports
Nature of Sports Service:
News, Sports, Talk.
Baseball:
MLB - Houston Astros.
College Sports:
Basketball, Football - Baylor Bears.
Football:
NFL - Dallas Cowboys.
Ice Hockey:
Minor League - Western Professional
Hockey League/WPHL - Central Texas
Stampede.

KTGR-AM
3215 LEMONE INDUSTRIAL BOULEVARD
SUITE 2
COLUMBIA, MO 65201
573-875-1099
Fax: 573-875-2439
• Shelley Tucker, News Director
(573) 875-1099
shelleyt@zrgmail.com

KTHN-FM
116 DALTON AVENUE
LA JUNTA, CO 81050
719-384-5456
Fax: 719-384-5450
kblj@rural-com.com
http://www.angelfire.com/cokbzzkblj
• Pat McGee, Sports Director
(719) 384-5456
Description:
Music.

KTIK SPORTS RADIO 1350
251 S. CAPITOL BLVD
BOISE, ID 83702
208-377-5845
Fax: 208-375-9248
jeff@ktik.com
www.ktik.com
• Jeff Caves, General Manager
• Pat Metzger, Sports Director
Nature of Sports Service:
Local. 24-hour sports radio programming.
Baseball:
Major League Baseball/MLB.
College Sports:
Basketball, Football.

KTIX-AM
2003 NORTHWEST 56TH DRIVE
PENDLETON, OR 97801
541-278-2500
Fax: 541-276-1480
• John Thomas, News/Sports Director
(541) 278-2500
Description:
News, Talk.

KTKC-FM
P.O. BOX 127
SPRINGHILL, LA 71075-0127
760-322-7890
Fax: 760-322-5493
• Ernest Pickens, Station Manager
epickings@hotmail.com
Description:
Music, News, Sports.

KTKR
6222 NW I H 10
SAN ANTONIO, TX 78201
210-736-9700
800-383-9624
Fax: 210-735-8811
www.ticketsports.com
• Bob Cohen, General Manager
• Jay Howard, Sports Director
Nature of Sports Service:
Local. 24-hour sports radio programming.
Baseball:
MLB - Texas Rangers.
College Sports:
Basketball - University of Texas; Football:
Texas Tech.
Football:
NFL.

KTMC-AM
1801 EAST GENE STAIPE BOULEVARD
MCALESTER, OK 74502-1068
918-423-1400
Fax: 918-423-7119
newsnan@mcalesterradio.com
• John Yates, News Director
(918) 429-2768
newsman@mcalesterradio.com
Description:
Music, News, Sports.

KTMT-AM
1438 ROSSANLEY DRIVE
MEDFORD, OR 97501-1751
541-779-1550
Fax: 541-776-2360
www.espn580.com
• Devin Harpole, Program Director
(541) 779-1550

Description:
Sports.

KTON-AM
P.O. BOX 1387
BELTON, TX 76513-5387
254-939-9377
Fax: 254-939-9458
• James Harrison, General Manager
cdavis940@vvm.com
Description:
Music, News, Sports.

KTRH-AM
2000 WEST LOOP SOUTH
HOUSTON, TX 77027-3510
713-212-8740
Fax: 713-212-8957
ktrh@aol.com
http://www.ktrh.com/main.html
• Melissa Brezner, Promotion Manager
• Ted DeLuca, Sports Director
(713) 212-8740
• Bryan Erickson, News Director
bryanerickson@clearchannel.com
Description:
News, Sports.

KTRS-AM
638 WEST PORT PLAZA DRIVE
SAINT LOUIS, MO 63146-3106
314-453-5500
888-550-5877
Fax: 314-453-9704
news@ktrs.com
http://www.ktrs.com/
• Jim Holder, Sports Director
(314) 453-5544
• Brian Kelly, News Director
(314) 453-5500
news@ktrs.com
• Craig Unger, Station Manager
(314) 453-5500
cunger@ktrs.com
Description:
News, Talk.

KTRS-FM
150 NICHOLS AVENUE
CASPER, WY 82601
307-266-5252
Fax: 307-235-9143
ktwo@clearchannel.com
http://www.kisscasper.com
• Vicki Daniels, News Director
vickidaniels@clearchannel.com
Description:
Music, News, Sports.

KTTT-AM
1418 25TH STREET
COLUMBUS, NE 68601
402-564-2866
800-651-5568
Fax: 402-564-2867
• Jim Dolezal, Sports Director
• Dean Johnson, Program Director
Description:
Music.

KTXT-FM
JOURNALISM BUILDING ROOM 201
LUBBOCK, TX 79409-0011
806-742-3916
Fax: 806-742-3906

pat.cates@ttu.edu
http://www.ttu.edu/~ktxt
• Josh Justice, Station Manager
(806) 742-3914
ktxtfm@yahoo.com
Description:
Music, News, Sports.

KTZN-AM
800 EAST DIMOND BOULEVARD SUITE
3-370
ANCHORAGE, AK 99515-2058
907-522-1515
Fax: 907-743-5184
anchorage@clearchannel.com
• Sezy Gerow, Marketing Director
(907) 743-5134
sezygerow@clearchannel.com

KUBL-FM
434 BEARCAT DRIVE
SALT LAKE CITY, UT 84115-2520
801-485-6700
Fax: 801-487-5369
http://www.kbull93.com
• Ed Hill, Program Director
(801) 464-8559
Description:
Music, News, Sports.

KUCD-FM
650 IWILEI ROAD SUITE 400
HONOLULU, HI 96817-5086
808-550-9200
Fax: 808-550-9510
jamiehyatt@clearchannel.com
• Christine Yasuma, Promotion Director
christineyasuma@clearchannel.com
Description:
Music, News, Sports.

KUKU-AM
983 US HIGHWAY EAST 160
WEST PLAINS, MO 65775
417-256-5976
Fax: 417-256-2208
http://www.ozarknewstalk.com
• Gary Lee, Program Director
• Tom Marhefka, Owner
Description:
Music, News, Sports.

KUPI-AM
854 LINDSAY BOULEVARD
IDAHO FALLS, ID 83402-1820
208-522-1101
Fax: 208-522-6110
http://www.kupi.com
• John Balginy, News Director
• James Garshow, Sports Director
Description:
Music, Sports.

KURE-FM
1199 FRILEY HALL
AMES, IA 50012-0001
515-294-4332
Fax: 515-294-8093
kure@iastate.edu
http://www.public.iastate.edu/~stu_org/kure
• Katie Pfeiffer, Program Director
Description:
Music, News, Sports.

media

KUSJ-FM
608 MOODY LANE
TEMPLE, TX 76504
254-547-8889
Fax: 254-773-0115
• Bourdon Wooten, General Manager
(254) 547-8889
bourdon.wooten@cumulus.com
Description:
Music, News, Sports.

KVAC-AM
260 CEDAR AVENUE
FORKS, WA 98331
360-374-6233
Fax: 360-374-6852
Description:
Music, News, Sports.

KVCU-AM
CAMPUS BOX 207
BOULDER, CO 80309
303-492-5031
Fax: 303-492-1369
http://www.radio1190.org
• Hunter Mancheck, Sports Director
• Schervin Revaie, Promotion Director
schervin@radio1190.org

KVHT-FM
210 WEST 3RD STREET
YANKTON, SD 57078
605-665-2600
Fax: 605-665-8875
sports@kvht.com
http://www.kvht.com
• Joe Van Goor, Sports Director
(605) 665-2600
Description:
Music, News, Sports.

KVIV-AM
6060 SURETY DRIVE
SUITE 100
EL PASO, TX 79905
915-565-2999
Fax: 915-562-3156
www.kviv1340.com
• Jesus Cruz, Program Director
Description:
Music, News, Sports.

KVOE-FM
1420 C OF E DRIVE
EMPORIA, KS 66801-2585
620-342-1400
800-279-1964
Fax: 620-342-0804
kvoe@kvoe.com
• Jeff O'Dell, News Director
• Greg Rahe, Sports Director
raheg@kvoe.com
Description:
Music, News, Sports.

KVOL AM/FM
PO BOX 3345
LAFAYETTE, LA 70502
337-232-1311
Fax: 337-233-3779
• Mary Galyean, General Manager
• Keith Leblanc, Program Director
• Jill Johnson, Station Sales Manager
Nature of Sports Service:
Sports, Talk Radio.
College Sports:

Baseball, Basketball, Football - Louisiana
State University/LSU.

KVON-AM
1124 FOSTER ROAD
NAPA, CA 94558
707-252-1440
888-252-1440
Fax: 707-226-7544
http://www.kvon.com
• Tracy Green, Office Manager
tracy@kvon.com
• Ira Smith, Sports Director
(707) 252-1440
ira@kvon.com
Description:
News, Talk.

KVOX-AM
1020 SOUTH 25TH STREET
FARGO, ND 58103-2312
701-237-5346
Fax: 701-235-4042
psa@kfgo.com
• Tank McNamara, Sports Director
• Paul Jurgens, News Director
Description:
Music, News, Sports.

KVRH-FM
7600 COUNTY ROAD 120
SALIDA, CO 81201-9423
719-539-2575
Fax: 719-539-4851
http://www.vtinet.com/kvrh
• Mike Kerrigan, Sports Director
Description:
Music.

KVTI-FM
4500 STEILACOOM BOULEVARD SW
TACOMA, WA 98499-4098
253-589-5884
Fax: 253-589-5797
http://www.i91.ctc.edu
• John Mangan, Program Director
Description:
Music, News, Sports.

KVTK-AM
210 WEST 3RD STREET
YANKTON, SD 57078
605-665-2600
Fax: 605-665-8875
www.kvtk.com
• Joe Van Goor, Sports Director
(605) 665-2600
sports@kvht.com
Description:
Sports.

KWAK-AM
1818 SOUTH BUERKLE STREET
STUTTGART, AR 72160
870-673-1595
800-737-5925
Fax: 870-673-8445
• Scott Siler, Sports Director
sasiler@yahoo.com
Description:
Music, News, Sports.

KWCR-FM
2188 UNIVERSITY CIRCLE
OGDEN, UT 84408-2188

801-626-6450
Fax: 801-626-6550
http://881weberfm.org
• Ashlie Johansen, General Manager
(801) 626-7424
kwcrradio@mail.weber.edu
• Nate Martinez, Sports Director
(801) 626-8817
Description:
Music, News, Sports.

KWDM-FM
1140 35TH STREET
WEST DES MOINES, IA 50266-2138
515-226-2660
Fax: 515-226-2609
kwdmradio@aol.com
http://www.kwdm.fm.net
• Brian D. Christensen, General Manager
Description:
Educational, Music, Sports.

KWFS-FM
2525 KELL BOULEVARD SUITE 200
WICHITA FALLS, TX 76308-1064
940-763-1111
Fax: 940-322-3166
http://www.lonestar103.com
• Chris Walters, Program Director
(940) 763-1111
chriswalters@clearchannel.com
Description:
Music, News, Sports.

KWHI-AM
P. O. BOX 1280
BRENHAM, TX 77833
979-836-3655
Fax: 979-830-8141
http://www.kwhi.com
• Frank Wagner, News Director
(979) 836-3655
news@kwhi.com
• Carolyn Warmke, Advertising Manager
(979) 836-3655
carolyn@ktex.com
• Ed Pothul, Sports Director
(979) 836-3655
doc@kwhi.com
Description:
Music, News, Sports.

KWIK
PO BOX 998
POCATELLO, ID 83204
208-233-1133
Fax: 208-232-1240
• Mike Hudson, General Manager
• Gary Shockley, Sports Director
Nature of Sports Service:
Local. 24 Hour Sports Station.
College Sports:
Basketball, Football - Idaho University.

KWIQ-AM
11768 KITTLESON ROAD
MOSES LAKE, WA 98837-9720
509-765-1761
Fax: 509-765-8901
http://www.kwiq.com
• Gary Patrick, General Manager
(509) 663-1586
gary.patrick@morris.com
Description:
Music, News, Sports.

KWKH
6341 WESTPORT AVE
SHREVEPORT, LA 71129
318-688-1130
Fax: 318-687-8574
• Barney Cannon, Sports Director
Office Address:
6341 Westport Ave, Shreveport, LA 71130.
Nature of Sports Service:
News, Sports.
College Sports:
Basketball, Football - Louisiana State University/LSU.

KWKH-AM
6341 WESTPORT AVENUE
SHREVEPORT, LA 71129-2415
318-688-1130
800-551-1130
Fax: 318-687-8574
http://www.kwkh1130.com
• John Lee, News Director
johnlee@clearchannel.com
Description:
Music, News, Sports.

KWMO-AM
511 WEST 5TH STREET
WASHINGTON, MO 63090
636-239-5432
Fax: 636-239-9735
studio@kslq.com
http://www.kwmo.net
• Chris Dieckhaus, News/Promotions Director
(636) 239-6800
chris@kslq.com
Description:
Music, News.

KWNO-FM
752 BLUFFVIEW CIRCLE
WINONA, MN 55987-2515
507-452-4000
800-584-6782
Fax: 507-452-9494
http://winonaradio.com/cdcountry/
• Darryl Smelser, News Director
• Paul Van Beek
(507) 452-4000

KWRD-AM
1101 KILGORE DRIVE
HENDERSON, TX 75652
903-655-1800
Fax: 903-655-1808
http://www.mykpxi.com
• Esther Melton, General Manager
Description:
Music, News, Sports.

KWSL-AM
1113 NEBRASKA STREET
SIOUX CITY, IA 51105-1438
712-258-5595
Fax: 712-252-2430
http://www.radio-works.com
• Curtis Anderson, Program/Sports Director
(712) 224-5487
curtisanderson@clearchannel.com
Description:
Music, News, Sports.

KWSN-AM
500 SOUTH PHILLIPS AVENUE
SIOUX FALLS, SD 57104-6825

605-331-5350
Fax: 605-336-0415
http://www.kwsn.com
• Greg Belfrage, News Director
(605) 271-5867
Description:
News, Talk.

KWTO-FM
3000 EAST CHESTNUT EXPRESSWAY
SPRINGFIELD, MO 65802-2528
417-862-3751
Fax: 417-869-7656
manager@radiospringfield.com
http://www.ktxrfm.com
• R. J. McAllister, News Director
(417) 862-5600
news@radiospringfield.com
• Art Hains, Sports Director
(417) 862-5600
sports@radiospringfield.com
Nature of Service:
All Sports

KWTS-FM
2501 4TH AVENUE
CANYON, TX 79016-0001
806-651-2797
Fax: 806-651-2818
kwtsgm@gmail.com
http://www.wtamu.edu/kwts
• Tony Collins, Sports Director
kwtssports@gmail.com
• Teresa Dunn, Sports Co-Director
kwtssports@gmail.com
• Ricky Mariscal, Program Director
(806) 651-2801
kwtspd@gmail.com
Description:
Educational, Music, News, Sports, Talk.
Sports Discussed:
West Texas A&M University sports, National sports, Local Sports
Frequency:
91.1

KWTX THE TICKER 1460AM
314 W. HWY 6
WACO, TX 76712
254-776-3900
Fax: 254-772-8708
• Michael Oppenheim, General Manager
• Rick May, Program Director
Nature of Sports Service:
24-hour sports radio programming station.

KXCA-AM
1525 SOUTHEAST FLOWERMOUND ROAD
LAWTON, OK 73501
580-355-1050
Fax: 580-355-1056
trebor1380@hotmail.com
http://1380theticket.4t.com
• Joy Chapman, General Manager
(580) 355-1050
Description:
Music.

KXDL-FM
221 CENTRAL AVENUE SUITE 6
LONG PRAIRIE, MN 56347
320-732-2164
Fax: 320-732-2284
hotrodfm@rea-alp.com
http://www.kxdlhotrodradio.com/

• Cliff Cline, News Director
Description:
Music, News, Sports.

KXIC-AM
3365 DUBUQUE STREET NORTHEASST
IOWA CITY, IA 52240
319-354-9500
Fax: 319-354-9504
royjustis@clearchannel.com
http://www.kxic.com
• Brent Balbinot, Sports Director
brentbalbinot@clearchannel.com
• Roy Justis, News Director
(319) 354-9500
Description:
News, Talk.

KXKX-FM
800 PCA ROAD
WARRENSBURG, MO 64093-9275
660-826-1050
800-748-7969
Fax: 660-827-5072
http://www.kxkx.com
• Danny Hampton, News Director
(660) 826-1050
Description:
Music, News, Sports.

KXLS-FM
PO BOX 952
ENID, OK 73702-0952
580-242-5957
Fax: 580-242-1390
• Geoff Haxton, News Director
(580) 237-1390
• Chad McKee, Sports Director
Description:
Music, News, Talk.

KXLY-AM
500 WEST BOONE AVENUE
SPOKANE, WA 99201-2404
509-324-4004
Fax: 509-327-3932
news4@kxly.com
http://www.kxly.com
• Gina Mauro, Promotions Manager
• Jerry Post, Assignment Editor
(509) 324-4004
jerryp@kxly.com
• Kirstin Votava, Marketing Director
• Rick Lukens, Sports Anchor
(509) 324-4000
rickl@kxly.com
Description:
News, Talk.

KXMO-FM
609 NORTH FRANKLIN
CUBA, MO 65453
573-885-0953
Fax: 573-364-5161
kxmo@misn.com
• Lee Buhr, Sports Director
• Joe Munsell, General Manager
(573) 364-2525

KXOW-AM
208 BUENA VISTA ROAD
HOT SPRINGS NATIONAL, AR 71913
501-525-4600
Fax: 501-525-4344
klaz@power1.net

639

• Eddie Tarpley, Advertising Manager
tarpley@klaz.com
Description:
Music.

KXOX-FM
1801 HOYT LANE
SWEETWATER, TX 79556-2663
325-236-6655
888-869-5969
Fax: 325-235-4391
http://www.members.tripod.com/~tatzel/wurm/kxox.ht
• Richard Ferguson, Sports Director
• Jeff Stein, News Director
Description:
Music.

KXPS-AM
1321 NORTH GENE AUTRY TRAIL
PALM SPRINGS, CA 92262-7992
760-322-7890
Fax: 760-322-5493
http://www.1010kxps.com
• Sara Regalado, Marketing Director

KXTA AM
3400 RIVERSIDE DR, #800
BURBANK, CA 91505
818-295-6400
Fax: 818-295-6475
• Roy Laughlin, General Manager
• Bill Lally, Sports Director
Nature of Sports Service:
Local. 24 Hour sports.
Basketball:
2002 signed a five year rights-fee deal with the Los Angeles Clippers.

KXTQ-AM
9800 UNIVERSITY AVENUE
LUBBOCK, TX 79423-4917
806-745-3434
Fax: 806-748-1949
dcampbell@ramarcom.com
• Jeff Klotzman, News Director
(806) 745-3434
jklotzman@ramarcom.com
Description:
Music, News, Sports.

KXTQ-FM
9800 UNIVERSITY AVENUE
LUBBOCK, TX 79423
806-745-3434
Fax: 806-748-1949
• Tony Samarripa, Program Director
(806) 745-3434
tsamarripa@ramarcom.com
Description:
Music, News, Sports.

KYAL-AM
2448 EAST 81ST STREET
SUITE 5500
TULSA, OK 74137-4248
918-492-2660
Fax: 918-492-8840
http://www.kxoj.com
• Bob Thornton, Program Director
bobt@kxoj.com
Description:
Music.

KYBG-AM SPORTS RADIO
5660 GREENWOOD PLAZA BLVD, STE 400
ENGLEWOOD, CO 80111-2402
303-721-9210
Fax: 303-721-1435
• Rob Quinn, General Manager
• Malcolm McClain, General Sales Manager
Nature of Sports Service:
Local. 24-hour sports radio programming.

KYCN-AM
450 EAST POLE
WHEATLAND, WY 82201
307-322-5926
Fax: 307-322-9300
http://kycn-kzew.com/
• Derek Barton, News Director
(307) 322-5926
Description:
Music, News, Sports.

KYCX-FM
1006-B MILAM
MEXIA, TX 76667-2527
254-562-5328
Fax: 254-562-6729
http://www.kycx.com
• David Campbell, Sports Director
kycxsports@aol.com
• Jan Phillips, News Director
brandi05@kycxfm.com
Description:
Music.

KYMN-AM
200 DIVISION STREET SUITE 260
NORTHFIELD, MN 55057
507-645-5695
Fax: 507-645-9768
contact@kymnradio.net
www.kymnradio.net
• Tor Ingstad, General Manager
Description:
Music, News, Talk.
Frequency:
1080 am

KYMO-AM
390 SOUTH HIGHWAY 102
EAST PRAIRIE, MO 63845
573-649-3597
Fax: 573-649-3983
• Michael Bennett, News Director
• Barney L. Webster, Advertising Manager
(573) 472-1080
Description:
Music.

KYTC-FM
402 19TH STREET, SW
MASON CITY, IA 50401-6435
641-423-8634
800-598-2858
Fax: 641-423-8206
http://www.klssradio.com
• Bob Fisher, News Director

KZEP SPORTS RADIO
427 9TH ST
SAN ANTONIO, TX 78215
210-226-6444
Fax: 210-225-5736
• Jay Levine, General Manager
• Chris Winston, Pro General Manager

Director
• Gary Isaacs, General Sales Manager
Nature of Sports Service:
Local. 24-hour sports radio programming.

KZEW-FM
450 EAST COAST
WHEATLAND, WY 82201-0248
307-322-5926
Fax: 307-322-9300
http://www.kycn-kzew.com/
• Derek Barton, News Director
• Catherine Smith, Advertising Manager
Description:
Music, News, Sports.

KZMQ-AM
2700 LANE 37 1/2
GREYBULL, WY 82426-9521
307-578-5000
Fax: 307-527-5045
http://www.bighornradio.com/
• Roger Gelder, Chief Operating Officer
rgelder@bhrnwy.com
• Thom Huge, News Director
(307) 578-5019
thuge@bhrnwy.com
Description:
Music, News, Sports.

KZMX-AM
WINDCAVENUE ROAD
HOT SPRINGS, SD 57747-0611
605-745-3637
Fax: 605-745-3517
kzmxrealcountry@email.com
• Gary Baker, News Director
Description:
Music, News, Sports.

KZNM-FM
2600A CAMINO ENTRADA
SANTA FE, NM 87505-9291
505-878-0980
Fax: 505-878-0098
• Rene Leon, Program Director
(505) 878-0980
dj977lobo@aol.com
Description:
Music, News, Sports.

KZXY-FM
12370 HESPERIA ROAD SUITE 17
VICTORVILLE, CA 92392
760-241-1313
Fax: 760-241-0205
• Chris Price, Advertising Manager
(760) 241-1313
chrisprice@clearchannel.com
Description:
Music, News, Sports.

MAGNUM BROADCASTING
PO BOX 448
PORTAGE, WI 53901
608-742-1000
Fax: 608-742-1688
www.magnumbroadcasting.com
• Ed Kramer, General Manager
• Brett Mathison, Program Director
Baseball:
MLB - Milwaukee Brewers (night games).

MARSHALL RADIO
1414 EAST COLLEGE DRIVE
MARSHALL, MN 56258-2027
507-532-2282
Fax: 507-532-3739
info@marshallradio.net
www.marshallradio.net
• Dan Paluch, News Director
Description:
Music, News, Sports.

MOTOR RACING NETWORK/MRN
555 MRN DRIVE
CONCORD, NC 28027
704-262-6700
Fax: 704-262-6811
www.motorracingnetwork.com
• David Hyatt, President
• Chris D'Aprile, Director
• Johns Singler, News Director
• Lauren Schweppe, Associate Producer
Nature of Sports Service:
National. Produces radio broadcasts for
NASCAR Sprint Cup, NASCAR Nationwide
Series, NASCAR Camping World Truck
Series, NASCAR K&N Pro Series, NASCAR
Whelen Modified Tour and GRAND-AM
Road Racing.

NEWSRADIO 1270 WFLA
325 JOHN KNOX RD, BLDG G
TALLAHASSEE, FL 32303
850-422-3107
Fax: 850-383-0747
www.wnls.com
• Judy Bailey, VP/General Manager Clear
Channel
• Rick Flagg, News Director
• J.L Dunbar, Program Director
Nature of Sports Service:
24 News and Sports.

POWELL BROADCASTING
2000 INDIAN HILLS DRIVE
SIOUX CITY, IA 51104
712-239-2100
Fax: 712-239-3346
www.kscj.com
• Dennis Bullock, General Manager
• Tim Meacham, Sports Director
(712) 239-2100
tmeacham@powelliowa.com
• Justin Barker, Production/Promotions
Director
(712) 239-2100
justinbaker@powelliowa.com
Nature of Sports Service:
Sports, Talk, News.
Baseball:
Minor League, American Association, IND -
Sioux City Explorers.
College Sports:
Basketball, Football - University of Iowa;
Basketball - NAIA Women's Division 2
National Championship (Basketball).

SNOCOUNTRY MOUNTAIN REPORTS
10 WATER STREET
SUITE 300
LEBANON, NH 03766
603-443-8812
Fax: 603-443-8838
info@snocountry.org
www.snocountry.com
• Tom Cottrill, President
• Chuck Devine, Director of Broadcast
Operations

(603) 443-8810
chuck.devine@snocountry.org
• Rob Werneer, Sales Representative West,
Midwest
(415) 305-7439
rob.werner@snocountry.org
• Andrew Davis, Radio Program Director
(603) 443-8823
andrew.davis@snocountry.org
• Sean Malaguti, Office Manager
(603) 443-8801
sean.malaguti@snocountry.org
• Bill Wadell, Web Developer
(604) 443-8822
bill.waddell@snocountry.org
• Tom Horrocks, Marketing Communications
Manager
(603) 443-8825
tom.horrocks@snocountry.org
Nature of Sports Service:
SnoCountry, a not-for-profit trade
association, collects and distributes snow
conditions and ski resort information,
serving media outlets, including web sites,
regional and national radio networks.
SnoCountry also provides snow sport
marketing and event management services

SPORTS 56 WHBQ
6080 MT. MORIAH
MEMPHIS, TN 38115
901-375-9324
Fax: 901-794-0041
www.sports56whbq.com

SPORTS RADIO 1080 THE FAN/KFXX
0700 SW BANCROFT
PORTLAND, OR 97239
503-250-1080
866-358-1080
Fax: 503-223-6909
www.1080thefan.com
• Dennis Glasgow, Program Director
(503) 535-0363
• Jack Hutchison, General Manager
(503) 535-0370
jhutchison@entercom.com
• Erin Hubert, Vice President/Market
Manager
(503) 535-0366
• Liz Kay, Promotions Director
(503) 535-0497
• Sam Hicks, General Sales Manager
(503) 535-0259
Nature of Service:
Local. 24-hour sports radio programming.
Year Founded:
1991
Baseball:
MLB - Seattle Mariners.
College Sports:
NFL, MLB, NCAA Football/Basketball, NBA,
BCS, March Madness

SPORTS RADIO 1260-AM WNDE
6161 FALL CREEK RD
INDIANAPOLIS, IN 46220
317-257-7565
Fax: 317-253-6501
www.wnde.com
• Rick Green, General Manager
• Buzz Casey, Program Director
• Mark Patrick, Sports Director
• Lee Anne Brooks, General Sales Manager
• Tad Williams, Promotions Director
Nature of Sports Service:
24 Hour Sports.

SPORTS RADIO 1510 KGA
1601 EAST 57TH AVENUE
SPOKANE, WA 99223-3026
509-448-1000
Fax: 509-448-7015
http://www.1510kga.com
• Pat Kenney, Producer
(509) 448-1000
• Toby Howell, Program Director
(509) 448-1000
thowell@radiospokane.com
• Jessica Foxx, Promotions Director
(509) 448-1000
jfoxx@radiospokane.com
Description:
Talk.
Teams:
Gonzaga University, Spokane Chiefs,
Spokane Indians, GSL FB & BB, NCAA BB
& FB, NFL

SPORTS RADIO 810/WHB-AM
UNION BRDCASTING INC.
6721 W. 121ST ST
OVERLAND PARK, KS 66209
913-344-1500
Fax: 913-344-1599
www.810whb.com
• Chad Boeger, General Manager/Program
Director
• Kevin Kietzman, Sports Director
• Todd Leabo, Asst Sports Director
Football:
NFL - Kansas City Chiefs.
College Sports:
NCAA - University of Kansas, Kansas State,
Missouri Tigers, UNKC Kangaroos.
Baseball:
MLB - Kansas City Royals.

SPORTS RADIO 97.1 THE FAN
605 S FRONT STREET
SUITE 300
COLUMBUS, OH 43215
614-460-3850
Fax: 614-460-3757
www.971thefan.com
• Keith Britton, Producer
(614) 460-3850
• Jay Taylor, Program Director
(614) 460-3829
• Scott Torgerson, Sports Director
(614) 460-3701
• Chris Spielman, Host, The Big Show
• Bruce Hooley, Host, The Big Show
• Scott Torgerson, Host, Common Man &
The Torg
• Mike Ricordati, Host, Common Man & The
Torg
Nature of Sports Service:
24 Hour Sports. ESPN radio network
Ice Hockey:
NHL - Columbus Blue Jackets.

SPORTS TALK 790 THE ZONE
(ATLANTA)
3350 PEACHTREE RD, STE 1610
ATLANTA, GA 30326
404-237-0079
Fax: 404-231-5923
• Matt Edgar, Program Director
(404) 564-4433
• Adam Klug, Executive
Producer/Operations Director
(404) 237-0079
• Andrew Saltzman, President/General
Manager

(404) 2237-007
asaltzman@790thezone.com
• Stephen Shapiro, President/Talk Show
Host
(404) 237-0079
sshapiro@790thezone.com
• Leslie Smith, Promotions Director
(404) 237-0079
lsmith@790thezone.com
• Evan Crocker, General Sales Manager
(404) 237-0079
• D'Ree Harris, Business Manager
(404) 237-0079
• Chris Young, National Sales Manager
(404) 237-0079
Station Covers:
Auto Racing, Boxing, Golf, MLB, NFL, NHL,
NBA, NCAA Football, NCAA Men's &
Women's Basketball, Olympics, Soccer,
Tennis, WNBA.
Frequency:
Daily.
Primary Audience:
Men 25-54
Sports:
All Sports.
Nature of Service:
Sports Talk Radio.

SPORTS TALK 980
8750 BROOKVILLE RD
SILVER SPRING, MD 20910
301-231-7798
Fax: 301-949-0142
• Marty Sheehan, Director of Sales

SPORTSRADIO 1460 KENO
8755 W. FLAMINGO
LAS VEGAS, NV 89147
702-876-1460
Fax: 702-876-6685
• Tony Bonnici, General Manager
• Jesse Leeds, General Sales Manager
• Art Breyfogle, Sports Sales Manager
• John Hanson, Program Director
Nature of Sports Service:
24 Hour Sports.

STAR 610 KILT SPORTS RADIO
24 GREENWAY PLAZA, STE 1900
HOUSTON, TX 77046
713-881-5100
houston.cbslocal.com
• Dickie Rosenfeld, General Manager
• Moose Rosenfeld, Local Sales Manager
Nature of Sports Service:
Local. 24-hour sports radio programming.

STILLWATER RADIO
408 EAST THOMAS AVENUE
STILLWATER, OK 74075
405-372-7800
Fax: 405-372-6969
stillwaterradio@coxinet.net
www.stillwaterradio.net
• Rex Holt, Sports Director
(405) 372-7800
• Bill Van Ness, News Director
Description:
We broadcast all Oklahoma State Men's
and Women's sports since 1947. Also
Stillwater High School and area high school
broadcasts. We also cover Coaches Shows
and a Daily Sports Talk Show.

TALK 1450 WMIQ RADIO
101 E. KENT
IRON MOUNTAIN, MI 49801
906-774-4321
Fax: 906-774-7799
talk1450wmiq@uplogon.com
• Veronica Roberts, General Manager
• Mike Carr, Sports Director
• Neal Peterson, Operations Manager
• Tom Hill, News Director
• Kevin Lynch, Production Director
• Randy Van Gasse, Colon Commentary
Nature of Sports Service:
News/Sports/Talk.
Circulation:
10,000
Primary Audience:
Men between 25-54 years old.
Sports:
Local, College & Pro.

TEAM 1200 SPORTS RADIO
87 GEORGE ST
OTTAWA, ON, CANADA K1N 9H7
613-729-1200
Fax: 613-739-4040
• Chris Gordon, Program Director
Nature of Sports Service:
24-Hour sports radio station. Carries
play-by-play coverage for the Ottawa
Senators, Ottawa 67's and Ottawa Lynx.

THE FAN 590
77 JARVIS ST
TORONTO, ON, CANADA M4Y 3B7
416-935-0590
Fax: 416-413-4116
www.fan590.com
LINEUP:
Marsden and Landry, The Bullpen, The Big
Show, Prime Time Sports.
Baseball:
MLB - Toronto Blue Jays.
Basketball:
Toronto Raptors.
Football:
AFL - Toronto Phantoms, CFL - Toronto
Argonauts, .
Ice Hockey:
NHL - Toronto Maple Leafs.
Lacrosse:
Toronto Rock.
Soccer:
Toronto Lynx:

THE GAME 730 AM/WVFN
3420 PINE TREE
LANSING, MI 48911
517-394-7272
Fax: 517-394-3388
• Rob Striker, General Manager
rob.striker@ctcomm.com
• Kelly Norton, Director Sales
kelly.norton@ctcomm.com
• Tony Conley, Program Director
tony.conley@ctcomm.com
• Mychal Grenawalt, Senior Account
Executive
mychal.grenawalt@ctcomm.com
• Kim Lozinc, GSM
kim.lozinc@ctcomm.com
Nature of Sports Service:
Local. 24-hour sports radio programming.

THE TICKET SPORTSRADIO 1310
3090 OLIVE STREET
WEST VICTORY PLAZA SUITE 400
DALLAS, TX 75219
214-526-2400
Fax: 214-520-4343
www.dfwradio.com

THE ZONE SPORTS RADIO 1300 AM
705 N. LAMAR BLVD
AUSTIN, TX 78703
512-684-7300
Fax: 512-684-7441
www.sportsradio1300.com
• Lise Hudson, Director of Sales
• Chuck Meyer, Program Director
• Marc Hoenig, Promotions Director
Nature of Sports Service:
24 Hour Sports.

TICKET760 KTKR
KTKR-AM
6222 NW IH-10
SAN ANTONIO, TX 78201
210-736-9700
Fax: 210-736-9738
www.ticketsports.com
• Nate Lundy, Program Director
natelundy@clearchannel.com
• Walter Pasacrita, Sports Director
walter@ticket760.com
• Jim Forsyth, News Director
jimforsyth@clearchannel.com
• Tim Merryman, Executive Producer
• Eric Gray, Afternoon Producer
ericgray@clearchannel.com
• Matt Martin, Vice President Market
Manager
mattmartin@clearchannel.com

WAAV-AM
3233 BURNT MILL DRIVE SUITE 4
WILMINGTON, NC 28403
910-251-9228
Fax: 910-762-0456
http://www.980waav.com/
• Rhonda Bellamy, News Director
(910) 332-2196
• Jennifer McLean, Advertising Manager
(910) 332-2142
Description:
Music, News, Sports.

WABI-AM
184 TARGET INDUSTRIAL CIRCLE
BANGOR, ME 04401-5113
207-947-9100
Fax: 207-942-0839
http://www.b97hits.com
• George Hale, Program/Sports Director
(207) 947-9100
georgehale@clearchannel.com
• Larry Pierce, Marketing Manager
larrypierce@clearchannel.com
Description:
Music.

WABO-AM
6746 HIGHWAY 184 WEST
WAYNESBORO, MS 39367-0507
601-735-4331
Fax: 601-735-4332
http://www.wabo105.com
• Jamie Heathcock, Program Director
Description:
Music, News, Sports.

WACA-AM
11141 GEORGIA AVENUE SUITE 301
WHEATON, MD 20902-4637
301-942-3500
Fax: 301-942-7798
http://www.radioamerica.net
• Herbert Baires, Sports Director
(301) 942-3500
• Alejandro Carrasco, President
(301) 942-3500
• Samuel Galvez, News Director
(301) 942-3500
• Wilson Romero, Sports Director
Description:
Music.

WACK 1420-AM HOMETOWN SPORTS
187 VIENNA RD
PO BOX 292
NEWARK, NY 14513
315-331-1420
Fax: 315-331-7101
wacknewsroom@gmail.com
www.1420wack.com
• John Tickner, General Manager
jtickner@rochester.rr.com
• Dick Reeves, Program Director
amdrive@rochester.rr.com
• Rus Jeffrey, News Director
(315) 381-7100
1420wack@rochester.rr.com
• John Oerleth, Local Sales Manager
• Larry Ann Evans, Producer
Nature of Sports Service:
News, Sports covering Rochester New York, and the Fingerlake Region. Primary audience age is from 25 through 54 years old.
Auto Sports:
NASCAR.
Baseball:
MLB - New York Yankees.
College Sports:
Syracuse University Football & Basketball.
Football:
NFL - Buffalo Bills; CBS Sunday & Monday Nights.
Ice Hockey:
NHL - Playoffs.

WADR-AM
239 GENESEE STREET SUITE 500
UTICA, NY 13501-3412
315-797-0803
Fax: 315-797-7813
adamgerstenhaber@clearchannel.com
http://www.starsradionetwork.com
• Brian Delaney, General Manager
briandelaney@clearchannel.com
Description:
Music, News, Sports.

WAEL-AM
GUANAJIBO HOMES
CALLA RAMIREZ PABON #600
MAYAGUEZ, PUERTO RIC 00682-1100
787-832-4560
Fax: 787-805-0800
• Luis Pirallo, Program Director
Description:
Music, News, Sports.

WAIK-AM
51 NORTH PRAIRIE STREET
GALESBURG, IL 61401-4613

309-342-3161
Fax: 309-342-0199
http://www.misslink.net/waik
• Dick Shimmin, News Director
(309) 342-3164
• Rob Strack, Sports Director
Description:
Music.

WAIT-AM
130 SOUTH JEFFERSON SUITE 200
CHICAGO, IL 60661
224-805-6868
Fax: 847-509-1677
wait@relevantradio.com
http://www.relevantradio.com
• Matt Nahigian, Program Director
(847) 400-3075
mnahigian@sportingnews.com

WAJZ-FM
6 JOHNSON ROAD
LATHAM, NY 12110-5641
518-786-6600
Fax: 518-786-6610
http://www.jamz963.com
• Rob Ryan, Program Director
Description:
Music, News, Sports.

WAKQ-FM
206 NORTH BREWER STREET
PARIS, TN 38242
731-642-7100
Fax: 731-644-9367
http://www.kf99kq105.com/
• Terry Hailey, President/Program Director
Description:
Music, News, Sports.

WAKR-AM
1795 WEST MARKET STREET
AKRON, OH 44313
330-869-9800
800-994-9973
Fax: 330-864-6799
http://www.wakr.net
• Ed Esposito, News Director
(330) 869-9800
eesposito@rcrg.net
• Joyce Lagios, Marketing/Promotion Director
(330) 869-9800
jlagios@rcrg.net
Description:
Music, News, Sports.

WALS-FM
3905 PROGRESS BOULEVARD
PERU, IL 61354
815-224-2100
Fax: 815-224-2066
wals102@theradiogroup.net
• Stuart Hall, News Director
stuart@theradiogroup.net
• Jared White, Sports Director
(815) 224-2100
radio1@theramp.net

WAMV-AM
132 SCHOOL ROAD
AMHERST, VA 24521
434-946-9000
888-946-1420
Fax: 434-946-2201

wamv1420@aol.com
http://www.wamvradio.com
• Robert K. Langstaff, Advertising Manager/Program Director
wamvradio@aol.com
Description:
Music, News, Sports.

WAMW-AM
104 EAST MAIN STREET
WASHINGTON, IN 47501-2908
812-254-6761
Fax: 812-254-3940
• Taylor Brown, News Director
Description:
Music, News.

WAMW-FM
104 EAST MAIN STREET
WASHINGTON, IN 47501-2908
812-254-6761
Fax: 812-254-3940
wamw@rtccom.net
http://www.wamwamfm.com
• Taylor Brown, News Director
Description:
Music, News, Sports.

WAPX-FM
AUSTIN PEAY STATE UNIVERSITY
CLARKSVILLE, TN 37044
931-648-7200
Fax: 931-648-5992
Description:
Music, News, Sports.

WAQE-AM
1859 21ST AVENUE
RICE LAKE, WI 54868-9502
715-234-9059
800-236-3698
Fax: 715-234-6942
info@waqe.com
• Ken Denucci, News Director
Description:
Music, News, Sports.

WAQE-FM
1859 21ST AVENUE
RICE LAKE, WI 54868-9502
715-234-9059
800-236-3698
Fax: 715-234-6942
info@waqe.com
• Ken Denucci, News Director
Description:
Music, News, Sports.

WAQI-AM
800 DOUGLAS ROAD
CORAL GABLES, FL 33134-3187
305-447-1140
Fax: 305-442-7676
http://www.univision.com
• Sarvelio Del Valle, Sports Director
(305) 447-1140
sarveliodelvalle@univision.com
Description:
News, Talk.

WARK-AM
880 COMMONWEALTH AVENUE
HAGERSTOWN, MD 21740-6836
301-733-4500
800-222-9279

Fax: 301-733-0040
http://www.warx.com
• Mike Krafthofer, News Director
(301) 733-4500
Description:
Music, News, Sports, Talk.

WARM-AM
600 BALTIMORE DRIVE 2ND FLOOR
WILKES BARRE, PA 18702-7901
570-824-9000
800-447-5000
Fax: 570-820-0520
http://www.590warm.com
• Brian Hughes, News Director
Description:
Music, News, Sports.

WASU-FM
332 WEY HALL
BOONE, NC 28608-0001
828-262-3170
Fax: 828-262-2543
• Richard Davis, General Manager
(828) 262-3170
• Bryce Johnson, Sports Director
(828) 262-3170
Description:
Music, News, Sports.

WATA-AM
738 BLOWING ROCK ROAD
BOONE, NC 28607
828-264-2411
Fax: 828-264-2412
info@wecr1023.com
• David Blank, News Director
(828) 264-2411
info@wataradio.com
Description:
Music, News, Sports.

WAUD-AM
2514 SOUTH COLLEGE STREET SUITE
104
AUBURN, AL 36830
334-887-9999
888-984-4379
Fax: 334-826-9599
info@thetiger.fm
• Chris Bailey, General Manager
chrisb@thetiger.fm
• Kevin Jackson, Program Director
kevin@thetiger.fm
• Bob Sanders, Advertising Manager
(334) 887-3401
• Bob Sanders, Sports Director
(334) 887-3401
Description:
Educational, Music, News, Sports, Talk.

WAUK ALL SPORTS RADIO
1801 CORAL DR
WAUKESHA, WI 53186
262-544-6800
Fax: 262-544-1705
wauk1510@execpc.com
www.doubleplay1510.com
• Ken Heinlein, Station Manager
• Scott Aebly, Pro General Manager Director
• Bill Johnson, Program Director
Nature of Sports Service:
Local. 24-hour sports radio programming.

WAVL-AM
P.O. BOX 277
APOLLO, PA 15613-0277
724-478-4020
http://www.praise910.com/
• Jeff Bogaczyk, News Director
Description:
Music, News, Sports, Talk.

WAVT-FM
212 SOUTH CENTER
POTTSVILLE, PA 17901
570-622-1360
Fax: 570-622-2822
news@pbcradio.com
http://www.pbcradio.com
• James A. Bowman, Advertising Manager
• Chad Gerber, Program Director
(570) 622-1360
Description:
Music, News, Sports.

WAVV-FM
11800 EAST TAMIAMI TRAIL
NAPLES, FL 34113-7909
239-775-9288
Fax: 239-793-7000
• Walt Tiburski, General Manager
w.tiburski@wavv101.com
Description:
Music. 2 minute sports report. M-F 7:30 &
8:30

WAXL-FM
501 OLD STATE ROAD
HUNTINGBURG, IN 47542
812-683-1215
Fax: 812-683-5891
waxl@psci.net
• Jim Anderson, News Director
(812) 683-1215
janderson@galgazette.com
• Kurt Gutgsell, Sports Director
(812) 683-1215
wbdc@psci.net

WAXO-AM/FM
217 COMMERCE STREET, W.
LEWISBURG, TN 37091-3337
931-359-6641
Fax: 931-270-9290
http://www.waxo.com
• Tim Atkinson, News Director
waxo@waxo.com
• Troy Cashion, Sports Director
(931) 359-6641
Description:
Music, News, Sports. Monday - Friday at
7:15 a.m. CST.

WAYC-FM
134 EAST PITT STREET 2ND FLOOR
BEDFORD, PA 15522-1311
814-623-1000
Fax: 814-623-9692
• Keith Bagley, News Director
• Jay B. Cessna, Sports Director
jaycessna@earthlink.net
Description:
Music.

WAYN-AM
1223 ROCKINGHAM ROAD
ROCKINGHAM, NC 28379

910-895-4041
Fax: 910-895-4993
wayninc@aol.com
• Jim Smith, News/Sports Director
Description:
Music.

WAYY-AM
944 HARLEM AVENUE
ALTOONA, WI 54720-1127
715-832-1530
800-866-9299
Fax: 715-832-5329
• Bruce Butler, Promotions Manager
• Dave Craig, Sports Director
davec@maverick-media.ws
• Dan Lea, News Director
• George Roberts, Advertising Manager
Description:
News, Talk.

WAYZ-FM
10960 JOHN WAYNE DRIVE
GREENCASTLE, PA 17225
717-597-9200
800-758-0838
Fax: 717-597-9210
http://www.wayz.com
• Scott Douglas, News Director
Description:
Music, News.

WAZZ-AM
3012 HIGHWOOD BLVD. #201
RALEIGH, NC 27604
910-484-1490
Fax: 910-323-5635
http://www.am1490wazz.com/
• Mac Edwards, Vice President
(910) 486-2002
mac@bbgi.com
• Val Jones, News Director
(910) 486-2085
Description:
Music, News, Sports.

WBAG-AM
1745 BIRCH BRIDGE ROAD
BURLINGTON, NC 27217
336-226-1150
Fax: 336-226-1180
• Bill Huff, Sports Director
1150@wbagradio.com
• Harry Myers, News Director
Description:
Music, News, Sports, Talk.

WBAL RADIO
3800 HOOPER AVE
BALTIMORE, MD 21211
410-338-6570
Fax: 410-366-4166
www.wbal.com
• Ed Kiernan, General Manager
• Steve Melewski, Sports Director
• Jeff Beauchamp, Vice President/Station
Manager
Nature of Sports Service:
News, Talk, Sports.
Baseball:
MLB - Baltimore Orioles.
College Sports:
University of Maryland - Basketball,
Football.

WBAX-AM
149 PENN AVENUE
SCRANTON, PA 18503
570-346-6555
Fax: 570-346-6038
http://www.wejl-wbax.com/
• Ruth Miller, News Director
(570) 207-8583
rmiller@shamrocknepa.com
Description:
Music.

WBBB-FM
3012 HIGHWOODS BOULEVARD
SUITE 201
RALEIGH, NC 27604
919-876-9600
Fax: 919-882-1746
info@curtismedia.com
http://www.radio961.com
• Jim Defontes, News Director
(919) 876-0674

WBBP-AM
250 EAST RAINES ROAD
MEMPHIS, TN 38109
901-278-7878
Fax: 901-344-0038
http://www.bbless.org/wbbp.home.htm
• G. E. Patterson, General Manager
Description:
Music, News, Sports.

WBCK - BATTLE CREEK
390 GOLDEN AVE
BATTLE CREEK, MI 49015
263-963-5555
Fax: 269-963-5185
• Jack McDervitt, General Manager
• Ken Ervin, Sports Director
Baseball:
MLB - Detroit Tigers.
Ice Hockey:
NHL - Detroit Red Wings.

WBCK-AM
390 GOLDEN AVENUE
BATTLE CREEK, MI 49015
269-963-5555
Fax: 269-963-5185
www.am930wbck.com
• Tim Collins, General Manager/Operations
Director
(269) 963-5555
• Ken Ervin, Sports Director
Description:
Radio: AM930, Football: NFL-Detroit Lions,
Football and Basketball: NCAA Michigan
State University

WBCN-FM
83 LEO BURMINGHAM PARKWAY
BOSTON, MA 02135
617-746-1400
Fax: 617-746-1408
http://www.wbcn.com
• Mark Hannon, General Manager
(617) 746-1400
mhannon@wbcn.com
Description:
Music.

WBCR-FM
700 COLLEGE STREET
PO BOX 39
BELOIT, WI 53511-5509

608-363-2402
Fax: 608-363-2718
wbcrmanager@gmail.com
http://www.beloit.edu/wbcr
• James Lynch, Program Director
Description:
Music, News, Sports.

WBCV-AM
P.O. BOX 68
BRISTOL, TN 37621-0068
423-968-5221
Fax: 423-968-7711
http://www.wbcv.com
• Cecil Reed, Program Director
Description:
Music, News, Sports.

WBDG-FM
1200 GIRLS SCHOOL ROAD, N.
INDIANAPOLIS, IN 46214-3403
317-244-9234
Fax: 317-243-5506
• Jon Easter, Station Manager
(317) 244-9234
jon.easter@wayne.k12.in.us
• Jason Adamson, Sports Director
(317) 244-9234
Description:
Music, News, Sports.

WBEC
211 JASON ST
PITTSFIELD, MA 01201
413-499-3333
Fax: 413-442-1590
• Joseph Gallagher, Owner
• Curt Preisser, Sports Director
• Laura Freed, Owner
Office Address:
211 Jason St, Pittsfield, MA 01202.
Nature of Sports Service:
News, Talk, Sports.
Baseball:
MLB - Boston Red Sox.
Basketball:
NBA Playoffs.
Football:
NFL - New England Patriots.
Ice Hockey:
NHL - Boston Bruins.

WBES-AM
817 SUNCREST PLACE
CHARLESTON, WV 25303-2302
304-342-3136
Fax: 304-342-3118
• Darrell Daniels, News Director
• John Dickensheets, Sports Director
Description:
Music.

WBET-AM
70808 SOUTH NOTTAWA ROAD
STURGIS, MI 49091-9731
269-651-2383
Fax: 269-659-1111
wmsh@wmshradio.com
• Tom Duke, Account Executive
(269) 651-2383
tduke@wbetfm.com
• Mike Stiles, News Director
mstiles@wmshradio.com
Description:
ESPN Radio 1230

WBEX-AM
45 WEST MAIN STREET
CHILLICOTHE, OH 45601-3104
740-773-3000
Fax: 740-774-4494
http://www.wbex.com
• Dan Ramey, Sports Director
danraney@clearchannel.com
• Mike Smith, News Director
Description:
Music, News, Sports, Talk.

WBFD-AM
134 EAST PITT STREET 2ND FLOOR
BEDFORD, PA 15522-1311
814-623-1000
Fax: 814-623-9692
• Keith Bagley, News Director
• Jay B. Cessna, President/Sports Director
Description:
Music.

WBFN-AM
390 GOLDEN AVENUE
BATTLE CREEK, MI 49015
269-963-5555
Fax: 269-963-5185
http://www.battlecreekradio.com
• Tim Collins, Program Director
(269) 963-5555
timcollins@clearchannel.com
Description:
Radio: AM 1400, Basebal: MLB-Detroit
Tigers, Ice Hockey: NHL-Detroit Red Wings

WBGG-AM
200 FLEET STREET
PITTSBURGH, PA 15220
412-937-1441
800-788-1067
Fax: 412-937-0323
http://www.970theburgh.com
• Bob McLaughlin, Program Director
(412) 919-8455
bobmclaughlin@clearchannel.com
Description:
Music.

WBGN-AM
901 LEHMAN AVENUE SUITE 1
BOWLING GREEN, KY 42101
270-843-0107
Fax: 270-782-0767
http://www.1340wbgn.com/
• Brad Hogan, Station Manager
Description:
Music, News, Sports.

WBGO-FM
54 PARK PLACE
NEWARK, NJ 07102-4302
973-624-8880
Fax: 973-824-8888
jazz88@wbgo.org
http://www.wbgo.org
• Doug Doyle, News Director
(973) 624-8880
ddoyle@wbgo.org
• Dorthaan Kirk, Promotion Manager
(973) 624-8880
dkirk@wbgo.org
Description:
Music, News, Sports.

media

WBHB-AM
601 WEST ROANOKE DRIVE
FITZGERALD, GA 31750
229-423-2077
Fax: 229-386-9866
• Brian Peters, Sports Director
Description:
Music.

WBHR-AM
1010 2ND STREET NORTH
SAUK RAPIDS, MN 56379
320-252-6200
Fax: 320-252-9367
http://www.660wbhr.com
• Gary Hoppe, Program Director
Description:
Music.

WBIG-AM
620 NORTH EOLA ROAD
AURORA, IL 60502
630-851-5200
Fax: 630-851-5286
mail@wbig1280.com
http://www.wbig1280.com
• Steve Marten, General Manager
(630) 851-5200
• Gerry Clarke, Sports Marketing
(630) 851-5200
• Ryan Gatenby, Program Director
(630) 851-5200
Description:
Music.
Description: Teams Sponsored
Chicago Bulls, Chicago Bears, Chicago
White Sox, Kane County Cougers(Cubs
Affiliate), Chicago Soul soccor

WBIZ-AM SPORTS RADIO
619 CAMERON ST
EAU CLAIRE, WI 54703
715-830-4000
Fax: 715-835-9680
• Rick Hencley, General Manager
• Dan Michaels, Program Director
• Mike Sullivan, Sports Director
• Kelly Lafky, Sales Manager
Nature of Sports Service:
Local. 24-hour sports radio programming.

WBLA-AM
512 PEANUT ROAD
ELIZABETHTOWN, NC 28337-8811
910-862-3184
Fax: 910-872-0100
http://www.wgqr1057.com
• Lee Hauser, Advertising Manager
• Al Radlein, Program Director
Description:
Music, News, Sports.

WBLJ-AM
613 SILVER CIRCLE
DALTON, GA 30721
706-278-5511
Fax: 706-278-9917
http://www.wbljl230.com
• Randal Davidson, Sports Director
randaldavidson@clearchannel.com
Description:
Music.

WBLK-FM
14 LAFAYETTE SQUARE SUITE 1300
BUFFALO, NY 14203-1928

716-852-9393
800-828-2191
Fax: 716-852-9390
http://www.wblk.com
• Chris Reynolds, Program Director
• Catherine Roberts, Promotion Director
Description:
Music, News, Sports.

**WBNS AM/FM - 1460 ESPN COLUMBUS &
97.1 THE FAN**
605 S FRONT STREET
SUITE 300
COLUMBUS, OH 43215
614-460-3850
Fax: 614-460-3757
www.971thefan.com
• Jay Taylor, Program Director
(614) 460-3829
• Todd Markiewicz, Director of Sales
(614) 460-2816
Description:
Founded in 1976, the station offers classic
country music, news, sports and local sports
play-by-play, Minnesota TWins, NFL
football, NCAA football and basketball.
Baseball:
Cleveland Indians
Football:
Monday Night Football
Hockey:
NHL - Columbus Blue Jackets
College Sports:
Basketball/Football - Ohio State University

WBNV-FM
740 EAST MAIN STREET
BARNESVILLE, OH 43713
740-425-9268
Fax: 740-432-1991
http://www.yourradioplace.com
• Reuben Perdue, Program/Sports Director
(740) 432-5605
Description:
Music, Sports.

WBOB-AM 1160 SPORTS RADIO
3656 EDWARDS RD
CINCINNATI, OH 45208
513-533-2500
Fax: 513-533-2527
• John Rohm, General Manager
• Doug Kidd, Interim Pro General
Manager/Director
• Roy Seransky, Sales Manager
• Ron James, Promotions Director
• Patti Marshall, Marketing Director
Nature of Sports Service:
Local. 24-hour sports radio programming.
Baseball:
MLB - Cincinnati Reds..
College Sports:
NCAA DIV I Xavier Musketeers, NCAA DIV I
Cincinnati Bearcats, NCAA Div I University
of Kentucky Wildcats
Football:
NFL - Cincinnati Bengals.
Ice Hockey:
American Hockey League/AHL - Cincinnati
Mighty Ducks

WBPZ-AM
21 EAST MAIN STREET
LOCK HAVEN, PA 17745-2443
570-748-4038
Fax: 570-748-0092

• John Lipez, Advertising Manager
• Mark Sohmer, News Director
Description:
Music.

WBRK 1340AM RADIO
100 NORTH ST
PITTSFIELD, MA 01201
413-442-1553
Fax: 413-445-5294
• Chip Hodgkins, General Manager
• Bob Shade, Sports Director
Baseball:
MLB - New York Yankees; Minor League -
Northern League - Berkshire Black Bears.
Basketball:
NBA - Boston Celtics.

WBRY-AM
P. O. BOX 7
WOODBURY, TN 37190
615-563-2313
Fax: 615-563-6229
askus@wbry.com
http://www.wbry.com
• Doug Combs, General Manager
dcombs@wbry.com
• Keith Ready, Sports Director
(615) 563-2313
askus@wbry.com
Description:
Music, News, Sports, Talk.

WBTI-FM
808 HURON AVENUE
PORT HURON, MI 48060-3705
810-982-9000
Fax: 810-987-9380
• Bill Gilmer, News Director
bgilmer@radiofirst.net
• Dennis Stuckey, Sports Director
(810) 982-9000
newsroom@bluewaternews.net
Description:
Music, News.

WBTM-AM
710 GROVE STREET
DANVILLE, VA 24541-1704
434-797-4290
Fax: 434-797-3918
wbtm1330@wbtm1330.com
http://www.wbtm1330.com/
• Carol Metz, Promotion Manager
• Chuck Vipperman, News Director
(434) 797-4290
Description:
Music, News, Sports, Talk.

WBUK-FM
667 WEST MARKET STREET
LIMA, OH 45801
419-223-2060
Fax: 419-229-3888
reneescott@clearchannel.com
http://www.wbuk.com
• Sou Boudriex, Advertising Sales
souboudrie@clearchannel.com
• Jeff Gunter, News Director
(419) 223-2060
jeffgunter@clearchannel.com
• Mike Mullen, Athletics Senior Editor/Sports
Director
mikemullen@clearchannel.com
• Todd Walker, Sports Director
toddwalker@clearchannel.com

WBUT-AM
252 PILLOW ST
BUTLER, PA 16001
724-287-5778
Fax: 724-282-9188
http://www.insidebutlercounty.com
• Bob Cupp, Sports Director
bobcupp@bcrnetwork.com
Sponsors:
Pittsburgh Steelers, Pittsburgh Pirates, Pittsburgh Penguins, Pitt Panthers as well as local high school leagues.

WBVP-AM
1316 7TH AVENUE
BEAVER FALLS, PA 15010-4217
724-846-4100
Fax: 724-843-7771
http://www.wbvp-wmba.com
• Bob Barrickman, Sports Director
• Pat Septak, News Director
Description:
Music, News, Sports, Talk.

WBXX-FM
390 GOLDEN AVENUE
BATTLE CREEK, MI 49015
269-963-9595
Fax: 269-963-5185
http://www.softrock953.com
• Tim Collins, General Manager/Operations Director
(269) 963-5555
• Nathan Adams, Overnight DJ/Sports Anchor
(269) 963-5555
NathanAdams@clearchannel.com
• Jeff Cassidy, Program Director
(269) 963-5555
Description:
Radio: FM95.3, Football and Basketball: NCAA University of Michigan

WBYL-FM
1559 WEST 4TH STREET
WILLIAMSPORT, PA 17701-5650
570-327-1400
Fax: 570-327-8156
kthomas@clearchannel.com
• Ken Sawyer, Sports Director
ksawyer@clearchannel.com
• Tom Scott, Promotion Manager
tscott@clearchannel.com
• Kathy Thomas, News Director
(570) 327-1400
Description:
Music.

WBYT-FM
237 WEST EDISON ROAD SUITE 200
MISHAWAKA, IN 46545-3137
574-258-5483
800-285-8646
Fax: 574-258-0930
b100@b100.com
http://www.b100.com
• Sahar Charisse, News Director
(574) 258-5483
Description:
Music, News, Sports.

WBZ-AM
1170 SOLDIERS FIELD ROAD
BOSTON, MA 02134

617-787-7000
Fax: 617-254-6383
http://www.wbz.com
• Peter Casey, News Director
(617) 787-7246
• Ted Jordan, Vice President
• Laurie Lamper, Promotions Director
(617) 787-7196
• Tony Nesbitt, Sports Executive Producer
(617) 787-7266
• Gil Santos, Sports Director
• Alan Segel, Sports Anchor (Weekend)
Description:
News, Talk.

WBZD-FM
1685 FOUR MILE DRIVE
WILLIAMSPORT, PA 17701-1938
570-323-8200
Fax: 570-323-5075
http://www.wbzd.com
• John Finn, News Director
john.fin@wilq.com
• Bob Pawlikowski, Advertising Manager
bobp@aol.com
Description:
Music, News, Sports.

WBZE-FM / WGLF.FM/ WWLD.FM / WHBX.FM
3411 WEST THARPE STREET
TALLAHASSEE, FL 32303-1139
850-201-3000
Fax: 850-561-8903
www.mystar98.com
Description:
Radio Stations : Music, News, Sports.
Sport Broadcasts:
Announces for FSU Volleyball, FSU and FAMU Basketball, and FAMU Football

WCAO-AM
1829 REISTERSTOWN ROAD SUITE 420
BALTIMORE, MD 21208-6320
410-366-7600
Fax: 410-467-0011
http://www.heaven600.com
• Yvonne Morton, News Director
(410) 261-7257
ymorton@wcao.com
Description:
Music, News, Sports, Talk.

WCBG-AM
10960 JOHN WAYNE DRIVE
GREENCASTLE, PA 17225
717-597-9200
800-758-0838
Fax: 717-597-9210
• Scott Douglas, News Director
Description:
Music, News, Sports, Talk.

WCBL-FM
P. O. BOX 387
BENTON, KY 42025
270-527-3102
Fax: 270-527-5606
http://www.bellsouth.net
• Sam Rickman, News Director
wcbl@bellsouth.net
• Jeff Waters, Sports Editor
(270) 527-3102
wcbl@bellsouth.net
Description:
Music.

WCBT-AM
3 EAST 1ST STREET
WELDON, NC 27890-1503
252-536-3115
Fax: 252-538-0378
http://www.wcbt1230.com
• Les Atkins, News Director
latkins@wnvnnews.com
• Mark Matthews, Sports Director
mark@firstmediarr.com
Description:
Sports.

WCCO
625 2ND AVE S.
SUITE 200
MINNEAPOLIS, MN 55402
612-370-0611
Fax: 612-370-0683
www.wcco.com
• Mike Max, Announcer
• Jay Dailey, GSM
• Lindsey Peterson, APD
Nature of Sports Service:
Local, 24-hour full-service programming. Broadcast station of the Minnesota Timberwolves and St. Thomas University.

WCCP
PO BOX 1560
CLEMSON, SC 29633
864-654-0606
800-499-1049
Fax: 864-654-9328
• George Clement, General Manager
• Tommy Powell, Sports Director
Nature of Sports Service:
Sports/70's Music.
Baseball:
MLB - Atlanta Braves.
College Sports:
Baseball, Basketball, Football - Clemson University.
Football:
NFL - Carolina Panthers.

WCCW-AM
RADIO CENTER-WCCW 300
SUITE 450
TRAVERSE CITY, MI 49684
231-946-6211
Fax: 231-946-1914
brianh@wccw.fm
• Annie Mac, News Director
• Brian Hale, ESPN Manager
(231) 946-6211
Description:
Music, News, Talk. ESPN Radio 1310 AM

WCDK-FM
2307 PENNSYLVANIA AVENUE
WEIRTON, WV 26062
304-723-1430
800-926-8255
Fax: 304-723-1688
• Tammie Beagle, News Director
(304) 723-1444
Description:
Music.

WCDO-AM
75 MAIN STREET
SIDNEY, NY 13838-1138
607-563-3588
Fax: 607-563-7805
http://www.wcdofm.com

media

647

• Rob Ray, News Director
rob@wcdofm.com
• Craig Stevens, Advertising Manager
craig@wcdofm.com
Description:
Music, News, Sports.

WCEM-AM
2 BAY STREET
CAMBRIDGE, MD 21613-0237
410-228-4800
Fax: 410-228-0130
http://www.mtsline.com
• Norm Elliott, News Director
(410) 228-4800
normelliott@hotmail.com
• Shan Shariff, Sports Director
Description:
Music, News, Sports.

WCFM-FM
WILLIAMS COLLEGE
WILLIAMSTOWN, MA 01267
413-597-3265
Fax: 413-597-2259
wcfmbd@wso.williams.edu
http://wcfm.williams.edu
• Adam Ain, General Manager
adam.s.ain@williams.edu
• Helena Johnson, Sports Director
(413) 597-3265
99mkm@williams.edu
Description:
Music, News, Sports, Talk.

WCFW-FM
318 WELL STREET
CHIPPEWA FALLS, WI 54729-1563
715-723-2257
Fax: 715-723-8276
• Patricia Bushland, Advertising Manager
• Roland Bushland, General Manager
Description:
Music, News, Sports.

WCGQ-FM
1820 WYNNTON ROAD
COLUMBUS, GA 31904
706-327-1217
Fax: 706-322-1077
http://www.q1073.com
• D.J. Jones, Sports Director
(404) 762-9942
• Chuck Thompson, Promotions Manager
Description:
Music, News, Sports.

WCHC-FM
COLLEGE OF THE HOLY CROSS
WORCESTER, MA 01610-2322
508-793-2475
Fax: 508-793-2471
http://www.holycross.edu/wchc
• Chris Delvicio, Program Director
Description:
Music, News, Sports.

WCHO-AM
1535 NORTH STREET
WASHINGTON COURT HOU, OH
43160-1111
740-335-0941
Fax: 740-335-6869
http://wwww.cho.com
• Dan Latham, General Manager
danlatham@clearchannel.com

• Randy L. Young, Sports Director
(740) 335-0941
randallyoung@clearchannel.com
Description:
Music.

WCHO-FM
1535 NORTH STREET
WASHINGTON COURT HOU, OH
43160-1111
740-335-0941
Fax: 740-335-6869
http://www.washingtonch.com
• Ed Helt, News Director
carlstaffan@clearchannel.com
• Randy L. Young, Sports Director
(740) 335-0941
randallyoung@clearchannel.com
Description:
Music.

WCJW-AM
3258 MERCHANT ROAD
WARSAW, NY 14569-0251
585-786-8131
Fax: 585-786-2241
• Jenny Snow, News Director
news@wcjw.com
Description:
Music, News, Sports.

WCKY-AM
8044 MONTGOMERY ROAD
SUITE 650
CINCINNATI, OH 45236
513-686-8300
800-749-9326
Fax: 513-241-0358
http://www.wcky.com/main.html
• Mike Kenney, General Manager
mikekenney@clearchannel.com
Description:
News, Talk.

WCLG-FM
343 HIGH STREET
MORGANTOWN, WV 26505
304-292-2222
Fax: 304-292-2224
http://www.wclg.com
Description:
Music

WCLH-FM
84 W. S. STREET
WILKES BARRE, PA 18766
570-408-4169
Fax: 570-408-5908
• Ariel Cohen, Assistant Marketing Director
(570) 408-4169
• Renee Loftus, Station Manager
(570) 408-4169
Description:
Educational, Music, News, Sports.

WCLN-AM
118 EAST MAIN STREET
CLINTON, NC 28328
910-592-8949
Fax: 910-592-3732
http://www.odies1170.com
• Thomas Elliott, Program Director
fly@oldies1170.com
Description:
Music, News, Sports.

WCLO-AM
1 SOUTH PARKER DRIVE
JANESVILLE, WI 53545-3928
608-752-7895
Fax: 608-752-4438
programming@wclo.com
http://www.wclo.com
• Tim Bremel, Program Director
(608) 752-7895
• Al Fagerli, Sports Director
(608) 752-7895
sports@wclo.com
• Mike O'Brien, Advertising Manager
mobrien@wclo.com
Description:
Music.

WCLT-AM
674 JACKSONTOWN ROAD, SOUTHEAST
HEATH, OH 43056
740-345-4004
Fax: 740-345-5775
http://www.wclt.com
• Eric Brown, News Director
• Tom Bunyard, General Sales Manager
(740) 345-4004
Description:
Sports radio programming.
Teams sponsored:
Ohio State Buckeyes, Columbus Blue
Jackets, Cleveland Indians, and High
School sports.

WCNC-AM
911 PARSONAGE STREET EXTENDED
ELIZABETH CITY, NC 27906-1246
252-335-4379
Fax: 252-338-5275
http://www.wcnc1240.com
• Sam Walker, Program/Sports Director
Description:
Music, News, Sports.

WCNC-AM / WZBO-AM
911 PARSONAGE EXTENDED
ELIZABETH CITY, NC 27909
252-335-4379
Fax: 252-338-5275
www.ecri.net
• Sam Walker, News Director
(252) 335-4379
swalker@ecri.net
Description:
Music, News, Sports.
Teams:
UNC Tarheels, Carolina Panthers,
Westwood One National Coverage NFL,
NCAA coverage of ACC and Big East.

WCOS
316 GREYSTONE BOULEVARD
COLUMBIA, SC 29210
803-343-1100
Fax: 803-748-9267
www.975wcos.com
• Steve Patterson, General Manager
• Kevin Cohen, Sports Director
Office Address:
56 Radio Lane, Columbia, SC 29210.
Nature of Sports Service:
Local. 24-hour sports radio programming.
Auto Sports:
NASCAR.
Baseball:
MLB - Atlanta Braves.

WCSL
PO BOX 370
CHERRYVILLE, NC 28021
704-435-3297
Fax: 704-435-1217
• Calvin Hastings, General Manager/Sales
• Andy Foster, Sports Director/Music
• Milton Baker, Office Manager
• Tim Biggerstaff, Product Director
• Larry Seagle, News Director
• Terresa Hastings, Traffic Director
Office Address:
1416 Shelby Hwy, Cherryville, NC 28021.
Nature of Sports Service:
Country; Sports.
Baseball:
MLB - Atlanta Braves.
College Sports:
Basketball, Football - University of North
Carolina Tarheels.
Football:
NFL - Carolina Panthers.

WCSL-AM
1416 SHELBY HIGHWAY
CHERRYVILLE, NC 28021
704-735-8071
877-638-7234
Fax: 704-435-1217
http://www.superstations.net
• Tim Biggerstaff, Program Director
tbiggerstaff@hrnb.com
• Larry Seagle, Sports Director
lseagle@hrnb.com
Description:
Music, News, Sports.

WCST-AM
440 RADIO STATION LANE
BERKELEY SPRINGS, WV 25411-4108
304-258-1010
Fax: 304-258-1010
• Mike Fagan, Promotion Manager/Sports
Director
c929@comcast.net
• Virgil Ruppenthal, Program Director
Description:
Music, News, Sports.

WCTA-AM
114 SOUTH JOHNSON STREET COURT
SQUARE
ALAMO, TN 38001-0246
731-696-2781
Fax: 731-696-5006
• Billy Williams, General/Advertising
Manager
Description:
Music, News, Sports.

WCTK-FM
75 OXFORD STREET SUITE 402
PROVIDENCE, RI 02905
401-467-4366
800-365-1037
Fax: 401-941-2795
http://www.wctk.com
• Rick Everett, Program Director
(401) 467-4366
reverett@hallradio.com
• Jamie Prevost, Promotion Manager
Description:
Music.

WCUM-AM
1862 COMMERCE DRIVE SUITE 2
BRIDGEPORT, CT 06605
203-335-1450
Fax: 203-337-1220
radiocumbre1450@aol.com
www.radiocumbre.com
• Migdalia Colon, Vice President
Description:
Music, News, Sports.

WCVM-FM
6200 EAST STATE ROAD 120
HOWE, IN 46746
260-562-3276
Fax: 260-562-2252
http://www.effectradio.com
• Banner Kidd, General Manager
banner@wqko.com

WCWT-FM
500 EAST FRANKLIN STREET
CENTERVILLE, OH 45459-5714
937-439-3558
Fax: 937-439-3574
• Bob Romond, Program Director
Description:
Music, News, Sports.

WCYJ-FM
51 WEST COLLEGE STREET
WAYNESBURG, PA 15370-1258
724-627-8191
http://www.waynesburg.edu
• Amy Sigmund, News Director
Description:
Music, News, Sports.

WDAE-AM 620
4002 GANDY BLVD
TAMPA, FL 33611
813-839-9393
Fax: 813-831-3299
www.620wdae.com
• Dave Reinhart, General Manager
• Scott Chase, Program Director
Office Address:
1416 Shelby Hwy, Cherryville, NC 28021.
Nature of Sports Service:
Local. 24-hour sports station.

WDAS-AM
23 WEST CITY AVENUE
BALA CYNWYD, PA 19004
610-617-8500
Fax: 610-617-8501
joetamburro@clearchannel.com
http://www.wdasam.com/main.html
• Erica Speed, Promotion Director
• Joe Tamburro, Program Director
Description:
Music, News, Sports.

WDBO-AM
4192 NORTH JOHN YOUNG PARKWAY
ORLANDO, FL 32804-2620
321-281-2030
Fax: 407-290-1076
news@wdbo.com
http://580wdbo.com/
• Scott Anez, Sports Director
(321) 281-2030
scott.anez@cox.com
Description:
Music, News, Sports.

WDBQ-AM
5490 SARATOGA ROAD
DUBUQUE, IA 52002-2593
563-583-6471
Fax: 563-583-4535
• Scott Lindahl, General Manager
Description:
Music, News, Sports.

WDDD-AM
1822 NORTH COURT
MARION, IL 62959
618-997-8123
Fax: 618-993-2319
brucefasol@clearchannel.com
• Bruce Fasol, Sports Director
(618) 997-8123
• April Ruebke, News Director
(618) 997-8123
aprilruebke@clearchannel.com
Description:
Music, News, Sports.

WDDD-FM
1822 NORTH COURT STREET
MARION, IL 62959
618-997-8123
Fax: 618-993-2319
rock105@accessus.net
http://www.w3dcountry.com/main.html
• Bruce Fasol, Sports Director
(618) 997-8123
• April Ruebke, News Director
(618) 997-8123
aprilruebke@clearchannel.com
Description:
Music.

WDDK-FM
1271-B EAST BROAD STREET
GREENSBORO, GA 30642-2335
706-453-4140
Fax: 706-453-7179
• Chip Lyness, Advertising Manager
Description:
Music, News, Sports.

WDEL-AM
P.O. BOX 7492
WILMINGTON, DE 19810
302-478-8898
Fax: 302-479-1532
wdelnews@wdel.com
http://www.wdel.com
• Janette Johnson, Marketing/Promotion
Director
(302) 478-2700
jjohnson@dbc1.com
• Don Voltz, Sports Director
(302) 478-8898
DVoltz@dbc1.com
• Len Holmquist, Sports Reporter
(302) 478-8898
Len@wdel.com
Description:
News, Talk.

WDFN
2930 E. JEFFERSON
DETROIT, MI 48207
313-259-5440
Fax: 313-259-9079
www.wdfn.com
• Peter Connolly, General Manager
• Jamie Samuelson, Sports Director

Office Address:
2909 Woodbridge, Detroit, MI 48207.
Nature of Sports Service:
Local. 24-hour sports radio programming.
Baseball:
CBS Package.
College Sports:
Basketball - NCAA; Football - University
Notre Dame.
Football:
Westwood One package.

WDFN - 1130 AM THE FAN
27675 Halsted Road
Farmington Hills, MI 48331
248-848-1130
Fax: 248-848-1422
www.wdfn.com
• Dave Pugh, General Manager
• Rona Danziger, Program Director
• Ellen Sawyer, Promotion and Marketing
Director
• Matt Dery, Sports Director
LINEUP:
Jamie Samuelson, Mike Stone, Bob
Wojnowski, Matt Dery. Brandon Tierney,
Greg Brady (not from the Brady Bunch),
Sabrina Black, Mark Spindler, Sean
Baligian.

WDHC-FM
440 RADIO STATION LANE
BERKELEY SPRINGS, WV 25411-4108
304-258-1010
Fax: 304-258-1976
• Mike Fagan, Promotion Manager/Sports
Director
• Virgil Ruppenthal, Program Director
Description:
Music, News, Sports.

WDKD-AM
51 COMMERCE STREET
SUMTER, SC 29151
803-775-2321
Fax: 803-773-4856
• Dave Baker, Program Director
(803) 775-2321
dave@vfastlink.com
• Derrick Rheims, Sports Director
drheims@miller.fm
Description:
Music, News, Sports.

WDKX-FM
683 EAST MAIN STREET
ROCHESTER, NY 14605-2740
585-262-2050
Fax: 585-262-2626
wdkx@wdkx.com
http://www.wdkx.com
• Andre Marcel, Program Director
• Mike Paz, Sports Editor
• Tariq Spence, Sports Director
Description:
Music, News, Sports.

WDLB
1712 NORTH CENTRAL AVENUE
MARSHFIELD, WI 54449
715-384-2191
800-236-1065
Fax: 715-387-3588
www.wdlbwosq.com
• Ken Rajek, General Manager
• Gene Delisio, Sports Director

(715) 384-2191
gene@wdlbwosq.com
• Arnie Peck, Sales Manager
(715) 384-2191
arnie@wdlbwosq.com
• Scott Johnson, Program Director
(715) 384-2191
Nature of Service:
Local over 100 high school events per year.
Year Founded:
1947
Basketball:
Marquette
Football:
NFL doubleheader on Sunday, college
game of the week
Office Address:
1712 North Central Ave, Marshfield, WI
54449.

WDLZ-FM
1714 WEST MAIN STREET
MURFREESBORO, NC 27855-0038
252-398-4111
Fax: 252-398-3581
frankk_00@hotmail.com
• Frank Knapper, Program Director
(252) 398-5688
Description:
Music.

WDNE-FM
WASHINGTON & DAVIS
ELKINS, WV 26241
304-636-1300
Fax: 304-636-2200
wdne@wvradio.com
• Zoe Ludski, News Director
Description:
Music, News, Sports.

WDOE-AM/FM
P.O. BOX 209
DUNKIRK, NY 14048-0209
716-366-1410
Fax: 716-366-1416
http://chautauquatoday.com
• Dan Palmer, Sports Director
dan@WDOE1410.com
• David Rowley, News Director
news@wdoe1410.com
Description:
Music, News, Sports, Talk.

WDOG-FM
2447 AUGUSTA HIGHWAY
ALLENDALE, SC 29810-0442
803-584-3500
Fax: 803-584-0202
wdog935@aol.com
http://www.wdog.fm
• Carl Gooding, Station Manager
wdog93@aol.com
Description:
Music.

WDOR-FM
P. O. BOX 549
STURGEON BAY, WI 54235
920-743-4411
Fax: 920-743-2334
• Roger Levendusky, News Director
(920) 743-4411
roger@wdor.com
• Chad Michaels, Sports Director
(920) 743-4411

chad@wdor.com
• Eddy Allen, General Manager
(920) 743-4411
eddy@wdor.com
Description:
Music, News, Sports, Talk.
Year Founded:
1947

WDOW-AM
26914 MARCELLUS HIGHWAY
DOWAGIAC, MI 49047-7444
269-782-5106
Fax: 269-782-5107
q92radio@yahoo.com
http://www.wdow.net
• Joe Jason, General Manager
Description:
Music, News, Sports.

WDPN-AM
393 SMYTH AVENUE NE
ALLIANCE, OH 44601-1562
330-821-1111
800-743-9293
Fax: 330-821-0379
• Charlotte Franko, Promotions Manager
• Clint Marshall, News Director
clint@q92radio.com
Description:
Music.

WDSL-AM
431 EATON ROAD
MOCKSVILLE, NC 27028-2582
336-751-9375
Fax: 336-751-5025
wdsl1520am@yahoo.com
• Garry Tilley, News Director
wdslradio@hotmail.com
Description:
Music, News, Sports.

WDSM SPORTS RADIO 710
715 E. CENTRAL ENTRANCE
DULUTH, MN 55811
218-722-4321
Fax: 218-722-5423
• Mark Fleischer, Sports Director/Program
Director
Nature of Sports Service:
News and sports radio programming.
College Sports:
Basketball - Univ of Wisconsin, Basketball &
Football.
Football:
NFL - Green Bay Packers.

WDSM-AM
715 EAST CENTRAL ENTRANCE
DULUTH, MN 55811-5596
218-722-4321
800-388-2428
Fax: 218-722-5423
http://www.wdsm.am/
• Roxanne Charles, General Manager
(218) 722-4321
• Mark Fleischer, Program/Sports Director
(218) 722-4321
• Dave Strandberg, News Director
(218) 722-4321
kdalnews@mwcradio.com
Description:
News, Sports.

WDUN-AM
P.O. BOX 10
GAINESVILLE, GA 30501-1706
770-532-9921
800-552-9386
Fax: 770-532-0506
http://www.wdun.com
• Jeff Hart, Sports Director
• John W. Jacobs, III, Owner
• Judd Hickinbotham, News/Sports Anchor
(770) 532-9921
Description:
Music, News, Talk.

WDUX-AM/FM
200 TOWER ROAD
WAUPACA, WI 54981
715-258-5528
Fax: 715-258-7711
mail@wdux.net
• Jack Barry, News/Sports Director
wdux@waupacaonline.net
Description:
Radio station broadcasting sports.

WDUX-FM
200 TOWER ROAD
WAUPACA, WI 54981
715-258-5528
Fax: 715-258-7711
wduxnews@waupacaonline.net
• Jack Barry, News Director
wdux@waupacaonline.net
• Jack Barry, Sports Director
wdux@waupacaonline.net
Description:
Educational, Music, News.

WDZN-FM
220 PACA STREET
CUMBERLAND, MD 21502
301-724-6000
Fax: 301-724-0617
http://www.disney.com
• Warren Gregory, Owner
(301) 724-0001
• Robin Jones, Program Director
(818) 955-6761
Description:
Music, News, Sports.

WEAI-FM
2161 OLD STATE ROAD, E.
JACKSONVILLE, IL 62650-6380
217-245-7171
Fax: 217-245-6711
weai@weai.com
http://www.weai.com
• Jerry Symons, Sports Director
• Gary Scott, General Manager
gscott@wlds.com
Description:
Music, News, Sports. Music format with
extensive coverage of Cardinal baseball and
over 270 local games a year.
Sports Discussed:
Cards-local
Frequency:
107.1

WEAQ-AM
944 HARLEM AVENUE
ALTOONA, WI 54720-1127
715-832-1530
800-866-9299
Fax: 715-832-5329

• Dave Craig, Sports Director
• Dan Lea, News Director
Description:
Music.

WEAS-FM
214 TELEVISION CIRCLE
SAVANNAH, GA 31406-4519
912-961-9000
888-567-0102
Fax: 912-961-7070
http://www.e93.com
• Lydis Syed, Advertising Manager
(912) 961-9000
Description:
Music, News, Sports.

WEDM-FM
9651 EAST 21ST STREET
INDIANAPOLIS, IN 46229-1706
317-532-6301
Fax: 317-532-6199
• Daniel J. Henn, General Manager
Description:
Music, News, Sports.

WEDO-AM
1985 LINCOLN WAY
MCKEESPORT, PA 15131
412-664-4431
Fax: 412-664-1236
• William Korch, News Director
bill@am81wedo.com
Description:
Music, News, Sports, Talk.

WEEB-AM
1650 MIDLAND ROAD
SOUTHERN PINES, NC 28388
910-692-7440
Fax: 910-692-7372
steve@weeb990.com
http://www.weeb990.com
• Steve Adams, News/Sports Director
Description:
News, Talk.

WEEI SPORTS RADIO
20 GUEST ST, THIRD FL
Brighton, MA 02135-2040
617-779-3500
Fax: 617-779-3557
www.weei.com
• Jim Rushton, Advertising
• Kerry Collins, Promotions
• Beverly Tilden, Integrated Marketing
Director

WEEO-AM
37 SOUTH MAIN STREET
CHAMBERSBURG, PA 17201
717-709-0801
Fax: 717-709-0802
Description:
Music.

WEEU-AM
34 NORTH 4TH STREET
READING, PA 19601-3943
610-376-7335
800-323-8800
Fax: 610-376-7756
weeu@weeu.com
http://www.weeu.com

• Mitch Gerhart, Sports Director
mgerhart@weeu.com
• Paul Roberts, Sports Talk Show Host
proberts@weeu.com
Description:
Talk, News, Sports.
Sports Discussed:
All Philadelphia Eagles and Phillies affiliate
Frequency:
830 AM

WEEX-AM
107 PAXINOSA ROAD, W.
EASTON, PA 18040
610-258-6155
Fax: 610-258-6292
http://www.espnlv.com
• Tom Fallon, Program Director
(610) 829-5528
• K. J. Zabali, Promotion Manager
Description:
Music.

WEIU-FM
600 LINCLON AVENUE
CHARLESTON, IL 61920
217-581-6116
Fax: 217-581-6650
hitmix@weiu.net
• Jeff Owens, Program/Sports Director
(217) 581-6954
jeff@weiu.net
Description:
Educational, Music, News, Sports, Talk.

WEJL-AM
149 PENN AVENUE
SCRANTON, PA 18503-2022
570-346-6555
Fax: 570-346-6038
http://www.wejl-wbax.com/main.htm
• Ruth Miller, News Director
(570) 207-8583
Description:
Music, News, Sports.

WEKS-FM
1523 KELL LANE SUITE 1
GRIFFIN, GA 30224-8878
770-412-8700
Fax: 770-412-8080
http://www.bear92.com
• Carl Pruett, Advertising Sales
• Chuck Tarkinton, Sports Director
• Stan Watson, Promotion Director
• Wanda Wilson, Office Manager

WEKT-AM
P.O. BOX 577
ELKTON, KY 42220-0577
270-265-5636
Fax: 270-265-5637
• Marshall Sidebottom, General/Advertising
Manager
wektam1070@yahoo.com
Description:
Music, News, Sports.

WEKX-FM
522 MAIN STREET
WILLIAMSBURG, KY 40769-1127
606-549-1027
Fax: 606-549-5565
wekx@bellsouth.net
http://www.hit102fm.com
• Rick Campbell, Program Director

media

WELM-AM
1705 LAKE STREET
ELMIRA, NY 14901-1220
607-733-5626
Fax: 607-733-5627
• E. D. Crum, Advertising Manager
(607) 733-5626
• Mike Jacobs, News Director
• Bob Michaels, Sports Director
(607) 733-5626
• Donna Van Debogart, Promotions
Manager
(607) 733-5626
Description:
Music, News, Sports.

WELW-AM
PO BOX 1330
WILLOUGHBY, OH 44096
440-946-1330
888-769-1330
Fax: 440-953-0320
http://www.welw.com
Description:
Talk and sports events
Sports Discussed:
Local high school and collegiate game
coverage; Lake County Captains minor
league baseball coverage

WEMJ-AM
COUNTRY CLUB ROAD VILLAGE W.
GILFORD, NH 03247
603-524-1323
Fax: 603-528-5185
• Allan Harrison, News/Programming
Director
Description:
Sports, Talk.

WENE
320 NORTH JENSEN ROAD
VESTAL, NY 13850
607-584—5800
Fax: 607-584-5900
http://1430theteam.com
• Jon Scaptura, Program Director
jonscaptura@clearchannel.com
• Joanne Aloi, General Manager
joannealoi@clearchannel.com
• Jim Free, Operations Manager
jimfree@clearchannel.com
• Michele Page Vojtisek, Sales Manager
(607) 584-5800
Year Founded:
1947
Frequency:
1430 KHz.
Primary Audience:
Men 25-54.
Baseball:
MLB - New York Yankees

WENG
PO BOX 1908
ENGLEWOOD, FL 34295
941-474-3231
888-434-1530
Fax: 941-475-2205
kenb@wengradio.com
www.wengradio.com
• Ken Birdsong, General Manager
• Rich Spedaliere, Sports Director
• Kyle Turner, Program Director
Nature of Sports Service:
News, Sports.
Basketball:

Orlando Magic
College Sports:
Basketball; Football - Florida State
University, Miami University, Notre Dame
University.
Football:
NFL - Tampa Bay Buccaneers, Miami
Dolphins.

WENK-AM
1729 NAILLING DRIVE
UNION CITY, TN 38261-2003
731-885-1240
Fax: 731-885-3405
http://www.1240wenk.com
• Robin Francis, Sports Director
(731) 885-1240
• Terry Hailey, Advertising
Manager/Program Director
Description:
Music, Talk.

WEPG-AM
105 NORTH ASH AVENUE
SOUTH PITTSBURG, TN 37380
423-837-8001
Fax: 423-837-8002
• Will Rodgers, News Director
willthevoiceman@aol.com
• Charles Rodgers, Owner
Description:
Music, News, Sports.

WERQ-FM
1705 WHITEHEAD ROAD
BALTIMORE, MD 21207
410-332-8200
Fax: 410-944-7182
http://www.92q.com
• Latoya Dixon, Promotions Director
(410) 907-0368
ladixson@radio-one.com
• Victor Starr, Program Director
(410) 332-8200
vstarr@radio-one.com
Description:
Music, News, Sports.

WEST-AM
436 NORTHAMPTON STREET
EASTON, PA 18042
610-258-9378
Fax: 610-250-9675
westnews1@verizon.net
http://www.am1400west.net
• Dick Hammer, Sports Director
• Pamela Richetta, Promotion Manager
richetta@verizon.net
Description:
Music, News, Sports.

WEVR-AM
178 RADIO ROAD
RIVER FALLS, WI 54022-8255
715-425-1111
• T. J. Campbell, News Director
Description:
Music, News, Sports.

WEVR-FM
178 RADIO ROAD
RIVER FALLS, WI 54022-8255
715-425-1111
• Carol Hanten, General Manager
Description:
Music, News, Sports.

WFAN SPORTS RADIO
345 HUDSON STREET
10TH FLOOR
NEW YORK, NY 10014
212-314-9200
877-337-6666
www.wfan.com
• Lee Davis, General Manager
• Eric Spitz, Program Director
• Theresa Beyer, Director of Marketing
• Brian Rooney, Promotions Manager
• Thomas Mansusi, General Sales Manager
Nature of Sports Service:
24-hour sports radio programming focusing
on New York metro area teams.
Baseball:
New York Mets
Basketball:
New York Knicks, New Jersey Nets
Football:
New York Giants
Ice Hockey:
New York Rangers, New Jersey Devils

WFAT-FM
6021 SOUTH WESTNEDGE AVENUE
KALAMAZOO, MI 49002
269-327-7600
Fax: 269-327-0726
http://www.wfat.com
• Jim Whelan, News Director
Description:
Music, News, Sports.

WFDF 910AM RADIO
6317 TAYLOR DR
FLINT, MI 48507
810-238-7300
Fax: 810-238-7310
• Nancy Dymond, General Manager
Nature of Sports Service:
News, Sports.
Basketball:
NBA - Detroit Pistons.
College Sports:
Basketball, Football - University of Michigan.
Football:
NFL - Detroit Lions.
Golf:
Local Coverage.

WFEB
1209 MILLERVILLE RD
SYLACAUGA, AL 35150
256-245-3281
Fax: 256-245-3050
• Bruce Carr, General Sales
Manager/Sports Director
Nature of Sports Service:
News, Sports.
Baseball:
MLB - Atlanta Braves.
College Sports:
Baseball, Basketball, Football - University of
Alabama.

WFEB-AM
1209 MILLERVILLE HIGHWAY
SYLACAUGA, AL 35150-0450
256-245-3281
Fax: 256-245-3050
http://www.wfeb1340.com
• Bruce Carr, Sports Director
Description:
Music, News, Sports, Talk.

WFFC-FM
ROUTE 40
FERRUM, VA 24088
800-868-9797
Fax: 540-365-4203
wffc@ferrum.edu
http://www.ferrum.edu/wffc
• Robert Glass, News Director
(800) 868-9797
rglass@ferrum.edu
Description:
Music, News, Sports.

WFFF-AM
P.O. BOX 550
COLUMBIA, MS 39429-0550
601-736-1360
Fax: 601-736-1361
• Ronnie Geiger, Sports Director
Description:
Music, News, Sports.

WFGN-AM
470 LEADMINE ROAD
GAFFNEY, SC 29340-4037
864-489-9430
Fax: 864-489-9440
• Eddie Bridges, Program Director
Description:
Music, News, Sports.

WFHR
645 25TH AVE N.
WISCONSIN RAPIDS, WI 54495
715-424-1300
800-424-9459
Fax: 715-424-1347
• Miles Knuteson, General Manager
• Terry Stake, Sports Director
Office Address:
645 25th Ave. North, Wisconsin Rapids, WI
54495.
Baseball:
MLB - Milwaukee Brewers.
College Sports:
Basketball, Football - University of
Wisconsin.
Football:
NFL - Green Bay Packers.

WFIN RADIO
551 LAKE CASCADES PKWY
FINDLAY, OH 45840
419-422-4545
Fax: 419-422-6736
wfin@wfin.com
www.wfin.com
• Sandra J. Kozlevcar, General Manager
• Chris Miller, Sports Director
Nature of Sports Service:
News.
Baseball:
MLB - Cleveland Indians.
College Sports:
Basketball, Football - Ohio State University.

WFIS-AM
1318 NORTH MAIN STREET
FOUNTAIN INN, SC 29644
864-963-5991
Fax: 864-963-5992
wfis16@aol.com
• Joe Lastringer, President/Sports & News
Director
• David Rich, Advertising Manager
contagioustalk@aol.com

Description:
Music, News, Sports.

WFLF-AM
2500 MAITLAND CENTER PARKWAY
SUITE 401
MAITLAND, FL 32751-4122
407-916-7800
Fax: 407-661-1940
http://www.540wfla.com
• Tom Morgan, Sports Director
tommorgan@clearchannel.com
Description:
News, Talk.

WFMB-AM SPORTS RADIO 1450
3055 S. 4TH ST
SPRINGFIELD, IL 62703
217-528-3033
Fax: 217-528-5348
sportsradio1450@sportsradio1450.com
www.sportsradio1450.com
• Kevin O'Dea, General Manager
• Jeff Hofmann, News Director
Nature of Sports Service:
24-hour sports.
Baseball:
MLB - Chicago Cubs.
Basketball:
NBA - Chicago Bulls.
Football:
NFL - Chicago Bears.

WFMQ-FM
1 CUMBERLAND SQ
LEBANON, TN 37087-3408
615-444-2562
800-467-0562
Fax: 615-444-2569
http://www.cumberland.edu
Description:
Music, News, Sports.

WFNR
7080 LEE HIGHWAY
RADFORD, VA 24141
540-731-6006
Fax: 540-633-2998
www.nrvtoday.com
• Ron Walton, General Manager
• Steve Gore, Sports Editor
• Rick Watson, Sports Director
• Scott Stevens, Program Director
Nature of Sports Service:
Local. Sports, News, Talk.
Auto Sports:
Indianapolis 500; Brick Yard 400.
Baseball:
MLB - Atlanta Braves.
College Sports
Football - University of Virginia.
Football:
NFL - Washington Redskins.

WFNR-AM
7080 LEE HIGHWAY
RADFORD, VA 24141-8503
540-731-6000
Fax: 540-633-2998
• Wes Watson, News Director
(540) 731-6015
Description:
News, Talk.

WFNZ-AM 610 SPORTS RADIO
1520 SOUTH BLVD, STE 300
CHARLOTTE, NC 28203
704-319-9369
Fax: 704-319-3933
www.wfnz.com
• Bill Schoening, General Manager
• DJ Stout, Operations Manager
Nature of Sports Service:
Local. 24-hour sports radio programming.

WFPR-AM
200 EAST THOMAS STREET
HAMMOND, LA 70401-3316
985-345-0060
Fax: 985-345-1110
• Ken Benitez, News Director
(985) 878-2265
Description:
Music, News, Sports, Talk.

WFRD-FM
DARTMOUTH COLLEGE 3RD FLOOR
HANOVER, NH 03755-0957
603-646-3313
Fax: 603-643-7655
wdcr-wfrd@dartmouth.edu
http://www.dartmouth.edu/community/broad
cast/wfrd
• Vikash Reddy, Program Director
Description:
Music, News, Sports.

WFRM-AM
9 SOUTH MAIN STREET
COUDERSPORT, PA 16915
814-274-8600
Fax: 814-274-0760
whks@verizon.net
• Jason Saulter
(814) 274-8600
• Pat Kostur
(814) 642-7004
Description:
Radio station broadcasting High School
sports, locally produced Sports Talk
programming and Pittsburgh Pirates
baseball.

WFRX-AM
1822 NORTH COURT
MARION, IL 62959
618-997-8123
Fax: 618-993-2319
brucefasol@clearchannel.com
http://wfrx-ampet.ip2m.com
• Bruce Fasol, Sports Director
(618) 997-8123
• April Ruebke, News Director
(618) 997-8123
aprilruebke@clearchannel.com
• Art Smith, Advertising Manager
artsmith@clearchannel.com
Description:
Music, News, Sports.

WFSE-FM
COMPTON HALL ROOM 102
EDINBORO, PA 16444
814-732-2641
timothychizmar@yahoo.com
http://www.edinboro.edu/cwis/wfse/
• Randy Schriber, General Manager
eupmetal@hotmail.com
• Rob Smith, Sports Director
wfsepsadept@hotmail.com

media

Description:
Music, News, Sports.

WFTG-AM
534 TOBACCO ROAD
LONDON, KY 40743
606-864-2148
Fax: 606-864-0645
• Brian Sizemore, News Director
(606) 280-2749
Description:
Music.

WFUV-FM
441 EAST FORDHAM ROAD
BRONX, NY 10458
718-817-4550
Fax: 718-817-5595
thefolks@wfuv.org
http://www.wfuv.org
• Bob Ahrens, Sports Producer
(718) 817-4550
bahrens@wfuv.org
• John Platt, Marketing Director
johnplatt@wfuv.org
• Julianne Welby, News Director
(718) 817-4557
Description:
Music, News, Sports.

WFXE-FM
2203 WYNNTON ROAD
COLUMBUS, GA 31906
706-576-3565
Fax: 706-576-3683
http://www.foxie105.com
• Carlos Williams, Sports Director
Description:
Music.

WFYY-FM
450 STATE ROUTE 204
SELINSGROVE, PA 17870
570-374-8819
800-871-9456
Fax: 570-374-7444
http://www.y106.fm
• Peggy Chamberlain, News Director
(570) 374-5711
maxmedianews@yahoo.com
Description:
Music, News, Sports.

WGAB
1180 MAPLE LANE
NEWBURGH, IN 47630
812-451-2422
• Don Davis, General Manager
• Nick Patrick, Director
Nature of Sports Service:
Local. 24-hour sports radio programming.

WGAD
750 WALNUT ST
GADSDEN, AL 35901
256-546-1611
Fax: 256-547-9062
www.wgad.com
• Mike McGowan, General Manager
(256) 546-1611
mike@wgad.com
• Angie Strawn, General Sales Manager
(256) 546-1611
angie@wgad.com
• Scott Chambers, News Director

(256) 546-1611
scott@wgad.com
Nature of Service:
News, Talk, Sports.
Primary Audience:
Adults 25-64.
Sports:
Braves Baseball, Alabama
Football/Basketball, High School Football.

WGAD-AM
PO BOX 1350
GADSDEN, AL 35902-1350
256-546-1611
Fax: 256-547-9062
http://www.wgad.com
• Dave Hedrick, President
(256) 546-1611
dhedrick@wgad.com
• Mike Hathcock, Sports Director
(256) 546-1611
Description:
Music, News, Sports, Talk.

WGAI-AM
PO BOX 1408
ELIZABETH CITY, NC 27906-1408
252-335-4371
Fax: 252-441-8063
• Mike Smith, General Manager
(252) 449-6074
mikesmith@beach104.com
Description:
Music, News, Sports, Talk.

WGAN
420 WESTERN AVE
SOUTH PORTLAND, ME 04106
207-774-4561
Fax: 207-774-3788
• Cary Pahigian, General Manager
• Doug Tribou, Program Director
Nature of Sports Service:
News, Talk, Sports.

WGAN-AM
420 WESTERN AVENUE
SOUTH PORTLAND, ME 04106
207-774-4561
Fax: 207-774-3788
http://www.56wgan.com
• Jeff Wade, Program Director
jwade@portlandradiogroup.com
Description:
News, Talk.

WGAP-AM
517 WATT ROAD
KNOXVILLE, TN 37933
865-675-4105
Fax: 865-675-4859
• Alex Carroll, Advertising Manager
• Brian Tatum, News Director
Description:
Music, News, Sports.

WGAW-AM
362 GREEN STREET 362 GREEN STREET
GARDNER, MA 01440
978-632-1332
Fax: 978-630-3011
http://www.1340.com
• Chris Thompson, General Manager
(978) 630-8700
Description:
Music.

WGBK-FM
4000 WEST LAKE AVENUE
GLENVIEW, IL 60025
847-486-4487
Fax: 847-486-4439
oswald@gbsradio.com
http://www.glenbrook.k12.il.us/gbsbro/wgbkhome.htm
• Daniel Oswald, General Manager
Description:
Educational, Music.

WGCM-AM
10250 LORRAINE ROAD
GULFPORT, MS 39503
228-896-5500
Fax: 228-896-0458
gwen@kicker108.com
• Pat McGowan, Program Director
pat@coast102.com
Description:
Music, News, Sports.

WGCY-FM
607 SOUTH SANGAMON AVENUE
GIBSON CITY, IL 60936-1720
217-784-8661
888-784-9429
Fax: 217-784-8677
• Jim Killian, News Director
jimkillian@hotmail.com
Description:
Music, News, Sports.

WGET
1560 FAIRFIELD RD
GETTYSBURG, PA 17325
717-334-3101
Fax: 717-334-5822
www.wget.com
• Cindy Ford, General Manager
• Dave Jackson, Sports Director
Nature of Sports Service:
Country Music, Sports.
Baseball:
MLB - Philadelphia Phillies.
College Sports:
Basketball, Football - Penn State University.
Football:
NFL - Washington Redskins.

WGFR-FM
640 BAY ROAD
QUEENSBURY, NY 12804-1408
518-743-2300
Fax: 518-745-1433
http://www.wgfr.org
• Kevin Ankeny, General Manager
(518) 743-2300
Description:
Music, News, Sports.

WGGA-AM
1102 THOMPSON BRIDGE ROAD
GAINESVILLE, GA 30501-1706
770-532-9921
800-552-9386
Fax: 770-532-0506
news@wdun.com
http://am1240wgga.com
• Tony Schiavone, Sports Director
Description:
News, Sports, Talk.

WGH-AM THE SCORE
5589 GREENWICH RD, STE 200
VIRGINIA BEACH, VA 23462
757-497-1310
Fax: 757-671-1010
• William Whitlow, General Manager
• Tony Mercurio, Program Director
• Jason Baker, Sports Sales
• Greg Hastings, Promotions
• Tony Mercurio, Sports Director
Nature of Sports Service:
Local. 24-hour sports radio programming.

WGHB-AM
PIRATE RADIO 1250 & 930
PO BOX 3333
GREENVILLE, NC 27836
252-317-1250
Fax: 252-753-4122
http://www.pirateradio1250.com
• Wes Hines, News Director
Description:
Music, News, Sports.

WGHT-AM
1878 LINCOLN AVENUE
POMPTON LAKES, NJ 07442-1611
973-839-1500
Fax: 973-839-2400
http://www.ghtradio.com
• Jonathan Fass, Sports Director
• John Silliman, President
info@wghtradio.com
• Debra Valentine, News Director
(973) 839-2424
Description:
Music, News, Sports.

WGL-AM
2000 LOWER HUNTINGTON ROAD
FORT WAYNE, IN 46819-1233
260-747-1511
Fax: 260-747-3999
http://www.wgl1250.com
• Dean Jackson, Sports Director
• B.J. Steele, Program Director
Description:
Talk.

WGLU-FM
2447 BEDFORD STREET SUITE 101
JOHNSTOWN, PA 15904-1405
814-534-8975
800-539-9458
Fax: 814-266-9212
http://www.power99online.com
• Mitch Edwards, Sports Director
(814) 534-8975
• Amy Wright, News Director
Description:
Music, News, Sports.

WGLV-FM
140 MAIN STREET
ESSEX JUNCTION, VT 05452
802-878-8885
Fax: 802-879-6835
http://www.thelightradio.net
• Rick McClary, General Manager
Description:
Music, News, Sports.

WGMA-AM
301 WEST MAIN STREET
SPINDALE, NC 28160-1234

828-287-5150
Fax: 828-287-0081
• Neil Murray, News Director
Description:
Music, News, Sports.

WGMN-AM
3807 BRANDON AVENUE
ROANOKE, VA 24018
540-725-1220
Fax: 540-725-1245
wgmn@clearchannel.com
http://www.wgmn.cc
• Steve Curtis, Sports Director
(540) 725-1220
stevecurtis@clearchannel.com
• Aaron Roberts, Program Director

WGN-AM
435 NORTH MICHIGAN AVENUE
CHICAGO, IL 60611-4099
312-222-4730
Fax: 312-222-5165
http://www.wgnradio.com
• Wes Bleed, News Director
wesbleed@wgnradio.com
• Lori Brayer, Marketing Director
• Dave Eanet, Sports Director
(312) 222-2141
• Mike Ferrin, Sports Producer
(312) 222-4730
mikeferrin@wgnradio.com
• Andy Masur, Sports Reporter
(312) 222-5094
andymasur@wgnradio.com
Description:
Music, News, Sports, Talk.

WGNC
1416 SHELBY HWY
CHERRYVILLE, NC 28021
704-435-3297
866-696-5343
Fax: 704-435-1217
netoldies@aol.com
• Calvin Hastings, General Manager/Sales
(704) 435-3297
netoldies@aol.com
• Andy Foster, Sports Director/Music
• Mike Hoyle, Operations Manager/Program Director
• Anna McGinnis, News Director
• Terresa Hastings, Traffic Director
Baseball:
MLB - Atlanta Braves.
College Sports:
Basketball, Football - University of North Carolina.
Football:
NFL - Carolina Panthers.

WGOM-AM
820 SOUTH PENNSYLVANIA STREET
MARION, IN 46953
765-664-7396
Fax: 765-668-6767
http://www.wmri.com
• Jim Brunner, Sports Director
(765) 664-7396
production@wmri.com
• Mike Jenkins, News Director
(765) 664-7396
• David Poehler, Vice President
(765) 664-7396
dpoehler@comtech.com
Description:
News, Sports, Talk.

WGOW-AM
821 PINEVILLE ROAD
CHATTANOOGA, TN 37405-2601
423-756-6141
Fax: 423-266-1652
wgow@wgow.com
http://www.wgow.com/am
• Kevin West, News Director
(423) 756-6141
• Kenneth Yamada, Advertising Sales
Description:
News, Talk.

WGR 55 SPORTS RADIO
500 CORPORATE PKWY, STE 200
AMHERST, NY 14226
716-843-0060
Fax: 716-832-3080
www.wgr55.com
• Tim Wenger, Operations Manager
• Bob Gaughan, Sports Director
• Andrea Glinski, Promotions Director
Nature of Sports Service:
24 Hour Sports.

WGRE-FM
609 SOUTH LOCUST STREET
GREENCASTLE, IN 46135-2047
765-658-4642
Fax: 765-658-4693
• Wes Anderson, Sports Director
• Lisa Chambers, News Director
Description:
Music, News, Sports.

WGRM-AM
1110 WRIGHT STREET
GREENWOOD, MS 38930
662-453-1240
Fax: 662-453-1241
• Tony Byrd, News Director
lmwh@netdoor.com
Description:
Music, News, Sports.

WGRM-FM
1110 WRIGHT STREET
GREENWOOD, MS 38930
662-453-1240
Fax: 662-453-1241
• Tony Byrd, News Director
Description:
Music, News, Sports.

WHAI-FM/WPVQ
81 WOODWARD ROAD
GREENFIELD, MA 01301
413-774-4301
Fax: 413-773-5637
www.whai.com
• Hugh Maffey, News Director
• Jeff Tirrell, Sports Director
(413) 774-4301
jtirrell@whai.com
Description:
Music, News, Sports.

WHAN-AM
11337 ASHCAKE ROAD
ASHLAND, VA 23005-0148
804-798-1010
Fax: 804-798-7933
info@whan1430.com
http://www.whan1430.com
• Skip Andrews, Program Director
skip@whan1430.com

media

• Bill Roberts, Advertising Manager
bill@whan1430.com
Description:
Music, News, Sports.

WHB-AM
6721 WEST 121ST STREET
OVERLAND PARK, KS 66209
913-344-1500
Fax: 913-344-1599
http://www.810whb.com
• Todd Leabo, News Director/Sports VP
toddleabo@810whb.com
Description:
Music, News, Sports, Talk.

WHBC-FM
550 MARKET AVENUE SOUTH
CANTON, OH 44702-2112
330-456-7166
Fax: 330-456-7199
pcook@whbc.com
http://www.mix941.com
• Pam Cook, News Director
• Jim Johnson, Sports Director
(330) 456-7166
Description:
Music.

WHBG-AM
130 MEDIA LANE
HARRISONBURG, VA 22801
540-434-0331
Fax: 540-432-0129
http://www.valleyradio.com
• Karl Magenhofer, News Director
news@valleyradio.com
Description:
ESPN Satellite Shows

WHBN-AM
2063 SHAKERTOWN ROAD
DANVILLE, KY 40422
859-236-2711
Fax: 859-236-1461
hometownradio@bellsouth.net
• Steve Bertram, Sports Director
(859) 236-2711
• Samantha Irvin, News Director
• Robert Wagner, Sports Director
Description:
Music, News, Sports.
Sports Discussed:
Local High School Teams and University of
Kentucky
Frequency:
1420

WHBQ SPORTS 56
SPORTS56 WJBQ
6080 MT. MORIAH
MEMPHIS, TN 38115
901-375-9324
888-360-8255
Fax: 901-794-5356
www.sports56whbq.com
• Dave Green, General Manager
Baseball:
MLB - St. Louis Cardinals, Memphis
Redbirds
Basketball:
NBA - Memphis Grizzlies.
College Sports:
Basketball, Football - Ole Miss, Notre Dame
Football

Football:
NFL - Tennessee Titans

WHBU 1240
9821 S. 800 W.
DALEVILLE, IN 47334
765-378-2080
Fax: 765-378-2090
www.whbu.com
• Doug Edge, General Manager
• John Fox, Sports Director
• Mike Michael, Program Director
Nature of Sports Service:
News/Sports.
Baseball:
MLB - Chicago White Sox, Chicago Cubs.
College Sports:
Purdue University - Football, Basketball.

WHBU-AM
9821 SOUTH 800 W.
DALEVILLE, IN 47334
765-378-2080
Fax: 765-378-2090
http://www.indianahoops.com/whbu
• Leland Franklin, Program Director
(765) 378-2080
• Jay Garrison, Sports Director
(765) 288-4403
Description:
News, Sports, Talk.

WHBY-AM
2800 EAST COLLEGE AVENUE
APPLETON, WI 54915-3200
920-733-6639
866-887-1150
Fax: 920-739-0494
whbyam@wcinet.com
http://www.whby.com
• Bill Scott, Sports Director
(920) 831-5646
• Dave Edwards, Talk Host/Program
Director
dedwards@wcinet.com
• Justin Hull, Talk Host
jhull@wcinet.com
Description:
Talk.
Sports Discussed:
Football, Baseball, basketball, hockey, golf -
most all
Frequency:
1150 AM

WHCC-FM
304 STATE ROAD 446
BLOOMINGTON, IN 47401-8837
812-336-8000
Fax: 812-336-7000
whcc105@whcc105.com
http://www.whcc105.com/
• Jeremy Gray, Sports/News Director
vina4pres04@yahoo.com
• Sheila Stephen, Promotions Director
Description:
Music, News.

WHCY-FM
45 MITCHELL AVENUE
FRANKLIN, NJ 07416
973-827-2525
Fax: 973-827-2135
http://www.max1063.com

• Alexandra Vallejo, News Director
(973) 823-6170
alexandravallejo@clearchannel.com
Description:
Music, News, Sports.

WHDL-AM
3163 NEW YORK STATE, ROUTE 417
OLEAN, NY 14760-1853
716-372-0161
800-877-9749
Fax: 716-372-0164
• Dick Hannon, Advertising Manager
• Gary Nease, Sports/News Director
wpig.production@bybradio.com
Description:
Music.

WHEN
500 PLUM ST, STE 100
SYRACUSE, NY 13204
315-472-9797
Fax: 315-472-2323
www.sybercuse.com/when
• Joel Delmonico, General Manager
• Ted Deluca, Sports Director
Nature of Sports Service:
24-hour sports.
Baseball:
MLB - New York Yankees; Minor League -
International League/AAA - Syracuse
SkyChiefs.
College Sports:
Basketball, Football, Ice Hockey - Syracuse
University.
Football:
NFL - New York Jets.

WHHB-FM
370 HOLLIS ST
HOLLISTON, MA 01746-1135
508-429-0681
http://www.whhb.com
• Chris Murphy, Advisor
(508) 429-0677
Description:
Music, News, Sports.

WHHS-FM
200 MILL ROAD
HAVERTOWN, PA 19083-3718
610-446-7111
Fax: 610-853-5952
http://www.whhs.org
• Gail Dornenberg, Sports Director
(610) 446-7111
• Kristy Jost, News Director
Description:
Educational, Music, News, Sports, Talk.

WHIP-AM
2432 HIGHWAY 115
MOORESVILLE, NC 28115-0600
704-664-9447
Fax: 704-664-5551
• Gary Trexler, News Director
Description:
Music, News, Sports.

WHIT
2740 SKI LANE
MADISON, WI 53713
608-273-1000
Fax: 608-271-8182
• Tom Walker, General Manager
• John Sylvester, Operations Manager

Program Director
• Chris Krok, Promotions Manager
Nature of Sports Service:
Local. 24-hour sports.

WHKS-AM
42 NORTH MAIN STREET
PORT ALLEGANY, PA 16743
814-642-7004
Fax: 814-642-9491
whks@verizon.net
Description:
Varsity sports, Music, News, Talk

WHOC-AM
1016 WEST BEACON STREET
PHILADELPHIA, MS 39350-3204
601-656-1490
Fax: 601-656-1491
wwslfm@yahoo.com
• Joe Vines, Advertising Manager/News &
Sports Director
(601) 656-7102
Description:
Music.

WHOL-AM
1125 COLORADO STREET
ALLENTOWN, PA 18103
610-434-4801
Fax: 484-223-0088
• Alfa Lopez, News Director
(610) 434-4081
Description:
Full Service, Music, News.

WHTC-AM
87 CENTRAL AVENUE
HOLLAND, MI 49423
616-392-3121
Fax: 616-392-8066
http://www.whtc.com
• Gary Stevens, News Director
Description:
Music, News, Sports, Talk.

WHTG-AM
2355 WEST BANGS AVENUE
NEPTUNE, NJ 07753-4111
732-918-1000
Fax: 732-774-4974
http://www.g1063.com
• John Dzuiba, General Manager
(732) 774-4755
johnd@g1063.com
Description:
Music, News, Sports.

WHTG-FM
2355 WEST BANGS AVENUE
NEPTUNE, NJ 07753-4111
732-774-4755
Fax: 732-774-7315
http://www.g1063.com
• Chris Brown, Promotions Director
• Keith Rella, News Director
(732) 774-4755
Description:
Music, News, Sports.

WHTK
207 MIDTOWN PLAZA
ROCHESTER, NY 14604

585-454-4884
Fax: 585-454-5081
www.wham1180.com
• Ken Spitger, General Manager
• Bob Mathews, Sports Director
Nature of Sports Service:
Local. Talk, Sports.
Baseball:
Minor League - International
League/AAA/Rochester Red Wings.
College Sports:
Football - Notre Dame University.

WHTK-AM
207 MIDTOWN PLAZA
ROCHESTER, NY 14604-2016
585-454-3942
Fax: 585-454-5081
• Randy Gorbman, News Director
(585) 454-3942
• Jeff Howlett, General Manager
(585) 454-3942
jeffhowlett@clearchannel.com
Description:
Talk.

WHTL-FM
PO BOX 66
WHITEHALL, WI 54773
715-538-4341
800-823-9485
Fax: 715-538-4360
marty@whtlradio.com
• Marty Little, Program/Sports Director
(715) 538-4341
Description:
Music.

WHTQ-FM
4192 JOHN YOUNG PARKWAY
ORLANDO, FL 32804-2620
407-422-9890
Fax: 407-291-4879
http://www.whtq.com
• Wes Halliwell, Promotion Manager
(321) 281-2053
wes.halliwell@coxradio.com
Description:
Music, News, Sports.

WHYN-AM
1331 MAIN STREET
SPRINGFIELD, MA 01103-1669
413-781-1011
Fax: 413-734-4434
johnbaicak@clearchannel.com
http://www.whyn.com
• John Baibak, News Director
(413) 781-1011
johnbaibak@clearchannel.com
Description:
News, Talk.

WIBC
40 MONUMENT CIRCLE
INDIANAPOLIS, IN 46204
317-266-9422
888-240-6397
Fax: 317-684-2021
www.wibc.com
• Tom Severino, General Manager
Football:
NFL - Indianapolis Colts.

WIBM-AM
1700 GLENSHIRE DRIVE
JACKSON, MI 49201-8302
517-787-9546
Fax: 517-787-7517
http://www.wkhm.com
• Marc Daly, Program Director
• Bruce Goldsen, Owner
bgoldsen@k1053.com
Description:
Music, News.

WIBN-FM
P.O. BOX 25
OXFORD, IN 47971-0025
765-385-2373
Fax: 765-385-2374
http://www.981wibn.com
• John Balvich, General Manager
(765) 385-2373
• Chris Wagner, Sports Director
(765) 385-2373
chriswagner@981wibn.com
Description:
Music, News, Sports.

WIBR
650 WOODALE BLVD
BATON ROUGE, LA 70806
225-926-1106
Fax: 225-928-1606
• Don Nelson, General Manager
• Charles Hanagriff, Sports Director
Nature of Sports Service:
24-hour sports.
Baseball:
MLB - Houston Astros.
College Sports:
Football, CBS; Basketball - Southeastern
Louisiana.
Football:
NFL - CBS Game of the Week.

WIBW AM 580 RADIO
1210 EXECUTIVE DR
TOPEKA, KS 66615
785-272-3456
Fax: 785-228-7282
• Craig Colboch, General Manager
• Greg Sharpe, Program Director/Sports
• Ed O'Donnell, Operations Director
Nature of Sports Service:
Fox Sports Radio.
Baseball:
MLB - Kansas City Royals.

WICK-AM
1049 NORTH SEKOL ROAD
SCRANTON, PA 18504-1040
570-344-1221
Fax: 570-344-0996
http://www.wick-am.com
• Dean Corwin, News Director
• Mike Remish, Sports Director
Description:
Music.

WICO-AM
919 ELLEGOOD STREET
SALISBURY, MD 21801
410-219-3500
Fax: 410-548-1543
http://www.wicoam.com
• Bill Reddish, News Director
billr@radiocenter.com

Description:
News, Talk.

WIGG-AM
959 NORTH MAGNOLIA DRIVE
WIGGINS, MS 39577-3630
601-928-7281
Fax: 601-528-5011
• A. R. Byrd, Advertising Manager
• Tony Coslik, Assignment Editor
Description:
Music, News, Sports.

WIKC-AM
PO BOX 638
BOGALUSA, LA 70427-2229
504-732-4190
Fax: 504-732-7594
• Gardner S. Adams, Jr., General Manager
timberlands@bellsouth.net
Description:
Music, News, Sports, Talk.

WILD-AM
90 WARREN STREET
BOSTON, MA 02119-3259
617-472-9447
Fax: 617-472-9474
http://www.wildam1090.com
• Rick Anderson, Program Director
(617) 472-9447
randerson@radio-one.com
• Willie Maye, Sports Director
(617) 472-9447
wmaye@radio-one.com
Description:
Music, News, Sports.

WILQ-FM
1685 FOUR MILE DRIVE
WILLIAMSPORT, PA 17701-1938
570-323-8200
800-377-1051
Fax: 570-323-5075
http://www.wilq.com
• John Finn, News Director
Description:
Music, News, Sports.

WILT-AM
22 SIXTH STREET
STROUDSBURG, PA 18360
570-421-2100
800-570-1013
Fax: 570-421-2040
http://www.wilk.microserve.net
• Joe Thomas, News Director
(570) 421-2100
Description:
News.

WIMA-AM
667 WEST MARKET STREET
LIMA, OH 45801
419-223-2060
Fax: 419-229-3888
davewoodward@clearchannel.com
http://www.1150wima.com
• Jeff Gunter, News Director
(419) 223-2060
jeffgunter@clearchannel.com
Description:
News, Talk.

WIMZ-FM
1100 SHARPS RIDGE ROAD
KNOXVILLE, TN 37917
865-525-6000
Fax: 865-525-2000
http://www.wimz.com
• Terry Gillingham, General Manager
(865) 329-8501
terry@sccradio.com
Description:
Music, News, Sports.

WINW-AM
4111 MARTINDALE ROAD, N.E.
CANTON, OH 44705-2727
330-454-3377
Fax: 330-492-5633
• Curtis Perry, General Manager/Promotion
Director
(330) 454-1520
Description:
Music, News, Sports.

WIP SPORTSRADIO 610
441 N. FIFTH ST
PHILADELPHIA, PA 19123
215-922-5000
Fax: 215-922-2434
www.610wip.com
• Marc Rayfield, Vice President/General
Manager
• Tom Bigby, Station Manager/Pro General
Manager
• Jon Latzer, General Sales Manager
• Brian Navy, National Sales Manager
• Will Chapman, Local Sales Manager
Nature of Sports Service:
Local, 24-hour sports radio programming.

WIQB-AM
11640 HIGHWAY 17 BYPASS
MURRELLS INLET, SC 29576
843-651-7869
Fax: 843-651-3197
• Kelly Broderick, Program Director
Description:
Music, News, Sports.

WIRO
134 4TH AVE
HUNTINGTON, WV 25701
304-525-7788
Fax: 304-525-3299
• Judy Jennings-Riffe, General Manager
• Paul Swan, Sports Director
Nature of Sports Service:
Local. 24-hour sports radio programming.

WIRQ-FM
260 COOPER ROAD
ROCHESTER, NY 14617-3049
585-336-3065
Fax: 585-336-2929
• Nick Graveoey, Program Director
finisher@musician.org
Description:
Music, News, Sports.

WIRY-AM
301 CORNELIA STREET
PLATTSBURGH, NY 12901-2308
518-563-1340
Fax: 518-563-1343
wiry@wiry.com
http://www.wiry.com

• Alan Drake, News/Sports Director
• Ann Tarasavage, Advertising Manager
yoe@yoe.com
• Ducky Drake, News Director ; Sports
Director
(518) 563-1340
wiry@wiry.com
Description:
Music, News, Sports.

WISK-FM
1028 ADDERTON STREET
AMERICUS, GA 31709
229-924-6500
Fax: 229-928-2337
http://www.americusradio.com
• Steve Lashley, Promotion Manager
Description:
Music, News, Sports.

WIUS-AM
815 E 8TH ST
BLOOMINGTON, IN 47408-3842
812-855-7862
Fax: 812-855-1073
http://www.wius.org
• Carl Gutierez, News Director
• Bryan Scheets, Sports Director
Description:
Music, News, Sports.

WIVQ-FM
3905 PROGRESS BOULEVARD
PERU, IL 61354
815-224-2100
Fax: 815-224-2066
lacom@theradiogroup.net
• Cole Studstill, Program Director
ostill@theradiogroup.net
• Jared White, Sports Director
jared@theradiogroup.net

WIVV-AM
1409 PONCE DE LEON AVENUE 4TH
FLOOR
SAN JUAN, PUERTO RIC 00907
787-724-1190
Fax: 787-722-5395
radio@therockradio.org
• Ruth Luttrel, General Manager
Description:
Music, News, Sports.

WIXX-FM
P.O. BOX 23333
GREEN BAY, WI 54301
920-435-3771
Fax: 920-444-1155
http://www.wixx.com
• Jerry Bader, News Director
Description:
Music, News, Sports.

WJAG-AM
309 BRAASCH AVENUE
NORFOLK, NE 68701-4113
402-371-0780
Fax: 402-371-6303
http://www.wjag.com/
• Jim Curry, News Director
• Joe Tjaden, Sports Director
jtjaden@wjag.com
Description:
Sports

WJAW-FM
PO BOX 708
MARIETTA, OH 45750
800-371-1490
Fax: 740-373-1717
news@morganco.net
http://www.wjawfm.com
• Andrew Rex, News Director

WJBC
236 GREENWOOD AVENUE
BLOOMINGTON, IL 61704
309-829-1221
Fax: 309-827-8071
newsroom@wjbc.com
www.wjbc.com
• Red Pitcher, General Manager
• Greg Halbleib, Sports Director
• R C McPride, Program Director
Auto Sports:
NASCAR.
Baseball:
MLB - St. Louis Cardinals.
College Sports:
Illinois State and Illinois Wesleyan FB and BB
Football
NFL - Monday Night Football

WJBO-AM
5555 HILTON AVENUE SUITE 500
BATON ROUGE, LA 70808-2564
225-231-1860
Fax: 225-231-1873
http://www.wjbo.com
• Robert Lee, News Director
• Jill Stokold, Promotions Director
Description:
News, Talk.

WJCI-AM
129 NORTH GARRARD
RANTOUL, IL 61866
217-893-1460
Fax: 217-893-0884
• Gary Voss, General Manager
whpo@whporadio.com
Description:
Music, Talk.

WJDB-FM
30280 HIGHWAY 43
THOMASVILLE, AL 36784
334-636-4438
800-245-9532
Fax: 334-636-4439
• Ivey Griffin, Marketing/Advertising Manager
wjdbradio@yahoo.com
Description:
Music, News, Sports.

WJDK-FM
219 WEST WASHINGTON STREET
MORRIS, IL 60450-2146
815-941-1000
Fax: 815-941-9300
• Mike Haensel, News Director
• Larry Nelson, President
(815) 941-1000
Description:
Music, News, Sports.

WJEL-FM
1901 EAST 86TH STREET
INDIANAPOLIS, IN 46240-2347

317-259-5278
• Rob Hendrix, Program Director
(317) 259-5278
Description:
Music, News, Sports.

WJFD-FM, INC.
651 ORCHARD STREET
SUITE 300
NEW BEDFORD, MA 02744
508-997-2929
Fax: 508-990-3893
claudia@wjfd.com
http://www.wjfd.com
• Manuel Calado, News Director
calado@wjfd.com
• Jorge Morais, General Manager
Description:
Music.

WJGA-FM
PO BOX 878
JACKSON, GA 30233
770-775-3151
Fax: 770-775-5153
• Don Earnhart, Sports Director
(770) 775-3151
• Don Earnhart, Sports Director
Description:
Music.

WJJB-AM
779 WARREN AVENUE
PORTLAND, ME 04103-1007
207-773-9695
Fax: 207-761-4406
morningjab@yahoo.com
http://www.bigjab.com
• Dave Shumacher, Program Director
(207) 773-9695
Description:
Talk.

WJJC-AM
153 BILL ANDERSON BOULEVARD
COMMERCE, GA 30529
706-335-3155
Fax: 706-335-1905
http://www.nbank.net/net/~wjjc/
• Rick Bennett, Sports Director
• Rob Jordan, Advertisin Sales/Sports Director

WJJO-FM
2740 SKI LANE
MADISON, WI 53711
608-273-1000
Fax: 608-271-8182
http://www.wjjo.com
• Randy Hawke, Program Director
(608) 441-3705
randy.hawke@wjjo.com
Description:
Music, News, Sports.

WJJQ-AM
81 EAST MOHAWK DRIVE
TOMAHAWK, WI 54487-8618
715-453-4482
Fax: 715-453-7169
wjjq@wjjq.com
http://www.wjjq.wjjq.com
• Gregg Albert, Program Director
galbert@wjjq.com
Description:
ESPN Sports Talk Event.

Year Founded:
1984

WJJT-AM
PO BOX 88
230 N FLORENCE AVE
JELLICO, TN 37762
423-494-1582
Fax: 423-784-5991
wjjtradio@gmail.com
www.jellicosgospellight.com
• James Kilgore, President & CEO
(423) 494-1582
• John Blankenship, Jr., General Manager
(606) 524-5123
johnsjsclean@gmail.com
Description:
Gospel music, news, sports and weather

WJOX-AM SPORTS RADIO
244 GOODWIN CREST DR
BIRMINGHAM, AL 35209
205-945-4646
Fax: 205-945-3999
• Terry Bond, General Manager
• Don Leo, Sports Director
Nature of Sports Service:
Local. 24-hour sports radio programming.
Baseball:
MLB - Atlanta Braves.
College Sports:
Baseball, Basketball, Football - Auburn University.

WJPF-AM
1431 COUNTRY AIRE DRIVE
CARTERVILLE, IL 62918-5118
618-985-4955
800-455-3243
Fax: 618-985-5904
http://www.wjpf.com
• Mike Reis, Sports Director
(618) 985-4955
• Steve Sine, News Director
• Mike Murphy, Sports Host
(618) 985-4955
mikemu@riverradio.net
Description:
Music, News, Talk.

WJPZ-FM
316 WAVERLY AVENUE
SYRACUSE, NY 13210-2437
315-443-4689
Fax: 315-443-2148
http://www.z89.org
• Joan Kump, Promotions Director
(315) 443-4689
promotions@v89.com
• Jon Versteeg, News Director
news@z89.com
• Andrew Gundling, Sports Director
(315) 443-4689
Description:
Music, News, Sports.

WJR-AM
3011 WEST GRAND BOULEVARD
DETROIT, MI 48202-9816
313-875-4440
800-859-0957
Fax: 313-875-9022
http://www.wjr.com
• Bridget Burns, Promotion Director
• Steve Courtney, Sports Director
(313) 875-4440

swrap760@hotmail.com
• Dick Haefner, News Director
(313) 873-9850
• Bob Schick, Advertising Sales
(313) 873-9752
• Jim Brandstatter, Sports
(313) 875-4440
Description:
Music, News, Sports.

WJRS-FM
P.O. BOX 800
JAMESTOWN, KY 42629-0800
270-343-4444
Fax: 270-866-2060
• Mike Scales, News Director
Description:
Music, News, Sports.

WJTN-AM
2 ORCHARD ROAD, WEST ELLICOTT
JAMESTOWN, NY 14701-8400
716-487-1151
800-879-7393
Fax: 716-664-9326
http://www.wjtn.com
• Matt Krieg, Sports Director
(716) 487-1151
• Merrill Rosen, General Manager
(716) 487-1151
Description:
Music, News, Sports.

WJUN-AM
OLD ROUTE 22 EAST
MEXICO, PA 17056
717-436-2135
Fax: 717-436-8155
wjun@acsworld.net
• Dan Roland, News Director
Description:
Music, News, Sports.

WJVL-FM
1 S PARKER DR
JANESVILLE, WI 53545-3928
608-752-7895
Fax: 608-752-4438
http://www.wjvl.com
• Tim Bremel, Promotions Director
(608) 752-7895
• Al Fagerli, Sports Director
(608) 752-7895
sports@wclo.com
• Mike O'Brien, Advertising Manager
mobrien@wclo.com
• Stan Stricker, News Director
news@wclo.com
Description:
Music.

WJVS-FM
3254 EAST KEMPER ROAD
CINCINNATI, OH 45241-1540
513-612-5816
Fax: 513-771-4928
• Dave Angeline, News Director
angelind@greatoaks.com
Description:
Music, News, Sports.

WKAN AM 1320
2 DEARBORN SQUARE
KANKAKEE, IL 60901

815-935-9555
Fax: 815-935-9593
www.wkan.com
• Gary Wright, General Manager
• Wyatt McKinstry, Sports Director
• Brendan Michaels, Operations Manager
Nature of Sports Service:
Local coverage of high school, college and
professional sports.
Auto Sports:
NASCAR
College Sports:
Basketball, Football - University of Illinois.
Football:
NFL - Chicago Bears.

WKAN-AM
70 MEADOW VIEW CENTER SUITE 400
KANKAKEE, IL 60901-3909
815-935-9555
Fax: 815-935-9593
wkan@staradio.com
http://www.wkan.com
• Bob Kersmarki, General Manager
bkersmarki@staradio.com
• Lee Schrock, Sports Director
Description:
Music, News.

WKAV-AM
1150 PEPSI PLACE SUITE 300
CHARLOTTESVILLE, VA 22901
434-978-4408
Fax: 434-978-0723
lindathomas@clearchannel.com
• Tommie McNeil, Jr., News Director
(434) 978-4408
tommiemcneil@clearchannel.com
Description:
Music.

WKBF-AM
3535 EAST KIMBERLY ROAD
DAVENPORT, IA 52807
563-344-7000
Fax: 563-344-7007
markminnick@clearchannel.com
http://www.qconline/wkbf.com
• Mark Minnick, News Director
Description:
Music.

WKBH-AM SPORTS RADIO
1407 SECOND AVE N.
LA CROSSE, WI 54602
608-779-9157
Fax: 608-782-8340
• Pat Delaney, Owner
Nature of Sports Service:
Local. 24-hour sports radio programming.
ESPN Radio.

WKBK-AM
69 STANHOPE AVENUE
KEENE, NH 03431-3641
603-352-9230
Fax: 603-357-3926
http://www.wkbkam.com/
• Bob Lund, Sports Director
(603) 352-9230
sports@wkbkwxod.com
• Paul Scheuring, News Director
(603) 352-9230
pscheuring@monadnockradiogroup.com
Description:
Music, News, Sports, Talk.

WKCL-FM
528 COLLEGE PARK ROAD
LADSON, SC 29456-3328
843-553-5420
Fax: 843-553-0636
• Carl Wiggins, Station Manager
(843) 553-8740
wkcl@msn.com
Description:
Music, News, Sports, Talk.

WKDE-FM
200 FRAZIER ROAD
ALTAVISTA, VA 24517-0390
434-369-5588
Fax: 434-369-1632
info@kdcountry.com
http://www.kdcountry.com
• David Hoehne, Advertising
Manager/Sports Director
• Kenny Shelton, Program
Director/Promotions Manager
• Dave Haney, Sports Director
(434) 369-1055
info@kdcountry.com
Description:
Music, News.

WKEE-FM
134 4TH AVENUE
HUNTINGTON, WV 25701
304-525-7788
800-544-9533
Fax: 304-525-3299
billcornwell@clearchannel.com
• Bill Cornwell, News Director
• Paul Swann, Sports Director
paulswann@clearchannel.com
Description:
Music, News, Sports.

WKEQ
PO BOX 740
SOMERSET, KY 42502
606-678-5151
Fax: 606-678-2026
• Nolan Kenner, General Manager
• Mike Tarter, Station Manager
Office address:
101 First Radio Lane, Somerset KY 42502.
Nature of Sports Service:
Local. 24-hour sports radio programming.
Baseball:
MLB - Cincinnati Reds.

WKGS-FM
207 MIDTOWN PLAZA
ROCHESTER, NY 14604-0840
585-454-4884
Fax: 585-454-5081
http://www.kiss1067.com
• Erick Anderson, Program Director
Description:
Music, News, Sports.

WKHS-FM
25301 LAMBS MEADOW ROAD
WORTON, MD 21678
410-778-4249
Fax: 410-778-3802
• Steve Kramarck, Program Director
Description:
Music, News, Sports.

WKIX-FM
2581 US HIGHWAY 70 WEST
GOLDSBORO, NC 27530-1934
919-736-1699
800-849-9582
Fax: 919-736-3876
info@curtismedia.com
http://www.kixonline.com/
• Thomas Vick, News Director
(919) 736-1699
tvick@curtismedia.com
Description:
Music, News, Sports.

WKJQ-FM 97.3
109 IRON HILL ROAD
PARSONS, TN 38363-0576
731-847-3011
Fax: 731-847-4600
ralphclenney@yahoo.com
• Ralph Clenney, Advertising Manager
ralphclenny@yahoo.com
• Steve Clenney, Program Director
Description:
We are now carrying all our sports on
WKJQ-FM 97.3. We do live broadcasts of
Tennessee Titans Football, U.T. Vols
Football, and local high school Football,
Basketbal, Baseball and Softball.
Year Founded:
1990

WKKJ-FM
45 MAIN STREET, W.
CHILLICOTHE, OH 45601-0244
740-773-3000
800-686-9555
Fax: 740-774-4494
newsroom@wkkj.com
http://www.wkkj.com
• Dan Ramey, Sports Director
(740) 773-3000
danramey@clearchannel.com
• Mike Smith, News/Sports Director
(740) 773-3000
mikesmith2@clearchannel.com
• Tracy Taylor, Advertising Manager
(740) 773-3000
tracytaylor@clearchannel.com
Description:
Music, News.

WKKS-FM
1106 FAIRLANE DRIVE
VANCEBURG, KY 41179-1208
606-796-3031
Fax: 606-796-6186
• Kathy Brown, News Director
Description:
Music, News, Sports.

WKLK-AM
1104 CLOQUET AVENUE
CLOQUET, MN 55720-1620
218-879-4534
888-404-9555
Fax: 218-879-1962
wklk@aol.com
http://www.wklk.com
• Jake Kachinski, News Director
Description:
Music, News, Sports, Talk.

WKLK-FM
1104 CLOQUET AVENUE
CLOQUET, MN 55720-1620

218-879-4534
Fax: 218-879-1962
wklk@aol.com
http://www.wklk.com
• Jake Kachinski, Program Director
Description:
Music, News, Sports.

WKLV-AM
P.O. BOX 192
BLACKSTONE, VA 23824
804-292-4146
800-849-4146
Fax: 804-292-7669
http://bobcatcountryradio.com
• Dennis Royer, General Manager
(804) 292-4146
bobcatcountry@hotmail.com
Description:
Music, News, Sports.

WKNH-FM
KEENE STATE COLLEGE
KEENE, NH 03431-4101
603-358-2734
Fax: 603-358-2131
• John Earl, News Director
(603) 358-2734
info@wknh.org
Description:
Music, News, Sports.

WKNR SPORTS RADIO
1301 EAST 9TH STREET
SUITE 252
CLEVELAND, OH 44114
216-583-9901
Fax: 216-583-9550
www.espncleveland.com
• Dave Urbach, General Manager
• Steve Legerski, Operations Manager
• Larry Gawthrop, General Sales Manager
• Bob Karlovec, Sports Director
• Jason Yarrow, Promotions Director
Nature of Sports Service:
Local. 24-hour sports radio programming.
Baseball:
MLB - Cleveland Indians.

WKNW-AM
1411 ASHMUN STREET
SAULT SAINTE MARIE, MI 49783
906-635-0995
800-866-8255
Fax: 906-635-1216
http://www.30below.com
• Dave Watson, News Director
(906) 632-1400
Description:
Music, News, Talk.

WKRK-AM
427 HILL STREET
MURPHY, NC 28906
828-837-4332
Fax: 828-837-8610
wkrk@1320am.com
http://www.1320am.com
• Tim Radford, Promotion Manager
tim@1320am.com
• Emma Ramsey, Advertising
Manager/News Director
Description:
Music, News, Sports, Talk.

WKRV-FM
P.O. BOX 100
VANDALIA, IL 62471-2810
618-283-2325
Fax: 618-283-1503
wkrv@sbcglobal.net
http://www.vandaliaradio.com
• John Harris, Advertising
Manager/Promotions Director
wkrv@sbcglobal.net
• Todd Stapleton, News & Sports Director
(618) 283-2325
wkrv@sbcglobal.net
Description:
Educational, Music, News, Sports, Talk.

WKUB-FM
2132 U.S. HIGHWAY 84
BLACKSHEAR, GA 31516-0112
912-449-3391
Fax: 912-449-6284
wkub@almatel.net
• Brian Blount, Sports Director

WKVG-AM
P.O. BOX 1474
JENKINS, KY 41537-1474
606-832-4655
Fax: 606-832-4656
• Jean Martin, Advertising Manager
wkvg@verizon.net
Description:
Music, News, Sports.

WKVM-AM
415 CALLE CARBONEL
SAN JUAN, PUERTO RIC 00918-2866
787-751-1018
Fax: 787-758-9967
• Alan Corales, General Manager
(787) 751-1013
Description:
Music, News, Sports.

WKVX-AM
P. O. BOX 39
WOOSTER, OH 44691
330-264-5122
800-833-9211
Fax: 330-264-3571
http://www.wqkt.com
• Mike Breckenridge, Program Director
events@wqkt.com
• Craig Walton, Advertising Manager
• Dan Earich, Sports Announcer
(330) 264-5122
events@wqkt.com
Description:
Music, News, Sports.

WKWF-AM
5450 MACDONALD AVENUE
KEY WEST, FL 33040-5738
305-296-7511
Fax: 305-296-0358
http://www.keysradio.net
• David Harris, General Manager
(305) 852-9085
daveharris@clearchannel.com
Description:
Music, News, Sports.

WKWZ-FM
70 SOUTH WOODS ROAD
SYOSSET, NY 11791-3204

516-364-5746
Fax: 516-364-5737
bigdave5@aol.com
• David Favilla, General Manager
(516) 364-5736
Description:
Music, News, Sports.

WKXQ-FM
108 EAST MAIN STREET
BEARDSTOWN, IL 62618
217-323-1790
800-704-9200
Fax: 217-323-1705
larry.bostwick@gmail.com
http://www.kool92.iscool.net
• Kevin Bonnard, General Manager
• Dean Ross, Sports Director
(217) 322-3396
wkkai@macomb.com
Description:
Music.

WKXW-FM
109 WALTERS AVENUE
TRENTON, NJ 08638-1812
609-771-8181
800-876-9599
Fax: 609-406-7956
http://www.nj1015.com
• Ray Handel, Promotions Director
• Eric Scott, News Director
ericscot@nj1015.com
Description:
Music, News, Sports, Talk.

WKYR-FM
HWY 90 EAST
BURKESVILLE, KY 42717-0340
270-433-7191
Fax: 270-433-7195
wkyr@mchsi.com
• Don Johnson, News Director
Description:
Music, News, Sports.

WKZO-AM
4200 WEST MAIN STREET
KALAMAZOO, MI 49006
269-345-7121
800-742-6590
Fax: 269-345-1436
http://www.wkzo.com
• Laura Lehman, News Director
• William J. Wertz, Vice President
Description:
News, Talk.

WKZS-FM
820 RAILROAD STREET
COVINGTON, IN 47932-1357
765-793-4823
Fax: 765-793-4644
newspsa@aol.com
http://www.kiss1031.com
• Greg Green, News Director/Sports Director
greg@kisscountryradio.com
Description:
Music, News, Sports.

WLAP-AM
2601 NICHOLASVILLE ROAD
LEXINGTON, KY 40503-3307
859-293-0563
Fax: 859-299-9527
http://www.wlap.com

• Karyn Czar, News Director/Reporter
(859) 293-0563
karynczar@clearchannel.com
Description:
News, Talk.

WLBR-AM
ROUTE 72 NORTH
LEBANON, PA 17046
717-272-7651
Fax: 717-274-0161
• Scott Bradley, Sports Director
• Gordon Weise, News Director
Description:
Music.

WLDY-AM
W8746 HIGHWAY 8
LADYSMITH, WI 54848-9565
715-532-5588
Fax: 715-532-7357
wldywjbl@yahoo.com
• Bob Krejcarek, Sports Director
• Jodi Long, News Director
jo_wldy_news@yahoo.com
• Chris Brooks, Station Manager
Description:
Ladysmith High school sports

WLER-FM
112 HOLLYWOOD DRIVE SUITE 203
BUTLER, PA 16001-4917
724-287-5778
Fax: 724-283-3005
newsdesk@bcrnetwork.com
http://www.wbut.com
• Victoria Hinterberger, Advertising Manager
vickih@bcrnetwork.com
• Cathy Martin, News Director
frontdesk@bcrnetwork.com
• Ron Willison, Sports Director
ronw@wbut.com
Description:
Music, News.

WLEY-AM
P.O. BOX 371300
CAYEY, PUERTO RIC 00737-1300
787-758-1300
Fax: 787-738-7744
• Joe Pagan, Station Manager
Description:
Music, News, Sports.

WLFN-AM
1407 2ND AVENUE NORTH
ONALASKA, WI 54650
608-782-8335
Fax: 608-782-8340
• Pat Smith, Station Manager
psmith@lacrosseradiogroup.net
Description:
Music, News, Sports.

WLGC
PO BOX 685
GREENUP, KY 41144
606-473-7377
Fax: 606-473-5086
• Rob Scheibly, General Manager
• Kent Robinson, Sports Director
Office Address:
Suite A, Main & Harrison, Greenup, KY
41144.
Nature of Sports Service:
Local. 24-hour sports radio programming.

College Sports:
Basketball - Game of the Week; Football -
Notre Dame.
Football:
NFL Game of the Week/Westwood One.

WLHT-FM
50 MONROE, NW SUITE 500
GRAND RAPIDS, MI 49503
616-451-4800
Fax: 616-451-0113
http://www.wlht.com
• Bruce Parrott, News/Promotions Director
Description:
Music, News, Sports.

WLKF-AM
404 WEST LIME STREET
LAKELAND, FL 33815
863-682-8184
800-227-9797
Fax: 863-683-2409
news@wpcv.com
http://www.wlkf.com
• Ed Kirkland, Advertising Manager
(863) 682-8184
Description:
Educational, News, Sports, Talk.

WLKL-FM
5001 LAKELAND BLVD.
MATTOON, IL 61938-5209
217-234-5271
Fax: 217-258-6459
• Ken Beno, Sports Director
(217) 234-5271
kbeno@lakeland.cc.il.us
Description:
Music, News, Sports.

WLKR-AM
10327 MILAN ROAD
MILAN, OH 44846
419-668-8151
800-686-9222
Fax: 419-668-9557
www.wlkrradio.com
• Bill Forthofer, Station Manager
• Mike Jeffries, Program Director
• Scott Truxell, News/Sports Director
Description:
News, Sports.
Frequency:
ESPN Radio Network 1510 am

WLKR-FM
10327 MILAN ROAD
MILAN, OH 44846
419-668-8151
800-686-9222
Fax: 419-609-2679
wlkr@accnorwalk.com
http://www.wlkrradio.com
• Scott Truxell, News Director
s.truxell@wkfm.com
Description:
Music, News, Sports.

WLLG-FM
7606 NORTH STATE STREET
LOWVILLE, NY 13367-1318
315-376-7500
Fax: 315-376-8549
sales@themoose.net
http://www.themoose.net

• Brian Best, News Director
(315) 376-7500
Description:
Music, News, Sports.

WLLL-AM
105 WHITE HALL ROAD
LYNCHBURG, VA 24501
434-385-9555
888-224-9809
Fax: 434-385-6073
wlllam930@aol.com
• Fletcher Hubbard, General Manager
(434) 385-4587
wlllam930@aol.com
• Bridgette Marie, Program Director
(434) 385-9555
wlllam930@aol.com
• Savanah Hubbard, Traffic Director
(434) 385-9555
wlllam930@aol.com
Description:
Music, News.
Year Founded:
1996

WLLN-AM
910 MCNEILL STREET 910 MCNEILL
STREET
LILLINGTON, NC 27546
910-893-2811
Fax: 910-893-2811
orlandohenao1@hotmail.com
• Orlando Hemau, Program Director
Description:
Music, News, Sports.

WLLY-AM
210 DEACON STREET
WILSON, NC 27895
252-237-5171
Fax: 252-237-5172
• Wallace Bullock, General Manager
Description:
Music, News, Sports.

WLMD-FM
119 WEST CARROLL STREET
MACOMB, IL 61455
309-833-5561
Fax: 309-833-3460
http://www.radiomacomb.com
• Beau Spencer, Sports Director
• Mike Weaver, News Director

WLOB-AM
779 WARREN AVENUE
PORTLAND, ME 04103-1007
207-773-9695
Fax: 207-761-4406
newstalkwlob@yahoo.com
• J.J. Jeffrey, Program Director
Description:
Music, News.

WLOH-AM
724 SOUTH COLUMBUS STREET
LANCASTER, OH 43130
740-653-4373
Fax: 470-654-7578
http://www.wloh.net
• Arlene Bohach, General Manager
Description:
Music, News, Sports.

WLOW-FM
1 SAINT AUGUSTINE PLACE
HILTON HEAD ISLAND, SC 29928-4717
843-785-9569
800-768-7600
Fax: 843-842-3369
http://www.wlow.com
• Chuck Cannon, Program Director
ccannon@adventureradio.fm
• Michelle Christensen, Marketing Director
(843) 785-9569
mchristensen@adventureradio.fm
Description:
Music, News, Sports, Talk.

WLQM-FM
320 NORTH FRANKLIN STREET
FRANKLIN, VA 23851
757-562-5650
Fax: 757-562-2345
wlqm@wlqmradio.com
http://www.wlqmradio.com
• Peter Clark, News Director
• Johnny Hart, Promotions Manager
• Tim Parsons, Sports Director
Description:
Music.

WLRT-AM
2845 NORTH ARMISTEAD AVENUE SUITE
C
HAMPTON, VA 23666-1657
757-766-9262
800-296-1490
Fax: 757-766-7439
http://www.racetalklive.com
• Chuck Hall, Advertising/General Manager
(757) 766-1960
Description:
Music, News, Sports.

WLSC-AM
4164 MAIN STREET
LORIS, SC 29569
843-756-1183
Fax: 843-756-0548
wlscradio@yahoo.com
www.wlsradio.com
• Jerry D. Jenrette, Program Director
Description:
Music, News, Sports, Talk.

WLTP-AM
6006 GRAND CENTRAL AVENUE
VIENNA, WV 26105
304-295-6070
Fax: 304-295-4389
http://www.wltp.com
• Steve Dougherty, Sports Director
(304) 295-6070
stevedougherty@clearchannel.com
• Lorri Ellman, Advertising Manager
(304) 295-6070
lorriellman@clearchannel.com
• Doug Hess, News Director
(304) 295-6070
douglashess@clearchannel.com

WLUR-FM
WEST WASHINGTON STREET
LEXINGTON, VA 24450-0303
540-458-4017
Fax: 540-458-4079
http://www.wlu.edu/~wlur
• Jeremy Franklin, Program Director
franklinj@wlu.edu

Description:
Music, News, Sports, Talk.

WLW
1111 ST. GREGORY ST
CINCINNATI, OH 45202
513-241-9597
Fax: 513-665-9700
www.700wlw.com
• Mike Kenney, General Manager
• Tom Horan, Vice President/Sports
Marketing
Nature of Sports Service:
News.
Baseball:
MLB - Cincinnati Reds.
College Sports:
Football - University of Cincinnati;
Basketball - University of Cincinnati, Xavier.

WMAM-AM
2880 ROOSEVELT ROAD, N.
MARINETTE, WI 54143
715-735-6631
Fax: 715-732-0125
http://www.quicksilverbroadcasting.com
• Kit Donaldson, Sports Director
Description:
Talk.

WMBA 1460
1316 7TH AVENUE
BEAVER FALLS, PA 15010
724-846-4100
Fax: 724-843-7771
• Donn Wuycik, General Manager
• Jim Frederick, Sports Director
Nature of Sports Service:
News/Sports.
Baseball:
MLB - Pittsburgh Pirates.
Ice Hockey:
NHL - Pittsburgh Penguins.

WMBE-AM AND WCLB
254 WINNEBAGO DRIVE
FOND DU LAC, WI 54935-2447
920-921-1071
Fax: 920-921-0757
• Chuck Freimund, Sports Director
(920) 921-1071
• Randy Hopper, General Manager
(920) 921-1071
rhopper@kfiz.com
• Mark Kastein, Station Manager
(920) 921-1071
• Bob Nelson, News Director
(920) 921-1071
bnelson@kfiz.com
• Ed Mueller, Sales
(920) 921-1071
Description:
Music, News, Sports.

WMCE-FM
501 EAST 38TH STREET
ERIE, PA 16546-0002
814-824-2261
Fax: 304-472-2571
• William Shannon, Advertising Sales
Manager/Program Director
(814) 824-2264
wshannon@mercyhurst.edu
• Steve Warzala, Sports Director
swarzala@mercyhurst.edu

media

Media: Sports Radio Stations

WMCR-FM
237 GENESEE STREET
ONEIDA, NY 13421-2701
315-363-6050
Fax: 315-363-9149
• Todd Emanuelli, Sports Director
wwmcrradio@aol.com
• Vivian Warren, General Manager
Description:
Music.

WMEB-FM
5748 MEMORIAL UNION WMEB FM
ORONO, ME 04469-5748
207-581-4340
Fax: 207-581-4343
www.umaine.edu/wemb
• Mathew Avery, Promotions Director
• Ben Jarvela, Promotion Director
benjamin.jarvela@umit.maine.edu
• Alfred Schulz, Program Director
alfred.schulz@umit.maine.edu
• Dustin Son, Sports Director
dustin.son@umit.maine.edu
Description:
Music, News, Sports.

WMEV-FM
1041 RADIO HILL ROAD
MARION, VA 24354
276-783-3151
800-653-3694
Fax: 276-783-3152
http://www.fm94.com
• Jim Mabe, Promotions Director
supercountry@fm94.com
• Lynn Rutledge, Program Director
lynnr@fm94.com
Description:
Music, News, Sports.

WMFD-AM
25 NORTH KERR AVENUE SUITE C
WILMINGTON, NC 28405-3403
910-791-3088
800-678-5991
Fax: 910-791-0112
http://www.am630.net
• Doug Carlisle, News Director
(910) 791-3088
Description:
News, Talk.

WMFR-AM
875 WEST 5TH STREET
WINSTON SALEM, NC 27101
336-777-3900
Fax: 336-777-3915
comments@triadsports.com
www.triadsports.com
• Mike Fenley, Program Director
(336) 777-3900
Description:
News, Talk.

WMHW-FM
180 MOORE HALL CENTRAL MICHIGAN
UNIV.
MOUNT PLEASANT, MI 48859
517-774-7287
Fax: 517-774-2426
wmhw@cmich.edu
http://www.cmich.edu
• Peter B. Orlik, General Manager
(517) 774-7279
wmhw@cmich.edu

Description:
Music, News, Sports.

WMIK-AM
NORTH 19TH STREET
MIDDLESBORO, KY 40965
606-248-5842
Fax: 606-248-7660
• Roy Shotton, General Manager
Description:
Music, News, Sports.

WMJI-FM
6200 OAK TREE BOULEVARD 4TH
FLOOR
INDEPENDENCE, OH 44131
216-520-2600
800-669-1057
Fax: 216-524-2600
http://www.wmji.com
• R. C. Bauer, News Director
(216) 520-2600
rbauer@wtam.com
Description:
Music, News, Sports.

WMJK-FM
1640 CLEVELAND ROAD
SANDUSKY, OH 44870-4357
419-625-1010
888-547-8792
Fax: 419-625-1348
http://www.wmjkradio.com
• Lisa Rice, General Manager
(419) 625-1010
lisajrice@clearchannel.com
Description:
Music.

WMJZ-FM
3687 SOUTH OTSEGO
GAYLORD, MI 49735
989-732-3446
Fax: 989-732-6202
• Mike Reling, Program Director
Description:
Music, News, Sports.

WMKX-FM
51 PICKERING STREET
BROOKVILLE, PA 15825-1245
814-849-8100
877-634-2765
Fax: 814-849-4585
• Kevin Heinrich, Program Director
(814) 849-8100
Description:
Music, News, Sports.

WMLM-AM
4170 NORTH STATE ROAD
ALMA, MI 48801-9316
989-463-4013
• Greg Siefker, General Manager
Description:
Music, News, Sports.

WMLN-FM
1071 BLUE HILL AVE
MILTON, MA 02186-2302
617-333-0311
Fax: 617-333-6860
• Holly Clark, Promotion Director
(617) 333-0500
• Jadd Naamani, Program Director

(617) 333-2370
• Nick Quinn, Sports Director
Description:
Music, News, Sports.

WMMC-FM
627 1/2 ARCHER AVENUE
MARSHALL, IL 62441
217-826-8017
Fax: 217-826-8519
wmmc106@aol.com
• Lori Spangler, Program Director

WMML-AM
89 EVERTS AVENUE
QUEENSBURY, NY 12804-2040
518-793-7733
Fax: 518-793-0838
http://www.wink105.com
• John Pratt, Program Director
(518) 793-7733

WMMS-FM
6200 OAK TREE BOULEVARD 4TH
FLOOR
INDEPENDENCE, OH 44131
216-520-2600
800-348-1007
Fax: 216-524-2600
http://www.wmms.com/main.html
• R. C. Bauer, News Director
(216) 520-2600
rbauer@wtam.com
Description:
Music, News, Sports.

WMNA-AM
P.O. BOX 730
GRETNA, VA 24557-0730
434-656-1234
Fax: 434-656-1235
• Devin Taylor, General Manager
(888) 881-8851
wmna730@hotmail.com
Description:
Music, News, Sports.

WMOI-FM
55 PUBLIC SQUARE
MONMOUTH, IL 61462-1755
309-734-9452
Fax: 309-734-3276
• David Klockenga, General Manager
Description:
Music, News, Sports.

WMOP-AM
343 NORTH EAST 1ST AVENUE
OCALA, FL 34470
352-732-2010
888-777-5765
Fax: 352-629-1614
http://www.wmop.com
• Adam Reardon, Sports Director
Description:
Music, News, Sports.

WMPX-WMRX AM AND FM
1510 BAYLISS STREET
MIDLAND, MI 48640
989-631-1490
Fax: 989-631-6357
http://www.wmpxwmrx.com
• Gary Williams, Program/Sports Director

Description:
Music, News, Sports.

WMRC-AM
258 MAIN STREET
MILFORD, MA 01757-2525
508-473-1490
Fax: 508-478-2200
• Edward Thompson, News Director
Description:
Music, News, Sports, Talk.

WMRN-AM
1330 NORTH MAIN STREET
MARION, OH 43302
740-383-1131
Fax: 740-387-3697
bensailor@clearchannel.com
http://www.wmrn.com
• Ben Failor, News Director
benfailor@clearchannel.com
Description:
Music, News, Sports, Talk.

WMRX-FM
1510 BAYLISS STREET
MIDLAND, MI 48640-1689
989-631-1490
Fax: 989-631-6357
wmpx@sbcglobal.net
• Gary Williams, Program/Sports Director
Description:
Music, News, Sports.

WMSR-AM
1030 OAKDALE STREET
MANCHESTER, TN 37355-2206
931-728-3526
Fax: 931-728-3527
Description:
Music, News, Sports.

WMSS-FM
214 RACE STREET
MIDDLETOWN, PA 17057-2242
717-948-9136
http://www.wmssfm.com
• Steve Leedy, Sports Director
• John Wilsbach, General Manager
Description:
Music, News, Sports.

WMTL-AM
2160 BRANDENBURG ROAD
LEITCHFIELD, KY 42754
270-259-5692
Fax: 270-259-5693
news@k105.com
• Jared Mitchell, News Director
(270) 259-5692
• David Thompson, Sports Director
(270) 259-5692
Description:
News, Talk.

WMTR-FM
303 NORTH DEFIANCE STREET
ARCHBOLD, OH 43502-1162
419-445-9050
Fax: 419-445-3531
http://www.961wmtr.com
• Larry Christy, Sports Director
• Mark Knapp, News Director/Promotion
Manager

Description:
Music, News, Sports.

WMUF 1047FM/97.5AM 1000, WRQR AM/FM, 94.1 FM
110 INDIA ROAD
PARIS, TN 38242-1239
731-644-9455
Fax: 731-644-9421
wmuf@bellsouth.net
• Janice Benton, Office Manager
• Howard Mcgill, News Director
radionews@bellsouth.net
• Lance Pierce, Sports Director
(731) 644-9455
wlzk@bellsouth.net
Description:
Educational, Music, News, Sports.

WMUH-FM
2400 CHEW STREET
ALLENTOWN, PA 18104
484-664-3239
Fax: 484-664-3539
wmuh@muhlenberg.edu
http://www.muhlenberg.edu
• Rich Gensiak, Program Director
Description:
Music, News, Sports.

WMVX-FM
6200 OAK TREE BOULEVARD
INDEPENDENCE, OH 44131
216-520-2600
800-829-1065
Fax: 216-901-8133
http://www.wmvx.com
• Don Hallett, Program Director
• Mike Snyders, Sports Director
(216) 696-4444
Description:
Music, News, Sports.

WNBH-AM
75 OXFORD STREET SUITE 402
PROVIDENCE, RI 02905
508-979-8003
Fax: 508-979-8009
bobcormier@catcountry.com
http://www.wnbh.com
• Rick Everett, Program Director
(508) 979-8003
• Ed Pereira, Promotion Manager
Description:
Music, News, Sports.

WNDE
6161 FALL CREEK RD
INDIANAPOLIS, IN 46220
317-257-7565
Fax: 317-253-6501
www.wnde.com
• Mark Patrick, Sports Director
markpatrick@clearchannel.com
Nature of Sports Service:
Local. Sports & Talk radio programming.
Frequency:
1260

WNDH-FM
709 NORTH PERRY STREET
NAPOLEON, OH 43545-1520
419-592-8060
Fax: 419-592-1085
wndh@clearchannel.com
http://www.wndh1031.com

• David Kleck, News Director
davekleck@clearchannel.com
• David Kleck, Sports Director
davekleck@clearchannel.com
Description:
Music, News, Sports.

WNEG-AM
145 H. ALEXANDER STREET
TOCCOA, GA 30577-1415
706-886-2191
Fax: 706-282-0189
www.wnegradio.com
• Ted Taylor, Sports Director
Description:
Music.

WNER-AM
134 MULLIN STREET
WATERTOWN, NY 13601-3616
315-788-0790
Fax: 315-788-4379
http://www.wuzz.com
• Nathan Lehman, News Director
(315) 788-0790
morning@790wtny.com
Description:
Music, News, Sports.

WNES-AM
1730 WEST EVERLY BROTHERS
BOULEVARD
CENTRAL CITY, KY 42330
270-754-3000
Fax: 270-754-3710
• Stan Barnett, Advertising Manager
ads@ky-leadernews.com
• Stan Barnett, Program Director
Description:
Music.

WNFL 1140-AM
1420 BELLEVUE STREET
GREEN BAY, WI 54305
920-435-3771
Fax: 920-321-2300
www.wnflam.com
• Dave Edwards, Program Director
(910) 435-3771
• John Maino, Sports Talk Show
(910) 435-3771
• Mark Daniels, Sports Director
(910) 435-3771
Nature of Sports Service:
Talk radio. 1140AM
College Sports:
Football, Basketball.

WNJC-AM
5 POINTS PLAZA
SEWELL, NJ 08080
856-227-1360
Fax: 856-232-9093
http://www.wnjc1360.com
• John Forsythe, General Manager
Description:
Music, News, Sports.

WNKT-FM
4230 FABER PLACE DRIVE SUITE 100
NORTH CHARLESTON, SC 29405
843-277-1200
800-225-9282
Fax: 843-277-1212
http://www.catcountry1075.com

media

• Brian Driver, Program Director
(843) 277-1200
Description:
Music, News, Sports.

WNLS
325 JOHN KNOX RD, BLDG G
TALLAHASSEE, FL 32303
850-422-3107
Fax: 850-383-0747
www.wnls.com
• J.L Dunbar, Program Director
• Brian Willard, Sports Director
• Rick Flagg, News Director
Nature of Sports Service:
24-hour sports.
Baseball:
MLB - Tampa Bay Devil Rays.
College Sports:
Baseball, Men's & Women's Basketball,
Football - Florida State University.
Football:
NFL - Tampa Bay Buccaneers.

WNMH-FM
206 MAIN STREET
NORTHFIELD, MA 01360-1050
413-498-3603
Fax: 413-498-0150
http://www.nmhschool.org
• Jo Grubman, Station Manager
(413) 498-5470
• Joe Ruscio, Sports Director
jruscio@nmhschool.org
Description:
Music, News, Sports.

WNML AM/FM
4711 OLD KINGSTON PIKE
KNOXVILLE, TN 37919
865-588-6511
Fax: 865-588-3725
sportsanimal99.com
• Mickey Dearstone, Program Director
mickey.dearstone@citcomm.com
• Frank Nystrom, Sales Manager
Description:
Music, News and All Sports

WNML-AM
4711 OLD KINGSTON PIKE
KNOXVILLE, TN 37919-5207
865-588-6511
Fax: 865-909-0254
http://www.sportsanimal99.com/
• Ed Brantley, General Manager
(865) 588-6511
• Mickey Dearstone, Program Director
Description:
News, Talk.

WNNJ-FM
45 MITCHELL AVENUE
FRANKLIN, NJ 07416
973-827-2525
Fax: 973-827-2135
http://www.wnnj.com
• Ken O'Brien, Program Director
(973) 823-6156
kenobrien@clearchannel.com
Description:
Music, News, Sports.

WNNZ-AM
1331 MAIN STREET
SPRINGFIELD, MA 01103-1669

413-781-1011
Fax: 413-858-1958
http://www.wnnz.com
• John Baibak, News Director
(413) 734-4432
Description:
Talk.

WNOI-FM
1001 NORTH OLIVE ROAD
FLORA, IL 62839
618-662-8331
Fax: 618-662-2407
http://www.wnoi.com
• Randy Poole, Advertising Manager
• Bill Thompson, News/Sports Director
Description:
Music, News, Sports.

WNPL-FM
10 MUSIC CIR E SUITE 901
NASHVILLE, TN 37203-4338
615-321-1067
Fax: 615-321-5771
• John Mountz, Program Director
(615) 321-1067
john.mountz@cumulus.com

WNPV-AM
1210 SNYDER ROAD
LANSDALE, PA 19446
215-855-8211
800-355-9678
Fax: 215-368-0180
jnolan@wnpv1440.com
• Jeff Nolan, Sports Director
jnolan@wnpv1440.com
Description:
News, Talk, Sports
Sports Broadcast:
NASCAR, Phillies, Lehigh Valley Iron Pigs,
Penn State Football & Basketball and high
school football broadcasts

WNSR/WMGC RADIO
435 37TH AVE N.
NASHVILLE, TN 37209
615-844-1039
Baseball:
Pacific Coast League: Nashville
College Sports:
Vanderbilt, Belmont University, University of
Tennessee, Tennessee State University.
Football:
NFL - Tennessee Titans.

WNSS-AM
1064 JAMES STREET
SYRACUSE, NY 13203-2704
315-472-0200
Fax: 315-472-1146
• Tom Mitchell, Station Manager
(315) 472-0200
Description:
News.

WNST-AM
1550 HART ROAD
BALTIMORE, MD 21286-1635
410-821-9678
Fax: 410-828-4698
http://www.nastyone.com
• Paul Kopelke, News Director
(410) 828-8088
Description:
Educational.

WNSV-FM
186 EAST SAINT LOUIS STREET
NASHVILLE, IL 62263
618-327-4444
Fax: 618-327-3716
wnsvfm@charter.net
• Brad Myer, Sports Director
wnsvfm@charter.net
Sports Discussed:
Baseball, football, volleyball, basketball
(local)
Description:
Broadcasts of local high school games in all
previous listed categories.

WNTR
516 WHITE AVE
CUMBERLAND, MD 21502
301-777-5400
Fax: 301-777-5404
www.wntr.com
• Dick Yoder, General Manager
• Pat Sullivan, Promotions Director
Nature of Sports Service:
News, Talk, Sports.
Baseball:
MLB - CBS Package.
College Sports:
Basketball - NCAA Final Four; Notre Dame
University sports.
Football:
NFL - Pittsburgh Steelers.

WNUS-FM
6006 GRAND CENTRAL AVENUE
VIENNA, WV 26105
304-295-6070
Fax: 304-295-4389
http://www.wnus.com
• Steve Daugherty, Sports Director
(304) 295-6070
steved@clearchannel.com
• Doug Hess, News Director
(304) 295-6070
douglashess@clearchannel.com
• Lori Ullmann, Promotion Manager
Description:
Music.

WNYG-AM
404 ROUTE 109
WEST BABYLON, NY 11704-6214
631-422-5973
Fax: 631-422-5992
http://www.studentradio1440.com
• Doug Edwards, Program Director
(631) 321-9694
Description:
Music, News, Sports.

WNYY
1751 HANSHAW RD
ITHACA, NY 14850
607-257-6400
Fax: 607-257-6497
www.1470wnyy.com
• Geoff Dunn, Program Director
• Peter Voorhees, Sports Director/ News
Director
• Susan Johnston, Marketing Director
Description:
Progressive talk radio.

WOAI
6222 NW IH 10 W.
SAN ANTONIO, TX 78201

210-736-9700
800-373-9700
Fax: 210-735-8811
• Bob Cohen, General Manager
• Jay Howard, Sports Director
Nature of Sports Service:
News, Talk, Sports.
Baseball:
CBS.

WOBN-FM
COWAN HALL
WESTERVILLE, OH 43081
614-823-1557
Fax: 614-823-1998
• Scott Bacon, Sports Director
• Cat Perlson, News Director
Description:
Music, News, Sports.

WOBT-AM
3616 HIGHWAY 47, N.
RHINELANDER, WI 54501-8819
715-362-1975
Fax: 715-362-1973
http://www.northwoodsespnsportszone.com
• John Burton, News Director
(715) 362-6140
Description:
Music, News, Sports.

WOES-FM
8989 COLONY ROAD
ELSIE, MI 48831-9724
989-862-4237
Fax: 989-862-4463
• Kevin Somers, Program Director
(989) 862-4237
somers@edzone.net
Description:
Music, News, Sports.

WOFX-AM
1 WASHINGTON SQUARE
ALBANY, NY 12205
518-452-4800
Fax: 518-452-4855
• Chuck Custer, News Director
(518) 452-4847
chuckcuster@clearchannel.com
• Peter Gimblette, Marketing Manager
petergimblette@clearchannel.com
Description:
Music.

WOHS
PO BOX 1590
SHELBY, NC 28151
704-435-3297
Fax: 704-435-1217
• Calvin Hastings, General Manager/Sales
netoldies@aol.com
• Andy Foster, Sports Director/Music
• Terresa Hastings, Office Manager
• Anna McGinnis, News Director
• Lori Deitz, Traffic Director
Office Address:
1511 W. Dixon Blvd, Shelby NC 28151.
Nature of Sports Service:
Country/Sports.
Baseball:
MLB - Atlanta Braves.
College Sports:
Basketball, Football - University of North
Carolina.

Football:
NFL - Carolina Panthers.

WOIC-AM
1900 PINEVIEW ROAD
COLUMBIA, SC 29209
803-695-8600
Fax: 803-695-8605
http://www.woic.com
• Dave Stewart, Program Director
Description:
Music.

WOIZ-AM
PO BOX 561130
GUAYANILLA, PUERTO RIC 00656-3130
787-835-1130
Fax: 787-835-3130
radioantillas@yahoo.com
• Luis A. Rodriguez, III, President/General
Manager
(787) 835-3130
radioantillas@yahoo.com
• Manuel Quinonez, Program Director
(787) 835-3130
radioantillas@yahoo.com
• Luis F. Mari, Technical Supervisor
(787) 835-3130
radioantillas@yahoo.com
• Erving Quinonez, Billing Director
(787) 835-3130
radioantillas@yahoo.com
• Rafael Acosta, Chief Executive
(787) 835-3130
radioantillas@yahoo.com
Description:
Music, News, Sports.
Year Founded:
1986

WONN-AM
404 WEST LIME STREET
LAKELAND, FL 33815
863-682-8184
Fax: 863-683-2409
news@wpcv.com
http://www.wonn.com
• Nancy Cattarius, Station Manager
(863) 682-8184
ncattarius@halllakeland.com
• Tunie Moss, Promotions Director
(863) 682-8184
• Mike James, Program Director
(863) 682-8184
• Andrea Oliver, News Director
(863) 682-8184
Description:
Music, News, Sports.

WONQ-AM
1033 STATE ROAD 436
SUITE 253
CASSELBERRY, FL 32707-5742
407-830-0800
Fax: 407-260-6100
• George M. Arroyo, Owner/President
• Josi Van Padilla, Sports Director
• Manuel Arroyo, Sports Director
(407) 830-0800
Description:
Music, News, Sports.

WOON-AM
1 SOCIAL STREET
WOONSOCKET, RI 02895-3136

401-762-1240
800-449-1240
Fax: 401-769-8232
studio@onworldwide.com
http://www.on-radio.com
• Lou Mandeville, Sports Director
(401) 762-1240
Description:
Music, News, Sports.

WOPP-AM
1101 CAMERON ROAD
OPP, AL 36467-2407
334-493-4545
Fax: 334-493-4546
wopp@wopp.com
http://www.wopp.com
• Joe Adams, Sports Director
(334) 453-4545
• Brett Ballard, Play-By-Play
(334) 453-4545
wopp@wopp.com
• Robert Boothe, General Manager
Frequency:
1290 AM

WORD
501 RUTHERFORD ST
GREENVILLE, SC 29609
864-271-9200
Fax: 864-242-1567
www.newstalkword.com
• Annell Kirkland, General Manager
• John Boone, Program Director/Sports
Director
Nature of Sports Service:
Local. News, Talk. Sports radio
programming.

WORD-AM
29 DARLINGTON ROAD
GREENVILLE, SC 29609-5313
864-271-6397
Fax: 864-242-1567
• Bob McLain, Program Director
bmclain@entercom.com
Description:
News, Talk.

WORG-FM
1675 CHESTNUT STREET
ORANGEBURG, SC 29115-3327
803-516-8400
Fax: 803-516-0704
psa@worg.com
http://www.worg.com
• Stu Wright, Program Director
gtw@worg.com
Description:
Music, News, Sports.

WORW-FM
1799 KRAFFT RD
PORT HURON, MI 48060
810-984-2675
Fax: 810-984-2747
• Carie Mertz, General Manager
Description:
Music, News, Sports.

WORX-FM
1224 EAST TELEGRAPH HILL ROAD
MADISON, IN 47250
812-265-3322
Fax: 812-273-5509

media

• Scott Davidson, News/Sports Director
manager@worxradio.com
Description:
Music, News, Sports.

WOSO-AM
52 PASEO COVADONGA PELLO
BUILDING C 3RD
SAN JUAN, PUERTO RIC 00901
787-724-4242
Fax: 787-723-9676
• Gary Tuominen, News Director
Description:
Music, News, Sports.

WOSQ-FM
1710 NORTH CENTRAL AVENUE
MARSHFIELD, WI 54449-1514
715-384-2191
Fax: 715-341-9744
Nature of Service:
ESPN Radio, over 100 local high school
events per year
Baseball:
ESPN games Saturday and Sunday
Basketball:
Milwaukee Bucks
College Sports:
Wisconsin Football, Men's and Women's
Basketball, ESPn Bowl games

WOWO-AM
2915 MAPLES ROAD
FORT WAYNE, IN 46816
260-447-5511
800-333-1190
Fax: 260-447-7546
news@wowo.com
http://www.wowo.com
• Jim Shovlin, Sports Director
(260) 447-5511
jshovlin@wowo.com
Description:
Radio broadcasting.
Frequency:
1190

WOYL-AM
1411 LIBERTY STREET
FRANKLIN, PA 16323-1696
814-432-2188
Fax: 814-437-9372
mytalkradio@yahoo.com
• Terry Deitz, General Manager
• Joseph Elan, Advertising Manager
joekool95@yahoo.com
• Tim Shaw, Sports Director
Description:
News, Talk.

WPAX-AM
117 REMINGTON AVENUE
THOMASVILLE, GA 31792-5520
229-226-1240
Fax: 229-226-1361
http://www.wpaxradio.com/
• Mark Brannan, Sports Reporter
wpaxwtuf@rose.net
• Len Robinson, Advertising Manager
lenrob@rose.net
Description:
Music, News, Sports, Talk.

WPCD-FM
2400 WEST BRADLEY AVENUE
CHAMPAIGN, IL 61821-1806

217-351-2450
wpcd@lycos.com
http://www.parkland.cc.il.us/wpcd
• Dan Hughes, News Director
dhughes@parkland.edu
Description:
Music, News, Sports.

WPCH-AM
500 CAROLINA SPRINGS ROAD
NORTH AUGUSTA, SC 29841
706-396-6000
800-816-1043
Fax: 803-279-0220
janasutter@clearchannel.com
• Charles McNeil, News Director
charles@wbbq.com
Description:
Music, News.

WPCV-FM
404 WEST LIME STREET
LAKELAND, FL 33815
863-682-8184
800-227-9797
Fax: 863-683-2409
news@wpcv.com
http://www.wpcv.com
• Nancy Cattarius, Advertising Manager
• Bob Crews, Sports Director
(863) 682-8184
• Tunie Moss, Promotions Manager
(863) 682-8184
Description:
Music, News, Sports.

WPDM-AM/WSNN-FM
7064 POTSDAM CANTON ROAD
POTSDAM, NY 13676
315-265-5510
Fax: 315-265-4040
hits@99hits.com
http://www.99hits.com
• Scott Dosztan, News Director
news@99hits.com
• Chris Engel, Sports Director
sports@99hits.com
Description:
Music.
Year Founded:
1955

WPDR RADIO
PO BOX 300
PORTAGE, WI 53901
608-742-8833
Fax: 608-742-1688
wpdr@jvlnet.net
• Ed Kramer, General Manager
• Mike Olson, Program Director
Nature of Sports Service:
Adult Contemporary, News, Talk. ESPN
Sports Talk (weekends)
Basketball:
NBA - Milwaukee Bucks
Baseball:
MLB - Milwaukee Brewers - Day Games.
Football:
NFL - Green Bay Packers.
College Sports:
Basketball, Football, Ice Hockey - University
of Wisconsin.

WPEN-AM
1 BALA PLAZA
BALA CYNWYD, PA 19004-1428

610-667-8500
Fax: 610-664-9610
http://www.sportstalk950.com
• Art Andrews, News Director
(610) 667-8500
aandrews@greatermediaphiladelphia.com
• Tony Bruno, Host - Morning Show
(610) 667-8500
wpen@sr950.com
• Bob DeBlois, Station Manager
(610) 667-8500
• Mike Sommers, Program Director
(610) 667-8500
Description:
Music.

WPEZ-FM
544 MULBERRY STREET 5TH FLOOR
MACON, GA 31201-8250
478-746-6286
Fax: 478-742-8061
http://z937.com/home.php
• John Sheftic, Marketing Manager
Description:
Music, News, Sports.

WPHM-AM
808 HURON STREET
PORT HURON, MI 48060
810-982-9000
Fax: 810-987-9380
http://www.wphm.com
• Bill Gilmer, News Director
bgilmer@radiofirst.net
• Al Tyrrell, Advertising Manager
(810) 982-9000
• Dennis Stuckey, Sports Director
Description:
Music, News, Sports, Talk.

WPIC-AM
2030 PINE HOLLOW BOULEVARD
SHARON, PA 16148-2520
724-346-4113
877-872-7737
Fax: 724-981-4545
http://www.wpic790.com
• Joe Biro, News Director
• Bob Greenburg, Sports Director
(724) 346-4113
bgreenburg@theradiocenter.com
Description:
Music, News, Sports, Talk.

WPIG-FM
3163 NEW YORK STATE, ROUTE 417
OLEAN, NY 14760
716-372-0161
800-877-9749
Fax: 716-372-0164
newsdesk@netsync.net
• Dick Hannon, Advertising Manager
• Gary Nease, News/Sports Director
Description:
Music.

WPKY-AM
108 WEST MAIN STREET
PRINCETON, KY 42445
270-365-2072
Fax: 270-365-2073
• Tom Rogers, General Manager
Description:
Music, News, Sports.

WPLO-AM
239 EZARD STREET
LAWRENCEVILLE, GA 30045-5936
770-237-9897
Fax: 770-237-8769
• Franco Vera, Promotion Director
Description:
Music, News, Sports, Talk.

WPMB-AM
232 SOUTH 4TH STREET
VANDALIA, IL 62471-2810
618-283-2325
Fax: 618-283-1503
• John Harris, Promotions Director
wkrv@sbcglobal.net
• Todd Stapleton, News/Sports Director
tstapleton@cromwellradio.com
Description:
Educational, Music, News, Sports, Talk.

WPMZ-AM
1270 MINERAL SPRING AVENUE
NORTH PROVIDENCE, RI 02904
401-726-8413
Fax: 401-726-8649
wpmz@aol.com
• Tony Mendez, Station Manager
(401) 726-8413
tmendez@poder1110.com

WPOP-AM SPORTS RADIO
10 COLUMBUS BLVD
HARTFORD, CT 06106
860-723-6000
Fax: 860-723-6079
www.espnradio1410.com
• Bob Plant, Program Director
Nature of Sports Service:
Local. 24-hour sports radio programming.

WPPA-AM
212 SOUTH CENTER
POTTSVILLE, PA 17901
570-622-1360
Fax: 570-622-2822
news@pbcradio.com
http://www.pbcradio.com
• Gene Starr, News Director
(570) 622-1360
• Bill Tidmore, Advertising & Promotion
Manager/Sports Director
Description:
Music, News, Sports.

WPRN-FM
909 WEST PUSHMATAHA STREET
BUTLER, AL 36904
205-459-3222
Fax: 205-459-4140
wprnfm1077@yahoo.com
http://www.wprnfm.com
• Henry Tyson, Sports Director

WPRO
1502 WAMPANOAY TRAIL
E. PROVIDENCE, RI 02915
401-433-4200
Fax: 401-433-1183
www.wpro.com
• Andrea Scott, General Manager
• Scott Cordischi, Sports Director
• Chris Gardner, Marketing Director
• Donna Callahan, Business Officer
Nature of Sports Service:
News, Talk, Sports.

Baseball:
MLB - Boston Red Sox; Minor League -
International League/AA/Pawtucket Red
Sox.
College Sports:
Basketball - Providence, Football - Brown
University; Ice Hockey - Providence.
Ice Hockey:
NHL - Boston Bruins; Minor League -
American Hockey League/AHL/Providence
Bruins.

WPRO-AM
1502 WAMPANOAG TRAIL
RIVERSIDE, RI 02915
401-433-4200
Fax: 401-433-5967
wprofm@aol.com
• David Bernstein, News Director
Description:
Music, News, Sports, Talk.

WPRZ-AM
7351 HUNTON STR WARRENTON
WARRENTON, VA 20187
540-349-1250
Fax: 540-349-2726
http://www.praisecommunications.org
• Sally L. Buchanan, Program Director
sally@wprz.org
Description:
Music, News, Sports.

WPXN-FM
361 NORTH RAILROAD AVENUE
PAXTON, IL 60957-1142
217-379-4333
http://www.wpxn.com
• Joel Cluver, News Director
• Dan Daugherity, Advertising
Manager/Sports Director
wpxn@hotmail.com
Description:
Music, News, Sports.

WQAL-FM
1041 HURON RADIO
CLEVELAND, OH 44115
216-578-0104
Fax: 216-363-7104
www.q104.cbslocal.com/
• Brian Conroy, Promotions Director
bconroy@q104.com
• Jim McIntyre, News Director
(216) 696-0123
jim@wdok.com
Description:
Music, News, Sports.

WQAM 560 SPORTS RADIO
20295 NW 2ND AVE
MIAMI, FL 33169
305-653-6796
Fax: 305-770-1456
• Greg Reed, General Manager
• Bill Mullon, Director of Sports Marketing
• Mike Eckstein, Director Sports Marketing
Nature of Sports Service:
Local. 24-hour sports radio programming.
Dolphins (NFL); Miami Hurricanes (NCAA),
Marlins (MLB), Florida Panthers (NHL);
Miami Heat (NBA).

WQBB-AM
1533 AMHERST ROAD
KNOXVILLE, TN 37909

865-824-1021
Fax: 865-824-1880
http://www.1040theticket.com
• Bruce Patrick, Program Director
(865) 824-1711
bpatrick@journalbroadcastgroup.com
• Chris Protzman, General Manager
(865) 824-1700
cprotzman@journalbroadcastgroup.com
Description:
News, Sports, Talk.

WQBX-FM
5310 NORTH STATE ROAD
ALMA, MI 48801
989-463-3175
Fax: 989-463-6674
http://www.wqbx.com
• Jim Sommerville, Program Director
wqbx@cmsinter.net
• Jim Sommerville, Sports Director
Description:
Music, News, Sports.

WQCM-FM
1250 MARYLAND AVENUE
HAGERSTOWN, MD 21740-7244
301-797-7300
Fax: 301-797-2659
• Mike Holder, Program Director
(717) 263-0813
Description:
Music, News, Sports.

WQDK-FM
443 HIGHWAY 42 WEST
AHOSKIE, NC 27910-9712
252-332-7993
Fax: 252-332-6887
• Don Upchurch, News Director
Description:
Music, News, Sports.

WQEL-FM
403 EAST RENSSELAER STREET
BUCYRUS, OH 44820-2438
419-562-2222
Fax: 419-562-0520
http://www.wbcowqel.com
• Debra J. Gifford, General Manager
• Jim Radke, Sports Director
jradke@wbcowqel.com
Description:
Music, News, Sports.

WQIC-FM
ROUTE 72 NORTH
LEBANON, PA 17046
717-272-7651
Fax: 717-274-0161
• Scott Bradley, Sports Director
• Gordon Weise, News Director
Description:
Music.

WQIO-FM
17421 COSHOCTON ROAD
MOUNT VERNON, OH 43050
740-397-1000
Fax: 740-392-9300
curtisnewland@basbroadcasting.com
www.wqioradio.com
• Curtis Newland, Operations Manager
(740) 397-1000

media

WQKE-FM
ALUMNI HALL
PLATTSBURGH, NY 12901
518-564-2000
Fax: 518-564-3994
http://137.142.200.27/wqke/
• Ashley Herington, News Director
• Seth Lindernen, Sports Director
Description:
Music, News, Sports.

WQKR-AM
100 MAIN STREET
PORTLAND, TN 37148
615-325-3250
Fax: 615-325-0803
www.wqkr.com
• Chris Ladd, Advertising Manager
chris@wqkr.com
• Chris Ladd, News Director
wqkr@comcast.net
• Chris Ladd, Sports Director
chris@wqkr.com
Description:
Music, News, Sports, Talk.

WQKT-FM
186 SOUTH HILLCREST DRIVE
WOOSTER, OH 44691
330-264-5122
800-833-9211
Fax: 330-264-3571
wqkt@aol.com
http://www.wqkt.com
• Mike Breckenridge, Program Director
events@wqkt.com
• Craig Walton, Advertising Manager
Description:
Music, News, Sports.

WQLA-FM
P.O. BOX 1530
LA FOLLETTE, TN 37766
423-566-1000
Fax: 865-457-5900
q105fm@bellsouth.com
• Cliff Jennings, Owner
q105fm@bellsouth.net
• Frank Scott, Program Director
q105fm@bellsouth.net
Description:
Music, News, Sports.

WQPM-AM
32215 124TH STREET
PRINCETON, MN 55371
763-389-1300
800-850-1061
Fax: 763-389-1359
• Troy Edwards, Program Director
Description:
Music, News, Sports, Talk.

WQSE-AM
201 HALL LANE
WHITE BLUFF, TN 37187
615-797-9785
Fax: 615-797-9788
duanedjwqse@aol.com
http://www.tngospel.com
• Duane Jeffrey, General Manager
Description:
Music, News, Sports.

WQSN AM 1660
4200 W. MAIN
KALAMAZOO, MI 49006
269-345-7121
800-873-1074
Fax: 269-345-1436
cyanm@wgsn.com
• Stephens C. Trivers, President/General
Manager
• Ryan Maguire, Programming/Promotions
Director
• Dennis Martin, VP Sales
• Geary Morrill, Chief Engineer
• Tammy Abramowski, Traffic Director
• Melissa Richard, Controller
Nature of Sports Service:
Local and ESPN 24-hour sports radio
programming. Jim Rome and 25 hours of
local programming weekly. Your local sports
leader.
Baseball:
MLB - Chicago Cubs, Chicago White Sox.
College Sports:
Basketball - Michigan State University,
Kalamazoo College: Football - Michigan
State University, Kalamazoo College.
Football:
NFL - Chicago Bears.
Ice Hockey:
NHL - Detroit Red Wings, UHL - Kalamazoo
Wings.
Baseball:
MLB - Chicago Cubs, Chicago White Sox.
College - Kalamazoo Kings.
Primary Audience:
Males 25-54 years old.

WQTM
2500 MAITLAND CENTER PKWY, STE 401
MAITLAND, FL 32751
407-916-7800
Fax: 407-916-0329
• Jenny Su Rhodes, General Manager
• Tom Morgan, Sports Director
Nature of Sports Service:
Local. 24-hour sports radio programming.
Baseball:
MLB - Atlanta Braves.
College Sports:
Basketball, Football - University of Florida,
University of Central Florida, University of
Miami.
Football:
NFL - Miami Dolphins.

WQXI 790
3550 PEACHTREE RD, NE PENTHOUSE
ATLANTA, GA 30326
404-238-3431
Fax: 404-365-9026
• Andrew Saltzman, General Manager
• Matt Edgar, Sports Director
Nature of Sports Service:
Sports radio. Pete Rose Show, Jim Rome,
Game Night.

WQXI-AM
3350 PEACHTREE ROAD, N.E.
ATLANTA, GA 30326-1040
404-237-0079
Fax: 404-231-5923
http://www.790thezone.com
• Leslie Rosetta-Smith, Marketing Director
lsmith@790thezone.com
• Leslie Rosetta-Smith, Promotions Director
• Andrew Saltzman, President
• Steven Shapiro, President

Description:
Music, Talk.

WQXX-FM
129 COLLEGE STREET
WEST LIBERTY, KY 41472-1156
606-784-4141
Fax: 606-743-9557
radio41472@yahoo.com
• Jim Forrest, Program Director
radio412@yahoo.com
Description:
Music, News, Sports.

WRAC-FM
114 MANCHESTER STREET, S.
WEST UNION, OH 45693-1262
937-544-9722
800-326-9722
Fax: 937-544-5523
• Donald J. Bowles, Owner
(937) 544-9722
• Ted Foster, News Director
c103country@yahoo.com
• Gary McClellen, Sports Director
(937) 544-9722
c103country@yahoo.com
Description:
Music, News, Sports.

WRAM-AM
55 PUBLIC SQUARE
MONMOUTH, IL 61462-1755
309-734-9452
Fax: 309-734-3276
• Tom Peterson, News Director
Description:
Music, News, Sports, Talk.

WRAY-AM
1900 WEST BROADWAY
PRINCETON, IN 47670-1095
812-386-1250
Fax: 812-386-6249
• Cliff Ingram, WRAY News Director
(812) 386-1250
cliff@wrayradio.com
Description:
Music, News, Sports.

WRAY-FM
P.O. BOX 8
PRINCETON, IN 47670-1095
812-386-1250
Fax: 812-386-6249
wray@wrayradio.com
http://www.wrayradio.com
• Cliff Ingram, News Director
(812) 386-1250
cliff@wrayradio.com
• Jeff Lankford, Sports Director
(812) 386-1250
jeff@wrayradio.com
• Lynn Roach, Promotion Director
(812) 386-1250
lynn@wrayradio.com
Description:
Music, News, Contests
Year Founded:
1950

WRCC-FM
390 GOLDEN AVENUE
BATTLE CREEK, MI 49015
269-963-5555
Fax: 269-963-5185

• Tim Collins, Operations Director
(269) 963-5555
• Jeff Jennings, Production Director
(269) 963-5555
• Kit Osborne, General Station Manager
(269) 963-5555
Description:
Radio: FM 104.9, Football and Basketball:
NCAA - Michigan Wolverine Football

WRCT-FM
1 WRCT PLAZA
500 FORBES AVENUE
PITTSBURGH, PA 15213
412-621-0728
Fax: 412-268-6549
news@wrct.org
http://www.wrct.org
• John Ketchpaw, Promotion Director
promotions@wrct.org
• Mike Rossman, Sports Director
sports@wrct.org
• Jason Tagyer, News Director
(412) 621-0728
news@wrct.org
Description:
Music, News, Sports.

WRCU-FM
13 OAK DRIVE
HAMILTON, NY 13346
315-228-7109
Fax: 315-228-7028
wrcu@mail.colgate.edu
http://www.wrcufm.com
• Darcy Benedict, General Manager
Description:
Music, News, Sports, Talk.

WRDL-FM
ASHLAND UNIVERSITY
ASHLAND, OH 44805-3702
419-289-5157
Fax: 419-289-5329
wrdl@ashland.edu
http://www.ashland.edu
• Tyler Miller, Sports Director
(419) 289-5157
wrdl@ashland.edu
• Kim Sweet-Buzzard, Program Director
wrdlashland@yahoo.com
• James Hana, Sports Director
(419) 289-5678
wrdl@ashland.edu
Description:
Music, News, Sports.

WRDU-FM
3100 SMOKETREE COURT SUITE 700
RALEIGH, NC 27604-1052
919-878-1500
Fax: 919-876-2929
http://www.1061rdu.com
• Josh Zach, News Director
joshzach@clearchannel.com
Description:
Music, News, Sports.

WRDW-AM
4051 JIMMIE DYESS PARKWAY
AUGUSTA, GA 30917
706-396-7000
Fax: 706-396-7100
maryliz@wgac.com
http://www.wrdwam.com

• Ashley Brown, Sports Director
(706) 396-7160

WREK-FM
350 FERST DRIVE, N.W.
ATLANTA, GA 30332-0630
404-894-2468
Fax: 404-894-6872
music.director@wrek.org
http://www.wrek.org
• Asif Heerji, Sports Editor
sports.director@wrek.org
• Eldon Stegall, Sports Director
(404) 894-2468
sports.director@wrek.org
Description:
Music, News, Sports, Talk.

WREV-AM
3025 WAUGHTOWN STREET SUITE G
WINSTON-SALEM, NC 27107
336-784-9004
Fax: 336-784-8337
http://www.quepasamedia.com
• Alfonso Fernandez, Station Manager
(336) 784-2774
Description:
Music, News, Sports, Talk.

WRFW-FM
306 N.HALL
RIVER FALLS, WI 54022-2882
715-425-3886
Fax: 715-425-3532
http://www.pureradio887.com
• Christine Duellman, News Director
• Steve Yeska, Sports Director
sports@pureradio887.com
Description:
Music, News, Sports.

WRGM SPORTS RADIO 1440
2900 PARK AVE W.
MANSFIELD, OH 44906
419-529-5900
Fax: 419-529-2319
comments@wrgm.com
www.wrgm.com
• Gunther Meisse, General Manager
Nature of Sports Service:
24-hour sports.
Auto Sports:
NASCAR.

WRGS-AM
211 BUREM ROAD
ROGERSVILLE, TN 37857
423-272-2628
Fax: 423-272-0328
http://www.wrgsradio.com
• Philip Beal, News Director
• Jay Phillips, Sports Director
(423) 272-3900
• J. Phillips, Sports Announcer
(423) 272-2628
stationmanager@wrgsradio.com
Description:
Music, News, Sports.
Sports Discussed:
Cherokee High School football, girls and
boys basketball, baseball and softball.
Frequency:
1370 am & 94.5 fm

WRHU-FM
111 HOFSTRA UNIVERSITY
HEMPSTEAD, NY 11549-1110
516-463-5667
Fax: 516-463-5668
mail@wrhu.org
http://www.wrhu.org
• Pete McCarthy, Sports Director
sports@wrhu.org
• Jamie Morris, Station Manager
(516) 463-5667
stationmanager@wrhu.org
Description:
Music, News, Sports.

WRIL-FM
P.O. BOX 693
PINEVILLE, KY 40977-0693
606-248-6565
877-724-4792
Fax: 606-248-6569
• Bob Dixon, Sports Director
• Elie Evans, Station Manager
wrilcountry@yahoo.com
Description:
Music, News, Sports.

WRJW-AM
2438 HIGHWAY 43 SOUTH
PICAYUNE, MS 39466-0907
601-798-4835
800-284-5036
Fax: 601-798-9755
www.wrjw.com
• Bo Moeller, News Director
(601) 798-4835
wrjw@charter.net
• Cary Meitzler, Sports Director
(601) 798-4835
wrjw@charter.net
• M. Delores Wood, General Manager
(601) 798-4835
wrjw@charter.net
• Caroline Randolph, Traffic Director
(601) 798-4835
wrjw@charter.net
• Denise Wilson, Public Service/Programs
(601) 798-4835
wrjw@charter.net
• Rebecca Barnes, Live Interviews
(601) 799-1900
wrjw@charter.net
• Roy Bunales, Music Director
(601) 799-1900
Nature of Service:
Music, News, Sports, Talk.
Year Founded:
1948

WRKD-AM
15 PAYNE AVENUE
ROCKLAND, ME 04841-2117
207-594-9400
Fax: 207-594-2234
matthewthompson@clearchannel.com
• Don Shields, Program Director
(207) 623-9000
donaldshields@clearchannel.com
• Donald Shields, Sports Director
(207) 623-9000
donaldshields@clearchannel.com
Description:
Music.

WRKR-FM
4154 JENNINGS DRIVE
KALAMAZOO, MI 49048

media

269-344-0111
Fax: 269-344-4223
http://www.wrkr.com
• Bill Anthony, News Director
• John Sterling, Market Manager
Description:
Music, News, Sports.

WRLS-FM
P.O. BOX 1008
HAYWARD, WI 54843-1008
715-634-4871
Fax: 715-634-3025
wrls@cheqnet.net
• Dick Bender, Sports Director
wrls-radio@cheqnet.net
• Stephanie Holman, News Director
sholman@cheqnet.net
Description:
Music, News, Sports.

WRMS-FM
108 EAST MAIN STREET
BEARDSTOWN, IL 62618-1241
217-323-1790
Fax: 217-323-1705
larry.bosiwick@gmail.com
• Larry Bosiwick, General Manager/Owner
Description:
Broadcasting local and national sports.
Affiliations:
Cubs, White Sox, Bulls, Bears, University of Illinois, University of Notre Dame and NASCAR.

WRNA-AM
633 PATTERSON STREET CHINA GROVE
KANNAPOLIS, NC 28083
704-857-1101
Fax: 704-857-0680
carl@fordbroadcasting.com
http://www.fordbroadcasting.com
• Carl Ford, Program Director
• Carl Ford, Sports Director
Description:
Music.

WRNL-AM
3245 BASIE ROAD
RICHMOND, VA 23228-3404
804-474-0000
800-432-9782
Fax: 804-474-0910
wrnl@clearchannel.com
http://www.sportsradio910.com
• Gary Hess, Sports Director
(804) 474-0155
garyhess@clearchannel.com
• Deanna Malone, News Director
(804) 474-0440
deannamalone@clearchannel.com
Description:
News, Sports.

WRNX-FM
98 LOWER WESTFIELD STREET
HOLYOKE, MA 01040-2744
413-536-1105
Fax: 413-536-1153
http://www.wrnx.com
• Glenn Cardinal, General Manager
glenn@wrnx.com
Description:
Music.

WRRG-FM
2000 5TH AVENUE
RIVER GROVE, IL 60171-1907
708-456-0300
Fax: 708-583-3121
• Kelli Lynch, Program Director
(708) 456-0300
wrrg@aol.com
• Tim McKinney, Sports Director
(708) 456-0300
wrrg@aol.com
Description:
Music, News, Sports.

WRSC
160 CLEARVIEW AVE
STATE COLLEGE, PA 16803
814-238-5085
Fax: 814-238-8993
• Joe Trimarchi, General Manager
(814) 238-5085
• Jeff Byers, Sports Director
(814) 238-5085
ironhead99@hotmail.com
• Dave Shannon, Program Director
(814) 238-5085
Nature of Sports Service:
News.
College Sports:
Basketball, Football, Wrestling - Penn State University.
Football:
NFL - Pittsburgh Steelers.

WRSE-FM
190 PROSPECT AVENUE
ELMHURST, IL 60126-3271
630-617-3500
Fax: 630-617-3313
http://www.elmhurst.edu/~jaywaves
• Dave Holder, Program Director
Description:
Educational, Music, News, Sports.

WRSN-FM
3100 SMOKETREE COURT SUITE 700
RALEIGH, NC 27604-1052
919-878-1500
Fax: 919-876-2929
briantaylor@clearchannel.com
http://www.sunny939.com
• Ken Spitzer, General Manager
(919) 874-9800
kenspitzer@clearchannel.com
• Rob Whiteside, Promotions Manager
robwhiteside@clearchannel.com
Description:
Music, News.

WRSW-AM
216 MARKET STREET, W
WARSAW, IN 46580-2800
574-372-3064
Fax: 574-267-2230
http://www.wrsw.net
• Roger Grossman, Sports Director
(574) 372-3064
roger@wrsw.net
• Jeremy Taylor, News Director
Description:
Music, News, Sports.

WRTK
4040 SIMON RD
YOUNGSTOWN, OH 44512

330-783-1000
Fax: 330-783-0060
• Pat Mulrooney, Program Director/Sports
Nature of Sports Service:
News, Talk, Sports.
Baseball:
MLB - Cleveland Indians.
College Sports:
Baseball, Basketball, Football - Youngstown State.
Football:
NFL - Pittsburgh Steelers.

WRUC-FM
REAMER CAMPUS CENTER
SCHENECTADY, NY 12308-2311
518-388-6151
Fax: 518-388-6790
http://wruc.union.edu/wruc/
• Matt Curtain, Sports Director
• Jennifer Mitchell, General Manager
Description:
Educational, Music, News, Sports.

WRUF
3200 WEIMER
GAINESVILLE, FL 32611
352-392-0771
Fax: 352-392-0519
gm@wruf.com
www.wruf.com
• Bob Clarke, Director General Manager
• Steve Russell, Sports Director
• Tom Krynski, News Director
Office Address:
3200 Weimer Hall, University of Florida Campus, Gainesville, FL 32611.
Nature of Sports Service:
News, Sports, Talk.
Baseball:
CBS.
College Sports:
Baseball - University of Florida, CBS; Basketball - University of Florida, CBS; Football - CBS.
Football:
NFL - Miami Dolphins.

WRXL-FM
3245 BASIE ROAD
RICHMOND, VA 23228-3404
804-474-0000
800-345-9436
Fax: 804-474-0168
http://www.wrxl.com
• Casey Krukowski, Program Director
(804) 474-0000
caseykrukowski@clearchannel.com
Description:
Music, News, Sports.

WRXX-FM
302 SOUTH POPLAR STREET
CENTRALIA, IL 62801-3922
618-533-5700
Fax: 618-533-5737
wrxx@mvn.net
• Aaron Fuchs, Operating Manager
• Brenda Robbins, Promotions Director
Description:
Music.

WSAL-AM
425, 2ND STREET
LOGANSPORT, IN 46947-3410

574-722-4000
Fax: 574-722-4010
http://www.wsal.com
• Mike Montgomery, Sports Director
• Joe Ulery, News Director
Description:
Music, News, Talk.

WSB-AM
1601 WEST PEACHTREE STREET, N.E.
ATLANTA, GA 30309-2663
404-897-7500
Fax: 404-897-7593
newstips@wsbradio.com
http://www.wsbradio.com
• Dave Baker, Executive Sports
Producer/Weekend Host
(404) 897-6282
dave.baker@wsbradio.com
• Michael Dobson, Promotions Director
(404) 897-7556
michael.dobson@wsbradio.com
• Larry Munson, Sports Host
• Tony Schiavone, Sports Reporter
(404) 897-7500
tony.schiavone@wsbradio.com
Description:
News, Talk.

WSBU-FM
PO BOX O
SAINT BONAVENTURE, NY 14778-2294
716-375-2307
Fax: 716-375-2583
wsbu@sbu.edu
http://wsbufm.net/p_cms.php?page_type=de
fault&CID=7
• Jen Anderson, Promotion Director
wsbu@sbu.edu
• Jeremy Noeson, Sports Director
• Elise Witz, News Director
Description:
Music.

WSCR THE SCORE SPORTSRADIO 670
455 N CITYFRONT PLAZA
CHICAGO, IL 60611
312-245-6000
Fax: 312-245-6072
www.wscr670am.com
• Mitch Rosen, Sports Director
• Rod Zimmerman, VP/General Manager
• Jackie Spencer, Director of Marketing
Nature of Sports Service:
24-hour sports radio programming.
Baseball:
MLB - CBS.
College Sports:
Basketball, Football - University of Illinois.

**WSDM-FM/WBOW-AM ESPN SPORTS
RADIO**
1301 OHIO STREET
TERRE HAUTE, IN 47807
812-234-9770
Fax: 812-238-1576
www.espnsportsradio.com
• Scott Jones, Station Director
(812) 234-9770
scott@espnsportsradio.com
Description:
ESPN Radio
Teams:
High school: Northview, Terre Haute North,
Terre Haute South, and West Vigo College:
Indiana State University, Purdue University,

and Butler University Professional: Indiana
Pacers

WSDP-FM
46181 JOY ROAD
CANTON, MI 48187-1316
734-416-7732
Fax: 734-416-7763
http://www.wsdpradio.com
• Bill Keith, General Manager
keithb@pccs.k12.mi.us
• Mike Schaffer, Sports Director
Description:
Educational, Music, News, Sports.

WSEW-FM
2 RIDGE ROAD
NEW DURHAM, NH 03855
603-859-9170
Fax: 603-859-8172
http://www.wsew.org
• Sharon Malone, Operations Manager
(603) 859-9170
smalone@wsew.org
Description:
Music, News, Sports.

WSFN-AM
7515 BLYTHE ISLAND HIGHWAY
BRUNSWICK, GA 31523
912-264-6251
Fax: 912-264-9991
www.thefansportsradio.com
• Gary Moss, Program Director
(912) 264-6251
wsfnradio@yahoo.com
• Kevin Willis, Sports Director
(912) 264-6251
wsfnradio@yahoo.com
Description:
Georgia's # 1 sports station. Featuring
ESPN Radio along with 4 hours of local,
regional sports programing.
Teams:
Atlanta Braves, Atlanta Falcons, Atlanta
Hawks, SECÃ†and ACCC sports.

WSFN-AM SPORTS RADIO
875 E. SUMMIT
MUSKEGON, MI 49444
231-733-2126
Fax: 231-739-9037
• Jill Gossett, General Manager
• Scott Siembida, Pro General Manager
Director
Nature of Sports Service:
Local. 24-hour sports radio programming.

WSHN-AM
3375 MERRIAM STREET
MUSKEGON, MI 49444
231-924-4700
800-386-9746
Fax: 231-924-9746
http://www.funcountry.com
• Jon Russell, News Director
jon.russell@muskegonradio.com
• Jon Russell, Sports Director
jon.russell@muskegonradio.com
Description:
Music, News, Sports.

WSHR-FM
212 SMITH ROAD
LAKE RONKONKOMA, NY 11779-2229

631-471-1400
Fax: 631-471-1408
wshr@sachem.edu
http://www.wshr.com
• Mark Laura, General Manager
mlaura@sachem.edu
Description:
Music, News, Sports.

WSHW-FM
PO BOX 545
FRANKFORT, IN 46041-0545
765-659-3338
800-447-4463
Fax: 765-659-3338
http://www.wshw.com
• Bern Kaspar, Chief Executive Officer
(765) 654-7000
vjk@casperradio.com
• Mike Reppert, News Director
• Greg Garrett, Sports Host
(765) 659-3338
Description:
Music, News, Sports.

WSIF-FM
1328 COLLEGIATE DRIVE
WILKESBORO, NC 28697
336-838-6179
Fax: 336-838-6277
• Al DeLachica, General Manager
(336) 838-6222
Description:
Music, News, Sports.

WSIG-FM
1866 EAST MARKET STREET SUITE 325
HARRISONBURG, VA 22801
540-432-1063
Fax: 540-433-9267
• Steve Walker, Program Director
Description:
Music, News, Sports.

WSJB-FM
278 WHITE BRIDGE ROAD
STANDISH, ME 04084-5270
207-893-7914
Fax: 207-893-7873
wyates@sjcme.edu
http://www.stjosephscollege.edu
• Bill Yates, General Manager
Description:
Music, News, Sports.

WSJM-AM
580 EAST NAPIER AVENUE
BENTON HARBOR, MI 49022
269-925-1111
Fax: 269-925-1011
aweston@wsjm.com
http://www.wsjm.com
• Joe Eauganno, Advertising Manager
(269) 925-1111
• Jim Gifford, Program Director
(269) 925-1111
gifford@wsjm.com
• Phil McDonald, Sports Director
Description:
Music, News, Talk.

WSKW
PO BOX 159, MIDDLE RD
SKOWHEGAN, ME 04976
207-474-5171
Fax: 207-474-3299

• Jason Roberts, General Manager/Program Director/Sports Director
Nature of Sports Service:
Local. 24-hour sports radio programming. ESPN Affiliate

WSLI-AM
5 TWELVE OAK CIRCLE SUITE A
JACKSON, MS 39209-6563
601-922-9307
888-848-9754
Fax: 601-922-5051
http://www.wslisports.com
• Bryan Eubank, General Manager
eubie@supersport930.com
Description:
Music, News, Sports.

WSLJ-FM
SAINT LAWRENCE UNIVERSITY
CANTON, NY 13617
315-229-5356
800-388-6758
Fax: 315-229-5373
radio@ncpr.org
http://www.ncpr.org
• Martha Foley, News Director
(315) 229-5304
martha@ncpr.org
Description:
Music, News.

WSLL-FM
SAINT LAWRENCE UNIVERSITY
CANTON, NY 13617
315-229-5356
800-388-6758
Fax: 315-229-5373
radio@ncpr.org
http://www.ncpr.org
• Martha Foley, News Director
(315) 229-5304
martha@ncpr.org
Description:
Music, News.

WSLO-FM
SAINT LAWRENCE UNIVERSITY
CANTON, NY 13617
315-229-5356
800-388-6758
Fax: 315-229-5373
radio@ncpr.org
http://www.ncpr.org
• Martha Foley, News Director
(315) 229-5304
martha@ncpr.org
Description:
Music, News.

WSMG-AM
1004 ARNOLD ROAD
GREENEVILLE, TN 37743
423-638-3188
Fax: 423-638-1979
wgrv@greeneville.com
http://www.greeneville.com/wsmg
• Leroy Moon, Advertising Manager
grv@greeneville.com
• Bobby Rader, News Director
• Bobby Rader, Sports Director
Description:
Music, News, Sports.

WSMI-AM
PO BOX 10
LITCHFIELD, IL 62056
217-532-5921
Fax: 217-532-2431
wsmi@wsmiradio.com
www.wsmiradio.com
• Kevin Talley, Promotions Director
• Terry Todt, Program Director
• Terry Todt, Sports Director
Description:
Music, News, Sports.

WSMK-FM
925 NORTH 5TH STREET
NILES, MI 49120-1601
616-683-4343
Fax: 269-683-7759
• Jeff Ryder, Program Director
(269) 683-4343
Description:
Music, News, Sports.
Year Founded:
1990

WSNV-FM
3807 BRANDON AVENUE S.W. SUITE 2350
ROANOKE, VA 24018
540-725-1220
Fax: 540-725-1245
http://www.j935.com
• Tammy Cazap, Advertising Manager
• Steve Cross, Program Director
stevecross@clearchannel.com
Description:
Music, News, Sports.

WSOU-FM
400 SOUTH ORANGE AVENUE
SOUTH ORANGE, NJ 07079-2646
973-761-9768
800-895-9768
Fax: 973-761-7593
wsou@shu.edu
http://www.wsou.net
• John Brickley, Sports Director
brickljo@shu.edu
• Aleks Tasic, News Director
(973) 313-6110
tasicale@shu.edu
• Brian Ciano, Sports Director
(973) 761-9768
wsousports@hotmail.com
Description:
Music, News, Sports.

WSPD
125 S. SUPERIOR ST
TOLEDO, OH 43602
419-244-8321
Fax: 419-242-2846
• Andy Stuart, General Manager
• Mellisa Richards, Marketing Director
Nature of Sports Service:
News, Sports, Talk.
Baseball:
MLB - Detroit Tigers.
College Sports:
Basketball, Football - University of Toledo.
Football:
NFL - Detroit Lions.

WSQR-AM
1851 COLTONVILLE ROAD
SYCAMORE, IL 60178-2663

815-899-1000
Fax: 815-899-9000
• Bob Costigan, News Director
Description:
Music, News, Sports.

WSRN-FM
500 COLLEGE AVENUE
SWARTHMORE, PA 19081-1306
610-328-8335
Fax: 610-328-8000
http://www.wsrnfm.org
• John C. Williams, General Manager
(610) 328-8340
jwillia3@swarthmore.edu
Description:
Music, News, Sports.

WSRW-AM
5675 STATE ROUTE 247
HILLSBORO, OH 45133
937-393-1590
Fax: 937-393-1611
http://www.wsrwam.com
• Damon Scott, Program Director
damonscott@clearchannel.com
Description:
Music, News, Talk.

WSRW-FM
5675 STATE ROUTE 247
HILLSBORO, OH 45133
937-393-1590
Fax: 937-393-1611
http://www.wsrw.com
• Damon Scott, Program Director
damonscott@clearchannel.com
Description:
Music, News, Sports.

WSSO-AM
601 2ND AVENUE NORTH
COLUMBUS, MS 39701
662-327-1183
Fax: 662-328-1122
chris.doughty@cumulus.com
• Greg Benefield, General Manager
(662) 327-1183
Description:
Music, News, Talk.

WSTP-AM
P. O. BOX 4157
SALISBURY, NC 28145
704-636-3811
Fax: 704-637-1490
newsradio1490@yahoo.com
http://www.1490wstp.com
• Mark Brown, News Director
• Howard Platt, Sports Director
(704) 636-3811
Description:
Music, News.

WSYL-AM
P.O. BOX 519
SYLVANIA, GA 30467-0519
912-564-7461
Fax: 912-564-7462
• Ann Jones, Advertising Manager
Description:
Music, News, Sports.

WSYY-AM
LAKE ROAD
PO BOX 1240
MILLINOCKET, ME 04462
207-723-9657
Fax: 207-723-5900
calendar@themountain949.com
http://www.angelfire.com/me2/wsyyfm/index.
html
• Michael Hale, Advertising Manager
mhale@themountain949.com
• Michael Hale, News Director
mhale@themountain949.com
• Michael Hale, Sports Director
mhale@themountain949.com
Description:
Music, News, Sports.

WTAD-AM
329 MAINE STREET
QUINCY, IL 62301
217-224-4102
Fax: 217-224-4133
http://www.wtad.com
• Mary Griffith, News Director
(217) 224-4102
mgriffith@staradio.com
Description:
News, Talk.

WTAW
2700 E. BYPASS, STE 5000
COLLEGE STATION, TX 77840
979-846-1150
Fax: 979-846-1933
www.wtaw.com/wtaw
• Ben Downs, General Manager
• Tom Turbiville, Sports Director
Nature of Sports Service:
News, Sports.
Baseball:
MLB - Houston Astros, CBS Baseball.
College Sports:
Football - University of Texas, CBS NCAA;
Baseball - Texas A&M; Basketball -
University of Texas, Texas A&M.
Football:
NFL - Dallas Cowboys.

WTBU-AM
BOSTON UNIVERSITY
BOSTON, MA 02215-2422
617-353-6401
Fax: 617-353-6403
wtbu@bu.edu
http://www.wtburadio.com/
• Matt Blanchette, Sports Director
sports@wtburadio.org
• Eden Kasle, News Director
news@wtburadio.org
Description:
Music, News, Sports.

WTCC-FM
P.O. BOX 9000
SPRINGFIELD, MA 01102-9000
413-746-9822
Fax: 413-755-6305
http://www.wtccfm.org
• Mark Lee, Program Director
(413) 746-9822
Description:
Music, News, Sports.

WTCH-AM
1456 GREENBAY STREET, E.
SHAWANO, WI 54166
715-524-2194
Fax: 715-524-9980
http://www.wtcham960.com
• Doug Erdman, News Director
(715) 524-2194
• Andy Richards, Sports Director
Description:
Music, News, Sports.

WTCO-AM
50 FRIENDSHIP PIKE
CAMPBELLSVILLE, KY 42718
270-789-2401
Fax: 270-789-1450
http://www.wtcoldies.com
• Marty Bagby, News Director
mbagby@commonwealthbroadcasting.com
• Marty Bagby, Sports Director
Description:
Music, News, Sports.

WTCQ-FM
1501 MOUNT VERNON ROAD
VIDALIA, GA 30474
912-537-9202
Fax: 912-537-4477
zfowler@vidaliacommunications.com
http://www.vidaliacommunications.com
• Collins Knighton, Sports Director
(912) 537-9202
• Martin McIntyre, Advertising Manager
Description:
Music.

WTCR-AM
134 4TH AVENUE
HUNTINGTON, WV 25701
304-525-7788
800-938-1033
Fax: 304-525-3299
billcornwell@clearchannel.com
http://www.havejoy.com
• Clint McElroy, Program Director
Description:
Music, News, Sports.

WTDK-FM
2 BAY STREET
CAMBRIDGE, MD 21613
410-228-4800
Fax: 410-228-0130
• Norm Elliott, News Director
(410) 228-4800
normelliott@hotmail.com
Description:
Music, News, Sports.

WTDY AM 1670
PO BOX 2058
MADISON, WI 53701
608-273-1000
Fax: 608-271-8182
• Tom Walker, General Manager
• John Sylvester, Operations
Manager/Program Director
• Chris Krok, Promotions Director
Nature Sports Service:
Sports and Talk Radio.

WTEM SPORTS RADIO
8750 BROOKVILLE RD
SILVER SPRING, MD 20910
301-231-7798

• Kristin Lewis, Asst Promotions Dir
Nature of Sports Service:
Local and National. 24-hour sports radio
programming.

WTGG-FM
200 EAST THOMAS STREET
HAMMOND, LA 70401
985-542-9844
Fax: 123-456-5679
ewdowdy@yahoo.com
http://www.tang965.com
• Ellise Dowdy, Promotions Director
(985) 345-0030
• Roger Gill, Sports Director
(985) 345-0060
• T. J. Maggio, Program Director
tjinthemorning@yahoo.com

WTGZ-FM
2514 SOUTH COLLEGE STREET SUITE
104
AUBURN, AL 36830
334-887-9999
888-984-4379
Fax: 334-826-9599
info@thetiger.fm
http://www.thetiger.net
• Kevin Jackson, Promotion Director

WTIG-AM
P.O. BOX 608
MASSILLON, OH 44647-9513
330-837-9900
Fax: 330-837-9844
espn@espn990.com
http://www.espn990.com
• Bill Caples, Sports Director
(330) 837-9900
espn@espn990.com
• Donovan Resh, Program Director
(330) 837-9900
espn@espn990.com
Description:
Music, News, Sports.

WTIV-AM
900 WATER STREET
MEADVILLE, PA 16335
814-724-1111
Fax: 814-333-9628
• Doug Metheney, News Director
radio@zoominternet.net
Description:
Music, News, Sports.

WTKG-AM
77 MONROE CENTER STEET, N.W. SUITE
1000
GRAND RAPIDS, MI 49503-2912
616-459-1919
Fax: 616-242-6599
http://www.wtkg.com
• Rich Jones, News Director
(616) 459-1919
richajones@clearchannel.com
Description:
Music, News.

WTKT-AM
600 CORPORATE CIRCLE
HARRISBURG, PA 17110
717-540-8800
800-500-9993
Fax: 717-671-9973

media

billmead@clearchannel.com
http://www.kool993.com
• Ron Roy, General Manager
ronroy@clearchannel.com
Description:
Music.

WTKY-FM
341 RADIO STATION ROAD
TOMPKINSVILLE, KY 42167
270-487-6119
Fax: 270-487-8462
• Bernice Whittimore, General Manager
• Bernice Whittimore, President
Description:
Music, News, Sports.

WTLC-FM
21 EAST SAINT JOSEPHS STREET
INDIANAPOLIS, IN 46204
317-266-9600
Fax: 317-328-3870
http://www.wtlc.com/contactus.asp
• Terri Durrett, News Director
tdurrett@radio-one.com
• Kay Feeney-Caito, Promotions Director
• Lakisha Knight, Promotions Director
(317) 266-9600
Description:
Music, News, Sports, Talk.

WTLX-FM
100 STODDART
BEAVER DAM, WI 53916-0902
920-885-4949
800-369-1005
Fax: 920-885-2152
• Evan Cohen, Program Director
(920) 885-4949
• Keith Williams, Sales Manager
(608) 245-9859
Description:
Music, News, Sports.

WTMJ
720 E. CAPITOL DR
MILWAUKEE, WI 53212
414-332-9611
Fax: 414-967-5298
www.620wtmj.com
• Carl Moll, Director Network Operations
• Tom Sheridan, General Sales Manager
• Jon Schweitzer, Senior VP/General Manager
Nature of Service:
News and score reporting for the bowling community in the greater Buffalo/Niagara Falls region.
Baseball:
MLB - Milwaukee Brewers.
Basketball:
NBA-Milwaukee Bucks
College Sports:
Basketball, Football - University of Wisconsin.
Football:
NFL - Green Bay Packers.
Publishing Company:
Westside News, Inc.
Primary Audience:
Bowling Community.
Frequency:
Weekly during bowling season.
Sports:
Bowling.

Circulation:
2,100

WTNS-FM
114 NORTH 6TH STREET
COSHOCTON, OH 43812
740-622-1560
Fax: 740-622-7940
• Ken Smailes, News Director
• Tom Thompson, Advertising Manager
Description:
Music, News, Sports.

WTNY-AM
134 MULLIN STREET
WATERTOWN, NY 13601-3616
315-788-0790
Fax: 315-788-4379
ltz93@hotmail.com
http://www.790wtny.com
• Nathan Lehman, News Director
(315) 788-0790
morning@790wtny.com
• George Nehr, Promotions Director
Description:
Music, News, Sports, Talk.

WTOD-AM
3225 ARLINGTON AVENUE
TOLEDO, OH 43614-2427
419-725-5700
Fax: 419-385-2902
• Brian Olsen, General Manager
• Tim Roberts, Advertising Manager
(419) 725-5700
Description:
Music, News, Sports.

WTON-AM
304 WEST BEVERLEY STREET
STAUNTON, VA 24401-4207
540-885-5188
800-978-2794
Fax: 540-885-1240
• Patrick Hite, News Director
(540) 885-5188
• J. G. Ratcliff, Owner
(540) 885-5188
Description:
Music.

WTOP-FM
3400 IDAHO AVENUE, N.W.
WASHINGTON, DC 20016-3046
202-895-5000
Fax: 202-895-5149
http://www.wtopnews.com
• Dave Johnson, Sports Director
(202) 895-5068
djohnson@wtopnews.com

WTOU-AM
1867 WEST MARKET STREET
AKRON, OH 44313-6901
330-836-4700
Fax: 330-836-5321
marvindurant@clearchannel.com
• Tom Duresky, News Director
tomduresky@clearchannel.com
Description:
Music.

WTPA-FM
2300 VARTAN WAY
HARRISBURG, PA 17110-9720

717-238-1041
800-946-5104
Fax: 717-234-7780
http://www.wtpafm.com
• John Paul Shaffer, News Director
Description:
Music, News, Sports.

WTPR-AM
206 NORTH BREWER STREET
PARIS, TN 38242
731-642-7100
Fax: 731-644-9367
http://www.wenkwtpr.com
• Terry Hailey, Advertising Manager
• Terry Hailey, News Director
(731) 642-7100
Description:
Music, News, Sports.

WTRN-AM
WASHINGTON AVENUE AND 1ST STREET
TYRONE, PA 16686
814-684-3200
Fax: 814-684-1220
amnet@aol.com
http://www.wtrn.net
• Jean Dixon, News Director
• Rich Saupp, Sports Director
Description:
Music, News, Sports, Talk.

WTRP-AM
806 NEW FRANKLIN ROAD
LAGRANGE, GA 30240-1844
706-884-7022
706-884-9877
Fax: 706-884-8612
http://www.wtrp.com
• Michael Buchanan, Sports Anchor
• Jennifer Jones, Advertising Sales
wtrp@charter.com

WTRS-FM
3357 SOUTHWEST 7TH STREET
OCALA, FL 34474
352-732-9877
Fax: 352-622-6675
http://www.wtrs.fm
• Sam Gerace, Advertising Manager
Description:
Music, News, Sports.

WTSX-FM
15 NEVERSINK DRIVE
PORT JERVIS, NY 12771
845-856-5185
888-967-9879
Fax: 845-856-4757
wtsx@frontiernet.net
http://www.wtsx.com
• Bob O., News Director
bobomorningshow@yahoo.com
Description:
Music, News, Sports.

WTTF-AM
167 MAIN STREET
TIFFIN, OH 44883
419-447-9883
Fax: 419-447-2212
www.wttf.com
• John Spahr, Operations Manager
• Steve Shoffner, News Director
• Jon Kerns, Sports Director

WTTR-AM
101 WTTR LANE
WESTMINSTER, MD 21158
410-848-5511
Fax: 410-876-5095
news@wttr.com
http://www.wttr.com
• Mark Woodworth, News Director
(410) 848-5511
news@wttr.com
• Charles Beckhardt, Sports Director
(410) 848-5511
info@wttr.com
Description:
Music, News, Sports, Talk.

WTXM-FM
P.O. BOX 3848
MARYVILLE, TN 47720
865-525-6000
Fax: 865-525-2000
http://www.knoxoldies.com/
• Brad Jeffries, Program Director
Description:
Music, News, Sports.

WTZN-AM
170 REDINGTON AVENUE
TROY, PA 16947
570-297-0100
800-326-9445
Fax: 570-297-3193
http://www.wiggle100.com/
• David Rockwell, News Director
news@wiggle100.com
Description:
Music.

WTZX-AM
520 NORTH SPRING STREET
SPARTA, TN 38583-1305
931-836-1055
Fax: 931-836-2320
donhoward@clearchannel.com
Description:
Music, News, Sports.

WUCZ-FM
104 Z COUNTRY LANE
CARTHAGE, TN 37030
615-735-1350
Fax: 615-735-0381
www.1041theranch.net
• Jim West, Sports Director
• John Wood, Sportsnuts Host
• Dennis Banka, Station Owner
dennis@1041theranch.net
Description:
Sports talk show dedicated to our local high
school football teams, with segments
dedicated to the Tennessee Volunteers and
the Tennessee Titans.
Sports Discussed:
Primary: local high school football;
Secondary: College & NFL Football,
Tennessee Titans and Tennessee
Volunteers, other sports as needed.
Frequency:
Sportsnuts airs Thrusday nights from August
thru November (High School Football
Season) from 6-8pm Central Time.

WUMP 730
PO BOX 389
ATHENS, AL 35612

256-830-8300
Fax: 256-232-6842
www.730ump.com
• Bill Dunnavant, General Manager
• Peter Thiele, Operations Manager/Sports
Director
Nature of Sports Service:
24 Hour sports.
Auto Sports:
NASCAR.
Baseball:
MLB Atlanta Braves.
College Sports:
Football, Basketball - Auburn University.

WUNR-AM
160 NORTH WASHINGTON STREET
BOSTON, MA 02114-2120
617-367-9003
Fax: 617-367-2265
• Velma May, News Director
Description:
Full Service, Music, News.

WUPR-AM
P.O. BOX 868
UTUADO, PUERTO RIC 00641-0868
787-894-2460
Fax: 787-894-4955
• Jose Martinez Giraud, General Manager
Description:
Music, News, Sports, Talk.

WUSB-FM
S.U.N.Y. AT STONY BROOK
STONY BROOK, NY 11794
631-632-6501
Fax: 631-632-7182
wusb@notes.cc.sunysb.edu
http://www.wusb.org
• Curt Hylton, Sports Director
(631) 632-6501
• Morton Mecklosky, News Director
(631) 751-2577
mecklom@sunysuffolk.edu
Description:
Music, News, Sports.

WUSI-FM
1100 LINCOLN DRIVE ROOM 1003 MAIL
CODE 6
CARBONDALE, IL 62901
618-453-4343
Fax: 618-453-6186
jeff.williams@wsiu.org
• Mike Zelten, Program Director
(618) 453-5020
mike.zelten@wsiu.org
Description:
Music, News, Sports.

WUVA-FM
1140 ROSE HILL DRIVE
CHARLOTTESVILLE, VA 22903-5128
434-817-6880
Fax: 434-977-3775
• Tanisha Thompson, Program Director
info@92.7kissfm.com
Description:
Music, News, Sports.

WVAC-FM
110 SOUTH MADISON STREET
ADRIAN, MI 49221-2518
517-265-5161
Fax: 517-264-3331

• Joe Elardo, Sports Director
• Ben McDuffee, News Director
Description:
Music, News, Sports.

WVBU-FM
P.O. BOX C-3956
LEWISBURG, PA 17837-2029
570-577-1174
Fax: 570-577-1174
wvbu@bucknell.edu
http://www.orgs.bucknell.edu/wvbu/
• Heather Franz, News Director
Description:
Music, News, Sports.

WVCH-AM
308 EAST DUTTONMILL ROAD
BROOKHAVEN, PA 19015-1109
610-872-8861
Fax: 610-872-8865
wvch@juno.com
http://www.wvch.com
• William Fenton, General Manager
(610) 279-9000
wvchtraffic@juno.com
Description:
Music.

WVEE-FM
1201 PEACHTREE STREET NORTHEAST
SUITE 80
ATLANTA, GA 30361-3500
404-898-8900
Fax: 404-898-8909
http://www.v-103.com
• Monique Davis, Marketing Director
monique.davis@infinitybroadcasting.com
• Monique Davis, Promotion Director
• Denise Meriwether, Promotions Assistant
denise.meriwether@infinitybroadcasting.co
m
• Denise Meriwether, Promotions
Coordinator
• Olivia Seymore, Promotions Coordinator
olivia.seymore@infinitybroadcasting.com
Description:
Music, News, Sports.

WVEI-AM
181 MORELAND STREET
WORCESTER, MA 01609
508-752-5611
Fax: 508-752-1006
• Jason Wolfe, Program Director
(617) 779-3541
Description:
Sports, Talk.

WVGM-AM
3305 OLD FOREST ROAD
LYNCHBURG, VA 24501
434-385-8298
Fax: 434-385-8991
• Tex Meyer, General Manager
(434) 385-8298
texmeyer@clearchannel.com

WVLZ-AM
802 SOUTH CENTRAL AVENUE
KNOXVILLE, TN 37902-1207
865-546-4653
Fax: 865-637-7133
• Gormon Collins, General Manager
Description:
Music.

media

WVMJ-FM
SETTLERS GREEN ROUTE 16
NORTH CONWAY, NH 03860
603-356-8870
Fax: 603-356-8875
office@wmwv.com
http://www.valley1045.com
• Ron Frizzel, General Manager
ronfrizzel@aol.com
Description:
Music, News, Sports.

WVMW-FM
2300 ADAMS AVENUE
SCRANTON, PA 18509-1514
570-348-6202
Fax: 570-961-4769
http://www.marywood.edu/departments/com
marts/WVMW.html
• Jessica Young, News Director
Description:
Music, News.

WVRY-FM
402 BNA DRIVE SUITE 400
NASHVILLE, TN 37217
615-367-2210
Fax: 615-367-0758
wmcshane@salemmusicnetwork.com
http://www.solidgospel.com
• Vance Dillard, Program Director
(615) 367-2210
vdillard@salemmusicnetwork.com
Description:
Music, News, Sports.

WVUM-FM
P.O. BOX 248191
CORAL GABLES, FL 33146
305-284-3131
Fax: 305-284-3132
info@wvum.org
http://www.wvum.org
• Jeremy Marks-Peltz, Sports Director
sports@wvum.org
Description:
Music, News, Sports.

WVXU-FM
1223 CENTRAL PARKWAY
CINCINNATI, OH 45214
513-352-9170
800-230-3576
Fax: 513-745-1004
wvxu@wvxu.org
www.wvxu.org
• Ann Thompson, News Director
(513) 745-3780
Description:
Educational, Music, News, Sports.

WWAG-FM
1680 STATE ROAD 1071
TOMPKINSVILLE, KY 42167
606-287-9924
1079fm@prtcnet.org
• Sherry Handy, Program Director

WWBF-AM
1130 RADIO ROAD
BARTOW, FL 33830-7600
863-533-0744
Fax: 863-533-8546
http://www.wwbf.com
• Susan Thornburg, Office Manager
susan@wwbf.com

• Tom Thornburg, Sports Director
tom@wwbf.com
Description:
Music, News, Sports.

WWCD-FM
503 SOUTH FRONT STREET SUITE 101
COLUMBUS, OH 43215-5666
614-221-9923
Fax: 614-227-0021
webmaster@cd101.com
http://www.cd101.com
• Randy Malloy, Marketing Director
(614) 221-9923
randym@cd101.com
• Randy Malloy, News Director
(614) 221-9923
randym@cd101.com
Description:
Music, News, Sports.

WWDW-FM
3 EAST 1ST STREET
WELDON, NC 27890
252-536-3115
Fax: 252-538-0378
• Les Atkins, News Director
• Mark Matthews, Sports Director
• Amy Moran, Advertising Sales Manager
(252) 538-9790
amymoran@yahoo.com

WWEL-FM
P.O. BOX 1988
LONDON, KY 40743
606-864-2148
Fax: 606-864-0645
http://www.1039thewolf.com
• Jerry Deaton, News Director
• Trevor Grigsby, Sports Director
• Frances Wilhoit, Account Executive
• Frances Wilhoit, Advertising Manager
• Frances Wilhoit, Promotions Manager
• Terry Harris, Sports Director
(606) 864-2148
Description:
Music.

WWFG-FM
351 TILGHMAN ROAD
SALISBURY, MD 21804-1126
410-742-1923
800-664-3764
Fax: 410-742-2329
salisburyproduction@clearchannel.com
http://www.delmarvaradio.com
• Brian Cleary, Program Director
(410) 572-6781
briancleary@clearchannel.com
Description:
Music, News, Sports.

WWIS-AM
W11573 TOWN CREEK ROAD
BLACK RIVER FALLS, WI 54615
715-284-4391
Fax: 715-284-9740
wwis@wwisradio.com
http://www.wwisradio.com
• Brian Brawner, Sports Director
• Bob Gabrielson, General Manager
Description:
Music.

WWIZ-FM
4040 SIMON ROAD
YOUNGSTOWN, OH 44512
330-783-1000
Fax: 330-783-0060
http://www.realrock104.com/
• Jim Loboy, News Director
(330) 783-1000
Description:
Music.

WWKA-FM
4192 NORTH JOHN YOUNG PARKWAY
ORLANDO, FL 32804
407-298-9292
Fax: 407-290-1076
http://www.k92fm.com
• Amy Jean Thompson, Promotion Director
(321) 281-2023
amyjean.thompson@cox.com
Description:
Music, News, Sports.

WWKC-FM
4988 SKYLINE DRIVE
CAMBRIDGE, OH 43725
740-432-5605
Fax: 740-432-1991
http://www.yourradioplace.com
• W. Grant Hafley, General Manager
• Reuben Perdue, Sports Director
(740) 432-5605
Description:
Music.

WWKY-FM
P.O. BOX 1310
MADISONVILLE, KY 42431
270-825-9779
Fax: 270-825-3260
• Keith Farrell, Account Executive
• Stephanie Vandygriff, Operations Manager
Description:
Music, News, Sports. Carries University of
Kentucky's football and men's basketball
games, Webster county high school games,
as well as the NFL's Tennessee Titans
games.
Publications:
High school football and high school
basketball schedules.

WWL
1450 PAYDRAS ST
NEW ORLEANS, LA 70112
504-593-6376
Fax: 504-593-1850
• Johnny Andrews, Vice President/General
Manager
• Buddy Deliberto, Sports Director
Nature of Sports Service:
News, Sports.
Baseball:
Minor League - Pacific Coast
League/PCL/New Orleans Zephyrs.
College Sports:
Basketball, Football - Louisiana State
University/LSU, Tulane.
Football:
NFL - New Orleans Saints.

WWLU-FM
LINCOLN UNIVERSITY
LINCOLN UNIVERSITY, PA 19352-0999
610-932-8300
Fax: 610-932-1905

Description:
Music, News, Sports, Talk.

WWTM
181 MORELAND ST
WORCESTER, MA 01609
508-836-9223
wwtm@hotmail.com
• Bruce Mittman, General Manager
• Chuck Perks, Program Director/Sports Director
Nature of Sports Service:
Local. 24-hour sports radio programming.
Baseball:
MLB - New York Yankees.
Basketball:
NBA Finals.
College Sports:
Basketball, Football - Holy Cross.
Ice Hockey:
NHL - Boston Bruins; Stanley Cup Finals.

WWTN-FM
10 MUSIC CIRCLE, E.
NASHVILLE, TN 37203-4338
615-291-7279
800-738-9986
Fax: 615-291-7268
http://www.997wtn.com
• Blake Fulton, Sports Director
(615) 291-7279
• John Mountz, Program Director
john.mountz@cumulus.com
• Lisa Valasquez, Promotions Director
(615) 321-1067
Description:
News, Sports, Talk.

WWVA-AM
1015 MAIN STREET
WHEELING, WV 30309
304-232-1170
Fax: 304-234-0041
http://www.newsradio1170.com
• Johnson Nixon, News Director
(304) 232-1170
johnsonnixon@clearchannel.com
• John Simonson, Sports Director
(304) 232-1170
johnsimonson@clearchannel.com
• Missy Tchappat, Advertising Director
• Missy Tchappat, Promotion Director
(304) 232-1170
missytchappat@clearchannel.com
Description:
News, Talk.

WXBD-AM
1909 EAST PASS ROAD SUITE D-11
GULFPORT, MS 39507
228-388-2001
Fax: 228-896-9736
• Suzanne Kelly, News Director
(228) 388-2001
mikesuzanne@hotmail.com
Description:
Music, News, Sports.

WXDU-FM
DUKE UNIVERSITY
DURHAM, NC 27708-0689
919-684-2957
Fax: 919-684-3260
wxdu@duke.edu
http://www.wxdu.duke.edu/

Description:
Music, News, Sports.

WXDX-AM
27675 HALSTED ROAD
FARMINGTON HILLS, MI 48331
248-324-5800
Fax: 248-848-0371
mschroeder@clearchannel.com
http://www.wxdx1310.com
• Mary Ann Schroeder-Barr, News Director
maryannschroeder@clearchannel.com

WXKS-FM
99 REVERE BEACH PARKWAY
MEDFORD, MA 02155
781-396-1430
Fax: 781-290-0722
http://www.kissfm.com
• Bill Costa, News Director
billcosta@clearchannel.com
• Dennis O'Heron, Promotion Manager
dennisoheron@clearchannel.com
Description:
Music, News, Sports.

WXLU-FM
SAINT LAWRENCE UNIVERSITY
CANTON, NY 13617
315-229-5356
800-388-6758
Fax: 315-229-5373
radio@ncpr.org
http://www.ncpr.org
• Martha Foley, News Director
(315) 229-5304
martha@ncpr.org
Description:
Music, News.

WXTB-FM
4002 GANDY BOULEVARD
TAMPA, FL 33611-3410
813-832-1000
Fax: 813-832-1090
http://www.98rock.com
• Meg Heimstead, Promotions Coordinator
Dirtbag@98rock.com
• Mike Oliviero, Promotion Director
mikeoliviero@clearchannel.com
Description:
Music, News, Sports.

WXXA-AM
4000 NUMBER 1 RADIO DRIVE
LOUISVILLE, KY 40218-4514
502-479-2222
Fax: 502-479-2225
http://www.wwky.com
• Ted Werbin, News Director
(502) 479-2201
tedwerbin@clearchannel.com
Description:
Music, News, Sports.

WXYT-AM
26495 AMERICAN DRIVE
SOUTHFIELD, MI 48034-6114
248-455-7350
Fax: 248-455-7369
http://www.wxyt.com
• Deb Spadafora, Promotions Director
daspadafora@cbs.com
• Dan Zampillo, Program Director
(248) 455-7350

Description:
Talk.

WYBF-FM
610 KING OF PRUSSIA ROAD
RADNOR, PA 19087-3623
610-902-8457
Fax: 610-902-8285
• Justin Hallman, Sports Director
(610) 902-5115
jjh722@cabrini.edu
• Krista Mazzeo, General Manager
(610) 902-8360
themazzspazz@hotmail.com
Description:
Educational, Music, News, Sports, Talk.

WYNT-FM
1330 NORTH MAIN STREET
MARION, OH 43302
877-472-3464
Fax: 740-387-3697
stevescott@clearchannel.com
http://www.majic959.com
• Ben Failor, News Director
benfailor@clearchannel.com
• Jeff Ruth, Sports Director
(877) 472-3464
jeffruth@clearchannel.com
Description:
Music, News, Sports, Talk.

WYRQ-FM
16405 HAVEN ROAD
LITTLE FALLS, MN 56345-2630
320-632-2992
800-568-7249
Fax: 320-632-2571
http://www.fallsradio.com
• Rod Grams, Program Director
(320) 632-5414
• Al Windsperger, Sports Director
(320) 632-2992
ads@fallsradio.com
Description:
Music, News, Sports.
Year Founded:
1980

WYSL-AM
P. O. BOX 236
AVON, NY 14414-9791
585-346-3000
Fax: 585-346-0450
info@wysl1040.com
http://www.wysl1040.com
• Robert Savage, News Director
savage@wysl1040.com
• Joe Centanni, Weekend And Sports Producer
(585) 346-3000
info@wysl1040.com
Description:
News, Talk.

WYTI-AM/FM
275 GLENNWOOD DRIVE
ROCKY MOUNT, VA 24151-0430
540-483-9955
Fax: 540-483-7802
wyti@wytiradio.com
www.wytiradio.com
• Susan Mullins, Vice President
Description:
Music, News, Sports.

Year Founded:
1957

WYXC-AM
1410 HIGHWAY 411 NE
CARTERSVILLE, GA 30121-5115
770-382-1306
Fax: 770-936-1967
• Chip Rogers, Owner
charles@wyxc.com
Description:
Music, News, Sports.

WYXY-FM
20 N.W. 3RD STREET
EVANSVILLE, IN 47708
812-424-8284
Fax: 812-426-7928
• Tim Huelfing, General Manager
Description:
Music, News, Sports.

WYYZ-AM
268 HOOD ROAD
JASPER, GA 30143-0280
706-692-4100
Fax: 706-692-4012
wyyz1490@aol.com
• Tania Clark, Station Manager
(706) 692-4100
radiomom@etcmail.com
Description:
Music, News, Sports, Talk.

WZBB-FM
10899 VIRGINIA AVENUE
BASSETT, VA 24055
618-564-2171
Fax: 618-564-3202
• Craig Richards, Program Director
crichards@wzbbfm.com
Description:
Music, News, Sports.

WZBO-AM
911 PARSONAGE STREET EXTENDED
ELIZABETH CITY, NC 27909
252-338-0196
Fax: 252-338-5275
http://www.ecri.net
• Chris Ling, Advertising Manager
(252) 441-2109
chris@ecri.net
• Rick Loesch, Advertising Manager
rloesch@ecri.net
• Rick Loesch, Owner
rloesch@ecri.net
• Sam Walker, News Director
Description:
Music, News, Sports, Talk.

WZCT-AM
1111 EAST WILLOW STREET
SCOTTSBORO, AL 35768
256-574-1330
Fax: 866-506-7181
www.southerngospelam1330.com/
• Rob Carlile, Sports Director
Description:
Music, News, Sports.

WZLX-FM
800 BOYLSTON STREET, SUITE 2450
BOSTON, MA 02199-8001

617-267-0123
Fax: 617-421-9305
http://www.wzlx.com/
• Chachi Loprete, Marketing Director
chachi@wzlx.com
• Chachi Loprete, Promotions Coordinator
chachi@wzlx.com
• Patrick Murray, News Director
(617) 267-0123
shatz@wzlx.com
• Tank Sferruzza, Sports Director
(617) 267-0123
tank@wzlx.com
Description:
Music, News, Sports.

WZMR-FM
6 JOHNSON ROAD
LATHAM, NY 12110-5610
518-786-6600
Fax: 518-786-6610
www.albanyedge.com
• Kevin Callahan, Program Director
(518) 786-6675
Description:
Music, News, Sports.

WZNJ-FM
1028 HIGHWAY 80, E.
DEMOPOLIS, AL 36732-3712
334-289-1400
Fax: 334-289-2156
• Amy Ward, Sports Director
Description:
Music, News, Sports.

WZTM
11300 4TH ST, STE 318
ST. PETERSBURG, FL 33716
727-871-1819
• Rob Weingarten, Program Director
• Al Dukes, Sports Director
• Tom Connolly, Executive Producer
Nature of Sports Service:
Local. 24-hour sports radio programming.
Baseball:
MLB - New York Yankees.
College Sports:
Baseball - University of South Florida;
Basketball - University of South Florida,
Florida State, Football - University of South
Florida, Florida State.
Football:
NFL - Jacksonville Jaguars.

WZVN-FM
6405 OLCOTT AVENUE
HAMMOND, IN 46320
219-462-6111
Fax: 219-989-8516
http://www.hitsandfavorites.com
• Laura Waluszko, News Director
(219) 462-6111
laura@radiooneindiana.com
Description:
Music, News, Sports.

WZXL-FM
8025 BLACKHORSE PIKE BAYPORT ONE,
SUITE
WEST ATLANTIC CITY, NJ 08232
609-484-8444
Fax: 609-646-6331
http://www.wzxl.com
• Steve Raymond, Program Director

Description:
Music, News, Sports.

WZZE-FM
P.O. BOX 5001
CONCORDVILLE, PA 19331-0004
610-459-8100
Fax: 610-459-4431
• Mark Smith, Program Director
(610) 459-8100
Description:
Music, News, Sports.

WZZT-FM
3101 FREEPORT ROAD
STERLING, IL 61081
815-625-3400
Fax: 815-625-6940
wsdr@theramp.net
• Cathy Wagner, Promotion Director
wsdrsd@theramp.net
• Brian Zschiesche, Program Director
(815) 625-3400
wsdrtm@theramp.net

XTRA SPORTS 910
645 E MISSOURI AVE, STE 119
PHOENIX, AZ 85012
602-798-9340
Fax: 602-798-9364
www.xtrasports910.com
• Susan Karis-Madigan, General Manager
Nature of Sports Service:
Local. 24-hour sports radio programming.

XTRA SPORTS RADIO (690 AM)
610 S. ARDMORE AVE
LOS ANGELES, CA 90005
213-385-0101
Fax: 213-427-7905
www.xtrasports690.com
• Greg Ashlock, General Manager
• Brian Blackmore, Sports Director
Nature of Sports Service:
Regional. 24-hour sports radio
programming. for all of Southern California.
Baseball:
ESPN Radio; CBS Baseball, World Series,
Playoffs.
Basketball:
Los Angeles Clippers; NBA Radio.
College Sports:
University of California Los Angeles (UCLA).
Arena Football League
Los Angeles Avengers.

XTRA SPORTS RADIO 1150 AM
610 S. ARDMORE AVE
LOS ANGELES, CA 90005
213-520-1150
800-522-1150
Fax: 213-427-7278
• Roy Laughlin, General Manager
• Bic Jacobs, Program Director
• Dan Kieley, Program Director
Nature of Sports Service:
Regional. 24-hour sports radio
programming, includes Los Angeles
Dodgers and UCLA.

Sports Television, Cable & Broadcasting

ABC SPORTS, INC.
47 W. 66TH STREET
13TH FLOOR
NEW YORK, NY 10023
212-456-7777
Fax: 212-456-2381
www.abcsports.com
• John Skipper, President, ESPN, Inc.

ANN LIGUORI PRODUCTIONS, INC.
3 PINE GROVE COURT
WESTHAMPTON, NY 11977-1324
631-325-8573
www.annliguori.com
• Ann Liguori, President/Executive
Producer/Host
Nature of Sports Service:
National. Cable TV producer, distributor and
broadcaster. Produces, sells and distributes
Sports Innerview with Ann Liguori, a weekly
show on Fox Sports networks, Ann also
hosts weekly, 5-hour, live sports call-in show
on WFAN - NY.

AUTOTRADER.COM, INC
3003 SUMMIT BLVD
SUITE 200
ATLANTA, GA 30319
404-568-8000
800-353-9350
Fax: 404-568-3060
www.autotrader.com
• Jimmy Hayes, Chairman
• Dallas Clement, Executive Vice
President/Chief Financial Offi
• Edward Smith, CTO
Football Media Sponsor:
NFL - broadcast sponsorship of Monday
Night Football on ABC, NFL Live on ESPN2,
and Sunday Night Football on ESPN
College Sports Media Sponsor:
TV broadcasts of NCAA basketball games
on CBS
Football Media Sponsor:
Superbowl Advertiser

BLACK ENTERTAINMENT TELEVISION
1 BET PLAZA
1235 WEST STREET NORTHEAST
WASHINGTON, DC 20018-1211
202-608-2000
Fax: 202-608-2589
www.bet.com
• Debra L Lee, Chairman/Chief Executive
Officer
• Paxton Baker, President, BET Event
Productions
• Vicky Free, EVP Marketing/Chief
Marketing Officer
• Stephen Hill, President, Music
Programming
Nature of Sports Service:
National. Cable TV
Programmer/broadcaster.

CABLE NEWS NETWORK/CNN
ONE CNN CENTER
ATLANTA, GA 30348
404-827-1700
Fax: 404-827-1099
www.cnn.com

• Jeff Zucker, President
• Janet Rolle, EVP/Chief Marketing Officer
• Ken Jautz, President, CNN US
Nature of Sports Service:
National. Cable TV 24-hour news station.
Sports news presented several times a day
with a 30-minute daily wrap-up during the
evenings; periodic features on sports
figures,. sports events. Heavy sports
programming on weekends.

**CANADIAN BROADCASTING
CORPORATION/CBC**
181 QUEEN STREET
OTTAWA, ON, CANADA K1Y 1E4
613-288-6000
866-306-4636
Fax: 613-288-6245
www.cbc.ca
• Hubert Lacroix, President/Chief Executive
Officer
• Hubert Lacroix, President/CEO/Director
• Johanne B Charbonneau, Vice
President/CFO
• Kirstine Stewart, Executive Vicep
President
• Sylvain Lafrance, EVP French Services
Nature of Sports Service:
National. Broadcasting network. Sales
function includes national, regional and
market-by market sales.
Notes:
CBC has been awarded Canadian
broadcast rights for the next three Olympic
games

CBS SPORTS
51 W. 52ND STREET
NEW YORK, NY 10019-6188
212-975-4321
Fax: 212-975-4516
www.cbscorporation.com
• David Berson, President, CBS Sports
• Summer Redstone, Executive Chairman
• Shari Redstone, Vice Chairman
• Joseph Ianniello, Executive Vice
President/CFO
• Doug Rousso, CTO/CIO
• Gil Schwartz, EVP/Chief Communications
Officer
• Peter Dunn, President, CBS Television
Studios
• David Berson, EVP, CBS
Sports/President, CBS College Sports
Nature of Sports Service:
National. TV network.

COMCAST SPORTSNET BAY AREA
370 3RD STREET
2ND FLOOR
SAN FRANCISCO, CA 94107
415-296-8900
http://www.csnbayarea.com
• Ted Griggs, President, Comcast SportsNet
Bay Area
• Janet Fern, Senior Vice President/General
Manager
• April Silvia, Director of Programming
• Brad Nau, Executive Producer
Nature of Sports Service:
Regional. Cable TV programmer. Current
properties: Oakland A's baseball, San
Francisco Giants baseball, Golden State
Warriors basketball, San Jose Sharks
hockey, the University of California and
Stanford sports, San Jose Earthquakes

soccer, Oakland Raiders football, San
Francisco 49ers football.

COMCAST SPORTSNET NEW ENGLAND
42 3RD AVENUE
BURLINGTON, MA 01803-4414
617-933-9300
• Laura Hannon, Director, Comcast
SportsNet New England
Nature of Sports Service:
Regional. Cable TV programmer. Current
programs: Boston Celtics, New England
Revoution, Boston Cannons, Maine Red
Claws.

COX CABLE - SAN DIEGO
5159 FEDERAL BOULEVARD
SAN DIEGO, CA 92105
619-262-1122
Fax: 619-266-5046
www.cox.com/sandiego
• James Robbins, President/CEO
• Jacqui Vines, Vice President
• William Geppert, Senior Vice President
Nature of Sports Service:
Regional. Cable TV programmer.
Broadcasts San Diego Padres games, San
Diego State University Aztecs and other
sports events to cable TV subscribers.

ESPN CLASSIC SPORTS NETWORK
935 MIDDLE STREET
BRISTOL, CT 06010-1099
860-585-2000
Fax: 860-585-2213
www.espnclassic.com
• George C Bodenheimer, President
• Christine Driessen, Chief Financial Officer
• Bob Regina, Director
Nature of Sports Service:
National. Cable TV network. Features
classic sports programming, series
documentaries, original productions.

ESPN TELEVISION
ESPN PLAZA
935 MIDDLE ST
BRISTOL, CT 06010
860-766-2000
www.espn.go.com
• John D Skipper, President
• Jodi Markley, Senior Vice President,
International Programm
• Michael Hill, Vice President/General
Manager
• David Weiler, Vice President of
Productions Operations
• Carol Pandiscia, Senior Vice President Of
Technology, Business
• Tim Orcutt, Vice President of Tax
• Steve Anderson, EVP, News, Talent, and
Content Operations
• Paul Richardson, SVP Human Resources
• David Pahl, Senior Vice President/General
Counsel
• Tony Waggoner, Senior Vice
President/Controller
• David Casamona, Director
• Linda Moore, Senior Director, Business
Administration
• Christina Lemay, Associate Director
• Jessica Martin, Director of Marketing
• Mike Soltys, Director of Communications
• Tomas Casabal, Producer
• Andy Bronstein, Senior Director, On Air
Promotions & Developm
• Mark Groeschner, Creative Director

• Brian Burns, VP Strategic Business Plan & Development
• Tim Bunnell, SVP International Programming & Marketing
Nature of Sports Service:
National. Cable TV Network, Sports coverage around the clock, including events, specials, news and information and lifestyle programming. ESPN, Inc. includes: ESPN, ESPN International, ESPN2, ESPN Enterprises, ESPNET, ESPN Radio Network, and ESPN Classic

---

EVENT SPECIALIST OF NEW ORLEANS
400 N. PETERS ST
VIEUX CARRE, SUITE 209
NEW ORLEANS, LA 70130
504-525-1115
877-917-1115
Fax: 504-525-1118
info@eventsno.com
www.eventsno.com
• Renee E. Ganucheau, President
(504) 525-1115
renee@eventsno.com
• Kimberly Zibilich, Sales Manager
(504) 525-1115
Services:
A destination Management Company specializing in arranging transportation, theme parties, entertainment, spouse programs, tours, hotel bookings and more
Clients:
AeroSpace General Counsel's Group, American Express Meetings & Incentives, American Institute of Chemical Engineers, BTI-Kuoni Event Solutions, CIMBAR Performance Minerals, Cole-Parmer Instrument Company, CRG Events, ECC Construction & Debris Removal Services, Entergy Corporation, EXXON-MOBIL, GMAC, Genesys Corporation, Hughes Network, Incentive Holland, The Innovation Group, International Association of Chiefs of Police, Laticrete International Inc., LA/MS Hospice & Palliative Care Organization, Microsoft, Milligan Events, Morris Meetings & Incentives, National Association of Gaming Regulators, National Association of State Boards of Account
Event Management Services:
Complete hotel negotiations for groups, entertainment, special events, speakers, tours, transportation.

FOX SPORTS ASIA
151 LORONG CHUAN
03-01
NEW TECH PARK, Singapore 556741
656-488-6500
Fax: 656-488-6470
http://www.foxsportsasia.com
• Ward Platt, President, Fox International Channels Asia Pacific
• Peter Hutton, Senior Vice President of Sports, Fox Internat
Nature of Sports Service:
Organization is joint venture between STAR TV and Fox International Channels. It is the official Asian station of the English Premier League.

FOX SPORTS INTERNATIONAL
TUDOR HOUSE
35 GRESSE ST
LONDON, ENGLAND W1T 1QY

+44-(0) 207 462 3400
info@foxsports.co.uk
• David Flowers, Director
• Richard Battista, Director
Nature of Sports Service
Operates the programming services Fox Soccer Channel and Fox Sports Middle East, as well as syndicating sports content worldwide.

FOX SPORTS NET ARIZONA
455 NORTH 3RD STREET
SUITE 290
PHOENIX, AZ 85004-2193
602-257-9500
Fax: 602-257-0848
www.foxsportsarizona.com
• Rebecca O'Sullivan, Vice President
• Ed Olsen, General Sales Manager
• Kathy Goodenough, On Air Presentation Manager
• Elizabeth Zall, National Sales Manager
• David Soble, Local Sales Manager
• Mike Connelly, Manager
• Amy Sun, Marketing Staff
Nature of Sports Service:
Regional. Cable TV broadcaster/programmer. Current properties include: Arizona Diamondbacks, Phoenix Coyotes, PAC-10, football and basketball, Arizona State University, University of Arizona, and FOX Sports News. An affiliate of FOX Sports Net.

FOX SPORTS NET CHICAGO
350 N. ORLEANS STREET
SUITE S1-100
CHICAGO, IL 60654
312-222-6000
csnchicagowebsite@comcastsportsnet.com
www.csnchicago.com
Nature of Sports Service:
Regional. Cable TV programmer. Basic cable sports network serving Iowa, Illinois and Indiana. Covers Chicago Bulls, Chicago Cubs, Bears, Blackhawks and White Sox; also college games from Notre Dame, DePaul, Northwestern, the Big 10, Missouri Valley Conference, plus high school events and championships. Also, professional golf and tennis, auto and horse racing, and sports talk shows.

FOX SPORTS NET DETROIT
26555 EVERGREEN ROAD
SUITE 90
SOUTHFIELD, MI 48076-4232
248-723-2000
Fax: 248-226-9740
http://www.foxsportsdetroit.com
• Greg Hammaren, Vice President/General Manager
• Karen Kanigowski, Manager
Nature of Sports Service:
Regional. Cable TV broadcaster/programmer. An affiliate of FOX Sports Net.

FOX SPORTS NET FLORIDA
500 EAST BROWARD BOULEVARD
SUITE 105
FT. LAUDERDALE, FL 33394
954-375-3634
Fax: 800-369-0073
infoFL@foxsports.net
www.foxsportsflorida.com

• Steve Tello, Vice President/General Manager
Nature of Sports Service:
Regional. Cable TV network.

FOX SPORTS NET MIDWEST
THE ANNEX BUILDING
700 ST. LOUIS UNION STATION
SUITE 300
ST. LOUIS, MO 63103
314-206-7000
Fax: 314-206-7070
midwest@foxsports.net
http://www.foxsportsmidwest.com
Nature of Sports Service:
Regional. Cable TV network. Current properties: St. Louis Cardinals, St. Louis Blues, Missouri Valley Conference basketball, Missouri Tigers sports, St. Louis Billikens men's basketball, Kansas State Wildcats basketball, Nebraska Cornhuskers basketball

---

FOX SPORTS NET NORTH
ONE MAIN STREET SOUTHEAST
SUITE 600
MINNEAPOLIS, MN 55414
612-486-9500
Fax: 612-486-9513
fsnnorthinfo@foxsports.net
http://www.foxsportsnorth.com
Nature of Sports Service:
Regional. 24-Hour sports cable channel - regional program producer, broadcaster. Metro feed (50-mile radius surrounding Minneapolis); Non-metro feed - cable companies in Minnesota, North Dakota, South Dakota, Iowa and parts of Wisconsin. Produces and distributes Minnesota Twins baseball; University of Minnesota and Big 10 basketball, volleyball and gymnastics; hockey; local college football; U. of Minnesota and WCHA hockey.

FOX SPORTS NET SOUTH
1175 PEACHTREE STREET, N.E.
SUITE 200
ATLANTA, GA 30361
404-230-7300
fssouth@foxsports.com
http://www.foxsportssouth.com
Nature of Sports Service:
Regional. Cable TV programmer. Owned and operated affiliate of FOX Sports Net. Coverage includes Atlanta Braves (MLB), Atlanta Hawks (NBA), Atlanta Dream (WNBA), Southeastern Conference, Atlantic Coast Conference, Conference USA, Southern Conference, Big South Conference.

FOX SPORTS NET WEST
1100 SOUTH FLOWER STREET
SUITE 2200
LOS ANGELES, CA 90015-2125
213-743-7800
http://www.foxsportswest.com
• Kathryn Cohen, General Manager
• Julien Quattlebaum, Vice President
• Andy Hubsch, Vice President of Finance
• Debbie Chavez, Director of Financial Reporting
• Ron Gralnik, Coordinating Producer
• Brad Kitchen, Management Information Systems Director
Nature of Sports Service:
Regional. Serves 4.8 million subscribers in

Southern California, Nevada and Hawaii. Properties include: C.D. Chivas USA (MLS), Los Angeles Angels of Anaheim (MLB), Los Angeles Kings (NHL), Big West Conference(NCAA), West Coast Conference (NCAA)

FOX SPORTS NETWORKS/FOX SPORTS NET
10201 W. PICO BOULEVARD
BUILDING 103
LOS ANGELES, CA 90035
310-369-1000
Fax: 212-354-6902
www.foxsports.com
• David Hill, Chairman/CEO
• Ed Goren, Vice Chairman
• Randy Freer, Co-President/Co-COO
• Eric Shanks, Co-President/Co-COO
• Doug Sellars, EVP Production/Executive Producer
• George Greenberg, EVP Programming & Production
• Mark Silverman, President, The Big Ten Network
• Robert Thompson, President, FOX National Cable Sports Networks
• Gary Hartley, Executive Vice President, Graphics
• Ray Bahrami, Senior Vice President, Sales
• Dennis Welsh, Vice President, Sales & Marketing
• Mike Gammone, Vice President of Advertising Sales
• Guy Weaton, Vice President/General Manager
• Sheila Bruce, Vice President, Sales
• Roy Seinfeld, Network Vice President
• Lauren Halpern, Vice President Sales Manager
• Natalie Murray, Vice President, Regional Sales Manager
• Tom Maney, Senior Vice President Advertising Sales
• Chris Tzianabos, Vice President, Sales & Marketing
• Raul De Quesada, Vice President, Marketing Communications
• Aaron Lowenberg, Vice President, Sales
• Dan Carlin, Vice President, Programming & Research
• Joe Viele, Vice President, Marketing Sales
• John Chalton, Vice President, Finance
• Jerry Carstens
Finance Director
Sports Service Founded:
2002
Nature of Sports Service:
Reaches over 78 million homes through its 21 regional sports channels, and it serves as the first truly national, regional and local supplier of sports programming. Fox Sports Net serves as the cable TV home to 70 of the 80 MLB, NHL and NBA teams based in the United States, and produces over 4,000 live events each year.

FOX SPORTS OHIO
9200 SOUTH HILLS BOULEVARD
SUITE 200
BROADVIEW HEIGHTS, OH 44147-3520
440-746-8000
Fax: 440-746-8700
www.foxsportsohio.com
• Charlie Knudson, Sales Executive
• Jeanmarie Fucci, Director of Marketing
• Steve Pawlowski, Communications Manager

• Melissa Simon, Production Manager
• John Kautz, Production Manager
• Janiak Bill, Finance Executive
• Steve Liverani, Principal
Nature of Sports Service:
Regional. Cable TV network.
Major Professional Teams:
Cleveland Cavaliers (NBA), Cincinnati Reds (MLB), Columbus Blue Jackets (NHL), Columbus Crew (MLS).
Other Professional Teams:
Lake Erie Monsters (AHL)

FOX SPORTS PRIME TICKET
1100 SOUTH FLOWER STREET
SUITE 2200
LOS ANGELES, CA 90015-2125
213-743-7800
http://www.foxsportswest.com
• Kathryn Cohen, General Manager
• Andy Hubsch, Vice President of Finance
• Julien Quattlebaum, Vice President
• Debbie Chavez, Director of Financial Reporting
• Ron Gralnik, Coordinating Producer
Nature of Sports Service:
Regional. Sports Network serves 2.1 million subscribers in Southern California and Nevada. Properties include: Los Angeles Dodgers, Los Angeles Clippers, Mighty Ducks of Anaheim, Live horse racing, Local high school sports, UCLA & USC athletic events, Xtra Live with Steve Mason & John Ireland and Fox Sports News.

FX NETWORKS, LLC
10201 WEST PICO BOULEVARD
BUILDING 103
LOS ANGELES, CA 90035
310-369-1000
Fax: 310-969-4688
www.fxnetworks.com
• John Landgraf, President/General Manager
• Nick Grad, EVP Original Programming
• Murray Jurgeleit, Managing Director
• Chuck Saftler, Executive Vice President
• Gerard Bocaccio, Senior Vice President, Advertising Sales
• Chris Carlisle, Senior Vice President, Marketing
• Julie Piepenkotter, Research Senior Vice President
• Todd Schoen, Senior Vice President Affiliate
• Eric Shiu, Vice President, Marketing Advertising
• Rick Haskins, Vice President of Marketing
• Scott Groneman, Vice President of Research
• Bruce Lefkowitz, Executive Vice President of Advertising
• Colette Wilson, Manager
• Derek Kuhn, Senior Director, Marketing & Business
• Audrey Capin, Director, Sales Research
• Leslie Hathaway, Director of Operations
• Jason Phipps, Director of Online Media
• Todd Heughens, Creative Director
• Monica Koyama, New Media Director
Nature of Sports Service:
National cable TV network with several hours of programming devoted to sports, particularly college football, college basketball and major league baseball.

GALAVISION
605 THIRD AVENUE
12TH FL
NEW YORK, NY 10158
212-455-5200
Fax: 212-867-6710
http://corporate.univision.com
• Haim Saban, Chairman
• Randel A. Falco, President/Chief Executive Officer/Director
• Andrew W. Hobson, Senior Executive Vice President/CFO
• Peter H. Lori, EVP/Controller/Chief Accounting Officer
• Roberto Llamas, EVP/Chief Human Resources Officer
• Jessica Rodriguez, Executive Vice President of Program Schedulin
• Keith G. Turner, President of Sales & Marketing
• Tonia O'Connor, President, Distribution Sales & Marketing
• Rick Alessandri, Senior Vice President, Business Development
• Richard Pacheco, Senior Vice President
• Rick Resnick, Vice President, Sports Marketing
Nature of Sports Service:
National. International. Cable network, with U.S. broadcast affiliates, broadcasting from Mexico to U.S., Europe, Northern Africa, Central and South America. Currently offers wrestling and boxing. Also offers ECO hour which includes results and summary of international sports events.

GLOBAL TELEVISION NETWORK, LTD.
289 GREAT RD
SUITE 307
ACTON, MA 01720-4766
978-264-9921
Fax: 978-264-9457
http://www.globaltv.com
• James A. Barisano, III, President
• Jackie Normand, General/Technical
• Al Viator, General/Technical
Nature of Sports Service:
National, International. Producer and distributor of automotive television series and automotive special reports.

HBO SPORTS
1100 AVE OF THE AMERICAS
NEW YORK, NY 10036
212-512-1000
Fax: 212-512-1182
www.hbo.com
• Ken Herschman, President, HBO Sports
• Shelley Wright Brindle, EVP, Domestic Network Distribution
• Pamela Levine, EVP, Marketing
• Joe Tarulli, Senior Vice President, Finance
• Sandra Chiles, Senior Vice President & GM, Affiliate Sales
• Barbara Thomas, Senior Vice President, Operations
• Stanley Fertig, Senior Vice President
• Royce Battleman, Senior Vice President, Business Affairs
• Melissa R. Barnett, Senior Vice President, Network Business Affai
• John Micale, Vice President, Sports Production
• Gena Desclos, Vice President, Post Production
• Gavin Doyle, Vice President, Finance
Nature of Sports Service:
National. Cable TV programmer, network.

media

Live televised programming and special events, magazine shows, retrospectives and highlight shows.

IN STORE SPORTS NETWORK
130 WEST 29TH STREET
NEW YORK, NY 10001
212-631-9800
Fax: 212-807-9297
skushner@mediaplace.us
www.mediaplace.us
• Scott Kushner, Chief Operating Officer
(212) 631-9800
skushner@mediaplace.us
• Jeremy Hopwood, Creative Director
(212) 631-9800
jhopwood@mediaplace.us
Nature of Sports Service:
Operators of the In-Store Sports Network. National Closed Circuit television network broadcasting in sport specialty retail, locations.

KING SPORTS & ENTERTAINMENT NETWORK, DON
501 FAIRWAY DRIVE
DEERFIELD BEACH, FL 33441-1865
954-418-5800
http://www.donkingtv.com
• Don King, President
• John Meehan, Vice President, Finance
• Celia Tuckman, Secretary

MADISON SQUARE GARDEN NETWORK/MSG
TWO PENNSYLVANIA PLAZA
FLOOR 19
NEW YORK, NY 10121-1703
212-465-6000
Fax: 212-465-6498
www.msg.com
• Michael Bair, President
• Jerry Passaro, SVP, TV Network Operations & Distribution
• Bobby Brown, Co-Director, Network Operations
• Michael Phillips, Co-Director, Network Operations
Nature of Sports Service:
National, Regional. Cable TV sports programming network. Reaches more than 6.5 million homes through 245 affiliates in New York, New Jersey, Connecticut, and Pennsylvania. Programming includes the New York Knickerbockers, New York Liberty, New York Rangers, New York Red Bulls, Buffalo Sabres, college basketball, college football, boxing, tennis, horse racing and more from Madison Square Garden and arenas around the country.

NBC SPORTS DIVISION
30 ROCKEFELLER PLAZA
NEW YORK, NY 10112
212-664-4444
Fax: 212-664-4085
www.nbc.com
• David Neal, EVP, NBC Olympics/Executive Producer, NBC Sports
• Mark H. Lazarus, President, NBC Sports
• Jonathan D. Miller, President of Programming, NBC Sports & VERSUS
• Dick D Ebersol, Chairman, NBC Universal Sports & Olympics
Nature of Sports Service:
National. Network.

NEW ENGLAND SPORTS NETWORK/NESN
480 ARSENAL STREET
BUILDING 1
WATERTOWN, MA 02472
617-536-9233
Fax: 617-536-7814
www.nesn.com
• John Henry, Principal Owner
• Sean McGrail, President
• Vanessa Brown, Managing Director
• Peter Plaehn, Vice President, Marketing
• Thomas C. Werner, Chairman
• Michael Narracci, Senior Coordinating Director
• Erik Haugen, Director of Program Development & Acquisition
• Holly Burgess, Manager
• Rick Booth, Creative Director
• Greg Mize, Promotions Coordinator
• Joel Feld, VP of Programming/Executive Producer
• Jamie Wentworth, Information Technologies Director
• Mary Overlan, Director, Finance
Nature of Sports Service:
Regional. A 24 hour, regional cable TV sports service. NESN delivers exclusive coverage of over 90 Boston Red Sox games each season including spring training coverage; Boston Bruins hockey including Stanley Cup playoff action from the TD BankNorth Garden; Pawtucket Red Sox baseball; ECAC Football Game of the Week; major conference college football, basketball baseball and volleyball; professional golf, tennis volleyball, auto racing, boxing, beach volleyball, soccer bowling and skiing; plus NESN SportsDesk, the network's morning sports news program.

NIPPON TELEVISION NETWORK CORPORATION
1-6-1 HIGASHI SHIMBASHI
MINATO-KU
TOKYO, JAPAN 105-7444
+81-3-6215-1111
http://www.ntv.co.jp
• Noritada Hosokawa, Chairman/President
Nature of Sports Service:
International. Commercial broadcasting network. Owns the Tokyo Verdy soccer team.

OUTSIDE TELEVISION
33 RIVERSIDE AVENUE
4TH FLOOR
WESTPORT, CT 06880
203-221-9240
Fax: 203-221-9283
http://www.outsidetelevision.com
Nature of Sports Service:
National. Creates and distributes outdoor lifestyle and resort-based sports programs such as Northface Expeditions, Outside Today, and Outside Television Presents.

PETRY MEDIA
200 PARK AVENUE
NEW YORK, NY 10017
212-230-5600
• Val Napolitano, President/CEO
(212) 230-5710
• Cindy Yantis, Vice President Group Sales Manager
• Rich Quigley, Manager

Nature of Service:
Media sales for live regional feed of Atlantic Coast Conference, Southeast Conference, Western Athletic Conference and Mountain West Conference NCAA Division 1 football and basketball.

PETRY TELEVISION
1 PENNSYLVANIA PLAZA
55TH FLOOR
NEW YORK, NY 10119
212-230-5600
Fax: 212-230-5876
• Val Napolitano, President & CEO, Petry Television
• Steve Berlin, Chief Financial Officer
• Steve Capozzoli, Senior Vice President/Managing Director
• Maureen Tillman, Vice President, Information Services
• Debbie Carter, Vice President/General Manager
• Kara D'Amato, Director of Creative Services
• Erica L. Grundfast, Vice President & Director of Human Resources
Nature of Sports Service:
Regional. TV advertising sales. Sales of sponsorships and promotions.

ROOT SPORTS NORTHWEST
3626 156 AVENUE SOUTHEAST
BELLEVUE, WA 98006
425-641-0104
Fax: 425-641-9811
northwest@rootsports.com
http://northwest.rootsports.com
• Liz Serrette, Principal
• Wayne Moss, Crew Coordinator
Nature of Sports Service:
Regional. Cable TV network. Provides programming for cable and other delivery systems throughout the Pacific Northwest in the states of Washington, Oregon, Idaho, Alaska, and Montana. Home of PAC-10 and Big Sky conferences, featuring college football, men's and women's basketball, baseball and a variety of Olympic sports and Fox Sports News. Professional sports include: the Seattle Mariners, Seattle Sounders, Portland Timbers, and pre-season Seattle Seahawks football.

ROOT SPORTS PITTSBURGH
323 NORTH SHORE DRIVE
SUITE 200
PITTSBURGH, PA 15212
412-316-3800
Fax: 412-316-3892
pittsburgh@rootsports.com
http://www.rootsports.com
Nature of Sports Service:
Regional. Program distributor for Cable TV. Provides coverage of Pittsburgh Pirates, Pittsburgh Steelers, and Pittsburgh Penguins; Big East basketball, Northeast Conference basketball, ACC basketball, Big 12 women's basketball, Pac-10 basketball, California University of Pennsylvania football and basektball, WPIAL high school football.

ROOT SPORTS ROCKY MOUNTAIN
2300 15TH ST
SUITE 300
DENVER, CO 80202

720-898-2700
rockymountain@rootsports.com
http://rockymountain.rootsports.com/
Nature of Sports Service:
Regional. Cable TV network. Current properties: Colorado Rockies, Utah Jazz, Denver Pioneer's men's ice hockey, Mountain West Conference, Conference USA, Western Athletic Conference, Big Sky Conference, and Big 12 Conference.

ROOT SPORTS UTAH
2300 15TH STREET
SUITE 300
DENVER, CO 80202
720-898-2700
rockymountain@rootsports.com
http://www.rootsports.com
Nature of Sports Service:
Regional. Cable TV network. Utah Jazz and other regional cable sports; TV broadcast of Utah Jazz games.

SPIKE TV
2600 COLORADO AVENUE
SANTA MONICA, CA 90404
310-907-2400
spike-feedback@spike.com
www.spiketv.com
• Jon Taffer, Owner
• Bjorn Rebney, Chief Executive Officer
• David Schwarz, Vice President, Communications
• Sammy Goldsmith, Accounts Payable
Nature of Sports Service:
National. Cable TV network. Programming focused on males ages 18-34.
Notes:
Formerly TNN, The National Network and The Nashville Network.

TELEMUNDO
2290 WEST 8TH AVENUE
HIALEAH, FL 33010
305-884-8200
Fax: 305-889-7980
http://www.telemundo.com
• Emilio Romano, President
• Javier Maynulet, Chief Financial Officer
• Susan Solano Vila, Executive Vice President, Marketing
• Mimi Belt, Vice President
• Dan Lovinger, EVP, Advertising Sales & Integrated Marketing
• Peter E. Blacker, EVP, Digital Media & Emerging Business
• Margaret Lazo, Vice President, Human Resources
• Jorge Hidalgo, Senior Executive Vice President, Sports
Nature of Sports Service:
National. TV Network for Hispanic audience.

THE SCORE TELEVISION NETWORK
370 KING ST WEST
SUITE 435
TORONTO, ON, CANADA M5V 1J9
416-977-6787
Fax: 416-977-0238
• John Levy, Chairman of the Board

THE SPORTS NETWORK
2200 BYBERRY ROAD
SUITE 200
HATBORO, PA 19040

215-441-8444
Fax: 215-441-5767
http://www.sportsnetwork.com

TSN - THE SPORTS NETWORK
9 CHANNEL NINE CT
SCARBOROUGH, ON, CANADA M1S 4B5
416-332-5000
Fax: 416-332-7656
audiencerelations@tsn.ca
www.tsn.ca
Nature of Sports Service:
National (Canadian). 24-hour Cable TV sports channel, distributed on cable in Canada. Covers all major and minor sports in Canada.

TURNER SPORTS, INC.
1015 TECHWOOD DRIVE
ATLANTA, GA 30303
404-827-1700
Fax: 404-827-5212
http://news.turner.com/section
display.cfm?section id=31
• Lenny Daniels, Executive Vice President/Chief Operating Officer
• Jon Diament, Executive Vice President, Sales & Marketing
• Sigal Moshe, Chief Information Officer
• Jackie Adams, Director, Marketing Promotions
• Zandra Teagle, Director, Finance & Accounting

UNIVISION TELEVISION NETWORK
9495 NORTHWEST 4141ST STREET
MIAMI, FL 33178
305-471-8277
www.univision.com
• Evelyn Ramirez, Vice President
• Rodrigo Salazar, Chief Financial Officer
• Eddy Davis, Director
• Sunil Vora, Controller
Nature of Sports Service:
National. Spanish language TV network. Live televised programming and special events.

USA NETWORK
30 ROCKEFELLER PLAZA
NEW YORK, NY 10112
212-664-4444
Fax: 212-664-6365
www.usanetwork.com
• Bonnie Hammer, Chairman
• Chris McCumber, Co-President
• Jane Blaney, EVP Programming, Acquisitions, Scheduling
• Jeff Wachtel, EVP, Original Programming
• Beth Roberts, EVP, Business Affairs, NBC Universal Cable

VIP COVERAGE, LLC
52 QUICKS LANE
KATONAH, NY 10536
914-767-0900
Fax: 914-232-3359
• Ben Harvey, Executive Producer
Year Founded:
2001
Nature of Service:
Three unique golf-related.

WHEELSTV
289 GREAT ROAD
SUITE 301
ACTON, MA 01720
978-264-4333
Fax: 978-264-9547
contact@wheelstv.net
http://wheelstvnetwork.com
• Jim Barisano, Chairman/CEO
• Lehel Reeves, President/Head Of Business Development
• Theresa Carlo, CFO
Nature of Sports Service:
National. Cable TV network. All auto sports, all the time. Creates and distributes exclusive original content for internet portals, websites, 3G mobile platforms, IPTV networks, OEM showrooms, VOD, and cable systems.

YANKEES ENTERTAINMENT & SPORTS NETWORK/YES
THE CHRYSLER BUILDING
405 LEXINGTON AVE
36TH FLOOR
NEW YORK, NY 10174-3699
646-487-3600
Fax: 646-487-3612
www.yesnetwork.com
• John Filippelli, President, Production & Programming
• Michael Wach, EVP, Advertising Sales
• Ed Deleney, Vice President, Operations
• Nicole Zussman, Vice President, Human Resources
• Jason Feneque, Senior Director of Sales & Marketing
• Reji Mathew, Director, Information Technology
Sports Service Founded:
2001

Sports Television Pay Per View

HBO SPORTS
212-512-1208
www.hbo.com/sports

INTEGRATED SPORTS MARKETING
8909 COMPLEX DRIVE
SUITE A
SAN DIEGO, CA 92123
858-836-0133
Fax: 858-836-0134
dm@ismsports.net
www.ismsports.net
• David Miller, President
dm@ismsports.net
• Cheryl Lemox, Senior Vice President, Marketing & Promotions
csmith@ismsports.net
• Doug Sampson, Vice President, Operations & Creative Service
doug@ismsports.net
• Kyle Mellor, Account Executive
kyle@ismsports.net
• Cassie Mnutz, Event Manager
cassie@ismsports.net
• Deanna Samson, Human Resources/Accounting Director
deanna@ismsports.net

media

M-NET TELEVISION
251 OAK AVENUE
FERNDALE
RANDBURG, SOUTH AFRI 2194
+27-011-289-2222
083-900-3788
Fax: +27-011-577-4901
enquiries@multichoice.co.za
http://www.mnet.dstv.com
• Tom Vosloo, Chairman
• Basil Sgourdos, Chief Financial Officer
• Imtiaz Patel, CEO, Supersport
• Eben Greyling, CEO, Pay-TV Platforms
• Antoine Adries Roux, CEO, Internet Operations
Nature of Sports Service:
International. Pay TV service.

SHOWTIME SPORTS
1633 BROADWAY, 15TH FL
NEW YORK, NY 10019
212-708-1600
Fax: 212-708-1217
www.sho.com
• Matthew C. Blank, Chairman/Chief Executive Officer
• Donald Buckley, EVP, Program Marketing, Digital Services
• Tim Delaney, Senior Vice President
• Geof Rochester, Senior Vice President, Marketing
• Nancy Glauberman, Senior Vice President, Business Development
• Jock McLean, Sports Vice President
Nature of Sports Service:
National. Pay-Per-View television programmer and distributor. Showtime Networks inlcude: Showtime, The Movie Channel and FLIX. Showtime also produces their own shows.

TIGERVISION
LSU ATHLETICS ADMINISTRATION BUILDING
BATON ROUGE, LA 70803
225-578-8001
http://www.LSUsports.net/tigervision
Nature of Sports Service:
Regional. Broadcaster, distributor (Pay-Per-View). TigerVision game broadcasts are on Pay-Per-View basis only. Other shows, including coaches shows and sports reports, are shown on both over-the-air and cable TV.

WILEN MEDIA CORPORATION
5 WELLWOOD AVE
E FARMINGDALE, NY 11735
631-439-5000
Fax: 631-439-4536
www.wilenmedia.com
• Richard Wilen, Chairman
• Darrin Wilen, President
• Corey Wilen, Executive Vice President
• John Diaz, Executive Vice President/Sales
Nature of Sports Service:
National. Provides video program promotions for Pay-Per-View sports to affiliates and publishes regional sports programming guides of SportsChannel, Prism and the New England Sports Network. Also authorized distributor of all print materials for PPV sporting events. Also publishes TV Blueprint, a national cable television publication.

Sports Television Programs, Local

13 SPORTS JAM
1000 NORTH MERIDIAN STREET
INDIANAPOLIS, IN 46204-1015
317-636-1313
Fax: 317-632-6720
13news@wthr.com
http://www.wthr.com
• Dave Calabro, Host
(317) 655-5754
dcalabro@wthr.com
Description:
Sports. Sunday at 11:20PM for 40 minutes.

27 SPORTS SPECTRUM
2851 WINCHESTER ROAD
LEXINGTON, KY 40509-4801
859-299-0411
Fax: 859-293-1578
news@wkyt.com
http://www.wkyt.com
• Barbara Carden, Program Director
• Dick Gabriel, Sports Director
(859) 566-1330
news27@wkyt.com
• David Patrick, Producer
Description:
Sports. Saturday at 11:20PM for 40 minutes. Program features information on local sports.

5 SPORTS LIVE
1100 BANYAN BOULEVARD
WEST PALM BEACH, FL 33401-5000
561-655-5455
800-930-9766
Fax: 561-653-5719
newstips@wptv.com
http://www.wptv.com
• Ben Becker, Sports Director
(561) 653-5729
bbecker@wptv.com
• Ben Becker, Producer
(561) 653-5729
bbecker@wptv.com
Description:
Sports. Sunday at 11:30PM for 30 minutes.

ARKANSAS OUTDOORS
350 SOUTH DONAGHEY STREET
CONWAY, AR 72034
800-662-2386
Fax: 501-682-4122
outdoors@aetn.org
http://www.aetn.org/arkansasoutdoors/
• Jim Holmes, Producer
(800) 662-2386
Description:
Educational, Interview, News. Thursday at 7:30PM for 30 minutes. Program covers topics of hunting, fishing, hiking, canoeing, and outdoor recreation.

BEARS KICK OFF LIVE
205 NORTH MICHIGAN AVENUE 2ND FLOOR
CHICAGO, IL 60601-5922
312-565-5532
Fax: 312-819-1332
http://www.foxchicago.com
• Corey McPherrin, Sports Anchor
(312) 565-5498
corey.mcpherrin@foxchicago.com

• John Eskra, Executive Producer
(312) 565-5478
john.eskra@foxchicago.com
Description:
Commentary, Interview. Sunday Program airs during football season.. Program is a sports talk show highlighting the Chicago Bears.

BIG BOARD SPORTS
15 NORTH PEARL STREET
ALBANY, NY 12204-1800
518-436-4791
800-999-9698
Fax: 518-434-0659
comments@wnyt.com
http://www.wnyt.com
• Rodger Wyland, Anchor
(518) 207-4818
rwyland@wnyt.com
• Rodger Wyland, Producer
(518) 207-4818
rwyland@wnyt.com
Description:
Interview, Talk. Sunday at 11:25PM for 30 minutes.

BIG SPORTS X-TRA
3701 SOUTH PEORIA
TULSA, OK 74105-3263
918-743-2222
800-727-5574
Fax: 918-748-1436
news@kjrh.com
http://www.kjrh.com
• Al Jerkens, Anchor
(918) 748-1539
jerkens@kjrh.com
• Al Jerkens, Producer
(918) 748-1539
jerkens@kjrh.com
Description:
Sports. Sunday at 10:30PM for 30 minutes.

BUCS ZONE
4045 NORTH HIMES AVENUE
TAMPA, FL 33607
813-354-2828
877-833-2828
Fax: 813-878-2828
news@wfts.com
http://www.wfts.com
• Al Keck, Anchor
(813) 354-2800
akeck@wfts.com
• Oscar Angulo, Producer
(813) 354-2843
news6tips@wfts.com
Description:
News, Sports, Weather. Sunday at 11:30PM for 30 minutes. Program recaps the week's sports events.

CAROLINA SPORTS FRIDAY
ONE JULIAN PRICE PLACE
CHARLOTTE, NC 28208-5211
704-374-3500 (ext 1)
Fax: 704-374-3889
assignmentdesk@wbtv.com
http://www.wbtv.com
• Delano Little, Host
dlittle@wbtv.com
Description:
Commentary, Sports, Talk. Friday at 11:35PM for 30 minutes. Includes in-depth segments on high school sports as well as coverage of college and professional sports.

EXTRA POINTS
3310 BISSONNET STREET
HOUSTON, TX 77005-2114
713-666-0713
Fax: 713-664-0013
ktrkwwwnews@abc.com
http://abc13.com/
• Tim Melton, Host
• Matthew Moore, Producer
matthew.moore@abc.com
Description:
Magazine. Saturday at 5:00PM for 30 minutes. Program is a weekly sports wrap-up show.

FIRST 4 SPORTS - SATURDAY
4 BROADCAST PLACE
JACKSONVILLE, FL 32207-8613
904-399-4000
Fax: 904-393-9822
jaxnews@news4jax.com
http://www.news4jax.com
• Chris Mullholland, Producer
(904) 399-4000
producer@wjxt.com
• Sean Woodland, Anchor
swoodland@wjxt.com
Description:
Sports. Saturday at 11:20PM for 15 minutes.

FIRST 4 SPORTS - SUNDAY
4 BROADCAST PLACE
JACKSONVILLE, FL 32207-8613
904-399-4000
Fax: 904-393-9822
jaxnews@news4jax.com
http://www.news4jax.com
• Sean Woodland, Anchor
• Matt Kingston, Producer
Description:
Sports. Sunday at 11:20PM for 20 minutes.

FISH MASTERS
1772 CALLE JOAQUIN
SAN LUIS OBISPO, CA 93405-7210
805-541-6666
Fax: 805-541-5142
ksby@ksby.com
http://www.ksby.com
Description:
Educational, Entertainment, Magazine, Music, Talk. Saturday at 1:00AM for 30 minutes. Program is a fishing and outdoor entertainment show.

FLY FISHING WITH GLEN BLACKWOOD
301 WEST FULTON STREET
GRAND RAPIDS, MI 49504-6430
616-331-6666
800-442-2771
Fax: 616-331-6625
http://www.wgvu.org
• Bill Cuppy, Producer
cuppyb@gvsu.edu
• Glen Blackwood, Host
(616) 331-6625
Description:
Educational. Thursday at 9:30PM for 30 minutes. Program features fly fishing tips for beginners and experts.

FOURTH DOWN ON FOUR
1024 NORTH RAMPART STREET
NEW ORLEANS, LA 70116-2406

504-529-4444
Fax: 504-529-6470
http://www.wwltv.com
• Juan Kincaid, Host
(504) 529-6297
Description:
Interview, Sports. Sunday at 10:35PM for 30 minutes.

FOX 13 SPORTS PAGE
5020 WEST AMELIA EARHART DRIVE
SALT LAKE CITY, UT 84116-2853
801-532-1300
Fax: 801-537-5335
http://www.fox13.com
• Mike Runge, Anchor
mrunge@fox13.com
Description:
Interview, Talk. Sunday at 9:30PM for 30 minutes.

FOX 59 OVERTIME
1440 NORTH MERIDIAN
INDIANAPOLIS, IN 46202-2305
317-632-5900
Fax: 317-687-6532
http://fox59.trb.com
• Allen Beckner, Producer
(317) 632-5900
• Tracy Forner, Anchor
(317) 687-6573
• Chris Hagan, Sports Broadcaster
(317) 687-6559
• Greg Kathary, Producer
(317) 632-5900
Description:
News, Talk. Sunday at 10:35PM for 30 minutes.

FOX SPORTS SUNDAY
400 NORTH GRIFFIN STREET
DALLAS, TX 75202-1901
214-720-4444
Fax: 214-720-3263
kdfw@foxinc.com
http://www.kdfw.com
• Kevin Morrell, Producer
• Mike Doocy, Host
(214) 720-3164
Description:
Call-In, Talk. Sunday at 10:00PM for 30 minutes.

FOX SPORTS XTRA
4261 SOUTHWEST FREEWAY
HOUSTON, TX 77027-7201
713-479-2600
Fax: 713-479-2859
http://www.fox26.com
• Keith Calkins, Host
(713) 479-2841
newsdesk@fox26.com
Description:
Sports. Sunday at 9:30PM for 30 minutes. Program is a sports talk show.

GV SPORTS
301 WEST FULTON STREET
GRAND RAPIDS, MI 49504-6430
616-331-6666
800-442-2771
Fax: 616-331-6625
http://www.wgvu.org
• Phil Lane, Producer
(616) 331-6791
lanep@gvsu.edu

Description:
Interview. Monday at 6:00PM for 30 minutes. Program features interviews with sports team coaches at Grand Valley State University and highlights of the week's games.

HIGH SCHOOL SPORTS FOCUS
2102 COMMERCE DRIVE
SAN JOSE, CA 95131-1804
408-953-3636
Fax: 408-953-3610
http://www.kicu.com
• Mike Sklut, Host
Description:
Interview. Sunday at 7:00PM for 1 hour; Saturday at 12:00PM for 30 minutes.

INSTANT REPLAY
1408 NORTH STREET MARY'S STREET
SAN ANTONIO, TX 78215-1739
210-351-1200
Fax: 210-351-1328
news@ksat.com
• Greg Simmons, Host
gsimmons@ksat.com
Description:
Entertainment, Interview, News, Play-by-Play, Sports. Sunday at 10:30PM for 30 minutes. Program offers sports recaps, one-on-one interviews, and sports-related features.

KTLA SPORTS ONLINE
5800 SUNSET BOULEVARD
LOS ANGELES, CA 90028
323-460-5500
Fax: 323-460-5333
http://www.ktla.com
• Tom Klimasz, Weekend Producer
(323) 460-5907
• Damon Andrews, Host
(323) 460-5443
dandrews@tribune.com
• Ted Green, Producer
(323) 460-5907
Description:
News, Sports. Sunday, Saturday at 10:40PM for 20 minutes.

MAXIMUM SPORTS
4335 NORTHWEST LOOP 410
SAN ANTONIO, TX 78229-5136
210-442-6318
Fax: 210-377-4758
kabbtv@kabb.com
http://www.kabb.com
• Chuck Miketinac, Host
(210) 442-6318
maxsport@kabb.com
Description:
Sports. Sunday at 9:30PM for 30 minutes.

NBC 5 SPORTS SUNDAY
NBC TOWER 454 NORTH COLUMBUS DRIVE
CHICAGO, IL 60611-5555
312-836-5555
Fax: 312-527-4238
http://www.nbc5.com/
• O'Meara McCormick, Sports Producer
(312) 836-5665
Description:
Commentary, Interview, Talk. Sunday at 10:35PM for 30 minutes. Program features a recap of the week in sports.

media

OKLAHOMA SPORTS BLITZ
302 SOUTH FRANKFORT STREET
TULSA, OK 74120-2422
918-732-6000
Fax: 918-732-6185
http://www.kotv.com
• John Holcomb, Host
(918) 732-6146
jholcomb@kotv.com
Description:
Information, Sports. Sunday at 10:30PM for 40 minutes.

OUTSIDE THE LINES
ESPN PLAZA
BRISTOL, CT 06010
866-377-6685
Fax: 860-766-2422
otlstoryideas@espn.com
http://sports.espn.go.com/espn/otl/index
• George Bodenheimer, President
• Christine Driessen, EVP & CFO
• Chuck Pagano, EVP & CTO
• Gary Hoenig, GM & Editorial Director, ESPN Publishing
• Kevin Ball, Director of Editorial Content & Copy Chief

PADRES MAGAZINE
1370 INDIA STREET 2ND FLOOR
SAN DIEGO, CA 92101-3418
619-266-5061
Fax: 619-595-0168
http://www.4sd.com
• Jerry Coleman, Host
(619) 266-5061
• Jason Bott, Coordinating Producer
• Jane Mitchell, Reporter
jane.mitchell@cox.com
Description:
Interview, Talk. Sunday, Monday, Tuesday, Wednesday, Thursday, Friday, Saturday Airtime varies; approximately 30 minutes.. Program profiles San Diego Padres players on and off the field.

Q IT UP SPORTS
1813 WESTLAKE AVENUE NORTH
SEATTLE, WA 98109-2706
206-674-1313
Fax: 206-674-1777
tips@q13.com
http://www.kcpq.com
• Dan Devone, Host
• Colin Resch, Producer
cresch@kcpq.com
Description:
Commentary, Talk. Sunday at 10:35PM for 30 minutes. Program analyzes the week in sports.

RICH BRENNER'S SPORTS SUNDAY
2005 FRANCIS STREET
HIGH POINT, NC 27263-1865
336-841-8888
Fax: 336-841-8051
news@wghp.com
http://www.fox8wghp.com
• Rich Brenner, Sports Anchor
• Rich Brenner, Host
• Rich Brenner, Producer
• Kevin Connolly, Anchor
(336) 821-1166
kconnolly@wghp.com
Description:
Sports. Sunday at 10:30PM for 30 minutes. Program covers local and national sports.

SPORTS CENTRAL
6121 SUNSET BOULEVARD
LOS ANGELES, CA 90028-6423
323-460-3000
Fax: 323-460-3733
kcbstvnews@cbs.com
http://www.kcbs-tv.com/
• Jim Hill, Sports Anchor
jhill@channel2000.com
Description:
Interview, Play-by-Play, Sports. Sunday Airtime varies to accommodate special programming.; Saturday Airtime varies to accommodate special programming.. Program is a weekend sports show covering local and national athletic events.

SPORTS EXTRA
5151 WISCONSIN AVENUE N.W.
WASHINGTON, DC 20016-4124
202-895-3000
Fax: 202-895-3133
http://www.fox5dc.com
• Dave Feldman, Host
assignment.desk@wttg.com
Description:
Commentary, Talk. Sunday at 11:00PM for 30 minutes. Program features analysis of the week in sports.

SPORTS FINAL
1001 VAN NESS AVENUE
SAN FRANCISCO, CA 94109-6982
415-441-4444
Fax: 415-561-8136
4listens@kron4.com
http://www.kron4.com
• Gary Radnich, Sports Director
Description:
Interview, Talk. Sunday at 11:30PM for 30 minutes. Program features sporting news and interviews.

SPORTS FINAL EDITION
550 WEST LAFAYETTE BOULEVARD
DETROIT, MI 48226-3123
313-222-0444
Fax: 313-222-0592
assignmentdesk@wdiv.com
http://www.clickondetroit.com/
• Fred McLeod, Anchor
(313) 222-0500
fredm@clickondetroit.com
• Fred McLeod, Producer
(313) 222-0504
fredm@clickondetroit.com
• Bernie Smilovitz, Sports Anchor
bernies@wdiv.com
Description:
Interview, Sports, Talk. Sunday at 11:35PM for 35 minutes. Program is a sports show with in-depth coverage of the week's action.

SPORTS JAM
4466 NORTH JOHN YOUNG PARKWAY
ORLANDO, FL 32804-1939
407-521-1200
Fax: 407-298-2122
desk@wkmg.com
http://www.wkmg.com
• Todd Lewis, Host
tlewis@local6.com
Description:
Play-by-Play, Sports. Sunday, Saturday at 11:30PM for 30 minutes. Program is a sports wrap-up-show.

SPORTS LINE LIVE
3556 LIBERTY AVENUE
SPRINGDALE, AR 72762
479-361-2900
888-777-9392
Fax: 479-361-2323
http://www.safetv.org
• Grant Hall, Host
• Noreen Dueck, Program Director
• Carlos Pardeiro, Producer
carlosp@ipa.net
• Rick Schaeffer, Host
Description:
Call-In, Interview, News, Sports, Talk. Thursday at 9:00PM for 1 hour. Program is a call-in talk show.

SPORTS LOCKER
1950 NORTH MERIDIAN
INDIANAPOLIS, IN 46202-1304
317-923-8888
Fax: 317-931-2242
newsdesk@wishtv.com
http://www.wishtv.com
• Jimmy Shumar, Producer
jshumar@wishtv.com
• Anthony Calhoun, Anchor
(317) 921-8686
acalhoun@wishtv.com
• Stacey Thorne, Executive Producer
(317) 956-8540
sthorne@wishtv.com
• Chris Widlic, Anchor
(317) 921-8536
cwidlic@wishtv.com
Description:
Interview, Talk. Sunday, Saturday at 11:22PM for 38 minutes. Program features sports updates and topical discussions.

SPORTS NIGHT
511 WEST ADAMS STREET
PHOENIX, AZ 85003-1608
602-257-1234
Fax: 602-262-0181
foxde602@fox.com
• Jude Lacava, Host
assignments@fox10.com
• Neil Wolf, Producer
assignments@fox10.com
Description:
Interview, News, Sports. Sunday at 9:30PM for 30 minutes.

SPORTS PAGE
624 WEST MUHAMMAD ALI BOULEVARD
LOUISVILLE, KY 40203-1915
502-584-6441
Fax: 502-589-5559
news@fox41.com
http://www.fox41.com
• Gary Montgomery, Host
(502) 561-7711
gmontgomery@fox41.com
Description:
Interview, Sports. Saturday at 12:30PM for 30 minutes.

SPORTS PLUS
7020 HEATHERHILL RD
BETHESDA, MD 20817
301-229-5401
Description:
Sports, Talk. Sunday at 10:35PM for 1 hour. Program is a sports talk show.

SPORTS RAP LIVE
99 DANVILLE CORNER ROAD
AUBURN, ME 04210-8693
207-782-1800
Fax: 207-783-7371
wmtw@wmtw.com
http://www.wmtw.com
• Norm Karkos, Anchor
nkarkos@wmtw.com
• Norm Karkos, Sports Director
nkarkos@wmtw.com
Description:
Call-In, Commentary, News, Sports. Monday at 7:00PM for 1 hour.

SPORTS SUNDAY
8181 SOUTHWEST FREEWAY
HOUSTON, TX 77074-1705
713-222-2222
Fax: 713-771-4930
desk@kprc.com
http://www.kprc.com
• Patsy Harris, Program Director
(713) 778-4751
• Patsy Harris, Producer
(713) 778-4751
Description:
News, Sports. Sunday at 10:20PM for 50 minutes.

SPORTS XTRA
1401 79TH STREET
CAUSOUTHEASTWAY
MIAMI, FL 33141-4104
305-795-2777
800-845-7777
Fax: 305-795-2746
newsdesk@wsvn.com
http://www.wsvn.com
• Steve Shapiro, Host
(305) 795-2777
sshapiro@wsvn.com
• Mike DiPasquale, Host
(305) 795-2777
mdipasquale@wsvn.com
Description:
Commentary, Talk. Sunday at 11:00PM for 30 minutes. Program analyzes the week in sports.

SPORTS ZONE
500 CIRCLE SEVEN DRIVE
GLENDALE, CA 91201-2331
818-863-7777
Fax: 818-863-7080
http://www.abc7.com
• Stan Radford, Producer
(818) 863-7649
stan.r.radford@abc.com
• Mike Parker, Producer
(818) 863-7648
mike.b.parker@abc.com
Description:
Commentary, Interview. Monday at 9:00PM for 1 hour. Program airs only during football season.

SPORTSBEAT SATURDAY
BROADCAST HOUSOUTHEAST 55 N. 300 W.
SALT LAKE CITY, UT 84180-1109
801-575-5555
Fax: 801-575-5830
feedback@ksl.com
http://www.ksl.com

• Tom Kirkland, Anchor
(801) 575-5500
tom.kirkland@ksl.com
Description:
Sports. Saturday at 10:30PM for 30 minutes.

SPORTSBEAT SUNDAY
BROADCAST HOUSOUTHEAST 55 N. 300 W.
SALT LAKE CITY, UT 84180-1109
801-575-5555
Fax: 801-575-5830
feedback@ksl.com
http://www.ksl.com
• Tom Kirkland, Anchor
(801) 575-5555
tom.kirkland@ksl.com
Description:
Sports. Sunday at 10:30PM for 30 minutes.

SPORTSFINAL
10 MONUMENT ROAD
BALA CYNWYD, PA 19004-1712
610-668-5510
Fax: 610-668-3700
wcaudesk@nbcuni.com
http://www.nbc10.com
• John Clark, Anchor
(610) 668-5534
Description:
Sports. Sunday at 11:35PM for 30 minutes.

SPORTSLINE
81 BARBER GREENE ROAD
DON MILLS, ON, CANADA M3C 2A2
416-446-5311
800-387-8001
Fax: 416-446-5447
newstips@globaltv.com
http://www.globaltv.com
• Don Martin, Host
(416) 446-5463
dmartin@globaltv.ca
• Jim Tatti, Host
sportsline.tor@globaltv.ca
Description:
News, Sports. Sunday, Monday, Tuesday, Wednesday, Thursday, Friday, Saturday at 11:30PM for 35 minutes. Program features sports highlights and commentary.

SPORTSLINE LIVE
721 BROADWAY
KINGSTON, NY 12401-3449
845-339-6397
800-824-3302
Fax: 845-339-6210
http://www.rnntv.com
• Kevin Connors, Sports Director
(845) 339-6397
kconnors@rnntv.com
• Kevin Connors, Host
(845) 339-6397
kconnors@rnntv.com
• Kevin Connors, Producer
(845) 339-6397
kconnors@rnntv.com
Description:
Call-In, Interview, Sports, Talk. Monday at 8:30AM for 30 minutes; Tuesday, Wednesday, Thursday, Friday at 8:30PM for 30 minutes. Program covers sports issues.

SPORTSWRAP AT 10:45
2 JACK LONDON SQUARE
OAKLAND, CA 94607-3727

510-834-1212
Fax: 510-272-9957
http://www.bayinsider.com
• Joe Fonzi, Anchor
(510) 874-0242
• Fred Inglis, Reporter
(510) 874-0164
• Pete Lupetti, Sports Editor
(510) 874-0252
Description:
News, Sports. Sunday, Saturday at 10:45PM for 15 minutes.

SUNDAY SPORTS EXTRA
3501 FARNAM STREET
OMAHA, NE 68131
402-346-6666
800-688-2431
Fax: 402-233-7888
sixonline@wowt.com
http://www.wowt.com
• Ross Jernstrom, Producer
(402) 346-6666
sixonline@wowt.com
Description:
Information, Sports. Sunday at 10:35PM for 30 minutes.

SUNDAY SPORTS FINAL
15000 SOUTHWEST 27TH STREET
MIRAMAR, FL 33027-4147
305-379-6666
Fax: 954-622-6107
newsroom@nbc6.net
http://www.nbc6.net
• Guy Rawlings, Host
(954) 622-6355
guy.rawlings@nbc.com
• Joe Rose, Host
(954) 622-6359
joe.rose@nbc.com
• Alex Suarez, Producer
(954) 622-6357
alex.suarez@nbc.com
Description:
Commentary, Interview, Talk. Sunday at 11:20AM for 40 minutes. Program analyzes the week in sports.

SUNDAY SPORTS REPLAY
1422 NEW BRITAIN AVENUE
WEST HARTFORD, CT 06110-1632
860-521-3030
800-523-9848
Fax: 860-521-4860
http://www.wvit.com
• Kevin Nathan, Anchor
• Don Laviano, Producer
(860) 521-3030
don.laviano@nbc.com
• Kevin Nathan, Sports Anchor
Description:
News, Sports. Sunday at 11:20PM for 20 minutes.

SUNDAY SPORTS SPECIAL
613 WOODIS AVENUE
NORFOLK, VA 23510-1017
757-625-1313
Fax: 757-628-6220
http://www.wvec.com
• Brian Smith, Host
(757) 628-6217
bsmith@wvec.com
Description:
Sports. Sunday at 11:20PM for 15 minutes.

THE FOX 8 10:00 PM WEEKEND NEWS
2005 FRANCIS STREET
HIGH POINT, NC 27263-1865
336-841-8888
Fax: 336-841-8051
news@wghp.com
http://www.fox8wghp.com
• Jeff Varner, Anchor
jvarner@wghp.com
• Alan Hobbs, Producer
(336) 841-1139
ahobbs@wghp.com
Description:
News, Sports, Weather. Sunday, Saturday
at 10:00PM for 30 minutes. 30 minute news
broadcast.

THE SCORE
5233 BRIDGE STREET
FORT WORTH, TX 76113
214-750-1111
888-654-5888
Fax: 214-696-9011
news@ktvt.com
http://www.cbs11tv.com
• Dandy Killeen, Producer
dandyk@ktvt.com
• Babe Laufenberg, Anchor / Sports Director
(214) 750-1111
babel@ktvt.com
Description:
Commentary, Talk. Sunday at 10:20PM for
30 minutes. Program highlights sports
scores and news.

WALL TO WALL SPORTS
770 TWIN RIVERS DRIVE
COLUMBUS, OH 43215
614-460-3700
Fax: 614-460-2891
http://www.wbns10tv.com
• Dom Tiberi, Host
(614) 460-3950
dom.tiberi@10tv.com
Description:
Sports. Sunday at 11:35PM for 25 minutes.

WBZ SPORTS FINAL
1170 SOLDIERS FIELD ROAD
BOSTON, MA 02134-1004
617-783-4444
Fax: 617-254-6383
http://www.cbs4boston.com
• Jackie Connally, Producer
(617) 787-7338
jaconnally@boston.cbs.com
Description:
Sports, Talk. Sunday at 11:35PM for 30
minutes.

Sports Television Programs, National

AROUND THE HORN
935 MIDDLE STREET
BRISTOL, CT 06010-1001
860-766-2000
800-999-9985
Fax: 860-766-2213
espn_inc@espn.com
http://www.espn.com
Description:
Information, Interview, Sports. Monday at
5:00PM for 30 minutes; Tuesday at 5:00PM

for 30 minutes; Wednesday at 5:00PM for
30 minutes; Thursday at 5:00PM for 30
minutes; Friday at 5:00PM for 30 minutes.
Program features a discussion of the day's
hot-butto

AZTEC SPORTS WEEKLY
1370 INDIA STREET 2ND FLOOR
SAN DIEGO, CA 92101-3418
619-266-5061
Fax: 619-595-0168
http://www.4sd.com
• Jason Bott, Producer
• Dennis Morgigno, Station Manager
dennis.morgigno@cox.com
Description:
Sports, Talk. Sunday, Monday, Tuesday,
Wednesday, Thursday, Friday, Saturday
Airtime varies; approximately 30 minutes..
Program focuses on San Diego State
University football and basketball.

BASEBALL TONIGHT
935 MIDDLE STREET
BRISTOL, CT 06010-1001
860-766-2000
800-999-9985
Fax: 860-766-2213
espn_inc@espn.com
http://www.espn.com
• Brian Kenny, Host
(860) 766-4816
brian.kenny@espn.com
• Chris Berman, Host
(860) 766-2147
chris.berman@espn.com
• Jay Levy, Senior Coordinating Producer
jay.levy@espn.com
• Karl Ravech, Anchor
karl.ravech@espn.com
• Karl Ravech, Host
karl.ravech@espn.com
• Ed Schimmel, Coordinating Producer
ed.schimmel@espn.com
• Mark Simon, Reporter
Mark.A.Simon@espn.com
• Norby Williamson, Managing Editor
(860) 766-2419
norby.williamson@espn.com
Description:
Commentary, Interview, Talk. Sunday,
Monday, Tuesday, Wednesday, Thursday,
Friday, Saturday Program airs daily March
through November for 60 minutes; airs
weekly November through March for 60
minutes; airtimes vary.. Program presents
the latest news from

BOB COSTAS NOW
1100 AVENUE OF THE AMERICAS
NEW YORK, NY 10036-6712
212-512-1000
Fax: 212-512-1751
http://www.hbo.com
• Rick Bernstein, Executive Producer
(212) 512-1438
rick.bernstein@hbo.com
• Bob Costas, Host
bob.costas@hbo.com
• Nick Dolan, Sports Director
(212) 512-1576
nick.dolan@hbo.com
• Ross Greenburg, Executive Producer
(212) 512-1013
ross.greenburg@hbo.com
Description:
Commentary, Current Events, Information,

Interview. Wednesday at 11:00PM for 1
hour. Program features interviews with
notable sports figures and celebrities.

BOXEO TELEMUNDO
2470 WEST 8TH AVENUE
HIALEAH, FL 33010-2020
305-884-8200
Fax: 305-884-6715
correo@telemundo.com
http://www.telemundo.com
• Robert Pardo, Producer
(305) 884-9640
• Rene Giraldo, Host
(305) 882-8782
rgfernan@telemundo.com
• Jessi Losada, Host
(305) 884-9683
• Guillermo Santa Cruz, Sports Director
(305) 882-8796
• Eli Velazquez, Executive Producer
(305) 889-7348
evelazquez@telemundo.com
Description:
Sports. Sunday, Monday, Tuesday,
Wednesday, Thursday, Friday, Saturday
Program airs on Saturday; time varies..
Program features live coverage of major
boxing matches.

CHARGERS PREVIEW
1370 INDIA STREET 2ND FLOOR
SAN DIEGO, CA 92101-3418
619-266-5061
Fax: 619-595-0168
http://www.4sd.com
• Michael Saks, Producer
(619) 263-9251
michael.saks@cox.com
• Billy Ra Smith, Host
Description:
Magazine, Sports. Sunday, Monday,
Tuesday, Wednesday, Thursday, Friday,
Saturday Airtime varies; approximately 30
minutes..

EMPIRE SPORTS REPORT
795 INDIAN CHURCH ROAD
WEST SENECA, NY 14224-1205
716-558-8444
800-357-3939
Fax: 716-558-8430
http://www.empiresports.com
• David Tasca, Producer
Description:
News, Play-by-Play, Talk. Sunday at
10:30PM for 1 hour; Monday at 10:30PM for
1 hour; Tuesday at 10:30PM for 1 hour;
Wednesday at 10:30PM for 1 hour;
Thursday at 10:30PM for 1 hour; Friday at
10:30PM for 1 hour; Saturday at 10:30PM
for 1 hour. Program fea

ESPN
545 MIDDLE STREET
BRISTOL, CT 06010-1001
860-766-2000
www.espn.com
• Trey Wingo, Anchor
(860) 766-4852
trey.wingo@espn.com
• John Anderson, Anchor
(860) 766-7239
john.anderson@espn.com
• Chris Berman, Anchor
(860) 766-2147
newseditors@espn.com

• Bruce Bernstein, Coordinating Producer
(860) 766-2156
bruce.bernstein@espn.com
• James Bowdon, Coordinating Producer
(860) 766-2675
james.bowdon@espn.com
• Linda Cohn, Anchor
(860) 766-2148
linda.cohn@espn.com
• Rece Davis, Anchor
(860) 766-2372
rece.davis@espn.com
• Rece Davis, Reporter
(860) 766-2372
rece.davis@espn.com
• Mark Gross, Assistant Managing Editor
(860) 766-7865
• Geoff Herman, Coordinating Producer
(860) 766-2552
geoff.herman@espn.com
• Brian Kenny, Anchor
(860) 766-4816
• Suzy Kolber, Anchor
suzy.kolber@espn.com
• Craig Lazarus, Senior Coordinating
Producer
(860) 766-2126
craig.lazarus@espn.com
• Steve Levy, Anchor
steve.levy@espn.com
• Jay Levy, Coordinating Producer
(860) 766-4457
jay.levy@espn.com
• Bob Ley, Anchor
otlweekly@espn.com
• Mark Malone, Reporter
• Julie Mariash, Coordinating Producer
(860) 766-2694
julie.mariash@espn.com
• Kenny Mayne, Anchor
(860) 766-2455
kenny.mayne@espn.com
• Chris McKendry, Anchor
(860) 766-4970
chris.mckendry@espn.com
• Mike McQuade, Coordinating Producer
(860) 766-2133
mike.mcquade@espn.com
• Dan Patrick, Anchor
• Bill Perry, Coordinating Producer
(860) 766-4872
• Bill Pidto, Anchor
(860) 766-2687
• Mark Preisler, (860) 766-7391
Coordinating Producer
• Gus Ramsey, Coordinating Producer
(860) 766-4568
• Karl Ravech, Anchor
karl.ravech@espn.com
• Tom Reilly, Coordinating Producer
(860) 766-2157
• Dave Revsine, Anchor
(860) 766-4066
• Ed Schimmel, Coordinating Producer
(860) 766-2118
Description:
Commentary, Talk. Sunday, Monday,
Tuesday, Wednesday, Thursday, Friday,
Saturday Program airs for 90 minutes;
airtimes vary.. Program features the latest
sports news, scores, game previews and
highlights, as well as sports history,
statistics, and trivia.

FRONT ROW
70 BROOKLINE AVENUE
BOSTON, MA 02215-3403

617-536-9233
Fax: 617-536-7814
sports@nesn.com
http://www.nesn.com
• Todd Kerrissey, Producer
tkerrissey@nesn.com
• Tom Caron, Host
tcaron@nesn.com
• Tom Larson, Assignment Reporter
tlarson@nesn.com
• Steve Sera, Executive Producer
ssera@nesn.com
Description:
Sports. Sunday at 12:30PM for 30 minutes;
Monday at 5:00PM for 30 minutes; Tuesday
at 5:00PM for 30 minutes; Wednesday at
5:00PM for 30 minutes; Thursday at 5:00PM
for 30 minutes; Friday at 5:00PM for 30
minutes. Program covers New England
sports.

FUTBOL TELEMUNDO
2470 WEST 8TH AVENUE
HIALEAH, FL 33010-2020
305-884-8200
Fax: 305-884-6715
correo@telemundo.com
http://www.telemundo.com
• Eli Velazquez, Executive Producer
(305) 889-7348
evelazquez@telemundo.com
• Guillermo Santa Cruz, Sports Director
(305) 882-8796
• Alejandro Blanco, Host
(305) 889-7373
• Andres Cantor, Host
(305) 889-7143
axcantor@telemundo.com
Description:
Sports. Sunday, Monday, Tuesday,
Wednesday, Thursday, Friday, Saturday
Airs on Sunday; times vary.. Program offers
live coverage of international soccer games.

HALLS OF FAME
TWO PENN PLAZA
NEW YORK, NY 10121-0091
212-465-6741
Fax: 212-465-4489
http://www.msgnetwork.com
• Francis X. Healy, Executive Producer
(212) 465-5926
francis.healy@thegarden.com
• Francis X. Healy, Host
(212) 465-5926
francis.healy@thegarden.com
Description:
Interview, Talk. Sunday, Monday, Tuesday,
Wednesday, Thursday, Friday, Saturday
Program airs weekly for 30 minutes; air
times vary.. Program features in-depth
discussions with athletes from a variety of
sports, all of whom are Hall of Fame
inductees in th

HIGH SCHOOL WEEKLY
4 PENN PLAZA
NEW YORK, NY 10001-2819
212-465-5949
Fax: 212-465-5944
http://www.msgnetwork.com
• Mike Quick, Producer
msgnetpr@msgnetwork.com
• Gene Golda, Associate Producer
gene.golda@thegarden.com
• Mike Quick, Host
msgnetpr@msgnetwork.com

Description:
Magazine. Thursday at 7:00PM for 30
minutes. Program features expanded
coverage of high school sports throughout
the fall and winter.

HOCKEY HOTLINE
795 INDIAN CHURCH ROAD
WEST SENECA, NY 14224-1205
716-558-8444
800-357-3939
Fax: 716-558-8430
http://www.empiresports.com
• Chrisanne Bellas, Producer
(716) 558-8470
• Chrisanne Bellas, Host
(716) 558-8470
• Mike Robitaille, Host
Description:
Commentary, Interview, News, Talk.
Sunday, Monday, Tuesday, Wednesday,
Thursday, Friday, Saturday Program airs
after each Buffalo Sabres game during the
NHL season, for 60 minutes..

INSIDE THE NFL
1100 AVENUE OF THE AMERICAS
NEW YORK, NY 10036-6712
212-512-1000
Fax: 212-512-1751
http://www.hbo.com/infl/
• Rick Bernstein, Executive Producer
(212) 512-1438
rick.bernstein@hbo.com
• Bob Costas, Host
bob.costas@hbo.com
• Dave Harmon, Coordinating Producer
(212) 512-5606
dave.harmon@hbo.com
• Brian Hyland, Coordinating Producer
(212) 512-1017
brian.hyland@hbo.com
Description:
Interview, Talk. Thursday at 8:00PM for 1
hour. Program covers the latest news in pro
football, reviews game highlights, and
features interviews and league history.

MONDAY NIGHT COUNTDOWN
935 MIDDLE STREET
BRISTOL, CT 06010-1001
860-766-2000
800-999-9985
Fax: 860-766-2422
espn_inc@espn.com
http://www.espn.com
• Stewart Scott, Host
(860) 766-2686
• Bob Rauscher, Senior Coordinating
Producer
(860) 766-2113
bob.rauscher@espn.com
• Melissa Stark, Correspondent
• Ed Werner, Reporter
Description:
Commentary, Interview, Talk. Monday at
7:00PM for 2.00 hours. Program features an
in-depth preview of the week's Monday
Night Football game, along with the latest
NFL news, Sunday game highlights, and a
look at the week's upcoming games; does
not air off-

NBA 2NIGHT
935 MIDDLE STREET
BRISTOL, CT 06010-1000

media

860-766-2000
Fax: 860-766-2422
http://www.espn.com
Description:
Magazine. Sunday, Monday, Tuesday, Wednesday, Thursday, Friday, Saturday Program airs weeknights for 30 minutes during basketball season; airtimes vary.. Program features the latest news from the NBA, as well as game highlights and analysis.

NBA INSIDE STUFF
450 HARMON MEADOW BOULEVARD
SECAUCUS, NJ 07094-3618
201-865-1500
800-635-4438
Fax: 201-865-8989
http://www.nba.com
• Ahmad Rashad, Executive Producer
(201) 974-6691
Description:
Talk. Sunday, Monday, Tuesday, Wednesday, Thursday, Friday, Saturday Program airtime varies.. Program features NBA news and interviews with NBA figures.

NBA TODAY
935 MIDDLE STREET
BRISTOL, CT 06010
860-766-2000
800-999-9985
Fax: 860-585-2400
espn_inc@espn.com
http://www.espn.com
• David Aldridge, Reporter
(202) 997-0035
• Barry Sacks, Senior Coordinating Producer
(860) 766-2187
Description:
Interview, Talk. Tuesday at 5:00PM for 30 minutes. Program features NBA news, plus game highlights and previews.

NESN SPORTSDESK
70 BROOKLINE AVENUE
BOSTON, MA 02215-3403
617-536-9233
Fax: 617-536-7814
sports@nesn.com
http://www.nesn.com
• Jamie Parker, Producer
jparker@nesn.com
• Hazel Mae, Anchor
hmae@nesn.com
Description:
News. Monday at 5:00AM for 4.00 hours; Tuesday at 5:00AM for 4.00 hours; Wednesday at 5:00AM for 4.00 hours; Thursday at 5:00AM for 4.00 hours; Friday at 5:00AM for 4.00 hours. Program covers the latest news in New England sports.

NESN SPORTSDESK: THE WEEKEND EDITION
70 BROOKLINE AVENUE
BOSTON, MA 02215-3403
617-536-9233
Fax: 617-536-7814
sports@nesn.com
http://www.nesn.com
• Jamie Parker, Producer
jparker@nesn.com
• Hazel Mae, Anchor
hmae@nesn.com

Description:
News. Sunday at 6:00AM for 6.00 hours; Saturday at 6:00AM for 6.00 hours. Program reviews the week in New England sports.

NFL 2NIGHT
935 MIDDLE STREET
BRISTOL, CT 06010-1001
860-766-2000
800-999-9985
Fax: 860-585-2400
espn_inc@espn.com
http://www.espn.com
• Trey Wingo, Host
trey.wingo@espn.com
• Hank Goldberg, Reporter
(860) 766-2000
• Suzy Kolber, Reporter
suzy.kolber@espn.com
• Andrea Kremer, Reporter
(818) 569-7500
• Sal Paolantonio, Reporter
sal.paolantonio@espn.com
• Bob Rauscher, Senior Coordinating Producer
(860) 766-2113
bob.rauscher@espn.com
• Ed Werder, Reporter
werdere@espn.com
Description:
Commentary, Information, Interview. Tuesday at 7:30PM for 30 minutes; Wednesday at 7:30PM for 30 minutes; Thursday at 7:30PM for 30 minutes; Friday at 7:30PM for 30 minutes; Saturday at 7:30PM for 30 minutes. Program provides daily NFL news, discusses cur

NFL COUNTDOWN
935 MIDDLE STREET
BRISTOL, CT 06010-1001
860-766-2000
800-999-9985
Fax: 860-585-2400
espn_inc@espn.com
http://www.espn.com
• Bob Rauscher, Senior Coordinating Producer
(860) 766-2113
bob.rauscher@espn.com
Description:
Interview, Talk. Sunday at 11:00AM for 2.00 hours. Program features football pre-game analysis along with updates and special reports.

NFL PRIMETIME
935 MIDDLE STREET
BRISTOL, CT 06010-1001
860-766-2000
800-999-9985
Fax: 860-585-2400
espn_inc@espn.com
http://www.espn.com
• Bill Fairweather, Producer
• Chris Berman, Host
(860) 766-2147
chris.berman@espn.com
• Bob Rauscher, Senior Coordinating Producer
(860) 766-2113
Description:
Commentary, Talk. Sunday at 7:30PM for 30 minutes. Program features football game highlights.

ONE-ON-ONE WITH JANE MITCHELL
1370 INDIA STREET 2ND FLOOR
SAN DIEGO, CA 92101-3418
619-266-5061
Fax: 619-595-0168
http://www.4sd.com
• Jane Mitchell, Producer
jane.mitchell@cox.com
• Jane Mitchell, Host
jane.mitchell@cox.com
Description:
Interview, Talk. Sunday, Monday, Tuesday, Wednesday, Thursday, Friday, Saturday Airtime varies; approximately 30 minutes.. Program features in-depth personal profiles of Padres stars and other local celebrities, business people and athletes.

PRIME TIME PADRES
1370 INDIA STREET 2ND FLOOR
SAN DIEGO, CA 92101-3418
619-266-5061
Fax: 619-595-0168
http://www.4sd.com
• Jason Bott, Producer
(619) 266-5061
• Tim Flannery, Host
• Jane Mitchell, Reporter
jane.mitchell@cox.com
• Dennis Morgigno, Station Manager
dennis.morgigno@cox.com
• Argy Stathopulos, Reporter
(619) 266-5024
argy.stathopulos@cox.com
Description:
Sports, Talk. Sunday, Monday, Tuesday, Wednesday, Thursday, Friday, Saturday Schedule varies; airs 15 to 30 minutes.. Program previews San Diego Padres baseball.

REAL SPORTS WITH BRYANT GUMBEL
1100 AVENUE OF THE AMERICAS
NEW YORK, NY 10036-6712
212-512-1000
Fax: 212-512-1751
http://www.hbo.com/realsports
• Kirby Bradley, Senior Producer
(212) 512-1469
kirby.bradley@hbo.com
• Rick Bernstein, Executive Producer
(212) 512-1438
rick.bernstein@hbo.com
• Rick Bernstein, Sports Director
(212) 512-1438
rick.bernstein@hbo.com
• Frank Deford, Correspondent
frankdeford@hbo.com
• Bernard Goldberg, Correspondent
(212) 512-1000
• Ross Greenburg, Executive Producer
(212) 512-1013
ross.greenburg@hbo.com
• Bryant Gumbel, Host
(212) 512-5235
Description:
Interview, Talk. Thursday at 10:00PM for 1 hour. Program presents in-depth and investigative reports covering issues from the sports world.

REPUBLICA DEPORTIVA
9405 NORTHWEST 41ST STREET
MIAMI, FL 33178-2301
305-471-3900
Fax: 305-471-4236
http://www.univision.net

• Fernando Fiore, Host
(305) 471-4070
Description:
Commentary, Interview, Play-by-Play, Sports, Talk. Sunday at 11:00AM for 2.00 hours. Program features interviews, the latest scores, and highlights of sporting events of interest to an Hispanic audience.

SPORTS CONNECTION
700 CARILLION PARKWAY
SUITE 9
SAINT PETERSBURG, FL 33716
727-329-2400
888-437-1239
Fax: 727-329-2434
http://www.baynews9.com
• Chris Elias, Producer
celias@baynews9.com
• Rock Riley, Host
rriley@baynews9.com
• Elliott Wiser, General Manager
ewiser@baynews9.com
Description:
Call-In, Interview, Sports, Talk. Program features live sports commentary and analysis.

SPORTS CORNER
4270 WEST MARDON AVENUE
LAS VEGAS, NV 89139-5854
702-361-2191
800-336-2225
Fax: 818-352-3229
http://www.cableradionetwork.com
• Jack Roberts, Executive Producer
jroberts@crni.net
• Jennifer Horn, Marketing Vice President
jhorn@crni.net
• Michael Horn, President
mhorn@crni.net
• Rod Myers, Host
rmyers@crni.net
Description:
Call-In, Sports, Talk. Sunday at 5:00PM for 2.00 hours; Monday at 5:00PM for 1 hour; Tuesday at 5:00PM for 1 hour; Wednesday at 5:00PM for 1 hour; Thursday at 5:00PM for 1 hour; Friday at 5:00PM for 1 hour. Program features audience call-in and guest inte

SPORTS LATENIGHT
160 WELLS AVENUE
NEWTON, MA 02459-3302
617-630-5000
Fax: 617-630-5057
newsdesk@necn.com
http://www.necn.com
• Chris Collins, Anchor
(617) 630-5000
ccollins@necn.com
Description:
Sports. Monday at 11:00PM for 30 minutes; Tuesday at 11:00PM for 30 minutes; Wednesday at 11:00PM for 30 minutes; Thursday at 11:00PM for 30 minutes; Friday at 11:00PM for 30 minutes. Program features highlights and scores from around the various sports l

SPORTS ON 1
75 NINTH AVENUE 6TH FLOOR
NEW YORK, NY 10011-7006
212-379-3311
Fax: 212-379-3575
http://www.ny1.com

• Kevin Garrity, Sports Anchor
• Marc Weingarten, Sports Director
marc.weingarten@ny1news.com
Description:
Call-In, Interview, Sports, Talk. Sunday at 11:30PM for 1 hour; Monday at 11:30PM for 1 hour; Tuesday at 11:30PM for 1 hour; Wednesday at 11:30PM for 1 hour; Thursday at 11:30PM for 1 hour; Friday at 11:30PM for 1 hour; Saturday at 11:30PM for 1 hour. Pro

SPORTS PAGE
2000 YORK ROAD SUITE 114
OAK BROOK, IL 60523-8863
630-368-4000
Fax: 630-368-4468
http://www.cltv.com
• L. J. Tabano, Producer
• Mike Bloomberg, Host
• Lou Canellis, Host
Description:
Call-In. Monday at 9:00PM for 1 hour; Tuesday at 9:00PM for 1 hour; Wednesday at 9:00PM for 1 hour; Thursday at 9:00PM for 1 hour; Friday at 9:00PM for 1 hour; Saturday at 9:00PM for 1 hour.

SPORTS REPORTERS II
935 MIDDLE STREET
BRISTOL, CT 06010-1001
860-766-2000
800-999-9985
Fax: 860-766-2213
espn_inc@espn.com
http://www.espn.com
• Joe Valerio, Producer
jovaler@optonline.net
Description:
Information, News, Talk. Tuesday at 7:30PM for 30 minutes. Program features a panel discussion of the day's hottest sports news.

SPORTSCENTURY
935 MIDDLE STREET BUILDING 7
BRISTOL, CT 06010-1001
860-585-2000
Fax: 860-766-2213
http://www.espn.com
Description:
Magazine. Monday at 8:00PM for 1 hour; Tuesday at 8:00PM for 1 hour; Wednesday at 8:00PM for 1 hour; Thursday at 8:00PM for 1 hour; Friday at 8:00PM for 1 hour. Program profiles the lives of sports legends of the 20th century.

THE SPORTS PAGE WITH LOU CANELLIS
2000 YORK ROAD SUITE 114
OAK BROOK, IL 60523-8863
630-368-4000
Fax: 630-368-4468
http://www.cltv.com
Description:
Call-In, Commentary, Interview. Sunday at 9:00PM for 1 hour. Program features games and humor along with sports news and analysis.

THE SPORTS REPORTERS
5 MINUTE MAN HILL
WESTPORT, CT 06880-6523
860-766-2000
800-999-9985

Fax: 203-226-3561
http://www.espn.com
• Joe Valerio, Producer
jovaler@optonline.net
• John Saunders, Host
jovaler@optonline.net
Description:
Commentary, Panel Discussion. Sunday at 10:00AM for 30 minutes. Program features discussions of current sports issues.

Sports Satellite Television

CAPITOL SPORTS NETWORK
2619 WESTERN BOULEVARD
RALEIGH, NC 27606
919-890-6000
Fax: 919-890-6095
www.cbc-raleigh.com
• James F. Goodmon, President/Chief Executive Officer
• Daniel P. McGrath, Vice President
• James F. Goodmon, Jr., Vice President, CBC New Media Group
• Michael Goodmon, Vice President, Real Estate
• Ardie Gregory, Vice President/GM, WRAL-FM
• George Habel, Vice President, Radio Networks/Sports 99.9 Th
• Angie Emerline, Vice President, Human Resources
• Steve Hammel, Vice President/GM, WRAL-TV
• Thomas McLaughlin, Assistant Treasurer
• Robert Matheny, Vice President, Police & Innovation
Nature of Sports Service:
Capitol Broadcasting Company, Inc. is a diversified communications company that owns and/or operates WRAL-TV, WRAL Digital, WRAZ-TV, WRAZ Digital, WRAL-FM, WRAL-HD2, WCMC-FM, WCMC-HD1, WDNC-AM, WCMC-HD2, WCMC-HD3, WCLY-AM, WCMC-HD4, Microspace, CBC New Media Group and Wolfpack Sports Properties (a joint venture with Learfield Sports) in Raleigh, NC; WJZY-TV and WMYT-TV in Charlotte, NC; WILM-TV and Sunrise Broadcasting in Wilmington, NC; The Durham Bulls Baseball Club in Durham, NC; and real estate interests including the American Tobacco Project and Diamond View office buildings in Durham, NC.
Additional Office:
229 N. Church St, Charlotte, NC 28202.

DIRECTV, INC.
2230 E. IMPERIAL HWY
EL SEGUNDO, CA 90245
310-964-5000
888-238-7177
800-531-5000
Fax: 877-580-2148
www.directv.com
• Michael White, Chairman/President/CEO
• Joseph A. Bosch, Executive Vice President/Chief HR Officer
• Brian B. Churchill, EVP/President, DIRECTV Latin America
• Patrick T. Doyle, Executive Vice President/Chief Financial Officer
• Larry D. Hunter, Executive Vice President/General Counsel
• Romulo C. Pontual, EVP/Chief Technology

Officer
• Fazal Merchant, Senior Vice President/Treasurer
• John F. Murphy, SVP/Controller/Chief Accounting Officer
• Ellen Filipiak, Senior Vice President, Customer Care
Baseball Sponsor:
MLB, Minor League
Auto Sports Sponsor:
NASCAR
Basketball Sponsor:
NBA
Football Sponsor:
NFL
Ice Hockey Sponsor:
NHL

DISH NETWORK
9601 SOUTH MERIDIAN BOULEVARD
ENGLEWOOD, CO 80112
303-723-1000
800-333-3474
888-743-5750
Fax: 303-723-1399
www.dish.com
• Charlie Ergen, Co-Founder/Chairman of the Board
• Joseph Clayton, President/Chief Executive Officer
• Michael Kelly, President of Blockbuster, L.L.C.
• Jim DeFranco, Co-Founder/EVP/Special Advisor to the CEO
• W. Erik Carlson, Executive Vice President, Operations
• Tom Cullen, Executive Vice President, Corporate Developme
• R. Stanton Dodge, EVP, General Counsel & Secretary
• Bernie Han, EVP/Chief Operating Officer
• Robert Olsen, EVP/Chief Financial Officer
• Dave Shull, EVP/Chief Commercial Officer
• Amir Ahmed, Senior Vice President, Sales & Distribution
• Vivek Khemka, Senior Vice President, Product Management
• Mike McClaskey, Senior Vice President, Chief Information Offi
• James Moorhead, Senior Vice President, Chief Marketing Office
• Brian Neylon, SVP, Sales Planning, Administration & Direct
• Warren Schlichting, Senior Vice President, Ad Sales

FOX SPORTS DIRECT
100 EAST ROYAL LANE
SUITE 250
IRVING, TX 75039
972-868-1400
800-766-6746
Fax: 972-868-1616
www.foxsports.com
• Glenn Gurgiolo, President
Description:
The nation's leading distributor of sports programming to the residential and commercial satellite dish marketplace by providing, NBA, NHL, MLB and NCAA action on more than 20 Regional Sports Networks via C-Band and Direct Broadcast Satellite (DBS). Networks represented: nine (9) FOX Sports Net regional networks, eight (8) from Sports Channel, plus Madison Square Garden, NESN, PASS Sports, HTS, Midwest Sports Channel, and Sunshine Network. Additional sports programming

represented includes NFL Sunday Ticket and the Golf Channel.

NASCAR
1 DAYTONA BOULEVARD
DAYTONA BEACH, FL 32114
386-253-0611
www.nascar.com
• Brian Z. France, Chairman/CEO
• Mike Helton, President
• Steve Phelps, Chief Marketing Officer
• Jim O'Connell, Chief Sales Officer/VP, Corporate Marketing
• Todd Wilson, Chief Financial Officer
• Gary Crotty, General Counsel
• Ed Bennett, SVP/Chief Administrative Officer
• Sabrina Macias, Director, Brand & Consumer Marketing Communic
• Chris Tropeano, Senior Manager, Business Communications
• Jon Schwartz, Senior Director, Business & Brand Communicati
• David Higdon, Managing Director, Integrated Marketing Comm.
• Jim Cassidy, Vice President
• Zane Stoddard, Vice President
• Kim Brink, Vice President
Products & Services:
The National Association for Stock Car Auto Racing, Inc. (NASCAR) is the sanctioning body for one of North America's premier sports. NASCAR races are broadcast in more than 150 countries and in 20 languages. In the U.S., races are broadcast on FOX, TNT, ABC/ESPN/ESPN2, SPEED, Motor Racing Network Radio, PRN Radio, and Sirius XM Satellite Radio. NASCAR fans are among the most brand-loyal in all of sports, and as a result more Fortune 500 companies participate in NASCAR than any other sport. NASCAR consists of three national series (the NASCAR Sprint Cup Series, NASCAR Nationwide Series, and NASCAR Camping World Truck Series), four regional

RFDTV
3201 DICKERSON PIKE
NASHVILLE, TN 37207
615-227-9292
patrick@rfdtv.com
www.rfdtv.com
• Patrick Gottsch, Founder/President
• Raquel Gottsch, EVP, Corporate Communications
• Gatsby Gottsch, EVP, Finance
• Randy Bernard, Chief Executive Officer
• Ed Frazier, Chief Operating Officer
• Steve Campione, Chief Financial Officer
• Michael E. LaBroad, Chief Marketing Officer
Nature of Sports Service:
RFD-TV is home to the most comprehensive lineup of agricultural-based programs ever assembled on one channel. Shows from around the world give agriculture professionals and hobbyists the widest variety of news and information available. Horses on RFD-TV is America's only daily block of high-quality and exclusive programs dedicated to the horse owner and horse lover, featuring the world's most respected and popular equine clinicians, breed features, competitions & event coverage. People who lvoe and respect the land make up the largest share of the RFD-TV audience. RFD-TV covers this growing

market with a wide variety of programs and featu

SHERIDAN BROADCASTING NETWORK
960 PENNSYIVANIA AVENUE
SUITE 200
PITTSBURGH, PA 15222
412-456-4086
800-456-4211
Fax: 412-456-4040
• Ty Miller, Director of Sports
• Jerry Lopes, President
Description:
National. Satellite distribution company.

SPORTS NEWSATELLITE
3 EMPIRE BOULEVARD
SOUTH HACKENSACK, NJ 07606
201-807-0888
Fax: 201-807-9007
• Joseph L. Podesta, Chairman
• James E. Holland, President
• Geoff Belinfante, Senior Vice President/Executive Producer
• Rich Domich, Senior Vice President/Sales/Marketing
• Jeanmarie Cap, Senior Vice President
• Tim Roberts, Vice President/Sports News Director
troberts@phoenixcomm.com
Description:
National. Program producer, distributor, syndicator. Produces sports news feeds for all NBC affiliates. Current properties include: Play It Up (For MSG Network).

STAR GROUP LIMITED
8th FLOOR, ONE HARBOURFRONT, 18 TAK FUNG STREET
HUNGHOM
KOWLOON
HONG KONG
corp-aff@startv.com
www.startv.com
• James Murdoch, Chariman/Chief Executive Officer
• Bruce Churchill, President/Chief Operating Officer
• Gary Walrath, Executive Vice President, STAR Group Limited
• Steve Askew, Executive Vice President/STAR Group Ltd.
Description:
International. Satellite programming network.

THE SPORTS NETWORK
2200 BYBERRY ROAD
SUITE 200
HATBORO, PA 19040
215-441-8444
Fax: 215-441-5767
http://www.sportsnetwork.com
• Mickey Charles, CEO/President
• Ken Zajac, Director of Sales
• Steve Cwikowitz, Account Executive
• Bernie Greenberg, Client Relations Coordinator
Nature of Sports Service
TSn is the largest privately owned international sports information company in North America and possibly, the world, servicing hundreds and hundreds of clients whose range multiplies that to, literally, millions of viewers/users worldwide. TSN covers the gamut of sports information,

ranging from NFL to Rugby, MLB to Cricket and virtually everything in between.

VERESTAR
3040 WILLIAMS DRIVE
SUITE 500
FAIRFAX, VA 22031
703-206-9000
Fax: 703-573-3522
• David Garrison, Chairman/Chief Executive Officer
• David Kagan, President/Chief Operating Officer
Description:
National, International. Satellite transmission service for sports programmers to broadcast and cable industries. Verestar has 11 satellite network access points, with gives them access to over 60 different satellites and manages 70 transponders.

Sports Television Stations

CLEAR CHANNEL ENTERTAINMENT, INC.
200 E BASSE ROAD
SAN ANTONIO, TX 78209
210-822-2828
Fax: 310-867-7001
www.clearchannel.com
• Mark P. Mays, Chairman
• Randall T. Mays, Vice Chairman
• Robert W. Pittman, CEO/Director
• Thomas W. Casey, Executive Vice President/Chief Financial Offi
• Robert H. Walls, Executive Vice President/General Counsel
• John E. Hogan, Chairman/CEO, Media & Entertainment
• Bob Stohrer, President
• Scott D. Hamilton, Senior Vice President/Chief Accounting Office
• Drew Fisher, Senior Vice President, Information

COX SPORTS/CHANNEL 9
17602 N. BLACK CANYON HWY, STE 111
PHOENIX, AZ 85023
602-866-0072
Fax: 602-547-8039
• Suzee Smith-Everhard, Director Televideo

GOLF CHANNEL, THE
7580 COMMERCE CENTER DRIVE
ORLANDO, FL 32819
407-363-4653
Fax: 407-363-7976
www.thegolfchannel.com
• Mike McCarley, President
• Jeff Dilley, Chief Financial Officer
• Robert Greenway, SVP Production/Programming/Ops
• Gene Pizzolato, SVP Advertising Sales
• Kevin Byrnes, Vice President Advertising Sales
• John Houde, Vice President New Media
• R. Andy Murphy, Vice President Network Operations
• Mark Oldham, Vice President Tournament Affairs
• Christine Sullivan, Vice President Marketing
• Tony Tortorici, Vice President Production
Description:
National. Cable Television programmer

offering 24-hour, 7 basic service. Live coverage of the PGA Tour, Champions Tour, LPGA, Nationwide, European and Australian Tours. Programming also includes: GOLF TALK LIVE, a call -in interview show with golfers. GOLF CHANNEL ACADEMY LIVE, a call-in instructional show. GOLF CENTRAL, a live news show, PROFILE OF A PRO, PASSAGE TO PARADISE, a golf travel program. The GOLF CHANNEL ACADEMY, an instructional series

KABC-TV
500 CIRCLE SEVEN DRIVE
GLENDALE, CA 91201-2331
818-863-7500
Fax: 818-863-7080
http://www.abclocal.go.com/kabc
• Bill Burton, Vice President
(818) 863-7261
• Rob Fukuzaki, Sports Anchor
(818) 863-7500
• Mike Parker, Sports Producer
(818) 863-7649
stan.r.radford@abc.com
• Stan Radford, Sports Producer
(818) 863-7649
stan.r.radford@abc.com

KAII-TV
88 PIIKOI STREET
HONOLULU, HI 96814-4245
808-591-2222
Fax: 808-593-8479
http://www.khon.com
• Kanoa Leahey, Sports Director
(808) 591-6359
news@khon.emmis.com
• Darlene Lee, Executive Assistant
• John Veneri, Sports Anchor
(808) 591-4289

KAMR-TV
1015 FILLMORE STREET, S.
AMARILLO, TX 79101-0751
806-383-3321
Fax: 806-349-9083
news@kamr.com
http://www.kamr.com
• Jeff Barger, Sports Director
(806) 383-3321
jeff.barger@kamr.com

KAPP-TV
P.O. BOX 10208
YAKIMA, WA 98902-1208
509-453-0351
Fax: 509-453-3623
kappnews@kapptv.com
http://www.kapptv.com
• Brad Reierson, Sports Director
(509) 453-0351

KARE-TV
8811 OLSON MEMORIAL HIGHWAY
MINNEAPOLIS, MN 55427-4762
763-546-1111
Fax: 763-546-8606
kare11@kare11.com
http://www.kare11.com
• Randy Shaver, Sports Director/Anchor
(763) 546-1111
rshaver@kare11.com
• Tim Stanko, Marketing Vice President
tstanko@kare11.com

• Tim Stanko, Promotion Vice President
tstanko@kare11.com
• Tim McNiff, Sports Anchor
(763) 546-1111
tmcniff@kare11.com

KARK-TV
1401 WEST CAPITOL AVENUE
LITTLE ROCK, AR 72201-2940
501-340-4444
Fax: 501-375-1961
news4@kark.com
http://www.kark.com
• Dean Hinson, President
• Mark Rushing, Sports Anchor
(501) 340-4525
mrushing@kark.com
• Bo Mattingly, Sports Anchor
(501) 340-4444

KATV-TV
PO BOX 77
LITTLE ROCK, AR 72201-3801
501-324-7777
Fax: 501-324-7899
tv7@katv.com
http://www.katv.com
• Paul Eells, Sports Director
(501) 324-7529
peells@katv.com
• Tim Vahsholtz, Promotions Director
(501) 324-7807
tvahsholtz@katv.com
• Steve Sullivan, Sports Anchor/Reporter
(501) 324-7777

KAUZ-TV
P.O. BOX 2130
WICHITA FALLS, TX 76309
940-322-6957
Fax: 940-761-3331
http://www.kauz.com/
• Adam Ostrow, Sports Director
aostrow@kauz.com
• Charlie Bartlett, Sports Reporter/Anchor

KBCI-TV
140 NORTH 16TH STREET
BOISE, ID 83702
208-472-2222
Fax: 208-472-2211
news@kbcitv.com
http://www.2news.tv/
• Vince Trimboli, Sports Director
(208) 472-2222
• Andrew Marden, Weekend Sports Anchor
(208) 489-1243

KBIM-TV
214 NORTH MAIN STREET
ROSWELL, NM 88201-4723
505-622-2120
Fax: 505-623-6606
• Mickey Winfield, Sports Director
mwinfield@kbimtv.com

KBMT-TV
525 INTERSTATE 10 SOUTH
BEAUMONT, TX 77701-3708
409-833-7512
Fax: 409-835-1617
• Dave Hofferth, Sports Director
12news@kbmt-tv.com
• Will Norman, Promotions Director

KBSH-TV
2300 HALL STREET
HAYS, KS 67601-3062
785-625-5277
Fax: 785-625-1161
cwalker_kbsh@yahoo.com
• Gerard Wellbrock, Sports Anchor
(785) 625-2578

KBTX-TV
PO BOX 3730
BRYAN, TX 77802-4305
979-846-7777
800-752-5289
Fax: 979-846-1888
news@kbtx.com
http://www.kbtx.com
• Jon Boaz, Advertising Manager
(979) 595-1580
• Darryl Bruffett, Sports Director
(979) 846-7777
bruffett@kbtx.com

KCAL-TV
6121 SUNSET BOULEVARD
LOS ANGELES, CA 90028
323-460-3000
Fax: 323-460-3733
kcbstvnews@cbs.com
http://www.kcal9.com/
• Jim Hill, Sports Reporter
• Alan Massengale, Sports Anchor

KCBS-TV
6121 SUNSET BOULEVARD
LOS ANGELES, CA 90028-6423
323-460-3000
Fax: 323-460-3733
kcbstvnews@cbs.com
http://www.kcbs-tv.com/
• Steve Hartman, Sports Reporter
• Jim Hill, Sports Director
jhill@channel2000.com

KCCW-TV
720 HAWTHORNE STREET
ALEXANDRIA, MN 56308-1866
320-763-5166
800-934-5226
Fax: 320-763-4991
http://www.kcco-tv.com
• Stacy Steinhagen, Sports Director
(320) 763-7189

KCEC-TV
777 GRANT STREET
DENVER, CO 80203
303-832-0050
800-725-8454
Fax: 303-318-6252
http://www.univision.com
• Luis Canela, Sports Director
(303) 832-0050
lcanela@entravision.com

KCEN-TV
PO BOX 6103
TEMPLE, TX 76503-6103
254-773-6868
Fax: 254-859-5831
news@kcentv.com
http://www.kcentv.com
• Steve Iandoli, Sports Director
(254) 859-5481
siandoli@kcentv.com
• Tyler Hedrick, Sports Reporter

(254) 773-6868
thedrick@kcentv.com

KCFW-TV
P.O. BOX 857
KALISPELL, MT 59901-4937
406-755-5239
Fax: 406-752-8002
news@kcfw.com
http://www.nbcmontana.com
• Matt Seigel, Sports Director
• Martin Ross, Sports Director
(406) 755-5239

KCNC-TV
1044 LINCOLN STREET
DENVER, CO 80203-2714
303-830-6464
Fax: 303-830-6380
kcncnews@cbs.com
http://www.kcncnews4.com
• Steve Cox, Executive Sports Producer
(303) 830-6464
scox@cbs.com

KCOP-TV
1999 SOUTH BUNDY DRIVE
LOS ANGELES, CA 90025
310-584-2000
Fax: 310-584-2024
http://www.mynetworktv.com
• Rod Cohen, Sports Assignment Editor
(310) 584-2030
• Rod Cohen, Sports Producer
(310) 584-2030
• Steve Jahnke, Sports Director
• Rick Garcia, Sports Anchor
(310) 584-2369

KCPQ-TV
1813 WESTLAKE AVENUE, NORTH
SEATTLE, WA 98109-2706
206-674-1305
Fax: 206-674-1713
tips@q13.com
http://www.kcpq.com
• Dan Devone, Sports Anchor
• Tony Ventrella, Sports Anchor
• Bill Wixey, Sports Anchor
(206) 674-1305

KCRA-TV
3 TELEVISION CIRCLE
SACRAMENTO, CA 95814-0794
916-444-7316
Fax: 916-441-4050
http://www.kcra.com
• Ron Hyde, Sports Director
(916) 325-3294
rbhyde@hearst.com
• Chris Lango, Sports Writer
(916) 444-7316
clango@hearst.com

KCRG-TV
501 2ND AVENUE, S.E.
CEDAR RAPIDS, IA 52401
319-398-8422
800-332-5443
Fax: 319-368-8505
newsreleases@kcrg.com
http://www.kcrg.com
• John Campbell, Sports Director
(319) 398-8325
john.campbell@kcrg.com
• Scott Saville, Weekend Sports

Anchor/Reporter
(319) 398-8422
Scott.Saville@kcrg.com
• Shawn Terrell, Sports Reporter
(319) 365-9999
shawn.terrell@kcrg.com
• David Welsh, Promotions Director
david.welsh@kcrg.com

KCTV-TV
4500 SHAWNEE MISSION PARKWAY
FAIRWAY, KS 66205
913-677-5555
Fax: 913-677-7135
kctv5@kctv5.com
http://www.kctv5.com
• Ken Bauer, Promotions Director
(913) 677-7129
kbauer@kctv5.com
• Leif Lisec, Sports Anchor
leif.lisec@twcable.com

KDAF-TV
8001 JOHN W. CARPENTER FREEWAY
DALLAS, TX 75247
214-252-9233
Fax: 214-252-3379
http://www.kdaf.com
• Dave Crome, Sports Anchor
(214) 252-9233
• Bob Irzyk, Sports Anchor
(214) 252-9233

KDF-TV
409 SOUTH STAPLES
CORPUS CHRISTI, TX 78401
361-886-6100
Fax: 361-886-6175
newsroom@kristv.com
http://www.kristv.com
• Art Mack, Sports Director
(361) 886-6172
amack@kristv.com
• Adela Paradero, Promotions Assistant
Director
(361) 886-6100
aparadero@kristv.com
• Adela Paradero, Promotions Director
(361) 886-6100

KDFW-TV
400 NORTH GRIFFIN STREET
DALLAS, TX 75202-1901
214-720-4444
Fax: 214-720-3263
http://www.kdfwfox4.com/
• Mike Doocy, Sports Anchor
(214) 720-3164
mdoocy@foxtv.com
• Max Morgan, Sports Anchor
(214) 720-3158
mmorgan@foxtv.com
• Nita Wiggins, Sports Reporter
(214) 720-3187
nwiggins@foxtv.com
• Chris Yates, Sports Reporter
(214) 720-4444
cyate032@foxtv.com

KDIN-TV
PO BOX 6450
JOHNSTON, IA 50131
515-281-4500
800-532-1290
Fax: 515-242-4113
http://www.iptv.org

• Jerry Grady, Sports Director
(515) 242-3111
• Dan Miller, Executive Director
(515) 242-3123
• Pat Rowan, Sports Director
(515) 281-4500

KDKA-TV
1 GATEWAY CENTER
PITTSBURGH, PA 15222
412-575-2200
Fax: 412-575-2871
newsdesk@kdka.com
http://www.kdka.com
• Mike Bukovcan, Sports Director
• Greg Jena, Promotions Director
(412) 575-2508
• Mike Zappone, Sports Director
• Bob Pompeani, Sports Director
(412) 575-2200

KDLH-TV
246 LAKE AVENUE, S.
DULUTH, MN 55802-1511
218-720-9600
Fax: 218-720-9660
http://www.northlandsnewscentre.com.com
• Christi Corbett, Promotion Manager
(218) 733-0303
christi@kdlh.com
• Chris Earl, Sports Director
(218) 720-9626
• Joe Dufek, Sports Anchor
(218) 727-9600

KDLT-TV
3600 SOUTH WESTPORT AVENUE
SIOUX FALLS, SD 57106-6325
605-361-5555
800-727-5358
Fax: 605-361-3982
news@kdlt.com
http://www.kdlt.com
• Mark Kitterman, Promotions Director
• Mark Ovenden, Sports Director
(605) 361-5555
sports@kdlt.com
• Jason Anschutz, Sports Anchor
(605) 361-5555
info@kdlt.com

KDRX-TV
4625 SOUTH 33RD PLACE
PHOENIX, AZ 85040-2861
602-268-2648
Fax: 602-470-0810
• Franciscio Romero, Sports Director
(602) 470-0507

KDTV-TV
50 FREMONT STREET 41ST FLOOR
SAN FRANCISCO, CA 94105-2240
415-538-8000
Fax: 415-538-8053
http://www.univision.net
• Tony Lopez, Sports Director
(415) 538-8010
• Sandra Thomas, Executive Director
(415) 538-8003
sthomas@univision.net

KECI-TV
340 WEST MAIN STREET
MISSOULA, MT 59802-4149
406-721-2063
Fax: 406-549-6507

news@keci.com
http://www.keci.com
• Kristian Read, Sports Director

KERO-TV
321 21ST STREET
BAKERSFIELD, CA 93301
661-637-2320
Fax: 661-323-5538
http://www.turnto23.com
• Joseph Fernandez, Sports Director
(661) 637-2323
joseph_fernandez@mcgraw-hill.com
• Steve McEvoy, Marketing Director
(661) 637-2323
steve_mcevoy@mcgraw-hill.com
• Steve Taylor, Promotions Director
(661) 637-2323
steve_taylor@mcgraw-hill.com
• Bryce Anslinger, Weekend Sports
Anchor/News Reporter
(661) 637-2320
bryce_anslinger@mcgraw-hill.com

KESQ-TV
42-650 MELANIE PLACE
PALM DESERT, CA 92211
760-773-0795
Fax: 760-773-5128
http://www.kesq.com
• Brad Hoffman, Sports Anchor
(760) 773-0795
bhoffman@kesq.com
• Brad Hoffman, Sports Reporter

KETK-TV
4300 RICHMOND ROAD
TYLER, TX 75703-1201
903-581-5656
800-594-5385
Fax: 903-561-2459
http://www.ketknbc.com/
• Danny Elzner, Sports Director
(903) 581-5656
delzner@nbc56.com
• Danny Elzner, Sports Director
(903) 581-5656
delzner@nbc56.com

KETV-TV
2665 DOUGLAS STREET
OMAHA, NE 68131
402-978-8954
Fax: 402-978-8931
http://www.ketv.com
• Jon Schuetz, Sports Director
(402) 345-7777
• Jon Schuetz, Sports Director
• Mike Sigmond, Sports Anchor
• Matt Schick, Weekend Sports Anchor
(402) 978-8954

KEVN-TV
2000 SKYLINE DRIVE
RAPID CITY, SD 57701
605-394-7777
Fax: 605-348-9128
news@kevn.com
http://www.fox7.blackhills.com
• Jamie Zepp, Sports Director
(605) 394-7777
sports@kevn.com

KEZI-TV
2975 CHAD DRIVE
EUGENE, OR 97408-7344

541-485-5611
Fax: 541-342-1568
kezi@kezi.com
http://www.kezi.com
• Carolyn S. Chambers, Chief Executive
Officer
• Scott Chambers, President
• Joe Giansante, Sports Director
(541) 485-5611
• Sam Adams, Sports Reporter
(541) 485-5778

KFBB-TV
3200 OLD HAVRE HIGHWAY
BLACK EAGLE, MT 59414-1139
406-453-4377
Fax: 406-727-9703
kfbb@kfbb.com
http://www.kfbb.com
• Jason Nitschke, Sports Director
(406) 453-4370
newsroom@kfbb.com

KFDA-TV
7900 BROADWAY DRIVE
AMARILLO, TX 79108
806-383-1010
Fax: 806-381-9859
newsroom@newschannel10.com
http://www.newschannel10.com
• Joyce Austin, Advertising Manager
jaustin@newschannel10.com
• Jason Zielinski, Sports Reporter ;
Weekend Anchor
(806) 383-1010
sports10@newschannel10.com
• Jeff Barger, Sports Director
(806) 383-1010
sports10@newschannel10.com

KFDM-TV
2955 INTERSTATE 10, E.
BEAUMONT, TX 77702-7128
409-892-6622
Fax: 409-892-6622
news@kfdm.com
http://www.kfdm.com
• Mike Friedman, Sports Director
(409) 895-4672
• Rix Garey, Advertising Manager
(409) 899-5544
rgarey@kfm.com
• Gina Hinson, Promotions Director
(409) 895-4628

KFDX-TV
P. O. BOX 4000
WICHITA FALLS, TX 76309
940-692-6273
Fax: 940-692-1441
kfdx@kfdx.com
http://www.kfdx.com
• Susan Knowles, Sports Director
(940) 692-1414
susan@kfdx.com

KFMB-TV
7677 ENGINEER ROAD
SAN DIEGO, CA 92111-1515
858-571-8888
Fax: 858-560-0627
yourstories@kfmb.com
http://www.kfmb.com
• John Howard, Sports Anchor
(858) 571-8888
jhoward@kfmb.com

media

• Kyle Kraska, Sports Director/Anchor
(858) 571-8888
kkraska@kfmb.com

KFOR-TV
PO BOX 14068
OKLAHOMA CITY, OK 73114-7515
405-424-4444
Fax: 405-478-6337
4warn@kfor.com
http://www.kfor.com
• Bob Barry, Sports Director
(405) 478-6366
bob.barrysr@kfor.com

KFSM-TV
PO BOX 369
FORT SMITH, AR 72901
479-783-3131
Fax: 479-783-1965
http://www.kfsm.com/
• Mike Irwin, Sports Director
(479) 783-3131

KFVE-TV
150 B PUUHALE ROAD
HONOLULU, HI 96819
808-847-3246
Fax: 808-845-3616
http://www.khnl.com
• Jim Leahy, Sports Director

KFYR-TV
P.O. BOX 1738
BISMARCK, ND 58501-4004
701-255-8105
Fax: 701-255-8220
news@kfyrtv.com
http://www.kfyrtv.com
• Lee Timmerman, Sports Director
(701) 255-8105
sports@kfyrtv.com

KGAN-TV
P.O. BOX 3131
CEDAR RAPIDS, IA 52402-2152
800-222-5426
800-222-5426
Fax: 319-395-0987
newsreleases@kgan.com
http://www.kgan.com
• Ruth Barnett, Promotions Manager
(319) 395-9060
rbarnett@kgan.com
• Kevin Hall, Sports Director
(800) 222-5426
• Jared Aarons, Sports Anchor
(319) 395-9060

KGMV-TV
1534 KAPIOLANI BOULEVARD
HONOLULU, HI 96814-3715
808-973-5462
Fax: 808-941-8153
http://www.kgmvnews.com
• Liz Chun, Sports Director
(808) 218-7696

KGO-TV
900 FRONT STREET
SAN FRANCISCO, CA 94111-1427
415-954-7926
Fax: 415-956-6402
abc7listens@kgo-tv.com
http://www.abc7news.com

• Bill Bacigalupi, Advertising Sales
• Larry Beil, Sports Anchor
larry.beil@abc.com
• Martin Wyatt, Sports Director
martin.wyatt@abc.com
• Mike Shumann, Sports Anchor
(415) 954-7926
mike.shumann@abc.com

KGPE-TV
4880 NORTH 1ST STREET
FRESNO, CA 93726-0514
559-222-2411
Fax: 559-225-5305
newsdesk@cbs47.tv
http://www.47tv.com
• Paul Loeffler, Sports Director
(559) 222-2411
paulloeffler@clearchannel.com
• George Takata, Sports Anchor
(559) 222-2411
georgetakata@clearchannel.com
• Rick Turner, Promotion Director
rickturner@clearchannel.com

KGTV-TV
4600 AIR WAY
SAN DIEGO, CA 92102-2528
619-527-6397
Fax: 619-527-0369
10news@10news.com
http://www.kgtv.com
• Jeff Cawley, Sports Director
(619) 237-6324
jeff_cawley@10news.com
• Wendy Simmons, Promotions Manager
wendy_urushima-simmons@10news.com
• Ben Higgins, Sports Anchor
(619) 527-6397
ben_higgins@10News.com

KGW-TV
1501 SW JEFFERSON STREET
PORTLAND, OR 97201-2549
503-226-5000
Fax: 503-226-5059
newsdesk@kgw.com
http://www.kgw.com
• Joe Becker, Sports Anchor
(503) 226-5000
• Ron Pivo, Sports Director
rpivo@kgw.com

KHAS-TV
P.O. BOX 578
HASTINGS, NE 68901
402-463-1321
Fax: 402-463-6551
http://www.khastv.com/
• Ed Littler, Sports Director
news5sports@khastv.com
• Scott Abraham, Sports Anchor
(402) 463-1321
scott.abraham@khastv.com

KHNL-TV
150-B PUHALE ROAD
HONOLULU, HI 96819-2233
808-847-3246
Fax: 808-845-3616
http://www.khnl.com
• Russell Yamanoha, Sports Anchor

KHON-TV
88 PIIKOI STREET
HONOLULU, HI 96814-4245

808-591-4278
Fax: 808-593-2418
news@khon.com
http://www.khon.com
• John Veneri, Weekend Sports Anchor
(808) 591-4278
jveneri@khon.com
• Kanoa Leahey, Sports Director
(808) 591-4278
kleahey@khon2.com

KHOU-TV
1945 ALLEN PARKWAY
HOUSTON, TX 77019-2506
713-526-1111
Fax: 713-520-7763
assignments@khou.com
http://www.khou.com
• Butch Alsandor, Sports Anchor
(713) 284-8781
balsandor@khou.com
• Carleton Cole, Sports Producer
(713) 521-4375
• Matt Musil, Sports Reporter
assignments@khou.com
• Gifford Nielsen, Sports Director/Anchor
(713) 284-8708

KHQA-TV
301 SOUTH 36TH STREET
QUINCY, IL 62301
217-222-6200
800-929-3518
Fax: 217-228-3164
khqa@khqa.com
http://www.khqa.com
• Chris Duerr, Sports Director
cduerr@khqa.com
• Kurt LaBelle, Sports Anchor
(217) 222-6200
klabelle@khqa.com
• Tyler Fulghum, Weekend Sports
Anchor/Reporter
(217) 222-6200
tfulghum@khqa.com

KICU-TV
2102 COMMERCE DRIVE
SAN JOSE, CA 95131-1804
408-953-3636
Fax: 408-953-3610
http://www.kicu.com
• Jeff Holub, Promotion Director
(510) 874-0542
• Mike Sklut, Anchor - High School Sports
Focus
(408) 953-3636
• Mike Sklut, Sports Producer
(408) 953-3636
• Brodie Brazil, Sports Reporter
(408) 953-3636

KIEM-TV
5650 SOUTH BROADWAY
EUREKA, CA 95503-6905
707-443-3123
Fax: 707-268-8109
http://kiem-tv.com
• Manny Machado, Sports Director
(707) 443-3123

KIII-TV
5002 SOUTH PADRE ISLAND DRIVE
CORPUS CHRISTI, TX 78411-4416
361-986-8300
Fax: 361-986-8311

news@kiiitv.com
http://www.kiiitv.com
• Dan McReynolds, Sports Director
(361) 986-8394

KIIN-TV
6450 CORPORATE DRIVE
JOHNSTON, IA 50131-1636
515-242-3100
800-532-1290
Fax: 515-242-4113
http://www.iptv.org
• Jerry Grady, Sports Director
(515) 242-3111
• Dan Miller, Executive Director
(515) 242-3123

KIMA-TV
2801 TERRACE HEIGHTS DRIVE
YAKIMA, WA 98901-1455
509-575-0029
Fax: 509-575-5526
tvnews@kimatv.com
http://www.kimatv.com
• Alan Sillence, Sports Director
(509) 575-0029
sillence@kimatv.com

KIMT-TV
112 NORTH PENNSYLVANIA AVENUE
MASON CITY, IA 50401-3404
641-423-2540
800-323-4883
Fax: 641-423-9309
http://www.kimt-tv.com
• Greg Berry, Sports Director
(641) 421-2620
• Jerome Risting, Promotion Director
(641) 421-2624
jristing@kimt.com

KING-TV
333 DEXTER AVENUE NORTH
SEATTLE, WA 98109-5107
206-448-3850
Fax: 206-448-4525
newstips@king5.com
http://www.king5.com
• Greg Bailey, Sports Anchor
gbailey@king5.com
• Michael King, Sports Reporter
mking@king5.com
• Katie Love, Promotion Coordinator
(206) 448-3890
klove@king5.com
• Paul Silvi, Sports Director/Anchor
(206) 448-3946
psilvi@king5.com
• D. J. Wilson, Advertising Sales Director
(206) 448-3882
• Lisa Gangel, Sports Reporter
(206) 448-3850

KION-TV
1550 MOFFETT STREET
SALINAS, CA 93905-3342
831-422-3500
800-321-5222
Fax: 831-422-9365
newstips@kion46.com
http://www.kion46.com
• Brent Calvin, Promotion Director
(831) 784-6401
brentcalvin@clearchannel.com
• Omar Ruiz, Sports Director
(831) 784-6411

omarruiz@clearchannel.com
• Hunter Finnell, Sports Director
(831) 784-1702
hunterfinnell@clearchannel.com

KIRO-TV
2807 THIRD AVENUE
SEATTLE, WA 98121
206-728-8308
800-777-5476
Fax: 206-441-4840
newstips@kirotv.com
http://www.kirotv.com
• Gaard Swanson, Sports Director
(206) 728-8308

KITV-TV
801 SOUTH KING STREET
HONOLULU, HI 96813
808-535-0400
Fax: 808-536-8993
http://www.kitv.com
• Rob DeMello, Sports Anchor (Weekend)
(808) 535-0400
• Robert Kekaula, Sports Anchor
(808) 535-0400

KIVI-TV
1866 EAST CHISHOLM DRIVE
NAMPA, ID 83687-6805
208-336-0500
Fax: 208-381-6681
news@todays6.com
http://www.todays6.com
• Joe Hughes, Sports Director
(208) 381-6855
jhughes@todays6.com

KJCT-TV
8 FORESIGHT CIRCLE
GRAND JUNCTION, CO 81505
970-245-8880
Fax: 970-245-8249
news8@kjct8.com
http://www.kjct8.com
• Josh Mitelman, Sports Director
jmitelman@kjct8.com
• Spencer Linton, Sports Reporter
(970) 245-8880
slinton@kjct8.com

KJRH-TV
P.O. BOX 2
TULSA, OK 74105-3263
918-743-2222
800-727-5574
Fax: 918-748-1436
news@kjrh.com
http://www.teamtulsa.com
• Marty Carpenter, Sports Reporter
sports@kjrh.com
• Al Jerkens, Sports Director
(918) 748-1539
jerkens@kjrh.com
• Jason Shackelford, Sports Reporter
(918) 743-2222
shackelford@kjrh.com
• Cayden McFarland, Sports Anchor
(918) 743-2222
news@kjrh.com

KKTV-TV
3100 NORTH NEVADA
COLORADO SPRINGS, CO 80907-5325
719-634-2844
Fax: 719-634-3741

ddownie@kktv11news.com
http://www.kktv.com
• Michelle Hughes, Promotions Manager
(719) 634-2844
mhughes@kktv11news.com
• Jesse Kurtz, Weekend Sports Anchor
(719) 634-2844
• John Owens, Sports Director
(719) 634-2844
jowens@kktv11news.com

KLAS-TV
3228 CHANNEL 8 DRIVE
LAS VEGAS, NV 89109-9000
702-792-8870
Fax: 702-792-2977
newsdesk@klastv.com
http://www.klastv.com
• Chris Maathuis, Sports Anchor
(702) 792-8895
cmaathuis@klastv.com
• Dave McCann, Sports Director
(702) 795-8896
• Michael Berk, Sports Reporter
(702) 792-8870

KLKN-TV
3240 S 10TH ST
LINCOLN, NE 68502-4401
402-434-8000
888-221-5556
Fax: 402-436-2236
8@klkntv.com
http://www.klkntv.com/
• Jon Wofford, Sports Director
(402) 436-2251
jwofford@klkntv.com

KMBC-TV
1049 CENTRAL STREET
KANSAS CITY, MO 64105-1619
816-760-9260
Fax: 816-421-4163
http://www.kmbc.com
• John Crumley, Sports Director
(816) 221-9999
jcrumley@hearst.com
• Len Dawson, Sports Anchor
ldawson@hearst.com
• Karen Kornacki, Sports Anchor/Reporter
(816) 760-9260
kkornacki@hearst.com
• Karen Kornacki, Sports Reporter
kkornacki@hearst.com
• Bill Pikus, Sports Anchor
(816) 221-9999
• Andy Fales, Weekend Sports Anchor
(816) 760-9260

KMEX-TV
5999 CENTER DRIVE
LOS ANGELES, CA 90045
310-216-3434
Fax: 310-348-3493
http://www.kmex.com
• Luis De La Parra, Promotions Director
(310) 348-3580
• Alejandro Luna, Sports Anchor
(310) 348-3478
aluna@univision.net
• Francisco Pinto, Sports Anchor
(310) 348-3497

KMGH-TV
123 SPEER BOULEVARD
DENVER, CO 80203-3417

303-832-7777
Fax: 303-832-0119
dennews@thedenverchannel.com
http://www.kmgh.com
• Lionel Bienvenu, Sports Anchor
(303) 832-0136
lionel_bienvenu@thedenverchannel.com
• Steve Gottsegen, Weekend Sports Anchor
(303) 832-7777
steve_gottsegen@kmgh.com
• Bobby Hayden, Sports Director
(303) 832-0169
bobby_hayden@kmgh.com
• Jay Maloney, Promotions Manager
(303) 832-0295
jay_maloney@kmgh.com
• Phil Aldridge, Sports Reporter
(303) 832-7777
phil_aldridge@thedenverchannel.com

KMIR-TV
72920 PARKVIEW DRIVE
PALM DESERT, CA 92260
760-568-3636
Fax: 760-341-7029
http://www.kmir6.com
• Cal Ahlers, Sports Anchor
(760) 568-3636

KMIZ-TV
501 BUSINESS LOOP 70 EAST
COLUMBIA, MO 65201-3909
573-449-0917
Fax: 573-875-7078
news@kmiz.com
http://www.kmiz.com
• Beau Baehnan, Sports Director
(573) 449-0917
sports@kmiz.com
• Beau Baehman, Sports Director
(573) 449-0917

KMOV-TV
ONE MEMORIAL DRIVE
SAINT LOUIS, MO 63102-2425
314-444-6333
Fax: 314-621-4775
pressrelease@kmov.com
http://www.kmov.com
• Dan Dillon, Promotions Director
(314) 444-3330
• Steve Savard, Sports Director
ssavard@kmov.com
• Jeff Skversky, Sports Anchor/Reporter
(314) 444-6333

KMPH-TV
5111 MCKINLEY AVENUE, E.
FRESNO, CA 93727-1985
559-453-8850
Fax: 559-255-9626
newsdesk@kmph.com
http://www.kmph.com
• Ken Felder, Advertising Manager
(559) 255-2600
kfelder@kmph.com
• Ralph Wood, Weeknight Sports Anchor
(559) 453-8850
rwoood@kmph.com
• Heidi Watney, Weekend Sports Anchor
(559) 453-8850
hwatney@kmph.com

KMSP-TV
11358 VIKING DRIVE
EDEN PRAIRIE, MN 55344-7238

952-946-5767
Fax: 952-942-0455
http://www.kmsp.com
• Jeff Grayson, Sports Director
• Dawn Mitchell, Weekend Sports
Anchor/Reporter
(952) 946-5767

KMTR-TV
3825 INTERNATIONAL COURT
SPRINGFIELD, OR 97477-1086
541-746-1600
Fax: 541-747-3429
newsdesk@kmtr.com
http://www.nbc16.com
• Dave Wenda, Sports Director
(541) 746-1600

KMTV-TV
10714 MOCKINGBIRD DRIVE
OMAHA, NE 68127
402-592-3333
Fax: 402-593-2737
news@km3news.com
http://www.kmtv3.com
• Ken Dudzik, Marketing Director
kdudzik@km3news.com
• Travis Justice, Sports Director
(402) 592-3333

KMVT-TV
1100 BLUE LAKES BOULEVARD, N.
TWIN FALLS, ID 83301-3305
208-733-1100
Fax: 208-733-4649
jmartin@kmvt.com
http://www.kmvt.com
• Eric Geller, Sports Director
(208) 733-6407
• Paul Johnson, Promotions Manager

KNBC-TV
3000 WEST ALAMEDA AVENUE
BURBANK, CA 91523
818-840-4444
Fax: 818-840-3535
knbc.desk@nbcuni.com
http://www.knbc.com
• Bob Long, Vice President
• Fred Roggin, Sports Director/Anchor
(818) 840-4444
fred.roggin@nbc.com
• Charlie Rosene, Senior Sports Producer
(818) 840-4444
• Kevin Applebaum, Sports Producer
(818) 840-4444

KNOE-TV
1400 OLIVER ROAD
MONROE, LA 71201
318-388-8888
Fax: 318-388-0070
knoetv@bayou.com
http://www.knoe.com
• Aaron Dietrich, Sports Director
(318) 388-8888
• Bill Elliott, Marketing Director
(318) 388-8888
• Bill Elliott, Promotions Manager

KNSD - NBC 7/39
8330 ENGINEER RD
SAN DIEGO, CA 92111
619-231-3939
Fax: 619-578-0202
www.nbcsandiego.com

• Phyllis Scwartz, President/General
Manager
• Jim Laslavic, Sports Director
Sports Covered:
All Major and minor league sports. Local
teams: San Diego Chargers San Diego
Padres San Diego Spirit San Diego Gulls
San Diego Sockers San Diego Riptide
University of San Diego Toreros SDSU
Aztecs UCSD Tritons.

KNSD-TV
225 BROADWAY
SAN DIEGO, CA 92101
619-578-0201
Fax: 619-578-0202
pressinquiries@nbcsandiego.com
http://www.nbcsandiego.com
• Jim Laslavic, Sports Director
(858) 279-3939
jim.laslavic@nbcuni.com
• Phyllis Schwartz, President

KNTV-TV
2450 NORTH FIRST STREET
SAN JOSE, CA 95110-2613
408-432-4780
Fax: 408-432-4425
newstips@nbc11.com
http://www.nbc11.com
• Craig Fierro, Sports Producer
(408) 432-4780
• Raj Mathai, Sports Director/Anchor
(408) 432-4780
raj.mathai@nbcuni.com
• Raj Mathai, Sports Director
(408) 297-8780
raj.mathai@nbc.com
• Jim Sanders, Vice President

KNXV-TV
515 NORTH 44TH STREET
PHOENIX, AZ 85008-6511
602-685-6397
Fax: 602-685-6363
assignmentdesk@abc15.com
http://www.phoenix360.com
• Craig Fouhy, Sports Director
(602) 273-1500
cfouhy@abc15.com

KOAA-TV
530 COMMUNICATIONS CIRCLE
COLORADO SPRINGS, CO 80905-1744
719-632-5030
Fax: 719-295-6677
news@koaa.com
http://www.koaa.com
• Richard Bouchez, Promotions Manager
(719) 544-5781
• Lee Douglas, Sports Director

KOAM-TV
2950 NORTHEAST HIGHWAY 69
PITTSBURG, KS 66762-0659
620-231-0400
Fax: 417-624-3158
http://www.koamtv.com
• Chad Plein, Sports Director
(620) 231-0400
cplein@koamtv.com
• Danny Thomas, President
(620) 231-0400
dwthomas@koamtv.com

KOAT-TV
P.O. BOX 25982
ALBUQUERQUE, NM 87107-4501
505-884-6324
Fax: 505-884-6282
koatdesk@hearst.com
http://www.thenewmexicochannel.com
• Bob Brown, Sports Director
(505) 884-6330
rbrown@hearst.com

KOBI-TV
125 SOUTH FIR STREET
MEDFORD, OR 97501-3115
541-779-5555
Fax: 541-779-5564
http://www.localnewscomesfirst.com
• Scott Gee, Promotion Director
sgee@kobi5.com
• Jordan Mason, Sports Director
(541) 842-4294
• Joe Camarlinghi, Sports Director
(541) 779-5555

KOCT-TV
3801 CARLISLE BOULEVARD, N.E.
ALBUQUERQUE, NM 87107
505-884-7777
Fax: 505-884-6282
koatdesk@hearst.com
http://www.thenewmexicochannel.com
• Bob Brown, Sports Director

KODE-TV
1928 WEST 13TH STREET
JOPLIN, MO 64801-3839
417-623-7260
Fax: 417-623-3736
http://www.kode-tv.com
• Brett Newtson, Sports Director
(417) 623-7260
bbrett@kode12.tv
• Bruce Vonde-Harr, Sports Director
(417) 623-7260

KOKI-TV
2625 SOUTH MEMORIAL DRIVE
TULSA, OK 74129
918-388-5100
Fax: 918-388-0516
news@fox23.com
http://www.fox23.com
• Deedra Determan, Marketing Director
drdeterman@fox23.com
• Ron Terrell, Sports Director
(918) 388-5263
rterrell@fox23.com

KOLR-TV
2650 EAST DIVISION STREET
SPRINGFIELD, MO 65803-5228
417-862-1010
Fax: 417-866-6397
http://www.ozarksfirst.com
• Dan Lucy, Sports Director
(417) 862-1010
dlucy@kolr10.com

KOMO-TV
140 4TH AVENUE NORTH
SEATTLE, WA 98109-4932
206-404-4145
Fax: 206-404-4422
tips@komo4news.com
http://www.komotv.com

• Colleen Brown, President
(206) 404-7000
• Eric Johnson, Sports Director
(206) 404-4145
ericj@komotv.com
• Eric Johnson, Sports Director
ericj@komotv.com
• Randa Minkarah, Marketing Director
rminkarah@komotv.com
• Derek Agnew, Sports Reporter
(206) 404-4000
dereka@komotv.com

KOMU-TV
5550 HIGHWAY 63, S.
COLUMBIA, MO 65201
573-882-8888
Fax: 573-884-5353
news@komu.com
http://www.komu.com
• Chris Grevino, Sports Director
grevinoc@komutv.com
• Monica Stoneking, Promotions Assistant
• Eric Blumberg, Sports Anchor ; Reporter
(573) 882-8888
EricBlumberg@komu.com

KOSA-TV
4101 EAST 42ND STREET
SUITE J7
ODESSA, TX 79762
432-580-5672
Fax: 432-580-8010
news@cbs7.com
http://www.cbs7.com/
• Whitney Harding, Sports Director
(915) 580-6397

KOTV-TV
PO BOX 6
TULSA, OK 74120-2422
918-732-6000
Fax: 918-732-6185
http://www.kotv.com
• John Holcomb, Sports Director
(918) 732-6146
• Donita Quesnel, Promotions Director
(918) 732-6070
bquesnel@kotb.com
• Mike Wolfe, Weekend Sports Anchor
(918) 732-6000

KOVR-TV
2713 KOVR DRIVE
WEST SACRAMENTO, CA 95605-1600
916-374-1313
Fax: 916-374-1304
news@kovr.com
http://www.kovr13.com
• Steve Harris, Promotions Manager
(916) 374-1429
• Jennifer Krier, Sports Anchor (Weekend)
• Arran Andersen, Sports Anchor
(916) 374-1313

KOVT-TV
3801 CARLISLE BOULEVARD, N.E.
ALBUQUERQUE, NM 87107
505-884-7777
Fax: 505-884-6282
koatdesk@hearst.com
• Bob Brown, Sports Director

KPIC-TV
P.O. BOX 1345
ROSEBURG, OR 97470-2955

541-672-4481
Fax: 541-672-4482
kpic4news@kpic.com
http://www.kpic.com
• Jason Hink, Sports Director
(541) 672-4481
• Connie Williamson, Advertising Manager
(541) 672-4481

KPIX-TV
855 BATTERY STREET
SAN FRANCISCO, CA 94111-1503
415-765-8610
Fax: 415-765-8916
newsdesk@kpix.com
http://www.kpix.com/
• Dennis O'Donnell, Sports Anchor
(415) 765-8610
newsdesk@kpix.com
• Dennis O'Donnell, Sports Director
• Rick Quan, Sports Anchor
(415) 765-8643

KPLR-TV
2250 BALL DRIVE
SAINT LOUIS, MO 63146
314-213-2222
Fax: 314-447-6430
http://www.kplr11.com
• Rich Gould, Sports Director
(314) 447-6438
• David Maul, Promotions Director
(314) 447-6359

KPNX-TV
1101 NORTH CENTRAL AVENUE
PHOENIX, AZ 85004-1818
602-257-1212
Fax: 602-257-6619
assignmentdesk@12news.com
http://www.kpnx.com
• Barry Orr, Sports Director
• Joe Pequeno, Sports
Producer/Reporter/Anchor
(602) 257-1212
• Bruce Cooper, Weekend Sports Reporter
(602) 257-1212

KPRC-TV
P.O. BOX 2222
HOUSTON, TX 77074-1705
713-778-4950
Fax: 713-771-4930
hounews@click2houston.com
http://www.click2houston.com/
• Katherine Harvin, Marketing Director
(713) 778-4831
kfuller@kprc.com
• Steve Mark, Sports Anchor
smark@click2houston.com
• Randy Mcilvoy, Sports Anchor
rmcilvoy@kprc.com
• Edward Ortelli, Advertising Manager
(713) 778-4893
• Michael Stewart, Promotions Director
(713) 778-4739
• Keith Norton, Sports Reporter
(713) 778-4950

KPRY-TV
300 NORTH DAKOTA AVENUE
SIOUX FALLS, SD 57104
605-336-1300
800-955-5739
Fax: 605-336-7936
ksfy@ksfy.com

media

• Eric Thorstenson, Sports Director
(605) 336-1300
ethorstenson@ksfy.com

KPTM-TV
4625 FAMAM STREET
OMAHA, NE 68132-3222
402-558-4200
Fax: 402-554-4279
news42@kptm.com
http://www.kptm.com/
• JJ Davis, Sports Director
(402) 558-4200
• Jeff Radcliffe, Sports Reporter
(402) 558-4200
• Donna Ridgley, Promotions Director
(402) 554-4232

KPTV-TV
14975 NW GREENBRIER PARKWAY
BEAVERTON, OR 97006-5731
503-906-1249
Fax: 503-548-6920
kptvnews@kptv.com
http://www.kptv.com/
• Tim Becker, Sports Director
(503) 906-1249
tbecker@kptv.com
• Matt Hyatt, Promotion Manager

KPVI-TV
902 EAST SHERMAN
POCATELLO, ID 83204-0667
208-232-6666
Fax: 208-233-6678
newsroom@kpvi.com
http://www.kpvi.com/
• Dave Reichelt, Sports Director
• Brad Shellgren, Sports Director
(208) 232-6666
bshellgren@kpvi.com

KQCA-TV
58 TELEVISION CIRCLE
SACRAMENTO, CA 95814-0750
916-447-5858
Fax: 916-554-4663
http://www.kqcachannel.com
• Ron Hyde, Sports Director
(916) 325-3294

KRBC-TV
4510 14TH STREET, S.
ABILENE, TX 79605-4737
325-692-4242
Fax: 325-692-8265
http://www.krbc.tv
• Amanda Campbell, Promotions Director
(325) 692-4242
acampbell@ktab.tv
• Caden McFarland, Sports Director
• John Wilson, Sports Director
(325) 692-4242
john@krbc9.com

KRCR-TV
755 AUDITORIUM DRIVE
REDDING, CA 96001-0920
530-243-7777
800-222-5727
Fax: 530-243-9382
http://www.krcrtv.com
• Mike Mangas, Sports Director
• Damae Thompson, Promotion Manager
• Eric Natkin, Sports Director
(530) 243-7777

KREM-TV
4103 SOUTH REGAL STREET
SPOKANE, WA 99223-7737
509-448-2000
Fax: 509-448-6397
newsdesk@krem.com
http://www.krem.com
• Tom Hudson, Sports Director
(509) 838-7370
tomh@krem.com

KRGV-TV
NEWSCHANNEL 5
WESLACO, TX 78596
956-631-5555
Fax: 956-973-5001
http://www.newschannel5.tv
• Dave Brown, Sports Director
(956) 631-5555
dave@klgv.com

KRIS-TV
P.O. BOX 840
CORPUS CHRISTI, TX 78401
361-886-6100
Fax: 361-886-6175
newsroom@kristv.com
http://www.kristv.com
• Art Mack, Sports Director
(361) 886-6172
• Sean Horejs, Weekend Sports Anchor
(361) 886-6100

KRIV-TV
4261 SOUTHWEST FREEWAY
HOUSTON, TX 77027-7201
713-479-2600
Fax: 713-479-2859
http://www.myfoxhouston.com/
• Mark Berman, Sports Director
(713) 479-2600
berman@fox26.com

KRON-TV
1001 VAN NESS AVENUE
SAN FRANCISCO, CA 94109-6982
415-561-8905
Fax: 415-561-8136
http://www.kron4.com
• Mark Antonitis, Vice President
• Jason Applebaum, Sports Producer
• Vernon Glenn, Sports Anchor
(415) 561-8905
• Dave Guingona, Sports Producer
(415) 561-8633
• Deb McDermot, President
(615) 369-7222

KRQE-TV
13 BROADCAST PLAZA SW
ALBUQUERQUE, NM 87104-1056
505-243-2285
Fax: 505-842-8483
newsdesk@krqe.com
http://www.krqe.com/
• Mike Powers, Sports Director
(505) 764-5240
mike.powers@krqe.com
• Mike Powers, Sports Director
(505) 764-5214
mike.powers@krqe.com
• Van Tate, Weekend Sports
Anchor/Reporter
(505) 243-2285
van.tate@krqe.com

KRTV-TV
3300 OLD HAVRE HIGHWAY
BLACK EAGLE, MT 59414-1079
406-791-5400
800-823-5788
Fax: 406-791-5479
krtvnews@krtv.com
http://www.krtv.com
• Heath Heggem, Sports Director
heath@krtv.com

KSBW-TV
P.O. BOX 81651
SALINAS, CA 93901-3339
831-758-8888
Fax: 831-422-0124
http://www.theksbwchannel.com
• Dennis Lehnen, Sports Director
(831) 758-8888

KSBY-TV
1772 CALLE JOAQUIN
SAN LUIS OBISPO, CA 93405-7210
805-541-6666
Fax: 805-597-8520
news@ksby.com
http://www.ksby.com
• Dave Alles, Sports Director/Anchor
(805) 541-6666
• Ryan Bennett, Sports Anchor
• Madeline Palaszewski, Promotion Director
(805) 597-8471

KSDK-TV
1000 MARKET STREET
SAINT LOUIS, MO 63101
314-421-5055
Fax: 314-444-5164
newstips@ksdk.com
http://www.ksdk.com
• Rene Knott, Sports Director
(314) 421-5055
• Frank Cusumano, Sports Reporter
(314) 421-5055

KSFY-TV
300 NORTH DAKOTA AVENUE
SIOUX FALLS, SD 57104
605-336-1300
800-955-5739
Fax: 605-336-2067
news@ksfy.com
http://www.ksfy.com/
• Erik Thorstenson, Sports Director
(605) 336-1300
ethorstenson@ksfy.com

KSHB-TV
4720 OAK STREET
KANSAS CITY, MO 64112-2236
816-932-4141
800-818-5742
Fax: 816-932-4145
desk@kshb.com
http://www.kshb.com
• Jack Harry, Sports Director
(816) 932-4141
harry@nbcactionnews.com

KSL-TV
5 TRIAD CENTER
SALT LAKE CITY, UT 84180-1109
801-575-5555
Fax: 801-575-5830
feedback@ksl.com
http://www.ksl.com

• Tom Kirkland, Sports Director
(801) 575-5555
tom.kirkland@ksl.com

KSNF-TV
PO BOX 1393
JOPLIN, MO 64802
417-781-2345
Fax: 417-782-2417
www.fourstateshomepage.com
• Eric Knecht, Sports Anchor
(417) 781-2345
eknecht@ksn16.tv
• Debora Palmer, Advertising Manager
(417) 781-2345
dpalmer@ksn16.tv
• Morgan Vance, Sports Ancor
(417) 781-2345
mvance@ksn16.tv

KSNT-TV
PO BOX 2700
TOPEKA, KS 66618
785-582-4000
Fax: 785-582-4783
27news@ksnt.com
http://www.ksnt.com
• Lance Veeser, Sports Anchor
(785) 582-3222
lveeser@ksnt.com
• Lance Veeser, Sports Director
(785) 582-3222
lveeser@ksnt.com
• Adam Alter, Sports Reporter
(785) 582-4000
aalter@ksnt.com

KSTP - KSTP 5/ABC
3415 UNIVESITY AVE
SAINT PAUL, MN 55114
651-646-5555
Fax: 651-642-4409
www.kstp.com
• Ed Piette, Vice President/General
Manager
• Joe Schmit, Sports Director

KSTS-TV
2450 NORTH FIRST STREET
SAN JOSE, CA 95131-1125
408-435-0327
Fax: 408-434-1046
info@ksts.com
http://www.ksts.com/
• Ramon Diaz, Sports Director
(408) 435-0327
noticias@ksts.com

KSTU-TV
5020 AMELIA EARHART DRIVE
SALT LAKE CITY, UT 84116-2853
801-532-1300
Fax: 801-536-1325
http://www.myfoxutah.com
• Mike Runge, Sports Director
• Rick Aaron, Sports Director
(801) 536-1313

KSWO-TV
P.O. BOX 708
LAWTON, OK 73501
580-355-7000
Fax: 580-357-3811
news@kswo.com
http://www.kswo.com

• Nathan Thompson, Sports Director
(580) 355-7000
• Todd Young, Promotions Director
tyoung@kswo.com
• Mike Straub, Sports Reporter
(580) 355-7000
mstraub@kswo.com

KTAL-TV
3150 NORTH MARKET STREET
SHREVEPORT, LA 71107-4005
318-629-6000
Fax: 318-629-7171
http://www.newschannel6.tv
• Dave Schwartz, Sports Director
(318) 629-6000
dschwartz@newschannel6.tv
• Scott Thomas, Advertising Manager
(318) 629-6000

KTBC-TV
119 EAST 10TH STREET
AUSTIN, TX 78701
512-476-7777
Fax: 512-495-7060
http://www.fox7.com
• Dave Cody, Sports Director
(512) 495-7708
sports@fox7.com

KTIV-TV
3135 FLOYD BOULEVARD
SIOUX CITY, IA 51108-1465
712-239-4100
800-234-5848
Fax: 712-239-2621
ktivnews@ktiv.com
http://www.ktiv.com
• Brad Pautsch, Sports Director
(712) 239-4100
bpautsch@ktiv.com
• Mike Orlando, Weekend Sports Anchor
(712) 239-4100
morlando@ktiv.com

KTLA-TV
5800 SUNSET BOULEVARD
LOS ANGELES, CA 90028
323-460-5500
Fax: 323-460-5333
http://www.ktla.com
• Damon Andrews, Sports Director/Anchor
(323) 460-5500
• Damon Andrews, Sports Director
(323) 460-5443
• Mark Brinks, Sports Writer
(323) 460-5907
• Ted Green, Sports Writer
(323) 460-5907

KTMD-TV
1235 NORTH LOOP WAY SUITE 125
HOUSTON, TX 77008-6405
713-974-4848
Fax: 713-266-6397
http://www.ktmd.com
• Lester Gretsh, Sports Director
• Carlos Munoz, Sports Reporter

KTNV-TV
3355 SOUTH VALLEY VIEW BOULEVARD
LAS VEGAS, NV 89102-8216
702-871-3345
Fax: 702-876-2237
ktnvnewsdesk@ktnv.com
http://www.ktnv.com

• Dennis Evans, Sports Anchor
(702) 257-8323
devans@ktnv.com
• Doug Kezirian, Sports Director
(702) 871-3345
dkezirian@ktnv.com

KTRE-TV
P.O. BOX 729
LUFKIN, TX 75902-0729
936-853-5873
Fax: 936-853-3084
ktrenews@ktre.com
http://www.ktre.com
• Shawn Clynch, Sports Director
(936) 853-5873
sClynch@ktre.com
• Mike Wiggins, Promotion Manager
mwiggins@ktre.com

KTRK-TV
P.O. BOX 13
HOUSTON, TX 77005-2114
713-666-0713
Fax: 713-664-0013
ktrk.newsalerts@abc.com
http://abc13.com/
• Bob Allen, Weekday Sports Director
(713) 663-4536
• Tim Melton, Weekend Sports Anchor
(713) 666-0713
• Bob Slovak, Weekend Sports Anchor
(713) 666-0713

KTTC-TV
6301 BANDEL ROAD NW
ROCHESTER, MN 55901-8798
507-280-5105
800-288-1656
Fax: 507-288-6324
http://www.kttc.com
• Pat Lund, Sports Director
(507) 280-5105
plund@kttc.com

KTTV-TV
1999 SOUTH BUNDY DRIVE
LOS ANGELES, CA 90025-5235
310-584-2025
Fax: 310-584-2023
http://www.myfoxla.com
• Rod Cohen, Sports Producer
• Jennifer Gould, Sports Anchor
(310) 584-2030
• Rick Garcia, Sports Director
(310) 584-2261
garcia@fox11la.com

KTUU-TV
701 EAST TUDOR ROAD
ANCHORAGE, AK 99503
907-762-9202
Fax: 907-563-3318
news_desk@ktuu.com
http://www.ktuu.com
• John Carpenter, Sports Director
(907) 762-9229
jcarpenter@ktuu.com

KTVB-TV
P.O. BOX 7
BOISE, ID 83706-1162
208-321-5614
800-559-7277
Fax: 208-375-7770

media

ktvbnews@ktvb.com
http://www.ktvb.com
• David Augusto, Sports Director
(208) 321-5614
daugusto@ktvb.com
• Kristi Edmunds, Marketing Director
kedmunds@ktvb.com
• P. J. Laws, Promotion Director
(208) 375-7277
plaws@ktvb.com

KTVE-TV
200 PAVILION ROAD
WEST MONROE, LA 71292
318-323-1972
Fax: 318-322-0926
http://www.region10.com
• Chris Mycoskie, Sports Director
(318) 323-1972
chrism@region10.com
• Esther Phillips, Promotions Manager
ephillips@region10.com

KTVH-TV
P.O. BOX 6125
HELENA, MT 59601
406-457-1212
Fax: 406-442-5106
http://www.ktvh.com
• Al Marks, Sports Director
amarks@ktvh.com
• Alan Marks, Sports Director
(406) 457-1212

KTVI-TV
2250 BALL DRIVE
SAINT LOUIS, MO 63146
314-213-2222
800-920-0222
Fax: 314-647-8960
ktvinews@foxtv.com
http://www.fox2now.com
• Rob Desir, Sports Reporter
• Susan Edwards, Executive Director
ktvinews@foxtv.com
• Martin Kilcoyne, Sports Director/Anchor
(314) 647-2222

KTVK-TV
5555 NORTH SEVENTH AVENUE
PHOENIX, AZ 85013-1701
602-207-3333
Fax: 602-207-3477
3tvnews@azfamily.com
http://www.azfamily.com
• Todd Kelly, Sports Director
todd_kelly@azfamily.com
• Brad Cesmat, Sports Reporter
(602) 207-3333

KTVM-TV
BOX 5268
BOZEMAN, MT 59715
406-586-0296
Fax: 406-586-0554
news@ktvm.com
http://www.ktvm.com/montana_news.php
• Steve Dent, Sports Director
(406) 586-0296

KTVN-TV
4925 ENERGY WAY
RENO, NV 89502-4105
775-861-4290
Fax: 775-861-4246

producers@ktvn.com
http://www.ktvn.com
• J. K. Metzker, Sports Director
(775) 861-4229
jmetzker@ktvn.com
• Garrett Dearborn, Weekend Sports Anchor
(775) 861-4290
gdearborn@ktvn.com

KTVT-TV
PO BOX 2495
FORT WORTH, TX 76113
817-451-1111
888-654-5888
Fax: 817-457-1897
news@ktvt.com
http://www.cbs11tv.com
• Dandy Killeen, Sports Director
dandyk@ktvt.com
• Babe Laufenberg, Sports Anchor
(817) 451-1111
• Chris Bullock, Sports Producer
(817) 586-7440
chrisb@ktvt.com

KTVU-TV
2 JACK LONDON SQUARE
OAKLAND, CA 94607-3727
510-874-0242
Fax: 510-451-2610
http://www.ktvu.com
• Mark Ibanez, Sports Director
(510) 874-0254
• Greg Rando, Advertising Writer
(510) 874-0375
• Joe Fonzi, Weekend Sports Anchor
(510) 834-1212

KTVX-TV
2175 WEST 1700 SOUTH
SALT LAKE CITY, UT 84104-4200
801-975-4401
800-766-1776
Fax: 801-973-4176
http://www.4utah.com
• Wesley Ruff, Sports Director
(801) 975-4444
wesley@abc4.com
• Wesley Ruff, Sports Director
(801) 975-4428
wruff@abc4.tv
• Dana Greene, Sports Reporter
(801) 975-4401
dana@abc4.com

KTVZ-TV
62990 OB RILEY ROAD
BEND, OR 97701
541-383-2121
800-331-8821
Fax: 541-382-1616
ktvz@ktvz.com
http://www.ktvz.com
• Vic Quick, Sports Director
sports@ktvz.com

KTXL-TV
4655 FRUITRIDGE ROAD
SACRAMENTO, CA 95820-5201
916-454-4548
Fax: 916-739-0559
http://fox40.trb.com/
• Jim Crandell, Sports Director
(916) 454-4548

KTXS-TV
P. O. BOX 2997
ABILENE, TX 79601
325-677-2281
800-588-5897
Fax: 325-672-5307
levesque@ktxs.com
http://www.ktxs.com
• David Caldwell, Promotions Manager
(325) 677-2281
• Jorge Montoya, Advertising Manager
(325) 677-2281
• Mark Rogers, Sports Anchor
(325) 677-2281

KUSA-TV
500 EAST SPEER BOULEVARD
DENVER, CO 80203-4187
303-871-1499
Fax: 303-698-4700
news@9news.com
http://www.9news.com
• Steve Carter, Promotions Director
(303) 871-1855
steve.carter@9news.com
• David Hunt, Sports Executive
Producer/Sports Directo
(303) 871-1499
david.hunt@9news.com

KUTV-TV
299 SOUTH MAIN STREET
SALT LAKE CITY, UT 84111
801-973-3000
Fax: 801-973-3349
news@kutv2.com
http://www.kutv.com
• Jeremy Castro, Sports Director
(801) 973-3327
castroje@kutv2.com
• John Greene, Marketing Director
(801) 973-3001
greenejr@kutv2.com
• Dan Sheldon, Sports Anchor/Reporter
(801) 973-3000

KUVN-TV
2323 BRYAN STREET SUITE 1900
DALLAS, TX 75201
214-758-2300
800-494-5886
Fax: 214-758-2351
noticias23dfw@univision.net
http://www.univision.net
• Louis Hernandez, Advertising Sales
Director
• Mario Montez, Sports Director
(214) 758-2344

KVAL-TV
P.O. BOX 1313
EUGENE, OR, 97405
541-342-4961
Fax: 541-342-5436
kvalnews@kval.com
http://www.kval.com
• Todd McKim, Sports Director

KVBC-TV
1500 FOREMASTER LANE
LAS VEGAS, NV 89101-1103
702-657-3150
Fax: 702-657-3152
http://www.kvbc.com
• Mitch Roberts, Sports Director
(702) 657-3150

• Rick Strasser, Sports Reporter/Director
(702) 657-3150

KVIA-TV
4140 RIO BRAVO
EL PASO, TX 79902-1002
915-496-7777
Fax: 915-532-0505
kvia@kvia.com
http://www.kvia.com
• Rick Cabrera, Sports Director
• Trini Parada, Promotions Assistant
• Raul Martinez, Sports Director
(915) 496-7777

KVII-TV
ONE BROADCAST CENTER
AMARILLO, TX 79101-4328
806-373-1787
Fax: 806-371-7329
pronews7@kvii.com
http://www.kvii.com
• Lee Baker, Sports Director
(806) 373-1787
lbaker@kvii.com
• Lee Baker, Sports Reporter
(806) 373-1787
lbaker@kvii.com
• Lisa Schmidt, Promotion Director
(806) 373-1787
lschmidth@kvii.com
• Lisa Schmidt, Promotions Manager
(806) 373-1787
lschmidt@kvii.com
• Paul Tubbs, Sports Reporter

KVLY-TV
P.O. BOX 1878
FARGO, ND 58103
701-237-5211
800-450-5844
Fax: 701-237-5396
news@kvlytv11.com
http://www.kvlytv11.com
• Scott Peters, Sports Director
(701) 237-5211

KVMD-TV
28202 CABOT ROAD
SUITE 300
LAGUNA NIGUEL, CA 92677
760-366-9881
888-550-5862
Fax: 949-365-5709
http://www.kvmdtv.com
• Larry Peterson, General Manager
lpeterson@kvmdtv.com
• Larry Peterson, Program Director

KVOA-TV
P.O. BOX 5188
TUCSON, AZ 85705-6539
520-624-2477
Fax: 520-884-4644
http://www.kvoa.com/
• Dan Ryan, Sports Director
• Jay Campbell, Sports Reporter
(520) 624-2477

KVUE-TV
PO BOX 9927
AUSTIN, TX 78757-8026
512-459-6521
Fax: 512-533-2233
news@kvue.com
http://www.kvue.com

• Mike Barnes, Sports Director/Anchor
(512) 459-2065
mbarnes@kvue.com

KVVU-TV
25 TV 5 DRIVE
HENDERSON, NV 89014
702-436-8256
Fax: 702-436-2507
5newsdesk@kvvu.com
http://www.ktvutv.com
• Dave Hall, Sports Anchor
(702) 436-8256
dhall3@kvvu.com
• Terri Peck, Marketing Director
• Kevin Bolinger, Sports Director
(702) 435-5555
kbolinger@kvvu.com

KWAB-TV
11320 COUNTY ROAD 127, WEST
MIDLAND, TX 79711
432-567-9999
Fax: 432-567-9993
• Donna Cooper, Account Executive
(432) 567-9999
dkcooper@kwes.com
• Scott Shields, Sports Director
(432) 567-9999
sshields@kwes.com
• Kathy Swindler, Promotions Director
(432) 567-9999
kswindler@kwes.com

KWES-TV
11320 COUNTY ROAD 127, WEST
MIDLAND, TX 79711
432-567-9999
Fax: 432-567-9993
http://www.kwes.com
• Donna Cooper, Account Executive
(432) 567-9999
dkcooper@kwes.com
• Scott Shields, Sports Director
(432) 567-9999
sshields@kwes.com
• Kathy Swindler, Promotions Director
(432) 567-9999
kswindler@kwes.com

KWEX-TV
411 EAST DURANGO
SAN ANTONIO, TX 78204-1309
210-227-4141
Fax: 210-227-0469
http://www.univision.net
• Jorge Rodriguez, Sports Director
(210) 242-7467
• Jaime Becerril, Sports Anchor
(210) 227-4141

KWGN-TV
6160 SOUTH WABASH WAY
GREENWOOD VILLAGE, CO 80111
303-740-2855
Fax: 303-740-2803
http://cw2.trb.com/
• Chris Riva, Sports Director
(303) 740-2855
• Mark Soicher, Sports Anchor
• Rob Venuski, Promotions Director
• Lisa Holbrook, Weekend Sports Anchor
(303) 740-2855

KWNB-TV
P.O. BOX 220
KEARNEY, NE 68848-0220
308-743-2494
Fax: 308-743-2644
• Becky Miller, Promotions Director
• Matt Schick, Sports Director
• Anita Wragge, Promotions Director
awragge@nebraska.tv

KWQC -TV6
805 BRADY ST
DAVENPORT, IA 52803
563-383-7000
Fax: 563-383-7131
www.kwqc.com
• Thom Cornelis, Sports Director
• Jim Graham, Vice President/General Manager
• Trish Tague, Marketing Director
Affiliate:
CBS.
Neilsen Market:
90

KWQC-TV
805 BRADY STREET
DAVENPORT, IA 52803-5211
563-383-7048
Fax: 563-383-7131
news@kwqc.com
http://www.kwqc.com/
• Jeff Bilyeu, Promotions Director
(563) 383-7075
• Thom Cornelis, Sports Director
(563) 383-7037

KWTV-TV
7401 NORTH KELLEY AVENUE
OKLAHOMA CITY, OK 73111-8420
405-841-9956
Fax: 405-841-9989
tv9@aol.com
http://www.newsok.com
• Dean Blevins, Sports Director
(405) 841-9956
• Joyce Reed, Vice President
• Mike Thomas, Marketing Director

KWTX-TV
P.O. BOX 2636
WACO, TX 76712-3976
254-776-1330
Fax: 254-776-4010
news@kwtx.com
http://www.kwtx.com
• Matt Iazzetti, Sports Director
(254) 741-5833
matt.iazzetti@kwtx.com

KWWL-TV
500 EAST FOURTH STREET
WATERLOO, IA 50703-5798
319-291-1200
Fax: 319-291-1255
http://www.kwwl.com/
• Rick Coleman, Sports Anchor/Reporter
(319) 291-1200
rcoleman@kwwl.com
• Raivan Hall, Promotions Assistant
(319) 291-1200
rhall@kwwl.com
• Matthew Hundley, Promotions Manager
(319) 291-1200
mhundley@kwwl.com

KXAM-TV
908 WEST MARTIN LUTHER KING JR.
AUSTIN, TX 78701
512-476-3636
Fax: 512-469-0630
news36@kxan.com
http://www.kxam.com
• Roger Wallace, Sports Director
(512) 476-3636
roger.wallace@kxan.com

KXAS - NBC 5
PO BOX 1780
FORT WORTH, TX 76101-1780
800-232-5927
Fax: 817-654-6325
www.kxas.com
• Tom O'Brien, General Manager
• Susan Tully, News Director
• Scott Murray, Sportscaster

KXAS-TV
P.O. BOX 1780
FORT WORTH, TX 76103-1400
817-429-5555
Fax: 817-654-6325
nbc5i@nbc.com
http://www.nbc5i.com
• Derek Castillo, Sports Anchor (Weekend)
derek.castillo@nbc.com
• Derek Castillo, Sports Reporter
• Newy Scruggs, Sports Director
(817) 654-6326
newy.scruggs@nbc.com
• Susan Tully, Vice President
susan.tully@nbc.com

KXII-TV
P. O. BOX 1175
SHERMAN, TX 75090-1935
903-892-8123
Fax: 903-892-4623
firstnews@kxii.com
http://www.kxii.com
• David Reed, Sports Director ; Anchor
(903) 892-8123
david.reed@kxii.com
• Mark Paasschen, Weekend Sports Anchor
(903) 892-8123
mvp@kxii.com

KXJB-TV
4302 13TH AVENUE S.W.
FARGO, ND 58103-3313
701-282-0444
Fax: 701-282-9331
http://www.cbs4you.com
• Rich Lodewyk, Sports Director
richl@kx4.com

KXLF-TV
1003 SOUTH MONTANA STREET
BUTTE, MT 59701-2839
406-496-8400
Fax: 406-782-8906
www.kxlf.com
• Shane Eqing, Sports Director
(406) 496-6427
• Aslan Hodges, Sports/News Reporter
(406) 496-8400
• Lennie Ambrose, Sports Anchor
(406) 496-8475
Description:
The above personnel also serve KBZK-TV
in Bozeman, MT, which is a sister station to
KXLF. A sports segment is part of the 5:30

p.m. and 10:00 p.m. newscast of
KXLF/KBZK.

KYIN-TV
6450 CORPORATE DRIVE
JOHNSTON, IA 50131-1636
515-242-3100
800-532-1290
Fax: 515-242-4113
http://www.iptv.org
• Jerry Grady, Sports Director
(515) 242-3111

KYTV-TV
P.O. BOX 3500
SPRINGFIELD, MO 65807-2443
417-268-3200
Fax: 417-268-3364
http://www.ky3.com/
• Peggy LaComfora, Promotion Manager
placomfora@ky3.com
• Peggy LaComfora, Promotions Manager
• Ned Reynolds, Sports Director
(417) 268-3200
nreynolds@ky3.com
• Joe Hickman, Weekend Sports
Anchor/Reporter
(417) 268-3200
jhickman@ky3.com

KYW-TV
1555 HAMILTON STREET
PHILADELPHIA, PA 19106-2517
215-977-5300
Fax: 215-977-5658
newsdesk@cbs3.com
http://www.cbs3.com
• Todd Ballantyne, Marketing Manager
ballantyne@kyw.com
• Steve Bucci, Sports Reporter
(215) 238-4660
bucci@kyw.com
• Gary Cobb, Sports Anchor (Weekend)
(215) 238-4612
cobb@kyw.com
• Michael Colleran, Vice President
colleran@kyw.com
• Beasley Reece, Sports Director
(215) 238-4700

LE RESEAU DES SPORTS (RSD) INC.
1755 BLVDRENE-LEVESQUE EST, BUR
300
MONTREAL, QUEBEC, CANADA H2K 4P6
514-599-2244
Fax: 514-599-2299
www.rds.ca
• Gerrry Frappier, President/General
Manager
(514) 599-2244
• Francois Messier, Vice President
Programming
(514) 599-2244
• Michel Gagnon, Vice President Marketing
(514) 599-2244
• Claude Dugre, Vice President Operations
• Lino Bramucci, Vice President Sales
Nature of Sports Service:
Regional. Cable TV broadcaster. 24-hour
French sports channel featuring major and
minor league sports and news shows.

OUTDOOR CHANNEL
43445 BUSINESS PARK DR
STE 103
TEMECULA, CA 92590-3670

800-770-5750
Fax: 909-699-6313
info@outdoorchannel.com
www.outdoorchannel.com
• Andrew J. Dale, President/Chief Executive
Officer
• Jake Hartwick, Executive Vice President
• Wade Sherman, Vice President Business
Development
• Amy Hendrickson, Vice President/Affiliate
Sales/Marketing
Nature of Sports Service:
Features quality programming designed to
educate and entertain sportsmen of all skill
levels. The channel promotes the traditional
outdoor activities that are a vital part of our
national heritage including fishing, hunting
and shooting sports.

TBO (WFLA) NEWS CHANNEL 8
200 S. PARKER ST
TAMPA, FL 33606
813-259-8010
www.tbo.com
• Kirk Read, General Manager
• Ray Trigony, Regional Sales Manager
• Sabina Espinet, Production Team Leader
• Karen Barr, Technical Manager
• Carl Lisciandrello, Weather/Sports Team
Leader
• Marty Strasen, Weather/Sports Producer

WAAY-TV
1000 MONTE SANO BOULEVARD, S.E.
HUNTSVILLE, AL 35801-6137
256-533-3131
Fax: 256-533-5191
newsroom@waaytv.com
http://www.waaytv.com
• T.W. Starr, Sports Director
(256) 533-3131
starr@waaytv.com
• Hugh Keeton, Sports Reporter
(256) 533-3131
keeton@waaytv.com

WAFB-TV
844 GOVERNMENT ST
BATON ROUGE, LA 70802-6030
225-383-9999
Fax: 225-379-7891
news@wafb.com
http://www.wafb.com
• Jacques Doucet, Sports Anchor
jdoucet@wafb.com
• Steve Schneider, Sports Anchor
(225) 383-9999
sschneider@wafb.com
• James Verrett, Sports Anchor
jverrett@wafb.com

WAFF-TV
1414 MEMORIAL PARKWAY, N.W.
HUNTSVILLE, AL 35801-5933
256-533-6397
Fax: 256-534-4101
news@waff.com
http://www.waff.com
• Will Kennedy, Sports Reporter
wkennedy@waff.com
• Lee Meredith, Vice President
justaminute@waff.com
• Kristen Talent, Sports Reporter
ktalent@waff.com
• Mike Aweau, Sports Producer
(256) 533-6397
maweau@waff.com

WAGA-TV
1551 BRIARCLIFF ROAD, N.E.
ATLANTA, GA 30306-2217
404-875-5555
Fax: 404-898-0169
newstipsatlanta@foxtv.com
http://www.fox5atlanta.com
• Chip Zeller, Sports Executive Producer
(404) 875-5555
czell593@foxtv.com
• Karen Graham, Weekend Sports
Anchor/Reporter
(404) 875-5555
karen.graham@foxtv.com

WAGT-TV
P.O. BOX 1526
AUGUSTA, GA 30901-1212
706-826-0001
800-924-8639
Fax: 706-724-4028
http://www.nbcaugusta.com
• Chris Kane, Sports Director
• Buddy Miller, Advertising Manager
(706) 826-0026
• Darien Wernig, Sports Anchor
• Stan Byrdy, Sports Director
(706) 826-0026

WAKA-TV
3251 HARRISON ROAD
MONTGOMERY, AL 36109
334-271-8888
800-467-0424
Fax: 334-244-6444
news@waka.com
http://www.waka.com
• Dee Jackson, Sports Director
(334) 271-8888
• Kayla Anderson, Sports Anchor
(334) 271-8888

WALA-TV
1501 FATCHEL PAIGE DRIVE
MOBILE, AL 36602-2614
251-434-1010
Fax: 251-434-1023
http://www.fox10tv.com
• Matt Pumo, Advertising Manager
• Eric Richey, Sports Director
(251) 434-1084
• Rob Lehocky, Sports Anchor ; Reporter
(251) 434-1010
rob.lehock@fox10tv.com

WALB-TV
1709 STUART AVENUE
ALBANY, GA 31707-1701
229-446-1010
Fax: 229-446-4000
http://www.walb.com
• Robert Hydrick, Sports Director
(229) 446-4042
robert.hydrick@walb.com

WAOW-TV
1908 GRAND AVENUE
WAUSAU, WI 54403-6870
715-842-2251
800-236-9269
Fax: 715-848-0195
http://www.waow.com
• Bryon Graff, Sports Director
bgraff@waow.com

WAPT-TV
P.O. BOX 10297
JACKSON, MS 39209-9634
601-922-1652
Fax: 601-922-8993
http://www.wapt.com
• Tony Bahou, Sports Anchor
(601) 922-1652

WATE - 6 WATE
1306 BROADWAY, NE
KNOXVILLE, TN 37917
865-637-6666
Fax: 865-523-3561
www.wate.com
• Jan Wade, General Manager
• Jim Wogan, Sports Director
Affiliation:
CBS.
Neilsen Market:
63
Sports:
All.
Local Sports:
KnoxPreps (High School) Sports. University
of Tennessee Men's & Women's Sports.

WAVE-TV
725 S. FLOYD STREET
LOUISVILLE, KY 40203-2337
502-561-4150 EXT 3
800-800-9283
Fax: 502-561-4105
newsrelease@wave3.com
http://www.wave3.com
• Kent Taylor, Sports Director
(502) 561-4126
ktaylor@wave3tv.com
• Bob Domine, Sports Anchor
(502) 585-2201
bdomine@wave3tv.com

WAVY-TV
300 WAVY STREET
PORTSMOUTH, VA 23704-5200
757-393-1010
Fax: 757-399-7628
newsdesk@wavy.com
http://www.wavy.com
• Bruce Rader, Sports Director
(757) 673-5370
wavy.sports@lintv.com
• Judy Triska, Promotion Manager
(757) 396-6164
promotions@wavy.com
• Chris Francis, Sports Anchor
(757) 397-8279
chris.francis@wavy.com

WB 32
10255 SW ARCTIC DR
BEAVERTON, OR 97005
503-644-3232
Fax: 503-626-3576
• Russel Cameron, Executive
Producer/Fishing The West
russc@wb32tv.com
• Steve Dant, General Manager
Nature of Sports Service:
National. Program producer and syndicator.
Current programs: Fishing The West,
Northwest Hunter.

WBAL-TV
3800 HOOPER AVENUE
BALTIMORE, MD 21211-1313

410-467-3000
Fax: 410-338-6526
http://www.thewbalchannel.com
• Gerry Sandusky, Sports Director/Anchor
(410) 467-3000
gsandusky@hearst.com
• Pete Gilbert, Sports Reporter
(410) 467-3000

WBAY - WBAY-TV 2
115 S. JEFFERSON ST
GREEN BAY, WI 54301
920-432-3331
Fax: 920-432-7808
www.wbay.com
• Tom McCarey, News Director
• Don Carmichael, General Manager
Nielsen Rank:
69
Affiliate:
ABC.
Sports:
University of Wisconsin Green Bay Men's
and Women's Local High School Sports.
Professional Teams:
Green Bay Packers NFL Green Bay Blizzard
Arena Football League.

WBAY-TV
115 SOUTH JEFFERSON STREET
GREEN BAY, WI 54301-4534
920-432-3331
800-242-8090
Fax: 920-432-1190
wbay@wbay.com
http://www.wbay.com/
• Chris Roth, Sports Director
(920) 438-3257

WBBH - NBC 2
3719 CENTRAL AVE
FORT MYERS, FL 33901
239-261-8820
www.nbc-2.com
• Darrel Adams, News Director
• Steven Pontius, Executive Vice
President/General Manager
Sports:
All.
Nielsen Market:
81
Affiliate:
NBC.

WBBH-TV
3719 CENTRAL AVENUE
FORT MYERS, FL 33901
239-939-2020
Fax: 239-939-3244
nbc2news@nbc-2.com
http://www.nbc-2.com
• Lori Grimaldi, Marketing Director
(239) 939-2020
• Dan Sheldon, Sports Anchor (Weekend)
• Grant Lodes, Weekend News and Sports
Anchor
(239) 939-2020

WBBJ-TV
346 MUSE STREET
JACKSON, TN 38301-3620
731-424-4515
Fax: 731-424-9299
7news@wbbjtv.com
http://www.wbbjtv.com

media

• Bart Barker, Sports Director
• Bret Barker, Sports Anchor
(731) 424-4515

WBBM-TV
630 NORTH MCCLURG COURT
CHICAGO, IL 60611-4536
312-202-2222
Fax: 312-202-3878
wbbm.programming@cbs.com
http://www.cbs2chicago.com
• Steve Goldberg, Sports Producer
(312) 202-2642
sjgoldberg@cbs.com
• Megan Mawicke, Sports Reporter
(312) 202-3601
mamawicke@cbs.com
• Norm Potash, Sports Producer
(312) 202-2653
nppotash@cbs.com
• Stephen Bardo, Sports Reporter
(312) 202-2222
sdbardo@cbs.com

WBFS-TV
8900 NORTHWEST 18TH TERRACE
MIAMI, FL 33172
954-523-3333
Fax: 305-628-3448
wfornews@wfor.cbs.com
http://www.cbs4.com
• Jim Berry, Sports Director

WBKB-TV
1390 NORTH BAGLEY STREET
ALPENA, MI 49707
989-356-3434
800-824-1092
Fax: 989-356-4188
http://www.wbkbtv.com
• Barbara Bowen, Advertising Manager
• Mark Kunz, Sports Director
markk@speednetllc.com
• Jeff Schaffer, Sports Director
(989) 356-3434
wbkbsports@yahoo.com

WBMA-TV
800 CONCOURSE PARKWAY SUITE 200
BIRMINGHAM, AL 35244-1889
205-403-3340
Fax: 205-403-3329
http://www.abc3340.com
• Mike Raita, Sports Director
(205) 982-3988
markr@abc3340.com

WBNG-TV
560 COLUMBIA DRIVE
JOHNSON CITY, NY 13790
607-729-8812
Fax: 607-729-4022
actionnews@wbngtv.com
http://www.wbng.com
• Brendan Oreilly, Sports Director
(607) 584-7283
wbng@wbngtv.com

WBOY-TV
904 PIKE STREET, W.
CLARKSBURG, WV 26301-2555
304-623-3311
Fax: 304-623-9269
news@wboy.com
http://www.wboy.com

• Greg Chandler, Sports Reporter
(304) 623-3311

WBRZ-TV
1650 HIGHLAND ROAD
BATON ROUGE, LA 70802-7018
225-387-2222
Fax: 225-336-2346
http://www.wbrz.com
• Michael Cauble, Sports Director
(225) 387-2222

WBZ-TV
1170 SOLDIERS FIELD ROAD
BOSTON, MA 02134-1004
617-787-7000
Fax: 617-254-6383
http://www.wbztv.com
• Steve Burton, Sports Reporter
(617) 787-7344
sjburton@boston.cbs.com
• Jackie Connally, Sports Producer
(617) 787-7338
jaconnally@boston.cbs.com
• Alice Cook, Sports Reporter
(617) 787-7340
• Bob Lobel, Sports Anchor
(617) 787-7022
• Dan Roche, Sports Reporter

WCAU-TV
10 MONUMENT ROAD
BALA CYNWYD, PA 19004-1712
610-668-5510
Fax: 610-668-3700
http://www.nbc10.com
• Howard Eskin, Sports Anchor (Weekend)
• Via Sikahema, Sports Anchor
• Colin Macaulay, Sports Producer
(610) 668-5660

WCAX-TV
30 JOY DRIVE
SOUTH BURLINGTON, VT 05403-6118
802-652-6300
Fax: 802-652-6399
channel3@wcax.com
http://www.wcax.com
• J. J. Cioffi, Sports Director
(802) 652-6340
sports@wcax.com

WCBI-TV
201 5TH STREET, S.
COLUMBUS, MS 39701-5729
662-327-4444
800-844-9224
Fax: 662-329-1004
news@wcbi.com
http://www.wcbi.com
• Susan Bell, Promotions Manager
• Jeff Shepard, Sports Director
(662) 327-4444
• Drew Powell, Sports Director
(662) 327-4444

WCBS-TV
524 WEST 57TH STREET
NEW YORK, NY 10019-2902
212-975-4321
Fax: 212-975-9387
desk@cbs2ny.com
http://wcbstv.com/
• Duke Castiglione, Sports Anchor
• Chris Scaglione, Sports Executive Producer

• Chris Wragge, Sports Correspondent
• John Discepolo, Sports Anchor/Reporter
(212) 975-4321

WCCB-TV
1 TELEVISION PLACE
CHARLOTTE, NC 28205-7038
704-372-1800
Fax: 704-358-4841
http://www.foxcharlotte.tv
• Kelli Bartik, Sports Reporter/Anchor
(704) 632-7517
kbartik@foxcharlotte.tv

WCCO-TV
90 SOUTH 11TH STREET
MINNEAPOLIS, MN 55403-2414
612-339-4444
Fax: 612-330-2767
http://www.wcco.com/
• Carry Clancy, Sports Producer
• Greg Littman, Sports Director
• Wendy McMahon, Promotions Director
• Mike Max, Sports Reporter
(612) 339-4444
mmax@cbs.com

WCFN-TV
118 WEST EDWARDS
SPRINGFIELD, IL 62704
217-544-3691
Fax: 217-544-3818
news@wcia.com
http://www.wcia.com
• Jason Elliott, Sports Director
(217) 373-3656
jelliott@wcia.com

WCHS-TV
1301 PIEDMONT ROAD
CHARLESTON, WV 25301-1426
304-346-5358
Fax: 304-345-1849
news@wchstv.com
http://www.wchstv.com
• Paul Fox, Promotions Director
(304) 346-5358
pfox@wchstv.com
• Alan Frank, Regional Manager
(412) 931-5300
afrank@sbgnet.com
• Josh Lewis, Sports Anchor
(304) 346-5358
jlewis@wchstv.com
• Mark Martin, Sports Director
(304) 346-5358
mmartin@wchstv.com
• Kennie Bass, Sports Reporter
(304) 346-5358
kbass@wchstv.com

WCIA-TV
509 SOUTH NEIL STREET
CHAMPAIGN, IL 61820
217-373-3650
Fax: 217-373-3663
news@wcia.com
http://illinoishomepage.net
• Peter Carlson, Promotions Manager
(217) 373-3638
promotions@wcia.com
• Jason Elliott, Sports Director
(217) 373-3650
news@wcia.com
• Aaron Bennett, Sports Reporter

(217) 356-8333
abennett@wcia.com

WCIV-TV
888 ALLBRITTON BOULEVARD
MOUNT PLEASANT, SC 29464-3033
843-881-4444
Fax: 843-849-2507
desk@wciv.com
http://www.wciv.com
• Josh Morton, Sports Director
(843) 881-4444

WCJB-TV
6220 NORTHWEST 43RD STREET
GAINESVILLE, FL 32653-3334
352-377-2020
Fax: 352-371-0747
tv20news@wcjb.com
http://www.wcjb.com
• Joe Girvan, Sports Director
(352) 377-2020
• Hank Astengo, Weekend Sports
Anchor/Weekday Sports Rep
(352) 377-2020

WCNC - NBC6
1001 WOOD RIDGE CENTER DR
CHARLOTTE, NC 28217
704-329-0898
Fax: 704-357-4980
www.nbc6.com
• Stuart Powell, Vice President/General
Manager
• Chuck Howard, Sports Director
• Keith Connors, Executive News Director
Professional Sports:
Carolina Panthers, (NFL), Carolina
Hurricanes (NHL), Carolina Cobras (Arena
Football League), NASCAR.
Network Affiliate:
NBC.
Nielsen Markett:
28

WCNC-TV
1001 WOOD RIDGE CENTER DRIVE
CHARLOTTE, NC 28217-1902
704-329-3636
Fax: 704-357-4975
http://www.wcnc.com
• Chuck Howard, Sports Director
• Greg Bailey, Sports Director
(704) 329-3636
gbailey@wcnc.com

WCPO-TV
1720 GILBERT AVENUE
CINCINNATI, OH 45202-2311
513-721-9900
Fax: 513-721-7717
newsdesk@wcpo.com
http://www.cincinow.com
• Paul Harper, Promotions Assistant
Director
• Sheila Obermeyer, Promotion Director
• John Popovich, Sports Director
(513) 852-4078
jpopovich@wcpo.com
• Lisa Cornwell, Weekend Sports
Anchor/Reporter
(513) 721-9900
lisa.cornwell@wcpo.com

WCSC-TV
2126 CHARLIE HALL BOULEVARD
CHARLESTON, SC 29414-5832
843-402-5755
Fax: 843-402-5744
talkback@live5news.com
http://www.wcsc.com
• Craig Birnbach, Sports Anchor
(843) 402-5750
cbirnbach@live5news.com
• Craig Birnbach, Sports Director
(843) 402-5750
cbirnbach@live5news.com
• Andy Pruitt, Sports Reporter
(843) 402-5755
apruitt@live5news.com
• Bob Behanian, Sports Reporter
(843) 402-5755

WCSH-TV
1 CONGRESS SQUARE
PORTLAND, ME 04101-3801
207-828-6666
800-464-1213
Fax: 207-828-6630
newscenter@wcsh6.com
http://www.wcsh6.com
• Bruce Glasier, Sports Director
(207) 828-6666
bruce.glasier@wcsh6.com

WCVB-TV
5 TV PLACE
NEEDHAM, MA 02494-2302
781-449-0400
Fax: 781-449-6681
http://www.thebostonchannel.com
• Mike Lynch, Sports Anchor
(781) 449-0400
mlynch@hearst.com
• Mike Dowling, Sports Reporter
(781) 433-4703

WDAF-TV
3030 SUMMIT STREET
KANSAS CITY, MO 64108-3312
816-753-4567
Fax: 816-561-4181
news@wdaftv4.com
http://www.wdaftv4.com/
• Frank Boal, Sports Director
(816) 753-4567

WDAM-TV
2362 HIGHWAY 11
MOSELLE, MS 39459
601-544-4730
Fax: 601-584-9302
info@wdam.com
http://www.wdam.com
• Jim Cameron, Vice President
jcameron@raycommedia.com
• Brenda Parker, Promotions Director
bparker@wdam.com
• Mitchell Williams, Sports Director
(601) 544-4730
mwilliams@raycommedia.com

WDAZ-TV
2220 SOUTH WASHINGTON STREET
GRAND FORKS, ND 58201-6346
701-775-2511
Fax: 701-746-4507
• Angela Cary, Promotions Director
• Pat Sweeney, Sports Director
(701) 775-2511

WDBJ-TV
P.O. BOX 7
ROANOKE, VA 24017
540-344-7000
Fax: 540-344-5097
news@wdbj7.com
http://www.wdbj7.com
• Mike Stevens, Sports Director
(540) 985-3623
mstevens@wdbj7.com
• Grant Kittelson, Sports Reporter
(540) 344-7000
gkittelson@wdbj7.com

WDEF
3300 BROAD ST
CHATTANOOGA, TN 37408
423-785-1257
Fax: 423-785-1273
www.wdef.com
• Cathy Gugerty, General Manager
• John Appicello, Sports Director
Office Address:
3300 Broad St, Chattanooga, TN 37401.
Nature of Sports Service:
Local. 24-hour sports radio programming.
Baseball:
MLB - Atlanta Braves.
College Sports:
Basketball, Football - University of
Tennessee.
Football:
NFL - Carolina Panthers.

WDEF-TV
3300 BROAD STREET
CHATTANOOGA, TN 37408-3061
423-785-1200
Fax: 423-785-1273
http://www.wdef.com
• Rick Nyman, Sports Director
(423) 785-1277
• Jason Law, Weekend Sports
Anchor/Reporter
(423) 785-1200

WDIV-TV
550 WEST LAFAYETTE BOULEVARD
DETROIT, MI 48226-3123
313-222-0500
Fax: 313-222-0592
assignmentdesk@wdiv.com
http://www.clickondetroit.com
• Fred Mcleod, Sports Reporter
fredm@clickondetroit.com
• Bernie Smilovitz, Sports Anchor & Director
(313) 222-0504
bernies@clickondetroit.com
• Katrina Hancock, Sports Anchor
(313) 222-0500
khancock@clickondetroit.com

WDJT-TV
809 S. 60TH STREET
MILWAUKEE, WI 53214-3363
414-607-8140
Fax: 414-777-5802
newsdesk@cbs58.com
http://www.cbs58.com
• Rock Rote, Sports Director
(414) 607-8140
• Ryan Nolan, Sports Reporter
(414) 607-8140

media

WEAR-TV
P.O. BOX 12278
PENSACOLA, FL 32506-3230
850-455-4599
Fax: 850-455-8972
newsroom@weartv.com
http://www.weartv.com
• Dan Shugart, Sports Director
(850) 455-4599
dshugart@weartv.com
• Mac McAllister, Sports
Producer/Photographer
(850) 455-4599

WEAU-TV
P.O. BOX 47
EAU CLAIRE, WI 54701-4551
715-835-1313
Fax: 715-832-3476
weau@weau.com
http://www.weau.com
• Emily Edwards, Promotions Director
• Bob Gallaher, Sports Director
(715) 835-1313
bob.gallaher@weau.com
• Paige Pearson, Weekend Sports Anchor
(715) 835-1313
paige.pearson@weau.com

WECT-TV
322 SHIPYARD BOULEVARD
WILMINGTON, NC 28412
910-791-6681
Fax: 910-791-9535
newsproducers@wect.com
http://www.wect.com
• Bob Bonner, Sports Director
(910) 791-6681
bbonner@raycommedia.com

WEEK-TV
2907 SPRINGFIELD ROAD
EAST PEORIA, IL 61611-4878
309-698-3737
Fax: 309-698-2070
news25@week.com
http://www.week.com
• Lee Hall, Sports Director
(309) 698-3737
lhall@week.com
• Mike Dimmick, Weekend Sports Anchor
(309) 698-3737
mdimmick@week.com

WEHT-TV
800 MARYWOOD DRIVE
HENDERSON, KY 42420-2431
812-424-9215
800-879-8542
Fax: 270-827-0561
http://www.abc25.com
• Mellissa Marks, Promotion Director
(812) 424-9215
mmarks@news25.us
• Lance Wilkerson, Sports Director
(800) 879-8574
lwilkerson@news25.us
• Drew Amman, Sports Anchor
(800) 879-8575
damman@news25.us

WENY-TV
474 OLD ITHACA ROAD
HORSEHEADS, NY 14845-7212

607-739-3636
Fax: 607-796-6171
http://www.weny.com
• Neille Gissune, Sports Director
(607) 739-3636
• Cory Hepola, Sports Director
(607) 739-3636

WESH-TV
1021 NORTH WYMORE ROAD
WINTER PARK, FL 32789-1717
407-645-2222
Fax: 407-539-7948
http://www.newschannel2000.com
• Pat Clarke, Sports Director
(407) 645-2222
pclarke@hearst.com
• Robert Fein, Vice President

WETM-TV
P.O. BOX 1207
ELMIRA, NY 14901
607-733-5518
Fax: 607-733-4739
news@wetmtv.com
http://www.wetmtv.com/
• Ed Bak, Sports Director
(607) 733-5518

WEWS-TV
3001 EUCLID AVENUE
CLEVELAND, OH 44115-2516
216-431-5555
Fax: 216-431-3666
news@newsnet5.com
http://www.newsnet5.com
• Tony Burke, Sports Producer
(216) 431-3441
burke@wews.com
• Chris Miller, Sports Director
miller@wews.com
• Andy Baskin, Sports Director
(216) 431-3700
abaskin@wews.com

WFAA-TV
606 YOUNG STREET
DALLAS, TX 75202-4895
214-748-9631
Fax: 214-977-6585
news8@wfaa.com
http://www.wfaa.com/
• Jim Glass, Promotions Director
• Dale Hansen, Sports Anchor
(214) 977-6214
dhansen@wfaa.com
• Gina Miller, Sports Reporter
(214) 748-9631
• David Muscari, Vice President
dmuscari@wfaa.com
• George Riba, Sports Director
(214) 977-6255
griba@wfaa.com
• Joe Trahan, Sports Reporter
jtrahan@wfaa.com

WFIE-TV
P.O. BOX 1414
EVANSVILLE, IN 47720
812-426-1414
Fax: 812-428-2228
http://www.14wfie.com
• Mike Blake, Sports Director
(812) 433-3404
mblake@14wfie.com

WFLA-TV
P.O. BOX 1410
TAMPA, FL 33606
813-221-5788
800-824-1695
Fax: 813-225-2770
news@wfla.com
http://www.wfla.com
• Dave Cook, Sports Producer
dcook@wfla.com
• J.P. Peterson, Sports Anchor
• Dan Lucas, Sports Reporter
(813) 221-5788
dlucas@wfla.com

WFLD TV CHANNEL 32 CHICAGO/FOX
205 N. MICHIGAN AVE
CHICAGO, IL 60601
312-565-5532
Fax: 312-819-1332
www.foxchicago.com
• Debra Juarez West, News Director

WFLD-TV
205 NORTH MICHIGAN AVENUE
CHICAGO, IL 60601-5922
312-565-5532
Fax: 312-565-5517
http://www.myfoxchicago.com
• Jill Carlson, Sports Anchor
• John Eskra, Sports Producer
(312) 565-5478
• James Marketti, Promotion Vice President
• Corey McPherrin, Sports Anchor
(312) 565-5529
• John Nuck, Vice President
(312) 565-5607

WFMJ-TV
101 WEST BOARDMAN STREET
YOUNGSTOWN, OH 44503-1305
330-744-8821
800-488-9365
Fax: 330-742-2472
news@wfmj.com
http://www.wfmj.com
• Mike Ackelson, Anchor
(330) 744-8611
mike@wfmj.com
• Dana Balash, Sports Director
(330) 744-8611
dana@wfmj.com
• Mike Case, Sports Anchor
(330) 744-8611
mcase@wfmj.com
• Joe Romano, Promotions Director
(330) 744-8611
jroma@wfmj.com
• Jack Stevenson, Marketing Director
jstev@wfmj.com

WFMY-TV
P.O. BOX TV-2
GREENSBORO, NC 27405
336-379-9369
800-237-1615
Fax: 336-230-0971
news@wfmy.com
http://www.digtriad.com/news/
• Greg Kerr, Sports Director
(336) 379-5780
gkerr@wfmy.gannett.com

WFMZ-TV
300 EAST ROCK ROAD
ALLENTOWN, PA 18103-7519

610-791-1111
Fax: 610-791-9994
news@wfmz.com
http://www.wfmz.com
• Dean Dallman, Advertising Coordinator
(610) 798-4000
deand@wfmz.com
• Troy Hein, Sports Reporter
(610) 791-1111
troyh@wfmz.com
• Dave Taveriner, Promotion Director
(610) 798-4000
davet@wfmz.com

WFRV-TV
P.O. BOX 19055
GREEN BAY, WI 54301
920-437-5411
Fax: 920-437-5769
http://www.wfrv.com
• Larry McCarren, Sports Director
(920) 437-5555
• Burke Griffin, Sports Anchor
(920) 437-5411
burke.griffin@wfrv.com

WFSB-TV
3 CONSTITUTION PLAZA
HARTFORD, CT 06103-1807
860-244-1700
Fax: 860-728-0263
newsdesk3@wfsb.com
http://www.wfsb.com
• Dina Falco, Sports Director
newsdesk3@wfsb.com
• Robert Montesi, Marketing Director
(860) 244-1736
newsdesk3@wfsb.com
• John Holt, Weekend Sports
Anchor/Reporter
(860) 244-1700
john.holt@wfsb.com

WFTS-TV
4045 NORTH HIMES AVENUE
TAMPA, FL 33607-6651
877-833-2828
Fax: 813-870-2828
newstips@wfts.com
http://www.wfts.com
• Oscar Angulo, Sports Producer
oangulo@wfts.com
• Al Keck, Sports Director
(813) 354-2800
akeck@wfts.com
• Donna Wilson, Promotion Director
dwilson@wfts.com
• Donna Wilson, Promotions Director
dwilson@wfts.com
• Dan Eassa, Sports Reporter/Producer
(877) 833-2828
deassa@wfts.com

WFTV-TV
490 EAST SOUTH STREET
ORLANDO, FL 32801-2816
407-841-9000
Fax: 407-481-2891
news@wftv.com
http://www.wftv.com
• Dan Hellie, Sports Director
dan.hellie@wftv.com
• Zach Klein, Weekend Sports
Anchor/Weekday Sports Rep
(407) 841-9000
news@wftv.com

Description:
Monday, Tuesday, Wednesday, Thursday,
Friday at 4:30AM for 2.00 hours.

WGAL-TV
P.O. BOX 7127
LANCASTER, PA 17603-3824
717-393-5851
Fax: 717-295-7457
http://www.wgal.com
• Mike Hostetler, Sports Anchor
(717) 393-5851
mhostetler@hearst.com
• Pat Principe, Sports Director ; Anchor
(717) 393-5851
pprincipe@hearst.com

WGBA-TV
1391 NORTH ROAD
GREEN BAY, WI 54313-9099
920-494-2626
800-800-6619
Fax: 920-494-9550
www.nbc26.com
• Ted Stefaniak, Sports Director
• John Burton, Sports Anchor
(920) 494-2626
jburton@nbc26.com
Sports Discussed:
All
Description:
News time.

WGCL-TV
425 14TH STREET, N.W.
ATLANTA, GA 30318-7965
404-327-3200
Fax: 404-327-3004
http://www.cbs46.com/
• Mark Harmon, Weekend Sports Anchor
(404) 327-3250
mharmon@mdp.com
• Sylvia McDonald, Sports Director
(404) 327-3250
• Corey Anderson, Sports
Producer/Reporter/Anchor
(404) 327-3250
Corey.Anderson@cbs46.com

WGEM-TV
P.O. BOX 80
QUINCY, IL 62301
217-228-6600
Fax: 217-228-6670
http://www.wgem.com
• Shawn Dickerman, Promotion Director
(217) 228-6632
sdickerman@wgem.com
• Ben Marth, Sports Director
(217) 228-6615
bmarth@wgem.com
• Ben Marth, Sports Reporter
(217) 228-6615
bmarth@wgem.com
• Bree Stewart, Sports Anchor
bstewart@wgem.com
• Tyler Tomlinson, Sports Anchor
(217) 228-6600

WGGB-TV
1300 LIBERTY STREET
SPRINGFIELD, MA 01104
413-733-8840
Fax: 413-788-7640
assignmentdesk@wggb.com
http://www.wggb.com/

• Jim Cline, Sports Reporter
(413) 733-4040
jcline@sbgnet.com
• Scott Coen, Sports Director
(413) 733-8840
scoen@sbgnet.com

WGME-TV
1335 WASHINGTON AVENUE
PORTLAND, ME 04103-3638
207-797-1313
Fax: 207-878-3505
http://www.wgme.com/
• Dave Eid, Sports Director
deid@wgme.sbgnet.com
• Dave Eid, Sports Reporter
(207) 797-1313
deid@wgme.sbgnet.com

WGN-9 CHICAGO'S CW
2501 WEST BRADLEY PLAZA
CHICAGO, IL 60618-4718
773-528-2311
Fax: 773-528-6050
www.wgntv.com
• Marty Wilke, Vice President/General
Manager
(773) 883-3383
• Bill Herriott, Director Sports Sales
(773) 883-3429
• Errol Gerber, Director Sales
(773) 883-3285
• Ken Reiner, Director Programming
• Bob Vorwald, Director Production
Baseball Sponsor:
MLB - Chicago Cubs, Chicago White Sox.
Basketball Sponsor:
NBA - Chicago Bulls.

WGXA-TV
599 MARTIN LUTHER KING JR.
BOULEVARD
MACON, GA 31201-3367
478-743-0742
800-592-4240
Fax: 478-745-6057
http://www.fox24.com
• Pete Cataldo, Sports Director
(478) 745-2424
• Marc Nash, Promotions Manager
(478) 745-2424
• Chace Ambrose, Sports
Reporter/Photographer
(478) 743-0742

WHAM-TV
4225 WEST HENRIETTA ROAD
ROCHESTER, NY 14623
585-334-8700
Fax: 585-359-1570
news@13wham.com
http://www.iknowrochester.com
• Mike Catalana, Sports Director
(585) 334-8700
mcatalana@13wham.com

WHBQ-TV
485 SOUTH HIGHLAND STREET
MEMPHIS, TN 38111-4398
901-320-1313
Fax: 901-323-0092
http://www.fox13whbq.com
• John Koski, Vice President
(901) 320-1310
• David Lee, Sports Director
(901) 320-1345

• Paul Sloan, Promotion Director
(901) 320-1311
fox13news@foxtv.com
• Greg Gaston, Sports Anchor/Reporter
(901) 320-1313

WHDH-TV
7 BULFINCH PLACE
BOSTON, MA 02114
617-725-0777
Fax: 617-723-6117
7news@whdh.com
http://www.whdh.com/
• Fred Nutter, Sports Director
(617) 725-0777
fnutter@whdh.com
• Joe Amorosino, Sports Director
(617) 725-0756
jamorosino@whdh.com

WHIO-TV
1414 WILMINGTON AVENUE
DAYTON, OH 45420-1543
937-259-2111
Fax: 937-259-2001
7online@whiotv.com
http://www.whiotv.com
• Mike Hartsock, Sports Director
(937) 259-2142
mike.hartsock@whiotv.com
• Margaret Brosko, Sports Anchor
(937) 259-2111
mbrosko@cox.com

WHIZ-TV
629 DOWNARD ROAD
ZANESVILLE, OH 43701-5108
740-452-5431
Fax: 740-452-6553
news@whizamfmtv.com
http://www.whizamfmtv.com
• Hank Littick, President
(740) 452-5431
hankcl@whizamfmtv.com
• Aaron Spragg, Sports Director

WHKY-TV
P.O. BOX 1059
HICKORY, NC 28602-1103
828-322-5115
Fax: 828-322-8256
news@whky.com
http://www.whky.com
• Jason Savage, Sports Director
(828) 322-5115
jsavage@whky.com

WHLA-TV
821 UNIVERSITY AVENUE
MADISON, WI 53706-1412
608-263-2121
800-422-9707
Fax: 608-263-1952
http://www.wpt.org
• Deb Piper, Sports Director
(608) 263-4222
piper@wpt.org

WHMB-TV
10511 GREENFIELD AVENUE
NOBLESVILLE, IN 46060
317-773-5050
Fax: 317-776-4051
http://www.lesea.com

• Dennis Kasey, Sports Director
(317) 773-5050
dkasey3535@aol.com

WHME-TV
61300 SOUTH IRONWOOD ROAD
SOUTH BEND, IN 46614
574-291-8200
Fax: 574-291-9043
broadcasting@lesea.com
http://www.lesea.com
• Charles Freeby, Sports Director
(574) 231-5260
cfreeby@lesea.com

WHNT-TV
P.O. BOX 19
HUNTSVILLE, AL 35801-4903
256-533-1919
800-533-8819
Fax: 256-536-9468
http://www.whnt.com
• Judy Cornelius, Promotions Manager
(256) 533-1919
judy.cornelius@whnt.com
• Lori Miller, Marketing Director
lori.miller@whnt.com
• John Pearson, Sports Director
(256) 533-1919
john.pearson@whnt.com

WHO-TV
1801 GRAND AVENUE
DES MOINES, IA 50309-3309
515-242-3500
Fax: 515-242-3796
news@whotv.com
http://www.whotv.com
• Tim Gardner, Promotions Director
(515) 242-3500
tim.gardner@whotv.com
• Keith Murphy, Sports Director
(515) 242-3739
keith.murphy@whotv.com
• Chris Hassel, Sports Reporter/Anchor
(515) 242-3500
chris.hassel@whotv.com

WHOI-TV
500 NORTH STEWART STREET
CREVE COEUR, IL 61610
309-698-1919
Fax: 309-698-4819
http://www.hoinews.com
• James Care, Promotions Producer
(309) 698-1919
jcare@whoitv.com
• Jim Mattson, Sports Director
(773) 838-7878
jmattson@whoitv.com

WHRM-TV
821 UNIVERSITY AVENUE
MADISON, WI 53706-1412
608-263-2121
800-422-9707
Fax: 608-263-1952
http://www.wpt.org
• Deb Piper, Sports Director
(608) 263-4222
piper@wpt.org

WHTM-TV
P.O. BOX 5860
HARRISBURG, PA 17110-2226

717-236-2727
Fax: 717-236-1263
news@abc27.com
http://www.abc27.com
• John Appicello, Sports Reporter
(717) 236-2727
jappicello@abc27.com
• Betty Fish, Promotions Manager
• Gregg Mace, Sports Director
(717) 236-2727

WHWC-TV
821 UNIVERSITY AVENUE
MADISON, WI 53706-1412
608-263-2121
800-422-9707
Fax: 608-263-1952
http://www.wpt.org
• Deb Piper, Sports Director
(608) 263-4222
piper@wpt.org

WIAT - CBS 42
2075 GOLDEN CREST DR
BIRMINGHAM, AL 35209
205-322—4200
Fax: 205-320-2722
newsrelease@cbs42.com
www.wiat.com
• J.D. Huey, Vice President/General
Manager
• Tod Buccelli, Marketing/Promotion Director
• Larry Ragan, News Director
Major Sports:
Major Sports Covered links to
sportsline.com.
Affiliate:
CBS.
Neilsen Market:
39

WICU-TV
3514 STATE STREET
ERIE, PA 16508
814-454-5201
Fax: 814-455-0703
http://www.wicu12.com
• Mike Ruzzi, Sports Director
(814) 454-5201
• Jay Puskar, Weekend Sports Anchor
(814) 454-5201

WIFR-TV
2523 NORTH MERIDIAN ROAD
ROCKFORD, IL 61101
815-987-5300
Fax: 815-965-0981
talkto23@wifr.com
http://www.wifr.com
• Mike Garrigan, anchor
(815) 987-5300
mike.garrigan@wifr.com

WILX-TV
500 AMERICAN ROAD
LANSING, MI 48911-5978
517-393-0110
Fax: 517-393-9180
news@wilx.com
http://www.wilx.com/
• Tim Staudt, Sports Director
(517) 393-0110
tim.staudt@wilx.com
• Dan Hedman, Sports Reporter
(517) 393-0110
dan.hedman@wilx.com

WINK-TV
2824 PALM BEACH BOULEVARD
FORT MYERS, FL 33916-1503
239-334-1131
800-886-6397
Fax: 239-334-0744
http://www.winktv.com
• Clayton Ferraro, Sports Director
(239) 334-1131
• Brian Simon, Sports Director

WIS-TV
P.O. BOX 367
COLUMBIA, SC 29201-3722
803-799-1010
Fax: 803-758-1155
countonwis@wistv.com
http://www.wistv.com
• Rick Henry, Sports Director
(803) 799-1010
rhenry@wistv.com

WISC-TV
7025 RAYMOND ROAD
MADISON, WI 53719-5053
608-273-3333
Fax: 608-271-0800
http://www.channel3000.com
• Eric Franke, Sports Director
(608) 277-5241
efranke@wisctv.com
• George Johnson, Sports Director
(608) 273-3333
gjohnson@wisctv.com

WISH-TV
1950 NORTH MERIDIAN STREET
INDIANAPOLIS, IN 46202-1304
317-923-8888
Fax: 317-931-2242
newsdesk@wishtv.com
http://www.wishtv.com
• Chris Widlic, Sports Director
cwidlic@wishtv.com
• Derek Daly, Sports Reporter
(317) 923-8888

WITN-TV
P.O. BOX 468
WASHINGTON, NC 27889
252-946-3131
Fax: 252-946-0558
• Billy Weaver, Sports Director
(252) 946-3131
• Brian Meador, Sports Reporter
(252) 946-3131

WIVB-TV
2077 ELMWOOD AVENUE
BUFFALO, NY 14207
716-876-7333
Fax: 716-874-8173
newsroom@wivb.com
http://www.wivb.com
• Dennis Williams, Sports Director
(716) 874-4410
dennis.williams@wivb.com

WIXT-TV
5904 BRIDGE STREET
EAST SYRACUSE, NY 13057-2941
315-446-9999
Fax: 315-446-0045
wixttv9@aol.com
http://www.wixt.com

• Steven Insanti, Sports Director
steveninsanti@clearchannel.com

WJBK-TV
16550 WEST NINE MILE ROAD
SOUTHFIELD, MI 48075-4705
248-395-3692
Fax: 248-557-1199
fox2newsdesk@foxtv.com
http://www.myfoxdetroit.com
• Dana McDaniel, Vice President
(248) 557-2000
• Glenn Therrien, Sports Executive Producer
(248) 522-5257
gther257@foxtv.com
• Ryan Ermanni, Sports
Anchor/Reporter/Producer
(248) 395-3692
ryan.ermanni@foxtv.com

WJFW-TV
3217 COUNTY HIGEWAY
RHINELANDER, WI 54501
715-365-8812
Fax: 715-365-8810
email@wjfw.com
http://www.wjfw-nbc12.com
• Matt Thompson, Sports Director
(715) 365-8812

WJHG-TV
8195 FRONT BEACH ROAD
PANAMA CITY BEACH, FL 32407-4820
850-234-7777
Fax: 850-233-6647
wjhg@wjhg.com
http://www.wjhg.com
• Scott Rossman, Sports Director
(850) 234-7777
scott.rossman@wjhg.com
• Adam Roland, Sports/News Reporter
(850) 234-7777
adam.roland@wjhg.com

WJHL-TV
P.O. BOX 1130
JOHNSON CITY, TN 37601-5730
423-926-2151
800-606-9545
Fax: 423-926-9080
http://www.wjhl.com
• Kenny Hawkins, Sports Director
(423) 434-4544
khawkins@wjhl.com

WJLA-TV
1100 WILSON BOULEVARD
ARLINGTON, VA 22209
703-236-9555
Fax: 703-236-2331
newsdesk@wjla.com
http://www.wjla.com
• Tim Brant, Sports Anchor
(703) 236-9555
• Stan Melcon, Promotions Director
(703) 236-9552
smelcon@wjla.com
• Howard Zeiden, Marketing Director
(703) 236-9552
hzeiden@wjla.com

WJTV-TV NEWS CHANNEL 12
1820 TV ROAD 1820
JACKSON, MS 39204-4148

601-372-6311
Fax: 601-372-8798
www.wjtv.com
• Jeff Platt, Sports Anchor/Reporter
(601) 944-4920
jplatt@wjtv.com
• Jason Hurst, Sports Anchor/Reporter
(601) 944-4921
jhurst@wjtv.com

WJW-TV
5800 SOUTH MARGINAL ROAD
CLEVELAND, OH 44103-1040
216-431-8888
888-847-6397
Fax: 216-391-9559
http://www.fox8cleveland.com
• Dan Coughlin, Sports Reporter
(216) 431-8888
• John Telich, Sports Reporter
(216) 432-4248

WJXT-TV
4 BROADCAST PLACE
JACKSONVILLE, FL 32207-8613
904-399-4000
Fax: 904-393-9822
jaxnews@news4jax.com
http://www.news4jax.com
• Sam Kouvaris, Sports Director
(904) 399-4000
skouvaris@wjxt.com
• John Dunlap, Sports Anchor/Reporter
(904) 399-4000

WJZ-TV
3725 MALDEN AVENUE
BALTIMORE, MD 21211-1322
410-466-0013
Fax: 410-578-0642
newsroom@wjz.com
http://www.wjz.com
• Mark Viviano, Sports Director
(410) 466-0013
• Mike Pupo, Sports Producer
(410) 466-0013
pupom@wjz.com

WKBN-TV
3930 SUNSET BOULEVARD
YOUNGSTOWN, OH 44512
330-782-1144
Fax: 330-782-3504
newsroom@wkbn.com
http://www.wkbn.com
• Ryan Allison, Sports Director
(330) 782-1144
newsroom@wkbn.com

WKBW-TV
7 BROADCAST PLAZA
BUFFALO, NY 14202-2611
716-845-6100
800-777-9645
Fax: 716-856-8784
news@wkbw.com
http://www.wkbw.com
• John Disciullo, Promotion Director
(716) 840-7860
johndis@wkbw.com
• John Murphy, Sports Director
(716) 840-7796
• Ginger Geoffery, Sports Anchor
(716) 845-6100

WKEF-TV
45 BROADCAST PLAZA
DAYTON, OH 45408
937-263-4500
Fax: 937-268-5265
http://www.daytonsnewssource.com
• Ray Crawford, Sports Director
(937) 262-1422
rcrawford@sbgnet.com
• Ryan Brant, Sports Director
(937) 262-1423

WKMG-TV
4466 JOHN YOUNG PARKWAY
ORLANDO, FL 32804-1939
407-521-1200
Fax: 407-298-2122
desk@wkmg.com
http://www.local6.com
• Todd Lewis, Sports Director
(407) 521-1215
tlewis@local6.com
• Kim Peoples, Marketing Director
(407) 521-1333
kpeoples@wkmg.com
• David Pingalore, Sports Anchor/Reporter
(407) 521-1200

WKOW-TV
5727 TOKAY BOULEVARD
MADISON, WI 53719-1219
608-273-2727
Fax: 608-274-9569
news@wkowtv.com
http://www.wkowtv.com/
• Jill Genter, Promotion Manager
(608) 274-1234
jgenter@wkowtv.com
• Jay Wilson, Sports Director
news@wkowtv.com
• Paul Garcia, Sports Anchor/Reporter
(608) 273-2727
pgarcia@wkowtv.com

WKRC-TV
1906 HIGHLAND AVENUE
CINCINNATI, OH 45219-3109
513-763-5500
Fax: 513-421-3820
http://www.wkrc.com
• Dennison Keller, Sports Reporter
• Elbert Tucker, Vice President
(513) 763-5447
• Brad Johansen, Sports Anchor
(513) 763-5500
bjohansen@wkrc.com

WKRN-TV
441 MURFREESBORO ROAD
NASHVILLE, TN 37210
615-248-7200
Fax: 615-248-7329
news@wkrn.com
http://www.wkrn.com
• John Dwyer, Sports Director
(615) 369-7240
sports@wkrn.com
• Mike Sechrist, President
news@wkrn.com
• Connie Sullivan, Advertising Manager
(615) 369-7222
csullivan@wkrn.com
• Tim Hardiman, Sports Producer
(615) 248-7200
timhardiman@wkrn.com

WKTV-TV
P.O. BOX 2
UTICA, NY 13503-0002
315-793-3475
Fax: 315-733-4893
newslink2@wktv.com
http://www.wktv.com
• Jason Powles, Sports Director/Sports Anchor
(315) 733-0404

WKYC-TV
1333 LAKESIDE AVENUE
CLEVELAND, OH 44114-1134
216-344-3300
Fax: 216-344-7493
news@wkyc.com
http://www.wkyc.com
• Mike Cairns, Sports Reporter
mikecairns@wkyc.com
• Jim Donovan, Sports Director
(216) 344-3406
jimdonovan@wkyc.com
• Joe Brown, Sports Reporter
(216) 344-3300
joebrown@wkyc.com

WKYT-TV
P.O. BOX 55037
LEXINGTON, KY 40509-4801
859-299-2727
Fax: 859-299-2494
http://www.wkyt.com
• Dick Gabriel, Sports Director
(859) 566-1330
dick.gabriel@wkyt.com
• Rob Bromley, Sports Anchor
(859) 299-2727
Rob.Bromley@wkyt.com

WLBT-TV
715 SOUTH JEFFERSON STREET
JACKSON, MS 39201-5622
601-948-3333
Fax: 601-355-7830
news@wlbt.com
http://www.wlbt.com
• Jackie Ellens, Promotions Director
jackiee@wlbt.net
• Rob Jay, Sports Director
(601) 948-3333
rob@wlbt.net
• Chuck Stinson, Sports Reporter
(601) 948-3333
chuck@wlbt.net

WLEF-TV
821 UNIVERSITY AVENUE
MADISON, WI 53706-1412
608-263-2121
800-422-9707
Fax: 608-263-9763
http://www.wpt.org
• Deb Piper, Sports Director
(608) 263-4222
piper@wpt.org

WLFI-TV
2605 YEAGER ROAD
WEST LAFAYETTE, IN 47906
765-463-1800
800-877-9534
Fax: 765-463-7979
newsroom@wlfi.com
http://www.wlfitv18.com

• Clayton Duffy, Sports Director
(765) 463-1800
• Deb McMahan, Promotions Director
(765) 237-5046
• Gage Butterbrodt, Sports Anchor
(765) 463-1800

WLIO-TV
1424 RICE AVENUE
LIMA, OH 45805-1949
419-228-5909
Fax: 419-225-6109
newsrelease@wlio.com
www.wlio.com
• Kevin Creamer, President/General Manager
(419) 228-8835
kevin@wlio.com
• Jeff Fitzgerald, News Director
fitz@wlio.com
• Jayson Geiser, Sports Director
jgeiser@wlio.com

WLS-TV
190 NORTH STATE STREET
CHICAGO, IL 60601-3302
312-750-7777
Fax: 312-899-8019
http://www.abc7chicago.com
• Emily L. Barr, President
• Jeff Blanzy, Weekend Sports Anchor
(312) 750-7777
• Mark Giangreco, Sports Director
(312) 750-7777
• Tom Hebel, Promotions Manager
• Mike Johnson, Sports Producer
• Brad Palmer, Sports Reporter
• Jim Rose, Sports Anchor
(312) 750-7777

WLS-TV CHANNEL 7 ABC (CHICAGO)
WLS TV
190 N. STATE ST.
CHICAGO, IL 60601
312-750-7777
Fax: 312-899-8019
www.abc7chicago.com
• Jennifer Graves, News Director
• Ben Koff, Marketing Account Executive

WLTV-TV
9405 NORTHWEST 41ST STREET
MIAMI, FL 33178-2301
305-471-3900
Fax: 305-471-3948
http://www.univision.net
• Manny Delafe, Sports Director
(305) 471-4362

WLVI-TV
75 MORRISSOUTHEASTY BOULEVARD
BOSTON, MA 02125-3316
617-265-5656
Fax: 617-265-0063
http://www.wb56.com
• Mike Ratte, Sports Director

WLWT-TV
1700 YOUNG STREET
CINCINNATI, OH 45210
513-412-5000
Fax: 513-412-6121
http://www.channelcincinnati.com
• Ken Broo, Sports Director
(513) 412-5089
• Jonathan Killian, Promotion Manager

(513) 412-5650
• George Vogel, Executive Sports Producer
(513) 412-5000
• George Vogel, Sports Director
(513) 412-5088

WMAQ TV CHICAGO
454 N. COLUMBUS DR, 1ST FL
CHICAGO, IL 60611-5514
312-836-5555
Fax: 317-527-5925
www.nbc5.com
• Larry Wert, NBC 5 President and General Manager
• Vicky Burns, News Director
• Sharon Brooks Buchanan, National Sales Manager
• Patricia Golden, VP/Dir Sls
• Toni Falvo, Dir Research Marketing and Press

WMAQ-TV
454 NORTH COLUMBUS DRIVE
CHICAGO, IL 60611-5555
312-836-5555
Fax: 312-527-5925
http://www.nbc5.com
• Jody Bajor, Marketing Manager
(312) 836-5551
jody.bajor@nbc.com
• Ryan Baker, Weekend Sports Anchor/Reporter
(312) 836-5555
• Tony Capriolo, Sports Executive Producer
(312) 836-5665
tony.capriolo@nbc.com
• V. Hannes, Sports Host
• Peggy Kusinski, Sports Reporter
(312) 836-5555
marion.brooks@nbc.com
• Mark Schanowski, Sports Reporter
• Frank Whittaker, Vice President
(312) 836-5654
frank.whittaker@nbc.com

WMAZ-TV
1314 GRAY HIGHWAY
MACON, GA 31211-1904
478-752-1313
Fax: 478-752-1429
eyewitnessnews@13wmaz.com
http://www.13wmaz.com
• Jeff Dudley, Marketing Manager
jdudley@13wmaz.com
• David Solano, Sports Director
(478) 752-1393
dsolano@13wmaz.com
• Suzanne Lawler, News/Sports Anchor/Reporter
(478) 752-1313

WMBB-TV
613 HARRISON AVENUE
PANAMA CITY, FL 32401
850-769-2313
Fax: 850-769-8231
http://www.wmbb.com
• Christian Ashley, Sports Director
• Kyle Burger, Sports Director
(850) 769-2313

WMC-TV
1960 UNION AVENUE
MEMPHIS, TN 38104-4031

901-726-0555
Fax: 901-278-7633
http://www.wmcstations.com
• Jarvis Greer, Sports Director
(901) 726-0568
jgreer@wmctv.com
• Carrie Anderson, Sports Reporter
(901) 726-0555

WMGM-TV
1601 NEW ROAD
LINWOOD, NJ 08221-1116
609-927-4440 EXT 200
Fax: 609-926-8875
http://www.nbc40.net
• Pete Thompson, Sports Director
(609) 927-4440
• Rob Brennan, Weekend Sports Anchor
(609) 927-4440
rbrennan@nbc40.net

WMTW-TV
P.O. BOX 8
AUBURN, ME 04210-8693
207-782-1800
Fax: 207-782-2165
news8wmtw@hearst.com
http://www.wmtw.com/
• Norm Karkos, Sports Director
• Dave Guthro, Sports Anchor/Reporter
(207) 782-1800

WMUR-TV
100 SOUTH COMMERCIAL STREET
MANCHESTER, NH 03101
603-669-9999
800-257-5151
Fax: 603-641-9005
news@wmur.com
http://www.thewmurchannel.com
• Jason King, Sports Anchor
(603) 669-9999
• Jamie Staton, Sports Anchor
(603) 669-9999
jstaton@hearst.com
• Naoko Funayama, Sports Anchor/Reporter/Producer
(603) 669-9999
nfunayama@hearst.com

WNBC-TV
30 ROCKEFELLER PLAZA
NEW YORK, NY 10112-0002
212-664-4444
Fax: 212-664-2994
newstips@wnbc.com
http://www.wnbc.com
• Bruce Beck, Weekend Sports Anchor
(212) 664-2903
Bruce.Beck@nbcuni.com
• Len Berman, Sports Anchor
(212) 664-4990
• Len Berman, Sports Director
newstips@wnbc.com
• Anna Carbonell, Vice President
newstips@wnbc.com
• Otis Livingston, Morning Sports Anchor
(212) 664-4444

WNCN-TV
1205 FRONT STREET
RALEIGH, NC 27609-7526
919-836-1717
Fax: 919-836-1687
http://www.nbc17.com

• Josh Adams, Sports Producer
(919) 836-1717
• Maryann Balbo, Marketing Director
(919) 835-6223
• Penn Holderness, Sports Reporter/Anchor
(919) 836-1717

WNEM-TV
P.O. BOX 531
SAGINAW, MI 48607
989-758-2044
800-522-9636
Fax: 989-758-2111
wnem@wnem.com
http://www.wnem.com
• Scott Kuhl, Sports Director
• Darryl Sellers, Sports Anchor/Reporter
(989) 758-2044

WNJU-TV
2200 FLETCHER AVENUE 6TH FLOOR
FORT LEE, NJ 07024
201-969-4047
Fax: 201-969-4120
http://www.telemundo47.com/index.html
• Veronica Contreras, Sports Anchor
veronica.contreras@nbcuni.com

WNWO-TV
300 SOUTH BYRNE ROAD
TOLEDO, OH 43615-6217
419-535-0024
Fax: 419-535-8936
news@nbc24.com
http://www.nbc24.com
• Jim Tichy, Sports Anchor
jtichy@nbc24.com
• Jim Tichy, Sports Director
• Ryan Fowler, Sports Reporter/Videographer
(419) 535-0024

WNYW-TV
205 EAST 67TH STREET
NEW YORK, NY 10021-6089
212-452-3808
Fax: 212-452-5512
http://www.myfoxny.com
• Lou Albanese, Sports Senior Producer
(212) 452-3784
lou.albanese@foxtv.com
• Ken Ashley, Promotion Director
• Scott Matthews, Vice President
fox5news@hotmail.com

WOAI-TV
P.O. BOX 2641
SAN ANTONIO, TX 78205-1321
210-226-4444
Fax: 210-224-9898
http://www.woai.com
• David Chancellor, Sports Anchor/Reporter
(210) 226-4444
davidchancellor@woai.com
• Don Harris, Sports Anchor
(210) 476-1036
donharris@woai.com
• Brooks Hogg, Vice President

WOFL-TV
35 SKYLINE DRIVE
LAKE MARY, FL 32746-6202
407-644-3535
Fax: 407-741-5189
http://www.fox35wofl.com

- Eric Clinkscales, Sports Anchor
- Eric Clinkscales, Sports Reporter
- Rick Snyder, Promotion Manager
- Thomas Forester, Sports Anchor
(407) 644-3535

WOI-TV
3903 WESTOWN PARKWAY
WEST DES MOINES, IA 50266
515-457-1026
800-858-5555
Fax: 515-457-1025
http://www.woi-tv.com
- Ray Cole, President
- Doug Sawyer, Promotions Manager
(515) 457-9645
- John Walters, Sports Director
- Eric Murphy, Weekend Sports Anchor
(515) 457-1026

WOIO-TV
1717 EAST 12TH STREET
CLEVELAND, OH 44114-3230
216-771-1943
800-929-0132
Fax: 216-436-5460
19tips@woio.com
http://www.woio.com
- Brian Duffy, Sports Anchor/Reporter
(216) 781-1900
bduffy@raycommedia.com

WOLO-TV
P.O. BOX 4217
COLUMBIA, SC 29223-7209
803-754-7525
Fax: 803-691-4015
http://www.wolo.com
- Jeff Floyd, Promotions Manager
(803) 754-7525
- Tim Hill, Sports Director
(803) 754-7525
THill@abccolumbia.com

WOWT-TV
3501 FARNAM STREET
OMAHA, NE 68131
402-346-6666
800-688-2431
Fax: 402-233-7888
sixonline@wowt.com
http://www.wowt.com
- John Chapman, Sports Anchor
(402) 346-6666
john.chapman@wowt.com
- Merlyn Klaus, Sports Producer
(402) 346-6666
merlyn.klaus@wowt.com
- Dave Webber, Sports Director
dave.webber@wowt.com

WPBN-TV
8513 M-72 WEST
TRAVERSE CITY, MI 49684
231-947-7770
800-968-7770
Fax: 231-947-0354
http://www.tv7-4.com
- Jerome Helminiak, Sports Director
(231) 995-5832
- Greg Johnson, Promotions Manager
(231) 995-5900
- Thom Pritz, Advertising Manager
(231) 995-5810
- Jayson Geiser, Sports Anchor/Reporter
(231) 947-7770

WPDE-TV
1194 ATLANTIC AVENUE
CONWAY, SC 29526
843-234-9733
800-698-4733
Fax: 843-234-9739
http://www.wpdetv.com
- Rich Chrampanis, Sports Director
(843) 234-9733
- Billy Huggins, Vice President

WPHL-TV
5001 WYNNEFIELD AVENUE
PHILADELPHIA, PA 19131-2504
215-878-1700
Fax: 215-879-7682
http://www.wb17.com
- Matt Biondi, Sports Anchor (Weekend)
- Wendy Kaiser, Promotion Director
(215) 883-3355
- Sabrina Pacifico, Publicity Coordinator
(215) 878-3334

WPIX-TV
220 EAST 42ND STREET
NEW YORK, NY 10017-5529
212-210-2411
Fax: 212-210-2591
http://cw11.trb.com
- Betty Ellen Berlamino, Vice President
(212) 210-2650
- Lolita Lopez, Sports Weekend Anchor
(212) 949-1100
- Sal Marchiano, Weeknight Sports Anchor
(212) 210-2411
- Bob Taute, Sports Director

WPLG-TV
3900 BISCAYNE BOULEVARD
MIAMI, FL 33137-3786
305-325-2370
Fax: 305-325-2480
newsdesk@wplg.com
http://www.local10.com
- Jimmy Cefalo, Sports Director
(305) 325-2484
jcefalo@wplg.com
- Henry Amor, Sports Producer
(305) 325-2370
hamor@local10.com

WPMI - NBC 15
661 AZALEA RD
MOBILE, AL 36609
251-602-1500
Fax: 251-602-1547
- Pat Greenwood, Sports Director
- Sharon Moloney, Vice President/General Manager
Alabama Collegiate Sports:
Alabama Athletics Auburn Athletics University of South Alabama Spring Hill College University of Mobile.
Neilsen Market:
62
Affiliate
NBC.
Professional Sports Teams:
New Orleans Saints (NFL), Mobile Reverlers (National Basketball Development League). Mobile BayBears (Southern League/AA) NASCAR Atlanta Braves (MLB) Mobile Wizards (Arena Football League).

WPNE-TV
821 UNIVERSITY AVENUE
MADISON, WI 53706
800-422-9707
Fax: 608-263-9763
comments@wpt.org
http://www.wpt.org
- Deb Piper, Sports Director
(608) 263-4222
piper@wpt.org

WPRI-TV
25 CATAMORE BOULEVARD
EAST PROVIDENCE, RI 02914-1203
401-438-7200
Fax: 401-431-1012
desk@wpri.com
http://www.wpri.com/
- Patrick Little, Sports Director
(401) 438-7200
plittle@wpri.com
- Robb Garofalo, Sports Anchor
(401) 438-7200
rgarofalo@wpri.com

WPTV-TV
1100 BANYAN BOULEVARD
WEST PALM BEACH, FL 33401-5000
561-653-5700
800-930-9766
Fax: 561-653-5719
newstips@wptv.com
http://www.wptv.com
- Ben Becker, Sports Director
newstips@wptv.com
- Jay Gilmore, Sports Reporter/Anchor
(561) 653-5700

WPTY-TV
2701 UNION AVENUE EXTENSION
MEMPHIS, TN 38112
901-323-2430
800-346-3030
Fax: 901-452-1820
http://www.abc24.com
- Greg Gaston, Sports Director
(901) 321-7617
greggaston@clearchannel.com
- Ari Bergeron, Sports Anchor/Reporter
(901) 323-2430

WPVI-TV
4100 CITY LINE AVENUE
PHILADELPHIA, PA 19131-1610
215-878-9700
Fax: 215-581-4530
cyber6@abc.com
http://www.wpvi.com
- Rebecca Campbell, President
- Paula McDermott, Marketing Director
(215) 581-4570
- Keith Russell, Sports Reporter/Weekend Sports Anchor
(215) 878-9700
- Kevin Russell, Sports Reporter
- Caroline Welch, Promotion Director
- Jamie Apody, Sports Reporter/Anchor
(215) 878-9700

WPXI-TV
4145 EVERGREEN ROAD
PITTSBURGH, PA 15214-4025
412-237-1100
800-237-9794
Fax: 412-237-4900

assignments@wpxi.com
http://www.wpxi.com
• John Fedko, Sports Director
(412) 237-1212
jfedko@wpxi.com
• Karen Lah, Promotions Director
(412) 237-1101
klah@wpxi.com

WQAD-TV
3003 PARK 16TH STREET
MOLINE, IL 61265-6060
309-764-8888
Fax: 309-764-5763
news@wqad.com
http://www.wqad.com
• Dan Burich, Sports Director
(309) 736-3325
dan.burich@wqad.com
• Mick Moninghoff, Sports Director
(309) 764-8888

WRBL-TV
1350 13TH AVENUE
COLUMBUS, GA 31901-2303
706-324-6397
Fax: 706-323-0841
news@wrbl.com
http://www.wrbl.com
• Stuart Webber, Sports Director
(706) 324-6397
swebber@wrbl.com

WRC-TV
4001 NEBRASKA AVENUE, N.W.
WASHINGTON, DC 20016-2733
202-885-4000
Fax: 202-885-4104
http://www.nbc4.com
• Wally Bruckner, Sports Reporter
(202) 885-4111
wally.bruckner@nbcuni.com
• Jeff Greenberg, Sports Producer
(202) 885-4870
• Joe Schreiber, Senior Sports Producer
(202) 885-3026
• Donna Weston, Promotions Vice President
donna.weston@nbcuni.com
• Nicole Zaloumis, Sports Reporter
• Lindsay Czarniak, Weekend Sports
Anchor/Reporter
(202) 885-4000

WRCB-TV
900 WHITEHALL ROAD
CHATTANOOGA, TN 37405-3247
423-267-5412
Fax: 423-756-3148
news@wrcbtv.com
http://www.wrcbtv.com
• Randy Smith, Sports Director
(423) 267-5412

WREG-TV
803 CHANNEL 3 DRIVE
MEMPHIS, TN 38103-4603
901-543-2333
800-766-3973
Fax: 901-543-2167
news@wreg.com
http://www.wreg.com
• Glenn Carver, Sports Director
(901) 543-2333
glenn.carver@wreg.com

WRGB-TV
1400 BALLTOWN ROAD
SCHENECTADY, NY 12309-4301
518-381-4988
Fax: 518-346-6249
news@cbs6albany.com
http://www.wrgb.com
• Doug Sherman, Sports Director
(518) 381-4988
• Tim Mack, Weekend Sports Anchor
(518) 381-4988

WRIC TV-8
301 ARBORETUM PLACE
RICHMOND, VA 23236-3464
804-330-8888
Fax: 804-330-8883
www.wric.com
• Tom Best, General Manager
• Dan Klintworth, Station Manager
• Bill Foy, News Director
Nielsen Rank:
60
Affiliate:
ABC.
Sports:
All.
Richmond Sports Teams:
Richmond Braves (Minor League Baseball)
Richmond Kickers (Soccer) Richmond
Renegades (Minor Lg Hockey) Richmond
Speed (Arena Football Lg)..

WRIC-TV
301 ARBORETUM PLACE
RICHMOND, VA 23236-3490
804-330-8888
Fax: 804-330-8883
news@wric.com
http://www.wric.com
• Chip Tarkenton, Sports Director
(804) 330-8888
ctarkenton@wric.com
• Dawn Davenport, Weekend Sports Anchor
; Reporter
(804) 330-8888
ddavenport@wric.com

WRNN-TV
721 BROADWAY
KINGSTON, NY 12401-3449
845-339-6397
800-824-3302
Fax: 845-339-6210
http://www.rnntv.com
• Kevin Connors, Sports Director
(845) 339-6397

WSAW-TV
1114 GRAND AVENUE
WAUSAU, WI 54403-6688
715-845-4211
Fax: 715-845-2649
news@wsaw.com
http://www.wsaw.com
• Mike Jacques, Sports Director
(715) 845-4211
mjacques@wsaw.com
• John Allee, Sports Reporter
(715) 845-4211
jallee@wsaw.com

WSAZ-TV
P.O. BOX 2115
HUNTINGTON, WV 25701

304-690-3069
800-426-1075
Fax: 304-208-3065
joe.wallace@wsaz.com
http://www.wsaz.com
• Matt Jaquinte, Advertising Manager
(304) 690-3003
matt.jaquinte@wsaz.com
• Keith Morehouse, Sports Director
(304) 697-4780
keith.morehouse@wsaz.com

WSB-TV
1601 WEST PEACHTREE STREET, N.E.
ATLANTA, GA 30309-2641
404-897-6270
Fax: 404-897-7370
assignmentdesk@wsbtv.com
http://www.wsbtv.com
• Chuck Dowdle, Sports Anchor
(404) 897-6270
chuck.dowdle@wsbtv.com
• Kevin Gerke, Sports Producer
(404) 897-7745
kevin.gerke@wsbtv.com
• Barry Sinnock, Promotions Director
(404) 897-7454
barry.sinnock@wsbtv.com

WSBK-TV
1170 SOLDIERS FIELD ROAD
BOSTON, MA 02134-1004
617-787-7000
Fax: 617-254-6383
http://tv38.com
• Angie Kucharski, Vice President
(617) 746-8353
• Bob Lobel, Sports Director
(617) 787-7000
• Julio Marenghi, President
(617) 787-7123

WSBT-TV
300 WEST JEFFERSON BOULEVARD
SOUTH BEND, IN 46601-1513
574-233-3141
800-872-3141
Fax: 574-288-6630
wsbtnews@wsbt.com
http://www.wsbt.com
• Charlie Adams, Sports Director
(574) 472-8119
nwsrm@wsbt.com
• Tom Lebuzienski, Advertising Manager
tom@wsbt.com
• Peter Byrne, Sports Anchor
(574) 233-3141
pmbyrne@wsbt.com

WSEE-TV
1220 PEACH STREET
ERIE, PA 16501
814-455-7575
Fax: 814-454-2564
http://www.35wsee.com
• Gary Drapcho, Sports Director
(814) 455-7575

WSFA-TV
P.O. BOX 251200
MONTGOMERY, AL 36105
334-284-5276
Fax: 334-613-8303
http://www.wsfa.com
• Edith Parten, Marketing Director
• Edith Parten, Promotions Director

• Jeff Shearer, Sports Director
(334) 284-5276
jshearer@wsfa.com

WSIL-TV
1416 COUNTRY AIR DRIVE
CARTERVILLE, IL 62918
618-985-2333
Fax: 618-985-6482
newsdesk@wsiltv.com
http://www.wsil3.com
• Darren Kinnard, Sports Director
sports@wsiltv.com

WSLS-TV
P.O. BOX 10
ROANOKE, VA 24011
540-981-9126
800-800-9757
Fax: 540-343-2059
news@wsls.com
http://www.wsls.com
• Justin Ditmore, Sports Director
(540) 981-9126

WSMV-TV
5700 KNOB ROAD
NASHVILLE, TN 37209-4523
615-353-4444
Fax: 615-353-2343
news@wsmv.com
http://www.wsmv.com
• Tim Hall, Promotions Manager
(615) 353-2203
thall@wsmv.com
• Rudy Kalis, Sports Director
(615) 353-4444
rkalis@wsmv.com
• Brad Hopkins, Sports Reporter/Host
(615) 353-4444

WSNS-TV
454 NORTH COLUMBUS DRIVE
CHICAGO, IL 60614-3877
312-836-3000
Fax: 312-836-3232
TelemundoChicagoAssignment@telemundo
.com
http://www.telemundochicago.com
• Oscar Guzman, Sports News Anchor
(312) 836-3000
TelemundoChicagoAssignment@telemundo
.com

WSOC-TV
P.O. BOX 34665
CHARLOTTE, NC 28206-2733
704-335-4871
Fax: 704-335-4736
assignment@wsoc-tv.com
http://www.wsoctv.com
• Harold Johnson, Sports Reporter
(704) 335-4746
assignment@wsoc-tv.com
• Jarod Latch, Sports Reporter
(704) 335-4871

WSPA-TV
P.O. BOX 1717
SPARTANBURG, SC 29303-6637
864-576-7777
Fax: 864-595-4600
newschannel7@wspa.com
http://www.wspa.com
• Bill Shatten, Advertising Manager
(864) 587-4455

bshatten@wspa.com
• Bill Shatten, Marketing Manager
(864) 587-4455
bshatten@wspa.com
• Pete Yanity, Sports Director
pyanity@wspa.com
• Ken Griner, Sports Photographer
(864) 576-7777
kgriner@wspa.com

WSVN-TV
1401 79TH STREET CAUSEWAY
MIAMI, FL 33141-4104
305-795-2777
800-845-7777
Fax: 305-795-2746
newsdesk@wsvn.com
http://www.wsvn.com
• Mike DiPasquale, Sports Anchor
(305) 795-2777
mdipasquale@wsvn.com
• Jim Goodman, Sports Producer
• Steve Shapiro, Sports Anchor
(305) 795-2777
sshapiro@wsvn.com
• Steve Shapiro, Sports Reporter
(305) 795-2777
sshapiro@wsvn.com
• Donovan Campbell, Sports
Reporter/Anchor
(305) 795-2777

WTAP-TV
1 TELEVISION PLAZA
PARKERSBURG, WV 26101-5373
304-485-4588
800-300-9827
Fax: 304-422-3920
news@wtap.com
http://www.wtap.com
• Joyce Ancrile, Promotion Manager
• James Wharton, Sports Director
(304) 485-6397
• Chris Brett, Weekend Sports Anchor
(304) 485-4588

WTEN NEWS 10/ABC
341 NORTHERN BLVD
ALBANY, NY 12204
518-436-4822
Fax: 518-426-4792
www.wten.com
• Bob Peterson, General Manager
• Dan Murphy, Sports Director
• Terry Kowalski, Marketing & Promotions
Director
Affiliate:
ABC.
Neilsen Rank:
56
Sports:
All.

WTEN-TV
341 NORTHERN BOULEVARD
ALBANY, NY 12204-1001
518-436-4822
Fax: 518-426-4792
news@wten.com
http://www.wten.com
• Terry Kowalski, Marketing Director
terry@wten.com
• Terry Kowalski, Promotions Director
terry@wten.com
• Dan Murphy, Sports Director
dan.murphy@wten.com
• Jamie Seh, Sports Reporter

(518) 436-4822
jamie.seh@wten.com

WTEV-TV
11700 CENTRAL PARKWAY
JACKSONVILLE, FL 32224-2600
904-642-3030
Fax: 904-642-5665
http://www.wtev.com
• Barry Buetel, Sports Director
barrybuetel@clearchannel.com

WTHI-TV
918 OHIO STREET
TERRE HAUTE, IN 47807
812-232-9481
Fax: 812-232-8953
action10news@wthitv.com
http://www.wthi.com
• Liam McHugh, Sports Director
(812) 232-4953
lmchugh@wthi.emmis.com
• Dick Telezyn, Advertising Manager
(812) 232-9481
dtelezyn@wthitv.com

WTHR-TV
P.O. BOX 1313
INDIANAPOLIS, IN 46204-1015
317-636-1313
Fax: 317-632-6720
http://www.wthr.com
• Dave Calabro, Sports Director
(317) 655-5754
dcalabro@wthr.com
• Rich Nye, Weekend Morning Sports
Anchor
(317) 636-1313
rnye@wthr.com
• Don Hein, Sports Reporter
(317) 636-1313
dhein@wthr.com

WTIC-TV
1 CORPORATE CENTER
HARTFORD, CT 06103-3290
860-527-6161
Fax: 860-727-0158
http://fox61.trb.com/
• Rich Coppola, Sports Director
(860) 723-2068
rcoppola@fox61.com

WTKR-TV
720 BOUSH STREET
NORFOLK, VA 23510-1502
757-446-1352
Fax: 757-446-1376
desk@wtkr.com
http://www.wtkr.com
• Ted Alexander, Sports Director
(757) 446-1361
ted.alexander@wtkr.com

WTMJ-TV
720 EAST CAPITOL DRIVE
MILWAUKEE, WI 53212-1308
414-332-9611
Fax: 414-967-5378
news@todaystmj4.com
http://www.todaystmj4.com
• Lance Allan, Sports Anchor
(414) 967-5368
jallan@todaystmj4.com
• Gregg Schraufnagel, Marketing Manager
(414) 332-9611

gschraufnagel@journalbroadcastgroup.com
• Erick Weber, Sports Reporter (Football NFL)

WTNH-TV
8 ELM STREET
NEW HAVEN, CT 06510-2006
203-784-8888
Fax: 203-789-2010
news8@wtnh.com
http://www.wtnh.com
• Noah Finz, Sports Director
(203) 784-8888
noah.finz@wtnh.com
• Paul Spingola, Promotions Director
• Mary Lee Weber, Marketing Director

WTOC-TV
P.O. BOX 8086
SAVANNAH, GA 31405
912-234-6397
Fax: 912-232-4945
http://www.wtoctv.com
• Rick Snow, Sports Director
(912) 234-1111
• Tiffany Greene, Sports Reporter
(912) 234-6397
tiffanygreene@wtoc.com

WTOL-TV
730 NORTH SUMMIT STREET
TOLEDO, OH 43604-1808
419-248-1111
800-248-9865
Fax: 419-244-7104
news@wtol.com
http://www.wtol.com
• Gary Albers, Promotion Manager
(419) 248-1170
galbers@wtol.com
• Gary Albers, Promotions Manager
(419) 248-1170
galbetrs@wtol.com
• Dan Cummins, Sports Director
(419) 248-1111
dcummins@wtol.com

WTOM-TV
8518 M-72 WEST
TRAVERSE CITY, MI 49684
231-947-7770
800-968-7770
Fax: 231-947-0354
http://www.tv7-4.com
• Jerome Helmeniak, Sports Director
(231) 995-5863

WTOV-TV
9 RED DONLEY PLAZA
MINGO JUNCTION, OH 43938
740-282-0911
800-288-0799
Fax: 740-282-0439
http://www.wtov.com
• Sherry Hansen, Promotions Manager
(740) 282-0911
shansen@wtov.com
• Don Sloan, Sports Director
(740) 282-0911
dsloan@wtov.com

WTRF-TV
96 16TH STREET
WHEELING, WV 26003-3660
304-232-7777
800-777-9873

Fax: 304-232-4975
http://www.wtrf.com
• Scott Nolte, Sports Director
(304) 230-6293
snolte@wtrf.com
• Mike Anthony, Sports Anchor
(304) 230-6286

WTSP-TV
P.O. BOX 10000
SAINT PETERSBURG, FL 33702-1908
727-577-1010
Fax: 727-576-6924
10news@tampabays10.com
http://www.wtsp.com
• John Nugent, Sports Director
(617) 474-5513
• Justin Allen, Sports Anchor/Reporter
(727) 577-1010

WTTG-TV
5151 WISCONSIN AVENUE, N.W.
WASHINGTON, DC 20016-4124
202-244-5151
Fax: 202-895-3133
wttg.desk@foxtv.com
http://www.fox5dc.com
• Dave Feldman, Sports Anchor
assignment.desk@wttg.com
• Dave Feldman, Sports Director
assignment.desk@wttg.com
• Lou Holder, Weekend Sports Anchor
(202) 244-5151

WTVC-TV
4279 BENTON DRIVE
CHATTANOOGA, TN 37406
423-756-5500
Fax: 423-757-7400
news@newschannel9.com
http://www.newschannel9.com
• Ronnie Minton, Marketing Director
rminton@newschannel9.com
• Darrell Patterson, Sports Director
(423) 757-7332
darrell@newschannel9.com

WTVD-TV
411 LIBERTY STREET
DURHAM, NC 27701-3407
919-687-2212
Fax: 919-687-4373
wtvdassignmentdesk@abc.com
http://www.abc11tv.com
• Drew Smith, Sports Director
• Mark Armstrong, Sports Anchor
(919) 687-2212
mark.armstrong@abc.com

WTVF-TV
474 JAMES ROBERTSON PARKWAY
NASHVILLE, TN 37219-1212
615-244-5000
Fax: 615-244-9883
newsroom@newschannel5.com
http://www.newschannel5.com
• Hope Hines, Sports Anchor
(615) 244-5223
hhines@newschannel5.com
• Hope Hines, Sports Director
(615) 244-5223
• Mark Howard, Sports Anchor
mhoward@newschannel5.com
• Mark Howard, Sports Reporter
mhoward@newschannel5.com
• Eric Yutzy, Sports Reporter

(615) 244-5000
sports@newschannel5.com
• Eric Yutzy, Sports Reporter
sports@newschannel5.com
• Kami Carmann, Sports Reporter
(615) 244-5000
sports@newschannel5.com

WTVH-TV
980 JAMES STREET
SYRACUSE, NY 13203-2503
315-425-5555
Fax: 315-425-0129
http://www.wtvh.com
• Kevin Maher, Sports Director
(315) 477-4637
• Rishi Barran, Sports Anchor
(315) 425-5555

WTVJ-TV
15000 SOUTHWEST 27TH STREET
MIRAMAR, FL 33027-4147
954-622-6000
Fax: 954-622-6107
newsroom@nbc6.net
http://www.nbc6.net
• Maria Khalil-Pagani, Promotions Manager
• Guy Rawlings, Sports Anchor
(954) 622-6355
• Joe Rose, Sports Anchor
(954) 622-6359
• Adam Kuperstein, Sports Anchor/Reporter
(954) 622-6000

WTVM-TV
P.O. BOX 1848
COLUMBUS, GA 31906-2931
706-324-6471
Fax: 706-322-7527
newsleader@wtvm.com
http://www.wtvm.com
• Adelaide Kirk, Advertising Manager
akirk@wtvm.com
• Dave Platta, Sports Director
dplatta@wtvm.com
• David Platta, Sports Director
(706) 322-5734
dplatta@wtvm.com

WTVO-TV
1917 NORTH MERIDIAN ROAD
ROCKFORD, IL 61101-9215
815-963-5413
Fax: 815-963-0029
newsdesk@wtvo.com
http://www.wtvo.com
• Scott Leber, Sports Director/Weekday Anchor - 5, 6 &
(815) 963-5413
sports@wtvo.com
• Vince Conway, Weekend Sports Anchor/Reporter
(815) 963-5413
vconway@wtvo.com

WTVT-TV
3213 WEST KENNEDY BOULEVARD
TAMPA, FL 33609-3006
813-876-1313
Fax: 813-871-5815
http://www.myfoxtampabay.com/myfox/
• Chip Carter, Sports Director
(813) 870-9733
• Chris Field, Sports Anchor
(813) 870-7105

- Mike House, Promotions Director
- Carrie Schroeder, Promotions Director

WTVW-TV
477 CARPENTER STREET
EVANSVILLE, IN 47708-1027
812-424-7777
800-511-6009
Fax: 812-421-7289
http://www.wtvw.com
- Mark McVicar, Sports Director
(812) 433-5572
- Doug Kufner, Sports Anchor/Reporter
(812) 424-7777

WTVY-TV
P.O. BOX 1089
DOTHAN, AL 36303
334-792-3195
Fax: 334-712-7452
http://www.wtvynews4.com
- Brad Sherwood, Sports Director
(334) 712-7419
bsherwood@wtvynews4.com
- Kelly O'Donnell, Sports Anchor
(334) 792-3195
kelly@wtvynews4.com

WTXF-TV
330 MARKET STREET
PHILADELPHIA, PA 19106-2706
215-925-2929
800-220-6397
Fax: 215-982-5494
http://www.foxphiladelphia.com
- Larry Fernchick, Marketing Director
(215) 925-2929
- Don Tollefson, Sports Director
(215) 925-7085
- Tom Sredenschek, Senior Sports Producer
(215) 925-2929

WUAB-TV
1717 EAST 12TH STREET
CLEVELAND, OH 44114-3230
216-771-1943
800-929-0132
Fax: 216-436-5460
19tips@woio.com
http://www.wuab.com
- Rob Boenau, Marketing Director
(216) 367-7111
rboenau@woio.com
- Chuck Galeti, Sports Reporter/Anchor
(216) 771-1943
cgaleti@woio.com

WUSA-TV
4100 WISCONSIN AVENUE, N.W.
WASHINGTON, DC 20016-2810
202-895-5999
Fax: 202-364-6163
http://www.wusa9.com
- Brett Haber, Sports Director
(202) 895-5999
bhaber@wusa9.com
- Levan Reid, Sports Anchor (Weekend)

WVEC-TV
613 WOODIS AVENUE
NORFOLK, VA 23510-1017
757-625-1313
Fax: 757-628-5855
http://www.wvec.com

- Scott Cash, Sports Director
(757) 628-6215
scash@wvec.com
- Matt Earl, Promotion Manager
(757) 625-1313
mearl@wvec.com

WVII-TV
371 TARGET INDUSTRIAL CIRCLE
BANGOR, ME 04401-5721
207-945-6457
800-499-9844
Fax: 207-945-6864
tv7news@wvii.com
http://www.wvii.com
- Gene Hardin, Promotions Director
ghardin@wvii.com
- Ted Lombardi, Sports Director
(207) 945-6457
sports@wvii.com

WVIT-TV
1422 NEW BRITAIN AVENUE
WEST HARTFORD, CT 06110-1632
860-521-3030
800-523-9848
Fax: 860-521-4860
newstips@nbc30.com
http://www.wvit.com/
- Kevin Nathan, Sports Anchor
- Persefone Contos, Sports Anchor
(860) 521-3030

WVLT-TV
P.O. BOX 59088
KNOXVILLE, TN 37919-4815
865-450-8880
Fax: 865-584-1978
wvltnews@wvlt-tv.com
http://www.volunteertv.com
- Dino Cartwright, Promotions Director
dino.cartwright@wvlt-tv.com
- Rick Russo, Sports Director
(865) 450-8880
rick.russo@wvlt-tv.com
- Daryl Hobby, Sports Anchor/Reporter
(865) 450-8880
daryl.hobby@wvlt-tv.com

WVTM-TV
1732 VALLEY VIEW DRIVE
BIRMINGHAM, AL 35209-1251
205-558-7300
800-947-6397
Fax: 205-323-3314
http://www.nbc13.com
- Rob Carlin, Sports Anchor
(205) 933-1313
- Jim Dunaway, Sports Director
(205) 933-1313
- Don Hawes, Sports Director
(205) 558-7300
dhawes@wvtm.com

WVUT-TV
1200 NORTH 2ND STREET
VINCENNES, IN 47591-2325
812-888-4135
Fax: 812-882-2237
- Tony Cloyd, Sports Director
(812) 888-5283
tcloyd@vinu.edu

WWAY-TV
615 NORTH FRONT STREET
WILMINGTON, NC 28402-3325

910-762-8581
Fax: 910-762-8367
http://www.wwaytv3.com
- Gene Motley, Sports Director
(910) 762-8581

WWBT-TV
P.O. BOX 12
RICHMOND, VA 23225-6116
804-230-1212
Fax: 804-230-2789
newsroom@nbc12.com
http://www.nbc12.com
- Eileen Cowel, Promotions Director
ecowel@nbc12.com
- Ben Hamlin, Sports Director
(804) 230-1212
bhamlin@nbc12.com
- Paula Hersh, Marketing Director
phersh@nbc12.com
- Nancy Kent, Vice President

WWLP-TV
ONE BROADCAST CTR.
CHICOPEE, MA 01013
413-786-2200
Fax: 413-377-2263
news@wwlp.com
http://www.wwlp.com
- Anna Giza, Promotion Manager
agiza@wwlp.com
- William M. Pepin, President
(413) 377-2236
bpepin@wwlp.com
- Rich Tettemer, Sports Director
(413) 786-2200
rtettemer@wwlp.com

WWMT-TV
590 WEST MAPLE STREET
KALAMAZOO, MI 49008-1926
269-388-9339
Fax: 269-388-8322
desk@wwmt.com
http://www.wwmt.com/
- Ed Kengerski, Sports Director
(269) 388-9339
ekengerski@wwmt.com

WWOR-TV
9 BROADCAST PLAZA
SECAUCUS, NJ 07096-2913
201-330-2215
Fax: 201-330-3844
http://www.my9ny.com/
- Rich Bagala, Sports Producer
(201) 330-2245
- Scott Matthews, Vice President
matthews@wwortv.com
- Russ Salzberg, Sports Anchor
(201) 330-2215

WWSB-TV
1477 10TH STREET
SARASOTA, FL 34236-4048
941-923-8840
Fax: 941-923-8709
wwsbnews@wwsb.tv
http://www.wwsb.com
- Kevin Negandhi, Sports Anchor
(941) 923-8840
knegandhi@wwsb.tv
- Don Brennan, Sports Director
(941) 923-6397
dbrennan@wwsb.tv

WWTV-TV
22320 130TH AVENUE
TUSTIN, MI 49688-8564
231-775-3478
800-782-7910
Fax: 231-775-3671
webmaster@9and10news.com
http://www.9and10news.com
• Tessia Clix, Promotions Director
tessiaclix@9and10news.com
• Mario Iacobelli, Owner
(231) 775-3478
marioiacobelli@9and10news.com
• Brian Lawson, Sports Director
(231) 775-3478
brianlawson@9and10news.com
• Luke Notestine, Sports Reporter/Anchor
(231) 775-3478
LukeNotestine@9and10news.com

WWUP-TV
22320 130TH AVENUE
TUSTIN, MI 49688-8564
231-775-3478
800-782-7910
Fax: 231-775-3671
webmaster@9and10news.com
http://www.9and10news.com
• Tessia Clix, Promotions Director
tessiaclix@9and10news.com
• Mario Iacobelli, Owner
(231) 775-3478
marioiacobelli@9and10news.com
• Brian Lawson, Sports Director
(231) 775-3478
brianlawson@9and10news.com
• Aaron Mills, Sports Director
(231) 775-3478
AaronMills@9and10news.com

WXIA-TV
1611 WEST PEACHTREE STREET, N.E.
ATLANTA, GA 30309-2641
404-873-9114
Fax: 404-881-0675
news@11alive.com
http://www.11alive.com
• Fred Kalil, Sports Anchor
(404) 873-9145
fkalil@11alive.com
• Fred Kalil, Sports Director
(404) 873-9114
• Kristy Revero, Sports Producer
krevero@wxia.gannett.com
• Sam Crenshaw, Weekend Sports Anchor
(404) 873-9114
screnshaw@11alive.com

WXOW-TV
3705 CTH25
LA CRESCENT, MN 55947
507-895-9969
Fax: 507-895-8124
wxow@wxow.com
http://www.wxow.com
• Scott Emerich, Sports Director
• Laramie McClurg, Promotions Manager
lmcclurg@wxow.com
• Brian Schumacher, Advertising Manager
bschumacher@wxow.com

WXVT-TV
3015 EAST REED ROAD
GREENVILLE, MS 38703-9452
662-334-1500
800-489-9988

Fax: 662-378-8122
http://www.wxvt.com
• Beverly Ford, Promotions Director
(662) 334-1500
• Stephen Robinson, Sports Anchor ;
Reporter
(662) 334-1500
stephen@wxvt.com
• Tony Byrd, Sports Anchor
(662) 334-1500
tbyrd@wxvt.com

WXXA-TV
28 CORPORATE CIRCLE
ALBANY, NY 12203-5121
518-862-0995
Fax: 518-862-0930
www.fox23news.com
• Rich Becker, Sports Director
(518) 862-0995
richbecker@clearchannel.com
• Scott Marlock, Sports Anchor / Reporter
(518) 822-0995
• Dani Stein, Sports Reporter /
Photographer
(518) 862-0995
Teams Covered:
NY Giants, Jets, Bills, Patriots, Siena,
UAlbany and Syracuse athletics, Union and
RPI athletics, NY Yankees, Mets, Red Sox,
NY Rangers, Isles, Sabres and Bruins, NY
Knicks and Nets

WYLN-TV
1057 TENTH STREET, E.
HAZLETON, PA 18201
570-459-1869
888-499-5635
Fax: 570-459-1383
http://www.wylntv.com
• Tim Thompson, Sports Director
(570) 459-1869

WYMT-TV
199 BLACK GOLD BOULEVARD
HAZARD, KY 41701
606-436-5757
Fax: 606-439-3760
http://www.wymtnews.com
• Brian Milam, Sports Director
(606) 436-5757
brian.milam@wymtnews.com
• Jeff Archer, Sports Reporter
(606) 436-5757
jeff.archer@wymtnews.com

WYTV-TV
3930 SUNSET BOULEVARD
YOUNGSTOWN, OH 44512
330-782-1144
Fax: 330-782-3504
jmarling@wytv.com
http://www.wytv.com
• Bob Hannon, Sports Director
bhannon@wytv.com
• Bill Castrovince, Sports Reporter
(330) 788-4046
bcastrovince@wytv.com

WZBN-TV
2600 EAST STATE STREET EXTENSION
HAMILTON, NJ 08619
609-587-2500
Fax: 609-587-0011
http://www.wzbn.com

• Greg Angelillo, Sports Reporter
(609) 587-2500

WZVN-TV
3719 CENTRAL AVENUE
FORT MYERS, FL 33901-8220
239-939-2020
Fax: 239-939-4801
http://www.abc-7.com
• Jason Kurtz, Sports Director
• Jason Kurz, Sports Director
(239) 939-2020

WZZM-TV
WZZM 13 BOX Z
GRAND RAPIDS, MI 49544-1601
616-785-1313
Fax: 616-785-1301
news@wzzm13.com
http://www.wzzm13.com/
• Henry Wofford, Sports Director
• Tom Clyde, Weekend Sports Reporter
(616) 785-1313

Sports on the World Wide Web

BLEACHER REPORT
info@bleacherreport.com
www.bleacherreport.com
• Bill McCandless, VP of Video
Programming and Production
• Dave Finocchio, Founder, VP of Content
• Dave Nemetz, Founder, VP of Business
Development
• Sam Parnell, Founder, VP of Engineering
• Joe Yanarella, Editor-in-Chief
Description:
b/r is an online medium for expert sports
writers to provide opinion and analysis of all
of the major US sports, including College,
MMA, Wrestling, and Motorsports, Cricket
and Rugby; content is provided by
thousands of professional sports writers,
and syndicated on CBSSports.com, the LA
Times, NHL.com, Hearst Newspapers,
USAToday.com, and Telegraph.co.uk. The
site also has the b/r Blog, as well as local
editions. Online subscriptions available.
Become a fan on Facebook, or follow on
Twitter
8294

CHICAGO TRIBUNE SPORTS
435 NORTH MICHIGAN AVE
CHICAGO, IL 60611
312-222-3478
800-874-2863
Fax: 312-828-9392
www.chicagosports.com
• Stuart W Courtney, Breaking Sports Editor
• Joel Boyd, Source Editor, Sports
• Tim Bannon, Deputy Sports Editor
• Christopher Boghossian, Sports Source
Editor
Description:
Focusing on 6 professional teams and
Illinois high school sports, site pools Tribune
Company media resources (Chicago
Tribune, WGN-TV, WGN Radio, and CLTV)
and others to deliver fast, accurate and
interesting sports news for Chicago sports
fans.

E-SPORTS MEDIA GROUP, INC.
3505 N. NORDICA
CHICAGO, IL 60634
773-736-7556
Fax: 775-263-1497
www.esportsmediagroup.com
• Dustin Klein, Publisher
• Rick Capone, Managing Editor
Features:
A growing number of contributing authors covering a wide variety of topics, an online sports wear super store with thousands of products, daily polls and contests, trivia and quotes, interactive games and fantasy leagues, and a portal (gateway/search engine) to other quality sports web sites on the Internet.
Description:
Owned by VSM, operator of e-sports! web site: www.e-sports.com, powered by a community of sports fans, athletes, coaches and sports media personalities.

GLOBAL REACH SPORTS
PO BOX 1417
WILLISTON, VT 05495
828-279-1674
Fax: 828-279-1674
info@globalreachsports.com
www.globalreachsports.com
• Geoff Elder, Co-Founder and Chief Technology Officer
• Katherine Ross, Co-Founder and Creative Director
• Stacy Luther, Director of Internet Development
Sports Service Founded:
1999
Description:
Organization offers Web site design and development, e-commerce solutions, content management, integrative software development, and participatory community tools and features. The organization's mission is to increase participation and services across an entire sport, starting with grassroots development on up to professional and elite-level performance. Parent organization of BikeResults.com.

GUESTMVP
104 W 4TH STREET
SUITE 301
ROYAL OAK, MI 48067
888-483-7868
Nature of Services:
GuestMVP powered by Konsyerzh, LLC. is the newest revolutionary device for the sports industry which maximizes the fan experience while providing sponsors with an interactive advertising portal - guests have the ability to order food and beverage, purchase merchandise, view instant replays, see live stats, search for local attractions, and much more.

INTERNET SPORTS AWARDS
EXCALIBUR MARKETING GROUP
4258 GERMANNA HWY, STE D-1
LOCUST GROVE, VA 22508
540-972-4690
Fax: 540-972-4691
www.isportsnet.com
Description:
Reaches over 18 million sports fans a year. Allows fans to vote for various awards.

IVRNET
1338-36TH AVENUE NE
CALGARY, AB, CANADA T2e 6T6
403-538-0400
800-351-7227
Fax: 403-538-2621
www.ivrnet.com
• David L Snell, President/Chief Executive Officer
• Chris D Groot, Vice President/Sales & Marketing
• Marcel Jacques, Senior Developer
• Frank Nemeth, Director and Developer
Description:
Organization specializes in the design and implementation of web-enabled league management software for recreational sports leagues.

MYTEAM.COM
400 UNICORN PARK, SUITE 300
WOBURN, MA 01801
781-376-9944
Fax: 781-376-8158
www.myteam.com
• Darko Dejanovic, Chief Executive Officer
• John Frascotti, President/Chief Operating Officer
• David Block, Director Technology/Development
• John Feldmeier, Director Product Development
• John Young, Vice President/Strategic Projects
• Reed Thompson, National Organization Initiatives
Description:
My Team is an online center for amateur sports.

ONLINE SPORTS
2060 WINERIDGE PLACE, SUITE C
ESCONDIDO, CA 92029
760-839-9363
800 856-2638
Fax: 760-839-9370
www.onlinesports.com
• Mike Farkas, President/Owner
• Chris Haupt, Chief Technology Officer
Nature of Sports Service:
National. On-line sports service. Serves as showplace for sports and recreation products and services on the Internet. Links to thousands of sports equipment, apparel, collectibles and services available online. Companies can list services or products directly for sale, or for promotional purposes.

ROTOWORLD
www.rotoworld.com
• Rick Cordella, Senior VP & General Manager, Digital Media
Nature of Sports Service:
Provider of Internet-based sports and financial games w/ over 30 games including full fantasy sports competitions, salary cap games, sports stock market simulations, pick'em style games and financial stock market simulations. 2 million members.

SI.COM
ONE CNN CENTER
ATLANTA, GA 30303
404-878-1600
Fax: 404-878-0011
www.si.com

• Matt Bean, Managing Editor
• Joey Trotz, Vice President, Operations, CNNSI,COM

SOCCER365.COM
3029 6TH AVE, SOUTH
BIRMINGHAM, AL 35233
205-323-3755
Fax: 205-323-2355
www.soccer365.com
• David Fleenor, Contributor

SPORTS NETWORK, THE
2200 BYBERRY RD
SUITE 200
HATBORO, PA 19040
215-441-8444
Fax: 215-441-5767
• Ken Zajac, Director of Sales
(215) 441-8444
• Bernie Greenberg, Sales
(215) 441-8444
bgreenberg@sportsnetwork.com
• Steve Cwitkowitz, Sales
(215) 441-8444
scwitkowitz@sportsnetwork.com
Description:
Organization offers real-time sports wire service furnishing sports content on a 24/7 basis using state-of-the-art technology. The data includes scores, trends, analysis, news, features, statistics, pre- and post-game reports, box scores, and historical data.

SPORTS STANDINGS, INC.
2514 TARPLEY RD, STE 104
CARROLLTON, TX 75006
972-416-8657
Fax: 972-478-7957
info@sportsstandings.com
Description:
The premier Internet athletic connection for amateur sports organizers, leagues and teams.

SPORTS XCHANGE, THE
PO BOX 918
NOVATO, CA 94948
415-897-8555
• Frank Cooney, President
Description:
National. Bulletin board information exchange service covering professional sports leagues. Information is submitted by beat writers and columnists across the country for each professional sport. Each participating group (NBA, NFL, MLB, etc.) has ability to exchange stories or features daily and in-depth notes weekly. Information remains on-line throughout the season and past seasons are archived. Participants have access to daily personnel moves and can download current rosters. Service is open to any group desiring to exchange information on a regular basis. Minimum of ten participants per group is preferred.

SPORTSNET
21 CHARLES ST
WESTPORT, CT 06880
800-226-7633
Fax: 203-226-7633
sales@sportsnet.com
www.sportsnet.com

Description:
National. Computerized trading card/information network. Services include SportsNet, SportsNet Stadium, SportsNet Today Magazine, SportsNet's Electronic Price Guide.

SPORTSNUTS, INC.
THE TOWERS AT SOUTH TOWNE, #2
10421 SOUTH 400 WEST, SUITE 550
SALT LAKE CITY, UT 84095
801-816-2500
Fax: 801-816-2599
• Chene Gardner, Chief Financial Officer
Description:
A leader in providing unique solutions to the challenges faced by athletes and the organizations in which participate. Helps organize and manage a wide variety of sports events providing online registration, event sponsorship, event coordination, online and offline promotion, and merchandise sales.

SPORTSPILOT, INC.
2514 TARPLEY RD
SUITE 104
CARROLLTON, TX 75006
214-472-3410
888-516-7249
Fax: 214-472-2641
www.sportspilot.com
• Ron Toupal, Chief Executive Officer
• Brad Cook, Founder
• Tim Adkison, Sales Manager
Description:
An Internet based company that provides Amateur Sport Organizations with sports office automation services, automated scorekeeping and real-time sports news and stats.

SPORTSWIRE/BUSINESS WIRE
44 MONTGOMERY STREET
39th FLOOR
SAN FRANCISCO, CA 94104
415-986-4422
800-381-9473
mike@bizwire.com
www.businesswire.com
• Cathy Baron Tamraz, Chairman/Chief Executive Officer
• Scott D. Goll, Editor
Description:
The leading source for full-text breaking news releases, multimedia and regulatory filings for companies and groups throughout the world.

STATS
2775 SHERMER ROAD
NORTHBROOK, IL 60062
847-583-2100
Fax: 847-583-2600

sales@stats.com
www.stats.com
• Gary Walrath, Chief Executive Officer

STAY IN THE ZONE
1060 MAIN STREET
SUITE 307
RIVER EDGE, NJ 07661
201-342-3663
800-580-9663
Fax: 201-342-2258
info@stayinthezone.com
www.stayinthezone.com
• Jay P. Granat, Founder
Description:
Blog focusing on sport psychology; resources, publications, and products for self-help.

TEAMLINK.COM, INC
200 NORTH COBB PARKWAY
SUITE 140
MARIETTA, GA 30062
770-514-0077
800-599-9402
Fax: 770-604-9520
www.tmlk.com
• David Supple, Chief Operating Officer
david@tmlk.com
• Heather Voight, Vice President/Collegiate Initiatives
heather@tmlk.com
Description:
Offers sports media professionals and team staffers access to team generated sports information from over 500 professional and collegiate sports organizations. This information is delivered to you via fax or e-mail the instant it is available or can be viewed directly from the site via the TeamLink Viewer.

THE ACTIVE NETWORK, INC.
1020 PROSPECT STREET
SUITE 250
LA JOLLA, CA 92037
858-551-9916
Fax: 858-551-7619
www.active.com
Description:
Active.com offers a one-stop shop for maintaining healthy lifestyles or setting and achieving fitness goals. THe site offers an online database of more than 100,000 events and activities in over 50 sports in 5,00 cities nationwide, from 5k runs to marathons to cycling races and triathlons. Finding events is easy and online registration makes participation fast and convenient.

THEPIT.COM
245 MAIN STREET
4TH FLOOR
WHITE PLAINS, NY 10601

866-374-8266
Fax: 212-376-0699
customer.service@thepit.com
www.thepit.com
Description:
An online marketplace that buys, sells or trades sport cards.

TURNER SPORTS
ONE CNN CENTER
ATLANTA, GA 30303
404-827-1700
www.turner.com
• David Levy, President
Description:
Exclusive producer of NASCAR.com.

VEGASINSIDER.COM
675 GRIER DRIVE
LAS VEGAS, NV 89119
702-892-0670
800-211-4759
Fax: 702-892-0682
www.vegasinsider.com
• Joseph Pesta, Webmaster
Description:
National. Sports information provider; on-line database sports service. Sports information service providing on-line database devoted to sports and horse racing. Including: Scores, standings, statistics, historical data, analysis, news, odds, and more updated and available 24 hours, seven days a week. Compatible with existing electronic, broadcasting newsroom systems. Customization available for individual markets, media, and promoters; also markets professional handicapping software for football and basketball.

YAHOO! SPORTS
701 FIRST AVENUE
SUNNYVALE, CA 94089
408-349-3300
Fax: 408-349-3301
www.sports.yahoo.com
• David Filo, Co-Founder
• Jerry Yang, Co-Founder
• Marissa Myer, Chief Executive Officer, President, Director
• Adam Cahan, SVP of Mobile and Emerging Products
• Henrique De Castro, Chief Operating Officer
• David Dibble, Executive Vice President, Technology & Operat
• Mikie Rosen, Senior Vice President, Global Media & Commerc
• Jay Rossiter, Executive Vice President, Platforms
• Kathy Savitt, Chief Marketing Officer
Baseball Sponsor:
MLB - San Francisco Giants.
Basketball Sponsor:
EA Sports Maui Classic.

media

5

sports sponsors

Air Sports Sponsors

COLUMBIA SPORTSWEAR COMPANY, 1128

Archery Sponsors

HYUNDAI MOTOR AMERICA, 737
INDIANA UNIVERSITY, 423

Auto Sports Sponsors

ARVINMERITOR, 1110
AT&T INC., 733
BANK OF AMERICA CORPORATION, 733
BOSE CORP., 734
BOWLING PROPRIETORS' ASSOCIATION OF AMERICA, 66
BRIDGESTONE AMERICAS, 734
BRITTEN-MEDIA, 1120
BUFFALO TURBINE, 1122
CHARTER COMMUNICATIONS, 735
COCA-COLA COMPANY, 735
COLEMAN COMPANY INC., 1128
COUCH DISTRIBUTING COMPANY, 1235
DIAMOND OIL COMPANY, 1236
DIRECTV, 693
FCA US, 736
GENERAL MOTORS, 736
GOODYEAR TIRE & RUBBER CO., 736
HEDMAN MANUFACTURING SOUTH, 1154
HEINEKEN USA, 737
HOLMATRO RESCUE EQUIPMENT, 1156
HONDA CANADA INC., 737
HYUNDAI MOTOR AMERICA, 737
J PATTON SPORTS MARKETING, 798
LAS VEGAS CONVENTION & VISITORS AUTHORITY, 237
MILLERCOORS, 738
MONSTER BEVERAGE CORPORATION, 739
NATIONWIDE FINANCIAL SERVICES, 739
NEW ERA CAP, 739
NISSAN CANADA, 739
NISSAN NORTH AMERICA, 739
PEPSICO, 740
PNC FINANCIAL SERVICES, 740
R.C.I., 1190
ROLEX WATCH USA, 740
SAM'S CLUB, 1248
SHELL OIL COMPANY, 741
SHERWIN-WILLIAMS CO., 741
SUNOCO, 741
THE HERSHEY CO., 742
TOYOTA MOTOR SALES, 742
UNILEVER USA, 742
VOLKSWAGEN GROUP OF AMERICA, 743
WALMART INC., 743

Auto Sports Sponsors - CART

GOODYEAR TIRE & RUBBER CO., 736
HOLMATRO RESCUE EQUIPMENT, 1156

Auto Sports Sponsors - IRL

HOLMATRO RESCUE EQUIPMENT, 1156
HONDA CANADA INC., 737
KROGER, 737
NEW ERA CAP, 739
PNC FINANCIAL SERVICES, 740
SHERWIN-WILLIAMS CO., 741

SIRIUS XM RADIO, 741
SUNOCO, 741

Auto Sports Sponsors - NASCAR

3M, 733
ADIDAS AMERICA, 733
ADVOCARE INTERNATIONAL, 733
AMERICAN HONDA MOTOR CO., 733
BANK OF AMERICA CORPORATION, 733
BURGER KING, 734
CANADIAN TIRE, 735
CATERPILLAR, 735
COCA-COLA COMPANY, 735
COLEMAN COMPANY INC., 1128
COMCAST CORPORATION, 735
DELL TECHNOLOGIES, 735
DIRECTV, 693
DRAFTKINGS, 736
EXXON MOBIL CORPORATION, 736
FEDEX CORPORATION, 736
FORD MOTOR COMPANY, 736
GENERAL ELECTRIC, 736
GOODYEAR TIRE & RUBBER CO., 736
KROGER, 737
LAS VEGAS CONVENTION & VISITORS AUTHORITY, 237
LOWE'S, 738
MARS NORTH AMERICA, 738
MICROSOFT CORPORATION, 738
MILLERCOORS, 738
MONSTER BEVERAGE CORPORATION, 739
NATIONWIDE FINANCIAL SERVICES, 739
RED BULL NORTH AMERICA, 740
SAM'S CLUB, 1248
SAMSUNG ELECTRONICS NA, 740
SHERWIN-WILLIAMS CO., 741
SIRIUS XM RADIO, 741
SONY CORP. OF AMERICA, 741
THE HERSHEY CO., 742
TOYOTA MOTOR SALES, 742
UNDER ARMOUR, 742
UNILEVER USA, 742
UNITED PARCEL SERVICE OF AMERICA, 743
VISA USA, 743
WALMART INC., 743

Auto Sports Sponsors - NASCAR Nationwide Race Series

CHARTER COMMUNICATIONS, 735
PEPSICO, 740
SAM'S CLUB, 1248

Badminton Sponsors

HL BADMINTON, 1155

Baseball Sponsors

ADIDAS AMERICA, 733
AMERICAN AIRLINES, 733
ANHEUSER-BUSCH INBEV, 733
ARAMARK CORPORATION, 1076
AVIS RENT A CAR SYSTEM, 935
BANK OF AMERICA CORPORATION, 733
BBVA COMPASS, 734
BP AMERICA, 734
BRIDGESTONE AMERICAS, 734
BULOVA WATCH COMPANY, 1122
CATERPILLAR, 735
CHEVRON CORPORATION, 735
COCA-COLA COMPANY, 735
COMCAST CORPORATION, 735
DELTA AIR LINES, 735
DIRECTV, 693

ENTERPRISE HOLDINGS, 736
FILA USA, 1143
GNC CORPORATION, 1148
GOODYEAR TIRE & RUBBER CO., 736
H-E-B, 1241
MASTERCARD, 738
MCDONALD'S CORPORATION, 738
MERCEDES-BENZ USA, 738
NEW ERA CAP, 739
NIKE, 739
PAPA JOHN'S INTERNATIONAL, 740
RAWLINGS SPORTING GOODS COMPANY INC., 1191
RED BULL NORTH AMERICA, 740
RINGOR, 1193
SCOTIABANK, 741
SHERWIN-WILLIAMS CO., 741
SIRIUS XM RADIO, 741
SUBWAY RESTAURANTS, 741
THE HERSHEY CO., 742
TICKETS.COM, 943
T-MOBILE USA, 741
TOPPS COMPANY, 1214
TOYOTA MOTOR SALES, 742
U.S. BANCORP, 742
UNDER ARMOUR, 742
VERIZON COMMUNICATIONS, 743
VOLKSWAGEN GROUP OF AMERICA, 743
WELLS FARGO & CO, 743
YAHOO! SPORTS, 723

Baseball Sponsors - Major League Baseball

ADIDAS AMERICA, 733
ALLSTATE INSURANCE, 733
AMERICAN HONDA MOTOR CO., 733
ANHEUSER-BUSCH INBEV, 733
ARAMARK CORPORATION, 1076
AVIS RENT A CAR SYSTEM, 935
BANK OF AMERICA CORPORATION, 733
BMO FINANCIAL GROUP, 734
BOSTON PIZZA, 734
BULOVA WATCH COMPANY, 1122
CAPITAL ONE FINANCIAL, 735
CHEVRON CORPORATION, 735
CITIGROUP, 735
COCA-COLA COMPANY, 735
COMCAST CORPORATION, 735
DELTA AIR LINES, 735
DIRECTV, 693
DR. PEPPER SNAPPLE GROUP, 736
DRAFTKINGS, 736
GENERAL ELECTRIC, 736
GENERAL MOTORS, 736
GNC CORPORATION, 1148
HONDA CANADA INC., 737
MACY'S, 738
MARS NORTH AMERICA, 738
MASTERCARD, 738
MCDONALD'S CORPORATION, 738
METLIFE, 738
MOLSONCOORS, 738
NESTLE USA, 739
NEW ERA CAP, 739
NIKE, 739
ORACLE CORPORATION, 739
PAPA JOHN'S INTERNATIONAL, 740
PEPSICO, 740
PNC FINANCIAL SERVICES, 740
ROGERS COMMUNICATIONS, 740
SAMSUNG ELECTRONICS NA, 740
SAP AMERICA, 740
SIRIUS XM RADIO, 741
SONY CORP. OF AMERICA, 741
SPORT CHEK, 741
SUBWAY RESTAURANTS, 741
TARGET STORES, 742
TIM HORTONS, 742
TOYOTA MOTOR SALES, 742
U.S. BANCORP, 742

UNDER ARMOUR, 742
UNITED CONTINENTAL HOLDINGS, 742
VERIZON COMMUNICATIONS, 743
WELLS FARGO & CO, 743
YAHOO! SPORTS, 723
YUM! BRANDS, 743

Basketball Sponsors

AMERICAN EXPRESS COMPANY, 733
ARAMARK CORPORATION, 1076
AT&T INC., 733
AUTOTRADER.COM, 681
BBVA COMPASS, 734
BULOVA WATCH COMPANY, 1122
BURGER KING, 734
COCA-COLA COMPANY, 735
COLONIAL LIFE & ACCIDENT INSURANCE COMPANY, 787
COMCAST CORPORATION, 735
FILA USA, 1143
GOODYEAR TIRE & RUBBER CO., 736
KAISER FOUNDATION HEALTH PLAN, 737
LG ELECTRONICS USA, 737
MCDONALD'S CORPORATION, 738
PAPA JOHN'S INTERNATIONAL, 740
SAP AMERICA, 740
TOPPS COMPANY, 1214
U.S. BANCORP, 742
YAHOO! SPORTS, 723
YUM! BRANDS, 743

Basketball Sponsors - National Basketball Associat

3M, 733
ALLSTATE INSURANCE, 733
AMERICAN AIRLINES, 733
AMERICAN EXPRESS COMPANY, 733
ANHEUSER-BUSCH INBEV, 733
BANK OF AMERICA CORPORATION, 733
BELL CANADA, 734
BMO FINANCIAL GROUP, 734
BULOVA WATCH COMPANY, 1122
CAPITAL ONE FINANCIAL, 735
CATERPILLAR, 735
CHARTER COMMUNICATIONS, 735
COCA-COLA COMPANY, 735
COMCAST CORPORATION, 735
DELTA AIR LINES, 735
DIAGEO NORTH AMERICA, 736
DIRECTV, 693
DRAFTKINGS, 736
EA SPORTS, 1225
ENTERPRISE HOLDINGS, 736
EXXON MOBIL CORPORATION, 736
FOOT LOCKER, 1240
FORD MOTOR COMPANY OF CANADA, 736
GENERAL ELECTRIC, 736
KIA MOTORS AMERICA, 737
LG ELECTRONICS USA, 737
LOWE'S, 738
MCDONALD'S CORPORATION, 738
MILLERCOORS, 738
MOLSONCOORS, 738
NESTLE USA, 739
NEW ERA CAP, 739
NIKE, 739
ORACLE CORPORATION, 739
PAPA JOHN'S INTERNATIONAL, 740
PEPSICO, 740
QUICKEN LOANS, 740
RED BULL NORTH AMERICA, 740
SAMSUNG ELECTRONICS NA, 740
SAP AMERICA, 740
SHERWIN-WILLIAMS CO., 741
SIRIUS XM RADIO, 741

sports sponsors

NCAA Sponsors

ADVOCARE INTERNATIONAL, 733
ALLSTATE INSURANCE, 733
AMERICAN EXPRESS COMPANY, 733
COCA-COLA COMPANY, 735
COMCAST CORPORATION, 735
DELTA AIR LINES, 735
ENTERPRISE HOLDINGS, 736
GOODYEAR TIRE & RUBBER CO., 736
HILTON HOTELS, 737
HOLLAND & KNIGHT, 893
JACKSONVILLE AND THE BEACHES CONVENTION AND VISITORS BUREAU, 235
LOWE'S, 738
MCDONALD'S CORPORATION, 738
MERCEDES-BENZ USA, 738
MICROSOFT CORPORATION, 738
NATIONWIDE FINANCIAL SERVICES, 739
NIKE, 739
NISSAN NORTH AMERICA, 739
NORTHWESTERN MUTUAL LIFE, 739
PAPA JOHN'S INTERNATIONAL, 740
PEPSICO, 740
PGA TOUR, 108
PNC FINANCIAL SERVICES, 740
SHERWIN-WILLIAMS CO., 741
SIRIUS XM RADIO, 741
ST. AUGUSTINE, 245
SUBWAY RESTAURANTS, 741
THE HERSHEY CO., 742
TICKET760 KTKR, 642
TOOLBOX STUDIOS, 823
TOYOTA MOTOR SALES, 742
U.S. BANCORP, 742
UNITED PARCEL SERVICE OF AMERICA, 743
VERIZON COMMUNICATIONS, 743
WELLS FARGO & CO, 743
WELLS FARGO & CO, 743
YUM! BRANDS, 743

Olympic Sponsors

AMJ CAMPBELL, 934
BELL CANADA, 734
BP AMERICA, 734
BURTON SNOWBOARDS, 1122
CANADIAN TIRE, 735
COCA-COLA COMPANY, 735
COMCAST CORPORATION, 735
EA SPORTS, 1225
FOOT LOCKER, 1240
GENERAL ELECTRIC, 736
KIA MOTORS AMERICA, 737
PROCTER & GAMBLE COMPANY, 740
SAMSUNG ELECTRONICS NA, 740
SWATCH GROUP, 741
THE HERSHEY CO., 742
TICKETS.COM, 943
TOYOTA MOTOR SALES, 742
UNITED CONTINENTAL HOLDINGS, 742
VISA USA, 743

Polo Sponsors

BMO FINANCIAL GROUP, 734

Racquetball Sponsors

EKTELON, 1138

Rodeo Sponsors

BMO FINANCIAL GROUP, 734
MONSTER BEVERAGE CORPORATION, 739

Rugby Sponsors

ADIDAS AMERICA, 733
EA SPORTS, 1225
HEINEKEN USA, 737
MASTERCARD, 738
SAMSUNG ELECTRONICS NA, 740

Running Sponsors

ALLSTATE INSURANCE, 733
AMERICAN AIRLINES, 733
ASICS AMERICA CORPORATION, 1111
BP AMERICA, 734
BROOKS, 1120
DELTA AIR LINES, 735
FILA USA, 1143
FOOT LOCKER, 1240
GNC CORPORATION, 1148
H-E-B, 1241
KAISER FOUNDATION HEALTH PLAN, 737
POWERCRANKS, 1187
SAUCONY, 1197
SCOTIABANK, 741
SPORT CHEK, 741
UNITED CONTINENTAL HOLDINGS, 742

Sailing Sponsors

SAP AMERICA, 740
SAUCONY, 1197
VANGUARD SAILBOATS, 1218

Shooting/Hunting Sponsors

WOOLRICH, 1223

Skateboard Sponsors

MONSTER BEVERAGE CORPORATION, 739
OCEAN PACIFIC APPAREL CORPORATION, 1181
VANS, 1251

Ski Sponsors

ATOMIC SKI USA, 1111
BOSE CORP., 734
BRIDGESTONE AMERICAS, 734
CANADIAN TIRE, 735
COLUMBIA SPORTSWEAR COMPANY, 1128
FILA USA, 1143
OLD DUTCH FOODS, 739
RELIABLE RACING SUPPLY, 1192
SPORT CHEK, 741
VISA USA, 743

Snowboard Sponsors

BOSE CORP., 734
BURTON SNOWBOARDS, 1122
MONSTER BEVERAGE CORPORATION, 739
OCEAN PACIFIC APPAREL CORPORATION, 1181
OLD DUTCH FOODS, 739
SPORT CHEK, 741
VANS, 1251
VISA USA, 743

Snowmobile Sponsors

CANADIAN TIRE, 735

Soccer Sponsors

ADIDAS AMERICA, 733
ADVOCARE INTERNATIONAL, 733
AMERICAN AIRLINES, 733
AMERICAN EXPRESS COMPANY, 733
AMJ CAMPBELL, 934
ANTIGUA GROUP, 1109
BARCLAYS, 734
BOSE CORP., 734
BRIDGESTONE AMERICAS, 734
BURGER KING, 734
CANADIAN TIRE, 735
FEDEX CORPORATION, 736
FILA USA, 1143
GNC CORPORATION, 1148
HEINEKEN USA, 737
HYUNDAI MOTOR AMERICA, 737
IBM, 737
KIA CANADA, 737
KIA MOTORS AMERICA, 737
MASTERCARD, 738
MCDONALD'S CORPORATION, 738
MICROSOFT CORPORATION, 738
NISSAN NORTH AMERICA, 739
SAMSUNG ELECTRONICS NA, 740
SAP AMERICA, 740
UMBRO U.S.A., 1217
UNILEVER USA, 742
VISA USA, 743
YAHOO! SPORTS, 723

Soccer Sponsors - Major League Soccer

ADVOCARE INTERNATIONAL, 733
ALLSTATE INSURANCE, 733
ANTIGUA GROUP, 1109
BMO FINANCIAL GROUP, 734
DRAFTKINGS, 736
KIA CANADA, 737
MARRIOTT INTERNATIONAL, 738
RED BULL NORTH AMERICA, 740
SAP AMERICA, 740
SIRIUS XM RADIO, 741
SPORT CHEK, 741
TARGET STORES, 742
TIM HORTONS, 742
TOYOTA MOTOR SALES, 742
UMBRO U.S.A., 1217
VOLKSWAGEN GROUP OF AMERICA, 743
YAHOO! SPORTS, 723

Softball Sponsors

RAWLINGS SPORTING GOODS COMPANY INC., 1191
RINGOR, 1193

Special Olympics Sponsors

COMCAST CORPORATION, 735
KIA MOTORS AMERICA, 737
MICROSOFT CORPORATION, 738
UNITED CONTINENTAL HOLDINGS, 742

Squash Sponsors

DUNLOP/MAXFLI/SLAZENGER GROUP AMERICAS, 1136
J.P. MORGAN CHASE, 737

Surfing Sponsors

KROGER, 737
OCEAN PACIFIC APPAREL CORPORATION, 1181
VANS, 1251

Swimming Sponsors

AQUA SPHERE US, 1109
BMW OF NORTH AMERICA, 734
COLORADO DISPLAY SYSTEMS, 1128

Tennis Sponsors

ADVOCARE INTERNATIONAL, 733
AMERICAN EXPRESS COMPANY, 733
BMW OF NORTH AMERICA, 734
CITIGROUP, 735
DELL TECHNOLOGIES, 735
FEDEX CORPORATION, 736
FILA USA, 1143
GENERAL ELECTRIC, 736
HYUNDAI MOTOR AMERICA, 737
IBM, 737
J.P. MORGAN CHASE, 737
KIA MOTORS AMERICA, 737
MASTERCARD, 738
PENN RACQUET SPORTS, 1184
PORSCHE CARS NORTH AMERICA, 1186
ROGERS COMMUNICATIONS, 740
SAP AMERICA, 740
WILSON SPORTING GOODS COMPANY, 1222

Track & Field Sponsors

BMW OF NORTH AMERICA, 734
BROOKS, 1120
FOOT LOCKER, 1240
REEBOK CANADA INC., 1192
THE HERSHEY CO., 742
VISA USA, 743

Triathlon Sponsors

AQUA SPHERE US, 1109
CLIF BAR, 1126
IRONMAN PROPERTIES, 175
IRONMAN WETSUITS, 1159
KAISER FOUNDATION HEALTH PLAN, 737
PANAMA CITY BEACH CONVENTION & VISITORS BUREAU, 242
POWERCRANKS, 1187
SAUCONY, 1197
TELUS CORPORATION, 742

Volleyball Sponsors

ASICS AMERICA CORPORATION, 1111
MIKASA SPORTS USA, 1173
SAMSUNG ELECTRONICS NA, 740
THE ORIGINAL BALL BAG LLC, 1182
WILSON SPORTING GOODS COMPANY, 1222

Walking Sponsors

GNC CORPORATION, 1148

Water Polo Sponsors

CAPITAL ONE FINANCIAL, 735
COLORADO TIME SYSTEMS, 1128
MIKASA SPORTS USA, 1173

Water Ski Sponsors

COLEMAN COMPANY INC., 1128

Wrestling Sponsors

AMERICAN AIRLINES, 733
ASICS AMERICA CORPORATION, 1111
LAS VEGAS CONVENTION & VISITORS AUTHORITY, 237
MONSTER BEVERAGE CORPORATION, 739

SAMSUNG ELECTRONICS NA, 740

Yacht Sponsors

NAUTICA INTERNATIONAL, 1177
SAUCONY, 1197
TOMMY HILFIGER, 1251
YAHOO! SPORTS, 723

Youth Sports Sponsors

ADVOCARE INTERNATIONAL, 733
DODGE, 736
GENERAL MOTORS, 736
LOWE'S, 738
MCDONALD'S CORPORATION, 738

SAMSUNG ELECTRONICS NA, 740
TIM HORTONS, 742
TOYOTA MOTOR SALES, 742

sports sponsors

Sports Related

3M
3M CENTER
ST. PAUL, MN 55144-1000
888-364-3577
www.3m.com
• Inge G. Thulin, Exec. Chairman
• Michael F, Roman, Chief Executive Officer
Total Spend:
$20M-$25M
Recent Sponsorships:
Minnesota Super Bowl Host Committee, 2018
Golf Sponsor:
PGA 3M Celebrity Challenge, Champions Tour 3M Championship
Football Sponsor:
NFL Minnesota Vikings
Auto Sports Sponsor:
NASCAR

ADIDAS AMERICA
ADIDAS VILLAGE
5055 N GREELEY AVENUE
PORTLAND, OR 97217
800-982-9337
Fax: 971-234-2450
customerservice@shopadidas.com
www.adidas-group.com/en/group/headquarters
• Kasper Rorsted, Chief Executive Officer
• Roland Auschel, Global Sales
• Eric Liedtke, Global Brands
Total Spend:
$195M-$200M
Recent Sponsorships:
NHL, 2016/17; US National Rugby Team, 2017; Sport Mediaset, 2016
Baseball Sponsor:
Minor League
Handball Sports:
EHF Champions League
Basketball Sponsor:
NBA, NBDL
College Sports:
NCAA Football, College Bowl
Lacrosse Sponsors:
National Lacross Classic
Soccer Sponsor:
U.S. Youth Soccer; FIFA World Cup; UEFA European Championship; Africa Cup of Nations; Olympic Games
Football Sponsor:
NFL, Indoor League

ADVOCARE INTERNATIONAL
2801 SUMMIT AVENUE
PLANO, TX 75074
800-542-4800
www.advocare.com
• Brian Connolly, Exec. Chairman
• Reid Ward, President and COO
Total Spend:
$20M-$25M
Recent Sponsorships:
WTA Stanford Classic being renamed the "Silicon Valley Classic", 2018
Tennis Sponsor:
Miami Open; Mubadala Silicon Valley Classic
Soccer Sponsor:
MLS; FC Dallas
Auto Motorsports Sponsor:
NASCAR; Ford Fusion
College Sports Sponsor:

AdvoCare Classic; AdvoCare Texas kickoff; AdvoCare Invitational

ALLSTATE INSURANCE
2775 SANDERS ROAD
NORTHBROOK, IL 60062
847-402-5000
www.allstate.com
• Thomas J. Wilson, Chairman, President & CEO
Total Spend:
$65M-$70M
Football Sponsor:
Pro Football Hall of Fame; American Football Coaches Association.
Hockey Sponsor:
NHL Chicago Blackhawks, Detroit Red Wings; AHL Chicago Wolves, Allstate Arena; National Hockey League Players Association
NCAA Sponsor:
Allstate Sugar Bowl; March Madness
Basketball Sponsor:
National Association of Basketball Coaches; Women's Basketball Coaches Association
Running Sponsor:
Allstate Life Insurance Chicago 13.1 Marathon
Soccer Sponsor:
Mexican National Soccer Team

AMERICAN AIRLINES
4333 AMON CARTER BLVD
FORT WORTH, TX 76155-2605
817-963-1234
www.aa.com
• Doug Parker, Chairman & CEO
• Robert Isom, President
Total Spend:
$25M-$30M
Endurance Sponsor:
Bank of America Chicago Marathon
Wrestling Sponsor:
USA Wrestling; WWE
Facility Sponsor:
American Airlines Center, Dallas, TX; American Airlines Arena, Miami, FL
Basketball Sponsor:
NBA Dallas Mavericks, Miami Heat
Football Sponsor:
NFL Dallas Cowboys, Philadelphia Eagles, Carolina Panthers
NCAA Sponsor:
Capital One Orange Bowl
Soccer Sponsor:
MLS Chicago Fire, DC United

AMERICAN EXPRESS COMPANY
WORLD FINANCIAL CENTER
200 VESEY STREET
NEW YORK, NY 10285-3106
212-640-2000
www.americanexpress.com
• Stephen J. Squeri, Chairman & CEO
Total Spend:
$50M-$55M
Basketball Sponsor:
NBA Los Angeles Lakers, Miami Heat, Washington Wizards, Utah Jazz
Facility Sponsor:
American Express community stadium, Falmer, UK; Staples Center; United Center
Tennis Sponsor:
US Open
Soccer Sponsor:
MLS Los Angeles Galaxy, Real Salt Lake
Hockey Sponsor:

NHL Chicago Blackhawks, Los Angeles Kings
Golf Sponsor:
PGA of America

AMERICAN HONDA MOTOR CO.
1919 TORRANCE BLVD
TORRANCE, CA 90501-2746
800-999-1009
Fax: 310-783-3023
www.honda.com
• Takahiro Hachigo, President & CEO, Honda Motor Co.
• Toshiaki Mikoshiba, Chairman & CEO, American Honda Motor Co.
Total Spend:
$40M-$45M
Auto Motor Sponsor:
NASCAR
Baseballe Sponsor:
Little League World Series, 2017; MLB, Toronto Blue Jays
Golf Sponsor:
The Honda Classic
Ice Hockey Sponsor:
NHL; Hockey Hall of Fame

ANHEUSER-BUSCH INBEV
ONE BUSCH PLACE
ST. LOUIS, MO 63118
800-342-5283
Fax: 314-577-2900
www.anheuser-busch.com
• Michel Doukeris, President & CEO, North America
Total Spend:
$350M-$355M
Baseball Sponsor:
MLB; Minor; Busch Stadium
Basketball Sponsor:
NBA
College Sponsor:
NCAA; College Bowl
Football Sponsor:
NFL
Golf Sponsor:
PGA; LPGA
Hockey Sponsor:
NHL

AT&T INC.
208 S AKARD STREET
DALLAS, TX 75202
210-821-4105
www.att.com
• Randall Stephenson, Chairman & CEO
Total Spend:
$195M-$200M
Golf Sponsor:
PGA
College Sponsor:
NCAA; College Bowl
Facility Sponsor:
AT&T Park; AT&T Center; AT&T Stadium; Jones AT&T Stadium; AT&T Performing Arts Center
Auto Car Sponsor:
Innovation Partner of Aston Martin Red Bull Racing
Football Sponsor:
NFL, Dalls Cowboys home stadium

BANK OF AMERICA CORPORATION
100 NORTH TRYON STREET
CHARLOTTE, NC 28255
www.bankofamerica.com

- Brian Moynihan, Chairman & CEO
- Dean Athanasia, Co-head, Consumer & Small Business
- Catherine P. Bessant, Chief Operations & Technology Officer
- Paul M. Donofrio, Chief Financial Officer
- Anne M. Finucane, Vice Chairman
- Geoffrey S. Greener, Chief Risk Officer
- Thomas K. Montag, Chief Operating Officer

Total Spend:
$75M-$80M
Baseball Sponsor:
MLB; Minor League
Auto Sports Sponsor:
NASCAR
Football Sponsor:
NFL; Bank of America Stadium
Basketball Sponsor:
WNBA; NBA
College Sponsor:
NCAA; College Bowl; NCAA Bank of America Arena at Hec Edmundson Pavilion
Running Sponsor:
Bank of America Chicago Marathon

BARCLAYS
745 SEVENTH AVE
NEW YORK, NY 10019
www.barclays.com
- John McFarlane, Group Chairman
- Jes Staley, Group CEO
Total Spend:
$35M-$40M
Soccer Sponsor:
Absa Premiership; Premier League through 2018-19 season

BBVA COMPASS
15 SOUTH 20TH STREET
BIRMINGHAM, AL 35233
www.bbvacompass.com
- Javier RodrÂ¡guez Soler, Chief Executive Officer
Total Spend:
$15-20 million
Recent Sponsorships:
2018 All-Star Chef Classic
8333

BELL CANADA
1 CARREFOUR
ALEXANDER-GRAHAM-BELL
BUILDING A, 4TH FLOOR
VERDUN, QC, CANADA H3E 3B3
www.bce.ca
- George Cope, President & CEO, BCE and Bell Canada
Basketball Sponsor:
Toronto Raptors
Facility Sponsor:
TIFF Bell Lightbox
Other:
Canadian Olympic/Paralympic Committees, Bell Let's Talk, TIFF

BERKSHIRE HATHAWAY, INC.
3555 FARNAM STREET
OMAHA, NE 68131
www.berkshirehathaway.com
- Warren E. Buffett, Chief Executive Officer
Total Spend:
$75M-$80M

BMO FINANCIAL GROUP
100 KING ST WEST
TORONTO, ON, CANADA M5X 1A1

416-867-3996
www.bmo.com
- Darryl White, Chief Executive Officer
Baseball Sponsor:
Chicago White Sox
Basketball Sponsor:
NBA (Chicago Bulls; Milwaukee Bucks; Toronto Raptors), NBA Canada, Jr. NBA
Hockey Sponsor:
Chicago Blackhawks
Soccer Sponsor:
MLS (Vancouver Whitecaps; Montreal Impact; Toronto FC)
Other:
Calgary Stampede, Polo for Heart, Stratford Festival, Kids Help Phone

---

BMW OF NORTH AMERICA, LLC
300 CHESTNUT RIDGE ROAD
WOODCLIFF LAKE, NJ 07677-7731
www.bmwusa.com
- Bernhard Kuhnt, President & CEO
  ext 4232
Total Spend:
$25M-$30M
Tennis Sponsor:
BMW Malaysian Open
Golf Sponsor:
PGA Tour BMW Championship; Web.com Tour BMW Charity Pro-Am
Sponsor:
U.S Olympic Committee, U.S Paralympics, U.S Speedskating, USA Bobsled and Skeleton, USA Swimming, USA Track and Field
Football Sponsor:
NFL Atlanta Falcons, Houston Texans

BOSE CORP.
THE MOUNTAIN
FRAMINGHAM, MA 01701
508-879-7330
800-460-9283
www.bose.com
- Phil Hess, President & Chief Executive Officer
Total Spend:
$30M-$35M
Recent Sponsorships:
Mumbai City FC, 2018
Football Sponsor:
NFL
Auto Motorsports Sponsor:
Formula 1; Mercedes-AMG Petronas Motorsport
Sponsor:
U.S. Ski & Snowboard Team; 261 Fearless

BOSTON PIZZA
100 - 10760 SHELLBRIDGE WAY
RICHMOND, BC, CANADA V6X 3H1
604-270-1108
Fax: 604-270-4168
bostonpizza.com
- Jim Treliving, Chairman & Owner
- Jordan Holm, President
Baseball Sponsor:
Toronto Blue Jays
Football Sponsor:
Edmonton Eskimos
Hockey Sponsor:
AHL, Hockey Canada, OHL, NHL (Calgary Flames; Edmonton Oilers; Vancouver Canucks; Winnipeg Jets), WHL
Other:
UFC

BP AMERICA
501 WESTLAKE PARK BLVD
HOUSTON, TX 77079
281-366-2000
800-333-3991
www.bp.com
- Bob Dudley, Group Chief Executive
- Susan Dio, Chairman and President, BP America
Total Spend:
$20M-$25M
Baseball Sponsor:
MLB Baltimore Orioles, Chicago Cubs, Cleveland Indians; MLB Crosstown Cup (Cubs-White Sox).
Sponsor:
U.S Olympic Committee; U.S Paralympics; BP MS 150 Bike Ride

BRIDGESTONE AMERICAS
200 4TH AVENUE S
NASHVILLE, TN 37201
615-937-1000
800-543-7522
Fax: 615-937-3621
www.bridgestoneamericas.com
- Gordon Knapp, President and CEO, Bridgestone Americas
- Bill Thompson, Chief Operating Officer
Total Spend:
$50M-$55M
Recent Sponsorships:
2018 Olympics; 2020 Olympics; Libertadores Cup, 2017
Auto Motor Sponsor:
World Solar Challenge; Firestone Racing
Sponsor:
Bridgestone Americas Tire Operations Latin America (BATO LA); South American Football Confederation (CONMEBOL); FIS Alpine Ski World Cup; Bridgestone Arena, Nashville, TN
Football Sponsor:
NFL; "Bridgestone Performance Moments"
Golf Sponsor:
Japan Golf Tour Bridgestone Open, PGA Tour WGC Bridgestone Invitational, PGA Tour, Web.com Tour, Champions Tour, World Golf Championship
Hockey Sponsor:
NHL Buffalo Sabres, Calgary Flames, Montreal Canadiens, Nashville Predators, Toronto Maple Leafs; NHL Players Association; Bridgestone NHL Winter Classic.

BUDWEISER CANADA
207 QUEEN'S QUAY WEST
SUITE 299
TORONTO, ON, CANADA M5J 1A7
416-361-5050
800-268-2337
Fax: 416-361-5200
www.budweiser.ca
- Marcelo Abud, President, Labatt Canada
Other:
Budweiser Stage (Ontario Place)

BURGER KING
5505 BLUE LAGOON DR
MIAMI, FL 33126
866-394-2493
www.bk.com
- Daniel S. Schwartz, Chief Executive Officer
- Jose E. Cil, President

Total Spend:
$15-20 million
Athlete Sponsor:
Conor McGregor (UFC)

CANADIAN TIRE
2180 YONGE STREET
TORONTO, ON, CANADA M4P 2V8
416-480-3000
Fax: 416-480-3970
www.canadiantire.ca
• Stephen Wetmore, President & CEO
• Dean McCann, Exec. Vice-Pres. & CFO
• Allan MacDonald, Exec. Vice-Pres., Retail
Auto Sports Sponsor:
NASCAR
Hockey Sponsor:
NHL
Amateur Sport Sponsor:
Canadian Olympic/Paralympic Committee,
Canadian Soccer Association, Skate
Canada, Hockey Canada, Alpine Canada,
Canada Snowboard
Other:
Canadian Tire Jumpstart Charities;
Canadian Sports Hall of Fame; Canada
Games

CAPITAL ONE FINANCIAL
1680 CAPITAL ONE DRIVE
MCLEAN, VA 22102
703-448-3747
877-383-4802
www.capitalone.com
• Michael C. Slocum, President, Commercial
Banking
• Darren Alcus, Head, Capital One
Corporate Banking group
Total Spend:
$55M-$60M
Recent Sponsorships:
Capital One Organe Bowl, 2018; Corporate
Champion of the NCAA
Baseball Sponsor:
MLB Texas Rangers, Washington Nationals
Basketball Sponsor:
NBA New Orleans Hornets, Washington
Wizards, Capital One Arena; Women's
Basketball Coaches Association
College Sponsor:
Capital One Cup; College Football Playoff
Hockey Sponsor:
NHL New York Islander, Washington
Capitals
Curling Sponsor:
Capital One Cup (curling), Capital One
Grand Slam of Curling, ASHAM World
Curling Tour
Sponsor:
USA Water Polo

CATERPILLAR
510 LAKE COOK RD
SUITE 100
DEERFIELD, IL 60015
309-675-2337
www.cat.com
• Jim Umpleby, Chairman and CEO
Total Spend:
$15-20 million
Motorsports Sponsor:
NASCAR (#31)

CHARTER COMMUNICATIONS
400 ATLANTIC ST
10TH FLOOR
STAMFORD, CT 06901
203-905-7800
888-438-2427
• Thomas M. Rutledge, Chairman and CEO
• John Bickham, President and COO
• Christopher Winfrey, Chief Financial
Officer
Total Spend:
$20M-$25M
Auto Sports Sponsor:
NASCAR, IndyCar, NHRA
Sponsor:
NFL St. Louis Rams; NBA Charlotte Hornets
(2016)

CHEVRON CORPORATION
6001 BOLLINGER CANYON ROAD
SAN RAMON, CA 94583
925-842-1000
www.chevron.com
• Michael K. Wirth, Chairman and CEO
Total Spend:
$20M-$25M
Baseball Sponsor:
Minor League. MLB Atlanta Braves, San
Francisco Giants
Sponsor:
NFL New Orleans Saints; MLS Vancouver
Whitecaps FC
Basketball Sponsor:
NBA Los Angeles Lakers, New Orleans
Hornets, Utah Jazz
Endurance Sports Sponsor:
Chevron Houston Marathon

CITIGROUP, INC.
388 GREENWICH ST
NEW YORK, NY 10013
800-285-3000
www.citigroup.com
• Michael Corbat, Chief Executive Officer,
Citigroup
Total Spend:
$70M-$75M
Recent Sponsorships:
Taste of Tennis, 2018; ProChamps, 2016
Facility Sponsor:
Citi Field, New York, NY - MLB New York
Mets

COCA-COLA COMPANY
ONE COCA-COLA PLAZA
ATLANTA, GA 30313
800-438-2653
www.coca-colacompany.com
• James Quincey, CEO
• Brian Smith, President and COO
Total Spend:
$265M-$270M
Auto Sports Sponsor:
NASCAR
Baseball Sponsor:
MLB; Minor League
College Sponsor:
NCAA; College Bowl
Football Sponsor:
NFL; Indoor League; CFL
Running Sponsor:
St. George Marathon; Twin Cities Marathon;
Grandma's Marathon
Basketball Sponsor:
NBA; WNBA; NBDL
Golf Sponsor:
PGA; LPGA

Hockey Sponsor:
NHL; AHL

COMCAST CORPORATION
COMCAST CENTER
1701 JFK BOULEVARD
PHILADELPHIA, PA 19103
www.xfinity.com
• Brian L. Roberts, Chairman and CEO
• Steve Burke, CEO, NBCUniversal and Sr.
EVP, Comcast Corp.
• Michael J. Cavanagh, Sr. EVP and Chief
Financial Officer
• David L. Cohen, Sr. EVP and Chief
Diversity Officer
Total Spend:
$55M-$60M
Recent Sponsorships:
USA Olympic Team; USA Paralympic Team,
2018; NASCAR Xfinity Series, 2017
College Sponsor:
NCAA; College Bowl; March Madness
Football Sponsor:
NFL Chicago Bears
Baseball Sponsor:
MLB Chicago Cubs, Chicago White Sox
Basketball Sponsor:
NBA
Hockey Sponsor:
NHL

DELL TECHNOLOGIES
ONE DELL WAY
ROUND ROCK, TX 78682
www.delltechnologies.com
• Michael Dell, Chairman and CEO
• Bill Scannell, President, Global Enterprise
Sales
Total Spend:
$25M-$30M
Recent Sponsorships:
International Tennis Hall of Fame Open,
2017; PGA Tour Dell Technologies
Championships, 2017
Auto Motorsports Sponsor:
NASCAR

DELTA AIR LINES
1030 DELTA BLVD
ATLANTA, GA 30354
404-715-2600
800-221-1212
www.delta.com
• Ed Bastian, Chief Executive Officer
• Glen Hauenstein, President
Total Spend:
$30M-$35M
Recent Sponsorships:
PGA Masters Tournament, 2017; Twin
Cities Marathon, 2016; Maxim Super Bowl
Party, 2018
Golf Sponsors:
LPGA
Baseball Sponsor:
MLB; NY Mets
Basketball Sponsor:
NBA; LA Lakers
College Sponsor:
NCAA
Running Sponsor:
Twin Cities Marathon
Football Sponsor:
NFL
Hockey Sponsor:
NHL

DIAGEO NORTH AMERICA
801 MAIN AVENUE
NORWALK, CT 06851
203-229-2100
www.diageo.com
• Ivan Menezes, Chief Executive Officer
• Deirdre Mahlan, President, Diageo North
America
Total Spend:
$30M-$35M
Recent Sponsorships:
Maxim Super Bowl Party, 2018
Basketball Sponsor:
NBA
Football Sponsor:
NFL
Golf Sponsor:
PGA; LPGA

DODGE
ONE RIVERSIDE DR W
WINDSOR, ON, CANADA N9A 5K3
519-973-2000
www.dodge.ca
• Reid Bigland, Chairman, President & CEO,
FCA Canada
Other:
Dodge Caravan Kids (hockey)

DR. PEPPER SNAPPLE GROUP, INC.
5301 LEGACY DRIVE
PLANO, TX 75024
972-673-7000
800-686-7398 (MEDIA)
800-696-5891 (CONSUMER)
www.drpeppersnapplegroup.com
• Larry D. Young, Chief Executive Officer
Total Spend:
$50M-$55M
Recent Sponsorships:
Title sponsor of the College Football Playoff
(CFP) series until 2026; MLB and MLB
Oakland A's, 2018
Football Sponsor:
NFL Los Angeles Rams

DRAFTKINGS, INC.
125 SUMMER ST
5TH FLOOR
BOSTON, MA 02110
support@draftkings.com
www.draftkings.com
• Jason Robins, Co-Founder & Chief
Executive Officer
• Paul Liberman, Co-Founder & Chief
Operating Officer
Total Spend:
$20M-$25M
Sponsor:
NBA Golden State Warrrios; World Poker
Tour European Championship; MLB; MLS;
NASCAR; NHL; CFL

ENTERPRISE HOLDINGS, INC.
600 CORPORATE PARK DR
ST. LOUIS, MO 63105
314-512-5000
800-RENT-A-CAR
www.enterprise.com
• Pamela Nicholson, CEO
• Christine Taylor, President and COO
Total Spend:
$25M-$30M
Recent Sponsorships:
MLB Kansas City Royals, Los Angeles
Angels, New York Mets, St. Louis Cardinals,

2015-2019; UEFA Europa League; PGA Jr.
League Championship, 2017
Soccer Sponsor:
UEFA Europa League
College Sponsor:
NCAA
Golf Sponsor:
PGA; PGA Jr. League
Hockey Sponsor:
NHL

EXXON MOBIL CORPORATION
5959 LAS COLINAS BLVD
IRVING, TX 75039-2298
972-940-6000
www.exxonmobil.com
• Darren W. Woods, Chairman and CEO
• Neil A. Chapman, Senior Vice President
• Jack P. Williams, Senior Vice President
• Andrew P. Swiger, Senior Vice President
Total Spend:
$30M-$35M
Recent Sponsorships:
NBA, WNBA, D-League, 2016
Auto Sports Sponsor:
NASCAR

FCA US, LLC
1000 CHRYSLER DRIVE
AUBURN HILLS, MI 48326
800-334-4920
www.fcagroup.com
• Michael Manley, CEO
• Reid Bigland, Head of U.S. Sales
Total Spend:
$20M-$25M
Recent Sponsorships:
Formula 1, 2018

FEDEX CORPORATION
942 SOUTH SHADY GROVE RD
MEMPHIS, TN 38120
901-369-3600
800-463-3339
www.fedex.com
• Frederick W. Smith, Chairman and CEO
• David J. Bronczek, President and COO
• Raj Subramaniam, President and CEO,
FedEx Express
Total Spend:
$95M-$100M
Soccer Sponsors:
UEFA European League
Football Sponsor;
NFL, FedEx Field
Tennis Sponsor:
ATP World Tour
Facility Sponsor:
FedExField (Landover, MD), FedExForum
(Memphis, TN)
Auto Sports Sponsor:
NASCAR

FORD MOTOR COMPANY
1 AMERICAN ROAD
DEARBORN, MI 48126
212-620-2200
www.ford.com
• William Clay Ford, Jr., Executive Chairman
• Jim Hackett, President and CEO
Total Spend:
$175M-$180M
Auto Motor Sponsor:
NASCAR
Facility Sponsor:

Ford Field, Detroit, MI; Ford Center,
Evansville, IN

FORD MOTOR COMPANY OF CANADA
1 THE CANADIAN ROAD
OAKVILLE, ON, CANADA L6H 1A7
www.ford.ca
• Mark Buzzell, President and CEO
Basketball Sponsor:
Toronto Raptors
Hockey Sponsor:
Toronto Maple Leafs

GENERAL ELECTRIC
41 FARNSWORTH ST
BOSTON, MA 02210
203-373-2211
Fax: 203-373-3131
www.ge.com
• H. Lawrence Culp, Jr., Chairman & CEO
Total Spend:
$15-20 million
Basketball Sponsor:
Boston Celtics
Motorsports Sponsor:
Formula 1
Other:
Olympic Games

GENERAL MOTORS
300 RENAISSANCE CTR
DETROIT, MI 48243
www.gm.com
• Mary T. Barra, Chairman and CEO
• Alan Batey, EVP and President, North
America
• Daniel E. Berce, SVP and President &
CEO, GM Financial
• Kimberly J. Brycz, SVP, Global Human
Resources
• Alicia Boler Davis, EVP, Global
Manufacturing
• Tony Cervone, SVP, Global
Communications
Total Spend:
$145M-$150M
Recent Sponsorships:
Chevy Youth Baseball, 2017; Chevy Youth
Soccer, 2017
Baseball Sponsor:
MLB, Minor League
College Sponsor:
NCAA, Bowl Games
Ice Hockey Sponsor:
NHL, AHL
Auto Sports Sponsor:
Grand AM Series for Trucks
Football Sponsor:
NFL
Golf Sponsor:
PGA

GOODYEAR TIRE & RUBBER CO., THE
200 INNOVATION WAY
AKRON, OH 44316-0001
330-796-2121
800-321-2136
Fax: 330-796-2222
corporate.goodyear.com
• Richard J. Kramer, Chairman, CEO and
President
• Steve McClellan, President, Americas
Total Spend:
$30M-$35M
Recent Sponsorships:
Pro Football Hall of Fame, 2016; Renewed

sponsorship for the NCAA Goodyear Cotton Bowl, 2017; NBA Cleveland Cavaliers, 2018
Auto Sports Sponsor:
NASCAR; NHRA
Baseball Sponsor:
MLB Cleveland Indians, Cincinnati Reds; Goodyear Ballpark, Phoenix, AZ

HEINEKEN USA
360 HAMILTON AVE
SUITE 1103
WHITE PLAINS, NY 10601
914-681-4100
www.heinekenusa.com
• Maggie Timoney, President and CEO
• Tim Tulfer, Chief Financial Officer
Total Spend:
$20M-$25M
Soccer Sponsor:
UEFA Champions League
Rudgy Sponsor:
Rugby World Cups
Golf Sponsor:
PGA CIMB Classic (2015)
Auto Motorshsports Sponsor:
Formula 1

HILTON HOTELS
7930 JONES BRANCH DR
MCLEAN, VA 22102
703-883-1000
Fax: 310-205-7880
www.hilton.com
• Christopher Nassetta, President and CEO
christopher.nassetta@hilton.com
Total Spend:
$15-20 million
Motorsports Sponsor:
McLaren-Honda (Formula 1)

HONDA CANADA INC.
180 HONDA BLVD
MARKHAM, ON, CANADA L6C 0H9
888-946-6329
www.honda.ca
• Dave Gardner, President & CEO
Auto Sports Sponsor:
Honda Indy (Toronto), Grand Prix of Canada (Montreal)
Baseball Sponsor:
Toronto Blue Jays
Hockey Sponsor:
NHL
Other:
Hockey Hall of Fame, Make-A-Wish© Canada

HYUNDAI MOTOR AMERICA
800-633-5151
consumeraffairs@hmausa.com
www.hyundaiusa.com
• William Lee, President & CEO, Hyundai Motor North America
Total Spend:
$85M-$90M
Recent Sponsorships:
Cricket World Cup; US PGA championship for its season opening title
Archery Sponsor:
Korea Archery Association since 1985
Soccer Sponsor:
FIFA World Cup since 2002
Auto Motor Sponsor:
World Rally Championship (WRC) since 2014

Tennis Sponsor:
Australian Open

IBM
1 NEW ORCHARD ROAD
ARMONK, NY 10504-1722
914-499-1900
800-426-4968
Fax: 914-765-6021
www.ibm.com
• Virginia M. Rometty, Chairman, President and CEO
Total Spend:
$20M-$25M
Golf Sponsor:
The PGA Masters 2018
Tennis Sponsor:
US Open; Wimbleton
Facility Sponsor:
Mercedes-Benz Stadium, Atlanta, GA
Soccer Sponsor:
MLS Los Angeles FC

J.P. MORGAN CHASE
270 PARK AVE
FLOOR 34
NEW YORK, NY 10017
212-270-6000
www.jpmorganchase.com
• James Dimon, Chairman and CEO
• Mary Callahan Erdoes, CEO, Asset and Wealth Management
• Douglas B. Petno, CEO, Commercial Banking
Total Spend:
$60M-$65M
Recent Sponsorships:
Awarded Sports Sponsor Of The Year, 2017; Chase Center arena, San Francisco, CA, 2019
Squash Sponsor:
Tournament of Champions
Tennis Sponsor:
US Open Tennis Championships
Facility Sponsor:
Lord's Cricket Ground, London; Amalie Arena, Tampa, FL; Amway Center, Orlando, FL

J.P. WISER'S
225 KING ST W
SUITE 1100
TORONTO, ON, CANADA M5V 3M2
416-479-2400
www.jpwisers.com
• Don Livermore, Master Blender
Other:
ESPN Fantasy Football, Women of Influence

KAISER FOUNDATION HEALTH PLAN
1 KAISER PLAZA
OAKLAND, CA 94612-3610
510-271-5800
Fax: 510-271-6493
healthy.kaiserpermanente.org
• Bernard J. Tyson, Chairman and CEO
Total Spend:
$15-20 million
Basketball Sponsor:
NBA

KIA CANADA
180 FOSTER CRESCENT
MISSISSAUGA, ON, CANADA L5R 4J5

905-755-6250
877-542-2886
Fax: 866-267-7424
www.kia.ca
• Kyle Lee, President & CEO
Soccer Sponsor:
FIFA, Toronto FC
Athlete Sponsor:
David Hearn (PGA)
Other:
Special Olympics

KIA MOTORS AMERICA
111 PETERS CANYON ROAD
IRVINE, CA 92606
949-468-4800
888-542-6334
Fax: 949-468-4515
kiamedia.com
• Sean Yoon, President and CEO
• Michael Cole, EVP and COO
Total Spend:
$35M-$40M
Recent Sponsorships:
Olympic Games, 2018; Special Olympics, 2018
Basketball Sponsor:
NBA; Kia NBA Tip-Off; Kia All-Star MVP; Kia NBA Performance Awards
College Sports Sponsor:
College Football Hall of Fame
Golf Sponsor:
LPGA; Bank of Hope Founders Cup; Kia Classic; ANA Inspiration; Volunteers of America LPGA Texas Classic; ShopRite LPGA Classic; Meijer LPGA Classic for Simply Give; KPMG Women's PGA Championship
Soccer Sponsor:
FIFA World Cup; UEFA Europa League; MLS
Tennis Sponsor:
Australian Open

KROGER
1014 VINE STREET
CINCINNATI, OH 45202-1100
513-762-4000
www.kroger.com
• Rodney McMullen, Chairman and CEO
Total Spend:
$25M-$30M
Recent Sponsorships:
U.S. Open of Surfing, 2017
Auto Sports Sponsor:
NASCAR, Indy Racing

LG ELECTRONICS USA
111 SYLVAN AVENUE
ENGLEWOOD CLIFFS, NJ
201-816-2000
Fax: 201-816-0636
www.lg.com
• William Cho, CEO, LG Electronics North America
Total Spend:
$15-20 million
Recent Sponsorships:
Olympic Winter Games 2018
Basketball Sponsor:
Los Angeles Lakers, Toronto Raptors
Hockey Sponsor:
Toronto Maple Leafs, Toronto Marlies (AHL), Montreal Canadiens
Soccer Sponsor:
English Premier League

sports sponsors

737

LOWE'S
1000 LOWE'S BLVD
MOORESVILLE, NC 28117
704-758-2917
800-445-6937
www.lowes.com
• Marvin R. Ellison, President and CEO
• David M. Denton, EVP and Chief Financial
Officer
• Sylvain Prud'homme, President and CEO,
Canada
Total Spend:
$40M-$45M
Sponsor:
NASCAR; NASCAR Hall of Fame; Boys &
Girls Club of America; NCAA; NBA Charlotte
Bobcats

LUCAS OIL
302 NORTH SHERIDAN ST
CORONA, CA 92880
951-270-0154
800-342-2512
Fax: 951-270-1902
lucasoil.com
• Forrest Lucas, Founder, President & CEO
Total Spend:
$15-20 million
Facility Sponsor:
Lucas Oil Stadium (Indianapolis)
Motorsports Sponsor:
Eight racing series, Lucas Oil Speedway
(Missouri)

MACY'S
7 WEST SEVENTH STREET
CINCINNATI, OH 45202
513-579-7000
Fax: 513-579-7555
www.macys.com
• Jeff Gennette, Chairman and CEO
• Hal Lawton, President
Total Spend:
$15-20 million
Event Sponsor:
Macy's Thanksgiving Day Parade

MARRIOTT INTERNATIONAL
10400 FERNWOOD ROAD
BETHESDA, MD 20817
301-380-3000
www.marriott.com
• J.W. Marriot, Jr., Exec. Chairman
• Arne M. Sorenson, President and CEO
Total Spend:
$35M-$40M
Recent Sponsorships:
FC Bayern, 2018; NHL Toronto Maple
Leafs, 2017

MARS NORTH AMERICA
6885 ELM STREET
MCLEAN, VA 22101
703-821-4900
www.mars.com
• Grant F. Reid, President and CEO
• Poul Weihrauch, President, Global Petcare
• Jean-Christophe Flatin, President,
Innovation, Science and Technology
• Fiona Dawson, President, Global Food,
Drinks & Multisales
• Andrew Clarke, President, Mars Wrigley
Confectionery
Total Spend:
$40M-$45M
Recent Sponsorships:

MLB Washington Nationals, 2017
Auto Motor Sponsor:
NASCAR
Football Sponsor:
NFL

MASTERCARD
2000 PURCHASE ST
PURCHASE, NY 10577
914-249-2000
www.mastercard.com
• Ajay Banga, President and CEO
• Craig Vosburg, President, North America
Total Spend:
$45M-$50M
Recent Sponsorships:
Rugby World Cup Japan 2019
Soccer Sponsor:
UEFA Champions League; Brazilian
National Team; Boca Juniors (Argentina);
NYC Football Club
Golf Sponsor:
PGA TOUR; Arnold Palmer Invitational;
Open Championship
Baseball Sponsor:
MLB; MLB Advanced Media; MLB Boston
Red Sox, Chicago Cubs, Los Angeles
Dodgers, New York Yankees
Hockey Sponsor:
The Mastercard Memorial Cup; NHL
Montreal Canadiens, Toronto Maple Leafs
Tennis Sponsor:
The Miami Open; The Australian Open

MCDONALD'S CORPORATION
1035 W RANDOLPH ST
CHICAGO, IL 60607
corporate.mcdonalds.com
• Steve Easterbrook, President & CEO
• Chris Kempczinski, President, McDonald's
USA
• David Fairhurst, Exec. VP and Chief
People Officer
• Robert Gibbs, Exec. VP and Chief
Communications Officer
• Jerry Krulewitch, Exec. VP and General
Counsel
• Silvia Lagnado, Exec. VP and Global Chief
Marketing Officer
• Kevin Ozan, Exec. VP and Chief Financial
Officer
Total Spend:
$50M-$55M
Recent Sponsorships:
McDonald's ends sponsorship with the
Olympic Games, 2017; Basketball Cape
Breton, 2017; College of Ozarks Basketball,
2018; FIFA World Cup, 2017 through 2021
Basketball Sponsor:
Maine McDonald's All-Star Basketball
Games; All American Games
Football Sponsor:
NFL
Ice Hockey Sponsor:
NHL; atoMc (minor hockey)
College Sports Sponsor:
NCAA, Bowl Games
Baseball Sponsor:
MLB, Minor League

MERCEDES-BENZ USA
ONE MERCEDES-BENZ DRIVE
SANDY SPRINGS, GA 30328
www.mbusa.com
• Dietmar Exler, President and CEO
Total Spend:
$55M-$60M

Recent Sponsorships:
Mercedes-Benz Stadium, Atlanta, GA, 2018;
Mercedes-Benz Dealer Championships
Baseball Sponsor:
Minor League
Golf Sponsor:
PGA
Football Sponsor:
NFL
College Sponsor:
NCAA, Bowl Games

METLIFE
METLIFE BUILDING
200 PARK AVENUE
NEW YORK, NY 10166
www.metlife.com
• Steven Kandarian, Chairman, President
and CEO
• Michel A. Khalaf, President, U.S. Business
Total Spend:
$25M-$30M
Golf Sponsor:
PGA; Metlife MatchUp Houston Open
Baseball Sposnor:
MLB
Facility Sponsor:
MetLife Stadium; NFL New York Giants,
New York Jets

MICROSOFT CORPORATION
ONE MICROSOFT WAY
REDMOND, WA 98052-7329
425-882-8080
Fax: 425-706-7329
www.microsoft.com
• Satya Nadella, Chief Executive Officer
• Brad Smith, President and Chief Legal
Officer
Total Spend:
$90M-$100M
Recent Sponsorships:
Special Olympics, 2018; Women's Soccer,
Seattle Reign FC, 2016
College Sports Sponsor:
NCAA, March Madness, 2016
Auto Sports Sponsor:
NASCAR
Football Sponsor:
NFL

MILLERCOORS
250 S WACKER DRIVE
CHICAGO, IL 60606
www.millercoors.com
• Gavin Hattersley, Chief Executive Officer
• Kevin Doyle, President, Sales & Distributor
Operations
Total Spend:
$120M-$125M
Recent Sponsorships:
FLW Tournament, 2016
Baseball Sponsor:
MLB - Colorado Rockies
Auto Sports Sponsor:
NASCAR, Coors Light
Basketball Sponsor:
NBA

MOLSONCOORS
33 CARLINGVIEW DR
TORONTO, ON, CANADA M9W 5E4
416-679-1786
www.molsoncoors.com
• Mark R. Hunter, President and CEO,
Molson Coors Brewing Company

- Frederic Landtmeters, President and CEO, Molson Coors Canada
- Gavin Hattersley, CEO, MillerCoors
Baseball Sponsor:
MLB (Canada)
Basketball Sponsor:
NBA (Canada)

MONDELEZ INTERNATIONAL
100 DEFOREST AVE
EAST HANOVER, NJ 07936
855-535-5648
www.mondelezinternational.com
- Dirk Van de Put, Chief Executive Officer
Total Spend:
$15-20 million
Recent Sponsorships:
Olympic Winter Games 2018
Soccer Sponsor:
MLS, English Premier League

MONSTER BEVERAGE CORPORATION
1 MONSTER WAY
CORONA, CA 92879
800-426-7367
info@monsterbevcorp.com
www.monsterbevcorp.com
- Rodney Sacks, Chairman and CEO
Total Spend:
$20M-$25M
Recent Sponsorships:
Monster Energy Cup Series, 2018; Monster Energy Boarderstyle Tour, 2018; PBR Monster Energy Tour, 2018; Monster Energy AMA Supercross, 2018
Auto Motorsports Sponsor:
NASCAR; Formula 1
Sponsor:
MMA Fighting

NATIONWIDE FINANCIAL SERVICES
ONE NATIONWIDE PLAZA
COLUMBUS, OH 43215
800-321-6064
www.nationwide.com
- Stephen Rasmussen, Chief Executive Officer
- Mark Thresher, Chief Financial Officer
Total Spend:
$45M-$50M
Auto Sports Sponsor:
NASCAR; No. 88 of Hendrick Motorsports
Golf Sponsor:
Memorial Tournament
Running Sponsor:
Nationwide Better Health Columbus Marathon
Baseball Sponsor:
Minor League, Columbus Clippers
College Sponsor:
Central Intercollegiate Athletic Association Tournament; Ohio State University athletics
Football Sponsor:
NFL
Hockey Sponsor:
NHL, Columbus Blue Jackets

NESTLE USA
1812 NORTH MOORE ST
ROSSLYN, VA 22209
818-549-6000
Fax: 818-553-3547
www.nestleusa.com
- Steve Presley, CEO, Nestle USA
Total Spend:
$25M-$30M

Baseball Sponsor:
MLB
Basketball Sponsor:
NBA
Football Sponsor:
NFL

NEW ERA CAP, CO
160 DELAWARE AVENUE
BUFFALO, NY 14202
716-604-9000
877-632-5950
Fax: 716-604-9299
www.neweracap.com
- Peter Augustine, President
- Christopher Koch, CEO
Total Spend:
$30M-$35M
Recent Sponsorships:
Schmidt Peterson Motorsports, 2018; NBA Brooklyn Nets, 2018
Auto Motor Sponsor:
IndyCar
Baseball Sponsor:
MLB; Minor League
Hockey Sponsor:
NHL
Basketbal Sponsor:
NBA
Football Sponsor:
NFL

NIKE
1 BOWERMAN DR
BEAVERTON, OR 97005
503-671-6453
800-344-6453
www.nike.com
- Phil Knight, Chairman Emeritus
- Mark Parker, Chairman/President/CEO
- Andy Campion, Chief Financial Officer
Total Spend:
$260M-$265M
Baseball Sponsor:
MLB; Minor League
Basketball Sponsor:
NBA; WNBA
College Sponsor:
NCAA; College Bowl
Running Sponsor:
Bank of America Chicago Marathon
Football Sponsor:
NFL
Golf Sponsor:
PGA; Champions Tour; LPGA

NISSAN CANADA
5290 ORBITOR DRIVE
MISSISSAUGA, ON, CANADA L4W 4Z5
800-387-0122
www.nissan.ca
- Joni Paiva, President
Recent Sponsorships:
Star Wars: The Last Jedi
Auto Sports Sponsor:
Nissan Micra Cup
Football Sponsor:
NFL

NISSAN NORTH AMERICA
ONE NISSAN WAY
FRANKLIN, TN 37067
615-725-1000
800-647-7261
www.nissanusa.com

- Denis Le Vot, Chairman, Nissan North America
Total Spend:
$35M-$40M
Recent Sponsorships:
Univision Deports/Mexican National Team, 2016
Auto Motor Sponsor:
Pirelli World Challenge
College Sponsor:
NCAA; College Bowl
Endurance Sports Sponsor:
Marine Corps Marathon

NORTHWESTERN MUTUAL LIFE
720 E WISCONSIN AVE
MILWAUKEE, WI 53202
414-271-1444
866-950-4644
www.northwesternmutual.com
- John E. Schlifske, Chairman, President and CEO
Total Spend:
$30M-$35M
College Sports Sponsor:
NCAA
Golf Sponsor:
PGA Champion Tour
Hockey Sponsor:
NHL St. Louis Blues

NRG ENERGY
804 CARNEGIE CENTER
PRINCETON, NJ 08540
609-524-4500
Fax: 609-524-4501
www.nrg.com
- Mauricio Gutierrez, President & CEO
Total Spend:
$15-20 million
Recent Sponsorships:
Coachella Valley Music & Arts Festival
Basketball Sponsor:
NBA (2)
Facility Sponsor:
NRG Stadium (Houston, NFL)
Football Sponsor:
NFL (8)
Soccer Sponsor:
MLS (2)

OLD DUTCH FOODS
100 BENTALL ST
WINNIPEG, MB, CANADA R2X 2Y5
800-351-2447
www.olddutchfoods.ca
- Steve Aanenson, President
Recent Sponsorships:
2017 FIG Artistic Gymnastics World Championships; 2017 Canada Summer Games
Football Sponsor:
Winnipeg Blue Bombers
Other:
MS Society Ontario; The Outdoor Adventure & Travel Show; World Ski & Snowboard Festival

ORACLE CORPORATION
500 ORACLE PKWY
REDWOOD SHORES, CA 94065
650-506-7000
800-392-2999
www.oracle.com

• Larry Ellison, Executive Chairman/Chief
Technology Officer
• Jeff Henley, Vice Chairman
Total Spend:
$25M–$30M
Sponsor:
MLB San Francisco Giants; Oracle Arena,
NBA Golden State Warriors

PAPA JOHN'S INTERNATIONAL
2002 PAPA JOHN'S BLVD
LOUISVILLE, KY 40299
www.papajohns.com
• Steve Ritchie, Chief Executive Officer
Total Spend:
$25M–$30M
Recent Sponsorships
Ending official sponsorship of the NFL, but
will continue sponsoring NFL teams locally,
2018.
Baseball Sponsor:
MLB
Basketball Sponsor:
NBA and WNBA
College Sponsor:
NCAA; March Madness
College Bowl Games Sponsor:
Sheraton Hawai'i Bowl, Texas Bowl
Facility Sponsor:
NCAA Papa John's Cardinal Stadium,
Louisville, KY
Hockey Sponsor:
NHL Tampa Bay Lightning

PEPSICO, INC.
700 ANDERSON HILL RD
PURCHASE, NY 10577
800-433-2652
www.pepsico.com
• Indra Nooyi, Chairman
• Ramon Laguarta, CEO
Total Spend:
$360M–$365M
Recent Sponsorships:
NFL, Super Bowl, 2018
Auto Sports Sponsor:
NASCAR; USAR
Baseball Sponsor:
MLB; Minor Leagues
Basketball Sponsor:
NBA
Bowling Sponsor:
PBA
College Sponsor:
NCAA; Bowl Games
Facilities Sponsor:
Auto Club Speedway of Southern California;
NBA/NHL Pepsi Center, Denver, CO; USHL
Pepsi Coliseum, Indianapolis, IN
Football Sponsor:
NFL; AF2; CIFL
Golf Sponsor:
LPGA Tour; PGA Tour
Hockey Sponsor:
NHL; AHL; CHL
Lacrosse Sponsor:
NLL

PNC FINANCIAL SERVICES
ONE PNC PLAZA
PITTSBURGH, PA 15222
888-762-2265
www.pnc.com
• William S. Demchak, Chairman, President
and CEO
• Robert Q. Reilly, Chief Financial Officer

• E. William Parsley, Chief Operating Officer
• Joseph E. Rockey, Chief Risk Officer
Total Spend:
$25M–$30M
Recent Sponsorships:
Verizon IndyCar Series; No. 9 Honda, 2018;
NFL New York Giants, 2016
College Sponsor:
NCAA
Facility Sponsor:
MLB PNC Park, Pittsburgh, PA; AAA PNC
Field, Moosic, PA; NCAA PNC Arena,
Raleigh, NC
Football Sponsor:
NFL
Hockey Sponsor:
NHL; Carolina Hurricanes

PROCTER & GAMBLE COMPANY
ONE PROCTER & GAMBLE PLAZA
CINCINNATI, OH 45202
513-983-1100
us.pg.com
• David S. Taylor, Chairman/President/CEO
Total Spend:
$75M–$80M
Recent Sponsorships:
NFL, 2018-2023
Golf Sponsor:
LPGA; Walmart NW Arkansas
Championship
Olympic Sponsor:
Team U.S.A.

QUICKEN LOANS
1050 WOODWARD AVE
DETROIT, MI 48226-1906
800-769-6133
www.quickenloans.com
• Dan Gilbert, Chairperson
Total Spend:
$15-20 million
Recent Sponsorships:
Lady Antebellum Wheels Up Tour 2015
Basketball Sponsor:
Cleveland Cavaliers
Facility Sponsor:
Quicken Loans Arena (Cleveland)
Football Sponsor:
Detroit Lions
Golf Sponsor:
PGA, Rickie Fowler
Hockey Sponsor:
Detroit Red Wings
Motorsports Sponsor:
NASCAR, Ryan Newman

RED BULL NORTH AMERICA
1740 STEWART STREET
SANTA MONICA, CA 90404
310-393-4647
Fax: 310-230-2361
www.redbull.com
• Stefan Kozak, Chief Executive Officer
Total Spend:
$20-25 million
Motosports Sponsor:
NASCAR, Formula 1
Extreme Sports Sponsor:
BMX, Motocross, Windsurfing,
Snowboarding, Skateboarding, Surfing

ROGERS COMMUNICATIONS
333 BLOOR ST EAST
TORONTO, ON, CANADA M4W 1G9

416-935-3548
www.rogers.com
• Joe Natale, President & CEO
Baseball Sponsor:
Toronto Blue Jays
Facility Sponsor:
Rogers Centre (Toronto)
Tennis Sponsor:
Rogers Cup
Other:
Writers' Trust of Canada, United Way,
Canadian Women's Foundation

ROLEX WATCH USA
665 FIFTH AVENUE
NEW YORK, NY 10022
212-758-7700
Fax: 212-980-2166
www.rolex.com
• Stewart Wicht, President & CEO
Total Spend:
$15-20 million
Golf Sponsor:
PGA/LPGA, The Masters, U.S. Open, U.S.
Women's Open, The Open, The Ryder Cup,
The Presidents Cup, The Solheim Cup
Motorsports Sponsor:
Formula 1, FIA World Endurance
Championship, The 24 Hours of Le Mans
Tennis Sponsor:
Wimbledon, Australian Open
Other:
Salzburg Festival, Teatro alla Scala, Royal
Opera House, Metropolitan Opera, Opera
National de Paris

SAMSUNG ELECTRONICS NA
3655 NORTH 1ST STREET
SAN JOSE, CA 95134
www.samsung.com
• Tim Baxter, President & CEO, Samsung
Electronics NA
• Young Hoon Eom, President & CEO,
Samsung Electronics America
Total Spend:
$40M–$45M
Sponsor:
Olympic Games; Youth Olympics; IAAF
World Championships in Athletics; IAAF
World Indoor Championships in Athletics;
FINA World Aquatic Championships; UCI
Track Cycling World Cup; World Rowing
Championships; Volleyball World League;
AFC Asia Cup; Africa Cup of Nations; NBA;
NBA Summer League; MLB; PGA
Championship; Samsung World
Championship; NASCAR; Super Rudgy

SAP AMERICA, INC.
3999 WEST CHESTER PIKE
NEWTOWN SQUARE, PA 19073
610-661-1000
800-872-1727
www.sap.com
• Bill McDermott, Chief Executive Officer
Total Spend:
$40M–$45M
Baseball Sponsor:
MLB New York Yankees
Basketball Sponsor:
FC Bayern Basketball; NBA; NBA New York
Nicks
Equestrian Sponsor:
CHIO Aachen; Event Rider Masters
Hockey Sponsor:
Alder Mannheim Hockey Club; NHL; NHL
New York Rangers; SAP Center - NHL San

Jose Sharks
Football Sponsor:
NFL New York Giants, New York Jets, San Francisco 49ers
Sailing Sponsor:
Extreme Sailing Series; U.S. Sailing
Soccer Sponsor:
City Football Group (CFG); FC Bayern Munich; German Football Association (DFB) World Cup Championship
Tennis Sponsor:
WTA

SCOTIABANK
SCOTIA PLAZA
44 KING STREET WEST
TORONTO, ON, CANADA M5H 1H1
416-866-6161
800-472-6842
Fax: 416-866-3750
www.scotiabank.com
• Brian J. Porter, President & CEO
Baseball Sponsor:
Minor League
Football Sponsor:
CFL (Edmonton Eskimos; Hamilton Tiger-Cats; Winnipeg Blue Bombers; BC Lions; Calgary Stampeders)
Hockey Sponsor:
NHL, Hockey Day in Canada
Facility Sponsor:
Scotiabank Arena (Toronto), Scotiabank Saddledome (Calgary)
Other:
Hot Docs, Giller Prize, Blue Nose Marathon, Calgary Marathon, Toronto Waterfront Marathon

SHELL OIL COMPANY
ONE SHELL PLAZA
910 LOUISIANA STREET
HOUSTON, TX 77002
713-767-5300
855-697-4355
www.shell.us
• Bruce Culpepper, President
Total Spend:
$40M-$45M
Auto Sports Sponsor:
NASCAR, Ferrari, Ducati, Shell-Pennzoil
Golf Sponsor:
PGA Shell Houston Open; World Golf Hall of Fame

SHERWIN-WILLIAMS CO.
101 W PROSPECT AVENUE
CLEVELAND, OH 44115
www.sherwin-williams.com
• John G. Morikis, President & CEO
Total Spend:
$15-20 million
Baseball Sponsor:
Los Angeles Angels
Hockey Sponsor:
CHL
Facility Sponsor:
Indianapolis Motor Speedway
Motorsports Sponsor:
IndyCar, NASCAR

SIRIUS XM RADIO
1221 AVENUE OF THE AMERICAS
36TH FLOOR
NEW YORK, NY 10020
866-635-5027
www.siriusxm.com

• James E. Meyer, Chief Executive Officer
Total Spend:
$35M-$40M
Auto Racing Sponsor:
IRL; NASCAR
Soccer Sponsor:
MLS
Golf Sponsor:
PGA
Football Sponsor:
NFL, CFL
Baseball Sponsor:
MLB; Minor Leagues
College Sponsor:
NCAA
Basketball Sponsor:
NBA
Hockey Sponsor:
NHL

SONY CORP. OF AMERICA
25 MADISON AVENUE
NEW YORK, NY 10010
212-833-6800
Fax: 212-833-6956
www.sony.com
• Howard Stringer, Chairman, President and CEO
Total Spend:
$15-20 million
Golf Sponsor:
Sony Open (Hawaii)

SPORT CHEK
824 41ST AVENUE NE
CALGARY, AB, CANADA T2E 3R3
403-717-1400
www.sportchek.ca
• T.J. Flood, President
Baseball Sponsor:
Toronto Blue Jays
Basketball Sponsor:
Toronto Raptors
Hockey Sponsor:
NHL (Calgary Flames; Edmonton Oilers; Ottawa Senators; Toronto Maple Leafs; Vancouver Canucks; Winnipeg Jets)
Soccer Sponsor:
MLS (Toronto FC; Vancouver Whitecaps FC)
Amateur Sport Sponsor:
Canadian Olympic/Paralympic Committee, Hockey Canada, Alpine Canada, Canada Snowboard
Other:
Canadian Sports Hall of Fame; Canada Games; Kamloops Marathon; SickKids Great Camp Adventure

SPRINT CORPORATION
6480 SPRINT PKWY
OVERLAND PARK, KS 66251
913-315-8081
www.sprint.com
• Marcelo Claure, Exec. Chairman
• Nestor Cano, Chief Operating Officer
• Michel Combes, CEO
Total Spend:
$55M-$60M
Facility Sponsor:
Sprint Center

STANLEY BLACK & DECKER
1000 STANLEY DR
NEW BRITAIN, CT 06053

860-225-5111
www.stanleyblackanddecker.com
• James M. Loree, President & CEO
Total Spend:
$15-20 million
Motorsports Sponsor:
NASCAR, Grand Prix motorcycle racing
Extreme Sports Sponsor:
Skateboarding, Snowboarding, Bull Riding, Mountain Biking, Motocross, BMX Flatland, BMX

SUBWAY RESTAURANTS
325 SUB WAY
MILFORD, CT 06461
203-877-4281
800-888-4848
www.subway.com
• Trevor Haynes, President & CEO
Total Spend:
$15-20 million
Recent Sponsorships:
NFL London Games, Subway Kids & Sports Golf Tournament
Baseball Sponsor:
Little League
College Football:
NCAA
Motorsports Sponsor:
Daniel Suarez (NASCAR)

SUNOCO
8020 PARK LANE
SUITE 200
DALLAS, TX 75231
800-786-6261
www.sunoco.com
• Joseph Kim, President and CEO
Total Spend:
$20-25 million
Motorsport Sponsor:
NASCAR, IndyCar, NHRA

SWATCH GROUP
SEERVORSTADT 6
PO BOX 2501
BIEL/BIENNE
41 32 343 6811
Fax: 41-32 343 6911
www.swatchgroup.com
• Nick Hayek, Jr., CEO
Total Spend:
$25M-$30M
Sponsors:
University of Miami Athletics, Miami Hurricanes; Olympic Games

T-MOBILE USA
12920 SE 38TH STREET
BELLEVUE, WA 98006
425-378-4000
Fax: 425-378-4040
www.t-mobile.com
• John Legere, CEO
Total Spend:
$50M-$55M
Recent Sponsorships:
T-Mobile Arena, Paradise, NV, 2016; Home Run Derby, since 2016
Baseball Sponsor:
MLB
Basketball Sponsor:
NWBA National Tournament
Ice Hockey Sponsor:
NHL; Vegas Golden Knights

TARGET STORES
1000 NICOLLET MALL
MINNEAPOLIS, MN 55403
612-304-6073
www.target.com
• Brian Cornell, Chairman and CEO
• Rick Gomez, EVP, Chief Marketing Officer
• John J. Mulligan, EVP, Chief Operating Officer
Total Spend:
$35M-$40M
Recent Sponsorships:
MLS; Minnesota United FC, 2017
Recent Sponsorships:
Nissan ends sponsorship with NASCAR, 2018
Baseball Sponsor:
MLB
Basketball Sponsor:
NBA
Facility Sponsor:
MLB Target Field, Minneapolis, MN; NBA/WNBA Target Center, Minneapolis, MN

TD CANADA TRUST
161 BAY ST
TORONTO, ON, CANADA M5J 2S1
www.td.com
• Bharat Masrani, Chief Executive Officer, TD Bank Group
Recent Sponsorships:
Landmarks 2017, Nature Conservancy, Park People
Facility Sponsor:
TD Garden (Boston), TD Place (Ottawa)
Other:
TD Montreal Jazz Festival, TD James Moody Democracy of Jazz Festival (New Jersey), Philadelphia International Festival of the Arts

TELUS CORPORATION
510 W GEORGIA ST
23RD FLOOR
VANCOUVER, BC, CANADA V6B 0M3
604-697-8044
Fax: 604-899-1289
www.telus.com
• Darren Entwhistle, President & CEO
• Doug French, CFO
Football Sponsor:
CFL (BC Lions; Calgary Stampeders; Edmonton Eskimos; Hamilton Tiger-Cats; Montreal Alouettes)
Hockey Sponsor:
Calgary Flames, OHL, WHL, Hockey Canada
Resort Sponsor:
Big White, Mont Tremblant, Resorts of the Canadian Rockies, Whistler-Blackcomb
Other:
IRONMAN Mont Tremblant, Nature Conservancy Canada, TELUS Science Centres, United Way Toronto, WWF - Canada

THE EMIRATES GROUP
www.emirates.com
• Tim Clark, President, Emirates Airline
Total Spend:
$15-20 million
Motorsports Sponsor:
Formula 1
Soccer Sponsor:
The Emirates FA Cup (English Premier League), Arsenal FC and The Emirates

Stadium, New York Cosmos, Real Madrid
Tennis Sponsor:
U.S. Open, Rogers Cup, ATP World Tour

THE HERSHEY CO.
100 CRYSTAL A DRIVE
HERSHEY, PA 17033
717-534-4200
Fax: 717-534-6550
www.hersheys.com
• Michele Buck, President & CEO
Total Spend:
$20-25 million
Olympic Sponsor:
Team USA

TIM HORTONS
EXCHANGE TOWER
130 KING ST WEST
TORONTO, ON, CANADA M5X 1A9
www.timhortons.com
• Sami Siddiqui, President
Baseball Sponsor:
Toronto Blue Jays
Basketball Sponsor:
Toronto Raptors
Football Sponsor:
CFL (BC Lions; Calgary Stampeders; Edmonton Eskimos; Hamilton Tiger-Cats; Montreal Alouettes; Saskatchewan Roughriders; Toronto Argonauts; Winnipeg Blue Bombers)
Hockey Sponsor:
NHL (Montreal Canadiens; Toronto Maple Leafs; Calgary Flames; Vancouver Canucks; Ottawa Senators; Winnipeg Jets; Edmonton Oilers), CHL, CWHL, Hockey Hall of Fame
Soccer Sponsor:
Toronto FC; Montreal Impact; Vancouver Whitecaps FC
Other:
Curling Canada, Tim Hortons Brier, Tim Hortons Roar of the Rings (Canadian Olympic Curling Trials)

TOYOTA MOTOR SALES, U.S.A.
800-331-4331
Fax: 310-468-7814
www.toyota.com/usa
• Jim Lentz, CEO
Total Spend:
$165M-$170M
Recent Sponsorships:
10-year Olympic sponsor, 2015
Auto Racing Sponsor:
NASCAR; USAC
Baseball Sponsor:
MLB; Minor Leagues; Michaels Toyota Youth Baseball
Basketball Sponsor:
NBA; WNBA; NBDL
College Sports Sponsor:
NCAA, Bowl Games, Broadcast sponsor
Facility Sponsor:
NBA Toyota Center, Houston, TX; NFL Toyota Stadium, Georgetown, KY; AF2/WHL Toyota Center, Kennewick, WA; AIFL/NAHL Town Toyota Center, Wenatchee, WA; CHL/AIFA Tim's Toyota Center, Prescott Valley, AZ; MLS/MLL Toyota Park, Bridgeview, IL; NBA/NHL Toyota Sports Center, El Segundo, CA
Football Sponsor:
NFL; AF2
Fishing Sponsor:
B.A.S.S.

Golf Sponsor:
PGA Tour; LPGA Tour
Hockey Sponsor:
AHL; CHL; NHL
Soccer Sponsor:
MLS

U.S. BANCORP
800 NICOLLET MALL
MINNEAPOLIS, MN 55402
651-466-3000
800-872-2657
Fax: 612-303-0782
www.usbank.com
• Richard Davis, President & CEO
Total Spend:
$20-25 million
Recent Sponsorships:
2017 U.S. Bank State Basketball Championships
Facility Sponsor:
U.S. Bank Stadium (NFL), U.S. Bank Arena (ECHL)

UNDER ARMOUR
PORT COVINGTON
BALTIMORE, MD
888-727-6687
Fax: 410-454-6535
mediarelations@underarmour.com
www.uabiz.com
• Kevin A. Plank, Founder, Chairman, President & CEO
 ext 6434
kplank@underarmour.com
• David E. Bergman, Chief Financial Officer
• Colin Browne, Chief Supply Chain Officer
• Kevin Eskridge, Chief Product Officer
• Paul Fipps, Chief Digital Officer
• Jason LaRose, President of North America
Total Spend:
$70M-$75M
Recent Sponsorships:
NASCAR, Hendrick Motorsports, 2014; Cancelled its 2013 8-year sponsorship with the USA Gymnastics Team, 2017
Baseball Sponsor:
MLB; Minor League
Basketball Sponsor:
NBA; WNBA
Golf Sponsor:
PGA; LPGA
Endurance Sports Sponsor:
Chevron Houston Marathon
Hockey Sponsor:
NHL; Toronto Maple Leafs

UNILEVER USA
800 SYLVAN AVENUE
ENGLEWOOD CLIFFS, NJ 07632
800-298-5018
www.unileverusa.com
• Alan Jope, Chief Executive Officer
• Graeme Pitkethly, Chief Financial Officer
Total Spend:
$25M-$30M
Recent Sponsorships:
Chelsea FC, 2017; Talladega Superspeedway, 2016
Auto Motorsports Sponsor:
NASCAR

UNITED CONTINENTAL HOLDINGS
WILLIS TOWER
CHICAGO, IL
newsroom.united.com

• Oscar Munoz, Chief Executive Officer
• J. Scott Kirby, President
Total Spend:
$30M-$35M
Baseball Sponsor:
MLB Chicago Cubs, Chicago White Sox, Kansas City Royals, Los Angeles Dodgers
Football Sponsor:
NFL Chicago Bears, Cleveland Browns, Denver Broncos, Houston Texans, Kansas City Chiefs, New Orleans Saints, New York Giants, New York Jets, Tampa Bay Buccaneers, Washington Redskins
Facility Sponsor:
United Center, Chicago, IL; NBA Chicago Bulls; NHL Chicago Blackhawks
Sponsor:
U.S. Olympic Committee; U.S. Paralympics; New York Road Runners Half Marathon

UNITED PARCEL SERVICE OF AMERICA, INC./UPS
55 GLENLAKE PKWY NE
ATLANTA, GA 30328
800-742-5877
www.ups.com
• David P. Abney, Chief Executive Officer
• Jim Barber, Chief Operating Officer
Total Spend:
$40M-$45M
Auto Sports Sponsor:
NASCAR; Ferrari Formula 1
College Sponsor:
NCAA
Golf Sponsor:
PGA; The Masters; The Open Championship

VERIZON COMMUNICATIONS
1095 AVENUE OF THE AMERICAS
NEW YORK, NY
www.verizon.com
• Hans Vestberg, Chief Executive Officer
Total Spend:
$155M-$160M
Baseball Sponsor:
MBL, Minor League
Basketball Sponsor:
NBA
College Sponsor:
NCAA; College Bowl
Football Sponsor:
NFL
Hockey Sponsor:
NHL; AHL

VF CORPORATION
105 CORPORATE CENTER BLVD
GREENSBORO, NC 27408
336-424-6000
www.vfc.com
• Steve Rendle, Chair, President & CEO
Total Spend:
$15-20 million

VISA USA
900 METRO CENTER BLVD
FOSTER CITY, CA 94404
800-847-2911
www.visa.com
• Alfred F. Kelly, Jr., Chief Executive Officer
• Lynn Biggar, EVP/Chief Marketing & Communications Officer
• Oliver Jenkyn, EVP/Regional President, North America
• Vasant Prabhu, EVP/Chief Financial Officer
• Ellen Richey, Vice Chairman/Chief Risk Officer
Total Spend:
$40M-$45M
Auto Sports Sponsor:
NASCAR
Football Sponsor:
NFL
Ice Hockey Sponsor:
NHL
Olympics Sponsor:
US Soccer; USA Track & Field; US Ski & Snowboarding; US Fencing; USA Gymnastics
Soccer Sponsor:
FIFA World Cup; FIFA World Football Museum

VOLKSWAGEN GROUP OF AMERICA
2200 FERDINAND PORSCHE DR
HERNDON, VA 20171
248-754-5000
Fax: 248-754-4930
www.volkswagengroupofamerica.com
• Scott Keogh, CEO & President
Total Spend:
$20-25 million
Recent Sponsorships:
UEFA EURO 2020

WALMART INC.
702 SW 8TH STREET
BENTONVILLE, AR 72716
800-WAL-MART
walmart.com
• Doug McMillon, President & CEO
Total Spend:
$20-25 million
Golf Sponsor:
Walmart NW Arkansas Championship (LPGA)
Fishing Sponsor:
Walmart FLW Tour (fly-fishing)

WELLS FARGO & CO
420 MONTGOMERY STREET
SAN FRANCISCO, CA 94163
866-249-3302
800-869-3557
www.wellsfargo.com
• Timothy J. Sloan, President & CEO
• John Shrewsberry, Chief Financial Officer

Total Spend:
$40M-$45M
Recent Sponsorships:
NFL Los Angeles Rams, 2017
Facility Sponsor:
Wells Fargo Arena, Des Moines, IA
Football Sponsor:
NFI
College Sponsor:
NCAA; College Bowl
Golf Sponsor:
PGA; Wells Fargo Championship
Baseball Sponsor:
MLB Colorado Rockies; Minor League
Basketball Sponsor:
NBA
Endurance Sports Sponsor:
St. George Marathon; Grandma's Marathon
Hockey Sponsor:
NHL

YUM! BRANDS
1900 COLONEL SANDERS LANE
LOUISVILLE, KY 40213
502-874-8300
www.yum.com
• Greg Creed, Chief Executive Officer
Total Spend:
$35M-$40M
Recent Sponsorships:
NFL, 2018; NCAA; FCS Division 1 College Football Championship, 2017
Facility Sponsor:
KFC Yum! Center, Louisville, KY - Louisville Cardinals (men's and women's basketball); American Airlines Center, Dallas, TX
Baskeball Sponsor:
NBA Dallas Mavericks
Baseball Sponsor:
MLB; MLB Cleveland Indians
Hockey Sponsor:
NHL Dallas Stars

ZURICH AMERICAN INSURANCE CO.
1299 ZURICH WAY
SCHAUMBURG, IL 60196-1056
800-382-2150
info.source@zurichna.com
www.zurichna.com
• Kathleen Savio, Chief Executive Officer
Total Spend:
$15-20 million
Hockey Sponsor:
Swiss National Team
Golf Sponsor:
PGA
Other:
World Economic Forum, Zurich Vitaparcours, Zurich Marato de Barcelona, German Olympic Team

6

professional services

professional services

Executive Search Services

ANDREA KIRBY COACHES, INC.
14364 NOLEN LANE
CHARLOTTE, NC 28277
704-541-4842
800-831-3883
Fax: 704-541-4816
www.andreakirby.com
Clients:
Sports Figures
Description:
Media workshops for players and management focusing on interview skills and media relationships. Also, skills for presentations and appearances. Broadcast coaching and evaluation for play-by-play and color commentators, announcers, and studio talent. Offers personal and team workshops for players, managers, coaches and front office personnel. Broadcast talent coach for networks and local stations.
Sports Service Founded:
1985

CHASEAMERICA, INC.
300 PARK AVENUE
17TH FLOOR
NEW YORK, NY 10022
646-706-7300
800-491-4980
• David E. Stefan, Chief Executive Officer
• Maria Dennison, President
Nature of Sports Service:
Executive search, M&A and management consulting services for sports apparel, footwear and equipment manufacturers, golf course and residential developers, hotels, spas, stadiums and other athletic facilities.

CORPORATE EXECUTIVE SERVICES
6 HUTTON CENTRE DRIVE
SUITE #1280
SOUTH COAST METRO, CA 92707
714-836-6742
Fax: 714-836-6816
www.corporateexecutive.com
• Warren Tempero, Chief Executive Officer
Services:
Provides career counseling and job placement firm for Corporate Executives in Southern California
Sports Service Founded:
1961
Description:
Executive search firm specializing in $40,000 - $200,000 accounting/financial/banking, technical - computer related, medical, legal and manufacturing.

CREATIVE GROUP
10 ALMADEN BOULEVARD
SUITE 900
SAN JOSE, CA 95113
408-961-2975
888-846-1668
Fax: 408-271-9487
san.jose@creativegroup.com
www.creativegroup.com
Description:
Expertise in creative staffing of freelance professionals. Provides freelance creative, advertising, marketing and Internet professionals to companies on a project basis. Creative Group for consultants who possess expertise in: Internet design, direct marketing, e-marketing and media relations

EASTMAN & BEAUDINE, INC.
7201 BISHOP ROAD
SUITE 220
PLANO, TX 75024
972-312-1012
• Bob E. Beadine, President & Chief Executive Officer
Services:
One of the country's leading executive searches for sports/entertainment/media, collegiate sports, marketing, board of directors, hospitality and leisure, technology/e-business, retail, manufacturing/operations, financial services.
Description:
Recognized as the premier search firm in sports recruiting. Exclusive affiliated partners in nine major cities throughout Europe and the Far East.
Year Founded:
1967

EXECUTIVE LEVELS INTERNATIONAL, LLC
4938 HAMPDEN LANE
#430
BETHESDA, MD 20814
301-320-3080
Fax: 831-306-3080
moreinfo@executivelevels.com
www.executivelevels.com
Nature of Service:
Performance based full service executive search firm specializing in management and executives for the following areas: Corporate Sports Properties, Media, Entertainment Sports Facilities, Live Event Producers, Professional Teams, All Leagues, Governing Bodies, Sports Apparel, Footwear, Sports Marketing and Advertising, Corporate Marketing, Sporting Goods, Consumer Goods: Manufacturers and Retailers, Online & Fantasy Related Sports, Arena Sports, College Athletics, Information Technology, E-Business, ECommerce, Networking, Telecommunications, Wireless, Internet, IT Consulting, Management Consulting, Media.
Year Founded:
1995

EXECUTIVE SPORTS PLACEMENT
74-923 HIGHWAY 111
#186
INDIAN WELLS, CA 92210
888-884-0495
Sports Service Founded:
1997
Services:
Placement of people in the sports industry.
Description:
Executive search and career consulting firm providing professional services in executive recruitment, career planning and resume preparation for entry to senior level management personnel.

GAME FACE, INC.
PO BOX 330
LEHI, UT 84043
503-523-8381
www.gamefaceinc.com
• Robert Cornilles, Founder/CEO
Description:
A sports executive training firm that specializes in enhancing sales and revenue, customer service, and personnel skills development for professional sports clubs, intercollegiate athletic departments, and individual executives.
Clients:
Clients include over 400 major and minor league professional sports organization, intercollegiate athletic departments, and fortune 1000 corporations.
Founded:
1995

GENERAL SPORTS TURF SYSTEMS
400 WATER STREET
SUITE 250
ROCHESTER, MI 48307
248-601-2200
Fax: 248-601-2400
www.generalsports.com
• Andrew D. Appleby, Chairman
• Robert Heinrich, Senior Vice President
• Ryan Copacia, Manager
• Shawn Vellek, Sales Representative
• Tyler Ingle, Controller

GRANT ASSOCIATES
301 SAYRE DRIVE
PRINCETON, NJ 08540-5826
609-514-8674
Fax: 212-684-4607
• David Grant, President
dave_grant@comcast.net
Nature of Service:
Executive recruiting, licensing management, sports/event promotion, strategic corporate growth consulting, U.S. market development.
Year Founded:
1997
Sports Service Founded:
1997

HEALTHANDWELLNESSJOBS.COM
3402 ENGLEWOOD DRIVE
PEARLAND, TX 77584
281-794-7879
www.healthandwellnessjobs.com
• Scott Hankosky, Chief Executive Officer
Services:
Provides health and wellness professionals national exposure to employment opportunities.
Nature of Sports Service:
A job posting web site for employers to post positions for Exercise Physiologist, Physical Therapist, Athletic Trainers, Personal Trainers, Academic Professors, Aerobic Instructors, Aquatic Instructors, Massage Therapist, Sports Administrators & Management and other health and wellness professionals.

HRESHKO CONSULTING GROUP
850 US HIGHWAY ONE
SUITE 2
NORTH BRUNSWICK, NJ 8902
732-545-9000
Fax: 732-545-0080
info@hcgusa.com
www.hcgusa.com
• Frank Hreshko, Managing Partner
Sports Service Founded:
1991

Marketing & Consulting Services:
Retained executive search firm specializing in recruiting, accounting, finance, licensing, sales, marketing, and senior management professionals for sporting goods manufacturers, professional sports teams and professional sports leagues and associations.

KORN/FERRY INTERNATIONAL
1900 AVENUE OF THE STARS
SUITE 2600
LOS ANGELES, CA 90067
310-552-1834
www.kornferry.com
• Paul C. Reilly, Chairman/Interim President, EMEA
(310) 843-4130
paul.reilly@kornferry.com
• Gary D. Burnison, CEO
(310) 226-2613
gary.burnison@kornferry.com
• Stephen Giusto, Executive Vice President/Chief Financial Offi
Services:
Premier provider of executive human capital solutions, with services ranging from corporate governance and CEO recruitment to executive search, middle-management recruitment and Leadership Development Solutions (LDS).
Description:
World-wide executive search firm with 71 offices in 40 countries. Specializes in assisting organizations locate high-caliber senior management in all aspects of the Sports Industry Including: Professional Sports, Collegiate Sports, Sporting Goods, Sports Finance, and Sports Technology

MiCa SPORTS
759 BLOOMFIELD AVENUE
SUITE 207
WEST CALDWELL, NJ 7006
973-618-9979
Fax: 973-618-9629
info@micasports.com
www.micasports.com
• Michelle Beidner, Co-Founder
michelle@micasports.com
• Caryn Snerson, Pricipal
(973) 618-9979
caryn@micasports.com
Sports Service Founded:
1999.
Nature of Service:
An executive search and placement firm servicing the national sports marketing industry. Concentrating exclusively on sports marketing opportunities, from corporate sponsorship and promotions to events, public relations, business development, sales, media, product licensing and more.

NEXT LEVEL EXECUTIVE SEARCH
24 CATHEDRAL PLACE
SUITE 500
SAINT AUGUSTINE, FL 32084
904-810-5177
866-810-5177
Fax: 904-810-6855
info@nextlevelexecutive.com
www.nextlevelexecutive.com
• Michael Garnes, President
Founded:
2003

Description:
Next Level Executive Search (NLES), is a focused global search firm specializing in recruitment and placement in the sports industry. The firm's functional areas of specialization are: sales, marketing, sponsorship and partnership leaders. The sectors NLES serves are companies, corporate sponsors and partnerships, associations, governing bodies, sports media, colleges, and professional teams and leagues.
Clients:
Retained and contingency executive search firm. Clients confidential

RUSSELL REYNOLDS ASSOCIATES, INC.
200 PARK AVENUE
SUITE 2300
NEW YORK, NY 10166-0002
212-351-2000
Fax: 212-370-0896
info@russellreynolds.com
www.russellreynolds.com
• Jim Bagley, Associate
jbagley@russellreynolds.com
• James Carpenter, Associate
Description:
A global executive recruitment and management assessment firm that delivers solutions to organizational challenges through the recruitment of exceptional leaders. Excels in finding uniquely qualified leaders for clients in all major markets.

SEARCH SYNERGY INC.
3004 NE 26TH AVENUE
PORTLAND, OR 97212-3547
503-288-2400
www.searchsynergy.com
• Ross Regis, Founder/President
ross@searchsynergy.com
• Ross Regis, Founder/President
(503) 288-2400
• Julie Yochim, Database Manager
Nature of Service:
Executive search firm specializing in mid-to-executive level positions within the sporting goods, outdoor, and action sports industries, for the product segments of footwear, apparel and equipment.

SPENCER STUART
353 N CLARK ST
CHICAGO, IL 60654
312-822-0080
Fax: 312-822-0116
www.spencerstuart.com
• Kenneth V Eckhart, Manager/Consultant
• Susan J. Baldwin, Consultant
Nature of Sports Service:
Firm offers management consulting and executive searches, specializing in finding top-level executives and board directors. Firm has nearly 300 consultants, who operate from 50 offices in 24 countries.

SPORT SEARCH.MVP GROUP
2990 E NORTHERN AVENUE
SUITE B101
PHOENIX, AZ 85028
602-485-5555
Fax: 602-458-3435
mt@sportsearch.net
www.sportsearch.net
• Marty McEvoy, Managing Director-International

martym@sportsearch.net
• Mark Tudi, President/Founder
mt@sportsearchonline.com
Services:
A premier Executive Search/Recruiting and Human Resource Consulting firm, sourcing the critical layer of management, completely focused in the Sports, Recreation and Entertainment Industries which provides retained executive search, customized recruiting assignments, on-line career management program, and sports & entertainment human resources forum

SPORTS GROUP INTERNATIONAL
7317 SPYGLASS WAY
SUITE 400
RALEIGH, NC 27615
919-855-0226
Fax: 919-855-0793
sgisearch@aol.com
www.sgisearch.com
• Joseph A. White, President
(919) 855-0226
sgisearch@aol.com
• Joseph White, President
(919) 855-0266
sgisearch@aol.com
• Dave Reinhart, Vice President
(413) 587-0022
• Rod Jahner, Vice President
(919) 435-7579
rjahner@gmail.com
• Alison White, Executive Search Consultant
(704) 466-0899
awhite.sgi@gmail.com
Nature of Service:
Retained Executive Search firm serving sporting goods, performance athletic footwear and apparel industries. Disciplines in which Sports Group International conducts search assignments include sales, marketing, product design, product development, supply chain management, international sales and marketing, general management, and sports marketing. Client scope is global. Sports Group International conducts search assignments in the USA, Canada, and overseas.
Year Founded:
1989

SPORTS GUIDES, LLC
13901 N 73RD STREET
SUITE 219
SCOTTSDALE, AZ 85281
480-948-8885
Description:
Assisted thousands of individuals in their pursuit of a career in the sports industry as well as thousands of companies to find the perfect employee. Offers many services such as job listings, a resume bank, industry contact, industry overviews, job description, salary information and chat sessions.

SPORTSEARCH, INC.
2990 E NORTHERN AVENUE
SUITE B101
PHOENIX, AZ 85028-4838
602-485-5555
Fax: 602-485-3435
www.sportsearchonline.com
• Mark Tudi, President
(602) 485-5555
mt@sportsearch.net
• Marty McEvoy, Managing Director

martym@sportsearch.net
• John Byrne, Search Consultant
john@sportsearch.net
• Mark Williamson, Manager Of Marketing Operations
mark@sportsearch.net
• Andy Sandler, Partner
Services:
Executive Search/Recruiting and Human Resource Consulting firm, sourcing the critical layer of management, completely focused in the Sports Recreation and Entertainment Industries, on a global basis.

STRATEGIC RESOURCES
19125 N CREEK PARKWAY
SUITE 120
BOTHELL, WA 98011
425-688-1151
Fax: 425-732-2112
corporate@strategicresources.com
www.strategicresources.com
• Ted Warren, President/Senior Partner
tedwarren@strategicresources.com
• Ted Warren, President and Senior Partner
tedwarren@strategicresources.com
• Marcus Williams, Vice President
mwilliams@strategicresources.com
• David Castelblanco, Vice President
dcastelblanco@strategicresources.com
• Daniela Chetan, Vice President
dchetan@strategicresources.com
• Allen Barron, Affiliated Partner
adb@strategicresources.com
Services:
National executive search firm specializing in senior-level executive search and Board of Director appointments. Also offers introductory services for M&A or strategic alliance.
Sports Service Founded:
1998
Nature of Sports Service:
Executive search firm recruiting for positions in middle to upper level management specializing in the sports industry. Services provided to professional leagues, stadium/arena operations, sporting goods manufacturers, sports marketing firms and sports broadcast media.

TALON GROUP INTERNATIONAL D/B/A/MANAGEMENT RECRUITERS OF MERCER ISLAND
9725 SE 36TH STREET
SUITE 312
MERCER ISLAND, WA 98040
206-232-0204
Fax: 206-232-6172
denise@mrmi.com
www.mrmi.com
• Vince Holt, President
(206) 232-0129
• Vanica Salvacruz, Project Coordinator
(206) 232-1624
vanica@mrmi.com
• Cheryl Cho, Director of Footwear
(206) 232-5047
cheryl@mrmi.com
• Jim Dykeman, Executive Recruiter
(206) 232-0211
jim@mrmi.com
• Denise Holt, Manager Administration
(206) 232-7051
denise@mrmi.com
• Vince Holt, President
(206) 232-0129

Sports Service Founded:
1980
Nature of Sports Service:
Specialize in employee placement in the wholesale apparel and footwear industry. Placements with major athletic and casual footwear and apparel companies such as Adidas, And 1, L.L. Bean, Brooks Sports, Diesel, XOXO, Mecca, Nautica, Reef Brazil and Teva. Positions include Product Design, Product Development, Marketing, Sales, and Sourcing.

TEAMWORK CONSULTING, INC.
22550 MCCAULEY ROAD
SHAKER HEIGHTS, OH 44122
216-360-1790
Fax: 216-292-9265
info@teamworkonline.com
www.teamworkconsulting.com
• Buffy Filippell, President
(216) 360-1790
Services:
Retained executive search firm focusing on mid-level to senior-level positions in the sports and live event industry.

THE GOULD GROUP
1471 ROUTE 9
ROME EXECUTIVE PLAZA
CLIFTON PARK, NY 12065
518-371-3052 EXT 301
Fax: 518-371-3953
www.thegouldgroup.net
• Tom Gould, Owner
Services:
Assists firms in sourcing outstanding performers in the field of sales management
Description:
Our professional placement assists firms in sourcing outstanding performers in the field of sales management. Works with client, companies and candidates throughout the United States.

TMP. WORLDWIDE/MONSTER GLOBAL HEADQUARTERS
622 THIRD AVENUE
39TH FLOOR
NEW YORK, NY 10017
212-351-7000
Fax: 646-658-0541
• Sal Iannuzzi, Chairman/Chief Executive Officer
sal.iannuzzi@monster.com
• Tim Yates, EVP/CFO
Services:
A global online careers and recruitment resource, known for connecting quality job seekers at all levels with leading employers across all industries and offers employers innovative technology and superior services that give them more control over the recruiting process.
Description:
Retained executive search firm servicing active apparel, sporting goods, athletic footwear and retail sports related companies. Recruit for positions from CEO to middle management sales, marketing, manufacturing, sourcing, finance and other functional areas.

TURNKEY SPORTS & ENTERTAINMENT
9 TANNER STREET
SUITE 8
HADDONFIELD, NJ 8033

856-685-1450
Fax: 856-685-1451
www.turnkeyse.com
• Len Perna, President/Chief Executive Officer
lenperna@turnkeyse.com
• Patrick Kuhlen, Marketing Director
patrickkuhlen@turnkeyse.com
• Haynes Hendrickson, Senior Vice President
• Michael Mayle, Vice President Information Technology
• Melissa Dean, Senior Vice President
• Dan Rossetti, Senior Vice President/Turnkey Search
Year Founded:
1996
Nature of Services:
Turnkey provides agency clients, brand clients and property clients comprehensive solutions that include marketing intelligence services in addition to recruitment services in the areas of live events, sports, sports media and entertainment.

WORK IN SPORTS
7010 E CHAUNCEY LANE
SUITE 115
PHOENIX, AZ 85054
480-905-7221
Fax: 480-905-7231
support@WorkInSports.com
www.WorkInSports.com
• John Mellor, President/Chief Executive Officer
jmellor@WorkInSports.com
• Jason Backs, EVP/Chief Operations Officer
jbacks@WorkInSports.com
• Robert Oakley, VP Interactive Marketing/Client Services
amyeaton@WorkInSports.com
• Amy Eaton, Director Employer Relations
amyeaton@WorkInSports.com
Nature of Services:
WorkInSports.com provides job board and employment resource services in the sports industry, working with teams, leagues, facilities, sponsors, agencies and other sports related organizations.
Year Founded:
2000

Event Planning & Services

ACTION MEDIA/VISION ENTERTAINMENT
2200 W ORANGEWOOD AVENUE
SUITE 230
ORANGE, CA 92868
949-789-7439
Fax: 949-789-7444
www.actionmediallc.com
• Rick Stark, Event Sales And Marketing
(989) 789-7439
rick.stark@apg-media.com
Services:
Action Media and its subsidiary Vision Entertainment is an integrated marketing and event production company that provides a unique, powerful gateway to the potent, yet elusive Gen X-Y audience. Provides compelling original concepts and turn-key solutions for an extensive list of clients.
Event Management Services:
Creates and manages sports events for

snowboarding, skateboarding and wakeboarding.

ADVANTAGE MARKETING GROUP, INC.
10030 N MACARTHUR BOULEVARD
SUITE 195
IRVING, TX 75063
972-869-2244
Fax: 847-952-3348
www.amgsports.com
• Werner Scott, President/Chief Executive Officer
wscott@amgsports.com

ADVERTISING WORLD SERIES
8117 MANCHESTER AVENUE
SUITE #198
PLAYA DEL REY, CA 90293
310-740-2195
michael@adworldseries.com
www.adworldseries.com
• Michael Meiches, Founder/Commissioner
(310) 740-2195
michael@adworldseries.com
Sports Service Founded:
1981
Event Management Services:
Produces Advertising Softball World Series Tournament for advertising media, and corporate teams plus other corporate events. Sponsored by Sports Illustrated.

AET LASERS
8124 NORRIS LANE
BALTIMORE, MD 21222
410-355-2055
800-771-7938
Fax: 410-355-2054
moreinfo@imageengineering.com
www.imageengineering.com
Event Management Services:
Special events and spectaculars, featuring lasers, lights pyro, and special effects, designed to enhance appeal and interest in sports events, as well as providing a unique, high profile vehicle for corporate sponsors.
Services:
Laser displays for events including: corporate, sporting, festival, broadcast media. Shows may include: pyrotechnics, confetti, intelligent lighting and CO2 for a fully integrated, turn-key production. Other services: hardware design, manufacturing, permanent installation. Created world's largest inflatable projection screen, the ITV.

Clients:
Anheuser Busch, Apple Computer, AT&T, Baltimore Blast, Boston Red Sox, Boy Scouts of America - Naitonal Jamboree, British Luxury Council, British Airways, Brooklyn Bridge - 120th Anniversary, Cannon, City of Peshtigo, WI, City of Rockville, MD, Coca-Cola, Detroit Red Wings, Digital Equipment Corporation, Discovery Channel, Fairfax, VA, Florida Sun Coast Dome, Ford Motor Company, General Motors, Georgia-Pacific
Sports Service Founded:
1979.

AMERICAN ADVERTISING SERVICES, INC./SPORTS MARKETING DIVISION
121 CHESTNUT STREET
PHILADELPHIA, PA 19106
215-923-9100
Sports Service Founded:
1986
Services:

Offers public relations, advertising, and marketing services which includes Sales Presentations, Commercials, Product Demonstrations, Training Tapes, and Shooting.
Athlete Management Services:
Promotion, contract negotiation, representation, accounting, legal and related services.
Event Management Services:
Full event management, including planning, sponsorship, traffic promotion and ticket sales, program books, exhibit areas, post event merchandising sales.
Marketing & Consulting Services:
Subsidiary of advertising agency, fully staffed to provide publicity and advertising services.

AMERICAN GRAPHITI
101 TREMONT STREET
BOSTON, MA 02108-5004
617-426-6668
Fax: 617-848-8950
elleng@americangraphiti.com
www.americangraphiti.com
• Ellen Gitelman, President
elleng@americangraphiti.com
Services:
Offers Public Relations and Marketing services.
Event Management Services:
Manages all aspects of events. Designs sponsorship programs, secures media sponsors, creates promotions, handles press and publicity, and obtains celebrity endorsements and appearances. Develops events from scratch or brings added value and fresh ideas to existing events.
Sports Service Founded:
1987

AMERICAN MARKETING AND MOTORSPORTS GROUP
26 GARDEN STREET
NEW YORK MILLS, NY 13417
315-736-8834
• Ralph Stoppiello, President/New Business Manager
• Dale Stoppiello, Vice President

ATHERTON COMMUNICATIONS, LP
705 BOSTON POST ROAD
GUILFORD, CT 6437
203-604-0028
Fax: 203-604-0028
www.athertoncommunications.com
• R. Kent Atherton, Founder/President
(203) 604-0028
Year Founded:
1994
Event Management Services:
Develops, produces and manages sports events for network broadcast including major college basketball invitational, The John R. Wooden Classic, Jet Jam (a 3 day extreme water sport and concert event, featuring professional personal watercraft racing), competing on the IJSBA tour and professional wakeboarding. Designs sponsorship opportunities with strategic marketing components to introduce advertising, merchandising and licensing rights.

AUTO SPORTS MARKETING GROUP
PO BOX 491
CLARKS SUMMIT, PA 18411
570-586-2198
Fax: 570-586-2198
sales@kidracers.com
www.kidracers.com
• Oscar Koveleski, Founder/Designer
Nature of Service:
50 years of organizing, managing events, contests, auto races (SCAA races at Pocono Raceway) model cars, slot cars, R/C cars, Battery Ride Ons, for SCCA, IMSA, NASCAR, IRL, SVRA, tracks and shows. Now offers consultant services for hire performed by hand picked special ops personnel. References include food industry, auto industry, toy industry, hobby industry, sanctioning bodies, track management.
Sports Service Founded:
1980
Athlete Management Services:
Auto racing sponsors.
Event Management Services:
Auto racing event promotion.
Brands:
Ferrari Monza, McLaren MK2, McLaren MK6, McLaren MK8B, 1914 Stutz Bearcat, Baby Ferrari 250, Type 52 Baby Bugatti Replica, Bugatti Vise

BEAR FOOT SPORTS
20 TOWNE DRIVE
PMB #200
BLUFFTON, SC 29910
843-757-8520
bfs@hargray.com
www.bearfootsports.com
• Mark Weisner, President/Founder
Sports Service Founded:
1991
Services:
Sports marketing and special event producer. Source for Adult Soccer Six Tournaments and Road Races. Publishes Coastal Sport & Wellness and provides Consultant Services for soccer, running and festival event planners.
Marketing & Consulting Services:
Consults with corporations with regard to corporate sponsorships, advertising and sales promotion related to sports and sports events. Also publishes COASTAL SPORT and WELLNESS. Corporate event planning.
Clients Include:
Universal Studios, Valsport, Select Sport, Tenet Health Systems, Nova Care, Hargray Communications, Pepsi, Old Navy.

BEWI PRODUCTIONS, INC.
240 BEAR HILL ROAD
SUITE 201
WALTHAM, MA 2451
781-890-3234
Fax: 781-890-0534
www.bewisports.com
• Bernard E. Weichsel, Founder/President
Nature of Service:
Producer of Ski and Snowboard Expos, Active Sports Events, Specialty Winter Promotions and The New England Youth Sports Festival.
Sports Service Founded:
1979
Clients:
U.S. Ski Team and other non-profit

Organizations
Event Management Services:
Complete production services - creation, implementation and on-site. Produces consumer snowsports expos in Boston; Denver. Specialists in skiing, outdoor wintertime activities. And the all new: New England Youth Sports Festival.

BLALOCK COMPANY, JANE
197EIGHTH STREET - FLAGSHIP WHARF
BOSTON, MA 2129
617-225-0008
800-466-1133
Fax: 617-621-8630
mbedrosian@jbcgolf.com
www.cowen-design.com/JBC
• Jane Blalock, President/Chief Executive Officer
• Jenn Shedd, Merchandise
jshedd@jbcgolf.com
• Mark Keaney, Sponsorship Sales
mkeaney@jbcgolf.com
• Megan Gardner, Marketing Opportunities
mgardner@jbcgolf.com
Services:
Produces top-quality, innovative golf programs and events.
Marketing & Consulting Services:
Primary focus in the area of golf. Specialists in corporate outings; creation and development of corporate programs; conference entertainment in golf, tennis and skiing. Organizer and creator of senior tournament featuring LPGA legends.
Event Management Services:
Organizers of the Gillette LPGA Golf Clinics and the Cadillac Golf Series for Women.
Sports Service Founded:
1990

BMK SPORTS
1207 BRIDGEWAY
SAUSALITO, CA 94965
415-289-5700
• Barry Mackay, Owner
• Rick Raducha, Owner
Services:
Sports Promotions
Sports Service Founded:
1970
Event Management Services:
Manages with SJAM ATP Tour Event, San Jose Arena, annually in February.

BRITTEN MEDIA
2322 CASS ROAD
TRAVERSE CITY, MI 49684
855-763-8204
Fax: 231-941-8299
• Paul Britten, President
Services:
Maker of unique banners, flags, and event solutions.
Clients:
University of Notre Dame, Tournament of Roses, ANC Sports, Anheuser-Busch, Indian Wells Tennis Center, Infineon Raceway, Atlanta Motor Speedway, Nasdaq 100 Tennis Open, Choice Hotels International, IMG, Dover Downs Entertainment, Gateway International Speedway, Bristol Motor Speedway, John Deer, Subaru of America, Crownline Boats, ATP Tennis, Paralyzed Veterans of America, Labatt USA, Mercedes-Benz Fashion Week, Pearle Vision, Purina,

General Motors Corporation, Clear Channel Entertainment, General Growth Properties, Simon Property Group and Daytona International Speedway
Description:
Specializes in banner graphics.

BROTMAN WINTER FRIED COMMUNICATIONS, INC.
111 PARK PLACE
FALLS CHURCH, VA 22046
703-534-4600
Fax: 703-536-2255
• Charlie Brotman, Board Chairman/Chief Executive Officer/Founder
• Steve Winter, President/Chief Operating Officer
swinter@bwfcom.com
• Kenny Fried, Executive Vice President
kfried@bwfcom.com
• Brian Bishop, Vice President
brian@bwfcom.com
Services:
Specializes in public and media relations, promotions, public service, community service, grass roots community outreach, special event management, artwork production, advertising and marketing campaigns.
Clients:
Booze Allen Classic Golf Tournament, DC United, D.C. Sports & Entertainment Commission, Legg Mason Tennis Classic, U.S. Soccer Foundation, RFK Stadium, California Tortilla, Bamboo Club, Coyote Ugly, Gordon Biersch Brewery Restaurant, Brasserie Les Halles, Starbucks, Tysons Corner Center, Foot Locker, Fahrney's Pens, Dulles Town Center, Hair Cuttery, Mervis Diamond Importers, DukesFest, Help the Homeless Walkathon, Sallie Mae 10K Road Race, McDonald's McSoccer Fest, Discovery Communications, Sport and Health Clubs, JK Moving and Storage, Mr. Wash's Brushless Car Wash, DC United's Kicks for Kids, Sallie Mae Fund, Hoop Dreams, Special Love, Most

---

BURWASH INTERNATIONAL, PETER
4200 RESEARCH FOREST DRIVE
SUITE 250
THE WOODLANDS, TX 77381
281-363-4707
800-255-4707
Fax: 281-292-7783
pbihq@pbitennis.com
www.pbitennis.com
• Chris Dyer, Chief Executive Officer
• Karen Kruse, Chief Financial Officer
• Chris Reid, Vice President
• Dave E. Neuhart, Tennis Director
• Chris Myrold, Director
Tennis Management Services:
Contracts with hotels, clubs and resorts all over the world to direct tennis operations. Also provides coaching services to national tennis teams in different countries, as well as on an individual basis to tournament players. Also manages and designs tennis facilities.
Event Management Services:
Produces International Tennis Show featuring entertainment and instruction. Produces tournaments, celebrity events, convention programs, grand openings.
Services:
Managing Professional Tennis Management and Staffing Hotels, Resorts and Clubs.

Products:
High Performance Tennis Apparel

CABELA'S SPORTSMAN'S QUEST
ONE CABELA DRIVE
SIDNEY, NE 69160
308-255-1347
800-243-6626
corporate@cabelas.com
www.cabelas.com
• Dennis Highby, Chief Executive Officer
Services:
Producer of competitive fishing, archery and sportsmen's events across the United States.
Clients:
People who enjoy the outdoor lifestyle
Event Management Services:
Develops and conducts shooting, angling, and outdoor sports promotions with participant and spectator appeal to hunters and anglers. Events include fishing tournaments, sporting clays, archery, sporting dogs, game calling, and all other related interests. Media exposure includes television coverage, a national radio network nation-wide and a magazine that is published six times a year. National sponsors include: Cabela's, Chevy Suburban-Tahoe, Starcraft, LaCrosse Footwear, VISA USA and Illinois DNR/DCCA.

CADWALADER, WICKERSHAM & TAFT
ONE WORLD FINANCIAL CENTER
NEW YORK, NY 10281
212-504-6000
Fax: 212-504-6666
www.cadwalader.com
• Marc A. Tolchin, Associate/Real Estate Finance
(212) 504-6019
marc.tolchin@cwt.com
• Andrew M. Troop, Partner/Financial Restructuring
(212) 504-6760
andrew.troop@cwt.com
Clients:
Financial Institutions, Industrial and Service Corporations, Governmental, Health Care and Not-For-Profit Entities, Individual Clients and Closely Held Companies
Description:
Project finance as been an integral component to the Firm's practice. Experience and expertise in ship, aircraft, electrical power generation, and sports arena financing. Represented banks financing the construction and renovation of the Golden State Warriors Arena, Oakland Raiders Coliseum, and Pasadena Rose Bowl.

CALIFORNIA CITYSPORTS/EVENT DIVISION
john@competitor.com
www.competitor.com
• John Smith, National Advertising Director
john@competitor.com
• Justin Sands, Regional Account Manager
justin@competitor.com
• Kelly Trimble, National Event Managing
kelly@competitor.com
• Geoff Barnett, Marketplace Advertising
geoff@competitor.com

professional services

Services:
Creates and manages sports events, focusing on lifestyle sports.

CAMEO MARKETING, INC
49 FARM VIEW DRIVE #302
SUITE 302
NEW GLOUCESTER, ME 4260
207-688-4580
Fax: 207-688-4581
www.cameomarketinginc.com
• Bob Tiernan, President
(207) 688-4580
• Bonnie Tirenan, COO
• Catriona Sumner, Director Account Services
Description:
Specializes in developing and managing sports, entertainment cause-related and media based event programs, Promotions and sponsorships. Cameo utilizes, mobile marketing and event execution.
Clients:
America Online, Castrol North America, United States Smokeless Tobacco, MCI / WorldCom Telecommunications, Schwans Sales Enterprises / Red Baron Frozen Pizza, Friendsly's Restaurant Corporation, Looking Glass Technologies, Ray Ban / Bausch & Lomb, Cadbury Beverages, Dynamix/Sierra Online, USPA & IRA, Hasbro Toys, Colgate Palmolive, Merryll Lynch Media, American Express / IDS Financial

CARD STUNTS BY KIVETT PRODUCTIONS
2543 SAINT HEATHER WAY
ORLANDO, FL 3206
407-342-0752
joe@cardstunts.com
www.cardstunts.com
• Joe Kivett, Owner
(407) 342-0752
joe@cardstunts.com
Founded:
1991
Nature of Service:
Audience participation flip card stunts

CARSON EVENTS INTERNATIONAL, INC.
323 LEWIS STREET
KETCHUM, ID 83340
208-726-5990
info@carsonevents.com
www.carsonevents.com
• Kathy Carson, President
• Paul Carson, Chief Executive Officer
• Dave Miglia, Operations Manager
• Art Daves, Vice President Operations/New Business
Services:
Event Management - Creation and concept design, Project management, Athlete liaison, Public relations, Venue procurement and site development, Vendor relations and contracting, Master scheduling, Staffing, Logistics and equipment management, Budgeting and accounting; Promotions - Merchandise programs, Product sampling, Consumer interactive programs, Celebrity endorsements, Public relations, Charity tie-ins, Fundraisers; Marketing - Creative elements, Print design and production, Corporate signage, Corporate functions and hospitality, Onsite branding design and production, Market and demographic

research, Web element design and integration
Sports Service Founded:
1981

CHAMPIONSHIP MANAGEMENT EVENTS, INC.
307 N EUCLID AVENUE
ONTARIO, CA 91762-3425
909-460-5500
Services:
Sports Promotions and Special Events
Athlete Management Services:
Manages and produces professional PGA Tour and Champions Tour events in Las Vegas.
Marketing & Consulting Services:
Sports marketing programs and consulting for corporate sponsors.

CHAMPIONSHIP SPORTS GROUP
1219 N STUART STREET
ARLINGTON, VA 22201-4809
703-875-9192
Fax: 703-875-9130
• Jonathan Rourke, Owner
Services:
Sports Marketing and Event Management services.

CIVIC ENTERTAINMENT GROUP
450 PARK AVENUE S
FLOOR 5
NEW YORK, NY 10016
212-426-7006
Fax: 212-426-7002
• Parke Spencer, President
Description:
CEG is a full-service event planning and marketing firm. Produces and oversees all elements of promotional events. Not limited to New York, CEG's clients and events are nationwide.

CLEAR CHANNEL ENTERTAINMENT - MOTORSPORTS
4255 MERIDIAN PARKWAY
AURORA, IL 60504
630-566-6100
Services:
Producer and promoter of The Speed Stick presents National Arenacross Series and the Arenacross Series of regional events.
Clients:
Monster Trucks, Grave Digger, Supper Cross, Freestyle Motocross,IHRA, Arenacross, Road Racing, Street Warriorz, Alpinestars, Thor, Snow Cross, Freestyle Snowcross

COMCAST-SPECTATOR
215-336-3600
• Peter A Luukko, President/Chief Operating Officer
Services:
Provides high quality sports and entertainment services anf facilities, provides sports programming for regional cable television.
Marketing & Consulting Services:
Owns the Philadelphia 76ers NBA team and the NHL's Philadelphia Flyers. Comcast Spectator also owns the Wachovia Center and Watchovia Spectrum sports and event arenas, three minor league baseball teams,

two soccer teams, one minor league hockey team, and one lacrosse team.

COMPASS COLLECTIVE
165 OTTLEY DRIVE NE
ATLANTA, GA 30324
404-875-6543
Fax: 404-875-7917
www.compasscollective.com
• David Peck, President/Chief Operating Officer
(404) 888-7723
david@compasscollective.com
• Robert A. Dailey, VP/Chief Executive Officer
(404) 888-7722
rob@compasscollective.com
• Scott Hughes, Project Manager
(404) 888-7730
scott@compasscollective.com
• David Peck, President
(404) 888-7723
• Rob Dailey, VP & CEO
(444) 888-7722
• Greg Oberholtzer, General Manager
(404) 888-7731
greg@compasscollective.com
Services:
Design: - two and three dimensional design, space planning, technology fulfillment, engineering. Primary expertise: tradeshow exhibits, permanent showrooms, corporate environments, meeting and event properties, museums, kiosks, large-format graphic presentations, banners, tension fabric structures, design conversant with American and European portable/modular exhibit systems. Production - wood, metal and plastics fabrication shops. Tradeshow program management - comprehensive logistics coordination, knowledgeable and responsible on-site supervision, shipping, warehousing. Content development/digital animation - development and production of
Event Marketing Services:
A full-service exhibit designs and fabrication company which specialize in customer service oriented design, fabrication, installation and logistics for product rooms, special events, tradeshow exhibits, specialty retail environments and museums. Provides presence marketing for large scale events, NFL teams and major sponsors.

CONCORD EXPO GROUP
PO BOX 885
EDEN, UT 84310
801-745-8804
Fax: 801-745-8803
conexpogrp@earthlink.net
www.concordexpogroup.com
• Kathy Donnelly, President
Marketing & Consulting Services:
Promotion and management of foreign trade shows, organizing American pavilions at these shows.
Clients:
People who wish to participate in trade shows in foreign countries.

CONE COMMUNICATIONS
855 BOYLSTON STREET
BOSTON, MA 2116
617-227-2111
Fax: 617-523-3955
jbang@coneinc.com

• Jens Bang, President/Chief Executive Officer
(617) 227-2211
jbang@coneinc.com
• Jens Bang, CEO
(617) 939-8324
• Tim Munroe, VP Business Development
(617) 939-8325
tmunroe@ConeComm.com
• Bill Fleishman, President
(617) 939-8340
Services:
Helps companies build their brands and develop a competitive market position through innovative programs that respond to the needs and passions of consumers through Brand Marketing, Cause Branding and Crisis and Issues Management.
Sports Service Founded:
1980
Marketing & Consulting Services:
Specializing in sporting goods marketing communications

CONFERENCE PLANNERS
3600 GIDDINGS ROAD
AUBURN HILLS, MI 48326
248-475-2500
Fax: 248-475-2325
careers@gpj.com
www.gpj.com
• Jeff Rutchik, Executive VP
(617) 535-9912
sales@gpj.com
• Tom Maher, Executive Director, Marketing
tom.maher@gpj.com
Description:
Provider of event management services and web-based registration tools that enable superior event performance.
Services:
Help clients improve event performance, reduce costs and deliver results throught the event portfolio, from tradeshows and conferences to road shows, mobile marketing and sponsorships.

CONVENTURES, INC.
ONE DESIGN CENTER PLACE
BOSTON, MA 2210
617-439-7700
Fax: 617-439-7701
info@conventures.com
www.conventures.com
• Ted Breslin, Vice President & CFO
tbreslin@conventures.com
• Kathleen Chrisom, Vice President, Sales & Marketing
kchrisom@conventures.com
• Dusty S. Rhodes, President
drhodes@conventures.com
• David Choate, Vice President & COO
dchoate@conventures.com
Nature of Service:
An special event agency focused on integrated event planning, public relations and marketing.
Event Management Services:
Marketing, promotion, publicity and on-site management of sporting events including road races, international soccer tournaments, track and field meets, golf tournaments, tennis celebrity series, exhibitions and seminars.

CORPORATE COMMUNICATIONS, INC.
108 S UNION STREET
ROCHESTER, NY 14607
585-262-3430
Fax: 585-262-3436
email@corp-com.com
www.corporatecomm.com
• Terry Palis, President
terry@corp-com.com
• Gil Fuqua, President
Services:
Full service advertising, marketing and public relations company that helps improve client's market share, positioning and corporate/public image.
Event Management Services:
Full service advertising, marketing, public relations, promotions, sponsor procurement and events administration. Consulting services available on per-project/event basis, as well as for entire event management.
Marketing & Consulting Services:
Marketing and consulting services for all areas of event management and business promotion.

COSTANTE GROUP SPORTS & EVENT MARKETING, LLC
4741 CENTRAL STREET
SUITE 117
KANSAS CITY, MO 64112
210-213-8792
don@costantegroup.com
www.costantegroup.com
• Don Costante, President
(210) 213-8792
don@costantegroup.com
• Kyle Hamrick, Producer and Video Specialist
• Zach Dierks, Producer, writer and editor
• Beth Roche, Client Services Specialist
• MIke Behymer, Business Development
• Jason Lodato, Event Management Specialist
• Kasey Schweitzer, Event Presentation
• Don Costante, Event Presentation & Production Specialist
Nature of Service:
The Costante Group offers a comprehensive solution for every aspect of athletic or corporate event production, designed to integrate seamlessly with your existing team in whatever capacity necessary. If specialized training or advice is all your staff requires, the Costante Group provides strategic consultations. If you're seeking more inclusive services, again, the Costante group steps up to meet your challenge.
Clients:
Jordan Brand Classic, NBA Entertainment, U.S. Army All-American Bowl
Year Founded:
2007

CREATIVE FACTOR, INC.
9805 HORTON RD. SW
CALGARY, ALBERTA, CANADA T2V 2X5
403-301-0811
403-719-3844
Fax: 403-301-0889
info@creativefactor.ca
www.creativefactor.ca
• Lynne DuVivier, President
Event Management Services:
Sales promotion, premium, and advertising specialty company that specializes in event

and sports promotions. Provides custom manufacturing, imprinting, packaging, fulfillment, etc.

CREATIVE GROUP, INC.
619 N LYNNDALE DRIVE
APPLETON, WI 54914
920-739-8850
800-236-2800
Fax: 920-739-8817
webmaster@creativegroupinc.com
www2.creativegroupinc.com
• Ron Officer, President/CEO
• Janet Traphagen, EVP, Sales
Description:
Expertise includes: Event planning, Meetings, sponsorship hospitality and event public relations programs. Works with clients on incentive programs with the ability to be flexible. Offers planning, imaginative promotion, reliable administration and budget management.
Services:
Provides a variety of marketing services specializing in building and managing incentive programs and planning corporate meetings and events. It also offers personal travel services including travel planning and emergency services that benefit from the company's large corporate travel business.

DEBOW COMMUNICATIONS, LTD.
350 W 31ST STREET
NEW YORK, NY 10001-2726
212-239-3000
Fax: 212-977-8376
info@debow.com
www.debow.com
• Thomas J. DE Bow, Owner
Services:
Creates, develops and implements effective integrated marketing solutions such as advertising programs, nationwide survey of real estate professionals, employee voluntary benefit enrollment program, corporate asset retention program, marketing program, on-line shopping and financial communications program.
Sports Service Founded:
1976
Event Management Services:
Creates and manages sports events with experience in billiards, football, and golf.
Marketing & Consulting Services:
Full service agency experienced in all facets of marketing strategy and communications, public relations, and advertising, including implementation services such as copy, art, and design.

DRIVER CONNECTION/RAPID RACEWAYS
161 WOODFORD AVENUE
UNIT 55
PLAINVILLE, CT 06062
860-793-1888
Fax: 860-229-3970
Services:
Provides renting of race cars as well as weekly competition events for every age and skill level. Features two state of the art racetracks supported by complete inventory of beginner cars to high performance cars, as well as parts and accessories for either the amateur or professional racer. Also features monthly major racing events.
Services:

Motorsports Marketing and Promotions
Clients:
Work with speedways, businesses and corporations in the field of sponsorship, marketing and promotions
Services:
Event Management Services: Development and organization of advertising, sponsorship, and entertainment programs at events, speedways, charity functions, trade shows, car shows, autograph sessions, etc.
Marketing & Consulting Services: Specializes in the development and fulfillment of advertising and promotional programs for businesses and corporations utilizing motorsports to build sales, improve credibility while strengthening brand loyalty to accomplish business goals
Services:
Event Management Services: Development and organization of advertising, sponsorship, and entertainment programs at events, speedways, charity functions, trade shows, car shows, autograph sessions, etc.
Marketing & Consulting Services: Specializes in the development and fulfillment of advertising and promotional programs for businesses and corporations utilizing motorsports to build sales, improve credibility while strengthening brand loyalty to accomplish business goals
Event Management Services:
Development and organization of advertising, sponsorship, and entertainment programs at events, speedways, charity functions, trade shows, car shows, autograph sessions, etc.
What We Offer:
Weekly Slot Car Events, Birthday Parties, Club Racing, Track & Car Rentals, Parts & Supplies, 1/24th and 1/32nd Scale Cars. We also feature monthly major racing events perfect for both the amateur and professional.

DSL GLOBAL EVENT MARKETING
94 VALLEY ROAD
MONTCLAIR, NJ 7042
336-924-1141
Fax: 336-924-1152
Description:
Specializes in mobile marketing tours, special events, event sponsorships and media events.
Services:
Provides integrated event marketing, development, consulting, and management services.
Clients:
The Upper Deck Company and Sony

EAGLE INTERNATIONAL TENTS & AIR DOMES
5620 E SHEA BOULEVARD
SCOTTSDALE, AZ 85254
480-219-9400
www.ei-tents.com
• Buford J. Dowell, Owner/Founder
• Rav.Buford Dowell, Founder
• Shannon Dowell, Associate
Services:
Offers a wide variety of products and services such as Giant Pole Tents, Frame Tents, Clear Span, Air Dome and like portable structures.
Event Management Services:
Agency for the design & production of pole

& metal frame tents, clear span portable structures, large air supported dome - arenas, sports covers for tennis - golf - soccer - hockey - basketball - volleyball - football - ice skating - skateboarding - driving ranges - storage - pools.

EDELMAN SPORTS/EVENT MARKETING
200 E RANDOLPH STREET
63RD FLOOR
CHICAGO, IL 60601
312-240-3000
Fax: 312-240-2900
www.edelman.com
• Daniel J. Edelman, Founder/Chairman
dan.edelman@edelman.com
• Richard Edelman, President/Chief Executive Officer
• Richard Edelman, President
Event Management Services:
All phases of public relations and other related activities designed to maximize the value of client-sponsored sports events. Clients include MVP.com.
Sports Service Founded:
1988

ELITE RACING, INC.
9477 WAPLES STREET
SUITE 150
SAN DIEGO, CA 92121
858-450-6510
800-311-1255
Fax: 858-450-6905
www.eliteracing.com
• Tim Murphy, Founder/Chief Executive Officer
Description:
Sports marketing and management company. Elite Racing organizes eight events each year, including the Rock 'n' Roll Marathon and the Carlsbad 5000, the world's fastest 5K.
Services:
Sports and management company that produces world-class running events.
Clients:
Produces Rock 'n' Roll Marathon and Carlsbad 5000

EPIC: STRATEGIC PLANNING & INTEGRATION WORLDWIDE
ATLANTA, GA
770-457-1145
ashaw@epic-usa.com
www.epic-usa.com
• Alan Shaw, Managing Director
• Steve Clark, Former Director
Year Founded:
1996
Description:
Provides strategic (and tactical) event planning & operations services with a focus on planning & execution of major sporting events. Assists corporations, organizing committees and association/federations who sponsor, own/operate and participate in a wide variety of large-scale sporting events, including Olympic Games, FIFA World Cups, Asian Games, Pan Am Games and Commonwealth Games. Established in 1996, by former Olympic/World Cup executive, Alan Shaw and purchased by LeadDog Marketing Group, Inc. in 2007. Core competencies and areas of expertise include: Strategic Planning, Event Ops

Planning & Auditing, Venue Management & Ops, Workforce

EVENT AUDIO VISUAL GROUP
45053 GRAND RIVER AVENUE
SUITE C
NOVI, MI 48375
800-935-2323
Fax: 800-935-8191
detroit@subrent.com
www.subrent.com
• Bret Tracey, President
(248) 867-4160
btracey@subrent.com
• Keith Solomon, Operations Manager
(248) 240-0519
ksolomon@subrent.com
Services:
Wholesale provider of LCD and DLP Projectors, lenses, video switchers and accessories for rental and resales.
Event Management Services:
Specializes in video displays for indoor and outdoor events.
Sports Service Founded:
1988

EVENTIVE MARKETING
488 MADISON AVE
4TH FLOOR
NEW YORK, NY 10022-5702
212-463-9700
Fax: 212-727-1716
www.eventivemarketing.com
• David Saalfrank, Senior Vice President Business Development
• David Saalfrank, Senior Vice President
• Ernie Kapanke, Vice President
• Raffi Grigorian, CEO
Services:
Event Marketing, Sampling Programs, Sponsorship Activation, Retail-tainment, Mobile Marketing, Multi-Cultural Marketing
Sports Service Founded:
1992
Event Management Services:
Design and implement programs geared toward a demographic audience from an athletes to weekend warriors. Marathons, triathlons, mountain biking or road racing, health clubs or ski resorts. Develops and execute integrated marketing programs that combine brand equity building elements.

EVENTS PROMOTIONS USA
1270 GLEN AVE.
MOORETOWN, NJ 08057
602-840-9005
800-378-6373
Fax: 602-840-9291
• Tim A. Owens, Chief Executive Officer/Event Producer
(602) 840-9005
towens@eventpromotionsusa.com
• Tom G. Tygett, President/Event Producer/Operations Director
(480) 941-1911
ttygett@eventpromotionsusa.com
Description:
Specializes in working with municipalities and non-profit organizations in the marketing, sales and production of major events on a public/private partnership. Integration includes: event marketing, sponsorship/partnership development, entertainment productions, special event food service and catering management, site

management, etc.
Sports Service Founded:
1987

EXTRAORDINARY EVENTS
13425 VENTURA BOULEVARD
SUITE 300
SHERMAN OAKS, CA 91423
818-783-6112
Fax: 818-783-8957
www.extraordinaryevents.net
• Andrea Michaels, President
amichaels@extraordinaryevents.net
• Jon Michaels, EVP Operations
jmichaels@extraordinaryevents.net
• Lauren Arnold, Associate producer
• Mandy Bianchi, Account Manager
• Taylor Black, Senior Account Manager
• Chris Clark, Senior Accoun Executive
• Brad Dawson, CPA-Accounting Manager
• Andrea Michaels, President of
Extraordinary Events
amichaels@extraordinaryevents.net
Description:
Specializes in entertainment marketing.
Headline entertainment, award
presentations, business theater, gala
events, theme events, music and
entertainment, product launches,
tradesshow-productions sponsorships and
sales support, tours and transportation,
venues.
Sports Service Founded:
1988

FELD ENTERTAINMENT
8607 WESTWOOD CENTER DRIVE
VIENNA, VA 22182
703-448-4000
Fax: 703-448-4100
information@feldinc.com
www.feldentertainment.com
• Kenneth Feld, Chairman/Chief Executive
Officer
• Mike Ruch, Chief Financial Officer
• Julie Robertson, Marketing SVP
• Jason Bitsoff, VP/GM
Sponsorship/Strategic Alliance
Event Management Services:
Produces show featuring world-class figure
skating and Disney starts showcased by
state-of-the-art staging and special effects.
Regular tour appears in over 90 markets
annually.

FLW OUTDOORS
30 GAMBLE LANE
BENTON, KY 42025
270-252-1000
info@flwoutdoors.com
• Jeff McCoy, Director Public Relations
jeff.mccoy@jacobs-mgmt.com
• Charlie Evans, President

FORESITE SPORTS
234 BRYN MAWR AVENUE
SUITE 101
BRYN MAWR, PA 19010-2133
610-525-8003
888-882-5440
Fax: 610-525-8004
info@foresitesports.com
www.foresitesports.com
Event Management Services:
Full service golf tournament supply firm
specializing in hole in one insurance, putting
contest coverage, shootout contests, event

signage and promotional products.
Services:
Specializes in supplying and organizing golf
outings and instructional clinics.

FRANKEL SPORTS GROUP
35 W WACKER DRIVE
CHICAGO, IL 60601
312-220-3200
• Marc Landsberg, Global President
• Bill Rosen, Chief Creative Officer
• Jeff Lupinacci, Chief Financial Officer
• Jenny Cacioppo, EVP/Managing Director
Services:
Sales promotion agency specializes in
motivating consumers to buy now.
Clients:
Allstate, AT&T, Coca-Cola, CDC, Cuervo,
Dreyers, GM, Mcdonald's, Kellogg's, P&G,
Symantec, Visa, Tylenol, United ,Whirlpool
Event Management Services:
Develops and implements national, regional
and local events. Coordinates and executes
cross promotions with event media partners,
co-sponsors and athletes. Advertising, New
Product Introduction, Brand Positioning,
Packaging, Direct/Database, Marketing,
Promotional Products & Services, Employee
Communications, Public Relations,
Entertainment Marketing, Retail Design and
Ethnic Marketing.
Sports Service Founded:
1984
Marketing & Consulting Services:
Sports marketing, strategic development
and consultation. Advises corporations
currently using or seeking to use sports as a
strategic marketing tool. Creates
sponsorships and marketing programs, with
major sports organizations, leagues, teams,
federations and networks. Plans and
develops sales promotion, public relations
and licensing programs relating to sports
marketing.
Services:
Advertising, New Product Introduction,
Brand Positioning, Packaging,
Direct/Database, Marketing, Promotional
Products & Services, Employee
Communications, Public Relations,
Entertainment Marketing, Retail Design,
Ethnic Marketing, Sports Marketing, Event
Marketing Sweepstakes, Contests and
Games, Fulfillment, Tie-in Partnerships,
Kids Marketing, Trade Promotion, Loyalty
Programs, Web Design, Marketing
Research.
Clients:
Allstate, AT&T Wireless, Coca-Cola, CDC,
Clorox, Cuervo, Dreyer's, General Motors,
Kellogg's, London Fog, McDonald's, Proctor
& Gamble, Symantec, Tylenol, United, Visa,
Whirlpool.
Other Locations:
103 Carnegie Center, Suite 106, Princeton,
NJ 08540. 609-720-1000; 303 Second
Street, South Tower, Fourth Floor, San
Francisco, CA 94107. 415-344-6400.

FRONT RUNNER
1665 9TH STREET
WHITE BEAR LAKE, MN 55110
651-653-7401
randy@frontrunnerusa.com
www.frontrunnerusa.com
Nature of Service:
Consulting firm in sport marketing, sports

promotion, sports public relations.
Specializing in running and fitness sports.
President is 3-time U.S. Olympic Distance
Runner and 2-time World Champion.
Sports Service Founded:
January 1980

GAMEDAY MANAGEMENT GROUP
315 E ROBINSON STREET
SUITE 505
ORLANDO, FL 32801
407-648-0213
Fax: 407-648-2418
www.gamedaymanagementgroup.com
• Tony Vitrano, President
tvitrano@gamedaymanagement.com
• Mike Witte, Senior VP Operations
• Mike Witte, Vice President
• Deborah McCandless, Vice President
• Cristine Paull, Vice President
• Jeff Hinton, Director Sales/Marketing
jhinton@gamedaymanagement.com
Nature of Service:
Gameday Management Group specializes in
the design and implementation of effective
transportation management solutions for
sporting and special events. Services
include event traffic plan design and
implementation, shuttle system design &
ground travel management.
Year Founded:
1994
Clients:
National Football League (Super Bowl), NFL
Europa, Major League Baseball,
International Speedway Corporation,
Daytona International Speedway, California
Speedway, Capital One Bowl, Champs
Sports Bowl, Arena Football League,
Soccer United Marketing, City of Glendale
(AZ), University of Florida, University of
Central Florida, 2005 Presidential
Inauguration, 2004 G8 Summit.

GCI GROUP
200 FIFTH AVENUE
NEW YORK, NY 10010
212-798-9700
Fax: 212-329-9900
jim.joseph@cohnwolfe.com
www.cohnwolfe.com
• Donna Imperato, President/Chief
Executive Officer
(212) 789-9800
• Tom Petrosini, EVP/CFO
(212) 789-9857
Services:
Areas of Expertise are Community
Relations, Consumer Marketing, Corporate
Communications, Events Marketing,
Healthcare Communications, Media
Relations, Multi-Cultural Marketing, New
Product Launches, Public Affairs, Youth
Marketing
Services:
Industry Knowledge: Automotive, Beauty &
Health, Biotechnology, Consumer Health
Products, Diet & Nutrition, Fashion &
Apparel, Financial Services, Food &
Beverage, Gas & Oil, Government
Agencies, Home Entertainment, Home
Improvement, Hospitality, Hospitals, Media
Organizations, Medical Devices,
Over-the-Counter Medications,
Payors/Providers, Pharmaceuticals, Retail,
Sports Organizations, Technology,
Telecommunications, Third Party
Organizations, Toys, and Transportation

Sports Service Founded:
1984
Event Management Services:
All facets of event marketing and management.

GIVING BACK FUND
6033 W CENTURY BOULEVARD
SUITE 350
LOS ANGELES, CA 90045
310-649-5222
Fax: 310-649-5070
main@givingback.org
www.givingback.org
• Marc Pollick, Founder/President
• Stephanie Sandler, Senior Vice President
Year Founded:
1997
Description:
To advise and mentor professional athletes, entertainers, business entrepreneurs, and others according to best practices in philanthropy and to leverage celebrity to raise funds for a wide range of charitable causes and important social issues.
Clients:
The Yao Ming Foundation, The Ben Roethlisberger Foundation, The Ben Gordon New Life Foundation, and others

GLOBAL EVENT MAKERS USA
11408 ORCHARD PARK DRIVE
SUITE 311
GLEN ALLEN, VA 23059
804-273-6731
800-476-8368
Fax: 804-273-6732
www.eventmakersusa.com
• Lawrence A. Creeger, Founder/President
(804) 273-6731
Event Management Services:
Rental equipment design, rental installation and management. Includes hospitality area concessions and spectator areas - tenting, heating, lighting, sound, crowd control, equipment for catering.

GLOBAL SPECTRUM
3601 S BROAD STREET
PHILADELPHIA, PA 19148
215-389-9587
Fax: 215-952-5651
tglickman@comcast-spectacor.com
www.global-spectrum.com
• Todd Glickman, Vp Business Development/Client Relations
tglickman@comcast-spectacor.com
• Tom Bradley, Box Office Manager
• Wayne Letson, Facility Engineer
• Todd Glickman, Senior Vp/COO
(215) 389-9587
jpage@comcast-spectacor.com
Nature of Service:
Provides innovative management, marketing, operations and event booking services for public assembly facilities, including arenas, civic and convention centers, stadiums, ice facilities, equestrian centers and theatres.
Marketing & Consulting Services:
Provides innovative, customized management and consulting solutions for the planning, start-up and operation of arenas, stadiums, convention centers and theaters worldwide.

GMR MARKETING
16155 W.STRATTON DR.
NEW BERLIN, WI 53151
262-786-5600
Fax: 262-786-0697
msmathers@gmrlive.com
www.gmrmarketing.com
• Gary Reynolds, Chief Executive Officer/Chairman
• Craig Connelly, President
• Bryan Buske, Chief Operating Officer
• Jay Lenstrom, Chief Marketing Officer
• Mike Boykin, EVP Sports
• Greg Busch, SVP Group Account Director
• Steve Dupee, Senior Director Sports
• Todd Fischer, Account Supervisor
• Tamera Green, Vice President
• David Martin, Account Director
• Dave Mullins, Account Executive
• Jonathan Norman, Sports Director
• Tyson Webber, Senior Account Director
Event Marketing Services:
Organization offers unique blend of event marketing strategic consulting and execution for Fortune 500 clients and brings expertise in key market segments including sports, music, entertainment, ethnic, lifestyle and mobile marketing.
Services:
Creates specialized event marketing programs for sports, music, lifestyle, and mobile marketing campaigns. The company produces product promotions at shopping malls, temporary retail locations, concerts, sports, and lifestyle events. It provides all-inclusive services - from concept and design to construction and site management.
Clients:
Alltel, DaimlerChrysler, Gillette, McDonald's, Microsoft, Miller Brewig Co., Nokia, Unilever and WM Wrigley Jr. Co.
Sports Service Founded:
1979
Clients Include:
Microsoft Corporation, Pepsi, Mercedes Benz, The Miller Brewing Company, Unilever, Intel, Kraft Food, Family Show.

GROUP DYNAMICS
411 US ROUTE
ONE FALMOUTH, ME 4105
207-781-8800
800-626-3539
Fax: 207-781-3841
info@groupdynamicsinc.com
www.groupdynamicsinc.com
• Robert Funk, President
Services:
A full service marketing and promotions company which specializes in the production and promotion of major national and international sporting and entertainment events. Provides operations, advertising, public relations, point-of sale production, marketing, sampling and event management services for major U.S. and International corporations. Organize MISS DANCE DIRLL TEAM COMPETITION.
Sports Service Founded:
1969
Marketing & Consulting Services:
Marketing consultation and sales promotion for sports and segmented marketing.

GROUP FIVE SALES, EVENT & SPORTS MARKETING
8701 MALLARD CREEK ROAD
CHARLOTTE, NC 28262
704-547-0683
Services:
Management Consulting and Event Marketing Services.
Description:
An event marketing company which is evolving to embrace the Internet to assist companies and their agencies to improve their results in the event marketing arena. Their software system that uses the Internet for the evaluation of a proposed event sponsorship in a fraction of the time it traditionally takes. The evaluation provides specific information in relation to the company's marketing goals. Specializing in the sports marketing and evaluation arena.

GUS MACKER BASKETBALL
107 EAST MAIN STREET
SUITE 3
BELDING, MI 48809
616-794-1445
Fax: 616-794-1472
www.macker.com
• Scott McNeal, Founder
Description:
The concept of Gus Macker 3-on-3 basketball tournament is being imitated across the USA but the Macker is still the one-and-only original game that is evolving as the hottest mass participation sport today.
Services:
Organizes 3-on-3 Basketball Tournaments which creates marketing opportunities for the sponsors.
Sports Service Founded:
1974

HAMILTON ASSOCIATES, SEENA
1161 YORK AVENUE
SUITE 12E
NEW YORK, NY 10065-7971
212-308-5368
Fax: 212-753-8742
• Seena Hamilton, President
Services:
Creative, PR-focused marketing firm specializing in the design and promotion of high-profile events, sponsorships, and multi-faceted marketing campaigns that meet a client's objectives.
Event Management Services:
Public relations focused events marketing firm that specializes in developing unique strategies for leveraging corporate sports and entertainment sponsorships with high-profile public relations and promotion programs

HCC SPECIALTY UNDERWRITERS, INC
401 EDGEWATER PLACE
SUITE 400
WAKEFIELD, MA 1880
781-994-6000
800-927-6306
Fax: 781-994-6001
inquiry@hccsu.com
www.hccsu.com
• Bill Hubbard, Chairman
• Marc Idelson, President/Chief Underwriting Officer
midelson@hccsu.com

• Matt Overlan, Chief Financial/Chief Operations Officer
moverlan@hccsu.com
• Mark Barry, Marketing Senior Vice President
mbarry@hccsu.com
Services:
Provides creative insurance solutions utilizing an ever-evolving portfolio of products and continuously expanding capabilities/leading provider of specialty insurance to the promotion marketing, sports and entertainment industries
Services:
Coverage includes disability, accidental death and dismemberment, life medical expense, team catastrophic, kidnap and ransom, and team stop/loss, event cancellation, weather insurance, special event liability insurance, prize indemnity insurance, contractual bonus insurance

HERITAGE CLASSIC FOUNDATION
71 LIGHTHOUSE ROAD
SUITE 4200
HILTON HEAD ISLAND, SC 29928
843-671-2448
800-234-1107
Fax: 843-671-6738
www.heritageclassicfoundation.com
• Simon Fraser, Chairman
• Ed Dowaschinski, VP Finance & Administration
• Rick Reichel, Treasurer
Sports Service Founded:
1990
Services:
Sponsor of the Verizon Heritage, South Carolina's only PGA TOUR event to generate funds for local and state charities and award grants to the Foundation's scholars.
Event Management Services:
Manages all aspects of sports events.

HIGHLINE SPORTS & ENTERTAINMENT
12 VAIL ROAD
SUITE 500
VAIL, CO 81657
970-476-6797
Fax: 970-476-6890
www.gohighline.com
• Jeff Brausch, President/Chief Executive Officer
(970) 476-6797
jeff@gohighline.com
• James Deighan, Vice President
(970) 476-6797
jamesd@gohighline.com
• Kelli Brausch, Controller
(970) 328-0905
kelli@gohighline.com
Sports Service Founded:
1996
Event Management Services:
A three-fold company focusing on the marketing and promotion of sporting events, media products, and organizations. The company offers expertise in sponsorship coordination, event production and management, event marketing, sales promotions and public relations.
Events include:
Vail Mogul Mania, Mountain Challenger, Vail Ultra 100, Fore SOS Par-Tee.
Services:
Leading provider of sports and

entertainment event marketing services. The company specializes in creating turn-key event marketing programs and successful partnerships with many of the world's leading brands.

HOMESTEAD MIAMI SPEEDWAY
ONE SPEEDWAY BOULEVARD
HOMESTEAD, FL 33035-1501
305-230-5000
866-409-7223
Fax: 305-230-5140
hmstix@homesteadmiamispeedway.com
www.homesteadmiamispeedway.com
• Sherry Adams, Corporate Partnerships/Hospitality Sponsorship
(305) 230-5209
• Matthew Becherer, President
Event Management Services:
Creates, manages and promotes auto racing events including, but not limited to, IndyCar, NASCAR, Formula One.
Services:
Creates, manages and promotes auto racing events. Home of the Ford 400 and Ford Championship Weekend, featuring the finales for the NASCAR NEXTEL Cup, Busch, and Craftsman Truck Series.

HURRICANE GOLF
203 E LINCOLN HIGHWAY
DEKALB, IL 60115
815-217-0110
866-955-3362
Fax: 815-787-3720
orders@hurricanegolf.com
www.hurricanegolf.com
• Mark Rankin, Sales
• Rob Lopez, Sales
(512) 385-4653
Services:
Event management for sporting events, production of large scale golf tournaments

ILTIS ASSOCIATES, JOHN
680 N LAKE SHORE DRIVE
SUITE 1328
CHICAGO, IL 60611-4546
312-787-8253
Fax: 312-337-1258
• John Iltis, President
Event Management Services:
Organize sport sponsorships and promote sports events.
Marketing & Consulting Services:
Licensing; coordination of corporations with sports events for promotion and sponsorship.

IMAGE IMPACT
4925 WYACONDA ROAD
ROCKVILLE, MD 20852
301-984-8283
800-336-0966
Fax: 212-208-4677
www.imageimpactinc.com
• Mickey Lawrence, President
• Olie Pirzadeh, President

IMPACT SPORTS, INC.
7322 E BROADWAY
SPOKANE, WA 99212
509-924-7768
Fax: 509-924-7668
www.tnb.net/impact-sports

• Paul Sorensen, Chief Executive Officer
• Gary Knudson, President
• Murray Walden, VP
Services:
A sports marketing company specializing in college athletics. Produces and markets radio and television broadcasts, handles game day promotions and markets on site signage at collegiate sporting venues.
Event Management Services:
Produces annual sports events in the Kingdome including the Kingbowl (High School State Championships), Washington State University TV, Eastern Washington University Radio Network, and World Indoor Paper Airplane Championship; plus, produces TV and radio sports packages of high school football and basketball; national cycling championships.

IMS PROPERTIES/INDY MOTOR SPEEDWAY
4790 W 16TH STREET
INDIANAPOLIS, IN 46222
317-492-6750
sales@brickyard.com
www.indianapolismotorspeedway.com
• Joie Chitwood, President/Chief Operating Officer
(970) 476-6797
jeff@gohighline.com
Marketing & Consulting Services:
Representation of the Indianapolis Speedway Corporation's trademarks for marketing, licensing, and sponsorship.
Event Management Services:
Manages all aspects of the Indianapolis 500 and the Brickyard 400.
Athlete Management Services:
Represents Indy Racing League drivers and teams in marketing, licensing, and sponsorship opportunities.

INTERBIKE
31910 DEL OBISPO STREET
SUITE 200
SAN JUAN CAPISTRANO, CA 92675
240-439-2986
866-221-7934
Fax: 949-226-5686
www.interbike.com
• Andria Klinger, Sales Manager
(949) 226-5745
• Pat Hus, Managing Director
• Sarah Timleck, Marketing Director
• Justin Gottlieb, Director Of Communications & PR
• Jennie Brewton-Dufur, Art Director
Marketing & Consulting Services:
Produces INTERBIKE, national trade show for bicycle products. Also publishes industry-wide bicycle market Interbike directory.

JAVELIN
1910 LOCUST STREET
ST LOUIS, MO 63103
314-361-1450
Fax: 314-361-1451
hello@javelin-inc.com
www.javelin-inc.com
• Donna Meier, Senior Partner
donnam@javelin-inc.com
• Jen Novak, Senior Partner
jenn@javelin-inc.com
• Jon Maurice, Executive Creative Director
jonm@javelin-inc.com

• Mark Lockwood, VP Bussiness
Development
markl@javelin-inc.com
• Tammy Derigan, Senior Dir of Cultural and
Consumer insights
tammyd@javelin-inc.com
• David Catron, Director of production
davidc@javelin-inc.com
• Mark Lockwood, Vice President Business
Development
(314) 361-1450
markl@javelin-inc.com
Services:
Concept development; creative design and
production; account and budget
management; end-to-end logistics
management/tour scheduling; set, activity
and exhibit design; fabrication and
production; venue/location/event research;
selection, negotiation and sell-in; sampling
goods management/warehousing; field
staffing, training and management; vehicle
leasing/insurance/maintenance/DOT
compliance; & Bulls-i ROI evaluation/project
reporting/recap
Nature of Service:
A worldwide event company specializing in
account specific and in-account events,
collegiate and youth marketing, corporate
events & incentive travel, mall tours, mobile
and custom vehicle tours, publicity stunts,
sampling and street intercept programs,
special events, sponsorship solicitation and
tie-ins.

JESSEN ASSOCIATES
9931 SW 61ST AVENUE
PORTLAND, OR 97219
503-977-3240
Fax: 503-977-3239
peterjj@peterjessen-gpa.com
www.peterjessen-gpa.com
Services:
Communication and Business Development
Consultation
Event Management Services:
Sports event photography company,
specializing in professional teams, leagues
& events.

KEYLIN & ASSOCIATES
2308 48TH AVENUE SW
SEATTLE, WA 98116
206-933-0339
• Ben Keylin, President
Services:
Marketing, Promotional, Public Relations &
Communications
Marketing & Consulting Services:
Serve as marketing consultants to minor
and major sports league teams and leagues,
including APSL, and Seattle SuperSonics.
Event Management Services:
Produces local and national sporting events
including National Cheerleading
Championship and the USA Spirit Squad
Cheerleading Tour.
Sports Service Founded:
1987

KORFF ENTERPRISES
250 W 57TH STREET
SUITE 1713
NEW YORK, NY 10107
212-691-2200
Fax: 212-691-6009

contact@korffenterprises.com
www.korffenterprises.com
• John Korff, President
john@korffenterprises.com
• Victoria Brumfield, Executive Director
victoria@korffenterprises.com
• Linsey Skalamara, Manager
linsey@korffenterprises.com
• Sarah Labawsky, Event Manager
sarah@korffenterprises.com
Services:
Sports and Special Events Marketing
Event Management Services:
Promotes and manages various types of
sporting events.

**KPMG CONVENTION, SPORTS &
ENTERTAINMENT PRACTICE**
100 N TAMPA STREET
SUITE 1700
TAMPA, FL 33602-5145
813-223-1466
Fax: 813-229-3976
www.kpmg.com
• Timothy P Flynn, Chairman Kpmg
International
• Michael Andrew, Chairman
• Alan Buckle, Deputy Chairman
Marketing & Consulting Services:
Specializes in development planning and
financial consulting for all forms of public
assembly facilities worldwide. Services
include market studies, operations analysis,
economic impact and financial assistance
including valuation services.

MARKETING EVENT PARTNERS
2711 PEACHTREE SQUARE
ATLANTA, GA 30360
404-522-7300
Fax: 404-255-6622
• Dennis Cooper, Chairman
• Paul Cooper, President
• Dominic Hoffman, Director Of Sales &
Event Staff
Event Management Services:
Conducts municipal event, management
and sports organization management audits.
Creates and implements sports events.
Marketing & Consulting Services:
Consults with cities and events regarding
bidding procedures. Develops programs and
sponsorship activities on behalf of sports
organizations.

MASON & MADISON
23 AMITY ROAD
BETHANY, CT 6524
203-393-1101
Fax: 203-393-2813
• Charlie Mason, President/Managing
Principal
mikec@javelin-inc.com
• Fran Onofrio, President
Services:
Advertising: Branding, Media, Print,
Broadcast, Direct, Collateral &
Unconventional
Clients:
Sun Connecticut, New Alliance Bank,
Emhart Tecknologies, Cookson Electronics,
SAS, Bruegger's, Adelphia, Braun, Cucina
di Carla, Krispy Kreme, Clear Channel,
Orrefors & Sprague
Services:
Public Relation: Research and Planning,
Media Relation, Community Relations,

Crisis Communication, Media Training,
Analyst Relations, Employee
Communication, Event Planning, Trade
Show Support & Ramp-Up Program
Event Management Services:
Multi-dimensional agency, includes
community service, international marketing,
interactive & multi-media, trade shows,
event planning, media buys, press relations
and media placement services. Provides
client service in automotive, electronics &
instrumentation, consumer products,
communications, transportation, utilities,
banking & finance, tourism, hospitality,
insurance healthcare and travel.

MAX-AIR PRODUCTIONS, INC.
9430 S RAINTREE DRIVE
SANDY, UT 84092
801-944-4849

MILLER & ASSOCIATES, CATHERINE
12 HOLLYWOOD ROAD
CHELSEA, LONDON, ENGLAND SW10
9HY
44-207-3511973
Fax: 619-234-8605
catherine@catherinemiller.com
www.catherinemiller.com
• Catherine Miller, Owner & Director
catherine@catherinemiller.com
• Claudia Kennaugh, Assistant Director
Services:
Advertising, Promotions, Public Relations &
Special Events

MIRAMAR EVENTS
1327 LIVINGSTON AVENUE
PACIFICA, CA 94044
650-726-3491
tim@miramarevents.com
www.miramarevents.com
• Timothy R. Beeman, Chairman/Chief
Executive Officer
(650) 726-3491
tim@miramarevents.com
Sports Service Founded:
1986
Event Management Services:
Strategic event planning; event
management and production; sponsorship
packaging and negotiation; TV packaging
and negotiation; sponsorship program
implementation; advertising and promotion;
publicity.
Services:
Media Relations, Marketing/Promotion,
Advertising, Project Coordination,
Sponsorship Sales Development,
Sponsorship Implementation & Strategic
Planning

MOBIVITY
58 W BUFFALO
SUITE 200
CHANDLER, AZ 85225
512-522-4710
Fax: 512-639-3375
info@mobivity.com
www.txtstation.com
• Michael Falato, Vice President Sales &
Business Development
(512) 535-5381
michael@txtstation.com
• Brook Paterson, Co-Founder
brook@txtstation.com
• Matthew Moulin, Chief Technology Officer

- Dennis Becker, President/CEO
- Michael Falato, SVP of Sales & Business Development
- Brad Dolian, VP ,Client Services
- Thi VanAusdal, Technical Lead
- Loyda Drew, Project Manager

Nature of Services:
Txtstation provides integrated campaigns that combine the passion of live broadcasts and events with the ubiquity of mobile messaging allowing broadcasters, event owners, sponsors and general media to communicate with viewers or fans directly through their mobile phones.

MOUNT UNION COLLEGE ANNUAL SPORTS SALES WORKSHOP
1972 CLARK AVENUE
ALLIANCE, OH 44601
800-992-6682
www.mountunion.edu
- Jim Kadlecek, Ph.D., Department Head
(330) 823-4045
- Richard F Giese, Ph.D., President
- James Thoma, Program Coordinator

Degrees Offered:
Sport Business

OVATION ENTERTAINMENT
7337 E SHOEMAN LANE
SCOTTSDALE, AZ 85251
480-946-9711
Fax: 480-941-1420

Services:
Develops and produces family shows and sports and entertainment special events.

PACIFIC SPORTFEST
12932 MOORPARK STREET
UNIT 2
STUDIO CITY, CA 91604
818-784-8077
Fax: 818-688-3863
www.playpsf.com
- Ingrid Moon, President/Chief Executive Officer
(888) 918-4938

Sports Service Founded:
2001

Services:
Event Consulting, Fundraising & Event Promotion

Event Management Services:
Organizes amateur sports events including tournaments, festivals, camps, and clinics. Specializes in women's and girls' sports, but also has co-ed events. Current focus is ice hockey; will be branching into soccer, inline hockey, and rugby.

PANOZ/SANCHEZ GROUP
14175 ICOT BOULEVARD
SUITE 300
CLEARWATER, FL 33760
305-670-4343
Fax: 305-670-4344
www.streetperformance.com

Marketing & Consulting Services:
Administers and manages professional motorsports including the Trans-Am Series.

Services:
Race promoter

PAULETTE WOLF EVENTS & ENTERTAINMENT
1165 N CLARK STREET
SUITE 613
CHICAGO, IL 60610
321-981-2600
Fax: 321-981-3600
events@pwe-e.com
www.pwe-e.com
- Paulette Wolf, Chief Executive Officer
- Jodi Wolf, President

Services:
Concept Development And Event Design, Event Production, Handling of All Logistics, Financial Management/Budgeting, Crowd Control/Security Plan, Organization Plan (Creating Timelines and Schedules), Food and Beverage Operations, Vendor Sourcing And Negotiation, Entertainment Negotiation, Booking and Production, Operational Planning and On Site Logistics, On Site Labour, Staging, Sound, Lighting, Video and Technical Staff, Custom Stage Design and Construction, Meeting Planning, Graphic Design, Blueprinting and Floor Plan Layout , Theme/Decor Design and Coordination, Set Up and Post Event Tear Down, Venue Selection

Clients:
AAML, ABC Sports, Adidas USA, Inc., Advocate Healthcare, AGFA, AIDS Foundation of Chicago, Aladdin Resort Casino, Alliant Foodservice, Allied Fibers, Amate House, American Beauty Association, American Red Cross, American Tobacco, AMOCO Corporation, Anheuser-Busch, Arlington Park Racetrack, Atlanta Committee For The Olympic Games, Avon, Beatrice Companies, Inc., Beckman-Coulter, Blue Cross/Blue Shield, The Rouse Company, The Borgata, Boyd Gaming, Breeder's Cup, Buena Vista Pictures, Burson Marsteller, Cannon USA, Inc., Catalina Conservancy, Charles Schwab, Chicago Architecture Foundation, Chicago Title & Trust, Children Defense Fund, Chris Cra

Services:
Coordination of City Services (i.e. Street Closure, Permitting, Police, EMT, Trash Removal, Etc.), Hotel Negotiations/Hotel Liaison, Space Management, Secure Celebrity Participation, Fashion Show Creative, Scheduling and Production, Premium Giveaways, Signage/Banners, Coordination and Production of Pyrotechnics, On Site Communications, Coordinate VIP Hospitality, General Liability Insurance From All Vendors, Secure Photographer and Video Services, Linen and Floral Design, Coordinate All Ground Transportation, Hotel, Hospitality and Backline Needs for Entertainment, Destination Management/Ground Transporatation.

PETER JACOBSEN PRODUCTIONS
9400 SW BARNES ROAD
SUITE 550
PORTLAND, OR 97225
503-526-9331
Fax: 503-641-2957
www.peterjacobsensports.com
- Mike Galeski, Executive Vp/ Managing Director
mike.galeski@peterjacobsensports.com
- Mike O'Donnell, Chief Operating Officer
- Monica Cruz, Chief Financial Officer

- Peter Jacobsen, President & Chief Executive Officer

Services:
Sports marketing and event management specializing in golf tournament management, marketing, and sponsorship

Event Management Services:
Specializes in event development, operations, sales, marketing and TV production. Produces and manages events in golf.

PIER 39 MARKET DEVELOPMENT
PIER 39, BEACH STREET & THE EMBARCADERO
STAIRWELL 2, LEVEL 3
SAN FRANCISCO, CA 94119-3730
415-705-5500
www.pier39.com
- Beth Schnitzer, Vice President Strategic Alliance
(415) 705-5500
- Tamara Goddard, Director Strategic Alliance
(415) 705-5500
tamara@pier39.com
- Mary Moffett, Partnership Marketing Account Executive
(415) 705-5563
mary@pier39.com
- Katie Gibbs, Sales Executive Partnership Marketing & Sales
(415) 705-5421
- Joe Ngammekchay, Coordinator Partnership Marketing & Sales
(415) 705-5566
- Ruth Tempest, Sales Administrator Partnership Marketing & S
(415) 705-5565

Sports Service Founded:
1979

Services:
A festival marketplace with more than 110 stores, 13 full-service restaurants with bay views and numerous fun-filled attractions. PIER 39's two-level design complements one of San Francisco's most unique shopping districts, featuring everything from NFL merchandise to jewelry and imported chocolates

Clients:
Coca-Cola, Crystal Geyser Alpine Spring Water, Discover Network, Dreyer's Grand Ice Cream, Shell Vacations Club

Event Management Services:
Official in-house sponsorship agency for Pier 39, its events and attractions and sponsorship representative for multiple high traffic venues in San Francisco. Purpose is to leverage the more than 10.5 million visitors annually to aid sponsors in reaching their marketing goals and objectives through Corporate or Event Sponsorship, Sampling and Display, Product Placement/Introduction or Outdoor Advertisement. Activities include, but are not limited to, Regattas, Hispanic Festival, July 4th Festival, Fleet Week, Snow Party/Ski exhibition. Annual event themes include Family, Civic, Cultural, Patriotic and Seasonal/Holiday Events.

POD PRODUCTIONS
20 BYRON ST
BANGALOW, NSW, 2479
612-6687-0411
Fax: 612-6687-0511
gallery@podproductions.com.au
www.podproductions.com.au

professional services

• Sean Watson, Photographer/Creative Director
Description:
Includes professionals with vast experiences in non-profit management, event planning, marketing, professional sports marketing, television production, and public relations.
Products:
Contemporary Image Gallery

PREMIERE RACING
67B FRONT STREET
MARBLEHEAD, MA 1945
781-639-9545
Fax: 781-639-9171
KWInfo@premiere-racing.com
www.premiere-racing.com
• Peter S. Craig, President
Peter@premiere-racing.com
• Jeanne Kleene, Manager
Jeanne@premiere-racing.com
• Alison Sipes, Office Manager
alison@premiere-racing.com
Description:
Management of sailboat regattas.
Services:
Management of sailboat regattas; involved in 2 major events: the January international regatta at Key West, Florida and Miami Race Week; manages other special events such as the Chesapeake stopover of the Volvo Ocean Race, the Drumbeat Regatta and other one-design regattas.

PRICEWATERHOUSECOOPERS
300 MADISON AVENUE
24TH FLOOR
NEW YORK, NY 10017
646-471-4000
Fax: 646-471-4444
• Bob Mortiz, Chairman, Senior Partner
• Mike Burwell, Operations Leader, Chief Financial Officer
• John Carter, Partner Affairs Leader, Chief Administrator
• Mitch Cohen, Strategic Execution Leader
• Scott Duncan, Marketing And Sales Leader
• Mike Davies, Director of Global Communications
Sponsor:
MLS Houston Dynamo. PGA Fall Finish, PGA Tour, PGA The Player's Championship, Champions Tour, Web.com Tour.

PRIMEDIA
3585 ENGINEERING DRIVE
SUITE 100
NORCROSS, GA 30092
687-421-3000
800-216-1423
Fax: 212-745-0121
• Dean B. Nelson, Chairman
• Charles Stubbs, President/CEO
• Michaelanne Discepolo, EVP, Human Resources
• Charles C. Stubbs, President & CEO
• Kim Payne, Senior Vice President & CFO
• Marlon Starr, Senior Vice President
• Mike Barber, Senior Vice President & Chief Accounting Offi
Services:
PRIMEDIA Enthusiast Media - encompasses the company's consumer magazine brands, including web sites and live events, as well as About.com

Services:
PRIMEDIA Consumer Guides - the country's largest publisher and distributor of free publications including Apartment Guide, New Home Guide and Auto Guide
PRIMEDIA Education - empowers millions of students to learn, includes Channel One, a propriety network to secondary schools; Films Media Group, a leading source of education videos; and Interactive Medical Network, a continuing medical education business.
Sports Service Founded:
1988
Event Management Services:
Total implementation of events from creative to on-site direction/management.
Marketing & Consulting Services:
Long and short-range marketing plan development; public relations counsel and direction; media placement; entertainment property and venue negotiation; customized retail/sales promotions; develop, license and merchandise products for distribution and on-site display.

PRO AM TOURNAMENTS
118 E MAPLE AVENUE
SUITE 2
LANGHORNE, PA 19047
800-357-1722
• Dennis M. O'Brien, President/Treasurer
Event Management Services:
Produces local, regional and national sports events.

PRO SPORTS & ENTERTAINMENT
1161 SAN VICENTE BOULEVARD
SUITE 304
LOS ANGELES, CA 90001
310-479-3806
• Paul H. Feller, President/Chief Executive Officer
Gabriella@prosportsinc.com
• Peter Ellsworth, Corporate Sales Manager
Peter@prosportsinc.com
• Jay Key, College Sports Marketing/Sales
Jay@prosportsinc.com
Nature of Sports Service:
Organization is an owner, producer, promoter, and operator of live entertainment events that generates revenue through selling corporate sponsorship, tickets, corporate hospitality, event merchandise, concessions, and athlete management, representation and endorsements.
Services:
Professional event marketing and management organization that owns, operates, manages, and promotes live sports and entertainment events. Specific services are: Sponsorship, Talent Representation, Marketing, Consultancy, Merchandise, Ticket / Entry, E-Commerce, Team League and Venue Rights, Television
Other Locations:
New York, Los Angeles, Seattle, Maui

PROFORMA SPORTS
810 PIONEER PARKWAY
PEORIA, IL 61615
309-692-6390
Fax: 309-692-6397
jeff.brookes@proforma.com
http://www.proforma.com/info

• Jeff Brookes, President
(309) 692-6390
jeff.brooke@proforma.com
Description:
Works with sports teams across the country producing their team programs.
Services:
Proforma specializes in serving the graphic communications needs of the sports and entertainment industry by partnering with our clients to develop innovative promotional campaigns, which build and support their brand identity, and most importantly, generate results for their organization and event.

QUICKFOOT
207 E HIGHWAY 80
PO BOX 29701
FORNEY, TX 75126
972-552-3800
Fax: 972-552-3810
info@quickfoot.com
www.quickfoot.com
Description:
Premier small-sided soccer tournament organizers.

RALEIGH CYCLE
6004 S 190TH STREET
SUITE 101
KENT, WA 98032
253-395-1100
Fax: 253-872-0257
www.raleighusa.com
• Sharon Robinson, CFO
Products:
Raleigh bicycles either for fitness, commuting, racing, or just cruising with family and friends.
Brands:
Raleigh Performance Comfort Road: Cadent 5.0 2006, Cadent 4.0 2006, Cadent 3.0 2006, Cadent 2.0 2006, and Cadent 1.0 2006. Raleigh Road: Rush Hour 2006, Team 2006, Prestige 2006, Competition 2006, Supercourse 2006, Grand Prix 2006, Grand Sport 2006, Sport 2006, Route 66 2006, Route 24 2006 and Route 1 2006. Raleigh Hybrid: Passage 5.0 2006, Passage 4.0 2006 and Passage 3.0 2006. Raleigh Full Suspension: Phase 2 2006, Phase 1 2006 and Phase 2006. Raleigh MTN Hardtail: Mojave 8.0 2006, Mojave 5.5 2006, Mojave 5.0 2006, Mojave 4.0 2006, Mojave 4.5 2006 and Mojave 2.0 2006. Raleigh Comfort: Venture 5.0 2006, Venture 4.0 2006, Venture 3.0 2006
Services:
Athlete Management: Bicycle racers/race teams and triathletes
Event Management Services:
Bicycle races.
Year Founded:
1896

RED SAIL SPORTS
PIER 5, THE EMBARCADERO
SUITE 102
SAN FRANCISCO, CA 94111
858-521-8244
877-733-7245
info@redsail.com
www.redsail.com
• Paul Lusk, Chief Operating/Financial Officer
plusk@redsail.com

• Lee Ann Wade, Corporate Marketing Director
lwade@redsail.com
Nature of Service:
Watersports centers, custom-built, luxurious catamarans, scuba diving, snorkeling and instruction, cruise passenger day trips, group travel expertise.

RIBER SPORTS MARKETING GROUP
7442 JAGER COURT
CINCINNATI, OH 45230
513-624-2100
Fax: 513-624-2110
www.ribersports.com
• Burch Riber, Founder
• Sam Riber, President
• Daryl Ellis, Director Of Business Development
• Burch R. Riber, President
Sports Service Founded:
1983
Event Management Services:
Creates, manages sports events. Develops and implements retail promotions based on events. Markets event sponsorships.
clients:
Prilosec OTC, ThermaCare, Pepto-Bismol, Metamucil, Pfizer, R+L Carriers, Sony, P+G BrandSAVER.

RICHLIN GROUP
13428 MAXELLA AVENUE
#278
MARINA DEL RAY, CA 90292
310-641-6477
Fax: 310-641-7250
www.trgolf.com
• Sandra Richlin, Founder/President
(310) 641-6477
sandra@trgolf.com
• Mark Gallandt, Operations Director
mark@trgolf.com
• Stacy Gallandt, Marketing/Public Relations
• Danny Garcia, Director Tournament Operations
Services:
Organizing golf events
Sports Service Founded:
1990
Event Management Services:
Specializes in producing golf events for corporations, tour groups, charities, and individuals. Full service agency includes management, promotional items, insurance and fundraising expertise.
Marketing & Consulting Services:
Consultation for sponsorship development.

RMY MANAGEMENT GROUP
5905 NW 54TH CIRCLE
CORAL SPRING, FL 33067
800-409-3813
Fax: 800-409-3813
roger@rmygroup.com
• Roger Yaffe, President
roger@rmygroup.com
Event Management Services:
Turnkey corporate event planning, association management and golf operations firm. Manages conferences, client entertainment and hospitality functions, sales meetings, incentives and golf events.
Services:
Association Management, Event Production, Professional Golf Services

SENIOR TOUR PLAYERS, INC.
1244 BOYLSTON STREET
SUITE 200
CHESTNUT HILL, MA 02467
617-266-3600

SFX/CLEAR CHANNEL ENTERTAINMENT
220 W 42ND STREET
NEW YORK, NY 10036
917-421-4000
Nature of Sports Services:
Producer and promoter of live entertainment. It produces concerts, touring Broadway shows, and sports events. Provides sports marketing and talent representation service through the SFX Sports Group.

SHOWPROCO, LLC
2915 BISCAYNE BOULEVARD
SUITE 303
MIAMI, FL 33137
305-893-8771
800-327-3736
Fax: 305-893-8783
www.showproco.com
• Sandra Lafrance, Operations/Productions
(305) 893-8771
• Christine Gomont, Accounting
(305) 893-8771
• Hardy C. C. Katz, Manager
Nature of Service:
Produces trade shows for sports licensed products and tailgate and picnic products: the Sports Licensing & Entertainment Marketplace and the Tailgate/Picnic Show.

SKYSIGNS UNLIMITED
302 3RD STREET
SUITE 7B
NEPTUNE BEACH, FL 32266
904-247-1241
Event Management Services:
Manages corporate balloon programs nationally and world wide. Creates and implements ballooning events including the Balloon Tour America professional hot air balloon racing circuit.

SMG
300 CONSHOHOKEN STATE ROAD
SUITE 770
WEST CONSHOHOKEN, PA 19428
610-729-7900
Fax: 610-729-1590
www.smgworld.com
• Wes Westley, President and CEO
• Maureen Ginty, Executive VP
• John Burns, Executive VP
• Gregg Caren, Sr.VP
Sports Service Founded:
Sports Service Founded: 1977
Event Management Services:
Production and marketing of sporting events.
Marketing & Consulting Services:
Stadiums, arenas, theaters, auditoriums and convention centers under its guidance worldwide. Divisions include SMG Productions, Network International, SMG sports advertising affiliate.

SOCCER MARKETING & PROMOTIONS, INC.
7444 SW 48 STREET
MIAMI, FL 33155

305-669-0101
Fax: 305-669-9979
www.copalatina.com
• Thomas Mulroy, Founder/President
• Paola Mulroy, VP Finance
• Marc Jacquemin, Operations Director/Tournament Coordinator
• Daniel Prenat, Competition Coordinator
• Rodrigo Oliva, Special Event Corrdinator
Services:
SM&P is a sports marketing firm that specializes in soccer events, has experience in the Hispanic market, international games, also experienced in corporate grass root implementation.
Clients:
Adidas USA, Inc., American Airline, Amateur Athletic Union, Anheuser Busch, Campbell's Soup Co., Chiquita, Dannon, Del Monte USA, Erima Sportswear, Eurosport, Gatorade, Hawaiian Punch, Hitachi America Ltd., Inca Kola, Just Say No Int., Ladeco Chilean Airlines, Lan Chile Airlines, Master Card, McDonalds Corp., Mlitre Sports, Motorola, M&M/Snickers, National Soccer Coaches Association, Nike, Shout, Soccer America Magazine, Soccer USA Partners, South Florida Olympic Committee, Terra Pro-Beach Soccer, The Academy, The Sports Authority, The Sports Chalet, TransAmerican Life, Transitions Optical, Uniroyal, United States Soccer Federation, Western U
Description:
SM&P is a sports marketing firm that specializes in soccer events, has experience in the Hispanic market, international games, also experienced in corporate grass root implementation.

SOUTHWIND KAYAK CENTER
17855 SKY PARK CIRCLE
#A
IRVINE, CA 92614
949-261-0200
800-768-8496
info@southwindkayaks.com
www.southwindkayaks.com
• John Upchurch, General Manager
info@southwindkayaks.com
Event Management Services:
Hosts sports events, focusing on environmental sports such as kayaking, canoeing, paddle surfing, etc.; also manages sea kayaking school and outfitter.

SPECIAL EVENT PRODUCTION
205 INDUSTRIAL DRIVE
CLEMMONS, NC 27012
336-764-2477
800-327-2352
Fax: 336-764-0684
information@sep-sports.com
www.sep-sports.com
Sports Service Founded:
1987
Event Management Services:
Transports, installs and operates portable electronic displays, scoreboards, video screens and scoring systems for the PGA Tour, Champions Tour, LPGA Tour, Nationwide Tour, ESPN X-Games, collegiate golf tournaments, celebrity golf tournaments, multi-sport events, and individual sports events (racing, waterski, horse shows, rodeos and promotions).

SPONSORWISE
info@sponsorwise.com
www.1.sponsorwise.com
- Burt Cummings, Chief Executive Officer
- Richard Raphael, Vice President Sales
- George Rassam, VP
Finance/Administration/CFO
- Russell Hinds, Founder
- Tad Williams, Marketing Director
Description:
Created to provide spohisticated tools need
in today'ssponsorship market. Based on our
collective experiences in corporations,
properties, agencies and the Internet, we set
out to design a platform that actively
supports everyone involved in the process.
Year Founded:
2002
Clients:
AirTran Airways, All State Insurance,
Amtrack, Bacardi, Bombay Sapphire,
Cingular Wireless, Columbia Sportswear,
ExxonMobil, Frontier Airlines, Gateway,
Gillette, Hershey's Food Company, Hyundai
Motor America, Hyundai Motor
Manufacturing/Alabama, Imperial Oil/Esso,
JetBlue Airways, Kawasaki, Kyocera
Wireless, L.G. Mobile Phones, Lexus,
Lowe's Companies, Marriott International,
MasterCard International, Mitsubishi Motors,
Motorola, Nintendo, Qwest
Communications, Reebok, SanDisk,
Staples, Toyota, Verizon Wireless, Wrigley.

SPORTHILL MARKETING
422 SPORT HILL ROAD
EASTON, CT 6612
203-261-5552
Fax: 203-452-2279
www.sporthillmarketing.com
- Bill Tustian, Owner/Founder
- Theresa S. Kelso, Office Manager
- Nancy Riling, Administrative Assistant
Clients:
ESPN, Equitable Life Assurance Co.,
Accessories Magazinne, Ski Magazine,
Skiing Magazine, Smith Corona, Inc.
Event Management Services:
Production, management of special events.

SPORTS AMERICA, INC.
10 S ADAMS STREET
ROCKVILLE, MD 20850
301-762-7100
sportsamerica@sportsamericainc.com
- Robert J Geoghan, President/Chief
Executive Officer/Founder
(301) 424-1080
robert.geoghan@sportsamericainc.com
- Wayne Ellis, VP Marketing
- Marc B. Steigerwalt, Events Manager
(301) 424-9354
marc.steigerwalt@sportsamericainc.com
Services:
Full-service event development and
management, including on-site execution,
pre-planning and post-evaluation,
promotion, public relations and all aspects of
project coordination.
Sports Service Founded:
1974
Marketing & Consulting Services:
Creation and management of sports
properties, strategic planning to integrate
sports into the marketing mix and creative
project development.

SPORTS MARKETING GROUP
47 MAIN STREET
#1
KEENE, NH 03431
603-358-5223
Fax: 509-756-3907
Services:
Specializes in international projects for
sports consulting for national/city
governments, corporations and
organizations
Products:
Racing Sportshirt, Polo, Long Sleve,
T-Shirts, Tank Tops, and Posters
Sports Service Founded:
1979
Event Management Services:
Financing, production and management of
major events, exclusively sports or including
sports activities.

SPORTS MEDIA ENTERPRISES
110 PEABODY DRIVE
STOW, MA 1775
978-897-5480
- John Clary, Contact
(978) 897-5480
Services:
Event Management: Organizing committee
for Emerald Isle Classic (Football), other
football games.

SPORTS PLUS
7020 HEATHERHILL ROAD
BETHESDA, MD 20817
301-229-5401
Fax: 301-229-2375
- Sara K. Fornaciari, Event Director
(301) 229-5401
sara@sportsplus.com
- Greg Chambers, Marketing Services
Director
Services:
Tournament promoter for IGA U.S. Indoors -
WTA Tour tennis event, MS Tennis Classic
in Denver, and the Owl Foundation Tennis
Fundraiser in Florida. Sports Promoters
Managers & Recruiters
Clients:
Express Sports, IGA, Multiple Sclerosis
Society - Colorado Chapter, National, The
Owl Foundation.
Sports Service Founded:
1990

SPORTSECONOMICS LLC
5847 HERON DRIVE
OAKLAND, CA 94618
510-387-0644
Fax: 510-295-2578
info@sportseconomics.com
www.sportseconomics.com
- Daniel Rascher, President
- Heather Rascher, VP
Nature of Services:
SportsEconomics is a professional services
firm that provides a broad range of
consulting services to the sports business
and entertainment communities. In the past
decade, SportsEconomics has provided
economic, financial, and marketing research
analysis to clients in a wide variety of fields
associated with sports. SportsEconomics is
based in the San Francisco Bay Area, but
serves clients throughout the United States
and the world. Our consultants offer
strategic analyses built on a base of intimate

knowledge of the institutions and economic
realities affecting the markets in which our
clients operate. We advise clients on topics
such as the
Description:
Marketing research is only as good as the
data collected. SportsEconomics offers a full
suite of custom business intelligence and
consulting solutions to address clients'
critical business issues and to enhance
organizational performance. Our research
not only provides clients with a better
understanding of the target customers and
markets in which they operate, but also
provides in-depth market analysis and
insight to put that information to optimal use.
We offer research and strategic analyses on
topics including effectiveness of marketing
projects and promotions, demand analysis,
ticket pricing optimization, media market
optimization, faci
Clients:
National Football League; National
Basketball Association; Major League
Baseball; National Hockey League;
American Hockey League; Major League
Soccer; Premier League (Soccer); National
Collegiate Athletic Association (NCAA);
Minor League Baseball Teams; NASCAR,
NHRA, Sports Commissions, PGA Tour.
Year Founded:
1998

SPORTSMARK MANAGEMENT GROUP
781 LINCOLN AVENUE
SUITE 380
SAN RAFAEL, CA 94901
415-461-5801
Fax: 415-461-5804
solutions@sportsmark.com
www.sportsmark.com
- Keith Bruce, Chief Marketing Officer
(415) 461-5801
keith@sportsmark.com
- Steve Skubic, CEO
Nature of Service:
All phases of event management including
creation, development, implementation and
hospitality. Hospitality services include
accomodations, transportation, tickets,
premiums, on-site communications, security,
and other aspects.

SPORTSMITH
5925 S 118TH E AVENUE
TULSA, OK 74146
918-307-2446
888-713-2880
Fax: 918-307-0216
www.sportsmith.net
Sports Service Founded:
1995
Event Management Services:
Develops, sets strategy, and implements
projects for clients utilizing local, regional or
international sports and special events to
promote their company's image and
corporate culture. Packages appropriate
tie-in promotions with media, retailers, and
major corporations. Events include trade
shows, running, walking, golf, water sports,
and track and field events.
Marketing & Consulting Services:
Complete corporate sponsorship planning,
management and on-site execution
including public relations, hospitality,
promotion and evaluation of companies.

SPORTSTARS, INC
1370 AVENUE OF THE AMERICAS
19TH FLOOR
NEW YORK, NY 10019
212-757-4044
Fax: 212-765-4833
marketing@sportstarsnyc.com
www.sportstarsnyc.com
Description:
Member contract advisor, represents professinoal athletes in contract negotiations in all major team sports.
Description:
Development and implementation of wide range of sports-related promotional programs, including special events, endorsement programs, and entertainment functions.

SPORTSVISIONS
29 QUAIL RUN
ORCHARD PARK, NY 14127-4611
716-639-8680
800-683-2880
Fax: 866-235-0566
• Terrence Murzynski, Owner
Nature of Sports Service:
Provides sports glasses that will enhance what the user wants to see and block out sunlight.

SPORTSYSTEMS CORPORATION
40 FOUNTAIN PLAZA
BUFFALO, NY 14202
716-858-5000
Fax: 716-858-5479
Services:
Manages all aspects of horse and greyhound racetrack operations. The largest owner and operator of pari-mutuel facilities in the United States. General Concessions: Offers upscale dining and services for suites and club seating areas through its premium catering division, Well Bread Restaurant Services Group, and retail sales through its Fan Zoner division, making Delaware North Companies Delaware North Companies Sportservice a true 'triple threat' operation.

SPURNEY ASSOCIATES, PETER
3701 LELAND STREET
CHEVY CHASE, MD 20015
301-652-7512
• Peter Spurney, President
Event Management Services:
An attraction and sports management firm. Services all segments of event/attraction management. Sets up attractions including from conceptual development, financing, sponsorship, implementation and management. Provides strategic partners with event association.
Sports Service Founded:
1973

SROBA & ASSOCIATES
8401 MAYLAND DRIVE
SUITE A
RICHMOND, VA 23294
804-965-5555
jsroba@sroba.com
• Joseph P Sroba, President
• Vern E. Inge, Jr., Legal Counsel
• Jose Ortega, Director of Player Development
• Miguel Nava, Director of Latin Operations

Sports Service Founded:
1985.
Nature of Sports Service:
Provides guidance and assistance in all areas of private personal and business management. Develops full marketing plans for image development and income generation. Coordinates financial plan, post-career consulting including business acquisition, new business formation, management and development.

STANDOUT SPORTS & EVENTS
205 W MAIN STREET
SOMERVILLE, NJ 08876-2834
908-725-7500
Fax: 908-725-7744
demarsport@aol.com
• John Demartini, President/Chief Executive Officer
Services:
Full Service sports and event company specializing in creating and producing charity fund-raising. Sports events include golf tournaments, dinners, galas, etc.

STARK EVENTS & ASSOCIATIONS
7510 W SUNSET BOULEVARD
LOS ANGELES, CA 90046
323-851-5446
www.starkeventsinc.com
• Rick Stark, Owner
(323) 851-5446
rick@becore.com
Services:
Develops and manages sponsorship and coordinates Extreme Sports Competition events nationally and internationally. Provides assistance to corporate clients and managing efficient sports sponsorships through extreme sports events.
Services:
Event Management : Promotion, production, marketing, and consulting for extreme sports events. Properties include Core Tour National Skate Series, United Skiboard Series, and the King of Dirt BMX Series. Also provides promotion and marketing for college and music events.
Sports Service Founded:
1993

STEINER SPORTS MARKETING
33 LECOUNT PLACE
NEW ROCHELLE, NY 10801
800-759-7267
Fax: 914-632-1102
generalinfo@steinersports.com
www.steinersports.com
• Brandon Steiner, Founder/Chairman/President/CEO
• Steve Weinreb, Managing Director
• Tony Cappa, Chief Financial Officer
• Jared Weiss, Executive Vice President
• Debbie Ebben, Vice President
• Jonathan Wolfsie, Director
Nature of Sports Service:
A full-service sports marketing agency that offers sponsorship consultation, management of consumer and trade promotions, development of point-of-sales materials, development of customer loyalty programs, creation of athlete fantasy experiences for key clients, and implementation of employee incentive programs.
Services:

Provides sportsmarketing services and authentic memorabilia
Products:
Producer of authentic autographed collectibles and the best source for all sports gift needs.
Clients:
Aetna US Healthcare; Alan Taylor Communications; Alcone Marketing Group; American Express; Anheuser-Busch; BBDO; Burson Marsteller; Cannon Business Solutions; Chase; Citi; Coca-Cola; Dannon; Davis Vision; DeMatteo Monness - Security Traders; Diageo Spirits; Kraft General Foods; eBay; ESPN; Fenway Partners - Investment Bankers; Fleishman - Hillard Public Relations; Foot Locker; Ford Motor Company; Gillette; J Brown, LMC Group; J.P. Morgan; Major League Baseball; MasterCard; Merck; Modell's Sporting Goods; New York Merchantile Exchange; Novartis; Schering - Plough; UBS Warburgh; Unilever; Yahoo; YPO; Baseball Athletes; Basketball Athletes; Foo
Sports Fantasy Division:
Offers sports fans the opportunity to meet athletes. The current packages feature players such as Mark Messier, NBA Legends Walt Clyde Frazier and others.
Strategic Sports Marketing & Consulting:
Provides corporations with expertise to help maximize the impact of their sports marketing efforts. Our focus is not only developing integrated marketing strategies, but also to provide a comprehensive program evaluation to determine the return on investment. Marketing, promotion, celebrity talent service with access to over 1,700 athletes available. Provides talent for events, appearances, public relations campaigns and endorsements.

STOWE AREA ASSOCIATION
51 MAIN STREET
PO BOX 1320
STOWE, VT 5672
802-253-7321
877-467-8693
Fax: 802-253-6628
askus@gostowe.com
www.gostowe.com
• Jo Sabel Courtney, Public Relations Manager
(802) 253-7321
Event Management Services:
Creates and manages summer sports events in the Stowe Mountain geographic area.
Services:
Miscellaneous: Child Care, Stowe Kinderhaus Home Day Care, Post Office, Western Union, Library, Meeting and Conferences, Weddings, Claire's Dog Camp, North Country Animal League, Stowe Kid's Stuff

STRATEGIC PLANNING CONCEPTS INTERNATIONAL
515 E FIRST STREET
SUITE A
TUSTIN, CA 92780
714-505-9353
888-895-3871
Fax: 714-505-4417
Andrew@spcintl.net
www.spcintl.net
• Andrew Strenk, President
(714) 505-9353

Andrew@spcintl.net
• Scott Klein, Fieldwork Manager and Research Associate
(714) 505-9353
Scott@spcintl.net
Services:
Provides services for sports facilities. Programs include site location and site analysis, feasibility studies, strategic plans, business plans, financial analysis, design development, entitlement procurement and traffic studies & tax assessments. International retail real estate consulting company: Strategy Formulation, Retail Format Selection, Project Sizing, Project Positioning, Tenant Strategies, Feasibility Studies, Market Analysis, Site Assessment, Evaluation of Conflicting Demographic and Psychodemographic Data, Trade Area Definitions, Cultural Context Assessment, Economic Trend Analysis, Labor Studies, Marketing Strategies, Site Analy
Clients:
Auto Zone, Avatar Development, Carlson Company, Carver Company, City of San Diego, Crumpler and Kruger, Donahue Schriber, Fenton Western, Forest City Development, Fransen Company, Hahn Company, Hechnger Company, Holsman International, Home Depot, Hoyts Cinema Corporation, Kornwasser Friedman, Mexus, Ross Dress for Less, Saks Fifth Avenue, San Diego National Sports Training Foundation, Southwestern Bell, Smart and Final, Sport Floor USA, Staubach Company, Strategic Edge, Thompson and Associates, Warner Bros.

SUMMIT SPORTS & EVENTS
9100 W JEWELL
SUITE 200
LAKEWOOD, CO 80232
303-989-4084
Fax: 303-989-0539
• Dan Cramer, President
Description:
Producer and manager of grassroots sporting events for amateur athletes in soccer, basketball and football.
Other Offices:
Atlanta, Boston, Pittsburgh.

TARGET SPORTS MARKETING
2811 UNIVERSITY AVENUE SOUTHEAST
#141050
MINNEAPOLIS, MN 55414
610-688-9233
Fax: 877-768-4164
info@tsmworldwide.com
Nature of Sports Service
A business consultancy and service partner focused on providing market and non-market strategic services to firms competing in the international shooting, hunting, and outdoor recreation industry.

TAYLOR WEST ADVERTISING
4040 BROADWAY
SUITE 302
SAN ANTONIO, TX 78209
210-805-0320
Fax: 205-805-9371
www.taylorwest.com
• Bill West, Chief Executive Officer/Owner
• Pat Roberson, VP/Chief Media Strategist
probeson@taylorwest.com

THE MCCRUM COMPANIES, INC.
3838 OAK LAWN
SUITE 200
DALLAS, TX 75219
214-526-5050
800-411-3756
Fax: 214-526-6050
www.gsrisk.com
• Douglas McCrum, President/Chief Business Officer
Event Management Services:
GSR provides special contingency insurance coverage to event promoters, sports teams, race tracks, broadcasters, agents and sponsors. Products include: prize indemnity for all contests, games and sweepstakes; coverage for cancellation, postponement, curtailment, abandonment or relocation of an event; non-appearance of artist(s), group(s) or teams(s) to cover abandonment of tours, film sessions and other events; failure to telecast pay-per-view, cable or other transmissions due to equipment failure, airwave disruption or pre-emption airtime; death and disgrace to cover costs in employing sports personalities in the promotion of a product, even

THINK TANK COMMUNICATIONS
Am SCHRAGEN WEG 19
POSTFACH 6
VADUZ, LICHTENSTE 9490
423-239-0145
Fax: 423-239-0146
office@thinktankag.com
www.thinktankag.com
• Jeffrey J. Stern, President
office@thinktankag.com
• Pablo G. Estela, Contact
• Colin Kuchy, Contact
• Manfred Frostner, Contact
Services:
Individual client management, corporate sponsorship and event management, sponsorship analysis, business partner network. Have offices in Europe and U.S. Organizers of Street Soccer Cup USA, a youth soccer tournament.

TOP RANK
3980 HOWARD HUGHES PARKWAY
SUITE 580
LAS VEGAS, NV 89109
702-732-2717
Fax: 702-733-8232
www.toprank.com
• Robert Arum, Founder/Chairman
Services:
Promotes championship fights and other major boxing matches throughout the world.
Clients:
Represents baseball players in all facets of sports representation / organizes and structures boxing matches

TOURNAMENT SPORTS
185 WEBER STREET S
WATERLOO, ONTARIO, CANADA N2J 2B1
519-888-6500
800-265-2454
Fax: 519-888-6540
info@tournament-sports.com
www.tournament-sports.com
Services:
Production and management services for professional golf events.

TRIPLE CROWN SPORTS
3930 AUTOMATION WAY
FORT COLLINS, CO 80525
970-223-6644
Fax: 970-223-3636
www.triplecrownsports.com
Sports Service Founded:
1982
Services:
Sports: Department for sponsor services include data base listings, research (surveys), publications, media and publicity, accounting service, travel agency. Publishes tournament brochures, direct mailing sales catalogues, event magazines.

TRITON SPORTS ASSOCIATES
325 MANVILLE ROAD
PLEASANTVILLE, NY 10570
914-747-5066
Fax: 914-747-5033
• Gordon Saint-Denis, President
• Ashish Raythatha, Principal
Services:
Services include Mergers and Acquisitions; Placement of Debt
Sports Service Founded:
2002
Nature of Sports Service:
Organization specializes in execution of complex transactions within the sports industry and maximizing the efficiency of the capital structure and operations of clients' sports properties. Services include Mergers and Acquisitions; Placement of Debt and Equity; Financial and Transactional Advisory; Restructuring, Turnaround, and Bankruptcy; Venue and Franchise Valuation; and Operational Advisory.

UBS FINANCIAL SERVICES
1285 AVENUE OF THE AMERICAS
NEW YORK, NY 10019
212-649-8000
www.ubs.com
• Marcel Ospel, Chairman
• Stephan Haeringer, Executive Vice Chairman
• Marco Suter, Executive Vice Chairman
• Rosemary Berkery, Vice Chairman of UBS Wealth Management Americ
• Bob McCann, CEO UBS Group Americas
• Dan Cochran, Chief Operating Officer, Wealth management
• John Dalby, Chief Financial Officer and Chief Risk Office
• Jonathan Eisenberg, General Counsel
• Paula Polito, Client Strategy Officer
• Anita Sands, Head of Change Leadership
Services:
Provides a full spectrum to institutional and corporate clients, governments and financial intermediaries globally.
Description:
Assists municipalities, government agencies, non-profit organizations and private entities in structuring, underwriting, trading and distributing tax-exempt and taxable bonds. The Group also provides a secondary market for these securities and develops and markets various financial products.

ULTRAFIT-USA
PO BOX 629
HILLIARD, OH 43026

614-332-5205
jeff@ultrafit-usa.com
www.ultrafit-usa.com
• Jeff Sheard, President
(614) 332-5205
jeff@ultrafit-usa.com
• Abby Sheard, Marketing
(614) 260-1452
abby@ultrafit-usa.com
Services:
Athlete Management: Sports marketing and management.
Services:
Event Management: Produces and coordinates triathlons and biathlons and other special event.
Sports Service Founded:
1985

UNITED RENTALS
5 GREENWICH OFFICE PARK
GREENWICH, CT 6831
203-622-3131
800-877-3687
Fax: 203-622-6080
www.unitedrentals.com
• Michael J Kneeland, President/Chief Executive Officer
• William B. Plummer, CEO/CFO
Event Management Services:
Manufactures, designs, coordinates and provides the rental of power generation, electrical distribution, portable air conditioning and mobile electric resistive heat for sporting events world wide. Also carries a line of complete catering kitchens, food trucks and mobile dish washing trucks for rental. Capable of servicing any size event. Provides professional service and technical advice. Complete turn-key operation.
Sports Service Founded:
1960

VAIL VALLEY FOUNDATION
90 BENCHMARK ROAD
SUITE 300
AVON, CO 81620
970-949-1999
888-920-2787
Fax: 970-949-9265
info@vvf.org
www.vvf.org
• Ceil Folz, President
• Heidi Elzinga, Assistant To President
helzinga@vvf.org
Nature of Service:
Through the organization of educational, cultural, historical, artistic and athletic performances, events and attractions for the education and benefit of the community. Providing the community with athletic educational and cultural events to enhance the quality of life in the Vail Valley.
Year Founded:
1981
Event Management Services:
World Cup Ski Racing, Pro-Am Ski Event/Fundraiser, Invitational Snowboard Event

VELOCITY SPORTS & ENTERTAINMENT
230 E AVENUE
NORWALK, CT 06855
203-831-2000
Fax: 203-831-2300

• Ed Beamon, CEO
(973) 285-9332
• Michelle Berg, Senior Vice President, Group Director
(973) 285-9332
Nature of Service:
Velocity Sports Management is a full-service, community minded, international sports marketing firm specializing in the concept, packaging, marketing and management of professional cycling teams and athletes. In addition, we provide the management of all related initiatives including on-site product demonstrations and sampling, athlete appearances for retail and corporate functions, and quantifying sponsorship effectiveness. Our mission is to maximize corporate and brand exposure by creating synergy between sponsors, consumers and the healthy, high-energy atmosphere that professional cycling creates.
Year Founded:
1994

WALSH ENTERPRISES , BOB
233 - 6TH AVENUE N
SEATTLE, WA 98109
206-903-6850
Fax: 206-903-6851
• Bob Walsh, President/Chief Executive Officer
Sports Service Founded:
1992
Services:
Event Management, Marketing & Consulting: Overall event planning, sponsorship development, creative direction, day-of-event management. Press and public relations direction and coordination.
Marketing & Consulting Services:
Specialists in the development of strategic affinity/lifestyle marketing programs for the corporate sector.
Other Location:
20 Telavi Street, Tbilisi, GA 38003.

WIRZ & ASSOCIATES
665-A NORTH TRAIL
STRATFORD, CT 6614
203-380-9931
203-858-4890
Fax: 612-465-5349
BWirz2@gmail.com
www.wirzandassociates.com
• Bob Wirz, Founder/President
(203) 858-4890
BWirz2@gmail.com
Services:
Sports: Full service media planning, publicity and management. Sports specialists experienced from amateur to major league All Star and World Series.
Clients:
American Baseball Coaches Association, Art Spaces, Inc., Bantam Doubleday Dell Publishing, Baseball America magazine, Bob's Stores, The City of NOrfolk, Virginia, Continental Basketball Association, Denver Baseball Commission, eNewsRelease.com, Fairfield Univ., Federacion Internationale De Volleyball, Glaucoma Foundation, Howe Sportsdata International, IBM, Independent Professional Baseball, Jessica Howard, Just For Men Haircolor (Combe, Inc.), Little League Baseball, Inc., Major League

Baseball, MCI, National Adult Baseball Association, New Haven County Cutters, Northern League, Oscar Mayer, Panini, Prodigy, Rotisserie League Baseball.
Sports Service Founded:
1985
Marketing & Consulting Services:
Wide-ranging public relations and marketing services in all sports.

WOHL & COMPANY
1630 JOSEPHINE
NEW ORLEANS, LA 70130
504-528-9900
kit@wohlco.com
www.wohlco.com
• Amy Wohl, Founder
Event Management Services:
On site event management.
Marketing & Consulting Services:
Full services as they relate to the sports event being managed, including consultation with the sports sanctioning organization.

WOMEN'S SPORTS LEGENDS
PO BOX 537
SAUSALITO, CA 94966-0537
415-331-7100
Fax: 415-331-7102
netres1@aol.com
www.wslegends.com
• Pam Shriver, President
Services:
Event Management: Athlete-owned sports promotion company, specializing in corporate events, tournaments and merchandising.
Sports Service Founded:
1995

WORLD BASKETBALL OPPORTUNITIES
W326 N9586 PERADELL CT
HARTLAND, WI 53029
262-966-9660
Fax: 262-966-9661
www.worldbasket.com
• Scott Woltzen, Contact
Services:
Marketing & Consulting: Independent scouting services provided for regional, national, and international professional and collegiate basketball games.
Services:
Event Management: Scheduling of inbound international men's and women's basketball games. Athlete Management: Representation of basketball players (male and female) from comprehensive contract negotiations, tax planning, financial planning, marketing, and summer sports camps to management of free agent camps to provide exposure to pro and international scouts.

WORLD GOLF HOSPITALITY
9755 DOGWOOD ROAD
SUITE 110
ROSWELL, GA 30075
770-998-3123
877-288-6719
Fax: 770-998-5515
• Brendan Lillis, President/CEO
• Martin Willis-Jackson, Chief Financial Officer
• Jess Taylor, Chief Operating Officer
• Aubrey Proud, Business Development

Nature of Service:
To offer the finest quality service to corporations in need of event, meeting, incentive, travel, hospitality and golf products.
Year Founded:
1992
Clients:
Absolut Vodka, The Absolut Spirits Company, Golf Magazine, Bridgestone, Level, Georgia-Pacific, AIG, Jim Beam, Coca-Cola

WORLD SPORTS GROUP, LTD.
419 E 57TH STREET
SUITE 9A
NEW YORK, NY 10022-3060
212-260-5001
Fax: 212-412-9022
• Rey Olsen, President

Event Security

ALPHA & OMEGA MOUNTED SECURITY PATROL
2906 W SOUTHLAKE BOULEVARD
SOUTHLAKE, TX 76092
817-379-6607
Fax: 817-379-5993
info@mountedpatrol.com
www.mountedpatrol.com
• Frank Keller, Founder/CEO
(817) 379-6607
info@mountedpatrol.com
• John DeRouen, Sr. Vice President, General Manager, A&O
(817) 379-6607
john.derouen@gmail.com
• Bruce Smith, VP of Operations, National Recruiting Directo
(817) 312-0164
equinesafety@aol.com
Description:
Pioneer of private mounted horse patrols in North America. Provides mounted patrol services to stadiums, arenas, auditoriums etc. Troopers specialize in weaponless security.
Services:
consulation for site selection and layout, advance work, tour security, review of staffing plans, on-site management of security teams, threat assessment, development of emergency response plans for multiple scenarios, analysis of manpower needs, integration of security plans with local law enforcement officials, emergency evacuation planning, consulation on people and package screening, consulation on venue surveillance needs and options, post-event evaluation and follow up plans, venue assessment and security planning.
Clients:
world cup soccer, super bowl xxviii houston,tx, united center chicago, il, bonnaroo music and camping festival, rothbury music festival, langerado music festival, phish music and camping festivals, virgin music festival, town and country village houston, tx, market street the woodlands township,tx, law enforcement units, g-8 summit savannah,ga, merriweather post pavilion, chronicle pavilion.

CONTEMPORARY SERVICES CORPORATION
17101 SUPERIOR STREET
NORTHRIDGE, CA 91325
818-885-5150
Fax: 818-885-0609
www.csc-usa.com
• Damon Zumwalt, CEO
dzumwalt@csc-usa.com
• Jim Granger, President
jgranger@csc-usa.com
• Mark Camillo, Sr. Vice President, Strategic Planning
• Mark Glaser, Sr. Vice President, Operations
• James H. Service, Vice President, General Counsel
• Jay Brock, Vice President, Operations
• Bruce Wagner, Vice President, Operations
Description:
CSC is the world leader in fully-managed event staffing, crowd management, security, and guest services for both the entertainment and sporting event industries. CSC's 42 years of experience have resulted in a loyal and esteemed client base, including more than 100 stadiums and arenas, over 70 universities and colleges, more than 20 convention centers, and numerous clients in the MLB, MLS, NBA, NFL, NHL, and NASCAR. CSC also has experience providing services to the world's largest special events, including the U.S. Open, 29 Super Bowls, 7 Olympic Games, 4 Presidential Inaugurations, and 2 World Cups.
Services:
Crowd management, security, ticket taking, ushering, parking services, box office services, and consulting.

GARDA WORLD
1101 WILSON BOULEVARD
SUITE 1725
ARLINGTON, VA 22209
703-253-8080
Fax: 703-592-1500
www.garda-world.com
• Lemarque Sheppard, President
• Steve Casteel, SVP, International Business Development
• Obie R Moore III, Seinor Vice President
• Rob Shuster, Senior Vice President
• Ray O'Hara, Senior Vice President
• Rolando P. Soliz, General Director
• Nicole A. Watson, Vice President Business Development
• Kevin Coughenour, Chief Information Officer
• Brent Wegner, General Counsel
• Christina Mansfield, Vice President Human Resources
Sports Service Founded:
1984.
Services:
Management: Help security professionals & event managers plan for, manage and respond to risks during events - including annual shareholders' meetings, sales conferences, product road shows, publicity events, conventions, and large-scale parties.
Services:
Event Integrity, Workplace Integrity, Litigation Integrity, Travel Integrity, Property Integrity, Product Integrity
Athlete Management Services:
Security services for athletes and their

families, such as residential security surveys, personal protection.
Event Management Services:
All types of security services for sports events.
Marketing & Consulting Services:
Advises corporations on security-related issues pertaining to events, athletes and sponsorship programs.

WACKENHUT SPORTS SECURITY
910 PAVERSTONE DRIVE
RALEIGH, NC 27615
561-622-5656
800-922-6488
www.g4s.com
• Grahame Gibson, COO/Divisional President Security
• Drew Levine, President Security Services
• William Hill, President Consulting & Investigation Services
• Susanne Jorgensen, Chief Financial Officer
• Julie Payne, Svp & General Counsel
• Dr. Michael Goodboe, Vp Human Resources/Corporate Learning Officer
• Brian McCabe, Chief Information Officer
• John Connolly, Chairman
• Nick Buckles, Group Chief Executive
• Trevor Dighton, Chief Financial Officer
Services:
Provides security, safety, crowd management, admissions, ushers, parking and related services to sports and entertainment venues throughout the United States.

Financial Services

A.P. SWANN INSURANCE SERVICES LLC
980 N MICHIGAN AVENUE
SUITE 1377
CHICAGO, IL 60611
312-274-0950
877-277-9266
Fax: 312-274-0955
info@apswann.com
www.apswann.com
Description:
nationally licensed insurance brokerage. A.P. Swann provides the ability and the experience to bring a vast array of surety bonds and insurance products,to both individual consumers and businesses.
specialties
meeting the unique needs of consumers seeking efficient, on-demand product purchase, and carriers desiring a cost-effective sales and delivery channel for low premium, low profit margin products.

ACTIVE INTERNATIONAL
ONE BLUE HILL PLAZA
PEARL RIVER, NY 10965
845-735-1700
800-448-7233
Fax: 845-735-0717
www.activeinternational.com
• Alan Elkin, Co-Founder/Chief Executive Officer
• Arthur Wagner, Co-Founder/President
• Richard Vendig, EVP/Chief Financial and Administrative Officer
• Fredrick Fuest, President, International Division

- Alan Brown, Evp Worldwide Media
- Elysa Gonzalez, Svp Marketing
- Barry M. Green, Evp Sales
- Sharon Marshall, General Counsel
- Jim Porcarelli, Chief Strategy Officer
- Thomas Ruderman, Chief Human Resource Officer
- Stu Allen, Svp Business Services
- Alan Elkin, Founder/CEO
- Mark Ordover, Evp Global Real Estate & Financial Assets

Description:
Enables a company to fund their sponsorship property without additional money. Offers customized corporate trading programs to assist in financing their racing team, golf outing, naming rights or sports and event sponsorships.

Services:
Provides a wide range of ways to help clients meet their business needs which includes advertising, printing, shipping and packaging, sports events marketing, etc.

ALLIED SPECIALTY INSURANCE
10451 GULF BOULEVARD
TREASURE ISLAND, FL 33706
727-367-6900
800-237-3355
Fax: 727-367-1407
rdaprile@alliedspecialty.com
www.alliedspecialty.com
- David Gallace, Contact
dgallace@alliedspecialty.com
- Rick D'Aprile, Contact
rdaprile@alliedspecialty.com
- Mark Jones, Contact
mjones@alliedspecialty.com
- Carol Perkins, Contact
cperkins@alliedspecialty.com

Services:
Provider of insurance solutions, which includes amusement facility, motorsports, outdoor amusement and specialty insurance.

Marketing & Consulting Services:
Specialists in sports and venue insurance needs, including but not limited to coverage of spectator and participant legal liability for athletic events, tenant-user liability programs for venue lessees, and group accident medical coverage for athletic teams and associations.

AMBAC ASSURANCE CORPORATION
ONE STATE STREET PLAZA
NEW YORK, NY 10004
212-658-7470
800-221-1854
Fax: 212-509-9190
www.ambac.com
- Michael A. Callen, Chair/Interim CEO
- Sean T. Leonard, Svp/CFO
- Douglas C. Renfield-Miller, Evp Europe & Asia/Pacific
- Diana N. W. Adams, President and Chief Executive Officer
- Robert B. Eisman, Senior Managing Director and Chief Accounting
- Stephen M. Ksenak, Senior Managing Director, General Counsel and
- David Trick, Senior Managing Director, Chief Financial Off
- Michael Fitzgerald, Managing Director
(212) 208-3222
mfitzgerald@ambac.com

Description:
Primarily engaged in insuring municipal and

structured finance obligations and is the successor of the oldest municipal bond insurance company. Financial guarantee insurance written by AMBAC, guaranteed payment when due of the principal and interest on the obligations insured. AMBAC has been assigned Triple A claims paying ability ratings from the 3 major rating agencies.

Services:
Primarily engaged in insuring municipal and structured finance obligations and is the successor of the oldest municipal bond insurance company. Financial guarantee insurance written by AMBAC, guaranteed payment when due of the principal and interest

AMERICA'S SCHOOLS PROGRAM
PO BOX 236
ATWOOD, CA 92601
800-345-4025
Fax: 951-344-8279
don@americas-schools.org
www.americas-schools.org/home.php
- Don Baird,
Sponsorships,Partnerships,Media Relationships
(800) 345-4025
don@americas-schools.org
- Vijay Kotrappa, Programs/General Information
(800) 345-4025

Marketing & Consulting Services:
Engaged in the business of generating additional discretionary revenues for schools, including high schools, grammar schools and community colleges via six primary revenue sources: corporate sponsors; an affinity credit card program; financial services; logo-licensing; non-logo licensing; and direct marketing.

AMERICAN HOLE 'N ONE
55 SCOTT STREET
BUFORD, GA 30518
800-499-2257
Fax: 770-271-4006
golf@ahno.net
www.americanholeinone.net

Services:
Leading resource for hole in one insurance, custom showroom promotions, sports risk insurance and superior sign packages

AON ENTERTAINMENT
707 WILSHIRE BOULEVARD
SUITE 2600
LOS ANGELES, CA 90017
213-630-3200
Fax: 213-627-6155
www.aon.com
- Mary Greening, Contact

Services:
All types of insurance services for the sports industry/creator innovative solutions in insurance and risk management, human capital consulting, and insurance underwriting to help clients

ASSURED GUARANTY CORPORATION
31 W 52ND STREET
NEW YORK, NY 10019
212-974-0100
Fax: 212-581-3268
info@fsa.com
www.assuredguaranty.com

- Robert P Cochran, Chairman/Chief Executive Officer
- Sean W McCarthy, President/Chief Operating Officer
- Joseph W Simon, Chief Financial Officer
- Bruno Deletre, Evp/Member Executive Committee
- Michele Colin, Head Risk Management

Services:
Triple A rated insurer of municipal bonds guaranteeing all types of general obligations and revenue bonds in both the new issue and secondary markets. Organization provides full service to the municipal market from its New York headquarters and regional area

BESSEMER TRUST
630 5TH AVENUE
NEW YORK, NY 10111
212-708-9100
Fax: 212-265-5826
www.bessemer.com
- George A. Wilcox, Jr., President
- Marc D Stern, Chief Executive Officer
- Rebecca H Patterson, Chief Investment Officer

Services:
Official Private Banking and Wealth Management Partner of NTRA/Breeders' Cup Limited.

BLACKROCK
60 STATE STREET
BOSTON, MA 02109
617-357-1200
800-531-0131
Fax: 617-951-9919
www2.blackrock.com
- Laurence Fink, Chairman/Chief Executive Officer
- James Rohr, Board Member
- Kenneth Dunn, Board Member
- Laurence D. Fink, Chairman and Chief Executive Officer
- Philipp Hildebrand, Vice Chairman
- Kendrick R. Wilson III, Vice Chairman
- Barbara Novick, Vice Chairman
- Robert S. Kapito, President
- Robert W. Fairbairn, Senior Managing Director
- Peter R. Fisher, Senior Managing Director

Description:
A new division within Private Client Group. Provides investment management for professional athletes.

Services:
Provides risk management, investment system outsourcing and financial advisory services to a growing number of institutional investors

BOLLINGER INSURANCE
101 JFK PARKWAY
SHORT HILLS, NJ 07078
973-467-0444
800-526-1379
Fax: 973-921-2876
www.bollingerinsurance.com
- Lori Windolf Crispo, Senior Executive Vice President, Sports Division
(800) 526-1379
lori@bollingerinsurance.com
- John A. Windolf, Chairman/CEO

Description:
Bollinger is a leading provider of Sports Insurance products and risk management

services in all 50 states. Insuring Amateur Sports Organizations has been our specialty for over 60 years. Bollinger provides a full array of coverages through A rated insurance companies for sports organizations and sports facilities.

Sports Service Founded:
1944

Year Founded:
1876

BWD GROUP LLC
45 EXECUTIVE DRIVE
PLAINVIEW, NY 11803
516-327-2700
www.bwdgroup.com

Sports Service Founded:
1929

Services:
Insurance products, risk management services and benefit programs for a diverse and distinguished clientele; sports and entertainment insurance; commercial and personal lines, individual and employee benefits, financial planning, consulting, program administration and claims services

CARPENTER, PETERSEN & ASSOCIATES - CPA'S
26020 TOWNE CENTRE DRIVE
FOOTHILL RANCH, CA 92610
949-951-3200
Fax: 949-951-3210
info@cpcpas.com
www.cpcpas.com
• John Carpenter, Owner
• David Petersen, Owner

Services:
Financial Statement consulting and preparation at all traditional levels, Tax Planning and compliance, Consulting Services, Accounting and Bookkeeping, and Industries and Professions Served

Description:
Provides financial and estate planning, money management services, income tax planning and preparation for over 30 years.

CHARLES SCHWAB & CO.
211 MAIN STREET
SAN FRANCISCO, CA 94105
415-667-1009
888-403-9000
800-435-4000
www.schwab.com
• Chuck Schwab, Founder
• Carol Benz, Investment Advisor
• Carolyn Clayton, Team Member
• Kirk Larson, Team Member
• Mike Dewitt, Management Team

Services:
Official investment firm of the PGA Tour, Champions Tour, and US Ski Team.

DELOITTE & TOUCHE LLP
100 KIMBALL DRIVE
PARSIPPANY, NJ 07054-2176
973-602-6000
Fax: 973-602-5050
www.deloitte.com

ERNST & YOUNG
5 TIMES SQUARE
NEW YORK, NY 10036-6530

212-773-3000
Fax: 212-773-6350
www.ey.com
• James Turley, Chairman/Chief Executive Officer
• John Ferraro, COO

Services:
Auditing, financial planning, accounting and consulting services for corporate involvement in sports franchises, sports facility management, or event management. Special purpose and compliance examinations; valuations and appraisals; tax planning

GAGLIARDI INSURANCE SERVICES
1302 LINCOLN AVE
SUITE 202
SAN JOSE, CA 95125
408-414-8100
800-995-9768
Fax: 408-414-8199
sales@gsportsinsurance.com
www.gisins.com
• Dominic Gagliardi, President
• Nicholas Gagliardi, Vp Sales / Marketing
• David Abhraham, VP
dabraham@gsportsinsurance.com
• MIchelle Valdivia, Director of Operations
mvaldivia@gsportsinsurance.com
• Patricia Chavez, Customer Service
pchavez@gsportsinsurance.com
• Rick Dukelow, Sales Representative
rdukelow@gsportsinsurance.com

Services:
Develop custom plans for organizations in specialty markets such as amateur and professional sports, special events, entertainment, prize indemnification, camps and conferences, and facilities

Description:
Providers of specialty insurance relating to sports and entertainment. Offer services in Sports Risk Management and Sports Leadership consultation. Experienced provider of league insurance, camp insurance and school athletic coverage.

JEFFREY M. BROOKS & CO, INC.
21207 CHAGRIN BOULEVARD
CLEVELAND, OH 44122
216-295-9530
Fax: 216-591-1656
• Jeffrey M Brooks, President

JPMORGAN CHASE BANK, N.A.
20201 E JACKSON DRIVE
SUITE 420
INDEPENDENCE, MO 64057
816-795-2914
866-281-9557
Fax: 816-795-2909
michael.a.dailey@chase.com
www.jpmorganchase.com
• Michael A. Dailey, Branch Manager
(816) 795-2914
michael.a.dailey@chase.com
• James A Bell, Audit Committee
• Laban P Jackson, Chairman of Audit Committee
• Stephen Burke, Compensation & Management Development Committ
• William C Weldon, Chairman of Corporate Governance & Nominating
• Crandall C Bowles, Chairman of Public Responsibilty Committee
• James S Crown, Chairman of Risk Policy

Committee
• Jamie Dimon, Chairman/Executive Committee

Description:
Specializes in providing mortgage loans, rookie lines of credit, equity lines, and pre-bonus lines of credit to professional athletes, family members, staff of athletic departments, as well as coaches. Also offers educational seminars on credit management and restoration, as well as identity theft protection.

K & K INSURANCE GROUP
1712 MAGNAVOX WAY
PO BOX 2338
FORT WAYNE, IN 46804
260-459-5000
800-237-2917
800-637-4757
Fax: 260-459-5800
lorena.hatfield@kandkinsurance.com
www.kandkinsurance.com
• Dan Johnson, Program Manager
• Stacie Helton, Underwriter
• Sheila Morton, Sales Director
• Lorena Hatfield, Marketing Resources Manager
(260) 459-5663
lorena.hatfied@kandkinsurance.com

Nature of Service:
Provides quality, professional commercial insurance products and services to virtually every aspect of the sports markets served, including professional and amateur sports teams, leagues, associations, events, facilities, coaches, camps, and clinics. Considered the leading provider of specialty sports, leisure and entertainment insurance in the industry.

M R COMART
450 FASHION AVENUE
SUITE 1701
NEW YORK, NY 10123
212-563-3100

Nature of Sports Service:
Organization offers all traditional accounting services, but with an emphasis on areas like royalties, taxation and advances that are unique and critical to entertainment and sports professionals.

MARCEL V. KUPER, CPA/PFS, CFE
500 W PALATINE ROAD
WHEELING, IL 60090
847-215-8630
Fax: 847-215-8632
mvkcpa@aol.com
www.ltplanning.com
• Marcel V Kupen, President
mvkruper@aol.com

Nature of Service:
Asset protection, cash management, business management, estate planning, investment management, risk management, retirement planning. In addition, representation for the Internal Revenue Service, tax preparation, fraud prevention and detection. A fee-based financial planner. We sell no products, and offer representation throughout the United States.

Services:
Corporate Web Application, e-Government Web Application, Customer Relation Management, Citizen Relation Management, Content Management for

Complex Organizations, Content Management for Less Complex Organizations, Subscription-based Broadcast Email System, e-Government Preparation.
Year Founded:
1980

MARSH & MCLENNAN
1166 AVENUE OF THE AMERICAS
NEW YORK, NY 10036
212-345-5000
www.mmc.com
• Oscar Fanjul, Director
• Leslie M Baker, Jr., Board of Directors
• Zachary W. Carter, Director
• Daniel S. Glaser, Director
• H. Edward Hanway, Director
Services:
Risk and Insurance Services and Risk Consulting and Technology
Marketing & Consulting Services:
Insurance brokerage firm providing consulting and transactional services in the management of risk for enterprises throughout the world, with offices in 70 countries.

MBIA INSURANCE CORPORATION
113 KING STREET
ARMONK, NY 10504
914-273-4545
info@mbia.com
www.mbia.com
• Cliff Corso, Managing Director
(914) 273-4545
• Anthony McKiernan, Managing Director
(914) 765-3611
• John Dare, Managing Director Structured Finance and St
(914) 765-3777
• Greg Diamond, Managing Director Head of Investor Relation
(914) 765-3190
• Kevin Brown, Managing Director Corporate Communications
• Tom Jordan, Managing Director
(914) 765-3428
Services:
Global Public Finance, Global Structured Finance, Asset Management, Revenue Finances
Description:
A leading insurer of municipal bonds and structured finance transactions. A leading provider of investment management services to the public sector. MBIA Insurance Corporation has a claims-paying rating of Triple-A from Moody's Investors Service, Inc., Standard & Poor's Ratings Group and Fitch Investors Service, L.P.

MOAG & COMPANY
323 WEST CAMDEN STREET
SUITE 400
BALTIMORE, MD 21201
410-230-0105
Fax: 410-230-0547
www.moagandcompany.com
• John A Moag, Jr., Chairman/Chief Executive Officer
jmoag@moagandcompany.com
• Thomas F Lang, Vice President
tlang@moagandcompany.com
• Marsha Russell, Administrator
mrussell@moagandcompany.com
• Nathaniel Wilson, Analyst

nwilson@moagandcompany.com
• Lauren Moag, Analyst
lmoag@moagandcompany.com
Description:
Dedicated team of investment bankers serving the sports, media and entertainment industries in ways that only a boutique firm can.
Sports Service Founded:
2001

MOODY'S INVESTORS SERVICE
ONE FRONT STREET
SUITE 1900
SAN FRANCISCO, CA 94111
212-553-1653
Fax: 415-274-1726
clientservices@moodys.com
www.moodys.com
Description:
Currently maintains over 40,000 ratings involving more than 20,000 local entities of government throughout the U.S. and Canada.
Services:
Provides independent credit ratings, research and financial information to the capital markets.

MZ SPORTS
3000 ATRIUM WAY
SUITE 101
MT LAUREL, NJ 08054-3910
856-778-9400
Fax: 856-778-8478
www.mzsports.com
• Mitchell H Ziets, President/Chief Executive Officer
Description:
Develops creative solutions for clients, due to an understanding of finance and sports, tremendous access to capital, both debt and equity and a developed web of relations with team, league and public officials, the financial community, architects, attorneys, tax advisors, consultants and other project vendors. These relationships are drawn upon to obtain for clients state-of-the-art information and ideas.
Services:
Acquisition Finance, Facility Finance, Lease Negotiation, Capital Structuring
Clients:
Anaheim Angels, Anaheim Mighty Ducks, City of Anaheim, Arena Football League, City of Arlington, Atlanta Falcons, Atlanta Hawks, Atlanta Thrashers, and Philps Arena, Boston Red Sox, Buffalo Sabres, Camden Couty Improvement Authority, Cleveland Cavaliers, Florida Marlins, Georgia Force, City of Grant Prairie, Hamilton County, Indiana University of Pennsylvania, Kansas City Royals, Los Angeles Dodgers, City of Los Angeles, City of Louisville, Middlesex County, Milwaukee Brewers, Minnesota Vikings, State of Minnesota, Minor League Baseball, New York City, NJ Sports and Exposition Authority - Giants Stadium, City of Oakland, Philadelphia City, Ph

NEUBERGER BERMAN
53 STATE STREET
SUITE 1303
BOSTON, MA 02109
212-476-8800
800-877-9700

866-497-4240
Fax: 781-796-2953
www.nb.com
Services:
Advisory Services (individuals), Advisory Services (institutions), Broker Advised Products, Close-End Funds, Institutional Separate Accounts, Mutual Funds(individuals), Mutual Funds (institutions), Private Asset Management, Professional Investor Clearing Services, Trust and Investment Management(individuals), Wealth and Fiduciary Services (individuals)
Description:
Offers a wide spectrum of investment products for a full range of clients, both individuals and institutional. Includes tax and financial planning, fiduciary services and financial advocacy for viturally any circumstances or need.

PARK LANE - INVESTMENT BANKING SERVICES
2029 CENTURY PARK E
SUITE 437
LOS ANGELES, CA 90067
310-201-8496
Fax: 310-388-5799
www.prkln.com
• Andrew W Kline, Founder and MD
• Carlos Silva, MD
• James A Shortill, Director ,Sports Media
• Robert Fasulo, Director , Corporate Development-Internationa
• Tarlin Ray, Director ,Entreprenuer in Residence
• Mark Abdou, Head General Counsel
• Chris Stuart, Principal , Sports Licensing & Estates
Nature of Service:
Park Lane is the preeminent small and middle market, investment bank providing clients with world class athletics corporate finance and M&A services. We advise clients when buying and selling sports related businesses and professional teams. Raise capital for emerging leagues and businesses involved in sports.

PATRICK M. CAPOZZI, CPA
3831 S PARK AVENUE
BLASDELL, NY 14219
716-824-4111
Fax: 716-825-6807
• Patrick Capozzi, Owner
pat@capozzicpa.com
Nature of Sports Service:
Financial services for professional athletes. Investment counseling, income tax planning and preparation.

PUBLIC FINANCIAL MANAGEMENT
ONE KEYSTONE PLAZA
SUITE 300
HARRISBURGH, PA 17101-2044
717-232-2723
Fax: 717-233-6073
www.pfm.com
• Dean Kaplan, Managing Director
Description:
Specializes in lease negotiations, financial planning and debt management, maintains an active strategic consulting and investment management practice.
Clients:
Alaska Industrial Economic Development

Authority; Arizona State University; Arizona School Facilities Board; Salt River Project; Arkansas State Highway Commission; California Asset Management Program; City and County of San Francisco; City of Anaheim; City of Newport Beach; City of Roseville; City of San Diego; Contra Coast Transportation Authority.

SADLER & COMPANY, INC.
3014 DEVINE ST.
PO BOX 5866
COLUMBIA, SC 29250-5866
800-622-7370
800-622-7370
Fax: 803-256-4017
sport@sadlersports.com
www.sadlersports.com
• John Sadler, President
(800) 622-7370
john@sadlerco.com
Description
Sadler & Company specializes in providing insurance solutions for the sports and recreation industries. Client base includes 12 national sports organizations and over 7000 community sports organizations such as teams & leagues, camps, outdoors, special events, health clubs, etc.

SADLER AND COMPANY INC
3014 DEVINE ST.
PO BOX 5866
COLUMBIA, SC 29250-5866
800-622-7370
800-622-7370
Fax: 803-256-4017
sport@sadlersports.com
www.sadlersports.com
• John Sadler, President
(800) 622-7370
john@sadlerco.com

SPORTS COVERAGE
5535 MILITARY PARKWAY
DALLAS, TX 75227
972-698-7329
888-844-3420
Fax: 214-381-4585
www.kentex.com
Sports Service Founded:
1988
Products:
America sports products
Brands:
America SP., JC Penney, NFL, Collegiate, NHL
Marketing & Consulting Services:
Provides insurance coverage for college athletic programs and sports camps, as well as disability income insurance for individual amateur and professional athletes and coaches.
Event Management Services:
Provides liability coverage for sports events.

SPORTSINSURANCE.COM
PO BOX 1155
LAKE PLACID, NY 12946
866-889-4763
Fax: 866-467-8770
info@SportsInsurance.com
www.sportsinsurance.com
• Mark DiPerno, President
mark@sportsinsurance.com
Nature of Sports Service:
Insurance organization focusing only on the

Sport, Special Event, Prize and Contingency Markets.
Sports Service Founded:
1997

TIAA CREF
PO BOX 1259
CHARLOTTE, NC 28201
800-842-2252
www.tiaa-cref.org
• Edward J. Grzybowski, Senior Managing Director, Chief Investment Of
Description:
Provides long-term financing in the construction and operational phases of projects worldwide, including major and minor league sports facilities, infrastructure, power, energy, telecommunications, and industrial operations.
Services:
Provides national financial services and retirement services in the academic, research, medical and cultural fields

TREATY OAK BANK
101 WESTLAKE DRIVE
AUSTIN, TX 78746
512-617-3600
888-387-3289
Fax: 512-617-3697
• Jeff Nash, President
• Coralie Pledger, Chief Financial Officer
• Randy Meeks, Executive Vice President
• Sheila Bostick Jagger, Senior Vice President
• Tommy Clark, Senior Vice President
• Steve Blackburn, Vice President
Nature of Sports Service:
Tax Strategy and Preparation, Small Business Consulting, Financial and Retirement Planning, Investment advisory, Asset management, Employee Benefits (Life, Health, Disability, 401k), Insurance & Annuities, Estate planning.

WELLS FARGO
1 NORTH JEFFERSON AVENUE
ST LOUIS, MO 63101-2205
877-879-2495
Fax: 314-955-2890
www.wachoviasecurities.com
Description:
The largest full services national securities firm. Services include: underwriting, financial advisory and private placement as well as, on-going services for public (state and local government) and private entities. Developed a sports and entertainment group.

WELLS FARGO INSURANCE INC.
10 S. WACKER
CHICAGO, IL 60606
312-920-9177
866-226-7342
Fax: 312-423-2508
• Ellen Sievert, National Director Of Communications
• Julien Smiley, Regional managing director
• Laura Schupbach, Executive VP
• Kevin Kenny, Executive VP Head of Insuarnce Brokerage
• H. David Wood, Executive VP Head of Insuarnce Operations Off
Services:
Provides insurance brokerage, administrative services, and financial and

consulting services with a unique blend of big-broker clout and local-broker service.

Marketing & Consulting Services

16W MARKETING, LLC
75 UNION AVENUE
RUTHERFORD, NJ 7070
201-635-8000
bnelson@16wmarketing.com
www.16wmarketing.com
• Ralph Vuono, Senior Director
(201) 635-8004
rvuono@16wmarketing.com
• Janice Miceli, VP
(201) 635-8005
jmecili@16wmarketing.com
• Kerry Kelly, Ass. To Partner
(201) 635-8006
kkelly@16wmarketing.com
• Shawn Flannelly, Manager - Business Develpoment
(201) 635-8007
sflannelly@16wmarketing.com
• Brian Nelson, Vp
(201) 635-8003
bnelson@16wmarketing.com
• Ralph Vuono, VP
(201) 635-8004
rvuono@16wmarketing.com
Nature of Service:
Sports Marketing firm specializing in talent marketing, corporate consulting, league/team services and corporate hospitality.

20/20 SPECIAL MARKETS
4650 BAKER STREET
CINCINNATI, OH 45212
513-561-9920
Fax: 513-569-0189
www.2020specialmarkets.com
Services:
Sales and marketing
Clients:
All-Clad Metalcrafters; J.A. Henckels; Enclume Design; Francis Francis

360 MANAGEMENT, LLC
8000 E DRIVE
SUITE 201
MIAMI, FL 33141
Fax: 734-372-6431
www.360mgt.com
• Morgan Menahem, Managing Director
morgan@360mgt.com
Services:
Serves as a managing and marketing representative for athletes and firms in the sporting world, with an emphasis in tennis; from sponsors to media and broadcasters.
Clients:
Tony Parker (Basketball); Jeanne-Marie Busutill (Golf); Jean-Francois Bachelot (Tennis); Ansley Cargill (Tennis); Peter Luczak (Tennis); Cyril Saulnier (Tennis); Christophe Rochus (Tennis); Lindsay Lee-Walters (Tennis)
Sports Service Founded:
2002
Sponsors Consulting & Sport Events:
Involved in the valuation of sponsors' partnership investments in various events as well as providing services, such as

consulting for marketing plans specificaly designed for companies involved in the world of sports.

361o EXPERIENTIAL
633 N ST CLAIR STREET
CHICAGO, IL 60611-3234
312-425-5053
inquiries@dfcbx.com
www.361experiential.com
• Brad Back, Senior Vice President Group Management Director
• Shannon Babcock, Management Director

4LICENSING CORPORATION
767 3RD AVENUE
17TH FLOOR
NEW YORK, NY 10017
212-758-7666
Fax: 212-754-5481
www.4licensingcorp.com
• Jay Emmett, Board of Directors
• Bruce M. Foster, Executive VP/CFO
Services:
Specializes in the areas of TV production and distribution, home video production, merchandise licensing, media planning and buying, music development, and Web site development.

A TEAM
232 MADISON AVENUE
NEW YORK, NY 10016
212-239-0499
Fax: 212-239-0575
acohen@ateampromo.com
www.theateamagency.com
• Andrew Cohen, Chief Executive Officer
(212) 239-0499
acohen@ateampromo.com
• Tom Sato, Executive VP
(212) 239-0499
• Bernie Lee, VP West Coast
blee@ateampromo.com
• Rick Krisburg, VP Account Director
rkrisburg@ateampromo.com
• Patti Villegas, Sr. Account Director
pvillegas@ateampromo.com
Description:
Strategic planning/concept development, creative development/execution, account management, event marketing and direct marketing.
Services:
Provides marketing services that helps strengthen and emphasize their client's brand image and unique attributes.
Clients:
Jaguar, Weight Wathcers, HIghfalls, Volvo, Skyy Spirits, Ricola, Vitamin Water, H-E-B
Other Location:
8001 Irvine Center Drive, 4th Floor, Irvine CA 92618. 949-754-3022; FAX: 949-754-4001.

A.D.D. MARKETING AND ADVERTISING
6600 LEXINGTON AVENUE
LOS ANGELES, CA 90038
323-790-0500
Fax: 323-790-0240
www.addmarketing.com
• Scott Leonard, CEO
• Elizabeth Baudoin, Client relation
• Lauren LeBlanc, Marketing and Advertising
Description:
Marketing Consultants, Advertising &

Promotional Product Dealers.
Services:
Specializes in developing communication solutions that seamlessly span from traditional to non-traditional.
Clients:
ABC Entertainment, America Online, Boost Mobile, Dreamworks, EA, ESPN, Fox Sports, Full Tilt Poker, Gravity Games, Haribo Gummie Bears, Head and Shoulders Shampoo, Levi's, Lexus, Mazda, Milk Processing Board, MTV, NBC Sports, Nestle, Nike, Nokia, Pantene, Paramount, Pringles, Razor Scooter, Sony, Toyota, Zumiez

AAA FLAG & BANNER
8955 NATIONAL BLVD
LOS ANGELES, CA 90034
310-836-3200
855-218-3300
Fax: 310-836-7253
sales@aaaflag.com
www.aaaflag.com
• Jay Jacoby, Representative
Nature of Services:
AAA Flag & Banner manufacturers and installs custom displays, banners and flags for Major Sporting Events and Fortune 500 Companies throughout the United States-services include concept creation, banner, sign and flag design, logos and corporate identity, layout and composition, marketing materials and event pageantry consultation.

AAI SPORTS INC. & AAI INTERNATIONAL, INC.
16000 DALLAS PARKWAY
SUITE 300
DALLAS, TX 75248
972-739-8401
Fax: 972-739-8495
gbass@aaisports.com
www.aaisports.com

ACC PROPERTIES
4512 WEYBRIDGE LANE
PO DRAWER ACC
GREENSBORO, NC 27407
336-854-8787
Fax: 336-854-8797
feedback@theacc.org
www.theacc.com
• John D Swofford, Commissioner
• Jeff Elliott, Finance/Administration
• Amy Yakola, Public Relations/Marketing
• Lynne Herndon, Director Of Business Operations
Marketing & Consulting Services:
Marketing Venture managed by ACC television partners Raycom Sports and Jefferson Pilot Sports & Entertainment. Serves to consolidate Conference-related marketing opportunities into a one-stop shopping format that will enhance the Raycom and Jefferson Pilot television packages. Oversees marketing, advertising merchandising, licensing and promotional opportunities for the Atlantic Coast Conference.

ACME MASCOTS, INC.
PO BOX 23831
BROOKLYN, NY 11202
718-722-7900
Fax: 718-770-7678

• Wayde Harrison, Development Director
• Bonnie Erickson, Creative Director
Services:
Provides a powerful character design, production, product development, and art direction and animation.
Clients:
Burger King, Swatch, AT&T, Sharp Electronics, American Dairy Association, Procter & Gamble, Budweiser, McDonald's, Montreal Expos, Hiroshima Carp, Chicago, White Sox, Philadelphia Phillies, New York Yankees, New Jersey Nets, Houston Rockets, Washington Wizards, Philadelphia 76ers, Orlando Magic, Charlotte Hornets, Kansas City Chiefs, Jacksonville Jaguars, Bell Telephone Company, TV Pilots, General Motors, State of Alaska, Sigma Marketing, Colorforms, Applause, Hasbro, Knickerbocker, etc.
Sports Service Founded:
1978
Marketing & Consulting Services:
Producers of Sport Consulting, design, construction and merchandising of mascot characters.

ACTION INK, INC.
14607 SAN PEDRO AVENUE
SUITE 130
SAN ANTONIO, TX 78232
210-490-1900
Fax: 210-490-1930
actionink@sbcglobal.net
www.actioninkresumes.com
• Tony Oliva, Contact
Year Founded:
1984
Description:
Offers complete resume preparation with writers who are degreed and have management, sales, personnel, and military experience.

ACTION SPORTS AMERICA
5263 PLACENTIA PARKWAY
SUITE 13
LAS VEGAS, NV 89118
610-832-7500
Fax: 612-465-1669
fun@actionsportsamerica.com
www.giantjersey.com
• Doug Verb, Founder & President
• Sam Sheckman, Vice President
(917) 767-7505
sam@giantjersey.com
Founded:
1983
Clients:
NHL, Scout Sports & Entertainment, Vegas Golden Knights
Nature of Service:
Sales promotion and event creation/management firm.

ACTION SPORTS INTERNATIONAL
4945 PRESIDENTS WAY
WESTWOOD GATEWAY
TUCKER, GA 30084
770-696-2575
Fax: 817-665-0047
• Jennifer Reese, Chief Operating Officer
jennifer@asiphoto.com
Marketing & Consulting Services:
Corporate and non-profit sports organization marketing, event management, sports art production and marketing, athlete

appearances, athletic fund raising, innovative marketing concepts. Dealer Kodak Dynamic Imaging.
Services:
Specializes in capturing an athlete's most memorable images through digital and film photography.

ACTION SPORTS MEDIA
3401 RUSS CIRCLE
SUITE E
ALCOA, TN 37701
865-379-0625
Fax: 865-379-9653
• Gordon Whitener, Chief Executive Officer
(865) 379-0625
• Jerry Felix, Chief Financial Officer
(865) 379-0625
Description:
A full service collegiate sports marketing company specializing in game day multimedia.
Clients:
The University of Alabama, The University of Iowa, Kansas State University, University of Kentucky/Rupp Arena, The University of Mississippi, Mississippi State University, Oklahoma State University, Oregon State University, Purdue University, The University of South Carolina, The University of Tennessee, The University of Texas, Texas A&M Uneversity, Gaderbilt University, University of Washington, Washington State University

ADLINK
WESTWOOD GATEWAY
11150 SANTA MONICA BOULEVARD
SUITE 1000
LOS ANGELES, CA 90025
310-477-3994
Fax: 310-477-8139
www.adlink.com
• Lisa Palmer, General Manager/Sales
Description:
Sells Television advertising in Los Angeles California encompassing 44 Cable Networks. Offer advertisng opportunities through marketing programs. Adtag - With Adtag, you can customize your commercials for unique geographic groups within the Los Angeles market. Adcopyâ„¢ Adcopy enables advertisers to sell different products to different market segments by running multiple commercials simultaneously, all with one buy.

ADRENALIN, INC.
54 W 11TH AVENUE
DENVER, CO 80204
888-454-8888
888-757-5646
Fax: 303-454-8889
info@goadrenalin.com
www.goadrenalin.com
• Daniel S Price, President
(303) 454-8888
dprice@goadrenalin.com
• Bryan Kimbell, Vice President, Partnership & Strategy
(303) 454-8888
bkimbell@goadrenalin.com
• Rick A Fillmon, Principal/Vice President Business Operations
(303) 454-8888
rfillmon@goadrenalin.com

Nature of Service:
Specializes in sports branding and marketing solutions. Develops and expands brands for sports and entertainment organizations.
Clients:
Altitude Sports Network,American Alpine Club, AEG, Broomfield Event Center, Chicago Fire, Cleveland Indians, Colorado Avalanche, Colorado Mammoth, Continental Basketball Assoc., Dallas Mavericks, Denver Broncos, Fox Sports Rocky Mountain, Gilco Sports & Entertainment Marketing, Gold Crown Foundation, Harlem Globetrotters, London Knights, Los Angeles Avengers, Major League Baseball Players Alumni Assoc., Major League Soccer, Memphis Redbirds, Metro Denver Sports Commission, National Basketball Association, National Hockey League, NYC2012, Phoenix Coyotes, Pikes Peak International Raceway, Sixth Man Solutions, Seattle Sonics, Team Builder Allia
Marketing & Consulting Services:
Specialize in designing logos, team uniforms, retail promotional materials, event tickets, advertising campaigns, game programs and brand architecture.
Year Founded:
1997

ADVANCED PROMOTIONAL CONCEPTS, INC.
2802 N HOWARD AVENUE
TAMPA, FL 33607
813-254-6600
Fax: 813-254-3526
apctampa@aol.com
www.apcpromotions.com
• Barbara Baker, Chief Executive Officer/President
Services:
Designs, negotiates and implements complete turn-key marketing services to clients such as Product Sampling, Product Demonstrations, Couponing, Mobile Marketing, Creative / Production, Point of Sale, Point of Sale Placement, Contests/Games, Promotion Planning, Sweepstakes / Fulfillment, Retail Merchandising, Name Generation, Sponsorship Negotiations, Premium Give-A-Ways, Field Research and Ethnic Marketing.
Clients:
Seagram Americas / Diageo, The Andrew Jergens Company, Universal Studios / CITYWALK, GMC / Cadillac, Con Agra Grocery Products, Clairol, Inc., Florida's Natural Growers, Gerber Products Co., Schering-Plough (Coppertone), The Rockport Co., Thomas J. Lipton Co., United Distillers, MCI Communications, Nutrogena, Ocean Spray Juices, Optyl, Inc. (Carrera), Procter and Gamble Co., Sara Lee Corp., Holiday Inn Worldwide, Jim Beam Brands Co., Joseph E. Seagram & Sons, MCA Music Group, M&M Mars, Whittle Communications, LP, General Motors Corp. (Cadillac), Van Camp's / Con Agra, R.J. Reynolds Tobacco Co. / Nabisco, Hiram Walker Group, Tech Data Corporat

ALAN TAYLOR COMMUNICATIONS, INC.
350 FIFTH AVENUE
EMPIRE STATE BUILDING
SUITE 3800
NEW YORK, NY 10118

212-714-1280
Fax: 212-695-5685
• Tony Signore, Chief Executive Officer and Managing Partner
(212) 714-1280
• Mark Beal, Contact
Services:
Provides a full range of public relations services that build brands and drive business.
Clients:
Gillette, MasterCard International, Yahoo!, Ameriquest, Best Western International, Inc., Duracell, Smirnoff, US Smokeless Tobacco, The History Channel, Reebok International, Levitra, AT&T Bank of America, Diageo North America Inc., Eight O'Clock Coffee, General Mills, Nestle Purina Petcare Company, GlaxoSmithKline/Schering Plough - Levitra, Pacific Health Laboratories, Inc., Staples, Pitney Bowes, Combe Inc., Sara Lee, Warner Bros., Boys Clubs of New York, Ironman Triathlon World Championships, JPMorgan Chase Corporate Challenge, The Miami Project to Cure Paralysis, International Tennis Hall of Fame, JPMorgan Chase, Pacific Life Open, Pilot

ALL TERRAIN PRODUCTIONS, INC.
2675 WEST GRAND AVENUE
CHICAGO, IL 60612
312-421-7672
www.allterrain.net
• Brook Jay, Co-President
• Sarah Eck-Thompson, Co-President
Year Founded:
1998
Description:
A hybird company of event management, field marketing & promotion and technical production.

ALL-CITY SPORTS MARKETING
1431 BROADWAY
11TH FLOOR
NEW YORK, NY 10018
212-221-7690
Fax: 212-719-9251
Sports Service Founded:
1995
Products:
Apparel and accessories
Marketing & Consulting Services:
Full service organization designed to handle three areas: manufacturing, marketing and media services.
Other Location:
85 NE Loop 410, Suite 600, San Antonio TX 78216. 800-235-8774; FAX: 210-341-2050.

ALLEN CONSULTING, INC.
89 MIDDLETOWN ROAD
HOLMDEL, NJ 07733
732-946-2711
Fax: 732-946-8032
Sylvia@allenconsulting.com
www.allenconsulting.com
• Sylvia Allen, Founder
sylvia@allenconsulting.com
Marketing & Consulting Services:
Advises on sponsorship development including developing marketing partners and strategic alliances, tailoring sports marketing programs and event sponsorship to best meet client needs, objectives and designing programs to achieve sales objectives.

On-site event and sports sponsorship and sales training.

ALLOY MARKETING & PROMOTION
77 N WASHINGTON STREET
8TH FLOOR
BOSTON, MA 02114
617-723-8929
Fax: 617-723-2188
info@ampagency.com
www.ampagency.com
• Gary Colen, President & CEO
• Steve McCall, Partner
• Erica Melia, Senior VP of Accounts Management
• Joel Breen, Digital Account Director
Services:
Provides urban, youth, and multicultural promotional marketing services, focuses grassroots marketing, promotional events, and web design and offers market research services to clients.

ALLOY MEDIA & MARKETING
10 ABEEL ROAD
CRANBURY, NJ 8512
609-655-8878
Fax: 609-395-0737
• Matthew Diamond, Chief Executive Officer/Managing Partner
• Chris Cassino, Vp
• Jodi Smith, VP of Public relations
• Gary Colen, President Of Agency
• James K. K. Johnson, COO/President/Co-Founder
Description:
Media and marketing arm of Alloy, Inc. Specializes in college and teen marketing. Sources include: MarketSource Corporation, CASS Communications, YouthStream Media, Market Place Media and others to provide sales and marketing solutions targeting young adults.
Clients:
MarketSource Youth Division, CASS Communications, YouthStream Media, Market Place Media and others to provide sales and marketing solutions targeting young adults.

AMERICAN DREAMS
3950 KOVAL LANE
SUITE 3029
LAS VEGAS, NV 89109
702-732-1971
Fax: 702-732-2815
www.usdreams.com
• Jim Bickford, President
Description:
To help celebrities and athletes share their stories and wisdom across America through the following: Books, Speeches, Seminars/Workshops, Speakers Bureau, Events, Foundation, TV Series and Web Site.
Products:
Books
Brands:
The Present Collage - Bill Gates, Quote, Reflections Of A Changing Era, From Homeless To Multi-Millionaire, Scaling The Summit Forward, Onward, Upward, Bouncing Back From Black Monday, High School Dropout To High Tech CEO, Turning Weakness Into Strength, From Iron Lung, To Illiterate, To Self-Made Millionaire, Community Hero, American Entrepreneur,

The Building Of Lucy's Cafe El Adobe, Hollywood Style, Fairy Tales Can Come True, Constructing A Better America, You've Got To Have A Goal Bigger Than You Are, The Journey To Freedom, Soaring To Success, I Am Focusing On God, Family And Domino's Pizza, I'm Proud To Be An American.
Services:
Conducts motivatiohal speeches, seminars/workshops, speakers bureau, and TV series.

AMERICAN HOLE 'N ONE
55 SCOTT STREET
BUFORD, GA 30518
770-271-1065
800-822-2257
Fax: 770-271-4006
info@ahno.net
www.americanholeinone.net
Services:
Leading resource for hole in one insurance, custom showroom promotions, sports risk insurance and superior sign packages

AMERICAN SPECIALTY
142 N MAIN STREET
ROANOKE, IN 46783
260-672-8800
800-245-2744
Fax: 260-672-8835
amerspec@amerspec.com
www.amerspec.com
• Drew Smith, Chief Marketing Official
(260) 673-1234
Description:
Providing insurance and risk management services to the Sports and Entertainment Industry.

AMERICAN SPECIALTY INSURANCE & RISK SERVICES, INC.
142 N MAIN STREET
PO BX 309
ROANOKE, IN 46783-0309
260-672-8800
800-245-2744
Fax: 260-672-8835
amerspec@amerspec.com
www.amerspec.com
• Tony Wittwer, SVP / Chief Marketing Officer
(260) 672-8800
twittwer@amerspec.com
Services:
Provides opportunities in management, marketing, underwriting, insurance service, risk consulting, crisis management, security, information services, finance, claims management, administration, regulatory compliance, and public relations - integrating it into one comprehensive program designed to protect the assets and enhance the financial performance of clients.
Clients:
Associations, organizing committees, events, facilities, intercollegiate and interscholastic organizations, sanctioning bodies, amusement, theme and water parks, family entertainment centers, carnivals, pari-mutuel facilities, venues, special and ancillary events, race teams, tracks, sponsors, drivers, driving schools and professional athletes.
Marketing & Consulting Services:

Provides a portfolio of specialized and risk management services for the sports and entertainment industry, including risk management insurance, claims management, loss control, and technology services.
Sports Service Founded:
1989

AMERICAN SPORTS DATA, INC.
51009 ARRIETA COURT
FORT MILL, SC 29707
914-461-3271
Fax: 914-461-3131
sportsdata@comporium.net
• Harvey Lauer, President
Services:
Provides syndicated and custom research to a wide array of major corporations, media and industry associations
Clients:
Adidas USA, Inc., Amateur Athletic Foundation, Bauer USA, Inc., Boston Consulting Group, Casio, Inc., Converse, Inc., Deutsche Banc, DDB Needham Worldwide, Nokia, Procter & Gamble, Sears, Roebuck & Co., Universal Gym Equipment, Wrangler
Sports Brand Intelligence Report:
Syndicated study of 186 U.S. sports brands. Awareness and ownership analyzed by demographics, product ownership, sports participation, magazine readership and sports viewership.
Health Club Trend Report:
Annual syndicated study of consumer behavior.
Sports Media Index:
Syndicated tracking study of athlete recognition, magazine readership, in-person spectator sports, TV sports viewership.
Sports Equipment Monitor:
Annual syndicated tracking study of consumer awareness of 24 sporting goods categories.
Athletic Footwear Monitor:
Tri-annual syndicated tracking study of the athletic footwear market.
American Sports Analysis:
Annual syndicated tracking study of sports participation monitoring 58 sports/activities.

AQUARIUS SPORTS AND ENTERTAINMENT
9801 WASHINGTONIAN BLVD
SUITE 310
GAITHERSBURG, MD 20878
301-604-2606
Fax: 240-328-6051
firstinitialLastname@aquarius-se.com
aquarius-se.com
• Marc Bluestein, President, Founder
(240) 547-3498
mbluestein@aquarius-se.com
• Jeff Goldscher, Executive VP, Marketing & Creative
jgoldscher@aquarius-se.com
• Sara Blum, VP, Finance & Operations
sblum@aquarius-se.com
• Eric Goldscher, Client Services Director
(240) 547-3483
egoldscher@aquarius-se.com
• Samantha Hooker, Client Services Coordinator
shooker@aquarius-se.com
Description:
Sports and entertainment marketing firm

that provides sponsorship consulting, sponsorhsip sales representation, corporate hospitality, and event and promotional marketing.
Nature of Services:
Sponsorship Consulting; Activation Consulting Services; Property Representation; Corporate Hospitality; Athlete Marketing; Entertainment Marketing

ARAMARK CORPORATION
1101 MARKET STREET
PHILADELPHIA, PA 19107
215-238-3000
800-272-6275
Fax: 215-238-3333
www.aramark.com
• Joseph Neubauer, Chairman
• L Frederick Sutherland, Executive Vice President/Chief Financial Officer
• Cathy Schlosberg, Vice President, Marketing/Education
• David Freireich, Media Relations Coordinator, Sports Entertainment
• Eric Foss, President
Baseball:
MLB; Minor League
College Sponsor:
NCAA; College Bowl
Basketball Sponsor:
NBDL
Football Sponsor:
Indoor League
Hockey Sponsor:
AHL

ARBITRON, INC.
9705 PATUXENT WOODS DRIVE
COLUMBIA, MD 21046
410-312-8000
www.arbitron.com
• Neal Bonner, Director, Custom Research
(410) 312-8594
neal.bonner@arbitron.com
Nature of Services:
Arbitron Inc., a media and marketing research firm serving the radio, television, cable, and advertising industries, measures network and local-market radio audiences across the United States by surveying the retail, media and product patterns of consumers and providing application software used for analyzing media audience and marketing information data.

ATLANTA INTERNATIONAL CONSULTING GROUP, INC. (AICG)
1401 PEACHTREE STREET
SUITE 500
ATLANTA, GA 30309
404-872-4884
Fax: 404-870-0440
sales@aicginc.com
www.aicginc.com
Services:
Specializes in creating programs that increase brand awareness, improve market share, and boost product profitability of clients through graphic design, printing, specialty merchandise and fulfillment services.
Services:
Graphic Design &Creative Direction, Custom Illustration & Artwork (Sports & Entertainment), Project Management, Corporate & Brand Identity (Logo Development), POS/POP & Custom

Packaging (Restaurant & Food Industry; Retail), Sales Collateral Support & Promotion (Desktop Publishing and Brochures), Internet Design & Implementation
Clients:
The Coca-Cola Company, Coca-Cola Enterprises, Bellsouth Corporation, McDonald's Corporation, AOL/Turner, S.C. Johnson, ARAMARK, MCI WorldCom
Athlete Management Services:
Exclusive representation of leading sports personalities. Representation of select entertainment properties. Full-service sports marketing firm for professional and amateur athletics. Provides career management consulting, contract advisement, endorsements, financial planning, promotions, entertainment representation and full-service merchandising.
Marketing & Consulting Services:
Provides strategic and tactical consultation in general sports marketing consultation, professional development, special segment, general market development, ethnic marketing development (African American, Hispanic, and Asian), youth marketing and female marketing development. Marketing representation for entertainers, musicians and broadcasters. Provides financial services through strategic alliances and affiliated company.
Event Management Services:
Creates grassroots or made-for-TV-sports/entertainment oriented events from concept to completion. Develops and implements integrated programs to assist clients in promoting their products and/or services. Full public relations and advertising capabilities, arranging for sponsorship of both new and existing sports events, developing tie-in promotions for such sponsorships, complete management of event. Experienced in targeting particular sales objectives through sports promotions. Develops event-driven sales promotion campaigns for corporate clients. Provides complete strategic planning, project management and promotional support services.

AURA360 VENTURES
28 DANFORTH STREET
SUITE 210
PORTLAND, ME 04101
207-699-2360
Fax: 207-699-2929
info@360mediaventures.com
www.aura360.com
• Lauren Panarese St. Clair, Marketing Director
• Parker Swenson, Properties Coordinator, Event Manager
• Ken Hess, Media Manager, Editor
• William Caswell, Editor & Videographer
• Rufus Frost, Managing Director
• Cathy Cooper, Partner, Production And Content
• Jessie Nickerson, Manager/Corporate Admin
Nature of Service:
Provides clients innovative brand integrated marketing services including property creation and development, property representation, event management, TV production and consultation.
Clients:
Jeep, Columbia Sportwear Company, Red

Bull, Honda, Lucas Oil Products Inc., BF Goodrich, Gillette, Amstel, Absolut Vodka, Sony, Rossignol, etc.

Next generation content marketing. Aura360 specializes in animating client brands through innovative event and media properties and related marketing ventures.

AUTO SPORTS MARKETING GROUP
PO BOX 491
CLARKS SUMMIT, PA 18411
570-586-2198
Fax: 570-586-2198
• Oscar Koveleski, Founder/Designer
Nature of Service:
50 years of organizing, managing events, contests, auto races (SCAA races at Pocono Raceway) model cars, slot cars, R/C cars, Battery Ride Ons, for SCCA, IMSA, NASCAR, IRL, SVRA, tracks and shows. Now offers consultant services for hire performed by hand picked special ops personnel. References include food industry, auto industry, toy industry, hobby industry, sanctioning bodies, track management.
Sports Service Founded:
1980
Athlete Management Services:
Auto racing sponsors.
Event Management Services:
Auto racing event promotion.
Brands:
Ferrari Monza, McLaren MK2, McLaren MK6, McLaren MK8B, 1914 Stutz Bearcat, Baby Ferrari 250, Type 52 Baby Bugatti Replica, Bugatti Vise

BAMBOO WORLDWIDE
30 NORTH RACINE
SUITE 300
CHICAGO, IL 60607
773-227-4848 EXT x 105
Fax: 773-227-2509
tracyt@bambooinc.com
www.bambooexperience.com
Description:
Marketing Consulting Services.
Services:
Provides strategic consulting, creative development and turnkey execution creating marketable experiences in the fields of retail design, costumer service, organizational development and sales force training.

BANSHEE MUSIC
5000 S TOWNE DRIVE
NEW BERLIN, WI 53151
262-501-2726
Fax: 262-786-0687
info@bansheemusic.com
• John Canaday, Director of Sports Marketing
• Jen DeBuhr, Digital Music Manager
• Chris Hanson, Musician
• Steve Knill, Manager
• Gary Reynolds, Member
• Kelly Schwanke, Manager
Nature of Services:
Banshee Music provides marketing services that focus on artist development, music publishing/administration, music producers for film and TV including sound design for professional and college sports teams, content development, music licensing, live

touring and creating brand marketing campaigns around a music platform.

BARNES MARKETING, INC.
15510 ROCKFIELD BOULEVARD
SUITE C
IRVINE, CA 92618
949-768-2942
Fax: 949-768-0630
info@barnesmarketing.com
www.barnesmarketing.com
Sports Service Founded:
1974
Services:
Specializes in marketing and consulting and event management services in motorsports marketing and race team sponsorship including comprehensive sales packages provided for potential sponsors, media coordination, and public relations and athlete management services which includes speaking engagements, personal appearances, product endorsements, radio and television, movies.
Athlete Management Services:
Speaking engagements, personal appearances, product endorsements, radio and television, movies.

BARRETT SPORTS GROUP
1219 MORNINGSIDE DRIVE
SUITE 101
MANHATTAN BEACH, CA 90266
310-802-8775
Fax: 310-802-8777
www.barrettsports.com
• Joshua C Cohen, Manager
jcc@barrettsports.com
Sports Service Founded:
2000
Services:
Provides high-quality and value-added consulting services such as in market demand, financial feasibility and economic impact analysis; finance; valuation; negotiations; operations; and politics and strategic planning to the sports and entertainment industry. Sports management consulting firm.

BDS MARKETING, INC.
10 HOLLAND
IRVINE, CA 92618
949-472-6700
www.bdsmktg.com
Services:
Provides sales promotion, field marketing, retail demonstrations/trainings and interactive services to clients.
Event Management Services:
Pavilion activities including product sampling, premium distribution, games and hospitality tents, IMSA Tour, LPGA Tour, NASCAR Nextel Cup Series.

BEAR ENTHUSIAST MARKETING GROUP
4520 E THOUSAND OAKS BOULEVARD
SUITE 200
WESTLAKE VILLAGE, CA 91362
818-371-7950
Fax: 818-371-7956
• Bruce Bear, President/Chief Executive Officer
• Rick Hauser, Senior Vice President/Account Director
• Jason Bear, Senior Account Executive
• Amy Brown, Public Relations Accounts

Supervisor
(818) 865-6464
Nature of Service:
Fully integrated marketing, advertising and public relations agency focused on the marketing needs of global and regional enthusiast brands.
Sports Service Founded:
1962
Clients:
Suzuki Marine, Dogloo, Body Glove, Trijicm, Buck Knives, Bowtech, Outdoor Products, Fiocdai, Corona Clipper, Marinco, Mothwing, Wiley X, Warn Industries, and Vivitar
Marketing & Consulting Services:
Advertising agency with 40+ years of branding experience and marketing expertise in sporting goods, hunting/fishing, outdoor boating, hardware, automotive and pet industries.

BENNETT GLOBAL MARKETING GROUP
1050 WINTER STREET
SUITE 1000, BAY COLONY CORPORATE CENTER
WALTHAM, MA 2451
781-839-7390
Fax: 781-530-3605
info@bennettglobal.com
• Jeffrey Bennett, Founder/President/Chief Executive Office
(781) 839-7390
jeff@bennettglobal.com
• Sean Barror, Partner
sean@bennettglobal.com
• Benjamin Sturner, Marketing Director
(781) 888-3530
ben@bennettglobal.com
• Leigh Chodos, Business Technology Development Director
leigh@bennettglobal.com
Nature of Sports Service:
Full-service marketing agency that specializes in sponsorship programs, naming rights, licensing rights and content distribution.
Sports Service Founded:
2003
Clients:
Dunkin Donuts, Reebok, Dunlop and Nike; world renowned sports franchise Manchester United Football Club and tennis sensations Anna Kournikova; leading music labels RCA and BMG Heritage of BMG Entertainment; and global Internet portal Terra Lycos.

BERRY & HOMER
2035 RICHMOND STREET
PHILADELPHIA, PA 19125
215-425-0888
Fax: 215-425-2701
info@berryandhomer.com
www.berryandhomer.com
• James Ely, Vice President Sales & Marketing
info@berryandhomer.com
Nature of Services:
Berry & Homer provides turnkey graphic imaging systems services, specializing in printed graphic and visual communications, tradeshow displays and materials, banners, double sided graphics, backlit displays, stadium & stage graphics - large format prints up to 150 feet long.
Locations:
Additional branch office at: 4390 Parliament

Place, Suite G, Lanham, MD, 20706; (Phone) 888-459-0888, 301-459-4500, (Fax) 301-459-9813.

BFG COMMUNICATIONS
6 ANOLYN
HILTON HEAD ISLAND
BLUFFTON, SC 29910
843-837-9115
Fax: 843-837-9225
info@bfgcom.com
www.bfgcom.com
• Kevin Meany, President
(843) 837-9115
• Neil Arlett, Account Director
(843) 837-0057
• Jill King, Production Director
(843) 837-0022
• Scott Seymour, VP, Chief Creative officer
• Sloane Kelly, Director of Interactive stratergy
• Steve Hamilton, VP Of Account Services
• Larry McGearty, Chief Creative Strategists
• Kyle Langley, Chief Research Officer
Services:
A full service marketing firm; handles everything from mobile marketing to the internet.
Clients:
Bailey's Irish Cream, Century 21 Real Estate, BC Wines, Alleton Rum, Guiness Brewing, Hyatt, Malibu Run, RTI Software. TGI Friday's Blenders.

BGA NEW MEDIA
230 PARK AVENUE
NEW YORK, NY 10169
212-808-3093
Marketing & Consulting Services:
Services range from B2B marketing to cutting-edge creative design. Specifically includes design, video production, branding, e-commerce, sponsorship sales, and strategic planning.

BILLBOARD TRAY
4355 COBB PARKWAY
SUITE J517
ATLANTA, GA 30339
678-444-4120
• Stephen Weinberger, CEO
Nature of Services:
Billboard Tray is THE walking billboard that delivers food with your advertising and promotional messages simultaneously to affluent, brand-loyal, and desireable spectators in marquee sports and entertainment venues nationwide.

BIRDZERK!
3715 KLONDIKE LANE
LOUISVILLE, KY 40218-1712
502-458-4020
800-219-0899
Fax: 502-458-0867
info@theskillvillegroup.com
www.birdzerk.com
• Dominic Latkovski, Owner
• Brennan Latkovski, Owner
brennan@theskillvillegroup.com
• Stephanie Fish, General Manager
stephanie@theskillvillegroup.com
Nature of Service:
The wildest, craziest show in sports featuring BirdZerk!, Zerk Jr., BabyZerk!, and BallZerk!
Year Founded:

1992
Sports Service Founded:
1992
Event Marketing Services:
Traveling mascot company.
Clients:
2002 AAA All-Star Game (Oklahoma City, OK), 2001 Southern League All-Star Game (Sevierville, TN), 2000 AAA All-Star Game (Rochester, NY), 2000 Southern League All-Star Game (Greenville, SC), 1999 AA All-Star Game (Mobile, AL), 1999 South Atlantic League All-Star Game (Salisbury, MD), 1998 AAA All-Star Game (Norfolk, VA), 1998 AAA World Series (Las Vegas, NV), 1998 NAIA Women's Final Four (Jackson, TN), 1994 California League All-Star Game (Adelanto, CA), 1994 AAA All-Star Game (Nashville, TN), 1993 Florida League All-Star Game (St. Petersburg, FL), 1991 AAA All-Star Game (Louisville, KY), Aberdeen Arsenal, Aberdeen Ironbirds.

BKB LTD.
PO BOX 4184
ENGLEWOOD, CO 80155
303-694-2202
Fax: 303-694-2278
www.bkbltd.com
• Kelley Creigh, President
(303) 694-2202
creigh@theendresultco.com
• Creigh Kelley, President
creigh@bkbltd.com
Services:
Provides the latest computerized Winning Time chip timing technology, creates a management plan and time line for a brand new recreational sporting event, manages recreational sporting events - from initial concept to full-race day staffing and equipment, provides event management and timing services for convention special events, assist with media contacts, direct-mail, and email campaigns, helps with brochure production and placement
Clients:
Houston Marathon, Runnin' of the Green 7K, Cozumel Marathon, and Colorado Springs Race for the Cure
Sports Service Founded:
1979.
Event Management Services:
Provides radio, TV, and public announcers for cycling, running events, triathlons.

BLIMP WORKS, INC.
156 BARNES AIRSHIP DRIVE
STATESVILLE, NC 28625
704-876-2378
Fax: 704-876-1251
www.theblimpworks.com
• Tracy Barnes, President/Designer
• Mollie Cook, Sales/Service Representative
• Tracey Barnes, President
Nature of Service:
Blimp Works advertising blimps and balloon products are ideal for outdoor advertising, grand openings, trade shows, marketing displays, promotional exhibits, promotional blimps, parade balloons, height visibility, indoor, outdoor attention.

BLIMPWORKS
9955 W ST MARTINS ROAD
FRANKLIN, WI 53132

414-305-3145
Fax: 414-425-8095
www.rcblimp.net
• Scott Fisher, President/Owner
Sports Service Founded:
1994
Event Mangement Services:
Blimp sales and marketing of radio-controlled indoor and outdoor advertising airship and cold-air inflatable, fethered blimps, Aerostats. tunnels and other shapes, for use at sporting events, games, arenas and sports fan-oriented fanfests.

BLUMENFELD AND ASSOCIATES PR, INC.
1877 BROADWAY
SUITE 100
BOULDER, CO 80302
203-326-1200
www.blumenfeldpr.com
• Jeff Blumenfeld, President
requests@blumenfeldpr.com
Year Founded:
1980
Nature of Service:
Special events, public relations and Web content.
Publications:
ExpeditionNews.com

BOARDWALK
116 N MARYLAND AVENUE
#220
GLENDALE, CA 91206
818-548-5639
Fax: 818-548-5931
www.boardwlk.com
• Kevin Walker, Account Supervisor
(818) 566-7007
info@boardwlk.com
• Harriet Breitborde, Creative Director
(818) 566-7007
info@boardwlk.com
Sports Service Founded:
1990
Services:
A branding, design and advertising agency that specializes in developing advantageous communication between sports/entertainment properties and their many constituencies.
Clients:
Anschutz Entertainment Group, Honda Racing, Los Angeles Dodgers, NASCAR, NFL Properties, STAPLES Center, Tony Hawk

BONHAM GROUP, INC.
6400 S FIDDLER'S GREEN CIRCLE
PLAZA TOWER ONE, SUITE 1600
SUITE 1600
GREENWOOD VILLAGE, CO 80111
303-592-4290
Fax: 303-592-4293
www.bonham.com
• Dean Bonham, Founder
(303) 592-4290
• Rob Vogel, President/Chief Operating Officer
(303) 592-4290
• David Ehrlich, EVP
(303) 592-4290
• Shawn Bradley, VP/Chief Operating Officer

(303) 592-4290
• Dick Albair, Vice President of Sales
Services:
Sponsorship evaluation, strategic consulting, market research, sponsorship sales, negotiation
Clients:
Adidas, Mervyn's, Ameriquest Mortgage Company, Miller Brewing Company, Bank of America, Motorola, Best Western National Car Rental, Boeing, Nationwide, Carolinas Healthcare, NEC, Centrix Financial, New York Life, Champ Sports, O2, Chick-fil-A, Office Depot, CITGO, Pacific Life, Corel Corporation, PETCO Animal Supplies, Datatix, Piedmont Hospital, Dell, PNC Bank, Delta Air Lines, Qwest, DeWalt, Reebok, DIRECTV, Schick, DSW Shoe Warehouse, Sears, Ericsson, Sprint, Enterprise Rent-a-Car, Suzuki Motor Corporation, FedEx, Target, General Mills, Tosco, Grainger, US Bank, IBM, U.S. Cellular, Invesco Funds, Verizon, Jeep, Xcel Energy, JPMorgan Chase
Services:
Naming rights analysis, TBG Property Analysis, sponsorship analysis, media analysis, soft drink analysis, and other analysis such as internet, food and beverage contracts, on-site events, and vendor relationships.
Marketing & Consulting Services:
Development of marketing plans, market analysis. Media analysis, food and beverage analysis, leverage sponsor benefits.
Clients:
Corporations, Entertainment Properties, Collegiate Properties, Sports Properties, Cultural Properties, Development Properties, Municipalities.

BORTZ MEDIA & SPORTS GROUP, INC.
5105 DTC PARKWAY
SUITE 200
GREENWOOD VILLAGE, CO 80111
303-893-9902
Fax: 303-893-9913
info@bortz.com
www.bortz.com
• Mark C Wyche, Managing Director
• Arthur B Steiker, Managing Director
• Arthur M Steiker, Managing Director
• Jim Trautman, Managing Director
• Mark Wyche, Managing Director
Description:
A 25 year leader in providing revenue enhancing services to the business of sports. Offers an aray of services to assist professional and collegiate clients competing more effectively in the rapidly changing sports world.
Nature of Services:
Media rights assessment, business plans/launch support for new national and regional sports networks, ticket pricing/gate revenue maximization and league scheduling
Clients:
Major League Baseball (MLB), National Basketball Association (NBA), National Hockey League (NHL), PGA Tour, Big East Conference, PAC-10 Conference and many individual franchises.
Media Consulting:
Offers financial analysis, market research and technological assessment to commercial broadcasters, cable television operators and programmers, wireless cable

operators, new media, and Internet companies.

BOZELL WORLDWIDE
1022 LEAVENWORTH
OMAHA, NE 68102
402-965-4300
Fax: 402-965-4399
info@bozell.com
www.bozell.com
• Robin Donovan, Managing Principal/Administration
rdonovan@bozell.com
Marketing & Consulting Services:
Public relations services.
Services:
Advertising Agencies, Advertising, Marketing and Direct Mail
Clients:
ShopVac, Plymouth and Chrysler

BRANDBUILDERS
PO BOX 1087
TENAFLY, NJ 07670-5087
201-266-8130
Fax: 973-575-6001
www.brandbuildersllc.com
• Richard L. Brown, President
richard@superpromotions.com
• Jeff Brown, Manager
Services:
Provider of best premiums, promotional products, ideas and professional services and direct-factory source of promotional needs
Year Founded:
1982
Clients:
American Airlines, American Express, Castrol Motor Oil, Citibank, Coca Cola, Colgate, Days Inn, Dun & Bradstreet, FILA, Harrah's, Harvey's, Hyatt Hotels, JVC, Lever Brothers, M&M Mars.
Event Management Services:
Provides variety of imprinted apparel items i.e. embroidered shirts, caps, etc., for events. Also provides site selection, travel, other event management services.

BRIAN J. MURPHY CONSULTANT
PO BOX 99
SOUTHPORT, CT 6490
203-259-3890
Fax: 203-255-1787
• Brian J Murphy
(203) 259-3890
Services:
Provides in-depth information about all types of sponsorship and sports marketing activities, provides covering of auto sports, team and individual sports events and sponsor activities
Consulting Services:
Provides objective opinions and analysis on sports-themed promotions, advertising, public relations, and all other areas of sports marketing. In-person consultation and/or written reports available.

CANAAN PUBLIC RELATIONS
75 S BROADWAY
SUITE 470
WHITE PLAINS, NY 10601
914-304-4080
Fax: 914-304-4083
• Lee Canaan, Founder
• Jed Canaan, President/CEO

Sports Service Founded:
1977
Services:
Media Relations, Audience Identification, Promotions, Marketing, Special Events, Launches and Openings, Press Conferences, Video News Releases, Audio News Releases, MAT Stories, Satellite Media Tours, Media Training, Press Releases/Press Kits/Speech Writing, Internal/External Communications (brochures, newsletters, etc.), Website Creation, Crisis Management, Printing, Photography

CARAT NORTH AMERICA
150 E 42ND ST
SUITE 14
NEW YORK, NY 10017
212-591-9100
Fax: 212-252-1250
mark.mylan@carat.com
www.carat.com
Description:
A multi-faceted marketing firm. An international marketing/media firm. Very versatile in approach and execution. Carat originates from Europe, and handles complex initiatives. Markets business/brand to consumer as well as Business to Business.
Services:
Carat delivers communications and media solutions and markets business/brand to consumer as well as Business to Business solutions such as advertiser-funded programming, barter, business to business, communication planning, communication strategy, communication/consumer insight, customer relationship management, data planning, event, face-to-face, interactive, international services, marketing management analysis, media buying, media planning, outdoor, product placement, sponsorship, and sport
Clients:
Adidas, Boost Mobile, Bank One, Festina Watches, Hyatt, Hyundai Motor America, Kia Motors America, New Line Cinema, Orbitz, Pernod, Ricard Philips Electronics, Rational Software, Siebel, TiVo, Warner-Lambert, Pfizer, RadioShack, and Philips, Midas, and Alberto-Culver

CATALYST COMMUNICATION
1515 WALNUT
SUITE 300
BOULDER, CO 80302
303-444-5545
800-444-5548
Fax: 303-444-0440
Info@catacom.com
www.catacom.com
• Lynn Guissinger, Chief Financial Officer/Legal
• Beth Prehn, Project-Ateer
• Billy Edward, List Magician
Services:
Advertising, communications and marketing agency, with specialty in cycling and fitness.

CATALYST MARKETING INTERNATIONAL
203-454-3168
bzappi@catalystnow.com
www.catalystnow.com

• Bob Zappi, Chief Executive Officer/Marketing Catalyst
(203) 256-5644
bzappi@catalystnow.com
Marketing & Consulting Services:
Integrated Marketing, Strategic Promotions, e-business, Co-marketing Strategic Partnerships, Person to Person, Mobile Mmarketing.
Description:
Catalyst approaches marketing with a Person to Person philosophy. Catalyst maintains a presence at events utilizing e-marketing and consumer data applications on site.
Services:
Integrated Marketing, Strategic Promotions, e-business, Co-marketing Strategic Partnerships, Person to Person Mobile Marketing.

CBS COLLEGIATE SPORT PROPERTIES
15320 E. MARIETTA
SUITE 2
SPOKANE VALLEY, WA 99216
509-892-4720
Fax: 509-892-4720
• Doug Paschal, Vice President/General Manager
(704) 541-5812
• Bill Cartwright, VP/Director Business Development
(605) 333-0417
• David Johnson, Director Sales/Marketing
• Rich Klein, Director Collegiate Properties
(434) 977-0239

CDM ENTERPRISES, INC.
4273 SANTOLINA WAY
MURRELLS INLET, SC 29576
843-357-3240
www.cdmenterprisesinc.com
Services:
Handles corporate licensing and consulting, for both the licenser and licensee, secures and consults on latest trends.

CELEBRITY FOCUS, INC.
1115 DEERFIELD RD
DEERFIELD, IL 60015
847-682-1234
ricbachrach@celebrityfocus.com
www.celebrityfocus.com
• Ric Bachrach, Chief Executive Officer
Nature of Services:
Provides celebrity sports and entertainment talent consultation and procurement services for corporations, public relations firms, advertising agencies and associations.
Year Founded:
1987
Clients:
Bustin & Company, Cohn & Wolfe, Edelman, Fallon McElligott, Fleishman Hillard, Golin Harris, Italia Advertising, Ketchum Public Relations, Leo Burnett, Lippe Taylor, Manning Selvage & Lee, Ogilvy Adams & Rinehart, Porter Novelli, Presence Euro RSCG, Rapp Collins, Publicis Consultants, Dig Communications, Marina Maher, R F Binder Dorland Communications
Marketing & Consulting Services:
Represents advertising, marketing, public relations agencies and corporations seeking

athletes and celebrities for promotional services and endorsements.

CENERGY SPORTS & ENTERTAINMENT
728 MAIN STREET
EAST AURORA, NY 14052
716-652-7400
Fax: 716-652-7161
• John D Cimperman, Managing Partner
• Duncan Shaw, Partner Agency Development
Services:
Offers a full range of sports and entertainment marketing services for professional sports teams, entertainment venues, municipalities, and brands.
Clients:
Agressive Skate Association (ASA), Bernie Kosar Enterprises, Charter Communications, Cleveland Indians, Court TV, DSR Motorsports, Meyer Products, Minnesota Twins, NASCAR Members Club, Ohio Historical Society, Superstation WGN, Toronto Blue Jays, Turner Network Television (TNT), Western Reserve Historical Society, World's Sports Center (Charlotte, NC), International Children's Games (Cleveland, 2004).

CHAMPIONS WORLD
250 MOONACHIE AVENUE
SUITE 102
MOONACHIE, NJ 07074
201-229-0175
Fax: 407-997-4503
• Charlie Stillitano, Chief Executive Officer
(201) 229-0175
• Frank Campagna, Special Assistant Chief Executive Office
(201) 229-0175
• Lino DiCuollo, Legal SVP/Finance
• Tim Kassel, SVP Administration
Services:
Provides unparalleled marketing, merchandising and operating expertise primarily in international football and other sports related events.

CHESTNUT COMMUNICATIONS INC.
15 E PUTNAM AVENUE
#3290
GREENWICH, CT 06830
203-629-9098
Services:
Creates marketing and advertising campaigns using sports personalities; recommends appropriate personalities for campaigns, negotiates terms, schedules appearances, etc.

CHOICE MARKETING SPORTSCARDS
369 TURNER INDUSTRIAL WAY
ASTON, PA 19014
610-494-1270
800-999-CHOICE (2464)
Fax: 610-494-8074
www.choicesportscards.com/
• Scott Smith, Vice President Sales & Operations
Nature of Services:
We design, print and package custom trading cards for sports teams and businesses nationwide.

CINI-LITTLE INTERNATIONAL
20251 CENTURY BOULEVARD
SUITE 375
GERMANTOWN, MD 20874
301-528-9700
Fax: 301-528-9711
www.cinilittle.com
• William V Eaton, Principal
(626) 441-1700
weaton@cinilittle.com
• Theodore E. Farrand, President/COO
tfarrand@cinilittle.com
• Kathleen M. Held, Vice President of Marketing & Business Dev.
kheld@cinilittle.com
• Michael W. Perigard, Director of CAD
mperigard@cinilittle.com
Year Founded:
1971.
Nature of Service:
Clients from all over the world have been coming to Cini-Little for over 50 years to find creative solutions for Foodservce, Laundry and Solid Waste/Recycling projects. Whether it be a management/operations issue, a remodeling or a new facility, Cini-Little has provided successful, operational and financial solutions to support clients in achieving their goals and objectives.
Representative Corporate Clients:
3-Com; Adobe Systems, Inc.; Allen-Bradley; Allstate Insurance Company; Alza Corporation; Anixter International, Inc.; Blue Cross Blue Shield; British Petroleum; Chase Mortgage Corporation; Cisco Systems, Inc.; Credit Suisse/First Boston; Debevoise & Plimpton; Discover Financial Services; Electronic for Imaging; Exxon Mobil; Fannie Mae; GAP, Inc.; Goldman Sachs; Hewlett Packard; Honda of America; IBM; International Monetary Fund; La Salle Bank Corporation/ABM AMRO Plaza; Lehman Brothers; MBNA America; Motorola; Oracle Corporation; Owens Corning; Philips Medical Systems; Principal Financial Group; QVC; Sherman & Sterling; The World Bank; Toys R

CLEAR BLUE MARKETING NETWORK
135 N OLD WOODWARD AVENUE
BIRMINGHAM, MI 48009
248-644-0800
todd@clearblue.biz
www.clearblue.biz
• Todd Smith, Founder/President/Chief Executive Office
todd@clearblue.biz
Description:
A full service marketing, event development and management firm. The organization researches targeted audiences, customers and media. They work understand the client needs and the atmosphere surrounding them. They look at communication as an event. This is used to develop more dynamic events or presentations. They also have the capabilities to organize press/trade show events.
Services:
Experiential Marketing, Public Relations, Branding, Launch Strategy, Online Communications

CLUB MARKETING AND MANAGEMENT SERVICES
5730 SOUTH
1050 EAST
OGDEN, UT 84405
801-390-3726
Fax: 888-541-0951
clubdoc@cms-clubweb.com
www.cms-clubweb.com
• Mark Davis, President
Services:
Offers personal consultations, training, marketing, advertising and multimedia publications services to independent club owners and operators run profitable clubs.
Description:
Sports and health club business advisors.

CMI
220 EAST 23RD STREET
SUITE 305
NEW YORK, NY 10010
212-598-4567
Fax: 212-598-4566
www.cminyc.com
Clients:
Coca-Cola, R.J. Reynolds, Kodak, Animal Planet, J. Walter Thompson, CMS, Revlon.

COHN & WOLFE
200 FIFTH AVENUE
NEW YORK, NY 10010
212-798-9700
Fax: 212-329-9900
resumes@cohnwolfe.com
www.cohnwolfe.com
• Donna Imperato, President/Chief Executive Officer
(212) 798-9800
donna.imperato@cohnwolfe.com
• Michael O'Brien, President/General Manager
• Tom Petrosini, Chief Financial Officer
Services:
Strategic marketing public relations firm creating, building and protecting the world's most prolific brands through corporate communications, product launches and positioning, sponsorships, special events, analyst relations, public affairs and more.
Clients:
Hampton Inn, Absolut, Chevron, Pfizer, Embassy Suites Hotel, Internet Security System, Lego, Tilley Endurables, ADP, UCP, Interwoven, Hilton, Aventis, The Medicines Company, Visa, Taco Bell, Epson, Endo Pharmaceuticals, Spirit Airlines, Pioneer Sound .Vision.Soul, Emcor, Samsung, Merck, LG Electronics, Colgate
Marketing & Consulting Services:
Provides counsel, creates sports sponsorship programs and executes public relations strategies designed to enhance media exposure, brand awareness, identity and image: Develops media programs for sports organizations as well as corporate and brand marketing initiatives.
Other Offices:
Dallas, London, Sydney.

COLLEGIATE LICENSING COMPANY
1075 PEACHTREE STREET
SUITE 3300
ATLANTA, GA 30309
770-956-0520
Fax: 770-955-4491

accounting@clc.com
www.clc.com
• Bill Battle, Founder / Chairman
wrb@clc.com
• Pat Battle, President / Chief Executive Officer
pbattle@clc.com
Services:
Brand Protection (Trademark Enforcement, Hologram Labeling, Labor Code Compliance); Brand Management (Brand Control Systems, Types of Licenses); Brand Development (Apparel and Non-Apparel Marketing, Retail Marketing, Promotional Licensing, Championship and Post-Season Licensing, Creative Services, External Communications)
Clients:
Colleges and Universities (Alabama A&M University, Alabama at Birmingham, The University of Alabama, The University of Alaska Anchorage, University of Alaska, University of Albany SUNY, University at Appalachian State University Arizona, The University of Arkansas Fayetteville, University of Arkansas Pine Bluff, University of Arkansas State University, Auburn University, Baylor University, Boise State University, Boston College, Boston University, Brigham Young University, California State University Northridge, California State University Sacramento, Central Florida, University of, Central Washington University Cincinnati, University of Cita

COLLEGIATE LICENSING COMPANY/CLC
1075 PEACHTREE STREET
SUITE 3300
ATLANTA, GA 30309
770-956-0520
Fax: 770-955-4491
iCLCcomments@clc.com
www.clc.com
• Bill Battle, Founder/Chairman
• Pat Battle, President/Chief Executive Officer
• Derek Eiler, Chief Operating Officer
• Doug Whitlock, President
Services:
Provides Accounting, Legal and Enforcement, Licensing Administration, Retail Marketing, Public Relations, and Promotional Licensing
Clients:
Alabama A&M University, The University of Alabama-Birmingham, The University of Alabama, University of Alaska-Anchorage, University of Alaska, University at Albany SUNY, Appalanchin State University, The University of Arizona, University of Arkansas Fayetteville, Univerity of Arkansas Pine Bluff, Arkansas State University, Auburn University, Baylor University, Boise State University, BostonCollege, Boston University, Brigham Young University, California State University Northridge, California State University Sacramento, University of Central Florida, Central Washington Universiy, University of Cincinnati, The Citadel, Clemson University, Col
Sports Service Founded:
1983
Marketing & Consulting Services:
Serves as collegiate licensing firm representing over 160 colleges, universities,

bowls and conferences and the NCAA. Assists groups with retail and promotional licensing opportunities. Partner with CollegeGear.com.

COLOGNE INTERNATIONAL TRADE FAIRS
8700 WEST BRYN MAWR AVE.
SUITE 640 NORTH
CHICAGO, IL 60631
773-326-9920
Fax: 773-714-0063
info@koelnmessenafta.com
www.koelnmessenafta.com
• Mette Petersen, President & Managing Director
• Ken Dickerson, Sales & Project Manager
• Rita Dommermuth, Sales & Project Manager
Sports Service Founded:
1982
Marketing & Consulting Services:
Represents the SPOGA Sports and Camping Equipment Trade Fair in Germany.

COLONIAL LIFE & ACCIDENT INSURANCE COMPANY
PO BOX 100195
COLUMBIA, SC 29202-3195
803-798-7000
800-325-4368
Fax: 803-213-7243
www.coloniallife.com
• Randall C Horn, President/CEO
• Dan Hughey, SVP National Sales
Facility/College Sports:
2004/12 year title - U. South Carolina's Basketball Arena.

COMSCORE MEDIA METRIX
7 PENN PLAZA
10TH FLOOR
NEW YORK, NY 10001-3967
212-497-1700
866-276-6972
Fax: 212-497-1701
www.comscore.com
• Magid M Abraham, President/Chief Executive Officer/Co-Founder
• Kenneth Tarpey, Chief Financial officer
• Serge Matta, President, Commercial Solutions
• Cameron Meierhoefer, Chief Operating Officer
• Gian M Fulgoni, Executive Chairman/Co-Counder

CONNECTIONS CONSULTING
1745 JEFFERSON DAVIS HIGHWAY
SUITE 612
ARLINGTON, VA 22202
703-416-6414
• Charlene Lefkowitz, Contact
Description:
Sports Marketing & Special Events.

CONSOLIDATED GRAPHICS
5858 WESTHEIMER
SUITE 200
HOUSTON, TX 77057
713-787-0977
Fax: 713-787-5013
www.cgx.com
• Ryan C. Farris, President
• Michael B. Barton, EVP/Chief Administrative Officer

• Aaron T. Grohs, National Sales & Marketing
• Joe R H. Davis, Chairman/CEO
• Jon C Biro, EVP, CFO
• Jim Cohen, EVP,Mergers and Acquisition
• M.Grae Griffin, EVP,Human Resources
• Aaron T Grohs, EVP, Sales and Marketing
Nature of Services:
Consolidated Graphics (CGX) offers web printing, industry-leading digital printing services, a rapidly growing number of fulfillment centers and proprietary Internet-based technology solutions.
Year Founded:
1985

COPELAND COMPANY, INC., HAL
5646 MILTON STREET
SUITE 330
DALLAS, TX 75206
214-361-8788
Fax: 214-361-5467
hecopeland@aol.com
• Harry E. Copeland, President
• Ann B. Copeland, Vice President
Services:
Public relations counsel and services, including sports authors for talk shows; marketing sports events, speech writing and ghostwriting for executives, coaches and athletes.
Description:
Ticket promotion and sponsor sales for sports team seasons and events, including publicity, advertising and media trade agreements.

CORNELL SPORTS MARKETING
CORNELL UNIVERSITY ATHLETICS
TEAGLE HALL, CAMPUS ROAD
ITHACA, NY 14853
607-255-6680
Fax: 607-255-2969
jwh33@cornell.edu
www.cornellbigred.com

CORPORATE SPORTS MARKETING GROUP/ATLANTA OFFICE
2120 RANGE ROAD
CLEARWATER, FL 33765
727-669-6972
866-550-5580
Fax: 727-669-2591
• Christopher King, Chairman/Chief Executive Officer
• Kevin Kieman, SVP Sales, Clearwater
• Christopher King, Chairman and CEO
• Holly King, Executive Vice President,Finance
• Carver Donaldson, Vice president, Sales
• Sheri Richards, Vice President, Cloent Relations
Description:
Sports related sponsorship and advertising opportunities for its clients, Major League Sports Advertising.
Clients:
MLB, NASCAR, NHL.

CORPORATE VISIONS
7-11 S BROADWAY
SUITE 406
WHITE PLAINS, NY 10601
914-761-9602
Fax: 914-761-9607
Services:
Domestic and International Promotional

Products and Premium Development and Sourcing, GWP/PWP Programs (Gift with purchase and Purchase with Purchase Programs), Brand Building, New Product Launches, Marketing and Promotional Program Consulting, Sales/Trade Incentives, Corporate Gifts

Description:
Bayer Pharmaceuticals, Bear Stearns, Breitling, Bristol-Myers Squibb Pharmaceuticals, Clairol Inc. (Herbal Essences,Aussie,Revitalique, Ultress, Nice'n Easy), NY Presbyterian Hospital, Cosmair/Ralph Lauren, Ebel, Eileen Fisher, Equitable Distributors, Inc., Good Housekeeping, Graham Windham, JP Morgan Chase, Jaeger Le Coultre, John Frieda, Judicial Title, Insurance, Manhattan Reporting Company, Matrix Essentials, MeadJohnson,Nutritionals, Mondera.com, Pepperidge, Farm, Redbook, Verizon, Warburg Pincus

Description:
To design innovative promotional programs that provide clients with the highest level of creativity and service in the business.

Sports Service Founded:
1989

CREATIVE SOLUTIONS GROUP
1250 N CROOKS
CLAWSON, MI 48017
248-288-9700
Fax: 248-288-0700
info@csgnow.com
www.csgnow.com

Description:
A full service marketing agency. Services include: Event marketing, trade show and auto show exhibits, product cutaways, animated displays, rental systmes and show management.

Services:
Provides Event Marketing, Trade Show and Auto Show Exhibits, Product Cutaways and Animated Displays, Rental Systems, Business Theater and Show Management.

CSMG INTERNATIONAL, LTD
20 W KINZIE
SUITE 1000
CHICAGO, IL 60610
312-242-2700
Fax: 312-242-2707
• Harry Hoopis, Chairman
anero@csmgsports.com
• Henry Thomas, President
• Marty Pereira, Chief Operating Officer
mpereira@csmgsports.com
• Ginger Gorden, Chief Financial Officer
• Andrew Stroth, Executive Vice President, Talent Marketing
• Nova Lanktree, Executive Vice President, Marketing Services
• Scott Pucino, Executive Vice President, Baseball
• Fletcher N Smtih, III, Executive Vice President, Football
• Kennard McGuire, Executive Vice President, Sports
• Melvin Roman, Vice President, Latin American Operations Bas

Nature of Service:
Talent management, talent marketing, corporate consultancy, event marketing and media production. International sports consulting and sports marketing. Offers personal financial planning and

comprehensive individual tax services for professional athletes.

Year Founded:
1981

Locations:
Chicago, Houston, Columbia, South Carolina, Atlanta, Scottsdale AZ.

CT MARKETING
10 WREN CT
MORRISTOWN, NJ 7960
973-267-6587
888-653-2645
Fax: 973-267-2490
www.ctmarketing.com

Description:
Advanced technology for market data and collection. Technology developed to handle event registration and management online. Build and manage a custom database also creates Web-based systems for inventive program tracking and award fulfillment.

CURTIS BIRCH, INC.
1547 10TH STREET
SUITE A
SANTA MONICA, CA 90401
310-394-2020
Fax: 310-496-1309
www.curtisbirch.com
• Richard Yelland, Founder/Director/Photographer
(310) 450-2020
richardy@curtisbirch.com

Year Founded:
2000.

Services:
Produces highly effective advertising, design, PR and marketing solutions from conception to execution, for major regional and national clients.

Clients:
Fox Sports, Fuel TV, Hot Wheels/Mattel, the Life Rolls Foundation, Surgi Count Medical.

Nature of Service:
Creative boutique providing full-service ad agency, public relations, and marketing services with a specialty in action and outdoor sports.

CUSTOM BUSINESS SOLUTIONS, INC.
12 MORGAN
IRVINE, CA 92618
949-380-7674
Fax: 949-380-7644
info@cbs-posi.com
www.cbs-posi.com
• Art Julian, Founder and CEO
(949) 609-6708
• Michael Block, Chief Financial Officer
(949) 609-6709
• Joseph Castillo, VP, Software Development
(800) 551-7674
• Rom V. Krupp, VP, Bisiness Development
(214) 924-1249
• Tammy Brown, VP, Support Services
(949) 609-6778
• Gary Henderson, Chief Technical Officer

Description:
Providing a cost efficient method to accommodate our clients with the products and services they need to make their businesses successful.

Services:
Complete POSitouch training, re-training and software upgrades, internet services,

automated pooling, web-basedemail, consolidated reports, advanced POS system, INetBlock

Clients:
The Cheesecake Factory, Stars, Ruby's Diner, Pat & Oscar's Restaurant, Riva Grill On the Lake, Ogden Entertainment, Sbarro

DANIEL BLACKMAN CONSULTING
7637 OAKBORO DRIVE
LAKE WORTH, FL 33467
561-965-1350
• Daniel Blackman, Chief Product Officer

Description:
Specializing in the use of computers and information systems by sport organizations.

DAXKO
600 UNIVERSITY PARK PLACE
SUITE 500
BIRMINGHAM, AL 35209
205-437-1400
877-729-4786
Fax: 205-437-0225
sales@daxko.com
www.daxko.com

DIRECTION
213 W INSTITITE PLACE
SUITE 506
CHICAGO, IL 60610-3128
312-943-2202
Fax: 312-943-2218
www.directiontourmarketing.com
• Micah Taylor, Nationwide Account Manager
(773) 404-4402
• Todd Kasten, Partner
• Joe Shanahan, Partner
• Chess Hubbard, Web Designer

Description:
Full service marketing company. Services Include: Retail marketing and promotion, Lifestyle Marketing, College and university marketing, event production, Graphic design, event promotion and market research.

Clients:
Chicago Department of Cultural Affairs, String Cheese Incident/ Sci-Fidelity Records, Museum of Contemporary Art, Clear Channel Entertainment, Kaiju Big Battel, Jam Productions, Resfest Digital Film Festival, Mayor's Office of Special Events; Chicago, Metro/Smart Bar/Double Door, Broadway in Chicago (Chicago's Leading Stage Producer), Quiksilver Clothing

Sports Service Founded:
1999.

Other Locations:
New York, Chicago.

DISSON SKATING
1420 BEVERLY ROAD
SUITE 350
MCLEAN, VA 22101
202-364-8500
Fax: 202-364-1997
• Stephen Disson, President/Founder/Chief Executive Officer
sdisson@dissonskating.com
• Stephen Disson, Director of Events
(703) 962-6640
• Pete Bockelman, Director of Operations & Sponsorships
(703) 962-6625
pbockelman@dissonskatingllc.com

• Alyssa Shane, Director of Events
(202) 903-0887
ashane@dissonskatingllc.com
Nature of Services:
Disson Skating was founded by the
company's President, Stephen Disson, a
sports marketing veteran who has been in
the business since 1976. Formerly with
Disson, Furst & Partners, as well as the
D&F Group and ProServ. He has created
and produced over 100 events for NBC,
CBS, USA Network, ESPN, Style Network,
Universal HD and Bravo.
Sports Service Founded:
1989.

**DOM CAMERA ASSOCIATES,
INC./NATIONAL ADVERTISING
NETWORK**
630 THIRD AVENUE
NEW YORK, NY 10017
212-370-1130
Fax: 212-370-1201
www.domcameracompany.com
• Dom Camera, Principal
• Jeanine Domich, Owner
Marketing, Media & Consulting Services:
Provides sports marketing, media buying
and consulting services.
Event Management Services:
Planning, development and execution.
Sports Service Founded:
1985

DON JAGODA ASSOCIATES, INC.
100 MARCUS DRIVE
MELVILLE, NY 11747
631-454-1800
Fax: 631-454-1834
www.dja.com
• Bruce Hollander, Executive Vice President
• Larry Berney, Chief Operating Officer
• Bruce Hollander, Executive Vice President
Description:
Award winning marketing services and sales
promotion agency. Specializing in
sweepstakes, contests, instant win games
and social media promotions.
Clients:
A&E Televeision Network Agency, AARP,
ABS-CBN, ACH Foods, ADI, Aeropostale,
America Online, Inc., American Express,
Ann Taylor, Apple & Eve, Applebees (NY &
NJ), Astoria Federal Savings Bank, AT&T,
Atlantic Bank, Best Western International,
kay Jewelers, Kayser-Roth Corp., Key
Foods Stores, Lime, Minolta, Neutrogena,
Newsday, NFO Plog, Nikon Inc, Olympus
America, Pepsi-Cola Company, Canon USA
Promotion/Marketing Services
Award-winning promotion planning &
strategy; creative & production;
sweepstakes, contests & games; refunds &
premium programs; merchandise & travel
incentive programs; club/loyalty/frequency
programs; interactive/Internet promotions;
database & telemarketing services; direct
response & fulfillment services.
Sports Service Founded:
1962.
Other Locations:
4370 Tujunga Avenue, Suite 330, Studio
City, CA 91604. 818-508-3000; FAX:
818-508-3034, 8125 Monetary Drive, Suite
G-5, West Palm Beach, FL 33404.
561-840-3333; FAX: 561-840-7772.

DORNA USA, LLC
800 THIRD AVENUE
28TH FLOOR
NEW YORK, NY 10022-7604
212-699-8400
Fax: 212-986-0927
lvillafane@vanwagner.com
• Michael J Levine, President
(212) 699-8603
mlevine@vanwagner.com
• Cliff Kaplan, President, Advertising and
Sponsorship S
(212) 699-8525
ckaplan@vanwagner.com
• John Haegele, Chief Operating Officer
(212) 699-8625
jhaegele@vanwagner.com
• John Massoni, Executive VP Operations &
Partner
Chicago Office:
601 S. Chaddick Drive, Wheeling, IL 60090.
847 465-8500; FAX: 847 465-8515
Services:
Offers national advertisers prominent
Placements within the game action in
full-view of the television cameras via its
Dorna rotational signage systems; optimal
Reach through a diverse offering of Media
and Sponsorship Sales opportunities for any
demographic; and Consulting and
Management services for advertisers
needing the Delivery of well-crafted strategic
plans.
Marketing & Consulting Services:
Full service sports marketing organization
specializing in rotational signage,
sponsorship sales, hospitality, and event
management and promotion. Marketing
agreement in place with over 90
professional and college properties in North
America. Signage is utilized along the
courts, fields and rinks of the NBA, MLB,
NHL and NCAA. Also provides custom-built
fascia signage for stadiums and areas.
Sports Promotion division, based in Virginia,
promotes, organizes, and markets sports
events in college football and basketball,
and pre-season NBA and MLB games.
22 NBA Basketball Teams:
Atlanta Hawks, Boston Celtics, Chicago
Bulls, Cleveland Cavaliers, Dallas
Mavericks, Denver Nuggets, Detroit Pistons,
Golden State Warriors, Houston Rockets,
Los Angeles Clippers, Los Angeles Lakers,
Miami Heat, Milwaukee Bucks, Minnesota
Timberwolves, New Jersey Nets, New York
Knicks, Orlando Magic, San Antonio Spurs,
Utah Jazz, Memphis Grizzlies, Washington
Wizards.
7 NHL Hockey Teams:
Calgary Flames, Carolina Hurricanes, Dallas
Stars, Detroit Red Wings, Minnesota Wild,
New York Islanders, Pittsburgh Penguins.
16 MLB Baseball Teams:
Anaheim Angels, Atlanta Braves, Chicago
White Sox, Cincinnati Reds, Detroit Tigers,
Florida Marlins, Houston Astros, Kansas
City Royals, Milwaukee Brewers, Minnesota
Twins, New York Mets, Oakland A's,
Pittsburgh Pirates, St. Louis Cardinals,
Tampa Bay Devil Rays, Texas Rangers.
Clients Include:
Ace Hardware, American Express,
Anheuser Busch, Armitron, AT&T,
AutoZone, carsdirect.com, Coca Cola,
Datek Online, Dean Witter, Discovery
Channel, Dunkin Donuts, FootAction,
FootLocker, Finish Line, GEICO,

hoopstv.com, IBM, Kraft, MasterCard,
McDonalds, Office Depot, Office Max,
Pepsi, Pfizer, Powerbar, Sears, Subway,
True Value and Volkswagen

DRAFTWORLDWIDE
633 N SAINT CLAIR STREET
CHICAGO, IL 60611-2897
312-425-5000
Fax: 312-944-3566
• Howard Draft, Executive Chairman
• Tod Tilford, Chief Creative Officer
• Daniel Bowens, Executive Creative
Director
• Micheal Fassnacht, President
Services:
Specializes in many disciplines including
Direct Marketing, Promotional/Retail
Marketing, Interactive Marketing, Media,
Data Technology Services,
Direct-To-Consumer Healthcare Marketing,
Customer Specific Marketing, Emerging
Media, Multi-cultural Marketing.
Description:
Marketing communications, branding, direct
marketing, promotions and retail.

DSN RETAILING TODAY
425 PARK AVENUE
SUITE 6
NEW YORK, NY 10022
212-756-5000
800-274-6951
Fax: 212-756-5209
• Tim Craig, Editor-in-Chief
(212) 756-5000
tcraig@dsnretailingtoday.com
• Bernadette Casey, Executive Editor
(212) 756-5000
bcasey@dsnretailingtoday.com
Products:
Business and finance magazine targeted to
retail professionals from CEOs to store
managers, in all incudsty, including sports.

DUFFY JENNINGS COMMUNICATIONS
SILICON VALLEY
SAN FRANCISCO, CA 94404
408-896-6900
duffy@duffyjennings.com
www.duffyjennings.com
• Tim Harrington, CEO
Services:
Offers Strategic Counsel, Public Relations,
Media Relations, Media Coaching,
Writing-Editing, Press Releases, Brand
Messaging, Reputation Management,
Employee Communications, Community
Affairs, Press Conferences, Trade Shows,
Publishing
Description:
Full service public relations firm and
marketing communications agency.

DVC WORLDWIDE
210 HEADQUARTERS PLAZA
MORRISTOWN, NJ 7960-6855
973-775-6700
Fax: 973-775-6703
Services:
Specializes in global marketing,
communications and digital solutions.
Utilizes advertising, merchandising and
co-marketing. Integrates promotional,
interactive, experiental, relationship and
healthcare marketing.

ELITE INTERNATIONAL SPORTS MARKETING, INC.
1049 BRISTOL MANOR DRIVE
BALLWIN, MO 63011
636-891-8028
Fax: 314-621-4449
• Jackie Joyner-Kersee, President
(314) 621-4448
• Della Gray, Operations Director
• Valerie Foster, Executive Assistant
Services:
Event Management: Create, plan, organize and execute special events. Marketing & Consulting: Specialized client research and development; program development; activity scheduling and travel coordination; and public relations.
Clients:
Football - Terry Fair, Ernest Blackwell, Matt Sherman, Baseball - Brian Jordan, Robert Kersee, Track & Field - Jackie Joyner-Kersee, Gail Devers, Greg Foster, Amy Acuff

ENDURANCE SPORTS MARKETING GROUP
801 MAIN STREET
SUITE 025
LOUISVILLE, CO 80516
303-926-1017
Fax: 425-920-5306
• Craig Mintzlaff, Principle
• Maggie Arnold, Directors Asst. Marketing & Registration
• Josh Caves, Sales & Field Marketing
• Jeff Stoner, Event Execution
Description:
Specializes in cycling and fitness expos held in conjunction with the countries largest bicycling, running, triathlon and fitness events.
Services:
Groundzero Sports specialty lies in producing, managing and promoting all aspects of the countries largest sports and fitness expos allowing race promoters and organizers to focus on what they do best - the race.

ENTRY MEDIA, INC.
127 W FAIRBANKS AVENUE
SUITE 417
WINTER PARK, FL 32789
407-678-4446
Fax: 407-679-1658
info@entrymedia.com
www.entrymedia.com
• Martin Hering, Founder/President
• Kenny Pober, Vice President, New York Market Manager
(212) 297-6400
Description:
Originator, manufacturer and marketer of Turnstile Advertising with Turnstile AdSleeve Armcovers. Converts ordinary turnstile units into revenue generators.

ENVIRONMENTAL OUTDOOR EDUCATION & RECREATION
29 WESTWOOD TERRACE
DEDHAM, MA 2026
617-326-2543
• David P Hodgdon, President/Executive Director
Sports Service Founded:
1966
Marketing & Consulting Services:

Recreational and educational consulting service including environmental analysis, Nordic skiing and mountain bike trail use, design, site evaluation, staff training, safety, workshops, etc. Historic, environmental and trail designation, documentation. State, national, world level capabilities. Also lecturer and photographer in out-of-doors for such activities as snow shoeing, ski touring, alpine and ski mountaineering, hiking, winter camping and survival, rock climbing, avalanche, training in the above listings.

EQUISURE INC,.
13790 E RICE PLACE
AURORA, CO 80015
303-614-6961
800-752-2472
Fax: 303-614-6967
www.equisure-inc.com
• Lesher Diane, Executive Vice President ext 302
Services:
Official Insurance Provider to United States Equestrian Federation members.

ESPN ABC SPORTS CUSTOMER MARKETING AND SALES
77 W 66TH STREET
NEW YORK, NY 10023
212-456-3654
www.espncms.com
• Ed Erhardt, President
Nature of Sports Service:
Provides detailed analysis on audience data, usage trends, industry news, and advertising case studies for customers looking to create a customized advertising plan.

EVENT STRATEGY GROUP
4070 BUTLER PIKE
#800
PLYMOUTH MEETING, PA 19462
610-260-2550
info@esg.us
www.esg.us
• Norman Aamodt, President/Chief Executive Officer
(610) 260-2551
• Renee Scullin, VP Event Management
(610) 260-2552
• Stefanie Turco, Strategic Development VP
(610) 260-2555
sturco@eventstrategygroup.com
• Pam Zelinski, Business Manager
(610) 260-2550
• Kathleen McKeever, Sr.Event Manager
(610) 260-2554
• Jennifer Scand, Sr.Event Manager
(610) 260-2556
• Melissa Edwards, Sr.Event Manager
(610) 260-9389
Description:
Full service marketing and sponsorship agency. Develops integrated and sponsorship programs. Their model is broken down five key components: strategic planning, information management, integrated maketing, event management and sponsorship marketing. Extensive experience in tradeshow management and hosted event management.
Clients:
Sungard, Plumtreet, QRS, Sungard Securities Processing, serena, dvHr Partnership, Lincoln Financial Group,

siteRock, K Rain, Siebel eBusiness, Coalition of Commercial Real Estate Associations, SeeBeyond, Ecom, Ziff Davis Media, GVFHRA, T-SIG, IDS Scheer Business Process Excellence

EVENTNET USA
1129 SE 4TH AVENUE
FORT LAUDERDALE, FL 33316
954-467-9898
Fax: 954-467-8252
info@EventNetUsa.com
www.eventnetusa.com
• Jill B Benson, Director ,Business Development
• Allison Wurstle, Associate Director, Business Development
• Joel Benson, Founder/Chief Executive Officer
(954) 467-9898
joelb@eventnetusa.com
• Ira Jaffe, Senior Vice President, Account Services
Services:
Specializes in mobile marketing, custom exhibit building, mall radio, pop-up marketing stores, targeted consumer sampling, spirit field services, targeted shows, mall billboards, guerrilla marketing, shopping malls.
Clients:
Adidas, Allstate Insurance, AARP, Almay, American Airlines, American Express, American Red Cross, American Tourister, Amoco Motor Club, Apple Computers Inc., Armstrong, AT&T, Barnes-Hind Inc., Best Buy, Better Homes & Gardens, Black & Decker, Blimpie, BMW, Boost, Borden, Inc., Bounty Microwave, Butterfingers, CBS Television, California Olive, California Pistachio, California Prune, Campbell Soup, Canon, Chevrolet, Citibank, Clairol, Inc., Coca Cola, Colgate, Converse, Coppertone, Corning, Dr. Pepper, DeBeers Diamonds, Discover Card, Disney Corp., Dole, Dove, Duncan Hines, Eastman Kodak, ELLE Magazine, Equal, Eureka, Ford Tractor, Frito Lay
Sports Service Founded:
1976
Promotional Tours:
CBS Sports Challenge, Apple Open House, Reebok Pump-up and Air-out campaign, NBA America's Tour, Olympic Games, the Turner Goodwill Games, the NBA All-Star Games, Major League Baseball, and the NFL Super Bowl Tour to malls, stadiums, and fairs.

EVENTORS
1030 N STATE STREET
SUITE 1-M
CHICAGO, IL 60610
312-944-6667
eventors@aol.com
• Jane E. Canepa, Owner
Sports Service Founded:
1976
Services:
Event Management Services: events, marketing and public relations company that focuses on special events
Event Management Services:
Public relations, promotion sponsorship, and event management of special events.

EXCALIBUR MARKETING GROUP
4258 GERMANNA HIGHWAY
SUITE D-1
LOCUST GROVE, VA 22508
540-972-4690
Fax: 540-972-4691
www.isportsnet.com
Sports Service Founded:
1992
Services:
Full service sports marketing firm specializing in all levels of the football industry, athlete management services, professional services, sports agents, market research services. Owns and operates the Dick Butkus Football Internet site (www.dickbutkus.com), dedicated to all levels of football. Also owns and operates Internet Sports Awards. Represents over 20 NFL Hall of Fame players available for corporate marketing programs.
Athlete Management Services:
Represents over 20 NFL Hall of Fame players available for corporate marketing programs.

EXCLUSIVE SPORTS MARKETING, INC.
6421 CONGRESS AVE
SUITE 103
BOCA RATON, FL 33487
561-241-3801
Fax: 561-241-3805
lorraine@exclusivesports.com
• Chris Colgan, President
(561) 241-3801
• Linda Meyer, VP of Finance
(561) 241-3801
lmeyer@exclusivesports.com
• Chris Carusone, Event Director
• Stevn J Tebon, CEO
• Katty Peraza, Design
Services:
Sports and event marketing/management which include road races, skating events, open water swims, and kids' events.
Clients:
Publix Supermarkets, Coca-Cola, PepsiCo, Anheuser-Busch, Gatorade, Toyota, Buick, Nike, Sunshine Network, Yamaha, Holiday Inn, Marriott, Ocean Properties, and Club Med.
Sports Service Founded:
1986
Nature of Sports Service:
Recreational based sports marketing firm.

EXHIBIT ENTERPRISES
1400 S LIVERNOIS
ROCHESTER HILLS, MI 48307
800-582-9250
800-582-9250
Fax: 248-601-9901
interest@eeiglobal.com
www.eeiglobal.com
• David M Gentile, Founder/Chairman
interest@eeiglobal.com
• Derek M Gentile, President/Chief Executive Officer
interest@eeiglobal.com
• Kirk A Brien, VP and General Manager
• Simon Fairweather, CCO
Services:
Specializes in major builds, permanent installations, private exhibitions, mobile marketing, animation, finishing and cut aways, modular displays, digital and large format graphics, trade shows and exhibits,

e-business solutions and event services
Clients:
BMW, GM ElectroMotive, BorgWarner, Visteon, Delphi, Dodge, Mini, Bendix, Eaton, Alcoa, Mitsubishi Electric, Daimler Chrysler, Rolls Royce, Detroit Zoological Institute, Ford Motor Company, GM Power Train, JTC Corporation, American Axle& Manufacturing, FAG, Wacker Ceramics, DTE Energy, DTE Energy Technologies
Description:
A globally-minded provider of creative marketing experiences. Curent reputation includes the auto industry, healthcare, aerospace and consumer goods. Increased capacity and service for both national and mobile business to business event groups. Utilizes animations/cutaways and large format graphics.
Sports Service Founded:
1981

FENWAY SPORTS GROUP
82 BROOKLINE AVENUE
BOSTON, MA 02215
617-226-6300
Fax: 617-226-6484
info@fenwaysportsgroup.com
www.fenwaysportsgroup.com
• Sam Kennedy, President
• Charles H. Steedman, Executive Vice President
• Jay Monahan, Executive Vice President
• Mark I. Lev, Co-Managing Director
Marketing & Consulting Services:
Specializes in development sponsorship and marketing programs for consumer product and industry-related companies seeking to leverage their sponsorships in auto racing.

FIELDHOUSE, INC.
1220 116TH AVENUE NE
SUITE 200
BELLEVUE, WA 98004
425-458-4200
877-232-9785
Fax: 425-467-0800
customerservice@fieldhouse.net
www.fieldhouse.com
• Carl Lombardi, Jr., President/Founder
• Carl Lombardi Jr., Founder
• Carl Lombardi Jr., Founder
 ext 203
Nature of Service:
Fieldhouse Store is a complete apparel, merchandise and fundraising site which offers the following services: Retail Store, Presale Online Bulk Ordering, Fan Poster, One Source, Tickets, Season Passes, Local Market and My Store
Year Founded:
2003
Marketing & Consulting Services:
Fieldhouse provides merchandise solutions to teams and leagues across the nation. Our benefits are our no-hassle bulk buying experience, and our free web stores for team logo wear.

FIRST PLUS SPORTS MARKETING
1600 VICEROY DR.
SUITE 325
DALLAS, FL 75235
954-475-2001
Fax: 954-475-8392
www.bizapedia.com/fl/FIRSTPLUS-SPORT S-MARKETING-INC.html

• Green Eric, Vice President
• Marino Daniel Cjr, Chief Executive Officer/ President
• Phillips Daniel T, Director
• Jim Roundtree, CFO
Services:
Marketing and consulting; represents professional athletes for marketing and endorsements.

FITPRO LIFESTYLE CONSULTANTS
121 HUBLEY MILL LAKE ROAD
UPPER TANTALLON, NS, CANADA B3Z 1E8
902-402-5466
866-4-FITPRO
Fax: 902-826-7230
• Paul Griffith, President
• Chris Tremblay, Director of Operations and Partner
• Sue Griffith, Consultant
• Paul Griffith, President and CEO
Description:
Is a health and lifestyle company that provides services to individuals, teams and organizations. We offer fitness programming and practical lifestyle management tools to assist individuals with thier personal goals and objectives.

FLAIR COMMUNICATIONS
214 W ERIE STREET
CHICAGO, IL 60654
312-943-5959
800-621-8317
Fax: 312-943-6049
• Allyn Miller, President
• Lee F Flaherty, Chief Executive Officer
lflaherty@flairagency.com
• Kevin Kennedy, EVP
(312) 943-5959
kkennedy@flairagency.com
• Bob Walz, Chief Operating Officer
Services:
Sales Promotion and Specialized Marketing Services; specializes in consumer brand marketing; develops program targeting consumers to brands and then build the relationship; utilizes the internet, events, instore promotions or home; PowerHouse marketing, account specific marketing, promotional media creating and buying, matchmaker database and tie-ins, ten-point plan to cut cost, incremental volume estimates and ROI models.
Description:
Specilizes in consumer brand marketing. Develops program targeting consumers to brands and then build the relationship. Utilizes the internet, events, ins tore promotions or home. Independently owned, results-oriented strategic planning and integrated marketing company handles everything from sponsorships, special events and grassroots field marketing.
Revenue:
$23.70 M

FRANKLIN COVEY
2200 W PARKWAY BOULEVARD
SALT LAKE CITY, UT 84119
801-817-5001
888-576-1776
800-827-1776
Fax: 801-817-8313
info@franklincovey.com
www.franklincovey.com

• Robert A Whitman, Chairman/Chief Executive Officer
• Stephen D. Young, Chief Financial Officer
• Scott Miller, Chief Marketing Officer
• Robert A. W. Whitman, Chairman
• Stephen Covey, Executive Vice President/Education/Training
• Todd R. Davis, Executive Vice President, Chief People & Oper

Services:
Franklin Covey is the global leader in effectiveness training ,productivity tools,and assessment services and orginizations,teams and indivduals.FranlinCovey helps companys succeed by unleashing the power of the work force to focus on top business priorities. FranlinCovey has 2,000 associates in 35 offices in 95 countries.

FULL HOUSE SPORTS MARKETING
FULL HOUSE
3215 GOLF ROAD #112
DELAFIELD, WI 53018
866-280-0637
866-280-0637
Fax: 312-360-0002
office@fillthehouse.com
www.fillthehouse.com
• Ron Contorno, President
Nature of Service:
Season tickets/Mini-plans, Group Sales, Consumer/Residential Databases, Subscription Files, Enthusiasts, Opt-In Email Databases
Clients:
Nashville Predators, Feld Entertainment, Washington Capitals, Providence Bruins, Comcast Spectacor, Harlem Globetrotters, Chicago Wolves, Louisiana IceGators, Los Angeles Galaxy, Milwaukee Bucks, Houston Comets, Toronto Raptors, New Orleans Saints, Minnesota Timberwolves, Grand Rapids Rampage, Oklahoma State University, Pittsburgh Pirates, Dayton Dragons, Houston Astros, Lexington Legends, Disney Sports Attractions, Maywood Park, DTE Energy Music Theatre, Memphis Grizzlies, Chicago Fire, Detroit Pistons, Chicago Blackhawks, Jacksonville Jaguars, Columbus Blue Jackets, Rochester Americans, Mandalay Sports Entertainment, Grand Rapids Griffins

FURMAN, INC., ANTHONY M.
250 W 57TH STREET
SUITE 1501
NEW YORK, NY 10107
212-956-5666
Fax: 212-956-5703
info@furmansports.com
www.furmansports.com
• Anthony Furman, President
tony@furmansports.com
• Joyce Keating, Office Manager
• Linda Torel, Account Consultant
• Evelyn Pate, Senior Account Consultant
Services:
Sports Marketing and Public Relations; marketing and consulting services which include programming, consultation and public relations activities to introduce clients to sports marketing and to enlarge and direct clients already having involvement.
Accounts Have Included:
American Express Travel Related Services, AT & T, Beneteau, Inc., Corning Optics, Ice Follies, International Toy Center,

Knickerbocker Cup, Lake Placid Film Forum, National Powerboat Association, New Jersey Special Olympics, Ski New Hampshire, Sportcraft, Vail Resorts, Hunter Mountain Resort, Wham-O Manufacturing Co., Woman's Pro Skiing, Liberty Cup, North Cove Yacht Harbor, Ski Utah Association.
Sports Service Founded:
1966
Marketing & Consulting Services:
Programming, consultation and public relations activities in sports to introduce clients to sports marketing and to enlarge and direct clients already having involvement with sports.

FUSE
431 PINE STREET
PO BOX 4509
BURLINGTON, VT 05406-4509
802-864-7123
Fax: 802-864-2595
rfp@fusemarketing.com
www.fusemarketing.com
• Bill Carter, Partner
• Brett Smith, Partner
• Issa Sawabini, Partner
• Julie C. Jatlow, Executive Director
Nature of Service:
A full-service youth culture marketing agency with capabilities in the following areas: Consulting, Event Marketing, Communications, Research, Creative Services
Sports Service Founded:
1995
Marketing & Consulting Services:
A promotional agency that connects corporate brands with the youth market through alternative sports such as snowboarding, wakeboarding, skateboarding, surfing, mountain biking, and BMX. Services include consultation and PR services, event sponsorship and management, athlete representation and promotion, and research services.
Clients:
180s, Association of Surfing Professionals, Battle Born Records, Billabong, Bula, Burton Snowboards, Dew Action Sports Tour , Dreaming Tree Films, Eastern Mountain Sports, Eastman Kodak, ESPN X Games Skateparks, Ford Motor Company, Motorola, Mountain Dew (Pepsi), Mr. Green (Pepsi), NBC Olympics, Polo Ralph Lauren, Powerpuff Girls (Cartoon Network), Quiksilver, Right Guard (Gillette), Sea-Doo (Bombardier Recreational Products), Sierra Mist (Pepsi), Ski-Doo (Bombardier Recreational Products), Slim Jim (Con Agra Foods), Stowe Mountain Resort, TAG Body Spray, Tony Hawk Clothing (Kohl's Department Stores), Toy Wishes, US Open Snowboarding Champion

GAGE MARKETING GROUP
10000 HIGHWAY 55
PLYMOUTH, MN 55441
763-595-3800
Fax: 763-595-3871
info@gage.com
www.gage.com
• Gregg Sampson, SVP Business Development/Media Relations
(763) 595-3846
businessdevelopment@gage.com

• Colleen Christensen, Project Manager
• Tom Belle, President, CEO
Nature of Service:
Promotional marketing programs in sports, including but not limited to Internet marketing.
Year Founded:
1992
Clients:
Alcoa Building Products, Allergan, American Express, Buca di Beppo Restaurants, Chino Latino Restaurant, Canon, Deli Express, Del Monte, ESPN, Formica, General Mills, Gerber, Goodyear, H J Heinz, Haagen Dazs, Healthy Choice, Hewlett Packard, Hunt Wesson, Kaiser Permanente, Knudson, Lee Jeans, Maxtor, M&M/Mars, Meredith, Nabisco, Orville Redenbacher, Pillsbury, Potlatch Corporation , Schwan's, Snapple, Steelcase, Toto USA, Trus Joint MacMillan, UPM-Kymmene, Whirlpool
Other Location;
4701 Von Karman, First Floor, Newport Beach, CA 92660

GAME DAY COMMUNICATIONS
700 W PETE ROSE WAY
CINCINNATI, OH 45203
513-929-4263
Fax: 513-929-0245
jreau@gamedaypr.com
www.gamedaypr.com
• Betsy Ross, President
bross@gamedaypr.com
Clients:
Anthony Munoz Foundation,Cincinnati Bengals, Cincinnati Flying Pigs Marathon, Cincinnati Kings and hart productions.

GAZELLE GROUP
475 WALL STREET
PRINCETON, NJ 08540
609-921-1300
Fax: 609-921-2332
gazelle@gazellegroup.com
www.gazellegroup.com
• Rick Giles, Founder/President
Description:
Represents, creates and consults across sports, entertainment and cultural activities. Committed to developing prioriteized business plans that achieve its clients' marketing and financial goals.
Services:
Professional athlete and coach representation, sponsorship representation and sales, corporate endorsements, personal appearances and motivational speaking, advertising, promotions and publicity, program production and advertising sales, conceptualization and development of individual events and series, merchandising and licensing, project and event implementation, rights acquisition, hospitality implementation and sales, creation of Internet presence, TV rights, packaging, representation and sales, signage and electronic imaging, budgeting
Clients:
Alliant Energy, American Airlines, Anaconda, Anheuser-Busch, AT&T Wireless, Big Y Supermarkets, Champion, Chevrolet, Cingular, Clear Channel, Coca-Cola, Continental Airlines, Crown Oil, Dell, Dish Network, First Union/Wachovia, First USA Bank, Fleet Bank, Foot Locker, Gillette, GlaxoSmithKline, Health Net,

Infiniti, IKON, Legg Mason, Merrill Lynch, Microsoft, Mohegan Sun, New York Life, Nike, Ocean Spray, Oldsmobile, Orbitz.com, Papa John's, Pennsylvania Lottery, Pepsi Cola, PNC Bank, Sony Playstation/, 989 Sports, Sports Illustrated, TIAA-CREF, Toyota, U.S. Marines, Warburg Pincus, Warrior Lacrosse, White Castle, Zebra Pen, Roto-Rooter, Roya
Sports Service Founded:
1994

GENESCO SPORTS ENTERPRISES, INC.
1845 WOODALL RODGERS FREEWAY
SUITE 1250
DALLAS, TX 75205-5412
214-826-6565
Fax: 214-826-6494
www.genescosports.com
• Charlie Torano, Co-Founder/Director
• John Tatum, Co-Founder/Director/Partner
• Mark Tatum, EVP
Description:
Sports Marketing Agency. Our mission is deceptively simple: to grow business by efficiently and effectively leveraging sports.
Services:
Sports marketing, negotiations and media, activation and execution of sports sponsorship programs
Clients:
Pepsi, Mountain Dew, Fortune magazine, Small World, Haggar Clothing, and awards.com
Sports Service Founded:
1994

GEOMETRY GLOBAL
636 11TH AVENUE
NEW YORK, NY 10036
212-537-3700
Fax: 212-537-3737
www.g2.com
• Jay Farrell, President
(312) 299-8500
jfarrell@g2.com
• Toby Hoare, Chairman
• Steve Harding, Global Chief Executive
Nature of Service:
Local event marketing. Develops customized events to complement localized brand marketing strategies. Concentration on grass roots participatory events, such as bicycling, beach volleyball, running, multi-sport, walking and youth sports.
Sports Service Founded:
1988
Clients:
Past and Present Clients: Dannon, Kraft/Nabisco, Yoo-Hoo, Dairy Management, Beef Council, Bic Pen, Guinness, Hewlett-Packard, Darden, Del Monte, FedEx, Kiwi, ABC News, Spectrum Brands, NBA Basketball, Scotties, Dr.Pepper/7-Up, Jose Cuervo, Smuckers, Avaya, Gerber, Nokia & The Knockout Group

GEORGE P. JOHNSON COMPANY
3600 GIDDINGS ROAD
AUBURN HILLS, MI 48326
248-475-2500
Fax: 248-475-2325
careers@gpj.com
www.gpj.com
• Robert Vallee, Sr., Chairman
• Laurence Vallee, President
• Robert G. Vallee, Jr, Chief Executive

Officer
• David Drews, EVP/Chief Financial Officer
• Jeff Rutchik, Executive VP
(617) 535-9912
• Tom Maher, Executive Director, Marketing
Clients:
CISCO, IBM, Rotary, Siebel, Saturn, Ford, Reebok, Scion, Acura, Lexus, Toyota, Honda
Description:
Specializes in integrated event marketing. Utilizes creative services, event marketing, event management and production. Incorporates event analysis and strategy to creative direction and design, architectural engineering and production and entertainment hospitality.
Other Locations:
18500 Crenshaw Boulevard, Torrance, CA 90504. 310-965-4300; FAX: 310-965-4696, 48 Wall Street, Suite 1100, New York, NY 10005. 212-918-4595; FAX: 212-918-4596, 999 Skyway Road, Suite 300, San Carlos, CA 94070. 650-226-0600; FAX: 650-226-0601.

GFK CUSTOM RESEARCH NORTH AMERICA
200 LIBERTY STREET
5TH FLOOR
NEW YORK, NY 10281
212-240-5300
Fax: 212-240-5353
www.gfkamerica.com
• Debra Pruent, Chief Operations Officer
• Thomas J. Finkle, Chief Client Services Officer
Services:
Offers a full spectrum of research products, strategic models and consulting services to address clients' key business needs on a global basis.
Sports Marketing Research:
Conducts research to test and evaluate all types of sports marketing and related activities. Custom marketing research of all types to answer specific objectives relating to events, promotions, personalities, ad campaigns, imagery, audience, demographics, attitudes, sponsorship, sampling and overall effectiveness. Weekly national and regional omnibus services available. Overnight custom research services.

GIGUNDA GROUP
540 N COMMERCIAL STREET
MANCHESTER, NH 3101
603-314-5000
Fax: 603-314-5001
info@gigundagroup.com
www.gigundagroup.com
• Ryan FitzSimons, Founder/Chief Executive Officer
(603) 491-3523
ryan@gigundagroup.com
• Dan Dewey, Chief Financial Officer
• Scott Schoessel, Sales VP/New Business Development
(603) 340-1940
• Michael B. Petran, Creative VP
michael_petan@gigundagroup.com
Description:
Provides marketing services to clients targeting the college crowd. Services include placement the Fall Welcome Gift(product samples, student offers) and In Your Face Memo Boards(small billboards).

Services:
Experiential / Mobile / Event / Field / Trade Marketing; Sponsorship Activation - Music / Sports / Entertainment; Brand Enhancement & Consultation — Strategy / Ideation / Positioning; Retail Activation / RetailTainment / EngageTainment; Trade & Consumer Hospitality Parties / VIP Packages; Viral / Interactive / Word-of-Mouth; PR / Stunts / Buzz; Product Sampling / Demonstration; Trade Shows & Sales Meetings - Design / Development / Execution. Total Program Management - Strategy, Design, Creation; Execution, Reporting; Field Staffing / Training / Management / CDL Drivers; Vehicle Design / Build Outs /Graphic Wraps /Procurement; Promotional Des
Clients:
Procter & Gamble, Kellogg's, Kraft/Nabisco, Campbell's, Cadbury Schweppes, Nestle, Just Born and TastyKake.
Other Locations:
Chicago, St. Louis, Denver.
Current projects:
Kroger 300. Formerly known as The Collegue Kit. Develops mobile marketing programs that clients visibility.

GILT EDGE SOCCER MARKETING, LLC
321 JEFFERSON STREET
FLOOR 2
CHICAGO, IL 60563
312-600-9710
contact@giltedgesoccer.com
www.giltedgesoccer.com
• John Guppy, Founder/President
(312) 600-9710
jguppy@giltedgesoccer.com
• Scott Hutchison, Managing Director/Partner
Description:
Marketing solutions agency for brand seeking to connect with the soccer consumer. We work with corporate, media, and industry brands.

GLOBAL PRODUCTIONS
550 POST OAK BOULEVARD
HOUSTON, TX 77027
713-681-5898
888-381-2861
Fax: 713-681-5220
service@globalindustrial.com
www.globalindustrial.com
Sports Service Founded:
1999
Marketing & Consulting Services:
An independent group of companies providing their clients with international reach and local implementation in the areas of public relations, sponsorship, and event marketing & management. Global has offices in the US, England, France, Italy, Spain, UAE and Japan.

GLOBAL SPORTS & ENTERTAINMENT
300 N CONTINENTAL BOULEVARD
SUITE 140
EL SEGUNDO, CA 90245
310-414-2690
Fax: 310-414-2693
admin@globalsports-ent.com
www.globalsports-ent.com
• Nick Zaccagnino, Founder & President
• Julie Matz, Senior Talent Producer
• Evan Levy, Senior Event Manager/Talent

Producer
• Cindy Katz, Talent Producer
• Ben Weiss, Athlete Relations/Jr. Talent Producer
Sports Service Founded:
1996
Marketing & Consulting Services:
Represents clients in all aspects of sports marketing. Develops or assists in the implementation of strategic marketing campaigns. Designs promotional campaigns to generate interest in targeted demographic groups. Promotes image enhancement and generates publicity for athletes and celebrities.

GO WITH A PRO, INC.
38 MILLER AVENUE P M B 241
MILL VALLEY, CA 94941
415-383-3907
www.gowithapro.com

GOLDEN BEAR INTERNATIONAL, INC.
11780 US HIGHWAY ONE
SUITE 500
NORTH PALM BEACH, FL 33408-3007
561-227-0300
Fax: 561-227-0548
www.nicklaus.com
• Jack Nicklaus, Chairman/Chief Executive Officer
• Bill O'Leary, President Landscape Design Services
Sports Service Founded:
1970
Marketing & Consulting Services:
Corporate services provided by eight operating divisions include: sports marketing and consulting; special events; television, video production and publishing; licensing and merchandising; public relations and promotion.
Services:
Marketing and Communications, Plan Documents, Specifications and Details, Computer Modeling, Landscape Design Services and Renovation Services.

GOLDEN BOY PROMOTIONS
626 WILSHIRE BOULEVARD
SUITE 350
LOS ANGELES, CA 90017
213-489-5631
Fax: 213-489-9048
info@goldenboypromotions.com
www.goldenboypromotions.com
• Oscar De La Hoya, President
(213) 489-5631
• Richard Schaefer, Chief Executive Officer
(213) 489-5631
Nature of Sports Service:
National boxing promotions firm.

GOLF SCORECARDS, INC
9735 SW SUNSHINE COURT
SUITE 700
BEAVERTON, OR 97005
503-352-0281
800-238-7267
Fax: 503-226-4501
information@golfscorecards.com
www.golfscorecards.com
• Cynthia Grant, President
(503) 352-0283
• Byron Grant, General Manager
(503) 352-0284
byron@golfscorecards.com

Products:
Quality design and printing: scorecards, yardage guides, other golf printed materials.

GOLFUTURES, INC.
7373 N SCOTTSDALE ROAD
SUITE B-100
PHOENIX, AZ 85253
480-315-8401
877-440-5360
Fax: 480-905-8705
www.golfutures.com
Services:
An employment service, serving both employers looking for golf educated personnel, as well as individuals searching for golf employment opportunities within the golf industry.
Marketing & Consulting Services:
Provides a variety of publishing and advisory services related to employment opportunities in the golf industry.
Sports Service Founded:
1991

GORILLA MARKETING, INC.
4100 FLAT ROCK DRIVE, #A
RIVERSIDE, CA 92505-5866
951-353-8133
800-464-6745
Fax: 951-353-1647
info@gorillamarketing.net
www.gorillamarketing.net
• Chris Arranaga, Chief Executive Officer/Sales
chris@gorillamarketing.net
• Bryce Arranaga, Art Department
• Rosslyn Forrester, Sales
• Joe Kalish, Sales
• Chris Arranaga, Owner & President
(951) 353-8133
chris@gorillamarketing.net
Services:
Delivers quality products and competitive prices along with unparalleled customer service.
Marketing & Consulting Services:
Promotional item supplier, stadium give-aways.

GRAND SLAM SPORTS MARKETING
625 MISSION VALLEY ROAD
NEW BRAUNFELS, TX 78132
830-625-5911
Fax: 830-625-5966
www.legendsoftennis.com
• Louanne Fischer, Director of Sales
Services:
Provides celebrity entertainment for tennis events to corporations, charity organizations, clubs, resorts, and tournaments. The company specializes in corporate outings and hospitality, charity events, club and resort programs, tournaments and product endorsements.
Event Management Services:
Event marketing through tennis events. Involved in setting up corporate events, sponsorship, endorsements, club and charity events.

GRANT ASSOCIATES
301 SAYRE DRIVE
PRINCETON, NJ 08540-5826
609-514-8674
Fax: 609-514-8673

• David Grant, President
dave_grant@comcast.net
Nature of Service:
Executive recruiting, licensing management, sports/event promotion, strategic corporate growth consulting, U.S. market development.
Year Founded:
1997
Sports Service Founded:
1997

GRAVITY TELEVISION & SPORTS MARKETING
1315 OAKRIDGE STREET
PO BOX 8189
FORT COLLINS, CO 80525
970-845-7979
Fax: 970-845-7991
• Mark Schelde, Founder/President
(970) 845-7979
mark@gravity.com
• Amit Kapur, CEO and Co Founder
• Jim Benedetto, CTO and Co-founder
• Steve Pearman, CPO and Co-founder
• Chris Bissell, Chief Software Architect
• Karl Rinderknecht, VP Business Development
Year Founded:
1998
Nature of Service:
A full service sports and entertainment company specializing in program development, strategic consulting, negotiation, planning, budgeting, activation and fulfillment. Gravity's biggest asset is the ability to create efficient and unique solutions in marketing & promotions, events & sponsorships and television products. Gravity has proven experience with national sponsorships like the PGA TOUR and NASCAR down to local sponsorships such as the San Francisco Giants and The Ski Tour. Gravity has extensive experience with the major sport governing bodies and their respective teams, athletes and events. Gravity is headquartered in Beaver Creek, C
Clients:
Charles Schwab & Company, World Championship Sports Network (WCSN), and Visionbytes. Past recent projects included Gillett Evernham Motorsports and Discovery HD Theater.

GRAVITY TELEVISION & SPORTS MARKETING
450 BRYANT STREET
SAN FRANCISCO, CA 94107-1303
415-495-5515
• Amit Kapur, CEO and Co Founder
• Jim Benedetto, CTO and Co-founder
• Steve Pearman, CPO and Co-Founder
• Chris Bissell, Chief Software Architect
• Karl Rinderknecht, VP Business Development
Year Founded:
1998.
Nature of Service:
A full service sports and entertainment company specializing in program development, strategic consulting, negotiation, planning, budgeting, activation and fulfillment. Gravity's biggest asset is the ability to create efficient and unique solutions in marketing & promotions, events & sponsorships and television production. Gravity has proven experience with national

sponsorhips like the PGA TOUR and NASCAR down to local sponsorships such as the San Francisco Giants and The Ski Tour. Gravity has extensive experience with the major sport governing bodies and their respective teams, athletes and events. Gravity is headquartered in Beaver Creek

Clients:
Charles Schwab & Company, World Championship Sports Network (WCSN), and Visionbytes. Past recent projects included Gillett Evernham Motorsports, and Discovery HD Theater.

HACHI INTERNATIONAL
444 PARK AVENUE S
7TH FLOOR
NEW YORK, NY 10016
212-696-1399
Fax: 212-696-1491
• Cammallere Kristi, Contact

Marketing Services:
Promotional, premium, ad specialty company. Sports Division sells promotional items of professional teams and college athletic programs.

Services:
Specializes in high perceived value gift ideas and direct sourced items from China. Advertising, Marketing and Sales, Player Development, Promotional Products, Premium Gifts: Catalog Merchandis Programs, Custom Design - Direct Import, Advertising Specialties, Award Programs, Redemption, Corporate Gifts, Direct Mail - Fulfillment.

HALO BRANDED SOLUTIONS
1980 INDUSTRIAL DRIVE
STERLING, IL 61081
815-625-0980
Fax: 815-632-6900
moreinfo@halo.com
www.halo.com
• Marc Simon, Chief Executive Officer and Director
• Jack Mewhirter, President
• Dale Moir, SVP - Information Technology, Programs O
• Dale Limes, Sales VP

Description:
Distributor of promotional marketing products and advertising specialities.

Services:
Effective in building brands through branded merchandise: an experienced sales force, online solutions, a diligent merchandising team, convenient distribution facilities, friendly customer service, marketing support, and the most efficient order processing technology in the industry.

HANG TEN INTERNATIONAL LICENSING CALIFORNIA CORPORATION
1400 BROADWAY
18TH FLOOR
NEW YORK, NY 10018
217-763-9200
Fax: 858-391-3386
info@hangten.com
www.hangten.com
• Paul Epner, Chief Executive Officer/President
paul_epner@hangten.com
• Michael Wakeman, General Manager
michael_wakeman@hangten.com

• Craig Kalter, Marketing VP
craig_kalter@hangten.com

Products:
Accessories, activewear, boys, denim, hosiery / underwear / loungewear, sportswear, swimwear and all types of casual sportswear.

Marketing & Consulting Services:
Licensing agency for the Hang Ten, Lightning Bolt, Ozzy and Cinderella brands.

HDS PROMOTIONAL MARKETING
1140 E WASHINGTON STREET
SUITE 206
PHOENIX, AZ 85034
602-635-6400
800-952-5339
Fax: 602-254-1212
info@hdsideas.com
www.hdsideas.com
• Scott Nash, General Partner
(602) 635-6387
• Ryan Niggel, COO
• Martin Bohinski, CFO
• Kelly Chiccitt, VP of Marketing
• Mark Algeri, VP of Sales
• Joss Witzel, Director Of Operations
• Michele Fausti, Assistant to CEO
• Howard Schwartz, Founder and CEO

Nature of Services:
Team Shop Premiums produces products for staff use, game day giveaways as well as sponsor and sports related gifts.

HEIDRICK & STRUGGLES
233 SOUTH WACKER DRIVE
WILLIS TOWER - SUITE 4200
CHICAGO, IL 60606-6303
312-496-1200
Fax: 312-496-1686
www.heidrick.com
• Joe Bailey, Managing Partner - Global Sport Leadership
(212) 551-3412
jbailey@heidrick.com
• John S Wood, Vice Chairman & Managing Partner
• Eric Olson, Managing Partner
• Rusty o' Kelley, Managing Partner
• Gareth McIlroy, Managing Partner

Description:
The world's first Leadership Advisory firm, blending executive search & leadership consulting. Heidrick & Struggles actively solves business problems for their clients every day. Through their leadership advisory framework, they help companies attract, develop and retain the world's most talented individuals. For nearly 60 years, they have helped the world to be better led.

Nature of Service:
The group serves as the trusted advisor on effective leadership and solving complex problems involving vision, strategy, and talent management. Our clients are selected from owners, boards, companies, associations, federations and government entities which are or have aspirations to become peak performance organizations in the global industry of sport. There is no other firm that offers this combined service of leadership consultation and executive search, known as Leadership Advisory.

HILL AND KNOWLTON PUBLIC RELATIONS
825 THIRD AVENUE
NEW YORK, NY 10022
212-885-0300
Fax: 212-885-0570
www.hillandknowlton.com
• Paul Taaffe, Chairman & Chief Executive Officer
(212) 885-0300
paul.taaffe@hillandknowlton.com
• Tony Burgess-Webb, Chief Marketing Officer/EV
tburgess@hillandknowlton.com
• Juan Capello, President and Managing Partner, Latin America
(212) 885-0334
juan.cappello@hillandknowlton.com
• Mike Coates, President and Chief Executive Officer, H
(416) 413-4606
michael.coates@hillandknowlton.ca
• Ian Bailey, Executive Vice President & General Manager

Event Management Services:
Event promotion/coordination; event publicity.

Services:
Public relations firm with services that range from marketing communications, corporate reputation management to political lobbying. Caters to the technology and health industries.

Clients:
Microsoft, Intel, Allied Bakeries, Ambev - Cerveceria Rio, Ariel P&G, baidu.com, Boots Nurofen, British Horseracing, Debswana, First Alert - Carbon Monoxide, Geox Respira, Heal Florida Healthcare, HP Elle, HP Photo Big Bang, i.Dolphin, International Truck, Labatt Sterling, Lock&Lock, London 2012, Lucky Loonie, Motorola Razr, Pacific Gas & Electric, Pfizer Detrol, SCIO, Sega Sonic, Smithsonian, Starbucks Muan Jai, The Maldives, The Palm, UK Trade & Investment, Ziggs

Marketing & Consulting Services:
Spokesperson identification/training.

Other Locations:
222 Merchandise Mart Plaza, Chicago, IL 60654. 312-255-1200; FAX: 312-255-3554, 808 Travis, Suite 2100, Houston, TX 77002. 713-752-1900; FAX: 713-752-1930, 10 Corporate Park, Suite 200, Irvine, CA 92606. 949-223-2300; FAX: 949-752-2130, 700 NE Multnomah, Suite 975, Portland, OR 97232. 503-248-9468; FAX: 503-274-7689, 2127 Fifth Avenue, Seattle, WA 98121. 206-728-1100; FAX: 206-728-1106, 421 W Riverside, Suite 450, Spokane, WA 99201. 509-744-3350; FAX: 509-744-3355, 106 E College Avenue, Suite 730, Tallahassee, FL 32301. 850-22-4100; FAX: 850-222-0075

HIVE
507 KING STREET E
UNIT 16
TORONTO, ONTARIO, CANADA M5A1M3
416-203-1339
www.thehive.ca

Services:
Advertising and promotion of the wares and services of others namely, conceiving, preparing, directing, and carrying out marketing promotions for others and conceiving, preparing, directing and carrying out advertising campaigns for others by: conceiving, preparing, directing and carrying

out events, meetings, and travel for others, advertising and promotion of wares and services of others, by mailings and printed matter for direct mail, print advertising, or outdoor media, dissemination on the internet, production of advertising messages for radio, television and the internet, copywriting, art direction, and concept generation

HOPE-BECKHAM, INC.
17 EXECUTIVE PARK DRIVE
SUITE 600
ATLANTA, GA 30329
404-636-8200
Fax: 404-636-0530
info@hopebeckham.com
www.hopebeckham.com
• Paul Beckham, Chairman
• Bob Hope, President, Co-Founder
bhope@hopebeckham.com
• Tom Hughes, Vice President
• Michael King, Vice President
• Garet Hayes, Vice President
• Ann Nelson, Vice President
Finance/Administration
anelson@hopebeckham.com
• Dick Stevens, Managing Director Event Marketing
• Chad Wallace, Project Director
• Dave Van Voorhis, Director Business Development
Nature of Service:
Public Relations, Event Marketing, Media Relations, Consulting and Web Integration.
Year Founded:
1994
Marketing & Consulting Services:
Consults on operations and marketing with leagues, teams, events and corporations on programming, financial and marketing issues with television and communications companies.
Clients:
Acuity, General Motors, Arcapita, Georgia Lottery Corporation, Atlanta Spirit LLC, Heavy Inc., Atlanta Sports Council, Help A Child Smile, BIKE - A division of Russell Corporation, Honduras Outreach Inc., Jones Day, Bugaboo Creek Steakhouse, LPGA (Ladies Professional Golf Association), Caribou Coffee, Learning Disabilities Association of Georgia, Channel One Network, McCormick & Schmick's Seafood Restaurant, ChoicePoint, Mount Bethel Christian Academy, Church's Chicken, Overtime Magazine, Coca-Cola Company, Southern Company, Comcast Cable Communications, Trinity House, Feld Entertainment, Women's Sports Foundation, Fisher & Phillips, Flagstar

HORROW SPORTS VENTURES
6800 SW 40TH STREET
SUITE 174
MIAMI, FL 33155
561-743-6408
Fax: 305-559-6737
info@horrowsports.com
www.horrowsports.com
• Rick Horrow, President
rhorrow@horrowsports.com
• Karla Swatek, Vice-President
Services:
Advisor to Teams and Leagues, Universities, Government Agencies, and Not-for-Profit Organizations. Experts in all aspects of Public/Private Partnership

Financing. Also, providers of solutions for complex team and entertainment facility development projects including coordination of public infrastructure objectives.
Clients:
NFL, NASCAR, Baltimore Orioles, New York Mets, National Association of Proffesional Baseball Leagues, CBS Sportsline USA, State of Virginia/ Virginia Tourism Corporation, Great White Shark Enterprises, Alabama Sports Foundation/City of Birmingham/Jefferson County Civic Center Authority, Hampton Roads Partnership, Metropolitan Richmond Business Foundation, Cleveland Indians, Columbus (OHIO) Community Development Council, Ladies Professional Golf Association and International Management Group.
Marketing & Consulting Services:
Specializes in serving in the creation of sports organizations and sports teams; facility development services for sports teams; and evaluating markets for expansion for sports organizations, leagues and teams.

HOST COMMUNICATIONS, INC.
546 E MAIN STREET
LEXINGTON, KY 40508
859-226-4678
imgassociations@imgworld.com
• Thomas J. Stultz, Senior Vice President/Managing Director
• David Bertram, VP National Priorities
• Tim Campbell, Vice President Sponsorship Sales - Western US
• Steve Cornwell, Executive Vice President Operations
• Lisa Fluty, Chief Information Officer
• Lawton Logan, Executive Vice President Sales
Nature of Service:
Creates opportunities for corporations to connect with specific audiences, who ultimately impact their growth and success.
Year Founded:
1972
College Bowl Game Sponsor:
Gator Bowl Foundation - The Patch Partner

HOST MANAGED EVENTS
546 E MAIN STREET
LEXINGTON, KY 40508
859-226-4678
imgassociations@imgworld.com
• Thomas Stultz, Senior Vice President/Managing Director
• David Bertram, VP National Priorities
• Dave Cawood, EVP, Administration and Collegiate Marke
• Tim Campbell, VP Media
Event Consulting Services:
Organization excels at staging and producing large, participatory grassroots sporting events domestically and internationally, and creating fully integrated marketing platforms, interactive events, tours, sampling programs, mobile marketing units, golf projects and fan fest events. Organization owns the NBA Hoop-It-Up, the official 3-on-3 basketball tour of the NBA, and Got Milk? 3v3 Soccer Shootout, the official 3v3 tour of Major League Soccer. Other projects include producing the NCAA Hoop CIty interactive events at the Men's Final Four and Women's Final Four, as well as at Frozen Fest during the Division I Men's Ice Hockey Championship.

Services:
One of the top five in the world of sports marketing. The company offers significantly diverse services with operating areas that include Collegiate Marketing and the NCAA, Association Management, Printing & Publishing, Radio and Television.

Clients:
Alltel, Coca Cola Deloitte & Touche, Dodge, Foot Locker, got milk?, IBM, Kraft Foods, New Balance, Pevonia Botanica, Methode Physiodermie, State Farm Insurance, Toys R Us

HUGHES SPORTS MARKETING
1141 S 7TH STREET
ST LOUIS, MO 63104
314-571-6300
Fax: 314-571-6300
• Jim Schnurbusch, Contact
Services:
Brand Positioning and Planning, Corporate Identity, Direct Marketing, Graphic Design, Guerrilla Marketing, Interactive Media Media Relations and Planning, Non-traditional Advertising (ambient and created media), Public Relations, Sales Promotion, Traditional Advertising (print, radio, TV), Web Site Design and Development

IEG, LLC
350 NORTH ORLEANS STREET
SUITE 1200
CHICAGO, IL 60654
312-944-1727
800-834-4850
Fax: 312-944-1897
www.sponsorship.com
• Jim Andrews, Senior Vice President, Content Strategy
• Shan Riggs, Vice President, IEG Client Solutions
Services:
IEG is the leading provider of consulting, valuation, measurement, research and training to the global sponsorship industry. IEG's sponsorship objective is to maximize sponsorship revenue for properties and maximize return on investment for sponsors.
Sports Service Founded:
1982
Marketing & Consulting Services:
From Sponsorship Valuation and Sponsorship Consulting Services to newsletters, conferences and customized research, IEG has the knowledge and resources to take yor sponsorship efforts to the next level. Because IEG neither sells sponsorship nor manages sponsors programs, they offer unbiased analysis and recommendations. IEG helps properties determine what their sponsorships are worth and hot to retain and grow current partnerships. As well as helps sponsors select the right opportunity, measure their sponsorship ROI and research their competitors' sponsorships.
Clients:
Dallas Cowboys, FIFA World Cup, NFL, MLS, U.S. Open Cycling Championship, Chicago Blackhawks, Miami Heat, Diageo, JPMorgan Chage, ING

IGNITION, INC.
101 MARIETTA STREET NW
6TH FLOOR
ATLANTA, GA 30303

678-701-0369
Fax: 678-701-0393
• Mark Driscoll, Founder
(678) 701-0369
dill@ignition-inc.com
• John Piester, Executive Vice President
• Susan Driscoll, Founder
• Dill Driscoll, Founder
• Mikey Hersom, Owner and President
• Cindy A Hersom, Owner and CMO
• Andi McWhorter, Chief Financial officer
• Amanda Daniels, VP
Services:
On the street activations, sampling
programs, mobile tours, sponsorship
management, motosports. Hospitality
programs include design, development and
implementation, merchandise, signage and
promotion.
Other Locations:
3 Harvest Lane, Tinton Falls, NJ 07724.
732-578-0035; FAX: 732-578-0089, 130
Taconic Business Park Road, Manchester,
VT 05255. 802-366-8200; FAX:
802-366-8220
Clients:
Coca-Cola, Fanta, Burger King, Delta,
AT&T, eBay, Sprite, CNN, Southern Fried
Football, Discovery Channel, Banquet, John
Deere, Microsoft, Indy Racing Gear

IMAGE MARKETING
1428 ORCHARD LAKE DRIVE
CHARLOTTE, NC 28270
704-849-2288
Fax: 704-849-2292
imarkinc@aol.com
• Don Doby, President/Media Relations
Marketing & Consulting Services:
Represents sponsors with respect to their
involvement in auto sports.

IMAGES USA
1320 ELLSWORTH INDUSTRIAL
BOULEVARD
BLDG. C
ATLANTA, GA 30318
404-892-2931
Fax: 404-892-8651
• Robert L McNeil, Jr., President/Chief
Executive Officer
• Robert L. McNeil, President & CEO
• John Lockyer, EVP Finance/Business
Management, Chief Operat
• Maria M. Moffitt, Vice President, Director
of Client Services
• Juan Quevedo, Director Market
Intelligence
• Shawn Arthur, Creative Director
• Hank Ernest, Director Public Relations
Nature of Service:
International and domestic advertising,
ethnic marketing, public relations, market
research and event marketing and
consulting
Year Founded:
1989
Event Management Services:
Provides event coordination, including
advertising for corporate sponsorship,
specialized promotions, and a wide range of
corporate hospitality services. Represents
sports events for sponsorship sales and
marketing.
Clients:
Army/ROTC, EPA, Georgia Lottery, Goody
Products, Atlanta DeKalb, Cox

Communications, Sprint, American Institute
for Managing Diversity, Fulton County Arts
Council, Scientific Games, CDC, DHR
Georgia Department of Human Resources,
Coca-Cola, McDonalds, United States
Environmental Protection Agency,
Compucredit, Roche, Wachovia

IMPACT MANAGEMENT GROUP, INC.
124 W CAPITOL AVENUE
SUITE 1886
LITTLE ROCK, AR 72201
501-244-9600
Fax: 501-244-9601
• Richard Bearden, Partner
bearden@img-partners.com
• Terry Benham, Owner & President
Marketing & Consulting Services:
Broad range of professional services for
corporations interested in using sports or
event marketing to increase sales and
awareness of their products. Also offers
consulting and administrative assistance to
sports organizations, including sales and
marketing planning, multimedia sales
representation and expense reduction
activities. Impact Management Group has
teamed up with Integrated Sports Partners,
for a consortium of 6 NCAA Div I
Conferences. IMG also administers
Kentucky High School sports awards
program.
Sports Service Founded:
1992

IMPRESS SPORTS INC
7800 THE BLUFFS
SUITE C
ATLANTA, GA 30336
678-391-6217
Fax: 678-428-0018
• Richard Wheeler, President
• Danny Jasiczek, Vice President Sales
Marketing & Consulting Services:
Specializing in the production and
distribution of custom point-of-sale displays,
in-store signs, pennants, banners, posters,
growth-charts, and more.
Description:
ImPress Sports is a print production
company focused on providing small to
large quantity promotional materials for
sports, event and product marketers.
ImPress Sports offers creative development,
production and distribution of custom
point-of-sale, posters, standees, banners,
growth posters, collateral, merchandisers,
pennant strings and more.

INFOUSA
1020 E 1ST STREET
PAPILLION, NE 68046
402-593-4500
800-835-5856
Fax: 402-331-1505
ir@infousa.com
www.infousa.com
• Edward C Mallin, President
• Bill L. Fairfield, President/CEO
• Mark Puljan, VP Central Region
• Jason Morris, Regional Manager Mid
Market Solutions
Nature of Services:
InfoUSA is a provider of sales leads, mail,
email and telemarketing lists that helps
companies manage their sales databases
through standardizing, updating, and

enhancing their current systems with
valuable, insightful information.

INNOVATIVE MARKETING CONSULTANTS
4284 SHORELINE DRIVE
SPRING PARK, MN 55384
952-252-1254
877-674-8206
Fax: 952-417-8146
info@imcsuccess.com
www.imcsuccess.com
• Shane Erickson, President/Chief Executive
Officer
• Paul Higgins, Operations Manager
• Paul Yahnke, National Sales Manager
• Adam Tschida, Senior Account Executive
adam@imcsuccess.com
• Robert Ed, Marketing Specialist
robert@imcsuccess.com
Nature of Services:
Innovative Marketing Consultants
manufactures on-premise promotional
marketing products for a variety of industries
including Sports Marketing (Sports Beads),
the Retail and Beverage Markets, and
Casinos.

INSIGHT SPORTS MANAGEMENT CO, LLC
8941 MILLER LANE
VIENNA, VA 22180
703-255-6588
Fax: 301-371-8095
• Anne Cook, Director, Club Operations
Marketing & Consulting Services:
Provides staffing, programming and
marketing services to tennis facilities in the
Mid-Atlantic region. Tennis event design,
promotion and management. Full range of
tennis club membership promotions and
sales efforts.

INTEGRITY SPORTS MARKETING, MEDIA & MANAGEMENT
228 ROUNDWAY DOWN
PO BOX 1064
DAVIDSON, NC 28036
704-896-8181
Fax: 704-896-8441
ContactUs@is3m.com
www.is3m.com
• Pat Millen, President, Chief Executive
Officer
(704) 896-8181
pmillen@is3m.com
• S. G. Pat Millen, President/CEO
patmillen@IS3M.com
Services:
Consultants to the soccer industry, ISM
provides strategic planning guidance,
creation and implementation for television,
print, video, digital and web-oriented
projects.
Clients:
US Youth Soccer, NSCAA, ACOG, FIFA,
CONCACAF, Caribbean Football Union,
NCAA, WUSA, ACC, Big East, Adidas,
MLS, Eurosport, Quokka Sports
Sports Service Founded:
1992
Event Management Services:
ISM is a multimedia sports marketing
consulting firm with an emphasis on soccer.

INTERFERENCE
611 BROADWAY
SUITE 819
NEW YORK, NY 10012
212-995-8553
info@interferenceinc.com
www.interferenceinc.com
• Sam Tr Ewen, Chief Executive Officer
• Michael Glickman, Event Marketing President
(212) 995-8553
Description:
Specializes in Guerilla/street marketing. Works to develop non-traditional Ad/marketing campaigns designed to grab the attention of others. Their style is considered alternative and unique in grabbing the attention of the consumers and forming a brand message.

INTERNATIONAL SPORTS MARKETING CONSULTANTS, LTD.
HAYBARN HOUSE
118 SOUTH STREET
DORKING, SURREY, ENGLAND RH4 2EZ
44-1306-743322
Fax: 44-1306-743007
jobs@ismsearch.com
www.ismsearch.com
• Jack McMahon, President
• Fred Steinberg, VP
Marketing & Consulting Services:
A full service agency with worldwide sports sponsorship experience. Provides strategic planning and program development for the integration of sports into a company's mainstream communications operation. ISMC develops and implements all aspects of event creation and management including negotiations, advertising, promotion, media relations and research. ISMC has extensive experience in Olympic games marketing and operations, the application of information technology for scoring and statistics, as well as sports-oriented Web Site development and marketing.
Sports Service Founded:
1994

INTERNATIONAL SPORTS PROPERTIES, INC.
540 N TRADE STREET
WINSTON-SALEM, NC 27101
336-831-0700
Fax: 336-768-7681
www.imgcollege.com
• Ben Sutton, Jr., Chairman of the Board/Chief Executive Officer
• Rick Barakat, Vice President
• Dan Barrett, Associate Regional Vice President
• Matthew Carlomagno, Vice President, Human Resources
• Ben C. Sutton Jr., President
Nature of Service:
General sports marketing work, event management, sales driven, handles sponsorship sales activities on behalf of broadcast media, colleges, college conferences, facilities, corporations, etc.
Year Founded:
1992
Clients:
Virginia Tech, Wake Forest University, Marshall University, University of Cincinnati, Georgia Tech, Southern Miss, Ohio University, Vanderbilt University, University of Alabama, University of Missouri, Syracuse University.

INTROMARK INC
217 NINTH STREET
PITTSBURG, PA 15222
800-851-6030
888-648-4332
Fax: 412-338-0497
licensing@intromark.com
www.intromark.com
Services:
Patent referral, submission of invention/ideas to industries for reviews. Offers inventors and entrepreneurs a variety of seminars, presentations and panel discussions to help pursue ideas.

INVENTION TECHNOLOGIES
2655 LE JEUNE ROAD
SUITE 550
CORAL GABLES, FL 33134-5846
786-437-8801
800-940-9020
Fax: 305-255-4515
info@invent-tech.com
Services:
Offers strategic marketing and global representation of inventors in the sale or license of their new product concepts; assists in the comprehensive research and documentation of product ideas and utilize aggressive and creative promotional techniques to introduce these ideas to industry; Handles all subsequent follow-up and negotiations with interested parties with the intent of securing a licensing agreement.

IRWIN BROH RESEARCH
1011 E TOUHY AVENUE
SUITE 450
DES PLAINES, IL 60018
847-297-7515
Fax: 847-297-7847
www.irwinbroh.com
• David L. Waitz, President/Chief Executive Officer
dwaitz@irwinbroh.com
• Thomas E. Jackowiak, Vice President
(847) 297-7515
tjockowiak@irwinbroh.com
• Robert J. Rowe, Executive Vice President
browe@irwinbroh.com
General Description:
Irwin Broh Research is a full-service marketing research firm based in Des Plaines, Illinois. For over 45 years, they have been providing insight to a wide variety of clients who want to know what their customers and prospects are thinking.
Sports Services Founded:
1971
Market Research & Consulting:
Specializing in the leisure time industry. Services include focus group research, market analyses, acquisition studies, sales forecasting, customer satisfaction, new product potential, market segmentation, awareness & usage, advertising research, retail site location and more. In-house facilities include focus group center, telephone interviewing center and data processing department.
Sporting Goods Market Database:
All major sports covered. Source is the annual consumer survey for NSGA'S THE SPORTING GOODS MARKET report.
Covers 63 individual sporting goods items, more than 20 sport categories. Other syndicated reports available for golf, sporting goods equipment, and sports footwear.

J PATTON SPORTS MARKETING
3450 RIVERGREEN COURT
DULUTH, GA 30096
770-612-0400
Fax: 770-612-0439
questions@jpattonsports.com
Auto Sports:
Indianapolis Motor Speedway - Digital Asst Management Services, Online Artwork Approval Systems, Holographic Brand Protection
Ice Hockey:
ECHL - Corporate Sponsor - Exclusive Supplier of Hologram Products.
The Collegiate Licensing Company:
Digital Asset Management Services, holographic Brand Protection
National Hockey League:
Digital Asset Management Services, Online Artwork Approval System
NASCAR:
Online Artwork Approval System
PGA Tour:
Digital Assest Management Services, Holographic Brand Protection

JACK ROUSE ASSOCIATES
600 VINE STREET
SUITE 1700
CINCINNATI, OH 45202
513-381-0055
Fax: 513-381-2691
www.jackrouse.com
• Keith James, President
kjames@jackrouse.com
• Jack Rouse, Chief Executive Officer
• Shawn McCoy, VP Marketing & Business Development
smccoy@jackrouse.com
• Amy Merrell, Chief Operating Officer
• Brian Donahue, Senior Project Director
• Randy Smith, Senior Project Director
Nature of Sports Service:
Creates attractions at sports venues designed to enhance fans' experiences and increase per caps revenue. Attractions include halls of fame, museums, interactive games/exhibitory, retail. Works with sponsor companies to design sponsored entertainment areas.
Services:
Provides a full range of planning, design, media and production management services.
Clients:
American Royal Museum and Visitor Center, Chisholm Trail Heritage Center, Columbus Zoo Pachyderm Exhibit, Enginuity, Texas Wild! at the Fort Worth Zoo, Fort Siloso at Sentosa Island, The National Underground Railroad Freedom Center, All About You, Cincinnati Museum of Natural History and Science, Head First! Theater at HealthSpace Cleveland, Journey to the Model T, The Arab American National Museum, Public Landing Gallery at The Cincinnati History Museum, The Wyoming Territorial Prison and End-of-Tracks Town, Western North Carolina Nature Center, AEGIS Theater, The National Park Service Washington Monument Interpretive Center,

African Rift Va
Current Projects:
Atlanta Braves Plaza & Scout's Alley;
Cincinnati Reds Museum & Hall of Fame;
Dayton USA; Green Bay Packers Hall of
Fame; Jack Nicklaus Museum; University of
Kentucky Basketball Museum; Ohio State
University Hall of Fame; San Diego Padres
Plaza.

JACKSON DAWSON MOTOR SPORTS
2 TASK INDUSTRIAL COURT
GREENVILLE, SC 29607
864-272-3000
800-722-3234
Fax: 864-272-3040
customer.service@jacksonmg.com
www.jacksonmg.com
Marketing & Consulting Services:
Locates sponsors for drivers, teams, and
sports events. Also produces decals for
sponsors, teams and events. Primary
specialty is motorsports.
Event Management Services:
Hospitality, catering and other services
involved in the implementation of sports
events. Display and promotion tours and
program implementation.

JHG TOWNSEND
6215 FERRIS SQUARE
SUITE 210
SAN DIEGO, CA 92121
888-246-2396
www.jhg.com
• Alex Benjamin, VP Finance & Operations
• Jayne Hancock, President/CEO
• Lisa Kendall, VP Business Partnerships
• Liya Sharif, VP Public Relations & Brand
Strategy
• Mary Fechtig, President/CEO
• Elizabeth E Cooper, Co-Founder
• Alex Benjamin, SVPof Finance &
Operations
• Cindy Subido, SVP
• Jacob Shea, EVP of Interactive &
technology
Nature of Services:
JHG is a San Diego-based marketing
agency serving the media, entertainment,
sports, and technology sectors that
integrates marketing strategy, branding,
public relations, interactive services, mobile
technology, and metrics to propel client
companies to success in the changing
marketplace.

JOYCE JULIUS AND ASSOCIATES, INC.
1225 EISENHOWER PLACE
SUITE 3
ANN ARBOR, MI 48108
734-971-1900
877-302-6389
Fax: 734-585-3451
www.joycejulius.com
• Cindy Shevrovich, President
cindy@joycejulius.com
• Robert Cotman, Chief Executive Officer
• Leslie Butler, Comptroller
• Jeff Meeson, IIT Director
• Laura Webb, Vice President Sales
(734) 971-1900
lwebb@joycejulius.com
• Eric Wright, Vice President
Research/Development
(734) 971-1900
ewright@joycejulius.com

• Cathie Joynt, Account Representative
(734) 971-1900
cathie@joycejulius.com
• David Yott, Managing Editor-Series
Reports
(734) 971-1900
dyott@joycejulius.com
• Raymond Howland, Managing
Editor-Special Reports
(734) 971-1900
rhowland@joycejulius.com
Services:
Provides comprehensive documentation of
in-broadcast brand exposure during sports,
special event, and entertainment television
programming. Provides complete
impression measurement of a sponsorship
program.
Sports Service Founded:
1985
Clients:
ABC, AFL, AMA, Anaheim Ducks, AVP,
Bank of America, Baylor University, Best
Buy, Boston Red Sox, Calgary Exhib. &
Stamp., Callaway, CBS, CFL, Champ Car,
Chicago Rush, Cotton Bowl Committee,
DaimlerChrysler, Detroit Lions, Eastman
Kodak, ESPN, FedEx, Ford Motor
Company, Fox, General Motors, GMR
Marketing, Gold Eagle Company, Golf
Channel, Gr. Phoenix Visit & Conv., Holiday
Inn, IMG, IRL, J. Walker Thompson, Just
Marketing, Latham Entertainment, Live
Nation, Miami Heat, Millsport LLC, MLB,
Momentum World Wide, NASCAR, National
Geographic, NBA, NBC, NCAA, N.O./Okh C.
Hornets, NFL, NHL, Octagon, Orlando
Predators, Palace of Auburn Hills, PGA Tour
Marketing & Consulting Services:
Consultation for corporate sponsors their
current programs and available program
options evaluating. Recommendations
based on corporate marketing objectives.
With marketing research service, NTIV can
provide pre and post event media analysis,
assistance with graphic design and
placement for optimum exposure.

JTR PRODUCTIONS
1515 MARLBOROUGH DRIVE
PO BOX 3056
ANN ARBOR, MI 48104-6222
734-994-0138
JTRProductions@sbcglobal.net
www.jtrproductions.com
• John T. Reid, President
(734) 994-0138
jreid66206@aol.com
Sports Service Founded:
1991
Event Management Services:
Produces football games for black colleges.
Specialists in all aspects of game
coordination, production and marketing.

JUMPIN' JACK SPORTS
333 OCEAN BOULEVARD
HAMPTON BEACH, NH 03842
603-957-6222
www.jumpinjacksjava.com
• Jack Fleming, President
College Bowl Game Sponsor:
College - University of North Carolina
through 2007-2008.

JUST MARKETING INTERNATIONAL
10960 BENNETT PARKWAY
ZIONSVILLE, IN 46077
317-344-1900
Fax: 317-344-1901
info@justmarketing.com
www.justmarketing.com
• Zak Brown, Founder, CEO
Nature of Service:
Strategic consultation, Research and
evaluation; Sponsorship development,
negotiation and management; Integrated
promotion planning and execution; Event
creation, Marketing and management;
Hospitality and corporate entertainment;
Customized driving events.

K & S PROMOTIONS
34 BAREFOOT HILL ROAD
SHARON, MA 2067
781-784-0100
• Bob Myerson, President
(781) 784-0100
Marketing & Consulting Services:
Develops and implements sports promotions
including corporate hospitality, sports
celebrity appearances, memorabilia
give-aways etc. Frequently utilized for client
entertaining, sales incentives, and
sweepstakes.

KAGAN WORLD MEDIA
40 RAGSDALE DRIVE
SUITE 250
MONTEREY, CA 93940
831-624-1536
800-307-2529
Fax: 831-641-0961
www.snl.com
• Paul Kagan, Chairman/Chief Executive
Officer
• Harvey Kraft, Marketing Director
• John Mansell, Senior Analyst/Consultant
• Robin Flynn, Senior Consultant
rflynn@kagan.com
Products:
Databooks, Newsletters, Conferences on
Kagan's CD, Industry Reports, Kagan
Events
Services:
Appraisals and Consulting
Sports Service Founded:
1969
Marketing & Consulting Services:
Appraisals and valuations of sports teams
and sports media interests.

KARLITZ & CO.
570 SEVENTH AVENUE
SUITE 1004
NEW YORK, NY 10018
646-289-8900
Fax: 646-289-8911
info@karlitz.com
www.karlitz.com
• Herb Karlitz, President/Founder
hkarlitz@karlitz.com
• Herb Karlitz, President
(646) 289-8901
hkarlitz@karlitz.com
Sports Service Founded:
1995
Services:
Entertainment/Lifestyle and Event Marketing
Clients:
A Better Chance, American Airlines,
American Film Institute, AT&T, Cendant,

799

Children Uniting Nations, CIT, Coca-Cola, Cohn & Wolfe, Entertainment Industry Foundation, Glaxo Smith Kline, IBM, Kraft Foods, The March of Dimes, Morgan Stanley, Nabisco, Napa Valley Vintners Association, The New York Times, The Rusty Staub Foundation, Scholarship America, Sentient Jet, Serta, Sony, Stamps.com, U.S. Postal Service, Vespa
Marketing & Consulting Services:
Serves in a continuing advisory capacity with clients relating to sports marketing involvement and sponsorship.

KART MARKETING INTERNATIONAL, INC
PO BOX 101
WHEATON, IL 60187
630-746-4164
Fax: 630-653-2637
karting@msn.com
• Darrell Sitarz, President/CEO
• Darrell Sitarz, President, CEO
• Len Manley, Sales
(859) 983-9234
Description:
Marketing for Go-Kart Industry (Motorsports); Trade Show Producer (Kart Expo International); News and Information website.
Sports Service Founded:
1990
Publications:
KARTING INDUSTRY BUYER'S GUIDE; KART MARKETING INTERNATIONAL (KMI).

KATZ MEDIA GROUP, INC/RADIO
125 W 55TH STREET
NEW YORK, NY 10019
212-424-6000
Fax: 212-424-6110
www.katz-media.com
• Stu Olds, Chief Executive Officer
(212) 424-6780
stu.olds@katz-media.com
• Robert Damon, Chief Financial Officer
(212) 424-6880
robert.damon@katz-media.com
• David Prager, Chief Information Officer
(212) 424-6704
david.prager@katz-media.com
• Theresa Frasca, Public Relations Manager
(312) 755-3817
Services:
Advertising
Sports Service Founded:
1992
Event Management Services:
Develops and implements integrated sports communication programs utilizing properties in the NFL, NBA, MLB, NHL and Division I college football and basketball to assist clients in achieving specific sales and marketing goals. Services include customized media, merchandising, and promotion.
Marketing & Consulting Services:
Exclusive broadcast marketing representative of college and professional sports franchises. Provides account servicing and consulting from concept to completion on national, regional and local sports marketing programs.

KCA ENTERPRISES INC
124 N MAIN STREET
ASHLAND CITY, TN 37015

615-792-2664
800-805-5654
• Jim Jackson, President
(800) 805-5654
Services:
Providing fund raising ideas and logoed products

KCSA PUBLIC RELATIONS WORLDWIDE
880 THIRD AVENUE
6TH FLOOR
NEW YORK, NY 10022
212-682-6300
Fax: 212-697-0910
www.kcsa.com
• Herbert L. Corbin, Founding Partner
hcorbin@kcsa.com
• Jeffrey Corbin, Managing Partner/Chief Executive Officer
jcorbin@kcsa.com
• Todd Fromer, Managing Partner/Investor Relations
tformer@kcsa.com
Services:
Corporate guidance, integrated financial/investor relations, and sophisticated business and consumer marketing communications services.
Sports Service Founded:
1952
Event Management Services:
Manages all aspects of sports event for public relations and marketing purposes - experienced in motorsports sponsorships, Pay-Per-View sports and entertainment, running, basketball, wrestling, all major league sports, sports publishing, corporate sponsorship and promotions. Works with organizations, corporations, publications, broadcasting, retail/apparel and travel related companies.
Clients:
Investor Relations Clients: 4Kids Entertainment, Inc. - (NYSE: KDE), Acies Corp. - (OTC BB: ACIE), ADDvantage Technologies Group, Inc - (Amex: AEY), Alexander & Baldwin, Inc. - (NASDAQ: ALEX); American Scientific Resources; American Stock Exchange; Arbitron Inc. - (NYSE: ARB); Authentidate - (NASDAQ: ADAT); Axiom Global Partners; Deutsche Telekom - (NYSE: DT); Dewey Electronics Corporation - (NASDAQ: DEWY); Docucorp International, Inc. - (NASDAQ DOCC); EVCI Career Colleges Holding Corp. - (NASDAQ: EVCI); General Steel Holdings Inc. - (OTC BB: GSHO.OB); Global Traffic Network

KETCHUM NEW YORK
1285 AVENUE OF THE AMERICAS
FOURTH FLOOR
NEW YORK, NY 10019
646-935-3900
ray.kotcher@ketchum.com
www.ketchum.com
• Rob Flaherty, Senior Partner/President
• Rob Flaherty, Senior Partner, CEO
rob.flaherty@ketchum.com
• Ray Kotcher, Senior Partner & Chairman
(646) 935-3902
ray.kotcher@ketchum.com
Description:
Ketchum Sports Network (KSN) - KSN creates and manages sponsorship programs. Organizations they have worked with includes but is not limited to: National Football League/NFL, College Football, NASCAR, Major League Baseball/MLB,

Olympic Games, Professional Soccer, Golf, Tennis and boating.
Services:
Brand marketing, Corporate communications, Food and nutrition communications, Healthcare communications, Media relations and strategy, Communications training and message development, Issues and crisis management, Change management consulting services, Entertainment marketing, Sports marketing, Multicultural marketing, Investor relations
Specialties:
Brand Marketing, Corporate, Food & Nutrition, Healthcare, Media Relations, Communications Training & Message Development, Issues & Crisis Management, Investor Relations, Ketchum Design, Ketchum Productions, Account Planning & Research, Knowledge Center, Concentric Communications, KEM(Ketchum Entertainment Marketing), Media Strategy, Creative Specialty Services, Global Research, Sports Marketing

KEYSTONE MARKETING, INC.
709 NORTH MAIN STREET
WINSTON-SALEM, NC 27101
336-777-3473
Fax: 336-354-0047
www.keystonemarketing.net
• Roger Bear, Chairman
rbear@keystonemarketing.net
• David Scheumann, President
dscheumann@keystonemarketing.net
• Candy Borreson, Marketing SVP
cborreson@keystonemarketing.net
• Mike Grice, President/Chief Creative Officer
(336) 354-0038
mike.grice@keystonemarketing.net
Services:
Research, Multimedia design and production, Graphic design services
Clients:
Kraft Foods, The Hershey Company, NTN Bearings, Checkers Restaurants, Jim Beam Brands, Dremel, Toyota Motor Sales USA, Inc.
Marketing & Consulting Services:
Complete sports marketing services including promotion, sponsorship consulting and management, account specific marketing, hospitality and public relations.
Event Management Services:
Manages sports marketing programs for the Planters' and Life Savers' Divisions of Nabisco Foods, Reckitt & Coleman, Rhodes Furniture, The Pfizer Company, Schneider National Trucking, Mallory Ignitions, Manager of Clarence Rose, PGA Tour. Heilig-Meyers Company, and golf activities for Northern Telecom. Also manages marketing efforts for Show Car programs for Heilig-Meyers Furniture and Barbasol Race Teams.
Sports Service Founded:
1989
Clients:
Kraft Foods, Jim Beam Brands, Pfizer, Hershey Foods Corporation, US Army, NVE Pharmaceuticals, Dremel, NTN Bearings, Toyota Motor Sales USA

KIKU OBATA & COMPANY
6161 DELMAR BOULEVARD
SUITE 200
ST LOUIS, MO 63112-1203
314-361-3110
www.kikuobata.com
• Kiku Obata, President
(314) 505-8414
kiku_obata@kikuobata.com
• Kevin Flynn, EVP
(314) 505-8418
kflynn@kikuobata.com
• David Leavey, Senior Architect
(314) 505-8440
dleavey@kikuobata.com
Year Founded:
1977
Description:
An expert at crafting fan experiences. For over thirty years, we have created strategies and design for sports, entertainment and retail brands and destinations around the world.
Clients:
Scottrade Center, Palace of Auburn Hills, St. Louis Cardinals, Sports Service, Comerica Park, Coors Field, AC St. Louis, Carolina Panthers, Target, Eco Shoppe, Whole Foods and Brown Shoe

KIVETT PRODUCTIONS
2543 SAINT HEATHER WAY
ORLANDO, FL 3206
407-342-0752
joe@cardstunts.com
www.giantamericanflag.com
• Joe Kivett, President
(407) 342-0752
joe@cardstunts.com
Services:
Kivett Productions manufactures giant American flags for major sporting events.
Founded:
1991
Clients Include:
NFL, MLB, NASCAR, NBA, NHL, NCAA, MLS, Coca-Cola, Nike, Pepsi, Home Depot, Australian Football League, Canadian Football League

KLINGE & ASSOCIATES, JOHN G.
25 STURGES HIGHWAY
WESTPORT, CT 6880
203-255-0829
• John G. Klinge, President
Sports Service Founded:
1986
Event Management Services:
Sponsor selection.
Marketing & Consulting Services:
Market analysis, media analysis, consumer research, sports premiums, promotions (trade and consumer), sports collectibles (cards, posters).

KNOX SPORTS MARKETING
13063 W LINEBAUGH AVENUE
TAMPA, FL 33626
813-891-6653
Fax: 813-891-6768
kmcmahon@knoxsports.com
• Paul Sickmon, President
(813) 891-6653
psickmon@knoxsports.com
• Kaitlyn McMahon, New Business Manager
(813) 891-6653
kmcmahon@knoxsports.com

• Jennifer Hope, Director, Client Services
(813) 891-6653
jhope@knoxsports.com
• Morgan Swem, Social Media Manager
(813) 891-6653
mswem@knoxsports.com
Specialties:
We assist clients in negotiating their sports sponsorships. Our expertise gives us the ability to think outside the box and create unique ways to meet our client's goals through the passionate fan base of sports teams and events.
Number of Members:
Four
Clients:
84 Lumber, Atlantic Coast Bank, BI-LO, CCM, Cirde K, Farm Bureau Insurance (Florida, Virginia, Texas, South Carolina), Huntington Bank, Hunters Kane's Furniture, Land o' Frost, Surgery Partners, St. Petersburg Times, Nash Finch.

LATINO SPORTS MARKETING, LLC
1901 FOURTH AVENUE
SUITE 300
SAN DIEGO, CA 92101
619-255-1027
Fax: 619-255-1504
• Anthony Eros, Chief Executive Officer and President
Description:
Full service sports marketing and consulting firm that creates vital relationships between companies and Latinos via sports.
Services:
Strategy/Consulting, Event Management
Clients:
Copa Tecate, U.S. Army, PGA Tour, Cartel Impacto, Inc., Curb Cup, Novamex, Sonrics, Latino Basketball Tournament, Host Communications, Heineken USA

LEADDOG MARKETING GROUP
440 9TH AVENUE
17TH FLOOR
NEW YORK, NY 10001
212-488-6530
Fax: 212-741-5013
www.leaddogmarketing.com
• Dan Mannix, President/CEO
(212) 488-6530
dan@leaddogmarketing.com
• Karen A Shnault, Sr.VP and Account Management
(212) 488-6530
karen@leaddogmarketing.com
• Lisa Hyman, Sr.VP and Integrated marketing
(212) 488-6530
lisa@leaddogmarketing.com
• Donna Providenti, COO
(212) 488-6530
donna@leaddogmarketing.com
• JG Robilotti, Sr. VP , Client Services
(212) 488-6530
jg@leaddogmarketing.com
• Dan Jahn, VP, Brand Promotions
(212) 488-6530
don@leaddogmarketing.com
• John Inguagiato, CFO
(212) 488-6530
Services:
Event Management and Production, Event Marketing, Magazine/Media Events, Sports Marketing, Promotions/Sweepstakes, Mobile Marketing, Design and Interactive Services.

Nature of Sports Service:
An independently-owned, NYC based full-service event marketing and brand promotion agency of 65 passionate people with satellite offices in Los Angeles, Chicago, Atlanta, Boston and Austin.LeadDog produces all aspects of consumer-focused experiences from ideation to execution, houses a full in-house design team and pays particular attention to developing turnkey strategies that deliver measurable results and align well with our clients' objectives.
Clients:
World Wrestling Entertainment, InStyle Magazine, American Cancer Society

LEADING IMAGE
54 KINGS FERRY ROAD
MONTROSE, NY 10548
914-739-5562
Fax: 914-739-5808
lsolomon@computer.net
• Lawrence Solomon, President
lsolomon@computer.net
Sports Service Founded:
1993
Marketing & Consulting Services:
Full range of sports, sporting goods and health and fitness marketing and promotion, public relations including publicity, new product introductions, strategic planning, special events, corporate sponsorships/celebrity endorsements, identity/image programs, infomercials, trade show/convention exhibit videos, VNR's, advertising, sales and marketing materials (print and video), marketing communications, internet marketing and World Wide Web ad design.
Other Office:
54 Main St., Terrytown, NY 10591 (Ph) 914-333-0722 (Fax) 914-333-0721.

LEIGH STOWELL & COMPANY
91 SOUTH JACKSON STREET
SUITE 4735
SEATTLE, WA 98194
206-727-2700
888-896-1641
Fax: 206-727-2898
main@stowellco.com
www.stowellco.com
• Leigh Stowell, Chief Executive Officer
• Sandy Schlee, EVP
• Craig Cripps, National Sales Director
Services:
Ascertainment, Market Roll-Out, Presentation Coaching, Market Visit Training, Weekly Video Email Training, Anytime Web-Based Software Training, Advanced Sales Skills Training, Visits with Key Clients and Agencies
Consulting Services:
Taking customized research to the next level integrating it around organizational objectives. Tactically assists North American sports, entertainment, and media organizations in the areas of sales, marketing, promotions, and business development based on proprietary annual surveys.
Sports & Entertainment:
Local customized research delivered in interactive software for sales, marketing, advertising, and promotional strategies. Conduct segmentation studies and measure

sports fan behaviors and attitudes. Focus on customer preferences and behavior in measuring event attendance, ticket purchases, media consumption, and product purchases. Also can analyze corporate, venue, talent, and brand attitudes. Discovering everything about customers and non-customers in local markets.

LESTER SPORTS & ENTERTAINMENT
PO BOX 481
HOPEWELL, NJ 08525
609-466-7905
Fax: 609-466-7562
pam.lester@lestersports.com
www.lestersports.com
• Pamela R. Lester, President
pam.lester@lestersports.com
Nature of Service:
Provides consulting services to the sports, entertainment, and licensing and merchandising industries, including, sports management and marketing, licensing and merchandising television.

LICENSING RESOURCE GROUP, INC.
442 CENTURY LANE
SUITE 100
HOLLAND, MI 49483
616-395-0676
Fax: 616-395-2517
www.lrgusa.com
• J. Lewis Hardy, President/CEO
(336) 896-7907
lewis@lrgusa.com
• Richard L. Rademaker, Founder/Chairman
(616) 395-0676
dick@lrgusa.com
• Gene Wandling, EVP/Chief Financial Officer
(319) 351-1776
gene@lrgusa.com
Nature of Service:
Provides its clients with the very best in service, from core management needs such as day-to-day administration, royalty management, compliance and enforcement, to marketing, merchandising, design and brand development.
Sports Service Founded:
1991
Clients:
University of Akron, University of Alabama in Huntsville, Alabama State University, Arizona State University, Austin Peay State University, Bemidji State University, Big East Conference, Bowling Green State University, Bradley University, Butler University, Cal State Fullerton, Cal State San Marcos, University of California Davis, University of California Santa Barbara, Campbell University, Canisius College, Case Western Reserve University, University of Central Arkansas, Central Colegiate Hockey Association, Central Connecticut State University, Central Michigan University, Charleston Southern University, Colorado College.
Marketing & Consulting Services:
Full service management company for college trademark licensing programs, including colleges, college conferences and college sports associations.

LIVE WIRE SPORTS GROUP
1260 N HANCOCK STREET
SUITE 105
ANAHEIM, CA 92807
714-777-7850
Fax: 714-777-7851
• Bill Hodson, Director
Nature of Services:
Advertising/Marketing, Custom Publishing, Digital Media, Sponsors Events, Media Planning/Buying, Market Research, Pilot Programs, Public Relations, Sports Management, Sponsor Development
Sports Service Founded:
2002

LOWENSTEIN EVENT MARKETING GROUP
11200 VALLEY HEIGHTS DRIVE
OWINGS MILLS, MD 21117
443-870-3657
Fax: 443-870-3547
info@lowensteinevents.com
www.lowensteinevents.com
• Lance Lowenstein, President
lance@lowensteinevents.com
• Barbara Bozzuto, Partner
Services:
Handles special event management, marketing and promotions, sponsorship packaging, and traveling tours.

MACKEY MARKETING GROUP, INC.
12 POWDER SPRINGS STREET
SUITE 220
MARIETTA, GA 30064
770-423-9593
info@mackeymarketing.com
www.mackeymarketing.com
• Brian C. Mackey, President
Services:
Specializes in event management, preparation, execution and publicizing of motorsports sponsorships.

MAKAI EVENTS AND PROMOTIONS
211 NEVADA STREET
EL SEGUNDO, CA 90245
310-546-9585
Fax: 310-321-7933
info@makaiinc.com
www.makaiinc.com
• Robbie Thain, President/Founder
• Linda Rosenberg, VP of Client Services
• Andrea Rackley, VP of Client Services
• Robbie Thain, Founder/President
Services:
Event Planning and Production, Guerilla Marketing, Product Sampling, Development and Execution of Promotional Campaigns, Warehouse Services and Equipment Rental, Integrated Media Services, Production services, Complete Creative Services, Cultural Marketing.
Nature of Sports Service:
Ch@lk T@lk is an online reporting system that gives clients real-time access to the events as the programs roll out.

MANDALAY ENTERTAINMENT COMPANY
4751 WILSHIRE BOULEVARD
3RD FLOOR
LOS ANGELES, CA 90010
323-549-4300
Fax: 323-549-9844
www.mandalay.com

• Peter Guber, Chairman/Chief Executive Officer
peterg@mandalay.com
• Paul Schaeffer, Vice Chairman/CEO
(323) 956-2400
pauls@mandalay.com
• Hank Stickney, Chief Executive Officer
• Ken Stickney, Managing Director
• Jon Spoelstra, President
Sports Service Founded:
1995
Services:
Specialize in managing professional sports franchises and venues throughout the country.
Clients:
Frisco Roughriders, Dayton Dragons, Erie Seawolves, Hagerstown Suns, Las Vegas 51s
Marketing & Consulting Services:
Movie production company that is using sports and specifically minor league baseball teams as a vehicle to create new entertainment channels, as well new markets for sponsors and advertisers to hit regional markets. Interested in producing sports movie productions. Owns the Dayton Dragons and Lake Elsinore Storm. Provides consulting services for TodaySports.com.

MARATHON
4655 S COACH DRIVE
TUCSON, AZ 85714-3467
520-202-2400
Fax: 520-202-2409
• Sue Brooks, President
• Susan Brooks, Owner
• Sharon Shearman, Consultant
Services:
A non-traditional marketing agency, specializing in event marketing, sponsorship sales, sponsorship activation, and non-profit event consulting.
Clients:
Chrysler, The Event, Ronald McDonald House Charities, The K Sean Elliot Charity Golf Classic, and Wildcat Dream Foundation
Sports Service Founded:
1986
Event Management Services:
Tournament sales, coordination, sponsorship and promotion for auto sports, golf, tennis, football, basketball, and other sports in the Tucson and Phoenix areas.
Marketing & Consulting Services:
Works with companies/products to develop an event or arrange special promotions within an existing event.

MARKET REACH
1010 WASHINGTON BOULEVARD
STAMFORD, CT 6901
203-352-0700
jtighe@market-reach.net
• Jim Tighe, President
(203) 257-6451
Services:
Specializes in event marketing, mobile marketing, mall marketing, retailtainment, sponsorship activation, hispanic sampling, college sampling, guerila marketing and product sampling.
Clients:
Qwest, Campbell's, Dannon, Hersheys, Hewlett Packard, American Express, Duracell, Pillsbury, Pfizer, Starbucks Coffee, AT&T, Yoohoo, Chock Fullo Nuts, Procter &

Gamble, Kraft,SC Johnson, AZO, Orangina, and BIC

MARKETING ARM
1999 BRYAN STREET
SUITE 1800
DALLAS, TX 75201
214-259-3200
Fax: 214-259-3201
info@themarketingarm.com
www.themarketingarm.com
• Gregg Hamburger, Chief Integration Officer
• Jennifer Henry, Chief Financial Officer
• Ray Clark, Founder/CEO
• Dan Belmont, President
Year Founded:
1993
Sports Service Founded:
1975.
Description:
A network of marketing services agencies building brands through emotionally powerful platforms,including sports, entertainment, music, events, promotions, and cause marketing. Based in Dallas, The Marketing Arm operates within Omnicom Group Inc (NYSE: OMC) and serves as the umbrella brand for four best-in-class agencies: Millsport, Davie Brown Entertainment, USMP, and ipsh.

MARKETING CONNECTIONS
712 N WELLS STREET
SUITE 200
CHICAGO, IL 60610
312-587-1465
Fax: 312-587-9883
www.mktgconnections.com
• Patrick Va Den Heuvel, Marketing Director
(312) 587-1465
pvanden@mktgconnections.com
Services:
Full service marketing agency that specializes in live field marketing. Offers pass-through pricing and online reporting.
Clients:
RJ Reynolds, Gatorade, Kellogg Co.

MARKETING DRIVE WORLDWIDE
800 CONNECTICUT AVENUE
3RD FLOOR E
NORWALK, CT 06854
203-857-6100
Fax: 203-834-1786
info@marketingdrive.com
www.marketingdrive.com
• Michael Harris, CEO, President
(203) 857-6100
michael.harris@marketingdrive.com
Services:
Provides the full spectrum of promotional marketing services such as strategic planning, national and regional promotions, co-marketing, channel marketing, retail menu marketing, promotional services, co-op advertising, co-op media, site development, e-marketing, CD and DVD authoring and design, customer acquisition programs, customer retention and loyalty programs, and database management; Interactive and Direct Response Services
Marketing & Consulting Services:
Assists clients to create national promotions, convert national sponsorships to local market promotions, create account-specific promotions and co-marketing programs.

Sports Service Founded:
1996

MARKETING WERKS
130 E RANDOLPH STREET
SUITE 2400
CHICAGO, IL 60601
312-228-0800
Fax: 312-228-0801
www.marketingwerks.com
• Betty Newman, President
• Scott Moller, VP
• Jason Vargas, Marketing Director
• T. J. Nolan, Sales Director
Services:
Event management, integrated experiential marketing; event, mobile and sports marketing; creative sampling solutions; brand launches, PR and media support; retail and sales promotion.
Clients:
Discover Card/ESPN Tailgate Tour, Hershey's Kissmobile Tour, LEGO Bionicle Find the Power Tour, Schick Shave Shack Tour, Snapple Dye Hard Tour

MARLIN ENTERTAINMENT GROUP, LTD
1720 POST ROAD E
WESTPORT, CT 06880
203-255-6100 EXT x 28
Fax: 203-255-6103
neal@marlinent.com
• Neal Frank, President
(203) 255-6100
neal@marlinent.com
Services:
Contest/Sweepstakes, Design/Production, Event Marketing/Tours, Entertainment Marketing, Cause Marketing, Sampling Programs, Guerilla/Buzz Marketing and Incentive/Loyalty Marketing ServicesProvides concept development, game play and design, registration, bonding, compliance, independent judging, online creative and hosting, and management, staffing, and event/tour production for mobile tours, mall tours, nightlife marketing, college events, fairs, festivals, and health clubs.
Clients:
We, Purina, MTV, History Channel, American Express, Comedy Central, Knowledge TV, GTE, MasterCard, Universal, A&E Network, Paramount, SEGA Channel, US West, NINTENDO, USWEST, VH1, ABC Family, Finlandia, Sci Fi, AMC, USA Network, Teen People, Sony, TAO, Toon Disney, Ragdoll, Ovation, NCC, NFL, The Weather Channel, CERTS, TCM, Music First, Game Show, Coca Cola, HBO, NBC Universal, and SOAP
Areas of Specialization:
Ambush, Cause, College, Entertainment Tie-ins, Experimental, Field Marketing, Interactive, Mall events, Mobile Marketing, Partnership Marketing, PR Stunts, Street Teams, Sponsorship Activation, Sweepstakes/Contests, Tours & Events

MATTEL SPORTS PROMOTION DEPARTMENT
333 CONTINENTAL BOULEVARD
MI-0836
EL SEGUNDO, CA 90245-5012
310-252-2000
Fax: 310-252-3866
corporate.mattel.com

• Daniel Roddick, Director
Description:
Program implementation center;develops and executes sports events and educational programs for flying disc(Frisbee) and foot bag play.

MAZZ MARKETING, INC.
287 COURTLAND AVENUE
BRIDGEPORT, CT 6605
203-260-4932
Fax: 866-209-1305
Wayne@WayneMazzoni.com
• Wayne Mazzoni, President
(203) 260-4932
wayne@waynemazzoni.com
• Gale Mazzoni, Marketing
mazzmarketing@aol.com
Company Description:
Helps high school athletes and their parents in their search for the right college, athletic program and athletic scholarships.
Nature of Service:
College recruiting seminars; Baseball Camps for high school athletes, consulting for high school athletes, books on getting college scholarships for high school athletes.
Products:
Books, video and apparel to learn more about the process in an effort to handle the process by themselves, camps, books, serminars, consulting.

MEDIA VISIONS
5875 OLD LEEDS ROAD
BIRMINGHAM, AL 35210
205-324-4600
800 254-0876
Fax: 205-324-4688
mcruce@mediavisions.com
www.mediavisions.com
• Michael K Cruce, Founder/President

MEDIAMARK RESEARCH INC./MRI
75 NINTH AVENUE
5TH FLOOR
NEW YORK, NY 10011
212-884-9200
800-310-3305
Fax: 212-884-9339
• Kathi Love, President/Chief Executive Officer
(212) 884-9257
• Alain Tessier, Chairman
(212) 884-9261
• Ian Jack, EVP/Chief Operating Officer
(212) 884-9252
• Ann Ma Kelly, VP/Marketing & Strategic Planning
(212) 884-9204
Magazine Research Product Volumes:
All major participation/spectator sports. Demographic/media cross-tabulated by sports annually. Cost depends upon purchaser.
Services:
Consumer Targeting, Brand Trial Loyalty, Promotional Opportunities, and Trade Marketing

MERCURY SPORTS MANAGEMENT
222 BLOOMINGDALE ROAD
WHITE PLAINS, NY 10605
914-683-0146
Fax: 914-683-1408

• Jay Schulthess, President
(914) 683-0146
Marketing & Consulting Services:
Provides management services to NASCAR
drivers. Consulting services to corporate
auto racing sponsors. Coordinates and
manages NASCAR licensing programs for
companies. Provides hospitality and public
relations services.
Specialty:
Auto Sports.
Clients:
Auto Sports, Nascar drivers, corporate auto
racing sponsors

METRO SIGNS ADVERTISING, INC.
4608 SCHUFF AVENUE
LOUISVILLE, KY 40213
502-452-2561
800-441-0627
Fax: 502-473-1286
www.1-metro.com

MILLSPORT, LLC
320 POST ROAD
DARIEN, CT 6820
203-662-4500
Fax: 203-662-9456
• Bob Basche, Chairman
(203) 662-4505
• Dan Belmont, President
(203) 662-4500
• Mike Bartelli, SVP-Millsport Motorsports
Division
(704) 262-6461
• Andrew Robinson, Senior Vice President
(214) 259-3200
• Daniel G. Belmont, President
• Andrew Robinson, Vice President
• Lisa Markham, Senior Vice President
• Mike Bartelli, Senior Vice President
Clients:
Frito-Lay, NASDAQ, Sunoco, Taco Bell,
AT&T, WalMart, Wells Fargo, Yahoo!, Pepsi
International, Tylenol, Elizabeth Arden
Sports Service Founded:
1975
Description:
The sports sponsorship and motorsports
consulting and activation division of The
Marketing Arm. Founded in 1975 as one of
the first sports marketing agencies in the
US, Millsport helps clients build marketing
advantage and drive business results
utilizing sports marketing assets. Based in
Stamford, Conn, with offices in Dallas (1999
Bryan Street, Suite 1800, Dallas, TX 75201,
Phone: 214-259-3200, Fax: 214-259-3201),
Chicago, and Los Angeles, Millsports
services include brand strategy,
property/media acquisition, integrated
program modeling, multi-channel activation,
hospitality, promotions, and evaluation. ROI
analytics.

MOBIVITY
58 W BUFFALO
SUITE 200
CHANDLER, AZ 85225
512-522-4710
Fax: 512-639-3375
sales@txtstation.com
www.txtstation.com
• Michael Falato, Director Sales & Business
Development
• Brook Paterson, Chief Financial
Officer/Director

• Matthew Moulin, Chief Technology Officer
• Dennis Becker, President/CEO
• Michael Falato, SVP of Sales & Business
Development
• Brad Dolian, VP ,Client Services
• Thi VanAusdal, Technical Lead
• Loyda Drew, Project Manager
Nature of Services:
Txtstation provides integrated campaigns
that combine the passion of live broadcasts
and events with the ubiquity of mobile
messaging allowing broadcasters, event
owners, sponsors and general media to
communicate with viewers or fans directly
through their mobile phones.

MODAK ILLUSTRATIONS
4225 JONATHAN LANE
CUMMING, GA 30130
828-368-8601
800-645-8165
• Ken Modak, Artist
Description:
Individuals and sports organizations have
sought out Modak's art talent.
Services:
Ken Modak is an artist whose ability to
capture the likeness of individuals is
exceptional. Many individuals and sports
organizations have sought out Modak's art
talent. Working primarily in a color pencil
technique, Ken feels this medium allows him
to best capture the feeling and detail he
looks for in his photo-realistic style. Ken's
knowledge of airbrush offers a perfect
complement to his pencil technique.
Clients:
Atlanta Falcons, Atlanta Junior Golf
Association, Coca-Cola, Country Music
Singer - Tracy Lawrence, Fellowship of
Christian Athletes, GTE Customer
Networks, PGA BellSouth Classic. Colleges:
Cleveland State, Florida, Florida State,
Gannon, Georgia, Georgia Southern,
Georgia Tech, Kentucky, Notre Dame,
Youngstown State

MOMENTUM IMC COMPANY
250 HUDSON STREET
2ND FLOOR
NEW YORK, NY 10013
646-638-5400
www.momentumww.com
Description:
Events and sponsorship unit of the
advertising agency McCann-Erickson North
America
Clients:
AT&T, General Motors, Coca-Cola,
Anheuser-Busch, Black & Decker, Sega of
America

MOTORSPORT CONCEPTS, LLC
2677 E. HWY 224
UNIT 11
DENVER, CO 80229
303-286-9498
motorsportconcepts@gmail.com
www.motorsport-concepts.com
Marketing & Consulting Services:
Provide marketing consulting, event
hospitality and coordination. Assist drivers
with obtaining sponsorship for motorsport
events.

MOUNTAIN NEWS CORPORATION
50 VASHELL WAY
SUITE 400
ORINDA, CA 94563
925-254-4456
Fax: 925-254-7923
info@mountainnews.com
www.mountainnews.com
Sports Service Founded:
1978
Marketing & Consulting Services:
Operates a separate recreation division
which represents a number of outdoor
recreation manufacturers, associations and
consumer show expositions with respect to
all facets of public relations, advertising and
sales promotion.

MULTI-AD
1720 W DETWEILLER DRIVE
PEORIA, IL 61615
309-692-1530
Fax: 309-692-8378
info@multiad.com
www.multi-ad.com
• Brian Jeske, Vice President, Sports
Operations
(770) 421-6461
bjeske@multi-ad.com
• Joe Dalfonso, Sports Consultant
(800) 348-6485
jdalfonso@multiad.com
• John F. Kocher, President
Year Founded:
1945
Sports Service Founded:
1990
Description:
Sports printer specializing in programs,
media guides, trading cards, promotional
material. Design, mailing, and warehouse
offered as well.

MURPHY & ORR EXHIBITS
564 MAIN STREET
FOREST PARK, GA 30297
404-366-2537
Fax: 404-366-2585
www.murphy-orr.com
• Art Hammerstrom, Account Executive
Nature of Services:
Murphy & Orr offers turnkey, custom exhibit
and display services including design and
space planning, exhibit and graphic
fabrication, interactive exhibit development,
as well as installation and updating services.
Year Founded:
1946

**NATIONAL ASSOCIATION OF SPORTS
COMMISSIONS**
9916 CARVER ROAD
SUITE 100
CINCINNATI, OH 45242
513-281-3888
Fax: 513-281-1765
info@SportsCommissions.org
www.SportsCommissions.org
• Don Schumacher, CSEE, Executive
Director
(513) 281-3888
don@sportscommissions.org
• Beth Hecquet, CMP, Meetings & Events
Director
(513) 281-3888
beth@sportscommissions.org
• Elizabeth Chaney, Director of Member

Services
(513) 281-3888
elizabeth@sportscommissions.org
Clients Include:
The National Association of Sports Commissions (NASC) is a non-profit membership based association for professionals in the sports event travel industry. Members include organizations that attract sporting events to their community (i.e. sports commissions and convention and visitors bureaus), event owners, and vendors and suppliers to the sports event industry.
Nature of Service:
The NASC provides networking opportunities, professional development, and industry best practices to sports event industry professionals. Nearly 550 organizations across the United States, Canada, and Puerto Rico are members of the NASC.
Sports Organization
For more than 20 years the National Association of Sports Commissions (NASC), a non-profit, 501(c) 3, membership based association , has served the sports event industry as its premier networkinf organization. The NASC is able to assit you in every way possible to meet all of your domestic and international event needs.

NATIONAL HOLE-IN-ONE ASSOCIATION
1840 N GREENVILLE AVENUE
SUITE 178
RICHARDSON, TX 75081-1898
972-808-9001
800-527-6944
888-527-6944
Fax: 972-808-9012
hio@hio.com
www.hio.com
Services:
Provider of golf-event prize services and offers the most complete hole-in-one promotion package which includes promotional materials.
Description:
We offer promotional programs to build traffic to your dealership through prize indemnification. Programs include golf, direct mail key matching, weather, basketball, football, baseball, hockey and fishing.

NATIONAL MEDIA GROUP, INC.
545 FIFTH AVENUE
SUITE 640
NEW YORK, NY 10017
212-424-0100
Fax: 212-867-1116
• Michael Goldberg, Chief Executive Officer
• Sid Schechter, Chief Operating Officer
• Adam M. Poe, Sales and Marketing Director
• Tina Gargiulo, Event Marketing Director
Services:
NMG and its affiliated agencies work with their clients to create integrated marketing platforms and campaigns incorporating one or more of the following elements sports sponsorship tie-ins, public relations, event management, consumer promotions, television production.
Clients:
IBM, Schick, AT&T, Nike, American Express, Reebok, Lucent Technologies,

Nestle, Sony, Dodge, Saturn, Schering-Plough, Warner-Lambert, Pfizer, Prudential Securities, EA Sports, KSwiss, Acclaim Entertainment, Fila, and Ocean Spray.
Year Founded:
1980
Description:
Sports marketing, Talent Representaton, Official Marketing Agency for NBA Coaches Association
Association Marketing:
Integrating sports personalities into sales and marketing platforms for corporate sponsors. Our creativity and contacts with some of the most high profile individuals in sports affords our clients the opportunity to leverage the assets of professional sports properties.
Event Marketing:
Maintains strategic relationships with experienced affiliated event management companies to implement affinity programs and insure the quality controls required for the event marketing components of our campaigns to achieve the established objective.
College Marketing:
The activities that NMG integrates into the college promotions are created by programming experts currently employed on college campuses throughout the United States who also serve our clients as supervisors on a regional level.
Talent and Television Production:
Has developed an in-depth knowledge of the television industry and a solid relationship with the major televison sports broadcast networks.

NATIONAL OUTDOOR SPORTS ADVERTISING
1200 POTOMAC STREET, NW
WASHINGTON, DC 20007-3211
202-965-9850
• W Micheal Gretschel, President

NATIONAL SCHOLASTIC ATHLETICS FOUNDATION, INC.
112 WIDGEON WAY
BRIDGEVILLE, DE 19933
919-414-8619
info@nationalscholastic.org
www.nationalscholastic.org
• James I. Spier, Executive Director
Description:
To support the development of junior age (under 20 years of age) athletes.
Sports Service Founded:
1990

NATIONAL SPORTING GOODS ASSOCIATION (NSGA)
1601 FEEHANVILLE DRIVE
SUITE 300
MOUNT PROSPECT, IL 60056
847-296-6742
800-815-5422
Fax: 847-391-9827
info@nsga.org
www.nsga.org
• Matt Carlson, President & Chief Executive Officer
Services:
The world's largest sporting good trade association consisting of retailers, suppliers, sales agent, media and industry associates.

Provides cost-saving services, information, and education for its members on a wide variety of sports also serves as the voice of the retailer/dealer, speaking out on issues that affect sporting goods retailers/dealers.
Fitness in America:
Analyzes adult frequent participants in seven fitness activities — aerobic, exercising, bicycling, calisthenics, exercise walking, exercising with equipment, running and swimming.
Lifestyle Characteristics of Sporting Consumers:
Using PRIZM analysis developed by Claritas, this report provides a versatile geo-demographic analysis of consumer purchasers of sporting goods. It addresses such questions as, Who are our target consumers?; Where do they live and shop?; How can we best reach them?. PRIZM clusters are organized into 12 broad social groups. In addition to analysis by individual product, product groupings are analyzed, e.g., all exercise equipment, in addition to home gyms, treadmills, etc. This report contains demographics on population, type of residence, household type (family, non-family, singles, etc.), size of HH, education and occupation of HH head.
Cost of Doing Business Survey:
Survey relates business costs for sporting goods stores. Contains income statements and productivity ratios by retail sales volume, number of stores, region, full line vs. specialty and team business. Productivity ratios included are: sales per employee, profit per employee, sales per total selling square foot, profit per total selling square foot and inventory turnover. Survey is free to NSGA retail members. Cost to non-members is $1,250.00.
Sport Equipment Expenditures:
Equipment expenditures presented for 28 sports. NSGA Brand Share Report: based on consumer recall of most recent purchase, NSGA Brand Share Studies report market share for 63 products. List of products available from NSGA. Cost is $425 for first product report, $375 for second, $275 for each additional report.
Year Founded:
1929

NATIONAL SPORTS FORUM
7290 NAVAJO ROAD
SUITE 204
SAN DIEGO, CA 92119
619-469-4101
Fax: 619-469-4007
info@sports-forum.com
www.sports-forum.com
• Ron Seaver, President
(619) 469-4101
r.seaver@sports-forum.com
• Erin Mooney, Communications Coordinator
(619) 469-4101
• Linsay Campbell, Operations Coordinator
(619) 469-4101
lindsay@sports-forum.com
• Bob Voight, Vice President
(619) 469-4101
bob@sports-forum.com
• Lindsay Campbell, Director of Operations
(619) 469.4101
lindsay@sports-forum.com
• Erin Mooney, Director of Communications
(619) 469.4101

erin@sports-forum.com
• Ryan Heidrich, Marketing Department
(619) 469.4101
ryan.h@sports-forum.com
• Nick Gilbert, Assistant Coordinator
Nature of Service:
Produce international team and event
marketing, promotions and sales
conferences that bring together top team
executives from both professional and
collegiate sports along with leading
corporate sponsors, advertisers and
agencies for the purpose of networking, idea
sharing and learning.
Sports Service Founded:
1994
Clients:
Budweiser, Winstead, Seachrest & Miuick,
Picture U Promotion, Txtstation, Garden
Fresh Restarants.
Marketing & Consulting Services:
Full service promotion and marketing
agency, creating developing and executing
national regional and local sponsorship
campaigns within teams, sports and events.

NELLIGAN SPORTS MARKETING, INC.
150 CLOVE ROAD
LITTLE FALLS, NJ 07424
973-812-5900
Fax: 973-812-8111
• T.J. Nelligan, Chairman / Chief Executive
Officer
tjn@nelligansports.com
• Tim Hofferth, President / Chief Operating
Officer
timh@nelligansports.com
• Mike Palisi, SVP
mikep@nelligansports.com
• TJ Nelligan, Chairman and CEO
(973) 812-5900
tjn@nelligansports.com
• Tim Hofferth, President and Chief
Operating Officer
(803) 945-2000
timh@nelligansports.com
• Mike Palisi, Executive Vice President
(973) 812-5900
mike@nelligansports.com
• Tom Varga, Senior Vice President
(973) 812-5900
tomv@nelligansports.com
• Mark Devine, Regional Senior Vice
President
(973) 812-5900
mdevine@nelligansports.com
Sports Service Founded:
1999
Services:
Provides sales and marketing expertise for
sports properties worldwide
Clients:
Hess, Geico, Lincoln Mercury, MBNA,
Pepsi, Aeropostale, Philips, Cooper Tires,
Cingular Wireless, Toyota, Nextel, 7-Up,
Verizon Wireless, Gatorade, Prudential
Financial, Pizza Hut, Oxford Health Plans,
Frontier, AMTRAK, Hilton, U.S. Army,
Coca-Cola, OppenheimerFunds, ING
Finacial Institutions, Pontiac, Bank of
America, US Airways, Wendy's Hamburger

**NETWORK FOUNDATON
TECHNOLOGIES (NFT)**
818 NELSON AVENUE
RUSTON, LA 71272

318-257-5432
888-262-9611
Fax: 318-257-5283
www.nft-tv.com
• Mike O'Neal, Founder/Chief Scientist
• Marcus Morton, Co-Founder/President
• Mike o' Neal, Founder and Chief Scientist
Nature of Services:
Network Foundation Technologies (NFT)
provides streaming media technology
services that harness the power of
distributed computing to bring the
economics of traditional broadcasting to the
world of online webcasting.

**NEW JERSEY SPORTS PRODUCTIONS,
INC./DBA MAIN EVENTS**
772 UNION BOULEVARD
TOTOWA, NJ 07512
973-200-7050
Fax: 973-200-7061
dtremblay@mainevents.com
www.mainevents.com
• Jolene Mizzone, Vice President,
Operations
• Kim Newman, Sports Scene Distributor
• Ellen Haley, Public Relations

NEW TIER COMMUNICATIONS
15875 N GREENWAY-HAYDEN LOOP
SUITE 109
SCOTTSDALE, AZ 85260
480-922-1711
Fax: 480-922-1733
www.newtier.com
• Michael D. Rossman, President & Chief
Executive Officer
• Mark Malenfant, VP Sales
• Steve Graber, Production Manager
Description:
Provides an integrated suite of multimedia
applications enabling clients to broadcast
real-time marketing messages to consumers
registered on the new Tier Network.
Nature of Services:
Services include development of interactive
multimedia development, web site
development, print and display advertising,
video and audio production, screen savers
and animation.
Clients:
IBM, Ticketmaster, TECO Energy, Adelphia,
Ohio Health, Verizon Electronics, Fox
Sports Net, SBC, Union Bank of California,
US Bank, American West Airlines, TD
Waterhouse, Solo, Philips, D.C. Lottery,
Major Leage Baseball, National Basketball
Assoc., National Hockey League, National
Football League, Collegiate, Specialty,
Southwest Airlines, Royals, Astros, Brewers,
Cardinals, University of Utah, Emerald
Downs.
Year Founded:
1994

NEWMAN COMMUNICATIONS
20 GUEST STREET
SUITE 150
BRIGHTON, MA 02135
617-254-4500
Fax: 617-923-2616
www.newmancom.com
• Bob Newman, Founder
• Robert K Newman, President
• Elise Bogdan, VP/Client Services Director
Services:
Provides public relations services

specializes in literary publicity and corporate
public relations necessary for planning a
public relations campaigns that target
specific media for any topic, and to any
market.
Description:
Founded 1991. NC is a national
publicity/media relations firm with a focus on
sports publicity. Many clients are former
athletes or sports authors.

NEXT LEVEL SPORTS, INC.
24 CATHEDRAL PLACE
SUITE 500
SAINT AUGUSTINE, FL 32084
904-810-5177
Fax: 904-810-6855
www.nextlevelsports.net
• Michael L. Garnes, Founder/President
info@nextlevelsports.net
Nature of Service:
Next Level Sports, Inc. (NLS) is a career
management, job placement and consulting
firm to college graduated 'scholar'
student-athletes. We provide a wide range
of career counseling, planning, assessment
and consulting services for college and
university student-athletes to help them
make a seamless transition from the world
of college to the business world. NLS
provides 'real life' skills and proven job
hunting tools through presentations,
seminars and workshops. Our programs
give student-athletes a laser-like focus on
how to approach, develop, manage and
execute effective job search with an
implementation plan. We help them to level
the pla
Year Founded:
1991
Consulting and Seminar Topics:
Clarifying career focus, Networking,
Creating resumes and letters, Analyzing
income potential, Understanding the job
market, Maximizing personal apperance,
Evaluating and negotiating offers. NLS
seminars are offered individually or as a
series. We can also customize seminars to
address the specific concerns or needs of
your student-athletes.

NEXT MARKETING
2820 PETERSON PALACE
NORCROSS, GA 30071
770-225-2200
Fax: 770-225-2300
info@nextmarketing.com
www.nextmarketing.com
• Henry Rischitelli, President
• Pat Conreaux, SVP, Creative Director
• Tim Leaumont, EVP, Finance and Agency
Business
Nature of Service:
Whether a brand is targeting large
audiences or singling out influencers, Next
Marketing creates brand experiences that
make profound and lasting impressions.
Event marketing, sponsorship activation,
guerila marketing, on-premise sampling and
retail demonstrations are just a few areas of
Next Marketing's expertise.
Year Founded:
1993
Clients:
U.S. Air Force, Air National Guard, General
Motors, Community Coffee, HPE, HPI, Cox,

General Tire, CDW, Webber Stevens and Ford amongst others.

NFL BUSINESS VENTURES
280 PARK AVENUE
NEW YORK, NY 10017
212-450-2000
Fax: 212-681-7573
• Roger Goodell, EVP/Chief Operating Officer
• Gary Gertzog, SVP, Business Affairs/General Counsel
• John Collins, SVP Marketing/Entertinment Programming
• Anthony Noto, Chief Financial Officer
• Kimberly A. Williams, CFO
• James W. Fields, Senior Strategic Analyst
• Paul J. Tagilabue, Consultant

NIELSEN SPORTS
85 BROAD STREET
NEW YORK, NY 10004
646-654 5000
800-864-1224
Fax: 646-654-8593
www.nielsensports.com
• Barbara Zidovsky, Director, Marketing
• Dan O'Toole, Director, New Products
• Earl Jeff, Account Manager
• Sara Erichson, General Manager, National Services
• Stephen Master, Vice President, Operations Manager Nielsen Sp
Description:
Nielson Sports, a division of Nielsen Media Research, specializes in creating best practices for the sports sponsorship industry. Nielsen Sports is committed to providing information that is results-oriented and objective for both buyers and sellers of sports sponsorships.
Sponsorship Scorecard:
Launched in January 2005, Sponsorship Scorecard is a service that measures television audience exposure to sponsor-placed media in all televised sporting events.
FANLinks:
The FANLinks service identifies changes in brand purchase habits of sports fans.
Nielsen Sports Quarterly:
Quarterly publication that is dedicated to best practices for the sports sponsorship industry. Topics include industry articles, scorecards, buyer insights, recent announcements, and glossary of terms.
Nielsen Media Research:
Provides media research and marketing services for sports and major events. Services include national and local television information services for networks and affiliates, independent stations, syndicates, cable networks and systems, advertisers and agencies.

NORDIC GROUP INTERNATIONAL
2727 NELSON ROAD
SUITE A107
LONGMONT, CO 80503
303-579-4739
Fax: 303-652-1709
jonathan@nordicgroupinternational.com
www.nordicgroupinternational.com
• Jonathan Wiesel, Principal
jonathan@nordicgroupinternational.com
• Jonathan Wiesel, Principal

(303) 579-4739
jonathan@nordicgroupinternational.com
Year Founded:
1981.
Clients:
Cross Country Ski Areas Association, NH, Viking Nordic, VT, Methow Valley Sport Trails Association, WA, Town of Breckenridge, CO, Breckenridge Nordic, CO, Crested Butte Nordic Council, CO, Eggshells in the Coffee (dude ranch seminars), CO, Great Glen Trails Outdoor Center, NH, Winding Trails Cross Country, CT and others
Nature of Service:
Site evaluations; Feasibility studies; Resort planning; Operations audits; Business planning; Four-season trail and facility design and construction; Recreation development; Staff selection and training; Program development; Marketing; Operations; Research; Approvals and permitting

NUVISIONS
259-263 GOFFLE ROAD
HAWTHORNE, NJ 7506
741-327-1650
888-239-3365
Fax: 949-752-9137
• George Carter, VP, Marketing
• Billy Carter, VP, Multi-Media
• Dominic Symes, Partner/Creative Director
Services:
Provides advertising, catalogue production, identity development, packaging and digital photography.
Other Location:
80 S. Yesler Way, Ste 310, Seattle, WA 98104.
Marketing & Consulting Services:
Advertising and design studio for footwear, sporting goods, outdoor, apparel & fitness products. Emphasis is on advertising, catalogue production, identity development, packaging and digital photography.

O'CONNOR COMMUNICATIONS
333 WARWICK ROAD
LAKE FOREST, IL 60045
847-615-5462
Fax: 847-615-5465
jimo@oconnorpr.com
• James O'Connor, President
(847) 615-5462
jimo@oconnorpr.com
• Jim O'Connor, President
• Lynda O'Connor, President
Year Founded:
1989
Nature of Service:
TV and Radio interviews, Website content, Speech writing, Press kits, Sales literature, Newsletters, Blogs, Seminar planning, New Product releases, Feature Stories, Case Studies, Trade Show support, Brochures.

OCTAGON MARKETING NORTH AMERICA
800 CONNECTICUT AVENUE
2ND FLOOR
NORWALK, CT 06854
203-354-7400
Fax: 203-354-7600
www.octagon.com
• Rick Dudley, President/CEO
• Phil D Picciotto, Founder & President

• Jeff Shifrin, President
• Lisa Murray, EVP
• Sean Nicholls, MD
• Simon Wardle, Chief Stratergy Officer
• Joan Cusco, President
Description:
Octagon is the world's largest sports and entertainment representation and marketing agency. Now affiliated with Ken Lindner & Associates to provide clients with multi-platform representation, and world-class services.

OCTAGON SPORTS
7100 FOREST AVENUE
SUITE 201
RICHMOND, VA 23226
804-285-4200
Fax: 804-285-4224
www.octagon.com
• Giff Breed, Managing Director Golf/Outdoors
• Phil De Picciotto, Founder & President
• Lisa Murray, Executive Vice President & Chief Marketing Of
• Simon Wardle, Chief Strategy Officer
• Rick Dudley, President & CEO
Nature of Service:
Octagon is uniquely poised to provide full service marketing solutions across the global platform. Octagon offers client expertise in the following areas: Angler Representation (endorsements, clinics, outings, appearances, licencing), Event Management (event ownership, creation & implementation), Sales/Property Management (package development & sponsorship management), Consulting (strategic sponsorship selection, contract negotiation, field marketing and implementation).

OKLAHOMA EVENTS, INC.
6465 AVONDALE DRIVE
NICHOLS HILLS, OK 73116
405-842-4141
Fax: 405-842-9674
• Lee Al Allan Smith, President
Services:
Full service event marketing & advertising
Sports Service Founded:
1990
Event Management Services:
Full service event marketing & management company, active in hockey, NBA, equestrian, and other sports.

OLYMPIA ENTERTAINMENT, INC.
2211 WOODWARD AVENUE
4TH FLOOR
DETROIT, MI 48201
313-471-3200
Fax: 313-471-3259
Info@olympiaentertainment.com
www.olympiaentertainment.com
• Steve Facione, SVP
Services:
Provides Advertising Sales/Corporate Partnerships, Event Booking and Development, Event, Facility & Team Marketing, including Publicity, Group Services, Sponsorship Sales, Promotions, Merchandising, Graphics, Subscriber Services, and Ticketing, Hospitality, Broadcasting, Merchandising, Food and Beverage Services, Specialty Food Concepts, Corporate Hospitality, Building

Operations: Security, Parking, Maintenance, Public Assembly, Facility Management, Sports Administration, Management Consulting, and Customized Business Communications & Presentations

Sports Service Founded:
1982

Event Management Services:
Manages Joe Louis Arena and Cobo Arena in Detroit, MI.

Marketing & Consulting Services:
Provides full marketing, management, sales, and booking services for Joe Louis Arena and Cobo Arena.

ONEWORLD COMMUNICATIONS
2001 HARRISON STREET
SAN FRANCISCO, CA 94110
415-355-1935
Fax: 415-355-0295
info@owcom.com
www.owcom.com
• Jonathan Villet, Director, Strategic & Creative Services
• Jonathan Villet, President & Founder
jonathan.villet@owcom.com
• Mark Allen, Lead Account Supervisor
• Dave Wren, Public Relations, Copywriting
david.wren@owcom.com
• Rose Tash, Art Director
• Alex Uncapher, Online Advertising Media Planner and Buyer
alex.uncapher@owcom.com
• Susan Barnes, Social Marketing/Social Media Manager
• Jonathan Villet, Founder, President

Services:
Full Service Communications Programs, from Planning to Evaluation, Strategic Planning, Positioning and Branding, Corporate Identity, Logo, Style, Marketing Organizational Development and Training, Call Center Service, Results Tracking and Analysis, Copywriting, Graphic Design, Website Design and Internet Services, Photography, Video Production, Radio and Television Commercials, Public Service Announcements, Displays and Conference Booths, Printing and Duplication, Print, Broadcast, Outdoor, Transportation, Web, Creative Production, Media Research and Analysis, Negotiation, Purchasing and Placement Tracking, Direct Mail and Fulfillment, Respon

Clients:
UNICEF, UNFPA Zimbabwe Press kit, IFAD, Atlanta Journal Constitution, The Age & Good Weekend Magazine, Australia, FAO Photo Library: permanent collection, Gourmet Magazine Australia, St. Stephens School, Rome, New Sociey, England, Pinto-Peira Brazil newspaper, Brazil, Australian Photography Yearbook, The Best of The Age, 1980 & 1981, 125 Years The Age Newspaper, Australia

ONSPORT STRATEGIES
8540 COLONNADE CENTER DR
RALEIGH, NC 27615-3052
919-256-1600
Fax: 919-256-1601
• Gary R Stevenson, President/Chief Executive Officer

Description:
Consulting practice dedicated to helping its clients leverage their investment in sports ownership, sports marketing, and sports television and new media.

Sports Service Founded:
1999

Clients:
American Express, National Basketball Association(NBA), PGA Tour, Simon Brand Ventures, Total Sports

ORIGINAL MEGAFAN
17410 MINNETONKA BOULEVARD
SUITE 164
MINNETONKA, MN 55345
952-334-4402
Fax: 952-473-2078
jonrichie@comcast.net
www.theoriginalmegafan.com
• Jon Richie, President

Nature of Services:
The MegaFan takes an ordinary, non-revenue driving concession container and combines it with a classic sports icon to transform it into the ideal container for popcorn, peanuts or chips.

OUTDOOR SPORTS MARKETING GROUP
822 LOCUST STREET
HENDERSONVILLE, NC 28792
866-893-8676
Fax: 866-336-542
info@outdoorsportsmarketing.com
www.outdoorsportsmarketing.com

Services:
Provides emerging and extreme sports marketing and development. Offers funding and sponsorship acquisition.

PAC-10 PROPERTIES
1021 W PICO BOULEVARD
BUILDING 103
SUITE 2146
LOS ANGELES, CA 90035
310-369-0598
Fax: 310-557-4455
www.pac-10.org
• Thomas C. Hansen, Commissioner
thansen@pac-10.org
• Mitch Huberman, SVP, Fox Sports Enterprises/Pac-10 Prope
(310) 369-0598
mhuberman@foxsports.net
• Renee Cohen, Marketing Manager
(310) 369-0083
• Shawn Culver, Account Executive
(310) 369-0631

Sports Service Founded:
1996

Marketing & Consulting Services:
Joint venture between FOX Sports Net and the Pac-10 collegiate conference. Manages all aspects of Conference marketing, including licensing, merchandising, publications and special events.
Coordinates with Fox Sports Net Sales in developing integrated marketing platforms for advertisers targeting adults 18-24 and 25-54 in some of the strongest DMA's (Demographics) in the country.

Services:
Manages all aspects of Conference marketing, including licensing, merchandising, publications and special events.

Clients:
Champion, Classic Sportswear, Electronic Arts, Fotoball, Killian Athletics, Nutmeg Mills, Sony, Spotlight, Stadium Sports, Whirley, Gear For Sports

PAOLISSO & ASSOCIATES, INC.
9051 BALTIMORE NATIONAL PIKE
ELLICOTT CITY, MD 21042
410-465-8930
• Paul Paolisso, President

Services:
Offers Sponsorship sales and event marketing. Produces sports programming for syndication, cable and non-broadcast use. Packages and markets sports properties and events

PARADIGM CONSULTING
26 RADCLIFFE DRIVE
GETZVILLE, NY 14068
716-688-1808
stephen@paradigmconsulting.ca
www.paradigmconsulting.ca

Services:
Provides business development, strategic planning, marketing and process consulting to indoor and outdoor sports and entertainment facility owners, operators, and developers of municipal, private and intercollegiate venues.

PATTERSON SPORTS VENTURES
2206 E LINCOLN DRIVE
SUITE 102
PHOENIX, AZ 85016
602-468-9700
Coach@Carlette.com
www.carlette.com
• Jack Sullivan, Creative Director
• Carlette Patterson, Founder/CEO
coach@carlette.com
• Dr. ralph Pim, 3D Coach
• Jackie R. Hutt, Player Development
• Elizabeth Lennon, Sports Life coach

Services:
Assists professional athletes develop, design and implement a Game Plan for life after the League. Specializes in marketing, management and special events, which includes, broadcast rights packaging, sponsorship sales, corporate imaging, board development, and community outreach and education.

Clients:
The Robert Wood Johnson Foundation, The Sports Philanthropy Project, The Athlete Legacy Network, Arizona State University, Phoenix Suns, Arizona Cardinals, Grand Canyon State Games, Fox Sports Net Arizona, Channel 3/Arizona Family.com, Arizona Republic, The Arizona Interscholastic Association, Arizona Tourism and Sports Authority, Cox Communications, Arizona Department of Health Services/Tobacco Education & Prevention Program, Blue Cross Blue Shield Arizona, Gatorade, Arizona Department of Commerce - Office of Sports Promotion, and Tempe Sports Authority

Sports Service Founded:
1998

Nature of Sports Service:
A full-service agency specializing in marketing, management and special events. Organization focus is on youth and community based sports programs and initiatives. Also has extensive experience in broadcast rights packaging, sponsorship sales, corporate imaging, board development, and community outreach and education. Expanded business to include life coaching for athletes transitioning from the

League to life and adults transitioning from success to significance.

PCA WORLDWIDE, INC.
23 MALA COMPRA ROAD
PALM COAST, FL 32137
386-446-8721
PCAF@PCAFhq.org
www.pcafhq.org
Marketing & Consulting Services:
A full service sports marketing, public relations and ad agency specializing in unique golf products & video production. Exclusive agent and lobbyist for the Tour Caddies Association Worldwide. Diverse, integrated marketing opportunities & database marketing.

PCGCAMPBELL
3200 GREENFIELD
SUITE 280
DEARBORN, MI 48120
313-336-9000
www.pcgcampbell.com
• David Scheinberg, President/Chief Executive Officer
(313) 336-9000
• John Scodellaro, Chief Financial Officer
(313) 336-9000
• Cheryl Kohs, Vice President Event Management
(313) 336-9000
• Kevin Kennedy, Vice President Public Relations
(313) 203-7108
Nature of Service:
Product marketing; public relations such as mass media and business-to-business publicity, corporate goodwill and community presence programs, professional sports media relations, product launches, event and program publicity.

PENN STATE SPORTS MARKETING
621 MAINSTREAM DRIVE, SUITE 230
NASHVILLE, TN 37228
615-742-6100
800-346-9467
Fax: 615-742-6124

PERFORMANCE PROMOTIONS SPORT PROMOTIONS
2010 NE 7TH AVENUE
PO BOX 350067
DANIA, FL 33004
954-462-3235
Fax: 954-462-3240
• David Benson, Operations Director
Sports Service Founded:
1986
Marketing & Consulting Services:
Specializes in motorsports marketing. Handles all aspects of sponsorship from inception to implementation, providing all services from publicity to team management.

PERFORMANCE RESEARCH
25 MILL STREET
QUEEN ANNE SQUARE
NEWPORT, RI 02840
401-848-0111
Fax: 401-848-0110
www.performanceresearch.com
• Jed Pearsall, President
jed@performanceresearch.com

• Bill Doyle, VP
bill@performanceresearch.com
• Marc Porter, Observational Research Manager
mporter@performanceresearch.com
• Larry Shannon-Missal, Reports Manager
Services:
Provide consulting services in order to maximize spending and ensure an appropriate match between corporate marketing objectives and proposed sponsorship packages such as On-Site/Event Research, Telephone Research, Focus Groups, On-Line Research, Web-based Sponsorships, Observational Research, Research in a box, Interantional Research and Sponsorship Consulting
Clients:
Cirque de Soleil, Daytona Properties, ESPN, Head of the Charles Regatta, Indy Racing League MLS, NCAA, Simon Properties, TNT, WTA,WTT WWE, X Games, Anheuser-Busch, AT&T, Bank of America, BF Goodrich, BP Amoco, Clorox, Coca-Cola, Colgate-Palmolive, Coors Brewing Company, Country Financial, Discover Card, Ford, General Foods, General Mills, General Motors, Harley Davidson, Hartford Insurance, Honda, Hyundai, KeyCorp, Kimberly Clark, Kodak, Lowes, Masterfoods, MCI Worldcom, Miller Brewing Company, Motorola, Nestle, Nike, Nissan, NTL, Ocean Spray, Pepsi-Cola, Philips Electronics, RJR, Saturn, Saucony, SmithKline Beecham, Sperry Topsider
Custom/Syndicated Studies:
Full-Service evaluation of cost, reach and impact of corporate sponsored sports and special events through proprietary and syndicated research studies. Focus group research of targeted sports audiences.
Consulting Services:
Provide consulting services related to event selection in order to maximize spending and ensure an appropriate match between corporate marketing objectives and proposed sponsorship packages.
Other Location:
95 Wilton Road, STE 375, London, UK IBZ; Phone: +44(0) 149I-410-822 Fax: +44(0) 20-7401-9234
Year Founded:
1985

PGI, INC.
220 WEST 42ND STREET
10TH FLOOR
NEW YORK, NY 10036
646-445-7000
Fax: 646-445-7001
• Lee Rubenstein, President/Chief Operating Officer
• Cindy Bell, EVP Meeting Services
Services:
The development of event marketing plans, sponsorship packages, sales strategies and solicitation plans for event or sports properties. Creation, design and management of promotional event concepts, displays and attractions and hospitality facilities for corporations and sports properties.
Event Management Services:
Creation, design and management of promotional event concepts, displays and attractions and hospitality facilities for corporations and sports properties.
Sports Service Founded:

1989
Other Location:
Atlanta Office: 5775 Peachtree Dunwoody Road, Bldg B, Ste 260, Atlanta, GA 30342; 404 256-1336; FAX: 404 256-1922

PHILLIPS MARKETING
1001 COOPER PT. RD. SW
SUITE 140-#189
OLYMPIA, WA 98502
360-596-9092
Fax: 360-596-9093
www.phillipsmarketing.net
• Robert B. Phillips, President
Sports Service Founded:
1989
Marketing & Communication Services:
Marketing, advertising, public relations, sales promotion, direct marketing, research, sales motivation, specializing in sports and sporting goods.

PHOTO FILE
333 NORTH BEDFORD ROAD
SUITE 130
MOUNT KISCO, NY 10549
914-375-6000
800-346-1678
Fax: 914-375-6009
customerservice@photofile.com
www.photofile.com
• Charles Singer, President
• Bill Cook, Chief Financial Officer
• Bryan Reilly, Photo Editor
Sports Service Founded:
1987
Services:
Manufactures licensed sports photography.
Clients:
Major League Baseball, the NBA and WNBA, NHL, NFL, and their respective player associations, as well as thousands of individual athletes.
Products:
Double Mat Mounted 8x10 Photos, Framed 8x10 Photos, Custom 11 x 14 and 16 x 20 Enlargements, Photoramics (12 x 36) Photos and Milestone & Memories-Double Matted Triple Image Commemorative.
Marketing & Consulting Services:
Specializes in the marketing and sales of sports photography, licensing with all major sports organizations including MLB, NFL, NBA, NHL, NASCAR in photos, key chains, plaques, and posters. Extensive photo library. Develops sports marketing and promotional programs for corporate clients through PF marketing services.

PITCH PR
39-43 BREWER STREET
LONDON, ENGLAND W1F 9UD
+44-(0) 20 7494 1616
Fax: 20-7437-5262
info@pitch.co.uk
www.pitch.co.uk
• Henry Chappell, Managing Director
henry@pitchpr.co.uk
Year Founded:
2001
Services:
Innovative public relations and marketing company specializing in representing sports-related clients - be it sponsorship activation, personalities, sponsorship consultancy and campaigns for clients. consumer PR, sponsorship activation,

corporate PR, sports PR, personalities, sponsorship consultancy

PLAYMAKER SPORTS ADVISORS
500 GRANT STREET
SUITE 5000
PITTSBURGH, PA 15219-2507
412-454-5000
Fax: 412-281-0717
phinfo@pepperlaw.com
www.pepperlaw.com
• Chuck Greenberg, President/Chief Executive Officer
Description:
Provides corporate, litigation and regulatory legal services to leading businesses, governmental entities, non-profit organizations and individuals throughout the nation and the world.
Services:
Assists owners and prospective owners of sports franchises with sports transaction structuring and negotiations
Other Locations:
100 Renaissance Center, 36th Floor, Detroit, MI 48243; Phone: 313-259-7110; 1180 Avenue of the Americas, 14th Floor, New York, NY 10036; Phone: 212-899-5090; 5 Park Plaza, Suite 1700, Irvine, CA 92614; Phone: 949-567-3500; Hamilton Square, 600 Fourteenth Street NW, Washington, DC 20005; Phone: 202-220-1200; Hercules Plaza, STE 5700, 1313 Market Place, P.O. Box 1709, Wilmington, DE 19899; Phone: 302-777-6500

PLB SPORTS
PENN CENTER W
BUILDING 3, SUITE 411
PITTSBURGH, PA 15276
412-787-8800
877-PLB-SPRT
Fax: 412-787-8745
info@plbsports.com
www.plbsports.com
• Ty Ballou, President
(412) 322-9409
info@plbsports.com
• Melissa Heher, Marketing VP
(412) 787-8800
info@plbsports.com
Description:
Marketer of Flutie Flakes named after Doug Flutie of the Buffalo Bills, and Ed's End Zone O's - A cereal named after Ed McCaffrey of the Denver Broncos.
Products:
Food products featuring athletes from the NFL, MLB, NBA, and NHL. Most recognized for the development and launch of Flutie Flakes for Doug Flutie and the Doug Flutie Foundation for Autism. Manages every aspect of its sports products from product development, sourcing through retail sales, marketing and public relations.
Brands:
Dan Marino, Ben Roethlisberger, David Ortiz, Carmelo Anthony, Doug Flutie, Ed McCaffrey, Pedro Martinez, Jerome Bettis, Bettis The Bus Barbecue Sauce, Bettis The Bus Mustard, Bettis The Bus Peanut Butter, Bettis The Bus Salsa, Bettis TheBus Pickles, Bucs Mustard, Buffalo Bills Mustard, Buffalo Bills Mustard, Dawg Pound FoodLine, Dilger'sDijon Mustards, Ed McCaffrey's Eddie Mac&Cheese, Ed McCaffrey'sEndzone O's, Elway's

Comeback Crunch, Falcons Mustard, Flutie Flakes, Flutie Flakes, Flutie Flakes SuperCharged, Flutie Fruitie, Grid Iron Fruit Snacks, Hines Ward 86 Steak Sauce, Holcomb's Hometown BBQ Sauce, Holcomb's Hometown Mustards, HotRod's
Sports Service Founded:
1996

POC MEDIA SPORTS & ENTERTAINMENT DIVISION
511 LINDSEY DRIVE
PATRICK O' CONNOR
WAYNE, PA 19087
610-636-5805
Fax: 610-971-0261
www.pocmedia.com
• Ashley Downey, General Manager
ashley.downey@pocmedia.com
• Pat O'Connor, Contact
(610) 636-5805
pat.oconnor@pocmedia.com
Services:
Integrated Marketing and Branding Initiatives, Development of Web Site, Multimedia and Interactive Marketing Communications Tools, Event Management, Planning and Staging and Non-Traditional Promotion for the Entertainment Industry

PORTER NOVELLI
250 GREENWICH STREET
36TH FLOOR
NEW YORK, NY 10007
212-601-8000
Fax: 212-601-8101
Darlan.Monterisi@porternovelli.com
www.porternovelli.com
• Anthony T Viceroy, President/Chief Financial Officer
(212) 601-8311
anthony.viceroy@porternovelli.com
• Gary Stockman, CEO
(212) 601-8114
gary.stockman@us.porternovelli.com
• Mike Gehb, Chief Financial Officer
mike.gehb@porternovelli.com
• Greg Waldron, Chief Talent Officer
greg.waldron@porternovelli.com
• Karen Van Bergen, CEO
Marketing & Consulting Services:
Public relations firm.
Services:
Strategic Planning & Research, Media & Influencer Relations, Multicultural, Alliance Building, Advertising & Corporate Identity, Direct Marketing, Interactive, Sports Marketing, CRM, Crisis & Issues
Clients:
Dannon, Gillette, Kellogg, Nissan, Schering-Plough, Tambrands and Wrigley's.
Sports Service Founded:
1972

PORTER PERFORMANCE SYSTEMS
PO BOX 5584
EUGENE, OR 97405
541-342-6875
kayporter1@comcast.net
www.thementalathlete.com
• Kay Porter, Owner
(541) 342-6875
kayporter1@comcast.net
Sports Service Founded:
1983
Description:
Author, The Mental Athlete, Inner Training

for Peak Performance, 2nd Edition (2000).
Marketing & Consulting Services:
Conducts sports psychology and mental training for peak performance seminars/workshops/clinics for athletes, teams, coaches and youths. General motivational speaking programs for companies and groups. Also offers wide range of seminars specializing in corporate fitness, mental training for peak performance, team building, customer relations, peak sales performance, conflict resolution and thriving on change. Also offers individual counseling/consultations for athletes and coaches.

POWER IMAGES
2333 STIRLING ROAD
FT LAUDERDALE, FL 33312
954-966-0260
800-207-9486
Fax: 954-963-2971
service@powerimages.com
• Mark Gompertz, SVP Video Services
(954) 966-0260
mark@medialab.tv
• Nadine Floyd, Jr, President, Operations
Services:
Provides design, digital photography and on demand printing, event signage and web sites. Provides video production services to corporations and television. Staging and production for on-site meetings and events.
Clients:
Power Images Media Lab produces marketing support materials for a large and prestigious client base. A partial list includes The Miami Dolphins, Spherion, Arby's, Motorola, DHL, Revlon, Concord Camera, Hunter Douglas, LaSalle Brokers, Convergsys, The Hackett Group

PREMIER PARTNERSHIPS
1148 4TH STREET
SANTA MONICA, CA 90403
310-656-2500
Fax: 310-656-2590
www.premierpartnerships.com
• Alan Rothenberg, Chairman
Alan@PremierPartnerships.com
• Randy Bernstein, President/Chief Operating Officer
Randy@PremierPartnerships.com
• Christopher Pepe, Western Operations VP
• Todd Parker, Eastern Operations VP
Todd@PremierPartnerships.com
• Alan I. Rothenberg, Chairman
• Randy Bernstein, President & CEO
• Jeff Marks, Managing Director
• Stephanie Cheng, Vice President, Marketing Services
• Todd Ferderer, Director, Finance
Nature of Sports Service:
Agency formed by top soccer executives that focuses on including sponsorship, marketing, naming rights and venue management.
Services:
Stadium/Venue Naming Rights Sales, Sports, Entertainment & Civic Sponsorship Sales, Broadcast Media & Internet Sales, Premium Ticket and Suite Sales, Sponsorship Sales Training Counsel on Prospective Opportunities, Sponsorship Analyses, Sponsorship Negotiation, Program Implementation Stadium/Venue Naming Rights, Sponsorship of stadium or property

Clients:
Rose Bowl, Major League Soccer, NBA, SUM, Pizza Hut Park, The Bard Capital Challenge, Hunt Sports Group, Los Angeles Dodgers, Kroenke Sports Enterprises, Clippers, Los Angeles Angels, Minnesota Timberwolves, Minnesota Twins, Lowes, MasterCard, Yahoo, Rochester Rhino Soccer, Worcester IceCats, Colorado Rapids, FC Dallas, The Fresno Grizzlies, Sacramento RiverCats, HBCU, Jacksonville, NAIA, Toronto Argonauts, North Texas Soccer, Music Center Speaker Series, Long Beach International Marathon, HOK, ASA Events, BlackHawk Marketing, Hoop It Up, Milwaukee Bucks, USL, Full, NTRA, Starfire Sports
Other Location:
New York

PREMIER SPORTS MANAGEMENT, INC.
7450 W 130TH STREET
SUITE 360
OVERLAND PARK, KS 66214
913-681-6990
Fax: 913-681-8864
www.premiersportsonline.com
• Gary Heise, President/Chief Operating Officer
gheise@premiersportsonline.com
• Lamar Hunt, Owner Sports Franchises
Marketing & Consulting Services:
Provides a full-service menu of marketing and communications services to sports properties, encompassing professional, amateur, corporate and private sectors. Services include sports marketing and promotions, event management, public relations, video production, creative services.
Services:
Provides a full-service include event management, marketing/communications, sponsorships, video production, and creatice services
Clients:
National Football League, Major League Soccer, National Collegiate Athletic Association (NCAA), Top Regional Clients:Kansas City Chiefs (NFL), Dallas Cowboys (NFL), Kansas City Wizards (MLS), Dallas Burn (MLS), Kansas City Royals (MLB), Big 12 Conference and University of Missouri. Corporate Sports Partners: Gatorade, Nike, New York Life, Pro Player, Nickelodeon, Associated Wholesale Grocers, Cellular One, Southwestern Bell, Time-Warner, Midland Dairy Association and American Airlines

PRINCE MARKETING GROUP
18 CARILLON CIRCLE
LIVINGSTON, NJ 7039
973-325-0800
800-987-7462
800-98-PRINCE
Fax: 973-243-0037
helpdesk@princemarketinggroup.com
www.princemarketinggroup.com
• Darren Prince, President/CEO
dprince@princemarketinggroup.com
• Steve Simon, Vice President and Talent representation
• Nicholas Cordasco, Talent representation
• Reggie Dance, Contact
• Daren Prince, President and CEO
(212) 585-0973

Nature of Service:
Full service sports and celebrity marketing firm. Public Appearances, Product Placement, Autograph Signing Sessions, Charity Events, Fantasy Camps and Tournaments available for athletes, Grand Openings and Promotions, Licensing and Product Endorsements, Motivational Speakers, Print Advertisements and Commercials and Voice-overs
Sports Service Founded:
1998
Clients:
Earin 'Magic' Johnson, Dennis Rodman, Hulk Hogan, Joe Frazier, Evel Knievel, Roy Jones Jr, Vinny Pazienza, Dave Winifield, Jenny McCarthy, Carmen Electra, Pamela Anderson, Nicollette Sheridan, Stacy Kiebler, Vince Neil, Marcus Schenkenberg, Brande Roderick, Symone Maree, Dave Prowse, Corbin Bernsen, Chuck Zito.

PRO MOTION, INC.
18405 EDISON AVENUE
CHESTERFIELD, MO 63005
314-997-0101
Fax: 314-997-6831
info@promotion1.com
www.promotion1.com
• Steve Randazzo, President
steve.randazzo@promotion1.com
Services:
Assist agencies in putting their Clients' products in the hands of potential customers where they live, work and play. Create the link between a Brand's advertising and its purchase with live commercials.
Clients:
Bandai, Gundam Invasion, Black & Decker, PartyMate Party Patrol, SnakeLight Tour, Bud Light, Bubble Zone, Maxim XXposure, Budweiser, NASCAR Brew Crew Challenge, SAM's CLUB Road Show, Wal-Mart and SAM's Club Grand Openings, Winner's Circle, Busch, Big Jake Million, Dollar Fish, Know Your Busch Racing
Description:
An independent , event/field/mobile marketing agency. Initiates personal encounters between consumers and products.
Sports Service Founded:
1995

PRO-REP, INC.
PO BOX 13176
CHESAPEAKE, VA 23325
757-222-9977
Fax: 330-308-8410
www.pro-rep.com
• Corinne Mastronardi, President
info@pro-rep.com
• Ellis Gillespie, Player Relations VP
info@pro-rep.com
• Loretta Journey, Accounting Manager
• Christopher Zambar, Player Protective Services Vice President
Description:
Full service marketing agency.
Services:
Corporate services include providing professional athletes for: Player Appearances, Player Endorsements, Speaking Engagements, Autographed Collectibles. Contract Negotiation, Pursuance of Endorsement Opportunities, Marketing and Public Relations (Public

Persona Development, Press Conferences, Press Releases), Financial Analysis (Budget Structuring, Income Tax Planning and Preparation, Insurance Coverage Analysis, Retirement Planning), Personal Services (Supervised off-season conditioning and diets; Concierge services, including temporary housing, transportation rentals, event tickets, limousine service)
Other Location:
South Florida Mid-Atlantic, PO Box 21234, Fort Lauderdale, FL 33335. 877-776-7376

PROFESSIONAL SPORTS MARKETING, INC.
2300 W WHITE AVENUE
MCKINNEY, TX 75071
214-544-0500
Fax: 214-544-0505
psm@professionalsportsmarketing.com
www.professionalsportsmarketing.com
• Kent Kramer, President
psm@professionalsportsmarketing.com
• Kurt Kramer, VP
psm@professionalsportsmarketing.com
Services:
Research, Creative Planning, Project Design and Implementation, Event Production and Staging, Sponsorship Evaluation and Negotiation, Sponsorship Sales, Public and Media Relations, Program Evaluation and Incentive Sports Travel. Totally integrated sports concept for sports events marketing, promotional programs, setup merchandising and advertising. Sports marketing consulting for corporate clients. Sports incentive travel programs including development and production of corporate.
Services:
Sport Marketing and Advertising
Clients:
Fritolay, Pepsi, Trimega, Ash Almond Associates
Sports Service Founded:
1985
Event Management Services:
Advertising and sales promotion. Specializes in special project events including project design, creative planning, research and event production, sponsorship evaluation and negotiation, public and media relations, program evaluation, incentive travel at major sporting events.

PROJECT SPORTS MARKETING
412 E MADISON STREET
SUITE 1218
TAMPA, FL 33602
813-442-4049
Fax: 509-756-3907
• Robert M. Bruni, Vice President Sales
(813) 442-4007
• Alan Weiss, Marketing Executive
(813) 442-4003
• Gabriel Guerrero, Sports Property Manager
(813) 442-4009
• Zach Levine, Creative Director
(813) 442-4006
Services:
Specializing in sports promotions, public relations and marketing services, including consultation with firms pursuing sports marketing strategies.
Event Management Services:
Event sponsorship negotiations.

Sports Service Founded:
1988

PROMARK ADVERTISING, INC.
3030 RED HILL AVENUE
COSTA MESA, CA 92626
714-641-1973
Fax: 714-641-3540
www.promarkadvertisinginc.com
• Brad Pilz, President
• David Major, Account Services
• Brad Pilz, President
Services:
Planning, development and activation of
mobile marketing programs, product
demonstrations, dealer/retail promotions,
contests, sweepstakes, hospitality and
special events, creative development and
production of exhibit properties, signage,
specialty advertising, promotional materials,
tour logistics, event staffing, venue and
sponsorship negotiation.
Description:
National promotional field-marketing
company. Their expertise is in the
development and implementation of
strategic, fully integrated, experiential mobile
marketing programs.
Sports Service Founded:
1981
Industry Expertise:
Automotive, motorcycles, marine,
automotive aftermarket, consumer
electronics, food and beverage

PROMONDE
12 CROMBIE STREET
SALEM, MA 1970
978-744-2654
• David Pelletier, President
(781) 639-8369
• Roland J. Regan Jr, Principal
(781) 639-8369
Marketing & Consulting Services:
A sports marketing and events development
management firm. Events include the
Mayors Cup racing series. Ride America,
and Action Lounge. ProMonde provides
strategic market planning, sponsorship
development, experiential marketing events,
investment analysis, public relations, media
negotiations, etc. The organization also
represents entertainers and or athletes.
Affiliated with the Cuban Charitable Classics
CCC. CCC is a 501C3 charitable entity
which promotes and directs sporting events
in Cuba for Cuban charity.

PROMOSPORT
76 CLARK ROAD
PO BOX 985
STOWE, VT 5672
802-253-5155
Fax: 802-253-9240
www.promosport.com
Sports Service Founded:
1981.
Marketing & Consulting Services:
Advises and performs independent
contractor projects for sports marketing
companies and public relation agencies;
Event management and promotion;
marketing and communication services for
sports events.

**PROMOTION EVENT & HOSPITALITY
EXCHANGE**
17212 N SCOTTSDALE ROAD
SUITE 1272
SCOTTSDALE, AZ 85255
480-699-8766

PROPERTYPORT
580 WHITE PLAINS ROAD
SUITE 620
TARRYTOWN, NY 10591
914-729-7231
866-729-7355
Fax: 914-729-7201
www.property-port.com
• Chris Thompson, Vice President Valuation
Services
cthompson@sponsoraid.com
• Mark F. Rockefeller, Board Chairman/CEO
Nature of Sports Services:
Organization is an application service
provider to consumer marketing companies
and their agencies that assists in crunching
down the time consuming and costly offline
processes that impede sponsorship
evaluation. The mission of SponsorAid is to
provide the necessary analytics that
facilitate sponsorship proposal
decision-making and negotiation for both
sponsors and properties.
Sports Service Founded:
2001

PROSPORTS MVP
225 E. CHEYENNE MOUNTAIN
BOULEVARD
SUITE 202
COLORADO SPRINGS, CO 80906
719-227-3920
Fax: 719-227-3922
general@prosportsmvp.com
www.prosportsmvp.com
• David Chavez, President, CEO
dchavez@prosportsmvp.com
• Mark Morley, Vice President
• Brian Lee, Director
blee@prosportsmvp.com
Nature of Service:
Pro Sports MVP is a full-service marketing
firm that specializes in events and
promotions which features sports and
entertainment personalities. We also provide
marketing services for over one thousand of
the sports world's most recognizable and
enduring athletes as well as a host of
Hollywood stars.
Year Founded:
1998

PSP SPORTS MARKETING
519 EIGHTH AVENUE
NEW YORK, NY 10018
212-697-1460
Fax: 212-286-8154
www.pspsports.com
• Martin Lewis, Executive Vice President
Business Development
(301) 315-0181
mlewis@pspsports.com
• David Gerschwer, Executive VP
(212) 697-1460
dgerschwer@pspsports.com
• Doug Kimmel, Marketing and Promotions
VP
dkimmel@pspsports.com
Services:
Provides marketers with a menu of fully

integrated services and marketing solutions
including print media, golf properties, sports
marketing services, custom publishing,
corporate hospitality and online media.
Clients:
Becks, Suzuki, Century 21, Thompson's
Waterseal
Sports Service Founded:
1971
Marketing & Consulting Services:
Full-service marketing agency handling the
development and implementation of a wide
range of sports-related promotional
programs, including sweepstakes, special
events, consumer promotions, point of sale,
sampling, single sponsor publications,
corporate hospitality and trade incentives.
Uniquely capable of coordinating
promotional programs with leading
professional and collegiate sporting events
across the country.
Other Locations:
New England Region: 151 Merrimac Street
#200, Boston, MA 02114. 617-367-5955;
FAX: 617-367-5831, Southeast Region:
3226 Leslie Lane, Atlanta, GA 30345.
770-414-9810; FAX: 770-414-9813, Midwest
Region: 20 North Wacker Drive, Suite 1330,
Chicago, IL 60606. 312-899-8098; FAX:
312-899-1252, Southwest Region: 12870
Hillcrest Road H226, Dallas, TX 75230.
972-387-2055; FAX: 972-387-2061, West
Region: 5200 West Century Boulevard,
Suite 810, Los Angeles, CA 90045.
310-410-5280; FAX: 310-342-7159

PUBLICIS DIALOG CHICAGO
111 E WACKER DRIVE
CHICAGO, IL 60601
312-552-4600
Fax: 312-552-4650
• Rose Ann Anschuetz, President / Chief
Executive Officer
(312) 522-4602
• Paul Fullmer, Chairman
(312) 373-7090
Description:
Full service public relations organization &
consultancy.
Services:
Research and strategic planning, media
relations, issues management, investor
relations, event and contest management,
and culinary services.
Clients:
ABC Radio, Abbott Labs, American
Express, Centers for Disease Control and
Prevention, Church and Dwight, ConAgra,
Geyser Peak Winery, Hewlett-Packard,
Microsoft, Nestle, Principal Financial Group,
Purina, Safeway Supermarkets, Samsung,
Siemens, Travelweb, UnitedHealthcare,
United Soybean Board, Whirlpool
Other Location:
Washington DC

PUBLICIS NEW YORK
950 3RD AVENUE
7TH FLOOR
NEW YORK, NY 10001
212-279-6950
Fax: 212-279-5560
www.publicis-usa.com
• Gill Duff, President / Chief Executive
Officer
• Debbie Yount, Chief Executive Officer
(212) 279-5815

• David Corr, EVP / Executive Creative Director
david.corr@publicis-usa.com
• Marta LaRock, EVP / Brand Planning Director
Services:
Creates highly acclaimed advertising campaigns such as research and strategic planning, media relations, issues management, investor relations, event and contest management, and culinary services to a wide range of industries.
Clients:
Ad Council, Amstel Light, Bermuda Tourism, BMW, Citizen, The Coca-Cola Company, Coinstar, Computer Discount Warehouse, COnsumer Electronics Association, Cranberry Marketing Committee, Urves, Denny's, DISH Network, FujiFilm, General Mills, GlaxoSmithKline, Hazelnut Council, Heifer International, Heineken, Hewlett-Packard, ISE, Kraft, L'Oreal, Legg Mason, Marriot Hotels, Nestle, Pernord Ricard, Power BAr, Procter & Gamble, Real Networks, Ross Products, Safeco, Sanofi-Aventis, Sara Lee, Siemens, Simon Property Group, TBS, T-Mobile, Thomson/RCA, Tumi, UBS, United Soybean Board, United Way, Vault, Washington's Lottery, Whirlpool, Wyeth
Marketing & Consulting Services:
Advertising and marketing communications.

PUBLICITY MATTERS
14644 MCKNEW ROAD
BURTONSVILLE, MD 20866
301-385-2090
matt@publicitymatters.net
www.publicitymatters.net
Services:
Full service public relations such publicity, media relations, media buying and media tours specializing in entertainment and sports events.

QUALITY REPETITION, THE
611 OLD WILLETS PATH
HAUPPAUGE, NY 11788-4105
631-232-1588
Services:
Provides guidance to athletes in all professional sports to create balanced physique that is more resistant to incidence and/or severity of on-the-field injury and improve physical ability to compete in specific sports.
Sports Service Founded:
1988

R. PANIAGUA, INC.
9 E 38TH STREET
SUITE 901
NEW YORK, NY 10016
212-679-6755
Fax: 212-679-6757
www.rpaniagua.com
• Ralph Paniagua, President
(212) 679-6755
ralph@rpaniagua.net
• Ralph A Paniagua Jr., President & CEO
Services:
Provides quality, integrated, media-leveraged Latino marketing community programs, tracks record of tying-in promotional marketing efforts with publishing, broadcast and grassroots programs that deliver measurable results to corporate partners.
Sports Service Founded:
1988
Athlete Management Services:
Promotion of Latino sports personalities for corporate sponsors, tying in with major sporting events and community projects. Promoters of major world Champion title fights on pay-per-view and closed circuit. Major League Baseball/stadium tie-ins, including the New York Yankees.
Event Management Services:
Manages events at baseball and other sports stadiums and sports facilities, small and large in capacity. Extensively involved in promotional events in the Hispanic market. Creates grassroots corporate promotional campaigns for boxing, baseball and soccer events. Broadcast rights holders of the Baseball Winter Leagues Caribbean World Series (TV, Cable).
Marketing & Consulting Services:
Hispanic marketing tied to retail and all levels of sports, including professional, on a regional and national level. Also provides international sports marketing. Creates and implements sports media and programs that increase the self-worth of Latinos, while delivering measurable success for corporate partners.

R.B. ROBERTSON & COMPANY
1350 COLLEGE POINT
WINTER PARK, FL 32789-5700
407-647-3963
800-835-7212
Fax: 407-644-1374
www.rbrobertson.com
• Randall B Robertson, President / Chief Executive Officer
(407) 647-3963
Sports Service Founded:
1987
Services:
Organization offers solutions to corporations to leverage golf events, specialize in corporate events, charity events, business golf seminars, and major championship hospitality.
Clients:
EMC, Fannie Mae, Golfweek, ITG Inc., Jefferies & Company, JPMorgan Chase, Lanny Wadkins, Marriott, McKesson HBOC, Pfizer Consumer Healthcare, Schering-Plough Corporation, Terrabrook, Trammell Crow Company, Thomas Weisel Partners
Services:
Corporate Events, Major Championships Hospitality, The Masters, Celebrity Appearances, Business Golf Seminars, Charity Events

RACING ENTERPRISES MOTOCROSS
13223 BLACK MOUNTAIN ROAD
SUITE 1-176
SAN DIEGO, CA 92129
858-484-1441
Fax: 858-484-7056
www.remsatmx.com
• Frank Thomason, President
fthomason@remsatmx.com
Services:
Promotes motocross racing
Description:
Helps promote pro and amateur riders from across the world.

Event Management Services:
Promotes motocross racing at Carlsbad Raceway.
Sports Service Founded:
1986

RADIAN 1
824 W.SUPERIOR STREET
SUITE 205
CHICAGO, IL 60642
312-492-9333
Fax: 312-372-0682
www.robinsonmaites.com
• Alan Maites, President
amaites@robinsonmaites.com
• Ryan Jarol, Vice President, Account director
• Paul Woolf, Vice President , Strategy and planning
pwoolf@robinsonmaites.com
• Bob Neff, Executive Creative Director
• Lowell Wallace, Account Director,Strategy
lwallace@robinsonmaites.com
Marketing & Consulting Services:
Full service, fully integrated sports and events consulting. Program development, execution and sponsorship sales.
Services:
Involvement and Action Incentives, Sales and Retailer Programs, Account-Specific Programs, Co-Marketing Programs, Merchandising, Site Design, Online Training/Education, E-mail Campaigns, On/Off Line Integration, Offline to Online Traffic Drivers, Text Message Marketing, Interactive Kiosks, Database Marketing - Development & Maintenance, Design and Modeling, Response Analysis, Direct Mail, List Acquisition, Relationship Marketing, Lead Generation and Qualification, Cross Sell and Upsell Marketing, Meeting and Convention ROI Optimization, Sports/Entertainment, Mobile Marketing, Sponsorship Activation and Leveraging, Product Sampling and Demonst
Clients:
BMG, Clorox, DHL, Discover Financial Services, MB Financial Bank, Minuteman International, Nakano, Nestle, Rand McNally, Sara Lee Intimates, Verizon Communications, Visa, World Space, Make A Wish Foundation, Big Brothers/Big Sisters, Better Business Bureau

RADIUS GROUP, INC.
545 E WESTFIELD BOULEVARD
INDIANAPOLIS, IN 46220
317-205-3500
Fax: 317-205-3501
• Kevin A. Davey, President
Description:
Manufacturer and martketers of die-cast replics vehicles for sporting and other evetns. Among recent custom die-cast projects include: Indianapolis 500, Indy Racing League, NASCAR, Minor Baseball, Kentucky Derby and more.

RAYCOM SPORTS
1900 W MOREHEAD STREET
SUITE 200
CHARLOTTE, NC 28208
704-378-4400
www.raycomsports.com
• Ken Haines, President / Chief Executive Officer
(704) 378-4400

khaines@raycomsports.com
• De Cordell, Sales and Marketing VP / ACC Properties
dcordell@raycomsports.com
• Brian Flajole, Golf & Business Development VP
(916) 645-7200
bflajole@raycomsports.com
• Ken Haines, President & CEO
• Jimmy Rayburn, Chief Operating Officer
• George Johnson, Senior Vice President
• Rob Reichley, Executive Producer
Services:
Leader in marketing, producing and distributing sports program and creating, managing and distributing special events

RCA GROUP EVENT MARKETING + MANAGEMENT
2310 W 75TH STREET
PRAIRIE VILLAGE, KS 66208
913-384-8920
Fax: 913-384-8921
www.rcagroup.com
• Russ Cline, President
russ@rcagroup.com
• Tom Boehm, Administration and Finance EVP
tom@rcagroup.com
• Mike Mathis, Operations EVP
mike@rcagroup.com
• David Pulford, EVP
dpulford@rcagroup.com
Services:
A sports and entertainment production/promotion company which provides turnkey event production/activation, sponsor management and marketing promotions services.
Marketing & Consulting Services:
Consults with businesses on marketing and managing sponsorships, sports and entertainment involvement.
Event Management Services:
Marketing, management and promotion firm providing event production, marketing, promotion, and operations for entertainment and sports events.
Clients Include:
ESPN, Inc., International Tennis Federation, Kansas City Chiefs Football Club, Inc., United States Tennis Association.
Year Founded:
1984

REESE SPORTS
955 BERKSHIRE BOULEVARD
WYOMISSING, PA 19610
610-378-1835
Fax: 610-378-1676
info@reeseadv.com
• Matt Golden, Managing Partner
(610) 378-1835
matt@reeseadv.com
• Greg Purcell, Director Brand Strategy/Managing Partner
Sports Service Founded:
1980
Marketing & Consulting Services:
Full service advertising, marketing and public relations agency. Areas of concentration include automotive racing, bicycling, boating, exercise/fitness, golfing, motorcycling, skiing, and tennis.

RELAY SPORTS AND ENTERTAINMENT MARKETING
222 MERCHANDISE MART PLAZA
SUITE 4-160B
CHICAGO, IL 60654
312-297-1212
Fax: 312-297-1401
• Wally Hayward, Chief Executive Officer
(312) 297-1400
• John Dolan, Chief Operating Officer
(314) 569-1977
• Jeannette Mueller, Chief Financial Officer
(314) 743-4718
• Tim Mauer, EVP/Managing Director
(312) 297-1400
Services:
Specializes in event production, mobile marketing, on-premise promotion, product sampling, trade shows and conventions, corporate hospitality, grassroots tournaments
Sponsorship Services:
League partnership, consumer promotions, made for tv-events, integrated sponsorship, athlete endorsement, motorsports
Year Founded:
2001
Other Locations:
303 E Wacker Drive, Chicago, Il 60601. 312-297-1423; FAX: 312-297-1401, 1675 Broadway, 3rd Floor, New York, NY 10019. 212-468-3916; FAX:212-468-4383, 1230 Peachtree Street NE, Suite 1825, Atlanta, GA 30309, 5200 Lankershim Boulevard, Suite 800, North Hollywood, CA 91601. 818-753-7268
Nature of Sports Service:
Provides strategic consulting and idea generation, program leveraging and management, and on-site event execution for its world-class brands. Expertise includes field marketing and research measurement, development and production of merchandising materials, event research/evaluation, event production and management, venue signage, naming rights, made-for-TV events, athlete endorsements, mobile marketing, mall tours, product sampling, hospitality, concert tours, equipment design and fabrication, and network sponsorships.
Clients:
Allstate, Anheuser-Busch, U.S. Army, Better Homes & Gardens, Coca-Cola, Delta Airlines, Hallmark, LEGO, McDonald's, MSN.IT, Nike, Nintendo and Ralston Purina.

RHINO SPORTS MARKETING
550 POST OAK BOULEVARD
SUITE 450
HOUSTON, TX 77027
713-681-6711
Fax: 713-681-5220
thensey@rhinomarketing.cc
www.rhinoworldwide.com
• Thomas Hensey, Head of USA Operations
thensey@rhinomarketing.cc
• Philip Lay, Head of UK Operations
Nature of Sports Service:
An independent consultancy specializing in sports marketing, sponsorship consultancy and sales, event marketing and management.
Services:
Consultancy (target audience analysis, role within the marketing mix, media evaluation, opportunity fit & analysis, sponsorship search and negotiation, contract advice,

future projections), Sponsorship Management & Exploitation, Sponsorship sales. Event Marketing, Event Management (Plans and budgets, construction, planning apparavals, project management, emergency services, media management and contracts, security, ticketing, hospitality
Clients:
KrisBrown's KickClub, Red Bull Master Class, Final 5, Shell Houston Open, Houston Golf Association, Giff Nielson/Roger Clemens Day of Golf For Kids

RHYS MILLEN RACING
17492 APEX CIRCLE
HUNTINGTON BEACH, CA 92647
714-847-2158
Fax: 714-848-6821
sales@rmrproducts.com
www.rodmillenstore.com

RMG3 EAST COAST
1801 W INTL SPEEDWAY BOULEVARD
DAYTONA BEACH, FL 32114
386-681-6124
www.rmg3.com
• Kevin Hindson, Vice President Marketing/Communications
(704) 377-7477
• Matt Heisley, VP Sales
(704) 377-7477
Services:
A full-service media, marketing and merchandising agency, providing such services as web site development, e-commerce consultation, and sponsorship solicitation.
Clients:
Alltel, Arena Football League, FIFA, Ford, FoxSports.com, Masterfoods, Mazda, MSNBC, National Guard, Speedway Motorsports (SMI), Speed Channel, US Men's National Soccer Team Players Association and West Coast Conference.
Sports Service Founded:
1998

ROBUSTELLI SPORTS MARKETING
1717 NEWFIELD AVE
STAMFORD, CT 06903
203-322-2790
Fax: 203-912-6487
www.rcsltd.com
• Richard Robustelli, Chairman/President
• Paul Salvatore, Chief Executive Officer
(203) 352-0500
• Dan DeFrancesco, Corporate Travel Management Division
(203) 352-0505
• Jim Robustelli, President
Sports Service Founded:
1958
Services:
Sports Marketing (sports related promotions, client entertainment, celebrity appearances, special event Ticketing), Merchandise Services, Motivation, Multimedia.
Event Management Services:
Sales meetings, incentive programs, celebrity appearances, sports related retail and trade promotions, sports memorabilia and major sporting event travel.
Business Revenue:
$10.60 M

ROUND ROBIN SPORTS
1415 N DEARBORN PKWY
SUITE 16C
CHICAGO, IL 60610
312-337-3790
Fax: 312-337-3996
• Robin Monsky, President
Nature of Services:
Provides media relations services to the
sports industry

ROWLAND COMPANY
1675 BROADWAY
3RD FLOOR
NEW YORK, NY 10019
212-527-8800
Fax: 212-527-8924
• Steve Bryant, Managing Director
• Maryanne Caruso, Senior Vice President
Services:
Public relations services for sporting goods,
sports marketing and sports sponsorship
clients.

RPR SPORTS & ENTERTAINMENT, LLC
23 VREELAND ROAD
FLORHAM PARK, NJ 7932
973-360-0600
Services:
Product placement/brand placement and
seamless brand/ brand message
integrations in feature films, television, and
world-class events. Strategically and
seamlessly integrate brands into the scripts
of tomorrow's blockbuster films.

RSR PARTNERS
600 STEAMBOAT ROAD
GREENWICH, CT 06830
203-618-7000
Fax: 203-618-7011
info@rsrpartners.com
www.rsrpartners.com
• Cameron Smith, Senior Associate, Global
Sport Leadership
(301) 675-8855

RUDER/FINN SPORTS, INC.
301 E 57TH STREET
NEW YORK, NY 10022
212-593-6400
info@ruderfinn.com
www.ruderfinn.com
• David Finn, Chairman
• Michael Schubert, Chief Innovation Officer
• Louise Harris, Chief Global Strategist
• Scott Schneider, Chief Digital Officer
• Rachel Spielman, Global Head of
Corporate Communications
(212) 593-6400
spielmanr@ruderfinn.com
• Emmanuel Tchividjian, Chief Ethics Officer
• John McInerney, Director, Consumer
Affairs
• Jen Long, Director, Technology &
Innovation
Nature of Sports Service:
A leading independent communications
agency whose expertise includes corporate
reputation management, branding, cultural
and social issues, and intent-driven social
media.

SADLER & COMPANY, INC.
3014 DEVINE ST.
PO BOX 5866
COLUMBIA, SC 29250-5866
800-622-7370
800-622-7370
Fax: 803-256-4017
sport@sadlersports.com
www.sadlersports.com
• John Sadler, President
(800) 622-7370
john@sadlerco.com
Description
Sadler & Company specializes in providing
insurance solutions for the sports and
recreation industries. Client base includes
12 national sports organizations and over
7000 community sports organizations such
as teams & leagues, camps, outdoors,
special events, health clubs, etc.

SAXTON COMMUNICATIONS INC.
1448 HOLLYWOOD AVENUE
LANGHORNE, PA 19047-7417
215-752-7797
Fax: 215-752-1518
ESAXTON144@AOL.COM
www.saxtonsponsormarket.com
• Ernie Saxton, President/Publisher
• Marilyn Saxton, Treasurer
• Joe McHugh, Advertising Staff
Nature of Sports Service:
A motorsports sponsorship firm specializing
in marketing, public relations,
representation, and media relations

SCA PROMOTIONS, INC.
3030 LBJ FREEWAY
SUITE 300
DALLAS, TX 75234
214-860-3770
888-860-3770
Fax: 214-860-3723
scainfo@scapromo.com
www.scapromotions.com
• Robert D. Hamman,
Founder/President/Chief Executive Office
info@scapromo.com
• Susan Hatfield, Marketing Director
(214) 860-3712
Services:
Jumbo prize coverage for contests, games
and other promotional programs, including
sports contests, gaming promotions, retail
contests, brand marketing programs and
media promotions, Guarantees for athlete
performance incentives
Clients:
BEN Marketing Group, Don Jagoda,
Promotion Group Central, The Integer
Group, The Properties Group, Ventura
Associates, Inc., Daimler Chrysler, Harley
Davidson, Mazda Motors of America, Inc.,
Mazda Motors of America, Inc., Nissan
North America, Inc., Toyota Motor Sales,
Bally's Las Vegas, Caesars Atlantic City,
Foxwoods Resort Casino, Harrah's, MGM
Grand Detroit Casino, Venetian Resort
Hotel, Harvard University, Ohio University,
Texas Tech University, University of
Arkansas, University of California-Berkeley,
University of Hawaii, Adidas American,
Blockbuster Inc., Hasbro Interactive, Sony
Electronics, Inc., WM Wrigley, American
Express Financ
Services:
Over-redemption protection for coupons and
premium offers, Internet and e-commerce

promotions, Packaged services where they
provide both the prize and materials to help
with the setup
Sports Service Founded:
1986
Event Management Services:
Contingent prize coverage, up to $1 million
in cash, of contests and sweepstakes,
contractual bonus awards, player incentives
and other promotional games; specializing
in sporting events. Contests such as football
toss and kick, basketball shots, hockey
shots, grand slam home runs, race tracks,
fishing tournaments, golf, track and field,
bowling, soccer, etc. Contractual incentive
bonuses with PGA, LPGA, Champion
player; NHL teams and NASCAR drivers.
Also specializes in promotional contests for
radio/TV stations and publications
associated with sports and sporting events.
Marketing & Consulting Services:
Provides consultation to sponsors,
advertisers, direct marketers,
manufacturers, event planners, and sports
teams for design, planning, and
implementation of promotional contests and
sweepstakes. Advises clients in contest
design and prize structuring, as well as the
latest concepts in promotional contests.
Clients:
Advertising/Promotions, Automotive,
Casinos & Lotteries, Colleges and
Universities, Consumer Products, Financial
Services, Food & Beverage, Insurance,
Internet, ESPN, Media, Non-Profit, Sports,
Technology & Telecommunications,
Microsoft Corporation

SCARBOROUGH SPORTS MARKETING
770 BROADWAY
NEW YORK, NY 10003
646-654-8400
855-80-SCARB
Fax: 646-654-8450
info@scarborough.com
www.scarborough.com
• Bob Cohen, President/Chief Executive
Officer
• Brian Condon, Executive VP, Commercial
Development
• Yvonne McHugh, Director of Marketing
and Communications
• Steve Seraita, Executive VP Sales
• Diana Illiano, Public Relations & Event
Coordinator
• Cary McFarland, Account Executive
• Tom Reutter, Account Manager
Nature of Service:
Provides consumer insights on sports fan
avidity; multi-media measures including
sports viewing and listening on a local,
regional and national level. Scarborough
measures over 1,700 categories and
brands, as well as media, demographics
and lifesytles of consumers. Corporate
sponsorhsip information including fans'
shopping and product/service usage.

SCHEERGAME SPORTS DEVELOPMENT
3127 W WISCONSIN AVENUE
MILWAUKEE, WI 53208
414-908-4252
Fax: 414-908-4259

SCREEN WORKS
2201 W. FULTON STREET
CHICAGO, IL 60612

professional services

312-243-8265
800-294-8111
Fax: 312-243-8290
screens@thescreenworks.com
www.thescreenworks.com
Services:
Creative Web site development and the maintenance

SEATS 3D
1150 BALLENA BOULEVARD
SUITE 250
ALAMEDA, CA 94501
510-521-0720
Fax: 510-521-3972
www.seats3d.com
• Steve Stonehouse, Senior VP Sales
• Jeff Sherratt, Director Business Development
jsherratt@ballenatech.com
• David Schwartz, Chief Operations Officer/Chief Technology Officer
• Richard H. Sherratt, Chairman of the Board/Chief Executive Officer
Nature of Services:
Using 3D visualizations of sports venues, Ballena Technologies creates realistic seating visuals to improve the online ticketing experience by familiarizing potential customers with a facility, creating excitement, sales, and customer satisfaction.

SFX/CLEAR CHANNEL COMMUNICATIONS
200 EAST BASSE ROAD
SAN ANTONIO, TX 78209-8328
210-822-2828
www.clearchannel.com
• Lowry Mays, Chairman of the Board
LLowryMays@clearchannel.com
• Mark Mays, Chief Executive Officer
MarkPMays@clearchannel.com
• Randall Mays, President and Chief Financial Officer
(210) 822-2828
RandallTMays@clearchannel.com
• Andrew W Levin, EVP and Chief Legal Officer
AndyLevin@clearchannel.com
Sports Service Founded:
1978
Marketing & Consulting Services:
Events and promotion, public relations/marketing communications for sports firms, associations, organizations and magazines, feature articles, brochures, news releases and newsletters on all aspects of sports medicine and participatory sports emphasizing prevention and treatment of athletic injuries; and athletic health/fitness research.

SHERRY GROUP INC.
TWO SYLVAN WAY
PARSIPPANY, NJ 7054
973-984-3000
Fax: 973-984-3088
• J. Gr Sherry, Chief Executive Officer
Services:
Public relations and sports marketing services for events, companies, institutions and individuals.
Clients:
Adams USA, Akadema, Amer Sports, Cendant Hotel Group, Commonfund, Danskin, Edgewood Country Club, Edwin

Watts Golf, Fender Footwear, GlaxoSmithKline, Higher One, Hollow Brook Golf Club, LG Electronics, Marriot Golf, Tennis Industry Association, The Peninsula, Promised Land Dairy, Roche Sports, Smith & Wesson, Snickers (Masterfoods), State Fair Meadowlands, Suunto USA, USA Fencing, Waeve Corporation, Wilson Golf, Wenger NA
Sports Service Founded:
1992
Marketing & Consulting Services:
Public relations and sports marketing services for events, companies, institutions and individuals.

SHOP
3195A AIRPORT LOOP
COSTA MESA, CA 92626
714-434-7467
Fax: 714-435-3599
• Nick Adcock, Contact
Services:
Provides a global view into the world of alternative sports marketing. Specializes in authentic and credible creative, promotional and marketing executions to the youth market.
Sports Service Founded:
1985

SHOT BLOCK PROMOTIONS
11 WESTFIELD ROAD
NATICK, MA 1760
508-651-7900
Sports Service Founded:
1992
Event Management Services:
Onsite promotions for amateur or semi-pro events and corporate promotions. Live event announcing and sponsor promotions.

SIGNATURES NETWORK
2 BRYANT STREET
SUITE 300
SAN FRANCISCO, CA 94105
415-247-7400
800-673-6136
Fax: 415-247-7407
info@signaturenetworks.com
www.signaturesnetwork.com
• Dell Furano, Chief Executive Officer
dfurano@signaturesnet.com
• Phil Cussen, President/ Chief Operating Officer
pcussen@signaturesnet.com
• Rick Fish, EVP, Artist Relations
rfish@signaturesnet.com
• Django Bayless, SVP, New Media Technology/ Artist Relation
dbayless@signaturesnet.com
Services:
SN holds the rights to market and license more than 125 superstars, artists, celebrities and entertainment properties.
Clients:
Aaron Carter, Alicia Keys, Bobby Brown, Bonnie McKee, Boyz II Men, Britney Spears, Kanye West, Kenny G, Kylie Minogue, Luther Vandross, Madonna, O-Town, The Monkees, Usher, Adan Chalino Sanchez, Gloria Estefan, Jennifer Lopez, Jon Secada, Luis Miguel, Mana, Marc Anthony, Shakira, Thalia, American Idols, Blues Brothers, Bridge School Benefit, Chicago, Curious George, Guys and Dolls, Happy Tree Friends, Hatewear, House of Blues, John

Belushi, Mavericks, Peter Pan, Robin Williams, The English Roses, The Osbourne Family, Yellow Submarine, Alan Parsons, Alice Cooper, Barbra Streisand, Billy Idol, Billy Joel, Black Sabbath, Bruce Springsteen, Dan F
Sports Service Founded:
1993

SILVERMAN MEDIA & MARKETING GROUP
2761 ELLEN RD
BELLMORE, NY 11710
516-781-1668
Fax: 516-679-1614
smmgsports@aol.com
www.silverman-media.com
• Ira H Silverman, President
(516) 495-5280
• Erica Quagliata, Account Executive
(516) 495-5280
Description:
Areas of service: public relations, integrated marketing, special event creation management, celebrity representation and charitable foundations. We are nationally recognized for our creativity, placement success, writing skills. Primary areas of specialization include: sports leagues, associations, charities, foundations, events, teams, venues, Halls of Fame, sponsors, equipment, toys, games, players (active and retired), sportscasters, managers, coaches, sports marketing, companies, agents, etc.
Services:
Public Relations, Integrated Marketing, Special Event Creation and Management, Celebrity/Personal Representation, Charitable Foundations, Creative Services.
Clients:
16W Marketing, Leslie Allen Foundation, Alzheimer's Association, Crohn's Colitis Foundation of America (CCFA), Tariq Abdul-Wahad, Current NBA Player, Leslie Allen, Retired WTA Tennis Player, Len Berman, WNBC-TV Sports Anchor, Bill Boggs, TV Personality.
Other Location:
245 5th Avenue, Room 64, New York, NY 10016. 212-686-5983
Year Founded:
1996

SILVERMAN SPORTS CONSULTANTS
900 PINE HALLOW ROAD
MOUNT PLEASANT, SC 29464
843-881-3383
Fax: 843-881-3387
• Stuart Fetter, Chief Executive Officer
Services:
Full-service provider of sales consulting and financial services for sporting goods retailers.
Sports Service Founded:
1945
Marketing & Consulting Services:
Full-service provider of sales consulting & financial services for sporting goods retailers.

SIMMONS MARKET RESEARCH BUREAU/SMRB
230 PARK AVENUE S
3RD FLOOR
NEW YORK, NY 10003
212-863-4500
Fax: 212-863-4495

• Evan Goldfarb, EVP, Media Services
(760) 992-9061
EvanG@smrb.com
• Chistopher Lubniewski, Managing VP, Media Services
(212) 863-4560
ChrisL@smrb.com
• Gary Warech, Managing VP, Media Services
(212) 863-4566
GaryW@smrb.com
• Jeromy Gabor, VP, Media Services
(212) 863-4554
JeremyG@smrb.com
Services:
Provides companies and advertising agencies with the critical marketing information, needed to target their products, brands and media to today's consuming public, including Adult Study (NCS/NHCS), Teens Study, Tweenz Study, Youth Study, Kids Study, Hispanic Study, Household Study, Gay and Lesbian Consumer Study, Simmons Local, Segmentation Systems, Database Integration, and Custom Research.

Study of Media and Markets:
All major sports covered. Sample size: 23,555 adults. Provides number/demographic characteristics of sports participants and spectators as well as their frequency of participation/attendance, equipment purchases and media exposure. Conducted annually, latest report - Oct, 1997. Subscription fee depends on size of company. More detailed information (brand preferences, attitudes, etc.) can be obtained via custom re-contact of 12,000 respondents, eliminating screening costs.
Other Location:
700 West Hillsboro Blvd., Bldg 4-201, Deerfield Beach, FL 3441; Phone: 954-427-4104; Fax: 954-427-3760

SLAM DUNK TO THE BEACH
ATTN: ROBERT F JACOBS
PO BOX 0133
FELTON, DE 19943
302-430-7526
Fax: 302-430-3865
www.slamdunktothebeach.com
• Robert F. Jacobs, Executive Director/Chief Executive Offic
Services:
Marketing & Consulting: Creates and manages Slam Dunk To The Beach National Holiday Basketball Invitational for high school basketball teams, as well as Slam Dunk To The Beach National Golf Invitational and Rockin' The Rim National Amateur Basketball Invitational.
Sports Service Founded:
1990

SLOANE VISION UNLIMITED
305 MADISON AVENUE
SUITE 1337
NEW YORK, NY 10017
212-922-0555
Fax: 212-922-1306
• Glenn Hendricks, VP Business Development/Licensing
(212) 922-0555
• Dave Landesberg, Director oF Licensing
Nature of Service:
Strategic targeting and product planning, Contract negotiations, Product concept development, Hand-in-hand working relationships with Licensors and Licensees, Billing, collections and Royalty reporting,

Integrated retail progams, Cross-marketing and Licensing opportunities, Quality control, Worldwide program implementation.
Sports Service Founded:
1939
Clients:
Chicken Soup for the Soul, DQ, J-14, Little League Baseball, Little Trees, Slinky Brand, TV Guide, Woman's World, Stuckeys
Marketing & Consulting Services:
Exclusive Worldwide Licensing agency for Little League Baseball.

SMART INDUSTRIES
1901 BELL AVENUE
SUITE 12
DES MOINES, IA 50315
515-265-9900
800-553-2442
Fax: 515-265-3148
www.smartind.com
Services:
Strategic planning and marketing services related to sports events, including, demand analysis, program development, financial feasibility, corporate sponsorship, and organization and staffing plans. Creates sponsorship collateral materials, sponsorship development, and media planning.

SME BRANDING
298 FIFTH AVENUE
5TH FLOOR
NEW YORK CITY, NY 10001
212-924-5700
Fax: 212-924-1941
www.smebranding.com
• Edward O'Hara, Chairman/Senior Partner
(212) 924-5700
eohara@smebranding.com
• Frederick S. Popp, CEO/Partner
(212) 924-5700
fpopp@smebranding.com
Year Founded:
1989.
Sports Service Founded:
1988
Services:
With over 2000 brand building solutions provided to sports, higher education, and corporate clients worldwide, SME has an unparalleled insight as to how brands must be built and communicated for maximum success. This experience is applied to each client engagement with highly successful results, increasing client revenue and building brand value.
Clients:
Adidas,Akebono, Amateur Softball Association, Anheuser-Busch, Anna Kournikova, Appalachian State University, Arena Football League, Asahi Beer, Atlanta Hawks, Atlanta Thrashers, Auburn University, Australian Football League, Bakersfield Blitz, Baltimore Bayhawks, Baylor University, Binghamton University, Boston Bruins, Boston Cannons, Boston College, The Boys Club of New York, Brand Asset Valuator, Brickyard 400, Brigham Young University, Cal State University - Northridge, Calgary Flames, California Cougars, Cadbury Schweppes, Cameron University, Canadian Football League, Chicago Rush, Chinese Football League, Churchill Downs, Classic Sports

SMITH ASBURY, INC.
225 N LIMA STREET
SUITE 6
SIERRA MADRE, CA 91024
626-836-3300
Fax: 626-836-5500
info@smithasbury.com
www.smithasbury.com
• Greg Asbury, Principal
gasbury@smithasbury.com
• Judy Smith Asbury, Founder
Services:
Delivers compelling marketing solutions through the use of strategic planning, identification of critical messages and target audiences, production of impactful designs, illustrations, and copywriting. Provides Strategic marketing, print design, e-marketing, and public relations.

SOCCER MARKETING & PROMOTIONS, INC.
7444 SW 48 STREET
MIAMI, FL 33155
305-669-0101
Fax: 305-669-9979
www.copalatina.com

SOCCER SPHERE
11140 ROCKVILLE PIKE (151)
ROCKVILLE, MD 20852
301-231-8022
Fax: 301-231-5261
ramsaysoccer@yahoo.com
• Graham Ramsay, President
(301) 231-8022
ramsaysoccer@yahoo.com
Description:
Specializing in both commercial and educationsl spheres of soccer marketing/consultancy activities worldwide
Year Founded:
1978

SPEEDWAY GROUP, INC.
19706 ONE NORMAN BOULEVARD
SUITE B12
CORNELIUS, NC 28031
704-904-4141
Fax: 704-987-5055
legal@speedwaygroup.com
www.speedwaygroup.com
• Mike Schriefer, President
Services:
Motorsports marketing and management group specializing in all forms of motorsports including INDYCAR and NASCAR Racing. Services include driving personnel for off-road or on-track demonstrations, ride and drives, driver training, sponsorship, and hospitality.

SPIKE/DDB PRODUCTIONS
55 WASHINGTON STREET
SUITE 650
BROOKLYN, NY 11201
718-596-5400
Fax: 718-596-7256
info@spikeddb.com
www.spikeddb.com
• Spike Lee, Chairman
slee@spikeddb.com
• Bola Esho, Account Supervisor
dwade@spikeddb.com
• Chad Mclean, Assistant Account Executive
• Felix Messina Jr., Account Executive

• Leah Hamilton, Senior Art Producer
• Jeison Rodriguez, Senior Art Director
Services:
Develops strategic and production of advertising and marketing programs. Develops and executes television, radio and print advertisements.
Clients:
Chanel, Pepsi, New York Knicks, Royal Caribbean, NFB, Clean&Clear, Exxon Mobil, Essence, Tanqueray, Doritos, State Palm Insurance, Frito Lay, Alltel, Foxwoods, Usta, TNT, Mountain Dew

SPONSORLOGIC, INC.
PO BOX 3728
MOORESVILLE, NC 28117
704-664-1714
Fax: 704-794-95796
MP@SponsorLogic.com
www.sponsorlogic.com
• Mel Poole, President
(704) 788-9915
MP@SponsorLogic.com
Year Founded:
1997.
Description:
Full service sponsorship management, coaching and sales agency
Clients:
National Electrical Contractors Assn, National Apartment Association, Sports Business Journal and Assn for Manufacturing Technology.

SPONSORSHIP RESEARCH INTERNATIONAL USA
230 E AVENUE
NORWALK, CT 06855
203-831-2061
Fax: 203-831-2301
hello@teamsri.com
www.teamsri.com
• Julie Zdziarski, EVP
(203) 831-2061
julie.zdziarski@teamsri.com
• Jeff Eccleston, VP
(203) 831-2060
jeff.eccleston@teamsri.com
Services:
Provides Event/Spectator Research, Custom Telephone Research, Web-based Research, Ethnography and Observation Research, Qualitative Research, Corporate Hospitality Evaluations, Impressions Analysis, Media Exposure and Valuation, and Property Valuation.
Clients:
ADT Security Services, Allstate, American Century, American Express, Anheuser-Busch, Bank One, Bell Sports, Canon, Cingular Wireless, Citizens Bank, Coca-Cola, ConAgra Foods, Delta Airlines, Eli Lilly, FedEx, Gateway Computers, Gillette, Hallmark, IBM, monster.com, Motorola, New Balance, Nike, Nissan, Nokia, Norelco, Pfizer, Philips, Reebok, Sprint, Sunoco, Texaco, The Home Depot, UBS, Wired Magazine, VISA, AFL, Dew Action Sports Tour, NASCAR, NBA, New York Jets, New York Mets, MLS, NFL, NTRA, New York Road Runners, San Francisco 49ers, US Open Tennis Series, WWE, AEG, Digitas, Edelman Public Relations, GMR Marketing, IMG, Jack Morton
Description:

Experience in spectator surveys, national sponsorship tracking studies, and national and international TV and press exposure reports, custom qualitative and quantitative sponsorship research.
Year Founded:
1996

SPORT & SOCIAL CLUBS OF THE U.S.
770 N HALSTED
SUITE #306
CHICAGO, IL 60622
312-850-8196
Fax: 312-850-3138
schedule@sportandsocialclubs.com
www.chicagosportandsocialclub.com
• Jason Erkes, President
jason@sportandsocialclubs.com
• Chris Hastings, VP
chris@sportandsocialclubs.com
Services:
Creates and sponsors events
Number of members:
15,000 participants.
Publications:
TAKE ACTION, 6 times annually.
Membership Requirements:
Dues of $30 per year.
Description:
Founded 1989. Event planning focusing on grass roots events. Over 150,000 participants in 20 cities across the U.S.

SPORT MANAGEMENT RESEARCH INSTITUTE
6965 EL CAMINO REAL
SUITE 105-228
CARLSBAD, CA 92009
954-389-9095
858-779-9291
info@go-smri.com
www.go-smri.com
• Kathleen A. Davis, President
kdavis@go-smri.com
• Sandy Keehn, Operations Director
skeehn@go-smri.com
Description:
Conducts all phases of market research projects. Works with sponsoring sports organizations the purpose, scope and methods for the project are determined. Marketing research projects data on: Sponsorship Impact, Service Deliver Assessment, Demographic Profiles, Event Satisfaction, Cross Event Preferences, Community Support/Public Relations. Marketing research projects conducted at consecutive annual events or intervals throughout a season. Research also includes trend analysis and industry comparisons.
Clients:
Giants Stadium, Florida Marlins, Florida Panthers, Cleveland Browns Coca-Cola Company, San Diego Chargers, San Diego Padres, University of Southern California, U.S. Tennis Open, USTA, Montreal Expos, NFL, AVP Tour, Super Bowls XXIV - XXVI.

SPORT SCAN INFO
2151 HAWKINS STREET
SUITE 200
CHARLOTTE, NC 28203
704-987-3450
Fax: 704-987-3455
sportscan@sportsonesource.com
www.sportscaninfo.com

Description:
Provider of weekly point-of-sale information on athletic footwear, apparel, licensed products, team sports equipment, outdoor products, golf, tennis, fitness equipment, inline skating and other sporting goods to the nation's leading retailers, manufacturers, financial institutions, sport agents and other interested third parties.
year founded
1989

SPORTAMERICA
PO BOX 95030
SALT LAKE, UT 84095
801-253-3360
800-467-7885
customerservice@sportamerica.com
www.sportamerica.com
• John W Scott, Chief Executive Officer
(801) 253-3360
john@sportAmerica.com
Marketing & Consulting Services:
Athletic educational and motivational products. Specializes in production, distribution and promotion of sports videos, books, camps, and clinics. Products focus on work ethic - from fundamentals, mental training, and fitness to X's and O's, skill development, team training, and individual workouts. Produces motivational audio products for business through the medium of the following sports: Basketball, golf, soccer, baseball, football, volleyball and fitness products.
Sports Service Founded:
1990

SPORTS & ENTERTAINMENT DIRECT, INC
2470 WINDY HILL ROAD
SUITE 300
MARIETTA, GA 30067
770-952-0025
Marketing & Consulting Services:
A promotional direct marketing company specializing in distribution of samples and advertising messages at major sports and entertainment events. Provides advertisers direct-to-sports-fan marketing programs through co-op fan bag distribution or solo sampling at major sports events.

SPORTS & FITNESS INDUSTRY ASSOCIATION
8505 FENTON STREET
SUITE 211
SILVER SPRING, MD 20910
301-495-6321
Fax: 301-495-6322
info@sfia.org
• Cove Tom, President & CEO
Description:
Trade association of leading sports and fitness brands.

SPORTS ADVERTISING NETWORK, INC.
366 N BROADWAY
JERICHO, NY 11753-2025
516-942-4215
• John Fugazy, VP
Services:
Sells advertising for professional teams, covering all aspects of professional team advertising media including broadcast, print, signage, official sponsorships and promotions. Also provides media buying

services for advertisers to gain access to sports venue.

SPORTS BUSINESS GROUP
1800 S PACIFIC COAST HIGHWAY
SUITE 24
REDONDO BEACH, CA 90277-6161
310-316-8825
Fax: 310-316-8826
info@sportsbusinessgroup.com
www.sportsbusinessgroup.com
• David M Carter, Founder/Business Consultant
david.carter@sportsbusinessgroup.com
• David M. Carter, Founder
david.carter@sportsbusinessgroup.com
• Jeff Marks, Senior Marketing Executive
jeff.marks@sportsbusinessgroup.com
Description:
Founded as a means to service the dynamic and increasingly volatile Southern California sports and entertainment industries. Provides consulting recommendations and advice to a broad range of corporations, the legal community, venues, the public sector, the media and academia. Is favorably and uniquely positioned as the premier provider of strategic marketing services for the sports industry.
Services:
Develops and implements business solutions for companies and organizations seeking strategic direction in the areas of sports marketing and management.
Year Founded:
1999

SPORTS BUSINESS RESEARCH NETWORK
PO BOX 2378
PRINCETON, NJ 08543
609-896-1996
Fax: 609-896-1903
richard@sbrnet.com
www.sbrnet.com
• Richard A Lipsey, President
(609) 896-1996
richard@sbrnet.com
Nature of Sports Service:
Provide marketing research on the sporting goods industry and a database of sixteen trade publications with articles indexed by subject and keyword. Market research information includes participation trends, consumer expenditures, import data, attendance data. Covers equipment, footwear, and apparel.

SPORTS DISPLAY
30051 COMMERCIO
RANCHO SANTA MARGARITA, CA 92688
800-854-3476
800-854-3476
Fax: 949-589-9247
www.sportsdisplay.com
• Janet Willingham, Recruiting Department Administrator
Sports Service Founded:
1977
Services:
International company specializing in advertising sales to businesses. Creates organization designs, builds and installs activity and information centers in over 4000 golf courses, tennis clubs, racquetball facilities and fitness centers across North America.

SPORTS INTERNATIONAL, INC.
9375 WASHINGTON BOULEVARD
LAUREL, MD 20723
301-575-9400
800-555-0801
Fax: 301-575-9439
www.footballcamps.com
• Chuck Bollweg, President
Sports Service Founded:
1982. Specializes in football camps for kids ages 8-18 hosted by NFL players past and present. Total marketing packages include: Supervision, location and player-position literature. Provides full coverage for all facets of camps.
Services:
Specializes in football camps for kids ages 8-18 hosted by NFL players past and present. Total marketing packages include: Supervision, location and player-position literature. Provides full coverage for all facets of camps.

SPORTS MANAGEMENT WORLDWIDE
1100 NW GLISAN STREET
SUITE 2B
PORTLAND, OR 97209
503-445-7105
888-95-AGENT
877-SMWW-Now
Fax: 503-445-9392
info@smww.com
www.smwwagency.com
• G. Lynn Lashbrook, President
(503) 407-2959
lynn@smww.com
• Liz Lashbrook, Executive Director
• Bill Kent, Director Operations
• John Print, Director of Soccer
• Trisonya Abraham, Director of Basketball
• Joe Bonahoom, Director of Baseball
Description:
Candidates complete an eight week SMW course, top performing students are offered the opportunity to stay on as Agent Advisors with Sports Management Worldwide.
Nature of Services:
New Agent Advisors have immediate access to the extensive infrastructure of the company, including certified professional sports team contract negotiations, financial planners, insurance counseling, accounting services, and marketing/endorsement resources for the athletes they represent.

SPORTS MARKET RESEARCH GROUP, INC.
1443 BEACON STREET
APT 808
BROOKLINE, MA 02446
617-277-5660
Nature of Service:
Creates consumer survey reports on bicycles, fitness equipment, Inline skates, ice hockey skates and golf equipment for U.S.
Year Founded:
1990

SPORTS MARKETING & ENTERTAINMENT, INC
11640 SAN VICENTE BOULEVARD
SUITE 204
LOS ANGELES, CA 90049
310-207-2233
800-288-0758
Fax: 310-207-0330

info@smenet.com
www.smenet.com
• Corey Shapoff, President/Chief Executive Officer
(310) 207-2233
cshapoff@smenet.com
• Matt Barnett, EVP
mbarnett@smenet.com
Services:
Secures entertainment, keynote speakers, and sports personalities for many of the world's most notable Fortune 500 companies.
Clients:
AFLAC, AMI, CONOCO, DirecTV, GTE, Ingram Alliace, Lucent Technologies, MCI, Merck, Nordstrom, Prudential, Sprint, Tyson, Warburg Dillon Read, etc.
Marketing & Consulting Services:
Provides sports personalities for personal appearances to corporations.
Sports Service Founded:
1991

SPORTS MARKETING ADMINISTRATORS
140 STREET ANDREWS WAY
ETTERS, PA 17319
717-932-0252
rick@sportsmarketingadmin.com
www.sportsmarketingadmin.com
Nature of Service:
Sports marketing company that creates and maintains sports websites and assists companies administer their sports marketing plans.

SPORTS MARKETING INTERNATIONAL
11 RAVEN ROAD
GLOUCESTER, MA 01931-0738
978-283-2030
• Bruton Smith, Chairman/Chief Executive Officer
Sports Service Founded:
1993
Marketing & Consulting Services:
International marketing; promotional planning and development; international communications; product development; product sourcing and logistics; full design services; international inventory movement; and sales and financial planning focusing on the tennis industry.

SPORTS MARKETING SURVEYS USA
6650 W INDIANTOWN ROAD
SUITE 220
JUPITER, FL 33458
561-427-0647
Fax: 561-427-0648
info@sportsmarketingsurveysusa.com
www.sportsmarketingsurveysusa.com
• Keith Storey, Vice President
(561) 427-0647
• Brandon Mason
• Carolyn Houston
• Stephen Proctor, Chairman
• Keith Storey, Vice President
(561) 427-0647
Keith.storey@sportsmarketingsurveysusa.com
Nature of Sports Service:
An independent company providing a specialist market research service to the sports and leisure industry. Provides full range of traditional and innovative market research techniques on a local, national, and international level.

Services:
Offers media research and market research, and also provides publications and consultancy service.
Clients:
Tennis: Wilson, Prince, Dunlop, Head, Yonex, Babolat, Volkl, United States Tennis Association, Tennis Industry Association Golf: Taylor Made, Callaway, Nike, Titleist/Cobra Cycling: Specialized, Giro Sport Design, Mavic, Michelin, Trek Snowsports: Snowsports Industries America, Salomon, K-2, Ride, Dalbello, Head, Dynastar, Nordica Soccer: adidas, Puma, Nike, Brine Hockey: National Hockey League, Mighty Ducks of Anaheim, Carolina Hurricanes, Washington Capitals, Chicago Blackhawks, Atlanta Thrashers, Columbus Bluejackets Baseball: Anaheim Angels Darts: Unicorn Rugged Outdoor Apparel: Salomon, Helly Hansen, Duofold Rugged Outdoor Footwear.

SPORTS PLACEMENT SERVICE INC
330 WEST 11TH STREET
SUITE 105
LOS ANGELES, CA 90015-2230
213-744-1308
Fax: 213-765-1871
www.sportsplacement.com
• Harlan Werner, President/Chief Executive Officer
Services:
Represents and markets the name, likeness and character of world-renowned, retired athletes, through Commercial Endorsement, Celebrity Placement, Public Speaking, Special Events, Licensing, Autograph Signing, Corporate Events.

SPORTS PROFILES
4711 GOLF ROAD
SUITE 900
SKOKIE, IL 60076
800-725-9423
800-725-9423 ext 10
info@sppsports.com
Description:
A promotions and publishing company that develops retail promotions and corporate entertainment.
Publications:
CHICAGO SPORTS PROFILES MAGAZINE, CALIFORNIA SPORTS PROFILES MAGAZINE.
Services:
Develops retail promotions and corporate entertainment.
Year Founded:
1983.

SPORTS RESEARCH CONSULTANTS
13 TERRACE CIRCLE
APT 2B
GREAT NECK, NY 11021-4145
516-487-0664
• Warren M. Shapiro, President
Nature of Sports Service:
Custom sports research of all types to answer specific objectives relating to sports promotions, personalities, and campaigns.

SPORTSALES
PO BOX 386025
BLOOMINGTON, MN 55438-6025
952-881-5280
800-466-4946

Fax: 866-733-9918
sportsales@aol.com
www.sportsalesinc.com
• David Rubinstein, President
Sports Service Founded:
1989
Marketing & Consulting Services:
Services include advertising and promotion sales, sports franchise consulting, corporate sponsor promotions, and purchasing and marketing of sports broadcast media.
Products:
Oudoor Gears
Brands:
Viking, Acorn

SPORTSCORP LTD.
875 N MICHIGAN AVENUE
SUITE 2325
CHICAGO, IL 60611
312-649-1799
888-296-1900
Fax: 312-649-1197
• Marc S. Ganis, President
Products and Services:
Sports facility development and consultation. Sells portable debit-card devices for concessions at St. Louis Rams
Clients/Brands:
St. Louis Rams, NCAA Final Four / FastBreak Concession Card
Sports Service Founded:
1984

SPORTSECONOMICS LLC
61 LOMBARDY LANE
ORINDA, CA 94563
510-387-0644
Fax: 510-295-2578
info@sportseconomics.com
www.sportseconomics.com
• Daniel A. Rascher, P.H.D., President
Nature of Sports Service
A professional services firm that provides a broad range of consulting services to the sports business and entertainment communities.

STARCOM MEDIAVEST GROUP
35 W WACKER DRIVE
CHICAGO, IL 60601
312-220-3535
Fax: 312-220-6530
• Laura Desmond, CEO
Services:
Starcom MediaVest Group encompasses an integrated network of nearly 3,800 contact architects specializing in media management, internet + digital communications, response media, entertainment marketing, sports sponsorships, event marketing and multicultural media
Description:
Mediavest researches and buys advertising space while Starcom provides media planning and marketing services.
Year Founded:
2000.

STEINER SPORTS MARKETING
145 HUGUENOT STREET
NEW ROCHELLE, NY 10801
914-307-1000
800-759-7267
Fax: 914-365-6428

generalinfo@steinersports.com
www.steinersports.com

STRATBRIDGE, INC.
BLANCHARD HOUSE
SUITE 304
249 AYER ROAD
HARVARD, MA 01451
978-772-4647
Fax: 617-977-8630
www.stratbridge.com
• Matthew Marolda, Founder/Chief Executive Officer
• Andrew H. Palmer, Strategy & Sales/Marketing
• Thomas L. Doorley, III, Strategy & Growth/Board of Directors
• Anthony J. Marolda, Strategy & Planning/Board of Directors
• Michael T. Horvath, Strategic Alliances/Board of Directors
Nature of Services:
StratBridge provides analytic solutions that enable professional sports managers to perform exhaustive diligence research at the touch of a button - StratBridge.net, a platform product, is a Web-native system that seamlessly extracts data from internal and external sources, regardless of format, and then visually renders it in high-resolution plasma displays.

STRATEGIC INSIGHT, LLC
11209 N. 26TH STREET
PHOENIX, AZ 85028
480-499-0466
info@strategicinsight.com
www.strategicinsight.com
• W. Lee Steele, President
lee@strategicinsight.com
Services:
Provide clients with practical, market-based, customer-oriented solutions designed to achieve specific sales and marketing goals
year founded
1991
Marketing & Consulting Services:
Specializing in maximization of clients' sales and marketing efforts in the sporting goods industry, through long range strategic planning, market research, new product development, trade and consumer promotions, communication plans, and internet marketing.
Internet Marketing:
We design and manage Pay-Per-Click Search Engine Ad Campaigns designed to generate a steady stream of pre-qualified sales prospects ready to buy your product or service. No ad budget is too big or too small.

STREET CHARACTERS, INC.
2-2828 18TH STREET NE
CALGARY, ALBERTA, CANADA T2E 7B1
888-627-2687
Fax: 403-250-3846
topdog@mascots.com
www.mascots.com
• Glenn Street, President
topdog@mascots.com
• Aubrey Fishman, Marketing Director
• Brendan Whitty, Concept Artist
Services:
Designs, manufactures, trains and manages mascot characters. Specialists in the manufacture of highly active, durable mascots for sports teams.

Notes:
888-MASCOTS and mascots.com are licensed trademarks of Street Characters, Inc.
Sports Service Founded:
1987
Clients Include:
MLB - Minnesota Twins, Pittsburgh Pirates; Texas Rangers; NFL - Arizona Cardinals, Denver Broncos, Detroit Lions, Houston Texans, Seattle Seahawks; NHL - Calgary Flames, Chicago Blackhawks, New York Islanders; NCAA - Georgetown University, Iowa State University, University of Nebraska, UNLV, San Jose State University.

STRIKE TEN ENTERTAINMENT, INC.
615 SIX FLAGS DRIVE
ARLINGTON, TX 76011
800-871-7869
Fax: 817-649-1918
striketen@bpaa.com
www.stemarketing.com
• John Berglund, President
(800) 871-7869
john@bpaa.com
• Toby Brown, Director
• Frank DeSocio, Vice President Sales/Activation
(316) 636-9494
frank@stemarketing.com
• Henry Lewczyk, Vice President Marketing/Research
(800) 871-7869
henry@bpaa.com
• John Harbuck, Executive Vice President/Managing Partner
(404) 606-2410
john@stemarketing.com
Nature of Service:
Centralized bowling marketing, bowling management, television, communications, merchandising, bowling promotions, bowling trade shows and events company representing the Bowling Proprietors Association of America, Strike Ten Entertainment and Strike Ten Select.

SUCCESS PROMOTIONS
14440 S OUTER FORTY ROAD
CHESTERFIELD, MO 63017
314-878-1999
Fax: 314-878-6663
• Colleen Wadley, Project Coordinator
• Andrea Everett, Customer Service
aeverett@successpromo.com
• Brandon Everett, Sales
beverett@successpromo.com
• Chris Hahs, Sales Executive
chahs@successpromo.com
• Dave Lois, Sales Executive
dlois@successpromo.com
• Diana Everett, President
deverett@successpromo.com
• Chad Everett, Sales Manager
ceverett@successpromo.com
Nature of Services:
Success Promotions provides professional sports with functional, retail-quality promotion merchandise to increase traffic, retain clientele and extend brand impressions long after an event.

SUMMIT SPORTS GROUP
3970 SADDLE ROCK ROAD
COLORADO SPRINGS, CO 80918

719-264-8112
Fax: 719-264-8243
www.summitsportsgroup.com
• Ron De Lorenzo, Founder/Owner/President
ron_summitsports@msn.com
Year Founded:
1986.
Sports Service Founded:
1986.
Services:
Provides advertising and marketing programs to reach golfers, both in Colorado and on a national scale.
Event Management Services:
Provides marketing, promotional, merchandising and broadcast plans for events, as well as for companies using the events as promotion/marketing vehicles.

SUPERLATIVE GROUP, INC.
26600 DETROIT ROAD
SUITE 250
CLEVELAND, OH 44145
216-592-9400
Fax: 216-592-9405
info@superlativegroup.com
www.superlativegroup.com
• Myles Gallagher, President and CEO

SWANSON COMMUNICATIONS
1025 VERMONT AVENUE NW
SUITE 1005
WASHINGTON, DC 20005
202-783-5500
Fax: 202-783-5516
contact@swansonpr.com
www.swansonpr.com
• Kelly Swanson, President
kswanson@swansonpr.com
• Lisa Milner, Manager
• Janet Cassar, Account Executive
Description:
Founded in 1997 and based in Washington DC, Swanson Communications is passionate about creating powerful communications strategies. They are experts in their field and a small agency by design. The agency establishes unique relationships with each of our clients while we develop and customize comprehensive marketing and communications plans that maximize investment and cut unnecessary costs. They maintain their client's integrity and keep them in the news through efficient follow-up strategies, commitment to market research, and active media contact. By forming solid partnerships, they generate positive public perception of their clients and
Clients:
HBO Sports/HBO Pay-Per-View™, Golden Boy Productions, Floyd Mayweather, Caron Butler (Dallas Mavericks), Bernard Hopkins, Washington Freedom
Nature of Services:
Public Relations, Marketing and Promotions, Event Planning and Management, and Research and Development

TAILWIND SPORTS/CYCLING DIVISION
88 KEARNEY STREET
4TH FLOOR
SAN FRANCISCO, CA 94108
415-705-6000
Fax: 415-705-6005

• Bill Stapleton, Chief Executive Officer
• Dan Osipow, General Manager / Operations Director
Description:
Sports marketing firm that owns United States Postal Pro Cycling Team, which is lead by six timer tour de France winner Lance Armstrong. The company is expanding into cycling event management.

TAYLOR RESEARCH & CONSULTING GROUP, INC.
500 MARKET STREET
PORTSMOUTH, NH 03801
603-422-7600
Fax: 603-422-7610
www.thetaylorgroup.com
• Scott Taylor, President
scott_taylor@thetaylorgroup.com
• Peter Fondulas, EVP
• Jason LaMountain, Senior Communications Consultant
• Scott Taylor PhD., President
• Jason Grucel, Communications Director/Research Consultant
jasong@thetaylorgroup.com
• Jason Lamountain, Senior Methodologist
• Joseph Hickey, Tracking Studies Director/Senior Research Con
• J. Scott Taylor, Client Service director/Research Consultant
Nature of Sports Service:
Estimates audience size and price/demand relationships for major pay-per-view events; analyzes brand equity of professional sports leagues; provides market estimates of sports licensed products; and identifies key target markets for clients.
Services:
Provides qualitative and quantitative market and opinion research and consulting services to businesses in a variety of industries

TBA ENTERTAINMENT CORPORATION
220 WEST 42ND STREET
10TH FLOOR
NEW YORK, NY 10036
646-445-7000
Fax: 646-445-7001
• Robert Geddes, Chief Executive Officer
• Lee Rubenstein, President/COO
• Jeff Kline, Business Affairs EVP
• Paula Balzer, CEO
Sports Service Founded:
1984
Clients:
Herbalife, SAP, Bristol-Myers Squibb, Motorola
Marketing & Consulting Services:
Specializing in managing merchandise concessions for sporting events and concerts.
Other Locations:
Los Angeles, London, Nashville, Chicago, San Diego, Salt Lake City, Atlanta, Omaha, Seattle.

TEAM FLORIDA MARKETING
PO BOX 13515
GAINESVILLE, FL 32604
352-372-1215
800-782-3216
Fax: 352-372-8944
• Dwight Johnson, President
Services:
Marketing representative for Florida Athletic

Coaches Association, the College Sports Publishers Association (CSPA) and other Florida sports properties. Full service firm specializing in sports publishing, sponsorship sales, event management and promotion
Sports Service Founded:
1992

TEAM SPORTS, INC.
6228 STATE STREET
WAUWATOSA, WI 53213
414-431-0559
Fax: 262-431-0585
www.teamsportsinc.com
• Tom Schuler, Director
tjsplow@aol.com
• Jack Hirt, Events Director
Services:
Provides team management and marketing service for some of the nation's most prestigious cycling and multisport team and events
Sports Service Founded:
1992
Marketing & Consulting Services:
Sports management for corporate sponsored team sports. Manages Volvo/Cannondale Mountain Bike Racing Team, Saturn Cycling Team, and the Rollerblade Racing Team.

TELE-SPORTS, INC.
PO BOX 232
ALLENTOWN, NJ 08501
800-410-9800
www.tele-sports.com
Marketing & Consulting Service:
Specializes in sports telemarketing and consulting for professional teams and organizations. Sells season and mini plan packages, sponsorship packages, appointment setting, and event management.

THE CHAPEL HILL NORTH GROUP
GLENN, MI
KENNETT SQUARE, PA 45140
877-887-0972
Fax: 267-908-9101
www.chapelhillnorth.com
• Stephen Frank, Contact
sfhughes@chapelhillnorth.com
Services:
market and industry analyses, competitor analysis, due diligence services.
Sports Service Founded:
2001
Nature of Sports Service:
assist organizations in understanding their competitive landscape in terms of competitors' costs structure and strategy.

THE KING PARTNERSHIP
1210 TRINITY ROAD
RALEIGH, NC 27607
919-828-2990
• George King, Chief Executive Officer
(919) 719-1319
• Jenny Martin, Account Director
Marketing & Consulting Services:
Full service advertising and sports marketing agency with experience in season ticket campaigns, sponsorship sales, team representation and event management.
Services:
Provides marketing services, including

media planning and placement, public relations and radio production.

THE Q SCORES COMPANY
1129 NORTHERN BLVD
SUITE 404
MANHASSET, NY 11030
516-365-7979
Fax: 516-365-9351
info@qscores.com
www.qscores.com
• Steven Levitt, President
steven@qscores.com
Nature of Service:
SPORTS Q: National survey on the familiarity and appeal Q SCORES of 500 active and retired sports personalities, among a sports fan audience, aged 12-64.
Nature of Service:
PERFORMER Q: National survey on the familiarity and appeal Q SCORES of over 1700 performers, including major sports personalities.
Year Founded:
1963

THE ROWERS' CODE
P.O. BOX 99613
SEATTLE, WA 98139
201-703-1020
855-ROW-CODE
Fax: 201-797-8769
info@rowerscode.com
www.rowerscode.com
• Rollinson Jane, President and CEO
• Marilyn Krichko, Founding Partner
• Jane Rollinson, Team Member
• Michael Roney, Sales and Marketing
(201) 703-1020
mr@michaelroney.net
Description of Sports Organization:
The Rowers' Code program includes both rowing and indoor elements- the ultimate in teambuilding impact. It is designed to let individuals, teams and leaders experience what it takes to pull together as a team. In this workshop you experience rowing with your fellow team members in a 60-foot Olympic-style boat, and then are challenged to apply the Rowers' Code to your sitation at work, allowing your team to achieve unprecedented success. The Rower's Code is a simple, actionable set of behaviors about teamwork and communication that can be applied to every workplace scenario. It is based on the premise that every
Teams:
Sessions available coast to coast.
Publications:
Book: The Rowers' Code: A Business Parable. How to Pull Together as a Team-And Win! Hardcover: 224 pages Publisher: Career Press ISBN-10: 1601631650
ISBN-13: 978-1601631657

THE SPORTS & FITNESS INDUSTRY ASSOCIATION (SFIA)
8505 FENTON STREET
SUITE 211
SILVER SPRING, MD 20910
301-495-6321
Fax: 301-495-6322
info@sfia.org
www.sfia.org
• Tom Cove, President/Chief Executive Officer
(202) 775-1762

jciambor@sgma.com
• Gregg Hartley, VP
(202) 349-9411
ghartley@sgma.com
• Andrea Cernich, Communications Director
(202) 349-9415
acernich@sgma.com
• Chris Strong, Business Development Director
(202) 349-9413
cstrong@sgma.com
• Robert Puccini, Chairman President, Mizuno USA
• Tom Cove, President & CEO, SFIA
• Chris Clawson, Secretary/Treasurer
• Carlos Ferraro, President Unisource Global Solutions
• Jon Letzler, President & CEO Augusta Sportswear Group
• Robert Parish, President & GM Jarden Team Sports
Services:
Sporting goods equipment, sports apparel, athletic footwear
Clients:
Outdoor Adventure Series Day Hiker Insoles, AquaSkipper, Golf Radar Timing Device, Spenco Medical, Inventist, Sports Sensors Inc.
Sports Equipment Monitor:
Brand recognition and ownership of 186 sports brands; $795. Monitors 24 types of sports equipment purchases; $365.
SGMA Marketing Expenditures Study:
Comprehensive report on manufacturers spending for communications, merchandising, promotion and other marketing expense items. A total of thirty items are reported by company size, major product, retail classes of trade. Report available at cost of $300 ($125 to SGMA members).
SGMA Sports Participation Index by ASD:
An abridged version of the American Sports Analysis sports participation study, available only to SGMA members free of charge. The 75-page report focuses on frequent sports participants.
SGMA Sports Apparel Market Index:
Detailed unit and dollar purchases by sex, retail channel of distribution for sweat pants, sweat shirts, shorts, thermals, athletic socks, jackets, swimwear, and sport shirts plus active sports report - three times per year. Annual demographic report. Free to SGMA members, $495 for four reports to non-members.
SGMA Athletic Footwear Market Index:
Tracking study of athletic footwear at retail. Total trends and separate trends for women, men and children. Trends by shoe type, price point, retail outlet, sale vs. regular price, primary use. Annual report on demographics of purchases. Free to SGMA members, $495 for non-members for four reports.
Recreation Market Report:
Statistical summary of manufacturers' shipments in wholesale dollars for the sporting goods/recreation industry and its products. Free.
Executive Compensation Study:
Report on compensation trends for key executives and middle managers employed by sporting goods companies. Based upon 120-plus company experiences totaling almost 700 positions.
Industry Financial Study:

Reports on overall industry sales trends and manufacturer's financial performance as measured by 26 key financial ratios.
Monthly U.S. Imports Report:
Major source for statistical report on flow of sporting goods to and from the U.S. Details volume trade from countries. Narrative summary and graphs show trends free to SMGA, every six months.
Other Location:
1150 17th Street, NW, STE 407, Washington, DC 20036; Phone: 202-775-1762

STRATEGIC AGENCY, THE
70 WEST 36TH STREET
10TH FLOOR
NEW YORK, NY 10018
212-869-3003
info@thestrategicagency.com
www.thestrategicagency.com
Description::
The primary goal is to influence your consumers' purchasing behavior. To do this, we must transfer equity between your brand and a relevant sports property. Here is the step-by-step process we use to facilitate this transfer: Client Research, Property Alignment, Activation, Management and Measurement.
Services:
Provide strategic method on how the sports marketplace can be leveraged to effectively help a brand achieve its objectives.
Clients:
Carolina Panthers, Russell Athletic, Fox Sports, Western Union, The History Channel, Gulf Oil, New England Patriots/Foxboro Stadium, GlaxcoSmithKline, OfficeMax, Merck, Bank of America, AltaVista.
Other Location:
One Baltimore Place, Suite 350, Atlanta, GA 30308. 404-885-9696; FAX: 404-885-9449.

TICKETMASTER
880 W. SUNSET BLVD
WEST HOLLYWOOD, CA 90069
213-639-6100
Fax: 213-386-1244
www.ticketmaster.com
• Michael Rapino, President & CEO
• Nathan Hubbard, Chief Executive Officer of Ticketing
Nature of Service:
Provides event ticket sales, marketing and distribution through Internet, phone, and retail outlets, along with online auctions, fan club ticketing, and venue-authorized fan resale ticketing services.
Brands:
TicketsNow; TicketExchange; Ticketmaster
Marketing & Consulting Services:
Works with professional and college sports teams to develop new programs designed to expand ticket sales by helping with marketing ideas and actual sales of tickets using outlets, telephones and Internet.
Sports Service Founded:
1995; Merged with Live Nation on January 25, 2010, creating Live Nation Entertainment, Inc

TNS SPORT - NORTH AMERICA
100 PARK AVENUE
4TH FLOOR
NEW YORK, NY 10017

212-991-6194
Fax: 914-684-6078
info-us@tns-global.com
www.tns-us.com
• Eric Salama, Global CEO
• MIke Gettle, Chief Financial Officer and Chief Operating o
• James Brooks, Global Operations Director
• Matthew Froggatt, Chief development Officer
• Tracy Schoenadal, VP
(203) 618-8621
tracy.schoenadel@intersearch.tnsofres.com
Description:
Leading provider of sports and sponsorship research. The only sports research company able to offer the complete research solution on a global scale, setting the industry standards utilising the latest research techniques and technologies. Regarded as a leader in evaluating sponsorships, providing customised, impartial and actionable research to over 200 of the World's leading corporate sponsors, teams, agencies, events and sports.

TOOLBOX STUDIOS
454 SOLEDAD STREET
SUITE 100
SAN ANTONIO, TX 78205
210-225-8269
877-225-8205
Fax: 210-225-8200
info@toolboxstudios.com
www.toolboxstudios.com
• Rob Simons, President
(210) 225-8269
rs@toolboxstudios.com
• Kathy Babb, Account Manager
(210) 225-8269
kb@toolboxstudios.com
• Ron Herrera, Account Executive
(210) 225-8269
rh@toolboxstudios.com
Nature of Service:
Toolbox Studios is a communication design firm that specializes in delivering creative solutions for highly complex marketing challenges. We offer strategy, design and execution services all under one roof. While we employ some of the most creative, award-winning minds in the industry, we are also uniquely staffed and equipped to execute any concept in virtually any medium - from podcast to broadcast, from outdoor boards to banner ads, from web design to web press. We are experts in branding, corporate identities, websites, advertising and publications. Our clients represent industries as diverse as financial services, youth media, museums, s
Year Founded:
1996

TOTAL SPORTS ENTERTAINMENT
PO BOX 5635
DEPERE, WI 54115
800-962-2471
Fax: 608-788-3864
info@yourtse.com
www.totalsportsentertainment.com
• Robert Masewicz, Founder/Owner
bob@totalsportsentertainment.com
• Bob Masewicz, Owner, Chief Consultant
(80) 962-24
bob@yourtse.com
• John Brostrom, Chief Executive Officer
(80) 962-24

john@yourtse.com
• Chris Mahal, Account Executive
Nature of Service:
Sports entertainment and promotions consulting company specializing in video board installation, training, and gameday entertainment enhancement. Developers of TSE GameTime game management computer program.

TRACK RECORD ENTERPRISES
11500 OLYMPIC BOULEVARD
OLYMPIC PLAZA BUILDING, SUITE 400
LOS ANGELES, CA 90064
310-839-1996
• Tom Mills, President
(310) 839-1996
Sports Service Founded:
1979
Services:
Music production and marketing company
Marketing & Consulting Services::
Full service sports marketing firm involved in hundreds of events, programs and projects featuring Olympians from the Southern California Olympians' alumni organization and a host of official sponsors, suppliers and licensees.

TRIPLE CROWN PRODUCTIONS
700 CENTRAL AVENUE
LOUISVILLE, KY 40208-1200
502-636-4405
triplecrown@kyderby.com
• Robert L. Evans, President
• Edward P. Seigenfeld, EVP
• Joseph A. De Francis, VP - Treasurer
• C. St Duncker, Secretary
Services:
Event Management Services specilizes in horseracing events.
Sports Service Founded:
1985
Event Management Services:
Company incorporated by Churchill Downs, Inc., the Maryland Jockey Club of Baltimore City and the New York Racing Association to coordinate marketing, sponsorship sales, publications, public relations and promotions for the Triple Crown (Kentucky Derby, Preakness Stakes, Belmont Stakes).

TSE SPORTS & ENTERTAINMENT
14 PENN PLAZA
SUITE 925
NEW YORK, NY 10122
212-695-9480
877-621-5243
Fax: 212-564-8098
www.tseworld.com
• Robert Tuchman, President
(212) 695-9480
• Brett Sklar, SVP
(877) 621-5243
• Andy Robb, Operations Director
(212) 695-9480
Services:
Provides marketing programs to reach and engage customers by leveraging the power of sports & entertainment to bring their brand messages to life. Provides athlete/celebrity talent for appearances, events, promotions, public relations projects and endorsements.
Services:
Specializes in working with corporations to provide them with marketing programs that

reach and engage their customers by leveraging the power of sports & entertainment to bring their brand messages to life. Focuses on Corporate Hospitality, Sales Promotions & Sweepstakes, Meeting & Event Planning, Athlete/ Celebrity Marketing, and Corporate Consulting.

Clients:
Anheuser-Busch, Bacardi Martini, Brown Forman, Coors, Deer Park, Geyser Peak Winery, InBev/Labatt USA, Miller Brewing Company, Diageo, Schieffelin & Somerset, Triarc Beverages, ABC Sports, Conde Nast Publications, Fox Network, GQ Magazine, HBO, NBC, ESPN, Maxim Magazine; Castrol, Daimler Chyrsler, ExxonMobil, Ford Motor Co., General Motors, Lexus, Pennzoil Products, Toyota; American Express, Bank of America, Merrill Lynch, JP Morgan Chase, KPMG, Bear Stearns, Hartford Financial, Morgan-Stanley Dean Whitter, AT&T, EMC, Ericsson, Hewlett-Packard, Lucent Technologies, Microsoft, IBM, Sony, Verizon; Bayer Corp., BIC USA, Bristol-Myers, Campbell's

Sports Travel:
Specializes in travel packages to major sporting events.

Athlete Management Services:
Provides athlete/celebrity talent for appearances, events, promotions, public relations projects and endorsements.

Event Management Services:
Specializes in providing hospitality and promotional services with multi-level involvement including consumer, trade and retail sales.

Promotional Services:
Specializes in fully integrated marketing promotions.

TSI SPORTS, INC.
2342 DANBURY LN
GAINESVILLE, GA 30507
678-717-1200
800-465-3461
Fax: 770-534-2233
golf@tsisports.com
www.tsisports.com
• Jennifer Sanders, Vice President

Description:
A leading, nationwide hole-in-one and promotional contest insurance company.

Services:
TSI Sports provides prize insurance services for hole-in-one and promotional contests, sweepstakes and games of chance and skill. The 800-Hole-in-1 brand is synonymous with quality and service. TSI Sports also has the latest in graphic and sign-making technology to put the promotional sponsors proudly in the spotlight. This includes printed fabric banners, signs and tabledrapes and direct UV printed signs on hard surfaces.

TURNKEY SPORTS & ENTERTAINMENT
9 TANNER STREET
SUITE 8
HADDONFIELD, NJ 08033
856-685-1450
Fax: 856-685-1451
www.turnkeyse.com
• Haynes Hendrickson, Senior Vice President - Turnkey Intelligence
• Kyle Mathiot, VP
• Michael Mayle, Chief Technical Officer

• Patrick Kuhlen, VP,Product Designing and marketing
• David Stys, SVP, Product Development
• Mellisa Dean, Chief Financial officer
• Len Perna, President
• Haynes Hendrickson, President, Turnkey Intelligence

Year Founded:
1996

UMBRELLA ENTERTAINMENT GROUP
1110 EUGENIA PLACE
SUITE 300
CARPINTERIA, CA 93013-2082
800-553-6637
Fax: 805-684-7808
info@airshownetwork.com
www.airshownetwork.com
• Jim Breen, President/Founder
(805) 684-0155
jim@airshownetwork.com

Services:
Develops and executes marketing campaigns for specific events which involves customer research, development of a marketing strategy, and design and implementation of all aspects of that strategy.

Clients:
Knudsen's, Kraft, Red Baron Pizza, Pontiac, Kodak, Metlife

Marketing & Consulting Services:
Creates, develops and executes relationship marketing strategies with key target audiences; specializes in college, air shows, military, family special events and recreation; sampling and coupon programs.

Event Management Services:
Creates events, develops sponsorships, provide turn-key services for these events.

Sports Service Founded:
1988

UNITED SPORTS ASSOCIATES/USA
170 ATLANTIC AVENUE
SWAMPSCOTT, MA 1907
781-477-0240
Fax: 781-598-4285
www.unitedsportsassociates.com
• Phil Sloan, Founder/President
(781) 477-0742
phil@unitedsportsassociates.com
• Craig Calcasola, VP/Director of Events
(781) 477-0240
craig@unitedsportsassociates.com

Description:
Develops and implements customer based sales initiatives. Produces and promotes proprietary sponsorship event properties. Plans and develops grassroots corporate hospitality programs. Manages and monitors audience acqusition strategies.

Year Founded:
2003

UNITED STATES SPORTS ACADEMY
ONE ACADEMY DRIVE
DAPHNE, AL 36526
251-626-3303
800-223-2668
Fax: 251-625-1035
academy@ussa.edu
www.ussa.edu
• Thomas Rosandich, President/CEO

Services:
An independent, non-profit, special mission school of sport offering sport-specific,

degree-granting residential and online distance learning programs to students, teachers and administrators around the world.

Nature of Services:
Offers Bachelor's, Master's, and Doctoral degrees and Continuing Education programs.

Sports Service Founded:
1972

UPSTARES MEDIA
184 S LIVINGSTON AVENUE
SUITE 9126
LIVINGSTON, NJ 07039
973-968-6666
Fax: 973-556-1999
stares@upstaresmedia.com
www.upstaresmedia.com
• Barry Roberts, President/CEO

USA COACHES CLINICS, INC.
4800 FALL BROOK DRIVE
COLUMBIA, MO 65203-9133
573-445-3843
800-COACH-13
Fax: 573-445-4224
www.usacoaches.com
• Bob Murrey, President, Owner
• Earl Hopper, Clinic Director
(314) 991-8600
info@usacoaches.com
• Craig Harbaugh, Director Sales/Operations
(314) 991-8600

Nature of Service:
Providing meetings set up to help coaches improve, and offers a sports library with books, and videos.

Year Founded:
1989

Marketing & Consulting Services:
Conducts seminars for high school coaches for basketball, football, track and field, baseball and volleyball. Also markets library of coaching books and videos, sold by mail order.

USA TODAY/SPORTS MARKETING
7950 JONES BRANCH DRIVE
MCLEAN, VA 22108-0605
703-854-3400
800-872-7073
accuracy@usatoday.com
www.usatoday.com
• Brent Jones, Reader Editor
(800) 872-7073
accuracy@usatoday.com

Services:
Sports Event Marketing Services

Marketing & Consulting Services:
Creates, evaluates and complements advertising programs of USA Today's major sports advertising accounts. Also develops integrated programs with various leagues, associations and numerous other sports-driven clients.

Sports Service Founded:
1987

USADATA.COM
477 MADISON AVENUE
SUITE 1220
NEW YORK, NY 10017
212-679-1411
800-599-5030
800-395-7707
Fax: 212-679-8507

info@usadata.com
www.usadata.com
• Ric Murphy, President/Chief Executive
Officer
(212) 679-1411
rmurphy@usadata.com
• Bruce Meberg, VP
(212) 679-1411
bmeberg@usadata.com
• Dominic Leclaire, List Integration Partner
dleclaire@usadata.com
Services:
Leading provider of Sales Leads and
On-Demand 1-to-1 Marketing Automation
solutions for customer acquisition and
relationship management for a wide range
of companies.
Clients:
A.I.G,A.D.P,A.D.T,All Nations
Church,American Cancer Society,Bankers
Life,Big Planet,BMW Excluservice,Bonetics
Corporation,Capital Financial,Castle
Press,Centers for Advanced
Medicine,Corcoran,Custom Exteriors,
Inc.,E.F.I,Farmers Insurance,Federal
Reserve Bank of Atlanta,Flexeprint,FX
STUDIOS,Hover Round,Hussman Corp.,JP
Morgan Chase,Kelley Solutions,Met
Life,Modern Postcard,Money Mailer,Morgan
Stanley,Nationwide,New England
Financial,New York Golf Center,New York
Life,Nu-Ear,Pinnacle Development
Partners,Press-Sense,RE/MAX,Restaurant.
com,Spectrum Bank,Sprint PCS,State Farm
Insurance,State University of New
York,Tampa Bay Buccaneers.
Products:
USADATA's application automate and
improve sales processes for organizations
ranging from networks of thousands of
decentralized users to a single, centralized
user.

VELOCITY SPORTS & ENTERTAINMENT
230 E AVENUE
NORWALK, CT 06855
203-831-2000
Fax: 203-831-2300
• David Grant, Principal
(203) 831-2000
grant@teamvelocity.com
• Alex Nieroth, Principal
(203) 831-2000
nieroth@teamvelocity.com
• Mike Reisman, Principal
(203) 831-2000
reisman@teamvelocity.com
• Harlan Stone, Principal
(203) 831-2000
stone@teamvelocity.com
• Bob Wilhelmy, Principal
Services:
Marketing agency specializing in helping
clients maximize the value of their sports
and entertainment sponsorship marketing
efforts. Assists clients in sponsorship
marketing process including strategic
planning, negotiation, program
development, leveraging, execution,
customer hospitality and pre-/post-event
evaluation.
Clients:
IBM, FedEX, Cingular Wireless, Texaco,
Novartis, The New York Times and
NASCAR
Description:
Sponsorship and event marketing agency.

VENUEWORKS
4611 MORTENSEN ROAD
SUITE 111
AMES, IA 50014
515-232-5151
888-232-5151
Fax: 515-663-2022
info@venuworks.com
www.venuworks.com

VISION PRO SPORTS, INC.
80 RIVER STREET
3RD FLOOR
HOBOKEN, NJ 7030
201-792-4111
Marketing & Consulting Services:
A full service creative marketing agency that
specializeds in the youth, sports and
entertainment industries.

VISION SPORTS & ENTERTAINMENT
PARTNERS
330 MADISON AVENUE
9TH FLOOR
NEW YORK, NY 10017
212-983-7250
look@vision.com
www.vision.com
• Billy Glennon, Group CEO
• Gerald Adams, Co-Founder and group
Director
• Charles Spinosa, Group Director
• Matthew Hancocks, Group Director
• Gianluca Romano, Group Director
• Graeme Toolin, Chief Financial Officer
Services:
Sports and Marketing firm and sports
agency for professional hockey players

WASHINGTON SPORTS &
ENTERTAINMENT
601 F STREET NW
WASHINGTON, DC 20004
202-628-3200
Fax: 202-661-5063
www.verizoncenter.com
• Abe Pollin, Chairman
• Susan O'Malley, President
• Brian Cawley, Director, Corporate
Marketing
• Judy Holland, SVP, Community Relations
Services:
Oversees marketing operations of
Washington Capitals, MCI Center, and the
Washington Wizards. Handles all aspects of
arena, event and team corporate
sponsorships, radio and TV sales, suite
sales, signage and other entertainment and
sports marketing.
Sports Service Founded:
1995

WEBER SHANDWICK WORLDWIDE
919 THIRD AVENUE
NEW YORK, NY 10022
212-445-8000
www.webershandwick.com
• Jack Leslie, Chairman
jleslie@webershandwick.com
• Harris Diamond, Chief Executive Officer
• Andy Polansky, President, Weber
Shandwick Worldwide
apolansky@webershandwick.com
• Colin Byrne, Chief Executive Officer,
Weber Shandwick
cbyrne@webershandwick.com

Description:
Public relations and communications
management firm.

WILKINSON GROUP
330 PRIMROSE ROAD
SUITE 205
BURLINGAME, CA 94010
650-375-7888
Fax: 650-340-8067
david@twgsponsorship.com
• David G. Wilkinson, President/Chief
Executive Officer
(650) 375-7888
david@twgsponsorship.com
• Krista Semotiuk, VP
(650) 375-7888
krista_semotiuk@twgsponsorship.com
• Louise M. Felsher, SVP Event Marketing
(650) 375-7883
lfelsher@twgsponsorship.com
Services:
Create marketing programs based on
strategies and built around events,
sponsorships or lifestyle activities;
entertainment, media, sport and cause
properties that are owned by clients for true
equity positioning; Create communications
strategies that make direct contact with
target markets in a focused manner; Add a
textured, human element to corporate
brands through alignment with lifestyle
activities; Stretch investments by creating
alliances (corporate, media, cause) that
decrease implementation costs; Generate a
direct return on investment for the sponsor
clients; Generate a direct return on
investment for the sponsor clients; Drive
custo
Clients:
Air Canada, Air Jamaica, Air New Zealand,
Akamai, Ast Computers, Bank of America,
Best Buy, Brugal, California Overnight,
Canadian Imperial Bank of Commerce,
Cisco Systems, Citibank, Clorox (Brita),
Coca-Cola Canada, Gateway,
Hewlett-Packard, Intel, Invensys, Jergens
(Biore), Manulife Financial, Pacific Bell,
Panasonic, Pepsi, Petro Canada, PG & E,
Proctor & Gamble, Reuters, Sears Roebuck
& Co, Teleglobe Canada, The New Power
Company, Wells Fargo, etc.
Sports Service Founded:
1982
Marketing & Consulting Services:
Sponsorship marketing seminars and
consulting for corporations; corporate
sponsorship consulting services;
educational materials; event creation and
production, propert, representation and
sales.

WINDY CITY SPORTS
1450 W RANDOLPH STREET
CHICAGO, IL 60607
312-421-1551
Fax: 312-421-1454
www.windycitysports.com
• Doug Kaplan, President/Publisher
doug@gen-a.com
• Kate Bongiovanni, Associate Editor
Sports Service Founded:
1992

professional services

WOLF GROUP-NY
4401 FAIR LAKES COURT
SUITE 310
FAIRFAX, VA 22033
703-502-9500
Fax: 703-502-3970
info@thewolfgroup.com
www.thewolfgroup.com
• Leonard S Wolf, Managing Partner
l.wolf@thewolfgroup.com
• Robert D. Len, Director
• Dale Mason, Senior International Tax
Manager
dmason@thewolf.com
• Robert D. Len, Partner
blen@thewolfgroup.com
• Dale Mason, International Tax Director and
Chief Operatin
• Sharif Mahfouz, Global Tax Director
• Michael Goodson, Chief Investment
Officer
• Leonard S. M. Wolf, Director
Description:
Fully integrated, brand-centric organization
with services in advertising, corporate
branding, interactive marketing, media
buying and planning, direct response, sales
promotion and public relations.
Services:
Offers a full range of marketing
communications services, including
advertising, strategic planning, sales
promotion, direct response, public relations,
package design, directory marketing and
interactive.
Clients:
Aamco, Canandaigua Wine Company,
Haagen-Dazs, HSBC Bank USA, I LOVE
NY, Scotts Company.
Other Locations:
Toronto, Cleveland, Atlanta, Buffalo,
Rochester NY

WOLF GROUP-OH
10860 KENWOOD ROAD
CINCINNATI, OH 45242
513-891-9100
800-222-4045
Fax: 513-792-3533
www.wolfgrp.com
• Steve Zweig, President
• Stuart Glassman, EVP
Services:
Provides promotional marketing
development of sports programs in the
promotion of client's name and/or products.
Full service and turn-key consumer and
trade promotions utilizing sports events,
media vehicles, premiums and
sweepstakes.
Sports Service Founded:
1984
Other Location:
New York

WORLD CLASS SPORTS
5777 W CENTURY BOULEVARD
SUITE 1070
LOS ANGELES, CA 90045
310-665-9400
Fax: 310-665-9844
wcsagent@pacbell.net
www.worldclass-sports.com
• Don Franken, President
wrldclssprts@earthlink.net
• Andrew Woolf, Vice President

(310) 665-9400
wcsagent@pacbell.net
Nature of Service:
Sports talent agency, sports celebrity
agency and sports speakers bureau. Began
in 1982. Professional and Olympic athletes,
legends and current stars.
Sports Service Founded:
1982
Marketing & Consulting Services:
Through Franken Enterprises advises
recommends and creates sports events
around a client's marketing objectives.
Creates fully integrated sports marketing
opportunities to increase client visibility and
sales.
Clients:
Pepsi, All Sport - Jerry Rice, Steve Young,
Hallmark - Bill Walton, Sprint - Dick Butkus,
Larry Czonka, Deacon Jones, ESPN
Extreme Games - Evel Knievel, Kellogg's -
Marion Jones, Ariba Computers - Marion
Jones, Gunze of Japan - Mike Piazza,
American Express - Evelyn Ashford,
American Express - Billy Mills, Got Milk -
Bob Burnquist, Mission Foods - Shannon
Miller, Dean Witter Reynolds - Bob Mathias,
Bayer Agriculture - Nolan Ryan, California
Dept. of Transportation - Joe Montana,
Panasonic - Nadia Comaneci, Sports
Illustrated - Deacon Jones and Conrad
Dobler, Black Star Bears Beer - Rollie
Fingers, Glaxo - Jim Ryun, Glaxo - Bob
Beamon, Dermik

WORLD PROMOTIONAL PRODUCTS, INC.
17751 SKY PARK CIRCLE
SUITE F
IRVINE, CA 92614
800-705-7796
Fax: 949-221-0693
• Chris Tyler, Vice President
ctyler@worldpromoproducts.com
Description:
World Promotional Products provides logo
and imprinted merchandise - services of
which include graphic and creative design,
screen print and embroidery.
Clients:
World Promotional Products works with
many NBA, MLB, NHL and Fortune 500
companies.
Nature of Services:
Trade Shows; Employee Incentives; Events
and Meetings; New Product Launches;
Brand Marketing Initiatives; Award
Programs; Golf and Charity Events.

WORLD SPORTS & MARKETING
460 N. ORLANDO AVE
SUITE 200
WINTER PARK, FL 32789
407-628-4802
Fax: 407-628-7061
www.wakeboardingmag.com

WSS EXECUTIVE SEARCH
7755 CENTER AVENUE
SUITE 1100
HUNTINGTON BEACH, CA 92647
714-848-1201
Fax: 714-848-5111
www.wssexecutivesearch.com
• Becky Heidesch, Founder & Chief
Executive Officer
• Mary Lou Youngblood, Sr.Partner

Clients:
Anaheim Angels, Hyundai Motor America,
Oshman's Sporting Goods, Gart Sports,
WNBA, Alta Dena Dairy, LPGA, Scudders
Private Investment Counsel, Monster, 24
Hour Fitness, Sports Illustrated for Women,
American Express, ESPN, Health Magazine,
Executive Women's Golf Association, Vans,
Golf Digest Companies, Golf Channel,
Burton Snowboards, O'Neil, SELF
Magazine, Healthsouth, WNBA LA Sparks,
Black Women in Sport Foundation,
Association for Women in Sports Media,
WUSA San Diego Spirit, California
Interscholastic Federation, etc.
Description:
WSS Executive Search, a division of
Women Sourcing Soltions, is a WBENC
certified, women-owned business
specializing in women and minority sourcing
solutions. WSS partners with their clients to
provide them with sourcing solutions to
solve their most challenging diversity hiring
efforts. WSS specializes in the sports,
financial and technology industry.
Nature of Service:
WSS customizes their recruitment and
management process for each client. By
offering personalized sourcing solutions,
WSS matches qualified professional
candidates with top-tier companies who are
often challenged in their industry in finding
women and minority candidates. WSS has
years of experience assisting companies in
reaching their diversity goals and
empowering candidates to realize their
career dreams!
Primary Audience:
Corporate America, specialty companies in
the sports, financial and technology sectors.
Candidate pool: Mid-management to
Executive Level.
Sports
All.

WTS INTERNATIONAL
3200 TOWER OAKS BOULEVARD
SUITE 400
ROCKVILLE, MD 20852
301-622-7800
800-229-8262
Fax: 301-622-3373
wts@wtsinternational.com
www.wtsinternational.com
• Gary J. Henkin, President
(301) 622-7800
ghenkin@wtsinternational.com
• Ralph Newman, Chief Operating Officer
(301) 622-7800
rnewman@wtsinternational.com
Services:
One of the world's leading spa, fitness, and
leisure consulting and management firms.
WTS provides: conceptual and strategic
planning; feasibility and needs assessment
studies; design consultation and space plan
development; pre-opening services; and
turnkey management or operational
consulting. Services spas, athletic and
tennis facilities, and leisure complexes of all
types and sizes throughout the United
States and abroad.
Clients:
The Sanderling Spa Resort and Spa,
Ashburn Village Sports Pavilion, Wyndham
Sugar Bay Resort and Spa, PGA Tour Spa
Laterra, Al Corniche Club, The Spa at
Southern Highlands, Peter Island Resort

and Spa, Hilton San Francisco Spa Fusion, Piedmont Community
Sports Service Founded:
1973
Marketing & Consulting Services:
Provides management, consulting services, personnel selection and program development for health/fitness facilities and spas of all types and sizes.

WUNDERMAN
285 MADISON AVENUE
NEW YORK, NY 10017
212-941-3000
Fax: 212-627-8342
www.wunderman.com
• Daniel Morel, Chairman/Global Chief Executive Officer
• Stewart Pearson, Chief Executive Officer/Wunderman EMEA
Services:
Promotional marketing programs. Achieves defined client objectives through the strategic and tactical application of sports as an integrated marketing medium, accomplished through programs that produce measurable results against brand objectives on nation
Clients:
American Institute of Certified Public Accountants, Astra-Zeneca, Canada Post, Caterpillar, Citibank, Coca-Cola, Danone, Diageo, Ford, Gannett, Hewlett-Packard, Hotels.com, Jaguar, Johnnie Walker, Land Rover, Lincoln Mercury, Lufthansa, M&G Investments, Mazda, Microsoft, Pfizer, Royal Canadian Mint, Royal Marsden Hospital, Sears, Star Alliance

XA, THE EXPERIENTIAL AGENCY
333 HUDSON STREET
SUITE 203
NEW YORK, NY 10013
646-688-6381
Fax: 212-274-1788
www.experientialagency.com
• Valerie Morel, EVP Marketing
(212) 625-9191
• Amanda Puck, Director Business Development/Public Relation
(312) 397-9100
Year Founded:
1989.
Clients:
ABN AMRO, Accenture, Aegis Insurance, Alberto-Culver, American Council of Life Insurers, Ameritech, Amoco, Anchor Food Products, Aramark, Astrazeneca, Avenue Q, Bank Calumet, Bank One, Biora, Black Clawson, Bristol-Myers Squibb, Burberry, Capri Capital Advisors, Cellular One, Chicago Stock Exchange, Citadel Investment Group, Clinical Insights, ComEd, Coors Brewing, Del Monte, Discount Tire Company, Enterprise Rent-A-Car, Ernst & Young, Eurex, ewireless, Exelon, Fairmont Hotels, The Fashion Group, Fleet Mortgage, Gardner Publishing, Chicago Gateway Green, GE Capital, General Growth Properties, Gilead Sciences, GlaxoWellcome, Goldman Sachs, Hea
Nature of Service:
Event Strategy Design/Production: Event Concepts, Design & Production, Multimedia Content Development, Talent Buying & Management, Celebrity Wrangling, Guest Management, Destination Management,

Data Capture & Measurement; Non-Traditional Marketing, Public Relations, Event Promotion.

YESAWICH, PEPPERDINE, BROWNE & RUSSELL
423 S KELLER ROAD
SUITE 100
ORLANDO, FL 32810-6121
407-875-1111
Fax: 407-875-1115
pyesawich@mmgyglobal.com
www.mmgyglobal.com
• Peter C. Yesawich, President/Chief Executive Officer
peter_yesawich@ypbr.com
• Larry Tolpin, President/Chief Creativer Officer
(407) 875-1111
larry_tolpin@ypbr.com
• Gary Sain, EVP/Chief Marketing Officer
(407) 875-1111
gary_sain@ypbr.com
• Clayton A. Ried, CEO & President
• Hugh McConnell, CFO & Executive Vice President
• Stewart Colowin, Executive Vice President
• Jeff Huggins, Senior Vice President
Sports Service Founded:
1993
Services:
Marketing, advertising and public relations agency that delivers extraordinary results for its clients through proprietary consumer insights, surprising strategies, big ideas and bold creative executions.
Clients:
Aero Mexico, Frontier, Mexicana, USAirways, Western Pacific Airlines , Dardens- Seasons 52, Ruth's Chris Steakhouse; Financial/Investment Banking: American Express, Bear Stearns and Company, Discover Card, MasterCard International, Merrill Lynch; Gaming: Bally Gaming, Belle Casinos, Caesar's Palace, Casino Rouge, Florida Lottery, Foxwoods Casino Resort, Grand Casinos, Hard Rock Hotels & Casinos, Hyatt Casinos, Wynn Las Vegas , etc.
Marketing & Consulting Services:
Advertising, public relations, marketing firm specializing in golf.

ZIP CELEBRITY, INC.
ONE COMMERCIAL WHARF WEST
BOSTON, MA 02110
617-350-5518
Fax: 508-647-5101
info@zipcelebrity.com
www.zipcelebrity.com
Description:
To match celebrity casting with corporate identity and goals. At the same time, we make sure that a portion of every talent fee goes to worthy charities. We give you the opportunity to match the true celebrity with your brands.
Services:
Matches celebrity casting with corporate identity and goals

ZOOPERSTARS!
PO BOX 36061
LOUISVILLE, KY 40233
502-458-4020
800-219-0899

Fax: 502-458-0867
www.zooperstars.com
• Brennan Latkovski, Co-Owner
(502) 458-4020
brennan@zooperstars.com
• Stephanie Fish, General Manager
stephanie@zooperstars.com
General Description:
Crazy Animals. Funny Stuff. Hilarious Routines. The hottest entertainment act in sports with characters such as LeBronco James, Peyton Manatee, Ken Giraffey, Jr., Tiger Woodschuck, Elephant Presley, Barack Ollama, Mia Hammster, Snail Earnhardt, Jr., Whale Gretzky, Shaquille O'Seal, Clammy Sosa, and other funny friends in a show the audience will love.
Year Founded:
1998
Sports Service Founded:
1998
Event Marketing Services:
An independent traveling troupe of inflatable mascots that perform during special events and half-time shows.
Clients:
Aberdeen Ironbirds, Adirondack Frostbite, Aguascalientes Railroadmen, Akron Aeros, Alabama Slammers, Albany Conquest, Albuquerque Dukes, Albuquerque Isotopes, Alexandria Aces, Altoona Curve, Amarillo Dillas, Arizona Rattlers, Arkansas RiverBlades, Arkansas Twisters, Asheville Tourists, Atlantic 10 Conference, Auburn Doubledays, Auburn University, Augusta Greenjackets, Augusta Lynx, Bakersfield Blitz, Bakersfield Condors, Bellarmine University, Big League World Series, Billings Mustangs, Binghamton Mets, Binghamton Senators, Birmingham Barons, Boise Hawks, Boise Power Series, Boston Celtics, Bowie BaySox, Brevard County Manatees.

Technical Services

A.V. CONCEPTS
1917 W 1ST STREET
TEMPE, AZ 85281
866-927-7590
800-473-6828
Fax: 480-894-8376
www.avconcepts.com
• Nick Smith, Owner/Founder
• Fred Mandrick, Owner/Founder
Nature of Service:
A provider of audio/video staging services including planning, technical support, coordination and execution of video audio and lighting for an event.
Year Founded:
1987
Other Locations:
7365 Mission Gorge Road, Suite A, San Diego, CA 92120; we also have office locations in Los Angeles, Scottsdale, Phoenix and Tucson.

ACCU-STATS VIDEO PRODUCTIONS
PO BOX 299
BLOOMINGDALE, NJ 07403
800-828-0397
Fax: 973-838-5771
accustats@accu-stats.com
www.accu-stats.com
Services:
Offers Professional Billiard Video Plays;

Also offers professional instructional videos.
Description:
Offers the best in professional billiard videos. Instructional videos by Buddy Hall, Grady Matthews, Bill Incardona, Mike Massey and Pat Fleming. Collections of books, instructional and biographical, essential to the avid pool and billiard fans.

ACENTECH INC.
33 MOULTON STREET
CAMBRIDGE, MA 02138
617-499-8000
Fax: 617-499-8074
info@acentech.com
www.acentech.com
• David Bowen, Senior Consultant
dbateman@acentech.com
• Carl Rosenberg, Principal
• Eric Wood, Principal
• J. Christopher Jaffe, Principal Consultant
• Christopher Savereid, Principal
Services:
Offers sound system design, mechanical noise and vibration control services, architectural acoustics, and video system design for sports facilities.
Nature of Sports Service:
Full service acoustical consulting firm. Sound system design, mechanical noise and vibration control services, architectural acoustics, and video system design for sports facilities.
Description:
Kenyon College Athletic Facility, Gambier OH; Quinnipiac College Recreation Center, Hamden CT; University of Maryland Recreation Center, College Park, MD

ACTIVE ALERT
15120 ENTERPRISE COURT
SUITE 100
CHANTILLY, VA 20151
703-227-9690
Fax: 703-803-3299
aasolutions@spectrarep.com
www.activeaccess.com
• Terrence Thomas, Interactive Marketing Manager
tterrence@bia.com
• Rodger Metchori, Sales Director
rmetchori@bia.com
Nature of Services:
BIA Information Network offers ActiveAccess, a private-label desktop application that gives a sports team a direct pipeline to fans to deliver the information they crave - scores, game videos, updated gameday information, local weather, and much more.

APUNIX COMPUTER SERVICES
17150 VIA DEL CAMPO
SUITE 308
SAN DIEGO, CA 92127
858-673-8649
800-827-8649
Fax: 858-673-8640
support@apunix.com
• Peter Berens, Founder/President
Peter.Berens@apunix.com
• Sylvia Berens, Founder/VP
Services:
Develops Kiosks and Photo ID systems. Offers instant issue employee photo ID system (which interfaces to time and attendance systems) and can be use to

create VIP or season ticket holder cards.
Description:
Develops Kiosks and Photo ID systems. Offers instant issue employee photo ID system (which interfaces to time and attendance systems) and can be used to create VIP or season ticket holder cards. Apunix's kiosk is the first Java touch screen multimedia kiosk.
Year Founded:
1981

ASAP SPORTS
225 BROADWAY
SUITE 700
NEW YORK, NY 10007
212-385-0297
info@asapsports.com
www.asapsports.com
• Peter P Balastrieri, CEO
(212) 385-0297
peter@asapsports.com
• Jeri Gargano, VP,Managing Director
(631) 425-2701
jeri@asapsports.com
• Vasili Timofeev, Director,Finance
(212) 385-0297
basil@asapsports.com
• Jaime Morrocco, Director,Technology ,Quality Control and Huma
(503) 317-8664
jaime@asapsports.com
Description:
Provides transcrpits and soundclips of press conferences at major sporting events around the world.

AUDIO VISUAL CONFERENCE TECHNOLOGIES
2 BARNES ST
PATTERSON, NJ 7501
973-345-5211
Description:
Provides professional audio visual services to convention centers and meeting facilities. Provides complete on-site audio/visual and business center departments. Specialists in operating and maintaining audio/visual systems.

BOSE CORPORATION
100 THE MOUNTAIN ROAD
FRAMINGHAM, MA 01701-9168
508-879-7330
800-999-2673
Fax: 508-820-3465
www.bose.com
• Sherwin Greenblatt, President
• Shari Goldman, Marketing Assistant
Services:
Develops total sound systems for any size facility.
Description:
Develops total sound systems for any size facility.

BRONSKILL & CO.
55 FIELDWAY RD
TORONTO, ON, CANADA M8Z 3L4
416-703-8689
Fax: 416-703-0740
info@bronskill.com
www.bronskill.com
• Michael Regan, President
(602) 722-5837
mregan@brejtfus.com
• Reg Bronskill, Chairman/CEO

Services:
Event creation, environmental design and entertainment.

BURNS ENTERTAINMENT & SPORTS MARKETING, INC
820 DAVIS STREET
SUITE 222
EVANSTON, IL 60201
847-866-9400
Fax: 847-491-9778
Bob.Williams@burnsent.com
www.burnsent.com
• Bob Williams, Chief Executive Officer
• Doug Shabelman, President
• Marc Ippolito, President/General Counsel
Services:
Burns Entertainment provides talent procurement services, linking entertainment and sports celebrities and properties with corporations, agencies, not-for-profits, colleges and associations. Provides leveraging experience and industry savvy to negotiate and execute deals in entertainment and sports. Also provides a propietary, state-of-the-art database to over 20,000 celebrities and properties for any request.
Sports Service Founded:
1970.

CALIFONE INTERNATIONAL, INC.
1145 ARROYO AVENUE
A
SAN FERNANDO, CA 91340
818-407-2400
800-722-0500
Fax: 818-407-2405
www.califone.com
• Roscoe Anthony, President
ross@califone.com
• Chase Stone, VP, Eastern Sales
chase@califone.com
• Terry Davis, VP, Central Sales
• Mike Morse, VP, Western & International Sales
mikem@califone.com
Products:
Califone manufactures a full line of educationally-focused audio/visual products including installed and portable PA's, wireless products,megaphones, multimedia player/recorders, document cameras, and computer peripherals for school uses.

CCI SOLUTIONS
1247 85TH AVENUE, SE
OLYMPIA, WA 98501
360-943-5378
800-426-8664
800-562-6006
Fax: 360-754-1566
info@ccisolutions.com
• Ronald L Simonson, Principal Consultant
(800) 426-8664
indepth@ccisolutions.com
• Joe Brannberg, Project Manager
(800) 426-8664
indepth@ccisolutions.com
• Rick Boring, Systems Consultant
(800) 426-8664
indepth@ccisolutions.com
• Greg Hearns, Systems Consultant
(800) 426-8664
indepth@ccisolutions.com
• Ronald L. Simonson, P.E., Principal Consultant

- Mark Pearson, Senior Systems Consultant
- Greg Hearns, Senior Systems Consultant
- Rick Boring, Senior Systems Consultant
Services:
Offers audio-visual consulting, products, technical systems and expertise; Offers custom solutions which includes: public and corporate facilities services, worship facilities services, retail product sales, cassette/CD duplication and replication services, architectural consulting, equipment rental, and equipment repair.
Description:
Develops and installs high definition arena sound systems. Exclusive source for the high definition KB-8 Arena audio system.
Clients Include:
Gund Arena, Cleveland OH; America West Arena, Phoenix AZ; Key Arena, Seattle WA; MCI Center, Washington DC

COACH D*A*V*E
1700 N HIGHLAND AVENUE
SUITE H-648
HOLLYWOOD, CA 90028
818-508-7578
Sports Service Founded:
1981. D*A*V*E is an acronym for Definitive Audio Video Education. Prepares athletes for endorsements and broadcasting, working one-on-one teaching fundamentals that help to develop greater marketability. Focuses on media training, oral presentation skills, speech therapy, image development, personal appearances, audio/video techniques, TV and radio commercials, endorsement training.

COMMUNITY PROFESSIONAL LOUDSPEAKERS
333 E 5TH STREET
CHESTER, PA 19013-4511
610-876-3400
800-523-4934
Fax: 610-874-0190
info@communitypro.com
www.communitypro.com
- Grace Paoli, Marketing Communications Manager
gpaoli@communitypro.com
Year Founded:
1968.
Nature of Service:
Supplier of professional sound systems for forty years.
Brands:
(Loudspeakers) Cloud Series; CPL; CSV; DnD Series; Horns & Drivers; I/O Series; iBox; M-Class; MVPII; R-Series; Solutions; STS; T-Class; Tandem Drive; WET; XLTE; (Electronics) DXP4800 Digital Controller; (Software) ULYSSES; (Discontinued Products) CBA/CBS; CSV8; CSV; CSX; DSC52 Digital Controller; MVP; SC21.1 System Controller; TANDEM DRIVE; VLF218; XLT; XLTPRO

EVENT AUDIO VISUAL GROUP
50888 CENTURY COURT
WIXOM, MI 48393
800-935-2323
Fax: 800-935-8191
detroit@subrent.com
www.subrent.com

GENUONE
3 COPLEY PLACE
SUITE 201
BOSTON, MA 02116
617-226-3000
866-436-8663
Fax: 617-226-3001
www.opsecsecurity.com
- Jeffrey Unger, Chief Executive Officer/Director
- Donn Worby, Chief Financial Officer
- Thomas Taylor, SVP Operations and Engineering
- Stephen Polinsky, VP of Sales
Description:
Provider of security technologies and solutions that enable companies to protect their products and value chain from counterfeiting, grey-market diversion, warranty fraud and intellectual property theft in the physical world and on the internet.
Brands:
SourceGuard, GenuNet, GenuGuard
Sports Service Founded:
1998.

GLOBAL SPECTRUM
41-B NEW LONDON TURNPIKE
SUITE 107
Glastonbury, CT 6033
860-657-0630
Fax: 860-657-0761
frusso@global-spectrum.com
www.global-spectrum.com
- Peter Luukko, President/Chief Operating Officer
- Frank E. Russo Jr, SVP, Sales and Client Services
frusso@global-spectrum.com
- John Page, SVP/Chief Operations Manager
jpage@global-spectrum.com
- Frank E. M. Russo Jr., Sr. Vice President
- Todd Glickman, Vice President
Clients:
Pre-opening clients Wachovia Center - Philadelphia, Pennsylvania; John Labatt Centre - London, Ontario; University of South Carolina Carolina Center - Columbia, South Carolina; The Budweiser Events Center at the Ranch - Loveland, Colorado; Bank United Center - Coral Gables, Florida; Overland Park Convention Center - Overland Park, Kansas; University of Rhode Island Ryan Center & Bradford R. Boss Arena - Kingston, Rhode Island; Old Dominion University Ted Constant Convocation Center - Norfolk, Virginia; Palm Beach County Convention Center - West Palm Beach, Florida; Hy-Vee Hall, Des Moines, Iowa; St. Charles Convention Center, St. Charles, Mis
Event Management Services:
Computer software for event scheduling, settlement, accounting, ticketing, fundraising.
Sports Service Founded:
1994
Other Location:
3601 South Broad Street, Philadelphia, PA 19147. 215-389-9587; FAX: 215-952-5651; 41B New London Turnpike, Glastonbury, CT 06033, Phone: 860-657-0630; 780 94th Avenue North, STE 107, St. Petersburg, FL 33702, Phone: 727-456-1170

GOLF SCORECARDS, INC
9735 SW SUNSHINE COURT
SUITE 700
BEAVERTON, OR 97005
503-352-0281
800-238-7267
Fax: 503-226-4501
information@golfscorecards.com
www.golfscorecards.com
- Cynthia Grant, President
(503) 352-0283
- Byron Grant, General Manager
(503) 352-0284
byron@golfscorecards.com
Products:
Quality design and printing: scorecards, yardage guides, other golf printed materials.

GRIP SALES & SERVICE TRAINING
2900 SE MARTINS STREET
PORTLAND, OR 97202
503-939-3927
Fax: 203-724-4331
www.gripinc.com
- Bret Polvorosa, President/Chief Executive Officer
Nature of Sports Services:
Help organization to generate more revenue and greater customer retention.

HENDERSON ENGINEERS INC.
8345 LENEXA DRIVE
SUITE 300
LENEXA, KS 66214
913-742-5000
Fax: 913-742-5001
info@hei-eng.com
www.hei-eng.com
- Russ L. Olsen, President
(913) 384-1261
- Ian Wolfe, VP
(913) 384-1261
ianw@adgkc.com
- Brian Kubicki, VP
(913) 384-1261
- George Damon, Senior Associate
(913) 384-1261
Services:
Provides a wide range of consulting and design services for all facility types. Consulting includes noise control, video playback, video production, television-distribution and multimedia systems design, and commissioning services.
Clients:
Athletics: GM Place, Vancouver Canada; Van Andel Arena, Grand Rapids, MI; Bob Devaney Arena, University of Nebraska - Lincoln; St. Charles Arena, St. Charles, MS; Gwinnett Arena, Duluth, Georgia; Memorial Coliseum, Fort Wayne, IN; MGM Grand Arena, Las Vegas, NV; Office Depot Center, Fort Lauderdale, FL; The Pyramid, Memphis, TN; Sovereign Center Arena, Reading, PA; Tyson Events Center Arena, Sioux City, Iowa; Dean Smith Center Arena, Chapel Hill, NC; America West Arena, Phoenix, AZ; Seabury Convocation and Recreation Center, Berea, Kentucky; Earlham Student Activities Center, Richmond, IN; Marietta College, Marietta, OH; Fulton and Susie Coll
Clients include:
Van Andel Arena, Grannett Civic & Cultural Center Arena, GM place, Dean Smith Center, Devaney Arena

Sports Service:
Provides a wide range of consulting and design services for all facility and venue types. Our services include architectural acoustics, facility analysis, sound & ALV design, noise & vibration control, TV distribution system design, systems commissioning, expert testimony.

INFORMATION & DISPLAY SYSTEMS, INC.
10275 CENTURION COURT
JACKSONVILLE, FL 32256
904-645-8697
Fax: 904-645-8496
marketing@ids-sports.com
www.ids-sports.com
• Rallis Pappas, President
• David Lunghino, VP
Services:
Technology vendor to the sports industry. Services focused on scoring/results systems, display, TV production, web production.
Sports:
Golf, Tennis, Basketball, hockey, Skiing, Olympics, Action Sports, Racing, Fighting

INNOVATIVE ELECTRONIC DESIGNS, INC.
9701 TAYLORSVILLE ROAD
LOUISVILLE, KY 40299
502-267-7436
Fax: 502-267-9070
info@iedaudio.com
www.iedaudio.com
• Jason Kleiman, Inside Sales Manager
• Mark Lewellyn, Sales and Marketing Director
• Matt Gray, Applications Engineer
• Rod Rupp, Applications Engineer
Brands:
500 Announcement Control Systems, 500 Visual Information Systems, 8000 Series Totally Integrated Processing System, 6000 Series Power Amplifier Systems, 3200 Series Digital Signal Processing Systems, 4400 and 4800 Series Automatic Mixers
Description:
Design and manufacturer of computer-controlled audio processing systems, including the 8000 series (TIPS Total Integrated Processing System) and the UDAPS-universal digital audio processing systems featuring all-digital equalizing, delay, attenuation, mixing, and routing. Other products include the 500ACS announcement control system, 4000 Series automatic microphone mixer systems, 4400/4800 stand-alone mixer systems, 5000 audio processing systems, 6000 power amplifier system, and 540 ambient analysis system. Applications include arenas and stadiums.

JHG TOWNSEND
6215 FERRIS SQUARE
SUITE 210
SAN DIEGO, CA 92121
888-246-2396
• Alex Benjamin, VP Finance & Operations
• Chris Hassett, VP Communications
• Lisa Kendall, VP Business Partnerships
• Liya Sharif, VP Public Relations & Brand Strategy
• Mary Fechtig, President/CEO
• Elizabeth E Cooper, Co-Founder

• Alex Benjamin, SVPof Finance & Operations
• Cindy Subido, SVP
• Jacob Shea, EVP of Interactive & technology
Nature of Services:
JHG is a San Diego-based marketing agency serving the media, entertainment, sports, and technology sectors that integrates marketing strategy, branding, public relations, interactive services, mobile technology, and metrics to propel client companies to success in the changing marketplace.

M.B.I. PRODUCTS CO., INC.
801 BOND STREET
ELYRIA, OH 44035-3118
440-322-6500
Fax: 440-322-1900
sales@mbiproducts.com
www.mbiproducts.com
• Emily Hoke, Marketing Director
sales@mbiproducts.com
• Andrew Ungar, Advertising Manager
sales@mbiproducts.com
• C. Boyd, Advertising Manager
sales@mbiproducts.com
• Chris Kysela, Sales
sales@mbiproducts.com
Brands:
Cloud-Lite Acoustical Baffles, Colorsonix Wall Panels, Lapendary Panels, San Pan Sanitary Panels, Shadow-Coustic Pads, Specialty Products (Colorsonix Floater Panel, Nubby Ceiling Panel, Rebounder Panel, Sound Stop Blanket)
Description:
Facilities - sound absorbers for arenas. High performance acoustical products that reduce reverberation and echo.

MODERNFOLD, INC.
215 W NEW ROAD
GREENFIELD, IN 46140
800-869-9685
Fax: 866-410-5016
info@modernfold.com
• Troy Pavy, Marketing
tpavy@modernfold.com
• Frank Mecklenburg, Customer Service Manager
fmecklenburg@modernfold.com
• Dan Popplewell, North East US Sales Manager
• Steve Molone, North Central US Sales Manager
smalone@modernfold.com
Brands:
Acousti-Seal operable partitions, Audio-Wall accordion partitions, Soundmaster accordion doors/partitions, ultra-seal, and moveable glass walls.
Description:
Owners and managers of arenas, convention centers, stadiums and theaters. Manufacturer of Modernfold movable wall systems, a complete line of acoustically operable partitions and accordion doors in a broad range of panel sizes and fabric finish options.

NEW TIER COMMUNICATIONS
15875 N GREENWAY HAYDEN LOOP
SUITE 109
SCOTTSDALE, AZ 85260

480-922-1711
Fax: 480-922-1733
• Michael D. Rossman, President & Chief Executive Officer
• Mark Malenfant, VP Sales
• Steve Graber, Production Manager
Description:
Provides an integrated suite of multimedia applications enabling clients to broadcast real-time marketing messages to consumers registered on the new Tier Network.
Nature of Services:
Services include development of interactive multimedia development, web site development, print and display advertising, video and audio production, screen savers and animation.
Clients:
IBM, Ticketmaster, TECO Energy, Adelphia, Ohio Health, Verizon Electronics, Fox Sports Net, SBC, Union Bank of California, US Bank, American West Airlines, TD Waterhouse, Solo, Philips, D.C. Lottery, Major Leage Baseball, National Basketball Assoc., National Hockey League, National Football League, Collegiate, Specialty, Southwest Airlines, Royals, Astros, Brewers, Cardinals, University of Utah, Emerald Downs.
Year Founded:
1994

ONE-ON-ONE SPORTS CONSULTANTS
4250 ALBANY DRIVE APT
SUITE F109
SAN JOSE, CA 95129
408-261-8480
Fax: 408-985-8341
jgr03@aol.com
• Jim Reardon, President
jgr03@aol.com
Nature of Sports Service:
Technical advisors.

PELTON MARSH KINSELLA
901 CARLETON DRIVE
RICHARDSON, TX 75081
214-814-5940
Fax: 206-495-1706
info@pmkconsultants.com
www.pmkconsultants.com
• Mollie Prince, Marketing Manager
• David E Marsh, VP
• Usman Bhatti, Principal - PMK International
• Dan Saenz, Acoustical Consultant
Manufacturer
Acoustics, theatrical planning, systems design including sound reinforcement, theatrical lighting, scoreboards, rigging, audio/visual and broadcast systems.

PHYSICIANS FOR QUALITY
808 W BLUEBONNET DRIVE
SAN MARCOS, TX 78666
800-284-3627
800-284-3627
Fax: 512-233-0642
Kim@PFQ.com
www.physiciansforquality.com
Description:
Founded 1987. Specialize in medical & fitness software consulting.

PILSON COMMUNICATIONS, INC.
160 KING STREET
CHAPPAQUA, NY 10514-3433

914-861-9216
• Neal H Pilson, President
Clients:
NASCAR, the International Olympic Committee, the Rose Bowl, UBS Bank, the Arena Football League and others
Sports Service Founded:
1995
Marketing & Consulting Services:
Active in all areas of sports television, media and marketing, providing representation, negotiation, consulting and packaging services for U.S. and international companies, organizations and associations.

PLAYING FIELD PROMOTIONS LLC
277 S FOREST STREET
DENVER, CO 80246
303-377-1109
800-966-1380
www.playingfieldpromotions.com
Description:
Athlete marketing and sports consulting with regard to athletes. Clients such as: Dusty Baker, Sean Casey, Drott Nixon, and Joe Mauer. Broadcasters John Miller, Kirby Puckett.

POC MEDIA SPORTS & ENTERTAINMENT DIVISION
511 LINDSEY DRIVE
MANOR HOUSE SUITE 301
WAYNE, PA 19087
610-636-5805
Fax: 610-971-0261
www.pocmedia.com
• Ashley Downey, General Manager
ashley.downey@pocmedia.com
• Pat O'Connor, Contact
(610) 636-5805
pat.oconnor@pocmedia.com
Services:
Integrated Marketing and Branding Initiatives, Development of Web Site, Multimedia and Interactive Marketing Communications Tools, Event Management, Planning and Staging and Non-Traditional Promotion for the Entertainment Industry

RAPIDTRON
3151 AIRWAY AVENUE
Bldg Q
COSTA MESA, CA 92626
949-798-0652
866-817-0127
Fax: 949-474-4550
www.rapidtron.com
• John Creel, President/Chief Executive Officer
• Peter Dermutz, Chief Technology Officer
• Larry Williams, Chief Operating Officer
• Chris Perkins, VP Sales & Marketing, Resorts
Brands:
AX 500 Smart Access Terminal, Panic Arms, Smart AX 500 reader, Smart Hand Held, Paper RFID Ticket, Smart Card, Printer, Smart TVM

SMITH, FAUSE, MCDONALD, INC.
351 8TH STREET
SAN FRANCISCO, CA 94103
415-255-9140
800-461-0660
Fax: 415-255-9180
info@sfmi.com
www.sfmi.com

• Peter A. McDonald, Principal/Founder/President
info@sfmi.com
• Kenneth R. Fause, Principal/VP
info@sfmi.com
• Ray Enriquez, Project Engineer
info@sfmi.com
Clients:
Partial list of organizations from Local Government (City of Berkeley, City of Phoenix, etc.); School and Community College Districts (Dublin Schools, Liberty Union high School District, etc.); Federal (Sandia National Labs); Developers (Cabot, Cabot & Forbes, Hines, etc.); Institutions (San Francisco Archdiocese, etc.); Corporations (Del Monte, Compaq, etc.); and Architects, Engineers and Constructions Managers (ADP, HMC Group, etc.)
Description:
Projects include college, NBA, NFL and NHL facilities.
Description:
Independent consulting services in acoustics, sound and MATV systems, broadcast and media facilities, large screen video displays, and event facilities for arenas and stadiums.

SPL INTEGRATED SOLUTIONS
6301 BENJAMIN ROAD
SUITE 101
TAMPA, FL 33634
813-884-7168
800-282-6733
Fax: 410-992-0758
sales@avispl.com
www.avispl.com
• Ashley Downey, General Manager
• Chad Gillenwater, Vice Chairman
• John Zettel, CEO
• Peter Grabowski, Chief Financial Officer
• Steve Benjamin, Executive VP
• Don Mastro, EVP, Sales
• Doug Carnell, EVP of Operations
• Martin Schaffel, Executive Chairman
Description:
Integrates audio and video systems, large-display videoconferencing systems, multimedia systems and large scale audio and video systems at sports venues. Has installed AV systems in over 40 professional sports stadiums and arenas.

SPORTS COMMUNICATIONS GROUP, LLC
831 HUNTERS GLN
ROCKWALL, TX 75032
972-772-8867
Marketing & Consulting Services:
Provides comprehensive communications support from experienced sports PR veterans for athletes, sports management firms, golf industry businesses and corporations with sports marketing initiatives. SCG has built its foundation in golf, but is currently exploring opportunities to expand into team sports.

SPORTS MEDIA CHALLENGE
7300 CARMEL EXECUTIVE PARK DRIVE
SUITE 120
CHARLOTTE, NC 28226
704-541-5942
800-929-4386
Fax: 704-541-5943

info@sportsmediachallenge.com
www.sportsmediachallenge.com
• Kathleen Hessert, Certified Speaking Professional
(704) 541-5942
khessert@sportsmediachallenge.com
• Joshua Baer, Chief Technology Consultant
Services:
Media Training, Crisis Communications, Public Speaking, Reputation Management, Online Word of Mouth and Conversation Tracking
Clients:
ASSOCIATIONS: American Football Coaches Association (AFCA), Black Coaches Association (BCA) College Sports Information Directors Association (CoSIDA), National Association of Collegiate Directors of Athletics (NACDA), Women's Basketball Coaches' Association (WBCA), NBA Coaches Associaiton; COLLEGES: Bowling Green UNiversity, Michigan State University, San Diego State University, University of Colorado, University of Connecticut, University of Florida, University of Maryland, University of North Carolina, University of Nortre Dame, University of Tennessee, University of Texas, University of Washington; ATHLETES, COACHES & PROFESSIONALS: Derek

SPORTS SYSTEMS SERVICES, INC.
2160 N CENTRAL ROAD
SUITE 104
FORT LEE, NJ 7024
201-429-9270
Fax: 201-585-3014
ContactUs@SportsSystems.com
www.sportssystems.com
• Jim Daigle, President
(201) 429-9288
Jim@SportsSystems.com
• Barb Hyde, VP of Operations
(201) 429-9280
barb.hyde@sportssystems.com
Sports Service Founded:
1987
IT Services:
Event sponsors and hospitality clients use our GuestPass to enchance guest communications and simplify complex or high-levelinvitation-registration for events. Companies with sponsorship or purchased tickets needing to increase usage (hence ROI) use our TicketTracker service to improve marketing, policy compliance, usage tracking and overall return on these investments. Our PressPass service is the far and away leader in online event accreditation management, serving nearly 1,100 worldwide events in 2010
Clients:
Most of our clients are the major sports marketing agencies- Agencies like IMG, Octagon, Genesco, Velocity/Team Epic, GMR and others rely on us because this is our core service - which helps them deliver their core service better.

SYNCHRON
15095 W 116TH STREET
OLATHE, KS 66062
913-338-4800
800-279-3874
Fax: 913-323-6049
www.synchron.com.hk
• Ben Cascio, Founder/President/Chief Executive Office

Description:
Provides audio conference calling services to sports organizations, teams and businesses world-wide. From an ad-hoc conference call for an impromptu meeting, to a Question-and-Answer session for a nation-wide press conferences.
Clients:
Microsoft, Starwood Hotels, Clear Channel and several other Fortune 2000 companies.
Year Founded:
1990

VENUE 1
489 DEVON PARK DRIVE
SUITE 310
WAYNE, PA 19087-1809
610-977-7700
• Jay T. Snider, Chairman/Chief Executive Officer
info@venueone.com
• Steve Weiss, President
info@venueone.com
• Jay R. Halbert, Chief Financial Officer/General Counsel
info@venueone.com
• Paul C. Frascella, Chief Operating Officer
info@venueone.com
Description:
Sports, entertainment, & recreational facility solutions. Designs facility management software. Enabling an arena/venue to keep track of all phases of facility management from ticket sales to concessions. Enables the customer to maintain fiscal control of concessions, suites, premium seat services, vending and retail operations.
Products:
Offer comprehensive, integrated venue management software and hardware solutions to the sports and entertainment sections.
Brands:
Tangent POS, FrontLine, TicketManager

WRIGHTSON, JOHNSON, HADDON & WILLIAMS, INC.
4801 SPRING VALLEY ROAD
SUITE 113
DALLAS, TX 75244
972-934-3700
Fax: 972-934-3720
info@wjhw.com
www.wjhw.com
• Jack Wrightson, Founder / Managing Principal
• Bill Haddon, Founder / Managing Principal
• Chris Williams, Founder / Managing Principal
• William B. Haddon, Co-Founder/Managing Principal
info@wjhw.com
• Jim Faber, Senior Associate
info@wjhw.com
Services:
Wrightson, Johnson, Haddon & Williams, Inc. is a 38-person M/WBE Certified firm offering state-of-the-art design services and consulting in audio, visual, video & scoring displays, broadcast provisions & video production, acoustics & noise control, theatre planning, lighting & rigging, distributed TV & satellite, video surveillance & access control, and tel/data structured cabling. Our strengths lie in the combined talents of our principals and employees, our diverse technical and business skills, and

experience accrued over the years from hundreds of successfully completed projects.
Clients:
We have a diverse range of project types including large sporting arenas and stadia, aviation, airports, health care facilities, high-tech edicational learning environments and athletic facilities, high-end performance arts, theatre and entertainment spaces, municipal facilities, and worship spaces.

Sports Agents

2X, INC.
413 SUNLIGHT WAY
CANON CITY, CO 81212
208-699-7696
Fax: 719-623-0020
jeanne@2xinc.com
www.2xinc.com
• Jeanne McNutty-King, Owner/Agent
jeanne@2xinc.com
Nature of Service:
Represents female athletes in all sports.
Services:
Full service sports agency representing women athletes.
Sports Service Founded:
1998

AAI SPORTS INC. & AAI INTERNATIONAL, INC.
16000 DALLAS PARKWAY
SUITE 300
DALLAS, TX 75248
972-739-8401
Fax: 972-739-8495
gbass@aaisports.com
www.aaisports.com
• George A Bass, Jr., Chief Executive Officer/President
gbass@aaisports.com
• George Bass, Partner
(972) 739-8490
gbass@aaisports.com
Services:
AAI's broad spectrum of services includes contract negotiation, commercial endorsements, marketing, media and public relations, as well as, an impressive range of services related to financial, business management, and tax preparation.
Clients:
Thomas Adams, Cory Alexander, Derrick Bryant, Jose Manuel Calderon, Larry Davis, KennyDye, Rick Hughes, Larry Johnson, Fredrik Jonzen, Federic Kammerichs, Mario Kasun, Pete Mickeal, Tyrone Nesby, Luis Scola, Tony Smith, Aaron Swinson, Nem Sovic, Tremaine Wingfield, John Woods, Angie Ball, Keisha Brown, Swin Cash, Camille Cooper, Katrina Crenshaw, Grace Daley, Helen Darling, Claudia Maria Das Neves, Keitha Dickerson, Adriana Dos Santos, Simone Edwards, Barbara Farris, Shauzinski Gortman, Julia Goureva, Dale Hodges, Kedra Holland-Corn, Joy Holmes-Harris, Shannon Johnson, Carolyn Jones-Young, Helen Luz, Clarisse Machanguana, Hamchetou Maiga, Izi
Services:
Marketing & Consulting Services, commercials print ads, publishing, radio shows, motion pictures, television, logo apparel.

Services:
Marketing & Consulting Services, commercials print ads, publishing, radio shows, motion pictures, television, logo apparel.
Marketing & Consulting Services Include:
Commericals print ads, publishing, radio shows, motion pictures, television, logo apparel.

ABBOTT MANAGEMENT GROUP
14 BEACON STREET
SUITE 814
BOSTON, MA 2108
617-723-4874
Fax: 617-723-8198
nabbott97@gmail.com
• Neil F Abbott, Founder/Partner
• Brittany Forgues, Associate
Services:
Offers: Pre-Draft Preparation, Off-Ice Training and Development, Contract Negotiation, Financial Management, Marketing/Public Relations, Insurance, Tax and Estate Planning and Post-Career Planning
Clients:
Some of Abbott Management's more successful clients include: Jeremy Roenick, Sergei Samsonov, Kyle McLaren, Mariusz Czerkawski, P.J. Axelsson, Nils Eksman
Description:
Contract negotiation, post career planning, investment contract negotiation, arbitration hearings, federal/state/international tax filings, provides securities advice, provides investment advice, licensing, endorsement exploration, tort actions/litigation.

AD CETERA SPORTS CELEBRITIES
2905 N SUMMIT AVENUE
MILWAUKEE, WI 53211-3441
414-967-7767
Fax: 414-967-7769
Nature of Service:
Provides a wide variety of personalities for just about any promotion or occasion. From product or service endorsements to appearances at corporate gatherings and grand openings, autograph signings to speaking engagements, Ad Cetera can find the perfect celebrity for your event.

ADVANCED ATHLETIC REPRESENTATION
5920 SAINT LAURENT DRIVE
AGOURA HILLS, CA 91301
818-889-3933
www.advanceathletics.com
• Michael C Moline, Chief Executive Officer
• Mike Mosa, Partner
Services:
All phases of athlete representation including contract negotiation, long-range planning, financial planning, and post-career counseling.

AKIN & RANDOLPH AGENCY
ONE GATEWAY CENTER
SUITE 2600
NEWARK, NJ 07102
973-353-8409
Fax: 973-353-8417
info@akinandrandolph.com
www.akinandrandolph.com
• Wanda Akin, Founder/Agent
(212) 581-7100

info@akinandrandolph.com
• Frank D. McIntyre, Sports Agent
(212) 581-7100
info@akinandrandolph.com
• Wanda Akin, Sports Agent, Literary Agent,
General Agent a
Description:
Full representation firm for athletes.
Services:
Review contracts with editors, publishers,
record producers and sports organizations,
Negotiate all aspects of contracts to obtain
the most beneficial terms, Create book
proposals and other image packages,
Negotiate/shop foreigh book rights, Review
book proposals and submit same to
publishers for review and bid, Receive and
review payment to clients and distribute
advances and royalties, Represent small
publishers on business/transactional
matters, Obtain recording contracts and film
deals, Arrange media exposure through
television, radio and magazine interviews
Clients:
Clients include Literary Division, Small
Press, Film, Music/Recordings,
Broadcast/TV, Sports

ALL PRO SPORTS & ENTERTAINMENT
36 STEELE STREET
THE SMITH CENTER, SUITE 100
DENVER, CO 80206
303-320-4004
800-783-4776
Fax: 303-320-4019
www.apse.net
• C. Lamont Smith, Founder/President
(303) 320-4004
• Peter J. Schaffer, Sports Agent
(303) 320-4004
• Grant Wittenwyler, Golf Director
(303) 320-4004
grantapse@comcast.net
Services:
All phases of athlete management, including
contract negotiation, financial planning,
post-career planning, endorsements, etc.
Clients:
Barry Sanders, LeCharles Bentley, Jonathan
Kaye, Jerome Bettis, Aaron Smith, Shane
Bertsch, Eddie George, David Diehl, Scott
Petersen, Braylon Edwards, Antonio Bryant,
Brian Kortan, Lito Sheppard, Jesse Palmer,
Ben Portie, Samari Rolle, Mike Anderson,
Chris Sessler, Derrick Mason, Dexter
Jackson, John Restino, Jason Gildon, Rudi
Johnson, Tom Woodard, Chad Brown, Willie
Roaf, Troy Riddle, Trevor Pryce, Mike
Rucker, Gavin Morgan, Tra Thomas,
Marques Anderson, Josef Marha, Jason
Ball, Tony Bryant, Tomas Divisek, Colin
Branch, Trung Canidate, Michal Sykora,
Bryce Fisher, Mario Edwards, Denise
Plante, Ray Green, Quinten Griffen, Vic
Lombardi, Kell

ALSTRAR INC. SPORTS & ENTERTAINMENT
25 REGAL DRIVE
NEW ROCHELLE, NY 10804
914-576-1943
Fax: 914-673-1282
Services:
Handles marketing and public relations for
businesses, organizations, athletes and
companies.

AMATEUR SPORTS GROUP, INC.
201 W. BALTIMORE STREET
SUITE 119
FIRST MARINER ARENA
BALTIMORE, MD 21201
410-962-7070
866-696-5425
Fax: 410-962-8777
www.asgsports.com
• Scott Westcoat, Director
(410) 962-7070
scott@asgsports.com
• Jonathan Reid, Operations Director
(443) 277-3125
• Damian Orencel, Event Specialist
(443) 834-6860
• Kerrie Eisenhauer, Senior Event Specialist
(410) 962-7070
• Sergio Luna, Multicultural Event Specialist
(410) 962-7070
• Denny Gordon, Event Specialist
(410) 962-7070
bullets52@aol.com
• Rob Spigone, DCU Event Specialist
(410) 962-7070
thebigspig@aol.com
• Scott Westcoat, President/CEO
scott@asgsports.com
• Derek Wilson, Executive Vice President,
derek@asgevents.com
• Keith Finnegan, Director of Operations &
Personnel
keith@asgevents.com
• Geoff Stinson, ASG Digital Event
Specialist
(410) 962-7070
• Warren Westcoat, Director of Enviroevents
• Charles Allen, Director of ASG Logistics
• Kristin Dempsey, Director of ASG
Fulfillment
kristin@asgevents.com
Services:
Event Management, Event Production,
Event Consulting, Marketing/Promotions
Marketing & Consulting Services:
Event Management and Production, Full
In-House Digital Media Division, Event
Marketing, Warehouse/Fulfillment Services.
Event Management Services:
Full event management, including planning,
sponsorship, traffic promotion and ticket
sales, program books, exhibit areas, post
event merchandising sales.
Athlete Management Services:
Promotion, contract negotiation,
representation, accounting, legal and related
services.
Sports Service Founded:
1994
Clients:
Ravens Fan Zone, Soccer Celebration,
Maryland Pepsi Pride, US Soccer
Federation, McDonald's McSoccerfest, DC
United's Just 4 Kicks, Soccer Seats,
MSYSA, Sand Duels, LAXFEST, Hoop it
Up, Copa Sears, Kicks Against Breast
Cancer, Twenty Plus Entertainment,
TerraGol Beach Soccer, Legacy Cup Soccer
Tournament.

ANSLOW, ESQ., RICHARD I.
195 ROUTE 9 S
2ND FLOOR
MANALAPAN, NJ 7726
732-409-1212
Fax: 732-577-1188
info@anslowlaw.com

• Richard I. Anslow, Managing Partner
(732) 409-1212
ranslow@anslowlaw.com
• Gregg E. Jaclin, Partner
(732) 409-1212
gjaclin@anslowlaw.com
Services:
Securities, Business & Corporate, Real
Estate, Wills & Estates, Sports &
Entertainment
Description:
Contract negotiation, post career planning,
investment contract negotiation, arbitration
hearings, federal/state/international tax
filings, licensing, endorsement exploration.

ARANDA GROUP
724 OLD YORK ROAD
JENKINTOWN, PA 19046-2833
215-576-6666
877-272-4033
Fax: 215-884-0356
www.arandagroup.com
• Arthur Rosenberg, President
(215) 576-6666
arthur@aranda.com
• Steven Rosenberg, VP/Chief Operating
Officer
(215) 576-6666
steven@aranda.com
• Arthur Rosenberg, Chairman of the Board
• Bill Alsberg, Associate VP
• Jacki Simmons, VP/Bookeeping
• Joanne Keller, Registered Investment
Assistant
• Tom Gallagher, Investment Assistant
• Erica Gurian, Client Services
Services:
Financial management firm; agents for
professional athletes and others.
Description:
Contract negotiation.

ARCTIC SPORTS
353 HUNTINGTON TURNPIKE
BRIDGEPORT, CT 6610
203-371-8326
Fax: 203-373-9655
• Rick Piccirillo, Owner
(203) 371-8326
Sports Service Founded:
1994.
Services:
Represents athletes who desire to play
abroad, handling all phases of contract
negotiations, team placement and
sponsorship opportunities.

ASCENSION ENTERPRISES INC.
PO BOX 301033
ARLINGTON, TX 76007-1033
817-633-7612
Fax: 817-633-7612
www.ascensionentinc.com
• Darren Deloatche, Founder
Year Founded:
1995
Services:
Contract Negotiation, Performance
Enhancement, Marketing Services, Personal
Services, Post-Athletic Career Planning,
Continuing Education
Clients:
Eddie Moore, Omari Hand, Keyon
Whiteside, Justin Brown, Troy Fleming,
Mark Jones, Steve Mascorro, Anthony
Hines, Delvin Hughley, Eric Houle, Jerome

Braziel, George Hudson, D'Wayne Taylor
Descripton:
Full service representation and management organization for professional athletes and entertainers.

ASSANTE SPORTS MANAGEMENT GROUP
2 QUEEN STREET EAST
19TH FLOOR
TORONTO, CANADA M5C 3G7
416-348-9994
888-348-9994
Fax: 416-364-2969
service@assante.com
www.assante.com
• Murray Oxby, Director Communications
(416) 681-3254
• James E. Ross L.L.B, Senior Vice President ,Wealth and Estate Plan
• Robert J. Dorrell CIIM,FCSI, Senior Vice President and Distribution Servic
• Steven J. C. Donald FCA, FCPA, President
OTHER LOCATIONS:
151 Yonge Street, 9th Floor, Toronto, Ontario, Canada M5C 2W7; Phone: 416-645-4000; Fax: 416-645-4005; 360 Main Street, STE 1900, Winnipeq, Manitoba, Canada R3C 3Z3; Phone: 204-957-1730; Fax: 204-947-2103
Description:
Our goal is to simplify and enhance the lives of our clients by serving as their primary financial advisor, managing their assets and lifestyle needs from the day we begin our relationship with them, through succeeding generations.

ATH-ELITE MANAGEMENT SERVICES
300 N MAIN STREET
BOWLING GREEN, OH 43402
419-352-4650
Fax: 419-354-4550

ATHLETIC RESOURCE MANAGEMENT, INC.
1100 RIDGEWAY LOOP ROAD
SUITE 500
MEMPHIS, TN 38120
901-761-8503
Fax: 901-763-3762
www.sextonsports.com
• Jim Sexton, President
(901) 763-4900
• Rick Landrum, Vice President
(901) 761-8505
• Jim Dutton, Director of Client Develoment
(901) 763-4900
• John Haur, Director of Marketing
(901) 763-4900
Services:
Sports agency representing NFL and Major League Baseball stars, golf and sports broadcasters.
Clients:

Nature of Sports Services:
Athlete represenatation.

ATLANTA INTERNATIONAL CONSULTING GROUP, INC. (AICG)
1401 PEACHTREE STREET
SUITE 500
ATLANTA, GA 30309
404-872-4884
Fax: 404-870-0440

sales@aicginc.com
www.aicginc.com
Services:
Specializes in creating programs that increase brand awareness, improve market share, and boost product profitability of clients through graphic design, printing, specialty merchandise and fulfillment services.
Services:
Graphic Design &Creative Direction, Custom Illustration & Artwork (Sports & Entertainment), Project Management, Corporate & Brand Identity (Logo Development), POS/POP & Custom Packaging (Restaurant & Food Industry; Retail), Sales Collateral Support & Promotion (Desktop Publishing and Brochures), Internet Design & Implementation
Clients:
The Coca-Cola Company, Coca-Cola Enterprises, Bellsouth Corporation, McDonald's Corporation, AOL/Turner, S.C. Johnson, ARAMARK, MCI WorldCom
Athlete Management Services:
Exclusive representation of leading sports personalities. Representation of select entertainment properties. Full-service sports marketing firm for professional and amateur athletics. Provides career management consulting, contract advisement, endorsements, financial planning, promotions, entertainment representation and full-service merchandising.
Marketing & Consulting Services:
Provides strategic and tactical consultation in general sports marketing consultation, professional development, special segment, general market development, ethnic marketing development (African American, Hispanic, and Asian), youth marketing and female marketing development. Marketing representation for entertainers, musicians and broadcasters. Provides financial services through strategic alliances and affiliated company.
Event Management Services:
Creates grassroots or made-for-TV-sports/entertainment oriented events from concept to completion. Develops and implements integrated programs to assist clients in promoting their products and/or services. Full public relations and advertising capabilities, arranging for sponsorship of both new and existing sports events, developing tie-in promotions for such sponsorships, complete management of event. Experienced in targeting particular sales objectives through sports promotions. Develops event-driven sales promotion campaigns for corporate clients. Provides complete strategic planning, project management and promotional support services.

AXELROD, BARRY
2236 ENCINITAS BOULEVARD
SUITE A
ENCINITAS, CA 92024
760-753-0088
Fax: 760-436-7399
baxy@msn.com
• Barry Axelrod, Owner
(760) 753-0088
Services:
Marketing of professional athletes and other sports-related entities.

Clients:
Legal, personal and financial management of professional and amateur athletes.
Sports Service Founded:
1977

BAKER SPORTS MANAGMENT
1750 MONTGOMERY STREET
1ST FLOOR
SAN FRANCISCO, CA 94111
415-433-3355
Fax: 415-433-4522
steve@bakersports.com
www.bakersports.com
• Stephen Baker, Owner
sbaker@bakersports.com
Description:
Contract negotiation, marketing, and endorsements.
SERVICES:
Sports Management
Clients:
Jeff Garcia, Ken Harvey, Brian Mitchell, Ray Brown, Kailee Wong, Nnamdi Asomugha, Eric Johnson, Jamie Winborn, Casey Moore, JT O'Suvillivan, Paul Smith, Adimchinobe Echemandu, Courtney Anderson, Brett Pierce, Will Svitek, Matt Giordano, Jon Ritchie, Greg Clark, Mike Croel & Shante Carver

BARNES MARKETING, INC.
1401 DOVE STREET
STUDIO 520
NEWPORT BEACH, CA 92660
949-553-0820
Fax: 949-768-0630
info@barnesmarketing.com
www.barnesmarketing.com
Sports Service Founded:
1974
Services:
Specializes in marketing and consulting and event management services in motorsports marketing and race team sponsorship including comprehensive sales packages provided for potential sponsors, media coordination, and public relations and athlete management services which includes speaking engagements, personal appearances, product endorsements, radio and television, movies.
Athlete Management Services:
Speaking engagements, personal appearances, product endorsements, radio and television, movies.

BARNNETT, HOWARD D
333 S MAIN STREET
POCATELLO, ID 83204
208-233-0845
Fax: 208-233-1304
www.hteh.com
• Howard D Burnett, Partner
(208) 233-0845
info@hawleytroxell.com
• Susan Olson, Executive Director
(208) 344-6000
solson@hawleytroxell.com
Description:
Contract negotiation, investment contract negotiation, federal/state/international tax filings.
Services:
Provides quality legal solutions for Business & Finance, Litigation, Real Estate,

Employment, Construction & Environmental Matters.

BATTLE, MICHAEL RAY
1801 LARKHILL LANE
RICHMOND, VA 23235
804-323-5041
Nature of Sports Service:
All phases of athlete representation including contract negotiation, long-range planning, financial planning, and post-career counseling.

BDA SPORTS MANAGEMENT
700 YGNACIO VALLEY ROAD
SUITE 330
WALNUT CREEK, CA 94596
925-279-1040
Fax: 925-279-1060
www.bdasports.com
• Bill A. Duffy, President/Chief Executive Officer
• Kevin Bradbury, Player Representation VP
• Merle Scott, Player Representative
• Bill Duffy, Chairman and CEO
• Billy Kuenzinger, President and General counsel
• Julie Neuman, Chief Financial Officer
• Shauna Smith, VP Client Relations
• Kevin Brabury, Sr. VP , Player Relations
• Michael Conley, Agent
• Todd Ramasar, Agent
Other Locations:
1000 North Kingsbury Street #105, Chicago, IL 60610; Phone: 312-467-9027; 655 Amsterdam Avenue, Uniondale, NY 11553; Phone:925-279-1040; 7402 SW 64th Place, Portland, OR 97219; Phone: 503-245-8989; 870 Commonwealth Avenue, STE 100, Venice, CA 90291; Phone: 310-581-4509
Services:
Draft Preparation & Positioning, Contract Negotiation, Career Management, Investment Planning, Global Management & Post-Career Guidance Sponsor Relations, Media Relations, Fan Relations, Camps & Clinics, Special Projects, Player Relationship, Family Relationship, Team Relationship & Role as Mentor/Role Model
Clients:
Carmelo Anthony, Leandro Barbosa, Andris Biedris, Zarko Cabarkapa, Anthony Carter, Speedy Claxto, Antonio Davis, Juan Dixon, Chris Duhon, Francisco Elson, Raymond Felton, Jeff Foster, Drew Gooden, Devin Green, Chuck Hayes, Mike James, Marko Jaric, Freddy Jones, Yao Ming, Steve Nash, Rasho Nesterovic, Michael Olowokandi, Travis Outlaw, Tayshaun Prince, Joel Przybilla, Zeljko Rebraca, Kareem Rush, Hakim Warrick, Louis Williams, Dorell Wright, Troy Bell, Jay Williams, Toby Bailey, Miroslav Beric, Andrew Betts, Ruben Boumtje-Boumtje, Yiannis Bouroussis, Louis Bullock, Robert Conley, Taylor Coppenrath, Vladimir Dasic, Bennett Davidson, Obinna Ekez

BECHTA, JACK D./JB SPORTS
7660 FAY AVENUE
SUITE H-502
LA JOLLA, CA 92037
858-454-9005
800-800-4775
Fax: 858-454-2330
sportsagent@NFLAdvisor.com
www.nfladvisor.com

• Jack D Bechta, Owner
Jack@NFLAdvisor.com
• Dominique Brutsche, Assistant
dominique@nfladvisor.com
Services:
Personalized pre-draft game plan; All Star and combine preparation; Coordination of individual pre-draft workouts; Pre-draft marketing, highlight films, and personalized assets; Draft day events coordination; Contract negotiations; Personal training
Clients:
Jonathan Babineaux, Matt Bowen, Tyrone Carter, Kerry Carter, Jared Clauss, Earl Dotson, Tim Dwight, Zeron Flemister, Kelly Gregg, Al Harris, Renaldo Hill, Brody Liddiard, Pete Lougheed, Jermane Mayberry, Mat McBriar, Larry Moore, Gene Mruczkowski, Scott Mruczkowski
Nature of Sports Service:
All phases of athlete representation including contract negotiation, long-range planning, financial planning, and post-career counseling.

BENJAMIN, GLEN
6 GLODE CT
AIRMONT, NY 10952
845-352-1449
Description:
Contract negotiation.

BERTHELSEN, RICHARD
280 PARK AVENUE
NEW YORK, NY 10017
212-450-2000
Fax: 212-681-7573
www.nfl.com
• Troy Vincent, President
tvincent@nfl.com
• Jerome Mertens, President
jmertens@nfl.com
• Harold Henderson, Labor Relation EVP
hhenderson@nfl.com
• Steve Bornstein, Media EVP
sbornstein@nfl.com
Services:
Collective bargaining agent for all players employed by clubs of the National Football League, governed by a volunteer board of active NFL players elected by their teammates on each team.
Description:
Represents sports organizations.

BEST IN SPORTS
138 RIVER ROAD
SHATTUCK OFFICE CENTER
ANDOVER, MA 01810
978-725-3581
Fax: 978-725-3582
• Thomas McLaughlin, Sports Agent
• Dwight Robinson, Sports Agent
Nature of Sports Service:
Athlete representation including contract negotiation, long-range planning, post-career counseling, endorsements contracts, European contracts.

BEVERLY HILLS SPORTS COUNCIL
9595 WILSHIRE BOULEVARD
SUITE 1010
BEVERLY HILLS, CA 90212
310-858-1935
Fax: 310-550-7980

• Daniel Lozano, Partner
• Rick Thurman, Chief Financial Officer
• Jeff Borris, General Counsel
Description:
Full representation of professional baseball players.
Services:
Professional sports club and promoter

BIG TEN ATHLETIC CONFERENCE
1500 W HIGGINS ROAD
PARK RIDGE, IL 60068-6300
847-696-1010
Fax: 847-696-1150
www.bigten.org
• James E Delany, Commissioner
jdelany@bigten.org
• Brad Traviolia, Associate Commissioner - Chief Operating
btraviolia@bigten.org
• Rich Falk, Associate Commissioner
rfalk@bigten.org
• James A. Delany, Commissioner
• Brad Traviolia, Deputy Commissioner
• Diane Dietz, Chief communications officer
• Wendy Fallen, Associate Commissioner
• Julie Suderman, Controller
Services:
Provide in excess of $63 million in athletic scholarship aid to 7,500 men and women student-athletes to compete for 25 championships, 12 for men and 13 for women. Conference institutions sponsor more than 250 athletic programs.
Description:
Represents sports organizations.

BIKE TAHOE
PO BOX 673
ZEPHYR COVE, NV 89448
775-586-9566
ty@biketahoe.org
www.biketahoe.org
• Ty Polastri, President
Founded:
2013
Clients Include:
State of Nevada, City of South Lake Tahoe, Sierra Nevada Media Group, The Tahoe Fund, Lake Tahoe Visitors Authority, El Dorado County, Zephyr Cove Lodge, Lakeside Inn, Hyatt Hotel, Flume Trail Bikes, South Shore Bikes, Tahoe Chamber of Commerce, North Lake Tahoe Resort Association
Nature of Service:
Multi-channel marketing, promotion and education using sport as a vehicle to drive consumers to business as to affect regional economic and environmental sustainability.

BLACKMAN & RABER, LTD.
123 E 54TH STREET
SUITE 9C
NEW YORK, NY 10022-4507
212-593-1803
Services:
Advertising Agency
Sports Service Founded:
1964
Athlete Management Services:
Consults with lawyers and agents on player endorsement negotiations. Placement of sports personalities in advertising and promotions.
Event Management Services:
Full service sales promotion agency.

Creates sweepstakes and contests, celebrity and special events. Negotiates sponsorships and licenses.
Marketing & Consulting Services:
Acts as talent consultants for advertising agencies specializing in sports campaigns. Assists with sales and trade incentive programs, advertising and promotional campaigns, and casting sports personalities.

BLACKSTAR SPORTS MANAGEMENT, INC.
2556 LAKESHORE BOULEVARD W
TRONTO, ONTARIO, CANADA M8V 1G1
416-399-6473
Fax: 416-252-4487
• Maurice C Martin, Agent
Nature of Sports Service:
All phases of athlete representation including contract negotiation, long-range planning, financial planning, tax service, endorsements and post-career counseling.
Clients Include:
Represents players from the National Football League (NFL), Arena Football League and Canadian Football League.

BLACKWELDER, MURRAY
IOWA STATE UNIVERSITY
1750 BEARDSHEAR HALL
AMES, IA 50011
515-294-4111
800-262-3810
Fax: 515-294-2592
contact@iastate.edu
www.iastate.edu
• Gregory L Geoffroy, President
(515) 294-2042
president@iastate.edu
• Elizabeth Hoffman, EVP/Provost
• Thomas L. Hill, Student Affairs VP
(515) 294-4420
tomhill@iastate.edu
• Warren R. Madden, Business and Finance VP
(515) 294-1530
wmadden@iastate.edu
Services:
Provides education services to their students.

BLYTHE, DONOVAN A.
595 INDUSTRIAL ROAD
SAN CARLOS, CA 94070
650-595-7797
donovan@blythesbasketball.com
www.blythesbasketball.com
• Donovan A Blythe, Director
(650) 341-3998
donovan@blythesbasketball.com
Nature of Sports Service:
All phases of athlete representation including contract negotiation, long-range planning, financial planning, and post-career counseling.

BODDICKER SPORTS MANAGEMENT
8333 DOUGLAS AVENUE
SUITE 975
DALLAS, TX 75225
214-369-9655
Fax: 214-369-9681
• Daniel J Boddicker, President
Nature of Sports Service:
All phases of athlete representation including contract negotiation, long-range

planning, financial planning, and post-career counseling.

BUSINESS ARENA, INC.
4720 MONTGOMERY LANE
SUITE 1010
BETHESDA, MD 20814
301-656-4800
Fax: 301-907-9494
• George Mavrikes, Sports Agent
Nature of Sports Service:
All phases of athlete representation including contract negotiation, long-range planning, financial planning, and post-career counseling.
SERVICES:
Contract Negotiations, Financial Services, Endorsements, Tax Advice - Referrals Only, Career Counseling, Post Career Counseling, Estate Planning, Marketing

CAFLISCH, ROBERT J.
301 SOUTH BEDFORD STREET
SUITE 7
MADISON, WI 53703
608-257-8280
Fax: 608-255-6010
www.ritzcaflisch.com
• Peter B. Ritz, Lawyer
• Robert J. Caflisch, Lawyer
Description:
Licensing, endorsement exploration.
Services:
Licensing, endorsement exploration.

CAMPBELL, JOHN RUSSELL (RUSS)
1901 SIXTH AVENUE N
SUITE 1500
BIRMINGHAM, AL 35203-4642
205-251-8100
Fax: 205-226-8799
rcampbell@balch.com
www.balch.com
• Russ Campbell, Partner
• Patrick Strong, Associate
Services:
Antitrust, Appellate, Business Litigation, Casualty Litigation, Civil Rights Litigation, Class Action Litigation, Coal and Fossil Fuels, Condemnation, Land Use and Water Rights, Construction, Consumer Financial Services, Corporate & Securities, Corporate Governance, Creditors Rights & Bankruptcy, Economic Development Incentives, Education, Employee Benefits & Executive Compensation, Energy, Energy and Utility Litigation, Energy Litigation, Finance, Lending and Leasing, Financial Institution Formations, Mergers & Acquisitions, Financial Institutions, Financial Products & Services, Financial Services Litigation, Financial Services Regulatory. R
Nature of Sports Service:
All phases of athlete representation including contract negotiation, long-range planning, and post-career counseling.
Other Locations:
1275 Pennsylvania Avenue, NW, 10th Floor, Washington, DC 20004; Phone: 202-347-6000; 40I East Capital Street, STE 200, Jackson, MS 3920I; Phone: 601-961-9900

CARDIOKICKBOXING.COM
91-1013 WAIPAA STREET
EWA BEACH, HI 96706-6499

808-457-7164
marcus.devalentino@cardiokickboxing.com
www.cardiokickboxing.com
• Marcus DeValentino, Program Director
marcus.devalentino@cardiokickboxing.com
• Frank Thiboutot, Cardio Kickboxing Creator
Description:
Created in 1992 as a fitness alternative and to preserve the integrity of the sport of kickboxing.

CAREER SPORTS & ENTERTAINMENT
150 INTERSTATE N PARKWAY SE
ATLANTA, GA 30339
770-955-1300
Fax: 770-226-5560
www.careersports.com
• Matt Kramer, Director Public Relations
(770) 955-1300
mkramer@careersports.com
• Lonnie Cooper, CEO
Sports Service Founded:
1986
Description:
Full service client representation, marketing and media services agency.
Clients:
Bellsouth, Cingular Wireless, The Home Depot, Kellogg Company, Aflac, Larry Coker, Bobby Cox, Billy Donovan, Mike Fratello, Paul Hewitt, Tom Izzo, Eddie Jordan, Nate Mcmillan, Sam Mitchell, Doc Rivers, Kelvin Sampson, Mark Slonaker, Reggie Theus, Isiah Thomas, Lennie Wilkens, Brian Winters , Randy Walker Clifford Warren, Brent Abernathy, Russ Adams, Michael Barrett, Kyle Davies, Mark DeRosa, Wes Helms, Richard Lewis, Kerry Ligtenberg, Ron Mahay, Mike Maroth, John Smoltz, TJ Tucker, Billy McCarthy, Briah Moehler, Derek Wathan, Roland Thatcher, Nick Cassini, Paul Claxton, David Denham, Ryuji Imada, Franklin Langham, Lee Williams, Allen Bestwic
Athlete Management Services:
Negotiation of player contracts - baseball, basketball and football.
Marketing & Consulting Services:
Endorsement marketing, personal appearances, speaking engagements, promotion of sports clinics. Internal & consumer promotions, event management, sponsorship negotiation and fulfillment.

CAREY, MICHAEL
SPORTS PERSONALITIES INC
16 TERRI RD
FRAMINGHAM, MA 1701
508-877-6150
Services:
Contract negotiation.

CASTLEREAGH, INC.
320 BUFFALO AVENUE
FREEPORT, NY 11520
516-379-2122
Fax: 516-379-2386
www.castlereaghpress.com
Sports Service Founded:
1992.
Services:
Commercial printers
Athlete Management Services:
Manages talent for appearances and endorsements.
Event Managment Services:

Represents corporations for event day sponsorships.
Marketing & Consulting Services:
Produces and markets sports memorabilia and collectibles; produces and manages theme travel related to DreamWeek and Fantasy Camp programs for golf and baseball.

CELEBRITY CONNECTIONS, L.L.C.
29 TROTTER LANE
NEWINGTON, CT 06111-5334
860-667-8290
Services:
Manages special events; handles athlete appearances and endorsements. Provides creative and cause marketing, entertainment and event management services. Serves as celebrity clearinghouse for charity events, providing celebrity personal appearances, talent development, and sport
Sports Service Founded:
1992
Athlete Management Services:
Handles athlete appearances and endorsements. Provides creative and cause marketing, entertainment and event management services. Serves as celebrity clearinghouse for charity events, providing celebrity personal appearances, talent development, and sports marketing. Specialty is niche marketing to African-American and Latino businesses.

CELEBRITY MARKETING GROUP
1701-1/2 BANKS
SUITE 1
HOUSTON, TX 77098
713-522-2230
• Mary Beggins, President
Services:
Provides public relations and administrative services to athletes. Specializes in endorsement opportunities, unique promotions, speaking engagements, personal appearances, merchandising and entertainment representation.
Sports Service Founded:
1993.

CELEBRITY SUPPLIERS OF LAS VEGAS
2756 N GREEN VALLEY PARKWAY
SUITE 449
LAS VEGAS, NV 89014-2100
702-451-8090
www.celebritysuppliers.com
• A.J. Sagman, President
(561) 362-0079
info@entertainmentservices.com
• Steve Rosenthal, Sales Manager
(561) 362-0079
info@entertainmentservices.com
• D. Manning, Marketing Director
Marketing & Consulting Services:
Supplying Half-time Visual Performers, TV Celebrities and Singing Impersonators for Teams Worldwide.
Services:
Provides top name performers, singers, dance bands, Motown bands, singing groups, oldies groups, disco groups, comedians, variety acts, magicians, jugglers, Celebrities, Speakers, Celebrity Athletes, musical and corporate entertainment for various types of events and venues worldwide.
Sports Service Founded:

1985
Other Location:
Boca Raton, FL. 561-362-0079

CENTRAL VIRGINIA SPORTS MANAGEMENT
117 SKYLARK DRIVE
DANVILLE, VA 24541
434-799-6426
Fax: 434-797-8857
• Kenneth Lewis, Sports Agent
Nature of Sports Service:
All phases of athlete representation including contract negotiation, long-range planning, financial planning, and post-career counseling.

CENTURY CITY SPORTS & ENTERTAINMENT
23679 CALABASAS ROAD
SUITE 151
CALABASAS, CA 91302
818-591-0295
Fax: 818-591-1140
• Ronald Glickman, Sports Agent
Nature of Sports Service:
All phases of athlete representation including contract negotiation, long-range planning, financial planning, and post-career counseling.

CHAMPIONSHIP GROUP, INC.
PO BOX 80489
ATLANTA, GA 30366
770-457-5777
info@champgrp.com
www.ChampionshipGroup.com
• Ardy Arani, CEO/Managing Director
• Larry Lubin, EVP Strategic Innovation
(770) 457-5777
• Roy Barudin, EVP Brand Development
(770) 457-5777
• Ray Curtis, Chief Financial Officer
(770) 936-3600
• Jeff Martin, Creative Services Director
(770) 457-5777
Year Founded:
1980
Services:
A strategic sports marketing and promotion resource with a twenty-eight year track record of creating innovative, high-impact business building campaigns, leveraged sponsorships, retail activation and lifestyle marketing programs for corporate clients.
Athlete Management Services:
Sports marketing and promotions for corporate clients with motorsports and lifestyle marketing.
Event Management Services:
Sports and special event marketing specialists. Develops and manages corporate sports promotion campaigns within motorsports, action sports, lifestyle and special events. Award winning strategy, flawless execution.

CHASE AMERICA
300 PARK AVENUE
17TH FLOOR
NEW YORK CITY, NY 10022
646-706-7300
800-491-4980
Fax: 561-491-5001
• David E Stefan, Jr., Chief Executive Officer / Palm Beach Office
(561) 491-5000

• Maria Dennison, President Corporate Office (New York)
• John Roy, Managing Director / Palm Beach Office
Services:
Executive search firm specializing in the home building industry.
Clients:
Fortune 500 companies to include chemical, mineral, oil and gas companies, land development, PUD, golf course communities and golf resort properties; home builders and land developers, commercial and multi-family real estate, the sports market place.
Sports Service Founded:
1996. Provides the highest quality professional education and image relations program for the emerging and professional athlete. Recognizes and meets the demands placed on the athlete's celebrity status; brings the best talent on the issues. Locations in New York, Palm Beach, Chicago, San Diego and Atlanta (Corporate Office).

CLARKE, ALLEN R.
40 N CENTRAL AVENUE
SUITE 1900
PHOENIX, AZ 85004
602-262-5311
Fax: 602-262-5747
www.lrlaw.com
• Jose A Cardenas, Chairman and Partner
(602) 262-5790
Jcardenas@lrlaw.com
• Kenneth Va Winkle Jr, Managing Partner
(602) 262-5357
Kvanwinkle@lrlaw.com
Description:
Contract negotiation, tort actions/litigation.
Services:
Appeals, Arbitration and Mediation, Banking and Lending, Bankruptcy, Broker/Dealer, Commercial Litigation, Construction, Corporate and Securities, Creditor's Rights, Criminal Defense, Government Regulation and Corporate Compliance, E-Discovery & Data Management, Education and Schools, Employee Benefits, Environmental and Natural Resources, Finance, Gaming, Government Contracts, Government Relations and Admnistrative, Health Care, Indian Affairs Law, Insurance, Intellectual Property, Labor and Employment, Mergers and Acquisitions, Personal Injury, Products Liability, Professional Liability and Discipline, Real Estate.

CLAYTON, LORINZO
43 THIRD AVENUE
WESTBURY, NY 11590
516-334-2767
Fax: 516-334-7282
Services:
All phases of athlete representation including contract negotiation, long-range planning, financial planning, and post-career counseling.

CLEAR CHANNEL ENTERTAINMENT, INC.
200 E BASSE ROAD
SAN ANTONIO, TX 78209
210-822-2828
Fax: 310-867-7001
www.clearchannel.com

• Randall T Mays, President/Chief Financial Officer
randalltmays@clearchannel.com
• John Hogan, CEO
Marketing & Consulting Services:
Integrates all components of the marketing mix to develop and implement full-service plans that meet the clients objectives. Expertise includes corporate consulting, stadium and arena naming rights, team and venue services, sponsorship sales, media sales, property marketing, retail licensing and merchandising, online strategies and public relations.
Services:
Promoters and producers of live entertainment events including music concerts, theatrical performances, and specialized motor sports events. Also provides event sponsorship and advertising.
Athlete Management Services:
Offering full-service representation of athletes, coaches and broadcasters. Services include contract negotiation and all marketing endeavours, including endorsements, licensing, promotions, charitable activities, speaking engagements and personal appearances.
Event Management Services:
Providing turnkey event development and management for a wide array of sports including tennis, golf, thoroughbred racing, soccer, figure skating and motor sports.
Television:
Develops, produces and distributes television and theatrical productions to meet the converging needs of sports and entertainment clients, including concept development and network negotiations. Organization has ongoing relationships with virtually every major broadcast and cable network and movie studio.

CMG WORLDWIDE
10500 CROSSPOINT BOULEVARD
INDIANAPOLIS, IN 46256
317-570-5000
Fax: 317-570-5500
www.cmgww.com
• Greg Thompson, Chief Operating Officer
• Maria Gejdosova, Vice President, Finance & Acquisitions
• Mark Roesler, Chairman/Chief Executive Officer
• Greg Thompson, COO
• Mark Vo Roesler, Chairman & CEO
Sports Service Founded:
1971
Services:
Worldwide representative of a wide range of athletic organizations, athletes, and estates. Negotiates personal appearances.
Services:
Merchandise Licensing, Advertising/Promotional Licensing, Brand Development/Extension, Sponsorship Negotiation, Professional Contract Negotiation, Product/Service Endorsements, Speakers Bureau, Personal Appearances, Autograph Signings, Interviews, Intellectual Property Strategies and Branding Services, Infringement, Policing and Enforcement Services, Domain Names Recovery and Internet Issues, Expert Witness Services, Consulting and Negotiation Services, Speakers, Lecturers and Presenters for Conferences, Programs and Commentary, Software Design for Licensing and

Marketing Companies, Web Development, Media Asset Management, Hardware Support
Clients:
Marilyn Monroe, James Dean, Sophia Loren, Ingrid Bergman, Ivana Trump, Lana Turner, Bette Davis, Tyrone Power, Errol Flynn, Montgomery Clift, Sir Laurence Olivier, Rock Hudson, Helen Hayes, Jean Harlow, Ginger Rogers, Josephine Baker, Lou Jacobs, Matthew Stymie Beard, Jr., George Spanky McFarland, William 'Buckwheat' Thomas, LillianGish, AlanLadd, Bettie Page, Telly Savalas, Peter Sellers, Jayne Mansfield, Marty Feldman, Mickey Rooney, Lee Strasberg, Tennessee Ernie Ford, Liza Minnelli, Carmen Miranda, Sharon Tate, Hedy Lamarr, Victoria Fuller, Redd Foxx, Gene Siskel, Holly Madison, Bridget Marquardt, Kendra Wilkinson, Dorothy Dandridge, Walter M
Consulting, Auction/Merchandise, Event Services:
Rights and Clearances, Auction, Location Shoots, Receptions/Event Venue, Exhibits.
Athlete Management Services:
Worldwide representative of a wide range of athletic organizations, athletes, and estates. Negotiates personal appearances.
Marketing & Consulting Services:
Provides management, marketing and advertising consultation for professional athletes.
Other Location:
8560 Sunset Boulevard, 10th Floor Penthouse, West Hollywood, CA 90069.
310-651-2000; FAX: 317-570-5500.

COLEMAN, DENNIS M.
800 BOYLSTON ROAD
PRUDENTIAL TOWER
BOSTON, MA 02199-3600
617-951-7000
Fax: 617-951-7050
www.ropesgray.com
• Dennis M Coleman, Partner
(617) 951-7361
dennis.coleman@ropesgray.com
• Mark V Nuccio, Partner
(617) 951-7368
mnuccio@ropesgray.com
Services:
All phases of athlete representation including contract negotiation, long-range planning, financial planning, and post-career counseling.
Clients:
National sports associations and foundations; Athletic footwear and licensed apparel manufacturers; A professional sports franchise; Coaches; Colleges and universities; and Sports marketing organizations.

CONDON, TOM
801 W 47TH STREET
SUITE 200
KANSAS CITY, MO 64112-1253
• Tom Condon, Lawyer
Services:
Personalized Representation, Contract Negotiation, Marketing and Endorsements, IMG Academies, Financial Services

CONSOLIDATED MANAGEMENT GROUP, INC.
237 PARK AVENUE
NEW YORK, NY 10017
212-551-3514
Services:
All phases of athlete representation including contract negotiation, long-range planning, financial planning, and post-career counseling.

CONWAY, MICHAEL W.
4 CAMPUS DRIVE
2ND FLOOR
PARSIPPANY, NJ 07054
973-285-3600
Fax: 973-285-3666
www.sfr1.com
• Michael W Conway, Financial Planner/Principal
(973) 285-3640
mconway@sfr1.com
• Nancy Chung, Director of Client Services
(973) 292-3710
• Joseph F Rowek, Vice President
(973) 285-3688
jrowek@sfr1.com
• Steven R Weinman, CPA, MBA, APC, Chairman of the Board & Chief Investment Offi
(973) 285-3660
fstubbs@sfr1.com
Services:
Separate divisions showcase specific strategies for sports stars and other celebrities, insurance planning for families and individuals, equities management that leaves no stone unturned, and wealth counseling that helps their clients make a difference in their communities

COOPER & COOPER LLD
1080 W. SHAW
SUITE 105
FRESNO, CA 93711
559-442-1650
Fax: 559-442-1659
joe@coopllp.com
• Joseph D Cooper, Member
(559) 442-1650
jcooper@cooper-hoppe.com
• Leah Ann Alcazar, Attorney
Year Founded:
1994.
Sports Service Founded:
1994.
Description:
Civil and insurance, which represents athletes and organizations.

CORBETT, KEVIN
220 JUANA AVENUE
SAN LEANDRO, CA 94577
510-357-4970
Fax: 510-357-1032

CORPORATE SPORTS INCENTIVES, INC.
7 NEW ENGLAND EXECUTIVE PARK
SUITE 610
BURLINGTON, MA 01803
800-627-7547
800-627-7545
Fax: 781-229-8886
• Marc H. Matthews, President/Chief Executive Officer
Services:
Marketing and consulting

Services:
Provides prepaid experience tickets to corporate and retail buyers offering first class access to a nationwide network of participating golf courses, ski resorts, movie theaters, and spas throughout the United States and Canada

CORRELL, P. KENT
102 E 10TH STREET
NEW YORK, NY 10003
212-475-3070
Fax: 212-475-2378

COTHERN, JOHN
1301 E MAIN STREET
MIDDLE TENNESSEE STATE UNIVERSITY
MURFREESBORO, TN 37132-0001
615-898-2300
Fax: 615-898-5671
www.mtsu.edu
• Sidney A McPhee, President
smcphee@mtsu.edu
• Kaylene Gebert, EVP/ Provost
(615) 898-2880
kgebert@mtsu.edu
• John W. Cothern, SVP
• Robert K Glenn, VP Student Affairs
Services:
Educational Services
Clients:
Students

CRACIUN III, JOSEPH
COLDWELL BANKER
27271 LAS RAMBLAS, SUITE 231
MISSION VIEJO, CA 92691
949-367-2082
Fax: 949-367-2080

CRAIGHILL, FRANCIS H., III
7950 JONES BRANCH DRIVE
SUITE 700N
MCLEAN, VA 22107
703-905-3300
Fax: 703-905-4495
www.octagon.com
• Kathy Connors, Director of Strategic Communications, At
• Lance Hill, VP
Description:
Contract negotiation, post career planning, endorsement exploration.
Services:
Contract negotiations; Marketing initiatives and endorsement programs; Public relations and charity involvement; Financial planning, wealth advisory and asset management; Television opportunities; Content creation; Property development; Event management; Speaking engagements
Clients:
NFL Hall of Famer and Super Bowl Champion John Elway; 8-time Olympic medalist Michael Phelps; Women's Soccer Icon Mia Hamm; Hot new musical act IL Divo; British Royalty The Duchess of York

CRANFORD, MICHAEL J.
913 WASHINGTON AVENUE
MACON, GA 31201
478-746-0704
Fax: 478-746-0927
• J. Michael Cranford, Law Attorney
(478) 746-0704

• Teresa M. Cranford, Paralegal/Mediator
(478) 746-0704
Services:
criminal defence of misdemeanor,DUI and felony cases. as well as personal injury and tort cases. including motorcycle related, automobile, pedestrian, premise liability and medical malpractice.

CRAVEN, JAMES B., III
349 W MAIN STREET
LIBERTY MARKET BUILDING
PO BOX 1366
DURHAM, NC 27701
919-688-8295
Fax: 919-688-7832
• James B. Craven III
Description:
Contract negotiation.

CRAWFORD LAW OFFICES
253 ALMENDRA AVENUE
LOS GATOS, CA 95030
408-395-9898
Fax: 408-395-4335
dcrawfordlaw@aol.com
www.dcrawfordlaw.com
• Dawson G. Crawford, Attorney
dcrawford@dcrawfordlaw.com
Description:
Business Litigation; Estate Planning; Business Transactions; Probate; Estate Litigation; Sports Law.

CRONSON TEAM, THE
336 W END AVENUE
SUITE 15A
NEW YORK, NY 10023
212-362-3322
• Don Cronson, President
Services:
Contract negotiation, post career planning, arbitration hearings, federal/state/international tax filings, provides investment advice, licensing, endorsement exploration and all other forms of financial management.

CROWE & DUNLEVY
20 N BROADWAY
SUITE 1800
OKLAHOMA CITY, OK 73102
405-235-7700
Fax: 405-239-6651
taylort@crowedunlevy.com
www.crowedunlevy.com
• Kevin D Gordon, Director
(405) 239-6619
kevin.gordon@crowedunlevy.com
• William G Paul, Advisory Director
(405) 239-6676
bill.paul@crowedunlevy.com
• D Ke Meyers, Chairman
(405) 235-7729
meyersd@crowedunlevy.com
• Clyde A Muchmore, Chairman Appellate Practice
(405) 235-7734
muchmore@crowedunlevy.com
• Zachary W. Allen, Director
(405) 235-7728
zach.allen@crowedunlevy.com
• Elliot P. Anderson, Associate
(918) 592-9844
elliot.anderson@crowedunlevy.com
Services:
represents clients in all aspects of the

general practice of law, including complex business transactions, litigation in both state and federal courts, natural resource law, and all types of alternative dispute resolution

CURRAN, RICHARD
REPRESENTATION INC
411 TIMBER LANE
DEVON, PA 19333
610-964-1062
Fax: 610-964-1007
Description:
Represents Hockey players.
Editor's note:
Mr. Curran also owns the Orr Hockey Group.

CURTIN, THOMAS R.
4 HEADQUARTERS PLAZA
PO BOX 1991
MORRISTOWN, NJ 07962
973-292-1700
Fax: 973-292-1767
• Thomas R. Curtin, Managing Partner
Description:
Contract negotiation, arbitration hearings, tort actions/litigation.

CURTIS MANAGEMENT GROUP
10500 CROSSPOINT BOULEVARD
INDIANAPOLIS, IN 46256
317-570-5000
Fax: 317-570-5500
www.cmgworldwide.com
• Greg Thompson, Chief Operating Officer
• Maria Gejdosova, Vice President, Finance & Acquisitions
• Mark Roesler, Chairman/Chief Executive Officer
• Greg Thompson, COO
• Mark Vo Roesler, Chairman & CEO
Sports Service Founded:
1971
Services:
Worldwide representative of a wide range of athletic organizations, athletes, and estates. Negotiates personal appearances.
Services:
Merchandise Licensing, Advertising/Promotional Licensing, Brand Development/Extension, Sponsorship Negotiation, Professional Contract Negotiation, Product/Service Endorsements, Speakers Bureau, Personal Appearances, Autograph Signings, Interviews, Intellectual Property Strategies and Branding Services, Infringement, Policing and Enforcement Services, Domain Names Recovery and Internet Issues, Expert Witness Services, Consulting and Negotiation Services, Speakers, Lecturers and Presenters for Conferences, Programs and Commentary, Software Design for Licensing and Marketing Companies, Web Development, Media Asset Management, Hardware Support
Clients:
Marilyn Monroe, James Dean, Sophia Loren, Ingrid Bergman, Ivana Trump, Lana Turner, Bette Davis, Tyrone Power, Errol Flynn, Montgomery Clift, Sir Laurence Olivier, Rock Hudson, Helen Hayes, Jean Harlow, Ginger Rogers, Josephine Baker, Lou Jacobs, Matthew Stymie Beard,Jr., George Spanky McFarland, William 'Buckwheat' Thomas,LillianGish,AlanLadd, Bettie Page, Telly Savalas, Peter Sellers,

Jayne Mansfield, Marty Feldman, Mickey Rooney, Lee Strasberg, Tennessee Ernie Ford, Liza Minnelli, Carmen Miranda, Sharon Tate, Hedy Lamarr, Victoria Fuller, Redd Foxx, Gene Siskel, Holly Madison, Bridget Marquardt, Kendra Wilkinson,Dorothy Dandridge, Walter M
Consulting, Auction/Merchandise, Event
Services:
Rights and Clearances, Auction, Location Shoots, Receptions/Event Venue, Exhibits.
Athlete Management Services:
Worldwide representative of a wide range of athletic organizations, athletes, and estates. Negotiates personal appearances.
Marketing & Consulting Services:
Provides management, marketing and advertising consultation for professional athletes.
Other Location:
8560 Sunset Boulevard, 10th Floor Penthouse, West Hollywood, CA 90069. 310-651-2000; FAX: 317-570-5500.

DAVIS, HOWARD E. (BEN)
6655 FIRST PARK TEN BOULEVARD
SUITE 250
SAN ANTONIO, TX 78213
210-738-8080
800-401-4619
Fax: 210-738-8088
• Howard E. Davis, Founder
(210) 738-8080
irish-x@att.net
Services:
Handles legal cases

DAVIS, TODD
10271 W PICO BOULEVARD
LOS ANGELES, CA 90064
310-277-4700
Fax: 310-201-0967
Description:
Represents professional sports teams.

DEKAI ENTERPRISES
440 RAMSEY ROAD
YARDLEY, PA 19067
215-321-4323
Fax: 215-321-3175
• Linda Bodley, VP
Nature of Sports Service:
All phases of athlete representation including contract negotiation, long-range planning, financial planning, and post-career counseling.
Services:
Contract Negotiations, Endorsements, Career Counseling, Post Career Counseling, Public Relations

DELL, DONALD L.
5335 WISCONSIN AVENUE NW
SUITE 850
WASHINGTON, DC 20015
202-721-7200
Fax: 202-721-7201
www.experiencebest.com
Nature of Services:
Sports marketing; television, events and representation

DENNIS CONNER SPORTS, INC.
2525 SHELTER ISLAND DRIVE
SUITE E
SAN DIEGO, CA 92106

619-523-5131
Fax: 619-263-1495
• Dennis Conner
Sports Service Founded:
1987.
Services:
Management, marketing and operations of large scale sailing, and related events including The America's Cup.
Marketing & Consulting Services:
Fundraising and sports.

DEPERSIA, ROBERT
35 KINGS HIGHWAY E
SUITE 102
HADDONFIELD, NJ 08033-2009
856-795-9688
Fax: 856-795-7944
info@depersialaw.com
www.depersialaw.com

DOMANN & PITTMAN
5 BURR OAKS CT
BOLINGBROOK, IL 60440-1285
630-783-9498
Fax: 630-783-9821
• Craig E. Domann, Co-founder
cdomann@dp-football.com
• Drew Pittman, Co-founder
dpittman@dp-football.com
Services:
Contract Negotiations, Marketing, Financial Guidance, Player Management, Career Transition, Vets Free Agency Contract Negotiation, Preparation for All-Star Games, Combine Training, Pre-draft Marketing
Clients:
Shaunard Harts, Quintin Williams, Billy Bajema, Marion Barber III, David Barrett, William Bartee, Jarrod Baxter, Monty Beisel, Ryon Bingham, Marc Boerigter, Alfonso Boone, Marko Cavka, Chris Chester, Tony Curtis, Trey Darilek, Glenn Earl, Makoa Freitas, Gilbert Gardner, Kelvin Garmon, Eric Ghiaciuc, Bobby Gray, MIke Green, Eric Green, Brock Gutierrez, Tyjuan Hagler, Ryan Hannam, Nick Hardwick, Drew Hodgdon, Jeb Huckeba, Frisman Jackson, Jeno James, Adrian Jones, Brandon Jones, Chris Kuper, Michael Lehan, Ryan Lilja, Kevin Mathis, David McMillan, Mike MInter, Jason Murphy, Chad Owens, Derek Pagel, Domata Peko, Duke Preston, John Standeford, Re
Sports Service Founded:
1991.
Other Office:
J. Drew Pittman, 2905 Maple Ave, Dallas, TX 75201. 214 855-1411; FAX: 214 954-1523

DRIVER CONNECTION/RAPID RACEWAYS
161 WOODFORD AVENUE
UNIT 55
PLAINVILLE, CT 06062
860-793-1888
Fax: 860-229-3970

EASTERN ATHLETIC SERVICES
11350 MCCORMICK ROAD
SUITE 800
EXECUTIVE PLAZA 1
HUNT VALLEY, MD 21031
410-229-0080
Fax: 443-212-5594
www.easfootball.com

• Anthony Agnone, Board of Directors
• Edward G Johnson, Board of Director
• Richard M Rosa, Board of Director
• Howard S Shotsky, Contract Researcher/Analyst
Services:
Combine Preparation/Pre-Draft Counseling, Contract Reviews and Negotiations, Player Marketing, Endorsements and Promotions, Financial Reviews and Planning, Tax Planning and Preparation, Insurance Planning, Personal Banking, Day-to-Day Needs
Clients:
John Abraham, Jason Babin, Tim Bulman, Trent Cole, Bill Conaty, Will Demps, Jason Fabini, Michael Gaines, Cornelius Griffin, Andrew Hoffman, Bhawoh Jue, Patrick Kerney, Dan Koppen, David Macklin, Sean McHugh, Antwan Odom, Shaun OHara, Jeffery Posey, Casey Rabach, Chris Roberson, Bryan Scott, Jamie Sharper, Chris Snee, Jerald Sowell, Michael Strahan, Kyle VandenBosch, Chris Villarrial, Bracy Walker, Rian Wallace, Reggie Wells, Ernest Wilford, Bobbie Williams
Description:
Contract negotiation, investment contract negotiation, federal/state/international tax filings, provides investment advice, endorsement exploration.
Year Founded:
1978

ECLIPSE SPORTS MANAGEMENT
675 SEMINOLE AVENUE
ATLANTA, GA 30307
404-853-5088
404-841-8223
• Scott Greenspun, Co-Founder/Principal
Services:
Sports and Event Marketing

EDELIN, KENTON S.
1200 BRADDOCK PLACE
SUITE 211
ALEXANDRIA, VA 22314
703-683-3961
Fax: 703-683-9696
marketing@mccuemortgage.com
www.mccuemortgage.com
• Kenton S Edelin, President
Nature of Sports Service:
All phases of athlete representation including contract negotiation, long-range planning, financial planning, and post-career counseling.

EDGE SPORTS INTERNATIONAL, INC.
1410 TECHNY ROAD
NORTHBROOK, IL 60062
847-291-4333
Fax: 847-498-6215
kreiter@edgesportsintl.com
www.edgesportsintl.com
• Keith Kreiter, President
kreiter@edgesportsintl.com
• Alessandro Barbalich, International Director
• Micheal Elman, General Counsel
• Keith Kreiter, Founder/CEO
• Greg Haenke, Vice President
Sports Service Founded:
1994.
Services:
Contract Negotiation, Wealth Management & Life Planning Service, The Marketing

Edge, Media Relations
Clients:
Maciej Lempe, Orien Greene, Kendall Gill, Marcello Hurtas, George Weah, Garrett Jones, Marcus Nettles, Jose Nieves
Description:
Athlete representation, marketing & consulting firm advising top athletes and corporations worldwide. Edge has been recognized as an industry leader in strategic marketing/branding campaigns. Business advisory arm counsels all athletes on creating a wealth preservation strategy insulating players with best in class service providers.
Athlete Management Services:
Manages careers of professional athletes in all sports, offering a package of services including contract negotiation, marketing/public relations, legal counsel, financial planning, product endorsement contract negotiations, and arranging for public appearances.
Marketing & Consulting Services:
Consults with corporations seeking to expand business through sports promotion, marketing, public relations, and licensing. Develops marketing plans and strategy implementation.
Clients include:
Rafer Alston, Cedric Ceballos, Mark Dalesandro, Matt Williams, Cathy Turner.

ELLIS, JIM
239 S FIFTH STREET
KENTUCKY HOME LIFE BUILDING, SUITE 1800
LOUISVILLE, KY 40202-3233
502-583-5547
Fax: 502-736-8150
Description:
Contract negotiation, endorsement exploration, tort actions/litigation/criminal law.

ELS MANAGEMENT INC.
39633 DORCHESTER CIRCLE
CANTON, MI 48188
734-446-4003
Fax: 734-727-0525
• Everett L. Stone, President
Nature of Sports Service:
All phases of athlete representation including contract negotiation, long-range planning, financial planning, and post-career counseling.
Services:
Contract Negotiations, Endorsements, Tax Advice - Referrals Only, Career Counseling, Post Career Counseling, Marketing

---

ENTER SPORTS MANAGEMENT
FIVE CONCOURSE PARKWAY
SUITE 3000
ATLANTA, GA 30328
770-350-8011
Fax: 770-350-8012
info@enter-sports.com
www.enter-sports.com
• Hadley Engelhard, President
(770) 350-8011
hadley@enter-sports.com
• Michael McGarvey, VP Marketing
• Ira Pernsley, Player Development
(770) 350-8011
irap@enter-sports.com
• James Story, Marketing & Player

Development
(770) 350-8011
pstory@enter-sports.com
Services:
Contract Negotiations; Marketing/Endorsements; Financial Services; Legal/Personal Services; and Conditioning/Training
Clients:
Travis Henry, Running Back, Buffalo Bills; Dorsey Levens, Running Back, Philadelphia Eagles; Dewayne Robertson, Defensive Tackle, New York Jets; Phillip Daniels, Defensive End, Washington Redskins; Tyrone Poole, Cornerback, New England Patriots; Nick Harper, Cornerback, Indianapolis Colts; Roosevelt Williams, Cornerback, Washington Redskins; Allen Rossum, Defensive Back/Returner, Atlanta Falcons; Kenyatta Jones, Offensive Tackle, Washington Redskins; Donte' Curry, Linebacker, Detroit Lions; Robert Mathis, Defensive End/ Linebacker, Indianapolis Colts; Nick Maddox, Running Back, Carolina Panthers;Joe Hamilton, Quarterback, Indianapolis Colts

---

ESTES, PETER R.
7108 EVANSTON ROAD
SPRINGFIELD, VA 22150
703-451-1254
Description:
Contract negotiation.

EUROSPORT ENTERPRISES, INC.
4810 JEAN TALON WEST
SUITE 203
QUEBEC
MONTREAL, CANADA H4P 2N5
514-875-1500
Fax: 514-875-2180
contactus@bamstrategy.com
www.bamstrategy.com
• Andrew Hertzog, President
(514) 369-2233
ahertzog@hllaw.ca
Nature of Service:
Full service sports agency, representing men and women basketball players from the United States and Canada. Handles basketball players ready to play overseas, as an alternative approach to gaining the experience to enter the NBA.
Year Founded:
1993

EXCALIBUR MARKETING GROUP
827 EASTOVER PARKWAY
LOCUST GROVE, VA 22508
540-972-7388
Fax: 540-972-4691
www.isportsnet.com
Sports Service Founded:
1992
Services:
Full service sports marketing firm specializing in all levels of the football industry, athlete management services, professional services, sports agents, market research services. Owns and operates the Dick Butkus Football Internet site (www.dickbutkus.com), dedicated to all levels of football. Also owns and operates Internet Sports Awards. Represents over 20 NFL Hall of Fame players available for corporate marketing programs.
Athlete Management Services:

Represents over 20 NFL Hall of Fame players available for corporate marketing programs.

FAMILIE
2052CORTE DEL NOGAL
SUITE 150
CARLSBAD, CA 92011
760-602-6200
Fax: 760-602-9800
info@wgmllc.com
www.wmgllc.com
• Steve Astephen, Principal Action Sports
steve@thefamilie.com
• Cris Whittaker
(760) 602-6200
cris@thefamilie.com
• Casey Wasserman, Chairman and CEO
• Arn Tellem, Vice Chairman
• David Kogan, Managing director
• Dean Christopher, Chief Financial officer
• Denise Durante, Co-managing Director of Consulting Division
• Elizabeth Lindsey, Co-Managing Director of Consulting Division
• John Brody, Managing Director
Services:
Marketing, public relations, creative, licensing, trend research and consulting.
Clients:
ESPN, Disney, Nike ACG, Jakks Pacific, Nestle, and DonJoy among others
Athlete Management:
Geared toward action sports athletes. Handles all phases of athlete management, contracts, endorsement opportunities, etc.
Public Relations & Marketing:
Develops public relations campaigns that includes extensive media coverage for products, athletes and event properties.

FAZZONE & BAILLIE
ONE TOWN CENTER
CHESHIRE, CT 6410
203-250-2222
Fax: 203-250-7388
info@fazzoneryan.com
www.fazzoneryan.com
• Joanne M Ryan, Attorney
(203) 250-2222
jryan@fazzoneryan.com
• Anthony J Fazzone, Attorney
afazzone@fazzoneryan.com
• Joanne M Ryan, Attorney
jryan@fazzoneryan.com
• Phillip Ricciuti, Attorney
pricciuti@fazzoneryan.com
Description:
Contract negotiation, post career planning, investment contract negotiation, arbitration hearings, federal/state/international tax filings, endorsement exploration, tort actions/litigation.
Services:
Real Estate Law, Business Services, Estate Planning, Estate and Probate Administration, Elder Law, Zoning and Land Use, Civil Litigation, Family Law

---

FEHR, STEVEN A.
204 W LINWOOD BOULEVARD
KANSAS CITY, MO 64111-1328
816-561-3755
Description:
Contract negotiation.
Services:

Labor and Employment Relations Attorneys, Probation Services, Professional Services.

FELDMAN, OSCAR
STONEBRIDGE W
41000 WOODWARD AVENUE
BLOOMFIELD HILLS, MI 48304
248-258-1616
Fax: 248-258-1439
feldman@butzel.com
www.butzel.com
• Richard E Rassel, Director, Global Client Relations
(313) 225-7014
rassel@butzel.com
• Philip J Kessler, President and Shareholder
(313) 225-7018
• Keefe A Brooks, VP and Shareholder
(248) 593-3010
brooks@butzel.com
• Richard B. C Brosnick, VP and Shareholder
brosnick@butzel.com
Description:
Represents professional sports teams. NBA - Detroit Pistons basketball.
Services:
Independent law firm, innovative solutions and advice. The firm strives to be on the cutting edge of new developments including advanced technology and manufacturing, e-commerce, internet law, intellectual property and cross-border operations and transactions.
Clients:
The firm's clients come from many business sectors, including automotive, manufacturing, banking and financial services, retail and wholesale distribution, insurance, professional services, health care, advertising, media, publishing, technology and computers, marine, transportation, construction, utilities and real estate.

FENTRESS, A. LEE
7950 JONES BEACH DR.
SUITE 700N
MCLEAN, VA 22107
703-905-3300
Fax: 703-905-4495
www.octagon.com
• Phil de Picciotto, Founder and President
• Rick Dudley, President & CEO
• Jeff Shifrin, President
• Lisa Murray, Executive Vice President Chief Marketing Offi
• Sean Nicholls, Managing Director
• Simon Wardle, Chief Strategy Officer
• Jeff Ehrenkranz, Managing Director
Description:
Contract negotiation, post career planning, endorsement exploration.
Services:
Contract negotiations, Marketing initiatives and endorsement programs, Public relations and charity involvement, Financial planning, wealth advisory and asset management, Television opportunities, Speaking engagements, Content creation, Property development, Event management

FINAL KICK MARKETING GROUP, INC.
2865 LYNNHAVEN DRIVE, C3
VIRGINIA BEACH, VA 23451
757-481-3400
800-789-6888
www.finalkick.com
Services:
Seeks endorsements for clients with equipment manufacturers, licensed goods, trading card companies, corporations; arranges personal appearances, television appearances, commercial deals, infomercials, speaking engagements; and conducts training. Represents professional and amateur athletes, Olympians and celebrities. Specializes in creating product media awareness of clients and the products they endorse. Services include contract negotiations, career management, tax preparation and post-career preparations.
Marketing & Consulting Services:
Seeks endorsements for clients with equipment manufacturers, licensed goods, trading card companies, corporations; arranges personal appearances, television appearances, commercial deals, infomercials, speaking engagements; and conducts a training and fitness program.
Athlete Management Services:
Represents professional and amateur athletes, Olympians and celebrities. Specializes in creating product media awareness of clients and the products they endorse. Services include contract negotiations, career management, tax preparation and post-career planning.
Sports Service Founded:
1996

FINAL KICK SPORTS
2865 LYNNHAVEN DRIVE
VIRGINIA BEACH, VA 23451
757-481-3400
800-789-6888
Fax: 757-481-3461
www.finalkick.com
Services:
Seeks endorsements for clients with equipment manufacturers, licensed goods, trading card companies, corporations; arranges personal appearances, television appearances, commercial deals, infomercials, speaking engagements; and conducts training. Represents professional and amateur athletes, Olympians and celebrities. Specializes in creating product media awareness of clients and the products they endorse. Services include contract negotiations, career management, tax preparation and post-career preparations.
Marketing & Consulting Services:
Seeks endorsements for clients with equipment manufacturers, licensed goods, trading card companies, corporations; arranges personal appearances, television appearances, commercial deals, infomercials, speaking engagements; and conducts a training and fitness program.
Athlete Management Services:
Represents professional and amateur athletes, Olympians and celebrities. Specializes in creating product media awareness of clients and the products they endorse. Services include contract negotiations, career management, tax preparation and post-career planning.
Sports Service Founded:
1996

FIRST DOWN PROMOTIONS
595 INDUSTRIAL ROAD
SAN CARLOS, CA 94070
650-595-7797
fdpromo@aol.com
• John Paye, President/Chief Executive Officer
(650) 326-7797
• Danielle Donahue, Marketing-Promotions VP
• Kristin Larios, Marketing And Promotions
Sports Service Founded:
1989.
Event Management Services:
Organizes and promotes the Benefit Basketball Association, a collection of NFL athletes who play basketball for charity. Manages celebrity golf tournaments, football clinics and softball fund-raisers.
Marketing & Consulting Services:
Promotes and markets products to directly increase sales and serve as product advertising.

FIRST STRING MANAGEMENT
85 ELLESMERE ROAD
UNIT 31
SCARBOROUGH, CANADA ON M1R 4B7
416-447-5991
• Kevin E. Fitzpatrick, Sports Agent
Nature of Sports Service:
All phases of athlete representation including contract negotiation, long-range planning, financial planning, and post-career counseling.

FITNESS PERFORMANCE CENTERS
280 ROUTE 513
SUITE V & W
GLEN GARDENER, NJ 08826
908-638-4687
Fax: 847-562-0386
s.cavitch@comcast.net
fitnessperformancecenter.com
• Robert Garza, Trainer
(847) 562-4386
rgarza@mybeyondfitness.com
• Michael Carnevali, Personal Trainer
• Shawn Cavitch, Owner

FOSTER & EASLEY SPORTS MANAGEMENT GROUP
13701 42ND AVENUE NE
SEATTLE, WA 98125
206-362-7780
800-326-3031
Fax: 206-362-0478
• Cameron Foster, President
• Kenny Easley, VP
• Courtney Foster, VP
Services:
Sports Promotions & Special Events. All phases of athlete representation including contract negations, commercial endorsements and tax planning. Member of NFLPA, NBAPA,CFLPA.
Clients:
Tom Ackerman, Archie Anderson, Kenyan Branscomb, Anthony Calvillo, Derrick Fenner, Napolean Kaufmann, Leon Neal
Description:
All phases of athlete representation including contract negations, commercial endorsements and tax planning. Member of NFLPA, NBAPA,CFLPA.

FRAZIER & FRAZIER
2399 UNIVERSITY BLVD.
4TH FLOOR
HOUSTON, TX 77005
713-655-7100
Fax: 713-655-7150
www.frazierlawhouston.com
• Kyle Frazier, Partner
• Bill Frazier, Partner
(281) 407-7910
Description:
Contract negotiation, post career planning, federal/state/international tax filings, investment advice, endorsement exploration, tort actions/litigation.

FRIED & COMPANY, P.C.
700 THIRTEENTH STREET NW
SUITE 990
WASHINGTON, DC 20005
202-331-3900
Fax: 202-331-3905
• Jeffrey Fried, President
• Nathan Peake, Sports Management Director
• Tanisha Howard, Sports/Entertainment Management
• Kiyo Ohen, Attorney
Description:
Athlete Management, contract negotiation, post career planning, licensing, endorsement commercialization, teaches sports law, Federal/state/International tax filings, Representing professional sports teams, Investment advice.

FUHRO, HANLEY & BEUKAS
36 MOUNTAINVIEW BOULEVARD
WAYNE, NJ 07470
973-686-1000
• Brian Fuhro, Esquire
Services:
Legal Services
Description:
Contract negotiation, post career planning, investment contract negotiation, arbitration hearings, federal/state/international tax filings, represents professional sports teams, provides securities advice, provides investment advice, licensing, endorsement exploration, tort actions/litigation.

FUTURE FOR KIDS
6991 E CAMELBACK ROAD
SUITE B - 100
SCOTTSDALE, AZ 85251
480-947-8131
Fax: 480-947-3729
info@futureforkids.org
www.FutureforKIDS.org
• Rodney Smith, President/Founder
info@futureforkids.org
• Beth Albrecht, Project Director/Grant Coordinator
info@futureforkids.org
• Sheehan McAuley, Program Director
info@futureforkids.org
• Madoona Bistany, Executive Director
• Regina LaPlante, Program Coordinator
• Becki Stephens, Office Assistant
• Bennett Conklin, Board Chair
• Michael Bankston, Vice Chair
• Tim Hyde, Secretary
Sports Service Founded:
1990.
Services:
Provides at-risk youth with mentorship and education through sports camps and technology centers.
Athlete Management Services:
Sports marketing firm specializing in the placement of past and present athletes and coaches for speaking engagements, appearances and endorsements.

GANIM ENTERPRISES
6449 LAKE TRAIL DRIVE
WESTERVILLE, OH 43082-8795
614-890-6073
Fax: 614-890-9986
• Doug Ganim, President
(614) 890-6073
ganim@earthlink.net
Sports Service Founded:
1984
Athlete Management Services:
Full professional representation of male and female racquetball players.
Event Management Services:
Sports marketing specialists in racquetball. Event production, administration and promotion nationwide. Professional, semi-pro and amateur events on both regional and national level.
Marketing & Consulting Services:
Sports marketing and consulting services offered with an emphasis in the sport of racquetball. Sponsorship procurement, industry consulting, and other specialized services available.

GARDA WORLD
5870 TRINITY PARKWAY
SUITE 300
CENTERVILLE, VA 20120
703-592-1400
Fax: 703-592-1500
www.vanceglobal.com
• Drew T. Ladau, President
• Steven W. Casteel, SVP, Intenational Business Development
• Oliver Westmacott, President and COO
• Pete Dordal Jr, Senior Vice President
• Adrian Blanchette, VP, Operations
• James Grimshaw, VP, Business Process and Integration
• Joe Hogan, Director, Emerging Markets
• Caroline Passey, Director, Marketing
Services:
Risk Analysis and Planning, Business Intelligence and Due Diligence, Uniformed Protection, Education and Training, Executive Protection, Contingency Planning and Response, Litigation Support, Labor Unrest Protection, Security and Intelligence in High-Risk Markets, Protection, Investigation, Monitoring and Compliance, Digital Security and Investigation
Sports Service Founded:
1984.
Nature of Sports Service:
Security services for athletes and their families.
Other Office:
Rio Nilo 74'4; Col Cuauhtemoc; Mexico, DF 06500. 525 514 2044

GARY PLAYER GROUP, INC
3930 RCA BOULEVARD
SUITE 3001
PALM BEACH GARDENS, FL 33410
561-624-0300
Fax: 561-624-0304
info@garyplayer.com
www.garyplayer.com
• Scott Ferrell, Gary Player Design President
(561) 624-0300
• Tim Smith, Gary Player Enterprises President
(561) 624-0300
Services:
Golf Course Design Service, Enterprises Service, Management Services & Golf Academy
Products:
Apparel, Accessories & Headwear, Golf Shoes, Equipment & Golf Accessories, Books, Videos & CDs, Special Items & Gifts & Memorabillia

GAUSDEN, THOMAS
ONE BREWERS WAY
MILWAUKEE, WI 53214
414-902-4400
Fax: 414-933-5474
www.milwaukeebrewers.com
Description:
Represents professional sports teams.

GAYLORD SPORTS MANAGEMENT
13845 N NORTHSIGHT BOULEVARD
SUITE 200
SCOTTSDALE, AZ 85260
480-483-9500
Fax: 480-483-9598
info@gaylordsports.com
• Steve Loy, Chief Executive Officer
(480) 483-9500
sloy@gaylordsports.com
• E.K. Gaylord, II, Chairman
(480) 483-9500
ek@gaylordsports.com
• David Yates, EVP/Chief Operating Officer
dyates@gaylordsports.com
• Steve Loy, President
sloy@gaylordsports.com
• David Yates, Senior VP
dyates@gaylordsports.com
• Jon Hartigan, Chief Financial Officer
jhartigan@gaylordsports.com
Nature of Sports Service:
A full-service professional management company with the proven ability to manage the careers of some of the best professional golfers in the world. Provides services for contract negotiations, corporate marketing and consulting, corporate outings and television and event opportunities. Specializes in the sport of golf.
Services:
Talent Representation, Corporate Sports Consulting, Media and Public Relations & Event Management (Tommy Bahama Challenge)
Clients:
Rich Beem, Mark Calcavecchia, Jim Carter, DavidGossett, Dudley Hart, Matt Hansen, Frank Lickliter II, Billy Mayfair, Rocco Mediate, Phil Mickelson, Ryan Moore, Arron Oberholser, Jeff Overton, Craig, Perks, Tom Pernice, Jr., Scott Piercy, Heath Slocum, Boyd Summerhays, Nick Watney, Jeremy Anderson, Ricky Barnes, Todd Demsey, Craig Lile, Bryce Molder, Chris Nallen, Chez Reavie, Tom Scherrer, Hale Irwin, Darren Clarke, David Howell, Stephen Leaney, Graeme McDowell, Paul McGinley, Peter O'Malley, Craig Parry, Lee Westwood, Robert Hamilton, Lee Williamson, Beth

Bauer, Catherine Cartwright, Rachel Hetherington, Brittany Lang, Cristie Kerr.

GEM GROUP
3 GATEAWAY CENTER
SUITE 1200
401 LIBERTY AVENUE
PITTSBURG, PA 15222
412-471-2885
800-242-8923
Fax: 412-471-2891
www.gemgroup.com
• Chuck Corcoran, Entertainment VP
(310) 843-3142
CCorcoran@gemgroup.com
Services:
Full service marketing communications agency specializing in Sport and Entertainment.
Areas of Sports Expertise:
Motorsports, soccer, horse raising, olympics, collegiate sports, tennis, figure skating, sailing, cricket, golf, rugby league, ice hockey, rugby union.
Services Include:
Contract negotiation, asset management, athlete recruitment, sponsorship consulting, promotion marketing, director marketing, public relations, internet, point-of-sale, hospitality services, event PR, media relations, special events, sampling, field marketing and alliance marketing.

GENERAL SPORTS TURF SYSTEMS
400 WATER STREET
SUITE 250
ROCHESTER, MI 48307
248-601-2200
Fax: 248-601-2400
www.generalsports.com
• Andy Appleby, Chairman/CEO
• Laurie Alpers, Director of administration and finance
• Melissa Priester, Director of Client Service
• Josh Hartman, Director of sales and marketing
• Lee Stacey, Executive Vice president
• Andrew D L. Appleby, Chairman and CEO
Services:
Executive Placement, Consulting Services, Hospitality & Event Management, Naming Rights & Sponsorships, Team Acquisition

GEORGE SPADORO
ONE BOLAND DRIVE
WEST ORANGE, NJ 07052
973-325-1500
Fax: 973-325-1501
info@wolffsamson.com
www.wolffsamson.com
• George Spadoro, Partner
(973) 530-2113
GSpadoro@wolffsamson.com
Nature of Sports Service:
All phases of athlete representation including: Marketing the athlete to professional teams, contract negotiation, endorsements, merchandising, tax/financial planning and post-career counseling.
Services:
Handles legal matters in the following practice areas: Corporate/Business, Administrative, Banking, Litigation, Labor, Commercial Real Estate, Creditors Rights, Partnerships, Mergers and Acquisitions, Municipal Law, Public and Private Real Estate Redevelopment.

GLASS, INC, KEITH
69 BROAD STREET
SUITE B
RED BANK, NJ 07701
732-741-9339
Fax: 732-741-3090
otgentertainment.net
• Laura Renae, Coordinator
(908) 741-9339
• Chuck Iarussi, Overseas/Placement Services
Services:
Legal Services
Clients:
Dale Ellis, Marty Conlon
Description:
Contract negotiation, endorsements, appearances & marketing.

GLOBAL ATHLETE MANAGEMENT ENTERPRISES
21031 VENTURA BOULEVARD
PENTHOUSE, 12TH FLOOR
WOODLAND HILLS, CA 91364
818-999-9127
Fax: 818-999-3354
• Jeffrey A. Slott, President/Agent/General Legal
• Nancy Hoover, Secretary/Director Operations
Description:
Offers legal and agent services to professional athletes.

GLOBAL SPORTS MARKETING & EVENTS
2432 W PEORIA AVENUE
SUITE 1163
PHOENIX, AZ 85034
602-943-6605
Services:
Marketing & Consulting Services: Sports sponsorship sales, event marketing, public relations, promotions, and athlete marketing.
Services:
Event Management Services: Full event management from consulting to full production.
Marketing & Consulting Services:
Sports sponsorship sales, event marketing, public relations, promotions, and athlete marketing.

GLOBAL SPORTS PRODUCTIONS, LTD.
16810 CRYSTAL DRIVE E
ENUMCLAW, WA 98022
310-454-9480
Fax: 253-874-1027
• Ed Kobak, President
edkobak@yahoo.com
Products:
Sports marketing and publishing firm that specializes in producing sports reference books and directories from around the world
Brands:
The Sports Address Bible & Almanac, Mascots!, The Celebrity Address Directory and Autograph Collector's Guide, The International Sports Directory, The Encyclopedia of Minor League Football, Sports Logo Guide, The National Directory of College Athletics, The Dream Job, The Career Guide to Sports Administration & The Encyclopedia of Sports Business Contacts

GOEPEL, ROBERT
1400 MAIN STREET
RACINE, WI 53403
262-637-5100
Fax: 262-637-8353
goepel@execpc.com
Services:
Legal Services
Description:
Contract negotiation, arbitration hearings, endorsement exploration, tort actions/litigation.

GOLDEN BEAR SPORTS MANAGEMENT
11780 US HIGHWAY ONE
N PALM BEACH, FL 33408
561-227-0300
Fax: 561-626-4104
• Keenan Delaney, Marketing Director
• Jack Nicklaus, Chief Executive Officer
jack.nicklaus@nicklaus.com
• Steve Nicklaus, Designer
stevenicklaus@nicklaus.com
Sports Service Founded:
1991.
Services:
Design services include Marketing & Communications; Plan Documents; Specifications and Details; Computer Modeling; Landscape Design Services; and Renovation Services.
Marketing & Consulting Services:
All phases of contract negotiation, financial management and planning for professional golfers.

GOWLING LAFLEUR HENDERSON
1600, 421 7TH AVENUE SW
CALGARY, ALBERTA, CANADA T2P 4K9
403-298-1000
Fax: 403-263-9193
webmaster@gowlings.com
www.gowlings.com
• Kenneth J. Warren, Managing Partner
(403) 298-1000
kenneth.warren@gowlings.com
• Greg Peterson, Partner
(403) 292-9812
• James S. Peacock, Partner
(403) 298-1011
james.peacock@gowlings.com
• Kerry R. Powell, Partner
(403) 292-9805
kerry.powell@gowlings.com
Services:
Aboriginal Law; Administrative & Public; Advertising; Banking Litigation; Business Law Charities & Not-For-Profit; Civil Fraud, Commercial Litigation; Construction Law; Copyright; Corporate Finance; Securities & Public M&A; Defamation & Media; Employment & Labour; Environmental; Estates & Trusts; Family; Financial Regulatory Law; Financial Services; Franchise and Distribution Law; Government Relations and Regulatory Affairs; Government Services; Immigration; Insurance; Professional Liability; Intellectual Property Litigation; Natural Resources; Occupational Health & Safety; Patent Prosecution; Privacy; Real Estate & Urban Development; Recover
Description:
Provides a full complement of legal services to national and international clients.

GRAND SLAM III
7160 ZIONSVILLE ROAD
INDIANAPOLIS, IN 46268
317-575-5900
Services:
Marketing Consultant Professional Athlete
Management

GRANT ASSOCIATES
301 SAYRE DRIVE
PRINCETON, NJ 08540-5826
609-514-8674
Fax: 609-514-8673
• David Grant, President
dave_grant@comcast.net
Nature of Service:
Executive recruiting, licensing management,
sports/event promotion, strategic corporate
growth consulting, U.S. market
development.
Year Founded:
1997
Sports Service Founded:
1997

GREG DAWLEY
1900 AVENUE OF THE STARS
SUITE 2350
LOS ANGELES, CA 90067
310-551-1700
Fax: 310-277-7062
Services:
Civil litigation and counseling in
business-related matters, business torts,
including banking, insurance, title insurance
and real estate
Description:
Tort actions/litigation, real estate contract
representative.

GROUP II COMMUNICATIONS
1311 W FOREST HOME AVENUE
FRANKLIN, WI 53132
414-425-2080
Fax: 414-425-7682
customerservice@groupii.com
www.groupii.com
• Laura Manion, Business Development
tom.feeney@groupii.com
• Tim Leahy, Client Services
tim.leahy@groupii.com
Services:
Merchandising services

GUNSTER, YOAKLEY & STEWART, P.C.
777 S FLAGLER DRIVE
SUITE 500 E
WEST PALM BEACH, FL 33401-6194
561-655-1980
800-749-1980
Fax: 561-655-5677
contact@gunster.com
www.gunster.com
• Stephen F. McDermott, Chief Financial
Officer/Chief Operations
(561) 650-0527
smcdermott@gunster.com
• H. William Perry, Managing Shareholder
(561) 650-0640
hperry@gunster.com
• Grant Sagear, Director of Information
Services
(561) 804-4354
gsagear@gunster.com
• William A. Adams, Shareholder
• David Atkinson, Practice Leader
• Davis D. Balz, Associate

Description:
Post career planning, licensing,
endorsement exploration.
Services:
Provide services to client relating to:
Corporate, Private Wealth Services,
Litigation Department, Real Estate Services
Clients:
Arvida/JMB Partners JM Family Enterprises,
Inc. SBA Communications Corporation,
AutoNation, Inc. J.P. Morgan Chase & Co.
Seven Springs Golf Club, Bank of America,
N.A. Jupiter Island Club Smiths Industries
PLC, Bankrate, Inc. Kellstrom Aerospace,
LLC Sonesta Hotels & Resorts, Boca Raton
Resort and Club Lee Munder Capital Group
The St. Joe Company, Capital City Bank
Group, Inc. Levenger Company Starwood
Hotels & Resorts, Chiquita International, Inc.
Lykes Bros., Inc. Teva Pharmaceutical Citrix
Systems, Inc. Murray Goodman Company
Todhunter International, Inc., First Citizens
Bank & Trust Park Avenue BBQ
Restaurants.
Areas of Practice:
Financial Services, Corporate Transactions,
Employment Law, Immigration, Land Use &
Environmental, Leisure & Resorts, Private
Wealth Services, Real Estate, Securities,
Mergers & Acquistions, Taxation &
International Taxation, Technology Law,
Urban Development, Litigation.

GURWIN, DAVID A.
301 GRANT STREET
ONE OXFORD CENTRE
20TH FLOOR
PITTSBURGH, PA 15219-1410
412-562-8800
Fax: 412-562-1041
info@bipc.com
www.buchananingersoll.com
• Thomas L. VanKirk, Chief Executive
Officer and Managing Dir
(412) 562-8875
vankirktl@bipc.com
• David A. Gurwin, Entertainment
Chair/Media Law Group/Technology
(412) 440-4493
david.gurwin@bipc.com
• Edward Jo Allera, Board of Director
(412) 562-8875
vankirktl@bipc.com
• John A. E. Barbour, CEO & Chairman of
the Board
(412) 392-2087
• Patrick C. Keane, Executive Shareholder
(703) 838-6522
• Steven E. Bizar, Executive Shareholde
(215) 665-3826
• Wendelynne J. Newton, Executive
Shareholder
(412) 562-8932
• Thomas S. Giotto, Executive Shareholder
(412) 392-2068
• Nolan W. Kurtz, Chief Operating Officer
(717) 237-4807
• Miles H. Simon, Chief Financial Officer
(412) 562-1809
Description:
Contract negotiation, post career planning,
investment contract negotiation, represents
professional sports teams, licensing,
endorsement exploration, represents college
athletic departments, represents sports
organizations.
Clients:
ABN Amro Bank N.V., Amerisourcebergen

Corp., Avecia, Bacardi, Ltd., Bank of
America, Bayer BioScience, N.V., Black Box
Corporation, Bush Brothers and Company
Catholic Health East, Cendant Corporation,
CFA Institute, Chevron, Children's Hospital
of Pittsburgh, Citigroup Inc., City of New
York, Concurrent Technologies Corporation,
Dale Carnegie & Associates Inc., Deere &
Co., Equitable Resources, Hearst-Argyle
Television Inc., Hershey Company, JER
Revenue Services, J.E. Robert Companies,
Johns Mansfield, J.P. Morgan Chase, Knoll
Inc., KV Pharmaceutical Company, Merck &
Company, Merrill Lynch, National City,
Oceania Cruises, Payment Protection S
Year Founded:
1850
Other Locations:
One Chase Manhattan Plaza, 35th Floor,
New York, NY 10005; Phone:
212-440-4400; 1776 K Street, NW STE 800,
Washington, DC 20006; Phone:
202-452-7900; Sun Trust Finance Center,
401 East Jackson Street, STE 2500,
Tampa, FL 33602; Phone 813-222-8180;
First National Bank Center, 401 West A
Street, STE 1900, San Diego, CA 92101;
Phone: 619-578-5000

GWINN & ROBY
1201 ELM STREET
4100 RENAISSANCE TOWER
DALLAS, TX 75270
214-698-4100
Fax: 214-747-2904
• Robert R Roby, Managing Partner
(214) 698-4198
• Robert A Gwinn, Of Counsel
(214) 698-4101
Services:
Represents both publicly and privately-held
corporations as well as individuals in
matters that include healthcare, HMO, and
medical malpractice defense; product
liability; complex multi-district class actions;
medical device and pharmaceutical
litigation; commercial litigation; construction
litigation; legal malpractice; securities
litigation; employment litigation on behalf of
management; insurance defense and
coverage matters; automobile litigation;
aviation litigation; general negligence
litigation; premises liability; family law; and
workers' compensation matters.
Clients:
Acme Trucking Company, Alcoa, Allstate,
Amarillo Globe News, American Red Cross,
American Welding Society, Baxter, Brinker
International, Bristol Hotel Co, Brookshire
Grocery Company, Brown & Brown, Inc.,
California State Auto Association, Carter
BloodCare, Inc., Coca-Cola Enterprises,
Inc., Coffee Memorial Blood Center,
Comcast, ConocoPhillips, ContiBeef, L.L.C.,
Core Data Resources, Inc., Covenant
Health System, Cracker Barrel, Crawford
and Co., Delphi Automotive Systems,
Eastern Livestock, L.L.C., EMCARE, Inc.,
Empire Fire & Marine Insurance Co.,
Fireman's Fund Insurance Cos., Friona
Industries, L.P., General Motors, Grove,
Worldwide, Guid
Nature of Sports Service:
All phases of athlete representation
including contract negotiation, long-range
planning and post-career counseling.

HACKLER, KENNETH P.
1700 SW COLLEGE AVENUE
TOPEKA, KS 66621-0001
785-670-1010
Fax: 785-233-2780
www.washburn.edu
• Jerry B. Farley, President
farley@washburn.edu
• Ron Wasserstein, VP for Academic Affairs
wasserstein@washburn.edu
• Wanda B. Hill, VPfor Administration and
Treasurer
hill@washburn.edu
• Denise C. Ottinger, VP for Student Life
ottinger@washburn.edu
Description:
Represents college athletic departments.
Services:
Provides High Academic Standards in a
Small Class Environment, Committed To
Student Success, Well Funded and
Affordable and Technologically
Sophisticated Environment

HAITBRINK, RICHARD F.
5208 ARGENTINE BOULEVARD
KANSAS CITY, KS 66106
913-328-1100
Fax: 913-287-1919
Services:
Promotion of tennis events, professional and
amateur, and corporate and fund raising
events. Consulting services for tennis
promoters, tennis clubs, resorts and
corporate departments seeking to utilize
tennis events in marketing strategy. Serves
as Executive Director for the National
Interscholastic Tennis Coaches Association.

HALL OF FAME SPORTS, INC.
14 BEACH DRIVE
PO BOX 2386
DARIEN, CT 6820
203-655-1023
Fax: 203-655-0799
www.halloffamesports.com
Athlete Management Services:
Manages business affairs of professional
athletes.
Marketing & Consulting Services:
Provides marketing, promotional material
and photographic services for organizations
with specific public relations objectives.

HAMAKAWA, CURT L.
1 OLYMPIC PLAZA
COLORADO SPRINGS, CO 80909-5760
719-866-4852
Fax: 719-866-2029
www.usolympicteam.com
• Jim Scherr, Chief Executive Officer
• Jeff Benz, General Counsel
• Walter Glover, Interim Chief Financial
Officer
• Larry Buendorf, Chief Security Officer
Larry.Buendorf@usoc.org
Services:
Organizes sports events, programs and
training centers to athletes
Description:
Amateur sports representation.

HAMBRIC SPORTS MANAGEMENT
3131 MCKINNEY AVENUE
SUITE 875
DALLAS, TX 75204

214-720-7179
Fax: 214-720-7787
www.hambricsports.com

HEALY, PAUL J.
1830 ATLANTIC BOULEVARD
HEALY, STONE & ZAHLER BUILDING
JACKSONVILLE, FL 32207
904-391-0029
Fax: 904-399-4540
contactus@paulhealylaw.com
www.paulhealylaw.com
• Paul J. Healy, Attorney
Nature of Service:
All phases of athlete representation
including contract negotiation, long-range
planning, financial planning, and post-career
counseling.
Year Founded:
1994

HERBERT L. RUDOY LTD.
230 W SUPERIOR STREET
SUITE 510
CHICAGO, IL 60654-3584
312-654-1717
Fax: 312-266-4220
chisport@aol.com
www.interperformances.com
• Herbert Rudoy, President
• Arturo Ortega, CEO
Services:
Contract negotiation.

HINSHAW & CULBERSON LLP
3200 N CENTRAL AVENUE
SUITE 800
PHOENIX, AZ 85012-2428
602-631-4400
Fax: 602-631-4404
www.hinshawlaw.com
• Donald L Mrozek, Chairman
(312) 704-3111
dmrozek@hinshawlaw.com
• J. William Roberts, Managing Partner
(312) 704-3918
broberts@hinshawlaw.com
Nature of Sports Service:
All phases of athlete representation
including contract negotiation, long-range
planning, financial planning, and post-career
counseling.
Services:
Construction Law, Corporate & Business
Law, Environmental, Government, Health
Care, Insurance Services, Labor &
Employment, Litigation, Professional
Liability, School Law

HINSHAW & CULBERTSON
222 N LASALLE STREET
SUITE 300
CHICAGO, IL 60601
312-704-3000
Fax: 312-704-3001
• Donald L. Mrozek, Chairman
(312) 704-3111
dmrozek@hinshawlaw.com
• J. William Roberts, Managing Partner
(312) 704-3918
broberts@hinshawlaw.com
Services:
Recruiting, retaining and promoting its
attorneys and staff members regardless of
gender, race, ethnicity, national origin,
physical ability, religion or personal
background

Nature of Sports Service:
All phases of athlete representation
including contract negotiation, long-range
planning, financial planning, and post-career
counseling.

HORROW, RICK
6800 SW 40TH STREET
SUITE 174
MIAMI, FL 33155
561-743-6408
Fax: 305-559-6737
info@horrowsports.com
www.horrowsports.com
• Rick Horrow, President
• Karla Swatek, VP
• Brian Finkel, Creative Director
• Betty Curbelo, Administrative assistant
Services:
Development and implementation of
facilities, properties, and projects for
communities, development entities, leagues,
franchises, and other businesses. Organizes
virtually every sport. Site selection, lease
negotiations, public/private partnership
financing and project implementation are
just some of the services HSV provides to
leagues, sanctioning organizations and
teams.

HS INTERNATIONAL
9871 IRVINE CENTER DRIVE
IRVINE, CA 92618
949-753-9153
Fax: 949-753-9253
info@hsi.net
www.hsi.net
• Daniel Escamilla, Track and Field
daniel@hsi.net
• Emanuel Hudson, Track &
Field/Football/Tennis, Attorney at La
((94)) 753-91
emanuel@hsi.net
Description:
To assist top athletes in their quest to
accomplish personal goals. Represents and
assists clients and athletes in business
ventures, including athletic endorsements,
public and media relations, marketing and
legal services.
Services:
Provide expert training and guidance along
with specialized management and
counseling

HUEBNER, ROBERT E. P.A.
2090 STADIUM DRIVE
SUITE A
BOZEMAN, MT 59715
406-586-4311
Services:
Represents and assists clients and athletes
in a wide range of ventures including: Speed
Training, Athletic Endorsements, Contract
Negotiations, Image and Brand
Enhancement, Legal Services, Public and
Media Relations Marketing, Events
Scheduling, Logistics Management and
Retirement Planning
Description:
Contract negotiation. Land Use;
Government; Sports Law.

HURSEY, RALPH MICHAEL
100 SE THIRD AVENUE
9TH FLOOR
FT. LAUDERDALE, FL 33394

954-761-8600
Fax: 954-463-6643
Services:
All phases of athlete representation including contract negotiation, long-range planning, financial planning, and post-career counseling.

ICON SPORTS MANAGEMENT
3916 CLOCK POINTE TRAIL
SUITE 101
STOW, OH 44224-2932
330-945-4234
Fax: 330-945-4371

IMAGE CIRCLE, THE
19 W 34TH STREET
PENTHOUSE FLOOR
NEW YORK, NY 10001
212-874-7394
Fax: 212-874-6607
dinah@dinahdayimagecoach.com
www.dinahdayimagecoach.com
• Dinah Day, Chief Executive Officer
(646) 339-9955
dinah@dinahdayimagecoach.com
Nature of Service:
Provides self-image and communication skills training. Group and individual workshops customized for athletes, coaches, and media spokespeople focusing on interpersonal skills, self-image awareness and public speaking, press for sucess training and improved overall confidence.
Sports Service Founded:
1985.
Clients:
Con Edison of New York, Inc., Continental Airlines, Baer Marks & Upham LLP, Avon Products, Inc., Pitney Bowes, Inc., American Express, Right Management Consultants, International Management Group, JPMorgan Chase, NCAA Division 1 Universities, Credit Suisse First Boston, RLR Associates, Lehman Brothers, Affiliations/Associations/Partnerships, Association of Fashion and Image Consultants, The Outplacement Institute, International Association of Career Management Professionals, The Fashion Group, International, Screen Actors Guild, Relapse Prevention Specialists, Publications

IMG
1360 E 9TH STREET
SUITE 100
CLEVELAND, OH 44114
216-522-1200
Fax: 216-522-1145
web.feedback@imgworld.com
www.imgworld.com
• Micheal J. Dolan, Chairman & CEO
• Chuck Bennett, President, IMG Golf/Tennis
• Michel Masquelier, President, IMG Media
• George Pyne, President, IMG Sports & Entertainment

Teams:

IMG CHICAGO
626 W JACKSON BLVD
SUITE 650
CHICAGO, IL 60661
312-275-8200
Fax: 312-327-2303
www.imgworld.com

• Theodore J Forstmann, Chairman/CEO
• Chuck Bennett, President IMG Golf , Tennis,Fashion and Event
• Michel Masquelier, President IMG Media
• Michael J J Dolan, President/CEO
• George Pyne, President IMG Sports & Entertainment
Description:
IMG connects brands to global opportunities in sports, fashion and media

Teams:

IMG FOOTBALL
123 W 8TH STREET
LAWRENCE, KS 66044
785-312-7555
Fax: 785-312-7557
www.imgworld.com
• Theodore J Forstmann, Chairman/CEO
• Chuck Bennett, President IMG Golf , Tennis,Fashion and Event
• Michel Masquelier, President IMG Media
• Michael J J Dolan, President/CEO
• George Pyne, President IMG Sports & Entertainment
Description:
IMG connects brands to global opportunities in sports, fashion and media.

Teams:

IMG LOS ANGELES/IMG X SPORTS
2049 CENTURY PARK E
SUITE 2480
LOS ANGELES, CA 90067
424-653-1960
Fax: 424-653-1914
www.imgworld.com
• Theodore J Forstmann, Chairman/CEO
• Chuck Bennett, President IMG Golf , Tennis,Fashion and Event
• Michel Masquelier, President IMG Media
• Michael J J Dolan, President/CEO
• George Pyne, President IMG Sports & Entertainment
Description:
IMG connects brands to global opportunities in sports, fashion and media.

IMPACT SPORTS MANAGEMENT
114-116 CURTAIN ROAD
1ST FLOOR
LONDON, ENGLAND EC2A 3AH
44-20-8905 1133
Fax: 44-20-8905-1020
impact-sports.com
• Mitchell Frankel, President
(407) 393-1475
Nature of Service:
Contract negotiation, endorsements and marketing for professional NFL, MLB and NBA athletes.

IMS SPORTS
2051 SAN ELIJO AVENUE
CARDIFF, CA 92007
Fax: 760-487-1368
• Circe Wallace-Hetzel, Sports Agent
(760) 487-1341
• Linnea Gibson, Sports Agent
(760) 487-1341
• Ashby Sorensen, Sports Agent
(760) 487-1342
• Peter A. Golden
golden@goldenew.com
Services:
Full-service agency which represents more than 40 alternative sports athletes.
Services:
Talent management to event operations, from broadcast ownership to retail

development
Clients:
Evan Hernandez, Jereme Rogers, Mike Taylor, Pat Channita, Paul Rodriguez, Ryan Sheckler, Tyler Adams Hawkins, Jake Brown, Lyn-Z Adams Hawkins, Rune Glifberg, Alexis Waite, Hana Beaman, Janna Meyen, Jeremy Jones, Jimi Tomer, Travis Rice, Wyatt Caldwell, Brad Gerlach, Jamie Sterling, Megan Abubo, Mike Losness, Taylor Knox, Dayne Kinnaird, Drake McElroy, Mary Osborne, Mike Carter, Fabiola Da Silva, Allan Cooke, Jamie Bestwick, Steve McCann
Sports Service Founded:
2000

INNOVATIVE SPORTS MARKETING & MANAGEMENT
720 MONROE STREET
SUITE #E303
HOBOKEN, NJ 7030-6352
201-610-0200
Fax: 201-610-9260

INTEGRATED SPORTS MANAGEMENT
6015 MIDDLEWATER CT
COLUMBIA, MD 21044
410-740-1147
Fax: 410-992-4999
Services:
Contract Negotiation and Business Management; Personality Marketing, Endorsements and Tax Refund Preparation; Combine and Draft Preparation; Preparation for Team Interviews; Real Estate Acquisition and Financing; Acquisition of Necessary Insurance; Assistance in Obtaining a Line of Credit; Individual Estate and Gift Tax Planning; Bank Account Reconciliation and Management; Post Sports Career Development
Nature of Sports Service:
All phases of athlete representation including contract negotiation, long-range planning, financial planning, and post-career counseling. Certified Athlete Agents in Florida, Tennessee and Mississippi. Member of the NFLPA since 1987. Associate member of Sports Lawyers Association.

INTEGRITY SPORTS PLAYER MANAGEMENT
26000 W 12 MILE ROAD
SOUTHFIELD, MI 48034
248-355-1727
800-887-6370
Fax: 248-355-5674
• Kevin T. Granader, President/Special Counsel
• Storm T. Kirschenbaum, VP/General Counsel
• Tim Walton, Founder
• Eugene Brown, Player Personnel VP
Services:
Asset Management, Securities Recordkeeping and Safekeeping, Annual Tax Information, Monthly Accounting Statement, Cash Flow Projections, Financial and Estate Planning, Real Property Management, Estate and Insurance Planning, Risk Management, Retirement Planning, Income Tax Returns for Federal, State and City Taxing Authorities, Assistance in Buying/Selling Homes, Cars and Other Assets, High School and College

Tuition Management Planning, Public Relations, Corporate Association, Merchandising, Equipment and Relocation Services

Clients:
Jermaine Brock, Nick DeBarr, Dan DeMent, Sean Dobson, Travis Gulick, Brian Hertel, Jared Hoerman, Tim Keinath, Gary Kinnie, Adam Moreno, Scott Koerber, Kevin Olore, Mike Prochaska, Johnny Poss, Dustin Shafer, Aaron Shrewsbury, Adam Sokoll, Doug Stasio, Chuck Van Robays, Chad Wiles, Joseph Yarbrough, Ruth Riley, Willie Burton, Clay Tucker, Bill Flowers, Ernest Jones, Earl Stephens, Adrian Jones, Victor Hobson, Marko Cavka, Stanley Wilson, David McMillan, Akarika Dawn, Jamar Landrom, Brian Alford, Bennie Blades, Brian Blades, Jovon Burkes, Tommie Boyd, Kevin Bryant, Mill Coleman, Lional Dalton, Dorsett Davis, Fred Foggie, Ricky Foggie, Dan Gibb

Nature of Service:
Full service sports representation firm. Represent athletes in Baseball, Football, Basketball, Hockey, Golf and Entertainers.

INTERNATIONAL CREATIVE MANAGEMENT, INC.
10250 CONSTELLATION BOULEVARD
LOS ANGELES, CA 90067
310-550-4000
careersla@icmpartners.com
www.icmtalent.com
• Jeffrey Berg, Chairman/Chief Executive Officer
jberg@icmtalent.com
• Jeffrey Berg, President
• Edward Limato, Co-President
• Chris Silbermann, Co-President
• Richard B. Levy, Chief Business Development Officer

Services:
Represents creative and technical talent in the fields of motion pictures, television, publishing, music, live performance, commercials and new media

Clients:
Allure, Amerie, Ashanti, Avant, DJ Beverley Bond, Bone Thugs N Harmony, Cam'ron, Case, Cash Money Millionaires, Crazy Al Cayne, Chico DeBarge, Mobb Deep, DJ Clue, DMX, Drag-On, En Vogue, Faith Evans, Fabolous, Fat man Scoop, Funk Master Flex, Anthony Hamilton, David Hollister, Joe, Patti LaBelle, Lil' Mo', Jennifer Lopez, Lost Boyz, LS-1, Memphis Bleek, Mr. Cheeks, Mystikal, Nas, New Edition, Nivea, Rah Digga, Ray J, Ron G, Royce Da 5'9, Ruff Endz, Ruff Ryders, Eric Sermon, Beanie Sigel, Smilez and Southstar, Special K 6 & Teddy Ted, Styles, Keith Sweat, The Lox, Usher

Sports Service Founded:
1975

Athlete Management Services:
Represent sports personalities for national television commercials and endorsements. Top athletes have been booked by this agency and have appeared in ads for Coca Cola, Gillette Right Guard, Pepsi, Nike, and many other products.

Other Locations:
40 West 57th Street, New York, NY 10019; Phone: 212-556-5600; 4-6 Soho Square, London WID 3PZ, England; Phone: 011-44-207-432-0800

Marketing & Consulting Services:
Marketing and management services for

athlete clients involved with television commercials.

INTERPERFORMANCES, INC.
230 W SUPERIOR STREET
SUITE 510
CHICAGO, IL 60654
312-654-1717
Fax: 312-266-4220
chrisport@aol.com
www.interperformances.com
• Luciano Capicchioni, President/Co-Chief Executive Officer
info@interperformances.com
• Luciano Capicchioni, President and Chief Executive Officers
• Manel Bosch, CEO Worldwide Operations
• Patricia A. Levine, Executive Administrator
• John Kern, Legal Counsel
• Herb Rudoy, President/Co-CEO

Other Office:
Via degli Aceri, 14, Gualdicciolo, 47892 Republic of San Marino, (Europe) 378 911007; Fax: 378 911008.

Services:
Full-service Marketing, Media Relations Advice, Public Relations, Post-Career Planning and Representation of Athletes, Corporations, Teams, Events, and Sponsors.

Clients:
Albert Alfonso, Amagou Pape-Philippe, Anderson Christian, Andriuskevicius Martynas, Angelopoulos Nikos, Angulo Alberto, Angulo Lucio, Argiropoulos Nikos, Baloggiannis Giorgos, Barcenas Enrique, Barlos Nikos, Barycz Wojciech, Becirovic Sani, Becka Pavel, Benevelli Andrea, Bianchi Alessandro, Bianco Gustavo, Blanda Marco, Bossini Thomas, Boudouris Nikos, Brana Carlos, Brkic David, Bryan Sylvere, Bueno Antonio, Caceres Juan, Callahan Dan, Carretta Luca, Causin Alberto, Cazorla Carlos, Cei Saverio, Charisis Kostas, Cinciarini Daniele, Coffin Mike, Coldebella Claudio, Conti Andrea, Cortesi Simone, Corvo Giuseppe, Cresnik Matej, Cusin Marco, D'Ayal

Description:
Full-service Marketing and Representation of Athletes, Corporations, Teams, Events, and Sponsors.

INTRASPORT MANAGEMENT GROUP
LEESBURG, VA 22075
703-861-0771
Fax: 703-777-2873
• Michael Draine, Sports Agent
• Caroline Roney, Attorney

Nature of Sports Service:
All phases of athlete representation including contract negotiation, long-range planning, financial planning, and post-career counseling.

IRWIN SPORTS MANAGEMENT, LLC
720 S GAY STREET
KNOXVILLE, TN 37902
865-637-5566
877-994-7946
Fax: 865-637-8819
• Timothy E. Irwin, President
(865) 637-5566
• Beth H. Riley, Office Manager

Services:
All phases of athlete representation including contract negotiation, long-range

planning, financial planning, and post-career counseling.

Clients:
Josh Burr, Tyson Clabo, Brennan Curtin, William dela Houssaye, Brad Hoover, Luke Lawton, Josh Mallard, Steve McKinney, Nick McNeil, Ben Nelson, Constantin Ritzmann, Larry Turner, Todd Yoder, Madison Hedgecock, Kelly Griffeth, Jonas Crafts, Amos Lamb, Brett Hodge, Brian Sump, Mike Woolridge

JACKSON WALKER LLP
777 MAIN STREET
SUITE 2100
FORT WORTH, TX 76102
817-334-7200
Fax: 817-334-7290
www.jw.com
• T. Michael Wilson, Firmwide Managing Partner
(214) 953-6020
mwilson@jw.com
• Albon O. Head, Jr., Managing Partner
(817) 334-7230
ahead@jw.com
• Jaymie D. Bell, Chief Marketing Officer
(214) 953-5812
jbell@jw.com
• Richard A. Herlan, Chief Financial Officer
(214) 953-5834
rherlan@jw.com
• Gail R. Horne, Administrator Dallas/Fort Worth
(214) 953-5879
ghorne@jw.com
• Sharon H. Kasachkoff, Director Operations
(214) 953-6048
skasachkoff@jw.com
• Steven W. McHargue, Chief Information Officer
(214) 953-5810
smchargue@jw.com

Nature of Service:
The firm regularly represents clients in such areas as corporate and securities, litigation, intellectual property, health care, labor and employment, legislative and regulatory, real estate, tax and estate planning, technology, bankruptcy, aviation and international law.

Year Founded:
1887

Clients:
Fortune 500 companies, multi-national corporations, major financial institutions, and a wide range of publicly traded corporations and closely held businesses.

Other Locations:
100 Congress Avenue, Suite 1100, Austin, Texas 78701; Bank of America Plaza, 901 Main Street, Suite 6000, Dallas, TX 75202; 1401 McKinney Street, Suite 1900, Houston, Texas 77010; 301 W. Beauregard Avenue, Suite 200, San Angelo, Texas 76903; Weston Centre, 112 E. Pecan Street, Suite 2400, San Antonio, Texas 78205.

JAMES CLIBANOFF BASKETBALL SERVICES
PO BOX 3267
MAPLE GLEN, PA 19002
215-793-4516
Fax: 215-793-4517
www.worldbasket.com
• Jim Clibanoff, President

JONES, IRIS
9430 RESEARCH BOULEVARD
ECHELON 1V, SUITE 400
AUSTIN, TX 78731
512-343-4564
Fax: 512-343-2351
Nature of Sports Service:
All phases of athlete representation including contract negotiation, long-range planning, financial planning, and post-career counseling.

JORDAN SPORTS MANAGEMENT - (LA)
2900 WESTFOLD DR, SUITE 200
BATON ROUGE, LA 70827
225-295-5624
Fax: 225-771-3272
Nature of Sports Service:
All phases of athlete representation including contract negotiation, long-range planning, financial planning, and post-career counseling.

JOSEPH ATHLETIC MANAGEMENT
104 W NORTHWOOD STREET, SUITE F
GREENSBORO, NC 27401
336-275-0863
800-826-7658
Fax: 336-275-6071
Nature of Sports Service:
All phases of athlete representation including contract negotiation, long-range planning, financial planning, and post-career counseling.

JUCKETT SPORTS & ENTERTAINMENT
3119 OAKES AVENUE
EVERETT, WA 98201
425-339-1559
Fax: 425-252-0798
staff@juckett.com
Sports Service Founded:
1986
Athlete Management Services:
International professional athlete representation, contract negotiation, world wide and regional endorsements, commercials, infomercials, personal appearances, speaking presentations and training, legal counsel.
Marketing & Consulting Services:
Marketing strategies provided for individual celebrity talent depending on area of recognition and location of talent. Legal counseling provided as needed. Sponsors road to Winning program.

KARIZMA SPORTS, LLC.
66 PROSPECT STREET
MANCHESTER, NH 3104
603-627-4666
Fax: 603-634-4347

KATZ MEDIA CORPORATION
125 W 55TH STREET
NEW YORK, NY 10019
212-424-6000
Fax: 513-721-3077
www.katz-media.com
• Stu Olds, Chief Executive Officer
• Robert Damon, CFO
Nature of Sports Service:
All phases of athlete representation including contract negotiation, long-range planning, financial planning, and post-career counseling.

KAUFFMAN SPORTS MANAGEMENT GROUP
5565 ADELINA COURT
SUITE 200
AGOURA HILLS, CA 91301
310-456-5400
818-991-1300
steve@kauffmansports.com
www.kauffmansports.com
• Steve Kauffman, Founder/President
• Larry Kauffman, Vice President of Finance
• Spencer Breecker, Partner
• John Hammond, General Manager
• Donnie Walsh, President of Basketball Operations
• Mike Born, Director of NBA Scouting
• Mike Bratz, Director of Player Personnel
• Steve Kauffman, Founder and President
steve@kauffmansports.com
Description:
Contract negotiation, post career planning, arbitration hearings, federal/state/international tax filings, provides investment advice, licensing, endorsement exploration.

KC SPORTS MANAGEMENT, INC.
23702 HARBOR VISTA DRIVE
SUITE 200
MALIBU, CA 90265
310-456-5400
Fax: 239-337-5364
Description:
All phases of athlete representation including contract negotiation, long-range planning, financial planning, and post-career counseling.

KCB SPORTS MARKETING
4000 ISLAND BOULEVARD
AVENTURA, FL 33160
kcbsportsmarketing.com
• Robert Bailey, Member
Description:
KCB is a full service marketing and athlete representation agency. Services include: endorsement exploration, personal appearnces, television and media appearances, radio, commercials, memorbilia products and show appearances.

KELLY ENTERPRISES, JIM
8207 MAIN STREET
SUITE 1
WILLIAMSVILLE, NY 14221
716-204-1212
Fax: 716-204-0999
dstupski@jimkelly.com
www.jimkelly.com
Sports Service Founded:
1986
Event Management Services:
Manages golf tournaments, camps, etc., working with athletes and corporate sports sponsors.
Athlete Management Services:
Provides contract negotiation and corporate sponsorship services.

KELMAN, LORIA, WILL HARVEY & THOMPSON
17000 W 10 MILE ROAD
SUITE 100
SOUTHFIELD
DETROIT, MI 48075

313-961-7363
Fax: 313-961-8875
• Charles Chomet, Attorney
• James Harvey, Attorney
• Alan Posner, Attorney
• Ann Thompson, Attorney

KING PRODUCTIONS, INC., DON
501 FAIRWAY DRIVE
DEERFIELD BEACH, FL 33441
954-418-5800
800-883-2288
Fax: 954-418-0166
www.donking.com
• Don King, President/Chief Executive Officer
Sports Service Founded:
1976
Athlete Management Services:
Handles athlete endorsements, promotional aspects for commercials, product endorsements.
Event Management Services:
Promotes and arranges for promotion of sports events of all types, specializing in boxing.

KIRKPATRICK, CRAWFORD
5300 MEMORIAL DRIVE, SUITE 520
HOUSTON, TX 77007
713-523-9500
Fax: 713-861-0079
• Crawford Kirkpatrick, Attorney

LAMPROS & ROBERTS CONSULTING
235 W. MAIN STREET
LOS GATOS, CA 95030
408-358-1125
800-841-7767
• Nick J Lampros, Member
• Jerry W. W. Roberts, Member
Description:
Contract negotiation, arbitration hearings, federal/state/international tax filings, endorsement exploration.

LANDMARK SPORT GROUP
10990 WILSHIRE BOULEVARD
LOS ANGELES, CA 90024
310-966-4101
Fax: 905-949-4984
admin@landmarksport.com
www.landmarksport.com
• Elliott Kerr, President
jekerr@landmarkspot.com
• Sharon Podatt, Director
• Adrian Sciarra, Director
• Lisa Dichiera, Director Of Advocacy
• Brian Hogg, Director
Sports Service Founded:
1987
Marketing & Consulting Services:
Advises clients on the most efficient way to utilize sports event marketing for commercial purposes. Advise clients already using sports event marketing on how to maximize investment. Assists corporations to determine speaker objectives and matches with speaker/personality to fulfill role of speaker.
Event Management Services:
Develops and implements all aspects of major sporting events on full-service, turn-key basis. Consultation, acquisition of sponsors, event coordination and management, negotiations with TV, facility contracts, etc.

professional services

Athlete Management Services:
Contract negotiation, financial management and endorsement negotiation services.
Clients:
Olympic Winter Athletes, Olympic Summer Athletes, Professional Athletes, Motivational Speakers. Event Management of the Mississauga Marathon, Oakville Half Marathon, and the Jane Rogers Championship Mississauga.

LANKTREE SPORTS CELEBRITY NETWORK, INC.
440 NORTH WELLS STREET
CHICAGO, IL 60610
312-266-9558
Fax: 312-242-2707
Sports Service Founded:
1991
Marketing & Consulting Services:
Comprehensive supplier of athletes for commercial and personal appearance projects from casting to negotiations.

LATIMER, TRACIE K.
11801 SW SECOND STREET
FT. LAUDERDALE, FL 33325
954-473-4964
Nature of Sports Service:
All phases of athlete representation including contract negotiation, long-range planning, financial planning, and post-career counseling.

LAW OFFICES OF JOSEPH R. CRUSE JR.
5541 DART COURT
SUITE 210
AGOURA HILLS, CA 91301
818-699-6282
Fax: 310-598-3876
• Joseph Cruse, Attorney at Law
(562) 833-5800
jcruse@jcruselaw.com
Founded:
1993
Services:
Handles legal matter in the following practice areas: Intellectual Property, Entertainment Law, Sports, Trademarks, Copyrights and Contracts

LEGACY SPORTS GROUP
500 NEWPORT CENTER DRIVE
SUITE 800
NEWPORT BEACH, CA 92660
949-720-8700
Fax: 949-720-1331
info@legacy-agency.com
www.legacy-agency.com
• Gregory Genske
(949) 720-8700
Description:
Contract negotiation, post career planning, arbitration hearings, and endorsement exploration.
Services:
A sports representation firm acting for professional athletes in a variety of sports, with emphasis on baseball and football. Legacy Sports Group also represents a number of media and other entertainment industry figures.

LINKS MANAGEMENT GROUP
PO BOX 2552
READING, RG4 8FR

44-1189-545045
Fax: 972-381-4228
info@linkmanagementgroup.com
www.linkmanagementgroup.com
• David K Parker, President
Athlete Management Services:
All phases of representation including endorsements, charity events, and other aspects of management, representing PGA Tour, Champions Tour, Nationwide Tour and LPGA Tour players.
Sports Service Founded:
1992

LISS, ARTHUR Y.
39400 N WOODWARD AVENUE
SUITE 200
BLOOMFIELD HILLS, MI 48304
248-647-9700
Fax: 248-647-0638
www.lissfirm.com
• Arthur Y Liss, Attorney
(248) 647-9700
• Jacqueline Benyo, Legal Assistant
Nature of Sports Service:
All phases of athlete representation including contract negotiation, long-range planning, financial planning, and post-career counseling.

LLOYD, ROBERT V.
10303 JASPER AVENUE
SUITE 1400
EDMONTON, ALBERTA, CANADA T5J 3N6
780-429-6220
Fax: 780-429-4453
www.ogilvie.com
Services:
Post career planning, arbitration hearings, federal/state/international tax filings.

LUMSDEN & MCCORMICK, LLP
369 FRANKLIN ST
THE CYCLORAMA BUILDING
BUFFALO, NY 14202
716-856-3300
888-586-7336
Fax: 716-856-2524
mailbox@lumsdencpa.com
www.lumsdencpa.com
• Louis Cercone, Jr., Partner
(716) 856-3300
• Dennis A. A Castiglia, Partner, Investment Management
(716) 856-3300
• Dale B. B Demyanick, Partner, Tax Planning
(716) 856-3300
ddemyanick@lumsdencpa.com
• Michael J. J Grimaldi, Partner, Health Care Organizations
(716) 856-3300
mgrimaldi@lumsdencpa.com
Nature of Sports Service:
All phases of athlete representation including contract negotiation, long-range planning, financial planning, and post-career counseling, accounting and tax and consulting services.
Year Founded:
1952
Sports Service Founded:
1985

LYLES, FREDERICK T.
3613 ADAVALE DRIVE
PLANO, TX 75025

972-335-8130
Nature of Sports Service:
All phases of athlete representation including contract negotiation, long-range planning, financial planning, and post-career counseling.

Other locations:

M.D. GILLIS & ASSOCIATES LTD.
154 EARL STREET
KINGSTON, ONTARIO, CANADA K7L 2H2
613-548-4917
Fax: 613-548-3991
• Michael Gillis, Agent
(613) 548-4917
• Dan Palango, Agent
(416) 816-3257
Services:
Organization is a sports representation firm catering exclusively to professional hockey players.
Clients:
Pavel Bure (NHL); Ulf Dahlen (NHL); Mathew Dandenault (NHL); Bobby Holik (NHL); Sergei Krivokrasov (NHL); Markus Naslund (NHL); Marcus Ragnersson (NHL); and Pat Verbeek (NHL).
Nature of Sports Service:
Organization is a sports representation firm catering exclusively to professional hockey players.
Clients Include:
Pavel Bure (NHL); Ulf Dahlen (NHL); Mathew Dandenault (NHL); Bobby Holik (NHL); Sergei Krivokrasov (NHL); Markus Naslund (NHL); Marcus Ragnersson (NHL); and Pat Verbeek (NHL).

MADIGAN CAPITAL MANAGEMENT
PO BOX 8
MONMOUTH BEACH, NJ 07750-1130
732-571-3132
• Ray Clark, Founder/CEO
• Dan Belmont, President, Sports
Services:
Athlete Management: Financial management, contract negotiation, marketing. Event Management: Product endorsement, corporate affiliations, golf outings.
Marketing & Consulting Services:
Product endorsement.

MAIN EVENTS
772 UNION BOULEVARD
TOTOWA, NJ 07512
973-200-7050
Fax: 973-200-7061
jmizzone@mainevents.com
www.mainevents.com
• Jolene Mizzone, Vice President of Operations
jmizzone@mainevents.com
• Kim Newman, Sports Scene Distributions
knewman@mainevents.com
• Ellen Haley, Public Relations
ehaley@mainevents.com
Year Founded:
1978
Description:
Professional boxing promotion
Clients:
Professional boxers

MAJOR LEAGUE BASEBALL PLAYERS ASSOCIATION
12 E 49TH STREET
24TH FLOOR
NEW YORK, NY 10017

212-826-0808
Fax: 212-752-4378
feedback@mlbpa.org
mlbplayers.mlb.com
• Donald M. Fehr, Executive
Director/General Counsel
• Martha Child, Managing Officer
• Judy Heeter, Director Business
Affairs/Licensing
• Greg Bouris, Director Communications
Services:
Contract negotiation.

MAKE IT HAPPEN SPORTS
108 N MAIN STREET
SUITE 800
SOUTH BEND, IN 46601
574-232-3025
Fax: 574-234-3363
• Andre B. Gammage, Sports Agent
Services:
All phases of athlete representation
including contract negotiation, long-range
planning, financial planning, and post-career
counseling.

MANAGEMENT ONE
7925A N ORACLE ROAD
#114
TUCSON, AZ 85704
513-651-1610
888-921-6663
Fax: 800-860-1984
info@management-one.com
• James M. Gould, Managing Partner
James.Gould@TheWalnutGroup.com
Services:
General Counsel for retail, service and
manufacturing industries

MANAGEMENT PLUS ENTERPRISES, INC.
6100 CENTER DRIVE
SUITE 900
LOS ANGELES, CA 90045
310-426-7500
888-483-2652
Fax: 310-426-8010
• Leonard Armato, President
Sports Service Founded:
1988.
Marketing & Consulting Services:
Representation of professional athletes in
marketing negotiation activities.

MARKETFORCE ONE, INC.
22353 SWEET JASMINE
THE SUMMIT
WOODLAND HILLS, CA 91367
818-279-2167
866-990-4440
Fax: 818-346-3105
bob@bobpritchard.com
www.bobpritchard.com
• Robert G. Pritchard, Chief Executive
Officer
• Susan Aird, Personnel Management
Services:
Business & marketing strategies, Planning
and implementation, Direct marketing,
Strategic Partner, Finance Acquisition,
Marketing for prolonged, sustainable growth
(domestic & global), Marketing Audits,
Complete business audits, Advertising,
Complete business audits, Advertising,
Consumer purchasing benefit, customer
service and added value programs, Project

management, Research, Sales Promotion,
Cause Related Marketing, Sponsorship
management, Event management, Training
& keynote addresses
Clients:
Formula One Motor Racing, Legends of
Tennis, McEnroe, Borg., Skins Golf with
Norman, Nicklaus., Pro-beach Volleyball,
Katarina Witt 18 Olympians Tour, World
Freestyle Skiing Championships, World
Series Cricket, Los Angeles International
Track Meet, Association of Surfing
Professionals, World Masters Games, Indy
Car Racing, Oakland Raiders, World
Heavyweight Champion, Evander Holyfield
Athlete Management Services:
Representation of athletes for corporate
endorsements including sales promotions
and public relations.
Other Office:
142 Cathedral St. Sydney New South Wales
2011 Australia
Sports Service Founded:
1978 (1986 in U.S.).
Event Management Services:
Marketing, sponsorship management, event
management, television production,
procurement and distribution, sport and
special event related promotions; event
staging hospitality, licensing.
Marketing & Consulting Services:
Lifestyle sponsorship packaging and
solicitation. Corporate sponsorship
management, sales promotion, public
relations, web site production, video
production.

MARKETING ARM
1999 BRYAN STREET
18TH FLOOR
DALLAS, TX 75201
214-259-3200
Fax: 214-259-3201
info@themarketingarm.com
www.themarketingarm.com
• Ray Clark, Founder/CEO
• Dan Belmont, President, Sports
Services:
Athlete Management: Financial
management, contract negotiation,
marketing. Event Management: Product
endorsement, corporate affiliations, golf
outings.
Marketing & Consulting Services:
Product endorsement.

MASTERPLAN GROUP INTERNATIONAL
122 S MICHIGAN AVENUE
SUITE 1220
CHICAGO, IL 60603
312-880-0340
Fax: 312-880-0346
www.masterplangroup.com
• Joseph D Wright, President/Chief
Executive Officer
• Steve Raquel, Director Marketing
Services:
Contract Negotiations, Preparing the
Athlete, Diet Assessment, Marketing the
Athlete, Financial and Tax Management,
Endorsements, Media and Community
Relations, Relocation Assistance, Personal
Organization
Clients:
National Football League, NFL Europe,
Motorsports
Sports Services Founded:

1990
Nature of Sports Service:
Contract and endorsement negotiations;
comprehensive financial management
services focused on risk management and
preservation of wealth; tax planning; public
relations; personal, professional, and
post-career counseling.

MATTGO ENTERPRISES, INC.
185 E 85TH STREET
APARTMENT 18G
NEW YORK, NY 10028-2146
212-427-4444
• Matt V Merola, President
(212) 427-4444
Services:
Representation of professional athletes in
off-the-field activities, excluding
investments.
Sports Service Founded:
1968.

MAUPIN, TAYLOR, P.A.
301 FAYETTEVILLE STREET
SUITE 1700
RALEIGH, NC 27601
919-981-4000
Fax: 919-981-4300
www.williamsmullen.com
• Julious P Smith, Jr., Chairman/Chief
Executive Officer
(804) 783-6408
jsmith@williamsmullen.com
• Keith M. Kapp, Vice President
(919) 981-4024
kkapp@williamsmullen.com
• William P Barrett, Staff
(919) 981-4043
• David D. W Addison, Partner
Services:
Labor and employment, environmental law
and real estate
Description:
Contract negotiation, endorsement
exploration.

MAX-AIR PRODUCTIONS, INC.
9430 S RAINTREE DRIVE
SANDY, UT 84092
801-944-4849
• Craig Peterson, President
Services:
Pioneered ski jumping and trampoline
shows and offers acrobatic thrill show
entertainment tosporting events, state and
county fairs, amusement parks and special
events worldwide. The company has
expanded into snowboarding and big air
jumping and leads the market with the latest
ramp and air bag innovations.
Event Management Services:
Design, production and implementation of
regional and national sponsorship and
marketing programs, including grass roots
product sampling and distribution programs,
extreme sport shows, events and
competitions. Owns and operates the
MAX-AIR SKI SHOW, the Vertical Thrill
Show Tour and Splash! Aerial Ski and
Snowboard water ramp competition series.
Marketing & Consulting Services:
Specializes in providing corporate marketing
opportunities and strategies through,
turn-key, event-driven sales promotion
campaigns for corporate clients. Provides

project management, public relations and promotional support services.

MAXIMUM SPORTS MANAGEMENT
6435 W JEFFERSON BOULEVARD
#197
FORT WAYNE, IN 46804
888-494-3330
Fax: 800-631-4380
www.maximumsports.com
• Rebecca Flaherty, General Manager
• Eugene Parker, Contract Advisor
Nature of Services:
All phases of athletes representation including contract negotiation, long-range planning, financial planning, and post-career counseling.
Services:
Based in Roanoke, Indiana, it is a sports representation firm with a significant client list of football athletes. The range of sports agency services includes negotiation of player contracts, performance bonuses and endorsement and marketing contracts and assists in linking professional athletes to endorsement, marketing and public relations opportunities.

MAXIMUM SPORTS MARKETING
196 N MAIN STREET
ROANOKE, IN 46783
260-672-9480
Fax: 260-672-1310
• Eugene Parker, Chief Executive Officer
Services:
All phases of athlete representation including contract negotiation, long-range planning, financial planning, and post-career counseling.

MCCARTHY TETRAULT
40 ELGIN STREET
THE CHAMBERS
SUITE 1400
OTTAWA, CANADA K1P 5K6
613-238-2000
Fax: 613-563-9386
info@mccarthy.ca
www.mccarthy.ca
• W. Lain Scott, Chair and Chief Executive Officer
(416) 601-7686
• Kenneth C. Morell, COO/Nationel Leader, Markets
(416) 601-7585
Services:
One of Canada's most prestigious law firms. Provides its clients with ready access to legal and related professional resources and representation on a national and international basis. offers legal services in communications, information technology, intellectual property, Internet and e-commerce, among other fields.
Description:
Represents college athletic departments, endorsement exploration.

MCCLELLAN SPORTS MANAGEMENT GROUP
20321 SW BIRCH STREET
SUITE 203
NEWPORT BEACH, CA 92660
949-752-6151
Services:
Sports Club/Manager/Promoter
Sports Service Founded:
1990
Athlete Management Services:
Sponsorship procurement; contract negotiation; legal and financial advising; career planning and development.
Event Management Services:
Event organization/planning; marketing strategies; advertising and promotion; sponsorship procurement.
Marketing & Consulting Services:
Organizational development; administration, etc.

MCCOY & ASSOCIATES, LLC
2381 E STADIUM BOULEVARD
ANN ARBOR, MI 48104
734-769-0001
Fax: 734-769-0056
info@mccoyandassociates.com
www.mccoyandassociates.com
• Robert McCoy
Services:
Legal services office
Nature of Sports Service:
All phases of athlete representation including contract negotiation, long-range planning, financial planning, and post-career counseling.

MCSHERRY, JR., WILLIAM J.
1675 BROADWAY
NEW YORK, NY 10019
212-484-3900
Fax: 212-484-3990
www.arentfox.com
• Jerrold S Abeles, Partner
• Jennifer Allen, Associate
Services:
Sports practice is one of the most experienced in the country. Serves as counsel to sports team franchises and provides legal advice to numerous purchasers and sellers of professional football, basketball, hockey and soccer teams, as well as team tennis.
Clients:
Charlotte Bobcats NBA franchise, the Washington Mystics WNBA franchise and the Charlotte Sting WNBA franchise.
Description:
Arbitration hearings, represents professional sports teams, licensing, tort actions/litigation.

MD STADIUM AUTHORITY
333 W CAMDEN STREET
SUITE 500
BALTIMORE, MD 21201
410-333-1560
877-637-8234
800-735-2258
Fax: 410-333-1888
www.mdstad.com
• Frederick W Puddester, Chairman
• Michael J. Frenz, Executive Director
• Gregory Smith, Chief Operating Officer
• Francoise Ca Hubschman, President
Year Founded:
July 1, 1986
Services:
Operation of baseball and football stadiums as well as other facilities.

MEDIA VISTA PRODUCTIONS
500 RAILWAY AVENUE
#306
CAMPBELL, CA 95008
408-282-1960
Fax: 408-549-9870
www.mediavista.com
• Peter Liebengood, President
• Cassandra Bellantoni, Executive Producer and Creative Director
• Gary Hinderliter, Engineering and Technology
• Jeanine Herrera, Graphic Artist and Designer
Services:
Specializes in Corporate Communications, provides on-camera talent, original music and production team to broadcast productions and various multimedia.
Clients:
Petroglyph, Mount Hermon Christian Conference Center, ADAC Laboratories, Dreamsports, Air Systems Inc., Lucent Technologies, Rentals.com, Naprotek, Inc., Hyatt San Jose, CPS, Graniterock, Santa Clara Valley Water District, NeoMagic Corporation, Featherlite Exhibits, Informatica, All Van Transportation, COM 21, ebay, Exodus, Santa Clara County Parks, SFS, The Business Journal, Casto Travel Inc., BJS.
Marketing & Consulting Services:
Provides image development training to athletes and sports personalities. Clients are trained on how to make the media work for them and to increase endorsement opportunities. Broadcast program features one-on-one coaching to assist athletes considering or making the transition from playing field to the broadcast booth.
Athlete Management Services:
Procures endorsements, personal appearances, and spokesperson roles for professional and amateur athletes. Creates and negotiates contracts for athlete marketing opportunities on a local, regional, national and global basis.
Sports Service Founded:
1991

MID-SOUTH SPORTS MANAGEMENT
• Stanley Morgan, President
(901) 523-2535
• Tim Jumper, Director of Basketball Operations
• Jay Laney, Chief Operating Officer
Sports Service Founded:
1995
Description:
All facets of athlete representation.
Services:
Athlete representation primarily in basketball.

MIDDLEBROOKS, WILLIAM T.
707 SE THIRD AVENUE
SUITE 600
FORT LAUDERDALE, FL 33316
954-462-4500
800-688-1054
Fax: 954-462-6597
info@middlebrookslaw.com
www.middlebrookslaw.com
Nature of Sports Service:
All phases of athlete representation including contract negotiation, long-range planning, financial planning, and post-career counseling.
Services:
Full-service law firm, specializing in Insurance Law, Medical Malpractice Law,

Personal Injury Law, and Product Liability Law.

MILLER CANFIELD SPORTS
150 W JEFFERSON
SUITE 2500
DETROIT, MI 48226
313-963-6420
Fax: 313-496-7500
www.millercanfield.com
• Michael W Hartmann, Chief Executive Officer
(313) 496-7554
hartmann@millercanfield.com
• David A. Robson, Office Manager
(313) 496-7575
robson@millercanfield.com
• Thomas Phillips, Managing Director
(517) 483-4902
phillipst@millercanfield.com
• Amanda Va Dusen, Managing Director
(313) 496-7512
vandusen@millercanfield.com
• Irene B. Hathaway, Resident Director
• James M. Angyan, Paralegal
Services:
Biggest and longest established law firm in Michigan. Makes use of dispute resolution, information technology, and many other innovative approaches in helping its clients solve their legal problems.
Description:
All phases of athlete management included but not limited to: Contract negotiations, business and career planning, estate planning, federal and state tax planning, protection of intellectual property.

MILLER, J. BRUCE
605 W MAIN STREET
LOUISVILLE, KY 40202-2921
502-587-0900
Fax: 502-587-9008
• J Br Miller
Description:
Contract negotiation.
Services:
Practices in the following areas of law: Civil and Commercial Litigation, Corporate Law, Sports and Entertainment Law, Governmental Law; Administrative Law and Health Care Law.
Clients:
Arvin Industries, Inc.; Buena Vista Distribution Co. (California/Kentucky); Columbia Pictures Industries, Inc. (California/Kentucky); D.A. Enterprises, Inc.; Derby Industries, Inc. (Kentucky); Dollar General Corporation, Inc.; Don King Productions, Inc.; Houghton Mifflin Co.; Humana, Inc.; Kentucky State Racing Commission; LGâ€™ Energy Corporation; Louisville (City of); Mabex Universal Film Corporation, Inc.; Maker's Mark Distillery; MGM/United Artists Communications Co.; Motion Picture Association of America; Paitco, Inc.; NTS Development, Inc.; Orion Pictures Distribution Corp.; Packaging Un-Limited, Inc.; R.Gene Smith Investments; Spectronic

MILLS, JR., ALVIN J.
1919 14TH STREET
ST# 410
PO BOX 187
BOULDER, CO
303-443-7770

• A Ja Mills Jr
Services:
All phases of athlete representation including contract negotiation, long-range planning, financial planning, and post-career counseling.

MITNICK, CRAIG R.
35 KINGS HIGHWAY E
HADDONFIELD, NJ 8033
856-427-9000
Fax: 856-427-0360
Description:
Contract negotiation, post career planning, investment contract negotiation, provides securities advice, provides investment advice, licensing, endorsement exploration, tort actions/litigation.
Services:
Specializing in State and Federal Criminal Defense. Preparation and Trial of Litigated Criminal Matters, the majority of which are venued in Superior Court and Federal Court. Extensive Knowledge and Experience involving indicatable/felony offenses, and Federal organized crimes, including all major crime prosecutions
Clients:
Matthew Lovett

MONFORE GROUP, INC
620 14TH STREET
SUITE C
TUSCALOOSA, AL 35402
205-750-8102
Fax: 205-750-8120
www.monforegroup.com
• Robert Monfore
rwm@monforegroup.com
Services:
Contract negotiation, post career planning, investment contract negotiation, provides investment advice.

MORRIS INTERNATIONAL
120 PARK AVE
SUITE 6
NEW YORK, NY 10017
917-663-2000
Fax: 704-896-3441
info@morrisinternational.com
www.morrisinternational.com
• Rick Hendrick, President
• Jaceb Olczak, Chief Financial Officer
Description:
The only AAAA advertising agency specializing in motorsports marketing and new product development has offered its clients a full range of professional expertise, including strategic planning, negotiations with teams, drivers & sanctioning bodies, car design, team management, public relations and event hospitality.
Services:
Morris International is the only AAAA advertising agency specializing in motorsports marketing and new product development. Morris International has offered its clients a full range of professional expertise, including strategic planning, negotiations with teams, drivers and sanctioning bodies, car design, team management, public relations and event hospitality. The company develops strategies that capture events, partnerships and media.
Clients:

AC-Delco, Alpha Sailboards, Anchorage Marine, Anheuser Busch, Busch Beer, Natural Light, Apache Stove Company, Apex Machine Tool Company, Tom Blackaller, Blue Bell, Inc./Wrangler Jeans, Boy Scouts of America, Buck Baker Driving School, Charlotte Motor Speedway, Charlotte Orioles, Cigarette Racing Boats, Consolidated Coin Caterers Corporation, Corning Glass Works/ Chameleon Sunglasses, Craftsman Motorsports, Dale Earnhardt Fan Club, Darlington International Raceway, Daytona International Speedway, Dixie Boat Company, Econo Lodges of America, Inc., John Force, GMAC, Grand National Scene, Grand National Illustrated, Griggs Publishing Company.
Sports Service Founded:
1971

NATIONAL FOOTBALL LEAGUE
280 PARK AVENUE
NEW YORK, NY 10017
212-450-2000
Fax: 212-681-7573
www.nfl.com
• Paul Tagliabue, NFL Commissioner
• Joe Browne, EVP Communications
• Jay E. Moyer, Special Counsel
• Troy Vincent, President-NFL Players Association
Services:
The exclusive collective bargaining agent for all players employed by clubs of the National Football League
Description:
Represents sports organizations.

NATIONAL FOOTBALL LEAGUE-LEGAL/NFL
280 PARK AVENUE
NEW YORK, NY 10017
212-450-2000
Fax: 212-681-7599
www.nfl.com
• Harold Henderson, EVP-NFL Management Council
• Dennis L. Curran, SVP/General Counsel-NFL Management Counc
Sponsors:
Merck-Zocor cholesterol reduction drug.
Services:
Represents all NFL Players

NATIONAL SPORTS AGENCY
5 LAKEVIEW COURT
LAKE SAINT LOUIS, MO 63367
636-265-1300
800-753-1245
Fax: 636-265-1303
• Harold C. Lewis, President
• Kevin J. Omell, VP / General Counsel
• Jonathan M. Caplin, Marketing and Player Relations Director
• Patty A. Midkiff, Controller
Nature of Sports Service:
All phases of athlete representation including contract negotiation, long-range planning, financial planning, and post-career counseling.
Clients:
Kenderick Allen, David Bowens, Kevin Carter, Shawn Cody, Travis Hall, Anthony Herron, Darrell Lee, CJ Mosley, Josh Buhl, Marlon Greenwood, Edgerton Hartwell, Bart Scott, Ellis Hobbs, Kevin House, Siddeeq Shabazz, Frank Walker, Bennie Anderson,

Thomas Barnett, Jason Brown, Rob Hunt, Bo Lacy, Fred Miller, David Allen, Nehemiah Broughton, ReShard Lee, Josh Scobey, Joe Smith, Derek Abney, James Adkisson, Richard Alston, Cortez Hankton, Harry Williams, Zach Hilton, Ben Steele, Roland Williams, Mike Scifres, Steve Atwater, Lewis Bush, Boby Christian, D Marco Farr, Mike Gruttadauria, Michael Jones, Randy Jordan, Max Lane, Stump Mitchell

---

NATIONAL SPORTS MANAGEMENT INC.
2425 E CAMELBACK
SUITE 1000
PHOENIX, AZ 85016
602-808-0404
Fax: 602-808-8788
www.nsmsports.com
• Todd Eley, President-Basketball
• George Sotos, President-Marketing
(602) 808-0404
• Ted Kritza, VP-Basketball
(602) 808-0404
• Michael Giorgio, Co-Owner, Agent
• John Massaroni, Co-Owner, General Counsel, Agent
• Tony Giorgio, Marketing Specialist
• Doug Lilly, Consultant / Agent
• David Segui, Baseball Consultant
Services:
Contract negotiation, post career planning, investment contract negotiation, arbitration hearings, federal/state/international tax filings, provides investment advice, endorsement exploration.
Year Founded:
1960

NATIONWIDE SPEAKERS BUREAU
1801 CENTURY PARK E
SUITE 460
LOS ANGELES, CA 90067
310-273-8807
Fax: 310-432-1181
• Jim Abott, Speaker
• Ed Adler, Vice President
Description:
Lecture Agency
Services:
Resource for booking speakers for conferences and special events, and talent for endorsements, product introductions and media tours
Clients:
AON Risk Services, Wal-Mart, kodak, lexus, mutual of omaha, hilton hotels, the national association of realtors, kinko's, the million dollar round table and fidelity investments.

NEOSTAR SPORTS AND ENTERTAINMENT
510 SHOTGUN ROAD
SUITE 520
SUNRISE, FL 33326
954-475-9311
Fax: 954-475-8392
www.neostarsportsandent.com
• Ralph Stringer, President / Chief Executive Officer
Sports Service Founded:
1989
Athlete Management Services:
Represents professional athletes for marketing and endorsement.
Event Management Services:
Production and management of sports and special events promotions, including

celebrity golf tournaments, 3-on-3 basketball.
Marketing & Consulting Services:
Evaluates sports marketing and endorsement opportunities for corporations in all areas.
Description:
Corporate sports marketing consultants.

NEWPORT BEACH
8000 W IH 10
SUITE 725
SAN ANTONIO, TX 78230-3868
210-342-9310
Services:
Contract negotiation, endorsement exploration.

NHLPA: NATIONAL HOCKEY LEAGUE PLAYERS' ASSOCIATION
20 BAY STREET
SUITE 1700
TORONTO, ONTARIO, CANADA M5J 2N8
416-313-2300
Fax: 416-313-2301
rparker@nhlpa.com
www.nhlpa.com
• Paul Kelly, Executive Director
• Mike Ouellet, Chief Of Business Affairs
• Craig Adams, Negotiating Committee
• Don Fehr, Executive Director
• Brandon Dubinsky, Negotiating Committee
• Douglas Murray, Negotiating Committee:
• George Parros, Negotiating Committee
Products:
Player Apparel, Collectibles, fantasy games, jersey customizers, novelties, player greetings, Printed Products, Trading Cards and video games.
Brands:
ccm/sport maska, activa consumer promotions corp.,enterplay llc, highland mint, mcfarlane toys,team beans, the promotions factory,beneway oy, chatham kent cyclones, espn, fantasy sports network, fantasy sport services, the sporting news, yahoo.com, all canadian emblem corporation, exclusive pro sports, great plains marketing, airborne entertainment, aminco international (usa) inc, burris, neiman & assosiates, frameworth sports marketing, gamewear, inglasco, minnesota wild hockey club, sababa toys, sports fx international cooperation,strat-o-matic game company inc., the meisner gallery inc., upi marketing inc.,wincraft inc., allstar greetings

---

OCTAGON ATHLETE REPRESENTATION (AGENTS)
800 CONNECTICUT AVENUE
2ND FLOOR
NORWALK, CT 06854
203-354-7400
Fax: 703-905-4495
www.octagon.com
• Rick Dudley, President /Chief Executive Officer
rick.dudley@octagon.com
• Phil De Picciotto, President-Athlete Representation
phil.depicciotto@octagon.com
• Chris Guinness, President-Octagon Television
• Mike Liut, Managing Director-Octagon Hockey
Services:
Career management/guidance, Contract

negotiations, Marketing and endorsements, Team relations, Public relations, Charitable activities, Financial planning and services
Clients:
Justin Leonard (golf), Davis Love III (golf), Anna Kournikova (tennis), Martina Hingis (tennis), Steffi Graf (tennis), Jana Novotna (tennis), Mark Philippoussis (tennis), Gustavo Kuerten (tennis), Amelie Mauresmo (tennis), David Robinson (basketball), Jerry Stackhouse (basketball), Sheryl Swoopes (basketball), Sergei Fedorov (hockey), Gareth Southgate (soccer), Ben Clarke (rugby), Steve Waugh (cricket), Jeanette Lee (billiards)
Description:
Contract negotiation, post career planning, arbitration hearings, federal/state/international tax filings, provides securities advice, provides investment advice, licensing, endorsement exploration. Sports marketing consulting agency.

OCTAGON ATHLETES & PERSONALITIES DIVISION
7950 JONES BRANCH DRIVE
SUITE 700N
MCLEAN, VA 22107
703-905-3300
• Nicola Murphy, Director Marketing, Athlete & Property Marketing
• Lisa Murray, Executive Vice President
• Sean Nicholas, Managing Director
• Simon Wardle, Chief Strategy Officer
• Rick Dudley, CEO, President
• Phillip DM DePicciotto, Founder and President, Octagon Worldwide
• Jeff Shirin, President, Octagon Marketing America
Services:
Athlete representation, financial consultancy, event management, property representation, tv rights sales and distribution, tv production and archive, rights ownership, and licensing and merchandising.

OCTAGON FOOTBALL
832 SANSOME STREET
1ST FLOOR
SAN FRANCISCO, CA 94111
415-318-4311
Fax: 415-646-0215
footballinfo@octagon.com
www.octagonfootball.com
• Mike Sullivan, Managing Director
• Ken Landphere, Director
Services:
All phases of athlete representation including contract negotiation, long-range planning, financial planning, and post-career counseling.

OCTAGON SPORTS
7231 FOREST AVENUE
SUITE 103
RICHMOND, VA 23226
804-285-4200
Fax: 804-285-4224
www.octagongolf.com
• Giff Breed, Managing Director Golf/Outdoors
• Phil De Picciotto, Founder & President
• Lisa Murray, Executive Vice President & Chief Marketing Of

- Simon Wardle, Chief Strategy Officer
- Rick Dudley, President & CEO

Nature of Service:
Octagon is uniquely poised to provide full service marketing solutions across the global platform. Octagon offers client expertise in the following areas: Angler Representation (endorsements, clinics, outings, appearances, licencing), Event Management (event ownership, creation & implementation), Sales/Property Management (package development & sponsorship management), Consulting (strategic sponsorship selection, contract negotiation, field marketing and implementation).

OKINAWAKENPODSSI.COM
91-1013 WAIPAA STREET
EWA BEACH, HI 96706-6499
808-457-7164
marcus.devalentino@okinawakenpodssi.com
www.OkinawaKenpoDSSI.com
- Marcus DeValentino, Program Director
marcus.devalentino@OkinawaKenpoDSSI.com

Nature of Service:
Promotes martial arts, training, certification, fitness and produces DVDs.

OLSEN, THOMAS
19000 MCCARTHER BOULEVARD
SUITE 500
IRVINE, CA 92612
714-440-7919
- Thomas Olsen, Attorney

Nature of Sports Service:
All phases of athlete representation including contract negotiation, long-range planning, financial planning, and post-career counseling.

OLSHER GROUP
2700 N MILITARY TRAIL
SUITE 210
BOCA RATON, FL 33431
561-338-7200

Nature of Sports Service:
All phases of athlete representation including contract negotiation, long-range planning, financial planning, post-career counseling, marketing & television.

Services:
Metal building industry

OUTSIDE THE BOX MARKETING, INC
ST MARY'S STREET
COUNTY HOUSE
WORCESTER, ENGLAND WR1 1HB
797-388-6417
Fax: 480-348-9678
- Scott Bartle, President
scott.bartle@otb-marketing.com

Sports Service Founded:
2000

Services:
Athlete representation, event management, sponsorship/marketing consulting.

OWENS, BRIGMAN
3524 K STREET NW
WASHINGTON, DC 20007-3503
202-625-3330
Fax: 202-337-0475
- Brigman Owens, Attorney

P.S. STARGAMES
40 SALEM STREET
SUITE 7
LYNNFIELD, MA 01940
781-224-9655
Fax: 781-224-9656
www.stargamesinc.com
- Jerry Solomon, President/Chief Executive Officer
(781) 224-9655
jerry@stargamesinc.com
- Michael Kerrigan, Director-Business Development/Affiliate
mstargames@aol.com
- Jess Smyser, Administrative Assistant
(781) 224-9655

Services:
Produces live and made-for-television sporting events

Year Founded:
1994

Description:
All phases of athlete representation including contract negotiation, long-range planning, and post-career counseling.

Clients Include:
Athletes: Nancy Kerrigan, Ivan Lendl, Vania King. Properties: Halloween on Ice, Nancy Kerrigan's World of Skating, Countdown to Draft Day, A New Year's Tradition: The Pure Bowl, Live the Dream: The Texas Longhorns Magical March: National Champions: The Story of the 2006 Florida Gators

---

PAIGE & RICE
9701 APOLLO DRIVE
SUITE 245
UPPER MARLBORO, MD 20774
301-925-4404
Fax: 301-925-4820
- Tony Paige, President/Chief Executive Officer
(301) 925-4404
- Kevin Glover, VP
(301) 925-4404
- Rodney Rice, Chief Financial Officer/Partner
(301) 925-4404
- Cherise Rhyns, Player Relations Director
(301) 925-4404

Description:
We are committed to conducting business with professionalism, honesty and integrity. Which is complimented by a full service approach to management that includes contract negotiation, marketing for endorsements, financial advising, investment counseling and career counseling.

Services:
All phases of athlete representation including contract negotiation, long-range planning, financial planning, and post-career counseling.

PALACE SPORTS & ENTERTAINMENT, INC.
6 CHAMPIONSHIP DRIVE
AUBURN HILLS, MI 48326
248-377-0100
Fax: 248-377-2154
www.palacenet.com
- Tom Gore, Owner
- Dennis Mannion, President
- Jeffrey Ajluni, Vice President

Description:
Owns and operates the NBA's Detroit Pistons, the WNBA's Detroit Shock, and the NHL's Tampa Bay Lightning.

PAOLI & SHEA, P.C.
257 W FRONT STREET
SUITE A
PO BOX 8131
MISSOULA, MT 59801
406-542-3330
800-816-9699
Fax: 406-542-3332
contact@paoli-law.com
www.paoli-law.com
- David R. Paoli, Member
- James Je Shea, Member
- Heather M. Latino, Associate
- Lance P. Jasper, Associate

Nature of Sports Service:
All phases of athlete representation including contract negotiation, long-range planning, financial planning, and post-career counseling.

Services:
Handles litigaton needs of clients in areas of Federal Employers' Liability Act (FELA), Serious injury and death cases, Product liability, Medical malpractice, Insurance, Criminal defense, and Employment disputes.

PENTRUST FINANCIAL SERVICES
3160 CAMINO DEL RIO S
B309
SAN DIEGO, CA 92108-3813
619-521-1458
- Joe E. Outlaw, President / Chief Executive Officer

Nature of Sports Service:
All phases of athlete representation including contract negotiation, long-range planning, financial planning, and post-career counseling.

PERFORMANCE SPORTS & ENTERTAINMENT
4615 SW FREEWAY
HOUSTON, TX 77027
713-965-0330

Services:
All phases of athlete representation including contract negotiation, long-range planning, financial planning, and post-career counseling.

PETER GREENBERG & ASSOCIATES
200 MADISON AVENUE
SUITE 2225
NEW YORK, NY 10016
212-334-6880
Fax: 212-334-6895
- Peter E. Greenberg, President

Services:
Sports promoter and managers, contract negotiation, post career planning, arbitration hearings, endorsement exploration and promotional marketing, specializing in baseball

---

PETER S. BRADLEY, ATTORNEY & COUNSELOR AT LAW
PO BOX 10904
NAPA, CA 94559
707-253-8838
Fax: 707-253-2962

- Brad S. Peter, Attorney & Owner
(707) 287-2661
- Mike Schumacher, Member
Description:
Contract negotiation, post career counseling, investment planning, arbitration hearings, federal/state/international tax filings, endorsement exploration, tort actions/litigation, estate planning, family law, business law.
Services:
Offers a complete list of career, financial, and image development services in the sports management field.
Year Founded:
1978

PETER SPORTS MANAGEMENT
PO BOX 10904
NAPA, CA 94581
707-253-8838
Fax: 707-253-2962
team_psm@sbcglobal.net
- Brad S. Peter, Managing Partner/Principal Owner
(707) 287-2661 m
- Mike Schumacher, Member
Nature of Sports Service:
All phases of athlete representation including contract negotiation, investment planning, arbitration hearings, federal/state/international tax filings, endorsement exploration, tort actions/litigation. Well known for its mentoring program - personal assistance, support and individual off season training programs with former professional athletes.
Year Founded:
1983
Services:
Offers a complete list of career, financial, and image development services in the sports management field.

PGA 20/20
100 PGA TOUR BOULEVARD
PONTE VEDRA BEACH, FL 32082
904-285-3700
Fax: 904-273-3512
www.pgatour.com

PHS, LTD.
401 WASHINGTON AVENUE
SUITE 902
TOWSON, MD 21204
410-296-2929
Fax: 410-296-2121
phsltd@abs.net
- Pam Shriver, Owner
- Marc Kantrowitz, Managing Director
Description:
Represents professional tennis player Pam Shriver.

PINNACLE ENTERPRISES, INC.
20121 S 172ND PLAZA CIRCLE
SPRINGFIELD, NE 68059-7186
402-677-3546
Fax: 703-893-3504
www.wiapt.com
- W D Denny Minami, President
- Peter M. Hill, Chairman/Chief Executive Officer
- Robert C. Morris, Founder / VP
- Brian L. Jo Katz, President
Services:
Management, Marketing Communications,

Leasing and Acquisitions, Development, Consulting
Sports Service Founded:
1988
Athlete Management Services:
Primarily represents golf professionals in all business opportunities including, but not limited to: corporate and product endorsements; personal, corporate and tournament appearances; financial management. Also works with major athletes in professional yachting, tennis, football, and with network sportscasters.
Event Management Services:
Provides turn-key management and consulting in areas of sports (especially golf) event conception, organization and implementation including, but not limited to: production, marketing and sponsor sales, financial management, public relations and operations. Specializes in procurement of professional golfers for event appearances.
Marketing & Consulting Services:
Specializes in serving designers, manufacturers and distributors of golf products worldwide. Critical and progressive intelligence in manufacturing, retail operations and wholesale marketing for established and start-up golf products and ventures. Expertise in product development and analysis, market analysis, market strategy and business development.

PLAYBOY ENTERTAINMENT GROUP
2706 MEDIA CENTER DRIVE
LOS ANGELES, CA 90065
323-276-4000
Fax: 323-276-4050
www.playboyenterprises.com
- Bob Meyers, Executive Vice President/President Media
- Jeffrey M. Jenest, EVP
- Scott N. Flanders, CEO
- Kristin Patrick, Chief Marketing Officer
- Rachel Sagan, Executive Vice President
- Matthew A. Nordby, Executive Vice Principal
Event Management Services:
Represents 75 Playboy Playmates, organized into 22 different sports teams, for celebrity promotions for corporations, event promoters, advertisers and charities.

PLAYPRO MANAGEMENT, INC.
1325 FRANKLIN AVENUE
SUITE 545
GARDEN CITY, NY 11530
516-741-0747
Fax: 516-741-1592
- Lloyd M. Friedland, President
Nature of Services:
Personal management services for professional athletes and broadcast professionals. Provides contract negotiation, endorsements, financial and personal planning, post career planning, and personal counseling services.
Sports Service Founded:
1992.

POITINGER REDMOND LYONS KURA & WALKER
2735 CRAWFIS BOULEVARD
SUITE 100
FAIRLAWN, OH 44333-2878

330-864-1144
Fax: 330-864-3002
www.prlkw.com
- Michael D. Poitinger, Shareholder
mpoitinger@prlkw.com
- James E. Redmond
jredmond@prlkw.com
- Richard W. Lyons
plan@prlkw.com
- Michael R. Kura
mkura@prlkw.com
Services:
Offers financial services such as fee-based financial, estate and non-qualified executive planning, charitable giving techniques, life and disability insurance, mutual funds and annuities and lifeime settlements.
Description:
Contract negotiation, post career planning, provides investment advice, licensing, endorsement exploration. Specialty is Financial Planning. Seeks opportunities to design creative solutions to both personal and business financial matters.

POLK, MARLIN A.
1650 FARNAM STREET
THE OMAHA BUILDING
OMAHA, NE 68102-2186
402-346-6000
Fax: 402-346-1148
www.kutakrock.com
Nature of Sports Service:
All phases of athlete representation including contract negotiation, long-range planning, financial planning, and post-career counseling.
Services:
Antitrust, Arbitrage Rebate Compliance, Banking and Commercial Lending, Bankruptcy, Blue Sky, Construction, Corporate, Corporate Finance, Emerging Companies, Employee Benefits, Employment Law, Environmental Law, Federal Practice and National Security Law, Government Contracts, Government Relations, Health Care Insurance, Intellectual Property and Technology Law, Litigation, Public Finance, Real Estate and Commercial Practice, Securities Law, Securities Litigation, Arbitration and Regulatory, Structured Finance, Tax, Tax Credits, Workouts and Surveillance

PONTON, WILLIE
PO BOX 2738
NEWPORT NEWS, VA 23609
757-988-0554
Nature of Sports Service:
All phases of athlete representation including contract negotiation, long-range planning, financial planning, and post-career counseling.

PORTER WRIGHT
41 S HIGH STREET
HUNTINGTON CENTER
COLUMBUS, OH 43215-6194
614-227-2000
800-533-2794
Fax: 614-227-2100
www.porterwright.com
- Robert W. Trafford, Managing Partner
(614) 227-2149
rtrafford@porterwright.com
- Robert S. Anderlen, Attorney
(216) 443-2554

• Jon M. Anderson, Attorney
(614) 227-2154
• William E. Arthur, Attorney
(614) 227-2056
warthur@porterwright.com
Nature of Sports Service:
All phases of athlete representation including contract negotiation, long-range planning, post-career counseling, endorsements, business transactions, estate planning (wills, etc.), and tax counseling.
Other Locations: :
250 East Fifth Street, STE 2200, Cincinnati, OH 45202; Phone 513-381-4700; 925 Euclid Avenue, STE 1700, Cleveland, OH 44115; Phone: 216-443-9000; One Dayton Centre, STE 1600, One South Main Street, Dayton, OH 45402; Phone: 937-449-6810; 5801 Pelican Bay Boulevard, STE 300, Naples, Fl 34108; Phone: 239-593-2900; 1919 Pennsylvania Avenue, NW, STE 500, Washington, DC 20006; Phone: 202-778-3000

POSITION SPORTS MARKETING
4852 E BASELINE RD.
SUITE 105
MESA, AZ 85206
480-248-6645
Fax: 480-240-5887
www.positionsports.com
• Kevin Foley, President
Sports Service Founded:
1975
Athlete Management Services:
Represents professional athletes for licensing, personal appearances.
Marketing & Consulting Services:
Consults, develops and executes sports promotion programs for corporations.

PPI MARKETING
15660 NORTH DALLAS PARKWAY
SUITE 1250
DALLAS, TX 75248
972-388-5300
800-937-5107
Fax: 972-388-5315
www.ppimarketing.com
• Roger Staubach, Founder/Partner
• Otis Birdsong, Events Director/Promotions
• Roz Cole, President
(972) 388-5307
• Kristopher Cumnock, Vice Persident, Creative Services, Event Mark
(972) 388-5304
• Tommy Finn, Vice President, Corporate Partnerships
(972) 388-5308
• Mary Barnes Knox, Vice President, Talent Marketing
(972) 388-5306
• Ward Eastman, Vice president, Strategic Alliances
(972) 388-5305
Sports Service Founded:
1993
Athlete Management Services:
Negotiates athlete/celebrity endorsement contacts.
Services:
Helps customize an alliance with one or any number of legends to fit client specific goals, strategies and objectives. Resource for business and motivational speakers, sports personalities and celebrities, entertainers

and bands.
Marketing & Consulting Services:
Speakers bureau and sports celebrity marketing firm. Specializes in marketing athletes and celebrities; plus scheduling public speakers and entertainers for a variety of events.

PREMIER MANAGEMENT GROUP
700 EVANVALE COURT
CARY, NC 27518
919-363-5105
Fax: 919-363-5106
evan@pmgsports.com
www.pmgsports.com
• Evan Morgenstein, President/Chief Executive Officer
(919) 363-5105
evan@pmgsports.com
• Bobby Brewer, Vice President
(520) 743-3979
bobby@pmgsports.com
• Laura Cutler, Corporate Communications Director
(919) 363-5105
laura@pmgsports.com
• Steven Weinreb
(919) 363-5105
steven@pmgsports.com
• Kelsey Morgan
(919) 363-5105
kelsey@pmgsports.com
Sports Service Founded:
1997
Sports Organization:
As an eliste marketing agency, PMG's goal is to create a space in the industry that is completely unique in the world of sports marketing throughits creativity and innovation. With over 35 exclusive Olympic and celebrity clients, PMG's goal is to provide each client with the same level of professional representation and service. Additionally, PMG is an industry leader in providing corporate consulting services. Each client, whether an athlete or a corporation, is treated with a personal touch.

PREMIERE MANAGEMENT
410 30TH AVENUE EAST
SUITE 107
ALEXANDRIA, MN 56308
320-762-6555
Fax: 903-297-8832
Premiere@premieremanagement.com
www.premiermanagement.com
• DuWayne Johnson, President
(320) 762-6555
djohnson@premiermanagement.com
Services:
Asset/Liability Management, Strategic Planning, Productivity Improvement, Financial Analysis and Reporting, Branch Acquisition/Mergers, Internal Control Programs, Leadership Development/Team Building, and Policy Writing
Clients:
First National Bank of Volga, Republic Bank, Duluth, MN, Independent Community Bankers of South Dakota, BankStar Financial, Elkton, SD, Reliabank, Estelline, SD
Nature of Sports Service:
All phases of athlete representation including contract negotiation, long-range planning, financial planning, and post-career counseling.

PRESKILL ROBERT
500 AIRPORT BLVD
SUITE 100
BURLINGAME, CA 94010
415-377-3919
preskilllaw@hotmail.com
• Robert Preskill, Founder
Services:
Provides assistance in licensing, purchase and sale of media-based or entertainment-based properties, and also in the areas of franchising, commercial leasing, purchase and sale of businesses and business assets, and trademark registration.
Description:
Publishing, entertainment, intellectual property, licensing agreements, sports law.

PRINCE MARKETING GROUP
18 CARILLON CIRCLE
LIVINGSTON, NJ 07039
973-325-0800
800-987-7462
800-98-PRINCE
Fax: 973-243-0037
helpdesk@princemarketinggroup.com
www.princemarketinggroup.com
• Darren Prince, President/CEO
dprince@princemarketinggroup.com
• Steve Simon, Vice President and Talent representation
• Nicholas Cordasco, Talent representation
• Reggie Dance, Contact
• Daren Prince, President and CEO
(212) 585-0973
Nature of Service:
Full service sports and celebrity marketing firm. Public Appearances, Product Placement, Autograph Signing Sessions, Charity Events, Fantasy Camps and Tournaments available for athletes, Grand Openings and Promotions, Licensing and Product Endorsements, Motivational Speakers, Print Advertisements and Commercials and Voice-overs
Sports Service Founded:
1998
Clients:
Earin 'Magic' Johnson, Dennis Rodman, Hulk Hogan, Joe Frazier, Evel Knievel, Roy Jones Jr, Vinny Pazienza, Dave Winifield, Jenny McCarthy, Carmen Electra, Pamela Anderson, Nicollette Sheridan, Stacy Kiebler, Vince Neil, Marcus Schenkenberg, Brande Roderick, Symone Maree, Dave Prowse, Corbin Bernsen, Chuck Zito.

PRIORITY SPORTS
325 N LA SALLE
SUITE 650
CHICAGO, IL 60654
312-664-7700
Fax: 312-664-5172
info@prioritysports.biz
www.prioritysports.biz
• Mark Bartelstein, Founder/Chief Executive Officer
mbart13@prioritysports.biz
• Brad Ames, President
• Rick Smith, President, Team Operations & General Cou
ricks@prioritysports.biz
• Jeff Roth
jeffr@prioritysports.biz
• Mike Mccartney, Football Operations Director

- Aaron Mintz
- Kenny Zuckerman, President, Athlete Representation
kennyz@prioritysports.biz
- Mark Bartelstein, CEO & Founder
Services:
Represents professional athletes in contract negotiations, endorsements, licensing, personal appearances. Provides clients with general career management and post-career planning. Consults businesses and organizations in all aspects of promotion and sponsorship.
Clients:
Robert Gallery, Marvel Smith, Kurt Warner, Kevin Mawae, Domanick Davis, Brad Hopkins, Alan Faneca, Jake Delhomme, Levi Jones, Adam Timmerman, Tory James, Olin Kreutz, Jon Jansen, Brandon Stokley
Sports Service Founded:
1985

PRIORITY SPORTS & ENTERTAINMENT
325 N LA SALLE
SUITE 650
CHICAGO, IL 60654
312-664-7700
Fax: 312-664-5172
info@prioritysports.biz
www.prioritysports.biz
- Mark Bartelstein, Founder/Chief Executive Officer
mbart13@prioritysports.biz
- Brad Ames, President
- Rick Smith, President, Team Operations & General Cou
ricks@prioritysports.biz
- Jeff Roth
jeffr@prioritysports.biz
- Mike Mccartney, Football Operations Director
- Aaron Mintz
- Kenny Zuckerman, President, Athlete Representation
kennyz@prioritysports.biz
- Mark Bartelstein, CEO & Founder
Services:
Represents professional athletes in contract negotiations, endorsements, licensing, personal appearances. Provides clients with general career management and post-career planning. Consults businesses and organizations in all aspects of promotion and sponsorship.
Clients:
Robert Gallery, Marvel Smith, Kurt Warner, Kevin Mawae, Domanick Davis, Brad Hopkins, Alan Faneca, Jake Delhomme, Levi Jones, Adam Timmerman, Tory James, Olin Kreutz, Jon Jansen, Brandon Stokley
Sports Service Founded:
1985

PRO FOOTBALL ASSOCIATES
10808 DEPOT STREET
WORTH, IL 60482
708-448-3768
Description:
All phases of athlete representation.

PRO FOOTBALL MANAGEMENT
434 NINTH STREET
SAN FRANCISCO, CA 94103
301-717-1748
Fax: 301-881-8642
- Michael Bernstein, Sports Agent

PRO IMAGE, INC.
4401 O'DONNELL STREET
THE CANTON TRADE CENTER
BALTIMORE, MD 21224
410-675-6775
Fax: 410-675-6776
- John Wright, President
Services:
Provides event services, including development, production, promotions, and management for a variety of related fields such as: Graphic Design, Archtecture, Promotions, Talent Negotiations, Entertainment and Marketing
Clients:
The Baltimore Orioles, The University of Maryland, The Baltimore Sun Newspaper, Helix Health Services, The Johns Hopkins University, The Rite Aid Corporation, The Center Club, The National Aquarium, The Maryland Science Center, The Washington Capitals, Signet Bank, The Hyatt Regency Hotel, The Baltimore Zoo, The Office of the Governor of Maryland, The Office of the Mayor of Baltimore, WBAL-TV 11, The Best Western Corporation, Towson University, Bayer Aspirin, The Baltimore Ravens, The Baltimore Arena, The Pier Six Concert Pavilion, etc.
Description:
All phases of athlete representation including contract negotiation, long-range planning, financial planning, and post-career counseling.

PRO PLAYER REPS (PPR, INC.)
34208 AURORA RD.
SUITE 250
CLEVELAND, OH 44139
440-665-1713
Fax: 440-498-1220
info@playersrep.com
www.playersrep.com
- Jerry Lastelick, Attorney
(972) 247-4327
Services:
Serves as Entertainment lawyers
Other Office:
PO Box 29333, Dallas, TX 75229-0333. 972 620-8050; 800 989-7377; FAX: 972 241-6430.
Sports Service Founded:
1989
Athlete Management Services:
Contract negotiation, legal services, general career management for professional athletes in football, basketball, baseball, and representation of Champions Tour golfers.
Marketing & Consulting Services:
Product endorsements, corporate outings, personal appearances, and special engagements.

PRO SPORT MANAGEMENT
8355 E HARTFORD DRIVE
SUITE 105
SCOTTSDALE, AZ 85255
480-368-8434
Fax: 480-368-1905
aa@prosportmanagement.com
www.prosportmanagement.com
- Geoff Ogilvy, Representative Player
- Aaron Baddeley, Representative Player
Golfers Represented:
Stephen Allan, Aaron Baddeley, Henrik Bjornstad, Maria Boden, Matthew Goggin, Richard Johnson, Jeff Klauk, Geoff Ogilvy,

Craig Spence, Henrik Stenson.
Services:
Provides player management services including career management, endorsement negotiations, secretarial services, personal and professional development
Clients:
Aaron, Baddeley, Anders Hansen, Lisa Holm, Steven Jeppesen, Jeff Klauk, John Klauk, Amanda Moltke-Leth, James Oh, Geoff Ogilvy, Aron Price, Craig Spence, Iben Tinning

PRO SPORT MANAGEMENT, INC.
8355 E. HARTFORD DRIVE
SUITE 105
SCOTTSDALE, AZ 85255
480-368-8434
Fax: 480-368-1905
www.prosportmanagement.com
- John F. Geletka, Sports Agent
Services:
Offers all phases of athlete representation including contract negotiation, long-range planning, financial planning, and post-career counseling.

PRO STAR MANAGEMENT, INC.
312 WALNUT STREET
1600 SCRIPPS CENTER
CINCINNATI, OH 45202
513-762-7676
Fax: 513-721-4628
Prostar@fuse.net
www.prostarmanagement.com
- Joe Bick, President
(513) 762-7676
prostar@fuse.net
- Joe Bick, President, Founder
Prostar@fuse.net
Services:
Representation of professional athletes (primarily baseball players) and media personalities. Services include contract negotiations, financial planning and management, endorsements and merchandising.
Year Founded:
1986.

PROFESSIONAL KICKING SERVICES, INC.
3121 JARBRIDGE WAY
SPARKS, NV 89434
775-626-5425
Fax: 775-626-3217
- Ray Pelfrey, Owner/Chief Executive Officer
- Rob Pelfrey, President
- Dusty Apocotos, Senior Staff Instructor
Services:
PKS is football's leading developer of college scholarship talent at all levels. Specific services are: Player Infor Database, Private Lessons, Pro/Free Agent Program
Services:
Provides Player Info Database, private lessons, and pro/free agent program. Creates Kicking shoes, accessories and training gear, and instructional videos.
Sports Service Founded:
1975
Athlete Management Services:
National kicking camps - college, high school free agents. NFL, private pro development program.

professional services

PROFESSIONAL SPORTS CONSULTANTS, INC.
ONE NORTHFIELD PLAZA
NORTHFIELD, IL 60093
847-441-1842
Fax: 847-441-1843
• Francis J. Murtha, President
• Matthew F. Murtha, VP, Stadium/Structures
• Brian Roy, VP, Marketing
Services:
Contract negotiations and financial management for the professional athlete and entertainer. Consulting services for the acquisition and sale of professional sports franchises and sports related assets.

PROFESSIONAL SPORTS MANAGEMENT GROUP
800 UNIVERSITY W
WINDSOR, ON, CANADA N9A 5R9
519-252-7771
Fax: 519-259-1831
www.prosportsmanagement.com
• Patrick J. Ducharme, Sports Agent
• Edward Ducharme, Sports Agent
Services:
Offers all phases of athlete representation including contract negotiation, long-range planning, financial planning, and post-career counseling.
Nature of Sports Service:
All phases of athlete representation including contract negotiation, long-range planning, financial planning, and post-career counseling.

PROFESSIONAL SPORTS MARKETING, INC.
2300 W WHITE AVENUE
SUITE 102
MCKINNEY, TX 75071
214-544-0500
Fax: 214-544-0505
psm@professionalsportsmarketing.com
www.professionalsportsmarketing.com
• Kent Kramer, President
psm@professionalsportsmarketing.com
• Kurt Kramer, VP
psm@professionalsportsmarketing.com
Services:
Research, Creative Planning, Project Design and Implementation, Event Production and Staging, Sponsorship Evaluation and Negotiation, Sponsorship Sales, Public and Media Relations, Program Evaluation and Incentive Sports Travel. Totally integrated sports concept for sports events marketing, promotional programs, setup merchandising and advertising. Sports marketing consulting for corporate clients. Sports incentive travel programs including development and production of corporate.
Services:
Sport Marketing and Advertising
Clients:
Fritolay, Pepsi, Trimega, Ash Almond Associates
Sports Service Founded:
1985
Event Management Services:
Advertising and sales promotion. Specializes in special project events including project design, creative planning, research and event production, sponsorship evaluation and negotiation, public and media relations, program evaluation, incentive travel at major sporting events.

PROFESSIONAL SPORTS PLANNERS
9140 IRVINE CENTER DRIVE
IRVINE, CA 92618
949-752-1010
Fax: 949-833-7960
www.prosportsplanners.com
• Michael M. Watkins, President
(949) 752-1010
• J.D. Sanchez, Esq, Sports Attorney
jdsanchez@prosportsplanners.com
Year Founded:
1985.
Services:
Provides complete contract negotiations, tax and billing services, investment guidance, product endorsement, arbitration and free agency.
Sports Service Founded:
1985.

PROFESSIONAL SPORTS PLANNING
909 FANNIN STREET
TWO HOUSTON CENTER, SUITE 2090
HOUSTON, TX 77010
713-659-2255
800-698-8680
Fax: 713-655-9545
• Carl C. Poston III, Agent
• Kevin D. Poston, President/CEO
Services:
Provides advice and representation for professional athletes.
Clients:
LaVar Arrington, Charles Woodson and Ty Law
Description:
Contract negotiation.

PROFILES SPORTS, INC.
3340 PEACHTREE ROAD, NE
16TH FLOOR
ATLANTA, GA 30326
404-842-7800
Fax: 404-842-7801
• Pat Dye, Jr., President
• Bill Johnson, Executive Vice President
billj500@aol.com
• Michael Perrett, VP Client Development/Marketing
michael@profilessports.com
• Chandra Vitale, COO/Executive Assistant to Pat Dye, Jr.
chandra@profilessports.com
• Randi Chapman, Director Client Services
randi@profilessports.com
• Kevin McGuire, Director Marketing
kevin@profilessports.com
Nature of Service:
At ProFiles, we want our clients to have more than just memories when they leave the game. We want them to be financially secure and prepared for life's challenges after sports.
Clients:
Jeff Backus, Fred Beasley, Michael Bennett, Keith Brooking, Mark Brown, Reggie Brown, Shawn Bryson , Tim Carter, Dexter Coakley, Antonio Cochran, Cosey Coleman, Rod Coleman, Russell Davis, Mike Degory, Heath Evans, Robert Geathers, Charles Grant, David Greene, Roman Harper, Garrison Hearst, Steve Herndon, Montrae Holland, Rueben Houston, Tommy Jackson, Sean Jones, Calvin Pace, Jermaine Phillips,

Mike Pucillo, Kelvin Pritchett, Izell Reese, Tony Richardson, Victor Riley, Dennis Rolland Jr., Justin Smiley, Jon Stinchcomb, Matt Stinchcomb, Demarcus Ware, Marcus Washington, Benjamin Watson, Fred Weary, Charlie Whitehurst, Ben Wilkerson.

PROFORMA SPORTS
810 W. PIONEER PARKWAY
PEORIA, IL 61615
309-692-6390
Fax: 309-692-6397
jeff.brookes@proforma.com
http://www.proforma.com/info

PROMOTION ASSOCIATES GROUP, INC.
3545 E LAYTON AVENUE
CUDAHY, WI 53110
414-747-1711
Fax: 414-747-1714

PROREPS AGENCY, INC./SPORTS STAR
2338 NW PROFESSIONAL DRIVE
CORVALLIS, OR 97330-3881
541-754-1440
Fax: 541-758-4019
• William B. Heck, Sports Agent
Nature of Sports Service:
All phases of athlete representation including contract negotiation, long-range planning, financial planning, and post-career counseling.

PROSTAR ENTERPRISES, INC.
5340 NE 32ND AVENUE
FORT LAUDERDALE, FL 33308
954-202-7792

PROTECT MANAGEMENT CORP.
30699 RUSSELL RANCH ROAD
SUITE 210
WESTLAKE VILLAGE, CA 91362
818-889-2121
Fax: 818-889-2141
www.protectmanagement.com
• Gary Wichard, President/ Chief Executive Officer
• Michael Sasson, VP / Certified MLB Agent
msasson@protectmanagement.com
• Jason Chinn, Public Relations/Marketing
jchinn@protectmanagement.com
• Jason Chinn, Vice President
• Jess Richman, Media and Marketing
• Beth Acker, Execuitve Assistant
Services:
Contract negotiations combined with marketing and public relations services.
Clients:
NFL Client: Jason Taylor, Terrell Suggs, Dwight Freeney, Keith Bulluck, Adam Archuleta, JP Losman, Teddy Lehman, Darren Howard, Tebucky Jones, Dyson Kevin, Stephen Alexander, Eric Hicks, Kevin Curtis, Andre Dyson, Kevin Mitchell, Justin Fargas, Chris Cooley, Brian Jennings, Cliff Russell, Brandon Moore, Johnnie Morant, Tommy Kelly, Grant Wiley, Travis Johnson and Darren Sproles. NBA Client: Wally Szczerbiak. MLB Client: Eric Byrnes, Justin Miller, Scott Cassidy, Jason Hart, Cody McKay, Matt Duff, John Gall, Dee Haynes, Nunez Jose, Gerald Laird and Josh Schmidt. Entertainment Client: Brian Bosworth.

QUATRINI, JAY
30 OLD BURLINGTON STREET
LONDON, ENGLAND W1S 3NL
+44-20-7468-2600
Fax: +44-20-7437-8216
• Vincent Calcara, Associate
(207) 468-5590
vcalcara@davenportlyons.com
• Catherine Baker, Professional Support Lawyer
(207) 468-2713
• Michelle Brown, Associate
(207) 468-5571
mbrown@davenportlyons.com
• Vincenza Calcara, Associate
(207) 468-5590
vcalcara@davenportlyons.com
Services:
Provides leagal services through its five departments, Company & Commercial, Litigation, Property, Employment and Private Client.
Clients:
ABTA, Agnes b, Aardman Animations, Armor Holdings Inc., Ask Central, Baker Street Media Finance Ltd, Barclays Bank plc, Bespoke Couture/Ozwald Boateng, Brand Connection Ltd, British Airways, British Greyhound Racing Board, Broadway Communications Ltd, Business Systems Group Holdings Plc, Capital Radio, Centaur Communications Ltd, Charlton Down Developments Ltd, CIT Group, Contender Entertainment Group, Counterpoint Systems Ltd, Derwent Valley Holdings Plc,Dorling Kindersley Ltd ,Dune ,Ed Victor Ltd, English & Pockett, Epson Europe Ltd, Express Newspapers,First Title Insurance Plc, French Connection Group plc, Fuller Smith & Turner, FX Corpora
Description:
Contract negotiation, represents professional sports teams, licensing, endorsement exploration, teaches sports law.

R.L.R. ASSOCIATES, LTD.
7 W 51ST STREET
4TH FLOOR
NEW YORK, NY 10020
212-541-8641
Fax: 212-541-6052
sgould@rlrassociates.net
www.rlrassociates.net
• Robert L. Rosen, President
rrosen@rlrassociates.net
• Gary I. Rosen, EVP
grosen@rlrassociates.net
• Craig Foster, VP
cfoster@rlrassociates.net
• Robert Rosen, Owner
• Eric Winchel, Manager
• Robert Lewis Rosen, President
Services:
Offers services on career management, talent marketing, content development and content rights sales.
Clients:
PGA, PGA Tour, America's Most Wanted, National Cheerleaders Association, CDT, NCSSE, Kelly Atkinson, Cathy Barreto, David Blatt, Peter Bleckner, Mike Cohen, Jennifer Danska, Chip Dean, Bob Fishman, Earl Freiman, Sandy Grossman, Jim Jennett, Jeff Kay, David Kiviat, Bob Matina, Jeff Mitchell, John Moore, Eric Neuhaus, April Rouge, etc.
Sports Service Founded:

1964
Athlete Management Services:
Full-service representation including, but not limited to, contract negotiation, financial and career planning, and endorsement opportunities for sports broadcasting executives and on-air professionals, sports associations, and sports authors, nationally and internationally.
Event Management Services:
Negotiates domestic and international television license fees and arranges for television sponsorship of events.
Marketing & Consulting Services:
Represents and negotiates television contracts for sportscasters, directors and producers.
Clients Include:
Dave Barnett (Announcer - ESPN), Tim Brando (CBS Sports), Bill Daughtry (Host, SportsDesk - MSG), Marques Johnson (FOX Sports Net), Ralph Kiner (Mets), Bob Ley (ESPN), Verne Lundquist (Turner Sports, CBS Sports), Tim McCarver (FOX Sports, SF Giants), Billy Packer (CBS Sports, ESPN), Gary Thorne (ESPN), Joe Torre (Mgr - NY Yankees).

RAD & ASSOCIATES
58 PARKWAY W
MOUNT VERNON, NY 10552
914-668-7898
Fax: 914-668-2575
rad58phd@aol.com
• Dick Dolce, President
• Glenn L Dolce, VP
Services:
Develops and provides licensing and merchandising consultation to professional athletes for product endorsements, promotions and media strategies.
Sports Service Founded:
1987
Athlete Management Services:
Develops and provides licensing and merchandising consultation to professional athletes for product endorsements, promotions and media strategies.
Event Management Services:
Secures corporate sponsorship for sports/special events. Manages, handle all aspects including licensing, merchandising and event concession sales in connection with event.
Marketing & Consulting Services:
Serve as consultant to national governing bodies, organizations, corporations and major manufacturers interested in achieving or maintaining specific licensing, merchandising or sales promotion goals through the use of sports. Consulting services include licensing feasibility, program objectives, licensing plans, policies and procedures. Assists manufacturers in search, evaluation, negotiation and acquisition of sport licenses.

RALEIGH CYCLE
6004 S 190TH STREET
SUITE 101
KENT, WA 98032
253-395-1100
800 222-5527
Fax: 253-872-0257
www.raleighusa.com
• Sharon Robinson, CFO

Products:
Raleigh bicycles either for fitness, commuting, racing, or just cruising with family and friends.
Brands:
Raleigh Performance Comfort Road: Cadent 5.0 2006, Cadent 4.0 2006, Cadent 3.0 2006, Cadent 2.0 2006, and Cadent 1.0 2006. Raleigh Road: Rush Hour 2006, Team 2006, Prestige 2006, Competition 2006, Supercourse 2006, Grand Prix 2006, Grand Sport 2006, Sport 2006, Route 66 2006, Route 24 2006 and Route 1 2006. Raleigh Hybrid: Passage 5.0 2006, Passage 4.0 2006 and Passage 3.0 2006. Raleigh Full Suspension: Phase 2 2006, Phase 1 2006 and Phase 2006. Raleigh MTN Hardtail: Mojave 8.0 2006, Mojave 5.5 2006, Mojave 5.0 2006, Mojave 4.0 2006, Mojave 4.5 2006 and Mojave 2.0 2006. Raleigh Comfort: Venture 5.0 2006, Venture 4.0 2006, Venture 3.0 2006
Services:
Athlete Management: Bicycle racers/race teams and triathletes
Event Management Services:
Bicycle races.
Year Founded:
1896

RAWLINGS, GEORGE R.
325 W MAIN STREET
SUITE 1700, WATERFRONT PLAZA
LOUISVILLE, KY 40202
502-587-1279
800-928-1279
Fax: 502-584-8580
Services:
Provides all phases of athlete representation including contract negotiation, long-range planning, financial planning, and post-career counseling.

RELLIHAN, JERRY J.
895 E WALNUT STREET
RAYMORE, MO 64083
816-322-6777
Fax: 816-322-6719
jerry@rellihanlaw.com
www.rellihanlaw.com
• Jerry Rellihan, Contact
jerry@rellihanlaw.com
Year Founded:
1984.
Services:
Provides legal assistance on Estate Planning.
Description:
Contract negotiation.

REMICK, LLOYD Z.
1650 MARKET STREET
56TH FLOOR
ONE LIBERTY PLACE
PHILADELPHIA, PA 19103-7334
215-790-1155
Fax: 215-575-3801
www.zanemanagement.com
• Lloyd Zane Remick, President/Chief Executive Officer
(215) 790-1155
remick@braverlaw.com
Nature of Service:
Provides personal management, contract negotiation, expert witness testimony, event planning, hospitality & tourism, appearances & endorsements and accounting & tax

services for Boxing, Football, Music, Authors, Movies and Television.
Year Founded:
1978

REYNOLDS SPORTS MANAGEMENT
3850 VINE STREET
SUITE 230
RIVERSIDE, CA 92507
951-784-6333
Fax: 951-784-1451
Info@Reynoldssports.com
www.reynoldssports.com
• Larry Reynolds, Founder/President
• Patrick Murphy, COO
• Mike Dillon, Executive Vice President
• Terry Jones, Vice President of Baseball Operations
• Doreen Hurtado, Director of Client Services
• Erika Moore, Executive Assistant / Director of Special Pro
• Larry Reynolds, President/CEO
Description:
Contract negotiation, post career planning, arbitration hearings, endorsement exploration, tort actions/litigation.
Services:
Provides assistance on Contract negotiation, Salary arbitration, Marketing and endorsement development, Income tax preparation assistance, Financial management coordination, Secondary career planning and management, Web page development and maintenance and Real estate and personal property purchasing assistance.
Clients:
Major League Roster: (40 man) Reggie Abercrombie: Florida Marlins,Boof Bonser: Minnesota Twins, Chad Cordero: Washington Nationals, Matt Diaz: Atlanta Braves, Carl Everett: Seattle Mariners, Joey Gathright: Tampa Bay Devil Rays, Chad Gaudin: Oakland Athletics, aTroy Hawkins: Baltimore Orioles, Ryan Howard: Philadelphia Phillies, Torii Hunter: Minnesota Twins, Scott Tyler: Florida Marlins, B.J. Upton: Tampa Bay Devil Rays and Mitch Wylie: NY Mets. Minor League Roster: Nick Bourgeois: Seattle Mariners, Ryan Christianson: Tampa Bay Devil Rays, Thomas Diamond: Texas Rangers, Clint Everts: Washington Nationals, Kiel Fisher: Philadelphia Phillies

RICE & RICE
100 E LINCOLNWAY
SUITE 1
VALPARAISO, IN 46383
219-462-0809
800-303-7423
Fax: 219-531-8644
www.riceandrice.com
• Bruce N. Adams, Partner
• Bruce Mi Rice, Attorney
Description:
Contract negotiation.
Services:
Provides legal assistance on Family Law.

RICHARD HOWELL SPORTS MANAGEMENT, INC.
2964 PEACHTREE ROAD
SUITE 330
ATLANTA, GA 30305

404-842-1556
Fax: 404-842-1586
• Richard S. Howell, Sports Agent
Nature of Sports Service:
Provides a full range of agency services to professional athletes including team contract negotiations, marketing endorsements and career counseling.

RILEY & HURLEY, P.C.
19853 W OUTER DRIVE
SUITE 100
DEARBORN, MI 48124
313-565-1330
Fax: 313-565-1318
rfrpc@rileyhurley.com
www.rileyhurley.com
• Robert F. Riley, Partner
rriley@rileyhurley.com
• William C. Hurley, Partner
whurley@rileyhurley.com
Services:
Represents sports associations and organizations; litigation, arbitration and negotiations.

RILEY, WILLIAM T., JR.
500 E PRATT STREET
SUITE 200
BALTIMORE, MD 21202
410-783-4900
Fax: 410-727-0460
www.reznickgroup.com
• William T. Riley Jr, Managing Principal
(410) 783-4900
bill.riley@reznickgroup.com
• Ryan Duckworth, National Conferences/Events
(404) 497-8960
Services:
All phases of athlete representation including contract negotiation, long-range planning, financial planning and income tax planning and preparation.
Clients:
Corporate Executives, Business Owners and Enterpreneurs; Government Professionals; Healthcare Administrators; Leadership and Investors; Nonprofit Professionals

RMI/ATLANTA
2498 JETT FERRY ROAD
SUITE 100
ATLANTA, GA 30338
770-399-9668
Fax: 770-391-9518
• Doug Messerlie, Founder
• Greg Thornton, Marketing Assistant
Services:
Research and Analysis, Marketing, Promotional ans Sponsorship Management, Event Management and Customer Entertainment, Public Relations, Media & Communications, Measurements and Return on Investment Documentation, Sponsorship Opportunities
Clients:
AT&T Racing, Siemens, Burger King, Dynoject, Ericsson, Dassault Systemes, PPG Industries, Perrier, Motorola Racing, Mighty, Turner, Cartoon Network, Caterpillar, Rotozip, Sylvania 300, Superchips, MSD Ignition, Stanley
Marketing & Consulting Services:
Creates and implements sports marketing strategies for corporations desiring to

promote their products and services through auto racing, events and related activities, including event management, public relations, promotions, research analysis and sponsor relations.
Sports Service Founded:
1989

ROSENBLATT, GERALD F.
2049 CENTURY PARK E
SUITE 3180
LOS ANGELES, CA 90067
310-393-5345
• Gerald F. Rosenblatt, Attorney
gerrysmusiclaw@aol.com
Services:
Contract negotiation, endorsement exploration. Represents athletes and entertainers.

ROSENHAUS SPORTS MANAGEMENT
6400 ALLISON ROAD
MIAMI BEACH, FL 33141-4540
305-936-1093
Fax: 305-864-3731
www.rosenhaussports.com
• Drew Rosenhaus, Chief Executive Officer
drosenhaus@aol.com
Services:
Contract negotiation, investment contract negotiation, provides investment advice.
Clients:
Clinton Portis (NFL Denver Broncos), Jeremy Shockey (NFL NY Giants), Wiillis McGahee (NFL Bullfalo Bills).

RUDER/FINN SPORTS, INC.
301 E 57TH STREET
NEW YORK, NY 10022
212-593-6400
www.ruderfinn.com
• David Finn, Chairman
• Kathy Bloomgarden, Chief Executive Officer
• Michael Schubert, Chief Innovation Officer
Services:
Health care marketing activities, developing a premier position in science programming, Corporate Relations, Public Affairs, Government Affairs, Professional and Financial Services, Investor Relations, Consumer/Product Marketing, Lifestyle Marketing, High Tech, Visual Technology, Design/Publishing, Crisis Communications, Travel/Hospitality, International
Services:
National network of event managers and promotional specialists help maximize sponsor identification with sporting events. Contacts with national and local print and broadcast media offers combination of event experience and publicity background. Aids clients in identifying which sports and events best fit marketing needs. Strong association with athletes and sports organizations gives R/F an ad hoc panel of experts to routinely approach for consulting services.
Sports Service Founded:
1986
Marketing & Consulting Services:
Aids clients in identifying which sports and events best fit marketing needs. Strong association with athletes and sports organizations gives R/F an ad hoc panel of experts to routinely approach for consulting services.
Other Offices:

professional services

861

Chicago, Washington DC, Beijing, Guangzhou, Hong Kong, Shanghai, Singapore, London and paris.

RUNGE, JOHN B.
2011 E. LAMAR BOULEVARD
SUITE 200
ARLINGTON, TX 76006
817-336-5355
Fax: 817-336-0432
www.rungefirm.com
Description:
Contract negotiation.

SAMMS, GREGORY A.
225 ALCAZAR AVENUE
CORAL GABLES, FL 33134
786-953-5802
Fax: 305-446-3538
sammslaw@gmail.com
www.gregsamms.com
Services:
All phases of athlete representation including contract negotiation, long-range planning, financial planning, and post-career counseling.

SANDERS, FREDRIC M.
120 BROADWAY
NEW YORK, NY 10271
212-810-2400
Fax: 212-810-2410
• Fredric M. Sanders, Partner
(212) 810-2400
Description:
Tax specialist.

SAXTON COMMUNICATIONS INC.
1448 HOLLYWOOD AVENUE
LANGHORNE, PA 19047-7417
215-752-7797
Fax: 215-752-1518
ESAXTON144@AOL.COM
www.saxtonsponsormarket.com
• Eric Saxton, Member
(267) 934-7286
ESAXTON144@AOL.COM
Other Offices:
Daytona Beach, FL; Norristown, PA
Sports Service Founded:
1970
Athlete Management Services:
Sponsorship representation, public relations, marketing, preparation of support materials (kits, releases, etc.), program books created, sponsorship and marketing consultation.
Event Management Services:
Brings together motorsports events and participants with sponsors, public relations, publicity, program books, newsletters, advertising, promotion.
Marketing & Consulting Services:
Advising clients on how they can fit into motorsports with sponsorship, merchandising and promotional programs. Publishes ERNIE SAXTON'S MOTORSPORTS SPONSORSHIP MARKETING NEWS, a monthly newsletter on marketing and sponsorship in motorsports.
Clients Include:
Eastern Motorsports Press Association, Grandview Speedway, Rising Star Publishing, Pennzoil Motorsports Show, Martin Brothers Tractor Racing Team, Ranger Joe Cyphen Monster Truck Team.

SCHAEFFER, RICHARD L.
8700 HEARTH STONE WAY
GRAND LEDGE, MI 48837
517-627-6530
Services:
Contract negotiation, post career planning, investment contract negotiation, arbitration hearings, endorsement exploration, tort actions/litigation.

SCHIFF HARDIN LLP
233 S WACKER DRIVE
6600 SEARS TOWER
CHICAGO, IL 60606
312-258-5500
Fax: 312-258-5600
www.schiffhardin.com
• Thomas W. Abendroth, Partner
(312) 258-5600
tabendroth@schiffhardin.com
• John F. Adams, Counsel
(312) 258-5541
jadams@schiffhardin.com
Description:
Represents professional sports teams (Chicago Bears).
Services:
Represents professional sports teams (Chicago Bears).
Year Founded:
1864
Other Locations:
Washington DC, New York NY, Lake Forest IL, Atlanta GA

SCHOEPPLER, KURT J.
1360 E 9TH STREET
IMG CENTER
SUITE #100
CLEVELAND, OH 44114-1737
216-522-1200
Fax: 216-522-1145
martin.jolly@imgworld.com
www.imgworld.com
• Ian Todd, President
• Theodore J. Forstmann, Chairman/CEO
tforstmann@imgworld.com
• Robert Ryder, EVP and Chief Financial Officer
rryder@imgworld.com
• Alastair Johnston, Co-Chief Executive Officer
ajohnston@imgworld.com
Services:
Contract negotiation.
Other Locations:
IMG MODELS, 304 Park Avenue South, Penthouse North 12th Floor, New York, NY 10010; Phone: 212-253-8884; 20 Guest Street, STE 400, Brighton Landing East, Brighton, MA 02135; Phone: 617-783-9032; 5301 Wisconsin Avenue, NW, STE 425, Washington, DC 20015; Phone: 202-964-8500; W - 2370 One PPG Place, pittsburgh, PA 15222; Phone: 412-391-4927; 175 Bloor Street East, STE 400, South Tower, Toronto, Ontario, CAN M4W 3R8; Phone: 416-960-5312; 2 Bryant Street, STE 150, San Francisco, CA 94105; Phone: 415-227-8000; 150 Athambra Circle, STE 825, Coral Gables, Fl 33134; Phone: 305-446-220

SCHULEFAND, KEITH
1301 N. FOREST ROAD
WILLIAMSVILLE, NY 14221

716-568-4453
888-499-1552
Fax: 716-565-1575
schulefand@hotmail.com
www.schulefandlawoffice.com
• Keith Schulefand, Esquire
(716) 632-5919
schulefand@hotmail.com
Services:
All phases of athlete representation including contract negotiation, long-range planning, financial planning, and post-career counseling.

SCOTT BORAS CORPORATION
2100 MAIN STREET
SUITE 300
IRVINE, CA 92714
949-833-1818
Fax: 949-833-1816
• Scott Boras, President and Owner
Services:
Agent for professional baseball players. It represented many of the highest-paid players in baseball.

SCRIMMAGE LINE SPORTS
917 E 543 ROAD
LAWRENCE, KS 66047
785-295-6275
Fax: 785-266-7819
• Aaron G. Hove, Sports Agent
Nature of Sports Service:
All phases of athlete representation including contract negotiation, long-range planning, financial planning, and post-career counseling.

SEA BROWN & ASSOCIATES
9200 BASIL COURT
SUITE 203
LANDOVER, MD 20785
301-322-8907
Fax: 301-322-4583
Services:
All phases of athlete representation including contract negotiation, long-range planning, financial planning, and post-career counseling.

SENIOR MANAGEMENT GROUP
125 STRAFFORD AVE
SUITE 112
WAYNE, PA 19087
610-293-1500
Fax: 610-293-1504
www.seniormg.com
• Brett W. Senior, Senior Partner
(610) 941-0770
Brett@seniormg.com
• D. Ch Le Vine, Financial Services Director
(610) 941-0770
Chris@seniormg.com
• Susan W. O'Donnell, Attorney
(610) 941-0770
susan@seniormg.com
• Terri V. McGrath, Manager
(610) 941-0770
tmcgrath@seniormg.com
Description:
Representing hundreds of professional athletes, coaches and management/owners from the sports industry.
Services:
Legal, tax, accounting and investment advisory services to actively and objectively advocate the clients' interest in the

marketplace - delivering superior service, performance and fiduciary peace of mind
Clients:
Joe Paterno: Penn State University Head Coach; Bill Parcells: Dallas Cowboys Head Coach; Robbie Gould: Placekicker, Chicago Bears; Frank Chamberlin: Linebacker, Houston, Texas; Jamie Bestwick: BMX X-Games Champion

SENIOR TOUR PLAYERS, INC.
1244 BOYLSTON STREET
SUITE 200
CHESTNUT HILL, MA 02467
617-266-3600
Services:
Represents and arranges for the services of the Champions Tour Golf Professionals. Events include corporate and charity pro-ams, speaking engagements, clinics, and golf community developments.
Services:
Event Management: Total golf event management and design; sponsorship sales. Marketing & Consulting: Specializes in residential golf course communities providing full marketing and consulting services in all aspects of the project including market studies, financial presentations, design, etc.

SENNET, CHARLES J.
435 N MICHIGAN AVENUE
TRIBUNE COMPANY
STE 600
CHICAGO, IL 60611
312-222-9100
Fax: 312-222-4206
www.tribune.com
• Samuel Zell, Chairman/Chief Executive Officer
• Chandler Bigelow, CFO
• Crane H. Kenney, SVP/General Counsel & Secretary
(312) 222-9100
• Thomas D. Leach, SVP, Development
(312) 222-9100
Services:
Publishing and broadcasting.
Description:
Contract negotiation, represents professional sports teams, licensing.

SFX SPORTS GROUP
5335 WISCONSIN AVENUE NW
SUITE 850
WASHINGTON, DC 20015
202-686-2000
Fax: 202-686-5050
www.sfxsports.com
• James R. Steiner, President
• David Falk, Chairman and Chief Executive Officer
• Tim J. Hoy, Executive Officer
• John Mascatello, President SFX Golf
• Bud Martin, Senior Vice President, SFX Sports
• Jim Lehman, Senior Vice President, SFX Golf
Nature of Service:
Provides full-service representation to its athlete clients. Our services include contract negotiation and all 'off-the-field' business and marketing endeavors, including endorsements, licensing, financial planning, promotions, charitable pursuits, speaking engagements, and personal appearances.

Events:
American Century Golf Championships, Heineken Classic, The Minnesota Golf Show, Rock-N-Racquets, Bob Hope Chrysler Classic, Legg Mason Tennis Classic, NFL Sporting Clays Team Challenge, Scholarship America Showdown.
Clients:
Jerry Rice, Cadillac Williams, Pedro Martinez, David Ortiz, Andre Agassi, Andy Roddick, Tom Lehman, and Andrew Bogut are just a few of the many top names in sports who choose SFX.

SFX SPORTS GROUP, INC.
5335 WISCONSIN AVENUE, NW
SUITE 850
WASHINGTON, DC 20015
202-686-2000
Fax: 202-686-5050
• Tim J. Hoy, Executive Officer
• David J Falk, Chairman and Chief Executive Officer
Services:
Baseball: Negotiation of Baseball Contracts (including winter ball, where appropriate); Representation in Salary Arbitration; Development and Updating of a Budget and Financial Plan; Preparation of All Tax Returns; Negotiation of Off-field Contracts, Including Product Endorsements & Appearances; Day-to-Day Personal & Financial Assistance
year founded:
1999
Nature of Sports Services:
Sports Marketing firm and talent agency representing athletes.

SHANNON PROFESSIONAL MANAGEMENT
313 N BIRCH AVENUE
SANTA ANA, CA 92701
714-542-3592
Services:
All phases of athlete representation including contract negotiation, long-range planning, financial planning, and post-career counseling.

SHAPIRO MANAGEMENT
2147 N BEACHWOOD DRIVE
LOS ANGELES, CA 90068
323-469-9452
Fax: 801-653-6571
burtjay@mail.com
www.burtshapiro.com
• Burt J. Shapiro, President
(323) 469-9452
burtjay@mail.com
Services:
Represents on-air broadcasters (anchors, sportscasters, weathercasters, reporters, hosts) news managers, producers,etc., represents actors, comedians, sports personalities, writers, directors, producers, etc.
Clients:
Ray Brune—-Exec. Prod./ABC's World News Now, Sr Prod/KTLA-TV;Lisa Darr—-Actress—numerous series, pilots, guest starring roles; Natasha Pavlova—numerous guest starring roles; Dorothy Malone—Oscar winning actress; Amy Jacobson—Reporter/WMAQ-TV; Jim Von Fleet—-Weathercaster/WOFL-TV; Tim Brando—-Host/Anchor, Play-by-Play/ESPN;

Karie Ross—-Anchor/Reporter/ESPN, Sports News Network, WTVJ-TV; Lola Martinez—-Weather Anchor/CNN Int.; Hiram Enriquez—Host/Anchor/Reporter/CNN en Espanol; Max Bretos—-Play-by-Play/Fox Sports Net; Mauricio Guevara—Play-by-Play/Fox Sports Net; Naibe Reynoso—Host/Radio Visa,Rep/Anchor/ KWGN-TV; Ricardo Fernan
Marketing & Consulting Services:
Sports management, marketing and leisure time marketing. Consultant to corporations and advertising agencies interested in achieving or maintaining specific marketing or sales promotions through the use of sports.
Event Management Services:
Summer camps, clinics, coordinates programs to assist companies in promoting their products and/or services.
Athlete Management Services:
Contract negotiation, appearances, endorsements, commercials, athlete career management and planning, theatrical planning, as well as financial management. In addition, represents sports broadcasters with network and local stations.
Sports Service Founded:
1986

SHAW SPORTS & ENTERTAINMENT
4819 S PARK AVENUE
HAMBURG, NY 14075
716-648-3020
Fax: 716-648-3730
www.shawsports.net
• Joseph H. Shaw, President
Nature of Sports Service:
All phases of athlete representation including contract negotiation, long-range planning, financial planning, and post-career counseling.

SHEEHY, NEIL K.
7760 FRANCE AVENUE SOUTH
SUITE 1100
MINNEAPOLIS, MN 55435
612-340-0261
neilksheehy@msn.com
• Neil K. Sheehy, Lawyer/Sports Agent
(612) 340-0261
NeilKSheehy@msn.com
• Timothy K. Sheehy, NHLPA Certified Agent
(508) 624-4556
tksheehy@aol.com
Description:
Contract negotiation, Endorsements, Career Advertisement
Services:
Represents professional athletes and media personalities, negotiates rookie contracts for first round draft choices in all four major sports- hockey, basketball, baseball and football.
Clients:
Sheehy Hockey, LLC.

SHEPLEY AGENCY
3109 W 6TH STREET
SUITE A
LAWRENCE, KS 66049
785-865-5200
Fax: 785-865-0643
• Vickie Shepley
(785) 865-5200

Description:
Contract negotiation.
Services:
Insurance Carriers

SHERMAN SPECIALTY COMPANY
300 JERICHO QUADRANGLE
SUITE 240
JERICHO, NY 11753
516-861-6420
800-645-6513
Fax: 516-861-1034
info@ShermanSpecialty.com
Products:
Toys and gifts with sports logos and
designs.

SHOENFELT SPORTS MANAGEMENT
2109 PERKINS ROAD
BATON ROUGE, LA 70808
225-336-4300
800-291-8452
Fax: 225-336-4350
info@shoenfeltlaw.com
• Oscar Shoenfelt, Owner/Sports Agent
(225) 336-4300
• Katie Shoenfelt, Partner
Services:
Medical malpractice, personal injury &
sports law firm
Clients:
Dwayne Missouri; Rufus Porter; and Willie
Williams, Ervin Johnson and Stanley
Roberts

SIMS, JR. JAMES A.
760 LONGRIDGE ROAD
OAKLAND, CA 94610
510-444-4974
Fax: 510-834-4456
JamesASims@aol.com
www.simssports.com
• James A. Sims Jr, President/Principal
(510) 444-4974
JamesASims@aol.com
• Jeremy Veit, Player Relations
Administrator
(510) 444-4974
JMVeit@aol.com
Services:
Full-service sports management firm
dedicated to providing the absolute highest
quality representation possible Contract,
Negotiation and Legal Services, Financial
and Investment Monitoring, Tax Services
and Estate Planning, Marketing,
Endorsements and Public Relations,
Combine Preparation, Career and Business
Planning, Talent Development, Charitable
and Philanthropic Services, Event Planning
and Coordination.
Clients:
Partial List of Players Represented in the
NFL, Jamal Anderson, Eugene Wilson,
Takeo Spikes, Rob Burnett, Tully
Banta-Cain, La'Roi Glover, Deltha O'Neal,
BJ Tucker, DeJuan Green, Wendell Hunter,
Johnny Johnson, First Rounders, Andre
Rison, Leonard Renfro, Takeo Spikes,
Deltha O'Neal, Second Rounders, Robert
Blackmon, Bruce Walker, Anthony Cook,
Dedric Mathis, Jeremy Newberry, Eugene
Wilson, Middle & Late Rounders, Fred
Beasley, Leonardo Carson, Troy Dumas,
Sam Garnes, Kahlil Hill, Monty Montgomery,
Pro Bowlers, Jamal Anderson, Robert

Blackmon, Rob Burnett, Johnny Johnson,
La'Roi Glover, Larry Whingham.

SMITH MOORE LEATHERWOOD, LLP
300 N GREENE STREET
SUITE 1400
GREENSBORO, NC 27401
336-378-5200
Fax: 336-378-5400
www.smithmoorelaw.com
• Erik Albright, Attorney
(336) 378-5368
erik.albright@smithmoorelaw.com
• Alan W. Duncan, Business Litigation
Nature of Sports Service:
Mr. Albright has represented sports
organizations and individuals for 20 years.
He represents collegiate conferences,
professional sports franchises, sports
venues, and event organizers. He previously
represented professional football and
baseball players.

SMITHERMAN, RODGER
2029 2ND AVENUE N
BIRMINGHAM, AL 35203
205-322-0012
Fax: 205-324-2000
rodger.smitherman@alsenate.gov
• Rodger Smithermanq, Senator
(205) 322-3768
rodger.smitherman@alsenate.gov

SPAIN & GILLON, LLC
2117 2ND AVENUE N
THE ZINSZER BUILDING
BIRMINGHAM, AL 35203
205-328-4100
Fax: 205-324-8866
www.spain-gillon.com
• David S. Maxey, Partner
(205) 581-6232
dsm@spain-gillon.com
• Scott B. Hannon, System
Administrator/Webmaster
• Jarrod Br Bazemore, Partner
(205) 581-6235
jbb@spain-gillon.com
• Steve R. Burford, Partner
(205) 581-6247
• Jarrod B. Bazemore, Attorney
• Brian V. Cash, Attorney
• James E. Ferguson, III, Attorney
(205) 581-6289
jef@spain-gillon.com
• Samuel H. Frazier, Of Counsel
(205) 581-6225
shf@spain-gillon.com
• Frederick M. Garfield, Partner
(205) 581-6259
fmg@spain-gillon.com
Services:
Administrative Law, Appellate Practice,
Arbitration and Mediation Services,
Bankruptcy, Business, Corporate Law &
Litigation, Civil Liability, Class Actions,
Commercial Transactions, Commercial
Transportation Litigation, Construction,
Consumer Fraud and Bad Faith, Corporate
Taxation, Environmental & Toxic Tort
Claims, ERISA, Errors & Omissions
Defense, Estate Planning and
Administration of Estates, Fidelity & Surety,
General Insurance Matters, Governmental,
Health & Hospital, Labor and Employment,
Life and Health Insurance Defense, Medical
& Professional Malpractice, Mergers and

Acquisitions, Pharmaceuticals and Medical
Devices.

SPARTA GROUP MEDIA/COACHES, INC.
140 LITTLETON ROAD
SUITE 100
PARSIPPANY, NJ 07054
973-335-0550
Fax: 973-335-2148
Frontdesk@thespartagroup.com
thespartagroup.com
• Craig E. Fenech, President
• Michael Nicotera, Senior Partner, Director
of Baseball Operatio
miken@thespartagroup.com
• Gene Casaleggio, Senior Partner, Director
of Player Developmen
Genec@thespartagroup.com
• William R. Boyd, Chief Financial Officer
Billb@thespartagroup.com
Clients:
Coaches: John Calipari (NCAA), Fran
Fraschilla (NCAA)
Media Personalities: Mike Breen, Mike Francesa,
John Sterling, Suzyn Waldman
Description:
All phases of athlete management.

SPITZ, ROBERT J.
204 N SAN ANTONIO AVENUE
ONTARIO, CA 91762
909-395-0909
Fax: 909-395-9535
TPLaw@aol.com
www.robertspitzlaw.com
• Robert J. Spitz, Attorney
tplaw@aol.com
Year Founded:
1975
Description:
Legal services, contracts and negotiations

SPORT MANAGEMENT, INC.
5805 CHANDLER COURT
WESTERVILLE, OH 43082
614-899-9476
Marketing & Consulting Services:
Sports marketing and management agency
representing athletes, venues and teams in
regard to sale promotions and sponsorship
procurement.

**SPORTRUST ASSOCIATES
INTERNATIONAL**
823 22ND STREET
SANTA MONICA, CA 90403
310-829-1747
Fax: 310-315-0424
• Ronald M. Del Duca Jr, Sports Agent
Nature of Sports Service:
All phases of athlete representation
including contract negotiation, long-range
planning, financial planning, and post-career
counseling.

SPORTS & SPONSORSHIPS, INC.
4000 HOLLYWOOD BOULEVARD
SUITE 755
SOUTH HOLLYWOOD, FL 33021
954-334-5930
Fax: 954-206-0360
info@sportsandsponsorships.com
www.sportsandsponsorships.com
• Scott Becher, President
scott@sportsandsponsorships.com
Services:
Strategic Planning, Representation, Event

Marketing
Clients:
Bristol-Myers Squibb Company, Cancun, Clairol, Skis Dynastar, Sports, FPL, Foot Locker, Fox Sports, Gillette, Hershey's, Sprint, FIFA, Florida Marlins, Crock Pot, Major League Baseball, NASCAR, NFL, NHL, NCAA

SPORTS BUSINESS ASSOCIATES, LLC
3 BENTLEY DRIVE
FRANKLIN LAKES, NJ 7417
201-697-2436
Fax: 201-581-0277
• James Santomier, Jr, PhD, Founder
(203) 697-2436
Description:
Provides critical intelligence to the sport industry and educational community worldwide. It offers a portfolio of in-depth reports and publications focusing on marketing, sponsorship, hospitality, media and broadcasting, new media, finance, globalization, licensed merchandise, and sport business education, as well as sport and country specific reports.

SPORTS IMPACT, INC.
60 E 42ND STREET
SUITE 726
NEW YORK, NY 10165-0721
212-697-0530
Fax: 212-697-0533
• Robert F. Corrao, Chairman/Chief Executive Officer
Services:
Offers sports celebrities as hosts of promotional events.
Other Address:
14 Diane Court, Katonah, NY 10536
Budget:
$1,000,000-$2,499,999
Sports Service Founded:
1984
Event Management Services:
Incorporates promotional opportunities in advertising packages.
Marketing & Consulting Services:
Produces and publishes magazines (NBA and NHL teams), distributed within the arenas and directly to season ticket holders homes.

SPORTS LINK, INC.
2033 W MCDERMOTT DRIVE
SUITE # 320-260
ALLEN, TX 75013
972-608-8818
888-727-7332
Fax: 972-608-8805
• Kyle Kramer, Founder
Services:
provides services and systems to maximize the usage and investments of companies that own or want to own season tickets, luxury suites of that sponsor teams and events.
year founded
1998

SPORTS LOOP
500 LAKE COOK ROAD
SUITE 350
DEERFIELD, IL 60015
847-797-0900
Fax: 888-253-5997

• Roy D. Kessel, President/General Counsel
rkessel@sportsloop.com
• Pete Force, VP-Business Development
pforce@sportsloop.com
• John Rudnick, VP-Technology
jrudnick@sportsloop.com
• John Morrison, Sports Management Associate
jmorrison@sportsloop.com
Services:
professional representation for athletes and entertainers, event management, sports marketing, corporate consulting, brand management, and hospitality services.
Description:
full service sports and entertainment firm providing innovative and sound approaches to meeting its clients objectives.

SPORTS MANAGEMENT AND MARKETING, INC.
1481 DOMINION COURT
PITTSBURGH, PA 15241
412-257-1900
Fax: 412-257-5939
SMMI@aol.com
www.sportsmmi.com
• John I. Nubani, President
SMMI@aol.com
• William Parise, Football Manager
SMMI@aol.com
• Jack Pierce, Track and Field Manager
SMMI@aol.com
Services:
Contract negotiations, Personal development of the athlete, Sports Promotions and Special Events
Clients:
Track and Field: Ibrahim Aden, Tacita Bass, Kameisha Bennett, Brahim Boulami, Khalid Boulami, Christian Cantwell, Lachlan Chrisholm, Jearl Miles Clark, Karol Damon, Dawn Ellerbe, Lindel Frater, Joe Greene, Abdelkader Hachlaf, MaryJayne Harrelson, Micah Harris, Kenny Harrison, Mohammed El Hattab, Aubrey Herring, Godfrey Herring, Nick Hysong, Denis Kholev, Kris Kuehl, Jeff Laynes, Nathan Leeper, Kevin Little, Jud Logan, Brian Miller, Virginia Miller, Maurice Mitchell, Emily Morris, Justin Norberg, Tracy O'Hara, Kjersti Platzer, Shanelle Porter, Mike Power, Connie Price-Smith, Rachid Ramzi, Todd Riech, Sean Robbins, Karol Rovelto, Tim Rusan, Sco

SPORTS MANAGEMENT GROUP WORLDWIDE, INC./SMGW
4041 UNIVERSITY DRIVE
SUITE 400
FAIRFAX, VA 22030
703-273-4640
Fax: 703-273-1130
www.smgwinc.com
• Dominick A Pilli, President and Chief Contract Advisor
dominick.pilli@gmail.com
Description:
SMGW, Inc. is a premier sports marketing and management firm consisting of clients from the major professional sports leagues and their respective Hall of Fames.
Year Founded:
1988
Nature of Services:
Contractional negotiations, representation agreements and marketing agreements.
Clients:

Clients originate from the major sports leagues and associations, not limited to MLB, NFL, NHL, NBA, and the Golf, Tennis, Soccer and Olympic areas.

SPORTS PERSONALITIES, INC.
3328 COMMERCIAL AVENUE
NORTHBROOK, IL 60062
508-877-6150
847-272-7892
info@personalitiesinc.com
www.personalitiesinc.com
• Michael Carey, President
Services:
All facets of athlete agency representation and management, including financial and marketing negotiations and contracts.

SPORTS STARS INTERNATIONAL, INC.
18485 MACK AVENUE
GROSSE POINTE FARMS
DETROIT, MI 48236-3242
313-886-9140
Fax: 313-886-0559
info@SportsStarsInternational.com
www.sportsstarsinternational.com
• Peter J. Huthwaite, President
Services:
Represent professional athletes in football, basketball, ice hockey, baseball, tennis. All phases of representation - negotiations, endorsements, financial planning and consulting.
Sports Services Founded:
1968.

SPORTS WEST FOOTBALL
27084 GRANDVIEW AVENUE
HAYWARD, CA 94542
510-888-9211
Fax: 510-581-6512
• Angelo Wright, President
(510) 553-7031
Services:
Contract negotiation

SPORTSTARS, INC
1370 AVENUE OF THE AMERICAS
19TH FLOOR
NEW YORK, NY 10019
212-757-4044
Fax: 212-765-4833
www.sportstarsnyc.com

SPORTSWORLD CONSULTANTS
14 SUPREME COURT
GAITHERSBURG, MD 20878
301-977-3735
• Leonard J. Levy, President
(301) 977-3735
Services:
Representation of athletes, including promotion, contract negotiation, and tax and financial services.
Sports Service Founded:
1984.

STANLEY & ASSOCIATES
200 12TH STREET
SUITE 800
ARLINGTON, VA 22202
703-310-5570
Fax: 703-310-5560
• Phil O. Nolan, Chairman/President/CEO
• Brian J. Clark, Executive Vice President/CFO/Treasurer

professional services

• Scott D. Chaplin, General Counsel/Secretary/Senior Vp
• Tom R. Fradette, Cheif Accounting Officer/Corporate Controller

STEPHENS SPORTS MANAGEMENT INC.
111 CENTER STREET
SUITE 300
LITTLE ROCK, AR 72201
501-377-2000
800-643-9691
Fax: 501-377-2470
www.stephens.com
• Kevin M. Scanlon, President
Services:
Contract negotiation, financial management, etc.
Sports Service Founded:
1987.

STERN, DAVID J.
590 FIFTH AVENUE
NEW YORK, NY 10036
212-515-6221
800-826-7050
Fax: 212-826-6197
dstern@nba.com
www.nba.com
• David J. Stern, Commissioner
Description:
Contract negotiations.

STINGER SPORTS GROUP
1200 S RESERVE STREET
SUITE F
MISSOULA, MT 59801
406-542-0119
Fax: 406-728-4631
• Ken Staninger, Owner/President
(406) 542-0119
ken@stingersportsgroup.com
• Ken Staninger, Member
(406) 544-3497
• Abdul Noah, Contect
(480) 234-5689
Description:
All phases of athlete representation.
Services:
All phases of athlete representation including talent evaluation, preparation for the draft, counseling, contract negotiations, public appearance and endorsements, and selectivity.

STITES & HARBISON
250 W MAIN STREET
SUITE 2300
LEXINGTON, KY 40507-1758
859-226-2300
Fax: 859-253-9144
general@stites.com
www.stites.com
• Marjorie A. Farris, Member
(502) 779-8258
mfarris@stites.com
• Stephen G. Allen, Member
(859) 226-2257
sallen@stites.com
Nature of Sports Service:
All phases of athlete representation including contract negotiation, long-range planning, financial planning, and post-career counseling.
Services:
Administrative Law, Airport Law, Alternative Dispute Resolution, Antitrust and Consumer Protection Litigation, Appellate Advocacy, Aviation Litigation, Bankruptcy, Business Expansions, Relocations, Joint Ventures & Government Incentive Procurement, Business Litigation, Capital Markets Lending, Charitable and Non-Profit Organizations, Civil Litigation, Class Action Defense, Commercial Disputes-Contracts and Business Torts, Commercial Finance, Community Development and Revitalization, Company Failure, Rehabilitation and Liquidation, Company Management, Governance and Control Litigation, Complex/Large Transaction Litigation Computer Law.
Clients:
AEGON USA Investment Management, Inc., Alcan Aluminum Corporation, The Alliance of Community Hospices & Palliative Care Services, Inc., Alternative Healthcare System, Inc., Ambrake Corporation, American Electric Power, American Institute of Steel Construction, Inc., Anthem Inc., Appriss, Inc., Aqua Tex, ArchVision, Ashland Inc., The Beck Group, BellSouth Corporation, Belo Corp., Bluegrass Conservancy, Robert Bosch Corporation, Boston Scientific Corporation, BrainstormUSA, LLC, Brown-Forman Corporation, Caldwell Tanks, Inc., Cingular Wireless, Columbus (Ohio) Airport Authority, Commonwealth Land Title Insurance Company, The Cordish Company.

STRIVERS GROUP
1100 INDUSTRIAL BOULEVARD
SUITE 3
SAN CARLOS, CA 94070
650-508-8078
Fax: 650-508-4411
• Kelly Cook, President
Services:
Represents professional athletes in contract negotiations, financial guidance, post-career exploration, development, and endorsement.
Sports Service Founded:
1989

SUNDHEIM, GEORGE M., III
DOTY SUNDHEIM & GILMORE
260 SHERIDAN AVENUE, SUITE 200
PALO ALTO, CA 94306
650-327-0100
Fax: 650-327-0101
duf@dotysund.com
www.dslaw.com
• Stanley E Doty, Partner
stan@dotylaw.com
• Annette Barlow, Partner
annette@dotylaw.com
Nature of Sports Service:
All phases of athlete representation including contract negotiation, long-range planning, financial planning, and post-career counseling.
Services:
Business Law, Employment Law and Real Estate Law.

SUNWEST SPORTS
7883 N PERSHING AVENUE
STOCKTON, CA 95207
209-952-9922
Fax: 209-951-3216
• Frank Bauer, President
(805) 773-0367

Services:
All phases of athlete representation.
Description:
All phases of athlete representation.

SUPERSTAR MANAGEMENT, INC.
7633 SUNKIST DRIVE
OAKLAND, CA 94605-3024
510-839-5400
Fax: 510-638-8889
info@superstarmanagement.com
www.superstarmanagement.com
• Abdul Jalil, President/Chief Executive Officer
(510) 839-5400
jalil@superstarmanagement.com
• Ian Faux, VP/Chief Operating Officer
info@superstarmanagement.com
• Kyle Peck, Sports Division
Services:
Provides PRE-DRAFT CONSULTATION. Utilizing the preseason, and post-season industry scouting reports, they market, push, and promote your interest to the selected pro teams they have determined are the best fit for you. SSM assesses the factors of ability and current production of Athlete, publicity and exposure quotient, level of competition, past performance of athlete, ability, needs and financial condition of the selected teams, public acceptance and marketability, desire of athlete, winning team, character and mental toughness, geographical preference of professional team.
Clients:
Muhammad Ali, Brian Taylor, U.S. Rep. J.C. Watts, Warner Bros. Records, Deion Sanders, Byron Stewart, Delvin Williams, Giant Records, Kareem Abdul-Jabbar, M.C. Hammer, Capitol Records, Lyman Bostock, Evander Holyfield, Spencer Haywood, Cliff Robinson
Nature of Sports Service:
Specialties include promoting, representing, advising, negotiating, and arbitrating contracts in the sports and entertainment field.

SYNERGY SPORTS INC.
14001 DALLAS PARKWAY
SUITE 1200
DALLAS, TX 75240
972-934-6562
Fax: 972-934-6508
gglick@synergysportsinc.com
www.synergysportsinc.com
Services:
NFL Pre-Combine Training, NBA Pre-Camp Training, Post-Combine Training, Market Research, Evaluation of Client Position, Development of Negotiation Position and Strategy, Education of Client Regarding Negotiations in Professional Leagues, Interface and Negotiate with Professional Team, Interface with Players Association, Contract Injury and Non-Injury Grievance Issues, Enforcement of Player Agreements, Coordination of Individual Workouts with Professional Teams, Specialized Weight, Speed, Flexibility and Strength Training, Post-Season Orthopedic Evaluations, Nutritional Consultations, Weight Loss Programs, Massage Therapy, Acupuncture and Chi
Sports Service Founded:
1997

TAFT, STETTINIUS & HOLLISTER
425 WALNUT STREET
SUITE 1800
CINCINNATI, OH 45202-3957
513-381-2838
Fax: 513-381-0205
webmaster@taftlaw.com
www.taftlaw.com
• Stephen M. Nechemias, Partner
(513) 357-9392
nechemias@taftlaw.com
• Marcia Voorhis Andrew, Partner
(513) 357-9671
andrew@taftlaw.com
Description:
Represents professional sports teams.
Services:
Offers legal services in areas of: (1) Business and Finance (which handles general business, corporate, mergers, and acquisitions, securities, private and public financing, real estate, banking, and insurance matters); (2) Laborand Employment; (3) Litigation (which includes bankruptcy, environmental and workers' compensation subgroups; and (4) Tax, Probate and Estate Planning.
Clients:
Businesses and individuals engaged in manufacturing, banking, finance, insurance, distribution, television and radio, professional sports, health care, advanced technology, energy, transportation, and real estate, as well as the New Economy.
Year Founded:
1924
Other Locations:
Twelfth Floor, 21 East State Street, Columbus, Ohio 43215-4221. 614-221-2838; FAX: 614-221-2007, 1717 Dixie Highway, Suite 340, Covington, Kentucky 41011-4704. 513-331-2838; FAX: 513-381-6613, 3500 BP Tower, 200 Public Square, Cleveland, Ohio 44114-2302. 216-241-2838; FAX: 216-241-3707, 110 North Main Street, Suite 900, Dayton, Ohio 45402-1786. 937-228-2838; FAX: 937-228-2816

TAGGART, WALTER J.
299 N SPRING MILL ROAD
VILLANOVA, PA 19085
610-519-7010
Fax: 610-519-5672
www.law.villanova.edu
• Nicole Garafano, Events Director
(610) 519-7066
garafano@law.villanova.edu
• Wendy C. Barron, Assistant Dean, Financial Aid
(610) 519-7015
• April ma Barton, Assistant Dean, Academic Computing
(610) 519-5201
• Colleen Belz, Alumni Relations Director
(610) 519-7036
cbelz@law.villanova.edu
• April Barton, Director for Academic Computing
(610) 519-5201
barton@law.villanova.edu
• Colleen Belz, Director of Development
(610) 519-7036
cbelz@law.villanova.edu
•Anthony Cancelli, Director of Business and Support Services
(610) 519-7833
cancelli@law.villanova.edu

• Elizabeth Dunn, Associate Director of Public Service Careers
(610) 519-7228
dunn@law.villanova.edu
• Christopher Dwyer, Associate Dean Finance & Administration
(610) 519-7083
• Diane Edelman, Director of International Programs and Associ
(610) 519-7047
edelman@law.villanova.edu
Description:
Contract negotiation.
Services:
Provides professional education that teaches student a probono legal service.

TALENT SPORTS MANAGEMENT
11141 ROSSER ROAD
DALLAS, TX 75229
214-369-2255
Fax: 210-417-4080
• Wollace DeSouza, Agent

TAYLOR, TODD
20 N BROADWAY
SUITE 1800
OKLAHOMA CITY, OK 73102
405-235-7700
Fax: 405-239-6651
taylort@crowedunlevy.com
www.crowedunlevy.com
• Jimmy Goodman, Director
(405) 235-7717
jimmy.goodman@crowedunlevy.com
• Lisa L. Rose, Director, HR and Administration
(405) 235-7777
lisa.rose@crowedunlevy.com
• Robb Pethick, Manager, Administrative Services
(918) 592-9826
rob.pethick@crowedunlevy.com
• Gail Huneryager, Director of Business Development and Marketin
(405) 239-6691
gail.huneryager@crowedunlevy.com
• Tom Keifer, Executive Director
(405) 235-7711
tom.keifer@crowedunlevy.com
• Jeanette Stanton, Business Development Manager
(405) 239-5481
jeanette.stanton@crowedunlevy.com
• Terry Hunter, IT Manager
(405) 239-6670
terry.hunter@crowedunlevy.com
Description:
Contract negotiation.
Services:
Practice areas include administrative and regulatory practice, alternative dispute resolution, antitrust, appellate practice, aviation/aircraft, bankruptcy and creditors' rights, commercial real estate, construction industry, corporate and securities/mergers and acquisitions, employee benefits and ERISA, energy law, environmental, financial institutions and finance, franchising and distribution, healthcare, healthcare litigation, hospitality industry, entertainment and gaming, initiative petition, insurance, intellectual property.

TERRIE WILLIAMS AGENCY
382 CENTRAL PARK W # 7R
SUITE 17U
NEW YORK, NY 10025
212-316-0305
Fax: 212-749-8867
www.terriewilliams.com
• Terrie M. Wiliams, President
Services:
Marketing & Consulting
Clients:
Andre Harrell, Daryl Simmons/Silent Partner Prod., Master P, George Howard, Janet Jackson, Miles Jaye, Kid n' Play, Donna McElroy, Rene McLean, Charnett Moffet, Eddie Murphy, Heavy D, Keith Sweat, Take 6, Jermaine Dupri, Russell Simmons, Boyz II Men, Carl Anderson, Anita Baker, Kathleen Battle, Bobby Brown, Miles Davis, Will Downing, Family Stand, Full Force, Richie Havens, Najee, Jay Hoggard, Lionel Richie, Sean Puffy Combs, NYC Grammy Committee, ASCAP, A Rage in Harlem/Miramax, The Inkwell/Touchstone, Cadence/Republic Pictures, The Five Heartbeats/20th Century Fox, House Party/New Line Cinema, The Meteor Man/MGM, Sarafina/Miramax, Tales fro

THEOFANOUS, PAUL
106 W 74TH STREET
NEW YORK, NY 10023
212-874-3043
Fax: 212-874-3997
• Paul Theofanous, President
Description:
Represents professional tennis players and professional hockey players.

THOMPSON HINE
3900 KEY CENTER
127 PUBLIC SQUARE
CLEVELAND, OH 44114-1291
216-566-5500
877-628-5500
Fax: 216-566-5800
www.thompsonhine.com
• Mark S Floyd, Vice Chair, Labor & Employment Practice
(216) 566-5836
• Robert B. Ford, Partner
(216) 566-5603
Nature of Sports Service:
Handles sports entertainment services, represents strategic investor in syndicated sports media content site.
Clients:
Alltel, Anthem Blue Cross/Blue Shield, Avery Dennison, Bank One Corporation, BIC Corporation, CH Energy Group, Central Hudson Gas & Electric Corporation, Charter One Bank FSB, Chemed, Davey Tree Expert Company, Duke Realty Corp., Eaton Corporation, Energizer/Eveready, Executive Jet Aviation, FirstMerit Corporation, FlowServe Corporation, Ford Motor Company, Ford Motor Credit, Forest City Enterprises, Inc., Formica Corp., Goodrich Corporation, Goodyear Tire and Rubber Co., Hobart Corporation, Howard Hanna Smythe Cramer, Indiana Insurance Co., Jo-Ann Stores, Inc., Kelly Services, Inc., KeyCorp/KeyBank, Lexis Nexis, Limited Brands, MeadWestvaco

THOMSON, WILLIAM R.
201 ONEAL STREET
BELTON, SC 29627-1410
864-338-7168
Fax: 864-338-7168
• William R. Thomson, Attorney
Description:
Contract negotiation.
Services:
Legal Services (Real Estate Law)

TOP NOTCH SPORTS MANAGEMENT
7324 SW FREEWAY
SUITE 349
HOUSTON, TX 77074
713-995-4681
800-903-9004
Fax: 713-995-4685
• Leroy M. Daniels, NFLPA Certified
Contract Advisor/Agent
Nature of Sports Service:
All phases of athlete representation
including contract negotiation, long-range
planning, financial planning, and post-career
counseling.

TRUE NORTH SPORTS MANAGEMENT
55 TABOR PLACE
SOUTH BURLINGTON, VT 05403
802-233-3478
info@truenorthsportsmgt.com
www.truenorthsportsmgt.com
• Erica Vessey, President/CEO
(802) 233-3478
info@truenorthsportsmgt.com
• Erica MacConnell, Marketing Director
(802) 233-3478
erica@kensowles.com
Description:
A full service athlete management and
sports promotion company representing
athletes and businesses in a variety of
action sports. Contract negotiation, post
career planning, endorsement exploration,
represents sports organizations. Turn Key
sports promotions and events.

TUDOR, DAVID F.
1047 MAPLE AVENUE
PO BOX 1775
NOBLESVILLE, IN 46060-2837
317-773-0600
Fax: 317-773-0610
Description:
Contract negotiation.

U/S SPORTS ADVISORS
250 EAST 96TH STREET
SUITE 450
INDIANAPOLIS, IN 46240
317-569-0300
Fax: 317-569-0393
dmartin@ussportsadvisors.com
www.ussportsadvisors.com
• Ungar Ken, President
(317) 569-0381
kungar@ussportsadvisors.com
• Krissi Edgington, Vice President of
Marketing
(317) 569-0202
kedgington@ussportsadvisors.com
• Teri Toler, Vice President, Administration
(317) 569-0351
ttoler@ussportsadvisors.com
• David Martin, Vice President, Business
Development
(704) 904-7872

dmartin@ussportsadvisors.com
• Ronda Hite, Controller
(317) 569-0220
rhite@ussportsadvisors.com

U/S Sports Advisors is a privately owned
sports and entertainment marketing agency.
Since 2006, our agency has served as a
partner and strategic advisors to sponsors,
leagues, governing bodies, teams, and
athletes. We are known for our steadfast
belief in their goals and our commitment to
showcasing their brands in authentic and
unexpected ways. Our experience in the
sports and entertainment industries help
clients connect to markets and fan bases
that constantly change. We like to win.
That's why we play smarter. We'll help you
play smarter.

UNIVERSAL SPORTS ASSOCIATES, INC.
12 S FIRST AVENUE
ST. CHARLES, IL 60174
630-377-7430
800-321-7430
Fax: 630-584-3081
• Tom Selakovich, President
Nature of Sports Service:
All phases of athlete representation
including contract negotiation, long-range
planning, financial planning, and post-career
counseling.

UPDIKE, THEODORE R.
4600 S MILL AVENUE
SUITE 130
TEMPE, AZ 85282-6758
602-820-4489
Fax: 602-820-8225
• Theodore R. Updike, Attorney

VANTAGE SPORTS MANAGEMENT
PO BOX 3140
WINTER PARK, FL 32790-3140
407-628-3131
Fax: 407-628-3121
• Scott Siegel, President
• Jeffrey Siegel, Chairman
• Alex Chehansky, Managing Director,
Business Development
• Davey Johnson, Senior Advisor, Baseball
Services:
Client Management, Strategic Alliances,
Sports and Event Marketing

**VECTOR SPORTS MANAGEMENT LTD.
CO.**
417 KELLER PARKWAY
KELLER, TX 76248-2302
817-337-4494
Services:
Contract Negotiation, Career Management,
Commercial Development, Training
Sports Service Founded:
1989

WALDON, GROUP THE
560 WHITE PLAINS ROAD
TARRYTOWN CORPORATE CENTER
TARRYTOWN, NY 10591
914-332-9700
Fax: 914-332-0020
office@waldenmed.com
www.waldenmed.com
• James A. W. Walden, Founder
• Richard S. Cohen, President

• Merle Symes, Leader
• Daniel J. Doyle, Chief Executive
• Steve Steiber, Executive
Services:
Guides the careers of such athletes and
entertainers

WALLACH ENTERTAINMENT
1400 BRAERIDGE DRIVE
BEVERLY HILLS, CA 90210
310-278-4574
Fax: 310-273-0548
wallach1@sbcglobal.net
• George Wallach, President
Services:
Contract negotiation, appearances,
endorsements, commercials, athlete career
management and planning, theatrical
planning, as well as financial management;
Summer camps, clinics. Designs programs
to assist companies in promoting their
products and/or services; Advises,
advertising agencies and companies on use
of athletes, as well as obtaining athletes for
such organizations. Also produces movies
and TV sport shows.

WARREN ASSOCIATES
2901 BRIGHTON ROAD
PITTSBURGH, PA 15212
412-766-5757
Fax: 412-766-6993
www.warrenassociates.net
• Mark Bolster, President
(412) 734-3757
mbolster@markbolster.com
Services:
Provide the highest quality production
services in photography
Clients:
Fortune 500 companies like Heinz, Disney,
and PPG, to non-profit organizations
including The Smithsonian and National
Geographic, and entertainment businesses
such as Universal Studios, IMG, the NFL,
and ESPN.

WEG & MEYERS
52 DUANE STREET
2ND FLOOR
FEDERAL PLAZA
NEW YORK, NY 10007
212-227-4210
Fax: 212-349-6702
• Dennis T. D'Antonio, Partner
• Joshua L. Mallin, Partner
• William H. Parash, Partner
Nature of Sports Service:
All phases of athlete representation
including contract negotiation, long-range
planning, financial planning, and post-career
counseling.
Services:
Represent the large and small property
owners in suits against third parties who are
responsible for causing damage to property,
the representation of public adjusters and
insurance brokers in suits against insurance
companies and the prosecution of claims
against insurance brokers in cases where
their negligence has caused or contributed
to coverage issues in connection with a
policyholder's claim.
Clients:
Tishman-Speyer Realty Helmsley-Spear
Inc., Witkoff Group Manocherian Real
Estate Developers, Industrial Acoustics Co.

William Zeckendorf, T.I.I. Industries Harry Macklowe, Adelphi University National Hockey League, The Gitano Group, Inc. Bank Leumi, Allou Distributors New York National Bank, Kenar Enterprises, Ltd. Proskauer, Rose, Goetz & Mendelsohn, LLP, Oleg Cassini Sol G. Atlas Realty Company, Inc, Berkshire Bank American Rice, Inc., Newmark & Co. Real Estate, Inc. Ranch One, Inc. and Ben Arnold-Sunbelt Beverage Company

WEINER LESNIAK LLP
629 PARSIPPANNY ROAD
PO BOX 438
PARSIPANNY, NJ 07054
973-403-1100
Fax: 973-403-0010
VFarrow@weinerlesniak.com
www.weinerlesniak.com
• Paul M Weiner, Senior Partner/Managing Partner
pweiner@weinerlesniak.com
• Raymond J Lesniak, Senior Partner/Corporate Law Department
rlesniak@weinerlesniak.com
• Howard E. Brecher, Partner/Tort Defense Division Head
hbrechner@weinerlesniak.com
• Louis I. Karp, Partner
lkarp@weinerlesniak.com
Nature of Sports Service:
All phases of athlete representation including contract negotiation, long-range planning, financial planning, and post-career counseling.
SERVICES:
Legal services to both the established business and the emerging technology company.

WEISS, ARTHUR B.
777 FRANKLIN AVENUE
SUITE 2
FRANKLIN LAKES, NJ 7417
201-891-6030
888-741-3206
Fax: 201-848-0311
• Arthur B. Weiss, Partner
Description:
Contract negotiation, appearances, endorsements, legal service, public relations.
Clients:
Football: Wayne Chrebet, Arlen Harris, Stephen Bowen, Devale Ellis, Mike Barr, Chas Gessner, Leon Johnson, Glen Foley, Dave Fiore, Gary Reasons, Blake Costanzo.

WHITE, STANLEY R.
10716 POT SPRING ROAD
COCKEYSVILLE, MD 21030
410-628-7543
Description:
Contract negotiation, arbitration hearings, endorsement exploration.

WIDENER UNIVERSITY SPORT MANAGEMENT
WIDENER UNIVERSITY ONE UNIVERSITY PLACE
CHESTER, PA 19013
610-499-1182
888-943-3637
888-WIDENER
Fax: 610-499-4614

bvlarson@widener.edu
www.widener.edu
• Brian Larson, Coodinator/ Sport Management
(610) 499-1182
brlarson@widener.edu
• Greg Cermignano, Faculty
(610) 499-4311
• Joe Fuhr, Faculty
(610) 499-1172
• Nicholas P. Trainer, Chairman
(610) 499-4512
• John H. Tilelli Jr., Vice Chair
• James T. Harris, President
• Joseph J. Baker, MBA, Senior Vice President for Administration and
(610) 499-4156
jjbaker@widener.edu
• Marcine Pickron-Davis, PhD, Chief Community Engagement and Diversity Offi
(610) 499-4566
mcpickron-davis@widener.edu
Nature of Service:
Widener's Sport Management program is one of the most rigorous and longest established program in the region. It is housed in the AAC5B-accredited School of Business Administration. Working with such teams as the Philadelphia Phillies, Sixers, Flyers and Eagles.
Year Founded:
1995
Description:
Academic, undergraduate program that works closely with industry experts from professional sport teams (Philadelphia Flyers; Philadelphia 76ers; Philadelphia Eagles; Philadelphia Union; Philadelphia Phillies), semipro teams (Wilmington Blue Rocks), retailers(Dick's Sporting Goods) and sporting goods manufacturer(Gore Tex).

WILDMAN, JOSEPH L.
1188 BISHOP STREET
SUITE 1811
HONOLULU, HI 96813-3307
808-521-5297

WILLIAMS & CONNOLLY
725 TWELFTH STREET, NW
WASHINGTON, DC 20005
202-434-5000
Fax: 202-434-5029
info@wc.com
• Richard M. Cooper, Partner
(202) 434-5466
rcooper@wc.com
• David E. Kendall, Partner
(202) 434-5145
dkendall@wc.com
• Jerry L. Shulman, Partner
(202) 434-5510
jshulman@wc.com
• James L. Tanner Jr, Partner
(202) 434-5104
jtanner@wc.com
Nature of Sports Service:
All phases of athlete representation including contract negotiation, long-range planning, financial planning, and post-career counseling.
Services:
Provide general business advice and representation, for assistance in negotiating contracts, leases, and league structures, for specific advice on how to structure their businesses to avoid controversy, and to

represent them in major litigation/arbitration disputes. Also includes radio, television, and cable broadcast agreements; stadium leases; stadium construction agreements; advertising and sponsorship agreements; and player arbitration; Provides legal services.

WITLIN PROFESSIONAL MANAGEMENT
7805 SW 6TH COURT
PLANTATION, FL 33324
954-473-4500
Fax: 954-473-1970
barrywitlin@gmail.com
• Barry Witlin, President
(954) 473-4500
barrywitlin@gmail.com

WONG, STANTON
733 BISHOP STREET
SUITE 2675
HONOLULU, HI 96813
808-536-3826
Fax: 808-536-3828
• Leighton Wong, President
(808) 536-3826
Services:
Contract negotiation

WOOLF ASSOCIATES, INC.
101 HUNTINGTON AVENUE
BOSTON, MA 2199
617-437-1212
Services:
Represents professional athletes and entertainment personalities

WORLD SPORTS GROUP, LTD.
419 E 57TH STREET
SUITE 9A
NEW YORK, NY 10022-3060
212-260-5001
Fax: 212-412-9022

WORLDWIDE SPORTS MANAGEMENT
45-14 30TH AVENUE
ASTORIA, NY 11103
718-204-2078
Fax: 718-204-2097
info@nysalamina.com
www.nysalamina.com

YEE & DUBIN LLP
725 S FIGUEROA STREET
SUITE 3085
LOS ANGELES, CA 90017-5430
213-892-7420
Fax: 213-892-7421
info@yeedubin.com
www.yeedubin.com
• Donald H. Yee, Partner
• Stephen L. Dubin, Partner
Description:
Contract negotiation; represents professional sports athletes and coaches; licensing; endorsement exploration; sports business consulting.

ZANE MANAGEMENT, INC.
1650 MARKET STREET
ONE LIBERTY PLACE, 56TH FL00R
PHILADELPHIA, PA 19103-7334
215-790-1155
Fax: 215-575-3801

lzr@braverlaw.com
www.zanemanagement.com
• Lloyd Zane Remick, President
• Christopher J. Cabott, Co-Founder
• Christopher J. Cabott, Associate Attorney
Services:
Provides Personal Management,
Legal-Expert Contract Negotiation and
Advice, Expert Witness Testimony
Hospitality, Tourism & Event Planning,
Appearances & Endorsements, Accounting
& Tax Services, Teamwork; Soliciting and
attracting sponsorships; Representing
corporations in virtually all of their celebrity
sales promotional and marketing needs.
Clients:
Merrill Reese, Lisa Natson p/k/a Golden
Girl, Pat Ciarrochi, Marc Howard, Phil
Andrews, Phil Jasner, Monica
Malpass,Joyce Evans, John Valerio, Lisa
Thomas-Laury, Vernon Odom, Wally
Kennedy, Dina Bair, Andrew Colton, Nicole
Fox, Denise James, Laura Jones, Don
Polec, Kathy Levine

Sports Attorneys

ABES & BAUMANN
810 PENN AVENUE
5TH FLOOR
PITTSBURGH, PA 15222-3614
412-228-4786
Fax: 412-765-0906
www.abesbaumann.com
• Edward Jaffee Abes, Esquire
eja@abesbaumann.com
• Thomas C Baumann, Esquire
tcb@abesbaumann.com
• Edward Jaffee Abes, Partner
(412) 228-4786
• Susan Paczak, Esquire
sp@abesbaumann.com
• Thomas C. Baumann, Partner
(412) 228-4786
• James R. Burn Jr., Associate
(412) 228-4786
• Douglas A. Williams, Associate
(412) 228-4786
Description;
Law Firm concentrating in representing
Workers' Compensation claimants in
Pennsylvania.
Services:
Representing professional athletes in
Worker's Compensation saces including, but
not limited to football, hoceky, baseball and
soccer players.
Clients:
Members of NFLPA, PHPA, NHLPA,
MLBPA and others

**ABRAHAM, WATKINS, NICHOLS,
SORRELS, MATTHEWS & FRIEND**
800 COMMERCE STREET
HOUSTON, TX 77002
713-222-7211
713-587-9668
Fax: 713-225-0827
www.abrahamwatkins.com
• Nick C. Nichols, Partner
(713) 222-7211
nnichols@abrahamwatkins.com
• Randall Owen Sorrels, Partner
(713) 222-7211
• Randall Ow Sorrels, Partner
(713) 222-7211

rsorrels@abrahamwatkins.com
• David P. Matthews, Partner
(713) 222-7211
dmatthews@abrahamwatkins.com
Services:
Provides legal services representing
individuals and families who suffer
catastrophic injuries and wrongful death
Description:
Tort actions/litigation.
Year Founded:
1951

ACKERMAN, VALERIE B.
645 5TH AVENUE
OLYMPIC TOWER
NEW YORK, NY 10022
212-407-8000
Fax: 212-750-9622
www.wnba.com
• Laurel J. Richie, President
(212) 407-8000
• Christine Godleski, Chief Operating Officer
• Renee Brown, Chief of Basketball
Operations and Player Rel
• Todd DeMoss, Senior Director, Basketball
Operations
• Dipali Ottaviani, Director, WNBA Team
Business Development:
• Dina Skokos, Director, WNBA
Communications
• Patrick Mulrenin, Director
Description:
Represents NBA.
Services:
Legal Services
Clients:
NBA

ADAMS & REESE
701 POYDRAS STREET, ONE SHELL
SQUARE
SUITE 4500
NEW ORLEANS, LA 70139
504-581-3234
Fax: 504-566-0210
www.adamsandreese.com
• Charles P Adams Jr, Managing Partner
(601) 353-3234
charles.adams@arlaw.com
• M. Ann Huckstep, Chairman/Executive
Committee
(205) 250-5009
ann.huckstep@arlaw.com
• Robert M Shofstahl, Chief Administrative
Officer
(225) 615-8400
• Paul J Lassalle, Chief Financial Officer
(225) 615-8400
paul.lassalle@arlaw.com
Description:
Contract negotiation, arbitration hearings,
endorsement exploration, tort
actions/litigation.
Other Locations:
450 Laurel Street, STE 1900, Baton Rouge,
LA 70801; Phone: 225-336-5200; Concord
CÃ†enter, 2100 Third Avenue North, STE
1100, Birmingham, AL 35203; Phone:
205-250-5000; One Houston Center, 1221
McKinney, STE 4400, Houston TX 77010;
713-652-5151; 111 East Capitol Street, STE
350, Jackson, MS 39201; Phone:
601-353-3234; One St. Louis Street, STE
4500, Mobile, AL 33602; Phone:
251-433-3234; Market Square North, 401

9th Street, STE 610 South, Washington, DC
20004; Phone: 202-737-3234

**ADAMSKI MOROSKI MADDEN & GREEN
LLP**
6633 BAY LAUREL PLACE
AVILA BEACH, CA 93424
805-543-0990
Fax: 805-543-0980
info@ammcglaw.com
• Steven J Adamski, Partner/Co-Founder
• Martin P. Moroski, Partner/Co-Founder
• Thomas J. Madden III, Partner
• Thomas D. Green, Partner
green@ammcglaw.com
• Steven J. Adamski, Partner
(805) 543-0990
adamski@ammcglaw.com
• Martin P. Moroski, Partner/Co-Founder
(805) 543-0990
moroski@ammcglaw.com
• Thomas J. Madden, Partner
tmadden@ammcglaw.com
• John Nicholson, Partner
• David Cumberland
(805) 543-0990
cumberland@ammcglaw.com
• Raymond A. Biering, Partner
(805) 543-0990
biering@ammcglaw.com
Description:
Business Litigation; Commercial Litigation;
Insurance Litigation; Real Property
Litigation; Intellectual Property Litigation;
Sports Law; Construction Defect Litigation;
Product Liability Litigation.
Other Locaation:
1200 Vine Street, Paso Robles, CA 93446;
Phone: 805-238-2300

ADELMAN, DANIEL W.
27 ELM STREET
NEW HAVEN, CT 06510
203-777-5007
Fax: 203-782-9830
heidi@adelmanlawct.com
www.adelmanlawct.com
• Daniel W. Adelman, President
(203) 777-5007
adelaw@aol.com
• Anne E. Epstein, Partner
adelaw@aol.com
Services:
Contract negotiation, arbitration hearings.
Description:
Family law

ADKINS, M. DOUGLAS
1601 ELM STREET
SUITE 3000
THANKSGIVING TOWER
DALLAS, TX 75201-4761
214-999-3000
Fax: 214-999-4667
www.gardere.com
• M. D. Adkins, Partner
(214) 999-4444
dadkins@gardere.com
• Michael A. Abbott, Partner
(713) 276-5571
mabbott@gardere.com
• James F Adama, Partner
(214) 999-4846
• Stephen Good, Managing Partner
(214) 999-4216
sgood@gardere.com

Other Locations:
One American Center, STE 3000, 600
Congress Avenue, Austin, TX 78707;
Phone: 512-542-7000; Fax: 512-542-7100;
1601 Elm Street, STE 3000, Dallas, TX
75201; Phone: 214-999-3000; Fax:
214-999-4667; 1000 Louisiana, STE 3400,
Houston, TX 77002; Phone: 713-276-5500;
Fax: 713-276-5555
Services:
Legal Services

ADLER & BLASS
89 FIFTH AVENUE
SUITE 902
NEW YORK, NY 10003
212-465-1718
Fax: 212-629-4005
• Norman Blass, Attorney
• Jonathan Blass, Attorney
Services:
Contract negotiation

ALCOX, PATRICK
75 PUBLIC SQUARE
SUITE 650
CLEVELAND, OH 44113
216-575-1560
Fax: 216-241-4851
• Patrick Alcox, Attorney/Owner
Services:
NFLPA worker's compensation panel
Cleveland Browns, Workers Compensation,
Sports Injury, Social Security Disability,
Personal Injury.

ALEXANDER & ASSOCIATES, P.C. MARY
44 MONTGOMERY STREET
SUITE 1303
SAN FRANCISCO, CA 94104
866-802-9497
877-454-9315
Fax: 415-433-5440
www.maryalexanderlaw.com
• Mary E. Alexander, Attorney/Principal
• Jennifer L. Fiore, Associate
• Mary E. Alexander, Attorney
• Sophia M. Aslami, Attorney
Description:
Courtroom preparation is the tademark of
our successful trial firm and we use
innovative courtroom exhibits to help juries
understand even the most complex legal
cases. Because the firm's strength has been
in innovation, creativity and preparation we
have been able to achieve an outstanding
record of success.
Services:
Legal Services

ALLMAN & MITZNER, LLC
1775 SHERMAN STREET
21ST FLOOR
DENVER, CO 80203
303-293-9393
Fax: 303-293-3130
www.allman-mitzner.com
• Robert L. Allman, Attorney
rallman@allman-mitzner.com
• John P. Mitzner, Attorney
Description:
NFLPA workers' compensation panel.
Services:
Legal Services

AMBROSE LAW GROUP, LLP
222 SW COLUMBIA STREET
SUITE 1670
PORTLAND, OR 97201-6616
503-222-0552
Fax: 503-222-0984
www.ambroselaw.com
• Christopher Ambrose, Attorney
crambrose@ambroselaw.com
• Janis K Alexander, Chief Operating Officer
(503) 222-0552
jkalexander@ambroselaw.com
• David R. Ambrose, Attorney
drambrose@ambroselaw.com
Services:
Legal Services

**ANAPOL, SCHWARTZ, WEISS, COHAN,
FELDMAN & SMALLEY, P.C.**
1710 SPRUCE STREET
PHILADELPHIA, PA 19103
215-735-1130
866-735-2792
Fax: 215-735-2211
www.anapolschwartz.com
• Nathaniel E. Ehrlich, Attorney
(610) 375-2750
nehrlich@anapolschwartz.com
• Alan Schwartz, Shareholder
(215) 735-0330
aschwartz@anapolschwartz.com
• Thomas R Anapol, Shareholder
(215) 790-4572
tanapol@anapolschwartz.com
• Sol H. Weiss, Shareholder
(215) 735-2098
sweiss@anapolschwartz.com
Services:
Arbitration hearings, tort actions/litigation.
Represents injured and terminated
professional athletes in collective bargaining
contract grievances, and in claims resulting
from their injuries.
Year Founded:
1977
Other Locations:
1900 Delancy Place, Philadelphia, PA
19103; Phone: 215-735-1130; 920 Trenton
Road, Fairless Hills, PA 19030; Phone:
215-945-6799; 1040 Kings Highway North,
STE 304, Cherry Hill, NJ 08034; Phone:
856-482-1600; 146 North 6th Street,
Reading, PA 19601; Phone: 610-375-2750;
334 West Front Street, Media, PA 19063;
Phone: 610-892-3714

ANDERSON & TUCKER
2101 FIFTH AVENUE N
PO BOX 360
ST. PETERSBURG, FL 33713
727-323-8886
800-458-6811
Fax: 727-323-3252
• Donald C. Anderson, Attorney
(727) 323-8886
• John V. Tucker, Attorney
(727) 323-8886
• Shannon Black, Staff
• Angela Jensen, Staff
• Stanice Anderson, Owner
• Mike Tucker, Owner
Services:
Legal Services

ANDREWS KURTH LLP
450 LEXINGTON AVENUE
NEW YORK, NY 10017

212-850-2800
Fax: 212-850-2929
webmaster@andrewskurth.com
www.andrewskurth.com
• Howard Ayers, CEO/Managing Partner
(713) 220-4044
• David Barbour, Partner
Corporate/Securities
(214) 659-4444
dbarbour@andrewskurth.com
• Richard Caldwell, Partner Litigation
(713) 220-4712
• Jason S Brookner, Partner
(214) 659-4457
• Andrew Feiner, Partner
(212) 850-2883
• Donna D Kim, Partner
(212) 850-2818
• Jessica Chue, Associate
(212) 850-2841
• Mathew A Gray, Associate
(212) 850-2834
• Rinat Hafizov, Associate
(212) 850-2810
• Brian M Clarke, Associate
(212) 850-2825
Services:
Provides services for corporate litigation,
bankruptcy reorganization, labor and
employment, environmental, real estate,
public law, securitization, benefits/executive
compensation, antitrust, corporate/securities
and a host of other legal problems.
Clients:
Clients includes private individuals and
corporations such as: Texas Water Dev.
Board, Texas Public Finance Authority,
Texas State Affordable Housing Corp., Univ.
of Houston, Harris County, City of Houston,
Houston Independent School Dist.,
Goldman Sachs, JP Morgan Securities,
Morgan Stanley, UBS Financial Services,
Coastal Securities, First Southwest
Company, Morgan Keegan & Co. and RBC
Dain Rauscher.

ARNET, WILLIAM F.
1100 CARRIE FRANCKE DRIVE
277 UNIVERSITY HALL
COLUMBIA, MO 65211-3020
573-882-2121
icshelpdesk@umsystem.edu
www.umsystem.edu
• Gary Forsee, President
(573) 882-2011
• Gordon H. Lamb, Executive Vice President
• Natalie Krawitz, Finance and
Administration VP
(573) 882-3611
krawitzn@umsystem.edu
• Stephen J. Owens, General Counsel
(573) 882-3211
owenssj@umsystem.edu
• Katharine S. Bunn, Counsel
(573) 882-3211
bunnk@umsystem.edu
• Susan M. Gardner, Counsel
(573) 882-3211
• Nancie D. Hawke, Counsel
(573) 882-3211
hawken@umsystem.edu
Services:
Learning institution committed to discover,
disseminate, preserve, and apply
knowledge. Promotes learning and fosters
innovation to support economic
development, and advances the health,
cultural, and social interests.

Description:
Represents college athletic departments.

ASHFORD & WRISTON
1099 ALAKEA STREET
ALII PLACE SUITE 1400
HONOLULU, HI 96813
808-539-0400
Fax: 808-533-4945
atty@awlaw.com
www.ashfordwriston.com
• A. Ja Wriston Jr, Of Counsel
(808) 539-0412
jwriston@awlaw.com
• Paul S. Aoki, Partner
(808) 539-0467
• Kirk W. Caldwell, Partner
(808) 539-0461
• Rosemary T. Fazio, Partner
(808) 539-0415
rfazio@awlaw.com
Services:
Provides legal expertise with emphasis in all
aspects of real property law and civil
litigation.
Clients:
Barnwell Industries, Bank of Hawaii, Dept. of
Hawaiian Homelands, Finance Realty Co.,
Ltd., First Hawaiian Bank, Ford Motor Credit
Corp., Hawaii Credit Union League, Hawaii
Medical Services Assoc., Hawaii Reserves,
Inc., Hawaii State Federal Credit Union,
Kahua Ranch Ltd., Kamehameha
Investment Corp., Kamehameha Schools,
Kaneohe Ranch, Knudsen Trust,
McCandless Ranch, Old Republic Title Co.,
Parker Ranch, Queen Liliuokalani Trust, The
Queen Emma Foundation, Queen's Medical
Center, State of Hawaii, Roman Catholic
Church in the State of Hawaii, The
Rehabilitation Hospital of the Pacific,
Territorial Savings & Loan Association.

AULTMAN, TYNER, ET AL
315 HEMPHILL STREET
PO DRAWER 750
HATTIESBURG, MS 39403
601-583-2671
Fax: 601-583-2677
• Thomas W. Tyner
Description:
Contract negotiation, licensing,
endorsement exploration, tort
actions/litigation.

BAIZLEY, DONALD
201 PORTAGE AVENUE
SUITE 2200
WINNIPEG, MB, CANADA R3B 3L3
204-957-1930
855-483-7529
Fax: 204-934-0570
info@tdslaw.com
www.tdslaw.com
• P. Mi Sinclair, Q.C., Managing Partner
(204) 934-2493
pms@tdslaw.com
• David J. Bailey, Executive Director
(204) 934-2500
djb@tdslaw.com
• Ainslie Brown, Comptroller
(204) 934-2510
ainslie@tdslaw.com
• Linda Balance, HR Administrator
(204) 934-2424
linda@tdslaw.com

Services:
Provides law services in the following areas:
aboriginal, administrative, alternative dispute
resolution, business, construction,
environmental, family, financial services,
government and regulatory, insolvency,
bankruptcy, insurance, intellectual property,
labor and employment, litigation, natural
resources and energy, property
development, municipal, securities, taxation,
sports and entertainment, technology and
trusts, estates and fiduciary obligations.

BAKER & DANIELS
300 N MERIDIAN STREET
SUITE 2700
INDIANAPOLIS, IN 46204-1750
317-237-0300
800-382-5426
Fax: 317-237-1000
webmaster@bakerd.com
www.bakerdaniels.com
• Brian K. Burke, Chair/Chief Executive
Officer
(317) 237-1242
Brian.Burke@bakerd.com
• Melanie S. Green, Director of Business
Development & Marketing
(317) 237-1334
melanie.green@bakerd.com
• Thomas C. Fox, Legal Administrator
(260) 460-1712
Tom.Fox@bakerd.com
• Jacqueline K. Kost, Legal Personnel
Director
(317) 237-1105
Jacqueline.Kost@bakerd.com
Description:
Represents professional sports teams
(Seattle Mariners).
Services:
Provides an array of integrated services in
the following fields of legal services, medical
technology, public affairs and federal
relations.
Clients:
Alimentation Couche-Tard Inc., American
Commercial Lines, Borg/Warner Inc.,
Bridgestone Corp., Bunge North America,
Inc., Central Indiana Corporate Partnership,
Circle K, Citizens Gas & Coke Utility, City of
Indianapolis, Clarian Health Partners,
Cummins Inc., Eli Lilly and Co., Fleetwood
Ent., Guidant Corp., Indiana Dept. of
Insurance, Indiana Univ., Indianapolis Bond
Bank, Indianapolis Public Schools, Integra
Bank Corp., JP Morgan Chase & Co.,
Kimball International Inc., Lear Corpo.,
Lehman Brothers, Lilly Endowment, Mac's
Convenience Stores LLC, Mittal Steel USA,
Inc., National Org. of Life and Health
Insurance Guaranty Associations, Pinna
Other Locations:
600 East 96th Street, STE 600, Indianapolis,
IN 46240; Phone: 317-569-9600; 111 East
Wayne Street, STE 800, Fort Wayne, IN
46802; Phone: 260-424-8000; First Bank
Building, 205 West Jefferson Blvd, STE 250
South Bend, IN 46601; Phone:
574-234-4149; 317 West Franklin Street,
Elkhard, IN 46515; Phone: 574-296-6000;
805 15th Street, NW, STE 700, Washington,
DC 2005; Phone: 202-312-7440

BAKER & MCKENZIE
130 E RANDOPLH DRIVE
ONE PRUDENTIAL PLAZA SUITE 2500
CHICAGO, IL 60601

312-861-8800
Fax: 312-861-8823
• John Conroy, Chairman
• David P. Hackett, Partner Chicago
(312) 861-6640
david.p.hackett@bakernet.com
• Nicholas F. Coward, Partner Washington
DC
(202) 452-7021
nicholas.f.coward@bakernet.com
• Eduardo C. M. Leite, Chairman of
execuitve board
• Raymundo E. Enriquez, Partner
• Greg C Walters, Global COO
• Peter Engstorm, Legal Counsel
• Michael Campbell, Global director of
knowledge
Description:
Arbitration hearings, endorsement
exploration.
Services:
Provides legal services in the following
areas: antittrust & trade, banking & finance,
corporate, dispute resolution, employment,
insurance, intellectual property,
international/commercial,
IT/communications, major projects & project
finance, pharmaceuticals & healthcare, real
estate, construction, environment & tourism
and tax matters.
Other Location:
One Prudential Plaza, STE 2500, Chicago,
IL 60601; Phone: 312-861-8800

BAKER, DAVID L.
1000 E UNIVERSITY AVENUE
LARAMIE, WY 82071
307-766-1121
www.uwyo.edu
• Thomas Buchanan, President
(307) 766-4121
tombuch@uwyo.edu
• Andrew Hansen, ACE Fellow
(307) 766-4121
hansen@uwyo.edu
• Shannon Sanchez, Executive
Administrative Assistant
(307) 766-4121
sanchez@uwyo.edu
• Kellie A. Southards, President's Staff
Associate
(307) 766-4122
ksouth@uwyo.edu
• Janet Lowe, Interim VP-Fiscal Admin
• Mark A. Collins, Interim VP-Operations
• Katy Hudson, Coord Financial Services
• Jeffery Greenwald, Manager
• Sheralyn Farnham, Analyst Executive
• Joshua Decker, Manager-Real Estate Ops
Description:
Represents college athletic departments.
Services:
Provider of baccalaureate and graduate
education, research, and outreach services.

BALTIMORE, BRYON
10088-102 AVENUE
2401 TD TOWER
EDMONTON, ALBERTA, CANADA T5J 2Z1
780-426-4660
Fax: 780-426-0982
lawyers@mccuaig.com
www.mccuaig.com
• Bryon Baltimore, Lawyer
(780) 441-3418
bbaltimore@mccuaig.com
• Robert M. Curtis, Lawyer
(780) 426-4660

rcurtis@mccuaig.com
• Branny M. Schepanovich, Lawyer
(780) 441-3404
bschepanovich@mccuaig.com
• Robert M. Curtis, Lawyer
rcurtis@mccuaig.com
Services:
Provides high quality legal services to individual, corporate and institutional clients in the following fields of expertise: aboriginal, corporate/commercial, employment, immigration & citizenship, labour, litigation, municipal, real estate, administrative, criminal, family law, intellectual property, landlord & tenant, mediation/ADR, personal injury and wills & estate law.
Clients:
Bryon Baltimore serves as certified agent for National Hockey Leage Player's Association.

BARRETT, WILLIAM A.
LAKE MERRITT PLAZA
1999 HARRISON ST.
SUITE 1700
OAKLAND, CA 94612-4700
510-465-7100
Fax: 510-465-8556
www.mcinerney-dillon.com
• William A. Barrett, Partner
(415) 558-4169
• Stacey Bales, Firm Administrator
Services:
Provides business & commercial legal services

BARTH, BERUS & CALDERON, LLP
333 CITY BOULEVARD W
SUITE 2050, CITY TOWER
ORANGE, CA 92868-2944
714-704-4828
800-548-8564
Fax: 714-704-1513
www.hmbfinlaw.com
• Harry M. Barth, Senior Partner
(714) 704-4828
harry@hmbfinlaw.com
• Joy Gi Berus, Partner
(714) 704-4828
• David R. Calderon, Attorney
(714) 704-4828
• Bradley G. Barth, Associate Attorney/Notary Public
(714) 704-4828
brad@hmbfinlaw.com
• Harry M. Barth, Founding Member/Senior Partner
(714) 704-4828
harry@barthattorneys.com
• David R. Calderon, Partner
(714) 704-4828
david@barthattorneys.com
• David M. Huynh, Associate
(714) 704-4828
• Matthew Amaro, Associate
(714) 704-4828
• Chris Barsness, Attorney/Finance & Business Management Consul
(714) 704-4828
• Darry C. Sheetz, Of Counsel
(949) 553-0300
Description:
Provides individual, family and business clients with legal representation that concentrates on asset protection planning. We address our client's immediate concerns while anticipating and safeguarding their

long-term business, financial and personal interests. Our clientele includes individuals as well as many leading companies in the healthcare, manufacturing and food-related industries.
Clients:
Seminars conducted: Banfield Charter Practice, Pet Hospitals/Petsmart, Burger King - Dallas/Fortworth Burger King Franchisee Association,Burger King - Mid-America Burger King Franchisee Association, Burger King - Mid-Atlantic Burger King Association, Burger King - National Franchisee Association Conventions,Burger King - Northern California Burger King Franchisee Association,Burger King - Northwest Burger King Franchisee Association,Burger King - Southern California Burger King Franchisee Association,Burger King - Southwest Burger King Franchisee Association, Burger King - Texas Franchisee Association.

BASSFORD, LOCKHART, TRUESDELL & BRIGGS, P.A.
33 S SIXTH STREET
SUITE 3800
MINNEAPOLIS, MN 55402-3707
612-333-3000
Fax: 612-333-8829
info@bassford.com
www.bassford.com
• Gregory P. Bulinski, Managing Partner/Chief Operating Officer
(612) 376-1610
greg@bassford.com
• Rebecca Egge Moos, Chief Executive Officer
(612) 376-1611
beckym@bassford.com
• Kevin P. Hickey, Chief Financial Officer
(612) 376-1620
kevinh@bassford.com
• Gregory P. J. Bulinski, Chief Executive Officer
(612) 376-1610
gbulinski@bassford.com
• Mark R. Whitmore, Chief Operating Officer/Managing Partner
(612) 376-1603
mwhitmore@bassford.com
• Michael A. Klutho, Chief Financial Officer
(612) 333-3000
mklutho@bassford.com
• Christopher R. Morris, Management Committee Member
(612) 376-1627
cmorris@bassford.com
• Kelly A. Putney, Management Committee Member
(612) 376-1605
kputney@bassford.com
• Robin Ann Williams, Management Committee Member
(612) 376-1631
rawilliams@bassford.com
• Jessica A. Gerhardson, Operations Manager
(612) 376-1642
jgerhardson@bassford.com
Services:
Provides a broad range of litigation services including: admiralty and maritime law, alternative dispute resolution, appellate practice, commercial litigation, construction law, environmental law, ERISA liability, Trust and estate, FDCPA, FCRA and privacy issues, health care and risk

management, hospital law, insurance, intellectual property, labor and employment, liquor liability, medical device, motor vehicle and no-fault, municipal, non-competition, trade secret and related claims, personal injury, products liability, professional ethics and liability, securities, shareholder and related corporate litigation and telecommunications.
Clients:
National recognized manufacturing corporations, insurance companies, healthcare providers.
Description:
Contract negotiation. Products Liability; Commercial Litigation; Insurance Litigation; Employment Litigation

---

BATE, PETERSON, DEACON, ZINN & YOUNG, LLP
888 S FIGUEROA STREET
15TH FLOOR
LOS ANGELES, CA 90017
213-362-1860
Fax: 213-362-1861
dlafond@bpdzylaw.com
• David H. Bate, Attorney
(231) 362-1860
dbate@bpdzylaw.com
• John W. Peterson, Attorney
• Linda Va Winkle Deacon, Attorney
• Harry A. A. Zinn, Attorney
(213) 362-1860
hzinn@yzblaw.com
• Julie A. Young, Attorney
(213) 362-1860
jyoung@yzblaw.com
• David H. Bate, Attorney
(213) 362-1860
dbate@yzblaw.com
• Lester F. Aponte, Attorney
(213) 362-1860
laponte@yzblaw.com
• Patricia M. Berry, Attorney
(213) 362-1860
pberry@yzblaw.com
• Stephanie M. Saito, Attorney
(213) 362-1860
ssaito@yzblaw.com
• Nirma Shivayi, Attorney
(213) 362-1860
nshivayi@yzblaw.com
Description:
Employment and Labor Law, Commercial Litigation, Business Law, Real Estate, Construction Law, Sports Law.
Services:
Represents clients in all aspects of employment and labor law and general business, insurance, securities, real estate and construction litigation.

BAUM, ETENGOFF & BUCKLEY
900 WASHINGTON STREET
VANCOUVER, WA 98660
360-693-2002
800-845-3099
Fax: 360-693-1407
• Mark Baum, Attorney
(360) 693-2002
Nature of Sports Service:
All phases of athlete representation including contract negotiation, long-range planning, financial planning, and post-career counseling.
Services:
Provides legal services in the fields of personal injury, family law and others.

BEALL & BURKHARDT
1114 STATE STREET
SUITE 200
LA ARCADA BUILDING
SANTA BARBARA, CA 93101-2716
805-966-6774
Fax: 805-963-5988
ArtyC@aol.com
beallandburkhardt.com
• William C. Beall, Partner
• Eric W. Burkhardt, Partner
Services:
Represent creditor, debtor and trustee
clients in bankruptcy
Clients:
Camarillo Community Bank and Bryant Sons
Jewelers
Description:
Contract negotiation, represents
professional sports teams, sports law, tort
actions/litigation.

BEAUTYMAN ASSOCIATES, P.C.
1201 BETHLEHEM PIKE
FLOURTOWN, PA 19031
215-836-7000
Fax: 215-836-6886
mbeauty@beautyman.com
www.beautyman.com
• Michael J. Beautyman, Chairperson
(215) 836-7000
michael@beautyman.com
• Stephen Alvstad, Counsel
• Robert J Nolan
• Jodi R Adelizzi
Description:
All phases of athlete representation
including contract negotiation, long-range
planning, financial planning, and post-career
counseling.
Services:
General Practice, all Courts. Insurance Law,
Estate Planning, Personal Injury, Family
Law, Taxation and Probate.

BECKER & POLIAKOFF, P.A.
1 EAST BROWARD BOULEVARD
SUITE 1800
FORT LAUDERDALE, FL 33301
954-987-7550
800-432-7712
Fax: 954-985-4176
care@bplegal.com
www.becker-poliakoff.com
• Alan S. Becker, Founding Shareholder
(954) 985-4127
abecker@becker-poliakoff.com
• Gary A. Poliakoff, Founding Shareholder
(954) 985-4150
gpoliakoff@becker-poliakoff.com
Services:
Provides a full range of legal services
including asset protection and estate
planning, homeowner and community
association law, civil and complex
commercial litigation, administrative law,
bancruptcy and creditors' rights, securities
law and litigation, custom and international
trade.
Clients:
AT&T, Broward County Schools, CBS
SportsLine.com, CVS Pharmacy, Florida
Memorial College, Engle Homes, Harley
Davidson, InterParfums, Inc., Isle of Capri
Casinos, Boston Proper, Miami Dade
County Schools, Miami Dade County, IKON
Office Solutions, Palm Beach County, Perry

Slingsby Systems, Inc., Raleigh Enterprises,
Ryder, Sprint PCS, TeleDanmark, Tishman
Speyer Properties, Inc., Ultimate Software
Group, Inc., Westin Diplomat Resort Hotel
Nature of Sports Service:
Entertainment Law; Sports Law; Intellectual
Property Law; Technology.

BECKER, WILLIAM F.X.
260 E JEFFERSON STREET
POTOMAC VALLEY BANK BUILDING, 2ND
FLOOR
ROCKVILLE, MD 20850-2333
301-340-6966
Fax: 301-309-6653
• William F. Becker, Attorney
(301) 340-6966
wfxbecker@aol.com
• Chelsea Drew, Legal Assistant
Nature of Sports Service:
All phases of athlete representation
including contract negotiation, long-range
planning, financial & estate planning,
post-career counseling. Licensed attorney in
Maryland, District of Columbia and West
Virginia.

BENDELOW LAW FIRM
1707 NORTH MAIN ST.
SUITE 301
LONGMONT, CO 80501
303-837-9600
Fax: 303-860-0311
www.bendelow.net
• Edward M. Bendelow, Managing Partner
(303) 837-9600
tedbendelow@bendelow.net
• Kenneth R. Hope, Attorney
(303) 837-9600
• Peter Scott, Attorney
(303) 837-9600
• Scott Watson, Attorney
(303) 837-9600
Description:
Experts in all aspects of commercial law,
real estate, land use and development,
water law, intellectual property. business
transactions and litigation. Represent
individuals, partnerships, business
governments and associations of all sizes
and types on issues small and large.
Services:
Business & Commercial Law, Contracts,
Business Organizations, Construction Law,
DUI/DWI, Entertainment, Sports & Leisure
Law, Environmental Law, Estate Planning,
Wills, Family Law, Divorce, Intellectual
Property Law, Trademarks, Litigation &
Appeals, Natural Resource Law, Real
Estate Law, Land Use and Zoning, Taxation
Law
Clients:
American Cancer Society, American Historic
Motorcycle Racing Association, American
Power Boat Association, Chenango
Homeowners Association, Sports Car Club
of America, Telluride Mountain Title
Company, Rocky Mountain Forest Products,
Sigma Dynamics
Other Location:
101 East Colorado Avenue, #201A, PO Box
726, Telluride, CO 81435; Phone:
970-728-4300; 79050 US Highway 40, STE
202C, PO Box 67, Winter Park, CO 80482;
Phone: 970-726-0600

BERMAN, HOWARD E.
1250 CENTRAL PARK AVENUE
YONKERS, NY 10708
914-423-8880
Fax: 914-423-8964
• Howard Berman, Partner
(914) 423-8880
• John P. Farrauto, Partner
(914) 423-8880
• Richard G. Fontana, Attorney
Services:
All phases of athlete representation
including contract negotiation,
endorsements, estate planning and legal
representation.

BERNARD M. RESNICK, ESQ, P.C.
TWO BALA PLAZA
SUITE 300
BALA CYNWYD, PA 19004
610-660-7774
bmresnick@gmail.com
www.bernardresnick.com
• Bernard M. Resnick, Sports Attorney
Description:
Entertainment law firm
Services:
Full-service entertainment, communications
and sports law firm which concentrates on
transactional work in various facets of the
entertainment industry.
Clients:
The Philadelphia Orchestra; Susan Milan;
The Budapest String Quartet; Piffaro, Ex
Umbris, and Fortune's Wheel; Peter Richard
Conte; Vitalij Kuprij; and The Amernet String
Quartet; Dave Mason; The Rembrandts;
Pink; Us3; The Alan Parsons Project, The
Cuffs, Pornosonic, Blink, The Naked Apes,
V.A., Peekaboo, Janita, Raje Shwari,
Anthrophobia, aboyandagirl, Autumn, Pete
Palladino, The Badlees, and Electron Love
Theory; Rich Gavalis (Bloodhound Gang);
and Chord Recordings, Tazmania Records,
Metropolitan Records, Dancesport Sounds
USA, DRP Records, BMP/Put It On A Disk
Records, 215 Records, Krush Unit, Inc.,
Chocolate Fireguard Music, Ltd., Ultimae

BERNARD, PAMELA J.
123 TIGERT HALL
PO BOX 113125
GAINESVILLE, FL 32611-3257
352-392-3261
Fax: 352-392-4387
www.generalcounsel.ufl.edu
• Pamela Bernard, VP/General Counsel
(352) 392-1358
pbernard@ufl.edu
• Karon Grabel, Senior Administrative
Assistant
(352) 392-1358
karon@ufl.edu
• James Be Machen, President
• Jamie Lewis Keith, Vice President and
General Counsel
jlkeith@ufl.edu
• Barbara C. Wingo, Associate Vice
President and Deputy General C
wingo@ufl.edu
• Amy M. Hass, Associate Vice President
and Deputy General C
amhass@ufl.edu
• Michael W. Ford, Sr. University Counsel
for Tax, Corporations
mwford@ufl.edu
Description:
Represents college athletic departments.

Services:
provides legal advice and representation to the University of Florida, its component units and affiliated entities, and to its employees while acting within the scope and course of their employment.
Clients:
Units and entities of University of Florida

BERNARD, WILLIAM DAVID
101 N COLUMBIA STREET
CHAPEL HILL, NC 27514-3502
919-968-1111
Fax: 919-968-1444
wbernard@brownandbunch.com
www.brownandbunch.com
• William Bernard, Partner
Services:
Contract negotiation, arbitration hearings, represents professional sports teams, endorsement exploration, tort actions/litigation. Commercial Law; Residential and Commercial Real Estate; Mediation.

BERRY, ROBERT C.
140 COMMONWEALTH AVENUE
CHESTNUT HILL, MA 02467
617-552-8550
Fax: 617-552-2615
bclawadm@bc.edu
www.bc.edu
• Robert Berry, Professor Emeritus
(617) 552-4360
• Filippa Ma Anzalone, Professor/Library and Computing Services
(617) 552-6809
filippa.anzalone@bc.edu
Services:
Prepares students to be among the best in law profession, both by giving them a thorough knowledge of the foundations of law through an extensive array of required and elective courses, and by encouraging them to think creatively in real-world situations, through advocacy programs, clinical programs, and student publications
Clients Include:
Impact Sports.
Description:
Contract negotiation, teaches sports law, handles publicity & private issues.

BERSHAD, LAWRENCE
SETON HALL UNIVERSITY SCHOOL OF LAW
ONE NEWARK CENTER
1109 RAYMOND BOULEVARD
NEWARK, NJ 7102
973-642-8500
888-415-7271
Fax: 973-642-8876
lawwebmaster@shu.edu
law.shu.edu
• Lawrence Bershad, Law Professor
(973) 642-8810
bershala@shu.edu
• Michelle Adams, Law Professor
(973) 642-8197
adamsmch@shu.edu
• Erik Lillquist, Vice Dean & Professor of Law
(973) 642-8844
erik.lillquist@shu.edu
• Terry Dealmedia, Assistant Dean for Administration and Finance
(973) 642-8732

terry.dealmeida@shu.edu
• Rose Marie Martins, Administrative Assistant to the Vice Dean & A
(973) 642-8378
rose.martins@shu.edu
• Gisele Joachim, Dean of Enrollment Management
(973) 642-8475
gisele.joachim@shu.edu
• Katya Valasek, Associate Director of Admissions
(973) 642-8848
katherine.valasek@shu.edu
• Mimi Huang, Associate Director of Admissions
(973) 642-8737
mimi.huang@shu.edu
Description:
Teaches sports law.
Services:
Educates health lawyers and health care professionals through its three degree programs: the Juris Doctorate with a concentration in health law (J.D.), the Master of Laws in Health Law (LL.M.), and the Masters of Science in Jurisprudence (M.S.J.). The program's faculty engages in original empirical and analytical research on emerging issues in health law and policy, and the program serves the wider community through frequent lectures and symposia

---

BERTUZZI, LAWRENCE
600 - 60 COLUMBIA WAY
MARKHAM, ON, CANADA L3R 0C9
905-415-6700
866-348-2432
Fax: 905-415-6777
markham@millerthomson.com
www.millerthomson.ca
• Lawrence Bertuzzi, Partner
(905) 415-6750
• Gerald D. E Courage, Chairman
• Paul Brace, Partner
(905) 415-6703
pbrace@millerthomson.com
• Peter McKelvey, Chief Operating Officer
• Chris Issar, Chief Financial Officer
• Richard Van Dyk, Chief Information Officer
• Katrina Stevens, National Director, Human Resources
• Monique Wijgerse, Chief Marketing & Business Development Office
Services:
Provides a complete range of business law, advocacy and personal legal services to Canadian and international corporations, entrepreneurs, institutions, governments and not-for-profit organizations

---

BEVERLY HILLS SPORTS COUNCIL
131 S. RODEO DRIVE
SUITE 100
BEVERLY HILLS, CA 90212
310-858-1872
Fax: 310-550-7980
info@bhscouncil.com
bhscouncil.com
• Daniel Lozano, Partner
• Rick Thurman, Chief Financial Officer
• Jeff Borris, General Counsel
Description:
Full representation of professional baseball players.
Services:
Professional sports club and promoter

BINGHAM MCCUTCHEN LLP
THREE EMBARCADERO CENTER
SAN FRANCISCO, CA 94111-4067
415-393-2000
Fax: 415-393-2286
• Jay S. Zimmerman, Chairman
(415) 393-2080
• Donn P. Pickett, Partner
(415) 393-2082
donn.pickett@bingham.com
• William A. Bachman, Chief Operating Officer
(617) 951-8216
• Sherri Bracken, Regional Director of Administration
(212) 705-7856
Services:
Endorsement exploration; provides a variety of legal services in areas of Corporate, Finance and Litigation law

---

BLACK, WILLIAM D., LAW OFFICES OF
ONE E CAMELBACK ROAD
SUITE 550
PHOENIX, AZ 85012
602-910-6144
888-349-3599
Fax: 602-265-3685
• William D. Black, Attorney/Principal
(602) 265-2211
• William D. Black, Attorney
• Bill Black, Attorney
• Stephen J. McFarlane, Of Counsel
• Robert E. Wisniewski, Of Counsel
• William D. J. Black, Founding Attorney
Year Founded:
1979
Services:
Personal Injury, Wrongful Death, Medical Malpractice, Workers Compensation, Employment Concerns, Intellectual Property Law, Computer Law, Restaurant & Liquor License Law, Hotel & Travel Law, Entertainment & Sports Law, Real Estate Law, Communications Law, 1st Amendment Law, General Business Law, Commercial Litigation

---

BLACKBOURN, LISLE W.
354 SEYMOUR COURT
ELKHORN, WI 53121
262-723-3220
Fax: 262-723-5091
godfrey@godfreylaw.com
www.godfreylaw.com
• Lisle Blackbourn, Attorney
(262) 723-3220
lblackbourn@godfreylaw.com
• Lisle W. Blackbourn, President & Managing Partner
(262) 723-3220
• Patrick S. DeMoon III, Associate
(262) 723-3220
• Michael J. Frazier, Associate
(262) 723-3220
• Kim A. Howarth, Partner
(262) 723-3220
• James P. Howe, Associate
(262) 723-3220
• Theodore N. Johnson, Partner
(262) 723-3220
• Robert C. Leibsle, Senior Partner
(262) 723-3220
Description:
Personal injury.
Services:
General Corporate Representation, Labor Negotiations, Arbitration, Financial &

Commercial Transactions, Business & Financial Planning, Employment Law and Practices, Trademarks, Trade Names and Licensing Agreements, Business Succession Planning, Personal Injury, Commercial, Employment Litigation, General Business Litigation, Product Liability, etc.

BLAIR, ROBERT W.
1155 DAIRY ASHFORD
SUITE 103
HOUSTON, TX 77079
281-870-9991
Fax: 281-870-9969
rwblair1@aol.com
• Robert Blair, Attorney
(281) 275-4275
Services:
Personal Injury, Business Disputes, Real Estate, Wills, Estates
Description:
Federal/state/international tax filings.

BLANC, DAVID
222 SE DORION AVENUE
PO BOX 218
PENDLETON, OR 97801
541-276-3331
800-994-3331
Fax: 541-276-3148
www.corey-byler.com
• David Blanc, Attorney
(541) 276-3331
blanc@corey-byler.com
• Steven H Corey, Attorney
corey@corey-byler.com
Services:
Civil Litigation, Estate Planning, Elder Law, Personal Injury, Divorce & Custody, Real Estate, Agricultural Law, Zoning & Land Use, Condemnation, Business, Water Law, Wills, Probate & Trusts

BLECHER & COLLINS
515 S FIGUEROA STREET
SUITE 1750
LOS ANGELES, CA 90071
213-622-4222
Fax: 213-622-1656
www.blechercollins.com
• Maxwell M. Blecher, Attorney/Founding Partner
(213) 622-4222
mblecher@blechercollins.com
• Harold R. Collins, Jr, Attorney/Founding Partner
(213) 622-4222
hcollins@blechercollins.com
• John E E. Andrews, Attorney/Partner
(213) 622-4222
jandrews@blechercollins.com
• Howard K Alperin, Attorney/Partner
halperin@blechercollins.com
• Gary M Joye, Attorney/Partner
gjoyr@blechercollins.com
• Alyson C Decker, Attorney/Partner
adecker@blechercollins.com
• William Hsu, Attorney/Partner
whsu@blechercollins.com
• Donald R Pepperman, Attorney/Partner
dpepperman@blechercollins.com
• Kristen M Peters, Attorney/Partner
kpeters@blechercollins.com
Services:
Antitrust, complex commercial litigation,

class actions, professional malpractice, intellectual property.

BOEHM, STEVE B.
1275 PENNSYLVANIA AVEUE, NW
WASHINGTON, DC 20004-2415
202-383-0100
Fax: 202-637-3593
steven.boehm@sablaw.com
• Steven B. Boehm, Attorney/Partner
(202) 383-0176
steven.boehm@sablaw.com
• Miranda K. Davis, Associate
(404) 853-8242
miranda.davis@sutherland.com
Nature of Sports Service:
All phases of athlete representation including contract negotiation, long-range planning, financial planning, and post-career counseling.
Services:
Represents national and regional financial service organizations in connection with the establishment and operation of public and private open and closed-end investment funds; assists insurance company and other financial services clients with the design and implementation of a variety of investment-oriented insurance products, including SEC-registered and unregistered variable life insurance products and other variable annuities

BOESCHE MCDERMOTT LLP
110 W 7TH STREET
SUITE 900
TULSA, OK 74119
918-583-1777
866-483-1777
Fax: 918-592-5809
• Bradley Beasley, Attorney
bbeasley@bme-law.com
• Michael Forsman, Attorney
• David Johnson, Attorney
Year Founded:
1927

BOSCH, GERARD R.
111 N 6TH STREET
READING, PA 19601
610-478-2000
Fax: 610-376-5610
Nature of Sports Service:
All phases of athlete representation including contract negotiation, long-range planning, financial planning, and post-career counseling. Assists universities in investigating violations of NCAA rules and regulations.

BOSE MCKINNEY & EVANS LLP
111 MONUMENT CIRCLE
SUITE 2700
INDIANAPOLIS, IN 46204
317-684-5000
Fax: 317-684-5173
webmaster@boselaw.com
www.boselaw.com
• Craig E. Pinkus, Partner/Co-Chair of the Intellectual Pro
(317) 684-5358
cpinkus@boselaw.com
• Lisa McKinney Goldner, Co-Chair Environmental Law
(317) 684-5124
lgoldner@boselaw.com

Services:
provides a full-range of legal services to privately owned businesses, publicly traded companies, high-tech organizations, and governmental entities
Clients:
Automotive Finance Corporation, Association of Indiana Life Insurance Companies, BMW Constructors, Inc., Brownsburg Community School Corporation, Chip Ganassi Racing Teams, Inc., Cinram, Inc., City of Indianapolis, Community Bankers Association of Indiana, Crowe Chizek and Company, LLP, Emmis Communications Corporation, Endress + Hauser, Fall Creek Regional Waste District, First Indiana Bank, Hillenbrand Industries, Indiana Bankers Association, Indiana Pork Producers Association, Indiana Soybean Board, Inc., Indiana University Anesthesiology Associates, Indiana Water & Wastewater Association, Indianapolis Colts, Inc., Johnson County REMC
Description:
Tort actions/litigation, represents college athletic departments, dispute resolution.
Other Locations:
2700 First Indiana Plaza, 135 North Pennsylvania Street, Indianapolis, IN 46204; Phone: 317-684-5000; 700 North One Lafayette Center, 1120 20th Street NW, Washington, DC 20036; Phone: 202-973-1229

BOUTIN, DENTINO, GIBSON, DI GUISTO, HODELL, INC.
555 CAPITOL MALL
SUITE 1500
SACRAMENTO, CA 95814
916-321-4444
Fax: 916-441-7597
info@boutinjones.com
www.boutinjones.com
• Stephen F. Boutin, Founder
(916) 321-4444
sboutin@boutindentino.com
• William Dentino, Principal
(916) 321-4444
• Chris Gibson, Principal
(916) 321-4444
• Jennifer E Lloyd, Paralegal
(916) 321-4444
• Elizabeth D Pullen, Paralegal
(916) 321-4444
epullen@boutinjones.com
• Sheryl S Stuckey, Paralegal
(916) 321-4444
sstuckey@boutinjones.com
• Penny R Brown, Attorney
(916) 321-4444
pbrown@boutinjones.com
• Kevin C Davis, Attorney
(916) 321-4444
kdavis@boutinjones.com
• Chris Gibson, Attorney
(916) 321-4444
• B.J Susich, Attorney
(916) 321-4444
bjsusich@boutinjones.com
Services:
Entity formation and consultation, corporate transactions, intellectual property, real estate, secured transactions, taxation, estate planning, and litigation
Description:
General business law, joint ventures, real estate, taxation, estate planning, sports, mergers, acquisitions.

BRADLEY & GMELICH
700 N BRAND BOULEVARD
10TH FLOOR
GLENDALE, CA 91203
818-243-5200
Fax: 818-243-5266
info@bglawyers.com
www.bglawyers.com
• Barry A. Bradley, Attorney/Managing
Partner
(818) 243-5200
bbradley@bglawyers.com
• Thomas Gmelich, Attorney/Partner
(818) 243-5200
tgmelich@bglawyers.com
• Mirth White, Associate
(818) 243-5200
• John K. Flock, Associate
(818) 243-5200
• Robert A. Crook, Associate
(818) 243-5200
• Lindy M. Bradley, Partner
(818) 243-5200
• Gary J. Bradley, Partner
(818) 243-5200
• Jonathan A. Ross, Partner
(818) 243-5200
• Barry A. Bradley, Managing partner
(818) 243-5200
Services:
General civil litigation, Private security,
Inadequate Security Liability, Premises
Liability Litigation, Sports & Recreational
Injury, Employment Law, Commercial
Business Litigation, Construction Claims &
Litigation, Alternative Dispute Resolution
Clients:
Brownyard Claims Management, Inc.,
Certain Underwriters at Lloyds of London,
Connecticut Specialty Insurance Company,
Crawford & Company, First Financial
Insurance Company, Frontier Pacific
Insurance Company, Great American
Insurance Company, Hartford Insurance
Company, Kemper Insurance Company,
National American Insurance Company of
California, Royal Insurance Company,
Schifrin, Gagnon & Dickey, Inc., Specialty
Risk Services, Inc., USF&G Insurance
Company, Zurich Insurance Company,
Albertsons/ Lucky Stores, Inc., Allied
Protection Services, American Stores, Inc.,
Arden Realty, Inc., Armguard Security,
Auburn Hills Racquet & Fitness Club

BREAUX, PAUL P.
3525 BANK DRIVE
ST GABRIEL, LA 70776-4616
225-642-5532
• Phil Breaux, Attorney
• Robert Hornstein, Attorney
Nature of Sports Service:
All phases of athlete representation
including contract negotiation, long-range
planning, financial planning, and post-career
counseling.

BRENNAN, PATRICK CAVANAUGH
324 E WISCONSIN AVENUE
MILWAUKEE, WI 53202
414-476-8707
• Brennan Patrick Cavanaugh, Attorney
Services:
Personal injury lawyer
Description:
Contract negotiation, endorsement
exploration, criminal law litigation specialist.

BRICK, ADAM
GEORGETOWN UNIVERSITY
MCDONOUGH ARENA
WASHINGTON, DC 20057
202-687-5414
Fax: 202-687-5366
www.georgetownuniversity.com
• Adam Brick, Senior Associate Athletic
Director Legal

BRICKER & ECKLER
100 S THIRD STREET
COLUMBUS, OH 43215-4291
614-227-2300
Fax: 614-227-2390
info@bricker.com
www.bricker.com
• Richard Simpson, Managing Partner
(614) 227-2354
rsimpson@bricker.com
• Richard King, Chief Operating Officer
(614) 227-2393
rking@bricker.com
• Charlotte Patin, Chief Information Officer
(614) 227-8882
cpatin@bricker.com
• Steve Odum, CFO
sodum@bricker.com
• Faith Williams, Administrative Partner
fwilliams@bricker.com
• Richard King, COO
rking@bricker.com
• Kurt Tunnell, Managing Partner
ktunnell@bricker.com
• Ahmad Sinno, CIO
asinno@bricker.com
Description:
Represents college athletic departments,
individuals, as well as corporations,
nonprofit organizations, government,
agencies, health care facilities, school
districts, and municipalities.

BRICKEY JAMES N. L.C.
8000 MARYLAND AVE
SUITE 750
CLAYTON, MO 63105
314-863-6178
Fax: 314-725-7075
• James N. Brickey, Attorney

BRIDGES, HAROLD A.
444 S FLOWER STREET
SUITE 2400
LOS ANGELES, CA 90071-2953
213-236-0600
800-333-4297
Fax: 213-236-2700
www.bwslaw.com
• Harold Bridges, Attorney
(213) 236-0600
• Lisa Arias, Secretary
Services:
All phases of athlete representation
including contract negotiation, long-range
planning, financial planning, and post-career
counseling.
Year Founded:
1927
Other Locatons:
2310 East Ponderosa Drive, STE 25,
Camarillo, CA 93010; Phone: 805-987-3468;
Fax: 805-482-9834; 5 Park Plaza, Ste 1280,
Irvine, CA 92614; Phone: 949-863-3363;
Fax: 949-863-3350; 3403 Tenth Street, STE
300, PO Box 1609, Riverside, CA 92501;
Phone: 951-788-0100; Fax: 951-788-5785;

701 B Street, Ste 1790, San Diego, CA
92101; Phone: 619-615-6672; Fax:
619-615-6673; 96 North Third Street, STE
620, San Jose, CA 95112; Phone
408-299-0422; Fax: 408-299-0429

BRIGGS, BUCK
CORNELL LAW SCHOOL
MYRON TAYLOR HALL
ITHACA, NY 14853-4901
607-255-4299
Fax: 607-255-7193
rfr4@cornell.edu
www.lawschool.cornell.edu
• Thomas R Bruce, Director Legal
Information Institute
• Richard F. Robinson, Associate Dean for
Administration and Finance
(607) 255-4299
rfr4@cornell.edu
• Richard D. Geiger, Associate Dean,
Communications & Enrollment
(607) 255-5141
rdg9@cornell.edu
• Peter Cronin, Associate Dean for Alumni
Affairs & Developme
(607) 255-3373
pc253@cornell.edu
• Martha Fitzgerald, Director of
Communications
(607) 255-6596
mpf28@cornell.edu
• Anne Lukingbeal, Associate Dean and
Dean of Students
(607) 255-5839
al50@cornell.edu
• Diane Cross, Director
(607) 255-1311
dsr2@cornell.edu
• William Buckley Briggs, Adjunct Professor
of Law
(607) 254-4765
william.briggs@nfl.com
Description:
Teaches sports law.

**BROWN, HALL, SHORE & MCKINLEY
LLP**
3031 W MARCH LANE
SUITE 230
STOCKTON, CA 95219
209-477-8171
888-583-7178
Fax: 209-477-2549
• Jerry Hall, Partner
(209) 477-8171
• Reed K Scott, Attorney
• John Conger, Attorney
• John McKinley, Attorney
• Dennis Shore, Attorney
• Scott L J. Harper, Attorney
Nature of Service:
Real Estate; Business and Corporate Law;
Commercial Law; Partnerships; Estate
Planning; Sports Law; Entertainment Law;
International Business Law; Intellectual
Property; Civil Litigation, Sports Agency
Law, Trademark infringement.
Year Founded:
1984
Sports Service Founded:
2002

BROWN, J. MICHAEL
500 W JEFFERSON STREET
PNC PLAZA, SUITE 2600
LOUISVILLE, KY 40202-2898

502-589-5235
Fax: 502-589-0309
Description:
Contract negotiation.
Other Locations:
2525 West End Avenue, STE 1500,
Nashville, TN 37203; Phone: 615-244-0020;
1600 Lexington Financial Center, 250 West
Main Street, Lexington, KY 40507; Phone:
859-233-2012; The Renaissance Center,
1715 Aaron Brenner Drive, STE 800,
Memphis, TN 38120; Phone 901-537-1000;
918 State Stree, Bowling Green, KY 42102;
Phone: 270-842-1050; 101 West Spring
Street, New Albany, IN 47150; Phone:
812-945-3561

BRUNINI, GRANTHAM GROWE & HEWES, P.L.L.C
190 E CAPITOL STREET
SUITE 100
PO DRAWER 119
JACKSON, MS 39201
601-948-3101
Fax: 601-960-6902
www.brunini.com
• Stephen Carmody, Attorney
(601) 960-6890
scarmody@brunini.com
• Christopher A. Shapley, Attorney
(601) 960-6875
Description:
Labor and Employment; Litigation; Workers
Compensation; Sports Law.
Services:
Handles a wide range of cases, including
litigation involving complex commercial
transactions, mass torts, construction
disputes, employment discrimination,
products liability, medical malpractice,
breach of contract, antitrust, securities fraud,
business torts, taxation, white collar crime,
and environmental issues
Clients:
AES Corporation, Aetna Casualty and
Surety, Adora Networks, Air2Lan, Allen
Canning Company, Amerada Hess
Company, American General, American
Home Shield, Inc., Amoco Business
Services, AmSouth Bank, Anderson-Tully
Company, Apache Corporation, Aquila
Energy, ARAMARK, Astec Industries, Inc.,
AT&T Corp., Athlon Pharmaceuticals, Inc.,
Ball-Foster Glass Company, Barksdale
Bonding and Insurance, Inc., Beazer East,
Inc., Beverly Enterprises, Birds Eye Foods,
Blue Cross & Blue Shield of Mississippi,
BOC Group, Inc., BP Amoco, Brothers of
the Sacred Heart, Brown and Williamson
Tobacco Corp., Browning-Ferris Industries,
Inc., Allied Waste Industries, B
Other Location:
1710 Jackson Avenue, Pascagula, MS
39567; Phone: 228-696-0040

BRUNO, CHRISTOPHER J.
855 BARRONE STREET
NEW ORLEANS, LA 70113
504-525-1335
800-966-1335
Fax: 504-581-1493
info@brunobrunolaw.com
www.brunobrunolaw.com
• Christopher J. Bruno, Partner/Attorney
(504) 525-1335
• Joseph M. Bruno, Managing Partner
(504) 525-1335
info@brunobrunolaw.com

Nature of Sports Service:
All phases of athlete representation
including contract negotiation, long-range
planning, financial planning, and post-career
counseling.

BRYANT-FIELDS, REGINA
555 CALIFORNIA STREET
SUITE 2000
SAN FRANCISCO, CA 94104
415-772-1200
Fax: 415-772-7400
www.brownwoodlaw.com
Services:
Contract negotiation, arbitration hearings,
represents professional sports teams,
endorsement exploration.
Clients:
Clients include numerous Fortune 100 and
500 companies in a wide range of industries
and business sectors, governments, banks,
insurance and financial institutions,
professional firms, foundations, institutions,
associations and individuals.
Description:
Contract negotiation, arbitration hearings,
represents professional sports teams,
endorsement exploration.

BRYENTON, GARY L.
1900 E 9TH STREET
3200 NATIONAL CITY CENTER
CLEVELAND, OH 44114-3482
216-621-0200
Fax: 216-696-0740
info@bakerlaw.com
www.bakerlaw.com
• R. St Kestner, Executive Partner
(216) 861-7558
skestner@bakerlaw.com
• Alec Wightman, Executive Partner
(614) 462-2636
awightman@bakerlaw.com
• John M. Gherlein, Partner/Chairperson,
Business
(216) 861-7398
jgherlein@bakerlaw.com
• Ronald G. Linville, Partner/Chairperson,
Employment and Labo
(614) 462-2647
rlinville@bakerlaw.com
• R. Steven Kestner, Executive Partner
(216) 861-7558
skestner@bakerlaw.com
Description:
Contract negotiation, post career planning,
investment contract negotiation, arbitration
hearings, federal/state/international tax
filings, represents professional sports teams
(Cleveland Indians), provides securities
advice, licensing, tort actions/litigation.
Other Locations:
666 Fifth Avenue, New York, NY 10103;
Phone: 212-589-4200; Washington Square,
STE 1100, 1050 Connecticut Avenue, NW,
Washington, DC 20036; Phone:
202-861-1500; 333 South Grand Avenue,
STE 1800, Los Angeles, CA 90071; Phone:
213-975-1600

BUCHANAN INGERSOLL ROONEY
301 GRANT STREET
ONE OXFORD CENTER, 20TH FLOOR
PITTSBURGH, PA 15219-1410
412-562-8800
Fax: 412-562-1041
www.bipc.com

• Arthur J. Rooney II, Of Counsel
(412) 392-2000
ajrooney@klettrooney.com
• Edwin L. Klett, Senior Lawyer/Shareholder
elklett@klettrooney.com
• William H. Schorling, Shareholder
(412) 392-2114
whschorling@klettrooney.com
• Robert J. Tyler Jr, Executive Director &
Chief Financial Off
rjtyler@klettrooney.com
Services:
Areas of practice include Bankruptcy and
Insolvency Practice, Corporate Practice,
Gaming Practice, General Liability Defense
Practice, Government Affairs Practice,
Higher Education Practice, International
Business Practice, Labor and Employment
Practice, and Real Estate Practice.
Description:
Contract negotiation, represents
professional sports teams, corporate law,
government affairs.

BUCHANAN INGERSOLL ROONEY PC
301 GRANT STREET
20TH FLOOR, ONE OXFORD CENTRE
PITTSBURGH, PA 15219-1410
412-562-8800
Fax: 412-562-1041
www.klettrooney.com
• Peter P. Ackourey, Shareholder
(609) 987-6807
peter.ackourey@bipc.com
• Nolan W. Kurtz, Executive
Director/Practice Operations
(717) 237-4807
nolan.kurtz@bipc.com
• Virginia L. O'Hare, Firm Administrator
vlohare@klettrooney.com
• Daniel F. Duffy Jr, Information Systems
Director
dfduffy@klettrooney.com
• Susan A. Yohe, Managing Shareholder
• Allyson J. Singel Aldous, Associate
(412) 0562-182
allyson.aldous@bipc.com
•
Lynn J. Alstadt, Shareholder
   (412) 562-1632
   lynn.alstadt@bipc.com
   • Christopher A. Amar, Associate
   (412) 562 8394
   christopher.amar@bipc.com
   • Bruce A. Americus, Shareholder
   (412) 562-8885
   bruce.americus@bipc.com
   • Margaret B. Angel, Shareholder
   (412) 562-3982
   margaret.angel@bipc.com
Description:
Represents college athletic departments.
Services:
Provides a full-service, general commercial
law services to corporations and other
business entities through interdisciplinary
practice .
Clients:
Clients range from leading Fortune 500
companies and closely-held businesses to
numerous colleges and universities,
hospitals and other health care institutions,
banks and other financial establishments,
software and technology companies,
minority businesses, charitable and
community organizations, and a National
Football League team.

BUNTING, ELIZABETH C.
910 RALEIGH ROAD
PO BOX 2688
OFFICE OF THE PRESIDENT
CHAPEL HILL, NC 27514
919-962-1000
www.northcarolina.edu
• Erskine B. Bowles, President
(919) 962-9000
• Jeffrey R. Davies, Chief of Staff
(919) 962-1591
• Jane Morton, Executive Assistant to the President
(919) 962-4622
• Tom Ross, President
(919) 962-9000
cparrish@northcarolina.edu
• Joni Worthington, Associate VP, Communications/Special Ass
(919) 962-4629
worthj@northcarolina.edu
• Celeste Parrish, Executive Assistant to the President
(919) 962-4622
• Kathy Jones, Administrative Assistant
(919) 962-462
kjones@northcarolina.edu
Description:
Represents college athletic departments.
Services:
Offers high quality education for the graduate and undergraduate studies.

BURELSON, PATE & GIBSON, L.L.P.
900 JACKSON STREET
SUITE 300
DALLAS, TX 75202
214-871-4900
Fax: 214-871-7543
www.bp-g.com
• John E. Agnew, Member
(214) 871-4900
jagnew@bp-g.com
• Timothy A. Duffy, Member
(214) 871-4900
tduffy@bp-g.com
• Michael P. Gibson, Partner
(214) 871-4900
mgibson@bp-g.com
• John E. E. Collins, Attorney
(214) 871-4900
jcollins@bp-g.com
• Paul Lund, Attorney
(214) 871-4900
plund@bp-g.com
• Tom Pappas, Attorney
(214) 871-4900
tpappas@bp-g.com
• John E. Agnew, Attorney
(214) 871-4900
jagnew@bp-g.com
• Carl D. Medders, Attorney
(214) 871-4900
cmedders@bp-g.com
Services:
Represents and advises clients in the areas of criminal defense, especially white collar crime, family law, personal injury, bankruptcy, tax, business litigation, labor and employment law, estate planning, probate, real estate, and insurance defense.

BURFORD, LLL, CHRIS W.
800 S BROADWAY
SUITE 400
WALNUT CREEK, CA 94596
925-937-4950
Fax: 925-937-0104

Services:
Licensing, endorsement exploration, represents sports organizations, tort actions/litigation, college conference representative.

BURG & ELDREDGE, P.C.
40 INVERNESS DRIVE E
ENGLEWOOD, CO 80112
303-792-5595
888-895-2080
Fax: 303-708-0527
info@burgsimpson.com
www.burgsimpson.com
• Michael S. Burg, Founder/Shareholder
(303) 792-5595
mburg@burgsimpson.com
• Peter W. Burg, Shareholder
(303) 792-5595
pburg@burgsimpson.com
• Alan K. Simpson, Shareholder
(307) 527-7891
asimpson@burgsimpson.com
• Scott J. Eldredge, Shareholder
(303) 792-5595
seldredge@burgsimpson.com
Services:
Athlete representation including contract negotiation, marketing, endorsements, estate planning and post career counseling.
Other Locations:
227 Massachusetts Avenue, NE, STE 1, Washington, DC 20002; Phone: 202-544-7600; 1135 14th Street, Cody, WY 82424; Phone: 307-527-7891; 7920 Belt Line Road, STE 650, Dallas, TX 75254; Phone: 972-934-1313; 2415 East Camelback Road, STE 700, Phoenix, AZ 85016; Phone: 602-508-6040

BURGOYNE, ROBERT A.
801 PENNSYLVANIA AVENUE NW
MARKET SQUARE
SUITE 500
WASHINGTON, DC 20004-2623
202-662-0200
Fax: 202-662-4643
info@fulbright.com
www.fulbright.com
• Robert A. Burgoyne, Partner
(202) 662-4513
rburgoyne@fulbright.com
• Danny Kim, Partner
• Selina Coleman, Senior Associate
(202) 662-4536
• Tracy DeMarco, Associate
(202) 662-4653
• Mark Thomas Emery, Senior Associate
(202) 662 0210
• Robert Owen, Partner
(212) 318-3070
rowen@fulbright.com
Description:
Represents college athletic departments.

BURT, JR., EDWARD C.
2583 WHITNEY AVENUE
HAMDEN, CT 06518
203-248-2182
Fax: 203-248-9466
www.burtlaw.us
• Edward C Burt, Attorney
• Christine Burt, Attorney
Description:
Contract negotiation.

BUSINESS LAW VENTURES
400 CAPITOL MALL
SUITE 900
SACRAMENTO, CA 95814
916-475-1272
Fax: 916-780-9838
info@businesslawventures.com
• Brent Lawrence, Chief Executive Officer/Managing Attorney
(916) 475-1272
brent@businesslawventures.com
• John Rosenbaum, Corporate Atorney
(916) 475-4212
john@businesslawventures.com
• Zuzana Bednarova, Business Development
(916) 475-1272
zuzana@businesslawventures.com
• Jordan Miller, Law Clerk
(916) 475-1272
jordan@businesslawventures.com
• Cindy Salwlyers, Bookkeeping
(916) 475-1272
cindi@businesslawventures.com
• Brent Lawrence, JD, MBA, Managing Atorney
((91)) 475-12
brent@businesslawventures.com
Services:
Mergers & Acquisitions, Real Estate (joint ventures and financing), Corporate Law Services (formation of Corporations and LLCs), Business Plans (including Marketing Plans), Assistance of early stage high-tech companies, Negotiation and Preparation of Contracts
Clients:
Sierra BG Office Supplies & Printing, California Family Fitness, Peabodys Coffee, FDI Collateral Management, PDF Development, Valley Air Express, Inc., TESCO Controls, Inc., Kiff Analytical, LLC, CWNet.com, RF Olmo & Associates, Air-Trak, ASK International, AP Thomas Construction, Jewel Fine Wines, TechCoire, Coastline Construction Corporation, Software Contract Solutions, Indicium Technologies, Heron Innovators, Murieta Health Club and others.
Nature of Sports Service:
All phases of athlete representation including contract negotiation, long-range planning, financial planning, and post-career counseling. 1) Mergers & Acquisitions, (2) Corporate Securities, (3) Business Planning and Contracts, and (4) Real Estate Development.
Year Founded:
1998

BUTLER. JAMES D., P.A.
591 SUMMIT AVENUE
JERSEY CITY, NJ 7306
201-653-1676
Fax: 201-653-3673
• James D. Butler, Attorney
• Alexander T. West, Associate
• Paul A. Liggio, Counsel
Description:
NFLPA. Handles the New York Giants/Jets workers compensation. Risk Management; Self-Insurance Law; Products Liability Law; Toxic Substances Law; Environmental Law; Construction Law; Transportation Law; Admiralty Law; Aviation Law; Sports Law.

**BUTZEL LONG, A PROFESSIONAL
CORPORATION**
41000 WOODWARD AVENUE
SUITE 200
STONERIDGE WEST BUILDING
BLOOMFIELD HILLS, MI 48304
248-258-1616
Fax: 248-258-1439
info@butzel.com
www.butzel.com
• Keefe A. Brooks, VP/Shareholder
(248) 593-3010
• James C. Bruno, VP/Shareholder
(313) 225-7024
bruno@butzel.com
• Carey A. DeWitt, VP/Shareholder
(313) 225-7056
dewitt@butzel.com
• Richard B. W. Brosnick, VP/Shareholder
brosnick@butzel.com
Services:
Admiralty, Marine and Waterfront
Development Practice,
Advertising/Marketing Law Practice,
Alternative Dispute Resolution Philosophy
and Practice, Appellate Practice, Bond
Practice, Business Litigation Practice,
Business, Corporate and Taxation Practice,
China Practice, Commercial and Industrial
Property Assessment Appeals, Commercial
Lending and Workout Practice, Commercial
Workout and Bankruptcy Practice,
Condemnation and Zoning Law Practice,
Corporate Compliance, Internal
Investigations and Criminal Defense, Family
Law Practice, Financial Institutions Practice,
Employee Benefits Practice, etc.
Description:
Represents sports organizations.
Other Locations:
150 West Jefferson, Ste 100, Detroit, MI
48226; Phone: 313-225-7000; Fax:
313-225-7080; 110 West Michigan, Ste
1100, Lansing, MI 48933; Phone:
517-372-6622; Fax: 517-372-6672; 350
South Main Street, Ste 300, Ann Arbor, MI
48104; Phone: 734-995-3110; Fax:
734-995-1777; 25 West 8th Street, Ste 200,
Holland, MI 49423; Phone: 616-396-8860;
Fax: 616-396-1771; 1200 North Federal
Highway, Ste 420, Boca Raton, FL 33432;
Phone: 561-368-2151; Fax: 561-368-4668;
801 Laurel Oak Drive, Ste 705, Naples, FL
34108; Phone: 239-593-1647; Fax:
239-593-1648

C. JAY ROBBINS
5115 HAMPTON BLVD.
NORFOLK, VA 23529
757-683-3144
Fax: 757-683-5041
www.odu.edu
• C. Ja Robbins, Special Assistant Attorney
General/Gener
Description:
Represents college athletic departments.

**CALIFORNIA WESTERN SCHOOL OF
LAW**
225 CEDAR STREET
SAN DIEGO, CA 92101
619-239-0391
Fax: 619-525-7092
www.cwsl.edu
• Jan Stiglitz, Law Professor/Co-Director,
Innocence Pro
(619) 525-1697
jstiglitz@cwsl.edu

• William J. Aceves, Law Professor/Director,
International Le
(619) 515-1589
waceves@cwsl.edu
• Richard J Finkmore, Law
Professor/Director, Louis M. Brown P
(619) 525-1687
tbarton@cwsl.edu
• Neils B. R. Schaumann, Dean
• Deborah Williams, Executive Assistant
Services:
Teaches sports law arbitration.

CALLAHAN, ROBERT E.
4041 MACARTHUR BOULEVARD
SUITE 350
NEWPORT BEACH, CA 92660
949-252-4615
Fax: 949-252-4616
rec@rcallahanlaw.com
• Robert Callahan, Attorney at Law
Nature of Services:
Legal Counsel
Clients include:
Big West Conference, Golden State Athletic
Conference, Pacific Sports LLC

CAMPBELL, ROBERT G.
2049 CENTURY PARK E
SUITE 2800
LOS ANGELES, CA 90067
310-284-2200
Fax: 310-284-2100
www.coxcastle.com
• Robert G. Campbell, Senior Counsel
(310) 284-2259
rcampbell@coxcastle.com
• Paul N. Dubrasich, Senior Counsel
(415) 262-5120
pdubrasich@coxcastle.com
• Edward C. Dygert, Senior Counsel
(949) 260-4642
edygert@coxcastle.com
• Ted M. Handel, Senior Counsel
(310) 284-2262
thandel@coxcastle.com
Services:
Represents and assists businesses,
institutions, and individuals in all aspects of
the real estate, finance, and construction
industries, including, acquisitions and
dispositions, affordable housing, bankruptcy,
workouts and commercial remedies,
commercial leasing, construction,
development risk management,
environmental, finance, institutional
investments, International and Emerging
markets, joint venture, labor and
employment, land use and entitlements,
litigation, property management, residential,
resort and hospitality properties, retail
development, and tax and estate planning.
Nature of Sports Service:
All phases of athlete representation
including contract negotiation and
post-career counseling.

**CANTOR, DAVID MICHAEL P.C., LAW
OFFICES OF**
2141 E BROADWAY ROAD
SUITE 220
TEMPE, AZ 85282
480-858-0808
888-822-6867
• David Michael Cantor, Attorney
Description:
Criminal Practice and General Civil

Litigation before State and Federal Courts.
Criminal Defense, Driving While Intoxicated,
Traffic Violations, Felonies, Drug Offenses,
Sexual Offenses, Assault and Battery,
Manslaughter, Murder, Capital Offenses,
Sports Law, with emphasis in Trial and
Appellate Practice.
Services:
Provides service in areas of Criminal Law,
DUI/DWI, Entertainment, Sports & Leisure
Law, Immigration & Naturalization Law,
Litigation & Appeals, Motor Vehicle
Accidents — Plaintiff, Personal Injury —
Defense, Personal Injury — Plaintiff, Traffic
Violations, and White Collar Crimes.

CARDWELL, VICTOR
10 S JEFFERSON STREET
SUITE 1400
ROANOKE, VA 24011
540-983-7600
800-552-4529
Fax: 540-983-7711
www.woodsrogers.com
• Heman Ma III, Principal
(540) 983-7654
marshall@woodsrogers.com
• Victor O. Cardwell, Principal
(540) 983-7529
cardwell@woodsrogers.com
• Nicholas C. R. Conte, Chairman of the
Board
• Thomas Bagby, President
(540) 983-7766
bagby@woodsrogers.com
• George Leloudis, Executive Director
(540) 983-7779
gleloudis@woodsrogers.com
• Paula Hess, Director of Human Resources
(540) 983-7534
phess@woodsrogers.com
• Lillian Crites, Marketing Director
(540) 983-7579
lcrites@woodsrogers.com
• Charles Helvey, IT Director
(540) 983-7572
chelvey@woodsrogers.com
• Cindi Harris, Accounting Manager
(540) 983-7573
charris@woodsrogers.com
Description:
Litigation, Sports and Entertainment Law.
Services:
Legal Representation
Other Locations:
823 East Main Street, Suite 1200,
Richmond, VA 23219; Phone:
804-343-5020; 825 Kemper Street,
Lynchburg, VA 24501; Phone:
434-846-4040; 530 Main Street, STE 201,
Danville, VA 24541; Phone: 434-797-8200

CARNEY & TROUPE
185 DEVONSHIRE ST.
SUITE 802
BOSTON, MA 2110
617-426-9797
Fax: 617-426-3816
• Gerard B. Carney, Attorney/Partner
Services:
Legal Representation
Description:
NFLPA workers' compensation panel.
Handles workers' compensation for the New
England Patriots.

CARTWRIGHT LAW FIRM, THE
222 FRONT STREET
5TH FLOOR
SAN FRANCISCO, CA 94111
415-433-0444
888-433-0440
Fax: 415-433-0449
www.cartwrightlaw.com
• Robert Cartwright, Partner
Services:
A personal injury law firm dedicated to providing high quality, aggressive legal representation to victims of personal injury.

CASHATT, BRENT A.
501 S.W. 7TH STREET
SUITE J
DES MOINES, IA 50309-2200
515-244-4300
Fax: 515-244-2650
lbabich@babichgoldman.com
www.babichgoldman.com
• Brent Cashatt, Attorney
• Leslie Babich, Attorney
• Todd E. Babich, Attorney
• Michael J. Carroll, Attorney
Description:
Contract negotiation, arbitration hearings, endorsement exploration, tort actions/litigation and financial planning.
Services:
Family Law; Domestic Relations; Litigation; Conflict Resolution; Mediation Services

CASTILLO, ANGEL
815 MORAGA DRIVE
LOS ANGELES, CA 90049
310-471-3000
Fax: 310-471-7990
ssmall@lsl-la.com
www.lsl-la.com
• Angel F. Castillo, Attorney
(310) 471-3000
acastillo@lsl-la.com
• Charles M. Levy, Attorney
(310) 471-3000
clevy@lsl-la.com
• Steven G. Small, Attorney
ssmall@lsl-la.com
• Tom Lallas, Attorney
tlallas@lsl-la.com
Services:
Represents commercial lenders

CELLI & ASSOCIATES
130 WEST LANCASTER AVENUE
SUITE 201
WAYNE, PA 19087
610-525-5380
Fax: 610-527-7659
rcelli@cellilaw.com
www.cellilaw.com
• Michael G. Celli, Jr, Attorney
Nature of Sports Service:
All phases of athlete representation including contract negotiation, long-range planning, financial planning, and post-career counseling.

CHAPMAN & CUTLER
111 W MONROE STREET
FLOOR 13
CHICAGO, IL 60603-4080
312-845-3000
Fax: 312-701-2361
www.chapman.com

• Richard A Cosgrove, Chief Executive Partner
(312) 845-3738
cosgrove@chapman.com
• Ann E. Acker, Partner
acker@chapman.com
• Daniel Johnson, Chief Operating Partner
• Kimberly L. Ahlgrim, Partner
ahlgrim@chapman.com
• Adrienne Ancheta, Associate
ancheta@chapman.com
• Anna M. Anderson, Associate
aanderso@chapman.com
• Laura E. Appleby, Associate
appleby@chapman.com
Services:
Asset Securitization, Banking, Bankruptcy, Restructuring and Workouts, Commercial Litigation and Dispute Resolution, Corporate Counseling, Corporate Finance and Securities, Intellectual Property, Investment Companies, Lease Finance, Public Finance, Real Estate and Environmenta, Sports Finance, Taxation, Trusts and Estates, Utility Finance
Clients:
World's largest banks, insurance companies, investment banks, corporate and governmental issuers, investors and credit providers.
Description:
Contract negotiation, investment contract negotiation.
Other Locations:
595 Market Street, STE 2600, San Francisco, CA 94105; Phone: 415-541-0500; 50 South Main Street, Salt Lake City, UT 84144; Phone: 801-533-0066

CHASEN & BOSCOLO CHARTERED
7852 WALKER DRIVE
SUITE 300
GREENBELT, MD 20770
301-220-0050
Fax: 301-474-1230
www.chasenboscolo.com
• Gerald Herz, Attorney
(301) 220-0050
gherz@chasenandboscolo.com
• Benjamin T. Boscolo, Attorney
(301) 220-0050
bboscolo@chasenandboscolo.com
• Barry Chasen, Attorney
bchasen@chasenandboscolo.com
• Thomas Teodori, Attorney
tteodori@chasenandboscolo.com
• Barry M Chasen, Attorney
bchasen@chasenandboscolo.com
• Gerald Herz, Attorney
gherz@chasenandboscolo.com
• W. David Falcon, Attorney
wfalcon@chasenandboscolo.com
• Matthew J. Peffer, Attorney
mpeffer@chasenandboscolo.com
• Michael D Reiter, Attorney
mreiter@chasenandboscolo.com
• Kevin H Stillman, Attorney
kstillman@chasenandboscolo.com
Services:
Represents professional athletes in disability and worker's compensation claims

CHERNESKY, RICHARD
10 N LUDLOW STREET
1100 COURTHOUSE PLAZA SW
DAYTON, OH 45402

937-449-2800
Fax: 937-449-2821
www.dinsmore.com
• Richard J. Chernesky, Managing Partner
(937) 449-2800
rjc@chklaw.com
• Edward M. Kress, Attorney
(937) 449-2800
emk@chklaw.com
• Richard A. Broock, Attorney
rab@chklaw.com
• Suellen J. Young, Executive Director
fjc@chklaw.com
• Kenneth L. Crooks, Chief Financial Officer
• Jennifer A. Davenport, Director of Marketing
• Christopher Flaherty, Chief Business Development Officer
• Stephanie Higgins, Director of Human Resources & Employee Benefi
• Mary Jo Merkowitz, Director of Library Services
• Frederick Caspar, Attorney
Description:
Business Law,Mergers & Acquisitions, Litigation, Estate Planning.
Services:
Corporate law, strategic planning, tax analysis, and litigation
Clients:
AAA Miami Valley Advantage Per Diem Staffing, LLC AK Steel Architectural Resources Corporation The Aristocrat Products Mfg. Co. Audi of America, Inc. The Berry Company Better Business Bureau of Dayton/Miami Valley, Inc. Bradstreet & Company, Inc. Bri Lyn, Inc. Brown Industrial, Inc. CBS Personnel Services, LLC Central State University Foundation CFA Holding, Inc. Chiropractic Health & Wellness Center, Inc. Church of the Messiah The Connor Group CSA Nutrition Services, Inc. Day International, Inc. Dayton Christian School, Inc. The Dayton Heart Center, Inc. The Dayton-Montgomery County Port Authority Digital Concepts, Inc. Digitron, Inc.
Year Founded:
1988

CINDRICH & COMPANY
552 WASHINGTON AVENUE
PITTSBURGH, PA 15106
412-429-1250
Fax: 412-429-1260
info@cindrich.com
www.cindrich.com
• Ralph E. Cindrich, Founder
(412) 429-1250
ralph@cindrich.com
• Gregory P. Diulus, Attorney
(412) 429-1250
gregory@cindrich.com
• Brian Ayrault, Attorney/Contract Advisor
brian@cindrich.com
• John Bermudez, Executive Director
john@cindrich.com
Services:
Assists clients in all football career related areas; deals with every significant company in the sporting goods, apparel and trading card industry; career counseling; media relations; legal advice and assistance; tax advice and preparation of tax returns; financial planning; represented Pro Football players from every team in the NFL and CFL
Clients:
Rookies: Greg Esligner, Erik Gill, Bruce Gradkowski, Ryan LaCasse, Matt Lentz,

Chris Morris, Jonathan Orr, Kai Parham, John Ritcher, Jason Spitz, Ative NFL clients: Eugene Baker, Ladell Betts, Martin Bibla, Jeff Blake, Jamaal Branch, Zach Bray, Ethan Brooks, Lang Campbell, Ben Claxton, Enoch DeMar, Daryl Dixon, Jeff Dugan, Mike Echols, Eric Edwards, James Farrior, Matt Farrior, Mike Flynn, Kynan Forney, John Paul 'JP' Foschi, Hank Fraley, Steven Gibbs, Tarik Glenn, Brian Griese, Michael Hawthorne, Ronney Jenkins, Adrian Klemm, Justin Kurpeikis, Mike Labinjo, Rien Long, Rasheed Marshall

CLARDY, DON S.
55 BEATTIE PLACE
ONE LIBERTY SQUARE, SUITE 1200, PO BOX 10589
SUITE 1200
GREENVILLE, SC 29601
864-271-9580
Fax: 864-271-7502
www.gwblawfirm.com
• Henry Mi Gallivan, Managing Shareholder
(864) 271-5341
mgallivan@gwblawfirm.com
• W. Howard Boyd, Jr., Shareholder
(864) 271-5343
hboyd@gwblawfirm.com
• Arthur L. Howson Jr, Shareholder
(864) 271-5352
ahowson@gwblawfirm.com
• Freda G. Lark, Human Resources Manager
(864) 271-5392
flark@GWBLawfirm.com
• Jeanette Behrens, Operations Assistant
(864) 271-5432
jbehrens@GWBlawfirm.com
• Tiffany Breeden, Billing & Collections Manager
(864) 241-7020
tbreeden@GWBlawfirm.com
• Kevin Dehlinger, Marketing Director
(864) 271-5369
kdehlinger@GWBlawfirm.com
• Kira DeLoache, Accounting Director
(864) 271-5388
kdeloache@GWBlawfirm.com
• Freda Lark, Human Resources Director
(864) 271-5392
flark@GWBlawfirm.com
• Rick Phillips, Operations Director
(864) 271-5393
rphillips@GWBlawfirm.com
Description:
Corporate law, Business Law, Estate Planning, Trusts & Estates.
Services:
Litigation, Administrative Law, Business and Commercial Law, Alternative Dispute Resolution
Clients:
ACE USA, AETNA, Air Products Polymers, L.P., American International Group, Baxter Healthcare Corporation, Bayer Corporation, BBA Nonwovens, Bell-Air, LLC, Blue Cross Blue Shield of South Carolina, BP America, Inc., Canal Insurance Company, Centex Homes, Central Carolina Bank, City of Greenville, CNA Insurance Companies, Coca-Cola Bottling Company Consolidated, CoLinx, LLC, Companion Healthcare, Companion Technologies, Crown Cork & Seal, CSX Transportation, Inc., DIRECTV, Inc., Dycos Staffing, Inc., The Dow Chemical Company, Empire Fire & Marine Insurance, Engelhard Corporation, ESIS,

Genuine Parts Company, GMAC Insurance, Greenville Airport C

CLARK, CAROL
1544 OLD ALABAMA ROAD
ROSWELL, GA 30076
770-804-0400
800-275-7171
Fax: 770-643-4080
www.mccalla.com
• Carol V. Clark, Attorney
(770) 804-0400
carol.clark@mccalla.com
• Timothy L. Geraghty, Attorney
(770) 804-0400
Services:
Contract negotiation

CLAYBORNE, COURTNEY
4020 JACKSON BOULEVARD
PO BOX 6900
RAPID CITY, SD 57709-6900
605-348-7300
800-998-3998
Fax: 605-348-4757
JohnsonEiesland@Rushmore.com
www.johnsoneiesland.com
• Courtney R. Clayborne, Attorney (Past)
• Glen H. Johnson, Attorney/Partner
gjohnson22@aol.com
• Gregory A. Eiesland, Attorney/Partner
geiesland@aol.com
• Kenneth R. Dewell, Attorney/Associate
Description:
Business Law, Commercial Litigation, Workers Compensation.
Services:
Laywer, Rapid City, SD, injury, Rapid City, medical, automobile, attorney, Rapid City, criminal, malpractice, Contracts, insurance, Defense, Rapid City

CLINARD, KEITH ASHFORD
ONE W FOURTH STREET
PO BOX 84
WINSTON-SALEM, NC 27101
336-721-3600
Fax: 336-721-3660
www.wcsr.com
• Keith A. Clinard, Attorney
(336) 721-3631
KClinard@wcsr.com
• William Sullivan, Senior Partner
(336) 721-3506
WSullivan@wcsr.com
• Deborah Hylton, Partner
DHylton@wcsr.com
• James B. Hunt Jr, Partner
JHunt@wcsr.com
Services:
Contract negotiation, arbitration hearings, tort actions/litigation.
Other Locations:
1401 Eye Street NW, 7th Floor, Washington, DC 20005; 8065 Leesburg Pike, 4th Floor, Tysons Corner, VA 22182; One Atlantic Center, STE 3500, 1201 West Peachtree Street, Atlanta, GA 30309

COHEN, ROBERT M.
4 FANEUIL HALL SQUARE
3RD FLOOR
BOSTON, MA 2109-1632
617-523-0505
• Robert M. Cohen, Founder
(617) 523-0505
• Steven D. Weil, Partner

(617) 523-0505
• Janet B. Fierman, Founding Partner
(617) 523-0505
• Thomas W. Evans, Partner
(617) 523-0505
• Robert M Cohen, Partner
Services:
Provides comprehensive business, real estate and litigation services
Clients:
Restaurants: Applebee's, Boston Market, Cinnabon, Inc., D'Angelos, Inc., Fuddruckers, Inc., McDonald's Corporation, Papa Gino's, Inc.; Retail & Service Companies: BÆ'loise-Holding, Bridgestone/Firestone, Dancing Deer Baking Company, Exxon/Mobil, HP, Kinkos, Inc., MBNA America Bank, N.A., Mercator Assurances S.A., Pitney Bowes, Zeltia S.A.; Real Estate: AIMCO, Alcourt Management Corporation, AvalonBay Communities, DMC Management Company, The Dolben Company, Inc., ELAW Corporation, Forest City, Homes Incorporated, Stuart Family Trust, Trammell Crow Company
Description:
Sports law.

COHN, WILLIAM A.
291 GERMANTOWN BEND COVE
CORDOVA, TN 38018
901-757-5557
888-LAWVOL1
Fax: 901-757-5535
info@cohnlawfirm.com
www.cohnlawfirm.com
• William Cohn, Principal Attorney
(901) 757-5557
info@cohnlawfirm.com
• Jeremy A. A Davis, Associate Attorney
Year Founded:
1981.
Sports Service Founded:
1985.
Nature of Service:
Focuses on personal injury, auto accidents, DUI, medical malpractice, family law, Real Estate Law, Bunkruptcy, Business Law, Account Collections, Social Security Disability and Sports Law.

COLE, DAYTON T.
BB DOUGHETHY ADMINISTRATION BUILDING
3RD FLOOR
PO BOX 32126
BOONE, NC 28608-2126
828-262-2000
Fax: 828-262-2556
www.appstate.edu
• Dayton T. Cole, University Attorney
(828) 262-2751
coledt@appstate.edu
• Dr. Kenneth E. Peacock, The Chancellor
• Dr. Lori Gonzalez, The Provost
• Cathy Bates, Chief Information Officer
• Charlie Cobb, Director of Athletics
• Hank Foreman, Associate Vice Chancellor for University Comm
• Lori Gonzalez, Provost & Executive Vice Chancellor
• Patrick McCoy, Director of Human Resources
Description:
Represents college athletic departments.

professional services

COLLINS, MESEREAU, REDDOCK & YU, LLP
10390 SANTA MONICA BOULEVARD
SUITE 220
LOS ANGELES, CA 90025
310-789-1177
Fax: 310-861-1007
info@mesereauyu.com
www.mesereauyu.com
• Susan C. Yu, Attorney
• Thomas A. Mesereau, Jr, Attorney
• Susan C Yu, Attorney
Services:
Litigation, criminal cases (state and federal court), civil rights, personal injury and sports/entertainment law, fraud, unfair competition, securities fraud, employment, breach of contract.

COMODECA, JAMES A.
255 E FIFTH STREET
SUITE 1900
CINCINNATI, OH 45202
513-977-8200
800-934-3477
Fax: 513-977-8141
info@dinslaw.com
• Alan H. Abes, Partner
(513) 977-8149
alan.abes@dinslaw.com
• James A. Comodeca, Partner
(513) 977-8358
jim.comodeca@dinslaw.com
Services:
Provides quality legal counsel to our clients
clients:
Public and private corporations to charitable organizations and encompass healthcare providers, local and state governments, financial institutions, real estate evelopers, franchisors and distributors and pharmaceutical companies.
Description:
General Litigation; Medical Malpractice Defense; Sports/Entertainment Law; Products Liability Defense.
Other Locations:
Lexington Financial Center, 250, West Main Street, STE 1400, Lexington, KY 40507; Phone: 859-425-1000; The Grant Building, 330 Grant Street, STE 2415, Pittsburgh, PA 15219; Phone: 412-281-5000

CONBOY, JOSEPH B.
1802 HARTFORD AVENUE
LUBBOCK, TX 79409-0004
806-742-3990 EXT 226
Fax: 806-742-1629
info.law@ttu.edu
www.law.ttu.edu
• Jon Whitmore, President
(806) 742-2121
tech.president@ttu.edu
• Jennifer S. Bard, Director of the Health Law Program
(806) 742-3990
• Martha McDaniel, Senior Business Assistant
(806) 742-3990
martha.mcdaniel@ttu.edu
• Dan Runge, Asst. Director, Admissions
(806) 742-3990
Description:
Teaches sports law.

CONBOY, MELISSA L.
317 MAIN BUILDING
113 JOYCE CENTER
NOTRE DAME, IN 46556
574-631-5000
Fax: 574-631-8212
newsinfo@nd.edu
www.nd.edu
• John Jerkins, President
(574) 631-3903
newsinfo@nd.edu
• Jack L Swarbrick, University Vice President/Director of Athleti
(574) 631-6107
• Missy Conboy, Senior Deputy Athletics Director
(574) 631-6107
• John Heisler, Senior Associate A.D./Media & Broadcast Relat
(574) 631-6107
• Tom Nevala, Senior Associate Athletics Director
(574) 631-6107
• Jill Bodensteiner, Associate Athletics Director
(574) 631-6107
• Michael Danch, Associate Athletics Director
(574) 631-6107
• Jim Fraleigh, Associate Athletics Director
(574) 631-6107
Services:
Represents college athletic departments NCAA Compliance.

CONNELL, MARY ANN
2094 OLD TAYLOR ROAD
SUITE 200
5 UNIVERSITY OFFICE PARK
OXFORD, MS 38655
662-236-0055
Fax: 662-236-0035
mconnell@mayomallette.com
www.mayomallette.com
• J. Ca Mayo Jr, Partner
(662) 236-0055
cmayo@mayomallette.com
• Pope S. Mallette, Partner
(662) 236-0055
pmallette@mayomallette.com
Description:
Represents college athletic departments.
Services:
Provides outstanding legal services to local, regional and national clients from its offices located in north Mississippi
Clients:
Amphenol Corporation, Baptist Memorial Health Care Corporation, Copeland Corporation, Emerson Electric Company, First National Bank of Oxford, Grisanti Ford, Inc., Grisanti Rebel Motors, Inc., Johnston-Tombigbee Furniture Manufacturing Company

CONNER & WINTERS, P.L.L.C.
4000 ONE WILLIAMS CENTER
TULSA, OK 74172-0148
918-586-5711
www.cwlaw.com
• John R. Elrod, Partner
(479) 582-5711
jelrod@cwlaw.com
• Greg S. Scharlau, Partner
(479) 582-5711
gscharlau@cwlaw.com
• Charles E. Scharlau, Jr, Attorney
(479) 582-5711
cscharlau@cwlaw.com

• Victor F. Di Albert, Partner
(405) 272-5733
valbert@cwlaw.com
• P. Bradley Bendure, Partner
(918) 586-8521
bbendure@cwlaw.com
• Mark H. Bennett, Partner
(405) 272-5718
mbennett@cwlaw.com
• Mark G. Berman, Partner
(918) 586-8961
mberman@cwlaw.com
• Gary L. Betow, Partner
(918) 586-5714
gbetow@cwlaw.com
• Debbie L. Blackwell, Partner
(918) 586-8970
dbleckwell@cwlaw.com
• Terri Chadick, Of counsel
(479) 582-5711
tchadick@cwlaw.com
Description:
Services extend from general, personal and business counseling to highly specialized assistance and advice. The firm offers a full range of legal services in each of our offices with regard to banking, real estate, trusts, probate, estate planning, litigation, income, gift taxation law and corporate finance.
Year Founded:
1933
Other Locations:
1627 I Street, NW STE 900, Washington, DC 20006; Phone: 202-887-5711; 1000 Louisiana, STE 1301, Houston, TX 77002; Phone: 713-355-5711; 1700 One Leadership Square, 211 North Robinson, Oklahoma City, OK 73102; Phone: 405-272-5711

COOK & FRANKE S.C.
660 E MASON STREET
MILWAUKEE, WI 53202
414-271-5900
Fax: 414-271-2002
• Steven L Nelson, Attorney
(414) 227-1220
• Jeffrey JP Conta, Attorney
(414) 227-1226
jconta@cf-law.com
• Lawrence Clancy, Attorney
(414) 227-1207
clancy@cf-law.com
• Paul D. Cranley, Attorney
(608) 251-0404
Services:
Contract negotiation, represents professional sports teams (Milwaukee Admirals).
Clients:
Companies and individuals working in the electronics, manufacturing, communications, utility and construction engineering, architectural, design and construction, commercial real estate, sports and entertainment industries.

COOLEY, GODWARD, LLP
101 CALIFORNIA STREET
5TH FLOOR
SAN FRANCISCO, CA 94111-5800
415-693-2000
Fax: 415-693-2222
www.cooley.com
• Gian-Michele A Marca, Partner
(415) 693-2148
gmamarca@cooley.com

• Stephen Neal, Chairman
• Joe Conoroy, CEO
• Mark Pitchford, Administrative and Legal Practice Partner
• Warren Martin, COO
• Gordon C Atkinson, Partner
(415) 693-2088
Services:
Represents professional sports teams.
Other Locatons:
380 Interlocken Crescent, STE 900, Bloomfield, CO 80021; Phone: 720-566-4000; One Freedom Square, Reston Tower Center, 11951 Freedom Drive, Reston, VA 20190; Phone: 703-456-8000

CORBETT & STEELMAN
18200 VON KARMAN AVENUE
SUITE 900
IRVINE, CA 92612-1023
949-553-9266
Fax: 949-553-8454
cvaughn@corbsteel.com
www.corbettandsteelman.com
• Bruce R. Corbett, Attorney
• Ken E. Steelman, Attorney
• Richard B. Spector, Attorney
• Christine Vaughn, Office Administration
cvaughn@corbsteel.com
Services:
Business litigation, entertainment litigation, media, sports law.

COWAN, DEBAETS, ABRAHAMS & SHEPPARD, LLP
41 MADISON AVENUE
34TH FLOOR
NEW YORK, NY 10010
212-974-7474
Fax: 212-974-8474
cdas@cdas.com
www.cdas.com
• Timothy Debaets, Partner
(212) 974-7474
tdebaets@cdas.com
• Anne C. Baker, Partner
(212) 974-7474
abaker@cdas.com
• Frederick P. Bimbler, Partner
fbimbler@cdas.com
Description:
Sports Law, Motion Picture; Television; Publishing.
Services:
Entertainment law, publishing, art law, copyright, trademark, and litigation
Clients:
Well-known organizations and individuals in motion pictures, television, book publishing, the visual arts and sports.

CRIVELLO, CARLSON, MENTKOWSKI S.C.
710 N PLANKINTON AVENUE
SUITE 500
MILWAUKEE, WI 53203
414-271-7722
Fax: 414-271-4438
www.milwlaw.com
• Nick Kotsonis, Attorney
(414) 271-7722
nkotsonis@milwlaw.com
• Donald H. Carlson, Attorney
(414) 271-7722
DCarlson@milwlaw.com

Description:
Contract negotiation.
Services:
Provides Trial, Appellate, Mediation and Arbitration Services in the following areas: Architectural and Engineering Litigation, Civil Rights Litigation, Commercial and Corporate Litigation, Construction Litigation, Electrical Accidents, Electronic Media and Privacy Law, Employee Benefits/ ERISA, Employment Law, Environmental Litigation, Errors and Omissions, Fire and Explosion, Fraudulent Insurance Claims, Industrial Accidents, Insurance Bad Faith Defense, Insurance Coverage Litigation, Labor Law, Legal Malpractice Defense, Libel, Slander and Defamation, Management Labor Relations, Mechanical Accidents

CROAK, FRANCIS R.
660 E MASON STREET
STE 300
MILWAUKEE, WI 53202
414-271-5900
Fax: 414-271-2002
• Francis R. Croak, Shareholder
• Lawrence Clancy, Attorney
(414) 227-1207
• Jeffrey JP Conta, Attorney
(414) 227-1226
Services:
Contract negotiation, represents professional sports teams (Milwaukee Admirals).
Clients:
Companies and individuals working in the electronics, manufacturing, communications, utility and construction engineering, architectural, design and construction, commercial real estate, sports and entertainment industries.

CULLEN, WESTON, PINES & BACH LLP
122 W WASHINGTON AVENUE
SUITE 900
MADISON, WI 53703-2718
608-807-0752
Fax: 608-251-2883
www.cwpb.com
• Lee Cullen, President/Attorney
(608) 251-0101
cullen@cwpb.com
• Carol Grob, Partner
(608) 251-0101
grob@cwpb.com
• Curt F. Pawlisch, Partner
pawlisch@cwpb.com
Services:
Includes labor and employment, energy and telecommunications, governmental relations, family law, civil and criminal litigation, and business and commerce
Description:
Contract Negotiation.

DALTON, MICHAEL
2200 ROSS AVENUE
SUITE 5200
DALLAS, TX 75201
214-665-3600
Fax: 214-665-3601
www.gtlaw.com
• Michael Dalton, Shareholder
(214) 665-3628
• Eric W Buether, Shareholder
(214) 665-3664

Services:
Provides advice and counsel to industry leaders worldwide

DANIELS, ERIC D.
280 TRUMBULL STREET
HARTFORD, CT 06103-3597
860-275-8200
Fax: 860-275-8299
ml@rc.com
www.rc.com
• Nancy A. Hayes, Operation Officer
(860) 275-8368
• Peter M. Merriman, Financial Officer
(860) 275-8368
• Wystan M. Ackerman, Partner
(860) 275-8388
wackerman@rc.com
• Shannon Holden, Legal Administrative Assistant
(860) 541-2645
sholden@rc.com
• Benjamin B. Adams, Member
(860) 275-8271
• Adam Anderson, Associates
(860) 275-8352
aanderson@rc.com
• Stephen W. Aronson, Partner
(860) 275-8281
saronson@rc.com
• Eileen P. Baldwin, Member
(860) 275-8277
ebaldwin@rc.com
Services:
Provides Trial, Appellate, Mediation and Arbitration Services in the following areas: Architectural and Engineering Litigation, Civil Rights Litigation, Commercial and Corporate Litigation, Construction Litigation
Description:
Contract negotiation.

DAVIS & KUELTHAU, S.C.
111 E KILBOURN AVENUE
SUITE 1400
MILWAUKEE, WI 53202
414-276-0200
lbevan@dkattorneys.com
www.dkattorneys.com
• Charles I. Henderson, Attorney/Shareholder
(414) 225-1479
chenderson@dkattorneys.com
• Lee A. M Bevan, Local Office Administrator
(414) 225-7503
lbevan@dkattorneys.com
• Dillon J. Ambrose, Associate
(414) 225-1410
dambrose@dkattorneys.com
• Patrick M. Bergin, Shareholder
(414) 225-7563
pbergin@dkattorneys.com
• James E. Braza, Shareholder
(414) 225-1421
jbraza@dkattorneys.com
• Rodney W. Carter, Shareholder
(262) 792-2405
rcarter@dkattorneys.com
• Peter W. Bruce, Of Counsel
(414) 225-1437
pbruce@dkattorneys.com
• Dianne S. Cauble, Of Counsel
(414) 225-1436
dcauble@dkattorneys.com
Description:
Contract negotiation, arbitration hearings, federal/state/international tax filings,

represents professional sports teams, endorsement exploration, tort actions/litigation, representing sports arenas and event sponsors.

Other Locations:
10 East Doty Street, STE 600, Madison, WI 53703; Phone: 608-280-8235; 318 South Washington Street, suite 300 Green Bay, WI 54301; Phone: 920-435-9378; 219 Washington Avenue,Oshkosh, WI 54901; Phone: 920-233-6050 605 North 8th Street, STE 610, Sheboygan, WI 53081; Phone: 920-451-1461; 300 North Corporate Drive, STE 150, Brookfield, WI 53045; Phone: 262-792-2400

DAVIS & WILKERSON
5113 SW PARKWAY
SUITE 115
AUSTIN, TX 78735
512-482-0614
Fax: 512-482-0342
www.dwlaw.com
• David M. Davis, Director/Shareholder
(512) 482-0614
ddavis@dwlaw.com
• Kevin Reed, VP
(512) 482-0614
kreed@dwlaw.com
• Leonard W Woods, Secretary/Treasurer
lwoods@dwlaw.com
• Robert L Hargett, Director
rhargett@dwlaw.com
Services:
All phases of athlete representation including contract negotiation, long-range planning, financial planning, and post-career counseling. Construction Litigation; First and Third Party Insurance Litigation; Products Liability.
Other Location:
1110 East Holland, Alpine, TX 79803; Phone: 432-837-5547
Year Founded:
1985

DEE, PAUL T.
5821 SAN AMARO DRIVE
PO BOX 248167
CORAL GABLES, FL 33146
305-284-2680
Fax: 305-284-2193
athleticdirector@miami.edu
www.hurricanesports.collegesports.com
• Paul T. Dee, Intercollegiate Athletics Director
(305) 284-2673
athleticdirector@miami.edu
• Blake James, Athletics Director
• Chris Freet, Associate AD
• Tony Hernandez, Deputy AD/Business Operations
• Jennifer Strawley, Sr Associate AD
Description:
Represents college athletic departments.

DEKAJLO LAW
1975 HEMPSTEAD TURNPIKE
SUITE 101
EAST MEADOW, NY 11554
516-542-9300
Fax: 516-542-9303
dekajlo@aol.com
dekajlo.com
• Oleh Dekajlo, Managing Partner
(516) 542-9300

• Orest R. Dekajlo, Attorney
(516) 542-9300
Services:
Tort actions/litigation.

DEMAYO, LAW OFFICES OF MICHAEL L.L.P.
1211 EAST MOREHEAD ST
CHARLOTTE, NC 28204
704-333-1000
877-529-1222
Fax: 704-333-6677
• Michael A. DeMayo, Principal/Founder
michael@demayolaw.com
• Michael J. McGinley, Chief Operating Officer
Nature of Service:
Represents auto accidents, workers' compensation, medical malpractices, personal injury and mass torts, social security disability, nursing home negligence, wrongful death, motocycle accidents, tractor trailer accidents, serious brain and spinal cord injuries. Guide our clients through the legal and financial challenges that they face after they are injured in a dignified and responsible manner.
Year Founded:
1992
Other Locations:
321 3rd Avenue NW, Hickory, NC 28601; 406 S Sutherland Avenue, Monroe, NC 28112

DENUNE, III, RALPH
5580 MONROE STREET
TOLEDO, OH 43560
419-885-3597
Fax: 419-885-3861
• John J. Callahan, Attorney
(419) 885-3597
• John F. McCarty, Attorney
(419) 885-3597
• Ralph De III, Attorney
(419) 885-3597
• John J. McHugh III, Attorney
(419) 885-3597
Services:
Provides Legal Services.

DEUTCH, ALLAN H
7670 N PORT WASHINGTON ROAD
STE 200
MILWAUKEE, WI 53217
414-247-9958
Fax: 414-247-9959
alan.deutch@deutch.com
www.deutch.com
• Alan H. Deutch, Attorney
alan.deutch@deutch.com
• Monte E. Weiss, Attorney
monte.weiss@deutch.com
• Alan H. Deutch, Attorney
• James L. McAlister, Attorney
• Nichole King, Legal Assistant
• G. Brighum, Legal Assisatant
Clients:
Real Estate Related: Re/Max Realty 100, Re/Max Preferred, Capitol Title, Inc. Title 100, Inc, Re/Max Executive Homes, Inc, American Southern Insurance Co., Home Insurance Co., Utah Fire and Home Insurance Co, Investors Insurance Co, Rupnow Homes, Bradley J. Kimmel Homes, M & M Home Builders, Meadow Homes, North Meadows, Park Meadows, Forest Hill Village, Cloisters of Greenforest Computer

Related: Innovative Software, Ltd, Web Emporium, LLC, Paramount Optical Laboratories, Allen-Knox Studios, Crownpoint Timesharing, Multiple Listing Service, Inc. Insurance Defense: Amerisure Insurance Company, American Family Insurance, American Southern Insur
Description:
Contract negotiation, teaches sports law, represents professional sports teams, licensing, endorsement exploration, tort actions/litigation, represents sports organizations.

DEWALD, SCOTT D.
201 EAST WASHINGTON
SUITE 1200
PHOENIX, AZ 85004
602-262-5311
Fax: 602-262-5747
clientservices@lrlaw.com
www.lewisandroca.com
• Scott D. DeWald, Partner
(602) 262-5333
Sdewald@lrlaw.com
• Nathalie M Daum, Marketing Director
(602) 528-4588
clientservices@lrlaw.com
Description:
Represents professional sports teams, provides securities advice, licensing.

DIFILIPPO, JAMES
2001 E FOURTH STREET
SUITE 104
SANTA ANNA, CA 92705
714-543-1770
• James Difilippo, Contact
description
real estate.

DINSMORE
101 S FIFTH STREET
2500 NATIONAL CITY TOWER
LOUISVILLE, KY 40202-3175
502-540-2300
Fax: 502-585-2207
• Donna King Perry, Managing Partner
(502) 581-8085
dperry@whf-law.com
• Glen Bagby, Partner
(859) 244-7100
gbagby@whf-law.com
Services:
Real property, probate, products liability, securities, health and hospital, medical malpractice, tax law, sports law and entertainment law.
Clients:
Norton Healthcare, CARITAS, Catholic Health Initiatives, CNA Pro, Chubb Insurance Company, Design Professionals Insurance Company, Interstate Insurance Company, Philadelphia Insurance Company, Pharmacists Mutual Insurance Company, Liberty Mutual Underwriters and AIG, American Commercial Lines Holdings LLC/Jeffboat LLC, Anderson Wood Products,Bank One Corporation ,Baptist Healthcare Systems , Brown-Forman Corporation, CARITAS Medical Center, CARITAS Peace Center, CARITAS Home Health, Catholic Health Initiatives, Center for Women and Families, Colgate-Palmolive Company, Ford Motor Company, Hill's Pet Nutrition, Kentucky Restaurant Association P

DREW, ECKL & FARNHAM, LLP
880 W PEACHTREE STREET
PO BOX 7600
ATLANTA, GA 30309
404-885-1400
Fax: 404-876-0992
jreale@deflaw.com
www.deflaw.com
• John P. Reale, Partner
(404) 885-6404
Description:
Civil, corporate or individual cases.
Services:
Provides company a wide variety of practice areas, including Civil rights/municipal liability, commercial law, construction law, employment and labor law, environmental law, federal workers' compensation, general liability, insurance coverage, major property subrogation, medical malpractice, nursing home litigation, personal injury, premises liability, products liability, professional athletes/ entertainment, professional liability, propety insurance, reinsurance, transportation cargo, transportation trucking, workers' compensation.
Year Founded:
1983

DRINKER BIDDLE
191 N WACKER DRIVE
SUITE 3700
CHICAGO, IL 60606-1698
312-569-1000
Fax: 312-569-3000
www.drinkerbiddle.com
• Harold L. Kaplan, Chairman/Partner
(312) 569-1204
• David L. Wolfe, Partner
(312) 569-1313
dwolfe@gcd.com
• Edwin A. Getz, Partner in Charge
• Matthew Farley, Counsel
(212) 248-3150
• Mark D. Nelson, Partner
(312) 569-1326
Services:
Practices and industries include Corporate Law, Corporate Restructuring & Financial Institutions, Customs and International Trade, Government Relations, Health, Higher Education, Indian Tribal Governments, Intellectual Property, Litigation, Pharmaceuticals, Real Estate, Wealth Planning & Philanthropy.
Clients:
Client base includes Fortune 1000 and middle market companies, investment advisory firms, financial institutions, hospitals and health care providers, universities, governmental entities, manufacturing companies and emerging technology companies.
Description:
Contract negotiation, post career planning, investment contract negotiation, federal/state/international tax filings, licensing, endorsement exploration.

DUANE MORRIS LLP
750 B STREET
SUITE 2900
SAN DIEGO, CA 92101-4681
619-744-2200
Fax: 619-744-2201
www.duanemorris.com

• Charles J. O'Donnell, Chief Operating Officer
(215) 979-1450
CJODonnell@duanemorris.com
• Michael A. Gillen, Tax Accounting Director
(215) 979-1635
MAGillen@duanemorris.com
• Mary Fa Robinson, Human Resources Director
(215) 979-1290
MFRobinson@duanemorris.com
• Marianne F M. Adriatico, Partner
(619) 744-2212
MFAdriatico@duanemorris.com
• P.Blake Allen, Partner
(619) 744-2231
• Ann K Bradley, Partner
(619) 744-2269
akbradley@duanemorris.com
• David A Charapp, Partner
(619) 744-2251
dcharapp@duanemorris.com
• Richard C kim, Partner
(619) 744-2294
RCKim@duanemorris.com
• Lisa H Chung, Associate
(619) 744-2272
LChung@duanemorris.com
• Courtney L Baird, Associate
(619) 744-2285
CLBaird@duanemorris.com
Clients:
From Fortune 500 companies to small entrepreneurial ventures, from public entities to individuals; domestic and international clients ranging from large multinational corporations to closely held entrepreneurial businesses.
Description:
Business law, business litigation, college and university law, commercial law, commercial litigation, sports law, trademarks, trademark licensing.
Other Locations:
1667 K Street, NW, Washington, DC 20006; Phone: 202-776-7800;380 Lexington Avenue, New York, NY 10168: Phone: 211-692-1000; 470 Atlantic Avenue, STE 500, Boston, MA 02210; Phone: 617-289-9200; 3200 Southwest Freeway, STE 3150, Houston, TX 77027; Phone: 713-402-3900

DUKE LEGAL COUNSEL
310 BLACKWELL STREET
4TH FLOOR, BOX 104124
DURHAM, NC 27710
919-684-3955
Fax: 919-684-8725
ogc-info@duke.edu
www.ogc.duke.edu
• Pamela J. Bernard, Vice President and General Counsel
pam.bernard@duke.edu
• Mark D. Gustafson, Deputy Counsel
• Kate S. Hendricks, Deputy Counsel for Duke University
kate.hendricks@duke.edu
• Ann E. Bradley, Associate University Counsel
ann.bradley@duke.edu
• Henry L. Cuthbert, Associate University Counsel
henry.cuthbert@duke.edu
Description:
Represents college athletic departments.

DURANTE, CHARLES J.
1007 N ORANGE STREET
NINTH FLOOR
PO BOX 2207
WILMINGTON, DE 19801
302-658-9141
Fax: 302-658-5614
• Charles J. Durante, Partner
(302) 888-6280
• Burton A. Amernick, Partner
(202) 331-7111
• D. Ro Casey, IS/Operations Manager
• Burton A. Amernick, Partner
(202) 331-7111
burton.amernick@novakdruce.com
• Richard C. Auchterlonie, Partner
(713) 571-3400
richard.auchterlonie@novakdruce.com
• Joseph W. Bain, Partner
(561) 847-7800
joseph.bain@novakdruce.com
• R. James Balls, Partner
(202) 572-0319
james.balls@novakdruce.com
• Katherine M. Basile, Partner
(408) 414-7330
katherine.basile@novakdruce.com
• Michael Bell, Partner
(202) 331-7111
michael.bell@novakdruce.com
• Jeffrey B. Bove, Partner
(302) 888-6241
jeff.bove@novakdruce.com
Other Location:
1990 M Street NW, STE 800, Washington, DC 20036; Phone: 202-331-7111
Services:
Provides wide range of legal disciplines in the fields of Intellectual Property, Commercial, Corporate, and Business Law, Transaction Services, International Trade Commission, Bankruptcy, Mergers and Acquisitions
Clients:
International, national and local corporate and individual clients.

EBERLE, BERLIN, KADING, TURNBOW & MCKLVEEN
1111 W JEFFERSON STREET SUITE 530
PO BOX 1368
BOISE, ID 83701
208-344-8535
Fax: 208-344-8542
webmaster@eberle.com
www.eberle.com
• R.M. Turnbow, Attorney
rturnbow@eberle.com
• William J. McKlveen, Attorney
wmcklveen@eberle.com
• Warren E. Jones, Attorney
wjones@eberle.com
• Thomas R. Linville, Attorney
tlinville@eberle.com
Services:
Provides Legal Services.
Clients:
Ada County Highway District; Agri-Beef Co.; AT&T; Bank United of Texas; Cessna Aircraft Co.; Chase Manhattan Leasing & Co.; C.I.T. Group Equipment Financing, Inc.; Citicorp Naitonal Services, Inc.; CRI Advantage, Inc.; The Dosen Companies; Deloitte & Touche; Employers Resource Management Company; First Banks; Franklin Building Supply Company; New Holland, North America; General Electric Co.; Investors Property Management;

Edward D. Jones & Co.; Key Bank National Association; Key Corp Leasing, Ltd.; DcDonnell Douglas Corporation; OX Ranch; Phillips Petroleum; Piper Jaffrey, Inc.; Prudential Securities; Shearson/American Express

ECKERT SEAMANS
600 GRANT STREET
US STEEL TOWER 44TH FLOOR
PITTSBURGH, PA 15219-2788
412-566-6000
Fax: 412-566-6099
info@eckertseamans.com
www.eckertseamans.com
• Timothy P. Ryan, Chief Executive Officer
(412) 566-5990
tryan@eckertseamans.com
• Scott D. Cessar, Attorney in Charge
scessar@eckertseamans.com
• Dan Abeles, Member
(412) 566-1295
dabeles@eckertseamans.com
• Jennifer Adams, Associate
(412) 566-6859
jadams@eckertseamans.com
• Brij K. Agarwal, Member
(412) 566-6183
bagarwal@eckertseamans.com
• Kevin P. Allen, Member
(412) 566-6866
kpallen@eckertseamans.com
• Kathryn C. Arbogast, Associate
(412) 566-6088
karbogast@eckertseamans.com
• Daniel C. P. Abeles, Member
(412) 566-1295
dabeles@eckertseamans.com
Clients:
Any local, regional, national or international corporations, individual, entrepreneurial, start-up, nonprofit and government clients.
Description:
Provides legal services to sports, entertainment and arts industry clients throughout the country. General representation of professional and college sports organizations. Advises on a number of sports-related issues, including player contracts and other labor law matters, broadcasting agreements, trademark, copyright and merchandising issues, as well as general corporate, finance and litigation matters
Other Locations:
1747 Pennsylvania Avenue, NW, STE 1200, Washington, DC 20006; Phone: 202-659-6600; Fax: 202-659-6699; The Towne Center, 4 East 8th Street, STE 200, Wilmington, DE 19801; Phone: 302-425-0430; Fax: 302-425-0432; U.S Steel Tower, 600 Grant Street, 44th Floor, Pittsburgh, PA 15219; Phone: 412-566-6000; Fax 412-566-6099; 1515 Market Street, 9th Floor, Philadelphia, PA 19102; Phone: 215-851-8400; Fax: 215-851-8383; 213 Market Street, 8th Floor, Harrisbury, PA 17101; Phone: 717-237-6000; Fax: 717-237-6019; 2400 Cranberry Square, 2nd Floor, Morgantown, WV 26508; Phone: 304-594-1000; Fax: 304-594-1181

ECKSTEIN LAW FIRM
1515 POYDRAS ST
SUITE 2195
NEW ORLEANS, LA 70112
504-527-0701
Fax: 504-566-0040
• Michael Eckstein, Member
Description:
Provides individual and corporate tax planning, closely held business law, estate and gift taxation, entrepreneurial business law, professional sports law, real estate tax practice, tax controversy work at city, state and federal level, high-tech/venture capital concerns, communication businesses, representation of professional athletes, licensing, mergers and acquisitions

EDELSTEIN, LAIRD & SOBEL
9255 SUNSET BOULEVARD
SUITE 800
LOS ANGELES, CA 90069
310-274-6184
Fax: 310-274-6185
Sobel@elsentlaw.com
www.elsentlaw.com
• Gerald F. Edelstein, Counsel/Attorney
Sobel@elsentlaw.com
• Peter Laird, Partners
Sobel@elsentlaw.com
• William R. Sobel, Partner
Sobel@elsentlaw.com
• Peter Laird, Partner
• Gerald. F. Edelstein, Partner
Services:
Provide clients with responsive service, quality legal work, the highest degree of confidentiality, and value.

EFRON, MORTON L.
5246 HOHMAN AVENUE
FIFTH FLOOR
HAMMOND, IN 46320
219-931-5380
Fax: 219-933-3180
mort@efronlaw.com
www.efronlaw.com
• Morton L. Efron, Attorney
(219) 931-5380
mort@efronlaw.com
• Marissa McDermott, Attorney
(219) 931-5380
Description:
Legal representation, including investment advice.
Services:
Provides expert legal skills and advice.
Year Founded:
1938

EGAN, ROBERT T.
33 EAST EUCLID AVENUE
ONE CENTENNIAL SQUARE
HADDONFIELD, NJ 08033
856-795-2121
Fax: 856-795-0574
webmaster@archerlaw.com
www.archerlaw.com
• Robert T. Egan, Partner
(856) 354-3079
regan@archerlaw.com
• Clint B. Allen, Associate
(856) 354-3017
callen@archerlaw.com
• Frank D. Allen, Partner
(856) 354-3075
fallen@archerlaw.com
• Robert. T. A. Egan, Partner
(856) 354-3079
regan@archerlaw.com
• Lynne Abraham, Partner
(215) 246-3113
labraham@archerlaw.com
• Kenneth E. Ahl, Partner
(215) 246-3132
kahl@archerlaw.com
• Clint B. Allen, Partner
(856) 354-3017
callen@archerlaw.com
• Frank D. Allen, Partner
(856) 354-3075
fallen@archerlaw.com
• James S. Asali, Partner
(215) 246-3112
jasali@archerlaw.com
• William M. Aukamp, Partner
(302) 356-6630
waukamp@archerlaw.com
Description:
Contract negotiation.
Services:
Provides highest quality, result-driven legal services to corporate and individual clients.
Clients:
Alliant Tech Systems, Associated Press, Avaya Inc., Bancroft Neurohealth, Bridgestone/Firesone Inc., Capital Blue Cross, City of Philadelphia, COIM USA, Inc., Cooper Hospital/UMC, Coriell Institute for Medical Research, Crown cork & Seal, Co.,Inc., Cumberland Farms, Inc., Cybex International, Delaware River Port Authority, Exxon Mobil Corporation, Fifth Third Bank, First American Marketing Corp., Gannett, Inc., Gloucester County College, Goucester County Imrprovement Authority, Hale Trailer Brake & Wheel, Heritage Building Group, Holman Enterprises, Hunterdon Medical Center, Lockheed-Martin Corp., Main Line Health System, Morgan Stanley DW

EHRHARDT, CHARLES W.
425 W JEFFERSON STREET
BK ROBERTS HALL, ROOM 205
TALLAHASSEE, FL 32306-1601
850-644-3400
Fax: 850-644-5487
www.law.fsu.edu
• Charles W. Ehrhardt, Emeritus Professor
(850) 644-5240
ehrhardt@law.fsu.edu
• Talbot D'Alemberte, President Emeritus/Professor
(850) 644-0800
Description:
Teaches sports law.

ELSWIT, LAWRENCE S.
1 SILBER WAY
BOSTON, MA 2215
617-353-2000
Fax: 617-353-5529
lelswit@bu.edu
www.bu.edu
• Robert A. Brown, President
(617) 353-2200
president@bu.edu
• Elizabeth B. Green, Executive Assistant to the President
(617) 353-2200
ebgreen@bu.edu
• Nancy K. Baker, Assistant to the President
(617) 353-2466
nbaker@bu.edu
• Tammy Egan, Administrative Manager
(617) 353-2200
tegan@bu.edu
Services:
Represents college athletic departments.

ELY, BETTINI, ULMAN & ROSENBLATT
3200 N CENTRAL AVENUE
SUITE 1930
PHOENIX, AZ 85012
602-230-2144
800-303-2144
Fax: 602-264-9337
eburlaw@eburlaw.com
www.eburlaw.com
• Herbert L. Ely, Attorney
Herbely@eburlaw.com
• Ronald Ozer, Attoney
(602) 230-2144
ronozer@eburlaw.com
• Alicia Funkhouser, Attoney
(602) 230-2144
afunkhouser@eburlaw.com
• Jenna Mandraccia, Attoney
(602) 230-2144
jenna@eburlaw.com
• Herb Ely, Attoney
(602) 230-2144
herbely@eburlaw.com
• Joseph M. M. Bettini, Attorney
(602) 230-2144
JoeBettini@eburlaw.com
• Walter R. R. Ulman, Attorney
(602) 230-2144
WaltUlman@eburlaw.com
• Burt Rosenblatt, Attoney
(602) 230-2144
burt@eburlaw.com
Services:
Specialists in personal injury, wrongful
death, workers' compensation cases,
medical malpractice, construction cases,
product liability cases by the Arizona Board
of Legal Specialization

EMERICK, WILLIAM E.
300 MAIN STREET
SUITE 900
PO BOX 1010
LAFAYETTE, IN 47902-1010
765-423-1561
Fax: 765-742-8175
www.stuartlaw.com
• William E. Emerick, Partner
(765) 428-7061
wee@stuartlaw.com
• Anthony S Benton, Partner
(765) 423-1561
asb@stuartlaw.com
• Nina B Kirkpatrick, Partner
nbk@stuartlaw.com
• James P Pratt, Firm Administrator
jep@stuartlaw.com
Description:
Represents college athletic departments.
Services:
Handles complex issues in nearly any area
of the law, banking and creditors rights,
business counselling, business
transactions, buying and selling
businesses, design and construction law,
education law, employment law,
environment law, estates and trusts, health
care law, insurance law, intellectual property
law, litigation, real estate, development and
zoning, taxation
Other Location:
8888 Keystone Crossing, STE 640,
Indianapolis, IN 46240; Phone:
317-574-7245

EMPLOYMENT LAW MANAGERS
225 E MASON STREET
SUITE 502
MILWAUKEE, WI 53202
414-276-0600
• James D. Thorne, President
Description:
Contract negotiation, post career planning,
investment contract negotiation, arbitration
hearings, federal/state/international tax
filings, provides investment advice,
licensing, endorsement exploration.

ENG & WOODS
903 E ASH STREET
COLUMBIA, MO 65201
573-874-4190
877-888-2345
Fax: 573-874-4192
info@engandwoods.com
www.engandwoods.com
• Patrick J. Eng, Partner
info@engandwoods.com
• Matthew B. Woods, Partner
info@engandwoods.com
• Larry M. Woods, Partner
info@engandwoods.com
• Patrick J. F. Eng, Senior Partner
• Matthew B. Woods, Senior Partner
• Douglas Pugh, Partner
info@engandwoods.com
• Thad R. Mulholland, Partner
• Jonathan D. McQuilkin, Partner
• Andrew D. Popplewell, Partner
• Adam Dowling, Associate
Description:
Contract negotiation.
Services:
Practice includes representing people who
are injured in auto accidents, by dangerous
or defective products, through the fault or
negligence of another person or at work:
criminal law, family law, probate law, and
general and commercial business law,
personal wills, damage lawsuits of all types,
product liability cases, auto accidents,
workers compensation cases and routine
consultations with business clients
Year Founded:
1953

ETTER, MCMAHON, LAMBERSON & CLARY, P.C.A.
618 W RIVERSIDE AVENUE
BANK OF WHITMAN BUILDING
SUITE 210
SPOKANE, WA 99201-0401
509-747-9100
Fax: 509-623-1439
ettermcmahon@ettermcmahon.com
www.ettermcmahon.com
• William F. Etter, Member
(509) 747-9100
ettermcmahon@ettermcmahon.com
• Michael J. McMahon, Member
(509) 747-9100
ettermcmahon@ettermcmahon.com
• Stephen M. Lamberson, Member
ettermcmahon@ettermcmahon.com
• William F. F. Etter, Managing Member
(509) 747-9100
• Michael J. McMahon, Member
(509) 747-9100
• Stephen M. Lamberson, Member
(509) 747-9100
• Raymond F. Clary, Member
(509) 747-9100

• Carl J. Oreskovich, Member
(509) 747-9100
• Ronald A. Van Wert, Member
(509) 747-9100
• Daniel E. Stowe, Associate
(509) 747-9100
Services:
Contract negotiation, post career planning,
investment contract negotiation,
endorsement exploration, tort
actions/litigation. Alcohol, Beverage Law,
Construction Law, Domestic Relations Law,
Estate Planning, Real Estate Law. Medical
Malpractice

EVANS, ESQ., THOMAS S.
110 WEST FAYETTE STREET
ONE LINCOLN CENTER
SYRACUSE, NY 13202-1355
315-218-8000
Fax: 315-218-8100
rhole@bsk.com
www.bsk.com
• Thomas S. Evans, Senior Member
(315) 218-8217
tevans@bsk.com
• John D. Allen, Attorney
(315) 343-9116
jdallen@bsk.com
• S. Pa Battaglia, Attorney
(315) 218-8277
sbattaglia@bsk.com
• Richard D. M. Hole, Chairman of the
Management Committee
(315) 218-8210
rhole@bsk.com
• Jordan C. Alaimo, Senior Counsel
(585) 362-4720
jalaimo@bsk.com
• John R. Aldrich, Member (Partner)
(518) 533-3240
jaldrich@bsk.com
• Jeffrey F. Allen, Senior Counsel
(585) 362-4709
jeffreyallen@bsk.com
• John D. Allen, Member (Partner)
(315) 218-8250
jdallen@bsk.com
• Kathleen M. Bennett, Member (Partner)
(315) 218-8631
kbennett@bsk.com
• Paul J. Avery, Associate
(315) 218-8238
pavery@bsk.com
Description:
Contract negotiation, arbitration hearings,
licensing, tort actions/litigation, represents
college athletic departments. NCAA
infractions and compliance matters.

FAGUE, TERENCE L.
33 W FIRST STREET
SUITE 600
DAYTON, OH 45402
937-223-8177
Fax: 937-223-6705
www.coollaw.com
• Douglas M. Ventura, Chief Operating
Officer
(937) 449-5545
ventura@coollaw.com
• Matthew L. Rauch, COO and CFO
(937) 449-1637
rauch@coollaw.com
• Alan J. Gusky, Controller
(937) 223-8177
gusky@coollaw.com
• Russell W. Jacox, IT Manager

(937) 223-8177
jacox@coollaw.com
• Elaine F. Reinert, Applications Support
(937) 223-8177
reinert@coollaw.com
Services:
Litigation: Business Litigation, Employment
Litigation, Real Estate Litigation. Represents
college athletic departments.
Description:
Represents college athletic departments.

FANEUIL, ROBERT A.
175 HIGHLAND AVENUE
NEEDHAM HEIGHTS, MA 2494
781-444-3838
Fax: 781-449-8240
RAF3838@aol.com
• Robert A. Faneuil, Attorney
(781) 444-3838
Services:
All phases of athlete representation
including contract negotiation, long-range
planning, financial planning, and post-career
counseling.
Clients:
Global Companies, LLC, Alliance Energy
Corp., The Education Resources Institute,
PMI Mortgage Insurance Co., New York
State Higher Education Service Corp.
Other Office:
Ritz Carleton Hotel, 2 Commonwealth Ave,
STE 15D, Boston, MA 02116

**FENNEMORE CRAIG, A PROFESSIONAL
CORPORATION**
2394 EAST CAMELBACK ROAD
SUITE 600
PHOENIX, AZ 85016-3249
602-916-5000
Fax: 602-916-5999
tberg@fclaw.com
www.fclaw.com
• Amy Abdo, Director
(602) 916-5399
aabdo@fclaw.com
• Bryan A. Albue, Director
(602) 916-5311
balbue@fclaw.com
• Scott L. Altes, Director
(602) 916-5323
saltes@fclaw.com
• Amy Abdo, Director
(602) 916-5399
aabdo@fclaw.com
• Robert D. Anderson, Director
(602) 916-5455
randerso@fclaw.com
• Gregory L. Adams, Associate
(602) 916-5474
gadams@fclaw.com
• Todd M. Allison, Associate
(602) 916-5391
tallison@fclaw.com
• Scott K. Ames, Of Counsel
(602) 916-5339
sames@fclaw.com
• Karen A. Curosh, Of Counsel
(602) 916-5458
kcurosh@fclaw.com
Other Locations:
One South Church Avenue, STE 1000,
Tucson, AZ 85701; Phone: 520-879-6800;
1891 North Mastick Way, STE A, Nogales,
AZ 85621; Phone: 520-761-4215; 1221
North Street, STE 801, Lincoln, NE 68508;
Phone: 402-323-6200

Services:
Substantial business practice covers real
estate, finance, public offerings, private
placements, corporate reorganizations,
mergers and acquisitions, dispositions,
entity formation, intellectual property, estate
planning, government relations and
numerous other practice areas.
Clients:
7-Eleven Inc.,Allied Waste Industries, Inc.,
America West Arena, Apple Computer Inc.,
Arizona Cattle Growers' Association,
Arizona Sports & Tourism Authority
(AZSTA), Arizona-American, Water
Company, Avnet, Inc., Banner Health
Arizona, BNSF Railway Company, The,
Bridgestone-Firestone, Cendant
Corporation, Christian Care, Circle G
Property Development LLC, ConocoPhillips
Company, D.R. Horton - Continental Series,
DMB Associates, Inc., Eurofresh, Exact
Flow/Flow Dynamics Inc.,Fairfield
Investments Inc., FINOVA Group Inc., First
Magnus Financial Corporation, Florida,
State of, Giant Industries Inc., Gila River
Power LP, Glendale, City of, Harlem

**FERGUSON, BRIG GEN/USA RET.,
MICHAEL L.**
4300 BAYOU BOULEVARD
SUITE 13
PENSACOLA, FL 32503
850-477-0660
Fax: 850-477-4510
• Michael Ferguson, Partner

**FERNANDEZ, SANTIAGO/SENIOR
VP/GENERAL COUNSEL LOS ANGELES
DODGERS, LLC**
1000 ELYSIAN PARK AVENUE
LOS ANGELES, CA 90012
323-224-1507
Fax: 323-224-1269
www.dodgers.com
• Sam Fernandez, Senior Vice President
and General Counsel
Services:
Contract negotiation, represents
professional sports teams, licensing.

FIDELIS COUNSEL ASSOCIATES
23 LACEWOOD COURT
OTTAWA, ONTARIO, CANADA K2E 7E2
613-226-8130
Fax: 613-224-3422
• Ed Ratushny, Agent
(613) 226-8130
• Rolland Hedges, Agent
(613) 795-9435
rhedges@magma.ca
Services:
Contract negotiation, arbitration hearings,
teaches sports law.
Year Founded:
1990

FIERBERG, IRA M. LAW OFFICES OF
1334 PARK VIEW AVENUE
SUITE 100
MANHATTAN BEACH, CA 90266-3788
323-546-8181
Fax: 310-546-8180
• Ira M. Fierberg, Member
• Craig S. Sunada, Member
Description:
Personal Injury, including Vehicular, Slip
and Fall, Major Bodily Injury, Dog Bites,

Wrongful Death. General Civil Litigation in
all State and Federal Courts, Trial, Business
Litigation, Sports Law, Motor Racing Sports
Representation and Motor Racing
Consulting.

**FILLENWARTH DENNERLINE GROTH &
TOWE**
429 E VERMONT STREET
SUITE 200
INDIANAPOLIS, IN 46202
317-353-9363
Fax: 317-351-7232
glohman@fdgtlaborlaw.com
www.fdgtlaborlaw.com
• William R. Groth, Attorney/Partner
wgroth@fdgtlaborlaw.com
Services:
NFLPA workers' compensation panel for the
Indianapolis Colts.

FINKELMEIER LAW FIRM
36 E SEVENTH STREET
SUITE 1660
CINCINNATI, OH 45202-4453
513-621-9921
(866) 781-5692
Fax: 513-621-9923
finkelmeier@fuse.net
www.finkelmeierlaw.com
• Louis J. Finkelmeier, Attorney at Law
• William I. Farrell, Partner/Attorney
(513) 621-9921
billfarrell@fuse.net
Services:
Workers Compensation, Sports Injury,
Social Security Disability and Probate Law.

FLY, WILLIAM L.
601 UNIVERSITY DRIVE
SAN MARCOS, TX 78666-4684
512-245-2111
www.txstate.edu
• William L. Fly, Staff
(512) 245-2530
• Denise M. T. Trauth, President
Description:
Represents college athletic departments.

FOGELGAREN, FORMAN & BERGMAN
277 BROADWAY
ROOM 1701
NEW YORK, NY 10007
212-962-1200
Fax: 212-608-5935
fofoberg@aol.com
• Eric I. Fogelgaren, Partner
(212) 962-1200
• Jonathan Forman, Partner
(212) 962-1200
• Robert Bergman, Partner
(212) 962-1200
Description:
Panel attorneys for NFLPA
Teams:
NY Jets and NY Giants

FOLEY & LARDNER
777 E WISCONSIN AVENUE
SUITE 3800
VEREX PLAZA
MILWAUKEE, WI 53202-5306
414-271-2400
Fax: 414-297-4900
www.foley.com

• Ralf-Reinhard Boer, Partner
(414) 297-5609
rboer@foley.com
• Mary K. Braza, Partner/Practice Chair
(414) 297-5505
mbraza@foley.com
• Irwin P. Raij, Partner/Practice Co-Chair
iraij@foley.com
• Linda E. A. Benfield, Office Managing
Partner
(414) 297-5825
lbenfield@foley.com
•Thomas N. Landgraf, Director,
Administration and Operations
(414) 297-5454
tlandgraf@foley.com
• Joshua A. Agen, Senior Counse
(414) 297-5703
jagen@foley.com
Nature of Service:
Recognized for its thorough understanding
of complex sports issues, Foley & Lardner
LLP is trusted by professionals in all
aspsects of the sports industry. The firm
represents professional franchises and
leagues, amateur and collegiate teams,
owners, stadium operators, sponsors,
promoters, developers and sporting goods
manufacturers. With an inside view of the
sports world, our attorneys have the
perspective and knowledge to help clients
identify and respond to emerging trends in
the industry. The firm's attorneys are
experienced in antitrust, public affairs,
litigation, intellectual property, public
finance, real estate, and labor and employ

FOSTER, DON
260 S BROAD STREET
PHILADELPHIA, PA 19102-5003
215-568-6060
Fax: 215-568-6603
www.klehr.com
• Don P Foster, Partner
(215) 569-4646
• Richard M Beck, Partner
(215) 569-2299
rbeck@klehr.com
• Keith W Kaplan, Partner
(215) 569-4143
KKaplan@klehr.com
• Heather I Levine, Partner
(215) 569-4398
hlevine@klehr.com
Services:
Workers Compensation
Clients:
NFLPA workers' compensation panel
Other Locations:
919 Market Street, STE 100, Wilmington,
DE 19801; Phone: 302-426-1189; 457
Hadonfield Road, STE 510, Cherry Hill, NJ
08002; Phone: 856-486-7900

FOSTER, SWIFT, COLLINS & SMITH, P.C.
313 S WASHINGTON SQUARE
LANSING, MI 48933-2114
517-371-8100
Fax: 517-371-8200
www.fosterswift.com
• Kimberly P. Hafley, Director of Marketing &
Recruitment
• Charles E. Barbieri, Shareholder
(517) 371-8155
CBarbieri@fosterswift.com
• Judith A. P. Salminen, Director of Human
Resources

(248) 538-6324
pasker@fosterswift.com
Services:
General Trial and Appellate Practice in all
State and Federal Courts. Administrative
Practice, Banking, Insurance, Corporation,
Real Estate, Municipal, Labor, Tax, Estate
Planning, Probate, ESOPs, Employee
Benefits, Environmental, Election, Oil and
Gas, Immigration, Motor Carrier,
Transportation, Licensing, Public Utility and
Securities Law, Litigation, Products Liability,
Professional Malpractice, Health and
Hospital Law, International, Intellectual
Property, Insurance Insolvency, Workers'
Compensation, Aviation Law, Construction,
Agricultural Law.

FOX & SPILLANE, LLP
1880 CENTURY PARK E
SUITE 1004
LOS ANGELES, CA 90067-1623
310-229-9300
Fax: 310-229-9380
• Jay Spillane, Attorney/Partner
• Gerard P Fox, Attorney/Partner
• Donald S Engel, Attorney
• Donald L Zachary, Attorney
Services:
Business litigation, copyright, trademark,
intellectual property, media, sports.

FRANK, MONTE E.
158 DEER HILL AVENUE
DANBURY, CT 06810
203-792-2771
Fax: 203-791-8149
cw@cohenandwolf.com
www.cohenandwolf.com
• Monte E. Frank, Principal
(203) 792-2771
mfrank@cohenandwolf.com
• Martin J. Albert, Principal
(203) 337-4121
malbert@cohenandwolf.com
• Richard L. Albrecht, Principal
(203) 368-0211
ralbrecht@cohenandwolf.com
• David A. Ball, Principal
(203) 368-0211
dball@cohenandwolf.com
Services:
All phases of athlete representation
including contract negotiation, long-range
planning, financial planning, and post-career
counseling.
Year Founded:
1951
Other Locations:
1115 Broad Street, Bridgeport, CT 06604;
Phone: 203-368-0211; 112 Prospect Street,
Stamford, CT 06904; Phone: 203-964-9907;
190 Main Street, Westport, CT 06880;
Phone: 203-222-1034

FRANKEL, PAUL D.
520 MADISON AVENUE
1030 SPITZER BLDG
TOLEDO, OH 43604
419-255-5111
419-255-3883
Fax: 419-255-3231
www.paulfrankellaw.com
Services:
Contract negotiation, endorsement
exploration.

**FRANKFURT, KURNIT, KLEIN & SELZ,
P.C.**
488 MADISON AVENUE
10TH FLOOR
NEW YORK, NY 10022
212-980-0120
Fax: 212-593-9175
www.fkks.com
• Michael Frankfurt, Senior Partner/Founder
(212) 826-5555
mfrankfurt@fkks.com
• Jeffrey A. Greenbaum, Partner in
Advertising, Marketing
• Michael Williams, Partner
(212) 826-5587
mwilliams@fkks.com
• Thomas D. Selz, Founding Partner
(212) 826-5535
• Cameron Myler, Associate
(212) 826-5545
• Edward Rosenthal, Partner
(212) 826-5524
erosenthal@fkks.com
Nature of Service:
All phases of athlete management. Contract
negotiation, arbitration/litigation, intellectual
property, trademark (U.S. and International)
issues for athletes, agents and
organizations. Represents athletes, sports
related sponsorship,
licensing/merchandising, television
producers.
Year Founded:
1977

**FRILOT, PARTRIDGE, KOHNKE &
CLEMENTS, L.C.**
1100 POYDRAS STREET
SUITE 3700
NEW ORLEANS, LA 70163
504-599-8000
Fax: 504-599-8100
contact@Frilot.com
• Miles Clements, Partner
(504) 599-8004
mclements@frilot.com
• Angela M. M. Bowlin, Partner
(504) 599-8215
abowlin@frilot.com
Description:
Contract negotiation, provides investment
advice, licensing, tort actions/litigation.
Admiralty and Maritime Law; Commercial
Litigation; Construction Litigation; Energy;
Environmental Litigation; Professional
Liability; Entertainment and the Arts; Mass
Torts; Litigation; Sports Law.

FULBRIGHT & JAWORSKI .L.L.P.
555 S FLOWER STREET
FORTY-FIRST FLOOR
LOS ANGELES, CA 90071
213-892-9200
Fax: 213-892-9494
www.fulbright.com
• Harry L. Hathaway, Counsel
(213) 892-9336
hhathaway@fulbright.com
• Peter H. Mason, Partner-In-Charge
(213) 892-9233
pmason@fulbright.com
Services:
Legal Services
Additional Offices United States:
Austin TX, Dallas, TX; Houston, TX; Los
Angeles, CA; Minneapolis, MN; New York,
NY, San Antonio, TX; Washington, D.C

Other Offices:
Hong Kong, London, Munich.
Year Founded:
1919
Description:
Our specifics deal with litigation, corporate, energy, intellectual, property, health law, public finance, international arbitration

GARVEY & STODDARD
634 W MAIN STREET
MADISON, WI 53703
608-256-1003
Fax: 608-256-0933
• Edward Garvey, Shareholder/Founder
• Kathleen McNeil, Shareholder
• Pamela McGillivray, Shareholder
• Christa Westerberg, Associate
Year Founded:
1997.
Services:
Teaches sports law, attorney training.
Description:
Emphasizing environmental, labor, employment, civil rights, Indian, local government, land, US and public interest law.

GARVEY, SCHUBERT & BARER
100 WALL STREET
20TH FLOOR
NEW YORK, NY 10005-3708
212-431-8700
Fax: 212-334-1278
www.gsblaw.com
• John K. Hoerster, Chairman
(206) 464-3939
jhoerster@gsblaw.com
• Keven J. Davis, Owner
(212) 431-8700
kdavis@gsblaw.com
• Lucinda D. Fernald, Executive Director
(206) 464-3939
cfernald@gsblaw.com
• Hillary H. L. Hughes, Owner
(212) 965-452
hhughes@gsblaw.com
• Andrew J. Goodman, Owner
(212) 965-4534
agoodman@gsblaw.com
• Matthew R. Schneider, Managing Director
(202) 298-1787
mschneider@gsblaw.com
• Seymour H. Bucholz, Of Counsel
(212) 965-4531
sbucholz@gsblaw.com
• MaryLyn R. Carabello, Associate
(212) 965.4509
mcarabello@gsblaw.com
• Je Jun Moon, Of Counsel
(212) 965-4524
jmoon@gsblaw.com
Description:
Contract negotiation, arbitration hearings, represents professional sports teams, licensing, endorsement exploration, tort actions/litigation, represents college athletic departments, represents sports organizations. Represents a large and diverse array of clients in the arts, entertainment and sports industries, both regionally and nationally.
Other Locations:
11th Floor, 121 SW Morrison Street, Portland, OR 97204; Phone: 503-228-3939; 18th Floor, Second & Seneca Building, 1191 Second Avenue, Seattle, WA 98101; Phone:

206-464-3939; 5th Floor Flour Mill Building, 1000 Potomac Street, NW, Washington, DC 20007; Phone: 202-965-7880

GEIGER & KEEN LLP
5405 N. PERSHING AVENUE
SUITE 2A
BUILDING C
STOCKTON, CA 95207
209-948-0434
Fax: 209-948-9451
www.bgrn.com
• Dennis Do Geiger, Partner
(209) 948-0434
• Laureen J. Keen
(209) 948-0434
lkeen@bgrn.com
• Timothy J. Kooy
(209) 948-0434
Description:
Contract negotiation, tort actions/litigation. General Civil and Trial Practice. Corporation, Probate, Estate Planning, Family Law, Estate Planning, Family Law, Banking, Real Property, Public Districts, Creditors' Bankruptcy and Commercial Transactions.

GOBER LAW FIRM
3200 WEST END AVENUE
SUITE 500
NASHVILLE, TN 37203-1322
615-783-2874
800-634-6237
Fax: 615-783-1606
gary@goberlaw.com
www.goberlaw.com
• Gary Gober, Principal Attorney/Founder
(800) 634-6237
gary@goberlaw.com
Description:
NFLPA. Handles workers compensation for the Tennessee Titans.
Clients:
Tennessee Titans and NFLPA.

GOLD, KEVIN M., ESQUIRE
ONE SOUTH MARKET SQUARE
M&T BANK BUILDING, 12TH FLOOR, PO BOX 1146
HARRISBURG, PA 17108-1146
717-862-4534
Fax: 717-238-8623
• Kevin Gold, Administrative Chair
(717) 237-6702
kgold@rhoads-sinon.com
• Richard E. Artell, Chairperson
(717) 237-6717
rartell@rhoads-sinon.com
Description:
Representation of professional football players.
Services:
Player Representation Services, Negotiation of the Player Contract, Counseling, Financial Management and Planning, Personal Training, Marketing, Career Planning
Clients:
NFLA players

GOLDMAN, LEE
4001 W. MCNICHOLS ROAD
DETROIT, MI 48221-3038
313-596-0264
Fax: 313-596-0280
www.udmercy.edu

• Lee Goldman, Law Professor
(313) 596-0203
goldmanl@udmercy.edu
• Antoine M. Garibaldi, Ph.D., President
(313) 993-1455
Description:
Teaches sports law.

GOLDSMITH, JAMES A.
1660 W 2ND STREET
SUITE 1100
CLEVELAND, OH 44113-1448
216-583-7000
Fax: 216-583-7001
infocleveland@ulmer.com
www.ulmer.com
• James Cowan, Executive Director
jcowan@ulmer.com
• Robert Horvath, Chief Financial Officer
rhorvath@ulmer.com
• Sam Shipley, Chief Information Officer
sshipley@ulmer.com
• Jennifer Lawry Adams, Partner
(216) 583-7052
jadams@ulmer.com
• John M. Alten, Partner
(216) 583-7354
• Mary Forbes Lovett, Partner
(216) 583-7074
mlovett@ulmer.com
Description:
Contract negotiation, post career planning, federal/state/international tax filings.
Other Locations:
600 Vine Street, STE 2800 Cincinnati, OH 45202; Phone: 513-698-5000; Fax: 513-698-500l; 88 East Broad Street, STE 1600, Columbus, OH 43215; Phone: 614-229-0000; Fax: 614-229-0001; One North Franklin Street, STE 1825, Chicago, IL 60606; Phone: 312-324-8000; Fax: 312-324-8001

GOPLERUD, III, C. PETER
2621 CARPENTER AVENUE
27TH & CARPENTER, OPPERMAN HALL
DES MOINES, IA 50311
515-271-2824
1-800-44-DRAKE x2824
Fax: 515-271-1958
www.law.drake.edu
• Allan W. Vestal, Dean
Description:
Teaches and consults in sports law, author.

GORDON, GEORGE B.
401 QUEEN CITY AVENUE
UNIVERSITY COUNSEL OF ALABAMA SYSTEM OFFICE
TUSCALOOSA, AL 35487
205-348-5681
Description:
Represents college athletic departments.

GOWEN, GEORGE W.
1359 BROADWAY
SUITE 600
NEW YORK, NY 10018
212-682-8811
Fax: 212-661-7769
DBM@dunnington.com
www.dunnington.com
• Marvin M Brown, Partner
mbrown@dunnington.com
• John T Dunlap, Partner
jdunlap@dunnington.com
• George W Gowen, Partner

ggowen@dunnington.com
• Michael J Kopcsak, Partner
mkopcsak@dunnington.com
Services:
Corporate, Estates, Trusts and Private Clients, Immigration, Litigation and Arbitration, Not-For-Profit, Religious and Charitable Institutions, Real Estate and Construction, Taxation
Description:
Represents sports organizations.

GRASSIA, ESQ., THOMAS C.
5 COMMONWEALTH ROAD
NATICK, MA 01760-1526
508-653-0054
Services:
Contract negotiation, post career planning, endorsement exploration.

GREENBERG TRAURIG, LLP
54 STATE STREET
6TH FLOOR
ALBANY, NY 12207
518-689-1400
Fax: 518-689-1499
info@gtlaw.com
www.gtlaw.com
• Henry W. Holmes Jr, Counsel
(310) 586-7858
• Paola A. Abello, Associate
(305) 579-0500
• Tricia A. Asaro, Shareholder
(518) 689-1400
• Michael A. Berlin, Shareholder
(212) 801-6424
• Christopher A. Cernik, Shareholder
(518) 689-1400
• Mark F. Glaser, Shareholder
(518) 689-1400
• Michael J. Grygiel, Shareholder
(518) 689-1400
• Hugh E. Hackney, Shareholder
(214) 665-3676
Services:
Artist and professional athlete management and representation.
Description:
Contract negotiation, post career planning, arbitration hearings, represents professional sports teams, licensing, endorsement exploration.
Specialty:
All phases of Motion pictures, television, sports.

GULAS LAW FIRM, P.C.
2031 SECOND AVENUE N
BIRMINGHAM, AL 35203
205-297-0005
877-453-4852
Fax: 205-879-1247
www.gulasandstuckey.com
• Ike Gulas, Attorney
• Jason Stuckey, Attorney
Services:
Personal Injury, Auto, truck or motor vehicle accident, Wrongful Death, Pharmaceutical, Drug or Medication Matters, Class actions or mass torts, Dangerous Products, Ephedra-related matters, Zyprexa use, Trucking, 18-wheeler accidents, Duragesic, Ortho-Evra, Vioxx, Unsafe Toys, Antidepressants, Car and tire defects

HAILE, SHAW & PFAFFENBERGER, P.A.
660 US HIGHWAY ONE
3RD FLOOR
NORTH PALM BEACH, FL 33408
561-627-8100
Fax: 561-622-7603
clientservices@hsplaw.com
www.haileshaw.com
• Robert G. Haile, Jr., Lawyer
rhaile@hsplaw.com
• David M. Shaw, Lawyer
dshaw@hsplaw.com
• William J. Pfaffenberger, Lawyer
wpfaffenberger@hsplaw.com
• Robert G. Haile Jr., Partner
rhaile@haileshaw.com
• David M. Shaw, Partner
dshaw@haileshaw.com
• Phillip M. Dicomo, Partner
pdicomo@haileshaw.com
• John Flanigan, Partner
jflanigan@haileshaw.com
• Lawrence C. Griffin, Partner
lgriffin@haileshaw.com
• Gerald L. Principe, Partner
gprincipe@haileshaw.com
Services:
Areas of practice include Trust and Estate Planning and Administration, Corporate Law and Business Planning, Real Estate Development, Environmental and Land Use, and Commercial and Civil Litigation
Description:
Contract negotiation, post career planning, investment contract negotiation, arbitration hearings, licensing, endorsement exploration, tort actions/litigation.

HANSEN, STEVEN W.
BELLFLOWER
LAKEWOOD, CA 90712-1347
562-866-6228
www.swhlaw.com
• Steven W. W. Hansen, Attorney
Other Locations:
1573 Indian Summer Road, San Marcos, CA 92069; Phone: 562-866-6228; 507 Sylvan Avenue, Mountain View, CA 94041; Phone 562-866-6228
Services:
Product Liability Defense / Sports Litigation Defense, Premises Liability Defense, Professional Liability Defense, Insurance Coverage and Bad Faith, Governmental Liability, Contract General Counsel/Third Party Administrator (TPA) services, Newsletter

HARBOUR, SMITH, HARRIS & MERRITT
404 N GREEN AT MAGRILL STREET
LONGVIEW, TX 75606-2072
903-757-4001
888-757-4001
Fax: 903-753-5123
emerritt@harbourlaw.com
www.harbourlaw.com
• Thomas W. Reardon, Esquire
(903) 757-4001
• John M Smith, Attorney
(903) 757-4001
• Jerry S Harris, Attorney
(903) 757-4001
jharris@harbourlaw.com
• Edward L Merritt, Attorney
(903) 757-4001
emerritt@harbourlaw.com
• Jessica M LaRue, Associate

(903) 757-4001
jlarue@harbourlaw.com
Services:
Contract negotiation, represents professional sports teams, endorsement exploration, tort actions/litigation.
Clients:
Regions Bank (formerly Longview National Bank) Spring Hill State Bank, Community Bank, General Accident Fire & Life Assurance Co.; Highlands Insurance Co.; Zurich-American Insurance Co.; Commercial Union Insurance Co.; State Farm Insurance Co.; ACE U.S.A. (formerly CIGNA Property & Casualty); ESIS, Inc.; Safeco Insurance Co.; Dairyland County Mutual Insurance Co.; Kemper Insurance Group; Mid-Continent Casualty Co.; National Surety Corp.; Ranger-Pan American Insurance Group; Sentry Insurance Co.; Scottsdale Insurance Co.; Nationwide Insurance; Farmland Insurance; Reliance Insurance Company; State & County Mutual Insurance Co.

HARRIS, ALAN E.
235 MONTGOMERY STREET
RUSS BUILDING
17TH FLOOR
SAN FRANCISCO, CA 94104
415-954-4400
Fax: 415-954-4480
www.fbm.com
• Alan E Harris, Counsel
(415) 954-4424
aharris@fbm.com
• John R Epperson, Special Counsel
(415) 954-4942
jepperson@fbm.com
Services:
Practices and Industries, Bankruptcy and Creditors' Rights, Business Litigation, Business Transactions, Construction, Employment, Environmental Law, Family Wealth, Hospitality, Insurance Coverage, Intellectual Property and Technology, Private Clients, Product Law, Real Estate, Securities, Tax, White Collar Crime.
Description:
Arbitration hearings, federal/state/international tax filings, licensing, tort actions/litigation.

HASLER, FONFARA AND MAXWELL, LLP
KEY BANK BUILDING, 6TH FLOOR, PO BOX 2267
FORT COLLINS, CO 80522
970-493-5070
Fax: 970-493-9703
www.hfglawfirm.com
• Timothy W Hasler, Attorney
• Joseph H Fonfara, Attorney
• Michael A Maxwell, Attorney
• Timothy L Goddard, Attorney
Description:
NFLPA workers' compensation panel, Denver Broncos. Estate Planning; Estate Administration; Business Law; Real Estate; Worker's Compensation.

HAUS & ROMAN, LLP
148 E WILSON STREET
SUITE 200
MADISON, WI 53703-3423
608-257-0420
Fax: 608-257-1383
hrbllp.com

• William Haus, Attorney/Partner
Services:
Worker's compensation
Clients:
NFLPA workers' compensation panel.

HAZLETT, WILKES & BAYHAM
310 S WILLIAMS BOULEVARD
SUITE 305
TUCSON, AZ 85711
520-790-9663
• Thomas Bayharm, Attorney/Partner
• James M Wilkes, Attorney/Partner
• Carl E. Hazlett, Attorney/Partner

HEAD, ALBON O., JR.
777 MAIN STREET
SUITE 2100
FORT WORTH, TX 76102
817-334-7200
Fax: 817-334-7290
www.jw.com
• Albon O Head Jr, Managing Partner
(817) 334-7230
ahead@jw.com
• Gail R. Horne, Administrator
(214) 953-5879
ghorne@jw.com
Services:
Antitrust, Appellate, Bankruptcy, Business Transactions, Corporate and Securities, Eminent Domain, Immigration, Intellectual Property, International, Labor and Employment, Litigation, Public Finance, Regulatory and Legislative, Tax
Description:
Represents professional sports teams (Texas Rangers).

HERMAN, HERMAN, KATZ & COTLAR, L.L.P.
820 O'KEEFE AVENUE
NEW ORLEANS, LA 70113
504-581-4892
Fax: 504-561-6024
info@hhkc.com
www.hhkc.com
• Leonard A Davis, Attorney/Partner
(504) 581-4892
ldavis@hhkc.com
• Maury, A. Herman, Founder
(504) 581-4892
mherman@hhklawfirm.com
• Morton. H. Katz, Founder
(504) 581-4892
mkatz@hhklawfirm.com
• Steven. J. Lane, Attorney
(504) 581-4892
slane@hhklawfirm.com
• Leonard. A. Davis, Attorney
(504) 581-4892
ldavis@hhklawfirm.com
• James. C. Klick, Partner
(504) 581-4892
jklick@hhklawfirm.com
• Stephen. J. Herman, Attorney
(504) 581-4892
sherman@hhklawfirm.com
• Russ M. Herman, Founder
(504) 581-4892
rherman@hhklawfirm.com
Description:
Contract negotiation, arbitration hearings, represents professional sports teams, licensing, endorsement exploration, tort actions/litigation, represents sports organizations. Corporate Law; Commercial

Law; Class Actions; Personal Injury; Business Litigation; Railroad Crossing and Derailment.

HERSHNER, HUNTER, ANDREWS, NEILL & SMITH L,L,P.
180 E 11TH AVENUE
EUGENE, OR 97401
541-686-8511
Fax: 541-344-2025
contact@hershnerhunter.com
www.hershnerhunter.com
• David N. Andrews, Attorney
contact@hershnerhunter.com
• William D. Brewer, Attorney
contact@hershnerhunter.com
• Melissa F. Busley, Attorney
contact@hershnerhunter.com
• Nancy K. Cary, Attorney
contact@hershnerhunter.com
• Jeffrey S. Cook, Firm Administrator
• Nancy Parks, Accounting Manager
• Crystal Harder, I.T. Manager
Services:
Contract negotiation, federal/state/international tax filings, licensing, endorsement exploration. Corporate Law; Estate Planning; Business Planning; Probate; Trust Administration; Tax Disputes.

HICKS, JERRY
2728 N. HARWOOD STREET
500 WINSTEAD BUILDING
DALLAS, TX 75201
214-745-5400
Fax: 214-745-5390
ksullivan@winstead.com
www.winstead.com
• W. Mike Baggett, Chairman Emeritus/Shareholder
(214) 745-5303
mbaggett@winstead.com
• Thomas R. Helfland, Chief Operating Officer
(214) 745-5342
thelfand@winstead.com
Nature of Sports Service:
Serves as lead counsel to a number of professional sports teams, international venue management companies, and governmental authorities responsible for the financing, developing, and operation of sports venues.
Project/Clients:
Reliant Stadium for the Houston Texans NFL franchise, SBC Center for thr San Antonio Spurs NBA franchise, New Houston downtown arena for the Houston Rockets and Houston Aeros, Sydney Olympic Arena for a management company, Various European arena venue; Appellate, Banking & Credit Transactions, Bankruptcy, Biotechnology, Business Restructuring, Construction, Corporate / Securities, Crisis Management, Emerging Business, Energy, Environmental, ERISA / Employee Benefits, Financial Institutions, Government Relations / Public Policy, Insurance, Intellectual Property, International, Labor & Employment, Litigation / Dispute Resolution, Nanotechnology

---

HITCHCOCK LAW FIRM
1465 ARCADE STREET
THE BARRISTER BUILDING
ST. PAUL, MN 55106

651-772-3401
Fax: 651-772-2115
• Edward J. Hitchcock, Attorney
(651) 772-3401
ehitchcock@hitchcocklaw.com
• Gene E Adkins, Attorney
(651) 772-3401
gadkins@hitchcocklaw.com
• Ralbern B Hitchcock, Attorney
rhitchcock@hitchcocklaw.com
• Gene E. Adkins, Attorney
• Edward J. Hitchcock, Attorney
• Raebern B. Hitchcock, Attorney
• Drew S. Slagle, Attorney
Services:
Represent and advise clients in the areas of estate planning, probate and trust administration, general litigation, and sports law
Description:
Contract negotiation, post career planning, investment contract negotiation, arbitration hearings, endorsement exploration, tort actions/litigation.

HODARI, AJILI
52 E GAY STREET
COLUMBUS, OH 43215
614-464-6400
Fax: 614-464-6350
www.vssp.com/hodari.html
• W. Jonathan Airey, Partner
(614) 464-6346
wjairey@vorys.com
• Raymond D. Anderson, Partner
(614) 464-6447
rdanderson@vssp.com
Nature of Sports Service:
All phases of athlete representation including contract negotiation, long-range planning, financial planning, and post-career counseling.
Services:
Represents clients in litigation, business and personal transactions involving virtually every legal subject
Other Locations:
First National Tower, 106 South Main Street, Akron, OH 44308; Phone: 330-245-1153; 277 South Washington Street, STE 310, Alexandria, VA 22314; Phone: 703-837-6999; Atrium Two, STE 2000, 22l EAst Fourth Street, Cincinnati, OH 45201; Phone: 513-723-4000; 2100 One Cleveland Center, l375 East 9th Street, Cleveland, OH 44114; Phone: 216-479-6100; 1828 L Street NW, 11th Floor, Washington, DC 20036; Phone; 202-467-8800

HOLLAND & KNIGHT
100 N TAMPA STREET
SUITE 4100
TAMPA, FL 33602
813-227-8500
Fax: 813-229-0134
fgrady@hklaw.com
www.hklaw.com
• Rod Anderson, Partner
(813) 227-6721
rod.anderson@hklaw.com
• Douglas A. Wright, Attorney
(813) 227-6536
doug.wright@hklaw.com
• Mark D. Austin, Associate
(813) 227-6535
mark.austin@hklaw.com
• Frederick J. Grady, Partner
(813) 227-6705

fred.grady@hklaw.com
• Bradford Kimbro, Partner
(813) 227-6660
brad.kimbro@hklaw.com
• Sylvia Stephens, Business Manager
sylvia.stephens@hklaw.com
College Sports/Football:
Gator Bowl Associaton, Chairman's Club
Member.
Services:
Efficient and responsive legal representation
anywhere in the world.
Newsletter:
Sports Law Subscription based.
Specialty:
Litigation - Commercial; Sports - Collegiate
Administration and Compliance; Education,
Government Contracts; Litigation -
Commercial: Construction and Design; Drug
and Medical Devices; Litigation -
Commercial: Entertainment. Taxation - State
and Local; Taxation: Federal; Sports
Practice.

HOLLER, J. EDWARD
1777 BULL STREET
COLUMBIA, SC 29201
803-765-2968
Fax: 803-252-8290
Services:
Contract negotiation, investment contract
negotiation, endorsement exploration, tort
actions/litigation - criminal.

HOLMES, RICH
4200 FIFTH AVENUE
PITTSBURGH, PA 15260
412-624-4141
Fax: 412-624-6688
usenate@pitt.edu
www.pitt.edu
• Irene Hanson Frieze, Professor
(412) 624-4336
frieze@pitt.edu
• Michael R. Pinsky, Vice President
mrpinsky@pitt.edu
• Ellen Ansell, Secretary
eansell@pitt.edu
• Nicholas G. Bircher, Immediate Past
President
ngbircher@pitt.edu
Description:
Represents college athletic departments.

HORLEN, HOLT & HOLLAS PLLC
2700 RUDDER FREEWAY, S
SUITE 5300
COLLEGE STATION, TX 77845-8142
979-696-1923
Fax: 979-696-2206
• Stephen R. Hollas, Attorney/Partner
Services:
All phases of athlete representation
including contract negotiation, long-range
planning, financial planning, and post-career
counseling.

HUGHES & LUCE
111 CONGRESS AVENUE
SUITE 900
AUSTIN, TX 78701
512-482-6800
Fax: 512-482-6859
• Edward O. Coultas, Partner
(512) 482-6823
• Philip M. Slinkard, Partner
(512) 482-6803

• Robert H Mow Jr, Partner
bob.mow@hughesluce.com
Clients:
Hillwood Development Corporation,
Electronic Data Systems, National Heritage
Insurance Company, SBC Communications,
H. Ross Perot, Sr., American Airlines,
Blockbuster, Dell, Dillard's, Ericsson,
Hillwood Development Corporation, Holly
Corporation, McAfee, VarTec Telecom,
Wal-Mart Stores, Worldspan, Sammons
Enterprises
Description:
Contract negotiation, arbitration hearings,
represents professional sports teams.
Other Location:
1717 Main Street, Ste 2800, Dallas, TX
75201; Phone: 214-939-5500

HUNEGS, STONE, LENEAVE, KYAS & THORNTON, P.A.
1000 12 OAKS CENTER DRIVE
SUITE 101
WAYZATA, MN 55391
612-568-0243
800-787-3453
Fax: 612-339-5150
www.hlklaw.com
• Richard Hunegs, Attorney
rhunegs@hlklaw.com
• Cortney S. LeNeave, Attorney
cleneave@hlklaw.com
• Cortney LeNeave, Attorney
• Randal W. LeNeave, Attorney
• Richard L. Carlson, Attorney
(612) 568-0243
• Richard J. Dinsmore PC, LLO, Attorney
(612) 568-0243
• Katie D. Figgins, Attorney
(612) 568-0243
• Richard G. Hunegs, Attorney
(612) 568-0243
• William Kvas, Attorney
(612) 568-0243
Description:
NFLPA. Handles the Minnesota Vikings
workers compensation.
Services:
Handle a variety of personal injury and
occupational illness claims
Other Location:
1000 Second Avenue, STE 3310, Seattle,
WA 98104; Phone: 206-448-7172;
800-525-3352

HUNT, ORTMANN, PALFFY & ROSSELL, INC.
301 N LAKE AVENUE
7TH FLOOR
PASADENA, CA 91101
626-440-5200
Fax: 626-796-0107
info@huntortmann.com
www.huntortmann.com
• Omel A. Nieves, Shareholder
(626) 440-5200
nieves@huntortmann.com
• Richard Mah, Principal
(626) 440-5200
mah@huntortmann.com
• Lawrence P Lubka, Principal
lubka@hobpr.com
• Richard E Blasco, Principal
blasco@hobpr.com
Clients:
City of Los Angeles, Alameda Corridor East,
Metropolitan Water District of Southern

California (MWD), Charles Pankow Builders,
Ltd., Sachs Electric Company, ACCO
Engineered Systems, R. D. Olson
Construction, W.E. O'Neil Construction Co.,
Tishman International Companies, Marcor
Environmental, Malcolm Drilling, Skidmore
Contracting Corporation, The Converse
Professional Group, Penhall Company, Los
Angeles County Metropolitan Transportation
Authority (MTA), City of Oxnard, Advanced
Structures, Inc., Building Industry Credit
Association, Salick Healthcare, Inc.,
Peterson Bros. Construction, Parr Lumber
Company, A. E. Schmidt Environmental,
Tetra
Description:
Contract negotiation, investment contract
negotiation, arbitration hearings,
federal/state/international tax filings,
licensing.

HUTCHISON, Q.C., J. MICHAEL
108-1218 WHARF STREET
VICTORIA, BC, CANADA V8W 1T8
250-388-6666
Fax: 250-389-0400
mhutchqc@bclawfirm.com
www.bclawfirm.com
Description:
Endorsement exploration, tort
actions/litigation, represents college athletic
departments, represents sports
organizations, player group and individual
athletes.

IAN C. PULVER
479 BEDFORD PARK AVENUE
TORONTO, ONTARIO, CANADA M5M 1K2
819-923-1034
Fax: 416-785-8032
ian@willsportsgroup.com
willsportsgroup.com
• Ian C. Pulver, Attorney
(416) 907-9801
ian@pulversports.com
Services:
Works in varied disciplines as labour law,
product licensing and community relations.
Description:
Represents sports organizations, tort
actions/litigation, Associate Counsel-NHL
Players Association.

IBACH, JOHN R.
1301 RIVERPLACE BOULEVARD
SUITE 1500
JACKSONVILLE, FL 32207
904-398-3911
Fax: 904-396-0663
bibach@rtlaw.com
www.rtlaw.com
• A. Gr Allen, Shareholder
(904) 346-5799
gallen@rtlaw.com
• Heather Ra Ambrose, Associate
(904) 346-5731
hambrose@rtlaw.com
Nature of Sports Service:
All phases of athlete representation
including contract negotiation, long-range
planning, financial planning, and post-career
counseling.
Clients:
Acosta Sales Co., Advanced Disposal
Services, Inc., Agri Dynamics, Inc., Alfred I.
Dupont Hospital for Children, American
Bio-Tech, Inc., American Coolair

Corporation, AmSouth Bank, Anchor Health Centers, Ascom Energy Systems, Inc., Atlantic Coast Asphalt Company, Atlantic States Bank, Bank of New York, The, Bartram Park, Ltd., BB&T, Inc., Ben Carter Properties, LLC, Borland - Groover Clinic, P.A., BPB America, Inc., Bremer Brace, Bremer Group, Brooks Health System, Brownfields Properties, LLC, Burkhardt Distributing Company, Celotex Corporation, Centex Homes Corporation of Florida, Chicago Title Insurance Company, City of Clearwater, Florida

Other Location:
170 Malaga Street, STE A, St. Augustine, FL 32084; Phone: 904-8241-0879

Year Founded:
1905

IRVING, PAUL H.
11355 W OLYMPIC BOULEVARD
LOS ANGELES, CA 90064
310-312-4000
Fax: 310-312-4224
pirving@manatt.com
www.manatt.com
• Paul Irving, Co-Chairman
(310) 312-4196
pirving@manatt.com
• Valentin G. Aguilar, Partner
(310) 312-4313
vaguilar@manatt.com
• Keith M. Allen Niesen, Partner
(310) 312-4105
kallen-niesen@manatt.com
• Dinesh R. Badkar, Associate
(310) 312-4266
dbadkar@manatt.com

Description:
Represents professional sports teams, licensing, endorsement exploration.

Services:
Advertising, Marketing & Media; Antitrust; Banking & Financial Industry; Bankruptcy & Financial Restructuring; Corporate & Finance; Energy, Environment & Resources; Government & Regulatory; Healthcare; Insurance; Intellectual Property & Internet; Employment & Labor; Litigation; Entertainment; Real Estate & Land Use; Tax, Benefits & Global Compensation; and Venture Capital & Technology.

Clients:
The Coca-Cola Company, Diageo North America, Den-Mat Corporation/Rembrandt Oral Care Products, D.L. Blair, DreamWorks, Dyson, Energizer Holdings, E. & J. Gallo Winery, Eveready Battery Company, Inc., Expedia, General Mills, Inc., Harley-Davidson, Jamba Juice, Kimberly-Clark Corporation, Martin Agency, MasterCard International, Mattel, Inc., Mead Johnson, Miller Brewing Company, Papa John's International, Inc., Reader's Digest Association, Inc., Schick Manufacturing, Inc., Thane International, Tommy Hilfiger, UniWorld Group, Inc., Yahoo! Inc., Zila Nutraceuticals, Amresco Commercial Finance, Bank of America Corp., California National Bank.

Other Locations:
121 State Street, Albany, NY 12207; Phone: 518-432-5990; 7 Times Square, New York, NY 10036; Phone: 212-790-4500; 695 Town Center Drive, 14th Floor, Costa Mesa, CA 92626; Phone: 714-371-2500; 1001 Page Mill Road, Building 2, Palo Alto, CA 94304; Phone: 650-812-1300; 1215 K Street, STE

1900, Sacramento, CA 95814; Phone: 916-552-2300; One Metro Center, 700 12th Street, NW, STE 1100, Washington, DC 20005; Phone 202-585-6500.

ISAAC, BRANT, LEDMAN & TEETOR
250 E BROAD STREET
SUITE 900
COLUMBUS, OH 43215-3742
614-221-2121
Fax: 614-365-9516
www.isaacbrant.com
• Timothy E. Miller, Attorney
timmiller@isaacbrant.com
• Scyld D. Anderson, Attorney
scyldanderson@isaacbrant.com
• Donald Anspaugh
donanspaugh@isaacbrant.com
• Douglas C. Boatright
douglasboatright@isaacbrant.com

Services:
Trial, Appellate & Federal Practice, General Business, Corporate, Estate Planning, Probate, Guardianship, Real Estate, Employment, Family, Negligence, Personal Injury, Transfusion-Related AIDS, Civil Arson, Insurance Defense, Insurance, Professional Malpractice, Premises Liability, Products Liability, Carrier Liability, Motor Sports Law, Commercial including Banking, Securities & OSHA Litigation, Risk Management

Nature of Sports Service:
All phases of athlete representation including contract negotiation, long-range planning, financial planning, and post-career counseling.

ISRAEL, FRIEDBERG & KORBATOV L.L.P.
11601 WILSHIRE BOULEVARD
SUITE 2200
LOS ANGELES, CA 90025
310-553-2200
Fax: 310-553-2280
www.ifklaw.com
• Igor Korbatov, Attorney
• James A. Friedberg
JFriedberg@ifklaw.com
• Igor Korbatov
IKorbatov@ifklaw.com
• Rudy Valner, Of Counsel
• Samuel Israel, Attorney
sisrael@ifklaw.com

JAFFE, RAITT, HEUER & WEISS, PC
500 GRISWOLD
SUITE 2400
DETROIT, MI 48226
313-961-1200
Fax: 313-961-1205
www.jaffelaw.com
• Arthur A. Weiss, Attorney
(248) 351-3000
aweiss@jaffelaw.com
• Joel Alam, Attorney
(248) 351-3000
jalam@jaffelaw.com
• Christopher A. Andreoff, Member
(248) 351-3000
candreoff@jaffelaw.com
• Patrice S. Arend, Member
(248) 351-3000
parend@jaffelaw.com

Description:
Contract negotiation, post career planning, investment contract negotiation, arbitration

hearings, federal/state/international tax filings, endorsement exploration, tort actions/litigation. Business Planning Law; Federal, State and Local Taxation Law.

Other Locations:
300 Park Street, STE 285, Birmingham, MI 48009; Phone: 248-540-1300; 201 South Main Street, STE 300, Ann Arbor, MI 48104; Phone: 734-222-4776

JANZER, JEROME M.
1000 N WATER STREET
SUITE 1700
MILWAUKEE, WI 53202
414-298-1000
800-553-6215
Fax: 414-298-8097
www.reinhartlaw.com
• Chad M. Anthony, Associate
(414) 298-8393
canthony@reinhartlaw.com
• Amy E. Arndt, Attorney
(414) 298-8300
aarndt@reinhartlaw.com

Description:
Post career planning, endorsement exploration, real estate investment.

Services:
Appellate, Banking and Finance, Bankruptcy and Creditors' Rights, Business Law, Computer & Technology, Crisis Management and Business Continuity, Employee Benefits, Entertainment Law, Environmental, Estate Planning, Executive Compensation, Government Relations, Health Care, Intellectual Property, International, Labor & Employment, Litigation, OSHA, Product Distribution and Franchise Law, Real Estate, Securities, Tax, Telecommunications and Energy

Other Locations:
22 East Mifflin Street, Madison, WI 53703; Phone: 608-229-2200; W233 North 2080 Ridgeview Parkway, Waukesha, WI 53188; Phone: 262-951-4500

JASEN & JASEN
69 DELAWARE AVENUE
SUITE 700
BUFFALO, NY 14202
716-848-9500
716-472-4444
www.jasenlaw.com
• Peter Jasen, Nsel, Couber
(716) 848-9500
lawyers@jasenlaw.com
• Mark M. Jasen, Member
(716) 848-9500
lawyers@jasenlaw.com

Nature of Sports Service:
All phases of athlete representation including contract negotiation, long-range planning, financial planning, and post-career counseling.

Services:
Provides high quality, responsive, cost effective and efficient legal services such as Auto/Motorcycle Accidents, Construction Accidents, Work Injuries, Neck/Back/Spine Injuries, Paraplegic, Quadriplegic, Paralysis, Wrongful Death, Boat Accidents, Railroad Accidents, Broken, Bones/Fractures, Head & Brain Injuries, Defective Products, Scaffold/Fall Injuries

JASPER, PATRICIA M.
405 HILGARD AVENUE
3149 MURPHY HALL
LOS ANGELES, CA 90024-1405
310-825-4321
Fax: 310-206-2390
www.ucla.edu
• Gene Block, Chancellor
(310) 825-2151
chancellor@conet.ucla.edu
• Gene G. Block, Chancellor
• Carole Goldberg, Vice Chancellor
Description:
Represents college athletic departments.
Services:
Provides cost-effective and high-quality
business support and administrative
services to campus customers such as
buying, facilities & operations, finance,
hospitality, housing, human resources,
public safety, technology and travel &
transportation.

JEANNIE BAUMGARTNER
2 PENNSYLVANIA PLAZA
14TH FLOOR
NEW YORK, NY 10121
212-465-6000
Fax: 212-465-6549
newyorkrangers@thegarden.com
www.newyorkrangers.com
• Glen Sather, President / General Manager
• Mike Golub, SVP-Marketing and Business
Operations
• Jeanie Baumgartner, VP-Marketing
• Rana Dershowitz, VP-Legal and Business
Affairs
Description:
Represents professional sports teams.

JENKENS & GILCHRIST PC
500 N AKARD
SUITE 1830
DALLAS, TX 75201
214-965-0776
Fax: 214-965-0780
Services:
Administrative & Legislative, Antitrust,
Bankruptcy, Construction, Corporate &
Securities, Energy, Environmental &
Administrative Advocacy, ERISA, ESOP,
Estate Planning, Financial Institutions,
Financial Services, Franchise & Distribution,
Health, Immigration, Intellectual Property,
International, Labor & Employment,
Litigation, Real Estate, Tax, Technology,
Transportation, White Collar
Description:
Contract negotiation, investment contract
negotiation, arbitration hearings,
federal/state/international tax filings,
represents professional sports teams,
provides securities advice, licensing,
endorsement exploration, tort
actions/litigation.

JENKINS & JONES
910 17TH STREET NW
SUITE 800
WASHINGTON, DC 20006-2606
202-223-2484
Fax: 202-331-3759
• Charles R. Jones Jr, Partner
(202) 223-2484
Services:
Contract negotiation, post career planning,
investment contract negotiation, Provides

investment advice, endorsement
exploration.

JERNIGAN LAW FIRM
2626 GLENWOOD AVENUE
SUITE 330
CAROLINA PLACE BUILDING
RALEIGH, NC 27608
919-833-0299
800-849-4478
(888) 877-3956
Fax: 919-256-2595
www.jernlaw.com
• Leonard T. Jernigan, Jr., Attorney
ltj@jernlaw.com
Description:
Practice focuses on people injured or
disabled, auto accidents, defective products,
on the job injuries, workers compensation
claims, exposure to asbestor and toxic
substances.

JOHNSON & BELL
33 W MONROE STREET
SUITE 2700
CHICAGO, IL 60603-5404
312-372-0770
Fax: 312-372-9818
info@jbltd.com
www.johnsonandbell.com
• William V. Johnson, President /
Shareholder
(312) 984-0218
johnsonw@jbltd.com
• John W. Bell, VP / Shareholder
(312) 984-0241
bellj@jbltd.com
• Jack T. Riley, VP / Shareholder
(312) 984-0269
rileyj@jbltd.com
• John A. Childers, VP / Shareholder
(312) 984-0262
childersj@jbltd.com
• John. W. Bell, Vice President
• Katherine J. Adamany, Associate
• Thomas J. Andrews, Shareholder
(312) 984-0239
• Joann T. Angarola, Shareholder
(312) 984-0201
• William G. Beatty, Shareholder
(312) 984-0232
• Daniel R. Bedell, Associate
(312) 984-0206
Services:
Apellate, Aviation litigation, Business
Litigation & Practice, Complex/Class
Litigation, Employment Law/ERISA,
Environmental, Financial Crimes, general
Negligence & Premises Liability, Hospitality
Law & Medical Liability, National
Coordinating Counsel, Product Liability,
Professional Liability Defense, Title
Insurance Defense, Toxic tort/Continuous
Exposure, Trucking & transportation Law,
Additional Practice Groups
Other Locations:
STE A, 9000 Indianapolis Blvd., Highland,
IN 46322; Phone: 219-923-5250; Fax:
219-923-6170; 325 Washington Street, STE
200, Waukegan, IL 60085; Phone:
847-662-7458; Fax: 847-662-7366
Year Founded:
1975

KAISER, RONALD A.
TEXAS A & M UNIVERSITY
156 FRANCIS HALL, CAMPUS 2261

FRANCIS HALL, SUITE 156
COLLEGE STATION, TX 77843-2261
979-845-3211
Fax: 979-845-0446
www.tamu.edu
• Jeffrey S. Vitter, EVP / Provost
(979) 845-4016
provost@tamu.edu
• R.Bowen A. Loften, President
(979) 845-5303
rkaiser@tamu.edu
• Karan Watson, EVP for academic affairs
• B.J. Crain, VP for finance and CFO
• Eric Hyman, Athletic Director
Clients:
Bookstore, Department of Student
Life-Off-campus, Department of Residence
Life-On-campus, Food Services, Health
Plan Provider, Housing Information,
Memorial Student Center, Memorial Student
Center Box Office, Print 'n' Copy, Student
Counseling Services, Student Health
Services , Transportation, University Police,
University Writing Center
Description:
Teaches sports law.

KALIS, CHRISTOPHER A.
5160 VILLAGE CREEK DRIVE
SUITE 100
PLANO, TX 75093
214-871-6005
Fax: 214-871-6050
chriskalis@kalislaw.com
• Christopher I. Kalis, Lawyer
(214) 871-6005
chriskalis@kalislaw.com
Nature of Sports Service:
All phases of athlete representation
including contract negotiation, long-range
planning, financial planning, and post-career
counseling.
Services:
Commercial Disputes, Trade Secret
Protection, Non-compete Agreements,
Athletes & Entertainers, Employment
Disputes, Personal Injuries, Defective
Products, Insurance Claims, Wrongful Death

KANAI, MARK A.
1101 15TH STREET
PO BOX 791
MODESTO, CA 95354
209-527-3650
Fax: 209-527-5518
mark@kanai-law.com
www.kanai-law.com
• Mark A. A. Kanai, Member
(906) 043-545
mark@kanai-law.com
Description:
Estate Planning, Trusts and Estates, Living
Trusts, Elder Law, Financial Planning,
Retirement Planning, Wealth Preservation,
Business Law, Employment Law, Corporate
Law, Partnership Law, Buying and Selling of
Businesses, Closely Held Business Law,
Emerging Growth Companies, Family
Business Successions, Real Estate,
Broadcast Radio, Sports Law.

KAPLAN, GARY L.
25 TAMALPAIS AVENUE
SUITE C
SAN ANSELMO, CA 94960
415-721-7584
• Gary L. Kaplan

Services:
Areas of practice include Personal Injury and Civil Litigation, Estate Planning and Probate, Labor and Employment Law, Commercial and Educational Loan Law, and Arbitration and Mediation

KARSNER & MEEHAN P.C.
128 DEAN STREET
TAUNTON, MA 2780
508-822-6600
877-684-0345
Fax: 508-822-8006
info@karsnermeehan.com
www.karsnermeehan.com
• James K. Meehan, Attorney
• Mark R. Karsner, Esquire
• David O. DeAbreu, Esquire
• Colleen C. G. Karsner, Attorney
(508) 822-6600
cck@karsnermeehan.com
• Mark R. Karsner, Attorney
(508) 822-6600
mrk@karsnermeehan.com
• James K. Meehan, Attorney
(508) 822-6600
jkm@karsnermeehan.com
• Robert C. Shea, Attorney
(508) 822-6600
rcs@karsnermeehan.com
• Karen L. Medeiros, Attorney
(508) 822-6600
klm@karsnermeehan.com
Description:
NFLPA. Handles workers compensation for the New England Patriots.
Services:
Areas of practice include Personal Injury, Workers' Compensation, Civil Litigation, Criminal Law, Wills & Estates, and Business Formation

KATZ, TELLER, BRANT & HILD
255 E FIFTH STREET
2400 CHEMED CENTER
CINCINNATI, OH 45202-4724
513-721-4532
Fax: 513-762-0000
ktbh@katzteller.com
www.katzteller.com
• Reuven J. Katz, Lawyer
(513) 977-3417
rkatz@katzteller.com
• Jerome S. Teller, Lawyer
(513) 977-3453
jteller@katzteller.com
• Andrew R. Berger, Attorney
(513) 977-3478
jcassity@katzteller.com
• Joel S. Brant, Attorney
(513) 977-3473
vschornak@katzteller.com
• Robert E. Brant, Attorney
(513) 977-3405
jcassity@katzteller.com
• Joseph A. Brant, Of Counsel
(513) 977-3408
jabrant@katzteller.com
• Adam D. Colvin, Attorney
(513) 977-3423
acolvin@katzteller.com
• Tedd H. Friedman, Attorney
(513) 721-4532
tfriedman@katzteller.com
Services:
Areas of practice include Creditors' Rights and Bankruptcy, Domestic Relations and Family Law, Employee Benefits and

Retirement Planning, Employment Law, Entertainment and Sports Law, Estate and Wealth Planning, Finance and Lending, General Business and Tax Matters, Health Care, Information Technology and e-Business, Insurance, Litigation, Probate, Real Estate and Environmental, Securities Law, and Title Insurance

KAY & MERKLE
100 THE EMBARCADERO
PENTHOUSE
SAN FRANCISCO, CA 94105-1217
415-357-1200
Fax: 415-512-9277
www.kaymerkle.com
• Steven Kay, Lawyer
(415) 357-1200
stevenkay@kmlaw100.com
• Walter F F. Merkle, Lawyer
(415) 357-1200
wmerkle@kmlaw100.com
• Steven Kay, Attorney
• W.Bruce Bercovich, Attorney
• John W Merkle, Attorney
• Lionel T. Aiken, Attorney
• Alan J Silver, Attorney
• Douglas A Marshall, Attorney
Services:
Areas of practice include business litigation, professional sports law, estate planning, entertainment law, and business law.

KEITH O. GREGORY
434 FAYETTEVILLE STREET MALL
SUITE 2030
RALEIGH, NC 27601
919-647-9728
877-297-6842
Fax: 919-832-4777
attykeithgregory@aol.com
• Keith O. Gregory, Member
attykeithgregory@aol.com
Services:
Areas of practice include Criminal Law, Driving While Intoxicated, Drug Crimes, Felonies, Homicide, Sexual Assault, Traffic Violations, Personal Injury, Automobile Accidents and Injuries, Wrongful Death, Divorce, Entertainment Law, Music Law, Sports Contracts, Separation Agreements, and Wills

KELLEY, MCELWEE & SCHMIDT, P.A.
2025 NORTH THIRD STREET
SUITE 150
PHOENIX, AZ 85004
602-230-1118
Fax: 602-230-9622
theresem@azfamilylaw.com
www.azfamilylaw.com
• Therese R. McElwee, Member
(602) 230-1118
theresem@azfamilylaw.com
• Brian E. Kelley, Member
(602) 230-1118
briank@azfamilylaw.com
• Paul G. Schmidt, Member
(602) 230-1118
pauls@azfamilylaw.com
Services:
Areas of practice include Complex Divorce, Prenuptial / Postnuptial Agreements, Mediation & Arbitration, Domestic Relations, and Child Custody Issues

KENYON & KENYON (DC OFFICE)
1500 K STREET NW
SUITE 700
WASHINGTON, DC 20005-1257
202-220-4200
Fax: 202-220-4201
www.kenyon.com
• Gwen Bey, Chief Administrative Officer
(212) 908-6396
gbey@kenyon.com
• John S. Barry, Chief Financial Officer
(212) 908-6468
jbarry@kenyon.com
• Kerstin Isaacs, Public Relations and Communications Mana
(212) 908-6853
kisaacs@kenyon.com
• Kathleen S. Lynn, Professional Recruiting Director
(212) 908-6177
klynn@kenyon.com
Services:
Provides litigation, prosecution, licensing and counseling services relating to patents, trademarks, copyrights, trade secrets and related matters, such as unfair business and unfair trade practices.
Other Office:
One Broadway, New York, NY 10004; Phone: 212-425-7200; 333 West San Carlos Street, STE 600, San Jose, CA 95110; Phone: 408-975-7500

KING & KELLEHER
4 EMBARCADERO CENTER
17H FLOOR
SAN FRANCISCO, CA 94111-4158
415-781-2888
Fax: 415-781-3011
• Edward V. King, Member
(415) 781-2888
evking@kingandkelleher.com
• Dirk V. Ausdall, Associate
(901) 868-914
• Alvin Lindsay, Associate
(415) 781-2888
alindsay@kingandkelleher.com
• Edward B. Vincent King, Jr., Partner
(905) 879-374
Description:
Litigation, Patents, Intellectual Property, Securities, Antitrust, Sports, Entertainment.
Services:
Areas of practice include Copyright, Patent & Trademark Attorneys, Corporate Business Attorneys, and Professional Services

KIRKPATRICK, WILLIAMS & MEEKS, L.L.P.
500 BROADWAY PLACE
SUPERIOR FEDERAL BUILDING, SUITE 404
LITTLE ROCK, AR 72201-3343
501-372-0401
Fax: 501-372-5277
• Joseph E. Kilpatrick Jr, Member
(501) 372-0401
joe@kawlaw.net
• Aylmer G. Ge Williams, Member
(501) 372-0401
gene@kawlaw.net
• Richard A. Smith, Managing Partner
• Charles H. Crocker, Associate
• W.Russell Meeks, Of Counsel

KORNBURG, HOWARD CRAIG
10880 WILSHIRE BOULEVARD
SUITE 1840
LOS ANGELES, CA 90024
310-474-5588
866-685-7259
Fax: 310-474-1078
www.kornberglawfirm.com
• Howard C. Kornberg, Sole Practitioner
hck@kornberglaw.com
Description:
Civil litigation, sports law, entertainment law, intellectual property, medical malpractice.
Services:
Areas of practice include Pedestrian & Bicycle Accidents; Elder Abuse; Birth Injuries; Dog bites; Slip and Fall Injuries; Trucking & Bus Accidents; Construction Site Accidents; Medical Malpractice; Sexual Harassment; Bad Faith Denial of Insurance Benefits; Motorcycle Accidents; Nursing Home Negligence; Death Claims; Burn Injuries; Fractures, Paralysis, Spinal Injuries; Aviation Accidents; Defective Products; Legal Malpractice; Civil Rights/Discrimination; and Fraud Claims.

KORZENIOWSKI, WALTER, ESQ.
688 WASHINGTON STREET
SOUTH EASTON, MA 2375
508-238-6200
Fax: 508-238-2899
walterkorzeniowski@hotmail.com
www.walterklaw.com
Description:
Handles workmans' compensation for the New England Patriots.
Services:
Provides legal services

KUPELIAN, ORMOND & MAGY
25800 NORTHWESTERN HIGHWAY
SUITE 950
SOUTHFIELD, MI 48075
248-357-0000
Fax: 248-357-7488
• Peter B. Kupelian, Lawyer
(248) 351-8351
• Peter B. P. Kupelian, Attorney
• David M. Blou, Associate attorney
Services:
Serves clients worldwide through the following departments: Litigation, Business and International, Commercial Property, and Municipal Law and Litigation.
Description:
Contract negotiation, licensing, endorsement exploration, tort actions/litigation.

LAING, DEAN P.
111 E WISCONSIN AVENUE
SUITE 1400
MILWAUKEE, WI 53202
414-276-5000
Fax: 414-276-6581
webmaster@wilaw.com
www.wilaw.com
• Jean M. Ansay, Lawyer
(262) 284-3407
jean.ansay@wilaw.com
• Dean P. Laing, Lawyer
(414) 276-5000
Services:
Areas of practice include Bankruptcy and Creditors Rights; Business Acquisitions and Dispositions; Business Succession

Planning; Commercial Litigation; Commercial Transactions; Construction Law; Corporations, Partnerships and Limited Liability Companies; Divorce, Custody and Marital Property Agreements; E-Commerce and Telecommunications Law; Employee Benefits and ERISA; Employment and Labor Law; Estate Planning and Probate; Intellectual Property Law; Municipal, Zoning and Administrative Law; Personal Injury and Products Litigation; Qualified Plans and Executive Compensation; Real Estate and Construction Law; Securities and Franchise Law; Tax
Description:
Contract negotiation, tort actions/litigation. Litigation; Products Liability; Personal Injury.
Other Location:
1329 West Grand Avenue, STE 200, PO Box 306, Port Washington, WI 53074; Phone: 262-284-3407
Year Founded:
1973

LAMPART, ABE
55 SECOND STREET
SUITE 1700
SAN FRANCISCO, CA 94105-3493
415-227-0900
Fax: 415-227-0770
www.buchalter.com
• Peter G. Bertrand, Shareholder
(415) 227-0900
pbertrand@buchalter.com
• Jonathan Y. Hawkins, Sr administrative director
• Kristy Sessions, HRM
• Judith Gordon, Marketing director
• David Bustle, Director of IT
Description:
Investment contract negotiation, represents sports organizations, arbitration hearings, provides securities advice, provides investment advice, endorsement exploration.
Services:
Provides transactional and litigation support for established and evolving businesses in the following practice areas: Bank and Finance; Business Practices; Insolvency; Intellectual Property; Labor & Employment; Litigation; Pro Bono; Real Estate; Tax.
Other Locations:
601 S Figueroa Street, STE 2400, Los Angeles, CA 90017; Phone: 213-891-0700; Fax: 213-896-0400; 18400 Von Karman Avenue, STE 800, Irvine, CA 92612; Phone: 949-760-1121; Fax: 949-72-0182; Anderson Brody Buchalter Nemer, 4600 East Shea Blvd., STE 100, Phoenix, AZ 85028; Phone: 602-234-0563; Fax: 602-234-2952

LAMPLEY, NATHANIEL
301 EAST FOURTH STREET
SUITE 3500
GREAT AMERICAN TOWER
CINCINNATI, OH 45202
513-723-4000
Fax: 513-723-4056
nlampley@vorys.com
www.vorys.com
• Terri Reyering Abare, Partner
(513) 723-4001
trabare@vorys.com
• TerriReyering Abare, Partner
(513) 723-4001
trabra@vorys.com

• T. Gregory Apocotos, Partner
(513) 723-8581
tgapocotos@vorys.com
• Melvin A. Bredre, Partner
(513) 723-4023
mabedre@vorys.com
• David E. Barnes, Paralegal
(513) 723-4815
debarnes@vorys.com
• Jessica K. Baverman, Associate
(513) 723-4092
jkbaverman@vorys.com
• Eric B Bond, Associate
(513) 723-4824
ebbond@vorys.com
• William P. DG Baldwin, Partner
(513) 723-4030
wdbaldwin@vorys.com
Nature of Sports Service:
All phases of athlete representation including contract negotiation, long-range planning, financial planning, and post-career counseling.
Services:
Areas of practice include Intellectual Property; International Law; Labor and Employment; Litigation; Probate and Estate Planning; Taxation, Technology; and Toxic Tort.

LANG, XIFARAS & BULLARD
115 ORCHARD STREET
NEW BEDFORD, MA 02740
508-992-1270
Fax: 508-993-8696
sfweiner@lxblaw.com
www.lxblaw.com
• Scott W. Lang, Attorney
(508) 992-1270
info@lxb-newbedford.com
• Scott W. D. Lang, Attorney
swlang@lxblaw.com
• Peter C. Bullard, Attorney
(508) 992-1270
pcbullard@lxblaw.com
• Susan Forgue Weiner, Attorney
(508) 992-1270
sfweiner@lxblaw.com
• Jennifer L. Davis, Attorney
(508) 992-1270
• Gigi D. D. Tierney, Attorney
(508) 992-1270
gdtierney@lxblaw.com
Description:
Providing quality legal services to families and businesses in the Greater New Bedford area.
Areas of Practice:
Administrative Law, Business Law, Consumer Protection, Employee Benefits, Estate Administration, Estate Planning, Family Law, Employment Law, Labor Law, Litigation, Personal Injury, Real Estate, Social Security, Workers' Compensation.

LATSHA DAVIS & MCKENNA, P.C.
1700 BENT CREEK BOULEVARD
SUITE 140
MECHANICSBURG, PA 17050
717-620-2424
Fax: 717-620-2444
www.ldylaw.com
• Latsha L. Kimber, Principal/Managing Shareholder
klatsha@ldylaw.com
• Kevin M. McKenna, Esq., Shareholder
(610) 524-8454

Description:
Tort litigation; sports law; workers'
compensation

LATTINVILLE, ROBERT H.
7700 FORSYTH BOULEVARD
SUITE 1100
ST. LOUIS, MO 63105
314-863-0800
Fax: 314-863-9388
www.stinson.com
• John W. Moticka, St. Louis Co-Managing
Partner
(314) 259-4562
jmoticka@stinson.com
• Charles G. Misko, St. Louis Co-Managing
Partner
(314) 259-4570
cmisko@stinsonmoheck.com
Services:
Areas of practice include real estate law,
mergers & acquisitions, labor &
employment, business litigation, financial
services, health care, sports law, and
products liability.

Nature of Sports Service:
All phases of athlete representation including
contract negotiation, estate planning,
endorsements, financial planning, compliance
matters, licensing matters and post-career
counseling.

LAURIA TOKUNGA GATES & LINN, LLP
1755 CREEKSIDE OAKS
#240
SACRAMENTO, CA 95833
916-492-2000
Fax: 916-492-2500
www.ltglaw.net
• Anthony D. Lauria, Lawyer
alauria@ltglaw.net
• Mark D. Tokunga, Lawyer
• Scott A. Linn, Lawyer
• Scott Andre, Sports Lawyer
Description:
Civil Practice, Construction Law, Insurance
Defense, Medical Malpractice, Personal
Injury, Products Liability, Bad Faith,
Recreation/Sports Law.

LAW OFFICE OF DONALD J STANTON
1185 WASHINGTON STREET
SUITE 6
NEWTON, MA 2465
617-964-1341
Fax: 617-964-6910
d4stanton@aol.com
• Donald J. Stanton, Esquire
(617) 964-1341
d4stanton@aol.com
Services:
Legal Services
Description:
Contract negotiation, arbitration hearings,
represents professional sports teams, tort
actions/litigation, estate planning.

LAW OFFICE OF WILLIAM D HOCHBERG
222 THIRD AVENUE N
EDMONDS, WA 98020
425-744-1220
Fax: 425-744-0464
info@hochberglaw.net
www.hochberglaw.net
• Bill Hochberg, Attorney
• Lillian Kaufer, Paralegal

Year Founded:
1996
Description:
Represents injured professional athletes in
Washington State.
Nature of Services:
Workers' compensation claims, social
security, disability, and personal injury
claims.

LAYMAN, MICHAEL L.
268 NEWMAN AVENUE
HARRISONBURG, VA 22801
540-433-2121
800-394-1646
Fax: 540-433-7296
info@layman-nichols.com
www.layman-nichols.com
• Michael L. Layman, Attorney/CPA
mlayman@layman-nichols.com
• Michael L. M. Layman, Attorney
• Lenora Fowler, Legal Secretary
• Carol B. Boutillier, Office Administrator
Services:
Areas of practice include tax planning,
estate and business succession planning,
elder law, wills and trusts, estate
administration, qualified retirement plans,
real estate, tax-deferred exchanges,
representation of closely-held businesses,
including professional practices, health law,
charitable planning, and employee benefits.

LEADBETTER, RONALD C.
527 ANDY HOLT TOWER
527 ANDY HOLT TOWER
KNOXVILLE, TN 37996-0184
865-974-1000
Fax: 865-974-4811
chancellor@utk.edu
www.utk.edu
• Susan Martin, Vice Chancellor Academic
Affairs
• Jimmy G. Cheek, Chancellor
(865) 974-3265
chancellor@utk.edu
Services:
Prides itself on adding value to
Tennessee—by educating its students,
doing research and creative work that
improves quality of life, and reaching out to
share expertise with Tennesseans.
Description:
Represents college athletic departments.

LEDBETTER, BEVERLY E.
ONE PROSPECT STREET
CAMPUS BOX 1860
PROVIDENCE, RI 2912
401-863-1000
Fax: 401-863-1199
SAC@brown.edu
www.brown.edu
• Ruth Simmons, President
(401) 863-2234
president@brown.edu
• Christina Paxson, President
Services:
A leading Ivy League institution with a
distinctive undergraduate academic
program, a world-class faculty, outstanding
graduate and medical students, and a
tradition of innovative and rigorous
multidisciplinary study.
Description:
Represents college athletic departments.

LEFKOWITZ, PAUL
55 PUBLIC SQUARE
SUITE 1950
CLEVELAND, OH 44113
216-621-8484
(800) 621-1062
Fax: 216-771-1632
www.climacolaw.com
• John R. Climaco, Founder
(216) 522-0265
jrclim@climacolaw.com
• John A. Peca, Managing Principal
(216) 522-0991
japeca@climacolaw.com
Services:
Areas of practice include Litigation,
Commercial Law, Municipal Law,
Employment Law, and Class Actions
Description:
NFLPA workers' compensation panel.

LEVIN, PAPANTONIO, THOMAS, MITCHELL, ECHSNER & PROCTOR, P.A.
316 S BAYLEN STREET
SUITE 600
PO BOX 12308
PENSACOLA, FL 32591
850-435-7000
888-435-7001
Fax: 850-435-7020
contact@levinlaw.com
www.levinlaw.com
• Brian Barr, Shareholder
• Robert Smith, Administrator
Nature of Sports Service:
All phases of athlete representation
including contract negotiation, long-range
planning, financial planning, and post-career
counseling.
Services:
Areas of practice include Personal Injury;
Medical Malpractice; Mass Tort / Product
Liability; Commercial Litigation; Insurance
Bad Faith; Workers' Compensation; Criminal
Law; Nursing Home Abuse; Environmental
Litigation.

LEVINSON, FRIEDMAN, P.S.
1001 FOURTH AVENUE
SUITE 4131
SEATTLE, WA 98154
206-624-8844
800-448-8008
Fax: 206-624-2912
www.admiralty.com
• Robert M. Kraft, Partner
(206) 624-8844
rmk@admiralty.com
• Lance E. Palmer, Partner
(206) 624-8844
Services:
Handles personal injury trials.
Clients:
Represents clients in following areas:
construction site injury; automobile injury;
motorcycle injury; workplace injury;
pedestrian injury; slip and fall injury; cruise
ship injury; fisherman injury; admiralty law;
maritime law; pharmaceutical injury;
fen-phen injury; wrongful death; product
liability; railroad injury; toxic products;
mesothelioma; redux injury; PPA Injury;
asbestosis.
Nature of Sports Service:
All phases of athlete representation
including contract negotiation, long-range
planning, financial planning, and post-career

counseling.
Year Founded:
1929

LEVY, HERMAN M.
500 EL CAMINO REAL
SANTA CLARA, CA 95053
408-554-4000
Fax: 408-554-5095
hlevy@scu.edu
www.scu.edu
• Paul Locatelli, Chancellor
• Lucia Albino Gilbert, Provost
Description:
Arbitration hearings, teaches sports law.
Services:
Areas of practice include arbitration
hearings and sports law.

LEWIS AND ROCA LLP
201 EAST WASHINGTON
SUITE 1200
PHOENIX, AZ 85004
602-262-5311
Fax: 602-262-5747
clientservices@lrlaw.com
www.lrlaw.com
• Emily Bayton, Partner
(602) 262-5768
ebayton@lrlaw.com
Other Locations:
One South Church Avenue, STE 700,
Tucson, AZ 85401; Phone: 520-622-2090;
Fax: 520-622-3088; 3993 Howard Hughes
Parkway, STE 600, Las Vegas, NV 89109;
Phone: 702-949-8200; Fax: 702-949-8398;
201 Third Street, NW, STE 1950,
Albuquerque, NM 87102; Phone:
505-764-5400; Fax: 505-764-5480
Services:
Areas of practice include Antitrust and Trade
Regulation, Appeals, Arbitration and
Mediation, Bankruptcy, Broker/Dealer,
Commercial Litigation, Construction,
Corporate and Securities, creditor's Rights,
Criminal Defense, Government Regulation
and Corporate Compliance, E-Discovery &
Data Management, Education and Schools,
Employee Benefits, Environmental and
Natural Resources, Finance, Gaming,
Government Relations and Administrative,
Healthcare, Indian Affairs Law, Insurance,
Intellectual Property, Labor and
Employment, Legal Risk Evaluation,
Mergers and Acquisitions, Personal Injury,
Products Liability

LEWIS, KING, KRIEG & WALDROP, P.C.
620 MARKET STREET
ONE CENTRE SQUARE, FIFTH FLOOR
PO BOX 2425
KNOXVILLE, TN 37901
865-546-4646
Fax: 865-523-6529
www.lewisking.com
• Charles B. Lewis, Lawyer
(865) 546-4646
• John K King, Lawyer
(865) 546-4646
jking@lewisking.com
• Richard W. Kreig, Lawyer
(865) 546-4646
Dkrieg@lkkwc.com
• Loy W Waldrop, Lawyer
(865) 546-4646
lwaldrop@lkkwc.com

Services:
Areas of practice include Appellate,
Arbitration, Aviation, Banking, Bankruptcy,
Business Organization and Litigation,
Casualty Defense, Construction and Surety
Law, Copyright and Trademark, Corporate,
Criminal, Domestic, Education,
Employment, Fire Loss, Health Care,
Insurance, Landlord/Tenant, Mediation,
Military, Municipal, Personal Injury, Products
Liability, Professional Liability, Regulatory,
Real Estate, Workers' Compensation, and
Zoning
Other Location:
Suntrust Bank Building, 201 Fourth Avenue
North, STE 1500, PO Box 198615,
Nashville, TN 37219; Phone: 615-259-1366

LIBRETT, FRIEDLAND & LIEBERMAN
1325 FRANKLIN AVENUE
SUITE 545
GARDEN CITY, NY 11530-1701
516-874-3523
866-427-5413
Fax: 516-741-1592
lfriedland@lfllaw.com
www.lfllaw.com
• Lloyd M. Friedland, Attorney
(516) 741-1040
lfriedland@lfllaw.com
• Richard A. Librett, Attorney
(516) 741-1040
rlibrett@lfllaw.com
• Edward L. Lieberman, Attorney
(516) 741-1040
elieberman@lfllaw.com
Year Founded:
1978
Description:
Contract negotiation, real estate, and
general practice law firm.

LICARI & WALSH, L.L.C.
322 E. MAIN STREET
SUITE 2B
BRANFORD, CT 06405
203-752-1450
Fax: 203-752-1401
www.licariwalsh.com
• Christopher M. Lucari, Member
(203) 752-1450
clicari@licari-walsh.com
• John M. Walsh Jr, Member
(203) 752-1450
jwalsh@licari-walsh.com
• Craig L. Manemeit, Associate
cmanemeit@licari-walsh.com
• Gary P. Sklaver, Counsel
gsklaver@licari-walsh.com
Services:
Areas of practice include: Personal Injury
(Automobile Collisions, Premises Liability,
Product Liability, Medical Malpractice,
Wrongful Death), Business Torts and
Commercial Litigation, Labor and
Employment Law, Workers' Compensation,
Small Business Law, Consumer Law,
Criminal Law, Real Estate (Commercial and
Residential), Wills and Probate.

**LIEBMANN, CONWAY, OLEJNICZAK &
JERRY**
231 S ADAMS STREET
PO BOX 23200
GREEN BAY, WI 54301

920-437-0476
Fax: 920-437-2868
www.lcojlaw.com
• Thomas M. Olejniczak, Partner
tmo@lcojlaw.com
• Herbect C. Liebmann III, Partner
• Geogory B. Conway, Partner
• Gregory Mi Conway, Attorney
Services:
Areas of practice include Adoptions,
Bankruptcy and Creditors' Rights,
Commercial Litigation, Computer and
Internet Law, Construction, Corporate/
Business Law, Development, Leasing,
Environment Issues, Estate/Retirement,
Planning and Probate, Hospital and Health
Care Law, Insurance Coverage/Defense,
Intellectual Property, Labor Employment
Matters, Litigation and Trials,
Meditation/Arbitration, Mergers/
Acquisitions, Municipal Law, Non-Profit
Institutions, Municipal Law, Non-Profit
institutions, Personal Injury Claims, Real
Estate and Construction, Tax, and Pension
and Employee Benefit Planning
Description:
Represents professional sports teams. On
the Board of Directors for the Green Bay
Packers.
Year Founded:
1976

LINDNER & MARSACK, S.C.
411 E WISCONSIN AVENUE
SUITE 1800
MILWAUKEE, WI 53202
414-273-3910
Fax: 414-273-0522
www.lindner-marsack.com
• Gary A. Marsack, President/Senior
Shareholder
(414) 273-3910
gmarsack@lindner-marsack.com
• Robert E. Schreiber, Jr., VP/Shareholder
(414) 273-3910
rschreiber@lindner-marsack.com
• Jonathan T. Swain, Board of Directors
jswain@lindner-marsack.com
• Chelsie D. R. Allan, Attorney
• Douglas M. Feldman, Attorney
• Alan M. Levy, Attorney
• Gary A. Marsack, Attorney
• John E. Murray, Attorney
• David C. Mckone, Attorney
Services:
Representation Matters (Maintaining
Non-Union Status, Union Organizing
Campaigns), Collective Bargaining and
Contract Administration (Labor Contract
Negotiations, Mediation, Interest Bargaining
(Win-Win), Public Sector Interest Arbitration,
Contract Interpretation, Discipline,
Grievance Handling, Arbitration), Labor
Dispute (Strike Preparations, Managing the
Labor Disputes, Public Relations and the
Labor Dispute), General Labor Matters
(General Consultation, Strategy
Development, OSHA and Safety and Health
Matters, WARN Act - Plant Closings - Mass
Layoffs), Labor Litigation (NLRB and
Related State Labor Agencies, Unfair Labor
Practice Matter

LOPEZ & FANTEL
2292 WEST COMMODORE WAY
SUITE 200
SEATTLE, WA 98199

206-322-5200
Fax: 206-322-1979
clopez@lopezfantel.com
• Carl Taylor Lopez, President
Services:
All phases of athlete representation
including contract negotiation, long-range
planning, financial planning, and post-career
counseling.

LOPEZ, PAT P.
6363 N SWAN ROAD
SUITE 151
TUCSON, AZ 85718
520-792-4800
Fax: 520-529-4262
rusingandlopez@aol.com
www.rusingandlopez.com
• Michael J. S. Rusing, Attornry
(520) 792-4800
mrusing@rusingandlopez.com
• Patricio P. Lopez III, Attorney
plopez@rusingandlopez.com
Clients:
AIMCO Properties, Alphagraphics, America
Online, Arizona Board of Regents, Arizona
Electric, Power Cooperative, Bank of
America, Big 5 Corp., Bob's Custom
Roofing, Brush Ceramic Products, Brush
Wellman Inc., Capin Car Wash, Charter
Funding, Chicanos por la Causa, Chubb
Group of Insurance Companies, Cintas
Citizens Transport and Storage, Cox
Communications, El Coronado Ranch,
Electronic Data Systems, Fairfield Homes,
First Magnus Financial Corporation,
Fresenius Medical Care North America,
Frontier Towing, Inc., Gates Learjet, Goettl
Air Conditioning, Inc., Guarantee Mutual
Life, Hydro Geo Chem, Jack in the Box, Inc.,
La Causa Construction, In
Nature of Sports Service:
All phases of athlete representation
including contract negotiation, long-range
planning, financial planning, and post-career
counseling.

LUBIN & ENOCH, P.C.
349 N 4TH AVENUE
PHOENIX, AZ 85003-1505
602-234-0008
Fax: 602-626-3586
www.lubinandenoch.com
• Nicholas J. Enoch, Attorney
• Stanley Lubin, Member
• Nicholas J. Enoch, Partner
• Jarrett J. Haskovec, Member
Services:
Areas of practice include Labor and
Employment Relations, Civil Service,
Employment Discrimination, Administrative
Law, and Arbitration. Civil Trial and
Appellate Practice
Clients:
Arizona State AFL-CIO; Local Unions 2859
& 3954, American Federation of
Government Employees, AFL-CIO; Local
Union 3190, American Federation of State,
County & Municipal Employees, AFL-CIO;
Local Union 93, American Postal Workers
Union, AFL-CIO; Community Legal Services
Attorney Union; Locals 266, 387, 570, 640,
769 and 1116, International Brotherhood of
Electrical Workers, AFL-CIO; Engineers and
Associate Employees of KTVK; United Farm
Workers, AFL-CIO; Professional Fire
Fighters of Arizona & Local Unions I-60,
3066, 3560, 3573, 3690, 3878, 3924 &

4191; International Association of Fire
Fighters, AFL-CIO

**LYNCH, GILARDI & GRUMMER, A
PROFESSIONAL CORPORATION**
170 COLUMBUS AVENUE
5TH FLOOR
SAN FRANCISCO, CA 94133
415-397-2800
Fax: 415-397-0937
www.lgglaw.com
• Kenneth F. Vierra, Partner
(415) 397-2800
kvierra@lgglaw.com
• Robert T. Lynch, Partner
(415) 397-2800
rlynch@lgglaw.com
Services:
Areas of practice include Commercial
Litigation & Advice Products Liability
Litigation, Construction Law & Litigation,
Professional Liability Litigation, Directors'
and Officers' Liability Real Estate Law and
Litigation, Employment Litigation and Advice
Sports Law & Athlete Representation,
Insurance Law And Litigation Toxic Tort and
Areas of practice include Environmental
Liability, and Intellectual Property
Transportation Law
Nature of Sports Service:
Sports Law, Real Estate, Landlord and
Tenant Law, Employment Law, Litigation,
Directors and Officers Liability.

MACDONALD, JAMES
709 S. DEAKIN STREET
PO BOX 442321
MOSCOW, ID 83844-2321
208-885-4977
888-884-3246
Fax: 208-885-5709
info@uidaho.edu
• James S. Macdonald, Professor
(208) 885-7947
jimmymac@uidaho.edu
• Michele Bartlett, Director, Development
(208) 364-4044
bartlett@uidaho.edu
Services:
Teaches sports law.

MAHONE, GLENN R.
435 SIXTH AVENUE
PITTSBURGH, PA 15219
412-288-3131
Fax: 412-288-3063
www.reedsmith.com
• Glenn R. Mahone, Partner
(412) 288-4240
gmahone@reedsmith.com
• Gary A. Sokulski, Chief Operating Officer
(412) 288-4232
gsokulski@reedsmith.com
Services:
All phases of athlete representation
including contract negotiation, long-range
planning, financial planning, and post-career
counseling.
Clients:
Advertising Research Foundation, AMION
Advertising & Marketing International
Network, ANA, Bank of America, Caithness
Energy, CIT, Dominion Resources, Inc.,
Federated Investors, FPL Energy LLC,
GMAC, H.R. Block, ICOM International
Communications Network, Interpublic
Group, JPMorgan Chase, Key Bank,

MAGNET Advertising Agency Network,
Mellon Financial Corporation, Merck, Inc.,
National Penn, NiSource, Inc., Ocwen,
Pfizer, Inc., PNC Bank, Sony Corporation of
America, Sony Electronics Inc., Sony
Pictures Entertainment, Starwood Capital
Group, TAAN Transworld Advertising
Agency Network, Wachovia, Wells Fargo,
N.A., WWP Wordwide Partners

**MAJOR LEAGUE BASEBALL
PROPERTIES**
75 NINTH AVENUE
5TH FLOOR
NEW YORK, NY 10011
212-931-7800
866-800-1275
Fax: 212-949-5654
www.mlb.com
• Allan H. Selig, Commissioner of Baseball
• Robert A DuPuy, President/Chief
Operating Officer
• Sandy Alderson, Executive VP of Baseball
Operations
• Carmen Julia Hunt, Information Contact
Person
• Jonathan Mariner, EVP,Finance
• Tim Brosnan, EVP,Business
Description:
The licensing agent for all of the Major
League Baseball entities the Office of the
Commissioner of Baseball, the American
and National Leagues of Professional
Baseball Clubs, the individual Major League
Baseball clubs and their affiliated and
related entities. MLBP secures protection for
and enforces the intellectual property rights
of all of the Major League Baseball entities
against infringers and counterfeiters
worldwide.

MALLOY, DOROTHY A.
800 E. LANCASTER AVENUE
206 TOLENTINE HALL, VILLANOVA
UNIVERSITY
VILLANOVA, PA 19085
610-519-4500
Fax: 610-519-7875
ogc@villanova.edu
www.villanova.edu
• Dorothy A. Malloy, VP/General Counsel
(610) 519-7857
dorothy.malloy@villanova.edu
• Debra Fickler, Deputy General Counsel
(610) 519-7857
debra.fickler@villanova.edu
Services:
Represents college athletic departments.

MANATT, PHELPS & PHILLIPS, LLP
7 TIMES SQUARE
NEW YORK, NY 10036
212-790-4500
Fax: 212-790-4545
wbernstein@manatt.com
www.manatt.com
• Mathew S. Rosengart, Partner
(212) 790-4565
mrosengart@manatt.com
• William S. Bernstein, Partner
(212) 830-7282
wbernstein@manatt.com
Services:
Areas of practice include Advertising,
Marketing & Media, Antitrust, Appellate,
Banking & Financial Industry, Bankruptcy &
Financial Restructuring, Corporate &

Finance, Criminal Defense & Investigations, Employment & Labor, Energy, Environmental & Natural Resources, Entertainment, Financial Services, Government & Regulatory, Healthcare Industry, Insurance Industry, Intellectual Property & Internet, International Trade & Policy, Litigation, Mergers & Acquisitions, Not-for-Profit Organizations, Real Estate & Land Use, Tax, Employee Benefits & Global Compensation, Unfair Competition Litigation, and Venture Capital & Technology

Clients:
The Coca-Cola Company, Diageo North America, Den-Mat Corporation/Rembrandt Oral Care Products, D.L. Blair, DreamWorks, Dyson, Energizer Holdings, E. & J. Gallo Winery, Eveready Battery Company, Inc., Expedia, General Mills, Inc., Harley-Davidson, Jamba Juice, Kimberly-Clark Corporation, Martin Agency, MasterCard International, Mattel, Inc., Mead Johnson, Miller Brewing Company, Papa John's International, Inc., Reader's Digest Association, Inc., Schick Manufacturing, Inc., Thane International, Tommy Hilfiger, UniWorld Group, Inc., Yahoo! Inc., Zila Nutraceuticals, Amresco Commercial Finance, Bank of America Corp., California National Bank, Cit

Description:
All phases of athlete representation including contract negotiation, long-range planning, financial planning, and post-career counseling.

MANDEL, IRWIN
1901 W MADISON STREET
UNITED CENTER
CHICAGO, IL 60612-2459
312-455-4000
Fax: 312-455-4189
sth@bulls.com
www.chicagobulls.com
• Jerry Reinsdorf, Chairman
• Irwin Mandel, SVP, Financial & Legal
Services:
Represents professional sports teams.

MANNING, MARDER, KASS, ELLROD, & RAMIREZ
801 S FIGUEROA STREET
15TH FLOOR
LOS ANGELES, CA 90017
213-624-6900
Fax: 213-624-6999
aje@mmker.com
• Anthony J. Ellrod, Partner
(213) 624-6900
aje@mmker.com
• Steven D. Manning, Partner
(213) 624-6900
sdm@mmker.com
Other Locations:
1 Park Plaza, Suite 500 Irvine, CA 92614 Phone: (949) 440-6690 Fax: (949) 474-6691; 550 W C Street, Suite 1900 San Diego, CA 92101 Phone: (619) 515-0269 Fax: (619) 515-0268; One California Street, Suite 1100 San Francisco, CA 94111 Phone: (415) 217-6990 Fax: (415) 217-6999; 14362 N Frank Lloyd Wright Boulevard, Suite 2300 Scottsdale, AZ 85260 Phone: (480) 477-5269 Fax: (480) 477-5268, 801 S Figueroa Street, 15th Floor, Los Angeles, CA 90017 Phone: (213) 624-6900 Fax: (213) 624-6999.

Description:
Insurance defense and coverage, business and commercial law, business transactions, sports and recreation, employment, wage and hour, professional, errors and omissions, appellate law, workers compensation, general civil defense, medical malpractice defense, construction defect, real estate litigation and transactions, police civil liability, government fort liability, immigration law.

MARGOLIS EDELSTEIN
170 S INDEPENDENCE MALL W
THE CURTIS CENTER
SUITE 400E
PHILADELPHIA, PA 19106-3337
215-922-1100
Fax: 215-922-1772
mail@margolisedelstein.com
www.margolisedelstein.com
• Joseph S. Bekelja, Partner
(215) 931-5807
jbekelja@margolisedelstein.com
• Peter D. Bludman, Partner
(215) 931-5879
pbludman@margolisedelstein.com
• Joseph S. Bekelja, Partner
(215) 931-5807
jbekelja@margolisedelstein.com
• Gordon Gelfond, Partner
(215) 931-5812
• Alan Wm. Margolis, Partner
(215) 931-5802
• Donald M. Davis, Partner
(215) 931-5813
ddavis@margolisedelstein.com
• William Longo, Partner
(215) 931-5861
wlongo@margolisedelstein.com
• Mark N. Cohen, Partner
(215) 931-5848
mcohen@margolisedelstein.com
Other Location:
Curtis Center, 4th Floor, Independence Square West, 601 Walnut street, Philadelphia, PA 19106; Phone: 215-922-1100
Services:
Automobile and Trucking Litigation, Aviation Litigation, Complex/Environmental/Toxic Tort Litigation, Construction Defect Litigation, Domestic Relations/Marital Law, Employment Practices Liability, ERISA and Employee Benefit Litigation , Fidelity and Surety Law, General Liability, Insurance Coverage, Insurance Fraud, Municipal Liability, Product Llability, Professional Liability, Worker's Compensation
Clients:
ACE Insurance Group, Allied Waste Industries, Inc., American International Group, Inc., Arch Insurance Group, Best Buy Company, Broadspire Services, Budget Rent-A-Car Corporation, CAMICO Mutual Insurance Co., Crawford & Company, Delta Air Lines, Inc., Erie Insurance Group, Federal Express Corporation, GAB Robins North America, Inc., Gallagher Bassett Services, General Star Management Company, Great American Insurance Company, Guideone Insurance Co., J & J Snack Food Corporation, K&K Insurance Group, Kingsway Insurance Group, Lennox International, Inc, Liberty Mutual Insurance Company, Navigators Insurance, New Jersey Manufacturers Insurance

---

MARISCAL, WEEKS, MCINTYRE & FRIELANDER, P.A.
2901 N CENTRAL AVENUE
SUITE 200
PHOENIX, AZ 85012
602-285-5000
Fax: 602-285-5100
• Gary L. Birnbaum, Managing Director
(602) 285-5009
gary.birnbaum@mwmf.com
• Ann Eastepp, Director of Administration
(602) 285-5050
Description:
General Civil Trial and Appellate Practice in all State and Federal Courts and Administrative Bodies. Corporate and Securities, Probate, Real Estate, Personal Injury, Insurance, Eminent Domain, Construction, Estate Planning, Family, Taxation, Health Care, Municipal, Native American, Administrative, Commercial, Financial Institution and Secured Lending, Bankruptcy, Employment, Environmental, Sports, Trademark and Intellectual Property, Title Insurance and Escrow Law, Professional Malpractice Defense, Alternative Dispute Resolution (Arbitration/Mediation).

MARKS, MARKS & KAPLAN
55 W MONROE STREET
SUITE 3300
CHICAGO, IL 60603
312-332-5200
Fax: 312-332-2952
• Arnee J Eisenberg, Partner
• Howard D. Galper, Partner
• Gilbert W. Gordon, Partner
• Spencer J. Marks, Partner
Services:
Civil Litigation, Commercial Litigation, Corporate and Business, Employee Benefits, Employee Relations, Estate Planning, Info Tech Law, Real Estate Law
Description:
NFLPA workers' compensation panel. Handles worker's compensation for the Chicago Bears. Complex Civil Litigation; Medical Malpractice; Class Actions; Professional Athletes' Injury Litigation; Appellate Practice; Sports Law.

MARRONE, ROBINSON, FREDERICK & FOSTER
111 N FIRST STREET
SUITE 300
BURBANK, CA 91502
818-841-1144
Fax: 818-841-0746
info@mrfflaw.net
www.mrfflaw.net
• Phillip R. Marrone, Member
• J. Alan Frederick, Member
• Thomas A. Foster, Attorney
• Gary D. Ellington, Attorney
Services:
All phases of athlete representation including contract negotiation, long-range planning, financial planning, and post-career counseling.
Clients:
Acceptance Risk Managers, Inc., Admiral Insurance Company, Argonaut Insurance Company, City of Burbank, Collier-Keyworth Company, Columbia Pictures Industries, Inc., Columbia Records, Dyna-Span Corporation, Emhart Industries, Inc., Epic Records, Euro Reinsurance Company,

Farmers Insurance Exchange, Fireman's Fund, Fireman's Insurance of Washington, D.C., Fremont Indemnity Company, Guaranty National Companies, Hyster Company, Investor's Insurance Group, L.A. Turf Club Incorporated, Leader Insurance Company, Magna Entertainment Corp., MCA Inc., Maxon Industries, Mustang Claim Service, Inc., NACCO Materials Handling Group, Inc., National Contine

MARSHALL, JR., HARRISON L.
201 N TRYON STREET
C/O SMITH, HELMS, MULLISS & MOORE
CHARLOTTE, NC 28202
704-343-2000
Fax: 704-343-2300
Services:
Represents college athletic departments.

MATHEWSON, ALFRED D.
1117 STANFORD NE
ALBUQUERQUE, NM 87131-0001
505-277-2146
Fax: 505-277-9958
mathewson@law.unm.edu
• Paul Biderman, Director - Institute of Public Law
(505) 277-8789
biderman@unm.edu
• Daniel Ortega, Director, International Law Programs
(505) 277-5723
ortega@law.unm.edu
Description:
Teaches sports law.

MAZZOTTA LAW OFFICES
24 WOODVILLE AVENUE
PITTSBURGH, PA 15220
412-471-0300
Fax: 412-471-3476
dmazzotta@mazzottalaw.com
www.mazzottalaw.com
• Donald S. Mazzotta, Attorney
dmazzotta@mazzottalaw.com
Services:
All phases of athlete representation including contract negotiation, long-range planning, financial planning, post-career counseling and all legal representation.

MCAFEE, ARTHUR
2021 L STREET NW
SUITE 600
WASHINGTON, DC 20036
202-463-2200
800-372-2000
Fax: 202-835-9775
Services:
Staff Counsel with the NFL Players Association.

MCBRIDE, B. GARY
FOUR SEAGATE
SUITE 400
TOLEDO, OH 43604-2622
419-241-2201
Fax: 419-241-8599
• B. Gary McBride, Partner
(419) 252-6231
gmcbride@snlaw.com
• Joel A Levine, Counsel
(419) 252-6274
Services:
Represents college athletic departments.

Special Education Law; School Law; Labor Relations Law.

MCCAREINS, R. MARK
35 W WACKER DRIVE
CHICAGO, IL 60601-9703
312-558-5600
Fax: 312-558-5700
www.winston.com
• R. Mark McCareins, Partner
(312) 558-5902
• Janis N Acosta, Partner
(312) 558-3711
Services:
Litigation, Corporate and Financial, Labor and Employment Relations, Tax, Real Estate, Intellectual Property, Governmental Relations and Regulatory Affairs, Energy, Environmental, Employee Benefits and Executive Compensation, Pro Bono, Health Care, Maritime and Admiralty, Trust and Estates
Clients:
Ameritech Corp., Tropicana Products, Inc., Abbott Laboratories, Monsanto Company, Hallmark Cards, Titan Wheel Co., Spiegel Co., The Marmon Group, Smurfit-Stone Container Co., Windmere Corp., Gannett Co., Hyatt Hotel Corp., Hinckley & Schmitt Co., Keebler Company, Western Union Corp., Luxottica Group (LensCrafters, Inc.), The Interlake Corp., Barr Laboratories, Dell Computer Co., Universal Outdoor, Marsulex Corp., Waste Management Corp., New Archery Products, Summation Legal Technologies, Integrated Machinery Systems, Inc. and Metals Service Center Institute.
Description:
Endorsement exploration, represents sports organizations, tort actions/litigation.
Other Locations;
333 South Grand Avenue, Los Angeles, CA 90071; 200 Park Avenue, New York, NY 10166; 101 California Street, San Francisco, CA 94111; 1400 L Street NW, Washington, DC 20005

MCCARTY & PRY
1655 W MARKET STREET
SUITE 400
AKRON, OH 44313
330-864-6611
Services:
All phases of athlete representation including contract negotiation, long-range planning, financial planning, and post-career counseling.

MCCLOUD, BARBARA
1450 JAYHAWK BOULEVARD
THE UNIVERSITY OF KANSAS
245 STRONG HALL
LAWRENCE, KS 66045-7535
785-864-2700
Fax: 785-864-4617
www.ku.edu
• Bernadette A. Gray-little, University chancellor
(785) 864-3131
chancellor@ku.edu
• Jeffrey Vitter, Executive Vice Chancellor, Provost
((78)) 864-49
jsv@ku.edu
Services:
Represents college athletic departments.

MCCULLOCH, JOSEPH M. JR.
1426 RICHLAND STREET
2ND FLOOR
COLUMBIA, SC 29201
803-779-0005
Fax: 803-779-0666
www.lawyers.com
• Joseph M. McCulloch Jr, Member
Description:
Represents college athletic departments.Criminal Defense; Driving While Intoxicated; Drug Crimes; Civil Litigation; Personal Injury; Wrongful Death.

MCDONALD, FLEMING, MOORHEAD & FERGUSON, GREEN & SMITH
25 W GOVERNMENT STREET
PENSACOLA, FL 32502-5813
850-477-0660
Fax: 850-477-4510
www.pensacolalaw.com
• Bruce A. McDonald, Founding Partner
brucemcdonald@pensacolalaw.com
• Edward P. Fleming, Partner
efleming@pensacolalaw.com
Description:
Develops agreements for sports organizations and individuals.
Services:
Personal Injury and Wrongful Death, Insurance Litigation, Mediation, Business Litigation, Construction Litigation, Real Estate Law, Real Estate Development, Community Association Law, Land Use, Planning and Zoning, Real Estate Closing, Probate, Business Law.

MCDONALD, SNYDER & WILLIAMS P.C.
1004 LIGONIER STREET
LATROBE, PA 15650
724-539-3511
Fax: 724-539-3527
http://mswlaw.lawoffice.com
• Gene E. McDonald, Attorney
(724) 539-3511
mswlaw@adelphia.net
• Donald J. Snyder Jr, Attorney
(724) 539-3511
mswlaw@adelphia.net
• Robert P. Lightcap, Attorney
(724) 539-3511
mswlaw@adelphia.net
• James J. Conte, Attorney
(724) 539-3511
Services:
Banking and Finance Law, Business and Commercial Law, Estate Planning, Family Law, Insurance Law, Municipal Law, Construction Law, Litigation and Appeals, Personal Injury Law, Real Estate Law, Eminent Domain Law and Workers' Compensation Law.
Description:
Endorsement exploration represents sports organizations, tort actions/litigation.

MCGUIREWOODS
101 W MAIN STREET
SUITE 9000
NORFOLK, VA 23510-1655
757-640-3700
Fax: 757-640-3701
www.mcguirewoods.com
• Robert L. Burrus, Jr., Partner/Chairman Emeritus
(804) 775-4306
rburrus@mcguirewoods.com

• William J. Strickland, Managing Partner
(804) 775-4350
wstrickland@mcguirewoods.com
Services:
Commercial Litigation, Complex Products Liability & Mass Tort Litigation, Corporate Services, Financial Services, Health Care & Pharmaceuticals, International Group, Labor & Employment, Real Estate & Environmental, Taxation & Employee Benefits, Technology & Business
Nature of Sports Service:
All phases of athlete representation including contract negotiation, long-range planning, financial planning, and post-career counseling.
Clients Include:
Baltimore Ravens, Virginia Baseball Stadium Authority.
Other Locations:
Washington Square, 1050 Connecticut Avenue NW, STE 1200, Washington, DC 20036; Phone 202-857-1700; 1324 Avenue of the Americas, Seventh Floor, New York, NY 10105; Phone: 212-548-2100; The Proscenium, 1170 Peachtree Street NE, STE 2100 Atlanta, GA 30309; Phone: 404-443-5500

MCINNIS, MALCOLM C.
1720 VOLUNTEER BOULEVARD
262 STOKELY ATHLETICS CENTER
KNOXVILLE, TN 37996-0184
865-974-1000
Fax: 865-974-4811
chancellor@utk.edu
www.utk.edu
• Jimmy G Cheek, Chancellor
(865) 974-3265
chancellor@utk.edu
• Malcolm C. McInnis, Staff
mmcinnis@utk.edu
Services:
Represents college athletic departments.

MCKENNA, LONG & ALDRIDGE, LLP
ONE MARKET PLAZA
SPEAR TOWER, 24TH FLOOR
SAN FRANCISCO, CA 94105
415-267-4000
Fax: 415-267-4198
cvolz@mckennalong.com
• Frank Kendo Berfield, Counsel
(415) 267-4048
fberfield@mckennalong.com
• Christopher Wood, Partner
(415) 267-4140
cwood@mckennalong.com
• S. Da Anderson, Executive Director
danderson@mckennalong.com
• Thomas Wardell, Corporate
(404) 527-4990
twardell@mckennalong.com
• Lynne Blair, Partner
(415) 267-4115
lblair@mckennalong.com
• Michelle Jackson, Partner
(415) 267-4132
mjackson@mckennalong.com
• John Vaughn, Partner
(619) 595-8030
jvaughn@mckennalong.com
• Daniel Hoye, Of Counsel
(415) 267-4055
dhoye@mckennalong.com
• Jennifer Lee, Partner
(415) 267-4126
jlee@mckennalong.com

• Lisa Oberg, Partner
(415) 267-4175
loberg@mckennalong.com
Services:
Offered in three areas: Corporate, Real Estate Finance and Development and Debt Restructuring and Bankruptcy. MLA's traditional Corporate practice ranges from day-to-day counseling to mergers & acquisitions to tax planning. Additionally, assist clients with conducting internal investigations and creating governance and regulatory compliance programs. The Corporate teams focus on helping clients meet their business objectives, while minimizing legal costs and complications.
Clients:
Serve local, regional, national and international clients, Fortune 500 corporations, private corporations, governmental agencies, non-profits, and high net worth individuals including: Affiliated Computer Computer Services, Inc., AFLAC, Inc., Agilent Technologies Inc., AGL Resources Inc., AT&T Corporation, Ball Corporation, Bank of America, NA, The Boeing Company, City of Atlanta, Canadian-American Business Council, Cisco Systems, Inc., Coca-Cola Enterprises Inc., Delta Air Lines, Inc., Dow AgroSciences LLC, Duke Energy Corporation, Eon Labs, Inc., General Motors Corporation, GMAC Commercial Mortgage Corporation, Hewlett-Packard Company
Other Locations:
303 Peachtree Street NE, Suite 5300, Atlanta, GA 30308. 404-527-4000; FAX: 404-527-4198, 1875 Lawrence Street, Suite 200, Denver, CO 80202. 303-634-4000; FAX: 303-634-4400, 444 South Flower Street, 8th Floor, Los Angeles, CA 90071-2901. 213-688-1000; FAX: 213-243-6330, 28 South Waterloo Road, Suite 101, Devon, PA 19333. 610-687-9750; FAX: 610-687-9755, Symphony Towers, 750 B Street, Suite 3300, San Diego, CA 92101-8105. 619-595-5400; FAX: 619-595-5450, 1900 K Street NW, Washington, DC 20006-1108. 202-496-7500; FAX: 202-496-7756

MCKENZIE, W. SHELBY
451 FLORIDA STREET
8TH FLOOR, CHASE TOWER S
BATON ROUGE, LA 70801
225-387-3221
Fax: 225-346-8049
info@taylorporter.com
www.taylorporter.com
• W. Shelby McKenzie, Partner
(225) 381-0243
shelby.mckenzie@taylorporter.com
• W. Arthur Abercrombie, Jr., Jr., Attorney
(225) 381-0259
arthur.abercrombie@taylorporter.com
Description:
Represents college athletic departments.
Clients:
Represent a variety of clients including established public and private companies, banks, insurance companies, governmental agencies, partnerships, individuals, estates, and not-for-profit organizations.

MCLOUGHLIN, STEPHEN J., LAW OFFICE OF
2555 RICHMOND AVENUE
STATEN ISLAND, NY 10314

718-983-1500
• Stephen J. McLoughlin PC, Attorney
Services:
Contract negotiation, post career planning, arbitration hearings, federal/state/international tax filings, provides investment advice.

MCPHERSON & KALMANSOHN
1801 CENTURY PARK E
24TH FLOOR
LOS ANGELES, CA 90067
310-553-8833
Fax: 310-553-9233
• Edwin F. McPherson, Attorney/Partner
emcpherson@m-klaw.com
• Mark E. Kalmansohn
markkal@earthlink.net
• Asha Dhillon
ashadhillon@m-klaw.com
• Anita Stephan
anibed@m-klaw.com
Services:
Represents numerous film, television and stage actors, professional athletes, screenwriters, directors, producers, stunt professionals, stunt Coordinators, authors, recording artists, musicians, songwriters, composers, record producers and engineers, personal managers, talent agents, business managers, attorneys, record companies, independent production companies, and major studios
Clients:
Music (Artists) - Stevie Nicks, The Beach Boys, Dan Fogelberg, Earth, Wind & Fire, Lou Rawls, Natalie Cole, Limp Bizkit, Fred Durst, Linkin Park, Weezer, Mya, Shakira, Jane's Addiction, Perry Farrell, Tool, Backstreet Boys, Porno For Pyros, Blink 182, Poison, Bret Michaels, Great White, Meat Loaf, Dr. Dre, Rage Against The Machine, Smash Mouth, Staind, Rufus, Ricky Martin, Santana, Megadeth, Faith No More, Russ Freeman, Wu Tang Clan, The The, Shai, Jeff Trott, Jonathan Butler, David Roback, Nashville Pussy, Record Labels - Interscope Records, Interscope Music, Death Row Records, Time Warner, Warner Music, Flawless Records, Priority Records
Nature of Sports Service:
All phases of athlete representation including contract negotiation, endorsements, and entertainment crossover.

MEYER, DARRAGH, BUCKLER, BEBENEK & ECK, PLLC
600 GRANT STREET
US STEEL TOWER
SUITE 4850
PITTSBURGH, PA 15219
412-261-6600
Fax: 412-471-2754
info@mdbbe.com
www.mdbbe.com
• Marie M. Jones, Attorney-at-Law
(412) 553-7103
mjones@mdbbe.com
• Eric N. Anderson, Executive Committee Member
(412) 553-7071
eanderson@mdbbe.com
• Daniel C Lawson, Executive Committee Member
(412) 553-7033
dlawson@mdbbe.com

• Dean Passodelis, Executive Committee Member
(412) 553-7145
dpassodelis@mdbbe.com
Nature of Sports Service:
All forms of litigation, including employment matters and contractual issues, with respect to athletes and sports organizations, including the representation of student athletes regarding their right to participate in sports.
Other Locations:
114 South Main Street, Greensburg, PA 15601. 724-836-4840; FAX: 724-836-0532, 120 Lakemont Park Boulevard, Altoona, PA 16602. 814-941-4600; FAX: 814-941-4605
Year Founded:
1913

MEYER, SUOZZI, ENGLISH & KLEIN
1350 BROADWAY
SUITE 501
PO BOX 822
NEW YORK, NY 10018
212-239-4999
800-734-0565
Fax: 212-239-1311
www.msek.com
• Barry J. Peek, Member
(212) 239-4999
bpeek@msek.com
• Linda E. Rodd, Of Counsel
(212) 239-4999
lrodd@msek.com
Description:
Contract negotiation, post career planning, arbitration hearings, provides investment advice, licensing, endorsement exploration, teaches sports law, tort actions/litigation.
Clients:
Allan Schneider Associates, Commerce, America's Most Convenient Bank, Conservation Services Group (CSG)
Year Founded:
1960

MEYER, UNKOVIC & SCOTT, LLP
535 SMITHFIELD STREET
SUITE 1300
HENRY W. OLIVER BUILDING
PITTSBURGH, PA 15222
412-456-2800
800-434-7765
Fax: 412-456-2864
postmaster@muslaw.com
www.muslaw.com
• Debra Z. Anderson, Counsel
(412) 456-2818
dza@muslaw.com
• W. Grant Scott, Partner
(412) 456-2893
wgs@muslaw.com
• Richard G. Kotarba, Partner
(412) 456-2841
rgk@muslaw.com
• Robert Mauro, Managing Partner
(412) 456-2826
rm@muslaw.com
• Joseph E. Bartoszewicz, Attorney
(412) 456-2865
jeb@muslaw.com
• Nicholas J. Bell, Attorney
(412) 456-2524
njb@muslaw.com
• Thomas A. Berret, Attorney
(412) 456-2828
tab@muslaw.com

• Peter J. Borghetti, Attorney
(412) 456-2817
pjb@muslaw.com
• Robert E. Dauer, Jr., Attorney
(412) 456-2835
red@muslaw.com
Description:
Contract negotiation.

MIDDLEBERG RIDDLE GROUP
909 POYDRAS STREET
SUITE 1400
NEW ORLEANS, LA 40112
504-525-7200
Fax: 504-581-5983
AdminNewOrleans@midrid.com
www.midrid.com
• Ira J. Middleburg, Managing Partner
imiddleb@midrid.com
• Dominic J. Gianna, Chair, Litigation Services
dgianna@midrid.com
• Edie Koonce, Administrator
(214) 220-6300
adminneworleans@midrid.com
• Carol Riddle, Administrator - Dallas
admindallas@midrid.com
• Darci Johnson, Director of Human Resources
(214) 220-6300
hrdallas@midrid.com
Services:
Contract negotiation. Environmental and Toxic Tort Law; Insurance Coverage Law; Drug and Medical Device Litigation; Product Liability.
Year Founded:
1980
Other Locations:
717 North Harwood, Suite 2400, Dallas, TX 75201. 214-220-6300, 450 Laurel Street, Suite 1101, Baton Rouge, LA 70809-1101. 225-381-7700

MILLER, KAGAN RODRIGUEZ AND SILVER, P.A.
515 N FLAGLER DRIVE
SUITE 1425
NORTH BRIDGE CENTRE
WEST PALM BEACH, FL 33401
561-833-1860
800-761-6577
Fax: 561-833-8848
www.mkrs.com
• H. George Kagan, Equity Partner
georgek@mkrs.com
• Robert J. Rodriguez, Equity and Managing Partner
• K. Kay Dodd, Attorney

MILLER, PEARSON, GLOE, BURNS, BEATTY & PARRISH, P.L.C.
301 W BROADWAY
PO BOX 28
DECORAH, IA 52101
563-382-4226
Fax: 563-382-3783
www.millerlawdecorah.com
• Marion L Beatty, Lawyer
Services:
Provides legal services; practices in the following areas of law: General Practice, all Courts. Insurance Law, Estate Planning, Personal Injury, Family Law, Taxation and Probate
Clients:
Luther College; Decorah Community School

District; Winneshiek County Memorial Hospital; Community First National State Bank; Viking State Bank; Waukon State Bank; Farmland Insurance Co.; Allied Mutual Insurance Co.; Royal Insurance Co.; Ohio Casualty Insurance Co.; Iowa Farm Mutual Insurance Cos.; Employers Mutual Liability Insurance Co. of Wisconsin; Continental Casualty Co.; Employers Mutual Casualty Co.; Employers Mutuals of Wausau, Wisconsin; Firemans Fund Group; Hawkeye Security Insurance Co.; The Atlantic Co.; Continental Insurance Co.; Iowa Mutual Insurance Co.; Motor Club of America; Auto Owners Insurance Co.; General Casualty; Grinne
Description:
Emphasis on personal injury, insurance law, estate planning, family law, taxation and probate. Represents college athletic departments.
Year Founded:
1940

MILLING BENSON WOODWARD, L.L.P.
909 POYDRAS STREET
SUITE 2300
NEW ORLEANS, LA 70012
504-569-7000
Fax: 504-569-7001
www.millinglaw.com
• Leon J. Bechet, Partner
(504) 549-7146
lbechet@millinglaw.com
• Hilton S. Bell, Managing Partner
(504) 569-7000
hbell@millinglaw.com
• J. Ti Betbeze, Partner
(504) 569-7196
jbetbeze@millinglaw.com
• Richard E. Santora, Partner
rsantora@millinglaw.com
Description:
Entertainment Law, Environmental, Governmental Relations, Health Care, Hospital Law, Intellectual Property, International, Labor, Legislative Practice, Mergers, Acquisitions, Oil and Gas, Professional Liability, Public Utility, Real Estate, Regulatory, Securities, Sports, Taxation, Tax Exempt Organizations, Technology, Telecommunications, Torts, Transportation, Trusts and Estates Law, Utility Law.
Year Founded:
1896
Other Locations:
101 La Rue France, Suite 200, Lafayette, LA. 337-232-3929; FAX: 337-233-4957, 214 Third Street, Suite 2B, Baton Rouge, LA. 225-291-7300; FAX: 225-291-4524

MINGLE, JAMES J.
GARDEN AVENUE
300 CCC BUILDING
ITHACA, NY 14853
607-255-5124
Fax: 607-255-2794
counsel-web@cornell.edu
counsel.cornell.edu
• James J. Mingle, Counsel/Secretary
(607) 255-3903
jjm19@cornell.edu
• David J. D. Skorton, President
Services:
Handles all aspects of the University's legal services including litigation, real property, commercial law, trusts and estates, tax,

employment, legal-policy issues and corporate legal advice to both the University administration and the University Board of Trustees
Description:
Represents college athletic departments.

MIZELL, CATHERINE
719 ANDY HOLT TOWER
1331 CIRCLE PARK
KNOXVILLE, TN 37996-0170
865-974-6538
Fax: 865-974-3074
bot.tennessee.edu
• Catherine Mizell, VP/General Counsel/Secretary
(865) 974-3245
cmizell@tennessee.edu
• Don C. Stansberry, Vice Chair
• Charles C. Anderson, Jr, Finance and Administration Chair
• Joe DiPietro, President
• Spruell Driver, Jr, Academic Affairs and Student Success (Chair)
• D. Crawford Gallimore, Member
• Bill C Haslam, Chair
Services:
Represents college athletic departments.

MONTGOMERY, MCCRACKEN, WALKER & RHODAS, LLP
1105 N MARKET STREET
SUITE 1500
WILMINGTON, DE 19801
302-504-7800
800-572-6697
Fax: 302-504-7820
info@mmwr.com
www.mmwr.com
• James G. McMillan, III, Associate
(302) 504-7879
• Virginia P. Sikes, Partner - PA
(215) 772-7275
vsikes@mmwr.com
• Louis A. Petroni, Partner - NJ
(856) 488-7757
lpetroni@mmwr.com
• Richard M M. Donaldson, Partner - DE
(302) 504-7840
• Sidney S Liebesman, Partner
(215) 772-7279
sliebesman@mmwr.com
• Richard G Placey, Partner
(302) 504-7880
rplacey@mmwr.com
• Natalie D Ramasey, Partner
(215) 772-7354
nramsey@mmwr.com
• Joanne T Semeister, Partner
(215) 772-7747
jsemeister@mmwr.com
• Mark A Fink, Of Counsel
(302) 504-7811
mfink@mmwr.com
• Laurie A Krepto, Associate
(215) 772-7410
lkrepto@mmwr.com
Areas of Specialization:
Litigation, corporate and securities, labor and employment law, tax, trust and estates, and antitrust. Practices in intellectual property, e-commerce and web-based business, computer and information technology, class action defense, toxic, long-term care, and sports law.
Other Locations:
123 South Broad Street, Avenue of the Arts, Philadelphia, PA 19109. 215-772-1500;

FAX: 215-772-7620, Liberty View, 457 Haddonfield Road, Suite 600, Cherry Hill, NJ 08002. 856-488-7700; FAX:856-488-7720, One Westlakes, Suite 200, 1235 Westlakes Drive, Berwyn, PA 19312. 610-889-2210; FAX: 610-889-2220.
Year Founded:
1912

MORRISON & FOERSTER LLP
370 SEVENTEENTH STREET
5200 REPUBLIC PLAZA
DENVER, CO 80202-5638
303-592-1500
Fax: 303-592-1510
info@mofo.com
www.mofo.com
• Randall J. Fons, Partner
(303) 592-2257
rfons@mofo.com
• Eric Elliff, Managing Partner - CO
(303) 592-2240
• A. Ma Olson, Managing Partner - CA
(213) 892-5362
aolson@mofo.com
• Mika L. Mayer, Partner
(650) 813-4298
mmayer@mofo.com
• Randall J. Fons, Managing Partner
(303) 592-2257
rfons@mofo.com
• Jordan Eth, Partner
(415) 268-7126
jeth@mofo.com
• Mark C. Zebrowski, Partner
(858) 720-5162
mzebrowski@mofo.com
• Craig D. Martin, Managing Partner
(415) 268-7681
cmartin@mofo.com
• Daniel R. Kahan, Associate
(703) 760-7306
dkahan@mofo.com
• Sherman W. Kahn, Of Counsel
(212) 468-8023
skahn@mofo.com
Description:
Corporate finance, project finance, institutional lending, financial services, real estate. Entertainment and Sports Law.
Clients:
Charles Schwab Corporation, Chiron Corporation, The Clorox Company, Converge Medical, Inc. , Digirad Corporation, Dynavax Technologies Corporation, EchoStar Communications Corporation, El Paso Corporation, Forward Ventures, Fujitsu Limited, GE Consumer Finance, The Hartford Financial Services Group, Inc., Hershey Foods Corporation, Hitachi, Ltd., JPMorgan Chase & Co., Kaiser Foundation Health Plan, Inc./Kaiser Foundation Hospitals, Kerr-McGee Corporation, Korn/Ferry International , LNR Property Corporation, Lucasfilm Ltd. , Medtronic, Inc., New York University, Nextel Communications, Inc., Nikon Corporation, Novell, Inc. , Oracle Corporation
Other Locations:
5200 Republic Plaza, 370 Seventeeth Street, Denver, Colorado 80202-5638. 309-592-1500; FAX: 303-592-1510, 555 West Fifth Street, Suite 3500, Los Angeles, California 90013-1024. 213-892-5200; FAX: 213-892-5454, 1290 Avenue of the Americas, New York, New York 10104-0050. 212-468-8000; FAX: 212-468-7900, 1650 Tysons Boulevard,

Suite 300, McLean, Virginia 22102. 703-760-7700; FAX: 703-760-777, 2000 Pennsylvania Avenue NW, Suite 5500, Washington, DC 20006-1888. 202-887-1500; FAX: 202-887-0763

MORTON & MCGOLDRICK, P.S.
820 A STREET
SUITE 600, PO BOX 1533
TACOMA, WA 98402
253-627-8131
Fax: 253-272-4338
bvmm@bvmm.com
www.bvmm.com
• Marc H. Cochran, Attorney
mhcochran@bvmm.com
• James H. Morton, Member
jhmorton@bvmm.com
• DAVID McGOLDRICK, Member
dmcgoldrick@bvmm.com
Services:
Contract negotiation, investment contract negotiation, arbitration hearings, federal/state/international tax filings. Tax Law; Estate Planning Law; Pension and Profit Sharing Law; Corporations Law; Securities Law.
Clients:
Apple, Bank of America Corporation, Beckman Coulter, Inc., Beijing Organizing Committee for the Games of the XXIX Olympiad, Calpine Corporation, Capital One Financial Corporation, The Columbia State Bank, Kemper Insurance Group, Chubb Group of Insurance Companies, Transport Insurance Company, Anglo American Insurance Co., McDonald's Corp., The Southland Corp., CRST Trucking Company, Markel Insurance Company, Cole & Weber (advertising agency), Edge Learning Institute, Inc., Cablecraft, Inc., Western Surety Co., Tacoma Telco Credit Union, Swanson-McGoldrick, Inc. (Realtor), Brandrud Manufacturing Company, Inc., Tacoma Cemeteries

---

MUNGO AND ASSOCIATES, P.C.
155 W CONGRESS
SUITE 404
DETROIT, MI 48226
313-963-0407
Fax: 313-963-0200
• Leonard Mungo, Regional Field Director
(313) 963-0407

MURPHY & DESMOND, S.C.
33 E MAIN STREET
SUITE 500
PO BOX 2038
MADISON, WI 53703
608-257-7181
877-619-5742
Fax: 608-257-2508
email@murphydesmond.com
www.murphydesmond.com
• Tim R. Valentyn, President/Managing Shareholder
(608) 268-5599
tvalentyn@murphydesmond.com
• Harvey L. Wendel, Member
(608) 268-5578
hwendel@murphydesmond.com
Services:
All phases of athlete representation including contract negotiation, endorsement exploration, long-range planning, financial planning, and post-career counseling.

Business Law; Real Estate; Sports Law; Entertainment Law.

MURRAY & MURRAY
2 CENTER PLAZA
SUITE 620
BOSTON, MA 02108
617-720-4411
Fax: 617-723-5370
• Vincent A. Murray Jr, Founding Member
vmurray@murraylawoffice.com
• Dino R. Santangelo, Associate
• Vincent A. H. Murray, Attorney
Services:
Contract negotiation.
Year Founded:
1975

NEW YORK YANKEES/BUSINESS OFFICE
E 161ST STREET
BRONX, NY 10451
718-293-4300
Fax: 718-681-1051
newyork.yankees.mlb.com
• Lonn A. Trost, COO
• Harold Z. Steinbrenner, Managing General Partner/Co-Chair
Services:
Represents sports organizations, arbitration hearings, represents professional sports teams, licensing, tort actions/litigation.

NIXON, PEABODY
437 MADISON AVENUE
NEW YORK, NY 10022-7039
212-940-3000
Fax: 212-940-3111
• Arthur Rosner, Office Managing Partner
(212) 940-3023
arosner@nixonpeabody.com
• Elizabeth Kennedy, Office Administrator
(518) 427-2657
ekennedy@nixonpeabody.com
• Andrew Glincher, Office Managing Partner
(617) 345-1222
• Susan Roney, Office Managing Partner
(716) 853-8101
sroney@nixonpeabody.com
• Lorraine McDonough, Office Adminstrator
(716) 853-8106
lmcdonough@nixonpeabody.com
• Mark Shea, Marketing Contact
(585) 263-1141
mshea@nixonpeabody.com
Services:
Include emerging and middle-market businesses, national and multinational corporations, financial institutions, public entities, educational and not-for-profit institutions, and individuals.
Other Locations:
100 Summer Street, Boston, MA 02110; Phone: 617-345-1000; one Embarcadero Center, San Francisco, CA 94111; Phone: 415-984-8200; 401 9th Street, NW, STE 900, Washington, DC 20004; Phone: 202-585-8000; two penn center 1500 jfk blvd ste 200 philadelphia, pa 19102 phone: 215-854-4096; one citizens plaza providence, ri 02903; phone: 401-454-1000.

NORONHA-ADVOGADOS CONSULTING
AV. ANTONIO AUGUSTO AGUIAR
LISBOA, PORTUGAL 1050-021
21-389-4178
Fax: 21-389-4179

noadlis@noronhaadvogados.com.br
www.noronhaadvogados.com.br
• Alexandre Laender Delgando, Director Stock Market/Insurance
• Durval De. Goyos, Senior partner, Partner and President
dng@noronhaadvogados.com.br
• Robert E. Williams, Partner-International Tax Dept
rew@noronhaadvogados.com.br
• Jun Zhang, Director
• Sherry Liu, Partner
shl@noronhaadvogados.com.br
• Stephen Logan, Partner
• Ramma Luthra, Partner
rtl@noronhaadvogados.com.br
• Joao Campos, Partner
Description:
Mergers and Acquisitions, Contracts, Corporations, Competition, Antitrust Law, Sports and Entertainment Law and Internet Law.
Services:
Offers a broad variety of legal services to clients with activities in the industrial, financial, commercial and service areas. It is capable and equipped to adequately assist the clients in the many different aspects of business law, particularly in the areas of aviation; banking, finance and insurance; corporate; contracts; environmental; international business transactions; labor; civil and tax litigation; maritime; mergers and acquisitions; mining, energy and oil; public administration; intelectual property; real estate; securities; taxation; trade; international tax planning; anti-trust; entertainment, internet and electronic commerce.

NORTH, PURSELL, RAMOS & JAMESON, PLC
414 UNION STREET
SUITE 1850
BANK OF AMERICA PLAZA
NASHVILLE, TN 37219
615-255-2555
Fax: 615-255-0032
• Michael F. Jameson, Lawyer
(615) 255-2555
mjameson@nprjlaw.com
• Edward A Hadley, Lawyer
(615) 255-2555
ehadley@nprjlaw.com
• Michael F. Jameson, Lawyer
(615) 255-2555
mjameson@nprjlaw.com
• Phillip North, Lawyer
(615) 255-2555
pnorth@nprjlaw.com
• Ronald H. Pursell, Lawyer
(615) 255-2555
rpursell@nprjlaw.com
• Ramos A. Gregory, Lawyer
(615) 255-2555
aramos@nprjlaw.com
• Lauren J. Smith, Lawyer
(615) 255-2555
lsmith@nprjlaw.com
• Renee L. Stewart, Lawyer
(615) 255-2555
rstewart@nprjlaw.com
Description:
NFLPA. Handles workers' compensation for the Tennessee Titans.
Services:
Areas of practice include, but are not limited to, civil trial practice, labor law, medical

malpractice defense, commercial litigation, sports law, products liability, taxation, real estate, and general business and corporate law.
Clients:
Current clients includes (listed alphabetically): Auto Owners' Insurance Company; Castle Recording Studio, Inc.; Castle Publishing, Inc.; National Football League Players' Association; Professional Hockey Players' Association; State Volunteer Mutual Insurance Company; Tennessee Urgent Care Associates; Tepro, Inc.; and The Yasuda Fire & Marine Insurance Company of America.

OBERMAYER, REBMANN, MAXWELL & HIPPEL, LLP
200 LOCUST STREET
SUITE 400
HARRISBURG, PA 17101-1508
717-234-9730
Fax: 717-234-9734
ark.clouser@obermayer.com
www.obermayer.com
• Louis B. Kupperman, Partner
(215) 665-3146
louis.kupperman@obermayer.com
• Martin Weinberg, Partner and Chairman
(215) 665-3196
martin.weinberg@obermayer.com
• Walter W Cohen, Attorney
(717) 234-9730
walter.cohen@obermayer.com
• Robart C Jubelirer, Attorney
(814) 942-3333
robert.jubelirer@obermayer.com
• Kevin J Kehner, Attorney
(717) 234-9730
kevin.kehner@obermayer.com
• Jay Evans, Attorney
(412) 288-2473
jay.evans@obermayer.com
• Bruce C Fox, Attorney
(412) 566-1500
bruce.fox@obermayer.com
• Beth Kirkpatrick, Attorney
(412) 288-2474
beth.kirkpatrick@obermayer.com
Description:
Certified contract advisor with the National Football League Players Association. Represents professional athletes in contract negotiations with professional sports teams. Also handles Major League Baseball Players.
Services:
Offers particular depth in the following practice areas: health, energy and utility, environmental, municipal finance, technology, employment, business and litigation, including criminal defense.
Year Founded:
1904
Other Locations:
One Penn Center, 19th Floor, 1617 John F Kennedy Boulevard, Philadephia, Pennsylvania 19103-1895. 215-665-3000; FAX: 215-665-3165, One Mellon Center, 500 Grant Street, Suite 5240, Pittsburg, Pennsylvania 15219-2502. 412-566-1500; FAX: 412-566-1508, 20 Brace Road, Suite 300, Cherry Hill, New Jersey 08034-2634. 856-795-3300; FAX: 856-795-8843, 1170 E Landis Avenue, Suite B, Vineland, New Jersey 08360-4230. 856-696-4600; FAX: 856-696-0501, 3 Mill Road, Suite 306A,

Wilmington, Delaware 19806.
302-655-9094; FAX: 302-658-8051

OCTAGON ATHLETE REPRESENTATION (ATTORNEYS)
7950 JONES BRANCH DRIVE
SUITE 700N
MCLEAN, VA 22107
703-905-3300
Fax: 703-905-4495
www.octagon.com
• Rick Dudley, President/Chief Executive Officer
• Phil de Picciotto, President, Athletes & Personalities
Services:
Helps clients reach their customers by leveraging relevant sports and entertainment content based on the company's proven expertise in: 1) Engagement marketing: consulting, events, promotions, public relations and property representation; 2) Athletes & personalities: management and procurement; 3) Television: rights, production, sales, distribution; and new media strategies, and; 4) Music and entertainment: management and production.
Description:
Endorsement exploration.

ORLANDO & ASSOCIATES
ONE WESTERN AVENUE
GLOUCESTER, MA 01930
978-283-8100
800-696-7111
Fax: 978-283-8507
firm@orlandoassociates.com
www.orlandoassociates.com
• Joseph M. Orlando, Lawyer
(978) 283-8100
jmorlando@orlandoassociates.com
• Joseph Orlando, Attorney
Services:
Specializes in personal injury litigation, with an emphasis on maritime personal injury law, but also including wrongful death and land-based personal injury tort law.

ORRICK, HERRINGTON & SUTCLIFFE LLP
777 S FIGUEROA STREET
SUITE 3200
LOS ANGELES, CA 90017-5855
213-629-2020
Fax: 213-612-2499
www.orrick.com
• Ralph H Baxter, Jr., Partner
(415) 773-5650
ralphbaxter@orrick.com
• J. Pe Coll Jr, Partner
(212) 506-3790
pcoll@orrick.com
• Karen G Johnson-McKewan, Partner
(415) 773-5917
kjohnson-mckewan@orrick.com
• Felicia B Graham, Partner
(202) 339-8486
fgraham@orrick.com
Description:
Maintains a substantial legal practice in the area of public finance for 100 years. Recognized as one of the nations leading counsel, acts as underwriters counsel, issuer counsel, swap/derivative counsel, and lender counsel in connection with the issuance of tax-exempt bonds. Maintains an active practice in advising public power entities, investor owned utilities and independent power producers on matters related to energy re-regulation.
Other Locations:
Orrick Building, 405 Howard Street, San Francisco, CA 94105; Phone: 415-773-5700; Fax: 415-773-5759; Washington Harbour, 3050 K Street NW, Washington, DC 20007; Phone: 202-339-8400; Fax: 202-339-8500; 666 Fifth Avenue, New York 10103; Phone: 212-506-5000; Fax: 212-506-5151; 400 Capital Mall, STE 3000, Sacramento, CA 95814; Phone: 916-447-9200

OSBORN MALEDON, P.A.
2929 N CENTRAL AVENUE
THE PHOENIX PLAZA, TWENTY-FIRST FLOOR
PHOENIX, AZ 85012-2793
602-640-9000
Fax: 602-640-9050
webmaster@omlaw.com
www.omlaw.com
• William J. Maledon, Lawyer
(602) 640-9331
wmaledon@omlaw.com
• Lynne C. Adams, Attorney
(602) 640-9348
ladams@omlaw.com
• Yaser Ali, Attorney
(602) 640-9349
• Jonathan F. Ariano, Attorney
(602) 640-9311
jariano@omlaw.com
• Ronda Beckerleg Thraen, Attorney
(602) 640-9303
• Maureen Beyers, Attorney
(602) 640-9305
mbeyers@omlaw.com
• John L. Blanchard, Attorney
(602) 640-9304
jblanchard@omlaw.com
• Timothy A. Nelson, Attorney
(602) 640-9388
nelson@omlaw.com
Description:
Intellectual Property; Mergers, Acquisitions and Divestitures; Probate; Products Liability; Professional Liability; Real Estate; Regulatory Law; Securities; Sports Law; Technology Business Startups; Technology Licensing; Technology and Science; Technology Transfers; Trusts and Estates.
Services:
Provides litigation, business and general counsel solutions for clients in the Southwest and nationwide.

PACKMAN, NEUWAHL & ROSENBERG
1500 SAN REMO AVENUE
SUITE 125
CORAL GABLES, FL 33146
305-665-3311
Fax: 305-665-1244
info@pnrlaw.com
www.pnrlaw.com
• Malcolm H. Neuwahl, Shareholder/Attorney
(305) 665-3311
mhn@pnrlaw.com
• Michael Rosenberg, Partner/Associate
(305) 665-3311
info@pnrlaw.com
Services:
Services provided: Estate Planning; General Taxation; International Taxation; Real Estate, Transactional and Commercial Practice; Immigration; Technology and Personal Service; Education.
Nature of Sports Service:
All phases of athlete representation including contract negotiation, long-range planning, financial planning, and post-career counseling.

PATTON BOGGS
2550 M STREET, NW
WASHINGTON, DC 20037
202-457-6000
Fax: 202-457-6315
www.pattonboggs.com
• Thomas Hale Boggs, Jr., Chairman/Partner
(202) 457-6040
• Edward J Newberry, Partner
(202) 457-5285
enewberry@pattonboggs.com
• Mary Be Bosco, Partner
(202) 457-6420
• Thomas S Hale Boggs , Jr., Chairman
(202) 457-6310
• Donald V. Moorehead, Vice Chairman
• Edward J. Newberry, Managing Partner
Services:
Administrative and Regulatory, Antitrust, Appropriations, Bankruptcy and Restructuring, Business, Corporate Finance, Defense and National Security, Employment Law, Energy, Environmental, Health and Safety, Estate Planning and Wealth Preservation, Federal Marketing, Firm Overview, Food and Drus, Government Contracts, Health Cate, Housing, Immigration, Intellectual Property, International Trade and Transactions, Litigation and Dispute Resolution, Mergers and Acquisitions, Middle East Practice, Municipal Representation, Native American Affairs, Political Law, Postal Regulation, Public Policy and Lobbying, Real Estate, Securities, Tax, Telecommun
Description:
Legislative, political and legal representation of private and public entities interested in the development or redevelopment of sports stadiums and arenas, including the public and/or private financing of stadiums, lease negotiations and drafting, economic generators, subcontracting with disadvantaged business entities, and state, local and federal tax issues.
Year Founded:
1962
Other Locations:
701 West 5th Avenue, STE 700, Anchorage, AK 99501; Phone: 907-263-6300; 2001 Ross Avenue, STE 3000, Dallas, TX 75201; Phone: 214-758-1500; 1660 Lincoln Street, STE 1900, Denver, CO 80264; Phone: 303-830-1776; Phone303-830-1776; 8484 Westpark Drive 9th Floor, McLean, VA 22102; Phone: 703-744-8000

PELLETTIERI RABSTEIN AND ALTMAN
100 NASSAU PARK BOULEVARD
SUITE 111
PRINCETON, NJ 8540
609-520-0900
800-432-5297
Fax: 609-452-8796
pra@pralaw.com
www.pralaw.com

- Tom Smith, Attorney
- Gary E. Adams, Lawyer
- Stephanie Testa, Marketing Coordinator
(609) 520-0900
- Gray E. Adams, Attorney
Services:
Specializes in Personal Injury & Accident; Medical Malpractice & Negligence; Workers Compensation & Disability; Class Action and Mass Tort; Divorce Litigation; Child Custody; Wills and Estate Planning; Tax Litigation; Elder Law; Real Estate; Criminal Law; Business Litigation; Contract Disputes; Shareholder & Partnership Disputes; Insurance Claims, Business Torts; Business Formation & Planning; Commerial Real Estate Litigation; Land Use; Labor & Employment.
Clients Include:
NCAA Div 1 Conference, The Northeast Conference, Metro Atlantic Athletic Conference, Atlantic 10 Conference, West Coast Conference and Patriot League, National Association of Sports Officials, Little League Baseball.
Year Founded:
1929

PERKINS COIE LAW FIRM
1201 THIRD AVENUE
SUITE 4900
SEATTLE, WA 98101-3099
206-359-8000
Fax: 206-359-9000
www.perkinscoie.com
- Nancy Williams, Managing Partner
NWilliams@perkinscoie.com
- Shylah R. Alfonso, Partner
(206) 359-3980
SAlfonso@perkinscoie.com
- Dannon Allbee, Associate
(206) 359-3496
- Anastasia K. Anderson, Associate
(206) 359-6760
- Stephen E. Arnett, Partner
(206) 359-6351
SArnett@perkinscoie.com
Services:
Provides national and international legal counsel and representation to leading aerospace, high-technology, manufacturing, natural resource, transportation and industrial companies as well as financial institutions. Also offers clients business-oriented advice in every major area of commercial and regulatory law, litigation, estate planning and trust services.

PHILLIPS & AKERS PC
3200 SW FREEWAY
SUITE 3200
HOUSTON, TX 77027
713-552-9595
Fax: 713-552-0231
contact@phillipsakers.com
www.phillipsakers.com
- Brock C. Akers, Shareholder
(713) 877-2555
Brock.Akers@phillipsakers.com
- Michael Phillips, Shareholder
(713) 552-9595
- Joe M. Allen, Associate
Services:
Practice areas include General Liability; Retailer Liability; Premises Liability and Security Cases; Healthcare Liability Defense; Non-Subscribers' Actions; Products Liability; Truck Litigation;

Insurance Litigation; Appellate; Labor and Employment; Commercial Litigation; Environmental Litigation; Consumer Litigation; and Oil Field/Construction/Industrial.
Description:
Contract negotiation, post career planning, investment contract negotiation, arbitration hearings, provides investment advice, endorsement exploration, tort actions/litigation.
Year Founded:
July 4, 1982

PIASECKI, MARK J.
511 S ST JOSEPH STREET
SOUTH BEND, IN 46601
574-233-7052
Fax: 574-233-7052
- Marl J. Piasecki, Lawyer
Description:
Contract negotiation, post career planning, federal/state/international tax filings, tort actions/litigation.
Services:
Areas of practice include Civil Litigation, Wills and Estates, and Business

PIERCE & HUGHES P.C.
17 VETERANS SQUARE
PO BOX 604
MEDIA, PA 19063-3217
610-566-9111
Fax: 610-566-0191
info@piercehughes.com
www.pierceandhughes.com
- Michael P. Pierce, Attorney
mppierce@piercehughes.com
- Paul Gordon Hughes, Attorney
pghughes@piercehughes.com
Services:
Handles legal matters in the following practice areas: Family Law, Divorce, Child Custody, Child Support, Domestic Violence, Visitation Rights, Personal Injury, Automobile Accidents, Slip and Fall, Wrongful Death, Medical Malpractice, Municipal Law, Workers Compensation, Social Security Disability, Unsafe Products, Consumer Law, Consumer Fraud, Civil Practice, Negligence, Criminal Law, Driving While Intoxicated, Drug Crimes, Juvenile Crimes, Parole and Probation, Traffic Violations, White Collar Crime, Trusts and Estates, Wills and Probate, Employment Law.
Description:
Pierce & Hughes is a boutique law firm with a focus on the sports world and a passion for serving those who excel in it.

PIPER MARBURY RUDNICK & WOLFE
203 N LASALLE STREET
SUITE 1900
CHICAGO, IL 60601-1293
312-368-4000
Fax: 312-236-7516
info@dlapiper.com
- Louis S Cohen, Partner
(312) 368-2171
- Deborah E Jennings, Partner/Chairman, Environmental Practice
(202) 861-3842
deborah.jennings@dlapiper.com
- Paul A Tiburzi, Managing Partner
(410) 580-4273
paul.tiburzi@dlapiper.com

- John G McJunkin, Managing Partner
(703) 773-4154
Services:
Provides an extensive range of legal services through seven global practice groups as follows: Commercial, Corporate and Finance, Human Resources, Legislative and Regulatory, Litigation, Real Estate, Technology, Media and Communications.
Description:
Full service national law firm. Sports facilities development proactive group has extensive experience representing and advising municipalities, counties, states and other political entities, professional sports teams, underwriters and financial consultants in connection with stadium and arena development, financing, construction, use and operation.
Other Locations:
One International Place, 21st Floor, Boston, MA 02110; Phone: 617-406-6000; 400 Capital Mall, STE 2400, Sacramento, CA 95814; Phone: 916-930-3200; 1221 South MoPac Expressway, STE 400, Austin, TX 78746; Phone: 512-457-7000; 1251 Avenue of the Americas, New York, NY 10020; Phone: 212-835-6000; One Liberty Place, l650 Market Street, STE 4900, Philadelphia, PA 19103; Phone: 215-656-3300; 117 Bay Street, Easton, MD 21601; Phone: 410-820-4460

POLSINELLI, SHALTON, FLANIGAN, SUELTHAUS PC
900 W. 48TH PLACE
SUITE 900
KANSAS CITY, MO 64112
816-753-1000
Fax: 816-753-1536
info@polsinelli.com
www.polsinelli.com/
- W. Russell Welsh, Chairman/Chief Executive Officer
(816) 360-4342
wrwelsh@polsinelli.com
- Jack M Epps, Partner
(913) 234-7455
jeppes@polsinelli.com
- Ron Patterson, Chief Operating Officer
rpatterson@polsinelli.com
- Julian Arredondo, Chief Financial Officer
jarrrendo@polsinelli.com
Nature of Sports Service:
All phases of athlete representation including contract negotiation, long-range planning, financial planning, and post-career counseling.
Other Locations:
100 South Fourth Street, STE 1100, St Louis, MO 63102; Phone: 314-889-8000; 400 Madison Avenue Suite 16C, New York NY 10017; Phone: 212-684-0199; 555 12th Street NW, STE 710, Washington, DC 20004; Phone: 202-783-3300.
Year Founded:
1972

POTTORFF, JAMES P. JR.
1450 JAYHAWK BLVD
LAWRENCE, KS 66045
785-864-2700
Fax: 785-864-4120
question@ku.edu
www.ku.edu
- James P. Pottorff, University General Counsel
(785) 864-3276

jpottorff@ku.edu
• Bernadette Gray E. Little, University
Chancellor
rhemenway@ku.edu
• Jeffery Vitter, Executive Vice Chancellor
and Provost
• Doug Girod, Executive Vice Chancellor
• Timothy Caboni, Vice Chancellor forPublic
Affairs
Description:
Represents college athletic departments.
Services:
A major public research and teaching
institution that operates through a diverse,
multicampus system.

PRESTON, GATES & ELLIS
925 FOURTH AVENUE
SUITE 2900
SEATTLE, WA 98104-1158
206-623-7580
Fax: 206-623-7022
kim.church@klgates.com
www.klgates.com
• Cabrelle M. Abel, Associate, Seattle
(206) 370-7812
• Ramona M. Emerson, Managing Partner,
Seattle
(206) 370-6748
• Jennifer S. Addis, Associate
(206) 370-8068
• Heidi Eckel Alessi, Partner
(206) 370-7983
• Carley Daye Andrews, Partner
(206) 370-7661
• James A. Andrus, Partner
(206) 370-8329
• Theodore J. Angelis, Partner
(206) 370-8101
• David A. Bateman, Partner
(206) 370-6682
Services:
Practice Areas: 1) Advocacy and Disputes:
Appellate, Constitutional and Governmental
Litigation; Commercial Litigation;
Competition Law and Economic Regulation;
Document Analysis Technology Group;
Government Contracts, Construction and
Procurement Policy; Intellectual Property
Litigation; Labor, Employment and Benefits.
2) Policy and Infrastructure: Energy and
Utilities; Environmental, Land Use and
Natural Resources; Global Telecom and
Media; Maritime; Policy and Public Law;
Public Finance; School Districts. 3)
Transactions: Alternative Investment
Management; Asia; Business Law;
Corporate Securities/Mergers and
Acquisitions
Description:
Contract negotiation, represents
professional sports teams, endorsement
exploration, tort actions/litigation.
Other Locations:
601 West Riverside Avenue, STE 1400,
Spokane, WA 99201; Phone: 509-624-2100;
55 Second Street, STE 1700, San
Francisco, CA 94105; Phone:
415-882-8200; 420 L Street, STE 400,
Anchorage, AK 99501; Phone:
907-276-1969; 222 SW Columbia Street,
STE 1400, Portland, OR 97201; Phone :
503-228-3200

PRINCE YEATES
15 WEST SOUTH TEMPLE
SUITE 1700
SALT LAKE CITY, UT 84101

801-524-1000
Fax: 801-524-1098
ronm@pyglaw.com
www.princeyeates.com
• Adam S. Affleck, Lawyer
asa@princeyeates.com
• Wilford A. Beesley III, Lawyer
wab@princeyeates.com
• Wilford A. Beesley, Lawyer
wab@princeyeates.com
• Richard L. Blanck, Lawyer
rlb@princeyeates.com
Services:
The firm provides a full range of services
with a particular focus on the practice of
business, litigation, real estate, bankruptcy
and employment law.

QUINN, JAMES W.
767 FIFTH AVENUE
ROOM 3501
NEW YORK, NY 10153
212-310-8000
Fax: 212-310-8007
www.weil.com
• James W. Quinn, Senior Partner
(212) 310-8385
james.quinn@weil.com
• Brad D. Scott, Executive Director
(212) 310-8271
• Scott Green, Chief Administrative Officer
(212) 310-6883
• Norman LaCroix, Chief Financial Officer
(212) 310-8359
Nature of Sports Service:
Arbitration hearings, represents professional
sports players associations, licensing,
represents other sports related
organizations, teaches sports law, tort
actions/litigation, anti-trust, and collective
bargaining.
Services:
Areas of practice include Business Finance
& Restructuring, Banking & Finance, Capital
Markets, Corporate Governance, Mergers &
Acquisitions, Private Equity, Real Estate
Transactions & Finance, Structured
Finance/Derivatives, Tax, Trusts & Estates,
Litigation/Regulatory, Antitrust/Competition,
Appellate, Bankruptcy Litigation, Complex
Commercial Litigation, Employment,
Financial Services, Global Dispute
Resolution, Intellectual Property & Media,
International Trade, Patent Litigation,
Product Liability/Mass Tort/Environmental,
and Securities/Corporate Governance

RAGSDALE, RICHARD A.
619 RIVER DRIVE
SUITE 200
ELMWOOD, NJ 7407
201-791-7797
Fax: 609-683-9501
www.nj-lawyer.com
• Richard A. Ragsdale, Managing Member
(609) 924-7179
richard.ragsdale@verizon.net
• Robert A. Sochor, Partner
(201) 791-7797
• Leonard E. Schwartz, Partner
(973) 301-1900
• Kenneth R. Cohen, Partner
(973) 301-1900
Services:
Provides expertise in the following areas:
Negotiating and closing a complete range of
commercial transactions, including business
acquisitions and sales, commercial real

estate leases and sales, and sophisticated
lending arrangements; Taxation: federal,
state, individual and corporate; Estate
planning and taxation, estate administration,
probate litigation and elder law; Asset
Protection. Using limited liability companies,
asset protection trusts and other creative
planning techniques to preserve assets from
the potential claims of creditors, State and
Federal taxing authorities, and other
governmental authorities.
Description:
Investment contract negotiation, represents
sports organizations, provides investment
advice, licensing, endorsement exploration,
represents college athletic departments,
sports complex.

RAUCH, JR., MARTIN W.
8742 MISTY CREEK DRIVE
SARASOTA, FL 34241
941-927-2722
Fax: 941-371-8388
martyrauch@aol.com
Services:
Provides services in contract negotiation,
arbitration hearings, endorsement
exploration, tort actions/litigation, and sports
management

RAWLE LAW OFFICES
1339 CHESTNUT STREET ONE S PENN
SQUARE
THE WIDENER BUILDING, 16TH FLOOR
PHILADELPHIA, PA 19107
215-575-4200
Fax: 215-563-2583
info@rawle.com
www.rawle.com
• John T. Donovan, Partner
(215) 575-4254
jdonovan@rawle.com
• Timothy J. Abeel, Partner
(215) 575-4280
tabeel@rawle.com
• Joshua Bachrach, Partner
(215) 575-4261
• Timothy J. S. Abeel, Partner
(215) 575-4280
tabeel@rawle.com
• Thomas A. Kuzmick, Partner
(215) 575-4262
tkuzmick@rawle.com
• John H. McCarthy, Partner
(215) 575-4359
jmccarthy@rawle.com
• Fred B. Buck, Partner
(215) 575-4317
fbuck@rawle.com
• William J. Carr, Partner
(215) 575-4221
wcarr@rawle.com
• Cynthia M. Certo, Partner
(215) 575-4284
• Maureen E. Daley, Partner
(215) 575-4293
mdaley@rawle.com
Services:
Represents manufacturers of industrial,
commercial and consumer products; drug,
pharmaceutical and chemical
manufacturers; life, health and disability
insurers and ERISA plans; owners and
architects, prime contractors, general
contractors, sub-contractors and
construction managers; nationally known
retail chains; and bus and trucking
companies. Defends insurers in coverage

actions and prosecute declaratory judgment actions on their behalf; municipalities, hospitals and public authorities; attorneys, accountants, architects and other professionals; shipowners here and abroad; nearly every industry, service and profession.

RAWLINGS, WILLIAM R.
11576 S STATE STREET
BUILDING 401
DRAPER, UT 84020-7122
801-553-0505
877-456-0505
Fax: 801-495-2122
www.brawlingslaw.com
• William R. Rawlings, Lawyer
(866) 329-0208
• Kenneth L. Christensen, Lawyer
(801) 553-0505
Services:
Areas of practice include business and commercial law, criminal defense, probate and estate administration, and a broad range of other legal matters.
Nature of Sports Service:
All phases of athlete representation including contract negotiation, long-range planning, financial planning, and post-career counseling.

REDWINE, THOMAS R.
116 S CROCKETT
SHERMAN, TX 75090
903-893-2133
Fax: 903-893-7889
• Thomas R. Redwine, Lawyer
(903) 893-2133
• John R. Mabary, Lawyer
(903) 893-2133
• Victoria E. Ingham, Partner
(903) 893-2133
• Bob Fleming, Lawyer
(903) 893-2133
Services:
Area of practice include contract negotiation, post career planning, investment contract negotiation, provides securities advice, provides investment advice, and endorsement exploration.

REED SMITH
225 FIFTH AVENUE
PITTSBURGH, PA 15222
412-288-3131
Fax: 412-288-3063
www.reedsmith.com
• Gregory B. Jordan, Global Managing Partner
(412) 288-4124
gjordan@reedsmith.com
• Gary A. Sokulski, Chief Operating Officer
(412) 288-4232
gsokulski@reedsmith.com
• David S. Egan, Chief Marketing Officer
(412) 288-4276
degan@reedsmith.com
• Kevin C. Abbott, Partner
(412) 288-3804
kabbott@reedsmith.com
• Gregory B. Jordan, Global Managing Partner
• Colleen T. Davies, Global Head of Legal Personnel
• Michael B Pollack, Global Head of Strategy
• Roger J. Parker, Europe, Middle East &

AsiaManaging Partner
• David J. Boutcher, Chair of Business & Finance Department
• Alexander Y. Thomas, Chair of Litigation Department
Services:
Areas of practice include Advertising & Marketing, Advocacy, Antitrust, Competition & Regulatory Litigation, Appellate, Arbitration, Associations, Aviation Litigation, Banking, Bankruptcy and Commercial Restructuring, Benefits, Class Action Defense, Communications, Construction, Corporate Services (U.K.), E-commerce, Employment, Energy & Natural Resources, Environmental Law, Executive Compensation, Export, Customs & Trade, Financial Services, Financial Services Litigation, Financial Services Regulatory, Fraud, French Group, German Group, Government Contracts, Government Relations, Health Care, Higher Education, Homeland Security, Immigration
Description:
Represents college athletic departments.
Other Locations:
599 Lexington Avenue, 29th Floor, New York, NY 10022; Phone: 212-521-5400; 1301 K Street NW, STE 1100, East Tower, Washington DC 20005; Phone: 202-414-9200; 355 South Grand Avenue, STE 2900, Los Angeles, CA 90071; Phone: 213-457-8000

REED SMITH LLP
599 LEXINGTON AVENUE
22ND FLOOR
NEW YORK, NY 10022
212-521-5400
Fax: 212-521-5450
www.reedsmith.com
• Gregory B. Jordan, Global Managing Partner
(412) 288-4124
gjordan@reedsmith.com
• Michael Pollack, Partner
(215) 851-8182
mpollack@reedsmith.com
• Thomas R. Amlicke, Partner
(212) 549-0341
tamlicke@reedsmith.com
• Douglas Wood, Partner
(212) 549-0377
dwood@reedsmith.com
• Jennifer L. Achilles, Associate
(212) 521 5412
jachilles@reedsmith.com
• James Andriola, Partner
(212) 205-6003
jandriola@reedsmith.com
• Jill N. Averett, Associate
(212) 205-6005
javerett@reedsmith.com
• Jason Barr, Associate
(212) 521-5428
jbarr@reedsmith.com
• Arnold L. Bartfeld, Partner
(212) 205-6008
abartfeld@reedsmith.com
• Oliver Beiersdorf, Partner
(212) 549 0415
obeiersdorf@reedsmith.com
• John B. Berringer, Partner
(212) 205-6010
jberringer@reedsmith.com
Description:
Representing sports organizations.
Services:

Areas of practice include Advertising & Marketing, Advocacy, Antitrust, Competition & Regulatory Litigation, Appellate, Arbitration, Associations, Aviation Litigation, Banking, Bankruptcy and Commercial Restructuring, Benefits, Class Action Defense, Communications, Construction, Corporate Services (U.K.), E-commerce, Employment, Energy & Natural Resources, Environmental Law, Executive Compensation, Export, Customs & Trade, Financial Services, etc
Other Location:
375 Park Avenue, Suite 17, New York, New York 10152-1799

REICH, ROBERT S.
345 PARK AVENUE
NEW YORK, NY 10154
212-407-4000
Fax: 212-407-4990
www.loeb.com
• David S. Schaefer, Managing Partner/Co-Chair
(212) 407-4848
dschaefer@loeb.com
• Kenneth B. Anderson, Partner
(212) 407-4856
kanderson@loeb.com
• Roger M. Arar, Partner
(212) 407-4906
rarar@loeb.com
• Michael D. Beck, Partner
(212) 407-4920
mbeck@loeb.com
Other Locations:
10130 Santa Monica Boulevard, STE 2200, Los Angeles, CA 90067; Phone: 310-282-2000; 321 North Clark Street, STE 2300, Chicago, Il 66610; Phone: 312-464-3100; 1906 Acklen Avenue, Nashville, TN 37212; Phone: 615-749-8300
Services:
Areas of practice include corporate and securities, litigation, entertainment and media, finance, real estate, intellectual property, private equity, employment, advertising and promotions, and tax and wealth services.

REINHART, BOERNER, VAN DEUREN S.C.
1000 N WATER STREET
SUITE 1700
MILWAUKEE, WI 53202
414-298-1000
800-553-6215
Fax: 414-298-8097
dsisson@reinhartlaw.com
www.reinhartlaw.com
• Richard A. Van Deuren, Chairman
(414) 298-8103
rvandeur@reinhartlaw.com
• Meg S. Pekarske, Shareholder
(608) 229-2216
mpekarsk@reinhartlaw.com
• James A. Pellegrini, Shareholder
(262) 951-4500
jpellegr@reinhartlaw.com
• David G. Hanson, Shareholder
(414) 298-8324
dhanson@reinhartlaw.com
• Wesley D. Anderson, Health Care Attourney
wanderson@reinhartlaw.com
• Joseph J. Balistreri, Real Estate/Banking & Finance Attourney
jbalistreri@reinhartlaw.com

• Thomas Burnett, Litigation Attourney
tburnett@reinhartlaw.com
• William R. Cummings, Real Estate
Attourney
tburnett@reinhartlaw.com
Description:
Contract negotiation.
Services:
Areas of practice include Appellate, Banking
and Finance, Bankruptcy and Creditors'
Rights, Business Law, Computer &
Technology, Crisis Management and
Business Continuity, Employee Benefits,
Entertainment Law, etc
Clients:
Resolute Systems, Allen-Edmonds, WTC,
Historic King Place, Sargento Cheese,
Carmelite Sisters, Riley Construction, GIC
Management, Inc., The Alliance, Ruud
Lighting, Skil-Tech of Madison, Inc.
Other Locations:
22 East Mifflin Street, Madison, WI 53703;
Phone: 608-229-2200; Phone:
608-229-2200; Ridgeview, Waukesha, WI
53188; Phone: 262-951-4500

REITER, ARNOLD E.
2 N BAYARD LANE
BOX 915
MAHWAH, NJ 7430
201-818-2333
Fax: 201-825-1509
Description:
Contract negotiation, post career planning,
investment contract negotiation, arbitration
hearings, federal/state/international tax
filings, licensing, endorsement exploration,
teaches sports law, tort actions/litigation.

RICHARDSON, DEAN
245 WINTER STREET SE
SALEM, OR 97301
503-370-6282
Fax: 503-370-6375
law-admission@willamette.edu
• Carol Long, Dean/Professor
(503) 370-6285
clong@willamette.edu
• Ann Nicgorski, Associate Dean &
Associate Professor of
(503) 370-6285
anicgors@willamette.edu
• Jerry D. Gray, Associate Dean
jgray@willamette.edu
• Dean Richardson, Professor
(503) 370-6410
drichard@willamette.edu
Services:
Provides comprehensive understanding of
the law, along with highly refined skills in
problem-solving, research and writing.
Offers a strong, integrated curriculum -
enhanced by extensive opportunities for
research and study.
Description:
Contract negotiation, post career planning,
arbitration hearings, endorsement
exploration, teaches sports law.

RIDENOUR, HIERDON, HARPER &
KELHOFFER P.L.L.C.
201 N CENTRAL AVENUE
CHASE TOWER
SUITE 3300
PHOENIX, AZ 85004

602-254-9900
Fax: 602-254-8670
www.rhlfirm.com
• Kurt Peterson, Member
(602) 254-9900
• Robert R. Beltz, Member
(602) 254-9900
• Jeffrey A. Bernick, Member
(602) 254-9900
• William G. Ridenour, Member
(602) 254-9900
Services:
Provides services in the following areas of
law: Alternate Dispute Resolution; Federal,
State and Local Taxation; Appellate
Advocacy Department; Government
Operations and Affairs; Banking,
Commercial Finance and Real Estate
Finance Group; Insurance and Financial
Services; Industry Regulation; Bankruptcy
Practice Group; Labor and Employment
Section; Business Services Group;
Legislative and Government Affairs
Services; Captive Insurance and Alternative
Risk Transfer; Municipal Liability;
Commercial Litigation; Personal Injury and
Insurance Defense Litigation; Construction
Litigation Real Estate Practice Group; and
Estate Planning Group
Nature of Sports Service:
All phases of athlete representation
including contract negotiation, long-range
planning, financial planning, and post-career
counseling. Commercial Transactions;
Banking; Real Estate Law; Leasing;
Mortgages.

RISMAN, MARC D.
10120 S EASTERN
SUITE 200
HENDERSON, NV 89052
702-388-8100
Fax: 702-492-4992
marcrisman@calneva-law.com
www.calneva-law.com
• Marc D. Risman, Lawyer
(702) 388-8100
marcrisman@calneva-law.com
Description:
Founded in 1979. Specializes in contract
negotiation, arbitration hearings, and
litigation in legal matters concerning boxing,
motor sports. and amateur athletics.
Services:
Practicing Intellectual Property, Sports Law,
Entertainment Law, Travel Law, Business
Law; Personal Injury, Gaming Law,
Trademarks, and Trade Names.
Publications:
Law of Boxing, Professionalism in the
Olympics, TAC Trust Fund, Legal aspects of
Major International Sporting Events,
Sports-Law Resolution of Disputes and
Litigation, Endorsement Contracts, Special
Event Security and Premises Liability

ROBINSON, WATERS & E'DORISIO
1099 18TH STREET
26TH FLOOR
DENVER, CO 80202
303-297-2600
Fax: 303-297-2750
info@rwolaw.com
www.rwolaw.com
• Otto K. Hilbert, III, Attorney
(303) 297-2600
ohilbert@rwolaw.com

• Stephen L. Waters, Attorney
(303) 297-2600
swaters@rwolaw.com
• John W. O'Doresio Jr, Shareholder
jodorisio@rwolaw.com
• Jeffrey A. Bartholomew, Shareholder
jbartholomew@rwolaw.com
Nature of Sports Service:
All phases of athlete representation
including contract negotiation, long-range
planning, financial planning, and post-career
counseling. Arbitration; Civil Litigation; Labor
and Employment; Securities Litigation;
White Collar Crime.

ROLAND, LENORA, R.
2000 TOWN CENTER
SUITE 900
SOUTHFIELD, MI 48075
248-355-0300
800-967-1234
Fax: 248-936-1971
info@sommerspc.com
• Leonard B. Schwartz, Lawyer
(248) 746-4064
lschwartz@sommerspc.com
• William M Brukoff, Senior Shareholder
(248) 746-4067
wbrukoff@sommerspc.com
• Steven J. Schwartz, Lawyer
(248) 746-4042
sjschwartz@sommerspc.com
• Norman S. Sommers, Lawyer
(248) 355-0300
nsommers@sommerspc.com
Nature of Sports Service:
All phases of athlete representation
including contract negotiation, long-range
planning, financial planning, and post-career
counseling.
Services:
Areas of practice include
ADR/Mediation/Arbitration, Age
Discrimination, Appellate Litigation, Auto
Negligence, Aviation Crash Litigation, Birth
Trauma, Business Litigation, Business
Transactions Law Civil Rights, Construction
Accidents, Corporate/Business
Transactions, Divorce/Family Law,
Employment and Labor Litigation, Estate
Planning/Probate, Medical Malpractice,
Mold Litigation/Toxic Torts

ROLLINS, RON
310 GROVELAND AVENUE
MINNEAPOLIS, MN 55403
612-874-8550
Fax: 612-874-9362
• David E. Krause, Attorney
(612) 874-8550
• Ronald L. Rollins, Partner
(612) 874-8550
• James B. Hovland, Lawyer
(612) 874-8550
Services:
Areas of practice include Products Liability,
Personal Injury, Transportation Law, Labor
Law, Pharmaceutical Law, Commercial Law,
Corporate Law, and Civil Law
Description:
NFLPA workers' compensation panel.

ROSENTHAL, ROBERT E.
787 MUNRAS AVENUE
PO BOX 1111
SUITE 200
MONTEREY, CA 93940

831-649-5551
Fax: 831-649-0272
info@brklegal.com
• Thomas P. Bohnen, Member
(831) 649-5551
tbohen@redshift.com
• Douglas K. Dusenbury, Member
(831) 649-5551
ddusenbury@mtrylegal.com
• Roger D. Bolgard, Partner
(831) 649-5551
rbolgard@redshift.com
• Thomas P. J. Bohnen, Associate
• Robert E. Rosenthal, Partner
• Andrew Kreeft, Partner
• Roger D. Bolgard, Associate
• Catherine J. Lee, Associates
• Sergio H. Parra, Associate
• Laura L. Franklin, Associate
Services:
Areas of practice include Commercial
Litigation, Family Law, Sports Law, Personal
Injury, Creditor Rights, Business Litigation,
Legal Malpractice, Real Property Litigation,
Entertainment Law, onstruction Litigation,
Collections, Criminal Law, Business
Transactions,and Medical Malpractice
Description:
Contract negotiation.

ROSS, STEPHEN F.
504 E PENNSYLVANIA AVENUE
CHAMPAIGN, IL 61820
217-333-0931
Fax: 217-244-1478
admissions@law.uiuc.edu
www.law.uiuc.edu
• Stephen F. Ross, Professor
sross@law.uiuc.edu
• Bruce P. M. Smith, Dean
• Margareth Etienne, Associate dean for
academic affairs
• John Rossi, Executive assistant dean
• Heather Ball, Director of events
• Jenny Carroll, Director of alumni relations
Description:
Teaches sports law.

ROUND, BRYAN E., ESQ.
PO BOX 480465
KANSAS CITY, MO 64148-0465
816-943-8383
Description:
NFLPA. Handles workers compensation for
the Kansas City Chiefs.

ROZIER LAW FIRM, P.C.
315 TOMBIGBEE STREET
1ST FLOOR
ST.JACKSON, MS 39201-4600
601-948-2779
Services:
Areas of practice include Personal injury,
Porbate, Property, Real Estate, Sports Law,
Torts, Wills and Estates, and Federal and
State Workers Compensation.

RUBENSTEIN, MARK A.
UNIVERSITY OF CALIFORNIA
545 STUDENT SERVICES BUILDING
BERKELEY, CA 94720- 1900
510-642-3580
Fax: 510-643-1420
www.haas.berkeley.edu/groups/finance/rubi
nste.html
• Steven Glazer, Of Counsel
• Mark A. Rubenstein, Member

• John D. Albright, Associate
• Eileen M. Burger, Associate
Services:
Handles legal matters in different practice
areas such as General Civil Practice before
State and Federal Courts, Real Estate,
Corporation, Commercial and Banking,
Personal Injury, Commercial Litigation,
Planning and Zoning Trials and Appeals.
Description:
Contract negotiation, licensing,
endorsement exploration, tort
actions/litigation.

RUBIN, ERIC M.
1201 CONNECTICUT AVENUE, NW
SIXTH FLOOR
SUITE 200
WASHINGTON, DC 20036
202-861-0870
Fax: 202-429-0657
www.rwdhc.com
• Frederick D. Cooke, Jr., Attorney
fcooke@rwdhc.com
• Walter E. Diercks, Esquire
wdiercks@rwdhc.com
• Eric M. Rubin, Esquire
erubin@rwdhc.com
• Steven J. Stone, Esquire
sstone@rwdhc.com
Services:
Areas of practice include Antitrust and Trade
Regulation, Banking, Business
Transactions, Communications, Corporate
Law and Governance, Criminal Law, Estate
Planning and Administration, Government
Relations, Homeland Security, litigation,
Media, Municipal Law, Outdoor Advertising,
and Real Estate and Land Use
Description:
Represents professional sports teams.

RUBIN, MICHAEL D.
611 ANTON BOULEVARD
SUITE 1400
COSTA MESA, CA 92626-1931
714-641-5100
Fax: 714-546-9035
learnmore@rutan.com
www.rutan.com
• Michael D. Rubin, Partner
(714) 641-3423
MRubin@rutan.com
• L. Ski Harrison, Partner
(714) 662-4641
sharrison@rutan.com
Services:
Areas of practice include: Business
Litigation, Competitive Business and
Advertising Practices,
Condemnation/Property Valuation,
Construction Law, Corporate/Securities,
Education Law, Employment/Labor,
Environmental, Financial Practices,
Intellectual Property/Technology, Land
Use/Natural Resources, Life Sciences,
Municipal & Government Agency Law, Real
Estate, Tax, Trusts/Estates
Description:
Represents sports facilities, equipment
manufacturers.
Year Founded
1906
Other Location:
50 West San Fernando Street, STE 320,
San Jose, CA 95113; Phone: 408-289-8777;
Fax: 408-289-8778

RUTGERS-NEWARK ATHLETICS
42 WARREN STREET
NEWARK, NJ 07102-1807
973-353-5474
Fax: 973-353-1431
www.rutgersnewarkathletics.com
• Mark Griffin, Director of Athletics
• Mary Stadelmann, Associate Director of
Athletics/Senior Woman
(973) 353-1460
mary.stad@rutgers.edu
Description:
Arbitration hearings.

RUXIN, ROBERT H.
676 ELM STREET
CONCORD, MA 1742
978-371-1732
Fax: 978-369-6223
• Richard W. Kazmaier Jr, President / Chief
Executive Officer
• Robert H. Ruxin, VP / General Counsel
Services:
Offering advisory services since 1975 to
sports product and sports marketing clients.

SAFFREN & WEINBERG
815 GREENWOOD AVENUE
SUITE 22
JENKINTOWN, PA 19046
215-576-0100
Fax: 215-576-6288
• Marc A. Weinberg, Lawyer / Partner
• Kenneth S. Saffren, Partner
Services:
All phases of athlete representation
including contract negotiation, long-range
planning, financial planning, and post-career
counseling.

SAPIR, EDDIE L., THE HONORABLE
1300 PERDIDO STREET
SECOND FLOOR WEST
NEW ORLEANS, LA 70112
504-658-1000
Fax: 504-658-1068
www.nocitycouncil.com
• Arnie Fielkow, Vice President
(504) 658-1060
afielkow@cityofno.com
• Stacy Head, President
• Jonathan Harris, Chief of staff
• Catrina Simmons, Executive administrative
assistant and schedu
• Barbara Lacen-keller, Director of
constituent services
• Greg Malveaux, Personal assistant

SASSOON & CYMROT LLP
84 STATE STREET
8TH FLOOR
BOSTON, MA 02109
617-720-0099
Fax: 617-720-0366
info@sassooncymrot.com
www.sassooncymrot.com
• Lewis Sassoon, Lawyer
lsassoon@sassooncymrot.com
• Jeffrey Cymrot, Lawyer
jcymrot@sassooncymrot.com
• William R Moriarty, Lawyer
• Anthony M. S Ambriano, Attorney
Services:
Provides local and multinational business
clients legal services on civil litigation, real
estate, bankruptcy and insolvency, business
and personal estate planning, bad debt

collection, divorce, construction, hotel and restaurant, personal injury/tort claims and patent and intellectual property

SAUER, JR., RUSSELL F.
355 S GRAND AVENUE
LOS ANGELES, CA 90071-1560
213-485-1234
Fax: 213-891-8763
www.lw.com
• Manuel A. Abascal, Partner
(213) 891-7889
manny.abascal@lw.com
• James L. Arnone, Partner
(213) 891-8204
james.arnone@lw.com
• LeeAnn Black, Chief Operating Officer
(212) 906-1218
leeann.black@lw.com
• Adrian F. Davis, Chief Attourney Development Officer
(415) 616-8335
adrian.davis@lw.com
• James E. Dow, Chief Real Estate Officer
(619) 238-2800
jim.dow@lw.com
• Joshua S. Friedlander, Chief Human Resources Officer
(212) 906-1286
josh.friedlander@lw.com
• Rod Harrington, Chief Administrative Officer
(004) 420-7710
• Alfred Harutunian, Chief Financial Officer
(213) 891-7253
alfred.harutunian@lw.com
Description:
Offers sophisticated corporate finance, mergers and acquisitions, company representation and corporated governance, private equity and investment funds, restructuring, internal investigations, intellectual property, and venture and technoloby transactions practices. Litigation department comprises commercial, securities and professional liability, antitrust, employment, insurance coverage, white collar and toxic tort. Finance department includes practice groups involved in all phases of lending work for banks and other lending insitutions and for borrowers, insolvency and creditors rights, project finance and public and tax-exempt finance
Other Locations:
Riverside Center, 275 Grove Street, 4th Floor, Newton, MA 02466; Phone: 617-663-5700; Sears Tower, STE 5800, 23 South Wacker Drive, Chicago, IL 60606; Phone: 312-876-7700; 885 Third Avenue, STE 1000, New York, NY 10022; Phone: 212-906-1200; 555 Eleventh Street, NW, STE 1000, Washington, DC 20004; Phone: 202-637-2200; Two Freedom Square, 11955 Freedom Drive, STE 500, Reston, VA 20190; Phone: 703-456-1000; 505 Montgomery Street, STE 200, San Francisco 94111; Phone: 415-391-0600

SCARINCI HOLLENBECK
1100 VALLEY BROOK AVENUE
PO BOX 790
LYNDHURST, NJ 07071-0790
201-896-4100
Fax: 201-896-8660
info@sh-law.com
www.sh-law.com
• Peter Moeller, Director Marketing & Communications

• Donald Scarinci, Managing Partner
(201) 896-4100
dscarinci@scarincihollenbeck.com
• Sheri K. Siegelbaum, Chair-Public Law Group
ssiegelbaum@njlegalink.com
Description:
Founded in 1988, Scarini Hollenbeck is a general practice law firm practice law firm focusing on real estate, business law, environmental and land use, public law, labor and employment law and litigation.
Nature of Service:
Legal industry.

SCHAFFER, S. ANDREW
70 WASHINGTON SQUARE S
NEW YORK, NY 10012
212-998-1212
Fax: 212-995-3048
www.nyu.edu
• John Sexton, President
(212) 998-2345
john.sexton@nyu.edu
• David W. McLaughlin, Provost
david.mclaughlin@nyu.edu
Services:
Represents college athletic departments.

SCHILL, JR., GILBERT E.
901 E CARY STREET
ONE JAMES CENTER
RICHMOND, VA 23219-4030
804-775-1000
Fax: 804-775-1061
www.mcguirewoods.com
• Gilbert E. Schill Jr, Partner
(804) 775-4345
gschill@mcguirewoods.com
• John V. Cogbill III, Managing Partner
(804) 775-4383
Description:
Represents college athletic departments.
Services:
Areas of practice include Complex Products Liability & Mass Tort Litigation, Corporate Services, Financial Services, Health Care & Pharmaceuticals, International Group, Labor & Employment, Real Estate & Benefits, taxation & Employee Benefits, and Technology & Business

SCHINE, JULIANEL, ANTONUCCI
830 POST ROAD E
WESTPORT, CT 6880
203-226-6861
Fax: 203-226-6866
• Francis Antonucci, Lawyer

SCHOENI, K. ROGER
201 E FIFTH STREET
PNC CENTER
SUITE 800
CINCINNATI, OH 45202-4190
513-381-0656
Fax: 513-381-5823
info@kplaw.com
www.kohnenpatton.com
• K. Roger Schoeni, Partner
(513) 381-0656
rschoeni@kplaw.com
• Peggy M. Barker, Partner
(513) 381-0656
pbarker@kplaw.com
• Joseph Beech, Partner
jbeech@kplaw.com
• Colleen M. Blandford, Partner

cblandford@kplaw.com
• John L. Campbell, Partner
jcampbell@kplaw.com
• Anthony J. Caruso, Partner
tcaruso@kplaw.com
• Ann R. Combs, Partner
acombs@kplaw.com
• Rebecca Cull, Partner
rcull@kplaw.com
Services:
Areas of practice include Corporate and Securities, Litigation, Employment Law, Estate Planning and Probate, Banking, Finance and Creditors' Rights, Real Estate and Construction, Government Relations, Franchising and Distribution, Computers and Technology, Tower Mediation, and Tower Land Title
Description:
Contract negotiation, arbitration hearings, federal/state/international tax filings, endorsement exploration, tort actions/litigation. Trial Practice; Products Liability Law.
Other Location:
211 Grandview Drive, STE 236, Fort Mitchell, KY 41017; Phone: 859-341-0009; Fax: 859-341-0344

SCHOONOVER, PAUL D.
4015 MAIN STREET
SUITE 200
DALLAS, TX 75226
214-712-4400
Fax: 815-572-9448
www.vialaw.com
• Paul D. Schoonover, Lawyer
(214) 712-4470
paul@klbf.com
Services:
Bankruptcy, Banking & Financial Institutions, Business Litigation, Commercial Litigation, Corporate & Securities, estate Planning & Probate, Family Law, Fidelity and Surety, Insurance Coverage, Insurance Defense, Labor & Employment, Products Liability, Real estate & Construction, School of Law, Sports & Entertainment, State & Local Government, Taxation

SCHUTTS & BOWEN
201 S BISCAYNE BOULEVARD
1500 MIAMI CENTER
MIAMI, FL 33131
305-358-6300
800-325-2892
Fax: 305-381-9982
• Kevin D. Cowan, Partner
(305) 379-9110
kcowan@shutts.com
• Carlos J. Abarca, Lawyer
(305) 347-7324
• Jeannette E. Albo, Partner
(305) 347-7381
Description:
Contract negotiation, endorsement exploration.
Services:
Areas of practice include Administrative Law, Admiralty, Antitrust, Appellate, Aviation, Commercial Finance, Community associations, Compliance Audits, Construction, Corporate, Corporate/Securities, Creditor's Right and Bankruptcy, Eminent Domain Inverse Condemnation, Environmental, Financial Institutions, Governmental Relations, Health Care, Immigration, Insurance, Insurance

Regulatory Practice, Intellectual Property, International Dispute Resolution, Internet, Labor & Employment, Land Use, Litigation, Public Finance and Local Government, Real Property and Development, Taxation, and Trusts and Estates

SCOTT A BLACKMUN
1750 E BOULDER STREET
UNITED STATES OLYMPIC TRANING CENTER
COLORADO SPRINGS, CO 80909-5760
719-632-5551
Fax: 719-866-4654
athleteservices@usoc.org
Services:
Amateur sports representation.

SCOTT, DAVID R.
7 COLLEGE AVENUE
WIANTES HALL, ROOM 324
NEW BRUNSWICK, NJ 08901-1259
732-932-7741
732-445-info (4636)
Fax: 732-932-6818
legal@oldqueens.rutgers.edu
www.rutgers.edu
• Richard L. McCormick, President
(732) 932-7454
koncsol@oldqueens.rutgers.edu
• Ralph R. Izzo, Chair
• Gerald C. Harvey, Vice Chair
• Robert Balchi, Ex Officio
• Bruce Fehn, Treasurer
• Leslie A. Fehrenbach, Secretary
• Mary Brennan, Assistant Secretary
Description:
Represents college athletic departments.
Services:
Dedicated to advanced learning, creating new knowledge and contributing to the growing vitality of the state

SEEKINGS, MICHAEL
29 MONTAGU STREET
CHARLESTON, SC 29401
843-513-1073
Fax: 843-853-8994
mseekings@leathbouchlaw.com
• Michael S. Seekings, Member
• Francis E. Grimball, Member
(843) 785-6969
Nature of Sports Service:
All phases of athlete representation including contract negotiation, long-range planning, financial planning, and post-career counseling.

SEGAL & LAX
501 FIFTH AVENUE
SUITE 2004
NEW YORK, NY 10017
212-922-0891
800-762-7852
Fax: 212-922-0896
www.segalandlax.com
• Mark Segal, Partner
(212) 922-0891
• Emil Lax, Lawyer
(212) 922-0891
• Patrick D. Gatti
Services:
Areas of practice include Personal Injury, Medical Malpractice, Slips & Falls, Motor Vehicle Accidents, Complex Litigation, Wrongful Death Claims, Construction site accidents, Immigration, Catastrophic Brain

Injury, Dental Malpractice, Electrical Accidents, Birth Trauma, Serious Injury Claims, Burn Injuries, Defective drugs, and Sports Law
Description:
Contract negotiation, arbitration hearings, endorsement exploration, tort actions/litigation.

SERGEANT, DAVID A.
1728 CENTRAL AVENUE
FORT DODGE, IA 50501
515-576-0333
Fax: 515-955-6388
• David A. Sergeant, Principal
Services:
Areas of practice include contract negotiation, investment contract negotiation, arbitration hearings, endorsement exploration, and sports law.

SHAPIRO, RONALD M.
1340 SMITH AVE
SUITE 200
BALTIMORE, MD 21209
410-779-1341
shapiro@shapiroadvisors-llc.com
• Ronald Shapiro, Founder
(410) 779-1341
shapiro@shapiroadvisors-llc.com
Nature of Service:
Deal coaching and negotiation consulting.
Clients:
San Antonio Spurs; Brooklyn Nets; Oklahoma City Thunder; Cleveland Browns
Description:
Founded in 2017, Shapiro Advisors is a negotiation deal coaching and consulting company.

SHEFSKY, LLOYD E.
111 E WACKER
SUITE 2800
CHICAGO, IL 60601
312-527-4000
Fax: 312-527-4011
www.shefskylaw.com
• Lloyd Shefsky, Counsel
(312) 836-4001
• Cezar M. Froelich, Partner
(312) 836-4002
cfroelich@shefskylaw.com
• Richard E. Aderman, Partner
(312) 836-4104
raderman@shefskylaw.com
• Sylvia D. Taylor, HRM
• Thomas Dal Compo, Litigation Paregal
• Dan Henderson, Sr litigation paralegal
• Kathy Deane, Firm administrator
• Amy Inlander, Paralegal manager
Description:
Post career planning, investment contract negotiation.
Services:
Areas of practice include Banking and Financial Institution, Bankruptcy, Corporate Finance, Creditors' Rights and Insolvency, Employment Law, Estate Planning and Probate, Government Regulation, Health Car, International Law, Litigation, Mergers & Acquisitions, Real Estate, Securities, and Technology
Clients:
TCB Development Corp.

SHEPHERD, JR., ROBERT E.
28 WESTHAMPTON WAY
UNIVERSITY OF RICHMOND
TC WILLIAMS SCHOOL OF LAW
RICHMOND, VA 23173
804-289-8189
Fax: 804-287-6516
www.law.richmond.edu
• Robert E. Shepherd Jr, Professor
• Margaret I. Bacigal, Professor/Administrative Director
(804) 289-8950
mbacigal@richmond.edu
• Ronald J. Bacigal, Professor
(804) 289-8194
rbacigal@richmond.edu
• John R. Barden, Head, Reference & Research Services
(804) 289-8727
Description:
Teaches sports law.

SHERMAN & NATHANSON, A PROFESSIONAL CORPORATION
9454 WILSHIRE BOULEVARD
A PROFESSIONAL CORPORATION
SUITE 900
BEVERLY HILLS, CA 90212
310-246-0321
Fax: 310-246-0305
rsherman@snmlaw.com
www.smnlawfirm.com
• Richard L. Sherman, Partner
(310) 246-0321
• Ken Nathanson, Partner
(310) 246-0321
knate@snmlaw.com
• Sheila Kadisha, Associate
• Abhay Khosla, Associate
• Maria Hall, Associate
• Richard Lloyd Sherman, Managing Partner
Services:
Areas of practice include Business Litigation, Entertainment Litigation, Real Estate Litigation, Civil Appeals, Business Transactions, Employment Law, and Intellectual Property Litigation

SHERRARD, GERMAN & KELLY
620 LIBERTY AVENUE
28TH FLOOR, TWO PNC PLAZA
PITTSBURGH, PA 15222
412-355-0200
Fax: 412-261-6221
sgk@sgkpc.com
www.sgkpc.com
• David R. Lowe, Shareholder/V.P.
(412) 355-0200
• Robert D. German, Managing Shareholder
(412) 355-0200
rdg@sgkpc.com
• Rita Kelly
(412) 258-6718
rk@sgkpc.com
• James R. Hankle
(412) 258-6712
jrh@sgkpc.com
Services:
Areas of practice include Corporate Services, Retail Financial Services, Commercial, Industrial and Real Estate Lending Services, Commercial Credit Recovery, Consumer Collection, Commercial Litigation, Litigation Management, and Estates and Trusts Services
Nature of Sports Service:
All phases of athlete representation

including contract negotiation, long-range planning, financial planning, and post-career counseling.

SHEUERMANN & JONES
701 POYDRAS STREET
41ST FLOOR
NEW ORLEANS, LA 70139
504-525-4361
888-525-4361
Fax: 504-525-4380
joneslaw@nola-law.com
www.nola-law.com
• Blake Jones, Managing Partner
• Arthel J Scheuermann, Partner
Nature of Sports Service:
All phases of athlete representation including contract negotiation, long-range planning, financial planning, and post-career counseling.

SHNEIDMAN, DANIEL L.
SHNEIDMAN LAW SC
PO BOX 442
MILWAUKEE, WI 53201
414-271-8650
Fax: 414-271-1054
Services:
Labor and sports law.

SHOR, ALAN P.
901 W WALNUT HILL LANE
MS 6A-6
IRVING, TX 75038-1003
972-580-5047
Fax: 972-580-5238
CustomerService@zales.com
www.zalecorp.com
• David H. Sternblitz, VP & Treasurer
(972) 580-4000
ir@zalecorp.com
• Sue E. Gove, EVP/Chief Operating Officer
• Mark R. Lenz, Group SVP/Chief Financial Officer
Description:
Contract negotiation, arbitration hearings, represents professional sports teams, licensing, endorsement exploration, tort actions/litigation, represents sports organizations.
Brands:
Zales Jewelers, Zales Outlet, Gordon's Jewelers, Bailey Banks & Biddle Fine Jewelers, Peoples Jewellers, Mappins Jewellers, Piercing Pagoda, Zales.com, BaileyBanksAndBiddle.com

SHOTWELLE, BROWN & SPERRY
1101 ROYAL AVENUE
PO BOX 14140
SUITE A
MONROE, LA 71201-4140
318-388-4700
Fax: 318-388-4736
sbs@shotwell-law.com
www.shotwell-law.com
• Marshall T. Napper, Shareholder
(318) 388-4700
mnapper@centurytel.net
• George M M. Wear, Jr, Jr., Shareholder
gmwjr@centurytel.net
Description:
Contract negotiation, tort actions/litigation, represents college athletic departments, represents sports organizations.

SHROPSHIRE, KENNETH L.
3730 WALNUT STREET, JON M
HUNTSMAN HALL
6TH FLOOR
SUITE 600
PHILADELPHIA, PA 19104
215-898-1393
Fax: 215-573-2006
sportsbusiness@wharton.upenn.edu
wsb.wharton.upenn.edu/
• Derrick L Hegans, Managing Director
Services:
Areas of practice include arbitration hearings, speaker, teaches sports law, author and expert witness

SHUMATE, FLAHERTY & EUBANKS & BAECHTOLD, P.S.C.
225 W IRVINE STREET
PO BOX 157
RICHMOND, KY 40475
859-623-3049
800-742-5830
Fax: 859-623-6406
lshouse@eblawfirm.com
www.eblawfirm.com
• Michael F. Eubanks, Lawyer
meubanks@eblawfirm.com
• James W. Baechtold, Lawyer
jbaechtold@eblawfirm.com
Services:
Areas of practice include Litigation, Personal Injury (Auto Accidents), Workers' Compensation, Criminal Law, Domestic Relations, Estates, Probate, General Practice, Real Estate, and Sports Law
Nature of Sports Service:
All phases of athlete representation including contract negotiation, long-range planning, financial planning, and post-career counseling. Criminal Law; Drugs and Narcotics; Personal Injury; Workers Compensation; Sports Law; Probate; Real Estate.

SICKING, RICHARD A., ESQ
1313 PONCE DE LEON BOULEVARD
SUITE 300
CORAL GABLES, FL 33134-3343
305-446-3700
800-431-4689
Fax: 305-446-4014
sickingpa@aol.com
• Richard A. Sicking, Attorney
Services:
NFLPA workers' compensation panel for the Miami Dolphins and Tampa Bay Buccaneers.

SIKORSKI, JR., EDMUND J.
29211 FORD ROAD
GARDEN CITY OFFICE
GARDEN CITY, MI 48135
734-422-2377
Fax: 734-423-1423
Firm@SikorskiLaw.com
www.sikorskilaw.com
Nature of Service:
Represents Michigan High School Athletic Association.
Year Founded:
1972

SILLS CUMMIS & GROSS P.C.
ONE RIVERFRONT PLAZA
THE LEGAL CENTER
NEWARK, NJ 07102

973-643-7000
Fax: 973-643-6500
sillsmail@sillscummis.com
www.sillscummis.com
• Anthony Caruso, Associate
• Peter A. Cross, Associate
• Lynne Anne Anderson, Member
(973) 643-5686
landerson@sillscummis.com
• Seth M. Apple, Associate
(973) 286-4815
sapple@sillscummis.com
Description:
Sills, Cummis & Gross is a premier law firm representing companies from Fortune 500 to emerging growth. Their entertainment and sports law group has represented artists and performers, coaches and athletes, sports marketing, sports leagues and investment groups involved in sports and entertainment projects.

SIMPSON, JACQUELINE
1360 E 9TH STREET
SUITE 100
CLEVELAND, OH 44114
216-522-1200
Fax: 216-436-3187
jsimpson@imgworld.com
• Jacqueline Simpson, Attorney
Description:
Contract negotiation.

SKODA, MINOTTI & CO.
6685 BETA DRIVE
MAYFIELD VILLAGE
CLEVELAND, OH 44143
440-449-6800
888-201-4484
Fax: 440-646-1615
www.skodaminotti.com
• Robert Barkett, Partner
(440) 449-6800
• Patrick T. Carney, Partner
(440) 449-6800
• Robert E. Coode, Partner
(440) 449-6800
• Kenneth M. Haffey, Partner
(440) 449-6800
khaffey@skodaminotti.com
Description:
Contract negotiation, post career planning, federal/state/international tax filings, represents professional athletes, provides investment advice, endorsement exploration, contract actions/litigation.
Services:
Offers Accounting, Consulting, Financial, Healthcare and Tax Services.

SLAUGHTER, FRED L.
411 W. 4TH STREET
8000 U.S COURTHOUSE
SANTA ANA, CA 92701
741-338-3500
Fax: 310-394-4243
Description:
Contract negotiation, post career planning, arbitration hearings, federal/state/international tax filings, endorsement exploration, teaches sports law, represents sports labor organizations.
Services:
Areas of practice include contract negotiation, post career planning, arbitration hearings, federal/state/international tax filings, endorsement exploration, teaches

sports law, and represents sports labor organizations.

SLOTT, JEFFREY LAW OFFICE
21031 VENTURA BOULEVARD
12TH FLOOR
WOODLAND HILLS, CA 91364
818-999-5859
Fax: 818-999-3354
• Jeffrey A. Slott, President/Agent/General Legal
(818) 999-5859
Description:
Offers legal and agent services to professional athletes.
Services:
Legal Services

SMITH & SMITH ATTORNEYS AT LAW
3838 OAK LAWN AVENUE
SUITE 1222
DALLAS, TX 75219
214-522-5571
Fax: 214-522-5009
pview.findlaw.com/view/1970123_1
• Robert B. Smith, Member
• Smith B. Robert, Member
Description:
Endorsement exploration, represents sports organizations, tort actions/litigation.
Services:
Areas of practice include endorsement exploration, represents sports organizations, and tort actions/litigation.

SMITH, CHARLES EDISON
640 NELSON STREET
DURHAM, NC 27707
919-530-6333
Fax: 919-530-6339
www.nccu.edu/law
• Phyliss Craig-Taylor, Professor
(919) 530-6333
pcraigt@nccu.edu
• Marshall Dayan, Professor
(919) 530-7816
mdayan@wpo.nccu.edu
• Jennifer Brobst, Clinical Supervising Lawyer
(919) 530-5371
jbrobst@nccu.edu
• Charles E. Smith, Professor, School of Law
(919) 530-6333
csmith@wpo.nccu.edu
Services:
Offers two programs leading to the Juris Doctor degree: a full-time day program and the only part-time evening program between Atlanta, Georgia, and the metropolitan Washington, DC area.
Description:
Teaches sports law.

SMITH, PAYTON
1201 THIRD AVENUE
SUITE 2200
SEATTLE, WA 98101-3045
206-622-3150
Fax: 206-757-7700
seattle@dwt.com
www.dwt.com
• Greg F Adams, Partner
(206) 757-8000
gregadams@dwt.com
• Keith Gormley Baldwin, Partner

(206) 757-8008
keithbaldwin@dwt.com
Description:
Represents sports organizations.
Services:
Serves regional, national and international clients, including Washington's largest newspaper, one of the nation's largest banks, leading hospitals and health care providers, retailers, telecommunications and other industry giants, many of which are involved in international transactions.

SOMERS & HODGES
TWO RAVINIA DRIVE
SUITE 310
ATLANTA, GA 30346
770-394-7200
Fax: 770-395-7698
Services:
Areas of practice include Golf industry legal matters; Private Club Law; Computer Software Law; Limited Liability Company; Tax Exempt Organizations; Golf Course Development; Country Club Law; Trade Association Law; and Nonprofit Organizations Law.
Description:
Golf industry legal matters. Private Club Law; Computer Software Law; Limited Liability Company; Tax Exempt Organizations; Golf Course Development; Country Club Law; Trade Association Law; Nonprofit Organizations Law.

SOOY, KATHLEEN T.
1001 PENNSYLVANIA AVENUE, NW
WASHINGTON, DC 20004-2595
202-624-2500
Fax: 202-628-5116
www.crowell.com
• Terry L. Albertson, Partner
(202) 624-2635
talbertson@crowell.com
• Shauna E. Alonge, Partner
(202) 624-2742
salonge@crowell.com
• Paul Alp, Counsel
(202) 624-2747
palp@crowell.com
• Katheryn W. Holmes Johnson, Director, media PR Communications
• Jessica O'Neil, Manager, media PR and communications
• Meredith Reilly, Specialist, PR
Description:
Represents college athletic departments.
Services:
Expertise: Administrative Law/Regulatory; Aerospace; Agriculture; Alternative Dispute Resolution; Antitrust; Appellate Practice; Associations; Automotive; Aviation; Bankruptcy; C&M; Capitolink; C&M International; Chemicals; Class Actions; Construction; Corporate Employee Benefits; Energy; European Practice; False Claims; Forest Products; Government Affairs; Government Contracts; Hazardous Materials; Health Care; Insurance; Intellectual Property; International Arbitration; Investment Management; Labor & Employment; Legislation; Life Sciences; Litigation; Mining; Natural Resources & Environmental; Pharmaceuticals; Plaintiff's Recovery Practice

SOROY, H. MICHAEL
11766 WILSHIRE BOULEVARD
SUITE 270
LOS ANGELES, CA 90025
310-444-7750
Fax: 310-312-1034
office@soroylaw.com
www.soroy.com
• H Michael Soroy, Firm Founder
(310) 444-7750
hms@soroylaw.com
• Fredrik Gran, Associate
(310) 444-7750
• H. Michael Soroy, Founder
(310) 444-7750
• Peter C Ver. Halen, Of Counsel
(310) 444-7750
• Asa Rosen, Business Operations Specialist
(310) 444-7750
• Iselin J. Tveitnes, Paralegal
(310) 444-7750
Description:
Entertainment, Sports and Leisure Law.
Services:
Handles cases in the areas of business & commercial law; business organizations; contracts; collections; international law; trademarks; travel, tourism & leisure law; estate planning; probate & estate administration; and residential & commercial real estate.
Year Founded:
1991

SQUIRE, SANDERS & DEMPSEY, LLP
127 PUBLIC SQUARE
4900 KEY TOWER
CLEVELAND, OH 44114
216-479-8500
Fax: 216-479-8780
www.ssd.com
• Frederick R. Nance, Managing Partner
(216) 479-8623
fnance@ssd.com
• Cipriano S. Beredo, III, Partner
(216) 479-8280
cberedo@ssd.com
• Rick Horrow, Counsel
(305) 577-2825
rhorrow@ssd.com
• Stephen Lerner, Partner
(513) 361-1220
slerner@ssd.com
Description:
Founded 1890, Squire, Sanders & Dempsey LLP has lawyers in 32 offices and 15 countries around the world. With one of the strongest integrated global platforms and their longstanding one-firm philosophy, Squire Sanders provides seamless legal counsel worldwide. Squire Sanders is ideally positioned to closely monitor legal developments that affect athletes, as well as sports teams, leagues, related businesses and goverments seeking to succeed in an increasingly global sports and entertainment marketplace. With a full range of legal services that assist clients in their management and marketing efforts, they have helped organizations and individ
Services:
All forms of dispute resolution including litigation; bond offerings and project financings; business, tax and estate planning issues for the post-career period; contract negotiations; how to maximize endorsement opportunities; legal aspects of

marketing and public relations activities; and protection of image and other intellectual property

STEARNS WEAVER MILLER
150 W FLAGLER STREET
SUITE 2200
MUSEUM TOWER
MIAMI, FL 33130
305-789-3200
Fax: 305-789-3395
info@stearnsweaver.com
www.stearnsweaver.com
• Alan H. Fein, Shareholder
(305) 789-3416
afein@swmwas.com
• Arturo J. Fernandez, Associate
(305) 789-3296
afernandez@swmwas.com
Nature of Service:
Represents professional sports franchises and athletes on a variety of subject matters and litigation.

STEIN, SPERLING, BENNETT, DE JONG, DRISCOLL & GREENFEIG, P.C.
25 W MIDDLE LANE
ROCKVILLE, MD 20850
301-340-2020
800-435-5230
Fax: 301-340-8217
info@steinsperling.com
www.steinsperling.com
• Fred A. Balkin, Principal
(301) 838-3225
fbalkin@steinsperling.com
• Millard S. Bennett, Principal
(301) 838-3203
mbennett@steinsperling.com
• Alexia Ke Bourgerie, Principal
(301) 838-3232
abourgerie@steinsperling.com
• David S. De Jong, Principal
(301) 838-3204
ddejong@steinsperling.com
• Fred Balkin, Principal
(301) 838-3225
fbalkin@steinsperling.com
• Millard Bennett, Principal
(301) 838-3203
mbennett@steinsperling.com
• Jolie Deutschman, Principal
(301) 738-2222
jdeutschman@steinsperling.com
• David Driscoll, Principal
(301) 838-3205
ddriscoll@steinsperling.com
• Monica Harms, Principal
(301) 838-3230
mharms@steinsperling.com
• Micah Bonaviri, Associate
(301) 838-3235
mbonaviri@steinsperling.com
Services:
Concentrates around various practice groups including business & tax, employment law, technology & e-commerce, estate planning & probate, family law, real property & commercial leasing, criminal law and injury law.
Description:
Contract negotiation, post career planning, investment contract negotiation, federal/state tax filings, IRS audits, appeals and litigation, endorsement exploration, tort actions. Tax Law; Tax Controversies; Estate Planning; Business Law; Professional Practices; Business Valuation.

STEINBERG, LEIGH
1280 BEACH AVENUE
SUITE 800
NEWPORT BEACH, CA 92660-4258
949-720-9121
Fax: 949-720-1331
• Leigh Steinberg
Services:
Areas of practice include contract negotiation, post career planning, arbitration hearings, and endorsement exploration.

STEPHEN D. LINETT, ATTORNEY AT LAW
1900 AVENUE OF THE STARS
SUITE 1100
LOS ANGELES, CA 90067
310-284-8277
Fax: 310-203-9428
linettemark@aol.com
• Steve Linett, Owner
Services:
Long time Attorney Agent representing athletes, coaches and sports broadcasters snce 1980. All phases of athlete representation including contract negotiations, financial planning, and post-career counseling, endorsement and legal advice.

STIMPERT & FORD, LLP
6300 WILSHIRE BOULEVARD
SUITE 1890
LOS ANGELES, CA 90048-5220
323-782-6782
888-907-3801
Fax: 323-677-2233
info@stimpertford.com
• Daniel P. Stimpert
(323) 782-6782
dpstimpert@stimpertford.com
• Daniel P. Stimpert, Attorney
• Ian J. J. Ford, Attorney
(323) 782-6782
ianjford@stimpertford.com
Services:
Real Estate Law, Real Estate & Construction Litigation, Commercial Collection & Commercial Law, Contract & Partnership Litigation, Tort Litigation, Insurance Defense
Clients:
The Arba Group, ICO Investment Group, La Curacao Business Center, Surety Trust Deed Services, Mika Company, Glendale Memorial Hospital and Health Center, Touring & Tasting Magazine, Lisanti, s.r.l., Travertini Paradiso s.r.l., Randolph International Trading Company, F&A Cheese/F&A Dairy

STINSON MORRISON HECKER LLP
1850 N CENTRAL AVENUE
SUITE 2100
PHOENIX, AZ 85004
602-279-1600
Fax: 602-240-6925
www.stinson.com
• Michael C. Manning, Partner
(602) 212-8503
mmanning@stinson.com
• James P. Armstrong, Partner
(602) 212-8605
jarmstrong@stinsonmoheck.com
• C. Ta Ashworth, Partner
(602) 212-8626
tashworth@stinsonmoheck.com

• Christian C. M. Beams, Associate
(602) 212-8609
cbeams@stinsonmoheck.com
• Mark D. Hinderks, Managing Partner
(816) 691-2706
mhinderks@stinson.com
• Terry E. Brummer, Chief Operating Officer
(816) 691-3366
tbrummer@stinson.com
• Allison M. Murdock, Deputy Managing Partner
(816) 691-3138
amurdock@stinson.com
• Doug Doerfler, Chief Financial Officer
(816) 691-3209
ddoerfler@stinson.com
• Vic A. Peterson, Chief Information Officer
(816) 691-2461
vpeterson@stinson.com
Services:
Delivers quality services from business litigation, commercial finance and business issues, to complex bankruptcy matters, intellectual property and media law, and banking matters.

STOCKTON & HING, P.A.
6609 N SCOTTSDALE ROAD
DEAUVILLE BUILDING
SUITE 202
SCOTTSDALE, AZ 85250
480-447-9649
Fax: 480-483-7721
Robert.Ong.Hing@webmail.azbar.org
www.martindale.com
• Robert On Hing, Member
(480) 951-0882
Robert.Ong.Hing@webmail.azbar.org
• Gregory Hing, Member
(480) 447-9649
Greg.Hing@azbar.org
• Robert Hing, Member
(480) 447-9649
• Henderson Stockton, Member
Year Founded:
1962.
Clients:
Representative Clients: Alliance of American Insurers; American Council of Life Insurance; Amica Mutual Insurance Company; Arizona Conference Corporation of Seventh-Day Adventists; Arizona Life & Disability Insurance Guaranty Fund; Arizona Property and Casualty Insurance Guaranty Fund; Chubb Life Insurance Co.; Cities West Publishing, Inc.; Equitable Insurance Services; Globe Life & Accident Insurance Co.; Great Republic Life Insurance Co.; Northwestern Mutual Life Insurance Co.; Pilgram Screw Corp.; Rancho Soledad Nurseries; Senate Insurance Co.; Scottsdale Athletic Club; Thunderbird Academy; United American Insurance Company; W.M. Grace.
Sports Service Founded:
1971.
Services:
General Practice. Probate, Estate Planning, Corporate, Real Estate, Insurance Regulatory Law and Legislative Law. General Civil Litigation, Administrative Law, Sports Law.

STOREY, MOYES
1850 N CENTRAL AVENUE
SUITE 1100
PHOENIX, AZ 85004
602-604-2141
Fax: 602-274-9135

• Jay I. Moyes, Member
(602) 604-2141
jimoyes@lawms.com
• Jeffrey L. Sellers, Member
(602) 604-2141
jlsellers@lawms.com
• William J. Sims III, Member
(602) 604-2141
• Jeffery L. A. Sellers, Attorney
jlsellers@law-msh.com
• Jay I. Moyes, Attorney
jimoyes@law-msh.com
• Keith Hendricks, Attorney
khendricks@law-msh.com
• Jeffery C. Zimmerman, Attorney
jczimmerman@law-msh.com
• Steve Wene, Attorney
swene@law-msh.com
Services:
Counsels clients throughout Arizona and the Southwest on a broad range of legal matters.

STRAYER & MIRABILE, P.C.
121 E GREGORY BOULEVARD
KANSAS CITY, MO 64114
816-363-3775
Fax: 816-221-4866
• Craig A. Strayer, Attorney/Partner
Services:
NFLPA workers' compensation panel

STUART LAW FIRM, P.L.L.C
1033 WADE AVENUE
SUITE 202
RALEIGH, NC 27605-1155
919-787-6050
Fax: 919-787-9988
main@stuartlawfirm.com
www.stuartlawfirm.com
• James L. Stuart, Principal
(919) 787-6050
jstuart@stuartlawfirm.com
• Catherine R. Stuart, Principal
(919) 787-6050
cstuart@stuartlawfirm.com
• Theresa S. Dew, Associate
(919) 787-6050
tdew@stuartlawfirm.com
• Charles C. Kyles, Associate
(919) 787-6050
ckyles@stuartlawfirm.com
• James L. Stuart, Member
jstuart@stuartlawfirm.com
• Catherine R. Stuart, Member
cstuart@stuartlawfirm.com
• Theresa S. Dew, Member
tdew@stuartlawfirm.com
• Charles C. Kyles, Member
Services:
Areas of practice include Bankruptcy, Business Law, Dispute Resolution/Mediation, Housing Finance, Insurance Regulatory, Intellectual Property, Municipal Bond Finance, Sports Law, Tax-Exempt Organizations, Workers Compensation
Clients:
North Carolina Self-Insurance Guaranty Association, U.S. Patent and Trademark Office

SULLIVAN FIRM, LTD., THE
2550 W GOLF ROAD
SUITE 101, THE MEADOWS CORPORATE CENTER - EAST TOWER
ROLLING MEADOWS, IL 60008-4501

847-228-1100
Fax: 847-228-5199
sullivan@thesullivanfirmltd.com
thesullivanfirmltd.com
• Terry Sullivan, President
thesullivanfirm@aol.com
• Judy Chessick, Member
thesullivanfirm@aol.com
• Nancy J. Nicol, Member
NJN96@aol.com
• Terry D. Sullivan, President
(847) 228-1100
sullivan@thesullivanfirmltd.com
• Michael Sullivan, Associate
(847) 228-1100
thesullivanfirm@aol.com
• Nancy J. Nicol, Associate
(847) 228-1100
nnicol@thesullivanfirmltd.com
• Judy Chessick, Associate
(847) 228-1100
jchessick@thesullivanfirmltd.com
• Martin J. Healy Jr, Counsel
Services:
Areas of practice include Litigation, Criminal Law, Family Law, Employment Law, Business Law, DWI and Real Estate
Description:
Contract negotiation.

SULLIVAN OLIVARIO & GIOIA LLP
665 MAIN STREET
SUITE 400
BUFFALO, NY 14202-3706
716-854-5300
Fax: 716-854-5299
• Kevin M. Carter, Attorney
• Horace A. Gioia, Attorney
• Charles H. Dougherty, Attorney
Services:
Areas of practice include General Practice, Family Law Adoption, Divorce, and Real Estate Law

SULLIVAN, WARD, BOME, TYLER & ASHER, P.C.
25800 NORTHWESTERN HIGHWAY
1000 MACCABEES CENTER
SOUTHFIELD, MI 48075-8412
248-746-0700
Fax: 248-746-2760
swappc@swappc.com
www.swappc.com
• Anthony A. Asher, Managing Partner
(248) 746-2701
aasher@swappc.com
• Lee C. Patton, Lawyer
(248) 746-2730
lpatton@swappc.com
• Robert E. Sullivan Jr, Lawyer
(248) 746-2738
• Sharon S. Almonrode, Senior Litigation Attorney/Partner
(248) 746-2732
Services:
Areas of practice include Complex Litigation & Creditors/Debtors Rights & Remedies, Business Planning and Licensing, Real Estate Transactions and Litigation, General Litigation, Labor (ERISA, Pension, and Governance), Tax and Estate Planning, Engineering Architectural Construction, Specialty Litigation
Clients:
Acura West, AEGON USA/Life Investors Insurance Company of America, AmerUs Annuity Group Co, Amurcon Corp, Arvo Group, LLC, Beztak Land Companies,

Disability Managerment Services, Inc., Diversified Chemical Technologies, Inc., Franklin Eye Consultants, P.C., Global Home Care, Inc., Hamon Research-Cottrell, Inc., Milacron Inc., Senior Benefit Services, Inc, Shenandoah Life Insurance Company The General Employees' Retirement System of the City of Pontiac, The Policemen's & Firemen's Retirement System of the City of Pontiac, Valenite LLC, Wedge-Mill Tool, Inc., American Dental Group; Community Bank of Dearborn, Cost Plus, Inc., Fifth Third Bank

SUNSERI, J. DOUGLAS
3000 18TH STREET
METAIRIE, LA 70002
504-837-1304
888-703-1304
Fax: 504-833-2843
• J. Douglas Sunseri, Lawyer
(504) 837-1304
• Albert J. Nicaud, Lawyer
(504) 837-1304
• Frank Th Fradella, Lawyer
(504) 837-1304
• James G. Washburn, Lawyer
(504) 837-1304
Services:
Areas of practice include General Liability, Coverage Issues, Worker's Compensation, Property & Casualty, Auto Liability, and Employer Liability
Clients:
Continental National Indemnity Company, Bridgefield Casualty Insurance Company, The Allen Insurance Group, Risk Management Services, Inc., The St. Paul Companies/USF&G, Louisiana State Board of Home Inspectors, Louisiana Department of Transportation and Development, Louisiana Nursing Home Association-Self-Insured Fund, Louisiana Employers Safety Association-Self Insured Fund, Louisiana Retailers Association-Self Insured Fund, Louisiana Hospital Association-Self Insured Fund, Hospital Services of Louisiana, Inc., Ashington University, Delgado University, The Bottle Water Company, Vinson Guard Service, B&I Welding and Consultants, Inc., AppleOn
Description:
Contract negotiation.

SWADOS, ROBERT
ONE CANAL SIDE
125 MAIN STREET
BUFFALO, NY 14203-2887
716-847-8400
Fax: 716-852-6100
www.phillipslytle.com
• Morgan G. Graham, Partner
(716) 847-7070
mgraham@phillipslytle.com
• Frederick G Attea, Partner
(716) 847-7010
fattea@phillipslytle.com
• Thomas C. Bailey, Partner
(716) 847-5410
tbailey@phillipslytle.com
• Robert O. Swados, Special Counsel
(716) 504-5728
rswados@phillipslytle.com
Description:
Represents professional sports teams.
Services:
Areas of practice include Commercial (Banking & Commercial, Bankruptcy &

Creditors' Rights, Real Estate, Telecommunications, Public Finance); Corporate (Corporate and Securities, Employee Benefits, Immigration, Intellectual Property, Franchise, Health Care, Tax, Family Wealth Planning(Family Wealth Planning); Labor & Employment(Labor & Employment, Education Law); Trial(Business Disputes, Antitrust, Accountants' Liability, Banking/Lender, Liability, Breach of Contract, Business Torts, Class Actions, ConstructionE-Commerce/Computer, Law, ERISA, Franchise and Distributorship, Relations, Fraud/RICO, Health Care, Insurance Coverage.

Clients:
ABB Automation, Inc., Archer Daniels Midland Company, BlueCross BlueShield of Western New York, Catholic Health System, Cello-Pack Corporation, Citibank, N.A., Coach, Inc., Davis Ulmer Sprinkler Company, Inc., DuPont, Emerson Electric Co., Ford Motor Credit Company, HSBC Bank USA, National Association, Keybank, N.A., Nassau County Industrial Development Agency, National Fuel, Platinum LLC, Rich Products Corporation, Sevenson Environmental Services, The Sovran Companies, UnumProvident Corporation, W.R. Grace & Co.

SWARBRICK, JR., JACK
UNIVERSITY OF NOTRE DAME
NOTRE DAME, IN 46556
574-631-5000
www.nd.edu
• John B. Swarbrick, Jr., Athletics Director
• John Affleck-Graves, Executive Vice President
• Terrill D. Albright, Partner
(317) 237-1262
Terry.Albright@bakerd.com
• James A. Aschleman, Partner
(317) 237-1131
Jim.Aschleman@bakerd.com
Services:
Areas of practice include Antitrust, Appellate Practice, Business Planning, China, Commercial, Financial and Bankruptcy, Construction, Corporate Finance, Education Law, Employee Benefits, Energy and Public Utilities Environmental Law, Government Affairs, Health Care, Immigration, Individual/Family, Insurance and Financial Services, Intellectual Property International, Labor and Employment, Life Sciences Litigation, Medical Device and Pharmaceuticals, Nonprofit Private Equity, Venture Capital and Investment Management, Product Liability, Public Finance, Real Estate/Land Use, Sports and Entertainment, Tax, Transportation, Trusts and Estates
Clients:
Alimentation Couche-Tard Inc. (ACT), American Commercial Lines, BorgWarner Inc., Bridgestone Corporation, Bunge North America, Inc. , Central Indiana Corporate Partnership, Circle K, Citizens Gas & Coke Utility, City of Indianapolis, Clarian Health Partners, Cummins Inc., Eli Lilly and Company, Fleetwood Enterprises, Guidant Corporation, Indiana Department of Insurance, Indiana University, Indianapolis Bond Bank, Indianapolis Public Schools, Integra Bank Corporation, J.P. Morgan Chase & Co., Kimball International Inc., Lear

Corporation, Lehman Brothers, Lilly Endowment, Mac's Convenience Stores LLC, Mittal Steel USA, Inc.
Description:
Represents major sports events.

TALLEY, ANTHONY, HUGHES & KNIGHT L.L.C.
322 COLUMBIA STREET
PO BOX 340
BOGALUSA, LA 70427
985-732-7151
866-517-8245
Fax: 985-732-1664
info@tahk.net
www.tahk.net
• E. B. Dittmer, II, Attorney
(985) 732-7151
ebd@tahk.net
• Charles M. Hughes Jr, Member
(985) 624-5010
cmhjr@tahk.net
• Craig J. Robichaux, Lawyer/Member
(985) 624-5010
cjr@tahk.net
• Paul S. Hughes, Lawyer
psh@tahk.net
Services:
Handles legal matters in the following practice areas: General Civil Practice, Trials, Probate, Real Property, Personal Injury, Banking and Corporate Law, Environmental Workers Compensation, Insurance, Banking, Real Estate, Trusts and Estates, and Litigation, as well as a general Corporate and Civil Practice.
Clients:
Aetna Casualty and Surety Co.; Audubon Insurance Co.; New Hampshire Indemnity Co.; South Carolina Insurance Co.; Trinity Insurance Co.; Security Insurance Co.; Hewitt-Coleman & Associates; Pacific Marine Insurance Co.; Employers National Insurance Co.; Louisiana Farm Bureau Casualty Insurance Co.; Louisiana Farm Bureau Mutual Insurance Co.; Southern Farm Bureau Casualty Insurance Co.; Southern Farm Bureau Mutual Insurance Co.; Mississippi Farm Bureau Casualty Insurance Co.; Texas Farm Bureau Casualty Insurance Co.; Louisiana Insurance Guaranty Association; State of Louisiana, Office of Risk Management; Houston General Insurance Co.
Nature of Sports Service:
All phases of athlete representation including contract negotiation, long-range planning, financial planning, and post-career counseling.

TARSHES, DAVID C.
1201 THIRD AVENUE
SUITE 2200
SEATTLE, WA 98101-3045
206-622-3150
Fax: 206-757-7700
seattle@dwt.com
www.dwt.com
• David C. Tarshes, Partner
(206) 622-3150
davidtarshes@dwt.com
• Greg F. Adams, Partner
(206) 622-3150
gregadams@dwt.com
Description:
Represents professional sports teams, tort actions/litigation, representation of leagues, associations, in litigation.

Services:
Areas of practice include Admiralty & Maritime, Advertising & Marketing Law, Aircraft Industry, Antitrust, Appellate Litigation, Business & Corporate, China Practice/Shanghai Office, Construction, Corporate Diversity Counseling, Corporate Finance, Credit Recovery & Bankruptcy, Education, eHealth/HIPAA, Emerging Business & Technology, Employment Related Services, Employee Benefits, Employment, Employment Litigation, Immigration Traditional Labor Energy, Entertainment, Environmental, Estate Planning, Finance & Commercial Law, Financial Services, Food & Agriculture, Government Contracts, Government Investigations & Criminal Defense, Governmental

---

TAULBEE, GEORGE M.
101 S TRYON STREET
SUITE 4000, BANK OF AMERICA PLAZA
CHARLOTTE, NC 28280-4000
704-444-1000
Fax: 704-444-1111
info@alston.com
www.alston.com
• Kenneth F. Britt, Executive Director
(404) 881-7000
ken.britt@alston.com
• Barbara J. Bryant, Chief Marketing Officer
(404) 881-7901
barbara.bryant@alston.com
• Cathy A. Benton, Chief Human Resources Officer
(404) 881-7202
cbenton@alston.com
• Scott Cotie, Chief Financial Officer
(404) 881-7562
scotie@alston.com
• John F. Baron, Partner in Charge
(704) 444-1434
john.baron@alston.com
• David M. Alban, Senior Associate
(704) 444-1174
david.alban@alston.com
• Malachi Alston, Associate
(704) 444-1129
malachi.alston@alston.com
• Blas P. Arroyo, Partner
(704) 444-1012
blas.arroyo@alston.com
Services:
Provides creative solutions to client challenges and an extraordinary skill base in more than a dozen areas of legal service, including a variety of transactional, litigational, tax, and intellectual property and technology services.
Clients:
Aflac, AIG, ALCOA, Allegiance Healthcare Corporation, Allied Systems, Altana Inc., ARCADIS, Arthritis Foundation, Assurant, Inc., BB&T, Belk Store Services, Inc., BellSouth Corporation, Bertelsmann AG, BGF Industries, Inc., BNP Residential Properties, Inc., Boral Industries, Inc., Borden, Inc., Bose Corporation, Cable News Network, CGW Southeast Partners & Affiliates, Cingular Wireless LLC, Delta Air Lines, Inc., Dimension Date Holdings, Inc., Duke University, Duke University Management Company, Emory Healthcare, Emory University, Genuine Parts Company, Georgia Hospital Association, Georgia-Pacific Corporation, Global Payments Inc., Gold Kist

Description:
Contract and license negotiation, trademark and copyright protection and enforcement (Auto Sports).

THACHER PROFFITT & WOOD
TWO WORLD FINANCIAL CENTER
NEW YORK, NY 10281
212-912-7400
Fax: 212-912-7751
www.tpw.com
• Paul D. Tvetenstrand, Managing Partner
(212) 912-7452
• Kofi Appenteng, Partner
(212) 912-7418
• Robert C. Azarow, Partner
(212) 912-7815
razarow@tpw.com
• Charles Do Bethill, Partner
(212) 912-8240
Services:
Designs innovative financial structures and deals for the major financial institutions. Practice focus in New York include Banking, Bankruptcy, Compensation & Benefits, Commercial Lending, M&A, Securities, Municipal Finance, Project Finance, Intellectual Property, Global Finance, International Arbitration, Latin America, Investment Company Act of 1940, Investment Advisers Act of 1940, Litigation & Dispute Resolution, Maritime, Real Estate, Structured Finance
Description:
Tort actions/litigation.

THE FERRARO LAW FIRM
600 BRICKELL AVENUE
38TH FLOOR
MIAMI, FL 33131
305-375-0111
800-275-3332
Fax: 305-379-6222
jlf@ferrarolaw.com
www.ferrarolaw.com
• James L. Ferraro, Shareholder
(305) 375-0111
jlf@ferrarolaw.com
• James L. Ferraro, Attorney/Share Holder
(305) 375-0111
• David A. Jagolinzer, Attorney/ Shareholder
• Juan P. Bauta, Attorney
• Sam Holland, Attorney
Services:
Contract negotiation, arbitration hearings, federal/state/international tax filings, tort actions/litigation.
Year Founded:
1985

THE UNIVERSITY OF TULSA COLLEGE OF LAW
3120 E FOURTH PLACE
TULSA, OK 74104
918-631-2401
Fax: 918-631-3126
www.law.utulsa.edu
• Janet Koven Levit, Dean
(918) 631-2400
janet-levit@utulsa.edu
• Martha Cordell, Assistant Dean for Student Compliance an
(918) 631-2445
martha-cordell@utulsa.edu
• Tom Arnold, Associate Dean for Assessment and Instit
(918) 631-3108

mark-arnold@utulsa.edu
• Ray Yasser, Professor
(918) 631-2442
raymond-yasser@utulsa.edu
• Jason Aamodt, Assistant Dean of Online Legal Education
(918) 631-305
jason-aamodt@utulsa.edu
Services:
Provides a unique student-centered environment designed to foster success at every step of the way from admission to placement
Description:
Contract negotiation, teaches sports law, tort actions/litigation, author.

THIES, DAVID
202 LINCOLN SQUARE
PO BOX 189
URBANA, IL 61803-0189
217-367-1126
Fax: 217-367-3752
www.webberthies.com
• Richard L. Thies, Shareholder
(217) 367-1126
rthies@webberthies.com
• Carl M. Webber, General Practice Lawyer/Member
(217) 367-1126
cwebber@webber.com
• David C. Thies, General Practice Lawyer/Member
(217) 367-1126
dthies@webber.com
• Holten D. Summers, General Practice Lawyer/Member
(217) 367-1126
hsummers@webber.com
Description:
Represents sports organizations.
Services:
Areas of practice include General, Appellate, Trial and Federal Practice, Complex Litigation, Probate, Trust, Family, Corporation, Labor/Employment (Management), Taxation, Real Estate, Zoning, Environmental, Health, Banking and Intellectual Property Law
Clients:
Porter Athletic Equipment Co. (Sporting Goods Mfg.); Village of Thomasboro; Illinois Crop Improvement Assoc.; GMS Management of Illinois, Inc. (Real Estate Development & Leasing); Frasca International; Heatlh Care Service Corporation, d/b/a Blue Cross/Blue Shield of Illinois; Regional Health Resource Center, Inc.; National Council of Teachers of English; Illinois-American Water Company; Durst Cycle.

THOMAS & TEAFF
7911 HERSCHEL AVENUE
SUITE 300
PO BOX 3100
LA JOLLA, CA 92038-3100
858-551-1980
Fax: 858-551-1988
www.lawyers.com
• Teaff F. Robert, Principal
(858) 551-1980
Description:
Entertainment and Sports Law, General Business.
Services:
Areas of practice include General Civil

Practice. Estates, Business, Real Property, Negligence, Entertainment and Sports Law, and Personal Injury

THOMAS M. COOLEY LAW SCHOOL
300 S CAPITOL AVENUE
PO BOX 13038
LANSING, MI 48933
517-371-5140
Fax: 517-334-5718
admissions@cooley.edu
www.cooley.edu
• Don LeDuc, President/Dean/Professor
(517) 371-5140
leducd@cooley.edu
• Brent V. Danielson, Chairman of the Board
(517) 371-5140
• Lawrence P. Nolan, Vice Chairman of the Board
(517) 371-5140
nolanl@cooley.edu
• Lawrence P. E. Nolan, Chair
• Louise Alderson, Vice Chair
• Don LeDuc, President and dean
• Cherie L. Beck, Corporate secretary, associate legal counsel
Services:
Focuses on skills training and practical legal education.
Description:
Teaches sports law, torts, product liability.

THOMAS PILACEK & ASSOCIATES
158 TUSKAWILLA ROAD
SUITE 2320
WINTER SPRINGS TOWN CENTER
WINTER SPRINGS, FL 32708
407-278-7243
800-569-8796
Fax: 407-660-8343
• Thomas J. Pilacek, Lawyer
(407) 660-9595
tpilacek@pilacek.com
• John C. Palmerini, Law Clerk
(407) 660-9595
• Deborah C. Brock, Firm Administrator/Paralegal
(407) 660-9595
dbrock@pilacek.com
• Jason Pilacek, Administrative Assistant
(407) 660-9595
Services:
Areas of practice include Private, Public and Federal Sector Employment, Federal & State Litigations, Appeals, Administrative Law & Arbitrations, Contract Preparation and Review, Severance, Non-Compete, and Retirement Agreements, Federal & State Labor, Fair Employment Practice & Civil Rights Laws, Business & Partnership Disputes
Nature of Sports Service:
All phases of athlete representation including contract negotiation, long-range planning, financial planning, and post-career counseling.

THOMAS S. BUSCH
6900 COLLEGE BLVD
SUITE 700
OVERLAND PARK, KS 66211
913-491-5500
Fax: 913-491-3341
www.fulbright.com
• Thomas S. Busch, Member
• Joseph Y. Holman, Member
• Brent A. Mitchell, Attorney

(316) 265-9311
bamitchell@martinpringle.com
• Sam Colville, Member
• Frank Basgall, Attorney
(316) 265-9311
fwbasgall@martinpringle.com
Description:
Sports licensing
Services:
Offers legal assistance in the area of sports organization governance.
Year Founded:
1982

THOMAS, MEANS & GILLIS, P.C.
60 COMMERCE STREET
SUITE 200
PO BOX 5058
MONTGOMERY, AL 36104
334-270-1033
800-626-9684
Fax: 334-260-9396
meansgillislaw.com
• Kenneth L. Thomas, Partner
(334) 270-1033
klthomas@tmgpc.com
• Tyrone C. Means, Managing Partner
(334) 270-1033
tcmeans@tmgpc.com
• H. Le Gillis, Managing Partner
(334) 270-1033
hlgillis@tmgpc.com
• Quinton S. Seay, Partner
(404) 222-8400
qsseay@tmgpc.com
Services:
Legal expertise spans the civil litigation spectrum, including personal injury and wrongful death, insurance law, consumer protection, and workers compensation, labor and employment law, education and government law and civil rights and Constitutional law
Description:
Contract negotiation, tort actions/litigation.

THORSNES, BARTOLOTTA & MCGUIRE
2550 FIFTH AVENUE
11TH FLOOR
SAN DIEGO, CA 92103
619-236-9363
800-577-2922
Fax: 619-236-9653
info@tbmlawyers.com
www.tbmlawyers.com
• Vincent J. Bartolotta Jr, Founding Partner
barlotta@tbmlawyers.com
• John F. McGuire, Jr., Founding Partner
mcguire@tbmlawyers.com
• Kevin F F. Quinn, Partner
quinn@tbmlawyers.com
• Vincent J Bartolotta, Partner
bartolotta@tbmlawyers.com
• John F McGuire, Partner
mcguire@tbmlawyers.com
• Karen R Frostrom, Partner
frostrom@tbmlawyers.com
• Ian Fusselman, Parner
fusselman@tbmlawyers.com
• Michael T Thorsnes, Of counsel
Services:
Services include the areas of Business Litigation, Personal Injury, Construction Defects, Wrongful Death, Medical Malpractice, ERISA, Class Action

TONKON TORP LLP
888 SW FIFTH AVENUE
1600 PIONEER TOWER
PORTLAND, OR 97204
503-221-1440
Fax: 503-274-8779
owen@tonkon.com
www.tonkon.com
• Owen D. Blank, Attorney
(503) 802-2011
owen.blank@tonkon.com
• Ryan M. Bledsoe, Attorney
(503) 802-2120
ryan.bledsoe@tonkon.com
Description:
Contract negotiation, post career planning, investment contract negotiation, arbitration hearings, represents professional sports teams, endorsement exploration. Business, commercial, constitutional, corporate, international, media, real estate, and sports law.
Year Founded:
1974

TREBATOSKI, CHRIS J.
100 E WISCONSIN AVENUE
SUITE 3300
MILWAUKEE, WI 53202
414-271-6560
Fax: 414-277-0656
info@michaelbest.com
www.michaelbest.com
• Thomas E. Obenberger, Managing Partner
(414) 225-4960
teobenberger@michaelbest.com
• David A. Krutz, Chairman, Management Committee
(262) 956-6550
dakrutz@michaelbest.com
• Scott C. Beightol, Partner
(414) 225-4994
scbeightol@michaelbest.com
• Robert J. Johannes, Partner
(414) 225-4954
rjjohannes@michaelbest.com
Description:
Represents professional sports teams.
Services:
Provides complete legal services related to Business, Employment Relations, Health Care, Intellectual Property, Land & Resources, Litigation, Taxation, and Wealth Planning Services.
Clients:
ABS Global, AE Business Solutions, Inc., AMEC Construction Company, American Transmission Company, LLC, Auto Glass Specialists, Inc., Bank of America, Berbee Information Networks Corporation, Blue Cross Blue Shield Association, Cedar Creek Partners LLC, Chicago Metallic Corporation, Clear Channel Outdoor, Inc., Cleary Gull, Coca-Cola Bottling Corp., Conley Publishing Group, Ltd., Derse, Inc., Envirotest Systems Corp., Earth Tech, Ltd., Ecker Enterprises, Inc., The F. Dohmen Company, U.S. Bank, National Association, Fiserv, Inc., Fort James Corporation, Freedom Plastics, Inc., Great Lakes Higher Education Corporation, HK Systems, Inc.

TRIBLER, ORPETT & CRONE
225 W WASHINGTON STREET
SUITE 1300
CHICAGO, IL 60606-3408
312-201-6400
Fax: 312-201-6401

info@tribler.com
www.tribler.com
• Mitchell A. Orpett, Director
(312) 201-6413
maorpett@tribler.com
• Willis R. Tribler, Director
(312) 201-6417
wrtribler@tribler.com
• Michael J. Meyer, Director
(312) 201-6435
mjmeyer@tribler.com
• Jeremy N. H. Boeder, Attorney
Services:
Areas of practice includes General Liability Defense, Labor and Employment, Insurance Coverage, Insurance Agents and Brokers, Construction Law, Directors and Officers Liability, Environmental Law & Toxic Torts, Insurance Insolvency and Regulatory Practice, Legal Malpractice, Medical Malpractice, Municipal Law, Petroleum Industries, Product Liability, Real Estate Agents and Brokers, Reinsurance
Description:
Arbitration hearings, tort actions/litigation.
Year Founded:
1978

VAINISI, JEROME R.
222 N LASALLE STREET
SUITE 300
CHICAGO, IL 60601
312-704-3000
Fax: 312-704-3001
info@hinshawlaw.com
www.hinshawlaw.com
• Paul R. Boken, Executive Managing Director
(312) 704-3208
pboken@hinshawlaw.com
• Donald L. Mrozek, Chairman
(312) 704-3111
dmrozek@hinshawlaw.com
• Jerome R. Vainisi, Partner
(312) 704-3166
jvainisi@hinshawlaw.com
Nature of Sports Service:
All phases of athlete representation including contract negotiation, income tax planning and preparation, estate planning, financial planning, and post-career counseling, marketing.
Services:
Provides a full-service practice with an emphasis in commercial litigation, products and general liability defense litigation, corporate, environmental and employment law, as well as the representation of professionals in their risk management and liability matters

VAN DER SMISSEN, BETTY
HPER 308
UNIVERSITY OF ARKANSAS
FAYETTEVILLE, AR 72701
Description:
Teaches sports law.
Services:
Provides Health, Physical Education and Leisure Services education in its 6 major divisions: Athletic Training; Health Promotion and Education; Leisure, Youth and Human Services; Physical Education; Graduate Studies; and Liberal Arts

professional services

VILLARINI & HENRY
16 MAIN STREET
HAMBURG, NY 14075
716-312-1136
888-834-8623
Fax: 716-648-1806
dhenry@villariniandhenry.com
www.villariniandhenry.com
• Robert M. Villarini, Lawyer and Partner
(716) 648-0510
bert@villariniandhenry.com
• Daniel John Henry, Jr., Lawyer & Partner
(716) 312-1136
dhenry@villariniandhenry.com
Services:
Offers high-quality representation based on a thorough understanding of the area of Criminal Law, Personal Injury/Negligence and Sports Law involving Professional Athletes' injury claims

VINET, MARK
63 DES FRENES
VAUDREUIL-SUR-LE-LAC
QUEBEC, CANADA J7V 8P3
450-510-1102
Fax: 450-510-1095
mark@markvinet.com
www.markvinet.com
• Mark Vinet, Author/Historian/Entertainment Lawyer
(450) 510-1102
markvinet@videotron.ca
Services:
Teaches college level history, entertainment business, contracts and copyright law courses.
Description:
Sports and entertainment law.

VLADECK WALDMAN ELIAS & ENGELHARD, P.C.
1501 BROADWAY
SUITE 800
NEW YORK, NY 10036-5560
212-403-7300
Fax: 212-221-3172
info@vladeck.com
www.vladeck.com
• Debra L. Raskin, Partner
(212) 403-7300
• Anne C. Vladeck, Partner
(212) 403-7327
avladeck@vladeck.com
• Debra L. Raskin, Partner
(212) 403-7300
draskin@vladeck.com
• Ivan D. Smith, Partner
(212) 403-7300
ismith@vladeck.com
Services:
Areas of practice includes Employment, Labor, Employee Benefits, General Litigation, Entertainment, Sports and the Arts, Non-profits and Pro Bono Commitment

VORYS, SATER, SEYMOUR & PEASE
52 E GAY STREET
PO BOX 1008
COLUMBUS, OH 43215
614-464-6400
www.vorys.com
• W. Jonathan Airey, Partner
(614) 464-6346
wjairey@vssp.com
• Raymond D. Anderson, Partner
(614) 464-6447

rdanderson@vssp.com
• Sandra J. Anderson, Partner
(614) 464-6405
sjanderson@vssp.com
• Julie K. R. Brown, Technology Executive Manager
(614) 464-5684
crauge@vssp.com
Description:
Contract negotiation, post career planning, federal/state/international tax filings, licensing, endorsement exploration, teaches sports law.
Services:
Areas of practice include Commercial & real Estate, Corporate & Finance, Energy& Utility, environment, Government & Lobbying, Health Care, intellectual Property, International, Labor 7 Employment, Litigation, Probate & Estate Planning, Tax, Technology, and Toxic Tort
Clients:
The Scotts Company, United States Shoe Corporation, Stringfellow, Tybouts Corner, ChemDyne, and Fields Brook, Honda of America, Mfg., Inc., Wendy's International, Inc., The Limited, Inc., Worthington Industries, Inc., Bob Evans Farms, Inc., and Eaton Corporation, Citibank, IBM, Columbia Gas Transmission Company, Nigerian National Petroleum Corporation

WAGENHEIM & WAGNER, P.A.
100 SOUTHEAST 3RD AVENUE
7TH FLOOR
ONE FINANCIAL PLAZA
FORT LAUDERDALE, FL 33394
954-564-4800
Fax: 954-564-5121
info@sportsinjurylaw.com
www.sportsinjurylaw.com
• Richard Wagenheim, Lawyer/Partner
(954) 564-4800
richw@sportsinjurylaw.com
• Barbara Wagner, Lawyer/Partner
(954) 564-4800
barbw@sportsinjurylaw.com
Clients:
List of professional athlete clients are players from the National Football League, Arena Football League, NFL Europe, Major League Baseball, Minor League Baseball, National Hockey League, East Coast Hockey League, International Hockey League and Major League Soccer.
Nature of Sports Service:
Workers' compensation injury and disability claims for professional athletes (members of NFLPA, AFLPA panel of workers compensation attorneys) Represent players from the NFL, AFL, NFLE, Major and Minor League Baseball, Hockey, Soccer, NHLPA and PHPA.

WALES, SCOTT A.
9001 N 76TH STREET
SUITE 310
MILWAUKEE, WI 53223-1911
414-357-7555
• Jerome T. Safer, Lawyer
(414) 357-7555
• Martin R. Stein, Lawyer
(414) 357-7555
• Scott A. Wales, Lawyer
(414) 357-7555
• Fredrick J. Safer, Attorney
• Martin R. Stein, Attorney

Services:
Areas of practice include contract negotiation, endorsement exploration, and tort actions/litigation

WALL LAW OFFICES, PLLC
4310 N 75TH STREET
SUITE B
SCOTTSDALE, AZ 85251
480-222-3888
Fax: 480-990-7860
Stephen.Wall@azbar.org
• Stephen M. M. Wall, Lawyer
(480) 222-3888
Stephen.Wall@azbar.org
Services:
Areas of practice include DUI/DWI, Extreme DUI, Aggravated DUI, Vehicular Homicide, All Criminal Offenses, Motorcycle & Auto Accidents, Serious Injury and Death

WARE, R. DAVID
504 BUTLER NATIONAL DRIVE
DULUTH, GA 30097
404-402-0204
Fax: 770-813-9776
• Robert Da Ware, Lawyer
(404) 402-0204
rdware@aol.com
Services:
Areas of practice include General Practice and Trial Law, Tort and Insurance Practice, and Local Government Law
Description:
Contract negotiation.

WARSHAFSKY LAW FIRM
839 N JEFFERSON STREET
SUITE 300
MILWAUKEE, WI 53202
414-276-4970
800-728-4970
Fax: 414-276-5533
www.warshafsky.com
• Frank T. Crivello, II, Lawyer
(414) 276-4970
• Ted M Warshafsky, Lawyer
(414) 273-4764
• Merton Rotter, Lawyer
(414) 276-4970
• Michael Tarnoff, Lawyer
(414) 276-4970
• Frank T. Crivello, Lawyer
• Gerald J. Bloch, Lawyer
• John R. Schatzman, Lawyer
Description:
Contract negotiation, endorsement exploration.
Services:
Areas of practice focus on personal injury law, including automobile accidents, medical malpractice, wrongful death and product liability

WATSON, RICHARD
925 EUCLID AVENUE
2000 HUNTINGTON BUILDING
CLEVELAND, OH 44115-1496
216-696-4700
Fax: 216-696-2706
law@spiethbell.com
www.spiethbell.com
• J. Talbot Young, Partner
(216) 535-1066
tyoung@spiethbell.com
• Richard T Watson, Lawyer
(216) 696-4700

923

richardtwatson@worldnet.att.net
• James R. Bright, Shareholder
(216) 696-4700
jbright@spiethbell.com
Description:
Represents professional sports teams.
Services:
Areas of practice include Business Law and Tax, Employment Law, Estate Planning & Personal Tax, Labor Law, liquor Control Law, Litigation, and Real Estate

WATTS, STEVEN R.
10 N LUDLOW STREET
1100 COURTHOUSE PLAZA, SW
DAYTON, OH 45402
937-449-2800
Fax: 937-449-2821
www.chklaw.com
• Richard J. Chernesky, Managing Partner
(937) 449-2804
richard.chernesky@dinslaw.com
• Edward M. Kress, Senior Partners
(937) 449-2830
edward.kress@dinslaw.com
• Richard A. Broock, Senior Partner
rab@chklaw.com
• Alexander A. R. Arestides, Associate
(937) 463-4935
alexander.arestides@dinsmore.com
• James E. Beyer, Partner
(937) 449-6438
james.beyer@dinsmore.com
• Richard A. Broock, Partner
(93-) 49-2840
richard.broock@dinsmore.com
• Frederick J. Caspar, Partner
(937) 449-2818
fred.caspar@dinsmore.com
• Joshua J. Chernesky, Associate
(937) 449-2811
joshua.chernesky@dinsmore.com
Description:
Contract negotiation.
Services:
Areas of practice include Business Law, Mergers and Acquisitions, Real Estate, Litigation, Securities, Taxation, Regulated Industries, Employment Law Counseling, Compensation, Retirement, and Employee Benefit Plans, Estate Planning and Administration, Probate Law, Banking, Product Liability, and Health Care Law
Clients:
AAA Miami Valley, Advantage Per Diem Staffing, LLC, AK Steel, Architectural Resources Corporation, The Aristocrat Products Mfg. Co., Audi of America, Inc., The Berry Company, Better Business Bureau of Dayton/Miami Valley, Inc., Bradstreet & Company, Inc., Bri Lyn, Inc., Brown Industrial, Inc., CBS Personnel Services, LLC, Central State University Foundation, CFA Holding, Inc., Chiropractic Health & Wellness Center, Inc., Church of the Messiah, The Connor Group, CSA Nutrition Services, Inc., Day International, Inc., Dayton Christian School, Inc., The Dayton Heart Center, Inc., The Dayton-Montgomery County Port Authority, Digital Concepts, Inc.

WEBB, WILLIAM Y.
1735 MARKET STREET
51ST FLOOR
PHILADELPHIA, PA 19103-7599

215-665-8500
Fax: 215-864-8999
www.ballardspahr.com
• Brian Walsh, Partner
(215) 864-8510
walsh@ballardspahr.com
• Arlene J Angelo, Partner
(215) 864-8133
angeloa@ballardspahr.com
• Steven Arbittier, Partner
(215) 864-8125
arbittier@ballardspahr.com
• Lynn Axelroth, Partner
(215) 864-8707
axelroth@ballardspahr.com
Description:
Represents professional sports teams, teaches sports law, mergers and acquisitions.
Services:
Areas of practice inclide Business and Finance, Construction, Employee Benefits, Energy and Project Finance, Environmental, Housing, Labor, Employment & Immigration, Litigation, Public Finance, Real Estate Leasing, Securities, Secularization, Tax, technology and emerging Companies, Telecommunications, Transactional Finance, Zoning and Land Use
Clients:
Comcast Corporation, Exelon Corporation, Going Global, Greka Energy Corporation, Leading the Way, Puratos Group, The Legal Services Corporation, Tractebel SA, Vision in a Virtual World, Overture to the Future, The Johns Hopkins University Downtown Center, The Philadelphia Phillies, The Ritz-Carlton, Exelon Corporation, Greka Energy Corporation, Leading the Way, An Urban Village, A League of Their Own.

WEBER & BAER, LLP
2029 CENTURY PARK E
SUITE 1400
LOS ANGELES, CA 90067
310-226-7570
Fax: 310-226-7571
jweber@weberbaer.com
www.weberbaer.com
• Jonathan S. Weber, Member
• Tracy Mi Baer, Member
• Andrew Treger, Member
• Jonathan S. Weber, Attorney
• Tracy Baer, Attorney
• Eric G. Rudin, Attorney
Services:
Provides services in the following areas: personal injury, plaintiffs personal injury, medical malpractice, products liability, negligence, automobile accidents and injuries, wrongful death, nursing home abuse.

WEIL, GOTSHAL & MANGES
767 FIFTH AVENUE
NEW YORK, NY 10153
212-310-8000
Fax: 212-310-8007
www.weil.com
• Stephen J. Dannhauser, Chairman
(212) 310-8326
stephen.dannhauser@weil.com
• Brad D. Scott, Executive Director
(212) 310-8271
brad.scott@weil.com
• Nancy L. Gray, Legal Recruiting Manager
(212) 735-4554

• Elizabeth A. Ventura, Senior director, communications
• Ashley Laputka, PR manager
• Meredith Moore, Director of global diversity
• Naima Walker-fierce, Director of legal recruiting
Description:
Contract negotiation, arbitration hearings, licensing, endorsement exploration, tort actions/litigation.
Services:
Areas of practice include Antitrust/Competition, Banking & Finance, Bankruptcy Litigation, Business Finance & Restructuring, Capital Markets, Complex Commercial, Litigation, Corporate, Corporate Governance, Employment, Financial Services, Global Dispute Resolution, Intellectual Property & Media, International Trade, Litigation/Regulatory, Mergers & Acquisitions, Patent Litigation, Private Equity, Product Liability/Mass Tort/Environmental, Real Estate Transactions & Finance, Securities/Corporate Governance, Structured Finance/Derivatives, Tax, and Trusts & Estates

WEILER, PAUL C.
1563 MASSACHUSETTS AVENUE
CAMBRIDGE, MA 2138
617-495-2955
Fax: 617-496-4865
pweiler@law.harvard.edu
www.law.harvard.edu
• Elena Kagan, Dean
(617) 495-4601
• Paul C. Weiler, Professor of Law
(617) 495-2955
pweiler@law.harvard.edu
• Henry J. Steiner, Director, Human Rights Program
(617) 495-3107
hsteiner@law.harvard.edu
• Paul C. Weiler, Henry J. Friendly Professor of Law
(617) 495-2955
pweiler@law.harvard.edu
Services:
Provides unparalleled opportunities to study law and related disciplines in an energetic and creative learning environment
Description:
Investment contract negotiation, represents sports organizations, teaches sports law.

WEINER, MICHAEL
12 E 49TH STREET
24TH FLOOR
NEW YORK, NY 10017
212-826-0808
Fax: 212-752-4378
feedback@mlbpa.org
www.mlbplayers.com
• Donald M. Fehr, Executive Director
(212) 826-0808
feedback@mlbpa.org
• Michael Weiner, General Counsel
(212) 826-0808
feedback@mlbpa.org
• Judy Heeter, Business Affairs and Licensing Director
(212) 826-080
feedback@mlbpa.org
• Gene Orza, Chief Operating Officer
(212) 826-080
feedback@mlbpa.org

Description:
Assistant General Counsel to Major League Baseball Players Association.
Services:
Aims to encourage citizen participation and direct action; promote economic justice and oppose corporate welfare; resist over-commercialization; foster informed and principled consumers; emphasize fan-friendliness; promote sustainability; cultivate personal and global responsibility; fight for inclusion, equal opportunity and respect for diversity; combat performance-enhancing drug use; encourage respectful fan behavior; resist network control; highlight physical fitness and participation; challenge media fusion with franchises, leagues and governing bodies.

WEISMAN, PAUL
15301 VENTURA BOULEVARD
SUITE # 300
SHERMAN OAKS, CA 91403-3129
818-986-9525
www.lagop.org
• Paul Weisman, Lawyer
(818) 986-9525
pweisman1@socal.rr.com
• Mark Vafiades, Chairman
mark@lagop.org
• Stephen C. Smith, First Vice Chairman
stephen@lagop.org
• Arturo Alas, Second Vice Chairman
arturo@lagop.org
Services:
Tax & Sports attortney, estate planning, tax controversy representation, corporate law, sports law and mediation.
Clients:
BNA Tax Management Portfolio on Federal Tax Collection Procedure 638 2d.
Description:
Taxation Law, Contract negotiation.

WEISS, STEPHEN L.
320 E VIRGINIA AVENUE
PHOENIX, AZ 85004
602-254-1977
888-650-4798
800-358-CATS
email@taylorandassociates.net
www.injuredworker.com
• Richard Taylor, Managing Attorney
(602) 254-2220
richard@taylorandassociates.net
• Thomas C. Whitley, Managing Attorney
(928) 526-4160
thomas@taylorandassociates.net
• Brian A. Weekley, Associate
(602) 254-1977
brian@taylorandassociates.net
• Roger A. Schwartz, Associate
(602) 257-5018
roger@taylorandassociates.net
Services:
Areas of practice include personal injury, workers' compensation, and social secuirty disability
Clients:
Kingman, Bullhead City, Lakeside, Payson, Mesa and Casa Grande
Description:
NFLPA workers' compensation panel.

WEISTART, JOHN C.
210 SCIENCE DRIVE
BOX 90362
DURHAM, NC 27708
919-613-7006
Fax: 919-613-7257
admissions@law.duke.edu
www.law.duke.edu
• David F. Levi, Dean
(919) 613-7006
levi@law.duke.edu
• William Hoye, Associate Dean, Admissions and Financial
(919) 613-8533
hoye@law.duke.edu
• Bruce A. Elvin, Assistant Dean, Career Services
(919) 613-7084
Elvin@law.duke.edu
• Theresa Newman, Associate Dean, Academic Affairs
(919) 613-7133
Newman@law.duke.edu
Description:
Post career planning, arbitration hearings, represents professional sports teams, teaches sports law, consulting.
Services:
Prepares students for responsible and productive lives in the legal profession, and, as a community of scholars, the Law School also provides leadership at the national and international levels in efforts to improve the law and legal institutions through teaching, research and other forms of public service

WELCH & CONDON
1109 TACOMA AVENUE S
PO BOX 1318
TACOMA, WA 98402
253-383-3427
Fax: 253-572-8957
info@welchcondon.com
www.welchcondon.com
• David B. Condon, Co-Founder
(253) 383-3427
dave@welchcondon.com
• Terri L. Herring-Puz, Associate
(253) 383-3427
therring@harbornet.com
Nature of Service:
Focuses on Workers' Compensation Law
Year Founded:
1978

WENDEL, CHRITTON, PARKS, AND DEBARI CHARTERED
5300 S FLORIDA AVENUE
PO BOX 5378
LAKELAND, FL 33813-4921
941-646-5091
Fax: 941-644-3477
• John F. Wendel, President/Shareholder
(941) 646-5091
• Charles P. Chritton, VP/Shareholder
Description:
Investment contract negotiation, represents sports organizations, arbitration hearings, represents professional sports teams, licensing, tort actions/litigation, stadium construction, team/league transactions.

WILLIAMS, BRIAN P.
501 MAIN STREET
SUITE 305, POST OFFICE BOX 3646
EVANSVILLE, IN 47735-3646

812-423-3183
Fax: 812-423-3841
evvlaw@k2d2.com
www.kddk.com
• Alan N. Shovers, Managing Partner
(812) 423-3183
ashovers@kddk.com
• Thomas O. Magan, Managing Partner
(812) 423-3183
shovers@k2d2.com
• Brian P. Williams, Partner
(812) 423-3183
williams@k2d2.com
• Larry R. Downs, Partner
(812) 423-3183
downs@k2d2.com
Description:
Represents college athletic departments.
Services:
Business Law Services, Bankruptcy, Collection & Creditors' Rights Services, Construction Law Services, Economic Development, Law Services, Education Law Services Environmental Law Services, Estate Planning Services, Family Law & Private, Adoption Services, Health Care Law Services, Immigration Law Services, Intellectual PropertyLaw Services, Labor & Employment
Law Services, Litigation & Trial Services, Real Estate Law Services, Tax & Employee Benefits Law Services
Clients:
Deaconess Hospital, Inc., American General Finance, University of Southern Indiana, Cresline Plastic Pipe Co., Inc., Keller Crescent Co., Inc., Red Spot Paint & Varnish Co., Inc., Lewis Bakeries, Inc., Buchta Leasing, Inc., Wabash General Hospital, The Rehabilitation Center, George Koch Sons, Inc., George Koch Sons, Inc., Toyota Motor Corporate Services of North America, Inc., AK Steel Corporation, Kaiser Aluminum Chemical Corporation, Card Management Corporation, Princeton Mining Company, Inc., Champion Laboratories, Inc., Raben Tire Co., Inc., Tyco Electronics Corporation, Mid-States Rubber Products, Inc., AES Corporation, DSM Engineering.

WILSON, ELSER, MOSKOWITZ ET AL
150 E 42ND STREET
NEW YORK, NY 10017-5639
212-490-3000
Fax: 212-490-3038
info@wilsonelser.com
www.wilsonelser.com
• Mark K. Anesh, Partner
(212) 490-3000
• Tracy J. Abatemarco, Partner
(212) 490-3000
• Bruce Ainbinder, Partner
(212) 490-3000
• Kevie An Aulbach, Partner
(212) 490-3000
• Larry Lum
(212) 490-3000
larry.lum@wilsonelser.com
• Robert T. Adams
(212) 490-3000
• Timothy P. Coon
(212) 490-3000
Services:
Offers counseling, litigation, arbitration and mediation, and other legal services. Represents Fortune 500 companies, including major insurers, and many other commercial, industrial, government and nonprofit entities. Areas of practice include aviation, admiralty and marine, corporate, commercial, professional liability, insurance

coverage, general liability, intellectual property, employment, product liability, real estate and construction.
Description:
Contract negotiation, investments, arbitration hearings, representation of professional sports teams, licensing, endorsement exploration, teaches sports law, tort actions/litigation, representation of sports promoters.

WINSTEAD ATTORNEYS
600 TRAVIS STREET
JPMORGAN CHASE TOWER
SUITE 1100
HOUSTON, TX 77002
713-650-8400
Fax: 713-650-2400
cporter@winstead.com
www.winstead.com
• Cindy Graves, Director of Administration
(713) 650-2777
cgraves@winstead.com
• Greg Erwin, Managing Shareholder
(Houston)
(713) 650-2781
gerwin@winstead.com
• Herb Albritton, Executive Director (Dallas)
• Allen Fuqua, Chief Marketing Officer
(Dallas)
• Glen Pryor, Chief Financial Administrator
(Dallas)
• Dominique Anderson, Director of Attorney
Recruiting (Dallas)
• Patty Stewart, Director of Human
Resources (Dallas)
• Joel Edwards, Director of Information
Technology (Dallas)
• Terri L. Lawrence, Director Library &
Information Resources (Dal
• Tom Forestier, Managing Shareholder
(713) 650-2749
tforestier@winstead.com
• Cindy Graves, Director of Administration
(713) 650-2777
 cgraves@winstead.com
• Zachary B Allie, Associate
(713) 650-2771
zallie@winstead.com
• Frank Amini, Associate
(713) 650-2795
famini@winstead.com
• Kenneth L Anderson, Associate
(713) 650-2648
kanderson@winstead.com
• Holly D Arnold, Associate
(713) 650-2723
harnold@winstead.com
Nature of Services:
The Sports Business and Public Venues Practice at Winstead Attorneys is counsel to major league and minor league teams in the development, operation and management of their franchises.
Clients:
Dallas Cowboys; Houston Texans; San Antonio Spurs; Texas Rangers; Portland Trail Blazers.
Sponsor:
National Sports Forum sponsor and partner.

WOLFE LAW, P.C.
200 W ADAMS STREET
SUITE 2200
CHICAGO, IL 60606
312-727-0403
Fax: 312-727-0406

ken@wolfelawpc.com
www.wolfelawfirmpc.com
• Kenneth Wolfe, President
ken@wolfelawpc.com
Description:
Law firm representing professional athletes in workers' compensation claims.
Year Founded:
2006

WOLOHAN, JOHN T.
953 DANBY ROAD
13 HILL CENTER
ITHACA, NY 14850
607-274-3011
Fax: 607-274-5792
admission@ithaca.edu
www.ithaca.edu
• Thomas R. Rochon, President
(607) 274-3111
president@ithaca.edu
Year Founded:
1893.
Description:
Teaches sports law, tort actions/litigation.

WOMBLE, CARLYLE, SANDRIDGE & RICE, PLLC
ONE W FOURTH STREET
PO BOX 84
WINSTON-SALEM, NC 27101
336-721-3600
Fax: 336-721-3660
mgunter@wcsr.com
www.wcsr.com
• Michael D. Gunter, Lawyer
(336) 721-3607
mgunter@wcsr.com
• Alfred G. Adams, Lawyer
(336) 721-3642
aadams@wcsr.com
• Jean T. Adams, Lawyer
(336) 721-3600
jadams@wcsr.com
• Patrick M. Allen, Lawyer
(336) 721-3574
PAllen@wcsr.com
• Alfred G. Adams, Lawyer
(336) 721-3642
• Jean T. Adams, Lawyer
• Mary Craven Adams, Lawyer
• Reid C. Adams, Lawyer
• Patrick M. Allen, Lawyer
(336) 721-3574
Description:
Contract negotiation, post career planning, federal/state/international tax filings, endorsement exploration.
Services:
Areas of practice include Antitrust, Distribution and Franchise Law; Appellate; Bankruptcy and Creditors' Rights; Capital Markets Business Group; Construction Law; Corporate and Securities; Economic Development; Employee Benefits; Environmental Law and Toxic Tort Litigation; Federal and State Government Affairs; Gaming Law; Government Contracts; Health Care; Insurance, Governmental and Tort Litigation; Intellectual Property; International Trade; Labor & Employment; Patent; Product Liability Litigation; Public Finance; Real Estate; Tax; Telecommunications, Cable & Broadcast; and Trusts & Estates

WONG, GLENN M.
121 PRESIDENTS DRIVE
UNIVERSITY OF MASSACHUSETTS
AMHERST, MA 1003
413-545-0441
Fax: 413-577-0642
www.isenberg.umass.edu
• John V. Lombardi, Chancellor/Professor
(413) 545-2211
lombardi@umass.edu
• Lisa Pi Masteralexis, Department Head
(413) 545-5061
lpmaster@sportmgt.umass.edu
• Carol A. Barr, Associate Department Head
(413) 545-5065
cbarr@sportmgt.umass.edu
• Glenn M. Wong, Professor
(413) 545-5053
gwong@sportmgt.umass.edu
Description:
Arbitration hearings, teaches sports law.
Services:
Offers undergraduate, masters and doctoral programs in a growing number of fields.

WOOD & LAMPING LLP
600 VINE STREET
SUITE 2500
CINCINNATI, OH 45202
513-852-6000
Fax: 513-852-6087
www.woodlamping.com
• Thomas M. Woebkenberg, Lawyer
(513) 852-6044
tmwoebkenberg@woodlamping.com
• Edward D. Bender, Lawyer
(513) 852-6000
edbender@woodlamping.com
• Paul R. Berninger, Lawyer
(513) 852-6000
prberninger@woodlamping.com
• Edward D. H. Bender, Partner
(513) 852-6002
edbender@woodlamping.com
• Paul R. Berninger, Partner
(513) 852-6002
prberninger@woodlamping.com
• Thomas J. Breed, Partner
(513) 852-6076
tjbreed@woodlamping.com
• Rayan F. Coutinho, Partner
(513) 852-6030
rfcoutinho@woodlamping.com
• Susan K. Cliffel, Partner
(513) 852-6040
skcliffel@woodlamping.com
• Gary J. Davis, Partner
(513) 852-6085
gjdavis@woodlamping.com
Services:
Works in the areas of litigation, business, government and land use, employment law, real estate, probate and estate planning, and domestic relations. Areas of practice include Admiralty, Bankruptcy, Business Reorganization, Civil / Commercial Litigation, Computer Law, Contract Negotiations, Construction, Corporate and Finance, Domestic Relations, Elder Law, Employee Benefits, ERISA, Estate Planning/Probate, Family Law, Health Care / Hospital, Insurance Defense, Financial Institutions/Banking, Labor/Employment, Medicaid Planning, Medical Malpractice, Mergers/Acquisitions, Municipal/Governmental, Personal Injury, Product Liability Defense, Pro

Description:
Contract negotiation.

WOOD, RICHARD
1400 R ST.
LINCOLN, NE 68588
402-472-2111
Fax: 402-472-2038
www.unl.edu
• Harvey S. Perlman, Chancellor
(402) 472-2116
hperlman1@unl.edu
• Richard Wood, VP/General Counsel
(402) 472-1201
Description:
Represents college athletic departments.
Services:
A research leader with a wide array of grant-funded projects aimed at broadening knowledge in the sciences and humanities

WORLEY, JAMES G.
727 E DEAN KEETON STREET
PO BOX 7399
AUSTIN, TX 78705
512-471-1232
Fax: 512-471-8102
www.utexas.edu
• William C. Powers Jr, President
(512) 471-1232
president@po.utexas.edu
• Patricia L. Clubb, VP, Employee & Campus Services
(512) 232-7742
• Richard B. Eason, VP, Resource Development
(512) 475-9609
• Sheldon Ekland-Olson, EVP and Provost
(512) 232-3301
seo@mail.utexas.edu
Description:
Represents college athletic departments.
Services:
From teaching and research to public service, the university's activities support its mission and core purpose: to transform lives for the benefit of society through the core values of learning, discovery, freedom, leadership, individual opportunity and responsibility

WRIGHT, DOUGLAS A.
100 N TAMPA STREET
SUITE 4100
TAMPA, FL 33602
813-227-8500
Fax: 813-229-0134
www.hklaw.com
• Bradford Kimbro, Executive Partner
(813) 227-6660
brad.kimbro@hklaw.com
• William Dufoe, Partner
(813) 227-6371
william.dufoe@hklaw.com
Nature of Sports Service:
All phases of athlete representation including contract negotiation, long-range planning, financial planning, and post-career counseling.

WYNN & WYNN, P.C.
90 NEW STATE HIGHWAY
RAYNHAM, MA 2767
508-823-4567
800-852-5211
Fax: 508-822-4097
www.wynnandwynn.com

• Thomas J. Wynn, Founding Partner
(508) 823-4567
twynn@wynnandwynn.com
• Paul F. Wynn, Founding Partner
(508) 823-4567
pwynn@wynnandwynn.com
• John J. O'Day Jr, Founding Partner
(508) 823-4567
joday@wynnandwynn.com
• Elizabeth K. Balaschak, Partner
(508) 823-4567
• Paul Wynn, Founding Partner
(508) 823-4567
• Thomas Wynn, Founding partner
(Ext) 435
• Kevin McRoy, Partner
(Ext) 422
• Charles Mulcahy, Partner
(Ext) 423
• William Rosa, Partner
(Ext) 412
• Andrew Toldo, Partner
(Ext) 411
Services:
Areas of practice include Business Litigation, Criminal Law, Insurance Defense, Estate Planning, and Wills, Bankruptcy, Estate Administration, Family and Marital Law, Real Estate, Personal Injury, and Workers' Compensation
Clients:
Fleet National Bank
Description:
NFLPA workers' compensation panel, handles workers' compensation for the New England Patriots.

WYRICK, ROBBINS, YATES & PONTON, L.L.P
4101 LAKE BOONE TRAIL
SUITE 300, THE SUMMIT
RALEIGH, NC 27607-7506
919-781-4000
Fax: 919-781-4865
www.wyrick.com
• Samuel T. Wyrick III, Lawyer
(919) 781-4000
swyrick@wyrick.com
• Larry E. Robbins, Lawyer
(919) 781-4000
lrobbins@wyrick.com
• James M. Yates Jr, Lawyer
(919) 781-4000
jyates@wyrick.com
• Thomas A. Allen, Attorney
Services:
Areas of practice include Appellate Advocacy, Banking Law, Business Law, Commercial Real Estate & Development Community & Homeowners' Associations, Construction Law, Creditors' Rights; Bankruptcy; Loan Work-Outs, Election Law, Employee Benefit, Environmental Law, Estate and Wealth Planning & Probate, Family Law, Franchise Law, Government Contracting Law, Health Care Law, Intellectual Property Protection & Licensing, Labor & Employment Law, Life Sciences & Biotechnology, Litigation, Mergers, Acquisitions & Divestitures, Securities Law, Taxation, Venture Capital & Private Equity Financings
Clients:
Adherex Technologies, Inc., Aeolus Pharmaceuticals, Inc., Argolyn Bioscience, Inc., Arius Pharmaceuticals, Inc., BioDelivery Sciences International, Inc., BioMarck Pharmaceuticals, Ltd, BioStratum,

Incorporated, Campbell Alliance Group, Inc., Chelsea Therapeutics, Inc., Container Graphics Corporation, DARA Biosciences, Inc., DarPharma, Inc., Encelle, Inc., Entegrion, Inc., Global Vaccines, Inc., Globus Medical, Inc., emocellular Therapeutics, Inc., Inspire Pharmaceuticals, Inc., Metabolon, Inc., Parion Sciences, Inc., Pentech Pharmaceuticals, Inc., Pharmaceutical Product Development, Inc. (PPD), PharmaNetics, Inc., Respirics, Inc.
Description:
Contract negotiation, tort actions/litigation. Community Association Law, Municipal Law, Creditor's Rights & Collections, Bankruptcy & Workouts, Litigation.

YONKE & POTTENGER, L.L.C.
1100 MAIN ST
SUITE 2450
KANSAS CITY, MO 64105
816-221-6000
877-221-8166
Fax: 816-221-6400
• Michael T. Yonke, Lawyer/Partner
(816) 221-6000
myonke@yplawfirm.com
• Jason M. Pottenger, Lawyer/Partner
(816) 221-6000
jpottenger@yplawfirm.com
• Albert J. Yonke, Of Counsel
(816) 221-6000
yplawfirm@yplawfirm.com
• Michael T. Yonke, Attorney
• Jason M. Pottenger, Attorney
• Thomas R. Onik, Attorney
• Albert J. Yonke, Attorney
• Tony Miller, Lawyer
(816) 221-6000
yplawfirm@yplawfirm.com
Services:
Areas of practice include Motor Vehicle Accidents, Construction Site Accidents, Medical Malpractice, Nursing Home Negligence, Trucking Accidents, Workers Compensation, and Criminal Defense

YOUNGER, TIMOTHY M.
10681 FOOTHILL BOULEVARD
SUITE 280
RANCHO CUCAMONGA, CA 91730
909-980-0630
www.youngerassociates.net
• Timothy M. Younger, Managing Partner
(909) 980-0630
• Melissa M. Thom, Associate
(909) 980-0630
• Timothy M. Younger, Attorney
Services:
Areas of practice include Civil Litigation including Personal Injury, Automobile accidents, Dog bites/attacks, Slip and fall accidents, Defective products, Wrongful death, Employment Law Matters, Workers' Compensation Subrogation, and Insurance Defense
Clients:
Liberty Mutual Insurance, Company Golden Eagle Insurance Corporation, Verizon, Crawford & Company, Southern California Risk Management Associates, Laidlaw Transit, Inc., Daewoo Motor Company, Stephen Daniels Real Estate Group, Zendejas Mexican Restaurants, Sunset Haven, Inc., CMAC Construction Company, Pacific Coast Funding, Michael J. Byrne Mfg. Co., Dean Foods Company, American Home Assurance Company

Description:
Contract negotiation and legal services.

ZIMMERMAN REED, P.L.LP.
1100 IDS CENTER
80 SOUTH 8TH STREET
MINNEAPOLIS, MN 55402
612-341-0400
800-755-0098
Fax: 612-341-0844
www.zimmreed.com
• Charles S. Zimmerman, Founding Partner
(612) 341-0400
csz@zimmreed.com
• Robert C. Moilanen, Partner
(612) 341-0400
• Timothy J. Becker, Lawyer
(612) 341-0400
• Carolyn G. G. Anderson, Attorney
Services:
Areas of practice include Consumer Fraud, Dangerous & Defective Drugs, Deceptive Insurance Practices, Securities & Investment Fraud, Employment Violations, Wage and Hour Litigation, Environmental & Toxic Torts, Healthcare Litigation, Improper Homeowner Charges, Mortgage Litigation, and Defective Medical Devices
Description:
All phases of athlete representation including contract negotiation, long-range planning, financial planning, and post-career counseling. Class Actions; Products Liability; Consumer Fraud; Mass Torts; Complex Litigation. Investment contract negotiation, represents sports organizations, arbitration hearings, licensing, endorsement exploration, tort actions/litigation, worker's comp.
Year Founded:
1982

Sports Medicine Services

ACCESS SPORTS MEDICINE & ORTHOPAEDICS
www.accesssportsmed.com
Description:
Locations in Exeter, Portsmouth, Plaistow, Raymond, Rochester and Dover.
Specialty:
Orthopaedic and sports medicine care.

ADVANCED ORTHOPEDICS AND SPORTS MEDICINE INSTITUTE
POND VIEW PROFESSIONAL PARK
301 PROFESSIONAL VIEW DRIVE
BUILDING 300
FREEHOLD, NJ 07728
advancedorthosports.com
Year Founded:
2007
Specialty:
Orthopedic and sports medicine care.

AEGIS SCIENCES CORPORATION
515 GREAT CIRCLE ROAD
NASHVILLE, TN 37228
800-533-7052
info@aegislabs.com
www.aegislabs.com
• David L. Black, Chief Executive Officer
• Timothy A. Robert, Chief Science Officer
Services/Products:
AEGIS is a federally certified forensic

toxicology laboratory providing services to corporations, colleges & universities, schools, government agencies, families, and individuals. AEGIS products and services will Deter and Detect substance abuse in your organization and, most importantly, Defend against the added costs and liability of drug abuse. Our goal is to provide you with accurate information and quality services that will help you insure a drug-free workplace, school, sports program, or family.
Brands:
Zero-Tolerance Drug Testingr; #9001 Zero-Tolerancer Substance Abuse Prevention Kit; #50277 Ensure Personal Breath Alcohol Tester; #50278 Disposable Mouthpieces; #50278 Disposable Mouthpieces.
Marketing & Consulting Services:
Drug and steroid testing for sports teams, conferences.
Year Founded:
1990

AMERICAN ACADEMY OF ORTHOPAEDIC SURGEONS
9400 W HIGGINS ROAD
ROSEMONT, IL 60018
847-823-7186
Fax: 847-823-8125
www.aaos.org
• Karen L. Hackett, Chief Executive Officer
• Richard J. Stewart, Chief Operating & Financial Officer
• Will Shaffer, Medical Director
Description:
Provides education and practice management services for orthopaedic surgeons.
Year Founded:
1933
Members:
39,000

AMERICAN ACADEMY OF PODIATRIC SPORTS MEDICINE
3121 NE 26TH STREET
OCALA, FL 34470
352-620-8562
info@aapsm.org
www.aapsm.org
• Rita Yates, Executive Director
Description:
Preventing and managing lower extremity sports and fitness injuries through scientific research, professional education and increasing public awareness.
Year Founded:
1970

AMERICAN COLLEGE OF SPORTS MEDICINE
401 W MICHIGAN STREET
INDIANAPOLIS, IN 46202-3233
317-637-9200
Fax: 317-634-7817
www.acsm.org
• Lawrence E. Armstrong, President
Description:
World's largest sports medicine and exercise science organization.

AMERICAN COLLEGE OF VETERINARY SPORTS MEDICINE AND REHABILITATION
PO BOX F
FORT COLLINS, CO 80522
info@vsmr.org
vsmr.org
• Andris J. Kaneps, President
Description:
A new College of the American Veterinary Medical Association, the ACVSMR was developed to care for athletic and working animals.
Year Founded:
2010

AMERICAN MEDICAL SOCIETY FOR SPORTS MEDICINE
4000 W 114TH STREET
SUITE 100
LEAWOOD, KS 66211
913-327-1415
Fax: 913-327-1491
www.amssm.org
• Jim Griffith, Executive Director
Description:
A forum for primary care non-surgical sports medicine physicians.
Year Founded:
1991

AMERICAN ORTHOPAEDIC FOOT & ANKLE SOCIETY
9400 W HIGGINS ROAD
SUITE 220
ROSEMONT, IL 60018-4975
847-698-4654
800-235-4855
Fax: 847-692-3315
aofasinfo@aofas.org
www.aofas.org
• Oster M. Susan, Executive Director
Description:
International organization of more than 2,000 orthopaedic surgeons specializing in treating injuries, diseases and conditions of the foot and ankle.
Year Founded:
1969

AMERICAN ORTHOPAEDIC SOCIETY FOR SPORTS MEDICINE
9400 W HIGGINS ROAD
SUITE 300
ROSEMONT, IL 60018
847-292-4900
877-321-3500
Fax: 847-292-4905
www.sportsmed.org
• Irvin E. Bomberger, Executive Director
Description:
Fosters, promotes, supports and augments investigative knowledge of sports medicine and its many ramifications. Develops and encourages the teaching of the same by developing, publishing and copyrighting educational material and providing specialized training for orthopaedic surgeons and others. Encourages education in allied professions in the prevention, recognition and orthopedic treatment of sports injuries.
Membership Requirements:
Five classifications of membership - Active, Associate, Affiliate, Honorary and Emeritus. Active members must be orthopaedic surgeons who are members of American

Academy of Orthopaedic Surgeons or Canadian citizens with similar qualifications, and must meet certain other requirements. Associate members must be orthopaedic surgeons either certified by American Board of Orthopaedic Surgery or eligible for certification or Canadian citizens with similar qualifications, and certain other requirements. Affiliate members are non-members of American Academy of Orthopaedic Surgeons or Canadian members with similar qualifications.
Member Services:
Interim Scientific meetings held each winter in conjunction with the American Academy of Orthopaedic Surgeons. Annual meetings held each summer.
Year Founded:
1972

AMERICAN OSTEOPATHIC ACADEMY OF SPORTS MEDICINE
2424 AMERICAN LANE
MADISON, WI 53704
608-443-2477
Fax: 608-443-2474
www.aoasm.org
• R. Scott Cook, President
• Shawn Kerger, Secretary & Treasurer
Description:
Forum for osteopathic sports medicine physicians.
Year Founded:
1984

AMERICAN PHYSICAL THERAPY ASSOCIATION
1111 NORTH FAIRFAX STREET
ALEXANDRIA, VA 22314-1488
703-684-2782
800-999-2782
Fax: 703-706-8536
www.apta.org
• J. Michael Bowers, Chief Executive Officer
Description:
Organization advancing the practice of physical therapy through education and research.

AMERICAN SPORTS MEDICINE INSTITUTE
833 ST. VINCENT'S DRIVE
SUITE 205
BIRMINGHAM, AL 35205
205-918-0000
www.asmi.org
• Lanier Johnson, Executive Director
(205) 918-2127
Services:
Provides medical education for physicians. Publisher of clinical and biomechanical research, surgical procedures, patient follow-up, and literature reviews, and audio/visual materials.
Year Founded:
1987

ANDREWS INSTITUTE FOR ORTHOPAEDICS & SPORTS MEDICINE
1040 GULF BREEZE PARKWAY
GULF BREEZE, FL 32561
850-916-8700
Fax: 850-916-8709
www.andrewsinstitute.com
• David M. Joyner, Executive Director
Year Founded:
2007

Specialty:
Musculoskeletal treatments and research.

ANDREWS SPORTS MEDICINE & ORTHOPEDIC CENTER
www.andrewssportsmedicine.com
Description:
Locations in Birmingham, Hoover and Pelham, Alabama.

ARTHROSCOPY ASSOCIATION OF NORTH AMERICA
9400 W HIGGINS ROAD
SUITE 200
ROSEMONT, IL 60018
847-292-2262
Fax: 847-292-2268
www.aana.org
• Laura M. Downes, Executive Director
Description:
New techniques and information defining the practice of arthroscopic surgery.
Year Founded:
1981

ASPEN ORTHOPAEDIC ASSOCIATES
0401 CASTLE CREEK ROAD
SUITE 2100
ASPEN, CO 81611
970-925-4141
866-925-4141
Fax: 970-925-4233
www.orthop.com
Specialty:
Orthopedic Sports Medicine

ATHLETICO PHYSICAL THERAPY
625 ENTERPRISE DRIVE
OAK BROOK, IL 60523
630-575-6200
Fax: 630-575-7400
info@athletico.com
www.athletico.com
• Mark Kaufman, President
Description:
Physical and occupational therapy.
Year Founded:
1991

AUSTIN SPORTS MEDICINE
900 W 38TH STREET
SUITE 300
AUSTIN, TX 78705
512-450-1300
www.austinsportsmed.com
Specialty:
Comprehensive care for active life style and sports related injuries.

BEACON ORTHOPAEDICS & SPORTS MEDICINE
513-354-3700
888-773-4353
www.beaconortho.com
Description:
Seven locations in the Cincinnati Tri-State area.
Year Founded:
1988

CAMPBELL CLINIC ORTHOPAEDICS
901-759-3100
www.campbellclinic.com
Description:
Five locations in the Memphis area with

after hours urgent care clinics at Germantown and Southaven locations.
Year Founded:
1909

CENTER FOR ATHLETIC MEDICINE
830 W DIVERSEY
SUITE 300
CHICAGO, IL 60614
773-248-4150
Fax: 773-248-4291
www.athleticmed.com
• Preston M. Wolin, Director
• Morgan Wolin, Sports Psychologist
Description:
Team Physicians for the Chicago Fire, DePaul University and University Illinois-Chicago.
Specialty:
Orthopedics/sports medicine; Knee, Shoulder, Elbow.
Year Founded:
1991

CHICAGO ORTHOPAEDICS & SPORTS MEDICINE
CHICAGO, IL
773-433-3130
www.chiorthosports.com
• Franni Huspen, Practice Administrator
Services:
Non-surgical procedures, minimally invasive surgery, traditional surgeries and physical therapy.
Year Founded:
1965

CINCINNATI SPORTSMEDICINE & ORTHOPAEDIC CENTER
10663 MONTGOMERY ROAD
CINCINNATI, OH 45242
513-347-9999
Fax: 513-792-3230
info@csmoc.com
www.cincinnatisportsmed.com
• Frank R. Noyes, Founder & Orthopaedic Surgeon
• Mark G. Siegel, Orthopaedic Surgeon
• Thomas N. Lindenfeld, Orthopaedic Surgeon
• Michelle Andrews, Orthopaedic Surgeon
• Marc T. Galloway, Orthopaedic Surgeon
• Samer S. Hasan, Orthopaedic Surgeon
• Matthew L. Busam, Orthopaedic Surgeon
• Sanjeev Bhatia, Orthopaedic Surgeon
• Rebecca E. Popham, Sports Medicine Physician
Board Certified:
Yes.
Fellowship Trained:
Yes.
Specialization:
Treatment of all musculoskeletal injuries, especially the knees and shoulder.
Services:
Specializes in the treatment of orthopaedic and sports injuries of joints and muscles of the knee, shoulder, elbow, ankle and hip. And internationally renown for its Cincinnati SportsMedicine Research and Education Foundation having published over 200 articles and 50 research studies.
Advanced Treatment:
Include meniscus allegrafts, repairs of the posterior cruciate ligament, repairing and reconstructing artifular cartilage in the knee, and complex knee disorders.

professional services

Year Founded:
1985

CLEVELAND CLINIC
9500 EUCLID AVENUE
CLEVELAND, OH 44195
800-223-2273
my.clevelandclinic.org
• Delos Cosgrove, President & Chief Executive Officer
Services/Products:
Services include Aging, Geriatrics, Eldercare, Allergy, Alcohol and Drug Dependency, Arthritis, Asthma, Back and Spine, Blood Disorders (Anemias), Breathing Problems, Bones, Joints, Muscles, Sports Injuries, Brain and Nervous System, Breast Disease, Cancer, Circulation, Colorectal Surgery, Diabetes, Endocrine, and Metabolism, Diabetic Foot Care, Digestive Diseases, including Liver, Ears, Nose, Throat and Mouth, Executive Health, Eyes, Gastric Bypass Surgery, General Surgery including Gall Bladder, Genetics and Inherited Diseases, Hearing Problems, Heart Disease, Hernias, Homecare, In Vitro Fertilization, Incontinence, Infertility, Inherited C
Specialty:
Orthopaedic Sports Medicine.
Year Founded:
1921

COASTAL ORTHOPAEDIC & SPORTS MEDICINE CENTER
www.coastal-orthopaedic.com
Services:
Minimally invasive surgery, sports injuries and rehabilitation, fracture care, viscosupplementation, joint replacement, urgent care, workers' compensation.

D1 SPORTS MEDICINE
www.d1sportsmedicine.com
• Geoffrey Connor, Founder & Medical Director
Description:
Integrated rehabilitation and training for a higher level of function post-injury. Locations in AL, AR, CO, FL, KS, KY, MS, NE, OK, TN and TX.

DISC SPORTS & SPINE CENTER
866-481-3472
discmdgroup.com
Description:
DISC is an integrated multidisciplinary practice with three locations in Southern California and is a medical services provider to the Los Angeles Kings and Red Bull North America.
Services:
Conservative and surgical spine and orthopedic care, interventional pain management, chiropractic care and sports medicine.

DMC ORTHOPAEDICS & SPORTS MEDICINE
DETROIT MEDICAL CENTER
3990 JOHN R STREET
DETROIT, MI 48201
313-745-6035
www.dmc.org
• Joe Mullany, President

Description:
The Detroit Medical Center is a network of nine specialty hospitals and is the healthcare services provider of the Detroit Tigers, Detroit Red Wings and Detroit Pistons.
Year Founded:
1886

DR. CHRIS STANKOVICH
1395 GRANDVIEW AVENUE
SUITE 6
COLUMBUS, OH 43212
614-561-4482
information@drstankovich.com
www.drstankovich.com
• Chris Stankovich
Services:
Provides athletes, coaches, parents, officials, and entire sport organizations with clinical and applied sport science peak performance training and counseling.

ELITE SPORTS MEDICINE & ORTHOPEDICS
www.eliteorthopaedic.com
• Burton Elrod, Founder
Description:
Elite has five locations in the Nashville area.

FONDREN ORTHOPEDIC GROUP
FONDREN MAIN AT TEXAS ORTHOPEDIC HOSPITAL
7401 MAIN STREET
HOUSTON, TX 77030
713-799-2300
Fax: 713-794-3380
www.fondren.com
Description:
The Group operates many offices in the Greater Houston area. Its main location is at Texas Orthopedic Hospital.
Year Founded:
1973

HEALTHSOUTH REHABILITATION
3660 GRANDVIEW PARKWAY
SUITE 200
BIRMINGHAM, AL 35243
205-967-7116
www.healthsouth.com
• Jay Grinney, President & Chief Executive Officer
• Doug Coltharp, EVP & Chief Financial Officer
• Mark J. Tarr, EVP & Chief Operating Officer
Description:
Network of post-acute healthcare service providers operating in 34 states and Puerto Rico.

ILLINOIS BONE & JOINT INSTITUTE
www.ibji.com
Description:
IBJI provides expert care in every orthopedic specialty at 20 locations throughout Chicago.
Year Founded:
1990

JACKSONVILLE ORTHOPAEDIC HOSPITAL
1325 SAN MARCO BOULEVARD
SUITE 701
JACKSONVILLE, FL 32207

904-346-3465
www.joionline.net
Description:
Sports medicine provider for the Jacksonville Jaguars, JOI operates out of six locations in the Jacksonville area.
Specialty:
Hand, foot & ankle, spine, joint replacement, sports medicine and rehabilitation.

KERLAN-JOBE ORTHOPAEDIC CLINIC
6801 PARK TERRACE
LOS ANGELES, CA 90045
310-665-7200
www.kerlanjobe.com
Specialty:
Sports medicine
Services:
Well known procedures that are available include Tendon Repair; Rotator Cuff Repair and Achilles Tendon Repair; Total Joint Replacement: Shoulder, Hip, Knee; Ligament Reconstructions: Tommy John Procedure and ACLR: Anterior Cruciate Ligament Reconstruction; Arthroscopic Surgery: Joint Debridement, Labral Repair, and Partial Menisectomy

KSF ORTHOPAEDIC CENTER
HOUSTON, TX
281-440-6960
www.ksfortho.com
Description:
Two locations serve Northwest Houston.
Services:
Spine & neck, shoulder, hand & wrist, hip, knee, foot & ankle, elbow and sports medicine.

LEMAK SPORTS MEDICINE & ORTHOPEDICS
720 MONTCLAIR ROAD
SUITE 101
BIRMINGHAM, AL 35213
866-252-3618
info@lemakhealth.com
www.lemaksports.com
• Matthew T. Lemak, Chief Executive Officer
Services:
Ankle, knee, elbow, hip, shoulder, spine, concussion clinics and Tenex Health procedure.

LENOX HILL HOSPITAL
100 E 77TH STREET
NEW YORK, NY 10075
212-434-2000
www.northwell.edu
• Michael J. Dowling, President & Chief Executive Officer
Specialty:
Internal medicine, cardiovascular disease, orthopaedics, sports medicine, otolaryngology/head and neck surgery and maternal/child health.
Services:
Anesthesiology, Cardiothoracic Surgery, Interventional Cardiology, Medicine, Medicine - Dermatology, Medicine - Division of Allergy & Immunology, Medicine - Division of Cardiovascular Disease, Medicine - Division of Critical Care Medicine, Medicine - Division of Emergency Services, Medicine - Division of Endocrinology/Metabolism, Medicine - Division of Gastroenterology, Medicine - Division of Hematology & Medical Oncology,

Medicine - Division of Infectious Disease, Medicine - Division of Internal Medicine/Primary Care, Medicine - Division of Nephrology, Medicine - Division of Neurology, Medicine.

MAYO CLINIC SPORTS MEDICINE
600 HENNEPIN AVENUE
MINNEAPOLIS, MN 55403
612-313-0520
sportsmedicine.mayoclinic.org
• Michael Stuart, Co-Director
• Edward Laskowski, Co-Director
• Jonathan Finnoff, Medical Director
Specialty:
Sports medicine
Services:
Sports and musculoskeletal injury prevention and rehabilitation.

MEDICAL CENTER ARLINGTON
3301 MATLOCK ROAD
ARLINGTON, TX 76015
817-465-3241
medicalcenterarlington.com
• Winston Borland, President & Chief Executive Officer
Year Founded:
1976

MEDSTAR UNION MEMORIAL SPORTS MEDICINE
201 E UNIVERSITY PARKWAY
BALTIMORE, MD 21218
410-554-2000
www.medstarunionmemorial.org
• Bradley S. Chambers, President
Services:
Regional center for sports medicine.
Clients:
Official medical team of the Baltimore Ravens.

MEMORIAL MEDICAL CENTER
701 N FIRST STREET
SPRINGFIELD, IL 62781
217-788-3000
www.memorialmedical.com
• Edgar J. Curtis, President & Chief Executive Officer
• Charles D. Callahan, EVP & Chief Operating Officer
• Rajesh G. Govindaiah, SVP & Chief Medical Officer
Services:
Cancer Services, Cardiovascular Services, Emergency Services, General Services, Home Health Care, Imaging Services, Orthopedic & Rehabilitation Services, Outpatient Services, Pediatric Services, Surgical Services, Wellness Programs, Women's Services

METHODIST SPORTS MEDICINE
201 PENNSYLVANIA PARKWAY
SUITE 100
INDIANAPOLIS, IN 46280
317-817-1200
Description:
Official team physicians for the Indianapolis Colts since 1984.
Specialty:
Concussion management, foot & ankle, hand, wrist & elbow, hip, joint replacement & arthritis, knee, pediatric sports medicine, physical medicine & rehabilitation, shoulder,

spine, sports performance and workers compensation.
Year Founded:
1984

MICHIGAN ORTHOPAEDIC INSTITUTE
248-663-1927
www.moimd.com

MIDWEST ORTHOPAEDICS AT RUSH
877-632-6637
www.rushortho.com
Description:
Regional center for orthopedic services and team physicians to the Chicago Bulls, Chicago White Sox and Chicago Fire Soccer Club.

NATIONAL ACADEMY OF SPORTS MEDICINE
1750 E NORTHROP BOULEVARD
SUITE 200
CHANDLER, AZ 85286-1744
800-460-6276
Fax: 480-656-3276
www.nasm.org
• Andrew Wyant, President & General Manager
Services:
Assessment, Optimum Performance Training, Recovery & Regeneration, Professional Consulting
Description:
Certification, continuing education and tools for personal trainers.
Member Services:
Job opportunities, referrals, insurance (liability and health), discounts from equipment manufacturers, and travel discounts.
Year Founded:
1987

NATIONAL ATHLETIC TRAINERS' ASSOCIATION
1620 VALWOOD PARKWAY
SUITE 115
CARROLLTON, TX 75006
214-637-6282
Fax: 214-637-2206
www.nata.org
• Dave Saddler, Executive Director
Description:
Professional association of athletic trainers dedicated to enhancing the quality of health care they provide.
Year Founded:
1950
Members:
35,000

NATIONAL CENTER FOR SPORTS SAFETY
1286 OAK GROVE ROAD
BIRMINGHAM, AL 35209
205-329-7535
866-508-6277
info@SportsSafety.org
www.sportssafety.org
• Lawrence Lemak, Founder
Description:
The NCSS is dedicated to the promotion of injury prevention and safety in youth sports.

NATIONAL SPORTS MEDICINE INSTITUTE
19455 DEERFIELD AVENUE
SUITE 312
LANSDOWNE, VA 20176
703-729-5010
Fax: 703-729-5833
contact@nationalsportsmed.com
www.nationsportsmed.com
Description:
State-of-the-art sports injury evaluation & treatment, diagnostic imaging and physical therapy in Lansdowne, Virginia.
Specialty:
Elbow, shoulder, knee, hip, ankle, sports medicine, wellness & human performance.

NATIONAL STRENGTH AND CONDITIONING ASSOCIATION
1885 BOB JOHNSON DRIVE
COLORADO SPRINGS, CO 80906
719-632-6722
800-815-6826
Fax: 719-632-6367
nsca@nsca.com
www.nsca.com
• Lee Madden, Sr. Director of Administrative Services
Description:
The Association exists to support the practical application of the latest research-based knowledge.
Year Founded:
1978

NEBRASKA ORTHOPAEDIC & SPORTS MEDICINE
CHI ST. ELIZABETH MEDICAL BUILDING
575 SOUTH 70TH STREET
SUITE 200
LINCOLN, NE 68510
402-488-3322
Fax: 402-488-1172
nebraskaortho.com
Services:
Foot & ankle, fracture clinic, general orthopaedics, hand & wrist, joint replacement, shoulder, spine care and sports medicine.

NEW ENGLAND BAPTIST HOSPITAL
125 PARKER HILL AVENUE
BOSTON, MA 02120
617-754-5000
www.nebh.org
• Trish Hannon, President & CEO
• Thomas Gheringhelli, Vice President, Finance
Services:
New England Baptist Hospital is the regional center for orthopedic surgery and musculoskeletal diseases and disorders.
Clients:
NEBH has been the official and exclusive hospital of the Boston Celtics for over 26 years.
Specialty:
Orthopaedic Surgery

NORTHWEST ORTHOPEDICS & SPORTS MEDICINE
350 HERITAGE WAY
SUITE 1200
KALISPELL, MT 59901
406-752-6784
Fax: 406-756-4111
www.kalispellregional.org

NYU LANGONE HOSPITAL FOR JOINT DISEASES
301 E 17TH STREET
NEW YORK, NY 10003
212-598-6000
nyulangone.org
• Robert I. Grossman, Chief Executive Officer
Services:
Provides the highest quality of surgical and therapeutic care in the treatment, rehabilitation, and prevention of musculoskeletal, rheumatic, immunological, neurological, and other related diseases and injuries. Programs and services include Ambulatory Care Services, Center for Arthritis & Autoimmunity, Diabetes Foot and Ankle Center, Harkness Dance Center, Initiative for Women with Disabilities, Occupational and Industrial Orthopedic Center, Osteoporosis Center, Comprehensive Pain Treatment Center, The Center for Children, Adult Orthopedic Service, Adult Reconstructive Services, Foot & Ankle Service, Trauma Fracture Service, Hand Service.
Year Founded:
1905

ORTHOCAROLINA
www.orthocarolina.com
• Daniel Murrey, Chief Executive Officer
• Steve Hendrick, Chief Operating Officer
• Jennifer Schenk, Chief Counsel & Chief Compliance Officer
• Brent Shear, Chief Financial Officer
Description:
Comprehensive musculoskeletal care.
Year Founded:
1922

ORTHOINDY
317-802-2000
orthoindy.com
Description:
Orthopedic practice in Central Indiana with more than 10 locations. Medical services provider to the Indiana Pacers.

ORTHOPAEDIC & SPORTS MEDICINE CENTER OF OREGON
orthosportsmed.com
Services:
Fracture care, joint reconstruction and arthroscopy.

ORTHOPAEDIC AND SPORTS MEDICINE CLINIC OF KANSAS CITY
3651 COLLEGE BOULEVARD
SUITE 100A
LEAWOOD, KS 66211
913-319-7500
www.osmckc.com
Services:
Cartilage restoration and repair, ligament reconstruction of the knee and knee replacement, shoulder surgery and replacement, elbow surgery and platelet rich plasma therapy.

ORTHOPAEDIC RESEARCH OF VIRGINIA
PO BOX 71690
RICHMOND, VA 23255-1690
804-527-5960
Fax: 804-527-5961
www.orv.com

• John F. Meyers, Physician
(804) 285-2300
• William R. Beach, Physician
(804) 285-2300
• Shannon Wolfe, Physician
(804) 285-2300
• Paul E. Caldwell, Physician
Services:
Performs various functions to advance musculoskeletal care, teaching, and research. Sponsors a one year fellowship in arthroscopy and sports medicine for residency-trained orthopaedic surgeons. Maintains a modern cadaver lab fully equipped with traditional and arthroscopic surgical instruments. Sponsors periodic educational programs for practicing orthopaedic surgeons and coordinates team coverage for local high school and collegiate athletic programs.

ORTHOPEDIC & SPORTS MEDICINE SPECIALISTS OF GREEN BAY
2223 LIME KILN ROAD
SUITE 1
GREEN BAY, WI 54311
920-430-8113
800-310-3877
Fax: 920-430-8124
www.osmsgb.com
Specialty:
Orthopedic and rheumatologic care.
Year Founded:
1963

ORTHOPEDIC ASSOCIATES OF HARTFORD
85 SEYMOUR STREET
SUITE 607
HARTFORD, CT 06106-5500
860-549-3210
www.oahct.com
Description:
Physicians providing comprehensive orthopedic and musculoskeletal healthcare.
Specialty:
Orthopedic surgery
Year Founded:
1970

ORTHOPEDIC PHYSICIAN ASSOCIATES
601 BROADWAY
SEATTLE, WA
www.opaortho.com
Description:
Regional center for orthopedic and musculoskeletal care. Medical services provider to the Seattle Mariners and Seattle Seahawks.
Year Founded:
1958

PEACHTREE ORTHOPAEDIC CLINIC
ATLANTA, GA
404-355-0743
www.pocatlanta.com
Description:
POC's clinics, rehabilitation locations and MRI facilities deliver a range of orthopaedic services to the Atlanta community. POC is the orthopaedic care provider to the Atlanta Braves and the Atlanta Hawks.
Year Founded:
1953

PHOENIX ORTHOPEDIC GROUP
602-277-1558
Description:
POG operates orthopedic surgery clinics in Phoenix and Scottsdale.
Specialty:
Orthopedic surgery, osteoporosis and osteoarthritis care, sports medicine and arthroplasty.

RESURGENS SPORTS MEDICINE CENTER
ATLANTA, GA
www.resurgenssportsmedicine.com
Description:
Georgia's largest orthopaedic practice.
Specialty:
Muscle strain, bone fracture, tendinitis, joint or ligament strain/tears, joint dislocation and MCL/ACL injuries.

ROTHMAN INSTITUTE
925 CHESTNUT STREET
5TH FLOOR
PHILADELPHIA, PA 19107
800-321-9999
www.rothmaninstitute.com
• Richard H. Rothman, Founder
• Alexander R. Vaccaro, President
Description:
Rothman Institute has twenty offices in the Greater Philadelphia area.
Specialty:
Sport medicine, rehabilitation, fracture care and orthopaedic oncology.

RUSH UNIVERSITY MEDICAL CENTER - SPORTS MEDICINE PROGRAM
1653 W CONGRESS PARKWAY
CHICAGO, IL 60612
888-352-7874
www.rush.edu
Description:
The pioneering specialists at Rush treat both the most common and the most complex conditions in athletes of all ages.

SLOCUM CENTER FOR ORTHOPEDICS & SPORTS MEDICINE
55 COBURG ROAD
EUGENE, OR 97401
541-485-8111
800-866-7906
Fax: 541-342-6379
www.slocumcenter.com
Specialty:
Ankle, elbow, foot, hand, hip, knee, shoulder, wrist, sports medicine.
Services:
MRI, digital X-ray, bone density/bone health, therapy center, on-site pharmacy.
Year Founded:
1939

SOUTHERN CALIFORNIA ORTHOPEDIC INSTITUTE
6815 NOBLE AVENUE
VAN NUYS, CA 91405
818-901-6600
moreinfo@scoi.com
www.scoi.com
Description:
Regional center for bone, joint and muscle injuries as well as musculoskeletal and spine disorders.
Specialty:

Orthopedic surgery
Services:
Provides a comprehensive range of orthopedic services, including Arthroscopic Surgery Sports Medicine, Worker's Compensation Injuries Knee Surgery, Shoulder Surgery Foot and Ankle Surgery, Hip Surgery Microsurgery and Limb Replantation, Hand and Upper Extremity Surgery, Arthritis Diagnosis and Treatment, Physical Medicine Total Joint Replacement, Fracture and Trauma Care Spinal Surgery & Scoliosis Treatment, Pediatric & Adolescent Orthopedics Electrodiagnostic Evaluations.

SOUTHERN ORTHOPAEDICS & SPORTS MEDICINE
3231 GLYNN AVENUE
BRUNSWICK, GA 31520
912-265-9006
Fax: 912-265-7200
www.sosmga.com
• Burton F. Elrod, Owner
Specialty:
Sports medicine
Services:
Orthopaedic specialties, particularly arthroscopic surgery, sports medicine/athletic injuries, reconstructive surgery of the knee, shoulder and elbow, surgical and non-surgical care of athletic injuries, spine surgery, joint replacement surgery, revision surgery for total joint problems, treatment of fractures, surgery of the hand, upper extremity/repetitive motion problems, and surgery of the foot and ankle.

SPORTS & ORTHOPAEDIC SPECIALISTS
952-946-9777
www.sportsandortho.com
Description:
Orthopedic surgery and sports medicine practice in Minneapolis and medical care provider to the Minnesota Twins.
Year Founded:
1999

SPORTS MEDICINE ASSOCIATES
TEXAS CENTER FOR ATHLETES
21 SPURS LANE
SUITE 300
SAN ANTONIO, TX 78240
210-699-8326
info@smasatx.com
sportsmedsa.com
Specialty:
Sports medicine, orthopaedics, concussion management, ligament repair and joint replacement.

SPORTS PHYSICAL THERAPY SECTION
PO BOX 431
ZIONSVILLE, IN 46077-431
877-732-5009
Fax: 317-669-8276
mwilkinson@spts.org
spts.org
• Mark S. De Carlo, Executive Director
• Mary Wilkinson, Director of Marketing
Description:
A component member of the American Physical Therapy Association, the SPTS is a forum for Association members with an interest in sports PT practice.

SPORTS, ORTHOPEDIC & REHABILITATION MEDICINE ASSOCIATES
650-851-4900
soarmedical.com
Description:
SOAR is a medical care provider for the San Francisco Giants.
Specialty:
Sports medicine, arthroscopy, ligament reconstruction, hand & foot surgery, joint replacement and pediatric and adolescent sports medicine.
Services:
Sports medicine, joint replacement, diagnostic radiology, spine rehabilitation, arthritis treatment and fracture care.

STAY IN THE ZONE
1060 MAIN STREET
SUITE 307
RIVER EDGE, NJ 07661
888-580-9663
Fax: 201-342-2258
stayinthezone.com
• Jay P. Granat, Founder
Description:
Sports psychology programs for athletes from many sports.
Year Founded:
1978
Teams:
High School, College, Professional

STEADMAN HAWKINS CLINIC - DENVER
8200 E BELLEVIEW AVENUE
SUITE 615
GREENWOOD VILLAGE, CO 80111
303-694-3333
Fax: 303-694-9666
www.shcdenver.com
Specialty:
Sports medicine & performance, physical & occupational therapy, upper extremity, hip & knee and foot & ankle.

STOP SPORTS INJURIES
9400 W HIGGINS ROAD
SUITE 300
ROSEMONT, IL 60018
847-655-8660
info@stopsportsinjuries.org
www.stopsportsinjuries.org
Description:
Stop Sports Injuries offers sport specific injury prevention resources for athletes, coaches, parents and healthcare providers.
Year Founded:
2008

TEMPLE ORTHOPAEDICS & SPORTS MEDICINE
MEDICAL OFFICE BUILDING
8815 GERMANTOWN PIKE
SUITE 14
PHILADELPHIA, PA 19118
215-248-9400
Fax: 215-248-9403
ortho.templehealth.org
• Eric J. Kropf, Chair
Specialty:
Regional center for the treatment of musculoskeletal disorders with five offices in the Philadelphia area.
Services:
Arthritis care, athletic care and treatment of

spinal disorders as well as fractures, foot and ankle problems and hand, wrist and elbow pain.

TEXAS SPORTS MEDICINE & ORTHOPAEDIC GROUP
214-369-7733
Fax: 214-369-7739
www.txsportsmed.com

THE AMERICAN PHYSIOLOGICAL SOCIETY
9650 ROCKVILLE PIKE
BETHESDA, MD 20814-3991
301-634-7164
Fax: 301-634-7241
www.the-aps.org
• Patricia E. Molina, President
Description:
The Society is dedicated to fostering education, research and the dissemination of information in the physiological sciences.
Year Founded:
1887

THE CARRELL CLINIC
9301 NORTH CENTRAL EXPRESSWAY
TOWER ONE
SUITE 500
DALLAS, TX 75231
214-220-2468
Fax: 469-232-9738
info@carrellclinic.com
www.carrellclinic.com
Specialty:
Pediatric orthopedics, sports injuries and arthroscopy.
Year Founded:
1921

THE ORTHOPAEDIC & SPORTS MEDICINE CENTER
888 WHITE PLAINS ROAD
TRUMBULL, CT 06611
203-268-2882
www.osmcenter.com
Services:
Hand, foot, ankle, knee, spine, hip and shoulder surgery. Joint reconstruction, podiatry and chiropractic care.
Year Founded:
1994

THE ORTHOPEDIC CENTER
410-820-8226
800-464-8226
Fax: 410-820-8405
www.theorthopediccenter.net
Description:
Multidisciplinary bone and joint care.
Year Founded:
1971

THE ORTHOPEDIC SPECIALTY HOSPITAL
5848 S FASHION BOULEVARD
MURRAY, UT 84107
801-314-4100
intermountainhealthcare.org
Services:
Orthopedic, physical therapy, sports medicine and sports training services.

THE STEADMAN CLINIC
181 W MEADOW DRIVE
VAIL, CO 81657
970-476-1100
thesteadmanclinic.com
• J. Richard Steadman, Founder & Managing Partner
• Marc J. Philippon, Managing Partner
Specialty:
Injuries of the knee, hip, shoulder, elbow, hand & wrist, foot & ankle and spine & neck.

THE STONE CLINIC
3727 BUCHANAN STREET
SUITE 300
SAN FRANCISCO, CA 94123
415-563-3110
www.stoneclinic.com

TRI-COUNTY ORTHOPEDICS
THE ADVANCED MEDICAL CENTER
197 RIDGEDALE AVENUE
SUITE 300
CEDAR KNOLLS, NJ 07927
973-538-2334
Fax: 973-829-9174
www.tri-countyortho.com

TRIA ORTHOPAEDIC CENTER
8100 NORTHLAND DRIVE
BLOOMINGTON, MN 55431
952-831-8742
tria.com
Services:
Sports medicine, physical therapy, orthotics & prosthetics, diagnostic imaging, bone densitometry and ambulatory surgery.

TRIHEALTH
619 OAK STREET
CINCINNATI, OH 45206
513-569-6111
www.trihealth.com
Description:
Regional network of sports medicine physicians, physical therapists and trainers. Medical services provider to the Cincinnati Bengals and Cincinnati Reds.

U.S. CENTER FOR SPORTS MEDICINE
333 S KIRKWOOD ROAD
SUITE 200
ST. LOUIS, MO 63122
314-909-1666
Fax: 314-909-7406

UBMD ORTHOPAEDICS & SPORTS MEDICINE
5500 MAIN STREET
SUITE 107
WILLIAMSVILLE, NY 14221
716-204-3200
contact@ubortho.com
www.ubortho.com
Description:
Team doctors to many high school and college teams in Western New York as well as professional teams such as the Buffalo Bills and Buffalo Sabres.

UHZ SPORTS MEDICINE INSTITUTE
786-268-6208
www.uhzsmi.com

Services:
Sports medicine; orthopedic, arthroscopic, knee, shoulder, elbow and ankle surgery.

UK HEALTHCARE ORTHOPAEDICS & SPORTS MEDICINE
800 ROSE STREET
ROOM C101
LEXINGTON, KY 40536
859-257-1000
800-333-8874
ukhealthcare.uky.edu
Description:
UK HealthCare is the brand name of the University of Kentucky's health care system offering advanced patient care to the people of Kentucky.
Year Founded:
1957

UNIVERSITY OF FLORIDA ORTHOPAEDICS & SPORT MEDICINE INSTITUTE
3450 HULL ROAD
GAINESVILLE, FL 32607
352-273-7002
Fax: 352-273-7293
www.ortho.ufl.edu
Description:
Orthopaedic care, rehabilitation and radiological services at the University of Florida College of Medicine.

UPMC SPORTS MEDICINE
200 LOTHROP STREET
PITTSBURGH, PA 15213-2582
412-647-8762
800-533-8762
www.upmc.com
Description:
Sports medicine provider for the Pittsburgh Penguins and Pittsburgh Steelers.
Services:
Athletic training; concussion, imaging, performance, bone & joint services; Young Athlete program.

VIRGINIA INSTITUTE FOR SPORTS MEDICINE
1849 OLD DONATION PARKWAY
VIRGINIA BEACH, VA 23454
757-422-8476
Description:
Providing surgical and non-surgical treatment of adult and pediatric patients.
Year Founded:
2003

WASHINGTON ORTHOPAEDICS & SPORTS MEDICINE
WASHINGTON, DC
www.wosm.com
• Laura Jensen, Chief Executive & Operating Officer

WELLINGTON ORTHOPAEDIC & SPORTS MEDICINE
CINCINNATI, OH
513-232-2663
wellingtonortho.com
Specialty:
Sports medicine, general orthopedics, joint replacement and concussion.
Year Founded:
1968

Sports Travel Services

AMATEUR SPORTS TRAVEL GROUP, INC
3808 OAK FOREST DRIVE
HIGH POINT, NC 27265
336-869-5954
888-541-5810
Fax: 888-541-5810
www.travel4sports.com
Services:
The world's largest sport travel directory aimed directly at youth and adult amateur athletes of all ages. It provides a discount travel source, free of charge for amateur athletes, parents, and coaches and intends to link amateur athletes with national sponsors who will offer discounts on travel, food, goods, and services to enhance and promote the world of amateur sports.

AMERICA OUTDOORS/AO
PO BOX 10847
KNOXVILLE, TN 37939
865-558-3595
800-524-4814
Fax: 865-558-3598
www.americaoutdoors.org
• Julie Kahlfeldt, Executive Director
• Robin Brown, Communications Director
Nature of Service:
A national association representing adventure travel outfitters, tour companies and outdoor educators, the mission of America Outdoors is supporting and developing outfitting businesses in the United States.

AMJ CAMPBELL
100 MILVERTON DRIVE
SUITE 830
MISSISSAUGA, ON, CANADA L5R-4H1
905-795-3785
888-AMJ-MOVE
Fax: 905-670-3787
contact@amjcampbell.com
www.amjcampbell.com
• Bruce D. Bowser, President/Chief Executive Officer
• Denis Cordick, VP Marketing
• Brian Farquhar, EVP Of Operations
• Bruce Bowser, President/CEO
• Dennis Frappier, President , Self Storage and Business develop
• Denis Cordick, VP, Marketing
Services
Official Mover for: BC Lions, Hamilton Tiger Cats, Winnipeg Blue Bombers; Toronto Maple Leafs; Canada Soccer Association; Toronto Raptors; Western Mustangs; Canadian Curling Association; World Curling Tour.

AMTRAK
60 MASSACHUSETTS AVENUE NE
SUITE 4E-315
WASHINGTON, DC 20002
202-906-3000
800-872-7245
Fax: 202-906-3560
mediarelations@amtrak.com
www.amtrak.com
• Joseph H. Boardman, President/Chief Executive Officer
• Linda Park, National Marketing Group Manager
(202) 906-4825

• Barbara Richardson, Executive Vice President
(202) 906-3610
• Karen Dunn, Media Relations Director
Regional Offices:
West - Oakland, CA; Midwest - Chicago, IL; Northeast - New York; South - New Orleans.

ANTHONY TRAVEL, INC.
7920 BELT LINE ROAD
SUITE 1010
DALLAS, TX 75254
214-363-0073
800-736-6377
Fax: 214-363-1180
www.anthonytravel.com
• Tina Acosta, International Travel Consultant
tinaacosta@anthonytravel.com
• Jean Anthony, Director, Notre Dame Events
• Normajean Baxter, Event Coordinator
normajeanbaxter@anthonytravel.com
• Dee An Bell, Marketing Manager
deeannbell@anthonytravel.com
Services:
Provides personal, professional travel service to all our clients, regardless of the size of the request.

AVIS RENT A CAR SYSTEM
6 SYLVAN WAY
PARSIPPANY, NJ 7054
973-496-3500
800-352-7900
Fax: 973-496-7584
www.avis.com
• Ronald L. Nelson, Chairman/CEO
• David B Wyshner, Sr.Executive VP, Chief Financial Officer
• Larry De Shon, President, EMEA
• Scott Deaver, Executive VP of Strategy
• Thomas M Gartland, President ,North America
• Mark J Servodidio, Executive VP and Chief Administrative Officer
• Gerard Insall, Sr.VP and CIO
• Ronald L Nelson, Chairman/Chief Operating Officer
Services:
MLB - New York Yankees Official rental car company

BLUE BIRD CORPORATION
402 BLUE BIRD BOULEVARD
PO BOX 937
FORT VALLEY, GA 31030
478-825-2021
800-486-7122
Fax: 478-822-2467
info@blue-bird.com
www.blue-bird.com
• Drew Hawkins, National Sales Manager
(770) 751-6755
wdhawkin@blue-bird.com
• Chris Payne, Bid and Contracts Administrator
(478) 822-2566
cdpayne@blue-bird.com
• Glenn Wilder, Sales Administration Manager
(478) 822-2904
ghwilder@blue-bird.com
• Phil Horlock, President nad CEO
• John Kwapis, Chief Operating Officer
• Dale Wendell, Senior VP of Global Bus Sales and marketing

• Phil Tighe, Chief Financial officer
• Steve Girardin, President and CEO
Products:
Provides innovative design and manufacturing of school buses, commercial buses and motor coaches.

BUSBANK
200 W ADAMS STREET
SUITE 1100
CHICAGO, IL 60606
312-476-6100
866-428-7226
Fax: 312-577-0947
sales@busbank.com
www.busbank.com/sportstravel/
• William R. Maulsby, President/CEO
• Don Sivesind, Vice President Sales
Nature of Services:
The BusBank is a group and event transportation specialist, services of which includes motorcoaches, school buses, mini buses, executive and sleeper coaches and other specialty vehicles, such as trolleys and double decker buses.

CAREY WORLDWIDE CHAUFFERED SERVICES
4530 WISCONSIN AVENUE NW
WASHINGTON, DC 20016
202-895-1200
800-336-4646
Fax: 904-223-9698
Customercare@carey.com
www.carey.com
• Diane M Ennist, Sr.VP ,General Counsel
• Rae D Fawcett, Sr.VP, Organisational Development and Human C
• Sally A Snead, Sr.Vp , Operations
• Joel J Barch, VP, Customer Experience
• Yolanda Carneiro, VP,Sales Development
• Gary L Kessler, President/CEO
• Mitchell J Lahr, Executive VP and Chief Financial Officer
Services:
Official Ground Transportation for the Gator Bowl.

CARLSON TRAVEL NETWORK
701 CARLSON PARKWAY
PO BOX 59159
MINNETONKA, MN 55305
763-212-5000
800-213-7295
Fax: 763-212-6664
info@carlson.com
www.carlson.com
• Marilyn C. Nelson, Chairman
mnelson@carlson.com
• Curtis C. Nelson, President and Chief Operating Officer
cnelson@carlson.com
• Trudy Rautio, EVP and Chief Financial Officer
trautio@carlson.com
• Jeffrey Balagna, EVP and Chief Information and Customer
jbalagna@carlson.com
Services:
Known as a global leader in the marketing, travel, and hospitality industries.
Brands:
Among the names in the Carlson family of brands and services are: Regent International Hotels r; Radisson Hotels & Resorts r; Park Plaza Hotels & Resorts ; Country Inns & Suites By Carlson; Park Innr

hotels; Radisson Seven Seas Cruisesr ; T.G.I. Friday'sr and Pick Up Stixr restaurants; Carlson Wagonlit Travel; Cruise Holidays; All Aboard Travel ; Cruise Specialists; Fly4Less.com ; CruiseDeals.com ; Results Travel; Carlson Destination Marketing Services; Carlson Leisure Travel Services; SeaMaster Cruisesr ; SinglesCruise.comr; CW Government Travel; Carlson Marketingr; Peppers & Rogers Groupr ; and Gold Points Reward Network.
Travel Services:
Team travel, special event travel, sports meetings and conventions, special event tour packages.
Sports Service Founded:
1986

CORPORATE AMERICA AVIATION, INC.
PO BOX 1978
BURBANK, CA 91507-1978
818-953-7206
800-521-8585
Fax: 818-563-2368
privatebizjets@aol.com
www.privatebizjets.com
• Daniel A. Darwish, President
Specializes in:
Private aircraft transportation for special events, promotional or personal tours; executive and celebrity travel, late-night flights. Worldwide scope of service.
Year Founded:
1989

FORSYTHE & ASSOCIATES, INC.
7770 FRONTAGE ROAD
SKOKIE, IL 60077
847-213-7000
800-843-4488
info@forsythe.com
www.forsythe.com
• Richard A. Forsythe, Chairman
rforsythe@forsythe.com
• William P. Brennan, President
wbrennan@forsythe.com
• Albert L. Weiss, Chief Financial Officer
aweiss@forsythe.com
• William P. Brennan, President & CEO
Event Management Services:
Specializes in providing management of all transportation for sports events, serving the needs of event producers, sponsors and broadcast media. Services include motor pool development, ground transportation and shuttle systems.
Services:
Technology infrastructure solutions provider, technology and business consulting services, leasing services, and value-added reseller services for all of the leading technology product manufacturers.
Services:
Provides technology and business consulting services, technology leasing services, and value-added reseller services for all of the leading technology product manufacturers.
Clients:
AFLAC, Archipelago, Education Management Corporation, H&R Block, NASDAQ, Outback Steakhouse, Snap-on Incorporated, Trizetto, US Bancorp, Visiting Nurse Service of New York

GO WITH A PRO, INC.
38 MILLER AVENUE P M B 241
MILL VALLEY, CA 94941
415-383-3907
• Tim Fitzpatrick, Cofounder/President/Chief Executive Officer
• Scot Schmidt, Co-Founder/Athlete Relations VP
• Jay Orlando, Co-Founder/Operations VP
• Robert Weaver, Surfing Director
Description:
We offer access to over 100 world-class professionals across a variety of today's most popular outdoor sports including skiing, snowboarding, surfing, climbing and mountain biking.
Services:
Provides a full line of services for companies looking to identify their products and corporate image with an active, exciting lifestyle. GowithaPro not only provides easy web-based access to an incredible pool of elite athletes ranging from Olympic heroes to action sport legends but also offers a complete line of professional services.

HAKINS MEETINGS & INCENTIVES
239 MADISON AVENUE
WYCKOFF, NJ 7481
201-848-7678
800-643-3977
Fax: 201-848-9210
info@hakins.com
www.hakins.com
• Paul Smith, President
psmith@hakins.com
• Florio Gay, VP
• Judy Zanetti, Director of Accounts
Other Locations:
Hakins West, 3541 Calle Gavanzo, Carlsbad CA 92009. 800 869-1873; FAX: 760 634-3219. E-Mail: bginnhakinswest@msn.com; William S. Ginn, Dir Bus Dev
Services:
Provides professional support in the design and execution of exceptionally successful group travel programs, supported by state-of-the-art group travel technology solutions. Delivers sound, value-based solutions to corporations involved in moving groups of people for meetings, incentives, promotions, hospitality, special events or sporting events.
Clients:
Weichert Realtors, Verizon, Ryan Partnership, Action/Emco
Sports Service Founded:
1986
Event Management Services:
Sports hospitality, special events, travel fulfillment of promotions, meetings, group and individual incentive travel.

HARMON TRAVEL SERVICE
1529 W WASHINGTON STREET
BOISE, ID 83702
208-388-3000
800-627-1315
Fax: 208-388-3003
vacations@harmontravel.com
www.harmontravel.com
• David Harmon, Group Dept Manager
• Mary E Cook, Corporate Dept Manager
• Kathleen Kelley, Accounting Manager
• Amee Bybee, Leisure Travel Consultant
• Anne Connors, Leisure Travel Consultant
• Bob E. Harmon, President, MCC, CTC
BobH@harmontravel.com
• Eleanor Harmon, Co-Founder
eleanorh@harmontravel.com

LUXECONCIERGE
404 CAMINO DEL RIO S
SUITE 601
SAN DIEGO, CA 92108
619-234-7766
800-964-6887
Fax: 619-234-2587
• Cynthia D. Adkins, Founder/President
• Jennifer Hecker, Operations Director
• Karen S. Somers, Conference Services Director
Services:
Provider of of luxury and corporate concierge services.
Description:
LuxeConcierge is a worldwide full service concierge and travel organization. A complete travel service. Skilled in booking, dinner reservations, local hotspots, tickets for sold out shows and events, car service, rental car booking, corporate travel gifts. Complete coordination and luxury.
Event Packages Include:
Super Bowl. NBA All-Star. Olympics. Final Four. The Masters. Wimbledon. World Series. Daytona 500. Ibiza. Essence Music Fest. Mardi Gras. Carnival. Cannes and more.
Services Include:
Travel Planning, Concierge Services, Event Tickets & Packages, Event Planning, Personal Shopping.

NEW DIRECTIONS
131 OLIVER STREET
BOSTON, MA 02110-3620
617-523-7775
Fax: 617-357-6482
info@newdirections.com
• David D. Corbett, Chief Executive Officer / Director
dcorbett@newdirections.com
• Jeffrey D. Redmond, President / Director
jredmond@newdirections.com
• Patricia B. Baillieul, VP
pbaillieul@newdirections.com
• Michael D. Jeans, President and Senior Consultant
mjeans@newdirections.com
• David D. Corbett, Founder and Senior Consultant
(617) 624-3333
dcorbett@newdirections.com
• Jeffrey D. Redmond, Partner, Director, and Senior Consultant
(617) 624-3334
jredmond@newdirections.com
• Patricia D. Smith, Senior Vice President
(617) 624.3359
psmith@newdirections.com
• Samuel C. Pease, Vice President and Senior Consultant
(617) 624-3302
spease@newdirections.com
Description:
Pre-eminent provider of career transition services exclusively for senior-level executives, professionals and their families. Helping clients find and create opportunities that not only meet their near-term career expectations and needs, but also advance their long-term work and life goals.

Year Founded:
1986

SENTIENT
100 GROSSMAN DRIVE
4TH FLOOR
WEYMOUTH, MA 02184
866-307-3684
800-760-4908
Fax: 631-756-0809
anicholas@sentientflight.com
www.sentient.com
• Steve M. Hankin, Chief Executive Officer
(866) 307-3684
• Tom Davis, President and Chief Executive Officer, A
(866) 307-3684
• John Bax, Chief Financial Officer
(866) 307-3684
• Charles Starkowsky, Chief Safety Officer
(866) 307-3684
Services:
Pioneers a unique membership program that offers the most flexible private jet solution for both individuals and corporations.

SEVEN CONTINENTS SPORTS, INC.
2340 S RIVER ROAD
DES PLAINES, IL 60018
847-699-8064
Sports Service Founded:
1985

SKYQUEST CHARTERS
1140 CORPORATE BOULEVARD
RENO, NV 89502-2330
775-746-5555
Fax: 775-746-5551
sales@skyquestcharters.com
www.skyquestcharters.com
• Kevin Gustafson, Chief Executive Officer
Services:
Serves tour operators, travel agents, cruise lines, collegiate sports teams and bands, and thousands of football fans. Fortune 500 companies, travel and leisure groups, also make up a small portion of its clientele.

SNOWMOBILE ADVENTURES
PO BOX 4167
DURANGO, CO 81302
970-259-7293
Fax: 970-749-5522
www.snowmobileadventures.com
• Pete Busby, Owner
Description:
Dispatch Snowmobile tours.

SNOWMOBILE ADVENTURES BCD, LC
1240 HARROP STREET
OGDEN, UT 84404-4641
801-394-5448
Description:
Rent our Snowmobiles, and provide guides for snowmobiling and racing.

SPORTS DESTINATION NETWORK, INC.
6501 E GREENWAY PARKWAY
SUITE 103-625
SCOTTSDALE, AZ 85254
480-767-3900
Fax: 480-767-6061
www.sdninc.com

• Dirk Smith, President/Founder
dsmith@sdninc.com
• Michelle McNally, Executive Asst
Services:
Services include: a) Initiate and formulate the site selection process of group events/meetings; b) Deliver collateral materials and SDN comments/information regarding potential hotels; c) Coordinate for client all appointment scheduling for any personal site inspection visits; d) Take responsibility for contract negotiation directly with hotels, yet the client signs the contracts for complete control, and; e) Assist with any ancillary requirements for group meetings (buses, limos, golf tournament, guest speaker, etc).
Clients:
Clients: 1) SPORTS WEAR / EQUIPMENT MANUFACTURERS, DISTRIBUTORS: Adidas America, Converse Sportswear, Easton Sports, Mizuno USA, Rawlings Sporting Goods, Reebok International, Russell Athletic, Taylor Made, The Sports Authority; 2) SPORTS TEAMS: Buffalo Sabres, San Francisco Giants, Sacramento Kings, San Jose Sharks, Seattle SuperSonics, St. Louis Blues, Tampa Bay Devil Rays; 3) SPORTS HEALTH AND FITNESS: American Youth Soccer Association, Gold's Gym Enterprises, HealthSouth; 4) SPORTS SERVICES AND PRODUCTS: H.O.K. Sports Facilities, Sega of America, Sony Signatures, Ticketmaster; 5) SPORTS BROADCASTING & COMMUNICATIONS: KNBR Radio, ESPN Radi
Nature of Sports Service:
A comprehensive sports travel consultant and management company uniquely designed to accommodate members of the sports community. Specializes in group and special projects.
Manufacturing Clients Include:
Adidas America — Professional / recreational sportswear Cleveland Golf — Golf Equipment Manufacturer Converse Sportswear — Professional / recreational sportswear Mizuno USA — Professional / recreational equipment Precept — Golf Equipment Manufacturer Rawlings Sporting Goods — Professional / recreational equipment Reebok International — Professional / recreational sportswear Russell Athletic — Professional / recreational sportswear Taylor Made — Golf Equipment Manufacturer The Sports Authority — Retail outlet chain

SPORTS EXPRESS, LLC
72 SUTTLE STREET
TRAVEL GUEST CARE
SUITE G
DURANGO, CO 81303
970-247-3048
800-357-4174
Fax: 970-385-8680
orders@luggageforward.com
www.sportsexpress.com
• Dave Welz, Media Relations Director
(970) 375-3405
dwelz@SportsExpress.com
• Jon Trevelise, Chief Executive Officer
• Mike Smedley, Media Relations
(970) 375-3405
Services:
Provides premier luggage and sports equipment delivery service; Partners with

leading firms including FedEx, UPS, national and regional airlines and numerous travel, resort and hospitality companies.
Clients:
Partners: West Coast Trends, Inc.; Fairmont Hotels & Resorts; Abercrombie & Kent Destination Clubs; Merrill +; America West Airlines; Northwest Airlines; United Airlines; Aspen/Snowmass; Adventure Cycling Association; The Executive Women's Golf Association;TSE Golf; Tri All 3 Sports.

SPORTS FANTASY TOURS & EVENTS
16633 DALLAS PARKWAY
SUITE 600
ADDISON, TX 75001
214-691-9476
Services:
Offers tours and programs at major sporting events including: Game tickets, Luxury suite rentals and hospitality, Hotel accommodations, Celebrity theme event, Ground transportation, Personalized gift amenities, On-site staffing & coordination; 2) Corporate hospitality events; 3) Consumer promotions (point of sale, sweepstakes, sports team tie-ins); 4) Golf tournament management & coordination; 5) Inter-active sporting events: Basketball Shoot-out, Football Toss, Golf Putting Contests; 6) Sports Celebrities & Professional Players (speakers, meet & greet, chalk talks, insider info); 7) Sales incentive awards; and 8) Trade show promotions.
clients
Sprint, Compaq, Fox SportsNet.
Sports Service Founded:
1994
Marketing & Consulting Services:
Specialists in the development and marketing of Inside The Game sports tour programs.

SPORTS TOUR CLASSICS
11150 SANTA MONICA BOULEVARD
#500
LOS ANGELES, CA 90025
310-777-2525
800-591-9198
Fax: 310-777-2524
info@primesport.com
www.primesport.com
Services:
A leader in the development, sales, and management of premium ticket packages to sold-out sport, concert and cultural events worldwide.
Sports Service Founded:
1989
Nature of Sports Service:
Travel tours for major sporting events. Specializing in incentive programs to major spectator sporting events (tickets, hotel, transportation, celebrity speakers).

SPORTS TRAVEL, INC.
9601 WHITE ROCK TRAIL
SUITE 101
DALLAS, TX 75238-5011
214-341-9777
800-528-5260
Fax: 214-341-8849
info@sportstravelinc.com
www.sportstravelinc.com
• Doug Hill, Sales Representative
(214) 341-9777
doug@sportstravelinc.com

• Tony Liscio II, President
(214) 341-9777
tony@sportstravelinc.com
• Jennifer Babisak, Sales Support
jennifer@sportstravelinc.com
• Tony Liscio II, President
tony@sportstravelinc.com
• Doug Hill, Sales Rep
doug@sportstravelinc.com
• Mary A. Hill, Administration Office
maryann@sportstravelinc.com
Sports Service Founded:
1982
Services:
Coordinates trips for all occasions and for any age group; arranges ski vacations for church groups, Young Life groups, and families.
Nature of Sports Service:
A full service travel agency specializing in ski trips for groups.

THS COMPANY
200 ROUTE 31
SUITE 204
FLEMINGTON, NJ 08822
908-979-0928
888-536-8326
Fax: 908-684-2456
tom@thsweb.com
www.thsweb.com
• Tom Berkman, General Manager
(908) 979-0928
tom@thsweb.com
• Kelli Orpen, Operations Director
(908) 850-5900
kelli@thsweb.com
• Briana Chapman, GM Championship Travel
(866) 790-8747
bri@thsweb.com
Services:
Offers a complete housing service that makes the booking of rooms easier for the hotels, the teams and the tournament.
Year Founded:
1998
Description of Sport Organization:
The premier sports housing service in the U.S. THS signs $25 million in hotel contracts per year as the official housing service for 80+ regional and national tournaments and championships each year.
Nature of Sports Service:
Provides free professional housing services for sports tournaments and other events. Organization handles all hotel-related responsibilities for an event including the signing of hotel contracts, negotiating headquarters hotel, comp rooms, reservations services, rebates and rebate collection.

TRANSPORTATION MANAGEMENT SERVICES, INC.
2870 PEACHTREE ROAD NW
ATLANTA, GA 30305
404-815-0551
• Tom Hastings, President
Florida Address:
4501 W. Cayuga Ave, Tampa, FL 33614. 813-873-8861; FAX: 813-873-8661
Event Management Services:
Transportation services including tour packaging, hotel accommodations, etc. Also provides receptive operator and charter bus services.

TSE SPORTS & ENTERTAINMENT
14 PENN PLAZA
SUITE 925
NEW YORK, NY 10122
212-695-9480
877-621-5243
Fax: 212-564-8098
www.tseworld.com
• Robert Tuchman, President
(212) 695-9480
• Brett Sklar, SVP
(877) 621-5243
• Andy Robb, Operations Director
(212) 695-9480
Services:
Provides marketing programs to reach and
engage customers by leveraging the power
of sports & entertainment to bring their
brand messages to life. Provides
athlete/celebrity talent for appearances,
events, promotions, public relations projects
and endorsements.
Services:
Specializes in working with corporations to
provide them with marketing programs that
reach and engage their customers by
leveraging the power of sports &
entertainment to bring their brand messages
to life. Focuses on Corporate Hospitality,
Sales Promotions & Sweepstakes, Meeting
& Event Planning, Athlete/ Celebrity
Marketing, and Corporate Consulting.
Clients:
Anheuser-Busch, Bacardi Martini, Brown
Forman, Coors, Deer Park, Geyser Peak
Winery, InBev/Labatt USA, Miller Brewing
Company, Diageo, Schieffelin & Somerset,
Triarc Beverages, ABC Sports, Conde Nast
Publications, Fox Network, GQ Magazine,
HBO, NBC, ESPN, Maxim Magazine;
Castrol, Daimler Chyrsler, ExxonMobil, Ford
Motor Co., General Motors, Lexus, Pennzoil
Products, Toyota; American Express, Bank
of America, Merrill Lynch, JP Morgan
Chase, KPMG, Bear Stearns, Hartford
Financial, Morgan-Stanley Dean Whitter,
AT&T, EMC, Ericsson, Hewlett-Packard,
Lucent Technologies, Microsoft, IBM, Sony,
Verizon; Bayer Corp., BIC USA,
Bristol-Myers, Campbell's
Sports Travel:
Specializes in travel packages to major
sporting events.
Athlete Management Services:
Provides athlete/celebrity talent for
appearances, events, promotions, public
relations projects and endorsements.
Event Management Services:
Specializes in providing hospitality and
promotional services with multi-level
involvement including consumer, trade and
retail sales.
Promotional Services:
Specializes in fully integrated marketing
promotions.

WESTERN SKI PROMOTIONS, INC.
4031 STONE WAY N
PO BOX 75298
SEATTLE, WA 98103
206-634-3620
Fax: 206-363-2114
Services:
Ski reports; European ski tours.

WORLDTEK TRAVEL
ONE AUDUBON
SUITE 400
NEW HAVEN, CT 6511
203-772-0470
800-243-1723
Fax: 203-865-2034
info@worldtek.com
www.worldtek.com
• Vito Luciani, Owner/Chairman
• Peter LeMay, Finance SVP
• Karen LaRose, Marketing and Special
Events SVP
• Dave Smith, Operations SVP
dave.smith@worldtek.com
Sports Service Founded:
1969
Services:
Offers comprehensive travel services for
associations, colleges, corporations,
meetings, universities and vacationers
Marketing & Consulting Services:
Manages travel arrangements for a wide
range of sports organizations, teams and
trade shows.
Clients Include:
Big Ten Conference, LPGA, NCAA, U.S.
Skiing, U.S. Volleyball.

Statistical Services

**ALL AMERICAN AMATEUR BASEBALL
ASSOCIATION**
331 PARKWAY DRIVE
ZANESVILLE, OH 43701
740-453-8531
• Douglas Pollack, President
• Len DiForte, 1st Vp
• Lou Tiberi, 2nd Vp
Services:
Supports and organizes amateur baseball
tournaments

ALL-PRO SOFTWARE
333 DOTY STREET
PO BOX 149
MINERAL POINT, WI 53565
608-987-4549
800-776-7859
Fax: 608-987-4553
info@allprosoftware.com
www.allprosoftware.com
Description:
Providing quality sports statics and
scheduling software. Offering quality
software thats easy to use for coachs,
scorekeepers, leagues and tournament
directors as well as YMCA's, city park and
recs, high school and colleges.
Products:
Quality Sports Statistics and Scheduling
Software
Brands:
Coaches, Scorekeepers, League &
Tournament Directors as well as YMCAs,
City Park & Recs, High Schools and
Colleges; StatTrak Address Manager v3.0;
StatTrak K-ForCE v3.0; League Scheduler
v6.0; Tournament Scheduler Pro; StatTrak
for Baseball; StatTrak for Hockey; StatTrak
for Volleyball; StatTrak for Soccerl; StatTrak
for Football

ELIAS SPORTS BUREAU
500 FIFTH AVENUE
SUITE 2140
NEW YORK, NY 10110
212-869-1530
Fax: 212-354-0980
www.esb.com
• Steve Hirdt, EVP
• Chris Thorn, VP
Services:
Statistical services in the field of
professional sports
Clients:
Major League Baseball Records, World
Series Records, Championship Series
Record, Division Series Records, All-Star
Game records, Hall of Fame Records, The
Elias Book of Baseball Records
Products:
Offers products on historical research in the
field of professional sports
Products:
Offers products on historical research in the
field of professional sports
Description:
Founded in 1913. Providing historical
research and statistical services in the field
of professional sports.
Clients Include:
All the major professional sports leagues in
North America, television networks,
newspapers and other publications, as well
as other providers of new media and
web-sites.
Publications:
The Elias Book of Baseball Records.

EQUIBASE COMPANY
821 CORPORATE DRIVE
LEXINGTON, KY 40503-2794
859-224-2860
800-333-2211
Fax: 859-224-2870
feedback@equibase.com
www.equibase.com
• Hank Zeitlin, President/Chief Operating
Officer
(859) 224-2860
hzeitlin@equibase.com
• Carlie Ambrose, Manager, Sales and
Contract
(859) 224-2868
cambrose@equibase.com
• Connie Brannen, Operations Manager
(859) 224-2854
cbrannen@equibase.com
• Hank Zeitlin, President and Chief
Operating Officer
(859) 224-2860
hzeitlin@equibase.com
• Shelby Cook, Online Service Coordinator
(859) 224-2863
scook@equibase.com
• Chris Dawahare, Manager , eBusiness
Operations and Developmen
(859) 224-2862
cdawahare@equibase.com
Sports Service Founded:
1991
Products:
Provides the Thoroughbred racetracks of
North America with a uniform,
industry-owned database of racing
information and statistics. Collects past
performance information from all
Thoroughbred racetracks in North America
through a network of chartcallers.
Brands:

Race Programs, Expert Selections, F.A.S.T. Sheets, Performance Cycle, Cycles Lite, FlashNet, Daily Racing Form, Track Bias Reports, SpeedGraph, ClassGraph, Premium Edited Pedigree, Five Generation Pedigree, ChartPlus, Harness Race Information, Harness Racing Products, Virtual Stable, Racing Leaders, All-Time Top 10 Leaders, Top Leaders by Track, Meet Statistics, Wireless Information, New Fan Information; Equibaser Race Programs, Virtual StableT

Nature of Sports Service:
Thoroughbred industry's official database for racing information and statistics. Through a network of chart callers, the company collects past performance information from all thoroughbred race tracks in North America. Its state-of-the-art database in Lexington, Kentucky processes, stores and makes available for retrieval over five million individual race starts containing well over a half billion items of information.

GOLFSTAT
PO BOX 399
BLOOMINGTON, IL 61702-0399
www.golfstat.com
• Mark Laesch, Founder
Description:
Developed and provided free tournament software for college golf tournments. Provides statistical services and software for men's and women's college golf programs. Compiles the MasterCard rankings for the College Golf Foundation and perform on side scoring at their national tournaments. Provides background information and scoring for Intersport Television for their productions of college golf. Created and provide the statistical information used by Golf World magazine in their college golf poll section. Wrote the first points system software for the AJGA.
Services:
Provides statistical services and software development services for college golf tournaments and events. Offers a customized statistical service for college golf teams on the web. Hosts and maintains personalized web pages for teams' and players' statistics
Clients:
Men's Golf Team of University of Alabama, Barry University, Baylor University, Boston College, University of California Riverside, University of Central Florida, Clemson University, Coastal Carolina University, University of Denver, East Tennessee State University, Fresno State University, University of Georgia, Georgia State University, Indiana University, Jacksonville State University, Kent State University, Long Beach State, Louisiana-Monroe, LSU, Mercer University, New Mexico, Savannah College of Art and Design, Southeastern Louisiana University, University of Southern California, University of South Florida, Southern Methodist, St. Mary'

ONNIDAN GROUP, THE
6122 RICKER ROAD
RALEIGH, NC 27610
919-329-7036
Fax: 919-747-4541
staff@onnidan.com
www.onnidan.com

• Eric Moore, Managing Editor
(919) 329-7036
staff@onnidan.com
Description:
Founded in 1987, The Onnidan Group is a partnership of individuals with backgrounds in sports information, marketing, journalism and telecommunication.
Services:
Statistical services, information brokering, personal computer operations and webite administration.

PLAYER HISTORY.COM
www.playerhistory.com
• Hakon An Winther, Founder
• Christian Holm, Technical Staff
Description:
Consists of a group of idealistic football fans with the intenion to making this web site the best place on the web to find information about players from all around the world as well as statistics about matches.

SPORTS REFERENCE, THE
6757 GREENE ST.
SUITE 315
PHILADELPHIA, PA 19119
215-301-9181
Fax: 800-660-5292
sf@sports-reference.com
www.sports-reference.com
• Sean Forman, Owner
sean-forman@baseball-reference.com
• Justin Kubatko, VP
• Doug Drinen, Football Operations
• Jay Virshbo, Business Development
• Neil Paine, User Affairs Coordinator
Services:
Provides statistical services and information services about baseball.

SPORTSLINE USA, INC./CBS.SPORTSLINE.COM
1401 W CYPRESS CREEK ROAD
FORT LAUDERDALE, FL 33309
954-351-2120
800-771-4616
Fax: 954-771-2807
ir@sportsline.com
www.cbssports.com
• Michael Levy, Founder/President/Chied Executive Office
• Mark J. Mariani, Sales/Marketing President
• Kenneth W. Sanders, Strategic and Financial Planning EVP
• Stephen E. Snyder, Product Development and Operations EVP
Services:
Provides online sports content, community and online sales of sporting equipment and supplies. Sports content includes multimedia sports news, information, entertainment
Clients:
CBSSportsLine.com, FANSTASY Sports, GolfWeb, NFL.com, PGATour.com, NCAA Sports.com
Products:
Fantasy sports products and merchandise
Nature of Sports Service:
Global on-line sports information service and media company. Devoted exclusively to sports information, entertainment and merchandising. Producers of CBS SportsLine. Produce the official League Web sites for Major League Baseball, the

PGA Tour, and NFL European League, and serves as the primary sports content provider for America Online, Netscape, and Excite.

STATS LLC
2775 SHERMER ROAD
NORTHBROOK, IL 60062
847-583-2100
Fax: 847-583-2600
sales@stats.com
www.stats.com
• Gary Walrath, Chief Executive Officer
• Susan Zamachek, Director, Human Resources
• Steve Byrd, Executive Vice President
• Bobby Schur, Executive Vice President
• Allan Spear, Director of Operations
• Brian Orefice, Editorial
• Jim Corelis, AVP, Applications
• Brian Kopp, Vice President, Strategic Planning
• John Sasman, Asst. VP, Commercial Products
• Nick Stamm, Director, Communications
• Greg Kirkorsky, VP- Sales
Nature of Service:
STATS is the world's leading sports technology, data and content company. The company passionately abides by a mission to revolutionize the way sports contests are viewed, understood and enjoyed. STATS' calling card consists of real-time scores, historical sports information, Associated Press editorial content, a turnkey fantasy sports operation and SportVU technology. Today, STATS' worldwide client network of media companies and professional sports leagues and teams utilize a broad spectrum of dynamic in-game broadcast presentations and virtual images, multimedia enhancements and game analysis and tactical coaching tools. STATS is owned join
Year Founded:
1981
Locations:
STATS recently opened satellite offices in Bangalore, Hong Kong and London to join an existing bureau in Mexico City.
Clients:
Professional teams, print and broadcast media, iTV platforms, software developers, fantasy game operators, publishers and interactive and wireless service providers around the globe, Yahoo!, EA Sports, Fox Sports, DIRECTV, CHIEFS

STRATBRIDGE, INC.
BLANCHARD HOUSE
SUITE 304
249 AYER ROAD
HARVARD, MA 1451
978-772-4647
Fax: 617-977-8630
www.stratbridge.com
• Matthew Marolda, Founder/Chief Executive Officer
• Andrew H. Palmer, Strategy & Sales/Marketing
• Thomas L. Doorley, III, Strategy & Growth/Board of Directors
• Anthony J. Marolda, Strategy & Planning/Board of Directors
• Michael T. Horvath, Strategic Alliances/Board of Directors
Nature of Services:
StratBridge provides analytic solutions that enable professional sports managers to

perform exhaustive diligence research at the touch of a button - StratBridge.net, a platform product, is a Web-native system that seamlessly extracts data from internal and external sources, regardless of format, and then visually renders it in high-resolution plasma displays.

TRAKUS, INC.
107 AUDUBON RD
BUILDING 3-10
WAKEFIELD, MA 1880
617-544-6070
Fax: 617-544-6071
info@trakus.com
www.trakus.com
• Bob McCarthy, President/Chief Executive Officer
• Barry Weisbord, Chairman
• Michael Ciacciarelli, Chief Operating Officer
• Patrick Cummings, Business Manager/Director, Racing Information
• Peter Gargalianos, Director, Field Operations
Sports Service Founded:
1997
Brands:
Trakus System 2.0
Nature of Sports Service:
System delivers motion characteristics like speed, acceleration, and impact of a collision. The resulting information will form new class of statistics, on-air graphics and coaching tools. Also creating a new way to record an event, providing a bridge between sports and emerging electronic media like the Internet, digital television, and video games.

Student Athlete Recruiting Services

ATHLETES ADVANCE
35 SALUTATION STREET
SUITE # 3
BOSTON, MA 2109
• Chris Teso, Chief Executive Officer
Description:
Promise to give student athletes exposure to collegiate athletic programs. Puts the power of search agents into the hands of coaches and allow them to search for talent on their own terms and contact the recruits that match their program.
Services:
Intends to be an online stat tracking and athletic community that acts as a conduit between college coach and student-athlete. Bridges geographic barriers that typically prevent a quality athlete from getting the recognition he/she deserves because they come from a small school that seldom elicits the same attention of a larger school. Athletes Advance puts the power of search agents into the hands of coaches and allows them to search for talent on their own terms and contact the recruits that match their program.

CERTIFIED ATHLETE
HOUSTON, TX 66216
913-905-5872
certifiedathlete@gmail.com
www.certifiedathlete.com

Description:
Set out to create a system that would allow academies to post athlete information and make it available to recruiters. The result of this effort is Certified Athlete.
Services:
A unique online network of athletes, schools, recruiters, and training academies that is revolutionizing the college recruiting process. CertifiedAthlete.com is designed to gain exposure for athletes and provide the tools for recruiters to review more athletes and in greater detail than was previously possible. Certified Athlete's Partner Academies offer Athlete Certifications, providing independent 3rd party tests and opinions.

COLLEGE PROSPECTS OF AMERICA
12682 COLLEGE PROSPECT DRIVE
LOGAN, OH 43138-0269
740-385-6624
888-275-2762
Fax: 740-385-9065
• Tracy Jackson, President & Chief Executive Officer
Year Founded:
1986.
Sports Service Founded:
1986
Services:
CPOA offers the following services:A custom profile form detailing athletic and academic achievements, Mailings of personalized reports to college coaches, Personal guidance throughout the recruiting process, Continuous internet marketing, Financial aid counseling, FAFSA preparation and electronic filing as well as enhancement and preparation of athletic videos for distribution to college coaches.

FIRST JOB IN SPORTS
201 N. ILLINOIS STREET
16TH FLOOR-SOUTH TOWER
INDIANAPOLIS, IN 46204
317-721-8134
Fax: 610-884-1800
www.firstjobinsports.com
• Brad Freeman, Executive Director
Nature of Service:
An online service to college students looking to find an internship or entry-level position in the sports industry. Students are able to insert criteria of positions they are looking for and only show jobs within that certain criteria. members are also able to submit their resume for hundreds of businesses to look at and members can receive daily job alerts directly in their email. Also offers advice regarding resume writing, cover letters, interview techniques, and other valuable information to help members land their first job in the sports industry.
Products:
Sports job board website for college students.

GLOBAL SPORTS CONNEXION
771 WEST END AVENUE
NEW YORK, NY 10025
212-967-0204
Fax: 212-656-1480
info@gsconline.net
www.gsconline.net
• Mark Ozer, Founder/Director
• Mark Ozer, Founder, Chairman

Sports Service Founded:
1990
Nature of Sports Services:
Assists high-level collegiate and professional athletes take advantage of global opportunities through their College Connexion and Tournament Connexion programs; heavy emphasis on Tennis.

NATIONWIDE SPORTS, INC.
1612 SHARON PLACE
CEDAR PARK, TX 78613-3563
512-249-2611
• Jeff Forster, President

NEW ENGLAND INTERACTIVE
3 SUNSET RIDGE
LEXINGTON, MA 2421
617-308-5094
info@NewEnglandInteractive.com
www.newenglandinteractive.com
• David Galehouse, Founder
(781) 862-3180
Products:
Creates and manages both local and national content websites.
Brands:
Varsityedge.com, Golfingnewengland.com, Newenglandathletics.com

RECRUIT, INC.
PO BOX 301
OWINGS MILLS, MD 21117
888-284-9227
Fax: 410-581-9513
Nature of Sports Service:
Recruiting and scouting service for high school athletes desiring to play college sports. Organization creates scouting reports on client athletes that can play at some level in college i.e., Division 1, 2, 3, or NAIA. Organization markets the athlete to the level that would get them the best response from college coaches. 100 scouts throughout the nation that work part and fulltime to find potential college prospects. Scouts are assigned to 20-30 schools to identify potential college prospects in their area. The regional scout interviews a potential college prospect to go over their academic and athletic background.

RECRUIT-ME
805-550-7566
support@recruit-me.com
www.recruit-me.com
• Jon Fugler, Founder
Founded:
2002
Nature of Service:
College recruitment and athletic scholarships.

SPORTS MEDIA CHALLENGE
7300 CARMEL EXECUTIVE PARK DRIVE
SUITE 120
CHARLOTTE, NC 28226
704-541-5942
800-929-4386
Fax: 704-541-5943
info@sportsmediachallenge.com
www.sportsmediachallenge.com
• Kathleen Hessert, Certified Speaking Professional
(704) 541-5942

khessert@sportsmediachallenge.com
• Joshua Baer, Chief Technology Consultant
Services:
Media Training, Crisis Communications, Public Speaking, Reputation Management, Online Word of Mouth and Conversation Tracking
Clients:
ASSOCIATIONS: American Football Coaches Association (AFCA), Black Coaches Association (BCA) College Sports Information Directors Association (CoSIDA), National Association of Collegiate Directors of Athletics (NACDA), Women's Basketball Coaches' Association (WBCA), NBA Coaches Associaiton; COLLEGES: Bowling Green UNiversity, Michigan State University, San Diego State University, University of Colorado, University of Connecticut, University of Florida, University of Maryland, University of North Carolina, University of Nortre Dame, University of Tennessee, University of Texas, University of Washington; ATHLETES, COACHES & PROFESSIONALS: Derek

VISION SPORTS, INC.
13236 WOODSEDGE WAY
CLERMONT, FL 34711-5916
407-654-6277
866-152-6418
Fax: 407-654-6269
• John Harris, Owner/President
Sports Service Founded:
2002
Services:
The College Sports Network for Recruiting High School Athletes
Nature of Sports Service:
Organization brings together student-athletes who are seeking scholarships with colleges that are seeking qualified student-athletes. Clients can monitor which colleges have visited their personal scouting report by using our innovative tracking feature.

Ticket Services

CITYSEATS.COM
1250 24TH STREET N.W 20037-1193
P.O 97180
WASHINGTON, DC 20090-7180
202-293-4800
• Carter Robertson, President and CEO
Nature of Sports Service:
Online marketplace to buy and sell tickets to hundreds of local events. Exchange tickets with other members through classifieds and auctions, or buy discounted tickets available exclusively through CitySeats.com.
Services:
Provides online marketplace to buy and sell tickets to hundreds of local events.

CYBERSEATS.COM
2995 VAN BUREN BOULEVARD
BUILDING A-13, SUITE 228
RIVERDALE, CA 92503-5606
951-637-8050
Fax: 951-637-8054
• Jim Lynskey, General Manager
jim@msintergate.com
Nature of Service:
Ticketing application that will allow fans to

see the views from the premium locations available in the stadium before they buy. Once fans have viewed the field they can then choose the exact seats they want, book them and pay for them in one easy transaction.

DESTINET LIMITED
BRADLEY HOUSE
7 PARK FIVE BUSINESS CENTRE, HARRIER WAY
EXETER, DEVON, ENGLAND EX2 7HU
44-01392-447-200
Fax: 44-01392-447-230
info@destinet.co.uk
www.destinet.co.uk
• Trevor Munday, Managing Director
• Ian Creek, Marketing Manager
Services:
Provides advanced online business solutions.
Clients:
The Royal Bank of Scotland Group Plc (Lombard), IDN Telecom Plc, English Regional Arts Board, Nationwide, Alpha Telecom and MyCallSavings.com
Description:
Delivers a full range of ticket sales service for special events, sporting events and performing arts clients. DESTINET provides an integrated agency/in-house ticketing service utilizing SQL dBASE management, networked Windows/NT and tandem servers.

DI/AN CONTROLS, INC.
530 W STREET
BRAINTREE, MA 02184
781-848-1299
• Robert Kodis, President,Treasurer and Director
Year Founded:
1958
Nature of Service:
Master System, Point of Sale Systems, Food Service Management System.

INTERNATIONAL MICRO SYSTEMS, INC.
200 RACOOSIN DRIVE
SUITE 110
ASTON, PA 19014
800-882-0627
800-882-0627
Fax: 484-574-8874
www.ims-pos.com
• Jeff Harvey, Director of Sales
• Rob Rae, Director of Marketing
Nature of Services:
International Micro Systems provides integrated POS (Point of Sales) and venue management solutions with a strong focus on sports arenas, convention centers, amusement facilities, and colleges/universities - products and services include inventory management, food and beverage POS systems, full-scale venue systems planning, installation and support, and pre-paid concession payment systems through ticketing.

INTERNATIONAL TICKETING ASSOCIATION (INTIX), THE
5868 EAST 71ST STREET
SUITE E 367
INDIANAPOLIS, IN 46220
212-629-4036
Fax: 212-629-8532

info@intix.org
www.intix.org
• Maureen Andersen, President
(212) 629-4036
• Kathleen O'Donnell, Deputy Director
• Mardi Dilger, Board Chair
(305) 480-1620
mdilger@marlins.com
Description:
The International Ticketing Association is a nonprofit membership organization committed to leading the forum for the entertainment ticketing industry. INTIX represents over 1000 ticketing, sales, technology, finance, and marketing professionals who work in arts, sports, and entertainment as well as a full range of public venues and institutions.

INTERTICKET, INC.
2 GLENRIDGE DRIVE
BEDFORD, MA 01730
781-275-5724
info@interticket.com
www.interticket.com

NATIONAL TICKET COMPANY
5562 SNYDERTOWN ROAD
PAXINOSN, PA 17860
570-672-2900
800-829-0829
Fax: 570-672-2999
ticket@nationalticket.com
www.nationalticket.com
• John Conway, VP Sales/Administration
ticket@nationalticket.com
• Ginger Seidel, Advertising/Marketing Coordinator
gseidel@nationalticket.com
(800) 829-0829
ticket@nationalticket.com
Year Founded:
1907
Description:
Manufacturer of tickets and wristbands. Season sheets, books and season wristband books. All printed in the USA!

NEIGHBORHOOD BOX OFFICE
3676 W CALIFORNIA AVENUE
BUILDING D
SALT LAKE CITY, UT 84104
801-887-7000
800-545-5776
Fax: 801-973-4188
www.nbo.com
• Keith A. Guevara, Chairman, Director, President and Chief
• Christopher Foley, Chief Financial Officer
Services:
Distributes and manages gift cards on all three platforms, MasterCard, Visa, and Discover. Provides Proprietary Technology, Transaction Processing, Client Services, Fulfillment, Order Processing, Tech Support, Call Center Support, Risk Management, Reporting, Marketing, Merchant and Mall Personnel Training.
Description:
Ticketing. Develops and markets transaction based interactive ticket & merchandise kiosks. Provides information and customer demographics to venues, promoters and retailers.

OMNICO GROUP
3100 SPRING FOREST ROAD
SUITE 125
RALEIGH, NC 27616
919-747-5700
Fax: 678-747-5799
www.omnicogroup.com
• Marc Bension, President
• Mark Kamiyama, Sales and Marketing SVP
Services:
Provides professional system solutions, service and consultancy for the leisure industry in the United States, North and South America, Europe, Asia and Africa. The world leaders in the design, development, implementation and service of specialized ticketing, concessions and merchandising point of sale systems for the leisure industry.
Description:
A Wembley TicketMaster joint venture, develops P.O.S. systems for stadium and arenas. The concession and merchandise systems include inventory control, suite catering and vending applications.

OPENSEATS, INC.
2805 WESTWOOD AVENUE
NASHVILLE, TN 37212
615-846-6750
866-789-1884
www.openseats.com
• Dan Maclellan, President
Sports Service Founded:
1999
Nature of Sports Service:
An online person-to-person trading community for people who want to buy or sell tickets to local sports and entertainment events.

PACIOLAN SYSTEMS, INC.
5171 CALIFORNIA AVENUE
SUITE 200
IRVINE, CA 92617
866-722-4652
Fax: 949-823-1610
www.paciolan.com
• Kothari Amit, CFO
(949) 823-1611
investors@paciolan.com
• Jane Kleinberger, Chairman
Services:
Online Ticketing, Enterprise Ticketing, Fund Development, Ticket Marketplace, Access Management, PACMail and Group Ticket Window; Implementation, Customer Support, Internet Adoption and eCommerce Services and Hosted Services

PEREY TURNSTILES, INC
308 BISHOP AVENUE
BRIDGEPORT, CT 6610
203-333-9400
877-TURNSTILE
Fax: 203-333-9410
perey@turnstile.com
www.turnstile.com
• Ed Hendrickson, VP
ehendrickson@turnstile.com
Products:
Waist High Passimeters, Optical Turnstiles, Drop Arm Turnstiles, Roto Gates, Mass Transit Turnstiles, Waist-High Traffic Control, Wheelchair Access, Automated Ticketing Turnstiles, Ticket Bo-Coin

OP-Railings, Custom Designs
Brands:
Model HD (#048), Model HDAC (#136), Model HDACR (#150), Model HDACMR (#150), Model TC (#055), Model HDACR-Optical (#152), Model HDACMR-Optical (#152), Model HD-Optical (#050), Model 151S Drop Arm, Model 151M Drop Arm, Model 49 Drop Arm, Customized Designs, Twin Roto-Gate, SA Roto-Gate, Type AA Roto-Gate, Type B Roto-Gate, Model 110, Model 109, Model 107, Impenetrable AA Roto-Gate, Super Kompak Controller (#055), #20 Traffic Controller, #80 Traffic Controller, Perey Railing, Swing Gate #1255, Swing Gate #1256, PAS-Gate Drop Arm Site, HD-OmniScan (#048), Model 138, Field Upgrade in Progress, Ticket Box, Internal Ticket Box, Kompak Coinpassor, P
Nature of Sports Service:
Turnstiles, automated ticketing support, ADA compliance, and life safety compliance.

QUICK TICK INTERNATIONAL, INC.
12902 HAYNES ROAD
SUITE 4
HOUSTON, TX 77066
832-249-6400
800-231-6144
Fax: 832-249-6424
www.quicktick.com
• Don C. Andrews, President
• Lisa Andrews, Assistant President
Services:
Commercial Ticket Printing

RAZOR GATOR, INC.
4094 GLENCOE AVE
SUITE A
MARINA DEL REY, CA 90292
310-481-3400
800-542-4466
Fax: 310-289-3010
www.razorgator.com
• Doug Knittle, Chief Executive Officer
• David Lord, Chief Operating Officer, President
• Thomas Swalla, Business Development Director
(310) 289-3000
Nature of Sports Service:
A leading secondary ticket distributor that provides its customers with sold-out and hard-to-find tickets to premium sports, concerts and theater events worldwide.
Sports Service Founded:
1958
Services:
Buying and Selling Sold-Out or Hard-to-Find Tickets

SEATS 3D
1150 BALLENA BOULEVARD
SUITE 250
ALAMEDA, CA 94501
510-521-0720
Fax: 510-521-3972
www.seats3d.com
• Steve Stonehouse, Senior VP Sales
• Jeff Sherratt, Director Business Development
• David Schwartz, Chief Operations Officer/Chief Technology Officer
• Richard H. Sherratt, Chairman of the Board/Chief Executive Officer
Nature of Services:
Using 3D visualizations of sports venues,

Ballena Technologies creates realistic seating visuals to improve the online ticketing experience by familiarizing potential customers with a facility, creating excitement, sales, and customer satisfaction.

SELECT TICKETING SYSTEMS, INC.
344 W GENESEE STREET
SUITE 102
SYRACUSE, NY 13202
315-479-6663
800-944-7277
Fax: 315-471-2715
• Renee Devesty
Products:
Ticketing - Designs, installs, and supports Ticket Wizard, PASS and PASS GOLD-software created for ticketing, marketing, and events management.
Description:
Select Technologies Corporation is the largest international vendor of in-house computerized ticketing systems in the world. Over 530 customers use Select's PASS system which operates over 2,000 venues (locations where arts, sports and entertainment events are viewed) around the world.

SPLITSEASONTICKETS, LLC
splitseasontickets.com
• Dan Bartlett, Founder/Owner
• Dan DeMato, Partner
• Brian De Vries, Partner
Nature of Services:
A season ticket sharing web-based service partnering with professional sports teams. SplitSeasonTickets provides: Matcher Service to match existing season ticket holders with share partners; Drafting Service that provides season ticket holders and share partners a simple, efficient way to divide their season tickets; and Partner Extranet access to real-time data and sharing activities. The services benefit the teams by allowing them to participate in providing the services, and track the sharer data.

STUBHUB
199 FREMONT STREET
SAN FRANCISCO, CA 94105
415-222-8400
866.788.2482
Fax: 415-222-8552
www.stubhub.com
• Jeff Fluhr, Co-Founder and Chief Executive Officer
customerservice@stubhub.com
• Carolyn Arend, Chief Financial Officer
customerservice@stubhub.com
• Colin Evans, Sales and Business Development VP
customerservice@stubhub.com
• Chris Tsakalakis, President
• Anne Robie, Director , Human resources
• Brigitte R. Bellan, GM, International
• Danielle Maged, Global Head of Partnership
Nature of Sports Service:
Web site that works as an intermediary between ticket buyers and sellers. Users can see what event tickets are available, purchase tickets or post tickets for sale. Site takes a ten percent listing fee on consummated sales and uses the

LiquidSeats technology platform. The LiquidSeats engine enables content sites, team sites and portals to easily integrate a secondary ticket market into their web site.
Services:
Buying and Selling Tickets

TICKET RESERVE, THE
20 N WACKER DRIVE
SUITE 1100
CHICAGO, IL 60606
312-357-4281
888-205-1611
Nature of Sports Service:
Organization utilizes technology to create new revenue streams for professional teams and organizations.
Services:
Seamless integration with teams' and event producers' existing technologies, providing secure transactions, reliable information and convenient use for fans worldwide; The Fan Forward, ConnectingPoint
Products:
Product that lets teams and leagues capitalize on potential contingent events

---

TICKET RETURN INC.
6407 IDLEWILD ROAD
CHARLOTTE, NC 28212
866-858-7876
info@ticketreturn.com
www.ticketreturn.com
• Aaron Clark, Account Executive
Brands:
ProTicket, ProScan, UTicket, UScan, Ustudent

TICKET TO GO, LLC
4124 CENTRAL PIKE
HERMITAGE, TN 37076
615-360-6700
877-282-8942
Fax: 615-874-8005
support@agiletix.com
• Caren Shaffer, President
• Michael Holt, EVP Product Development And Client support Se
• John Lemon, Director, System Implementation and Customer
• Julien McBride, Director, Software and System Development
• Shane A. Burkett, Director, Strategic Marketing
• Richard Steward, EVP Operations/Sales
Nature of Sports Service:
Offers online ticketing, software for box office operations, and portable ticket selling and printing kiosks. Also offers Interactive

Voice Response system, allowing customers to place orders by telephone and listen to pre-recorded information on events, venues and payment and shipping options.
Services:
Full-featured Box Office and Call Center sales, Robust venue and event management, Fully integrated, highly customizable security, Express Sales, Web sales seamless integrated into your website, Kiosk sales, Reserved seating and general admission ticketing, Table seating, Catalog sales, Flexible packaging for season ticket and tour package sales, Group Sales, Unique ticket bar coding, Data mart, data mining and decision support services, Accounting support, 24/7 call center, Fulfillment services, Application and web hosting, System administration management, Implementation, conversion, training services

---

TICKETMASTER
880 W. SUNSET BLVD
WEST HOLLYWOOD, CA 90069
213-639-6100
Fax: 213-386-1244
www.ticketmaster.com
• Michael Rapino, President & CEO
• Nathan Hubbard, Chief Executive Officer of Ticketing
Nature of Service:
Provides event ticket sales, marketing and distribution through Internet, phone, and retail outlets, along with online auctions, fan club ticketing, and venue-authorized fan resale ticketing services.
Brands:
TicketsNow; TicketExchange; Ticketmaster
Marketing & Consulting Services:
Works with professional and college sports teams to develop new programs designed to expand ticket sales by helping with marketing ideas and actual sales of tickets using outlets, telephones and Internet.
Sports Service Founded:
1995; Merged with Live Nation on January 25, 2010, creating Live Nation Entertainment, Inc

---

TICKETS.COM
555 ANTON BOULEVARD
PO BOX 272127
COSTA MESA, CA 92626
714-327-5400
888-397-3400
Fax: 714-327-5410
sales@tickets.com
www.tickets.com

• Larry Witherspoon, Chief Executive Officer
• John Walker, CEO, President
• Daniel Wu, Chief Financial Officer
• Joe Choti, Chief Technology Officer
• Joe DeMots, Senior Vice President of Business Development
• John Rizzi, Senior Vice President of Project Management
• Ed Gow, Vice President of Sales and Marketing
• Doug Lyons, Vice President of Product Marketing
• Danielle Nagao, Vice President of Financial Operations
• Jan Yerzik, Chief Marketing Manager
• Chaeli Walker, Marketing Manager
• John Walker, President, CEO
Description:
Online, offline ticketing software and services.
Baseball Sponsor:
Chicago Cubs, New York Mets

WEBTICKETS.COM
4651 ROSWELL ROAD NE
SUITE F-503
ATLANTA, GA 30342-3051
404-843-1344
800-846-2407
Fax: 404-303-1574
cto@webtickets.com
www.webtickets.com
• Carl White, Chief Ticket Officer
cto@webtickets.com
Services:
Buying and Selling Event Tickets

WORLDWIDE TICKET CRAFT
3606 QUANTUM BLVD
BOYNTON BEACH, FL 33426
954-426-5754
877-426-5754
Fax: 954-426-5761
online@wwticket.com
www.worldwideticketcraft.com
• Erik Covitz, President
erikc@wwticket.com
• Mark Turner, Vice President of information Systems
mturner@wwticket.com
• Alan Tonks, Chief Financial Officer
atonks@wwticket.com
• George Scher, Chief Operations Officer
Description:
Ticket Manufacturer. Designer and developer of event tickets, custom tickets, etc.
Services:
Ticket Printing

7
facilities

7

facilities

facilities

facilities

Arenas & Stadiums

A.J. MCCLUNG MEMORIAL STADIUM
600 4TH STREET
COLUMBUS, GA 31901
706-653-4500
Fax: 706-653-4549
• Anthony L. Ford, General Manager
Seating Capacity:
15,000

A.J. PALUMBO CENTER
600 FORBES AVENUE
PITTSBURGH, PA 15282
412-396-6632
800-456-0590
Fax: 412-396-5855
harperd1@duq.edu
www.goduquesne.com/facilities/duqu-facil-p
alumbo.html
• Bob Derda, General Manager
bderda@duqssportsproperties.com
Seating Capacity:
4,406

ABILENE CIVIC CENTER
1100 NORTH 6TH STREET
ABILENE, TX 79601
325-676-6211
Fax: 325-676-6343
abilene@abilenetx.com
www.abilenetx.com
Seating Capacity:
2,121

ACADEMIC-ATHLETIC CENTER
195 ACADEMIC-ATHLETIC CENTER
MOREHEAD, KY 40351
606-783-2088
Fax: 606-783-5035
www.msueagles.com
• Randy Stacy, Athletic Media Relations
Director
r.stacy@moreheadstate.edu
• Brian Hutchinson, Director of Athletics
(606) 783-2089
b.hutchinson@moreheadstate.edu
• Rhonda Ferguson, Administrative
Assistant to the AD
(606) 783-2089
r.ferguson@moreheadstate.edu
• Harry Floyd, Athletic Secretary
(606) 783-2088
hbfloyd@moreheadstate.edu
• Peggy Osborne, Faculty Athletics
Representative
(606) 783-2755
p.osborne@moreheadstate.edu
Seating Capacity:
6,500

ADAMS CENTER
32 CAMPUS DRIVE
MISSOULA, MT 59812
406-243-5355
Fax: 406-243-4265
tristin.flint@mso.umt.edu
www.gogriz.com/facilities/
• Brad Murphy, Executive Director
(406) 243-4261
brad.murphy@mso.umt.edu
• Brandon Kress, Assistant Director,
Operations
(406) 243-5357
brandon.kress@mso.umt.edu
• Adrien Wingard, Events & Promotion
Coordinator
(406) 243-5403
adrien.wingard@mso.umt.edu
• Kelsi Plante, Client Technology Support
Manager
(406) 243-5329
kelsi.plante@mso.umt.edu
Seating Capacity:
7,500 sporting events; 6,000 concerts, 7,655
concerts in the round.
Year Founded:
1955

AGGIE MEMORIAL STADIUM
3035 WILLIAMS AVENUE
ROBERTS HALL
LAS CRUCES, NM 88003
575-646-4413
Fax: 575-646-2099
www.nmstatesports.com
• Bobbie Welch, Booking and Marketing
Director
(505) 646-7630
• Gary Rachele, Assistant Director
(505) 646-4413
• Will Lofdahl, Special Events Director
(505) 646-4413
• Barbara A. Welch, Special Events
Coordinator
(505) 646-7525
Seating Capacity:
30,343
Year Founded:
1978

AL F. CANIGLIA FIELD
60TH & DODGE STREET
UNIVERSITY OF NEBRASKA AT OMAHA
OMAHA, NE 68182
402-554-2305
Fax: 402-554-3694
www.omavs.com
• Kevin Brady, Assistant Operations
Coordinator
(402) 554-2606
knbrady@unomaha.edu
Services
Located in the heart of the UNO campus,
the stadium's infield is Field Turf while the
track is a Seal-Flex surface. The stadium is
the home field for the Maverick football
team, and also hosts UNO's outdoor track &
field events.
Seating Capacity
3,0+8

AL G. LANGFORD CHAPARRAL CENTER
3600 NORTH GARFIELD
MIDLAND COLLEGE
MIDLAND, TX 79705
432-685-4500
Fax: 432-685-4740
www.midland.edu
• Mike Stevens, Director
(416) 685-4583
mstevens@midland.edu

ALAMODOME SAN ANTONIO
100 MONTANA STREET
SAN ANTONIO, TX 78203
210-207-3663
Fax: 210-207-3646
dmarketing@alamodome.com
www.alamodome.com
Services:
The Alamodome is what is known as a 'third
generation' facility. It features the very latest
in dome architecture and engineering
technology, with column-free spans for
unobstructed viewing and a curtain wall
system for configuration flexibility. The
Alamodome has 160,000 gross square feet
of contiguous exhibit floor space. The
Alamodome has two 24.5' X 32.5'
Daktronics ProStarr 16.5mm end zone
displays, a center hung arena scoreboard
with four 9' X 12' Daktronics ProStar 10mm
displays, and a brand new dual sided
Daktronics ProStarr 23mm outdoor marquee
located in Parking Lot A.
Seating Capacity:
65,000

ALBANY CIVIC CENTER
100 WEST OGLETHORPE BOULEVARD
ALBANY, GA 31701-6808
229-430-5200
Fax: 229-430-5163
www.albany.ga.us
• Joel Holmes, Director
(229) 430-5222
• Derrell Smith, Deputy Director
(229) 430-5222
• Shanice Howard, Event Manager
(229) 430-1804
• Uy Tram, Administrative Manager
(229) 430-1805
Arena Seating Capacity:
10,240

ALBERT LEA CITY ARENA
701 LAKE CHAPEAU DRIVE
ALBERT LEA, MN 56007
507-377-4374
Fax: 507-377-4336
cityofalbertlea.org/departments/parks-and-re
creation/city-arena/
• Robert Furland, Facility Manager
(507) 377-4374
Services:
The facility is home to the boys and girls
high school hockey teams, the Albert Lea
Figure Skaters, the Albert Lea Youth Hockey
Association and the Waldorf College Hockey
Team.

ALERUS CENTER
1200 42ND STREET SOUTH
GRAND FORKS, ND 58201
701-792-1200
Fax: 701-746-6511
www.aleruscenter.com
• Tami Pearson, Marketing Manager
• Vione Jordheim, Senior Administrative
Assistant
• Wendy Nimens, Business Manager
wnimens@aleruscenter.com
• Jeremy Linstad, Director of Operations
Services
Able to accommodate a variety of sporting
events, the Alerus Center is home to the
University of North Dakota Fighting Sioux
Football team and hosts soccer, wrestling,
basketball, monster trucks, rodeos, and
Super Snowcross. This remarkable facility
has the capacity to host local, regional and
national sporting events.
Seating Capacity
Footbal seating capacity: 13,400 concert
seating capacity: 22,000 145,000 square
feet of exhibit space

facilities

ALEX BOX STADIUM
SKIP BERTMAN DRIVE
BATON ROUGE, LA 70803
225-578-8001
800-469-8781
Fax: 225-578-2430
www.lsusports.net
• Ronnie Haliburton, Sr. Associate AD, Facility Management
(225) 578-4712
rhalibu@lse.edu
• Todd Jeansonne, Director of Facilities & Grounds
(225) 578-5519
tjeans2@lsu.edu
• Flo Williams, Manager of Facilities & Grounds
(225) 578-6729
fwilli3@lsu.edu
Services:
Since 1985, it has been the site of four SEC tournaments, 16 NCAA regional tournaments, three NCAA super regional series and one ABCA Hall of Fame tournament. Each year, The Box undergoes facility-improvement projects designed to enhance the comfort and enjoyment of LSU baseball fans.
Seating Capacity:
10,326

ALFOND ARENA
COLLEGE AVENUE
ORONO, ME 04473
207-581-1104
Fax: 207-581-3297
www.goblackbears.com
• Deb Leavitt, Athletic Ticket Manager
(207) 581-2327
• Jason Hoyt, Account Executive
(207) 584-4103
jhoyt@blackbearsportsproperties.com
Arena Seating Capacity:
5,712
Year Founded:
1977

ALFRED LAWSON JR. MULTIPURPOSE CENTER
1800 WAHNISH WAY
TALLAHASSEE, FL 32307
850-412-5966
Fax: 850-599-3810
www.famu.edu
• Robert D. Carroll, Director of Multipurpose Facility
(850) 599-8081
Arena Seating Capacity:
8,470

ALLEN COUNTY WAR MEMORIAL COLISEUM
4000 PARNELL AVENUE
FORT WAYNE, IN 46805
260-482-9502
Fax: 260-484-1637
www.memorialcoliseum.com
• Randy Brown, General Manager
(260) 482-9502
rbrown@memorialcoliseum.com
• Bryan Christie, Vice President of Operations
(260) 482-9502
bchristie@memorialcoliseum.com
• Rich Thoma, Plant Facilities Manager
(260) 482-9502
rthoma@memorialcoliseum.com

Services:
Allen County War Memorial Coliseum can be configured with a 1/10 mile paved indoor oval for special events. The facility has most recently been used for an indoor USAC event.
Seating Capacity:
10,240

ALLSTATE ARENA
6920 NORTH MANNHEIM ROAD
ROSEMONT, IL 60018
847-635-6601
Fax: 847-635-6606
www.rosemont.com/allstate/
• Patrick Nagle, Executive Director
(847) 635-6601
Seating Capacity:
18,500

ALLTEL ARENA
ONE VERIZON ARENA WAY
NORTH LITTLE ROCK, AR 72114
501-340-5660
Fax: 501-340-5668
www.verizonarena.com
• Michael Marion, General Manager
Services:
In addition to being the home court for UALR Basketball, this facility also hosts the Arkansas Twisters Arena Football 2 Team, Ringling Brothers Barnum and Bailey Circus, Champions on Ice Figure Skating exhibition, concerts and a number of other exciting quality attractions.
Seating Capacity:
18,000

ALOHA STADIUM
99-500 SALT LAKE BLVD
HONOLULU, HI 96818
808-483-2500
Fax: 808-483-2823
alohastadium@hawaii.gov
alohastadium.hawaii.gov
• Scott Chan, Stadium Manager
Seating Capacity:
50,000
Teams:
Hawaii Rainbow Warriors, Hawai'i Bowl

ALUMNI COLISEUM
521 LANCASTER AVENUE
RICHMOND, KY 40475
859-622-3654
Fax: 859-622-5108
michael.clark@eku.edu
www.ekusports.com
• Sean Hamilton, General Manager
(859) 622-6372
shamilton@ekusportsproperties.com
• Lynn Tyler, Athletics Administrative Coordinator
(859) 622-2120
Stadium Seating Capacity:
6,500

ALUMNI FIELD STADIUM, BOSTON COLLEGE
140 COMMONWEALTH AVENUE
BOSTON COLLEGE ATHLETICS
CHESTNUT HILL, MA 02467
617-552-3000
www.bceagles.com
• Matt Conway, Associate Athletics Director, Operations

(617) 552-6672
conwayml@bc.edu
Stadium Seating Capacity:
45,000

ALUMNI FIELD STADIUM, VIRGINIA MILITARY INSTITUTE
VIRGINIA MILITARY INSTITUTE
116 SMITH HALL
LEXINGTON, VA 24450
540-464-7253
Fax: 540-464-7622
igoec@vmi.edu
www.vmikeydets.com
• Elizabeth Igo, Assistant Athletic Director, Facilities
(540) 464-7266
igopec@vmi.edu
Stadium Seating Capacity:
10,000

AMARILLO CIVIC CENTER COMPLEX
401 SOUTH BUCHANAN
AMARILLO, TX 79101
806-378-4247
amarillociviccenter.com
• Sherman Bass, General Manager
(806) 378-4247
sherman.bass@amarillo.gov
• Bo Fowlkes, Assistant General Manager
(806) 378-9460
bo.fowlkes@amarillo.gov
• Christopher Post, Operations Manager
(806) 378-9480
christopher.post@amarillo.gov
Seating Capacity:
4,870

AMERICAN AIRLINES ARENA
601 BISCAYNE BOULEVARD
MIAMI, FL 33132
786-777-1000
Fax: 786-777-1600
guestservices@heat.com
www.aaarena.com
Seating Capacity:
19,600

AMERICAN AIRLINES CENTER
2500 VICTORY AVENUE
DALLAS, TX 75219
214-222-3687
800-745-3000
www.americanairlinescenter.com
Tenant(s):
Dallas Mavericks, Dallas Stars

AMON G. CARTER STADIUM
2850 STADIUM DRIVE
FORT WORTH, TX 76129
817-257-7000
Fax: 817-257-7656
www.gofrogs.com/facilities/tcu-facilities-football.html
• Jay Fields, General Manager
• Sean Conner, Assistant Athletics Director, Ticket Operations
s.conner@tcu.edu
Seating Capacity:
45,000
Team:
Texas Christian University Horned Frogs

ANDY KERR STADIUM
13 OAK DRIVE
HAMILTON, NY 13346

315-228-1000
Fax: 315-228-7008
www.gocolgateraiders.com
• Kenny Copps, Ticket Manager
(315) 228-7600
kcopps@colgate.edu
• Emmett House, Grounds Supervisor
(315) 228-7577
ehouse@colgate.edu
Seating Capacity:
10,221

ANGELS STADIUM OF ANAHEIM
2000 GENE AUTRY WAY
ANAHEIM, CA 92806
714-940-2000
Fax: 714-940-2266
robert.alvarado@angelsbb.com
losangeles.angels.mlb.com/ana/ballpark/
• Billy Eppler, General Manager
• Calvin Ching, Sr. Manager, Stadium
Events & Operations
• Brian Sanders, Sr. Director, Ballpark
Operations
Team:
Los Angeles Angels
Seating Capacity:
45,050

APPALACHIAN POWER PARK
601 MORRIS STREET
SUITE 201
CHARLESTON, WV 25301
304-344-2287
Fax: 304-344-0083
• Ken Fogel, Executive Vice-President
(304) 344-BATS
kfogel@wvpower.com
• Tim Mueller, General Manager
(304) 344-BATS
tmueller@wvpower.com
• Gary Olson, Director of Ticketing
(304) 344-BATS
Sport:
Minor League Baseball
Team:
WV Power - a single A affiliate of the
Pittsburgh Pirates.
Seating Capacity:
4,300

ARIZONA STADIUM
545 NORTH NATIONAL CHAMPION DRIVE
TUCSON, AZ 85721-0096
520-621-2200
Fax: 520-621-9323
www.arizonawildcats.com
• Joe Moeller, General Manager
(520) 626-5538
joe.moeller@imgworld.com
Seating Capacity:
56,029
Tenants:
Arizona Wildcats; Arizona Bowl

ARKANSAS STATE FAIR
2600 HOWARD STREET
LITTLE ROCK, AR 72206
501-372-8341
Fax: 501-372-4197
www.arkansasstatefair.com
• Ralph Shoptaw, President and General
Manager
rshoptaw@asfg.net
• Tiffany Wilkerson, Commercial Exhibit
Coordinator
tiffany@asfg.net

• Will Hornburg, Director of Sales &
Promotions
(501) 372-8341
will.h@asfg.net
Arena Seating Capacity:
10,000

**ARKANSAS STATE UNIVERSITY
CONVOCATION CENTER**
217 OLYMPIC DRIVE
JONESBORO, AR 72401
870-972-3870
Fax: 870-972-3825
www.astateconvo.com
• Tim Dean, Director
(870) 972-3870
timd@astate.edu
• Lesa Carmack, Booking Coordinator
(870) 972-3870
lesac@astate.edu
• Haley Stout, Box Office Manager
(870) 972-2781
hstout@astate.edu
• Dennis Timms, Operations Foreman
(870) 972-3870
dennis@astate.edu
Seating Capacity:
10,529
Seating Capacity:
30,000

ARMSTRONG STADIUM
100 EAST QUEEN STREET
HAMPTON, VA 23668
757-727-5641
Fax: 757-728-6995
www.hamptonpirates.com/sports/2006/8/8/a
rmstrongstadium.aspx
• John Jackson, Director of Facilities
(757) 727-5516
john.jackson@hamptonu.edu
• John Brown, Assistant Director of Facilities
(757) 728-6665
john.brown@hamptonu.edu
Seating Capacity:
12,000

ARROWHEAD STADIUM
ONE ARROWHEAD DRIVE
KANSAS CITY, MO 64129
816-920-9300
Fax: 816-924-4570
www.kcchiefs.com
• Tim Hassett, Vice President of Stadium
Operations
• Rocco Mazzella, Stadium Services
Manager
• Brandon Hamilton, Director of Facilities
Tenants:
Kansas City Chiefs
Seating Capacity:
76,416

ARTHUR ASHE STADIUM
124-02 ROOSEVELT AVENUE
FLUSHING, NY 11368
718-760-6200
Fax: 718-592-9488
www.usta.com
Note:
Arthur Ashe Stadium is a part of the USTA
National Tennis Center.
Seating Capacity:
23,771

ASSEMBLY HALL
1001 EAST 17TH STREET
BLOOMINGTON, IN 47408-1590
812-855-2794
Fax: 812-855-0488
iuad@indiana.edu
iuhoosiers.com
• Eric Neuburger, Associate Athletic
Director, Facilities
(812) 855-2127
eneuburg@indiana.edu
Seating Capacity:
17,484

AT&T CENTER
ONE AT&T CENTER PARKWAY
SAN ANTONIO, TX 78219
210-444-5140
www.attcenter.com
Seating Capacity:
19,000
Tenant(s):
San Antonio Spurs (NBA), San Antonio
Stars (WNBA), San Antonio Rampage
(AHL), San Antonio Stock Show & Rodeo
(PRCA).

AT&T FIELD
201 POWER ALLEY
CHATTANOOGA, TN 37402
423-267-2208
Fax: 423-267-4258
web.minorleaguebaseball.com/index.jsp?sid
=t498
• Rick Mozingo, President
rmozingo@lookouts.com
• Steve Sullivan, Director, Food & Beverage
ssullivan@lookouts.com
• Anastasia McCowan, Business & Ticket
Operations Manager
amccowan@lookouts.com
• Alex Tainsh, Marketing & Promotions
Manager
atainsh@lookouts.com
Sport:
Minor League Baseball.
Team:
Chattanooga Lookouts.
Year Founded:
2000
Capacity:
6,362

AT&T PARK
24 WILLIE MAYS PLAZA
SAN FRANCISCO, CA 94107
415-972-2000
Fax: 415-947-2800
sanfrancisco.giants.mlb.com/sf/ballpark
Stadium Seating Capacity:
41,915
Tenant(s):
San Francisco Giants (MLB).

ATWOOD STADIUM
1700 UNIVERSITY AVENUE
FLINT, MI 48504
810-766-7463
Fax: 810-766-7468
• Thomas W. Ayers, Vice President for
Administration & Finance
(810) 762-9787
tayers@kettering.edu
Stadium Seating Capacity:
11,000

facilities

Arena Seating Capacity:
11,000

AUTOZONE PARK
200 UNION AVENUE
MEMPHIS, TN 38103
901-721-6050
Fax: 901-328-1102
• Craig Unger, General Manager
cunger@cardinals.com
• Gian D'Amico, Ticket Operations Manager
gdamico@cardinals.com
• Mark Anderson, Director of Operations
manderson@cardinals.com
Year Opened:
2000
Team:
Memphis Redbirds.
Capacity:
10,000

AUTZEN STADIUM
2700 MLK JR. BOUELVARD
EUGENE, OR 97401
541-346-4481
Fax: 541-346-5031
tigersoccercamp@yahoo.com
www.goducks.com
• Rob Mullens, Athletic Director
(541) 346-5455
• Mike Duncan, Sr. Associate Athletic
Director, Facilities
(541) 346-5326
Stadium Seating Capacity:
54,000
Team:
University of Oregon Ducks (NCAA)

AVISTA STADIUM
602 NORTH HAVANA STREET
SPOKANE, WA 99202
509-343-6886
Fax: 509-534-5368
mail@spokaneindians.com
• Chris Duff, General Manager
cduff@spokaneindians.com
• Josh Roys, Vice President, Tickets
jroys@spokaneindians.com
• John Tibbett, Stadium Operations
Manager
• Larry Blumer, Assistant Director of
Stadium Operations
Sport:
Baseball
Tenant(s):
Spokane Indians (NWL)
Year Founded:
1958
Capacity:
6,803

BAKER ATHLETICS COMPLEX
533 WEST 218TH STREET
NEW YORK, NY 10034
212-942-0431
Fax: 212-854-2988
jar14@columbia.edu
www.gocolumbialions.com
• Steve Figueroa, Manager of Facilities
Operations
(212) 851-0113
sf2317@columbia.edu
• Erich Ely, Associate Athletics Director,
Facilities Op.
(212) 854-5911
ee2133@columbia.edu

Stadium Seating Capacity:
17,000

BALLPARK AT HARBOR YARD
500 MAIN STREET
BRIDGEPORT, CT 06604
203-345-4800
Fax: 203-345-4830
info@bridgeportbluefish.com
bridgeportbluefish.com/stadium/
• Frank Boulton, Principal Owner, CEO
• Jamie Toole, General Manager
(203) 416-1705
jtoole@bridgeportbluefish.com
• Dan Gregory, Director of Stadium
Operations
(203) 416-1704
dgregory@bridgeportbluefish.com
• Drew LaBoy, Director of Operations
(203) 416-1719
dlaboy@bridgeportbluefish.com
Sport:
Minor League Baseball, Lacrosse
Tenant(s):
Bridgeport Bluefish (ALPB), Sacred Heart
Pioneers (NCAA).

BANCORP SOUTH ARENA
375 EAST MAIN STREET
TUPELO, MS 38804
662-841-6573
Fax: 662-841-6413
thunt@bcsarena.com
www.bcsarena.com
• Todd Hunt, Executive Director
thunt@bcsarena.com
• Craig Russell, Director of Operations
crussell@bcsarena.com
• Kevan Kirkpatrick, Director of Marketing
kkirkpatrick@bcsarena.com
Arena Seating Capacity:
10,000
Year Founded:
1993

BANK OF AMERICA STADIUM
800 SOUTH MINT STREET
CHARLOTTE, NC 28202
704-358-7000
1-888-297-8673
Fax: 704-358-7619
feedback@panthers.nfl.com
www.panthers.com/stadium
• Jerry Richardson, Owner, Founder
• Dave Gettleman, General Manager
• Matthew Getz, Facility Manager
Stadium Seating Capacity:
75,412
Description:
Home Stadium for the Carolina Panthers.
Owned by:
Carolinas Stadium Corp.

BANKERS LIFE FIELDHOUSE
125 SOUTH PENNSYLVANIA STREET
INDIANAPOLIS, IN 46204
317-917-2500
Fax: 317-917-2599
pacersinsider@pacers.com
www.bankerslifefieldhouse.com
• Herbert Simon, Owner, Chairman and
CEO
(317) 917-2500
• Kevin Pritchard, EVP Basketball
Operations, General Manager
(317) 917-2500
• Mel Raines, Sr. Vice President Facilities

Operations
(317) 917-2500
• Tom Rutledge, Vice President, Production
& Operations
(317) 917-2500
Seating Capacity:
18,165
Home Arena for:
NBA-Indiana Pacers, WNBA-Indiana Fever

BARCLAYS CENTER
620 ATLANTIC AVENUE
BROOKLYN, NY 11217
917-618-6100
800-745-3000
Fax: 718-942-9595
www.barclayscenter.com
• Brett Yormark, Chief Executive Officer
• Fred Mangione, Chief Operating Officer
• Stephen Rosebrook, General Manager
• Richard Vartigian, Director, Operations
Seating Capacity:
19,000 for shows & events; approximately
17,732 for Brooklyn Nets
Opened:
September 28, 2012
Tenant(s):
Brooklyn Nets (NBA), New York Islanders
(NHL)

BASEBALL GROUNDS OF
JACKSONVILLE
301 A. PHILIP RANDOLPH BOULEVARD
JACKSONVILLE, FL 32202
904-358-2846
Fax: 904-358-2845
www.jaxsuns.com
• Harold Craw, General Manager
harold@jaxsuns.com
• Christian Galen, Director of Field
Operations
christiang@jaxsuns.com
• Weill Casey, Stadium Operations Manager
weill@jaxsuns.com
Tenant(s):
Jacksonville Suns, Jacksonville Armada FC
Year Founded:
2003
Capacity:
11,000

BASKETBALL CITY
PIER 36 AT 299 SOUTH STREET
NEW YORK, NY 10002
212-233-5050
Fax: 212-233-6161
info@basketballcity.com
www.basketballcity.com
• Bruce Radler, President
bruce@basketballcity.com
• Lee Isenstein, COO, Corporate Events
lee@basketballcity.com
• Christopher Kenny, Director of Youth
Programs
chris@basketballcity.com
Description:
A basketball facility geared toward, league
set ups, and an NBA practice facility.
Equipped with 6 basketball courts on the
main floor, as well as a weight training
facility.
Year Founded:
1997

BAYONNE VETERANS MEMORIAL STADIUM
WEST 26TH STREET
BAYONNE, NJ 07002
201-858-6164
Fax: 201-858-6092
Stadium Seating Capacity:
8,000

BB&T BALLPARK
324 SOUTH MINT STREET
CHARLOTTE, NC 28202
704-274-8300
Fax: 704-274-8330
knights@charlotteknights.com
www.milb.com
• Dan Rajkowski, Chief Operating Officer
danr@charlotteknights.com
• Scotty Brown, General Manager
scottb@charlotteknights.com
• Matt Parrott, Head Groundskeeper
mattp@charlotteknights.com
Stadium Seating Capacity:
10,200

BB&T BALLPARK AT HISTORIC BOWMAN FIELD
1700 WEST FOURTH STREET
WILLIAMSPORT, PA 17701
570-326-3389
Fax: 570-326-3494
mail@crosscutters.com
www.crosscutters.com
• Doug Estes, VP, General Manager
doug@crosscutters.com
• Gabe Sinicropi, Jr, VP, Marketing & Public Relations
gabe@crosscutters.com
• Bill Gehron III, Director of Food & Beverage
bill@crosscutters.com
• Sarah Budd, Director of Ticket Operations/Community Relations
sarah@crosscutters.com
• Nate Schneider, Director of Partner Services
nate@crosscutters.com
Sport:
Minor League Baseball.
Tenant(s):
Williamsport Crosscutters baseball.
Year Founded:
1926
Seating Capacity:
4,200

BB&T CENTER
ONE PANTHER PARKWAY
SUNRISE, FL 33323
954-835-7000
Fax: 954-835-8012
info@floridapanthers.com
www.thebbtcenter.com
• Adam Fullerton, Director, Arena Operations
• Brian Gilner, Operations Manager
• Tom Embrey, Director of Events & Guest Services
Arena Seating Capacity:
20,737
Year Founded:
1998
Nature of Service:
Sports, Entertainment, Concerts, and more.
Tenant(s):
Florida Panthers (NHL).

BC PLACE
777 PACIFIC BOULEVARD
VANCOUVER, BC, CANADA V6B 4Y8
604-669-2300
www.bcplace.com
• Patricia Jelinski, General Manager
• Brian Griffin, Director, Facility Operations
• Wayne Smith, Director, Human Resources & Labour Relations
• Milad Sakiani, Director, IT Services
Owned and Operated:
BC Pavilion Corp.
Year Opened:
1983
Seating Capacity:
54,500
Tenant(s):
BC Lions (CFL), Vancouver Whitecaps FC (MLS)

BEARD-EAVES-MEMORIAL COLISEUM
329 SOUTH DONAHUE DRIVE
AUBURN, AL 36849
334-844-4750
Fax: 334-844-0515
athletics@auburn.edu
www.auburntigers.com
• Jay Jacobs, Director of Athletics
(334) 844-9891
athldir@auburn.edu
• David Benedict, Chief Operating Officer
(334) 844-1411
dpb0013@auburn.edu
• Jeff Steele, Associate Athletic Director, Facilities
(334) 844-2389
steelmj@auburn.edu
• Ben Thomas, Director of Facilities
(334) 844-9176
thomabe@auburn.edu
• Sarah Stallkamp, Manager of Operations
(334) 844-9622
ses0032@auburn.edu
Seating Capacity:
10,500

BEARS & EAGLES RIVERFRONT STADIUM
450 BROAD STREET
NEWARK, NJ 07102
973-848-1000
Fax: 973-621-0095
• Garry Templeton, General Manager
Year Founded:
1999
Capacity:
6,200

BEAVER STADIUM
ONE BEAVER STADUIM
UNIVERSITY PARK
STATE COLLEGE, PA 16802
814-863-1000
www.gopsusports.com
• David M. Joyner, Director of Athletics
(814) 865-1086
Athletic_Director@athletics.psu.edu
• Fran Ganter, Associate Athletic Director for Football Admi
(814) 865-0411
fxg2@psu.edu
• Charmelle Green, Associate Athletic Director/Senior Woman Admi
(814) 865-1104
• Mark Bodenschatz, Associate Athletic Director - Facilities & Op
(814) 863-3489

• Greg Myford, Associate Athletic Director of Business Relat
(814) 865-1757
gjm14@psu.edu
• Joe Battista, Associate Athletic Director of Ice Arena & Ho
(814) 863-203
• Jan Bortner, Assistant Athletic Director
(814) 863-0420
jeb12@psu.edu
Seating Capacity:
106,572
Team:
Pennsylvania State University football.

BEEGHLY GYM
224 WEST SPRING STREET
YOUNGSTOWN, OH 44502
330-941-2962
800-468-6978
Fax: 330-941-3191
ysusports@ysu.edu
ysusports.com/information/facilities/beeghly_center
• Ron Strollo, Executive Director of Intercollegiate Athletics
(330) 941-2385
• Tim Stuart, Assistant Athletic Director
(330) 941-2887
testuart@ysu.edu
• Alvy Armstrong, Head Equipment Manager
(330) 941-3725
adarmstrong@ysu.edu
Seating Capacity:
6,300

BELL MTS PLACE
300 PORTAGE AVENUE
WINNIPEG, MB, CANADA R3C 5S6
info@tnse.com
www.bellmtsplace.ca
• Mark Chipman, Executive Chairman, TNSE
• Kevin Donnelly, Sr. Vice President, Venues & Entertainment
Owners:
True North Sports & Entertainment
Year Opened:
2004
Seating Capacity:
Hockey - 15,294; End-Stage Concert - 16,170; Center-Stage Concert - 16,345; Rodeo/Motocross - 13,198; Basketball - 15,570
Tenant(s):
Winnipeg Jets (NHL)

BENDER ARENA
4400 MASSACHUSETTS AVENUE NW
WASHINGTON, DC 20016-8005
202-885-3001
Fax: 202-885-3033
walker@american.edu
www.aueagles.com
• Billy Walker, Director of Athletics
(202) 885-3001
walker@american.edu
• Jordan Tobin, Assistant Athletic Director, Facilities
(202) 885-3074
jtobin@american.edu
Arena Seating Capacity:
6,000

BERNARD G. JOHNSON COLISEUM
1964 BOBBY K. MARKS
HUNTSVILLE, TX 77340

facilities

936-294-1111
Fax: 936-294-1913
www.gobearkats.com
• Bobby Williams, Athletic Director
(936) 294-4205
bwilliams@shsu.edu
• Greg Hinze, Associate Athletic Director
Operations
(936) 294-1725
ghinze@shsu.edu
Coliseum Seating Capacity:
6,110

BERRY EVENTS CENTER
1401 PRESQUE ISLE AVENUE
NORTHERN MICHIGAN UNIVERSITY
ATHLETICS
MARQUETTE, MI 49855-5301
906-227-2850
800-682-9797
Fax: 906-227-2855
www.nmuwildcats.com
• Forrest Karr, Director of Athletics
(906) 227-1826
fkarr@nmu.edu
• Carl Bammert, Associate Athletic Director,
Facilities
(906) 227-2465
cbammert@nmu.edu
• Kathy Malay, Principal Secretary, Facilities
(906) 227-2851
kmalay@nmu.edu
Seating Capacity:
4,300
Tenant(s):
Northern Michigan Wildcats (Hockey &
Basketball).

BETHPAGE BALLPARK
3 COURT HOUSE DRIVE
CENTRAL ISLIP, NY 11722
631-940-3825
Fax: 631-940-3800
info@liducks.com
www.liducks.com
• Frank Boulton, Founder/CEO
• Michael Pfaff, President, General Manager
mpfaff@liducks.com
• Doug Cohen, Assistant General Manager
dcohen@liducks.com
• Gerry Anderson, Director of Administration
ganderson@liducks.com
Sport:
Minor League Baseball
Tenant(s):
Long Island Ducks baseball
Year Founded:
2000
Seating Capacity:
6,002

BIG SANDY SUPERSTORE ARENA
ONE CIVIC CENTER PLAZA
HUNTINGTON, WV 25701
304-696-5990
Fax: 304-696-1777
www.bigsandyarena.com
• Rik Edgar, General Manager
(304) 696-5566
redgar@bigsandyarena.com
• Cara Hedrick, Marketing and Sales
Manager
(304) 696-5990
cara@bigsandyarena.com
• Steve Kessick, Director of Operations
(304) 696-5990
skessick@bigsandyarena.com

• Sherry Sias-Lyell, Finance and Human
Resources Manager
(304) 696-5990
slyell@bigsandyarena.com
Seating Capacity:
9,000
Nature of Service:
Facility can accommodate concerts, flat
exhibitions, sales events, seminars, live
performances, indoor sporting events
including football, basketball, hockey, ice
skating, rodeo, motor sports, wrestling.
Venue also offers full-service conference
center ad
Year Founded:
1977

BILL SNYDER FAMILY STADIUM
1800 COLLEGE AVENUE
BRAMLAGE COLISEUM
MANHATTAN, KS 66502
785-532-6910
1-800-221-CATS
www.kstatesports.com/facilities
• John Currie, Director of Athletics
(785) 532-6912
jcurrie@kstatesports.com
• Clint Dowdle, Chief Of Staff
(785) 532-7056
cdowdle@kstatesports.com
• Scott Garrett, Sr. Associateathletic
Director, External Ops.
(785) 532-2880
sgarrett@kstatesports.com
• R.J. Bokelman, Director of Facilities
Operations
(785) 532-7601
rjb@kstatesports.com
Team:
Kansas State University
Seating Capacity:
50,000

**BILLINGS MUSTANGS PROFESSIONAL
BASEBALL CLUB**
DEHLER PARK
2611 9TH AVENUE NORTH
BILLINGS, MT 59101
406-252-1241
Fax: 406-252-2968
mustangs@billingsmustangs.com
www.billingsmustangs.com
• Gary Roller, General Manager
groller@billingsmustangs.com
• Chris Marshall, Sr. Director, Corporate
Sales
cmarshall@billingsmustangs.com
• Matt Schoonover, Sr. Director, Stadium
Operations
mschoonover@billingsmustangs.com
• John Barta, Sr. Director, Field
Maintenance & Facilities
Seating Capacity:
3,071
Year Founded:
1948

BISMARCK EVENT CENTER
315 SOUTH 5TH STREET
BISMARCK, ND 58504
701-355-1370
Fax: 701-222-6599
www.bismarckeventcenter.com
• Charlie Jeske, General Manager
(701) 355-1370
cjeske@bismarcknd.gov
• Ron Staiger, Operations Director

(701) 355-1381
rstaiger@bismarcknd.gov
Seating Capacity:
10,100
Nature of Service:
Arena, Exhibit Hall, Belle Mehus Theatre.

BLACKHAM COLISEUM
444 CAJUNDOME BOULEVARD
LAFAYETTE, LA 70506
337-482-5393
Fax: 337-482-5830
www.lafayettetravel.com
• Cindy Dermenstein, Convention Services
Coordinator
Seating Capacity:
9,800

BLUE CROSS ARENA
ONE WAR MEMORIAL SQUARE
ROCHESTER, NY 14614
585-758-5300
Fax: 585-758-5327
info@bluecrossarena.com
www.bluecrossarena.com
• Jeff E Calkins, General Manager
jcalkins@bluecrossarena.com
Tenant(s):
Rochester Americans (AHL), Rochester
Knighthawks (NLL), Rochester Razorsharks
(PBL)
Seating Capacity:
10,669

BMO FIELD
170 PRINCES' BLVD.
TORONTO, ON, CANADA M6K 3C3
416-263-5700
Fax: 416-815-6050
fanservices@mlse.com
www.bmofield.com
• Michael Friisdahl, President/CEO
Owners:
City of Toronto.
Operators:
Maple Leafs Sports & Entertainment.
Year Opened:
2007
Seating Capacity:
30,991
Tenant(s):
Toronto FC (MLS), Canada men's national
soccer team, Canada women's national
soccer team, Canada national rugby union
team, Toronto Argonauts (CFL).

BOB CARPENTER CENTER
631 SOUTH COLLEGE AVENUE
UNIVERSITY OF DELAWARE
NEWARK, DE 19716
302-831-4016
Fax: 302-831-8653
athletics@udel.edu
www.bluehens.com
• Joe Shirley, Sr. Associate Athletic Director,
Facilities
(302) 831-8586
jshirley@udel.edu
• Alica Greco-Walker, Associate Athletic
Director, Events & Ops.
(302) 831-8660
agreco@udel.edu
Arena Seating Capacity:
5,100
Organization:
University of Delaware Athletics

BOBBY BOWDEN FIELD AT DOAK CAMPBELL STADIUM
PENSACOLA STREET & STADIUM DRIVE
FLORIDA STATE UNIVERSITY
TALLAHASSEE, FL 32306
850-645-2527
Fax: 850-644-7293
www.seminoles.com/facilities
• Stan Wilcox, Director of Athletics
(850) 644-1079
• Bernie Waxman, Associate Athletics Director, Facilities
(850) 644-9940
bwaxman@fsu.edu
• Ryan Zornes, Assistant Director of Event Management
(850) 228-7589
rzornes@fsu.edu
Seating Capacity:
82,300
Teams:
Florida State University football.

BOBBY DODD STADIUM AT HISTORIC GRANT FIELD
155 NORTH AVENUE NORTHWEST
GEORGIA INSTITUTE OF TECHNOLOGY
ATLANTA, GA 30332
404-894-5400
Fax: 404-894-1300
www.ramblinwreck.com
• Derek Grice, Associate Athletic Director, Facilities
(404) 894-6668
dgrice@athletics.gatech.edu
• Cheryl LaFoy, Director of Event Operations
(404) 894-5431
clafoy@athletics.gatech.edu
• Jackson Matthews, Facilities Manager
(404) 894-5474
jmathews@athletics.gatech.edu
• Doc Hill, Facility Manager, Bobby Dodd Stadium
(404) 894-8490
dhill@athletics.gatech.edu
Stadium Seating Capacity:
55,000

BOBCAT STADIUM
101 BRADDOCK ROAD
FROSTBURG STATE UNIVERSITY
FROSTBURG, MD 21532-2303
301-687-4000
Fax: 301-687-4201
tadell@frostburg.edu
www.frostburgsports.com
• Troy Dell, Athletic Director
(301) 687-4455
• Rubin Stevenson, Associate Athletic Director
(301) 687-4086
rstevenson@frostburg.edu
Seating Capacity:
4,000
Year Founded:
1974
Track Size:
8 Lane, 400m (42)

BOBCAT STADIUM (MSU)
#1 BOBCAT CIRCLE
MONTANA STATE UNIVERSITY
BOZEMAN, MT 59717
406-994-7117
Fax: 406-994-2278

www.msubobcats.com/sports/2009/9/20/Facilities.aspx
• Peter Fields, Director of Athletics
(406) 994-3499
pfields@msubobcats.com
• Quinn Pacini, General Manager
(406) 994-4244
qpacini@bobcatsportsproperties.com
• Melanie Stocks, Director of Sports Facilities
(406) 994-6997
mstocks@montana.edu
Stadium Seating Capacity:
20,767

BOBCAT STADIUM TEXAS STATE
1100 AQUARENA SPRINGS
TEXAS STATE UNIVERSITY
SAN MARCOS, TX 78666
512-245-2114
Fax: 512-245-8387
athletics@txstate.edu
www.txstatebobcats.com
• Jeremy Stolfa, Assistant Athletic Director, Facilities
(512) 245-2023
stolfa@txstate.edu
• Chris Hannah, Director of Facilities and Game Ops.
(512) 245-9027
c_h165@txstate.edu
• Cody Farr, Director of Sports Turf Maintenance
(512) 245-2404
cf24@txstate.edu
Stadium Seating Capacity:
30,000

BOJANGLES' COLISEUM
2700 EAST INDEPENDENCE BOULEVARD
CHARLOTTE, NC 28205
704-372-3600
Fax: 704-335-3118
www.bojanglescoliseum.com
• Michael Crum, Chief Operating Officer
Permanent Seating Capacity:
8,600

BON SECOURS WELLNESS ARENA
650 NORTH ACADEMY STREET
GREENVILLE, SC 29601
864-241-3800
Fax: 864-250-4939
info@bswarena.com
www.bonsecoursarena.com
• Roger Newton, President / General Manager
• Randy Collins, Food & Beverage General Manager
• Beth Paul, Director of Finance and Administration
• Chris Williams, Operations Manager
cwilliams@biloctr.com
• Dwight Rust, Director of Operations
• Rik Knopp, Director of Sales and Marketing
Seating Capacity:
15,000
Tenant(s):
Greenville Road Warriors/Swamp Rabbits (ECHL).

BOONE PICKENS STADIUM
700 WEST HALL OF FAME AVENUE
OKLAHOMA STATE UNIVERSITY
STILLWATER, OK 74078

405-744-7301
877-227-6773
Fax: 405-744-9084
posse@okstate.edu
www.okstate.com/facilities/boone-pickens-stadium.html
• Shan Rains, Associate Athletic Director, Facilities Ops.
(405) 744-3012
shan.rains@okstate.edu
• Douglas Beach, Assistant Director of Athletic Facilities
(405) 744-6142
douglas.beach@okstate.edu
• John Houck, Manager, Cowboy Athletic Facilities
(405) 780-0004
john.houck@okstate.edu
• Monty Karns, Sr. Associate Athletic Director, Facilities
monty.karns@okstate.edu
Seating Capacity:
60,218
Tenant(s):
Oklahoma State Cowboys (NCAA).

BOSSE FIELD
23 DON MATTINGLY WAY
EVANSVILLE, IN 47711
812-435-8686
Fax: 812-435-8688
www.evansvilleotters.com
• Joel Padfield, General Manager
(812) 435-8686
jpadfield@evansvilleotters.com
• Jake Riffert, Director of Operations
(812) 435-8686
jriffert@evansvilleotters.com
• Lance Adler, Sports Turf Manager
(812) 435-8686
• Casie Williams, Controller
Tenant(s):
Evansville Otters (FL).
Seating Capacity:
5,181

BOUTWELL MUNICIPAL AUDITORIUM
1930 8TH AVENUE NORTH
BIRMINGHAM, AL 35203
205-254-2820
Fax: 205-254-2926
opi@birminghamal.gov
www.birminghamal.gov/about/city-directory/boutwell-auditorium
• Kevin G. Arrington, Director
(205) 254-2820
• Charlotte Latham, Concessions Supervisor
(205) 254-7762
• Charles Williams, Building Maintenance Superintendent
(205) 254-7733
• Jesse McElroy, Stage Manager
(205) 254-7761
Seating Capacity:
5,000

BOWEN FIELD
2003 STADIUM DRIVE
BLUEFIELD, WV 24701
304-324-1326
Fax: 304-324-1318
www.milb.com/index.jsp?sid=t517
• George McGonagle, President
(304) 324-1326
• Jeff Gray, General Manager
jeff.gray@bluefieldjays.com
• Mike White, Director of Fields Operations

Tenant(s):
Bluefield Blue Jays
Capacity:
3,000

BRADLEY CENTER
1001 NORTH 4TH STREET
MILWAUKEE, WI 53203
414-227-0797
Fax: 414-227-2400
• Brad Harrison, General Manager
(414) 288-1679
brad.harrison@marquette.edu
Seating Capacity:
20,000
Tenant(s):
Milwaukee Bucks (NBA), Milwaukee
Admirals (AHL), Marquette Golden Eagles
(NCAA).

BRAGG MEMORIAL STADIUM
1835 WAHNISH WAY
TALLAHASSEE, FL 32307
850-599-3000
Fax: 850-599-3810
michael.smith@famu.edu
www.famuathletics.com
• Milton Overton, Director of Athletics
(850) 599-3868
• Rose Garrison, Event Manager
(850) 599-3868
rose.garrison@famu.edu
• LaNorris Hayes, Grounds and
Maintenance Staff
(850) 599-3983
Seating Capacity:
25,500

BRAMLAGE COLISEUM
1800 COLLEGE AVENUE
MANHATTAN, KS 66502
785-532-7600
Fax: 785-532-7655
bramlage@ksu.edu
www.kstatesports.com
• John Currie, Director of Athletics
(785) 532-6912
jcurrie@kstatesports.com
• Jim Muller, Director of Facilities
Maintenance
(785) 532-7602
jmuller@kstatesports.com
• Charlie Thomas, Sr. Associate AD, Capital
Project Development
(785) 532-7609
cthomas@kstatesports.com
• Casey Scott, Sr. Associate AD, Operations
& Event Management
(785) 532-5263
caseys@kstatesports.com
• R.J. Bokelman, Director of Facilities
Operations
(785) 532-7601
rjb@kstatesports.com
• Brian Cordill, Director of Event Operations
(785) 532-7713
bcordill@kstatesports.com
Seating Capacity:
12,528

BRENT BROWN BALLPARK
970 W UNIVERSITY PARKWAY
OREM, UT 84058
801-377-2255
Fax: 801-377-2345
www.oremowlz.com

• Rick Berry, General Manager
rick@oremowlz.com
• Julie Hatch, Assistant General Manager
julie@oremowlz.com
Sport:
Baseball
Opened:
2005
Team:
Orem Owlz (Pioneer League); Utah Valley
Wolverines (NCAA)
Seating Capacity:
2,500

BRICK BREEDEN FIELDHOUSE
1 BOBCAT CIRCLE
BOZEMAN, MT 59717
406-994-7117
800-808-5940
mstocks@montana.edu
brickbreeden.com
• Chris Hayden, Director of Operations
(406) 994-4238
christopher.hayden@montana.edu
• Melanie Stocks, Director
(406) 994-6997
mstocks@montana.edu
• Ron Perrin, Director of Concessions
(406) 994-7741
rperrin@montana.edu
Arena Seating Capacity:
8,900

BRIDGESTONE ARENA
501 BROADWAY
NASHVILLE, TN 37203
615-770-2000
Fax: 615-770-2010
www.bridgestonearena.com
• Hugh Lombardi, SVP/General Manager
(615) 770-2002
• Jim Green, Assistant General Manager
(615) 770-2051
Arena Seating Capacity:
20,000
Year Founded:
1996
Tenant(s):
Nashville Predators

BRIGHT HOUSE NETWORKS STADIUM
4000 CENTRAL FLORIDA BOULEVARD
BUILDING 39
ORLANDO, FL 32816
407-823-3213
adoffice@athletics.ucf.edu
www.ucfknights.com
• Danny White, Director of Athletics
(407) 823-2261
adoffice@athletics.ucf.edu
• Lauren Perez, Director of Executive
Operations
(407) 823-2261
lperez@athletics.ucf.edu
• Tom Snyder, Associate AD, Facilities &
Event Operations
(407) 823-4954
tsnyder@athletics.ucf.edu
• Matt Oberlin, Director, Event Operations
(407) 823-4299
moberlin@athletics.ucf.edu
• Robert Sample, Director of Sports Turf and
Grounds
(407) 823-4598
rsample@athletics.ucf.edu
Seating Capacity:
44,206

Tenant(s):
The University of Central Florida

BRINGHURST FIELD
1 BABE RUTH DRIVE
ALEXANDRIA, LA 71301
318-473-2237
Fax: 318-473-2229
• Andrew Aguilar, General Manager
Year Founded:
1933
Capacity:
3,500
Tenant(s):
Alexandria Aces baseball.

BROADMOOR WORLD ARENA
3185 VENETUCCI BOULEVARD
COLORADO SPRINGS, CO 80906
719-477-2100
Fax: 719-477-2199
www.broadmoorworldarena.com
• Dot Lischick, General Manager
dlischick@broadmoorworldarena.com
• Tuesday Heslop, Assistant General
Manager
tuesday@broadmoorworldarena.com
• Claudean Brooks, Executive Assistant
gmassist@broadmoorworldarena.com
Arena Seating Capacity:
9,000
Year Founded:
1998
Clients:
Colorado College Tigers (NCAA)

BRONCO STADIUM
1910 UNIVERSITY DRIVE
BOISE STATE UNIVERSITY
BOISE, ID 83725
208-426-1000
Fax: 208-426-1998
www.broncosports.com
• Curt Apsey, Executive Director of Athletics
(208) 426-1826
• Bob Carney, Associate Athletic Director,
Facilities & Ops.
(208) 426-2570
robertcarney@boisestate.edu
• Joey King, General Manager
(208) 426-4999
jking@broncosportsproperties.com
• DJ Guimento, Assistant Athletic Director,
Facility Ops.
(208) 426-1513
Stadium Seating Capacity:
76,125

BROOME COUNTY VETERANS
MEMORIAL ARENA
ONE STUART STREET
BINGHAMTON, NY 13901
607-778-1528
Fax: 607-778-1528
www.broomearenaforum.com
• Robert Warner, Chairman of the Board
Seating Capacity:
6,925
Tenant(s):
Binghamton Senators (AHL)

BROWN COUNTY VETERANS MEMORIAL
ARENA
2420 NICOLET DRIVE
UNIVERSITY OF WISCONSIN -

GREENBAY
GREEN BAY, WI 54311-7001
920-465-2145
Fax: 920-465-2652
athletics@uwgb.edu
www.greenbayphoenix.com
• Mary Ellen Gillespie, Director of Athletics
(920) 465-2145
• Jeff Krueger, Director of Operations
(920) 465-2189
kruegerj@uwgb.edu
• Brent Tavis, Assistant AD for Events and
Operations
(920) 465-2064
tavisb@uwgb.edu
Seating Capacity:
5,248

BROWN STADIUM
235 HOPE STREET
BROWN UNIVERSITY ATHLETICS
PROVIDENCE, RI 02912
401-863-2295
Fax: 401-863-1436
thomas_bold@brown.edu
www.brownbears.com
• Jack Hayes, Director of Athletics
(401) 863-2972
jack_hayes@brown.edu
• Tom Bold, Sr. Associate Director of
Athletics, Facilities
(401) 863-2295
thomas_bold@brown.edu
• AJ Kizekai, Facilities & Operations
Coordinator
(401) 863-1869
• Dave Longo, Manager, Facilities &
Operations
(401) 863-9647
david_longo@brown.edu
Stadium Seating Capacity:
20,000

BROWNWOOD COLISEUM
500 EAST BAKER
HOWARD PAYNE UNIVERSITY
BROWNWOOD, TX 76801
325-649-8111
Fax: 325-649-8960
achoate@hputx.edu
www.hpusports.com
• John Nickols, Director of Athletics
jnickols@hputx.edu
• Troy Drummond, Associate Director of
Athletics, Operations
(325) 649-8103
tdrummond@hputx.edu
• Abram Choate, Assistant Director of
Athletics, Sports Info.
(325) 649-8111
achoate@hputx.edu
Arena Seating Capacity:
4,000

BRYANT DENNY STADIUM
BOX 870323
UNIVERSITY OF ALABAMA
TUSCALOOSA, AL 35487
205-348-3600
Fax: 205-348-2196
www.rolltide.com
• Bill Battle, Director of Athletics
(205) 348-3600
fgaston@ia.ua.edu
• Brandon Sevedge, Assistant Athletics
Director, Facilities
(205) 348-3573

bsevedge@ia.ua.edu
• Jonathan DeWitt, Director, Athletic
Grounds
Stadium Seating Capacity:
101,821

BRYCE JORDAN CENTER
127 BRYCE JORDAN CENTER
UNIVERSITY PARK, PA 16802
814-865-5555
Fax: 814-863-5705
bjc.psu.edu
• Mark Bodenschatz, Associate Athletic
Director, Facilities
(814) 863-3489
mab163@psu.edu
• Cory Chapman, General Manager
(814) 867-1337
• Shawn Shaible, Athletic Equipment &
Facilities Worker
(814) 865-2723
Arena Seating Capacity:
15,000

BUDWEISER GARDENS
99 DUNDAS STREET
LONDON, ON, CANADA N6A 6K1
519-667-5700
judy.sullivan@spectraxp.com
www.budweisergardens.com
• Dave Scott, CEO, Spectra Venue
Management
• John Page, President, Spectra Venue
Management
Owners:
London Civic Centre Corporation.
Operator:
Comcast Spectacor.
Year Founded:
2002
Seating Capacity:
10,200
Tenant(s):
London Knights (OHL), London Lightning
(NBL).

BULLDOGS STADIUM
1794 EAST BARSTOW AVENUE
FRESNO, CA 93740
559-431-3647
Fax: 559-278-7003
www.gobulldogs.com
• Jim Bartko, Director of Athletics
(559) 278-3178
athleticdirector@mail.fresnostate.edu
• Thomas Beach, Director of Athletics
• Betsy Mosher, Deputy Director
• Paul Ladwig, Sr.Associate
• John Kriebs, Associate A.d
• Steve Robertello, Associate A.d
• Ryan Reggiani, Assistant A.d
• Betsy Mosher, Sr. Associat AD,
Administration
(559) 879-4876
Stadium Seating Capacity:
41,031
Team:
Fresno State football.

**BURGESS-SNOW FIELD AT JSU
STADIUM**
700 PELHAM ROAD N
JACKSONVILLE, AL 36265
www.jsugamecocksports.com/sports/2008/8
/4/FB_0804082618.aspx

• Greg Seitz, Athletic Director
• John Grass, Head Coach, Football
(256) 782-5365
jsufootball@jsu.edu
Opened:
1947
Team:
Jacksonville State Gamecocks
Seating Capacity:
24,000

BURICH ARENA
950 HARRINGTON STREET SW
HUTCHINSON, MN 55350
320-234-5640
Fax: 320-234-4243
www.hutchinsonprce.com
Arena Seating Capacity:
3,500

BURKE FIELD
9550 16TH STREET NORTH
SAINT PETERSBURG, FL 33716
727-822-6937
800-582-6953
Fax: 727-821-5819
admin@minorleaguebaseball.com
www.minorleaguebaseball.com
• Steve Mullins, Athletic Director
(479) 968-0245
smullins@atu.edu
• Sam Bernabe, Chairman
• Randy Mobley, President
(614) 791-9300
• Branch Rickey, President
(719) 636-3399
• Lee Landers, President (Appalachian
League)
(704) 873-5300
Stadium Seating Capacity:
6,000

BURLINGTON ATHLETIC STADIUM
1450 GRAHAM STREET
BURLINGTON, NC 27217
336-222-0223
Fax: 336-226-2498
info@burlingtonroyals.com
www.burlingtonroyals.com
• Miles Wolff, President
info@burlingtonroyals.com
• Dan Moushon, Vice President
info@burlingtonroyals.com
• Ryan Keur, General Manager
rkeur@burlingtonroyals.com
• Miranda Ervin, Assistant General Manager
• Mikie Morrison, Director of Operations
mmorrison@burlingtonroyals.com

BURLINGTON BEES
2712 MOUNT PLEASANT STREET
BURLINGTON, IA 52601
319-754-5705
Fax: 319-754-5882
www.gobees.com
• Chuck Brockett, General Manager
chuck@gobees.com
• Kim Parker, Assistant General Manager
kim@gobees.com
Arena Seating Capacity:
3,200
Year Founded:
1947

BURTON MEMORIAL COLISEUM
7001 GULF HIGHWAY
LAKE CHARLES, LA 70607
337-721-4090
www.burtoncomplexevents.com
• Jason A. Barnes, General Manager
jbarnes@burtoncomplex.com
• Jared LeBlue, Operations Manager
jleblue@burtoncomplex.com
• Emily Porche, Event Coordinator
eporche@burtoncomplex.com
Arena Seating Capacity:
7000

BUSCH STADIUM
700 CLARK STREET
SAINT LOUIS, MO 63102
314-345-9600
stlouis.cardinals.mlb.com/stl/ballpark
• William O. DeWitt, Jr., Chairman & CEO
(301) 345-9600
• Joe Abernathy, Vice President, Stadium
Operations
(301) 345-9600
Description:
Home of the St. Louis Cardinals, Major
League Baseball team; inaugural game April
10, 2006.
Tenant(s):
MLB - St. Louis Cardinals baseball.
Permanent Seating Capacity:
43,975

BUTLER BOWL
SUNSET AVENUE & WEST 46TH STREET
BUTLER UNIVERSITY
INDIANAPOLIS, IN 46208
317-940-9375
Fax: 317-940-9734
info@butler.edu
www.butlersports.com
• Willis Cheaney, General Manager
(317) 940-8279
wcheaney@butlersportsproperties.com
• Chandler Prince, Manager, Business
Development
(317) 940-8278
cprince@butlersportsproperties.com
Permanent Seating Capacity:
5,647

C.E. GAINES CENTER
601 SOUTH MARTIN LUTHER KING JR.
DRIVE
WINSTON-SALEM STATE UNIVERSITY
WINSTON-SALEM, NC 27110
336-750-2141
Fax: 336-750-8880
wssurams.com
• Tonia Walker, Director of Athletics
(336) 750-2141
• Ariel Germain, Director of Marketing and
Special Events
(336) 750-2936
germaina@wssu.edu
Arena Seating Capacity:
3,200

C.O. BROWN STADIUM
1392 CAPITAL AVENUE NORTHEAST
BATTLE CREEK, MI 49017
269-962-0735
northwoodsleague.com
• Dick Radatz, Jr., Owner
(269) 962-0735
info@battlecreekbombers.com
• Anthony Iovieno, General Manager

(269) 962-0735
info@battlecreekbombers.com
• Kyle Harvey, Corporate Marketing
Manager
• Andrea Weed, Director of Marketing
andrea@battlecreekbombers.com
• Patrick Bielec, Director of Ballpark
Operations
patrick@growlersbaseball.com
Stadium Seating Capacity:
4,701

CAJUN FIELD STADIUM
201 REINHARDT DRIVE
LAFAYETTE, LA 70506
337-482-5393
Fax: 337-482-6649
www.ragincajuns.com
• Scott Farmer, Director of Athletics
(337) 482-5393
sfarmer@louisiana.edu
• David Faber, Assistant Athletics Director of
Operations
(337) 482-1835
dfaber@louisiana.edu
Stadium Seating Capacity:
36,900

CAJUNDOME
444 CAJUNDOME BOULEVARD
LAFAYETTE, LA 70506
337-265-2100
Fax: 337-265-2311
gdavis@cajundome.com
www.cajundome.com
• Greg Davis, Director
(337) 265-2100
gdavis@cajundome.com
• Phil Ashurst, Operations Director
(337) 265-2143
phila@cajundome.com
Arena Seating Capacity:
11,550

CALFEE PARK
700 SOUTH WASHINGTON AVENUE
PULASKI, VA 24301
540-980-1070
Fax: 540-980-1850
info@pulaskiyankees.net
www.milb.com
• Blair Hoke, General Manager
bhoke@pulaskiyankees.net
Arena Seating Capacity:
2,500

CALGARY STAMPEDE
1410 OLYMPIC WAY SE
CALGARY, AB, CANADA T2G 2W1
403-261-0101
Fax: 403-265-7197
info@calgarystampede.com
www.calgarystampede.com
• Warren Connell, Chief Executive Officer

CALIFORNIA MEMORIAL STADIUM
76 CANYON ROAD
BERKELEY, CA 94720-4422
510-642-0580
Fax: 510-642-3399
www.calbears.com
• H. Michael Williams, Director of Athletics
(510) 642-0580
athletic.director@berkeley.edu
• Chris Pezman, Associate AD of Facilities
& Operations

cpezman@berkeley.edu
• Matthew Gallagher, General Manager
matthew.gallagher@img.com
• Katie Fontes, Coordinator Sponsor
Services
katie.fontes@img.com
Seating Capacity:
62,467
Teams:
University of California football.

CALIHAN HALL
4001 WEST MCNICHOLS ROAD
UNIVERSITY OF DETROIT MERCY
DETROIT, MI 48221
313-993-1700
Fax: 313-993-2449
www.detroittitans.com
• Robert C. Vowels, Jr., Director of Athletics
(313) 993-1700
vowelsrc@udmercy.edu
• Clifford Sims, Director of Operations
(313) 993-1714
simsc1@udmercy.edu
• Tim Fair, Assistant Director of Operatinos
(313) 993-1700
fairtr@udmercy.edu
Arena Seating Capacity:
8,295

CAM HENDERSON CENTER
MARSHALL UNIVERSITY
PO BOX 1360
HUNTINGTON, WV 25715
304-696-5408
Fax: 304-696-6448
www.herdzone.com
• Mike Hamrick, Director of Athletics
(304) 696-5408
• Tom Ponietowicz, Director of Events
(304) 696-7280
ponietowicz@marshall.edu
• Andrew Brown, Director of Facilities
(304) 696-3665
brown613@marshall.edu
Seating Capacity:
62,467

CAMBRIA COUNTY WAR MEMORIAL
326 NAPOLEON STREET
JOHNSTOWN, PA 15901-1704
814-536-5156
800-243-8499
Fax: 814-536-3670
www.warmemorialarena.com/
• Stephen St. John, General Manager
(814) 536-5156
steve@warmemorialarena.com
• Karen Gregorchik, Assistant General
Manager
(814) 536-5156
kgregorchik@warmemorialarena.com
• Brian Levandoski, NCRC Arena Manager
(814) 915-0430
operations@warmemorialarena.com
Seating Capacity:
4,001

CAMERON HALL
401 NORTH MAIN STREET
VIRGINIA MILITARY INSTITUTE
LEXINGTON, VA 24450
540-464-7251
Fax: 540-464-7622
www.vmikeydets.com

• Dave Diles, Athletic Director
(540) 464-7251
dilesdl@vmi.edu
Seating Capacity:
5,000

CAMP RANDALL STADIUM
1440 MONROE STREET
UNIVERSITY OF WISCONSIN
MADISON, WI 53711
608-262-1866
800-GO-BADGERS
Fax: 608-265-3036
contactus@uwbadgers.com
www.uwbadgers.com
• Barry Alvarez, Director of Athletics
(608) 262-1866
• Glenn Betts, Building Operations
(608) 262.3354
Tenant(s):
NCAA - University of Wisconsin football.
Stadium Seating Capacity:
80,321

CAMPANELLI STADIUM
1 FEINBERG WAY
BROCKTON, MA 02301
508-559-7000
Fax: 508-584-1620
roxfun@brocktonrox.com
www.brocktonrox.com
• Chris English, Owner and President
cenglish@brocktonrox.com
• Todd Marlin, General Manager
tmarlin@brocktonrox.com
• Ben Rapaport, Assistant General Manager
Ben@Brocktonrox.com
Stadium Seating Capacity:
4,750
Year Founded:
2002
Track Type:
Natural grass.

CANADIAN TIRE CENTRE
1000 PALLADIUM DRIVE
OTTAWA, ON, CANADA K2V 1A5
613-599-0100
www.canadiantirecentre.com
Year Opened:
1996
Seating Capacity:
20,041
Tenant(s):
NHL - Ottawa Senators

CANAL PARK
300 SOUTH MAIN STREET
AKRON, OH 44308
330-253-5151
1-855-977-8225
Fax: 330-253-3300
information@akronrubberducks.com
www.milb.com
• Ken Babby, Owner, CEO
kenbabby@akronrubberducks.com
• Jim Pfander, General Manager
jim@akronrubberducks.com
• Adam Horner, Director, Ballpark
Operations
ahorner@akronrubberducks.com
Sport:
Minor League Baseball.
Team:
Akron Aeros baseball
Year Founded:
1997

Capacity:
7,630

CANTON MEMORIAL CIVIC CENTER
1101 MARKET AVENUE NORTH
CANTON, OH 44702
330-489-3090
Fax: 330-471-8840
www.cantonciviccenter.com
• Blake Schilling, General Manager
blake.schilling@cantonohio.gov
• Geoff Tompkins, Assistant General
Manager
geoff.tompkins@cantonohio.gov
• Steve Meadows, Operations Manager
steve.meadows@cantonohio.gov
• Monica Johnson, Box Office Manager
monica.johnson@cantonohio.gov
• Wilbur Allen, Finance Manager
wilbur.allen@cantonohio.gov
Seating Capacity:
5,200

CAPITAL CITY STADIUM
301 SOUTH ASSEMBLY STREET
COLUMBIA, SC 29201
803-705-4784
Fax: 803-705-4842
www.benedicttigers.com
• Willie Washington, Athletic Director
(803) 705-4734
washingtonw@benedict.edu
• William Hatten, Intramurals and Facilities
Coordinator
(803) 705-4965
hattenw@benedict.edu
Tenant(s):
Benedict Tigers

CARL WOOTEN STADIUM
PO BOX 430
OKLAHOMA PANHANDLE STATE
COLLEGE
GOODWELL, OK 73939
580-349-2611
800-664-6778
Fax: 580-349-2302
www.opsu.edu
• R. Wayne Stewart, Athletic Director
(580) 349-1408
rwstewart@opsu.edu
Stadium Seating Capacity:
5,000

CARLSON CENTER
2010 2ND AVENUE
FAIRBANKS, AK 99701
907-451-7800
Fax: 907-451-1195
info@carlson-center.com
www.carlson-center.com
• Kristin Baysinger, General Manager
kbaysinger@fnsb.us
• Adam Powell, Operations Manager
apowell@fnsb.us
• Camille Relatado, Marketing & Box Office
Manager
crelatado@fnsb.us
• Sarah Nolan, Bookkeeper
snolan@fnsb.us
Seating Capacity:
4,595
Year Founded:
1990
Tenant(s):
Alaska Nanooks (WCHA), World Eskimo
Indian Olympics, WWF/WWE

Nature of Service:
Entertainment and sports arena.

**CARNIE SMITH
STADIUM/BRANDENBURG FIELD**
1701 SOUTH BROADWAY
PITTSBURG STATE UNIVERSITY
PITTSBURG, KS 66762
620-231-7000
800-854-7488
Fax: 620-235-4661
psuinfo@pittstate.edu
www.pittstategorillas.com
• Jim Johnson, Athletics Director
(620) 235-4389
jjohnson@pittstate.edu
• Tom Myers, Associate Athletic Director,
Facilities
(620) 235-4640
ltmyers@pittstate.edu
• Lacie Anderson, Office and Special Events
Manager
(620) 235-4389
landerson@pittstate.edu
Stadium Seating Capacity:
8,343

CARRIER DOME
900 IRVING AVENUE
SYRACUSE UNIVERSITY
SYRACUSE, NY 13244
315-443-4221
888-366-3849
Fax: 315-443-3692
www.carrierdome.com
• Pete Sala, Vice President & Chief
Facilities Officer
(315) 443-4221
pesala@syr.edu
• John DeFrancisco, Facility Systems
Specialist
(315) 443-4221
jadefran@syr.edu
• Lacey Kohl, Operations
lmkohl@syr.edu
• Mark Barbuto, Event Staff Manager
(315) 443-4634
mbarbuto@syr.edu
• Jeremiah Maher, Assistant Athletics
Director, Ticket Sales
(315) 443-2121
jjmaher@syr.edu
Permanent Seating Capacity:
49,262

CARTER FINLEY STADIUM
4600 TRINITY ROAD
RALEIGH, NC 27607
919-515-2101
Fax: 919-515-1161
www.gopack.com
• Jeff Dunlap, Director of Operations
(919) 515-2104
jsdunlap@ncsu.edu
• Deborah A. Yow, Director of Athletics
(919) 515-2109
d_yow@ncsu.edu
• Chris Boyer, Deputy Athletic Director,
External Ops.
(919) 513-8085
ccboyer@ncsu.edu
• James Bowling, Carter-Finley Stadium
Facilities
(919) 515-7369
jhbowlin@ncsu.edu
• Christopher Norris, Facilities Maintenance
Supervisor

facilities

(919) 515-7369
cwnorris@ncsu.edu
• Nathan Abraham, Assistant Director of Turf & Grounds
(919) 515-7369
ntabraha@ncsu.edu
Stadium Seating Capacity:
57,583
Tenant(s):
North Carolina Wolfpack football (NCAA).

CARVER-HAWKEYE ARENA
1 ELLIOT DRIVE
UNIVERSITY OF IOWA
IOWA CITY, IA 52242-1020
319-335-9743
Fax: 319-335-9333
www.hawkeyesports.com
• Gary Barta, Director of Athletics
(319) 335-9435
gary-barta@uiowa.edu
• Damiam Simcox, Director, Facilities
(319) 335-9410
• Katie Ortmann, Attendant, Facilities Operations
(319) 335-9406
katie-ortmann@uiowa.edu
Arena Seating Capacity:
15,400
Tenant(s):
Iowa Hawkeyes men's and women's basketball, gymnastics, volleyball, and wrestling

CASHMAN FIELD
850 LAS VEGAS BOULEVARD NORTH
LAS VEGAS, NV 89101
702-943-7200
Fax: 702-386-7214
info@lv51.com
www.lv51.com
• Don Logan, President, COO
(702) 943-7200
dlogan@lv51.com
• Nick Fitzenreider, Vice President, Operations
fitzstadium@aol.com
• Chip Vespe, Operations Manager
chip@lv51.com
Stadium Seating Capacity:
9,334
Year Founded:
1983

CASPER EVENTS CENTER
200 NORTH DAVID
CASPER, WY 82601
307-235-8400
800-442-2256
Fax: 307-235-8445
www.caspereventscenter.com
• Brett Dovala, Building Manager
(307) 235-8441
• Paul Hanson, Operations Supervisor
(307) 235-8458
• Matt Hinds, Events Coordinator
(307) 235-8449
• Cody Lawson, Maintenance Crew Chief
(307) 235-8434
Arena Seating Capacity:
8,395

CASSELL COLISEUM
675 WASHINGTON STREET SOUTHWEST
BLACKSBURG, VA 24061
540-231-9963
Fax: 540-231-3060

hokipoki@vt.edu
www.hokiesports.com
• Whit Babcock, Director of Athletics
(540) 231-9984
hokipoki@vt.edu
• Tom Gabbard, Sr. Associate Athletics Director, Facilities
(540) 231-6265
tgabbard@vt.edu
• James Torgersen, Director, Facilities
(540) 231-7584
jamest08@vt.edu
• Jerry Cheynet, Coordinator, Operations
(540) 231-6067
msoccer@vt.edu
• Pete Pool, Director, Stadium and Fields
(540) 231-6067
ppool@vt.edu
Coliseum Seating Capacity:
10,052

CENTENE STADIUM
1015 25TH STREET NORTH
GREAT FALLS, MT 59401
406-452-5311
Fax: 406-454-0811
voyagers@gfvoyagers.com
www.gfvoyagers.com
• Scott Reasoner, General Manager
(406) 452-5311
scott@gfvoyagers.com
• Matt Coakley, Assistant General Manager
(406) 452-5311
matt@gfvoyagers.com
• Scott Lettre, Director of Sales
(406) 452-5311
slettre@gfvoyagers.com
Team:
Great Falls Voyagers
Year Founded:
1969
Capacity:
4,500

CENTRE BELL
1909 AVENUE DES CANADIENS-DE-MONTREAL
MONTREAL, QC, CANADA H4B 5G0
514-989-2841
855-310-2525
www.centrebell.ca
• Geoff Molson, President/CEO
Owners:
Geoff, Andrew and Justin Molson
Year Opened:
1996
Seating Capacity:
21,288
Tenant(s):
Montreal Canadiens (NHL).

CENTURYLINK CENTER OMAHA
455 NORTH 10TH STREET
OMAHA, NE 68102
402-341-1500
Fax: 402-991-1501
bdrass@creighton.edu
www.centurylinkcenteromaha.com
• Bruce Rasmussen, Athletic Director
(402) 280-2720
bdrass@creighton.edu
• Brandon McCarville, Director of Facilities
brandonmccarville@creighton.edu
• JJ Borecky, Assistant Director of Facilities
jjborecky@creighton.edu
Seating Capacity:
18,975

Owned by:
City of Omaha
Year Opened:
2003
Facility Management:
Metropolitan Entertainment & Convention Authority.

CESSNA STADIUM
1845 FAIRMOUNT
WICHITA STATE UNIVERSITY
WICHITA, KS 67260-0018
316-978-3265
Fax: 316-978-3336
mediarelations@goshockers.com
www.goshockers.com
• Darron Boatright, Interim Director of Athletics
(316) 978-5498
dboatright@goshockers.com
• Brad Pittman, Associate Athletic Director, Facilities & Ops.
(316) 978-5556
bpittman@goshockers.com
• Mike Sandbo, Director of Facilities and Operations
(316) 978-5512
msandbo@goshockers.com
• Jesse Torres, Director of Equipment Operations
(316) 978-7471
jtorres@goshockers.com
• Mark Rogers, General Manager
(316) 978-7552
mrogers@goshockers.com
• Sheri Jans, Senior Acount Executive
(316) 978-7554
sjans@goshockers.com
Arena Seating Capacity:
24,000

CFE ARENA
12777 GEMINI BOULEVARD NORTH
ORLANDO, FL 32816
407-823-3070
Fax: 407-823-0248
www.cfearena.com
• Brian Hixenbaugh, General Manager
(407) 823-3070
brian.hixenbaugh@ucf.edu
• Lavar Smith, Assistant General Manager
lavar.smith@ucf.edu
• Mike Terrell, Operations Manager
michael.terrell@ucf.edu
• Jack Wentzell, Assistant Operations Manager
jack.wentzell@ucf.edu
• Ryan Fitzgerald, Event Manager
ryan.fitzgerald@ucf.edu
Arena Seating Capacity:
10,072

CHAMPION STADIUM
700 SOUTH VICTORY WAY
LAKE BUENA VISTA, FL 34747
407-938-3500
Fax: 407-938-3442
www.espnwwos.com/complex/champion-stadium
• Vinny O'Leary, Director, Stadium Ops.
Sport:
Minor League Baseball/Major League Baseball Training.
Tenant(s):
Atlanta Braves, USSSA Pride (NPF).
Year Founded:
1997

Capacity:
9,500

CHARLES E. SMITH CENTER
600 22ND STREET, NW
GEORGE WASHINGTON UNIVERSITY
WASHINGTON, DC 20052
202-994-6650
Fax: 202-994-6818
gwad@gwu.edu
www.gwsports.com
• Patrick Nero, Director of Athletics
(202) 994-6650
gwad@gwu.edu
• Michael Aresco, Assistant Athletics
Director, Administration
(202) 994-5480
msa05002@gwu.edu
• Andrew Lundt, Assistant Director of
Operations, Facilities
(202) 994-3151
andrew_lundt@gwu.edu
• Autumn Glowacki, Coordinator of
Operations, Events and Facilities
(202) 994-5959
athsched@gwu.edu
Seating Capacity:
5,000
Sports:
Men's & Women's Basketball, Vomen's
Volleyball, Women's Gymnastcs

CHARLES KOCH ARENA
1854 FAIRMOUNT
WICHITA STATE UNIVERSITY
WICHITA, KS 67260
316-978-3456
Fax: 316-978-3345
mediarelations@goshockers.com
www.goshockers.com
• Darron Boatright, Interim Director of
Athletics
(316) 978-5498
dboatright@goshockers.com
• Rege Klitzke, Sr. Associate AD, Business
Ops.
(316) 978-3251
rklitzke@goshockers.com
• Brad Pittman, Associate Athletic Director,
Facilities & Ops.
(316) 978-5556
bpittman@goshockers.com
• Mike Sandbo, Director of Facilities and
Operations
(316) 978-5512
msandbo@goshockers.com
• Jesse Torres, Director of Equipment
Operations
(316) 978-7471
jtorres@goshockers.com
Arena Seating Capacity:
10,506

**CHARLES M. MURPHY ATHLETIC
CENTER**
MURPHY CENTER ROOM G100
MIDDLE TENNESSEE STATE
UNIVERSITY
MURFREESBORO, TN 37132
615-904-8258
Fax: 615-904-8101
rita.whitaker@mtsu.edu
www.mtsu.edu/murphycenter
• Darrell Towe, Director
(615) 904-8258
darrell.towe@mtsu.edu
• Rita Whitaker, Manager

(615) 904-8129
rita.whitaker@mtsu.edu
• Sherrie Murray, Administrative Assistant &
Office Manager
(615) 904-8258
sherrie.murray@mtsu.edu
• Chris Gannar, Event Coordinator
(615) 898-5189
chris.gannar@mtsu.edu
Arena Seating Capacity:
11,520

CHARLESTON CIVIC CENTER
200 CIVIC CENTER DRIVE
CHARLESTON, WV 25301
304-345-1500
Fax: 304-345-3492
john.robertson@charlestonwvciviccenter.com
www.charlestonwvciviccenter.com
• John Robertson, General Manager
(304) 345-1500
john.robertson@cityofcharleston.org
• Jim Smith, Assistant Manager, Director of
Operations
jim.smith@charlestonwvciviccenter.com
• Betty Tinney, Business Manager
betty.tinney@charlestonwvciviccenter.com
• Anna Campbell, Director of Marketing
(304) 345-1500
anna.campbell@charlestonwvciviccenter.com
Arena Seating Capacity:
13,500
Year Founded:
1959
Nature of Service:
Spectator concert, family events, sporting
events, meetings, conventions, banquets.

CHASE FIELD BALL PARK
401 EAST JEFFERSON STREET
PHOENIX, AZ 85004
602-462-6500
Fax: 602-462-6600
ballparktours@dbacks.com
arizona.diamondbacks.mlb.com
• Ken Kendrick, Managing General Partner
(602) 462-6500
• Dave Stewart, SVP & General Manager
(602) 462-6500
• Russ Amaral, VP, Facilities & Event
Services
(602) 462-6500
• Bryan White, Director, Event Services
(602) 462-6500
Owned by:
Maricopa County Stadium District.
Seating Capacity:
48,519
Year Founded:
1998
Team:
Arizona Diamondbacks MLB baseball.

CHENEY STADIUM
2502 SOUTH TYLER STREET
TACOMA, WA 98405
253-752-7707
Fax: 253-752-7135
aartman@tacomarainiers.com
www.milb.com/index.jsp?sid=t529
• Aaron Artman, President
(253) 752-7707
aartman@tacomarainiers.com
• Cameron Badgett, Director of Ticket
Operations

(253) 752-7707
cbadgett@tacomarainiers.com
• Ryan Schutt, Sr. Director of Ballpark
Operations
(253) 752-7707
rschutt@tacomarainiers.com
• Nick Cherniske, Stadium Operations
Manager
(253) 752-7707
ncherniske@tacomarainiers.com
Stadium Seating Capacity:
6,800
Year Founded:
1960
Clients:
Tacoma Rainiers Baseball Club

CHESAPEAKE ENERGY ARENA
100 WEST RENO AVENUE
OKLAHOMA CITY, OK 73102
405-602-8700
info@chesapeakearena.com
www.chesapeakearena.com
Seating Capacity:
18,203
Year Founded:
2002
Tenant(s):
Oklahoma City Thunder

CHICKASAW BRICKTOWN BALLPARK
2 SOUTH MICKEY MANTLE DRIVE
OKLAHOMA CITY, OK 73104
Founded:
1998
Team:
Oklahoma City Dodgers
Seating Capacity:
13,066

CHRISTENSEN STADIUM
4300 NORTH LAMESA ROAD
MIDLAND, TX 79706
432-685-4500
Year Founded:
1952
Capacity:
5,000

CHRISTL ARENA
639 HOWARD ROAD
WEST POINT, NY 10996
845-938-6332
Fax: 845-938-8707
www.goarmywestpoint.com
• Boo Corrigan, Director of Athletics
(845) 938-3701
• Steve Tucker, General Manager
(845) 446-2500
stucker@awpsportsproperties.com
• Jillian Mazza, Sponsorship Coordinator
(845) 446-2500
Arena Seating Capacity:
5,043

CHUKCHANSI PARK
1800 TULARE STREET
FRESNO, CA 93721
559-320-4487
Fax: 559-320-1216
info@fresnogrizzlies.com
www.fresnogrizzlies.com
• Derek Franks, President
(559) 320-2524
dfranks@fresnogrizzlies.com
• Andrew Melrose, VP, Partnership

Marketing
(559) 320-2502
amelrose@fresnogrizzlies.com
• Andrew Milios, VP, Ticket Sales
(559) 320-2533
amilios@fresnogrizzlies.com
Stadium Seating Capacity:
12,500
Year Founded:
1994, new stadium opened 2002
Nature of Service:
Triple A Affiliate of the Washington
Nationals.
Teams:
Fresno Grizzlies

CINCINNATI GARDENS
2250 SEYMOUR AVENUE
CINCINNATI, OH 45212
513-631-7793
Fax: 513-351-5898
info@cincygardens.com
www.cincygardens.com
• Gerry Robinson, Owner/Chairman
• Pete Robinson, President/CEO
(513) 351-3999
• Joe Jagoditz, General Manager
(513) 351-3999
• Greg Waddell, Director of PR/Media
Relations
(513) 351-3999
gwaddell@cincygardens.com
• Jerry Henderson, Operations Manager
(513) 351-3999
jhenderson@cincygardens.com
Arena Seating Capacity:
10,208

CITI FIELD
120-01 ROOSEVELT AVENUE
FLUSHING, NY 11368
718-565-1542 EXT 4360
newyork.mets.mlb.com/nym/ballpark
• Fred Wilpon, Chairman of the Board &
Chief Executive Officer
• Saul Katz, President
• Jeff Wilpon, Chief Operating Officer
• Sandy Alderson, General Manager
• Sue Lucchi, Vice President, Ballpark
Operations
Seating Capacity:
41,922
Team:
New York Mets MLB baseball.

CITIZENS BANK PARK
ONE CITIZENS BANK WAY
PHILADELPHIA, PA 19148
215-463-6000
www.citizensbank.com/ballpark
• Andy MacPhail, President
(215) 463-6000
• David Montgomery, Chairman
(215) 463-6000
• Mike DiMuzio, Director, Operations/Facility
• Eric Tobin, Director, Operations/Events
• Sal DeAngelis, Director,
Operations/Security
Year Opened:
2004
Permanent Seating Capacity:
43,651
Tenant(s):
MLB - Philadelphia Phillies baseball

CIVIC CENTER COMPLEX
701 MAIN STREET
BEAUMONT, TX 77701
409-838-3435
800-782-3081
Fax: 409-838-3715
discoverbeaumont@beaumonttexas.gov
www.discoverbeaumont.com
• Lenny Caballero, Event Facilities Director
lcaballero@beaumonttexas.gov
• Tommie Minkins, Operations Division
Manager
tminkins@beaumonttexas.gov
• Emily Wheeler, Marketing Division
Manager
ewheeler@beaumonttexas.gov
Arena Seating Capacity:
6,500

CIVIC CENTER OF ANDERSON
3027 MLK JR. BOULEVARD
ANDERSON, SC 29625
864-260-4800
Fax: 864-260-4847
asec@andersoncountysc.org
www.andersonevents.com
• Terry Gaines, Events Coordinator
(864) 260-4800
• Shelly Callahan, Receptionist, Business
Office
(864) 260-4800
Seating Capacity:
3,200

CLASSIC PARK
35300 VINE STREET
EASTLAKE, OH 44095
440-975-8085
Fax: 440-975-8958
ask@lakevisit.com
www.captainsbaseball.com
• Peter Carfagna, Chairman,
Secretary/Treasurer
• Rita Murphy, Vice Chairman of Captains
Charities
Sport:
Baseball.
Tenant(s):
Lake County Captains baseball
Capacity:
7,273

CLEMSON MEMORIAL STADIUM
100 PERIMETER ROAD
CLEMSON, SC 29634
864-656-2564
Fax: 864-656-0415
www.clemsontigers.com
• Dan Radakovich, Director of Athletics
(864) 656-1935
• Graham Neff, Deputy Athletics Director
(864) 656-0128
neffg@clemson.edu
• Gary Wade, Assistant Athletic Director of
Facilities
(864) 643-6004
wgary@clemson.edu
Stadium Seating Capacity:
81,500

**CLEVE L. ABBOTT MEMORIAL ALUMNI
STADIUM**
1200 WEST MONTGOMERY ROAD
TUSKEGEE, AL 36088
334-724-4545
Fax: 334-724-4233
www.goldentigersports.com

• Curtis Campbell, Director of Athletics
(334) 724-4545
ccampbell@mytu.tuskegee.edu
• Dave Lunn, Manager, Athletics Facilities
and Transportation
dlunn@mytu.tuskegee.edu
Stadium Seating Capacity:
10,000

CMC-NORTHEAST STADIUM
2888 MOOSE ROAD
KANNAPOLIS, NC 28083
704-932-3267
Fax: 704-938-7040
info@intimidatorsbaseball.com
kannapolis.intimidators.milb.com
• Brad Smith, President
bsmith@intimidatorsbaseball.com
• Randy Long, General Manager
rlong@intimidatorsbaseball.com
• Josh Feldman, Director of
Communications
jfeldman@intimidatorsbaseball.com
• Darren Cozart, Director of Operations
dcozart@intimidatorsbaseball.com
Sport:
Baseball.
Tenant(s):
Kannapolis Intimidators baseball.
Year Founded:
1995
Capacity:
4,700

COBO ARENA
1 WASHINGTON BOULEVARD
DETROIT, MI 48226
313-877-8777
Fax: 313-877-8577
www.cobocenter.com
• Thom Connors, Regional Vice President
SMG
• Claude Molinari, General Manager Cobo
Center
• Cedric Turnbore, Director of Operations
• Greg DeSandy Turnbore, Director of Sales
and Event Services
Arena Seating Capacity:
12,141

COCA-COCA FIELD
1 JAMES D. GRIFFIN PLAZA
BUFFALO, NY 14203
716-846-2000
Fax: 716-852-6530
info@bisons.com
www.bisons.com
• Joseph W. Segarra, Vice President, Chief
Operating Officer
• Jonathan A. Dandes, President, Rich
Baseball Operations
• Michael Buczkowski, Vice President,
General Manager
• Tom Sciarrino, Director, Stadium
Operations
• Robert Free, Director of Foodservice
Operations
Seating Capacity:
18,025

COCA-COLA COLISEUM
45 MANITOBA DRIVE
TORONTO, ON, CANADA M6K 3C3
416-263-3900
Fax: 416-263-3901
www.coca-colacoliseum.com
• Bryan Leslie, Director, Building Operations

Owners:
City of Toronto.
Operators:
Maple Leafs Sports & Entertainment Ltd.
Seating Capacity:
Hockey: 7,851; Concerts: 9,250
Tenant(s):
AHL - Toronto Marlies.

COHEN STADIUM
9700 GATEWAY N. BOULEVARD
EL PASO, TX 79924
915-755-2000
Seating Capacity:
9,725

COLEMAN COLISEUM
BOX 870323
TUSCALOOSA, AL 35487
205-348-3600
Fax: 205-348-2196
www.rolltide.com
• Bill Battle, Athletic Director
(205) 348-3600
• Brandon Sevedge, Assistant Athletics
Director, Facilities
(205) 348-3573
bsevedge@ia.ua.edu
Arena Seating Capacity:
15,383

COLLEGE OF WILLIAM & MARY
751 UKROP WAY
WILLIAMSBURG, VA 23185
757-221-3400
Fax: 757-221-3412
www.tribeathletics.com
• Terry Driscoll, Athletic Director
(757) 221-3332
• Michael Pritchett, Assistant Athletics
Director, Facilities & Ops.
(757) 221-3355
mapritchett@wm.edu
• Adam Andrusyszyn, Assistant Director,
Facilities & Ops.
(757) 221-3345
anandrusyszyn@wm.edu
• Shane Vernarsky, Head Athletic
Equipment Amanager
(757) 221-3335
sjvernarsky@wm.edu
• Vicki Collier, Facilities & Operations
Coordinator
(757) 221-1039
vmcollier@wm.edu
Arena Seating Capacity:
8,600
**Walter J. Zable Stadium Seating
Capacity:**
11,686

COLONIAL LIFE ARENA
801 LINCOLN STREET
COLUMBIA, SC 29208
803-576-9200
Fax: 803-576-9299
www.coloniallifearena.com
• Sid Kenyon, General Manager
(803) 576-9200
• Lexie Boone, Sr. Assistant General
Manager, Director of Ops.
(803) 576-9200
• Curt Derrick, Assistant General Manager,
Director of Ticketing
(803) 576-9200
• Julie Carter, Director of Business

Operations
(803) 576-9200
Year Opened:
2002
Arena Seating Capacity:
18,000
Tenant(s):
NCAA - University of South Carolina
basketball.

COMERICA PARK
2100 WOODWARD AVENUE
DETROIT, MI 48201-3470
313-962-4000
Fax: 301-985-6254
• Michael Illitch, Detroit Tigers
Owner/Director
(313) 471-2000
• Al Avila, EVP of Baseball Ops & General
Manager
(313) 471-2000
• Brian Skipinski, Director, Park Operations
(313) 471-2000
• Heather Nabozny, Head Groundskeeper
(313) 471-2000
• Ed Goward, Sr Manager, Park Operations
(313) 471-2000
Stadium Seating Capacity:
41,574
Tenant(s):
MLB - Detroit Tigers baseball.

**COMMONWEALTH STADIUM
(EDMONTON)**
11000 STADIUM ROAD NW
EDMONTON, AB, CANADA T5H 4E2
780-442-5311
311@edmonton.ca
Owners:
City of Edmonton
Year Opened:
1978
Seating Capacity:
60,000
Tenant(s):
CFL - Edmonton Eskimos.

**COMMONWEALTH STADIUM
(KENTUCKY)**
338 LEXINGTON AVENUE
LEXINGTON, KY 40506-0604
859-257-8000
mbarn@uky.edu
www.ukathletics.com
• Mitch Barnhart, Athletics Director
(859) 257-8015
mbarn@uky.edu
• Elizabeth Briggs, Assistant Athletic
Director, Premium Seating
(859) 257-1757
elizabeth.briggs@uky.edu
• Kevin Saal, Sr. Associate Athletic Director,
Operations
(859) 254-2788
kevin.saal@uky.edu
• Donnie Mefford, Assistant Athletic
Director, Facilities
(859) 257-7124
donnie.mefford@uky.edu
Seating Capacity:
61,000

COMMUNITYAMERICA BALLPARK
1800 VILLAGE WEST PARKWAY
KANSAS CITY, KS 66111

913-328-2255
Fax: 913-328-5674
www.tbonesbaseball.com
• John Ehlert, Owner
• Matt Fulks, Director of Media Relations
(913) 328-5639
mfulks@tbonesbaseball.com
• Adam Ehlert, President
aehlert@tbonesbaseball.com
• Chris Browne, General Manager
cbrowne@tbonesbaseball.com
• John Massarelli, Manager, Director of
Baseball Operations
• Kyle Disney, Stadium Operations
Coordinator
(913) 328-5655
kdisney@tbonesbaseball.com
Tenant(s):
Kansas City T-Bones baseball.
Seating Capacity:
10,385

CONSOL ENERGY CENTER
1001 FIFTH AVENUE
PITTSBURGH, PA 15219
412-642-1800
Fax: 412-642-1925
info@consolenergycenter.com
www.consolenergycenter.com
• Jay Roberts, General Manager
(412) 642-1893
Seating Capacity:
18,000
Tenant(s):
Pittsburgh Penguins (NHL).

CONVOCATION CENTER: EMU
799 NORTH HEWITT ROAD
EASTERN MICHIGAN UNIVERSITY
YPSILANTI, MI 48197
734-487-1050
Fax: 734-487-6898
www.emich.edu/bookemu/convo/
• Heather Lyke, Vice President, Director of
Athletics
(734) 487-1050
hlyke@emich.edu
• Mike Malach, Sr. Associate AD for
Finance/Operations
(734) 487-7174
michael.malach@emich.edu
• Adam Martin, Director of Facilities and
Operations
(734) 487-1050
amarti54@emich.edu
• Andrew Hensley, Assistant Director of
Facilities
(734) 487-1050
ahensle3@emich.edu
Seating Capacity:
8,824
Year Founded:
1998

CONVOCATION CENTER: NIU
1525 WEST LINCOLN HIGHWAY
NORTHERN ILLINOIS UNIVERSITY
DEKALB, IL 60115-2854
815-752-6800
Fax: 815-753-7700
convocenter@niu.edu
www.niuconvo.com
• Sean T. Frazier, Director of Athletics
(815) 753-9473
• John Cheney, Sr. Associate Athletics
Director, Facilities
(815) 753-1801

967

jcheney2@niu.edu
• Kiera Miller, Assistant Athletics Director,
Compliance
(815) 753-8339
kmiller4@niu.edu
Arena Seating Capacity:
10,000
Year Founded:
2002

COOLEY LAW SCHOOL STADIUM
505 E MICHIGAN AVENUE
LANSING, MI 48912
517-485-4500
Fax: 517-485-4518
www.lansinglugnuts.com
• Nick Grueser, General Manager
ngrueser@lansinglugnuts.com
• Dennis Busse, Stadium Operations
Manager
 ext 459
dbusse@lansinglugnuts.com
Founded:
1996
Team:
Lansing Lugnuts
Seating Capacity:
7,527

COORS EVENTS CENTER
950 REGENT DRIVE
BOULDER, CO 80309
303-492-5319
Fax: 303-492-4801
www.cubuffs.com
• Rick George, Athletic Director
(303) 492-6843
rick.george@colorado.edu
• Steve Pizzi, Assistant Athletics Director,
Coors Events Center
(303) 492-4749
stephen.pizzi@colorado.edu
• Jason DePaepe, Associate Athletic
Director, Facilities
(303) 492-4749
jason.depaepe@colorado.edu
• Marco Amrbiz, Custodail Maintenance
Staff, Coords Events Center
(303) 492-4749
Seating Capacity:
11,064

COORS FIELD
2001 BLAKE STREET
DENVER, CO 80205
303-292-0200
Fax: 303-296-2068
colorado.rockies.mlb.com
• Richard L. Monfort, Owner, CEO
• Jeff Bridich, Sr. Vice President & General
Manager
• Lenus Lucero, Assistant VP, Balpark
Operations
Permanent Seating Capacity:
50,398
Owned by:
State of Colorado.

COPELAND PARK
800 COPELAND AVENUE
LA CROSSE, WI 54603
608-796-9553
Fax: 608-796-9032
info@lacrosseloggers.com
www.lacrosseloggers.com
• Dan Kapanke, Owner
• Chris Goodell, General Manager

• Ben Kapanke, Assistant General Manager
• Elizabeth Kapanke, Director of
Merchandising
Sport:
Minor League Baseball.
Tenant(s):
Lacrosse Loggers baseball (NWL), UW-La
Crosse (NCAA).
Year Founded:
2003
Capacity:
3,550

CORN PALACE
604 NORTH MAIN STREET
MITCHELL, SD 57301
605-995-8430
Fax: 605-996-8273
cornpalace.com
• Scott Schmidt, Director
(605) 995-8427
sschmidt@cornpalace.com
Arena Seating Capacity:
3,200

COTTON BOWL/FAIR PARK
3921 MARTIN LUTHER KING JR.
BOULEVARD
DALLAS, TX 75210
214-565-9931
info@bigtex.com
bigtex.com
Seating Capacity:
92,100
Team:
Heart of Dallas Bowl (NCAA)

COW PALACE
2600 GENEVA AVENUE
DALY CITY, CA 94014
415-404-4111
Fax: 415-469-6111
info@cowpalace.com
www.cowpalace.com
• Mara Kopp, President
• Barbara Wanvig, 1st Vice President
• Paul Wattis, 2nd Vice President
• Ken Alstott, CEO
Seating Capacity:
16,500
Year Founded:
1941

COWBOY STADIUM
700 EAST MCNEESE STREET
LAKE CHARLES, LA 70605
337-475-5000
800-622-3352
Fax: 337-475-5202
www.mcneesesports.com
• Bruce Hemphill, Director of Athletics
(337) 475-5563
bhemphill@mcneese.edu
• Steve Gugliucci, Director of Marketing,
Ticket Operations
(337) 475-5208
sgugliucci@mcneese.edu
• Tommy McClelland, Director
Stadium Seating Capacity:
17,410

COWBOYS STADIUM
ONE AT&T WAY
ARLINGTON, TX 76011

817-892-4000
800-745-3000
stadium.dallascowboys.com
• Jeff Stroud, General Manager
• Jud W. Heflin, Director of Planning and
Logistics
• Paul Turner, Director of Event Operations
& Security
• Scott Woodrow, Director of Stadium
Engineering
• Tod Martin, Director of Stadium Projects
Seating Capacity:
80,000
Tenant(s):
Dallas Cowboys (NFL), Cotton Bowl Classic
(NCAA)

COWELL STADIUM
145 MAIN STREET
DURHAM, NH 03824
603-862-1850
Fax: 603-862-4069
unhwildcats.com
• Marty Scarano, Director of Athletics
(603) 862-2013
marty.scarano@unh.edu
• Jon Danos, Sr. Associate Athletic Director,
External Affairs
(603) 862-4677
jon.danos@unh.edu
• Carrie Kimball, Associate Athletic Director,
Operations
(603) 862-2774
carolynn.kimball@unh.edu
• Ciaran Cullen, Associate Athletic Director,
Business Development
(603) 862-0287
ciaran.cullen@unh.edu
• Jean Mitchell, Athletic Facilities,
Housekeeping Manager
(603) 862-4746
jeanm@hopper.unh.edu
Seating Capacity:
6,500

COWTOWN COLISEUM
121 EAST EXCHANGE AVENUE
FORT WORTH, TX 76164
817-625-1025
888-269-8696
Fax: 817-625-1148
stockyardsrodeo.com
• Hub Baker, General Manager
(817) 625-1025
hub@cowtowncoliseum.com
• Clay Barlow, Facilities Manager
(817) 625-1025
groupsales@cowtowncoliseum.com
• Nate Krieger, Marketing Director
(817) 625-1025
nate@cowtowncoliseum.com
Coliseum Seating Capacity:
3,418

CRANDON PARK TENNIS CENTER
7300 CRANDON BOULEVARD
KEY BISCAYNE, FL 33149
305-365-2300
www.miamidade.gov/parks/crandon-tennis.a
sp
Seating Capacity:
13,800

CRISLER CENTER
333 EAST STADIUM BOULEVARD
UNIVERSITY OF MICHIGAN
ANN ARBOR, MI 48104

734-647-2583
Fax: 734-764-3221
info@umich.edu
www.mgoblue.com
• Mark S. Schlissel, President
(734) 764-6270
• Rob Rademacher, Executive Sr. Associate
Athletic Director, COO
(734) 647-9763
Seating Capacity:
12,707

DAKOTADOME
414 EAST CLARK STREET
DEPARTMENT OF ATHLETICS
VERMILLION, SD 57069
605-677-5309
Fax: 605-677-5618
www.goyotes.com
• David Herbster, Athletics Director
(605) 677-5943
david.herbster@usd.edu
• Dan Gaston, Sr. Associate Athletic
Director, Operations
dan.gaston@usd.edu
• Gary Madsen, Operations Manager
gary.madsen@usd.edu
Stadium Seating Capacity:
10,000

DAMASCHKE FIELD
95 RIVER STREET
ONEONTA, NY 13820
607-432-6326
Fax: 607-432-1965
• Nader John, Assistant GM/Business
Manager
Tenant(s):
Oneonta Outlaws
Year Founded:
1905

DARRELL K ROYAL - TEXAS MEMORIAL STADIUM
2139 SAN JACINTO BOULEVARD
AUSTIN, TX 78712
512-471-9405
www.texassports.com
• Dave Marmion, Executive Sr. Associate
Athletic Director
(512) 471-4067
• Nick Voinis, Sr. Associate Athletics
Director, Communications
(512) 471-2151
• Ed Goble, Executive Sr. Associate AD,
Facilities
(512) 471-6848
Seating Capacity:
100,119

DAVIS WADE STADIUM AT SCOTT FIELD
90 B.S. HOOD DRIVE
MISSISSIPPI STATE, MS 39762
662-325-2532
Fax: 662-325-7904
www.hailstate.com
• Scott Stricklin, Director of Athletics
(662) 325-0863
scottstricklin@athletics.msstate.edu
• Don Williams, General Manager
(662) 325-4171
dwilliams@learfield.com
• Bobby Tomlinson, Associate AD, Facility
Planning
(662) 325-7452
btomlinson@athletics.msstate.edu
• Jay Logan, Associate AD, Event &

Facilities Management
(662) 325-2877
jlogan@athletics.msstate.edu
Stadium Seating Capacity:
61,337
Year Founded:
1914
Track Type:
Prescription Athletic Turf

DAYTONA BEACH LEISURE SERVICES
301 SOUTH RIDGEWOOD AVENUE
DAYTONA BEACH, FL 32114
386-671-8337
Fax: 386-671-3410
www.codb.us
• Percy Williamson, Director
Permanent Seating Capacity:
10,000

DEAN E. SMITH CENTER
300 SKIPPER BOWLES DRIVE
UNIVERSITY OF NORTH CAROLINA
CHAPEL HILL, NC 27514
919-962-6000
Fax: 919-966-3173
www.goheels.com
• Bubba Cunningham, Athletic Director
(919) 962-6000
bubba.cunningham@unc.edu
• Angie Bitting, Director of Smith Center
(919) 962-6000
abitting@uncaa.unc.edu
• Curt Brossman, Smith Center Operations
Assistant
(919) 962-6000
cbrossman@unc.edu
Permanent Seating Capacity:
21,750

DEE EVENTS CENTER
3870 STADIUM WAY DEPT. 2701
OGDEN, UT 84408
801-626-6817
Fax: 801-626-6490
www.weberstatesports.com
• Jerry Bovee, Director of Intercollegiate
Athletics
(801) 626-6817
jerrybovee@weber.edu
• Ron Goch, Associate Athletics Director,
External Operations
(801) 626-6731
rongoch@weber.edu
• Paul Grua, Director of Athletic
Communications
(801) 626-7414
pgrua@weber.edu
Arena Seating Capacity:
11,500

DEE GLEN SMITH SPECTRUM
7400 OLD MAIN HILL
LOGAN, UT 84322
435-797-1850
Fax: 435-797-2615
john.hartwell@usu.edu
www.utahstateaggies.com
• John Hartwell, Athletics Director
(435) 797-2060
john.hartwell@usu.edu
• Landon Day, General Manager, Aggie
Sports Properties
(435) 797-8991
lday@aggiesportsproperties.com
• Reed Capener, Director of Event
Operations

(435) 797-7186
reed.capener@usu.edu
• Jana Doggett, Deputy Athletics Director,
External Operations
(435) 797-3907
kana.doggett@usu.edu
Stadium Seating Capacity:
10,270

DELL DIAMOND
3400 EAST PALM VALLEY BOULEVARD
ROUND ROCK, TX 78665
512-255-2255
Fax: 512-255-1558
info@rrexpress.com
www.roundrockexpress.com
• Reese Ryan, Owner & CEO
dbowman@rrexpress.com
• JJ Gottsch, Chief Operating Officer
jjgottsch@rrexpress.com
• Tim Jackson, General Manager
tjackson@rrexpress.com
• David Powers, Senior Director, Stadium
Operations
dpowers@rrexpress.com
• Aurelio Martinez, Director, Stadium
Maintenance
amartinez@rrexpress.com
Team:
Round Rock Express
Year Founded:
2000
Capacity:
8,631

DELMAR STADIUM COMPLEX
1900 MANGUM ROAD
HOUSTON, TX 77455
713-957-7700
Fax: 713-957-7704
• Mike Truelove, Stadium Supervisor
Field Seating Capacity:
12,000

DELTAPLEX ENTERTAINMENT & EXPO CENTER
2500 TURNER AVENUE NORTHWEST
GRAND RAPIDS, MI 49544
616-364-9000
Fax: 616-559-8001
events@deltaplex.com
deltaplex.com
• Joel Langlois, President
(616) 364-9000
joel@deltaplex.com
• Erin Spaanstra, Assistant General
Manager & Event Director
(616) 559-7927
erin@deltaplex.com
• Adam Sturt, Operations Manager
(616) 365-5759
operations@deltaplex.com
Arena Seating Capacity:
7,000

DENVER COLISEUM
4600 HUMBOLDT STREET
DENVER, CO 80216
720-865-2475
tad.bowman@denvergov.org
www.denvercoliseum.com
• Tad Bowman, Venue Director
(720) 865-2488
tad.bowman@denvergov.org
• Steve Jorgensen, Guest Services
Manager
(720) 865-2477

steven.jorgensen@denvergov.org
• Jeannette Murrietta, Booking Manager
(720) 865-2484
jeannette.murrietta@denvergov.org
• Jordan Bishop, Assistant Director of
Marketing & Communications
(720) 865-4309
jordan.bishop@denvergov.org
Seating Capacity:
10,500

DEVAULT MEMORIAL STADIUM
BOX 1434
BRISTOL, VA 24203
276-206-9946
Fax: 276-669-7686
gm@bristolbaseball.com
www.bristolbaseball.com
• Mark Young, Vice President of Community
Relations
marky@bristolbaseball.com
• Craig Adams, Vice President of Game Day
Operations
ballparkoperations@bristolbaseball.com
• Lucas Hobbs, Vice President of Marketing
and Communications
marketing@bristolbaseball.com
Seating Capacity:
2,000
Team:
Bristol White Sox

DIAMOND FIELD
3001 NORTH BOULEVARD
RICHMOND, VA 23230
804-359-3866
Fax: 804-359-1373
info@squirrelsbaseball.com
• Chuck Domino, Chief Executive Officer
• Ben Rothrock, Assistant General Manager
of Operations
ben.rothrock@squirrelsbaseball.com
• Steve Pump, Director of Stadium
Operations
steve.pump@squirrelsbaseball.com
• Steve Ruckman, Director of Field
Operations
stever@squirrelsbaseball.com
Tenant(s):
Richmond Braves baseball
Year Founded:
1985
Capacity:
12,134

DICKEY-STEPHENS PARK
400 WEST BROADWAY STREET
NORTH LITTLE ROCK, AR 72114
501-664-1555
travs@travs.com
• Greg Johnston, Park Superintendent
greg@travs.com
Opened:
April 12, 2007
Team:
Arkansas Travelers
Sport:
Baseball
Seating Capacity:
5,800 fixed seats; 7,200 seating capacity for
baseball

DIDDLE ARENA
1605 AVENUE OF CHAMPIONS
BOWLING GREEN, KY 42101-6412
270-745-3542
www.wkusports.com

• Todd Stewart, Director of Athletics
(270) 745-5276
• Craig Biggs, Associate AD, Administration
(270) 745-5279
craig.biggs@wku.edu
• Lee Forsythe, Assistant Athletic Director,
Facilities
(270) 745-2903
les.forsythe@wku.edu
• Chris Bloomfield, General Manager
(270) 745-6462
chris.bloomfield@imgworld.com
Seating Capacity:
7,326

DODGE PHYSICAL FITNESS CENTER
WEST 119TH STREET & BROADWAY
NEW YORK, NY 10027
212-854-2548
Fax: 212-854-6200
www.gocolumbialions.com
• Bill Ebner, Facilities Operations Director
• Patrick Desir, Manager Of Facilities
Operations
(212) 854-3441
pd2227@columbia.edu
Seating Capacity:
3,405

DODGER STADIUM
1000 ELYSIAN PARK AVENUE
LOS ANGELES, CA 90012
866-800-1275
Fax: 323-224-1269
www.dodgers.com
• Steve Ethier, Sr. Vice President, Stadium
Operations
• Josh Byrnes, Sr. Vice President, Baseball
Operations
• David Edford, Director of Facilities
Permanent Seating Capacity:
56,000
Description:
Home Stadium For: Los Angeles Dodgers
Owned by:
Los Angeles Dodgers

DON MCBRIDE STADIUM
201 NW 13TH STREET
RICHMOND, IN 47374
765-983-7291
Fax: 765-962-7529
Year Founded:
1995
Capacity:
1,787

DONALD E. YOUNG FITNESS CENTER
1200 UNIVERSITY STREET
UNIT 9409
SPEARFISH, SD 57799-9424
605-642-6096
800-255-2478
Fax: 605-642-6539
www.bhsu.edu/StudentLife/YoungCenter.as
px
• Jhett Albers, Director of Athletics
(605) 642-6885
jhett.albers@bhsu.edu
• Melissa Christensen, Assistant Athletic
Director, External Operations
(605) 642-6460
melissa.christensen@bhsu.edu
• Brock Anundson, Assistant Athletic
Director, Facility Operations
(605) 642-6882
brock.anundson@bhsu.edu

• Brock Anundson, Assistant Athletic
Director, Facility Operations
(605) 642-6882
brock.anundson@bhsu.edu
Arena Seating Capacity:
4,000

DONALD L. TUCKER CIVIC CENTER
505 WEST PENSACOLA STREET
TALLAHASSEE, FL 32301
850-645-2527
Fax: 850-644-7293
www.seminoles.com
• Stan Wilcox, Director of Athletics
(850) 644-1079
vcupp@admin.fsu.edu
• Karl Hicks, Deputy Athletics Director,
External Operations
(850) 645-2014
kphicks@fsu.edu
• Brandon Kendrick, Assistant Director of
Facilities
(850) 228-9316
bkendrick@fsu.edu
Seating Capacity:
13,500

DONALD W. REYNOLDS RAZORBACK STADIUM
350 NORTH RAZORBACK ROAD
FAYETTEVILLE, AR 72701
479-575-6533
Fax: 479-575-4904
raztk@uark.edu
www.arkansasrazorbacks.com
• Jeff Long, Vice Chancellor and Director of
Athletics
(479) 575-7641
athldir@uark.edu
• Pat Berger, Director of Sports Turf
(479) 575-6887
pberger@uark.edu
• Chris Freet, Sr. Associate AD, External
Operations
(479) 575-6533
cjfreet@uark.edu
• Chris Pohl, Associate AD, Event
Management
(479) 575-7312
cpohl@uark.edu
• Justin Maland, Associate Athletic Director,
Facilities
(479) 575-6768
jmaland@uark.edu
Seating Capacity:
72,000

DORT FEDERAL CREDIT UNION EVENT CENTER
3501 LAPEER ROAD
FLINT, MI 48503
810-744-0580
Fax: 810-744-2906
www.dorteventcenter.com
• Jeremy Torrey, General Manager
jeremy@dorteventcenter.com
Opened:
1969
Team(s):
Flint Firebirds (OHL); Waza Flo (MASL)
Seating Capacity:
Hockey 4,021; Boxing 5,109; Concerts
6,469

DOYT PERRY FIELD STADIUM
1610 STADIUM DRIVE
BOWLING GREEN, OH 43403

419-372-2401
Fax: 419-372-0475
ckingst@bgsu.edu
www.bgsufalcons.com
• Chris Kingston, Director of Athletics
(419) 372-7052
ckingst@bgsu.edu
• Jamie Baringer, Assistant AD, Arena
Operations
(419) 372-2764
jbaring@bgsu.edu
• Steve Messenger, Assistant AD,
Operations & Events
(419) 372-7263
smessen@bgsu.edu
• Chuck Spicer, Falcon Sports Properties
General Manager
(419) 372-4007
cspicer@falconsportsproperties.com
Stadium Seating Capacity:
24,000

DOZER PARK
730 SW JEFFERSON STREET
PEORIA, IL 61605
peoria.chiefs.milb.com/index.jsp?sid=t443
Founded:
2002
Team:
Peoria Chiefs
Seating Capacity:
7,500

DR. PEPPER BALLPARK
7300 ROUGHRIDERS TRAIL
FRISCO, TX 75034
972-334-1900
Fax: 972-731-7455
info@ridersbaseball.com
www.ridersbaseball.com
• Chuck Greenberg, CEO & General Partner
chucku@ridersbaseball.com
• Jason Dambach, General Manager
jason@ridersbaseball.com
• Scott Burchett, Chief Operating Officer
sburchett@ridersbaseball.com
• Gina Pierce, Director, Game Entertainment
gpierce@ridersbaseball.com
Sport:
Minor League Baseball.
Tenant(s):
Frisco RoughRiders (TL), TXU Energy
Winter Games of Texas
Year Founded:
2003

DRAKE STADIUM
2507 UNIVERSITY AVENUE
DES MOINES, IA 50311
515-271-2889
Fax: 515-271-4189
godrakebulldogs.com
• Sandy Hatfield, Director of Athletics
(515) 271-2889
sandra.clubb@drake.edu
• Dave Haskin, Associate Athletic Director,
External Affairs
(515) 271-4628
dave.haskin@drake.edu
• Brady Randall, Assistant Athletic Director,
Operations
(515) 271-3849
brady.randall@drake.edu
• Greg Ellis, General Manager
(515) 271-4894
greg.ellis@img.com

Stadium Seating Capacity:
14,557

DRAKE STADIUM/UCLA
325 WESTWOOD PLAZA
LOS ANGELES, CA 90095
310-825-8699
Fax: 310-206-7047
www.uclabruins.com
• Dan Guerrero, Director of Athletics
ad@athletics.ucla.edu
• Jake Kuennen, Facilities Manager
jkuennen@athletics.ucla.edu
• Mike Dowling, Associate Athletic Director,
Operations
mdowling@athletics.ucla.edu
• Kevin Borg, Assistant Athletic Director,
Facilities
kborg@athletics.ucla.edu
Tenant(s):
Drake Relays, Drake University football
(NCAA).
Seating Capacity:
14,557

**DUDY NOBLE STADIUM, POLK-DEMENT
STADIUM**
145 LAKEVIEW DRIVE
MISSISSIPPI STATE UNIVERSITY
MISSISSIPPI, MS 39762
662-325-5232
Fax: 662-325-7904
rice@athletics.msstate.edu
www.hailstate.com
• Scott Stricklin, Director of Athletics
(662) 325-0863
scottstricklin@athletics.msstate.edu
• Don Williams, General Manager, Bulldogs
Sports Properties
(662) 325-4171
• Mike Nemeth, Sr. Associate AD,
Administration
(662) 325-2300
Stadium Seating Capacity:
7,200
Year Founded:
1967
Track Type:
Tiflawn 419 Hybrid Bermuda Grass

DUNN CENTER
WINFIELD DUNN CENTER
CORNER OF MARION STREET & DRANE
STREET
ROOM 141417
CLARKSVILLE, TN 37040
931-221-7127
877-861-2778
Fax: 931-221-7980
gov@apsu.edu
letsgopeay.com
• Ryan Ivey, Director of Athletics
(931) 221-7904
iveyr@apsu.edu
• Josh Jorgensen, Assistant Athletics
Director, External Affairs
(931) 221-7672
jorgensenj@apsu.edu
• Bud Jenkins, Facilities Director
(931) 221-7700
jenkinsc@apsu.edu
Arena Seating Capacity:
7,257

DUNN FIELD
546 LUCE STREET
ELMIRA, NY 14904

607-734-2690
Fax: 607-734-0891
www.theelmirapioneers.com
• Don Lewis, Owner
(607) 734-2690
donspioneers@gmail.com
• Robbie Nichols, Owner
(607) 734-2690
generalmanagernichols@yahoo.com
• Chris P. Bacon, Director of Fan
Entertainment
(607) 734-2690

DURHAM BULLS ATHLETIC PARK
409 BLACKWELL STREET
DURHAM, NC 27701
919-687-6500
Fax: 919-687-6560
info@durhambulls.com
www.durhambulls.com
• Mike Birling, General Manager
(919) 687-6500
mbirling@durhambulls.com
• Scott Strickland, Director of Stadium
Operations
(919) 687-6500
sstrickland@durhambulls.com
• Cortlund Beneke, Operations Manager
cbeneke@durhambulls.com
• Peter Wallace, Director of Ticketing
(919) 687-6500
pwallace@durhambulls.com
Sport:
Baseball.
Tenant(s):
Durham Bulls baseball.
Capacity:
10,000

DUTCHESS STADIUM
1500 ROUTE 9D
WAPPINGERS FALLS, NY 12524
845-838-0094
Fax: 845-838-0014
www.hvrenegades.com
• Jeff Goldklang, President
• Eben Yager, Senior Vice President &
General Manager
eben@hvrenegades.com
• Vicky DeFreese, Director of Business
Operations
vicky@hvrenegades.com
• Jon Basil, Director of Ticket Sales
jbasil@hvrenegades.com
• Joe Ausanio, Director of Baseball
Operations
joe@hvrenegades.com
Sport:
Baseball.
Tenant(s):
Hudson Valley Renegades baseball.
Capacity:
4,494

DWYER STADIUM
299 BANK STREET
BATAVIA, NY 14020
585-343-5454
Fax: 585-343-5620
www.muckdogs.com
• Travis Sick, General Manager
(585) 343-5454
tsick@muckdogs.com
• Mike Ewing, Assistant General Manager
(585) 343-5454
mewing@muckdogs.com
• Don Rock, Director of Stadium Grounds

(585) 343-5454
rockhead44@hotmail.com
• Kathy Bills, Director of Merchandising
(585) 454-1001
bmoore@redwingsbaseball.com
Sport:
Baseball.
Team:
Batavia Muckdogs
Capacity:
2,600

EAGLEBANK ARENA
4500 PATRIOT CIRCLE
FAIRFAX, VA 22030
www.eaglebankarena.com
• Brad Edwards, Asst. Vice President, Director of Athletics
bedwards@gmu.edu
• Dave Paulsen, Head Coach, Men's Basketball
dpaulsen@gmu.edu
• Nyla Milleson, Head Coach, Women's Basketball
nmilleso@gmu.edu
Team:
George Mason Patriots
Seating Capacity:
10,000

ECCLES COLISEUM
351 WEST UNIVERSITY BOULEVARD
SOUTHERN UTAH UNIVERSITY
CEDAR CITY, UT 84720
435-865-8354
Fax: 435-586-5444
www.suutbirds.com
• Jason Butikofer, Athletic Director
jasonbutikofer@suu.edu
• Andrew Parrish, Chief Operating Officer
andrewparrish@suu.edu
• David Thompson, Director for Business Operations
(435) 865-8263
davidthompson6@suu.edu
Coliseum Seating Capacity:
8,500

ED & RAE SCHOLLMAIER ARENA
2800 STADIUM DRIVE
FORT WORTH, TX 76109
817-257-7000
Fax: 817-257-7656
www.gofrogs.com
• Chris Del Conte, Director of Intercollegiate Athletics
delconte@tcu.edu
• T. Ross Bailey, Sr. Associate Athletic Director, Facilities
r.bailey@tcu.edu
Seating Capacity:
6,800

ED SMITH STADIUM/SPORTS COMPLEX
2700 12TH STREET
SARASOTA, FL 34237
941-893-6300
Fax: 941-365-1587
baltimore.orioles.mlb.com
• Peter G. Angelos, Chief Executive Officer
• Robert A. Ames, Chief Financial Officer
• Kevin Cummings, Director, Ballpark Operations
Owned by:
City of Sarasota, Florida
Sport:
Baseball.

Team:
Sarasota Red Sox.
Stadium Seating Capacity:
8,500

EL PASO COUNTY COLISEUM
4100 EAST PAISANO DRIVE
EL PASO, TX 79905
915-534-4229
Fax: 915-532-4048
• Brian Kennedy, President/CEO
bkennedy@elpasosports.us
• James Smith, VP, Director of Operations
jsmith@elpasosports.us
• Thea Chambers, Marketing Director
(915) 494-4907
Fixed Seating Capacity:
5,250

EMENS AUDITORIUM
2000 WEST UNIVERSITY AVENUE
BALL STATE UNIVERSITY
MUNCIE, IN 47306
765-285-1539
Fax: 765-285-3719
emens@bsu.edu
https://cms.bsu.edu/web/emens/
• Mark Sandy, Director of Intercollegiate Athletics
(765) 285-5131
• Pat Quinn, Deputy Athletics Director, Operations
(765) 285-8907
• Chris Ulm, General Manager, Ball State Sports Properties
(765) 285-1434
Auditorium Seating:
3,575

ENMAX CENTRE
2510 SCENIC DRIVE SOUTH
LETHBRIDGE, AL T1K 1N2
403-320-4040
Fax: 403-327-3620
www.enmaxcentre.ca
• Kim Gallucci, General Manager
(403) 320-4086
• Jordan Dekens, Sales & Marketing Manager
(403) 320-3807
jordan.dekens@lethbridge.ca
• Len Overbeeke, Operations Manager
(403) 320-4055
len.overbeeke@lethbridge.ca
• Becky Little, Events Manager
(403) 320-4119
becky.little@lethbridge.ca
• Jennifer Norsworthy, Account & Ticket Manager
(403) 328-7361
jennifer.norsworthy@lethbridge.ca
Seating Capacity:
5,479
Tenants:
Lethbridge Hurricanes (WHL)

ERIE INSURANCE ARENA
809 FRENCH STREET
ERIE, PA 16501
814-453-7117
Fax: 814-455-9931
casey@erieevents.com
www.erieinsurancearena.com
• John A. Wells, Executive Director
(814) 453-7117
casey@erieevents.com
• Ray Williams, Director of Sports Facilities

rwilliams@erieevents.com
• Jeff Esposito, General Manager
• Barry Copple, Operations Manager
barry@erieevents.com
Seating Capacity:
9,000
Year Founded:
1983
Nature of Service:
Multi-purpose facility.
Tenant(s):
Erie BayHawks (NBA D-League), Erie Otters (OHL).

ESPN WIDE WORLD OF SPORTS COMPLEX
PO BOX 10000
LAKE BUENA VISTA, FL 32830
407-938-3398
Fax: 407-938-3478
www.espnwwos.com/complex/
Date opened:
1997

EVERETT MEMORIAL STADIUM
3802 BROADWAY
EVERETT, WA 98201
425-258-3673
Fax: 425-258-3675
info@aquasox.com
www.aquasox.com
• Danny Tetzlaff, General Manager
dannyt@aquasox.com
• Dustin Coder, Director of Tickets
dustinc@aquasox.com
• Pat Dillon, Director of Corporate Partnerships
patd@aquasox.com
• Rick Maddox, Director of Food and Beverage
rickm@aquasox.com
Sport:
Baseball.
Tenant(s):
Everett Aqua Sox baseball.
Year Founded:
1984
Capacity:
12,000

EXHIBITION PLACE
100 PRINCES' BOULEVARD
SUITE 1
TORONTO, ON, CANADA M6K 3C3
416-263-3000
info@explace.on.ca
www.explace.on.ca
• Mark Grimes, Chair
Owners:
City of Toronto.
Year Opened:
1879.

EXPO NEW MEXICO
300 SAN PEDRO NE
ALBUQUERQUE, NM 87108
505-222-9700
Fax: 505-266-7784
www.exponm.com
• Dan Mourning, General Manager
(505) 222-9700
• Erin Thompson, Deputy Manager
• Ken Salazar, Operations Manager
• Sally Mayer, Senior Manager
Permanent Seating Capacity:
12,000

EXPOCITE
250, BOULEVARD WILFRID-HAMEL
EDIFICE F
QUEBEC, QC, CANADA G1L 5A7
418-691-7110
888-866-3976
info@expocite.com
www.expocite.com
• Vincent Dufresne, President
• Simon Lachance, Operations Director
Owners:
Quebec City.
Operators:
ExpoCite.
Year Founded:
1898

FAIR GROUNDS FIELD
2901 PERSHING BOULEVARD
SHREVEPORT, LA 71109
318-636-5555
Fax: 318-636-5670
Sport:
Baseball
Year Founded:
1986
Seating Capacity:
Stadium/Arena 4,200

FAIR PARK COLISEUM
1012 AVENUE A
LUBBOCK, TX 79408
806-763-2833
Fax: 806-744-5903
info@southplainsfair.com
southplainsfair.com
Sports Arena Seating Capacity:
8,513

FALCON PARK
130 NORTH DIVISION STREET
AUBURN, NY 13021
315-255-2489
Fax: 315-255-2675
info@auburndoubledays.com
www.milb.com/index.jsp?sid=t458
• Mike Voutsinas, General Manager
• Andrew Sagarin, Operations Manager
• Paul Mullin, Sponsorship Services
Manager
Sport:
Baseball.
Tenant(s):
Auburn Doubledays baseball.
Year Founded:
1995
Capacity:
2,800

FALCON STADIUM
2169 FIELD HOUSE DRIVE
US AIR FORCE ACADEMY
COLORADO SPRINGS, CO 80840-9500
719-333-4008
www.goairforcefalcons.com
• Jim Knowlton, Director of Athletics
(719) 333-4008
• Col. Tony McKenzie, Director of Staff
(719) 333-4008
tony.mckenzie1@usafa.edu
• Mitch Mann, Associate AD, External
Operations
(719) 333-2626
mitch.mann@airforceathletics.org
• Gary Sheffield, Stadium Manager

(719) 333-4924
gary.sheffield@airforceathletics.org
Seating Capacity:
46,692

FAMILY ARENA, THE
2002 ARENA PARKWAY
ST. CHARLES, MO 63303
636-896-4200
Fax: 636-896-4205
info@familyarena.com
familyarena.com
• Jim Knowlton, Director of Athletics
(719) 333-4008
rickn@familyarena.com
Arena Seating Capacity:
10,467

FANT-EWING COLISEUM
308 WARHAWK WAY
MONROE, LA 71209-9900
318-342-5360
Fax: 318-342-5367
www.ulmwarhawks.com
• Brian Wickstrom, Director of Athletics
(318) 342-5360
wickstrom@ulm.edu
• Phil Shaw, Associate Athletics Director,
Internal Ops.
(318) 342-5442
• Kevin VanDerzee, Assistant Athletics
Director, Business Ops.ra
(318) 342-5380
vanderzee@ulm.edu
• Joe Domingos, General Manager
(318) 342-3556
jdomingos@warhawksportsproperties.com
Seating Capacity:
7,085

FARGODOME
1800 UNIVERSITY DRIVE NORTH
FARGO, ND 58102
701-241-9100
Fax: 701-237-0987
dome.info@fargodome.com
www.fargodome.com
Seating Capacity:
26,700

FARREL STADIUM
855 SOUTH NEW STREET
WEST CHESTER, PA 19383
610-436-3555
Fax: 610-921-7566
www.wcupagoldenrams.com
• Edward Matejkovic, Director of Athletics
(610) 436-3555
ematejkovic@wcupa.edu
• Terry Beattie, Associate Athletic Director,
Facilities
(610) 436-3317
tbeattie@wcupa.edu
• Chris Frey, Facilities, Operations Manager
(610) 430-4416
cfrey@wcupa.edu
Stadium Seating Capacity:
7,500

FAUROT FIELD AT MEMORIAL STADIUM
MIZZOU ATHLETICS
MIZZOU ARENA
1 CHAMPIONS DRIVE
COLUMBIA, MO 65205
573-882-6501
www.mutigers.com

• Mack Rhoades, Director of Athletics
(573) 882-2055
• Allen Frost, Mizzou Sports Park Facils.
Mgr. - Memorial Stadium
frosta@missouri.edu
• Barry Odom, Head Coach, Football
Seating Capacity:
71,168
Team:
University of Missouri Tigers

FEDEXFIELD
1600 FEDEX WAY
LANDOVER, MD 20785
301-276-6000
Fax: 301-276-6002
www.redskins.com
• Daniel Snyder, Owner
• Scot McCloughan, General Manager
• Dennis Greene, President of Business
Operations
Description:
Home Stadium for the Washington Redskins
Permanent Seating Capacity:
82,000

FENWAY PARK
4 YAWKEY WAY
BOSTON, MA 02215
617-226-6000
Fax: 617-226-6394
events@redsox.com
boston.redsox.mlb.com
• Sam Kennedy, President
(617) 226-6000
• Mike Hazen, Sr. Vice President, General
Manager
(617) 226-6000
• Frank Wren, Sr. Vice President, Baseball
Operations
(617) 226-6000
• Pete Nesbit, Vice President, Ballpark
Operations
(617) 226-6000
• Raquel Ferreira, Vice President, Baseball
Administration
Tenant(s):
MLB - Boston Red Sox baseball.
Permanent Seating Capacity:
37,227

FERRELL CENTER
1500 SOUTH UNIVERSITY PARKS DRIVE
WACO, TX 76706
254-710-1234
Fax: 254-710-1968
www.baylorbears.com
• Ian McCaw, Director of Athletics
(254) 710-1222
• Nick Joos, Executive Associate AD,
External Affairs
(254) 710-3043
nicholas_joos@baylor.edu
• Wes Yeary, Director of Sports Ministries
(254) 710-3027
wes_yeary@baylor.edu
Arena Seating Capacity:
12,000

FIFTH THIRD BALLPARK
4500 WEST RIVER DRIVE NE
COMSTOCK PARK, MI 49321
616-784-4131
800-277-7946
Fax: 616-784-4911
playball@whitecapsbaseball.com
www.fifththirdballpark.com

- Lew Chamberlin, CEO
lchamberlin@whitecapsbaseball.com
- Denny Baxter, Chief Financial Officer
dbaxter@whitecapsbaseball.com
- Chad Sayen, Director of Ticket Sales
chads@whitecapsbaseball.com
- Michael Craven, Operations Manager
mcraven@whitecapsbaseball.com
Sport:
Baseball.
Team:
West Michigan Whitecaps
Year Founded:
1994
Capacity:
9,684

FIFTH THIRD FIELD
220 NORTH PATTERSON BOULEVARD
DAYTON, OH 45402
937-228-2287
Fax: 937-228-2284
dragons@daytondragons.com
dayton.dragon.milb.com
- Robert Murphy, President and General Manager
teampresident@daytondragons.com
- John Wallace, Sr. Director of Operations
john.wallace@daytondragons.com
- Joe Elking, Director of Facility Operations
joe.elking@daytondragons.com
- Britt Barry, Sports Turf Manager
britt.barry@daytondragons.com
Seating Capacity:
7,230
Year Founded:
2000

FIRST AMERICAN BANK BALLPARK
5514 CHAMPIONS DRIVE
MIDLAND, TX 79706
432-520-2255
Fax: 432-520-8326
rockhounds@nwol.net
www.midlandrockhounds.org
- Miles Prentice, President
- Monty Hoppel, General Manager
(432) 520-2255
mhoppel@midlandrockhounds.org
- Andrew Brown, Director of Ticket Operations
(432) 520-2255
- Ray Fieldhouse, Assistant General Manager, Operations
(432) 520-2255
rfieldhouse@midlandrockhounds.org
- C.J. Bahr, Director of Stadium Operations
(432) 520-2255
cbahr@midlandrockhounds.org
Team:
Midland Rockhounds
Sport:
Baseball
Year Founded:
2002
Capacity:
6,669

FIRST ENERGY STADIUM
100 ALFRED LERNER WAY
CLEVELAND, OH 44114
440-891-5050
Fax: 440-891-5051
www.firstenergystadium.com
- Alec Scheiner, President
- Sashi Brown, Executive Vice President, Footbal Ops.

- Phil Dangerfield, Vice President, Football Operations
Stadium Seating Capacity:
67,431
Description:
Home stadium for NFL - Cleveland Browns

FIRSTENERGY STADIUM
1900 CENTRE AVENUE/RT 61 SOUTH
READING, PA 19605
610-375-8469
Fax: 610-373-5868
info@fightins.com
www.milb.com/index.jsp?sid=t522
- Scott Hunsicker, General Manager
shunsicker@fightins.com
- Matt Hoffmaster, Executive Director of Operations
mhoffmaster@fightins.com
- Kevin Sklenarik, Executive Director of Baseball Operations
ksklenarik@fightins.com
- Mike Becker, Executive Director of Tickets
mbecker@fightins.com
- Eric Scarcella, Director of Public Relations
escarcella@fightins.com
Sport:
Baseball.
Team:
Reading Phillies
Year Founded:
1951
Capacity:
9,000

FLORENCE CIVIC CENTER
3300 WEST RADIO DRIVE
FLORENCE, SC 29501
843-679-9417
Fax: 843-679-9429
info@florenceciviccenter.com
www.florenceciviccenter.com
- Paul Beard, Jr., Director of Operations
pbeard@florenceciviccenter.com
- Tony Rogers, Operations Manager
trogers@florenceciviccenter.com
- Mark Wade, Director of Sales and Marketing
mwade@florenceciviccenter.com
Arena Seating Capacity:
9,736

FNB FIELD
245 CHAMPION WAY
HARRISBURG, PA 17101
717-231-4444
Fax: 717-231-4445
information@senatorsbaseball.com
www.milb.com/index.jsp?sid=t547
- Randy Whitaker, General Manager
(717) 231-4444
whitaker@senatorsbaseball.com
- Tim Foreman, Director of Stadium Operations
(717) 231-4444
Sport:
Minor League Baseball.
Tenant(s):
Harrisburg Senators, Harrisburg City Islanders
Year Founded:
1987
Capacity:
6,187

FOLSOM FIELD
2400 COLORADO AVENUE
BOULDER, CO 80302
303-492-2200
Fax: 303-492-1700
www.cubuffs.com
- Rick George, Athletic Director
(303) 492-6843
rick.george@colorado.edu
- Lance Gerlach, General Manager
(303) 469-9600
lgerlach@buffalosportsproperties.com
- Steve Pizzi, Assistant AD, Coors Events Center
(303) 492-1994
stephen.pizzi@colorado.edu
- Jason DePaepe, Associate AD, Facilities & Operations
(303) 492-1994
jason.depaepe@colorado.edu
Stadium Seating Capacity:
50,183

FORD FIELD
2000 BRUSH STREET
DETROIT, MI 48226
313-262-2000
Fax: 313-262-2808
www.detroitlions.com
- Michael Singer, Sr. Director of Corporate Partnership
- Veronica Bonner, Sr. Manager of Human Resources
- Jared Kozinn, Director of Business Development
- Mark Graham, Director of Ticket Operations
- Fred Reddig, Director of Facilities
Year Opened:
2002
Seating Capacity:
65,000
Tenant(s):
NFL - Detroit Lions football.

FORUM FIELD
84 MECHANIC STREET
PRESQUE ISLE, ME 04769
207-764-0491
Fax: 207-764-2525
theforum@pirec.org
www.pirec.org
Arena Seating Capacity:
4,800

FOSTER FIELD
1600 UNIVERSITY AVENUE
SAN ANGELO, TX 76904
325-942-6587
Fax: 325-947-9480
www.angelosports.com
- James Reid, Interim Director of Athletics
(325) 942-2267
james.reid@angelo.edu
- Troy Hill, Assistant Athletics Director, Sports Medicine
(325) 486-6055
troy.hill@angelo.edu
- Brandon Ireton, Assistant Athletics Director of Athletic Comm.
(325) 942-2378
brandon.ireton@angelo.edu
Arena Seating Capacity:
4,200
Year Founded:
2000

Tenant(s):
Angelo State Rams (NCAA)

FOX CITIES STADIUM
2400 NORTH CASALOMA DRIVE
PO BOX 7464
APPLETON, WI 54912
920-733-4152
Fax: 920-733-8032
info@timberrattlers.com
www.milb.com/index.jsp?sid=t572
• Rob Zerjav, President
rzerjav@timberrattlers.com
• Aaron Hahn, Vice President, Assistant
General Manager
ahahn@timberrattlers.com
• Ryan Moede, Director of Tickets
rmoede@timberrattlers.com
• Ron Kaiser, Director of Stadium
Operations
rkaiser@timberrattlers.com
• Aaron Johnson, Stadium Operations
Manager
ajohnson@timberrattlers.com
Sport
Baseball.
Capacity:
5,900

FRANK ERWIN CENTER
1701 RED RIVER
AUSTIN, TX 78701
512-471-7744
Fax: 512-471-9652
comments@erwin.utexas.edu
www.uterwincenter.com
• John M. Graham, Executive Sr. Associate
Athletics Director
(512) 471-4716
john.graham@athletics.utexas.edu
• Thom Ramirez, Assistant Director for
Operations
(512) 471-2645
thom.ramirez@athletics.utexas.edu
• Chris Reynolds, General Manager
(512) 471-2646
christopher.reynolds@sodexo.com
Arena Seating Capacity:
16,540

**FRANK HOWARD FIELD AT MEMORIAL
STADIUM**
1 AVENUE OF CHAMPIONS
CLEMSON, SC 29634
800-253-6766
www.clemsontigers.com
• Dan Radakovich, Director of Athletics
(864) 656-1935
danrad1@clemson.edu
• Graham Neff, Deputy Athletics Director
(864) 656-0128
• Dabo Swinney, Head Coach, Football
(864) 656-2796
Seating Capacity:
80,301
Team:
Clemson Tigers

FRANKLIN FIELD
235 SOUTH 33RD STREET
UNIVERSITY OF PENNSYLVANIA
PHILADELPHIA, PA 19104
215-898-6151
Fax: 215-573-2095
www.pennathletics.com
• M. Grace Calhoun, Director of Athletics
and Recreation

(215) 898-7215
athdir@pobox.upenn.edu
• Alanna Shanahan, Deputy Director of
Athletics
(215) 898-9828
awren@upenn.edu
• Roger Reina, Sr. Associate AD, External
Affairs
(215) 898-6602
rreina@upenn.edu
• Michael J. Diorka, Associate AD, Facility
Management
(215) 898-6121
diorka@upenn.edu
• Scott Ward, Assistant AD, Operation
(215) 898-6153
sward2@upenn.edu
• Noah Gustkey, Assistant AD, Facilities
(215) 573-4025
gustkey@upenn.edu
Stadium Seating Capacity:
52,958
Team:
University of Pennsylvania football.

FRASER FIELD
365 WESTERN AVENUE
LYNN, MA 01904
781-595-9400
Fax: 781-583-5025
navigatorsgm@gmail.com
www.nsnavs.com
• Bill Terlecky, General Manager
• Ashley Laramie, Assistant General
Manager
• Pete Laven, President, Salvi Sports
Sport:
Baseball.
Tenant(s):
North Shore Spirit baseball
Year Founded:
1940
Capacity:
3,804

FREEDOM HALL CIVIC CENTER
1320 PACTOLAS ROAD
FREEDOM HALL CIVIC CENTER
JOHNSON CITY, TN 37604
423-461-4855
Fax: 423-461-4867
www.johnsoncitytn.org
• Lisa Chamness, Director
(423) 461-4855
Arena Seating Capacity:
19,200
Year Founded:
1956

FREEMAN COLISEUM
3201 EAST HOUSTON STREET
SAN ANTONIO, TX 78219
210-226-1177
Fax: 210-226-5081
www.freemancoliseum.com
• Derrick Howard, Executive Director
(210) 226-1177
derrickh@freemancoliseum.com
• JC Hrubetz, General Manager
(210) 226-1177
jc@freemancoliseum.com
• John Kinard, Assistant Operations
Manager
(210) 225-2562
johnk@freemancoliseum.com
• Jeanne Janes, Marketing Director
(210) 226-1177

jeanne@freemancoliseum.com
• Anna Harrier, Events Director
(210) 226-1177
annah@freemancoliseum.com
Arena Seating Capacity:
11,700

**FRESNO CONVENTION &
ENTERTAINMENT CENTER**
848 M STREET
2ND FLOOR
FRESNO, CA 93721
559-445-8100
800-788-0836
Fax: 559-445-8110
fresnoconvention-entertainmentcenter@smg
fresno
www.fresnoconventioncenter.com
• William Overfelt, General Manager
(559) 445-8150
bill.overfelt@smgfresno.com
• Lyn Higginson, Director of Finance
(559) 445-8152
lyn.higginson@smgfresno.com
• Matt Heinks, Box Office Manager
(559) 445-8200
matt.heinks@smgfresno.com
• Skyla Souza, Event Manager
(559) 445-8171
skyla.souza@smgfresno.com
• Israel Morales, Utility Manager
(559) 445-8169
israel.morales@smgfresno.com
Arena Seating Capacity:
11,300

FRONTIER FIELD
ONE MORRIE SILVER WAY
ROCHESTER, NY 14608
585-454-1001
Fax: 585-454-1056
info@redwingsbaseball.com
www.redwingsbaseball.com
• Naomi Silver, President, CEO & COO
nsilver@redwingsbaseball.com
• Dan Mason, General Manager
dmason@redwingsbaseball.com
• Rob Dermody, Director of Ticket
Operations
rdermody@redwingsbaseball.com
• Jeff Dodge, General Manager, Food &
Beverage
jdodge@redwingsbaseball.com
Sport:
Baseball.
Team:
Rochester Red Wings.
Year Founded:
1996
Capacity:
13,500

G. RICHARD PFITZNER STADIUM
7 COUNTY COMPLEX COURT
WOODBRIDGE, VA 22192
703-590-2311
Fax: 703-590-5716
info@potomacnationals.com
• Art Silber, Chairman, CEO
• Lani Silber Weiss, President, COO
lsweiss@potomacnationals.com
• Zach Prehn, Vice President, General
Manager
zprehn@potomacnationals.com
• Chris Bentivegna, Director of Ticket
Operations
cbentivegna@potomacnationals.com

facilities

• Arthur Bouvier, Director of Stadium
Operations
abouvier@potomacnationals.com
Stadium Seating Capacity:
6,000
Nature of Service:
Minor League Baseball.

GARCELON FIELD
130 CENTRAL AVENUE
LEWISTON, ME 04240
207-786-6411
Fax: 207-786-8232
athletics.bates.edu
• Kevin McHugh, Director of Athletics
(207) 786-6341
kmchugh@bates.edu
• Tommy Verdell, Assistant Athletic Director
(207) 786-6357
tverdell@bates.edu
Stadium Seating Capacity:
3,000

GARRETT COLISEUM
1555 FEDERAL DRIVE
MONTGOMERY, AL 36109
334-356-6866
Fax: 334-272-6835
www.thegarrettcoliseum.com
• Bill Hardin, Director of Events and
Marketing
(334) 356-6866
bill@thegarrettcoliseum.com
• Connie Luckie, Office Manager
(334) 356-6866
connie@thegarrettcoliseum.com
Arena Seating Capacity:
10,500

GARY SOUTH SHORE RAILCATS
U.S. STEEL YARD
ONE STADIUM PLAZA
GARY, IN 46402
219-882-2255
Fax: 219-882-2259
www.railcatsbaseball.com
• Pete Laven, President, Salvi Sports
Enterprises
plaven@salvisports.com
• Brian Lyter, General Manager
blyter@railcatsbaseball.com
• David Kay, Assistant General Manager
(219) 882-2255
dkay@railcatsbaseball.com
• Phil West, Director of Food and Beverage
(219) 882-2255
pwest@railcatsbaseball.com
• Noah Simmons, Head Groundskeeper,
Operations
(219) 331-9833
nsimmons@railcatsbaseball.com
Team:
Gary Southshore Railcats
Year Founded:
2002
Capacity:
6,139

GCS BALLPARK
2301 GRIZZLIE BEAR BOULEVARD
SAUGET, IL 62206
618-337-3000
Fax: 618-332-3625
www.gatewaygrizzlies.com
• Steve Gomric, General Manager
sgomric@gatewaygrizzlies.com
• Kurt Ringkamp, Director of Stadium

Operations
kringkamp@gatewaygrizzlies.com
Sport:
Baseball.
Tenant(s):
Gateway Grizzlies (Frontier League).
Year Founded:
2002
Seating Capacity:
6,000

**GEORGE J. SHERMAN FAMILY-SPORTS
COMPLEX**
2095 HILLSIDE ROAD
UNIT 1173
STORRS, CT 06269
860-486-2725
Fax: 860-486-3300
athleticdirector@uconn.edu
www.uconnhuskies.com
• David Benedict, Director of Athletics
(860) 486-2725
athleticdirector@uconn.edu
• Neal Eskin, Sr. Associate Director of
Athletics, External
neal.eskin@uconn.edu
• Maureen O'Connor, Associate Director of
Athletics, Business Services
(860) 486-4142
• Evan Feinglass, Associate Director of
Athletics, Facilities
(860) 486-4712
evan.feinglass@uconn.edu
• Tom Murphy, General Manager
(860) 834-3339
tom.murphy@img.com

GEORGE M. STEINBRENNER FIELD
ONE STEINBRENNER DRIVE
TAMPA, FL 33614
813-673-3055
Fax: 813-673-3174
www.steinbrennerfield.com
• C. Vance Smith, Director of Florida
Operations, General Manager
vsmith@yankees.com
• Matt Gess, Assistant General Manager,
Marketing
mgess@yankees.com
• AmySue Manzione, Operations
Coordinator
amanzione@yankees.com
• Jennifer Magliocchetti, Assistant Director,
Ticket Operations
jmagliocchetti@yankees.com
Sport:
Baseball
Tenant(s):
New York Yankees (spring training), Tampa
Yankees (FSL), Gulf Coast Yankees (GCL)
Year Founded:
1996
Capacity:
11,026

GEORGIA DOME
ONE GEORGIA DOME DRIVE NW
ATLANTA, GA 30313-1591
404-223-9200
Fax: 404-223-8011
• Frank Poe, Executive Director
(404) 223-4000
fpoe@gwcc.com
• Kevin Duvall, Chief Operating Officer
(404) 223-4000
kduvall@gwcc.com
• Carl Adkins, Chief Commercial Officer

(404) 223-4000
cadkins@gadome.com
Tenants:
Peach Bowl (NCAA), Georgia State
Panthers (NCAA)
Permanent Seating Capacity:
80,000

GEORGIA INSTITUTE OF TECHNOLOGY
N AVENUE
GEORGIA INSTITUTE OF TECHNOLOGY
ATLANTA, GA 30332-0255
404-894-2000
Fax: 404-894-4243
finaid@gatech.edu
www.gatech.edu
• Dan Radakovich, Athletic Director
(404) 894-5411
• Mike Edwards, Athletics
Director/Recreation Facilities
Coliseum Seating Capacity:
10,000

GIANT CENTER
550 WEST HERSHEYPARK DRIVE
HERSHEY, PA 17033
717-534-3911
Fax: 717-534-8996
info@hersheypa.com
www.hersheyentertainment.com
• Vikki Hultquist
(717) 534-8966
vhultquist@hersheypa.com
Seating Capacity:
12,500

GILL COLISEUM
114 GILL COLISEUM
OREGON STATE UNIVERSITY
CORVALLIS, OR 97331
541-737-7373
Fax: 541-737-7363
wecare@oregonstate.edu
www.osubeavers.com
• Todd Stansbury, Vice President, Director
of Athletics
(541) 737-7373
• Zack Lassiter, Deputy Athletics Director,
External Operations
(541) 737-7373
zack.lassiter@oregonstate.edu
• Steve Sullivan, General Manager
(541) 737-8364
ssullivan@beaversportsproperties.com
• Matt Kolasinski, Associate General
Manager
• Jake Gibson, Assistant Athletic Director,
Facilities
(541) 737-1618
jake.gibson@oregonstate.edu
Arena Seating Capacity:
9,604

GILLETTE STADIUM
ONE PATRIOT PLACE
FOXBOROUGH, MA 02035-1388
508-384-4378
Fax: 508-384-4339
www.gillettestadium.com
Tenant(s):
New England Patriots (NFL), New England
Revolution (MLS), UMass Minutement
(NCAA), Boston Cannons (MLL)
Seating Capacity:
65,829

GLASS BOWL STADIUM
2801 WEST BANCROFT STREET
TOLEDO, OH 43606-3390
419-530-2945
Fax: 419-530-4428
www.utrockets.com
Stadium Seating Capacity:
26,248

GLENS FALLS CIVIC CENTER
ONE CIVIC CENTER PLAZA
GLENS FALLS, NY 12801
518-798-0366
Fax: 518-793-7750
www.glensfallscc.com
• Jeff Mead, General Manager
(518) 798-0366
• Alyssa Aufiero, Event Manager
(518) 798-0366
• Avery Giroux, Box Office Manager
(518) 798-0366
• Ron Russell, Operations Manager
(518) 798-0366
• Larry Didio, Assistant Operations Manager
(518) 798-0366
Arena Seating Capacity:
4,794

GOLDEN LION STADIUM
1200 NORTH UNIVERSITY DRIVE
PINE BLUFF, AR 71601
870-575-7950
Fax: 870-575-7880
www.uapblionsroar.com
• Lonza Hardy, Jr., Director of Athletics
(870) 575-7950
• Stephanie Smith-Brown, Athletics
Business Manager
(870) 575-8273
smithbs@uapb.edu
• Carolyn Nance, HPER Complex Facilities
Manager
(870) 575-7184
nancec@uapb.edu
Stadium Seating Capacity:
16,000

GRAYSON STADIUM
1401 EAST VICTORY DRIVE
SAVANNAH, GA 31404
912-712-2482
thesavannahbananas.com
• Jared Orton, President
(336) 675-1066
jared@thesavannahbananas.com
• Marie Gentry, Director of Sponsor Services
(336) 312-3421
marie@thesavannahbananas.com
• Austin Glasscox, Director of Fan
Development
(704) 507-7092
Stadium Seating Capacity:
4,000
Year Founded:
1941
Clients:
Savannah Bananas

GREAT AMERICAN BALLPARK
100 JOE NUXHALL WAY
CINNCINATI, OH 45202
513-765-7000
cincinnati.reds.mlb.com
• Robert H. Castellini, President and Chief
Executive Officer
• Mike Saverino, Operations Manager

• Tim O'Connell, Vice President of Ballpark
Operations
Seating Capacity:
42,319
Teams:
Cincinnati Reds baseball.

GREAT PLAINS COLISEUM
920 SOUTH SHERIDAN ROAD
LAWTON, OK 73505
580-357-1483
Fax: 580-357-1192
gpc64@swbell.net
www.gpcoliseum.com
• Phillip Humble, Executive Director
(580) 357-1483
gpc64@swbell.net
• Joe Kirk, Office Manager
(580) 357-1483
• Brandy Jaurez, Executive Assistant
Arena Seating Capacity:
3,000

GREENSBORO COLISEUM COMPLEX
1921 WEST GATE CITY BOULEVARD
GREENSBORO, NC 27403
336-373-7400
Fax: 336-373-2170
www.greensborocoliseum.com
• Matt Brown, Managing Director
(336) 373-7400
matt.brown@greensboro-nc.gov
• Scott Johnson, Deputy Director
(336) 373-7449
scott.johnson@greensboro-nc.gov
• Mike Frost, General Manager
(336) 373-7466
mike_frost@comcastspectacor.com
Seating Capacity:
23,500
Team:
UNC Greensboro Men's Basketball

GREYHOUND STADIUM
1500 SOUTH AVENUE K
PORTALES, NM 88130
575-562-2088
Fax: 505-562-2822
athletics@enmu.edu
www.goeasternathletics.com
• Jeff Geiser, Athletic Director
(575) 562-2153
jeff.geiser@enmu.edu
• Karen Doherty, Facilities Coordinator
(575) 562-2153
karen.doherty@enmu.edu
Stadium Seating Capacity:
5,200

HADLOCK FIELD
271 PARK AVENUE
PORTLAND, ME 04102
207-874-9300
Fax: 207-780-0317
seadogs@seadogs.com
www.milb.com/index.jsp?sid=t546
• Charlie Eshbach, President
ceshbach@seadogs.com
• Geoff Iacuessa, Executive Vice President
& General Manager
geoff@seadogs.com
• Chris Cameron, Director of Media
Relations
ccameron@seadogs.com
Arena Seating Capacity:
7,368
Team:

Portland Sea Dogs
Year Founded:
1994

HAMMONS STUDENT CENTER
901 SOUTH NATIONAL AVENUE
SPRINGFIELD, MO 65807
417-836-5240
www.missouristate.edu/hsc
• Keith Boaz, Executive Director
keithboaz@missouristate.edu
• Laree Moore, Associate Director
lareemoore@missouristate.edu
Arena Seating Capacity:
8,846

HAMPTON COLISEUM
1000 COLISEUM DRIVE
HAMPTON, VA 23666
757-838-4203
Fax: 757-838-2595
www.hamptoncoliseum.org
Arena Seating Capacity:
13,800

HANCOCK STADIUM
ILLINOIS STATE UNIVERSITY
CAMPUS BOX 2660
NORMAL, IL 61790-2660
309-438-8000
Fax: 309-438-2220
www.goredbirds.com
• Larry Lyons, Director of Athletics
(309) 438-3636
lelyons@ilstu.edu
• Bryan Goodall, Assistant Athletics
Director, Ticket Operations
(309) 438-8787
bsgooda@ilstu.edu
Arena Seating Capacity:
13,391

HANK AARON STADIUM
755 BOLLING BROTHERS BOULEVARD
MOBILE, AL 36606
251-479-2327
Fax: 251-476-1147
www.mobilebaybears.com
• Chris Morgan, General Manager
chris@mobilebaybears.com
• Ari Rosenbaum, Assistant General
Manager
ari@mobilebaybears.com
• Matt Baranofsky, Director of Ticket
Operations
matt@mobilebaybears.com
• Nathan Breiner, Director of Stadium
Operations
nathanb@mobilebaybears.com
Sport:
Baseball
Team:
Mobile BayBears
Year Founded:
1997
Capacity:
6,000

HARA ARENA
1001 SHILOH SPRINGS ROAD
DAYTON, OH 45414
937-278-4776
Fax: 937-278-4633
www.haracomplex.com
• Rose Cory, General Manager
(937) 278-4776

crose@haracomplex.com
• Karen Wampler, Public Relations Director
(937) 278-4776
harapr@haracomplex.com
• Tom Shade, Food Service Manager
(937) 278-4776
tshade@haracomplex.com
• Kimberly Wampler, Event Coordinator
(937) 278-4776
kswampler@haracomplex.com
Arena Seating Capacity:
5,500

HARBOR PARK
150 PARK AVENUE
NORFOLK, VA 23510
757-622-2222
Fax: 757-624-9090
receptionist@norfolktides.com
www.norfolktides.com
• Ken Young, President
(757) 622-2222
kyoung@norfolktides.com
• Joe Gregory, General Manager
jgregory@norfolktides.com
• Mike Zeman, Director of Stadium
Operations
mzeman@norfolktides.com
• Gretchen Todd, Director of Ticket
Operations
gtodd@norfolktides.com
Sport:
Baseball
Team:
Norfolk Tides
Year Founded:
1993
Capacity:
11,856

HARBOUR STATION
99 STATION STREET
SAINT JOHN, NB, CANADA E2L 4X4
506-632-6103
Fax: 506-632-6121
www.harbourstation.ca
• Michael Caddell, General Manager
• Ewen Cameron, Operations Director
Year Opened:
1993, renovated 2005.
Seating Capacity:
7,205
Tenant(s):
Saint John Sea Dogs (QMJHL), Saint John
Mill Rats

HARDER STADIUM
STADIUM ROAD
UNIVERSITY OF CALIFORNIA, SANTA
BARBARA
SANTA BARBARA, CA 93106
805-893-4011
Fax: 805-893-8640
www.ucsbgauchos.com
• John McCutcheon, Director of
Intercollegiate Athletics
(805) 893-8320
jmccutch@athletics.ucsb.edu
• Lee Pike, General Manager, Gaucho
Sports Properties
(805) 893-7875
Permanent Seating Capacity:
17,000

HARRY GROVE STADIUM
21 STADIUM DRIVE
FREDERICK, MD 21703

301-662-0013
Fax: 301-662-0018
info@frederickkeys.com
www.frederickkeys.com
• Dave Ziedelis, General Manager
dziedelis@frederickkeys.com
• Ben Sealy, Director of Ticket Operations
bsealy@frederickkeys.com
• Kari Collins, Director of Stadium
Operations
kcollins@frederickkeys.com
Sport:
Baseball
Tenant(s):
Frederick Keys baseball
Year Founded:
1990

HARVARD UNIVERSITY - BRIGHT ARENA
65 NORTH HARVARD STREET
HARVARD UNIVERSITY
BOSTON, MA 02163
617-495-3454
Fax: 617-496-2270
harvtix@fas.harvard.edu
www.gocrimson.com
• Bob Scalise, Director of Athletics
(617) 495-2204
scalise@fas.harvard.edu
• Patricia Henry, Sr. Associate Director of
Athletics
(617) 495-2201
pwhenry@fas.harvard.edu
• Patricia Henry, Sr. Associate Director of
Athletics
(617) 495-2201
pwhenry@fas.harvard.edu
Seating Capacity:
3,095

HAYMARKET PARK
403 LINE DRIVE CIRCLE
LINCOLN, NE 68508
402-474-2255
Fax: 402-474-2254
www.saltdogs.com
• Jim Abel, Chairman
• Charlie Meyer, President, General
Manager
(402) 474-2255
charliem@saltdogs.com
• Dave Aschwege, Director of Stadium
Operations
(402) 441-4191
davea@saltdogs.com
• Dan Busch, Assistant Director of Stadium
Operations
(402) 441-4186
danielb@saltdogs.com
• Josh Klute, Athletic Turf Manager
(402) 441-4189
joshk@saltdogs.com
Capacity:
2,500
Year Founded:
2002
Team:
Lincoln Saltdogs
Sport:
Baseball

HEC EDMUNDSON PAVILION
218 GRAVES BUILDING
BOX 354070
SEATTLE, WA 98195-4070
206-543-2210
Fax: 206-616-1761

tickets@u.washington.edu
www.gohuskies.com
• Jennifer Cohen, Athletic Director
huskyad@uw.edu
• Chip Lydum, Associate AD Operations
(206) 616-2026
• Dan Erickson, Director of Events & Guest
Services
(206) 685-2570
dgerick@uw.edu
• Tyler Clay, Facilities Manager
(206) 616-9331
Arena Seating Capacity:
10,000

HEINZ FIELD
100 ART ROONEY AVENUE
PITTSBURGH, PA 15212
412-432-7800
Fax: 412-432-7878
www.steelers.com
• Arthur J. Rooney II, President
• Kevin Colbert, General Manager
• Jim Sacco, Director of Stadium
Management
• Steve Eyerman, Facilities Manager
Owned by:
Sports & Exhibition Authority of Pittsburgh
and Allegheny County.
Tenant(s):
NFL - Pittsburgh Steelers football; NCAA -
Univ. of Pittsburgh football.
Seating Capacity:
65,000

**HELENA AREA CHAMBER OF
COMMERCE**
225 CRUSE AVENUE
SUITE A
HELENA, MT 59601
406-442-4120
Fax: 406-447-1532
info@helenachamber.com
helenachamber.com
• Cathy Burwell, CEO/President
• Mike Mergenthaler, Vice President
• Margaret Hennen, Office &
Communication Director
Sport:
Baseball
Team:
Helena Brewers
Year Founded:
1939

**HERITAGE FIELD AT MAVERICK
STADIUM**
12000 STADIUM ROAD
ADELANTO, CA 92301
760-246-6287
Fax: 760-246-3197
• Ben Hemmen, General Manager
ben@hdmavs.com
• Sarah Bosso, Assistant General Manager
sarah@hdmavs.com
• Eric Smith, Stadium Operations Manager
esmith@hdmavs.com
• David Barry, Director of Tickets and
Finance
david@hdmavs.com
Sport:
Baseball
Team:
High Desert Mavericks
Year Founded:
1991

Capacity:
3,808

HESTAND STADIUM FAIRGROUNDS
ONE CONVENTION CENTER PLAZA
PINE BLUFF, AR 71601
870-536-7600
Fax: 870-850-2105
pbinfo@pinebluff.com
www.pinebluffcvb.org
• Greg Gustek, Director
(870) 536-7600
• Susie Madsen, Visitor and Group Tour
Information
(870) 536-7600
Seating capacity:
7,000

HI CORBETT FIELD
1 NATIONAL CHAMPIONSHIP DRIVE
TUCSON, AZ 85721-0096
520-621-2200
Fax: 520-327-2371
www.arizonawildcats.com/facilities/hi-corbett
-field.html
• Greg Byrne, Vice President for Athletics
(520) 621-4622
uofaad@arizona.edu
• James Francis, Sr. Associate Director of
Athletics, External Ops.
(520) 621-8001
jfrancis@arizona.edu
• Joe Moeller, General Manager
(520) 626-5538
joe.moeller@imgworld.com
• Suzy Mason, Sr. Associate Director of
Athletics, Facilities
(520) 621-6484
masons@arizona.edu
Stadium Seating Capacity:
9,500

HINKLE FIELDHOUSE
510 WEST 49TH STREET
BUTLER UNIVERSITY
INDIANAPOLIS, IN 46208
317-940-9375
Fax: 317-940-9734
info@butler.edu
www.butlersports.com
• Barry Collier, Director of Athletics
(317) 940-9878
athleticdirector@butler.edu
• Mike Freeman, Associate Athletic Director,
External Ops.
(317) 940-6452
msfreema@butler.edu
• Neal Smith, Assistant Athletic Director,
Facilities
(317) 940-9316
nasmith@butler.edu
Permanent Seating Capacity:
9,100

HIRAM BITHORN STADIUM
AVE FRANKLIN DELANO ROOSEVELT
SAN JUAN, PUERTO RIC 00920
787-725-2110
Fax: 787-725 2133
Permenant Seating Capacity:
18,264
Tenant(s):
Santurce Crabbers

HOBART ARENA
255 ADAMS STREET
TROY, OH 45373
937-339-2911
Fax: 937-335-0046
www.hobartarena.com
• Ken Siler, Arena Manager
ken.siler@troyohio.gov
• Cheryl Terry, Office Manager
cheryl.terry@troyohio.gov
• Phill Noll, Operations Manager
phill.noll@troyohio.gov
Seating Capacity:
3,782

HOFHEINZ PAVILION
3204 CULLEN BOULEVARD
HOUSTON, TX 77204-6002
713-743-9370
Fax: 713-743-9375
directorofathletics@uh.edu
www.uhcougars.com
• Hunter Yurachek, Vice President for
Athletics
(713) 743-9370
directorofathletics@uh.edu
• Marvin Julich, Jr., Sr. Associate Athletics
Director, External Relatio
mjulich@central.uh.edu
• Jeremy McDonald, Facilities General
Manager
mcdonald-jeremy@aramark.com
• Valerie Roux, S&E General Manager
roux-valerie@aramark.com
Arena Seating Capacity:
8,918

**HOFSTRA UNIVERSITY STADIUM &
ARENA**
245 HOFSTRA NORTHERN BOULEVARD
HOFSTRA UNIVERSITY
HEMPSTEAD, NY 11549
516-463-6633
800-463-7872
Fax: 516-463-6520
www.gohofstra.com
• Jay Artinian, Sr. Associate Director of
Athletics Facilities
(516) 463-7931
jay.m.artinian@hofstra.edu
• Ann Baller, Associate Director of Athletic
Facilities
(516) 463-6671
ann.m.combes-baller@hofstra.edu
• Maria Corvino, Assistant Director of
Athletics, Ticket Ops.
(516) 463-8499
maria.corvino@hofstra.edu
Stadium Seating Capacity:
1,600

HOHOKAM STADIUM
1235 NORTH CENTER STREET
MESA, AZ 85201
mesaaz.gov/things-to-do/hohokam-stadium
Year Founded:
1997
Seating Capacity:
10,500
Team:
Spring training home of Oakland Athletics.

HOLMAN STADIUM
67 AMHERST STREET
NASHUA, NH 03064
603-718-8883
Fax: 603-718-1305

info@nashuasilverknights.com
www.nashuasilverknights.com
• Victoria Cookson, General Manager
• Michael Broderick, General Manager
• Cheryl McCardell, Front Office Coordinator
Sport:
Baseball
Team:
Nashua Silver Knights
Capacity:
4,000

HOLT ARENA
550 MEMORIAL DRIVE
POCATELLO, ID 83201
208-282-3398
Fax: 208-233-1553
• George Casper, Director of Events
(208) 282-3398
caspgeor@isu.edu
• Erin Joy Fisk, Director of Ticketing
(208) 282-4093
joyerin@isu.edu
• Julie McKnight, Box Office Manager
(208) 282-3330
mcknjuli@isu.edu
• Mike Dooley, Concession Manager
(208) 282-4170
doolmike@isu.edu
Arena Seating Capacity:
12,000

HOMER BRYCE STADIUM
712 HAYTER STREET
NACOGDOCHES, TX 75962
936-468-3501
Fax: 936-468-7601
sfajacks.com
• Robert Hill, Director of Athletics
(936) 468-4540
rhill@sfasu.edu
• John Branch, Associate Athletic Director,
External Affairs
(936) 468-4334
jbranch@sfasu.edu
• Greg Payne, Director of Facilities
(936) 468-4200
gpayne@sfasu.edu
Stadium Seating Capacity:
14,575

HOMER STRYKER FIELD
251 MILLS STREET
KALAMAZOO, MI 49048
269-492-9966
Fax: 269-388-8333
northwoodsleague.com/kalamazoo-growlers
/team/ballpark
Sport:
Baseball
Tenant(s):
Kalamazoo Growlers
Year Founded:
1963
Capacity:
4,000

HOMEWOOD FIELD
3400 NORTH CHARLES STREET
BALTIMORE, MD 21218
410-516-7490
Fax: 410-516-5376
www.hopkinssports.com
• Tom Calder, Director of Athletics &
Recreation
(410) 516-7490
tcalder@jhu.edu

• Jon Gregory, Assistant Director of
Athletics, Facilities
(410) 516-5053
jon.gregory@jhu.edu
• Brad Mountcastle, Director of Sports
Performance and Wellness
(410) 516-6176
bmountcastle@jhu.edu
Stadium Seating Capacity:
8,500
Year Founded:
1906

HONDA CENTER
2695 EAST KATELLA AVENUE
ANAHEIM, CA 92806
714-704-2400
Fax: 714-704-2443
contactus@hondacenter.com
www.hondacenter.com
Owned by:
City of Anaheim
Tenant(s):
Anaheim Ducks (NHL), Los Angeles Kiss
(AFL)
Seating Capacity:
18,900

HOOKER FIELD
450 EAST COMMONWEALTH
BOULEVARD
MARTINSVILLE, VA 24112
276-403-5250
Fax: 276-403-5376
www.martinsvillemustangs.com
• Brian McConnell, General Manager
(276) 403-5250
brian@martinsvillemustangs.com
Sport:
Minor League Baseball
Team:
Martinsville Mustangs
Year Founded:
1988
Capacity:
3,200

HOOPER EBLEN CENTER
1100 MCGEE BOULEVARD
TTU BOX 5057
COOKEVILLE, TN 38505
931-372-3940
Fax: 931-372-3114
www.ttusports.com
• Mark Wilson, Director of Athletics
(931) 372-6306
mwilson@tntech.edu
• Matt Dexter, Sr. Facilities and Events
Coordinator
(931) 372-3945
mmdexter@tntech.edu
Arena Seating Capacity:
9,280

HOOVER METROPOLITAN STADIUM
100 BEN CHAPMAN DRIVE
HOOVER, AL 35244
205-444-7500
Fax: 205-988-9698
www.hooveral.org
Sport:
Baseball
Team:
Hoover High School football
Year Founded:
1988

Capacity:
10,800

HOWARD C. GENTRY COMPLEX
3500 JOHN A MERRITT BOULEVARD
NASHVILLE, TN 37209
615-963-5000
Fax: 615-963-5911
www.tnstate.edu
• Teresa Lawrence Phillips, Athletics
Director
(615) 963-1545
• Wilson Lee, Center For Extended Ed
Director
(615) 963-7362
Seating Capacity:
10,500

HOWARD J. LAMADE STADIUM
539 U.S ROUTE 15 HWY
P.O. BOX 3485
S. WILLIAMSPORT, PA 17701
570-326-1971
www.springfieldchallenger.org
Teams:
Little League World Series
Seating Capacity:
40,000

HP PAVILION AT SAN JOSE
525 W SANTA CLARA STREET
SAN JOSE, CA 95113
408-287-9200
800-366-4423
Fax: 408-999-5797
• Goddard Jim, Executive Vice
President/General Manager
• Jim Goddard, EVP/General Manager
• Kent Russell, VP Sales/Marketing
• Steve Kirsner, Booking & Events Director
(408) 999-5834
Owned by:
City of San Jose
Seating Capacity:
17,496

HSBC ARENA
ONE SEYMOUR H KNOX III PLAZA
BUFFALO, NY 14203-3096
716-855-4100
Fax: 716-855-4122
info@firstniagaracenter.com
www.firstniagaracenter.com
• Makowski Stan, Director of Arena
Operations
• Edward Thompson, Director Concessions
• Christye Peterson, SVP Marketing
• Jennifer Stich, Event Booking Manager
Owned by:
Crossroads Arena L.L.C.
Tenant(s):
AFL - Buffalo Destroyers Football, NHL -
Buffalo Sabres Hockey, NLL - Buffalo
Bandits Lacrosse
Permanent Seating Capacity:
20,000. AFL- 18,200

HUMBERT HUMPHREY METRODOME
900 S 5TH ST.
MINNEAPOLIS, MN 55415
612-332-0386
Fax: 612-332-8334
www.msfc.com
• Ted Mondale, CEO/Executive Director
(612) 335-3315
ted.mondale@msfa.com

• Steve Maki, Director of
Facilities/Engineering
(612) 335-3313
steve.maki@msfa.com
• Mary C. Fox-Stroman, Director of Finance
(612) 335-3311
mary.fox-stroman@msfa.com
• Jennifer Hathaway, Director of
Communications
(612) 335-3308
jenn.hathaway@msfa.com
• Bobbi Ellenberg, Events Services Manager
(612) 335-3318
bobbi.ellenberg@msfa.com
Seating Capacity:
64,000
Teams:
Minneapolis Vikings NFL football.

HUGH MILLS MEMORIAL STADIUM
ALBANY STATE UNIVERSITY
601 NORTH VAN BUREN STREET
ALBANY, GA 31705
229-430-4600
csmith@oceancenter.com
www.oceancenter.com
• John I. Davis, Athletic Director
• Henry Rivers, Sports Medicine Director
• Pam Hill, Concessions Coordinator
Physical Address:
601 N. Van Buren, Albany, GA.
Seating Capacity:
10,000

HUGHES STADIUM (CA)
3835 FREEPORT BOULEVARD
SACRAMENTO, CA 95822
916-558-2111
Fax: 916-558-2030
www.scc.losrios.edu
• Mitchell Campbell, Dean / Athletic Director
• Kathryn E. Jeffery, Ph.D, President
Seating Capacity:
22,240
Owned by:
Metropolitan Sports Commission (City of
Minneapolis)

HUGHES STADIUM (CO)
COLORADO STATE UNIVERSITY
FORT COLLINS, CO 80523-0120
970-491-5300
800-491-RAMS
Fax: 970-491-1348
csurams.cstv.com
• Max Doug, Assistant Athletic
Director/Facilities
(970) 491-2706
dmax@lamar.colostate.edu
• Paul Kowalczyk, Director of Athletics
(970) 491-3350
karen.taylor@colostate.edu
• Jim McElwain, Head Coach
• Jack Graham, Director of athletics
• Jim Francis, Faculty
• David Crum, Sr.Associate Director
• Doug Max, Sr.Associate Director

HUGHES STADIUM (MD)
1700 E COLD SPRING LANE
BALTIMORE, MD 21251
443-885-3333
Fax: 410-319-4011
info@morgan.edu
www.morgan.edu
• Kevin M. Banks, Vice President for
Student Affairs

kevin.banks@morgan.edu
• Tanya V. Rush, Associate Vice President for Student Affairs
tanya.rush@morgan.edu
• Seymour E. Chambers, Chief Judicial Officer
seymour.chambers@morgan.edu
• Marsha M. Price, Administrative Assistant
marsha.price@morgan.edu
• Sharon R. Taylor, Administrative Assistant
Sharon.taylor@morgan.edu
• Floyd Kerr, Athletic Director
Stadium Seating Capacity:
7,500

HULMAN CENTER
200 N SEVENTH STREET
TERRE HAUTE, IN 47809-1902
812-237-3737
800-468-6478
Fax: 812-237-3741
www.indstate.edu/hctaf
• Jennifer Cook, Business Manager
(812) 237-3770
j-cook@indstate.edu
• Jennifer Cook, Facility Marketing/Ticket Sales Manager
• Judith Price, Operations/Event Services Manager
• Julia Kirkpatrick, Administrative Assistant/Reservations
Year Founded:
1973
Arena Seating Capacity:
10,220

HUMPHREY COLISEUM
PO BOX HY
MISSISSIPPI STATE, MS 39762
662-325-4201
Fax: 662-325-7456
msuinfo@ur.msstate.edu
www.humphreycoliseum.msstate.edu
• Todd Hunt, Humphrey Coliseum Director
(662) 325-4201
• Duffy Neubauer, Operations Coordinator
(662) 214-4201
Permanent Seating Capacity:
10,500

HUNNICUTT FIELD
205 OLD BLUEFIELD ROAD
PRINCETON, WV 24740
304-487-2000
Fax: 304-487-8762
www.princetonrays.net
• Jim Holland, General Manager
• Mick Bayle, Director - Stadium Operations
• Dewey Russell, President
Arena Seating Capacity:
1,950
Year Founded:
1988
Teams:
Princeton Rays Professional Baseball, Mercer County Public Schools

HUNTER WRIGHT STADIUM
800 GRANDBY ROAD
KINGSPORT, TN 37600
423-224-2626
Fax: 423-224-2625
info@kmets.com
web.minorleaguebaseball.com
• Spivey Rick, Kingsport Mets President
• Pat O'Conner, President & CEO
admin@minorleaguebaseball.com

• Stan Brand, Vice President
admin@minorleaguebaseball.com
• Scott Poley, Senior Vice President, Legal Affairs
• Tim Brunswick, Vice President, Baseball & Business Operation
timbrunswick@minorleaguebaseball.com
• Brian Earle, Vice President, BIRCO & Business Services
brianearle@minorleaguebaseball.com
• Tina Gust, Vice President, Business Development
tinagust@minorleaguebaseball.com
• Steve Densa, Executive Director, Communications
Sport:
Baseball
Tenant(s):
Kingsport Mets baseball
Year Founded:
1995
Capacity:
2,000

HUNTINGTON PARK
330 HUNTINGTON PARK LANE
COLUMBUS, OH 43215
614-462-5250
Fax: 614-462-3271
info@clippersbaseball.com
www.clippersbaseball.com
• Ken Schnacke, President/GM
kschnacke@clippersbaseball.com
Sport:
Minor League Baseball.
Team:
Columbus Clippers.
Seating Capacity:
10,000

HUNTSVILLE STARS
3125 LEEMAN FERRY ROAD
PO BOX 2769
HUNTSVILLE, AL 35801
256-882-2562
Fax: 256-880-0801
info@huntsvillestars.com
web.minorleaguebaseball.com
• Rogers Va Buck, General Manager
tom@huntsvillestars.com
• Pat O'Conner, President & CEO
admin@minorleaguebaseball.com
• Stan Brand, Vice President
admin@minorleaguebaseball.com
• Scott Poley, Senior Vice President, Legal Affairs
• Tim Brunswick, Vice President, Baseball & Business Operation
timbrunswick@minorleaguebaseball.com
• Brian Earle, Vice President, BIRCO & Business Services
brianearle@minorleaguebaseball.com
• Tina Gust, Vice President, Business Development
tinagust@minorleaguebaseball.com
• Steve Densa, Executive Director, Communications
stevedensa@minorleaguebaseball.com
Nature of Service:
Minor League Baseball.
Year Founded:
1985
Nature of Service:
AA affiliated of Milwaukee Brewers.

HURON ARENA
150 5TH STREET SW
HURON, SD 57350
605-353-6970
Fax: 605-353-6973
www.huron.k12.sd.us
• Terry Rotert, Arena Activities Director/Arena Manager
• Colette Habbena, Administrative Assistant
Arena Seating Capacity:
5,448

HUSKY STADIUM
218 GRAVES BUILDING
UNIVERSITY OF WASHINGTON BOX 354070
3910 MONT LAKE BLVD
SEATTLE, WA 98195
206-543-2200
Fax: 206-616-1761
tickets@u.washington.edu
www.gohuskies.com
• Scott Woodward, Athletic Director
(206) 543-2212
huskyad@u.washington.edu
• Chip Lydum, Associate Athletic Director/Facilities &
(206) 543-7373
clydum@washington.edu
• Larry White, Facilities Manager
• Jim Daves, Facilities Manager
(206) 543-2230
jdaves@washington.edu
• Larry White, Facilities Manager
Year Founded:
1920
Stadium Seating Capacity:
72,500
Track Type:
Synthetic
Track Size:
400 meters
Team:
University of Washington football.

HYSLOP SPORTS CENTER
ROOM 120
2751 2ND AVEUE N STOP 9013
GRAND FORKS, ND 58202-9013
701-777-2237
Fax: 701-777-2285
www.fightingsioux.com
• Steve Brekke, Director of Athletic Development
(701) 777-6426
steveb@undalumni.net
• Kathleen McCann, Assistant Director
Arena Seating Capacity:
6,000

I WIRELESS CENTER
1201 RIVER DRIVE
MOLINE, IL 61265
309-764-2001
Fax: 309-764-2192
www.iwirelesscenter.com
• Steve R Hyman, Executive Director
(309) 764-2001
• Rocky R Jones, Director Finance
(309) 764-2001
• Brett Cornish, Marketing/Sales Director
• Scott Mullen, Executive Director
(309) 277-1309
• John Watts, Director Operations
Home Arena for:
AF2 - Quad City Steamwheelers.

Arena Seating Capacity:
10,700 Basketball, 9,800 Hockey.

INDEPENDENCE STADIUM
3301 PERSHING BLVD.
LA STATE FAIRGROUNDS
SHREVEPORT, LA 71109
318-673-7758
independencebowl.org
• John Hubbard, Chairman
• Troy J. Broussard, Vice-Chairman
• Kyle McInnis, 1st Vice-Chairman
• Paul Pratt, 2nd Vice-Chairman
• Darin Seal, Treasurer
• Missy Setters, Executive Director
• John Cordaro, Assistant Executive
Director for Ticketing
john@advocarev100bowl.org
Seating Capacity:
51,000
Teams:
Independence Bowl football.

INGALLS RINK
20 TOWER PARKWAY
YALE UNIVERSITY
NEW HAVEN, CT 6511
203-432-4747
Fax: 203-432-7772
www.yalebulldogs.com
• Thomas Beckett, Director of Athletics
(203) 432-1414
thomas.beckett@yale.edu
• Jennifer O'Neil, Assistant to the Director
(203) 432-1414
jennifer.oneil@yale.edu
• Dan Silverman, Director of Compliance
(203) 436-8309
daniel.c.silverman@yale.edu
• Amy Backus, Senior Associate Athletics
Director for Compl
(203) 432-7668
amy.backus@yale.edu
• Barbara Chesler, Senior Associate
Athletics Director for Capit
(203) 432-1437
barbara.chesler@yale.edu
• Francine Georges, Senior Associate
Athletics Director for Human
(203) 432-1442
francine.georges@yale.edu
• Edward Mockus, Senior Associate Athletic
Director Facilities
(203) 432-2494
edward.mockus@yale.edu
Arena Seating Capacity:
3,486.00
Year Founded:
1958

INVESCO FIELD AT MILE HIGH STADIUM
1701 BRYANT STREET
SUITE 700
DENVER, CO 80204
720-258-3000
Fax: 720-258-3050
parking@broncos.nfl.net
www.sportsauthorityfieldatmilehigh.com
• Freeman Mac, Stadium Operations VP
• Gail Stuckey, Stadium Operations Director
• Andy Gorchov, Events Director
• Lorraine Spargo, Premium Seat Sales
Director
Tenant(s):
NFL - Denver Broncos football, MLS -
Colorado Rapids soccer.

Permanent Seating Capacity:
76,125

INVESTORS GROUP FIELD
315 CHANCELLOR MATHESON RD.
WINNIPEG, MB, CANADA R3T 1Z2
204-784-2583
bbombers@bluebombers.com
Owners:
Winnipeg Blue Bombers; City of Winnipeg;
University of Manitoba.
Operators:
Winnipeg Blue Bombers.
Year Opened:
2013.
Seating Capacity:
33,422; expandable to 40,000.
Tenant(s):
CFL - Winnipeg Blue Bombers. CIS -
Manitba Bisons. CJFL - Winnipeg Rifles.

IOWA STATE CENTER
SCHEMAN BUILDING SUITE 102
IOWA STATE UNIVERSITY
AMES, IA 50011-1113
515-294-3347
877-843-2368
Fax: 515-294-3349
iscinfo@iastate.edu
www.center.iastate.edu
• Mark North, Executive Director
• Scott Wycoff, Business Finance Director
• Sara Barr, Marketing Director
• Hilton Coliseum, Management
• Randy Baumeister, Operations Director
Arena Seating Capacity:
15,000
Stadium Seating Capacity:
56,000

IOWA STATE UNIVERSITY ATHLETICS
1800 S 4TH STREET
JACOBSON ATHLETIC BUILDING
AMES, IA 50011-1140
515-294-3662
Fax: 515-294-0558
www.cyclones.com
• Jamie Pollard, Athletic Director
(515) 294-0123
bvelde@iastate.edu
• Rebecca Hornbacher, Women's Soccer
Coach
(515) 294-5328
• Bobby Douglas, Wrestling Coach
(515) 294-4643
bobbyd@iastate.edu
• Jamie Pollard, Director of Athletics
(515) 294-0123
jbp@iastate.edu
• Julie Bright, Sr. Assoc. AD/Administration
(Apr) 10
jabright@iastate.edu
• David Harris, Sr. Assoc. AD/Student
Services
(Apr) 41
dwh@iastate.edu
• Chris Jorgensen, Sr. Assoc. AD/Facilities,
Planning and Manage
(4-0) 07
cjorg@iastate.edu
Stadium Seating Capacity:
15,000

ISOTOPES PARK
1601 AVENIDA CESAR CHAVEZ SE
ALBUQUERQUE, NM 87106

505-924-2255
Fax: 505-242-8899
web.minorleaguebaseball.com
• Young Ken, President
• Daniel Luna, Ticketing Director
• Pat O'Conner, President & CEO
admin@minorleaguebaseball.com
• Stan Brand, Vice President
admin@minorleaguebaseball.com
• Scott Poley, Senior Vice President, Legal
Affairs
• Tim Brunswick, Vice President, Baseball &
Business Operation
timbrunswick@minorleaguebaseball.com
• Brian Earle, Vice President, BIRCO &
Business Services
brianearle@minorleaguebaseball.com
• Tina Gust, Vice President, Business
Development
tinagust@minorleaguebaseball.com
• Steve Densa, Executive Director,
Communications
stevedensa@minorleaguebaseball.com

ITHACA COLLEGE ATHLETICS
953 DANBY ROAD
ITHACA COLLEGE
ITHACA, NY 14850
607-274-3209
Fax: 607-274-1667
mlindberg@ithaca.edu
www.ithaca.edu
• Ken Kutler, Intercollegiate Athletics
Director
(607) 274-3209
kkutler@ithaca.edu
• Ernie McClatchie, Asst Director of
Intercollegiate Athletics
(607) 274-5708
emcclatchie@ithaca.edu
• Mike R. Lindberg, Asst Director of
Intercollegiate Athletics
(607) 274-3199
mlindberg@ithaca.edu
Stadium Seating Capacity:
5,000
Track Type:
All-Weather (synthetic)
Track Size:
400 Meters.
Tenants:
Ithaca College football.

IZOD CENTER
THE MEADOWLANDS SPORTS COMPLEX
50 STATE ROUTE 120
EAST RUTHERFORD, NJ 7073
201-935-8500
contact@metlifestadium.com
www.izodcenter.com
• Minish Jim, SVP
(201) 460-4203
jminish@njsea.com
• Kathleen Francis, Sales/Marketing &
Communications SVP
(201) 842-5010
kfrancis@njsea.com
• Ron Va DeVeen, VP/Associate General
Manager
(201) 460-4387
rvandeveen@njsea.com
• Karen Sullivan, Ticketing VP
(201) 842-5325
ksullivan@njsea.com
Arena Seating Capacity:
40,000
Year Founded:
1981

Nature of Service:
Arena.
Tenants:
NJ Devils (NHL), NJ Nets (NBA), Seton Hall Pirates (College Basketball).

J LAWRENCE WALK-UP SKYDOME
PO BOX 15400
FLAGSTAFF, AZ 86011
928-523-3449
Fax: 928-523-7588
• Dave Brown, Skydome Director/Color Commentator
dave.brown@nau.edu
• Steve Holton, Athletic Director/Northern Arizona Unive
Arena Seating Capacity:
16,500

J. LAWRENCE WALKUP SKYDOME
NORTHERN ARIZONA UNIVERSITY
PO BOX 15096
FLAGSTAFF, AZ 86011
928-523-3449
Fax: 928-523-7588
www.nauathletics.com/information/facilities/skydome
• Lisa Campos, Vice President for Intercollegiate Athletics
• Rob Morrison, Director of Facilities
• Jerome Souers, Head Coach, Football
• Jack Murphy, Head Coach, Men's Basketball
• Sue Darling, Head Coach, Women's Basketball
Team:
NAU Lumberjacks
Seating Capacity:
11,230

JACK BRESLIN STUDENT EVENTS CENTER
534 BIRCH ROAD
MICHIGAN STATE UNIVERSITY
EAST LANSING, MI 48824
517-432-1989
800-968-2737
Fax: 517-432-1510
www.breslincenter.com
• Scott H Breckner, Director
• Gavin J Smith, Operations Assistant Director
Permanent Seating Capacity:
15,130

JACK RUSSELL MEMORIAL STADIUM
800 PHILLIES DRIVE
CLEARWATER, FL 33755
727-797-9090
727-781-2224
Fax: 727-447-3924
• Timberlake John, General Manager
• Dianne Gonzalez, Busines Manager/Florida Operations
Sport:
Baseball
Tenant(s):
Clearwater Phillies

JACK SPINKS STADIUM
1000 ASU DRIVE
#510
ALCORN STATE, MS 39096
601-877-6500
Fax: 601-877-3821

asu_sportsinfo@yahoo.com
www.alcornsports.com
• Wiley H Jones, Interim Athletic Director
• LaToya G Shields, Sports Information Director
(601) 877-6466
latoya@alcorn.edu
• Johnny Thomas, Football Coach
• Samuel West, Men's Basketball Coach
Stadium Seating Capacity:
22,500
Arena Seating Capacity:
7,000

JACK TRICE STADIUM
1800 S. 4TH STREET
AMES, IA 50011-1140
515-294-3662
Fax: 515-294-0104
mtodd@iastate.edu
www.cyclones.com
• Julie Bright, Sr. Assoc. AD/Administration
(515) 294-5410
jabright@iastate.edu
• David Harris, Sr. Assoc. AD/Student Services
(515) 294-3141
dwh@iastate.edu
• Chris Jorgensen, Sr. Assoc. AD/Facilities, Planning and Manage
(515) 294-0307
cjorg@iastate.edu
• Steve Malchow, Sr. Assoc. AD/Communications
(515) 294-5095
sdm@iastate.edu
• Frank Nogel, Sr. Assoc. AD/External Relations
(515) 294-6463
fnogel@iastate.edu
• Jamie Pollard, Director of Athletics
(515) 294-0123
jbp@iastate.edu
• Mike Green, Assoc. Director
(515) 294-2008
mgreen@iastate.edu
Seating Capacity:
55,000
Teams:
Iowa State University football.

JACKIE ROBINSON BALLPARK
110 E ORANGE AVENUE
DAYTONA BEACH, FL 32114
386-257-3172
Fax: 386-257-3382
www.milb.com
• Bill Papierniak, General Manager
• Michael Swope, General Manager
• Pat O'Conner, President / CEO
admin@minorleaguebaseball.com
• Brady Ballard, General Manager
Sport:
Baseball
Team:
Daytona Cubs
Year Founded:
1914
Capacity:
4,000

JACKSONVILLE VETERANS MEMORIAL ARENA
300 A. PHILIP RANDOLPH BOULEVARD
JACKSONVILLE, FL 32202
904-630-3900
howcanwehelp@jaxevents.com

jaxevents.com/venue/veterans-memorial-arena
• Bill McConnell, General Manager
(904) 630-3900
• Sandy Avery, Box Office Manager
(904) 630-3900
savery@smgjax.com
• Val Glanton, Senior Event Manager
• Lyle Klemmt, Senior Operations Manager
(904) 630-3934
lklemmt@smgjax.com
• Alex Alston, Director of Sales & Marketing
(904) 630-4055
alexa@smgjax.com
• Whitney Oxnard, VIP Services Coordinator
(904) 630-3953
woxnard@smgjax.com
Home Arena for:
AF2 - Jacksonville Tomcats.
Coliseum Seating Capacity:
10,276

JACOBS FIELD
2401 ONTARIO STREET
CLEVELAND, OH 44115
216-420-4444
Fax: 216-420-4396
access@website.mlb.com
cleveland.indians.mlb.com
• Lawrence J Dolan, Owner and Chief Executive Officer
• Scott Sterneckert, Ticket Sales Director
• Jerry Crabb, Ballpark Operations Director
• Gloria Carter, Assistant Ballpark Operations
• Paul J. Dolan, Chairman/Chief Executive Officer
• Mark Shapiro, President
• Chris Antonetti, Executive Vice President & General Manager
• Bob DiBiasio, Senior Vice President, Public Affairs
• Victor Gregovits, Senior Vice President, Sales & Business Devel
• Sara Lehrke, Vice President, Human Resources/Chief Diversi
Permanent Seating Capacity:
42,400
Description:
Home Stadium For: Cleveland Indians.
Owned by:
Gateway Economic Development Corp.

JADWIN GYMNASIUM
PRINCETON UNIVERSITY
PRINCETON, NJ 8544
609-258-3000
Fax: 609-258-4477
www.princeton.edu
• Gary D Walters, Athletic Director
Seating Capacity:
7,500

JAMES A. RHODES ARENA
373 CARROLL STREET
UNIVERSITY OF AKRON
AKRON, OH 44325-5104
330-972-6920
Fax: 330-972-5847
athfac@uakron.edu
www.gozips.com
• Paul Hammond, Assistant Athletic Director/Facilities O
• Tom Wistrcill, Director of Athletics
(330) 972-7080
krex@uakron.edu
• Mary Lu Gribschaw, Senior Associate

Athletics Director/Senior Wo
(330) 0972-708
marylu@uakron.edu
• Dan Satter, Senior Associate Athletics
Director for Exter
(330) 972-7468
dsatter@uakron.edu
• J. Dean Carro, Faculty Athletics
Representative
(330) 972-7751
carro1@uakron.edu
• Kathy Rex, Sr. Administrative Assistant to
the Director
(330) 972-6689
krex@uakron.edu
• Kyra Lobbins, Coordinator of Programming
(330) 972-8355
kyralob@uakron.edu
Arena Seating Capacity:
4,984

JAMES E. O'NEILL JR. ARENA
7400 BAY ROAD
SAGINAW VALLEY STATE UNIVERSITY
UNIVERSITY CENTER, MI 48710-0001
989-964-4000
800-968-9500
Fax: 989-964-7389
javogl@svsu.edu
www.svsu.edu
• Mike Watson, Athletic Director
Arena Seating Capacity:
6,000

JAMESTOWN CIVIC CENTER
212 3RD AVENUE NE
JAMESTOWN, ND 58401
701-252-8088
Fax: 701-252-8089
www.jamestownciviccenter.com
• Pam Fosse, Director
(701) 252-8088
pfosse@daktel.com
• Crystal Diestler, Administrative Assistant
cdiestler@daktel.com
• Chastity Mikkelson, Secretary
cmikkelson@daktel.com
Permanent Seating Capacity:
Stadium/Arena 6,500

JAX EVENTS PRESENTED BY SMG
ONE EVER BANK FIELD DRIVE
JACKSONVILLE, FL 32202
904-633-6100
Fax: 904-633-6190
www.jaxevents.com
• Gerry Albert, Senior Vice President of
Stadium Operations
galbert@smgjax.com
• Tracey Evans, Director
• Nan Coyle, Director Marketing
• Sandy Avery, Box Office Manager
(904) 630-3974
savery@smgjax.com
• Barry Milligan, Sales & Marketing Manager
(904) 630-4056
• Christina Castle, Assistant Marketing &
Media Manager
(904) 630-4026
• Angela Green, VIP Services Manager &
Group Sales
(904) 630-3958
Permanent Seating Capacity:
73,000
Home Stadium for:
Jacksonville Jaguars.

JAYNE STADIUM
112 PLAYFORTH PLACE
MOREHEAD STATE UNIVERSITY
MOREHEAD, KY 40351
606-783-2088
800-585-6781
Fax: 606-783-5035
athletics@moreheadstate.edu
www.msueagles.com
• Brian Hutchinson, Athletic Director
b.hutchinson@moreheadstate.edu
• Randy Stacy, Athlete/Media Relations
Director
• Rhonda Ferguson, Administrative
Assistant to the AD
(606) 783-2089
r.ferguson@moreheadstate.edu
• Harry Floyd, Athletic Secretary
(606) 783-2088
hbfloyd@moreheadstate.edu
• Peggy Osborne, Faculty Athletics
Representative
(606) 783-2755
p.osborne@moreheadstate.edu
Stadium Seating Capacity:
10,000

JEKYLL ISLAND SOCCER COMPLEX
700 SOUTHVILLE BEACHVIEW DRIVE
JEKYLL ISLAND, GA 31527
877-453-5955
Fax: 912-635-4004
admin@goldenislesoccer.com
www.goldenislesoccer.com
• Eric Garvey, Soccer Marketing Director
egarvey@jekyllisland.com
Description:
7 Soccer fields, prescription Bermuda turf,
concession pavilion.

JERRY UHT PARK
110 E 10TH STREET
ERIE, PA 16501
814-456-1300
Fax: 814-456-7520
seawolves@seawolves.com
www.seawolves.com
• Mark Pirrello, Director of Merchandise/Box
Office Manager
mpirrello@seawolves.com
• Amy McArdle, Director of Accounting and
Finance
• Cody Herrick, Director of Ticket Sales
• Dan Torf, Director of Group Sales
• Kevin Forte, Group Sales Coordinator
• Greg Coleman, President
Sport:
Baseball
Team:
Erie Seawolves
Year Founded:
1995
Capacity:
6,000

JOAN C. EDWARDS STADIUM
2001 3RD AVENUE
HUNTINGTON, WV 25755
www.herdzone.com
• Mike Hamrick, Director of Athletics
• Doc Holliday, Head Coach, Football
Seating Capacity:
38,016

JOE AILLET STADIUM
305 WISTERIA STREET
PO BOX 3046
RUSTON, LA 71270-9985
318-257-4111
Fax: 318-257-3757
vandevelde@latech.edu
www.latechsports.com
• Tommy Sisemore, Director Athletic
Facilities
(318) 257-53223
• Derek Dooley, Athletics Director
(318) 257-4547
• Marie Gilbert, Associate A.D./Chief
Financial Officer
(318) 257-3637
mgilbert@latech.edu
• James Liberatos, Faculty Athletics
Representative
(318) 257-4287
jamesl@latech.edu
• Leah Beasley, Associate A.D./Marketing
and Game Management
(318) 257-5332
lbeasley@latech.edu
• Malcolm Butler, Associate A.D./Media
Relations
(318) 257-3145
mbutler@latech.edu
• Mary Kay Hungate, Deputy Athletics
Director - SWA
(318) 257-5654
usmkh@latech.edu
• Bruce Van De Velde, Athletics Director
(318) 257-3247
vendevelde@latech.edu
Seating Capacity:
30200
Tenant(s):
Louisiana Tech Bulldogs

JOE ALBI STADIUM
4918 W EVERETT
SPOKANE, WA 99205
509-326-4625
Fax: 509-326-0636
abuck@spokaneshadow.com
• Jeff Robbins, General Manager
Stadium Seating Capacity:
22,000

JOE FABER FIELD
5001 VETERANS DRIVE
SAINT CLOUD, MN 56303
320-240-9798
Fax: 320-255-5228
info@stcloudrox.com
www.stcloudrox.com
• Nelson Jim, Director of Broadcasting
• Scott Schreiner, Vice President &
Co-owner
Scott@StCloudRox.com
• Wes Sharp, General Manager
Wes@StCloudRox.com
• Kyle Kohls, Assistant General Manager
Wes@StCloudRox.com
• Andy Sailer, Media & Public Relations
Manager
• Scott Schreiner, Co-Owner & VP
scott@stcloudrox.com
Sport:
Collegiate Professional Baseball
Tenant(s):
St. Cloud River Rats baseball
Year Founded:
1971

Capacity:
2,200

JOE L. REED ACADOME
915 S JACKSON STREET
MONTGOMERY, AL 36104
334-229-4100
800-253-5037
Fax: 334-229-4988
www.alasu.edu
• John Knight, Executive Director of Marketing & ommunications
• William H. Harris, President
Arena Seating Capacity:
8,000

JOE MARTIN FIELD
1221 POTTER STREET
BELLINGHAM, WA 98229
360-527-1035
bellinghambells.com
• Nick Caples, Vice President of Operations
(360) 746-0406
nick@bellinghambells.com
• Stephanie Morrell, General Manager
(360) 746-0409
stephanie@bellinghambells.com
• Levi Stewart, Sales & Marketing Coordinator
(360) 527-1035
levi@bellinghambells.com
Capacity:
1,600

JOE O'BRIEN FIELD
136 S SYCAMORE STREET
ELIZABETHTON, TN 37643
423-547-6441
Fax: 423-547-6442
www.milb.com/index.jsp?sid=t576
• Jim Rantz, Director
• David Nanney, Head Groundskeeper
Sport:
Minor League Baseball.
Team:
Elizabethton Twins.
Year Founded:
1974
Capacity:
1,500

JOHN E. TUCKER COLISEUM
1306 N EL PASO AVENUE
RUSSELLVILLE, AR 72801
479-968-0389
Fax: 479-968-0647
kdavis@atu.edu
athletics.atu.edu
• Brent Linker, Athletic Facilities Director
(479) 968-0212
• Steve Mullins, Athletic Director
(479) 968-0245
smullins@atu.edu
• Paul smith, Information Director
(479) 968-0645
psmith@atu.edu
• Kristy Bayer, Administrator
(479) 968-0513
kbayer@atu.edu
• Amy White, Compliance Officer
(479) 968-6071
awhite@atu.edu
• Bryan Fisher, Director of Athletic Relations
(479) 968-0674
bfisher@atu.edu
• Ben Greenberg, Sports Information

Director
bgreenberg@atu.edu
Arena Seating Capacity:
3,500

JOHN F. SAVAGE HALL
2801 W BANCROFT STREET
UNIVERSITY OF TOLEDO
TOLEDO, OH 43606-3390
419-530-4226
800-586-5336
Fax: 419-530-8429
utmarcom@utoledo.edu
www.utoledo.edu
• John Adams, Director, University Marketing
(419) 530-2676
john.adams@utoledo.edu
• C. Vernon Snyder, Vice President for Institutional Advancement
(419) 530-4249
• Ron Beczynski, Facilities Director
• Chris Spengler, Director of Advancement Relations
(419) 530-4927
• Daniel Stong, Major Gifts Officer, Athletics
(419) 530-5525
• Jeff Barton, Director of Development, College of Pharmacy
(419) 530-5413
• Patricia Keller, Director of Prospect Research
(419) 530-5409
• Laura Robinson, Senior Major Gift Officer
(860) 989-9652
Arena Seating Capacity:
9,600

JOHN O'QUINN FIELD AT ROBERTSON STADIUM
3100 CULLEN BOULEVARD
UNIVERSITY OF HOUSTON
HOUSTON, TX 77204-6002
713-462-6647
877-268-4275
Fax: 713-743-9449
support@uh.edu
www.uhcougars.com
• Dave Maggard, Athletic Director
dmaggard@uh.edu
• John Robinson, Deputy Athletics Director
jrobinson@uh.edu
• Darren Dunn, Athletics Director
• T.J. Meagher, Associate Athletics Director for Internal Ope
• DeJuena Chizer, Associate Athletics Director/SWA
• Barbara Stone, Executive Administrative Assistant
• Pat A. Streko, Jr., Assistant Vice President/General Manager
(713) 743-1446
Stadium Seating Capacity:
22,000

JOHN THURMAN FIELD
601 NEECE DR. ROAD
MODESTO, CA 95351
209-572-4487
Fax: 209-572-4490
fun@modestonuts.com
www.modestonuts.com
• Eric Rauber, Director of Group Sales
• Ryan Thomas, Director of Operations
• Alex Margulies, Director of Broadcasting
• Justin McKissick, Director of Public Relations

• Ed Mack, Assistant General Manager - Operations
ed@modestonuts.com
• Tyler Richardson, Assistant General Manager - Sales & Marketing
tyler@modestonuts.com
• Steven Almanza, Production Manager
steven@modestonuts.com
• Mike Gorrasi, Executive Vice President-HWS Baseball
mike@modestonuts.com
Sport:
Baseball
Team:
Modesto A's
Year Founded:
1952
Capacity:
3,870

JOHNNY RED FLOYD STADIUM
MTSU BOX 20
MURFREESBORO, TN 37132
615-898-2450
Fax: 615-898-5626
www.goblueraiders.com
• Darrell Towe, Director
(615) 494-7699
dtowe@mtsu.edu
• Boniface Amuzu, Operations Coordinator
(615) 898-5189
bamuzu@mtsu.edu
• Todd Wyant, Director, Student Athlete Enhancement Center
(615) 898-5610
twyant@mtsu.edu
• Wynnifred Counts, Associate Director/Coordinator of Life Skills
(615) 898-5581
wcounts@mtsu.edu
• Chris Massaro, Director of Athletics
(615) 898-2452
cmassaro@mtsu.edu
• Diane Turnham, Associate Athletic Director/SWA
(615) 898-2938
dturnham@mtsu.edu
• Graham Neff, Associate Athletic Director
(615) 898-5563
gneff@mtsu.edu
• Zackie Sanderson, Associate Athletic Director/Business
(615) 898-2207
zsanders@mtsu.edu
Stadium Seating Capacity:
30,788
Sport:
Football

JOHNSON HAGOOD STADIUM
171 MOULTRIE STREET
THE CITADEL FOUNDATION
CHARLESTON, SC 29409
843-953-5277
Fax: 843-953-5124
ron.ginyard@citadel.edu
www.citadelsports.com
• Mike Hoffman, Communications & Marketing Asst Dir
mhoffma1@citadel.edu
• Noelle Orr Blaney, Director Media Relations
(843) 953-5353
noelle.orr@citadel.edu
• Larry Leckonby, Director of Athletics
(843) 953-5030
larry.leckonby@citadel.edu

• John McAleer Sr., Associate Athletic
Director/Development
(843) 953-1354
john.mcaleer@citadel.edu
• Kelly Simpson, Associate Athletic
Director/SWA
(843) 953-6604
kelly.simpson@citadel.edu
• Geoff Von Dollen, Associate Athletic
Director/Business
(843) 953-5352
geoff.vondollen@citadel.edu
• Andy Solomon, Associate Athletic
Director/Marketing
(843) 953-6300
solomona@citadel.edu
• Robby Bennett, Assistant Athletic
Director/Ticket Office
(843) 953-7181
robert.bennett@citadel.edu
Stadium Seating Capacity:
21,000

JOKER MARCHANT STADIUM
2125 North Lake Avenue
#A
LAKELAND, FL 33805
863-686-8075
Fax: 863-688-9589
www.milb.com
• Myers Ron, Director of Florida Operations
• Don Miers, Florida Operations Director
Sport:
Baseball
Tenant(s):
Detroit Tigers; Spring Training Facility
Lakeland Tigers.
Year Founded:
1966, Renovated 2002
Capacity:
8,500

JON M. HUNTSMAN CENTER
1825 E S CAMPUS DRIVE
UNIVERSITY OF UTAH
SALT LAKE CITY, UT 84112-0900
801-581-8171
Fax: 801-581-6670
utahutes.cstv.com
• Chris Hill, Director of Athletics
(801) 581-3508
• Liz Abel, Assistant Athletic Director/Sports
Infor
Basketball Seating Capacity:
15,000

JONES AT&T STADIUM
6TH STREET
BOX 43021
LUBBOCK, TX 79409
806-742-3355
Fax: 806-742-1856
www.texastech.com
• Ron Damron, Associate Athletic
Director/Facility Operations
• Liz Parke, Assistant Athletic
Director/Facility Operations
• Tim Walker, Facilities Manager
• Gerald Myers, Director of Athletics
• Kirby Hocutt, Athletic Director
Coliseum Seating Capacity:
52,000

JONES SBC STADIUM
6TH STREET
TEXAS TECH ATHLETIC DEPARTMENT
LUBBOCK, TX 79409

806-742-3355
Fax: 806-742-7856
www.texastech.com
• Steve Uryasz, Senior Associate Athletic
Director
• Tim Walker, Facilities Manager
• Kirby Hocutt, Athletic Director
• Gerald Myers, Director of Athletics
Stadium Seating Capacity:
50,500

JOSEPH L. BRUNO STADIUM
80 VANDENBURGH AVENUE
TROY, NY 12180
518-629-2287
Fax: 518-629-2299
info@tcvalleycats.com
www.tcvalleycats.com
• Rick Murphy, General Manager
(518) 629-2287
rickmurphy@tcvalleycats.com
• Matt Callahan, Assistant General Manager
(518) 629-2287
matt@tcvalleycats.com
• Ryan Burke, Account Executive
(518) 629-2287
• Chris Chenes, Media/Production Manager
(518) 629-2287
chrischenes@tcvalleycats.com
• Keith Sweeney, Stadium Operations
Manager
(518) 629-2287
keith@tcvalleycats.com
• Jessica Kaszeta, Box Office/Ticket
Manager
(518) 629-2287
jessicakaszeta@tcvalleycats.com
• William L. Gladstone, President/Principal
Owner
 ext 21
Stadium Seating Capacity:
4,500.00
Year Founded:
2002
Track Type:
Grass.
Track Size:
L 330, C 400, R 330.

JOSEPH P. RILEY, JR PARK
360 FISHBURNE STREET
CHARLESTON, SC 29403
843-723-7241
Fax: 843-723-2641
admin@riverdogs.com
www.riverdogs.com
• Mike Veeck, President
admin@riverdogs.com
• Dave Echols, VP/General Manager
• John Schumacher, Director of Stadium
Operations
• Marvin Goldklang, Chairman
• Kristen Wolfe, Special Events Manager
• Mike Veeck, President
• Dr. Gene Budig, Co-Owner
• Peter Freund, Co-Owner
• Al Phillips, Co-Owner
• Bill Murray, Director of Fun
• Michael DeAntonio, Director of
Merchandise
Sport:
Baseball
Team:
Charleston River Dogs
Year Founded:
1996
Capacity:

7,880
Sports Organization:
The Charleston RiverDogs are a Minor
League Baseball team who serve as the
Class A Affiliate of the New York Yankees,
and are a proud member of the South
Atlantic League.

**JOYCE ATHLETIC & CONVOCATION
CENTER**
C113 JOYCE CENTER
NOTRE DAME UNIVERSITY
NOTRE DAME, IN 46556
574-631-5030
Fax: 574-631-8596
www.und.com
• Kevin White, Athletics Director
(574) 631-7277
• Patricia Bellia, Faculty Athletics
Representative
(574) 631-3866
• Missy Conboy, Senior Deputy Athletics
Director
(574) 631-6107
• John Heisler, Senior Associate Athletics
Director (Media an
(574) 631-6107
• Jill Bodensteiner, Associate Athletics
Director (Compliance and
(574) 631-6107
• Michael Danch, Associate Athletics
Director (Facilities)
(574) 631-6107
• Jack Swarbrick, University Vice
President/Director of Athleti
(574) 631-6107
Arena Seating Capacity:
11,400

JPS FIELD AT MALONE STADIUM
ULM ATHLETICS
308 WARHAWK WAY
MONROE, LA 71209
318-342-5360
www.ulmwarhawks.com
• Brian Wickstrom, Director of Athletics
• Matt Viator, Head Coach, Football
Seating Capacity:
30,427

JS DORTON ARENA
1025 BLUE RIDGE BOULEVARD
RALEIGH, NC 27607
919-821-7400
Fax: 919-733-5079
claudine.davis@ncagr.gov
www.ncstatefair.org/dorton.htm
• Wyatt V Wesley, Manager
• Claudine Davis, Facility Sales Director
claudine.davis@ncagr.gov
• Pam Moore, Budget and Human
Resources Director
• Dudley Baggett, Landscaping Director
• Ray Frost, Assistant Manager for
Operations
• Peter Green, Maintenance Office Manager
• Angie Crone, Sponsorship Coordinator
Arena Seating Capacity:
5,110
Number of Members:
52
Affiliations:
Carolina Roller Derby, Inc, aWFTA member
Teams:
Carolina Rollergirls- Caroline Rollar Derby,
Inc. Womens Flat Track Derby

Association(WFTDA)
www.carolinarollergirls.com

JUDY JOHNSON FIELD AT DANIEL S. FRAWLEY STADIUM
801 SHIPYARD DRIVE
WILMINGTON, DE 19801
302-777-5772
Fax: 302-777-5657
info@bluerocks.com
www.delawarestadiumcorp.com
• Steve Gold, Field Operations Director
sgold@bluerocks.com
• Jared Forma, Ticket Sales Director
Sport:
Baseball.
Tenant(s):
Wilmington Blue Rocks baseball.
Year Founded:
1993
Capacity:
6,532

KANSAS COLISEUM
1279 E 85TH STREET
PARK CITY, KS 67147
316-440-0888
Fax: 316-440-0928
www.kansascoliseum.com
• Sam Fulco, Director
Arena Seating Capacity:
11,652

KAUFFMAN STADIUM
1 ROYAL WAY
PO BOX 419969
KANSAS CITY, MO 64129
816-504-4040
Fax: 816-504-4142
ticketservices@royals.com
kansascity.royals.mlb.com
• Dan Glass, Director Stadium Operations
• Charlie Seraphin, VP Sales & Marketing
• Rob Stoltz, General Manager/Volume Services
• Tonya Mangels, Marketing/Sales Director
• Allan H. Selig, Commissioner of Baseball
• Tim Brosnan, Executive Vice President, Business
• Rob Manfred, Executive Vice President, Economics & League
• Jonathan Mariner, Executive Vice President and Chief Financial
• John McHale, Jr, Executive Vice President, Administration & Ch
• Joe Torre, Executive Vice President of Baseball Operatio
• Frank Robinson, Executive Vice President of Baseball Developm
Owned by:
Jackson County Sports Authority
Description:
Home Stadium For: Kansas City Royals.
Permanent Seating Capacity:
40,625

KAY RODGERS PARK
4400 MIDLAND BOULEVARD
FORT SMITH, AR 72904
479-783-6176
cindy@kayrodgerspark.com
www.kayrodgerspark.org
• Rebecca, Accounting - Administration
rebecca@kayrodgerspark.com
• Cindy, Futurity - Administration
cindy@kayrodgerspark.com

KELLOGG ARENA
ONE MCCAMLY SQUARE
BATTLE CREEK, MI 49017
269-963-4800
Fax: 269-968-8840
www.kelloggarena.com
• Kevin M. Scheibler, General Manager
(269) 963-4800
kscheibler@kelloggarena.com
• Treasa Sylvester, Finance Director
(269) 963-4800
tsylvester@kelloggarena.com
• Bill Evans, Sports Promotion
• Ben Randels, Operations Manager
(269) 963-4800
brandels@kelloggarena.com
• Lindsay Lerette, Sales and Marketing Manager
(269) 963-4800
llerette@kelloggarena.com
• Jimmy Biggs, Food and Beverage Manager
(269) 963-4800
jbiggs@kelloggarena.com
Permanent Seating Capacity:
6,000

KELLY/SHORTS STADIUM
1200 FRANKLIN STREET
MT. PLEASANT, MI 48859
989-774-4000
Fax: 989-774-7957
cmsports@cmich.edu
www.cmich.edu
• Keith Voeks, Assistant Director
voeks1ke@cmich.edu
• Cal Seelye, Director, Events and Conference Services
seely1ch@cmich.edu
• Chad Garland, Assistant Director, Events and Conference Ser
(989) 774-7675
garla1ce@cmich.edu
• Emily Tritschler, Coordinator, Events and Conference Services
mcclu1es@cmich.edu
• Scott Harrington, Technical Specialist, University Events
(989) 774-3355
harri3sr@cmich.edu
• Connie Camp, SR Specialist Clerk, Bovee University Center
(989) 774-7477
highe1cl@cmich.edu
• Brittany Cornwell, Graduate Assistant, Events and Conference Ser
cornw1ba@cmich.edu
Stadium Seating Capacity:
Football - 30,000.

KENAN MEMORIAL STADIUM
78 STADIUM DRIVE
UNIVERSITY OF NORTH CAROLINA
CHAPEL HILL, NC 27514
919-962-5555
Fax: 919-966-3173
www.goheels.com
• Dick E Baddour, Athletic Director
(919) 962-6000
dbaddour@uncaa.unc.edu
• Karlton Creech, Sr. Assoc. Athletic Director/Chief of Staff
(919) 843-8432
kcreech@unc.edu
• Beth Miller, Sr. Associate Athletic Director/Senior Woman
• Paul Pogge, Assoc. Athletic Director/Risk Management

(919) 962-6000
ppogge@uncaa.unc.edu
• Larry Gallo, Exec. Associate Athletic Director
(919) 962-6000
athgallo@uncaa.unc.edu
• Molly Norton, Executive Assistant to Bubba Cunningham
(919) 962-8200
mbnorton@uncaa.unc.edu
• Kathy Griggs, Administrative Assistant
(919) 843-5834
kgriggs@uncaa.unc.edu
• Bubba Cunningham, Athletic Director
(919) 962-8200
bubba.cunningham@unc.edu
Permanent Seating Capacity:
60,000

KENT STATE UNIVERSITY ATHLETICS
PO BOX 5190
KENT, OH 44242
330-672-5974
Fax: 330-672-5978
info@kent.edu
www.kentstatesports.com
• Laing Kennedy, Director of Athletics
(330) 672-3120
lkennedy@kent.edu
• Cynthia Stone, Facilities/Operations Assistant
(303) 672-7493
cstone1@kent.edu
Stadium Seating Capacity:
30,520
Memorial Gym Capacity Seating:
6,327

KEYSPAN PARK
1904 SURF AVENUE
BROOKLYN, NY 11224
718-382-2600
Fax: 718-449-6368
info@brooklyncyclones.com
www.brooklyncyclones.com
• Rebecca Schwartz, Marketing & Entertainment Manager
rebecca@brooklyncyclones.com
• Steve cohen, General Manager
steve@brooklyncyclones.com
• Kevin Mahoney, Assistant General Manager
kevin@brooklyncyclones.com
• Gary J. Perone, Director of New Business Development
gary@brooklyncyclones.com
• Billy Harner, Director of Communications
(718) 382-2610
BHarner@BrooklynCyclones.com
• Greg Conaway, Manager, Ticket Operations
gconway@brooklyncyclones.com
• Danny Diaz, Manager, Group Sales
ddiaz@brooklyncyclones.com
• Josh Mevorach, Community Relations Manager
(718) 382-2603
JMevorach@BrooklynCyclones.com
Sport:
Baseball
Team:
Brooklyn Cyclones
Year Founded:
2001
Capacity:
8,000

KIBBIE DOME
PO BOX 442307
UNIVERSITY OF IDAHO
MOSCOW, ID 83844
208-885-7928
888-884-3246
Fax: 208-885-2862
info@uidaho.edu
www.govandals.com/
• Scott Gadeken, Head Strength &
Conditioning Coach
• Joy Francis, Assistant Manager/Kibbie
Dome
Arena Seating Capacity:
8,500
Stadium Seating Capacity:
16,500

KIDD BREWER STADIUM
111 RIVERS STREET
GEORGE M HOLMES CONVOCATION
CENTER
BOONE, NC 28608
828-262-2079
Fax: 828-262-2556
www.goasu.com
• Charlie Cobb, Athletic Director
(828) 262-4010
robinsonlk@appstate.edu
• Mike Flynn, Sports Information Director
(828) 262-2268
flynnmh@appstate.edu
• Troy Heustess, Athletics Facilities
Coordinator
(828) 262-7768
Stadium Seating Capacity:
18,000

KIMBROUGH MEMORIAL STADIUM
BUFFALO STADIUM ROAD AT I-27
CANYON, TX 79016
806-651-4400
Fax: 806-651-4409
www.gobuffsgo.com
• Ed Harris, Athletic Director
• Kent Johnson, Assoc. Dir for Event
Operations
(806) 651-4406
• Patrick O' Brien, President University
(806) 651-2100
pobrien@wtamu.edu
• Michael McBroom, Director of Intercollege
Athletics
(806) 651-4400
• David Rausch, Faculty
(806) 651-2423
drausch@wtamu.edu
• John Hasse, Ass.Director
(806) 651-2766
jhasse@wtamu.edu
• Debra Carter, Administration
(806) 651-4400
dcarter@wtamu.edu

KIRBY SPORTS CENTER
700 WEST PIERCE STREET
EASTON, PA 18042
610-330-5470
Fax: 610-230-5702
www.goleopards.com
• Bruce McCutcheon, Director of Athletics
(610) 330-5470
mccutchb@lafayette.edu
Arena Seating Capacity:
3,500

KNIGHTS STADIUM
2280 DEERFIELD DRIVE
FORT MILL, SC 29715
704-357-8071
Fax: 704-329-2155
charlotteknights@charlotteknights.com
www.charlotteknights.com
• Mike Riviello, Director of Marketing &
Advertising
miker@charlotteknights.com
• Kelly Crawford, Ticket Office Coordinator
• Sean Owens, Group Sales Director/Ticket
Operations
• Dan Rajkowski, Executive Vice President,
Chief Operating Off
danr@charlotteknights.com
• Chris Semmens, Vice President of Sales
chriss@charlotteknights.com
• Mark Smith, Vice President of Marketing
marks@charlotteknights.com
• Julie Clark, Director of Special Programs &
Events
juliec@charlotteknights.com
• Sean Owens, Director of Ticket Sales &
Hospitality
• Matt Millward, Director of Ticket
Operations
mattm@charlotteknights.com
Stadium Seating Capacity:
10,002.00
Nature of Service:
Baseball Entertainment.

KNOLOGY PARK
373 DOUGLAS AVENUE
#A
DUNEDIN, FL 34698
727-733-9302
Fax: 727-734-7661
shelby.nelson@bluejays.com
www.dunedinbluejays.com
• Janette Donoghue, Assistant General
Manager
(727) 738-7019
ken.carson@bluejays.com
• Shelby Nelson, Director and General
Manager
(727) 738-7020
shelby.nelson@bluejays.com
• Gayle Gentry, Accounting Manager
(727) 738-7002
gayle.gentry@bluejays.com
Sport:
Baseball.
Team:
Dunedin Blue Jays baseball.
Year Founded:
1990
Capacity:
6,106

**KNOXVILLE CIVIC
AUDITORIUM/COLISEUM**
500 HOWARD BAKER JR AVENUE
PO BOX 2603
KNOXVILLE, TN 37915
865-215-8900
Fax: 865-215-8989
www.knoxvillecoliseum.com
• Dale Dunn, General Manager
(865) 215-1454
ddunn@cityofknoxville.org
• Robbie Sandoval, Assistant General
Manager / Booking
(865) 215-8911
rsandoval@cityofknoxville.org
• Greg Mackay, Director of Public Facilities

(865) 215-1454
gmackay@cityofknoxville.org
• Dale Dunn, General Manager
(865) 215-8910
ddunn@cityofknoxville.org
• Doug Simmons, Operations Manager
(865) 215-8931
dsimmons@cityofknoxville.org
• Elizabeth Morrow, Box Office Manager
(865) 215-8922
• Salina Garrett, Financial Analyst
(865) 215-8913
• Jamie Cunningham, Executive Secretary
(865) 215-8914
jacunningham@cityofknoxville.org
Arena Seating Capacity:
7,000

KNUTE NELSON MEMORIAL FIELD
503 5TH AVENUE W
ALEXANDRIA, MN 56308
320-763-8151
Fax: 320-763-8152
• Shawn Reilly, Owner
(320) 763-8151
• Mitch Kluver, Assistant General Manager
(320) 763-8151
Sport:
Baseball
Tenant(s):
Alexandria Beetles baseball
Year Founded:
1939, Renovated 1967
Capacity:
1,500

KOHL CENTER
601 W DAYTON STREET
UNIVERSITY OF WISCONSIN
MADISON, WI 53715
608-263-5645
866-788-2482
Fax: 608-265-4700
webmaster@uwbadgers.com
www.uwbadgers.com
• Zach Wagne, General Manager
• Ryan Sedevie, Assistant Director of
Marketing & Promotions
• Barry Alvarez, Administration Director of
Athletics
(608) 262-1866
• Michael Cerniglia, Administration Assistant
To The Athletic Dire
(608) 262-0147
• Sean Frazier, Administration Deputy
Athletic Director
(608) 890-2017
Tenant(s):
NCAA - University of Wisconsin athletics.
Seating Capacity:
17,230

KYLE FIELD
WELBORN ROAD
TEXAS A&M UNIVERSITY
KOLDUS BLDG
COLLEGE STATION, TX 77843
979-845-5129
Fax: 979-845-6825
webmaster@tamu.edu
www.tamu.edu
• Antonio Cepeda-Benito, Associate Dean of
Faculties
(979) 845-5129
bbyrne@athletics.tamu.edu
• Eddie J. Davis, Interim President

Arena Seating Capacity:
82,600.00
Year Founded:
1927

L.P. FRANS STADIUM
2500 CLEMENT BOULEVARD NW
HICKORY, NC 28601
828-322-3000
Fax: 828-322-6137
crawdad@hickorycrawdads.com
www.hickorycrawdads.com
• Mark Seaman, General Manager
(828) 322-3000
mseaman@hickorycrawdads.com
• Charlie Downs, Assistant General
Manager of Operations
cdowns@hickorycrawdads.com
Team:
Hickory Crawdads
Year Founded:
1993
Seating Capacity:
5,062

LA CROSSE CENTER
300 HARBORVIEW PLAZA
LA CROSSE, WI 54601
608-789-7400
Fax: 608-789-7444
office@lacrossecenter.com
www.lacrossecenter.com
• Art Fahey, Director
(608) 789-7413
afahey@lacrossecenter.com
• Sue Weiman, Business Manager
• Mike Ferris, Sales Representative
• Sue Wieman, Business Manager
(608) 789-7411
swieman@lacrossecenter.com
• Dave Guepfer, Food and Beverage
Manager
(608) 789-7428
dguepfer@lacrossecenter.com
• Nikki Kimpton, Box Office Supervisor
(608) 789-7426
nkimpton@lacrossecenter.com
• Dave Follansbee, Assistant Food and
Beverage Supervisor
(608) 789-7428
dfollansbee@lacrossecenter.com
• Thao Moua, Accountant/Bookkeeper
(608) 789-7449
Arena Seating Capacity:
8,000

LACKAWANNA COUNTY STADIUM
235 MONTAGE MOUNTAIN ROAD
MOOSIC, PA 18507
570-969-2255
Fax: 570-963-6564
www.lackawannacounty.org
• Jeremy Ruby, General Manager/Red
Barons
(570) 969-2255
• Ann Ma Nocera, Director/Ticket
Operations
• Curt Camoni, Director/Stadium Operations
(570) 969-2255
Sport:
Baseball
Team:
Scranton Wilkes-Barre Red Barons
Year Founded:
1989
Capacity:
10,800

LADD PEEBLES STADIUM
1621 VIRGINIA STREET
PO BOX 66721
MOBILE, AL 36604
251-208-2500
Fax: 251-208-2514
www.laddpeeblesstadium.com
• Paul Christopher, Manager
• Allen Chapman, Director
allen.chapman@hubinternational.com
• Ann Davis, Director
• Richard Davis, Director
davis230@bellsouth.net
• Clyde Dumas, Director
clydedumas@comcast.net
• Thelma Cooke Thrash, Director
thelmathrash@aol.com
• David Wilhelm, Director
• Randy Gould, Chairman
lq6070gm@laquinta.com
Stadium Seating Capacity:
41,000
Team:
Southern Alabama football, Senior and
GMAC Bowls.

LAFAYETE COLLEGE
PIERCE & HAMILTON STREETS
KIRBY SPORTS CENTER
EASTON, PA 18042
610-330-5470
Fax: 610-330-5702
www.goleopards.com
• Bruce McCutcheon, Director of Athletics
mccutchb@lafayette.edu
• George Bright, Associate Director Of
Athletics
brightg@lafayette.edu
Field Seating Capacity:
13,745

LAKE ELSINORE STORM
500 DIAMOND DRIVE
LAKE ELSINORE, CA 92530
951-245-4487
Fax: 951-245-0305
info@stormbaseball.com
www.stormbaseball.com
• Bruce Kessman, VP/Director/Stadium
Operations
• Jake Burch, Assistant Director/Stadium
Operations
• Gary Jacobs, Owner
• Len Simon, Owner
• Dave Oster, President
doster@stormbaseball.com
• Chris Jones, Chris Jones VP/General
Manager
• Tracy Kessman, Assistant General
Manager
• Kasey Rawitzer, Account Executive
krawitzer@stormbaseball.com
Sport:
Baseball
Tenant(s):
Lake Elsinore Storm baseball
Year Founded:
1994
Capacity:
7,866

LAKE OLMSTEAD STADIUM
78 MILLEDGE ROAD
AUGUSTA, GA 30904
706-736-7889
Fax: 706-736-1122

info@greenjacketsbaseball.com
www.greenjacketsbaseball.com
• Tom Denlinger, General Manager
tdenlinger@greenjacketsbaseball.com
• Brandon Greene, Assistant General
Manager
bgreene@greenjacketsbaseball.com
• Billy Nowak, Supervisor, Stadium
Operations
bnowak@greenjacketsbaseball.com
Year Founded:
1988
Capacity:
4,800
Nature of Service:
Minor league baseball facility.

LAKELAND CENTER
701 W LIME STREET
LAKELAND, FL 33815
863-834-8100
800-200-4870
Fax: 863-834-8101
tlcclientservices@lakelandgov.net
www.thelakelandcenter.com
• Mike LaPan, Executive Director
(863) 834-8133
mike.lapan@lakelandgov.net
• Scott Sloman, Assistant Director
(863) 834-8144
scott.sloman@lakelandgov.net
• Tim Holloway, Client Services Manager
• Scott Sloman, Assistant Director/Booking
Director
(863) 834-8144
• Lori Powell, Director of Sales
(863) 834-6116
• Lisa Parker, Sales Administrative Assistant
(863) 834-5110
• Lindsay Hansen, Executive Administrative
Assistant
(863) 834-8145
• Jennifer Clark, Box Office Manager
(863) 834-8136
• Shirley Greife, Assistant Box Office
Manager
(863) 834-8121
Owned by:
City of Lakeland.
Arena Seating Capacity:
10,000

LAKELAND CENTER, THE
701 W LIME STREET
THE LAKELAND CENTER
LAKELAND, FL 33815
863-834-8100
800-200-4870
Fax: 863-834-8125
tlcinfo@lakelandgov.net
www.thelakelandcenter.com
• Mike LaPan, Executive Director
(863) 834-8133
• Scott Sloman, Assistant Director
• John Oney, Director of Sales
John.Oney@lakelandgov.net
• Jason Refermat, Director Of Markering
Jason.refermat@lakelandgov.net
• Jennifer Clark, Box Office Manager
Jennifer.Clark@lakelandgov.net
• Allison Jones, Director Of Event Services
Allison.Jones@lakelandgov.net
• Steven Collazo, Director Of Event
Services
Steven.Collazo@lakelandgov.net
Description:
The Lakeland Center is multi-purpose
entertainment complex featuring the 10,000

facilities

seat Jenkins Arena, 2,300 seat Youkey Theatre and 100,000 square feet of meeting and exhibition space.
Arena Seating Capacity:
10,000 - Jenkins Arena. 2,300 - Youkey Theatre

LAKEVIEW ARENA
300 WEST BARAGA AVE.
MARQUETTE, MI 49855
906-228-0490
Fax: 906-228-0493
www.mqtcty.org
• Leslie Hugh, Parks/Recreation Director
Permanent Seating Capacity:
3,500

LAKEWOOD BLUECLAWS
2 STADIUM WAY
LAKEWOOD, NJ 8701
732-901-7000
Fax: 732-901-3967
lakewood.blueclaws.milb.com
• Rich Mozingo, Assistant General Manager
(732) 901-7000
• Brandon Marano, General Manager
(732) 901-7000
• Joe Harrington, Assistant General Manager of Ticket Sales
(732) 901-7000
• Amy DeMichele, Marketing Manager
(732) 901-7000
• Andrew Gilberti, Ticket Sales Manager
(732) 901-7000
• Annmarie Clifford, Ticket Sales Manager
(732) 901-7000
Clients:
Lakewood BlueClaws (Professional Baseball)
Nature of Service:
Single-A Affiliate of the Philadelphia Phillies

LAMBEAU FIELD
1265 LOMBARDI AVENUE
GREEN BAY, WI 54304
920-569-7500
Fax: 920-569-7301
www.packers.com
• Ted Eisenreich, Packers Director of Facility Operations
• Tim Connolly, Packers VP Sales/Marketing
• Jim Boettcher, Director of Operations-Levy Restaurants
• Larry L. Weyers, Vice President and Lead Director
• Mark H. Murphy, President
• Daniel T. Ariens, Secretary
• Mark J. McMullen, Treasurer
Owned by:
City of Green Bay
Tenant(s):
NFL - Green Bay Packers football
Permanent Seating Capacity:
73,128; 166 Private Suites; 6,000 Club Seats

LANE STADIUM/WORSHAM FIELD
122 LANE STADIUM - WEST SIDE
VIRGINIA TECH (0502)
BLACKSBURG, VA 24061
540-231-6796
800-828-3244
Fax: 540-231-3060
hokipoki@vt.edu
www.hokiesports.com

• Jim Weaver, Director Athletics
(540) 231-3977
jim.weaver@vt.edu
• Kent Sheets, Facilities Manager
(540) 231-2199
ksheets@vt.edu
• Tim East, Associate Director of Athletics for External
(540) 231-6600
easttim@vt.edu
• Tom Gabbard, Associate Director of Athletics for Internal
(540) 231-6265
tgabbard@vt.edu
• Mike Gentry, Associate Director of Athletics for Athletic
(540) 231-2984
gentrym@vt.edu
• Mike Goforth, Associate Director of Athletics for Sports Me
(540) 231-6410
ab8631@vt.edu
• Tom Gabbard, Assoc. Director of Athletics, Internal Affair
(540) 231-6265
tgabbard@vt.edu
Stadium Seating Capacity:
66,000
Team:
Virginia Tech football.

LANGLEY EVENTS CENTRE
7888 200 STREET
LANGLEY, BC, CANADA V2Y 3J4
604-882-8800
www.langleyeventscentre.com
Opened:
2009
Tenant(s):
Vancouver Giants (WHL)

LANTZ ARENA
2024 LANTZ ARENA
CHARLESTON, IL 61920
217-581-6408
Fax: 217-581-7001
bvrettberg@eiu.edu
www.eiu.edu
• Rich D McDuffie, Director Athletics
• Rodger D Jehlicka, Associate Athletic Director
Arena Seating Capacity:
5,200

LAS VEGAS CONVENTION & VISITOR'S AUTHORITY
3150 PARADISE ROAD
LAS VEGAS, NV 89109
702-892-0711
877-847-4858
Fax: 702-386-7126
www.lvcva.com
• Vince Alberta, APR, Vice President of Public Affairs
(702) 892-7663
PR@lvcva.com
• Joey Campbell, Business Marketing Manager
(702) 892-7638
• Dawn Christensen, Director of Communications
(702) 892-2984
• Jeremy Handel, Senior Manager, Public Affairs
(702) 892-7640
jhandel@lvcva.com
• Courtney Fitzgerald, Public Relations

Manager - Leisure
(702) 892-7686
cfitzgerald@lvcva.com
• Lisa Jacob, Senior Manager, Las Vegas News Bureau
(702) 892-7641
ljacob@lvcva.com
• Jesse Davis, APR, Director, International Public Relations
(702) 892-7655
Stadium Seating Capacity:
9,370

LAVELL EDWARDS STADIUM
A-41 ASB
Brigham Young University
PROVO, UT 84602
801-422-4636
Fax: 801-422-0806
marriottcenter@byu.edu
home.byu.edu
• Larry R Duffin, Director
• David Miles, Assistant Director- Booking
Stadium Seating Capacity:
65,000
Team:
Brigham Young University football.

LAWLOR EVENTS CENTER
1500 N VIRGINIA STREET
MAIL STOP 230
LEGACY HALL/MS-264
RENO, NV 89557
775-784-4659
Fax: 775-784-4428
lawlorinfo@yahoo.com
www.unr.edu/lawlor
• Chris Orheim, Facilities/Events
(775) 784-6900
corheim@unr.edu
• Jeff Rabedeaux, Facilities Coordinator
(775) 784-6900
Arena Seating Capacity:
12,400

LAWRENCE A. WIEN STADIUM
411 W 116 STREET
MAIL CODE 1902
NEW YORK, NY 10027
212-854-2538
Fax: 212-854-2988
www.columbia.edu
• Patrick Desir, Manager of Facilities Operations
(212) 854-3441
pd2227@columbia.edu
• Mark Monty, Director of Athletics Department
(212) 851-7458
Stadium Seating Capacity:
3,405

LAWRENCE JOEL VETERANS MEMORIAL COLISEUM
2825 UNIVERSITY PARKWAY
WINSTON-SALEM ENTERTAINMENT SPORTS COMPLEX
WINSTON-SALEM, NC 27105
336-758-2410
Fax: 336-727-2922
jeff.salisbury@img.com
www.ljvm.com
• Benjamin Dame, Complex Director
(336) 725-5635
bdame@ljvm.com
• Charlie R Vestal, Assistant Director Event Services

(336) 725-5635
cvestal@ljvm.com
• Benjamin P Dame, Director, Public
Assembly Facilities
(336) 725-5635
• Dewey Williard, Finance Director
(336) 725-5635
• Chuck Webster, Complex Marketing
Director
(336) 725-5635
• Brian Day, Operations Director
(336) 725-5635
• David Sparks, Dixie Classic Fair Director
(336) 725-5635
• Brian Candler, General Manager Aramark
Sports & Entertainmen
(336) 725-5635
• Leigha Cordell, Event Sales Coordinator
(336) 725-5635
Arena Seating Capacity:
15,290
Tenant(s):
NCAA - Wake Forest University basketball,
SEHL - Winston-Salem Moosehead ice
hockey

LAWRENCE-DUMONT STADIUM
300 S SYCAMORE STREET
WICHITA, KS 67213
316-264-6887
Fax: 316-264-2129
www.wichitawingnuts.com
• Robertson Josh, Asst. GM/Director,
Stadium/Baseball Operations
• David Poppleton, Assistant
Stadium/Baseball Operations

LEE ARENA
1700 SW COLLEGE AVENUE
TOPEKA, KS 66621
785-670-1010
Fax: 785-670-1028
webmaster@washburn.edu
www.washburn.edu
• Loren Ferre, Athletic Director
(785) 670-1794
loren.ferre@washburn.edu
• Gilbert Herrera, Facilities Manager
• Loren Ferre, Director Athletics
• Gene Cassell, Director Sports Information
Stadium Seating Capacity:
3,818

LEE CIVIC CENTER
11831 BAYSHORE ROAD
N FORT MYERS, FL 33917
239-543-8368
Fax: 239-543-4110
swffair@leeciviccenter.com
www.leeciviccenter.com
• Alta Mosley, General Manager
• Simon Train, Operations Manager
• Al Bertoni, Concessions Manager
Arena Seating Capacity:
8,000

LEGION FIELD STADIUM
400 GRAYMONT AVENUE W
BIRMINGHAM, AL 35204-4008
205-254-2391
Fax: 205-254-2515
wegarre@ci.birmingham.al.us
• Melvin Miller, Stadium Manager
melvin.miller@birminghamal.gov
Seating Capacity:
71.594
Team:

University of Alabama football; Papa Johns
Bowl.

LEGION STADIUM COMPLEX
302 WILLARD STREET
WILMINGTON, NC 28401
910-341-7855
Fax: 910-341-7854
amy.beatty@wilmingtonnc.gov
www.wilmingtonnc.gov
• Marian Doherty, Manager
(910) 341-3237
marian.doherty@wilmingtonnc.gov
• Amy Beatty, Concessions & Facilities
(910) 341-4604
amy.beatty@wilmingtonnc.gov
Stadium Seating Capacity:
6,500

LELACHEUR PARK
450 AIKEN STREET
LOWELL, MA 01854
978-459-2255
Fax: 978-459-1674
info@lowellspinners.com
www.lowellspinners.com
• Drew Weber, Owner & CEO
• Tim Bawmann, President & General
Manager
• Jon Healy, Vice President, Ticket
Operations
• Jeff Cohen, Director of Merchandising
• Gareth Markey, Vice President, Facilities
Sport:
Baseball
Tenant(s):
Lowell Spinners baseball
Year Founded:
1998
Capacity:
5,030

LEWIS AND CLARK PARK
3400 LINE DRIVE
SIOUX CITY, IA 51106
712-277-9467
Fax: 712-277-9406
www.xsbaseball.com
• Ashley Schoenrock, Director of Ticket
Sales
• Shane Tritz, General Manager
tritz@xsbaseball.com
• Luke Nielsen, Assistant General Manager
• Shane Tritz, General Manager
(712) 277-9467
tritz@xsbaseball.com
• Ashley Schoenrock, Assistant General
Manager
(712) 277-9467
• Dave Nitz, Director of Broadcasting
d_nitz@hotmail.com
• Julie Stinger, Office Manager
Team:
Sioux City Explorers
Year Founded:
1993
Sport:
Baseball
Seating Capacity:
3,650

LIACOURAS CENTER
1776 N BROAD STREET
PHILADELPHIA, PA 19121
215-204-2400
800-298-4200

Fax: 215-204-2405
www.liacourascenter.com
• Fran Rodowicz, Regional Vice President
(215) 204-2401
• James Grafstrom, Assistant General
Manager
(215) 204-2407
• Scott Walcoff, Marketing Manager
(215) 204-2403
Arena Seating Capacity:
10,200
Year Founded:
1997
Nature of Service:
Multi-purpose arena
Tenant(s):
Temple University Basketball

LIBERTY BOWL MEMORIAL STADIUM
335 S HOLLYWOOD STREET
MEMPHIS, TN 38104
901-729-4344
Fax: 901-678-4134
www.libertybowl.org
• Patti Shannon, Chairman of the Board
• Ray Pohlman, President
• Billy Hicks, Jr, Vice President
• Steve Ehrhart, Executive Director
sehrhart@libertybowl.org
• Perry Winstead, Chief Financial Officer
perry.winstead@ldcom.com
• Patrick Byrne, Director of Sales and
Marketing
Patrick.byrne@libertybowl.org
• Kevin Alexander, Operations Manager
kevin.alexander@libertybowl.org
Seating Capacity
62,384
Team:
Memphis Tigers football.

LINCOLN FINANCIAL FIELD
ONE NOVACARE WAY
PHILADELPHIA, PA 19145
215-463-2500
Contact@lincolnfinancialfield.com
www.lincolnfinancialfield.com
Seating Capacity
68,532
Tenants
NFL - Philadelphia Eagles football; NCAA -
Temple University football

LINCOLN PARK STOCKER STADIUM
250 N 5TH STREET
GRAND JUNCTION, CO 81501
970-244-1542
Fax: 970-242-1637
Seating Capacity
5,500
Seating Capacity:
Suplizio Field: 6600

LINDBORG-CREGG FIELD
700 CREGG LANE
MISSOULA, MT 59801
406-543-3300
Fax: 406-543-9463
info@missoulaosprey.com
www.missoulaosprey.com
• Jared Amoss, General Manager Ogren
Park Allegiance Field
• Mike Ellis, Executive Vice President
mellis@missoulaosprey.com
• Jeff Griffin, Vice President/General
Manager
jgriffin@missoulaosprey.com

• Jared Amoss, General Manager-Operations
jamoss@missoulaosprey.com
• Kim Johns, Retail Manager
kimj@missoulaosprey.com
• Grant Warner, Sales Assistant/Account Executive
gwarner@missoulaosprey.com
• Nola Hunter, Office Manager
nhunter@missoulaosprey.com
Sport
Baseball
Team:
Missoula Osprey
Year Founded:
1999
Seating Capacity
2,200

LINDQUIST FIELD
2330 LINCOLN AVENUE
OGDEN, UT 84401
801-393-2400
Fax: 801-393-2473
• Kenny Kppinski, Head Groundskeeper
(864) 656-2308
butch@clemson.edu
• Dave Baggott, President
• Damon Berryhill, Manager
• Doug Mientkiewicz, Hitting Coach
• Bill Simas, Pitching Coach
Seating Capacity
5,000
Sport
Baseball
Team:
Ogden Raptors
Year Founded:
1997

LISTON B. RAMSEY REGIONAL ACTIVITY CENTER
92 CATAMOUNT ROAD
WESTERN CAROLINA UNIVERSITY
CULLOWHEE, NC 28723
828-227-7677
828-227-7677
www.wcu.edu/ramsey/
• Laura Huff, Director of Marketing
• Debbie Hyatt, Box office manager
dhyatt@wcu.edu
• Ryan Fisher, Assistant director of operations
jrfisher@wcu.edu
• Bill Clarke, Director
clarke@wcu.edu
Arena Seating Capacity:
8,100

LLOYD NOBLE CENTER
660 PARRINGTON OVAL
NORMAN, OK 73019-0390
405-325-0311
Fax: 405-325-4583
lnc@ou.edu
www.ou.edu
• Kenny Gajewski, Athletic Facilities
• Greg Smith, Athletic Facilities
• David L. Boren, President
• Kevin McIntyre, Director of Operations
• Loida Haffener-Salmond, Director of Events
Seating Capacity
12,000
Sports Organization
Division 1 arena hosting University of Oklahoma Men's and Women's Basketball,

Women's Gymnastics, Graduations, Concerts and any other large event.

LOANMART FIELD
8408 ROCHESTER AVENUE
RANCHO CUCAMONGA, CA 91730
909-481-5000
Fax: 909-481-5005
info@rcquakes.com
www.rcquakes.com
• Brent Miles, President
(909) 481-5000
info@rcquakes.com
• Grant Riddle, Vice President, General Manager
Sport:
Baseball
Team:
Rancho Cucamonga Quakes
Year Founded:
1993
Capacity:
6,588

LOS ANGELES MEMORIAL COLISEUM SPORTS ARENA/STADIUM
3939 S FIGUEROA STREET
LOS ANGELES, CA 90037
213-747-7111
www.lacoliseum.com
• Pat Lynch, General Manager
(213) 265-6317
• Harold Zoubul, General Manager Food/Beverage
(213) 765-6380
• Yrene Asalde, Event Manager
(213) 765-6362
yasalde@lacoliseum.com
• Jonathan Lee, Director Of Marketing, Filmings Manager
(213) 765-6357
jlee@lacoliseum.com
Seating Capacity
93,607
Seating Capacity
16,500

LOS ANGELES TENNIS CENTER
420 CHARLES E YOUNG DRIVE WEST
LOS ANGELES, CA 90095
310-825-4546
www.recreation.ucla.edu

LOUIS BROWN ALTHETIC CENTER
83 ROCKAFELLER ROAD
PISCATAWAY, NJ 8854
732-445-4220
Fax: 732-445-2752
www.scarletknights.com
• Robert E Mulcahy, Athletic Director
(732) 445-8610
Seating Capacity
8,400

LOUISIANA SUPERDOME
SUGAR BOWL DRIVE
NEW ORLEANS, LA 70112
504-587-3663
800-756-7074
Fax: 504-587-3848
ada@superdome.com
www.superdome.com
• Doug Thornton, General Manager
• Danny Vincens, Assistant General Manager
• David Weidler, Director

Finance/Administration
• Bill Curl, Director Public Relations
Owned by:
State of Louisiana
Description:
NFL - New Orleans Saints football, NCAA - Tulane University football
Seating Capacity
72,000

LOUISVILLE METRO HALL
601 W JEFFERSON ST.
LOUISVILLE, KY 40202
502-574-3521
Fax: 502-574-0065
• Alvin Hampton, Sales/Marketing Director
Mary Helen Byck Arena Seating Capacity:
6,850

LOUISVILLE SLUGGER FIELD
401 E MAIN STREET
LOUISVILLE, KY 40202
502-212-2287
Fax: 502-515-2255
www.batsbaseball.com
• James Breeding, Director Ticket Sales
jbreeding@batsbaseball.com
• Scott Shoemaker, Director Stadium Operations
sshoemaker@batsbaseball.com
• Gary Ulmer, President/CEO
gulmer@batsbaseball.com
• Dale Owens, Sr. Vice President of Corporate Sales
dowens@batsbaseball.com
• Greg Galiette, Sr. Vice President of Marketing
ggaliette@batsbaseball.com
• Scott Shoemaker, Vice President of Operations & Technology
sshoemaker@batsbaseball.com
• James Breeding, Vice President of Business Operations
jbreeding@batsbaseball.com
• Michele Anderson, Controller
manderson@batsbaseball.com
Sport
Baseball
Tenants
Lousville Bats baseball
Year Founded:
2000
Seating Capacity
13,131

LP FIELD
460 GREAT CIRCLE ROAD
NASHVILLE, TN 37228
615-565-4000
Fax: 615-565-4175
www.titansonline.com
• Mike Reinfeldt, Executive Vice President and General Manager
• Dempsey Henderson, Facilities Manager
• K.S. Adams, Jr., Founder, Owner, Chairman of the Board, Presid
• Don MacLachlan, Executive Vice President of Administration an
• Ruston Webster, Executive Vice President/General Manager
• Elza Bullock, Senior Vice President and General Counsel
• Lake Dawson, Vice President of Player Personnel
• Bob Hyde, Vice President of Community Relations
• Jenneen Kaufman, Vice President/CFO

Tenant(s):
NFL - Tennessee Titans football.
Stadium Seating Capacity:
68,804

LT SMITH STADIUM
1 BIG RED WAY
WESTERN KENTUCKY UNIVERSITY
BOWLING GREEN, KY 42101
270-745-6062
Fax: 270-745-6187
pam.herriford@wku.edu
www.wkusports.com
• Camden Wood Selig, Athletic Director
(270) 745-5276
• Craig Biggs, Associate Athletics Director
(270) 745-5729
craig.biggs@wku.edu
• Jim Clark, Associate Athletics Director
(270) 745-5321
jim.clark@wku.edu
• Todd Stewart, Director of Athletics
(270) 745-5276
todd.stewart@wku.edu
• Lindsay Boyden, Assistant AD (Marketing)
(270) 745-6562
• Debbie Carroll, Business Operations
Specialist
(270) 745-5038
debbie.carroll@wku.edu
Stadium Seating Capacity:
17,000

LUCAS OIL STADIUM
500 S CAPITOL AVENUE
INDIANAPOLIS, IN 46225-1117
317-262-8600
Fax: 317-262-5757
losinfo@icclos.com
www.lucasoilstadium.com
• Barney Levengood, Executive Director
(317) 262-3400
• Eric Neuburger, Stadium Director
(317) 262-8600
Seating Capacity:
Football 63,000; Basketball, Conventions,
Concerts, Superbowl, etc 70,000
Tenants:
Indianapolis Colts
Owned by:
Indiana Stadium and Convention Building
Authority (ISCBA) but leased and operated
byt the Capital Improvement Board of
Managers of Marion County (CIB).
Nature of Service:
Large Sports and Convention Arena.
Year Founded:
2008

LYNCHBURG CITY STADIUM
3180 FORT AVENUE
LYNCHBURG, VA 24501
434-528-1144
Fax: 434-846-0768
info@lynchburg-hillcats.com
www.lynchburg-hillcats.com
• Bonnie Roberts, Assistant General
Manager/Hillcats
(434) 528-1144
rroberts@lynchburg-hillcats.com
• Darren Johnson, Director of Sales
djohnson@lynchburg-hillcats.com
• Brad Goodale, Director of Group Sales
bgoodale@lynchburg-hillcats.com
• Erik Wilson, Director of Broadcasting
• Ashley Stephenson, Director of
Promotions

astephenson@lynchburg-hillcats.com
• John Hutt, Director of Ticketing
jhutt@lynchburg-hillcats.com
• Paul Sunwall, General Manager
psunwall@lynchburg-hillcats.com
• Rex Angel, President
Sport
Baseball
Team:
Lynchburg Hillcats
Year Founded:
1940
Seating Capacity
4,000
Description:
Minor League professional baseball team,
member of the Class A Advanced Carolina
League.

M.M. ROBERTS STADIUM
118 COLLEGE DRIVE
HATTIESBURG, MS 39406
601-266-5017
www.southernmiss.com
• Bill McGillis, Director of Athletics
• Tim Atkinson, Assistant Athletic Director
(601) 266-5025
• Jay Hopson, Head Coach, Football
(601) 266-4567
Team:
Southern Miss Golden Eagles
Seating Capacity:
36,000

MABEE CENTER ARENA
7777 S LEWIS AVENUE
TULSA, OK 74171
918-495-6400
Fax: 918-495-6478
www.mabeecenter.com
• Tony Winters, General Manager
(918) 495-6404
twinters@oru.edu
• Vick Barker, Operations Director
(918) 495-6406
vbarker@oru.edu
• James D. Smith, Director of Marketing &
Business Development
jasmith@oru.edu
Seating Capacity
11,763

MACKAY STADIUM
RENO, NV
Fax: 775-784-4497
www.nevadawolfpack.com/facilities/mackay-
stadium.html
Seating Capacity:
30,000

MACKEY ARENA
900 JOHN R. WOODEN DRIVE
WEST LAFAYETTE, IN 47907
765-494-3194
800-497-7678
Fax: 765-494-5447
www.purduesports.com
• Steve Simmerman, Snr. Associate
Athletics Director - Facilities
(765) 494-3143
simmerman@purdue.edu
• Paul Horsley, Operations Superintendent
(765) 494-6773
phorsley@purdue.edu
Seating Capacity:
14,264

MADISON SQUARE GARDEN
4 PENNSYLVANIA PLAZA
NEW YORK, NY 10001
212-465-6741
msgfeedback@msg.com
www.thegarden.com
• Dolan L James, Executive Chairman
• Hank Ratner, President, Chief Executive
Officer
• Lawrence Burian, EVP, General Counsel,
Secretary
• Steve Collins, Executive VP Facilities
• Robert Pollichino, Executive Vice
President, Chief Financial Officer
• Barry Watkins, Executive Vice President of
Communications
Seating Capacity:
18,200
Home Arena for:
New York Knicks, New York Rangers, New
York Liberty.

MAGNOLIA FIELD
MISSISSIPPI VALLEY STATE
UNIVERSITY, DEPT. OF ATHLETICS
14000 HIGHWAY 82 WEST
BOX 7246
ITTA BENA, MS 38941
662-254-3550
Fax: 662-254-3639
www.mvsusports.com
• Dianthia Ford-Kee, Director of Athletics
(662) 254-3550
• Lee Smith, Associate Athletic Director &
Head Coach, Softball
(662) 254-3721
• Aaron Stevens, Head Coach, Baseball

MANNING FIELD AT JOHN L. GUIDRY STADIUM
906 EAST 1ST STREET
THIBODAUX, LA 70310
www.geauxcolonels.com
• Rob Bernardi, Director of Athletics
• Tim Rebowe, Head Coach, Football
Team:
Nicholls State Colonels
Seating Capacity:
10,500

MAPFRE STADIUM
ONE BLACK & GOLD BOULEVARD
COLUMBUS, OH 43211-2091
614-447-2739
Fax: 614-447-4109
mapfrestadium.com
• Dan Lolli, Director of Stadium Operations
• Meredith Ley, Stadium Operations
Manager
mley@columbuscrewsc.com
• Jordan Enke, Director of Facilities
jenke@columbuscrewsc.com
Stadium Seating Capacity:
19,968
Tenant(s):
MLS - Columbus Crew soccer.

MARIUCCI ARENA
1901 4TH STREET SE
MINNEAPOLIS, MN 55455
612-625-8365
Fax: 612-624-5887
www.gophersports.com
• Beth Goetz, Interim Director of Athletics
• Don Lucia, Head Coach, Men's Hockey
• Brad Frost, Head Coach, Women's
Hockey

Seating Capacity:
9,800

MARRIOTT CENTER
500 E UNIVERSITY PARKWAY
PROVO, UT 84602
801-422-2981
byucougars.com/facilities/basketball
• Tom Holmoe, Director of Athletics
(801) 422-1508
• Dave Rose, Head Coach, Men's
Basketball
(801) 422-3612
• Jeff Judkins, Head Coach, Women's
Basketball
(801) 422-1265
Seating Capacity:
20,900

MARYLAND STADIUM
90 STADIUM DRIVE
UNIVERSITY OF MARYLAND
COLLEGE PARK, MD 20742
301-314-7070
www.umterps.com/facilities
• Kevin Anderson, Director of Athletics
(301) 314-7075
dorourke@umd.edu
• Joshua Kaplan, Associate AD, Facilities
Operations & Events
(301) 314-9729
jkap@umd.edu
• P.J. Ellis, Director of Grounds
(301) 314-7383
pellis@umd.edu
Seating Capacity:
51,802
Teams:
University of Maryland football.

MARYVALE BASEBALL PARK
3600 N 51ST AVENUE
PHOENIX, AZ 85031
623-245-5500
www.mlb.com/springtraining
Description:
Spring training home of the Milwaukee
Brewers.
Seating Capacity:
10,000

MATTHEW KNIGHT ARENA
1390 VILLARD STREET
EUGENE, OR 97403
541-346-4461
800-932-3668
www.goducks.com
• Rob Mullens, Athletic Director
Seating Capacity:
12,364

MATTHEWS ARENA
238 ST. BOTOLPH STREET
BOSTON, MA 02115
617-373-2691
www.gonu.com
• Peter Roby, Athletic Director
• Jim Madigan, Head Coach, Men's Hockey
• Dave Flint, Head Coach, Women's Hockey
• Bill Coen, Head Coach, Men's Basketball
• Kelly Cole, Head Coach, Women's
Basketball
Seating Capacity:
6,000

MAVERICK STADIUM
1307 W MITCHELL STREET
ARLINGTON, TX 76019-0079
817-272-2033
Fax: 817-272-2922
www.uta.edu/maverickstadium
• Tom Kloza, Stadium Director
Seating Capacity:
12,500

MCCARTHY STADIUM
1900 W OLNEY AVENUE
PHILADELPHIA, PA 19141
www.goexplorers.com
• Bill Bradshaw, Interim Director of Athletics
(215) 951-1425
• Pat Farrell, Head Coach, Men's Soccer
(215) 951-1993
• Paul Royal, Head Coach, Women's
Soccer
(215) 951-1523
• Candace Taglianetti Bossell, Head Coach,
Women's Lacrosse
(215) 951-1994
Seating Capacity:
7,500

MCCORMICK FIELD
30 BUCHANAN PLACE
ASHEVILLE, NC 28801
828-258-0428
Fax: 828-258-0320
asheville.tourists.milb.com/index.jsp?sid=t57
3
• Brian DeWine, President
• Larry Hawkins, General Manager
• Brandon Reeves, Director, Stadium
Operations
Sport:
Baseball
Team:
Asheville Tourists
Year Founded:
1992
Seating Capacity:
4,100

MCCOY STADIUM
1 COLUMBUS AVENUE
PAWTUCKET, RI 02860
401-724-7300
Fax: 401-724-2140
info@pawsox.com
www.milb.com/index.jsp?sid=t533
• Charles Steinberg, President
• Dan Rea, SVP & General Manager
Sport:
Baseball
Team:
Pawtucket Red Sox
Year Founded:
1942. Renovated 1999
Seating Capacity:
10,031

MCKALE MEMORIAL CENTER
1721 E ENKE DRIVE
TUCSON, AZ 85721
www.arizonawildcats.com
• Greg Byrne, Vice President, Athletics
• Sean Miller, Head Coach, Men's
Basketball
• Niya Butts, Head Coach, Women's
Basketball
Seating Capacity:
14,000

MEADOWLANDS SPORTS COMPLEX
50 STATE HIGHWAY 120
EAST RUTHERFORD, NJ 07073
201-935-8500
www.njsea.com

MEMORIAL COLISEUM
201 AVENUE OF CHAMPIONS
LEXINGTON, KY 40506-0019
www.ukathletics.com/page/facilities-memori
al-coliseum
• Mitch Barnhart, Athletics Director
(859) 257-8015
• Matthew Mitchell, Head Coach, Women's
Basketball
• Tim Garrison, Head Coach, Gymnastics
• Craig Skinner, Head Coach, Volleyball
Seating Capacity:
8,500

MEMORIAL FIELD
4 CROSBY STREET
HANOVER, NH 03755
603-646-1110
www.dartmouthsports.com
• Harry Sheehy, Director of Athletics &
Recreation
• Richard Whitmore, Sr. Assoc. Athl. Dir. of
Facilities & Operations
• Buddy Teevens, Head Coach, Football
Seating Capacity:
11,000

MEMORIAL GYM
210 25TH AVENUE S
NASHVILLE, TN 37240
615-322-1793
www.vucommodores.com
• David Williams, II, Athletics Director
• Kevin Stallings, Head Coach, Men's
Basketball
(615) 322-6530
• Melanie Balcomb, Head Coach, Women's
Basketball
(615) 343-8482
Seating Capacity:
14,326

MEMORIAL GYMNASIUM
GRAMBLING UNIVERSITY
GRAMBLING, LA
www.gram.edu
• Obadiah Simmons, Interim Athletic
Director
(318) 274-2374
• Demetria Keys-Johnson, Head Coach,
Volleyball
(318) 274-3216
Seating Capacity:
2,200

MEMORIAL STADIUM (ILLINOIS)
1402 S FIRST STREET
CHAMPAIGN, IL 61820
217-333-1400
www.fightingillini.com
• Josh Whitman, Director of Athletics
(217) 333-3631
• Lenny Willis, Director of Facilities
(217) 333-2303
• Lovie Smith, Head Coach, Football
Seating Capacity:
60,670
Team:
University of Illinois Fighting Illini

MEMORIAL STADIUM (INDIANA)
1001 E 17TH STREET
BLOOMINGTON, IN 47408
812-855-1966
iuhoosiers.com
• Fred Glass, Vice President & Director of Athletics
iuad@indiana.edu
• Scott Dolson, Deputy Director of Athletics
sdolson@indiana.edu
• Eric Neuburger, Assoc. Athl. Dir. for Facilities & Ext. Alliances
eneuburg@indiana.edu
• Kevin Wilson, Head Coach, Football
football@indiana.edu
Seating Capacity:
52,929
Team:
Indiana Hoosiers

MEMORIAL STADIUM (KANSAS)
1101 MAINE STREET
LAWRENCE, KS 66045
785-864-3141
www.kuathletics.com
• Sheahon Zenger, Director of Athletics
kuathletics@ku.edu
• Jay Ellis, Assistant Athletic Director - Facilities
ajellis@ku.edu
• David Beaty, Head Coach, Football
kansasfootball@ku.edu
Seating Capacity:
50,071
Team:
Kansas Jayhawks

MEMORIAL STADIUM (NEBRASKA)
ONE STADIUM DRIVE
LINCOLN, NE 68588
402-472-2263
www.huskers.com
• Shawn Eichorst, Director of Athletics
• Mike Riley, Head Coach, Football
Team:
Nebraska Cornhuskers
Seating Capacity:
85,000

MERRILL FIELD AT YUNEVICH STADIUM
1 SAXON DRIVE
ALFRED, NY 14802
800-541-9229
saxons@alfred.edu
www.alfred.edu
• Paul Vecchio, Athletic Director
(607) 871-2030
vecchio@alfred.edu
• Bob Rankl, Head Coach, Football
(607) 871-2302
ranklr@alfred.edu
• Jason Lockner, Head Coach, Men's Lacrosse
(607) 871-2890
locknerj@alfred.edu
• Erynn Anderson, Head Coach, Women's Lacrosse
(607) 871-2628
andersonel@alfred.edu
• Matt Smith, Head Coach, Men's Soccer
(607) 871-2899
smithma@alfred.edu
• Aileen Ascolese, Head Coach, Women's Soccer
(607) 871-2896
ascolese@alfred.edu

Seating Capacity:
1,355

MESQUITE ARENA
1818 RODEO DRIVE
MESQUITE, TX 75149
972-285-8777
Fax: 972-289-2999
info@mesquiterodeo.com
www.mesquiterodeo.com
Seating Capacity:
5,500
Convention/Expo Center:
35,000 sq. ft.

METRAPARK
308 6TH AVENUE N
BILLINGS, MT 59101
406-256-2400
info@metrapark.com
www.metrapark.com
Rimrock Auto Arena Seating Capacity:
12,000

METRO BANK PARK
245 CHAMPIONSHIP WAY
HARRISBURG, PA 17101
717-231-4444
information@senatorsbaseball.com
www.senatorsbaseball.com
Sport:
Baseball
Team:
Harrisburg Senators, AA affiliate of the Washington Nationals.
Year Founded:
1987
Seating Capacity:
6,187

MGM GRAND HOTEL & CASINO
3799 LAS VEGAS BOULEVARD SOUTH
LAS VEGAS, NV 89109
877-880-0880
Fax: 702-891-3036
guestservices@lv.mgmgrand.com
www.mgmgrand.com
Year Founded:
1993

MICHIE STADIUM
700 MILLS ROAD
WEST POINT, NY 10996
877-849-2769
www.goarmywestpoint.com
• Boo Corrigan, Director of Athletics
• Jeff Monken, Head Coach, Football
Seating Capacity:
38,000
Teams:
Army Black Knights

MICHIGAN STADIUM
1201 S MAIN STREET
ANN ARBOR, MI 48104-3722
734-647-2583
Fax: 734-764-3221
www.mgoblue.com
• Warde Manuel, Director of Athletics
• Jim Harbaugh, Head Coach, Football
(734) 763-4422
• John Paul, Head Coach, Men's Lacrosse
(734) 763-3679
• Jennifer Ulehla, Head Coach, Women's Lacrosse
(734) 647-9856

Seating Capacity:
107,601
Team:
University of Michigan Wolverines

MILLER PARK
ONE BREWERS WAY
MILWAUKEE, WI 53214
414-902-4400
milwaukee.brewers.mlb.com
Team:
Milwaukee Brewers
Seating Capacity:
41,900

MILLETT HALL
500 E SYCAMORE STREET
OXFORD, OH 45056
www.miamiredhawks.com
• David Sayler, Director of Athletics
(513) 529-7286
• John Cooper, Head Coach, Men's Basketball
(513) 529-1650
• Cleve Wright, Head Coach, Women's Basketball
(513) 529-3300
• Carolyn Condit, Head Coach, Volleyball
(513) 529-6922
Team:
Miami University RedHawks
Seating Capacity:
6,400

MINUTE MAID PARK
501 CRAWFORD STREET
SUITE 400
HOUSTON, TX 77002
houston.astros.mlb.com
Team:
Houston Astros
Seating Capacity:
40,963

MISSISSIPPI COAST COLISEUM AND CONVENTION CENTER
2350 BEACH BOULEVARD
BILOXI, MS 39531
228-594-3700
800-726-2781
Fax: 228-594-3812
www.mscoastcoliseum.com
• Matt McDonnell, Executive Director
• Gregg Blaize, Assistant Executive Director
Seating Capacity:
15,000

MISSISSIPPI VETERANS MEMORIAL STADIUM
2531 NORTH STATE STREET
JACKSON, MS 39216
601-354-6021
www.ms-veteransstadium.com
• Tom Cooper, Event Manager
(601) 345-6021
thomas.c.cooper@jsums.edu
Seating Capacity:
60,492
Team:
Jackson State University Tigers

MITCHELL HALL GYMNASIUM
1820 PINE STREET
LA CROSSE, WI 54601
608-785-8616
Fax: 608-785-8674

facilities

athletics@uwlax.edu
www.uwlathletics.com
• Kim Blum, Director of Athletics
(608) 785-8616
kblum@uwlax.edu
• Jason Murphy, Facilities Director
• Ken Koelbl, Head Coach, Men's
Basketball
• Lois Heeren, Head Coach, Women's
Basketball
• Dave Malecek, Head Coach, Wrestling
• Barbara Gibson, Head Coach, Gymnastics
Seating Capacity:
2,880

MOBILE CIVIC CENTER
401 CIVIC CENTER DRIVE
MOBILE, AL 36602
251-208-7261
www.mobilecivicctr.com
• Bob Brazier, General Manager
(251) 208-2111
• Joe Delaronde, Director of Operations
(251) 208-7937
Seating Capacity:
10,112

MOBY ARENA
951 W PLUM STREET
FORT COLLINS, CO 80523
970-491-5300
800-491-RAMS
www.csurams.com
• Joe Parker, Athletics Director
(970) 491-3350
• Doug Max, Snr. Assoc. Athl. Dir. for
Facilities & Scheduling
• Larry Eustachy, Head Coach, Men's
Basketball
(970) 491-6232
• Ryun Williams, Head Coach, Women's
Basketball
(970) 491-6569
• Tom Hilbert, Head Coach, Volleyball
(970) 491-6410
Team:
Colorado State Rams
Seating Capacity:
8,745

MOHEGAN SUN ARENA
1 MOHEGAN SUN BOULEVARD
UNCASVILLE, CT 06382
888-226-7711
information@mohegansun.com
mohegansun.com
Team:
Connecticut Sun
Seating Capacity:
9,518

MONTAGNE CENTER
4400 SOUTH MLK PARKWAY
BEAUMONT, TX 77705
409-880-1810
Fax: 409-880-1814
www.montagnecenter.com
• Jason Henderson, Director of Athletics
(409) 880-8303
jason.henderson@lamar.edu
• Tic Price, Head Coach, Men's Basketball
(409) 880-8301
tic.price@lamar.edu
• Robin Harmony, Head Coach, Women's
Basketball
(409) 880-2238
robin.harmony@lamar.edu

Team:
Lamar University Cardinals & Lady
Cardinals
Seating Capacity:
10,080

MONTANA EXPOPARK
400 3RD STREET NW
GREAT FALLS, MT 59404
406-727-8900
Fax: 406-452-8955
goexpopark.com
• Randy Bogden, Advisory Board Chairman
Description:
Home of the Montana State Fair, the
Montana ExpoPark is a 133-acre fairground
consisting of exhibition pavilions, a horse
racing track and a multi-purpose sports
arena. The six original, Art Deco buildings
were added to the National Register of
Historic Places.

MOODY COLISEUM
6024 AIRLINE ROAD
DALLAS, TX 75205
214-768-2000
www.smumustangs.com
• Rick Hart, Director of Athletics
(214) 768-4301
rlhart@smu.edu
• Larry Brown, Head Coach, Men's
Basketball
(214) 768-3501
• Lisa Dark, Associate Head Coach,
Women's Basketball
(214) 768-3681
Team:
Southern Methodist University Mustangs
Seating Capacity:
7,000

MOSAIC STADIUM
1700 ELPHINSTONE STREET
REGINA, SK, CANADA S4P 2Z6
306-781-9200
www.evrazplace.com/facilities/mosaic-stadium
Opened:
1936
Team:
Saskatchewan Roughriders
Seating Capacity:
33,350

MOUNTAINEER FIELD AT MILAN PUSKAR STADIUM
1 IRA ERRETT RODGERS DRIVE
MORGANTOWN, WV 26505
www.wvusports.com
• Shane Lyons, Director of Athletics
• April Messerly, Asst. AD for Facilities &
Operations
• Dana Holgorsen, Head Coach, Football
Team:
West Virginia Mountaineers
Seating Capacity:
60,000

MULLINS CENTER
200 COMMONWEALTH AVENUE
2ND FLOOR
AMHERST, MA 01003
413-545-3040
www.mullinscenter.com
• Brian Caputo, General Manager
(413) 545-3129

• Sean Dolan, Director of Operations & Asst.
GM
(413) 545-3336
• Derek Kellogg, Head Coach, Men's
Basketball
• Sharon Dawley, Head Coach, Women's
Basketball
• John Micheletto, Head Coach, Ice Hockey
Team:
UMass Minutemen
Seating Capacity:
10,500

MUNICIPAL STADIUM
274 EAST MEMORIAL BOULEVARD
HAGERSTOWN, MD 21740
301-791-6266
Fax: 301-791-6066
info@hagerstownsuns.com
www.hagerstownsuns.com
• Bruce Quinn, President
• Travis Painter, General Manager
travis.painter@hagerstownsuns.com
• Brian Saddler, Grounds Keeper
brian.saddler@hagerstownsuns.com
Sport:
Baseball
Team:
Hagerstown Suns
Year Founded:
1930

MUSSELMAN STADIUM
300 N WASHINGTON STREET
GETTYSBURG COLLEGE
GETTYSBURG, PA 17325
717-337-6300
Fax: 717-337-6666
tmyers@gettysburg.edu
www.gettysburg.edu
• David Wright, Athletic Director
(717) 337-6530
• Susan Fumagalli, Assistant Director of
Athletics
(717) 337-6401
sfumagal@gettysburg.edu
Stadium Seating Capacity:
6,000

MYRL H. SHOEMAKER CENTER
2700 O'VARSITY WAY
SHOEMAKER CENTER, UNIVERSITY OF
CINCINNATI
CINCINNATI, OH 45221
513-556-2170
Fax: 513-556-0619
uccheerleading@yahoo.com
www.gobearcats.com
• Mike Thomas, Director of Athletics
(513) 556-4603
bearcat.ad@uc.edu
• Bob Arkeilpane, Deputy Director of
Athletics
(513) 556-2449
bob.arkeilpane@us.edu
• David Szymanski, Faculty Athletics
Representative
(513) 556-3935
david.szymanski@uc.edu
• Omar Banks, Sr. Associate AD/CFO
(513) 556-0608
• Brendan Fouracre, Sr. Associate
AD/Facilities & Operations
(513) 556-3541
brendan.fouracre@uc.edu
• Andy Hurley, Sr. Associate AD/External
Relations

(513) 556-9302
• Santa Ono, University President
(513) 556-2201
president@uc.edu
Arena Seating Capacity:
13,176
Nippert Stadium Seating Capacity:
35,000

N.E.C. ARENA BIRMINGHAM
NATIONAL EXHIBITION CENTRE
BIRMINGHAM, ENGLAND B4O 1NT
44-(0) 121 780 4141
Fax: -44-767-3700
info@necgroup.co.uk
www.necgroup.co.uk
• Martin C Angle, Non-Executive Chairman
• Paul Thandi, Chief Executive
• John Hornby, Chief Operating Officer
• Nick Waight, Chief Executive of the
Convention Centre
• Kevin Watson, Managing Director
Amadeus
• Kathryn James, Managing Director,
National Exhibition Centre
• Phil Mead, Managing Director, Arenas
Permanent Seating Capacity:
12,500

NASHVILLE MUNICIPAL AUDITORIUM
417 4TH AVENUE N
NASHVILLE, TN 37201
615-862-6390
Fax: 615-862-6394
www.nashvilleauditorium.com
• Bob Skoney, General Manager
bob.skoney@nashville.gov
• Derrick Pentico, Event Manager
derrick.pentico@nashville.gov
Description:
A multipurpose sports arena and
entertainment venue located in downtown
Nashville. Houses Musicians Hall of Fame &
Museum.
Seating Capacity:
8,000

NASSAU VETERANS MEMORIAL COLISEUM
1255 HEMPSTEAD TURNPIKE
UNIONDALE, NY 11553
www.nassaucoliseum.com
Description:
Multi-purpose indoor arena on Long Island.
Until 2015 the Nassau Coliseum was the
home of the New York Islanders of the NHL.
Current renovations are expected to be
completed in 2017.
Seating Capacity:
18,000

NATIONALS PARK
1500 SOUTH CAPITOL STREET SE
WASHINGTON, DC 20003
202-675-6287
Fax: 202-640-7999
nationals.com
• Theodore N. Lerner, Managing Principal
Owner
• Mike Rizzo, General Manager & President
of Baseball Operations
Teams:
Washington Nationals
Seating Capacity:
41,546

NATIONWIDE ARENA
200 W NATIONWIDE BOULEVARD
COLUMBUS, OH 43215
614-246-2000
Fax: 614-246-4300
www.nationwidearena.com
Description:
Multi-purpose sports and entertainment
revue. Nationwide Arena hosts more than
150 events annually.
Founded:
2000
Team(s):
Columbus Blue Jackets (NFL); Columbus
Destroyers (AFL)
Seating Capacity:
20,000

NAVY-MARINE CORPS MEMORIAL STADIUM
550 TAYLOR AVENUE
ANNAPOLIS, MD 21401
410-263-4783
www.navysports.com
• Chet Gladchuk, Director of Athletics
(410) 293-8910
gladchuk@usna.edu
• Tom McKavitt, Assoc. AD, Facilities &
Maintenance
(410) 293-8770
tmckavit@usna.edu
• Ken Niumatalolo, Head Coach, Football
(410) 293-2241
tully@usna.edu
• Rick Sowell, Head Coach, Men's Lacrosse
(410) 293-8779
sowell@usna.edu
• Cindy Timchal, Head Coach, Women's
Lacrosse
(410) 293-8746
timchal@usna.edu
Team:
Navy Midshipmen
Seating Capacity:
34,000

NBT BANK STADIUM
300 NBT BANK PARKWAY
SYRACUSE, NY 13208
315-474-7833
www.syracusechiefs.com
Team:
Syracuse Chiefs
Founded:
1997
Seating Capacity:
11,071

NELSON W. WOLFF MUNICIPAL STADIUM
5757 US HWY 90 WEST
SAN ANTONIO, TX 78227
210-675-7275
Fax: 210-670-0001
sainfo@samissions.com
www.milb.com/index.jsp?sid=t510
• Dave Gasaway, General Manager
Team:
San Antonio Missions
Seating Capacity:
9,200

NEW BRITAIN STADIUM
230 JOHN KARBONIC WAY
NEW BRITAIN, CT 06051

860-826-2337
info@nbbees.com
nbbees.com
• Patrick Day, General Manager
Team:
New Britain Bees
Founded:
1996
Seating Capacity:
6,146

NEWMAN OUTDOOR FIELD
1515 15TH AVENUE NORTH
FARGO, ND 58102
701-235-6161
800-303-6161
Fax: 701-297-9247
redhawks@fmredhawks.com
www.fmredhawks.com
• Brad Thom, President & CEO
• Tim Jallen, Director of Field & Stadium
Operations
tjallen@fmredhawks.com
Founded:
1996
Team:
Fargo-Moorhead RedHawks
Seating Capacity:
4,513

NEYLAND STADIUM
1600 PHILLIP FULMER WAY
SUITE 201
KNOXVILLE, TN 37996
www.utsports.com
• Dave Hart, Director of Athletics
(865) 974-1224
athleticdirector@utk.edu
• Kevin Zurcher, Asst. AD for Athletic
Facilities & Grounds
(865) 974-8479
kzurcher@tennessee.edu
• Butch Jones, Head Coach, Football
Team:
Tennessee Volunteers
Seating Capacity:
102,455

NICKERSON FIELD
285 BABCOCK STREET
BOSTON, MA 02215
617-353-4630
Fax: 617-353-5286
gobu@bu.edu
www.goterriers.com
• Drew Marrochello, Director of Athletics
(617) 353-4631
• Ryan Polley, Head Coach, Men's Lacrosse
(617) 358-0365
• Liz Robertshaw, Head Coach, Women's
Lacrosse
(617) 353-2094
• Neil Roberts, Head Coach, Men's Soccer
(617) 358-3793
• Nancy Feldman, Head Coach, Women's
Soccer
(617) 353-8456
Team:
BU Terriers
Seating Capacity:
10,412

NIPPERT STADIUM
2700 BEARCATS WAY
CINCINNATI, OH 45221
513-556-2287
www.gobearcats.com

• Mike Bohn, Director of Athletics
(513) 556-4603
• Brendan Fouracre, Sr. Assoc. AD,
Facilities & Operations
(513) 556-3541
• Tommy Tuberville, Head Coach, Football
(513) 556-4110
Team:
Cincinnati Bearcats
Seating Capacity:
35,000

NORTH CHARLESTON COLISEUM
5001 COLISEUM DRIVE
NORTH CHARLESTON, SC 29418
843-529-5000
www.northcharlestoncoliseumpac.com
Team:
South Carolina Stingrays (ECHL)
Seating Capacity:
14,000

NOTRE DAME STADIUM
MOOSE KRAUSE CIRCLE
SOUTH BEND, IN 46616
574-631-7356
www.und.com
• Jack Swarbrick, Univ. VP & Director of
Athletics
(574) 631-6107
• Dan Brazo, Facility Manager, Notre Dame
Stadium
(574) 631-7962
Team:
Notre Dame Fighting Irish
Seating Capacity:
80,795

NRG STADIUM
1 NRG PARK
HOUSTON, TX 77054
832-667-1400
Fax: 832-667-1748
www.reliantpark.com/nrg-park-facilities/nrg-stadium
Seating Capacity:
72,000
Teams:
Houston Texans NFL football; Texas Bowl.

NYSEG STADIUM
211 HENRY STREET
BINGHAMTON, NY 13901
607-723-6387
Fax: 607-723-7779
bmets@bmets.com
www.bmets.com
• Jim Weed, General Manager
• Richard Tylicki, Director of Stadium
Operations
Team:
Binghamton Mets
Year Founded:
1992
Seating Capacity:
6,012

O'BRIEN FIELD
GRANT AVENUE & 4TH STREET
CHARLESTON, IL 61920
www.eiupanthers.com
• Tom Michael, Athletic Director
• Kim Dameron, Head Coach, Football
(217) 581-5031
rkdameron@eiu.edu
• Tom Akers, Director, Track & Field

(217) 581-2625
tlakers@eiu.edu
Team:
Eastern Illinois Panthers
Seating Capacity:
10,000

O'NEILL CENTER
43 LAKE AVENUE EXTENSION
DANBURY, CT 06811
203-837-9015
Fax: 203-837-9050
www.wcsuathletics.com/information/Western
_Athletic_Facilties
• Scott Ames, Interim Athletic Director
(203) 837-9014
• Bob Campbell, Head Coach, Men's
Basketball
(203) 837-9017
• Kimberley Rybczyk, Head Coach,
Women's Basketball
(203) 837-9018
rybczykk@wcsu.edu
• Don Ferguson, Head Coach, Women's
Volleyball
(203) 837-9022
fergusond@wcsu.edu
Team:
WestConn Colonials
Seating Capacity:
4,500

O.co COLISEUM
7000 COLISEUM WAY
OAKLAND, CA 94621
510-569-2121
www.coliseum.com
Teams:
Oakland Athletics (MLB); Oakland Raiders
(NFL)
Seating Capacity:
Baseball 35,067; Football 56,057; Soccer
63,132

OCEAN CENTER
101 N ATLANTIC AVENUE
DAYTONA BEACH, FL 32118
386-254-4500
800-858-6444
Fax: 386-254-4512
frontdesk@oceancenter.com
www.oceancenter.com
• Don Poor, Director
dpoor@oceancenter.com
Owner:
Volusia County
Seating Capacity:
Hockey/Arena Football 6,176; Basketball
8,362; Wrestling 8,582

ODEUM EXPO CENTER
1033 NORTH VILLA AVENUE
VILLA PARK, IL 60181
630-941-9292
Fax: 630-832-9183
www.odeumexpo.com
• Phil Greco, President
phil@odeumexpo.com
• Brad Walsh, Facility Manager
brad@odeumexpo.com
Team:
Chicago Blitz (AIF)
Seating Capacity:
Indoor Soccer/Football, Lacrosse 2,500;
Boxing/Wrestling 5,500

OHIO STADIUM
411 WOODY HAYES DRIVE
COLUMBUS, OH 43210
614-292-6330
Fax: 614-292-3585
www.ohiostatebuckeyes.com
• Gene Smith, Athletics Director
• Don Patko, Assoc. AD, Facilities
Operations
• Urban Meyer, Head Coach, Football
Team:
Ohio State Buckeyes
Seating Capacity:
104,944

OKLAHOMA MEMORIAL STADIUM
180 WEST BROOKS
NORMAN, OK 73019
405-325-8000
www.soonersports.com
• Joe Castiglione, Director of Athletics
(405) 325-8208
• Kenny Mossman, Sr. Associate AD,
External Operations
(405) 325-8228
kmossman@ou.edu
• Zac Selmon, Sr. Associate AD, Operations
(405) 325-3396
zacselmon@ou.edu
• Greg Tipton, Sr. Associate AD, Internal
Operations
(405) 325-8379
gtipton@ou.edu
• Eric Barnhart, General Manager
(405) 352-2407
ebarnhart@oussp.com
Seating Capacity:
82,112
Teams:
University of Oklahoma football.

OLYMPIC CENTER
2634 MAIN STREET
LAKE PLACID, NY 12946
518-523-1655
800-462-6236
info@orda.org
www.whiteface.com
Description:
Sports complex in Lake Placid, NY,
comprising a conference center, Olympic
museum, two arenas, and speed skating
and figure skating rinks.

OMAN ARENA
179 LANE AVENUE
JACKSON, TN 38301
731-425-8580
Fax: 731-425-8589
info@cityofjackson.net
www.cityofjackson.net
Founded:
1967
Seating Capacity:
5,600

ONEOK FIELD
201 NORTH ELGIN AVENUE
TULSA, OK 74120
918-744-5998
Fax: 918-747-3267
mail@tulsadrillers.com
www.tulsadrillers.com
• Mike Melega, President/GM
mike@tulsadrillers.com
• Mark Hilliard, Vice President, Operations
mark@tulsadrillers.com

• Marshall Schellhardt, Stadium Operations Manager
marshall@tulsadrillers.com
Founded:
2010
Team:
Tulsa Drillers
Seating Capacity:
7,833

ORACLE ARENA
7000 COLISEUM WAY
OAKLAND, CA 94621
510-383-4801
www.coliseum.com
Team:
Golden State Warriors (NBA)
Seating Capacity:
Basketball 19,596; Concert 20,000; Hockey 17,200

ORIOLE PARK AT CAMDEN YARDS
333 WEST CAMDEN STREET
BALTIMORE, MD 21201
410-685-9800
baltimore.orioles.mlb.com/bal/ballpark
• Kevin Cummings, Director, Ballpark Operations
Team:
Baltimore Orioles (MLB)
Seating Capacity:
45,971

ORLANDO CITRUS BOWL
1 CITRUS BOWL PLACE
ORLANDO, FL 32805
407-440-7000
Fax: 407-440-7001
www.orlandocitrusbowl.com
• Allen Johnson, Executive Director
• Charles P. Leone, Operations Division Manager
charles.leone@cityoforlando.net
• John Sparks, Stadium Operations Assistant Division Manager
john.sparks@cityoforlando.net
• Matthew Larsen, Stadium Manager
matthew.larsen@cityoforlando.net
• Ollie Rives, Facility Manager
ollie.rives@cityoforlando.net
Tenant(s):
Citrus Bowl (NCAA), Florida Classic (NCAA), Orlando City SC (MLS), Cure Bowl (NCAA), Orlando Pride (NWSL)
Seating Capacity:
70,000

ORLEANS ARENA
4500 W TROPICANA AVENUE
LAS VEGAS, NV 89103
702-284-7777
888-234-2334
Fax: 702-284-7778
www.orleansarena.com
Team:
Las Vegas Sin (LFL)
Seating Capacity:
9,500

OSCEOLA COUNTY STADIUM
631 HERITAGE PARK WAY
KISSIMMEE, FL 34744
321-697-3201
www.osceolastadium.com
• Erik Anderson, Facility Superintendent

Team:
Astros (GCL)
Seating Capacity:
5,300

OZARK CIVIC CENTER
320 EAST COLLEGE STREET
PO BOX 789
OZARK, AL 36361
334-774-2618
877-622-2322
civic@ozarkalabama.us
www.ozarkalabama.us
• Lauren Hohbach, Area Supervisor
• Steve Sherrill, Director of Leisure Services
• Kassidy Reeder, Administrative Assistant
Built:
1975
Seating Capacity:
3,600

PACIFIC COLISEUM
PACIFIC NATIONAL EXHIBITION
2901 E HASTINGS STREET
VANCOUVER, BC, CANADA V5K 5J1
604-253-2311
Fax: 604-251-7753
info@pne.ca
www.pne.ca
• Shelley Frost, President/CEO
Opened:
1968
Seating Capacity:
Ice hockey: 16,281; Concerts: 17,500

PALACE OF AUBURN HILLS, THE
6 CHAMPIONSHIP DRIVE
AUBURN HILLS, MI 48326
248-377-0100
www.palacenet.com
• Dennis Mannion, President & CEO
• Mario Etemad, EVP, Operations
Team:
Detroit Pistons (NBA)
Seating Capacity:
24,276

PALESTRA, THE
235 SOUTH 33RD STREET
PHILADELPHIA, PA 19104-6322
215-898-6151
Fax: 215-573-2161
www.pennathletics.com
• Calhoun M. Grace, Director of Athletics & Recreation
• Steve Donahue, Head Coach, Men's Basketball
• Mike McLaughlin, Head Coach, Women's Basketball
• Kerry Carr, Head Coach, Women's Volleyball
• Alex Tirapelle, Head Coach, Wrestling
Team:
Penn Quakers
Seating Capacity:
8,722

PAN AMERICAN CENTER
1810 EAST UNIVERSITY AVENUE
LAS CRUCES, NM 88003
575-646-4413
panam.nmsu.edu
• Mario Moccia, Director of Athletics
moccia@nmsu.edu
• Marvin Menzies, Head Coach, Men's Basketball

mtrakh@nmsu.edu
• Mark Trakh, Head Coach, Women's Basketball
mtrakh@nmsu.edu
• Michael Jordan, Head Coach, Volleyball
micjorda@nmsu.edu
Founded:
1968
Team:
New Mexico State Aggies
Seating Capacity:
12,482

PAPA JOHN'S CARDINAL STADIUM
2800 SOUTH FLOYD STREET
LOUISVILLE, KY 40209
• Michael J. Ortman, Stadium Manager
(502) 852-3893
Team:
Louisville Cardinals
Seating Capacity:
56,000

PARC OLYMPIQUE
4141, AVENUE PIERRE-DE COUBERTIN
MONTREAL, QC, CANADA H1V 3N7
514-252-4141
Fax: 514-252-0372
rio@rio.gouv.qc.ca
parcolympique.qc.ca
• Michel Labrecque, President/CEO
Founded:
1976
Seating Capacity:
56,040

PARKVIEW FIELD
1301 EWING STREET
FORT WAYNE, IN 46802
260-482-6400
Fax: 260-471-4678
www.parkviewfield.com
Sport:
Baseball
Opened:
2009
Team:
Fort Wayne TinCaps
Seating Capacity:
8,100

PARSONS FIELD/FRIEDMAN DIAMOND
178 KENT STREET
BROOKLINE, MA 02446
617-373-2672
Fax: 617-373-8988
gonu.com
• Peter Roby, Athletic Director
• Mike Glavine, Head Coach, Baseball
(617) 373-3657
• Chris Gbandi, Head Coach, Men's Soccer
(617) 373-7581
• Ashley Phillips, Head Coach, Women's Soccer
(617) 373-2335
Opened:
1930
Team:
Northeastern Huskies
Seating Capacity:
7,000

PAUL BROWN STADIUM
1 PAUL BROWN STADIUM
CINCINNATI, OH 45202
www.bengals.com

facilities

- Mike Brown, President
- Katie Blackburn, Executive Vice President
Team:
Cincinnati Bengals
Seating Capacity:
65,535

PAULEY PAVILION
301 WESTWOOD PLAZA
LOS ANGELES, CA 90024
310-825-4546
Fax: 310-825-8664
www.uclabruins.com
- Dan Guerrero, Director of Athletics
- Steve Alford, Head Coach, Men's
Basketball
- Cori Close, Head Coach, Women's
Basketball
- Valorie Kondos Field, Head Coach,
Women's Gymnastics
- John Speraw, Head Coach, Men's
Volleyball
- Michael Sealy, Head Coach, Women's
Volleyball
Team:
UCLA Bruins
Seating Capacity:
13,800

PENDLETON CONVENTION CENTER
1601 WESTGATE
PENDLETON, OR 97801
541-276-6569
800-863-9358
Fax: 541-278-1317
www.pendletonconventioncenter.com
- Kathy Marshall, Operations
kathy.marshall@ci.pendleton.or.us
Seating Capacity:
5,000

PENSACOLA BAY CENTER
201 E GREGORY STREET
PENSACOLA, FL 32502
850-432-0800
www.pensacolabaycenter.com
- Cyndee Pennington, General Manager
cpennington@smgpcola.com
- Scott Cornwell, Director of Operations
scornwell@smgpcola.com
Team:
Pensacola Ice Flyers (SPHL)
Seating Capacity:
Hockey 8,150; Non-hockey 10,000

PEOPLES NATURAL GAS FIELD
1000 PARK AVENUE
ALTOONA, PA 16602
814-943-5400
Fax: 814-943-9050
www.altoonacurve.com
Opened:
1999
Team:
Altoona Curve (EL)
Seating Capacity:
7,210

PEORIA CIVIC CENTER
201 SW JEFFERSON STREET
PEORIA, IL 61602
309-673-8900
www.peoriaciviccenter.com
- Anne Clayton, General Manager
aclayton@peoriaciviccenter.com

- Jason Bain, Operations Manager
jbain@peoriaciviccenter.com
Opened:
1982
Seating Capacity:
Hockey/Indoor Football 9,919; Basketball
11,433; Concerts 12,036

PEORIA SPORTS COMPLEX
16101 N 83RD AVENUE
PEORIA, AZ 85382
623-773-8700
Fax: 623-773-8716
sportscomplex@peoriaaz.gov
peoriasportscomplex.com
Opened:
1994
Team(s):
Seattle Mariners and San Diego Padres
Seating Capacity:
12,339

PEPSI CENTER
1000 CHOPPER CIRCLE
DENVER, CO 80204
303-405-1100
Fax: 303-575-1920
customerservice@altitudetickets.com
www.pepsicenter.com
- E. Stanley Kroenke, Owner
- Martin Jim, President & CEO
Team(s):
Denver Nuggets (NBA); Colorado
Avalanche (NHL); Colorado Mammoth
(NLL); Colorado Crush (AFL)
Seating Capacity:
Basketball 19,155; Hockey/Lacrosse
18,007; Arena Football 17,417

PERCIVAL MOLSON MEMORIAL STADIUM
475, AVENUE DES PINS
MONTREAL, QC, CANADA H2W 1S4
Owners:
McGill University
Year Opened:
1919
Seating Capacity:
25,012.
Tenant(s):
CFL - Montreal Alouettes. McGill Redmen

PERKINS STADIUM
910 WEST SCHWAGER DRIVE
UNIVERSITY OF WISCONSIN
WHITEWATER, WI 53190
262-472-1234
Fax: 262-472-2791
webmaster@uww.edu
www.uww.edu
- Amy Edmonds, Director of Intercollegiate
Athletics
(262) 472-4661
edmondsa@uww.edu
- Bob Lanza, Associate AD/Finance &
Business Operations
(262) 472-3190
lanzar@uww.edu
- Kirby Mills, Assistant AD/Development
(262) 472-5646
millsk@uww.edu
- Chris Lindeke, Director of Athletic
Communications
(262) 472-1147
lindekec@uww.edu
- Kay Bradley, Athletic Administrative
Assistant

(262) 472-4661
bradlekf@uww.edu
- Reid Gibbs, Assistant Coach/Equipment
Room Manager
(262) 472-3189
gibbsr@uww.edu
Year Founded:
1970
Seating Capacity:
11,000

PERSHING CENTER
226 CENTENNIAL MALL S
LINCOLN, NE 68508
402-441-8744
Fax: 402-441-7913
- Tom Lorenz, General Manager
- Derek Andersen, Marketing Director
- Fred McCoy, Operations Director
- Sharon Mandery, Event Services Director
Arena Seating Capacity:
6,818

PETE MARAVICH ASSEMBLY CENTER
PETE MARAVICH ASSEMBLY CENTER
LOUISIANA STATE UNIVERSITY
BATON ROUGE, LA 70803
225-578-8025
Fax: 225-578-8437
athletics@lsu.edu
www.maravichcenter.com
- Brendan Fouracre, Director
(225) 578-8424
bdfour@lsu.edu
- Jeff Campbell, Associate Director
- Nathan Hanson, Assistant Operations
Manager
- Dwight Johnson, Assistant Operations
Manager
Arena Seating Capacity:
14,500

PETE MATHEWS COLISEUM
700 PELHAM ROAD N
JACKSONVILLE STATE UNIVERSITY
JACKSONVILLE, AL 36265-1602
256-782-5368
800-231-5291
Fax: 256-782-5666
info@jsu.edu
www.jsu.edu
- Pete Conroy, Director
Arena Seating Capacity:
6,000

PETE TAYLOR BASEBALL PARK
THE UNIVERSITY OF SOUTHERN
MISSISSIPPI
118 COLLEGE DRIVE
HATTIESBURG, MS 39406-0001
601-266-4468
Fax: 601-266-6595
www.southernmiss.com
- Richard C Giannini, Athletic Director
(601) 266-5422
richard.giannini@usm.edu
- Diane Stark, Senior Associate Athletic
Director
(601) 266-5422
- Scott Carr, Associate Athletic
Director/External Ope
(601) 266-5017
scott.carr@usm.edu
- Sonya Varnell, Associate Athletic
Director/Olympic Spor
(601) 266-5017
sonya.varnell@usm.edu

• Christi Holloway, Chief Financial Officer
(601) 266-5299
• Jeremy McClain, Senior Associate Athletic
Director for Extern
(601) 266-5017
• Kent Hegenauer, Senior Associate Athletic
Director/Director o
(601) 266-5017
• Brian Morrison, Associate Director of
Athletics/Major Gifts
(601) 266-5055
• Jeff Hammond, Athletics Director
(601) 266-5422
Clients:
Colleges, Universities nationwide.
Nature of Service:
Baseball diamond for colleges and
universities as part of Institutions of Higher
Learning.
Seating Capacity:
37,000

PETERSEN EVENTS CENTER
3719 TERRACE STREET
UNIVERSITY OF PITTSBURGH
PITTSBURGH, PA 15261
412-648-3054
Fax: 412-648-3285
PECHelp@pitt.edu
www.peterseneventscenter.com
• John Abrams, Facilities/Operations
Manager
(412) 648-8204
jabrams@athletics.pitt.edu
• Anthony Smith, Operations Manager
• Steve Haught, Accounting Manager
• Jodi Hummert, Events & Guest Services
Manager
• Scott Michaels, General Manager
Year Opened:
2002
Arena Seating Capacity:
12,500
Tenant(s):
University of Pittsburgh basketball.

PETERSON EVENTS CENTER
3719 TERRACE STREET
UNIVERSITY OF PITTSBURGH
PITTSBURGH, PA 15261
412-648-8230
Fax: 412-648-8306
www.pittsburghpanthers.com
• Jeff Long, Athletic Director
(412) 648-8230
• Carol Sprague, Senior Associate Athletic
Director
• Mike Pratapas, Senior Associate Athletic
Director
• Steve Pederson, Athletic Director
(412) 648-8230
spederson@athletics.pitt.edu
• Donna Sanft, Executive Associate Athletic
Director
(412) 648-8209
dsanft@athletics.pitt.edu
• Marcus Bowman, Assistant Athletic
Director for Administratio
(412) 648-7181
mbowman@athletics.pitt.edu
• Stephanie Armstrong, Executive Secretary
for the Athletic Director
(412) 648-8230
sarmstrong@athletics.pitt.edu
• Sue George, Secretary to Executive
Associate AD
(412) 648-8209
sgeorge@athletics.pitt.edu

• Maureen Anderson, Associate Athletic
Director, Development
(412) 648-8738
manderson@athletics.pitt.edu
Arena Seating Capacity:
6,798

PGE PARK
1844 SW MORRISON
PORTLAND, OR 97205
503-553-5400
Fax: 503-553-5405
• Ben Hoel, Director, Ticket Operations
Team:
Portland Beavers
Sport:
Baseball
Capacity:
30,500

PHILIP B. ELFSTROM STADIUM
34W002 CHERRY LANE
GENEVA, IL 60134
630-232-8811
Fax: 630-232-8815
info@kanecountycougars.com
www.kccougars.com
• Woleben Mike, President
• Jeff Sedivy, VP/General Manager
• Mary Almlie, Business Manager
• R. Michael Patterson, Senior Director,
Ticketing
rmpatterson@kanecountycougars.com
• Douglas Czurylo, Senior Director - Finance
and Administration
dczurylo@kanecountycougars.com
• Amy Mason, Director of Ticket Services,
Director, Commun
amason@kanecountycougars.com
• Dan Klinkhamer, Director of Security
dklinkhamer@kanecountycougars.com
• Shawn Touney, Director of Public
Relations
stouney@kanecountycougars.com
• Mike Klafehn, Director of Stadium
Operations
mklafehn@kanecountycougars.com
• Robin Hull, Business Manager
rhull@kanecountycougars.com
Sport:
Baseball
Team:
Kane Country Cougars
Year Founded:
1991
Capacity:
5,900

PHILIPS ARENA
1 PHILIPS DRIVE
ATLANTA, GA 30303
404-878-3000
Fax: 404-878-3020
www.philipsarena.com
• Bob Williams, President/General Manager
• Danny Ferry, President of Basketball
Operations and Genera
• Phil Ebinger, Executive Vice President and
Chief Financial
• Scott Wilkinson, Executive Vice President,
Chief Legal Officer
• Ailey Penningroth, Senior Vice President
and Chief Marketing Off
• Andrew Steinberg, Senior Vice President
and Chief Revenue Offic
• Trey Feazell, Senior Vice President and
General Manager

Arena Seating Capacity:
Arena Football 18,500; Basketball 20,007;
Concerts 21,000; Hockey 18,559.
Arena Football:
Georgia Force.
NBA:
Atlanta Hawks.
NHL:
Atlanta Thrashers.

PHOENIX MUNICIPAL STADIUM
5999 E VAN BUREN
PHOENIX, AZ 85008
602-495-7240
800-550-2827
Fax: 602-392-0225
www.phoenix.gov/parks/sports
• Huss Chad, Groundskeeper
Team:
Oakland Athletics Spring Training.
Year Founded:
1965
Capacity:
8,500

PICO RIVERA SPORTS ARENA
350 SOUTH BIXEL STREET
SUITE 250
LOS ANGELES, CA 90017
213-482-6333
Fax: 213-482-6340
www.lasports.org
• Ralph Hauser, Manager
• Anthony Hauser, Concessions Manager
• Scott L London, Chairman
• David Simon, President
• Karen Brodkin, SVP
• Ben Stilp, Controller
• Mark Meyers, Director of Communications
• Monica Maldonado, Director of Special
Events
• Mona Green, Executive Assistant
Arena Seating Capacity:
4,500.00
Year Founded:
1979
Nature of Service:
Rodeo style arena, catering to the Latin
Charro Rodeos.

PINNACLE BANK ARENA
PINNACLE ARENA DRIVE
400 PINNACLE ARENA DRIVE
LINCOLN, NE 68508
402-904-4444
info@pinnaclebankarena.com
www.pinnaclebankarena.com
• Tom Lorenz, General Manager
• Charlie Schilling, Assistant General
Manager

PIONEER FIELD
1 UNIVERSITY PLAZA
UNIVERSITY OF WISCONSIN
PLATTEVILLE, WI 53818-3099
608-342-1491
800-362-5515
Fax: 608-342-1576
athletics@uwplatt.edu
www.uwplatt.edu
• Mark Molesworth, Athletic Director
(608) 342-1567
molewom@uwplatt.edu
• Daus Hap, Event Manager
(608) 342-1567
• Curt Fatzinger, PAC/Intramural Director
(608) 342-1568

facilities

• Tom Antczak, Head Cross Country Asst. Track
(608) 342-1504
• Ryanne Breckenridge, Asst. Athletic Trainer
(608) 342-6015
• Eric Frese, Head Baseball Coach
(608) 342-1843
• Enzo Fuschino, Head Men's Soccer Coach
(608) 342-1343
• Jeff Gard, Head Men's Basketball Coach
(608) 342-1278
Stadium Seating Capacity:
10,000

PK PARK
2760 M.L. KING JR. BOULEVARD
EUGENE, OR 97405
541-342-5367
Fax: 541-342-6089
info@emeraldsbaseball.com
www.milb.com/index.jsp?sid=t461
• Allan Benavides, General Manager
allan@emeraldsbaseball.com
• Matt Dompe, Assistant General Manager
matt@emeraldsbaseball.com
• Chris Bowers, Event Manager
chris@emeraldsbaseball.com
• Peter Billups, Director of Tickets
peter@emeraldsbaseball.com
Stadium Seating Capacity:
4,000
Year Founded:
2009
Tenant(s):
Eugene Emeralds, Oregon Ducks

PLASTER SPORTS COMPLEX
901 S NATIONAL AVENUE
SPRINGFIELD, MO 65897
417-836-5000
Fax: 417-836-7660
www.missouristate.edu
• Blackwood Randy, Executive Director
• Brad Brown, Associate Director
• Keith Boaz, Assistant Director
• Randy Blackwood, Executive Director
RandallBlackwood@missouristate.edu
• Laree Moore, Associate Director
• Beverly Nickols, Facility Supervisor
• Keith Boaz, Director
KeithBoaz@missouristate.edu
• Laree Moore, Associate Director
LareeMoore@missouristate.edu
• Melissa Blankenship, Assistant Director
MelissaBlankenship@missouristate.edu
• Brenda O'Connell, Administrative Secretary
BrendaOConnell@missouristate.edu
Stadium Seating Capacity:
16,000

PNC PARK
115 FEDERAL STREET
PNC PARK AT N SHORE
PITTSBURGH, PA 15212
412-323-5000
• Dennis DaPra, Operations VP
• Frank Coonelly, President
• Bryan Stroh, Vice President and General Counsel
• Tyrone Brooks, Director of Player Personnel
• Joe DelliCarri, Director of Amateur Scouting
• Rene Gayo, Director of Latin American Scouting
• Larry Broadway, Director of Minor League Operations
• Bob Nutting, Chairman of the Board
Tenant(s):
Pittsburgh Pirates

POHLMAN FIELD
2301 SKYLINE DRIVE
PO BOX 855
BELOIT, WI 53511
608-362-2272
Fax: 608-362-0418
snappy@snappersbaseball.com
www.snappersbaseball.com
• Jeff Vohs, General Manager
• Dennis Conerton, Chairman
• Perry Folts, President
• Jeff Klett, VP/Director
• Natalie Tobey, Director of Community Relations
• Mark Inserra, Director of Media Relations
• Bill Czaja, Director, Corporate Sales/Promotions
• Katie Pietrowiak, Director, Tickets/Merchandise
Capacity:
3,501
Year Founded:
1982
Sport:
Baseball
Team
Beloit Snappers

POINT STADIUM
401 MAIN STREET
CITY HALL RECREATION DEPARTMENT
JOHNSTOWN, PA 15901
814-533-2104
Fax: 814-533-2111
• Karl Kittner, Recreation Director
• Rich Horvath, Stadium Manager
Stadium Seating Capacity:
10,500

PONTIAC SILVERDOME
1200 FEATHERSTONE ROAD
PONTIAC, MI 48342
248-338-7000
Fax: 248-499-6754
• Walker Eric, Executive Director
Owned by:
City of Pontiac
Permanent Seating Capacity:
80,311

PRATHER COLISEUM
NSU ATHLETIC FIELDHOUSE
220 S JEFFERSON
NATCHITOCHES, LA 71497
318-357-5251
Fax: 318-357-4221
athleticsinfo@nsula.edu
www.nsudemons.com
• Greg Burke, Athletics Director
(318) 357-5251
burkeg@nsula.edu
• Haley Taitano, Assoc. AD for Ext. Relats./Sr. Women's Advisor
(318) 357-4278
blounth@nsula.edu
• Doug Ireland, Asst. AD, Media Relations
(318) 357-6467
ireland@nsula.edu
• Mike Jaworski, Director of Development and Engagement
(318) 357-4295
jaworskim@nsula.edu
• Mike Doty, Director of Athletic Facilities and Event Mgmt.
(318) 357-6898
dotym@nsula.edu
• Chance Creppel, Asst. Director of Facilities and Event Mgmt.
(318) 357-4265
creppelc@nsula.edu
Coliseum Seating Capacity:
3,400
Nature of Service:
Basketball and volleyball arena

PRINCE GEORGE'S STADIUM
4101 CRAIN HIGHWAY
BOWIE, MD 20716
301-805-6000
Fax: 301-464-4911
info@baysox.com
www.baysox.com
• Shallcross Brian, General Manager
• Brandan Kaiser, Director of Marketing
bkaiser@baysox.com
• Charlene Fewer, Director of Ticket Operations
cfewer@baysox.com
• Matt McLaughlin, Director of Corporate Sponsorships
mmclaughlin@baysox.com
• Darlene Mingioli, Director of Game Day Staff
dmingioli@baysox.com
• Brian Shallcross, General Manager
bshallcross@baysox.com
• Phil Wrye, Assistant General Manager
pwrye@baysox.com
• Andrew Jackson, Stadium Operations Manager
Sport:
Baseball
Team:
Bowie Baysox
Year Founded:
1994
Seating Capacity:
10,000

PRINCE WILLIAM CO. STADIUM
7 COUNTY COMPLEX COURT
WOODBRIDGE, VA 22192
703-590-5900
Fax: 703-590-0209
www.pwcparks.org
• Rich Artenian, Director
• Marvin Vann, Sports Marketing Coordinator
(703) 792-4005
mvann@pwcgov.org

PROGRESSIVE AUTO SALES ARENA
255 CHRISTINA STREET N
SARNIA, ON, CANADA N7S 7N2
519-332-0330
parksandrecreation@sarnia.ca
www.progressiveautosalesarena.com
Owners:
City of Sarnia.
Year Opened:
1998
Seating Capacity:
Hockey - 5,000. Concerts - 6,000.
Tenant(s):
OHL - Sarnia Sting.

PROGRESSIVE FIELD
2401 ONTARIO ST
CLEVELAND, OH 44115
216-420-4487
cleveland.indians.mlb.com
Seating Capacity:
43,345
Teams:
Cleaveland Indians MLB baseball.

PROVOST UMPHREY STADIUM
4400 MLK PARKWAY
LAMAR UNIVERSITY
BEAUMONT, TX 77705
409-880-1715
800-687-9962
Fax: 409-880-7542
www.lamarcardinals.com
• Brad McGowan, Assistant Athletic Director for Development
(409) 880-1881
• Jason Henderson, Athletic Director/Compliance Director
(409) 880-8303
jason.henderson@lamar.edu
• Sharon Williams, Executive Associate
(409) 880-2248
Sharon.Williams@lamar.edu
• Scott Reeves, Sport Performance Director
(409) 880-7427
• Joshua Miller, Sport Performance Assistant
(409) 880-7445
joshua.miller@lamar.edu
• Billy Tubbs, Athletic Director
(409) 880-2248
billy.tubbs@lamar.edu
Arena Seating Capacity:
17,000. Football; 10,200 Basketball.

QUAD CITIES RIVER BANDITS
209 S GAINES STREET
DAVENPORT, IA 52802
563-324-3000
Fax: 563-324-3109
bandit@riverbandits.com
www.riverbandits.com
• Nick Harvey, Ticket Manager
(563) 333-2737
Sport:
Minor League Baseball, Midwest League, Class A Affiliate of the Houston Astros.
Year Founded:
1931
Capacity:
5,500

QUALCOMM STADIUM
9449 FRIARS ROAD
SAN DIEGO, CA 92108
619-641-3100
Fax: 619-283-0460
stadium@sandiego.gov
www.sandiego.gov
• Michael McSweeney, Stadium General Manager
(619) 641-3126
• Michele Kelley, Special Events Coordinator
(619) 641-3187
Stadium Seating Capacity:
70,000.00
Year Founded:
1967
Clients:
San Diego Chargers, San Diego State Aztecs.

QUICKEN LOANS ARENA
1 CENTER COURT
CLEVELAND, OH 44115
216-420-2000
800-332-2287
888-894-9424
Fax: 216-420-2101
www.theqarena.com
• Boland Jim, Vice Chairman
• Len Komoroski, President
• Roy Jones, Executive VP/General Manager
• Edward Markey, Communications VP
• Gordon Gund, Chief Executive Officer
• John Wolf, Chief Financial Officer
• Roy Jones, Executive Vice President
• Sue Katalinas, President
• David Katzman, Vice Chairman
• Rod Hollen, Vice President
Owned by:
Gordon Gund & Gateway Economic Development Corp.
Permanent Seating Capacity:
20,500
Tenant(s):
AHL - Cleveland Barons ice hockey, NBA - Cleveland Cavaliers basketball, WNBA - Cleveland Rockers basketball.

QWEST FIELD
800 OCCIDENTAL AVENUE S
SUITE 100
SEATTLE, WA 98134
206-381-7555
888-NFL-HAWK
Fax: 425-893-5108
customerservice@seahawks.com
www.qwestfield.com
• Jeff Klein, VP/General Manager
Year Opened:
2002
Seating Capicity:
67,000
Team:
Seattle Seahawks NFL football.

RACER ARENA
218 STEWART STADIUM
ATHLETIC DEPARTMENT, MURRAY STATE UNIVERSITY
MURRAY, KY 42071
270-762-6800
800-272-4678
Fax: 270-762-6814
www.murraystate.edu
• Allen Ward, Athletic Director
(270) 809-3164
allen.ward@murraystate.edu
• Matt Kelly, Senior associate AD
(270) 809-4424
matt.kelly@murraystate.edu
• Paul Bubb, Associate AD (External affairs)
(270) 809-3369
paul.bubb@murraystate.edu
• Steve Harrell, Associate AD - Compliance & Administrative Af
(270) 809-3430
sharrell4@murraystate.edu
Seating Capacity:
5,500

RALEIGH CONVENTION AND CONFERENCE CENTER COMPLEX
500 S SALISBURY STREET
RALEIGH, NC 27601

919-996-8500
Fax: 919-996-8550
www.raleighconvention.com
• Laurie Okun, Director of Sales and Marketing
• Mickey Barbour, Operations Director
• Dave Chapman, IT Director
• Hazel Cockram, Assistant Director, Business and Finance
• Doug Grissom, Assistant Director, Outdoor Events and Festiv
• Mara Craft, National/International Convention Senior Sale
Permanent Seating Capacity:
3,800

RALEY FIELD
400 BALLPARK DRIVE
W SACRAMENTO, CA 95691
916-376-4700
Fax: 916-376-4710
reception@rivercats.com
www.raleyfield.com
• Matt LaRose, Stadium Operations VP
• Matt Fucile, Stadium Operations Director
Sport:
Baseball
Team:
Sacramento River Cats
Year Founded:
2000
Seating Capacity:
19,111

RALPH ENGELSTAD ARENA
ONE RALPH ENGELSTAD ARENA DRIVE
GRAND FORKS, ND 58203
701-777-4167
Fax: 701-777-6643
fans@theralph.com
www.theralph.com
• Michael Bergeron, Chief Financial Officer
(701) 777-4930
michaelb@theralph.com
• Charlie Muus, Director of Maintenance & Operations
(701) 777-0807
charliem@theralph.com
• Sadie Steenerson, Administrative Assistant
(701) 777-6609
sadies@theralph.com

RALPH WILSON STADIUM
1 BILLS DRIVE
ORCHARD PARK, NY 14127
716-648-0658
877-228-4257
888-283-4327
Fax: 716-312-8603
www.buffalobills.com
• William G Munson, Operations VP
• Joe Frandina, Vice President, Stadium Operations
• Russ Brandon, Business Development/Marketing VP
Permanent Seating Capacity:
73,967
Team:
Home Stadium for the Buffalo Bills
Owned by:
County of Erie

RANGERS BALLPARK
1000 BALLPARK WAY
ARLINGTON, TX 76011

817-273-5222
texas.rangers.mlb.com
Seating Capacity:
49,115
Teams:
Texas Rangers MLB baseball

RANKIN WILLIAMS FIELD HOUSE
100 CAMPUS DRIVE
SOUTHWESTERN OKLAHOMA STATE
UNIVERSITY
WEATHERFORD, OK 73096
580-772-6611
www.swosu.edu/athletics
• Todd Thurman, Athletic Director
todd.thurman@swosu.edu
• Justin Tinder, Sports Information Director
(580) 774-7162
justin.tinder@swosu.edu
Stadium Seating Capacity:
9,000

RAPIDES PARISH COLISEUM
5600 COLISEUM BOULEVARD
ALEXANDRIA, LA 71303
318-442-9581
Fax: 318-442-9582
rapidescoliseum@gmail.com
www.therapidesparishcoliseum.com/
• Don Guillory, Executive Director
Permanent Seating Capacity:
6,000

RATCLIFFE STADIUM
1101 E UNIVERSITY AVENUE
FRESNO, CA 93741
559-442-4600
Fax: 559-489-2281
www.fresnocitycollege.edu
• Susan Yates, Athletic Director
susan.yates@fresnocitycollege.edu
• Tony Cantu, President
• Dr.Tim Woods, VP
• Dr.Chris Villa, VP
• Cheryl Sullivan, VP of Administrative
Services
• Tony A. Cantu, President
Stadium Seating Capacity:
13,500

**RAYMOND CHABOT GRANT THORNTON
PARK**
302 COVENTRY ROAD
OTTAWA, ON, CANADA K1K 4P5
Founded:
1993
Team:
Ottawa Champions (Can-Am League)
Seating Capacity:
10,332

RAYMOND JAMES STADIUM
4201 N DALE MABRY HIGHWAY
TAMPA, FL 33607
813-350-6500
Fax: 813-673-4312
bcasey@tampasportsauthority.com
www.raymondjamesstadium.com
• Mickey Farrell, Dir. of Operations
(813) 350-6507
mfarrell@tampasportsauthority.com
• Jeanette Baker, Vice President of
Finance/Administration
(813) 350-6517
jbaker@tampasportsauthority.com
• Bobby Silvest, Vice President of Marketing

& Communications
(813) 350-6504
bsilvest@tampasportsauthority.com
• Kennie Sims, Vice President of Golf
Operations
(813) 350-6510
ksims@tampasportsauthority.com
• Kevin Kenny, Director of Golf
(813) 673-4316
kkenny@tampasportsauthority.com
• Laura Beuhring, Director of Golf
(813) 641-4374
lbeuhring@tampasportsauthority.com
• Eric Hart, President & CEO
(813) 350-6500
ehart@tampasportsauthority.com
Owned by:
Tampa Sports Authority.
Tenant(s):
NFL - Tampa Bay Buccaneers football,
NCAA - Outback Bowl football, NCAA -
Univ. of South Florida football, Monster Jam
Permanent Seating Capacity:
65,890

RBC CENTER
1400 EDWARDS MILL ROAD
RALEIGH, NC 27607
919-861-2300
Fax: 919-861-2310
www.thepncarena.com
• Emma Bennett, Arena Marketing Director
• Davin Olsen, Director Arena Operations
• Sims Hinds, Arena Management VP
Arena Seating Capacity:
Basketball 21,000; Hockey 18,500; AFL
16,985.
Home Arena for:
NHL - Carolina Hurricanes; NCAA - North
Carolina State University.

RE/MAX FIELD
10233 96TH AVENUE NW
EDMONTON, AB, CANADA T5K 0A5
780-717-6739
ryan@edmontonprospects.com
www.remaxfield.com
Owners:
City of Edmonton
Year Opened:
1995
Seating Capacity:
9,200
Tenant(s):
WMBL - Edmonton Prospects.

RED BULL ARENA
600 CAPE MAY STREET
HARRISON, NJ 7029
888-370-7287
fanservices@newyorkredbulls.com
www.newyorkredbulls.com/redbullarena
Seating Capacity:
25,000
Teams:
New York Red Bulls soccer.

RED MC EWEN BASEBALL FIELD
4202 E FOWLER AVENUE
UNIVERSITY OF SOUTH FLORIDA
TAMPA, FL 33620
813-974-2011
Fax: 813-974-4028
help@usf.edu
www.usf.edu
• Carl Carlucci, Chief Financial
Officer/President

• Clark Bruuns, Marketing/Promotions
Manager
• Kelly C Hickman, Event Operations
Assistant Director
• Doug Woolard, Director of Athletics
(813) 974-1442
• Bill McGillis, Executive Associate Director
of Athletics
(813) 974-8930
• Barry Clements, Senior Associate Director
of Athletics / Spor
(813) 974-4144
clements@usf.edu
• Craig Angelos, Associate Director of
Athletics / Compliance
(813) 974-3528
• Scott Glaser, Associate Director of
Athletics / Facilities
(813) 974-3110
sglaser@usf.edu
• Brett Huebner, Associate Director of
Athletics / CFO
(813) 974-3227
• Amy Perkins, Associate Director of
Athletics / SWA / Stude
(813) 974-3007
Stadium Seating Capacity:
3,000

REDBIRD ARENA
CAMPUS BOX 2660
ILLINOIS STATE UNIVERSITY, COLLEGE
AT DELAINE
NORMAL, IL 61790-2660
309-438-2000
Fax: 309-438-3513
www.goredbirds.com
• Cheahon Zenger, Athletic Director
(309) 438-3636
sjzenge@ilstu.edu
• Gary Friedman, Director of Athletics
(309) 438-3636
gafried@ilstu.edu
• Larry Lyons, Executive Associate Athletics
Director
(309) 438-5626
lelyons@ilstu.edu
• Leanna Bordner, Senior Associate
Athletics Director/SWA
(438) 3639
lkbordn@ilstu.edu
• Cindy Harris, Senior Associate Athletics
Director/Complianc
(309) 438-2677
caharri@ilstu.edu
Arena Seating Capacity:
10,500

**REED GREEN COLISEUM
(BASKETBALL)**
118 COLLEGE DRIVE
PO BOX 5017, UNIVERSITY OF
SOUTHERN MISSISSIPPI
HATTIESBURG, MS 39406-5142
601-266-6085
Fax: 601-266-4445
• Richard Giannini, Athletic Director
(601) 266-5422
• Scott Carr, Deputy Director of Athletics
(601) 266-5422
scott.carr@usm.edu
• Denis Wiesenburg, Provost
• Bob Pierce, Vice President-Advancement
• Tom Estes, Interim Vice President-Finance
& Administrati
• Frances Lucas, Vice President-Gulf Coast
• Joseph S. Paul, Vice President-Student

Affairs
• Aubrey K. Lucas, Interim President
Arena Seating Capacity:
8,095

RELIANT ASTRODOME
8400 KIRBY LANE
HOUSTON, TX 77054
832-677-1400
Fax: 832-667-1410
guestservices@reliantpark.com
www.reliantpark.com
• Guinn Shea, President
• Eric Jones, Marketing/Sales Director
• Mark Miller, General Manager
• Mary Majorwitz, Client Relations
Coordinator
• Barbara Beaton, Director of Sales
• Justin White, Executive Sales Manager
• Craig Chapman, Event Coordinator
• Ejah Praag, Event Coordinator
Permanent Seating Capacity:
58,000
Owned by:
Harris County

RELIANT ASTRODOME COMPLEX
8400 KIRBY DRIVE
HOUSTON, TX 77054
832-667-1400
Fax: 832-667-1748
guestservices@reliantpark.com
www.reliantpark.com
• Guinn Shey, General Manager
• Mark Miller, GM
• Jeff Gaines, Ass. GM
• Barbara Beaton, Sales Direcor
• Justin White, Executive Sales Manager
• Liz Conner, Contract Manager
• Lydia Parker, Booking Manager
• Pam Jones, Sales Administrative
Event Management Services:
Manages Astrodome/Astrohall/Astroarena.
Sports Complex-trade shows, consumer
shows, and exhibitions.
Seating Capacity:
65,000

RENSSELAER POLYTECHNIC INSTITUTE/HOUSTON FIELD
110 8TH STREET
TROY, NY 12180-3590
518-276-6000
www.rpi.edu
• Norris Pearson, Manager
(518) 276-6121
• Brian Darby, Operations Supervisor
darbyb@rpi.edu
Seating Capacity:
6,900

RENTSCHLER FIELD
615 SILVER LANE
EAST HARTFORD, CT 6118
860-610-4700
info@rentschlerfield.com
www.rentschlerfield.com
• Michael Fresher, General Manager
Seating Capacity:
40,000
Teams:
Univertisy of Conneticut football; Hartford
Colonials, United Football League

RESER STADIUM
114 GILL COLISEUM
OREGON STATE UNIVERSITY
CORVALLIS, OR 97331
541-737-2547
Fax: 541-737-7895
www.osubeavers.com
• Bob Cheney, Interim Operations Director
• Matt Arend, Ticket Operations Director
Stadium Seating Capacity:
35,000
Team:
Oregon State University football.

REYNOLDS COLISEUM
2500 WARREN CARROLL DRIVE
CAMPUS BOX 8502
WEISIGER BROWN BUILDING
RALEIGH, NC 27695
919-515-3050
Fax: 919-515-1161
www.gopack.com
• Billy Ray Dunn, Manager
(919) 515-2108
brdunn3@unity.ncsu.edu
• David Bowles, Maintainence Supervisor
(919) 515-2108
Arena Seating Capacity:
12,400

RICE STADIUM
6100 MAIN STREET
RICE UNIVERSITY
HOUSTON, TX 77005
713-348-0000
Fax: 713-348-6019
www.riceowls.com
• Chris DelConte, Athletic Director
(713) 348-4077
• Rick Greenspan, Director of Athletics
(713) 348-4077
• Rick Mello, Senior Executive Athletics
Director
(713) 348-8872
• Stacy Mosely, Senior Associate Athletics
Director, SWA
(713) 348-5829
• Dr. Jack Garrett, Senior Associate
AD/Sport Admin. and Support
(713) 348-6921
• Tina Villard, Director of Recreation Center
and Activities
(713) 348-5398
tvillard@rice.edu
• Andy Platt, Associate Athletics
Director/Business & Finan
(713) 348-509
• David Sayler, Sr. Executive Athletics
Director
(713) 348-4077
Arena Seating Capacity:
70,000
Team:
Rice University football.

RICE-ECCLES STADIUM
451 SOUTH 1400 EAST
6TH FLOOR
SALT LAKE CITY, UT 84112
801-581-5445
Fax: 801-585-1417
info@stadium.utah.edu
www.stadium.utah.edu
Seating Capacity:
45,600
Teams:
Utah Utes football.

RICE-TOTTEN STADIUM
MISSISSIPPI VALLEY STATE
UNIVERSITY, DEPT. OF ATHLETICS
14000 HIGHWAY 82 WEST
BOX 7246
ITTA BENA, MS 38941
662-254-3550
Fax: 662-254-3639
www.mvsusports.com
• Dianthia Ford-Kee, Director of Athletics
(662) 254-3550
• Rick Comegy, Head Coach, Football
rick.comegy@mvsu.edu
Seating Capacity:
10,000

RICHARD M BORCHARD REGIONAL FAIRGROUNDS/SPECTRA
1213 TERRY SHAMSIE BOULEVARD
ROBSTOWN, TX 78380
361-387-9000
Fax: 361-387-9077
jgreen@rmbfairgrounds.com
www.rmbfairgrounds.com
• Jason Green, General Manager
(361) 387-9000
jgreen@rmbfairgrounds.com
Teams:
Hurricane Alley Roller Derby Team
Seating Capacity:
Central Pavilion Arena: 2,000
Year Founded:
2003
Capacity:
4,000
Track Type:
Flat Track

RICHMOND COLISEUM
601 E LEIGH STREET
RICHMOND, VA 23219-1431
804-780-4970
Fax: 804-780-4606
info@richmondcoliseum.net
www.richmondcoliseum.net
• Dwight Johnson, Assistant General
Manager/Director of Operations
(804) 780-4970
djohnson@richmondcoliseum.net
• Lesa Williams, Assistant General Manager
Arena Seating Capacity:
13,523
Home Arena for:
AF2 - Richmond Speed.
Sports Organizations
Richmond Raiders-AIFA-Arena Football;
Arena Racing

RICHMOND COUNTY BANK BALLPARK
75 RICHMOND TERRACE
STATEN ISLAND, NY 10301
718-720-9265
Fax: 718-273-5763
www.siyanks.com
• Brown Robert, Manager, Stadium
Operations
• Dominic Costantino, Tickets Director
• Jane M. Rogers, President, General
Manager
jrogers@siyanks.com
• Kerry Atkinson, Senior Vice President of
Corporate Sales
• Brian Levine, Vice President of Ticket
Sales
blevine@siyanks.com
• Matt Gulino, Director, Ticket Sales &
Operations

facilities

- Tom Phillips, Finance Manager
- Jillian Wright, Manager, Sponsor Services
- Bob Brown, Facility Manager
(718) 313-1345
Sport:
Baseball
Team:
Staten Island Yankees
Year Founded:
2001
Capacity:
6,500

RICKENBRODE STADUIM
800 UNIVERSITY DRIVE
NW MISSOURI STATE UNIVERSITY
MARYVILLE, MO 64468
660-562-1562
Fax: 660-562-1493
www.nwmissouri.edu
- Gene Steinmeyer, Women's Basketball Coach
(660) 562-1299
- Bob Boerigter, Athletic Director
(660) 562-1306
- James Redd, Athletic Director
- Andy Seely, Sports Information Director
Rickenbrode Stadium Seating Capacity:
7,000
Lampkin Arena Seating Capacity:
3,000

RIPKEN STADIUM
873 LONG DRIVE
ABERDEEN, MD 21001
410-297-9292
Fax: 410-297-6653
www.ironbirdsbaseball.com
- Aaron Mozser, General Manager
(410) 297-9292
- Amy Venuto, Sales Director
(410) 297-9292
- Aaron Moszes, Assistant General Manager
(410) 297-9292
- Cal H Ripken, Jr., Principal Owner/Chairman & Founder
- Bill Ripken, CO-Owner/Executive Vice President
- Amy Venuto, Executive Director
Amy@ripkenbaseball.com
- Brad Cox, Assistant General Manager
bcox@ripkenbaseball.com
- Jason Vaughn, Production & Game Entertainment Manager
- Christopher Stieber, Account Executive
- Elly Ripken, Accounting Manager
elly@ripkenbaseball.com
Stadium Seating Capacity:
5,800.00
Year Founded:
2002
Clients:
MBNA, Coca-Cola, Baltimore Sun, Mercantile Bank, ComCast, Wingate Inn, Close Call America.
Nature of Service:
Baseball Stadium, Event Destination (Concerts/Shows/Games/etc.)
Teams:
Aberdeen Iron Birds

RIVERFRONT STADIUM
850 PARK ROAD
WATERLOO, IA 50703

319-232-0500
Fax: 319-232-0700
www.waterloobucks.com
- John Marso, Co-Owner
- Dan Corbin, General Manager
(319) 232-0500
corbin@waterloobucks.com
- Aaron Rustad, Assistant General Manager
- Kendall Hughson, Asst. GM/Dir of Stadium Operations
(319) 232-0500
Sport:
Summer collegiate baseball team.
Capacity:
5,000
Teams:
Waterloo Bucks, Northwoods League

RIVERSIDE ARENA
900 HARRINGTON STREET
HUTCHINSON, MN 55350
320-234-5640
Fax: 320-234-4243
Information@ci.hutchinson.mn.us
www.ci.austin.mn.us
- Dale Madison, Chairperson
(507) 433-1881
- Randy Queensland, Vice-Chairperson
- Lindy Rider, Secretary/Treasurer
- Tony Bennett, Director
- Tim Gabrielson, Director
- Marian Clennon, Director
- Steve Leif, Director
Arena Seating Capacity:
3,500.00
Year Founded:
1976
Track Type:
Concrete.
Track Size:
85x200.

ROANOKE CIVIC CENTER
710 WILLIAMSON ROAD
ROANOKE, VA 24016
540-853-2241
Fax: 540-853-2748
- Boyd Mina, Director
- Robyn Schon, Assistant Director
Arena Seating Capacity:
11,000.00
Year Founded:
1971
Clients:
Clear Channel Entertainment/Motorsports, Outback Concerts, Feld Entertainment.
Nature of Service:
Full-service public assembly facility.

ROBERT F. KENNEDY MEMORIAL STADIUM
2400 EAST CAPITOL ST, SOUTH EAST
WASHINGTON, DC 20003
202-587-5000
www.dcunited.com/matchday/stadium/faq
Seating Capacity:
57,000
Teams:
DC United soccer.

ROBERTS STADIUM (IA)
3201 PETERS AVENUE
SIOUX CITY, IA 51102
712-279-6651
Fax: 712-279-6099
- Ray Rowe, Facility Manager

Stadium Seating Capacity:
7,000

ROBINS CENTER
ROBINS CENTER
UNIVERSITY OF RICHMOND
RICHMOND, VA 23173
804-289-8363
Fax: 804-289-8820
www.cbssports.com
- Jim Miller, Athletic Director
(804) 289-8694
jmiller@richmond.edu
- Ruth M Goehring, Associate Athletic Director/Events & Fac
- Tanya Cornwell, Ticket Manager
Arena Seating Capacity:
9,171

ROBINS STADIUM
ROBINS CENTER
UNIVERSITY OF RICHMOND
RICHMOND, VA 23173
804-289-8363
Fax: 804-289-8820
athletic@richmond.edu
www.richmondspiders.com
- Jim Miller, Athletic Director
(804) 289-8694
- Keith M Gill, Director of Athletics
(804) 289-8694
athleticdirector@richmond.edu
- Robbie Brinkley, Assistant to the Director of Athletics
(804) 289-8694
- David Walsh, Deputy Athletic Director
(804) 289-8009
dwalsh@richmond.edu
- Cathy Rossi, Assistant Director of Athletics/Business
(804) 289-8368
- Bob Black, Assistant Director of Athletics/Communication
(804) 287-6885
bblack@richmond.edu
Stadium Seating Capacity:
22,319

ROCKFORD AVIATORS
4503 INTERSTATE DRIVE
LOVES PARK, IL 61111
815-885-2255
Fax: 815-885-2204
- Brad Sholes, General Manager
(815) 885-2255
- Rich Austin, Manager
(815) 885-2255
- Jacob Wise, Director of Media/Broadcasting
(815) 885-2255
Sport:
Baseball.
Team:
Rockford Aviators.
Year Founded:
2001
Seating Capacity:
3,500
Description:
Independent baseball team; member of Frontier league.

ROGER DEAN STADIUM
4751 MAIN STREET
JUPITER, FL 33458
561-775-1818
Fax: 561-691-6886

f.desk@rogerdeanstadium.com
www.rogerdeanstadium.com
• Jorge Toro, Stadium Building Manager
(561) 630-1852
j.toro@rogerdeanstadium.com
• Marshall Jennings, Facility Operations
Manager
(561) 630-1854
m.jennings@rogerdeanstadium.com
• Rob Rabenecker, General Manager
(561) 630-1848
r.rabenecker@rogerdeanstadium.com
• Mike Bauer, General Manager
(561) 630-1840
m.bauer@rogerdeanstadium.com
• Carol McAteer, Executive Assistant to the
General Manager
(561) 630-1850
c.mcateer@rogerdeanstadium.com
• Lisa Fegley, Assistant GM
(561) 799-1389
l.fegley@rogerdeanstadium.com
• Melissa Kuper, Assistant GM
(561) 630-1848
m.kuper@rogerdeanstadium.com
• David Vago, Office Manager
(561) 775-1818
d.vago@rogerdeanstadium.com
• Angie Albert, Accounting Assistant
(561) 630-1849
a.albert@rogerdeanstadium.com
• Alex Inman, Event Services Manager
(561) 630-1855
a.inman@rogerdeanstadium.com
Sport:
Baseball
Team:
Jupiter Hammerheads
Year Founded:
1998
Capacity:
6,600

ROGERS ARENA
800 GRIFFITHS WAY
VANCOUVER, BC, CANADA V6B 6G1
604-899-7400
rogersarena.com
Owners:
Canucks Sports & Entertainment.
Year Opened:
1995
Seating Capacity:
Hockey - 18,910. Basketball - 19,700.
Concerts - 19,000.
Tenant(s):
NHL - Vancouver Canucks

ROGERS CENTRE
1 BLUE JAYS WAY
TORONTO, ON, CANADA M5V 1J1
416-341-1000
guestservices@rogerscentre.com
Owners:
Rogers Communications, Inc.
Operators:
Rogers Stadium Limited Partnership.
Year Opened:
1989
Seating Capacity:
Baseball - 49,282. Canadian football -
31,074-52,230. American football - 54,000.
Soccer - 47,568. Basketball -
22,911-28,708. Concerts - 10,000-55,000.
Tenant(s):
MLB - Toronto Blue Jays

ROGERS PLACE
10220 104 AVENUE NW
EDMONTON, AB, CANADA T5H 2X6
780-414-5483
info@rogersplace.com
www.rogersplace.com
• Susan Darrington, Exececutive VP,
Rogers Place
Owners:
City of Edmonton.
Operators:
Oilers Entertainment Group.
Tenant(s):
NHL - Edmonton Oilers. WHL - Edmonton
Oil Kings.

ROGERS STADIUM
1 HAYDEN DR.
VIRGINIA STATE UNIVERSITY
PETERSBURG, VA 23806-2096
804-524-5000
Fax: 804-524-5763
www.vsu.edu
• Peggy Davis, Athletic Director
• Andrea C. Tatum, Director of Alumni
Relations
(804) 524-5973
atatum@vsu.edu
• Sharna D. Gannaway, Alumni Relations
Assistant
(804) 524-6935
sgannaway@vsu.edu
Permanent Seating Capacity:
13,500

RON STEPHENS STADIUM
1400 NW DEARBORN AVENUE
LAWTON, OK 73507
580-357-5672
• Jerry Cauthern, Athletic Director
Stadium Seating Capacity:
9,900

ROSE BASKETBALL ARENA
1200 FRANKLIN STREET
CENTRAL MICHIGAN UNIVERSITY
MOUNT PLEASANT, MI 48859
989-774-4000
Fax: 989-774-7957
cmsports@cmich.edu
www.cmich.edu
• Cal Seelye, Director, Events and
Conference Services
seely1ch@cmich.edu
• Chad Garland, Assistant Director, Events
and Conference Ser
(989) 774-7675
garla1ce@cmich.edu
• Emily Tritschler, Coordinator, Events and
Conference Services
mcclu1es@cmich.edu
• Scott Harrington, Technical Specialist,
University Events
(989) 774-3355
harri3sr@cmich.edu
• Connie Camp, SR Specialist Clerk, Bovee
University Center
(989) 774-7477
highe1cl@cmich.edu
• Brittany Cornwell, Graduate Assistant,
Events and Conference Ser
cornw1ba@cmich.edu
Description:
Additional Website:
www.cmuchippewas.com
Arena Seating Capacity:
5,200

ROSE BOWL STADIUM
1001 ROSE BOWL DRIVE
PASADENA, CA 91103
626-577-3100
Fax: 626-405-0992
rosebowlstadium@yahoo.com
www.rosebowlstadium.com
• Darryl Dunn, General Manager
ddunn@ci.pasadena.ca.us
• Larry Madden, CFO
(626) 577-3100
• Charles Thompson, HR Manager
(626) 577-3100
• George Cunningham, Chief Operating
Officer
• Larry Madden, Chief Financial officer
• David Sams, Director of Golf Course
Operations
• Charles Thompson, Corp Communications
• Julie Benavidez, Event Manager
• Paul Engl, Sponsorship Director
Home Stadium for:
NCAA - Rose Bowl, UCLA Bruins Football,
MLS - Los Angeles Galaxy.
Stadium Seating Capacity:
92,542
Description:
Sports/Entertainment stadium

ROSE GARDEN, THE
ONE CENTER COURT
SUITE 150
PORTLAND, OR 97227
503-797-9619
Fax: 503-236-4906
facilitymarketing@rosequarter.com
www.rosegarden.com
• Hubert Erin, EVP
• J Isaac, SVP Business Affairs
• Jim Kotchik, SVP/Chief Financial Officer
• Jim McCue, VP Facility Sales/Marketing
Permanent Seating Capacity:
20,300
Tenant(s):
NBA - Portland Trail Blazers basketball;
WHL - Portland Winter Hawks hockey.

ROSE QUARTER BOX OFFICE
ONE CENTER COURT
SUITE 150
PORTLAND, OR 97227
503-235-8771
Fax: 503-736-2187
Feedback@RoseQuarter.com
www.rosequarter.com
• Erin Hubert, EVP
• J Isaac, SVP Business Affairs
• Jim Kotchik, SVP/Chief Financial Officer
• Chris Oxley, General Manager
Arena Seating Capacity:
12,000

ROSENBLATT STADIUM
12356 BALLPARK WAY
WERNER PARK
PAPILLION, NE 68046
402-734-2550
Fax: 402-734-7166
www.oroyals.com
• Kyle Fisher, Vice President/Baseball
Operations
• Erich Hover, Ticket Sales
Director/Operations
• Gary Green, Chief Executive Officer
• Martie Cordaro, President and General
Manager
• Laurie Schlender, Assistant General

Manager
• Matthew Rau, Director of Corporate Sales
• Dave Endress, Director of Business Development
• Mark Nasser, Director of Broadcasting
• Brett Pollock, Director of Baseball Operations
Sport:
Baseball
Team:
Omaha Royals
Year Founded:
1948
Capacity:
24,000

ROSS-ADE STADIUM
850 BEERING DRIVE
PURDUE UNIVERSITY
W LAFAYETTE, IN 47907
765-496-2005
800-497-7678
Fax: 765-496-1842
www.purduesports.com
• Morgan Burke, Athletic Director
(765) 494-3189
mjb@purdue.edu
• Roger Blalock, Senior Associate Athletic Director
(765) 494-3203
Stadium Seating Capacity:
62,500

ROY STEWART STADIUM
217 STEWART STADIUM
MURRAY STATE ATHLETICS
MURRAY, KY 42071-3351
270-809-6858
Fax: 270-762-6800
www.goracers.com
• Miles Chambers, Equipment Manager
(270) 809-3430
• Allen Ward, Administration - Director of Athletics
(270) 809-3164
allen.ward@murraystate.edu
• Matt Kelly, Administration - Senior Associate AD
(270) 809-4424
matt.kelly@murraystate.edu
• Paul Bubb, Administration - Associate AD - External Affa
(270) 809-3369
• Steve Harrell, Administration - Associate AD - Compliance &
(270) 809-3430
sharrell4@murraystate.edu
• Velvet Milkman, Administration - Senior Woman Administrator
(270) 809-5408
vmilkman@murraystate.edu
• Crystal Morrow, Administration - Assistant to the Athletic Di
(270) 809-3746
crystal.morrow@murraystate.edu
Permanent Seating Capacity:
16,800

ROY WILKINS AUDITORIUM
199 WEST KELLOG BLVD.
SAINT PAUL, MN 55102
651-265-4800
Fax: 651-265-4899
info@xcelenergycenter.com
www.theroy.org
• Jim Ibister, Vice President
(651) 265-4801

• Jim Ibister, General Manager
(651) 265-4801
• Susan Hubbard, Director of Booking and Administration
(651) 265-4806
• Mark Stoffel, Senior Director of Operations
(651) 265-4807
• Kristina Meier, Director of Box Office Operations
(651) 726-8264
• Kate Steley, Director of Event Management and RiverCentre
(651) 265-4810
• John Koehler, Event Manager
(651) 265-4849
• Jill Mastel, Event Manager
(651) 265-4809
Seating Capacity:
10,000

ROYAL FARMS ARENA
201 WEST BALTIMORE STREET
BALTIMORE, MD 21201
410-347-2020
Fax: 410-347-2042
www.royalfarmsarena.com
• Jason Smith, Director of Operations
Arena Seating Capacity:
11,271
Year Founded:
1962
Nature of Service:
Entertainment, sporting events.

RUPP ARENA
430 W VINE STREET
LEXINGTON, KY 40507
859-233-4567
Fax: 859-253-2718
boxoffice@rupparena.com
www.rupparena.com
• Bill Owen, President and CEO
bowen@rupparena.com
• Carl Hall, Director Arena Management
chall@rupparena.com
• Carl Hall, Director of Arena Management
• Cathy Derr, Senior Manager, Arena Events
• Theresa Lloyd, Manager, Arena Events
• Neal Werner, Director of Business Affairs
• Merrill Richardson, Director of Facilities Administration
• Bob Stoops, Technical Services Manager
Year Founded:
1976
Arena Seating Capacity:
2,300-23,000
Clients Include:
University of Kentucky Men's Basketball, Clear Channel Entertainment, Lexington Horsemen, Outback Concerts

RUSHMORE PLAZA CIVIC CENTER
444 N. MT. RUSHMORE ROAD
RAPID CITY, SD 57701
605-394-4111
800-468-6463
Fax: 605-394-6621
gotmine@rushmore.com
www.gotmine.com
• Brian Maliske, General Manager
(605) 394-4115
• Jayne Kraemer, Assistant General Manager
(605) 394-4115
jaynek@rushmore.com
• Steve Montgomery, Marketing Sales Manager

• Paul Sterling, Operations Manager
• Tom Barber, Asst operations Manager
• Brian Maliske, General Manager
• Tracy Heitsch, Asst General Manager / Finance
• Jayne Kraemer, Asst General Manager / Events
• Tanya Gray, Director of Events Services
• Larry Dale, Life Safety & Events Coordinator
Arena Seating Capacity:
11,000

RUSSELL E. DIETHRICK JR. PARK
485 FALCONER STREET
RUSSELL E DIETHRICH, JR PARK
JAMESTOWN, NY 14702-0638
716-664-0915
Fax: 716-664-4175
www.jamestownjammers.com
• Matt Drayer, General Manager
matt@jamestownjammers.com
• George Sisson, Sales/Marketing Director
george@jamestownjammers.com
Sport:
Baseball
Team:
Jametown Jammers
Year Founded:
1941
Capacity:
3,300

RUTGERS ATHLETIC CENTER
83 ROCKAFELLER ROAD
PISCATAWAY, NJ 08854
732-445-4223
Fax: 732-445-2990
www.scarletknights.com
• McK Williams, Associate Athletic Director
• Tim Pernetti, Athletic Director
(732) 445-7839
ad@scarletknights.com
• Jason Baum, Senior Associate AD, Communications
(732) 445-4200
jbaum@scarletknights.com
• Geoff Brown, Senior Associate AD/Chief Marketing Officer
(732) 445-7868
gbrown@scarletknights.com
• Doug Fillis, Senior Associate AD, Administration
(732) 445-7816
dfillis@scarletknights.com
• Kate Hickey, Senior Associate AD/Senior Woman Administrato
(732) 445-7899
khickey@scarletknights.com
• Douglas Kokoskie, Senior Associate AD for Facilties/Events/Oper
(732) 445-4223
koko@scarletknights.com
• Tim Thiess, Accounting Assistant
Permanent Seating Capacity:
9,000

RYAN CENTER
ONE LINCOLN ALMOND PLAZA
THE RYAN CENTER
KINGSTON, RI 02881
401-788-3200
Fax: 401-788-3210
info@theryancenter.com
www.theryancenter.com

• Ron Petro, Athletic Director
• Diana Zanetto, Director Sales & Marketing
(401) 788-3230
Year Opened:
2002
Tenant(s):
NCAA - University of Rhode Island
basketball.
Permanent Seating Capacity:
7,571
Team:
Northwestern football

RYAN FIELD
1501 CENTRAL STREET
EVANSTON, IL 60208
847-491-7887
www.nusports.com
• Jim Phillips, Vice President for Athletics &
Recreation
• Scott Arey, Assoc. AD, Facilities
• Pat Fitzgerald, Head Coach, Football
Team:
Northwestern Wildcats
Seating Capacity:
47,130

SAFECO FIELD
1250 1ST AVENUE
SEATTLE, WA 98154
206-346-4000
800-332-3226
Fax: 206-346-4250
www.safeco.com
• Geffrey Craig, Manager
• Jackie Cram, Assistant
Manager/Operations
• Cindy Hum, Assistant Manager/Services
• Moose Clusen, Safeco Site Sales
Stadium Seating Capacity:
47,000
Team:
Seattle Mariners major league baseball.

SAINT JOSEPH CIVIC ARENA
100 N 4TH STREET
SAINT JOSEPH, MO 64501
816-271-4717
800-821-5052
Fax: 816-232-9213
kbrock@stjoemo.org
civicfac@ci.st-joseph.mo.us
• Kathy Brock, Manager Civic Facilities
(816) 271-4717
kbrock@stjoemo.org
• Chad Bumphrey, Operations Supervisor
cbumphrey@stjoemo.org
• Carolyn Thomas, Operations Coordinator
cathomas@stjoemo.org
Arena Seating Capacity:
4,222 concert style; 3,800 basketball style
Year Founded:
1980
Nature of Service:
Multi-use facility hosting events such as
trade shows, banquets, circus, meetings,
basketball, bull riding, roller derby,
conventions, concerts, wrestling,
gymnastics, etc.

SALEM CIVIC CENTER
1001 ROANOKE BOULEVARD
SALEM, VA 24153
540-375-3004
Fax: 540-375-4011
www.salemciviccenter.com

• Harveycutter C. Carey, Director of Civic
Facilities
charveycutter@salemva.gov
• John E Saunders, Assistant Director
• Peggy Dickerson, Sales Director
Arena Seating Capacity:
8,500
Stadium Seating Capacity:
6,100 (Baseball).
Stadium Seating Capacity:
8,000 (Football).

SAM BOYD STADIUM
4505 S MARYLAND PARKWAY
LAS VEGAS, NV 89154
702-895-3011
Fax: 702-895-1099
• Gayle Juneau, Ed.D., Executive Director of
Academic Advising
• Tricia Lozano, M.Ed., Academic Advising
Administration Coordinator
• Roy Hessinger, B.S., Advising Database
Analyst
• Eric Lee, UNLV Transition Advisor
• Janet Hollinger, UNLV Transition Advisor
Stadium Seating Capacity:
42,500
Owned by:
Univ of Nevada, Las Vegas.

SAM LYNN BALLPARK
4009 CHESTER AVENUE
BAKERSFIELD, CA 93301
661-716-4487
Fax: 661-322-6199
• Noren Craig, Stadium Operations Director
• Cricket Whitaker, Ticket Sales Director
• Dan Besbris, Director of Broadcasting and
Media Relations
(424) 248-0866
DBesbris@BakersfieldBlaze.com
• Dale Billodeaux, Director of Sales and
Merchandise
• Elizabeth Martin, General Manager
EMartin@BakersfieldBlaze.com
• Philip Guiry, Assistant General Manager
• Mike Candela, Assistant General
Manager, Ticketing
• Megan Murphy, Event and Group Manager
• Brianne Gidcumb, Ticket Sales Manager
Sport:
Baseball
Team:
Bakersfield Blaze
Year Founded:
1941
Capacity:
4,200

**SAMUEL J. PLUMERI FIELD AT MERCER
COUNTY WATERFRONT PARK**
ONE THUNDER ROAD
TRENTON, NJ 8611
609-394-3300
Fax: 609-394-9666
fun@trentonthunder.com
www.trentonthunder.com
• Matt Pentima, Ticket Operations Director
(609) 394-3300
mattp@trentonthunder.com
• Will Smith, General Manager/ Chief
Operating Officer
will@trentonthunder.com
• Eric Lipsman, Senior Vice President of
Corporate Sales and
(609) 394-3300
eric@trentonthunder.com

• Ryan Crammer, Vice President,
Operations
(609) 394-3300
ryan@trentonthunder.com
• Matt Pentima, Director of Ticket
Operations
(609) 394-3300
matt@trentonthunder.com
• Bill Cook, Director of Public Relations
(609) 394-3300
bill@trentonthunder.com
• Joe Pappalardo, Director of Merchandising
(609) 394-3300
joe@trentonthunder.com
• Patience Purdy, Director of Community
Relations
(609) 394-3300
Sport:
Baseball
Team:
Trenton Thunder
Year Founded:
1994
Capacity:
6,440

SAN JOSE MUNICIPAL STADIUM
588 E ALMA AVENUE
SAN JOSE, CA 95112
408-297-1435
Fax: 408-297-1453
www.sjgiants.com
• Linda Pereira, Director, Player Relations
(408) 297-1435
• Chris Lampe, Chief Operating Officer
(408) 297-1435
chrislampe@sjgiants.com
• Mike Wilson, General Manager
(408) 297-1435
markwilson@sjgiants.com
• Zach Walter, Assistant General Manager
(408) 297-1435
zachwalter@sjgiants.com
• Terry Mylor, Operations
Capacity:
4,000

SANFORD STADIUM
1 SELIG CIRCLE
UNIVERSITY OF GEORGIA, PO BOX 1472
ATHENS, GA 30602
706-542-9036
Fax: 706-542-2980
www.georgiadogs.com/facilities/sanford-sta
dium.html
• Vince Dolley, Athletic Director
• Charles Whittemore, Assistant Athletic
Director/Facilities
• Ray McEwen, Assistant Director/Facilities
• Michael Adams, UGA President
• Jere W. Morehead, Vice Chairman
• Greg McGarity, Director of Athletics
ad@sports.uga.edu
• Frank Crumley, Executive Associate
Athletic Director - Finan
fcrumley@sports.uga.edu
• Carla Williams, Executive Associate
Athletic Director
cwilliams@sports.uga.edu
• Claude Felton, Senior Associate Athletic
Director - Sports C
cfelton@sports.uga.edu
• Alan Thomas, Associate Athletic Director -
External Operat
athomas@sports.uga.edu
Stadium Seating Capacity:
92,746

SAVVIS CENTER
1401 CLARK AVENUE
SAINT LOUIS, MO 63103
314-622-5400
Fax: 314-622-2588
webmaster@scottradecenter.com
www.scottradecenter.com
• Dennis Petrullo, SVP/General Manager
• Fred Corsi, Operations VP
• Dave Coverstone, Human Resources VP
• David Born, Guest Service Director
Arena Seating Capacity:
19,022
Tenant(s):
NHL - St. Louis Blues ice hockey; NCAA -
Saint Louis University men's basketball

SCHAUMBURG BOOMERS STADIUM
1999 SOUTH SPRINGSGUTH ROAD
SCHAUMBURG, IL 60193
847-461-3695
Fax: 630-493-3501
info@boomersbaseball.com
www.boomersbaseball.com
• Pete Laven, President, General Manager
(847) 461-3695
plaven@salvisports.com
• Mike Tlusty, Director of Facilities
(847) 461-3695
mtlusty@boomersbaseball.com
• Ryan Kukla, Director of Ticket Operations
(847) 461-3695
rkukla@boomersbaseball.com
Services
It is primarily used for baseball and cricket,
and is the home field of the Schaumburg
Boomers.
Seating Capacity
7,365

VALUE CITY ARENA/JEROME SCHOTTENSTEIN CENTER
555 BORROR DRIVE
COLUMBUS, OH 43210
614-688-3939
800-273-6201
800-ARENA-01
Fax: 614-292-5067
osuarena@osu.edu
www.schottensteincenter.com
• Vicki L Chorman, Associate Director
• Justin Doyle, Manager Marketing
Promotions
• Michael Gatto, Director Events
Administration
• Scott Dickson, Director of Event Services
and Security
• Carolyn Speicher, Guest Services
Manager
• Andy Geiger, Athletics Director
Arena Seating Capacity:
13,276

SCOPE ARENA
201 E BRAMBLETON AVENUE
NORFOLK, VA 23510
757-664-6464
Fax: 757-664-6990
www.sevenvenues.com/about/mission/scop
e
• John Rhamstine, Director
Arena Seating Capacity:
13,800
Home Arena for:
NCAA - Old Dominion University, AF2 -
Norfolk Nighthawks

SCOTIABANK ARENA
40 BAY STREET
TORONTO, ON, CANADA M5J 2L2
416-815-5500
www.scotiabankarena.com
• Michael Friisdahl, President/CEO, Maple
Leaf Sports & Entertainment
• Cynthia Devine, Chief Financial Officer
• Nick Eaves, Chief Venues & Operations
Officer
Owners:
Maple Leaf Sports & Entertainment Ltd.
Year Opened:
1999
Tenant(s):
NBA - Toronto Raptors, NHL - Toronto
Maple Leafs, NLL - Toronto Rock.
Seating Capacity:
Basketball - 19,800. Hockey - 18,800.
Lacrosse - 18,819. Concerts - 19,800.
Theater - 5,200.

SCOTIABANK SADDLEDOME
555 SADDLEDOME RISE SE
CALGARY, AB, CANADA T2G 2W1
403-777-4646
Fax: 403-777-2171
customerservice@calgaryflames.com
www.scotiabanksaddledome.com
• Libby Raines, VP, Building Operations
• Trent Anderson, Director, Building
Operations
Owners:
City of Calgary.
Operators:
Saddledome Foundation/Calgary Flames
LP.
Year Opened:
1983
Seating Capacity:
19,289
Tenant(s):
NHL - Calgary Flames. NLL - Calgary
Roughnecks. WHL - Calgary Hitmen.

SCOTT STADIUM
UVA ATHLETIC DEPT
PO BOX 400825
CHARLOTTESVILLE, VA 22904-4825
434-982-5200
Fax: 434-982-5213
ece3k@virginia.edu
www.virginiasports.com
• Keith Te VanDerbeek, Associate Director
of Athletics for Business Opera
(434) 982-5200
kdv@virginia.edu
• Jon Oliver, Executive Assistant Athletics
Director
(434) 243-5114
jko3b@virginia.edu
• Craig Littlepage, Director of Athletics
(434) 982-5100
• Becky Davis, Executive Assistant
(434) 982-5100
• Jon Oliver, Executive Associate Athletics
Director
(434) 243-5114
• Sharon McCauley, Administrative
Assistant to the Executive Ass
(434) 243-5114
• Jane Miller, Senior Associate Director of
Athletics for Pr
(434) 982-5151
• Kyle Denzel, General Manager
Stadium Seating Capacity:
61,500

Team:
University of Virginia football.

SCOTTSDALE STADIUM
7408 E OSBORN ROAD
SCOTTSDALE, AZ 85251
480-312-2586
Fax: 480-312-2888
tnichols@ScottsdaleAZ.gov
www.scottsdaleaz.gov/stadium
• Clifford Craig, Financial services general
manager
• Jeff Cesaretti, Stadium Co-ordinator
(480) 312-2380
jcesaretti@ScottsdaleAZ.gov
• Stephanie Johnson, Assistant Stadium
Co-ordinator
(480) 312-2856
stejohnson@ScottsdaleAZ.gov
Sport:
Minor League Baseball
Team:
Scottsdale Scorpions.
Year Founded:
1992
Capacity:
3688 Stadium seats; 4500 Bleacher seats;
3012 Berm seats

SEAGATE CENTRE
401 JEFFERSON AVENUE
TOLEDO, OH 43604
419-255-3300
Fax: 419-255-7731
cdupuis@meettoledo.org
www.toledo-seagate.com
• Carol E DuPuis, Director of Sales and
Marketing
(419) 392-0937
cdupuis@meettoledo.org
• Jim Thielman, Director Operations
• Carol Dupuis, Director
Sales/Marketing/Booking
(419) 392-0937
cdupuis@meettoledo.org
• Steve Miller, General Manager
(419) 321-5010
smiller@meettoledo.org
• J.T. Theilman, Director of Operations
(419) 321-5025
jthielman@meettoledo.org
• Agnes Rock, Director of Finance
(419) 321-5015
• Terry Huerta, Human Resource & Payroll
Manager
(419) 321-5018
THuerta@meettoledo.org
• Launren O'neill, Sales Manager
(419) 321-5006
• Michael Mccall, Event Services Manager
(419) 321-5029
Arena Seating Capacity:
7,500

SEC TAYLOR STADIUM
ONE LINE DRIVE
PRINCIPAL PARK
DES MOINES, IA 50309
515-243-6111
800-464-2827
Fax: 515-243-5152
www.iowacubs.com
• Tom Greene, Director Stadium Operations
tgreene@iowacubs.com
• Jim Nahas, VP, Assistant General
Manager
jnahas@iowacubs.com

• Chris Schlosser, Head Groundskeeper
• Michael Gartner, Chairman
mgartner@iowacubs.com
• Sam Bernabe, President / General Manager
sbernabe@iowacubs.com
• Michael Giudicessi, Corporate Secretary
mikeg@iowacubs.com
• Nate Teut, VP / Assistant General Manager
(515) 280-2652
natet@iowacubs.com
• Jim Nahas, VP / Assistant General Manager
(515) 243-6019
jnahas@iowacubs.com
• Sue Tollefson, VP / Chief Financial Office
(515) 243-6015
suet@iowacubs.com
• Deene Ehlis, VP / Director of Broadcast Operations
(515) 280-2648
dehlis@iowacubs.com
Stadium Seating Capacity:
11,500.00
Year Founded:
1992
Track Type:
Grass.
Track Size:
335-400-335.

SELBY STADIUM
61 S SANDUSKY STREET
DELAWARE, OH 43015
740-368-3200
Fax: 740-368-3751
www.owu.edu
• Roger Ingles, Athletic Director
(740) 368-3738
rdingles@owu.edu
• Seth McGuffin
(740) 368-3756
Seating Capacity:
9,800
Sports:
Track & Field, Field Hockey, Football, Track, Men's & Women's Lacrosse.
Track:
1/4 mile Defango

SHAW PARK
ONE PORTAGE AVENUE E
WINNIPEG, MB, CANADA R3B 3N3
204-982-2273
Fax: 204-982-2274
contact@goldeyes.com
goldeyes.com/shaw-park
• Sam Katz, President, Winnipeg Goldeyes
Sport:
Baseball
Team:
Winnipeg Goldeyes; Winnipeg Wesmen
Year Founded:
1999
Capacity:
7,461

SHIRK STADIUM
13TH & BERN STREETS
PO BOX 15234
READING, PA 19612
610-921-2381
Fax: 610-921-7566
athletics@alb.edu
www.albright.edu

• Robert J. Beall, President & Chief Executive Officer
• W. C. Jack Miller, Vice Chair
• Steve George, Athletic Director
• Karen A. Rightmire, Secretary
• John T. Baily, Chair
Stadium Seating Capacity:
9,000

SHOEMAKER CENTER
2600 CLIFTON AVENUE
UNIVERSITY OF CINCINNATI
CINCINNATI, OH 45221
513-556-6000
Fax: 513-556-0601
reccenter@uc.edu
www.uc.edu
• Kendra Violet, Associate Director of Facilities and Operations
• Francisco Hiawath, Coordinator Operations/Facilities
• Bob Bauer, Operations/Maintenance Director
Arena Seating Capacity:
13,164

SHOW ME CENTER
1333 N SPRIGG STREET
CAPE GIRARDEAU, MO 63701
573-651-2297
Fax: 573-651-5054
smc@semo.edu
www.showmecenter.biz
• Ross David, Director
dross@semo.edu
• Greg Talbut, Business Manager
(573) 651-2297
gtalbut@semo.edu
• Brad Gentry, Marketing Director
bgentry@semo.edu
• Jack Davis, Event Supervisor
Arena Seating Capacity:
10,000
Tenant(s):
NCAA - Southeast Missouri State University athletics

SHUFORD GYM/STADIUM
625 7TH AVENUE NE
HICKORY, NC 28601
828-328-1741
Fax: 828-328-7329
• Todd Lawing, Associate Athletics Director
• Caroline Cauthen, Director
Shuford Gym Seating Capacity:
3,000
Stadium Seating Capacity:
10,000

SILVER CROSS FIELD
1 MAYOR ART SCHULTZ DRIVE
SILVER CROSS FIELD
JOLIET, IL 60432
815-722-2287
Fax: 815-726-4304
info@jolietslammers.com
www.jolietslammers.com
• Kelly Sufka, Executive Vice President/General Manager
(815) 774-2885
ksufka@jackhammerbaseball.com
• Jeff Eckert, Director of Field/Stadium Operations
Team:
Joliet Jackhammers
Sport:
Baseball

Year Founded:
2003
Capacity:
6,915

SILVIO O. CONTE FORUM
140 COMMONWEALTH AVENUE
CHESTNUT HILL, MA 2467
617-552-8520
Fax: 617-552-4903
gene.d@bc.edu
www.bceagles.com
• Gene DeFilippo, Athletic Director
• Brad Bates, Director of Athletics
(617) 552-4681
• Beth Mahoney, Administrative Assistant to the Director of A
(617) 552-4680
mahonebe@bc.edu
• John Kane, Senior Associate Athletic Director
(617) 552-8840
kano@bc.edu
• Jody Mooradian, Senior Associate Athletics Director - SWA
(617) 552-4801
Arena Seating Capacity:
8,606

SIMMONS FIELD
330 N GLENVIEW AVENUE
MILWAUKEE, WI 53143-3379
414-453-4567
Fax: 414-453-3001
www.wlhs.org
• Jeff Sitz, Athletic - Director
(414) 453-4567
• Ryan Walz, Physical Education/Religion
(414) 453-4567
• Rev. Kenneth Fisher, President
ext 2161
ken.fisher@wlhs.org
Sport:
Baseball
Team:
Kennosha Mammoths
Year Founded:
1933
Capacity:
3,000

SIOUX FALLS ARENA
1201 N W AVENUE
SIOUX FALLS, SD 57104-1334
605-367-7288
800-338-3177
Fax: 605-338-1463
info@sfarena.com
www.sfarena.com
• Russ DeCurtins, General Manager
• Terry Torkildson, General Manager
terry@sfarena.com
• Jeff Gortmaker, Director of Operations
• Carmen Giles, Director of Event Services
• Dusty Plaugher, Operations Manager
• Nicole Nogosek, Box Office Manager
• Rick Huffman, Director of Sales & Marketing
• Kelly Zamora, Director of Finance
Arena Seating Capacity:
8,000

SIOUX FALLS STADIUM
1001 N W AVENUE
SIOUX FALLS, SD 57104
605-333-6060
Fax: 605-333-0139

info@sfcanaries.com
www.sfcanaries.com
• John Kuhn, President
jkuhn@canariesbaseball.com
• Tom Garrity, President/CEO
• Gary Weckwerth, Managing Partner
garyweck@aol.com
• Jim Loria, Senior Vice President of
Corporate Sponsorshi
(605) 336-6060
• Jim Olander, Vice President of Broadcast
& Communications
(605) 336-6060
olander@sfstampede.com
• Nate Welch, Vice President of Operations
(605) 336-6060
• Matt Ferguson, Vice President of Ticket
Sales
(605) 336-6060
• Kim Hipple, Director of Ticketing
(605) 336-6060
Sport:
Baseball.
Team:
Sioux Falls Canaries.
Year Founded:
1941
Capacity:
4,500

SKY SOX STADIUM
4385 TUTT BOULEVARD
SECURITY SERVICE FIELD
COLORADO SPRINGS, CO 80922
719-597-1449
Fax: 719-597-2491
www.skysox.com
• Rai Henniger, Senior Vice President
Marketing & Promotions
• Steve DeLeon, Vice President of Field
Operations
sdeleon@skysox.com
Sport:
Baseball
Team:
Colorado Springs Sky Sox
Year Founded:
1988
Capacity:
8,500

SKYHAWK ARENA
15 MT PELIA ROAD
1022 ELAM CENTER
UT MARTIN
MARTIN, TN 38238
731-881-7660
Fax: 731-881-7962
www.utmsports.com
• Kevin Creech, Sales & Marketing Assistant
(731) 881-7694
kcreech@utm.edu
• Phil Dane, Athletics Director
(731) 881-7661
pdane@utm.edu
• Bill Kaler, Assistant Athletics
Director/Compliance Offic
(731) 881-7662
bkaler@utm.edu
• Danelle Fabianich, Assistant Athletics
Director for Administrati
(731) 881-7663
danellef@utm.edu
• Tracie Moss, Athletics Secretary &
Insurance
(731) 881-7660
tmoss@utm.edu

• Trudy Henderson, Administrative
Specialist
(731) 881-7630
trudyh@utm.edu
• Joe Lofaro, Sports Information Director
(731) 881-7632
jlofaro@utm.edu
• Bart Belew, Assistant Athletics Director for
Athletic Tra
(731) 881-7679
bbelew@utm.edu
Arena Seating Capacity:
6,600

SKYHAWK STADIUM
15 MT PELIA ROAD
1022 ELAM CENTER
UT MARTIN
MARTIN, TN 38238
731-881-7660
Fax: 731-881-7962
www.utmsports.com
• Phil Dane, Athletic Director
(731) 881-7661
pdane@utm.edu
• Danelle Fabianich, Assistant Athletics
Director for Administrati
(731) 881-7663
danellef@utm.edu
• Tracie Moss, Athletics Secretary &
Insurance
(731) 881-7660
tmoss@utm.edu
• Trudy Henderson, Administrative
Specialist
(731) 881-7630
trudyh@utm.edu
• Joe Lofaro, Sports Information Director
(731) 881-7632
jlofaro@utm.edu
• Bart Belew, Assistant Athletics Director for
Athletic Tra
(731) 881-7679
bbelew@utm.edu
Stadium Seating Capacity:
7,500

SLEEP TRAIN ARENA
ONE SPORTS PARKWAY
SACRAMENTO, CA 95834
916-928-0000
Fax: 916-928-0727
www.sleeptrainarena.com
Seating Capacity:
17,317
Tenants:
Sacramento Kings

SMITH'S BALLPARK
77 WEST 1300 SOUTH
SALT LAKE CITY, UT 84115
801-350-6900
Fax: 801-485-6818
www.milb.com/index.jsp?sid=t561
• Clark Whitworth, President
(801) 350-6900
• Steve Starks, President, Miller Sports
Properties
(801) 350-6900
• Marc Amicone, Vice President, General
Manager
Sport:
Baseball.
Tenant(s):
Salt Lake Bees baseball.
Year Founded:
1994

Capacity:
15,411

SMITH-WILLIS STADIUM
200 LAKELAND DRIVE
JACKSON, MS 39216
601-968-5956
Fax: 601-965-7025
slittle@belhaven.edu
• Aguilar Andrew, Assistant General
Manager
• Amanda Stringer, Group Sales/Ticket
Marketing Director
Team:
Jackson Senators
Sport:
Baseball

SMITH-WILLS STADIUM
1200 LAKELAND DRIVE
JACKSON, MS 39216
601-362-2294
Fax: 601-362-9577
www.jacksonsenators.com
• Brasfield Craig, VP/General Manager
(601) 362-2294
• Chet Carey, Assistant General
Manager/Sales Marketin
(601) 362-2294
• Scott Jacobs, Group Sales Director/Ticket
Operations
(601) 362-2294
• Carrie Brasfield, Merchandising Director
(601) 362-2294
Sport:
Baseball
Capacity:
5,200

SMOKIES PARK
3540 LINE DRIVE
KODAK, TN 37764
865-286-2300
Fax: 865-523-9913
info@smokiesbaseball.com
www.smokiesbaseball.com
• Rennie Leon, Director of Marketing
Development
• Doug Kirchhofer, President
dkirchhofer@smokiesbaseball.com
• Mick Gillispie, Director, Broadcasting
mgillispie@smokiesbaseball.com
• Lauren Chesney, Director, Community
Relations
lchesney@smokiesbaseball.com
• Matt Strutner, Director, Corporate Ticket
Development
mstrutner@smokiesbaseball.com
• Ryan M. Cox, Director, Entertainment &
Client Services
rcox@smokiesbaseball.com
• Stuart Morris, Director, Field Operations
smorris@smokiesbaseball.com
• Tony DaSilveira, Director, Food and
Beverage
tdasilveira@smokiesbaseball.com
Sport:
Baseball
Team:
Tennessee Smokies
Year Founded:
2000
Capacity:
6,412

SMOOTHIE KINGS CENTER
1501 DAVE DIXON DRIVE
NEW ORLEANS, LA 70113
504-587-3663
800-756-7074
www.smoothiekingcenter.com
Team:
New Orleans Pelicans (NBA)
Seating Capacity:
18,500

SOLDIER FIELD
1410 S MUSEUM CAMPUS DRIVE
CAMPUS DRIVE GATE14
CHICAGO, IL 60605
312-235-7000
Fax: 312-235-7030
www.soldierfield.net
• Kate McGregor, Director of Sales & Marketing
• Tim LeFevour, GM
• Michael Ortman, Director of Operations
• Kevin Walsh, Director of Events
• Luca Serra, Director of Sponsership Media
• Marty McAndrew, finance
• Scott Rendell, Event Coordinator
Owned by:
Chicago Park District (City of Chicago)
Tenant(s):
NFL - Chicago Bears football, MLS - Chicago Fire soccer.
Permanent Seating Capacity:
61,500

SOUTH CAROLINA STATE UNIVERSITY
300 COLLEGE STREET NE
ORANGEBURG, SC 29117
803-536-7000
800-260-5956
Fax: 803-533-3988
admissions@scsu.edu
www.scsu.edu
• Carolyn M Free, ASSOCIATE DIRECTOR
• David O. Igiozee, Accountant/Manager
digiozee@scsu.edu
• Angelia P. Jackson, Administrative Assistant
ajackson@scsu.edu
• Gloria Lott, Fiscal Technician
• Gwendolyn Love, Fiscal Technician
glove@scsu.edu
• Kay Snider, Interim Director
ksnider@scsu.edu
• Andrea S. Milford Williams, Project Director
• Charlene Johnson, Director of Athletics
Bulldog Stadium:
2,500
S.H.M Memorial Center Seating Capacity:
2,500

SPACE COAST STADIUM
5800 STADIUM PARKWAY
SUITE 101
VIERA, FL 32940
321-633-9200
Fax: 321-633-4418
www.manateesbaseball.com
• Tom Winters, Chairman
• Jeff Weinhold, Tickets Manager
• Tom Winters, Chairman
• Dewight Titus, Vice Chairman
• Charlie Baumann, President
• Frank Longobardo, Director of Ticketing and Media
(321) 633-9200
flongobardo@spacecoaststadium.com

• Kelley Wheeler, Director of Business Operations and Finance
(321) 633-9200
ksoto@spacecoaststadium.com
• Kevin Soto, Director of Promotions and Community Relation
(321) 633-9200
ksoto@spacecoaststadium.com
• Kyle Smith, General Manager
(321) 633-9200
ksmith@spacecoaststadium.com
Sport:
Baseball
Team:
Montreal Expos spring training facility; Brevard County Manatees.
Year Founded:
1994
Capacity:
8,100

SPARTAN STADIUM
ONE BIRCH ROAD
JACK BRESLIN STUDENT EVENTS CENTER
E LANSING, MI 48824
517-432-1989
Fax: 517-432-1510
alliance@msu.edu
www.msuspartans.com
• Mark Hollis, Athletic Director
(517) 355-1623
ad@ath.msu.edu
• Greg Ianni, Deputy Athletic Director
(517) 355-5263
ianni@ath.msu.edu
• Shelly Appelbaum, Senior Associate AD
(517) 355-8849
appelbau@ath.msu.edu
• Chuck Sleeper, Senior Associate AD
(517) 432-4611
sleeper@ath.msu.edu
Stadium Seating Capacity:
72,027
Team:
Michigan State University football.

SPECIAL OLYMPICS STADIUM
350 NEW CAMPUS DRIVE
THE COLLEGE AT BROCKPORT
BROCKPORT, NY 14420-2914
716-395-2211
Fax: 716-395-2160
mandriat@brockport.edu
www.brockport.edu
• Mike Andriatch, Sports Information Director
(585) 395-5809
• Lee J. Cohen, Head Athletic Trainer
(585) 395-2251
lcohen@brockport.edu
Stadium Seating Capacity:
10,000

SPECTRUM
7400 OLD MAIN HILL
UTAH STATE UNIVERSITY
LOGAN, UT 84322
435-797-1000
800-488-8108
Fax: 435-797-2615
registrar@usu.edu
www.usu.edu
• Doug Hoffman, Athletic Media Relations Director
(435) 797-3714
doug.hoffman@usu.edu

• Scott Randall, Assistant AD
(435) 797-7186
scott.randall@usu.edu
• Justin Williams, Event Services Manager
(435) 797-2995
justin.williams@usu.edu
Seating Capacity:
Romney Stadium (Football) 25,513; Dee Glen Smith Spectrum (Basketball) 10,270

SPOKANE VETERANS MEMORIAL ARENA
720 W MALLON AVENUE
SPOKANE, WA 99201
509-279-7000
Fax: 509-279-7050
ktwohig@spokanearena.com
www.spokanearena.com
• Kevin Twohig, General Manager
(509) 279-7002
• Kevin B Twohig, CEO, Spokane Public Facilities District
ktwohig@spokanearena.com
• Matt Gibson, Arena General Manager
mg@spokanearena.com
• Stephanie Huff, Hr and Contract Services Manager
shuff@spokanearena.com
• Dave Gebhardt, Operations Manager
dgebhardt@spokanearena.com
• Shardell Shrum, Operations Supervisor
sshrum@spokanearena.com
• Casey Booey III, Tech Specialist
cbooey@spokanearena.com
• Monte Koch, Tech Specialist
mkoch@spokanearena.com
Arena Seating Capacity:
12,500

SPORTS PAVILION
1925 UNIVERSITY AVENUE SE
MINNEAPOLIS, MN 55455
612-625-3007
Fax: 612-625-7788
dale0099@umn.edu
gophersports.com
• Scott P. Ellison, Associate Athletic Director
(612) 624-4497
ellis004@umn.edu
• Norwood Teague, Director of Athletics
(612) 624-4497
• David Benedict, Executive Associate
(612) 624-4497
• Mike Ellis, Sr. Associate AD
(612) 624-4497
• Beth Goetz, Sr. Associate AD/SWA
(612) 624-4497
Arena Seating Capacity:
5,700

ST JOHN'S UNIVERSITY
8000 UTOPIA PARKWAY
CARNESECCA ARENA, ROOM 157
QUEENS, NY 11439
718-990-6217
Fax: 718-990-2063
webmaster@stjohns.edu
redstormsports.collegesports.com
• Erin McDonnell, Associate Athletics Director for Facilities and Op
(718) 990-1690
mcdonnee@stjohns.edu
• Neftali Collazo, Associate Athletic Director/Facilities
(718) 990-5951
collazon@stjohns.edu
• Dennis Myron, Ticket Operations Director

facilities

Alumni Hall Seating Capacity:
6,008
Stadium Seating Capacity:
3,000

ST LAWRENCE UNIVERSITY
23 ROMODA DRIVE
CANTON, NY 13617
315-229-5011
800-285-1856
Fax: 315-229-5589
lcania@stlawu.edu
www.stlawu.edu/sports
• Margie Strait, Athletic Director
(315) 229-5784
mstrait@stlawu.edu
• Bob Durocher, Assistant Athletic
Director/Facilities
(315) 229-5870
bdur@stlawu.edu
Field Stadium Seating Capacity:
5,000
Sports Center Seating Capacity:
3,500
Ice Arena:
3,500

ST PAUL SAINTS
360 BROADWAY
SAINT PAUL, MN 55101
651-644-3517
Fax: 651-644-1627
www.saintsbaseball.com
• Derek Sharrer, Executive Vice President /
General Manager
dsharrer@saintsbaseball.com
• Tom Whaley, Executive Vice President
twhaley@saintsbaseball.com
• Chris Schwab, Senior Vice
President/Assistant General Manager
cschwab@saintsbaseball.com
• Sean Aronson, Vice President/Director Of
Broadcasting/Media
saronson@saintsbaseball.com
• Tyson Jeffers, Director Corporate Sales
tjeffers@saintsbaseball.com
• Sierra Bailey, Director
Marketing/Promotions
sbailey@saintsbaseball.com
Year Founded:
1993
Team:
St. Paul Saints
Sport:
Baseball
Capacity:
7,210

STABLER ARENA
124 GOODMAN DRIVE
LEHIGH UNIVERSITY
BETHLEHEM, PA 18015
610-758-3770
Fax: 610-866-8070
www.stablerarena.com
• Richard H Fritz, Director of Events
• Allen Biddinger, Facilities/Events Manager
• Ed Barndt, Facilities/Events Manager
• Jason Gall, Facilities/Events Coordinator
Arena Seating Capacity:
6,700

STADE CANAC
100 CARDINAL MAURICE-ROY
QUEBEC, QC, CANADA G1K 8Z1
418-521-2255
877-521-2244

Fax: 418-521-2266
info@capitalesdequebec.com
capitalesdequebec.com
• Michel Laplante, President
Year Opened:
1938, renovated 1999
Seating Capacity:
4,800
Tenant(s):
Quebec Capitales; Quebec Diamants

STADE SAPUTO
OLYMPIC PARK
4750 SHERBROOKE STREET E
MONTREAL, QC, CANADA H1V 3S8
info@impactmontreal.com
www.impactmontreal.com/en/stadium/stade-
saputo
• Joey Saputo, Owner, Montreal Impact &
Stade Saputo
• Kevin Gilmore, President & CEO, Montreal
Impact
• Eric Girouard, Director, Stadium
Operations
Owner:
Saputo Inc.
Operator:
Montreal Impact
Year Opened:
2008, expanded 2012.
Seating Capacity:
20,801

STAMBAUGH STADIUM
ROOM 1003
ONE UNIVERSITY PLAZA
YOUNGSTOWN, OH 44555
330-941-2962
800-468-6978
Fax: 330-941-3191
ysusports@ysu.edu
www.ysusports.com
• Grant Springer
(330) 941-3671
• Tom Morella
(330) 941-2351
tmorella@ysu.edu
Seating Capacity:
Stadium 20,630; Arena 6,300
Tenants:
Youngstown State Athletics
Track:
Becoming an indoor facility

STANFORD STADIUM
625 NELSON RD
STANFORD, CA 94305
650-723-4591
Fax: 650-725-8642
www.gostanford.com
Seating Capacity:
50,000
Teams:
Stanford University football.

**STANLEY COVELESKI REGIONAL
STADIUM**
501 W S STREET
COVELESKI REGIONAL STADIUM
S BEND, IN 46601
574-235-9988
Fax: 574-235-9950
• Peter Argueta, Director of Stadium
Operations
• Alan Levin, Principal Owner
• Tony Wittrock, Sales Director

• Andrew Berlin, Owner
hawks@silverhawks.com
• Joe Hart, President
jhart@silverhawks.com
• Nick Brown, Director of Corporate
Sales/Business Developm
nbrown@silverhawks.com
• Cheryl Carlson, Director of Finance and
Human Resources
cherylcarlson@silverhawks.com
• Kelly Knutson, Director of Marketing
kknutson@silverhawks.com
• Ben Hayes, Director of Food and
Beverage
bhayes@prosportscatering.com
• Peter Argueta, Assistant General Manager
- Operations
pargueta@silverhawks.com
Sport:
Baseball.
Team:
South Bend Silver Hawks.
Year Built:
1987
Seating Capacity:
5,000

STANLEY J MARSHALL HPER CENTER
11TH STREET AND 16TH AVENUE
SDSU BOX 2820
BROOKINGS, SD 57007-1497
605-688-5817
Fax: 605-688-5999
• Matt Thorn, Assistant AD
• Erin Breczinski, Athletic Tickets Manager
Arena Seating Capacity:
9,000

**STAPLES CENTER/ANSCHUTZ
ENTERTAINMENT GROUP**
1111 S FIGUEROA STREET
SUITE 2350
LOS ANGELES, CA 90015
213-742-7100
Fax: 213-742-7889
www.staplescenter.com
• Tim Leiweke, President & CEO,AEG
• Kathy Carter, Sales/Marketing-AEG
Marketing VP
Tenant(s):
AFL - Los Angeles Avengers football; NBA -
Los Angeles Clippers basketball; NBA - Los
Angeles Lakers basketball; NHL - Los
Angeles Kings hockey; WNBA - Los
Angeles Sparks basketball.
Arena Seating Capacity:
19,282

STARR RINK
13 OAK DRIVE
HAMILTON, NY 13346
315-228-1000
Fax: 315-824-7544
www.colgate.edu
• Dave Roach, Athletic Director
• Robert D. Cornell, Director
Arena Seating Capacity:
2,200

STATE MUTUAL STADIUM
755 BRAVES BOULEVARD
ROME, GA 30161
706-368-9388
Fax: 706-368-6525
rome.braves@braves.com
www.romebraves.com

- Michael Dunn, General Manager
- Jim Jones, Assistant General Manager
- Eric Allman, Director of Stadium Operations
- Dave Atwood, Director of Culinary Services
- Brad Smith, Director of Food and Beverage
- Jeff Fletcher, Ticket Manager
- Michael Dunn, General Manager
Team:
Rome Braves
Date:
2003
Capacity:
5,000
Sport:
Baseball

STATE UNIVERSITY OF NEW YORK
102 ALUMNI ARENA
UNIVERSITY OF BUFFALO, DIVISION OF ATHLETICS
BUFFALO, NY 14260
716-645-3141
Fax: 716-645-2438
ub-athletics@buffalo.edu
- Bob Maxwell, Assistant Athletic Director for Facility Operation
(716) 645-3486
rmax@buffalo.edu
- Sue Kurkowski, Director, Facility Operations
(716) 645-3992
kurowski@buffalo.edu
- Linda Billups, Facilities/Events Operations Assistant
- Nicolas Titus, Coordinator Facilities
UB Stadium:
17,200
Stadium Seating Capacity:
4,000
Alumni Arena Seating Capacity:
8,500
Natatorium Seating Capacity:
2,000

STEPHEN C O'CONNELL CENTER
2132 STADIUM ROAD
GAINESVILLE, FL 32611
352-392-5500
Fax: 352-392-7106
scoc-marketing@ufl.edu
www.oconnellcenter.ufl.edu
- Lynda Reinhart, Director
lyndar@ufl.edu
- Jeremy Cynkar, Operations Director
(352) 392-5507
cynkar@ufl.edu
- Renne Musson, Associate Director
(352) 392-5506
musson@ufl.edu
- Anthony Rizo, Production Manager
(352) 392-0408
arizo15@ufl.edu
- Lynda Reinhart, Director
(352) 392-5510
lyndar@ufl.edu
- David Lucier, Assistant Director
(352) 392-5505
dlucier@ufl.edu
Seating Capacity:
11,500
Sports:
Men's & Women's basketball, women's volleyball, women's gymnastics, men's & women's swimming & diving, men's &

women's indoor track.
Home Team:
University of Florida Gators

STRAHAN COLISEUM
601 UNIVERSITY DRIVE
SAN MARCOS, TX 78666
512-245-2114
Fax: 512-245-8387
athletics@txstate.edu
www.txstatebobcats.com
- Derek Grice, Facility/Game Operations Director
(512) 245-2023
pg13@txstate.edu
- Adam Alonzo, Assistant Director - Facility & Game Operatio
(512) 245-2404
aa08@txstate.edu
- Larry Teis, Director Of Athletics
(512) 245-2963
lt10@txstate.edu
- Don Coryell, Administration - Associate Athletics Director
(512) 245-2220
dc32@txstate.edu
- Tracy Shoemake, Administration - Associate Athletics Director
(512) 245-2114
ts23@txstate.edu
- Travis Comer, Administration - Associate Athletics Director
(512) 245-2247
tc26@txstate.edu
- Paul Gowens, Administration - NCAA Faculty Representative
(512) 245-3252
pg01@txstate.edu
- Jessica Henry, Support Staff - Administrative Assistant - At
(512) 245-2963
jh81@txstate.edu
Coliseum Seating Capacity:
7,200

STRAWBERRY STADIUM
SLU 10309
HAMMOND, LA 70402
985-549-2253
Fax: 985-549-3495
sportsinfo@selu.edu
www.lionsports.net
- Andrew Bechae, Facility Director
(985) 549-3419
- Dennis Roland, Head Football Coach
(985) 549-5550
droland@selu.edu
- Bart Bellairs, Athletics Director
(985) 549-2395
athletics@southeastern.edu
- Linda Alford, Administrative Coordinator
(985) 549-5599
lalford@southeastern.edu
- Andrew Bechac, Senior Associate AD for Internal Operations
(985) 549-3419
Andrew.Bechac@southeastern.edu
- Tim Baldwin, Head Golf Coach/Assistant AD for Special Even
(985) 549-5186
tbaldwin@southeastern.edu
- Chris Bentley, Assistant to the AD/Lifeskills and Academic L
(985) 549-3393
cbentley@southeastern.edu
- Mary Kathryn Borland, Assistant AD for Academic Services/SWA
(985) 549-2256

MaryKathryn.Borland@southeastern.edu
- Carley Cryer, Marketing and Promotions
(985) 549-3227
Carley.Cryer@southeastern.edu
Stadium Seating Capacity:
8,396

SULLIVAN ARENA
1600 GAMBELL STREET
ANCHORAGE, AK 99501
907-279-0618
Fax: 907-274-0676
www.sullivanarena.com
- Tanya Pont, Marketing Director
pontt@sullivanarena.com
- Joe Wooden, General Manager
woodenj@sullivanarena.com
- Penny McKibbon, Director of Finance
- Tanya Pont, Director of Marketing
- Greg Stubbs, Director of Operations
Permanent Seating Capacity:
8,935

SUN BOWL
151 GLORY ROAD
EL PASO, TX 79908
915-747-5481
Fax: 915-747-5228
dhc@utep.edu
www.utepspecialevents.com/
- Michael Spence, Facility Director
mspence@utep.edu
- Jorge Vazquez, Executive Director of Special Events
(915) 747-5481
vazquezj@utep.edu
- Mike Spence, Director of Special Facilities Management
(915) 747-5481
mspence@utep.edu
- Ricky Nichols, Assistant Director
(915) 747-5481
rlnichols@utep.edu
- Eileen Laidler, Business Manager
(915) 747-5481
eclaidler@utep.edu
- Julian E. Valdes, Marketing Coordinator
(915) 747-5481
jevaldes@utep.edu
- Fernie Mabini, Technical Supervisor
(915) 747-5481
fmabini@utep.edu
- Bradley Serrao, Technical Coordinator
(915) 747-5481
blthomas@utep.edu
Stadium Seating Capacity:
52,000.00
Year Founded:
1963
Clients:
Clear Channel Entertainment, AEG, Stargate, Stone City Attraction.
Nature of Service:
University Venue.

SUN DEVIL STADIUM
500 EAST VETERANS WAY
TEMPE, AZ 85287
480-965-2381
888-786-3857
Fax: 480-965-6006
sundeviltickets@asu.edu
thesundevils.cstv.com
- Jeff O'Connor, Athletic Facilities Manager
(480) 965-0950
jeff.oconner@asu.edu
- Michael Chismar, Senior Associate AD

facilities

(480) 965-1287
michael.chismar@asu.edu
• John McClees, Athletic Facilities
Maintenance Coordina
• Lyn Music, Facilities/Events Management
Director
Owned by:
Arizona State University
Tenant(s):
Arizona State University football, NCAA -
Tostitos Fiesta Bowl football game.
Permanent Seating Capacity:
73,379

SUN LIFE STADIUM
2269 NW 199TH STREET
MIAMI GARDENS, FL 33056
305-943-8000
• Stephen M. Ross, Owner/Managing
General Partner
• Tom Garfinkel, President/Chief Executive
Officer
• Jeremy Walls, Sr., Vice President/Chief
Revenue Officer
• Claudia Lezcano, Sr., Vice President,
Chief Marketing Officer
• Terry Howard, Sr., Vice President/Chief
Technology Officer
• Todd Boyan, Vice President/General
Manager, Sun Life Stadium
Tenant(s):
MLB - Florida Marlins baseball, NFL - Miami
Dolphins football, NCAA - Florida Atlantic
University football, NCAA - FedEx Orange
Bowl football game.
Permanent Seating Capacity:
75,540 (football); 36,331 (baseball).

SUN NATIONAL BANK CENTER
81 HAMILTON AVENUE
ROUTE 129
TRENTON, NJ 08611
609-656-3200
Fax: 609-656-3201
www.sunnationalbankcenter.com
• Claudio Oliveira, General Manager
• Tim Moore, Event Manager
tim_moore@comcastspectacor.com
• Robert Coughlin, Director of Operations
robert_coughlin@comcastspectacor.com
Arena Seating Capacity:
8,600

SUPERIOR DOME
1401 PRESQUE ISLE AVENUE
NORTHERN MICHIGAN UNIVERSITY
MARQUETTE, MI 49855
906-227-2850
800-682-9797
Fax: 906-227-2855
brberube@nmu.edu
www.nmu.edu
• Carl Bammert, Associate
Director-Facilities
• Forrest Karr, Athletic Director
(906) 227-1826
fkarr@nmu.edu
• Steve Reed, Senior Associate Director
(906) 227-1183
sreed@nmu.edu
• Carl Bammert, Associate
Director-Facilities
(906) 227-2465
cbammert@nmu.edu
• Bridget Berube Carter, Associate
Director-Compliance

(906) 227-2371
brberube@nmu.edu
Stadium Seating Capacity:
9,000

SYDNEY ENTERTAINMENT CENTRE
35 HARBOUR STREET
PO BOX K10
DARLING HARBOUR, NSW 2000, 2000
-61-02-9320-4200
Fax: -61-02-9281-2682
• Tegan Pryce, Venue Services Manager
(029) 320-4207
tegan@sydentcent.com.au
• Natalie Cutcliffe, Marketing Manager
• Joe Brex, Business Manager
• Lee Kessler, Events Manager

TACO BELL ARENA
1910 UNIVERSITY DRIVE
BOISE STATE UNIVERSITY
BOISE, ID 83725
208-426-1900
Fax: 208-426-1998
www.tacobellarena.com
• Joyce Grimes, Executive Director
(208) 426-1600
jgrimes@boisestate.edu
• Leslie Pass, Events Assistant Director
(208) 426-1982
lpass@boisestate.edu
• Lisa Cochran, Marketing Director
(208) 426-2546
lcochran@boisestate.edu
• Lisa Cochran, Executive Director
lcochran@boisestate.edu
• Ron Janeczko, Associate Director
Facilities & Production
rjaneczk@boisestate.edu
• Leslie Pass, Assistant Director of Events
lpass@boisestate.edu
• John Roberts, Assistant Director, Booking
and Scheduling
• Micki Courtney, Assistant Director,
Ticketing and Guest Servi
mickicourtney@boisestate.edu
• Alex Satterlee, Office Manager
• Rodney Miller, Production Manager
rodneymiller@boisestate.edu
Seating Capacity:
12,428

TACOMA DOME
2727 EAST D STREET
TACOMA, WA 98421
253-272-3663
Fax: 253-593-7620
info@tacomadome.org
www.tacomadome.org
• Rob Henson, Deputy Director/Booking
Manager
• Hillary Brenner, Marketing Assistant
hbrenner@tacomadome.org
• Beth Sylves, Marketing Manager
(253) 593-7602
• Kim Bedier, Director
• Rob Henson, Booking Manager
• Nancy Green, Administrative Assistant
• Angela Tamajka, Marketing Manager
• Hillary Brenner, Marketing Coordinator
• Jeff Brown, Event Coordinator
Arena Seating Capacity:
23,000
Year Founded:
1983
Events:

Concerts, Exhibitions/Trade Shows, Family
Events, High School Sports

TAD SMITH COLISEUM
908 ALL-AMERICAN DRIVE
UNIVERSITY, MS 38677
662-915-7241
1-800-467-3235
www.olemisssports.com
• Ross Bjork, Director of Athletics
(662) 915-7546
• Joe Swingle, Associate Athletic Director,
Facilities
(662) 915-7508
jswingle@olemiss.edu
• Neal Mead, Assistant Director for Event
Management Ops.
(662) 816-2699
nmead@olemiss.edu
Coliseum Seating Capacity:
8,867

TAMPA BAY TIMES FORUM
401 CHANNELSIDE DRIVE
TAMPA, FL 33602
813-301-6500
Fax: 813-301-1480
sponsorship@tampabaytimesforum.com
• Jay Goulde, Executive Director
• Rob Higgins, Executive Director, Tampa
Bay Sports Commissi
Tenant(s):
AFL - Tampa Bay Storm football, NHL -
Tampa Bay Lightning hockey.
Permanent Seating Capacity:
20,000

TARGET CENTER
600 FIRST AVENUE N
MINNEAPOLIS, MN 55403-1416
612-673-1600
Fax: 612-673-1370
info@targetcenter.com
www.targetcenter.com
• Kevin McHale, Basketball Operations VP
• Sandy Sweetser, Marketing Director
• Dana Warg, Executive Director
• Ajay Sekhran, Concessions Manager
Description:
Home Arena For: Minnesota Timberwolves.
Permanent Seating Capacity:
19,006

TARGET FIELD
1 TWINS WAY
MINNEAPOLIS, MN 55403
612-375-1366
minnesota.twins.mlb.com
• Alfton Dennis, Operations Director
(612) 335-3314
• Dave Horsman, Senior Director, Ballpark
Operations
davehorsman@twinsbaseball.com
• Lisa Knutson, Event Operations Assistant
lisaknutson@twinsbaseball.com
• Dick Dugan, Security Manager
dickdugan@twinsbaseball.com
• Jim Pohlad, Chief Executive Officer,
Minnesota Twins
• Dave St. Peter, President, Minnesota
Twins
• Terry Ryan, Executive Vice President,
General Manager
• Laura Day, Executive Vice President,
Business Developmen
• Kip Elliott, Executive Vice President,
Business Administra

• Matt Hoy, Senior Vice President,
Operations
Owned by:
Minnesota Ballpark Authority in conjunction
with the Twins-Hennepin County ballpark
legislation.
Tenant(s):
MLB - Minnesota Twins baseball, NCAA -
University of Minnesota football
Seating Capacity:
39,504

TAYLOR STADIUM
ONE CHAMPIONS DRIVE
COLUMBIA, MO 65211
573-256-4004
Fax: 573-256-4003
www.mutigers.com
• Wendt Gary, President/Co-Owner
• Karen Watson, Office Director/Ticket
Operations
• Melissa Wheeler, Business Affairs Director
(573) 256-4004
mwheeler@midmomavs.com
• Rick Stonelang, Sales/Marketing Director
rstonelang@midmomavs.com
Capacity:
3,331
Year Founded:
2002
Team:
Missouri Tigers
Sport:
Baseball

TCF BANK STADIUM
2009 SOUTH EAST UNIVERSITY AVE
MINNEAPOLIS, MN 55455
612-624-8080
Fax: 612-625-0003
fans@gopherfanrelations.com
www.mygophersports.com
Seating Capacity:
50,000
Teams:
University of Minneapolis Gophers

TD BANKNORTH GARDEN
100 LEGENDS WAY
BOSTON, MA 2114
617-624-1050
Fax: 617-523-7184
customerservice@tdgarden.com
www.tdbanknorthgarden.com
• Rusty Sullivan, Executive Director
(617) 624-1237
rsullivan@dncboston.com
• John Wentzell, SVP/General Manager
• David Splaine, SVP Sales
• Christopher W Maher, VP/Boston Garden
Dev
• John Ratoff, SVP Corporate Partnerships
• Christopher Johnson, VP Corporate
Partnerships
• Caryn Kelly, Client Services Manager
• Michele Savage, Corporate Partnerships
Permanent Seating Capacity:
19,580
Description:
Home Arena For: Boston Bruins, Boston
Celtics.
Owned by:
Delaware North Inc.

TD PLACE
1015 BANK STREET
OTTAWA, ON, CANADA K1S 3W7

613-232-6767
877-489-2849
www.tdplace.ca
• Chris Wynn, Director, Operations
• Brian Giles, Facilities Manager
Owner:
City of Ottawa
Operator:
Ottawa Sports and Entertainment Group
Year Opened:
1908
Seating Capacity:
24,000
Tenant(s):
Ottawa Redblacks (CFL), Ottawa Fury
(USL)

TD WATERHOUSE CENTRE
600 W AMELIA STREET
ORLANDO CENTROPLEX
ORLANDO, FL 32801-1113
407-849-2000
Fax: 407-849-2329
• Allen Johnson, Executive Director
(407) 849-2012
allen.johnson@cityoforlando.net
• Jon Dorman, Deputy Director
(407) 849-2088
jon.dorman@cityoforlando.net
• Tanya Bowley, Marketing Director
(407) 849-2590
tanya.bowley@cityoforlando.net
• Cindy Mitchum, Business Manager
(407) 849-2150
cindy.mitchum@cityoforlando.net
Permanent Seating Capacity:
17,320 AFL 15,595
Tenant(s):
ACHL - Orlando Seals hockey; NBA -
Orlando Magic basketball; AFL - Orlando
Predators football.

**SEMINOLE COUNTY SPORTS TRAINING
CENTER**
1000 AAA DRIVE
SUITE 200 MS14
HEATHROW, FL 32746
407-665-2900
800-800-7832
Fax: 407-665-2920
dtrosset@seminolecountyfl.gov
www.visitseminole.com
• Sharon Sears, Executive Director
(407) 665-2901
ssears@seminolecountyfl.gov
• Danny Trosset, Sales and Marketing
Manager
(407) 665-2913
dtrosset@seminolecountyfl.gov
• Rosangela Santiago, Senior Staff
Assistant
(407) 665-2908
rsantiago@seminolecountyfl.gov
• Sarah Collins, Customer Service
Representative
(407) 665-2900
SCollins@seminolecountyfl.gov
Year Founded:
1993
Description:
Team Seminole event experts make events
smoth, gratifying, and a memorable
experience. Goal is not to simply meet
expectations, but to go above and beyond
all expectations and make events
extraordinary. Paying attention to the little
things, the team makes certain all

participating teams, coaches, family
members, and spectators want to come
back to Seminole County for the next big
event.

TEAMWORKS CENTERS
30 GREAT ROAD
ACTON, MA 01720
978-287-5533
Fax: 508-287-0211
info@twcenters.com
www.twcenters.com
• Kevin O'Connell, CEO/President
(978) 287-0212
koconnell@twcenters.com
• Peter Corbet, Co-Chief Executive Officer
• Bill Disandro, General Manager/Bay State
Description:
Multi-purpose family and corporate indoor
sports and entertainment complexes
featuring a wide variety of activities such as
sport leagues, tournaments, birthday
parties, instructional programs, corporate
and other special events for all ages. The
faciliti

**TED CONSTANT CONVOCATION
CENTER**
4320 HAMPTON BOULEVARD
NORFOLK, VA 23529
757-683-5762
Fax: 757-683-6544
tedconstantcenter@gmail.com
www.constantcenter.com
• Mike Fryling, General Manager
mike_fryling@comcastspectacor.com
• Chase Hathway, Assistant General
Manager
• Jordan Avant, Director of Events and
Operations
jordan_avant@comcastspectacor.com
• Matthew Gibb, Event Manager
Year Opened:
2002
Tenant(s):
NCAA - Old Dominion University basketball.
Permanent Seating Capacity:
9,520

TEXAS RANGERS BASEBALL CLUB
1000 BALLPARK WAY
SUITE 400
ARLINGTON, TX 76011
817-273-2222
Fax: 817-273-5110
www.texasrangers.com
• Ryan Nolan, President
(817) 273-5233
mcramer@texasrangers.com
• Rick McLaughlin, Business Operations
EVP
(817) 436-5944
rmclaughlin@texasrangers.com
• Casey Shilts, General Counsel SVP
(817) 273-5235
cshilts@texasrangers.com
• Jeff Cogen, Marketing EVP
(817) 273-5196
jcogen@texasrangers.com
• Jay Miller, Senior Vice President
(817) 273-5233
jmiller@texasrangers.com
Owned by:
City of Arlington
Home Stadium for:
Texas Rangers.
Permanent Seating Capacity:

49,115 (Ballpark in Arlington)
Year Founded:
1972

THE BALLPARK AT JACKSON
4 FUN PLACE
JACKSON, TN 38305
731-988-5299
Fax: 731-988-5246
www.milb.com

THE CROWN COMPLEX
1960 COLISEUM DRIVE
FAYETTEVILLE, NC 28306
910-438-4100
Fax: 910-323-0489
contactus@crowncoliseum.com
www.crowncomplexnc.com
• Karen Long, Chief Executive Officer
• Dionne Hill, Director Of Sales
• Max Speers, Sales Manager
• Karen Long, General Manager
klong@crowncoliseum.com
• Chris Ragland, AGM / Director of Operations
cragland@crowncoliseum.com
• Lisa Foster, Director of Finance
• Marshall Perry, Director of Marketing & Sales
• Victor Landry, Director of Event Services
vlandry@crowncoliseum.com
• Rita Perry, Executive Administrative Assistant to the GM
rperry@crowncoliseum.com
• Chris Ragland, AGM / Director of Operations
Crown Coliseum Seating Capacity:
13,500
Arena Seating Capacity:
5,500
Tenant(s):
ACHL - Cape Fear FireAntz ice hockey,
AFL2 - Cape Fear Wildcats indoor football,
NBDL - Fayetteville Patriots basketball.

THE DOME AT AMERICA'S CENTER
901 NORTH BROADWAY
ST. LOUIS, MO 63101
314-342-5036
Fax: 314-621-7729
convention@explorestlouis.com
explorestlouis.com
Permanent Seating Capacity:
66,000
Description:
St. Louis Rams

THE DOME CENTER
2695 EAST HENRIETTA ROAD
HENRIETTA, NY 14467
585-334-4000
Fax: 585-334-3005
• Fran Tepper, Executive Director
Seating Capacity:
4,700

THE UNIVERSITY OF MONTANA ATHLETIC DEPARTMENT
32 CAMPUS DRIVE
UNIVERSITY OF MONTANA-MISSOULA
MISSOULA, MT 59812-8496
406-243-4749
888-666-8262
Fax: 406-243-2264
grizzlymarketing@mso.umt.edu
www.gogriz.com

• Christie Anderson, Director of Marketing and Promotions
(406) 243-4336
chrisite.anderson@mso.umt.edu
• Jimmy Martinez, Assistant Director/Facilities
Arena Seating Capacity:
15,400

THE WINNIPED BLUE BOMBERS
315 CHANCELLOR MATHESON ROAD
WINNIPEG, MB, CANADA R3T 1Z2
204-784-2583
Fax: 204-783-5222
bbombers@bluebombers.com
www.bluebombers.com
• Garth Buchko, President and Chief Executive Officer
• Jim Bell, Vice-President and Chief Operating Officer
• Jerry Maslowsky, Vice President of Marketing & Brand Developme
• Fin Paterson, Vice President and Director of Sales
• Bill Watchorn, Chairperson - Board of Directors
• Darren Cameron, Director of Communications and Media Relation
• Jeffrey Bannon, Director of Marketing
Seating Capacity:
29,503
Playing Surface:
Artificial
Teams:
Winnipeg Blue Bombers

THOMAS ASSEMBLY CENTER
1650 W ALABAMA
PO BOX 3046
RUSTON, LA 71270
318-257-4111
Fax: 318-257-3757
vandevelde@latech.edu
www.latechsports.com
• Tommy Sisemore, Facilities Director
(318) 257-5323
sisemore@latech.edu
• Bruce Van De Velde, Athletics Director
(318) 257-3247
vendevelde@latech.edu
• Marie Gilbert, Associate A.D./Chief Financial Officer
(318) 257-3637
mgilbert@latech.edu
• James Liberatos, Faculty Athletics Representative
(318) 257-4287
jamesl@latech.edu
• Leah Beasley, Associate A.D./Marketing and Game Management
(318) 257-5332
lbeasley@latech.edu
• Malcolm Butler, Associate A.D./Media Relations
(318) 257-3145
mbutler@latech.edu
• Mary Kay Hungate, Deputy Athletics Director - SWA
(318) 257-5654
usmkh@latech.edu
• Derek Dooley, Athletics Director
(318) 257-4547
Seating Capacity:
8,000

THOMAS J. DODD MEMORIAL STADIUM
14 STOTT AVENUE
NORWICH, CT 6360
860-887-7962
Fax: 860-886-5996
info@cttigers.com
www.cttigers.com
• Andrew Weber, General Manager
• Eric Knighton, Vice President & Assistant General Manager
(860) 887-7962
eric@cttigers.com
• Eric Knighton, Assistant General Manager
• C J Knudsen, Vice President & General Manager
(860) 887-7962
cj@cttigers.com
• Heather Bartlett, Director of Concessions and Merchandise

(860) 887-7962
heather@cttigers.com
• Bryan Barkley, Director of Facilities and Turf Management
(860) 887-7962
bryan@cttigers.com
• Dave Schermerhorn, Director of Community Relations and Promotion
(860) 887-7962
dave@cttigers.com
• Jon Versteeg, Director of Media Relations
(860) 887-7962
jon@cttigers.com
• Minna DeGaetano, Accounting Manager
Sport:
Minor League Baseball
Seating Capacity:
6,270
Year Founded:
1995

THOMPSON ARENA
6083 ALUMNI GYM
DARTHMOUTH ATHLETICS
HANOVER, NH 03755-3512
603-646-3074
Fax: 603-646-3348
sportspub@dartmouth.edu
www.dartmouth.edu
• Richard Whitmore, Operations/Facilities Director
(603) 646-2673
• Randy Meck, Operations/Facilities Assistant Director
(603) 646-9299
Seating Capacity:
3,500; 4,500 SR.

THOMPSON-BOLING ARENA
1600 PHILLIP FULMER WAY
SUITE 202
KNOXVILLE, TN 37996
865-974-0953
Fax: 865-974-2800
treese@utk.edu
www.tbarena.com
• Tim Reese, Manager
(865) 974-0953
treese@utk.edu
Arena Seating Capacity:
24,451

TICKETRETURN.COM FIELD
1251 21ST AVENUE NORTH
MYRTLE BEACH, SC 29577
843-918-6002
info@myrtlebeachpelicans.com
www.myrtlebeachpelicans.com

• Chuck Greenberg, Chairman and Managing Partner
chuck@myrtlebeachpelicans.com
• Andy Milovich, President/General Manager
andy@myrtlebeachpelicans.com
• Mike Snow, Assistant General Manager, Operations
msnow@myrtlebeachpelicans.com
• Corey Russell, Sports Turf Manager
crussell@myrtlebeachpelicans.com
Year Founded:
1999
Permanent Seating Capacity:
6,599
Team:
Myrtle Beach Pelicans

TIGER STADIUM
ATHLETIC ADMINISTRATION BUILDING
5TH FLOOR
PO BOX 25095
BATON ROUGE, LA 70803
225-578-8826
800-469-8781
Fax: 225-578-2430
webmaster@lsu.edu
www.lsu.edu
• Ronnie Haliburton, Associate Athletic Director
(225) 578-4712
• Skip Bertman, Athletic Director
(225) 578-3600
• David D. Kurpius, Associate Vice Chancellor for Enrollment Mana
kurpius@lsu.edu
• Norma Riles, Assistant to the Associate Vice Chancellor fo
nriles@lsu.edu
• Amy Marix, Associate Director - Federal Aid & Scholarshi
amarix@lsu.edu
• Amy Prejean, Associate Director - Athletics, Customer Serv
apreje1@lsu.edu
• Christine Day, Associate Director - Business Unit
ctday@lsu.edu
• Lupe Lamadrid, Associate Director - Undergraduate Admissions
glamadrid@lsu.edu
• Melanie Thornton, Associate Director - Technology
mverre2@lsu.edu
Seating Capacity:
92,400
Team:
Louisiana State University football.

TIMES UNION CENTER
51 S PEARL STREET
ALBANY, NY 12207
518-487-2000
Fax: 518-487-2020
www.timesunioncenter-albany.com
• Bob Belber, General Manager
Arena Seating Capacity:
17,000, AFL-13,652.
Tenant(s):
AF2 - Albany Conquest football, AHL - Albany River Rats hockey, NLL - Albany Attack lacrosse.

TOLEDO MUD HENS
406 WASHINGTON STREET
TOLEDO, OH 43604
419-725-4367
Fax: 419-725-4368

webmaster@milb.com
www.milb.com
• Kirk Sausser, Manager Stadium Operations
• Joe Napoli, President/General Manager
• Neil Neukam, Assistant G.M./Director of Corporate Partners
• Erik Ibsen, Assistant G.M./Ticket Sales & Operations
• Pam Alspach, Chief Financial Officer
• Kim McBroom, Chief Marketing Officer
Sport:
Baseball.
Tenant(s):
Toledo Mud Hens baseball.
Year Founded:
2002
Capacity:
8,500

TOOMEY FIELD
ONE SHIELDS AVENUE
HICKEY GYM 264
DAVIS, CA 95616
530-752-1011
Fax: 530-752-6681
www.ucdavis.edu
• Greg Warzecka, Athletic Director
(530) 752-4557
gwarzecka@ucdavis.edu
• Bob Bullis, Associate Athletic Director
(530) 752-4806
rebullis@ucdavis.edu
• Russell Randall, Event Manager
• P.B Katehi, Chancellor
• Ralph Hexter, Executive Vice Chancellor
• JOhn Meyer, Vice Chancellor
• Shaun Keister, Vice Chancellor
• Claire Pomeroy, Vice Chancellor
• Harris Lewin, Vice Chancellor
Stadium Seating Capacity:
10,111

TOP OF THE THIRD
440 N GIDDINGS STREET
VISALIA, CA 93291
559-625-0480
Fax: 559-739-7732
oaksbaseball@hotmail.com
• Drietz Tom, Head Groundskeeper
• Jennifer Whiteley, General Manager
• John Drigotas, Group Sales Director
• Ira Liebman, Broadcasting & Media Relations Director
Arena Seating Capacity:
1,612.00
Nature of Service:
Minor League Baseball.
Year Founded:
1998, Recreation Park 1946

TOYOTA CENTER
1510 POLK STREET
HOUSTON, TX 77002
713-758-7200
Fax: 713-758-7315
guestservices@rocketball.com
www.houstontoyotacenter.com
• Hall Doug, General Manager
• Tad Brown, Corporate Development VP
tadb@rocketball.com
Tenant(s):
AHL - Houston Aeros hockey, NBA - Houston Rocket basketball, WNBA - Houston Comets basketball.
Permanent Seating Capacity:
18,500 basketball 17,800 hockey

Year Opened:
2003. Home arena for Houston Rockets.
Owned by:
Harris County-Houston Sports Authority.

TR HUGHES BALLPARK
900 TR HUGHES BOULEVARD
OZZIE SMITH SPORTS COMPLEX
O'FALLON, MO 63366
636-240-2287
Fax: 636-240-7313
www.rivercityrascals.com
• John Kuhn, President
• Lou Siville, Assistant General Manager, VP of Corporate Sales
• Dan Dial, Executive Vice President & General Manager
ddial@rivercityrascals.com
• Ashley Phillips, Sr. Account Executive
• Courtney Oakley, Sr. Director of Ticket Operations
coakley@rivercityrascals.com
• Greg Talbott, Director of Broadcast/ Media Relations
• Jody Sellers, Assistant General Manager
• Mo Stranz, Director of Food & Beverage
mstranz@rivercityrascals.com
• Sheri Livingston, Business Manager
Sport:
Baseball.
Team:
River City Rascals.
Year Founded:
1999
Capacity:
4,989

TRADITION FIELD SPORTS COMPLEX
525 NW PEACOCK BOULEVARD
PORT ST LUCIE, FL 34986
772-871-2115
Fax: 772-785-6878
info@stluciemets.com
www.stluciemets.com
• Paul Taglieri, President & CEO
• Jack Brenner, Clubhouse Manager
• Benny Distefano, Hitting Coach
• Phil Regan, Pitching Coach
•Jose Carreno, Coach
• Ryan Ellis, Manager
Sport:
Baseball
Tenant(s):
New York Mets Spring Training. St. Lucie Mets baseball.
Capacity:
7,800
Year Founded:
1988

TRI-CITIES STADIUM
6200 BURDEN BOULEVARD
PASCO, WA 99301
509-544-8789
Fax: 509-547-9570
info@dustdevilsbaseball.com
www.dustdevilsbaseball.com
• Monica Ortega, Vice President/General Manager
• Brent Miles, President
bmiles@dustdevilsbaseball.com
• Derrel Ebert, Vice President - General Manager
debert@dustdevilsbaseball.com
• Tim Gittel, Vice President - Business Operations
tgittel@dustdevilsbaseball.com

• Dan O'Neill, Assistant General Manager - Tickets
doneill@dustdevilsbaseball.com
• Anne Brenner, Director of Sponsorships
abrenner@dustdevilsbaseball.com
• Andrew Klein, Group Sales Manager
aklein@dustdevilsbaseball.com
• Austin Redman, Ticket Operations Manager
aredman@dustdevilsbaseball.com
Sport:
Baseball
Team:
Tri-City Dust Devils
Capacity:
3,750
Year Founded:
1995

TRINITY MOTHER FRANCES ROSE STADIUM
609 FAIR PARK DRIVE
TYLER, TX 75701
903-262-1000
Fax: 903-262-1168
www.tylerisd.org
• Danny Long, Athletic Director
(903) 590-4084
• Sharon Roy, Executive Director of Human Resources
• Nancy Swanson, Executive Director of Curriculum & Instructio
• Kim Tunnell, Executive Director of Strategic Planning & Co
• Dawn Parnell, Director of Communications
• Tosha Bjork, Chief Financial Officer
• Cecil McDaniel, Deputy Superintendent
• Darlene Marshall, Executive Director of Elementary Education
(903) 262-3080
maryellen.reed@tylerisd.org
Stadium Seating Capacity:
11,500.00
Nature of Service:
Football Games, Track Meets.
Track Type:
All weather rubber composite.
Track Size:
7 Lanes.

TROPICANA FIELD
ONE TROPICANA DRIVE
SAINT PETERSBURG, FL 33705
727-825-3137
888-326-7297
Fax: 727-825-3300
www.devilrays.com
• David Auker, Business Operations SVP
• Brian Richeson, Vice President of Sales & Service
• Rick Nafe, Operations/Facilities VP
• Rick Vaughn, Public Relations VP
Arena Seating Capacity:
42,500
Year Founded:
1995
Team:
Tampa Bay Rays MLB baseball.

TSONGAS CENTER
300 MARTIN LUTHER KING JR. WAY
LOWELL, MA 01852
978-934-5760
Fax: 978-934-5743
www.tsongascenter.com
Opened:
1996

Team:
UMass Lowell River Hawks
Seating Capacity:
6,496

TUCKER STADIUM
1151 STADIUM DRIVE
PO BOX 5057, TENNESSEE TECH ATHLETICS
COOKEVILLE, TN 38505
931-372-3961
Fax: 931-372-3114
MailAdmin@tntech.edu
www.tntech.edu
• Frank Harrell, Interim Athletic Director
(931) 372-3939
fharrell@tntech.edu
• John Wheeler, Director
(931) 372-3945
bshannon@tntech.edu
• Randy Smith, Assistant Interim Athletic Director/Faci
Stadium Seating Capacity:
16,500

TUCSON ELECTRIC PARK
2500 E AJO WAY
TUCSON, AZ 85713
520-546-5566
Fax: 520-434-1159
info@kinosportscomplex.com
www.kinosportscomplex.com
• Burke Matthew, Stadium Operations Director
• David Whatton, Program Manager
(520) 243-6350
david.whatton@pima.gov
Sport:
Baseball.
Team(s):
Chicago White Sox Spring Training; Arizona Diamondbacks Spring Training; Tucson Sidewinders baseball.
Year Founded:
1998
Capacity:
11,000

TULANE UNIVERSITY
6823 SAINT CHARLES AVENUE
NEW ORLEANS, LA 70118
504-865-5000
Fax: 504-862-8961
www.tulane.edu
• Rick Dickson, Executive Director
(504) 865-5569
• Scott S Cowen, President
(504) 865-5201
ssc@tulane.edu
Arena Seating Capacity:
3,600

TURNER FIELD
755 HANK AARON DRIVE SE
ATLANTA, GA 30315
404-522-7630
Fax: 404-614-1329
www.atlantabraves.com
• Larry Bowman, Senior Director Stadium Operations & Security
• Mike Glisson, Stadium Operations Manager
Seating Capacity:
50,000
Permanent Seating Capacity:
52,007
Tenants:

Home Stadium For: Atlanta Braves.
Notes:
Site of the 2000 MLB All-Star game.

TURPIN STADIUM
NSU ATHLETIC FIELDHOUSE
220 S JEFFERSON
NATCHITOCHES, LA 71497
318-357-5251
Fax: 318-357-4221
athleticsinfo@nsula.edu
www.nsudemons.com
• Mike Doty, Director of Facilities
(318) 357-6898
dotym@nsula.edu
• Chance Creppel, Asst. Director of Facilities
(318) 357-4265
creppelc@nsula.edu
• Greg Burke, Director of Athletics
(318) 357-5251
burkeg@nsula.edu
• Haley Taitano, Assoc. AD, External Relations & Sr. Women's Adv.
(318) 357-4278
blounth@nsula.edu
• Doug Ireland, Asst. AD, Media Relations
(318) 357-6467
ireland@nsula.edu
• Mike Jaworski, Director of Development and Engagement
(318) 357-4295
jaworskim@nsula.edu
Stadium Seating Capacity:
15,971
Description:
The football stadium for Northwestern State University. Two local high schools also use the field for their home football games.
Teams:
Northwestern State Demons Football; High Schools: Natchitoches Central High School and St. Mary's High School

TUSKEGEE UNIVERSITY
1200 W. MONTGOMERY ROAD
TUSKEGEE, AL 36088
334-727-8500
800- 622- 6531
Fax: 334-727-5750
www.tuskegee.edu
• Dr. Benjamin F. Payton, President
(334) 727-8501
• Shamima Amin, Chief of Staff
(334) 727-8503
• Luther S. Williams, President
(334) -727-802
• Cecil Lucy, Vice President for Finance
(334) 724-4733
• Gilbert S L. Rochon, President's Office
(334) 727-8501
Seating Capacity
3,000

U.S. CELLULAR CENTER
87 HAYWOOD STREET
ASHEVILLE, NC 28801
828-259-5736
Fax: 828-259-5777
ccorl@ashevillenc.gov
www.uscellularcenterasheville.com
• Chris Corl, General Manager
(828) 259-5452
ccorl@ashevillenc.gov
• Dan Dover, Operations Manager
(828) 259-5741
ddover@ashevillenc.gov

• Cassandra Marcelo, Marketing and Box Office Coordinator
(828) 259-5739
cmarcelo@ashevillenc.gov
Seating Capacity:
7,200

UAA SPORTS ARENA
3211 PROVIDENCE DRIVE
UNIVERSITY OF ALASKA-ANCHORAGE
ANCHORAGE, AK 99508
907-786-1250
Fax: 907-786-1142
goseawolves@uaa.alaska.edu
www.goseawolves.com
• Steve Cobb, Athletic Director
(907) 786-1225
ansrc@uaa.alaska.edu
• Nate Sagan, Sports Information Director
(907) 786-1295
• Tim McDiffett, Associate Athletic Director
(907) 786-1307
tim@uaa.alaska.edu
• Steve Cobb, Director of Athletics
(907) 786-1225
srcobb@uaa.alaska.edu
• Dede Allen, Assoc. Athletic Director
(Compliance & Academ
(907) 786-4803
dmallen@uaa.alaska.edu
• Jane Pallister, Assoc. Athletic Director
(Internal Affairs)
(907) 786-1225
jane@uaa.alaska.edu
• Kevin Silver, Assoc. Athletic Director
(WFSC)
(907) 786-4809
kevin.silver@uaa.alaska.edu
• Tlisa Northcutt, Director of Development
(907) 786-1211
tanorthcutt@uaa.alaska.edu
• Margot Ferguson, Marketing Specialist
(907) 786-1307
margot@uaa.alaska.edu
Arena Seating Capacity:
1,500

UAB ARENA
617 13TH STREET S, BRTW 134
BRTW 134
BIRMINGHAM, AL 35294-1160
205-934-7296
Fax: 205-975-8015
BartowArena@uab.edu
www.uab.edu
• Steve Mitchell, Director
(205) 934-7748
stemitch@uab.edu
Arena Seating Capacity:
8,460
Year Founded:
1987
Nature of Service:
This facility accommodates most of the UAB athletic teams and is used as the official site to see Blazer Basketball and Lady Blazer Basketball and Volleyball. Bartow Arena seats 8,460 for basketball and there are other configurations ranging from 1,200 s

UD ARENA
1801 EDWIN C. MOSES BOULEVARD
DAYTON, OH 45408
937-229-1000
Fax: 937-229-4461
info@udayton.edu
http://udayton.edu

Arena Seating Capacity:
14,000
Nature of Service:
Full service multi-purpose sports and entertainment facility.
Tenants:
University of Dayton Flyers (NCAA).

UNI-DOME
1227 WEST 27TH ST.
CEDAR FALLS, IA 50614
319-273-2311
877-216-3663
Fax: 319-273-5966
UNIDOME@uni.edu
www.vpaf.uni.edu
• Andre Seoldo, Assistant Athletic Director
(319) 273-6636
andre.seoldo@uni.edu
• Dave Kohrs, Assistant Director for Facilities
(319) 273-2865
david.kohrs@uni.edu
• Michael Hager, Vice President for Administration & Financial
(319) 273-2382
michael.hager@uni.edu
• Jan Hanish, Assistant Vice President for Administration &
(319) 273-3526
jan.hanish@uni.edu
• Jennifer Hansmann, Administrative Assistant to Vice President
(319) 273-2382
jenny.hansmann@uni.edu
• Brenda Neff, Account Specialist
(319) 273-2383
brenda.neff@uni.edu
• Bruce Rieks, Budget System Development/Reporting Director
(319) 273-7498
bruce.rieks@uni.edu
Arena Seating Capacity:
24,196
Stadium Seating Capacity:
16,300

UNITED CENTER
1901 W MADISON STREET
CHICAGO, IL 60612
312-455-4500
Fax: 312-455-4511
webmaster@unitedcenter.com
www.unitedcenter.com
• Jim Koehler, General Manager
(312) 455-4501
• Steve Schanwald, Senior Vice President of Operations
(312) 455-4110
sschanwald@bulls.com
• Terry Savarise, Operations Senior VP
• Terry Savarise, Sr. VP of Operations
• Jim Koehler, General Manger
• Steve Schulze, Chief Information Officer
• Greg Hanrahan, Sr.Director of Premium Seating
• Jim Bare, Sr.Director Box Office
• Troy Brown, Sr.Director Youth Service
• Valerie Toth, Seating Manger
Owned by:
United Center Joint Venture.
Tenant(s):
NBA - Chicago Bulls basketball; NHL - Chicago Blackhawks hockey.
Permanent Seating Capacity:
20,500 (ice hockey); 22,500 (basketball).

UNIVERSITY ARENA
1414 UNIVERSITY BOULEVARD SE
COLLEEN J MALOOF ADMINISTRATION BUILDING
ALBUQUERQUE, NM 87106
505-925-5500
Fax: 505-925-5955
www.golobos.com
• Scott Dotson, Associate Athletic Director Facilities
(505) 925-5925
• Jimmy Martinez, Assistant Director
(985) 925-5954
jdmartin@unm.edu
• Jeff Salmond, Head Sports Turf Manager
Arena Seating Capacity:
18,018

UNIVERSITY CENTER
800 GALLOWAY DRIVE
SLU 10309
HAMMOND, LA 70402
985-549-5091
Fax: 985-549-2504
sportsinfo@selu.edu
www.lionsports.net
• Joel Erdmann, Athletic Director
(985) 549-2359
jerdmann@selu.edu
• Bart M Bellairs, Athletics Director
(985) 549-2395
athletics@southeastern.edu
• Linda Alford, Administrative Coordinator
(985) 549-5599
lalford@southeastern.edu
• Andrew Bechac, Senior associate
(985) 549-3419
Andrew.Bechac@southeastern.edu
• Tim Baldwin, Head Golf Coach/Assistant AD for Special Even
(985) 549-5186
tbaldwin@southeastern.edu
Arena Seating Capacity:
7,500

UNIVERSITY HALL
295 MASSIE RD.
PO BOX 400862
CHARLOTTESVILLE, VA 22903
434-22904-4862
888-575-8497
Fax: 434-243-4959
Linda@rmcevents.com
www.johnpauljonesarena.com
• Liz Flynn, Director of Marketing
(434) 243-4957
• Scott Cornwell, Director Of Operations
(434) 243-2077
Arena Seating Capacity:
8,450

UNIVERSITY OF CHARLESTON
2300 MACCORKLE AVENUE SE
CHARLESTON, WV 25304
304-357-4800
800-995-4682
Fax: 304-357-4781
admissions@ucwv.edu
www.ucwv.edu
• Edwin H Welch, Dr, President
• Dr. Edwin H. Welch, President
(304) 357-4713
edwinwelch@ucwv.edu
Stadium Seating Capacity:
22,000

facilities

UNIVERSITY OF HARTFORD SPORTS CENTER
200 BLOOMFIELD AVENUE
W HARTFORD, CT 6117
860-768-5050
Fax: 860-768-4229
www.hartford.edu/athletics/SPORTSCTR//hours.html
• Ted Stavropoulos, Sports Center Director
tstavropo@hartford.edu
• Kelli Cullen, Assistant Facility Director
kcullen@hartford.edu
• Chris Wilk, Assistant Facility Director/Events
• Shaun Krafthofer, Assistant Facility Director/Evening Superviso
krafthofe@hartford.edu
Arena Seating Capacity:
3,545

UNIVERSITY OF KANSAS
1651 NAISMITH DRIVE
SLU 10309
LAWRENCE, KS 66045
785-864-3143
Fax: 785-864-5035
KUAthletics@KU.edu
www.kuathletics.com
• Lew Perkins, Athletic Director
(785) 864-3143
• Debbie Van Saun, Associate Athletic Director/Senior Woman
(785) 864-7903
dvansaun@ku.edu
• John Hadl, Associate Athletic Director/Development
• Chris Howard, Associate Athletics Director
(785) 864-7993
choward1@ku.edu
• Paul Buskirk, Associate Athletics Director - Student Athlet
(785) 864-7960
• Glenn Quick, Associate Athletics Director - Academic and C
(785) 864-7961
• Scott Ward, Ph.D., Associate Athletics Director - Academic and C
(785) 864-7696
• Shanda Hayden, Associate Director, Academic and Career Couns
(785) 864-7695
• Laura Jacobsen, Associate Director, Academic and Career Couns
(785) 864-4035
• Katie Martincich, Associate Director, Academic and Career Couns
(785) 864-7795
Seating Capacity:
50,000

UNIVERSITY OF NORTH TEXAS-COLISEUM
1155 Union Circle
310857
DENTON, TX 76203
940-565-2557
Fax: 940-565-3671
coliseum@unt.edu
• Rick Villarreal, Athletic Director
(940) 565-3646
rick.villarreal@unt.edu
• Steven Bartolotta, Assistant Sports Information Director
(940) 369-8329
steve.bartolotta@unt.edu
• Bill Michael, Football Coach
• Jessica Hulsebosch,, Director of Mean Green Club

(940) 369-8916
• Dan Johnston, Associate Athletic Director, Development
(940) 369-7034
• Andy Williams, Assistant Athletic Director - Business Operat
(940) 565-4067
• Jamie Adams, Assistant Athletic Director, Marketing & Prom
(940) 369-7169
• Mike Ashbaugh, Senior Associate Athletic Director, Business
(940) 565-2068
• Chaunte Baldwin, Assistant Athletic Director, Student Services
(940) 891-6834
Arena Seating Capacity:
10,000

UNIVERSITY OF PHOENIX STADIUM
1 CARDINALS DRIVE
GLENDALE, AZ 85305
623-433-7102
Fax: 623-433-7199
www.universityofphoenixstadium.com
Seating Capacity:
63,400
Teams:
Arizona Cardinals NFL football.

UNIVERSITY OF PORTLAND
5000 N WILLAMETTE BOULEVARD
CHILES CENTER, THE
PORTLAND, OR 97203-5798
503-943-8000
Fax: 503-943-8082
www.up.edu
• Julie Lapomarda, Sports Information Director
Seating Capacity:
5,000

UNIVERSITY OF WYOMING ARENA-AUDITORIUM
1000 E UNIVERSITY AVENUE
UNIVERSITY OF WYOMING
DEPARTMENT 3414
LARAMIE, WY 82071
307-766-2292
Fax: 307-766-5414
wyosid@uwyo.edu
www.gowyo.com
• Tom Burman, Athletic Director
(307) 766-2292
• Kevin McKinney, Senior Associate AD, External Affairs
(307) 766-2444
kevinm@uwyo.edu
• Tom Burman, Director of Athletics
(307) 766-2292
• Matt Whisenant, Deputy Director of Athletics
(307) 766-5551
mwhise@uwyo.edu
• Molly Moore, Sr. Assoc. AD, Internal Operations/SWA
(307) 766-4092
mmoore30@uwyo.edu
• Phil Wille, Assoc. AD, Academic Services
(307) 766-2391
pwille@uwyo.edu
• Sara Ray, Assoc. AD, Academic Services
(307) 766-2391
sray3@uwyo.edu
• Bill Sparks, Sr. Assoc. AD, Business Operations

(307) 766-5771
bsparks@uwyo.edu
Arena Seating Capacity:
15,028

UNIVERSITY STADIUM
1414 UNIVERSITY BOULEVARD SE
COLLEEN J MALOOF ADMINISTRATION BUILDING
MSC04 2680
ALBUQUERQUE, NM 87131-0001
505-925-5500
Fax: 505-925-5955
www.golobos.com
• Tim Cass, Senior Associate Athletic Director
(505) 925-5508
tcass@unm.edu
• Greg Remington, Associate AD/Media Relations
(505) 925-5925
gregrem@unm.edu
• Rocky Long, Football Coach
• Fran Fraschilla, Men's Basketball Coach
Stadium Seating Capacity:
30,000

UNK SPORTS CENTER
HEALTH AND SPORTS CENTER 102
UNIVERSITY OF NEBRASKA AT KEARNEY
KEARNEY, NE 68849
308-865-8514
Fax: 308-865-8832
www.lopers.com
• Jon McBride, Athletic Director
(308) 865-8332
mcbridejl@unk.edu
• Amy Perko, Associate AD Director
(308) 865-8863
lundgrenjl@unk.edu
Arena Seating Capacity:
5,842

UNLV TICKETS
4505 S MARYLAND PARKWAY
BOX 450003
LAS VEGAS, NV 89154-0003
702-895-3761
866-388-3267
Fax: 702-895-1099
customer.service@unlvtickets.com
www.unlvtickets.com
• Daren Libonati, Arena Director
(702) 895-3761
daren@thomasandmack.com
• Joe Carter, Food & Beverage Director
(702) 895-4172
joe.carter@thomasandmack.com
• Dale Eeles, Corporate Relations Director
• Elizabeth Swallia, Director of UNLVtickets Operations
• Chuck Soberinsky, Director of Ticketing for Thomas & Mack Cente
(702) 895-3905
• Susan Schwartz, Director of Athletic Ticketing
(702) 895-3679
Arena Seating Capacity:
18,500
Owned by:
University of Nevada, Las Vegas.
Boxing Capacity:
19,522
Tenant(s):
AFL - Las Vegas Gladiators football, NCAA - UNLV basketball.

UNM ARENA
1 UNIVERSITY OF NEW MEXICO
COLLEEN J MALOOF ADMINISTRATION
BUILDING
MSC04 2680
ALBUQUERQUE, NM 87131-0001
505-925-5500
Fax: 505-925-5955
rita@unm.edu
www.golobos.com
• Tim Cass, Senior Associate Athletic
Director
(505) 925-5508
tcass@unm.edu
• Greg Remington, Associate AD/Media
Relations
(505) 925-5925
gregrem@unm.edu
• Mark Koson, Stadium Manager
• Paul Krebs, Vice-President, Athletics
(505) 925-5510
rita@unm.edu
• Tim Cass, Deputy Athletic Director
(505) 925-5508
tcass@unm.edu
• Janice Ruggiero, Senior Associate
AD/Administration & Senior W
(505) 277-5067
ruggiero@unm.edu
• Kurt Esser, Senior Associate AD/External
(505) 925-5544
kesser@unm.edu
• Henry Villegas, Associate AD/Student
Development
(505) 277-6538
hvillega@unm.edu
• Brad Hutchins, Associate AD/Marketing &
Revenue Generation
(505) 925-5606
hutchins@unm.edu
• Lee De Leon, Associate AD/Development
(505) 925-5919
Stadium Seating Capacity:
30,000

US AIRWAYS CENTER
201 E JEFFERSON STREET
PO BOX 433
ST. PHOENIX, AZ 85004
602-379-7878
800-800-9494
Fax: 602-379-2002
webmaster@phxses.com
• Colangelo Jerry, Chairman/Chief
Executive Officer
• Bob Machen, President
• Paige Peterson, General Manager
• Alvan Adams, VP Facility Manager
Owned by:
City of Phoenix
Home Arena for:
Phoenix Suns, Phoenix Coyotes, Arizona
Rattlers, Phoenix Mercury
Seating Capacity:
Basketball: 19,023; Football: 16,285

US BANK ARENA
100 BROADWAY
CINCINNATI, OH 45202
513-421-4111
Fax: 513-333-3040
info@usbankarena.com
www.usbankarena.com
• Chuck Kemp, General Manager
• Bill Barrett, Director Marketing/Booking
• Matt Dunne, Building Manager
Arena Seating Capacity:
17,000

US CELLULAR ARENA
400 W KILBOURN AVENUE
MILWAUKEE, WI 53203
414-908-6000
800-745-3000
Fax: 414-908-6010
boxoffice@wcd.org
• Richard A Geyer, President/CEO
(414) 908-6050
rgeyer@wcd.org
• David Schneider, Sales Manager
(414) 908-6098
dschneider@wcd.org
• Jason Borders, Event Services Director
(414) 908-6079
jborders@wcd.org
• Donna Hrobsky, Box Office Manager
(414) 908-6035
dhrobsky@wcd.org
• Allan Ray, Technical
(613) 966-2972
Seating Capacity:
Maximum-12,418; Basketball-11,119;
Hockey-9,652; Indoor
Soccer/Football-9,600;
Boxing/Wrestling-12,146; Open Floor
(indoor motorsports, rodeo etc) -8,910.
Tenants:
Milwaukee Wave (Major Indoor Soccer
League); University of Wisconsin-Milwaukee
Panthers Men's Basketball team (NCAA
Division I, Horizon League conference).
Events:
Disney on Ice; Tripoli Shrine Circus;
Universal Cheerleaders competitions

US CELLULAR CENTER
370 1ST AVENUE NE
CEDAR RAPIDS, IA 52401-1197
319-398-5211
Fax: 319-362-2102
info@uscellularcenter.com
www.uscellularcenter.com
• Schoenike Scott, Executive Director
d.herting@uscellularcenter.com
• Terry Dederich, Assistant Executive
Director
• Thomas Fesenmeyer, Director Operations
• Gene Felling, Executive Director
(319) 398-5211
g.felling@uscellularcenter.com
• Taya Roos, Director of Finance
(319) 398-5211
t.roos@uscellularcenter.com
• Scott Piquard, Director of Event
Operations
(319) 398-5211
s.piquard@uscellularcenter.com
• Sarah Mandalinski, Marketing Director
(319) 398-5211
s.madalinski@uscellularcenter.com
• Deena Rupalo, Ticket Office Manager
(319) -398-521
d.rupalo@uscellularcenter.com
• Jason Lester, Event Manager
(319) 398-5211
j.lester@uscellularcenter.com
Seating Capacity:
10,000

US CELLULAR FIELD
333 WEST 35TH ST
CHICAGO, IL 60616
312-674-1000
Fax: 312-674-5103
chicago.whitesox.mlb.com
Seating Capacity:
41,000

Teams:
Chicago White Sox MLB baseball.

USA HOCKEY ARENA
14900 BECK ROAD
PLYMOUTH, MI 48170
734-453-6400
www.usahockeyarena.com
• Scott Monaghan, Sr. Director, Operations
scottm@usahockey.org
• Denise Ronayne, Director of Sales &
Marketing
denise.ronayne@usahockeyarena.org
Seating Capacity:
3,504; 4,500 for concerts.

USF SOCCER STADIUM
4202 EAST FOWLER AVENUE
ATH 100
TAMPA, FL 33620
813-974-2125
Fax: 813-974-4028
www.gousfbulls.com
• Mark Harlan, Director of Athletics
(813) 974-1442
markharlan@usf.edu
• Barry Clements, Deputy Director of
Athletics
(813) 974-4144
clements@usf.edu
• Jocelyn Fisher, Senior Associate Director
of Athletics
(813) 974-6885
jafisher1@usf.edu
• Marquita Armstead, Associate Director of
Athletics/Compliance
(813) 974-4061
marmstead@usf.edu
• Scott Glaser, Senior Associate Director of
Athletics/Facilities
(813) 974-3110
sglaser@usf.edu
• Dan Krone, Director of Facilities
(813) 974-8935
dkrone@usf.edu
Permanent Seating Capacity:
3,000

USF SUN DOME
4202 EAST FOWLER AVENUE
SUN 130
TAMPA, FL 33620
813-974-3111
Fax: 813-905-9813
sundomearena@usf.edu
www.sundomearena.com
• Trent Merritt, General Manager
tmerritt1@usf.edu
• Jack Ligon, Assistant General
Manager/Director of Operations
jligon@usf.edu
• Allison Dobin, Director of Marketing
dobin@usf.edu
• Nicole Williams, Director of Finance
nicolew@usf.edu
• Tom Bradley, Box Office Manager
tbradley2@usf.edu
• Dennis Perez, Senior Operations Manager
dennisperez@usf.edu
• Michele Harhut, Senior Event Manager
mharhut@usf.edu
• Tyler Hine, Operations Manager
tylerhine@usf.edu
• Eric McDade, Event Manager
mcdade@usf.edu
• Wayne Letson, Facility Engineer
wletson@usf.edu

• Whitney Henry, Marketing & Sales
Coordinator
whitneyhenry@usf.edu
Permanent Seating Capacity:
10,411
Year Founded:
1980
Tenants:
USF Athletics.

**USTA BILLIE JEAN KING NATIONAL
TENNIS CENTER**
FLUSHING MEADOW-CORONA PARK
FLUSHING, NY 11368
718-760-6200
Fax: 718-592-9488
www.usta.com
Description:
The largest public tennis facility in the world
and home to the US Open. Twenty outdoor
and twelve indoor courts.

UTC MCKENZIE ARENA
720 EAST 4TH STREET
DEPT 3403
615 MCCALLIE AVENUE
CHATTANOOGA, TN 37403
423-425-4706
Fax: 423-425-4783
mckenziefan@utc.edu
www.utc.edu/mckenzie-arena
• Obie Webster, Executive Director,
Entertainment & Sports Venues
(423) 425-4706
obie-webster@utc.edu
• Kyle Askew, Technical Director
(423) 425-4746
• Arland Jenkins, Operations Coordinator
(423) 425-4648
• Sandra Farris, Event
Coordinator/Accounting
(423) 425-4030
• Brent McMillan, Box Office Supervisor
(423) 425-5273
Arena Seating Capacity:
11,557
Year Founded:
1982
Nature of Service:
Multi-purpose arena.
Tenant(s):
University of Tennessee at Chattanooga,
men's & women's basketball.

UTEP SPECIAL EVENTS
151 GLORY ROAD
EL PASO, TX 79908
915-747-5481
Fax: 915-747-7469
events@utep.edu
www.utepspecialevents.com
• Jorge Vazquez, Executive Director
vazquezj@utep.edu
• Mike Spence, Director of Special Facilities
Management
mspence@utep.edu
• Ricky Nichols, Assistant Director
rlnichols@utep.edu
• Julian E. Valdes, Marketing Manager
jevaldes@utep.edu
• Christina Garay, Building Supervisor
cvgaray@utep.edu
Arena Seating Capacity:
12,000
Clients:
AEG, Stardate, Stone City Attractions.

Nature of Service:
University venues

VA MEMORIAL STADIUM
17273 STREET ROUTE 104
CHILLICOTHE, OH 45601
740-773-7117
Fax: 740-773-8338
paints@bright.net
www.chillicothepaints.com
• Chris Hanners, Owner
• Shirley Bandy, President
• John Wend, Director of Sales &
Marketing/PA Announcer
• Maleine Davis, Director of Finance
• Brian Mannino, Director of Baseball
Operations
• Greg Cypret, Manager
• Jim Miner, Stadium Operations/Clubhouse
Manager
• Toni Diehl, Stadium Supervisor
Capacity:
3,000

VALLEY VIEW CASINO CENTER
3500 SPORTS ARENA BOULEVARD
SAN DIEGO, CA 92110-4919
619-224-4171
Fax: 619-224-3010
info@valleyviewcasinocenter.com
www.valleyviewcasinocenter.com
• Ernie Hahn, General Manager
Seating Capacity:
15,000

**VALUE CITY ARENA/JEROME
SCHOTTENSTEIN CENTER**
555 BORROR DRIVE
COLUMBUS, OH 43210
614-292-3231
800-273-6201
Fax: 614-292-5067
osuarena@osu.edu
www.schottensteincenter.com
• Michael Gatto, Director
(614) 688-5579
• Bredan Buckley, Booking & Scheduling
Director
(614) 688-8400
• Tracy Hedrick, Promotions Director
(614) 247-0008
• Tim Flipovich, Arena Supervisor
(614) 688-5411
• Sarah Reissig, Arena Supervisor
(614) 688-5411
Seating Capacity:
17,500-20,000.

VAN ANDEL ARENA
130 WEST FULTON
GRAND RAPIDS, MI 49503-2601
616-742-6600
Fax: 616-742-6197
webmaster@smggr.com
www.vanandelarena.com
• Richard MacKeigan, General Manager
• Jim Watt, Assistant General Manager
jwatt@smggr.com
• Lynne Ike, Director of Marketing
(616) 742-6198
like@smggr.com
• Hilarie Szarowicz, Marketing Manager
hszarowicz@smggr.com
• Kevin Abbott, Operations Manager
• Marcus Scott, Box Office Manager
Year Founded:
1996

Seating Capacity:
12,000.
Nature of Service:
Sports Arena for Arenacross, Basketball,
Football, Wrestling and other events.
Clients Include:
Grand Rapids Griffins - AHL, Harlem
Globetrotters, WWE, Arenacross, Thunder
Nationals, Freestyle.
Tenant(s):
Grand Rapids Griffins - AHL.

VANDERBILT STADIUM
2601 JESS NEELY DRIVE
NASHVILLE, TN 37212
615-322-4653
Fax: 615-343-7064
www.vucommodores.com
• David Williams II, Athletics Director
(615) 343-1107
• Brock Williams, Assistant Vice Chancellor,
Facilities & Game Ops
(615) 343-4411
brock.williams@vanderbilt.edu
• Ed Higgins, Director, Facilities & Game
Operations
(615) 343-2012
ed.higgins@vanderbilt.edu
• Eric Chaffin, Associate Director, Game
Operations & Facilities
(615) 322-1793
eric.chaffin@vanderbilt.edu
Stadium Seating Capacity:
40,550
Team:
Vanderbilt college football.

**VAUGHT-HEMINGWAY
STADIUM/HOLLINGSWORTH FIELD**
908 ALL-AMERICAN DRIVE
PO BOX 1848
UNIVERSITY, MS 38677
662-915-7241
Fax: 662-915-7683
www.olemisssports.com
• Ross Bjork, Director of Athletics
(662) 915-7546
• Joe Swingle, Associate Director, Facilities
& Game Operations
(662) 915-7508
jswingle@olemiss.edu
• Kerry Page, Associate Director, Facilities
& Sports Turf
kcpage@olemiss.edu
• Durrell Buford, Associate Superintendent,
Athletics Grounds
Stadium Seating Capacity:
60,580

VERIZON CENTER
601 F STREET NORTHWEST
WASHINGTON, DC 20004
202-628-3200
www.verizoncenter.com
• Ted Leonis, Founder/Chairman/Majoriy
Owner/CEO
• Dick Patrick, Vice Chairman/Chief
Operating Officer
• Raul Fernandez, Vice Chairman
• Sheila Johnson, Vice Chairman
Tenant(s):
NHL - Washington Capitals hockey, NBA -
Washington Wizards basketball.
Owned by:
Monumental Sports & Entertainment
Seating Capacity:
20,000

VERIZON WIRELESS CENTER
ONE CIVIC CENTER PLAZA
MANKATO, MN 56001
507-389-3000
Fax: 507-345-1627
verizonwirelesscentermn.com
• Burt Lyman, Executive Director
(507) 389-3000
blyman@verizonwirelesscentermn.com
• JoAnn Hoffmann, Ticket Office Specialist
(507) 387-8456
jhoffman@verizonwirelesscentermn.com
• Steve Conover, Operations Manager
(507) 387-8440
sconover@verizonwirelesscentermn.com
Seating Capacity:
5,280

VERMONT LAKE MONSTERS
1 KING STREET FERRY DOCK
BURLINGTON, VT 05401
802-655-4200
Fax: 802-655-5660
info@vermontlakemonsters.com
www.vermontlakemonsters.com
• Raymond C. Pecor Jr., President
• Kyle Bostwick, Vice President
• Nate Cloutier, General Manager
nate@vermontlakemonsters.com
• Joe Doud, Asst. General Manager
nate@vermontlakemonsters.com
Sport:
Minor League Baseball.
Team:
Vermont Expos baseball
Year Founded:
1922
Capacity:
4,000

VERNON KENNEDY FIELD/WALTON STADIUM
203 MULTIPURPOSE BUILDING
500 SOUTH WASHINGTON STREET
WARRENSBURG, MO 64093
660-543-4250
877-729-8266
Fax: 660-543-8034
www.ucmathletics.com
• Jerry Hughes, Athletics Director
hughes@ucmo.edu
• Kathy Anderson, Senior Associate Athletic Director
(660) 543-4310
klanderson@ucmo.edu
• Scott Thomason, Assistant Athletic Director, Facilities
(660) 543-4011
sthomason@ucmo.edu
Stadium Seating Capacity:
12,000

VETERANS MEMORIAL COLISEUM
300 NORTH WINNING WAY
PORTLAND, OR 97227
503-235-8771

VETERANS MEMORIAL COLISEUM (IN)
300 COURT STREET
EVANSVILLE, IN 47708
812-424-5879
Coliseum Seating Capacity:
4,055

VETERANS MEMORIAL STADIUM
2531 NORTH STATE STREET
JACKSON, MS 39216
601-354-6021
Fax: 601-354-6019
www.ms-veteransstadium.com
• Thomas Cooper, Interim Stadium Manager
Stadium Seating Capacity:
60,492

VETERANS MEMORIAL STADIUM (CEDAR RAPIDS)
950 ROCKFORD ROAD SOUTHWEST
CEDAR RAPIDS, IA 52404
319-363-3887
Fax: 319-363-5631
doug@kernels.com
www.kernels.com
• Doug Nelson, Chief Executive Officer
(319) 896-7614
doug@kernels.com
• Scott Wilson, General Manager
(319) 896-7612
scott@kernels.com
• Andrea Brommelkamp, Director of Tickets & Group Sales
(319) 896-7603
andrea@kernels.com
• Jesse Roeder, Sports Turf Manager
(319) 896-7637
jesse@kernels.com
• Sammy Brzostowski, Ticket Office Manager
(319) 896-7622
sammy@kernels.com
Stadium Seating Capacity:
5,300
Year Founded:
2002
Tenant(s):
Cedar Rapids Kernels.

VICTORY FIELD
501 WEST MARYLAND STREET
INDIANAPOLIS, IN 46225
317-269-3545
Fax: 317-269-3541
indians@indyindians.com
www.indyindians.com
• Max B. Schumacher, Chairman/President
(317) 269-3548
• Cal Burleson, Vice President, Baseball & Administrative Affairs
burleson@indyindians.com
• Randy Lewandowski, General Manager
rlewandowski@indyindians.com
• Joel Zawacki, Director of Corporate Sales & Marketing
(317) 532-6935
jzawacki@indyindians.com
• Tim Hughes, Director of Facilities
(317) 532-6779
thughes@indyindians.com
• Matt Guay, Director of Tickets & Operations
(317) 532-6784
mguay@indyindians.com
Sport:
Baseball
Team:
Indianapolis Indians
Year Founded:
1996
Capacity:
14,230

VIKING HALL CIVIC CENTER
1100 EDGEMONT AVENUE
PO BOX 3563
BRISTOL, TN 37620
423-764-4171
423-764-0188
Fax: 423-764-3299
• Darlene Cole, Venue Manager
vikhall@vikinghall.com
• Terrie Talbert, Department Manager
tsmith-talbert@bristoltn.org
• Sarah Rhymer, Box Office Manager
• Eddie Abbott, Operations Manager
• Lisa Beckner, Office Manager
• Terrie Talbert, Department Manager
• Tommy Baker, City Web Master
• Angie Rutherford, Box office Manager
Arena Seating Capacity:
6,200

VINES CENTER
1971 UNIVERSITY BOULEVARD
LYNCHBURG, VA 24515
434-582-2000
866-447-2084
Fax: 434-582-2205
www.liberty.edu
• Jeff Barber, Director of Athletics
jbarber2@liberty.edu
• Mickey Guridy, Senior Associate AD, Internal Operations
maguridy@liberty.edu
• Tim East, Senior Associate AD, External Operations
• Dan Maxam, Assistant Athletics Director, Facilities
• Anna Hutchinson, Assistant Athletics Director, Ticket Operations
Capacity:
8,085

VIRGINIA BEACH SPORTSPLEX
2044 LANDSTOWN CENTRE WAY
VIRGINIA BEACH, VA 23456
757-427-2990
Fax: 757-430-8895
chuck@beachsportsplex.com
www.thevirginiabeachsportsplex.com
• Nick Senti, Contact
Built:
1999
Operated by:
Hometown Sports Management
Seating Capacity:
10,000
Nature of Service:
Color Me Rad, USA Field Hockey, Division 3 College Lacrosse, High School Football, Soccer, Field Lacrosse and Rugby

VIVINT SMART HOME ARENA
301 WEST SOUTH TEMPLE
SALT LAKE CITY, UT 84101
801-325-2000
Fax: 801-325-2516
comments@vivintarena.com
www.vivintarena.com
Permanent Seating Capacity:
20,000
Tenant(s):
Utah Jazz (NBA)

VOLCANOES STADIUM
6700 FIELD OF DREAMS WAY
NORTHEAST
KEIZER, OR 97303

503-390-2225
Fax: 503-390-2227
info@volcanoesbaseball.com
www.volcanoesbaseball.com
• Jerry Walker, Co-Owner/General Manager
(503) 390-2225
jwalker@volcanoesbaseball.com
• Rick Nelson, Stadium Operations
(503) 390-2225
rnelson@volcanoesbaseball.com
• Jerry Howard, Senior Account Executive
• Bea Howard, Ticket Office
Stadium Seating Capacity:
4,254
Year Founded:
1997
Nature of Service:
Sports facility.
Tenant(s):
Salem-Keizer Volcanoes, Single A Affiliate
of the San Francisco Giants.

VON BRAUN CENTER
700 MONROE STREET
HUNTSVILLE, AL 35801
256-533-1953
Fax: 256-551-2203
vbcinfo@vonbrauncenter.com
www.vonbrauncenter.com
• Steve Maples, Executive Director
stevemaples@vonbrauncenter.com
• Mike Vojticek, Assistant Director
vojticek@vonbrauncenter.com
• Ron Grimes, Director of Operations
rgrimes@vonbrauncenter.com
• Marie Arighi, Director of Sales & Marketing
marighi@vonbrauncenter.com
• Johnny Hunkapiller, Director of Special
Projects
jhunkapiller@vonbrauncenter.com
• Shawn McCown, Director of Finance
smccown@vonbrauncenter.com
• Bruce Mitchell, Director of Food &
Beverage
bmitchell@vonbrauncenter.com
• Byron Clanton, Director of Facilities
bclanton@vonbrauncenter.com
Capacity:
10,000

WAGNER FIELD/KSU
1800 COLLEGE AVENUE
BRAMLAGE COLISEUM
MANHATTAN, KS 66502
785-532-5876
800-221-1187
Fax: 785-532-2004
sportsinfo@k-state.edu
www.kstatesports.com
• Bob Krause, Athletics Director
(785) 532-6912
vpia@ksu.edu
• John Currie, Director of Athletics
(785) 532-6912
• Reid Sigmon, Senior Associate AD/Chief
Operating Officer
(785) 532-6913
• Vicki Jones, Executive Assistant to Athletic
Director
(785) 532-6912
• Jana Buehler, Academic Learning
Specialist
• Jim Muller, Associate Director
jamesbm@ksu.edu
Stadium Seating Capacity:
50,000

WAKE FOREST BASEBALL PARK
401 DEACON BOULEVARD
WINSTON-SALEM, NC 27115
336-758-4620
Fax: 336-759-2042
www.wakeforestsports.com
• Ron Wellman, Director of Athletics
(336) 758-5753
• Steve Adams, Associate AD, Internal
Operations
(336) 758-4908
adamss@wfu.edu
• Pete Fisch, Associate AD, Venue
Management
(336) 758-2659
fischpj@wfu.edu
• Corey Jenkins, Associate AD, Events and
Facilities
(336) 758-6166
jenkinca@wfu.edu
Arena Seating Capacity:
6,280
Year Founded:
1956
Nature of Service:
Minor League Baseball.

WALKER ARENA
955 4TH STREET
MUSKEGON, MI 49440
231-726-2939
www.lcwalkerarena.com
• John Vanbiesbrouck, General Manager
• Tim Taylor, President of Business
Operations
• Dan Devowe, Sales Director
Tenant(s):
USHL - Muskegon Lumberjacks.
Arena Seating Capacity:
5,000

WALTER J. ZABLE STADIUM AT CARY FIELD
100 STADIUM DRIVE
COLLEGE OF WILLIAM & MARY
WILLIAMSBURG, VA 23185
757-221-3400
Fax: 757-221-7691
www.tribeathletics.com
• Terry Driscoll, Athletic Director
(757) 221-3332
• Steve Cole, Associate Athletics Director,
Internal Affairs
(757) 221-3361
slcole@wm.edu
• Chelsey Burk, Assistant Athletics Director,
Business Affairs
(757) 221-3373
cpburk@wm.edu
• Michael Pritchett, Assistant Athletics
Director, Facilities
(757) 221-3355
mapritchett@wm.edu
• Pete Kresky, Director of Corporate Sales
and Sponsorship
(757) 221-3353
pmkres@wm.edu
• Jaime LaBianco, Executive Secretary
(757) 221-3332
jllabi@wm.edu
• Sarah Smith, Administrative Assistant
(757) 221-3327
smsmith@wm.edu
Seating Capacity:
11,686

WAR MEMORIAL AUDITORIUM
800 NORTHEAST 8TH STREET
FORT LAUDERDALE, FL 33304
954-828-5380
Fax: 954-763-1769
rstried@fortlauderdale.gov
www.fortlauderdale.gov/wma
• Karen Newhart, Marketing Specialist
(954) 828-4352
knewhart@fortlauderdale.gov
Seating Capacity:
2,110
Sports:
MMA, Boxing, Wrestling, Karate, Judo,
Gymnastics

WAR MEMORIAL STADIUM
1 STADIUM DRIVE
LITTLE ROCK, AR 72225
501-663-0775
Fax: 501-663-6387
www.wmstadium.com
• Jerry Cohen, Executive Director
• Danny-Joe Crofford, Marketing Director
• J.O. Bailey, Assistant Stadium Manager
jobailey@arkansas.gov
• Nancy Toland, Office Manager
nancy.toland@arkansas.gov
• Dinah Soderling, Stadium Fiscal Manager
dinah.soderling@arkansas.gov
• Emily Martin, Special Events Manager
emily.martin@arkansas.gov
Seating Capacity:
54,120
Team:
Arkansas college football.

WAR MEMORIAL STADIUM (WY)
1000 EAST UNIVERSITY AVENUE
UNIVERSITY OF WYOMING
DEPARTMENT 3414
LARAMIE, WY 82071
307-766-2292
Fax: 307-766-6729
www.gowyo.com
• Tom Burman, Director of Athletics
(307) 766-2292
uwad@uwyo.edu
• Matt Whisenant, Deputy Director of
Athletics
(307) 766-5551
mwhise@uwyo.edu
• Kevin McKinney, Senior Associate AD,
External Affairs
(307) 766-2444
kevinm@uwyo.edu
• Bill Sparks, Senior Associate AD,
Business Operations
(307) 766-5771
bsparks@uwyo.edu
• Phil Wille, Associate AD, Internal
Operations
(307) 766-2391
pwille@uwyo.edu
• Tyson Drew, Associate AD, Facility
Operations/Event Management
(307) 766-2007
tdrew@uwyo.edu
• Albert Reiser, Assistant AD, Academic
Services
(307) 766-2075
areiser@uwyo.edu
Stadium Seating Capacity:
29,181
Year Founded:
1950

WAYNE STATE COLLEGE
1111 MAIN STREET
WAYNE, NE 68787
402-375-7520
Fax: 402-375-7271
migrosz1@wsc.edu
www.wscwildcats.com
• Mike Powichi, Athletic Director
• Mike Barry, Associate Athletic Director
(402) 375-7521
mibarry1@wsc.edu
• Steve Schafer, Sports Information Director
Rice Fieldhouse Seating Capacity:
2,500
Memorial Stadium Seating Capacity:
3,500
Sports:
Football, Volleyball, Women's Soccer, Golf, Cross Country, Basketball, Track and Field, Baseball, Softball
Track Types:
Mondo Sports Surface: indoor, 160 meters; Polyurethane: Outdoor, 400 meters

WEEDE ARENA
1701 SOUTH BROADWAY
PITTSBURG STATE UNIVERSITY
PITTSBURG, KS 66762-7504
620-231-7000
Fax: 620-235-4661
psuinfo@pittstate.edu
www.pittstate.edu
• Steve Scott, President
• Jim Johnson, Athletics Director
(620) 235-4389
jjohnson@pittstate.edu
• Dan Wilkes, Associate Athletic Director/Communications
(620) 235-4147
dwilkes@pittstate.edu
• Tom Myers, Associate Athletic Director/Facilities
(620) 235-4640
ltmyers@pittstate.edu
• Heidi Johnson, Director of Media Relations & Promotions
(620) 235-4138
hjohnson@pittstate.edu
Arena Seating Capacity:
6,500

WELLS FARGO CENTER
3601 SOUTH BROAD STREET
PHILADELPHIA, PA 19148
215-336-3600
800-298-4200
www.wellsfargocenterphilly.com
• John Page, President, Wells Fargo Complex
Owned by:
Ed Snider.
Tenant(s):
NBA - Philadelphia 76ers Basketball, NHL - Philadelphia Flyers Hockey.
Permanent Seating Capacity:
19,500

WELSH RYAN ARENA
2705 ASHLAND AVENUE
NORTHWESTERN UNIVERSITY
EVANSTON, IL 60208
847-491-3205
Fax: 847-491-4659
d-robert@northwestern.edu
www.nusports.com
• Jim Phillips, Vice President, Athletics & Recreation

• Steve Green, Deputy Director of Athletics (Internal Affairs)
(847) 467-6827
sag411@northwestern.edu
• Carrie Forsman, Director of Facilities
(847) 491-8686
c-forsman@northwestern.edu
• Rachel Gunn, Department Assistant
(847) 467-6827
r-gunn@northwestern.edu
• Debbie Robert, Administrative Assistant
(847) 491-4795
d-robert@northwestern.edu
Arena Seating Capacity:
8,117

WEST VIRGINIA UNIVERSITY/WVU COLISEUM
3450 MONONGAHELA BOULEVARD
WEST VIRGINIA UNIVERSITY
MORGANTOWN, WV 26505
304-293-5621
Fax: 304-293-4105
www.wvusports.com
• Shane Lyons, Director of Athletics
(304) 293-5621
• Keli Cunningham, Executive Senior Associate Athletic Director
(304) 293-6758
keli.cunningham@mail.wvu.edu
• Matt Borman, Senior Associate AD/Executive Director
(304) 293-2294
matt.borman@mail.wvu.edu
• Terri Howes, Senior Associate AD/Sports Administration
(304) 293-2889
terri.howes@mail.wvu.edu
• Michael Szul, Senior Associate AD/Business Operations
(304) 293-2101
michael.szul@mail.wvu.edu
• Michael Fragale, Associate Athletic Director/Communications
(304) 293-2821
michael.fragale@mail.wvu.edu
• April Messerly, Assistant Athletic Director for Facilities
(304) 293-3056
april.messerly@mail.wvu.edu
Coliseum Seating Capacity:
14,000

WESTERN HALL
1 UNIVERSITY CIRCLE
WESTERN ILLINOIS UNIVERSITY
MACOMB, IL 61455
309-298-1190
Fax: 309-298-2009
www.goleathernecks.com
• Matt Tanney, Director of Athletics
(309) 298-1190
m-tanney@wiu.edu
• Patrick Osterman, Assistant Athletic Director for Communications
(309) 298-1133
pr-osterman@wiu.edu
• Nancy Sprout, Assistant Athletic Director for Business Operation
(309) 298-1591
nk-sprout@wiu.edu
Arena Seating Capacity:
5,139
Tenant(s):
NCAA - Western Illinois University basketball

WHITAKER BANK BALLPARK
207 LEGENDS LANE
LEXINGTON, KY 40505
859-252-4487
Fax: 859-252-0747
lexington.legends.milb.com
• Shannon Kidd, Director, Stadium Operations
skidd@lexingtonlegends.com
• Mark Costagliola, Ticket Operations Manager
mcostagliola@lexingtonlegends.com
Sport:
Baseball
Team:
Lexington Legends
Year Founded:
2001
Seating Capacity:
6,994

WHITTEMORE CENTER ARENA
128 MAIN STREET
DURHAM, NH 03824
603-862-4000
campus.recreation@unh.edu
campusrec.unh.edu/whittemore-center-arena
• Marty Scarano, Director of Athletics
(603) 862-2013
marty.scarano@unh.edu
• Steve Metcalf, Deputy Athletic Director
(603) 862-2596
steve.metcalf@unh.edu
• Kate McAfee, Associate Athletic Director for Event Management
(603) 862-0173
kate.mcafee@unh.edu
• AJ Lewis, Box Office Manager
(603) 862-1763
aj.lewis@unh.edu
Arena Seating Capacity:
6,500

WHITTIER FIELD
9000 COLLEGE STATION
BOWDOIN COLLEGE
BRUNSWICK, ME 04011-8490
207-725-3326
Fax: 207-725-3019
• Tim Ryan, Director of Athletics
(207) 725-3247
tryan@bowdoin.edu
• Alice Wiercinski, Associate Director of Athletics
(207) 798-4342
awiercin@bowdoin.edu
• Terry Meagher, Associate Athletic Director
(207) 725-3328
tmeagher@bowdoin.edu
• Lynn Ruddy, Associate Athletic Director
(207) 725-3623
lruddy@bowdoin.edu
• James Caton, Assistant AD for Communications
(207) 725-4254
jcaton@bowdoin.edu
• Micki Manheimer, Sports Information Associate
(207) 725-3701
mmanheim@bowdoin.edu
Stadium Seating Capacity:
9,000

facilities

WILKINS STADIUM
100 EAST UNIVERSITY
OFFICE OF THE PRESIDENT
MAGNOLIA, AR 71753-5000
870-235-4000
Fax: 870-235-5005
www.muleriderathletics.com
• Steve Browning, Director of Athletics
(870) 235-4132
dsbrowning@saumag.edu
• Michael Westbrook, Associate Director of
Athletics for Operations
(870) 235-5090
• Daniel Gallegos, Sports Information
Director
(870) 235-4104
sausid@saumag.edu
Stadium Seating Capacity:
6,000

WILLIAM & MARY HALL
751 UKROP WAY
WILLIAMSBURG, VA 23185
757-221-3340
Fax: 757-221-7691
www.tribeathletics.com
• Terry Driscoll, Athletics Director
(757) 221-3332
• Steve Cole, Associate Athletics Director,
Internal Affairs
(757) 221-3361
slcole@wm.edu
• Chelsey Burk, Assistant Athletics Director,
Business Affairs
(757) 221-3373
cpburk@wm.edu
• Tiffany Christian, Assistant Athletics
Director, Compliance
(757) 221-7601
ttchristian@wm.edu
• Michael Pritchett, Assistant Athletics
Director, Facilities
(757) 221-3355
• Spencer Milne, Assistant Athletics
Director, Marketing/Promotions
(757) 221-3356
shmiln@wm.edu
• Jason Simms, Assistant Athletics Director,
Academic Services
(757) 221-3241
jlsimms@wm.edu
• Jaime LaBianco, Executive Secretary
(757) 221-3332
jilabi@wm.edu
Arena Seating Capacity:
11,300

WILLIAM R. JOHNSON COLISEUM
712 HAYTER STREET
NACOGDOCHES, TX 75962
936-468-4540
www.sfajacks.com
• Robert Hill, Director of Athletics
(936) 468-4540
rhill@sfasu.edu
• Matt Fenley, Associate Athletics Director,
Compliance
(936) 468-4570
mfenley@sfasu.edu
• John Branch, Associate Athletics Director,
External Affairs
(936) 468-4334
jbranch@sfasu.edu
• Rob Meyers, Assistant Athletics Director,
Business
(936) 468-4080
rmeyers@sfasu.edu

• Rob McDermand, Assistant Athletics
Director, Academic Services
(936) 468-4429
mcdermanrd@sfasu.edu
• Payton Adams, Coordinator of Athletic
Operations
(936) 468-5183
adamsp@sfasu.edu
• Pam Cole, Administrative Assistant
(936) 468-4540
colepd@sfasu.edu
Coliseum Seating Capacity:
7,200

WILLIAMS ARENA
1925 UNIVERSITY AVENUE SOUTHEAST
MINNEAPOLIS, MN 55455
612-625-3007
Fax: 612-625-7788
icaadmin@umn.edu
www.gophersports.com
• Beth Goetz, Interim Director of Athletics
(612) 624-4497
• Tom McGinnis, Senior Associate AD/CFO
(612) 624-4497
• Marc Ryan, Senior Associate AD
(612) 624-4497
• Jeremiah Carter, Director of Compliance
(612) 626-5480
Arena Seating Capacity:
14,625

WILLIAMS COLLEGE ATHLETICS
22 SPRING STREET
LASELL GYMNASIUM
WILLIAMSTOWN, MA 1267
413-597-4982
Fax: 413-597-4158
webfeedback@williams.edu
athletics.williams.edu
• Harry Sheehy, Chair & Director of
Athletics/PE/Recreation
(413) 597-2366
hsheehy@williams.edu
• Bud Fisher, Associate AD/Head Coach of
Nordic Skiing
(413) 597-2340
rfisher@williams.edu
• Gary Guerin, Associate Director for
Operations
(413) 597-3321
gguerin@williams.edu
• Jennifer Chuks, Assistant Athletic
Administrator
(413) 597-4085
Jennifer.E.Chuks@williams.edu
• Lisa Melendy, Athletic Director
(413) 597-3511
lmelendy@williams.edu
Stadium Seating Capacity:
8,000

WILLIAMS STADIUM
1971 UNIVERSITY BOULEVARD
LYNCHBURG, VA 24515
434-582-2100
Fax: 434-582-2205
www.liberty.edu
• Jeff Barber, Director of Athletics
jbarber2@liberty.edu
• Mickey Guridy, Senior Associate Athletics
Director
maguridy@liberty.edu
• Tim East, Senior Associate Athletics
Director
tmeast@liberty.edu
• Mike Minyard, Associate Athletics Director,

Sales & Promotions
• Dan Maxam, Assistant Athletics Director,
Facilities
dlmaxam@liberty.edu
Stadium Seating Capacity:
19,200

WILLIAMS-BRICE STADIUM
1125 GEORGE ROGERS BOULEVARD
COLUMBIA, SC 29201
803-777-4202
www.gamecocksonline.com
• Ray Tanner, Athletics Director
• Charles Waddell, Deputy Athletics Director
• Josh Waters, Assistant AD/Marketing
• Duane Grooms, Assistant AD/Facilities
Services
• Lance Grantham, Assistant AD/Ticket
Operations
Stadium Seating Capacity:
80,250
Team:
University of South Carolina football.

WINGS EVENT CENTER
3600 VANRICK DRIVE
KALAMAZOO, MI 49001
269-345-1125
Fax: 269-345-6584
www.wingseventcenter.com
• Toni Daniels, Director of Sales
• Rob Underwood, Director of Entertainment
runderwood@wingseventcenter.com
• Holly Rinal, Operations Manager
hrinal@wingseventcenter.com
• Emilie Vanderlaan, Special Events
Coordinator
evanderlaan@wingseventcenter.com
Arena Seating Capacity:
5,113

WISCONSIN CENTER DISTRICT
400 WEST WISCONSIN AVENUE
MILWAUKEE, WI 53203
414-908-6000
Fax: 414-908-6010
www.wcd.org
• Russell Staerkel, President/CEO
• Jeffrey Sinkovec, Director of Finance and
Accounting
(414) 908-6071
jsinkovec@wcd.org
• Thomas Paul, Director of Information
Technology
(414) 908-6090
tpaul@wcd.org
• Trace Goudreau, Director of Sales &
Marketing
(414) 908-6072
tgoudreau@wcd.org
• Robert Seefeld, Director of Building
Services
(414) 908-6054
rseefeld@wcd.org
• Tony Dynicki, Director of Sports &
Entertainment Sales
(414) 908-6084
tdynicki@wcd.org
• Elizabeth Unruh, Sales Manager
(414) 908-6079
eunruh@wcd.org
Description:
A convention center used for basketball,
volleyball, gymnastics, fencing and other
tournaments.

WISCONSIN-MADISON FIELDHOUSE
1450 MONROE STREET
UNIVERSITY OF WISCONSIN
MADISON, WI 53706
608-262-3354
Fax: 608-265-3036
webmaster@uwbadgers.com
www.uwbadgers.com
• Barry Alvarez, Director of Athletics
• Walter Dickey, Deputy Athletic Director
(608) 265-2973
wjd@athletics.wisc.edu
• Justin M Doherty, Senior Associate
Athletic Director
(608) 262-9023
jmd@athletics.wisc.edu
• Terry Gawlik, Senior Associate Athletic
Director/SWA
(608) 265-4987
tlg@athletics.wisc.edu
• Mario Morris, Director of Financial
Operations
(608) 265-4134
mgm@athletics.wisc.edu
Arena Seating Capacity:
10,600
Tenant(s):
University of Wisconsin.

WJ HALE STADIUM
3500 JOHN A MERRITT BOULEVARD
NASHVILLE, TN 37209
615-963-5000
www.tsutigers.com
• Teresa L Phillips, Director of Athletics
(615) 963-5034
tphillips@tnstate.edu
• Daniel Kuhn, Director of Operations
(615) 963-2136
dkuhn@tnstate.edu
• Zellina Anderson, Ticket Office Manager
(615) 963-5841
zanderson@tnstate.edu
Stadium Seating Capacity:
10,000
Tenant(s):
Tennessee State University.

WL ZORN ARENA
121 GARFIELD AVENUE
EAU CLAIRE, WI 54701
715-836-4636
service_center@uwec.edu
www.blugolds.com
• Dan Schumacher, Director of Athletics
(715) 836-5858
schumadj@uwec.edu
• Jill Millis, Assistant Athletic Director,
Sports Information
(715) 836-4184
millisjl@uwec.edu
Year Founded:
1952
Arena Seating Capacity:
2,500

WOLSTEIN CENTER
2000 PROSPECT AVENUE
CLEVELAND, OH 44115
216-687-9292
Fax: 216-687-5450
www.wolsteincenter.com
• Jennifer Kelly, Executive Director
(216) 687-9292
j.r.kelly1@csuohio.edu
• Nicole Taylor, Fiscal Manager
(216) 687-9292

n.m.taylor79@csuohio.edu
• Karey Clarke, Box Office Manager
(216) 687-9292
k.a.clarke@csuohio.edu
• Vicki Wetzler, Event Manager
(216) 687-9292
v.wetzler@csuohio.edu
Arena Seating Capacity:
8,500

WORLD WAR MEMORIAL STADIUM
510 YANCEYVILLE STREET
GREENSBORO, NC 27405
336-274-0462
www.greensborosports.org/war-memorial-st
adium
• Billy Edringston, Associate Athletics
Director/Facilities/Operations
Sport:
Baseball
Tenant(s):
NCAA - North Carolina A&T State University
athletics, Greensboro College athletics.
Year Founded:
1926
Capacity:
7,500

WORTHEN ARENA (WR)
1699 WEST BETHEL AVENUE
BALL STATE UNIVERSITY
MUNCIE, IN 47306
765-285-8708
Fax: 765-285-5353
cms.bsu.edu
• Mark Sandy, Director of Intercollegiate
Athletics
• Daniel P Byrnes, Director, Sports Facilities
& Recreation Services
• Brian Hardin, Deputy Athletics Director
• Karin Lee, Senior Associate Athletics
Director
(765) 285-5127
kalee2@bsu.edu
• Joe Hernandez, Associate Athletics
Director for Sports & Alumni
(765) 285-1282
jhernand@bsu.edu
• Mark Serrao, Assistant Director of
Ticketing & Premium Seating
(765) 285-1474
maserrao@bsu.edu
Permanent Seating Capacity:
11,500
Tenant(s):
NCAA - Ball State University athletics.

WRIGHT STATE UNIVERSITY RAIDERS
3640 COLONEL GLENN HIGHWAY
SUITE 430
DAYTON, OH 45435-0001
937-775-3498
Fax: 937-775-2060
nutterguest@wright.edu
www.nuttercenter.com
• John Cox, Facilities Manager
(937) 775-4672
john.cox@wright.edu
• Becky Sparks, Business Manager
(937) 775-4785
becky.sparks@wright.edu
• Misty Cox, Booking/Marketing Manager
(937) 775-4674
misty.cox@wright.edu
• Kiley Fleming, Box Office Manager
(937) 775-4786
kiley.fleming@wright.edu

Arena Seating Capacity:
11,200
Arena events:
Southwest Ohio's hottest sports and
entertainment venue.
Tenant(s):
NCAA - Wright State University athletics.
Founded:
1990
Description:
Location for national touring acts and
sporting events.

WRIGLEY FIELD
1060 WEST ADDISON STREET
CHICAGO, IL 60613-4397
773-404-2827
Fax: 773-404-4129
chicago.cubs.mlb.com
• Alex Sugarman, SVP, Strategy & Ballpark
Operations
• Matt Kenny, Senior Director, Event
Operations
• Patrick Meenan, Senior Director, Facilities
& Procurement
• Miguel DeJesus, Ticket Office Manager
Permanent Seating Capacity:
41,160
Team:
Chicago Cubs MLB baseball.

XCEL ENERGY CENTER
199 WEST KELLOGG BOULEVARD
SAINT PAUL, MN 55102
651-265-4800
Fax: 651-265-4899
info@xcelenergycenter.com
www.xcelenergycenter.com
• Jack Larson, Vice President/General
Manager
• Mark Stoffel, Senior Director Operations
(651) 265-4807
Stadium Seating Capacity:
17,954
Tenant(s):
NHL - Minnesota Wild ice hockey.

XL CENTER
ONE CIVIC CENTER PLAZA
HARTFORD, CT 06103
860-249-6333
877-522-8499
Fax: 860-241-4226
xlcenterinfo@xlcenter.com
www.xlcenter.com
• Chris Lawrence, General Manager
• Bryan Dooley, Vice President, Corporate
Sales
Permanent Seating Capacity:
15,564
Owned by:
City of Hartford.
Year Founded:
1975
Tenants:
University of Connecticut Men's and
Women's Basketball (NCAA/Big East),
Hartford Wolf Pack (AHL).

YACK ARENA
3131 THIRD STREET
WYANDOTTE, MI 48192
734-324-7292
agarbin@wyandottemi.gov
www.wyandotte.net

facilities

• Justin Lanagan, Superintendent
(734) 324-4507
jnlanagan@wyan.org
Description:
Youth hockey and youth figure skating.
Home Teams:
Wyandotte Warriors, Wyandotte Roosevelt
High School Hockey, Wyandotte Figure
Skating Club

YAGER STADIUM AT MOORE BOWL
1700 SW COLLEGE AVENUE
TOPEKA, KS 66621
785-670-1134
Fax: 785-670-1091
www.wusports.com
• Loren Ferre, Director of Athletics
(785) 670-1794
loren.ferre@washburn.edu
• Gil Herrera, Facilities Director
(785) 670-1304
gilbert.herrera@washburn.edu
• Craig Schurig, Head Coach, Football
(785) 670-1340
craig.schurig@washburn.edu
• Chris Jones, Head Coach, Women's
Soccer
(785) 670-1756
Teams:
Washburn University Ichabods football &
Lady Blues soccer.
Seating Capacity:
7,200

YAKIMA COUNTY STADIUM
1220 PACIFIC AVENUE
YAKIMA, WA 98901
509-575-4487
Fax: 509-469-2105
info@pippinsbaseball.com
• Zachary Fraser, President
• Jeff Garretson, General Manager
• Marcus McKimmy, Assistant General
Manager
marcus@pippinsbaseball.com
• Andy Jones, Director of Hospitality
andy@pippinsbaseball.com
Stadium Physical Address:
1301 S Fair Ave, Yakima, WA 98901.
Sport:
Baseball
Tenant(s):
Yakima Valley Pippins baseball
Year Founded & Description:
Club founded in 2014. The Pippins are a
member of the 11-team West Coast League,
a summer wood-bat collegiate league with
teams in Washington state, Oregon and
British Columbia.
Arena Seating Capacity:
2,800

YAKIMA VALLEY SUNDOME
1301 SOUTH FAIR AVENUE
YAKIMA, WA 98901
509-248-7160
Fax: 509-248-8093
www.statefairpark.org
• Trent Marquis, Chairman
• Sid Morrison, Vice Chairman
• Greg Stewart, President & General
Manager
(509) 248-7160
cwsf@fairfun.com
• Greg Lybeck, Assistant General Manager
(509) 248-7160
gregl@fairfun.com

• Steve Sires, Facilities Manager
steves@fairfun.com
• Willard Nelson, Operations Manager
willardn@fairfun.com
• Ray Mata, Events & Production Manager
raym@fairfun.com
• Ruth Anglin, Fair Activities Manager
• Jill Rodgers, Fair Activities Assistant
jillr@fairfun.com
Arena Seating Capacity:
6,195
Year Founded:
1990

YALE BOWL
20 TOWER PARKWAY
YALE UNIVERSITY
NEW HAVEN, CT 06511
203-432-4747
Fax: 203-432-7772
support.athletics@yale.edu
www.yalebulldogs.com
• Thomas Beckett, Director of Athletics
(203) 432-1414
thomas.beckett@yale.edu
• Christian Bray, Director of Compliance
(203) 432-7668
christian.bray@yale.edu
• Edward Mockus, Senior Associate Athletic
Director Facilities
(203) 432-2494
edward.mockus@yale.edu
• Patrick O'Neill, Associate Athletic Director
Marketing/Licensing
(203) 432-2205
patrick.oneill@yale.edu
• Jennifer O'Neil, Assistant to the Director
(203) 432-1414
jennifer.oneil@yale.edu
• Francine Georges, Human Resources
Generalist, Athletics
(203) 432-1442
francine.georges@yale.edu
Arena Seating Capacity:
61,466
Year Founded:
November 21, 1914

YALE FIELD
252 DERBY AVENUE
WEST HAVEN, CT 06516
203-432-1423
scott.griffin@yale.edu
www.yalebulldogs.com
• Scott Griffin, General Manager
(203) 432-1423
scott.griffin@yale.edu
Sport:
Baseball
Team:
Yale Bulldogs
Year Founded:
1928
Capacity:
5,000

YANKEE STADIUM
ONE EAST 161ST STREET
BRONX, NY 10451
718-293-4300
Fax: 718-293-8431
newyork.yankees.mlb.com
• Joan Steinbrenner, Vice Chairperson
• Randy Levine, President
• Lonn A Trost, Chief Operating
Officer/General Counsel
• Brian Cashman, Senior Vice President,

General Manager
• Deborah A Tymon, Senior Vice President,
Marketing
• Cindy Kamradt, Stadium Planning &
Special Projects Director
• Carol Laurenzano, Stadium Operations
Director
Year opened:
2009
Permanent Seating Capacity:
52,325
Description:
Home stadium for New York Yankees.

YOGI BERRA STADIUM
8 YOGI BERRA DRIVE
LITTLE FALLS, NJ 07424
973-746-7434
Fax: 973-655-8006
info@jackals.com
www.jackals.com
• Floyd Hall, Owner and Chairman
ext 8068
• Gregory L. Lockard, President
• Larry Hall, Executive Vice President
• Jennifer Fertig, Vice President of Finance
& Operations
• Jeff Palladino, Director of Group Sales &
Ticket Operations
(973) 655-8009
• Jarrett Schack, Group Sales & Operations
Coordinator
(973) 655-8038
• Aldo Licitra, Facilities Manager
• Eric McConnell, Concessions Manager
(973) 655-8053
emcconnell@jackals.com
Sport:
Baseball
Tenant(s):
New Jersey Jackals baseball
Year Founded:
1998
Capacity:
3,784

YOST ICE ARENA
1116 SOUTH STATE STREET
UNIVERSITY OF MICHIGAN
ANN ARBOR, MI 48109
734-764-4600
Fax: 734-764-0247
yostice@umich.edu
www.umich.edu
• Mark S. Schlissel, President
• Andrew Hicks, Facility Manager
adhicks@umich.edu
• Jill Feudi, Business Office Manager
jfeudi@umich.edu
• Trey Garant, Associate Manager
tgarant@umich.edu
• Rob Ramsburgh, Operations Manager
robram@umich.edu
Arena Seating Capacity:
6,603
Tenant(s):
NCAA - University of Michigan ice hockey.

iWIRELESS CENTER
1 UNIVERSITY CIRCLE
WESTERN ILLINOIS UNIVERSITY
MACOMB, IL 61455
309-298-1190
Fax: 309-298-2009
SID@wiu.edu
www.goleathernecks.com

• Tim Van Alstine, Director of Athletics
(309) 298-1190
t-vanalstine@wu.edu
• Matt Tanney, Associate Athletics Director
(309) 298-1964
m-tanney@wiu.edu
• Claire Smalzer, Assistant Director of
Academic Services
• Chris Wlezien, Interim Director of
Compliance
(309) 298-2221
cm-wlezien@wiu.edu
• Becky Schluter, Administrative Assistant to
the Associate Athletic
(309) 298-1964
rs-schluter@wiu.edu
• Patrick Osterman, Assistant Athletics
Director for Media Services
(309) 298-1133
pr-osterman@wiu.edu
• Nancy Sprouy, Asst. Director Of Athletics,
Business Operations
(309) 298-1190
NK-Sprout@wiu.edu
Tenant(s):
NCAA - Western Illinois University football.
Stadium Seating Capacity:
15,368

Race Tracks - Auto

ALABAMA INTERNATIONAL DRAGWAY
1245 CRUMP ROAD
PO BOX 426
STEELE, AL 35987
256-538-7223
Fax: 256-354-5014
www.alabamainternationaldragway.com
• Colins Jason, General Manager/Promoter
Track Type:
Dragstrip

ALABAMA STATE FAIRGROUNDS
2331 BESSEMER ROAD
BIRMINGHAM, AL 35208
205-786-8100
Fax: 205-786-8222
opi@birminghamal.gov
www.informationbirmingham.com
• Leroy R Cowan, Director
State Fair Arena Seating Capacity:
6,000
**Birmingham International Speedway
Seating Capacity**
10,000

ALASKA RACEWAY PARK
3900 ENGLISH BAY DRIVE
WASILLA, AK 99654
907-746-7223
Fax: 907-376-0733
www.akracewaypark.com
• Rickey Rogers, Promoter
Track Length:
1/8 mile.
Track Type:
Dragstrip.

ALL AMERICAN SPEEDWAY
800 ALL AMERICAN CITY BOULEVARD
ROSEVILLE, CA 95678
916-786-2025
Fax: 916-786-2139
info@allamericanspeedway.com
www.allamericanspeedway.com

• Rick Poppert, Director Competition
(916) 786-2025
Track Size:
1/4 mile.
Track Type:
Semi-Banked Oval.

AMAROO PARK
ANNANGROVE ROAD
AUSTRALIAN RACING DRRS CLUB
NSW, 2156
-3-5952 2548
Fax: -61-9678-1184
www.amaroopark.com
• Beck Damon, Member, Ardc Committee

ATLANTA DRAGWAY
500 E RIDGEWAY ROAD
COMMERCE, GA 30529
706-335-2301
Fax: 706-423-9261
www.atlantadragway.com
• Ray Wilkings, General Manager
(706) 335-2301
• Crystal Wilson, Sales& Marketing Manager
(706) 423-9252
cwilson@nhra.com
• Joanne Lineberry, Sales/Marketing
Manager
• Mike Savage, Track Manager
(706) 335-2301
msavage@nhra.com
• Jodee Kennedy, Administrative Assistant
(706) 423-9253
jkennedy@nhra.com
Description:
Drag Racing Track.
Seating capacity:
30,000

ATLANTA MOTOR SPEEDWAY
PO BOX 500
HAMPTON, GA 30228
770-946-4211
877-926-7849
Fax: 770-946-3928
amstix@atlantamotorspeedway.com
www.atlantamotorspeedway.com
• Ed Clark, President/General Manager
(770) 946-3921
• Dave Mullison, Manager
Marketing/Communications
(770) 707-7980
davem@atlantamotorspeedway.com
• Juanita Martin, Assistant to the President
• Greg Walter, VP Sales
(770) 946-3918
gregw@atlantamotorspeedway.com
• Kristi Wilson, Director of Client Services
• Brad Harrison, Web Content Manager
• Allison Fillmore, Corporate Sales Manager
• Nicole Fowler, Sales Executive
Description:
Auto race track.
Series:
NASCAR Nextel Cup Series; NASCAR
Busch Series.

ATMORE DRAGWAY
PO BOX 912
FLOMATON, AL 36441-1915
251-368-8363
Fax: 904-212-6597
karen@atmoredragway.com
www.atmoredragway.com
• Ed Clark, President and General Manager

Size:
1/8 mile
Type of Track:
Dragstrip

AUTO CLUB FAMOSO
33559 FAMOSO ROAD
MCFARLAND, CA 93250
661-399-5351
Fax: 661-399-2608
famosoraceway@gmail.com
www.famosoraceway.com
• Clake Bowser, Operator

CALIFORNIA SPEEDWAY
9300 CHERRY AVENUE
FONTANA, CA 92335
909-429-5000
800-944-7223
Fax: 909-429-5500
sales@autoclubspeedway.com
www.autoclubspeedway.com
• Gillian Zucker, President
• Fritz Maskrey, Senior Director of Corporate
Sales & Marketing
• Jason Klein, Marketing Director
• Gillian Zucker, President
president@autoclubspeedway.com
• Dave Allen, Vice President of Sales and
Marketing
• Otis Greer, Director of Community Affairs
• Art Avila, Director of Accounting
• Fritz Maskrey, Sr. Director of Corporate
Sales & Marketing
• Curt Jacey, Director of Business
Development
• Deanna Ingram, Director of Ticketing
Track Length:
2 miles
Front Straight:
3,100 feet
Back Straight:
2,500 feet
Banking:
11 degrees

BAKERSFIELD SPEEDWAY
PO BOX 82184
BAKERSFIELD, CA 93380-2184
661-393-3373
Fax: 661-393-7085
www.bakersfieldspeedway.com
• Scott Schweitzer, Owner
(661) 393-3373
scott@bakersfieldspeedway.com
Track Type:
High Banked Oval.
Track Size:
1/3 mile.

BANDIMERE SPEEDWAY
3051 S ROONEY ROAD
MORRISON, CO 80465
303-697-6001
800-664-8946
Fax: 303-697-0815
www.bandimere.com
• John C. Bandimere, Jr., President
(303) 697-6001
johnjr@bandimere.com
• John C. Bandimere, III, Executive Vice
President, General Manager
(303) 697-6001
sporty@bandimere.com
• Larry Crispe, Executive VP Operations
(303) 697-6001
larry@bandimere.com

• Sandy Newton, C.F.O.
(303) 697-6001
• Bruce Kamada, Director of
Sales/Sponsorship Developmen
(303) 697-6001
• Debbra Parker, Director of Hospitality
(303) 697-6001
• Paul Lombardi, Food & Beverage Director
(303) 697-6001
Track:
1/4 concrete drag strip
Seating Capacity:
Track: 23,000

BARC LIMITED
THRUXTON CIRCUIT
ANDOVER HAMPSHIRE, ENGLAND SP11
8PN
-44-1264 882200
Fax: 44-1264 882233
info@barc.net
www.barc.net
• Dennis Carter, Chief Executive
dcarter@barc.net
• Trevor Swettenham, Press Officer
press@barc.net
• Dale Wells, Competition Manager
dwells@barc.net
• Mark Jones, Chief Executive
mcurley@barc.net
• Ian Watson, Business Development
Manager
iwatson@barc.net
• Pat Blakney, Thruxton Operations Manage
(012) 4 774918
pat@thruxtonracing.co.uk
• Angie Kew, Membership Secretary
akew@barc.net
• Mark Youngs, Thruxton Catering Manager
(044) 01554 89
pembrey@barc.net
• Tom Jones, Thruxton Facilities Supervisor
(044) 01264 88
tjones@barc.net
Rallycross:
0.9 miles.
Track Length:
1.456 miles.

BARONA SPEEDWAY
1794 WILDCAT CANYON ROAD
LAKESIDE, CA 92040
619-749-8115
Salz944@cox.net
www.baronaspeedway.com
• Jim Scribellito, Promoter
Type of Track:
High-Banked Oval.
Track Length:
1/6 mile.

BATESVILLE MOTOR SPEEDWAY
5090 HEBER SPRINGS ROAD
BATESVILLE, AR 72501
870-251-0011
www.batesvillemotorspeedway.net
• Connie Starr, Ticket sales and Promotions
(870) 613-1337
• Wimp Reed, Technical Support
(870) 251-1566
wreed31@gmail.com
• Starr Mooney, Promoter
Type of Track:
High-Banked Oval.
Track Length:
3/8 mile.

BEACON HILL SPEEDWAY
400 GOBATTI PL
PUEBLO, CO 81008-9667
719-542-2277
www.beaconhillspeedway.com
• Sparks Dall, Promoter
Type of Track:
Semi-Banked Oval
Track Length:
1/4 mile

BIRMINGHAM INTERNATIONAL RACEWAY
2321 BESSEMER ROAD
BIRMINGHAM, AL 35208
205-781-2471
Fax: 205-424-5537
• Ray Tennyson, Director of Public Relations
• Carolyn Harvey, General Manager
Arena Seating Capacity:
8,000.00
Year Founded:
1914
Track Type
Asphalt.
Track Size
5/8.

BRAINARD INTERNATIONAL RACEWAY
5523 BIRCHDALE ROAD
BRAINERD, MN 56401
218-824-7223
866-444-4455
Fax: 218-824-7240
www.brainerdraceway.com
• Scott Quick, General Manager
Description:
Auto race track.

BRISTOL MOTOR SPEEDWAY & DRAGWAY
151 SPEEDWAY BOULEVARD
BRISTOL, TN 37620
423-989-6933
Fax: 423-764-1646
www.bristolmotorspeedway.com
• Jeff Byrd, President/General Manager
(423) 989-6999
jeff@bristolmotorspeedway.com
• Wayne Estes, VP/Communications &
Events
(423) 989-6935
wayne@bristolmotorspeedway.com
• Logan McCabe, VP Marketing
(423) 989-6934
Logan@bristolmotorspeedway.com
• O.Bruton Smith, Chairman
• Jerry Caldwell, General Manager
(423) 989-6912
• DeDe Hash, VP Security /Asset
Management
(423) 989-6928
• Julie Bennett, VP General Counsel
(423) 989-6912
• Fred King, VP Finances
(423) 989-6927
• Wayne Estes, VP Events
(423) 989-6935
• Kevin Triplett, VP/Public Affairs
(423) 989-6905
ktriplett@bristolmotorspeedway.com
Series:
NASCAR Nextel Cup Series; NASCAR
Busch Series.
Description:
Auto race track.

BUTTONWILLOW RACEWAY PARK
24551 LERDO HIGHWAY
BUTTONWILLOW, CA 93206
661-764-5333
Fax: 661-764-5334
info@buttonwillowraceway.com
www.buttonwillowraceway.com
• Les Phillips, Contact
(661) 764-5333
lesrace@aol.com
• Carrie Hester, Administrator
carrie@buttonwillowraceway.com
• Mike Miserendino, Business Development
Manager
mike@buttonwillowraceway.com
• Laura May Booker, Food & Gift Shop
Manager
lauramay@buttonwillowraceway.com

CALEXPO
1600 EXPOSITION BOULEVARD
SACRAMENTO, CA 95815
916-263-3000
877-225-3976
Fax: 916-263-3250
info@calexpo.com
www.calexpo.com
• Norbert J. Bartosik, CEO & General
Manager
• Don Henry, Marketing Director
• Jerry Brown, Govenor
• Cynthia Bryant, Director
• Willie Pelote, Director
• Sonney Chong, Director
• Jeffrey Azoff, Dirctor

CANYON SPEEDWAY
9777 W CAREFREE HIGHWAY
PEORIA, AZ 85345
602-258-7223
Fax: 623-465-7131
www.canyonspeedwaypark.com
• Jeff Stafford, Promoter
Track Type:
High-Banked Oval.
Track Length:
3/8 mile.

CAPITOL SPEEDWAY
MILE 75.5 PARKS HIGHWAY
WILLOW, AK 99688
907-495-6420
Fax: 907-495-5819
www.capitolspeedway.org
• Lackey Karen, Owner
• Earl Lackey, Owner
• Michelle Maynor, Business Manager
(907) 354-7223
Track Size:
1/4 mile.
Track Type:
Dragstrip.

CARLSBAD RACEWAY
649 DAISY
ESCONDIDO, CA 92069
760-480-8369
Fax: 760-727-4390
carlsbadraceway@carlsbadraceway.org
www.carlsbadraceway.org
• Jim LeVold, Promoter

CENTERVILLE DRAGWAY PARK INC
10239 DRAGSTRIP LANE
PO BOX 160
CENTERVILLE, AR 72829

479-576-4001
cvdrag@arkwest.com
www.centervilledragway.com
• Wayne Styles, President
• Patty Styles, Promoter
Track Length:
1000 feet.
Track Type:
Dragstrip.

CHARLOTTE MOTOR SPEEDWAY
5555 CONCORD PARKWAY S
CONCORD, NC 28027
704-455-3200
800-455-3267
Fax: 704-455-2547
tickets@charlottemotorspeedway.com
www.charlottemotorspeedway.com
• Marcus Smith, President/General Manager
• Doug Stafford, Executive Vice President
• Jerry Gappens, Promotions/Public
Relations VP
• Dan Farrell, Corporate Sales/Marketing
Director
Description:
Founded 1960. Auto race track.
Series:
NASCAR Nextel Cup Series; NASCAR
Busch Series.
Year Founded:
1960
Seating Capacity:
165,000

CHICAGOLAND SPEEDWAY
500 SPEEDWAY BOULEVARD
JOLIET, IL 60433
815-722-5500
888-629-7223
Fax: 815-724-0520
marketing@chicagolandspeedway.com
www.chicagolandspeedway.com
• Tim Carey, President
timcarey@hawthorneracecourse.com
• Scott Paddock, President
• John Brokopp, Public Relations/Publicity
Director
• Edward Duffy, Chief Executive Officer
• Lori Whalen, Director of Accounting
• Lisa Bhender, Office Coordinator
• Julyn Stiff, Director of Guest Services
• Erin Barry, Hospitality Manager
Description:
Horse race track.
Description:
Horse race track.

YUMA SPEEDWAY PARK
3450 W COUNTY 15TH STREET
YUMA, AZ 85365
620-344-1563
Fax: 520-726-7280
www.cocopahspeedway.com/
Track Type:
Semi-Banked Oval.
Track Length:
3/8 mile.

COLORADO NATIONAL SPEEDWAY
4281 GRADEN BOULEVARD
DACONO, CO 80514
303-665-4173
303-665-4173
Fax: 303-828-2403
info@coloradospeedway.com
www.coloradospeedway.com

• Mindy Harkins, Marketing
(303) 231-9460
• Sue Nordhougen, Track Operations
(303) 828-0116
• Joe Star, Track Photographer
(303) 828-0116
• Randy Wolf, Food And Beverage
(303) 828-0116
• Marc Mooser, Track Announcer
• Darrell Smith, CNS Tech
Description:
Track Operates 28 events running April -
September. Average Attendance 6,300.
Weekly car count exceeds 100. Divisions
include late models, protracts, figure-eight's,
grand american modified, super stocks,
trains.
Description:
Auto race track (3/8 mile paved oval)
hosting the following NASCAR series:
NASCAR Craftsman Truck Series/NASCAR
Nextel Cup Series, Featherlite Southwest
Tour.
Track Size:
3/8 mile
Track Type:
Semi-Banked Oval

COMPETITION PARK MOTOCROSS
96 SUGAR SHACK LANE
BEAR CREEK, NC 27207
919-224-7237
speedcompound@yahoo.com
www.speedcompoundmx.com
• Jim Neese, Rider Development
• Dan Rodgers, Promoter

COSTA MESA SPEEDWAY
88 FAIR DRIVE
PO BOX 3334
COSTA MESA, CA 92674
949-492-9933
Fax: 949-492-2547
www.costamesaspeedway.net
• Brad Oxley, Promoter
• John Creith, Track Staff
Seating Capacity:
8,750

CRAWFORD COUNTY SPEEDWAY
7118 N HIGHWAY 59
VAN BUREN, AR 72956
479-632-2749
Fax: 479-632-4450
www.crawfordcountyspeedway.net
• Donnie Watson, Promoter
Track Type:
Slightly banked, 3/8 of a mile, red clay oval
Seating Capacity:
4,500
Sport:
Stock Car Racing (Modified, Street Stock,
Mini Stock, Grand National, Front Wheel
Drive and 360 E Modified).

CROFT CLASSIC & HISTORIC
MOTORSPORTS LTD (CCHM)
WEST LANE
DALTON ON TEES
N YORKSHIRE, ENGLAND DL2 2PN
-44-01325 721815
Fax: -44-01325 721819
www.croftcircuit.co.uk
• Tara Horn, Contact person

CROWLEY'S RIDGE RACEWAY
1708 HIGHWAY 351
PARAGOULD, AR 72450
870-236-3141
Fax: 805-398-0467
www.crraceway.com

CYCLELAND SPEEDWAY
47 NELSON ROAD
OROVILLE, CA 95965
530-342-0063
Fax: 530-892-9213
www.cyclelandspeedway.com
• Moural Lowell, Promoter

DALLAS COUNTY DRAGWAY
3182 COUNTY ROAD 63
PO BOX 110651
SELMA, AL 35211
334-418-6900
• Alexander Marvin, Promoter
Size:
1/8 mile.
Track Type:
Dragstrip

DARLINGTON RACEWAY
1301 HARRY BYRD HIGHWAY
DARLINGTON, SC 29532
843-395-8900
Fax: 843-393-3911
tickets@darlingtonraceway.com
www.darlingtonraceway.com
• Chris Browning, President
• Mac Josey, Vice President & General
Manager
• Josey Mac, Ticket Operations Director
Description:
Founded 1950. NASCAR Auto race track.
Series:
NASCAR Nextel Cup Series NASCARA
Busch Series NASCAR Craftsman Truck
Series

DAYTONA INTERNATIONAL SPEEDWAY
1801 W INTERNATIONAL SPEEDWAY
BOULEVARD
DAYTONA BEACH, FL 32114
386-254-2700
866-472-8725
Fax: 386-257-0281
www.daytonainternationalspeedway.com
• Kenny Kane, Media &Communications
Senior Director
• Robin Braig, President
• Brian Harper, Corporate Sales Senior
Manager
• Debbie Weller, Marketing
Partnerships/Sales Director
Arena Seating Capacity:
170,000 and infield.
Year Founded:
1953
Track Type:
Superspeedway.
Track Size:
2.5 miles, 3.56 mile road course.

DEL MAR SPEEDWAY
1001 N PACIFIC AVENUE
SAN PEDRO, CA 95928
310-547-9898
Fax: 310-547-9900
• Chris Agajanian, Promoter

DELTA SPEEDWAY
1658 S AIRPORT WAY AT CHARTER WAY
STOCKON, CA 95206
1-4-595-8922
Fax: 209-823-2928
info@deltaraceway.com
www.deltaraceway.com
• Mick Evans, President
(209) 239-3079
Nature of Service:
Micro sprint race track, 600 cc multi, 600 cc
Stock, 250 cc, 600 cc Restrictor, Stock
appearing, beginning box stock.
Track Type:
Dirt Oval.
Track Size:
1/8 Mile.

DIXIE SPEEDWAY
150 DIXIE DRIVE
WOODSTOCK, GA 30189
770-926-5315
Fax: 770-926-8339
dixiespeedway@aol.com
www.dixiespeedway.com
• Mickey Swims, President
• Mike Swims, VP
Description:
Founded 1968.
Seating capacity:
10,000.00
Auto Racing:
Sprint cars; stock cars' Hav-A-Tampa late
models.

DOVER INTERNATIONAL SPEEDWAY
1131 N DUPONT HIGHWAY
DOVER, DE 19901
302-883-6500
800-441-7223
Fax: 302-672-0100
info@doverspeedway.com
www.doverspeedway.com
• Denis McGlynn, President/Chief Executive
Officer
• Jerry Miraglia, Dover Motorsports VP
• Jerry Dunning, VP/General Manager
• Mark Rossi, Sales/Marketing VP
• Craig Amhaus, Business Development
Manager
Description:
Auto race track.
Series:
NASCAR Nextel Cup Series; NASCAR
Busch Series; NASCAR Craftsman Truck
Series.

EAST ALABAMA MOTOR SPEEDWAY
4238 US HIGHWAY 80 W
PHENIX CITY, AL 36870
334-297-2594
Fax: 334-297-2699
eams@bellsouth.net
www.eamsdirt.com
• Billy Thomas, President
Description:
Auto race track.
Track Type:
High-Banked Oval.
Size:
3/8 mile.

FAASST MOTORSPORTS INC.
719-761-1372
fmi@faasst.com
www.faasst.com

• Judy Faass, CEO
Track Length:
2.5 miles
Type of Track:
Road course
Founded:
2005
Description:
Faasst Motorsports offers educational
driving and racing programs in a race track
environment for teens, high performance car
owners and novice racers. Faasst is also an
authorized dealer of driving gear, racing
gear and equipment.
Nature of Service:
Racing Operations - Racing Schools -
Product Development - Equipment Sales

FAIRBANKS RACING LIONS
PO BOX 74762
FAIRBANKS, AK 99707
907-452-3833
• Wes Wallace, Promoter
(907) 495-6420
• Nancy Wallace, Promoter
(907) 495-6420
• Jamie Bodenstadt, President
akgrizzly@gci.net
Track Length:
3/8 mile.
Track Type:
Slightly-Banked Oval.

FAIRPLEX
1101 W MCKINLEY AVENUE
POMONA, CA 91768
909-623-3111
Fax: 909-865-3602
info@fairplex.com
www.fairplex.com
• Wendy Talarico, Communications
Manager
(909) 865-4263
• Melissa DeMonaco-Tapia, Director of
Sales
(909) 865-4042
demonaco@fairplex.com
Description:
Founded 1922. Home of thoroughbred and
quarter horse racing during the Los Angeles
County Fair each September-October.
Horse shows held regularly throughout the
year. Also hosts National Hot Rod
Association Winternationals (February), and
Winston World Fi
Description:
Founded 1922. Home of thoroughbred and
quarter horse racing during the Los Angeles
County Fair each September-October.
Horse shows held regularly throughout the
year. Also hosts National Hot Rod
Association Winternationals (February), and
Winston World Fi
Seating Capacity
10,000

FIREBIRD INTERNATIONAL RACEWAY
20000 S MARICOPA ROAD
BOX 5023
CHANDLER, AZ 85226
602-268-0200
Fax: 520-796-0531
teamfirebirdinfo@aol.com
www.firebirdraceway.com
• Charlie Allen, President
• Franki Buckman, Vice President
• Charlie Allen, President

(602) 268-0200
info@firebirdraceway.com
Track Length:
1.6 mile, 1.2 mile, 1.1 mile.
Track Type:
Road Course (multiple).

FLOMATON SPEEDWAY
913 HWY 113
FLOMATON, AL 36441
251-296-2233
flomaton.racing@gmail.com
www.flomatonspeedway.com
• Jimmy Goodwin, Promoter
• Pete Arnold, Promoter
• Freddie McCall, Track Owner
(850) 554-3848
• Nascar Ron, Promoter
(251) 538-0546
• Micha McCall McCall, Track Operations
• Tim Wood, Chief Technical Inspector
(251) 727-1513
• Bo McCall, Fuel/ Tire Sales
(251) 655-0971
Track Type:
High-Banked Oval.
Size:
1/4 mile.

GATEWAY MOTORSPORTS PARK
700 RACEWAY BOULEVARD
PO BOX 200
MADISON, IL 62060
618-875-7550
866-357-7333
www.gatewaymsp.com
• Denis F McGlynn, president and CEO of
Dover Motorsports
• Lenny Batycki, General Manager
• Linda Thornton, Administration Manager
• Curtis Francisco
• Mike Stambaugh, COO
• Allison Dziadus, Corporate Sales ,
Hospitality & NHRA
• Jeff Zelenovich, Ticketing Manager
• Mark Fourier, Digital Marketing & Social
Media
• Jeanne Lachmiller, Event Planning &
Executive Assistant
• Dan Harman, Opertaing Manager
Series:
NASCAR Busch Series; NASCAR
Craftsman Truck Series.
Description:
Motorsports facility.

GEORGE RAY'S DRAGSTRIP
485 HIGHWAY 135 S
PARAGOULD, AR 72450
870-236-8247
• Charles Joliffs, Contact
Track Type:
Dragstrip.
Track Size:
1/8 mile.

HALLETT MOTOR RACING CIRCUIT
59901 E 55 ROAD
JENNINGS, OK 74038
918-356-4814
Fax: 918-356-4815
www.hallettracing.com
• Scott Stephens, Contact
(918) 356-4814
• Connie Stephens, Contact Person
(918) 356-4814

Description:
Auto race track. NHRA sanctioned drag racing.

HICKORY MOTOR SPEEDWAY
3130 HIGHWAY 70 SE
NEWTON, NC 28658
828-464-3655
Fax: 828-465-5017
hickorymotor@bellsouth.net
www.hickorymotorspeedway.com
• Kevin Piercy, Promoter
• Alan Kanupp, Race Director
alan91557@yahoo.com
• Scott Kilby, Technical Director
(704) 880-8003
scott.kilby@ecmd.com
• Bobby Everhart, Website
(336) 692-5131
redd@sgionline.net
Description:
Auto race track for NASCAR/Busch Grand National Series, Goody's Dash, and Nextel Cup Series.

HOLIDAY RACEWAY
20105 HWY 11
WOODSTOCK, AL 35188
205-938-2123
www.holidayraceway.com
• Jason Beams, Track Promoter
jason@holidayraceway.com
• Chris Batech
chris@holidayraceway.com
• Jonathan Beams
jonathan@holidayraceway.com
Track Type:
Dragstrip.
Size:
1/8 mile.

HOLTVILLE AERODOME INTERNATIONAL RACEWAY
2975 E NORRISH ROAD
HOLTVILLE, CA 92250
619-356-4641
Fax: 205-672-2186
• Jeanne Matthews, Promoter

HOMESTEAD MOTORSPORTS COMPLEX
ONE SPEEDWAY BOULEVARD
HOMESTEAD, FL 33035-1501
305-230-5000
866-409-7223
Fax: 305-230-5140
HMSguestservices@homesteadmiamispeedway.com
www.homesteadmiamispeedway.com
• Nathalie Salas, Community Relation Manager
• Hope Mees, Operations/Track Rentals
(305) 230-5174
hmees@homesteadmiamispeedway.com
• Phil de Montmollin, Public Relations
• Matthew Becherer, Track President
• Albert Garcia, Vice President, Operations
• Shawn McGee, Vice President, Sales and Marketing
• Art Cordova, Director, Accounting & Finance
• William Donnay, Director of Facility Operations
• Ali Bradshaw, Director, Ticket Sales
• Kevin Gregory, Director, Marketing
Track Length:
1.5 miles, 8 degrees.

HOMESTEAD-MIAMI SPEEDWAY, LLC
ONE RALPH SANCHEZ SPEEDWAY BOULEVARD
HOMESTEAD, FL 33035-1501
305-230-5000
866-409-7223
Fax: 305-230-5140
HMSguestservices@homesteadmiamispeedway.com
www.homesteadmiamispeedway.com
• Gray Curtis, President
• Al Garcia, Vice President of Operations
• Mayra Soto, Controller
• Matthew Becherer, Track President
• Albert Garcia, VP/Operations
• Shawn McGee, VP/Sales and Marketing
• Ali Bradshaw, Director,Ticket Sales
• Art Cordova, Director, Accounting & Finance
• Jay Fraioli, Director, Security
• Kevin Gregory, Director, Marketing
Description:
Founded 1995. Auto race track.
Series:
NASCAR Nextel Cup Series, NASCAR Busch Series, NASCAR Craftsman Truck Series, Indy Racing League.

HUNTSVILLE DRAGWAY
502 QUARTER MOUNTAIN ROAD
HARVEST, AL 35749
205-852-4505
Fax: 205-251-7375
www.huntsvilledragway.com
• George Howard, Promoter
Track Type:
Dragstrip
Track Size:
1/8 mile.

HUNTSVILLE SPEEDWAY
357 HEGIA BURROW ROAD
HUNTSVILLE, AL 35803
256-882-9191
Fax: 256-882-9131
huntsvillespeedway@gmail.com
www.huntsvillespeedway.com
• Ben David Atkinson, Promoter
(256) 539-4484
• Elizabeth Lee, General Manager
(256) 882-9191
Arena Seating Capacity:
3,000.00
Year Founded:
1959
Clients:
Racing Divisions: Late Models, Super Modifieds, Super Streets, Mini Modifieds, Hobby Cups, Huntsville Buzz, Mini Cups, Southern All Stars, USCS Winged Sprint Cars.
Track Type:
High banked asphalt.

I-70 SPEEDWAY
12773 N OUTER ROAD
ODESSA, MO 64070
816-230-0080
Fax: 913-230-8222
I70Speedway@hotmail.com
www.i70speedway.net
• Marc Olson, General Manager
• Craig Hover, Marketing/Public Relations Director
Track Address:
12773 Outer Road, Odessa, MO 64076
Description:

Auto Racing Facility featuring ASA AcDello Series and NASCAR weekly racing series. Hosts the biggest racing events in Missouri, with a 28-degree bank.

I-76 SPEEDWAY
16359 COUNTY ROAD S
FORT MORGAN, CO 80701
970-867-2101
Fax: 970-867-2101
i76speedway@fmweb.us
www.i-76speedway.com
• Butch Speicher, Owner
(970) 867-2101
Track:
1/4 mile dirt
Seating Capacity:
1,000
Event:
Stock Car races
Description:
The premier destination for sports events in Chicago's Northwest suburbs, convenient to downtown Chicago and O'Hare Airport. We will assist with locating venues and housing. Our area features a 100,000 sq. ft. Convention Center, soccer & baseball/softball fields, local college facilities and indoor park district complexes.

INDIANAPOLIS MOTOR SPEEDWAY CORPORATION
4790 W 16TH STREET
INDIANAPOLIS, IN 46222
317-492-8500
Fax: 317-492-6482
imspr@brickyard.com
www.indianapolismotorspeedway.com
• George H Anton, President/Chief Executive Officer
• Joie Chitwood, President/Chief Operations Officer IMS
• Jeff Belskus, EVP
• Fred Nation, EVP/Corporate Communications
• David Strahan, Account Executive
Series:
NASCAR Nextel Cup Series; NASCAR Busch Series; NASCAR Craftsman Truck Series.
Description:
Owns and operates race track and related facilities. Home of the Indianapolis 500 (Indy Racing League); Brickyard 400 (NASCAR); United States Grand Prix (Formula One).
Publications:
INDIANAPOLIS 500 OFFICIAL PROGRAM, annual; MAY INDY REVIEW, annual; BRICKYARD 400 OFFICIAL PROGRAM, annual; UNITED STATES GRAND PRIX OFFICIAL PROGRAM, annual; RECORD BOOK OF INDIANAPOLIS 500, annual; RECORD BOOK OF BRICKYARD 400, annual.

INDIANAPOLIS RACEWAY PARK
10267 E US HIGHWAY 136
PO BOX 34300
INDIANAPOLIS, IN 46234
317-291-4090
Fax: 317-291-4220
wcollier@nhra.com
www.lucasoilraceway.com
• Angela Eaton, Business Administration Director
• Jeff Dakin, Director Operations
• Brad Horn, Communications Manager

Sports Service Founded:
Sports Service Founded: 1960.
Nature of Service:
Motorsports Park.

INTERNATIONAL SPEEDWAY CORPORATION
ONE DAYTONA BOULEVARD
DAYTONA BEACH, FL 32114
386-254-2700
www.internationalspeedwaycorporation.com

JENNERSTOWN SPEEDWAY
224 RACE STREET
PO BOX 230
PO Box 230
JENNERSTOWN, PA 15547
814-629-6677
Fax: 814-629-7121
www.jennerstown.com
• Dave Wheeler, President
(814) 629-6677
dave@jennerstown.com
• Jen Wheeler, Secretary/Treasurer
(814) 629-6677
jen@jennerstown.com
• Joseph Dirienzo, Sales/Marketing Director
(814) 629-6677
joe@jennerstown.com
• Larry Mattingly, General Manager
(814) 629-6677
larrymatt@jennerstown.com
Arena Seating Capacity:
9,000.00
Clients
Weekly Nascar-sanctioned races, Hooters
Pro Cup 250, ASA, ISMA.
Nature of Service:
Automobile racetrack.
Track Type:
Asphalt.

JULESBURG DRAGSTRIP
98 KANSAS STREET
CHEYENNE, WY 82009
970-631-4490
Fax: 970-474-9999
• Bill Schneider, Promoter
Track Type:
Dragstrip
Track Size:
1/4 mile

KANSAS SPEEDWAY
400 SPEEDWAY BOULEVARD
KANSAS CITY, KS 66111
913-328-3380
866-460-7223
Fax: 913-328-3380
www.kansasspeedway.com
• Jamie Bodenstadt, President
• Greg Fritze, Vice President
• Travis Watson, Business Manager
• Sue Bodenstadt, Treasure
• Jeff Anderson, Secretary
• Anna M Watson, Site Admin
• Jamie Bodenstadt
(907) 322-8359
• Jamie Bodenstadt, President
akgrizzly@gci.net
Track Type:
Dragstrip.
Track Length:
1/4 mile.

KENNEDY RACEWAY
912 6TH STREET NE
SUITE 10
KENNEDY, AL 35073
205-674-8088
• Kathy Hills, Promoter
Developers:
International Speedway Corp.
Size:
3/8 mile.
Track Type:
High-Banked Oval.

KENTUCKY SPEEDWAY
ONE SPEEDWAY DRIVE
SPARTA, KY 41086
859-578-2300
888-652-7223
Fax: 859-647-4307
www.kentuckyspeedway.com
• Andy Vertrees, Director Operations
• Dan Stuart, Director of Sponsorship
Development & Client Svcs.
dstuart@kentuckyspeedway.com
• Tim Bray, Communications Director
(859) 567-3400
tbray@kentuckyspeedway.com
• Mark Simendinger, GM
mSimendinger@kentuckyspeedway.com
• Karen Bannick, Office Manager
kbannick@kentuckyspeedway.com
• Pam Mylor, Service Coordinator
pmylor@kentuckyspeedway.com
• Kara Spencer, Front Desk
kspencer@kentuckyspeedway.com
• John Cox, VP Of sales
(859) 578-2328
jcox@kentuckyspeedway.com
Series:
Busch Series, Craftsman Truck Series, Indy
Racing League, ARCA RE/MAX Series, Hills
Bros All Pro Series, Goody's Dash Series,
K.O.I.L. Tour.

KERN COUNTY RACEWAY PARK
PO BOX 816
ROSAMOND, CA 93560
805-272-1234
Fax: 805-266-0584
• Rusty Fields, Promoter

KNOXVILLE RACEWAY
1000 N LINCOLN STREET
PO BOX 347
KNOXVILLE, IA 50138
641-842-5431
Fax: 641-842-2899
info@knoxvilleraceway.com
www.knoxvilleraceway.com
• Brian Stickel, General Manager, Promoter
bstickel@knoxvilleraceway.com
Description:
Races most Saturday nights from May to
October. Featured events include 50th
Goodyear Knoxville Nationals provided by
Lucas Oil, 20th Annual Arnold Motor Supply
360 Knoxville Nationals, Lucas Oil Late
Model Knoxville Nationals.
Events:
Knoxville Nationals
Track:
1/2 mile banked dirt oval.

LAKEPORT SPEEDWAY
401 MARTIN STREET
PO BOX 1411
LAKEPORT, CA 95453

707-279-9577
Fax: 707-279-9677
lakeportspeedway@TheSnakePitDev.com
www.lakeportspeedway.com
• Dave Swindell, Promoter
• Danny McIntire, President
Description:

Track Size:
1/4 mile.

LAKESIDE SPEEDWAY
5615 WALCOTT DRIVE
KANSAS CITY, KS 66109
913-299-2040
Fax: 913-299-1105
www.lakesidespeedway.net
• Marc Olson, Owner
Track Size:
3/8 mile.
Track Type:
High-Banked Oval.

LAS VEGAS MOTOR SPEEDWAY/LVMS
7000 LAS VEGAS BOULEVARD N
LAS VEGAS, NV 89115
702-644-4444
800-644-4444
Fax: 702-644-7774
media@lvms.com
www.lvms.com
• Ricky May, Sales/Marketing VP
(702) 632-8241
rmay@lvms.com
• David Stetzer, Vice President of
Operations
(702) 632-8234
dstetzer@lvms.com
• Chris Powell, President/General Manager
(702) 632-8030
cpowell@lvms.com
• O. Bruton Smith, Chairman of the Board
• Chris Powell, President and General
Manager
(702) 644-4444
media@lvms.com
• Bill Soard, Vice President of Finance
(702) 632-8042
wsoard@lvms.com
• David Stetzer, Vice President of
Operations
(702) 632-8234
dstetzer@lvms.com
• Jeff Motley, Vice President of Public
Relations
(702) 632-8266
jmotley@lvms.com
• Kevin Camper, Senior Vice President of
Sales and Marketing
(702) 632-8241
kcamper@lvms.com
• Bobby McKenna, Director of Facility
Operations
(702) 632-8128
bckenna@lvms.com
Series:
NASCAR Nextel Cup Series; NASCAR
Busch Series; NASCAR Craftsman Truck
Series.
Back Straight:
3 degrees.
Front Straight:
8 degrees.
Banking:
Corners: 12 degrees.

LASSITER MOUNTAIN DRAGWAY
PO BOX 934
GARDENDALE, AL 35071
205-849-2778
lassitermountain@gmail.com
www.lassitermountain.net
• John Howard, Track Manager
(205) 849-2778
lassitermountain@gmail.com
• Matt Howard, Advertising
(205) 746-6616
matt.howard58@gmail.com
• Anthony Brown, Promoter
Track Size:
1/8 mile.
Track Type:
Dragstrip.

LEMOORE RACEWAY
1750 HIGHWAY 41
LEMOORE, CA 93245
559-924-2536
Fax: 559-217-8832
info@stoneysllc.com
www.lemooreraceway.com
• Nadine Strauss, Manager
• David Furia, Co-manager
• Danny McIntire, President
Year Founded:
1949
Arena Seating Capacity:
1,800.00
Nature of Service:
Auto Racing.
Track Type:
Asphalt.

LIME ROCK PARK
60 WHITE HOLLOW ROAD
LAKEVILLE, CT 6039
860-435-5000
Fax: 860-435-5010
info@limerock.com
www.limerock.com
• Steve Potter, General Manager/VP
(860) 435-5000
stevepotter@limerock.com
• William McMinn, Marketing/Sales Director
(860) 365-0047
wmcminn@limerock.com
• Petra Willig, Track Sales Manager
(860) 435-5000
petra@limerock.com
• Skip Barber, President and Owner
• Nancy Eppley, Operations Manager
(860) 432-5011
nancy@limerock.com
• Donnia A Hamzy, Office Manager
(860) 432-5000
• Rick Roso, Press, PR & Editorial Director
(860) 432-5000
rick@limerock.com
• Georgia Blades, CEO
(860) 432-5000
georgia@limerock.com
• Walter Irvine, Director Business
Development
(860) 432-5000
walter@limerock.com
• Renea Topp, Director of Marketing & PR
(860) 432-5000
renea@limerock.com
Year Founded:
1957
Track Type:
Paved Road Race Track.
Seating Capacity:

Unlimited Hillside viewing.
Track Size:
1.53 Miles.

LOS ANGELES COUNTY RACEWAY
6850 E AVENUE T
PALMDALE, CA 93550
661-533-2224
Fax: 661-533-2226
lacountyraceway@hotmail.com
www.lacr.net
• Bernard Longjohn, Promoter
Track Size:
1/4 mile.
Track Type:
Dragstrip.

MADERA SPEEDWAY
1850 W CLEVELAND AVENUE
MADERA, CA 93637
209-356-1968
Fax: 209-356-1968
tickets@racemadera.com
www.racemadera.com
• Kye Evans, Promoter
(559) 924-2536
kyle@ke-promotions.com
• Kenny Shephard, President / GM
(209) 769-9581
kshephard@racemadera.com
Track Size:
1/8 mile.
Track Type:
Semi-Banked Oval.

MANZANITA SPEEDWAY
3417 W BROADWAY ROAD
PHOENIX, AZ 85041
602-276-7575
Fax: 602-276-2328
• Keith Hall, Promoter
• Ladd Hall, Promoter
Track Type:
Semi-Banked Oval.
Track Size:
1/2 mile and 5/8 mile.

MARBURY DIRT TRACK & KART SHOP
3098 GO KART ROAD
MARBURY, AL 36051
205-755-0465
• Jeff Scott, Promoter
Track Type:
High-Banked Oval.
Track Size:
1/8 mile.

MARTINSVILLE SPEEDWAY
340 SPEEDWAY ROAD
RIDGEWAY, VA 24148
276-956-1543
Fax: 276-956-2820
www.martinsvillespeedway.com
• W. Clay Campbell, President
• Mike Smith, Public Relations Director
(276) 956-1543
msmith@martinsvillespeedway.com
• Karen Parker, Marketing/Business
Development Director
(276) 956-8460
kparker@martinsvillespeedway.com
• Hope Perry, Promotions/Publications
Director
(276) 956-1148
• Karen Parker, VP Marketing
• Rob Gehman, Sr.Director of Accounting

• Henry Williams, Sr.Director of Facility
Operations
• Billy Moore, Track Suprintendent
• Gordon Wilson, Director, Track Operations
Year Founded:
1947
Track Type:
Oval.
Track Size:
.526 mile.

MAZDA RACEWAY LAGUNA SECA
1021 MONTEREY-SALINAS HIGHWAY
SALINAS, CA 93908
831-242-8201
800-327-7322
Fax: 831-373-0533
media@mazdaraceway.com
www.mazdaraceway.com
• Jeanie Sumners, Marketing Manager
(831) 242-8252
jeanie@MazdaRaceway.com
• Steve Fields, Executive Director of
Corporate Development
(831) 277-5798
steve@mazdaraceway.com
• Ann Bixler, Events VP
annb@laguna-seca.com
• Gill Campbell, CEO/General Manager
• Melvyn Record, VP Marketing and Sales
• Ann Bixler, VP Event Operations
• Barry Toepke, VP Communications &
Historic Racing
• Bo Beresiwsky, VP Facility Operations
• Jim Harris, Chief Financial officer
• Steve Fields, Executive Director of
Corporate Development
Description:
Founded 1957. Auto and motorcycle road
race track.

MEMPHIS MOTORSPORTS PARK (MMP)
5500 VICTORY LANE
MILLINGTON, TN 38053
901-969-7223
866-40-77333
Fax: 901-969-8012
www.racemir.com
• Jason Rittenberry, VP/General Manager
(901) 354-2530
• Aaron Hitchcock, Business Development
Manager
• Doug Franklin, Director Public
Relations/Marketing
• Blake Barnes, Ticket Manager
• Daniel Carpenter, Director of Business
Development
• Christi Carson, Corporate Account
Executive
• Jerry Pennington, Corporate Account
Executive
• Jason Rittenberry, General Manager
• Garett Story, Corporate Account Executive
• Pam Kendrick, Vice President & General
Manager
(901) 969-0811
Pkendrick@racemir.com
• Paul Cartwright, Director of Operations
(901) 969-0661
Pcartwright@racemir.com
• Kate Armitage, Director of Public Relations
& Communication
(901) 969-0667
karmitage@racemir.com
• Sharon Nix, Concessions & Facility
Manager
(901) 969-0669
snix@racemir.com

facilities

• Mike Fry, Maintenance Manager
(901) 969-0668
• Glynn Williford, Account Executive /
Sponsor Relations
(901) 969-0777
gwilliford@racemir.com
• Dan Carpenter, Sponsorship Sales
(901) 969-7223
dcarpenter@racemir.com
Series:
NASCAR Busch Series; NASCAR
Craftsman Truck Series.

MERCED FAIRGROUNDS SPEEDWAY
900 MARTIN LUTHER KING JR HIGHWAY
(HIGWAY 59)
MERCED, CA 95301
209-383-3802
Fax: 209-383-3802
• Chuck Griffin, Promoter
(209) 383-3802
ccmrchuck@att.net
• Marylee Griffin, Manager/Treasurer
(209) 383-3802
ccmrmarylee@att.net
• John Bass, Announcer
Track Type:
Semi-Banked Oval.
Track Size:
1/4 mile.
Tracks:
Paved Oval, Dirt Track, Dragstrip, Road
Course.

MESA MARIN RACEWAY
9520 TAFT HIGHWAY
BAKERSFIELD, CA 93311
661-397-7333
Fax: 661-831-2582
• Marion Collins, President/Owner
• Larry Collins, Operations VP
• Judy Salamacha, Public
Relations/Marketing VP
Description:
Auto race track hosting the following
NASCAR racing series: NASCAR West,
Featherlite Southwest Tour, Supertruck,
NASCAR Craftsman Track Series, NASCAR
Winston West, NASCAR Featherlite
Southwest Tour, NASCAR Nextel Cup
Series, Ultra Wheel Spec Trucks, WSMR

MICHIGAN INTERNATIONAL SPEEDWAY
(MIS)
12626 US HIGHWAY 12
BROOKLYN, MI 49230-9068
517-592-6666
Fax: 517-592-3848
contact@mispeedway.com
www.mispeedway.com
• Roger Curtis, President
• Keith Karbo, Marketing Director
• Bill Janitz, Public Relations/New Manager
• Roger Curtis, President
• Kelly Daniels, Director of Accounting
• Jennifer Hutchinson, Director of Business
Development
(517) 592-1128
• Sammie Lukaskiewicz, Sr.Director of
Communications
• Karen Hively, Sr.Executive Ass to the
President
• Barry Gibson, Sr.Director of Operations
• Jim Hobbs, Security Director
Descriptin:
Auto race track.
Series:

NASCAR Nextel Cup Series; NASCAR
Busch Series; NASCAR Craftsman Truck
Series.
Year Founded:
1968
Seating capacity:
136,373

MID-OHIO SPORTS CAR COURSE
7721 STEAM CORNERS ROAD
LEXINGTON, OH 44904-0108
419-884-4000
Fax: 419-884-0042
info@midohio.com
www.midohio.com
• Craig Rust, President
crust@midohio.com
• Adam Fisher, Director Of Operations &
Facility
afisher@midohio.com
• Kathy Nolan, Business Development
Director
knolan@midohio.com
• Steve Bidlack, Marketing And
Communications Manager
sbidlack@greensavoree.com
Year Founded & Description:
A comprehensive motorsports facility
openedin 1962, Mid-Ohio Sports Car
Course features a permanent road-racing
circuit with two primary configurations: a
2.4-mile, 15-turn, and a 2.25-mile, 13-turn
circuit. Located 60 miles north of Columbus
and 75 miles south of Cleveland near
Mansfeild, the track has been called the
most competitive in the U.S. and annually
hosts a diversity of locally, regionally and
nationally sanctioned racing events for
amateur, club and professional drivers and
riders.
Track Type:
Permanent road course.
Track Size:
2.4 miles.
Seating Capacity:
Unlimited general admission and
approximately 5,000 grandstand seats.
Clients Include:
American Honda Motor Co. Inc; Cooper
Tires; Summit Racing; Sunoco.
Nature of Service:
Motorsports entertainment and driving;
riding school.

MILWAUKEE MILE
7722 W GREENFIELD AVENUE
W ALLIS, WI 53214
414-453-5761
Fax: 414-453-9920
• Claude Napier, President/CEO
• Steve Jones, General Manager/Chief
Operating Officer
• Gary Girard, Operations Director
• Cheryl Kuchinskas, Office
Manager/Business Manager
Arena Seating Capacity:
45,000
Track Type:
1 mile paved.
Track Size:
1 mile.
Year Founded:
1903

MITCHELL RACEWAY
4075 PEGER ROAD
FAIRBANKS, AK 99709

907-479-4266
Fax: 907-457-5063
• Jessica Bain, Secretary
(907) 479-5655
• Mark (Doc) Davos, President
Track Type:
Slightly-Banked Oval.
Track Length:
1/4 mile.

MOBILE DRAGWAY
7800 PARK BOULEVARD
IRVINGTON, AL 36544
251-957-3054
MobileDragway@aol.com
www.mobiledragway.com
• Gary Moore, Promoter
(251) 957-3054
gary@MobileDragway.com
Track Size:
1/8 mile.
Track Type:
Dragstrip.

MOBILE INTERNATIONAL SPEEDWAY
7800 PARK BOULVARD
IRVINGTON, AL 36544
251-957-2063
Fax: 251-957-2026
www.mobilespeedway.net
• Bill Roth, Promoter
Track Size:
1/2 mile.
Track Type:
High-Banked Oval.

MONTEZUMA COUNTY FAIRGROUNDS
107 N CHESTNUT
CORTEZ, CO 81321
970-565-1000
• Dante Sena, Promoter
Track Type:
Semi-Banked Oval
Track Size:
3/8 mile

MONTGOMERY MOTORSPORTS PARK
(MMP)
2600 N BELT DRIVE
MONTGOMERY, AL 36110
334-260-9660
Fax: 334-260-9320
jim@mmpdragracing.com
www.mmpdragracing.com
• Anthony Oehler, Manager
• Phillips Chris
• Jim Howard
Track Size:
1/4 mile.
Track Type:
Dragstrip.

MOUNTAIN VIEW MOTORSPORTS PARK
3692 26TH STREET
BOULDER, CO 80304
970-535-9999
• Andrew Rosen, Promoter
• Travis Rosen, Promoter
Track Size:
1.3 miles
Track Type:
Road Course (9 turns)

MYRTLE BEACH SPEEDWAY(MBS)
455 HOSPITALITY LANE
MYRTLE BEACH, SC 29579

843-236-0500
Fax: 704-886-2410
stevez@mbspeedway.com
www.myrtlebeachspeedway.com
• Billy Hardee, Owner
• Nick Lucas, Owner
• Bill Hennecy, Track Manager
bhennecy@aol.com
Description:
Auto race track for NASCAR Weekly Racing
Series presented by Dodge, Hills Bros All
Pro Series, Goody's Dash and SMART
Open Wheel Modified.
Seating Capacity:
12,500
Year Founded:
1958
Track Type:
Asphalt.

NASHVILLE SUPERSPEEDWAY
4847-F MCCRARY ROAD
LEBANON, TN 37090
615-547-7500
Fax: 615-547-7575
Info@nashvillesuperspeedway.com
www.nashvillesuperspeedway.com
• Connie Boshers, Director of Administration
• Griffin Colvert, Director Business
Development
• Cliff Hawks, General Manager
Nature of Service:
Track Rental, Road Course, Community
Events.
Year Founded:
2001
Clients:
NASCAR Busch Series(2), Indy Car Series,
NASCAR Craftman Truck Series, 40th
Anniversary of the Ford Mustang.
Arena Seating Capacity:
25,000.00

NATIONAL HOT ROD ASSOCIATION
2035 FINANCIAL WAY
GLENDORA, CA 91741
626-914-4761
Fax: 626-963-5360
nhra@nhra.com
www.nhra.com
• Tom Compton, President
• Dallas Gardner, Board Chairman
Track Type:
Dragstrip.
Track Size:
1/4 mile.

NATIONAL ORANGE SHOW EVENTS CENTER
689 S E STREET
SAN BERNANDINO, CA 92408
909-888-6788
Fax: 909-889-7666
info@nosevents.com
www.nosevents.com
• Steve Larsen, General Manager
(909) 888-6788
Type of Track:
Semi-Banked Oval.
Track Size:
1/4 mile.

NATIONAL TRAIL RACEWAY
2650 NATIONAL ROAD SW
HEBRON, OH 43025

740-928-5706
Fax: 740-928-2922
www.nationaltrailraceway.com
• Jim Layton, General Manager
(740) 928-5706
jlayton@nhra.com
• Mike Fornataro, Sales/Marketing Manager
(740) 928-5706
MFornataro@nhra.com
• Christoper Stilwell, Facility and Operations
manager
(740) 928-5706
CStilwell@nhra.com
• Janice Hagg, Administrative Assistant
(740) 928-5706
JHagg@nhra.com
Seating Capacity:
12,000
Sports:
National Trail Raceway is a division of
NHRA Drag Racing.
Track Type:
1/4 mile drag strip.
Description:
NHRA Drag Race Track
Events:
Chrysler Classic, MOPAR Nationals, NMRA,
Buick Performance Nationals, NHRA
Unleashed, Jegs Northern Sports Nationals,
ET Racing

NEA SPEEDWAY
1512 WOFFORD STREET
JONESBORO, AR 72401
870-935-3749
• Hugh Cornelison, Promoter
• Edna Cornelison, Promoter
Track Type:
Semi-Banked Oval.
Track Size:
1/4 mile.

NELSON LEDGES ROAD COURSE
10342 STATE ROUTE 305
GARRETTSVILLE, OH 44231
330-977-0111
info@nelsonledges.com
www.nelsonledges.com
• Fred Wolf, Manager
(330) 977-0111
Description:
Automobile and motorcycle race track.
Year founded
1958.
Track type and size
Road course; 2.0 miles.
Seating capacity:
10,0000.

NEW HAMPSHIRE MOTOR SPEEDWAY
1122 ROUTE 106 N
LOUDON, NH 3307
603-783-4744
Fax: 603-783-9691
info@nhms.com
www.nhms.com
• O Bruton Smith, Chairman of the Board
• Jerry Gappens, EVP/General Manager
• Susan Colby, VP Guest Services
(603) 783-4744
scolby@nhms.com
• Troy Taylor, VP Sales/Marketing
(603) 783-4744
ttaylor@nhms.com
Track:
1.058 Mile Oval & 1.6 Mile Road Course.
Seating Capacity:

93,521
Year Built:
1989-1990
Events:
Inaugural Sno Bowl (Snowmobile Racing);
Annual Vintage Racing Celebration; Annual
Loudon Classic (Motorcycle Racing); Annual
LENOX Industrial Tools 301 (NASCAR);
Annual SYLVANIA 300 (NASCAR).
Description:
NHMS features a wide variety of racing
sanctioned by NASCAR, including the
NASCAR Sprint Cup Series, NASCAR
Nationwide Series, the NASCAR Camping
World Truck Series, the NASCAR K&N Pro
Series East, and the NASCAR Whelen
Modified Tour. The American-Canadian
Tour late models compete in an
invitation-only event during the September
NASCAR SYLVANIA 300 race weekend.
Festures sanctioned racing with the
American SportBike Racing Association, the
Championship Cup Series, the Sports Car
Club of America, the World Karting
Association, the Vintage Racing Group, the
Sidecar Racers Association, and the United
States Classic Racing Association.

NORTH ALABAMA SPEEDWAY
12200 HIGHWAY 247
TUSCUMBIA, AL 35674
256-381-0881
northalabamaspeedway@hotmail.com
• Sam Bates, Owner
Track Type:
Dragstrip.
Track Size:
1/8 mile.

NORTHWEST ARKANSAS SPEEDWAY
1804 SLACK STREET
PEA RIDGE, AR 72751
479-451-8636
Fax: 501-451-1900
• Darla Nix, Track operator
• Gary Wilbur, Promoter
• Butch Wilbur, Promoter
Track Size:
3/8 mile.
Track Type:
High-Banked Oval.

OCEAN SPEEDWAY
2601 E LAKE AVENUE
WATSONVILLE, CA 95010
831-662-9466
Fax: 831-668-0708
OceanSpeedway@aol.com
www.oceanspeedway.com
• John Prentice, Promoter
(831) 464-1500

PENTON RACEWAY, INC.
PENTON KARTING KOMPLEX
LAFAYETTE, AL 36862
334-864-0967
• Edge Bill & Debbie, Promoter
(334) 864-9641
• Mike Edge
(334) 864-9448
Arena Seating Capacity:
1,200.00
Year Founded:
1980
Track Type:
Clay round track.

facilities

Track Size:
1/8 mile.

PERRIS AUTO SPEEDWAY
18700 LAKE PERRIS DRIVE
PERRIS, CA 92571
951-940-0134
800-595-4849
Fax: 909-940-0634
openwhchic.kim@aol.com
www.perrisautospeedway.com
• Dan Kazarian, Promoter
Track Type:
High-Banked Oval.
Track Size:
1/2 mile.

PETALUMA SPEEDWAY
PO BOX 6
PETALUMA, CA 94953
707-763-7223
Info@Petaluma-Speedway.com
www.petaluma-speedway.com
• Jim Soares, Promoter
Track Type:
Semi-Banked Oval.
Track Size:
3/8 mile.

PHOENIX INTERNATIONAL RACEWAY
7602 S. AVONDALE BOULEVARD
AVONDALE, AZ 85323
623-772-2000
Fax: 623-932-0416
ticketoffice@phoenixinternationalraceway.com
www.phoenixintlraceway.com
• Bryan Sperber, President
• Marie Jarnlof-Carey, Accounting & Ticketing Operations Direct
• Jim Kofakis, Director Sales
• Bryan Sperber, President
• Jennifer Wentzel, Execuive Assistant
• James Hamilton, Director of Government Affairs
• Marie Isabell, Sr.Director of Business Directions
• Jay Wagner, Director of Ticket Operations
• Gale Powers, Sr.Management Member
• Terrie Ball, Accounting and Payroll Manager
Sponsor
Checker Auto Parts 500.
Description:
Founded 1964. One-mile oval track for auto racing. Stages four events annually, including NASCAR Nextel Cup weekend, Copper World Indy 200, Grand American Road Racing, NASCAR Winter Heat.
Track Address:
7602 S. 115th Ave, Avondale, AZ 85323

PIKES PEAK INTERNATIONAL RACEWAY
16650 MIDWAY RANCH ROAD
FOUNTAIN, CO 80817
719-382-7223
888-306-7223
Fax: 719-382-9180
info@ppir.com
www.ppir.com
• Bob Boileau, President
(719) 382-7223
• Jared Thompson, Track Manager
jared@ppir.com
Special Events:
USAC Silver Crown Championship Series;

USAC National Midget Series; NASCAR West Series; ARCA Bondo/Mar-Hyde Series; NASCAR Busch Series; ASA ACDelco Challenge Series; USAC Western States Midget Series; USAC Western States Sprint Car Series; Late Model St
Seating Capacity:
10,000
Track Type:
Oval; Road Course; Autocross Lot; Dirt Road Course
Track Size:
1-Mile Oval; 1.3 Mile Road Course; 12 Acre Autocross Lot; 2-mile Dirt Road Course
Nature of Service:
Homegrown festival and motor-sports events and Facility Rentals

PLACERVILLE SPEEDWAY
100 PLACERVILLE DRIVE
SUITE #3
PLACERVILLE, CA 95667
530-626-3680
Fax: 916-783-7223
placervillespeedwaymedia@yahoo.com
www.placervillespeedway.com
• John Padjen, Sullivan
• Alan Handy, Track Manager
• Mike Andreeta, Director of Competiton
• Cindy Jones, Scorekeeping
• Kristina Coffey, Business Office
• Bill Sullivan, Director of Communications
Track Distance:
1/4 mile.
Track Type:
High-Banked Oval.

PLAZA PARK RACEWAY
1820 W. LACEY BLVD.
HANFORD, CA 93230
559-651-5114
plazaparkraceway@gmail.com
www.plazaparkraceway.com
• Brandon Morse, Promoter
Track Type:
Semi-Banked Oval.
Track Distance:
1/5 mile.

POCONO RACEWAY
PO BOX 500
LONG PONG ROAD
LONG POND, PA 18334
570-646-2300
800-722-3929
Fax: 570-646-2010
www.poconoraceway.com
• Dr Joseph R. Mattioli, Chief Executive Officer/Chairman
• Rose Mattioli, Secretary/Treasurer
• George Ewald, VP/Track Superintendent
• Daniel Dougherty, VP Track Services/Leases
Description:
Auto race track.
Sponsors:
Pocono 500; Pennsylvania 500.

PORTLAND INTERNATIONAL RACEWAY
1940 N VICTORY BOULEVARD
PORTLAND, OR 97217
503-823-7223
Fax: 503-823-5896
pir@portlandoregon.gov
www.portlandraceway.com
• E.C. Mueller, Racetrack Manager

Description:
Founded 1961. Auto, on- & off-road motorcycle racing, drag racing, bicycle racing, Swap Meets, police training, driver training, action sports events, runs/walks.
Track Type:
1/4 mile & 1/8 mile drag strips incorporated in to a Road Course whose track length without "Festival Turns" is 1.915 miles and nine turns. With the "Festival Turns" it is 1.967 miles and 12 turns. The track surface is asphalt with a concrete surface for the "Festival Turns." There are no banked turns.
Seating Capacity:
18,000 seating plus additional 8,000 General Admission
Clients:
INDYCAR, Pirelli World Challenge, SCCA, NHRA Summit Series, Cascade Sports Car Club, Oregon Motorcycle Road Racing Association, Thursday Night Motocross, SOVREN, SVRA
Nature of Service:
Portland International Raceway hosts sports car and motorcycle road racing, INDYCAR, USAC, NHRA drag racing, motocross, bicycle racing and running/walking events. Portland International Raceway is owned and operated by the City of Portland through its bureau of Parks and Recreation. The raceway is operated as an Enterprise Fund, meaning that it is self-sustaining. Operating expenses and capital improvements are covered by the revenues that it generates, as the raceway receives no general fund tax dollars. The raceway's varied, year-round activities bring between 30 and 40 million dollars into the surrounding community each year.

PORTLAND SPEEDWAY
9727 N MARTIN LUTHER KING JR BOULEVARD
PORTLAND, OR 97217
508-285-2881
Fax: 281-447-3915
houevents@aol.com
• Craig Armstrong, General Manager
• Shannon Derrick, Public Relations Director
• Fred Armstrong, Marketing Director
• Kim Mitchell, Administration/Operations Manager
Description:
Auto race track hosting the NASCAR Weekly Racing Series, (Friday nights; April-September), plus the Pennzoil World of Outlaws sprint car series, Northern Sprint Tour; Dirt Late Models; National Championships Flat Track Motorcycles.

PRAIRIE CITY SVRA RACEWAY PARK
191 WALKER LANE
OROVILLE, CA 95965
530-532-1014
Fax: 503-532-9180
info@hangtownmx.com
• Jerry W Ahrens, Promoter
(530) 532-1014
amp@cncnet.com
Track Type:
Semi-Banked Oval.
Track Size:
1/8 mile.

PRESCOTT RACEWAY
5121 HIGHWAY 53 E
PRESCOTT, AR 71857

870-887-3984
Fax: 501-332-4413
jackie-lewis@live.com
www.prescottraceway.net
• Jackie Lewis, Owner
(870) 904-5952
jackie-lewis@live.com
• Velvet Lewis, Owner
(870) 234-2184
Track Size:
1/8 mile.
Track Type:
Dragstrip.

REDWOOD ACRES FAIRGROUNDS
3750 HARRIS STREET
EUREKA, CA 95501
707-445-3037
Fax: 707-445-1583
www.redwoodacres.com
• Richard Olson, Chairman and co-founder
• Terry Coltra, President
tcoltra@ncidc.org
• Cindy Bedingfield, CEO
• Scott Downie
sdownie@dfg.ca.gov
• Ed Laidlaw
egllge@yahoo.com
• Meredith Biasca
• Connie Stewart
conniestew@humboldt.edu
Type of Track:
Semi-Banked Oval.
Track Length:
3/8 mile.

RICHMOND INTERNATIONAL RACEWAY
600 E LABURNUM AVENUE
RICHMOND, VA 23222
866-455-7223
866-455-7223
Fax: 804-321-3833
ririnfo@rir.com
www.rir.com
• Douglas Fritz, President
• Brett Adams, Senior Operations Director
• Roger Curtis, Seniorr Marketing/Sales Director
• Dennis Bickmeier, President
• John Moreland, VP, Sales and Marketing
• Justin DuBrueler, Sr.Director Accounting
• Jeff Hedrick, Sr.Director of Operations
• Deborah Clemons, Director of Community Affairs
• Diane Cahoon, Director of Ticket Operations
• Louis Gilmore, Director of Business Developmetn
Arena Seating Capacity:
107,000.00
Clients:
NASCAR Nextel Cup Series, NASCAR Busch, MASCAR Craftsman Truck, IRL IndyCar Series.
Track Type:
D-shaped oval.
Track Size:
3/4 mile.

ROAD AMERICA
N7390 STATE HIGHWAY 67
PLYMOUTH, WI 53073
920-892-4576
800-365-7223
Fax: 920-892-4550
info@roadamerica.com
www.roadamerica.com

• George Bruggenthies, General Manager/President
(920) 892-4576
george@roadamerica.com
• Mary Lo Haen, Marketing
(920) 893-3704
marylou@roadamerica.com
• Gail Bartelt, Corporate Hospitality/Rentals
(920) 892-4576
• Tonya Gosse, Finance
• Gail Barteilt, Hospitality & Track Trends
• Mary L Haen, Marketing & Promotions
• John Ewert, Communications
• Kathy Kiesau, Administration & Retail
• Mike Kertscher, Group Programs & Schools
• Carson Wilkinson, Safety Director
(920) 892-4576
safety@roadamerica.com
Arena Seating Capacity:
250,000.00
Year Founded:
1955
Clients:
Top professional, amateur motorcycle, sports car, open wheel, kart series.
Nature of Service:
Road America provides a full service, first class road race facility; anemities include VIP suites, gourmet catering, camping, motor home area, internationally acclaimed permanent road racing track.

ROAD ATLANTA
5300 WINDER HIGHWAY
BRASELTON, GA 30517
770-967-6143
800-849-7223
Fax: 770-967-2668
info@roadatlanta.com
www.roadatlanta.com
• Geoff Lee, President
(770) 967-6143
glee@roadatlanta.com
• Joey Greene, Vice President of Operations
(770) 967-6143
jgreene@roadatlanta.com
• Steve Lanier, Facility Manager
slanier@roadatlanta.com
• Ken Grogan, Director of Security
kgrogan@roadatlanta.com
• Angie Griffin, Corporate Sales Coordinator
agriffin@roadatlanta.com
• Lisa Stewart, Accounting Manager
lstewart@roadatlanta.com
Description:
Road racing track and entertainment facility. Features Professional SportsCar, AMA, NASB & WERA Motorcycles, Vintage and Historic Racing. Operates Driver Training Center offering Advanced Handling and Road Racing courses.

ROCKY HILL SPEEDWAY
312 W BELLVIEW
PORTERVILLE, CA 93257
209-784-4660
Fax: 870-773-2243
WhoWon.com
• Issac Vallejo, Promoter
Track Length:
1/4 mile.
Track Type:
Slightly-Banked Oval.

ROYAL PURPLE RACEWAY
2525 SOUTH FM 565
BAYTOWN, TX 77523
281-383-7223
281-383-2666
Fax: 281-383-3777
media@royalpurpleraceway.com
www.royalpurpleraceway.com/
• Seth Angel, Executive VP/General Manager
• LaRhonda Aron, Director of Business Affairs and Ticketing
laron@royalpurpleraceway.com
• Fern Davis, Director of Sales & Business Development
fdavis@royalpurpleraceway.com
• Nayeli Pacheco, Executive Administrative Assistant & Hospital
npacheco@royalpurpleraceway.com
• Don Neal, Food & Beverage Coordinator
npacheco@royalpurpleraceway.com
• Kenny DeLaughter, Facili es Manager
• John Wood, Photographer
• Seth Angel, EVP & General Manager
seth@royalpurpleraceway.com
Description:
Auto race track. NHRA sanctioned drag racing.
Permanent seating capacity:
30,000

SACRAMENTO RACEWAY PARK (DRAGSTRIP/MX)
5305 EXCELSIOR ROAD
SACRAMENTO, CA 95827
916-363-2653
Fax: 916-368-8772
sacramentoraceway@zetabb.com
www.sacramentoraceway.com
• D. L Smith, Track Owner
nitrofeverracing@zetabb.com
• Cynthiia C Crump, Concession Manager
(916) 708-8811
• Jennifer A Trimp, General Manager
(916) 416-0545
• Tony A Trimp, Events Manager
(916) 416-0545
• Roger Williams, Drag Racing Director
red99nb@yahoo.com
• David Smith, Promoter
(916) 416-1689
• David Smith Jr., Test & Tune
davejr@zetabb.com
• Cindy Crump, Track Rental Info.
sacramentoraceway@zetabb.com
• Ken Breneisen
FriNightMX@techemail.com
Teams Sponsored:
Dragstrip, dirt oval.
Track Size:
1/4 mile.
Teams Sponsored:
SRP ET Drag Racing Finals team NHRA

SANAIR SUPER SPEEDWAY
830 GRAND RANG SAINT-FRANCOIS
SAINT-PIE, QC, CANADA J0H 1W0
450-772-6400
www.sanair.ca
Description:
Motorsports park

SAND HILL RANCH
50 CAMINO DIABLO ROAD
BRENTWOOD, CA 94513
925-634-3328
prsports@silcon.com

• Tom Anderson, Promoter
Track Size:
1/5 mile.
Track Type:
Semi-Banked Oval.

SEBRING INTERNATIONAL RACEWAY
113 MIDWAY DRIVE
SEBRING, FL 33870
863-655-1442
800-626-7223
Fax: 863-655-1777
info@sebringraceway.com
www.sebringraceway.com
• Tres Stephenson, President and General Manager
(941) 655-1442
tstephenson@sebringraceway.com
• Tres Stephenson, President and GM
• Jesse McClelland, Director of Operations
• Ken Breslauer, Communications Director/Track Historian
(727) 895-3482
sebring12pr@aol.com
• Kristie Scottile, Director of Sales and Amrketing
• David Gourley, Ass Director of Sales and Marketing
• Greg Marcotte, Director of Finance and HR
• Toni Feo, Ass.Director of Finance and HR
Description:
Auto race track.

SECOND CREEK RACEWAY (OVAL)
17010 E 88TH AVENUE
ROUTE 1
BOX 113
COMMERCE CITY, CO 80022
303-371-6661
Fax: 303-371-6662
www.na-motorsports.com/Tracks/CO/SecondCreek.html
• Bob McClusky, Track Manager
Track Types:
Semi-Banked Oval; Airport Road Course (8 turns)
Track Length:
1/5 mile; 1.7 miles

SHANNONVILLE MOTORSPORT PARK
7047 OLD HIGHWAY #2
PO BOX 259
SHANNONVILLE, ON, CANADA K0K 3A0
613-969-1906
800-959-8955
Fax: 613-966-6890
www.shannonville.com
Description:
Race track
Long Track:
4.03 km
Pro Track:
2.47 km
Fabi Circuit:
2.23 km

SHASTA DISTRICT FAIR
1890 BRIGGS STREET
ANDERSON, CA 96007
530-378-6789
Fax: 530-378-6788
• Sciarani Trish, Shasta District Fairgrounds/Chief Execut
• George Wade, Raceway Park Operations General Manager
(530) 378-6789

• Chris Workman, CEO
• Stina Deatley, Representative
• Melanie Silva, Business Assistant
• Ken Scheeler, Maintainace Supritendent
• Tom Atkinson, Maintainance
Seating Capacity:
3,800

SILVER DOLLAR SPEEDWAY
704 VINE AVENUE
ROSEVILLE, CA 95678
530-891-6535
Fax: 916-891-6535
www.na-motorsports.com
• Alan Padjen, Track Manager
Track Type:
Semi-Banked Oval.
Track Size:
1/4 mile.

SISKAYOU MOTOR SPEEDWAY
1712 FAIRLANE ROAD
YREKA, CA 96097
530-842-2767
Fax: 530-842-4724
siskiyoumotorspeedway@gmail.com
www.siskiyoumotorspeedway.com
• Josh Cullen, President
• Rick Weber, Vice President
• Rebecca Desmond, CEO
• Julie Phillips, Secretary
• Chris Cullen, Director
• Jim Rohn, Director
• Linda Carlin, Treasurer
Track Type:
Semi-Banked Oval.

SONOMA RACEWAY
29355 ARNOLD DRIVE
SONOMA, CA 95476
707-938-8448
800-870-7223
Fax: 707-938-8691
trackinfo@racesonoma.com
www.racesonoma.com
• Frank Gullum, VP Sales
(707) 933-3914
fgullum@infineonraceway.com
• Melvyn Record, VP Marketing
(707) 933-3937
mrecord@infineonraceway.com
• Bobby O'Gorman, Operations Director
(707) 933-3906
• Brad Lawrence, Group Sales
(707) 933-3939
blawrence@infineonraceway.com
Description:
Founded 1988. Auto race track. Features all types of racing including NASCAR Nextel Cup, NASCAR West Featherlite Southwest Tour, and Craftsman Truck Series, AMA Vintage Motorcycles and superbikes, NHRA Drag Racing, SCCA Trans-Am, Professional SportsCar Ra
Series:
NASCAR Nextel Cup Series

SOUTH ALABAMA SPEEDWAY
189 WEST HWY 52
KINGSTON, AL 36453
334-774-3161
speedway.SAS@gmail.com
www.southalabamaspeedway.com
• John Dykes, owner
(334) 774-3161
southalabama@charter.net
• Sandra Dykes, Promoter

• John Dykes
(334) 774-3161
• MaLeah Hill
(334) 432-0211
MaLeah.SAS@gmail.com
• Edward Berry, Tech
(334) 379-4457
Track Size:
4/10 mile.
Track Type:
High-Banked Oval.

SOUTH BOSTON SPEEDWAY
1188 JAMES D HAGOOD HIGHWAY
PO BOX 1066
S BOSTON, VA 24592
434-572-4947
877-440-1540
Fax: 434-575-8992
info@southbostonspeedway.com
www.southbostonspeedway.com
• Cathy Rice, General Manager
• Nick Iqdalsky, Sr.VP
• Jenny Morris, Office Assistant
• Helen Barksdale, Office Manager
• Terry Daniels, Maintainace Supritendent
• John A Evans, Speedway Announcer
Description:
Auto race track for NASCAR and NASCAR All-Pro Series. Hosting NASCAR Hills Bros.. All-Pro Series, ASA Series, ARCA RE/MAX Series, NASCAR Goody's Dash Series, Extreme Motor-X, USAR Hooter's Pro Cup Series, USAC Midgets, NASCAR Craftsman Truck Series and NA

EL MIRAGE DRY LAKE
2517 SYCAMORE DRIVE
SUITE 353
SIMI VALLEY, CA 93065
805-526-1805
Fax: 805-584-8518
office@scta-bni.org
www.scta-bni.org
• Lonnie Martin, El Mirage Maintenance Club Liaison
• Scott Andrews, President
(818) 419-8074
scott.andrews@scta-bni.org
Location:
El Mirage, CA

SOUTHWESTERN INTERNATIONAL RACEWAY
12000 S HOUGHTON ROAD
TUCSON, AZ 85747
520-762-9700
Fax: 520-762-9777
sirace97@yahoo.com
• Dennis Scheepstra, Track manager
(520) 429-0397
• Dan Owens, Events
(520) 869-7772
dowens@merlesauto.com
• Paul Smith, Events
(520) 850-0353
Track Size:
1/4 mile.
Track Type:
Dragstrip.

STAFFORD MOTOR SPEEDWAY
55 W STREET
STAFFORD SPRINGS, CT 6076
860-684-2783
Fax: 860-684-6236
www.staffordspeedway.com

• Mark Arute, COO/General Manager
markarute@staffordspeedway.com
• Lisa Arute, Executive Vice President
lisaarute@staffordspeedway.com
• Scott Running, Sr.Director
scottrunning@staffordspeedway.com
• Mike Young, Manager
Description:
Auto race track hosting the following
NASCAR racing series: Busch North Series,
Featherlite Modified Series. Also hosts SK
Modifieds, Late Models, D.A.R.E. Stocks,
U.S. Hot Rods, Monster Trucks, Harley
Davidson Jamboree, Automotive Swap
Meets, and motorcy

SUMMERVILLE SPEEDWAY
1896 CENTRAL AVENUE
SUMMERVILLE, SC 29483-9325
843-761-1428
Fax: 843-761-2772
www.na-motorsports.com/Tracks/SC/Summ
erville.html
• Charlie Powell, Promoter
Description:
Auto race track hosting the following
NASCAR racing series: Slim Jim All Pro
Series, Goody's Dash Series.

SUMMIT POINT MOTORSPORTS PARK
201 MOTOR PARK CIRCLE
PO BOX 190
SUMMIT POINT, WV 25446
304-725-8444
Fax: 304-728-7124
office@bsr-inc.com
www.summitpoint-raceway.com
• Bill Scott, President
Description:
Auto, motorcycle, kart race track.

SYDNEY MOTORSPORT PARK
PO BOX 6747
BLACKTOWN DC, NSW, 2148
61—2 9672 1000
Fax: 61—9672-0208
www.sydneymotorsportpark.com
• Brian Goulding, Race Operations Manager
brian@ardc.com.au
• Phil Harrison, Marketing Manager
phil@ardc.com.au
• Brian Goulding, Race Operations Manager

TALLADEGA GRAN PRIX RACEWAY
46 PILGRIM LANE
MUNFORD, AL 36268
256-493-0302
Fax: 256-362-3718
www.tgprace.com
• David Upchurch, President
• Michael Upchurch, VP
• Katrina Upchurch, Administrator
katrina@tgprace.com
Track Type:
Road Course (9 turns).
Track Length:
1.3 miles.
Sports:
Motorcycle races, testing, riding schools,
limited car tune & test, driving schools

TALLADEGA SHORT TRACK
4343 SPEEDWAY BVLD
EASTABOGA, AL 36260
256-831-1413

• Lynn Phillips, Promoter
(256) 454-5414
• Alfred Gurley, Promoter
Track Type:
High-Banked Oval.
Track Length:
1/3 mile.

TALLADEGA SUPERSPEEDWAY
3366 SPEEDWAY BOULEVARD
TALLADEGA, AL 35160
877-462-3342
Fax: 256-761-4717
www.talladegasuperspeedway.com
• Kristi R King, Director Public Relations
(256) 761-4705
• Andrew Smith, Public Relations Assistant
(256) 761-4706
Description:
Founded 1969. Tri-oval race track.
Seating Capacity:
With approximately 143,000 grandstand
seats and a 212-acre infield, Talladega
Superspeedway hosts two major stock car
racing weekends each year. The Talladega
500 in April and Alabama 500 in October.
Both are NASCAR Nextel Cup Series
events.

TEXAS MOTOR SPEEDWAY/TMS
3545 LONE STAR CIRCLE
FORT WORTH, TX 76177
817-215-8500
Fax: 817-491-3749
www.texasmotorspeedway.com
• Eddit Gossage, President/General
Manager
• Kenton Nelson, Assistant General
Manager
• Kevin Camper, Director of Sales & Bus.
Dev.
• Mike Zizzo, Director Public Relations
Sponsor
DIRECTV
Back Straight:
1,330 feet
Front Straight:
2,250 feet
Banking:
24 and 8 degrees

TEXAS MOTORPLEX
7500 W. HIGHWAY 287
ENNIS, TX 75119
972-878-2641
Fax: 972-878-1848
www.texasmotorplex.com
• Ryan Haas, General Manager
• Gregg Griffin, Marketing Services
• Elon Werner, Media Relations Director
• Arthur O'Bright, Marketing Services/Sales
Description:
Founded 1986. Drag racing track.

THE LEGENDARY DARLINGTON
2056 E BOBO NEWSOME HWY
SC 151
HARTSVILLE, SC 29550
843-383-0008
Fax: 843-383-9933
www.darlingtondragway.com
• Bill Wilson, President
(843) 383-0008
Description:
Dragstrip (1/4 mile).
Seating Capacity:
15,000

**THOMPSON SPEEDWAY
MOTORSPORTS PARK**
205 E THOMPSON ROAD
THOMPSON, CT 06277
860-923-2280
Fax: 860-923-2398
oval@thompsonspeedway.com
www.thompsonspeedway.com
• Donald J Hoenig, Owner/Promoter
pitcrew@thompsonspeedway.com
• Russ Dowd, Operations Director/Media
Contact
• Donald J Hoeing, President
• D.R Hoeing, VP
• Jeff Zuidema, Race Director
• Russ Dowd, Director of Operations
• Mary Ann Rossi, Office Manager
pitcrew@thompsonspeedway.com
• Richard Sprague, Chief Inspector
• Josh Vanada, Competition Director
Track:
5/8 mile high banked asphalt oval
Seating Capacity:
15,000

**THUNDER MOUNTAIN SUPER
SPEEDWAY**
10151 SPEEDWAY LANE
PO BOX 13
CENTERVILLE, AR 72829
479-576-2593
Fax: 479-576-2432
• Wayne Tidwell, Owner/Promoter
(479) 970-0160
Track Type:
High-Banked Oval.
Track Size:
1/4 mile.

THUNDER RACEWAY, INC.
4701 E DEUCE OF CLUBS
SHOW LOW, AZ 85901
928-978-0428
Fax: 520-532-0170
www.thunderraceway.com
• Bob Livingston, Promoter
(928) 242-1384
Track Size:
1/4 mile.
Track Type:
High-Banked Oval.

THUNDER RIDGE MOTOR SPEEDWAY
1601 49TH AVENUE SW
LANNETT, AL 36863-3655
334-576-7233
Fax: 334-576-7233
Track Length:
1/8 mile.
Track Type:
Banked Oval.

THUNDER VALLEY RACEWAY
JUMPER'S BROOK ROAD
PO BOX 681
BISHOP'S FALLS, NL, CANADA A1V 1W5
205-487-3199
• Floyd Dillard, Promoter
Track Length:
1/4 mile.
Track Type:
Slightly-Banked Oval.

facilities

THUNDER VALLEY SPEEDWAY
1588 SHADE CHURCH RD
CENTRAL CITY
CENTRAL CITY, PA 15926
240-382-0526
thundervalleyrace@gmail.com
• Tiffany Trollinger, Contact
• Morgan Padula, General Manager
• Joe Padula, Promoter
• Mark Lashley, Head Flagman
• Mark Moore, Chief Steward
Track Length:
3/8 mile.
Track Type:
Semi-Banked Oval.

THUNDERBOWL RACEWAY
BARDSLEY & K STREET
TULARE, CA 93274
559-688-0909
Fax: 559-687-1957
www.thunderbowlraceway.com
• Steve Faria, Promoter
(559) 688-0909
• Don Sharp, Marketing/Advertising
(559) 734-9246
Track Type:
Oval- Dirt Track (Clay) Big events- World of
Outlaws & Torphy Cup
Track Size:
1/3 mile.

THUNDERHILL RACEWAY PARK
5250 HWY
PO BOX 966
WILLOWS, CA 95988
530-934-5588
888-995-7222
Fax: 530-934-8794
office@thunderhill.com
www.thunderhill.com
• David Vodden, Chief Executive
Officer/Promoter
(530) 934-5588
dvodden@thunderhill.com
• Shannon Ell, General Manager
(530) 934-5588
shannon@thunderhill.com
• Terry Taylor, Accounting Manager
(530) 934-5588
office@thunderhill.com
• Ray Mudd, Events Manager
(530) 934-5588
ray@thunderhill.com
• Bob Maybell, Facilities Manager
(530) 934-5588
• Terry Taylor, Personnel and Accounting
(530) 934-5588
• Sean Crandall, Maintenance
(530) 330-2188
Year Founded:
1993
Seating Capacity:
On Hills, 10,000.
Track Type:
3 Mile, 15 Turn Road Course.
Track Size:
Six Configurations: 1.0, 1.3, 1.5, 1.7, 1.9
and 3.0 Miles.

TRI CITY SPEEDWAY
5100 NAMEOKI ROAD
PONTOON BEACH, IL 62040
636-448-9111
800-617-9077
Fax: 618-931-3217

tricityspeedway@msn.com
www.tricityspeedway.net
• Anita Ratliff, Contact person
Description:
Dirt track stock car racing.

TUCSON RACEWAY PARK
11955 S HARRISON ROAD
TUCSON, AZ 85747
520-762-9200
Fax: 520-762-5053
www.tucsonracewaypark.com
• David Deery, General Manager
(520) 762-9200
• Mark Ebert, Director
speed@theracingschool.com
Year Founded:
1968
Track Size:
3/8 mile & 1/4 mile.
Track Type:
Banked-Asphalt Oval.
Seating Capacity:
6,500

TWIN CITY RACEWAY
7075 SHOTGUN DRIVE
KENAI, AK 99611
907-283-9078
• Ed Kobak, Media and Promotions
(907) 260-6292
globalnw@earthlink.net
• Bill Jackson, Promoter
Track Type:
Semi-Banked Oval.
Track Length:
3/8 mile.

VENTURA RACEWAY
10 WEST HARBOUR BLVD.
VENTURA, CA 93001
805-985-5433
Fax: 805-984-3095
info@venturaraceway.com
• Jim Naylor, Promoter
(805) 985-5835
jnaylor@ucnet.com
• Cliff Morgan, General Manager
(805) 985-5433
cmorgan428@hotmail.com
• Mike Sweeney
mike@venturaraceway.com
Arena Seating Capacity:
4,000.00
Year Founded:
1977
Clients:
Motorsports Teams and Fans.
Nature of Service:
Motorsports Racing weekly series, Ventura
Racing Associates Sprint Cars, VRASR
Sprints Cars, VRA Pony Stocks, VRA
Modifieds, VRA Dwarf Cars, IMCA
Modifieds, USAC Midgets, Focus Midgets,
USAC/CRA 410 Sprint Cars.

WATKINS GLEN INTERNATIONAL
2790 COUNTY ROUTE 16
WATKINS GLEN, NY 14891
607-535-2486
866-461-7223
Fax: 607-535-8918
racing@theglen.com
www.theglen.com
• Kevin Gundaker, Contact
kevin@tricityspeedway.net

• Tammy Gundaker, Contact Person
tammy@tricityspeedway.net
• Brandy Gundaker, Marketing Incharge
Seating Capacity:
4,500
Description:
Founded 1963. Auto race track. Features
Super Stock, Stock, Winged Sprint, Oval
Track and Midget Car Racing.

WESTERN COLORADO DRAGWAY
115 32 RD
GRAND JUNCTION
CLIFTON, CO 81520
970-523-1720
wcdra@hotmail.com
www.wcdra.com
• Doug Styers, President
• Dale Umberger, VP
• Mike McCallum, Executive Board
(970) 260-7430
• Chris McCallum, Executive Board
(970) 986-5401
• John Cozzette, Executive Board
(970) 242-5955
• Bryan Carmack, Executive Board
(970) 523-1720
• Bud Preuss, Executive Board
(970) 250-2217
• Mike Hansen, Treasurer
Track Length:
1/4 mile
Track Type:
Dragstrip

**WILLOW SPRINGS INTERNATIONAL
RACEWAY**
3500 75TH STREET W
ROSAMOND, CA 93560
661-256-6666
Fax: 661-256-9140
info@willowspringsraceway.com
www.willowspringsraceway.com
• Rick Romo, Contact
(661) 256-8974
Physical Address:
3500 75th St West, Rosamond, CA 93560.
Nature of Service:
Auto, motorcycles, and karts racetrack.
Features Sprint Car, Oval Track, Indy Car,
Stock Car, and Midget Car racing.
Seating Capacity:
10,000+.
Publications:
WILLOW SPRINGS SPECTATOR, monthly.

Race Tracks - Equestrian Downs & Parks

ALABAMA STATE FAIRGROUNDS
2331 BESSEMER ROAD
BIRMINGHAM, AL 35208
205-786-8100
Fax: 205-786-8222
opi@birminghamal.gov
www.informationbirmingham.com
• Leroy R Cowan, Director
State Fair Arena Seating Capacity:
6,000
**Birmingham International Speedway
Seating Capacity**
10,000

ALAMEDA COUNTY FAIRGROUNDS
4501 PLEASANTON AVENUE
PLEASANTON, CA 94566
925-426-7600
Fax: 925-426-7599
info@alamedacountyfair.com
www.alamedacountyfair.com
• Janet Lockhart, President
• Dean Schenone, Vice President
Seating capacity racing grandstand:
6,500

ARIZONA EXPOSITION & STATE FAIR
1826 W MCDOWELL ROAD
PHOENIX, AZ 85007
602-252-6771
Fax: 602-495-1302
info@azstatefair.com
www.azstatefair.com

ARKANSAS STATE FAIRGROUNDS
2600 HOWARD STREET
LITTLE ROCK, AR 72206
501-372-8341
Fax: 501-372-4197
www.arkansasstatefair.com
• Ralph Shoptaw, President / General
Manager
rshoptaw@asfg.net
Barton Coliseum Seating Capacity:
10,219

ARLINGTON INTERNATIONAL
2200 WEST ELUCID AVENUE
ARLINGTON HEIGHTS, IL 60006
847-385-7500
Fax: 309-792-0522
eaglemotz@aol.com
www.arlingtonpark.com
• Richard Duchossois, Chairman
• Ed Jamison, VP/General Manager
Year Founded:
1973
Seating capacity:
3,500
Nature of Service:
Harness horse race track.

ASSINIBOIA DOWNS
3975 PORTAGE AVENUE
WINNIPEG, MANITOBA, CANADA R3K
2E9
204-885-3330
800-282-8053
Fax: 204-831-5348
info@assiniboiadowns.com
www.assiniboiadowns.com
• Harvey D. Warner, President
(204) 885-3330
info@assiniboiadowns.com
• Norm Elder, Vice President
(204) 885-3330
info@assiniboiadowns.com
• Barry Anderson, Secretary
(204) 885-3330
info@assiniboiadowns.com
• Sharon Gulyas, General Manager
(204) 885-3330
sgulyas@assiniboiadowns.com
Seating capacity:
5,000
Year Founded:
1958
Track Type:
Thoroughbred Dirt Track.
Track Size:
13/16 mile.

ATLANTIC CITY RACE COURSE
4501 BLACK HORSE PIKE
MAYS LANDING, NJ 8330
609-641-2190
Fax: 609-645-8309
www.acracecourse.com
• James J. Murphy, President/General
Manager
• Robert P. Levy, Chief Business
Description:
Founded 1944. Thoroughbred race track.
Seating capacity:
16,000

BAY MEADOWS
901 MARINES ISLAND BOULEVARD
SUITE 125
SAN MATEO, CA 94404
650-573-4600
650-574-7223
Fax: 650-573-4670
www.baymeadows.com
• Jack Liebau, President

BELMONT PARK
3146 MISSION BOULEVARD
PO BOX 90
SAN DIEGO, CA 92109
858-228-9283
Fax: 858-488-4316
www.belmontpark.com
• Nancie No Geller, PRESIDENT
• Terrence Meyoucks, President/Chief
Operating Officer
• Alec Ingle, Chief Financial Officer/Asst to
the Pres
• Glen Mathes, Director, Communications

BELTERRA PARK
6301 KELLOGG ROAD
CINCINNATI, OH 45230-5237
513-354-8246
800-699-7558
Fax: 513-232-1412
• Jack Hanessian, General Manager
(513) 232-8000
jackh@riverdowns.com
• John Engelhardt, Director, Public
Relations
(513) 232-8000
johne@riverdowns.com
• Vincent Cyster, Simulcast Coordinator
• Ed Vomacka, Secretary, Racing
• Shannon Fink, Group Sales
(513) 354-8246
• Terry Moore, Bookeper
(513) 354-8265
Description:
Thoroughbred horse race track.
Seating capacity:
15,000.00
Nature of Service:
Year-Round Simulcasting.

**BERGERON RODEO GROUNDS AND
ENTERTAINMENT CENTER**
6591 ORANGE DRIVE
DAVIE, FL 33314
954-797-1000
Fax: 954-797-2061
citizens_response@davie-fl.gov
www.davie-fl.gov
• Joan Kovac, Chairperson
• Phillip R. Holste, Intergovernmental Affairs
Manager
• Giovanni Moss, Housing and Community
Development Director

Seating Capacity:
7,000
Description:
Rentals: 954-797-1163

BETFAIR HOLLYWOOD PARK
1050 S PRAIRIE AVENUE
INGLEWOOD, CA 90301
310-419-1549
Fax: 310-672-4664
www.hollywoodpark.com
• Eual M. Eual, Vice President & General
Manager
• Eual Wyatt, General Manager
• Steve Arnold, VP, Finance
• Alan Gutterman, VP, Marketing
Description:
Founded 1938. Thoroughbred horse race
track.
Seating capacity:
50,000

BEULAH PARK
3811 SW BOULEVARD
PO BOX 850
GROVE CITY, OH 43123
614-871-9600
Fax: 614-871-0433
www.beulahpark.com
• Charles Ruma, President
• Michael A. Weiss, General Manager
• Vic Mason, Publishing Director
• Jim McKinney, GM
(614) 871-9400
• Gina Schmidt, Coordinator
(614) 871-9400
• Ed Vomacka, Racing Secreatary
(614) 871-9400
• Larry Shipley, Food and Beverage
(614) 871-9400
• Holly Chandler, Admissions Incharge
(614) 871-9400
• David Hardy, Plant Supritendent
(614) 871-9400
Description:
Thoroughbred horse race track, simulcast
and banquet facility.
Seating capacity:
9,000

BIG FRESNO FAIR (BFF)
1121 CHANCE AVENUE
FRESNO, CA 93702
559-650-3247
Fax: 559-650-3226
info@fresnofair.com
www.fresnofair.com
• John C C Alkire, Chief Executive Officer
(559) 650-3247
jalkire@fresnofair.com
• Debbie Nalchajian-Cohen,
Communications/Media Relations
Arena Seating Capacity:
5,000.00
Year Founded:
1883
Clients:
Local residents, racing enthusists.
Nature of Service:
Horseracing Facility.

BIRMINGHAM RACE COURSE
1000 JOHN ROGERS DRIVE
BIRMINGHAM, AL 35210
205-838-7500
800-998-8238

facilities

Fax: 205-838-7407
www.birminghamracecourse.com
• Joe E. O'Neill, Operations Manager
• W. M. Russell, VP, Operations
• S. Le Yates, Chief Financial Officer
• Linda Butler, Human Resources Officer
• Brian Carpenter, Director of Racing
• Elaine Lucas, Director of Mutuels
• Bennie Polo, Manager
• Barabara Hummel, Group Sales
Description:
Horse Racing Track.

CALDER CASINO & RACE COURSE
21001 NW 27TH AVENUE
PO BOX 1808
MIAMI GARDEN, FL 33056
305-625-1311
800-333-3227
Fax: 305-624-6284
customerservice@calderracecourse.com
www.calderracecourse.com
• Tom O'Donnell, President
• John Marshall, General Manager/Vice
President
• Michael Cronin, Director, Marketing
Description:
Founded 1972. Sporting
event/entertainment facility, thoroughbred
race track.
Permanent Seating capacity:
15,000

CALIFORNIA EXPOSITION & STATE FAIR
1600 EXPOSITION BOULEVARD
SACRAMENTO, CA 95815
916-263-3000
877-225-3976
Fax: 916-263-3304
info@calexpo.com
www.calexpo.com
• Marko Mlikotin, Chairman
emanuel@calexpo.com
• Norbert Bartosik, General Manager
(916) 263-3061
nbartosik@calexpo.com
• David Dhillon, Assistant General Manager,
Marketing
(916) 263-3219
ddhillon@calexpo.com
• Dave Elliott, Assistant General Manager,
Racing
(916) 263-3283
delliott@calexpo.com
• Jerry Brown, Goveror
• Willie Pelote, Director
• Sonney Chong, Director
• Jeffery Azoff, Director
• Rima Barkett, Director
• Rex Hime, Director
Description:
Founded 1854 as an agricultural fair. Offers
entertainment and exhibits with broad public
appeal.

CALGARY STAMPEDE
1410 OLYMPIC WAY SE
CALGARY, AB, CANADA T2G 2W1
403-261-0101
800-661-1767
www.calgarystampede.com
• Warren Connell, Chief Executive Officer

CANTERBURY PARK
1100 CANTERBURY ROAD
SHAKOPEE, MN 55379

952-445-7223
800-340-6361
Fax: 952-496-6400
cbypark@canterburypark.com
www.canterburypark.com
• Randy D. Sampson, President/Chief
Executive Officer
• John Harty, VP, Marketing
• Michael J. Garin, VP, Hospitality
• Mark A. Erickson, VP Facilities

CHURCHILL DOWNS
700 CENTRAL AVENUE
LOUISVILLE, KY 40208
502-636-4400
Fax: 502-636-4430
customerservice@kyderby.com
www.churchilldowns.com
• Carl Pollard, Chairman
• Thomas H. Meeker, Chief Executive
Officer/President
• Steve Sexton, President
• Karl Schmitt, SVP Corporate
Communications
• Tricia Amburgey, Senior Director
Sponsorship Sales
Description:
Owns Arlington International Racecourse.

CLINTON RACEWAY
PO BOX 778
147 BEECH STREET
CLINTON, ON, CANADA N0M 1LO
519-482-5270
Fax: 519-482-1489
cdejong@clintonraceway.com
clintonraceway.com
• Jessica Carnochan, Marketing Director
jessicacarnochan@gmail.com
Description:
Horse race track

DEL MAR THOROUGHBRED CLUB
2260 JIMMY DURANTE BOULEVARD
DEL MAR, CA 92014
858-755-1141
Fax: 858-792-1477
marys@dmtc.com
www.dmtc.com
• Joe W. Harper, President/General
Manager
(858) 755-1141
joeh@dmtc.com
• Craig R. Fravel, EVP
(858) 755-1141
craig@dmtc.com
• Michael R. Ernst, VP/Chief Financial
Officer
(858) 755-1141
mike@dmtc.com
• Joe Harper, President & GM
joeh@dmtc.com
• Mike Ernst, EVP & CFO
mike@dmtc.com
• Tom Robbins, EVP, Racing & Industry
Realtions
tomr@dmtc.com
• Josh Rubinstein, SVP , Development
josh@dmtc.com
• Craig Dado, SVP, Marketing
(858) 755-1141
craigd@dmtc.com
• Ann Hall, VP Humann resources&
Administration
annh@dmtc.com
• Tim Read, VP , Operations & Collective

Bargain
timr@dmtc.com
Year Founded:
1937
Track Type:
Dirt, Turf.
Track Size:
1 mile dirt, 7/8 turf.

DELAWARE COUNTY FAIR
236 PENNSYLVANIA AVENUE
PO BOX 1278
DELAWARE, OH 43015
740-362-3851
800-335-3247
Fax: 740-363-4132
fair@delawarecountyfair.com
www.delawarecountyfair.com
• Kent Hastings, PRESIDENT
wthomson@delgazette.com
• Gary Must, General Manager
garymust@midohio.net
• Phil Terry, Marketing Director & fair
manager
pterry@littlebrownjug.com
• Steve Vaughn, Grounds
• Jennifer Keysor, Reserve Tickets &
Admissions
• Sheila Hemans, Reserve Tickets &
Admissions
Description:
Harness race track.
Seating capacity:
17,500

**DELAWARE PARK RACETRACK &
SLOTS**
777 DELAWARE PARK BOULEVARD
WILMINGTON, DE 19804
302-994-2521
800-417-5687
Fax: 302-355-1292
programs@delawarepark.com
www.delawarepark.com
• William Rickman, president and general
manager
• Andrew Gentile, General Manager
• Bill Fasy, EVP/Chief Operating Officer
• John Rooney, VP, Finance/Racing

DRESDEN RACEWAY
1244 N STREET
DRESDEN, ONTARIO, CANADA NOP 1M0
519-683-4466
Fax: 519-683-4038
www.windsorraceway.com
• Lorrie Brown, General Manager
• Paul Hawman, Race Secretary
Description:
Harness horse race track.

DUQUOIN STATE FAIR
655 EXECUTIVE DRIVE
DU QUOIN, IL 62832
618-542-1515
Fax: 618-542-1541
www.agr.state.il.us/dq
• John Rednour Jr., Fairground Director
Description:
Home of the World Trotting Derby.

EL COMANDANTE RACE TRACK
ROAD NO 3, KM 15.3
PO BOX 1643
CANOVANAS, PUERTO RIC 00729-1643

787-641-6060
Fax: 787-641-6085
• Juan M. Rivera, President/Chief Executive
Officer
• Alejandro Fuentes, EVP/General Manager
• Carlos A. Pena, VP, Racing Operations
• Stanley Pinkerton, VP/Chief Financial
Officer
Description:
Horse race track.

ELLIS PARK
3300 US HIGHWAY 41
HENDERSON, KY 42420
812-425-1456
800-333-8089
Fax: 812-425-3725
ellispark@ellisparkracing.com
www.ellisparkracing.com
• Ron Geary, Owner/President
ron.geary@ellisparkracing.com
• Ron Geary, Owner/President
• Joe Rudisill, General Manager
• Bob Jackson, Operations Manager
• Eric Lemerand, IRM Operations Manager
• Robyn Oglesby, Marketing Manager
• Chad Keown, Food & Beverage Manager
Year Founded:
1922
Description:
Founded 1922. Pari-mutuel wagering on
horse racing; conducts live thoroughbred
racing.
Nature of Service:
Pari-mutuel wagering on horse racing; live
thoroughbred racing.

EMERALD DOWNS
2300 EMERALD DOWNS DRIVE
AUBURN, WA 98001
253-288-7000
888-931-8400
Fax: 253-288-7010
info@emeralddowns.com
www.emeralddowns.com
• Ron Crockett, President
• Bob Fraser, Director, Operations
• Ron Crockett, President
• Jack Hodge, Vice President
• Emerald Downs, Vice President of
Operations
Description:
Thoroughbred horse race track.

EVANGELINE DOWNS
2235 CRESWELL LANE EXTENSION
PO BOX 90270
OPELOUSAS, LA 70570
866-472-2466
877-770-7867
Fax: 337-594-3166
www.evangelinedowns.com
• Mike As Howard, General Manager
• Charles As Jr, VP

EXHIBITION PARK
37 MCALLISTER DRIVE
PO BOX 284
SAINT JOHN, NB, CANADA E2L 3Y2
506-636-2020
Fax: 506-636-6958
blair.macdonald@nb.aibn.com
• Blair MacDonald, Administration
• Paul Gilbride, President
• Frank McCarey, VP
• Williard Jenkins, Treasurer
• J.Charles Swanton, Secretary

• Gerry Lowe, BOD
• Stan Fielding, BOD
Year Founded:
1890
Nature of Service:
Harness race track; part of The Exhibition
Association of the City and County of Saint
John.

EXIBITION PARK - LETHBRIDGE
3401 PARKSIDE DRIVE S
LETHBRIDGE, CANADA ABT1J 4R3
403-328-4491
Fax: 403-320-8139
events@exhibitionpark.ca
www.exhibitionpark.ca
• Rudy Friesen, General Manager
(403) 328-4491
rudy@exhibitionpark.ca
• Rudy Friesen, GM
(403) 328-4491
rudy@exhibitionpark.ca
• Diana DiRocco, Executive Assistant
(403) 328-3201
diana@exhibitionpark.ca
• Bridget Mearns, Developmetn Coordinator
(403) 328-3218
bridget@exhibitionpark.ca
• Bruce Larson, Controller
(403) 328-3203
bruce@exhibitionpark.ca
• Shawn Anderson, Product Supervisor
(403) 317-3207
shawan@exhibitionpark.ca
• Bryan Litchfield, Manager Operations
(403) 894-0418
bryan@exhibitionpark.ca
• Don Young, President
Description:
Thoroughbred, quarter horse race track.
Seating capacity:
3,750

FAIR GROUNDS CORPORATION
1751 GENTILLY BOULEVARD
NEW ORLEANS, LA 70119
504-944-5515
Fax: 504-948-1160
www.fairgroundsracecourse.com
• Bryan G. Krantz, President
• Gordon M Robertson, Director, Mutuels

FAIRMOUNT PARK RACETRACK
9301 COLLINSVILLE ROAD
COLLINSVILLE, IL 62234
618-345-4300
Fax: 314-436-1516
info@fairmountpark.com
www.fairmountpark.com
• Greg Graves, Mutuel Manager
(618) 345-4300
• Nikki Tanner, Group Sales Director
(618) 345-4300
groupsales@fairmountpark.com
• Rajni Kumar, Manager
(618) 345-4300
• Bobby Pace, Racing Secretary
(618) 345-4300
Description:
Founded 1925. Year-round thoroughbred
and harness racing track.
Publications:
THE INSIDE TRACK NEWSLETTER,
quarterly.

FAIRPLEX
1101 W MCKINLEY AVENUE
POMONA, CA 91768
909-623-3111
Fax: 909-865-3602
info@fairplex.com
www.fairplex.com
• Wendy Talarico, Communications
Manager
(909) 865-4263
• Melissa DeMonaco-Tapia, Director of
Sales
(909) 865-4042
demonaco@fairplex.com
Description:
Founded 1922. Home of thoroughbred and
quarter horse racing during the Los Angeles
County Fair each September-October.
Horse shows held regularly throughout the
year. Also hosts National Hot Rod
Association Winternationals (February), and
Winston World Fi
Description:
Founded 1922. Home of thoroughbred and
quarter horse racing during the Los Angeles
County Fair each September-October.
Horse shows held regularly throughout the
year. Also hosts National Hot Rod
Association Winternationals (February), and
Winston World Fi
Seating Capacity
10,000

FINGER LAKES GAMING & RACETRACK
5857 ROUTE 96
PO BOX 25250
FARMINGTON, NY 14425
585-924-3232
Fax: 585-924-3967
smartin@dncinc.com
www.fingerlakesracetrack.com
• Steve Martin, Sr. Director of Marketing and
Gaming
(585) 924-3232
smartin@dncinc.com
• Brad Lewis, Director, Racing
blewis@dncinc.com
• Steve Martin, Director, Publicity/Marketing
smartin@dncinc.com
• Chris Riegle, President and GM
• Vieden Zahariev, Sr.Director of Finance
• Philip Palermo, Director of Operations
• Steve Martin, Sr.Director of Marketing
• Mike Struzyk, Controller
• Charles Petersen, Gaming Manager
• Brian Moore, Director of Marketing
Arena Seating Capacity:
6,000 Seating; 10,000 Total Capacity.
Year Founded:
1962
Track Type:
Dirt, Thoroughbred (no turf course).
Track Size:
1 mile oval.

FINISH LINE MANAGEMENT
1700 JOE YENNI BOULEVARD
KENNER, LA 70065
504-466-8521
Fax: 504-466-3908
• Nick Leggio, Director
Description:
Horse race track.

FONNER PARK
700 E STOLLEY PARK ROAD
PO BOX 490
GRAND ISLAND, NE 68802
308-382-4515
Fax: 308-384-2753
fonnerpark@aol.com
www.fonnerpark.com
• Hugh M. Miner Jr, EVP/Chief Executive Officer
• Bruce Swihart, Chief Operating Officer
• Todd Otto, Assistantt Manager
Description:
Founded 1954. Thoroughbred horse race track. Also serves as civic center for activities throughout the year. Home of the Hall County Fair.
Seating capacity:
8,000

FOUR STATES FAIR & RODEO
3700 E 50TH STREET
TEXARKANA, AR 71854
870-773-2941
800-776-1836
Fax: 870-772-0713
lisab@fourstatesfair.com
www.fourstatesfair.com
• Jimmy Curtis, Chairman of the Board
(870) 773-2941
• Ken Curtis, Concession Manager
(870) 773-2941
kenc@fourstatesfair.com
• Sharon Hays, Office Manager
(870) 773-2941
sharonh@fourstatesfair.com
• Tammy Turk, Marketing Director
(870) 773-2941
tammy@fourstatesfair.com
Arena Seating Capacity:
6,800.00
Year Founded:
1945
Nature of Service:
Multi-purpose entertainment center, fairgrounds and RV year-round parking available.
Track Type:
Ampitheater.

FRASER DOWNS
17755 60TH AVENUE
SURREY, BC, CANADA V3S 1V3
604-576-9141
Fax: 604-576-9821
www.fraserdowns.com
• Chuck Keeling, Vice President Racing Operations
• Keith Quinlan, Racing Secretary
• Dan Jukich, Simulcast Coordinator
• Francis Penny, Marketing Manager/Publicist

FREDERICTON CAPITAL EXHIBIT CENTRE
361 SMYTHE STREET
STATION A
FREDERICTON, NB, CANADA E3B 4Y9
506-458-8819
Fax: 506-458-9294
www.frex.ca
• Joe Bilrout, General Manager/Secretary
• Mike Vokey, Executive Director
mvokey@frex.ca
Year Founded:
1827
Nature of Service:

Harness race track; trade and convention center; ice arena.

FREEHOLD RACEWAY
130 PARK AVENUE
FREEHOLD, NJ 7728
732-462-3800
Fax: 732-462-2920
www.freeholdraceway.com
• Howard Bruno, General Manager
• Mark Rosenthal, Controller
Description:
Located in central New Jersey in the historic town of Freehold, Freehold Raceway was established in 1853 and features live Standardbred barness races for trotters and pacers from August through early June. Also open seven days a week and seven nights year round for thoroughbred and harness racing simulcasts from tracks throughout North America.
Track:
1/2 mile harness racetrack

FREMONT CO. FAIRGROUNDS
1004 LEGION ROAD
SIDNEY, IA 51652
712-374-2715
Fax: 712-374-3286
• Doug Doty, Extension Director
Rodeo Arena Seating Capacity:
8,500
Grandstand Seating Capacity:
5,500

GEORGIA INTERNATIONAL HORSE PARK (GIHP)
1996 CENTENNIAL OLYMPIC PARKWAY
CONYERS, GA 30013
770-860-4190
888-860-4224
Fax: 770-602-2500
www.georgiahorsepark.com
• Darlene Partain, Sales Manager
(770) 860-4198
Seating Capacity:
Grand Prix Stadium 8,000 (plus additional); Charles Walker Arena 25,00 (plus additional)

GREAT CANADIAN GAMING CORPORATION
7485 5TH SIDEROAD
INNISFIL, ONTARIO, CANADA L9S 3S1
705-726-9401
866-915-9400
Fax: 705-726-8364
www.georgiandowns.com
• Chris Roberts, Director of Operations
(705) 726-9401
croberts@georgiandowns.com
• Bruce Barbour, Director of Racing Operations
• Linda Prosser, Pari-Mutuel Manager
(705) 726-9401
lprosser@georgiandowns.com
• Barb Rafuse, Accounting Manger
brafuse@georgiandowns.com
• Jackie Warner, Public Relations
jwarner@georgiandowns.com
• Dexter Hunte, Security Manager
dhunte@georgiandowns.com
• Peter Musgrove, Facilities/Operations Manager
(705) 726-9401
pmusgrove@georgiandowns.com

Arena Seating Capacity:
2,000
Year Founded:
2001
Nature of Service:
Harness Racing, Restaurants, Tele Theatre Lounge, Meetings, Conferences, Slots, Casino.
Tenant(s):
Ontario Lottery and Gaming Corporation, Slots at Georgian Downs.
Description;
Standardbred Racetrack.

GIANTS STADIUM
50 STATE ROUTE 120
E RUTHERFORD, NJ 7073
201-935-8500
Fax: 201-935-7646
publicaffairs@njsea.com
www.njsea.com
• James Minish, SVP, Stadium/Arena
(201) 460-4204
jminish@njsea.com
• Ron Va Veen, VP/Associate General Manager, Booking/Ev
(201) 460-4387
rvandeveen@njsea.com
• Helen Strus, VP, Stadium/Arena Event Marketing
(201) 460-4355
hstruc@njsea.com
• Eric Stover, AVP, Stadium Ops
(201) 460-4299
estover@njsea.com
Description:
Home of the Hambletonian.

GOLDEN GATE FIELDS (GGF)
1100 EASTSHORE HIGHWAY
BERKELEY, CA 94710
510-559-7330
Fax: 510-559-7460
www.goldengatefields.com
• Jack Liebau, General Manager
Seating capacity:
14,750
Year Founded:
1941
Nature of Service:
Thoroughbred race track.

GRAND RIVER RACEWAY (GRR)
7445 WELLINGTON COUNTY ROAD 21
ELORA, ONTARIO, CANADA N0B 1S0
519-846-5455
Fax: 519-846-0206
info@grandriverraceway.com
www.grandriverraceway.com
• Ted Clarke, General Manager
(519) 846-5455
tclarke@GrandRiverRaceway.com
• Kelly Spencer, Marketing/Communications Manager
(519) 846-5455
kspencer@GrandRiverRaceway.com
• Susan Ellis, Administrative Assistant
(519) 846-5455
sellis@grandriverraceway.com
• Helen Bogl, CFO
(519) 846-5455
hbogl@GrandRiverRaceway.com
• Doug McCaig, Facilities manager
(519) 846-5455
• Diane Twasnick, Race Office
(519) 846-1106
raceoffice@GrandRiverRaceway.com

• Amy Clarke, Gift Shop Manager
(519) 846-5455

GULFSTREAM RACING & CASINO PARK
901 S FEDERAL HIGHWAY
HALLANDALE BEACH, FL 33009
954-454-7000
800-771-8873
Fax: 954-457-6510
www.gulfstreampark.com
• Bernie Hettel, Director of Racing
Operations
(954) 457-6138
• David Rovine, Director, Marketing
• Joe Tanenbaum, Director,
Communications
• Dennis Testa, Director, Operations
Description:
Manages Gulfstream Horse Race Track
sponsorships & special events.

HANOVER RACEWAY
265 5TH STREET
HANOVER, ONTARIO, CANADA N4N 3X3
519-364-2860
Fax: 519-364-7314
hanoverraceway@wightman.ca
www.hanoverraceway.com
• Diane Twasnick, Race Secretary
(519) 846-1106
• Gord Dougan, General Manager
• Linda MacDonald, Food and Beverage
Manager

HARRAH'S LOUISIANA DOWNS
8000 E TEXAS STREET
BOSSIER CITY, LA 71111
318-742-5555
800-427-7247
Fax: 318-741-2615
www.harrahslouisianadowns.com
• Lori Megown, Vice President
• Thomas Roberts, General Manager
Description:
Horse race track.

HARRINGTON RACEWAY & CASINO
15 W RIDER ROAD
HARRINGTON, DE 19952
302-398-7223
Fax: 302-398-3056
hri@harringtonraceway.com
www.harringtonraceway.com
• Patricia Key, Chief Operating Officer
pkey@harringtonraceway.com
• James Boese, General Manager
jboese@harringtonraceway.com
• Jim Boese, Director Simulcast/Publicity
Year Founded:
1946
Nature of Service:
Pari-Mutuel harness racing.

HASTINGS RACECOURSE
PNE GATE 8 OR 9
VANCOUVER, BC, CANADA V5K 3N8
604-254-1631
877-677-7702
Fax: 604-251-0411
info@hastingsracecourse.com
www.hastingsracecourse.com
• Mutti Raj, General Manager
ckeeline@gcgaming.com
• Michael Brown, General Manager
mbrown@hastingsracecourse.com
• Geoff Mussellam, Communications

Manager
gmussellam@hastingsracecourse.com
• Raj Mutti, Marketing Manager
rmutti@hastingsracecourse.com
Description:
Thoroughbred horse race track.
Seating capacity:
7,800

HAWTHORNE RACE COURSE
3501 S LARAMIE
STICKNEY/CICERO, IL 60804
708-780-3700
Fax: 708-780-3677
www.sportsmanspark.com
• Tim F. Carey, President & General
Manager
• Howard Fagan, Director, Marketing
• David Zenner, Director Publicity

**HAZEL PARK HARNESS RACEWAY
(HPHR)**
1650 E 10 MILE ROAD
HAZEL PARK, MI 48030
248-398-1000
Fax: 248-398-5236
hazelparkharness@yahoo.com
hazelparkraceway.com
• Ken Marshall, Director Operations
ken.marshall@hazelparkraceway.com
• Ladd Biro, Race Secretary
ladd.biro@hazelparkraceway.com
• Bernard Hartman, VP
• Mike Bozich, Ass. Director of Operations
• Bobbie Walker, Horseman's bookeeper
bobbie.walker@hazelparkraceway.com
• Kathy Deluge, Comptroller
kathy.deluge@hazelparkraceway.com
• Mary Matuszak, Plant Supritendent
• Pete Marvin, Security Director
Description:
Harness horse race track.
Seating capacity:
12,200

HESTAND STADIUM FAIRGROUNDS
420 N BLAKE
PINE BLUFF, AR 71601
870-535-2900
Fax: 870-534-2864
www.pinebluffchamber.com
• Greg Gustek, Director
(870) 536-7600
• Susie Madsen, Visitor and Group Tour
Information
(870) 536-7600
Seating capacity:
7,000

HIALEAH PARK RACING & CASINO
105 E 21ST STREET
PO BOX 158
HIALEAH, FL 33013
305-885-8000
Fax: 305-887-8006
• John J. Brunetti, Chairman
• Janet Diaz, Media & Website Coordinator
Description:
Founded 1925. Thoroughbred race track.
Seating capacity:
32,000

**HIAWATHA HORSE PARK &
ENTERTAINMENT CENTRE**
1730 LONDON LINE
SARNIA, ONTARIO, CANADA N7T 2H2

519-542-5543
Fax: 519-542-3538
info@hiawathahorsepark.com
www.hiawathahorsepark.com
• James R. Henderson, Owner
• Ryan Trusler, General Manager
• Brian Tominson, Chef
• Linda Fisher, Special Event Manager
• Mary Edwards, Bar Manager
• Becky Ramasay, Bookeeper
Sports Organizaton
Dring Range- 27 automated stations and
expansive grass tee deck; 6 beach volley
ball courts; 2 baseball diamonds; F1 Go
Karting

**HOLLYWOOD CASINO AT PENN
NATIONAL RACE COURSE**
777 HOLLYWOOD BOULEVARD
GRANTVILLE, PA 17028
717-469-2211
Fax: 717-469-2910
Fred.Lipkin@pngaming.com
www.hollywoodpnrc.com
• Gary Luderitz, General Manager
(717) 469-2211
• Fred Lipkin, Publicity Director
(717) 469-2211
Description:
Horse race track.

HOOSIER PARK
4500 DAN PATCH CIRCLE
ANDERSON, IN 46013
765-642-7223
800-526-7223
Fax: 765-644-2754
info@hoosierpark.com
www.hoosierpark.com
• Richard B. Moore, President/General
Manager
• Thomas F. Bannon, VP, Communications
• Donna R. Smith, VP, Marketing
• Brian Elmore, General Manager
Arena Seating Capacity:
3,500.00
Year Founded:
1994
Nature of Service:
Horse Racing, Simulcasting.
Track Type:
Standardbred, Thoroughbred, Quarter
Horse.

HUMBOLDT COUNTY FAIR ASSN
1250 FIFTH STREET
FERNDALE, CA 95536
707-786-9511
Fax: 707-786-9450
humcofair@frontiernet.net
www.humboldtcountyfair.org
• Stuart Titus, General Manager
• Ella Robinson, Racing Secretary
• George Vidak, Mutuel Manager

ILLINOIS OFF TRACK BETTING
13148 RIVERCREST DRIVE
CRESTWOOD, IL 60445
708-489-4700
800-826-3344
Fax: 708-672-5932
• Mike Belmonte, General Manager
• Ken Churilla, Marketing
• Michelle Milligan, Group Sales
Description:
1 mile horse racing facility

facilities

INDIANA STATE FAIR/FAIRGROUNDS
1202 E 38TH STREET
INDIANAPOLIS, IN 46205
317-927-7500
Fax: 317-927-7695
www.in.gov
• Cindy C. Hoye, Executive Director
(317) 927-7500
• Michelle Leavell, Entertainment & Events
Manager
(317) 927-7530
• Andy Klotz, Publicity Coordinator
Year Founded:
1852
Nature of Service:
Horse, quarter midget auto and motorcycle
race tracks; horse shows, ice skating, figure
skating, and rollerblading.

ISLAND GROVE REGIONAL PARK (IGRP)
501 N 14TH AVENUE
GREELEY, CO 80634
970-350-9390
Fax: 970-350-9344
www.greeleygov.com
• Tom Welch, Facility Manager
(950) 350-9522
• Kathy Dilbeck, Scheduling Coordinator
Pro-Rodeo Arena Seating Capacity:
9,300

ISLE CASINO RACING POMPANO PARK
777 ISLE OF CAPRI CIRCLE
POMPANO BEACH, FL 33069
954-972-2000
800-843-4753
Fax: 954-972-7894
www.pompanopark.com
• Doug Shipley, General Manager and the
Corporate Vice President
• Kathleen Jenny, VP Finance
• Steven Wolf, Director,
Marketing/Communications
• Mark Loewe, Director,
Racing/Simulcasting

JEFFERSON COUNTY FAIRGROUNDS (JCF)
15200 W 6TH AVENUE
SUITE A
GOLDEN, CO 80401
303-271-6600
Fax: 303-271-6606
www.co.jefferson.co.us
• Mark A Danner, Director
mdanner@jeffco.us
• Sherry Burgener, Administrative
Coordinator
• Scott L. Gales, Director
sgales@jeffco.us

KANSAS STATE FAIR (KSF)
2000 N POPLAR STREET
HUTCHINSON, KS 67502-5562
620-669-3600
800-362-3247
Fax: 620-669-3640
info@kansasstatefair.com
www.kansasstatefair.com
• Lori Mulch, Assistant General Manager
• Denny Stoecklein, General Manager
• Mary Holmes, Director, Special Events
Horse Exhibition Seating Capacity:
1,500
Grandstand Seating Capacity:
10,000

KAWARTHA DOWNS & SPEEDWAY
1382 COUNTY ROAD
SUITE 28
FRASERVILLE, ONTARIO, CANADA K0L
1V0
705-939-6316
Fax: 705-939-6342
race@kawarthadowns.com
www.kawarthadowns.com
• Derek Lynch, Speedway Manager
(705) 939-6316
derekL@kawarthadowns.com
• Jenn Fraser, Manager of Security Services
(705) 939-6316
jfraser@kawarthadowns.com
Seating capacity:
2,000
Description:
Harness horse race track.

KAY ROGERS PARK
4400 MIDLAND BOULEVARD
FORT SMITH, AR 72904
479-783-6176
800-364-1080
Fax: 479-782-9944
www.kayrogerspark.com
• Rebecca, Accounting - Administration
rebecca@kayrogerspark.com
• Cindy, Futurity - Administration
cindy@kayrogerspark.com

KEENELAND ASSOCIATION, INC
4201 VERSAILLES ROAD
PO BOX 1690
LEXINGTON, KY 40510
859-254-3412
800-456-3412
Fax: 859-255-2484
webmaster@keeneland.com
www.keeneland.com
• Nick C. Nicholson, President/Chief
Executive Officer
• Harvie Wilkinson, VP
• W.B. Ro Beasley, Director, Racing
• Bill Thomason, President and CEO
• Vince Gabbert, VP, COO
• Walt Robertson, VP of Sales
• Brad Lovell, VP, Chief Information Officer
• Rogers Beasley, VP of racing
• Connie V Onselder, VP, CFO
Year Founded:
1936
Nature of Service:
Thoroughbred race course and auction
company.

LAKE COUNTY FAIR
889 S COURT STREET
PO BOX 327
CROWN POINT, IN 46308
219-663-3617
Fax: 219-662-6013
lcfsecretary@lake-county-fair.com
www.lake-county-fair.com
• Bub Wise Roland, President
• Zern Hayden, 1st VP
• Tom Lump, VP
• Arlene Marcinek, Secretary
Horse Arena Seating Capacity:
1,500
Grandstand Seating Capacity:
2,000

LAUREL PARK
ROUTE 198 & RACETRACK ROAD
PO BOX 130
LAUREL, MD 20725
301-725-0400
800-638-1859
Fax: 301-725-4561
info@marylandracing.com
www.laurelpark.com
• Joe De Francis, President/Chief Executive
Officer
• Ron Charles, COO
• Douglas J. Illig, Chief Financial Officer
• John Mooney, President, Racing Services
Year Founded:
1911
Nature of Service:
Thoroughbred race track.

LES BOIS PARK
5610 GLENWOOD STREET
GARDEN CITY, ID 83714
208-258-2177
800-376-3991
Fax: 208-321-4820
• Duayne Dideriksen, General Manager
• Roger White, Director, Racing
• Ron Andreoli, Simulcast Coordinator
• Kerry Lawson, GM
(208) 258-2177
• Tim Thibert, Racing secretary
(208) 258-2181
• Melinda Nothern, Marketing & Public
Relations
(208) 867-5847
Description:
Horse race track.

LOS ALAMITOS RACE COURSE
4961 KATELLA AVENUE
LOS ALAMITOS, CA 90720
714-820-2800
Fax: 714-995-6276
larace@losalamitos.com
www.losalamitos.com
• Ed Allred, Chairman & CEO
eallred@losalamitos.com
• Orlando Gutierrez, Marketing Director &
Media
(714) 820-2690
larace@losalamitos.com
• Jeff TRUE, Director, Marketing
• Ed Allred, Owner
Description:
Horse race track.

MARSHFIELD FAIR
140 MAIN STREET
PO BOX 5
MARSHFIELD, MA 2050
781-834-6629
Fax: 781-834-6750
www.marshfieldfair.org
• Ray McKay, Fair Director
• Carleton Chandler, Secretary/Treasurer
• Leonardo S. LaForest, President
• Richard Harlfinger, Vice President
• William Frugoli, Auditor
Description:
Founded 1867.

MAYWOOD PARK
8600 W N AVENUE
MELROSE PARK, IL 60160
708-343-4800
800-748-5782

Fax: 708-343-2564
www.maywoodpark.com
• Jim Hannon, Director, Public Relations
• Duke Johnston, President
duke@maywoodpark.com
Description:
Horse race track.

METRAPARK
308 6TH AVENUE N
PO BOX 2514
BILLINGS, MT 59103
406-256-2400
800-366-8538
Fax: 406-256-2479
www.metrapark.com
• Wood Faye, President
• Sandra Hawke, Marketing Director
Grandstand Seating:
8,500

MOHAWK RACETRACK
9430 GUELPH LINE
CAMPBELLVILLE, ON, CANADA L0P 1B0
416-675-7223
888-675-7223
Fax: 416-213-2128
jss@woodbineentertainment.com
www.woodbineentertainment.com
• David Willmot, Chairman and Chief
Executive Officer
• Nick Eaves, President
• Jamie Martin, EVP Racing
• Steve Koch, VP Thoroughbred Racing
• Bruce Murray, VP Standardbred Racing
Seating capacity:
7,000
Description:
Harness horse race track.

MOHEGAN SUN POCONO DOWNS
1280 HIGHWAY 315
WILKES-BARRE, PA 18702
570-831-2100
888-878-3696
Fax: 570-823-9407
mythoughts@mohegansunpocono.com
www.poconodowns.com
• Conrad Sonkowiak, VP of Racing
• John Zimich, Public Relations Director
• Dale Rapson, Operations Manager

MONMOUTH PARK
175 OCEANPORT AVENUE
OCEANPORT, NJ 7757
732-222-2100
Fax: 732-571-5240
monmouthinfo@njsea.com
www.monmouthpark.com
• Dennis O. Dowd, SVP, Racing
(201) 842-5027
bgarland@njsea.com
• Robert Kulina, VP/General Manager
(732) 571-5545
bkulina@njsea.com
• Bob Juliano, Director, Facilities
(732) 571-5486
bjuliano@njsea.com
• James Jeamas, VP, Finance
(732) 571-5551
jjeamas@njsea.com
Description:
Thoroughbred horse race track.
Seating capacity:
50,000

MONTICELLO RACEWAY
204 ROUTE 17B
PO BOX 5013
MONTICELLO, NY 12701
845-794-4100
Fax: 845-791-7060
swiles@empireresorts.com
www.monticelloraceway.com
• Cliff Ehrlich, Executive VP & GM
(845) 794-4100
cehrlich@empireresorts.com
• Shawn Wiles, General Manager
(845) 794-4100
swiles@empireresorts.com
• Eric Warner, Director of Racing
(845) 794-4100
• John Manzi, Director, Public Relations
(845) 794-4100
jmanzi@empireresorts.com
Description:
Harness Race Track.

MOUNTAINEER CASINO, RACE TRACK & RESORT
MOUNTAINEER CIRCLE, ROUTE 2
CHESTER, WV 26034
304-387-8000
800-804-0468
info@mtrgaming.com
www.moreatmountaineer.com
• Tim Ameault, President/Chief Executive
Officer
• Tamara Pettit, Director, Public Relations
• Rosemary Williams, Director of Racing
• Jeffery J Dahl, President and CEO
• John W Bittner, EVP and CFO
• Joseph L Billhimer, EVP and COO
• Fred A Buro, VP and Chief Marketing
Officer
• Steven M Biilik, Chairman
• Rober A Blatt, Vice Chairman
Description:
Founded 1951. Thoroughbred race track
with mini-resort.
Permanent seating capacity:
7,000

NEBRASKA STATE FAIR
1811 WEST 2ND STREET
GRAND ISLAND, NE 68803
308-382-1620
Fax: 308-384-1555
info@statefair.org
www.statefair.org
• Joseph McDermott, Executive Director
• Connie Decker, Ticket Manager
cdecker@statefair.org
• Jana Kruger, Chairperson
• Joseph McDermott, Executive Director
• Kelly O' Brien, Administrative Assistant
• Chelsey Junqck, Entairtainment Director
• Valerie Brewer, Entairtainment Assistant
• Scott Yound, Maintainance Director
• Bill Angell, Supritenent
Description:
Thoroughbred horse race track. Late model
car races.
Seating capacity:
6,000
Seating Capacity:
1,860

NEW MEXICO STATE FAIR
300 SAN PEDRO NE
ALBUQUERQUE, NM 87108

505-222-9700
Fax: 505-266-7784
www.exponm.com
• Mike Cerletti, General Manager
• Kathy Duffy, Marketing Director
• Dan Mouring, General Manager
• John C Jaramillo, Deputy Manager
• Ken Salazar, Operations Manager
• Sally Mayer, Sr. Manager
• Bill Nordin, CFO
• Alison Haxton, Event Coordinator
Description:
Founded 1938, to hold 17-day agricultural
exposition.

AQUEDUCT
110-00 ROCKAWAY BOULEVARD
PO BOX 90
JAMAICA, NY 11420
718-641-4700
800-221-6266
Fax: 718-843-0054
nyra@nyrainc.com
www.nyra.com
• Barry K K. Schwartz, Chairman/Chief
Executive Officer
• Terrence Meyocks, President/Chief
Operating Officer
• Alec Ingle, Chief Financial
Officer/Assistant to the
• David Skorton, Chairman
• Anthhony J Bonomo, President
• Rick Cotton, EVP
• Michael J Giudice, Sr .M.D
• Michael Dubb, Principal
• Bobby Flay, Team
• Robert Megna, Budget Director
Description:
Thoroughbred horse race track.

NORTHVILLE DOWNS
301 SOUTH CENTER STREET
NORTHVILLE, MI 48167
248-349-1000
800-270-7117
Fax: 248-348-8955
www.northvilledowns.com
• Zayti Margaret, Executive Manager
• Louis E. Carlo, Director, Operations
• Michael Janchick, Race Secretary
Description:
Horse race track.

OAKLAWN JOCKEY CLUB
2705 CENTRAL AVENUE
PO BOX 699
HOT SPRINGS, AR 71901
501-624-4950
800-625-5236
Fax: 501-623-4088
winning@oaklawn.com
www.oaklawn.com
• Charles J. Cella, Owner/President
• Eric Jackson, General Manager
ejackson@oaklawn.com
• Bobby Geiger, Director
Mutuels/Simulcasting
• Craig Holtz, Operations Director
Description:
Founded 1904. Thoroughbred horse race
track.
Seating capacity:
27,000

PAXRACING
3001 STREET ROAD
PO BOX 1000
BENSALEM, PA 19020
215-639-9000
888-238-2946
Fax: 215-639-0337
www.parxracing.com
• Joe Wilson, Chief Operating Officer
• Len Carey, Senior Vice President/Facilities
• Bill Barnes, Director Mutuels
Description:
Founded 1974. Thoroughbred horse race track.
Seating capacity:
9,400

PENN NATIONAL RACECOURSE
777 HOLLYWOOD BOULEVARD
PO BOX 32
GRANTVILLE, PA 17028
717-469-2211
Fax: 717-469-2910
Fred.Lipkin@pngaming.com
www.hollywoodpnrc.com
• Gary Luderitz, General Manager
(717) 469-2211
• Fred Lipkin, Publicity & Marketing Director
(717) 469-2211
Description:
Thoroughbred horse race track.
Seating capacity:
6,500

PIMA COUNTY FAIR
11300 S HOUGHTON ROAD
TUCSON, AZ 85747
520-762-9100
Fax: 520-762-5005
Office@Pimacountyfair.com
www.pimacountyfair.com
• Jon Baker, Executive Director
(520) 762-9100
Jon@pimacountyfair.com
• Jon Baker, Executive Director
ext 14
• Bryon Lopez, CFO
• Peggy Bauernfeind, Administrative
Assistant, Interim Events
• Diane McDonald, Accountant
• Launa Rabago, Marketing Manager
(520) 762-9100
launa@pimacountyfair.com
• Phyllis Armbruster, Concession Manager
• Bert Rodriguez, Maintenance Manager
Horse Arena Seating Capacity:
3,000
Livestock Arena Seating Capacity:
3,000
Rodeo Arena Seating Capacity:
3,000
Super Stage Field:
64,000

PIMLICO RACE COURSE
5201 PARK HEIGHTS AVENUE
BALTIMORE, MD 21215
410-542-9400
800-638-3811
Fax: 410-542-1221
info@marylandracing.com
www.pimlico.com
• Karen A. Weiss, Director of Group Sales
(301) 470-5439
kweiss@marylandracing.com
• Robert Dipietro, EVP

• James Mango, Chief Operating Officer
• Martin Jacobs, General Counsel
Year Founded:
1870
Nature of Service:
Thoroughbred race track.

PLATTE COUNTY AGRICULTURAL SOCIETY
822 15 STREET
COLUMBUS, NE 68601
402-564-0133
Fax: 402-564-0990
www.agpark.com
• Gary Wiese, President
• Patty Laska, Office Manager
• Leon Ebel, Mutuels Manager
(402) 564-9711
Seating capacity:
4,000.00
Year Founded:
1941
Track Type:
Dirt.
Nature of Service:
Thoroughbred horse racing. Live from July - September. Simulcast year-round.

PORTLAND MEADOWS
1001 N SCHMEER ROAD
PORTLAND, OR 97217
503-285-9144
800-888-7576
Fax: 503-737-1038
www.portlandmeadows.com
• William Alempijevic, General Manager
• William Alamplijevlc, General Manager
• Patrick J. Kerrison, Director, Operations
• Cheryl Jones, Director/Off Track Wagering/OTBs
• Jerry P Kohls, Director of racing
jerry.kohls@portlandmeadows.com
• Kelth Jones, Mutuel Manager
• Kent Hunter, Manager
kent.hunter@portlandmeadows.com
• Brlan Vierck, Manager of Guest Services
• John McSwain, Security Manager
Description:
Thoroughbred horse race track.
Seating capacity:
5,000

PRAIRIE MEADOWS RACETRACK AND CASINO, INC
1 PRAIRIE MEADOWS DRIVE
PO BOX 1000
ALTOONA, IA 50009
515-967-1000
800-325-9015
chuck.schott@prairiemeadows.com
www.prairiemeadows.com
• Gary Palmer, President / CEO
gary.palmer@prairiemeadows.com
• Ann Atkin, VP Operations
ann.atkin@prairiemeadows.com
• Derron Heldt, Director, Racing
• Tom Manning, Director, Marketing/Sales/Public Relatio
Year Founded:
1989
Nature of Service:
Horse race track.
Seating capacity:
5,000
Overall capacity:
8,000

QUINTE EX FALL FAIR
18 YEOMAN STREET
BEN BLEECKER BUILDING
BELLEVILLE, ONTARIO, CANADA K8P 3X2
613-968-3266
Fax: 613-968-3956
info@qer.ca
www.qer.ca
• Marilynne Cotten, President
(613) 966-3266
• Liz Muldoon, Second VP
(613) 475-8890

RACEWAY PARK
5700 TELEGRAPH ROAD
TOLEDO, OH 43612
419-476-7751
Fax: 419-476-7979
racewayparkinfo@pngaming.com
• John McNamara, Director of Marketing & Guest Services
john.mcnamara@pngaming.com
• Craig Laginess, Finance Director
craig.laginess@pngaming.com
• Bruce Patterson, Facilities Director
bruce.patterson@pngaming.com
• Ron Hornyak, Mutuels Manager
ron.hornyak@pngaming.com
• Matt Clark, Simucast Director
matt.clark@pngaming.com
• Mark Loewe, General Manager
Description:
Harness horse race track.
Seating capacity:
5,700

RED MILE, THE
1200 RED MILE ROAD
LEXINGTON, KY 40504
859-255-0752
Fax: 859-231-0217
info@theredmile.com
www.theredmile.com
• Joe Costa, President & CEO
• Donna Bradford, Director Operations
• Nick Salvi, Race Secretary
• Connie Hochstetler, Racing Secretary
• Shannon Cobb, CFO
• Julie Sorrell, Director of Mutuels

REMINGTON PARK
ONE REMINGTON PLACE
OKLAHOMA CITY, OK 73111
405-424-1000
800-456-4244
Fax: 405-425-3234
contact@remingtonpark.com
www.remingtonpark.com
• Frank Stronach, Chairman
• Mike Corey, Chief Steward
• Fred Hutton, Director, Racing
• Matt Vance, Director, Operations
Year Founded:
1988
Nature of Sports Service:
Founded 1988. Thoroughbred, quarter horse race track.
Seating capacity:
12,000
Publications:
THE REMINGTON POST, monthly during racing seasons.

RETAMA PARK
1 RETAMA PARKWAY
SELMA, TX 78154

210-651-7000
Fax: 210-651-7097
run@retamapark.com
www.retamapark.com
• Brian P. Brown, Chief Executive Officer
• Joe R. Straus, Jr., Board Chairman
• Larry Craft, Director, Racing
• Jackie F. Hart, Director, Mutuels
Physical Address:
1 Ratama Pkwy, Selma, TX 78265-7535
Description:
Thoroughbred and Quarter Horse race track.

RIDEAU CARLETON RACEWAY
4837 ALBION ROAD
OTTAWA, ON, CANADA K1X 1A3
613-822-2211
Fax: 613-822-1586
www.rcr.net
• Alexei Vidal, Marketing Coordinator
(613) 822-2211
alexei.vidal@hrcottawa.com
• Monica Boudreau, Account Manager
(613) 236-5444
monica@blackiron.agency
• Kenzie Scott, Account Manager
(613) 236-5444
kenzie@blackiron.agency
Year Founded:
1962
Nature of Sports Service:
Harness race track.

ROCKINGHAM PARK
ROCKINGHAM PARK BOULEVARD
PO BOX 47
SALEM, NH 3079
603-898-2311
Fax: 603-893-7284
• Ozzie Cole, Racing Secretary
(603) 898-2311
raceoffice@rockinghampark.com
• Ed Callahan, President/General Manager
(603) 898-2311
ECallahan@rockinghampark.com
• Edward Keelan, VP
• Ed Ca Callahan, President/GM
(603) 898-2311
ecallahan@rockinghampark.com
• Kathleen Brothers, Vp/Mutuel Manager
(603) 898-2311
Mutuels@rockinghampark.com
• John Vitale, Ass.Genaral Manage
(603) 898-2311
admissions@rockinghampark.com
• Robert Black, Admissions Director
(603) 898-2311
admissions@rockinghampark.com
• Ron Oldeman, TV Control
(603) 898-2311
RockTV@rockinghampark.com
• Bob Tolman, Comptroller
(603) 898-2311
BTolman@rockinghampark.com
• Skip Burbine, Money Room Settlement
(603) 898-2311
Mutuels@rockinghampark.com
Year Founded:
1906
Seating capacity:
10,000
Nature of Service:
Thoroughbred horse track.
Track Type:
Harness

ROSECROFT RACEWAY
6336 ROSECROFT DRIVE
FORT WASHINGTON, MD 20744
301-567-4500
Fax: 301-567-9267
www.rosecroft.com
• Scott Warren, Director of Racing & Simulcasting
• Lisa Watts, VP Mutuels & Operations
• Greg Boehmer, Simulcast Manager
• Christopher M McErlean, VP
christopher.mcerlean@pngaming.com
• Lisa Watts, Director of Operations
lisa.watts@pngaming.com
• Lisa White, Director of Finance
lisa.white@pngaming.com
• Michael Wandishin, Racing Secretary
michael.wandishin@pngaming.com
Description:
Harness horse race track.
Seating capacity:
3,000

RUIDOSO DOWNS RACE TRACK CASINO
26225 US HWY 70
RUIDOSO DOWNS, NM 88346
575-378-4431
Fax: 505-378-4631
info@raceruidoso.com
www.ruidownsracing.com
• R. D. Hubbard, Owner
• Bruce Rimbo, President
• Rick Baugh, General Manager
• Vicki McCabe, Director, Personnel

SAN JOAQUIN COUNTY FAIR
1658 S AIRPORT WAY
STOCKTON, CA 95206
209-466-5041
Fax: 209-466-5739
www.sanjoaquinfair.com
• Mitch Slater, President
• Victoria Salazar, Vice President
• George Vidak, Manager, Mutuel
• Nanett Martin, President
• Tori Verber, President
• Joe Valente, VP
• Sam Fant, BOD
Description:
Thoroughbred, quarter horse race track.
Seating capacity:
5,000

SANDOWN PARK
1810 GLAMORGAN ROAD
PO BOX 2370
SIDNEY, BC, CANADA V8L 3Y3
250-656-1631
Fax: 250-656-7422
• Jackie Ballas, Director, Operations
• Chuck Keeling, General Manager
• Keith Quinlan, Secretary, Racing
Description:
Horse race track.

SANTA ANITA PARK
285 W HUNTINGTON DRIVE
PO BOX 60014
ARCADIA, CA 91007
626-574-7223
888-338-7223
Fax: 626-446-1456
info@santaanita.com
www.santaanita.com
• Charles Ron, President
• Jim McAlpine, Chief Financial Officer

• Chris McCarron, VP and General Manager
• Stuart Zanzille, Marketing Manager
Description:
Founded 1934. Thoroughbred horse race track.
Seating capacity:
26,000

SARATOGA RACETRACK
NYRA
PO BOX 90
JAMAICA, NY 11417
718-641-4700
888-285-5961
Fax: 518-581-4064
info@southernsaratoga.org
www.saratogaracetrack.org
• George Hathaway, Facilities Manager
Description:
Horse race track.

SCIOTO DOWNS
6000 S HIGH STREET
PO BOX 7823
COLUMBUS, OH 43207
614-295-4700
800-723-6967
Fax: 614-295-8871
www.sciotodowns.com
• Ryan T. Edward, President
• Jerry Kalb, Assistant General Manager
• Anne Doolin, Director, Publicity and Marketing
Description:
Harness horse race track.

SIKESTON JAYCEE BOOTHEEL RODEO ARENA
1220 N INGRAM ROAD
PO BOX 5
SIKESTON, MO 63801
573-471-7196
800-455-2855
Fax: 573-471-1540
info@sikestonrodeo.com
www.sikestonrodeo.com
• Jason Pounds, President
• Ron Payne, VP
• Jon Gilmore, Secretary
Seating Capacity:
7,000

SOLANO COUNTY FAIRGROUNDS
900 FAIRGROUNDS DRIVE
VALLEJO, CA 94589
707-551-2000
Fax: 707-642-7947
bdill@scfair.org
www.scfair.org
• Michael Paluszak, General Manager
(707) 551-2000
mpaluszak@scfair.org
• Trina Gonzalez, Executive Assistant to General Manager
• Patrick Skelton, Deputy General Manager
• Michael Passey, GM
• Kim Mini, Events Coordinator
(707) 551-2006
• Eric Burke, Food Department
(707) 551-2014
• Mark Coffman, Security Supervisor
(707) 551-2013
• Rene Edens, Place Manager
(707) 551-2030
Description:
Founded 1940.

facilities

SONOMA COUNTY FAIRGROUNDS
1350 BENNETT VALLEY ROAD
PO BOX 1536
SANTA ROSA, CA 95404
707-545-4200
Fax: 707-573-9342
info@sonomacountyfair.com
www.sonomacountyfair.com
• Tawny J. Tesconi, Fair Manager
(707) 545-4200
• Mike Runyan, President
Description:
Horse race track.
Stadium Seating Capacity:
4,000
Track Seating Capacity:
5,000
Track Size:
1.25 miles

SPORTS CREEK RACEWAY
4290 MORRISH ROAD
PO BOX 207
SWARTZ CREEK, MI 48473
810-635-3333
Fax: 810-635-9711
www.sportscreek.com
• Chris Locking, General Manager
Description:
Harness horse race track.

SUDBURY DOWNS
400 BONIN ROAD
CHELMSFORD, ON, CANADA P0M 1L0
705-855-9001
sudburydowns@gmail.com
www.sudburydowns.com
Year Founded:
1974
Nature of Sports Service:
Harness horse race track.

SUFFOLK DOWNS
525 MC CLELLAN HIGHWAY
EAST BOSTON, MA 2128
617-567-3900
800-225-3460
Fax: 617-567-7511
www.suffolkdowns.com
• John Hall, II, President
• Chip Tuttle, Chief Operating Officer
• John Morrissey, Racing Secretary
• Sam Elliott, Assistant Racing Secy
Description:
Thoroughbred horse race track.
Seating capacity:
60,000.00

SULKY TROIS RIVIERES
1850 RUE DE L HIPODROME
PO BOX 1565
TROIS RIVIERES, QC, CANADA G9A 5L6
819-374-6734
Fax: 819-376-4453
• Frenette Benoit, Race Secretary
• Ginette Ricard, SC Field Representative

SUNLAND PARK RACETRACK & CASINO
1200 FUTURITY DRIVE
SUNLAND PARK, NM 88063-9057
505-874-5200
800-572-1142
Fax: 505-589-1518
sunlandinfo@sunland-park.com
www.sunland-park.com

• Harold Payne, Resident Manager
• Adeline Rogers, Director, Marketing
• Linda Robb, Facilities Manager
• Bruce Bruebaker, Director, Human
Resource

TAMPA BAY DOWNS
11225 RACETRACK ROAD
TAMPA, FL 33626
813-855-4401
866-823-6967
Fax: 813-854-3539
customerservice@tampabaydowns.com
www.tampabaydowns.com
• Margo Flynn, VP Marketing
Description:
1 mile dirt/turf track

THE DOWNS RACETRACK & CASINO AT ALBUQUERQUE
201 CALIFORNIA STREET NE
ALBUQUERQUE, NM 87108
505-266-5555
Fax: 505-268-1970
michaell@abqdowns.com
www.abqdowns.com
• Craig Smith, General Manager
• Don Cook, Director Racing

THE SHOW PLACE ARENA & PRINCE GEORGE'S EQUESTRIAN CENTER
14900 PENNSYLVANIA AVENUE
UPPER MARLBORO, MD 20772
301-952-7900
Fax: 301-952-8167
showplacearena@pgparks.com
www.showplacearena.com
• Bill Chambers, General Manager
(301) 952-7906
william.chambers@pgparks.com
• Nancy Weiman, Marketing Manager
(301) 952-7913
nancy.weiman@pgparks.com
Seating Capacity:
Stadium/Arena 5,500
Sports:
Basketball, horse shows, other
Events:
Capital Challenge Horse Show, Atlantic 10
Women's Basketball Championship, Fall &
Spring Home Shows and Concerts. Host of
the 2012 CAA Women's Basketball
Championship.
Description:
The Show Place Arena and Prince George's
Equestrian Center, suburban Washington
D.C.'s most versatile sports & entertainment
venue - creates a unique setting for sporting
events. With flexible seating, concessions,
parking, air conditioning, and banquet rooms
available. Also available outdoor equestrian
lighted show rings, stabling, schooling rings,
and secretaries booth with PA system.

THISTLEDOWN RACINO
21501 EMERY ROAD
CLEVELAND, OH 44128
216-662-8600
800-289-9956
Fax: 216-662-5339
www.caesars.com
• Brent D. Reitz, General Manager
• Heather McColloch, Publicity Director
• Greg Davis, Simulcasting
• Bob Hickey, Simulcasting
Description:
Thoroughbred horse race track.

Seating capacity:
7,500

THREE COUNTY FAIR
3 COUNTY FAIR
HAMPSHIRE
NORTHAMPTON, MA 01060-0305
413-584-2237
info@3countyfair.com
www.3countyfair.com
• Alan Jacque, President
Description:
Founded 1818.

THUNDER RIDGE RACING AND ENTERTAINMENT COMPLEX
164 THUNDER ROAD
PRESTONBURG, KY 41653
606-886-7223
Fax: 606-886-7225
asratliff@yahoo.com
www.thunderridgeharness.com
• Ann Reeder, General Manager/President
• Wilma Foley, Mutuels
• Anita Ratliff, GM
Description:
Harness horse race track.

TURF PARADISE
1501 W BELL ROAD
PHOENIX, AZ 85023
602-942-1101
Fax: 602-942-8659
tp@turfparadise.net
www.turfparadise.com
• Jerry Simms, Chairman
• Dave Johnson, VP & Assistant General
Manager
Description:
Horse race track.

TURFWAY PARK
7500 TURFWAY ROAD
PO BOX 8
FLORENCE, KY 41042
859-371-0200
800-733-0200
Fax: 859-647-4730
spinson@tpark.com
www.turfway.com
• Robert N. Elliston, President & CEO
• Clifford Reed, VP/Chief Financial Officer
• Daniel Bach, General Manager
• Rick Leigh, Racing Secretary
• Sherry Pinson, Director of
Communications
• Tyler Picklesimer, Assistant Racing
Secretary
Description:
Horse race track established in 1959.
Stabling for 1,000 horses. One-mile
Polytrack racing surface with quarter-mile
and 6 1/2-furlong chutes. Live racing
December-March. Simulcast racing
year-round.

VERNON DOWNS
4229 STUHLMAN ROAD
VERNON, NY 13476
315-829-2201
877-88-3766
Fax: 315-829-3320
info@vernondowns.com
www.vernondowns.com
• Pete Savage, President
• Paul V. Noyes, Secretary

- James R. Wise, Chief Financial Officer/Treasurer
- Don Hoover, Director, Racing/Simulcasting

WESTERN FAIR ENTERTAINMENT CENTRE
316 RECTORY STREET
PO BOX 7550
LONDON, ONTARIO, CANADA N5W 53V9
519-438-7203
800-619-4629
Fax: 519-679-3124
- Hugh Mitchell, CEO
- Dave Taylor, Senior Marketing Manager
dtaylor@westernfair.com
- Ian Fleaming, Acting Raceway Manager
ifleaming@westernfair.com
- Reg Ash, CFO
- Mike Woods, COO
- Michelle Campbell, Chairperson
- Don McCallum, Vice Chairman
- Janet Carr, Member
- Pam Kelly, Assistant Raceway Manager
pkelly@westernfair.com
Description:
Founded 1960. Harness horse race track.
Seating capacity:
4,500

WOODBINE ENTERTAINMENT
555 REXDALE BOULEVARD
PO BOX 156
TORONTO, ON, CANADA M9W 5L2
416-675-7223
888-675-7223
Fax: 416-213-2129
kbm@woodbineentertainment.com
www.woodbineentertainment.com
- David Willmot, Chairman/Chief Executive Officer
- Nicholas Eaves, President/Chief Operating Officer

WOODLANDS RACE PARK
9700 LEAVENWORTH ROAD
PO BOX 12036
KANSAS CITY, KS 66109
913-299-9797
Fax: 913-299-9804
www.woodlandskc.com
- Jayme A LaRocca, General Manager
- Howard T. Grace, President
Description:
Quarter horse and thoroughbred horse racetrack (one-mile Oval).
Seating capacity:
20,000. The Woodlands racing complex is a dual-horse and greyhound racing facility with two separate tracks.

WOODSTOCK RACEWAY
875 NELLIS STREET
WOODSTOCK, ON, CANADA N4S 8Z9
519-537-4808
woodstock@gatewaycasinos.ca
woodstock.gatewaycasinos.com

YONKERS RACEWAY
810 YONKERS AVENUE
YONKERS, NY 10704
914-968-4200
Fax: 914-968-4479
www.empirecitycasino.com
- Timothy J J Rooney, President
- Robert J. Galterio, General Manager

- Denis Moran, Assistant General Manager
- Jack Moran, Mutuel Director, Live Racing

Race Tracks - Greyhound

BEST BET
201 MONUMENT ROAD
PO BOX 54249
JACKSONVILLE, FL 32225
904-646-0001
Fax: 904-646-0420
www.bestbetjax.com
- Howard Korman, President
- Jamie Shelton, CFO
jamies@bestbetjax.com
- Howard Korman, President
howardk@bestbetjax.com
- Matt Kroetz, COO
mattk@bestbetjax.com
- Deborah Giardina, Executive Director of Poker
deborahg@bestbetjax.com
- Jesse Hollander, Associate Director
jesseh@bestbetjax.com
- Brett Howard, Room Manager
bretth@bestbetjax.com
- Marty Fontes, Race Director
martyf@bestbetjax.com
- Howard Korman, CEO
Description:
Greyhound racing track.

BLUFFS RUN
2701 23RD AVENUE
COUNCIL BLUFFS, IA 51501
712-323-2500
800-238-2946
Fax: 712-322-9354
- Weien Peter J, SVP/GM
- Julie Pritchard, Director, Marketing
- Dianne Wegley, Human Resource Director
Description:
Greyhound racing track.

CORPUS CHRISTI GREYHOUND RACE TRACK
5302 LEOPARD STREET
ST.CORPUS CHRISTI, TX 78408
361-289-9333
Fax: 361-289-4307
CCGRT1@yahoo.com
www.corpuschristidogs.com
- Triplett Jacques, General Manager
(361) 289-4301
cccrt@aol.com
- Michelle Gonzalez, Administrative Assistant
(361) 289-4306
- Jim Austin, Mutuels Manager
(361) 289-4321
- Norman T. Campbell, Simulcast Coordinator and Decoder
(305) 649-3000
Arena Seating Capacity:
1,952.00
Year Founded:
1990
Track Type:
Greyhound.
Track Size:
1/4 mile.

DAIRYLAND GREYHOUND PARK, INC
5522-104TH AVENUE
KENOSHA, WI 53144

262-657-8200
800-233-3357
Fax: 262-657-8231
dgpinfo@dairylandgp.com
- William O. Agpar, Jr., VP Operations/General Manager
- Danny Crouch, Director Mutuels/Asst General Manager
- Paul Lu Jr, Director, Publicity and Marketing
Description:
Greyhound racing track.

DAYTONA BEACH KENNEL CLUB
960 S WILLAMSON BOULEVARD
PO BOX 11470
DAYTONA BEACH, FL 32114
386-252-6484
Fax: 386-255-6075
breid@dncinc.com
www.daytonagreyhound.com
- Daniel Francati, General Manager
(386) 252-6484
dfrancat@dncinc.com
- Michael Stringer, Asst General Manager/Food & Beverage Manager
(386) 252-6484
mstringe@dncinc.com
Description:
Greyhound racing track.

DERBY LANE
10490 GANDY BOULEVARD NORTH
SAINT PETERSBURG, FL 33702-2395
727-812-3339
Fax: 727-579-4362
marketg@derbylane.com
www.derbylane.com
- David Tiano, Chief Operations Officer
- Bill Van Hoogen, Director of Racing
- Stephen P. Hlas, Secretary/Treasurer
Description:
Greyhound racing track.

DUBUQUE GREYHOUND PARK AT MYSTIQUE
1855 GREYHOUND PARK ROAD
DUBUQUE, IA 52004-3190
563-582-3647
800-373-3647
Fax: 563-582-9074
joeya@mystiquedbq.com
www.mystiquedbq.com
- Brian Carpenter, Racing Director
(563) 585-2970
brianc@mystiquedbq.com
Seating Capacity:
Grandstand 400; Outdoor 200
Track:
Greyhound Track; 3/19 of a mile, 5/16 of a mile, 3/8 of a mile, 7/16 of a mile.

FLAGLER DOG TRACK
450 NW 37TH AVENUE
PO BOX 350940
MIAMI, FL 33125
305-649-3000
888-56-MAGIC
Fax: 305-631-4525
info@magiccitycasino.com
www.magiccitycasino.com
- Hutchinson William, General Manager
(305) 649-3000
whutchinson@flaglerdogs.com
- Fred Havenick, President and Chief Executive Officer
(305) 649-3000

Arena Seating Capacity:
2,000
Year Founded
1934
Nature of Service:
For simulcasting, live greyhound racing and poker.
Track Type:
Sand and Marl greyhound track.

GENEVA LAKES GREYHOUND TRACK
1600 E GENEVA STREET
INTERSTATE 43 HIGHWAY 50
DELAVAN, WI 53115
262-728-8000
800-477-4552
Fax: 262-728-6103
www.genevagreyhounds.com
• Roth Milt, General Manager
• Rebecca Krahn, Mutuel Manager and Assistant General Man
• Mae Mohr, Director, Racing
Description:
Greyhound racing track.
Seating capacity:
2,950 indoors; 900 outdoors.

GREENETRACK INC.
PO BOX 471
EUTAW, AL 35462
205-372-9318
800-633-5942
Fax: 205-372-0579
www.greenetrackpaysyoumoney.com
• Herlecia Hampton, General Manager
herleciaher@yahoo.com
• Jimmie Paster, Operations Director
gteutowal@aol.com
Seating Capacity:
Track 1,800

GREYHOUND PARK & EVENT CENTER
5100 RIVERBEND AVENUE
POST FALLS, ID 83854
208-773-0545
800-828-4880
Fax: 208-773-2049
ContactUs@GPEventCenter.com
www.gpeventcenter.com
• Oaks Randy, General Manager
Description:
Greyhound racing track.

LINCOLN PARK
100 TWIN RIVER ROAD
LINCOLN, RI 02865
401-723-3200
877-827-4237
Fax: 401-727-4770
• Dan Bucci, General Manager
• Lauren Quinn, Park Supervisor
• Craig Sculos, Marketing Director and Assistant General
• Gary Liberatore, Director, Racing
Description:
Thoroughbred race track and Greyhound racing track.
Description:
Thoroughbred race track and Greyhound racing track.

LUCKY'S CARD ROOM
8300 N NEBRASKA AVENUE
PO BOX 8096
TAMPA, FL 33609

813-932-4313 Ext 301
Fax: 813-932-5048
www.tampadogs.com
• Mike Hater, President/General Manger
• Hillary Fellenz, Marketing
• Theresa Hughes, Racing Secretary
Description:
Greyhound racing track.

MACON COUNTY GREYHOUND PARK, INC.
8680 COUNTY ROAD 40
PO BOX 128
SHORTER, AL 36075
334-727-0540
800-688-2946
Fax: 334-727-0737
www.victoryland.com
• James W. Baker, Raing Manager
jim.baker@mcgp.us
• Victory Land, Contact
Description:
Greyhound racing track.

MARDI GRAS CASINO
831 N FEDERAL HIGHWAY
HALLANDALE BEACH, FL 33009
954-924-3200
877-557-5687
Fax: 954-457-4229
www.mardigrascasinofl.com
• Berg Howard, Director, Public Relations and Marketing

MEADOWLANDS RACING & ENTERTAINMENT
50 STATE ROUTE 120
E RUTHERFORD, NJ 7073
201-935-8500
800-782-2537
Fax: 201-460-4244
www.thebigm.com
• Dennis Dowd, SVP Racing
(201) 460-4183
ddowd@njsea.com
• Chris McErlean, VP Racing Operations
(201) 460-4184
cmcelean@njsea.com
• Vernard Bennett, Assistant VP, Wagering Guest Services
(201) 460-4115
vbennett@njsea.com
• Marcello Esposito, Assistant VP, Operations
(201) 842-5034
mesposito@njsea.com
• Darin Zoccali, Director of Racing Operations
dzoccali@newmracing.com
• Sam McKee, Director of Simulcasting & TV Production
smckee@newmracing.com
• Mona Vaccarella, Director of HR
mvaccarella@newmracing.com
• James Patalano, Director of Purchasing
jpatalano@newmracing.com
• Jessica Wester, Asst. Director
jwester@newmracing.com
• Bill Kudlacik, Director of Security
bkudlacik@newmracing.com
Arena Seating Capacity:
Track 40,000, Grandstand 25,000, Clubhouse 10,000.
Year Founded:
1971
Nature of Service:
Harness, Thoroughbred, Simulcasting

Horseracing.
Track Type:
Harness, Thoroughbred, Simulcasting Horseracing.

MELBOURNE GREYHOUND PARK & CLUB 52 POKER
1100 N WICKHAM ROAD
MELBOURNE, FL 32935
321-259-9800
Fax: 321-259-3437
info@mgpark.com
www.mgpark.com
• Patrick T. Biddix, General Manager
Description:
Greyhound racing track.

MILE HIGH RACING & ENTERNTAINMENT
10750 E LLIFF AVENUE
AURORA, CO 80014
303-751-5918
Fax: 303-289-1640
www.mihiracing.com
• Bruce Seymore, Director Racing Operations
Description:
Greyhound racing track.

MOBILE GREYHOUND PARK
7101 OLD PASCA GOULA ROAD
PO BOX 43
THEODORE, AL 36582-4011
251-653-5000
800-272-5000
Fax: 251-653-9185
info@pcigaming.com
www.mobilegreyhoundpark.com
• David L. Jones, General Manager
djones1@pcigaming.com
• Paula Justice, Simulcast Director
pjustice@pcigaming.com
• Vivian Reynolds, Group Sales
• Barbara Holt, Mutuels
• Carol Mitchell, Bookeeping
cmitchell@pcigaming.com
• Ellis Hardy, Director of Racing
ehardy@pcigaming.com
• John Rooks, Food Director
Description:
Greyhound racing track.

NAPLES-FORT MYERS GREYHOUND TRACK
10601 BONITA BEACH ROAD
PO BOX 2567
BONITA SPRINGS, FL 34135-2567
239-992-2411
Fax: 239-947-9244
www.naplesfortmyersdogs.com
• Larry Mosher, Director Racing Operations
• James Schwartz, Security Director
(239) 992-2411
• Larry Baldwin, Executive Manager
(239) 992-2411
• Juan Fra, General manager
(239) 992-2411
• Michael Hernandez, Ass.General manger
(239) 992-2411
• David Sonenstahl, Facilities Director
(239) 992-2411
• Cindy Fra, Room Manger
(239) 992-2411
• Bob Dorris, Mutuel Manager
(239) 992-2411
• Tammy Gaida, Admissions Incharge
(239) 992-2411

• Vered Ullman, Office Manager
(239) 992-2411
Description:
Greyhound racing track.

PALM BEACH KENNEL CLUB
1111 NORTH CONGRESS AVENUE
W PALM BEACH, FL 33409
561-683-2222
Fax: 561-471-9114
www.pbkennelclub.com
• Arthur J. Laughlin, General Manager
(561) 683-2222
• Joe Love, Government Affairs
• Micheal Glenn, General Manager
• San Catalfano, Director of Mutuels
• Rick Domian, Racing Director
• Theresa Hume, Publicity Director
• Renne Lampman, HR
• Patrick J Rooney Sr., CEO, President
Description:
Greyhound racing track.

PENSACOLA GREYHOUND TRACK
951 DOG TRACK ROAD
PENSACOLA, FL 32506
850-455-8595
800-345-3997
Fax: 850-453-8883
www.pensacolagreyhoundtrack.com
• Schlikin Nick, General Manager
• Mary Utterbach, Director Racing
Description:
Greyhound racing track.

PHOENIX GREYHOUND PARK
3801 E WASHINGTON STREET
PO BOX 20300
PHOENIX, AZ 85034
602-273-7181
Fax: 602-273-6176
www.phoenixgreyhoundpark.com
• Daniel A. Luciano, General Manager
dluciano@dncinc.com
• Mike Hillard, Director Racing
• Dennis Young, Operations
• Bac Tran, Director Marketing
• Mike Hillard, Racing Director
Description:
Greyhound racing track.
Permanent seating capacity:
6,500

PUEBLO GREYHOUND PARK
3215 LAKE AVENUE
PUEBLO, CO 81004-3895
719-566-0370
Fax: 719-566-0450
www.wembleyco.com
• Rose Steve, General Manager
• Dave Montoya, Mutuel Manager
• Frank Provenza, Marketing Director
Description:
Greyhound racing track.

SANFORD-ORLANDO KENNEL CLUB, INC.
301 DOG TRACK ROAD
LONGWOOD, FL 32750
407-831-1600
Fax: 407-831-3997
info.sokc@pngaming.com
www.sanfordorlandokc.com
• Collins Jack, Track Manager
• Mike Newlin, General Manager

Description:
Greyhound racing track.

SARASOTA KENNEL CLUB, INC.
5400 BRADENTON ROAD
SARASOTA, FL 34234
941-355-7744
Fax: 941-351-2207
info@sarasotakennelclub.com
www.sarasotakennelclub.com
• Collins Jr. Jack, Track Manager
Description:
Greyhound racing track.

SEABROOK PARK
319 NEW ZEALAND ROAD
PO BOX 219
SEABROOK, NH 03874-4119
603-474-3065
866-732-2766
Fax: 603-474-2438
www.seabrookgreyhoundpark.com
• Carney James, President
• Glenn Jones, Racing Secy
• Neil Casey, Director Racing
• Bill Modie, Publicity
• Edward J Keelan, President
• Joseph Carney, General Manager
Description:
Greyhound racing track.

SOUTHLAND PARK
1550 N INGRAM BOULEVARD
PO BOX 2088
I-40 & I-55 Exit 279 A
W MEMPHIS, AR 72301
870-735-3670
800-467-6182
Fax: 870-732-8335
www.southlandgreyhound.com
• Troy Keeping, President/General Manager
(870) 735-3670
tkeeping@dncinc.com
• Gayla Allen, Executive Assistant
(870) 735-3670
gallen@dncinc.com
• Maurice Cummings, Controller
• Troy Keeping, President and GM
• Osi Imomoh, Sr.Director of Operations
• Maureen Finley, Director of Finance
• Jlm Wilson, Director of Gaming
• Shane Bolender, Director of Racing
• Bobbi Jones, Marketing
• Estell Wilson, Food Director
Year Founded:
1956
Track Type:
Greyhound Racing.

TUCSON GREYHOUND PARK, INC.
2601 S THIRD AVENUE
TUCSON, AZ 85713
520-884-7576
800-704-5218
Fax: 520-624-9389
info@tucsongreyhound.com
www.tucdogtrak.com
• Tom Taylor, CEO/General Manager
• Joseph Zappala, President/Owner
Description:
Greyhound racing track.

WHEELING ISLAND GAMING, INC.
1 S STONE STREET
WHEELING, WV 26003-2009

304-232-5050
877-946-4373
Fax: 304-231-1834
www.wheelingisland.com
• Campbell R. Lesley, Publicity Director
Description:
Greyhound racing track.
Permanent seating capacity:
3,500

WICHITA GREYHOUND PARK
1500 E 77TH STREET N
VALLER CENTER
WICHITA, KS 67147-0277
316-755-4000
800-535-0482
Fax: 316-755-2405
www.wgpi.com
• Ruffin G Phil, Owner
• Shelli Baker, Interim General Manager/Simulcast
• Todd Dennett, Director Mutuels
• Phillip Ru Jr, Director Operations
Description:
Greyhound racing track.

WOODLANDS, THE
9700 LEAVENWORTH ROAD
PO BOX 12036
KANSAS CITY, KS 66109-3551
913-299-9797
800-695-7223
Fax: 913-299-9804
www.woodlandskc.com
• Jayme LaRocca, General Manager
• Howard T. Grace, President
Description:
Greyhound racing track.

Facility Architects & Developers

360 ARCHITECTURE
300 W 22ND STREET
SUITE 400
KANSAS CITY, MO 64108
816-472-3360
Fax: 816-531-3388
360architects.com
• Tracy Stearns, Senior Principal
• George M. Heinlein, Senior Principal
Nature of Service
Architectural Design, interior design, visioning & strategic design, building & site evaluation, programming & space planning, graphics & way finding, 3D illustration & animation, and sustainability consulting
Clients
Cutler Residence, KC Power & Light, Burnham Square Condominium, Nationwide Arena District, Bernstein-Rein Advertising Atrium, H&R Block Center, Boulevard Brewery Expansion, Johnson County Sunset Drive, Valencia Place/Lockton, IRS Service Center, Midland Loan Services, C3, University of Dayton Arena, American Airlines Arena, Nationwide Arena, Mizzou Arena, New York Sports & Convention Center, Sprint Center, UCF Football Stadium, KCK Baseball, KU Hall Center for the Humanities, Graceland University, Carter Art Center

facilities

ABEL BANNISON BUTZ
80 8TH AVENUE
SUITE 1105
NEW YORK, NY 10011
212-206-0630
Fax: 212-645-0048
info@abbnyc.com
www.abbnyc.com
• Terri-Lee Burger, Prinicipal
• John S. Butz, Principal
(212) 206-0630
• Terri-Lee Burger, Registered Landscape
Architect
• John S. Butz, Registered Landscape
Architect
Services:
Park design, campus planning, and outdoor
sports and athletic facility design
Specialties:
Public Parks, Waterfront Parks, Athletic
Facilities, Campus Planning and Design,
Streetscape Improvements, Master
Planning/Site Planning
Projects:
1998-2001 Hudson River Park - Segment 4,
New York, NY; 2001 Madison Square Park,
New York, NY; 2000 Community Rock
Garden, Bronx, NY; 1998 Fountain of Youth
Playground, Bronx, NY; 1993 Riverbank
State Park, New York, NY; 1991 Broadway
Malls, 61st to 168th Street, New York, NY;
1990-1996 East River Esplanade: Phase I -
94th to 103rd Street,Phase II - 63rd to 71st
Street, Phase IV - 90th to 94th Street; 1999
Grand Central North End District
Streetscape, New York, NY; 1999 47th
Street Improvements, Diamond District, New
York, NY; 1999 Raul Wallenberg Memorial,
New York, NY; 1998 South Broadway,
Yonkers, NY; 1995 Citicorp/Court Square,
Long Islan

ACKERMAN MCQUEEN ADVERTISING
1601 N W EXPRESSWAY
1100 THE TOWER
OKLAHOMA CITY, OK 73118
405-843-7777
Fax: 405-848-8034
debby-johnson@am.com
www.am.com
• Agnes McQueen, Chief Executive Officer
• Bill Winkler, Chief Financial Officer/Chief
Operating
• Edmund O. Martin, Board Chairman
• David Lipson, President
Services:
Marketing, Advertising and Research
agency
Clients:
Kerr-McGee Corporation, Juniper Networks,
Inc., LeapFrog, BancFirst, Integris Health,
Integris Heart Hospital, Caymus Vinyards,
WinStar Casinos, OGE Energy Corporation,
Air Force Memorial Foundation, TownCenter
Booksellers, Chickasaw Nation, Oklahoma
Tourism and Recreation Department, Shark
Jaw Toys, American Indian Cultural Center,
Texas Alliance of Energy Producers, Big
Boing Toys, The Oklahoman, Bickel &
Brewer, Oklahoma Parks, Resorts & Golf,
Oklahoma State Fair, Greater Oklahoma
City Chamber of Commerce, Oklahoma
Capitol Complex & Centennial
Commemoration, River Parks Authority,
Xirrus

ADOLFSON & PERTSON, INC.
6701 WEST 23RD STREET
MINNEAPOLIS, MN 55426
952-544-1561
Fax: 952-525-2333
contactMN@a-p.com
www.a-p.com
• David Adolfson, Chairman Emeritus
• Michael C. Peterson, Chief Growth Officer
• Scott A. Weicht, President/Chied Financial
Officer
• William Bradford, President/CEO
• Marc W. Boatwright, Seior Vice President
• Mark Dixon, President & Owner
• Kevin Gott, President
Services:
General Construction, Construction
Management Services, Design and Build
Services, Facilites Maintenance Services.
Operates as a contractor of commercial
construction
Clients:
CenturyTel,Duke-weeks Realty,Carlson
Real Estate
Company,SunCor,360Networks,SuperValu,
Inc.,Lang Associates,The Trammell Crow
Company,The Chute Companies,Prudential
Insurance Co.,Wal-Mart,Dayton Hudson
Corporation,Target Stores,Amerimar
Enterprises,Saks Fifth Avenue,Federated
Department Stores,General
Growth,REI,Home Depot,JC Penney
Corporation,Safeway,Hutchinson
Technology, Inc.,Andersen Windows,Control
Data Corporation,Donatelle Plastics,
Inc.,Cannon,Equipment Company,Green
Giant Company,Green Bay Packaging,ADC
Telecommunications,Midwest Coca-Cola
Bottling,Pepsi-Cola
Mid-Wisconsin,Beverage, Inc.,Kaiser
Permanente,Howard Young Medical Center

AECOM
800 LA SALLE AVENUE
MINNEAPOLIS, MN 55402
612-376-2000
Fax: 612-376-2271
• Rick Lincicome, Chief Executive Officer
• Welton Becket, Founder
• Jon Buggy, Managing Principal-Healthcare
• Maggie Walsh, Associate Vice President,
Marketing
asktransportation@aecom.com
Service
Architectural and planning services for sport
facilities
Client
Alfa Development Corporation, Allina Health
System, American University in Cairo,
Amtrak Consolidated National Operations
Center, Atlanta Braves, Augsburg Fortress
Publishers, Bay Area Medical Center, Blue
Stream Ventures, Bovis Lend Lease,
Bozeman Deaconess Hospital, Brasil
Telecom, Buffalo Sabres, Capital Projects,
Charlotte Bobcats/Charlotte Sting,
Children's National Medical Center, City of
Grand Forks, City of Kansas City, City of
Sioux City, City Public Service Energy
Management Center, Cleveland Cavaliers,
Cleveland State University, Crescendo
Ventures, Crozer Keystone Health System,
Dai-Ichi Resort Company, Drug
Enforcement Agency (D
Clients
E*TRADE, East Texas Medical Center, El
Paso Diablos, Elon University, ERCOT
(Electric Reliability Council of Texas),

Federal Reserve Bank of Kansas City, First
& Goal Inc. (FGI), Florida Hospital Orlando,
Gearworks, Georgetown University Law
Center, Gonzaga University, Grand Action
Committee, GSA (U.S. General Services
Administration), Gustavus Adolphus
College, Hae Song Company International
Ltd., Hammes Company, Hays Medical
Center, Health Care Systems,
Hewlett-Packard, HI-WIRE, Huizenga
Holdings Inc., IHMS - Welcare, Indiana
Pacers, Iowa State University, JP Morgan
Chase H&Q

ALBANESE/BROOKS/ASSOCIATES P.C.
1001 N ALVERNON WAY
SUITE 175
TUCSON, AZ 85711
520-881-4512
Fax: 520-881-7505
• Kim Fernandez, Principal
• Kim Ferranti, Treasurer
• Paty Marquez, Project Architect
• Rob Bass, Project Architect
Services:
Design and master planning of indoor and
outdoor recreational facilities. Specialty
includes recreation centers and pools
Clients:
City of Tucson, Pima County, United
Methodist Church, Lutheran Church of the
Ascension, Catalina American Baptist
Church, Holy Way Presbyterian Church,
Cottonwood Elementary, Mesquite
Elementary, Catalina High Magnet School,
Sycamore Elementary

ALFRED GOBAR ASSOCIATES
300 S HARBOR BOULEVARD
SUITE 900
ANAHEIM, CA 92805
714-772-8900
Fax: 714-772-8911
www.gobar.com
• Alfred J Gobar, President and Chairman
• Alonzo Pedrin, Principal
• James Wolf, Principal
• Ryan Early, Senior Research Associate
Services:
Consultants that specialize in economic
feasibility analyses and market analyses for
recreation and mass spectator facilities
Clients:
Kaufman & Broad, Greystone Homes, S & S
Construction, Presley Homes, Centex
Homes, Lewis Homes, The Irvine Company,
Catellus Development Corp., CT Realty
Corp., Birtcher, Mission Viejo Company, Del
Webb Corporation, Pacific Gulf Properties,
Rancho Mission Viejo, Tejon Ranch, Santa
Margarita Company, Triquest Development,
Rose Hills Company, Pohl-Brown
Associates, Polygon Homes, Greystone
Homes, Instorage, ICI Development,
Majestic Realty, The Koll Company, the
Lusk Companies, Wrather Corporation,
DoubleTree Inns, TraveLodge, All Seasons
Inn

AMERICAN LEISURE CORPORATION
414 AIRPORT EXECUTIVE PARK
NANUET, NY 10954
845-371-5670
Fax: 845-371-5680
www.americanleisure.com
• Steve Kass, Founder/Chief Executive
Officer

- Wendy Bosalavage, President
wbosalavage@americanleisure.com
- Terri Barbaria, EVP
- Wendy Bosalavage, President
- Tom Johnston, COO
- Beth Caplan, Chief Financial Officer
bcaplan@americanleisure.com
- Jason D Verney, VP , Operations
- Don Amblo, VP , Operations
- Joann Patrello, VP
Services:
Provides expert assistance and services in
the design, development, marketing and
management of recreational and lifestyle
facilities such as Fitness Clubs, Corporate
Fitness Centers, Wellness Centers, Spas,
Medical Spas, Golf & Country Clubs, JCC's
& YMCA's
Clients:
The Fitness Center at Atlantic
Apartments,The Bay Club,BelleFair at Rye
Brook,The Bromley Fitness Center,Carlton
House Club,The Channel Club,The Estates
at Chapel Hill Lifestyle Center & Spa,The
Lifestyle Center, Spa & Lake Club at Chapin
Estates,The Lifestyle Center at Clinton
Green,The Columbia Fitness Center,The
Lifestyle Center at Columbus
Tower,Connaught Tower Club,The Copley
Lifestyle Center,The Lifestyle Center at The
Devonshire,The Esplanade Lifestyle
Center,The Exchange Fitness Center,Affinia
Fitness Spa at The Dumont Hotel,Affinia
Wellness Spa at The Benjamin Hotel,The
Spa at The Aruba Grand Hotel,The Spa at
Ballys at Bally's Casino

AQUATIC DESIGN GROUP, INC.
2226 FARADAY AVENUE
CARLSBAD, CA 92008
760-438-8400
800.938.0542
Fax: 760-438-5251
info@aquaticdesigngroup.com
www.aquaticdesigngroup.com
- Randy Mendoroz, President
Services:
Planning, architecture and engineering
services for competitive, recreation and
leisure aquatic facilities
Clients:
Four Seasons Hotels,Gravity Fitness Center
and Spa at Le Parker Meridien
Hotel,Hampton Retreats,The Rock Spa at
The Hard Rock Hotel,The Thalossotherapy
Spa, Fitness & Tennis Club at The Marbella
Hotel,Millenium Hilton Hotel Fitness
Center,The Spa & Fitness Center at Ocean
Point Hotel,R & A Hotels,The Spa & Salon
at The Ritz Carlton San Juan,Sheraton
Health Club, Sheraton Manhattan,Sheraton
Health Club, Sheraton New York,Starwood
Hotels,Sutton Place Hotels,The Spa &
Fitness Center at The Victor Hotel,Villa
Roma Resort & Country Club,The Spa at
The Aruba Grand Hotel,The Spa at Ballys at
Bally's Casino Hotel etc

ARC ARCHITECTS
1101 E PIKE STREET
FLOOR 3
SEATTLE, WA 98122
206-322-3322
Fax: 206-322-9323
www.arcarchitects.com
- Dave Rutherford, Principal
- Rex Bond, Principal
- Stan Lokting, Principal

Services:
Provides architectural services such as
feasibility studies, master planning,
programming, design & construction
administration, sustainable design, special
needs & diverse communities, and
renovations & additions
Clients:
Camp Easter Seals, Lake Sammamish
State Park, Port Townsend City Hall,
Sammamish Commons, Lake City Library,
WSU Agricultural Research & Technology
Building, UW Golf Driving Range, South
Bellevue Community Center, William Shore
Memorial Pool, St. Andrews East Village
Housing

ARC ICESPORTS & ENTERTAINMENT
50 S LAWN COURT
ROCKVILLE, MD 20850
301-315-5660
Fax: 301-315-5665
- John Cook, President
(416) 675-7604
Nature of Sports Service:
Developers of hockey and figure skating
facilities. Focus on developing ice rinks in
the United States

ARCHITECHNICS INC.
510 MAINE STREET
10TH FLOOR
QUINCY, IL 62301
217-222-0554
Fax: 217-223-3361
archeng@architechnicsinc.com
www.architechnicsinc.com
- Anthony E Crane, Partner
- Todd J. Moore, Professional Engineer
- Martin E Meyer, Partner
Description:
Architects providing architectural design as
well as utility studies, budget analysis and
services for buildings, HVAC, mechanical
and electrical components

ARCHITECTS DELAWIE WILKES RODRIGUES BARKER
2265 INDIA STREET
SAN DIEGO, CA 92101
619-299-6690
Fax: 619-299-5513
info@delawie.com
www.delawie.com
- Michael B. Wilkes, Chief Executive Officer
- M. Andrew An Rodrigues, President
- James Barker, VP
- M. Andrew Rodrigues, Principal
- Paul E. Schroeder, Principal
- Frank Ternasky, Principal
- Michael Asaro, Principal
Description:
Architectural planning
Services:
Architecture, Master Planning, Programming
& Facilities Analysis, Computer Graphics

ARCHITECTURAL ASSOCIATES, LTD.
5801 WASHINGTON AVENUE
SUITE 203
RACINE, WI 53402
262-886-1700
Fax: 262-886-5885
architect@aaltd.com
www.aaltd.com
- John Murphy, President
johnm@aaltd.com

Description:
Recreation and aquatic centers

ARCHITECTURAL RESOURCES CAMBRIDGE INC.
FIVE CAMBRIDGE CENTER
CAMBRIDGE, MA 2142
617-547-2200
Fax: 617-547-7222
ARCmail@arcusa.com
www.arcusa.com
- Henry S. Reeder, President/Principal
- Colin L. Smith, Principal
- Arthur Cohen, Principal
Services:
Provides professional services in the fields
of architecture, planning, and interior design
Clients:
Terry Sanford Institute of Public Policy,John
Pappajohn Business Building,Kennedy
School of Government,Jaharis Family
Center for Biomedical and Nutrition
Sciences,Olin Center for Language &
Culture,Isenberg School of
Management,George S. Dively Executive
Education Center, Leeds School of
Business Design,Blake Hall Renovation and
Addition,Research & Development
Building/Manufacturing Building,New
Research Building,R&D Facility/Office and
Laboratory Renovations,Jaharis Family
Center for Biomedical and Nutrition
Sciences,Five Mountain Road-Laboratory
Conversion,Research
Building,Pharmaceutical Production and
R&D Expansion,Hauser Center for Nonpr
Description:
Amherst College, Boston University, Boston
College, Princeton University, Yale
University, Berkshire School, Milton
Academy, Noble & Greenough School and
Phillips Exeter Academy

BALLARD KING & ASSOCIATES
2743 E RAVENHILL CIRCLE
HIGHLANDS RANCH, CO 80126
303-470-8661
Fax: 303-470-8642
BKA@ballardking.com
www.ballardking.com
- Jeffrey L. King, President & Founding
Partner
- Kenneth S. Ballard, President & Founding
Partner
- Darin J. Barr, Senior Associate
Services:
Recreation facility planning and operation
consultants specializing in needs
assessment studies, feasibility reports,
design review operations pro formas,
marketing plans, audits and operations
planning
Clients:
Wheat Ridge Recreation Center, Sylvester
Powell Community Center, Red Mountain
Multigenerational Center, Greater Plymouth
Community Center, Sherwood Family
YMCA, The Pointe at Ballwin Commons

BARKER RINKER SEACAT ARCHITECTURE
3457 RINGSBY COURT
UNIT 200
DENVER, CO 80216
303-455-1366
866-646-1980
Fax: 303-455-7457

brs@brsarch.com
www.brsarch.com
• Steve Blackburn, Principal
• Keith Hayes, Principal
• Roz Schneider, Principal
• Craig Bouck, President, CEO
(303) 455-1366
craigbouck@brsarch.com
• Chuck Musgrave, Principal, CFO
(303) 455-1366
chuckmusgrave@brsarch.com
• Frank Buono, Principal, CIO
(303) 455-1366
frankbuono@brsarch.com
• Katie Barnes, Principal, COO
(303) 455-1366
katiebarnes@brsarch.com
• Dave Hammel, Principal
(303) 455-1366
davehammel@brsarch.com
• Keith Hayes, Principal
(303) 455-1366
keithhayes@brsarch.com
Description:
Program and design of community
recreation centers throughout the United
States

BERNIER, CARR & ASSOCIATES
327 MULLIN STREET
WATERTOWN, NY 13601
315-782-8130
Fax: 315-782-7192
kreinhardt@thebcgroup.com
www.thebcgroup.com
• Bernard H Brown Jr, Chief Executive
Officer
• Rick W. Tague, President
rtague@thebcgroup.com
• Bernard H Brown, CEO
• Pamela S Beyor, Chairperson
• Rick W Tague, President
• Mari L Cecil, VP
• Shawn M Travers, Principal
• Lynette Beck, Marketing Director
• Mickey G Lehman, VP

BETA DESIGN GROUP, INC.
2534 ROYAL PL
C
GRAND RAPIDS, MI 49503
770-491-9250
800-235-6299
Fax: 616-235-6393
• Doug Brant, President
• Liz English, Marketing Director
• Carolyn DuBuis, Human Resources
Director
Description:
Comprehensive architectural, mechanical
and electrical design services including
interior design, site planning, community
planning, graphic design construction
administration and civil engineering

**BLUNDEN BARCLAY ROBBIE
ASSOCIATES ACHITECTS**
200 PUBLIC SQUARE
BP TOWER, SUITE 200
CLEVELAND, OH 44114
216-566-7888
Fax: 216-566-9023
• Robert A Barclay, President, Marketing,
Human Resources
Description:
Athletic facilities including gymnasiums,

fitness centers, field houses and outdoor
education facilities.

BMK ARCHITECTS
323 CENTRAL AVENUE
SARASOTA, FL 34236
941-365-6056
Fax: 941-955-2592
• Darrell Mclain, President/Principal
• Charles Kuykendall, SVP/Principal
• William J. Tyle, SVP/Financial Principal
• Richard Opalinsky, VP/Principal
• James Robison, Chief Information Officer

BOND ARCHITECTS
200 S CENTRAL AVENUE
SUITE 100
SAINT LOUIS, MO 63105
314-863-4994
Fax: 314-863-4996
www.bondwolfe.com
• Susan Pruchnicki, Principal
• Art Bond, Principal
abond@bondarchitectsinc.com
Description:
Full range of professional design services
with expertise in private municipal and
institutional sports and recreation facilities.

BOWEN WILLIAMSON ZIMMERMAN INC.
2211 PARMENTER STREET
MIDDLETON, WI 53562
608-831-2900
Fax: 608-831-5800
info@bwzarchitects.com
www.bwzarchitects.com
• Frederick E Zimmerman, Project Director
Description:
Facility engineers.

BRAILSFORD & DUNLAVEY
1140 CONNECTICUT AVENUE, NW
SUITE 400
WASHINGTON, DC 20036
202-289-4455
Fax: 202-289-6461
info@programmanagers.com
• BJ Ruddell, Marketing Director
• Will Mangrum, Senior Vice President
• Brad Noyes, Senior Vice President
• Jeff Turner, Senior Vice President
• Kevin Keegan, Vice President
• Bill Mykins, Vice president
• Alan Resnick, Vice President
• Chris A Dunlavey, President
Year Founded:
1993
Nature of Service:
Facility planning and project management
firm to a variety of clients including major
and minor league athletic teams, collegiate
athletics and recreation, and community
recreation. Organization conducts market,
financial, and programming analysis, site
Clients Include:
Baltimore Ravens, Ohio Arts and Sports
Commission, DC Sport & Entertainment
Commission, Duke University, University of
Maryland and the Unviersity of Rhode
Island.

BRAUN & STEIDL ARCHITECTS INC
1041 W MARKET STREET
AKRON, OH 44313

330-864-7755
Fax: 330-864-3691
www.bsa-net.com
• Charles Schreckenberger
cschreckenberger@bsa-net.com
• Rachel Schwarz
rschwarz@bsa-net.com
• Phillip Steinberg
psteinberg@bsa-net.com
• Paula Ryan, Media
pryan@bsa-net.com
• Robert Habel, Vice President
rhabel@bsa-net.com

**BRESLIN, RIDYARD, FADERO
ARCHITECTS**
1226 UNION BOULEVARD
ALLENTOWN, PA 18109
610-437-9626
Fax: 610-437-4769
BRFA@breslinarchitects.com
www.breslinarchitects.com
• Robin W Breslin, President
(610) 437-9626
robinbreslin@breslinarchitects.com
• Robert J. Hayes, Senior Associate
(610) 437-9626

**BROSSO, WILHELM & MCWILLIAMS,
INC.**
1001 CROMWELL BRIDGE ROAD
SUITE 200
BALTIMORE, MD 21286
410-321-6760
Fax: 410-321-6782
• Robert A A. Brosso, President
Description:
Architects/interior designers/consultants of
fitness, recreational, wellness and athletic
facilities in the U.S., Great Britain and
Canada.

**BROWNING DAY MULLINS DIERDORF
ARCHITECTS**
626 N ILLINOIS STREET
INDIANAPOLIS, IN 46204
317-635-5030
Fax: 317-634-5409
info@bdmd.com
www.bdmd.com
• Craig W Mullins, Chairman of the Board
• Uohn JA Dierdorf, Chief Executive Officer
• Jonathan Hess, EVP
• Cynthia Richmond, Senior Marketing
Coordinator
Description:
Architectural design and consulting.

BRUNER/COTT & ASSOCIATES INC.
130 PROSPECT STREET
CAMBRIDGE, MA 2139
617-492-8400
Fax: 617-876-4002
info@brunercott.com
www.brunercott.com
• Henry Moss, Prinicpal
• Leland Cott, Founding Principal
• Lynne Brooks, Principal
• Daniel Raih, Principal
• Lawrence Cheng, Associate Principal
• Robert Simmons, Associate Principal
• Simeon Bruner, Founding Principal
Description:
Architecture and interior design of athletic,
recreational and multi-purpose spaces,
specializing in the renovation and adaptive
reuse of older buildings.

Services:
Campus planning, with specialities in Student Amenities: Dormitories, Dining Halls, and Student Center

BRUNGARDT ENTERPRISES, L.L.C.
2195 S TELLURIDE COURT
AURORA, CO 80013
303-537-1285
888-740-2223
Fax: 303-537-1293
info@b-ent.com
www.b-ent.com
• Peter Brungardt, Owner
(303) 537-1285
info@b-ent.com
• Noreen Brungardt, Business Manager
(303) 537-1285
info@b-ent.com
Description:
Computer drafting services, and event layouts.

BSA ARCHITECTS
300 MONTEGOMERY STREET
SUITE 1135
SAN FRANCISCO, CA 94104
415-281-4720
Fax: 415-281-4721
smergy@bsaarchitects.com
www.bsaarchitects.com
• Robert E Allen, Principal
(415) 781-1526
ballen@bsaarchitects.com
• Michael Pattinson, Int'l Assoc AIA, RIBA, IIDA, BIID Principal
• John Ashworth, Principal
• David D. Ross, Principal
• Sarah Mergy, Senior AssociateDirector of Marketing and Off
• Dillon Parker, Associate
• George Janson, Senior Associate
• Henrik Bull, Principal Emeritus
Year Founded:
1967
Clients:
City, County, State, Federal municipalities, Independent districts, agencies, public and private colleges, universities, private resort, recreation clients.
Nature of Service:
Facility planning and architectural services.

BURBACH AQUATICS - ARCHITECTS & ENGINEERS, INC.
5974 STATE HIGHWAY 80 S
PLATTEVILLE, WI 53818
608-348-3262
Fax: 608-348-4970
baae@centurytel.net
www.burbachaquatics.com
• David Burbach, President
• Roger Schamberger, VP Marketing
Year Founded:
1978
Clients:
Municipal Clients, Park Districts, County Park and Recreation, Local Units of Government.
Nature of Service:
Indoor, outdoor family aquatic centers, technical evualations, feasibility to marketing studies, design of specification construction administration.

BURLEY'S
1500 WESTEC DRIVE
EUGENE, OR 97402
814-262-7313
800-311-5294
Fax: 814-262-7610
burley@burley.com
www.burley.com
• W Graeme Roustan, Owner
c.lawery@burleys.com
• Robert Heffernan
bheffernan@burleys.com
Year Founded:
1985
Clients:
Anybody with a dream to own their own ice or inline rink. Domestic and International.
Nature of Service:
Design, manufacture, install and supply ice and inline rink facilities.

BURNHAM REAL ESTATE SERVICES
4435 EASTGATE MALL
SUITE 200
SAN DIEGO, CA 92121
858-452-6500
Fax: 858-452-3206
• Malin Brunham, Chairman
(619) 525-2172
• Stath Karras, President & CEO
(858) 334-4001
stath.karras@cushwake.com
Description:
Specializing in projects and construction management for athletic facilities.

BUTLER HEAVY STRUCTURES
HEAVY STRUCTURES
1540 GENESSEE STREET
KANSAS CITY, MO 64102
816-245-6500
Fax: 816-245-6055
heavystructures@bucon.com
www.heavystructures.com
• Mark Cogley, General Management
(816) 245-6777
macogley@heavystructures.com
• Mark Mazzoni, Project Management
(816) 245-6914
mdmazzoni@heavystructures.com
• Melessia Jones, Marketing and Website Feedback
(816) 245-6957
mkjones@heavystructures.com
• Mike Gravino, Business Development Manager
(727) 934-6805
dmgravino@heavystructures.com
Description:
General contractor.

C.H. GUERNSEY & CO.
5555 N GRAND BOULEVARD
OKLAHOMA CITY, OK 73112
405-416-8100
Fax: 405-416-8111
www.guernsey.us
• Michael K Moore, President/CEO
• Justin Proctor, Marketing Director
(405) 416-6805
justin.proctor@chguernsey.com
Description:
Architects, engineers, consultants.

CAMBRIDGE SEVEN ASSOCIATES INC.
1050 MASSACHUSETTS AVENUE
CAMBRIDGE, MA 2138
617-492-7000
Fax: 617-492-7007
www.c7a.com
• Peter Kuttner, President
• Dagmar Vonschwerin, Director Marketing
• Ronald Baker, Principal
• Stefanie Greenfield, Principal
• Steven Imrich, Principal
• Patricia Intrieri, Principal
• Gary Johnson, Principal
• Timothy Mansfield, Principal
Description:
Architecture, interiors and graphic design.
Services:
Architectural Design, Urban, Design, Master Planning, Adaptive Reuse/Renovation, Sustainable Design, Feasibility Analysis, Interior Design, programming Exhibit Design, Habitat Design, Graphic Design, Marketing Communications Design, Construction Administration

CARLSON DESIGN/CONSTRUCT CORP.
34 EXECUTIVE PARK
SUITE 250
IRVINE, CA 92614
949-251-0455
Fax: 949-251-0465
www.carlson-dc.com
• Bill Fraser, President
• Kari-ann Godberson, Human Resources Director
• William B. Fraser, PE Chief Executive Officer
• John L. Watts, President
• Tom Ryan, Director of Sales and Marketing
• Sean Suzuki, Director of Operations
• Joe Huebner, Director of Business Development
• Jeanne-Marie Pate, Controller
Service
Provide clients with highest level of services such as consulting, design and construction and offers industry's top skills for the most demanding projects and building programs which includes technologically challenging projects, multi-site rollouts, and projects with aggressive schedules
Clients
Charles Schwab, American Express, Accredited Home Lenders, Washington Mutual, First Tennessee, Mellon Bank One, Bank of America, Bank of New York, Wells Fargo, SAFECO Corp., Dime Savings Bank, Fidelity, State Street, Deutsche Bank, Pershing/DLJ Direct, Citicorp, John Hancock, Boatmen's Bancshares, Inc. Fleet Financial Services

CEI ARCHITECTURE
500 - 1500 W GEORGIA STREET
VANCOUVER, BRITISH COLUMBIA, CANADA V6G 2Z6
604-687-1898
888-922-2088
Fax: 604-682-5398
tpow@ceiarchitecture.com
www.ceiarchitecture.com
• Mark Hentze, Director Recreation/Culture/Community
mhertze@ceiarchitecture.com
• John Scott, Senior Partner
• Mark Hentze, Partner
• Conrad Boychuk, Senior Director, Recreation and Venue Develop
• Heidi Matthews, Director of Interior Design

facilities

• Michael McNaught, Director of
Post-Secondary
• Hugh Jansen, Associate, Manager of
Operation
• Troy Ransdell, Partner
Service
Provides planning, urban design,
architectural and interior design services for
an extensive range of individual companies
and institutions including hospitals and
laboratories.
Clients
Alcan Canada Ltd., BC Hothouse Ltd., B C
Rail, BCR Properties, B C Sugar, Beutel
Goodman Real Estate, Canada Lands
Corporation, Canadian Occidental
Petroleum, CB Richard Ellis, CN Real
Estate Management, Colliers International,
Concert Properties Ltd., Chrysler Canada
Ltd., Grosvenor International Ltd.,
Greyhound Canada Ltd., Intrawest
Development Corporation, Metropolitan Life
Assurance, Morguard Investments Ltd.,
NISSAN Canada Ltd., Penreal Capital
Management Ltd., Pilot Pacific
Developments Inc., Progressive Properties,
Safeway Canada, Scotiabank, Shell
Canada, Slough Estates Canada Ltd.,
Toronto Dominion Bank, Yaohan USA
Corporation, Glen

CHICAGO SCENIC STUDIO
1315 N NORTH BRANCH STREET
CHICAGO, IL 60642
312-274-9900
Fax: 312-274-9901
www.chicagoscenic.com
• Robert F Doepel, President
bdoepel@chicagoscenic.com
• Wayne Sorensen, Chief Financial Officer
• Henry Ng, Controller
• Pete Rahill, Director
• Robert F Doepel, President
• Henry Ng, Comptroller
• Wayne Sorensen, CFO
• Diane Langhorst, Marketing Manager
• Ross Hamilton, Project Manager
• Jean Burch, Project Manger
Sports Service Founded:
1979

CLARK ENTERPRISES
7500 OLD GEORGETOWN ROAD
BETHESDA, MD 20814
301-272-8100
Fax: 301-272-1928
www.clarkus.com
• Alice K. Patterson, Community Relations
Officer
• Christie Goldman, Business Development
Executive
• Kasey Repass, Office Manager
Service
Offers expertise in the development,
financing, construction and/or design-build
delivery of major sports facilities from coast
to coast; sports facility development
professionals highly experienced in
preconstruction consultation and
construction administration; and unique
project delivery methods and project
completion guarantees.

THE COLLABORATIVE, INC.
500 MADISON AVENUE
TOLEDO, OH 43604

419-242-7405
Fax: 419-242-7400
TCI@thecollaborativeinc.com
www.thecollaborativeinc.com
• Michael J. DiNardoi, Managing Partner
(419) 242-7405
mdinardo@thecollaborativeinc.com
• Frank G. Beans, Managing Principal
(419) 242-7405
fbeans@thecollaborativeinc.com
• Ray Micham, Senior Associate
(419) 242-7405
rmicham@thecollaborativeinc.com
• Frank G. Beans, Partner
• Dan Tabor, Architect/Partner
• Mike DiNardo, Architect/Partner
• Ray Micham, Architect/Partner
• Micheal. A Muse, Architect/Partner
• Paul.R Hollenbeck, Architect/Partner
Emertius
• Susan Armstrong, Senior Associate
(419) 242-7400
sarmstrong@thecollaborativeinc.com
Service
Provide services in architecture, landscape
architecture, planning, interior design,
contract furnishings and graphic design
such as programming, space planning,
zoning process/presentations, site selection
and planning and interior architectural
detailing
Clients
Adrian College, Adrian, Michigan, University
of Akron, Akron, Ohio, Alma College, Alma,
Michigan, Ashland University, Ashland,
Ohio, Ashland Theological Seminary,
Ashland, Ohio, Barton College, Wilson,
North Carolina, Bluffton College, Bluffton,
Ohio, Bowling Green State University,
Bowling Green, Ohio, Centenary College,
Hackettstown, New Jersey, Central Ohio
Technical College, OSU Newark, Ohio,
Columbus Academy, Gahanna, Ohio,
Evergreen Schools, Metamora, Ohio, Family
Learning Center of NW Ohio, Genoa
Schools, Genoa, Ohio, Gesu Parish, Toledo,
Ohio, Henry County Board of Co.
Commissioners (HOPE School, McClure,
Ohio), Leipsic Local Schools

**COMMUNICATION ARTS
INCORPORATED**
1112 PEARL STREET
BOULDER, CO 80302
303-447-8202
Fax: 303-440-7096
• Daniel Aizemann, Senior Designer
• Richard Foy, Co-Chairman
• Janet A. Martin, President
• Mike Doyle, Vice President/Architect
• Mark Jasin, Senior Designer
Service
Responsible for the development of overall
project character as well as planning and
retail design for retail environments,
adaptive re-use projects and urban spaces
and provides strategic services and
solutions for internet enabled environments.
Clients
AMC Theaters, Ballys Hotel and Casino,
BankBoston, Bass Pro Shops, Ben Carter
Properties, CBL & Associates Properties,
Centerra Properties, LLC, Century Theaters,
Crescent Development, Denver Museum of
Natural History, Doubletree Guest Suites,
Downtown Denver Partnership, Inc.,
Famous Players Theaters, Gaylord
Entertainment Company, Genesco, Gerald

Hines Interests, Horizon Organic Dairy, JFK
International Air Terminal LLC, KSL
Recreation, L.A. Arena Company, LCOR
Incorporated, Madison Square Garden, Ltd,
MMI Realty, NASA Human Habitation
Module, Port Authorities of New York & New
Jersey, Prime Retail, Inc., Prudential Realty
Group, Publix, Sa

COOKE DOUGLASS FARR LEMONS/LTD.
3100 N STATE STREET
SUITE 200
JACKSON, MS 39216
601-366-3110
Fax: 601-366-3181
www.cdfl.com
• Robert E. Farr II, Prinicpal/Corporate
President
rfarr@cdfl.com
• David A Lemons, Principal
dlemons@cdfl.com
• Jody G. Coleman, Principal
jcoleman@cdfl.com
• Jesse R. Browning, Principal
jbrowning@cdfl.com
• Robert E. Farr, Principal
rfarr@cdfl.com
• David A. Lemons, Principal
dlemons@cdfl.com
• Jody G. Coleman, Principal
jcoleman@cdfl.com
• Ann Somers, Principal
asomers@cdfl.com
• Robert O. Byrd, Principal
• Gene E. Crager, Principal
gcrager@cdfl.com
Service
Provides services on
architecture/engineering, planning, interior
design, design-build management and
facility commissioning. It works
collaboratively to provide innovative
planning, landscape architecture, campus
and urban design solutions, develop ideas,
strategies and concepts on diverse and
challenging sites, offers a complete range of
services for the planning, design and
delivery of interior environments and
specializes in the master planning and
design of sports complexes.

COUNSILMAN-HUNSAKER
10733 SUNSET OFFICE DRIVE
4TH FLOOR
SAINT LOUIS, MO 63127
314-894-1245
Fax: 314-894-0109
www.counsilmanhunsaker.com
• Scot Hunsaker, President
(314) 894-1245
scothunsaker@chah2o.com
• Doug Cook, Chairman of the Board
• Darren Bevard, Principal
• Jeff Nodorft, Principal
• Carl Nylander, Principal
• Kevin Post, Principal
• Matt Cappello, Studio Director
Service
Offers an extensive services from existing
facility evaluation to comprehensive concept
development from project visioning through
design, engineering and construction
administration to business management and
aquatic operations.
Clients
Chandler Unified School District, Cheyenne
Mountain High School, Clayton County
Aquatic Center, Cleveland State University,

Delta State University, The City of Dallas, Great America-Paramount, The City of Cleburne, Collinsville Area Recreation, Baylor University, Boston University, Oklahoma State University, Fort Valley State University, George Mason University, Georgia Institute of Technology, Kent State University, Kenyon College, Massachusetts Institute of Technology, Middleburry College, Georgetown Preparatory School, Haslett Public School District, Hastings Community Center, Keller Independent School District, Lakeview High School, New S

CPG ARCHITECTS
ONE DOCK STREET
STAMFORD, CT 6902
203-967-3456
Fax: 203-353-1863
cpgarchitects@hotmail.com
www.cpgarch.com
• Gary Unger, Principal/Founder
gary_unger@cpgarch.com
• Robert Mi Tieni, Principal/President
robert_tieni@cpgarch.com
• Karen Lika, SVP
karen_lika@cpgarch.com
• Karen M. Lika, Principal
• Jenny Paik, Principal
• Carl Mirbach, Creative Director
• Mickey Mallardi, VP-Architecture
mickey_mallardi@cpgarch.com
• James Sackett, VP, Director of Design
Service
Provides unique, future-focused process and comprehensive array of services such as creative management solutions as well as providing design solutions for pre-lease, architectural and interior planning
Clients
100 Wall Street, NYC, 300 Park Avenue, NYC, 666 Fifth Avenue, NYC, Amdocs, Ann Taylor, Bloomberg, Breitling, Chrysler Building, Citibank, North America, Comedy Central, Commonfund, Continental Airlines, Cornell Medical University, Edison Schools, Ford Motor Company, G.E. Capital, Greenwich Hospital, Guinness UDV, Honeywell, IBM, IRS, JP Morgan, Knights of Columbus, Lincoln Building, Louis Vitton, Madge Networks, McDonalds, McGraw Hill, Mitsui, Modern Media, Morgan Stanley, NBC Olympics, Nine est, Opticare, Paloma partners, physicians Health Services, PriceWaterHouseCoopers,, provident Bank, reader's Digest, Riggs bank, DC, REI Medical Center

CRADDOCK-CUNNINGHAM ARCHITECTURAL PARTNERS
10 9TH STREET
LYNCHBURG, VA 24504
434-846-8456
Fax: 434-846-4534
• Hal C. Craddock, Principal
• Lynn Cunningham, Principal
• Tara Cunningham, Marketing Director
• Mark W. Smith, Architect
• Gary Harvey
• Mark Smith
• Matt Tyree
Service
Specializes on master planning and architectural design for private schools,and universities, and historical redevelopment and renovation, with follow-up building design documents and construction administration

Clients
Fork Union Military Academy; Estes Athletic Center, Aquatics Center; Virginia Episcopal School, Van Avery Athletic Center, Weight Room, Carrington Tennis Courts, Alumni Hall, Football Stadium; Averett University North Campus-Athletics Master

CRP ARCHITECTS, P.C.
100 E SAINT VRAIN STREET
SUITE 300
COLORADO SPRINGS, CO 80903
719-633-5901
Fax: 719-633-5903
www.christiansenreece.com
• Holger Christiansen, Principal Architect
• Leland Reece, Principal Architect
Service
Architectural services

CSHQA
ARCHITECTS/ENGINEERS/PLANNERS
250 S 5TH STREET
CW MOORE PLAZA
BOISE, ID 83702
208-343-4635
Fax: 208-343-1858
www.cshqa.com
• Jeffrey A. A. Shneider, President
• Kent A. Hanway, EVP - Board of Directors
• John D. Maulin, Operations VP - Board Director
• Jeffrey A. A. Shneider, Principal Emeritus
• John D. Maulin, Executive VP - Director
• Craig Slocum, Corporate Secretary - Board of Directors
• James G. Murray, Principal/Director
• J. Michael Brady, Principal/Director
• Patrizia Morgan Norberg, Principal - Director
Service
Offers complete in-house design services specializes in commercial design, architecture & urban planning, civil, structural electrical & mechanical engineering and interior design.
Clients
Boise Airport, Rogue Valley International, Fresno Yosemite International Airport, Idaho Air National Guard, CW Moore Plaza, Blue Cross of Idaho, First National Bank of Idaho, Farmers and Merchants State Bank, Key Bank, Spink Butler, Boise Telco Federal Credit Union, CRI Advantage, KPMG, Stoel Rives, IPC General Office Complex, Lewis-Clark State College, BSU Pavilion, BSU Engineering Technology Complex, Boise Schools, Nampa Schools, Belgrade Schools, Lithia Motors, Albertsons, Safeway, McMillans Corner

DAHLIN GROUP ARCHITECTS PLANNERS
5865 OWENS DRIVE
PLEASANTON, CA 94588
925-251-7200
Fax: 925-251-7201
pleasanton@dahlingroup.com
www.dahlingroup.com
• Doug Dahlin, President/Founder
• Alan J. Burrell, Principal
• Harris P. Pierson, Principal / General Manager
• Mario Aiello, Architect
• Al Burrell, Architect
• Karl Danielson, Architect
• Mark Day, Architect

• Kurt Donnelly, Architect
• Nancy Keenan, Architect
Service
Build and sustain professional design expertise in planning resedential, and community serving architecture.

DAUER HASWELL ARCHITECTS
1748 PLATTE STREET
DENVER, CO 80202
303-458-9600
Fax: 303-458- 9666
• Brad Haswell, RA
• Jim Dauer, partner
Description:
Recreation architects specializing in planning and design of community recreation centers.

DAVIS DESIGN
1221 N ST
SUITE 600
LINCOLN, NE 68508
402-476-9700
Fax: 402-476-9722
www.davisdesign.com
• Matt S Metcalf, Principal
• Mike Wachal, Principal
• Wade Stange, Principal
• Jon Dalton, Principal
• Mike Marsh, Principal
• Ed Bukacek, Senior Associate
• Marilyn Larson, Director of Marketing/Public Relations
(402) 476-9700
marilyn.larson@davisdesign.com
Services
Full-service architecture, engineering and interior design firm with experience in the design of stadiums, auditoriums, gymnasiums, swimming facilities, and health, fitness and recreation centers.
Clients
Heritage Park, Husker Auto Group, Electronic Contracting, Inc., Lochland Country Club, Kawasaki Motors Mfg. Corp., West Gate Bank Center, A.G. Edwards & Sons, Inc,, Security Financial Life, National Research Corporation, First National Bank, TierOne Center, Our Savior Lutheran Church, Norfolk Arts Center, First-Plymouth Church, Mid-America Union Conference, Living Water Church, Morrison Cancer Center, Tabtiha LifeQuest Center, Crete Area Medical Center, BryanLGH West Medical Plaza, Sioux Valley Memorial Hospital, Nebraska Orthopaedic & Sports Medicine, SVMH Wellness Center, Ortner Center, Union College, BryanLGH College of Health Sciences, Ha

DES ARCHITECTS/ENGINEERS, INC.
399 BRADFORD STREET
THIRD FLOOR
REDWOOD CITY, CA 94063
650-364-6453
Fax: 650-364-2618
marketing@des-ae.com
www.des-ae.com
• Susan Eschweiler, Principal
seschweiler@des-ae.com
• C. Thomas Gilman, President & Principal
tgilman@des-ae.com
• Craig Ivancovich
• Tom Gilman, President
• Steve Mincey, Principal/CEO
• Jana Gunsul, Associate Principal

facilities

• Melanie Rogers, Associate
Principal/Director of Human Resourc
Services
Provides architecture, design and
engineering services to corporations,
developers, schools, governments and civic
organizations through innovative solutions
for all types of project.
Clients
BMC (Roche), Genentech Inc, Oral B, Alza
Pharmaceuticals, Matrix Pharmaceuticals,
Borland (Inprise), Openwave, Hewlett
Packard Agilent, Britannia East Grand,
PacificShores Center, Moffett Park, Phillips,
Verifone, Jefferson Place, Carlmont High
Scool, Woodside High School, Sequoia High
School, Wilbur Hall, Stern Hall, San Carlos
Youth Center, Foster City Government
Center, Redwood City Firestation #20,
Redwood City Firestation #9, Sequoia
Hospital Birthing, Sequoia Hospital Cardiac
Cath, Sequoia Hospital Acute Care, 2900
Medical Office Building, Sequoia Hospital
Endoscopy, Sequoia House, San Leandro
Hospital, Apple Ireland, Claris Software

DESIGNS IN FITNESS, INC.
1919 N LOOP W
SUITE 435
HOUSTON, TX 77008
910-306-3142
Fax: 713-862-2189
• John Velandra, Personal Trainer

DILULLO ASSOCIATES INC.
16 CRYSTAL STREET
MELROSE, MA 2176
781-662-3498
Fax: 781-662-8389
• Dan Dilullo, contact
Service
Athletic facilities for colleges and high
schools

DLR GROUP
6457 FRANCES
SUITE 200
OMAHA, NE 68106
402-393-4100
866-357-8600
Fax: 402-393-8747
www.dlrgroup.com
• Dale Hallock, Principal
• Ken West, Chairman
kwest@dlrgroup.com
• Bryce Pearsall, Principal
• Griff Davenport, Principal
• Jon Petit, Principal
• Griff Davenport, AIA Managing Principal
Service
offers architectural, engineering, and
planning services

DLZ
157 EAST MARYLAND STREET
INDIANAPOLIS, IN 46204
317-633-4120
800-336-5352
Fax: 317-633-4177
info@dlz.com
www.dlz.com
• Vikram Rajadhyaksha, Chairman
Service
transportation engineering, architecture,
field services, civil engineering, landscape
architecture, construction administration,
environmental services, and geotechnical

engineering
Client
City of Columbus, Department of Public
Utilities; U.S. Army Corps of Engineers,
Detroit District; Ohio Department of Natural
Resources, Department of Engineering;
Indiana Department of Natural Resources;
U.S. Army Corps of Engineers, Huntington
District; Northern Indiana Commuter,
Transportation District; City of Cleveland,
Department of Port Control; City of Lansing;
City of Indianapolis, Department of Capital
Asset; Ohio Department of Transportation;
Michigan Department of Transportation; Ivy
Tech State College; U.S. Postal Service,
Facilities Service Office; Lake Michigan
College; Indiana Department of Correction;
Greater Cleveland Regiona

DON CAREY & ASSOCIATES
9441 NE 16TH STREET
CLYDE HILL, WA 98004
425-454-8166
Fax: 425-462-6188
• Don Carey, Owner
Service
Aquatic design consultants specializing in
feasibility studies, permits, funding
alternatives and aquatic design

DONALD DEMARS INTERNATIONAL
24201 HIGHLANDER ROAD
WEST HILLS, CA 91307-1245
818-773-6540
Fax: 818-773-8803
• Donald DeMars, Chairman & CEO
• Collin Jones, Controller
• Jay Martinez, Executive Architect
• Dave Hurt, General Manager
Service
Development consulting and
architectural/interior design services for
sports, fitness, and wellness center
developments
Client
Scripps Clinic Integrative Medicine Center
Hospital, Braemar Country Club, Pinnacle
Fitness, Inc., Georgetown Physical Therapy
and Fitness Center, Downtown Athletic
Club, The Pomona Healthplex, Manhattan
Athletic Club

**E.G.A. SITE PLANNING/LANDSCAPE
ARCHITECTS**
42 MAIN STREET
NYACK, NY 10960
914-358-6444
Fax: 914-358-7403
• Edward Gaudy, Landscape Architect
vega@tco.com
Service
Site planning of athletic fields, playing courts
and playgrounds at schools and colleges

**ED2 INTERNATIONAL
ARCHITECTS/PLANNERS**
1426 FILLMORE STREET
SUITE 302
SAN FRANCISCO, CA 94115
415-474-1400
Fax: 415-474-9110
contact2@ed2intl.com
• Frank S Fung, President
Service
planning and design of veterinary medical
facilities

EDMOND N. ZISOOK AIA & ASSOCIATES
630 DUNDEE ROAD
SUITE 110
NORTHBROOK, IL 60062
847-564-8333
Fax: 847-564-9989
arenson@sasarch.com
www.sasarch.com
• Edmond N. Zisook, Owner
Service
Fitness and rehabilitation center design and
park facilities in the U.S., Canada, U.K. and
the Far East

ELLENZWEIG ASSOCIATES, INC.
1280 MASSACHUSETTS AVENUE
CAMBRIDGE, MA 2138
617-491-5575
Fax: 617-868-2318
hunt@ellenzweig.com
www.ellenzweig.com
• Miltos Catmoeris, Principal
catomeris@ellenzweig.com
• Harry Ellenzweig, Principal
harry@ellenzweig.com
• Michael Lauber, Principal
lauber@ellenzweig.com
• Catherine Hunt, Associate Principal and
Director of Marketing
hunt@ellenzweig.com
• James Blount, Principal
blount@ellenzweig.com
• Shrine Boulos Anderson, Principal
boulos@ellenzweig.com
• Neil Cahalane, Principal
cahalane@ellenzweig.com
• Steve Mahler, Principal
mahler@ellenzweig.com
• Janet Ross, Principal
ross@ellenzweig.com
Service
Architects for colleges and universities;
Master planning, programming, Feasibility
study preparation, Architectural design,
Laboratory planning and design,
Construction administration
Client
Allegheny College, Ariad Pharmaceuticals,
Augustana College, Babson College, Blue
Cross and Blue Shield of Connecticut,
Boston College, Bowdoin College, Brandeis
University, Bryn Mawr College, Charitable
Leadership Foundation, Charles Stark
Draper Laboratory, Childrens Hospital,
Childrens Hospital of Philadelphia, Clark
University, Connecticut College, Dartmouth
College, Dayton International Airport,
Dickinson College, Dixie State College,
Eisai Research Institute of Boston, EMD
Pharmaceuticals, Emory University, Fidelity
Corporate Real Estate, Friends of Post
Office Square, Hamilton College, Harvard
medical School, Harvard University, Hobart
Clients
Johns Hopkins University, Joslin Diabetes
Center, Lafayette College, Lawrence
University, Lexigen Pharmaceuticals, Loyola
University Chicago Stritch School of
Medicing, Massachusetts Bay Transporation
Authority, Massachusetts Institute of
Technology, Memphis Biotech Foundation,
Millikin University, Rhodes college, Rowan
University, Syracuse University, Tufts
University, University of British columbia,
University of Chicago, University of Florida,
University of Kentucky, University of
Massachusetts, University of Miami,
University of New England, University of

New Hampshire, University of North Carolina Greensboro, University of Notre Dame, Un

ELS ARCHITECTURE AND URBAN DESIGN
2040 ADDISON STREET
BERKELEY, CA 94704
510-549-2929
Fax: 510-843-3304
info@elsarch.com
www.elsarch.com
- Barry Elbasani, Founding Principal
- Carol Shen, Managing Principal
- Bruce Bullman, Principal
- David Fawcett, Principal
- Clarence D. Mamuyac, Jr., Principal
- David Petta, Principal
- Jamie Rusin, Principal
- Kurt Schindler, Principal
- Connie Nitta Curtis, Associate Principal
Service
Architectural Services: Pre-Design Assistance, Capital Campaign Support, Public Process and Facilitation, Site Planning and Programming, Urban Design, Master Planning, Sustainable Design Analysis, LEED Certification, Conceptual Design, Schematic Design, Design Development, Construction Documents, Bidding Assistance, Construction Administration, Post Occupancy Assistance

ERICKSON MCGOVERN
101 E 26TH STREET
SUITE 300
TACOMA, WA 98421
253-531-0206
Fax: 253-531-9197
mail@ericksonmcgovern.com
www.ericksonmcgovern.com
- Jay Peterson, Partner
- Steve Storaasli, Principal
Steve@EricksonMcGovern.com
- Wayne Lerch, Principal
Wayne@EricksonMcGovern.com
- Steve Storaasli, Partner
Service
Architects specializing in educational facilities

EWING COLE CHERRY BROTT
FEDERAL RESERVE BANK BUILDING
100 N 6TH STREET
PHILADELPHIA, PA 19106-1590
215-923-2020
Fax: 215-574-9163
mhenden@ewingcole.com
www.ewingcole.com
- John C. Gerbner, President and COO
(215) 625-4135
jgerber@ewingcole.com
- James A Wilson, Managing Principal
jwilson@ewingcole.com
- S. Mark Hebden, President
mhebden@ewingcole.com
- Donald H. Dissinger, Senior Vice President
ddissinger@ewingcole.com
- James A. Wilson, Senior Vice President
jwilson@ewingcole.com
- Jared Loos, Director of Operations
jloos@ewingcole.com
- Robert McConnell, Director of Architecture
- Pradeep Patel, Director of Engineering
- Joseph Kelly, Chief Executive Officer
jkelly@ewingcole.com

Service
Pre-Design Services, Architectural Design, Interior Design, Engineering, Services to Building Owners and Developers, Presentation Service
Client
Atlantic City Racecourse, Atlantic City, NJ; Birmingham Turf Club, Birmingham, AL; Boyd Gaming, Venton, LA; Bucknell University, Lewisburg, PA; Canterbury Downs Shakopee, MN; Churchill Downs, Louisville, KY; The City of Philadelphia, Philadelphia, PA; Clearwater Phillies, Clearwater, FL; Emerald Downs, Auburn, WA; Empire City Trotting Club, Yonkers, NY; Garden State Park, Cherry Hill, NJ; George Mason University, Fairfax, VA; Hamilton College, Clinton, NY; Hollywood Park Racetrack, Los Angeles, CA; Horseshoe International Taipei, Taiwan; Hubbard Enterprises, Ruidoso, NM; LaSalle University, Philadelphia, PA; Lone Star Jockey Club, Grand Prair
Clients
New Jersey Sports and Exhibition Authority, East Rutherford and Atlantic City, NJ; Penn National Racecourse, Grantham, PA; Penn State University, State College, PA; Philadelphia Park, Philadelphia, PA; Philadelphia Phillies, Philadelphia, PA; Remington Park, Oklahoma City, OK; River Downs, Cincinnati, OH; Rosecroft Raceway, Fort Washington, MD; Sam Houston Race Park, Houston, TX; Singapore Turf Club, Kranji, Singapore; United Horseman of Alberta, Calgary, Alberta, Canada; University of Delaware, Newark, DE; University of Indianapolis Indianapolis, IN; University of Pennsylvania, Philadelphia, PA; University of the Sciences Philadelphia, Phila

FANNING/HOWEY ASSOCIATES, INC.
540 EAST MARKET STREET
CELINA, OH 45822
419-586-7771
888-499-2292
Fax: 419-586-2141
www.fhai.com
- Dan H Mader, President/Chief Executive Officer
- Clair E. Howey, Vice-Chairman of the Board
- Randall L Sprunger, AIA, Chief Operating Officer
- Michael E Hall, AIA, Chief Marketing Officer
- Daniel R. Mader, President and Chief Executive Officer
- Michael E. Hall, Vice President and Chief Marketing Officer
- Douglas M. Wickstrom, Secretary/Treasurer and Chief Technology Offi
- Bruce T. Runyon, Chief Operations Officer
- Randall L. Sprunger, Director
- Steve A. Wilczynski, Director
Service
Architects, engineers, consultants specializing in educational facility design

FENTRESS ARCHITECTS
421 BROADWAY
DENVER, CO 80203
303-722-5000
Fax: 303-722-5080
studio@fentressbradburn.com
www.fentressbradburn.com

- Jim Bradburn, Architect/Principal
- Agatha Kessler, Chief execuitve officer and Principal
- Karen Gilbert, Director Marketing
- Sue Rossberg, Human Resources Director
jobs@fentressbradburn.com
- Colin Lewis, Chief Financial Officer
- Bob Louden, Principal
- Brian. H. Chaffee, Principal and Director
- Jack Cook, Principal
- Jeff Olson, Principal
- Curt Frentress, President and Principal-in-Charge of Design
Fentress@FentressBradburn.com
Service
Architects specializing in interiors and planning
Client
(Projects) Transportation: Incheon International Airport, Denver International Airport, Seattle-Tacoma International Airport, Raleigh-Durham International Airport, Doha International Airport, Ronstadt Transit Center Civic: Cape Girardeau Federal Courthouse, Oakland Administration Buildings, Clark County Government Center, California Dept of Education HQ, Sacramento City Hall Building, Jefferson County Gov't Center, RTC/RFCD Headquarters, Loveloand Police & Courts Building, Colorado State Capitol Renovations Commercial: Dubai Mixed-Use Towers, Arraya Class A Office Tower, alDiera Tower, 421 Broadway, Norwest Bank Tower, Gulf Canada Resources
Clients
(Projects) Laboratory: David E Skaggs Federal Center, Natural Resources Building, UCDHSC Research Complex 1&2; Public Assembly: Colorado Convention Center Exp, Palm Springs Convention Center Exp, Vail Conference and Civic Center, Pasadena Conference Center Exp, INVESCO Field at Mile Hi, Santa Fe Civic Center, Eccles Conference, Peery's Theater, Arvada Center Expansion; Education: Tennyson Center for Children, Denver Academy High School, CU Math Bldg & Engineering Library; Hospitality: Tritch Building Renovation, Palmetto Bay Plantation, One Polo Creek, One Wynkoop Plaza, The Watermark

FFKR ARCHITECTS
BOGUE BUILDING
730 PACIFIC AVENUE
SALT LAKE CITY, UT 84104
801-521-6186
Fax: 801-539-1916
contactus@ffkr.com
www.ffkr.com
- Richard K. Frerichs, Principal
- Franklin T. Ferguson, Founding Principal
- Kenneth E. Louder, President/Chief Execuitve Officer
- Jeffrey L. Fisher, Principal
- Kenneth Louder, Principal
- James. W. Lewis, Principal
- Mark. R. Wilson, Principal
- Roger P. Jackson, Principal
- J. David Gilis, Principal
- Kevin Mass, Principal
Service
Architectural services include feasibility studies, programming, design-build, conceptual design, architectural design, sustainable design, construction documents, construction administration, and

facilities

specifications. Interior design services include feasibility studies, programming, space planning, schematic design, design development, construction documents, furnishings, fixtures and equipment, purchasing, construction administration, wayfinding, graphics, and move management

Client
(Projects) Current: Eyring Planetarium, Joseph F. Smith Building BYU, Valley JH Addition/Remodel; Arts and Entertainment: Randall Jones, Abravanal Hall, Sevier Valley Center; College and University: Harold B. Lee Library Expansion, Spori Building Replacement, Sorenson Physical Education Building; Historic and Restoration: Vernal Temple, Joseph Smith Memorial Building, Bogue Supply Building; Hospitality: Aspen Grove Lodge, Orangerie, Casino Arizona at Salt River; Interior Design & Space Planning: Passages, River Rock Casino, Prestige Financial; Laboratories and Technical: Eccles Genetics Building, Moran I, Benson Science Building

Clients
(Projects) Master Planning: Palace Indian Gaming, SUU Master Plan, UVSC West Campus; Office Buildings: Kimball at BYU Idaho, JVWCD, Northwest Pipeline; Parking: River Rock Parking, Jordan Commons, Northwest Pipeline Parking; Religious: Jerusalem Center, John Taylor Building BYU Idaho, Nauvoo Temple; Retail and Commercial: Larry H. Miller Truckland, Megaplex at The Gateway, Jordan Commons; Schools: Viewmont High School, Olympus Junior High, Whittier Elemetary; Sports and Recreation: Cougar Stadium, The Delta Center, Salt Lake Sports, Fairmont

FGM ARCHITECTS & ENGINEERS
475 REGENCY PARK
SUITE 200
O'FALLON, IL 62269
618-624-3364
Fax: 618-624-3369
www.fgmarchitects.com
• Jr Ha James, EVP (Past)
• John Ochoa, President/Chief Executive Officer
john.ochoa@fgm-inc.com
• Kathleen Miles, Chief Financial Officer
kathleen.miles@fgm-inc.com
• John Ochoa, President and Chief Executive officer
• Mike Caraker, Chief Information Officer
mike.caraker@fgm-inc.com
• Joe Chronister, Director of Higher Education
• John Dzarnowski, Director of Municipal and Recreation
Service
Predesign Consulting, Architectural Planning and Design, Engineering, Interior Architecture
Client
Commercial: Des Plaines Multi-Use, Drake Hotel, General Life Building, Life Insurance Data Processing, Marriott Courtyard Hotels, Meijer Food Stores, Motomart, One Technology Center; K12 Education: Berwyn North SD 98 Prairie Oak Elementary School, Cicero SD 99 Unity Junior High Schook, Cicero SD 99 District Administrict Offices, Frankfort CCSD 157-C Grand Prairie Addition, Grayslake CHSD #127 New High

School, Highland CUSD 5 New Middle School, McHenry CHSD 156 East High School Addition & Renovation, McHenry CHSD 156 West High School Addition & Renovation; Higher Education: Kaskaskia College, Olivet Nazarene University Track, SIUC Softball Com

Clients
State/Federal: Bachelor Enlisted Quarters 27 - Historic Rehabilitation, Forrestal Village - Wholehouse Repairs, Ft. Campbell Guest House - new facility, Scott AFB Collocated Club - new facility, Scott AFB TACC Global Decision Center - new facility, United States Postal Service - team contract; Municipal: Addison Village Hall, Huntley Community Center, Kildeer Village Hall, Lake in the Hills Village Hall, New Lenox Village Hall, Warren Town Hall; Public Safety: Addison Fire Station #3, Addison Police Department, Algonquin/Lake in the Hills Fire Headquarters, Algonquin/Lake in the Hills Fire Stations, Arlington Heights Fire Department Headquart

FINK ROBERTS & PETRIE
4040 VINCENNES CIRCLE
SUITE 300
INDIANAPOLIS, IN 46268
317-872-8400
800-875-3307
Fax: 317-876-2408
frp@frpinc.com
www.frpinc.com
• Michael C Natali, President, Structural Engineering Department Head
• David Lash, VP, Civil Department Head
• Scott E. Rouse, Vice President, Senior Project Manager
• William G. T. Horton, President, Senior Project Manager
Description:
Specializing in structural engineering for professional, collegiate and recreational sports facilities.

FLAD ARCHITECTS
644 SCIENCE DRIVE
MADISON, WI 53711
608-238-2661
Fax: 608-238-6727
flad@flad.com
www.flad.com
• Laura Stillman, Executive Vice President
• Laura Serebin, Principal
• Rachel Nelan, Principal
• Davis Black, Principal
• Mark Corey, Principal
• Jim Gazvoda, Principal
• Jerry Polly, Principal
• Jeffery Raasch, Principal
Description:
Architects specializing in high technology facilities; structural engineers.
Services:
Interior Design, Landscape, Structural, Master Planning, Sustainable Design

FLEWELLING & MOODY
815 COLORODO BLVD
SUITE 200
LOS ANGELES, CA 90041
626-449-6787
Fax: 323-543-8198
www.flewelling-moody.com
• Scott Gaudineer, President/Principal
• Matthew C. Buchanan, Principal

Services:
Specialize in master planing, new construction, modernization and facilities assessment of K-12, community college and higher education facilities

FLUOR CORPORATION
6700 LAS COLINAS BOULEVARD
IRVING, TX 75039
469-398-7000
Fax: 469-398-7255
www.fluor.com
• Alan L L. Boeckmann, Chairman/Chief Executive Officer
• Lawrence N. Fisher, Chief Legal Officer/Secretary
• D. Mi Steuert, SVP/Chief Financial Officer
• Kenneth H. Lockwood, VP, Corporate Finance & Investor Relations
Services:
Global engineering, construction, maintenance and diversified services company
Clients:
KoSa, DSM Elastomers Europe, AECI Lysine Project, BF Goodrich, Yanpet Expansion

FOREMAN ARCHITECTS ENGINEERS INC.
525 W NEW CASTLE STREET
PO BOX 189
ZELIENOPLE, PA 16063
724-452-9690
Fax: 724-452-0136
faeinfo@foremangroup.com
www.foremangroup.com
• Phillip G. Foreman, CEO and President
• David E. Foreman, Vice President
Description:
Architects and engineers specializing in educational facilities.
Services:
Design buildings

FORESITE DESIGN, INC.
3269 COOLIDGE HIGHWAY
BERKLEY, MI 48072
248-547-7757
800-732-0611
Fax: 248-547-0218
info@foresitedesign.com
www.foresitedesign.com
• Bruce C S Lemons, President
• Bruce S. Lemons, President
• Mike Sims, Project Manager
Description:
Landscape architectural/site planning firm specializing in site evaluation, design, construction documents and contract administration of outdoor sports facilities.
Services:
Design services

FOUNTAINHEAD ASSOCIATES
609 DEEP VALLEY DRIVE
SUITE 200
ROLLING HILLS ESTATES, CA 90274
310-378-1410
Fax: 310-378-0719
jerry.papazian@fountainheadassoc.com
www.fountainheadassoc.com
• Jerry Papazian, Managing Director
Description:
Architects and construction managers specializing in ice skating facilities, swimming pools and pre-engineered

buildings.
Services:
Assists exisiting business and organizations develop, implement, manage and sustain their strategic goals; assists entrepreneurs in organizing and structuring new business ventures; provides personal clothing and mentoring services to executives.

FRIBERG ASSOCIATES INC.
2001 BEACH STREET
SUITE 530
FORT WORTH, TX 76103
817-336-0543
Fax: 817-429-0119
• Emil E Friberg, President
• Larry W. Akers, President/Senior Mechanical Designer/Project
• Bobby G. Alexander, Vice President/Secretary
• David W. McDonald, Principal/Electrical Engineer
• Joshua D. Schmidt, Principal/Mechanical Engineer
• Will Martin, Plumbing/Fire Protection Designer
• Emil E. Friberg, Chairman of the Board
Description:
Mechanical, electrical plumbing consultants.
Services:
Offers a range of services that includes strategic consulting, master planning, energy studies, systems design, maintenance analysis, and construction administration

FTL DESIGN ENGINEERING STUDIO
44 E EAST 32ND STREET
3RD FLOOR
NEW YORK, NY 10016
212-732-4691
Fax: 212-385-1025
www.ftlstudio.com
• Nicholas S Goldsmith, Senior Principal
• Mercedes Gonzalez, CFO
• Ashish Soni, Principal
• Joseph Schedlbauer, Engineering Principal
Description:
Specializes in lightweight, deployable design and construction technologies. Offers consulting and design services.
Services:
Urban iconic, performance building, building skins, event buildings, and transportation buildings

GAUDREAU, INC. ARCHITECTS/PLANNERS/ENGINEERS
810 LIGHT STREET
BALTIMORE, MD 21230
410-837-5040
Fax: 410-837-8093
info@gaudreauinc.com
www.gaudreauinc.com
• William A L Gaudreau, President
• David G. Gaudreau, Senior Vice President
• Randal Gaskins, Vice President
Description:
Architecture, planning, engineering for athletic and recreational facilities ranging from large college and university complexes to small corporate executive centers and community parks
Services:
Comprehensive architectural services,

ranging from site searches, master planning, strategic planning, programming and design

GEIGER ENGINEERS
2 EXECUTIVE BOULEVARD
SUITE 410
SUFFERN, NY 10901
845-368-3330
Fax: 845-368-3366
dor@geigerengineers.com
www.geigerengineers.com
• David Chen, Principal
• Paul A.Gossen, Principal
• Paul Gossen, Principal
• Mike Liao, Principal
• Stephen P.Emery, Principal
• Timothy D.Mills, Principal
• David M.Campbell, Principal
Nature of Sports Service:
Consulting engineers specializing in sports structures, long-span roofs, entertainment events engineering venue evaluations and rigging.
Other Office:
Geiger Engineers, P.C. Bellingham Office 114 W. Magnolia St. Suite 505 Bellingham WA 98225 phone: 360-734-7194 fax: 360-734-7399
Services:
Structural design, computer-aided design and diversified applies science research

GLASS ARCHITECTS
200 E STREET
SUITE 100
SANTA ROSA, CA 95404
707-544-3920
Fax: 707-544-2514
info@glassarchitects.com
www.glassarchitects.com
• Anne Glass, Human Resources Director aglass@glassarchitects.com
• Eric Glass, Principal eric@glassarchitects.com
• Charlie Sikes, Associate csikes@glassarchitects.com
• Jeff Bousfield, Associate jbousfield@glassarchitects.com
• Dave Zaro, Associate dzaro@glassarchitects.com
Description:
Architects specializing in community recreation, sports and aquatic centers

GOODY CLANCY
420 BOYLSTON STREET
BOSTON, MA 02116-3866
617-262-2760
Fax: 617-262-9512
www.goodyclancy.com
• Roger Goldstein, Principal (617) 850-6537 roger.goldstein@goodyclancy.com
• David Dixon, FAIA, Principle for Planning & Urban Design
• David Spillane, AICP, RIBA, Principal, Director of Planning
• Bernard Dooley, AIA, LEED, Director of Laboratory Planning
Description:
Architecture, planning and urban design firm specializing in academic facilities, campus planning, residential communities and historic preservation

GOSSEN LIVINGSTON ARCHITECTURE
1525 E. DOUGLAS
WICHITA, KS 67211
316-265-9367
Fax: 316-265-5646
• William B Livingston, President/CEO
Description:
Architecture, planning, programming, landscape architecture and interior design for university, college and high school sports facilities
Services:
Provides services in every major architectural field, including discovery/programming, master planning, interior design and landscape architecture

GRAHAM/MEUS, INC. ARCHITECTS
SIX EDGERLY PLACE
BOSTON, MA 2116
617-423-9399
Fax: 617-482-8506
• Daniel L Meus, Principal
• Gary Graham, Principal
• Carolyn Tacelli, Director of Finance
• Melissa Vaillancourt, Director of the Boston Studio
• Linda Tetreault, Project Manager
• Cordelia Dawson, Project Manager/Designer
• Bethany Robertson, Drafting Programs
• Andrew Sikorski, Designer
Year Founded:
1980
Clients:
Institutional, Private Fitness, YMCA, YWCA, Community Fitness, College and University Healthcare.
Nature of Service:
Provide planning, architecture, and interior design services

GREENWAY GROUP, THE
25 TECHNOLOGY PARKWAY SOUTH
SUITE 101
NORCROSS, GA 30092
678-879-0929
800-726-8603
Fax: 678-879-0930
www.greenway.us
• James P Cramer, Principal and Chairman
• Dough Parker, Managing Principal
• Bob Fisher, Principal
• David R. Zimmerman, Consulting Principal
• Lorna Rein, Consulting Principal
• Tonya Smith, Membership Manager and Executive Assistant
• Dave Zimmerman, Consulting Principal
• James P. Cramer, Chairman & Principal
Description:
Natural sport turf specialists; installs and renovates athletic playing fields.
Services:
Consulting and business networking firms for the design and construction industry

GREMMER ASSOCIATES
120 WILSHIRE BOULEVARD NORTH
STEVENS POINT, WI 54481
715-341-4363
Fax: 715-341-1856
www.gremmerassociates.com
• Dave Glodowski, Vice president
Description:
Firm provides transportation engineering, recreational and athletic facility design, municipal engineering, site design,

construction services and surveying in the Midwest and West. Specialties include urban and rural highways, bridges, sewage collection
Services:
Transportation design, municipal design, site design, surveying services, construction management, and storm water management

GRILLIAS PIRC ROSIER ALVES
15707 ROCKFIELD BOULEVARD
SUITE 300
IRVINE, CA 92618
949-951-4774
Fax: 949-250-4912
• Peter Grillias, President
Services:
Specializing in planning, architecture, engineering and interior design

GROUNDS MAINTENANCE SERVICES
16982 W. NATIONAL AVE.
NEW BERLIN, WI 53151
262-784-8219
800-227-9381
Fax: 866-236-1546
info@groundsmaintenancewi.com
www.groundsmaintenancewi.com
• Floyd Perry, Marketing Director
Nature of Service
Athletic field risk, injury and prevention consultant and author/lecturer on sports fields, athletic field maintenance, quality supplies and equipment. Instructional groundskeeping books and videos, workshops, retail tools and equipment

HAMMEL, GREEN AND ABRAHAMSON INC.
420 5TH STREET NORTH
SUITE 100
MINNEAPOLIS, MN 55401
612-758-4000
888-442-8255
Fax: 612-758-4199
info@hga.com
www.hga.com
• Daniel Avchen, Chairman/CEO
davchen@hga.com
• Dan Rectenwald, Chief Operating Officer
• Stephen Fiskum, Principal
• Hal Henderson, Principal
• Kent Mainquist, Chief Financial Officer
• Paul Asp, Director of Structural Engineering
• Deb Barnes, Director of Interior Design
Nature of Service
Full service architecture, engineering and planning firm. HGA offers design and engineering expertise for healthcare, corporate, the arts, community and education clients.
Clients
3M, Accenture, ADC Telecommunications, Affinity - Mercy Medical Center, Ag-Chem, Agricultural and Food Sciences Academy, Albermarle County School District, Virginia, All Saints - St. Luke's Hospital, Allina Health System, American Express, American Medical Systems, American Red Cross, American River College, Andersen Windows Corporation, Andrews University, Anoka Hennepin School District, Anoka Technical Institute, Antioch Public Library, Artspace, Aspen Medical Group, Associated Eye Physicians, Augsburg College, Aurora Health System, Aurora University, Austin

Junior College, B.F. Goodrich Aerospace, Baycare Surgery Center, Beaumont Clinic, B

HASTINGS + CHIVETTA ARCHITECTS, INC.
622 EMERSON ROAD
SUITE 200
SAINT LOUIS, MO 63141
314-863-5717
888-659-2724
Fax: 314-863-2823
info@hcarchitects.com
www.hastingschivetta.com
• James R Capps, Principal.
jcapps@hcarchitects.com
• Erik J. Kochner, Principal
ekochner@hcarchitects.com
• James B. Favier, Principal
jfavier@hcarchitects.com
• Christopher Chivetta, President /Principal
cchivetta@hcarchitects.com
• Erik J.Kocher, Design Principal
• James R.Capps, Principal
Nature of Service
Provides a full range of architectural services to institutional, educational, municipal, and corporate clients. Portfolio of experience includes master planning, college and university facilities, community centers, educational, commercial, and sports and recreation facilities.
Clients
MASTER PLANNING (Centre College, Charminade College Preparatory School, Community School of Naples, Fontbonne University, Forsyth School, Hanover College, Lindenwood University, Lutheran North High School, Nebraska College of Technical Agriculture, Pulaski Academy, Rossman School, St. Joseph's Academy, The Bolles School, Union University, University of Tulsa, University of Utah, Villa Duchesne School, Wabash Colege);
COLLEGIATE (Central Missouri State University, Centre College, Fontbonne College, Hanover College, Illinois Wesleyan University, Juniata College, Lindenwood College, Longwood University, Missouri State University, Morehead State
Clients
Private K-12 Projects (Chaminade College Preparatory School, Community School Naples, Community School of Naples, Darlington School, Forsyth School, Girls Preparatory School, St. Joseph's Academy, The McCallie School, The Westminster School, Villa Duchesne School); Public K-12 Projects (Ferguson-Florissant School District, Okemos Public Schools, South Lyon Community Schools; MUNICIPAL (City of Arnold, City of Des Peres, City of Farmington, City of Fort Collins, City of Liberty, City of Mission, City of Richmond Heights, City of St. Peters, City of Thornton, Jewish Community Center, Peoria Park District & OSF Saint Francis Medical Center, St.
Clients
COMMERCIAL/CIVIC (City of Town & Country, Enterprise Rent-A-Car, Federated Foods, Jefferson Smurfit, Missouri Ahletic Club, National Super Markets, Inc., Roosevelt Federal Savings & Loan, Sachs Properties, St. Louis County, St. Louis County Library

HAYES LARGE ARCHITECTS
LOGAN BOULEVARD & FIFTH AVENUE
SUITE 700
ALTOONA, PA 16602
814-946-0451
888-809-6134
Fax: 814-946-9054
www.hayeslarge.com
• S. Dwight Knouse, AIA, Executive Partner
• Mark Shrift, RSLA, Director of Landscape Architecture
• Randy Hudson, Principal
grhudson@hayeslarge.com
• Ron Miller, Principal
• W. Joe Mollenauer, Chief Financial Officer
• Bradford J. Furey, Director, Educational Planning Resources
• Mark S. Shrift, Director, Landscape Architecture
• Karl H. Kessler, Director, Electrical Engineering
• Carmen L. Wyckoff, Principal
• Randy Hudson, Director Of Design
Nature of Service
One of America's leading architecture, engineering and planning firms, providing superior client service from six offices in Pennsylvania, Virginia.
Clients
St Louis Cardinals New Ballpark, Comerica Park, Coors Field, The Palace of Auburn Hills, The Coliseum, Edward Jones Dome, Gaylord Entertainment Center, Pro Player Stadium, Raymond James Stadium
Clients
Healthcare: Health Sciences Center Library/Classroom (West Virginia University); Lewistown Hospital (Lewistown, PA); Miners Hospital (Hastings, PA); New Outpatient Center, Atrium and parking Garage Addition (Altoona Hospital, Altoona, PA); Trauma Center (Altoona Hospital)
Clients
Cultural/Civic: (Government) Keystone Building, Department of General Services - Harrisburg, PA; Rachael Carson State Office Building, Harrisburg, PA; (Museum) Baker Mansion, Altoona, PA; The National Civil War Museum, City of Harrisburg - Harrisburg, PA; (Religious) St. John the Evangelist Roman Catholic Church; (Community) Frank J. Paquerilla Conference Center, Johnstown, PA; Mishler Theatre, Altoona, PA; Pennsylvania College of Technology, Community Arts Center - Williamsport, PA; Private Retirement Residence - Central PA; Planning/Studies: DoDea Educational Specifications, US Department of Defense Educational Activity/VA; Loudoun County
Services:
Athletic facility design; synthetic turf; stadium design

HEALTH FITNESS CORPORATION
1700 WEST 82ND STREET
SUITE 200
MINNEAPOLIS, MN 55431
612-831-6830
800-639-7913
Fax: 952-897-5096
info@hfit.com
www.hfit.com
• Gregg V. Lehman, President/Chief Executive Officer
• Paul W. Lotharius, President and Chief Executive Officer
• Mark Totts, Senior Vice President

- Sean McManamy, Senior Vice President
- Brian Harrigan, Vice President
- Kelly Merriman, Vice President
- Tina Loskota, Vice President, Human Resources
- Debra Marshall, Vice President, Marketing

Nature of Service

Consultants/managers specializing in corporate and hospital health and fitness facilities and programs including feasibility studies, facility planning, physical therapy services and ergonomics.

Clients

Waukesha Memorial Hospital, Waukesha, WI; Hewlett-Packard; Health Benefits Wellness and Recognition Services, Texas Instruments, Dallas, TX; Wilton P. Herbert Health and Wellness Center, St. Elizabeth Hospital, Beaumont, TX

Services:

Provider of integrated health and fitness management services for employees and individuals

---

HEALTH FITNESS DYNAMICS, INC.
1012 N. OCEAN BLVD
SUITE 103
POMPANO BEACH, FL 33062
954-942-0049
Fax: 954-941-0854
hfd@hfdspa.com
www.hfdspa.com
- Judith L Singer, President & Co-Owner
(954) 942-0049
judysinger@hfdspa.com
- Judy A Singer, Founder & Co-Owner
- Patty Monteson, Founder & Co-Owner
- Patricia Monteson, Principal
pattymonteson@hfdspa.com

Nature of Service

Specializing in spa design, planning, and marketing to luxury spa hotels, spa resorts, day spas, and other spa related companies.

Clients

Resorts and Hotels: The Spa at Sawgrass, Alderbrook Resort & Spa, Four Seasons Jackson Hole, Four Seasons New York, Little Dix Bay, Malliouhana, Four Seasons Biltmore Santa Barbara, Ballantyne Resort, Cranwell Resort, Pinehurst Resort, Sandestin Hilton, Mandarin Oriental, Sonesta Key Biscayne, Hotel Cresent Court, Bacara, Royal Sands, Agua at Sanderson, Portofino Bay Hotel, Monterey Plaza Hotel, La Posada de Santa Fe, Silverado Country Club & Resort, The Homestead, Double Tree Islander, Agua at Delano, Wind Spa, The Breakers, Scottsdale Princess, Four Seasons Resort, Hawaii at Hualalai, The Coeur d'Alene, The Salish Lodge, The Disney Institute

---

HEERY INTERNATIONAL, INC.
999 PEACHTREE STREET NE
ATLANTA, GA 30309-3953
404-881-9880
Fax: 404-946-2398
Corporate@heery.com
www.heery.com
- Jim J. Moynihan, Chairman & CEO
jmoynihan@heery.com
- Bill Heitz, President
- Greg Pierce, Regional Manager

Nature of Service

Architecture, engineering, master planning, design and construction management of sports facilities.

Description:

Architecture, engineering, master planning, design and construction management of sports facilities.

Clients

Architecture: Atlanta Botanical Gardens; Atlanta History Center Museum; Atlanta History Center Parking Deck; Bosch Corporation; Central Michigan University; Citadel; Coca-Cola; Comdisco; Conoco Headquarters, Cumberland County Civic Center; Dare County; Dare County Justice Center; Dekalb County Courthouse; Emory University School of Law; Erie Seawolves Stadium; Franklin Templeton; Georgia Dome; Georgia World Congress Center; Heery D.C. Office; Hotel Thayer; Jacksonville Baptist Hospital; James Madison University; Kennesaw State University; Mayo Clinic; MBNA Multiple Locations; McCoy Stadium; Memorial Mission Parking Deck; Metlife; Missoula Sta

Services:

Architecture, Construction Managemetn, Engineering, Facilities Management, Interior Design, and Program Management

---

HERBERT LEWIS KRUSE BLUNCK ARCHITECTURE
500 EAST LOCUST
SUITE 300
DES MOINES, IA 50309
515-288-9536
Fax: 515-288-5816
arch@hlkb.com
www.hlkb.com
- Kirck V V. Blunk, Principal
kblunck@hlkb.com
- Doug Fey, Senior Architect
dfey@hlkb.com
- J. Ma Schmidt, Senior Architect
mschimdt@hlkb.com

Nature of Service

Offers master planning, architectural design, interior design, and landscape architecture.

Clients

(Parking): Newton Road Parking + Chilled Water Facility, Center Street Park + Ride, Wells Fargo Financial Parking Facility; (Education): Visitor Center/Hall of Fame, University of Iowa; Roosevelt Practice Facility, Roosevelt High School; Kimmel Theatre/Youngker Hall, Cornell College; Academic Building, Palmer College of Chiropractic Florida; Mowethy Hall, Cornell College; John Chrystal Center; Grinnell College; Palmer Center for Chiropractic Research, Palmer College of Chiropratic; Palmer Friendship Court, Palmer College of Chiropratic

Clients

(Workplace): Meredith Corporate Expansion; Coppola Enterprises Office; Landscape Architect's Office; Marakon Associates, New York; Metro Waste Authority; Renaissance Granite, Marble, + Tile; Two River Marketing; Wells Fargo Financial Corporate Expansion; Faegre + Benson Law Office; (Private) Fingerman Residence, Moen Residence, Seely Residence, Rents Loft

Clients

(Renewed): Glove Factory, Herndon Hall Restoration, Ola Babcock Miller Building, Mowethy Hall, Finkbine Mansion; (Retail) Sticks, M.C, Ginsberg; (Landscape) American College Testing, Grays Lake Pedestrian Bridge, Kautz Plaza, Hilltop

Pedestrian Mall, Drake - West Campus; (In Progress) Blank Honors Center, Melrose Parking Ramp Addition, Papajohn Higher Education Center, ITTC, McLeod, 420 East Locust

---

HKS INC
1919 MCKINNEY AVENUE
DALLAS, TX 75201
214-969-5599
Fax: 214-969-3397
www.hksinc.com
- H Ralph Hawkins, President/Chief Executive Officer
rhawkins@hksinc.com
- Nunzio M. DeSantis, EVP
ndesantis@hksinc.com
- Ralph Hawkins, Chairman and CEO

Nature of Service

Provides services in architecture, structural engineering, interior design, master planning, project management, architectural programming, multi-media production, graphic design and model services.

Clients

(Aviation): Dallas/Fort Worth International Airport Terminal D; Dallas/Fort Worth International Airport Terminal B Concourse Addition & Renovation; Phoenix Sky Harbor International Airport Consolidated Rental Car Facility; Orlando International Airport - North Terminal Station BP - S010; Orlando International Airport Airside One FIS Corridor and In-Transit Lounge; (Commercial): Hall Office Park, Frisco, TX; Kilroy San Diego Corporate Center; Whole Foods Market; Frost Bank Tower; CNL Center at City Commons; Gallery Place; 3883 Howard Hughes Parkway; Five Houston Center; (Corporate): Fidelity Investments; Sabre Holdings Headquarters; Nissan Mot

Clients

(Education): Texas A&M Foundation Jon L. Hagier Center; Southern Methodist University Cox School of Business; University of Kansas Medical Center; Dallas ISD Jesse Owens Memorial Complex; Grand Prairie ISD Gopher-Warrior Bowl; Birdville Independent School District; Garland ISD Special Events Center; (Governmental): Pinellas County Forensic Science Center; Federal Bureau of Prisons; Henry Wade Juvenile Justice Center; Seminole County Criminal Justice Center; Colorado Department of Corrections San Carlos Special Needs Unit; George H. Mahon Federal Building & Courthouse; Idaho Juvenile Observation and Assessment Center; U.S. Census Headquarters

Clients

(Graphics): La Vid, Makara, Aikman's Enzone, HKS Recruitment, Whataburger Field, Miami Children's Hospital, St. Rose Dominican Hospital; (Healthcare): Emory Crawford Long Hospital, Obici Hospital, M.D. Anderson Cancer Center, Utah Valley Regional Medical Center, Children's Hospital Central California, Abbott Northwestern Heart Hospital, George Washington University Hospital, Clarian West Medical Center, St. Rose Dominican Hospital, Parker Adventist Hospital, Seattle Children's Hospital, Cleveland Clinic Florida Weston Hospital

HNTB CORP
715 KIRK DRIVE
KANSAS CITY, MO 64105
816-472-1201
Fax: 816-472-4516
www.hntb.com
• Ken Graham, CEO
(816) 742-1201
• Mike Handelman, Chief Sales Officer
(816) 472-1201
• Mike Scott, Chief Operating Officer
(816) 472-1201
• Harvey Co Hammond, Executive
Chairman
• Paul Yarossi, Executive Vice President
• Ed Mcspedon, Executive Vice President
• Becky Zahner, Chief Planning Officer
(816) 472-1201
Nature of Service
Provides architectural service with clients in
the aviation, corporate, education, federal
and local government/civic markets.
Provides design and project management
expertise focused by market and by
discipline. Design studios include: Aviation,
Civic, Convention Centers, Corporate,
Education, Federal, Historic Preservation,
Interiors, Parking Facilities, Program
Management, Sports Architecture, Structural
Engineering, Transportation Architecture.
Clients
(Aviation): Chicago Midway Airport,
Dallas/Forth Worth International Airport
Terminal D, T.F. Green Airport,
Wilkes-Barre/Scranton International Airport,
Kansas City International Airport, Tucson
International Airport Terminal Expansion,
McGhee Tyson Airport Renovation, Bradley
International Airport; (Civic) Union Station;
Kansas City Public Library, Central Library;
Bartle Hall Convention Center, Boston
Convention and Exhibition Center, San
Diego Convention Center, Washington D.C.
Convention Center Program Management,
Rhode Island Convention Center
Clients
(Corporate): Shook, Hardy & Bacon LLP,
Polsinelli Shalton Welte Suelthaus PC,
HNTB Headquarters, Kansas City Public
Library, Central Library; Sprint ION;
(Education): The Ohio State University Ohio
Stadium, University of Southern California
Galen Center, Oregon State University
Reser Stadium, Purdue University Ross-Ade
Stadium, University of Georgia Sanford
Stadium, University of Kentucky
Commonwealth Stadium, University of
Tennessee Aquatics Center, University of
Kentucky Basketball Training Facility
Clients
(Federal): Naval Air Systems Command
Headquarters, U.S. Air Force Academy
Athletic Complex Expansion, The Mary E.
Switzer Memorial Building; (Historic
Preservation): Union Station, Kansas City
Public Library, Central Library; (Sports
Architecture) INVESCO Field at Mile High;
The Ohio State University Ohio Stadium,
U.S. Air Force Academy Athletic Complex
Expansion, Mid-America Center, Council
Bluffs; Fifth Third Field, University of
Southern California Galen Center, Oregon
State University Reser Stadium, Purdue
University Ross-Ade Stadium, University of
Georgia Sanford Stadium, University of
Kentucky Commonwealth Stadium,
University of Tenness

HOLABIRD & ROOT
140 S DEARBORN STREET
SUITE 700
CHICAGO, IL 60603
312-357-1771
Fax: 312-357-1909
holabird@holabird.com
www.holabird.com
• Greg Cook, Principal
gcook@holabird.com
• Jeff Case, Principal
• Jim Miller, Principal
• James Baird, Principal
Description:
Professional architectural design services

INTEGRATED DESIGN SOLUTIONS
425 CASHMAN DRIVE
SUITE 100
CHIPPEWA FALLS, WI 54729
715-723-6500
Fax: 715-723-6523
info@integrateddesign.com
www.integrateddesign.com
• Scott Olson, President
• Stacy Olson, Operations Manager
• Jason Revelle, Buisness Development
Manager
• Dave Keys, Industrial Designer
• Bob Fehr, Product Development Engineer
• Katie Remaly, Industrial Designer
• Matt Ludvigson, Graphic Designer
Services:
Industrial designs, Engineering, Graphic
Design, Prototyping, Project Management

JOHN M.Y. LEE/MICHAEL TIMCHULA ARCHITECTS
320 W 13TH STREET
NEW YORK, NY 10014-1280
212-929-3131
Fax: 212-463-8964
• John MY Lee
• Michael Timchula
Description:
Gymnasium, natatorium and tennis stadium
architecture
Description:
Gymnasium, natatorium and tennis stadium
architecture.

KIKU OBATA & COMPANY
6161 DELMAR BOULEVARD
SUITE 200
ST LOUIS, MO 63112
314-361-3110
www.kikuobata.com

KINSEY ASSOCIATES
HASTINGS COMMONS BUILDING 2A
486 SCHOOLEYS MOUNTAIN ROAD
SUITE 207
HACKETTSTOWN, NJ 07840
908-850-6488
Fax: 908-788-6788
• John L Jo Belle, President
• Gordon A. Raupp, VP
Sports Service Founded:
1962
Design & Consulting Services:
Recreation Master Plan Planning, Site
Studies, Working Drawings and
Specifications, Construction Contract
Administration, Permitting, and Funding
Assistance.

L. ROBERT KIMBALL & ASSOCIATES
615 W HIGHLAND AVENUE
PO BOX 1000
EBENSBURG, PA 15931
814-472-7700
Fax: 814-472-7712
aande@lrkimball.com
• Joel V McCamley, Senior Vice President
• Jeff Kimball, Principal & CEO
• Richard E. Genday, Senior Vice President
• Adam S. Henger, Senior Vice President
• E. Jack Lerch, Senior Vice President
• Rick Taormina, Senior Vice President

• Karen G. Maul, Vice President
Description:
Consulting services for indoor, outdoor and
rooftop tennis facilities for tournaments,
clubs, resort and institutional projects in U.S.
and international markets

LEHMAN-SMITH-MCLEISH PLLC
1212 BANKS NW
WASHINGTON, DC 20007
202-295-4800
Fax: 202-295-4856
info@lsm.com
www.lsm.com
• Debra Lehman-Smith, Partner
• James Black McLeish, III, Partner
Description:
Architectural and interior design services

LMN ARCHITECTS
801 SECOND AVENUE
SUITE 501
SEATTLE, WA 98104
206-682-3460
Fax: 206-343-9388
design@lmnarchitects.com
www.lmnarchitects.com
• Chris Eseman, Partner
• Kristy Kimura, Principal
Nature of Sports Service:
Architectural firm with expertise in the
design of public assembly facilities

LOCKWOOD, ANDREWS, AND NEWNAM/LAN
2925 BRIARPARK DRIVE
SUITE 400
HOUSTON, TX 77042
713-266-6900
Fax: 713-266-2089
info@lan-inc.com
www.lan-inc.com
• Dennis Petersen, President
• Jeremy Nakashima, P.E, Senior Project
Manager
• Daniel B. McCausland, Director of
Program
• Randall C. Hill, Director of Engineering

LOHMANN COMPANIES
18250 BECK ROAD
MARENGO, IL 60152
815-923-3400
Fax: 815-923-3662
design@lohmann.com
www.lohmann.com
• Robert M Lohmann, president and
principal architect
• Todd A. Quitno, Golf Course Architect
Marketing & Consulting Services:
Full-service golf course architectural firm.
Administrates and supervises the complete
golf course construction process

MAHG ARCHITECHTURE
6400 RILEY PARK DRIVE
FORT SMITH, AR 72916
479-782-1051
Fax: 479-782-6019
info@mahgarch.com
www.mahgarch.com
• Hunter Galen D, Partner
Description:
Consultants that specialize in economic
feasibility analyses and market analyses for
recreation and mass spectator facilities

MILTON POWELL & PARTNERS
PO BOX 600984
SUITE 200
DALLAS, TX 75360-0984
214-213-7862
Fax: 214-520-3005
mpowell@mpparchitects.com
www.mpparchitects.com
• Milton Powell, Principal
• Richard C. Robinson, Principal
Description:
Professional services include architectural
design and planning

MITCHEL ABRAMOWITZ, A.I.A.
2526 ROSEWOOD AVENUE
ROSLYN, PA 19001-3012
215-368-9133
Fax: 215-368-8232
faramitch@comcast.net
• Mitchell Abramowitz, President/Owner
Nature of Sports Service:
Architects and designers of ice skating
facilities, swimming pools, and recreational
facilities. Consultants and construction
managers

MURAKAMI/NELSON
100 FILBERT STREET
OAKLAND, CA 94607
510-444-7959
Fax: 510-893-5244
office@murakaminelson.com
www.murakaminelson.com
• Michael Murakami, Principal
• Takane Eshima, Principal Emeritus
• John S. Nelson, Principal
Nature of Service
Architectural, planning, exterior and interior
design for athletic and recreational facilities;
new and remodeling and seismic
strengthening for university, institutional and
private clients.
Clients
City of Alameda, County of Alameda, Bank
of America, Berkeley Unified School District,
Lowell Berry Foundation, Brickyard Cove
Investments, E.D. Bullard Company, C & H
Development Company, California Coastal
Conservancy, California State University,
San Jose; California Department of
Transportation, Contra Costa County, Tom
Dannenberg, Doten Motors, Dinwiddie
Construction, Degenkolb Engineers, Deleuw
Cather, DMJM, Doric Development, City of
Dublin, Duffel Financial & Construction
Company, Duwo Partners, East Bay
Municipal Utility District, East Bay Regional
Park District, East Bay Asian Local
Development Corporation, ED2
International, EDAW

NBBJ
523 W 6TH STREET
SUITE 300
LOS ANGELES, CA 90014
213-243-3333
Fax: 213-243-3334
losangeles_office@nbbj.com
www.nbbj.com
• Scott Hunter, Principal
(213) 243-3333
• Patrick Winters, Senior Associate
• Robert Mankin, Senior Associate
• Jonathan Ward, Principal
• Paul Becker, Senior Associate
Current Projects:
Milwaukee Brewers, Seattle Mariners,
Cincinnati Bengals, San Francisco 49ers,
LG Twins baseball team in Seoul, Korea,
new arenas for the Los Angeles
Kings/Lakers, Xavier University.
Nature of Sports Service
Architectural design for sports facilities.
Year Founded:
1995

NBBJ SPORTS
2 RECTOR STREET
25 TH FLOOR
NEW YORK, NY 10006
212-924-9000
Fax: 212-924-9292
info@nbbj.com
www.nbbj.com
• Jane Ayers, Principal
(614) 224-7145
sports@nbbj.com

OSBORN ENGINEERING
1300 E 9TH STREET
SUITE 1500
CLEVELAND, OH 44114
216-861-2020
Fax: 216-861-3329
www.osborn-eng.com
• Kurt K. Rim, Chairman
• Eugene P. Baxendale, President
eugene.baxendale@osborn-eng.com
Description:
Planning, design, engineering for new or
renovations, expansions, restorations of
stadiums, arenas, and recreation facilities

PAIGE DESIGN GROUP
5 PEARSE WYND ROAD
BAHAMA, NC 27503
919-620-0300
Fax: 919-620-0091
dpaige@paigedesigngroup.com
www.paigedesigngroup.com
• Don Paige, President and OWNER
dpaige@paigedesigngroup.com
• Tim Murphy, P.E., Associate & Project
Manager
tmurphy@paigedesigngroup.com
• Don Paige, President
dpaige@paigedesigngroup.com
Nature of Sports Service:
Planners, developers, renovators of athletic
facilities including stadiums, arenas, indoor
multi-sport complexes, outdoor fields, park
and recreation facilities; specializes in
synthetic sport surfacing and flooring

PARSONS
401 DIAMOND DRIVE NW
HUNTSVILLE, AL 35806-2192

256-837-5200
Fax: 256-830-0287
www.parsons.com
• Charles L Harrington, Chairman of the
Board & CEO
• Curtis A Bower, Vice Chairman Of The
Board
• William Turner, EVP/Chief Operating
Officer
• Gary Boyd, EVP/Chief Development
Officer
Service
Architecture, Interiors, Construction
Management, Facility Condition
Assessment, Information Technology,
Master Planning, Program and Project
Management

PIPER RUDNICK LLP
2000 AVENUE OF THE STARS
SUITE 400
NORTH TOWER
LOS ANGELES, CA 90067-4704
310-595-3000
Fax: 310-595-3300
info@dlapiper.com
www.dlapiper.com
• Brian C. Lusaght, Partner
• Jannet Abboud, Special Counsel
• Maurad Abida, Practice Group Head
• Therese Zeid, Sr.Consultant
• Norman Abrams, Partner
• Jakub Adam, Partner
• Stephen Abreu, Associate
• Frank Burch, Global Chairman
Nature of Service:
Sports facilities development

RAWHIDE PAVILION & RODEA ARENA
23023 N SCOTTSDALE ROAD
SCOTTSDALE, AZ 85255
480-502-1880
Fax: 480-502-1301
• Trudel St Sandy, Sales/Marketing Director
• Danelle Newton, Event Manager
• Steve Feld, Special Projects Manager
Year Founded:
1970
Seating Capacity:
Pavilion 6,000; Arena 6,800
Track Type:
Dirt track.
Track Size:
1/4 mile

ROSSER
TWO PEACHTREE POINTE
1555 PEACHTREE STREET, NE
SUITE 800
ATLANTA, GA 30309
404-876-3800
Fax: 404-888-6861
frothbard@rosser.com
www.rosser.com
• Ray Ashe, Project Management Director
Description:
Architectural design for sports facilities

SH GROUP
11 W 42ND STREET
NEW YORK, NY 10036-2300
800-328-1600
800-858-2478
Fax: 212-556-3333
info@syska.com
www.syska.com

• John Magliano, Chairman / Chief Executive Officer
• Harvery Goldman, President/Chief Operating Officer
• Robert Dusconi, Chief Financial Officer
• Ann Banning-Wright, Chief Strategy Officer
Services:
Consulting, engineering, technology and construction services
Clients:
World's leading private and public corporations, fast-growing and high tech companies, colleges and universities, real estate owners and developers, as well as local, state and federal government agencies, architects and design professionals.

SHEN MILSON & WILKE
33 NEW MONTGOMERY STREET
10TH FLOOR
SAN FRANCISCO, CA 94105
415-391-7610
800-221-1444
Fax: 415-391-0171
www.smwinc.com
• Dennis A Paoletti, Principal
dpaoletti@sf.smwinc.com
• Kevin Eldredge, Associate Principal
Other Office:
5263 South 300 West, Salt Lake City, UT 84107. 801 266-3605; FAX: 801 266-1151
Description:
Professional services include acoustical and audiovisual consulting

SINK COMBS DETHLEFS, A PROFESSIONAL CORPORATION FOR ARCHITECTURE
475 LINCOLN STREET
SUITE 100
DENVER, CO 80203
303-308-0200
866-535-5653
Fax: 303-308-0222
marketing@sinkcombs.com
www.sinkcombs.com
• Donald L. Dethlefs, Chief Executive Officer (303) 308-0200
• B. Stephen King, Project Manager
• Brian Parish, Director of Media Development
• Jennifer Stephens, Marketing Director
• Jamie Ryan, Director of Accounting and Human Resource Adm
• Karen Stanzyk, Contract Manager
• April Luxner, Marketing Coordinator
• Kevin Armstrong, Associate
Description:
Sink Combs Dethlefs has had a long standing reputation for quality design, creativity, cost effectiveness, innovation, efficiency and excellence had long characterized the process and designs of the firm for more than four decades.

STANMAR INC.
321 COMMONWEALTH ROAD
SUITE 201
WAYLAND, MA 1778
508-310-9922
Fax: 508-310-0479
www.stanmar-inc.com
• Mark Snider, President
sthompson@stanmar-inc.com
Description:
Professional services include architectural

design and construction
Clients:
Tufts University, Philadelphia University, Nantucket Boys & Girls Club, Eagle Hill School & more

STANTEC
2335 W HIGHWAY 36
SAINT PAUL, MN 55113
651-636-4724
800-880-4700
Fax: 651-636-1311
www.bonestroo.com
• Sorvala Marvin, President
• Chris Peterson, Human Resources Director
• David Loskota, Director Marketing
Description:
Architects, engineers and construction managers specializing in the planning design and construction administration of ice arenas and family aquatic centers.

TBSA
27001 US HIGHWAY 19 N
CLEARWATER, FL 33761
727-723-7785
Fax: 727-723-0605
www.funleaguegroup.com
• Terry Killian, Rink Manager
• Kathy Winter, Asst. Skating Director
• Diane Paul, Marketing Director
• Nadine Pearen, Skating Director
nadine@funleaguegroup.com
Description:
Develops combination ice skating, hockey and inline skating/hockey facilities.
Services:
Specializing in the ownership and management of ice sports and family entertainment centers

THA ARCHITECTS ENGINEERS
817 E KEARSLEY STREET
FLINT, MI 48503
810-767-5600
Fax: 810-767-1650
info@tha-flint.com
www.tha-flint.com
• Jeffrey L. Bennett, Architects Engineer
• Madonna L. Bennett, Project Director
• George S. Anannich, Operations Director
• Donald E. Lee, Project Manager
Services:
Planning Services, Architectural Services, Interior Design Services, Mechanical Engineering Services, Electrical Engineering Services, Structural Engineering Services, Construction Services, Post Construction Services

THE DAVIS EXPERIENCE
60 E RIO SALADO PARKWAY
SUITE 200
TEMPE, AZ 85281-9130
480-638-1100
Fax: 602-381-4844
www.thedavisexperience.com
• Michael R Davis, Chief Executive Officer/Director of Desi
mdavis@dfdch.com
• Lisa Davis, Board Member
ldavis@dfdch.com
• Timothy Sprague, Board Member
tsprague@dfdch.com
• Rory A. Carder, Managing Director, Principal

(480) 638-1150
rcarder@thedavisexperience.com
• Jamie Moore, Chief Operating Officer
jmoore@dfdch.com
Service
Architecture, Interior Architecture, Space Planning, Land Planning, Landscape Architecture, Facilities Management, Graphic Design

THORNTON-TOMASETTI ENGINEERS
51 MADISON AVENUE
NEW YORK, NY 10010-1603
917-661-7800
Fax: 917-661-7801
Careers@TheTTGroup.com
www.thorntontomasetti.com
• Daniel A Cuoco, President/CEO
• Aine M. Brazil, Managing Principal
• Joseph G. Burns, Managing Principal
• Jim C. Kent, Director of Communications
• John Fairbairn, Director of Human Resources
Services:
Provides designs and engineering services for the structural component of major facilities throughout the world.

TVS DESIGN
1230 PEACHTREE STREET NE
2700 PROMENADE TWO
ATLANTA, GA 30309
404-888-6600
Fax: 404-888-6700
www.tvsa.com
• Roger L. Neuenschwander, President
• Marc Hirsch, Marketing Manager
• Kristi Patterson, Information Technology Manager
Services:
International architecture and interior designs services
Clients:
Retail, workplace interiors, hospitality and entertainment markets

U.S. TENNIS COURT & TRACK BUILDERS ASSOCIATION
8480 BALTIMORE
SUITE 307
NATIONAL PIKE
ELLICOT CITY, MD 21043
410-
866-501-2722
Fax: 410-730-8833
info@sportsbuilders.org
www.sportsbuilders.org
• Todd George, Chairman
(813) 645-2315
george@welchtennis.com
• Gordy Pierce, President-Tennis Division
(508) 759-5636
gpierce@tennisandtrack.com
• Sam Fisher, President-Tract Division
(800) 432-3191
sfisher@fishertracks.com
• Alex Levitsky, President-Professional Division
(732) 747-9050
Services:
ASBA is a national organization for builders, designers and suppliers of materials for tennis courts, running tracks, synthetic turf fields, indoor and outdoor synthetic sports surfaces. It is recognized as a centralized source for technical information, including consumer-oriented information.

VALLEY CREST
24151 VENTURA BOULEVARD
CALABASAS, CA 91302
818-223-8500
Fax: 818-223-8142
webmaster@valleycrest.com
www.valleycrest.com
• Burton S. Sperber, Founder / Chief Executive Officer
• Richard A. Sperber, President / CEO
• Po Chen, General Manager
(714) 327-5374
pchen@valleycrest.com
Services:
Sport field consulting, construction and maintenance.

VOA ASSOCIATES INCORPORATED
224 S MICHIGAN AVENUE
SUITE 1400
CHICAGO, IL 60604
312-554-1400
Fax: 312-554-1412
www.voa.com
• Rebel Roberts, PRESIDENT
Services:
Strategy and planning services, architectural design, landscape architecture and comprehensive planning, interior design, graphical services and coputer applications services.
Clients:
Amtrak, Brookfield Zoo, Burlington Northern/Santa Fe Railroad, CB Richard Ellis, Citibank Commercial Development, City of Chicago, Federal Express, Curitiba International Trade Center, Insigna/ESG, Sullivan Building Foundation, Central Florida Communioty Collection, Florida International University, Lawrence University.

WALTER P MOORE
1301 MCKINNEY
SUITE 1100
HOUSTON, TX 77010
713-630-7300
Fax: 713-630-7396
info@walterpmoore.com
www.walterpmoore.com
• Ray Messer, President / Chairman of the Board
rmesser@walterpmoore.com
• Larry Griffis, Senior Principal & Division President
lgriffis@walterpmoore.com
• Jerry Marcus, Parking Consulting Services Executive Di
jmarcus@walterpmoore.com
• Raymond Messer, President and Chairman of the Board
• Lee Slade, Senior Principal/Executive Director
• Dennis Wittry, Principal/Managing Director
• Dilip Choudhuri, Principal/Executive Director
• Gabriel A. Jimenez, Principal/Managing Director/ Director of Oper
• Charles Penland, Senior Principal/Executive Director
• Doug Coenen, Principal/Managing Directo
Services:
Parking Consulting, Research & Development, Structural Diagnostics, Structural Engineering Services
Clients:
Architects, Colleges and Universities, Corporations, Government Agencies, Hospitals, Institutions, Management

Districts, Real Estate Developers, Regional Development Authorities, Tax Increment Reinvestment Zones

WESLEY MEDICAL CENTER
550 N HILLSIDE
WICHITA, KS 67214
316-962-2000
Fax: 316-962-8040
www.wesleymc.com
• Helen Thomas, Director, Marketing and Public Relations
• Mary Singleton, employer relations director
Nature of Service
Health promotion and facility management services.
Services:
Provides a full range of diagnostic and treatment services

WISS, JANNEY, ELSTNER ASSOCIATES, INC./WJE
330 PFINGSTEN ROAD
NORTHBROOK, IL 60062
847-272-7400
Fax: 847-291-9599
info@wje.com
www.wje.com
• William Nugent, President/Senior Principal
wnugent@wje.com
• Gary.J. Klein, Executive Vice president and senior principal
(847) 753-6572
gklein@wje.com
• Brady Thomas, Dir of Corp Ops, Assoc Dir of Proj Ops, Princ
(847) 272-7400
• Calabrese Flora, Associate Principal
(847) 272-7400
fcalabrese@wje.com
• Douglas Crampton, Associate Principal
(847) 272-7400
dcrampton@wje.com
• Timothy Crowe, Associate Principal
(847) 272-7400
tcrowe@wje.com
• Richard Arnold, Associate Principal
(847) 272-7400
rarnold@wje.com
Sports Facility Services Include:
Structural and architectural assessments, repair and rehabilitation design, annual condition surveys; water leakage investigations; concrete deterioration's evaluations, corrosion investigations, seismic analysis and upgrade; testing and instrumentation

WRIGHTSON, JOHNSON, HADDON & WILLIAMS, INC.
4801 SPRING VALLEY ROAD
SUITE 113
DALLAS, TX 75244
972-934-3700
Fax: 972-934-3720
info@wjhw.com
www.wjhw.com

WSP
512 7TH AVENUE
NEW YORK, NY 10018
212-532-9600
Fax: 212-689-7489
www.wspgroup.com
• Randy Meyers, President and CEO
• Norman D Kurtz, Chairman

Facility Management

ACCESS DATA SUPPORT SERVICES & FACILITY MANAGEMENT GROUP
2425 W LOOP S
SUITE 855
HOUSTON, TX 77027
713-439-0370
800-206-0931
Fax: 713-439-0376
ads@access-data.com
www.access-data.com
• Andrea Renee Logans, President & CEO
• Tom Logans, Support Services VP
• Renee Re Logans, President/Chief Executive Officer
• Tom Logans, Vice President
Nature of Sports Service:
A multi-disciplined, minority-owned service company that provides facility support services, construction management and specialized personnel placement. Organization has years of experience in providing facilities maintenance and management services.

ARAMARK CORPORATION
1101 MARKET STREET
PHILADELPHIA, PA 19107
215-238-3000
800-272-6275
Fax: 215-238-3333
www.aramark.com
• Joseph Neubauer, Chairman
• L Frederick Sutherland, Executive Vice President/Chief Financial Officer
• Cathy Schlosberg, Vice President, Marketing/Education
• David Freireich, Media Relations Coordinator, Sports Entertainment
• Eric Foss, President
Baseball:
MLB; Minor League
College Sponsor:
NCAA; College Bowl
Basketball Sponsor:
NBDL
Football Sponsor:
Indoor League
Hockey Sponsor:
AHL

BARTON MALOW COMPANY
26500 AMERICAN DRIVE
SOUTHFIELD, MI 48034
248-436-5000
Fax: 248-436-5001
info@bartonmalow.com
www.bartonmalow.com
• Ben Maibach, III, President
• Sheryl Mailbach, Chief Marketing Officer & Senior Vice Preside
Description:
Recognized as an innovator of construction and program management, and one of the premier sports builders in the country. Offers comprehensive building services such as general contracting, design/building, construction management and facility management.

BIGELOW COMPANIES, THE
6501 E COMMERCE AVENUE
SUITE 120
KANSAS CITY, MO 64120

facilities

1073

816-483-5553
Fax: 816-483-5510
chrisbigelow@bigelowcompanies.com
www.bigelowcompanies.com
• Chris Bigelow, President
(816) 994-3261
chrisbigelow@bigelowcompanies.com
• Lee Roberts, Director of Design
(816) 994-3262
leeroberts@bigelowcompanies.com
• Jason Simpson, Design and Technology
Specialist
(816) 994-3268
jasonsimpson@bigelowcompanies.com
• Laurie Roark, Director of Administration
(816) 994-3263
laurieroark@bigelowcompanies.com
Year Founded:
1988
Clients:
Denver Broncos, Kroenke Sports &
Entertainment, Quicken Loans Arena,
Monumental Sports
Services:
Foodservice design

CENTERPLATE
2187 ATLANTIC ST
STAMFORD, CT 68902
864-598-8600
800-698-6992
Fax: 864-598-8686
info@centerplate.com
www.centerplate.com
• Des Hague, President and Chief Executive
Officer
• Kenneth R Frick, VP/Chief Financial
Officer
• Steve Trotter, VP, New Business
Development
Sports Service Founded:
1973
Description:
The largest hospitality partner to North
America's sporting and entertainment
venues.
Marketing & Consulting Services:
Food, beverage, merchandise and
management provider for sports facilities.

DELOITTE & TOUCHE LLP
100 KIMBALL DRIVE
PARSIPPANY, NJ 07054-2176
973-602-6000
Fax: 973-683-7459
www.deloitte.com
• William G Parrett, Global CEO
• Stewart Rog, Principal
Description:
Management consultants with expertise in
all aspects of sports facilities development
and operations, including feasibility studies,
financing, lease negotiation assistance,
premium seating and seat license market
analyses, economic impact studies, and ev

FINISH LINE EVENTS
5725-E CONCORD PARKWAY S
CONCORD, NC 28027
704-455-3235
Fax: 704-454-4744
Sports Service Founded:
1960
Nature of Sports Service:
Currently operates at six of the largest
sports venues in the United States - Atlanta
Motor Speedway, Bristol Motor Speedway,

Lowe's Motor Speedway in Charlotte, Texas
Motor Speedway in Fort Worth and Infineon
Raceway in Sonoma, California.

FIRST AND GOAL, INC.
PO BOX 941176
HOUSTON, TX 77094
713-571-9121
Fax: 206-381-7572
info@teamfirstandgoal.org
www.teamfirstandgoal.org
• Paul G Allen, Chairman
• Jody Patton, Vice Chairman
• Bob Whitsitt, President
• Tyrone Smith, President
Sports Service Founded:
1997
Nature of Sports Service:
Organization founded by Paul G. Allen to
manage the development, construction and
operation of the Washington State
Football/Soccer Stadium and Exhibition
Center. Dedicated to working in partnership
with the community to build and operate a
world-class.

GLOBAL SPECTRUM
3601 SOUTH BROAD STREET
PHILADELPHIA, PA 19148
215-389-9587
Fax: 215-952-5651
tglickman@comcast-spectacor.com
www.global-spectrum.com

HEERY INTERNATIONAL, INC.
999 PEACHTREE STREET NE
ATLANTA, GA 30309-3953
404-881-9880
Fax: 404-892-8479
Corporate@heery.com
www.heery.com
• Jim J. Moynihan, Chairman & CEO
jmoynihan@heery.com
• Bill Heitz, President
• Greg Pierce, Regional Manager
Nature of Service
Architecture, engineering, master planning,
design and construction management of
sports facilities.
Description:
Architecture, engineering, master planning,
design and construction management of
sports facilities.
Clients
Architecture: Atlanta Botanical Gardens;
Atlanta History Center Museum; Atlanta
History Center Parking Deck; Bosch
Corporation; Central Michigan University;
Citadel; Coca-Cola; Comdisco; Conoco
Headquarters, Cumberland County Civic
Center; Dare County; Dare County Justice
Center; Dekalb County Courthouse; Emory
University School of Law; Erie Seawolves
Stadium; Franklin Templeton; Georgia
Dome; Georgia World Congress Center;
Heery D.C. Office; Hotel Thayer;
Jacksonville Baptist Hospital; James
Madison University; Kennesaw State
University; Mayo Clinic; MBNA Multiple
Locations; McCoy Stadium; Memorial
Mission Parking Deck; Metlife; Missoula Sta
Services:
Architecture, Construction Managemetn,
Engineering, Facilities Management, Interior
Design, and Program Management

IMS PROPERTIES/INDY MOTOR SPEEDWAY
4790 W 16TH STREET
INDIANAPOLIS, IN 46222
317-492-8500
sales@brickyard.com
www.indianapolismotorspeedway.com

INTERNATIONAL MICRO SYSTEMS, INC.
200 RACOOSIN DRIVE
SUITE 110
ASTON, PA 19014
484-482-1600
800-882-0627
Fax: 484-574-8874
sales-marketing@ims-pos.com
www.ims-pos.com
• Jeff Harvey, Director of Sales
• Rob Rae, Director of Marketing
Nature of Services:
International Micro Systems provides
integrated POS (Point of Sales) and venue
management solutions with a strong focus
on sports arenas, convention centers,
amusement facilities, and
colleges/universities - products and services
include inventory management, food and
beverage POS systems, full-scale venue
systems planning, installation and support,
and pre-paid concession payment systems
through ticketing.

JOHN M.Y. LEE/MICHAEL TIMCHULA ARCHITECTS
320 W 13TH STREET
NEW YORK, NY 10014-1280
212-929-3131
Fax: 212-463-8964
www.aecdaily.com
• John MY Lee
• Michael Timchula
Description:
Gymnasium, natatorium and tennis stadium
architecture
Description:
Gymnasium, natatorium and tennis stadium
architecture.

LUNDY'S SPECIAL EVENTS
1385 PRIDEMORE COURT
LEXINGTON, KY 40505
859-255-0717
Fax: 859-253-9790
www.lundyscatering.com
• Abigail Dobson, BOD
• Alissa Tibe, VP
• Jerry Lundergan, Principal Catering
Development
Year Founded:
Lundy's: 1965
Event Food Management Services:
National, mobile, full-service special event
firm providing corporate hospitality catering,
general concessions and facilities
management for sports and special events.

MEADOWLANDS/NEW JERSEY SPORTS & EXPOSITION AUTHORITY
50 STATE ROUTE 120
EXECUTIVE OFFICES
E RUTHERFORD, NJ 7073
201-935-8500
Fax: 201-507-8130
www.izodcenter.com
• George R Zottinger, Chairman
• Bruce H Garland, SVP/Racing Operations
• Joseph R Consolazio, SVP/Chief Financial

Officer
• Barbara Lampen, SVP/Strategic Planning/Development
Meadowlands Stadium:
Home field for NY Giants and NY Jets football teams. Robert Castronovo, Exec VP/Gen Mgr; Robert E. Carney, Asst Gen Mgr Ops; William Squires, Dir Stad Ops; Leo Ehrline, Asst Gen Mgr Mktg; 201 935-8500; FAX: 201 460-4294; Gen Mgr FAX: 201 507-8122.
Continental Airlines Arena:
Home field for NY Nets basketball team. Robert Castronovo, Exec VP/Gen Mgr; Robert E. Carney, Asst Gen Mgr Ops; Leo Ehrline, Asst Gen Mgr Mktg; 201 935-8500; FAX: 201 460-4294; Gen Mgr FAX: 201 507-8122.

MORSE DIESEL INTERNATIONAL INC.
148 STATE STREET, 7TH FLOOR
BOSTON, MA 2109
617-725-2788
800-698-4002
Fax: 617-725-4925
• O'Marah Eamon, Business Development Director
• Kevin Collins, Sports Director
• Dave Kersey, Project Executive
Projects Include:
United Center, Fleet Center, Broward County Arena, Tampa Bay Ice Palace, Tampa NFL Stadium, Chicago (AHL) Arena, U. Cal Berkeley Arena, Ohio State Stadium, Philadelphia Eagles Training Center, SF 49ers Stadium, Miami Heat Arena, Pittsburgh Pirates Ballpar
Description:
Premiere Construction Manager, Consultant and Owner's Representative of Major Sports Facility projects. Expertise includes: Site & Foundation, Truss Erection, False-work Framing, Roof/Canopy , Mechanical, Electrical & Plumbing (MEP) Coordination, Precast

PATRON SOLUTIONS, LP
701 LEE ROAD
SUITE 305
WAYNE, PA 19087
610-408-9460
Fax: 610-408-9551
info@patronsolutions.com
www.patronsolutions.com
• Fred Maglione, President/CEO
• Dave Homan, VP/COO
• Christian Varano, New Business Development Director
(610) 854-1104
• Stephen Scalese, Development/Marketing Director
(610) 854-1103
scalese@patronsolutions.com
• Thomas Greco, Call Center Operations Director
tgreco@patronsolutions.com
• Daniel Durso, Finance Director
ddurso@patronsolutions.com
• Dave Homan, Vice President

PRITCHARD INDUSTRIES, INC
4040 DIRECTORS ROW
HOUSTON, TX 77092
713-957-1387
Fax: 713-957-1574
psperduti@pritchardindustries.com
www.pritchardindustries.com

• Peter Sperduti, VP/General Manager
Nature of Sports Service:
Provides industry specific facility services for sports and entertainment complexes including General Cleaning, Intensive Training, Pressure Washing, Quality Control and Recycling.

R.I.C. CORPORATION
6215 CONSTITUTION DRIVE
FORT WAYNE, IN 46804-1517
260-432-0799
Fax: 260-432-9155
sales@riccorp.com
www.riccorp.com
• Rick Kriscka, President
Description:
Developed windows based Facility Management Software system. A completely integrated system with applications for all phases of the operation from initial marketing through to final billing. Each application is licensed separately per user, so you only pa

RODER USA, INC.
1954 N 30TH ROAD
HOLLYWOOD, FL 33021-4401
954-894-6400
Fax: 954-964-1700
www.roderusa.com
• Andrew Soffe, Account Executive (West Coast)
(800) 258-8368
• Keith Krzeminski, Accountt Executive (Northeast)
(540) 992-3377
• Robert Kraak, President
• Russ Sell, Account Executive (Southeast I)
(954) 894-6400
Nature of Sports Service:
Create temporary facilities including; tents, lightweight-construction halls, and steel halls, for golf tournaments, tennis tournaments, etc.

SMG
300 CONSHOHOKEN STATE ROAD
SUITE 450
WEST CONSHOHOKEN, PA 19428
610-729-7900
Fax: 610-729-1590
www.smgworld.com
• Wes Westley, President and CEO
• Maureen Ginty, Executive VP
• John Burns, Executive VP
• Gregg Caren, Sr.VP
Sports Service Founded:
Sports Service Founded: 1977
Event Management Services:
Production and marketing of sporting events.
Marketing & Consulting Services:
Stadiums, arenas, theaters, auditoriums and convention centers under its guidance worldwide. Divisions include SMG Productions, Network International, SMG sports advertising affiliate.

SPEEDWAY MOTORSPORTS, INC.
5555 CONCORD PARKWAY S
CONCORD, NC 28027
704-455-3239
Fax: 704-455-2168
www.speedwaymotorsports.com
• Cary Tharrington, SVP & General Counsel
• Donald Hawk, Chief Racing Development

Officer
• Jerry Caldwell, EVP & General Manager
Nature of Sports Services:
A marketer and producer of motorsports entertainment in the United States. The company owns and operates six motorsports facilities including Atlanta Motor Speedway, Bristol (TN), Motor Speedway, Lowe's Motor Speedway, Las Vegas Motor Speedway, Infineon Raceway, and New Hampshire Speedway

SPORTSERVICE CORPORATION
FOUNTAIN PLAZA
40 FOUNTAIN PLAZA
BUFFALO, NY 14202
716-858-5000
800-828-7240
800-441-5645
Fax: 716-858-5479
info@delawarenorth.com
www.delawarenorth.com
• Wendy Watkins, Vice President Corporate Communications and Market
• Jeffrey Hess, Director Retail/Marketing Services
• Nancy Parker, President
• Jeremy Jacobs, Chief Executive Officer
Description:
Provides food, beverage and retail services at sports and recreational facilities as well as glittering, upscale, one-of-a-kind events.

VENUEWORKS
4611 MORTENSEN ROAD
SUITE 111
AMES, IA 50014
515-232-5151
888-232-5151
Fax: 515-663-2022
info@venuworks.com
www.venuworks.com
• Steve L Peters, Founder/President
(515) 232-5151
speters@venuworks.com
• Andy Long, Vice President of Events and Entertainment
(515) 232-5151
along@venuworks.com
• Doug Kuhnel, Senior VP Operations
(515) 232-5151
dkuhnel@venuworks.com
• Tammy Roolbeck, Venue Services VP
• Larry Gawronski, Southern Region VP
• Andy Long, National Director Business Development
• Betty Beisker, Human Resources VP
• Joseph Briglia, Vice President of Development
(609) 505-4226
jbriglia@venuworks.com
• Paul Putter, National Director Programming
• Sharon Cummins, National Director of Planning and Development
scummins@venuworks.com
Description:
Provides comprehensive management for arenas, convention centers and theaters, specializing in territory markets. Also provides consulting services for facility planning, feasibility studies and sponsor development.
Managed Facilities Include:
Midwest Wireless Civic Center, Mankato, MN; RiverCenter/Adler Theater, Davenport, IA; Alerus Center, Grand Forks, ND; U.S. Cellular Center/Paramount Theater, Cedar

facilities

Rapids, IA; and Brookings Area MultiPlax, SD.

VENUWORKS
4611 MORTENSEN ROAD
SUITE 111
AMES, IA 50014
515-232-5151
Fax: 515-663-2022
info@venuworks.com
www.venuworks.com
• Peters Steve, Founder/President
(515) 232-5151
speters@venuworks.com
• Joseph Briglia, Vice President of Development
(609) 505-4226
jbriglia@venuworks.com
• Andy Long, Vice President of Events and Entertainment
(515) 232-5151
along@venuworks.com
• Sharon Cummins, National Director of Planning and Development
scummins@venuworks.com
• Russell Ferguson, Vice President of Food and Beverage Services
rferguson@venuworks.com
• Doug Kuhnel, Senior Vice President
(515) 232-5151
dkuhnel@venuworks.com

WILLIAM CARUSO & ASSOCIATES, INC.
8055 EAST TUFTS AVENUE
SUITE 1320
DENVER, CO 80237
303-649-1600
Fax: 303-649-1660
wcaruso@wcarusoassoc.com
www.wcarusoassoc.com
• William J Caruso, President
(303) 649-1600
wcaruso@wcarusoassoc.com
• Stephen K Young, Principal & Director Of Design
(303) 649-1600
syoung@wcarusoassoc.com
Sports Service Founded:
1987
Consulting Services:
Independent consulting firm specializing in the planning and design of food/beverage facilities for the public assembly building industry.

Facility Concession Services

ARAMARK CORPORATION
1101 MARKET STREET
PHILADELPHIA, PA 19107
215-238-3000
800-999-8989
Fax: 215-238-3333
www.aramark.com
• Joseph Neubauer, Chairman
• L Frederick Sutherland, Executive Vice President/Chief Financial Officer
• Cathy Schlosberg, Vice President, Marketing/Education
• David Freireich, Media Relations Coordinator, Sports Entertainment
• Eric Foss, President
Baseball:
MLB; Minor League

College Sponsor:
NCAA; College Bowl
Basketball Sponsor:
NBDL
Football Sponsor:
Indoor League
Hockey Sponsor:
AHL

BIGELOW COMPANIES, THE
6501 E COMMERCE AVENUE
SUITE 120
KANSAS CITY, MO 64120
816-483-5553
Fax: 816-483-5510
chrisbigelow@bigelowcompanies.com
www.bigelowcompanies.com
• Chris Bigelow, President
(816) 994-3261
chrisbigelow@bigelowcompanies.com
• Lee Roberts, Director of Design
(816) 994-3262
leeroberts@bigelowcompanies.com
• Jason Simpson, Design and Technology Specialist
(816) 994-3268
jasonsimpson@bigelowcompanies.com
• Laurie Roark, Director of Administration
(816) 994-3263
laurieroark@bigelowcompanies.com
Year Founded:
1988
Clients:
Denver Broncos, Kroenke Sports & Entertainment, Quicken Loans Arena, Monumental Sports
Services:
Foodservice design

C. CRETORS & CO.
3243 N CALIFORNIA AVENUE
CHICAGO, IL 60618
773-588-1690
800-228-1885
Fax: 773-588-7141
Solesen@Cretors.com
www.cretors.com

CENTERPLATE
2187 ATLANTIC STREET
STAMFORD, CT 6902
800-698-6992
Fax: 864-598-8686
info@centerplate.com
www.centerplate.com
• Des Hague, President and Chief Executive Officer
• Kenneth R Frick, VP/Chief Financial Officer
• Steve Trotter, VP, New Business Development
Sports Service Founded:
1973
Description:
The largest hospitality partner to North America's sporting and entertainment venues.
Marketing & Consulting Services:
Food, beverage, merchandise and management provider for sports facilities.

CENTURY INDUSTRIES, LLC
PO BOX C
SELLERSBURG, IN 47172
812-246-3371
800-248-3371

Fax: 812-246-5446
www.centuryindustries.com
• Michelle McRae, Marketing Director
michelle@centuryindustries.com
• Robert Uhl, President
Manufacturer:
Mobile Concessions - Portable Stands, Seating, Bleachers.
Services:
Vendor Special Event Service, Goldrush Concession, Kiosk, Tail Cater, P.O.P Cup Merchandisers, Mobile Kitchens, Ticket Booths, Special Purpose Trailers, Goldrush, Mobile Staging, Mobile Bleacher Seating, Self Service Centers, Drive-Thru Retail Service Centers, USPS, Expanding Trailers and Merchandising
Clients:
Sausage Grill, Fried Dough, Elephant Ears, Route 66 Diner, Cafeteria

CHECKERS DRIVE-IN RESTAURANTS
4300 WEST CYPRESS STREET
SUITE 600
TAMPA, FL 33607
813-283-7000
800-275-3628
Fax: 813-283-7001
www.checkers.com
• Terri Snyder, Executive Vice President and Chief Marketing
• Adams Noyes, Executive Vice President Of Operations and Te
• Todd Lindsey, Senior Vice President/ Chief Financial Office
• Enrique Rick Silva, President & CEO
Services:
Official Burger for MLB - Tampa Bay Rays; Minor League Baseball - Louisville Bats; University of Florida Gators; Florida State University Seminoles; University of Louisville Cardinals.

CONCESSION SOLUTIONS, INC.
16022 26TH AVENUE NE
SHORELINE, WA 98155
206-440-9203
Fax: 206-440-9213
info@concessionsolutions.com
www.concessionsolutions.com
• Theresa Traulsen, President
theresa@concessionsolutions.com
• Bob Traulsen, Vice President
• Hope Kaser, Vice President Operations
• Sandi Burton, Associate
Consulting Services:
Onsite Evaluations; Profitability Analysis; Product Evaluations; Audit Program; Facility Design and Systematization; Management and Staff Training; Request for Proposal Review and Development; Website Design and Development; and Concession Management for

CUSTOM MOBILE FOOD EQUIPMENT
275 SOUTH 2ND ROAD
HAMMONTON, NJ 8037
609-561-6900
800-257-7855
Fax: 609-567-9318
www.customsalesandservice.com
• Cathy Chartier, Contact
(800) 257-7855
lynda.sikora@foodcart.com
Products:
Mobile food equipment - catering trucks,

specialty and general food carts, hot/cold food equipment.

DAVID & SONS, INC.
PO BOX 7907, 5626 E SHIELDS
FRESNO, CA 93727-7818
209-291-0231
800-876-0231
Fax: 209-291-8239
• Bobby Shehorn, VP Sales
Food Category:
Appetizers and Snacks.

DI/AN CONTROLS, INC.
530 W STREET
BRAINTREE, MA 2184
781-848-1299
Fax: 781-848-1659

EXECUTIVE RESTROOM TRAILERS
1093 A1A BEACH BOULEVARD
SUITE 421
SAINT AUGUSTINE, FL 32080
888-445-4928
888-445-4928
Fax: 904-461-5588
www.exrt.com
• Tim Haszard, President
• Sharon L Haszard, VP
sharon@exrt.com
Sports Service Founded:
1971
Event Management Services:
Manufactures and leases upscale restroom facilities for sporting events; also handles coordination of portable sanitation for sports events. Provides services for the Brickyard 400-NASCAR, NFL Quarterback Challenge, Super Bowl, Family Circle Tennis Tourna

GAME TIME FOOD & BEVERAGE SERVICES, INC.
355 W DUNDEE ROAD
BUFFALO GROVE, IL 60089
847-243-4263
Fax: 847-243-2155
• Blumenthal Steve, Business Development
• Alan Day, Director Operations
Description:
Specializes in minor league facility concessions.

INTERNATIONAL MICRO SYSTEMS, INC.
200 RACOOSIN DRIVE
SUITE 110
ASTON, PA 19014
484-482-1600
800-882-0627
Fax: 484-574-8874
sales-marketing@ims-pos.com
www.ims-pos.com
• Jeff Harvey, Director of Sales
• Rob Rae, Director of Marketing
Nature of Services:
International Micro Systems provides integrated POS (Point of Sales) and venue management solutions with a strong focus on sports arenas, convention centers, amusement facilities, and colleges/universities - products and services include inventory management, food and beverage POS systems, full-scale venue systems planning, installation and support, and pre-paid concession payment systems through ticketing.

LEVY RESTAURANTS SPORTS & ENTERTAINMENT
980 NORTH MICHIGAN AVENUE
LEVEL 2
CHICAGO, IL 60611-4501
312-664-8200
Fax: 312-280-2739
www.levyrestaurants.com
• Larry Levy, Chairman/Founder
• John Swanson, SVP Operations
Nature of Sports Service:
Brings restaurant-quality dining from its base of award-winning restaurants to the premium food service at 56 sports and entertainment venues across the country.
Sports Service Founded:
1982

LUNDY'S SPECIAL EVENTS
1385 PRIDEMORE COURT
LEXINGTON, KY 40505
859-255-0717
Fax: 859-253-9790
www.lundyscatering.com
• Abigail Dobson, BOD
• Alissa Tibe, VP
• Jerry Lundergan, Principal Catering Development
Year Founded:
Lundy's: 1965
Event Food Management Services:
National, mobile, full-service special event firm providing corporate hospitality catering, general concessions and facilities management for sports and special events.

OVATION FOOD SERVICES LP
18228 US HIGWAY 41 N
LUTZ, FL 33549
813-948-6900
Fax: 813-948-6565
www.ovationsfoodservices.com
• Kenneth J Young, President
• Ken Young, President
(813) 948-6900
Ken.Young@ovationsfs.com
• Todd Wickner, Founder
Todd.Wickner@ovationsfs.com
• Doug Drewes, Executive Vice President
Doug.Drewes@ovationsfs.com
• Charlie Neary, Executive Vice President
(925) 426-5128
Charlie.Neary@ovationsfs.com
• Mark Healey, Vice President
(617) 733-5505
• Adrienne Hanson, Chief Financial Officer
(813) 948-6900
• Todd Wickner, Founder
Nature of Sports Service:
Organization specializes in concessions, catering, and other services for arenas, stadiums, and similar large venues.

PERFECTION EQUIPMENT, INC.
4259 LEE AVENUE
GURNEE, IL 60031
847-244-7200
800-356-6301
Fax: 847-244-7205
www.perfectequip.com
• Sandy Hahn, President
sand@perfectequip.com
• Alan Hale, Operations Manager
alanhale@perfectequip.com
• Sandy Hahn, President
• Alan Hale, Operations Manager/R&D
• Kathy Pino, Sales/Administration

• Robert Barnhisel, Director of Sales and Installation
• Gene Wood, Purchasing
Description:
Concessions including carbonated beverage dispensing systems; powered condiment dispensing systems; self contained/ sealed system and constant temperature, remote beer system; glycol chillers.

PIONEEER FAMILY BRANDS, INC.
12674 PONY EXPRESS ROAD
SUITE 1
DRAPER, UT 84020
801-523-3850
800-975-4766
Fax: 801-523-3815
sales@pioneerfamilybrands.com
www.tropicalsno.com
• Donald Griffiths, President
(801) 523-3850
donald@pioneerfamilybrands.com
• Steve Griffiths, Assistant Controller
(801) 523-3850
steve@pioneerfamilybrands.com
• David Griffiths, VP Manufacturing/Purchasing
• Debra Didier, Secretary/Treasurer/Chief Financial Offi
Year Founded:
1973
Nature of Service:
Manufacturer, distributor of Tropical Sno Hawaiian Shave Ice products.

SPORTSERVICE CORPORATION
FOUNTAIN PLAZA
40 FOUNTAIN PLAZA
BUFFALO, NY 14202
716-858-5000
800-828-7240
Fax: 716-858-5479
www.delawarenorth.com
• Wendy Watkins, Vice President Corporate Communications and Market
• Jeffrey Hess, Director Retail/Marketing Services
• Nancy Parker, President
• Jeremy Jacobs, Chief Executive Officer
Description:
Provides food, beverage and retail services at sports and recreational facilities as well as glittering, upscale, one-of-a-kind events.

TANGENT ASSOCIATES, INC.
5000 SW 52ND, SUITE 501
FORT LAUDERDALE, FL 33314-5514 Â
954-797-9883
866-287-4736
Fax: 954-797-9887
info@micros.com
www.micros.com
• A.L. Giannopoulos, Executive Chairman
• Peter A. Altabef, President and Chief Executive Officer
• Daniel J. Bell, Senior Vice President, Hotels & Leisure and E
• Don DeMarinis, Vice President, Leisure and Entertainment
• Dan Harley, Vice President, West Major Account Restaurant
• Cynthia A. Russo, Executive Vice President, Chief Financial Off
• James T. Walsh, Chief Information Security Officer
Description:
Provides Point-of-sale and inventory control

facilities

systems for food and beverage concessions management in the US and Canada. Systems accummulate the volumes of transactions which occur for every event or function at a major stadium and arena.

WILLIAM CARUSO & ASSOCIATES, INC.
8055 EAST TUFTS AVENUE
SUITE 1320
DENVER, CO 80237

303-649-1600
Fax: 303-649-1660
wcaruso@wcarusoassoc.com
www.wcarusoassoc.com
• William J Caruso, President
(303) 649-1600
wcaruso@wcarusoassoc.com
• Stephen K Young, Principal & Director Of Design

(303) 649-1600
syoung@wcarusoassoc.com
Sports Service Founded:
1987
Consulting Services:
Independent consulting firm specializing in the planning and design of food/beverage facilities for the public assembly building industry.

8
manufacturers & retailers

Apparel Manufacturers

5TH AND OCEAN CLOTHING, 1099
A4, 1099
A-B EMBLEM, 1099
ABC ACTIVEWEAR LLC, 1100
ACTION SPOT SPORTS, 1227
ADAMS USA, 1103
ALL STAR PRO GOLF, 1105
ALLIAN SNOWBOARDS, 1106
ALPS SPORTSWEAR MFG. COMPANY, 1106
AMF BOWLING WORLDWIDE, 1108
AND 1, 1109
ANTIGUA GROUP, 1109
ANVIL KNITWEAR INC., 1109
ASHWORTH, 1110
ASICS AMERICA CORPORATION, 1111
ATHENA GOLF, 1111
ATHLETIC KNIT, 1111
AUDERO SPORTS SUPPLY, 1111
AUTHENTIC FITNESS CORP., 1112
AVIA AMERICAN SPORTING GOODS, 1112
B' WARMER THERMAL PRODUCTS, 1112
BABY FANATIC, 1113
BALLGIRL ATHLETIC, 1114
BETHEL INTERNATIONAL, 1116
BIG BOY HEADGEAR, 1116
BIG TIME SPORTS APPAREL, 1116
BLUE FISH, 1118
BLUEFLY, 1231
BOAST, 1118
BODY GLOVE INTERNATIONAL, 1118
BODY WRAPPERS/ANGELO LUZIO, 1119
BOGNER, 1119
BRISTOL ATHLETIC, 1120
BRUTE WRESTLING, 1121
BUFFALO EXPORT, 1122
BVT PRODUCTS, 1122
CAMOFACE, 1123
CAMPUS OUTFITTERS, 1123
CASTAWAY COLLECTIBLES, 1125
CENTRALIA KNITTING MILLS, 1125
CEO MANUFACTURERS, 1125
CLUBHOUSEKIT, 1127
CMS SPORTS, 1235
COBBLESTONES ACTIVEWEAR, 1127
COED SPORTSWEAR INC, 1127
COLLEGE CONCEPTS, 1235
COLLEGIATE LICENSING COMPANY, 786
COLLEGIATE PACIFIC, 1235
COLUMBIA SPORTSWEAR COMPANY, 1128
COMFYFEET, 1129
CROSS CREEK APPAREL, 1131
CROWN PRINCE, 1131
CUSTOM SPORTSWEAR CORP/DBA
    SPORTSWEAR UNLIMITED, 1132
DAEWOO INTERNATIONAL CORPORATION,
    1236
DALCO ATHLETIC LETTERING, 1133
DANSKIN, 1133
DC SPORTS, 1236
DEHEN, 1134
DELTA APPAREL COMPANY, 1134
DESCENTE NORTH AMERICA, 1134
DEVENTER'S CHEER & DANCEWEAR
    FACTORY, 1134
DIVOTS SPORTSWEAR COMPANY, 1135
DODGER INDUSTRIES INC., 1135
DUCK HEAD APPAREL COMPANY, 1136
DUNBROOKE, 1136
DYNASTY APPAREL INDUSTRIES, 1136
E.P. PRO, 1137
EARBAGS, 1137
EASTBAY, 1237
EASTERN MOUNTAIN SPORTS, 1237
EIGER SPORTSWEAR, 1138
ELITE SPORTSWEAR, 1139
ELLESSE U.S.A., 1139
EVERLAST WORLDWIDE, 1140
FERA, 1142
FITNESS TECH INTERNATIONAL, 1144
FRANCO APPAREL GROUP, 1145
FUBU THE COLLECTION, 1146
FUN-TEES, 1146
G GIRL, 1240
G III SPORTS, 1146
GAIAM, 1146
GAME TIME LLC, 1146
GAMETIME PLUSH, 1147
GAMEWEAR, 1147

GARAN, 1147
GEAR FOR SPORTS, 1147
GOTCHA INTERNATIONAL, 1150
GRAVEL GEAR SKATEBOARD CLOTHING, 1151
GTM SPORTSWEAR, 1151
GUESS? INC, 1151
GULBENKIAN SWIM, 1151
HAGGAR CORPORATION, 1152
HANES BRANDS, 1152
HARPER INDUSTRIES INC, 1153
HARTWELL SPORTS, 1153
HASCALL SPORTSWEAR, 1153
HATCHERS MANUFACTURING INC., 1153
HEAD/PENN USA, 1153
HEADMASTER INC, 1153
HELLY HANSEN, 1154
HI STYLE LETTERED SPORTSWEAR
    COMPANY, 1154
HIND, 1155
HOLLOWAY SPORTSWEAR, 1156
HOLOUBEK, 1156
INSPORT INTERNATIONAL, 1158
INVENTION TECHNOLOGIES, 798
IRONMAN PROPERTIES, 1159
JACQUES MORET, 1159
JAMMIN APPAREL, 1159
JANTZEN, 1160
JEFF HAMILTON COLLECTION, 1160
JEM SPORTSWEAR INC., 1160
JH DESIGN GROUP, 1160
K2 INC., 1162
KAEPA USA, 1162
KAMPALA INDUSTRIES, 1162
KAPPA INC, 1162
KEY SPORTZ-WEAR, 1163
KING LOUIE INTERNATIONAL, 1163
L&L GROUP/FOREMOST ATHLETIC APPAREL,
    1164
L.A. GEAR, 1164
L.A.T SPORTSWEAR, 1164
LEGEND SPORTS, 1166
LEON LEVIN, 1166
LEO'S DANCEWEAR, 1166
LIEBE ATHLETIC LETTERING, 1166
LILY'S OF BEVERLY HILLS, 1167
LIQUID BLUE, 1167
LITTLE KING MANUFACTURING COMPANY INC,
    1167
LOCUST INC., 1167
LONE STAR ATHLETIC DESIGNS, 1168
LOST ARROW CORPORATION, 1168
MARCIA ORIGINALS, 1170
MECA SPORTSWEAR, 1172
MITCHELL & NESS NOSTALGIA COMPANY,
    1174
MOPRO, 1175
MOTORSPORTS AUTHENTICS, 1175
MOVING COMFORT, 1176
MTC MARKETING INC, 1176
NATIVE SUN SPORTSWEAR, 1177
NCED SAHARA, 1177
NEUEDGE SPORTSWEAR, 1178
NEW AGENDA BY PERRIN, 1178
NEW BALANCE ATHLETIC SHOE, 1178
NEW ENGLAND CAP CO., 1178
NEWTEX USA, 1179
NIKE, 1179
NIKE GOLF, 1179
NO FEAR, 1180
NORDICA USA, 1180
NORTH FACE, 1180
NUMBERALLS, 1181
NYX GOLF, 1181
OCEAN PACIFIC APPAREL CORPORATION,
    1181
OLD TIME SPORTS, 1182
OMEGA GEAR INC, 1182
O'NEILL, 1181
ONFIELD APPAREL, 1182
OT SPORTS, 1183
PEARL IZUMI (USA), 1184
PERFORMANCE SPORTS APPAREL, 1184
PHI-TEN USA INC, 1185
PINE SPORTS, 1185
POLO BY RALPH LAUREN, 1186
POMCHIES LLC, 1186
PONY INTERNATIONAL INC., 1186
PREMIUMWEAR, 1187
PRINCE SPORTS, 1188
PROGEAR, 1189

PSC/ENCORE SELECT INC, 1189
PVH CORP., 1190
QUIKSILVER, 1190
RAMSTAR MILLS, 1191
REEBOK APPAREL GROUP, 1192
REEBOK CANADA INC., 1192
REEBOK INTERNATIONAL LTD.-RETAIL, 1247
RENNOC, 1192
REYN SPOONER INC, 1193
RINGOR, 1193
RIPON ATHLETIC, 1194
ROCKY SHOES & BOOTS, 1194
ROOTS APPAREL, 1194
RUGGERS RUGBY SUPPLY, 1195
RUSSELL ATHLETIC, 1195
SEVEN SONS AND COMPANY INC, 1198
SHYDA'S, 1199
SIDEOUT SPORT, 1200
SIGNATURE DESIGNS, 1200
SMACK APPAREL, 1201
SOFFE COMPANY, 1202
SOLAR TAN THRU SUITS, 1202
SOYAD BROTHERS TEXTILE CORPORATION,
    1203
SPEEDLINE ATHLETIC WEAR, 1203
SPORT FACE, 1204
SPORT OBERMEYER, 1204
SPORTIF U.S.A., 1204
SPORTS-FASHION, 1206
SPRY SPORTS USA, 1206
STAMINA PRODUCTS INC, 1207
SUNDAY PLAYERS, 1209
SURE FOOT CORPORATION, 1209
T3K INC, 1210
TEAM CALIBER, 1211
TEAMLINE, 1211
TEN SECONDS, 1211
TENACIOUS LTD, 1212
TEXTILE REVOLUTION, 1212
TKO SPORTS GROUP, 1213
TONIX, 1213
TOP OF THE WORLD CAPS, 1214
TOP-FLITE COMPANY, 1214
TOYQUEST, 1214
TRANS APPAREL, 1214
TROY CORPORATION, 1215
TURFER SPORTSWEAR, 1216
TYCA CORPORATION, 1216
TYR SPORT, 1216
UMBRO U.S.A., 1217
VF BRAND SOLUTIONS, 1219
VF CORPORATION, 1219
V-FORMATION\THE NEXED LIFE, 1218
VITAL/PROMARX, 1220
VITRONIX PROMOTIONAL GROUP, 1220
WARPT INDUSTRIES, 1220
WEEKEND EXERCISE COMPANY, 1221
WINDJAMMER INC., 1222
WINTERLAND PRODUCTIONS, 1222
WOMEN'S GOLF UNLIMITED, 1223
WOOLRICH, 1223
YARRINGTON MILLS CORPORATION, 1224
ZERO GLOVES, 1224
ZORREL INTERNATIONAL, 1224

Archery Manufacturers

BEAR ARCHERY, 1115
BROWNING, 1121
CINCINNATI GAMES, 1126
DARTON ARCHERY, 1236
EASTON TECHNICAL PRODUCTS, 1137
HOYT USA, 1156
SAUNDERS ARCHERY COMPANY, 1197
SPORTS SENSORS INC, 1205
TC SPORTS, 1211

Auto Sports Manufacturers

BUTLER BUILT MOTORSPORTS EQUIPMENT,
    1122
PRO SPECIALTIES GROUP, 1188

Badminton Manufacturers

ADA TENNIS, 1103
CINCINNATI GAMES, 1126
CLASSIC SPORT COMPANIES INC, 1126
DUNLOP/MAXFLI/SLAZENGER GROUP
    AMERICAS, 1136

PRO PERFORMANCE SPORTS, 1188
PRO-LINE CAP COMPANY, 1188
PROMARX/VITAL, 1189
PUMA NORTH AMERICA, 1189
PUTTERMAN ATHLETICS, 1190
PW ATHLETIC COMPANY, 1190
RAINBOW IMPORTS, 1191
RAWLINGS SPORTING GOODS COMPANY
    INC., 1191
REEBOK INTERNATIONAL LTD.-RETAIL, 1247
REGENT SPORTS CORPORATION, 1192
RICHARDSON SPORTS, 1193
RIDDELL, 1193
RIPKEN BASEBALL LLC, 1194
ROYAL TEXTILE MILLS, 1195
RUSSELL ATHLETIC, 1195
S.M. ATHLETICS, 1196
SARANAC GLOVE COMPANY, 1196
SAUCONY, 1197
SCHUTT SPORTS INC, 1197
SEAGULL INTERNATIONAL, 1197
SHAMROCK SPORTS BAG COMPANY, 1199
SHOCK DOCTOR INC, 1199
SIPES COMPANY, 1200
SOFFE COMPANY, 1202
SOUTHERN BLEACHER COMPANY, 1202
SOUTHLAND ATHLETIC MANUFACTURING
    COMPANY, 1203
SPECIALTY NETS, 1203
SPEEDLINE ATHLETIC WEAR, 1203
SPORTCAP, 1204
SPORTDECALS, 1204
SPORTIME, 1204
SPORTLINE INC, 1204
SPORTS BELLE INC., 1205
SPORTS SENSORS INC, 1205
SPORTS SUPPLY GROUP, 1205
SPORTS TUTOR INC, 1205
SPORTS WEST SALES, 1206
SPRI PRODUCTS INC, 1206
STACKHOUSE ATHLETIC EQUIPMENT, 1207
STALKER RADAR, 1207
STALL & DEAN MFG. COMPANY, 1207
STANDARD MERCHANDISING COMPANY, 1207
SUPERIOR EXERCISE PRODUCTS, 1209
SWING AWAY SPORTS PRODUCTS, 1210
T3K INC, 1210
TACKI-MAC GRIPS, 1210
TC SPORTS, 1211
TEAMLINE, 1211
TIDE-RIDER, 1213
TINY TOTS SPORTS, 1213
TOP-COMFO ATHLETIC SOX, 1214
TRENWAY, 1215
TROPHY GLOVE COMPANY, 1215
TUF-WEAR, 1216
TURFER SPORTSWEAR, 1216
TWIN CITY KNITTING COMPANY, 1216
U.S. GAMES, 1217
ULTRA PLAY SYSTEMS, 1217
UNIQUE SPORTS PRODUCTS, 1217
VARSITY BRANDS, 1218
VICTORY SPORTS NETS, 1219
VIKING TECHNOLOGY INC., 1219
VITRONIX PROMOTIONAL GROUP, 1220
WEST COAST NETTING, 1221
WILSON SPORTING GOODS COMPANY, 1222
WINN, 1222
WITTE GROUP, 1222
WITTEK GOLF SUPPLY COMPANY, 1222
ZERO GLOVES, 1224

Basketball Manufacturers

AALCO MANUFACTURING CO. INC., 1100
ADASTRA DESIGNS INC., 1103
ADP LEMCO, 1103
ALCHESTER MILLS COMPANY, 1104
ALGOMA NET COMPANY, 1104
ALL STAR KNITWEAR, 1105
ALL STAR SPORTING GOODS, 1105
ALPHA SPORTSWEAR, 1106
AMERICAN PLAYGROUND CORPORATION,
    1108
AND 1, 1109
AWARD DECALS, 1112
B' WARMER THERMAL PRODUCTS, 1112
BADEN SPORTS, 1113
BALLSTARS, 1114
BANKSHOT SPORTS ORGANIZATION, 1229

BISON, 1117
BSN SPORTS, 1121
CANNON SPORTS INC., 1233
CHAMPION BALL COMPANY, 1125
CLASSIC SPORT COMPANIES INC, 1126
DANDY PRODUCTS, 1133
DC SPORTS, 1236
DOUGLAS INDUSTRIES, 1135
ESCALADE SPORTS, 1140
EVERLAST WORLDWIDE, 1140
E-Z GARD INDUSTRIES, 1137
FILA USA, 1143
FIRST SERVICE, 1143
FISHER ATHLETIC EQUIPMENT, 1143
FRANKLIN SPORTS, 1145
GAME MASTER ATHLETIC COMPANY, 1146
GAME TIME, 1146
GARED SPORTS, 1147
GOALSETTER SYSTEMS, 1149
GUMRUNNERS, 1151
H E HODGE COMPANY, 1151
HAMMETT COMPANY, 1152
HARVEST VICTORY LTD, 1153
HUFFY SPORTS COMPANY, 1157
HYDRA-RIB, 1157
JAYPRO SPORTS, 1160
JJ ACCESSORIES, 1160
K2 INC., 1162
KORNEY BOARD AIDS, 1164
LIFETIME, 1166
MARKWORT SPORTING GOODS COMPANY,
    1170
MARTY GILMAN, 1171
MICHAEL JORDAN BRAND/NIKE, 1173
MIKASA SPORTS USA, 1173
MILLERBERND MANUFACTURING COMPANY,
    1174
MIRACLE RECREATION EQUIPMENT
    COMPANY, 1174
MOOSE MOUNTAIN SPORTS & GAMES LTD,
    1175
MOPRO, 1175
NUMBERALLS, 1181
PERFORMANCE SPORTS SYSTEMS, 1184
PORTER ATHLETIC EQUIPMENT COMPANY,
    1186
PRO BOUND SPORTS, 1188
PW ATHLETIC COMPANY, 1190
R.A.M. SPORTS, 1190
RAINBOW IMPORTS, 1191
REGENT SPORTS CORPORATION, 1192
RICHARDSON SPORTS, 1193
ROBBINS SPORTS SURFACES, 1194
SCHELDE NORTH AMERICA, 1197
SCHUTT SPORTS INC, 1197
SHOCK DOCTOR INC, 1199
SOL-EFFECT ENTERPRISE COMPANY LTD,
    1202
SPORTSPLAY EQUIPMENT, 1206
STACKHOUSE ATHLETIC EQUIPMENT, 1207
SUPERIOR EXERCISE PRODUCTS, 1209
SWEDE-O, 1210
TC SPORTS, 1211
TEAMLINE, 1211
THE ORIGINAL BALL BAG LLC, 1182
TINY TOTS SPORTS, 1213
U.S. GAMES, 1217
ULTRA PLAY SYSTEMS, 1217
VICTORY SPORTS NETS, 1219
WEST COAST NETTING, 1221

Billiards Manufacturers

DMI SPORTS INC, 1135
GLD PRODUCTS, 1148
HALEX, 1152
IMPERIAL INTERNATIONAL, 1158
KING COBRA GAMING, 1163
LION SPORTS INC, 1167
MOOSE MOUNTAIN SPORTS & GAMES LTD,
    1175
MURREY INTERNATIONAL, 1176

Boat Manufacturers

ABSOLUTELY NEW, 1100
BOSTON WHALER, 1119
BRUNSWICK CORPORATION, 1121
CANAMER INT'L, 1123
FROST MOTORSPORTS, 16

INVENTION TECHNOLOGIES, 798
JOHNSON OUTDOORS, 1161
KOOLATRON, 1164
MERCURY MARINE, 1173
NASH MANUFACTURING INC, 1177
NATIONAL MARINE MANUFACTURERS
    ASSOCIATION, 64
PELICAN INTERNATIONAL INC, 1184
SEVYLOR USA INC., 1198
SHAW & TENNEY, 1199
WATER SPORTS LLC, 1221

Bowling Manufacturers

ACE MITCHELL BOWLERS MART, 1101
ALL AMERICAN BOWLING PRO SHOP, 1105
AMF BOWLING WORLDWIDE, 1108
BEGNI'RS TO PRO'S, 1230
BOWLERSPARADISE.COM, 1232
BOWLINGSHIRT.COM, 1119
CLASSIC PRODUCTS, 1126
COLUMBIA 300, 1128
EBONITE INTERNATIONAL, 1138
MASTER INDUSTRIES WORLDWIDE, 1171
MELO CO., 1172
MOOSE MOUNTAIN SPORTS & GAMES LTD,
    1175
MURREY INTERNATIONAL, 1176
SATURNIAN 1 INC., 1197
SOYAD BROTHERS TEXTILE CORPORATION,
    1203

Boxing Manufacturers

BALAZS, 1113
CLUBHOUSEKIT, 1127
HEAVY HANDS, 1154
IMPACT TRAINING SYSTEMS INC, 1157
MARTY GILMAN, 1171
OMEGA GEAR INC, 1182
SHOCK DOCTOR INC, 1199
SUPERIOR EXERCISE PRODUCTS, 1209
TKO SPORTS GROUP, 1213

Climbing Manufacturers

BLACK DIAMOND EQUIPMENT, 1117
BOUNTY HUNTER, 1119
BREWER'S LEDGE, 1120
ENTRE-PRISES USA, 1139
FILA USA, 1143
JEEP ELECTRONICS, 1160
LIBERTY MOUNTAIN SPORTS, 1166

Croquet Manufacturers

CINCINNATI GAMES, 1126
FUNLINE MERCHANDISE COMPANY INC, 1146
KING COBRA GAMING, 1163

Curling Manufacturers

REPUBLIC PACKAGING CORPORATION, 1192
TROPHY GLOVE COMPANY, 1215

Cycling Manufacturers

ABSOLUTELY NEW, 1100
ADVANTAGE SPORTS RACK, 1104
AMERICAN PLAYGROUND CORPORATION,
    1108
AMERICAN RECREATION PRODUCTS, 1108
ASA PRODUCTS, 1110
BELL SPORTS INC., 1116
BIKE USA INC., 1116
BION INCORPORATED, 1117
BRUNSWICK BICYCLE DIVISION, 1121
BRUNSWICK CORPORATION, 1121
CANNONDALE BICYCLE CORPORATION, 1123
CHUCK ROAST EQUIPMENT, 1126
DANSKIN, 1133
DESCENTE NORTH AMERICA, 1134
DIAMONDBACK BICYCLES, 1135
EARBAGS, 1137
EASY RACERS, 1138
GIRO SPORT DESIGN, 1148
GRANDOE CORPORATION, 1150
GUMRUNNERS, 1151
HARVEST VICTORY LTD, 1153
HIND, 1155

Dart Manufacturers

Diving Manufacturers

Equipment Manufacturers

Exercise/Fitness Manufacturers

MARK OF FITNESS INC, 1170
MAXIMUS FITNESS PRODUCTS, 1171
MEDI-DYNE HEALTHCARE PRODUCTS LTD, 1172
MIRACLE RECREATION EQUIPMENT COMPANY, 1174
NAUTILUS HPS, 1177
NIELSEN-KELLERMAN, 1179
NORDICTRACK, 1180
NORSK FITNESS PRODUCTS, 1180
OKLAHOMA LEATHER PRODUCTS, 1181
OLYMPIA SPORTS, 1182
OMEGA GEAR INC, 1182
OOLTEWAH MANUFACTURING COMPANY, 1182
OSSUR AMERICAS, 1183
PADDLE COMPANY INC, 1183
PARAMOUNT FITNESS CORPORATION, 1183
POLAR ELECTRO INC., 1186
POMCHIES LLC, 1186
PRECOR, 1187
PRO PERFORMANCE SPORTS, 1188
PRO STAR SPORTS, 1188
PROFESSIONAL GYM, 1189
PROMARX/VITAL, 1189
RAINBOW IMPORTS, 1191
SAVAGE FITNESS, 1197
SHINN FU COMPANY OF AMERICA, 1199
SMC INNOVATIONS, 1201
SOYAD BROTHERS TEXTILE CORPORATION, 1203
SPIRIT MANUFACTURING, 1203
SPORTS SPECIFIC SCIENCES, 1226
SPORTS SUPPLY GROUP, 1205
SPORTSPLAY EQUIPMENT, 1206
SPRI PRODUCTS INC, 1206
STAIRMASTER HEALTH AND FITNESS PRODUCTS, 1207
STAMINA PRODUCTS INC, 1207
STARTRAC BY UNISEN, 1207
STRENGTH, 1208
SUNDAY PLAYERS, 1209
SUPERIOR EXERCISE PRODUCTS, 1209
T3K INC, 1210
TASK INDUSTRIES, 1211
TINY TOTS SPORTS, 1213
TRUE FITNESS TECHNOLOGY, 1215
TUNTURI, 1216
UNIVERSAL GYM EQUIPMENT INC., 1218
VALEO, 1218
VECTRA FITNESS CORPORATION, 1219
VISION FITNESS, 1220
WAI LANA YOGA, 1220
WALKER & COMPANY, 1220
WORLD FAMOUS TRADING COMPANY LTD., 1223
WORLD SPORTING GOODS, 1223
YORK BARBELL COMPANY, 1253

Eyewear Manufacturers

ALLAN ENTERPRISES, 1106
BALLCO PRODUCTS, 1114
BAUSCH & LOMB, 1115
BUSHNELL CORPORATION, 1122
BUSHNELL SPORT OPTICS, 1122
CAPO INC./PANAMA JACK, 1124
CHAPMAN WALTERS INTERCOASTAL GROUP, 1234
CROAKIES, 1131
FGX DIRECT LLC., 1142
HEAD DOWN TRAINERS.COM, 1153
NIKON SPORTS & RECREATIONAL OPTICS, 1179
OAKLEY, 1181
OLYMPIC OPTICAL COMPANY, 1182
SMITH SPORT OPTICS, 1201
STYLE EYES, 1209
SUNDOG EYEWEAR USA, 1209
SWISS ARMY BRANDS, 1210
UNIQUE SPORTS PRODUCTS, 1217
UVEX SPORTS, 1218
VUARNET, 1220

Facility Manufacturers

A&H ATHLETIC FLOOR SERVICES, 1099
AACER FLOORING, 1099
AALCO MANUFACTURING CO. INC., 1100
A-B ASSOCIATES, 1099

ACADEMY SPORTS TURF, 1100
ACO POLYMER PRODUCTS, 1101
ACOUSTICAL INTERIORS, 1102
ACT ONE COMMUNICATIONS, 1102
ACTION FLOOR SYSTEMS, 1102
AD ART SIGN COMPANY, 1103
ADIRONDACK RUBBER PRODUCTS, 1103
ADOLPH KIEFER & ASSOCIATES, 1103
ADP LEMCO, 1103
ADVANCED EQUIPMENT CORPORATION, 1104
ALL AMERICAN SCOREBOARDS, 1105
ALUMINUM SEATING, 1107
ALVARADO MANUFACTURING COMPANY, 1107
AMERICAN ELECTRIC LIGHTING, 1107
AMERICAN SEATING, 1108
ANC SPORTS ENTERPRISES, 1228
ASCENSION, 1110
ATHLETIC & PERFORMANCE RIGGING/APR, 1111
ATHLETIC FIELD SERVICES, 1111
A-TURF, 1099
B & G EQUIPMENT COMPANY, 1112
B&R ERECTORS/BLEACHERS, 1112
BACHARACH RASIN SPORTING GOODS, 1113
BARCO MEDIA, 1114
BASIC COATINGS, 1115
BEACON ATHLETICS, 1229
BEST PORTABLE FENCE, 1116
BIEBER LIGHTING CORPORATION, 1116
BOSS GRAPHICS, 1119
BOYLE & COMPANY, 1119
C. CRETORS & CO., 1122
CABLEFORM INC., 1123
CANAMER INT'L, 1123
CIMCO REFRIGERATION, 1126
COLBOND, 1128
COLORADO DISPLAY SYSTEMS, 1128
COLORADO TIME SYSTEMS, 1128
COMMUNITY PROFESSIONAL LOUDSPEAKERS, 829
CONNOR SPORTS FLOORING CORPORATION, 1129
CONTOUR SEATS, 1129
COOPER LIGHTING, 1129
CORSAIR DISPLAY SYSTEMS, 1130
COURT COMPANY, 1130
COVER SPORTS USA, 1130
COVERMASTER, 1235
CROSSFIELD PRODUCTS CORPORATION, 1131
CROWN INDUSTRIES, 1131
DAKTRONICS, 1133
DLF INTERNATIONAL SEEDS, 1236
DRAPER INC., 1135
DYNAMIC TEAM SPORTS, 1136
E.B. ROTONDI & SONS, 1137
ELECTRA TARP, 1138
ELECTRO-MECH SCOREBOARD COMPANY, 1138
ENDURA RUBBER FLOORING, 1139
ENDURANCE NET, 1139
EQUIPTO, 1140
EVAN FALL PROTECTION SYSTEMS, 1140
EVERSAN, 1141
EXMARK MANUFACTURING, 1141
EZ-LINER INDUSTRIES, 1141
FAIR-PLAY SCOREBOARDS, 1142
FAIRTRON, 1142
FIBERESIN INDUSTRIES, 1142
FISHER ATHLETIC EQUIPMENT, 1143
FLEXCO, 1144
FN THOMPSON COMPANY, 1144
GAME TIME, 1146
GE LIGHTING SYSTEMS, 1147
GENERAL SPORTS VENUE ASTROTURF, 1147
GEORGIA MARBLE COMPANY, 1148
GETZ CORPORATION, 1148
GREENTECH, 1151
GUSTAFSON MANUFACTURING COMPANY, 1151
H&B SPECIALIZED PRODUCTS, 1151
HIGH END SYSTEMS, 1155
HINES III, 1155
HOLLMAN, 1155
HORNER FLOORING COMPANY, 1156
HT TENNIS, 1156
HUBBELL LIGHTING, 1156
HUFCOR, 1157
HUMMER TURFGRASS SYSTEMS, 1157
HUSSEY SEATING COMPANY, 1157

INTERKAL INC., 1158
INTERNATIONAL SPORTS TIMING, 1159
IRWIN SEATING COMPANY, 1159
JIFFY LINE STRIPERS, 1160
JOHNSONITE, 1161
KRUEGER INTERNATIONAL, 1164
LAM LIGHTING SYSTEMS, 1165
LANDSCAPE STRUCTURES, 1165
LAWRENCE METAL PRODUCTS, 1165
LEE TENNIS PRODUCTS, 1165
LESCO, 1166
LINEAR RUBBER PRODUCTS, 1167
LITHONIA LIGHTING, 1167
LSI INDUSTRIES, 1169
LSI LIGHTING INDUSTRIES, 1169
LYCIAN STAGE LIGHTING, 1169
MATEFLEX-MELE CORPORATION, 1171
MCARTHUR TOWELS & SPORTS, 1172
METRO SIGNS ADVERTISING, 1173
MICROLITE, 1173
MILLERBERND MANUFACTURING COMPANY, 1174
MIRACLE RECREATION EQUIPMENT COMPANY, 1174
MITCHELL RUBBER PRODUCTS, 1174
MITSUBISHI DIAMOND VISION, 1174
MONDO AMERICA, 1174
MONOLITHIC DOME INSTITUTE, 1175
MOTZ GROUP, 1176
MUSCO SPORTS-LIGHTING, 1176
NATARE CORPORATION, 1177
NEIL ENTERPRISES, 1178
NET RESULTS SPORTS MARKETING/NRSM INC., 1178
NEVCO, 1178
NGI SPORTS, 1179
NO FAULT SPORT GROUP, 1180
NORA SYSTEMS, 1180
NORTH STAR LIGHTING, 1180
NOVA SPORTS USA, 1181
OFF THE WALL PRODUCTS, 1181
PARTAC PEAT CORPORATION/BEAM CLAY, 1184
PAWLING CORPORATION/STANDARD PRODUCTS DIVISION, 1184
PHILIPS LIGHTING COMPANY, 1185
PIONEER NEW MEDIA TECHNOLOGIES, 1185
PLAYFIELD INTERNATIONAL INC., 1186
POLEMAX L.L.C., 1186
PORTAFLOOR, 1186
RELIABLE RACING SUPPLY, 1192
REVERE PLASTICS, 1193
RHINO SPORTS, 1193
RIP FLAG, 1194
RLS LIGHTING, 1194
ROBBINS SPORTS SURFACES, 1194
RODER USA, 1075
RPTC, 1195
SACO TECHNOLOGIES INC./SMARTVISION, 1196
SAFEGUARD FLOOR SYSTEMS, 1196
SAFWAY SERVICES, 1196
SANDSTROM PRODUCTS COMPANY, 1196
SEALFLEX INDUSTRIES, 1197
SEATING SERVICES INCORPORATED, 1198
SETCOM CORPORATION, 1198
SIGNCO, 1200
SMITHCO, 1201
SONY SPORTS, 1202
SOUTHERN BLEACHER COMPANY, 1202
SPECTRUM CORPORATION, 1203
SPORT COURT, 1204
S'PORTABLE SCOREBOARDS, 1196
SPORTGRASS, 1204
SPORTMASTER, 1204
SRI SPORTS, 1206
STAGERIGHT CORP., 1207
STRONGWALL SYSTEMS INC., 1208
STURDISTEEL COMPANY, 1208
SUNTEC PAINT, 1209
SUPERIOR FLOOR COMPANY, 1209
SYNTHETIC SURFACES, 1210
T.C. THILON USA, 1210
TAIYO BIRDAIR CORPORATION, 1210
TENNIS SURFACES COMPANY, 1212
TERRAPLAS USA RENTALS, 1212
TOMCAT USA, 1213
TOMSED CORPORATION, 1213
TRACKLITE SYSTEMS, 1214
TRANS-LUX SPORTS, 1214

TRUSCO MFG. COMPANY, 1216
TUFLEX RUBBER PRODUCTS, 1216
U.S. TRAFFIC CORPORATION, 1217
UNIVERSAL FABRIC STRUCTURES, 1218
UNIVERSAL SPORTS LIGHTING, 1218
VELVETOP PRODUCTS, 1219
VIBRA-WHIRL & COMPANY, 1219
VIKING ICE, 1219
VIRCO MANUFACTURING CORPORATION, 1219
WESTERN GOLF, 1221
WORLD DRYER CORPORATION, 1223
XL VIDEO, 1223
YEADON FABRIC STRUCTURES LTD., 1224
ZAMBONI & COMPANY, 1224

Fencing Manufacturers

AMERICAN FENCERS SUPPLY, 1107
COVER SPORTS USA, 1130
EVENT PROMOTION SUPPLY, 1140
RELIABLE RACING SUPPLY, 1192

Field Hockey Manufacturers

ACADEMY SPORTS TURF, 1100
ALUMINUM ATHLETIC EQUIPMENT COMPANY (AAE), 1107
BISON, 1117
CRAN BARRY INC., 1131
CUTTERS GLOVES, 1132
JUGS COMPANY, 1161
JUGS INC/JKP SPORTS, 1161
LEADER SPORTS USA/THE HILSINGER COMPANY, 1165
MOOSE MOUNTAIN SPORTS & GAMES LTD, 1175
RAGE CAGE, 1191
SHOCK DOCTOR INC, 1199
WEST COAST NETTING, 1221

Fishing Equipment Manufacturers

ABSOLUTELY NEW, 1100
ABSOLUTELY NEW, 1100
ABU GARCIA, 1100
BASS PRO SHOPS, 1229
CABELA'S, 1233
DAIWA CORPORATION, 1133
FLAMBEAU OUTDOORS, 1144
GUMRUNNERS, 1151
HARVEST VICTORY LTD, 1153
HOOK & HACKLE, 1156
INDUSTRIAL OPPORTUNITIES, 1158
INTROMARK INC, 798
INVENTION TECHNOLOGIES, 798
JOHNSON OUTDOORS, 1161
LOWRANCE ELECTRONICS, 1168
MCNETT CORPORATION, 1172
NYX GOLF, 1181
OLYMPIC OPTICAL COMPANY, 1182
PENN FISHING TACKLE COMPANY, 1184
PURE FISHING, 1189
SEAGULL INTERNATIONAL, 1197
SHAKESPEARE FISHING TACKLE DIVISION, 1198
SHIMANO AMERICAN CORPORATION, 1199
ZEBCO, 1224

Flag Manufacturers

ABC FLAG MANUFACTURING CO., 1100
BSI PRODUCTS, 1121
FREMONT DIE CONSUMER PRODUCTS INC, 1145
HIREV, 1155
JTD ENTERPRISES INC, 1161
ONPOINT VISUALS, 1182
PARTY ANIMAL INC., 1184

Floor Manufacturers

A&H ATHLETIC FLOOR SERVICES, 1099
AACER FLOORING, 1099
AALCO MANUFACTURING CO. INC., 1100
A-B ASSOCIATES, 1099
ACTION ATHLETIC EQUIPMENT, 1102
ACTION FLOOR SYSTEMS, 1102
ADIRONDACK RUBBER PRODUCTS, 1103
ADOLPH KIEFER & ASSOCIATES, 1103

ADP LEMCO, 1103
A-TURF, 1099
BASIC COATINGS, 1115
BOYLE & COMPANY, 1119
CELLO PROFESSIONAL PRODUCTS, 1125
CENTAUR FLOOR SYSTEMS, 1125
COLBOND, 1128
CONNOR SPORTS FLOORING CORPORATION, 1129
COVER SPORTS USA, 1130
COVERMASTER, 1235
CROSSFIELD PRODUCTS CORPORATION, 1131
ENDURA RUBBER FLOORING, 1139
EPIC METALS, 1140
FIRST SERVICE, 1143
FLEXCO, 1144
FLOORBOARDZ RUGS, 1144
GERSTUNG/GYM-THING, 1148
H E HODGE COMPANY, 1151
H&B SPECIALIZED PRODUCTS, 1151
HORNER FLOORING COMPANY, 1156
IMPEX INC, 1158
JOHNSONITE, 1161
KIEFER U.S.A., 1163
MATEFLEX-MELE CORPORATION, 1171
MITCHELL RUBBER PRODUCTS, 1174
MONDO AMERICA, 1174
MYLEC, 1176
NATARE CORPORATION, 1177
NO FAULT SPORT GROUP, 1180
NORA SYSTEMS, 1180
PAIGE DESIGN GROUP, 1071
PAWLING CORPORATION/STANDARD PRODUCTS DIVISION, 1184
PORTAFLOOR, 1186
PRO STAR SPORTS, 1188
PUTTERMAN ATHLETICS, 1190
REVERE PLASTICS, 1193
RHINO SPORTS, 1193
RIP FLAG, 1194
SAFEGUARD FLOOR SYSTEMS, 1196
SPORT COURT, 1204
SPORTS SPECIFIC SCIENCES, 1226
SRI SPORTS, 1206
STRONGWALL SYSTEMS INC., 1208
SUNTEC PAINT, 1209
SUPERIOR FLOOR COMPANY, 1209
SURFACE AMERICA, 1209
TENNIS SURFACES COMPANY, 1212
TRACKLITE SYSTEMS, 1214
TUFLEX RUBBER PRODUCTS, 1216
WORLD CLASS ATHLETIC SURFACES, 1223

Football Manufacturers

ACTION ATHLETIC EQUIPMENT, 1102
ADAMS USA, 1103
ALGOMA NET COMPANY, 1104
ALL AMERICAN SPORTS CORP/RIDDELL ALL AMERICAN, 1105
ALL STAR SPORTING GOODS, 1105
ALUMINUM ATHLETIC EQUIPMENT COMPANY (AAE), 1107
ANTIOCH SPORTS, 1109
AUSTIN ATHLETIC COMPANY, 1112
AWARD DECALS, 1112
B' WARMER THERMAL PRODUCTS, 1112
BALLSTARS, 1114
BISON, 1117
BRINE, 1120
BSN SPORTS, 1121
CANNON SPORTS INC., 1233
CHAMPION BALL COMPANY, 1125
CLASSIC SPORT COMPANIES INC, 1126
CLUBHOUSEKIT, 1127
COVERMASTER, 1235
CUSTOM DECAL & EMBLEMS, 1132
CUTTERS GLOVES, 1132
CYRK, 1132
DALCO ATHLETIC LETTERING, 1133
DANDY PRODUCTS, 1133
DEBEER LACROSSE, 1134
DIAMOND SPORTS, 1134
DMI SPORTS INC, 1135
DOUGLAS INDUSTRIES, 1135
EASTON SPORTS, 1137
E-Z GARD INDUSTRIES, 1137
FISHER ATHLETIC EQUIPMENT, 1143
FRANKLIN SPORTS, 1145

GAME MASTER ATHLETIC COMPANY, 1146
GATOR ATHLETIC INC., 1147
GEAR PRO-TEC, 1147
GENERAL SPORTCRAFT COMPANY, 1147
GERRY COSBY & COMPANY, 1148
GOAL SPORTING GOODS, 1149
GUMRUNNERS, 1151
HADAR ATHLETIC MFG. COMPANY, 1152
HAMMETT COMPANY, 1152
HARVEST VICTORY LTD, 1153
IMPACT TRAINING SYSTEMS INC, 1157
JAYPRO SPORTS, 1160
JJ ACCESSORIES, 1160
JUGS COMPANY, 1161
JUGS INC/JKP SPORTS, 1161
LAFAYETTE INSTRUMENT COMPANY, 1165
LEADER SPORTS USA/THE HILSINGER COMPANY, 1165
MARKWORT SPORTING GOODS COMPANY, 1170
MARTY GILMAN, 1171
MIKASA SPORTS USA, 1173
MOOSE MOUNTAIN SPORTS & GAMES LTD, 1175
NOCONA ATHLETIC GOODS COMPANY, 1180
OMNI BODYWORK, 1182
POINT BLANK SOLUTIONS, 1186
PW ATHLETIC COMPANY, 1190
R.A.M. SPORTS, 1190
RAE CROWTHER COMPANY, 1191
RAINBOW IMPORTS, 1191
RAWLINGS SPORTING GOODS COMPANY INC., 1191
REEBOK INTERNATIONAL LTD.-RETAIL, 1247
REGENT SPORTS CORPORATION, 1192
REPUBLIC PACKAGING CORPORATION, 1192
RIDDELL, 1193
RIDDELL ATHLETIC FOOTWEAR, 1193
ROGERS ATHLETIC COMPANY, 1194
ROYAL TEXTILE MILLS, 1195
SAFE-T-GARD CORPORATION, 1196
SCHUTT SPORTS INC, 1197
SHOCK DOCTOR INC, 1199
SOL-EFFECT ENTERPRISE COMPANY LTD, 1202
SOUTHERN BLEACHER COMPANY, 1202
SPORTDECALS, 1204
SPORTLINE INC, 1204
SPORTS SUPPLY GROUP, 1205
SPORTSPLAY EQUIPMENT, 1206
STACKHOUSE ATHLETIC EQUIPMENT, 1207
SUPERIOR EXERCISE PRODUCTS, 1209
SWEDE-O, 1210
T3K INC, 1210
TC SPORTS, 1211
TINY TOTS SPORTS, 1213
TRIMAN TELE-GOAL, 1215
TROPHY GLOVE COMPANY, 1215
TUF-WEAR, 1216
U.S. GAMES, 1217
VARSITY BRANDS, 1218
WELLS LAMONT SPORTS & SPECIALTIES, 1221
WILSON SPORTING GOODS COMPANY, 1222
WORLD SPORTING GOODS, 1223

Footwear Manufacturers

ACOR, 1101
ACORN PRODUCTS COMPANY, 1101
ADVANCED DESIGN CONCEPTS, 1104
ALL STAR KNITWEAR, 1105
AMERICAN ATHLETIC SHOE COMPANY, 1107
AMERICAN SPORTING GOODS COMPANY, 1228
AMF BOWLING WORLDWIDE, 1108
AND 1, 1109
ASICS AMERICA CORPORATION, 1111
AUDERO SPORTS SUPPLY, 1111
BIRKENSTOCK FOOTPRINT SANDALS INC., 1231
BROOKS, 1120
BRUTE WRESTLING, 1121
CMS SPORTS, 1235
CONVERSE, 1235
DECKERS OUTDOOR CORPORATION, 1134
DEXTER SHOE COMPANY, 1134
DIADORA AMERICA, 1134
DOCKER'S FOOTWEAR, 1135
E.S. ORIGINALS, 1137

General Manufacturers

SLAZENGER GOLF PRODUCTS CO, 1201
SMYTH SYSTEMS, 1201
SOLE CHOICE, 1202
SOYAD BROTHERS TEXTILE CORPORATION, 1203
SPORT HALEY INC., 1204
SPORTS SENSORS INC, 1205
STURM, 1208
STX INC., 1208
SUN MOUNTAIN SPORTS, 1209
SUNDERLAND OF SCOTLAND, 1209
SUNTIME/LINKSWALKER, 1209
SUPERIOR EXERCISE PRODUCTS, 1209
TACKI-MAC GRIPS, 1210
TAYLORMADE-ADIDAS GOLF, 1211
TEN SECONDS, 1211
TEXTILE REVOLUTION, 1212
THE ORIGINAL BALL BAG LLC, 1182
TINY TOTS SPORTS, 1213
TITANIUM SPORTS TECHNOLOGIES, 1213
TITLEIST (COBRA/PINNACLE), 1213
TKO SPORTS GROUP, 1213
TOMIC GOLF & SKI MFG., 1213
TOP-FLITE COMPANY, 1214
TOWN TALK CAP MFG. COMPANY, 1214
TR GEAR/PROTONIC, 1214
TRANS APPAREL, 1214
TROPHY GLOVE COMPANY, 1215
TRUE TEMPER SPORTS, 1215
TRUEX GOLF, 1215
TURFCO MFG., 1216
UNIQUE SPORTS PRODUCTS, 1217
UNITED SPORTS TECHNOLOGIES/UST, 1217
UT GOLF, 1218
WESTERN GOLF, 1221
WILSON SPORTING GOODS COMPANY, 1222
WITTEK GOLF SUPPLY COMPANY, 1222
WOMEN'S GOLF UNLIMITED, 1223
WOMENS GOLFWORKS, 1223
WOODS TO WEDGES, 1223
YONEX CORPORATION, 1224
ZERO GLOVES, 1224

Gymnastics Manufacturers

ACTION ATHLETIC EQUIPMENT, 1102
ALGOMA NET COMPANY, 1104
CABANA BANNERS, 1123
CANAMER INT'L, 1123
COURT-1 SPORTS INC., 1130
ELITE SPORTSWEAR, 1139
FISHER ATHLETIC EQUIPMENT, 1143
H E HODGE COMPANY, 1151
INDUSTRIAL OPPORTUNITIES, 1158
MANCINO MANUFACTURING CO., 1170
RESILITE SPORTS PRODUCTS, 1193
SEAWAY MATS, 1198
TROPHY GLOVE COMPANY, 1215

Hat Manufacturers

A-B EMBLEM, 1099
ALCHESTER MILLS COMPANY, 1104
AMERICAN NEEDLE & NOVELTY INC., 1108
ANTIGUA GROUP, 1109
APSCO ENTERPRISES, 1109
BIG TIME SPORTS APPAREL, 1116
BRONER, 1232
BUFFALO EXPORT, 1122
COED SPORTSWEAR INC, 1127
CROAKIES, 1131
CUSHEES, 1131
DORFMAN-PACIFIC COMPANY, 1135
DREW PEARSON MARKETING, 1237
EARBAGS, 1137
EDDY BROS. HAT CO. INC., 1138
FOAMHEADS, 1145
GAMETIME PLUSH, 1147
GAMEWEAR, 1147
GOLF & TENNIS HEADWEAR COMPANY, 1149
GOORIN BROS., 1150
H&C HEADWARE/KC CAP, 1152
HAT WORLD/LIDS CORP., 1241
HYP HATS, 1157
IMPERIAL HEADWEAR, 1157
KANGOL HEADWEAR, 1162
KRYPTONICS U.S.A., 1164
LEADER MANUFACTURING COMPANY, 1165
LEADER SPORTS USA/THE HILSINGER
   COMPANY, 1165

LEGEND SPORTS, 1166
LONE STAR ATHLETIC DESIGNS, 1168
MILLER GOLF, 1174
MOUNTAIN HIGH HOSIERY, 1176
MPC PROMOTIONS, 1176
MTC MARKETING INC, 1176
NEW ENGLAND CAP CO., 1178
NEW ERA CAP, 1178
NIKE GOLF, 1179
OLD TIME SPORTS, 1182
ONFIELD APPAREL GROUP, 1182
PARAMOUNT HEADWEAR, 1183
PIONEER INDUSTRIES, 1185
PRO-LINE CAP COMPANY, 1188
RAINBOW IMPORTS, 1191
SCHUESSLER KNITTING MILLS, 1197
SEAGULL INTERNATIONAL, 1197
SKEA, 1200
SOLAR BLOC HATS, 1249
SPORTCAP, 1204
STANLY HEADWEAR, 1207
SUN SHADER INTERNATIONAL, 1209
SUNTIME/LINKSWALKER, 1209
TEXACE CORP., 1212
TOWN TALK CAP MFG. COMPANY, 1214
TWINS ENTERPRISES, 1216
TYCA CORPORATION, 1216
VIKING TECHNOLOGY INC., 1219
VITRONIX PROMOTIONAL GROUP, 1220
VOYAGER CUSTOM PRODUCTS, 1220
ZERO GLOVES, 1224

Horse Shoe Manufacturers

ST. PIERRE MANUFACTURING CORPORATION, 1207

Ice Hockey Manufacturers

ABI TAPE PRODUCTS, 1100
ALL STAR SPORTING GOODS, 1105
ALPHA SPORTSWEAR, 1106
AMERICAN ATHLETIC SHOE COMPANY, 1107
BAUER NIKE HOCKEY, 1115
BLADEMASTER, 1118
C.N. IS BELIEVING, 1122
CCM HOCKEY, 1125
CHRISTIAN BROTHERS, 1126
CLASSIC SPORT COMPANIES INC, 1126
COURT-1 SPORTS INC., 1130
CUSTOM DECAL & EMBLEMS, 1132
CUTTERS GLOVES, 1132
DMI SPORTS INC, 1135
DOUGLAS INDUSTRIES, 1135
DR SPORTS EQUIPMENT, 1135
EASTON SPORTS, 1137
GERRY COSBY & COMPANY, 1148
HIGH 5 SPORTSWEAR, 1155
HILLERICH & BRADSBY COMPANY, 1155
IN GLAS COMPANY, 1158
INDUSTRIAL OPPORTUNITIES, 1158
IRWIN SPORTS, 1159
ITECH SPORT PRODUCTS, 1159
JAYPRO SPORTS, 1160
JOFA HOCKEY/THE HOCKEY COMPANY, 1161
KARHU U.S.A. LIMITED, 1162
KEYBEC SUBLIME, 1163
KITCHENER HOCKEY STICKS LTD., 1163
LEADER SPORTS USA/THE HILSINGER
   COMPANY, 1165
MCCARTHY-SORENSEN ATHLETIC, 1172
MDF INDUSTRIES INC, 1172
OCEAN HOCKEY SUPPLY COMPANY, 1181
OMNI BODYWORK, 1182
PHOENIX VENTURES CORPORATION, 1185
REEBOK APPAREL GROUP, 1192
RIEDELL SHOES, 1193
ROYAL TEXTILE MILLS, 1195
SAFE-T-GARD CORPORATION, 1196
SHER-WOOD HOCKEY INC, 1199
SHERWOOD-DROLET CORPORATION, 1199
SHIELD, 1199
SOL-EFFECT ENTERPRISE COMPANY LTD, 1202
STRAUSS SKATES & BICYCLES, 1208
TERRAMAR SPORTS WORLDWIDE, 1212

Ice Skating Manufacturers

BLADEMASTER, 1118

CCM HOCKEY, 1125
CUTTERS GLOVES, 1132
REEBOK APPAREL GROUP, 1192
SENECA SPORTS INC., 1198
SOL-EFFECT ENTERPRISE COMPANY LTD, 1202
WISSOTA MANUFACTURING COMPANY, 1222

Inline Skating Manufacturers

ATOMIC SKI USA, 1111
BAUER NIKE HOCKEY, 1115
BLADEMASTER, 1118
BRAVO SPORTS, 1120
BVT PRODUCTS, 1122
CREATIVE URETHANES, 1131
DEVENTER'S CHEER & DANCEWEAR
   FACTORY, 1134
EASTON SPORTS, 1137
EVOL SNOWBOARDS, 1141
FRANKLIN SPORTS, 1145
GUMRUNNERS, 1151
HARBINGER, 1153
K2 INC., 1162
KAPPA USA, 1162
KWIK GOAL LTD., 1164
NATIONAL SPORTING GOODS CORPORATION, 284
NIGHT SPORTS, 1179
NOVA SPORTS USA, 1181
NYX GOLF, 1181
POMCHIES LLC, 1186
PRECISION SPORTS, 1187
PRINCE SPORTS, 1188
PRO-TEC, 1189
RIEDELL SHOES, 1193
ROCES USA, 1194
ROLLER DERBY SKATE CORPORATION, 1194
ROLLERBLADE INC., 1194
SAUCONY, 1197
SELECT DISTRIBUTION/VISION STREET
   WEAR, 1198
SENECA SPORTS INC., 1198
SHANGHAI WINGO INTERNATIONAL, 1199
SOL-EFFECT ENTERPRISE COMPANY LTD, 1202
SPEED SKATELUBE, 1203
VARIFLEX INC., 1218
V-FORMATION\THE NEXED LIFE, 1218

Lacrosse Manufacturers

ACADEMY SPORTS TURF, 1100
ALL LACROSSE, 1105
ALUMINUM ATHLETIC EQUIPMENT COMPANY
   (AAE), 1107
BISON, 1117
CINCINNATI GAMES, 1126
CLASSIC SPORT COMPANIES INC, 1126
CRAN BARRY INC., 1131
CUTTERS GLOVES, 1132
DMI SPORTS INC, 1135
FOAMHEADS, 1145
FUNLINE MERCHANDISE COMPANY INC, 1146
INNOVA-CHAMPION DISCS INC, 1158
K2 INC., 1162
LACROSSE UNLIMITED, 1164
LEADER SPORTS USA/THE HILSINGER
   COMPANY, 1165
MOHAWK INTERNATIONAL LACROSSE, 1174
RAGE CAGE, 1191
SHOCK DOCTOR INC, 1199
SOUTHERN BLEACHER COMPANY, 1202
TC SPORTS, 1211
WEST COAST NETTING, 1221

Licensed Products Manufacturers

5TH AND OCEAN CLOTHING, 1099
ABSOLUTELY NEW, 1100
ACTION SPORTS IMAGE, 1102
ACTION SPORTS SYSTEMS INCORPORATED, 1102
AMINCO INTERNATIONAL (USA)
   INCORPORATED, 1108
AUTHENTIC STREET SIGNS, 1112
B' WARMER THERMAL PRODUCTS, 1112
BABY FANATIC, 1113
BACON & COMPANY, 1113
BASS IND INCORPORATED, 1115

Light Manufacturers

Martial Arts Manufacturers

Miscellaneous Manufacturers

PROMARK EMBLEMS LLC, 1189
PROMARX/VITAL, 1189
PROZRELIEF, 1189
PSC/ENCORE SELECT INC, 1189
Q-RAY INC, 1190
RACING REFLECTIONS INC, 1191
RAINBOW IMPORTS, 1191
RAVENSBURGER FX SCHMID, 1191
RAZOR USA LLC, 1192
REEBOK APPAREL GROUP, 1192
REYN SPOONER INC, 1193
RIPKEN BASEBALL LLC, 1194
RYNO ATHLETICS, 1196
SATURNIAN 1 INC., 1197
SEVEN SONS AND COMPANY INC, 1198
SHIRTS & SKINS INC, 1199
SHOCK DOCTOR INC, 1199
SIGNATURE DESIGNS, 1200
SILVER KNIGHT SALES & MARKETING, 1200
SISKIYOU GIFTS, 1200
SKI SKOOT INC, 1200
SMACK APPAREL, 1201
SMC INNOVATIONS, 1201
SOCCEREDGE INC, 1201
SOCCERPAL, 1201
SOF SOLE, 1201
SOLE CHOICE, 1202
SOL-EFFECT ENTERPRISE COMPANY LTD, 1202
SOUTHERN UMBRELLA COMPANY, 1203
SOYAD BROTHERS TEXTILE CORPORATION, 1203
SPORT CARD CREATIONS INC., 1203
SPORT COLLECTORS GUILD INC, 1203
SPORT FACE, 1204
SPORT HELMETS, 1204
SPORT SEARCH.MVP GROUP, 756
SPORTING GOODS AGENTS ASSOCIATION (SGAA), 288
SPORTLINE INC, 1204
SPORTS COVERAGE, 1205
SPORTS INC, 1205
SPORTS SENSORS INC, 1205
SPORTS SPECIFIC SCIENCES, 1226
SPORTS TUTOR INC, 1205
SPRY SPORTS USA, 1206
STACKS OF PLAQUES, 1207
STAMINA PRODUCTS INC, 1207
STICK COMPANY/RPI OF ATLANTA, 1208
STORIS MANAGEMENT SYSTEMS, 1226
SUNDAY PLAYERS, 1209
SUNTIME/LINKSWALKER, 1209
SUPERIOR EXERCISE PRODUCTS, 1209
SUTTERS MILL SPECIALTIES, 1210
T3K INC, 1210
TANDEM SPORT, 1210
TANITA CORPORATION OF AMERICA, 1211
TEAM SPORTS AMERICA, 1211
TEXTILE REVOLUTION, 1212
TICKETS.COM, 943
TINY TOTS SPORTS, 1213
TOYQUEST, 1214
TR GEAR/PROTONIC, 1214
TRAILER CORPORATION OF AMERICA, 1214
TRAVELERS CLUB LUGGAGE, 1214
UNIVERSAL NUTRITION, 1218
VITAL/PROMARX, 1220
WATER SPORTS LLC, 1221
WHAM-O, 1221

Motorcycle Manufacturers

CUSTOM DECAL & EMBLEMS, 1132
UVEX SPORTS, 1218

Mountainboard Manufacturers

MONGOOSE ALL-TERRAIN BOARDS, 1175

NASCAR Truck Series Manufacturers

HIREV, 1155
HUNTER MANUFACTURING GROUP INC, 1157

Outerwear Manufacturers

ALPS SPORTSWEAR MFG. COMPANY, 1106
AMERICAN RECREATION PRODUCTS, 1108

ANTIGUA GROUP, 1109
BIRKENSTOCK FOOTPRINT SANDALS INC., 1231
BRUTE WRESTLING, 1121
BUCK KNIVES, 1121
BVT PRODUCTS, 1122
CAMOFACE, 1123
CARHARTT INC., 1234
CARIBOU MOUNTAINEERING, 1124
COLEMAN COMPANY INC., 1128
COLLEGIATE LICENSING COMPANY, 786
DEVENTER'S CHEER & DANCEWEAR FACTORY, 1134
DR SPORTS EQUIPMENT, 1135
EARBAGS, 1137
EXXEL OUTDOORS, 1141
FEDERAL PREMIUM AMMUNITION, 1142
FRANCO APPAREL GROUP, 1145
G III SPORTS, 1146
GEORGIA BOOT, 1148
HEADMASTER INC, 1153
HIGH SIERRA SPORT COMPANY, 1155
HI-TEC SPORTS USA INC., 1154
IGLOO PRODUCTS CORPORATION, 1157
JEFF HAMILTON COLLECTION, 1160
JH DESIGN GROUP, 1160
JOHNSON WORLDWIDE ASSOCIATES/CAMPING DIVISION, 1161
KAMPALA INDUSTRIES, 1162
KARHU U.S.A. LIMITED, 1162
KEY SPORTZ-WEAR, 1163
K-SWISS INC., 1162
LEGEND SPORTS, 1166
LOWE ALPINE SYSTEMS, 1168
MARLIN FIREARMS COMPANY, 1170
MARMOT, 1170
MARMOT MOUNTAIN LTD., 1170
MCNETT CORPORATION, 1172
MONTRAIL, 1175
MOSSBERG & SONS, 1175
MOUNTAIN HARDWEAR, 1176
MOUNTAIN SAFETY RESEARCH, 1176
MTC MARKETING INC, 1176
NATURAL SPORT, 1177
NEWTEX USA, 1179
NIKE, 1179
NORTH FACE, 1180
NUMBERALLS, 1181
PATAGONIA, 1184
PHI-TEN USA INC, 1185
PINE SPORTS, 1185
POMCHIES LLC, 1186
REEBOK INTERNATIONAL LTD.-RETAIL, 1247
REMINGTON ARMS COMPANY, 1192
ROCKY SHOES & BOOTS, 1194
RUBBERMAID INCORPORATED, 1195
S.L. OUTERBANKS LLC, 1196
SEVEN SONS AND COMPANY INC, 1198
SIERRA DESIGNS, 1200
SKB SHOTGUNS, 1200
SOYAD BROTHERS TEXTILE CORPORATION, 1203
SPORT FACE, 1204
SPRY SPORTS USA, 1206
SURE FOOT CORPORATION, 1209
SWISS ARMY BRANDS, 1210
T3K INC, 1210
TEVA BRAND, 1212
TRIUS PRODUCTS, 1215
U.S. REPEATING ARMS COMPANY/WINCHESTER, 1217
VF CORPORATION, 1219

Paddle Ball Manufacturer

PADDLE COMPANY INC, 1183

Racquet Manufacturers

BABOLAT VS NORTH AMERICA, 1113
BALLCO PRODUCTS, 1114
DAEWOO INTERNATIONAL CORPORATION, 1236
MARTIN-KILPATRICK, 1170
MICHIGAN LADDER COMPANY, 1173
PRO-LINE CAP COMPANY, 1188
SPORTMASTER INTERNATIONAL, 1250
TROPHY GLOVE COMPANY, 1215
UNIQUE SPORTS PRODUCTS, 1217
WEST COAST NETTING, 1221

WEST RIDGE DESIGNS, 1221

Racquetball Manufacturers

ADAMS USA, 1103
ALGOMA NET COMPANY, 1104
BABOLAT VS NORTH AMERICA, 1113
E-FORCE, 1137
EKTELON, 1138
LEADER SPORTS USA/THE HILSINGER COMPANY, 1165
TECNIFIBRE USA, 1211
TROPHY GLOVE COMPANY, 1215
UNIQUE SPORTS PRODUCTS, 1217
WEST COAST NETTING, 1221

Radar Gun Manufacturers

ADASTRA DESIGNS INC., 1103
BASEBALL FIT HITTING & PITCHING ACADEMY, 1114
DECATUR ELECTRONICS, 1134
STALKER RADAR, 1207

Retailers, Sporting Goods

24 HOUR FITNESS CENTERS, 1227
A&N STORES, 1227
ABERCROMBIE & FITCH CO., 1227
ACADEMY SPORTS & OUTDOORS, 1227
ACE HARDWARE, 1227
ADVENTURE 16, 1227
ALTREC.COM, 1227
AMERICAN EAGLE OUTFITTERS, 1228
ANACONDA SPORTS, 1228
ANY MOUNTAIN, 1228
ATHLETA, 1228
ATHLETE'S FOOT, 1228
ATHLETIC DEALERS OF AMERICA, 1228
AUSTAD'S GOLF STORE'S, 1228
AUSTAD'S GOLF/CATALOG, 1229
BASE MOUNTAIN SPORTS, 1229
BASEBALLJUNK.COM, 1229
BASS PRO SHOPS, 1229
BEALLS ENTERPRISES DEPARTMENT STORES, 1230
BEI GROUP, 1230
BELK STORES SERVICES, 1230
BEST BIKE BUYS, 1230
BICYCLE EXCHANGE, 1230
BIG 5 SPORTING GOODS, 1231
BIGG'S HYPER SHOPPES, 1231
BIKE LINE, 1231
BI-MART, 1230
BJ'S WHOLESALE CLUB, 1231
BLUE RIBBON BLANKETS, 1231
BOATER'S WORLD, 1231
BOB WARD & SONS, 1231
BOB'S STORES, 1232
BON TON STORES, 1232
BOSCOV'S DEPARTMENT STORES, 1232
BRANCH BROOK COMPANY, 1232
BREEZE SKI RENTAL, 1232
BROOKSTONE COMPANY, 1232
BUILDING #19, 1232
BUNKER JONES GOLF, 1232
BURDINE'S, 1232
BUSYBODY, 1233
BUY.COM SPORTS STORE, 1233
C M T SPECIALTY SPORTS, 1233
CABELA'S, 1233
CAMPING WORLD, 1233
CAMPMOR, 1233
CANAL JEAN CO., 1233
CHAMPS SPORTS, 1234
CHICK'S SPORTING GOODS, 1234
CHRISTY SPORTS/SPORTSTALKER, 1234
CITY SPORTS, 1234
CLARKS COMPANIES NA, 1234
COLOR INC., 1235
CRAZY SHIRTS, 1235
DALEBOOT U.S.A., 1133
DECATHLON USA SPORTS MEGASTORE, 1236
DICK'S SPORTING GOODS INC., 1236
DILLARD DEPARTMENT STORES, 1236
DIXIE SPORTING GOODS, 1236
DOLLAR GENERAL CORPORATION, 1236
DR. JAY'S, 1237
DUCKWALL ALCO STORES, 1237
DUNHAM'S ATHLEISURE CORPORATION, 1237

Roller Hockey Manufacturers

Roller Skating Manufacturers

Rowing/Crew Manufacturers

Rugby Manufacturers

Running Apparel/Supplies Manufacturer

Scoreboard Manufacturers

COVERMASTER, 1235
CUSHEES, 1131
DUNLOP/MAXFLI/SLAZENGER GROUP AMERICAS, 1136
DYNAFLEX INTERNATIONAL, 1136
EVERLAST WORLDWIDE, 1140
FILA USA, 1143
FIRST SERVICE, 1143
GAME TIME, 1146
GETZ CORPORATION, 1148
GEXCO ENTERPRISES, 1148
GOLD MEDAL RECREATIONAL PRODUCTS, 1149
GOLF & TENNIS HEADWEAR COMPANY, 1149
GRAPHITE MASTER, 1151
GUMRUNNERS, 1151
GUTERMAN INTERNATIONAL, 1151
HAR-TRU, 1153
HEAD/PENN USA, 1153
HT TENNIS, 1156
JJ ACCESSORIES, 1160
JUGS COMPANY, 1161
JUGS INC/JKP SPORTS, 1161
LEE TENNIS PRODUCTS, 1165
LITTLE MISS TENNIS/TV SPORTS, 1167
LOBSTER SPORTS, 1167
LUMASTROBE WARNING LIGHTS, 1169
MARTIN SPORTS, 1170
MASTER SPORTS, 1171
MATCH POINT, 1171
MAXLINE EAGNAS, 1171
METALTEK, 1173
MEYCO PRODUCTS, 1173
MOPRO, 1175
N.J.P. SPORTS, 1177
NYX GOLF, 1181
PADDLE COMPANY INC, 1183
PENN RACQUET SPORTS, 1184
PERFORMANCE SPORTS SYSTEMS, 1184
POMCHIES LLC, 1186
POWERS COURT/TOA, 1187
PRINCE SPORTS, 1188
PRO INNOVATIVE CONCEPTS, 1188
PRO KENNEX, 1188
PROMARX/VITAL, 1189
PVH CORP., 1190
RAINBOW IMPORTS, 1191
RODER USA, 1075
ROL-DRI, 1194
SALAUN SPORTS, 1196
SOLAR BLOC HATS, 1249
SOYAD BROTHERS TEXTILE CORPORATION, 1203
SPORTMASTER INC., 1204
SPORTMASTER INTERNATIONAL, 1250
SUPERIOR EXERCISE PRODUCTS, 1209
TACKI-MAC GRIPS, 1210
TECNIFIBRE USA, 1211
TENNIS MACHINES, 1212
TENNIS SURFACES COMPANY, 1212
TOP OF THE WORLD CAPS, 1214
TOWN TALK CAP MFG. COMPANY, 1214
WEED U.S.A., 1221
WILSON SPORTING GOODS COMPANY, 1222
WINN, 1222
YONEX CORPORATION, 1224

Timing Device Manufacturers

ACUMEN, 1102
ALL AMERICAN SCOREBOARDS, 1105
ARISTO IMPORT COMPANY, 1110
BACHARACH RASIN SPORTING GOODS, 1113
BALLANDRA CORPORATION, 1114
BARCO MEDIA, 1114
B-BALL LIGHTS, 1113
CEI, 1234
COLOR SIGN SERVICE, 1128
COLORADO DISPLAY SYSTEMS, 1128
COLORADO TIME SYSTEMS, 1128
DAKTRONICS, 1133
ELECTRO-MECH SCOREBOARD COMPANY, 1138
ERIC ARMIN INC./EAI, 1140
EVERSAN, 1141
FAIR-PLAY SCOREBOARDS, 1142
FELDMAR WATCH COMPANY, 1142
FREESTYLE USA, 1145
GETZ CORPORATION, 1148
GRALAB, 1150

INTERNATIONAL SPORTS TIMING, 1159
MARSHALL-BROWNING INTERNATIONAL CORPORATION, 1170
NATARE CORPORATION, 1177
NEVCO, 1178
PRECISE INTERNATIONAL, 1187
SOCCER SPORT SUPPLY CO., 1201
SPECTRUM CORPORATION, 1203
SPRINGCO, 1206
SWISS ARMY BRANDS, 1210
TIMEX CORPORATION, 1213
U.S. GAMES, 1217
WEBSTER WATCH CO., 1221
WEST COAST NETTING, 1221

Track & Field Manufacturers

ACTION ATHLETIC EQUIPMENT, 1102
ADIRONDACK RUBBER PRODUCTS, 1103
ALGOMA NET COMPANY, 1104
ALUMINUM ATHLETIC EQUIPMENT COMPANY (AAE), 1107
BLAZER MANUFACTURING, 1118
DAEWOO INTERNATIONAL CORPORATION, 1236
FISHER ATHLETIC EQUIPMENT, 1143
KAPPA USA, 1162
MARSHALL-BROWNING INTERNATIONAL CORPORATION, 1170
MARTY GILMAN, 1171
M-F ATHLETIC COMPANY, 1169
PORTAPIT/CATAPOLE, 1186
RED LION PRODUCTS, 1192
REPUBLIC PACKAGING CORPORATION, 1192
SOUTHERN BLEACHER COMPANY, 1202
SPORTLINE INC, 1204
SPRINGCO, 1206
TC SPORTS, 1211
VIBRA-WHIRL & COMPANY, 1219

Trading Card/Collectible Manufacturers

D.P.M. ENTERPRISES, 1132
FLEER/SKYBOX INTERNATIONAL, 1144
HENWAY SPORTS & SPECIALTIES, 1154
MEIGRAY GROUP, 1244
MULTI-AD, 1176
PLAYOFF CORP., 1186
PRESS PASS INC, 1187
PSC/ENCORE SELECT INC, 1189
SPORT PINS INTERNATIONAL, 1204
SPORTS IMMORTALS MUSEUM, 1205
STEINER SPORTS MEMORBILIA, 1208
THEPIT.COM, 723
TOPPS COMPANY, 1214
UPPER DECK COMPANY, 1218

Training Supply Manufacturers

A-ATHLETIC AND MEDICAL SUPPLY COMPANY, 1227
ABI TAPE PRODUCTS, 1100
ABSOLUTE FITNESS, 1100
ACCELERATED CARE PLUS, 1100
ACCUFITNESS, 1101
ACTIVE ANKLE SYSTEMS, 1102
AIRCAST, 1104
ALCHESTER MILLS COMPANY, 1104
ARI-MED PHARMACEUTICALS, 1110
ARTHRON, 1110
BAILEY MANUFACTURING COMPANY, 1113
BIOFREEZE/PERFORMANCE HEALTHPRODUCTS, 1117
BIOGRIP, 1117
BIOLIFE, 1117
BSN-JOBST, 1121
CANNON SPORTS INC., 1233
CASCO/USA, 1124
CDM SPORT, 1125
CERASPORT, 1125
CRAMER PRODUCTS, 1130
CREATIVE CUSTOM PRODUCTS, 1131
DARBY ATHLETIC HEALTH, 1133
EMERGENCY MEDICAL SUPPLY, 1139
EMPI, 1139
ENDLESS POOLS, 1139
ETCHASOFT, 1140
EXERTOOLS, 1141

FASTECH LABS, 1142
FERNO PERFORMANCE POOLS, 1142
FITBALL USA, 1143
HAFER CASE, 1152
JOHNSON & JOHNSON CONSUMER PRODUCTS INC., 1161
KEN YOUNG COMPANY, 1162
LOGAN INC., 1168
MCDAVID, 1172
MEDIC FIRST AID INTERNATIONAL, 1172
MUELLER SPORTS MEDICINE, 1176
NDL PRODUCTS, 1178
NORSK FITNESS PRODUCTS, 1180
PARAMOUNT FITNESS CORPORATION, 1183
PARKER LABORATORIES, 1183
PRO ORTHOPEDIC DEVICES, 1188
PROTEAM BY HAUSMANN, 1189
QUEST TECHNOLOGIES, 1190
RED LION PRODUCTS, 1192
SEATTLE SYSTEMS/LENOX HILL BRACE COMPANY, 1198
SEIRUS SPORTS ACCESSORIES, 1198
SOLE CUSTOM FOOTBEDS, 1202
SPORT CARD CREATIONS INC., 1203
SPORTS HEALTH, 1205
STANDARD MERCHANDISING COMPANY, 1207
STROMGREN SUPPORTS, 1208
SWING AWAY SPORTS PRODUCTS, 1210
THOUGHT TECHNOLOGY, 1212
TROPHY GLOVE COMPANY, 1215
UNIQUE SPORTS PRODUCTS, 1217
VIBRA-WHIRL & COMPANY, 1219
WITTE GROUP, 1222

Trophy Manufacturers

A-B EMBLEM, 1099
AD MFG. COMPANY, 1103
ALKAHN LABEL, 1105
ALL STAR INDUSTRIES, 1105
AMPROS TROPHIES, 1109
AUBURN LEATHER COMPANY, 1228
AWARDS ETC., 1112
BLUE RIDGE MOUNTAIN WOODCRAFTS, 1118
CLASSIC MEDALLICS, 1126
COYLE & GREER AWARDS CANADA LTD., 1130
CREATIVE AWARDS BY LANE, 1131
CREATIVE TROPHIES COMPANY, 1131
CROWN TROPHY COMPANY, 1235
CUSTOM DECAL & EMBLEMS, 1132
FREEMAN PRODUCTS, 1145
GENERAL AWARDS, 1147
GOLD CREST ENGRAVING, 1149
GOLF-ART.COM, 1150
GRAHAM EMBROIDERY COMPANY, 1150
IRA K. MEDALS & AWARDS INC., 1159
JEBCO, 1160
KING COBRA GAMING, 1163
LACROSSE UNLIMITED, 1164
LORIA AWARDS, 1168
MAIN TROPHY SUPPLY COMPANY, 1170
MEIER AND FRANK MDSE. COMPANY, 1172
MIDWEST TROPHY MANUFACTURING, 1173
MOPRO, 1175
MOSLOW & BRO., 1175
NEW HERMES INC., 1179
NEW YORK EMBLEMS & AWARDS, 1179
OLYMPIA TROPHY COMPANY, 1182
OWENS & CO., 1190
PADDLE TRAMPS MFG. COMPANY, 1183
PLASTIMAYD CORPORATION, 1185
POWERS EMBROIDERY/ CHENILLE, 1187
PSC/ENCORE SELECT INC, 1189
RHODES WOOD COMPANY, 1193
RUDIG TROPHIES, 1195
SMITH WOOD SPECIALTIES, 1201
SPORT CARD CREATIONS INC., 1203
SPORTDECALS, 1204
SPORTS ACCESSORIES AMERICA INC., 1205
STERLING TROPHIES, 1208
SUMMIT - GARDNER & GELDMACHER, 1209
TROPAR MANUFACTURING COMPANY, 1215
TROPHY WORLD, 1215
TROPHYLAND USA, 1215
VOYAGER CUSTOM PRODUCTS, 1220
WILSON TROPHY COMPANY OF CALIFORNIA, 1222
YARBOROUGH TIME LTD., 1224

manufacturers/retailers

Turf Manufacturers

ACADEMY SPORTS TURF, 1100
ASTRO TURF MANUFACTURING COMPANY, 1111
AVERY SPORTS TURF, 1112
BANNERMAN LTD., 1114
COVERMASTER, 1235
EARTH & TURF, 1137
FIELD TURF TARKETT, 1143
GENERAL SPORTS TURF SYSTEMS, 844
GENERAL SPORTS VENUE ASTROTURF, 1147
GREENTECH, 1151
HUMMER TURFGRASS SYSTEMS, 1157
KIEFER U.S.A., 1163
LESCO, 1166
NGI SPORTS, 1179
SPORTGRASS, 1204
SYNTHETIC SURFACES, 1210
UNITED TURF, 1217
UNITED TURF INDUSTRIES, 1217
WEST COAST TURF, 1221

Uniform Manufacturers

A-B EMBLEM, 1099
AD MFG. COMPANY, 1103
ADVANCED CUTTING SYSTEMS, 1103
AEF EMBLEMS, 1104
ALLESON ATHLETIC, 1106
ANTIGUA GROUP, 1109
AUGUSTA SPORTSWEAR, 1111
BETLIN INC., 1116
BRISTOL ATHLETIC, 1120
CLASSIC PRODUCTS, 1126
CLIFF KEEN ATHLETIC INC., 1127
CLUBHOUSEKIT, 1127
COBBLESTONES ACTIVEWEAR, 1127
COED SPORTSWEAR INC, 1127
COLLEGIATE LICENSING COMPANY, 786
CRAN BARRY INC., 1131
CUSTOM SPORTSWEAR CORP/DBA
    SPORTSWEAR UNLIMITED, 1132
CUTTERS GLOVES, 1132
DEVENTER'S CHEER & DANCEWEAR
    FACTORY, 1134
DODGER INDUSTRIES INC., 1135
EARBAGS, 1137
EMPIRE SPORTING GOODS MFG. COMPANY, 1139
G GIRL, 1240
GAME TIME LLC, 1146
GAMETIME PLUSH, 1147
GAMEWEAR, 1147
GATOR ATHLETIC INC., 1147
HEADMASTER INC, 1153
HI STYLE LETTERED SPORTSWEAR
    COMPANY, 1154
JEFF HAMILTON COLLECTION, 1160
KEY SPORTZ-WEAR, 1163
LETRELL SPORTS, 1166
LIEBE ATHLETIC LETTERING, 1166
LIQUID BLUE, 1167
MAJESTIC ATHLETIC, 1170
MCCARTHY-SORENSEN ATHLETIC, 1172
MEIGRAY GROUP, 1244
MERRYGARDEN ATHLETIC WEAR, 1173
NEUEDGE SPORTSWEAR, 1178
NEWSOUTH ATHLETIC COMPANY INC., 1179
NUMBERALLS, 1181
OLD TIME SPORTS, 1182
OMEGA GEAR INC, 1182
ONFIELD APPAREL, 1182
PINE SPORTS, 1185
PINNACLE SPORTS EQUIPMENT INC, 1185
POMCHIES LLC, 1186
RUGBY IMPORTS, 1195
S.M. ATHLETICS, 1196
SHIRTS & SKINS INC, 1199
SIPES COMPANY, 1200
SMACK APPAREL, 1201
SOFFE COMPANY, 1202
SOUTHLAND ATHLETIC MANUFACTURING
    COMPANY, 1203
SOYAD BROTHERS TEXTILE CORPORATION, 1203
SPEEDLINE ATHLETIC WEAR, 1203
SPORT FACE, 1204
SPORTS BELLE INC., 1205
SPRY SPORTS USA, 1206

STAHLS, 1207
STALL & DEAN MFG. COMPANY, 1207
SUNDAY PLAYERS, 1209
SUPERIOR UNIFORM GROUP INC., 1209
T3K INC, 1210
TEAMLINE, 1211
TM ATHLETICS, 1213

Volleyball Manufacturers

AALCO MANUFACTURING CO. INC., 1100
ALGOMA NET COMPANY, 1104
ALL STAR SPORTING GOODS, 1105
ALLESON ATHLETIC, 1106
ALPHA SPORTSWEAR, 1106
AMERICAN ATHLETIC INC., 1107
ASICS AMERICA CORPORATION, 1111
AUDERO SPORTS SUPPLY, 1111
AUGUSTA SPORTSWEAR, 1111
BADEN SPORTS, 1113
BALLSTARS, 1114
BETLIN INC., 1116
BISON, 1117
BLAZER MANUFACTURING, 1118
BRINE, 1120
C.N. IS BELIEVING, 1122
CARBONMAX SPORTS TECHNOLOGY, 1124
CARRON NET COMPANY, 1124
CHAMPION BALL COMPANY, 1125
CLASSIC SPORT COMPANIES INC, 1126
CLIFF KEEN ATHLETIC INC., 1127
CONVERSE, 1235
CUSTOM SPORTSWEAR CORP/DBA
    SPORTSWEAR UNLIMITED, 1132
DODGER INDUSTRIES INC., 1135
DOUGLAS INDUSTRIES, 1135
DRYBRANCH, 1136
DYNAMIC TEAM SPORTS, 1136
EIGER SPORTSWEAR, 1138
EMPIRE SPORTING GOODS MFG. COMPANY, 1139
EXCEL VOLLEYBALL PRODUCTS, 1141
E-Z GARD INDUSTRIES, 1137
FIRST SERVICE, 1143
FRANKLIN SPORTS, 1145
GAME MASTER ATHLETIC COMPANY, 1146
GAME TIME, 1146
GENERAL SPORTCRAFT COMPANY, 1147
GEORGI-SPORTS, 1148
GERRY COSBY & COMPANY, 1148
GILL ATHLETICS, 1148
GOAL SPORTING GOODS, 1149
GOLD MEDAL RECREATIONAL PRODUCTS, 1149
HANCO-M. HANDELSMAN COMPANY, 1152
HI STYLE LETTERED SPORTSWEAR
    COMPANY, 1154
HIND, 1155
HORNER FLOORING COMPANY, 1156
INTERNATIONAL SEAWAY TRADING
    CORPORATION, 1159
J&B SALES, 1159
JAYPRO SPORTS, 1160
JEFFERIES SOCKS, 1160
KAEPA USA, 1162
KORNEY BOARD AIDS, 1164
K-SWISS INC., 1162
LOGAN INC., 1168
LOVING ASSOCIATES INC., 1168
MARKWORT SPORTING GOODS COMPANY, 1170
MARTIN SPORTS, 1170
MERRYGARDEN ATHLETIC WEAR, 1173
MIKASA SPORTS USA, 1173
MINIHANE & ASSOCIATES, 1174
MOLTEN USA, 1174
NIKE, 1179
PARTAC PEAT CORPORATION/BEAM CLAY, 1184
PERFORMANCE SPORTS SYSTEMS, 1184
PORTER ATHLETIC EQUIPMENT COMPANY, 1186
PRO FEET, 1188
PUMA NORTH AMERICA, 1189
PW ATHLETIC COMPANY, 1190
R.A.M. SPORTS, 1190
REGENT SPORTS CORPORATION, 1192
RICHARDSON SPORTS, 1193
RIDDELL, 1193
ROYAL TEXTILE MILLS, 1195

RUSSELL ATHLETIC, 1195
S.M. ATHLETICS, 1196
SALAUN SPORTS, 1196
SCHELDE NORTH AMERICA, 1197
SENECA SPORTS INC., 1198
SHAMROCK SPORTS BAG COMPANY, 1199
SIDEOUT SPORT, 1200
SOCCER SPORT SUPPLY CO., 1201
SOL-EFFECT ENTERPRISE COMPANY LTD, 1202
SOUTHLAND ATHLETIC MANUFACTURING
    COMPANY, 1203
SPECIALTY NETS, 1203
SPEEDLINE ATHLETIC WEAR, 1203
SPORTIME, 1204
SPORTMASTER INC., 1204
SPORTS IMPORTS, 1205
SPORTS TUTOR INC, 1205
SPORTS WEST SALES, 1206
SPRY SPORTS USA, 1206
STACKHOUSE ATHLETIC EQUIPMENT, 1207
SUPERIOR EXERCISE PRODUCTS, 1209
TACHIKARA USA INC., 1210
TANDEM SPORT, 1210
TC SPORTS, 1211
TOP-COMFO ATHLETIC SOX, 1214
TRACE ATHLETIC CORPORATION, 1214
TRENWAY, 1215
TWIN CITY KNITTING COMPANY, 1216
U.S. GAMES, 1217
ULTRA PLAY SYSTEMS, 1217
VICTORY SPORTS NETS, 1219
VIKING TECHNOLOGY INC., 1219
WEST COAST NETTING, 1221
WILSON SPORTING GOODS COMPANY, 1222
WITTE GROUP, 1222

Water Ski Manufacturers

BADEN SPORTS, 1113
CONNELLY SKIS, 1129
HEDSTROM CORPORATION, 1154
HO SPORTS INC., 1155
NASH MANUFACTURING INC, 1177
O'BRIEN INTERNATIONAL, 1181
O'NEILL, 1181
ORION ROPEWORKS, 1182
WEST RIDGE DESIGNS, 1221

Water Sports Manufacturers

COMFORT LINE PRODUCTS, 1128
EMPIRE SPORTS/SISCO SPORTS, 1139
FERNO PERFORMANCE POOLS, 1142
FROST MOTORSPORTS, 16
MIKASA SPORTS USA, 1173
MOREY BODYBOARDS, 1175
NASH MANUFACTURING INC, 1177
OMEGA MARINE PRODUCTS, 1182
ORION ROPEWORKS, 1182
PELICAN INTERNATIONAL INC, 1184
POOLMASTER, 1186
REPUBLIC PACKAGING CORPORATION, 1192
SHAW & TENNEY, 1199
WELLINGTON LEISURE PRODUCTS, 1221

Weightlifting Manufacturers

ABSOLUTE FITNESS, 1100
CANNON SPORTS INC., 1233
CAP BARBELL, 1123
CERASPORT, 1125
FITNESS EM, 1143
FITTER INTERNATIONAL INC, 1144
GEAR PRO-TEC, 1147
GRIPWEIGHTS, 1151
HARBINGER, 1153
HEAVY HANDS, 1154
HOIST FITNESS SYSTEMS, 1155
HORIZON FITNESS, 1156
IMPACT TRAINING SYSTEMS INC, 1157
IMPEX INC, 1158
IRON GLOVES INC, 1159
JUMP ROPE TECH INC, 1161
KAMPALA INDUSTRIES, 1162
LION SPORTS INC, 1167
MEDI-DYNE HEALTHCARE PRODUCTS LTD, 1172
OMEGA GEAR INC, 1182
SMC INNOVATIONS, 1201

SPORTLINE INC, 1204
SPORTS SPECIFIC SCIENCES, 1226
SPRI PRODUCTS INC, 1206
STAMINA PRODUCTS INC, 1207
SUPERIOR EXERCISE PRODUCTS, 1209
TKO SPORTS GROUP, 1213
TROPHY GLOVE COMPANY, 1215

Windsurfing Equipment Manufacturers

BIC SPORT NORTH AMERICA, 1116
CONCEPT II, 1129
NORTH SPORTS, 1180

Wrestling Manufacturers

ACTION ATHLETIC EQUIPMENT, 1102
ADIDAS WRESTLING, 1103
ALGOMA NET COMPANY, 1104
BRUTE WRESTLING, 1121
CANNON SPORTS INC., 1233
CLUBHOUSEKIT, 1127
E-Z GARD INDUSTRIES, 1137
FISHER ATHLETIC EQUIPMENT, 1143
IMPACT TRAINING SYSTEMS INC, 1157
MATMAN WRESTLING COMPANY, 1171
REPUBLIC PACKAGING CORPORATION, 1192
RESILITE SPORTS PRODUCTS, 1193

SHOCK DOCTOR INC, 1199
SMC INNOVATIONS, 1201
SUPERIOR EXERCISE PRODUCTS, 1209
TC SPORTS, 1211

manufacturers/retailers

Equipment & Product Manufacturers

5TH AND OCEAN CLOTHING
160 DELAWARE AVENUE
BUFFALO, NY 14202
716-604-9000
Fax: 716-604-9299
info@5thocean.com
www.5thocean.com
• Alex Leiter, President / Chief Executive Officer
alex@5thocean.com
• Luis Leiter, Vice President
luisl@5thocean.com
• Ralph Garcia, Chief Operations Officer
ralphg@5thocean.com
Products:
Manufacturers clothing for water sports.

600 RACING, INC.
5245 NC HIGHWAY 49 S
HARRISBURG, NC 28075
704-455-3896
Fax: 704-455-3820
www.uslegendcars.com
• GE Chapman, General Manager
(704) 455-3896
gechapman@uslegendcars.com
• Joe Maylish, 600 West Manager
(702) 643-4386
jmaylish@600racing.com
• James Michael Spink, 600 Kentucky Manager
(859) 567-4423
jspink@600racing.com
• Kris Perry, Purchasing
(704) 455-3896
kperry@600racing.com
• Haven Kerchner, Communications Manager/Magazine
(704) 455-3896
hkerchner@600racing.com
• Foxworthy, Parts
(704) 455-1424
jfoxworthy@600racing.com
Nature of Sports Service:
The largest manufacturer of race cars in the world, and is the exclusive producer of the Legends Car, Bandolero and Thunder Roadsters.
Year Founded:
1992

A&H ATHLETIC FLOOR SERVICES, INC.
PO BOX 55502
INDIANAPOLIS, IN 46205
317-598-0159
Fax: 317-845-9139
• Byron Haflich, President/Owner
• James Taylor, Product Manager
Nature of Service:
Sanding & Finishing; Screening & Recoating; Logos, Lettering; Graphics, & Emblems; Court Lining; Repair and/or Replacement; TyKote Dustless Refinishing System; and Traditional Refinishing System
Year Founded:
1988
Products:
Basic Coatings, Court Clean Maintenance Systems, Rubbermaid Microfiber Dust Systems, Ulti Mats Weight Room Flooring, Humane Rubber Floors, Action Wood Floor Systems, Action Herculan Synthetic Floors.

A-B ASSOCIATES, INC.
12300 OLD TESSON ROAD
SUITE 300-E
SAINT LOUIS, MO 63128
314-842-1819
800-783-2358
Fax: 314-842-1526
• Rob Amelung, Marketing
Products:
General Sporting Goods.

A-B EMBLEM
291 MERRIMON AVENUE
PO BOX 695
WEAVERVILLE, NC 28787
828-645-3015
800-438-4285
Fax: 800-355-3581
sales@abemblem.com
www.abemblem.com
• Bernie Conrad, President
berniec@abemblem.com
• Andrew Nagle, EVP
andrewn@abemblem.com
• Jackie Reece, Accounting Executive
(888) 438-4024
jackier@abemblem.com
• Leisa Williams, Accounting Executive
Products:
NASA Patches; American Flags; Mouse Flags; Corporate Use; Scout Patches; Fotografick Emblems; Soccer Patches; Cap Collection; Key Fobs; Municipal Emblems; Youth Patches; Pins & Jewelry; Blazer Crests; Needlecut Patches; Soccer Pins; Luggage Tags; Appliques
Clients:
NASA; Boy Scout Troops; and Bowling Clubs

A-TURF
505 AERO DRIVE
PO BOX 157
CHEEKTOWAGA, NY 14225
716-204-0748
888-777-6910
Fax: 716-204-0189
info@aturf.com
www.aturf.com
• Jim Dobmeier, President & Founder
Products:
Artificial turf for sports facilities.

A.D. STARR
61 S 4TH STREET
PITTSBURGH, PA 15219
412-488-7233
800-487-2448
Fax: 800-487-2448
info@adstarr.com
www.adstarr.com
Products:
Baseballs; Softballs; Batting Helmets; Uniforms; Catcher's Gear; Women's Softball; Field Equipment; Umpire Gear; Bas & Accessories; Pitching Machines; Bats & Training Aids; Gloves & Mitts; and Safety & First-aid
Clients:
BPA Baseball; National Club Baseball Association; USSSA Baseball; Pnoy Baseball; Dixie Baseball & Softball; Little League Baseball & Softball; Cal Ripken & Babe Ruth Baseball; Dizzy Dean Baseball; American Fastpitch Association; NASI; USSSA Slow & Fast Pitch; NFHS Baseball Fast Pitch Softball; American Legion Baseball; Adult & Federation Leagues; Palamino Leagues; NSA Slow & Fast Pitch Softball

A4
6199 MALBURG WAY
VERNON, CA 90058
323-585-0550
888-464-3824
Fax: 323-583-6565
info@a4.com
www.a4.com
• Mark Mertens, Owner
(323) 585-0550
mark@a4.com
• Mike Owings, Vice President Sales
(323) 585-0550
mike@a4.com
Services:
Designing and manufacturing of high quality athletic gear for onfield and Retail Sales. Performance gear, PE uniforms, Polos, Warm-Ups and Bags.
Sports:
Baseball, softball, basketball, football, soccer, lacrosse, track & field.
Year Founded:
1969
Clients:
6,500 Professional, College & High School Teams, Chick's, Sports Chalet, M C Sports, Pomida, 24 Hour Fitness and Hillfits.

AAA FLAG & BANNER
8955 NATIONAL BOULEVARD
LOS ANGELES, CA 90034
310-836-3200
855-218-3300
Fax: 310-836-7253
sales@aaaflag.com
www.aaaflag.com
• Jay Jacoby, Representative
Nature of Services:
AAA Flag & Banner manufacturers and installs custom displays, banners and flags for Major Sporting Events and Fortune 500 Companies throughout the United States-services include concept creation, banner, sign and flag design, logos and corporate identity, layout and composition, marketing materials and event pageantry consultation.

AACER FLOORING
970 OGDEN ROAD
PO BOX 151
PESHTIGO, WI 54157
715-582-1181
877-582-1181
Fax: 715-582-1182
www.aacerflooring.com
• Kevin Barker, Vice President of Marketing
kbarker@aacerflooring.com
• Nick Larson, MidWestern Regional Distribution Sales
nickl@aacerflooring.com
• Kelly Kahara, Customer Service Manager
kellyk@aacerflooring.com
• Laurn Fontaine, Customer Service Representative
laurnf@aacerflooring.com
• Laura Thomson, Human Resource Manager
laurat@aacerflooring.com
• Koko Thaw, International Sales Manager
kokot@aacerflooring.com
• Jason Nieminksi, Technical Manager

manufacturers/retailers

jnieminski@aacerflooring.com
• Kevin Barker, VP of Sales & Marketing
kbarker@aacerflooring.com
Sports Products:
Performance sports flooring systems -
maple & synthetic.

AALCO MANUFACTURING CO. INC.
1650 AVENUE H
SAINT LOUIS, MO 63125
314-544-4300
800-537-1259
Fax: 314-544-2386
sales@aalcomfg.com
www.aalcomfg.com
• Richard Pohrer, President
rpohrer@aalcomfg.com
Products:
Basketball and Volleyball Curtains
Brands:
Basketball: Wall Swing-up: 24WS; Side
Fold: 22 SF; Wall Stationary: 20SW; Series
100 Center Strut; Roll Fold; Series 2000
Solo-Glide; Series 300 Clear View; Series
200 Double Drop Volleyball: Swingline
Ceiling Suspended Volleyball; Spikeline
System; Power Post Gold System: APPS;
Aluminum Standards: PV-35A; Curtains:
Top Roll Divider Curtain: TRU-110; Fold-up
Divider Curtain: VSCM; Slope Fold Divider
Curtain:VSCM-C; Radius Fold-Up Divider
Curtain: VSCM-R; Walk Draw Curtain:WDC

AARDVARK MASCOTS
1199 CHERRYBROOKE COMMONS
SAN LEANDRO, CA 94578
818-508-7900
aardvarkmascots@gmail.com
www.aardvarkmascots.com
• Cindy Maniates, Costume Artist
(818) 508-7900
aardvarkmascots@gmail.com
Products:
Custom made mascot costumes since 1985.

ABC ACTIVEWEAR LLC
16112 NW 13TH AVENUE
SUITE A
MIAMI, FL 33169
305-625-5778
Fax: 305-622-2872
Products:
Activewear; Swimwear

ABC FLAG MANUFACTURING CO.
212 S MAIN STREET
FORT WORTH, TX 76104
817-335-2548
800-288-9625
Fax: 817-877-1610
www.lonestarbannersandflags.com
• Mike Tettleton, President
• Mark Buechele, General Manager
(817) 335-2548
markb@abcflag.com
Products:
Flags, banners (U.S., state, custom, sports).
Distributor and installer of flag poles.

ABI TAPE PRODUCTS
105 WHITTENDALE DRIVE
MOORESTOWN, NJ 8507
856-778-0700
Fax: 888-224-6325
info@abitape.com
www.abitape.com

• Roger S Marcus, Chairman / Chief
Executive Officer
• Richard G Marcus, President / Chief
Operating Officer
• Willaim M Marcus, EVP/Treasurer
• Howard N. Feist III, Chief Financial Officer
/ Finance VP
Products:
Tape Products
Brands:
Ideal Tape Co., Inc.; Transfer Rite; Protect
Rite; Autowrap

ABSOLUTE FITNESS, INC
149 INTERLOCHEN DRIVE NE
ATLANTA, GA 30342-3711
770-933-8987
Fax: 770-980-9751
• Jeff Kushner, Marketing Director
• Tami Roe, President
Products:
Aquatic Exercise Equipment, Balance
Training Equipment, Barbells,
Cable-Attached Bars, Curling Bars, Olympic
Bars, Power Bars, Specialty Bars, Standard
Weight Bars, Bicycles, Stationary, Body
Composition Analyzers, Skinfold Calipers,
Boxes, Breathing Aids, Conditioning Charts,
Injury Treatment Charts, Nutrition Charts,
Plyometrics Charts, Rehabilitation Charts,
Speed Charts, Strength Charts, Computer
Systems/Software for Athletic Equipment,
Fitness Assessment, and Nutrition,
Conditioning Aids, Conditioning Certification
Programs, Cord Devices, Dumbbells, Power
Hooks, Pro-Style, Educational Books &
Videos, Elevated Shoes, Equipment Storage
Sys

ABSOLUTELY NEW
650 TOWNSEND STREET
SUITE 475
SAN FRANCISCO, CA 94103
415-865-6200
888-946-8368
800-627-5382
Fax: 415-865-6210
• Richard S. Donat, Chief Executive Officer
• Henry Lo, Chief Financial Officer
• Bill Feroe, Executive Vice President
• Steve Lee, Manufacturing Director
Products:
Portable Grills; Trolley; Kitchen Wares;
Grassland Gears; Food Supplements;
Cleaning Materials; Lightings; Christmas
Decorations
Brands:
Porta-Q; Brief Tote, Tuff Tote, Micro Tote,
Shop Tote, Shop Tote Tinted, Travel Tote,
Classic Cart Tote, Click Tote; Roasting
Wand, Shrimp Sheller; Compact Utility
Chair, Garden Tote; First Call; X-Tendo Mitt,
Bucket Wringer, Deco Fresh Brush, Way
Beyond Lint; Solar Camping Light, Areama
Pipe Tool, Candle Cuts; Wonderland Box,
Auto Wreath, Car Get-Ups, Magic Santa
Tracks, Pop-Down Christmas Tree, Magic
Fold Box

ABU GARCIA, INC.
1900 18TH STREET
SPIRIT LAKE, IA 51360
800-228-4272
abugarcia@purefishing.com
www.abu-garcia.com
Products:
Accessories, Baitcast Reels,

Spinning-Spincast Reels, Combos, Clothing
Brands:
Power Handle Accessory, Reel Lube;
Ambassadeur Morrum, Ambassadeur 2005
Low-Profile, Ambassadeur 4007 Low-Profile,
Ambassadeur 5600WS, Ambassadeur D5
Series, Ambassadeur D6 Series,
Ambassadeur C3 Series, Ambassadeur Big
Game Collection, Ambassadeur Trophy
Series, Ambassadeur 1003 Low-Profile,
Ambassadeur B Series, Ambassadeur B
Series; Abumatic 1276, Abumatic
Underspin, Cardinal 500 Series, Cardinal
300 Series, Cardinal 100 Series, Cardinal
170 Saltwater Series, Cardinal 170
Saltwater Series, Cardinal 770 Series,
Cardinal 770 Series; Abumatic Combo,
Agenda Combo, Ambassadeur TGC
Baitcast Combo, Ambassadeur 1003
Low-Profile Combo, Ambassadeur

ACADEMY SPORTS TURF
3740 S JASON STREET
ENGLEWOOD, CO 80110
800-372-6639
Fax: 303-762-8190
steve@academysportsturf.com
www.academysportsturf.com
• Steve Jewell, Marketing
steve@academysportsturf.com
• Paul Kelley, Director
steve@academysportsturf.com
Products:
Turf
Brands:
Academy Sports Turf

ACCELERATED CARE PLUS, LLC
4850 JOULE STREET
SUITE A-1
RENO, NV 89502
775-685-4000
800-350-1100
Fax: 775-685-4013
customersupport@acplus.com
www.acplus.com
• John Beach, Chief Executive Officer
johnbeach@acplus.com
• Chris Castel, President
chriscastel@acplus.com
• Richard Taylor, Chief Operating Officer
richardtaylor@acplus.com
• John Beach, Chief Executive Officer
• Antony Ricketts, Chief Financial Officer
• Debbie Koepsel, Chief Operating Officer
• Richard Taylor, Chief Sales Officer
• Tony Taylor, Chief Marketing Officer
• Curtis Beach, Marketing Director
curtisbeach@acplus.com
• Joe Cummings, Marketing Manager
joecummings@acplus.com
Products:
Electrical Stimulation Products, Ultrasound
Products, Shortwave Diathermy, Infection
Control Supplies, Electrotherapy Supplies
Brands:
OMNISTIM 500A, OMNISTIMr 500B,
OMNISTIM FX2, OMNISTIMr FX2 GOLD,
OMNISTIM FX2 PRO, OMNISTIM FX2
PRO, OMNISOUND 3000E, OMNISOUND
3000C, SHORTWAVE DIATHERMY
MEGAPULSE II, Delta T Automatic Tissue
Temperature Dose Control, Pulsed
Shortwave Diathermy, GDWP - Germicidal
Disposable Wipe (50/bx), UBF-0406B -
ProBarrier Film (600ft/rl), 20303 - Ultrasound
Probe Sheaths (75/bx), 20325 - Ultrasound
Probe Sheaths (25/bx), 10060-25 - Elastic

Bands (25/bg), SC100 - Megapulse Applicator Head Cover (100/bx), 3X004 - Poly Tubing (500ft/rl), ERC2X2, ERC2X4, ERC3X5, ERC4X4, ULTRASOUND GEL

ACCESSORY TIME
3500 SUNSET AVENUE
OCEAN, NJ 7712
732-918-2201
800-826-1355
Fax: 732-918-2203
ikegemal@aol.com
Products:
Watches, Clocks, Watchcases

ACCUFITNESS, LLC
PO BOX 4411
GREENWOOD VILLAGE, CO 80155-4411
303-799-4721
800-866-2727
Fax: 303-799-4778
info@accufitness.com
www.accufitness.com
• Shawn M Gillespie, President
info@accufitness.com
• Carol Fitzgerald, Customer Service Representative
Products:
Accu-Measure Fitness 3000 Personal Body Fat Tester, FatTrack Gold Digital Body Fat Caliper, FatTrack Pro Digital Body Fat Management System, MYOTape - Body Tape Measure, HYDRYX - Hardcore workout towel, Body Tracker - Body composition tracking software, My Workout Trainer - Body composition and workout tracking software, BOA - High speed professional jump ropes, Bowflex - Heart rate monitors, Bowflex
Description:
AccuFitness is a worldwide leader in consumer fitness and body measurement devices along with other outstanding fitness products. Likewise we provide industry leading software packages designed to help you reach and maintain your fitness goals! Try My Workout Trainer to accurately track your workouts, macro-nutrition information, and body composition measurements & calculations. If you want to focus solely on tracking body composition and conditioning information only - Body tracker software is the ticket. AccuFitness products are designed and selected to help you burn more fat and build cardiovascular strength during your favorite physical a
Our products are ideal for:
Fitness enthusiasts who want to maximize fat loss and cardiovascular benefits; Individuals who are just starting to exercise or fat burning regimen; Military personnel maintaining physical readiness; Figure and Bodybuilding competitors who want to maintain peak competition form; Those who want to improve their current health & fitness status; People who want to monitor their decrease in body fat and/or increase in lean muscle mass.
Brands:
Accu-Measure Fitness 3000 Personal Body Fat Tester, FatTrack GOLD Digital Body Fat Caliper with MyoTape, Accu-Measure FitKid Caliper for Children, FatTrack PRO DIGITAL Body Fat Measurement System, New MyoTape Body Tape Measure, MyoTape D, HYDRYX Hard-Core

ACCUSPLIT
3090 INDEPENDENCE DRIVE
SUITE 150
LIVEMORE, CA 94551
925-226-0888
800-965-2008
800-935-1996
Fax: 925-463-0147
sales@accusplit.com
www.accusplit.com
• W. Ron Sutton, Founder
(925) 226-0888
ron@accusplit.com
• Yasuji Kato, Partner
• Yoshiro Hatano, Partner
• W. Ron Sutton, Founder
Products:
Pedometers, Sportswatches-Digital, Timers, Time-Out Clocks.
Year Founded:
1972
Brands:
AAS420 Steps to Healthy Bones, AAS440 The Step Diet Program, AAS475 Stepping Out with Stanford, AAS411 Walk Yourself Thin, AAS416 Walk with Byron Nelson, AAS480 Tom Lehnan's Family Golf, AAS413 Walk With Notah, AAS410 Pedometer Walking, Accusplit Eagle, Accusplit X, Accusplit 10K-A-Day, Accusplit Healthengine, Accusplit Alliance, Accusplit Survivor, Accusplit Pro Survivor, Gra Lab.

ACE MITCHELL BOWLERS MART
1946 S ARLINGTON STREET
PO BOX 3168
CUYAHOGA FALLS, OH 44223
330-920-6200
800-321-0309
Fax: 330-785-1060
dbehra@acemitchell.com
www.acemitchell.com
• Dave Grau, Owner
dgrau@acemitchell.com
• Todd Williams, Vice President
(800) 321-0309
twilliams@acemitchell.com
Products:
Bags, Balls, Birthday Party Supplies, Bowlers Aids and Towels, Bowlers Tape and Shur Hooks, Gloves and Supports, Grips, Lane Machines and Parts, Lane Supplies, Pinsetter Parts, Pro shop supplies, Rental Shoes/House Balls, Shoes
Brands:
Thunder Alley

ACME WHISTLES/HIATT - THOMPSON CORPORATION
7200 W 66TH STREET
BEDFORD PARK, IL 60638
724-932-2177
Fax: 724-932-2166
sales@combinedsystems.com
www.combinedsystems.com
• Charles Thompson, Director
(708) 496-8595
htsb@sbcglobal.net
• Dawn Thompson, President
(708) 496-8595
Products:
Handcuffs, Chainwork, Transportation Security, Training Equipment and Accessories, Legcuffs
Year Founded:
1988

ACO POLYMER PRODUCTS, INC.
12080 RAVENNA ROAD
PO BOX 245
CHARDON, OH 44024
440-285-7000
800-543-4764
Fax: 440-285-7005
info@acousa.com
www.acousa.com
• Josef-Severin Ahlmann, Founder
info@acousa.com
• Hans-Julius Ahlmann, Managing Partner
info@acousa.com
Products:
Drainage Systems for Sports Tracks, Elastic Railing, Elastic Curb, Sand Traps and Water Jumps.
Brands:
PowerDrain S100K/S300K, KlassikDrain K100S/KS100S, FlowDrain FG100/FG200, Fastform FF300/FF600, SlabDrain, ChemDrain, Brickslot, Membrane Drain, MiniKlassik, Cross Sidewalk Drain, Series 600 Catch Basins, Fiberglass Catch Basins, Sump Boxes, System 1000 Track Trench Drainage, System 2000 Track Trench Drainage, System 3000 Track Trench Drainage, System 4000 Open Trench Drainage, System 6000 Synthetic Turf Trench Drainage, System 7000 Sandpit & Curb System, System 8000 Steeple Chase Jumps, System 9000 Bleacher System, HomeDrain, Raindrain, Oil/Water/Sand Separator, Spill Containment Curbs, AT200 Tunnel, AT500 Tunnel, Amphibian Tunnel Entrance

ACOR, INC.
18530 S MILES PARKWAY
CLEVELAND, OH 44128
216-662-4500
800-237-2267
Fax: 216-662-4547
cs@acor.com
www.acor.com
• Greg Alaimo, CP, Co-Owner/Founder
• Jeffrey Alaimo, CPO, Co-Owner/Founder
Products:
Shoes, Orthotic Product Lines, Fabricating Materials, Accessories, Custom Footwear
Brands:
Spring Street, Activz, Broadway, Comfort Street, River Walk, Quikfit, QuikFormables, Sole Defense, KidFits, Rigids, Modification Components, Top Covers

ACORN PRODUCTS COMPANY, INC.
2 CEDAR STREET
PO BOX 1190
LEWISTON, ME 04240-7874
207-786-3526
800-872-2676
Fax: 800-280-4127
www.acornearth.com
• John Donnelly, President
info@acornearth.com
• David K. Quinn, Founder & Chief Executive Officer
info@acornearth.com
• John Donnelly, President
Products:
Comfort Footwear Products, Sheepskin Boots, Sheepskin Slippers and Accessories
Brands:
Toggle Slipper, Highlander, Textured Moc, Polar Moc, Polar Pair, Summit Slipper, Slipper Sock, Boiled Wool Moc, Euro Clog,

Euro Closed Clog, Easy Does It, Big Easy, Big Easy Sheepskin, Dakota Moc, Ultra Moc, Lifetime Toaster, Sheepskin Romeo, Sheepskin Bootie, Sheep-On, Sheepskin Venetian Moc, Sheepskin Woven Moc, Sheepskin Penny Moc, Short Boot, Tall Boot, Felt Dorm Scuff, Felt Dorm Bootie, Cool Down, Chill Out, Unwind, Take Five, Sundal Thong, Sundal Slide, Spa Mule, Knotty Girl, Travel Slipper, Den Slipper, Hampton, Cashmere Ballerina, Cashmere Mule, Cozy Scuff, Ocelot Scuff

ACOUSTICAL INTERIORS
2247 TOMLYN STREET
RICHMOND, VA 23230-3334
804-342-2900
888-765-2900
Fax: 804-342-1107
info@acousticsfirst.com
www.acousticsfirst.com
• Nick Colleran, Principal
Products:
Ceiling Treatments, Wall Treatments, Absorbers: Foam, Glass Fiber, Fabric, Diffusers, Barriers, Industrial, Vibration
Brands:
Cloudscape Hanging Baffles, Cloudscape Banners, FireFlex Baffle, Double Duty Diffuser, Art Diffusors, Respond & Sonora, Quiet Louver, Pyramid Acoustical Foam Panel, Geometrix, Bermuda Triangle Traps, Polyurethane Pyramid, CuttingWedge, Fireproof (Class 1) Wall Panels, Hanging Baffles, Sound Cylinder, Respond & SonoraT Wall Panels & Ceiling Treatment, Sound Channels, Guilford of MainerFR701, Quiet Louver Panels, Cloudscape Ceiling Banners & Baffles, Double Duty Diffuser, Art Diffusors, Pyramidal Diffuser, QuadraPyramid, BlockAid Vinyl Sound Barrier, Foam/Barrier Composites, Blankets & Enclosures

ACT ONE COMMUNICATIONS
314 PASEO TESORO
WALNUT CREEK, CA 92812
909-595-6818
888-228-6631
Fax: 909-595-7388
• Daniel Shih, President
danshih@aol.com
• Christine Lien, Vice President
clien@actone1.com
• Jason Chin, Sales
jason@actone1.com
• Ethan Lin, Marketing Manager
ethan@actone1.com
Products:
LED Video Displays and Screens, LED Fascia Displays, LED Architectural Lighting
Brands:
Act One

ACTION ATHLETIC EQUIPMENT
3144 21ST STREET
ZION, IL 60099-1426
847-746-2042
Fax: 847-746-2071
• Tim Higgins, Production Manager
matman@ix.netcom.com
• Joe Higgins, Founder
matman@ix.netcom.com
• Jane Craig, Sales Manager
Products:
General Sports Equipment.

ACTION FLOOR SYSTEMS, LLC
4781 N US HIGHWAY 51
MERCER, WI 54547-9708
715-476-3512
800-746-3512
Fax: 715-476-3585
info@actionfloors.com
www.actionfloors.com
• Gary Stephenson, President
info@actionfloors.com
• Tom Abendroth, Vice President
• Tom Mitchell, General Manager
(410) 838-5318
• Dan Corullo, Secretary
Products:
Premium Sports Floor Systems and Residential Floors
Brands:
ProAction Thrust, ProAction Flex, ChannelFlex Plus, ChannelFlex II, ChannelFlex, ActionThrust I, ActionThrust II, Concorde, Concorde II, Vari-Flex, Vari-Flex Plus Action Interloc I, Action Interloc II, Action Interloc II Plus, Anchored VariFlex, Anchored VariFlex Plus, ActionCush I, ActionCush II, ActionCush II Plus, Anchored ActionCush II, Anchored ActionCush II Plus ActionLoc, ActionFast, ActionFlex, ActionTech I, ActionChannel I, ActionChannel II, Action Fixed-Sleeper, ActionWood, ActionWood Plus, ActionWood Flex, Herculan Synthetic, Action ReFlex, Maple, Cherry, Beech, Birch, Ash

ACTION GRAPHIX
2623 COMMERCE DRIVE
JONESBORO, AR 72401
870-931-7440
800-762-9807
Fax: 870-931-7528
www.actiongraphix.com
• Blant Hurt, President
(870) 931-7440
Products:
Provides graphic images for a variety of sports related accessories.

ACTION IMAGES
33 ALDGATE HIGH STREET
1ST FLOOR, ALDGATE HOUSE
LONDON, ENGLAND EC3N 1DL
-44-7003-5820
www.actionimages.com
• Alan Whiter, Head of Sales/Marketing
alan.whiter@actionimages.com
• Monique Villa, Chairman
• Philip Kelly, Chief Executive
• David Jacobs, Managing Director
Services:
Photography capturing the spirit and passion of sport.
Clients:
FIFA, Coca-Cola, Barclays, Carslberg

ACTION SIGNS AND BILLBOARDS
720 HILLSIDE AVENUE
CHANDLER, MN 56122
507-677-2568
Fax: 507-677-2568
Loren@ActionSignsAndBillboards.com
www.actionsignsandbillboards.com
• Loren Vander Woude, President
loren@frontiernet.net
Products:
Manufacturing of tri-paneled rotating signs, rotating billboards, rotating mobile billboard trucks and trailers

ACTION SPORTS IMAGE
6301 PERFORMANCE DRIVE
CONCORD, NC 28027
704-454-4000
800-952-0708
Fax: 704-454-4030
www.lionelnascarcollectables.com
• Ruth Crowley, President
• Lesa France Kennedy, ISC President
• Marcus Smith, SMI Executive VP, National Sales and Mar
Products:
Produces racing collectibles. Products include a broad range of motorsports-related die-cast car replica collectibles, apparel, souvenirs and other memorabilia.
Brands:
Action Racing Collectables (ARC), the Racing Collectables Club of America (RCCA), Revell Collection, Winner's Circle, and Chase Authentics

ACTION SPORTS SYSTEMS INCORPORATED
617 CARBON CITY ROAD
MORGANTON, NC 28655
828-584-8000
800-631-1091
Fax: 828-584-8440
action_sports@bellsouth.net
www.actionsportsuniforms.com
Description:
Provides support for audio and video systems that record sporting events.

ACTIVE ANKLE SYSTEMS, INC.
233 QUARTERMASTER COURT
JEFFERSONVILLE, IN 47130
812-258-0663
800-800-2896
info@activeankle.com
www.activeankle.com
Products:
General Sports Products for Training & Conditioning, specializing in Ankle Braces.
Brands:
T1 Trainer Ankle Brace, Active Ankle - T2, Active Ankle - CF Pro, Trainer Overhaul Kit, T2 Overhaul Kit, Exercise Pads, EVA Pads, Trainer Strap Kit and T2 Strap Kit.

ACUMEN, INC.
101A EXECUTIVE DRIVE
SUITE 100
STERLING, VA 20166
703-437-7333
Fax: 703-904-0218
Products:
Exercise Accessories, Heart Rate Monitors, Sporting Goods and Sports Equipment.

ACUSHNET COMPANY
333 BRIDGE STREET
FAIRHAVEN, MA 2719
508-979-2000
866-389-2658
Fax: 508-979-3927
ebizhelp@acushnetgolf.com
www.acushnetgolf.com
• Joe Gomes, Director of Communications
Products:
Provides golf products of superior performance and quality.
Brands:
Acushnet Company's primary brands are the Titleist, FootJoy and Cobra. Pinnacle and

Scotty Cameron are sub-brands used for specific Titleist products.

AD ART/ELECTRONIC SIGN COMPANY
5 THOMAS MELLON CIRCLE
SUITE 260
SAN FRANCISCO, CA 94134
415-869-6460
Fax: 415-869-6485
www.adart.com
• Bob Kierejczyk, President
• Duane Contento, Senior Vice President
• Jeremy Anderson, Executive Vice President
• Terry Long, Chief Executive Officer

AD MFG. COMPANY
248-44 JERICHO TURNPIKE
BELLEROSE, NY 11001
516-352-6161
800-841-6790
Fax: 516-352-8502
www.adtrophy.com
• Ronald Karmitz, VP
Products:
Trophies, Medals, Ribbons, Plaques, Keychains, Pins, Dog Tags, Gift Items and Mascots.

ADA TENNIS
2925 CHRYSLER ROAD
KANSAS CITY, KS 66115
913-371-2664
800-234-0460
Fax: 913-371-2663
adatennis1@aol.com
• Ray D. Jones, Jr, Owner
• Randy Kempke, Sales Representative
Products:
Tennis, Badmitton, Basketball, Football, and Soccer - Supplies and Equipment.

ADAMS GOLF GP CORPORATION
2801 EAST PLANO PARKWAY
SUITE 572
PLANO, TX 75074
972-673-9000
800-709-6142
Fax: 972-398-8818
• Barney Adams, Chairman of the Board
• John Ward, President
• Russell L. Fleischer, Director
• John M. Gregory, Director
Products:
Golf related products.
Brands:
Air Assault, Assault, VMI, Tight Lies

ADAMS USA, INC.
610 S JEFFERSON AVENUE
COOKEVILLE, TN 38501
931-526-2109
800-251-6857
Fax: 931-526-8357
www.adamsusa.com
• Vaughn Howard, Owner
• Garry McNabb, Stockholder
(931) 526-2109
• Rose Postic, President
Products:
Football helmets, Shoulder pads, Chin straps
Brands:
Adams USA, Trace

ADASTRA DESIGNS INC.
8345 W 16TH AVENUE
LAKEWOOD, CO 80215
303-274-9035
800-638-4667
Fax: 303-274-9038
info@adastran.com
www.adastran.com
Products:
Basketball, Radar Speed Measurement, Music, Interactive Electronic Football, Metaphaser, Sports Score Boards, Custom Products and Electronic Golf Targets.

ADER SPORTING GOODS INC.
10969 SHADY TRAIL
SUITE 105
DALLAS, TX 75220
214-352-7343
800-733-2338
Fax: 214-352-7360
sales@aderfitness.com
www.aderfitness.com
• Cathay Kang, President
Products:
Exercise Equipment
Brands:
ASI Olympic Plates, ASI Dumbbells, ASI Slectorized Parts, ASI Machine Parts and Lat Pull Down Machines.

ADIDAS WRESTLING
8 CORPORATE BOULEVARD
SINKING SPRING, PA 19608
610-678-4050
800-486-2788
Fax: 887-879-4040
info@brute.com
www.brute.com
• Josiah (J Henson, Founder
• Jeff Bowyer, Co-Founder / National Sales Manager
Products:
Wrestling products and apparel to sporting goods dealers; amateur and professional athletic clubs and teams. Singlets: Phenom 2, Vapor 2, Bionic 2, Freedom 2, Lehigh 2, Solid and Phenom; Earguards: ZerO g Earguard, Quad II Earguard, Shockwave Earguard, Brute ClassiX, LE 03 Earguard, MM3 Earguard and Butt Pad; Kneepads: Sublitek Custom, Adidas, VW01, Equalizer, Youth Predator, Lycra Custom, Nylon Custom and Lyrca Knee Pad; Footwear: Mat Hog, Combat Speed II, adiStar Wrestling, adiStar SL Super Light John Smith Sig., Response Wrestling, A'ttaak, Tyrint II and A'ttaak Womens.
Brands:
Adidas and CCS READY

ADIRONDACK RUBBER PRODUCTS
5633 ROUTE 31
VERONA, NY 13478
315-363-3726
Fax: 315-363-7214
• Debra Parkin, Marketing
• Steven Joanis, Sales
Products:
Baseball/Softball Pitchers Mound Pad; Gymnastics Mats; Non Slip Floors; Interlocking Rubber Mats; Weight Room Flooring; Locker Room Flooring and Tiles; Martial Arts Mats; Indoor Tracks; Weight Room Flooring; Ice Rink Rubber Flooring.

ADOLPH KIEFER & ASSOCIATES
1700 KIEFER DRIVE
ZION, IL 60099
847-872-8866
800-323-4071
Fax: 847-746-8888
info@kiefer.com
www.kiefer.com
• Adolph Kiefer, Founder
(847) 872-8866
adolph@kiefer.com
• Edita Emini, National Team Sales Manager
Products:
Swimwear, Technical Suits, Goggles, Training, Books & Videos, Swimmer's Gear, Lifeguard Shop, Kiefer Guard, TYR Guard, Speedo Guard, Guard Wear, Guard Gear, Rescue Gear, Lifesaving Equipment, Rescue Training, Kiefer Guard Chairs ,Water Safety, AEDs, Kid's Swim Suits, Kid's Kickboards, Kid's Goggles, Pool Games, Learn-To-Swim, Swim Diapers, Ruth Sova Products, Resistance Workout, T & F Books & Videos, T & F Accessories, T & F Suits, Pool Lifts, TYR Triathlete
Brands:
Speedo, TYR, Dolphin Suits, Kiefer suits, Nike, Grab Bag, Workout, Optical, Masks, Finis

ADP LEMCO, INC.
5970 W DANNON WAY
W JORDAN, UT 84081-6203
801-280-4000
800-575-3626
Fax: 801-280-4040
customerservice@adplemco.com
www.adplemco.com
• Mark McCormack, President & Chief Operating Officer
(801) 307-4230
mmccormack@adplemco.com
• David L Hall, Vice President
(801) 280-4000
sales@adplemco.com
• Schyler Sommer, Sales Manager
(807) 307-4230
ssommer@adplemco.com
Products:
Basketball Backstops, Backboard Padding, Portable Backboard, Stationary Backboard, Nets, Breakaway Rims, Goals, Shot Clocks, Gym Divider Curtains, Wall Padding, Scoreboards, Tennis & Volleyball Equipment, and Posts

ADVANCED CUTTING SYSTEMS, INC.
17578 76TH STREET
LIVE OAK, FL 32060
386-330-6889
800-874-8674
Fax: 386-330-6610
beverlyyagins@acsystem.us
www.acsystem.us
• Beverly Yagins, Sales Manager
(800) 874-8674
beverlyyagins@acsystem.us
• Carolyn Miller, Sales & Product Information
info@acsystem.us
Products:
Die Cutter, Steel Rule Dies for Making Lettering & Logos for Uniforms, Computerized Sign Making Equipment.
Year Founded:
2005

ADVANCED DESIGN CONCEPTS
N27 W23655 PAUL ROAD
PEWAUKEE, WI 53072-5793
262-523-1010
Fax: 262-523-1011
• Edward J. Norton, Partner
• Mark O. Schaefer, President & Chief Of Innovation
• Jim Marschalek, Vice President
• Patrick Woodzick, Designer
Services:
Research, design, development, marketing, sourcing of athletic shoes.

ADVANCED EQUIPMENT CORPORATION
2401 W COMMONWEALTH AVENUE
FULLERTON, CA 92833
714-635-5350
Fax: 714-525-6083
www.advancedequipment.com
• Wesley Dickson, Founder / Chief Executive Officer
Products:
Operable walls. Produces manual and electric walls with heights over 40 feet, panel constructions and tracks. Produces Vision, a micro-processor controlled rear projection screen cover which creates a flush wall.
Brands:
Vision

ADVANTAGE SPORTS RACK
2222 QUEEN STREET
BELLINGHAM, WA 98229-4753
360-756-2411
888-722-5240
Fax: 360-756-2414
support@heininger.biz
www.heininger.biz
• Jeffrey V. Heininger, Founder
• Nick Homes, Marketing
Services:
Cycling - Bike Car Racks; Skiing-Alpine - Ski Car Racks.

ADVANTAGE TENNIS SUPPLY
235 ARCADIA STREET
RICHMOND, VA 23225
804-276-0011
800-476-5432
Fax: 804-276-0557
• Toni McDavid, President
toni@advantagetennissupply.com
• Amy Ward, Manager
Year Founded:
1978.
Brands:
Edwards Sports Products, M Putterman, Igloo Coolers, Penn Tennis Balls, Advantage Tennis Products
Products & Services:
Manufacturer, Distributor of Tennis Court Equipment, Ball Machines, Balls, Divider Nets, Net Center Straps, Net Posts, Nets, Tennis Backdrop Curtains, Windscreens.

AEF EMBLEMS
8770 GUION ROAD
SUITE C
INDIANAPOLIS, IN 46268
317-802-5743
800-983-6662
Fax: 317-802-5750
www.aefemblem.com
• Andrew E. Falender, President
• Phil Stillerman, National Account Manager

Products:
Custom-made Lapel Pins, Commemerorative Coins/Medallions, Trading Pins, Zipper Pulls, Embroidered Patches, PVC Key Tags, Pins.

AEROBICS INC.
34 FAIRFIELD PLACE
WEST CALDWELL, NJ 7006
973-276-9700
Fax: 973-794-6395
www.pacemaster.com
• Gerald J Staub, President
• Thomas N Staub, VP
(973) 276-9700
Products:
Training & Conditioning - Treadmills.
Brands:
Pacemaster

AEROBIE, INC
744 SAN ANTONIO ROAD
SUITE 15
PALO ALTO, CA 94303
650-493-3050
800-999-3565
Fax: 650-493-7050
aerobie@aerobie.com
www.aerobie.com
• Alex Tennant, General Manager
aerobie@aerobie.com
• Charlene Myers, Domestic Customer Service
aerobie@aerobie.com
• Greg Baker, Operations Manager
• Michelle Smith, International Customer Service
aerobie@aerobie.com
• Don Abbott, National Sales Manager
aerobie@aerobie.com
Products:
Flying discs, boomerang, yo-yo, balls
Year Founded:
1984
Brands:
Aerobie, Orbiter, Squidgie, AeroSpin, Skylighter, Epic, SharpShooter, Superdisc

AEROMAT
48541 WARM SPRINGS BLVD
SUITE 503
FREMONT, CA 94539
877-278-6158
Fax: 707-221-4040
info@aeromats.com
www.aeromats.com
Products:
Yoga Block, Yoga Wedge, Yoga Mat Carrying Harness, Yoga Straps, Yoga Aeromats, Yoga/Pilates Aeromats, Foam Roller, Pilates/Body Toning Rings, Smooth Surface Aeromat, Dual Surface Aeromat, Aeromat Work-out Mat, Balance Dome, Balance Board, Balance Board with Pad, Balance Disc Cushion, Balance Pad, Fitness Ball, Fitness Ball Kit, Fitness Ball Resistance Kit, Fitness Ball Stacker, De Luxe Figure 8 Tube, Exercise Flex Bar with Tube, Power Flex Bar, APF Aeromat, APL Aeromat, Dual Surface Aeromat, Smooth Surface Aeromat, Workout Mat and more.

AIRCAST, INC.
1430 DECISION STREET
VISTA, CA 92081

760-727-1280
800-336-6569
Fax: 800-936-6569
• Mike S. Zafirovski, Chairman
• Sidney Braginsky, Director
• John Chiminski, Director
• Chinch E. Chu, Director
• Leslie H. Cross, Director
• Julia Kahr, Director
• James R. (Ron) Lawson, Director
Products:
Cryo/Cuff Ankle Sprain Care, Forearm Rotational Brace Arm Immobilizer, AutoChill System with Adjustable Docking Station, Back/Hip/Rib Cryo/Cuff, Calf Cryo/Cuff for Walking Brace Diabetic Replacement, Elbow Cryo/Cuff, Foot Cryo/Cuff FP Walker (foam pneumatic), Hand and Wrist Cryo/Cuff, Hand Bulb with Pressure Gauge Heel Supports, Knee Cryo/Cuff, Knee Immobilizer Leg Brace, Mayo Clinic Elbow Brace Pneumatic Armband, Pneumatic Walker, Diabetic System Pressure Verification Kit, Shoulder Cryo/Cuff, Thigh Cryo/Cuff Tube Assembly
Brands:
AirHeel, AirLift, CryoCuff, Autochill

AJAY SPORTS
37735 ENTERPRISE CT
SUITE 600
FARMINGTON HILLS, MI 48331
248-994-0553
800-776-4653
Fax: 248-489-9334
www.progolfamerica.com
• Thomas W. Itin, Chairman / Chief Executive Officer
• Brian T Donelly, President / Chief Operating Officer
Products:
Golf Clubs - Iron or Wood Sets.
Brands:
Palm Springs Golf, Inc., Prestige Golf Corp., Pro Golf International, Inc., Pro Golf of America, Inc and ProGolf.com, Inc.

ALCHESTER MILLS COMPANY, INC.
1125 WRIGHT AVENUE
CAMDEN, NJ 8103
856-964-9700
Fax: 856-964-9135
• M. Tarnoff, President
Products:
Baseball: Caps, Socks; Basketball: Supporters, Cup Supporters, Gripping Aids, Hats/Caps/Visors, Protective, Socks; Field Hockey: Stick Grips; Football: Knee/Elbow Pads, Socks.

ALDILA
1945 KELLOGG AVE
CARLSBAD, CA 92008
sales@aldila.com
www.aldila.com
• Steve Gandolfo, Customer Service Manager
Products:
Golf Equipment
Brands:
Aldila

ALGOMA NET COMPANY
1525 MUELLER STREET
ALGOMA, WI 54201

920-487-5577
Fax: 920-487-2852
www.algomanet.com
• James L Westrich, VP / General Manager
Products:
Bags and Equipment for Baseball, Basketball, Field Hockey, Football, Gymnastics, Martial Arts, Racquet Sports, Rugby, Soccer, and Field and Track.

ALKAHN LABEL
1430 BROADWAY
7TH FLOOR
NEW YORK, NY 10018
212-768-7700
Fax: 212-768-7794
info@paxar.com
www.alkahn.com
• Max L Kahn, Chairman
• Philip Kahn, President
• Jeff Stern, National Retail Sales Manager
Products:
Variable Data Tickets & Labels, Brand Promotion & Merchandising Tags, Fabric Labels & Collections, Brand Protection & Security, Printers, Accessories, & Supplies, Monarch Brand Bar Code & RFID Products, Handheld Labels, Tags, & Attachers

ALKALINE INSTITUTE
915 W FOOTHILL BOULEVARD
SUITE J
CLAREMONT, CA 91711
888-225-6452
www.alkalineinstitute.com

ALL AMERICAN BOWLING PRO SHOP
1148 PULASKI HIGHWAY #152
BEAR, DE 19701
888-626-2695
allamericanbowling@yahoo.com
www.allamericanbowling.com
Products:
AMF Balls, Brunswick Balls, Columbia Balls, Dexter Mens Shoes, Dynothane Balls, Ebonite Shirts, Hammer Balls, Linds Mens Shoes, NXT Ladies Shoes, Roto Grip Balls, Storm Shirts, Ball Spinners, Brunswick Shirts, Columbia Shirts, Dynothane ABS Shoes, Ebonite Bags, Etonic Ladies's Shoes, K-R Bags, MoRich Balls, NXT Mens Shoes, Storm Bags, Track Balls, Brunswick Bags, Columbia Bags, Dexter Ladies Shoes, Dynothane ABS Shoes LADIES, Ebonite Balls, Etonic Men's Shoes, Linds Ladies Shoes, NFL Hand Grip Bags, Nu Line Balls, Storm Balls, Track Shirts

ALL AMERICAN GOLF SALES, INC.
550 BROOKFOREST AVENUE
SHOREWOOD, IL 60431
815-744-0440
Fax: 815-744-0444
• Edward Rhee, President
Products:
Golf Bags, Drivers/Woods, Irons/Hybrids/Wedges, Putters, Packaged Club Sets
Brands:
Pro Fantom, Tour System III, True Flite, Trueline, Unix

ALL AMERICAN SCOREBOARDS
401 SOUTH MAIN STREET
PO BOX 100
PARDEEVILLE, WI 53954

608-429-2121
800-356-8146
Fax: 877-505-9405
scoreboardsales@everbrite.com
www.allamericanscoreboards.com
• Fred Foster, Sales Service
score@everbrite.com
• Scott Carter, President
• Chris Stark, Sales Manager
score@everbrite.com
Products:
Scoreboards for Football, Baseball, Basketball, Soccer, Multi-Sport, Hockey and Racing, Scoretables, Portable, Scoreboard, Accessories

ALL AMERICAN SPORTS CORP/RIDDELL ALL AMERICAN
669 SUGAR LANE
ELYRIA, OH 44035
440-366-8225
800-275-5338
Fax: 440-366-6292
help@riddellsports.com
www.riddell.com
• Don Gleisner, President
• Bill Sherman, President / Chief Executive Officer
Products:
Football: Helments, Helment Accessories, Shoulder Pads, Footballs & Accessories
Brands:
Maxpror Shockblocker II, Mini Jaw Cutters, Mox Box Refill, Mox Box Repair Hardware Kit, Kra-Liter IV Facemasks, Z-Bar Steel Thick-Coat, Z-Bar Titanium Thin Coat, Power Varsity Pads, Ultra Varsity Pad, Evolution Varsity Pads, Air Pac Varsity Pads, Warrior Varsity/Junior Pads, Warrior II Youth Pads, X-ForceT Youth Pads, Power Pad Accessories, Air Pac Pad Accessories

ALL LACROSSE, INC.
147 VALLEY ROAD
MONTCLAIR, NJ 7042
973-509-0303
800-522-7693
Fax: 973-509-1345
www.alllacrosse.com
• Yogi Trivedi, President
Products:
Sticks, Pads, Helmets, Gloves, Accessories, Shorts and Shirts, Stringing Kits, Stringing Kits, Lacrosse Cleats & Goals & Nets
Brands:
Brine, DeBeer, STX, Warrior

ALL PRO EXERCISE PRODUCTS, INC.
ALL PRO EXERCISE PRODUCTS INC.
HILLSBOROUGH, NJ 8844
908-281-7100
800-735-9287
Fax: 908-281-5793
support@allproweights.com
www.allproweights.com
• Edie Winston, President
• Scott Winston, President
Brands:
All Pro, Hands Free, Power Walker, Aqua Power, Thighaciser, Power Stride, Power Vest, Weight to Jump, Weight-A-Band, Contour Foam, Weight-A-Toner
Products:
Weight-adjustable exercise & fitness products including: ankle weights, wrist weights, vests, belts, thigh weights, upper arm weights, aquatic ankle weights,

weighted resistance bands, and weighted jump ropes.

ALL STAR FOWNES
5728 MAJOR BOULEVARD
SUITE 612
ORLANDO, FL 32819
407-351-1611
800-654-5683
Fax: 407-351-1703
• Leslie Armstrong, National Sales Manager
fownes@bellsouth.net
• Robin Morgan, Customer Service / Credit Manager
fownes@bellsouth.net
• Delila Smalley, Customer Service
Products:
Golf Equipment.
Brands:
Deluxe All Weather, Polartec Winter Pairs, Shur Soft Crown, Sof-Tac, Super Crown, SuperTech

ALL STAR INDUSTRIES, INC.
7001-T W 20TH AVENUE
HIALEAH, FL 33014
305-823-4830
800-432-3528
Fax: 305-823-4836
www.asisupplier.com/allstar
• Paul Fields, President
• Clara Zeinfield, VP
Products:
Trophies, Plaques, Medals, Cups & Bowls, Desk Sets, Specialty Items & name tags (metal or plastic).

ALL STAR KNITWEAR, INC.
841 E BROADWAY STREET
GRIFFIN, GA 30223
770-227-5016
800-241-0246
Fax: 770-412-6264
www.allstarknit.com
• Robert W. Willis, Sr., President
• Bobby Willis, Jr., Vice President
bobbyjr@allstarknit.com
• Jimmy Willis, Secretary/Treasurer
Products:
Athletic Hosiery, including Football and Soccer Socks.
Year Founded:
1955
Brands:
All-Star Knitwear

ALL STAR PRO GOLF, INC.
1501 35TH AVENUE WEST
SPENCER, IA 51301-0155
712-262-8891
800-247-4830
Fax: 712-262-8891
sales@allstarprogolf.com
www.allstarprogolf.com
• Jay Horton, National Account Manager
horton@allstarprogolf.com
• Clark Smith, National Account Representative
clark@allstarprogolf.com
Products:
Golf clubs & accessories

ALL STAR SPORTING GOODS
1 MAIN STREET
PO BOX 1356
SHIRLEY, MA 1464

978-425-6266
800-777-3810
Fax: 978-425-4068
customerservice@all-starsports.com
www.all-starsports.com
• Stanley Jurga, President
(978) 425-6266
jurga@all-starsports.com
• Carol Jurga, Vice President/General
Manager
(978) 425-6266
cjurga@all-starsports.com
• Jeff Johnson, Vice President Sales
(978) 425-6266
jjohnson@all-starsports.com
• Kathie Fontaine, Customer Relation
Director
(978) 425-6266
kfontaine@all-starsports.com
Products:
Baseball & Softball: MVP Head Gear,
Catcher's Equipment, Umpire's Equipment,
Accessories, Baseball Helmets,
Women's/Girl's Softball, Gloves & Mitts,
Baseballs, Equipment Bags, Cups &
Supporters, Bases & Plates. Football:
JR.Lite Helmets, Girdles, Shoulder Pads,
Hands & Forearm Guards & Accessories.

ALL-SPORT BRUSH LLC
7316 E 38TH STREET
PO BOX 4769
TULSA, OK 74145
918-749-3368
Fax: 918-749-5133
www.causecare.com
• Ed Conn, Chief Executive Officer
(918) 749-3368
• James Evans, Director of Sales/Marketing
(918) 749-3368
Products:
Toothbrushes
Year Founded:
2003

ALLAN ENTERPRISES
7517 N SENECA ROAD
MILWAUKEE, WI 53217
414-352-6152
• Allan Fefer, Owner
Products:
Eyewear
Brands:
All-Guards, Over-Guard, Pro-Guard,
Pro-Tector, Sport-Specs, Varsity, Victoria

ALLESON ATHLETIC, DON
2921 BRIGHTON-HENRIETTA TOWN LINE
ROAD
ROCHESTER, NY 14623
585-272-0606
800-641-0041
Fax: 800-836-0775
• Todd Levine, VP Marketing / Sales
• Bill Lolas, VP Retail Sales
• Steve Schwarz, VP Manufacturing
• Elena OLiveri, VP Operation
• Steve Schwarz, Head Of Manufacturing
Unit
• Yvonne Dailey, Assistant
Products:
Apparel and Uniforms for Baseball/Softball,
Football, Basketball, Volleyball, Track and
Field, Soccer, Official, Shorts, Field Hockey,
Ice HOckey and Cheerleading

ALLIAN SNOWBOARDS
PMB #513 18335 NW W UNION
SUITE C
PORTLAND, OR 97229
mikemiya@alliansnowboards.com
www.alliansnowboards.com
• Mike Miyazawa, President
Products:
Snowboards: Signature Series, Pro Series,
Freedom Series, Soft Wear, Tech Points
and Line Up
Brands:
Backman 146, Backman154, Backman 157,
Backman 160, Stephens 145, Stephens
150, Stephens 155, Stephens 159,
Stephens 165, Peter Strom 55, Peter Strom
58, Peter Strom 63, Knock Out 142, Knock
Out 153, Knock Out 155, White Out 146,
151, 155, 157, Black OUt 157W, 159, 161,
161W, 163, 165, 167, Freedom Series 136,
142, 146, 136, Freedom Series 150, 155

ALPHA RACQUET SPORTS
7208 MCNEIL DRIVE
207
AUSTIN, TX 78729
512-250-1499
800-922-9024
Fax: 512-279-9454
info@alphatennis.com
www.alphatennis.com
• Mark Gonzalez, Sales Manager
• Greg Gonyea, Customer Sales Manager
Products:
Racquet Sports - Badminton Equipment,
Racquet Grips, Racquet String, Racquet
Stringing Machines, Tennis Court
Equipment.
Brands:
Orbitor, BLU-DC Plus, PIONEER DC,
Firecable, Synthetic, Viper, Patriot, GUT200
POLY, COMFORT PLUS, CLAYCOURT
PLUS, HARDCOURT SG, GUT 2000,
PRODIGY, ELEMENT, ULTRA SPIN SOLID
CORE, FIREWEB, FLEXEL,
POWERCABLE, POLYCABLE,
TOURNABLEND, RAB ENDURA, RAB
MONOFLEX, EXCEL I, EXCELL II,
AQUAZORB, ALL PLAYER, TRAX,
WRAPTOR, IGUANA, GRIP TUBEZ, GRIP
BUCKETS, Curved Awl, Scalpel, Digital
Calipers, Stringed Cutters, Straight Awl,
Alpha RAB, Accuswing, Viper Balance
Beam, ALPHA BAll Clip, ALPHA Balancer,
ALPHA String Savers, Open Mesh
Polypropylene, ALPHA Cap, STRING IT
T-Shirt, TOURNAMENT Shuttlecocks,
XP-90, XP-80, XP-85

ALPHA SPORTSWEAR, INC.
PO BOX 3652
BLAINE, WA 98231-3652
604-873-2621
866-888-2621
Fax: 604-873-4652
custserv@alphasportswear.com
Products:
Sportswear for Hockey, Basketball, Football,
Baseball and Volleyball
Brands:
Superstar Mesh Jersey; Tech Knit Jersey

ALPINA SPORTS CORPORATION
98 ETNA ROAD
LEBANON, NH 3766
603-448-3101
800-425-7462

Fax: 603-448-1586
www.alpinasports.com
• Rolf Schaer, President / Chief Executive
Officer
info@alpinasports.com
• Steve Kvinlaug, Sales VP
info@alpinasports.com
• Gary Fleming, President
Products:
Racing Skis, Boots, Bindings; Sports Skis,
Boots, Bindings & Touring Skis, Boots,
Bindings, Poles and other kinds of Boots
Brands:
SCL, SK, NNN R3 CLASSIC, NNN NIS
CLASSIC, HYPERSONIC C3 CLASSIC
COLD, CCS: CARBON CONTROL SKATE,
HYPERSONIC C3 MGV, HYPERSONIC C3
CLASSIC WET, NNN NIS SKATE,
HYPERSONIC C3 CLASSIC COLD NIS,
HYPERSONIC 3X3 SKATE NIS SC,
HYPERSONIC 3X3 SKATE SC,
HYPERSONIC 3X3 SKATE NIS R,
HYPERSONIC 3X3 SKATE R,
HYPERSONIC 3X3 SKATE NIS HP,
HYPERSONIC 3X3 SKATE HP,
SUPRASONIC SKATE, SUPRASONIC
CLASSIC, DIABLO, CRISPI X-R, Rottefella
Cobra

ALPS SPORTSWEAR MFG. COMPANY,
INC.
15 UNION STREET
LAWRENCE, MA 1840
978-683-2438
800-262-7010
Fax: 978-686-8051
• Marvin Axelrod, President
alps@alps-sportswear.com
• David Lane, Merchandising VP
alps@alps-sportswear.com
• Jerry Stone, Sales VP
Products:
Ladies Sweater & Shirts, Dream Wear,
Men's Sweaters & Shirts, Tees & Hats,
Afghans & Mukluk
Brands:
Simple Pleasures, Flirtacious Crew, Crystal
Cove Hoodie, Cornucopia Crew, Cornucopia
Scarf, Cherry Grove Cardigan, Fox Ridge
Vest, Frosty Ridge, Sweet Violet, Jubilee
Vee, Holly Hill Vee, Maybell, Kaleidoscope
Cardigan, Kaleidoscope Cardigan, Cloud
Nine Crew, Tularosa, Apple Valley Vest,
Serenade Hoodie #1821, Ariel, Long Haul
Vee, Break Away Zip, Crooked Creek, Call
of the Road Crew, Moose Trail Crew, Laid
Back Henley, Moose River Henley, Laid
Back Henley, Moose Ball Cap, Black Label
Cap, Aspen Leaf, Shenandoah, Heirloom,
Tumbleweed, Eldorado, Holiday Mukluk,
Catalina Mukluk, Super Mukluk, Backpacker
Mukluk, Sunset Dream Mukluk, Catchin'
Som

ALTUS ATHLETIC MFG. COMPANY
709 SOUTH VETERANS DRIVE
PO BOX 736
ALTUS, OK 73521
580-482-0891
800-654-9873
Fax: 580-482-2760
www.altusathletic.com
• John Hetzel, Director Marketing/Product
Development
• Bill Goodbread, National Sales Manager
• Felicia Rogers, Customer Service
• Curt Underwood, VP Of Sales

Products:
Belts, Weightlifting Accessories, Gloves, Ankle and Wrist Weights, Hands & Forearm Development, Home Fitness Equipment, Jump Ropes, Combo Packs, Stretching & Toning, Yoga/Pilates, and Fitness Balls

ALUMINUM ATHLETIC EQUIPMENT COMPANY (AAE)
1000 ENTERPRISE DRIVE
ROYERSFORD, PA 19468-1298
610-825-6565
800-523-5471
Fax: 610-825-2378
info@myaaeworld.com
www.aaesports.com
• Timothy W. Driscoll, President / Chief Executive Officer
(610) 825-6565
timd@aaesports.com
• Tom Syron, Sales Director
(610) 825-6565
toms@aaesports.com
Products:
Accu-Kick Practice Football Goal; Air Horn; Aluminum Pit Cover; Award Stands; Ballstopper System, Football; Ballstopper System, Self-Standing Model; Bell-Lap Counters; Ballstopper System, Ground Sleeve Model; Ballstopper System, Soccer; Benches; Ballstopper System, Multi-Sport; Batons; Bleachers; Batting Tunnels; Bottomboard Cushionong System; Cages; Circles; Combination Football/Soccer Goals, Rollaway; Corner Flags; Crowd Control Fencing; Camera Support Post; Coach's Clipboard; Competition Equipment; Crossbars; Curbing; Canopies; Coach's Lecterns; Cone Makers; Crossbar Lifters; Carts & Carriers; Combination football/Soccer, Goals; Conversion

ALUMINUM SEATING, INC.
555 TENNIS COURT LANE
SAN BERNARDINO, CA 92408
909-884-9449
800-757-7328
Fax: 909-388-2187
sales@aluminumseating.com
www.aluminumseating.com
• Bonnie Gaudesi, Sales Manager
(800) 757-7328
sales@aluminumseating.com
Products:
Aluminum seating products, bleachers, benches, picnic tables, aluminum planks, accessories
Brands:
Aluminum Seating, Inc.
Clients:
Schoools, Municipalities, Little League

ALVARADO MANUFACTURING COMPANY
12660 COLONY STREET
CHINO, CA 91710
909-591-8431
800-423-4143
Fax: 909-628-1403
www.alvaradomfg.com
• Bret Armatas, President
(909) 549-8431
barmatas@alvaradomfg.com
• Brian Dilard, Director of Marketing
(909) 591-8431
swillhoft@alvaradomfg.com

Products:
Post and Rail Systems, Eclipse Retractable Belt, Escort Retractable Belt, FP-14 Rope Stanchions, Ultima Retractable Belt, Waist High Turnstiles, Full Height Turnstiles, Optical Turnstiles, Security Gates, 3-arm and 4-arm Turnstiles, self-closing gates, manual swing gates, bumper systems, case guards/posts, Ticket Scanning Turnstiles/Mobile Handheld Scanning, GateLinkT Validation Admission Control Software, Associated Professional Services, Three-Arm and Optical Turnstiles for Patron Counting, GateWatchT Patron Counting Software, ParkWatchT Vehicle Counting System.
Brands:
Supervisor, Defender

AMA GOLF
208 MICHELLE COURT
S SAN FRANCISCO, CA 94080
650-952-2286
800-635-8062
Fax: 650-952-5131
orders@amagolf.com
www.amagolf.com
• Ryan Chin, Owner
ryan@amagolf.com
Products:
Manufacturer, Distributor, Importer/Exporter of golf products.

AMERICAN ATHLETIC INC.
200 AMERICAN AVENUE
JEFFERSON, IA 50129
515-386-3125
800-247-3978
Fax: 515-386-4566
www.americanathletic.com
• Mark Shaw, Vice President/General Manager
mshaw@americanathletic.com
• Scott Roth, Gymnastics Divisional Director
sroth@americanathletic.com
• Kevin Murphy, Team/Sports Construction Sales
kmurphy@americanathletic.com
• Les Arp, Engineering/Materials Divisional Director
larp@americanathletic.com
Products:
Vault, Uneven Bars, Balance Beams, Floor Exercise, Pommel Horse, Rings, Parallel Bars, Horizontal Bar, Accessories, Adapters, Cheer floors, Mats & Pads, Training, Skill Shapes.
Brands:
Infinity ELITE, TAC/10 International LZT, ELITE, CLASSIC

AMERICAN ATHLETIC SHOE COMPANY
15 S STREET
PO BOX 777
WARE, MA 1082
413-967-3511
Fax: 413-967-3585
www.americanathleticshoe.com
• Paul M Opalinski, President
Products:
Figure Skates, Hockey Skates, Rental Skates, Inline Skates & Water Shoes
Brands:
Classic Rentskates, OkeRent Skates, SoftRent Skates, SoftRent Sport Skates, SoftRent Hockey, SoftRent Figure, SoftRent Sport, RentSkate Figure, RentSkate

Hockey, OkeRent Figure, OkeRent Hockey, Figure Skates, Beginner Skates, Hockey Skates

AMERICAN CORD & WEBBING COMPANY, INC.
88 CENTURY DRIVE
WOONSOCKET, RI 2895
401-762-5500
Fax: 401-762-5514
www.acw1.com
• Mark Krauss, President
mkrauss@acw1.com
• Dennis Smith, Advertising / Marketing Director
dsmith@acw1.com
Products:
Webbing, Cord, Plastic Fasteners, Metal Fasteners, Assemies, Buckles
Brands:
Webbing - Comanche, Wave, Custom Logo, Apache, ZZ, Chain, Braid Weave, Flying Saucer; West Havel Plastic Buckles & Fasteners

AMERICAN ELECTRIC LIGHTING
3825 COLUMBUS ROAD SW
BUILDING F
GRANVILLE, OH 43023
770-483-6014
800-754-0463
866-465-6742
Fax: 740-349-4490
customerservice@holophane.com
www.americanelectriclighting.com
Products:
Roadway Luminaries, Decorative Post Top, Security Lighting, Area and Site Lighting, Flood Lighting, Dark to Light Photocontrols, Poles
Brands:
Roadway Lighting Luminaries - DuraStar Series 20, DuraStar Series 30, Wall Pack 882, Roadway-Area-SP2, Roadway-Area-SRP, Roadway-Area-SRX; Decorative Post Top - ConTempo-245, American Revolution 247 Cutoff, American Revolution-247, Cresthill Classic, Cresthill Centennial

AMERICAN FENCERS SUPPLY
1027 TERRA NOVA BOULEVARD
PACIFICA, CA 94044
650-359-7911
Fax: 650-359-7913
www.amfence.com
Products:
Foils, Sabers, Epees, Foil Parts, Saber Parts, Epee Parts, Blades, Jackets, Gloves, Shoes, Stockings, Knickers, Masks and Equipment Bags, Children's Equipment and Clothing, Tools, Shirts and Apparel, Scoring Equipment, Instructors Equipment, Cards & Stickers, Posters & Prints, Videos and DVDs, Starter and Competition Sets, Books, Swords, Broadswords, Daggers, Small, Town and Court Swords, Fencing Weapons modified for theatrical use, Blades, Rapiers, Armour from the Old Met Opera
Brands:
Standard French, Standard Children's French, Leather French, Rubber over Metal French, Standard Belgian, Olympic, Schultz, Visconti, Gerdere, Schermasport, Rambeau, Leon Paul FIE Blade, Leon Paul Blade, Vnti FIE Blade, Leather Thumb Pad, Vniti Guard, German Point Parts, German Guard Socket,

manufacturers/retailers

Renaissance, Heavy Italian, Florentine, Late Dutch, Medieval Valencia, Zweihander w/parrying hooks, Spanish Fishtail, Claymore

AMERICAN FITNESS EQUIPMENT LLC
412 WASHINGTON STREET
D
NORWELL, MA 02061
781-659-0006
800-244-2856
Fax: 301-770-2104
amfit@gis.net
• Joe Cedrone, Founder/Chief Executive Officer
(781) 659-0006
amfit@gis.net
• Don Cedrone, General Manager
(781) 659-0006
amfit@gis.net
• Mark Cedrone, Warehouse/Service Manager
(781) 659-0006
amfit@gis.net
Products:
Treadmills, Rowers, Bikes, Strength Training, Free Weights, Benches, Accessories, Multi-Gyms, Ellipticals, Mirrors, Sport Flooring, Mats, Steam Generators, Sauna Rooms and Stoves, Boxing
Brands:
Pace Master, Landice, Blades, Spirit, Nautilus-Schwinn, Keys, Life-Span, Evo, Body Craft, and Fitnet, Sports Art, Kettler, Lamar, Ignite, Monarx, Schwinn Spinners, Water Rower, Body Craft, First Degree Boxing, Everlast, TKO, Century, Balaz

AMERICAN NEEDLE & NOVELTY INC.
1275 BUSCH PARKWAY
BUFFALO GROVE, IL 60089
847-215-0011
800-356-7589
Fax: 847-215-0013
www.americanneedle.com
• Robert Kronenberger, President
ronald@amer-needle.com
• Michael Smucker, Corporate Sales VP
michael@amer-needle.com
• Ronald Kronenberger, Manufacturing VP
• Jason Franklin, Corporate Sales Director
Products:
Embroidered headwear for various sports.
Brands:
CAP B-024, Pose 2, Pose 3

AMERICAN NON-SLIP PRODUCTS
4530-F PATTON DRIVE
EAST ATLANTA, GA 30336
800-221-4329
www.americannonslip.com
Products:
Non Slip Rug Pads, Multi-Purpose Liners, Specific Purpose Liners & Mats, Bath/Kitchen Mats & Liners, Laminate Underlayment
Brands:
Cush-n-Hold, Hold Tight, Miracle Hold Plus, Rug Saver, Slip Not, Sultan, Super Movenot, Wicker Loc, Miracle Hold, Rug Hold Natural, Rug To Rug, Lok Lift, Stay In Place, Patio Pad, Multi-Grip Natural, Cushion-Aire, Double Grip, Rug Preserver, Tiger Grip Blue, Tiger Grip Plus, Cush-N-It Sink Mats, Cush-N-It-Bath Mats, Cush-N-It-Shower Mats, Line It, Super Line It, Line All, Super Line It, Line It

AMERICAN PLAYGROUND CORPORATION
6406 PRODUCTION DRIVE
ANDERSON, IN 46013
765-642-0288
800-541-1602
Fax: 765-649-7162
www.american-playground.com
Products:
Slides, swings, climbers, basketball, soccer, see saws, merry-go-rounds, bike racks, park amenities, bleachers, flags and flag poles
Brands:
Junior Slide, Senior Slide, Straight Slide, Wave Slide, Step Climber, Freedom Climbers, Climbing Ladders, Arched Ladders, Arched Climbers, Friendly Turtles, Critters

AMERICAN RANGE COMPANY
4 VAN AUKER STREET
ROCHESTER, NY 14608
585-328-2480
800-324-9769
Fax: 585-328-2503
salesinfo@arcgolf.com
www.arcgolf.com
Products:
Golf driving range equipment and services, spare parts for any equipment used in the golf range business
Brands:
ARC-Eliminatore Ball Picker, ARC Glider Nylon Disc Pickers, ARC-Ultra Range Mats, ARC Natural Turf, ARC Trays, SOFTEE Ball Tray, Bell Tee Marker and Tee Receptacle, Circular Marker, Hollow Dimple Tee Marker, Lock Nylon Flag, ARC Solid Polymer Blended Putters, ARC Vision Distance Markers, ARC Range Clubs

AMERICAN RECREATION PRODUCTS, INC.
1224 FERN RIDGE PARKWAY
SAINT LOUIS, MO 63141
314-576-8000
800-325-4121
Fax: 314-576-8072
www.instabed.com
• George J. Grabner Jr, President
• W Le Capps III, CFO
Products:
Subsidiary of Kellwood Company, makes outdoor gear including tents, backpacks, sleeping bags, outdoor clothing, and related camping accessories

AMERICAN SEATING
801 BROADWAY AVE NW
GRAND RAPIDS, MI 49504-4499
616-732-6600
800-748-0268
800-748-0353
Fax: 616-732-6401
info@amseco.com
www.americanseating.com
• Edward Clark, Chief Executive Officer
eclark@americanseating.com
• Owen Fritz, Sales VP
Products:
Public and commercial venue seating
Brands:
Dimension, Omnia by Ares, Spirit, Sports Seating, Stellar, Viva by Sebel, Whirl, Framework Segway, Framework, Accuwerks, Brilliance, Credence, Acton

AMERICAN SOCCER COMPANY, INC.
726 E ANAHEIM STREET
WILMINGTON, CA 90744
800-626-7774
Fax: 800-426-1222
sales@scoresports.com
www.scoresports.com
Products:
Jerseys, shorts, socks, goalkeeper gear, warm-ups, coaches gear, accessories, soccer balls, shin guards, field equipment, bags and referee gear
Brands:
USA #509, Chicago #508, Japan #505, England #535, Brazil #520, Estonia #570, Switzerland #545, Sydney #117A, Milan #155A, Lisbon #115A, Rio #175A, Zurich #120A, Turin # 130A, Edinburgh #153A, Dublin #145A, Vienna # 150A, Striped #810, Solid #800, Flying Feet #825, Ankle Sock #830, GALAPAGOS - #325, MAUI - #330, BORA BORA - #350, TASMANIA PANT - #900A, BAHAMAS SHORT - #903A, BEAR CLAW - #920, FIRE GLOVES - #925, DENALI - #3300, SANTIAGO - #3400, ATHENS - #163A, LONDON - #167A, PORTFOLIO - #817, COACH/REFEREE BAG - #850, ACCESSORY BAG - #852, SHOE/GLOVE BAG - #853, SPORT BAG - #864, PLAYER BAG - #865, TEAM TRAVEL - #867, SACK PACK - #871, DAY P

AMERICAN WHISTLE CORPORATION
6540 HUNTLEY ROAD
COLUMBUS, OH 43229
614-846-2918
800-876-2918
Fax: 614-846-4821
custserv@americanwhistle.com
www.americanwhistle.com
• Ray Giesse, CEO
rgiesse@americanwhistle.com
Products:
Whistles, Award Whistles, Retail Packages, Lanyards, Safe-T-Tips, Police Accessories
Brands:
American Classic, Patriot Whistle, American Spirit, Safe-T-Tip, Nylon Woven Lanyard, Custom Blister, Snake Chain, Whistle Hook

AMF BOWLING WORLDWIDE
7313 BELL CREEK RD
MECHANICSVILLE, VA 23111
804-730-4000
800-342-5263
Fax: 804-730-1313
benefits@amf.com
www.amf.com
• Fred Hipp, President / Chief Executive Officer
• William McDonnell, Chief Financial Officer
• John Walker, Chief Operating Officer
(804) 730-4301
• David Hankin, Chief Executive Officer
• Farah Boroomand, Chief Financial Officer
• Mark Chamberlain, Chief Operating Officer
Products:
Bowling Centers, Bowling and Billiard Products, Shirts, Ladies Wear, Jackets, Accessories
Brands:
Polo

AMINCO INTERNATIONAL (USA) INCORPORATED
20571 CRESCENT BAY DRIVE
LAKE FOREST, CA 92630-8825

949-457-3261
800-929-4004
Fax: 949-457-3279
www.amincousa.com
• William Wu, President
Products:
Emblematic jewelry, collectible pins, key tags, magnets, zipper pulls, coasters, luggage tags, belt buckles
Brands:
Unforgettaballs, All Star Game, World Series, NHL All-Stars, NBA Championship, Zoo Animals Collection, Wildlife Collection

AMPROS TROPHIES
4830 N FRONT STREET
PHILADELPHIA, PA 19120
215-324-5565
Fax: 215-324-0417
trophywon@aol.com
ampros.com
• Scott Borman, President
Products:
Trophies, Awards - Components, Emblems, Jewelry, Medals, Plaques, Ribbons, Trophies.

ANCHOR INDUSTRIES INC.
1100 BURCH DRIVE
PO BOX 3477
EVANSVILLE, IN 47725
812-867-2421
800-544-4445
Fax: 812-867-1429
corp@anchorinc.com
www.anchorinc.com
• Bill Kinman, International Sales Representative
(812) 867-4637
bill_kinman@anchorinc.com
• Pete Mogavero, Chairman & President ext 322
Products:
Tents, Awnings, Pool Covers, Contract Sewing, Factory Outlet, Field Covers, Circus Tents, Carnival Ride Tops
Brands:
Clearspan Structures, Camp & Retreat Tents, Llazar Retractable Awnings, New Llazar Retractable Awnings

AND 1
101 ENTERPRISE
SUITE 100
ALISO VIEJO, CA 92656
610-249-2255
866-866-1232
customerservice@and1.com
www.and1.com
• Bart Houlahan, President
• Seth Berger, Chief Executive Officer
• James Fox, Chief Financial Officer
• Christina Houlahan, Chief Operating Officer
Products:
Mens Footwear, Apparel, Kids Footwear, PreSchool Footwear
Brands:
Lockdown, Grip Mid, Devastate, Phenom, Fly Mid, In Rande, Tochillin Camput, Playmaker Low, Haywood, Kids Lockdown, Kids Grip Mid, Kids Phenom Low, Kids Desparate, Kids Fly Mid, Diggy Dish Tee, Diggy Game Tee, Diggy Game Short, Groupies Tee, Your Girl Tee, Mixtape, Bag O Chips Pocketed Game Short, Trash 101 Tee, I'm Sorry Tee, Player Original Game

Short, Taste of Defeat Tee, Triple Threat Tee, Player Practice Fleece Hoody, LTWT, In Ball We Trust

ANTIGUA GROUP, INC.
16651 N 84TH AVENUE
PEORIA, AZ 85382
623-523-6000
800-528-3133
Fax: 623-523-6016
www.antigua.com
• Ron McPherson, President/CEO
• Jerry K. Whitley, Finance VP
• Joe Blanchette, Information Technology VP
• Micheal P. Whitley, Director Of Operations
• Penny Larson, Director Of Human Resources
• Joseph M. Blanchette, VP Of Information Technology
Products:
Lifestyle apparel, including golf and various other sports.

ANTIOCH SPORTS
16083 N. 75TH AVENUE
PEORIA, AZ 85382
800-350-7019
Fax: 866-607-9918
• Ryan Coulter, Vice President
(623) 486-7462
Nature of Services:
Product manufacturer of sporting goods.

ANVIL KNITWEAR INC.
NEWTON
CHRIST CHURCH
BARBADOS, 17047
212-476-0300
800-223-0332
Fax: 212-808-4790
www.anvilknitwear.com
• Anthony Corsano, CEO
info@anvilknitwear.com
• Christopher Levesque, Marketing VP
info@anvilknitwear.com
Products:
Long and short sleeve T-shirts, polo shirts, ringers/baseballs, henleys, athletic shorts, caps, towels, robes, bags
Brands:
chromaZONE

APEX ATHLETIC EQUIPMENT INC.
160 KIPP AVE
ELMWOOD PARK, NJ 7407
201-475-8282
• Mike Lanzano, General Manager
Products:
Baseball - Bases, Protective-Catcher, Protective-Umpire; Football - Practice Equipment; Gymnastics - Mats; Track & Field/Running - Vaulting Pits or Mattresses; Wrestling - Mats.

APSCO ENTERPRISES
50TH STREET & FIRST AVENUE
BUILDING 57, 5TH FLOOR
BROOKLYN, NY 11232
718-965-9500
Fax: 718-965-3088
• Philip DiPietro, Owner
• Philip Livoti, President
Products:
Screen Printing, Embroidery, RF Welding, Graphic Design, Garment Manufacturing

AQUA LEISURE IND., INC.
525 BODWELL STREET EXTENSION
PO BOX 239
AVON, MA 02322-1098
508-587-5400
866-807-3998
Fax: 508-587-5318
customercare@aqualeisure.com
www.aqualeisure.com
• Simon C. Fireman, Chairman
• Steven M. Berenson, President
• Richard Moeller, Sales Asst VP
Products:
Pools, Lounges & Floats, Toys & Games, Swim & Dive Gear, Sun Protection, Learn to Swim 1-2-3, Fitness, Winter Fun
Brands:
Simple-Set Pools, SwimSchool, SunSmart, Dolfino, AquaPools, AquaFitness, Uncle Bob's, AquaPLay, AquaSport, AquaPro, AquaGames, Inflatables

AQUA SPHERE US
2340 COUSTEAU COURT
VISTA, CA 92081
760-597-5082
800-775-3483
Fax: 760-597-4914
support@aqualung.com
www.aquaspthereusa.com
• Laguette Olivier, Director Marketing
Products:
Regulators, instrumentation, buoyancy devices, masks, fins, snorkels, wet suits, and gear bags
Brands:
Seal Mask, Seal XP, Seal Kid, Kaiman Goggles, Sphera, Sphera Jr., Zip Fin, SideDraft Snorkel, Aqua FM Snorkel, Aqua Skins, Stingray, Wet/Dry Duffel, Anti Fog, Dry Towel, Kickboard, Protective Case, Strap, Strap Cover, Aqua Glide Cap, Swim Glove, Swim Paddles
Swimming Sponsor:
Ford Ironman World Championship

AQUAJOGGER
4660 MAIN STREET
UNIT B270
SPRINGFIELD, OR 97478
541-484-2454
800-922-9544
Fax: 541-484-0501
info@aquajogger.com
www.aquajogger.com
• Steve Bergstrom, Vice President Sales & Marketing
Nature of Services:
Manufacturer of aquatic exercise equipment.
Brands:
AquaJogger

AQUASPORT CORPORATION
1651 WHITFIELD AVENUE
SARASOTA, FL 34243
941-751-7886
Fax: 941-751-7851
• Dean Samuelson, President

ARBOR
102 WASHINGTON BOULEVARD
VENICE, CA 90292
310-577-1120
Fax: 310-577-1121
www.arborcollective.com
• Bob Carlson, President/Founder
info@arborsports.com

- Greg Bergen, Sales Manager
- Brad Farmer, Marketing Director
Products:
Snowboards, Skateboards, Gears
Brands:
A-Frame, Element, Abacus, Draft, Formula, Mystic, Crossbow, Roundhouse, Push, Stance, Basich Series, Mini, Cruiser, Carver, Hats & Beanies, Men's Tees, Men's Hoodies, Women's Tees & Hoodies

ARCOA INDUSTRIES
911 S. ANDREASEN DR.
ESCONDIDO, CA 92029
760-599-6915
888-637-1926
Fax: 760-599-6986
info@arcoa.com
www.arcmate.com
- Chet Warfel, Chief Executive Officer
info@arcoa.com
- Marty Ziegenfuss, President
info@arcoa.com
Products:
Labor Saving Devices
Brands:
E-Z Reacher, E-Z Grabber, E-Z Litter Stick

ARI-MED PHARMACEUTICALS
1615 W UNIVERSITY DRIVE
SUITE 135
TEMPE, AZ 85281-3257
480-966-9802
800-527-4923
Fax: 480-966-9806
info@ari-med.com
www.ari-med.com
- Jim Bilas, Director of Marketing
bilas@ari-med.com
Products:
Medical products used for sports training, topical analgesic. Market Flex-All pain relieving gels to the sports medicine marketplace.
Brands:
Flexall 454

ARISTO IMPORT COMPANY, INC.
85 HUNT ROAD
ORANGEBURG, NY 10962
845-359-0720
800-352-6304
Fax: 845-359-0020
aristoinc@aol.com
Products:
Chronographs, Pedometers, Stop Clocks, Stopwatches-Digital, Mechanical, Timers.
Brands:
Apollo, Aristo

ARMOUR GOLF COMPANY
40 KING STREET W
TORONTO, ONTARIO, CANADA M5H 3Y2
416-361-6336
800-723-4653
Fax: 416-785-4276
mail@hilcocc.com
www.tommyarmourgolf.com
- James Salter, Chief Executive Officer
Products:
Golf Apparel, Bags, Balls, Clubs Iron or Wood Sets, Clubs Putters, Clubs Utility, Gloves, Headcovers, Umbrellas.
Brands:
Diamond Scot, Dual Force, Golden Scot, Odyssey, Silver Scot, Soft Scot, Tommy Armour, Tommy Gun, T-Line

ARROYO COMBINATION EXERCISE BIKE
1295 E ATHENS
FRESNO, CA 93720
916-977-0112
Fax: 229-433-0718
- Joe Arroyo, President
Products:
Exercise bicycles.

ARTHRON, INC.
PO BOX 1627
BRENTWOOD, TN 37024
800-758-5633
Fax: 615-371-5405
www.sportsinjuries.com
- Denis Rowe, Director
(615) 377-6595
denisro@comcast.net
- Steven Antonopoulos, Head Athletic Trainer
Products:
Sports Medicine products.
Brands:
Impact Pads, Impact AC Pad, Impact Hip Pad, Impact Quad Pad, Impact Delt Pad, Impact O-S Pad, Impact Clavicle Pad

ARVINMERITOR
2135 W MAPLE ROAD
TROY, MI 48084
248-435-1000
800-535-5560
Fax: 248-435-1393
- Charles G McClure, Chairman, CEO and President
- James Donlon, Senior Vice President and Chief Financial Officer
- Lin Cummins, Senior Vice President and Communications
- Rakesh Sachdev, Senior Vice President/President-Asia & Pacific
- Kevin Nowlan, Vice President and Chief Financial Officer
- Jeffrey A. Craig, Senior Vice President and President, Commerci
- Pedro Ferro, Senior Vice President and President, Aftermar
- Vernon G. Baker II, Senior Vice President and General Counsel
- Barbara G. Novak, Vice President and Corporate Secretary
- Larry E. Ott, Senior Vice President, Human Resources and Co
Products/Services
Manufacturer of automotive/vehicle parts, systems and technologies including: chassis systems; door systems; roof systems, and steel wheels, etc.

ASA PRODUCTS, INC.
532 CORALRIDGE PLACE
CITY OF INDUSTRY, CA 91746
626-855-0900
877-869-6451
Fax: 626-855-0931
sales@mobocruiser.com
www.asaproducts.com
- Melody Hsieh, President/Owner
(626) 855-0900
melody@asaproducts.com
- Jessie Wu, Accounting Manager
jessie@asaproducts.com
- Stephen Collier, Customer Care Specialist
- Harun Riyanto, Executive Administrator
harun@asaproducts.com
Products:
Ultimate Three Wheeled Cruisers: Mobo

Shift, Mobo Triton, Mobo Triton pro, Mobo Mobito, Helmets, Combination lock, Bicycle Pump, Pedals, Triton Cruiser Basket, Flashlight, Bottle Holder, Flash Pin and Water Ball.
Year Founded:
1998
Brands:
Mobo

ASCENSION
3526 E FORT LOWELL ROAD
TUCSON, AZ 85716
520-881-3993
800-459-0400
Fax: 520-881-4983
sales@wheelchairlift.com
www.wheelchairlift.com
- Megan Ehrnard, Inside Sls Rep
(800) 459-0400
sales@wheelchairlift.com
- Timothy C. Mabe, President & CEO
(520) 881-3993
ramos@wheelchairlift.com
- Andrew Brown, Event Services Manager
Products:
Portable wheelchair lifts for sporting events, vehicle transporting, etc.
Brands:
Ascension

ASERTA SPORTS
1660 MABURY ROAD
SAN JOSE, CA 95133
408-251-PUTT (7888)
- Michael D Bonneau, Founder
- Richard J Selmeier, President & CEO
- Steve Sacks, Vice President Operations
- Steven Gray, National Director Sales
- Richard Parente, Design & Product Development
Products and Services
Aserta Sports, Inc. is in the business of designing, manufacturing and marketing innovative golf products that enhance performance and enjoyment of the game.

ASHAWAY LINE & TWINE MFG. COMPANY
24 LAUREL STREET
ASHAWAY, RI 2804
401-377-2221
800-556-7260
Fax: 401-377-9091
sales@ashawayusa.com
www.ashawayusa.com
- Pamela A. Crandall, Chairperson of the Board
- Kathryn C. Crandall, President
- Steven J. Crandall, VP
Products:
Racquet Sports - Racquet Strings.
Brands:
Crossfire, Dynamite, Flex, Killfire, Microlegend, Powerkill, Powernick, Rally Super-Kill, Super Nick, Super Nick XL, Vantage

ASHWORTH, INC.
5545 FERMI COURT
CARLSBAD, CA 92008-7324
760-438-6610
866-530-8624
Fax: 760-438-6657
- Christa McNamara, Director Public Relations
(760) 918-6466

• Allan Fletcher, Chief Executive Officer
• Greg Slack, Chief Financial Officer/
Treasurer
Products:
Golf Apparel.
Brands:
Ashworht.Corporate, Callaway, The Game

ASICS AMERICA CORPORATION
29 PARKER
SUITE 100
IRVINE, CA 92618
800-678-9435
800-333-8404
Fax: 949-453-0292
consumer@asicsamerica.com
www.asicsamerica.com
• Masaaki Uetsuki, Chmn, CEO, ASICS
Tiger
• Kiyomi Wada, Pres / Rep Dir
• Richard Bourne, President
• Motoi Oyama, President & CEO
Products:
Baseball - Shoes; Basketball - Shoes;
Warm-Up Suits; Racquet Sports - Apparel,
Bags-Equipment, Shoes; Softball - Shoes;
Track & Field - Apparel, Bags, Shoes;
Training & Conditioning - Cross-training
Apparel, Shoes; Volleyball - Shoes,
Uniforms; Wrestling; Cheering - Apparels,
Footwear, Bag
Brands:
GEL-Lyte, GELS, GT-Intensity

**ASTRO TURF MANUFACTURING
COMPANY**
701 LEANDER DRIVE
LEANDER, TX 78641
706-277-8873
877-723-8873
help@astroturf.com
www.astroturf.com
• Jim Savoca, VP Sales / Marketing
info@astroturf.com
• William La Starks, Manager Golf Products
info@astroturf.com
• Regina Duckett, Administrative Asst
info@astroturf.com
Products:
Synthetic turf products
Brands:
AstroLawnr, AstroPlayr, AstroTurfr, NeXturfr
and PureGrassTM

ATHENA GOLF
55706 BRAE BURN
LA QUINTA, CA 92253
760-564-7554
877-328-4362
Fax: 760-771-0321
• Debbie Behlman, Director Marketing
Products:
Women's golf apparel.
Brands:
Athena Golf Apparel

**ATHLETIC & PERFORMANCE
RIGGING/APR**
146 RIVERSIDE DRIVE
TIFFIN, OH 44883-1644
419-443-0500
800-445-1546
Fax: 419-447-5969
www.athleticrigging.net
• Steve Maiberger, VP
Products:
Motorized Netting Systems.

ATHLETIC FIELD SERVICES, INC.
PO BOX 215
GENESEE DEPOT, WI 53127
262-968-9101
Fax: 262-968-9102
www.afstrack.com
• Gwenn Zerull, President
• Bob Zerull, Vice President of Sales &
Marketing
• Russell Hansen, Vice President of
Production
• Devin Wheat, Project Manager
Products:
Running Track Facilities Surfaces
Brands:
Seal Flex

ATHLETIC KNIT
2 SCARLETT ROAD
TORONTO, ONTARIO, CANADA M6N 4J6
416-766-6151
888-818-5648
Fax: 416-766-7381
www.athleticknit.com
• Bernard Sliwin, President
• David Sliwin, Vice President
(416) 766-6151
david.sliwin@athleticknit.com
• Daniel Sliwin, Vice President
daniel.sliwin@athleticknit.com
• John Larin, Sales Manager
johnl@athleticknit.com
• Aaron Sellon, Sales and Customer Service
aarons@athleticknit.com
• Brian Edwards, Sales and Customer
Service
briane@athleticknit.com
• Blair Mcinnins, Sales and Customer
Service
blairm@athleticknit.com
• Maria Mcinnins, Sales and Customer
Service
Products:
Baseball, Basketball, Football, Hockey,
Lacrose and Volleyball Apparel

**ATHLETIC TRAINING EQUIPMENT
COMPANY/ATEC**
655 SPICE ISLAND DRIVE
SPARKS, NV 89431
800-998-2832
800-755-5100
Fax: 800-959-2832
askATEC@wilson.com
www.atecsports.com
• Eugene Grant, President
• Larry Leukhardt, Dir Sls
Products:
Baseball Bags Equipment, Batting
Ranges/Indoor/Outdoor, Cages/Backstops,
Nets, Pitching Machines; Softball
Balls-Molded Urethane, Cages/Backstops,
Nets, Pitching Machines, Field Maintenance,
Protective Equipment.
Brands:
ATEC, Casey, Hummer, Tuffy, Soft Toss,
Hitting Streak, Rookie, Catch Net

ATLANTIC FITNESS PRODUCTS
PO BOX 300
LINTHICUM, MD 21090
410-859-3538
800-445-1855
Fax: 410-859-3907
www.atlantic-fitness.com

• Ronald E. Overby, VP
• Faye Miller, Secretary
• Richard Stone, Sales Manager
Products:
Fitness Equipment.
Brands:
Atlantic

ATOMIC SKI USA
9 COLUMBIA DRIVE
AMHERST, NH 03031
603-880-6143
800-258-5020
Fax: 436-4523900120
info@atomicski.com
www.atomicski.com
• Peter Juric, International Race Director
• Eduardo Guzman, US National Race
Director
Products:
Alpine Accessories, Bindings, Boots, Poles,
Skis. Nordic Accessories, Mountain Boots,
Snowboards, Skis.
Brands:
Atomic, Koflach, Oxygen
Skiing Sponsor:
NYSSRA - New York State Ski Racing
Association

ATSKO INC.
2664 RUSSELL S E
ORANGEBURG, SC 29115
803-531-1820
800-845-2728
Fax: 803-531-2139
info@atsko.com
www.atsko.com
• Kurt Besser, President
Kurt@atsko.com
• Kurt Baumgartner, National Sales
Manager
Description:
Products to restore performance of outdoor
clothes, footwear, and equipment.
Products:
Manufacturer of SNO-SEAL, Sport-Wash,
Water-Guard, U-V-Killer, Sensi-Clean,
No-O-Dor and other brands to care for
clothing, footwear and outdoor gear.
Clients:
Distributors and Retailers of Sporting Goods
accessories and equipment.
Brands:
Sno-Seal, Rapid Rod, Sport-Wash,
U-V-Killer, U-V Shield, U-V Block,
N-O-DOR, Pro-Tech-Skin, Water-Guard

AUDERO SPORTS SUPPLY, INC.
4935 MCCONNELL AVENUE
SUITE 11
LOS ANGELES, CA 90066
310-822-3637
800-443-5037
Fax: 310-822-6308
olympussoc@aol.com
• Jose C. Audero, President
Products:
Soccer equipment and accessories
Brands:
Olympus

AUGUSTA SPORTSWEAR
425 PARK W DRIVE
GROVETOWN, GA 30813
706-860-4633
800-237-6695
Fax: 706-868-5672

sales@augustasportswear.com
www.augustasportswear.com
• Mike Holliman, Vice President Human Resources
• Chad Trollinger, Director Marketing
Products:
Athletic Jerseys, Shorts & Pants, Athletic Fleece, Outerwear, Sport Shirts, Woven Shirts, Corporate Casual, Aprons, Totes, Bags, Headwear and Accessories
Year Founded:
1977
Brands:
Augusta

AUSTIN ATHLETIC COMPANY
1005 E 39TH STREET
SHAWNEE, OK 74804
405-273-8681
800-813-7706
Fax: 405-275-5859
• Orville Austin, Owner
• Craig Ansell, Manager Production
Products:
Shoulder, Hip, Thigh and Knee Pads and accessories and football equipment reconditioning
Brands:
Austin Lok-Cup and Air-Lok shoulder pads, RC-PRO, RC-P, RC-F, HYL, BSI and SSI hip pads, ATP-R thigh pad, KYL knee pad, A-SYM and A-SYW sideline markers, A-SFW pylons, A-GPR goal post pad, A-GPD deluxe goal post pad, TPZ-8, RRD and STP-8 dummy, SRD-5 CRD-5 and SHD-6 blocking shield

AUTHENTIC FITNESS CORP.
501 7TH AVENUE
NEW YORK, NY 10018
212-287-8250
800-547-8770
Fax: 323-721-3613
• Joseph C. Gromek, President / Chief Executive Officer
• Lawrence Rutkowski, EVP / Chief Financial Officer
• Helen McCluskey, Warnaco Intimate Apparel President
• Frank Tworecke, CFO & Executive Vice President
Products:
Swimwear, fitness apparel and swin accessories
Brands:
Speedo, Ann Cole, Nautica, Sandcastle and Sunset Beach

AUTHENTIC STREET SIGNS
183 MAIN STREET
SAINT PETER, IL 62880
618-349-8878
800-289-4042
Fax: 618-349-6245
www.authenticstreetsigns.com
• Ed Onorato, National Sales Manager
Products:
Authentic street signs, LED night light, Neon signs
Brands:
Chicago Bulls, Denver Broncos, New York Yankees, St. Louis Cardinals, Philadelphia Flyers and Texas Longhorns

AUTOMATED BATTING CAGES CORPORATION
4897 INDIAN SCHOOL ROAD NE
SUITE 150
SALEM, OR 97305
503-304-8899
800-854-3140
Fax: 503-304-1899
parts@jjamusements.com
www.battingcages.com
• Doug Spray, President / Sales Construction
doug@battingcages.com
• Jim Peper, Plant Supervisor
jim@battingcages.com
• Darrin Lenz, Service Manager
Products:
Baseball and softball wheel-style pitching machines, coin/token boxes, conveyor/ball feeding and sorting systems, sign packages, light boxes, control panels, main mast slide collar, complete netting systems, design consultation and more
Brands:
ABC equipments

AVALANCHE SNOWBOARDS INC.
991 TYLER STREET
SUITE 200
BENICIA, CA 94510-2914
707-746-6982
800-541-0218
Fax: 707-746-5769
• Chris Sanders, President
Products:
Snowboards and accessories.
Brands:
MBA, Universal

AVERY SPORTS TURF, INC.
9 RIVERSIDE INDUSTRIAL PARK NE
ROME, GA 30161-8434
706-802-1970
800-765-3034
Fax: 706-802-1737
www.averysportsturf.com
• George Avery, President
Products:
Turf for fairways, target greens, range mats, athletic fields and tennis courts

AVIA AMERICAN SPORTING GOODS
7525 IRVINE CENTER DR
Suite 150
IRVINE, CA 92618
888-855-2842
800-848-8698
service@avia.com
www.avia.com
Products:
Basketball Shoes, Basketball Apparel; Running Shoes; Running Apparel; Women's Fitness Apparel

AWARD DECALS
14802 W 114TH TERRACE
LENEXA, KS 66215
913-677-6681
800-525-9395
Fax: 913-677-4250
order@awarddecals.com
www.awarddecals.com
• Clay Hirner, Partner
• Mallory Hirner, Partner
Products:
Custom decals and signs with mascot or logo, including football helmet decals.

AWARDS ETC.
4333 WELBORN ROAD
BRYAN, TX 77801
979-268-0981
Fax: 979-268-0985
• Robert E. Earle, Owner
Products:
Diploma Plaques, Framing, Laser, Engraving, Plaques, Trophies

B & G EQUIPMENT COMPANY
135 REGION S DRIVE
JACKSON, GA 30233
678-688-5601
800-544-8811
Fax: 678-688-5633
salesdept@bgequip.com
www.bgequip.com
• Bob Mathews, VP Manufacturing (678) 688-5601
• George Brehm, VP Sales and Marketing (678) 688-5601
• Lynn Donato, VP Sales - Retail Products
• Cecil Patterson, President, CEO
• Sargent Mark, Senior Vice President of Sales Industrial & J
• Amy Gwara, Pest Control, Industrial & Export Sales Distr
• Heiney Bob, Pest Control Products Sales & Tech Support
Products:
B&G Water Fountain Model WB-45
Brands:
PistrolPro 700 Series, VersaFoamer 4000, Borate 5000 & 5400 Sprayer, 1151-M Mini, 1152-A Hand, Long Reach Granular and 2250 Electric Dust-R, Perimeter Patrol System, 2600 Flex-A-Lite fogger, Robco Perimeter Spray Gun, MultiDose 3000, PestPro2000 Operator, B&G Acid, B&G Chemical Resistant and B&G Industrial Sprayer, Dura Spray, AquaMate, PetWash, PetFood Protectors, Easy Hose, Watering Wand

B&R ERECTORS/BLEACHERS
14200 WASHINGTON STREET
WOODSTOCK, IL 60098
866-253-2247
800-451-0638
Fax: 877-994-1715
bleachers@brbleachers.com
www.brbleachersonline.com
• Roger Be Jr, President (866) 253-2247
• Terry O'Hagan, Vice President, Operations (866) 253-2247
tohagan@brbleachers.com
Products:
Seats and Bleachers, including Covers, Mobile Seats, Permanent, Portable and Replacement Seats, as well as Bleacher Repair, Maintenance, Inspection and Consulting
Brands:
BR Bulldog Power System, BR Aisle Way Solutions, BR Rail Systems, BR Closure Systems, BR Surface Components, BR Bleacher R&D Products and BR Bleacher Seating Options

B' WARMER THERMAL PRODUCTS
10828 139TH STREET
EDMONTON, ALBERTA, CANADA T5M 1P7
780-482-6401
888-426-2224

Fax: 780-488-6182
info@bwarmer.com
• Dirk De Man, Chief Financial Officer
• Gordon Red Batty, Equipment Manager
Products:
Hand warmer, mitts and pants that will keep
you warm and comfortable
Brands:
B' Warmer Hand Warmer, B' Warmer Hand
Dryer, B' Warmer Sideliner Mitts, B' Warmer
Tear-Away Pants and B' Warmer Boot Sock

B-BALL LIGHTS
6911 PALMER ROAD
GREENS FORK, IN 47345
800-515-9049
Fax: 765-886-5471
• Bruce Watts, Marketing
Products:
Basketball Facilities; Shot Clocks,
Scoreboard Systems; Portable Scoreboards
Brands:
B-Ball Lights

BABOLAT VS NORTH AMERICA, INC.
1775 CHERRY STREET
SUITE 100
LOUISVILLE, CO 80027-3139
720-542-6290
877-316-9435
Fax: 303-444-2088
www.babolat.us
• Jean-Louis Boyre, President
Nature of Service:
Wholesale to dealers
Year Founded:
1999
Products:
Tennis Equipment and Products, Rackets,
Strings, Shoes, Bags and Accessories.
Brands:
Babolot

BABY FANATIC, LLC
1901 E FRANKLIN STREET
SUITE 114
RICHMOND, VA 23223
804-644-4707
Fax: 804-644-4709
www.babyfanatic.com
• Tricia Woodson, Chief Executive Officer
(804) 833-3131
twoodson@babyfanatic.com
Products:
Amusement, decorations, entertainment,
toys, embroidered pillow and comforter,
shirts and other accessories related to
sports teams and events. NCAA, MLB, &
NFL-themed baby products.

**BACHARACH RASIN SPORTING GOODS,
INC.**
802 GLEN EAGLES COURT
TOWSON, MD 21204
410-825-6747
800-726-2368
Fax: 410-321-0720
• Chris M. Hutchins, President
Products:
Durable goods, boys clothing & furnishings,
apparel & garments, women's apparel,
men's clothing & furnishings and sporting
goods

BACON & COMPANY
200-208 W SUMMIT HILL
KNOXVILLE, TN 37902
865-523-9181
Fax: 865-546-2212
info@baconco.com
www.baconco.com
Products:
Writing Instruments, Office Essentials,
Corporate Events, Employee & Client
Rewards, Clothing Accessories
Brands:
Anvil, Ashworth, Augusta, Bic,
BlueGeneration, The Brand Book Online,
Carhartt, Custom Crest, Cutter & Buck,
Gemline, Leeds, Sanford, Port Authority,
Vantage, VF Imagewear

BADEN SPORTS, INC.
3401 LIND AVE SW
RENTON, WA 98057
253-925-0500
800-544-2998
Fax: 253-925-0570
info@badensports.com
www.badensports.com
• Michael Shindler, Chief Executive Officer
Products:
Athletic balls for baseball, basketball,
football, playgrounds, rugby, soccer,
softball, volleyball, water polo, etc.
Notebooks, ball bags, soccer socks.
Brands:
Baden Perfection, Baden Lexum, Play
ground, Baden Officials

BADGE-A-MINIT LTD.
345 N LEWIS AVENUE
OGLESBY, IL 61348
800-223-4103
800-223-4103
Fax: 815-883-9696
questions@badgeaminit.com
www.badgeaminit.com
• Malcolm Roebuck, Chairman of the Board
• Cindy Kurkowski, President
Products:
Training & Conditioning - Benches, Exercise
Boards, Exercise Tables, Leg Elevation
Boards, Stall Bars, Incline Boards; Training
Room Supplies - Benches, Taping Tables

BAG BOY COMPANY
2701 EMERYWOOD PARKWAY
SUITE 101
RICHMOND, VA 23294
800-955-2269
Fax: 888-822-4269
bagboycs@bagboy.com
www.bagboyllc.com
• David Boardman, President & CEO
Products:
Golf Carts, Golf Bags, Travel Cases and
Accessories
Brands:
Bag Boy, AMF, Baby Jogger

BAGGO
600 MID AMERICA BLVD
HOT SPRINGS, AR 71913
501-767-3855
888-323-1813
Fax: 501-767-5173
customerservice@baggo.com
www.baggo.com

• Kirk Conville, President
(888) 323-1813
kirk@baggo.com
Products:
Bag Toss Game; Apparel and Accessories,
Bean Bags
Brands:
BAGGO, BAGGO #1, BAGGO #2, BAGGO
Build Your Own!, BAGGO Fan, BAGGO
Guy, BAGGO Mouth, BAGGO Themed

BAILEY MANUFACTURING COMPANY
PO BOX 130
LODI, OH 44254-0130
800-321-8372
Fax: 800-224-5390
baileytables@gmail.com
www.baileymfg.com
• Larry Strimple, President
Products:
Parallel Bars, Work Tables, Mat Tables,
Treatment Tables, Examination Tables, Tilt
Tables, Standing Tables, Sports Medicine
Tables, Couches/Lounges, Exercise
Devices, Weights, Stools, Chairs,
Wheelchair Aids, Aids, Posture Mirrors,
Training Stairs, Positioning Equipment,
Positioning Pillows, Professional Modular
Training Room Furniture, Classic Modular
Training Room Furniture, Deluxe Taping
Table, Whirlpool Tables, Back Extension
Treatment Table, Hand Therapy Table &
Desk, Economy Electric Hi-Lo Adjustable
Back Treatment Table, Economy Electric
Treatment Table, Training Room Furnitures

BALAZS, INC.
625 TODD ROAD
HONEY BROOK, PA 19344
610-433-4515
888-466-6765
Fax: 610-433-4695
info@balazsboxing.com
www.balazsboxing.com
• Brian DeMaris, President
brian@balazsboxing.com
Nature of Service:
Boxing and Fitness Equipment
Products:
Bag Mounts, Bags, Gloves, Protective Gear,
Training Accessories, Instructional Videos
Brands:
Balazs, Everlast, Century

BALFOUR CO.
7211 CIRCLE S ROAD
BUILDING A
AUSTIN, TX 78745
877-225-3687
800-225-3687
Fax: 512-443-5213
rings@balfour.com
www.balfour.com
• David G. Fiore, President / Chief Executive
Officer
• Sherice P. Bench, Chief Financing Officer
• Parke H. Davis, VP, Retail
Products:
Certificates, medals, rings, high quality
jewelry, announcements, and frames for
athletics and sporting events.

BALL & HELMET HOLDER, LLC
126 SMITH STREET
DERBY, CT 6418
203-627-6351
• Nicholas Donofrio, Founder

Products:
Ball holder, Helmet holder

BALL DYNAMICS INTERNATIONAL
14215 MEAD STREET
LONGMONT, CO 80504
800-752-2255
800-752-2255
Fax: 877-223-2962
• Joanne Posner-Mayer, Founder
• Cheryl Soleway, Master Trainer
Products:
Balance Tools, Books, DVDs & Videos,
Seating, Exercise Mats and Accessories,
Exercise Balls, Massage and Sensory
Tools, Therapy Mats and Tools, Yoga and
Pilates Mats
Brands:
FitBALL, AIREX, Gymnic, ChiBALL

BALLANDRA CORPORATION
3800 BAYVIEW STREET STEVESTON
VILLAGE
SUITE 202
RICHMOND, BC, CANADA 90670
604-274-5774
Fax: 604-274-5775
www.balandra.ca
• Caleb Law, President
Products:
Timing Devices - Chronographs,
Pedometers, Stopwatches-Digital, Timers
Brands:
Becona, Pateau, Quartz

BALLCO PRODUCTS, INC.
114 W POPLAR AVENUE
SAN MATEO, CA 94402-1152
650-343-2918
Fax: 650-343-0614
• Count Ja Lewenhaupt, President
Products:
Eyewear - Goggles; Racquet Sports -
Racquet Strings, Racquet Grips, Tennis
Balls, Tennis Racquets; Skiing-Alpine -
Bags, Gloves, Poles, Ski Brakes
Brands:
Bota

BALLGIRL ATHLETIC
225 WESTCHESTER AVENUE
PORT CHESTER, NY 10573
877-268-7778
877-268-7778
Fax: 800-385-7804
• Henry Norley, Jr, General Manager
Products:
Sports apparel, team uniforms, jerseys, and
bottoms
Brands:
Athena Dazzle Jersey, Excela Short, Game
Short, Lightning Rip Away Pant, Lightning
Shooting Shirt, Olympia Sleeveless,
Competitor Short Sleeve, Medalista 3 Short,
Medalista 5 Short, Valda Short Sleeve,
Performa Sleeveless

BALLQUBE, INC.
12146 CR 4233 W
CUSHING, TX 75760
903-863-5572
800-543-1470
Fax: 903-863-5571
sales@ballqube.com
www.ballqube.com
• Steve Castleberry, General Manager

Products:
Hat Holder, Baseball Holder,
Basketball/Soccer Ball, Bat Rack Holder,
Cereal Box Holder, Figure Holder,
Grandstand Football Holder, Football
Helmet Holder, Golf Ball Holder, Hockey
Stick Holder, Hockey Stick Holder, Golf Ball
Holder, Jersey Holders, Mini-Helmet Holder,
Softball Holder, Three Ball & Three Puck
Holders, Team Roster Cabinets, Laser
Engraved Team Logo Displays, Card
Holders
Brands:
PRO BOX, T-N-T, BallQube, Cap It

BALLSTARS
100 MISSION WOODS DRIVE
NEW CENTURY, KS 66031
913-764-7738
800-237-0653
Fax: 913-254-7803
sales@ballstars.com
www.photoball.com
• Nicole Gresham Perry, Chief Executive
Officer
(913) 764-7738
• Marshall Widman, Founder
• Devlan Reeves, Vice President Of
Marketing
Description:
Group holds global patents for imprinting
photos and logos on balls.sports balls.
Products:
Heat Transfer Systems for imprinting
photos, text, logos and other graphics on
actual sports balls; Accessories - Baseball
Display, Softball Display, Hockey Puck
Cube Display/Case, Baseball or Softball
Holder, Wire Ornament Hanger, Ornament
Tree

BAMBOO & RATTAN WORKS INC.
470 OBERLIN AVENUE S
LAKEWOOD, NJ 8701
732-370-0220
800-422-6266
Fax: 732-905-8386
bambooman1@aol.com
• Arthur Leon Maison, President/Chief
Operating Officer
bambooman1@aol.com
• Suzanne M. Maison, Vice
President/Marketing Director
Suzbamboo@comcast.net
Services:
Supplier of Manau rattan for martial arts and
SCA, whipping poles for greens, fencing
materials - custom and stock.
Clients:
Walt Disney, Macy's, Polo Ralph Lauren,
African Lion Safari, Six Flags Great
Adventure, American National Can, Ball
Metal Beverage, Crown Cork and Seal,
Henredon Furniture, Ficks Reed, Bauer
International, City of Virginia Beach,
Cincinnati Zoo, Brooklyn Botanic, Bronz
Zoo, Cleveland Botanical, Garden, Como
Park Conservatory, Columbia University,
Denver Black Arts Festival.
Year Founded:
1880

BANNERMAN LTD.
41 KELFIELD STREET
REXDALE, ONTARIO, CANADA M9W 5A3
416-247-7875
800-665-2696

Fax: 416-247-6540
info@sportsturfmagic.com
www.sportsturfmagic.com
• George Bannerman, Sales
• Ron Bannerman, Sales
Nature of Service:
Equipment for professional turf
management.
Year Founded:
1958
Products:
Aeriation equipment, Shaver Mowers, Drag
Mats, Seeding Equipment, Lawn Thatchers,
Trimmers/Blowers, Turf Comb, Turf Drainer,
Top Dressing Equipment, Lawn Bowls
Pusher, Greens Thatchers, Rakes, Turf
Rollers.

BARCO MEDIA
3059 PREMIERE PARKWAY
DULUTH, GA 30097
678-475-8000
webmaster@barco.com
www.barco.com
• Herman Daems, Chairman
• Eric VanZele, President & CEO
• Filip Pintelon, Chief Operating Officer
• Carl Peeters, Chief Financial Officer
• Jan Van Acoleyen, Chief Human
Resources Officer
• Jacques Bertrand, Chief Sales Officer
• Dave Scott, General Manager Defense &
Aerospace Division
• Herman Daems, Chairman
Products:
Visual Displays, Controllers, Graphical
Cards, Display Management Service

BARRECRAFTERS
700 BERNARD
GRANBY, CANADA J2G 9H7
800-451-3240
Fax: 800-361-6389
• Mark Snelling, President
• Robert Finnegan, Engineering VP
• Mark Comcowich, National Sales Manager
Products:
Automotive and Rack Accessories, Sport
Lockers & Car-Go Boxes, Bike Racks, Hitch
Racks
Brands:
Sierra Ski Racks, SB-4 Snowboard Rack,
SX-22 Mini-Roof Kit, US-276 - 299 Specialty
Hooks, Aerro B-4 & B-6, US-454 Horizontal
Ski Kit, SX-53 Sierra Ski Racks, US-243
Factory Mount Snowboard Kit, EL-1 The
Elevator, Snap-Around-Mounts, US-207
Mini-Winch Kit, KI-16 Permanent Mounting
Gutter, A857 Piranha Upright Bike Rack,
US-231 Upright Bike Kit/Locking, US-311
Locking Fork Mount Bike Kit, US-301 Wheel
Carrier, A859 Piranha Fork Mount Bike
Rack, RP-1 Bike RackPack, A1145 Super
Touring, A1166 Super Voyager, A1122
Super Pacer, BSR-1 Hang 2 Bike Storage
Rack, A825 Pro Mount Fork Block, APK-400
Pickup Bike Rack, A30503T Hitch N Drive
3-Bike Ball Mo

BASEBALL FIT HITTING & PITCHING
ACADEMY
11204 DOVER CT
YUKON, OK 73099
405-373-3253
support@baseballfit.com
www.baseballfit.com

• Steve Zawrotny, Director of Training
(405) 373-3253
steve@baseballfit.com
Products:
Throwing Velocity Booklet, Bat Speed
Booklet, Strength & Conditioning Booklet,
E-BOOKLETS, Weighted Softballs, BIG Z
Bat, Softball Videos, Metal Baseball Bats,
Metal Softball Bats, Wood Baseball Bats,
Throwing Strikes Booklet, Baseball Videos
Brands:
Baseball Fit, BIG Z

BASIC COATINGS, INC.
1001 BROWN AVENUE
PO BOX 3126
TOLEDO, OH 43607
515-288-0231
800-241-5471
Fax: 800-488-5800
bcinfo@basiccoatings.com
www.basiccoatings.com
• Nels Ingebrigtsen, President
• Mark Vick, Director ofSales
Products:
Water based wood floor coatings, Oil based
wood floor coatings, Dustless systems,
Maintenance products
Brands:
StreetShoe, Flo-cat, Commercial Catalyzed
Sealer, Hydroline Sealer, TyKote, Squeaky,
Dustline Dust Mop Treatment, Basic Oil
Modified Urethane MSDS, Heavy Duty
OMU, Amberizer MSDS

BASS IND INCORPORATED
3485 NE 65TH STREET
MIAMI, FL 33147
305-751-2716
800-346-8575
Fax: 305-756-6165
sales@bassind.com
www.bassind.com
• Robert Baron, President
(305) 751-2716
rmb@bassind.com
• Eric Finnegan, VP
(305) 751-2716
sales@bassind.com
Products:
Theatre Display Systems, Transparency
Showcases, Casino Display Systems, Video
Store Displays, Home Cinema Accessories,
Sports Cinema Seating & Accessories

BASS PRO SHOPS
2500 E KEARNEY
SPRINGFIELD, MO 65898
417-873-5000
800-976-6344
Fax: 417-873-4672
www.basspro.com
• John Morris, Founder
• James Hagale, CEO/President
• Stan Lippelman, Vice President Of
Marketing
• Larry Whitely, Manager Of
Communications and Outdoor Education
• Jenna Kendall, Media Informations
Coordinator
Baseball Sponsor:
MLB St Louis Cardinals
Fishing Sponsor:
National Hunting and Fishing Day.
Brands:
Johnny Morris Signature Series Trigger
Rods, Qualifier XPSTM Trigger R, Tourney

Special Graphite Rods, ExtremeTM XPSTM
Woo Dav, ExtremeTM XPSTM Trigger,
Browning Fishing Citori Trigger Rods,
Browning Fishing SilaFlex Trigger Rods,
Bass Pro Shops Johnny Morris Signature
Series Spinning Rods, Bass Pro Shops Pro
Qualifier XPSTM Spinning, Bass Pro Shops
ExtremeTM XPSTM Spinnin, Bass Pro
Shops ExtremeTM XPSTM Travel, Bass Pro
Shops ExtremeTM XPSTM Woo Dav, Bass
Pro Shops Micro LiteTM Graphite Spinning
Rod, Browning Fishing Citori Spinning Rods,
Browning Fishing SilaFlex Spinning Rods,
Bass Pro Shops Tourney Special Premium
Graphite Casting, Bass P
Products:
Rods, Reels, Combos, Lures, Rainwear &
Footwear, Flies & Kits, Watercraft, Fly
Fishing Apparel, Waders & Accessories,
Sunglasses, Optics, Black Powder, Shooting
Accessories, Decoys & Calls, Treestands,
Hunting Videos & Books, Hunting Clothing,
Hunting Outerwear, Hunting Boots, Tents,
Packs & Bags, Sleeping Bags & Beds, Metal
Detectors, Canoes & Kayaks, Paddles &
Oars, Canoe & Kayak Accessories, GPS
Units, GPS Accessories, Radio &
Accessories, Lanterns, Headlamps,
Spotlights, Flashlights, Dehydrators,
Vacuum Sealers, Kitchen Accesories,
Apparel, Footwear.
Sponsor:
Bass Pro Shops Bassmaster Open

BATTLE CREEK EQUIPMENT COMPANY
702 S REED
PO BOX 629
FREMONT, IN 46737
269-962-6181
800-253-0854
www.battlecreekequipment.com
• David Underhill, President
orders@battlecreekequipment.com
Description:
Maker of hot- and cold-therapy products for
managing pain.
Brands:
Automatic Moist Heat Pads, Joint-specific
Cold Therapy wraps, Microwaveable Moist
Heat wraps, Joint-specific Pain
Management Kits

BAUER NIKE HOCKEY, INC.
150 OCEAN ROAD
GREENLAND, NH 3840
603-430-2111
Fax: 603-430-3010
• Chris Zimmerman, Chief Executive Officer
• Bob Colburn, VP / General Manager
Products:
Ice Hockey - Apparel, Goalie Equipment,
Protective, Skates, Sticks; Ice Skating -
Skates; In-Line Skating - Accessories,
Apparel, Protective, Roller Hockey Skates,
Skates; USA Hockey - Official authentic
competitive apparel provider.
Brands:
Nike N-Dorfin, Tuuk

BAUERFEIND USA INCORPORATED
3005 CHASTAIN MEADOWS PARKWAY
SUITE 700
MARIETTA, GA 30066
770-429-8330
800-423-3405
Fax: 770-429-8477

info@bauerfeindusa.com
www.bauerfeindusa.com
• Bea Bauerfeino, Chief Executive Officer
(770) 429-8330
Products:
Medical equipment and supplies for athletic
applications.

BAUSCH & LOMB
ONE BAUSCH & LOMB PLACE
ROCHESTER, NY 14604-2701
585-338-6000
800-828-1430
Fax: 585-338-6896
www.bausch.com
• Fred Hassan, Chairman
• Brent L. Saunders, President & Chief
Executive Officer
Products:
Eyewear and sunglasses for all uses,
including for athlethes.
Brands:
Ray-Ban, Wayfarer

BD
ONE BECTON DRIVE
FRANKLIN LAKES, NJ 7417
201-847-6800
Fax: 201-847-5741
marilyn_miller@bd.com
www.bd.com
• Edward J. Ludwig, President / Chief
Executive Officer
(201) 847-6800
Products:
Medical Supplies, Devices, Laboratory
Equipment and Diagnostic Products for
competitive athletes and other applications.
Brands:
ABG Syringes, BD Q-SyteT, BD PosiflowT,
Interlinkr System, BD TwinpakT, BD
IntegraT, BD Safety-LokT, BD SafetyGlideT
, BD BBLT CHROMagarT, BD BBLT MI
Agar, BD BBLT Modified mTEC Agar, BD
OptiluxT, BD Auto ISO-FilterT, BD FalconT
6-well Multiwell Plate, BD FalconT HTS
FluoroBlokT, BDT Safety Knife with BD
Xstar BladeT, BD BeaverT, BD XstarT, BD
PocketT, LeVEEN Shunt, BD Insyte-NT
AutoguardT, BD AngiocathT AutoguardT,
BD Autoguard ProT, BD Saf-T-IntimaT, BD
Vacutainerr

BEAR ARCHERY
817 MAXWELL AVENUE
EVANSVILLE, IN 47711
812-467-1200
800-694-9494
Fax: 812-467-1300
bearcustomercare@beararcheryproducts.com
• Jim Allshouse, President
• Jack Bowman, Direcotr Of Business
Development
Products:
Compound Bows, Traditional Bows,
Crossbows

BEARCOM GROUP
4009 DISTRIBUTION DRIVE
BUILDING 200
GARLAND, TX 75041
214-340-8876
800-449-6171
800-252-1691
Fax: 214-340-1738

info@bearcom.com
www.bearcom.com
• Jerry Denham, President/CEO/Founder
• Brest Bisnar, Executive Vice President & Founder
• John Watson, Chairman

BELL FOUNDRY CO./BFCO FITNESS PRODUCTS
5310 SOUTHERN AVENUE
PO BOX 1070
SOUTHGATE, CA 90280
323-564-5701
Fax: 323-564-9717
info@bfco.com
www.bfco.com
• Cesar Cappellini, President / Chief Executive Officer
(323) 564-5701
info@bfco.com
• Greg Hach, Marketing Director / Sales Director
• Edgar Cruz, Aluminum-Marketing Director
ecruz@bfco.com
Products:
Barbells; Weightlifting Equipment and Accessories.

BELL SPORTS INC.
735 PACESETTER DRIVE
RANTOUL, IL 61866
800-456-2355
800-456-2355
Fax: 800-888-9009
consumersupport@bellsports.com
Products:
Auto Racing and cycling helmets.
Brands:
BSI, CPC, Mongoose, Blackburne, Bellistic, Faction, Metropolis, Citi, Alibi, Trigger, Amigo, Lil' Bell Shell, Boomerang, X-Ray, Influx, Ghisallo, Furio, Sweep R, Sweep XC

BERCO PRODUCTS, INCORPORATED
2437 E. 53RD ST.
LOS ANGELES, CA 90058
323-587-7263
800-858-7444
Fax: 941-927-3699
bercoproducts@sbcglobal.net
• Fred Berger, CEO
Products:
Licensed collegiate bobble head dolls, chain pulls, holiday ornaments, salt & pepper shakers, wind chimes, stepping stones garden stones, and picture frames, including sports related memoribilia.
Brands:
Big Nasty Bobble Head Dolls

BERGAMOT, INCORPORATED
820 WISCONSIN STREET
DELAVAN, WI 53115
262-728-5572 EXT 204
800-922-6733
Fax: 262-728-3750
customerservice@bergamot.net
www.bergamot.net
• Wayne Smith, President
• Craig Halvorsen, Wholesale Sales VP
(262) 728-5572
craigh@bergamot.net
Products:
Hitch Covers, Logo plates, Travel Mugs, VIP Coffee Mug, S & P Shaker Set, Fluted Shot Glass, Stainless Shot, Square Shot, Key Tags, Hitch Locks, NASCAR Logo

Collection, Lapel Pin, Beverage Holders, Belt Buckles, Retro Gas Pump Machine, Reflectors, NFL and MLB Accessories
Brands:
Alfred Hitch Cover, Meridian Metal Works, Logo Plates, Bergamot Buckle and Accessories

BEST PORTABLE FENCE
PO BOX 8434
GOLETA, CA 93118
805-637-6696
866-637-6329
Fax: 805-685-2688
sportfence@yahoo.com
• Donn Zellet, President
info@dazsports.com
• Bill Rozich, VP Marketing
Products:
Manufacturer of foul poles, gates, a full line of picket and lattice fences, and custom tents and canopies

BETHEL INTERNATIONAL
4610 BRAGG BOULEVARD
FAYETTEVILLE, NC 28303
910-868-4554
Fax: 910-868-3658
www.bethelwholesale.com
Products:
Jewelry, apparel, and gifts for the sports industry.
Brands:
Alabama Crimson Tide, Alabama, Arkansas, Auburn, Clemson Tigers, Duke Blue Devils, East Carolina Pirates, Florida Gators, Georgia Bulldogs, Georgia Tech, Kentucky Wildcats, Louisiana State Tigers, Louisville, Marshall, Maryland, Miami Hurricanes, Michigan Wolverines, Nebraska Cornhuskers, North Carolina Tar Heels, Ohio State Buckeyes, Oklahoma State, Penn State, Oklahoma Sooners, UCLA, Virginia Tech

BETLIN INC.
1445 MARION ROAD
COLUMBUS, OH 43207
614-443-0248
800-923-8546
Fax: 614-443-4658
www.betlin.com
• Robert Archer, President
• Vanda Burdette, External VP
• Pat Silk, Administrative VP
• John Archer, Sales / Marketing VP
Products:
Baseball Uniforms; Basketball Uniforms; Football Uniforms; Warm-Up Suits; Ice Hockey Uniforms; Lacrosse Uniforms; Soccer Uniforms; Softball Uniforms; Track & Field/Running Apparel; Volleyball Uniforms; Wrestling Apparel, Uniforms.
Brands:
Adidas, Mudcats, Wildcats

BIC SPORT NORTH AMERICA
2380 CRANBERRY HIGHWAY
WEST WAREHAM, MA 2576
508-291-2770
Fax: 508-291-2772
• Chris Decerso, Director of Sales and Marketing
(508) 291-2770
chris.decerso@bicworld.com
Products:
Water Sports Equipment: Windsurfing,

Surfing, Kayaks, Stand-Up Paddling, Junior Sailboats, Dinghies.
Brands:
Bic, Okespor, Nautix
Year Founded:
1979

BIEBER LIGHTING CORPORATION
970 W MANCHESTER
INGLEWOOD, CA 90301
310-645-6789
800-243-2375
Fax: 310-216-0333
• Joe Fuhrman, Vice President
Products:
Manufacturer of outdoor lighting, poles for tennis courts, parking lots, walkways, and other professional, recreational and commerical applications
Brands:
Bieber Lighting

BIG BOY HEADGEAR
711 E GARDENA BOULEVARD
GARDENA, CA 90248
214-388-2744
866-244-2692
Fax: 310-715-1526
joanne@bigboygear.com
www.bigboygear.com
• Joanne Kim, Co-Owner
Products:
Hats/Headwear, Leather Apparel, Outerwear, Pants/Slacks, Private Label, Sportswear, Printed T-shirts

BIG LEAGUE PROMOTIONS
1974 NW 82 AVENUE
MIAMI, FL 33126
305-640-9606
Fax: 305-640-9845
INFO@RICOINC.COM
Products:
Checkers, Magnetic Darts, Tic Tac Toe, and Chess game sets with sports team logos.
Brands:
Checkers: NFL Checkers, College Rival Checkers, MLB Checkers, Golf and Soccer Checkers; Magnetic Darts: NFL Magnetic Darts, MLB Magnetic Darts, College Magnetic Darts; NFL Tic Tac Toe; Chess: NFL Chess, City Chess, Sport Chess, Theme Chess

BIG TIME SPORTS APPAREL, INC.
3750 W MAIN STREET
NORMAN, OK 73072
405-447-3300
Fax: 405-573-7716
• Tom Lawson, President / Chief Operating Officer
Products:
Athletic Apparel and Collegiate Sportswear - Jerseys, Sweatshirts, Pants, Hats

BIKE USA INC.
2811 BROADHEAD ROAD
BETHLEHEM, PA 18020
610-868-7652
800-225-2453
Fax: 610-868-6335
customerservice@bikeusainc.com
www.bikeusainc.com
• Ssu-Liu Liu, President
• Steve Green, General Manager
• Marc Weiner, Vice President of Sales

(972) 556-1803
marc@bikeusainc.com
Products:
Bikes, Folding Table
Brands:
Bikes: Punisher, Screamin' Eagle, Docksider, Trailblazer, Freestyle BMX, Tomcat BMX, Fold-A-Bike, Scooters, Stabilizer

BILLBOARDS ON WHEELS
2090 FIFTH AVENUE
RONKONKOMA, NY 11779
631-580-7772 EXT 808
Fax: 631-580-3725
mikecutino@aol.com
www.bow1.com
• Michael Cutino, Publisher
Description:
Manufactures outdoor billboards and printing designs for the Tri-State area.

BIODEX MEDICAL SYSTEMS
20 RAMSAY ROAD
SHIRLEY, NY 11967-4704
631-924-9000
800-224-6339
Fax: 631-924-8355
info@biodex.com
www.biodex.com
• James Reiss, President
jreiss@biodex.com
• John Bennett, VP and Chief Financial Officer
info@biodex.com
Products:
Physical Medicine and Rehabilitation Products; Nuclear Medicine Supplies and Accessories - Dose Calibrators, Lead-Lined Laboratory Furniture Lung Ventilation Systems, PET Positron Emission Tomography Systems, Storage Cabinets, Radiation Shields, Syringe Shields and Vial Shields
Brands:
System 3, Balance System SD, Gait Trainer 2, Atomlab, Pulomonex II Xenon System, Venti-Scan IV Radioaerosol Administration System, Phantom

BIOFREEZE/PERFORMANCE HEALTH PRODUCTS
2230 BOYD ROAD
EXPORT, PA 15632
724-733-9500
800-246-3733
Fax: 724-733-4266
web@biofreeze.com
www.biofreeze.com
Products:
Topical pain relieving products in tubes, pump bottles, spray or roll-on
Brands:
Biofreeze

BIOGRIP, INC.
213 LATHROP WAY
SUITE I
SACRAMENTO, CA 95815
916-483-2686
888-590-4747
Fax: 916-483-1654
www.biogrip.com
• Stephen Tamaribuchi, President
• Rebecca Tamaribuchis, Chief Financial Officer

Products:
Fitness, sports medicine, and medical rehabilitation products
Brands:
e3 Fitness Grips, e3 Tricep/Lat, e3 Cable Resist, e3 Elastic Resist, e3 Ski Poles

BIOLIFE, LLC
8163 25TH COURT EAST
SARASOTA, FL 34243
941-360-1300
800-722-7559
Fax: 941-360-1310
customer.care@biolife.com
www.biolife.com
• Douglas Goodman, President
customer.care@biolife.com
• Tim Kelly, VP Sales
tim.kelly@biolife.com
• Andrew McFall, VP Marketing
andrew.mcfall@biolife.com
• Sam Shake, Chief Executive Officer
sam.shake@biolife.com
• Michele Slingluff, Chief Financial Officer
michele.slingluff@biolife.com
• Claudia Masselink, Director of Quality
claudia.masselink@biolife.com
• Kelly Keene, Director of Research & Development
kelly.keene@biolife.com
• Nick Wright, Director Sales
nick.wright@biolife.com
Products:
QR Powder for bleeding control (for Consumers, Medical Professionals), QR Powder for bleeding control (QR Powder for Occupational Health / Worksites, Sports Medicine)
Brands:
UrgentQR, NosebleedQR, SportsQR, KidsQR

BION INCORPORATED
14656 59TH AVENUE
BRITISH COLUMBIA, CANADA V3S 0V7
604-599-8609
Fax: 604-599-8201
bion_inc@yahoo.com
Products:
HRM, Velometer, Cycle Computer, Body Fat Moniftor, Pedometer

BIOSIG INSTRUMENTS, INC.
PO BOX 860
CHAMPLAIN, NY 12919
514-637-0016
800-463-5470
Fax: 514-637-1353
biosig@biosig.net
www.biosiginstruments.com
• Gregory Lekhtman, President
Products:
Insta-Pulse Fitness Heart Rate Monitors, Antense-Fitness Anti-Tension Device, Exerlopers No-Impact Running/Jogging Shoes, Body Trim-Home Exerciser, Insta-Runner Revolutionary Cardio Exerciser, Electronic Gym-Muscle Strength Monitor, Sea Logger-Water Walking System No Impact Exerciser, OEM Custom Designed Fitness Sensors/Electronics and products.
Year Founded:
1975
Clients:
Fitness equipment dealers, schools, universities, museums, exports worldwide.

BISON, INC.
603 L STREET
LINCOLN, NE 68508
800-247-7668
Fax: 800-638-0698
www.bisoninc.com
• Nick Cusick, President
Nature of Service:
Sporting goods manufacturer represented by 1500 dealers across the US
Brands:
Arena, Baseline 180 degrees, CarbonMax, CenterCourt, Centerline, Club Court, Competitor, Court Protector, Dura Steel, DuraSkin, DuraSkin for Soccer, Easy Reach, Easy Store, Easy-Up, Elite, Fail-Safe, FlexCourt, Glass Max, Kids Hoops, Lady CarbonMax, Lifeguard, Magnum, Match Point, PerfectGoal, Perpetual, Playtime, Power Adjust, ProTech, Protector, QwikChange, QwikPrint, Rapid Adjust, ReAction, Ruff Play, Safe Stuff, Sand Bar, Shooting Station, ShootOut, Side Court, Sidecourt, SideLine, Sport Pride, Street Hoops, The Patriot, TimeKeeper, T-Rex, TruFlex, Tuffglass, Ultimate, Ultimate Jr, Weatherbeater, Web Net, Zip Crank
Products:
Manufacturer of goals, gym and field accessories for basketball, volleyball, soccer, football, rugby, lacrosse, field hockey and futsal. Bison has equipment for every level of indoor and outdoor competition and recreation: portable basketball systems, wall mount basketball structures, goal height adjusters; competition, rec and playground basketball goals and backboards; backboard padding; ball carts; competition, rec and outdoor volleyball systems; player's benches; gymnasium wall padding and scorer's tables; youth goals; portable game bases; tetherball and badminton sets; soccer, fotball, rugby, lacrosse and futsal goals and accessories; sa

BLACK DIAMOND EQUIPMENT, LTD.
2084 E 3900 S
SALT LAKE CITY, UT 84124
801-278-5552
800-775-5552
Fax: 801-278-5544
bdmo@bdel.com
www.bdel.com
• Peter Metcalf, President / Chief Operating Officer
peter@bdel.com
• Colleen Graham, VP Marketing
(801) 365-5522
• Meredith Saarinen, VP Production
Products:
Carabiners/Draws, Protection, Harnesses, BigWall, Belay/Rappel, Helmets, Pads/Bags/Chalk, Rope/Cord/Webbing, Ice Gear, Skis/Bindings, Poles, Backcountry Gear, Gloves/Gaiters, SCARPA Ski Boots, Packs, Trekking Poles, Lightware/Headlamps, Tents/'Mids/Bivys, Clothing, Accessories, Spare Parts, Specials
Brands:
Carabiners/Draws - LiveWire, Dynotron; Protection - Camalots, Camalot C3s, Harnesses - Blizzard, Chaos; Belay/Rappel - ATC-Guide, ATC-XP; Helmets - Tracer, Half Dome; Pads - Mondo II, Drop Zone II; Rope/Cord/Webbing - Rando, Ice Twin; Backcountry Gear - AvaLung II; Glove -

Patrol, Patrol Mitt, Prodigy, Kingpin; SCARPA Ski Boots - T1, T2X Men's, T2X Women's; Packs - Predator, Jackal, Revelation; Trekking Poles - Terra CF, Contour; Lightware/Headlamps - Soliras, SpaceShot 2; Tents - Guilding Light, Skylight; Clothing - Alpine Shirt, Alpine Pants, BDYs; Accessories - Microns, JiveWires; Nut Tool; Spare Parts - Rock, Snow

BLADEMASTER
566 RIVERVIEW DRIVE
CHATHAM, ONTARIO, CANADA N7M 5L5
519-352-4550
888-648-7776
Fax: 519-352-7676
blademaster@guspro.com
www.blademaster.ca
• August Sunnen, President
(519) 352-4550
augusts@guspro.com
• Paul Sunnen, Chief Operating Officer
(519) 352-4550
pauls@guspro.com
• Bob Moon, Sales Manager
(519) 352-4550
bobm@guspro.com
• Marcel Michaud, Customer Service Associate
(519) 352-4550
marcelm@guspro.com
Products:
Skate Sharpening Machines (Triples Station, Wheel/Diamonds, Double Station, Sharpening Accessories), Skate Sharpening Machines (Single Station, Service Accessories, Portables, Holders/Contouring), Boot expander tools and accessories.
Brands:
Blademaster, Lil Red, Big Red

BLADEZ, INC
20155 ELLIPSE
FOOTHILL RANCH, CA 92610
949-206-0330
888-325-2339
Fax: 949-206-0013
• Stephen Wilkins, President / Chief Operating Officer
• Lenny Vainberg, VP
Products:
Powered Personal Transportation products (Electric Powerboards, Gas Powerboards, Treadmills, Ellipticals, Mobility Vehicles)
Brands:
QCS (Quick Change System, SPS (Smart Power System), GSEV (Electric Vehicle Rated), XTR Comp, XTR Street, XTR SE 450, eLite 300s, eLite 250, XTR-S 450, XTR-Lite 250, XTR-HD 550)

BLAZER MANUFACTURING, INC.
5109 W. 26TH STREET
W INDUSTRIAL SITE
PO BOX 266
COLUMBUS, NE 68601
800-322-2731
Fax: 800-257-4045
info@blazerathletic.com
www.blazerathletic.com
• Gordon Blaser, VP
• Sheila Gottsch, National Sales Manager
Products:
Athletic Equipment (Dryline Marker, Steel High School Vault Std., Steel Adjustable

Vault Std., Quick Measure, Alum. SJ. Std. w/Alum., Alum. SJ. Std. w/Round Base, SS Long Jump Tray, Discus Ring, Web Throwing Circles, Shot Put Ring, Hammer Ring, Pole Vault Boxes, Transport Cart; Team Sportswear; Industrial Products
Brands:
Stock Velocity, IO-Skin, 15 & 16, Conquest, 3-Color, Solid, Victory, Triumph, Millenium, Paramax, Duo-MAX Pants, Stock IO-Skin, Amibition, Duo-MAX, 2-Color, Knit Trim Option, All-American, Achiever, Tri-Sleeve, Contender

BLUE FISH
5738 SUNSET DRIVE
SUITE 2044
SOUTH MIAMI, FL 33143
305-381-5024
Fax: 786-953-5690
customerservice@bluefishsport.com
www.bluefishsport.com
Products:
Accessories, Tops, Outerwear, Bottoms
Brands:
8203 Spaghetti Top, 6108 BF Jersey Top, 8176 BF Silk Top, 621 Basic Tank, 6142 Surprise Tank, 6138 BF Straps Tank, 8428 Umberella Top, 8170 V Top, 8476 Fit Top, 3/4 Sleeves Top, 8486 Action Top, 8313 T Shirt, 8478 - Justin Top, 6155 - Tic Tac Bra, 8481 Don Top, 8491, Gus Top, 6158 Action Bra, 6156 Tic Tac Top, 8489 Spa Top, 8482 Strong Top, 8484 Sherah Top, 8495 Diamond Top, 8486 Tennis Top, 8497 Silver Top; 8333 Poly Jacket, 8159 Basic Jacket, 8425 Zip Jacket, 8499 Gus Jacket, 8490 Funky Jacket, 8514 Polka Dot Jacket, 8503 Diamond Jacket; 9160 Stud Pant, 9219 Zip Capri, 9249 Tiki Pants, 9289 - Action Pant, 942 - Dual Screen Pant, 841 - Stron

BLUE RIDGE MOUNTAIN WOODCRAFTS, INC.
71 MERK DAVIS STREET
PO BOX 566
ELLIJAY, GA 30540
706-276-2222
800-348-0748
Fax: 800-348-9798
sales@blueridgewoodcrafts.com
www.blueridgewoodcrafts.com
• Fred Stahl, Chief Operating Officer
sales@blueridgewoodcrafts.com
Products:
Heavy weight and plastic extrusion columns, wood plaques and accessories, trophy base sets, cup bases, Italian marble and steel rods, figurines and mylars
Brands:
Pro-Wood

BMORE SPORTS
1430 JOH AVENUE
BUILDING M
BALTIMORE, MD 21227
410-247-2345
gandracchio@ptcintl.com
www.bmoresports.com or www.ptcintl.com
• Gianni Andracchio, Account Executive
gandracchio@ptcintl.com
Nature of Services:
Bmore Sports is a manufacturer of a variety of game-day promotional products including sports leather binders and jotters, wood ticket boxes, custom coolers and dog tag collectibles.

Year Founded:
1980

BOAST, INC.
53 W 36TH STREET
SUITE 302
NEW YORK, NY 10018
212-695-6424
800-327-7666
Fax: 561-863-5321
questions@boastusa.com
www.boastusa.com
• Bill St John, President
• Heather Burrows, Credit Manager
Products:
Golf, Tennis, Racquet Sports Apparel and Outerwear.

BOBBY JONES INTERNATIONAL
7406 RT 487 THE MATTERN BLDG
PO BOX 214
MILDRED, PA 18632-9015
585-467-7240
800-767-1260
Fax: 585-467-0854
rochester@hickeyfreeman.com
www.bobbyjones.com
• Carol O'Grady, Director Corporate Tour Sales
Products:
Golf Apparel.

BODY GLOVE INTERNATIONAL, INC.
504 N. BROADWAY
REDONDO BEACH, CA 90277
310-374-3441
Fax: 310-372-7457
pr@bodyglove.com
www.bodyglove.com
• Robbie Meistrell, Founder
• Russel Lesser, President
• Celeste Berouty, Sales Director
• Scott Daley, Director Marketing
Products:
Wetsuits, men's apparel, jr. swimwear, technology accessories, personal flotation devices (life vests), snorkeling gear, bags, water sports, sunglasses
Brands:
Vapor, Matrix, Storm Trooper, Stealth Short Zip, Pro 2, Axis, Formula, Arc, Rashguard, Java, Rover, Vibe, Aura

BODY SOLID, INC.
1900 S DES PLAINES AVENUE
FOREST PARK, IL 60130
708-427-3555
800-833-1227
Fax: 708-427-3556
sales@bodysolid.com
www.bodysolid.com
• Andy Huck, Eastern Sales Manager
(708) 427-3555
ahuck@bodysolid.com
• Duane Abbott, Western Sales Manager
(708) 427-3555
dabbott@bodysolid.com
• Jeff Estopellan, MidWest Sales Manager
(708) 427-3555
jestopellan@bodysolid.com
Products:
Weightlifting - Benches, Dumbbell Racks, Home Gyms, Power Racks, Lat Machines, Selectorized Single Station Machines for Clubs, Weight Trees.
Brands:
Endurance T3 Treadmill, Endurance Tf3i

Treadmill, Endurance T4i Treadmill, Endurance T6iHRC Treadmill, Endurance TF6iHRC Treadmill, Endurance E4 Elliptical, Endurance Cardio E5HRC Elliptical, Endurance Cardio E7 Elliptical, Endurance Cardio E7HRC Elliptical, Endurance B3R Recumbant Bike, Endurance B3U Upright Bike, Body-Solid G1S Home Gym, Body Solid G2B Home Gym, Body-Solid G3S Home Gym, Body Solid G5S Home Gym, Bod-Solid G6B Home Gym, Body-Solid G8I Home Gym, Body-Solid G9S Home Gym, Body-Solid G10B Home Gym, Body-Solid EXM4000S Pro Gym, Body-Solid EXM1500S Home Gym, Body-Solid EXM3000LPS Home Gym, Body-Solid Series

BODY WISE INTERNATIONAL
17101 ARMSTRONG AVENUE
SUITE 101
IRVINE, CA 92614
714-505-6121
800-830-9596
Fax: 714-368-1296
services@bodywise.com
www.bodywise.com
• William F Farley, CEO
• Tom Tierney, Founding Chairman
• Debra Meyer, VP Operations
• Kathy Martino, Vice President Community Relations/Consultant
• Leslie Boyd-Bradley, Vice President Business Development
Products:
Sports & dietary supplements.
Brands:
BW365 Shakes, BW365 Lean Support, One Bite, Right Choice - Am Formula, Right Choice - PM Formula, Beta-C, Essential Calcium, Omega Complete, Cardio-Wise, COmfort Tea, CoQ10, Revitalizing Tea, Glucomine, Male Advantage, MemX2, OptimEyes, Oxy-G2, Super Cell, AG-Immune, NK-Immune, Relief, Aller Wise, Female Advantage Balance, Female Advantage Transitions, Estrenol, Pro Pure, Tiger Vites, Workout Formula, Electro Aloe.

BODY WRAPPERS/ANGELO LUZIO
107 TRUMBULL STREET
ELIZABETH, NJ 07206-2165
908-354-7218
800-323-0786
Fax: 908-354-4023
info@bodywrappers.com
www.bodywrappers.com
• Marie West, President
• Nicholas Karant, Vice President
• Trudy Christ, Marketing Director
Products:
Manufacturer of dance and team dance apparel and distributors of Angelo Luzio dance shops.
Brands:
Body Wrappers, Totalstretch, Princess Aurora, Premiere Collection, Dance Between, totalSTRETCH tights and undergarments

BOELTER BRANDS, LLC
4200 NORTH PORT WASHINGTON RD
GLENDALE, WI 53212
877-233-7287
800-233-7287
Fax: 414-967-4399

sales@boelterbrands.com
www.boelterbrandsproducts.com
Products:
Plastic cups, coasters, glassware, pitchers, buckets.

BOGNER
185 ALLEN BROOK LANE
SUITE 201
WILLISTON, VT 5495
802-861-6900
800-801-0372
Fax: 802-861-6909
www.bogner.com
• Peter Born, President
• Konstantin Brandstetter, Executive Vice President
• Homeira Lane, Bogner Sport Sales & Marketing
• Hannes Bogner, Chief Financial Officer
Products:
Golf - Apparel; Skiing-Alpine - Accessories, Outerwear-Jackets, Vests, Pants; Skiing-Nordic - Accessories, Outerwear-Suits, Tops, Pants.
Nature of Services:
Wholesale sales and marketing of men's and ladies' skiwear and sportswear.

BOSS GRAPHICS, INC.
2668-A HONOLULU AVENUE
MONTROSE, CA 91020
818-248-7066
Fax: 626-398-5123
larry@bossgraphics.com
www.bossgraphics.com
• Larry Lousen, President
Products:
Graphics and Murals for Auditoriums, Gym/Sport Arenas, Stadiums, Pool Areas, and other Commercial Applications; also Floor Graphics.

BOSS MANUFACTURING COMPANY
221 W FIRST STREET
KEWANEE, IL 61443
309-852-2131
800-447-4581
Fax: 309-852-0848
bossmfg1893@bossgloves.com
• David Hunter, Marketing Director
• Gerry Stockerman, Operations Director
Products:
Gloves, Boots, Protective Wear and Rainwear
Brands:
Boss, Foot Glove, Mesh, Morris Feel, Morris Zip Flap

BOSTON WHALER, INC.
100 WHALER WAY
EDGEWATER, FL 32141
386-428-0057
877-294-5645
Fax: 386-423-8589
www.whaler.com
• John Ward, President
• Tim Schiek, President
Products:
Fiberglass Boats.
Brands:
Sport/Montauk, Dauntless, Ventura, Outrage, Conquest

BOTTELSEN DART COMPANY
945 W MCCOY LANE
SANTA MARIA, CA 93455
805-922-4519
800-537-2164
Fax: 805-922-5961
info@bottelsendarts.com
www.bottelsendarts.com
• Jeff Bryan, Director
Products:
Dart and Related Accessories
Brands:
Megathrust Hammerhead, Buzzbomb, Precision Grip, Precision Grip Hammerhead, G.T., Ohh...Aah!, Mega Thrust, Devastators, Heavy Weights, Tough Koat, Black Knights, Gorilla Grip, 80% Tungsten, Kick Ass Tungsten, Kick Ass Brass, G.T. Stubbies, Buzz BOmbs Tungsten, Buzz Bomb Brass, Skinny's, Skinny's Colors, Gap, Nemesis, Berzerker Brasss, Hammer Head Spinning, Classic G.T. Shafts, New G.T. Shafts, Aluminum Shafts, Nylon, Combo Crackers, Deflectors, Wrenches, O-Rings, Sharpening Stones, Point Protectors, Soft Tip Points, Jug O'Darts, Pro Packs, Quad Cases, Solo Cases, Wedge Cases, Hard Cases, DartBoards, Books, Metallized Polyester Film, Metallize

BOUNTY HUNTER
1465-H HENRY BRENNAN
EL PASO, TX 79936
915-633-8354
800-413-4131
Fax: 915-633-8175
info@frsttx.com
www.detecting.com
Products:
Metal Detector
Brands:
Bounty Hunter Junior, VLF, Gold Digger, Fast Tracker, Tracker II, Quick Silver, Tracker IV, Lone Star, Quick Draw II, Sharp Shooter II, Land Star, Camo-LS, Land Ranger, Time Ranger.

BOWLINGSHIRT.COM
6262 OLIVE BOULEVARD
SAINT LOUIS, MO 63130
314-426-4886
800-444-1685
Fax: 314-426-1713
Sales@CruisinUSA.com
www.bowlingshirt.com
• Alan Spetner, Chief Cruisin' Officer
(314) 336-0607
Alan@cruisinusa.com
• Helene Spetner, President
(314) 336-0608
Helene@cruisinusa.com
• Tim Coggeshall, VP of Sales
(314) 336-0610
Tim@cruisinusa.com
Products:
Unisex Bowling Shirts in many styles and colors, Gifts and Accessories
Brands:
Classic Bowlers, Retro Bowlers, Loungemasters, Fifties Bowlers, Swingmasters, The Imperial Line, Slick Daddys

BOYLE & COMPANY, INC.
1803 SALISBURY HIGHWAY
STATESVILLE, NC 28677

704-872-8151
800-438-1061
Fax: 888-867-1337
marketing@johnboyle.com
www.johnboyle.com
• John Bo Bell Jr, Chairman
• Paul B Stelzner, Chief Executive Officer
• Michael B Dorfman, President
• William W White, VP, Sales & Marketing
Products:
Awnings, Banners, Industrial, Marine, Mining, Speacialty, Tents
Brands:
Gulf Stream, Main Street, Pyrotone, Sunbrella, Sunbrella Plus, Sunbrella firesist, Sunbrella firesist plus, Gottschalk Fibers, Signmaster Supreme, Canopy FS, Canopy Plus, Cool Glo, Cool Glo Ultra, BTF-19, Nite Lite, Eradi-Lite, Patio 500, Veranda, Tenara, Star Ultra Dee, Polymatic, Dabond, RIRI Decor, YKK Vislon, YKK Ziplon, YKK Uretex, Zippy Cool Cleaner/Lubricant, Monterey Lateral Arm System, Catalina & Santa Barbara Retractable Systems, Ventura Sun Screen System, Ibiza Retractable Arm System, Robusta Heavy Duty Window System, Siesta Window System, Steel Stitch, Gatorstitch, Armadillo, Stimpson, Fasnap, Dot, Bendarc Bender, Crownarc Crowner

BRAVO SPORTS
12801 CARMENITA ROAD
SANTA FE SPRINGS, CA 90670
562-484-5100
800-234-9737
Fax: 562-484-5183
www.bravosportscorp.com
• Leonardo Pais, Chief Executive Officer
• Cameron Adamson, Chief Financial Officer
• Drew Brassard, Chief Information Officer
Products:
Decks, wheels, components, helmets, longboard skateboards, protective
Brands:
Natural VI, Natural Charcoal VI, Natural Red V2, Natural Blue V2, Standard, Eagle, Skull-n-Wings, Trucks, ABEC 5 Bearings, Grip Tape, Mounting Bolts, Riser Pads, Transparent Skateboard Helmet, Spiked Helmet, Kore Series Matte Black Helmet, Kore Series Elbow Pads, Kore Series Wrist Guards, Kore Series Knee Pads , Elbow Pads, Wrist Guards, Knee Pads.

BRAZOS SPORTSWEAR
4101 FOUNDERS BOULEVARD
BATAVIA, OH 45103
513-753-3400
Fax: 513-563-6692
Products:
Sports apparel for professional competititon and recreational activities.

BREWER'S LEDGE, INC.
87 YORK AVENUE
RANDOLPH, MA 2368
617-983-5244
800-707-9616
Fax: 781-961-5204
Sales@Treadwall.com
www.brewersledge.com
• Conant Brewer, President
(800) 707-9616
conant@treadwall.com
• Jeff Brewer, Vice President
(800) 707-9616

jeff@treadwall.com
• Howard Richardson, Operations
Products:
Exercise and Fitness Equipment, including Rotating Climbing Walls, Portable Climbing Walls and Rock Climbing Simulators.
Brands:
LedgeWall, WingWall, KidWall, TreadWall, TreadWall Trailers, KidWall Trailers, Climbco
Year Founded:
1990
Description:
Since 1989, Brewer's Ledge has provided over 900 facilities with climbing systems. Brewer's Ledge is a family company offering a full line of fixed, rotating, and portable climbing walls, focusing on kids programs and fitness training. This includes self-installed, textured panels, Treadwall™ and KidWall™ rotating walls, adjustable playground walls, towers, racquetball conversions, custom walls and portable walls. They support customers fully, helping with design, training and equipment needs. Specifications, free quotes and videos are always available.

BRIDGESTONE SPORTS (U.S.A.), INC.
15320 INDUSTRIAL PARK BOULEVARD NE
COVINGTON, GA 30014
770-787-7400
800-358-6319
Fax: 770-786-6416
• Yasuhiko Moteki, President
(822) 558-2235
• Stephen Graham, New Product Manager
• Randy Eaton, Senior Sales Director
Products:
Golf Accessories, Bags, Balls, Clubs-Wood/Iron Sets, Gloves.
Brands:
Precept

BRIGADE QM
1025 COBB INTERNATIONAL DRIVE NW
SUITE 100
KENNESAW, GA 30156-9217
770-428-1234
800-663-7487
Fax: 770-426-7726
brigade@brigadeqm.com
www.brigadeqm.com
• Mitchell L Werbell IV, President
(770) 428-1248
• Mark Smith, Marketing Director
• Geoffrey W. Werbell, Chief Financial Officer
• Mike McCourt, Director Of Merchandising
Products:
Adventure Clothing, Military Field Gear, Bags, Foot, Head & Handwear, Rain Gear, Logo Apparel, Repair Supplies, Survival & First Aid, Vitamins & Body Building Supplements, Eyewear, Books & Manuals, Novelty Items
Brands:
3MT Products, 5.11 Tactical Seriesr, 7.62 Designsr, ACCUSHARPT, Accusplitr, ACRr, ActcelT, Adventure Medical Kits, Adventure ReadyT, Aerko Chemical Defense OC Sprays, Aerobic Oxygen, AimSHOTT, Al Mar KnivesT, All Weather Safety Whistle, Alliance Rubber Company, Alpenr Outdoor, ALTAr Protection Products, Altamar Combat Boots, American Optical, AOSafetyr

Products, ASPr, A-TeamT Apparel, ATN Night Vision, Austri-Alpin, AZORAr

BRIGHT SITES, INC
17935 SW LAKE HAVEN DRIVE
LAKE OSWEGO, OR 97035
503-639-0594
800-458-9055
Fax: 503-620-1189
www.brightsights.com
• Marie Mann, President
marie@spiritone.com
• Robert Mann, Chief Executive Officer
Products:
Gun Sight Coatings and Application Kit
Brands:
Bright Sights Glow Kit, Bright Sights Kit, Bright Sights High Visibility Coatings, Ghost Glow Luminescent Coatings, Application Kit, Ghost Glow Luminescent Coatings

BRINE, INC.
47 SUMNER STREET
MILFORD, MA 1757
508-478-3250
800-968-7845
Fax: 586-446-1162
www.brine.com
• Sean Fox, President
• Erica Cronan, Senior Media & Communications Manager
(508) 902-2283
Products:
Men's Lacrosse, Women's Lacrosse, Soccer Apparel, Equipment & Accessories, Field Hockey Apparel, Equipment & Accessories
Brands:
Brine, Guru Series, Phenom Series, Prodigy Series

BRISTOL ATHLETIC
700 SHELBY STREET
PO BOX 158
BRISTOL, TN 37620
423-968-4140
800-336-8775
Fax: 423-968-2084
www.bristolproducts.com
• Richard C Horner Jr, President
• Richard Horner, Finance VP
• Chris Horner, Sales VP
• Jan Rainero, Cheerleader Coordinator
Products:
Athletic Socks, Baseball uniforms, Cheerleading uniforms & accessories, Football uniforms, Basketball uniforms, Game Officials uniforms
Brands:
Bristol

BRITTEN-MEDIA
2322 CASS ROAD
TRAVERSE CITY, MI 49684
855-763-8204
800-426-9496
Fax: 231-941-8299
• Tom Britten, President
Auto Sports:
Mazda Raceway Laguna Seca - Preferred Facility Banner and Signage Production and Installation Vendor.

BROOKS
4300 ROOSEVELT WAY NE
SEATTLE, WA 98105

425-488-3131
800-227-6657
Fax: 425-489-1975
www.brooksrunning.com
• James M Weber, President / Chief Executive Officer
• David Bohan, EVP & COO
• Stan Mavis, Senior VP Apparel / Accessories
Products:
Athletic Footwear, Apparel & Accessories.
Brands:
HydroFLX, Diagonal Rollbar, Ethylene Vinyl Acetate, Podular Technology, HydroFlow and Substance 257, Powerpro, Silc, Aireplex and Vapor Dry

BROOKWOOD COMPANIES, INC.
25 W 45TH STREET
11TH FLOOR
NEW YORK, NY 10036
212-551-0100
800-426-5468
Fax: 212-472-0294
webmaster@brookwoodcos.com
www.brookwoodcos.com
• Amber Brookman, President / Chief Executive Officer
Products:
Consumer Fabrics, Industrial/Medical Fabrics, Military Fabrics
Brands:
Cordura, MicroFiber, MicroSupplex, Supplex, Sympatex, Tactel

BROWNELL & CO., INC.
423 E HADDAM-MOODUS ROAD
PO BOX 362
MOODUS, CT 06469-0362
860-873-8625
800-222-4007
Fax: 860-873-1944
www.brownellco.com
• Anthony Ferraz, President
• Cynthia Stakowitz, VP
Products:
Cargo Nets, Posts & Court equipment, Bowstrings, Cordage products for commercial fishing, Wire & Cable, and Industrial Applications.
Brands:
TS-1, Fast Flight, S4 Thin, D-75, D-75 Thin, Ultra-CAM, Tri-Colors, B50, TCD-150, Diamondback, Excellerant Braided, #5 Polyester Braid, #4 Twisted, #4 Sherwood Forest, Monofilament, CAM EZ and Liquid Lok, String Loop, Brownell Bowstring Server, Brownell Bowstring Jig, Bowstring Video, Wax Stick,30 DS, 30 DS DT, 40 DS

BROWNING
ONE BROWNING PLACE
MORGAN, UT 84050
801-876-2711
800-333-3288
Fax: 801-876-3331
www.browning.com
• Charles Guevremont, President
• Kraig Walker, Chief Financial Officer / Secretary
• Travis Hall, Senior VP
Products:
Firearms, Apparel, Gun Safes, Gun Cases, Knives, Lights, Accessories, Signature & Gifts, Footwear, Sport Optics
Brands:
T-Bolt, Cynergy, Silver, A-Bolt, Citori, BPS, BAR, Gold, BLR, Centerfire, Buckmark, BT-99

BRUNSWICK BICYCLE DIVISION
4902 HAMMERSLY ROAD
MADISON, WI 53711
847-573-0686
800-626-2811
Fax: 847-573-0602
www.mongoose.com
• George W Buckley, Chairman / Chief Executive Officer
• Dave Duecker, Brand Director
Products:
Bicycles, Protective Gear, BikeBoard, Bike Accessories, Saddles, Electric Scooters, Skateboards, Skateboard Gear
Brands:
Mongoose

BRUNSWICK CORPORATION
1 N FIELD COURT
LAKE FOREST, IL 60045-4811
847-735-4700
Fax: 847-735-4765
services@brunswick.com
www.brunswick.com
• Peter Hamilton, SVP/CFO
• Victoria Reich, VP / President - Brunswick European Grou
• Kathryn Chieger, VP Corporate / Investor Relations
• George W Buckley, Chairman / Chief Executive Officer
Products:
Boats, Marine Engines, Fitness Equipment, Bowling & Billiards Equipment, Brunswick New Technologies
Brands:
Albermatrie, Baja, Bayliner, Boston Whaler, Cabo, Crestliner, HarrisKayot, Hatteras, Lowe, Lund, Maxum, Meridian, Palmetto, Princecraft, Sea Boss, Sea Ray, Sealine, Triton, Trophy, Brunswick CGP, Attwood, Kellogg Marine, Land 'N' Sea, Mercury, MerCruiser, Mariner, Teignbridge, MotorGuide, Cummins-MerCruiser, Mercury Castings, Life Fitness, Hammer Strength, ParaBody, Brunswick Bowling, Brunswick Billiards, Valley-Dynamo, Navman, Northstar Technologies, IDS/Monolith, MotoTron, MX Marine

BRUTE GROUP
8 CORPORATE BOULEVARD
SINKING SPRING, PA 19608
610-678-4050
800-486-2788
Fax: 877-879-4040
info@brute.com
www.brute.com
• John W Purnell, Chief Executive Officer
• Tim Gardner, Sales Manager
Products:
Athletic Goods

BRUTE WRESTLING
8 CORPORATE BOULEVARD
SINKING SPRING, PA 19608
610-678-4050
800-486-2788
Fax: 610-678-4040
info@brute.com
www.brute.com
• Jeff Bowyer, National Sales Manager
• Mary Mallis, Director of Marketing and Communication

(610) 898-1705
mmallis@hensongroupsports.com
Products:
Wrestling Apparel and Accessories
Brands:
Adidas

BSI PRODUCTS
9510 BERGER ROAD
COLUMBIA, MD 21046
410-381-2596
888-381-2596
Fax: 410-995-6268
sales@bsiproducts.com
www.bsiproducts.com
Products:
Motorsports Licensed Products, Collegiate Licensed Products, NFL Licensed Products
Brands:
NASCAR, Nextel, Greg Biffle #16, Kyle Busch #5, Jack Daniels #7, Dale Earnhardt #3, Dale Earnhardt Jr. #8, Carl Edwards #99, Jeff Gordon #24, Kevin Harvick #29, Dale Jarrett #88, Jimmie Johnson #48, Kasey Kahne #9, Matt Kenseth #17, Mark Martin #6, Ryan Newman #12, Elliot Sadler #38, Tony Stewart #20, Brian Vickers #25, Rusty Wallace #2, Checkered, Chevy Racing, Ford Racing, Dodge Racing

BSN SPORTS
1901 DIPLOMAT
PO BOX 7726
DALLAS, TX 75209
972-484-9484
800-527-7510
Fax: 800-899-0149
feedbsn@sportssupplygroup.com
www.bsnsports.com
• John Walker, President
(972) 484-9484
• Dave Jones, Marketing Director
Products:
Athletic Goods
Brands:
Multisport Tabletop Electric Scoreboard, Jugs Lite Flite Practice Baseball, FenceMate, MacGregor, Voit, Easton, Rawlings, Micro-Mesh, GameCraft, Compact, Cramer, Wilson, Penn, PORTaPiT

BSN-JOBST, INC.
5825 CARNEGIE BOULEVARD
CHARLOTTE, NC 28209
704-554-9933
800-537-1063
Fax: 800-835-4325
BSN.Orders@BSNmedical.com
www.jobst-usa.com
• Claus Wiegel, President
• Jake Newman, Marketing Director
(704) 554-9933
jake.newman@bsnmedical.com
Products:
Support Wear, Sensifoot, Medical Legwear, Custom, Compression Bandages, Plastic/Post-Surgical Garments
Brands:
Jobstr

BUCK KNIVES, INC.
660 S LOCHSA STREET
POST FALLS, ID 83854-5200
208-262-0500
800-326-2825
Fax: 208-262-0738

pfstore@buckknives.com
www.buckknives.com
• Charles T Buck, Chairman / Chief
Executive Officer
• Charles B Buck, President
• Richard Konopasek, Finance VP / Chief
Financial Officer
• C J. Buck, CEO
Products:
Knives, Accessories, Apparel
Brands:
Buck Knives

BUFFALO EXPORT, LLC
99 S SPOKANE STREET
SEATTLE, WA 98134
206-682-9900 EXT 206
Fax: 206-682-9907
Larry@BuffaloExportLLC.com
www.buffaloexportllc.com
• Larry Benezra, President / Chief Executive
Officer
larry@buffaloexportllc.com
• Adam Benezra, Vice President
Products:
Baseball Caps; General Sports Products -
Imprinted Apparel, Sweatclothes.
Description:
Five-generation, family-owned business
selling used baseball caps and sports
equipment.

BUFFALO TURBINE
180 ZOAR VALLEY ROAD
SPRINGVILLE, NY 14141
716-592-2700
Fax: 716-592-2460
info@buffaloturbine.com
www.buffaloturbine.com
• Jody Smith, Advertising, Marketing
Auto Sports:
Official Debris Blower of the International
Hot Rod Association
Description of Company/Product Line:
Debris Blowers, Sprayers, Dusters, Dust
Suppression Systems, Top Dressers and
the SANDEVIL™ Attachment

BUGATTI
100 CONDOR STREET
BOSTON, MA 2128
617-567-7600
800-284-2887
Fax: 617-567-5541
www.bugatti.com

BULOVA WATCH COMPANY
ONE BULOVA AVENUE
WOODSIDE, NY 11377
718-204-3222
800-233-3350
Fax: 718-204-3546
service@bulova.com
www.bulova.com
• Fae Druiz, Vice President
fdruiz@bulova.com
Services:
Manufactures watches featuring the NBA
logo on the face of the watch. Bulova has a
complete line of NBA sports watches. Logos
include all NBA teams

BURTON SNOWBOARDS
80 INDUSTRIAL PARKWAY
BURLINGTON, VT 5401

800-881-3138
Fax: 802-660-3250
info@burton.com
global.burton.com
• Jake Burton, Chief Executive Officer
info@burton.com
• Laurent Potdevin, President / Chief
Operating Officer
info@burton.com
• Mike Abbott, Chief Financial Officer
info@burton.com
Products:
Snowboards, Snowboard Apparel,
Snowboard Accessories.

BUSHNELL CORPORATION
9200 CODY
OVERLAND PARK, KS 66214-1734
913-752-3400
800-423-3537
Fax: 913-752-3550
www.bolle.com
• Joe Messner, President
• Philip Gyori, VP Marketing / Bushnell
Products:
Eyewear - Sunglasses; Skiing-Alpine -
Goggles.
Brands:
Bounce, Demeanor, Heetseeker, J-Walker,
Limit, Meanstreak, Meltdown, Mercuria,
Pharmium, Sin City, Thunderstruck,
Valorium, Vanadium, Zyrium, Canebrake,
Chill, Envy, Groove, Mongrel, Morph, Orvet,
Piraja, Sidney, Sizzle, Spright, Spry,
Swisher, Downdraft, Slipstream, Windshear,
Kickback, Kicker, Parole, Supercell,
Turbulence, Upshot, Vigilante, Atlantic,
Laguna, Santa Marta, Tarpon, Scream, Jinx,
Nova, Shark, Zark, Nebula, Simmer, Stoke,
Boost, X500, Boost OTG, Bolle 1.0, Bolle
2.0, Shellmet

BUSHNELL SPORT OPTICS
9200 CODY
OVERLAND PARK, KS 66214-1734
913-752-3400
800-423-3537
Fax: 913-752-3550
www.bushnell.com
• Joseph Messner, Chief Executive Officer
• Dave Broadbent, Chief Financial Officer
• Blake Lipham, President & CEO
Products:
Binoculars, Night Vision, Laser
Rangefinders, Digital Products, Telescopes,
Spotting Scopes, Riflescopes, and Sports
Imaging.
Brands:
Bushnell, Browning, and Tasco.

**BUTLER BUILT MOTORSPORTS
EQUIPMENT**
70 PITTS SCHOOL ROAD NW
CONCORD, NC 28027
704-784-1027
800-621-7328
Fax: 704-784-1024
sales@butlerbuilt.net
www.butlerbuilt.net
• Brian Butler, President
sales@butlerbuilt.net
• Jeannie Butler, Secretary Treasury
sales@butlerbuilt.net
• Robert DeRosa, Sales Manager
sales@butlerbuilt.net
• Mark Linkous, Dealer-Wholesale Sales

Director
sales@butlerbuilt.net
Products:
Custom Seating, Standard Seating,
Accessories, Replacement Covers, Air
Management Systems, Aluminum Steering
Wheels, Restraint Systems, Technical
Assistance, Oil Tanks.

BVT PRODUCTS, LLC
8143 BRUMBY COURT
TRINITY, FL 34655
727-834-8944
Fax: 727-834-8722
vicki@bvtproducts.com
www.bvtproducts.com
• Vicki Forster, President
(727) 834-8944
vicki@bvtproducts.com
Products:
Water Bottle Carriers: The Go Caddy™ and
the Golfing Caddy™

C & H BASEBALL
2215 60TH DRIVE E
BRADENTON, FL 34203
941-727-1533
800-248-5192
Fax: 941-727-0588
sales@chbaseball.com
www.chbaseball.com
• Torrey Spears, Operations Manager
torrey@chbaseball.com
• Rob Huff, President
rob@chbaseball.com
• Danielle Huff, Vice President/Owner
danielle@chbaseball.com
• Torrey Spears, Operations Manager
Products:
Batting cages, fielding screens, batting
tunnels, windscreen, tarps, wallpadding,
bases, and pitching machines.
Year Founded:
1968
Description:
C&H Baseball is the industry leader in
supplying field equipment & batting cages
for Major League, minor league, colleges
and high schools around the nation.
Brands:
Schutt, Spalding, Jugs, Atec, C&H, Wilson

C. CRETORS & CO.
3243 N CALIFORNIA AVENUE
CHICAGO, IL 60618
773-588-1690
800-228-1885
Fax: 773-588-2171
solesen@cretors.com
www.cretors.com
• Gino A Nardulli, Marketing Director
Nature of Service:
Concessions Equipment and Portable
Stands.
Products:
Suspended Kettles, Pedestal Poppers,
Enclosed Cabinet, Open Cabinet, Giants
with Tables, Small Concession Poppers,
Cotton Candy, Warmer Cabinets, Hotdog
Grills & Bun Warmers, Topping &
Dispensing Systems, and Gourmet Retail
Equipment

C.N. IS BELIEVING
18 UNION STREET
WOLFEBORO, NH 3894

617-520-4079
Fax: 603-515-1181
www.nitelitesports.com
• Corky Newcomb, Owner/President
corkyn@cnisbelieving.com
• Nolan Antonucci, Marketing & PR
Co-ordinator
Products:
Baseball Balls, Metal and Wood Bats,
Pitching Machines; Field Hockey Balls;
Football Balls; Golf Ball Retrievers, Balls;
Ice Hockey Pucks; Lacrosse Balls; Tennis
Balls; Rugby Balls; Soccer Balls; Softball
Balls, Pitching Machines,lighted
glasses,light sticks

CABANA BANNERS
46946 217TH STREET
BROOKINGS, SD 57006
605-692-4580
800-697-3139
Fax: 605-692-6113
info@cabanabanners.com
www.cabanabanners.com
• Patti Nash, President / Chief Executive
Officer
info@cabanabanners.com
• Troy Dubois, Sales/Marketing
info@cabanabanners.com
• Jeff Pitts, Production Manager
info@cabanabanners.com
Products:
Athletic Banners

CABELA'S
ONE CABELA DRIVE
SIDNEY, NE 69160
308-254-6745
800-237-4444
800-237-4444
Fax: 308-254-7345
www.cabelas.com
• Dennis Highby, President / Chief
Executive Officer / Di
• Michael Callahan, SVP
• James Cabela, President
• Patrick A. Snyder, Merchandising SVP
• Dave Roehr, Finance VP
• Ralph Castner, VP / Chief Financial Officer
• Steven Krajewski, Real Estate Manager
Products:
Hunting, Fishing and Skiwear

CABLEFORM INC.
8845 THREE NOTCH ROAD
TROY, VA 22974
434-589-8224
Fax: 434-589-3803
sales@cableform.com
www.cableform.com
• Andrew L. Thexton, President
athexton@Cableform.com
Products:
Field Communications Equipment; Battery
Powered Electronic Megaphones.
Brands:
Alert Hailer, Audio Guider, Audio Hailer,
Hailer Alert, Hailer Jr., Little Yeller, Super
Hailer

CALLAWAY GOLF
2180 RUTHERFORD ROAD
CARLSBAD, CA 92008-7328
760-931-1771
800-588-9836
Fax: 760-930-5015

info@callawaygolf.com
www.callawaygolf.com
• George Fellows, President / Chief
Executive Officer
gfellows@callawaygolf.com
• Oliver S. Brewer III, Chief Executive
Officer, President & Director
Products:
Golf Clubs - Wood/Iron Sets.
Brands:
Big Bertha Metal Woods and Irons, Great
Big Bertha II Titanium Drivers and Fairway
Woods, Big Bertha Steelhead(TM) III
Stainless Steel Drivers and Fairway Woods,
Hawk Eye VFT Tungsten Injected(TM)
Titanium Irons, Big Bertha Stainless Steel
Irons

CAMERA SPORTSEAT, INC.
5517 STATE ROAD
WADSWORTH, OH 44281
330-425-3035
800-649-5261
Fax: 480-990-2088
www.camerasportseat.com
• Hob A. Zabarsky, President
(440) 582-0122
camerasportseat@hotmail.com
• Bill Heideman, Design Engineer
(480) 874-3359
camerasportseat@hotmail.com
Products:
Manufacturer of low profile portable and
permanent camera mounts for TV broadcast
with seated operator which reduces or
eliminates sightline problems for spectators
seated behind cameras.
Year Founded:
1994

CAMOFACE
4275 THUNDERBIRD LANE
CINCINNATI, OH 45246
877-671-2800
www.camoface.com
Services:
Sports team/design face and body painting.

CAMPUS OUTFITTERS
2525 DRANE FIELD RD.
SUITE 11
COLLEGE PARK, MD 20740
888-923-0700
Fax: 301-220-0368
www.rissebrothers.com
Products:
Collegiate Embroidered Sportswear

CANAMER INT'L, LLC
5701 INDUSTRIAL PARK ROAD
WINONA, MN 55987
507-452-1700
800-533-8020
Fax: 507-452-1784
info@canamer.com
www.canamer.com
• Marie Eglinton, Area Sales Representative
ext 104
marier@canamer.com
• Thomas Scott, Sales Manager
ext 105
Products:
Athletic Field Covers, Gym Floor Covers,
Wind Screens, Tennis Courts, Gym
Curtains, Golf Courses and Pond Liners.
Brands:
Polycan™

CANNONDALE BICYCLE CORPORATION
16 TROWBRIDGE ROAD
BETHEL, CT 6801
203-749-7000
800-245-3872
Fax: 203-748-4012
custserv@cannondale.com
www.cannondale.com
• Dan Alloway, Sales and European
Operations VP
custserv@cannondale.com
• Scott Montgomery, Marketing VP
custserv@cannondale.com
Products:
Cycling - Apparel, Bicycles, Bike Bags,
Components, Pumps, Racks, Trailers,
Water Bottles.
Brands:
Coda

CANON U.S.A.
ONE CANON PARK
MELVILLE, NY 11747
631-330-5000
Fax: 516-328-5069
pr@cusa.canon.com
www.usa.canon.com
• Joe Adachi, President & CEO
• Fujio Mitarai, Chairman & CEO
Services:
NFL - Cameras & Equipment, Binoculars;
PGA Tour - Official Copier, Fax,
Multi-Function Printer, Printer, Scanner,
Camera and Binocular of the PGA Tour and
Champions Tour.

CANVAS NURSERY INC
2130-A ANDREA LANE
FORT MYERS, FL 33912
239-433-3335
800-226-3335
Fax: 239-790-2617
canvas@thecanvasnursery.com
www.thecanvasnursery.com
Products:
Handcrafted artificial trees, plants and
foliage in tropical styles using cotton canvas
for interior facilities and stadiums.

CAP BARBELL
3400 ROGERDALE ROAD
HOUSTON, TX 77042
713-977-3090
877-227-0955
Fax: 713-977-3099
CustomerService@capbarbell.com
www.capbarbell.com
Products:
Bar & Handles; Benches & Racks; Free
Weights; Home Gym Accessories;
Additional Manufacturers Parts

CAPITOL PARTITIONS, INC
9199 RED BRANCH ROAD
COLUMBIA, MD 21045
410-740-8870
Fax: 410-740-8865
info@capitolpartitions.com
www.capitolpartitions.com
• James Arnaiz, President
info@capitolpartitions.com
• Patricia Arnaiz, Marketing VP
emsis@smart.net
Products:
Toilet partitions, unit showers, washroom
vanities and related products. Flooring
products and finishes. Cubicles, Modular

manufacturers/retailers

Office Furniture, Office Chairs, Office Partitions

CAPO INC./PANAMA JACK
2 SUNSHINE BOULEVARD
ORMOND BEACH, FL 32174
800-282-7696
Fax: 386-672-8720
www.capo.com
• Jack Hewitt, VP
jhewitt@capo.com
• Teresa Cox, President
Products:
Sunglasses and visors for athletes and fans alike.
Brands:
Angler Eyes, Crown, Crystal Vision, Extreme Optiks, Healthwear, Just Add Kids, Junior Varsity, Lensis by Polaroid, NASCAR, Visual

CARAVAN PROTECTIVE CASES
25 HAWTHORNE STREET
ELYRIA, OH 44035
800-477-6780
Fax: 440-366-1809
• Richard Galbraith, President / Sales
(800) 477-6780
• Chuck Patton, Sales / Engineering
(800) 477-6780
Products:
Athletic Cases, Audio Cases, Classical Instrument Cases, Computer Cases, Drawer Cases, Lighting Cases, Medical Cases, Category Cases, Production/Office, Truck Pack Utility Cases, Video Cases

CARBITE GOLF COMPANY
5816 DRYDEN PLACE
CARLSBAD, CA 92008
760-929-1410
800-272-4325
Fax: 760-929-1360
www.carbitegolf.com
• Chuck Jones, President/Chief Executive Officer
info@carbitegolf.com
• Donna Carson, National Sales Manager
info@carbitegolf.com
• Peter Maglaque, Vice President
• Mike Nelson, Customer Service
Nature of Service:
Manufacturer
Products:
Putters and Wedges - Putterballs
Brands:
Carbite

CARBONMAX SPORTS TECHNOLOGY, INC.
603 L STREET
LINCOLN, NE 68508
800-247-7668
Fax: 800-638-0698
www.carbonmax.com
Products:
Volleyball - Net Systems; Nets, Padding, Posts
Brands:
CarbonMax

CARD EMPORIUM
8028 HIGHWAY 55
GOLDEN VALLEY, MN 55427
763-541-1340
877-709-9585

Fax: 952-417-8146
info@sportbeads.com
www.sportbeads.com
Products:
Collectible cards of sports figures.

CARDIOSPORT
DRAGOON HOUSE, HUSSAR COUR
WATERLOOVILLE, PO7 7SF
-44-225-7388
888-760-3059
Fax: -44-225-7399
• Russell Baier, Vice President
(631) 274-3248
Products:
Heart rate monitors. GO Range, GT Range, Fusion Range, Accessories range. Contour lite chest belt with changeable battery system.
Brands: Reebok: RS1, RS11, RS111, Cardiosport

CARDS PLUS
PO BOX 131551
STATEN ISLAND, NY 10308
718-966-4250
800-231-9454
Fax: 718-966-4250
cardsplus01@aol.com
www.cardsplus.com
Products:
Collectible cards of sports and other celebrity figures.

CARIBOU MOUNTAINEERING
400 COMMERCE ROAD
ALICE, TX 78332
361-668-3766
800-824-4153
Fax: 361-668-3769
• Richard Current, President
Products:
Camping/Outdoor Products - Accessories, Daypacks, Fanny Packs, Hiking Packs, Luggage, Sleeping Bags.

CARROM COMPANY
218 E DOWLAND STREET
PO BOX 649
LUNDINGTON, MI 49431-2309
231-845-1263
800-223-6047
Fax: 231-843-9276
customerservice@carrom.com
www.carrom.com
• Terri Dima, Sales/Marketing Coordinator
(231) 845-1263
dima@carrom.com
• Michael McAvay, Sales
(231) 845-1263
mcavay@carrom.com
• Robert Fortuna, Sales
(231) 845-1263
fortuna@carrom.com
Products:
Air Powered Hockey, Foosball, Stick Hockey, Basketball
Brands:
Carrom®, Dueke®, Rochelle®

CARRON NET COMPANY, INC.
1623-17TH STREET
PO BOX 177
TWO RIVERS, WI 54241-0177
920-793-2217
800-558-7768

Fax: 920-793-2122
sales@carronnet.com
www.carronnet.com
• Bill Kiel, Jr, President/CEO
Year Founded:
1934.
Products:
Sports nets, Volleyball nets, Basketball nets, Tennis nets & tennis posts, Soccer nets & goal nets, Baseball batting cage nets, Backstop & foul ball nets, Golf nets, Wallyball nets, Nets to enclose athletic courts, Nets to enclose soccer fields, Stadium.

CARTS OF COLORADO, INC.
5420 S QUEBEC
SUITE 204
GREENWOOD VILLAGE, CO 80111
303-329-0101
800-227-8634
Fax: 303-329-6577
carts@cartsofcolorado.com
www.cartsofcolorado.com
• Dan Gallery, Sales
(800) 227-8634
dagallery@cartsofcolorado.com
• Jeff Clark, Parts & Service
Products:
Produce mobile and modular merchandising units used in retailing of food and beverages, hard goods, and various specialty products. Specialize in custom designs, free-standing kiosk units, and modular designs can be disassembled.

CASCO/USA
RR 7 BOX 1972
AUGUSTA, ME 04330
207-623-2918
Fax: 724-746-8500
• Peter J. Tambone, President / Chief Executive Officer
• Barbara Tambone, VP Sales
Products:
Training Room Supplies - Ankle Wraps, Finger Splints, Leg Guards, Rib Guards, Neoprene Supports.
Brands:
Casco, Castiglia

CASSEMCO, INC.
1595 LEMON FARRIS ROAD
COOKEVILLE, TN 38506
931-528-6588
800-844-3626
Fax: 931-528-2290
www.cassemco.com
• Jerry G. Samon, General Manager
(931) 528-6588
jsamon@live.com
• Sam Moody, Director of Operations
(931) 528-6588
• Ernie Julian, Director of Engineering & Q.A.
(931) 528-6588
• Scott Ward, Director of Business Development
(931) 528-6588
• Stuart Norris, Midwest Territory Manager
(931) 528-6588
• Eleanor Hooks, Production Coordinator/Shipping/Rec.
(931) 528-6588
ewhite@cassemco.com
• Mary Smith, Accounting Supervisor/ Office Manager

(931) 528-6588
msmith@cassemco.com
Services:
Foam and soft-goods fabricator offering die
cut and profiled products made from all
types of foam. Areas of expertise: Die
Cutting, Profile Cutting,
Sheeting/Convoluting, Contract Sewing,
Private Label Packaging, Adhesive
Application

CASTAWAY COLLECTIBLES
1480 S HOHOKUM
TEMPE, AZ 85281
602-337-3700
800-952-0708
Fax: 602-337-3790
RCCAInfo@lionelnascar.com
www.lionelnascarcollectibles.com
• Howard Hitchcock, Vice President and
General Manager
Products:
Produces the most respected racing
collectibles in the industry.
Brands:
Action Racing Collectables (ARC), the
Racing Collectables Club of America
(RCCA), Revell Collection, Winner's Circle,
and Chase Authentics

CATEK SNOWBOARD BINDINGS
PO BOX 5111
NEWPORT, RI 2841
401-624-8999
Fax: 401-624-8999
info@catek.com
Products:
Snowboard bindings, parts, accessories and
late model parts
Brands:
Coiler, Donek, Madd, Pogo, Prior, Virus

CCM HOCKEY
3400 RAYMOND-LASNIER
MONTREAL, QC, CANADA H4R 3L3
800-451-4600
800-636-5895 (CAN)
Fax: 514-461-8020
ccmhockey.com/en
• Matthew O'Toole, CMO, Head of Global
Marketing
• Philippe Dube, President and Chief
Executive Officer
• Jamie Coughlin, VP Of Sales
Products:
Ice Hockey - Bags-Equipment, Gloves,
Helmets, Masks, Protective, Skates,
Uniforms.
Brands:
CCM, JOFA, KOHO, Heaton

CDM SPORT
816 LADERA DRIVE
FORT WORTH, TX 76108
817-448-8908
800-400-7542
Fax: 817-448-8701
steve@cdmsport.com
www.cdmsport.com
• Steve McGee, President
steve@cdmsport.com
• Wren Barnett, Office Manager
wren@cdmsport.com
Products:
Monitored Rehab Systems, Instant Replays,
BackSystem, Core Strength Rack,
Electro-Therapy

Brands:
Backsystems, Shark, FMS, Pneumex,
Stronglite, Flexmonitor, Monitored Rehab
Systems, Rehab Education, The Golf
Channel, Angler

CELLO PROFESSIONAL PRODUCTS
1354 OLD POST ROAD
HAVRE DE GRACE, MD 21078
800-638-4850
800-638-4850
Fax: 410-939-3028
RBlankenship@carrollco.com
www.cello-online.com
• Thomas Ferraro, Account Manager
(631) 271-8578
• David Hazman, Sales Manager
(800) 638-5990
• Leon Ewell, Sales Manager
(800) 638-5990
• Larry F Nedrow, Executive Vice President
Products:
Floor Care Products, Carpet Care Products,
Cleaners/Degreasers,
Disinfectants/Restroom, Specialty Products,
& Dilution Control
Brands:
Armakote, Commander, Perma-Gloss Plus,
20 Plus, HTF High Traffic Floor Finish, HTF
25 High Traffic Floor Finish, Dimensions,
Victory, Paramount, Cellobrate, Oracle,
Hi-Production Spray Buff, About Face Spray
Buff, Hi-Beam, Dress Up, Silver Streak,
Glitz, Cello Seal, Cellothane 25, Clear
Concrete Seal, Down & Up, Kleen Strip,
Pulverize Dimensions Floor Finish Striper,
Mop 'n Strip, Deep Strip, Neutra Strip,
Ammoniated Cleaner Striper, On & Off,
Floor Care Neutralizer, Carpet Restoration
Pre-Spray, Grease-X Traffic Lane Cleaner &
Pre-Oil Break, The Natural, Freeze Gum &
Candle Wax Remover

CENTAUR FLOOR SYSTEMS, LLC
963 N. SAN MAREAS RD
SANTA BARBARA, CA 93111
805-957-0182
800-536-9007
Fax: 805-957-0125
www.centaurfloors.com
• John Donati, Owner
(800) 536-7007
john@centaurfloors.com
• Jim Langhorn, Co-Owner
• Terri Cruz, Order Processing
• Peter Hernandez, Bookkeeper
Products:
Flooring - Fitness, Recreational. Flooring
Surfaces Include: Rubber, Wood, Multi
Sport, Tracks, Specs.
Brands:
Boflex, Rubberflex, Gymlastic Sports Floor,
Sportweave, Bolon
Year Founded:
1997

CENTRALIA KNITTING MILLS, INC.
1002 W MAIN STREET
CENTRALIA, WA 98531
360-736-3994
Fax: 800-723-4317
• Dorothy Thoreson, President
• Ralph E. Thoreson, Vice President
Products:
Letterman Jackets, Corporate Apparel,
Embroidery, Sweaters, Chenille, Blankets
and Banners

Brands:
Frank Troeh, Octonek, Skookum Sportswear

CENTURY INDUSTRIES, LLC
299 PRATHR STREET
SELLERSBURG, IN 47172
812-246-3371
800-248-3371
Fax: 812-246-5446
www.centuryindustries.com

CENTURY SPORTS, INC.
1995 RUTGERS UNIVERSITY
BOULEVARD
PO BOX 2035
LAKEWOOD, NJ 08701-8035
732-905-4422
800-526-7548
Fax: 732-905-7766
sales@centurysportsinc.com
www.centurysportsinc.com
• Timothy Fogarty, President
Products:
Eyewear - Protective; Racquet Sports,
Badminton Equipment, Gloves, Platform
Tennis Equipment, Racquet Grips, Racquet
Strings, Racquet Stringing Machines,
Shoes, Socks, Squash Equipment, Wilson
Tennis Court Equipment
Year Founded:
1972
Brands:
Wilson
Clients:
All tennis end-user facilities in US and
around the world.

CEO MANUFACTURERS
1111 BUNKER HILL ROAD
HOUSTON, TX 77055
713-467-6899
800-231-3568
Fax: 713-467-2505
• Carlos Kuri, President
Products:
General Sports Products - Ladies
Coordinates & Short Sets.
Brands:
Manufacturer, Custom House

CERASPORT
55 MATHEWS DRIVE
SUITE 220
HILTON HEAD, SC 29926
842-842-2600
888-237-2598
customerservice@ceraproducts.us
www.ceraproductsinc.com
• Charlene Da Riikonen, Founder
(410) 309-1000
• Esko Riikonen, Founder
• Mark Perlotto, Executive Vice President
and General Manager
• Jennifer Rapp, Director of Marketing
(410) 309-1000
Products:
Nutritional supplements and energy drinks.
Brands:
CeraLyte 50, CeraLyte70, CeraLyte 90,
CeraLyte 50 Ready-to-drink, CeraLyte Cera
Mixed Sampler Pack, Cera Sport Berry
Sport Flavor Powder Pouch

CHAMPION BALL COMPANY
3800 DURBIN STREET
IRWINDALE, CA 91706

626-960-2100
888-464-5646
Fax: 626-960-2050
info@championball.com
www.championball.com
• Andrew Barajas, Sales Executive & Trade
Show Manager
andrew@championball.com
Products:
Basketballs, Footballs, Volleyballs, Soccer
Balls, Playground Balls, Playball, Tether
Balls, and Customized Balls
Brands:
Western Star, Mavericks, Outback
Steakhouse, Kid Size PVC Soccer, Cheez
It, Soccor (Galaxy), Soccor(Otto)

CHAOS SNOWBOARDS
8614 ARGENT STREET
SUITE E
SANTEE, CA 92071
619-258-9911
888-4424-267
Fax: 619-258-1383
web@chaossnowboards.com
www.chaossnowboards.com
• Roselynn Brown, President
web@chaossnowboards.com
• Frank Saputo, Owner
Products:
Snowboarding - Apparel, Bindings,
Snowboards.
Brands:
Bratz, Carbon, Dead Knight, Fat Boy, Kaos,
Phantom, Poison, Pure Carbon, Snow
Goddess, Snow Princess

CHECKERED FLAG SPORTS
545 HOLLIE DRIVE
MARTINSVILLE, VA 24112
276-666-3000
800-278-1940
Fax: 800-240-3382
info@southprintinc.com
www.checkeredflagsports.com
• Debbie Simmons, Customer Service
(276) 666-3000

CHEER KIDS
1315 SUNDAY DRIVE
INDIANAPOLIS, IN 46217-9334
317-780-0609
800-869-0609
800-864-6315
Fax: 317-780-4188
www.cheerkids.com
• Kaitlyn Keller, Contact
• Chuck Pugh, Executive VP Sales &
Marketing
(317) 780-0609
• Tina Mollis, Product Manager of Dance
Products:
Cheer Uniforms, Jewelry, and Accessories

CHRISTIAN BROTHERS, INC.
416 PIRKLE FERRY ROAD
BUILDING I
CUMMING, GA 30040
770-619-2855
Fax: 770-619-0123
contact@cbigc.com
www.cbigc.com
• Thomas Slaird, Chief Operating Officer
• Bill Christian, VP
(800) 346-5055
• Daniel Nielsen, President

Products:
Activewear; Ice Hockey Protective, Sticks;
In-Line Hockey Protective, Sticks.

CHUCK ROAST EQUIPMENT, INC.
ODELL HILL ROAD
PO BOX 2080
CONWAY, NH 03818-2080
603-447-5492
800-533-1654
Fax: 603-447-2277
custserv@chuckroast.com
www.chuckroast.com
• Charles Henderson, President
• Laurie Perkins, Marketing
Products:
Cycling Apparel; Skiing-Alpine
Apparel-Outerwear; Skiing-Nordic
Apparel-Outerwear.
Brands:
UNH, New Hampshire, Camp Belknap,
Stonyfield Farm, Maranacook Nordic, Dave
Matthews Band, The HBOMax, NHS,
Calumet, NH Public Radio, Wausau Papers
Safety, Jen's Friends Cancer Foundation

CIMCO REFRIGERATION
65 VILLIERS STREET
TORONTO, CANADA M5A 3S1
416-465-7581
Fax: 416-465-8815
www.cimcorefrigeration.com
• Steve McLeod, President
smcleod@toromont.com
Products:
Refrigeration equipment, such as heat
exchangers and pressure vessels,
packaged refrigeration systems, electrical
control panels and microprocessor control
systems for sports facilities.
Brands:
H.A. Phillips, Alco, Henry, Penn, Hubbell,
Refrigeration Specialties, Honeywell, Lau,
Danfoss, Paragon, Sporlan, Hansen
Technologies

CINCINNATI GAMES
PO BOX 18
KINGS MILLS, OH 45034
513-298-1123
866-574-9330
Products:
Tally Table, Premium Quality Wood Game
Boards, Premium Heavy Duty Bags
Brands:
The Cincinnati Corn Bag Game

CLASSIC MEDALLICS, INC.
520 S FULTON AVENUE
MOUNT VERNON, NY 10550
914-530-6259
800-221-1348
Fax: 800-541-3821
sales@classic-medallics.com
www.classic-medallics.com
• Gerald Singer, President
sales@classic-medallics.com
Year Founded:
1941.
Products:
Medallions Inserts; Medals; Ribbons;
Keyrings with Medals; Pins; Plaques,
Frames, Clocks; Traditional Trophies; Resin
Stoned Trophies; Scholastic Resin Trophies;
Sports & Fireman Trophies; Trophy Cups;
Bowls & Trays; Mugs & Coasters; Corp.
Gifts & Awards; Custom Products.

CLASSIC PRODUCTS
4617 INDUSTRIAL ROAD
FORT WAYNE, IN 46825
260-484-2695
800-444-0123
Fax: 260-483-7421
webmaster@classicproducts.com
www.classicproducts.com
• Robert Gudorf, EVP
webmaster@classicproducts.com
Products:
Bowling supplies

CLASSIC SPORT COMPANIES INC
5151 BANNOCK STREET
SUITE D
DENVER, CO 80216
303-991-8010
800-225-5712
Fax: 720-294-8333
Products:
Table Hockey, Table Soccer, Rod Hockey,
Combo Tables, Billiards, Table Tennis,
Basketball Games, Basketball, Soccer,
Football, Vollyball, Accessories, Goals,
Specialty Balls & Games, Croquet, Bocce,
Horseshoes, Combination Games,
Tetherball

CLEVELAND GOLF COMPANY
5601 SKYLAB ROAD
HUNTINGTON BEACH, CA 92647
714-889-1300
800-999-6263
Fax: 714-889-5890
www.clevelandgolf.com
• Bruno Cercley, Chairman
• Greg Hopkins, President
Products:
Clubs (Woods, Irons, Wedges, Hybrids,
Putters, Women's, Juniors)
Brands:
Woods (Launcher 460 Comp Driver,
Launcher Comp Fairway Woods); Irons (CGI
Black Pearl Irons, CGI Irons); Wedges
(CG11 Wedges, CG11 Black Pearl
Wedges); Hybrids (HALO Hybrid Utility,
LDI); Putters (Design By 1905, Design by
1948); Women's (Launcher Ti460, Launcher
Steel, W-Series Launcher Irons, W-Series
TA6 irons, W-Series CG11, 588W's,
W-Series Halo); Juniors (Gold Model, Silver
Model)

CLIF BAR
1610 5TH STREET
BERKELEY, CA 94710-1715
800-254-3227
800-254-3227
www.clifbar.com
• Gary Erickson, Owner
Nature of Service:
Energy bar maker that uses a healthy
combination of protein, carbohydrates,
vitamins and minerals, that delivers a
moderate, sustained increase in blood sugar
levels, the nutrition for sustained energy that
athletes and other active people need for
peak performance.
Brands:
Clif Bar, Luna Bar, Mojo Bar and Clif Shot.
Cycling Sponsor:
Reach the Beach, Deathride, Seattle to
Portland Bicycle Classic, Hotter-N-Hell 100.
Mountain Biking: WORS MTB Series, 24
Hours of Adrenaline, Niketown Run for the
Parks, Sea Otter Classic, 24 Hours of

Adrenaline at Laguna Seca, Pedro's Mountain Bike Festival, 24 Hours of Adrenaline Idyllwild.
Marathons:
LA Marathon, Canyonlands Half Marathon, Catalina Marathon, John Hancock Sports & Fitness Expo (Boston Marathon), SLC Marathon and 5k, Flying Pig Marathon, Helvatia Half Marathon, Grandma's Marathon, Seafair Marathon, AFC Half Marathon, Twin Cities Marathon, Tucson Marathon, California International Marathon, Dallas White Rock Marathon.
Triathlons:
Escape from Alcatraz Triathlon, San Diego International Triathlon, River Cities Triathlon, Los Angeles Triathlon.

CLIFF KEEN ATHLETIC INC.
4480 VARSITY DRIVE
SUITE B
ANN ARBOR, MI 48108
734-975-8800
800-992-0799
Fax: 800-590-0759
info@cliffkeen.com
www.cliffkeen.com
• James C. Keen, Chief Executive Officer
info@cliffkeen.com
• Thomas P. Keen, President
info@cliffkeen.com
• Barry Bellaire, General Manager
info@cliffkeen.com
• Mary Tolle, Controller
info@cliffkeen.com
• Chad Clark, Vice President/ Sales & Marketing
• James Ralston, Sales Manager
• Jan Dobbs, Executive Administrator
Description:
Leading manufacturer of wrestling equipment and officials wear.

CLIMAX MANUFACTURES
3820 OCEANIC DRIVE
SUITE 311
OCEANSIDE, CA 92056
760-722-1455
Fax: 760-967-0554
www.trackertrucks.com
• Larry Balma, Founder
Products:
Tracker Trucks, Accessories, Gear, Decks, Quads, Books/Mags & Movies Orion Trucks, Replacement Parts, Hardware
Brands:
Tracker Axis, Tracker Red and White, New Kevin Staab Purple Signature Tracker, Slalom Tracker Custom Offset Limited Edition Racetrack Model, Tracker RT-S & RT-X Models, Magnesium, New Tracker, Classic Wing

CLOUDBURST INC.
707 E. HUENEME ROAD
SUITE B
OXNARD, CA 93033
805-986-4125
800-800-5479
Fax: 805-715-0514
info@cloudburst.com
www.cloudburst.com
• Mike Davis, President
mdavis@cloudburst.com
• Steve Wright, President / Public Relations
Sports Dire
swright@cloudburst.com

Products:
Electric Housewares and Fans (Misting Fan Kits, Pump Modules, Fixed Lined Systems, Portable Coolers, Sideline Systems, Satellite Fans, Misting Nozzles, Mist Rings, Mist Lines, Water Filtration, Brass Fittings, Hoses, Water Tanks, Starter Systems & Kits, Extensions & Hoses, Misting Nozzles, Compression Fittings, Accessories, Merchandising Displays)
Brands:
Cloudburst, Mist&Cool

CLUB CAR, INC.
4125 WASHINGTON ROAD
PO BOX 204658
EVANS, GA 30809
706-863-3000
800-258-2227
Fax: 706-863-5808
www.clubcar.com
• Philip Tralies, President / Chief Executive Officer
p.tralies@clubcar.com
• Marc A. Dufour, President & CEO
Products:
Golf Cars, Turf Vehicles
Brands:
Precedent, DS Electric Golf Car-IQ System, DS Gas Golf Car, Carryall 294, Carryall Turf 1, Carryall Turf 2, Carryall Turf 272, Turf 252, Carryall Turf 6

CLUB GLOVE
17811 JAMESTOWN LANE
HUNTINGTON BEACH, CA 92647
714-843-9288
800-736-4568
info@clubglove.com
www.clubglove.com
• Jim Jamison, Director of Operations
(714) 843-9288
Products:
Golf Bags
Brands:
Elephant Vinyl Cart Bag, Ballistic Nylon Cart Bag, Hotstepper, Aficionado III

CLUBHOUSEKIT
1545 HIGHWAY 9
TOMS RIVER, NJ 8755
732-240-6900
800-553-4726
Fax: 732-240-3599
www.clubhousekit.com
• Brad Singer, President
(877) 258-2548
Nature of Service:
Full line of amenities for the clubhouse or lockerroom including industrial strength cleaning products designed exclusively for the outdoor sports market.
Products:
Grass & Blood Eliminator, Athletic Equipment Cleaner, Protective Headgear Disinfectant, Athletic Equipment Polish, Claymate Clay Remover, Pro-Detergent with Color-safe Bleach, Duffel Bag Deodorizer, Pine Tar, Glove Oil, Rosin Bag, Shoe Polish, Pine Tar Remover, Hat Cleaner
Brands:
Clubhouse Kit

COBBLESTONES ACTIVEWEAR
7095 W 3500 S
WEST VALLEY CITY, UT 84128

801-250-1865
800-592-7195
Fax: 801-250-6099
CustomerService@cobblestones.com
www.gamegear.com
• Mark Osborn, President
(801) 382-6514
• Clayton Osborn, Marketing, Sales
(801) 382-6564
• Patti Osborn-Bell, Accounting
(801) 382-6513
• Randy Haun, Information System
(801) 250-4500
• Cade Osborn, President
(801) 382-6566
Products:
Activewear for Baseball, Softball, Basketball, Aerobics / Cheerleader, Football, Phys Ed/Camp

COBRA PUMA GOLF
1818 ASTON AVENUE
CARLSBAD, CA 92008
800-917-3300
800-843-5464
Fax: 760-929-0374
customerservice@cobragolf.com
www.cobragolf.com
• Robert Dubiel, President
robert@cobragolf.com
• Mark C. McClure, Chief Executive Officer & Director
• Jeff Harmet, President
• Robert K. Bruning, Chief Financial Officer
• David A. Schaefer, Senior VP & Chief Operating Officer
Products:
Drivers, Fairways, Utility Metals Irons
Brands:
Drivers - King Cobra X/Speed, King Cobra F/Speed, King Cobra M/Speed, King Cobra M/Speed Seniors', King Cobra M/Speed Women's, King Cobra 454 COMP, King Cobra 414 Comp, King Cobra 414 Comp Tour; Fairways - King Cobra X/Speed, King Cobra F/Speed, King Cobra M/Speed, King Cobra M/Speed Seniors', King Cobra M/Speed Women's, King Cobra COMP Fairways, Utility Metals - King Cobra Baffler Men's & Seniors', King Cobra Baffler Women's; Irons - King Cobra Men's 2300 I/M, King Cobra Men's 3400 I/XH, King Cobra Senior's 3400 I/XH, King Cobra Women's 3400 I/XH, King Cobra Men's 3100 I/H, King Cobra Senior's 3100 I/H, King Cobra Women's 3100 I/H, King Cobr

COED SPORTSWEAR INC
27 PLEASANT STREET
NEWFIELDS, NH 3856
603-772-1990
800-926-6578
Fax: 603-772-0351
donl@coedsportswear.com
www.coedsportswear.com
• Mark Lane, Co-Founder/ President
ext 106
mark@coedsportswear.com
• Scott MacHardy, Co-founder / VP
(603) 772-1990
• Selim Tobey, Vice President- Sales
selim@coedsportswear.com
Products:
Imprinted T-shirts, sweatshirts, and various other tops; boxer shorts; athletic shorts and headwear
Brands:
It's All About, The Power of a Girl, Coed

manufacturers/retailers

Naked, Corona, Rebel Flag, Soccer Mom, Post Card Past, Life's A Bass, Go Figure, Miller Lite, Miller High Life, Snuggleball, Definitions, Coots & Biddy's

COLBOND, INC.
PO BOX 1057
ENKA, NC 28728
828-665-5050
800-365-7391
Fax: 828-665-5009
info@colbond-usa.com
www.colbond-usa.com
• Axel Poscher, Vice President
• Tim Woodlee, Sales and Marketing Manager, NAFTA
(828) 665-5016
tim.woodlee@colbond.com
• Heather Rohde, Profile Products LLC - Exclusive Distributor
(847) 215-3454
• Don Brown, Sales, Automotive, Filtration Colback Support
(828) 665-5075
don.brown@colbond.com
• Greg Wood, Composites Media, Filtration Enkamat Spacer M
(828) 665-5084
greg.wood@colbond.com
• Richard Goodrum, Geosynthetics
(828) 665-5023
richard.goodrum@colbond.com
• Shelia Snyder, Geosynthetics, Roofing Membrane Reinforcement
(828) 665-5069
shelia.snyder@colbond.com
• Debbie Bailey, Customer Service, Athletic Fields
(828) 665-5013
debbie.bailey@colbond.com
Products:
Matrix and nonwoven products
Brands:
Colback Original, Colbonddrain, Easy Tuft, Enkadrain, Enkadri & Drain, EnkaFusion, EnkagridGolf Drain, Enkagrid, Enkamat, Enkamat II, EnkamatPlus, EnkaPath, Enkaroof Vent, Enkaroof VM, EnkaShoreline, Enkasonic, EnkaTrap, Enkaturf Drain, Enkavent, Home Slicker, MFM, Mortar Break, Mortar Break II, Mortar Catch

COLEMAN COMPANY INC.
1767 DENVER W BOULEVARD
SUITE 200
GOLDEN, CO 80401
316-832-2700
800-835-3278
Fax: 316-832-3060
newsroom@coleman.com
www.coleman.com
• Gary A. Kiedaisch, President / Chief Executive Officer
gary@coleman.com
• Nancy Paulson, Global Human Resources SVP
nancy@coleman.com
• Robert A. Markovitch, President & CEO
Products:
Tents and Shelters, Stoves Lighting, Inflatables, Sleeping Bags, Sleeping Pads, Roadtrip Grill, Heaters, Outdoor Fireplaces, Coolers, Gear for Pets, Water Recreation, Mosquito Control, Hot Water Systems, Furniture, Grills & Accessories, Backpacks, Accessories, Storage, Cookware, Emergency Gear, Boats, Outlet Store, Spas,

Footwear, Sunglasses, Heating & Cooling, Watches, Cargo Carriers, Exponent, Airpumps, Blankets, Coolers, Airbeds, Cookware, Emergency Gear, Beds & Cots, Inflatable Boats & Kayaks
Brands:
Coleman

COLOR SIGN SERVICE, INC.
11096 61ST STREET NE
PO BOX 124
ALBERTVILLE, MN 55301
763-497-1374
800-497-2141
Fax: 763-497-1375
www.colorsign.com
Products:
Color Sign Systems (Message Centers, Time & Temp, Scoreboards, I.D. Signs, Ground Directional, Signs)

COLORADO DISPLAY SYSTEMS
1551 E 11TH STREET
LOVELAND, CO 80537
970-667-1000
800-299-0111
Fax: 970-667-5876
www.coloradodisplay.com
• Anita Sayed, President / Chief Executive Officer
Commercial Products:
Billboards/Video Display; Marquees; Information Boards; Highway Transportation Signage; Flight Information System

COLORADO TIME SYSTEMS
1551 E 11TH STREET
LOVELAND, CO 80537
970-667-1000
800-299-0111
Fax: 970-667-5876
info@coloradotime.com
www.coloradotime.com
• Anita Sayed, President/Chief Executive Officer
Products:
Arena: Full Matrix LED Socreboards; Light-reflective Scoreboards and Products. Ribbon and Fuscia Boards, same for Stadiums and Natatoriums.

COLUMBIA 300, INC.
1813 W 7TH STREET
PO BOX 13430
HOPKINSVILLE, KY 42240
270-881-1300
800-626-8350
Fax: 270-881-1201
www.columbia300.com
• Ronald J. Herrmann, Chief Executive Officer
• Mike Allbritton, President / Chief Operating Officer
• Roger Vessell, Sales VP
• Bob Ried, Vice President
Products:
High Performance Balls; Mid Range Balls; 3-Piece Balls; Polyester Balls; Retired Balls; Houseballs; 1-Ball Bags; 2-Ball Bags; 3-Ball Bags; 4-Ball Bags; 5-Ball Bags; 6-Ball Bags; Cleaners/Polishers; Gloves; Grips; Shoe Accessories; Tape Products; Columbia 300 Wear; Ball Wear; Active Wear; Towels
Brands:
(High-Performance) Action; Action Packed; Backyard Bully; Big Bully; EPX T1; Full Throttle; (Mid-Performance Balls) Dr.Jekyll;

Hyde; Messenger To Low Rg; Messenger Ti Pearl; Overdrive; Panic; Power Drive; Power Drive Sanded; Shock; Super Trooper; U Turn; U Turn; Particle; UTurn Particel Pearl; (3-Piece Balls) Scout; Scout Hi-Flare Particle; Scout Hi-Flare Reactive; Scout Hi-Flare Urethane; Scout Reactive; (Polyester Balls) Blue Dot; White Dots; (Retired Balls) AfterShock; AfterShock Pearlized; Alter Ego; Beast Master; Beast Pearl with MICA; Beast with MICA; Black Knight; Black Knight; Black Shadow; Blue Beast; Blue Knight; Blue Shadow; Boss T

COLUMBIA PARCAR CORP.
1115 COMMERCIAL AVENUE
REEDSBURG, WI 53959
608-524-8888
800-222-4653
Fax: 608-524-8380
info@parcar.com
www.parcar.com
• William R. Sauey, Chairman
• Todd Sauey, President
Products:
Passenger Vehicles
Brands:
Summit; Eagle

COLUMBIA SPORTSWEAR COMPANY
14375 NW SCIENCE PARK DRIVE
PORTLAND, OR 97229-5418
503-985-4000
800-622-6953
Fax: 503-985-5800
www.columbia.com
• Gertrude Boyle, Chairwoman
• Timothy P. Boyle, President & Chief Executive Officer
• Patrick D. Anderson, Chief Operating Officer
Products:
Sportswear
Brands:
Cloud-Bound Jacket; Grangeville Pant; Springbrook Long Sleeve Tee; Skamania Pass; ROC Ball Cap; Delphine Creek Jacket; Sand Creek Pant; Mesa Ridge Lite Long Sleeve Shirt; Tigertooth; Ladies Logo Ball Cap; Switchback Trail Jacket; Challenger II Convertible Pants; Challenger II Shirt; Magneto; ROC Ball Cap; Peak to Creek Shell; Million Mile II Pant; Titanium Diablo Pass; Splendor Peak Shell; Saber XCR; Staubio; Panther Ridge; Boorad; Columbia Logo II Ball Cap; Challenger Tech Organizer; Insulated Products; Tents & Sleeping Bags; Willow Creek; Bugaboo; Omni Released Sheets; Freedom Trail Throws

COMFORT LINE PRODUCTS
2717 N TAMIAMI TRAIL
N FORT MYERS, FL 33903
239-997-6366
866-891-5585
888-997-6366
Fax: 239-997-6312
www.clpusa.com
• Richard Doyle, President
Products:
Whirlpools and spa accessories.

COMFORT PRODUCTS, INC.
931 RIVER ROAD
CROYDON, PA 19021

215-781-0300
800-822-7500
Fax: 215-785-5737
info@comfortoandp.com
www.comfortoandp.com
• Harold Bernhardt, President
hbernhardt@comfortoandp.com
• Cathy Brown, Customer Service
cbrown@comfortoandp.com
Products:
Athletic socks, outdoorsmen socks, thermal socks, liner socks, antimicrobial socks, lacrossse socks, logo socks
Brands:
Footwarmer III, ThermaFlex K

COMFYFEET
105 N BROADWAY AVE
PO BOX 352
HARTINGTON, NE 68739
402-999-0371
888-515-6677
Fax: 402-215-0803
www.comfyfeet.biz
Products:
College Slippers; NFL Color Slippers; College Scuff Slippers; College Baby Slippers; College Baby Blanket Set; College Baby Blanket; College Yard Signs; College Hanging Laser Cut Signs; Generic Slippers; Bird Feeders; Bird Houses; Spirit Spirals; Tumblers; Blanket, Throws, and Pillows; Door Mats; Freezer Mugs; Trash Cans; Wall Clocks; Ornaments and Figurines; Snack Helmets; Helmet Piggy Banks; Biederlack; Helmets; Batting Helmets; Banners; Schutt Full Size Replica Helmets
Brands:
Alabama Crimson Tide Original Comfy Feet Slippers; Arizona State Sun Devils Original Comfy Feet Slippers; Arizona Wildcats Original Comfy Feet Slippers; Arkansas Razorbacks Original Comfy Feet Slippers; Auburn Tigers Original Comfy Feet Slippers; Bobby Labonte Original Comfy Feet Slippers; Cincinnati Bearcats Original Comfy Feet Slippers; Clemson Tigers Original Comfy Feet Slippers; Colorado Buffaloes Original Comfy Feet Slippers; Connecticut Huskies Original Comfy Feet Slippers; Duke Blue Devils Original Comfy Feet Slippers; East Carolina Pirates Original Comfy Feet Slippers; Florida Gators Original Comfy Feet Slippers

COMMUNITY PROFESSIONAL LOUDSPEAKERS
333 E 5TH STREET
CHESTER, PA 19013-4511
610-876-3400
800-523-4934
Fax: 610-874-0190
info@communitypro.com
www.communitypro.com

CONCEPT II, INC.
105 INDUSTRIAL PARK DRIVE
MORRISVILLE, VT 5661
802-888-7971
800-245-5676
Fax: 802-888-4791
rowing@concept2.com
www.concept2.com
• Richard A. Dreissigacker, President
• Bev Incledon, President
Products:
Indoor Rowers; Oars; DYNO; Slides; Heart

Rate Monitors; Clothing
Brands:
(Rower) Model D Indoor Rower; (Oars) Dreissigacker Oars; (DYNO) Dynamic Strength Training; (Slides) TeamBoat Slides; Single Rower Slide; (Clothing) C2 Lightweight Workout T-Shirt; C2 Logo Black T; Women's Tank Top; Men's Tank Top; Performance Shirt; Ladies Scoopneck T

CONCEPT ONE ACCESSORIES
119 W 40TH STREET
NEW YORK, NY 10018
212-868-2590
Fax: 212-868-2595
www.concept1.com
• Sam Hafif, President / Chief Executive Officer
(212) 868-2590
sam@concept1.com
• Harvey Mallis, Sales VP
(212) 868-2590
harvey@concept1.com
• Bernie Hafif, Finance VP / Operations
(212) 868-2590
bernie@concept1.com
• Jason Colin, Director of Communications
(212) 381-3937
Products:
Backpacks; Gloves; Headwear; Umbrellas
Brands:
Akademiks; Blue Marlin; Levi Strauss Signature; Cooperstown Collection; Major League Baseball; Original Penguin; Corona Extra; Sean John; Private Label / C1 Design; U.S. Polo Association; Concept rock (80's Band)

CONCORD INDUSTRIES
19 WILLARD ROAD
NORWALK, CT 6851
203-810-4188
888-441-1603
Fax: 203-286-1188
www.sp-us.com
• Karen Condron, Founder
kcondron@concordind.com
Products:
Corporate Gifts; Sports Licensed Products; Carriage House Leather; Premium Key Holders; Auto Accessories; Outdoor Licensed Products; Postal Products; Belt Buckles

CONNELLY SKIS
20621 52ND AVENUE W
PO BOX 716
LYNNWOOD, WA 98036
425-775-5416
Fax: 425-778-9590
infobox@connellyskis.com
www.connellyskis.com
• Thomas Stephens, President
tstephens@connellyskis.com
• Gordy Holmes, Marketing VP
(425) 775-5416
• Gordy Holmes, President & CEO
Products:
Water skis, bindings, kneeboards, ropes, vests, gloves, and apparel for the recreation industry.
Brands:
Concept, HC Jumpers, HC Trick, Revolution, Rocket, Silhouette, Team 2, Proline, Ski Warm
Year Founded:
1965

CONNOR SPORTS FLOORING CORPORATION
1830 HOWARD STREET
SUITE F
ELK GROVE VILLAGE, IL 60007
847-290-9020
800-283-9522
Fax: 847-890-9034
www.connorfloor.com
• Ron Cerny, President
• Doug Grove, National Sales Manager
dgrove@connorfloor.com
Products:
Synthetic Athletic Surfacing, Wood Flooring
Brands:
Duracushion, Grip-Tite, Permalock, Powerstrip, Rezill-CHANNEL

CONROY GLOVES
110 S MARKET STREET
JOHNSTOWN, NY 12095
518-762-9444
Fax: 518-762-0900
• Brian Conroy, President
Products:
Skiing-Alpine - Gloves

CONTINENTAL SPORTS SUPPLY, INC.
3981 S DECATUR STREET
ENGLEWOOD, CO 80110
800-877-5053
Fax: 720-833-0814
info@reuschusa.com
www.reuschusa.com
• David D. Banning, President
Products:
Soccer - Bags-Equipment, Balls-Rubber, Cleats, Corner Flags, Gloves-Goalie, Protective, Shinguards, Socks, Uniforms. Rugby: uniforms, balls, bags. Ski: gloves.
Brands:
Continental, Vici, Reusch
Year Founded:
1980.

CONTOUR SEATS, INC.
6530 CHAPMANS ROAD
ALLENTOWN, PA 18106
610-395-5144
800-247-4509
Fax: 610-398-7099
info@contourseats.com
www.contourseats.com
• Carl A. Gross, President/CEO
c.gross@contourseats.com
• Janine Gross, Officer Manager
j.gross@contourseats.com
Products:
Contour Seats, Stadium Seats, Spectator Seating

COOPER LIGHTING
1121 HIGHWAY 74 S
PEACHTREE CITY, GA 30269
770-486-4680
Fax: 770-486-4318
www.cooperlighting.com
• David Feldman, President
• Terry A Klebe, SVP / Chief Financial Officer
• Donnie Miller, National Account Director
(770) 486-4471
• Wayne Blanton, National Accounts Sales / Marketing Mana
(770) 486-4365
Products:
Incandescent, HID and fluorescent fixtures

to architectural, emergency, outdoor and exit lighting

Brands:
Fail-Safe high-abuse, clean room and vandal-resistant lighting. Halo recessed and track lighting. Iris lighting systems. Lumiere outdoor architectural and landscape lighting. McGraw-Edison and Lumark indoor and outdoor HID lighting. Metalux florescent lighting. MWS modular wiring systems. Portfolio architectural recessed lighting. Sure-Lites and AtLite exit and emergency lighting.

COOPSPORT INTERNATIONAL LP
1335 PARK CENTER DRIVE
SUITE B
VISTA, CA 92081
760-727-8697
815-22-515
Fax: 760-727-8699
www.coop.no
• Scott Cooper, Owner / President
Products:
Sporting goods and toys for adult and children such as: CoopSport, CoopKIds, CoopHydro, CoopImpulse, CoopSport Pool and Coop Premium
Brands:
Air Rocket, Air Sted, Air Tube, Surfster, Gription Football, WetBall, WetVolley, WetFoot, WetDisk, WetSmash Paddles, Wet Glove, Wet Hoop, Coop Accessories, Hit-A-Way Jr., Tumble Jumbo, Big Time Soccer, First Toss Glove n' Ball, First Pitch Bat n' Ball, First Goal Hockey Set, First Goal Soccer Goal, First Strike Bowling Set, Nuf Nuf, Hydroball Football, HydroBall All Purpose, HydroCatch Game, HydroDisk Flying DIsk, HydroGlove Ball Game, HydroSmash Paddled, HydroVolley Volleyball, Zip Stix, SlingBall Tail Ball, Micro Revolution Set, Rookie Hoop, Rookie Football, Rookie Soccer, Rookie Volleyball, Tumble Playball, Revolution Flying Disk, SunSport

CORPORATION FOR LASER OPTICS RESEARCH
47 DURHAM STREET
PORTSMOUTH, NH 3801
603-430-2023
Fax: 603-430-2058
• Masayuki Karakawa, President/Chief Technology Officer
• Robert Zielstorff, Vice President of Finance
• George Naumann, Senior Vice President Operations
Products:
Solid state laser systems for laser video displays.

CORSAIR DISPLAY SYSTEMS, INC.
1236 N. 18TH STREET
SHEBOYGAN, WI 53081-3201
920-457-4851
800-624-2051
Fax: 585-396-5953
sales@corsairdisplay.com
www.vollrath.com
• David W Mansfield, President
sales@corsairdisplay.com
• Nancy Bryan Role, Account Manager
nrole@corsairdisplay.com
Products:
Designing and manufacturing custom and

standard carts, kiosks, inline systems, merchandisers and pastry cases
Brands:
BBQ Cart NFL Jaguars All Tel Stadium, Beer Cart MLB Astros, Cleveland Zoo Food Service, Cocktail Cart Mudhens, Deli Cart Bilo Center, Kiosk - 8x10 - Red Wings, Kiosk - St. Petersburg Times, Merchandise Cart - Beaver Stadium, Retail Merchandise Box - Cardinal Stadium, Retail Program Cart - Invesco Field, Locker Box - Pac Bell, Chesapeake Bay Hyatt, LuLu's Bait Shack, Lulu's Bait Shack, Murphys Bar and Grill, 12x10 Kiosk Joker's Wild Six Flags, Cold Beverage Cart - Six Flags, Italian Ice Cart - Lodge - Jay Vending, Cart - Italian Ice - Fifties, Gazebo Roseland Waterpark, Lemonade Cart - Jay Vending, Cold Beverage Cart - Pepsi - Six Flags, Hot D

COURT COMPANY
5440 S 900 E
MURRAY, UT 84117
801-288-8979
877-273-1172
Fax: 801-266-2949
www.courtcompany.com
• Randy Stafford, Co-Owner/President
thecountco@aol.com
Products:
Racquetball and squash courts along with other types of athletic court systems.

COURT-1 SPORTS INC.
156 LAWRENCE PAQUETTE
CHAMPLAIN, NY 12919
514-731-3607
800-363-3591
Fax: 514-731-2929
info@court-1.com
www.court-1.com
• Matthew LiLi, President
(514) 731-3607
lili@court-1.com
Products:
Sporting Equipment for Hockey; Tennis; Soccer Nets & GoalFrames, Marathon & Gym Mats

COVER SPORTS USA
5000 PASCHALL AVENUE
PHILADELPHIA, PA 19143
215-724-3582
800-445-6680
Fax: 215-724-8706
sales@coversports.com
www.coversports.com
• Ronald Nissenbaum, President
• Victoria Christinzio, Credit Manager
Products:
Field and fence covers and other related products.
Brands:
FieldSaverT Field Covers, FieldSaverT Protective Rain Covers, FieldSaverT Football Sideline Covers, GymGuardT Gym Floor Covers, SafeFoamT Fence Padding, Oval Poly Mesh, Soft Knit Mesh, TempFenceT Pole, 50' Fence Kit, 100' Fence Kit, 150' Fence Kit, FenceCrownT Safe, Good-Looking Fence Tops, FenceMateT Windscreen and Privacy Screen

COYLE & GREER AWARDS CANADA LTD.
383 SOVEREIGN ROAD
LONDON, ENGLAND N6M 1A3
519-659-5862
800-265-2607
Fax: 519-659-7052
info@talbot-promo.com
www.talbot-promo.com
• Brenda MacDonald, President
• Steve Levschuk, President
Products:
Recognition Awards, Jewelry, Writing Instruments, Lapel Pins, Medals & Ribbons, Glassware, Cast Products, Business Gifts & Wearables, Service & Safety Awards

COYOTE PROMOTIONS
300 NORTHERN BOULEVARD
SUITE 26
GREAT NECK, NY 11021
516-487-5696
800-726-9683
Fax: 516-482-7425
www.coyotepromotions.com
• Marc Simone, Vice President Sales
marc@coyotepromotions.com
Nature of Services:
Adobe Graphics and Design, Inc. are suppliers of premium and promotional items to the media industry that includes custom-imprinted products and sports pins to both the college and professional sports market.

CRAMER PRODUCTS, INC.
PO BOX 1001
GARDNER, KS 66030
913-856-7511
800-345-2231
Fax: 913-884-5626
info@cramersportsmed.com
www.cramersportsmed.com
• Tom Rogge, President / Chief Executive Officer
trogge@cramersportsmed.com
• Matt Conway, Vice President
• Rob Mogolov, Director Of Marketing
Products:
Sports medicine and athletic training room supplies including tape, athletic trauma kits, braces & supports and educational products.
Brands:
CRAMER CO STRETCH NON ADHESIVE TAPE, SKIN LUBEr LUBRICATING OINTMENT STICK, CRAMER 1000 ATHLETIC TRAINER'S TAPE, CRAMER 250 ATHLETIC TRAINER'S TAPE, CRAMER NON-TEAR STRETCH TAPE, DE-HESIVET TAPE REMOVER SPRAY, QDAr TAPING BASE, TAPE UNDERWRAP, AT 2470 SOFT SIDED KIT, AT BACKPACK DELUXE, AT 1782 / AT 1577 / AT 819 / SOFT SIDED KITS, AT 273 DELUXE FANNY PACK, AT 166 FANNY PACK, AT MESSENGER PACK, ACTIVE ANKLEr CHAMELEON ANKLE BRACE, ACTIVE ANKLEr T1, ACTIVE ANKLEr T2, ACTIVE ANKLEr AS1 ANKLE BRACE, ACTIVE ANKLEr PRO LACERT ANKLE BRACE, DELUXE HINGED KNEE BRACE, DELUXE KNEE STABILIZER, HINGED KNEE BRACE, PATELLAR SUPPORT, KNEE SUPPORT, FOOTBALL

CRAN BARRY INC.
3 GRIFFIN WAY
CHELSEA, MA 2150
617-884-6290
800-992-2021
Fax: 617-567-9953
service@cranbarry.com
www.cranbarry.com
• John Vinton, Chief Executive Officer & President
service@cranbarry.com
Products:
Sports Team Uniforms

CREATIONS BY ALAN STUART
49 W 38 STREET
NEW YORK, NY 10018
212-719-5511
800-866-4424
Fax: 212-719-5267
Products:
Toothbrushes, Collegiates, Bath Supplies & Bags

CREATIVE AWARDS BY LANE
1713 ELMHURST ROAD
ELK GROVE VILLAGE, IL 60007
847-593-7700
Fax: 847-593-1155
• John P. Erskine, President/CEO
Products:
Trophies/Plaques/Jewelry/Advertising
Special Ties/Engraving/Lasering

CREATIVE CUSTOM PRODUCTS
PO BOX 414
CEDARBURG, WI 53012
800-368-8182
Fax: 262-375-9465
www.creativecustomproducts.com
• John Ochsenwald, Chief Executive Officer
Products:
Athletic training equipment and supplies
Brands:
IC WRAP, I.C. Bags, Tape Tube, CaviCide, Plastic Ice Bags, Foam Rolls, White

CREATIVE TROPHIES COMPANY
437 AVENUE U
BROOKLYN, NY 11223
718-339-8266
888-807-7835
Fax: 718-998-7082
creativetrophies@aol.com
www.creativetrophies.com
• Joe Minuto, General Manager
(718) 339-8266
creativetrophies@aol.com
Products:
Trophies, Trophy Cups, Plaques, Lucite Awards, Great Awards, Great Gifts & Desk Ideas, Promotional Items, Scholastic Awards, Ribbons, Airflyte & Related Products
Brands:
American Eagle, Copper Look Figure Awards, Economical Trophies, Jumbo Figure Awards, Oscar Like Awards, Resin Sport Display Dishes, World Series Trophy, 964 SERIES, DA01 SERIES, DA 03 SERIES, DA 04 SERIES, DA 05 SERIES, DAO6 SERIES, DA 07 SERIES, DA 08 SERIES, Elegant Plaques, Clock Plaques, Copper Creations, Picture Plaques, A2276, A2966, A3808, A5960, A5968, BC1, BC2, BC6, BC18, BC46, BC850, Walnut Name Block, Walnut Name Block w/ Pen, Wood

Pen Box and Pen, Economical Pens, Elite Custom Pens, AP Series Pins, EP Series Pins, Stars & School Pins, NA70G, NA70S

CREATIVE URETHANES
250 INDEPENDENCE DRIVE
WINCHESTER, VA 22602
540-542-6676
888-338-7139
Fax: 540-542-6678
cuinfo@creativeurethanes.com
www.creativeurethanes.com
• Dan Maxwell, Owner
Services:
Reaction Injection Molding, Plastic Pipe - Durothane AR Piping System, Custom Urethane Wheels & Urethane Molding Services
Products:
Urethane wheels and surfaces for rollerskaing and skateboarding.

CROAKIES
88 LIFE LINK WAY
BOZEMAN, MT 59718
307-733-2269
800-443-8620
Fax: 406-587-4303
croakies@croakies.com
www.croakies.com
• John Krisik, President
• John Scott, EVP
jscott@croakies.com
• Fred Bowditch, Manager
• Dinah Delaney, Chief Financial Officer
Products:
Bag Packs, Shovels, Poles, Probes, Accessories, Skis, Bindings, Boots, Clothing and Accessories
Year Founded:
1978

CROSMAN CORPORATION
7629 ROUTES 5 & 20
EAST BLOOMFIELD, NY 14469
418-682-3000
800-724-7486
Fax: 418-682-3343
www.crosman.com
• Ken D'Arcy, President / Chief Executive Officer
• Robert Beckwith, Vice President, Finance
• Steve Upham, Vice President Sales
• Phil Dolci, President & CEO
Products:
Airguns, Rifles, pistols, kits, soft air, ammo/CO2, slingshots & ranges
Brands:
AirSource, Break Barrel, Co2, Pneumatic; 2240, 3576 Revolver, American Classic pump pistol, Auto Air II Red Dot, Repeat Air 1008B CO2 pistol, Repeat Air 1008BRD, 1008 Shooter's Kit, 1008S Air Pistol Kit, 1008S Shooter's Kit, 357 Shooter's Kit, 781 Action Kit, Pumpmaster Starter Kit, Air Mag P50, Pulse R70, Stinger P32, Stinger R34, Stinger R36, Stinger Shotgun, Wingmaster, .177 cal. Hollow Point pellets, .177 cal. Super Match pellets, Model VTS, Model CSS, Model FSS, Large Range, Medium Range, Small Range, Legacy 1000, Legacy Pro Pak

CROSS CREEK APPAREL, INC.
755 LEE STREET
SUITE 1000
ALEXANDER CITY, AL 35011

800-321-1138
• W Ha Spires Jr, President
cc_custservice@russellcorp.com
• John Meis, Sales / Merchandising VP
cc_custservice@russellcorp.com
• Dick Younger, Merchandising General Manager
cc_custservice@russellcorp.com
Products:
General Sports Products - Apparel; Golf - Apparel.
Brands:
Cross Creek

CROSSFIELD PRODUCTS CORPORATION
140 VALLEY ROAD
ROSELLE PARK, NJ 7204
908-245-2800
Fax: 908-245-0659
www.crossfieldproducts.com
• Charles R. Watt, President
dexotex@crossfieldproducts.com
• Richard M. Watt, VP
Services:
Flooring for Sports Facilities.
Brands:
Dex-O-Tex Gym-Flor

CROWN INDUSTRIES, INC.
155 N PARK STREET
EAST ORANGE, NJ 7017
973-672-2277
877-747-2457
Fax: 866-200-5546
www.gocrown.com
Products:
Stanchions and Ropes for crowd control, Pipe & Drape, Brass Rails and Brass Fittings, Aluminum Easels, Brass Easels, Bellman's Carts, Luggage Carts, Pedestal Tables, and Folding Table Legs
Brands:
DPendaPull (tm) retractable, King, Crown, Plastic Stanchions, Ropes and Rods, Snap Ends & Wallplates, Signs and sign frames, Tops, Brass Polish, Foot rails, Glassracks, Tubing, Accessories, Ball Fittings, Brackets, Fancy Brackets (animal heads), Finials, Flanges, Flush Fittings, Posts, Bellman's Carts and Luggage Carts, Folding Table Legs Pedestal Tables

CROWN PRINCE, INC.
3670 N 126TH STREET
BROOKFIELD, WI 53005
262-781-7580
800-727-7580
Fax: 800-434-7411
www.greatshirts.com
• Tom Reutman, Chairman
• Scott Roberts, President
• Joe Reutman, VP Sales / Marketing
Products:
Baseball Jerseys; General Sports Products Award and Coaches Jackets, Die Cut Letters-Numerals, Hats/Caps/Visors, Heat Transfers, Sweatclothes, T-shirts, Towels; Golf Shirts.
Brands:
Anvil, Auburn, Cannon, Fruit of the Loom, Hanes, Health Knit, Screen Stars, Signal, Sneakers, Sportowels

CUSHEES, INC.
6590 E ROGERS CIRCLE
BOCA RATON, FL 33487

561-994-3001
800-327-5012
Fax: 561-994-3009
cushees@bellsouth.net
www.cushees.com
• Robert Kenny, President
cushees@bellsouth.net
• Robert F. Kenny, Jr, Assistant Account
Manager
• Rose Saul, Controller
Products:
Golf socks, tennis socks, wristbands,
headbands, cloth hats, straw hats, sparkle
caps, sparkle visors, sequin hats, cowboy
hats, gambler hats, fedoras.
Clients:
Golf shops, Tennis shops, sporting goods
dealers
Brands:
Solarbloc, Cushees

CUSTOM DECAL & EMBLEMS, INC.
9446 BOND AVENUE
EL CAJON, CA 92021
619-449-5611
800-637-5802
Fax: 619-449-5713
custom@customdecal.com
• Matthew Smoke, President
• Donna Archuletta, Manager
Services:
Helmet Decals for Baseball, Football,
Hockey, Motocross
Clients:
High School and College athletics, Surf and
Snowboard industries, AMA Supercross and
Motocross Teams, No Fear, and DYE
Paintball Products

CUSTOM PIN & DESIGN
245 IVANHOE STREET
DENVER, CO 80220-5862
877-307-7467
Fax: 720-524-7376
www.custompin.com
• John Stevenson, Owner
Products:
Lapel Pins. Specializing in custom design.
Badges and Buttons

**CUSTOM SPORTSWEAR CORP/DBA
SPORTSWEAR UNLIMITED**
8 ENTERPRISE CT
SEWELL, NJ 8080
856-589-3303
800-697-0330
www.customsportswear.net
• Helen Bowers, General Manager
Products:
Baseball - Socks, Stirrups, Uniforms;
Basketball - Uniforms; Bowling - Shirts; Field
Hockey - Uniforms; Football - Jerseys;
General Sports Bags, Equipment, Screen
Printing, T-shirts, Warm-Up Suits; Golf -
Apparel; Gymnastics - Apparel; Ice Hockey -
Jersey

CUTTER AND BUCK, INC.
701 N 34TH STREET
SUITE 400
SEATTLE, WA 98103
206-622-4191
800-713-7810
Fax: 206-830-6278
help@cutterbuck.com
www.cutterbuck.com

• Douglas G. Southern, Chairman
help@cutterbuck.com
• John T. Wyatt, President / Chief Operating
Officer / Di
help@cutterbuck.com
• Ernie Johnson, SVP / Chief Financial
Officer
Products:
Men and women's shirts, pants, sweaters &
vests, shorts & swimwear, outerwear,
sweaters & vests. Golf Apparels.
Brands:
Annika, Signature, CB ProTec, Super Bowl
XL, Texas Longhorns

CUTTERS GLOVES
110 CHESIRE LANE
SUITE 120
MINNETONKA, MN 55305
602-381-5434
800-233-6956
Fax: 602-381-5658
www.cuttersgloves.com
Products:
Innovator of performance grip material
(football, batting, golf, fitness, racquet,
accessories)

CY YOUNG INDUSTRIES, INC.
16201 W 110TH STREET
LENEXA, KS 66219
913-438-1776
800-729-2610
Fax: 913-888-1774
cyyounginc@aol.com
www.cyyoungind.com
• Carrie Yo Sr, President
cyyounginc@aol.com
Services:
Seat renovations in theatres, auditoriums,
arenas, and stadiums.

CYBEX INTERNATIONAL, INC.
10 TROTTER DRIVE
MEDWAY, MA 2053
508-533-4300
Fax: 508-533-5500
www.cybexintl.com
• John Aglialoro, Chairman
• Arthur W Hicks Jr, President & COO
• Joan Carter, Vice Chairman and Secretary
• John McCarthy, Director
Products:
Training Products, including total body, arc,
recumbent, free weights, treadmills.
Brands:
Trotter, Cybex, Cyclone, Elite

CYGNET TURF & EQUIPMENT
4711 INSLEY ROAD
NORTH BALTIMORE, OH 45872
419-354-1112
888-285-0722
Fax: 419-352-1244
www.cygnetturf.com
• John Noe, Marketing Director
Services:
Stripping old turf and installing new
turf/grass.
Clients:
Cleveland Browns, Cleveland Indians,
Chicago Bears, Toledo Mudhens, New
England Patriots, St. Louis Cardinals.

CYRK, INC.
100 CUMMINGS CENTER
SUITE 250-C
BEVERLY, MA 1915
978-998-7100
800-426-3125
Fax: 978-998-6840
• Jeffrey Werner, Chief Executive Officer
Products:
Athletic Jackets/Parkas, Bags-Equipment,
Hats/Caps/Visors, Screen Printing,
Shoelaces, Shorts, Sweatclothes, Sweaters,
T-shirts, Wristbands/Headbands; Golf
Gloves, Umbrellas; Gymnastics Apparel;
Racquet Sports Apparel, Bags-Equipment;
Skiing-Alpine Gloves
Brands:
Cyrksport, Sondico, Lil Teamwear

D.P.M. ENTERPRISES
128 REGIONAL PARK DRIVE
KINGSPORT, TN 37966
423-349-4129
www.dpmenterprises.net
• Dino Miliotis, Owner
• Pam Peters, VP
Products:
Collectibles - Sports Celebrity Collector
Plates; Signed Sports Art; Signed Sports
Memorabilia; Sports-Related Corporate
Premiums/Gifts.

DA KINE
408 COLUMBIA STREET
HOOD RIVER, OR 97031
541-386-3166
Fax: 541-386-6199
info@dakine.com
www.dakine.com
• Randy Torcom, Snow Team & Marketing
Manager
(541) 386-3166
randyt@dakine.com
Products:
Builds gear for board sport enthusiasts
including bags, snowboarders, surfers,
kiteboarders and windsurfers
Brands:
Leashes: Kanui, Kanui Team, Pro Comp,
Super Lite, Kanui Girls, Longboard, Easy
Clip Leash Release Pin, Surf Packs: Patrol,
Channel, Interval, Point

DACON
3686 SE DIXIE HIGHWAY
STUART, FL 34997
772-288-3111
Fax: 772-288-1893
dacon@daconmfg.com
www.daconmfg.com
• Laurie Cummings, Marketing
Products:
Air Pumps, Flag Markers, Equipment
Hanger, Ball Rack, Bat Cart, Relay Batons

DACOR CORPORATION
1 SELLECK STREET
SHORE POINTE
NORWALK, CT 6855
203-852-7079
Fax: 203-853-2892
dacor@us.head.com
www.divedacor.com
• Carlo Bertozzi, President
• Rob Cairns, Business Development VP
• Matt Mulryan, Sales Manager

Products:
General Sports Products - T-shirts, Warm-Up Suits, Windbreakers; Water Sports - Apparel-Fashion, Buoyancy Compensators, Depth Gauges, Diving Masks, Fins, Scuba Regulators, Scuba Valves, Snorkels.

DACOR SPORT
1 SELLECK STREET
SHORE POINTE
NORWALK, CT 6855
203-852-7079
800-323-3483
Fax: 203-853-2892
dacor@us.head.com
www.divedacor.com
• Matt Mulryan, Sales Manager
Products:
Water Recreational Gear Accessories, Fins, Masks, Snorkels.

DAHLGREN FOOTWEAR INC.
19636 SW 90TH COURT
TUALATIN, OR 97062
503-612-9581
888-870-1156
Fax: 503-885-1821
www.dahlgrenfootwear.com
• Ray Dahlgren, Founder
info@dahlgrenfootwear.com
• Diane Dahlgren, Founder
info@dahlgrenfootwear.com
Products:
Socks for sports.

DAIWA CORPORATION
11137 WARLAND DRIVE
CYPRESS, CA 90630
562-375-6800
800-736-4653
Fax: 800-736-4653
admail@daiwa.com
www.daiwa.com
• Tad Suzuki, President
admail@daiwa.com
• Cynthia Young, VP
admail@daiwa.com
• Terry Pederson, National Sales Manager
admail@daiwa.com
• Taka Inagaki, President
• Tad Kojima, Chairman
Products:
Clothing Accessories, including fighing gear.

DAKTRONICS, INC.
201 DAKTRONICS DRIVE
PO BOX 5128
BROOKINGS, SD 57006-5128
605-692-0200
800-843-5843
Fax: 800-325-8766
sales@daktronics.com
www.daktronics.com
• Aelred J Kurtenbach, Chairman
sales@daktronics.com
• Jay Parker, National Sales Manager
• Tom Coughlin, Sales Manager/High School Sports
• Dean Dodge, Sales Manager/Audio Division
• Jim Morgan, President & Chief Executive Officer
sales@daktronics.com
• Philip Pikelny, Vice President & Chief Marketing Officer
• Frank Kurtenbach, Vice President Sales

sales@daktronics.com
• Bill Retterath, Chief Financial Officer/Treasurer
sales@daktronics.com
• Mark Steinkamp, Marketing Manager
Nature of Services:
Daktronics is the world's leading designer and manufacturer of electronic scoreboards and LED video displays for all levels of sports.
Customer Demographic:
Thousands of high school and college facilities, and a majority of professional sports teams and facilities in the US.
Year Founded:
1968
Products:
Large Screen Video Systems, Scoreboards, Electronic Message Centers, Variable Message Signs, Display Control Systems, Sports Sound Systems.
Brands:
ProStar 190 Video Displays, ProAd 190 Digital Advertising Displays, All Sport 190 Scoreboards, OmniSport 190 Timing Systems, Venus 190 Display Controller.

DALCO ATHLETIC LETTERING, INC.
3719 CAVALIER DRIVE
GARLAND, TX 75042
972-487-1200
800-288-3252
Fax: 972-276-9608
sales@dalcoathletic.com
www.dalcoathletic.com
• Gene Feil, Chief Operating Officer
gfeil@dalcoathletic.com
• Linda Feil, Co-Owner
lfeil@dalcoathletic.com
• Michael D Carter, Sales VP
mcarter@dalcoathletic.com
• Alvion Caywood, Manager
Products:
Official/Umpire Clothing and Accessories, Athletic Lettering

DALEBOOT U.S.A.
2660 S 300 W
SALT LAKE CITY, UT 84115
801-487-3649
Fax: 801-487-3880
daleboot@dalebootusa.com
www.dalebootusa.com
• Adam Olson, General Manager
(801) 487-3649
daleboot@dalebootusa.com
Products:
Boots, Bags, Caps

DAMASCUS WORLDWIDE, INC.
63 WALES STREET
RUTLAND, VT 5701
805-639-0746
800-451-4167
Fax: 800-305-2417
info@damascusgear.com
www.damascusgear.com
• Lawrence J Welton, President
Products:
Gloves, Tactical Gear, Swat Gear

DANDY PRODUCTS, INC.
PO BOX 1980
WESTERVILLE, OH 43086-1980
740-881-2790
800-591-2284
Fax: 740-881-2791

dlc@dandyproducts.com
www.dandyproducts.com
• Dan Reed, Marketing Officer
Products:
Florr and Wall Padding
Year Founded:
1989
Brands:
Protective Wall Pads

DANSKIN, INC.
1411 BROADWAY
8TH FLOOR
NEW YORK, NY 8810
212-764-4630
877-443-2121
Fax: 212-764-7265
edanskin@danskin.com
www.danskin.com
• Carol J Hochman, President / Chief Executive Officer
contact_us@danskin.com
• John A Sarto, Chief Financial Officer
contact_us@danskin.com
• Barbara Khouri, President
Products:
Dancewear, Active Wear, Comfortable clothes

DANT CLAYTON CORPORATION
1500 BERNHEIM LANE
LOUISVILLE, KY 40210-7408
800-626-2177
Fax: 502-637-9983
info@dantclayton.com
www.stadiumbleachers.com

DARBY ATHLETIC HEALTH
300 JERICHO QUADRANGLE
JERICHO, NY 11753
800-247-4768
Fax: 800-430-5612
www.darbymedical.com
Products:
Emergency & First Aid Products, Exam Room Equipment, Medical Spa Supplies, Nutritional Products, Orthopedic Products, Pharmaceuticals, Physical Therapy/ Massage Therapy Aids, Practice Builders, Sutures, Syringes and Needles, Vitamins and Supplements, X-Ray Supplies

---

DART WORLD INC
140 LINWOOD STREET
LYNN, MA 1905
781-581-6035
800-225-2558
Fax: 781-592-8760
info@dartworld.com
www.dartworld.com
• Mark Amirault, Principal
mamirault@dartworld.com
• Brian Dower, National Sales Manager
Products:
Steel/Soft Tips , Flights, Shafts, Cabinets, Dartboards, Backboards; Indoor and Outdoor games
Brands:
Dart World; Harrows; Target

DARTFISH USA
6505 SHILOH ROAD
SUITE 110-B
ALPHARETTA, GA 30005
404-685-9505
888-655-3850

Fax: 404-685-9130
usa@dartfish.com
www.dartfish.com
• Victor Bergonzoli, President/CEO
victor.bergonzoli@dartfish.com
• Ron Imbriale, Sales VP
usa@dartfish.com
• Mark Matoza, Golf Director
usa@dartfish.com
Products:
Sports electronics, including software programs.

DATREK PROFESSIONAL BAG
2701 EMERYWOOD PKWY
SUITE 101
RICHMOND, VA 23294
804-726-1328
800-955-2269
Fax: 888-822-4269
datrekcs@datrek.com
www.datrek.com
• Craig Ramsbottom, President
Products:
Golf Bags and Accessories

DAVID CLARK CO., INC.
360 FRANKLIN STREET
PO BOX 15054
WORCESTER, MA 1604
508-751-5800
800-298-6235
800-900-3434
Fax: 508-753-5827
service@DavidClark.com
www.davidclark.com
• Bob Daigle, Product Manager
(508) 751-5888
bdaigle@davidclark.com
• John Farr, National Sales Manager
• Dennis Buzzell, Market Manager, Aviation
and Airline
(508) 751-5889
DBuzzell@DavidClark.com
• John Tasi, Product Manager,
Government/Military
(508) 751-5886
JTasi@DavidClark.com
• Robert A. Vincent, President
Year Founded:
1935.
Products:
Communication headsets, intercoms,
two-way radios and accessories.

DEBEER LACROSSE
510 MARYVILLE UNIVERSITY DR.
SUITE 110
ST. LOUIS, MO 63141
800-833-3535
• James L Muhlfelder, President / Chief
Executive Officer
info@debeerlacrosse.com
• Regy Thorpe, General Manager
info@debeerlacrosse.com
Products:
Sticks, Handles, Eyemasks, Gloves,
Equipment Bags, Accesories

DECATUR ELECTRONICS, INC.
3433 EAST WOOD STREET
PHOENIX, AZ 85040
602-428-4315
888-428-4315
Fax: 602-621-4200
www.decaturelectronics.com
• Cody Caldwell, Bids Specialist

Products:
Speed radar for sports applications,
including motorcycles, snowmobiles, boats
and others.
Year Founded:
1955

DECKERS OUTDOOR CORPORATION
250 COROMAR DRIVE
GOLETA, CA 93117
805-967-7611
Fax: 805-967-9722
www.deckers.com
• Angel R Martinez,
CEO/President/Chairman
• Zohar Ziv, Chief Operating Officer
• Thomas A George, Chief Financial Officer
• Graciela Montgomery, Chief Human
Resources Officer
Products:
Sports Sandals and Shoes.

DEHEN, INC.
1040 NE 44TH AVENUE
SUITE 3
PORTLAND, OR 97213
503-222-3871
800-544-8819
Fax: 503-222-2751
www.dehen1920.com
• Jim Artaiz, VP Marketing / Sales
(503) 222-3871
jamesartaiz@dehen.com
• Beezie Lasseigne, Sales
(503) 222-3871
• Gary Hilde, President
ext 15
• Jim Artaiz, Vice President
Products:
Activewear, Cheerleading Uniforms and
Supplies, Wool and Leather Varsity Jackets,
Custom apparel and outerwear.
Year Founded:
1920

DELTA APPAREL COMPANY
2750 PREMIERE PARKWAY
SUITE 100
DULUTH, GA 30097
678-775-6900
800-285-4456
Fax: 800-588-0199
www.deltaapparel.com
• Robert Humphreys, President / Chief
Executive Officer
• Steve Cochran, President
Products:
Athletic Apparel, Fleecewear.

DELTA GOLF COMPANY
4727 W MONTROSE AVENUE
CHICAGO, IL 60641
773-777-7877
800-909-4653
Fax: 773-777-6543
• Joseph R Morisco, President / Chief
Executive Officer
• Randy Turner, Sls Mgr
Products:
Golf Bags for Clubs, Clubs - Iron or Wood
Sets, Putters, Utility Clubs, Clubheads,
Grips, Shafts.

DESCENTE NORTH AMERICA, INC.
334 MARSHALL WAY N
LAYTON, UT 84041

801-317-0017
800-999-0475
Fax: 801-317-0020
info@descente.com
www.descente.com
• Guy Christie, President
• Johnny Miller, National Sales Manager /
Golf Division
• Curt Geiger, National Sales Manager / Ski
Division
• Nori Higuchi, President
Products:
Team apparel for skiing, cycling, volleyball,
swimming, and speed skating

**DEVENTER'S CHEER & DANCEWEAR
FACTORY, INC.**
105 BASSET HIGHWAY
DOVER, NJ 7801
973-366-7097
Fax: 973-366-7098
• Susan Zakosky, Vice President
(973) 366-7097
Year Founded:
1974
Products:
Dance and activewear.

DEXTER SHOE COMPANY
71 RAILROAD AVE
DEXTER, ME 4930
207-924-7341
Fax: 603-595-2337
www.dextershoe.com
• Jerry Hyde, President
• Theodore Alfond, EVP
• Stephen Tucker, VP Sales / Marketing
• Peter Lunder, Director
Products:
Bowling Shoes and Golf Shoes.

DIADORA AMERICA
2129 67TH AVENUE S
KENT, WA 98032
253-520-8868
800-342-3672
Fax: 253-520-6372
info@gvsamerica.com
www.diadoraamerica.com
• Mauro Visentin, Chief Executive Officer
• Linda Walker, VP Distribution / Customer
Service
• Stephanie Nelson, Director Apparel
Marketing
• William Nutall, President
Products:
Tennis Shoes; Soccer Shoes, Apparel;
Running Shoes-Run/Jog, Shoes-Cross
Training, Sandals.

DIAMOND SPORTS
1880 E. ST. ANDREW PL
SANTA ANA, CA 92705
714-415-7600
Fax: 714-415-7601
www.diamond-sports.com
• Andrea Gordon, President
Products:
Baseballs, softballs, batting gloves, batter's
helmets & accessories, mitts, catcher's gear
& accessories, bags & buckets,
merchandise and apparels. Foot ball
shoulder pads, apparel/accessories. Field
equipment.

DIAMONDBACK BICYCLES
6004 S 190TH STREET
SUITE 101
KENT, WA 98032
253-395-1100
800-776-7641
Fax: 800-851-0807
www.diamondback.com
• Jon Kennedy, Marketing Manager
Products:
Cycling Accessories, Bicycles, BMX, Fitness
Equipment.

DIEBOLD INCORPORATED
5995 MAYFAIR ROAD
N CANTON, OH 44720-8077
330-490-4000
800-999-3600
Fax: 330-490-3794
www.diebold.com
• Kevin J Krakora, Executive VP/CFO
• George S. Mayes, Executive Vice
President and Chief Operating
• Bradley C. Richardson, Executive Vice
President and Chief Financial
• Frank A. Natoli, Executive Vice President
and Chief Innovation
• Henry D.G. W. Wallace, Executive
Chairman of the Board
Sports Related Products:
Kiosks, ATMs, etc. for sports facilities.

DIVERSA PRODUCTS GROUP
1615 W UNIVERSITY DRIVE
SUITE 135
TEMPE, AZ 85281-3257
480-966-9802
800-527-4923
Fax: 480-966-9806
info@bushwalkerbags.com
www.bushwalkerbags.com
• Jim Bilas, Marketing Director
info@bushwalkerbags.com
Products:
Athletic Trainers' Bags, Beltpacks and equip
bags
Brands:
Bushwalker Bags

DIVOTS SPORTSWEAR COMPANY, INC.
5903-A PEACHTREE INDUSTRIAL
BOULEVARD
NORCROSS, GA 30092
770-447-4800
800-847-3467
Fax: 770-448-3244
info@divots.com
www.divots.com
• Bob Friedman, President
info@divots.com
Products:
Golf Apparel
Brands:
Divots
Clients:
Golf Shops

DJ ORTHOPEDICS
1430 DECISION STREET
VISTA, CA 92081
760-727-1280
800-336-6569
Fax: 800-936-6569
officecare@djortho.com
• Chinh E Chu, Chairman of the Board
• Leslie H Cross, President & Chief
Executive Officer

• Vickie L Capps, Finance SVP / Chief
Financial Officer
Products:
Knee Braces, Foot & Ankle Braces, Upper
Extremities & Back Braces

DMI SPORTS INC
1300 VIRGINIA DRIVE
SUITE 401
FORT WASHINGTON, PA 19034
215-283-0153
800-423-3220
Fax: 215-283-9573
www.dmisports.com
• Jeremy Stork
(215) 283-0153
Products:
Indoor games, featuring complete lines of
Billiard, Dart and Table Tennis Equipment,
Soccer Tables, Hockey Tables, Garage
Door Sports, and Casino

DOCKER'S FOOTWEAR
1415 MURFREESBORO ROAD
SUITE 190
NASHVILLE, TN 37217
800-654-2371
888-324-6189
Fax: 800-654-2371
www.dockersshoes.com
• Hal N. Pennington, Chairman / President /
Chief Executive O
• Robert J. Dennis, EVP / Chief Operating
Officer
• James C. Estapa, SVP, Genesco Retail
• Jonathan D. Caplan, SVP, Genesco
Branded
Products:
Athletic and casual footwear, under a
license agreement with Levi Strauss & Co.
Brands:
Dockers

DODGER INDUSTRIES INC.
2705 STULTZ ROAD
PO BOX 711
MARTINSVILLE, VA 24112-07411
800-247-7879
Fax: 276-638-7161
sales@dodgerindustries.com
www.dodgerindustries.com
• Joe Throssel, Vice President
(641) 939-5464
jthrossel@dodgerindustries.com
• Steve Throssel, Chief Executive Officer
(641) 939-2335
sthrossel@dodgerindustries.com
• Clark Lawler, Executive VP
• Mark Adams, Marketing
Products:
Athletic apparel for teams and fans

DOLOMITE AMERICA, INC.
5 COMMERCE AVENUE
WEST LEBANON, NH 3784
800-257-2008
Fax: 203-855-1360
www.dolomiteusa.com
• Erika Smith, Sales / Marketing Director
(800) 257-2008
Products:
A variety of boots, including ski boots.

DORFMAN-PACIFIC COMPANY, INC.
2615 BOEING WAY
STOCKTON, CA 95206

866-304-5468
800-367-3626
Fax: 800-437-4287
custservice@dorfman-pacific.com
www.dorfman-pacific.com
• Doug Highsmith, President / Chief
Executive Officer
(209) 982-1400
custservice@dorfman-pacific.com
• John Callanan, VP
Products:
Hats and caps for men, women and
children, including those used for a variety
of sporting activities.

DOUGLAS INDUSTRIES, INC.
3441 S 11TH AVENUE
ELDRIDGE, IA 52748
800-553-8907
800-553-8907
Fax: 800-443-8907
sales@douglas-sports.com
www.douglas-sports.com
• Brad Fandel, Director of Sales
(800) 553-8907
• Jerry Douglas, CEO & President
jdouglas@douglas-sports.com
Products:
Douglas is a manufacturer of Sport Nets &
Equipment for a variety of sports including:
Tennis, Baseball, Soccer, Volleyball,
Basketball, Hockey, and Golf. Products
include: Tennis Nets and Posts, Backdrop
Curtains, Gym Dividers, Customer Netting,
Protective Padding, Volleyball Posts and
Nets, Baseball and Softball Products,
Windscreen, and much more.

DR SPORTS EQUIPMENT
5790 PARE
MONTREAL, QUEBEC, CANADA H4P 2M2
514-731-6841
800-567-6777
Fax: 514-342-4059
www.drxsports.com
• Todd Weaving, Sales / Marketing VP
Products:
Hockey, Ski and Baseball Equipment.

DRAPER INC.
411 S PEARL STREET
PO BOX 425
SPICELAND, IN 47385
765-987-7999
800-238-7999
Fax: 765-987-7142
drapercontract@draperinc.com
www.draperinc.com
• Debbie Searcy, Accounts Receivable and
Traffic Manager
(765) 856-1224
dsearcy@draperinc.com
• Robert Mathes, AV / Video Market
Manager
(765) 987-7999
bmathes@draperinc.com
• Chris Broome, Contract Market Manager
(765) 987-7999
cbroome@draperinc.com
• Neal Turner, Gymnasium Equipment
Manager
(800) 238-7999
nturner@draperinc.com
• Lee Denhart, Field Sales Manager
(765) 856-1211
ldenhart@draperinc.com
• Amy Bradway, AV/Video Sales

(765) 856-1252
abradway@draperinc.com
• Steve Cook, National AV Consultant
Manager
(765) 987-7999
scook@draperinc.com
• Amy Madden, Sales Support Manager,
Lifts Product Manager
(765) 856-1212
amadden@draperinc.com
Products:
Basketball Backstops, Gym Divider
Curtains, Gym Wall Pads, & Volleyball
Equipment
Brands:
EZ Fold Backstop
Nature of Service:
Manufacturer of Athletic Equipment.

DRYBRANCH, INC./SPORT DESIGN
1 COMMERCIAL COURT
PLAINVIEW, NY 11803-1600
516-576-7000
800-645-7722
Fax: 516-576-7008
www.drybranch.com
• Arthur Miller, President
Products:
Game Design-Better Quality Adult Games
Featuring Chess, Dominoes, Backgammon
and More. Sport Design: Smashball &
Kadima Racquet Sets. Scatch Reach Volley
Toss & Catch Products. Beach and Lawn
Games. Soft Smash-Foam Toys and Sports
Products.

DUCK HEAD APPAREL COMPANY
1020 BARROW INDUSTRIAL PARKWAY
PO BOX 688
WINDER, GA 30680
770-867-3111
800-933-0680
Fax: 770-307-1800
• Robert Rockey, President
• Billy Mattison, VP Merchandise
• Bill Reese, President
Products:
Men's and boys' casual sportswear
products, including shirts, shorts and pants
and other apparel and accessory products

DUCK HOUSE INC
4651 STATE STREET
#1 TOPLINE PLAZA
MONTCLAIR, CA 91763
909-628-0720
800-354-3655
Fax: 909-628-0382
sales@duckhouse.com
www.duckhouse.com
• Jeff Sherman, Sales / Marketing EVP
(909) 628-0720
jeff@duckhouse.com
Products:
Freezer Mugs, Glow Mugs, Tumblers,
Dinner Sets, Party Packs, Glow Pens, Paper
Weights, Placemats, Floor Merchandiser,
Availability Charts

DUNBROOKE
4200 LITTLE BLUE PARKWAY
INDEPENDENCE, MO 64057
816-795-7722
800-641-3627
Fax: 816-795-0321
greatservice@dunbrooke.com
www.dunbrooke.com

• Dave Hausen, President
(816) 795-7722
hausen@dunbrooke.com
• Jay Jones, Chief Financial Officer
(816) 795-7722
jones@dunbrooke.com
• Bob Pierce, EVP Sales / Marketing
(816) 795-7722
pierce@dunbrooke.com
Products:
Athletic Jackets/Parkas; Fashion Jackets &
Activewear, Knit Shirts, Woven Shirts,
Fleece

DUNLOP/MAXFLI/SLAZENGER GROUP AMERICAS
100 MAXFLI DRIVE
WESTMINSTER, SC 29693
864-241-2200
800-768-4727
Fax: 864-647-4087
www.maxfli.com
• David Beanon, Chairman
• Mike Rizzo, President
• Steve Ryan, VP Finance
• Edward Hughes, VP Marketing
Products:
Golf: Bags for Clubs, Luggage, Balls,
Clubs-Iron or Wood Sets, Putters, Utility
Clubs, Gloves, Hats/Caps, Headcovers,
Rainwear. Raquet Sports: Badminton and
Tennis equipment, Racquet Grips, Racquet
Strings, Shoes

DUNN'S
PO BOX 539
SYDNEY, NE 69162
308-233-5862
800-353-8621
Fax: 308-255-2450
www.dunns.com
• Parker Overton, President / Chief
Executive Officer
(308) 233-5862
customerservice@dunns.com
• Larry Carrol, Chief Operating Officer
(308) 233-5862
customerservice@dunns.com
• Brian Moen, Marketing Director
(308) 233-5862
Products:
Hunting apparel and products, footwear and
sporting dog equipment

DURHAM BOAT COMPANY
220 NEWMARKET ROAD
ROUTE 108
DURHAM, NH 3824
603-659-7575
Fax: 603-659-2548
cfuerst@durhamboat.com
www.durhamboat.com
• Coleen Fuerst, President
(603) 659-7575
Cfuerst@durhamboat.com
• James Dreher, VP General Manager
Products:
Boat racing equipment and accessories,
including Dreher Carbon Sculls, Dreher
Carbon Sweeps, Dreher Carbon
Footstretchers, Dreher Carbon Riggers,
Dreher Carbon Seats, BBG Racing Shells,
Racing Shells, Recreational Shells, Travel
Accessories, Books, Videos & DVDs,
Rowing Clothing, Rigging Accessories,
Rowing Electronics, Indoor Rowing Products

DYNAFLEX INTERNATIONAL
1144 N GROVE STREET
ANAHEIM, CA 92806
714-630-0909
800-480-8084
Fax: 714-632-5470
• Farren Mataele, Vice President
(714) 630-0909
farren@dynaflexpro.com
• Tom Smith, Chief Executive Officer
(714) 630-0909
dynaflexus@aol.com
• Tiffany Ludwig, Sales Manager
(714) 630-0909
tiffany@dynaflexpro.com
Products:
Health and exercise equipment, Dynamax
Core Trainer, Yoga Pilates kits, Powerball
Blue gyro-hand wrist exerciser, Body
Secrets massage rollers, Extreme Grip.
Description:
Unique line of gyro exercisers and many
other products to offer on the market today.

DYNAMIC TEAM SPORTS
454 ACORN LANE
DOWNINGTOWN, PA 19335
610-518-3300
800-437-6223
Fax: 610-518-9200
info@dynamicteamsports.com
www.dynamicteamsports.com
• Scott A Samter, President
• Richard Nigro, Sales/Operations Director
(610) 518-3300
sales@dynamicteamsports.com
Products:
Manufactures uniforms for basketball,
baseball, softball, soccer, wrestling,
lacrosse, field hockey, volleyball, track &
field, tennis and cheerleading, football,
swimming, ice hockey and rugby.

DYNASTY APPAREL INDUSTRIES
13000 NW 42ND AVENUE
MIAMI, FL 33054
305-685-3490
800-833-8337
Fax: 305-687-1393
hector@dynastyapparel.com
• Ignacio Mendez, President
imendez@dynastyapparel.com
• Armando Mendez, CEO
armendez@dynastyapparel.com
• Lorenzo Mendez, COO
Lorenzo@dynastyapparel.com
• Felix Hernandez, CFO
fhernandez@dynastyapparel.com
• Hector Rodriguez, Executive of Sales and
Marketing
Hector@dynastyapparel.com
• Lissette Padron, Marketing Coordinator
Lissette@dynastyapparel.com
• Erica Mendez, Licensing Coordinator
Erica@dynastyapparel.com
Products:
Manufactures sports apparel: T-shirts,
pullovers, tank tops; embroidery and screen
printing services

DYNASTY DESIGNS, LLC
1101 N WARSON ROAD
SAINT LOUIS, MO 63132
314-429-2220
866-892-2225
Fax: 314-429-2234
www.dynastydesigns.com

- Craig Albrecht, CEO
- Ted Albrecht, President & Chief Operations Officer
- Drew Caylor, Vice President
Products:
Collegiate Furniture, Pub Stools, PUb Tables, Gifts, and Holiday Accessories.
Year Founded:
2002

E&D SPECIALTY STANDS INC.
2081 FRANKLIN STREET
PO BOX 700
N COLLINS, NY 14111
800-525-8515
800-525-8515
Fax: 716-337-2903
info@edstands.com
www.edstands.com
- Doug Bigelow, Vice Presidnet
(800) 525-8515
dougb@edstands.com
- Jon Williams, National Sales Manager
(800) 525-8515
jonw@edstands.com
Products:
Design, fabrication and installation of bleachers, grandstands, stadium seating and portable seating units (Permanent Beam Design, Angle Frame Design, Portable Bleachers, Seat Boards, Seat Backs, Foot Boards, Riser Boards, Decking Types, VIP Suites & Pressboxes).

E-FORCE
2151 LAS PALMAS DRIVE
SUITE D
CARLSBAD, CA 92011
800-433-6723
Fax: 760-804-0225
warranty@e-force.com
www.e-force.com
- Ron Grimes, President
Products:
Racquetball - Accessories, Bags, Eyewear, Gloves, Racquets, String.

E-Z GARD INDUSTRIES
3405 ANNAPOLIS LANE N
SUITE 200
PLYMOUNTH, MN 55447
800-233-6956
866-253-1314
Fax: 888-446-5999
- Steven J. Washburn, President / Chief Executive Officer
- John McCartan, SVP of Sales
- Jay Turkbas, VP of Marketing and Product Development
Products:
Offers a comprehensive line of innovative performance products, including core protective gear for hockey, football and baseball, lacrosse equipment, and bio-mechanic insoles.

E-Z GO
1451 MARVIN GRIFFIN ROAD
AUGUSTA, GA 30906
706-798-4311
800-241-5855
Fax: 706-771-4609
www.ezgo.com
- Kathleen C Searle, VP Communications
- Kevin Holleran, President
- Jon Phillips, Director International Sales
- Chris Spencer, VP

Products:
Oldest manufacturer of golf cars and utility vehicles, and produces the #1 selling golf car.

E.B. ROTONDI & SONS, INC.
21 MANISON STREET
STONEHAM, MA 02180-3111
781-438-5005
Fax: 781-438-5006
www.ebrotondi.com
- Michael J. Rotondi, Vice President
mjr@ebrotondi.com
- Michael J. Rotondi, Vice President
- Dennis Lawhorne, Project Manager
- Lawrence Schofield, Engineer
- A. Joseph B. Rotondi, President
rbg@ebrotondi.com
Nature of Service:
General Contractor Sports Facility Construction
Year Founded:
1932
Products:
Surfaces Floor and Court Sports Facilities
Brands:
Har Tru Nova

E.P. PRO
8 W 40TH STREET
2ND FLOOR
NEW YORK, NY 10018
855-924-2228
800-926-8010
Fax: 212-302-5982
www.eppro.com
- Larry Mathe, President / Chief Executive Officer
- Stuart Warshaw, Chief Financial Officer
- Sandy Martinelli, VP Operations
- Rebecca Ryan, VP Sales
Products:
Providing high quality, classic, golf specific sportswear

E.S. ORIGINALS
450 W 33RD STREET
NEW YORK, NY 10001
212-736-8124
800-677-6577
Fax: 212-736-8366
www.esoriginals.com
- John Otis, Marketing Director
Products:
Manufacturers and importers of fashion footwears: Athletic Shoes, Canvas Sneakers, Plush Character Slippers, Quilted Fabric Slippers, Knit Slippers Socks, Rain and Snow Boots, Hiker-Style Boots, Clear Plastic Jelly Shoes, Aqua Socks, Beach Sandals

EAGLES WINGS
2101 OLD HICKORY TREE ROAD
SAINT CLOUD, FL 34772
407-892-6358
Fax: 407-892-6759
www.eagleswings.com
Products:
Offer a variety of themed ties (Inspirational ties, Sports ties, Specialty ties, Fashion Essentials) and men's accessories

EARBAGS
45 KENSICO DRIVE
2ND FLOOR
MOUNT KISCO, NY 10549
914-242-8566
888-327-2241
Fax: 914-242-8567
Julie@sprigsville.com
www.sprigs.com
- Valerie Ciptak, President
val@sprigsville.com
- Dawn Chaskin, VP, Sales & Marketing
dawn@sprigsville.com
Products:
Swedish bandless earmuff for cycling, riding, and professional athletes in windy or cold weather.

EARMARK
1125 DIXWELL AVENUE
HAMDEN, CT 06514
203-777-2130
888-327-6275
Fax: 203-777-2886
sales@earmark.com
www.earmark.com
- Andy Cowell, Contact
(203) 777-2130
Founded:
1973
Description:
Earmark designs and manufactures wireless communication systems.

EARTH & TURF
112 S RAILROAD AVENUE
NEW HOLLAND, PA 17557
717-355-2776
888-693-2638
Fax: 877-243-2442
www.earthandturf.com
- John Bentley, President
Products:
Manufactures Topdressers and Aerators for the Turgrass Industry.

EASTON SPORTS, INC.
7855 HASKELL AVENUE
SUITE 200
VAN NUYS, CA 91406-1902
800-632-7866
800-632-7866
Fax: 818-782-4407
customerservice@eastonsports.com
www.eastonsports.com
- Jim Easton, Chairman
customerservice@eastonsports.com
- Tony Palma, President
customerservice@eastonsports.com
- Gerry Maurizio, Chief Information Officer
customerservice@eastonsports.com
- Mike Zlatek, VP Bsbl / Softball
Products:
Privately owned manufacturer, marketer, and distributor of sports equipment.

EASTON TECHNICAL PRODUCTS
5040 HAROLD GATTY DRIVE
SALT LAKE CITY, UT 84116-2897
801-539-1400
Fax: 801-533-9907
techinfo@eastontp.com
www.eastonarchery.com
- Chris Oswald, Director, Marketing & Sales
- Greg Easton, President
Products:
Unparalleled leader in the arrow industry,

delivering the most technologicaly advanced arrows and components for target archers and bowhunters alike.

EASTPAK CORPORATION
PO BOX 1817
APPLETON, WI 54912-1817
800-222-5725
Fax: 920-735-1933
www.eastpak.com
• Gwen Wisler, President / Chief Executive Officer
• Mark Goldman, Chairman
• Henry Friedman, SVP Sales
• Jim Salzenstein, EVP
Products:
Outdoor Products, Backpacks, Bag.

EASY RACERS
10 HANGAR WAY
WATSONVILLE, CA 95076
831-722-9797
Fax: 831-768-9623
info@easyracers.com
www.easyracers.com
• Denton Worthy Coetzee, Chief Executive Officer & President
Products:
Industry leader in cutting edge recumbent bicycle design and manufacture.

EATON GOLF PRIDE
440 MURRAY HILL ROAD
SOUTHERN PINES, NC 28387
910-695-2900
Fax: 910-277-3700
ContactGolfPride@Eaton.com
www.eaton.com
• Jeff Fiorini, General Manager
• Dwight Miles, Director, Sales & Marketing
• Dan Koehler, Global Marketing Manager
• Wright Chandler, Sales Manager
Products:
Leading supplier of grips to the club manufacturing industry and the top choice for grip replacement.

EBBETS FIELD FLANNELS
119 S JACKSON STREET
SEATTLE, WA 98104
206-382-7249
888-896-2936
Fax: 206-382-4411
customerservice@ebbets.com
www.ebbets.com
• Jerry Cohen, Founder
(206) 382-7249
jcohen@ebbets.com
Products:
Vintage Baseball Uniforms, Jackets, Jersys, Ballcaps, Fungo Shirts, T-shirts, Utility Jersy, Practical Jersy, Gridiron Shirts
Year Founded:
1988

EBONITE INTERNATIONAL, INC.
1813 W 7TH STREET
HOPKINSVILLE, KY 42240
270-881-1200
800-626-8350
Fax: 270-881-1201
www.ebonite.com
• Mike Quitter, VP International
• Carl Rogers, CFO & Treasurer
• Bob Reid, VP, Marketing
• J M. Quitter, VP Sales

Products:
Manufacturer of bowling balls for professionals and style-concious bowlers. It also manufactures ball bags and other accessories.

ECLECTIC PRODUCTS, INC.
101 DIXIE MAE DRIVE
PINEVILLE, LA 71360
318-640-5116
800-349-4667
Fax: 547-746-1983
info@eclecticproducts.com
www.eclecticproducts.com
• Sheila Ecker, Sales Coordinator
• Ken Barton, Vice President, Industrial Sales and Manufacturing
Description:
Adhesives for the sports and outdoor markets.
Brands:
Shoe Goo; Sport & Outdoor Goop; Marine Goop
Clients:
Wal-Mart, Academy Sports, Home Depot, K-Mart, Dick's Sporting Goods, Bass Pro Shops

EDDY BROS. HAT CO. INC.
314 E BIDWELL STREET
FOLSOM, CA 95630
916-983-2668
www.eddybros.com
• Jack Eddy, Founder
Products:
Headwear

EIBACH SPRINGS, INC
264 MARIAH CIRCLE
CORONA, CA 92879
951-256-8300
800-507-2338
Fax: 951-256-8333
eibach@eibach.com
Products:
Automotive Suspension Products, as well as Industrial Springs, Dynaflex Die-Springs and Seal Components, High Performance Valve Springs, Children's Play Ground Components.

EIGER SPORTSWEAR, INC.
4775 S BUTTERFIELD DRIVE
155
TUCSON, AZ 85714
800-527-3757
800-527-3757
Fax: 520-571-0733
• Bruce Caris, Sales Manager
• Wolfgang Weber, Marketing Director
Products:
Custom Apparel, including Soccer Uniforms (Men's/Women's) Volleyball Uniforms, Sweatsuits, Bags and Socks.

EKTELON
17110 Marcy Street
LL02
Omaha, NE 68118
402-884-7600
800-283-2635
Fax: 402-884-6286
www.ektelon.com
• Scott Winters, Director
• Jon Panno, Product Manager

Products:
Racquets, Powerpacks, Gloves, Eyeguards, Footwear, Sportbags, Strings and Grips, Accessories

ELASCO, INC.
11377 MARKON DRIVE
GARDEN GROVE, CA 92841
714-891-1795
800-827-7887
Fax: 714-895-7031
info@elascourethane.com
www.elascourethane.com
• Henry Larrucea, Partner
info@elascourethane.com
• David Schindler, President
Products:
Electrical, water and pneumatic cable guards.

ELBY GIFTS
879 INDUSTRIEL
BOIS DES FILION, QUEBEC, CANADA J6Z 4T3
450-965-8288
877-352-9462
Fax: 450-965-8688
info@elbygifts.com
www.elbygifts.com
• Robert Lio, President
(450) 965-8288
robertlio@elbygifts.com
• Sonja Coia, Operating Manager VP
(450) 965-8229
scoia@elbygifts.com
• Jonathan Lio, Sales Coordinator
(450) 965-8242
jonathanlio@elbygifts.com
• Linda Sirois, Customer Service
(450) 965-8222
orders@elbygifts.com
• Barbara Sheppard, Claims Department
(450) 965-8240
claims@elbygifts.com
• Marzieh Tandel, Account Receivables, Compte Clients
(450) 965-8228
marzieh@elbygifts.com
Products:
Giftware, home d,cor, collectibles, and licensed products

ELECTRA TARP
2900 PERRY DRIVE SW
CANTON, OH 44706
330-477-7168
800-274-1003
Fax: 330-477-7702
electratarp@sbcglobal.net
www.electratarp.com
• Robert Fulmer, President
• Bitsy Paul, President's Assistant
bitsy@electratarp.com
• Michele Minock, Sales Representative
Products:
All Purpose Tarpaulins & Accessories, Football Safeline Covers, Anti-Static Polyethylene, Athletic Covers, Awana Game Floors, Colorguard Floor, Industrial and Commercial Tarpaulins, Floor Covers, Greenhouse Covers, Mobile Storage Racks, Gym Floor Covers.

ELECTRO-MECH SCOREBOARD COMPANY
72 IINDUSTRIAL BLVD
WRIGHTSVILLE, GA 31096

478-864-3366
800-445-7846
Fax: 478-864-0212
score@electro-mech.com
www.electro-mech.com
• Allen McMichael, President
• Tim Branton, Outside Sales
score@electro-mech.com
• Jim Ledford, National Sales Manager
• Allen McMichael, Internet Sales
• Leslie Lawrence, Inside Sales
Products:
Timing Devices - Scoreboards.

ELITE SPORTSWEAR, L.P.
2136 N 13TH STREET
PO BOX 16400
READING, PA 19612-6400
800-345-4087
Fax: 888-866-9884
info@gkelite.com
• Sallie Weaver, President
• Paul Honig, Finance VP
• Birgitte Sorensen, Marketing Manager
• Kelly McKeown, Executive VP
Products:
GK Competitive Gymnastics Apparel, GK
Workout Gymnastics Apparel, GK
Essentials Apparel, GK Dancewear, GK
Skating Wear, GK Synchro Team Skating
Wear

ELLESSE U.S.A., INC.
3333 NEW HYDE PARK ROAD
SUITE 200
NEW HYDE PARK, NY 11042
516-365-1333
800-ELLESSE
Fax: 516-365-2333
info@ellesse.com
www.ellesse.com
• Stuart Hudson, National Sales Manager
(516) 643-0445
stuartmhudson@aol.com
Products:
Sportswear, Footwear and watches
Year Founded:
1959

EMBROIDERY STORE
3929-A WESTPOINT BOULEVARD
SUITE 100
WINSTON-SALEM, NC 27103
336-765-0910
800-504-9757
Fax: 336-765-0920
info@embstore.com
www.embstore.com
• Bill Fenimore, VP
BFenimore@embstore.com
Products:
Backings and Toppings, Bobbin Cases &
Sewing Hooks, Clearance, Embroidery
Starter Kit, Embroidery Supplies, General
Parts, Gift Card, Hooping Systems, Hoops
and Frames, Logo Builder Software,
Meistergram Designs and Alphabets,
Needles, Scissors and Snips, Stock
Designs, Threads and Bobbins

EMERGENCY MEDICAL SUPPLY
238 SALTWELL ROAD
PO BOX 99
SHEPHERDSVILLE, KY 40165
502-543-2401
Fax: 502-543-5032

• Chip Brake, National Sales Manager
(800) 720-4119
Products:
Clearance Items, Special Items, Airway
Management Items, Apparel, Bags and
Cases, Bandaging, Dressing & Tapes,
Blood Collection, Cold and Hot Packs, Cots,
Defib and Pacing Pads, Diagnostics, ECG
Electrodes, Extrication/Splints, Gloves, Glow
Stick Chemical Lights, Immobilization,
Incident Command/Mass Casualty, Infection
Control, Infusion, Injection, Instruments &
Tools, Monitors & Accessories, Pandemic
Bio Kits, Patient Assesment, Patient Care
Disposable Items, Patient Transport, Sharps
Containers, Stocked Kits, Training
Equipment

EMPI, INC.
599 CARDIGAN ROAD
PO BOX 64640
SAINT PAUL, MN 55126-4099
615-415-9000
800-328-2536
Fax: 800-450-3593
support@empi.com
• John Velure, Senior Director of Marketing
• Mark Francois, Director of Corporate
Communications
(760) 734-4766
Products:
Transcutaneous Electrical Nerve
Stimulation, Interferential Current Pain
Management, Clinical Portable Multifunction
Electrotherapy System, Neuromuscular
Electrical Stimulation, Non-invasive drug
delivery system, Non-invasive drug delivery
system, Cervical and Lumbar traction,
Dynamic Splinting Orthoses, Pelvic Floor
Stimulation devices, TENS / NMES
electrodes and accessories

EMPIRE SPORTING GOODS MFG.
COMPANY, INC.
301 MT PLEASANT AVENUE
NEWARK, NJ 07104-3723
973-497-5600
800-221-3455
Fax: 212-941-7113
www.empiresportinggoods.com
• Charles Rauch, President
Products:
Baseball - Caps, Socks, Stirrups, Uniforms;
Basketball - Socks, Uniforms; Boxing -
Trunks; Football - Socks, Uniforms; General
Sports Products - Athletic Jackets/Parkas,
Athletic Supporters, Complete Lettering
Department, Referee Uniforms, Warm-Up
Suits

EMPIRE SPORTS/SISCO SPORTS
1639 ABBOT KINNEY BOULEVARD
VENICE, CA 90291
310-450-4114
Fax: 310-301-7962
• Chou Windsor, Owner
• Ray Flores, Product Manager
Products:
1995

ENDLESS POOLS, INC.
1601 DUTTON MILL ROAD
ASTON, PA 19014
610-497-8676
800-910-2714
Fax: 610-497-9328

swim@endlesspools.com
www.endlesspools.com
• James Murdock, Founder/President
swim@endlesspools.com
• Tim Plummer, VP
swim@endlesspools.com
Products:
Workout training pool that uses water-flow
resistance in small scale training pools.

ENDURA RUBBER FLOORING
2250 SOUTH TENTH STREET
SAN JOSE, CA 95112
800-669-7010
800-447-8442
Fax: 781-647-4543
info@burkeindustries.com
www.burkeflooring.com
• Dan Kelly, President
• Joseph Balfe, Sales Administration
Manager
Products:
Floor tile, stair treads, SRT series spike and
skate resistant tile, cove base, stair nosing,
accessories, adhesives, maintenance
products, and special products.

ENDURANCE NET
PO BOX 127
PO BOX 127
ROEBLING, NJ 8554
609-499-3450
800-808-6387
Fax: 609-499-3520
EnduranceNet@aol.com
www.endurancenetinc.com
• Mike Thompson, Sales Manager
Manufacturer:
Nets - Game Bird Netting, Bird & Wildlife
Netting, Barrior Nets for all types of Sports.
Fabric Net.

ENELL, INC.
319 SECOND STREET
PO BOX 808
HAVRE, MT 59501
406-265-8250
800-828-7661
Fax: 406-265-5909
info@enell.com
www.enell.com
• Renelle Braaten, Founder and President
(406) 265-8250
renelle.braaten@enell.com
• Mara Bronson, Marketing Director
(406) 265-8250
• Nicole Knowlton, Customer Service
(406) 265-8250
nicole.knowlton@enell.com
Description:
Manufacture, market & distribute
high-performance apparel for well-endowed
women.
Sports Products Manufactured:
Enell Sports Bra & Enell Lite Bra
Brands:
Enell

ENTRE-PRISES USA
63085 18TH STREET
SUITE 101
BEND, OR 97701
541-388-5463
800-580-5463
Fax: 541-388-3248
Info@epusa.com
www.epusa.com

- Eric Meade, Co-Owner/CEO
- Antoine Richard, CEO / President

Products:
Manufactures, designs, installs and distributes the most diverse line of climbing walls and handholds in the industry.

EPIC METALS
11 TALBOT AVENUE
RANKIN, PA 15104
412-351-3913
877-696-3742
Fax: 412-351-2018
info@epicmetals.com
www.epicmetals.com
- Ed Thomas, General Manager Sales
- Thomas Hartman, Vice President Sales

Products:
Architectural roof and floor deck ceiling systems.

EQUALIZER EXERCISE MACHINES
DEER PARK PO
PO BOX 25105
RED DEER, ALBERTA, CANADA T4R 2M2
403-309-5551
Fax: 403-342-5509
james@equalizerexercise.com
www.equalizerexercise.com

Products:
6000 Series, Home Gym with Gripless, 1000 Series, Single Station, Pec Fly Rear Delt,Leg Curl/ Leg Extension, Free Weights, Half Rack, Pro Power Rack, Flat to Military Bench and Cable Crossover.

EQUIPTO
225 MAIN STREET
TATAMY, PA 18085
610-253-2775
800-323-0801
Fax: 888-859-2121
www.equipto.com
- Tom Matyas, President and Chief Executive Officer
- Joe Gianfalla, Marketing & Sales VP
- Tom Matyas, President and CEO

Products:
Provider of automotive workbench and of complete storage space solutions offering shelving & racks, modular drawer cabinets, mobile aisle systems, mezzanines, workcenters, cabinets and carts

ERIC ARMIN INC./EAI
118 BAUER DRIVE
PO BOX 7046
OAKLAND, NJ 07436-7046
201-891-9466
800-272-0272
Fax: 201-891-5689
info@eaiusa.com
www.eaiusa.com
- Eric Guglberger, President
eguglberger@eaiusa.com

Products:
Calculators, watches, workbooks; vernier probes, manipulatives and EAI science related products; chronographs, stopwatches, timing products and atomic watches.

ERIK SPORTS, INC.
18 INDUSTRIAL AVENUE
MAHWAH, NJ 7430

201-825-2434
800-247-6579
Fax: 201-825-2414
info@eriksports.com
www.eriksports.com
- Michael Messler, President
(800) 247-6579
mmessler@eriksports.com

Products:
Boots, bindings, poles, skis, waxes & accessories and youth equipment; Snowshoe and Snowshoe poles; and Snowboards, bindings, boots and waxes & accessories.

ESCALADE SPORTS
817 MAXWELL AVENUE
EVANSVILLE, IN 47711
812-467-1200
800-467-1421
Fax: 812-467-1245
customerservice@escaladesports.com
www.escaladesports.com
- Bob Keller, President
- Dave Fetherman, Vice President, Sales & Marketing
- Philip J. Piccolo, Executive VP
- Kirk Williams, VP Of Strategic Analysis & Development

Products:
Producer of table tennis tables and accessories; billiards tables; darts, dartboards, cabinets and accessories; Aerobic step products; Full line of Archery Equipment; basketball, volleyball, badminton, croquet, bocce and soccer products.

Brands:
Goalrilla, Stiga, Ping-Pong, The Step, USW, Woodplay, Oasis, Bear Archery, Trophy Ridge, Musclesmith

ESPORTSMAN.COM
8116 S TRYON STREET
SUITE B3#212
CHARLOTTE, NC 28273
877-343-7767
888-776-7811
Fax: 704-248-8151
- David Singh, Founder

ETCHASOFT, INC.
13400 SUTTON PARK DRIVE S
SUITE 1501
JACKSONVILLE, FL 32224
904-493-0701
Fax: 904-493-0704
info@etchasoft.com
www.etchasoft.com
- Ben Balke, President

Products:
Commercial Product, Commercial Product & Spin Off company and Beta Product for commercial use.

ETONIC
350 FIFTH AVENUE
SUITE 6617
NEW YORK, NY 10118
212-273-3301
Fax: 212-273-3345
www.shopetonic.com/
- Tom Elwell, Chief Executive Officer
- Dan Ladd, Global Sales VP
- Karen Pitts, Global Marketing VP
- Dan Werremeyer, President

Products:
Shoes and gloves.

EVAN CORPORATION
22 SW AVENUE
JAMESTOWN, RI 2835
401-423-2230
Fax: 401-423-2785
info@evancorp.com
www.evancorp.com
- David P. Evangelista, President & Chief Executive Officer

Year Founded:
1995.

Nature of Service:
Provider of rigging and rooftop fall protection systems for public assembly facilities with installations in more than 95 facilities nationwide.

EVENT PROMOTION SUPPLY
11420 E 51ST AVENUE
DENVER, CO 80239
303-371-1717
800-227-0337
Fax: 303-371-9149
allisont@eps-doublet.com
www.eps-doublet.com
- Jon Leasia, President
jleasia@eps-doublet.com

Products:
Banners, Instant Advertising, Flags, Point of Purchase, Tradeshow Graphics, Display Frames, Graphic Tents, Event Supplies, Contestant Number and Bibs, Fences and Barricades, Fleet and Transit, Traffic and Safety and Design and Installation .

EVERLAST WORLDWIDE INC
1350 BROADWAY
SUITE 2300
NEW YORK, NY 10018
212-239-0990
Fax: 212-239-4261
info@everlast.com
www.everlast.com
- Adam Geisler, President

Products:
Manufacturer: Boxing - Pro Boxing Gloves, Training Gloves, Bag Gloves, Evergel Glove Wraps, Handwrap, Tape, Gauze, Punch Mitt, Shield, Protector, Boxing Head Gear, Mouthpiece, Protective Cups, Shoes, Rings, Punching Bags, Heavy Bags, Speed Bags; Training & Exercise Equipment.

EVERLAST WORLDWIDE, INC.
1350 BROADWAY
SUITE 2300
NEW YORK, NY 10018
212-239-0990
Fax: 212-239-4261
www.everlast.com
- George Q. Horowitz, Chairman / President / Chief Executive O
- Matthew F. Mark, Chief Financial Officer
- Rita Cinque-Kriss, VP / Director
- Wayne Nadorf, Sales Assistant VP / Director

Products:
Women's activewear, sportswear, swimwear and coverups and men's activewear, sportswear and outerwear; line of boxing related sporting goods such as boxing gloves, heavy bags, speed bags, boxing trunks, and miscellaneous gym equipment; men's, women's and children's apparel,

sleepwear, underwear, hosiery, footwear, leatherwear, cardiovascular equipment, eyewear, sports bags, hats and other accessories.

EVERSAN, INC/UNITEC MFG DIVISION
34 MAIN STREET
WHITESBORO, NY 13492
315-736-3967
800-383-6060
Fax: 315-736-4058
sales@eversan.com
www.eversan.com
• Mustafa Evke, Chief Executive Officer
• Allan Roberts, VP
Products:
Timing Devices - Message Board Systems, Electronic Scoreboards, Stopwatches-Digital, Timers, Shot Clocks, Ski Race Timing.

EVOL SNOWBOARDS
7130 CONVOY COURT
SAN DIEGO, CA 92111
858-874-4970
888-674-7478
Fax: 858-278-3274
• Tony Magnusson, President
• Tony Chen, VP
• Doug Weston, National Sales Manager
Products:
Snowboards, Skateboards, Skateboard Shoes, Apparel, Wakeboards

EXCALIBUR ELECTRONICS
555 TAXTER ROAD
SUITE 210
ELMSFORD, NY 10523-2336
914-964-5200
800-592-4337
Fax: 914-476-3068
service@excaliburelectronics.com
www.excaliburelectronics.com
• Shane Samole, President
• Mike Catena, EVP
• Andy Stathopolus, Operations VP
• Al Lawrence, Product Development VP
Products:
Sports, Casino & Parlor Games, Chess and Poker Games.
Brands:
Exploring the Universe, Keepsake Corner, Master Series

EXCEL VOLLEYBALL PRODUCTS, INC.
15545 COMPUTER LANE
HUNTINGTON BEACH, CA 92649
714-898-7720
800-677-3669
Fax: 714-892-4730
info@excelsportsproducts.com
www.excelsportsproducts.com
• Cherry Blaine, President
• Sharon Shroyer, Marketing Director
Products:
Ankle Protection: ankle braces, Boxes, Carts, Equipment Storage, Jump-Training Device, Portable Scoring & Press Tables, Recreation Swim Equipment

EXCLUSIVELY EXPO, INC.
1225 NAPERVILLE DRIVE
ROMEOVILLE, IL 60446
630-378-4600
Fax: 630-378-4617
Sales@exclusivelyexpo.com

• Jim Buehner, Owner
(630) 378-4600
sales@exclusivelyexpo.com
• Marie Buehner, Marketing Manager
marieb@exclusivelyexpo.com
Products:
Soccer Nets, Volleyball Equipment: Serving Machines; Net Systems; Padding; Posts; Volleyballs; Water Polo Equipment

EXECUTIVE DIVERSIONS
1870 COLT ROAD
SUITE 110
MEDIA, PA 19063
610-566-1171
Fax: 610-565-2289
www.edigolfevents.com
• Kevin M. Scanlon, President/CEO
(610) 566-1171
kevin@edigolfevents.com
• Rachel Kane, Development & Marketing Director
(516) 668-2739
Nature of Service:
Manufacturer
Description:
EDI provides sports event management to corporate, charity and private industries. EDI manages up to twenty golf events annually including corporat, charity and Pro-Am golf outings.
Year Founded:
1987
Products:
Cheer Uniforms - Budget to High End, Cheer Apparel, Warm up Jackets and Pants, Dance Team and Dance Recital Costumes.
Brands:
Deventers Cheer, Dancewear Factory.

EXERCYCLE CORPORATION
31 HAYWARD STREET
FRANKLIN, MA 2038
508-528-3100
800-367-6712
Fax: 508-528-8454
www.theracycle.com
• Michael Dugan, President / Chief Executive Officer
• David St. Germain, President
Products:
Stationary Bikes and Exercise Machines for the Physically Challenged

EXERTOOLS
170 EAST MEADOWS
PETALUMA, CA 94952
800-235-1559
Fax: 707-585-8404
customersupport@exertoolsinc.com
www.exertools.com
• Eric Parsells, President
(800) 235-1559
Products:
Exertools manufactures and distributes products to the fitness, therapeutic and rehabilitation markets. Exertools has been a product innovator for years. Products include the industry standard Plyoback rebounder - a market leader in the field of plyometric exercise, DynaDisc balance cushions - a staple in training & conditioning protocols, DynaBoard Balance Boards - used with DynaDiscs to increase the challenge of balance & core training, the Dual Mult-Slant stretching device, and three

lines of Medicine Balls designed for a variety of applications. Exertools has expanded their webstore to offer products from other top manufacturers concentra

EXMARK MANUFACTURING
INDUSTRIAL PARK NW
PO BOX 808
BEATRICE, NE 68310-0808
402-223-6300
Fax: 402-223-6384
www.exmark.com
• John Cloutier, Marketing Communications Manager
(402) 223-6308
john.cloutier@exmark.com
• John Swanson, Product Manager
• Daryn Walters, Director of Marketing
• Garry Busboom, Director of Research and Development
• Dave Converse, Director of Engineering
Products:
Mowing systems

EXXEL OUTDOORS
300 AMERICAN BOULEVARD
HALEYVILLE, AL 35565
205-486-5258
Fax: 205-486-9882
www.exxel.com
• Harry Kazazian, CEO
• Armen Kouleyan, President
• Torry H. Upham, VP
Products:
Exporter of high quality camping gear, such as fishing apparel, sleeping bags, hunting apparel, water sports, tents, military apparel

EZ-LINER INDUSTRIES
1920 ALBANY PLACE SE
ORANGE CITY, IA 51041
712-737-4016
800-373-4016
Fax: 712-737-4148
sales@ezliner.com
www.ezliner.com
• Rob Krommendyk, Marketing Manager
Products:
Pavement and field paint striping equipment.
Year Founded:
1965
Description:
EZ-Liner manufactures high-quality striping equipment for rugged use and dependability.

F.I.T. VENTILATION
104 MECO LANE
OAK RIDGE, TN 33760
646-475-2249
Fax: 865-298-0199
www.exai.com
• Eran Shatzman, VP Business Development
• Yosh Sagie, VP Sales
• Gal Moran, Partner and CEO/CFO
gal@exai.com
• Tzvika Agassi, COO
• Shy Rosenzweig, CMO
• Ethan Pogrebizsky, CTO
Products:
Multiple ventilations such as: FIT Fan Models, Single Fan Models, Athletic Model, Wall Mount Model, Misting Option, Compact Model

FABRICATION ENTERPRISES
PO BOX 1500
WHITE PLAINS, NY 10602
914-345-9300
800-431-2830
Fax: 914-345-9800
info@fab-ent.com
www.fab-ent.com
• Elliott Goldberg, President
elliott@Fab-Ent.com
• Andrew Goldberg, Catalog Marketing
andrew@Fab-Ent.com
• Jason Drucker, Sales
jason@Fab-Ent.com
• Linda Goldberg, Director Of Sales
• Andrew Goldberg, Director Of Marketing
Products:
Medical and nutritional products for Physical Therapy, Rehabilitation, Homecare and Sports Medicine

FAIR-PLAY SCOREBOARDS
1700 DELAWARE AVENUE
DES MOINES, IA 50317
515-265-5305
800-247-0265
Fax: 515-265-3364
sales@fair-play.com
www.fair-play.com
• J.M. Allain, President & CEO
• Jeff Reeser, National Sales Manager
Products:
Scoreboards, Control Systems, Sports Message Centers, Accessories, Information Displays, Signage, Scoring & Video Systems
Brands:
Fair-Play and TL Vision

FAIRTRON
26 PEARL STREET
NORWALK, CT 6850
860-269-1578
Fax: 203-852-0836
sales@trans-lux.com
www.trans-lux.com
• Michael R Mulcahy, President/Chief Executive Officer
• Thomas Brandt, EVP / Co-Chief Executive Officer
• Jean-Marc L. D Allain, President & Chief Executive Officer
• Brian Laroche, President, TL Energy
• Karl P. Hirschauer, Vice President
• Thomas F. Mahone, Vice President
• Todd Dupee, Vice President and Controller
• Jay A. Forlenzo, Vice President
• Jane Bauer, Assistant Vice President, Human Resources
Products:
Indoor Programmable LED Signs, Electronic Outdoor Displays, Scoreboards,Electronic Outdoor Displays

FANATICS UNLIMITED
5507 FOXVALE COURT
MIDLOTHIAN, VA 23112
804-739-2392
Fax: 804-601-2820
• Chuck Bajnai, Creator / Executive Manager
Products:
Fun collectibles with sports team and desgins.

FANMATS LLC
3255 SHAWNEE INDUSTRIAL WAY
SUITE 100
SUWANEE, GA 30024
678-730-0600
800-525-5923
Fax: 678-730-0604
sales@FANMATS.com
www.fanmats.com
• Bob Roche, Owner
bob@fanmats.com
• GM Onur
(678) 730-0600
• Iteace Davila, Accounts Receivable
(678) 730-0592
Products:
Tufted floor mats and rugs including athletic mats, entrance mats, area mats, car, truck, tailgate and garage mats
Description;
A licensed MLB, NFL, NBA, NHL and college manufacturer of fangear out of Georgia, developing and making a range of sports licensed mats, mirror covers, fanbrands and official yoga mats.
Teams;
NFL, MLB, NHL, & NBA. Plus 800 College teams as well as Military teams.

FASTECH LABS
1100 OWENDALE
SUITE J
TROY, MI 48083
248-244-9000
800-986-3668
Fax: 248-528-9801
www.fastechlabs.net
• Glenn Cumberland, Founder
(800) 351-3668
fastglenn@aol.com
Products:
Pedorthic Foot Support Products - Arch Cushions & Supports, Foot Orthotics, Heel Supports.

FEDERAL PREMIUM AMMUNITION
900 EHLEN DRIVE
ANOKA, MN 55303-7503
800-379-1732
Fax: 763-323-2506
www.federalpremium.com
• Gerald W. Bersett, President
• Margaret McDonald, VP
Products:
Complete line of shotshell, centerfire, rifle, pistol, slug, buckshot and rimfire ammunition and components

FELDMAR WATCH COMPANY, INC.
9000 W PICO BOULEVARD
LOS ANGELES, CA 90035
310-274-8016
Fax: 310-274-2081
info@feldmarwatch.com
www.feldmarwatch.com
• Sol Meller, President
smeller@feldmarwatch.com
Products:
Watches, Stopwatches, Fine Pens, Accessories

FENWICK GOLF COMPANY
1900 18TH STREET
SPIRIT LAKE, IA 51360
712-336-1520
800-554-4653
Fax: 712-336-5183

Products:
Golf - Graphite Golf Shafts.

FERA
3521 CHALLENGER STREET
TORRANCE, CA 90503
310-370-8538
800-828-3372
Fax: 310-214-3668
info@ferastyle.com
www.ferastyle.com
• Eric Tung, Founder
Products:
Skiing-Alpine - Apparel-Activewear, Outerwear, Sweaters, Base layers.

FERNO PERFORMANCE POOLS
70 WEIL WAY
WILMINGTON, OH 45177
888-206-7802
888-206-7802
Fax: 937-382-0895
www.fernoperformancepools.com
Products:
Commercial and Home Pools, Underwater Treadmills and Water Bike, Pool Accessories and Safety Products, Whirlpool Tanks

FGX DIRECT LLC
500 GEORGE WASHINGTON HIGHWAY
SMITHFIELD, RI 02917
401-231-3800
800-426-6396
crinfo@fgxi.com
gargoyleseyewear.com/
• Don Wanat, President
• Synthia Pope, VP
• Clair Tucker, Advertising Director / Public Relations
Products:
Eyewear - Sunglasses.

FIBERESIN INDUSTRIES, INC.
37031 E WISCONSIN AVENUE
PO BOX 88
OCONOMOWOC, WI 53066-3146
262-567-4427
800-450-0051
Fax: 262-567-4814
info@fiberesin.com
www.fiberesin.com
• Jeff Bahr, Director of Manufacturing
jbahr@fiberesin.com
• Sandy Higgins, Customer Service Manager
(262) 560-4429
shiggins@fiberesin.com
• David Callies, Quality Assurance Manager
dcallies@fiberesin.com
• Jim Schwind, Technical Services Director
(262) 560-4457
jschwind@fiberesin.com
• Lonie Wise, National Sales Manager
(262) 560-4460
lwise@fiberesin.com
• Glenda Kieso, Accounts Payable and Human Resources
(262) 560-4424
gkieso@fiberesin.com
• Jim Lawrence, Controller
jlawrence@fiberesin.com
• Mike MacDougal, President and CEO
(262) 560-4439
mmacdougal@fiberesin.com
Products:
Develops custom solutions for utilizing wood

composites, paper, specialty formulated plastics, and resins in laminated products in the athletics facilities and equipment industries.

FIBEROPTIC LIGHTING INC.
950 SE M STREET
GRANTS PASS, OR 97526
541-476-6900
800-543-2533
Fax: 541-476-0796
• Hyla Lipson, President / Chief Executive Officer
• Sam Moon, Sales Consultant
hyla@flisign.com
• Carol Porter, Sales Consultant
hyla@flisign.com
• John Jones, Structural Consultant
Products:
Custom fiber optic signs and displays

FIELD GENERAL LLC
5662 N. MILLER CIRCLE
STANSBURY PARK, UT 84074
479-872-5388
888-822-3352
Fax: 479-872-5388
info@field-general.com
www.field-general.com
Products:
Baseball and Softball Gloves

FIELD TURF TARKETT
8088 MONTVIEW
MONTREAL, QUEBEC, CANADA H4P 2L7
514-340-9311
800-724-2969
Fax: 514-340-9374
info@fieldturf.com
www.fieldturf.com
• Joe Fields, Chief Executive Officer
• Troy Squires, VP Marketing
(800) 724-2969
• Jim Petrucelli, VP Marketing
(800) 724-2969
• Darren Gill, Director Marketing
(800) 724-2969
dgill@fieldturf.com
Products:
Turf, Hardwood Courts, Running Tracks, PVC Flooring, Tennis Courts.
Year Founded:
1994
Brands:
Field Turf, Prestige, Omnisports, Atlas Resisport, Field Turf Playground, Le Monde

FIELDMASTER INFIELD GROOMER
15551 W 109TH
LENEXA, KS 66219
913-492-7303
800-728-3581
Fax: 913-492-8532
www.fieldmaster.com
• Dan Goldblatt, President
info@fieldmaster.com
Products:
Grooming system that helps maintain a baseball/softball fields, including level infields.

FILA USA
1 FILA WAY
SPARKS GLENCOE, MD 21152
410-773-3000
800-845-3452
Fax: 410-773-4989
ecommUSA@fila.com
www.fila.com
• Jon Epstein, President
• Young-Chan Cho, Chief Financial Officer
• Lauren Mallon, Global Marketing Manager
• Yoon-Soo Yong, Chairman & CEO
Products:
Basketball Shoes; Golf Apparel, Hats/Caps, Rainwear; Racquet Sports Apparel, Bags, Equipment, Shoes, Socks; Skiing-Alpine Pants, Parkas, Sweaters, Vests, Underclothing; Track & Field/Running Apparel, Shoes; Training & Conditioning Aerobic Shoes; Water Sports
Sponsor:
Tennis Players: James Blake, Anna Chavetadze, Kim Clijsters, Marina Erakovic, Karin Knapp, Svetlana Kuznetsova, Andreas Seppl, and Janko Tipsarevic.

FILIPPI IMPORTERS/ELITE ROWING, INC
233 ASH STREET
WESTON, MA 2493
617-783-8442
Fax: 617-783-8442
info@eliterowing.com
www.eliterowing.com
• Selvig Alex, President
Products:
Provides boats to International rowing teams.

FIRST SERVICE
737 SOUTHPOINT BOULEVARD
SUITE D
PETALUMA, CA 94954
707-781-1960
800-227-1742
Fax: 800-809-9172
firstservice@clubstuff.com
www.clubstuff.com
• Dan Goldblatt, President
(800) 227-1742
dan@clubstuff.com
• Tom Helms, Sales Manager
(800) 227-1742
tom@clubstuff.com
Products:
Aerobic Flooring, Aerobic Studio Equipment, Court Conversion Systems, Mats, Noise Reduction Systems, Climbing Walls, Locker Room Furnishings, Playground Surfacing, Protective Padding, RCA Rubber Flooring, Seating Solutions, Basketball Equipment, Bleachers, Gym Divider Curtains, Multi-Play Tiles, Player Benches, Protective Floor Covers, Scoreboards, Scorer's Tables & Scorekeepers, Volleyball Equipment, Site Furnishings.
Year Founded:
1974

FISHER ATHLETIC EQUIPMENT, INC.
2060 CAUBLE ROAD
SALISBURY, NC 28147
800-438-6028
800-438-6028
Fax: 800-272-4448
customerservice@fisherathletic.com
• Robert Pritchard, President
(704) 636-5713
bobpritchard@fisherathletic.com
• Brian Pritchard, VP
(704) 636-5713
brianpritchard@fisherathletic.com
• Bill Keeler, Marketing Manager
(704) 636-5713
billkeeler@fisherathletic.com
• Bob Pritchard, President
Products:
Equipments and Accessories for Football, Baseball, Track & Field, Basketball, Soccer; Exercise Mats, Training Equipments, Protective Padding, Gym Dividers, Wind Screen, Rail Padding and Bags

FIT-TRAIL BY SOUTHWOOD CORPORATION
PO BOX 38900
CHARLOTTE, NC 28278
704-588-5000
800-727-6884
Fax: 704-588-5017
vickydwight@southwoodcorp.com
www.fittrail.com
• Vicky Dwight, VP & Account Executive
(704) 588-5000
• Patsi Sheets, Office Manager
(704) 588-5000
Products:
FitTrail outdoor exercise system fitness trail courses (10 or 20-station models)

FITBALL USA
14215 MEAD STREET
LONGMONT, CO 80504
800-752-2255
800-752-2255
Fax: 877-223-2962
• Dale Mayer, Chief Executive Officer
• Gloria Miller, Marketing
Products:
Balance tools, books, DVDs, Videos, Fragrances, Ergonomic Seating, Exercise Mats, Accessories, Body Therapy, Exercise Balls, Massage and Sensory Tools, Therapy Mats, Therapy Tools, Yoga and Pilates Overball and Mats

FITNESS EM, LLC
660 DOUGLAS STREET
UXBRIDGE, MA 01569
508-278-3209
800-704-5561
Fax: 508-278-6145
info@empowerfitness.com
www.fitnessem.com
• Donna Savage, President/Co-Founder
info@fitnessem.com
• Kathy O'Connel Johnson, VP Sales/Marketing
info@fitnessem.com
Products:
Fitness Equipment
Brands:
Danskin Fitness Accessories, Empower Fitness Equipment

FITNESS FLOORING
6199 NORWALDO AVENUE
INDIANAPOLIS, IN 46220
317-849-6181
800-428-5306
Fax: 317-842-5384
info@fitnessfloors.com
www.exerflex.com
• Mark Center, President / National Sales Manager
mark@exerflex.com
• Dave Osborn, Sales Manager
dave@exerflex.com
Products:
Surfacing for aerobics, basketball, weight

rooms. Different products such as Group Exercise, Rubber Flooring, Modular Flooring

FITNESS MASTER INC
11419 MATHIS
#200
DALLAS, TX 75234
214-350-8884
866-434-8639
Fax: 214-350-8876
• Eric R Dick, Manager
info@fitnexonline.com
• Ed Banasky, Vice President
info@fitnexonline.com
• Joe Ramirez, Manager
Products:
Fitness equipment and accessories

FITNESS TECH INTERNATIONAL
40 RONSON DRIVE
UNIT 3
ETOBICOKE, ONTARIO, CANADA M9W 1B3
416-573-0701
800-844-4019
www.thepowersuit.com
• Lebert Veira, CEO and President
Products:
Cross training system

FITTER INTERNATIONAL INC
3050, 2600 PORTLAND STREET SE
CALGARY, ALBERTA, CANADA T2G 4M6
403-243-6830
800-348-8371
Fax: 403-229-1230
orders@fitter1.com
www.fitter1.com
• Louis Stack, President/Founder
(403) 243-6830
louisstack@fitter1.com
Products:
Leading the World to better balance through Retail and WHLS distribution of Exercise balls, balance boards, cobblestone mat, trikke, Boardrock, Bongo board, blideboard, Bosu Ball, Pro Fitter, Indo Board, kid's toys, active sitting.

FLAGS INTERNATIONAL
10845 MCKINLEY HIGHWAY
OSCEOLA, IN 46561
574-674-5125
800-627-3524
Fax: 574-674-5134
info@flagsinternational.com
www.flagsinternational.com
• Cathy M Bolinger, President / Owner
• Michael Shidler, Customer Service Director
info@flagsinternational.com
• David Aker, VP
Products:
Flags, Banners, Custom Designed Flags & Banners, Flagpoles and Flag Items (hats, books, bunting, fans, pulldowns, windsock, arm patches, decals and static clings, lapel pins, stringed flags and fandangles, car window flags, bumper stickers, license plates, keychains, mini-banners, tabletop flags, gravemakers, display cases

FLAMBEAU OUTDOORS
15981 VALPLAST ROAD
MIDDLEFIELD, OH 44062

440-632-1631
800-457-5252
Fax: 440-632-1581
consumer@flambeauoutdoors.com
www.flambeauoutdoors.com
• Jason Sauey, President
Products:
Fishing and hunting gear and accessories.

FLEER/SKYBOX INTERNATIONAL
5909 SEA OTTER PLACE
CARLSBAD, CA 92010-6621
Fax: 760-929-3194
customer_service@upperdeck.com
sports.upperdeck.com
• Roger Grass, President / Chief Executive officer
• Chris Tobias, Chief Financial Officer
• Lloyd Powlak, SVP Marketing / Sales
• Bill Bordegon, VP Marketing / Sales
Products:
Trading Cards

FLEXCO
1401 E 6TH STREET
TUSCUMBIA, AL 35674
800-633-3151
Fax: 800-346-9075
info@flexcofloors.com
www.flexcofloors.com
• Bart Rogers, VP Sales/Marketing
brogers@roppeholdingcompany.com
• Ron Tait, National Sales Manager
rtait@flexcofloors.com
• Norman J. Freebeck, Executive Director of Manufacturing
njfreebeck@flexcofloors.com
• Jeremy Whipple, Marketing Manager
• Don Blazer, Director of Manufacturing
dblazer@flexcofloors.com
• Brent Fike, Technical Installation Training Manager
bfike@flexcofloors.com
• Rex Smallwood, Technical - Quality Assurance
rsmallwood@flexcofloors.com
• Dale Gross, Director of International Sales & ESD Product
dgross@flexcofloors.com
Products:
Rubber flooring, wall base, stair treads, vinyl accessories, floor finishing accessories, vinyl flooring

FLOATING SWIMWEAR INC
1970 S W STREET
WITCHITA, KS 67216-2143
316-942-8899
800-705-1959
Fax: 316-524-0411
www.floatwear.com
• Don Royer, President
Products:
Swimwear, beachwear and protective playwear

FLOORBOARDZ RUGS
970 CALLE AMANECER
SUITE A
SAN CLEMENTE, CA 92673
949-281-7304
866-585-4886
Fax: 866-680-1061
• Jillian Mintz, Sales Manager
(916) 858-1177

Products:
Tufted and printed rugs in the shape of surfboards

FLYBAR
PO BOX 563
ELLENVILLE, NY 12428
845-647-8400
800-764-6784
irwin@flybar.com
www.flybar.com
Products:
Pogo Sticks

FN THOMPSON COMPANY
5605 CARNEGIE BOULEVARD
SUITE 200
CHARLOTTE, NC 28209
704-551-2700
Fax: 704-551-2799
www.bekbuildinggroup.com
• Luther P Cochrane, Chairman / Chief Executive Officer
• Larry M Beasley, President / Chief Operating Officer
• Trilby Carriker, Chief Financial Officer
• Philip Southerland, President
• Mike Pierle, Executive Vice President
• Trilby Carriker, Chief Administration Officer/Chief Financial
• Frank Holley, Executive Vice President , Food & Beverage, L
• Chuck Lewis, General Counsel
• Garland Burton, Director of Diversity and Community Affairs
• Candace Watson, Human Resources Director
Services:
Commercial, healthcare, industrial and institutional construction

FNF ENT/STELLAR TOYS
18308 WARD STREET
FOUNTAIN VALLEY, CA 92708
949-722-8377
877-354-7635
Fax: 714-963-3387
www.flipnflyer.com
• Larry Huset, President
(949) 722-8377
• Debbie Swanson, Director Marketing
(949) 233-7160
sales@stellartoys.com
Nature of Service:
Manufacturer and Wholesaler Distributor of Flying Discs
Year Founded:
2002
Products:
Gyroscopic Flying Disc, Flip N Flyer, Freestyle Spin Sport
Brands:
Flip N Flyer

FNT INDUSTRIES, INC.
1805 PIERCE AVENUE
MARINETTE, WI 54143
715-732-2511
800-338-9860
Fax: 715-732-2574
• Werner Haberl, President
Products:
Netting, twine, rope, cordage, sports nets & accessories.

FOAMHEADS, LLC
663 S LUCILE STREET
SEATTLE, WA 98108
206-624-5222
Fax: 206-624-5229
info@foamheads.com
www.foamheads.com
• Jeff Richey, Chief Executive Officer
(206) 624-5222
jeffr@foamheads.com
• Jim Bell, Founder
(206) 624-5222
jimb@foamheads.com
• Kevin Hilisman, Sales Manager
(206) 624-5222
kevinh@foamheads.com
Products:
Foamheads, Action Figures, and 4-in-1
Toppers
Brands:
Foamheads & Actionheads
Clients:
Retailers, stadiums and fan shops

FOCUS GOLF SYSTEMS, INC.
25 DRAPER STREET
GREENVILLE, SC 29611
864-271-0201
800-235-5516
Fax: 864-271-3258
info@focusgroup.com
www.dunlopsportsonline.com
• William Emery, President
info@focusgroup.com
• Brandon Mill, Director
info@focusgroup.com
Products:
Golf, Tennis and Sqaush sports equipments
and accessories.

FOGDOG SPORTS
1075 FIRST AVENUE
KING OF PRUSSIA, PA 19406
650-980-2500
800-624-2017
Fax: 610-265-6099
Products:
Sports apparel, accessories and equipment.

FOOTJOY
333 BRIDGE STREET
PO BOX 965
FAIRHAVEN, MA 02719-0965
800-225-8500
800-225-8500
Fax: 508-979-3909
www.footjoy.com
• Jim Connor, President
• John Peal, European Marketing Director
Products:
Golf shoes, gloves, outerwear, socks,
spikeless shoes, belts, hats, and
miscellaneous

FOR BARE FEET INC
1201 SOUTH OHIO STREET
PO BOX 159
MARTINSVILLE, IN 46151
765-349-7474
800-669-0674
Fax: 765-349-7470
fbf@fbforiginals.com
www.forbarefeet.com
Products:
Novelty socks, team socks, university socks,
headbands, and wristbands

FOREFRONT GOLF
835 BILL JONES INDUSTRIAL DRIVE
SPRINGFIELD, TN 37172
615-384-1230
800-247-9651
Fax: 615-384-1290
• Stan J Harris, Chief Executive Officer
sharris@forefrontgolf.com
Products:
Stand bags, Cart bags, Classic, Ladies, and
Customize golf bags.
Brands:
Stand Collection: Alphine, Triad, Trek,
Scout; Cart Collection: Cart Blanche Maxim;
Classic Collection: Destin, Premier,
Signature; Ladies Collection: Lexa,
Platinum, Cloud Nine

FOX 40 INTERNATIONAL INC.
4645 WITMER INDUSTRIAL ESTATE
NIAGARA FALLS, NY 14305-1360
716-298-1129
888-663-6940
Fax: 716-298-1204
foxinfo@fox40world.com
www.fox40world.com
• Ron Foxcroft, Founder/CEO
foxinfo@fox40world.com
• Dave Foxcroft, President & COO
Products:
Fox 40 Whistles (Referee & Coach, Sport &
Safety), Lanyards & Flex Coils, Don Cherry
Products (Hockey sticks & Mouthguards),
Fox 40 Coaching Boards, Fox 40 Marine,
Kliptek Intelight, FoxMed, Fox 40
Mouthguards, Protex/PTX/Longdon

FOX RIVER MILLS, INC.
227 POPLAR STREET
PO BOX 298
OSAGE, IA 50461-0298
641-732-3798
800-247-1815
Fax: 641-732-5128
www.foxsox.com
• Jeff Lessard, Executive Vice President
(641) 732-3798
• John Lessard, President
 ext 221
Products:
Socks and handwear
Brands:
Fox River Socks & Handwear
Clients:
Sporting Goods and outdoor retailers

FRAMEWORTH SPORTS MARKETING
1198 CALEDONIA ROAD
TORONTO, ONTARIO, CANADA M6A 2W5
416-781-1115
Fax: 416-781-1038
info@frameworth.com
www.frameworth.com
• Brian Ehrenworth, President
• Carmelo Notaro, Retail Store Manager
(416) 781-1115
carmelo@frameworth.com
Products:
NHL, NHL, MLB, NBA, NASCAR, plus golf,
soccer and boxing memorabilia and
collectibles.

FRANCO APPAREL GROUP
100 W 33RD STREET
SUITE 911
NEW YORK, NY 10001

212-967-7272
Fax: 212-967-7395
info@francoapparel.com
www.francoapparel.com
• Ike Franco, President / Chief Operating
Officer
info@francoapparel.com
• Joanne Guglielmo, Chief Financial Officer
• Allen Franco, Sales VP
• Desiree Scialpi, Marketing / Licensing
Director
Products:
Childrenwear and sports licensed apparel

FRANKLIN SPORTS, INC.
17 CAMPANELLI PARKWAY
PO BOX 508
STOUGHTON, MA 02072-0508
781-344-1111
800-225-8649
Fax: 781-341-0333
www.franklinsports.com
• Irving Franklin, Chairman/Founder
• Larry Franklin, President / Chief Executive
Officer
• Rich Ferenz, Sales VP
Products:
Batting gloves, fielding gloves,
fielding/pitching practice, batting practice,
balls/accessories, volleyball sets, badminton
sets, combination sets, croquet sets, bocce
sets, horseshoe sets, coleman sets,
tetherball sets, yard games, accessories,
table tennis, darts, table top, ready to go,
future champs, MLB, soft sport, learn to
play, soccer balls, soccer shinguards,
soccer goals & rebounders, accessories,
playground balls, basketballs, volleyballs,
footballs, and fan products

FREEMAN PRODUCTS, INC.
715 PARK N BOULEVARD
CLARKESTON, GA 30021
404-297-9083
800-537-3362
Fax: 201-475-4818
info@fpworldwide.com
www.freemanproductsworldwide.com
• Vince Cariello, President
• George Ercolino, VP
Products:
Trophies, Awards - Clocks, Components,
Engraving Machines, Incentives and
Recognition Awards, Medals, Plaques,
Ribbons, Trophies.

FREESTYLE USA
47-14 32ND PLACE
LONG ISLAND, NY 11101
805-484-1216
800-874-0907
Fax: 800-776-5997
customerservice@genevawg.com
www.freestyleusa.com
• Jimmy Olmes, President
• Brett Ritter, Brand Manager
• John Katker, National Sales Manager
Products:
Men's and Women's Watches and
Accessories with sports logos and designs.

FREMONT DIE CONSUMER PRODUCTS INC
1709A ENDEAVOR DRIVE
WILLIAMSBURG, VA 23185
757-872-6438
800-336-8847

Fax: 757-872-6958
cs@fremontdie.com
www.fremontdie.com
• James B. Hotze, President
(757) 872-6438
jhotze@fremontdie.com
• Sharon Weinberg, Vice President
sweinberg@fremontdie.com
• Wanda Pullom, General Manager
wpullom@fremontdie.com
• Wally Morgan, Operations/EDI/Shipping
wmorgan@fremontdie.com
• David Hotze, Marketing/Sales
dhotze@fremontdie.com
Products:
House flags, steering wheel covers, fuzzy
dice, license plate frames, wastebaskets,
tire covers, car flags, car socks, mini
banners, antenna flags, bike flags, magnets,
plastic parking signs, street signs, and stop
signs, desk toppers, fight song plaques, wall
banners, bar stool covers (top cover with
logo), visor organizer, CD/DVD holder, litter
bag, tailgate net and tackle buddy/bop bag
(inflatable).
Year Founded:
1982

FUBU THE COLLECTION
350 5TH AVENUE
SUITE 6617
NEW YORK, NY 10118
212-273-3300
Fax: 212-273-3333
www.fblegacy.com
• John Daymond, Chief Executive Officer
• Carl Brown, Co-Founder
• Keith Perrin, Co-Founder / VP
• J. Al Martin, VP / Head Designer
Products:
Men's shoes, tuxedos, suits and collectible
apparel; Ladies and Children's shoes and
apparel and accessories

FULL 90 SPORTS, INC.
10251 VISTA SORRENTO PARKWAY #300
SAN DIEGO, CA 92191
877-438-5590
Fax: 858-777-6592
Questions@Full90.com
www.full90.com
• Jeff Skeen, Founder/Chief Executive
Officer
• Dennis Piper, Corporate Affairs VP
• Mark Skeen, Marketing VP
• Tim Killeen, Vice President, Sales
(858) 777-6528
Description:
Manufacturer of state-of-the-art soccer
products designed to extend the enjoyment
of soccer for players of all ages. Developed
unique padded headboard.
Products:
Soccer Headgear
Clients:
Sporting Goods and soccer specialty
retailers

FUN & FITNESS LLC
PO BOX 5241
SACRAMENTO, CA 95817
916-599-0490
888-995-4273
Fax: 916-361-5432
playnosweat@aol.com
www.playnosweat.com

Products:
Playground and fitness equipment.

FUN-TEES, INC.
4725 CORPORATE DRIVE NW
SUITE 100
CONCORD, NC 28027
704-788-3003
Fax: 704-795-9300
• Lewis Reid, President
clientserv@funtees.com
• Mark Weibel, CFO
• Brendi Hensley, Office Manager
Products:
Manufacturer of knitted apparel

FUNLINE MERCHANDISE COMPANY INC
7751 CHERRY AVENUE
FONTANA, CA 92336
909-357-7988
Fax: 626-336-7982
www.musclemachines.com
Products:
Gymnasium apparatus such as trampolines

G III SPORTS
512 SEVENTH AVENUE
NEW YORK, NY 10018
212-403-0500
Fax: 212-403-0551
info@g-iii.com
www.g-iii.com
• Morris Goldfarb, Chief Executive Officer /
Chairman
• Jeanette Nostra-Katz, President
• Sammy Aaron, Vice Chairman
• Wayne Miller, Chief Operating Officer
• Neal Nackman, Chief Financial Officer
• Jeffrey Goldfarb, Director of Strategic
Planning
Products:
Introduced women's leather outerwear,
men's leather apparel, women's textile
outerwear and sportswear, men's textile
outerwear, and NFL team logo outerwear

G-PUSH SPORT, INC.
277 GLADSTONE AVENUE
ONTARIO, CANADA M6J 3L9
416-532-3870
Fax: 416-530-4826
• Anita Stephan, Communications
Products:
Sports Supplements.

G. LOOMIS INC.
1 HOLLAND DRIVE
IRVINE, CA 92618
877-577-0600
Fax: 360-225-7169
loomis@gloomis.com
www.gloomis.com
• Gary Loomis, Founder
loomis@gloomis.com
• Bruce Holt, Executive Director
loomis@gloomis.com
• Mark Landry, Sales Manager
loomis@gloomis.com
Products:
General Tackle, Fly, Blanks, Clothing, Hats,
Collectibles, Travel Gear

GAIAM
833 W S BOULDER ROAD
PO BOX 3095
BOULDER, CO 80307-3095

303-222-3600
877-989-6321
800-254-8464
Fax: 303-222-3700
customerservice@gaiam.com
www.gaiam.com
• Jirka Rysavy, Chairman / Chief Executive
Officer
customerservice@gaiam.com
• Lynn Powers, President / Chief Operating
Officer
customerservice@gaiam.com
• Janet Mathews, Chief Financial Officer
customerservice@gaiam.com
Products:
Towels, Shower & Bath Filters, Cleaners,
Shower Curtains, Bathroom Accesories,
Storage & Organization, Laundry, Cleaning
Tools, Seventh Generatioh Products,
Batteries & Chargers, Energy Efficient
Bulbs, Lamps, Light Therapy, Natural
Spectrum Bulbs, Heating, Energy Savers,
Humidifiers & Dehumidifiers, Fans & Cooling

GAME MASTER ATHLETIC COMPANY
1624 DOLWICK DRIVE
ERLANGER, KY 41018
859-746-9800
800-646-4225
Fax: 859-746-5636
info@gamemasterathletic.com
www.gmasterathletic.com
• Garrett Kamstra, President/CEO
Products:
Softball Pitching Machine, Dual Portable
Screen, Synthetic Leather Gloves, Ultimate
Bat and Ball, Junior Size College Logo
Rubber Footballs, Official Size College Logo
Synthetic Leather Autograph Footballs, Mini
Size College Logo Rubber Footballs, Logo
Footballs in Blister Packs on Clip Strips,
Official Size College Logo Rubber
Basketballs, Official Size College Logo
Autograph Basketballs, Mini Size College
Logo Rubber Basketballs, and more.

GAME TIME LLC
181 BOYD STREET
MONTGOMERY, NY 12549
888-249-9627
cs@genevawg.com
Products:
Watches

GAME TIME, INC.
150 PLAYCORE DRIVE SE
FORT PAYNE, AL 35967
256-845-5610
800-235-2440
800-235-2440
Fax: 256-845-9361
dking@gametime.com
www.gametime.com
• Bob Farnsworth, President
dking@gametime.com
• Tom Norquist, Senior Vice President
dking@gametime.com
• Craig Bierley, GMC Advertising and Sales
Promotion Director
Products:
KidTime Slides, WallCan Climbers, Links
and Bridges, Panels, Roofs, Swings, Riding,
Hands on Playsets, StreetScape, TuffClad,
Playground Pets, Benches, Tables,
Accessories, FitKid Equipment, Basketball
Equipmentss, Baseball Equipment, Soccer
Equipment, Volleyball Equipment, Tennis

Equipment, Tetherball Equipment, Surfacing, Shade Structures, Spray Parks

GAMETIME PLUSH
9540 PATHWAY STREET
SUITE 101
SANTEE, CA 92071-4178
619-596-6161
888-817-5874
Fax: 619-596-1198
Products:
Officially licensed collegiate fan toys and apparel

GAMEWEAR
79 HUDSON STREET
SECOND FLOOR
HOBOKEN, NJ 7030
973-954-2413
Fax: 973-529-0242
www.gamewear.com
• Frank Cerullo, CEO
• Nick Iovacchini, President
Year Founded:
2003.
Nature of Service:
Products are officially licensed and made from the most iconic element in sports- the ball used in play -so they more closely connect the wearer to their favorite teams and players than any other product.

GARAN, INC.
350 FIFTH AVENUE
NEW YORK, NY 10118
212-563-2000
Fax: 212-971-2250
• Seymour Lichtenstein, Chairman & Chief Executive
• Alexander Sistarenik, Treasurer
• William J Wilson, Finance VP & Chief Financial Officer
• Jerald S Kamiel, President
Products:
Shirts & Blouses, Suits Career, Skirts, Size - Junior, suits, Pants & Trousers, Sportswear, Dresses Casual, Shorts, dresses

GARED SPORTS - SSI VOLLEYBALL
707 N 2ND STREET
SUITE 202
SAINT LOUIS, MO 63102
314-421-0044
800-325-2682
Fax: 314-421-6014
customerservice@garedsports.com
www.garedsports.com
• Dean Baker, Sales / Marketing VP
(314) 421-0044
• Laura St George, National Sales Manager
(314) 421-0044
laura@garedsports.com
• Kevin Needler, Operations Manager
(314) 421-0044
kara@garedsports.com
Products:
Indoor Badminton Systems & Nets, Tether Ball Indoor/Outdoor Sets, Basketball Accessories, Backboards - Glass, Backboards - NOn-Glass, Goals - Breakaway, Goals - Fixed Institutional & Playground, NBA Arena Backboard & Goals, Outdoor, Portables, Residential/Playground Basketball Systems, Scorebooks, Training Aides/Skill Development, 3 POint Wall Mount, 4 Point Wall Mounts, 4 Point Wall Mounts - Side

Fold, 4 Point Wall Mounts - Swing Up, Ceiling Suspended Backstops, Electric Adjust-a-Goals, Gym Accessories, Manual Adjust-A-Goals, Wall Padding, Benches, Bike Racks, Bleachers, Official Round Soccer Goals, Official Soccer Goals, Recreational Soccer

GARMONT USA, INC.
170 BOYER CIRCLE
SUITE 20
WILLISTON, VT 5495
802-658-8322
Fax: 802-658-0431
www.garmontusa.com
• John Schweizer, Division Manager / Exel / President
info@garmontusa.com
• Bill Hill, Chief Financial Officer
info@garmontusa.com
• Gord Bailes, Sales VP
Products:
Footwear, Socks, Winter Gear

GATOR ATHLETIC INC.
1243 IND PARKWAY, IND PARK
PO BOX 1243
CLARKSDALE, MS 38614
662-627-7413
800-572-2470
www.gator-athletics.com
• Billie N Strohm, President
Products:
Football - Jerseys; Softball - Jerseys.

GE LIGHTING SYSTEMS
3010 SPARTANBURG HIGHWAY
EAST FLAT ROCK, NC 28726
800-305-1372
Fax: 800-305-1373
www.ge.com
• Maryrose Sylvester, President / Chief Executive Officer
lighting.systems@lighting.ge.com
Products:
Lighting Fixtures

GE MARQUETTE
3000 N GRANDVIEW BOULEVARD
WAUKAESHA, WI 53188
262-544-3011
800-643-6439
Fax: 262-544-3384
www.gemedicalsystems.com
• David Zachman, National Sales Training & Marketing Officer
Products:
Training & Conditioning - Stress Testing Equipment, Treadmills.

GEAR FOR SPORTS
9700 COMMERCE PARKWAY
LENEXA, KS 66219
913-693-3200
800-255-1065
Fax: 913-693-3917
www.gearforsports.com
• Larry Graveel, President / Chief Operating Officer
• Randy Stabenow, GEAR Manufacturing VP
Products:
Sportswear, Headwear and Accessories

GEAR PRO-TEC
1901 DIPLOMAT DRIVE
DALLAS, TX 75234
800-859-8625
Fax: 888-858-8337
www.gearprotec.com
• Ed Tobergte, President
• Stanley L. Bryant, President
Year Founded:
1992.
Products:
Z-Cool, Z-Accessories, Z-Cool Youth, X-2 Air, Air-Tech, The Gamer, Youth Pads, Accessories, Chin Straps.

GENERAL AWARDS, INC.
7715 NW 64TH STREET
MIAMI, FL 33166
305-592-3346
800-327-2846
Fax: 305-592-9304
• Cinthia Waas-Russiyan, President / Owner
sales@generalawardsinc.com
• Nicholas Russiyan, Owner
Products:
Awards, Medals, Pins, Ribbons, Color Flex, Trophy Hardware

GENERAL SPORTCRAFT COMPANY, LTD.
313 WATERLOO VALLEY ROAD
BUDD LAKE, NJ 7828
973-347-3800
800-526-0244
Fax: 973-347-5711
www.sportcraft.com
• Michael J J. Nally, Chief Executive Officer & President
• Frank Ginolfi, Chief Financial Officer
Products:
Dartboards, Billiard Tables, Table Tennis, Foosball Tables, Turbo Hockey, Multi-games Tables, Casino Games, Volleyball Systems, Combination Badminton/Volley, Badminton Systems, Croquet sets, Horseshoes, Bocce, Tetherball Sets, Monster Games, Bounces houses, Treadmills

GENERAL SPORTS VENUE ASTROTURF
11550 COMMON OAKS DRIVE
SUITE 206
RALEIGH, NC 27614
919-488-5819
800-723-8873
Fax: 919-488-5802
help@astroturf.com
www.astroturf.com
• Jon L Pritchett, President / Chief Executive Officer
(919) 488-5800
jpritchett@gsvenue.com
• Dan Fuhrman, SVP / Chief Finacial Officer
• Jim Petrucelli, Vice President of Business Development
(919) 488-5800
• Troy Squires, Global Director of Sales and Marketing
• Vince Yoos, Project Director - Northeast
• Bryan Jones, Project Manager - Northwest/Southwest
• Mitchell Truban, Project Manager
• Cab Bramlett, Design Engineer
• Robert Staten, Controller
Products:
Synthetic Turf, Fusion Turf, Transition Turf, Venue Projects.

manufacturers/retailers

1147

GEORGI-SPORTS
2191 EMBASSY DRIVE
LANCASTER, PA 17603
717-291-8924
800-338-2527
Fax: 717-291-9188
• George Matthew, President
Products:
Accessories, Field Hockey Balls, Field
Hockey Sticks, Goals and Nets, Protective
Equipment, Referee's Equipment, Stick and
Team Bags, Uniforms

GEORGIA BOOT
39 EAST CANAL STREET
NELSONVILLE, OH 45764
866-442-4908
Fax: 615-790-8005
info@georgiaboot.com
www.georgiaboot.com
• Gerald M Cohn, Chief Executive Officer
info@georgiaboot.com
• Tommy Morrison, President
info@georgiaboot.com
Products:
Outdoor Footwear

GEORGIA MARBLE COMPANY
200 GEORGIA MARBLE LANE
PO BOX 238
TATE, GA 30177
770-735-2611
800-334-0122
Fax: 770-735-2236
www.polycor.com
• Richard Ryan, President
• Brian Mills, VP
• Craig Garland, Sales Manager
• Shari Kort, Advertising Manager
Products:
Granite, Marble, Tiles and Slabs for various
applications, including sports arenas

GERRY COSBY & COMPANY, INC.
11 PENNSYLVANIA PLAZA
NEW YORK, NY 10001
212-563-6464
877-563-6464
Fax: 212-967-0876
gcsmsg@cosbysports.com
www.cosbysports.com
• Michael Cosby, Owner/President
Products:
Professional team bags and equipment; All
equipment bags and football protective
equipment. Professional factory located at
103 Under Mountain Road, Sheffield, MA
01257.
Brands:
Cosby Bags, Mr. Tops Football shoulder
pads, 'The Professionals Choice™'
Clients:
Pro Teams (NY Yankees), College Teams,
High School and Pee Wee Teams, and
individuals

GERSTUNG/GYM-THING, INC.
1400 COPPERMINE TERRACE
BALTIMORE, MD 21209
410-337-7781
800-922-3575
Fax: 410-337-0471
info@gerstung.us
www.gerstung.com
• Siegfried Gerstung, Founder/Owner
(800) 922-3575
sg@gerstung.com

• Jeff Tarleton, General Manager
(800) 922-3575
info@gerstung.com
• Fran Ice, Sales Advisor
(800) 922-3575
floors@gerstung.com
Products:
Manufacturer of aerobic and dance floors,
weight room flooring, fitness products,
gymnastics equipment.

GETZ CORPORATION
539 WEST WALNUT AVENUE
ORANGE, CA 92868-2232
800-854-7447
Fax: 800-660-6040
www.getzcorp.net
• Micheal Paulsen, President
Year Founded:
1971.
Products:
Score Board, Gameboards, Bullhorns,
Airhorns, Poms, Megaphones, Accessories,
Bags, Puncture Seal, Pine Tar, Water
Bottles, Spirit Items, Miscellaneous

GEXCO ENTERPRISES
PO BOX 6514
NORCO, CA 92860
951-735-4951
800-829-8222
Fax: 800-281-1748
www.gexcoenterprises.com
• Gex Coons, Chief Executive Officer
• Jeff Olsen, President
• Walt Sendziak, Sales Manager
Products:
Ankle Supports, Ball Pressurizers, Elbow
Supports, Gripping Aids, Head Bands, Knee
Supports, Shoe Repair, Shorts, Socks, Sun
Lotion, Wrist Bands; Racquet Sports - Ball
Pick-Up Baskets, Ball Pressurizers, Court
Equipment, Gripping Aids, Racquet Strings

GIACONA CONTAINER
121 INDUSTRIAL AVENUE
NEW ORLEANS, LA 70121
504-835-5465
800-299-4332
Fax: 504-835-5581
giacona@giacona.com
www.giacona.com
• Corrado Giacona, II, President
(504) 835-5465
• Gina Giacona Lynch, Vice President
Products:
Cups, Sculptured Drinkware,
Lanyards/Lasos, Lite-Up Products, Deli
Tubs & Pails, Shots, Insulated Drinkware,
Sipper Bottles, Pubware, Cup Accessories,
CD Music Medallions
Nature of Service:
Manufacturer, Designer and Custom Printer
Brands:
Giacona Container Brand

GILL ATHLETICS
601 MERCURY DRIVE
CHAMPAIGN, IL 61822-9648
212-367-8438
800-367-3090
Fax: 217-367-8440
sales@gillathletics.com
www.gillathletics.com
• Fred Dixon, National Sales Manager
(800) 637-3090

fdixon@gillathletics.com
• David Hodge, President
Products:
Athletic Field Construction Equipment,
Steeple Chase, Track Buring, Cages, Ball
Stop Systems, Goal Posts, Communications
Boxes, Sand Trap Forms, Soccer Goals,
Track & Field/Running Crossbars, Disci,
Hammers, Hurdles, Javelins, Landing Pits,
Shot Puts, Standards, Starting Blocks,
Take-Off Boards, Toe Boards, Vaulting
Boxes, Vaulting Poles; Strength & Training
Equipment.

GIRO SPORT DESIGN
380 ENCINAL STREET
SANTA CRUZ, CA 95060
831-420-4010
800-969-4476
Fax: 831-457-4444
www.giro.com
• Greg Shapleigh, SR. Vice President
• Rob Wesson, R&D Director
Products:
Bicycles, Helmets, Accessories

GLD PRODUCTS
S84W19093 ENTERPRISE DRIVE
MUSKEGO, WI 53150
262-679-8730
800-225-7593
Fax: 262-679-8730
info@gldgames.com
www.gldproducts.com
• Nick Voden, President
GLD@gldmfg.com
Nature of Service:
Wholesale and distributing in the sporting
goods industry.
Year Founded:
1981
Products:
Darts, Billiards, Table Games, Home Casino
Brands:
Fat Cat, Viper

GNC CORPORATION
300 6TH AVENUE
PITTSBURGH, PA 15222
412-288-4600
877-462-4700
Fax: 412-288-8379
www.gnc.com
• Jennifer Brinker, Senior Director of
Advertising
(412) 288-4688
• Mary Breunig, Sales and Promotions
Manager - Midwest
(847) 240-1301
• Mandy Kiggins, Sales and Promotions
Manager - Northeast
(412) 288-2028
• Jim Brooks, Sales and Promotions
Manager - Southern
(727) 572-6338
• Paul Katz, Sales and Promotions Manager
- Western
(949) 458-2700
• John Depcrymski, Advertising/Promotions
Manager
Exercise/Fitness Sponsor:
NPC, Mr. Pittsburgh.

GO FLOW, INC.
2323 CLEAR LAKE CITY BOULEVARD
SUITE 180-232
HOUSTON, TX 77062

281-480-7698
888-463-5699
Fax: 877-849-1406
go4flow@gmail.com
• Monica Barrera, President
Products:
Misting, Heating, Apparel, Bags, Flow
Drinking Device, Air Conditioners

GO FLY A KITE
21749 BAKER PARKWAY
WALNUT, CA 91789
877-875-2557
Products:
Single Line Kites, Diamonds, Dragons,
Flying Wonders, Frameless Flyers, Inflatable
Kites, Interactive Kites, Performance Kites,
Traction Kites, Wind Designs
Brands:
Joel Scholtz, Poldeltas, Superflyers,
Parastunters, Pro Series, Storm Series

GOAL SPORTING GOODS, INC.
37 INDUSTRIAL PARK ROAD
PO BOX 236
ESSEX, CT 6426
860-767-9112
800-334-4625
Fax: 860-767-9121
Goal@GoalSports.com
www.goalsports.com
• Andrew Turek, President
Products:
Soccer - Official Goals / Round, Official
Goals / Square, Official Unpainted Goals,
Recreational Goals, Official Indoor/Outdoor
Goals, Futsal Soccer/Handball Goals,
Patented Telescoping Design, Soccer
League Goals, Transportable/Adjustable
Goals, PowerGoal, Lacrosse, Field Hockey
Goals, Benches and Bleachers.
Year Founded:
1983

GOALSETTER SYSTEMS, INC.
1041 CORDOVA AVE
LYNNVILLE, IA 50153
641-594-4625
800-362-4625
Fax: 641-594-3343
www.goalsetter.com
• Teryl Ver Ploeg, Development & Marketing
• Faye Brand, Sales & Marketing Manager
• Bryan De Jong, Purchasing
• Andy Edwards, Dealer & Inside Sales,
Warranty
• Jennifer Morris, Shipping & Accounting
• Stefanie VanWyk, Graphic Design
• Wayne Woollums, Dealer & Inside Sales,
Scheels Account Manager
Products:
"Made in USA in ground and wall mounted
adjustable height basketball goal systems.
Additional products include: basketball rims,
basketball goals, backboards, wall mounted
basketball goals, basketball pole pads for
6-inch, 5-inch and 4-inch square poles and
other basektball accessories, collegiate
products.
Year Founded:
1991

GOLD CREST ENGRAVING
8847 WILBUR AVENUE
NORTHRIDGE, CA 91324
818-764-3231
888-423-9623

Fax: 818-765-8851
info@goldcrest1.com
www.blazercrests.com
• Bob Harvey, President
• Harvey Parker, Chief Executive Officer
• Steve Parker, EVP
Products:
Trophies, Awards - Bullion Blazer Crests,
Emblems, Jewelry, Plaques, Custom
Trophies.

GOLD MEDAL RECREATIONAL PRODUCTS
20 BLUE MOUNTAIN AVENUE
ANNISTON, AL 36201
800-633-2354
Fax: 256-240-2509
www.gold-medal-rec.com
• Bob Jones, National Sales Manager
Products:
Golf - Indoor safe No Shag Golf Practice
System, Outdoor No Shag Golf Practice
Cage, Safe Stroke-Shaver Practice Net,
Stylish Indoor No Shag Practice Net,
Portable No Shag Indoor/Outdoor Practice
System, Gold Medal Tee Mat, Gold Medal
Commercial Tee Mat, Protective Golf
Netting, Turf Maintenance, Baseball Batting
Cage Nets, Baseball Field fence Screening,
Teammate Patented Baseball/Softball
Pitchback Practice System, Pitchback,
TeamMate Patented Tee Ball Practice Net,
Tennis - Tennis Nets, Tennis Posts, Tennis
Court Divider Netting, Net Court Tennis
Rebound Net, DeLuxe Tennis Rebound Net
and Frame, Volleyball - Invincible
Tournament Volleybal

GOLD'S GYM INTERNATIONAL, INC.
125 E JOHN CARPENTER FWY
SUITE 1300
IRVING, TX 75062
310-392-6004
Fax: 310-396-1065
www.goldsgym.com
• Mike Feinman, COO
• Gene LaMott, President / Chief Executive
Officer
• Jim Snow, President
• Randy Schultz, Chief Financial Officer
Products:
Outerwear, Tanks, Pants, Tees, Shorts,
Tops, Sports Bag, Fitness Accessories,
Books, Caps and Accessories

GOLF & TENNIS HEADWEAR COMPANY
8315 W 20TH AVENUE
HIALEAH, FL 33014
305-558-4310
800-327-4287
Fax: 305-558-2093
• Bernard Maeroff, President/Owner
(305) 558-4310
bmaeroff@triangleheadwear.com
• Jim Miller, Finance Executive
Products:
General Sports Products: Hats, Caps,
Visors; Golf: Hats, Caps, Towels &
Umbrellas; Racquet Sports: Hats, Caps,
Visors.

GOLF DESIGN USA
11591 MARKON DRIVE
GARDEN GROVE, CA 92841
800-854-6148
800-854-6148
Fax: 800-824-0699

mcheek@golfdesignusa.com
www.golfdesignproducts.com
• John R Tate, President
jrtate@golfdesignusa.com
• David Wung, VP Operations
• Jim Tate, VP Advertising
Products:
Ball Mark Repair Tools, golf accessories,
custom packaging, putters, bag tags and
Point of Purchase displays

GOLF GEAR INTERNATIONAL
5285 INDUSTRIAL DRIVE
HUNTINGTON BEACH, CA 92649
801-364-3885
Fax: 714-899-4284
• Peter H Pocklington, Chairman
• Don Anderson, Chief Executive Officer
• Michael Piraino, President / Chief
Operating Officer / Ch
• Chris Holiday, Sales / Marketing SVP

GOLF SOLUTIONS WORLDWIDE
5070 CHANDUS WAY
TOBYHANNA, PA 18466
570-243-8555
855-251-6474
Fax: 570-243-8555
• Frank Kohuth, President
• Barbara Kohuth, VP
Products:
Drivng Range Products: Ball Pickers,
Washers & Dispensers, Tees Dividers, Mats
& Barrier Netting, Drivers, Balls, Tees &
Baskets, Miniature Golf Products: Rubber
Putters, Balls & Dispensers, Blacklight
Miniature Golf Supplies, Carpet, Obstacles
& Other Course Supplies, Carpet, Obstacles
& Other Course Supplies, Score Cards,
Pencils & Other Supplies, Course
Equipment Supplies: Balls, Washers &
Custom Tees, Litter Caddies, Flags,
Flagpoles, Pennant Makers, Prefabricated
Driving Range Shelters, Paintball Target
Range, Soft Swipe Spike Cleaner, Blacklight
Miniature Golf Supplies, New Scorecard
Stand

GOLF WAREHOUSE
8851 E 34TH STREET N
WICHITA, KS 67226
888-746-7849
888-838-5551
Fax: 316-838-5557
www.tgw.com
• Brian Jones, Manager
bjones@tgw.com
Products:
Golf Equipment (Clubs,Bags, Balls),
Apparel/Shoes (Men's Apparel,
Men'sBusiness Casual, Apres Golf,
Women's Apparel, Headwear, Junior
Apparel, Rainwear, Mens Shoes, Womens
Shoes, Junior Shoes, Shoe Accessories,
Lucky Size Sale), Accessories(Gloves, On
Course Accessories, Electric/Pull Carts,
Learning/Training, Rangefinders, GPS
Systems, Travel Covers, Luggage,
Sunglasses, Watches, Wood/Iron/Putter
Gloves, Health Fitness, Bag Accessories,
Shoes Accessories, Club Repair),
Multimedia(Books, Videos, DVDs,
Software), Home/Gift (Artwork, Home,
Accessories, Office, Personal Items, Gift
Ideas, Memorabilia, Golf Cards/Gift Wrap,
Calendars), Specialty

manufacturers/retailers

GOLF-ART.COM, INC.
632 DANBURY ROAD
WILTON, CT 67897
203-438-8989
800-283-3344
Fax: 203-438-8959
www.golf-art.com
• Skip Rooney, Owner/President
(203) 438-8989
skiprooney@mac.com
• Scott Newton, General Manager
(203) 468-8989
• Warren Beardow
(203) 515-8566
bradbsr@comcast.net
Year Founded:
1986.
Nature of Service:
Classic photos, limited edition lithographs, memorabilia, prints, awards, gifts, decors, originals, golf club decorations, tournament awards, auctions.

GOLFSMITH INTERNATIONAL, INC.
11000 N IH35
SHOWROOM
AUSTIN, TX 78753
512-837-5210
800-925-7709
Fax: 512-837-1245
http://www.golfgalaxy.com
• James D Thompson, President / Chief Executive Officer
• Virginia Bunte, VP / Chief Financial Officer
• Kiprian Miles, VP / Chief Information Officer
• Ginger Bunte, Chief Financial Officer
• Sue E. Gove, President
Products:
Golf and Tennis accessories, balls, clubs, custom club fitting, gifts, gift cards, gloves, grips, Golf Bags & Travel, Home & Office, Outlet, Personalized Gear, Practice and Training, Pre-Owned Clubs, Shoes, Teams and Collegiate, Video & Books
Products:
Golf Clubs, Golf Bags, Golf Balls, Golf Gifts, Golf Shoes, Golf Apparel, Accessories, Custom Club Fitting, Gift Cards, Gloves, Grips, Personalized Gear
Brands:
Callaway, TaylorMade, Cleveland, Cobra, Odyssey, Adidas, Maxfli, Ashworth, Adams, Lynx, MacGregor, Nike, Zevo, Snake Eyes, Golfsmith, Killer Bee, GearForGolf, GiftsForGolf

GOLFWORKS
4820 JACKSONTOWN ROAD
PO BOX 3008
NEWARK, OH 43056-3008
740-323-0311
800-800-3290
Fax: 740-323-0311
golfworks@golfworks.com
www.golfworks.com
• Ralph Maltby, Founder
• Mark McCormick, Chief Executive Officer
Products:
Drivers, Iron Sets, Fairways and Hybrids, Wedges, Putters, Full Sets, Golf Balls, Golf Bags, Golf Buddies, Ladies Club & Sets, Left Hand, Junior Gear, Golf shoes, Accessories

GOOD STUFF CORPORATION
47-00 33RD STREET
LONG ISLAND CITY, NY 11101
718-937-3333
888-768-2094
Fax: 718-937-1037
contact@goodstuff.com
www.goodstuff.com
• Josh Parker, Vice President Sales
(719) 937-3333
jparker@goodstuff.com
• Eric Lashin, Sales Manager
(718) 937-3333
elashin@winstuff.com
Nature of Service:
Wholesale
Year Founded:
1988
Products:
Balls, Baseball Caps, Candy Toys, Everyday Plush, Licensed Plush, Novelties, Novelty Hats, Pillows, Private Label, Sports Sets, Towels
Brands:
MLB, NBA, NFL, NHL, Looney Tunes, Sesame Street, Tootsie Roll, Shrek The Third, Hasbro Brands, Superman, Care Bears, Rock-N-Roll Bands.

GOODE SKI TECHNOLOGIES
2450 WALL AVENUE
OGDEN, UT 84401
801-621-2300
888-464-6633
Fax: 801-621-1434
goode@goode.com
www.goode.com
• David Goode, President
Products:
Water Skis, Water Ski Accessories, PowerShell Boots, Ruber Boots, Snow Skis, Snow Ski Gloves, Close-Outs

GOORIN BROS., INC.
1269 HOWARD STREET
SAN FRANCISCO, CA 94103
800-862-0100
Fax: 415-431-9199
info@goorin.com
www.goorin.com
• Cassel Goorin, Founder
Products:
Unique custom pieces with special packaging including individual hat boxes, exclusive satin tip stickers, hard-to-find fabrics and linings

GOTCHA INTERNATIONAL
15255 ALTON PARKWAY
SUITE 300
IRVINE, CA 92618
949-221-0990
www.gotcha.com
• Michael Tomson, Founder
• Joel Cooper, Founder
Products:
Surf/Sport Shops, junior, girls, footwears, beach towels, surfboard, wet suit and accessory products

GOTTA HAVE IT GOLF INC
4231 SW 71ST AVENUE
MIAMI, FL 33155
305-665-7475
888-446-5757
Fax: 305-446-6276
www.gottahaveitgolf.com

Products:
Sports, Entertainment and Historical collectibles

GRAFALLOY CORPORATION
8275 TOURNAMENT DRIVE
SUITE 200
MEMPHIS, TN 38125
800-355-8783
matt.savard@truetemper.com
www.grafalloy.com
• Graeme Horwood, VP
Products:
Manufacturer of state of the art carbon fiber wood and iron golf shafts

GRAHAM EMBROIDERY COMPANY
5045 FRANKLIN AVENUE
WACO, TX 76710
888-996-8678
Fax: 888-996-8693
www.grahamembroidery.com
Products:
Embroidery and chenille emblems hand crafted by artisans for more than 60 years.

GRALAB
900 DIMCO WAY
CENTERVILLE, OH 45458
937-433-7600
800-876-8353
Fax: 937-433-0520
www.gralab.com
• Mike Sieron, President / Chief Executive Officer
(934) 433-7600
Products:
Ball knobs, push-pull-lift knobs, oval and tapered knobs, tapered handles, fluted torque knobs, knurled clamping knobs, three and four pronged clamping knobs, T-handle knobs.
Year Founded:
1924

GRAMAN USA, INC.
25 SPECTRUM POINTE
SUITE 403
LAKE FOREST, CA 92630
949-916-3300
800-429-0333
Fax: 949-916-3301
• Ken Chai, President
Products:
Golf Graphite Shafts

GRANADA PITCHING MACHINES
1557 N PENRITH PL
MERIDIAN, ID 83642
800-547-5032
Fax: 208-416-6598
granada@battingpractice.com
www.battingpractice.com
• Norman R. Bruce, President
Products:
Baseball Polyball, Pitching Machines; Softball Polyball, Pitching Machines, Electronic instantaneous mixing/Programmable

GRANDOE CORPORATION
11 GRANDOE LANE
GLOVERSVILLE, NY 12078
518-725-8641
800-472-6363
Fax: 518-773-3388

• Eric Freidman, President
Products:
Gloves for the ski, golf, outdoor and fashion industries.

GRAPHITE MASTER
3815 MEDFORD STREET
LOS ANGELES, CA 90063
323-261-1107
Fax: 323-261-4813
info@graphitemaster.com
www.graphitemaster.com
• Hank Johns, VP
(323) 261-1107
hjohns@graphitemaster.com
Products:
Fiberglass and composite fabrics for surfboards, kayaks, boats, marine and sport applications, industrial, aircraft, prototype, hobbyists, and more

GRAVEL GEAR SKATEBOARD CLOTHING
PO BOX 60127
SAINT PETERSBURG, FL 33784-0127
727-321-7027
877-752-8344
Fax: 727-321-2124
• Laura Mitchell, Marketing Director
(727) 560-0340
• Marty Martinez, Midwest Sales Manager
(214) 282-5877
dallasmarty@hotmail.com
• Stacey Foster, Art Director
(727) 321-7027
Products:
Full line of skateboarding clothing and sporting goods accessories.

GREAT AMERICAN PRODUCTS
1661 S SEGUIN AVENUE
NEW BRAUNFELS, TX 78130
830-620-4400
800-341-4436
Fax: 830-620-8430
wally@gap1.com
www.gap1.com
• Roger Tuttle, Sales Representative
(830) 643-8007
rogerk@gap1.com
• Kevin T. Ulbert, VP of Sales
(830) 643-8024
kevin@gap1.com
• Wally Gullick, VP of Licensed Sports
(830) 643-8023
wally@gap1.com
• Ralph Gabriel, Director of Merchandising
(830) 643-8053
ralph@gap1.com
Products:
NFL, NBA, MLB, MLS, NHL licensed drinkware with dimensional metal logos, custom manufacturing.

GREENTECH
470 CLUBFIELD DRIVE
ROSWELL, GA 30075
804-363-5048
Fax: 770-587-2445
info@greentechitm.com
www.greentechitm.com
• Christopher P. Scott, Founder
• John Patton, VP
(770) 587-2522
info@greentechitm.com
Brands:
GreenTech Systems

Products:
Natural turf for athletic fields and gold tees.

GRIPWEIGHTS
4889 CULVER ROAD
ROCHESTER, NY 14622
585-314-5161
• Steve Nothnagle, Inventor
(585) 314-5161
Products:
Hand weights

GTM SPORTSWEAR
520 MCCALL ROAD
MANHATTAN, KS 66502
877-558-6510
800-377-8527
Fax: 877-908-7033
Customer_service@igtm.com
• Dave Dreiling, Owner
Customer_service@igtm.com
• Larry Harper, VP of Sales
Products:
Uniforms, warm-ups, performance wear, t-shirts, shorts, trophies & awards.

GUESS? INC
1444 S ALAMEDA STREET
LOS ANGELES, CA 90021
213-765-3100
800-224-8377
Fax: 213-744-7838
www.guess.com
• Paul Marciano, Co-Founder
• Frederick G. Silny, SVP
Products:
Tees & Tanks, Sweaters, Wraps, Skirts, Shorts, Capris, Pants, All Jeans, Jackets, Guess Collection, Guess Swimwear, accessories, Wedges, Dress, Sandals, Athletic

GULBENKIAN SWIM, INC.
16 BEAVER BROOK ROAD
DANBURY, CT 6810
203-790-0800
800-431-2586
Fax: 203-791-1449
info@gulbenkianswim.com
www.gulbenkianswim.org
• Edward Gulbenkian, CEO
• Lauren Druckman, Sales Manager
Description:
Manufacture and distribution of cutting edge aquatic products for over 50 years.

GUMRUNNERS
333 WASHINGTON STREET
PO BOX 392
JERSEY CITY, NJ 7302
201-678-9300
Fax: 201-884-1026
info@gumrunners.com
www.gumrunners.com
• Kevin Gass, Co-Founder
kevin@gumrunners.com
• Laurence Molloy, Co-Founder / VP
lmolloy@joltgum.com
Products:
Energy gum and beverages.

GUSTAFSON MANUFACTURING COMPANY
101 44TH STREET
PO BOX 4335
CORPUS CHRISTI, TX 78469

361-882-4025
800-372-4653
Fax: 361-887-7396
gustafsonmfg@earthlink.net
www.lineking.com
• William H. Carney, President
lineking@rangeking.com
Products:
Athletic field line marker, golf ball retriever

GUTERMAN INTERNATIONAL, INC.
603 PLEASANT STREET
PAXTON, MA 1612
508-852-8206
800-343-6096
Fax: 508-856-0632
www.gutermanintl.com
• Peter S. Guterman, President
Products:
Court Equipment & Ball Throwing Machines, Balls, Racquets, String, & Stringing Machines, Bags, Sports Nutrients, Footwear & Sport Socks, Badminton, Court Equipment, Platform, Squash, Tennis & Racquetball

H E HODGE COMPANY
5971 PARKWAY NORTH BLVD
SUITE 200B
CUMMING, GA 30040
770-205-8312
800-282-2248
Fax: 770-205-8318
jhodge@hehodge.com
www.hehodge.com
• Byron Ebersole, VP Sales
• Eric Bourrie, Sales Representative
• Jody Stage, Accounting Manager
jstage@hehodge.com
• Ron Saren, Sales Representative
ronsaren@bellsouth.net
• Tucker Green, Project Manager
• Tony Johnson, Project Manager
• Jim Arthurs, President/CEO
Products:
Basketball goals, volleyball equipment, bleachers, cabinets, lockers, library furniture, office furniture, handicap lifts, computer tables and cafeteria tables

H&B SPECIALIZED PRODUCTS
2629 30TH AVENUE S
MINNEAPOLIS, MN 55406
612-721-5031
800-328-4852
Fax: 952-374-6111
info@hbsponline.com
www.hbsponline.com
• Robert Johnston, President
info@hbsponline.com
• Sherry Ringberg, Chief Finanacial Officer
info@hbsponline.com
• Tom Lerick, General Manager / Construction
info@hbsponline.com
• Stephen Duncan, General Manager, Specialized Products
info@hbsponline.com
Products:
Athletic Equipment, Bleachers, Stadium Seating, Athletic Flooring Systems, Lockers, Athletic & Corridor, Auditorium Seating, Operable Walls, Panel Partitions & Accordion Doors

H & C HEADWARE/KC CAP
17145 MARGAY AVENUE
CARSON, CA 90746
310-324-5263
800-321-9888
Fax: 310-324-8763
CA@KCCAPS.com
www.kccaps.com
• Ken Feldman, Vice President - Sales
CA@KCCAPS.com
Products:
Mfg. Headwear: 6 panel, 5 panel, Beanies
Winter Gear: Blankets, scarves Apparel:
Polos, aprons

H&H ENTERPRISES
PO BOX 585
GRAND HAVEN, MI 49417
616-846-8972
800-878-7777
Fax: 616-846-1004
www.bleacherpeople.com
• John Heinritz, President
• Dwight Ralya, Operations Manager
• Jim Harding, Sales Manager
• Dan DeVries, Estimating
• Deb Vanderstelt, Administrative Assistant
• Richard Crace, Inspections
• Brad Heinritz, General Manager
Products:
Outdoor aluminum bleachers and
grandstands
Brands:
Porter, Gill, Power Max and Pacer

H.H. BROWN SHOE COMPANY
124 W PUTNAM AVENUE
GREENWICH, CT 6830
203-661-2424
888-444-2769
Fax: 203-661-1818
bornservice@hhbrown.com
www.hhbrown.com
• Carmine Iandiorio, General Manager
• Scott Bohling, Chief Financial Officer
• Francis C. Rooney, Jr., Chairman of the
Board
Products:
Manufactures and distributes premier work
shoes and boots, rugged recreational
footwear and comfort casual shoes for men
and women

H.S.T. INC.
8985 CRESTMAR POINT
SAN DIEGO, CA 92121-3222
858-689-0552
800-444-6075
Fax: 858-689-4094
www.hst-inc.com
• Randy M. Beck, Co-Founder / Chief
Executive Officer
sales@hst-inc.com
• Gary D. Beck, Co-Founder / Director
Products:
Golf Shafts, Golf Club Heads, Laser
Machined Putter Inserts, Arrows, Speaker
Baffles, Bicycle Tubes, Ice Axes, Tie Rods,
Industrial Tubes, and more

HAAS-JORDAN COMPANY
1447 SUMMIT STREET
TOLEDO, OH 43604
419-243-2189
800-536-0283
Fax: 419-243-8401

info@haas-jordan.com
www.haas-jordan.com
• Thomas Waltz, President (F.J. Westcott
Co.)
• Todd Blackmar, Sales / Marketing Director
• Janet Ritson, Senior Customer Service
Representative
• Kelly Mondora, Operations Director
Products:
Golf Ball Retrievers, Umbrellas

HADAR ATHLETIC MFG. COMPANY
1515 N 11TH STREET
PO BOX 218
HUMBOLDT, IA 50548
515-332-5312
888-655-1606
Fax: 515-332-1448
general@hadarathletic.com
www.hadarathletic.com
• Mary Miner, President / Finance Director
(888) 655-1606
mary@hadarathletic.com
• Wayne Miner, General Manager
wayne@hadarathletic.com
Products:
Baseball, Basketball, Football, Rugby,
Soccer, Softball, Tract & Field, Volleyball,
Wrestling Equipments and Accessories.
Gym & Playground Equipment. Matts

HAFER CASE
1018 MULCAHY
ROSENBERG, TX 77471
281-341-5070
800-990-8860
Fax: 281-239-7410
bhafer@hafercase.com
www.hafercase.com
Description:
Design, manufacture and sell ATA
re-useable shipping and storage cases.

HAGGAR APPAREL COMPANY
11511 LUNA ROAD
DALLAS, TX 75234
214-352-8481
877-841-2219
Fax: 214-956-0216
www.haggar.com
• Micheal Stitt, CEO
• Frank Bracken, President / Chief
Operating Officer
• Dr. Michelle A. Haggar, MD
Products:
Men's & Women's Casual & Dress Wear

HALEX
45 RANICK ROAD
PO BOX 11357
HAUPPAUGE, NY 11788
631-234-2800
800-645-5190
Fax: 631-234-2948
www.regent-halex.com
Products:
Sporting Good Equipment

HAMILTON ATHLETIC
1605 STANLEY RUSS ROAD
CONWAY, AZ 72034
501-327-0706
Fax: 501-327-0706
www.hamiltonathletic.com
• Bobby Hamilton, Founder

Products:
Pocket Sports Bra

HAMMAKA
PO BOX 837
KAYSVILLE, UT 84037
877-375-4647
877-375-4647
Fax: 877-426-6252
www.hammaka.com
• Braydon Bailey, Chief Executive Officer
Products:
Chairs & Hammocks

HAMMETT COMPANY, J.L.
PO BOX 89057
BRAINTREE, MA 02185-9057
781-848-1000
800-955-2200
Fax: 888-262-1054
• Richmond Y Holden Jr, President
Products:
Arts & Crafts Materials, Teachers Helpers,
Teachers Resources, Bilingual Education
Materials, Children's Books, Classroom
Decor, Game Materials and Accessories,
Learning Toys, Office Supplies, Educational
Music & Video

HANA TIME
226 PUBLIC STREET
PROVIDENCE, RI 2905
800-362-9896
Fax: 401-330-4201
orders@logoart.com
www.logoart.com
Products:
Jewelry, Watch, Clocks & Binoculars

HANCO-M. HANDELSMAN COMPANY
3067 N ELSTON AVENUE
CHICAGO, IL 60618
773-303-1800
800-621-4454
Fax: 773-303-0012
customerservice@hancotee.com
www.hancotee.com
• Ana B. Monzon, Customer Service
(773) 303-1800
• Wilma McDaniel, Customer Service
(773) 303-1800
Products:
Aprons, Bandannas, Baseball Shirts, Bibs,
Bikinis, Blankets, Camouflage Sweat Shirts,
Camouflage T-Shirts, Camouflage Tank,
Caps, Ear Band, Football Shirts, Golf Shirts,
Hav-A-Dannas, Jackets, Jersey, Baseball
Apparel, Pants, Scarf, Scrubs, Shorts,
Smock, Soccer Shirts, Sports Bra, Sports
Shirts, Sweat Pants, Sweat Shirts, Sweat
Bands, Tank Tops, Ties, T-Shirts, Thermal
Underwear, Tote Bags, Towels, Turtleneck,
Underwear, Vests, Visors, Zipper Hoods
Brands:
MLB Apparel, Baseball Caps, NHL Apparel,
NFL Apparel & Caps

HANES
1000 EAST HANES MILL ROAD
WINSTON SALEM, NC 27105
800-503-6702
800-832-0594
contact_us@hanesbrands.com
www.hanes.com
• Rich Noll, Chairman/CEO
• Gerald W Evans, Jr., Chief Operating

Officer
• Richard D Moss, Chief Financial Officer
Products:
Undergarments, Socks, Ladys' Shoes &
Casualwear

HAR-TRU
2200 OLD IVY ROAD
SUITE 100
CHARLOTTESVILLE, VA 22903
877-442-7878
hartru.com
• David Morgen, President
Products:
Tennis Court Products, Tennis Windscreen,
Tennies Nets, Backboard & Rebound Units,
Tennis Ball Machines, Court Accessories,
Sports Nets, Batting Cages/Screens,
Basketball Goal Netting, Indoor and Outdoor
Field Covers, Golf Ball Barrier Netting,
Soccer Goal Netting
Brands:
Royale-Screen, Air Master, Mastershade,
Courtmaster, Tidyfit

HARBINGER
801 CHADBOURNE ROAD
SUITE 103
FAIRFIELD, CA 94534
707-438-7777
800-729-5954
Fax: 800-729-5947
sales@harbingerfitness.com
www.harbingerfitness.com
• David McCrane, President
• Michele Gaedke, Vice President
Product/Marketing
Nature of Service:
Wholesale supplier of fitness accessories.
Year Founded:
1988
Products:
Fitness Accessories & Training Aids
Brands:
Harbinger Fitness

HARBOR SPORTS GEAR
2810 CANON STREET
SAN DIEGO, CA 92106
619-222-5891
Fax: 619-222-5228
sales@harborsportsgear.com
www.harborsportsgear.com
• Pete Slaughter
Products:
Sports & Travel Bags

HARDMAN COMPANY
11/12 TOKENHOUSE YARD
LONDON, ENGLAND EC2R 7AS
20-7929-3399
Fax: 20-7929-3377
hardmanco@aol.com
www.hardmanandco.com
• John Holmes, Chairman
• Roger Hardman, Founder
• Keith Hiscock, Chief Executive Officer
• Steve Clapham, Non-Executive Director
Products:
Athletic Equipment Bags

HARPER INDUSTRIES INC
136 CENTRAL AVENUE
CLARK, NJ 07066
732-815-3200
Fax: 620-896-7129

• Thomas S Friedland, President
• Laura Friedland, VP
Products:
General Sports Products - Shorts,
Sweatclothes, T-shirts, Warm-Up Suits;
Water Sports - Swimming Suits

HARRISON SPORTS, INC.
11247 ILEX AVENUE
PACOIMA, CA 91331
818-834-7600
800-347-4646
Fax: 818-834-7601
info@harrison.com
www.harrison.com
• Michael H Cheng, President
mike@harrison.com
• Eileen S. Lai, VP
eileen@harrison.com
• Chris Elson, Marketing Director
elson@harrison.com
Products:
Golf Shaft & Accessories

HARRISON-HOGE INDUSTRIES, INC.
19 N COLUMBIA STREET
PORT JEFFERSON STATION, NY 11777
631-473-7308
800-748-8066
Fax: 631-473-7398
www.seaeagle.com
• Navneet Syal, Export Manager
navneet@seaeagle.com
Products:
Training & Conditioning Exercise Machines,
Inflatable Boats with Floorboards

HARRISS & COVINGTON INC.
1250 HICKORY CHAPEL ROAD
PO BOX 1909
HIGH POINT, NC 27260
336-882-6811
Fax: 336-889-2412
customerservice@harrissandcov.com
www.harrissandcov.com
• Ned Covington, President/CEO
ncovington@harrissandcov.com
• Darrell Frye, Finance and Administration
VP
dfrye@harrissandcov.com
• Danny McNair, Manufacturing VP
dmcnair@harrissandcov.com
• Edward Harris Covington, President
Products:
Socks

HARTWELL SPORTS, INC.
97 WINFIELD CIRCLE
HARTWELL, GA 30643
706-856-4900
800-849-5555
Fax: 800-849-2121
customerservice@hartwell.com
www.hartwell.com/
• Rick Cesere, Chief Executive Officer
• Ray Titus, President
• Michael Snyder, Sales VP
• Ray Ferrell, VP Of Sales
Products:
Mens apparel, womens apparel, shirts,
outwear, athletic, companion styles, new
styles and closeouts

HARVEST VICTORY LTD
4809 E 49TH STREET
VERNON, CA 90058

323-588-9880
Fax: 323-588-9886
info@harvestvictoryusa.com
www.harvestvictoryusa.com
Products:
Backpack, sport bag, hiking backpack, duffle
bag, school bag, laptop backpack, computer
briefcase, traveling bag, waist bag & fanny
pack

HASCALL SPORTSWEAR, INC.
PO BOX 213
BOSTON, MA 02128-0002
617-567-4160
Fax: 617-567-4195
• Carl R Hascall, President
• Linda Hascall, VP
Products:
General Sports Products - Athletic
Jackets/Parkas

HATCHERS MANUFACTURING INC.
130 CONDOR STREET
E BOSTON, MA 2128
617-568-1262
800-225-6842
Fax: 617-567-9953
• John Vinton, Chief Executive Officer
• Peter Spillane, Production Manager
• Katie Dinsmore, Sales Manager
• Jennifer Clark, Marketing Manager
Products:
General Sports Products Athletic
Jackets/Parkas, Cheerleading Uniforms &
Accessories, Warm-Up Suits

HEAD DOWN TRAINERS.COM
888-422-2768
888-422-2768
Fax: 610-455-0495
www.headdowntrainers.com
• Tom O'Connell, Coach
• Andy Lopez, Head Baseball Coach
Products:
Training glasses

HEAD/PENN USA
306 S 45TH AVENUE
PHOENIX, AZ 85043
602-269-1492
800-289-7366
Fax: 602-484-0533
www.head.com
• Johan Eliasch, Chairman and Chief
Executive Officer, He
headinvestors@aol.com
• Ralf Bernhart, Chief Financial Officer
headinvestors@aol.com
• Klaus Hotter, EVP, Winter Sport Division
headinvestors@aol.com
• Georg Kroell, EVP, Licensing Division
Products:
Tennis, squash and racquetball racquets;
alpine skis and ski boots; snowboarding
boards, bindings and boots; accessories
and apparel; Alpine ski bindings; and Diving
equipment

HEADMASTER INC
3310 S FAIRVIEW STREET
SANTA ANA, CA 92704
714-556-5244
800-241-4442
Fax: 714-556-5243
• Johan Eliasch, Chairman
• Klaus Hotter, Executive Vice President

Products:
Caps, hats, visors, closeout products, bags, beanies and boxers

HEART RATE, INC.
RATE INC. 1411 E WILSHIRE AVENUE
SANTA ANA, CA 92705
714-850-9716
800-237-2271
Fax: 714-850-9716
email@heartrateinc.com
www.versaclimber.com
• Richard Charnitski, President
webmaster@heartrateinc.com
• Dan Charnitski, General Manager
webmaster@heartrateinc.com
• Kimberly DuBois, National Sales Manager
webmaster@heartrateinc.com
Brands:
Versaclimber: 108 H, 108 HP, 108 CM, 108 SM, 108 CMA, 108 SMA, 108 LX, 108 LXP, 108 ALX, 108 SRM and ExerVibe, Climber; VersaPulley: Portable VersaPulley, Wall Mount VersaPulley and ArmBlaster; 1-2-3 Heart Rate Monitors: Hand-Held, Equipment Mounted, Wall Mounted and Floor Stand
Products:
Training Equipment

HEARTLINE FITNESS PRODUCTS, INC.
8041 CESSNA AVENUE
SUITE 200
GAITHERSBURG, MD 20879
301-921-0661
800-262-3348
Fax: 301-330-5479
sales@heartlinefitness.com
www.heartlinefitness.com
• Robert F Burgess Jr, President
(301) 921-0661
bob@heartlinefitness.com
• Jason Malecki, Territory Manager, DC/MD
(703) 493-9405
jason@heartlinefitness.com
• Joe Purpura, Territory Manager, Pennsylvania
(412) 609-6507
joe@heartlinefitness.com
• Doug Meadows, Key Accounts Manager
Products:
CoreRack Training Series, Auxiliary Training Series, Circuit Training Series, Free Weight Essentials, Cardiovascular Training Series

HEAVY HANDS
140 FELL COURT
SUITE 120
HAUPPAUGE, NY 11788
631-300-3500
Fax: 631-300-3501
customerservice@lionsportsinc.com
www.heavyhandsfitness.com
• Len Schwartz, Heavyhands Father
customerservice@lionsportsinc.com
Products:
Heavyhands Walking Book / DVD / 2 lb Combo Special, Heavyhands instructional DVD, Special: DVD and 2-lb. Combo-Pac Black Heavyhands, YogaHands Combo Special, AeroAbs DVD, Heavyhands Walk Plus DVD #45510, YogaHands DVD and 10-lb. Heavyhands

HEAVY HITTER INDUSTRIES, INC.
PO BOX 2344
VALLEY CENTER, CA 92082

760-749-7833
800-283-1717
Fax: 760-749-7829
info@heavyhitter.com
www.heavyhitter.com
• Margie Nybye, Owner/Vice President
(760) 749-7833
• Lance S Nybye, Marketing Director
info@heavyhitter.com
Products:
Baseball Bats
Year Founded:
1977

HEDMAN MANUFACTURING SOUTH
730 BRANCH DRIVE
ALPHARETTA, GA 30004
770-664-8880
562-921-0404
Fax: 770-664-6885
techsupport@hedman.com
www.hedman.com
• Robert Vandergriff, Chief Executive Officer/Chairman
• Chris Vandergriff, President

HEDSTROM CORPORATION
3436 N KENNICOTT AVENUE
ARLINGTON HEIGHTS, IL 60004-7801
847-259-4468
800-323-5999
Fax: 847-259-4633
www.hedscape.com
• Michael Johnston, President
• Kenneth J Giacomino, EVP / Chief Financial Officer
• Susan Meek, Corporate VP
Products:
Basketball - Balls-Vinyl; Football - Balls-Vinyl; Racquet Sports - Platform Tennis Equipment; Softball - Balls-Rubber; Volleyball - Balls-Vinyl. Water Sports - Personal Flotation; Gym Sets - Balls, Spring Horses, Trampolines

HELLY HANSEN, (U.S.) INC.
4104 C STREET NE
SUITE 200
AUBURN, WA 98002
866-376-4183
800-435-5901
Fax: 253-852-1481
www.hellyhansen.com
• Ric Long, President
Products:
Men and Women: jackets, pants, thermal, life base layer, footwear and off hill; Kids: jackets, pants, suits and accessories; Accessories: gloves, beanies and bags

HENRY-GRIFFITTS
827 W PRAIRIE AVE.
HAYDEN, ID 83835
208-772-8505
800-446-0036
Fax: 208-772-9632
www.henry-griffitts.com
• Billy McDonald, Board Chairman
• Randy Henry, Founder
• Jim Hofmeister, Chief Executive Officer
• Randall Henry, President
Products:
Model 82 Driver, RDH Fairway Series, RDH3 irons, GreenBack$ irons, GLII, youth woods, RHD Wedge Series, Fit2Aim Putter System, Shafts, Accessories(sun hat, visor, junior bag, towels, umbrella), golf bags and

travel bags, RDH Deep Fairway Woods, TS-1 Irons, Evergreen Rescue Woods, RDH 460 Driver.
Nature of Service:
Dynamic Cutoms-Fit Golf Clubs

HENWAY SPORTS & SPECIALTIES, INC.
5693 W HOWARD STREET
NILES, IL 60714
847-588-3500
800-901-0700
Fax: 847-588-1218
• Steve Wilneff, President
• Myron Gruenberg, VP
• Laurence Wilneff, VP
• Evan Alston, Promotions VP
Products:
Corporate and event sales of authentic sports game items and autographed items

HERE'S FRED GOLF COMPANY, INC.
2205 SAINT JOHNS BLUFF ROAD
JACKSONVILLE, FL 32246-2309
904-645-9790
800-874-7395
Fax: 904-645-9493
info@heresfredgolf.com
www.heresfredgolf.com
• Douglas Kirchloff, President
(904) 645-9790
dougk@heresfredgolf.com
Products:
Caddy Bibs, Golf Flags, Embroidered Screen Printing, Headcovers, Tees, Spikes, Pencils, Golf Towels.

HI STYLE LETTERED SPORTSWEAR COMPANY, INC.
HIGHWAY 65 N
CARROLLTON, MO 64633
660-542-3410
800-821-3610
Fax: 660-542-3467
• Jean Arp, President
• Troy A Howell, VP
Products:
Baseball - Uniforms; Basketball - Uniforms; Field Hockey - Uniforms; Football - Uniforms; Soccer - Uniforms; Softball - Caps, Uniforms; Track & Field/Running - Apparel-Track & Field; Volleyball - Uniforms

HI-TEC SPORTS USA INC.
4801 STODDARD ROAD
MODESTO, CA 95356
209-545-1111
800-521-1698
Fax: 209-545-2543
retailinfo@hi-tec.com
www.hi-tec.com
• Frank Van Wezel, Chairman / Founder
retailinfo@hi-tec.com
• Paul Brooks, Chief Executive Officer
info@hi-tec.com
Products:
Footwear for Outdoors, Golf, and Court sport activities

HICKORY BRANDS, INC.
429 27TH STREET NW
PO BOX 429
HICKORY, NC 28601
828-322-2600
800-438-5777
Fax: 800-422-3279
www.hickorybrands.com

• Bob Bell, Chief Executive Officer
• Joseph Nissan, President
• Josh Higgins, Retail Sales Director
Products:
General Sports Products - Athletic Shoe Cleaners, Waterproofers, Shoelaces, Leather. Athletic Socks - Over the Calf, Mid Calf, Anklet, Crew, Quarter, Cushion Sole Yarns Used Cotton, Acrylic, Nylon, Performance Fibers

HIGH 5 SPORTSWEAR
18300 CASCADE AVENUE
SUITE 200
SEATTLE, WA 98188
206-574-0123
800-222-4016
Fax: 206-574-0276
customercare@high5sportswear.com
www.high5sportswear.com
• Tom Mercer, Vice President, Sales & Marketing
tom.mercer@high5sportswear.com
• John Moore, Owner
Products:
Uniforms, Bags, Jerseys, Shorts, and Warm-Ups.

HIGH END SYSTEMS, INC
2105 GRACY FARMS LANE
AUSTIN, TX 78758
512-836-2242
800-890-8989
Fax: 512-837-5290
jeff.pelzl@barco.com
www.highend.com
• Merritt Belisle, Chairman
• Richard Belliveau, Co-Founder & Chief Technology Officer
Year Founded:
1986.
Products:
Digital Lighting, Lighting Consoles, and Automated Luminaires.

HIGH SIERRA SPORT COMPANY
880 CORPORATE WOODS PARKWAY
VERNON HILLS, IL 60061
847-913-1100
800-323-9590
Fax: 800-323-9591
customerservice@highsierrasport.com
www.hssc.com
• Hank Bernbaum, President
Products:
Outdoor Products - Backpacks, Outerwear, Polar Fleece, Luggage, Duffels.

HILLERICH & BRADSBY COMPANY, INC.
800 W MAIN STREET
LOUISVILLE, KY 40202
877-775-8443
800-282-2287
Fax: 502-585-1179
www.slugger.com
• John A. Hillerich IV, President / Chief Executive Officer
• Marty Archer, President, Louisville Slugger Division
• Chuck Schupp, Sales / Promotions Director, Pro Basebal
• Bill Williams, Public Relations / VP
Products:
Baseball - Bat Racks/Hangers, Bat Tape, Bat Weights, Bats-Metal, Bats-Wood, Gloves-Batter, Gloves-Catcher, Gloves-Fielder, Gloves-First Base, Glove

Oil; Golf - Bags-For Clubs, Clubs-Iron Or Wood Sets, Clubs-Utility, Headcovers; Ice Hockey - Sticks

HIND, INC.
191 SPRING STREET
PO BOX 9191
LEXINGTON, MA 2420
800-365-4933
Fax: 800-797-4248
www.hind.com
• Kenneth L. Minton, President
• Gregory W. Hind, Chairman
• Bruce W. Dixon, Chief Executive Officer
Products:
Cycling - Apparel; General Sports Products - Bags-Equipment, Silk-screening, Tights, Training Aids, Warm Global Suits; Gymnastics - Apparel; Racquet Sports - Apparel, Bags-Equipment; Track & Field/Running - Apparel-Run/Jog, Apparel

HINES III
3653 REGENT BOULEVARD
SUITE 405
JACKSONVILLE, FL 32224
904-645-6500
877-645-6501
Fax: 904-645-6655
www.hinesiii.com
• Samuel J. Hines, VP Sales/Marketing
• Judith K. Hines, President
Products:
Benches, Planters and Receptacles for athletic stadiums and other large facilities.

HIREV
364 WILLIAMSON ROAD
SUITE 301
MOORESVILLE, NC 28117
888-329-4658
Fax: 035-191-0243
productsupport@hirev.com
www.hirev.com
Products:
Tribute Hoods, Replica Hoods, Computer Kits, Absorbent Coasters, Computer Mice, and Computer Mouse Pads with sports logos and designs.

HL CORPORATION
PO BOX 3327
MANHATTAN BEACH, CA 90266
310-546-3652
800-457-7678
Fax: 310-372-7443
hlcorp7@hotmail.com
www.hlbadminton.com
• Dean Schoppe, President
hlcorp7@hotmail.com
• Dean Schoppe, President
hlcorp7@hotmail.com
Products:
Manufacturer and distributor of badminton rackets and shuttlecoks.

HO SPORTS INC.
7926 BRACKEN PLACE SE
SNOQUALMIE, WA 98065
425-885-3505
800-938-4646
Fax: 425-867-5327
info@hosports.com
www.hosports.com
• Brian Gardner, VP

Products:
Skiing - Alpine - Snowboards; Water Sports - Water Skis, Wet Suits; Knee Boards, Vests, Gloves, Bags and Apparel.

HOCKEY COMPANY
3400 RAYMOND-LASNIER
SAINT-LAURENT, CANADA H4R 3L3
514-461-8000
Fax: 514-937-8276
• Robert A. Desrosiers, Finance and Administration VP / Chief Fi
Products:
Skates, Sticks, Helmets and protective equipment products.

HOGGAN HEALTH INDUSTRIES
8020 S 1300 W
PO BOX 488
WEST JORDAN, UT 84088
801-572-6500
800-678-7888
Fax: 801-572-6514
contact@hogganhealth.com
www.hogganhealth.com
• Lynn Hoggan, President
lynn@hogganhealth.com
Products:
Training & Conditioning Exercise Machines.

HOIST FITNESS SYSTEMS
11900 COMMUNNITY ROAD
POWAY, CA 92064
858-578-7676
800-548-5438
Fax: 858-578-9558
webprodsupport@hoistfitness.com
www.hoistfitness.com
• Jeffrey Partrick, Chief Executive Officer
• Roger Cloyd, President / Founder
• Rany Webber, VP / Founder
• Mario Lopez, Product Support Manager
(858) 578-7676
mlopez@hoistfitness.com
• Jeremy Miller, International Sales/ Director of Marketing
(858) 578-7676
jmiller@hoistfitness.com
Products:
Home Gyms, Freeweights, and HD-HS Series.

HOLE IN NONE, INC.
1247 W WEBB AVENUE
BURLINGTON, NC 27217-1150
336-228-1758
800-444-8933
Fax: 336-228-0703
holeinnone@aol.com
• B H. Bridgers Jr, President
• W O. Shaw, VP
Products:
Baseball - Socks, Stirrups; Basketball - Socks; Football - Socks; General Sports Products - Socks; Golf - Socks; Soccer - Socks; Softball - Socks, Stirrups; Track & Field/Running - Socks.

HOLLMAN, INC.
1825 WALNUT HILL LANE
SUITE 110
IRVING, TX 75038
972-815-4000
800-433-3630
Fax: 972-815-2921
www.hollman.com

- Joseph H. Hollman, President
- Vi Ho, Chief Financial Officer
- Sue Hwang, VP Locker Division
- Travis Hollman, VP
travish@hollman.com
Products:
Plastic Laminate and Wood Lockers,
Panelized Racquetball and Squash Courts,
and Athletic Glass Wall Systems.

HOLLOWAY SPORTSWEAR, INC.
2633 CAMPBELL ROAD
PO BOX 4489
SIDNEY, OH 45365
937-497-7575
800-331-5156
Fax: 937-497-8080
sales@hollowayusa.com
www.hollowayusa.com
- Mark S Vondenhuevel, President
Year Founded:
1964.
Products:
Teamwear & Warm-Ups, Sweatshirts,
Pullovers & Windshirts, Canyon Fleece,
Performance Wear/Shirts, Outerwear, Wool
Variety Jackets, Blankets and Bags

HOLMATRO RESCUE EQUIPMENT
505 MCCORMICK DRIVE
GLEN BURNIE, MD 21061
410-768-9662
Fax: 410-768-4878
- William Swayne, President
- Jaap G. Meijer, Chairman

HOLOUBEK, INC.
W238 N1800 ROCKWOOD DRIVE
WAUKESHA, WI 53188-1198
262-547-0500
800-886-4759
Fax: 262-547-6580
- Verne Holoubek, Founder
- Doug Konriff, National Sales Manager
Products:
General Sports Products - Apparel-Screen
Printed, Heat Transfers, Lettering, Transfer
Equipment.

HOOK & HACKLE
607 ANN STREET REAR
HOMESTEAD, PA 15120
412-476-8620
800-552-8342
Fax: 412-476-8639
ron@hookhack.com
www.hookhack.com
Description:
Fly fishing tackle, rod building and fly tying
specialists.

HORIZON FITNESS
1620 LANDMARK DRIVE
COTTAGE GROVE, WI 53527
800-962-3596
www.horizonfitness.com
- Bob Whip, President
- Bill Sotis, Executive Vice President Of
Sales
Products:
Commercial-quality treadmills, ellipticals and
stationary bicycles

HORNER FLOORING COMPANY
23400 HELLMAN DRIVE
PO BOX 380
DOLLAR BAY, MI 49922
906-482-1180
800-380-0119
Fax: 906-482-6115
info@hornerflooring.com
www.hornerflooring.com
- Doug Hamar, President / Chief Executive
Officer
dhamar@hornerflooring.com
- Mark Young, VP Operations
myoung@hornerflooring.com
- Lew Bosco, Director Horner Study Center
lbosco@hornerflooring.com
Products:
Basketball, Racquetball, Squash, Volleyball
courts and flooring.

HORNUNG'S GOLF PRODUCTS, INC.
815 MORRIS STREET
FOND DU LAC, WI 54935
920-922-2640
800-323-3569
Fax: 920-922-4986
info@hornungs.com
www.hornungs.com
- Robert Hornung, President
(800) 323-3569
bob@hornungs.com
Products:
Golf Course Maintenance. Equipment,
Apparel, Bags-For Clubs, Balls,
Cleats/Spikes, Clubs-Iron Or Wood Sets,
Clubs-Putters, Clubs-Utility, Clubheads,
Club Grips, Club Shafts, Driving Nets/Mats,
Flag Poles, Gloves, Grip Waxes, Hats/Caps,
Headcovers, Mechani

HOT SAUCE HARRYS, INC.
1077 INNOVATION AVENUE
SUITE 109
NORTH PORT, FL 34289
214-902-8552
800-588-8979
Fax: 214-956-9885
info@HotSauceHarrys.com
www.hotsauceharrys.com
- Dianne Harris, Owner/President
Dianne@HotSauceHarrys.com
- Bob Harris, Vice President
Bob@HotSauceHarrys.com
- Lauren Smith, Vice President
lauren@hotsauceharrys.com
Products:
Distributor of Licensed gourmet products for
NCAA, MLB, OCC, Pedregon Racing Team,
Don Garlits, US Duck Stamps
Year Founded:
1995

HOT SOX, INC.
95 MADISON AVENUE
NEW YORK, NY 10016
212-957-2000
Fax: 212-957-1050
inquiries@hotsox.com
www.hotsox.com
- Gary Wolkowitz, President
- Ellie Gordon, Founder / Senior EVP
Products:
Baseball, Basketball, Soccer, Softball, Track
& Field/Running Socks.

HOYT USA
593 NORTH WRIGHT BROTHERS DRIVE
SALT LAKE CITY, UT 84116
801-363-2990
Fax: 801-537-1470
- Randy Walk, President
- Tom Driffill, Human Resource Manager
Products:
Archery - Bows, Accessories
Archery/Bow Hunting Sponsor:
Professional Archers and Bow Hunters;
Team Hoyt and Team Hoyt Recurve.

HT TENNIS
12932 SALEM AVENUE
PO BOX 569
HAGERSTOWN, MD 21741
301-739-3077
800-842-7878
Fax: 301-739-6104
- Richard N Funkhouser Jr, President
(301) 739-3077
Products:
Surfaces and Tennis Court Equipment,
Tennis Nets, Tennis Facility Products

HUBBELL LIGHTING, INC.
701 MILLENIUM BOULEVARD
SUITE L
GREENVILLE, SC 29607
864-678-1000
800-627-3377
Fax: 864-678-1065
info@hubbell.com
www.hubbelllighting.com
- Scott Muse, President
Products:
Boxes and Fittings, Cable/HOse
Management, COmmunication Solutions,
Enclosures, Hazardous Environment,
Industrial Controls, Lighting, Lighting
Controls/Sensors, Telecom and Data,
Testing Equipment, Utility Products and
Tools, Wiring Products and Workstations

HUDSON BOAT WORKS INC.
2519 FANSHAWE PARK ROAD E
LONDON, ON, CANADA N5X 4A1
519-473-9864
Fax: 519-473-2861
hbw@hudsonboatworks.com
www.hudsonboatworks.com
- Jack Coughlan, President/Founder
(519) 473-9864
hbw@hudsonboatworks.com
- Dallas Coughlan, Director
- Hugh Hudson, Sales Manager
(519) 473-9864
hugh@hudsonboatworks.com
- Jeff McIntyre, Sales and Service
(519) 473-9864
hbw@hudsonboatworks.com
- Glen Burston, Operations Manager
(519) 473-9864
glen@hudsonboatworks.com
- Chris McCully, Technical Services
Products:
High Performance Rowing Equipment:
Olympic class racing boats: 1x, 2-, 2x, 4-,
4+, 4x, 8+
Nature of Service:
Customer direct sales, service & delivery; on
site service at select regattas and events

HUFCOR, INC.
2101 KENNEDY ROAD
PO BOX 591
JANESVILLE, WI 53547-0591
608-756-1241
800-542-2371 Ext 214
Fax: 608-758-8253
info@hufcor.com
www.hufcor.com
• Jim Landherr, VP Manufacturing
Products:
Facilities - partial & full height, acoustically rated operable walls/partitions

HUFFY BICYCLE COMPANY
6551 CENTERVILLE BUSINESS PARKWAY
CENTERVILLE, OH 45459
937-865-2800
800-872-2453
Fax: 937-865-5470
service@huffy.com
www.huffybikes.com
• John A Muskovich, Chief Executive Officer / President
• Nancy A Michaud, Senior VP, General Counsel - Secretary
• Robert L Diekman, Senior VP, Operations - Logistics
• Steven D Lipton, Senior VP, Chief Financial Officer
Products:
Bicycles

HUFFY SPORTS COMPANY
PO BOX 90015
BOWLING GREEN, KY 42103-7932
800-558-5234
Fax: 262-820-6757
service@huffysports.com
www.huffysports.com
• Randy Schickert, President / General Manager
• Patrick Ehren, VP of Sales and Marketing
Products:
Basketball Systems, Sports balls, Youth products, Pool Sports, Accessories

HUGGER-MUGGER YOGA PRODUCTS
1190 S PIONEER ROAD
SALT LAKE CITY, UT 84104
801-268-9642
800-473-4888
Fax: 801-268-2629
comments@huggermugger.com
www.huggermugger.com
• Sara Chambers, Founder
• Earl Loveless, Sales Manager
sales@huggermugger.com
Products:
Yoga, Pilates and Meditation Products.

HUMMER TURFGRASS SYSTEMS, INC.
1527 S COLEBROOK ROAD
MANHEIM, PA 17545
717-898-5000
800-872-8873
Fax: 717-898-0770
info@usaturf.com
www.usaturf.com
• Robert Hummer, President
bob@usaturf.com
• Matt Wimer, Director of Field Operations
matt@usaturf.com
Year Founded:
1968.
Products:

Natural grass sports surfaces
Description:
Producing high-quality natural grass playing surfaces for over 40 years. Specializing in design, build and construction of first class athletic fields.

HUNTER MANUFACTURING GROUP INC
201 W LOUDON AVENUE
LEXINGTON, KY 40508
859-254-7573
800-237-1869
Fax: 859-254-7614
keith.spaulding@huntermfg.com
• Keith Spaulding, Sales Contact
(800) 237-1869
keith.spaulding@huntermfg.com
• Bill Brown, Director of Motorsports
bill.brown@huntermfg.com
• John Miller, Credit Manager
bill.brown@huntermfg.com
• Bob Johnson, Purchasing Manager
bob.johnson@huntermfg.com
Products:
Bottoms Up Collection, Collector Glasses, Collector Glasses, Glass Mugs, Stemware, Coffee Mugs, Specialty Mugs, Sublimated Coffee Mugs, Ceramic Steins, Stainless Steel Collection, Collector Plates, Leaded Crystal, Cooperstown and Heritage Jersey, Player Products, Game Day Products, Sporting Goods

HUSSEY SEATING COMPANY
38 DYER STREET EXTENSION
NORTH BERWICK, ME 3906
207-676-2271
800-341-0401
Fax: 207-676-2222
info@husseyseating.com
www.husseyseating.com
• Timothy Hussey, President / Chief Executive Officer
Thussey@husseyseating.com
• Jack Rogers, Sales VP
jrogers@husseyseating.com
Products:
Auditorium Seating, Stadium Seating, Telescopic Gym Seats, Telescopic Platforms

HYDRA-RIB, INC.
PO BOX 90015
BOWLING GREEN, KY 42103-7932
800-558-5234
Fax: 262-820-6757
service@huffysports.com
Products:
Basketball Apparatus

HYDRO SPA
6101 N 45TH STREET
ST PETERSBURG, FL 33714
727-573-9611
877-237-8772
Fax: 727-525-5659
CustomerService@PremiumLeisure.com
• Tammie Colombotti, National Sales Coordinator
(727) 573-9611
tammie.colombotti@premiumleisure.com
• Bill Piontek, International Sales
Products:
Luxury Hot Tubs &Personal Hydrotherapy products, Portable Spas & Backyard Leisure products

HYP HATS, LTD
10 E 34TH STREET
6TH FLOOR
NEW YORK, NY 10016
212-684-7717
800-331-1181
Fax: 212-684-7589
sales@hyphats.com
• Howard Levy, President
howardl@hyponline.com
• Rob Weingard, Sales VP
• Mike Pascal, Chief Financial Officer and VP Operations
• Rob Weingard, Accessories Businesses
Products:
Branded & Custom caps, headwear, cold weather accessories, hair accessories & hosiery.

ICON HEALTH & FITNESS, INC.
1500 S 1000 W
LOGAN, UT 84321
435-750-5000
866-506-9095
Fax: 435-750-3917
service@iconfitness.com
www.iconfitness.com
• David J Watterson, Chairman / Chief Executive Officer
• Joseph Brough, Chief Operating Officer
• Fred Beck, Chief Financial Officer
• Matthew N Allen, President / Chief Merchandising Officer
Products:
Home Fitness Equipment, Accessories, Spas, Commercial Fitness Gear

IGLOO PRODUCTS CORPORATION
777 IGLOO ROAD
KATY, TX 77494
713-584-6800
800-364-5566
Fax: 713-935-7732
www.igloocoolers.com
• Jim Morley, President
• Eve Heim-Grubb, Marketing Director
Products:
Plastic ice chests and beverage coolers

IMAGE INNOVATIONS INC
432 PARK AVENUE
NEW YORK, NY 10016
518-589-9400
• Michael Preston, Chief Executive Officer / Director
• Derick Sinclair, Chief Financial Officer / Director
Services:
Sports-, entertainment- and cause-related artwork and collectibles

IMPACT TRAINING SYSTEMS INC
8722 LANYARD COURT
RANCHO CUCAMONGA, CA 91730
909-946-1617
877-467-2285
Fax: 909-946-8370
• Richard Pumerantz, President
richard@impacttrainingsystems.com
Products:
Training products

IMPERIAL HEADWEAR, INC.
ONE PARAMOUNT DRIVE
BOURBON, MO 65441

303-597-0206
800-950-1916
Fax: 800-755-5121
www.imperialsports.com
• John Bond, President
jbond@imperialheadwear.com
• Rick White, President/CEO
Products:
Full service line of men's and ladies
headwear. Custom art, embroidery, sun
protection and technical offering

IMPERIAL INTERNATIONAL
303 PATERSON PLANK ROAD
CARLSTADT, NJ 7072
201-288-9199
800-526-6261
Fax: 201-288-8990
inquiries@imperialusa.com
www.imperialusa.com
Products:
Billiard Tables, Pool Accessories, Furniture,
Cues & Cases

IMPEX INC
2801 S. TOWNE AVE.
POMONA, CA 91766
626-961-8686
800-999-8899
Fax: 626-961-9966
info@impex-fitness.com
www.impex-fitness.com
Products:
Home Fitness equipment

IN GLAS COMPANY
1060 CHERBOURG STREET
SHERBROOKE, QC, CANADA J1K 2N8
819-563-2202
800-563-2202
Fax: 819-566-1846
www.inglasco.com
• Denis Drolet, President / Chief Executive
Officer
• Marc-Andre Watson, Chief Financial
Officer
• Jose Cloutier, Information Technology
Director
Products:
Hockey souvenir pucks, sticks, and other
promotional items

INDUSTRIAL OPPORTUNITIES, INC.
2586 BUSINESS HIGHWAY 19
PO BOX 1649
ANDREWS, NC 28901
828-321-4754
Fax: 828-321-4784
info@elasticproducts.com
www.industrialopportunities.com
• Harry Baughn, Sales / Marketing Director
(828) 321-4754
• Tom O'Brien, President/CEO
 ext 211
Products:
suspenders and sewn items
Brands:
Hold-Up Gang

**INFORMATION & DISPLAY SYSTEMS,
INC.**
10275 CENTURION COURT
JACKSONVILLE, FL 32256
904-645-8697
Fax: 904-645-8496

marketing@ids-sports.com
www.ids-sports.com

INLAND ASSOCIATES
18965 W 158TH STREET
OLATHE, KS 66062
913-764-7977
800-888-7800
Fax: 913-764-8721
www.inlandassoc.com
• Peggy Meader, President
Products:
Video displays.

INNOVA-CHAMPION DISCS INC
900 S DUPONT AVE
ONTARIO, CA 91761
909-481-6266
800-408-8449
Fax: 909-481-6263
info@innovadiscs.com
www.innovadiscs.com
Products:
Golf Discs & Accessories

**INNOVATIVE MARKETING
CONSULTANTS**
4282 SHORELINE DRIVE
SPRING PARK, MN 55384
952-252-1254
877-674-8206
Fax: 952-417-8146
info@imcsuccess.com
www.imcsuccess.com
• Shane Erickson, President/Chief Executive
Officer
• Paul Higgins, Operations Manager
• Paul Yahnke, National Sales Manager
• Adam Tschida, Senior Account Executive
adam@imcsuccess.com
• Robert Ed, Marketing Specialist
robert@imcsuccess.com
Nature of Services:
Innovative Marketing Consultants
manufactures on-premise promotional
marketing products for a variety of industries
including Sports Marketing (Sports Beads),
the Retail and Beverage Markets, and
Casinos.

**INNOVATIVE SPORTS
TECHNOLOGIES/IST**
819 18TH STREET
PO BOX 1311
BEDFORD, IN 47421
800-505-2319
Fax: 812-277-0315
Products:
Golf Shafts

INNOVO GROUP INC.
5901 S EASTERN AVENUE
SUITE 1560
COMMERCE, CA 90040
310-786-1789
800-627-2621
Fax: 310-786-1792
• Samuel J Furrow, Chairman of the Board
innovo@innovogroup.com
• Marc Crossman, Interim Chief Executive
Officer / Presid
innovo@innovogroup.com
• Kelly Hoffman, Director
Products:
Private Label and Branded Apparels &
Accessories

INSPORT INTERNATIONAL, INC.
2929 E COMMERCIAL BOULEVARD #205
FORT LAUDERDALE, FL 33308
800-652-5200
• Eric Merk, President
Products:
Cycling, Track & Field/Running, Training &
Conditioning Apparel and Accessories

INSTA GRAPHIC SYSTEMS
13925 E 166TH STREET
CERRITOS, CA 90703
562-404-3000
800-421-6971
Fax: 562-404-3010
sales@instagraph.com
www.instagraph.com
• Janet Wells, President/Chief Executive
Officer
info@instagraph.com
• Larry Johnson, Vice President-Engineering
info@instagraph.com
Nature of Service:
A leader in heat transfer and machine
technology for 48 years designs, develops,
manufactures and sells innovative custom
heat transfers and quality machines
worldwide. Applications in various
industries, including sports apparel and
supplies.
Year Founded:
1959
Products:
Heat seal machines, custom transfers, die
cut letters and numbers

**INSTA-BENCH/CARRY GEAR
SOLUTIONS**
2125 WESTERN AVENUE
SUITE 300
SEATTLE, WA 98121
206-957-6801
Fax: 206-441-4464
info@carrygear.com
www.carrygear.com

INTERKAL INC.
5981 E CORK STREET
KALAMAZOO, MI 49048
269-349-1521
Fax: 269-349-6530
sales@interkal.com
www.interkal.com
• Kevin Hemler, Vice President - Sales and
Marketing
Products:
Gymnasiums, Multipurpose Facilities,
Stadiums & Arenas Seating Systems &
Accessories

**INTERNATIONAL MASCOT
CORPORATION**
125 ROYAL WOODS COURT
SUITE 145
TURKER, GA 30084
770-723-9000
800-834-8588
Fax: 770-723-9007
imcservice@imcmascots.com
www.imcmascots.com
• Jonathan Schloss, Director of US
Operations
jschloss@imcmascots.com
• Joel Leveille, Marketing Director
• David Swangel, Operations Manager
Products:
Costumes, Mascot & Accessories

INTERNATIONAL MICROTECH, INC.
642 ROUTE 109
LINDENHURST, NY 11757
850-897-8666
800-327-1033
Fax: 305-599-0936
• Frank Bianco, President
info@petbehave.com
• J Zabala, Marketing / Sales Manager
Products:
Pet Traning Tools and Gadgets; Pet
Grooming Kit

**INTERNATIONAL SEAWAY TRADING
CORPORATION**
7100 W CAMINO REAL
SUITE 110
BOCA RATON, FL 33433-5510
561-447-4433
Fax: 561-447-4488
seaway222@aol.com
• Larry Satz, SVP
lsatz@aol.com
• Harvey K. Girdy, CEO
• Peter Grzybowski, CFO/VP
Products:
Footware

INTERNATIONAL SPORTS TIMING
3286 KENTLAND COURT SE
GRAND RAPIDS, MI 49548
616-247-1033
800-835-2611
Fax: 616-247-0086
info@istime.com
www.istime.com
• Richard Farnsworth, President
(800) 835-2611
• Jane Farnsworth, Director Marketing
(800) 835-2611
Products:
Scoreboards, Software and Timing Devices
(Swimming & Water Polo).
Year Founded:
1982

IPANEMA WEAR
SAN DIEGO, CA
760-576-6500
Fax: 858-759-5016
• Patricia Martins, Founder, Designer,
President
Products:
Swimming/Diving Apparels

IRA K. MEDALS & AWARDS INC.
4584 AUSTIN BOULEVARD
ISLAND PARK, NY 11558-1695
516-431-2131
Fax: 516-431-2412
• Ira Kartiganer, President
Products:
Trophies, Awards Components, Crests,
Cups, Emblems, Jewelry, Medals, Patches,
Plaques, Ribbons, Trophies.

IRON GLOVES INC
15863 N GREENWAY HAYDEN LOOP
SUITE 117
SCOTTSDALE, AZ 85260
480-905-1109
Fax: 480-905-1112
info@irongloves.com˜
www.irongloves.com
• Dominick Cirone, President
lsatz@aol.com

Products:
Golf Club Covers, Iron Covers, Putter
Covers, Insulated Water Bottle Holders,
Licensed Beverage holders, Soft Sided
Cooler Bags, Baseball Bat Warmers and
Protectors, complete line of Custom Logo
Neoprene
Nature of Services:
Sporting Goods Designer and Manufacturer
Brands:
Iron Gloves, The Gripp, Gravity Gripp, Putter
Gloves, Therasqueeze, the Bottle Glove,
Tag-A-Longs, Magnacover

IRONMAN PROPERTIES
2701 N ROCKY POINT DRIVE
SUITE 1250
TAMPA, FL 33607
813-868-5940
866-859-3343
Fax: 813-868-5930
bill.potts@ironman.com
www.ironman.com
• Bill Potts, Global Licensing
Services:
Identifies, develops, manufactures and sells
Ironman-Triathlon-branded product.

IRONMAN WETSUITS
3131 WESTERN AVENUE, SUITE 316
SEATTLE, WA 98121
206-632-1994

IRWIN SEATING COMPANY
3251 FRUIT RIDGE AVENUE NW
PO BOX 2429
GRAND RAPIDS, MI 49544
616-574-7400
866-464-7946
Fax: 616-574-7411
sales@irwinseating.com
www.irwinseating.com
• Bruce Cohen, Vice President,
Sales/Marketing
(616) 574-7306
cohenb@irwinseating.com
Products:
Manufacturer of fixed seating and telescopic
bleachers- fixed audience seating for
stadiums and arenas.
Year Founded:
1908

IRWIN SPORTS
43 HANNA AVENUE
TORONTO, ON, CANADA M6K 1X6
800-268-1732
Fax: 800-268-6399
• George Irwin, President
• Greg Anger, Marketing Director
• Dave Callon, Sales Manager
• Susan Pryde, Human Resources Director
Products:
Baseball Bags-Equipment, Balls,
Bats-Metal, Bats-Wood, Batter's Gloves,
Batting Helmets, Catcher's Helmet,
Gloves-Catcher, Gloves-Fielder,
Gloves-First Base, Glove Oil, Masks, Nets,
Pine-Tar Cloths, Protective-Catcher,
Protective-Umpire, Umpire Indicators

ITECH SPORT PRODUCTS, INC.
18103 TRANSCANADA HIGHWAY
KIRKLAND, QUEBEC, CANADA H9J 3Z4
514-697-9900

• Robin Burns, President
• Dave Smallwood, Director United States
Sales VP
Services:
Manufacturer of Hockey equipment bags,
helmets, gloves, sticks, goalie equipment
and accessories.

IVANKO BARBELL COMPANY
PO BOX 6224
RENO, NV 89513
775-624-0177
800-759-6399
Fax: 775-624-0188
info@ivanko.com
www.ivanko.com
• Tom I Lincir, President
• Chet Groskreutz, Sales / Marketing VP
Products:
Training and Conditioning Barbells,
Dumbells, Free Weights, Olympic plates,
Weightlifting bars, Plates, Collars, Benches,
and Accessories

J&B SALES, INC.
2307 ROOSEVELT DRIVE
ARLINGTON, TX 76016
817-461-5421
Fax: 817-459-0501
• Jim Reeder, President
Products:
Baseball Bags-Equipment, Bat Tape,
Bats-Metal, Gloves-Batter, Gloves-Catcher,
Gloves-Fielder, Gloves-First Base, Masks,
Protective-Catcher, Shoes-Metal Cleats,
Shoes-Rubber Cleats, Socks, Umpire
Indicators; Basketball - Backboards, Hoops,
Nets, Shoes

JACKSTER COMPANY
670 SURF AVENUE
STRATFORD, CT 6615
203-378-4023
800-225-8370
Fax: 203-378-4605
www.jacksterinc.com
• Jack Kramer, President
Products:
General Sports Products - Athletic Socks,
Belts, Gloves, Hats/Caps, Suspenders

JACQUES MORET
1411 BROADWAY
8TH FLOOR
NEW YORK, NY 10018
212-354-2400
800-441-1999
Fax: 212-354-1052
info@moret.com
www.moret.com
• Joseph Harary, President
• Ron Mangini, SVP
• Irwin Luxemburg, Chief Finance Officer
• Gary D Herwitz, EVP
Products:
General sports apparel for athletes and
fans.

JAMMIN APPAREL
335 TECHNOLOGY DRIVE
ROCKY MOUNT, VA 24151
540-484-4600
800-852-6646
Fax: 540-484-4601
customercare@jammin.com
www.jammin.com

- Mark Grinde, Partner / Administration
- Brian Grinde, Partner / Production
- Steve Weil, Partner / Sales

Products:
General Sports Products - Accessories, Sport Shirts, Warm Up Suits, Windshirts, Softball Uniforms, Hockey Jerseys, Arctic Fleece, Jackets, Parkas, Swim Parkas, Caps, Bags, and Accessories

JANTZEN, INC.
3000 NW 107TH AVENUE
MIAMI, FL 33172
800-626-0215
www.jantzen.com
- Carl Jantzen, Founder
- John Zehntbauer, Founder

Products:
Swimwear, resortwear, beachwear, accessories and footwear.

JAYPRO SPORTS, LLC
976 HARTFORD TURNPIKE
PO BOX 400
WATERFORD, CT 6385
860-447-3001
800-243-0533
Fax: 860-444-1779
info@jaypro.com
www.jaypro.com
- Robert Ferrara, President
- Bill Wild, CEO

Products:
Archery - Nets, Target Stands; Baseball - Batting Tees, Cages/Backstops, First Base Safety Protectors, Infield Drag Mats, Nets, Pitcher Safety Protectors; Basketball - Backboards, Hoops, Nets, Standards; Facilities - Benches, Divider Nets, Wall Mats

JB SPORTS & HAIRDRESSING
701 BILTMORE STREET
SAN LEANDRO, CA 94577
510-205-3628
Fax: 510-568-3688
www.88288.com
- Rayn Li, Contact
(510) 205-3628

Products:
Manufacturers of skateboard, inline skate, ice skate, roller skates, agressive skates, inline speed skates, kid's skates, scooters, inline hockey skates, skateboard set, high frequency heat transfer paper, skateboard bags, inline skate bag, Mountain Bicycles, Multi-functional Folding Bicycles, and related protective products including helmets, knee and elbow pads, and wrist guards.

JEBCO
125 ADVANCED DRIVE
SPRINGBORO, OH 45066
937-746-2268
800-635-3226
Fax: 800-701-9487
- John Cole, President

Products:
Manufacturer of licensed collectible Motorsports wall clocks, wall thermometers, desk clocks, custom clocks, custom plaques and awards.

JEEP ELECTRONICS
80-A E JEFRYN BOULEVARD
DEER PARK, NY 11729

631-389-5642
800-357-8785
Fax: 631-242-6177
www.kngamerica.com
- Kash Gobindram, President / Chief Executive Officer

Products:
Novelty and collectible telephones, personal audio electronics, universal remotes, and home decor products.

JEFF HAMILTON COLLECTION
2340 E OLYMPIC BOULEVARD
LOS ANGELES, CA 90021
213-747-1818
Fax: 213-747-4343
jhjackets@aol.com
www.jeffhamilton.com

Products:
Men's and Boy's Collectible Clothing.

JEFFERIES SOCKS
2203 TUCKER STREET
BURLINGTON, NC 27215
336-226-7315
800-334-6831
Fax: 800-727-5502
socks@jefferiessocks.com
www.jefferiessocks.com
- Kenneth Hamby, President

Products:
Infants Socks; Boys Socks; Girls Socks; Ladies' socks

JEM SPORTSWEAR INC.
459 PARK AVENUE
SAN FERNANDO, CA 91340
818-365-9361
Fax: 818-361-8055
info@jemsportswear.com
www.jemsportswear.com
- Randi Kagan, VP, Licensing and Marketing
randi.spieker@jemsportswear.com

Products:
Golf Apparel; Gymnastics Apparel; Racquet Sports Apparel; Track & Field/Running Apparel-Run/Jog; Water Sports Apparel.

JERSEY NAPS
1954 AIRPORT ROAD
SUITE 207
ATLANTA, GA 30341
678-720-0702
Fax: 678-720-0704
www.JerseyNaps.com
- William Katz, Chief Marketing Officer

Nature of Services:
Jersey Naps are high quality napkins folded into a patented shape that replicates a sports jersey, entertainment character, brand icon or seasonal costume.

JH DESIGN GROUP
940 W WASHINGTON BOULEVARD
LOS ANGELES, CA 90015
213-747-5700
800-353-1010
Fax: 213-747-3648
www.jhdesigngroup.com
- Albert Elkouby, Chief Executive Officer
albert@jhdesigngroup.net
- Jacob Nisim, General Manager
jacob@jhdesigngroup.net
- Vered Nisim, Vice President of Marketing

- Omer Hadad, Sports Division
- Charles Alloun, Controller

Products:
Reversible wool and leather jacket with embroidered logos; Kids twill racing style jacket with embroidered logos; Adults twill racing style jacket with embroidered logos; Leather racing jacket with embroidered logos.

JIFFY LINE STRIPERS
611 KNIGHTSBRIDGE ROAD
PO BOX 35
WAUNAKEE, WI 53597
608-849-4770
800-844-5002
Fax: 608-849-7456
- Peder Bach, President
- Geri Carlson, Vice President

Description:
Manufacturer of line painting equipment for athletic fields; manufacturer of athletic field paints.

Year Founded:
1961

JJ ACCESSORIES
7057 MARCELLE STREET
PARAMOUNT, CA 90723
562-630-6310
Fax: 562-630-6343
sales@jjshoelace.com
www.jjshoelace.com

Products:
Shoelaces; Accessories

JKP SPORTS
11885 SW HERMAN RD.
TUALATIN, OR 97062
503-692-1635
800-547-6843
Fax: 503-691-1100
info@jugssports.com
www.jugssports.com
- Butch Paulson, President
- John Paulson, Service Manager
- Ed Dechenne, Sales Manager
- Curtis Kawasaki, Controller

Products:
Pitching Machines; Protective Screens; Radar Guns; Feeders; Batting Cage Nets; Frames; Baseballs & Softballs; Packages

JOE RAPP, INC.
835 LONGVIEW AVENUE
N WOODMERE, NY 11581
516-792-0230
Fax: 516-792-0131
joerappinc@aol.com
www.therapper.com
- Joe Rapp, President/Owner
joerappinc@aol.com

Nature of Services:
Stadium hand clapper, concession and promotional products.

Year Founded:
1992

Brands:
The Rapper

Description:
Producer of THE RAPPER and THE RAPPER THUNDERSTIX, two of the best spirit products produced today.

JOFA HOCKEY/THE HOCKEY COMPANY
3400 RAYMOND-LASNIER
SUITE 800
MONTREAL(QUEBEC), CANADA H4R 3L3
514-461-8000
Fax: 514-937-8276
• Robert A. Desrosiers, Finance and
Administration VP / Chief Fi
Products:
Skates, Sticks, Helmets and protective
equipment products.

JOG-A-LITE, INC.
18 HIGH STREET
PO BOX 149
SILVER LAKE, NH 3875
603-367-4741
800-258-8974
Fax: 603-367-8098
www.jogalite.com
• Barclay Huntington, Founder
hbarclay@jogalite.com
• Peter Lang, President
plang@jogalite.com
Products:
New Reflective Safety Vest; Reflective
Safety Vest; Arm & Leg Bands; Reflective
Stick-Ons; Lights & Sound; Pet Savers; Gift
Packs; Runner's Log

**JOHN R. GREEN COMPANY INC., OLD
MASTER PUTTERS**
411 W 6TH STREET
COVINGTON, KY 41011
859-431-5568
800-354-9737
Fax: 859-431-0266
www.johnrgreenco.com
• Tom Green, President
Products:
Supplies; Teaching Materials; Furnitures

**JOHNSON & JOHNSON CONSUMER
PRODUCTS INC.**
ONE JOHNSON & JOHNSON PLAZA
NEW BRUNSWICK, NJ 8933
732-524-0400
Fax: 908-874-1123
www.jnj.com
• Mary Sue Coleman, President
• James G. Cullen, Chief Operating Officer
• Alex G. Gorsky, Chairman
Products:
Sports and nutritional supplements.

JOHNSON OUTDOORS
555 MAIN STREET
RACINE, WI 53403
262-631-6600
800-227-6433
Fax: 262-631-6601
corporate@johnsonoutdoors.com
www.johnsonoutdoors.com
• Helen Johnson-Leipold, Chairman / Chief
Executive Officer
• Cynthia Georgeson, VP Worldwide
Communications
(262) 631-6600
cgeorgeson@johnsonoutdoors.com
• David Johnson, VP Chief Financial Officer
Products:
Outdoor Equipment; Watercraft; Marine
Electronics; Diving; JOI Boilerplate.
Nature of Services:
Johnson Outdoors is a global outdoor
recreation company that turns ideas into
adventure with innovative, products. The

company designs, manufactures and
markets a portfolio of consumer-preferred
brands across four categories: Watercraft,
Marine Electronics, Diving and Outdoor
Equipment. Johnson Outdoors' familiar
brands include among others: Old Town
Canoes and Kayaks; Ocean Kayak and
Necky Kayaks; Lendal Paddles; Carlisle and
Extrasport Padding Accessories; Minn Kora
Motors; Cannon Downriggers; Humminbird
Fishfinders; Geonax Chartplotters;
SCUBAPRO UWATEC and Seemann Dive
Equipment; Silva Compasses; Tech O
Digital Instruments; and Eureka Ten

**JOHNSON WORLDWIDE
ASSOCIATES/CAMPING DIVISION**
1326 WILLOW ROAD
STURTEVANT, WI 53177
262-884-1500
Fax: 262-884-1703
www.jwa.com
• Helen Johnson-Leipold, Chairman / Chief
Executive Officer
hjohnson@johnsonoutdoors.com
• Terry E. London, Board of Director
Products:
Outdoor Equipment; Watercraft; Motors;
Fishing; Diving

JOHNSONITE
16910 MUNN ROAD
CHAGRIN FALLS, OH 44023
440-543-8916
800-899-8916
Fax: 440-543-8920
info@johnsonite.com
www.johnsonite.com
• Laurey Banker, Director of Product
Management
Products:
Triumph Skate & Spike-Resistant Tile;
Replay Skate & Spike-Resistant Recycled
Sports Flooring; Inertia Sport Flooring Tiles

JOSLIN DISPLAYS INC
10 UPTON DRIVE # 8
WILMINGTON, MA 1887
978-284-6660
800-325-1030
Fax: 978-658-4263
sales@joslindisplays.net
www.joslindisplays.net
Products:
Slatwall; Gridwall; Mannequins; Hangers;
Showcases; Wall Hardware; Store Supplies;
Jewelry Displays; Plexi Displays; Shoe
Displays; Wood Fixtures; Packaging; Racks;
Signholders

JOY ENTERPRISES/FURY CUTLERY
1862 MLK JR BOULEVARD
PORT COMMERCE CENTER III
WEST PALM BEACH, FL 33404
561-863-3205
800-500-3879
Fax: 561-863-3277
mail@joyenterprises.com
www.joy-247.com
Products:
Folding Knives; Hunting Knives; Collector's
Knives

JTD ENTERPRISES INC
4 WALNUT STREET
CHILTON, WI 53014

920-849-2900
888-595-5833
Fax: 586-427-1329
jtdenterprises@frontier.com
www.jtdent.com
Products:
Flagpoles; Search N' Rescue Retrievers

JUGS COMPANY
11885 SW HERMAN RD.
PO BOX 365
TUALATIN, OR 97062
503-692-1635
800-547-6843
Fax: 503-691-1100
info@thejugscompany.com
• Steve Candello, Marketing Director
stevec@jkpsports.com
Products:
Pitching Machines, Accessories, baseballs,
softballs, protective screen, nets, batting
cage frames, ball feeders, tennis ball, spin
tennis machine, spin remote tennis
machine, field hockey machine, radar
equipment, football passing machine, and
soccer machine

JUGS INC/JKP SPORTS
11885 SW HERMAN RD.
PO BOX 365
TUALATIN, OR 97062
503-692-1635
800-547-6843
Fax: 503-691-1100
jugsusa@aol.com
www.jugssports.com
Products:
Pitching Machines; Protective Screens;
Radar Guns; Feeders; Batting Cage Nets;
Frames; Baseballs & Softballs; Packages

JUMP ROPE TECH INC
PO BOX 5238
WOODBRIDGE, VA 22194
703-580-6302
800-953-5867
Fax: 703-680-2826
Jump4Speed@aol.com
www.jumpropetech.com
• Buddy Lee, President/CEO
• Elvis Malcolm, Technical Advisor
Products:
Patented Swivel Bearing Jump Ropes;
Jump Rope Sets; Total Fit Travel Gym;
Olympic Kids Gym Sets; Training Aids -
Video/Audio; Double Dutch, Beaded and
Long Ropes; Toy Ropes with Counter,
Music, Lights; Jump Rope Toys - Animal
Characters

JUMPSPORT
2055 S 7TH STREET
SUITE A
SAN JOSE, CA 95112
408-213-2551
888-567-5867
Fax: 408-213-2930
www.jumpsport.com
• Mark Publicover, Product Safety
Inventor/CEO
(408) 866-3120
Products:
Trampolines; Safety Nets; Rebounders

K-SWISS INC.
31248 OAKCREST DRIVE
WESTLAKE VILLAGE, CA 91361
818-706-5100
800-938-8000
Fax: 818-706-5390
Kscs@k-swiss.com
www.kswiss.com
• Steven Nichols, President/Chairman
Kscs@k-swiss.com
• Preston Davis, VP Sales
Kscs@k-swiss.com
• Tom Harrison, SVP Sales / Georgia
Kscs@k-swiss.com
• George Powlick, VP Finance / Chief
Financial Officer
Kscs@k-swiss.com
Products:
Shoes

K2 INC.
4201 6TH AVENUE S
SEATTLE, WA 98108
800-426-1617
info@k2sports.com
www.k2sports.com
• Richard J. Heckmann, Chairman / Chief
Executive Officer
• J Wa Merek, EVP / Chief Operating Officer
• John J. Rangel, SVP
• Anthony W. DeRocco, President
Products:
Equipment and supplies for skiing,
snowboarding, skating and biking

KAEPA USA, INC.
9050 AUTOBAHN DRIVE
SUITE 500
DALLAS, TX 75237
972-296-7300
800-880-9200
Fax: 972-296-7319
webcontact@kaepa-usa.com
www.kaepa.com
• Russell Shimomura, Product / Creative
Director
(972) 296-7300
russells@kaepa-usa.com
• Sharon McCord, Sales Director
(972) 296-7300
sharonm@kaepa-usa.com
• John Atkinson, President
(972) 296-7300
johnat@kaepa-usa.com
Products:
Footwear, Apparel and Accessories for
Volleyball, Cheer, Auxiliary Dance and
Fitness

KAMPALA INDUSTRIES
19 CUMMINGS ROAD
MONMOUTH JUNCTION, NJ 08852-2915
732-438-9750
877-526-7762
Fax: 732-438-9752
kampalaind@hotmail.com
www.kampala.com.pk
Products:
Gloves, garments and tanned leather

KANGAROO PRODUCTS COMPANY
111 KANGAROO DRIVE
PO BOX 607
COLUMBUS, NC 28722-0607
828-894-8241
800-438-3011

Fax: 828-894-2718
www.kangaroogolf.com
• Michael McCue, President
(828) 894-8241
caddie@kangaroogolf.com
• Timothy R. Pope, VP New Product
Development
(828) 894-8241
• Michael Whitt, Sales Manager
mikewhitt@kangaroogolf.com
Products:
Golf Cart Battery Chargers, Carts-Electric
(for walking golfers), Motorized Golf Bag
Carriers

KANGOL HEADWEAR, INC.
411 FIFTH AVENUE
SECOND FLOOR
NEW YORK, NY 10016
212-981-9900
800-431-1802
Fax: 212-981-9901
inquiries@kangolheadwearusa.com
www.kangol.com
• David Heys, Chief Executive Officer
Products:
Headwear, Eyewear, Footwear, Bags,
Apparel, Wristwear, Accessories

KAPPA USA
350 5TH AVENUE
SUITE 6617
NEW YORK, NY 10118
212-273-3399
Fax: 212-273-3333
info@kappa.com
• Simon Bamber, President
info@kappa.com
• Mike Callahan, Chief Financing Officer /
Chief Operatin
info@kappa.com
• Doug Gordon, VP Sales / Marketing
info@kappa.com
• Peter Milone, Director Business
Development
Products:
Sports Apparel, Footwear and Accessories

KARHU U.S.A. LIMITED
208 FLYNN AVENUE
STUDIO 3H
BURLINGTON, VT 5401
802-864-4519
888-288-2668
Fax: 800-422-8454
customerservice@kahru.com
www.karhu.com
• Douglas Barbor, President / Chief
Executive Officer
customerservice@kahru.com
• David Smallwood, VP Hockey Division
customerservice@kahru.com
• Jacques Lavertue, General Manager /
Outdoor Division
customerservice@kahru.com
• Casey Sheahan, VP Marketing Outdoor
Division
customerservice@kahru.com
Products:
Hiking - Outdoor Footwear; Ice Hockey -
Equipment, Sticks; In-Line Skating - Skates;
Skiing-Nordic - Accessories, Bindings,
Boots, Skis.

KASCO CORPORATION OF AMERICA
2171 KINGSTON COURT
SUITE H
MARIETTA, GA 30067
770-303-4500
800-431-2560
Fax: 770-303-0044
www.kascogolf.com
• Keiko Morii, Director Of Marketing And
Public Relations
• Yoshihiro Sato, Contact
Products:
Golf Gloves, Clubs, Balls and Bags

KAYSER-ROTH INC.
102 CORPORATE CENTER BOULEVARD
GREENSBORO, NC 27408
800-575-3497
800-327-8769
Fax: 336-854-4352
customerservice@kayser-roth.com
www.kayser-roth.com
• Kevin Toomey, President / Chief Executive
Officer
customerservice@nononsense.com
Products:
Women's athletic undergarments.

KEDS CORPORATION
4200 SOUTH A STREET
RICHMOND, IN 47374
617-824-6000
800-680-0966
Fax: 800-446-1339
customerservice@keds.com
www.keds.com
• Kristin Burrows, President, Keds
• Matthew E Rubel, Chairman of the Board,
President & CEO
Products:
Athletic and casual footwear for children and
adults

KEISER CORPORATION
2470 S CHERRY AVENUE
FRESNO, CA 93706
800-888-7009
Fax: 559-256-8100
info@keiser.com
www.keiser.com
• Dennis L. Keiser, President/Founder
info@keiser.com
• Randy J. Keiser, VP
info@keiser.com
• Tony Peterson, VP International Sales &
Marketing
(425) 402-8509
tonyp@keiser.com
• Anthony A. Peterson, VP
Products:
Training & Conditioning - low-impact
variable resistance exercise machines;
Stretching stations, Indoor Group Cycling
Bikes, Children Play Products

KEN YOUNG COMPANY, INC.
147 HALLS COURT
CAIRO, GA 39828
229-377-9444
800-251-1800
Fax: 229-377-6446
snewmons@kenyoungco.com
www.kenyoungco.com
• Ken Young, Sales
kyoung@kenyoungco.com
• Kim Chelsey, Sales
• LeAnn Maxwell Vickers, Customer Service

Products:
Athletic Apparel

KENYON CONSUMER PRODUCTS, INC.
141 FAIRGROUNDS ROAD
PO BOX 458
W KINGSTON, RI 02892
401-792-3704
800-537-0024
Fax: 401-782-4870
kcp@KenyonConsumer.com
www.kenyonconsumer.com
• Andrew Curtis, President
kcp@kenyonconsumer.com
• Beth Curtis, VP
kcp@kenyonconsumer.com
• David Kenyon, Owner
Products:
Camping accessories, technical thermal
underwear, and fleece and pile garments
and accessories

KENYON INDUSTRIES
25 WEST 45TH STREET
11TH FLOOR
NEW YORK, NY 10036
212-551-0100
Fax: 646-472-0294
www.brookwoodcos.com
• Amber Brookwood, President/CEO
Products:
Performance fabrics specializing in lifestyle
markets, including Activewear, outerwear,
luggage, and specialty bag markets

KEY SPORTZ-WEAR
3301 S GALLOWAY STREET
SUITE 293
PHILADELPHIA, PA 19145
215-339-0605
888-339-0605
Fax: 215-339-8250
liaconijr@aol.com
Products:
Sports apparel.

KEYBEC SUBLIME, INC.
9031 DU PARC
MONTREAL, QC, CANADA H2N 1Z1
514-858-7582
800-516-0396
Fax: 514-858-7597
www.groupetrium.com
• Pierre Bellemarre, Co-founder
• Pierre Gendron, President
Distributor:
Baseball Uniforms; General Sports Products
Athletic Jackets, Headwear; Ice Hockey
Protective, Skates, Socks, Sticks, Sweaters;
Soccer Uniforms.

KEYS FITNESS PRODUCTS
PO BOX 357
HUGHES SPRINGS, TX 75656
888-320-7885
866-962-0173
Fax: 214-340-1768
• Tim Chen, President and Chief Executive
Officer
• Ken Kruebbe, Public Relations Officer
• Kevin Brady, Export Sales Manager
Products:
Treadmills, home gyms, racks, cable
columns, weight storage, benches, ellipticals
and accessory equipment such as weights,

reading racks, medicine balls, bars and
apparel.

KI
1330 BELLEVUE STREET
GREEN BAY, WI 54308
920-468-8100
800-424-2432
Fax: 920-468-0280
salesadvance@ki.com
www.ki.com
• Richard J. Resch, President and Chief
Executive Officer
salesadvance@ki.com
• Mark Olsen, Chief Financial Officer,
Treasurer
salesadvance@ki.com
• Brian Krenke, President
salesadvance@ki.com
• Andy McGregor, Executive Vice President
Products:
AGI Benches, AGI Guest Seating, AGI
Lounge Seating, AGI Multiple Seating, AGI
Occasional Tables, AGI Professional
Seating, Airport Gatehold Seating,
Auditorium/Lecture Hall, Desks -
Accessories, Desks - Adjustable Height,
Desks - Carrels, Desks - Circulation/Library,
Desks - Classroom, Desks - Office, Files,
GS-27F-0513H Household & Quarters
Contract, GS-28F-2002D Special Use
Contract, GS-28F-8022H Office Furniture
Contract, Healthcare Furniture

KIEFER U.S.A.
2910 FALLING WATERS BOULEVARD
LINDENHURST, IL 60046-6799
847-245-8450
800-322-5448
Fax: 847-245-8590
info@kieferusa.com
• Brion Rittenberry, President & CEO
• Dan Kehoe, Vice President, Sales
Year Founded:
1977
Nature of Service:
Sports flooring contractors & distributors
Brands:
Mondo Sports, Connor Sport Surfacing,
PaviGym.

KING COBRA GAMING
4045 NEWBURG ROAD
EASTON, PA 18045
610-762-7335
Fax: 610-614-1066
Products:
Regulation Rubber Quoits, Quoit Slate
Boards, Horseshoes Outfit, Bocce, Darts,
Bar & Shield Darts Kit, Poker Tables,
Blackjack Tables, Roulette / Craps Tables,
Table Game & Accessories (Table Brush,
Cup Holder, Playing Cards, Card Shuffler
and Poker Table Top), Poker Chips

KING LOUIE INTERNATIONAL, INC.
2700 ROBERTS RD.
BAXTER SPRINGS, KS 66713
620-856-2341
800-521-5212
Fax: 816-765-3228
kloffice@kinglouie.com
www.kinglouie.com
• Robert Palan, President
• Roger P. Carroll, Marketing VP
• Dick MccLearen, Manufacturing Executive
• Ruth Ann Shelton, Human Resources

Executive
• Teresa Buchanan, Purchasing Executive
Nature of Sports Services:
Bowling Shirts; Activewear, Athletic
Jackets/Parkas, Fashion Jackets, Fleece,
T-shirts; Golf Apparel; Skiing-Alpine
Outerwear/Jackets-Vests-Pants; Track &
Field/Running Apparel-Run/Jog.

KING PAR CORPORATION
G-5140 FLUSHING ROAD
FLUSHING, MI 48433
810-732-2470
888-502-4653
Fax: 810-732-6662
custserv@kingpar.com
• William J. Baird, Chief Executive Officer
custserv@kingpar.com
• Ryan Coffell, Controller
(810) 410-1840
rcoffell@kingpar.com
• L. Toups, Operations Manager
(810) 410-1875
ltoups@kingpar.com
• Doug Hinton, General Sales Manager
(810) 410-1835
dhinton@kingpar.com
Products:
Clubs, bags, balls, tees, accessories,
apparel, gloves, hats and shoes for every
age group. Types of clubs includes
individual woods, fairway wods, hybrids,
junior irons.
Brands:
Orlimar, Affinity, InTech.

KITCHENER HOCKEY STICKS LTD.
176 FORFAR AVENUE
KITCHENER, ONTARIO, CANADA N2B
3A1
519-743-9325
888-548-7849
Fax: 519-579-4817
• Sandy Watson, President
(519) 743-9325
info@kitchenerhockeysticks.com
• Bob Pastway, General Manager
Products:
Hockey sticks

KOLDER INC
1601 N CLOSNER BOULEVARD
EDINBURG, TX 78541
956-381-9851
877-817-0288
Fax: 956-383-0502
jody@kolder.com
www.kolder.com
• Charlie Meyer, President
(956) 318-9851
• Jody Hancock, Retail Sales Manager
(956) 318-9851
• Brenda Rios, CSR
  ext 204
• Vennessa Flores, CSR
  ext 250
• Ruby Rivera, CSR
  ext 7159
Products:
Licensed & Novelty Items- beverage, bags,
computer accessories, glassware, etc.
Teams;
MLB, NHL, NFL, College Teams.

KOOLATRON
27 CATHARINE AVENUE
BRANTFORD ONTARIO, CANADA N3T
1X5
519-756-3950
800-265-8456
Fax: 519-756-3725
service@koolatron.com
www.koolatron.com
• Arun Kulkarni, President
• Carol Murtland, Purchasing Manager
• Gary Sitton, Info Systems Manager
• George Verghese, Operations VP
Products:
Car Accessories, 12V Coolers and
Warmers, 12V Spotlight/Lamps, Auto Fans
and Power Inverters, Kitchen Appliances,
Total Chef Oven, Robatic Vacuum Cleaner,
Wine Cooler and Aerobeds, Toothbrush,
sleeping aid and snore stopper and
hairbrush, Revolutionary home
gym,abdominal exerciser, Yoga Mat,
Magnetic Elliptical Trainer, Land Rider Bike
and Body Bow, Pet Dish Six Days, Pet Dish,
Pet Fountain etc., Mosquito Control,
Electronic Pest Control and Ultrasonic Pest
Control Products for indoor and outdoor
control of pest, mosquitoes, flies etc.,
Portable Sonar Fish Finder, High Power
Dynamo Torch and First Alert Eternal
Flashlight

KORNEY BOARD AIDS, INC.
312 HARRISON AVENUE
PO BOX 264
ROXTON, TX 75477
903-346-3269
800-842-7772
Fax: 877-488-3920
sales@kbacoach.com
www.kbacoach.com
• Jeff Reed, President
(800) 842-7772
jcreed65@yahoo.com
Products:
Coaching boards, basketball coaching aids,
basketball equipment and training, volleyball
coaching and training equipment, coaching
and training videos and books for basketball
and volleyball, ball racks and ball carriers,
gym supplies and equipment
Nature of Service:
Retail & Wholesale
Brands:
Spalding, Korney Boards, Shoot-Away Toss
Back, Cramer, Tachikara & Muller

KRUEGER INTERNATIONAL
1330 BELLEVUE STREET
GREEN BAY, WI 54302
920-468-8100
800-424-2432
Fax: 920-468-0280
salesadvance@ki.com
www.ki.com
• Richard J. Resch, President and Chief
Executive Officer
salesadvance@ki.com
• Mark Olsen, Chief Financial Officer,
Treasurer
salesadvance@ki.com
• Mark Christopher, Sales / Marketing VP
salesadvance@ki.com
Products:
Accessories, Adjustable Worksurfaces, AGI
Collections, Auditorium Seating, Classroom
furniture, Folding Chairs, Guest Seating,
Lecture Hall Furniture, Library Furniture,

Lounge Seating, Powered Tables, Public
Seating, Residence Hall Furniture, Site
Furnishing, Stools, Tables, Healthcare
Furniture, Task Seating, Desking, Files and
Storage and more.

KRYPTONICS U.S.A.
12801 CARMENITA ROAD
SANTA FE SPRINGS, CA 90670
562-484-5100
800-248-5327
Fax: 562-484-5183
mjoines@bravocorp.com
www.kryptonics.com
• Samuel Kratish, President
• Esther Kratish, Treasurer
Products:
Baseball Caps; Softball Caps.

KTM SPORTMOTORCYCLE USA
1119 MILAN AVENUE
AMHERST, OH 44001
440-985-3553
Fax: 330-645-1586
www.ktmusa.com
• Stefan Pierer, CEO
Description:
KTM Sportmotorcycle is a growing
motorcycle company that specializes in dirt
bikes. KTM is an international business with
numerous locations including several within
the United States. KTM has a newly
constructed development centre in
Mattighofen, Austria that includes an
integrated motor sports department in
addition to a modern engine factory in
Munderfing which has doubled their
production capacities in recent years.
Thanks to tremendous research and
development, competent, highly-motivated
staff and innumerable motor sports
successes, KTM manufactured
approximately 80,400 motorcycles during
2005.

KUNNAN GOLF
470 CLOVERLEAF DRIVE
UNIT B
BALDWIN PARK, CA 91706
626-934-0388
800-399-8599
Fax: 626-934-0377
• Frank Zou, Sales Manager
Description:
Golf - Clubs-Wood/Iron Sets, Individual
Woods, Irons.

KWIK GOAL LTD.
140 PACIFIC DRIVE
QUAKERTOWN, PA 18951
215-536-2200
800-531-4252
Fax: 800-778-8869
info@kwikgoal.com
www.kwikgoal.com
Products:
Decks, wheels, components, helmets,
Elbow Pads, Wrist Guards and Knee Pads.

**L&L GROUP/FOREMOST ATHLETIC
APPAREL**
1307 E MAPLE ROAD
TROY, MI 48083
248-689-3850
Fax: 248-689-4653

mijgl@llgroup.net
www.llgroup.net
• John G Levy, President/CEO
(248) 689-3850
mijgl@llgroup.net
• Mike Burns, Vice President/Finance
Brands:
Auburn, Augusta, Bike, Crystal Springs,
Dunbrooke, Gatorade, Hanes, Lee, New Era
Products:
Sports apparel.

L.A. GEAR
5900 RODEO ROAD
LOS ANGELES, CA 90016-4313
310-822-1995
800-253-7740
Fax: 310-581-7709
www.lagear.com
• William L Benford, President
• David F Gatto, Chairman/CEO
• Bruce Macgregor, SVP Product Marketing
Products:
Basketball - Shoes; Racquet Sports -
Shoes; Training & Conditioning - Aerobic
Shoes, Cross Training Shoes

L.A.T SPORTSWEAR
1200 AIRPORT DRIVE
BALL GROUND, GA 30107
770-479-1877
800-414-5650
Fax: 770-479-4078
www.latsportswear.com
• Isador Mitzner, Chief Executive Officer
• Gina Watson, President / COO / CEO
• Mickie Schneider, EVP / Chief Financial
Officer
• Chuck Phares, Executive VP Of Sales
Products:
General Sports Activewear and T-shirts for
infants, toddlers, youths, ladies, juniors, and
teams

LACROSSE FOOTWEAR, INC.
17634 NE AIRPORT WAY
PORTLAND, OR 97230
503-262-0110
800-323-2668
Fax: 503-262-0115
customerservice@lacrossefootwear.com
www.lacrossefootwear.com
Products:
All Purpose Shoes Leather, Rubber
Footwear, Boots

LACROSSE UNLIMITED
363 NESCONSET HIGWAY
HAUPPAUGE, NY 11788
631-366-5299
800-366-5299
Fax: 631-406-6381
nick@lacrosseunlimited.com
www.lacrosseunltd.com
• Nick Gallagher, Manager
nick@lacrosseunlimited.com
• Sam Desimone, Co-President
Products:
Equipments: Custom Stringing, Custom
Dyed Heads, Unstrung & Factory Sticks,
Handles, Helmets, Gloves, Arm Pads,
Shoulder Pads, Rib Pads, Goalie Pads,
Women's Equipment, Goals & Targets,
Cleats & Footwear, LU Originals Apparel:
Under Armor/Performance Gear, Shorts,
Shirts, Bags, Hats

LAFAYETTE INSTRUMENT COMPANY
3700 SAGAMORE PARKWAY N
PO BOX 5729
LAFAYETTE, IN 47903
765-423-1505
800-428-7545
Fax: 765-423-4111
info@lafayetteinstrument.com
www.lafayetteinstrument.com
• Terry Echard, President / General
Manager
• Chris Fausett, VP/Manager/Sales/Trained
Polygraph Examiner
• Jennifer Rider, Vice President/Chief
Information Officer
• Mike Greene, Operations Manager
• Brent Smitley, Engineering Manager
• Todd Hooker, Traffic Control Manager
• Judy Gledhill, Accounts Receivable
Products:
Instrumentation for Strength Testing, Range
of Motion, Anthropometrics, Sensibilities,
Physiological Measures, Exercise Testing,
Dexterity and Coordination

LAM LIGHTING SYSTEMS
938 S GREEN STREET
TUPELO, MS 38804
714-549-9765
800-234-1890
Fax: 662-680-6619
www.daybrite.com
• Craig Brauks, General Manager
(714) 549-9765
craig.brauks@philips.com
• Bill Busch, Senior Product Manager
• Brandi Sears, Director, Specification
Marketing
(662) 680-6634
Brandi.Sears@philips.com
Products:
Indoor Lighting for Sports Facilities such as
Curvilinear(Pendant Mount), Wall & Cove,
Asymmetrical, Linear

LAMKIN LEATHER & RUBBER COMPANY
6530 GATEWAY PARK DRIVE
SAN DIEGO, CA 92154
619-661-7090
800-642-7755
Fax: 619-661-0014
info@lamkingrips.com
www.lamkingrips.com
• Bob Lamkin, President / Chief Executive
Officer
• Thomas Lamkin, EVP
• Mike Lamkin, Engineering VP
Products:
Golf Grips

LANDS' END, INC.
1 LANDS' END LANE
DODGEVILLE, WI 53595
608-935-9341
800-356-4444
800-963-4816
Fax: 608-935-4291
www.landsend.com
• Donald R Hughes, Senior VP / Chief
Financial Officer
hughes@landsend.com
• Gary C Comer , Founder
comer@landsend.com
• Mindy C Meads , Merchandising Design
EVP
meads@landsend.com
• Kelly A Ritchie, Senior VP, Employee

Services
ritchie@landsend.com
• Michele Casper, Senior Director of Public
Relations
• Jim Kennedy, Senior Director of Integrated
Marketing
• Adam Weil, Director
• J Henley, Design Director
Products:
Swimwear, Beach Towels & Totes,
Women's Regular: All Styles, Little Black
Suits, Mix & Match Separates, Tankinis &
Bikinis, 1-piece Tanks, Slenderizing Suits,
Swimfinity Suits, Shop by Anxiety Zones,
Shop by Bra Style, Shop by Body Shape,
Mastectomy, Long Torso, Cover-ups,
Women's Plus, Shoes & Sandals, Men's,
Girls', Boys', Outdoor Living

LANDSCAPE STRUCTURES, INC.
601 7TH STREET S
PO BOX 198
DELANO, MN 55328-8605
763-972-5200
888-438-6574
Fax: 763-972-3185
www.playlsi.com
• Barbara King, Co-Founder
• Young Climbers, Manufacturing VP ,
Human Resources
Products:
Facilities - Benches, Fitness Trails/Circuits,
Playground Equipment

LANDWAVE PRODUCTS INC
ONE COREWAY DRIVE
PIONEER, OH 43554
419-737-9584
800-922-6956
Fax: 419-737-2130
fun@landwaveproducts.com
www.landwaveproducts.com
• Michael A Nowakowski, Vice President,
Sales & Marketing
(419) 737-9584
mnowakowski@landwaveproducts.com
Products:
Landwave ramp systems and skateboards.

LASER MAGIC
946 CENTURY LANE
APOPKA, FL 32703
407-880-7151
800-771-7151
Fax: 407-880-7150
www.lasermagic.net
Products:
LASER CUT Mirrored License Plates and
other laser cut or engraved products with
sports logos and designs.

LAWRENCE METAL PRODUCTS
260 SPUR DRIVE S
PO BOX 400
BAY SHORE, NY 11706
631-666-0300
800-441-0019
Fax: 631-666-0336
sales@tensator.com
www.tensator.com
• David Lawrence, President
• Betty Castro, Sales / Marketing VP
• Jim Stumpf, Sales Director
Products:
Crowd control and hospitality products,
including Stancions, Post and Ropes,

TensaBarriers, Signage, Barriers, Food
Shields, Sneeze Guards and Railing

**LEADER MANUFACTURING COMPANY,
INC.**
11861 WESTLINE INDUSTRIAL DRIVE
SUITE 100
SAINT LOUIS, MO 63146
314-567-1000
800-325-2666
Fax: 314-567-1006
customerservice@leadermanufacturing.com
www.leadermanufacturing.com
• Marc Tenzer, President
Products:
Baseball - Caps; Softball - Caps

**LEADER SPORTS USA/THE HILSINGER
COMPANY**
33 W BACON STREET
PO BOX 1538
PLAINVILLE, MA 02762-0538
508-699-4406
800-847-2001
Fax: 800-959-4452
kpeever@zleader.com
Products:
Eyewear products such as: Swim Goggles,
Water Sports Goggles, Snorkeling, Swim
Accessories, Racket Sports, Team Sports

LEADING BRANDS
1500 W GEORGIA
SUITE 1800
VANCOUVER BC, CANADA V6G 2Z6
604-685-5200
866-685-5200
Fax: 604-685-5249
info@LBIX.com
• Ralph McRae, Chairman and Chief
Executive Officer
• Dave Read, Executive Vice-President
• Robert Mockford, VP of Operations
• Sinan al Zubaidi, VP of Bottling Operations
• R. Thomas Gaglardi, President, Northland
Properties Corporation
• Darryl Eddy, President, Radale Inc.
• James Corbett, President & CEO,
Canadian Outback Adventures
• Ralph D. McRae, Chairman and Chief
Executive Officer
Brands:
TREK Natural Sports Drink
Nature of Service:
The largest independent, fully integrated
premium beverage company in Canada.
NITRO
Energy Drink by Trek

LEE TENNIS PRODUCTS
650 PETER JEFFERSON PARKWAY
SUITE 300 B
CHARLOTTESVILLE, VA 22911
434-295-6167
877-442-7878
Fax: 434-971-6995
• John Welborn, General Manager
(434) 531-9763
jwelborn@leetennis.com
• Randy Futty, Sales Engineer
futty@leetennis.com
• Ed Montecalvo, Contractor Services
montecalvo@leetennis.com
Products:
Facilities - Courts -Tennis; Racquet Sports -
Tennis Court Equipment, Tennis
Nets/Standards

LEE'S LICENSED ENAMELWARE
2242 HIGHWAY 182
INWOOD, IA 51240
712-753-4403
800-736-6530
Fax: 712-753-4542
information@soynuts.com
Products:
Enamelware kettles for commercial
popcorn-making

LEGEND SPORTS
3080 W WILLETLE CIRCLE
W JORDAN, UT 84084
801-964-5600
800-448-4680
Fax: 801-964-5500

LEO'S DANCEWEAR, INC.
1170 TRADEMARK DRIVE
SUITE 112
RENO, NV 89521
773-889-7700
800-736-5367
Fax: 800-736-5330
www.leosdancewear.com
• Glenn Baruck, President
info@leosdancewear.com
• Barbara Kanies, National Sales Manager
bkanies@leosdancewear.com
• Sherri Giacone, Marketing /
Communications Manager
info@leosdancewear.com
• Leo Harris, Founder
• Nancy Thomas, Human Resource
Manager
Products:
Dance Tights / Liners, Dance Tutus, Nylon
Dancewear, Dance Skirts, Performancewear
/ Dresses, Cotton / Prima-Cotton
Dancewear, Performance Spandex Dance,
Powerwear, Liturgical Dancewear, Jazz
Shoes, Tap Shoes, Ballet / Pointe Shoes,
Gymnastic Shoes, Lyrical / Modern Shoes,
Shoe Accessories, Performancewear,
Kiddazzle, Starlettes, Ballet & Lyrical, Jazz
& Taps, Alternatives

LEON LEVIN
CORPORATE PARK DRIVE
SUITE 240
300 OAK STREET
PEMBROKE, MA 02359
212-575-1900
866-937-5366
Fax: 212-944-1482
customerservice@leonlevin.com
www.leonlevin.com
Products:
Sports, golf apparel and casual wear.

LESCO, INC.
650 STEPHENSON HIGHWAY
SUITE 1300
TROY, MI 48083-1110
800-321-5325
800-820-4848
Fax: 800-673-3030
• Jefferey L Rutherford, Chief Execuitve
Officer
jrutherford@lesco.com
• Bruce K Thorn, Chief Operating Officer
CustomerService@LESCO.com
• Michael Weisbarth, VP / Chief Financial
Officer / Treasurer
CustomerService@LESCO.com
• Ron E Brown, Branch Manager

CustomerService@LESCO.com
• Chris Marsh, Category Manager
Products:
Equipment, Irrigation, Golf Accessories, Turf
Grass Seed, Parts, Fertilizers, Pest Control,
Merchandise, Combo Products, Control
Products

LETRELL SPORTS
3004 INDUSTRIAL PARKWAY W
KNOXVILLE, TN 37921
865-546-8070
800-325-3975
• Dick Jacobstein, Chief Execuitve Officer /
Sales Manager
Products:
Athletic Uniforms and Garments for
basketball, baseball, and football

LIBERTY MOUNTAIN SPORTS, LLC.
9816 SOUTH JORDAN GATEWAY (500 W)
SANDY, UT 84070
801-307-9200
800-366-2666
Fax: 801-307-9300
sales@libertymtn.com
www.libertymountain.com
• Gary E Heward, President
Products:
Climbing & Mountaineering, Add-on Sales,
Soft Goods, Gear Maintenance, First Aid &
Personal Care, Camp & Trail Gear,
Coghlans, Backpacks, Tents, & Bags, Biking
Accessories, Compasses & Instruments,
Lights, Knives & Tools, Matches & Fire
Starters, Stoves & Lanterns, Food &
Cookware, Water Products, Water Sports,
Optics, Kids, Books & Maps, Travel, Gifts,
Games, & Toys, Emergency Essentials

LIEBE ATHLETIC LETTERING
582 GODDARD AVENUE
CHESTERFIELD, MO 63005-1109
636-530-3700
800-845-4323
Fax: 636-530-3890
info@liebe.com
www.liebe.com
• Robert Liebe, III, President
• Jeanette James, Customer Service
Manager
jjames@liebe.com
• Ron Deters, CFO
• Greg Deniszczuk, Marketing Director
• Rob Knoll, Sales/Marketing Manager
rknoll@liebe.com
Products:
Sewing, Embroidery, Patches, Twill Letters,
Vinyl Letters, Finishing, Corporate Apparel

LIFE FITNESS, INC.
5100 N RIVER ROAD
SCHILLER PARK, IL 60176
847-288-3300
800-351-3737
Fax: 800-216-8893
glynis@gibsoncommunications.com
www.lifefitness.com
• John Stransky, President
glynis@gibsoncommunications.com
• Steven Drickey, General Counsel
glynis@gibsoncommunications.com
• Judy L Gustafson, VP Human Resources
glynis@gibsoncommunications.com
• Matthew Johnson, VP Global Strategic
Planning & Business
glynis@gibsoncommunications.com

Products:
Treadmills, Elliptical Cross Trainers,
Exercise Bikes, Stair Climbers, Home Gms,
Free Weight System, Specialized Workout
Stations

LIFE PRIORITY, INC.
11184 ANTIOCH RD OULEVARD
#417
OVERLAND PARK, KS 66210
913-438-5433
800-787-5438
Fax: 913-438-5444
www.lifepriority.com
• Greg Pryor, President
gprior@lifepriority.com
• Michelle Pryor, Marketing Director
• Tracey Budz, Public Relations
Products:
Health supplements - Durk Pearson &
Sandy Shaw designer foods, creatine,
glucosamine

LIFEGEAR INC
9858 BALDWIN PLACE
EL MONTE, CA 91731
626-456-8300
Fax: 626-452-9692
Products:
Fitness equipment and machines.

LIFELINE INTERNATIONAL, INC.
5424 W. ROOSEVELT ROAD
CHICAGO, IL 60644
608-288-9252
800-553-6633
Fax: 312-265-6789
www.lifelineusa.com
• Bobby Hinds, CEO
(800) 553-6633
info@lifelineusa.com
• Jon Hinds, National Sales Manager
info@lifelineusa.com
• Joy Hinds, Secretary
joy@lifelineusa.com
• Paul Flowers, President
Products:
Equipments for Sports Training - Core
Strength & Agility, Sports Training - Sports
Specific, Chin Up Devices, Rehab/Fitness
Equipment, Portable Gyms, Resistance
Cables, Jump Ropes, Accessories, Shape
Aerobic Products, Wall Gyms, Balls, Books
and Videos.
Products:
Lifeline's Train Station is a total fitness
rehab center that is quick and convenient
with unlimited exercise possibilities, at a low
cost that is small enough to fit in your back
pocket; The Lifeline USA WHEEL GYM has
been created to maximize the ability of the
wheelchair user to perform an incredible
variety of resistance exercises properly,
conveniently, and independently; Lifeline
USA Kettleballs are effective for fat loss,
strength training, and building muscle -
powerfully train the entire body anytime and
virtually anywhere; Lifeline Portable Gym is
a 2 lb. gym that can tone and shape all the
muscle groups of your body in 1/4 the time
Year Founded:
1973

LIFETIME PRODUCTS, INC.
PO BOX 160010
FREEPORT CENTER BUILDING D-11
CLEARFIELD, UT 84016-0010

801-776-1532
800-242-3865
Fax: 801-776-4397
info@lifetime.com
www.lifetime.com
• Vince Rhoton, Senior Vice President Of
Sales And Marketing
• Richard Hendrickson, President
pmickey@lifetime.com
• Mark Whiting, CFO
• Katie Salter, Communications Manager
Products:
Tables & Chairs, Basketball Equipment,
Outdoor Storage, Recreation

LIGHTNING GOLF DISCS
1402 CORTO
DALLAS, TX 75218
214-328-9017
Fax: 214-328-9088
www.lightninggolfdiscs.com
Products:
Golf Discs, Golf Bags, DB5-Basktet,
Fixtures

LIGHTWEAR
924 KENTUCKY STREET
BELLINGHAM, WA 98225
360-734-8798
800-213-3926
Fax: 360-676-8773
sales@lightwear.com
www.lightwear.com
• Jack Hovenier, Founder
Products:
NFL, MLB, NHL, NASCAR, NBA, NCAA
apparel and accessories.

LILY'S OF BEVERLY HILLS
20314 GRAMERCY PLACE
TORRANCE, CA 90501
310-781-2200
Fax: 310-781-2206
lbhonline@lbhgroup.com
www.lbhgroup.com
Products:
Warm-Up Suits, Golf Apparel, Tennis
Apparel

LIND SHOE COMPANY
501 LASER DRIVE
SOMERSET, WI 54025
800-950-4568
800-328-5463
Fax: 715-247-5440
info@linds.com
www.linds.com
• Jeffrey Lind, President
info@linds.com
Products:
Specializes in the importation, selling, and
distribution of a variety of quality bowling
products including rental shoes, resale
shoes, house balls, resale balls, bowling
bags, bowling pins, steel bowling lockers,
and a variety of pro shop accessories.

LINEAR RUBBER PRODUCTS, INC.
5416 46TH STREET
KENOSHA, WI 53144
262-652-3912
800-558-4040
Fax: 262-657-6705
info@rubbermats.com
www.rubbermats.com

• Beth Lane, Sales Director
info@rubbermats.com
Products:
Manufacturer of genuine rubber flooring for
weight rooms and fitness areas to absorb
the impact of free weights, secure exercise
equipment and provide acoustical qualities.
All products are sold at factory-direct pricing.
Brands:
Power Pad Flooring is available in
single-piece mats up to 6' x 16', the largest
in the industry. Gymatts are available in
48-inch x 72-inch sections. Top Mat II
Flooring System comes in black or
color-flecked roll stock, interlocking tiles and
squares.
Year Founded:
1972

LION SPORTS INC
701 KOEHLER AVENUE
SUITE 2
RONKONKOMA, NY 11779
631-580-5010
877-244-5466
Fax: 631-580-7660
www.heavyhandsfitness.com
Products:
Manufacturer of hand weights for exercise
and fitness, weight-loss, sports training,
walkers, and those seeking strength or
endurance training

LIQUID BLUE
ONE CROWNMARK DRIVE
LINCOLN, RI 2865
401-333-6200
866-450-2583
Fax: 401-333-0340
retail@liquidblue.com
www.liquidblue.com
Products:
Manufacturer of T-Shirts, Tie-Dye shirts, and
all kinds of hard to find music and sports
stickers, hats, and collectible memorabilia.

LITHONIA LIGHTING
PO BOX A
CONYERS, GA 30012
770-922-9000
Fax: 770-483-2635
comments@lithonia.com
www.lithonia.com
• Ken Honeycutt, President
comments@lithonia.com
Products:
Manufacturer of lighting equipment for
commercial, industrial, outdoor and
residential applications

LITTLE KING MANUFACTURING COMPANY INC
114 EAST WALNUT
PO BOX 287
ALAMO, TN 38001
731-696-5517
800-530-7024
Fax: 731-696-2289
gail@littlekingmfg.com
• Gail Hart, Sales Manager
(731) 696-5517
gail@littlekingmfg.com
Year Founded:
1955
Products:
Manufacturer of apparel and childrens sport
wear.

Brands:
Little King

LITTLE MISS TENNIS/T.V. SPORTS
PO BOX 17442
MEMPHIS, TN 38187-0442
901-371-0291
800-388-0291
Fax: 901-371-0293
customerservice@littlemisstennis.com
www.littlemisstennis.com
• Marilyn Kosten, Founder/President
customerservice@littlemisstennis.com
• Herb Kosten, Finance VP
Products:
Manufacturer of tennis player apparel for
boys and girls

LITTLE RIVER MARINE COMPANY
250A SE 10TH AVENUE
GAINESVILLE, FL 32601
352-378-5025
800-247-4591
Fax: 352-378-5025
info@littlerivermarine.com
www.littlerivermarine.com
• Bill Larson, President
info@littlerivermarine.com
• Steve Larson, Marketing VP / Sales
Director
info@littlerivermarine.com
Products:
Manufacturer of hand crafted rowing craft,
rowing shells and rowboats

LJO, INC.
401 HAMBURG TURNPIKE
SUITE 305
WAYNE, NJ 07470-2139
973-956-6990
Fax: 973-956-6991
ljo@ljoinc.com
www.ljoinc.com
• Leif J. Ostberg, Chief Executive Officer
ljo@ljoinc.com
• Louis Destefano, Chief Operating Officer
ljo@ljoinc.com
• Barbara Koetsier, Chief Financial Officer
ljo@ljoinc.com
Services:
Specializes in designing, developing,
sampling, sourcing and the manufacturing of
high-end branded or designer footwear

LOBSTER SPORTS
7340 FULTON AVENUE
NORTH HOLLYWOOD, CA 91605
818-764-6000
800-210-5992
Fax: 818-764-6061
www.lobstersports.com
• Tony Potter, President
info@lobstersports.com
Products:
Manufacturer of Baseball - Baseball Bucket;
Racquet Sports - Tennis Ball Throwing
Machines, Tennis Balls, Tennis Racquets;
Street Hockey (DEK) - Hockey Bucket.

LOCUST INC.
11-1155 NORTH SERVICE ROAD
W. OAKVILLE, ONTARIO, CANADA L6M
3E3
905-820-0303
800-284-8079
Fax: 905-820-8220

• Michael R Krog, Founder/CEO
(905) 820-0303
investors@locust.com
• George Azcurra, Sls / Marketing (Canada)
gazcurra@locust.ca
• Luke Deneau, Sales Director / Marketing
(Canada)
ldeneau@locust.ca
Products:
Manufacturer and Designer of Soccer
Apparel

LOG HOUSE DESIGNS, INC.
HCR-68, BOX 248
CENTER CONWAY, NH 3813
603-694-3300
Fax: 603-694-3374
• Kenyon King, President
• Janice Purslow, VP
Products:
General Sports Products including Bags,
Equipment, Apparel and Accessories for
Golf, Skiing-Alpine/Nordic.

LOGAN INC.
546 VALLEY ROAD
UPPER MONTCLAIR, NJ 7043
973-509-3190
Fax: 973-509-3191
info@loganandco.com
www.loganandco.com
• Kate Logan, President & CEO
Products:
Bags and Equipment for Baseball,
Basketball, Football, Ice Hockey,
Skiing-Alpine, Soccer, Softball, Track &
Field/Running , Volleyball and Wrestling.
Also Dummies for Blocking, Whirlpool
Baths, and Training Room Supplies.

LOGO ART
226 PUBLIC STREET
PROVIDENCE, RI 2905
800-362-9896
800-362-9896
Fax: 401-330-4201
Logoartsales@herffjones.com
www.logoart.com
Products:
Manufacturer of jewelry utilizing logos of
colleges, sports teams and corporations

LOGO CHAIR, INC.
117 SE PARKWAY
FRANKLIN, TN 37064
615-261-2100
888-959-3030
Fax: 615-261-9240
• Bill McCauley, Founder
Products:
Manufacturer of high quality sporting goods
and tailgating products. Specializing in
officially licensed college merchandise.

LOGOART
226 PUBLIC STREET
PROVIDENCE, RI 2905
800-362-9896
Fax: 401-330-4201
orders@logoart.com
www.logoart.com
Products:
Jewelry, Team Logo Watches, Clocks and
Binoculars
Brands:
LogoArt, Prospect, TeamTime

LOMMA GOLF
305 CHERRY STREET
SCRANTON, PA 18505
570-346-5555
Fax: 570-346-5580
info@lommagolf.com
www.lommagolf.com
• Gary Knight, Executive VP
• Ralph Lomma, Founder and President
info@lommagolf.com
• Joyce C. Lomma, Esq, Vice President
AOO/PR
joylomma@icontech.com
Products:
Pre-fabricated miniature golf courses.
Provides design services for both upscale
and turnkey solutions for all miniature
golfing needs, with waterfalls, caves, ponds,
creeks, mountains and more.
Year Founded:
1955

LONE STAR ATHLETIC DESIGNS, INC.
512 W MAIN STREET
PALESTINE, TX 75801
903-729-1643
800-527-2178
Fax: 903-729-4599
www.lonestarathleticsinc.com
• Charles McCullough, President / Sales
Director
Products:
Baseball - Caps; General Sports Products -
Award Jackets, Embroidery, Heat Transfers,
Lettering, Screen Printing, T-shirts.

LORIA AWARDS
1876 CENTRAL PARK AVENUE
YONKERS, NY 10710
914-779-3377
800-540-2927
Fax: 914-779-3587
customerservice@loriaawards.com
www.loriaawards.com
• Roger V. Loria, President
customerservice@loriaawards.com
Products:
Trophies, Awards, Emblems, Medals,
Patches, Plaques, Ribbons.

LOST ARROW CORPORATION
259 W SANTA CLARA ST
PO BOX 32050
VENTURA, CA 93001
805-643-8616
800-638-6464
Fax: 805-653-6355
customer_service@patagonia.com
www.patagonia.com
• Michael Crooke, Chief Executive Officer
patagonia@news.patagonia.com
• Bob Kelleher, Chief Operating Officer
patagonia@news.patagonia.com
• Perry Klebahn, EVP
• Casey Sheahan, President
• Martha Groszewski, VP/Chief Executive
Officer
Products:
Manufacturer of outdoor apparel, rugged
clothing and accessories to mountain
climbers, skiers, and other extreme sports.
Products:Rowing/Crew - Underclothing;
Rugby - Jerseys; Skiing-Nordic - Gaiters,
Shells, Sweaters, Underclothing; Track &
Field/Running - Apparel-Run/Jog.

LOUISVILLE GOLF
2320 WATTERSON TRAIL
LOUISVILLE, KY 40299
800-456-1631
Fax: 502-491-6189
sales@louisvillegolf.com
www.louisvillegolf.com
• Josh Fischer, VP Marketing / Marketing
Director
• Larry Fischer, VP, Sales
• Mike Just, President
mjust@louisvillegolf.com
• Nancy Silk, Office Manager
Products:
A leader in design and production of
persimmon wood golf clubs

LOUISVILLE SLUGGER
800 W MAIN STREET
LOUISVILLE, KY 40202
502-585-5226
800-282-2287
Fax: 502-585-1179
www.slugger.com
• John A. Hillerich IV, President / Chief
Executive Officer
• Marty Archer, President, Louisville Slugger
Division
• John A. Jack Hillerich III, Chairman of the
Board
Products:
Baseball, Fastpitch Softball, Slowpitch
Softball pitching systems.

LOVING ASSOCIATES INC.
3711 KENNEBEC DRIVE
SUITE 100
EAGAN, MN 55122
952-912-2500
888-796-4997
Fax: 651-379-4082
info@rti-inc.com
www.laloving.com
• Jeffery K Kiesel, President / Chief
Executive Officer
• Darla Czech, Purchasing Director
Products:
Apparel for sports, active and casual wear
for women.

LOWE ALPINE SYSTEMS
ANN STREET
KENDAL, ENGLAND LA9 6AA
44-1539-740840
Fax: 44-1539-726314
www.lowealpine.com
• Ann Ma Tewey, VP, Operations / Finance
lowecs@lowealpine.com
• Jeff Lowe, President
Products:
Technical Outerwear Jackets, Pants, Shirts
& Tees, Pants & Shorts, Baselayer, Clothing
Accessories, Technical Mountain Packs,
Multi-day Packs, Hyperlite Packs, Activist
Packs, Day Packs, Travel Packs, Belt
Packs, Pack Accessories, Military Packs

LOWRANCE ELECTRONICS, INC.
12000 E SKELLY DRIVE
TULSA, OK 74128
918-437-6881
800-628-4487
Fax: 918-234-1705
• Darrell J. Lowrance, President / Chief
Executive Officer / Di
• Mark C. McQuown, VP, Sales

- Bob G. Callaway, VP, Marketing
- Leif C. Ottoson, President
Products:
High-quality sport fishing SONAR and Global Positioning System (GPS) mapping instruments

LSI INDUSTRIES
10000 ALLIANCE ROAD
CINCINNATI, OH 45242
513-793-3200
800-436-7800
Fax: 800-373-9998
www.lsi-industries.com
- James Sferra, EVP, Manufacturing / Secretary / Directo
courtsider@lsi-industries.com
Products:
Sharp cutoff products that provide environmentally friendly lighting solutions for the tennis and sports markets

LSI LIGHTING INDUSTRIES
10000 ALLIANCE ROAD
CINCINNATI, OH 45242
513-793-3200
800-794-3448
Fax: 513-984-1335
www.lsi-industries.com
- Robert J. P. Ready, Chairman and Chief Executive Officer
- David W. McCauley, President, LSI Graphics Solutions
- Ronald S. Stowell, VP / Chief Financial Officer / Treasurer
Products:
LSI Lighting Solutions Plus (Accent & Downlights, Architectural Indoor Lighting, Architectural Outdoor Lighting, Automotive Lighting, Courtsider Sports Lighting, Indoor Lighting, Outdoor Lighting, Petroleum Lighting, QSR Lighting, Retail National Accounts Lighting, International Lighting); LSI Graphic Solutions Plus (Active Digital Signage, Menu Boards, Floor Graphics, Fleet Graphics, Kiosks, P.O.P Displays, Fixtures, Channel Letters, Architectural Elements, Dimensional Letters, OEM Products)

LUMASTROBE WARNING LIGHTS
33 GREENWOOD AVENUE
MIDLAND PARK, NJ 7432
201-444-7041
800-775-5862
Fax: 201-445-8575
info@lumastrobe.com
www.lumastrobe.com
- Peter H. Zecher, President
info@lumastrobe.com
- George Shabet, Sales Manager
info@lumastrobe.com
- Jill Opermann, Advertising Director
(201) 444-0600
jill@pmcontrols.com
Products:
Solar and Portable Battery Powered Warning Lights. Marshalling wands and flashing warning lights.

LYCIAN STAGE LIGHTING
PO BOX 214
SUGAR LOAF, NY 10981
845-469-2285
Fax: 845-469-5355
slerman@lycian.com
www.lycian.com

- Steve Lerman, Director, Sales and Marketing
(845) 469-2285
slerman@lycian.com
Products:
Lycian Followspots

LYNX GOLF, INC.
11000 NORTH IH 35
AUSTIN, TX 78753
512-837-4810
800-813-6897
www.golfsmith.com
- Barry King, VP Marketing
comments@golfsmith.com
- Steve Jones, VP, Marketing
Products:
Retailer for golf clubs, accessories, balls, shoes

M-F ATHLETIC COMPANY
11 AMFLEX DRIVE
CRANSTON, RI 2921
401-942-9363
888-556-7464
Fax: 401-942-7645
mfathletic@mfathletic.com
www.everythingtrackandfield.com
- Bill Falk, Founder
bill.falk@mfathletic.com
- Eric Falk, VP, Administrative
eric.falk@mfathletic.com
- Mark Strawderman, General Manager, Track & Field Division
Products:
Throwing Equipment, Jumping Equipment, Shoes & Apparel, Books & Videos, Timing & Measuring, Tents, Sprints/Hurdles Equipment, Training Equipment, Meet Management, In-Ground Equipment

MACGREGOR GOLF COMPANY
11000 NORTH IH 35
AUSTIN, TX 78753
512-837-4810
800-813-6897
Fax: 800-455-1220
www.golfsmith.com
- Barry Schneider, Chairman / Chief Executive Officer
Products:
Driver, wood, shaft, hybrid, iron, wedge, putter, and golf accessories

MACHO PRODUCTS, INC.
10045 102ND TERRACE
SEBASTIAN, FL 32958
772-388-9892
800-327-6812
888-388-9892
Fax: 772-388-9859
sales@macho.com
www.macho.com
- Amir Shadab, President / Chief Executive Officer
- Nancy Grossbart, VP, Marketing
(888) 388-9892
nancy@macho.com
Products:
Sparring Gear such as Universal Face Shield, Warrior, Dyna, Chest Protectors, Cloth Guards, XP, Rival, Sewn Vinyl, Ringstar Shoes & Shins, and XP Cloth Guards, Belts, Uniforms, Mouth Protectors, Groin Protectors, Shoes, Chat Kama, Training Mats, Equipment Bags, Promotional Items (Headband, Macho Logo

T-Shirts, Macho Towel), TC Training Line, and Everlast Training Gear

MACKENZIE COMPANY
1066 WEST HASTINGS STREET
SUITE 1240
OCEANIC PLAZA
VANCOUVER, BC, CANADA V6E 3X1
604-685-9227
Fax: 604-685-4060
mackenz@telus.net
www.mackenziecompany.com
- Jim Stewart, Owner
(503) 246-7330
- Daniel Ramsey, Owner
mackenziecompany@yahoo.com
Products:
Golf - Bags, Headcovers, Trophies/Tee Prizes

MACNEILL ENGINEERING-CHAMPS GOLF SPIKES
140 LOCKE DRIVE
PO BOX 735
MARLBOROUGH, MA 1752
508-481-8830
800-652-4267
Fax: 508-303-4923
sales@macneillusa.com
www.champspikes.com
- Harris MacNeill, President / Chief Executive Officer
- Jeffrey Dow, Chief Operating Officer
- Rich Locke, Chief Financial Officer
Products:
Golf: Spikes, ball markers, cleaning tools, divot tools, shoe trees, wrenches; Football& Soccer: spikes and wrenches; Baseball: Cleats; Track: spikes and wrenches

MAGNET SOLUTIONS
5827 LONG
SHAWNEE, KS 66216
913-631-3528
888-875-8768
Fax: 913-631-3528
- Bridget Sossaya, Owner
Products:
Team Schedule Magnets, Promotional Magnets, Player Card Magnets, Mouse Pads, Other Promotional Items

MAGNETSTREET
3890 PHEASANT RIDGE DRIVE NE
Suite 190
BLAINE, MN 55449
763-786-9400
800-788-8633
Fax: 763-786-9393
info@magnetstreet.com
www.magnetstreet.com
- Carrie Biddle, Vice President of Sales
Products:
Manufacturer of the highest quality full-color refrigerator magnets. Creates custom magnets such as Save the Date magnets, calendar magnets, wedding magnets or business card magnets.

MAGNUM FITNESS SYSTEMS
2201 12TH AVENUE
S MILWAUKEE, WI 53172
414-764-4068
800-372-0554
Fax: 414-768-7047

sales@magnumfitness.com
www.magnumfitness.com
• Larry Nelson, VP
Products:
Bikes, steppers, ellipticals, treadmills, upper body, handles, dumbbells, olympic bars, olympic plates, and other fitness equipments

MAIN TROPHY SUPPLY COMPANY
1691 W IMPERIAL COURT
MOUNT PROSPECT, IL 60056
847-439-2550
800-323-6054
Fax: 847-439-5199
sales@maintrophysupply.com
www.maintrophy.com
• Dennis Hoggstrom, General Manager
(847) 435-2550
sales@maintrophysupply.com
• Karen Jones, Production Manager
(847) 435-2550
sales@maintrophysupply.com
• Dan Maxinson, Salesperson
(847) 435-2550
sales@maintrophysupply.com
Products:
Metal, Plastics, Plaques, and award covers.

MAJESTIC ATHLETIC WEAR LIMITED
2320 NEWLINS MILLS RD.
EASTON, PA 18045
610-746-6800
866-471-6861
Fax: 610-588-9958
www.majesticathletic.com
• Faust Capobianco, Founder & Chairman
• Rob Brodersen, VP & General Manager
• Jim Pisani, President
Products:
Baseball Jerseys, Uniforms; Basketball Uniforms; Football Uniforms, Fleece, Shorts; Softball Uniforms, Licensed Apparel.
Brands:
MLB Authentic Collection, MLB Genuine Merchandise, Majestic Select, Home Base, Majestic Threads.

MAJESTIC ATHLETIC WEAR LIMITED
2320 NEWLINS MILL ROAD
EASTON, PA 18045
610-588-0100
888-824-9470
Fax: 610-588-3800
www.majesticathletic.com
• John Wilson, Director Sales
Football:
AFL - Official Replica Jersey Supplier.

MAKOTO USA INC
5689 S OURAY STREET
CENTENNIAL, CO 80015
303-766-3971
Fax: 303-547-3373
info@makoto-usa.com
www.makoto-usa.com
• Dave Shaw, Vice President
Description:
Manufacturer of the Makoto Sports Arena - used for training cognitive function and reaction time.

MANCINO MANUFACTURING CO.,INC.
4700 WISSAHICKON AVENUE
BUILDING E SUITE 109
PHILADELPHIA, PA 19144

800-338-6287
800-338-6287
Fax: 800-949-3595
info@mancinomats.com
www.mancinomats.com
• Robert P. Mancino, President
(800) 338-6287
• Wayne L. Agnew, Digital Media Director
(800) 338-6287
Products:
Manufacturer of folding mats, training shapes, wall padding and custom safety cushioning.

MARCIA ORIGINALS
20740 PLUMMER STREET
CHATSWORTH, CA 91311-5001
818-993-1003
800-423-5208
Fax: 818-993-1977
• Marcia Grey, Owner
Products:
Golf Apparel; Racquet Sports Apparel; Track & Field/Running Apparel-Run/Jog.

MARK OF FITNESS INC
850 ROUTE 1 N
NORTH BRUNSWICK, NJ 8902
732-565-0333
800-438-9260
Fax: 732-565-0335
Products:
Manufacturer of precision products including: blood pressure monitors, pillbox timer, medical products, heart rate monitors and other medical instruments.

MARKWORT SPORTING GOODS COMPANY
1101 RESEARCH BOULEVARD
SAINT LOUIS, MO 63132-1711
314-942-1711
800-280-5555
Fax: 314-942-1179
sales@markwort.com
www.markwort.com
• Glenn Markwort, Chief Executive Officer / VP
(314) 652-8935
• Bob Herman, General Manager
• Jim Tieszen, Advertising Director
Products:
Manufacturer and distributor of sporting goods equipment and accessories, like baseballs, softballs, gloves and mitts, protective equipment, batter's gloves, uniforms, socks, laces, glove oil and training accessories.

MARLIN FIREARMS COMPANY
PO BOX 1871
MADISON, NC 27025
203-239-5621
800-544-8892
Fax: 203-234-7991
www.marlinfirearms.com
• Robert W. W. Behn, President
Products:
Manufacturer of firearms.

MARMOT
5789 STATE FARM DRIVE
SUITE 100
ROHNERT PARK, CA 94928
707-544-4590
888-357-3262

Fax: 707-544-1344
www.marmot.com
• Simon Marmot, Director
Products:
Backpacks, Shelter Tents

MARMOT MOUNTAIN LTD.
5789 STATE FARM DRIVE
SUITE 100
ROHNERT PARK, CA 94928
707-544-4590
888-357-3262
Fax: 707-544-1344
info@marmot.com
www.marmot.com
• Stephen Crisafulli, President / Chief Executive Officer
• Mark Martin, Chief Operating Officer
Products:
Manufacturer of clothing, sportswear, base layer, gloves, packs, bags, tents and various accessories.

MARSHALL-BROWNING INTERNATIONAL CORPORATION
353 CHRISTIAN STREET
SUITE 3
OXFORD, CT 6478
203-264-2702
800-336-6756
Fax: 203-264-0543
sales@robictimers.com
www.robictimers.com
Products:
Manufacturer of handheld timers and stopwatches.

MARTIN SPORTS, INC.
495 INDUSTRIAL ROAD
PO BOX 6532
CARLSTADT, NJ 7072
800-221-1993
Fax: 201-438-7113
orderdesk@martinsports.com
www.martinsports.com
• Don Martin, Principal
Products:
Manufacturer and importer of sports equipment and apparel, including beach balls, bean bags, bowling equipment, cageballs, coated foam balls, cones, custom balls, flag footballs, girdles, etc.

MARTIN STONE QUARRIES
1355 N READING AVENUE
BECHTELSVILLE, PA 19505
610-367-2011
Fax: 610-367-8613
sales@martinstone.com
www.martinstone.com
• Glenn Martin, President
• Dave Martin, President, Gable
• Rod Martin, VP
Products:
Produces material used for sports fields and other surfaces.

MARTIN-KILPATRICK TABLE TENNIS COMPANY
4482 TECHNOLOGY DRIVE
WILSON, NC 27896
800-334-8315
Fax: 252-291-8203
sales@butterflyna.com
www.butterflyna.com
• Bowie Martin, President

Products:
Provider of table tennis equipment.

MARTY GILMAN, INC. DBA GILMAN GEAR
30 GILMAN ROAD
GILMAN, CT 06336-0097
800-243-0398
Fax: 860-823-1859
sales@gilmangear.com
www.gilmangear.com
• Neil Gilman, President
(860) 383-1980
neil@gilmangear.com
• Shirley Gilman, Chief Executive Officer
• Nadine Parker, Finance Director
accounting@gilmangear.com
• Jon Macrina, Purchasing Manager
purchasing@gilmangear.com
Products:
Manufacturer of football practice equipment and football field equipment. In addition, manufacturer of basketball training equipment, wrestling training equipment and strength and conditioning equipment.
Teams;
All teams in the NFL and CFL. 600 college teams and 7,000 high school teams.

MASTER HOME PRODUCTS
7520 N SAINT LOUIS AVENUE
SKOKIE, IL 60076
888-710-7206
888-710-7206
Fax: 847-674-9400
customerservice@mhpinternational.com
• Michael Friedman, Founder and President
Products:
Imports Portable Massage Tables and Chairs

MASTER INDUSTRIES WORLDWIDE, LLC
1001 S LINWOOD AVE
SANTA ANA, CA 92705
714-361-9767
Fax: 949-660-1678
sales@masterindustries.com
www.masterindustries.com
• Cathy Kay, General Manager/Controller
Products:
Manufacturer of over 100 premium high-performance bowling accessories for serious amateur and professional enthusiasts.

MASTER SPORTS
6206 EASTGATE MALL
SAN DIEGO, CA 92121
www.mastersports.com
• Eric Doden, General Manager
Products:
Products include Machines, Essential Tools, Accessories, Professional Tracking System

MATCH PLAY OF PINEHURST
695 SW BROAD STREET
SOUTHERN PINES, NC 28387
910-692-3741
888-252-4939
Fax: 910-401-1143
• Doug Smith, Founder
Products:
Golf Clubs and Accessories, Bag Tags, Ball Retrievers, Christmas Items, Clothing & Headwear, Club Repair Materials, Divot Repair Tools, Gloves, Golf Bags, Golf Balls,

Golf Clubs, Headcovers, Home/Gift Items, Jewelry, Navika Accessories, Night Golf, Novelty Items, Practice Equipment, Purses & Totes, Rain Protection, Shafts, Socks, Spikes, Team Sport Items, Tees, Towels

MATCH POINT
PO BOX 1211
WAUKESHA, WI 53187
262-827-0206
800-670-4964
Fax: 262-827-0771
jhill47733@aol.com
www.match-point.biz
• Jack Hill, President
(262) 827-0206
jhill47733@aol.com
• Peter Adams, President
Products:
Tennis accessories
Clients:
Schools; Tennis Facilities

MATEFLEX-MELE CORPORATION
2007 BEECHGROVE PLACE
UTICA, NY 13501
315-733-1412
800-926-3539
Fax: 315-735-4372
info@mateflex.com
www.mateflex.com
• Gabe Martini, Sales Manager
(315) 733-1412
gmartini@mateflex.com
• Fred Jones, Vice President, Products & Services
(800) 926-3539
fjones@mateflex.com
• Tony Sardelli, General Manager
(800) 926-3539
ts@mateflex.com
• Sandra Radell, Office Manager
(800) 926-3539
sradell@mateflex.com
• John Gleason, Manager of Field Services
(800) 926-3539
jgleason@mateflex.com
• Kevin Wheelock, Sales Representative
(800) 926-3539
kwheelock@mateflex.com
• Dan Spinella, Sales Representative
(800) 926-3539
dspinella@mateflex.com
Products:
Mat,flex II, Mat,flex III, ProGym, TileFlex, Inline Arena Tile

MATMAN WRESTLING COMPANY
12724 PACIFIC HIGHWAY SW
TACOMA, WA 98499
253-582-5555
800-426-3999
Fax: 253-582-2591
info@matmanwrestling.com
www.matmanwrestling.com
• Warren Deprenger, President
Products:
Uniforms/Singlets, Warmups, Youth, Accessories, Kneepads, Shoes, Ear Guards

MATZIE GOLF COMPANY, INC.
2271 W. MALVERN AVENUE
SUITE 197
FULLERTON, CA 92833
800-783-2255
www.matzie.com

• Fred Matzie, Founder
• Don Gibas, President
Products:
Amazing Assist, Swing Perfecter, E-Z Tempo trainer, Novelty Putters, Training Grips, Long Putters, Logo Putters

MAXIMUS FITNESS PRODUCTS
4752 W MISSION BOULEVARD
SUITE D
MONTCLAIR, CA 91762
909-364-9099
800-634-6294
Fax: 909-364-9033
Products:
Specializes Home, Hotels, YMCA's, Schools Military Resorts, Apartments, Universities, Physical Therapy, Corporate Fitness Recreation Centers, Correctional Facilities, Personal Training Studios, Police & Fire Departments, Rehab Centers & Hospitals Equipment

MAXLINE EAGNAS
18116 S HOBART BOULEVARD
GARDENA, CA 90248
310-523-4641
Fax: 310-523-2851
maxline@eagnas.com
www.eagnas.com
Products:
Portable Electronic, Stringing Machines, Portable Manual, Stringing Machines, Table-top Electronic, Stringing Machines, Table-top Manual, Stringing Machines, Professional Electronic Stringing Machines, Professional Manual, Stringing Machines, Badminton Machines, Stringing Tools, Strings, Grips, Accessories, Bags, Training Devices, Ball Pick Up Devices, Ball Machines

MAXX GROUP
1200 FORUM WAY S
PO BOX 40610
FORT WORTH, TX 76140
817-336-5671
866-362-3904
Fax: 817-551-0698
www.themaxxgroup.com
• Sasha Denman, Licensing Coordinator
(817) 336-5671
sasha@themaxxgroup.com
Nature of Service:
Manufacturer of Licensed NASCAR Collectibles
Products:
Barstools, Pub Tables, Car Tackers, Signature Tackers, Big GoGriller, Neon Clocks, Night Lights, Plasma Clocks.

MCARTHUR TOWEL AND SPORTS
700 MOORE STREET
PO BOX 448
BARABOO, WI 53913
608-356-8922
800-356-9168
Fax: 608-356-7587
sales@mcarthurtowels.com
www.mcarthur-towels.com
• Vern Fowler, Divisional Sales Manager
(800) 356-9168
vfowler@mcarthurtowels.com
Products:
Designs and distributes blank and printed terry products and sports-related gift items under licenses with professional teams in

the NFL, NHL, NBA, MBL, NCAA and NASCAR. Also sells blank towels and terry products.
Year Founded:
1885

MCARTHUR TOWELS & SPORTS
700 MOORE STREET
PO BOX 448
BARABOO, WI 53913
608-356-8922
800-356-9168
Fax: 608-356-7587
sales@mcarthurtowels.com
www.mcarthurtowels.com
• Gregg H. McArthur, President
(608) 356-8922
gmcarthur@mcarthurtowels.com
• Neil Mattson, VP, Operations
(800) 356-9168
nmattson@mcarthurtowels.com
• Don Carroll, Manager, Athletic Sales
(800) 356-9168
• Kelly Borchert, Manager, Retail Sales
(800) 356-9168
Description:
Brings affordable quality towels to schools, health clubs and retail stores across the U.S. Carries a full line of bath, bench, sweat and workout towels and offers a line of licensed sports products for the NFL, MLB, NHL and NBA. The extensive licensed product line includes beach towels, baby bibs, game day essentials, golf towels and golf accessories that feature professional team logos from acros the nation. The high profile Gatorade Beach Towel, Super Bowl Trophy Towel and the Steelers' Terrible Towel are a few examples of McArthur's many programs.
Year Founded:
1885
Teams:
All NFL, MLB, NHL, NBA and NCAA

MCCARTHY-SORENSEN ATHLETIC, INC.
1700 PIERCE AVENUE
PO BOX 232
MARINETTE, WI 54143
800-521-3153
Fax: 715-735-7193
• Don Sorensen, President
(800) 521-3153
Products:
Manufactures custom jerseys, custom socks, custom football jerseys, custom lacrosse jersey, custom baseball jersey, referee jerseys, cordura garment bags

MCDAVID SPORTS MEDICAL PRODUCTS
10305 ARGONNE DRIVE
WOODBRIDGE, IL 60517
630-783-0600
800-237-8254
Fax: 630-783-1270
• Rey Corpuz, Marketing Director
rcorpuz@mcdavidinc.com
• Bob McDavid, President
bmcdavid@mcdavidinc.com
Products:
Sports Medicine, Braces, Supports, Athletic Tape, Hot & Cold Therapy, Cups & Supporters, Performance Apparel, Protective Apparel and Hexpad Technology.
Brands:
McDavid, Cowboy Collar, Hexpad Technology.

Clients:
Major Sporting Goods Retailers, Independent Retailers and Team Dealers.

MCNETT CORPORATION
1411 MEADOR AVENUE
BELLINGHAM, WA 98229
360-671-2227
Fax: 360-671-4521
customerservice@mcnett.com
www.mcnett.com
• Duane McNett, President
• Karen Robins, Human Resources Executive
• Liz Mathias, Sales Executive
• Travis Huisman, CFO
Products:
Adhesives & Seam Sealers, Water Repellents, Cleaners & Rejuvenators, Water Treatment, Tape & Patches

MDF INDUSTRIES INC
127 SHELDON DRIVE
UNIT 1
CAMBRIDGE, ONTARIO, CANADA N1R 6T7
800-452-2154
Fax: 519-624-0339
flemgray@sentex.net
• Ted E Gray, President/Owner
• Gerry Blasioll, Operations Officer
Products:
Skate Sharpeners, Boot Maintenance, Sharpeners Supplies and Paint Shakers.

MECA SPORTSWEAR, INC.
1120 TOWNLINE ROAD
TOMAH, WI 54660
651-638-3800
800-729-6322
Fax: 608-374-6405
infoweb@mecasportswear.com
www.mecasportswear.com
• Tom A. Bramwell, President
• Sue Faulkner, Human Resources Executive
• Rick Zimmerman, Sales Executive
• Joe Clary, Purchasing Executive
Products:
School Jacket, Custom Letter Jacket, Award Letters & Patches, Stock Wool Jackets, Stock nylon Jackets, School Apparel, School Accessories, Corporate Items

MEDI-DYNE HEALTHCARE PRODUCTS LTD
1812 INDUSTRIAL BOULEVARD
PO BOX 1649
COLLEYVILLE, TX 76034
817-251-8660
800-810-1740
Fax: 817-488-6616
customersupport@medi-dyne.com
www.medi-dyne.com
• Craig DiGiovanni, Contact
(817) 251-8660
craig@medi-dyne.com
Products:
Tuli's Shock Absorbers for your feet including heel cups, arch supports, insoles and more. StretchRite multipurpose stretching tool. CoreStretch - an effective device for stretching the back, hips. Skin-on-Skin Blister prevention products.
Brands:
Tulis, Skin-On-Skin, ProStretch, StretchRite, CoreStretch.

MEDIC FIRST AID INTERNATIONAL, INC.
1450 WESTEC DRIVE
PO BOX 21738
EUGENE, OR 97402
541-284-3898
800-447-3177
Fax: 541-344-7429
info@medicfirstaid.com
www.hsi.com
• Bill Clendenen, Chief Executive Officer
• Frank Powers, Chief Operating Officer
• Jeff Jackson, Chief Financial Officer and VP of Production
• Steve Barnett, Marketing Director
(541) 344-7099
Description:
MEDIC FIRST AID is the source for your emergency care needs-from CPR, AED, and First Aid Training, to entire AED implementation programs. MEDIC FIRST AID will help you meet federal, state and local regulatory requirements for workplace safety and health.
Nature of Service:
CPR, AED, First Aid Training, Automated External Defibrillator (AED) implementation
Brands:
MEDIC FIRST AID, American Heart Association

MEIER AND FRANK MDSE. COMPANY, INC.
5641 WASHINGTON STREET
DENVER, CO 80216
303-295-1368
800-525-3569
Fax: 303-293-3814
Products:
Direct importers and distributors of wholesale flags of the world, cloisonn, pins (hat tacs), pencil sharpeners, custom lapel pins, fire emblems, embroidered patches, custom glassware and promotional mugs. Also importers, manufacturers and distributors of bowling, golf and soccer motif items.

MELEX PRODUCTS INTERNATIONAL, II, INC./DBA MELEX GOLF CARS
3900 BUSINESS HIGHWAY 70 W
CLAYTON, NC 27520
800-334-8665
Fax: 304-748-2700
www.melex.com
• Andrzej Jesionek, Chief Executive Officer
• K. S. Mallory, VP / Chief Financial Officer
• Andy Kielawa, Research / Development Director
Products:
Assembles and sells golf cars and utility vehicles. Also offers a diverse line of utility vehicles for commercial, industrial and personal use.

MELO CO., INC. AND XS BAGGAGE
1848 STATE ROUTE 9J
STUYVESANT, NY 12173
518-732-7791
Fax: 518-684-2688
melobags@att.net
• Jim Melville, President
Products:
Manufacturer of backpacks,duffles/dance bags, messenger bags, shoulder bags, sling bags, small stuff/add-ons, and tote bags.

MEMORY COMPANY
PO BOX 610
PHOENIX CITY, AL 36868
334-448-0708
888-448-1480
Fax: 334-480-0197
info@memorycompany.com
www.memorycompany.com
• Charles Sizemore, CEO
• Randy Brown, President
Products:
Non apparel gifts within college teams, the
NFL, MLB, NHL, NASCAR
Year Founded:
1997

**MERCURY INTERNATIONAL
CORPORATION**
19 ALICE AGNEW DRIVE
N ATTLEBORO, MA 2761
508-699-9000
www.mercuryfootwear.com
• Gary Gorsuch, President
• Irving Wiseman, Chairman / Founder
• Howard Wiseman, Chief Executive Officer
• Nicloas De Santis, President
Products:
General Sports Products - Athletic Shoes,
Outdoor Casual Shoes, Workboots.

MERCURY LUGGAGE MFG. CO.
4843 VICTOR STREET
PO BOX 47558
JACKSONVILLE, FL 32207
904-733-9595
800-874-1885
Fax: 904-733-9671
www.mercuryluggage.com
Products:
Manufacturer of trunks and footlockers, as
well as the largest supplier of luggage and
military logo embroidered bags.

MERCURY MARINE
W6250 W PIONEER ROAD
PO BOX 1939
FOND DU LAC, WI 54936-1939
920-929-5040
Fax: 920-929-5893
www.mercurymarine.com
• Patrick Mackey, President
• Coy Sabel, Communications Manager
• Douglas Pietrowski, Finance Director
Products:
A leading manufacturer of marine propulsion
systems.

MERRYGARDEN ATHLETIC WEAR
97 WINFIELD CIRCLE
HARTWELL, GA 30643
706-856-4900
800-849-5555
Fax: 800-849-2121
customerservice@hartwell.com
• Burt Severns, VP Sales / Marketing
Products:
Baseball Uniforms; Basketball Uniforms;
Jerseys, Shorts, T-shirts; Soccer Jerseys,
Uniforms; Softball Uniforms; Track &
Field/Running Apparel-Track & Field;
Volleyball Uniforms.

METALTEK
455 KITTY HAWK DRIVE
MORRISVILLE, NC 27560

919-544-0344
800-776-6770
Fax: 919-544-1430
metaltek@msn.com
www.playmatetennismachines.com
Products:
Manufacturer of sporting and athletic goods.

METRO SIGNS ADVERTISING, INC.
4608 SCHUFF AVENUE
LOUISVILLE, KY 40213
502-452-2561
800-441-0627
Fax: 502-473-1286
www.1-metro.com
• C.J. Bud Theobald, President
cjt@1-metro.com
• A Kent Brown, VP Operations
(502) 608-9650
• Hank Allgeier, Senior Graphic Tech
(502) 551-3546
hank@1-metro.com
Products:
Banners (Fabric, Vinyl, Mesh), Feather
Banners & Harware, Flags, Media
Backdrops, 100% Foam Sideline Banner
Stands, Collapsible/Expandable
Banner/Panel Frames, Retractable Banner
Stands.
Nature of Business:
Concept Creation, Design, Large Format
Printing, Portable Frame Systems, Custom
Metal Fabrication
Brands:
Transframe, AdCades, AdPads
Year Founded:
1984

MEYCO PRODUCTS, INC.
1225 WALT WHITMAN ROAD
MELVILLE, NY 11747
631-421-9800
800-446-3926
Fax: 631-421-8621
sales@meycoproducts.com
www.meycoproducts.com
• David Weissner, President
• John Ciniglio, VP
Products:
Manufacturer of swimming pool covers.

MICHAEL JORDAN BRAND/NIKE
ONE BOWERMAN DRIVE
BEAVERTON, OR 97005
503-671-6453
800-344-6453
Fax: 503-671-6300
www.jordanbrand.com
• Larry Miller, President, The Jordan Brand
• Howard White, VP, The Jordan Brand
Products:
Designs and markets a wide variety of
athletic footwear, apparel and related items
for competitive and recreational uses.

MICHIGAN LADDER COMPANY
12 E FOREST AVENUE
PO BOX 981307
YPSILANTI, MI 48198
734-482-5946
800-444-6704
Fax: 734-482-8424
sales@michiganladder.com
www.michiganladder.com
• R. F. Nissly, President
• Tom Harrison, Owner & President

Description:
Racquet Sports - Table Tennis Equipment.

MICROLITE
100 1ST AVENUE WEST
PO BOX 808
OSKALOOSA, IA 52577
641-673-0411
800-825-6020
Fax: 641-673-6360
service@musco.com
www.musco.com
• Heidi Tegtmeier, Partnership Program
Manager
Products:
Designs and manufactures lighting control
systems for indoor arenas, outdoor
stadiums, college facilities, and
multi-purpose civic centers.

MIDWEST LETTERING COMPANY
645 BELLEFONTAINE AVENUE
MARION, OH 43302
740-382-1905
800-848-8289
Fax: 740-387-2788
midwestlettering@midohio.twcbc.com
• Richard Vance, President
Products:
Manufactures Sports Lettering Products,
including Die Cut Lettering, Heat Transfers,
Digi-Cut Names/Numbers, Heat Seal
Presses/Supplies, and Screen Printing
Equipment & Supplies.

**MIDWEST TROPHY MANUFACTURING,
INC.**
3405 S E 29TH STREET
DEL CITY, OK 73115
405-670-4545
877-686-7464
Fax: 405-672-0964
info@mytrophy.com
www.mwtrophy.com
• David Smith, Founder / Chief Executive
Officer
• Roger Mashore, President
Products:
Manufacturer of medals, ribbons,
promotional items, apparel, awards, special
recognition, banners/certificates and jewelry.

MIKASA SPORTS USA
1821 KETTERING STREET
IRVINE, CA 92614-5617
800-854-6927
Fax: 800-854-6960
info@mikasasports.com
www.mikasasports.com
• Richard McCoy, President
Products:
Manufacturer of basketball, soccer, football,
water polo, rugby, tetherballs, kickballs,
dodgeballs, and playground balls.

MIKEN SPORTS
131 BISSEN ST
CALEDONIA, MN 55921
877-807-5291
Fax: 507-725-3675
info@mikensports.com
www.mikensports.com
• Jim Hoschert, Business Manager
jhoschert@mikensports.com
• Joe Krage, Chief Financial Officer
jkrage@mikensports.com

• Mike Rommes, Sales Manager
mrommes@mikensports.com
Products:
Manufacturer of high-performance softball
and baseball bats; fielding gloves; batting
gloves; bags and accessories.

MILLER GOLF
835 BILL JONES INDUSTRIAL DRIVE
SPRINGFIELD, TN 37172
615-384-1286
800-343-1000
Fax: 615-384-1290
www.millergolf.com
• Mike Hedge, President
• Max Waits, Chief Operating Officer
Products:
A leading supplier of customized golf
accessories and awards, including bag tags,
tees, divot tools, ball markers, towels,
umbrellas, head-covers, luggage, and
tournament prizes and awards.

MILLER SNOWBOARD SPECIALTIES
PO BOX 1510
OREM, UT 84059
801-223-9500
801-223-9500
Fax: 801-223-9105
millerfree@aol.com
• Matthew Miller, Owner
Products:
Snowboards - Releasable Snowboard
Binding, Snowboard Retaining Straps, and
Ski Bibs.

**MILLERBERND MANUFACTURING
COMPANY**
622 SIXTH STREET S
PO BOX 98
WINSTED, MN 55395
320-485-2111
Fax: 320-485-4420
www.millerberndmfg.com
• David Millerbernd, President
• Dick Clark, Marketing Manager
(320) 485-2111
• Jim Goodwin, Eastern Regional Sales
Manager
(802) 362-5346
• Mike Wendolek, Inside & Area Sales, Key
Account Manager
(320) 485-2111
• Steve Klobb, Inside Sales, Regional
Manager
(320) 485-2111
sklobe@millerberndmfg.com
• Betty Johnson, Inside Sales,
Representative Quotations, Cust
(320) 485-2111
bmj@millerberndmfg.com
Products:
Lighting poles & bases, golf carts,
floodlighting poles, decorative lighting poles,
high mast lighting poles, heavy-duty hinged
camera poles and monopole
communications towers

MINIHANE & ASSOCIATES
2 WINTER STREET
WALTHAM, MA 2451
781-891-0460
Fax: 781-891-3629
• Robert Minihane, President
Products:
Baseball - Uniforms; Basketball - Goals,
Shoes, Uniforms; Football - Helmets,

Uniforms; General Sports Products -
Hats/Caps, Referee Uniforms, T-shirts
(Licensed); Racquet Sports - Shoes; Softball
- Uniforms; Track & Field/Running -
Apparel-Track & Field

**MIRACLE RECREATION EQUIPMENT
COMPANY**
878 HIGHWAY 60
MONETT, MO 65708
417-235-6917
888-458-2752
Fax: 417-235-3551
play@miraclerec.com
www.miracle-recreation.com
• Mark Burgess, VP, Sales / Marketing
• Dan Guthrie, President
• Don Hemingway, Vice President of
Business Development
Products:
KidRox, Webscapes, Mega Towers, Center
Stage, City Park Series, Big Timber, Kids
Choice, Tots Choice, Toddlers Choice,
Outdoor Fitness, Climbers, Decks,
Convertibles, Play Panels, Overhead
Challenges, Ramps and Bridges, Roofs,
Slides, Stairs and Steps, Climbers, KidRox,
Overhead Challenges, Slides, Swings,
Spring Riders, Sand and Water, Backstop,
Basketball, Pool Slides, Water Slides,
Benches, Bike Racks, Bleachers, Litter
Receptacles, Grills, Tables

MIRACLE-GRIP LETTERING
440 SPEEDWELL AVENUE
MORRIS PLAINS, NJ 7950
973-267-3240
Fax: 973-540-1589
• Lou Culmone, Partner
Products:
Velcro Removable Lettering.

**MITCHELL & NESS NOSTALGIA
COMPANY**
1201 CHESTNUT STREET
PHILADELPHIA, PA 19107
267-273-7622
866-879-6485
Fax: 215-731-0131
www.mitchellandness.com
Products:
Products include authentic vintage jerseys
from MLB, the NBA, NFL, and NHL

MITCHELL RUBBER PRODUCTS, INC.
10220 SAN SEVAINE WAY
MIRA LOMA, CA 91752
800-453-7526
Fax: 909-968-2026
sales@mitchellrubber.com
www.mitchellrubber.com
• Jeffrey Mitchell, President
Products:
Heavy Duty Truck Accessories, Safety
Surfacing, Weight Room Flooring, and
Flooring for Gymnasiums.

MITSUBISHI DIAMOND VISION
530 KEYSTONE DRIVE
WARRENDALE, PA 15086
724-772-2555
Fax: 724-772-2146
DiamondVisionSales@meppi.com
www.diamond-vision.com
• Steve Mathews, VP, Development /
Diamond Vision Systems

• Dave Belding, VP, Technical Operations
• Mark Foster, National Sales Manager
• Marian Loveless, Marketing Coordinator
Products:
Provides a variety of screen sizes and
resolutions for Stadiums or Outdoor Sports
Applications, Arenas or Indoor Sports
Applications, Commercial Applications,
Transportable, LEDerAD, HDTV

MITSUSHIBA INTERNATIONAL, INC.
2300 E WALNUT AVENUE
FULLERTON, CA 92831
714-870-1900
800-722-4061
Fax: 714-870-1921
www.mitsushiba.com
Products:
Golf - Graphite Shafts, Golf Clubs, Golf
Bags.

MIZOTT
245 N. ERIE ST.
SUITE 1704
TOLEDO, OH 43604
419-537-3401
Fax: 419-536-0008
www.mizott.com
• Stevie D Lott, Founder
• Phyllis Lott, Business Development

MOHAWK INTERNATIONAL LACROSSE
BOX 13
ROOSEVELTOWN, NY 13683
613-936-1175
Fax: 613-936-2283
• Mark Mitchell, President
Products:
Lacrosse: Field Sticks, Goalie Sticks and
Clothing, Mini Lacrosse Sticks , Aluminum
and Wood Shafts, Ball Caps, Titanium
Shafts, NLL Pro Cage
Brands:
The Mission Extreme, The Mission, The
Thunder, Lightning

MOLTEN USA, INC.
1170 TRADEMARK DRIVE
SUITE 109
RENO, NV 89521
775-353-4000
800-477-1994
Fax: 775-358-9407
info@moltenusa.com
www.moltenusa.com
• Melissa Dawson, President
Products:
Baseketball, Football, Volleyball
Accessories, Tetherball, Water Polo Ball,
Soccer Accessories, Soccer Match Balls,
Soccer Practice Balls, Soccer Recreational
Balls, Shinguards Award Balls, Bags, Ball
Carts, Marker Cones/Carrier, Miscellaneous,
Protective Gear, Scoreboards

MONDO AMERICA, INC.
2655 FRANCIS HUGHES
LAVAL, QUEBEC, CANADA H7L 3S8
450-967-5800
800-663-8138
Fax: 450-663-7927
mondo@mondousa.com
www.mondousa.com
• Diane Zupicic, Sales Coordinator
dzupicic@mondousa.com

• Bill Mylett, Sales Manager
mondo@mondousa.com
Products:
Healthcare, Education, Fitness &
Recreation, Track & Field , Mondoturf
Systems, Ice Arena surfaces

MONGOOSE ALL-TERRAIN BOARDS
110 E 59TH STREET
SUITE 3201
NEW YORK, NY 10022
212-688-5600
Fax: 212-688-6683
www.flashrollers.com
• Evan Lipstein, President
Products:
Skateboards, Wheel Sets, Helmets, Pads,
T-shirts, and High Performance All-Terrain
Boards and All-Terrain Board Accessories.

MONITOR PREMIUMS
11045 DONNER PASS ROAD
SUITE 2B
TRUCKEE, CA 96161
530-582-5484
866-288-7893
Fax: 530-579-3266
info@monitorpremiums.com
• Drew Tornga, Managing Director
(530) 582.5484
info@monitorpremiums.com
Products:
Flying Disc, Skateboard Grip Tape, Foam
Trucker Hat, Custom BBQ Apron, Poker
Set, Beverage Koozie, Cell Phone Signal
Enhancer, Flashlight Radio, Messenger
Bag, all with sports logos and desgins.

MONOLITHIC DOME INSTITUTE
177 DOME PARK PLACE
ITALY, TX 76651
972-483-7423
Fax: 972-483-6662
email@monolithic.com
www.monolithic.com
• David South, President
Products:
Gymnasiums, Arenas, Sports Halls, Rinks,
Domes & Buildings
Brands:
Monolithic

MONTRAIL, INC.
1414 HARBOUR WAY SOUTH
SUITE 1005
RICHMOND, CA 94804
206-621-9303
855-698-7245
Fax: 206-621-0230
www.montrail.com
• Menno Vanwyk, Chief Executive Officer
• Scott Tucker, SVP, Financial Planning /
Production
• Greg Meyer, Director
Products:
Outdoor Products - Hiking Boots, Running
Shoes, Trail Shoes.

MOOSE MOUNTAIN SPORTS & GAMES LTD
8 WOOD HOLLOW ROAD
SUITE 302
PARSIPPANY, NJ 7054
973-884-8900
888-666-7388
Fax: 973-884-8999

Products:
Manufacturer of electronic toys and games

MOPRO
1024 N COUNTY ROAD W
ODESSA, TX 79763
432-550-2633
866-245-2497
Fax: 432-550-0605
• Reggie Lawrence, Contact
(432) 550-2633
Products:
Leading innovator in hat accessories and
related items to distributors in the
promotional products industry and retailers.

MORETZ SPORTS
514 W 21ST STREET
PO BOX 580
NEWTON, NC 28658
828-464-0751
866-714-8486
Fax: 828-464-8078
www.goldtoe.com
• John Moretz, President / Chief Executive
Officer
(828) 464-0751
info@moretzsports.com
• Jeff Wheeler, President, Sales
(828) 464-0751
jwheeler@moretzsports.com
• Denise Yow, President, Design /
Merchandising
(828) 464-0751
dyow@moretzsports.com
• Paul Delmonico, President
• Dave Johnson, CFO
Products:
Dominant sockwear manufacturer in the
sporting goods trade channel.

MOREY BODYBOARDS
5903 CHRISTIE AVENUE
EMERYVILLE, CA 94608
510-596-4200
888-942-6650
Fax: 510-596-4292
www.moreybodyboards.com
• Greg Lehr, SVP, Manufacturing / Logistics
• Steve Simes, SVP
Products:
Manufacturer of bodyboards, swinfins,
skimboards, gear and surfboards.

MOSLOW & BRO., INC., M.A.
375 NORFOLK AVENUE
BUFFALO, NY 14215
716-896-2950
800-828-7140
Fax: 716-896-2699
sales@moslowbros.com
www.moslowbros.com
• William M. Moslow, President
Products & Services:
Provides products in wood, jade and clear
crystal, acrylic, and marble to the award,
recognition and giftware industries. Also
provides custom product design and
manufacturing, and personalized services
such as drop shipment and custom
packaging.

MOSSBERG & SONS, INC.
7 GRASSO AVENUE
NORTH HAVEN, CT 6473

203-230-5300
800-363-3555
Fax: 203-230-5420
service@mossberg.com
www.mossberg.com
• Alan Iver Mossberg, CEO
• Linda Powell, Director Of Media Relations
• Thomas L. Taylor, VP Of Sales &
Marketing
Products:
Hunting/shooting firearms.

MOTION IMAGING
975 MAIN STREET
FARMINGDALE, NY 11735
516-777-3700
Fax: 516-777-5627
• Robert Thompson, President
• John Conkling, Vice President
Products:
Producer of high quality lenticular posters,
magnets, cups and point of purchase
displays with brilliant 3D imagery.
Year Founded:
1999

MOTORHEAD PRODUCTS
PO BOX 1338
CULLMAN, AL 35056
256-775-6337
866-542-6337
Fax: 256-775-3605
info@motorheadproducts.com
www.motorheadproducts.com
• Mike Rogus, Chief Executive Officer
(256) 775-6337
ceo@motorheadproducts.com
• Jeff Lamote, President
(256) 775-6337
jeff@motorheadproducts.com
Products:
Manufactures fine gift and novelty items
under license from NASCAR, Inc, NASCAR
Racing Teams and Drivers, General Motors
and Dodge Classic Automobiles (Muscle
Cars), Monster Garage, Monster House,
John Deere, NFL, BBQ accessories,
beverage accessories, keychains, leather
accessories and pins
Year Founded:
1999

MOTORSPORTS AUTHENTICS
6301 PERFORMANCE DRIVE
CONCORD, NC 28027
704-454-4000
800-952-0708
RCCAInfo@lionelnascar.com
www.lionelnascarcollectables.com
• Mark Dyer, President/CEO
• Howard Hitchcock, Vice President and
General Manager
Products:
Produces racing collectibles with ten years
experience in the design, manufacture, and
marketing of racing merchandise. Its
products include a broad range of
motorsports-related die-cast car replica
collectibles, apparel, souvenirs and other
memorabilia.
Brands:
Action Racing Collectables (ARC), the
Racing Collectables Club of America
(RCCA), Revell Collection, Winner's Circle,
and Chase Authentics

manufacturers/retailers

1175

MOTZ GROUP
3607 CHURCH STREET
SUITE 300
CINCINNATI, OH 45244
513-533-6452
800-871-3992
Fax: 513-871-5889
info@themotzgroup.com
www.themotzgroup.com
• Joseph Motz, President/Chief Executive Officer
• Mark Heinlein, Senior Vice President
• John Lill, MCC General Manager
• Zach A. Burns, President
Products:
Designs and constructs quality natural grass adn synthetic turf field systems.
Brands:
Pat®-Moisture Management System for sports fields, 24/7®-Infilled Synthetic Turf, HPG®-Custom Designed Field Systems, TS-II®-Synthetically Stabilized Natural Turf.

MOUNTAIN HARDWEAR
1414 HARBOR WAY S
SUITE 105
RICHMOND, CA 94804
510-558-3000
800-953-8375
877-927-5649
Fax: 510-559-6709
www.mountainhardwear.com
• Topher Gaylord, President
Products:
Manufacturer of men's and women's apparel and outdoor products like outerwear, sleeping bags, tents and other accessories.

MOUNTAIN HIGH HOSIERY, INC.
1791 W DAIRY PLACE
TUCSON, AZ 85705
800-528-5355
• Gerald Birin, Chief Executive Officer
Products:
Manufactures hosiery for men and women.

MOUNTAIN SAFETY RESEARCH
4000 1ST AVENUE S
SEATTLE, WA 98134
205-505-9500
800-531-9531
Fax: 206-682-4184
info@msrgear.com
https://www.msrgear.com/
• Dave Bartholomew, President / Chief Executive Officer
• Ken Meidell, VP
Products:
Manufacturer of Tents, Stoves & Fuel, Cookware, Hydration, Water Treatment, Packtowl, Snow Equipment, and Poles.

MOUNTED MEMORIES INC
5000 NW 108 AVENUE
SUNRISE, FL 33351
954-742-8544
800-749-7529
Fax: 954-742-7044
www.mountedmemories.com
Products:
An industry leader in sports memorabilia collectibles and acrylic cases. Line of products include baseballs, footballs, basketballs, jerseys and other hand-signed memorabilia.

MOVING COMFORT, INC.
19910 N CREEK PARKWAY
SUITE 200
BOTHELL, WA 98011-8223
800-763-6000
Fax: 425-489-1975
www.movingcomfort.com
• Ellen Wessel, President
Products:
Offers a variety of women's sport bras, sport underwear, shorts, tops, tights and outerwear for running, hiking, walking, weight training, yoga, martial arts, kayaking, skiing and snowshoeing, rock climbing, horseback riding, golf, tennis, basketball, volleyball, soccer, inline skating, etc.

MPC PROMOTIONS
4300 PRODUCE ROAD
LOUISVILLE, KY 40218
502-451-4900
800-331-0989
Fax: 888-451-8475
customerservice@mpcpromotions.com
www.mpcpromotions.com
• Donald V Dobina, President
Products:
Producer of top quality promotional products that can be customized with company logo for promotions, advertising incentives, trade shows, business gifts and employee recognition programs. MPC also designs corporate incentive and licensed apparel programs.

MTC MARKETING INC
1624 WEST CROSBY ROAD
CARROLLTON, TX 75006
972-488-0577
800-295-4995
Fax: 972-488-8595
customerservice@mtcmarketinginc.com
• Odalis Perez, Administrative Assistant
(972) 488-0577
adalis@mtcmarketing.com
Products:
Manufacturer of Sports Jackets and Caps.

MUELLER SPORTS MEDICINE, INC.
ONE QUENCH DRIVE
PO BOX 99
PRAIRIE DU SAC, WI 53578
608-643-8530
800-356-9522
Fax: 608-643-2568
sportcare@muellersportsmed.com
www.muellersportsmed.com
• Brett Mueller, President
• Curt Mueller, Chief Executive Officer
• Herb Raschka, Senior Vice President
• Rick Olson, National Sporting Goods Sales Manager
• Jeff Mueller, VP
• Jane Volts, National Key Account Rep
Products:
Abrasion Control/Padding, Analgesics, Blood spill/Biohazard Products, Bottles & Bottle Carriers, Braces & Supports, Cleaners/Disinfectants, Cold/Hot Therapy, Grip Enhancers, Mouthguards, Protective Gear, Quench Sports Gum, Sports Accessories, Tapes & Wraps, Trainers Kits
Nature of Service:
Manufacture and distribute complete line of Sports Medicine Products worldwide.
Brands:
No Glare, M-Tape, M-Wrap, Quench, Sport

Care, Hg80 (Mueller Mercury), ATF Ankle Brace, and Whizzer

MULTI-AD
1720 W DETWEILLER DRIVE
PEORIA, IL 61615
309-692-1530
800-348-6485
Fax: 309-692-8378
info@multiad.com
www.multi-ad.com
• Brian Jeske, Vice President, Sports Operations
(770) 421-6461
bjeske@multiad.com
• Joe Dalfonso, Sports Consultant
(800) 348-6485
jdalfonso@multiad.com
• Ron Fauss, Sports Consultant
(309) 648-0531
rfauss@multiad.com
Year Founded:
1945
Sports Service Founded:
1990
Description:
Sports printer specializing in programs, media guides, trading cards, promotional material. Design, mailing and warehouse services offered as well.

MURREY INTERNATIONAL
14150 S FIGUEROA STREET
LOS ANGELES, CA 90061
310-532-6091
800-421-1022
Fax: 310-217-0504
sales@murreybowling.com
www.murreybowling.com
• Patrick Murrey, President
Products:
Bowling Lanes, Seats, Ball Returns, Combo Tables, Food Court Tables, Masking Units, Rack 'N Rolls, Graphics, Pinsetting Machines, Rental Shoes.

MUSCO SPORTS-LIGHTING
100 1ST AVENUE W
PO BOX 808
OSKALOOSA, IA 52577
641-673-0411
800-825-6030
Fax: 641-673-4852
lighting@musco.com
www.musco.com
• Joe Crookham, President
joe.crookham@musco.com
• Jeanie Bieri, Director, Marketing
• Heidi Tegtmeier, Partnership Program Manager
heidi.tegtmeier@musco.com
Products:
Lighting for Sports Fields.

MYLEC, INC.
37 COMMERCIAL DRIVE
WINCHENDON, MA 1475
978-297-0089
Fax: 978-297-1359
berdmann@mylec.com
www.mylec.com
• Ricky Laperriere, President
(978) 297-0089
ricky@mylec.com
• Ken Cashman, Vice President
(978) 297-0089

Products:
Street Hockey - Balls, Goals, Flooring, Protective Equipment, Sticks and Blades.

N CASE IT
19 INDUSTRIAL DRIVE
PACIFIC, MO 63069
636-257-6655
800-536-6655
Fax: 636-257-0531
support@ncaseit.com
www.ati-1.com
• Keith Skubic, Area Sales Representative
(636) 257-6655
keith.skubic@ati-1.com
• Vicki Stone, Area Sales Representative
(636) 257-6655
vicki.stone@ati-1.com
• Thomas C. White, President
• Dave Ambrose, Sales
(636) 257-8929
• Jeff Novak, Outside Sales
(415) 665-6934
jeff.novak@ati-1.com
Products:
Largest stocking distributor/fabricator of thermosets and thermoplastics.

N.J.P. SPORTS, INC.
548 W ARDEN AVENUE
GLENDALE, CA 91203
818-247-3914
800-773-4657
Fax: 818-247-2605
njpsports@earthlink.net
www.njpsports.com
• Norman J. Perry, President
(818) 247-3914
njpsports@earthlink.net
• Regina Perry, VP
(818) 247-3914
njpsports@earthlink.net
Products:
Fabricates and installs windscreens, netting, and other items related to tennis, baseball, and sports. Provides builders with tennis posts, sleeves and other court items.

NASH MANUFACTURING INC
315 W RIPY STREET
PO BOX 11526
FORT WORTH, TX 76110
817-926-5223
800-433-2901
Fax: 817-924-5111
help@nashmfg.com
• Russ Miller, President
Products:
Manufactures skateboards, waterboards, bodyboards, waterskis and wakeboards.

NATARE CORPORATION
5905 W 74TH STREET
INDIANAPOLIS, IN 46278-1786
317-290-8828
800-336-8828
Fax: 317-290-9998
natare@natare.com
www.natare.com
• Michael Walsh, President
(800) 336-8828
• David L. Keim, VP
• Scott C. Calwell, Natare Product Manager
(800) 336-8828
scalwell@natare.com
Products:
Seen as one of the world's most respected

manufacturers and suppliers in the pool industry, Natare offers equipment, complete systems, and services for commercial and public swimming pools, water parks, and aquatic facilities. Our products and systems include stainless steel pools and spas, PVC pool membrane lining, pool gutters, filtration systems, bulkheads, and more.

NATIONAL BATTING CAGES, INC
PO BOX 250
FOREST GROVE, OR 97116-0250
800-547-8800
Fax: 503-357-3727
sales@nationalbattingcages.com
www.nationalbattingcages.com
• Fred Schmidtke, President
(503) 357-6615
Products:
Manufacturer of baseball equipment such as Portable Batting Cages, Batting Tunnel Nets, Protective Screens, Batting Tunnel Frames, Pitching Mounds, Windscreen Stadium Netting, Accessories, Pitching Machines, Outdoor Support Frame, and Hitting Cages.

NATIONAL EMBLEM INC
17036 S AVALON BOULEVARD
PO BOX 5325
CARSON, CA 90746-5325
310-515-5055
800-877-6185
Fax: 310-515-5966
bids@nationalemblem.com
www.nationalemblem.com
• David Wilson, Regional Sales Executive
Products:
Manufacturer of custom embroidered emblems, flags, baseball caps, key rings and woven labels for Major League Baseball, National Football League, NBA and NHL.

NATIVE SUN SPORTSWEAR
4590 62ND AVENUE N
PINELLAS PARK, FL 33781
727-528-2111
800-777-5800
Fax: 727-528-8441
info@nativesunsports.com
www.nativesunsports.com
• George A. Mitcheson, President
(727) 528-2111
info@nativesunsports.com
Products:
Caps and Visors, T-Shirts, Lapel Pins, Polos, and Wind Jackets.

NATURAL BALANCE, INC.
3130 N COMMERCE COURT
CASTLE ROCK, CO 80109
800-833-8737
800-624-4260
Fax: 800-661-9890
www.naturalbalance.com
• Mark Owens, Founder
• Caroline Owens, Founder
Products:
Producer of quality herbal and natural products, nutritional supplements for athletes.

NATURAL SPORT
8300 MARYLAND AVENUE
PO BOX 29
SAINT LOUIS, MO 63105
314-854-4000
800-766-6465
Fax: 314-854-2037
www.brownsshoecompany.com
• Ronald A. Fromm, Chairman and Chief Executive Officer
(314) 854-4000
• Diane M. Sullivan, President
• Kenneth W. Gilberton, President
• Richard C. Schumacher, VP
Products:
A leading consumer-driven footwear company and a marketer and supplier of branded, private label and licensed footwear to department stores, mass-merchandisers, independent and specialty stores.

NAUTICA INTERNATIONAL
40 W 57TH STREET
NEW YORK, NY 10019
866-376-4184
Fax: 212-887-8136
www.nautica.com
• Zach Augustine, Vice President/Creative Services Director
• Anne Lacombe, Vice President Marketing
Boating/Yachting:
2003 Dennis Conner Stars & Stripes.

NAUTILUS HPS, INC.
17750 SE 6TH WAY
VANCOUVER, WA 98683
360-859-2900
800-782-4799
800-605-3369
Fax: 360-694-7755
sales@nautilus.com
www.nautilusgroup.com
• Gregg Hammann, President and Chief Executive Officer
• Bill Meadowcroft, Chief Financial Officer
• Tim Hawkins, Chief Customer Officer & Chief Marketing
• Darryl Thomas, SVP, Strategic Planning and Internationa
Products:
Provides tools and education necessary to help people achieve a fit and healthy lifestyle. Manufactures and markets a complete line of innovative health and fitness products through direct, commercial, retail, specialty and international channels.

NCED SAHARA
12100 ESTHER LAMA DRIVE
EL PASO, TX 79936
915-833-1145
800-669-5646
Fax: 800-473-4190
• Robert E. Jones, President and Chief Executive Officer
• Ernie Lopez, VP / Chief Operations Officer
• Brian Keiser, Chief Financial Officer
• Steve Wilson, General Manager
Products:
T-Shirts and Sweatshirts, Warm-Ups, Windshirts, Jackets, Caps and Hats, and Bags

NCR
6060 PRIMACY PARKWAY
SUITE 460
MEMPHIS, TN 38119

901-681-2800
800-852-5852
Fax: 901-681-2802
www.counterpointpos.com
• Andee Pure Williamson, Marketing Manager
(901) 681-2800
andee.williamson@radiantsystems.com
• Mike Phelan, Marketing Analyst
(901) 681-2800
mike.phelan@radiantsystems.com
• Joanna Cravens, Account Manager
(901) 681-2800
joanna.cravens@radiantsystems.com
• Beverly Emerson, Account Manager
(901) 681-2800
beverly.emerson@radiantsystems.com
Products:
CounterPoint Point of sale/inventory management software and accompanying services include CPOnline (integrated Ecommerce package) and CPGateway (2-second card processing)

NDL PRODUCTS, INC.
4031 NE 12 TERRACE
OAKLAND PARK, FL 33334
954-566-0040
800-979-4343
Fax: 954-568-6906
• Joseph Giaquinto, President
(954) 566-0040
Products:
Sports medicine and health care products for the mass-merchant, chain drug and chain food national distribution channels. NDL's collection of brands service specific segments of the sporting goods and health care markets with its sports medicine, protective gear, health supports and magnetic therapy products. NDL also offers private label or house brand programs to major retailers and large wholesalers along with specific OEM programs to outside brands that service the same markets.

NEFF - DEALER DIVISION
645 PINE STREET
PO BOX 218
GREENVILLE, OH 45331
937-548-3194
800-232-6333
Fax: 800-544-9030
www.neffco.com
• Bruce Hines, President
• Micky Sullivan, Athletic Director
Products:
Offers a comprehensive line of awards that includes Plaques, Chenille Letters, Medals, Certificates, Banners, and more, including staff and student apparel, Letter Jackets, and custom scholastic graphics.

NEIL ENTERPRISES
450 E BUNKER COURT
VERNON HILLS, IL 60061
847-549-7627
800-621-5584
Fax: 847-549-0349
info@neilenterprises.com
www.neilenterprises.com
• Neil Fine, President
(847) 549-7627
nfine@neilenterprises.com
• Ted Swiss, Sales Manager
(847) 549-7627
• Micheal Sheck, VP

Products:
Promotional product/photo novelty manufacturer and also a supplier/distributor of Sony Printers and Media. Manufactures a proprietary line of Easy Snapins which can be assembled on the spot. Included are buttons, key tags, mugs, resin sports frames, memory notes, sponsor plaques, water bottles, metal button machines and much more.
Year Founded:
1961

NET RESULTS SPORTS MARKETING/NRSM INC.
3405 OAK STREET
Chicago, IL, 60606
MYRTLE BEACH, SC 29577
843-916-8218
Fax: 843-916-8210
info@netsportsplus.com
www.netsportsplus.com
• Max Davis, President
Nature of Service:
Sports Construction: Includes Paving, Sports Lighting, Sports Fencing, Sport Specific Accessories and Landscaping. Specialize in Tennis Courts, Basketball Courts and Running tracks. Certified Professionals for all applications and projects. Windscreens, Fence Capping, Custom Logos, Sports Netting and Sports Padding for indoor and outdoor applications. Seating (Benches, Custom Sports Seating, Bleachers and Stadium Seating). Also we can supply and install high tech Shade Structures for all types of seating applications. Tennis Accessories: Clay Court Equipment and Supplies, Courts Awning and Cabanas, Nets and Net Posts, and Teaching Equipment.

NEUEDGE SPORTSWEAR
8 CORPORATE BOULEVARD
SINKING SPRING, PA 19068
610-678-4050
800-486-2788
Fax: 610-678-4040
Products:
Manufacturer of uniforms for basketball, soccer, softball and volleyball

NEUMANN & COMPANY, R.
300 OBSERVER HIGHWAY
PO BOX MD
HOBOKEN, NJ 7030
201-659-3400
800-372-4141
Fax: 201-659-6655
• Richard Bernheim, President
Products:
Golf - Leather Grips; Tennis - Leather Grips

NEVCO
301 E HARRIS AVENUE
GREENVILLE, IL 62246-2151
618-664-0360
800-851-4040
Fax: 618-664-0398
sales@nevco.com
www.nevco.com
• Scott Moore, VP Sales & Marketing
• Gary Robert, President and COO
• Paul R. Peterson, Marketing Manager
(800) 851-4040
ppeterson@nevco.com

Products:
Scoreboards for Baseball/Softball, Basketball, Football, Hockey, Soccer, Swimming, Track, Volleyball, Wrestling; Video Displays, Accessories, Signage, Controls, Shot Clocks/Timers

NEVER SUMMER SNOWBOARDS
5077 COLORADO BOULEVARD
DENVER, CO 80216
303-320-1813
Fax: 303-320-0771
info@neversummer.com
www.neversummer.com
• Nick Giancamilli, President
Products:
Snowboards and Clothing

NEW AGENDA BY PERRIN
5320 RUSCHE DRIVE
COMSTOCK PARK, MI 49321
616-785-9091
800-243-6361
Fax: 616-785-9312
canderson@perrinwear.com
www.perrinwear.com
• Todd Dufford, National Sales Manager
(800) 243-6326
Products:
Apparel: Athletic, Children's, Imprinted, Licensed Collegiate apparel, Screen Print and Embroidery.
Year Founded:
1992

NEW BALANCE ATHLETIC SHOE, INC.
BRIGHTON LANDING 20 GUEST STREET
BOSTON, MA 02135-2088
617-783-4000
800-595-9138
Fax: 617-787-9355
info@newbalance.com
www.newbalance.com
• James S. Davis, Chairman and Chief Executive Officer
• Jim Tompkins, President and Chief Operating Officer
Products:
Footwear, Apparel, Accessories and Equipment for all Sports, including Basketball, Outdoor Sports, Hiking, Racquet Sports, Track & Field, Volleyball, Golf, Baseball, Tennis, Football, Training

NEW ENGLAND CAP CO.
756 DERBY AVENUE
SEYMOUR, CT 6483
203-736-6184
Fax: 203-732-5105
service@newenglandcap.com
www.newenglandcap.com
• Eric Black, Operations Manager
Products:
Clothing, Hats, Caps, Jackets, T-shirts

NEW ERA CAP, CO
160 DELAWARE AVENUE
BUFFALO, NY 14202
716-604-9000
877-NEC-5950
Fax: 716-604-9299
www.neweracap.com
• Gary Matos, Senior Vice President, Marketing
ext 1169
• John DeWaal, Vice President, Global

Marketing
 ext 1137
john.dewaal@neweracap.com
• Jim Wannemacher, Vice President,
Advertising
 ext 1286
jim.wannemacher@neweracap.com
• Dana Marciniak, Manager, Corporate
Communications
(716) 604-9259
dana.marciniak@neweracap.com
• Katherine Kulczyk, Media Contact
 ext 1463
katherine.kulczyk@neweracap.com
Products:
Manufacturer of sports-licensed headwear.

NEW HERMES INC.
2200 NORTHMONT PARKWAY
DULUTH, GA 30096
770-623-0331
800-543-7637
800-533-7637
Fax: 770-814-7203
www.gravograph.us
• Ben Anderson-Ray, Chief Executive
Officer
• Gerard Guyard, Chairman
Products:
Manufacturer of engraving machines,
marking equipment, signage and other
engraving products.

NEW YORK EMBLEMS & AWARDS, INC.
4644 ELEVENTH STREET
3RD FLOOR
LONG ISLAND CITY, NY 11101
718-786-8852
Fax: 718-786-8857
• David Srebnik, President
Products:
Trophies, Awards - Components, Emblems,
Jewelry, Medals, Plaques, Ribbons

NEWSOUTH ATHLETIC COMPANY INC.
301 E MAIN STREET
PO BOX 604
DALLAS, NC 28034
704-922-1557
800-438-9934
Fax: 704-922-5324
• Randy Harris, VP and Chief Operating
Officer
Products:
Softball and Baseball Pants, Jerseys and
Accessories

NEWTEX USA
8050 VICTOR MENDON ROAD
VICTOR, NY 14564
585-924-9135
800-836-1001
Fax: 585-924-4645
sales@newtex.com
www.newtex.com
• Doug Bailey, President
(716) 909-3477
Products:
Manufacturer of high-tech, heat resistant
products for the industrial and safety
markets.

NGI SPORTS
2807 WALKER ROAD
CHATTANOOGA, TN 37421

423-499-5546
800-835-0033
Fax: 423-499-8882
info@ngisports.com
www.ngisports.com
• Rick Burke, Owner/Manager/CEO/COO
• David Burke, East Coast Sales
• Terri West, Office Manager/Sales &
Service
• Corey Brisbin, Western States
Sales/Technical Manager
Products:
Synthetic Turf Surfaces for Golf, Soccer,
Tennis, and Field Sports.
Brands:
Nova Pro Court XP; Nova Pro Bouncer;
Nova Pro Clay; Nova Pro Xtreme; Titan Trax
Shield

**NICKLAUS GOLF EQUIPMENT
COMPANY, L.C.**
951 US HIGHWAY ONE
SUITE 500
NORTH PALM BEACH, FL 33408
561-691-3434
800-322-1872
Fax: 561-227-0548
contact@nicklausgolf.com
www.nicklaus-golf.com
• Jack Nicklaus, Chairman
• Robert P. Kelly, Chief Executive Officer
• Robert Cook, Chief Financial Officer
• William Henwood, Chief Sales and
Marketing Officer
Products:
Golf Clubs

NIELSEN-KELLERMAN
21 CREEK PARKWAY
BOOTHWYN, PA 19061
610-447-1555
800-784-4221
Fax: 610-447-1577
info@nkhome.com
www.nkhome.com
• Richard Kellerman, President
• Katie Gofrey, Kastrel Sales Manager
khorn@nkhome.com
Nature of Service:
Provides electronic equipment for the United
States Rowing team.

NIELSEN-KELLERMAN
21 CREEK CIRCLE
BOOTHWYN, PA 19061
610-447-1555
800-784-4221
Fax: 610-447-1577
info@nkhome.com
www.nkhome.com
• Katie Horn, Kastrel Sales Manager
khorn@nkhome.com
• Chris Mesigian, Internal Sales Manager,
Rowing
• Michael Naughton, Product Manager
mnaughton@nkhome.com
• Richard Kellerman, President
• Paul Nielsen, VP
• Alix Kocher, Administrator
• Alix James, Marketing
Products:
Rowing/Padding Equipment, Wind/Weather
Instruments, Interval Timing Systems,
Watches, and other Waterproof Intruments
for active lifestyles and technical
applications

NIGHT SPORTS
952-935-9140
800-933-7825
Fax: 952-935-9142
info@nightsportsusa.com
www.nightsportsusa.com
• John Gill, President
• David Shirley, European Office
davidshirley@nightsportsuk.com
Products:
Glow in the dark golf/mini putt balls.

NIKE GOLF
ONE BOWERMAN DRIVE
BEAVERTON, OR 97005
503-671-6453
Fax: 503-671-6376
info@nike.com
www.nikegolf.com
• Bob Wood, President
• David Pillsbury, U.S. General Manager
• John Springer, Director, General
Operations
Products:
Golf apparel, footwear, headwear, balls, and
bags

NIKE, INC.
ONE BOWERMAN DRIVE
BEAVERTON, OR 97005-6453
503-671-6453
800-344-6453
Fax: 503-646-6926
www.nike.com
• Philip H. Knight, Chairman
• Mark Parker, President and Chief
Executive Officer
• David Ayre, EVP, Global Human
Resources
• Don Blair, EVP/Chief Financial Officer
• Trevor Edwards, President, Nike Brands
• Jeanne P Jackson, President, Product &
Merchandising
Products:
Sports footwear, apparel and equipment

**NIKON SPORTS & RECREATIONAL
OPTICS**
1300 WALT WHITMAN ROAD
MELVILLE, NY 11747-3064
631-547-4200
800-645-6678
Fax: 631-547-4025
www.nikonusa.com
• Toshiyuki Masai, Chief Executive Officer &
President
• David C. Lee, Senior VP
• Richard LoPinto, Senior VP Of Product
• Joseph Carfora, VP Of Sales
Products:
Photography Equipment, Binoculars,
Microscopes, Optical Instruments with
special features for use in the sports
industry.

NILS, INC.
3550 CADILLAC AVENUE
COSTA MESA, CA 92626
877-412-7467
800-933-6457
Fax: 866-756-4463
info@nils.us
www.nilsskiwear.com
• Lane Fowler, Marketing and Customer
Service Manager
• Nils Anderson, Owner & Chief Executive
Officer

Products:
Manufacturer and designer of Women's Skiwear and Sportswear.

NIRVE SPORTS
15401 ASSEMBLY LANE
HUNTINGTON BEACH, CA 92649
714-892-5795
888-296-4783
Fax: 714-963-6762
info@nirve.com
www.nirve.com
• Linda Reed, National Sales Manager
(714) 593-8301
Products:
Designer of collectible lifestyle cruiser and chopper bicycles, components, and accessories.

NO FAULT INDUSTRIES
3112 VALLEY CREEK DRIVE
SUITE C
BATON ROUGE, LA 70808
225-215-7760
866-637-7678
Fax: 225-291-3821
info@nofault.com
www.nofault.com
• David Brantley, President and Owner
(225) 215-7760
• Jennifer Smith, Vice President of Sales & Administration
(225) 215-7760
• Jay Ratelle, Vice President of Operations
Products:
Sport and Safety Surface Products, Rubber Mulch, Safety Tile, Sport Floor

NO FEAR
183 MADISON AVE
SUITE 1701
NEW YORK, NY 10016
760-931-9550
877-796-7842
Fax: 760-931-9741
www.nofear.com
• Larry Collette, President
• Anthony Miranda, Sports Marketing
Products:
General Sports Activewear, Athletic Footwear, T-shirts, Eyewear, Watches, Accessories

NOCONA ATHLETIC GOODS COMPANY
2650 SOUTH 46TH STREET
SUITE 105
PHOENIX, AZ 85034
602-381-5434
800-433-0957
Fax: 940-825-4994
info@nokona.com
www.nokona.com
• Robert M. Storey Jr, President
Products:
Baseball - Bases, Batting Helmets, Gloves/Catcher/Fielder/First Base, Protective-Catcher/Umpire; Football - Bags, Equipment, Helmets, Knee/Elbow Pads, Masks, Shields, Shoulder Pads; Softball - Bases, Gloves-Catcher/Fielder/First Base

NOLIMITZ
1265 NORTH MAIN
WHITE SALMON, WA 98672

509-493-4484 Ext 222
Fax: 509-493-4485
www.nolimitz.com
• Jason Lemieux, Recreational Sales & Marketing
Products:
Windsurfing masts

NORA SYSTEMS, INC.
9 NORTHEASTERN BLVD
SALEM, NH 03079
978-689-1021
800-332-6672
800-332-NORA
Fax: 603-894-6615
www.nora.com/us
• Christine Mousseau, Marketing Specialist
(978) 689-0530
christine.mousseau@nora.com
Description:
Durable rubber flooring in a wide range of colors and patterns to create appealing designs. Offering a high degree of slip resistance to ensure safe footing and low maintenance for floors that look as good as they perform.
Year Founded:
1986 (U.S.)
Products:
norament™ grano, norament™ 992
Brands:
norament™, noraplan™

NORDICA USA
VIA FANTE D'ITALIA 56
31040
GIAVERA DEL MONTELLO, TREVISO, ITALY 3784
+39-
800-892-2668
www.nordica.com
• Andy Knittle, President
• Wendy Reger, Marketing Communications Manager
• Kirk Langford, Vice President Sales
• Theresa Powell, Customer Service Manager
Products:
Skiing-Alpine - Accessories, Apparel, Boots, Gloves

NORDICTRACK
1500 S 1000 W
LOGAN, UT 84321
888-308-9616
877-993-7999
Fax: 435-786-3987
service@iconfitness.com
www.nordictrack.com
• Patrick J Hald, President/COO
• Michael Larson, VP, Sales
• Colleen Logan, VP, Marketing
Products:
Treadmills, Ellipticals, Exercise Bikes, Strength Training, Incline Trainers, Skiers, Steppers, Accessories, Men's Apparel, Women's Apparel, Jogging Strollers, Yoga, Relaxation, Pilates, Commercial Grade Equipment

NORSK FITNESS PRODUCTS, INC.
2100 SAINT PATRICK STREET
MONTREAL, QC, CANADA H3K 1B2
514-931-3635
800-667-7510
Fax: 514-932-2779

info@thera-p.com
www.thera-p.com
• Mark Chaimberg, Vice President
info@thera-p.com
• Eric Chaimberg, VP Graphic Design
echaimberg@swingpaints.com
Products:
Manufactures fitness products, including cold and heated compression wraps, and gel packs.
Year founded:
1993.

NORTH FACE
14450 DOOLITTLE DRIVE
SAN LEANDRO, CA 94577
888-863-1968
855-500-8639
Fax: 510-618-3531
tnf_consumerservices@vfc.com
www.thenorthface.com
• Steve Rendle, President
• Dan Templin, Chief Finnacial Officer
• Jody Kalmbach, VP, Marketing
• Dave Sweet, VP, Operations
Products:
Men's apparel, Women's Apparel, Footwear, Tents, Bags, Sleeping Bags, Accessories

NORTH SPORTS, INC.
1 N SHORE DRIVE SE
WHITE SALMON, WA 98672
509-493-4938
Fax: 509-493-4966
www.northsports.com
• David Johnson, President
• Aaron Carpenter, VP
Importer:
Sailboards, Snowboards.

NORTH STAR LIGHTING, INC.
835 INDUSTRIAL DRIVE
ELMHURST, IL 60126
708-681-4330
800-229-4330
Fax: 708-681-4006
www.northstar-lighting.com
• Sobit Inan, President
• Jeffrey Sanders, Marketing Manager
Products:
Sports lighting, Area lighting, Industrial lighting, Floodlighting, Roadway lighting, Commercial lighting, Poles and Accessories, Security Lighting, Tunnel Lighting, Marine & Hazardous lighting

NORTHERN LITES
300 S 86TH AVENUE
WAUSAU, WI 54401
715-848-0490
800-360-5483
Fax: 715-848-0386
www.northernlites.com
• Russell Post, Designer/Founder
• Charles Post, VP
Products:
Snowshoes

NORTHWESTERN GOLF COMPANY
835 N CHURCH COURT
ELMHURST, IL 60126
630-530-1424
800-224-6532
Fax: 630-530-1610
golf.ps@mcimail.com
www.proselectsports.com

• Brian Birkan, VP, Finance
Products:
Golf Bags for Clubs, Clubs-Iron or Wood Sets, Putters, Utility Clubs, Shafts.

NOVA SPORTS USA
6 INDUSTRIAL ROAD
BUILDING 2
MILFORD, MA 1757
508-473-6540
800-872-6682
Fax: 508-473-4077
bill@novasports.com
www.novasports.com
• Robert Righter, President
• Bill Righter, Chief Financial Officer
• Dave Commito, Operations Director
• Laurie Swanfeldt, Office/Credit Manager
• Jacob Righter, Director of Sales & Marketing
Products:
Surfacing for Inline Sports, Basketball, Tennis Courts; Repairs to Surfaces; Tennis Court Nets and Posts.

NTN COMMUNICATIONS, INC.
2231 RUTHERFORD RD
SUITE 200
CARLSBAD, CA 92008
877-963-9200
800-745-4686
Fax: 760-438-3505
www.buzztime.com
Products:
Sports trivia games.

NUMBERALLS
82 B MCKEE DRIVE
MAHWAH, NJ 7430
201-512-3338
888-788-7133
Fax: 201-512-3240
www.numberalls.com
Products:
Football, Baseball/Softball, Basketball, Soccer, Volleyball, Classic, Alphabet, Continental, Champion, Euro, One Color, Two Color, Mascot Rhinestone, Mascot Names, Sports Fans, Sports Sheets, Puff Glitter

NYX GOLF
15936 MIDWAY RD.
ADDISON, TX 75001
972-991-5511
800-505-4699
Fax: 972-385-8607
Sales@nyxgolf.com
www.nyxgolf.com
Products:
NYX Golf Vision System

O'BRIEN INTERNATIONAL
7926 BRACKEN PLACE SE
PO BOX 97087
SNOQUALMIE, WA 98065
425-202-2100
800-662-7436
Fax: 425-831-1052
customerservice@obrien.com
www.obrien.com
Products:
Water Sports - Gloves, Inflatables, Kneeboards, Personal Flotation, Ropes, Wakeboards, Water Skis.

O'NEILL, INC.
1071 41ST aVENUE
PO BOX 6300
SANTA CRUZ, CA 95063
866-663-4551
800-538-0764
INFO@ONEILL.COM
www.oneill.com
• Pat O'Neill, President
• Mark Tinkess, Director, Sales
Products:
Jackets, Bags, Full Suits(Cold-Frigid), Full suits (Warm-Cool), Rash & U.V. Guards, Spring Suits, Neoprene Tops & Bottoms, Boardshorts, Thermal Layering, Walkshorts, Hoods, Knits & Wovens, Gloves, Boots, Denim, Tees, Footwear

OAKLEY, INC.
ONE ICON
FOOTHILL RANCH, CA 92610
949-951-0991
800-403-7449
Fax: 949-699-3500
customercare@oakley.com
www.oakley.com
• Colin Baden, CEO
Products:
Sunglasses, Wearable Electronics, Apparel, Watches, Footwear, Bags & Backpacks, Goggles, Prescription Eyewear, Towels, Stickers, Posters, Keychains, Lanyards, Medusa, Umbrellas, Videos

OCEAN HOCKEY SUPPLY COMPANY
197 CHAMBERS BRIDGE ROAD
BRICKTOWN, NJ 08723-3492
732-477-4411
800-631-2159
Fax: 732-477-1167
info@oceanhockey.com
www.oceanhockey.com
• Joan Dwulet, President
Products:
Helmets; Facemasks; Throat & Neck Guards; Shoulder Pads; Elbow Pads; Gloves; Jocks; Pants/Girdles; Shin Guards; Senior Skates; Junior/Youth Skates; Figure/Recreational Skates; Chest & Arm; Catch Gloves; Blockers; Goal Pads; Sr Sticks/Shafts; Intermediate/ Junior/ Youth Sticks; Goal Sticks; Senior Blades; Junior Blades; Bags; Performance Wear; Jerseys/Hose; Apparel; Roller Hockey; Referee; Gifts/Games; Accessories.

OCEAN PACIFIC APPAREL CORPORATION
3 STUDEBAKER
IRVINE, CA 92618
949-580-1888
Fax: 949-580-1870
www.op.com
• Michael Marcky, VP, Marketing and Advertising
• Richard A. D. Baker, Chairman
• Jim Jenks, Founder
• Ute Pelzer, Chief Financial Officer
Products:
Product lines: Swimwear & Beachwear, Coats, Sportswear, Accessories, Outerwear, Resort Wear, Luggage & Travel Goods, Jackets, Hair Accessories, Hats & Caps, Jeans, Dresses Casual, Skirts, Size - Young Mens, dresses, Headwear, Skiwear, Jog Suits, Pants & Trousers, T Shirts, Knitwear

& Sweaters, Shorts, Shirts & Blouses, Athleticwear, Sweaters.

OCEANIC USA
2002 DAVIS STREET
SAN LEANDRO, CA 94577
510-562-0500
800-435-3483
Fax: 510-569-5404
hello@oceanicusa.com
www.oceanicworldwide.com
• Robert Hollis, CEO
• Paul Elsinga, Chief Financial Officer
• Nestor A. Palmero, VP
Products:
Regulators, Computers, Gauges, BCDs, Masks, Snorkels, Fins, Boots, Gloves, Hoods, Wetsuits, Bags, Knives, Lights, Vehicles, Safety Devices, Snorkeling, H2O Audio.

OCEANTIS SPORTS
12362 BEACH BOULEVARD
SUITE 14D
STANTON, CA 90680
239-217-3150
855-772-6269
Fax: 714-889-7066
• Chuck Flathers, Vice President Of Sales (360) 808-1861
chuckflathers@oceantis.com
Products:
Wholesaler of bodyboards, skimboards, soft surfboards and kickboards.

OFF THE WALL PRODUCTS, LLC
PO BOX 1461
SALT LAKE CITY, UT 84110
801-363-7740
877-659-7245
Fax: 801-363-6372
www.multi-barrier.com
• Judd Grayzel, Marketing & Sales Manager judd@multi-barrier.com
• Marc Christensen, Managing Member marc@multi-barrier.com
Products:
Specializes in plastic water ballast and crowd-control barricades, including construction barricades, roadway barricades, airport barricades, event barricade, and military use barricades.

OKLAHOMA LEATHER PRODUCTS, INC.
500 26TH STREET NW
MIAMI, OK 74354
918-542-6651
Fax: 918-542-4340
• Richard Platt, President
Products:
Single Action and Black Powder Holsters, Cartridge Belts, and Accessories; Tool Pouches and Holders.

OLD KENTUCKY LEATHERS
125 CALDWELL STREET
AUBURN, KY 42206-0338
270-542-7107
800-635-0617
Fax: 270-586-4100
www.auburnleather.com
• Lisa Howlett, President
Products:
Leather dyeing and retanning and leather products and accessories for a variety of sports.

OLD TIME SPORTS
10 FANARAS DRIVE
SALISBURY, MA 1952
978-499-1844
888-829-2400
Fax: 978-499-3844
Questions@oldtimesports.com
www.oldtimesports.com
Products:
Team Hats, Team Tees, Sweatshirts, Stanley Cap, NHL League, Team Women's Tees, Team Graphics, Garments for Men, Women, and Youth.

OLYMPIA SPORTS
5 BRADLEY DRIVE
WESTBROOK, ME 4092
207-854-2794
Fax: 207-854-4168
www.olympiasports.net
• Dick Coffey, President
• Ed Manganello, Chairman
Products:
Sports equipment, fitness equipment and apparel, athletic footwear, popular sports/leisure wear and accessories.

OLYMPIA SPORTS COMPANY, INC.
500 EXECUTIVE BOULEVARD
ELMSFORD, NY 10523
914-347-4737
800-645-6124
Fax: 914-347-2029
www.olympiagloves.com
• Fred Heumann, Chairman
• Roger Heumann, President
• Paul Janis, Administration
Products:
Manufacturer of quality performance sports gloves.

OLYMPIA TROPHY COMPANY
605 FORREST DRIVE
HAGERSTOWN, MD 21742
301-739-5811
888-448-1305
800-957-6604
Fax: 301-739-8955
olympiatrophy@myactv.net
www.olympiatc.com
• Charles L. Kight, President
Products:
Dash Plaques, Trophies and Awards

OLYMPIC OPTICAL COMPANY
123 EXPLORER STREET
POMONA, CA 91768
909-468-3636
800-423-4277
Fax: 909-468-3640
www.jacksonsafety.com
• Winston Wolfe, President
• Jim McCarty, VP, Sales
• Freida Bushart, National Sales Manager, Key Accounts
• Tom Burns, President & CEO
Products:
Manufacturer of safety eyewear and hearing protection products.

OMEGA GEAR INC
2437 COYLE STREET
BROOKLYN, NY 11235
718-743-7740
866-400-6342

Products:
Kick Shields/Mitts/Pads, Martial Arts Uniforms, Boxing Gloves, Boxing Equipment, Mixed Martial Arts Gloves, Head Guard, Kickboxing Gear, Kickboxing Pants/Shorts, Punching Bags/Balls, and Accessories.

OMEGA MARINE PRODUCTS
18 HALLOCK MEADOW DRIVE
STONY BROOK, NY 11790
631-246-9082
800-966-6342
Fax: 631-246-9084
• Rosemary Gubista, Owner
Products:
Transportation Equipment and Supplies

OMNI BODYWORK
50 O'CONNELL WAY
EAST TAUNTON, MA 2718
508-824-2444
800-448-6664
Fax: 508-822-6030
sales@omnils.com
www.omnils.com
• Richard D Nikolaev, Chairman of the Board
• George B. B. Cipolletti, President & CEO
• David L. LaSalle, Chief Operations Officer
• Edward J. Cheal, Chief Science Officer
• James V. Barrile, Chief Financial Officer
Products:
Designer, manufacturer and distributor of high quality orthotic devices. Also a leader in knee bracing and measurement systems.

ONFIELD APPAREL
8677 LOGO ATHLETIC COURT
INDIANAPOLIS, IN 46219
317-895-7000
Fax: 317-895-7252
• David Baxter, President and Chief Executive Officer
• Edward Ed White, VP, Marketing
Products:
Manufacturer of uniforms, sweatsuits, performance apparel and accessories for professional teams of the NBA, NFL, NHL, and other sports leagues.

ONFIELD APPAREL GROUP, LLC HEADWARE DIVISION
5 INDUSTRIAL DRIVE
MATTAPOISETT, MA 02739-1300
508-758-6101
800-453-3341
Fax: 508-758-3298
• Rick Bednarz, VP, Sales
Products:
Licensed Headwear.

ONPOINT VISUALS
325 POGY PLACE BLDG. B6
FERNANDIAN BEACH, FL 32034
904-206-3299
Fax: 904-491-1286
www.tradeshowsensations.com
• George Nicholas, General Manager
(866) 860-1892
gnicholas@onpointvisuals.com
• Bill Anderson, Director Marketing/Business Development
(866) 860-1892
banderson@onpointvisuals.com

Nature of Service:
Custom Large Format Graphics/Trade Show Displays
Year Founded:
1892
Products:
Manufacturer of quality, custom large-format graphics such as trade show displays, signage, indoor/outdoor banners on fabric and vinyl substrates, also offer a line of hardware that includes a variety of mounting systems, displays, pop-up tents, and Tension Fabric Structures.
Brands:
onPoint visuals

OOLTEWAH MANUFACTURING COMPANY
5722 MAIN STREET
PO BOX 587
OOLTEWAH, TN 37363
423-238-5388
Fax: 423-238-5387
chuck@ooltewah.com
www.ooltewah.com
• Chuck Daniels, President
chuck_daniels@ooltewah.com
Products:
Wholesale distributor of Medical Soft Goods, Bathroom Mats, and other products. Also specializes in Motorcycle Equipment sales, and Web Design.

THE ORIGINAL BALL BAG LLC
125 INDUSTRIAL WAY
COSTA MESA, CA 92627
949-548-2277
Fax: 949-722-1370
sales@ballbag.com
www.ballbag.com
• Doug Rugg, President & CEO
Products:
Official NBA Licensee: NBA Ball Bag, NBA Team logoed BallBags, NBA Jersey Pack, Transporter; BallBags and Packs for all major sports, including baseball, soccer, tennis, football, volleyball, and water polo; a complete line of Golf Bags and accessories with NBA and NBA Team logos.

ORIGINAL MAPLE BAT COMPANY
110 INDUSTRIAL AVE
SUITE 2
CARLETON PLACE, ONTARIO, CANADA
K7C 3T2
613-257-3060
888-726-2287
Fax: 613-257-8577
bats@sambat.com
www.sambat.com
• Sam Holman, Founder
• Arlene Anderson, President
abaca@sambat.com
• Blair Quinn, National Sales Manager
quinnitr@rogers.com
• Lee Carswell, Sales
lcarswell@sambat.com
• Alisa Luoma, Head Office Sales
alisa@sambat.com
Products:
Manufacturer of baseball bats.

ORION ROPEWORKS
953 BENTON AVENUE
WINSLOW, ME 4901
888-537-7673
888- 537-7673

Fax: 888-412-7763
sales@orionropeworks.com
• Floyd Kierstead, Vice President Industrial
Products
(800) 848-4405
fkierstead@orionropeworks.com
• Floyd Kierstead, Vice President Industrial
Products
Products:
Bulk rope for netting applications, dock and
anchor lines.

ORLIMAR GOLF COMPANY
G-5140 FLUSHING ROAD
FLUSHING, MI 48433
810-732-0454
888-502-4653
Fax: 810-732-6662
custserv@kingpar.com
www.orlimar.com
• William J. Baird, Chief Executive Officer
custserv@orlimar.com
• Ryan Coffler, Controller
custserv@orlimar.com
• L. Toups, Operations Manager
custserv@orlimar.com
• John Runyon, President
Products:
Golf Clubs - Iron or Wood Sets, Putters.

OSSUR AMERICAS
27412 ALISO VIEJO PARKWAY
ALISO VIEJO, CA 92656
949-382-3883
800-223-6263
Fax: 800-831-3160
ossurusa@ossur.com
www.ossur.com
• Jon Sigurdsson, President/CEO
• Jon Sigurosson, President and Chief
Executive Officer
Products:
Knee, Foot & Ankle, Upper Extremity
Braces, Suppport & Accessories

OT SPORTS
172 BOONE STREET
BURLINGTON, NC 27215
336-222-8774
800-988-6285
Fax: 336-227-5116
info@otsports.com
www.otsports.com
• Scott Gollnick, VP Sales/Marketing
(336) 222-9774
scott@otsports.com
Products:
Products include: baseball, basketball,
football, hockey, socccer and lacrosse
jerseys
Year Founded:
1994
Brands:
OT Sports, Brine

OTOMIX ATHLETIC GEAR
7585 COMMERCIAL WAY
SUITE E
HENDERSON, NV 89011
otomix7@aol.com
www.otomix.com
• Mitchell Bobrow, President
• Nancy Barrett, VP, National Sales
otomix3@aol.com
• Belinda Field, International Sales
Products:
General Sports Footwear, Fitness/Street

Active Apparel, Training/Martial Arts
Accessories, Wrestling Footwear.

PACIFIC CYCLE, LLC
4902 HAMMERSLEY ROAD
MADISON, WI 53711
608-268-2468
800-666-8813
Fax: 608-268-2466
info@pacific-cycle.com
www.pacificcycle.com
• Byron Smith, President / Chief Operating
Officer
Products:
Bicycles and accessories for the cyclist.

PACIFIC TRAIL
1700 WESTLAKE AVENUE N
SUITE 200
SEATTLE, WA 98109
206-270-5300
800-622-6953
Fax: 206-270-5301
Info@pacifictrail.com
www.columbia.com
• Gary E Hansen, President
• Todd Gilmer, Marketing Manager
Products:
Casual Outerwear, Active Outerwear and
Performance Outerwear. Ski and
Snowboard Apparel.

PADDLE COMPANY INC
27 E BROAD STREET
HOPEWELL, NJ 8525
609-466-8000
Fax: 609-466-8834
Products:
Tennis paddles

PADDLE TRAMPS MFG. COMPANY
1317 UNIVERSITY AVENUE
LUBBOCK, TX 79401
806-765-9901
Fax: 806-763-9148
sales@paddletramps.com
www.paddletramps.com
• Thomas Abraham, Owner
Products:
Manufacturer and wholesaler of decorative
wood products and paddles custom
designed with sports logos and other
information.

PAIGE DESIGN GROUP
5 PEARSE WYND ROAD
BAHAMA, NC 27503
919-451-1641
Fax: 919-620-0091
dpaige@paigedesigngroup.com
www.paigedesigngroup.com

PARAGON SPORTS
2300 E WALNUT AVENUE
FULLERTON, CA 92831
714-870-1900
800-722-4061
Fax: 714-870-1921
www.mitsushiba.com
• Richard Tcheng, President
Products:
Golf - Club Components, Shafts.

PARAMOUNT FITNESS CORPORATION
6450 E BANDINI BOULEVARD
LOS ANGELES, CA 90040
323-721-2121
800-721-2121
Fax: 323-724-2000
www.paramountfitness.com
• Steve Rhodes, President
• Jim McIntyre, Vice President of Sales &
Marketing
Products:
Training & Conditioning - Benches, Single
and Multi Station Exercise Machines.

PARAMOUNT HEADWEAR, INC.
1 PARAMOUNT DRIVE
BOURBON, MO 65441
573-732-4411
800-255-4287
Fax: 573-732-5211
www.paramountapparel.com
• Bruce Levinson, Vice Chairman/Chief
Executive Officer
• Steve Lefler, President
• Mark Rubenstein, Chairman & Co-Chief
Executive Officer
Products:
Knit Hats and Caps, Screened and
Embroidered Tees and Sweats.

PARICON, LLC.
52 PARK STREET
PO BOX 157
SOUTH PARIS, ME 04281
207-743-6896
Fax: 207-743-2530
info@pariconsleds.com
www.pariconsleds.com
• Ted Morton, Partner
ted@pariconsleds.com
• Tom Morton, Partner
tom@pariconsleds.com
Nature of Service:
Wholesales and distributes winter products
(Flexible Flyer sleds and snow toys) and
summer toss games to major retailers, toy
stores, grocery stores, hardware stores,
sporting goods stores and webstores.
Products:
Sleds, snowboards, foam sliders, inflatable
tubes, wooden toboggans and snow toys
Brands:
Flexible Flyer

PARKER LABORATORIES, INC.
286 ELDRIDGE ROAD
FAIRFIELD, NJ 7004
973-276-9500
800-631-8888
Fax: 973-276-9510
parker@parkerlabs.com
www.parkerlabs.com
• Neal Buchalter, President
• Carol Buchalter, Chairman
• Martin King, Director, International Sales
• Tom Rodenberg, National Sales Manager
• Joan Bartello, Advertising Manager
• Nick Economou, Operations Manager
• Kathleen Tirch, Quality Assurance
Manager
• Diane Sharkey, Human Resources
Manager
Products:
Manufacturer of electromedical contact
media

PARSONS OFFICIALS SUPPLIES
515 W LUNT AVENUE
PO BOX 847
ELGIN, IL 60120
866-664-8840
Fax: 847-352-3375
customerservice@pluspos.com
www.pluspos.com
• Buck Parsons, President
• Sylvia Parsons, Sales Manager
Products:
Baseball, Basketball, & Football coach and
Umpire supplies.

**PARTAC PEAT CORPORATION/BEAM
CLAY**
ONE KELSEY PARK
GREAT MEADOWS, NJ 7838
908-637-4191
800-247-2326
Fax: 908-637-8421
sales@partac.com
www.beamclay.com
Products:
Baseball and sports turf surfaces and
supplies
Nature of Service:
Manufacturer/Distributor
Brands:
Beam Clay, Partac, All Sports, Fence
Guard, Permanent Foul Line

PARTY ANIMAL INC.
909 CROCKER RD.
WESTLAKE, OH 44145
440-471-1030
800-456-0145
Fax: 440-617-9476
sales@partyanimalinc.com
www.partyanimalinc.com
Description:
Manufacturer of high quality flags, banners,
& collectible toys licensed for NFL, MLB,
NBA, NHL and over 65 colleges.
Products:
Applique & embroidered flags, banners, tall
team flags, team decorating strips & Lil'
Teammates collectible toys.

PATAGONIA
8550 WHITE FIR STREET
PO BOX 32050
RENO, NV 89523-2050
775-746-6878
800-638-6464
Fax: 775-746-6827
customer_service@patagonia.com
www.patagonia.com
• Ric Hatch, North American Sales Director
• Bill Kulczycki, Sales Director
Products:
Outdoor Sports Apparel.

**PAWLING CORPORATION/STANDARD
PRODUCTS DIVISION**
32 NELSON HILL ROAD
WASSAIC, NY 12592
845-373-9300
800-431-3456
Fax: 845-855-1139
sales@pawling.com
www.pawling.com
• Roger W Smith, Chairman / President
• Rich C Raible, VP / General Manager
Products:
Wall Protection Systems, Entrance Mats &
Gratings, Athletic Flooring Systems, Heavy

Duty Impact Protection Systems, Parking &
Traffic Safety Products, Prespray Watertight
Doors and Barriers, Prespray Airtight Doors,
etc.

PEARL IZUMI (USA)
1886 PRAIRIE WAY
LOUISVILLE, CO 80027
303-460-8888
800-328-8488
Fax: 303-466-4237
info@pearlizumi.com
www.pearlizumi.com
• Tom Adams, VP, Salels
• Josh Parker, Marketing Coordinator
Products:
Apparel for cycling, general sports, track &
field.

PELICAN INTERNATIONAL INC
1000, PLACE PAUL-KANE
LAVAL, QC, CANADA H7C 2T2
450-644-1222
888-669-6960
Fax: 450-664-4522
service@pelicansport.com
www.pelicansport.com
• Christian Elie, President
Products:
Canoes, Kayaks, Pedal Boats, Fishing
Boats and Accessories, Toys
Brands:
Pelican

PENN FISHING TACKLE COMPANY
7 SCIENCE COURT
COLUMBIA, SC 29203
215-229-9415
800-892-5444
Fax: 215-223-3017
www.pennreels.com
• Herbert O Henze, President
• Brent Kane, Marketing Director
• Viola Bird, VP
• Bryan Nelson, VP
Products:
Manufacturer of fishing reels, rods, combos,
downriggers, hooks, line, accessories,
tackle storage, Ltd Ed Prints, Apparel

PENN RACQUET SPORTS
306 S 45TH AVENUE
PHOENIX, AZ 85043
800-289-7366
Fax: 888-329-7366
askus@us.head.com
www.pennracquet.com
• Gregg Weida, President
• Johan Elisch, Chairman
• David Haggerty, President
• Kevin Kempin, VP
Products:
Racquet Sports - Apparel, Bags-Equipment,
Racquetball Balls, Racquetball Racquets,
Shoes, Tennis Balls.

PEPCO POMS SPORTS
9611 HIGHWAY 60 S
PO BOX 950
WHARTON, TX 77488
979-523-3116
800-527-1150
Fax: 800-762-5532
sales@pepcopoms.com
www.pepcopoms.com

Products:
Producer of cheerleader and promotional
pom pons and spirit accessories.

PERFECT CURVE, INC.
200 LINCOLN STREET
5TH FLOOR
BOSTON, MA 2111
617-224-1600
800-244-7733
Fax: 617-224-1601
customerservice@perfectcurve.com
www.perfectcurve.com
• Gregg Myles Levin, President
gregg@perfectcurve.com
• Barry M Levin, Sales VP
• Jason Seavey, Sales Director
jason@perfectcurve.com
• David Carey, Account Executive
Products:
Perfect Curve Cap Curver, Cap Cleaner &
Deodorizer, Perfect Curve CapRack, Water
& Stain Repellent.

PERFORMANCE SPORTS APPAREL
2201 NORTH FRONT STREET
HARRISBURG, PA 17110
877-263-0350
800-543-8952
Fax: 717-213-6977
info@medalist.com
www.medalist.com
• David Ferguson, President/CEO
(610) 373-5300
dferguson@medalist.com
• Richard Heck, National Sales Manager
Products:
General Sports Products Performance
Apparel, including Silk Underwear, Sport
Underwear, Thermal Underwear,
Turtlenecks.

**PERFORMANCE SPORTS SYSTEMS,
INC.**
9200 E 146TH STREET
SUITE A
NOBLESVILLE, IN 46060
317-774-9840
800-848-8034
Fax: 317-774-9841
info@perfsports.com
www.perfsports.com
• David Byrne, General Manager
Products:
Manufacturer of sporting equipment

HOGAN COMPANY
3000 NW 107TH AVENUE
MIAMI, FL 33172
305-592-2830
Fax: 305-594-2307
info@pery.com
www.pery.com
Products:
Golf - Apparel, Bags-for Clubs,
Bags-Luggage, Balls, Clubs-Iron or Wood
Sets, Clubs-Putters, Clubs-Utility, Gloves,
Headcovers, Umbrellas.

PETER DAVID INC
10890 THORNMINT ROAD
SUITE A
SAN DIEGO, CA 92127
858-385-2680
800-369-7467

Fax: 858-385-2690
www.peterdavid.com
Products:
Sports collectibles such as lapel pins, earrings, necklaces, key chains, magnets, collector sets

PHI-TEN USA INC
980 KNOX STREET
TORRANCE, CA 90502
310-328-8585
888-774-4836
Fax: 310-328-0716
www.phitenusa.com
• Yoshihiro Hirata, President
• Katashi Santo, Vice President
Products:
Titanium Necklace, Titanium Bracelet, Titanium Discs, Titanium Tape, Liquid Titanium, Titanium Wrap, Titanium Waist Belt, Aqua Titanium Belt, Titanium Insole, Titanium Support, Moisture Soap, Titanium Socks, Titanium Shorts, Titanium Compress Pants, Titanium Shirts

PHILIPS LIGHTING COMPANY
200 FRANKLIN SQUARE DRIVE
PO BOX 6800
SOMERSET, NJ 08875-6800
732-563-3000
800-555-0050
Fax: 732-563-3229
www.lighting.philips.com
• Frans Van Houten, Chairman
• Jim Andrew, Chief Strategy & Innovation Officer
• Eric Coutinho, Chief Legal Officer
Products:
Manufacturer of lighting for sports Facilities.

PHOENIX VENTURES CORPORATION
777 ALEXANDER ROAD
PRINCETON, NJ 8540
609-734-4999
Fax: 609-734-4994
• Gail C O'Denise, President
Products:
Hunting/Fishing - Equipment; Ice Hockey - Equipment; Tennis - Equipment.

PHOTO FILE
333 BEDFORD ROAD
SUITE 130
MOUNT KISCO, NY 10549
914-375-6000
800-346-1678
Fax: 914-375-6009
customerservice@photofile.com
www.photofile.com
Products:
Manufacturer of licensed sports photography

PIANTEDOSI OARS, INC.
PO BOX 643
W ACTON, MA 1720
978-263-1814
Fax: 978-263-5940
rowalden.com
• Gary G Piantedosi, Partner
Products:
Rowing/Crew - Oars, Shells, Sculls

PINCKARD BASEBALL GLOVES
PO BOX 52026
SALT LAKE CITY, UT 84106

385-232-6460
Fax: 626-683-3103
atozinc@earthlink.net
• Bill Pinckard, Founder
Products:
Baseball and Softball balls and gloves.

PINE SPORTS
208 S MAIN STREET
PO BOX 98
STAR, NC 27356
910-428-2185
800-342-2948
Fax: 910-428-9367
www.pinesports.com
Products:
Provides a variety of products that represent sports teams and players that includes NASCAR drivers as part of their product listings.

PING, INC.
2201 W DESERT COVE
PO BOX 82000
PHOENIX, AZ 85071-2000
800-474-6434
Fax: 602-687-5037
www.ping.com
• John Solheim, Chairman/President
• Mike Trueblood, Chief Financial Officer
• Allan Solheim, EVP
• Stacey Solheim, VP
Products:
Golf Equipment - Metal Woods Setm Hybrids, Irons, Wedges, Putters, Bags for Clubs, Accessories.

PINNACLE SPORTS EQUIPMENT INC
3801 VICTORY BOULEVARD
STATEN ISLAND, NY 10314
718-698-0775
Fax: 718-494-1583
info@bamboobat.com
www.bamboobats.net
• Thomas M Verrengia, Chief Executive Officer / Co-Founder
tverrengia@bamboobat.com
• Hsu Yanshen, President / Founder
yhsu@bamboobat.com
Products:
Manufacturer of Adult BamBooBat, Youth BamBooBat, Fungo BamBooBat, Softball BamBooBat, Hardwood Bat, and Equipment Bag.

PIONEER INDUSTRIES, INC.
171 S NEWMAN STREET
HACKENSACK, NJ 7601
201-933-1900
Fax: 201-933-9580
mdorf@pioneerindustries.com
www.pioneerindustries.com
• Jeffrey Haversat, General Partner
jhaversat@pioneerindustries.com
• Ralph Tarzia, VP Operations
• Mitchel Dorf, President
mdorf@pioneerindustries.com
• Mitchell Dorf, President
• Bill Zerby, Plant Manager
• Gaeton Di Napoli, Controller
Products:
Manufacturer of Hollow Metal Doors, Frames and Sticks

PIONEER NEW MEDIA TECHNOLOGIES, INC.
1925 E DOMINGUEZ STREET
LONG BEACH, CA 90810
310-952-2000
800-421-1404
Fax: 310-952-2960
www.pioneerelectronics.com
• Michael Townsend, Mobile Entertainment Marketing VP
• Amy Friend, Public Relations Director
Products:
Plasma, DVD Players & Recorders, A/V Receivers & Amplifiers, CD & Cassette Players, Home Theater Systems, Speakers & Headphones, Turntables, Computer Drives.

PLASTIMAYD CORPORATION
14151 FIR CITY
OREGON CITY, OR 97045-6806
503-654-8502
800-348-2600
Fax: 503-654-7935
www.plastimayd.com
• Martin Samuelson, President
• Todd Mulvaney, President
• Tim Hartford, Engineer/Technical
• Ron Uenberg, Finance Executive
Products:
Manufacturer of Pool Liners, Safety Covers and Winter Domes for Swimming Pools.

PLAY VISIONS
19180 144TH AVENUE NE
WOODINVILLE, WA 98072
425-482-2836
800-678-8697
Fax: 425-482-2842
laurab@playvisions.com
www.playvisions.com
• Kiley Rose, Sales Manager
(425) 482-2836
kileyr@playvisions.com
• Mark Chernick, CEO
Products:
Product lines include Horror Balls, Animags, Stress Balls, Hyperflex, Squishy Stuff, StuntMaster, Club Earth, Zibbies, Thredz, OddBall, ZooLights.

PLAYERS GOLF
145 S ORLANDO AVENUE
SUITE 8
MAITLAND, FL 32751
800-550-2223
Fax: 407-677-4878
info@playersgolf.com
www.playersgolf.com
Products:
Golf Equipment: Wood Sets, Irons, Putters, Utility/Hybrid Clubs, Logo Club Grips, Golf Bags, Golf Balls, Accessories, Training Aids, Fitness.

PLAYERS PUBLISHING
7316 ROCHELLE WAY
FAIR OAKS, CA 95628
916-202-9747
800-548-3500
Fax: 916-314-8006
rick@playerspublishing.com
www.playerspublishing.com
Products:
Offers quality artwork of the NBA's top players.

PLAYFIELD INTERNATIONAL INC.
1220 GREEN ROAD
CHATSWORTH, GA 30705
706-695-4581
800-221-7449
Fax: 706-695-4755
www.playfieldinternational.com
• Steve Linville, President
• Darrel Turner, Chief Operating Officer
Products:
Global supplier of the finest Artificial Turf Surfaces for landscaping, pet areas & kennels, play areas, golf courses, and playing fields.

PLAYOFF CORP.
2300 E RANDOL MILL ROAD
ARLINGTON, TX 76011
817-983-0300
• Larry Blackwell, President
• Stanley St Mayer, Chief Financial Officer
• Steve Peek, Score Entertainment SVP
• Art Young, Managing Director, Donruss Promotions Gr
Products:
Manufacturer of sports trading cards.

POCOCK RACING SHELLS
615 - 80TH STREET SW
EVERETT, WA 98203
425-438-9048
888-762-6251
Fax: 425-438-9043
niki@pocock.com
www.pocock.com
• Bill Tytus, President
bill@pocock.com
• John Tytus, Sales
• Amy Winner, Marketing
• Dave Haworth Jr., Customer Relations
Products:
Manufacturer of Racing Shells/Boats.

POINT BLANK SOLUTIONS
2102 SW 2ND STREET
POMPANO BEACH, FL 33069
954-630-0900
800-413-5155
Fax: 954-630-9225
www.pointblanksolutionsinc.com
• Larry H Ellis, President/CEO
• Michael Foreman, VP, Government and International Sales / Prod
(407) 448 6139
mforeman@pbearmor.com
• Bryant Halstead, Government Sales - Federal and Department of
(954) 629-5920
bhalstead@body-armor.com
• Michael Foreman, VP, Government and International Sales / Prod
(407) 448-6139
mforeman@pbearmor.com
• Paul Raspino, Military Sales - U.S. Army and National Guard
(910) 964-6808
praspino@pbsinc.com
• Corey Provenzano, Private Military Contractor Sales, OEM Busine
(754) 581-2758
cprovenzano@pbsinc.com
• Mark T. F. Smith, Vice President, Sales
(859) 620-2344
salesinquiries@pbsinc.com
Products:
Sports medicine, health supports, protective gear and magnetic therapy products.

POLAR ELECTRO INC.
1111 MARCUS AVENUE
SUITE M15
LAKE SUCCESS, NY 11042-1034
800-227-1314
Fax: 516-364-5454
customer.service.usa@polar.com
www.polar.com
• Burt Birnbaum, President
• Herb Baer, President
Products:
Manufacturer of Sports Equipment and Personal Fitness Solution - Heart Rate Monitors, Team System, Precision Performance Software, Accessories.

POLEMAX L.L.C.
8214 WESTCHESTER
SUITE 500
DALLAS, TX 75225
214-692-3532
800-458-0884
Fax: 214-692-3540
• Mac Fuller, Owner
Products:
Padded cover that is placed over poles or ground columns that may include symbols, an advertiser's logo, etc.

POLO BY RALPH LAUREN
625 MADISON AVENUE
11TH FLOOR
NEW YORK, NY 10022
212-318-7000
888-475-7674
Fax: 212-888-5780
www.ralphlauren.com
• Ralph Lauren, Chief Executive Officer
• Roger N Farah, President / Chief Operating Officer
• Tracey Travis, Senior VP and Chief Financial Officer
• Christopher H. Peterson, Chief Financial Officer & Senior VP
Products:
Manufacturer and importer of Polos, Chinos, Denim, Pants, Sweaters, Sweats & Tees, Sport Shirts, including sport apparel.

POMCHIES LLC
4900 E. ARROYO VERDE DRIVE
PARADISE VALLEY, AZ 85253
602-493-1745
888-576-6244
Fax: 602-404-0577
sales@pomchies.com
www.pomchies.com
Products:
Manufacturer of ponytail holders, pomchies, pomsnaps and pomclips for cheerleaders, sports teams, dance, swimming spirit, gymnastic.

PONY INTERNATIONAL INC.
9465 WILSHIRE BOULEVARD
6TH FLOOR
BEVERLY HILLS, CA 90212
866-766-9669
800-826-2205
info@pony.com
www.pony.com
• David Orr, Sales VP
(212) 459-2433
dorr@pony.com
Products:
General Sporting Goods.

POOLMASTER, INC.
770 DEL PASO ROAD
SACRAMENTO, CA 95834-1117
916-567-9800
800-854-1492
Fax: 916-567-9880
www.poolmaster.com
• Lee Tager, President
(916) 567-9800
lee@poolmaster.net
• Kim Levin, VP Of Sales
Products:
Water Sports Caps, Diving Masks, Goggles, Fins, Personal Flotation, Snorkels, Games for Swimming Pools, Pool & Spa Digital Clock Thermometers

PORSCHE CARS NORTH AMERICA
980 HAMMOND DRIVE
SUITE 1000
ATLANTA, GA 30328
770-290-3500
800-767-7243
Fax: 770-290-3700
www.porsche.com
• Robert Carlson, General Manager/Public Relations
• Tim Mahoney, General Manager/Marketing
• Matthius Muller, President
• Thomas Edig, Deputy Chairman

PORTAFLOOR
939 S 700 W
SALT LAKE CITY, UT 84104
801-972-0260
800-421-8112
801-657-5260
Fax: 801-401-3504
info@portafloor.com
www.portafloor.com
• Jon Isaacs, VP/General Manager
• Ronald N. Cemy, President & CEO
Products:
Grass and Stadium Protection System, Synthetic Surface Covering, Ice Protection Covering, Dirt Covering.

PORTAPIT/CATAPOLE
1901 DIPLOMAT DRIVE
PO Box 7726
DALLAS, TX 75209
800-527-7510
800-899-0149
feedgym@sportsupplygroup.com
www.portapit.com
• Gordon Klunkert, Portapit Advertising
• Robert K Mitchell, Chief Financial Officer
(972) 406-3484
bmitchell@sportsupplygroup.com
Products:
Track & Field - Crossbars, Discs, Hurdles, Landing Pits, Pole Vault Poles, Shots.

PORTER ATHLETIC EQUIPMENT COMPANY
601 MERCURY DRIVE
CHAMPAIGN, IL 61822-9648
217-367-8438
800-637-3090
Fax: 217-367-8440
www.porterathletic.com
• Greg Hege, President
• Edward Schroeder, Product Development VP
• Dan Morgan, Sales / Marketing VP
• David Hodge, President
• Mary Kotelly, Human Resources Executive

• Mike Schendel, Purchasing Executive
• Steve Vogelsang, Chief Marketing Officer
Products:
General Sports Equipment

POWELL GOLF, INC., JOE
1781 BARBER ROAD
SARASOTA, FL 34240
941-377-7742
800-237-4660
Fax: 941-377-7036
joepowellgolf@verizon.net
www.joepowellgolf.com
• John Powell, President
joepowell@acun.com
Products:
Golf - Clubs - Wood/Iron Sets, Putters

POWER SOURCE SPORTS INC
23207 STELLING AVENUE
PORT CHARLOTTE, FL 33980
941-764-9000
Fax: 941-764-0613
Brands:
Power Source
Products:
Sports electronics.

POWERBRANDS LLC
80-A E JEFRYN BOULEVARD
DEER PARK, NY 11729
631-389-5642
800-354-8785
Fax: 631-242-6177
kngny@aol.com
www.kngamerica.com
• Kash Gobindram, President / Chief
Executive Officer
Products:
Phones, clocks, Picture Frames, Lamps, CD
Players, remotes, Headsets, Solar Lanterns,
Radio Coolers, Flashlights, Radios,
Boomboxes, Phonographs, Night Lights

POWERCRANKS
365 PIMLICO DRIVE
WALNUT CREEK, CA 94597
925-480-7697
888-733-2572
Fax: 419-710-8477
customerservice@powercranks.com
www.powercranks.com
• Frank Day, Founder
• Andrew L Weber, Sales / Marketing
Director
• John McKenna, Chief Operating Officer /
Chief Financial Officer
Products:
PowerCranks, PowerCranks xLite,
Stationary Bikes, PowerCranks Training
Tools, PowerCranks Clothing

POWERS COURT/TOA
40 S MAIN STREET
NEW CITY, NY 10956
212-691-3888
800-728-3664
Fax: 212-255-7129
• Mark Sterns, President
Services:
The official U.S. agent for four of the finest
tennis manufacturers from around the globe:
TOA, Kirschbaum, BDE, ISO-Speed. As a
full line distributor we also offer competitive
pricing on all major brands of tennis strings

and accessories, including Wilson, Prince,
Gamma, Tecnifibre and Babolat.

**POWERS EMBROIDERY/ CHENILLE,
INC., USA**
11330 HILLGUARD RD.
DALLAS, TX 75243
214-343-0888
800-227-2040
Fax: 214-349-8884
info@powersembroidery.com
www.chenille.com
• Bob Powers, President / Chief Executive
Officer
• David Gooch, VP
• Jay Powers, Marketing VP
• Ken Gilmer, President
• Theresa Jacks, Human Resources
Executive
• Melissa Dennis, Sales Executive
• Marla Platt, Finance Executive
Products:
Cheerleader Emblems; Awards, Banners,
Chenille Award Emblems, Custom Swiss
Patches, Varsity Jackets.

**PRAIRIE ROSE PERSONALIZED
PRODUCTS**
1941 HIGHWAY 86
MILFORD, IA 51351
712-337-8119
877-337-8119
Fax: 712-337-0184
www.prairierose.com
Products:
Picture Frames with sports logos and
designs.

PRECISE INTERNATIONAL
15 CORPORATE DRIVE
ORANGEBURG, NY 10962
800-267-3577
800-267-3577
Fax: 800-438-5806
www.wengerna.com
• Tom Abbott, Chief Executive Officer
Products:
Manufactures knives, watches, swiss army
fragrance, swiss business tool, knife & swiss
business, tool accessories, watchbands,
tents, backpacks, sleeping bags and air
mattresses, casual travel bags, duffel bags
and travel accessories, computer cases,
leather folios and other business
accessories, corporate gifts.

PRECISION COMPOSITES
19138 WALNUT DRIVE
SUITE 201
ROWLAND HEIGHTS, CA 91748
626-964-4276
800-422-3838
Fax: 626-964-9436
www.precisioncomposites.com
• Peter A'Costa, National Sales Manager
Products:
Offers a complete line of 100% filament
wound graphite golf shafts designed to fit
golfers of all skill levels-from beginner to
professionals.

PRECISION SPORTS
29910 OHANA CIRCLE
LAKE ELSINORE, CA 92532
951-674-1665
800-524-5892

Fax: 951-674-2518
sherri@labeda.com
www.labeda.com
• Sherri Labeda, Corporate Secretary
(951) 674-1665
sherri@labeda.com
• Shelly Labeda, Chief Financial Officer
(951) 674-1665
shelly@labeda.com
• Kevin Labeda, Chemist/Director Of
Operations
kevinl@labeda.com
• Robert Chornomud, National/OEM Sales &
Marketing Manager
Products:
Specializes in high end high rebound
formulas to provide companies the very best
skateboard wheels on the market, from
blank economy wheels, dual durometer
wheels, to super high end four color process
printed wheels.

PRECOR, INC
20031 142ND AVENUE NE
PO BOX 7202
WOODINVILLE, WA 98072-4002
425-486-9292
800-786-8404
Fax: 425-486-3856
commsls@precor.com
www.precor.com
• Robert Baker, President
• Serge Dupuis, Vice President of Finance
• Bill Dixon, Vice President of Operations
• Jim Birrell, Chief Innovation Officer
• Elisa Humphrey, Senior VP of Consumer
Division
Products:
Elliptical Fitness Crosstrainers (EFX),
Treadmills, Cycles, Climbers,
StretchTrainers, Strength Training Systems

PREMIUMWEAR
4375 WILLOW DR.
HAMMEL, MN 55340
952-912-2500
800-488-4800
800-370-8706
Fax: 800-370-8706
sales@riversendtrading.com
www.riversendtrading.com
• Jayme Weber, President Promotional
Products
• Cynthia L Boeddeker, Operations VP
Products:
Sports Apparel and Accessories

PRESS PASS INC
9805 NORTHCROSS CENTER CT.
SUITE H
HUNTERSVILLE, NC 28078
704-942-3060
800-618-0683
Fax: 704-942-3070
www.presspassinc.com
• DJ Kazmiercak, Senior Vice President,
Sales & Marketing
Products:
Collectible trading cards and diecast
vehicles.
Description:
Press Pass, Inc. is a leading designer,
producer, and manufacturer of innovative,
high-quality trading cards and die-cast
collectibles. Press Pass reaches consumers
through multiple channels of distribution
supporting approximately 10,000 retail

outlets.
Brands:
Press Pass, Wheels

PRESTON LEATHER PRODUCTS
44 MITCHELL ROAD
PO BOX 594
IPSWICH, MA 1938
978-356-5701
800-343-8120
Fax: 978-356-9832
www.prestonleather.com
• C.A. Ebinger, General Manager
Products:
Bags, Belts, Dog Collars, Ribbons with
sports logos and designs.

PRIME TIME TOYS
PO BOX 256
POMPTON LAKES, NJ 7442
973-839-5711
Fax: 973-839-5811
pttllc@worldnet.att.net
www.primetimetoys.com
Nature of Service:
Distributor
Year Founded:
1993
Products:
Manufacturers of toys such as Boss Bow,
Rocket Blaster, Sky Diver, Squeeze Blaster,
Target, Lite-Up Sub, Max Liquidator and
Eliminator, Underwater Scramble, Splash
Bombs 4 Pack, Basketball Challenge, and
Glack Blaster.
Brands:
Max Liquidator Splash Bombs

PRINCE SPORTS GROUP, INC.
116 HIGH STREET
HAMPTON HILL, LONDON, ENGLAND
TW121NT
+44-
800-283-6647
Fax: 609-291-5900
• George Napier, Chairman / Chief
Executive Officer
• David Evins, EVP / Chief Financial Officer
• Tom Dye, Operations VP / General
Manager
• Howard Lay, Product Management VP
Products:
Racquet Sports - Apparel,
Bags-Necessities, Racquet Strings,
Racquetball Equipment & Shoes, Shoes,
Rollerblade Skates & Protective Gear,
Squash Racquets, Stringing Machines,
Tennis Racquets, Tennis Ball Machines,
Tennis Shoes

PRO BOUND SPORTS
428 HIGHWAY 40
DORRANCE, KS 67634
785-666-4207
800-525-8580
Fax: 785-666-4410
proboundspts@hbcomm.net
www.proboundsports.com
• Thomas Mahoney, President/Owner
(785) 666-4267
tom.mahoney@proboundsports.com
• Julie Dauber, Sales Representative
(785) 666-4207
Nature of Service:
Manufacturing, sporting goods,
wholesale/retail.
Year Founded:

1993
Products:
Designer and manufacturer of portable
roll-in and stationary basketball goal
supports along with ball returns, ball carts,
bleachers, score tables, and other main line
sporting goods.
Brands:
Ultra-Pro, Pro-Fold II, Pro-Bounder, Hot
Shot, Bull Dog, Score Pro.
Clients:
Colleges, High Schools, YMCA, YWCA,
Recreational Facilities, Residential/Home
Recreation

PRO FEET, INC.
PO BOX 2720
BURLINGTON, NC 27215-2720
336-226-0237
800-334-1101
Fax: 800-811-3338
info@profeet.com
www.profeet.com
• Russell Wilson, CEO
• Callum Brown, Vice President Operations
• Taylor Wilson, Vice President Sales
Year Founded:
1979.
Products:
Socks for Baseball, Basketball, Cycling,
Bowling, Boxing, Curling, Football, Golf,
Gymnastics, Handball, Racquet Sports,
Soccer, Softball, Track & Field, Volleyball,
Wrestling; Universal Tube Socks;
Wristbands/Headbands, Cheerleading.

PRO INNOVATIVE CONCEPTS
3836 E WATKINS STREET
PHOENIX, AZ 85034-7265
602-437-5100
800-858-4121
info@proinnovative.com
www.proinnovative.com
• Mark Scatterday, President
• Andrew Reichlin, Chief Executive Officer
• Bryan Christie, Sales / Marketing Director
info@proinnovative.com
Products:
Benders, Close Outs, Desk & Office
Accessories, Highlighters, Keychains,
Mirrors & Magnifiers, Noisemakers & Music
Related, Pens, Stress Relief, Toys.

PRO KENNEX
1159 MONTEREY PLACE
SUITE A
ENCINITAS, CA 92024-1340
800-778-1755
Fax: 619-635-9205
www.prokennex.com
• Jeff Yao, Chief Executive Officer
• Kevin Gilbert, President
Products:
Manufacturer, distributor and marketer of
various products for tennis, hockey, golf,
racquetball, squash and badminton.

PRO ORTHOPEDIC DEVICES, INC.
2884 E GANLEY ROAD
TUCSON, AZ 85706
520-294-4401
800-523-5611
Fax: 520-294-6116
info@proorthopedic.com
www.proorthopedic.com
• Gerald Detty, President
(800) 323-5611

• Jackie Ingrahm, Team Specialist
(800) 323-5611
jackie@proorthopedic.com
• Gerald Detty, President
• Karl Walton, Finance Executive
• Mark Ellisor, Operations Executive
Products:
Professional Products: Knee Supports,
Patella Stabilizers, Hinged Braces, Thigh
and Groin Supports, Ankle & Calf Supports,
Low Back Supports, Elbow Supports, Wrist
& Shoulder Supports, Training Aids, and
Scuff Pads.

PRO PERFORMANCE SPORTS
12375 WORLD TRADE DRIVE
PO BOX 500127
SAN DIEGO, CA 92128
858-675-3350
877-448-2929
Fax: 858-618-3330
www.properformancesports.com
Products:
Manufacturer, distributor and marketer of
innovative high performance sports products
and trainers.

PRO SELECT SPORTS*USA
19638 EAGLE RIDGE LANE
NORTHRIDGE, CA 91326
877-774-4228
Fax: 866-240-4257
www.proselectsports.com
• Nat C Rosasco, Chairman
• Nat G Rosasco, President
Products:
Bag & Club Sets, Golg Bags, Golf Gear,
Golf Irons & Hybrids, Golf Putters, Golf
Shoes, Golf Wedges, Drivers & Woods

PRO SPECIALTIES GROUP
8221 ARJONS DRIVE
SUITE F
SAN DIEGO, CA 92126
858-541-1100
800-544-564
Fax: 858-268-5801
info@psginc.com
www.psginc.com
• Steven Mendoza, VP, Business
Development
stevenm@psginc.com
• Charles Cooper, Sales Manager
charlesc@psginc.com
• Elizabeth Sanchez, Marketing Manager
info@psginc.com
Products:
Marketers and manufacturers of advertising
specialties and licensed sports products.

PRO STAR SPORTS, INC.
1133 WINCHESTER
KANSAS CITY, MO 64126
816-241-9737
800-821-8482
Fax: 816-241-2459
www.prostarsports.com
Products:
Weight Training Equipment - Racks,
Benches, Olympic Benches

PRO-LINE CAP COMPANY
1332 N MAIN STREET
FORT WORTH, TX 76106
817-246-1978
800-227-2456

Fax: 817-367-1585
charris@prolinecap.com
• Charles Harris, Sales / Marketing VP
(817) 246-1978
charris@prolinecap.com
• Joel Taylor, Sales / Marketing Manager
(817) 246-1978
jtaylor@prolinecap.com
• Steve Henning, Art Director
(817) 246-1978
shenning@prolinecap.com
• Charles Harris, VP Of Sales & Marketing
charris@prolinecap.com
• Alan Beam, Art Director
abeam@prolinecap.com
Products:
Caps and hats for Baseball, General Sports, Racquet Sports, Softball

PRO-TEC
6550 KATELLA AVE.
CYPRESS, CA 90630
310-318-5897
888-691-8889
Fax: 310-318-8807
www.pro-tec.net
Products:
Offers a wide variety of sports helmets and protection gear.

PROFESSIONAL GYM
805 CHEROKEE
PO BOX 188
MARSHALL, MO 65340
660-886-9628
800-821-7665
Fax: 660-886-3041
• Greg Mach, President
• Dale Thomas, Sales Director
Products:
Training, Conditioning and Physical Fitness Equipment

PROGEAR, INC.
11828 SLATER AVENUE NE
SUITE 150
KIRKLAND, WA 98034
425-814-3900
Fax: 425-814-3902
info@marketsync.com
www.marketsync.com
• Michael Bauer, SVP Marketing/Sales
• Tom Malone, Director
• Bob Wiggins, Director
• Jeremy Whiteley, Founder
• Bill Koszewski, Chief Technology Officer & Interim CEO
Products:
Promotional Products: Apparel & Accessories, Awards & Recognition, bags & Backpacks, Gifts, Golf, Sports & Outdoors

PROMARK 1
6730 N CMINO PDRE ISIDORO
TUCSON, AZ 85718
520-297-2246
aaleamoni@aol.com
• Aran S Aleamoni, President / Chief Executive Officer
Products:
Premium promotional products for golf.

PROMARK EMBLEMS LLC
14052 VALLEY DRIVE
PO BOX 872
LONGMONT, CO 80504

303-926-1328
888-287-0056
Fax: 303-926-1450
www.teampromark.com
Products:
Offers specialty emblems for clubs, organizations or teams.

PROMARX/VITAL
7 NORDEN LANE
HUNTINGTON STATION, NY 11746
631-673-1084
800-777-8482
Fax: 866-326-4478
VitalTeam@Vital-Apparel.com
Products:
Matching Accessories, Sports Themed Apparel, Team Sports Apparel. Matching Accessories include Hair Ribbons, Hair Bows, Hair Scrunchies, Headbands, Knit Hats & Matching Knit Gloves, Mesh Top Socks, Non Terry Socks, Sleeve Holders, Dazzle Tote Bags, Polar Fleece Blankets and Flip Flops

PROMOS - SPORTS & CORPORATE PROMOTIONS LLC
513 W MT PLEASANT AVENUE
SUITE 208
LIVINGSTON, NJ 07039-1721
973-422-0004
800-394-7196
Fax: 973-422-0114
info@PROMOSLLC.com
www.promosllc.com
• Russel Steinberg, President
(973) 422-0004
russel@promosllc.com
Products:
Producers of any promotional item with a logo. Also producers of personalized party favors and gifts like Sweats, Compressed T-shirts, Towels, Hats, Mugs, Candles, Bags, Scrubs, Sport Balls, Mousepads, Blankets, Banners, Posters, Socks, etc.

PROPET USA INC.
2415 W VALLEY HIGHWAY N
AUBURN, WA 98001
253-854-7600
800-877-6738
800-877-6738
Fax: 253-854-7607
customerservice@propetusa.com
www.propetusa.com
• Jack Hawkins, President
• Ali Altaf, EVP
• Rick Wang, Office Manager
Products:
General Sports Products - Walking Shoes

PROTEAM BY HAUSMANN
130 UNION STREET
NORTHVALE, NJ 7647
201-767-0255
888-428-7626
Fax: 201-767-1369
sales@proteamtables.com
www.proteamtables.com
• George Batchelor, Sales / Marketing Director
(201) 767-0255
sales@proteamtables.com
• Joe Patten, National Sales Manager
(201) 767-0255
joep@hausmann.com

Products:
Modular Taping Stations, Treatment Tables, Taping Tables, Benches, Lockers, Cabinets, Stools, Weight Racks

PROZRELIEF
115 PERIMETER CENTER PLACE
SUITE 945
ATLANTA, GA 30346
678-990-8002
877-286-7074
Fax: 770-206-2389
Products:
Glucosamine Chondroitin MSM, ProzRelief Joint Formula

PSC/ENCORE SELECT INC
5019 W NASSAU STREET
TAMPA, FL 33607
813-282-7073
800-310-9428
Fax: 813-282-7079
www.encoreselect.com
Products:
Apparel, Autograph Memorabilia, Awards/Trophies, Collectible Wall D,cor, Custom Framing, Display Cases, Game-Used Products, Matted Prints, Stadium Products, and Trading Cards

PUMA NORTH AMERICA
1 CONGRESS ST.
SUITE 110
BOSTON, MA 2114
617-488-2900
Fax: 978-698-1174
info@puma.com
www.puma.com
• Jochen Zeitz, Chairman of the Board/CEO
• Dieter Bock, Chief Financial Officer
• Eric Safin, Classics Category Manager
• Donna Deane, Apparel Category Manager
Products:
Baseball - Shoes-Metal Cleats, Shoes-Rubber Cleats; Basketball - Shoes; Football - Shoes-Cleated; General Sports Products - All-Purpose Shoes, Bags-Equipment, T-shirts; Soccer - Shoes; Softball - Shoes-Metal Cleats, Shoes-Rubber Cleats; Track & Field/Runn

PURE FISHING
7 SCIENCE COURT
COLUMBIA, SC 29203
803-754-7000
800-334-9105
Fax: 712-336-5183
purefishinginquiries@purefishing.com
www.purefishing.com
• Tom Bedell, Owner
Products:
Line, Lures, Reels, Rods, Soft Bait, Terminal Tackle.

PUTT-PUTT GOLF COURSES OF AMERICA, INC.
300 S LIBERTY STREET
SUITE 110
WINSTON-SALEM, NC 27101
336-714-3950
866-788-8788
Fax: 336-714-3955
www.putt-putt.com
• David Callahan, President
• Teresa Greco, Chief Operating Officer

Products:
General Sports Products including Game Rooms and Miniature Golf Courses.

PUTTERMAN ATHLETICS
4834 S OAKLEY PLACE
CHICAGO, IL 60609
773-927-4120
800-621-0146
Fax: 773-650-6046
www.mputterman.com
• Alan Berman, Chief Business
• Edward E Reicin, President
• Benjamin Beiler, President and CEO
Products:
Windscreens, gym floor covers, wall padding
Description:
90-year old manufacturer of quality sports equipment.
Brands:
Putterman

IZOD CLUB GOLF & TENNIS
1001 FRONTIER ROAD
BRIDGEWATER, NJ 08807
610-374-4242
800-866-7292
Fax: 610-478-1989
pvh.com
• Mark Webber, Chief Executive Officer
• Robert Rully, Sales VP
• Pam Smith, Marketing / Advertising Manager
Products:
Golf apparel, hats, caps, visors, socks, umbrellas, premium knit golf shirts, sweaters and sweater vests, fleece country club design sweatshirts, golf windshirts and rain suits, as well as twill pants and shorts.

PW ATHLETIC COMPANY, INC.
140 N GILBERT ROAD
PO BOX 8760
MESA, AZ 85203-9028
480-962-5289
800-687-5768
Fax: 800-729-2483
info@pwathletic.com
www.pwathletic.com
• Dave Bang, Owner
• Wayne Anderson, Marketing
Products:
Baseball - Cages/Backstops, Dugouts, First Base Safety Protectors, Foul Line Poles; Basketball - Backboards, Backstops, Hoops, Nets, Standards; Bike - Racks; Facilities - Soccer Field Equipment; Football - Goal Posts; Racquet Sports - Tennis Court Nets

Q-RAY INC
PO BOX 9
ARLINGTON HEIGHTS, IL 60006
866-5441825
Fax: 847-228-5195
QRay@QRay.com
www.qray.com
Products:
Q-Ray Ionized Bracelets

QUABAUG CORPORATION
DAMON MILL SQUARE
SUITE H3
CONCORD, MA 1742
508-867-7731
Fax: 508-867-4600

sales@vibramusa.com
www.vibram.us
• Robert E Varnum, Chairman
• Michael Gionfriddo, VP
• Tony Post, President & CEO
Products:
General Sports Products - Athletic Footwear

QUANTUM ROCK ENTERPRISES
PO BOX 4032
ROLLING HILLS ESTATES, CA 90274
310-378-2171
Fax: 310-378-9383
QuantumRock@QuantumRock.com
www.quantumrock.com
• Fred Willis, Owner
fredwillis@quantumrock.com
Nature of Services:
Mobile Rock Climbing Walls For Special Events, Trade Shows, Marketing Promotions, Corporate Events, Film/TV Productions.

QUEST TECHNOLOGIES, A 3M COMPANY
1060 CORPORATE CENTER DRIVE
OCONOMOWOC, WI 53066
262-567-9157
800-245-0779
Fax: 262-567-4047
• Melissa Wesemann, Marketing Manager
Products:
Noise Dosimeters, Sound Level Meters, Gas Detection Monitors, Vibration Monitors, Indoor Air Quality Monitors, Audiometric Equipment, Heat Stress & Thermal Environment Monitors, Applications Software
Year Founded:
1947

QUIKSILVER
15202 GRAHAM STREET
HUNTINGTON BEACH, CA 92649
714-889-2200
800-435-9917
Fax: 714-889-3700
customerservice@quiksilver.com
www.quiksilverinc.com
• Robert B McKnight Jr, Chairman / Chief Executive Officer
(714) 889-2200
robert.mcknight@quiksilver.com
• Bernard Mariette, President / Director
(714) 889-2200
bernard.mariette@quiksilver.com
• Steven L Brink, Chief Financial Officer
(714) 889-2200
steven.brink@quiksilver.com
• Robert B. McKnight Jr., Executive Chairman
• Andrew P. Mooney, Chief Executive Officer & President
Products:
General Sports Apparel

R.A.M. SPORTS, INC.
4640 ADMIRALTY WAY
SUITE 50
MARINA DEL REY
CALIFORNIA, CA 90292
310-496-5728
800-225-5712
Fax: 310-496-5729
• Mike Oister, President
• Matt Torson, Special Accounts Manager

• Mike Gloden, Operations Manager
• Randy Jones, Treasurer
Products:
Balls for volleyball, soccer and football.

R.C.I.
12001 CR 1114
TYLER, TX 75709
903-939-1908
Fax: 903-939-2202
sales@rciracing.com
www.rciracing.com
• Steve Crane, Marketing

R.S. OWENS & CO., INC.
5535 N LYNCH AVENUE
CHICAGO, IL 60630
773-282-6000
800-282-6200
Fax: 773-545-4501
salesinfo@rsowens.com
www.rsowens.com
• Scott Siegel, President
• Dave Kryan, Pubic Relations Manager
• George Sorpremant, Marketing Manager
• Larry Maloney, VP Sales & Marketing
• Jacqueline Duda, Customer Service Manager
• Lawrence Maloney, VP Of Sales & Marketing
• Kristen Groote, VP Of Sales & Marketing
Products:
Trophies, Awards, Medals, Plaques, Ribbons.
Year Founded:
1938

RACEAMERICA, INC.
105 BONVENTURA DRIVE
SAN JOSE, CA 95134
408-988-6188
Fax: 408-988-1603
info@raceamerica.com
www.raceamerica.com
• Phillip Briseno, Sales Manager
• Dennis Laczny, President
• Tina Bozarth, Operations Manager
Nature of Service:
The industry leader in advanced event critical timing electronics. Designs and manufactures a complete line of portable timing systems, software and LED-based scoreboards and displays for use in both single and multi-lane snowmobile, autocross, mud bog, soap boxz derby, ATV, and drag racing. Also provides a variety of customized timing solutions for private, commercial, and industrial applications. Produces the world's state-of-the-art, fully wireless drag racing timing system and continues to innovate with flexibility to match uniwue customer needs.
Year Founded:
1991
Products:
Timing systems and LED scoreboards for drag race, autocross, downhill skiing, ATV and Mudbog racing, soap box derby and racetracks. track marshalling equipment including corner safety lights, blag flag displays and track marshall software. Race management software, counting displays, countdown clocks, speed trap, lap timers and auto timers. Also manufacture custom timing solutions for a variety of applications.

RACEBRICKS MEMORABILIA LLC DBA CLEAR COLLECTIBLES
21515 ROSCOE BOULEVARD
CANOGA PARK, CA 91304
818-676-1612
877-790-0990
Fax: 818-676-1614
cyracebricks@yahoo.com
• Charles Yacobian, General Manager
(818) 676-1612
cyracebricks@yahoo.com
Year Founded:
2004
Products:
Collegiate logo/image glass and acrylic items.

RACING COMMUNICATIONS
3860 MOON STATION ROAD
KENNESAW, GA 30144
770-429-8783
Fax: 770-429-8835
info@racingcommunications.com
www.racingcommunications.com
• Kraig Pechenino, Marketing Director
Products:
Radio Systems, 2-Way Radios, Headsets, Intercom Systems, Scanners, Racing Helmets, In-Car Accessories

RACING REFLECTIONS INC
556 S MAIN STREET
MARION, VA 24354
276-783-9017
800-883-9017
Fax: 276-783-5939
www.racingreflections.com
• Robert Battaglia, President
Products:
Licensed NASCAR Merchadise

RAE CROWTHER COMPANY
2273 BURKETT DR.
ROCK HILL, SC 29730
800-841-5050
800-841-5050
Fax: 803-366-3633
www.raecrowther.com
• Hans Krause, President
(800) 841-5050
Products:
Football - Dummies, Field Equipment, Shields, Protective Pads, Sleds, Chutes, Running Ropes.
Nature of Service:
Full line of strength equipment for all levels of play.
Brands:
S-Advantage Tackler, S-Advantage Sleds, Attack Sled, Zig-zag Sled, Hit-Tech Station, Classic Two Man Sled, Classic 5 & 7 Man Sled, Classic tackling Sled, Defensive Reaction Machine, Tunch Punch Sled, Cruncher Sled, Run Tunnel, Monster Ropes, Maskill Sled, Parts 2-5-7 sled, parts DFR 1950-2000, Parts DFR 2001-2002, Parts Tackling, Super Chute, Jam Tent, Chutes Stalls, Center Machine, QB Throwing Net, Hanging Net, Tunch Punch Ladder, Pop Up Dummies, Hand Shields, Stand Up Dummies, Step-Overs

RAGE CAGE
357 COUNCIL OAK DRIVE
SEVERN, MD 21144
410-672-0282
Fax: 410-672-0689

info@ragecage.com
www.ragecage.com
• Frank Reeves, President
frank@ragecage.com
Products:
Lacrosse, Hockey Goals, Lacrosse Ground Bracket with hardware, Shot Blocker, ProTraction Feet, Lacrosse Carrying Strap

RAINBOW IMPORTS
421 NE ALDEN AVENUE
BEND, OR 97701
541-389-7129
800-628-7440
Fax: 541-389-7770
Products:
General sporting goods.

RAISINS COMPANY INC.
COSTA MESA, CA 92649
949-493-0651
800-472-4746
Fax: 949-645-0313
• Steve Tully, Raisins Corporate Operations EVP
• Marty Samuels, Sales / National Marketing EVP
Products:
Sports and Team Products: Swimming & Diving

RALEIGH CYCLE
6004 S 190TH STREET
SUITE 101
KENT, WA 98032
253-395-1100
800 222-5527
Fax: 253-872-0257
www.raleighusa.com
• William Austin, President
Products:
Bicycles and cycling accessories

RAMSTAR MILLS, INC.
1107 COMMERICIAL ST.
ATHENS, TX 75751
903-292-1724
800-327-2303
Fax: 903-292-1726
sales@ramstar.com
www.ramstaronline.com
• Bob Wielenga, President
(800) 327-2303
bobw@ramstar.com
• Kenneth Holt, General Manager
(800) 327-2303
Products:
Manufacturer of T-shirts, Tank Tops and Shorts. Also a manufacturer of HydroWick by AmeriTeesr high performance moisture management apparel in short and long sleeve tees, tanks, safety vests and sweatshirts. Made in USA apparel.

RAND INTERNATIONAL
51 EXECUTIVE BOULEVARD
FARMINGDALE, NY 11735
631-249-6000
Fax: 631-249-6015
• Allen Goldmeier, President
• Steven Goldmeier, VP
Products:
Bicycles, Wheel Goods, Bicycle Accessories.

RAPIDRIBBONS
505 S 9TH STREET
PO BOX 222
GOSHEN, IN 46526-3446
800-752-6595
Fax: 800-365-0064
sales@rapidribbons.com
www.rapidribbons.com
• Milton Thomas, Chief Operating Officer
milt.rapidribbons@verizon.net
Products:
Ribbons, Ribbon Logos, Ribbon Tags, Medals, Pins, Certificates, Trophies, Watches, Clothing/Blankets, Gold Awards, Graduation/Honors, Badges/Holders/Tags.

RAPPORT COMPOSITES
8802 BASH STREET
SUITE E
INDIANAPOLIS, IN 46256
866-286-7322
800-783-0196
Fax: 877-783-0196
www.swingscience.net
• Michael Perryman, President
• Connie Nielson, VP Operations
• Caleb Smith, Sales Director
Products:
Supplier of premium golf club components.

RAVENSBURGER FX SCHMID
1 PUZZLE LANE
NEWTON, NH 3858
855-257-1500
800-886-1236
Fax: 603-382-3366
www.ravensburger.com
• Karsten Schmidt, Speaker
• Frank Mallet, Chief Financial Officer / Chief Operatin
Products:
Distributor of children's, adult and family games and puzzles throughout the U.S. and Canada.

RAWLINGS SPORTING GOODS COMPANY INC.
510 MARYVILLE UNIVERSITY DRIVE
SUITE 110
SAINT LOUIS, MO 63141
314-819-2800
800-729-5464
Fax: 314-819-2988
contact@rawlings.com
www.rawlings.com
• Mike Thompson, SVP, Sports Marketing & Bus Development
• David Zumbach, VP Marketing
• Scott Siebers, Product Manager, Baseball
ssiebers@rawlings.com
Products:
Baseballs, Custom Bats, MiniBats, Socks, Sport Belts, Shin Guards, Golf Clubs, Golf Balls, Golf Bags, Non-motorized Golf Carts, Golf Club Heads, Leather and Synthetic Golf Gloves.

RAY COOK GOLF COMPANY
2212 GATLIN CREEK ROAD
DRIPPING SPRINGS, TX 78620
512-782-8245
Fax: 817-326-5514
www.raycook.com
• Jack Lynch, Chief Operating Officer
Products:
Golf Clubs and Putters

manufacturers/retailers

RAZOR USA LLC
16200-A CARMENTIA ROAD
PO BOX 3610
CERRITOS, CA 90703
562-345-6000
866-467-2967
Fax: 562-345-6087
www.razor.com
• Carlton Calvin, President
• Katherine Mahoney, VP, Marketing
• Katy Fletcher, Brand Manager
Products:
Dirt Bike, Miniature Electric Motorcross Bike, Electric Motorcycle, Electric Scooter

RED LION PRODUCTS
1125 WRIGHT AVENUE
CAMDEN, NJ 8103-1615
856-964-9700
800-526-2363
Fax: 856-964-9135
www.standardmerchandisingco.com/RED-LION-C58.aspx
• Lee Tarnoff, VP
Products:
Baseball, Soccer, Volleyball Socks & Accessories, Wristbands/Headbands, Reflective Running Accessories, Training & Conditioning Tape.

REDLINE PERFORMANCE PRODUCTS, INC.
42670 450TH STREET
PO BOX 399
PERHAM, MN 56573
218-346-7790
Fax: 760-598-0167
www.1redline.com
• Kent H. Harle, Chief Executive Officer / Founder / Dire
• Mark A. Payne, President / Chief Financial Officer / Di
• Chris B. Rodewald, Sales / Marketing VP
• Stanley R. Herman, Director
Products:
Designer and manufacturer of snowmobiles.

REEBOK APPAREL GROUP
1895 J W FOSTER BOULEVARD
CANTON, MA 2021
781-401-5000
800-382-3823
Fax: 781-401-7402
www.reebok.com
• Paul Harrington, President / Chief Executive Officer
• Uli I. Becker, President
• David Baxter, President, Sports Licensed Division
• John Warren, General Manager, Sports Licensed Division
• Kenneth Watchmaker, EVP / Chief Financial Officer
Products:
Manufacturers of sportswear and accessories. Also sports men's casualwear and shoes.

REEBOK CANADA INC.
3400 RAYMOND-LASNIER
ST-LAURENT(QUEBEC), CANADA H4R 3L3
514-461-8000
866-870-1743
www.reebok.com
• Paul Harrington, President/CEO

Products:
Sporting apparel, footwear, accessories.

REGENT SPORTS CORPORATION
45 RANICK ROAD
PO BOX 11357
HAUPPAUGE, NY 11788
631-234-2800
800-645-5190
Fax: 631-232-0124
• Harvey Feldman, President
Products:
Sporting goods equipment. Offers products for outdoor games, baseball gloves and equipment, basketballs, soccer balls, soccer equipments and accessories, volleyballs, table tennis balls, table tennis products and footballs.

RELIABLE OF MILWAUKEE
6737 W. WASHIONGTON STREET
SUITE 3200
MILWAUKEE, WI 53214
414-272-5084
800-336-6876
Fax: 414-272-6443
www.reliableofmilwaukee.com
• Mark Blutstein, President/CEO
(414) 238-2622
markb@relknit.com
• Janice Betchkal, Chief Financial Officer
(414) 238-2628
Janice@relknit.com
• John Johnson, Chief Operations Officer
(414) 238-2623
johnjohnson@relknit.com
• Kathleen Caylor, EVP Design
(414) 238-2623
kathleenc@relknit.com
• Tanya Thorson, VP Marketing
(414) 238-6359
Tanya@relknit.com
Products:
Headwear, slippers, fashion accessories, robes, golf accessories or promotional products, Nitco new and recycled golf balls. Promotional products distributor.
Year Founded:
1911
Description:
Fifth generation family owned company headquartered in Milwaukee, producing brands Muk Luks, Golf Balls Direct and Nitro, Express Promotions, and Quietwear.
Clients Include:
Kohl's, Walmart, Target, Bon-Ton, Macy's, JcPenney, QVC, Zulilly, Groupon, DSW, Dicks Sporting Goods, Cabela's, American Eagle Outfitters, Urban Outfitters, Dry Goods, Tilly's, Free People.

RELIABLE RACING SUPPLY, INC.
643 UPPER GLEN STREET
QUEENSBURY, NY 12804
518-793-5677
800-223-4448
Fax: 800-585-4443
customerservice@reliableracing.com
www.reliableracing.com
• John Jacobs, President
(800) 223-4448
john@reliableracing.com
• Kathleen Spear, Vice President Operations
(800) 223-4448
kathy@reliableracing.com
• Kelli Evans, Creative Desing

(800) 223-4448
kelli@reliableracing.com
Year Founded:
1969.
Nature of Service:
Supplier to ski resorts, golf courses, recreation facilities and event promoters. Manufacturer of Break-A-Way® slalom poles, Porta-flex® - temporary crowd-control solutions for sports facilities and event venues. Custom racing bibs, numbers and banners. US distributor of TAG Heuer and ALGE sports timing systems and athletic scoreboards. Full range of golf course and golf tournament supplies. Direct consumer source via internet and catalog of ski and snowboard competition gear and accessories.

REMINGTON ARMS COMPANY, INC.
870 REMINGTON DRIVE
PO BOX 700
MADISON, NC 27025-0700
800-243-9700
Fax: 336-548-7801
info@remington.com
www.remington.com
• Tommy Millner, President / Chief Executive Officer
• John Dwyer, Ammunition VP
Products:
Sporting goods products for the hunting and shooting sports markets, as well as military, government and law enforcement markets.

RENAISSANCE GOLF DESIGN, INC.
530 E EIGHTH SREET
TRAVERSE CITY, MI 49686
231-941-7499
Fax: 231-941-2114
renaissancegolf@aol.com
www.renaissancegolf.com
• Tom Doak, Principal / Founder
renaissancegolf@aol.com
• Bruce Hepner, VP
renaissancegolf@aol.com
Services:
Golf course design and architecture in the minimalist style.

RENNOC
645 PINE STREET
GREENVILLE, OH 45331
856-327-5400
800-372-7100
Fax: 800-675-1727
www.rennoc.com
• Richard Conner, Founder / Chief Executive Officer
• Mike Hess, Co-Chief Executive Officer
Products:
General Sports Products - Manufactures athletic jackets and warm-up suits

REPUBLIC PACKAGING CORPORATION
9160 S GREEN STREET
CHICAGO, IL 60620
773-233-6530
Fax: 773-233-6005
reppack@repco.com
www.repco.com
• Charles Wood, President / Chief Executive Officer
reppack@repco.com
• Rose Wood, VP
reppack@repco.com

• Edward Olszewski, Chief Financial Oficer
reppack@repco.com
Services:
Designs, tests, manufactures and delivers
cushion packaging solutions to meet the
unique needs of customers.

RESILITE SPORTS PRODUCTS, INC.
PO BOX 764
SUNBURY, PA 17801
570-473-3529
800-843-6287
800-326-9307
Fax: 570-473-8988
resilite@resilite.com
www.resilite.com
• Paul Gilbert, President
(800) 843-6287
• Jeff Baker, Director of Marketing
Year Founded:
1959.
Nature of Service:
Specializes in customized padding
solutions, for post, columns, and other
hard-to-cover obstructions. We've solved
padding dilemas for thousands of
customers!

REVERE PLASTICS, INC.
19 HAMPDEN STREET
BOSTON, MA 2119
617-442-3100
800-226-8374
Fax: 617-442-1152
athleticcovers@revereplastics.com
www.revereplastics.com
• Edward Smith, President
athleticcovers@revereplastics.com
• Tina Walsch, Office Manager
athleticcovers@revereplastics.com
Products:
Produces protective covering for athletic
surfaces.

REVGEAR SPORTS CO.
15073 KESWICK STREET
VAN NUYS, CA 91405
818-847-1100
800-767-8288
Fax: 818-781-7833
info@revgear.com
www.revgear.com
• Paul Reavlin, Founder
paulr@revgear.com
Products:
Training tools, aids, apparels, accessories
for sparring, boxing and kickboxing, self
defense and grappling and aerobic
kickboxing such as gloves, shin guards,
chest protectors, rib and ab guards,
chestguards, groin and abdominal
protectors, athletic cup supporters, hand
wraps, training aids, mitts and shields,
heavy bags, mats and flooring and
instructional videaos and DVDs

REYN SPOONER INC
66-1600 LALAMILO ROAD
PO BOX 1509
KAMUELA, HI 96743
808-842-4793
888-289-7396
Fax: 808-847-5296
info@reyns.com
www.reyns.com
• Tim McCullough, President / Chief
Executive Officer

info@reyns.com
• Kirk Hubbard, Chief Operating Officer
info@reyns.com
Products:
Manufactures a large and unique selection
of authentic Hawaiian aloha shirts printed
with Automotive, Major League Baseball
and Collegiate Athletics themes.

RHINO SPORTS
15029 N 74TH STREET
SCOTTSDALE, AZ 85260-2406
480-719-8585
800-585-0922
Fax: 480-315-9217
www.rhinocourts.com
• John Shaffer, President
info@rhinocourts.com
• Jay Abraham, EVP
info@rhinocourts.com
• Bob Hemming, National Sales Manager
• Joe Kreigbaum, Local Sales/Dealer
Support
• Eric Keef, Project Manager
• Ted Waldrup, Dealer, Orange Country
Services:
Rhino Court basketball provides for court
flooring and court construction for basketball
courts, tennis courts, gym flooring,
basketball gym floors and athletic fitness
sports.

RHODES WOOD COMPANY, INC.
5909 EVERGREEN BOULEVARD
SAINT LOUIS, MO 63134
314-522-1600
Fax: 314-522-0000
• Marvin Rhodes, President
• Joyce Rhodes, VP
Services:
Trophies, Awards and Components.

RICHARDSON SPORTS, INC.
500 INTERNATIONAL WAY
PO BOX 2440
SPRINGFIELD, OR 97477
541-687-1818
Fax: 541-687-1130
sales@richardsoncap.com
www.richardsoncap.com
• Neil Richardson, President
sales@richardsoncap.com
• Donna Richardson, VP
sales@richardsoncap.com
Products:
Caps, hats, visors

RICO INDUSTRIES/TAG EXPRESS
7000 N AUSTIN AVENUE
NILES, IL 60714
312-427-0313
800-423-5856
Fax: 312-427-1887
info@ricoinc.com
www.ricoinc.com
• Daniel Schack, Contact
info@ricoinc.com
Products:
Licensed MBL, NBA, NFL, NHL, NASCAR
and Collegiate Athletics novelty items and
accessories for the home, office and car.

RIDDELL ATHLETIC FOOTWEAR
669 SUGAR LANE
ELYRIA, OH 44035

440-366-8225
800-275-5338
Fax: 440-366-6292
www.riddell.com
• Ernie Wood, President
webmaster@riddellfootwear.com
• Ed Travis, SVP
webmaster@riddellfootwear.com
• Chip Walther, Sales VP
webmaster@riddellfootwear.com
• Bill Sherman, President / Chief Executive
Officer
Products:
Cleated footwear and other athletic shoes

RIDDELL, INC.
9801 W HIGGINS ROAD
SUITE 800
ROSEMONT, IL 60018
773-794-1994
800-275-5338
Fax: 773-794-6155
help@riddellsports.com
www.riddell.com
• Bill Sherman, President / Chief Executive
Officer
Products:
Baseball Batting Helmets, Cycling Helmets,
Football Helmets, General Sports Products,
Collectibles.

RIEDELL SHOES, INC.
122 CANNON RIVER AVENUE
PO BOX 21
RED WING, MN 55066
651-388-8251
800-698-6893
Fax: 651-385-5500
customerservice@riedellskates.com
www.riedellskates.com
• Bob Riegelman, President / Chief
Executive Officer
customerservice@riedellskates.com
• Scott Riegelman, VP
customerservice@riedellskates.com
• Dan Riegelman, Marketing VP
customerservice@riedellskates.com
• Dustin Glebe, Coordinator
customerservice@riedellskates.com
Products:
Ice and roller skates

RIGHT GARD CORPORATION
531 N 4TH STREET
PO BOX 286
DENVER, PA 17517
717-336-2700
800-535-1122
Fax: 717-484-2180
• Richard A. McGrath, President
ra@ultimatesport.net
• Julie Kelly, General Manager
• Stacey Bidges, National Sales Manager
stacey@ultimatesport.net
• Richard A. Mc Grath, President
ra@ultimatesport.net
Products:
Soccer shin guards, mouth guards,
protective gear, soccer shorts, perfromance
wear, sports apparel, accessories

RINGOR
7929 SW BURNS WAY
WILSONVILLE, OR 97070
503-582-9889
800-746-4670
Fax: 503-582-9899

manufacturers/retailers

Questions@Ringor.com
www.ringor.com
• Carol Ihlenburg, President
Products:
Baseball & Softball, Non Metal Cleats, Metal
Spikes, Athletic Apparel, Turf Shoes/Cross
Trainers, Sandals/Shoes Accessories, Bags

RIP FLAG
408 S FEDERAL
MASON CITY, IA 50401
641-423-0044
888-747-3524
Fax: 507-625-5111
customercare@ripflag.com
www.ripflag.com
Products:
Flag, Football, Belts

RIPKEN BASEBALL LLC
1427 CLARKVIEW ROAD
SUITE 100
BALTIMORE, MD 21209
410-823-0808
800-486-0850
Fax: 410-823-0850
www.ripkenbaseball.com
• Cal Ripken, President / Chief Executive
Officer
• Bill Ripken, Co-Owner / Executive Vice
President
• Karen Desantis, Executive Assistant
• Chris Flannery, Chief Operating Officer
• Brian Thornton, Director of
Marketing/Corporate Development
• Jeff Eiseman, Vice President
Products:
Athletic Shorts, Caps, Casual Wear,
Children's Apparel, Jackets & Sweatshirts,
Jerseys, Mascot Apparel, Novelties,
T-shirts, Women's Apparel, Instructional
Products, JUGS Equipment like
Accessories, Baseballs, Pitching machines,
Protective Screens

RIPON ATHLETIC
290 JUNCTION STREET
PO BOX 25
BERLIN, WI 54923
920-361-1500
Fax: 866-997-4766
www.riponathletic.com
• Henry M. Derleth, President
Products:
Athletic Jackets, Athletic Uniforms

RLS LIGHTING, INC.
203 ANSIN BOULEVARD
HALLANDALE, FL 33009
954-458-0345
800-226-1757
Fax: 954-983-3691
info@rlslighting.com
www.rlslighting.com
Products:
Sports Lighting, Street Lighting, Parking
Lighting, Area Lighting, Landscape Lighting
and Decorative Lighting, Aluminum Park
Benches, Bicycle Racks, Mail Boxes, Trash
Receptacles & Liners, Street Signs, Sign
Lighting

ROBBINS SPORTS SURFACES
4777 EASTERN AVENUE
CINCINNATI, OH 45226

513-871-8889
800-543-1913
Fax: 513-871-7998
info@robbinsfloor.com
www.robbinsfloor.com
• James H. Stoehr, Jr, Owner/Chairman of
Board
• Ken Thomas, VP Marketing
(513) 619-5964
• Ken Thomas, Vice President of Marketing
(513) 619-5932
Products:
Maple and synthetic sports flooring

ROBOT FACTORY
3740 INTERPARK DRIVE
COLORADO SPRINGS, CO 80907-5058
719-447-0331
800-717-6268
Fax: 719-447-0332
info@robotfactory.com
www.robotfactory.com
• Skip Engelbrecht, President
• Eileen Engelbrecht, VP
Products:
Robots and robotic devices for education,
entertainment, advertising and promotions.
Year Founded:
1966

ROCES USA, INC.
10 TECHNOLOGY DRIVE
UNIT 1B
W LEBANON, NH 3784
603-298-2137
800-770-8750
Fax: 603-298 2139
info@rocesusa.com
www.rocesusa.com
• Dave Smallwood, General Manager
davesmallwood@rocesusa.com
Description:
Inline Skates/Protective Gear, Ice Skates,
Quad Skates and Adjustable Ski Boots

ROCKPORT COMPANY
1895 JW FOSTER BOULEVARD
CANTON, MA 2021
781-401-5000
800-828-0545
Fax: 781-401-7402
www.rockport.com
• Paul Fireman, Chairman / Chief Executive
Officer
• Jay M. Margolis, President / Chief
Operating Officer
• Martin Coles, EVP / President / Chief
Operating Office
• Terry R. Pillow, SVP / Chief Executive
Officer-Ralph Laur
Products:
Walking shoes

ROCKY SHOES & BOOTS, INC.
39 E CANAL STREET
NELSONVILLE, OH 45764
740-753-1951
866-442-4908
Fax: 740-753-4024
www.rockyboots.com
• Mike Brooks, Chairman of Board / Chief
Executive Offi
• David Sharp, President / Chief Operating
Officer
• James E. McDonald, EVP / Chief Financial
Officer
• David R. Sharp, President

Products:
Premium quality rugged outdoor,
occupational, and casual footwear, as well
as branded clothing and accessories

ROGERS ATHLETIC COMPANY
3760 W LUDINGTON DRIVE
FARWELL, MI 48622
989-386-2950
800-457-5337
Fax: 888-549-9659
www.rogersathletic.com
Products:
Football practice and field equipments such
as sleds, chutes and dummies, strength
training equipment, dumbells and weight
plates, multi station strength machines.

ROL-DRI, INC.
2048 WIRT ROAD
HOUSTON, TX 77055
Products:
Tennis Court Equipment

ROLLER DERBY SKATE CORPORATION
311 W EDWARDS
PO BOX 249
LITCHFIELD, IL 62056
217-324-3961
Fax: 217-324-2213
info@rollerderbyskates.com
www.rollerderby.com
• Edwin C. Seltzer, President
Products:
Wheeled skates

ROLLERBLADE INC.
VIA FANTE D'ITALIA 56
31040
GIAVERA DEL MONTELLO, ITALY
03784-1673
800-232-7655
www.rollerblade.com
• Nicholas J. Skally, Public Relations and
Marketing Manager
nskally@rollerblade.com
• Jeremy Stonier, VP / General Manager
• Stephen Charrier, President
Products:
In-Line Skating Protective Gear, Skates

ROOTS APPAREL
1400 CASTLEFIELD AVENUE
TORONTO, ONTARIO, CANADA M6B 4C4
416-781-3574
866-297-6687
866-297-4327
B2Bsales@roots.com
www.roots.com
• Michael Budman, Co-Founder
• Don Green, Co-Founder
• Robert Sarner, Director Of
Communications/Public Affairs
rsarner@roots.com
• Jennifer Cornwell, Marketing Director
Products:
Activewear, Backpacks, Bedding & Bath
Linens and Accessories , Belts, Camping
Gear and Outdoor Accessories, Casual
Bags and Sporting Equipment

ROSSIGNOL SKI COMPANY, INC.
1413 CENTER DRIVE
PO BOX 981060
PARK CITY, UT 84098

371-6762-6025
800-437-6771
Fax: 371-6789-2053
inforossiusa@rossignol.com
www.rossignol.com
• Laurent Boix-Vives, Chairman
• Francois Goulet, President
• Daniel Mornet, VP
• M. Bruno Cercley, President
• Angelo Maina, Director, Racing Department
• Yann Laphin, Communications Director
Products:
Winter Sports Goods like board, binding, boot, pole and clothing

ROYAL PRECISION, INC.
8275 TOURNAMENT DRIVE
#200
MEMPHIS, TN 38125
860-489-9254
800-920-4747
Fax: 860-489-5454
• John C Lauchnor, President / Chief Executive Officer
Sales@RoyalPrecision.com
• Ronald L Chalmers, Manufacturing EVP
Sales@RoyalPrecision.com
• Ray Lucas, SVP Sales / Marketing
Sales@RoyalPrecision.com
• Scott Hennessy, President and CEO
Products:
Component Supply to Golf Club Manufacturers and Distributors.

ROYAL ROBBINS
1524 PRINCETON AVENUE
MODESTO, CA 95350
209-529-6913
800-587-9044
800-336-8661, CA ONLY
Fax: 209-522-5511
rrmail@royalrobbins.com
www.royalrobbins.com
• Royal Robbins, President / Owner
rrmail@royalrobbins.com
• Dan Costa, Chief Executive Officer
rrmail@royalrobbins.com
Products:
Manufacturer and Distributor of Activewear; Outdoor Products Apparel.

ROYAL TEXTILE MILLS, INC.
929 FIRETOWER ROAD
PO BOX 159
YANCEYVILLE, NC 27379
800-334-9361
Fax: 800-934-9360
info@dukeathletic-tactical.com
www.dukeathletic-tactical.com
• Mark Atwater, President
Products:
Baseball Protective-Catcher; Basketball Protective; Football Knee/Elbow Pads; General Sports Products Athletic Socks, Athletic Supporters, Support Products-Joint, T-shirts (Blank), Wristbands/Headbands; Ice Hockey Protective; Soccer Protective, etc.

ROYCE UNION BICYCLE COMPANY, INC.
6551 CENTERVILLE BUSINESS PARKWAY
CENTERVILLE, OH 45459
937-865-2800
800-872-2453
Fax: 937-856-5470

service@huffy.com
www.huffy.com
• John A Muskovich, Chief Executive Officer / President
customer.service@huffy.com
• Nancy A. Michaud, SVP, General Counsel / Secretary
customer.service@huffy.com
• Robert L Diekman, SVP, Operations / Logistics
customer.service@huffy.com
• Bill D Smith, President andCEO
customer.service@huffy.com
Products:
A diversified sporting goods company, marketing bicycles and wheeled products.

RPTC, LLC
300 BOSTON POST ROAD
ORANGE, CT 06477-3505
203-795-5696
800-950-5049
Fax: 203-795-9120
rgmtennis@aol.com
www.platformtennis.com
• Christopher Casiraghi, President / Chief Business
rgmtennis@aol.com
• Chris Casiraghi, President
Products:
Manufactures and Constructs Tennis Courts and Platform Tennis

RUBATEX CORPORATION
1001 BROAD STREET
BEDFORD, VA 24523
540-587-5870
800-782-2839
Fax: 866-532-4200
www.fostek.com
• Lynn Bakker, Technical Services VP
rubatexsales@rubatex.com
• Roger Schmidt, Manager Marketing / Technology
(800) 348-3428
rubatexsales@rubatex.com
• Stephanie Crisara, Sales VP
rubatexsales@rubatex.com
Products:
Closed cell rubber for use in pads and water sportswear.

RUBBERMAID INCORPORATED
3124 VALLEY AVENUE
WINCHESTER, VA 22601
540-542-8695
Fax: 540-542-8770
www.rubbermaid.com
• Mark D. Ketchum, Chief Executive Officer
• Hartley Blaha, President, Corporate Development
• Paul G. Boitmann, President, North American Sales Operatio
• Gino de Biondi, VP of Marketing
• Steve Pawl, VP of Marketing
Products:
Global marketer of consumer products for homes, commercial purposes and medical.

RUDIG TROPHIES
580 N 108TH PLACE
PO BOX 26429
WAUWATOSA, WI 53226
414-773-9000
Fax: 414-773-9181
rudigtrophy@sbcglobal.net
www.rudigtrophy.com

• Tom Rudig, President
• Nick Karegeannes, General Manager
Products:
Engravable Trophies, Awards, Components, Dealer Programs, Emblems, Expert Engravers, Medals, Plaques, Ribbons, Signs, Silkscreening.

RUFFOLO ENTERPRISES, INC.
2926 75TH STREET
KENOSHA, WI 53143
262-652-3126
800-877-7025
Fax: 262-652-3188
sales@fktools-us.com
www.fktools-us.com
• Ralph J Ruffolo, President
• Mary Ruffolo, Vice President
sales@fktools-us.com
Products:
Skiing-Alpine - Ski/Snowboard Car Racks; Skiing-Nordic - Ski Car Racks, FK/SKS Ski and Snowboard tuning tools, Wax, Irons and Vises, Diamond Stones.
Year Founded:
1975
Brands:
Ski-Hiker, FK, SKS, DMT

RUGBY IMPORTS, LTD.
885 WARREN AVENUE
E PROVIDENCE, RI 2914
401-438-2727
800-431-4514
Fax: 401-438-8260
gear@rugbyimports.com
www.rugbyimports.com
• Robert J Hoder, President
gear@rugbyimports.com
• Mark Hoder, VP
mark@rugbyimports.com
Products:
Rugby Balls, Jerseys, Shoes/Boots, Shorts, Socks, Uniforms.

RUGGERS RUGBY SUPPLY
121 UNION STREET
WEST SPRINGFIELD, MA 1089
413-746-9554
877-784-4377
Fax: 413-746-9526
sales@ruggers.com
www.ruggers.com
• Vic Thomas, President
vic@ruggers.com
Products:
Rugby shirts and equipment.

RUSSELL ATHLETIC
PO BOX 90015
BOWLING GREEN, KY 42104
877-879-8410
888-606-5520
Fax: 877-729-4800
www.russellathletic.com
• John F Ward, Chairman / Chief Executive Officer, Russ
• Calvin Johnston, Chief Executive Officer, Russell Athleti
• Mike Thorne, President, Russell Athletic Team and Bik
Products:
Baseball Uniforms; Basketball Uniforms; Football Uniforms; General Sports Products Athletic Jackets/Parkas, Sweat Clothes, Warm-Up Suits; Ice Hockey Uniforms; Lacrosse Uniforms; Soccer Uniforms;

Softball Uniforms; Track & Field/Running Apparel

RYKA, INC.
101 ENTERPRISE ROAD
SUITE 100
ALISO VIEJO, CA 92656
978-897-8744
888-295-8864
Fax: 503-525-7953
www.ryka.com
• Lance Rist, President
info@RYKA.com
Products:
Designs, develops and markets leading performance fitness products including performance athletic footwear and apparel.

RYNO ATHLETICS
1902 BRANDON DRIVE
TYLER, TX 75703
903-526-4140
888-609-6725
Fax: 800-574-0008
orders@ryno.com
ryno.com
• Brandon Steele, President/Chief Executive Officer
• Phil Steele, National Sales Manager
Products:
Products include backpacks and garment bags, baseball bags, premium duffels, specialty sport bags, team/travel duffels.
Year Founded:
1996

S'PORTABLE SCOREBOARDS
106 MAX HURT DRIVE
MURRAY, KY 42071
270-759-1600
800-323-7745
Fax: 270-759-4112
sales@sportablescoreboards.com
www.sportablescoreboards.com
• Michael C. Cowen, Chairman
mikecowen@scoreboard1.com
• Peter Cowen, President / Chief Executive Officer
Products:
Scoreboard Manufacturer, Timing Devices, Numeric Displays.

S.L. OUTERBANKS LLC
1000 EAST HANES MILL RD.
WINSTON-SALEM, NC 27105
800-685-7557
Fax: 800-289-1870
hbi_service@hanesbrands.com
• John Marsh, President
Products:
Manufacturer, Importer, Exporter of Knitted Polo Shirts; Golf Apparel.

S.M. ATHLETICS
10421 LEXINGTON DRIVE
KNOXVILLE, TN 37932
865-966-3434
800-332-3458
Fax: 865-966-3448
sales@smathletics.com
www.smathletics.com
• R. F. Saraceni, President
• John Sewell, VP
Products:
Baseball - Uniforms; Basketball - Uniforms; Football - Uniforms; General Sports

Products - Cheerleading, Warm-Up Suits; Ice Hockey - Uniforms; Soccer - Uniforms; Softball - Uniforms; Track & Field/Running; Volleyball - Uniforms.

SACO TECHNOLOGIES INC./SMARTVISION
7809 TRANS CANADA
MONTREAL, QUEBEC, CANADA H4S 1L3
514-745-0310
800-991-7226
Fax: 514-745-0315
www.lsi-industries.com
• Fred Jalbout, President/CEO
Products:
Large video screens for stadiums and other venues.

SAFE-T-GARD CORPORATION
12980 W. CEDAR DRIVE
PO BOX 1468
LAKEWOOD, CO 80228
303-763-8900
800-356-9026
800-382-6789
Fax: 303-763-8071
www.safetgard.com
• Scott Jacobs, President
• Kathy Jensen, Treasurer
Products:
Accessory equipment, ankle protection/stabilizers, bandages, athletic supporters, compression/sliding shorts, hot packs, mouth/nose/shin guards, fans, knee/elbow/forearm/ankle pads & supports, tape underwrap, volleyball padding, whistles, wraps

SAFEGUARD FLOOR SYSTEMS
5617 CROWNDALE DRIVE
PLANO, TX 75093
972-473-6746
Fax: 972-473-6746
• Lisa Willis, President
(972) 473-6746
lisawillis@safeguardfloors.com
Products:
Protective floor panel system.

SAFWAY SERVICES, LLC
N19 W24200 RIVERWOOD DRIVE
WAUKESHA, WI 53188
262-523-6500
800-558-4772
Fax: 262-523-9808
www.safway.com
• Jim Walters, Executive Vice President & CFO
• Jerry Johns, EVP / Chief Operating Officer
marketing@safway.com
• Robert Sukalich, VP / Chief Financial Officer
marketing@safway.com
• Jon Weber, VP / Controller
• Bill Hayes, President and CEO
• Chris Wells, Senior Vice President of Acquisitions & Corpo
• Marty McGee, Senior Vice President of Industrial Services
• Dana Valentine, Senior Vice President & Chief Human Resources
• Jon Weber, Vice President & Controller
• Curt Paulsen, VP Human Resources/General Counsel
Products:
Scaffolds and accessories
Year Founded:

1936
Description:
Safway Services rents and sells scaffolding, access equipment, and accessories, and provides labor and service support from project start to finish.

SALAUN SPORTS, INC., HENRI
210 W ROAD
PORTSMOUTH, NH 3801
603-436-0150
800-258-7255
Fax: 603-436-2869
sales@salaunsports.com
www.salaunsports.com
• Henri R Salaun, President
• Pamela Begdan, Manager
Products:
Basketball - Balls-Rubber, Nets; Football - Knee/Elbow Pads; General Sports Products - Athletic Supporters, Ball Inflators, Cones, Markers, Coaches Supplies, Junior and Official Size Goals, Wristbands/Headbands; Racquet Sports, Badminton Equipment, Gloves

SANDSTROM PRODUCTS COMPANY
224 MAIN STREET
PORT BYRON, IL 61275
309-523-2121
800-747-1084
Fax: 309-523-3912
mark@sandstromproducts.com
www.sandstromproducts.com
• Rick J Hartsock, Chairman
(309) 523-2121
• Brian Suhl, VP / Chief Operating Officer
(309) 523-2121
brian@sandstromproducts.com
• Brian Suhl, President
(309) 523-2121
• Mark Lousberg, Director of Sales
• Rick Wahlig, Purchasing Manager
• Dave Steele, Plant Manager
• Russ Burt, Technical Director
• Heather White, Director of Operations
• Linda Hocker, Customer Service
Products:
Solid film lubricants, piston skirt coatings, OEM coatings & product finishes, UV & energy cured coatings, floor coatings & resurfacers.

SARANAC GLOVE COMPANY
999 LOMBARDI AVENUE
GREEN BAY, WI 54304
920-435-3737 EXT 204
800-727-2622
Fax: 920-435-7618
jimz@saranacglove.com
www.saranacglove.com
• John Fabry, President / Chief Executive Officer
johnf@saranacglove.com
• Dan Small, Executive VP Sales / Marketing
dans@saranacglove.com
• Tina Rooks, Controller
tinar@saranacglove.com
• Judy Lundin, VP Sales Eastern Region
judyl@saranacglove.com
Products:
Sports, winter, motorcycle, industrial/work, home & garden gloves, mechanics, law enforcement gloves and accessories.

SATURNIAN 1 INC.
PO BOX 700538
PLYMOUTH, MI 48170
800-653-2719
Fax: 734-454-6514
info@sat1sport.com
www.sat1sport.com
• Mark Sassak, President
info@sat1sport.com
Products:
Tye dye kites & spinners. Indoor/outdoor games (trapp ball, thumb ball, basketball, beanbag shuffle, hip hopscotch, bat, ball & glove sets, golf, bowling, soft shoes, muckers, toss & target, flyer golf, basketball toss, soccer goal & ball, roll to score, tent & tube EZ twist games. Fun Gripper Balls, Toys and Collegiates.

SAUCONY
4200 SOUTH A STREET
RICHMOND, IN 47374
800-282-6575
Fax: 978-532-6105
customerservice@saucony.com
www.saucony.com
• Richie Woodworth, President
• Charles Gottesman, Vice Chairman / EVP Business Development
• Arthur E Rogers Jr, President Saucony Domestic
• Richie Woodworth, President
• John H. Fisher, Chief Executive Officer/Chairman
• Micheal Umana, Chief Operating Officer/Chief Financial Offic
Products:
Athletic footwear, casual footwear, apparel, and accessories.

SAUNDERS ARCHERY COMPANY
1874 14TH AVENUE
PO BOX 1707
COLUMBUS, NE 68601
402-564-7177
800-228-1408
Fax: 402-564-3260
www.sausa.com
• Gene Saunders, President
• Tom Saunders, Director, Plant 3, Screw Machine Operations
• Charles Saunders, Director, Product Development & Marketing
Products:
Archery equipments and accessories

SAVAGE FITNESS
39 PLEASANT VALLEY ROAD
PO BOX 488
SUTTON, MA 1590
508-865-0097
800-682-8416
Fax: 508-865-1925
• Michael Savage, President
• Donna Savage, VP Marketing
Products:
Treamdill accessories

SCHELDE NORTH AMERICA, LLC
4180 44TH STREET SE
SUITE C
GRAND RAPIDS, MI 49512-4057
616-554-4945
800-823-0182
Fax: 616-554-1623
www.scheldesports.com

• David Noe, Vice President Sales & Marketing
(616) 554-4945
dnoe@scheldesports.com
• David Noe, VP - Sales & Marketing
(616) 554-4945
• Bob Howell, National Sales Manager
(800) 820-7780
• Madelyn Meneghetti, Regional Product Specialist
(616) 554-4945
• John Connors, Service Manager
(616) 554-4945
• Ronna Russell, Regional Sales Manager
(800) 823-0182
• Logsdon, Regional Sales Manager
(800) 823-0182
Products:
Manufacturer of gymnasium equipment: basketball portables, ceiling and wall mounts, volleyball systems, wall pads, scorers tables, etc.

SCHOENBROD RACING SHELLS
596 ELM STREET
BIDDEFORD, ME 4005
207-283-3026
Fax: 207-985-6814
• Charles Dibble, President
Manufacturer & Distributor:
Rowing/Crew - Shells/Sculls.

SCHUESSLER KNITTING MILLS
301 MUNSON AVENUE
MCKEES ROCKS, PA 15136
412-331-6660
800-245-6111
Fax: 412-331-6347
Products:
Knitted Headwear

SCHUTT SPORTS INC
710 S INDUSTRIAL DRIVE
PO BOX 426
LITCHFIELD, IL 62056
217-324-2712
800-426-9784
Fax: 217-324-2732
www.schuttsports.com
• Dave Rossi, VP Marketing
(217) 324-2712
sales@schutt-sports.com
• Robert Erd, Chief Executive Officer
(217) 324-2712
sales@schutt-sports.com
• Kip Meyer, VP and General Manager
• Robert Erb, President and CEO
• Pete Reinke, VP Regional Development
• Mark Watts, Regional Sales Manager
(217) 324-2712
Products:
Baseball Batter's Guards, Catcher's Masks, Helmets; Basketball Backboards, Hoops, Nets, Padding, Rebounders; Football Faceguards, Helmets, Sports Collectibles, Softball Batter's Helmets, Catcher's Helmets. Baseball, Softball, Rec Bases.
Year Founded:
1918

SCHWINN CYCLING & FITNESS
1690 38TH STREET
BOULDER, CO 80301
800-605-3369
800-868-5764
Fax: 303-939-0260

customerservice@schwinnfitness.com
www.schwinn.com
• Jeff Sinclair, Chief Executive Officer
• Pat Warner, Fitness Director
• Charity Emmons, Marketing Manager
Products:
Bikes

SCOTT USA
110 LINDSAY CIRCLE
KETCHUM, ID 83340
208-622-1000
Fax: 208-622-1005
www.scott-sports.com
• Shauna Unser, Sales/Product Manager
• Larry Morton, Winter Sports Vice President/General Manager
• Lance Levy, Sales/Public Relations Coordinator
• Gabe Glosband, Marketing Manager
• Pascal Ducrot, President
Products:
Wintersport - Goggles, Poles, Skis, Protection, Gloves, Apparel, Hats; Motorsport - Goggles, Works system, Goggle Accessories, Replacement Lenses, Grips, Apparel, Sunglasses, Bags & Packs; Bike - Mountain, Road, Junior, Frames, Accessories, Bike wear, Mechanical wear, Eyewear; Paintball - Goggles, Replacement Lenses, Sunglasses, Apparel

SCOTTISH CHRISTMAS
6111 N PERIMETER ROAD
OSCODA, MI 48750
989-739-1600
800-259-6785
Fax: 248-391-5777
www.scottish-christmas.com
• Stan Aldridge, President / Owner
• Kevin Aldridge, Contact
Products:
Licensed Sports Ornaments

SEAGULL INTERNATIONAL, INC.
1220 SPRING GARDEN STREET
PHILADELPHIA, PA 19123
215-922-2100
800-666-9300
Fax: 215-922-0970
info@seagullintl.com
www.seagullintl.com
• Steven A Segal, President
info@seagullintl.com
Products:
Headwear, Bandannas & Headwraps, Tote Bags, Rainwear & Umbrellas, Footwear, Beach & Swim Accessories, Nylon Jackets, Gloves, Custom Designs, Product Display Racks, Souvenirs

SEALFLEX INDUSTRIES, INC.
3303 HARBOR BOULEVARD
SUITE C2
COSTA MESA, CA 92626
714-708-0850
800-651-2098
Fax: 714-708-2711
www.sealflex.com
• Dennis Davis, President
(800) 651-2098
• John Schneider, Vice President
(888) 378-4621
• Joe Luperico, Shipping
(714) 708-0850
• Cindi Miraldi Litecher, National Sales

manufacturers/retailers

Manager
(623) 376-9231
Nature of Service:
Moisture Mitigation Protecting Flooring
Materials
Year Founded:
1985
Products:
Floor Moisture Protection Products, Flooring
Adhesives (Moisture resistant) to 8 lbs, 5
year warranty.
Brands:
PH Blocker Primer 100, SL Ultratac 200, SL
Ultratac 255, SealFlex Membrane System,
MDK Kits.

SEATING SERVICES INCORPORATED
131 AVA DRIVE
HEWITT, TX 76643-2906
254-666-5155
800-433-3116
Fax: 254-666-4472
info@sturdisteel.com
www.sturdisteel.com
• Diane Cooke, President / Chief Executive
Officer
(800) 552-9470
• Timothy B Cooke, Sales & Marketing VP
(716) 549-9003
Services:
Seats, Arena & Auditorium, Replacement
Seating, Stadium Seating

SEATTLE BIKE SUPPLY
6004 S 190TH STREET
SUITE 202
KENT, WA 98032
425-251-1516
800-283-2453
Fax: 425-251-6041
www.seattlebikesupply.com
• Brent Carlson, Marketing / Sales Director
• Chuck Hooper, President
Products:
Bikes, Bike Parts

**SEATTLE SYSTEMS/LENOX HILL BRACE
COMPANY**
26296 TWELVE TREES LANE NW
POULSBO, WA 98370
360-697-5656
Fax: 360-697-5876
• Anthony Diemont, National Direct Sales
Supervisor
(360) 598-8955
adiemont@seattlesystems.com
• Dave Adams, EVP
(360) 598-8941
dadams@seattlesystems.com
• Anna Re Potts, Marketing / Customer
Service Director
(360) 598-8990
AReyes@seattlesystems.com
Products:
Orthotic Bracing, Cold Therapy, Sports
Medicine & Artificial Limb Components &
Systems

SEAWAY MATS, INC.
252 PARK STREET
MALONE, NY 12953
518-483-2560
800-361-0464
Fax: 518-207-0120
www.quedltd.com

• Gary Madden, Manager
(800) 361-0464
gary@queltd.com
Products:
Gym Mats, Divider Curtains, Goals & Post,
Padding, Protective Nets, Sport Nets,
Transporters, Wall Pads, Tike Site

SECONDWIND PRODUCTS, INC.
429 27TH STREET NW
HICKORY, NC 28601
828-322-2600
800-438-5777
Fax: 828-328-1700
info@tenseconds.com
www.tenseconds.com
• Steven W Lee, President
• Kevin Hansen, Operations VP / Chief
Financial Officer
• Bob Applegate, Marketing VP
• William A Blythe, Research &
Development Director
Products:
Insoles, Shoe Care, Cleats/Spikes, Shoe
Laces, Custom Laces/Lanyards, Sport
Socks

SEIRUS SPORTS ACCESSORIES
13975 DANIELSON STREET
POWAY, CA 92064
858-513-1212
800-447-3787
Fax: 858-513-7878
www.seirus.com
• Mike Carey, President
• Wendy Carey, VP
• Joe Edwards, VP
Products:
Neoprene, Fleece & Weatherproof
tri-laminate products

**SELECT DISTRIBUTION/VISION STREET
WEAR**
1763 PLACENTIA AVENUE
COSTA MESA, CA 92627
949-722-8556
800-854-7370
Fax: 949-722-1257
www.selectsk8.com
• Brad Dorfman, Owner
Products:
General Sports Products - Athletic Shoes;
Skates; Skateboards; Snowboarding
Apparel, Snowboards

SELECT SPORT AMERICA
1015 UNION CENTER DRIVE
SUITE 200
ALPHARETTA, GA 30004
770-751-9930
888-238-3097
Fax: 770-751-9940
info@selectsportamerica.com
www.selectsportamerica.com
• Peter Eigil Nielsen, Chairman
• Soren Nielsen, President
(888) 239-3097
info@selectsportamerica.com
• Peter Knap, CEO in Select Sport A/S
• Finn Martensen, Attorney at law
Nature of Service:
North American Distributor
Year Founded:
1997
Products:
Soccer Balls, Gloves, Shinguards,
Club/Camp/Training Apparel & Equipment,

Bags
Brands:
Select

SENECA SPORTS INC.
75 FORTUNE BOULEVARD
PO BOX 719
MILDFORD, MA 1757
508-634-3616
800-861-7867
Fax: 508-634-8154
• David L Landay, President
davidl@seneca.com
• Carl Fritz, Marketing Manager
carlf@seneca.com
• Robert Montolio, Sales Manager / Slumber
Bags & Tents
robertm@seneca.com
• Kevin Black, Sales Director / Brookfield
Division
kevinb@seneca.com
Products:
Ice Skates; In-Line Skating Accessories,
In-Line Skating Protective, In-Line Skating
Skates; Skateboarding Protective;
Skateboards; Soccer Balls, Soccer
Protective; Street Hockey Equipment, Street
Hockey Skates: Volleyball Balls

SETCOM CORPORATION
3019 ALVIN DE VANE BOULEVARD
SUITE 560
AUSTIN, TX 78741
650-965-8020
888-673-8266
Fax: 650-965-1193
info@setcomcorp.com
www.setcomcorp.com
• Bob Vo Buelow, Sales / Marketing Director
info@setcomcorp.com
• Donna Gallant, Sales / Marketing
Administrator
• Gordon Arnold, Account Executive
• James Roberts, President
Products:
Communication Equipment for firefighters,
police motorcycle officers, military, auto
racing, entertainment, and public safety and
industrial applications

SEVEN SONS AND COMPANY INC
139 INTERSTATE PARK
SPARTANBURG, SC 29303
864-587-5511
800-722-5794
Fax: 864-587-0745
info@sevensons.com
Products:
Sports apparel

SEVYLOR USA INC.
3600 N HYDRAULIC
WINCHITA, KS 67219
320-252-1642
800-835-3278
Fax: 316-832-6201
sevylor@coleman.com
www.sevylor.com
Products:
Kayaks, Canoes, Inflatables and Personal
Watercraft

**SHAKESPEARE FISHING TACKLE
DIVISION**
7 SCIENCE COURT
COLUMBIA, SC 29203

800-466-5643
800-334-9105
Fax: 803-786-8902
www.shakespeare-fishing.com
• David Lund, Vice President of Marketing
(803) 754-7000
Products:
Fishing Equipment & Accessories

SHAMROCK SPORTS BAG COMPANY
1000 MERIDIAN STREET
HUNTSVILLE, AL 35807
256-533-0210
800-447-8038
Fax: 256-772-2386
• Tim McCormick, President
Products:
Baseball Bags-Equipment; Basketball
Bags-Equipment; Fencing Bags; Football
Bags-Equipment; General Sports Products
All-Purpose Bags; Golf Bags-Luggage; Ice
Hockey Bags-Equipment; Ice Skating Skate
Bags; Racquet Sports Bags-Equipment;
Soccer Bags-Equipment

SHANGHAI WINGO INTERNATIONAL
NO 1438 SHANXI N ROAD
FORTUNE TIMES BUILDING
UNIT 1507
SHANGHAI, 200060
-86-6231-8482
Fax: -86-6232-0583
wingo@wingointernational.com
www.wingointernational.com
• Chris Young, Director
chris@wingointernational.com
Products:
Roller Skates and Scooters

SHAW & TENNEY
20 WATER STREET
PO BOX 213
ORONO, ME 4473
207-866-4867
800-240-4867
info@shawandtenney.com
www.shawandtenney.com
• Steven Holt, Owner
• Nancy Forster-Holt, Owner
Products:
Rowing Oars; Specialty and Sculling Oars;
Classic Paddles; For Adirondack Guide
Boats; Marine Hardware; Masts and Spars;
Boat Hooks; Pack Baskets; Canoe Parts &
Accessories; Apparel (Jackets, Hats,
T-shirts); Awards & Gifts (Souvenir and
Trophy Paddles, Souvenir and Trophy
Canoes, Paddle & Canoe Wall Plaque,
Canoe Plaque); Flag Poles and Yardarms

SHER-WOOD HOCKEY INC
2745 RUE DE LA SHERWOOD
SHERBROOKE, QUEBEC, CANADA J1K
1E1
866-563-2205
Fax: 819-821-4848
info@sher-wood.ca
• Bill Clark, President
(502) 588-7303
bill.clark@slugger.com
• Lou Candusso, Director of Operations
(519) 627-2248
• Graham Watson, VP Business
Development / USA Sales Mana
(734) 397-8324
gwlouisville@aol.com

• Dave Timbeck, Import Products Manager
dtimbeck@aol.com
Products:
Ice hockey players and goalies equipment,
bags, apparel and accessories

SHERMAN SPECIALTY COMPANY
300 JERICHO QUADRANGLE
SUITE 240
JERICHO, NY 11753
516-861-6420
800-645-6513
Fax: 516-861-1034
info@ShermanSpecialty.com

**SHERPA INC./DBA MOHN SKI RACK
COMPANY**
6580-B BELLEAU WOOD LANE
SACRAMENTO, CA 95822
916-395-9600
800-543-6646
Fax: 916-395-9625
www.mohnsportracks.com
• Jeff Zimmerman, President / Owner
info@mohnsportracks.com
Products:
Ski, Snowboard, Wakeboard, Skateboard
Racks

**SHERWOOD-DROLET CORPORATION,
LTD.**
2745 SHERWOOD BOULEVARD
QC, CANADA J1K 1E1
819-563-2202
866-563-2202
Fax: 819-821-4848
www.sher-wood.com
• Genevieve Therrien, Marketing Manager
Products:
Players (Player Sticks, Hockey Sticks,
Shafts, Blades, Blades Style, Protective
Equipment, Elbows Pads, Hockey Gloves,
Hockey Pants, Neckguard, Shinguards,
Shoulders Pads); Goalies (Goalie Sticks,
Protective Equipment, Goal Pads, Catch
Mitts, Blockers, Chest & Arm, Goal Pants)

SHIELD MFG, INC.
425 FILLMORE AVENUE
TONAWANDA, NY 14150
716-694-7100
800-828-7669
Fax: 716-694-8652
info@shieldsports.com
www.shieldsports.com
• David Berghash, Chief Executive Officer
dberghash@shieldsports.com
• James Geraci, President
(716) 694-7100
Products:
Team Hockey (Hockey Stick Sizing Chart,
Elementary, Middle School, Senior High
School/Collegiate Indoor, Senior High
School/Collegiate Outdoor); Accessories
(Hockey, Pucks & Balls, General and
Gymnasium).

SHIMANO AMERICAN CORPORATION
ONE HOLLAND DRIVE
IRVINE, CA 92618
949-951-5003
877-577-0600
Fax: 949-768-0920
www.shimano.com
• Yoshizo Shimano, President
• Yozo Shimano, President

Products:
Reels (Conventional Reels, Low Profile
Baitcasting Reels, Round Baitcasting Reels,
Spinning Reels, Saltwater Spinning Reels);
Rods (Freshwater Rods, Muskie Rods,
Salmon/Steelhead Rods, Freshwater
Trolling Rods, Inshore Rods, Butterfly
Jigging, Saltwater Rods, Kingfish Rods)

SHINN FU COMPANY OF AMERICA, INC.
10939 N POMONA AVENUE
KANSAS CITY, MO 64153
816-891-6390
888-332-6419
Fax: 816-891-6599
sfakc@shinnfuamerica.com
www.shinnfuamerica.com
• Joey Su, Executive VP
Products:
Lifting equipment (sevice jacks, jacks
stands, truck jacks, transmission jacks,
engine cranes, end lifts); Collision repair
equipment (porto-power kits, foot and hand
pumps, hydraulic rams, frame straightening
equipment and chainless anchor system)

SHIRTS & SKINS INC
10820 SW TUALATIN SHERWOOD ROAD
TUALATIN, OR 97062
503-646-4263
Fax: 503-646-4261
info@shirtsandskinsinc.com
www.shirtsandskinsinc.com
• Tamer Kiykiuglu, Vice President
(503) 646-4263
Products:
Team Uniforms (Reversible Uniforms -
Reversible Game Jersey, Reversible Game
Short, Reversible Practice Jersey, Practice
Short (non-reversible); Varsity Collection
Uniforms - Varsity Game Jersey, Varsity
Game Short, Varsity LS, Varsity Team
Jacket, Varsity Team Pant), Team Apparel.

SHOCK DOCTOR INC
3405 ANNAPOLIS LANE N
SUITE 200
PLYMOUTH, MN 55447
800-233-6956
866-253-1314
Fax: 888-446-5999
Products:
Lacrosse - Shoulder Pads, Arm Pads,
Gloves, Shorts, Equipment Bag, Backpack,
SlingPack, Impact Shirt, Rib Pads, Slash
Guard, Chin Cup; Baseball -Sliding Shorts,
Insoles; Hockey - Hockey Shorts, Insoles;
Football - Football Chin Cup, Turf Insole

SHYDA'S
1635 S LINCOLN AVENUE
LEBANON, PA 17042
717-274-2551
Fax: 717-274-6702
info@shydas.com
www.shydas.com
• Doris Shyda, Owner
info@shydas.com
• Segmund Sh Jr, President
info@shydas.com
Products:
Line of hunting and shooting clothing
(Hunting - Boots, Down, Fleece,
Hats/Caps/Neck Gaiters/HeadNet,
Jackets/Parkas, Lightweight, Long
Underwear, Pants/Bibs/Coverall, Rain Wear,
Supprescent, Sweaters/Shirts, Upland

Clothing, Vest; Wool -
Pants/Jacket/Shirt/Bib/; Shooting Sports -
Duffles/Backpack, Gloves, Waders/Rubber
Boots, Shirts/Sweaters, Jackets, Vests;
Boots - Boots/Shoes/Chest Waders, Boots,
Waders/Rubber Boots,
Casual/Hunting/Hiker/Snow,
Casual/Hiker/Uniform/Snow/Work,
Laces/Footbeds/Boot Care/Repla,
Hunting/Hikers/Rubber/Snow

SIDEOUT SPORT, INC.
6835 VALJEAN AVENUE
VAN NUYS, CA 91406
818-908-9868
Fax: 818-908-9191
The_Cherokee_Group@cherokeeusa.com
• Robert Margolis, Chairman of the
Board/CEO
• Howard Siegel, President
• Russell Riopelle, Chief Financial Officer
• Sandi Stuart, EVP, Brand Development
Products:
Tank, Hoodie, Tees, Long-sleeve Shirts,
Shirts and Pants, Cargos, Cords, Screen
Tees, Tees and Board Shorts, Skateboard,
Volleyball

SIERRA DESIGNS
2011 CHERRY STREET
SUITE 202
LOUISVILLE, CO 80027
510-450-9555
800-635-0461
Fax: 800-504-2745
www.sierradesigns.com
• Mark Mathews, Director of Sales
mmathews@sierradesigns.com
• Bob Swanson, Founder
Products:
Tents (Tents, Tarps, Accessories); Sleeping
Bags (Sleeping Bags, Bivies, Accessories)

SIGNATURE DESIGNS
798 RAYS ROAD
SUITE 105C
STONE MOUNTAIN, GA 30083
404-297-0028
866-525-0550
Fax: 706-266-3822
Products:
Full Color Printing for Flyers and Postcards,
Posters, Brochures, Business Cards,
Presentation Folders, Door Hangers, Rack
Cards, CD Inserts Tickets, Print Packages;
Apparel Printing for T-shirts and Baby Doll
Tees; CD Manufacturing, DVD
Manufacturing, Web Design, Cover Design

SIGNCO
5831 NORTH 58th STREET
LINCOLN, NE 68522
402-474-6646
866-848-6646
Fax: 402-474-3212
• Jim Graham, General Manager
(402) 474-6646
sales@signco.com
Products & Services:
LED Products & Services - LED Scoring
Table, Ribbon Board); Rotating/Static
Products & Services - Basketball Signs,
Baseball Signs, Football Signs; Concourse
Renovations - Corporate Sponsor Halo, Wall
Mounted Static Light Boxes, Retail Store &
Fixtures, Interactive Kiosks, Custom Signs &
Marquee, Customize Recognition Wall

Customize Recognition Wall/Timeline Wall,
Trophy Display Cases; Retail Printing
Products & Services - Banners, Vinyl Decals

SILVER KNIGHT SALES & MARKETING
576 GEORGESVILLE ROAD
COLUMBUS, OH 43228
614-274-1141
Fax: 614-274-1284
Products:
Athletic apparel

SIMS SPORTS, INC.
22105 23RD DRIVE, SE
BOTHELL, WA 98021
451-951-2700
Fax: 425-951-2740
www.simsnow.com
• John Textor, Chief Executive Officer
Products:
Snowboards

SIPES COMPANY, INC., HOWE K.
249 E MALLORY AVENUE
MEMPHIS, TN 38109-2598
901-948-0378
800-238-2682
Fax: 901-774-4380
• Howe K Sipes Jr, President
Products:
Athletic apparel - baseball and softball
uniforms, satin and wool jackets

SISKIYOU GIFTS
3551 AVION DRIVE
MEDFORD, OR 97504
800-866-7475
Fax: 800-650-9926
CustomerService@siskiyougifts.com
www.siskiyougifts.com
Products:
Belt Buckles, Key Chains, Jewelry and
Accessories, Money Clips, Zippos,
Beverage Ware, Leather Ware, Gifts, Cell
Phone Accessories, MP3 Holders,
Toothbrushes, and BBQ Sets.

SKANE LTD.
125 HIGH STREET
FARMINGTON, ME 04938-1929
207-778-9508
800-848-0468
Fax: 207-778-5043
skane@mainewest.com
• Leonard J Widen, President
• Kurt J Widen, VP
Products:
Skiing-Alpine - Apparel.

SKB SHOTGUNS
4441 S 134TH STREET
OMAHA, NE 68137-1107
800-752-2767
Fax: 402-330-8040
www.skbshotguns.com
• Robert Johansen, President
Products:
SKB Hunting Shotguns,
Accessories/Apparel & Parts/Wood

SKEA, LTD.
41184 HIGHWAY 6
SUITE 240
AVON, CO 81620

970-949-4815
800-338-6303
Fax: 970-949-1592
customersvc@skealimited.com
www.skealimited.com
• Diane J Boyer-Irwin, President
• Jocelyn M Boyer, Owner / Fashion
Coordinator
• Georges Boyer, Co Owner
Products:
Skiwear, Outerwear, Shimmies, Accessories

SKECHERS USA
228 MANHATTAN BEACH BOULEVARD
MANHATTAN BEACH, CA 90266
310-318-3100
800-746-3411
Fax: 888-566-5746
info@skechers.com
www.skechers.com
• Robert Greenberg, Chairman / Chief
Executive Officer
info@skechers.com
• Michael Greenberg, President / Director
info@skechers.com
• David Weinberg, EVP / Chief Operation
Officer
info@skechers.com
• Mark Nason, Merchandising EVP
info@skechers.com
Products:
Footwear for Women, Men & Kids

SKI SKOOT INC
2240 275 COURT
SAMMAMISH, WA 98075
425-557-8985
800-600-6945
Fax: 425-557-8907
www.skiskoot.com
• Dawn Carlton
(425) 941-3765
sales@skiskoot.com
Products:
Scooters for Summer and Winter Seasons

SKILLBUILDERS, INC.
1312 W GRANGER
BROKEN ARROW, OK 74012
918-258-9987
800-580-4314
Fax: 918-355-7412
sales@skillbuilder.com
www.skillbuilder.com
• Andi Upson, Office Manager
• Roy Hanks, Sales
roysellssports@gmail.com
• Heidi Robison, Sales
heidisellssports@gmail.com
• Selma Hamlin, IT/Internet Manager
Products:
Batting cages, pitching machines, field turf
and equipment, protective screens,
windscreen, fence crowns, stance mats,
pitching mounds, uniforms, putting greens,
flags, cups, golf nets and mats, uniforms.
Founded:
1997

SKIS DYNASTAR INC.
1413 CENTER DRIVE
PO BOX 981060
PARK CITY, UT 84098
435-252-3300
Fax: 435-252-3301
www.dynastar.com

Products:
Ski, Bindings, Ski Boots, Snowboards, Apparel and Accessories

SKYLINE NORTHWEST CORPORATION/DBA BARRACUDA SPORTS PRODUCTS
117 FOOTHILLS ROAD
LAKE OSWEGO, OR 97034
503-697-3225
800-547-8664
FAX: 800-238-4658
Fax: 800-238-4658
skyline@skylinenw.com
• John Runckel, Chief Executive Officer
skyline@skylinenw.com
• Rick Runckel, President
skyline@skylinenw.com
Products:
Ski, Snowboard, Swimwear, Swimming goggles andAccessories for Motorsports, Watersports, Wintersports, Swimwear, googles & fins and eye protection gear

SKYWAY
4451 CATERPILLAR ROAD
REDDING, CA 96003
530-243-5151
800-332-3357
Fax: 530-243-5104
generalinfo@skywaywheels.com
• Kenneth Coster, Chief Executive Officer
ken@skywaywheels.com
• Parrey Cremeans, Sales Deparment
sales@skywaywheels.com
• Ken Coster, Sales Deparment
• Rein Stolz, Engineering Department
• Patrick McEachen, Customer Service
Products:
Different kinds of Wheels such as: BEAD-LOK Wheels, Bicycle Wheels, Caster Wheels, Utility Wheels, Wheelchair Wheels, Standard Hubs, & other wheel accessories

SLAZENGER GOLF PRODUCTS CO
16651 N 84TH AVENUE
PEORIA, AZ 85382
623-523-6000
800-528-3133
• Tony Smith, National Sales Manager -Golf Division
• Dan Moore, National Sales Manager -Corporate Division
• Chris D Daltorio, President and CEO
Products:
Golf Apparel, Balls, Clubs-Wood/Iron Sets, Gloves, Hats/Caps/Visors.

SMACK APPAREL
2310 W STATE STREET
TAMPA, FL 33609
813-250-0627
877-762-2511
Fax: 813-251-4539
smacksales@smackapparel.com
www.smackapparel.com
Products:
Designed and Printed high quality sports apparel

SMC INNOVATIONS
103 PARK AVENUE WEST
PO BOX 269
WOODVILLE, WI 54028
715-698-3050
866-450-0200

Fax: 715-698-3061
customerservice@smc-innovations.com
Products:
High-precision injection molds and plastic parts for sporting goods and other applications.

SMITH SPORT OPTICS, INC.
280 NORTHWOOD WAY
BOX 2999
KETCHUM, ID 83340
208-726-4477
888-206-2995
Fax: 208-726-9584
smith@smithoptics.com
www.smithoptics.com
• Blair Clark, SVP Sales & Marketing
• Ned Post, President
• Ned Post, President
smith@smithoptics.com
Products:
Sunglasses, Snow Goggles, Snow Helmets, Motorsport Goggles, Accessories, Apparel.
Brands:
Smith Optics, Smith Helmets, SunCloud Polarized Optics

SMITH WOOD SPECIALTIES
6150 NW HIGHWAY
CHICAGO, IL 60631
708-209-6401
800-621-6450
Fax: 773-774-1753
jim@smith-wood.com
www.smith-wood.com
• James Smith, President
custserv@smith-wood.com
Products:
Laser and Color Plaques, Rectangular Plaques, State Plaques, Acrylic Awards, Bases and Sets, Certicate and Photo Plaques, Tablets and Trophies

SMITHCO
34 W AVENUE
WAYNE, PA 19087
610-688-4009
800-891-9435
Fax: 610-688-6069
smithco_home@msn.com
www.smithco.com
• Ted Smith, Founder
• Don Smith, President
ds@smithco.com
• Bill Kenney, VP Sales and Marketing
• Scott Taylor, Chief Engineer
Products:
Bunker Rakes, Athletic Field Conditioners, Field Markers, Turf Sweeper, Dedicated Spray Vehicles, Utility Vehicles, Specialized Greens Care Machinery & Other Spayers

SMYTH SYSTEMS, INC.
5 WALNUT GROVE DRIVE
SUITE 100
HORSHAM, PA 19044
888-789-9073
800-462-4372
Fax: 905-763-0527
www.smythsystems.com
• Barry Symons, Chief Executive Officer
Services:
Club Management Software for Country Clubs, Athletic Clus, City Clubs, Golf Coarses, Resorts

SOCCER PAL
1624 CROSBY ROAD
SUITE 124
CARROLLTON, TX 75006
469-574-1300
Fax: 469-574-1350
www.soccerpal.com
• Steve Ferguson, President
• Tina Amason, Marketing / Promotions Director
Products:
Soccer training equipment and accessories.

SOCCER SPORT SUPPLY CO., INC.
1745 FIRST AVENUE
NEW YORK, NY 10128
800-223-1010
Fax: 212-427-8769
soccersport@verizon.net
www.doss-soccer.com
• Hermann Doss, President
(212) 427-6050
• Dorothy Doss, President
• Scott Davidson, Manager
(212) 427-6050
Products:
Everything for soccer: Shoes, Uniforms, Balls, Playground Equipment, Practice Nets, Official Size Nets, Goalie Equipment, Goalie Uniforms, Goalie Gloves, Referee Uniforms, Referee Equipment.

SOCCEREDGE INC
35 MARLBOROUGH STREET
SUITE 7
BOSTON, MA 2116
617-267-0333
Fax: 617-267-0210
mail@socceredge.com
Products:
SoccerEdge Bungee Cord Training Tool

SOCCERMALL.NET
13747 MONTFORT DRIVE
SUITE 300
DALLAS, TX 75240
972-503-5501
866-762-2376
Fax: 972-404-9287
info@soccermall.net
www.soccermall.net

SOCCERPAL
1624 W CROSBY ROAD
SUITE 124
CARROLLTON, TX 75006
469-574-1300
800-676-2237
Fax: 469-574-1350
www.soccerpal.com
Products:
Training devices in Soccer, retail products, player's equipment, coach's equipment

SOF SOLE
9221 GLOBE CENTER DRIVE
MORRISVILLE, NC 27560
919-544-7900
800-446-7587
Fax: 919-314-1960
help@4implus.com
www.sofsole.com
• Todd Vore, President
(919) 544-7900
todd@4implus.com
• Kurt Wineman, Vice President Sales

(919) 544-7900
kurt@4implus.com
• Steve Head, Executive Vice President
Sales
(919) 544-7900
steve@4implus.com
• John Andrews, Vice President Marketing
(919) 544-7900
john@4implus.com
Products:
Performance Insoles, Comfort Insoles,
Technical Socks, Fashion Accessories,
Shoe Care, Traction Devices.
Brands:
Sof Sole®, Yaktrax®, Apar™, Airplus®, Sof
Comfort®

SOFFE COMPANY, INC.
ONE SOFFE DRIVE
PO BOX 2507
FAYETTEVILLE, NC 28312
888-257-8673
800-444-0337
Fax: 910-486-9030
www.soffe.com
• Ken Spires, President
customerservice@mjsoffee.com
• James Soffe, Chief Executive Officer
customerservice@mjsoffee.com
• Tony Cimaglia, Operations VP
customerservice@mjsoffee.com
• Dick Soffe, Manufacturing EVP
• Ray Edwards, VP of Strategic
• Evan Gettenberg, Director - Sales
Inventory Management
• Greg Roscoe, Midwest Regional Sales
Manager
groscoe@mjsoffe.com
• Tim Wann, Southern Regional Sales
Manager
twann@mjsoffe.com
Products:
T-shirts, jerseys, shorts, fleece wear

SOFTBALL RAMPAGE
2177 WESTBELT DR.
COLUMBUS, OH 43228
614-629-9934
877-868-8945
Fax: 614-527-8565
service@softballrampage.com
http://www.softballrampage.com
Nature of Sports Service:
Softball Rampage is the official online retail
partner of the National Pro Fastpitch.

SOFTRIDE
4201 MERIDIAN STREET
BELLINGHAM, WA 98226
360-647-7420
888-258-7286
Fax: 360-647-1884
info@softride.com
www.softride.com
• Mike Allsop, Chief Executive Officer
info@softride.com
• Glen Morgan, Business Development VP
info@softride.com
Products:
Bikes, Indoor Cycling Bike, Racks, Towing,
Accessories

SOL-EFFECT ENTERPRISE COMPANY LTD
11878 CLARK STREET
ARCADIA, CA 91006

626-599-8277
888-626-2999
Fax: 626-599-9897
sol@soleffect.com
Products:
Balls, Skates, Fitness, Sports Toys,
Accessories

SOLAR TAN THRU SUITS
5455 W WATERS AVENUE
SUITE 215
TAMPA, FL 33634-1208
813-886-6800
888-826-8478
Fax: 813-889-9900
sales@solartanthru.com
www.solartanthru.com
• Dale Sanders, President
• Helen Katrnak, VP
Products:
Manufacturers, Distributors, Importers and
Exporters of Water Sports Accessories, and
Fashion Apparel

SOLE CHOICE, INC.
830 MURRAY STREET
PORTSMOUTH, OH 45662
740-354-2813
800-848-8696
Fax: 740-353-4669
sales@solechoiceinc.com
www.solechoiceinc.com
• Steven Keating, President & Chief
Executive Officer
• Bryan Davis, VP Sales
• Beth Minton, Marketing Director
• Michael Keating, Regional Sales Manager
Products:
Blister Pak, Sports Laces, Boot, Work &
Military Laces, Hiking & Hunting Laces, Self
Shining Liquids, Athletic Creams, Mink Oil
and Saddle Soap, Suede & Nubuck Cleaner
and Protector, Rain & Stain Repellent,
Water Repellent, Silicone Water Repellent,
Athletic Shoe Shampoo, Athletic Gel
Cleaner, Shoe Deodorizers, Shoe Goo, Boot
& Shoe Cleaning Tool
Brands:
MPRO
Year Founded:
1902

SOLE CUSTOM FOOTBEDS
608 CRESCENT CIRCLE
GREAT FALLS, MT 59404
403-204-0907
866-949-7653
Fax: 888-691-0714
sales@yoursole.com
www.yoursole.com
• Mike Baker, President
• Greg Davidson, Web Developer
• Rob Nathan, Product Director
Products:
Heat moldable custom footbeds,
performance socks
Nature of Service:
Manufacturer and Distributor of premium
custom insoles.
Brands:
SOLE Custom Footbeds, SOLE
Performance Socks

SONY COMPUTER ENTERTAINMENT AMERICA, INC.
989 E HILLSDALE BOULEVARD
2ND FLOOR
FOSTER CITY, CA 94404
650-655-8000
800-345-7669
Fax: 650-655-8001
www.us.playstation.com
• Jack Tretton, CEO
Products:
Electronic sports devices.

SONY SPORTS
64-A HALI ROAD
SIE
SIALKOT-4, PAKISTAN 51340
-92-355-6642
Fax: -92-355-4323
info@sony-sports.com
www.sony-sports.com
• M Younus Sony, Chief Executive Officer
info@sony-sports.com
• M Yo Sony, Partner
info@sony-sports.com
• Faisal Yo Sony, Partner
info@sony-sports.com
• M. Younus Sony, Chief Executive
• Yousaf Sony, Director
Products:
Fitness Accessories, Boxing Gloves,
Weightlifting Belts, Boxing Accessories,
Punching/Boxing Mitts, Sadal/Tool Bags,
Motocross Gloves, Sailing Gloves, Cycling
Gloves, Weightlifting Gloves, Martial Art
Uniforms and track suits, Protection
Equipment, Karate Protection Gears

SOUND & VIDEO CREATIONS, INC
2408 FELTS AVE
NASHVILLE, TN 37211
615-460-7330
Fax: 615-460-7331
support@clickeffects.com
www.clickeffects.com
• Ed Filmia, Senior Director
Products:
Click Effects Pro-AV, Click Effects Audio,
Click Effects Replay

SOUTHERN BLEACHER COMPANY, INC.
801 FIFTH STREET
PO BOX ONE
GRAHAM, TX 76450
940-549-0733
800-433-0912
Fax: 940-549-1365
www.southernbleacher.com
• Jo Ann Pettus, President
(800) 433-0912
jpettus@southernbleacher.com
• Bill Duckworth, Operations Manager
• Andy Smith, Project Coordinator
• Randy Wray, Installation Manager
• Rusty Hughes, Project Coordinator
• Justin Campbell, Project Coordinator
• Garrett Pettus, VP of Southern Bleacher
(800) 433-0912
gpettus@southernbleacher.com
• Wyatt Pettus, Director Special Events
(800) 433-0912
wpettus@southernbleacher.com
Products:
Stadiums, Grandstands, Decking Systems,
Seating Options, Coatings, Bleachers, Press
Boxes, High School Facilities
Clients:

School districts and colleges throughout the U.S.
Year Founded:
1946

SOUTHERN UMBRELLA COMPANY, INC./DBA SOUTHERN PLUS
1611 ZION CME CHURCH ROAD
HARTWELL, GA 30643
706-376-5151
800-241-7107
Fax: 706-376-1244
www.southernplus.com
• Grethe Adams, President
• Brannon Craig, National Sales Manager
Products:
Umbrellas, Chairs, Coolers, Blankets, Picnic, Bags, Totes, Fitness, Collections

SOUTHLAND ATHLETIC MANUFACTURING COMPANY
714 E GROVE STREET
PO BOX 280
TERRELL, TX 75160
972-563-3321
800-527-7637
Fax: 972-563-0943
• William C Sturgeon, President
• Armando DeLeon, Plant manager
Products:
Baseball uniforms, Softball uniforms, Basketball uniforms, Track uniforms, Football uniforms

SOYAD BROTHERS TEXTILE CORPORATION
24011 HOOVER ROAD
WARREN, MI 48089
586-755-5700
800-922-9923
Fax: 586-755-3790
quality@soyadsocks.com
www.soyadsocks.com
• Tom Soyad, President
quality@soyadsocks.com
Products:
Sport Socks

SPECIALIZED BICYCLE COMPONENTS, INC.
15130 CONCORD CIRCLE
MORGAN HILL, CA 95037
408-779-6229
877-808-8154
Fax: 408-779-1631
store_customerservice@specialized.com
www.specialized.com
• Mike Sinyard, President / Founder
customerservice@specialized.com
• Michael Haynes, Chief Financial Officer
customerservice@specialized.com
• Bob Margevicius, EVP
customerservice@specialized.com
Products:
Bikes, Equipment

SPECIALTY NETS
535 BRAGATO ROAD
SUITE B
SAN CARLOS, CA 94070
650-591-0505
800-645-6790
Fax: 800-645-6791
info@specialtynets.com
• Victor K. Saiz, General Manager

Nature of Service:
Private labeling - sports and industrial netting, finished and/or unfinished, knit to domestic manufactures and importers specifications - product development department available.
Year Founded:
1975
Products:
Baseball Nets, Field Hockey Nets, Golf Driving Nets/Mats, Ice Hockey Nets, Lacrosse Nets, Racquet Sports Tennis Nets, Soccer Nets, Softball Nets, Volleyball Nets, Wind Screens, Bird Protection Nets. Products also include baseball and combination baseball/golf batting tunnel nets.

SPECTRUM CORPORATION
10048 EASTHAVEN BOULEVARD
HOUSTON, TX 77075
713-944-6200
800-392-5050
Fax: 713-944-1290
info@spectrumscoreboards.com
www.spectrumscoreboards.com
• Jim B. Bishop, President
(713) 944-6200
jim@specorp.com
• Gary Liddell, Sales/Marketing VP/Vice President/Treasurer
(713) 944-62
info@specorp.com
• Tyson Swan, Office Manager
(713) 944-6200
info@specorp.com
• Tim Kyle, Athletic Director
Products:
Scoreboards, Display Solutions, Software Solutions, Outdoor Message Centers
Nature of Service:
Manufacturer, Sales and Service

SPEED SKATELUBE
5858 ENGINEER DRIVE
HUNTINGTON BEACH, CA 92649
714-898-4377
Fax: 714-891-7467
tiodize@tiodize.com
www.tiodize.com
• Tom Adams, President
(714) 902-0501
tom.adams@tiodize.com
• Wades Friedrichs, Marketing
(714) 902-0507
wade.friedrichs@tiodize.com
• Thomas R. Adams, President
(714) 898-4377
tom.adams@tiodize.com
• Wade Friedrichs, Marketing
(714) 898-4377
wade.friedrichs@tiodize.com
• Tom Moore, Purchasing
(714) 898-4377
tom.moore@tiodize.com
• Gary Wittman, Technical Director
(714) 902-0506
gary.wittman@tiodize.com
• Rudy Villegas, Material Processing Control Shipping & Reciev
(714) 902-0510
customerservice@tiodize.com
• Patty Enna, Controller
(714) 898-4377
patty.enna@tiodize.com
Products:
Composite Fasteners, Self-Lubricating Composites, Anodizing, Emissivity, Dry Film

Lubricants, Corrosion Coatings, Sport and Consumer Products, Racing Products

SPEEDLINE ATHLETIC WEAR, INC.
1804 N HABANA AVENUE
TAMPA, FL 33607
813-876-1375
Fax: 813-873-8714
service@speedlineathletic.com
www.speedlineathletic.com
• Steven Malzone, President
smalzone@propakspeedline.com
Products:
Baseball Uniforms; Basketball Uniforms; Football Uniforms; General Sports Products Athletic Jackets/Parkas, Referee Uniforms, Warm-Up Suits; Soccer Uniforms; Softball Uniforms; Track & Field/Running Apparel-Track & Field; Volleyball Uniforms

SPEEDPLAY, INC.
10151 PACIFIC MESA BOULEVARD
SUITE 107
SAN DIEGO, CA 92121
858-453-4707
800-468-6694
Fax: 858-453-5871
email@speedplay.com
www.speedplay.com
• Richard Bryne, Chief Executive Officer
email@speedplay.com
• Sharon Worman, President
email@speedplay.com
Products:
High-performance pedal systems for on-road and off-road cyclists

SPIRIT MANUFACTURING
3000 NESTLE ROAD
JONESBORO, AR 72401
870-935-1107
800-258-4555
Fax: 800-935-7611
www.spiritfitness.com
• Roger Hurt, President
Products:
Treadmills, Ellipticals, & Bikes

SPORT CARD CREATIONS INC.
131 S MAIN STREET
NATICK, MA 1760
508-653-1731
Fax: 508-655-7758
ddds11@aol.com
www.sportcardcreations.com
• Denise LePage, President / Chief Executive Officer
(508) 653-1731
ddds11@aol.com
Products:
Sells sport card displays for sport cards, collectibles etc.

SPORT COLLECTORS GUILD INC
7310 W ROOSEVELT STREET
SUITE 32
PHOENIX, AZ 85043-2219
623-478-0007
800-950-0320
Fax: 602-233-9490
www.replicastadiums.com
Products:
Unique handicrafted replicas, memorabilia, and military items

SPORT COURT, INC.
939 S 700 W
SALT LAKE CITY, UT 84104
800-421-8112
Fax: 801-401-3504
www.sportcourt.com
• Ronald N Cerny, President / Chief
Executive Officer
info@sportcourt.com
• Ronald Yokubison, VP Finance / Chief
Financial Officer
• Troy Mohr, VP Manufacturing
• Ron Cerny, President
• Andrew Gettig, VP International
• Ryan Burke, International Business
Manager
Products:
Manufacturer of flooring systems, from
outdoor game courts to indoor gymnasiums,
roller hockey rinks to synthetic putting
greens (Tennis-Courts; Racquet Sports;
Flooring; Lighting Systems; Nets)

SPORT FACE
4275 THUNDERBIRD LANE
FAIRFIELD, OH 45014
513-671-2800
877-611-2800
Fax: 513-671-2830
info@sportface.com
www.sportface.com
Products:
Face and body paint in convenient
easy-to-use tubes

SPORT HALEY INC.
4600 E 48TH AVENUE
DENVER, CO 80216
303-320-8800
800-627-9211
800-701-6478
Fax: 303-320-8820
customerservice@sporthaley.com
www.sporthaley.com
• Patrick Hurley, SVP / Chief Financial
Officer
info@SportHaley.com
• Robert Haley, President / Director
• Cathy Blair, President and Creative
Director
• Lisa Langas, National Sales Manager
(303) 320-8915
• Erin Scrimshaw, National Key Accounts
Manager
(303) 946-1254
Products:
Fashion golf apparel and outerwear

SPORT HELMETS, INC.
4635 CROSSROAD PARK DRIVE
LIVERPOOL, NY 13088
315-453-3073
800-537-1702
Fax: 315-453-3762
helmets@cascadehelmets.com
• Stephen Moore, President
• Bill Brine, Founder
Products:
Large manufacturer of lacrosse helmets and
eyemasks, including a water rescue helmet

SPORT OBERMEYER, LTD.
115 AABC
ASPEN, CO 81611
970-925-5060
800-525-4203
Fax: 970-925-9203

custserv@obermeyer.com
www.obermeyer.com
• Klaus Obermeyer, President
(970) 925-5060
lindage@obermeyer.com
• Klaus Obermeyer, Founder and President
(970) 920-6663
lindage@obermeyer.com
• Robert Yturri, Senior VP, Brand
Management
Products:
Mens collection, ladies collection, juniors
collection and preschool collection of
performance clothing.

SPORT PINS INTERNATIONAL, INC.
888 BERRY COURT
UPLAND, CA 91786-8439
909-985-4549
800-949-7467
Fax: 909-982-0912
www.sportpins.com
• Connie Bivens, President
(800) 949-7467
• Jon Bivens, CEO/CFO
(800) 949-7467
jonbivens@sportpins.com
• Jeff Bivens, Director Sales
(800) 949-7467
jeffbivens@sportpins.com
• Maria Bivens, Marketing Manager
• Mike Bivens, Vice President Operations
(800) 949-7467
mbivens@sportpins.com
Nature of Service:
Provider of recognition products to the
sports and corporate markets, with special
emphasis on the youth and professional
soccer markets.
Year Founded:
1980
Products:
Manufacturer of top quality lapel pins,
medallions, commemorative coins,
embroidered patches, key chains, jewelry
and other recognition products, laser
engraved glass, wood, and acrylic awards.

SPORTCAP, INC.
3314 INDUSTRY DRIVE
SIGNAL HILL, CA 90755
562-494-8950
877-337-2282
Fax: 562-494-8920
authsportcap@gmail.com
www.authenticsportcap.com
Products:
Baseball Caps/Visors/Hats; General Sports
Products Caps/Hats/Visors; Softball Caps

SPORTDECALS
PO BOX 860
SPRING GROVE, IL 60081-0860
815-675-2471
800-435-6110
Fax: 800-557-3322
sports@sportdecals.com
www.sportdecals.com
• Donald Metivier, Founder
Products:
Baseball Helmet Decals; Football Helmet
Decals; Athletic Jackets; Cheerleading
Supplies; Decals; Die Cut; Letters;
Numerals and Illustrations/Calendars;
Screen Printing; Sweatclothes; T-shirts; Ice
Hockey Helmet Decals; Lacrosse Helmet
Decals and Banners

SPORTGRASS, INC.
6718 WHITTIER AVENUE
SUITE 220
MCLEAN, VA 22101
703-288-1800
Fax: 703-288-1873
• William Ward, Chairman
• Brian Wood, General Manager
Services:
Provides construction and installation of
SportGrass for athletic field

SPORTIF U.S.A.
1415 GREG STREET
SUITE 101
SPARKS, NV 89431
775-359-6400
800-921-1655
Fax: 775-353-3400
customerservice@sportif.com
www.sportif.com
Products:
Manufacturer of tennis shorts, fishing,
nautical and outdoor apparel

SPORTIME
4671 E AIRPORT DRIVE
ONTARIO, CA 91761-7869
909-390-0334
800-472-7790
Fax: 800-497-1444
order@sptdistctr.com
www.sptdistctr.com
• Troy Niswander, President
troy@sptdistctr.com
• Tanya Purcell, Secretary / Treasurer
• Charlie McWilliams, Wholesale Manager
Products:
Distributor: Sporting goods

SPORTLINE INC
4 EXECUTIVE PLAZA
YONKERS, NY 10701
914-964-5200
800-338-6337
Fax: 914-964-1283
www.sportline.com
• Larry Livingston, Founder
Products:
Manufacturer and distributor of sports timing
and fitness products such as stopwatches,
pedometers and sport watches

SPORTMASTER
2520 S CAMPBELL STREET
PO BOX 2277
SANDUSKY, OH 44870
419-626-4375
800-395-7325
Fax: 419-626-5477
info@sportmaster.net
www.sportmaster.net
• Jeff Earheart
info@sportmaster.net
Products:
Sport Surfacing, Traffic Paints, Crack Fillers,
Tools/Accessories

SPORTMASTER INC.
521 MADISON AVENUE
COVINGTON, KY 41011
606-431-3555
Fax: 606-431-3556
• Mark Wheatley, President
Products:
Distributor: Logowear

1204

SPORTS ACCESSORIES AMERICA INC.
4935 IRIS STREET
WHEAT RIDGE, CO 80033
303-431-0875
800-321-7245
Fax: 303-431-9873
• Phil Seifert, Chief Executive Officer
Products:
Trophies, Awards Crests, Emblems, Jewelry, Patches

SPORTS AUTHORITY, INC.
1050 W HAMPDEN AVENUE
ENGLEWOOD, CO 80110
303-200-5050
800-589-0483
Fax: 303-863-2240
www.sportsauthority.com
• Doug Morton, Chairman and Chief Executive Officer
dmorton@thesportsauthority.com
• Paul Gaudet, Executive Vice President/Store Operations
• Darrell Webb, Chairman of the Board/Chief Executive Officer
• Thomas Hendrickson, Executive Vice President, Chief Financial Off
• Greg Waters, Executive Vice President/Merchandising
clee@thesportsauthority.com
Products:
Sporting goods and information such as apparel, footwear, team sports, golf/racquet, outdoor, action sports, fan shop, games, accessories and women's shop

SPORTS BELLE INC.
6723 PLEASANT RIDGE ROAD
KNOXVILLE, TN 37921
865-938-2063
800-888-2063
Fax: 865-947-4465
www.sportsbelle.com
• Royd Walker, Sales / Marketing Director
Products:
Baseball Jerseys, Uniforms; Basketball Uniforms; Football Uniforms; General Sports Products Apparel

SPORTS COVERAGE
5535 MILITARY PARKWAY
DALLAS, TX 75227
214-381-3096
800-460-8234
Fax: 214-381-4585
www.sportscoverageinc.com
Products:
Shower Curtain, Comforter, Sham, Valance, Drape, Bedskirt, Jersey Sheet Set, Pillow Case, Tail Gate Kit (Apron & Mitt), Apron, Sham Pillow, Box Toss Pillow, Box Floor Pillow, Bath Set

SPORTS HEALTH
865 MUIRFIELD DRIVE
HANOVER PARK, IL 60133
866-323-5465
800-323-1305
Fax: 866-235-1305
info@schoolhealth.com
• John Miller, National Sales Manager
(800) 367-8319
• Gina Streepy, Product Director
(800) 323-1305
gstreepy@schoolhealth.com
• Susan Rogers, President
(800) 323-1305

• Tory L., MA ATC, Associate Athletic Director
• Phil V. MSEd, ATC/L, Assistant Athletic Director
• Scott O., Assistant Athletic Trainer
• Pat B., Office Assistant
Products:
Asthma and Allergy Products, Diabetic Products and Syringes, Asthma Treatment and Response Products, CPR and Automated External Defibrillators, Fire Safety, Mobile Communications, Training Manikins and Resuscitation Devices, First Aid and Bandages, Furniture and Equipment, Health Education Resources, Hot/Cold and Hydro Therapy, Hydration and Nutrition Products, Infection and Infestation Control, Paper and Plastic Products, Pharmacy, Rehab Equipment and Supplies, Sports Medicine Supplies, Vision and Hearing products, Vital Statistics and Health Assessment

SPORTS IMMORTALS MUSEUM
6830 N FEDERAL HIGHWAY
BOCA RATON, FL 33487
561-997-2575
Fax: 561-997-6949
www.sportsimmortals.com
• Jim Platt, Vice President
(561) 997-2575
legends@sportsimmortals.com
• Jim Platt, Vice President
(561) 997-2575
legends@sportsimmortals.com
Year Founded:
1992.
Description:
Sports Immortals Museum contains over one million mementos from the world's greatest athletes.
Sports Products Manufactured or Sold:
Retail store offers a selection of over 20,000 unique sports collectible items for sale.

SPORTS IMPORTS
PO BOX 21040
COLUMBUS, OH 43221
614-771-0246
800-556-3198
Fax: 614-771-0750
info@sportsimports.com
www.sportsimports.com
• Brad Underwood, President
info@sportsimports.com
• Tom Johnson, Athletic Director
Products:
Volleyball, badminton and tennis equipment

SPORTS INC
333 2ND AVENUE N
LEWISTOWN, MT 59457
406-538-3496
Fax: 800-227-7207
Info@hq.sportsinc.com
www.sportsinc.com
Description:
Sporting goods buying group.

SPORTS MEDIA, INC.
520 8TH STREET
QUAD CITIES, IL 61282
309-755-6557
Fax: 801-981-2566
CustomerService@SportsMedia.net
www.sportsmedia.net

• Dan Kosth, Chief Executive Officer
(312) 436-0500
dan@sportsmedia.net
• Scott Posnanski, CIO & CFO
(262) 456-5629
scott@sportsmedia.net
Products:
Sports media stadium concession products such as CD Cup Lids, 3D Lenticular Cups, Photo Cups, Plastic Cups, Cup Holders and Concession Trays
Description:
Sports Marketing Agency

SPORTS POSTER WAREHOUSE
55 QUEEN'S PLATE DRIVE
UNIT 9
TORONTO, ONTARIO, CANADA M9W 6P2
416-696-8353
888-650-3455
Fax: 416-352-5418
info@sportsposterwarehouse.com
www.sportsposterwarehouse.com
• Niel Flagg, President
Products:
sports posters

SPORTS SENSORS INC
11351 EMBASSY DRIVE
PO BOX 46198
CINCINNATI, OH 45420
513-825-5745
888-542-9246
Fax: 513-825-8532
adilz@cinci.rr.com
www.sportssensors.com
• Al Dilz, President
(888) 542-9246
adilz@cinci.rr.com
Year Founded:
1998.
Services:
Affordable, portable supplier radar training aids and doppler radars for sports applications.
Products:
Glove radar, swing speed radar, paintball radarchron, arrowspeed radarchron, swing speed radar with tempo timer, kickspeed radar

SPORTS SUPPLY GROUP
1901 DIPLOMAT DRIVE
DALLAS, TX 75234
972-484-9484
800-527-7510
Fax: 972-406-3467
feedgym@sportsupplygroup.com
www.sportsupplygroup.com
• Geoffrey P. Jurick, Chairman / Chief Financial Officer
feedgym@sportsupplygroup.com
• John P. Walker, President / Director
jwalker@sportsupplygroup.com
• Robert Mitchell, Chief Financial Officer
(972) 406-3484
bmitchell@sportsupplygroup.com
• Michael P. Glassman, Sales / Marketing VP
mglassman@sportsupplygroup.com
Products:
Recreational equipments, athletic and sports equipment products

SPORTS TUTOR INC
3300 WINONA AVENUE
BURBANK, CA 91504

manufacturers/retailers

1205

818-972-2772
800-448-8867
Fax: 818-972-9651
intl-sales@sportstutor.com
www.sportstutorinc.com
• Thomas Kekalos, Sales Manager
(818) 972-2772
Products:
Sports machines for baseball, volleyball,
soccer and tennis
Year Founded:
1988

SPORTS WEST SALES, INC.
999 OAKCREST AVENUE
BREA, CA 92821
714-671-0895
800-996-2811
Fax: 714-255-0571
normsws@aol.com
• Norm Lamming, President
Products:
Baseball Equipment, Jackets, Socks,
Uniforms, Basketball Equipment, Football
Equipment, Socks, Uniforms, Athletic
Jackets, Nets, Sweatclothes, T-shirts,
Bags-Equipment, Racquet Sports Apparel,
Soccer Bags-Equipment, Balls, Uniforms,
Softball Bags-Equipment

SPORTS-FASHION
5381 RIVERWALK TRAIL
COMMERCE TOWNSHIP, MI 48382
248-310-9462
Fax: 248-366-9779
www.sports-fashion.com
Products:
Fitness and sport wear

SPORTSPLAY EQUIPMENT, INC.
8505 DELMAR BLVD
SUITE G
SAINT LOUIS, MO 63124
314-389-4140
800-727-8180
Fax: 314-389-9034
smeyer@sportsplayinc.com
www.sportsplayinc.com
• Scott Meyer, Director of Marketing
smeyer@sportsplayinc.com
Products:
Basketball backboards and sports
equipment, playground equipment, merry go
rounds, swings, see saws, ADA play
products, spring riders, independent slides,
fitness equipment, and site amenities.
Description:
Known for fun equipment of exceptional
safety and durability since 1996. Offers a full
sports line as well as modern playground
equipment.

SPORTSPRINT
6197 BERMUDA ROAD
SAINT LOUIS, MO 63135
314-521-9000
800-325-4858
Fax: 314-521-0395
www.sportsprint.com
• Ralph Rockamann, Owner / President
ralph@sportsprint.com
• Lance Walker, Sales Manager
lance@sportsprint.com
• Connie Bailey, Sales Contact
connie@sportsprint.com
• Tim Bennett, Production Manager
tim@sportsprint.com

SPRI PRODUCTS INC
1769 NORTHWIND BOULEVARD
LIBERTYVILLE, IL 60048
847-968-7917
800-222-7774
Fax: 847-680-7539
customerservice@spri.com
• Adam Zwyer, Marketing Manager
Products:
SPRI Products, Inc. is the leading
manufacturer and distributor of rubberized
resistance exercise products for the health
and fitness industry and develops a wide
range of innovative, affordable fitness tools
and supportive educational materials for
everyone from the casual exerciser to the
professional athlete. Equipment and
accessory offerings include those for fitness
training for strength, balance, sports
conditioning, and many more applications.

SPRINGCO
1450 W 228TH STREET
8
TORRANCE, CA 90501
800-676-7463
888-415-5212
Fax: 805-781-6092
Custserv@vsathletics.com
www.vsathletics.com
• Brian Springer, Owner
brian@vsathletics.com
• Billy Smith, President
rich@vsathletics.com
• Peanut Harms, VP of Marketing/Sales
• Jack Smith, Marketing
• David Ulibarri, Sales, Screening
• Kristin Tumulak, Accounting
Products:
Footwear/Spikes, Apparel/Uniforms, Youth
Items, Bags, Repl. Spikes, Misc., Track
Equipment, Field Event Equipment, Pole
Vault/High Jump, Throwing Equipment,
Timing Equipment, Cross Country
Equipment, Training Equipment, Books,
Videos & Camps

SPRINT AQUATICS
ROTHHAMMER INTERNATIONAL INC,
DBA SPRINT AQUATICS
PO BOX 3840
SAN LUIS OBISPO, CA 93403
805-541-5330
800-235-2156
Fax: 805-541-5339
info@sprintaquatics.com
www.sprintaquatics.com
• Dianne Rothhammer, President
(805) 541-5330
info@sprintaquatics.com
• Chuck Sheetz, VP
info@sprintaquatics.com
Products:
Aquatic and therapy supplies such as Bags,
Balance Boards, Balls, Bells and Bars,
Belts, Caps, Children's Therapy, Clothing,
Collars and Pillows, Competitive Training,
Ear and Nose Protection, Fins, Fitness and
Exercise Education, Floatation Devices,
Gloves, Goggles, Kickboards, Masks and
Snorkels, Personal Care, Pool Equipment,
Safety, Shoes, Teaching, Therapy and
Exercise Equipment, Therapy Education,
Toys and Games, Water Polo, Weights,
Whistles and Lanyards

SPRY SPORTS USA
842 E 9TH STREET
SUITE 1K
BROOKLYN, NY 11230
718-434-3505
Fax: 718-434-0297
spryusa@sprysports.net
www.sprysports.net
Products:
Sporting products such as Footballs,
Volleyballs, Soccer balls, Handballs, Sports
wears, Goalkeeper shirts & gloves, knee
pad, track suit, soccer uniform, fleece shirts,
goal keeper set, shorts and pent, t-shirts,
rain coat

SPYDER ACTIVE SPORTS
4725 WALNUT STREET
BOULDER, CO 80301
303-544-4000
800-333-0302
Fax: 303-449-1404
spyder-info@spyder.com
www.spyder.com
• David L Jacobs, Founder
spyder-info@spyder.com
• John Walbrecht, VP Sales / Marketing
spyder-info@spyder.com
• Doug Saunders, VP Operations
spyder-info@spyder.com
• Tom McGann, President and Chief
Executive Officer
spyder-info@spyder.com
• JJ Collier, VP of Design and
Merchandising
• Russ Rowan, Vice President of Sales and
Marketing
• Cees De Witte, President, Spyder Europe
AG
• Doug Hood, Chief Financial Officer
Products:
Alpine-Skiing, Freeskiing and Outdoor
Apparels and Outerwear

SRI SPORTS, INC.
701 LEANDER DRIVE
LEANDER, TX 78641
706-517-5891
800-723-8873
Fax: 512-259-2952
• Thomas DeNova, President
info@srisport.com
• Kevin Swank, Chief Operating Officer /
Track / Tennis
info@srisport.com
• Charles Fleishman, Chief Marketing
Officer
info@srisport.com
• Robert Allison, EVP Special Facilities
Products:
Field, Track, Indoor and Tennis Systems

ST. LOUIS BRAID COMPANY
2035 LUCAS AVENUE
SAINT LOUIS, MO 63103
314-231-0540
800-231-0540
Fax: 314-231-0551
sales@stlouisbraid.com
www.stlouisbraid.com
• Thomas Goltermann, President
sales@stlouisbraid.com
• Chris Goltermann, VP
sales@stlouisbraid.com
Products:
Quality Braided Shoelace, Drawcord,
Industrial Braid, Cordage

ST. PIERRE MANUFACTURING CORPORATION
317 E MOUNTAIN STREET
WORCESTER, MA 01606
508-853-8010
800-926-2342
Fax: 508-853-3860
info@stpierreusa.com
www.stpierreusa.com
• Edward St. Pierre, Chief Financial Officer
(508) 853-8010
edstpierre@stpierreusa.com
• Peter St. Pierre, Sales
(508) 853-8010
pstpierre@stpierreusa.com
Products:
Made in the USA, Official Forged Pitching Horseshoes
Year Founded:
1920
Brands:
Royal; American; American Presidential; and Wonde

STACKHOUSE ATHLETIC EQUIPMENT, INC.
1450 MCDONALD STREET NE
SALEM, OR 97301
503-363-1840
800-285-3604
Fax: 503-363-0511
sales@stackhouseathletic.com
www.stackhouseathletic.com
• Greg Henshaw, President
greg@stackhouseathletic.com
• Larry D'Amato, Senior Sales/Development Manager
larry@stackhouseathletic.com
Products:
Athletic Equipments, Discus, Shotputs, Hammers, Starting Blocks, Javelins, High Jump, Pole Vault Misc., Pole Vault Poles, Take Off Boards, Toe Boards Rings, Cages, Measurements, Start Pistols, Surfacing, Batons, Stop Watches, Hurdles
Nature of Service:
Manufacturer and Wholesaler of Team Sports Athletic Goods.
Brands:
Newton, Nordic and Ate

STACKS OF PLAQUES
5019 WEST NASSAU STREET
TAMPA, FL 33607
813-282-7073
Fax: 813-282-7079
mkovel@encoreselect.com
www.stacksofplaques.net
• Lou Scalia, President/Owner

STADIUM ROLL
36250 EASTERDAY WAY
FREMONT, CA 94536-1670
510-792-7655
• Dean Valentine, Owner
Products:
Manufactures security-friendly, alternative carryall for fans to take personal items into stadiums and arenas

STAGERIGHT CORP.
495 PIONEER PARKWAY
CLARE, MI 48617
989-386-7393
800-438-4499
Fax: 989-386-3500
info@stageright.com
www.stageright.com
• Sean M Langer, Director Facility Services
info@stageright.com
• O D Rogers, President
info@stageright.com
Products:
Portable staging; portable seating risers; sound (acoustical) shells and music shells; choral risers and band risers; ADA ramps and infills; fold-and-roll stages; meeting room risers; crowd control barricades; pit fillers and stage extensions; and platforms for outdoor performances

STAHLS
20600 STEPHENS STREET
ST CLAIR SHORES, MI 48080
586-772-5551
800-478-2457
Fax: 586-772-6237
info@stahlsid.com
www.stahlsid.com
• Ted Stahl, Chief Executive Officer
info@stahlsid.com
Year Founded:
1932.
Nature of Service:
Specializes in the development, manufacturing, and distribution of heat printing technologies and equipment. Your source for athletic and personal customization including: pre cut letters and numbers, pre-spaced player names and numbers, CAD-COLOR® Solutions™ digital print media, Hotronix® heat presses, CAD-CUT® heat applied materials by the yard, transfer papers, custom cut applique, computerized cutting systems, and more.

STAIRMASTER HEALTH AND FITNESS PRODUCTS
12421 WILLOWS ROAD NE
SUITE 100
KIRKLAND, WA 98034-8736
425-823-1825
800-635-2936
Fax: 425-821-3794
commericialsales@stairmaster.com
www.stairmaster.com
• Brian Cook, Chief Executive Officer
commericialsales@stairmaster.com
• Tom Bryant, President
commericialsales@stairmaster.com
Products:
Aerobic Benches, Cardio Equipment, Climbers, Stairclimbers, Step Masters, Steppers

STALKER RADAR
2609 TECHNOLOGY DRIVE
PLANO, TX 75074-7467
972-398-3780
800-782-5537
Fax: 972-398-3781
sales@stalkerradar.com
www.stalkerradar.com
• Alan Mead, Chairman / Chief Executive Officer, Appl
sales@stalkerradar.com
• Stan Partee, President
sales@stalkerradar.com
• George Snarr, Field Sales Representative
Products:
Advanced radar and laser speed measurement equipment for many different customers and applications, including: The

Law Enforcement Community, Sports and Testing Applications, O.E.M. Applications
Brands:
Stalker Sports Radar

STALL & DEAN MFG. COMPANY, INC.
120 COMMERCE ROAD
CARLSTADT, NJ 7072
201-729-0333
Fax: 201-729-1222
• CH Dean, Founder
• WT Stall, Founder
Products:
Baseball Uniforms; Hockey Uniforms; Soccer Uniforms; Rugby Jerseys

STAMINA PRODUCTS INC
2040 N ALLIANCE AVENUE
SPRINGFIELD, MO 65803
417-889-7011
800-375-7520
Fax: 417-889-8064
customerservice@staminaproducts.com
www.staminaproducts.com
• Brent Swanson, Vice President of Sales
(417) 889-7011
brents@staminaproducts.com
• Bob McBride, Vice President
(417) 889-7011
bobm@staminaproducts.com
Products:
Fitness Equipments, Apparel and Accessories
Brands:
Stamina, Aero Pilates, Gyrotonic, Avari

STANDARD MERCHANDISING COMPANY
1125 WRIGHT AVENUE
CAMDEN, NJ 08103-1615
856-964-9700
800-526-2363
Fax: 856-964-9135
webmaster@stanmerch.com
www.standardmerchandisingco.com
• Jeff Tarnoff, Owner
thuanbui@gis.net
• Lee Tarnoff, Owner
thuanbui@gis.net
Products:
Socks for Baseball, Soccer, and other sports, Sports accessories

STANLY HEADWEAR
119 W MARION STREET
SHELBY, NC 28150
800-438-1526
Fax: 800-643-8531
• Phillip Johnson, President
traceyp@stanlyapparel.com
• Gay Martin, Sales Coordinator
Products:
Knit Caps, Cloth Caps, Safety Headwear, Straw Hat, Towels, Visors, Hunting and Camo

STARTRAC BY UNISEN, INC.
14410 MYFORD ROAD
IRVINE, CA 92606
714-669-1660
800-228-6635
Fax: 714-508-3303
sales@startrac.com
www.startrac.com
• Keith White, Director
sales@startrac.com
• Steve Nero, President

Products:
Cardio Equipment, Computerized Ellipticals, Computerized Equipment, Computerized Treadmills, Running Simulators, Stairclimbers, Treadmills

STEAMBOAT SKI & BIKE KARE INC.
442 LINCOLN AVENUE
STEAMBOAT SPRINGS, CO 80477
970-879-9144
800-525-5374
Fax: 970-879-9111
info@steamboatskiandbike.com
www.steamboatskiandbike.com
• Harry Martin, Partner
info@steamboatskiandbike.com
• Mike Parra, Partner
info@steamboatskiandbike.com
Products:
Ski and bike equipments, clothing and accessories

STEINER SPORTS MEMORBILIA
145 HUGUENOT STREET
NEW ROCHELLE, NY 10801
914-307-1000
800-759-7267
Fax: 914-632-1102
generalinfo@steinersports.com
www.steinersports.com
• Brandon Steiner, CEO
info@steinersports.com
• Jared Weiss, EVP
info@steinersports.com
• David Fiderer, VP Special Markets
(800) 759-7267
• Scott Rue, VP Operations
info@steinersports.com
Products:
Memorabilia signed by legendary athletes, and current sports figures

STERLING TROPHIES, INC.
373 MAIN ST
BOX 345
CATSKILL, NY 12414
518-943-3707
Fax: 763-576-9156
sterentinc2@aol.com
• John De Giorno, President
sterentinc2@aol.com
Products:
Award Ribbons, Bronze Plaques, Clocks, Desk Sets, Engraved Wall Signs, Flags and Banners, Lead Crystal Awards, Medals and Medallions, NamePlates/Badges, Ribbon Magnets, Sports Magnets, Trophies, Wood Plaques

STICK COMPANY/RPI OF ATLANTA
120 INTERSTATE N PARKWAY E
SUITE 440
ATLANTA, GA 30339-2158
770-850-0750
888-882-0750
Fax: 775-258-2090
www.thestick.com
• Patrick Materna, Vice President
Sales/International Markting
patrick@thestick.com
Nature of Service:
Manufacturer of The Stick - a self massage tool often seen on TV used by NFL, NBA, MLB, and NHL players.
Year Founded:
1991
Products:

Stick, Stick Systems, Footwheel, TriggerWheel, Little Stick, Posture Curve, Wellness Video, Instructional DVD
Brands:
The Stick, Biostick, Intracell Stick, Posture Curve, FootWheel, TriggerWheel.

STRAUSS SKATES & BICYCLES
1751 E COPE AVENUE
MAPLEWOOD, MN 55109
651-770-1344
888-770-1344
www.straussskatesandbicycles.com
• Donald H. Eyinck, President
Products:
Hockey skates and protective equipment, team uniforms, figure skating clothing, figure skates, in-line skates, letter jackets, lacrosse, broomball, NHL jerseys, factory authorized repair department, bicycles, bicycle repair.
Year Founded:
1887

STRENGTH SYSTEMS, INC.
1344 DANVILLE ST.
SUITE B
KENNER, LA 70062
504-468-9595
800-549-0341
Fax: 504-468-9120
• David Bouza, President
strength@earthlink.net
• Kevin Bouza, Marketing / Operations VP
Products:
Shoes, Jump Ropes, Weighted Vests, Weighted Shorts, Training Videos and Manuals, and Chute.

STRENGTH, INC.
164 3RD AVE SOUTH
TWIN FALLS, ID 83301
208-735-8940
800-370-3307
Fax: 208-735-8940
www.strengthequipment.net
• Stephen DeWitt, Owner, Designer, & Builder
Products:
Weight Lifting and Body Building Equipment

STROMGREN SUPPORTS, INC.
600 MAIN ST.
SUITE 201
HAYS, KS 67601
785-625-4674
800-527-1988
Fax: 785-625-9036
www.stromgren.com
• John Flynn, President
info@stromgren.com
• Terry Karlin, VP Team Sales
• Carl Wilhite, VP National Sales Manager
(888) 567-5083
Products:
Compression wear and support products, including football protection, neoprene products, sliding shorts for baseball and softball, ankle and knee support products, exercise clothing, back and wrist support and performance apparel system

STRONG INTERNATIONAL, INC.
13710 FNB PARKWAY
SUITE 400
OMAHA, NE 68154

402-453-4444
800-424-1215
Fax: 402-453-7238
www.strong-cinema.com
• John P. Wilmers, President / Chief Executive Officer
info@strong-cinema.com
• Ray Boegner, SVP
info@strong-cinema.com
• Pat Moore, VP, Cinema Products
info@strong-cinema.com
• Gary L. Cavey, President & CEO
Products:
35mm and 70mm film projection, Xenon Consoles and Lamphouses, Film Projection Systems, Platter Transports, CineNet Automation Systems and Digital Projection Systems

STRONGWALL SYSTEMS INC.
107 CHESTNUT STREET
RIDGEWOOD, NJ 7450
201-445-4633
800-535-0668
Fax: 201-447-2317
info@strongwall.com
www.strongwall.com
• John L. Maggi, National Sales Manager
strongwall@strongwall.com
• George Va Dyk, Sales VP
strongwall@strongwall.com
• Bill Kokoletsos, President
strongwall@strongwall.com
Products:
Sports Surfacing System: Courts-Racquetball, Courts-Squash, Flooring-Racquetball, Flooring-Anti Slip, Flooring-Squash, Flooring-Gymnasium, Flooring/Multi-Purpose

STURDISTEEL COMPANY
PO BOX 2655
WACO, TX 76702-2655
254-666-5155
800-433-3116
Fax: 254-666-4472
jbledsoe@sturdisteel.com
www.sturdisteel.com
• Johnny Bledsoe, President / Director Marketing
jbledsoe@sturdisteel.com
Services:
Manufactures and designs outdoor stadium seating, bleachers and grandstands

STURM, RUGER & COMPANY, INC.
411 SUNAPEE STREET
NEWPORT, NH 3773
203-259-7843
Fax: 203-256-3367
www.ruger.com
• James E. Service, Chairman
• Stephen L. Sanetti, Vice Chairman, President, Chief Operatin
• Stephen L. M. Sanett, Vice-Chairman, President and Interim Chief Ex
• Christopher Killoy, Vice President of Sales and Marketing
Products:
Golf Club Heads, Hunting/Shooting Firearms

STX INC.
1500 BUSH STREET
BALTIMORE, MD 21230
410-837-2022
800-368-2250

Fax: 410-539-3908
www.stx.com
• Richard Tucker, President
info@stxlacrosse.com
• Jason Goger, President
Products:
Field Hockey Equipment, General Sports Products, Backyard Games, Golf Clubs and Putters, Lacrosse Apparel, Balls, Gloves, Nets, Pockets-Nylon, Sticks, Goalie, Handles, Bags, and Apparel.

STYLE EYES, INC.
824 W 18TH STREET
COSTA MESA, CA 92627
949-548-5355
800-227-6246
Fax: 949-548-5655
info@StyleEyes.com
www.styleeyes.com
• Philip Kahn, President
info@StyleEyes.com
Products:
Sunglasses-Skiing, Sunglasses-Water Sports

SUMMIT - GARDNER & GELDMACHER
960 MAPLEWOOD DRIVE
ITASCA, IL 60143
866-237-0400
Fax: 630-775-0132
info@summitmg.com
www.summitmg.com
• Dan Renz, Chief Executive Officer
chicago@summitmarketing.com
• Mike Harper, President - DC
• Steve Bawden, EVP / General Manager
• Michael Tritt, President - Kansas City
Services:
Provides marketing services such as promotional products, catalog programs, recognition/incentive, sales promotion, direct marketing

SUN MOUNTAIN SPORTS
301 N 1ST STREET W
MISSOULA, MT 59802-3625
406-728-9224
800-227-9224
Fax: 406-728-8998
www.sunmountain.com
• Rick Reimers, Founder
• Ed Kowachek, President
• Blake Ludwig, Chief Financial Officer
Products:
Golf Bags, Outerwear, Carts, Accessories

SUN SHADER INTERNATIONAL, INC./WASHINGTON SQUARE GARDEN, INC
4601 10TH AVENUE N
LAKE WORTH, FL 33463
561-433-9996
wsginc@hotmail.com
• Robert Boswell, President
wsginc@hotmail.com
Products:
Tennis Visors, Golf Visors, Headbands

SUNDAY PLAYERS
1400 BROADWAY
10TH FLOOR
NEW YORK, NY 10018
972-934-6565
Fax: 212-329-3486

info@sundayplayers.net
www.sundayplayers.net
Products:
Performance apparel for athletes: Compression Gear, Pro-Series Compression Gear, Performance Tees, Off-Field Gear

SUNDERLAND OF SCOTLAND
30 WATERWORKS ROAD
GUNTERSVILLE, AL 35976
256-264-0210
800-999-6599
Fax: 256-264-0215
info@sunderlandgolf.com
www.sunderlandgolf.com
• Paul Sunderland, President
info@sunderlandgolf.com
Products:
Golf Apparel

SUNDOG EYEWEAR USA
75 SKYLINE CRES NE
CALGARY, AB, CANADA T2K 5X2
877-205-5722 EXT 3
800-771-4310
Fax: 403-516-3018
Products:
Eyewear, Sunglasses

SUNTEC PAINT, INC.
PO BOX 2278
GAINESVILLE, FL 32602-2278
352-372-3421
800-333-1104
Fax: 352-376-4579
www.suntecpaint.com
• Joseph H. Anderson, President
sales@suntecpaint.com
Products:
Provides athletic field marking paints to professional, college and high school athletic stadiums; Coatings for Racquetball Walls, Field Marking Paint, Gym Floors

SUNTIME/LINKSWALKER
4800 126TH AVENUE N
CLEARWATER, FL 33762
727-572-8443
800-659-2824
Fax: 727-573-4814
info@suntime.com
www.suntime.com
• Janet Lawson, Vendor Support and Custom Sales Manager
Products:
Supplier and manufacturer of quality sports related timepieces, specializes in logo 'd watches and clocks and collegiate products

SUPERIOR EXERCISE PRODUCTS
947 CLOVER STREET
LAKE GENEVA, WI 53147
262-249-8787
Fax: 262-248-9430
www.superiorexerciseproducts.com
Products:
Revolutionary stretching devices

SUPERIOR FLOOR COMPANY, INC.
PO BOX 151
970 OGDEN ROAD
PESHTIGO, WI 54157
715-582-1181
877-582-1181

Fax: 715-582-1182
www.aacerflooring.com
• Michael Kobielak, Chief Operating Officer
mikek@aacerflooring.com
• Kevin Barker, Vice President Of Sales/Marketing
kbarker@aacerflooring.com
• Kelly Kahara, Customer Service Manager
kellyk@aacerflooring.com
• Nick Larson, MidWestern Regional Distribution Sales
nickl@aacerflooring.com
• Koko Thaw, International Sales Manager
kokot@aacerflooring.com
• Laurn Fontaine, Customer Service Representative
laurnf@aacerflooring.com
• Jason Nieminksi, Technical Manager
jnieminski@aacerflooring.com
• Laura Thomson, Human Resource Manager
laurat@aacerflooring.com
Products:
Indoor Flooring. Sports Flooring

SUPERIOR UNIFORM GROUP INC.
10055 SEMINOLE BOULEVARD
SEMINOLE, FL 33772
727-397-9611
800-727-8643
Fax: 727-393-0238
info@superioruniformgroup.com
www.superioruniformgroup.com
• Alan Schwartz, President
(727) 397-9611
info@superioruniformgroup.com
Products:
Sports uniforms.

SURE FOOT CORPORATION
1401 DYKE AVENUE
GRAND FORKS, ND 58203-2049
701-775-9560
800-722-3668
Fax: 701-775-4867
info@surefoot.net
www.surefoot.net
• Jon Larson, Founder/Partner
info@surefoot.net
• Van Larson, Vice President
info@surefoot.net
• Wayne Waege, General Sales Manager
wayne@surefoot.net
Products:
Manufacturer, Distributor of specialty branded outdoor apparel and footwear accessories

SURFACE AMERICA
PO BOX 157
WILLIAMSVILLE, NY 14231
716-632-8413
800-999-0555
Fax: 716-204-0189
info@surfaceamerica.com
www.surfaceamerica.com
• Jim Dobmeier, President & Founder
(716) 632-8413
surface@surfam.com
• Tom Discipio, Sales
Products:
Manufactures Playground Surfacing, Gymnasium Flooring, Fitness Flooring, Specialty Surfacing, Synthetic Grass

SUTTERS MILL SPECIALTIES
921 SOUTH PARK LANE
TEMPE, AZ 85281
602-437-5550
800-824-0594
Fax: 602-437-5551
sales@suttersmill.com
www.suttersmill.com
Products:
Apparel, Beverage, Blankets, College, Desk,
Gifts, Golf, Key Tags, Pen & Writing
Instruments, Seasonal, Tools, Travel,
Wallets and Money Clips, Watches

SWEDE-O, INC.
6459 ASH STREET
NORTH BRANCH, MN 55056
651-674-8301
800-525-9339
Fax: 651-674-8425
• Tom Traver, Vice President
Sales/Marketing
(651) 674-8301
ttraver@swedeo.com
• Michael Kenny, Sales Director
• Dan Kline, Sales Manager
Products:
Swede-O is recognized as a worldwide
leader providing innovative products
designed to prevent or rehabilitate soft
tissue injuries for over 25 years.
Brands:
Swede-o, Thermoskin

SWIM OUTLET
1165 E 230TH STREET
CARSON, CA 90745
310-522-2700
Fax: 310-952-8444
www.swimoutlet.com
• John Wickham, President
• Amber Delecce, Marketing Director
Products:
Swimwear for all swimmers, including
competitive athletes.
Brands:
Jag, Esprit Beach, Daffy Waterwear, Rebel
Beach, Silver Swim, L.E.I., Summer Girl,
Swim Systems, Baja Blue, Sun Blush

SWING AWAY SPORTS PRODUCTS, INC.
4206-A 50TH STREET #7
LUBBOCK, TX 79413
800-999-1968
Fax: 602-801-3300
service@swingaway.com
www.swingaway.com
• John J Flading, President/CEO
• Mark Zender, Sales VP
(360) 825-4299
getgood@swingaway.com
• Trisha Summers, National Sales Support
Manager
(360) 825-4299
getgood@swingaway.com
• John J Flading, President and CEO
(360) 825-4299
getgood@swingaway.com
Products:
Baseball/Softball Pitching/Protection
Screen, Training Aids, Accessories, Upper
Hand Batting Gloves.

SWISS ARMY BRANDS, INC.
1 RESEARCH DRIVE
SHELTON, CT 06484-0874

203-929-6391
800-442-2706
Fax: 203-926-2640
service@trggrp.com
www.victorinox.com
• Rick Taggart, President
• Thomas M Lupinski, SVP / Chief Financial
Officer
info@swissarmy.com
• Cheri McKenzie, SVP / Chief Marketing
Officer
• Pete Mitchell, VP Corporate Markets
Products:
Sunglasses; General Sports Products;
Compasses; Outdoor Products; Knives;
Timing Devices; Watches

SYNTHETIC SURFACES, INC.
PO BOX 241
SCOTCH PLAINS, NJ 07076-0241
908-233-6803
Fax: 908-233-6844
info@nordot.com
www.nordot.com
• Norris Legue, President/Founder
(908) 233-6803
info@nordot.com
Services:
Makers of NORDOT© Adhesives for
installing synthetic turf athletic fields and
other sport, recreational and aquatic
surfaces since 1973.

T.C. THILON USA
1131 BROADWAY STREET
DAYTON, TN 37321-1802
423-775-0792
800-251-1033
Fax: 423-775-5813
www.tencate.com
• Mark Edwards, President
• Ian Petrie, Manager Director
Products:
Artificial Yarn for Sports Fields

T3K INC
6515 CLINTON HIGHWAY
SUITE 207
KNOXVILLE, TN 37912
865-859-9212
www.t3kwear.com
Products:
Apparel that provides flexibility,warmth, and
breathe ability to all who work or play in cold
weather. It comes as no surprise that snow
boarders, skiers, snowmobilers, joggers,
skaters, ice climbers, and other outdoor
enthusiasts find that T3K is the superior
choice for cold weather protection

TABATA USA, INC.
2380 MIRA MAR AVENUE
LONG BEACH, CA 90815
562-498-3708
800-482-2282
Fax: 562-498-0415
info@tusa.com
www.tusa.com
• Eiji Kimura, President
info@tusa.com
Products:
Skiing Goggles; Scuba Equipment;
Swimming Goggles

TACHIKARA USA INC.
100 IRELAND DRIVE
MCCARRAN, NV 89434
775-352-3500
800-729-8224
Fax: 775-352-3518
office@tachikara.com
www.tachikara.com
• Dan Burke, President
office@tachikara.com
• Roger Revelle, SVP
office@tachikara.com
Products:
Volleyballs, Soccerballs, Basketballs,
Footballs, Playground, Tetherballs, Neo-Glo
Balls, Wallyballs, Specialty, Accessories,
Ball carts

TACKI-MAC GRIPS, INC.
22000 NORTHPARK DRIVE
KINGWOOD, TX 77339
800-334-7477
debbie@tackimac.com
www.tackimac.com
Products:
Baseball Metal Bat Grips; Golf Club Grips;
Ice Hockey Grips; Racquet Sports Racquet
Grips

BIRDAIR, INC.
65 LAWRENCE BELL DRIVE
SUITE 200
AMHERST, NY 14221
716-633-9500
800-622-2246
Fax: 716-633-9850
www.birdair.com
• Yasuyki Kono, President
• David C Capezzuto, Sales VP
sales@taiyobirdair.com
Products:
Birdair, Inc. produces lightweight structural
support for multi-sports facilities offering
unique design and climate controlled
interiors creating comfortable environments.
These lightweight roof solutions are
economical, durable and noncombustible

TANDEM SPORT
440 BAXTER AVENUE
LOUISVILLE, KY 40204
502-582-3530
800-766-1098
Fax: 502-582-1344
www.tandemsport.com
• Anne Brown, President / Owner
(800) 766-1098
anne@tandemsport.com
• Dan Evans, Chief Operating Officer /
Owner
(800) 766-1098
dan@tandemsport.com
• Tammy Allgeier, National Sales Manager
(800) 766-1098
tammy@tandemsports.com
• Anne Brown, President/Owner
• Dan Evans, CEO, Owner
dan@tandemsport.com
• Mike Ryan, Owner
• Lindsay Tucker, Sales/Marketing
(800) 766-1098
• Tammy Allgeier, National Sales Manager
• Shelley Benson, Operations Manager
• Heather Isgrigg, Customer Service
Manager
Products:
Sports Medicine, Sports Accessories,

Tandem Sport Volleyball Equipment, Official Supplies, Cups and Keychains, Tandem Sport Volleyball Apparel, Miller Lite Volleyball Products
Nature of Service:
Distributor and manufacturer of sports medicine and sport accessory
Brands:
Active Ankle, Pro-Tec, Suede-O, Security Equipment, Skids, Tandem Sport
Year Founded:
1989

TANITA CORPORATION OF AMERICA
2625 S CLEARBOOK DRIVE
ARLINGTON HEIGHTS, IL 60005
847-640-9241
800-826-4828
Fax: 847-640-9261
4health@tanita.com
www.tanita.com
• Jeff Kahn, VP Sales
• Keith Erickson, Sales Manager
Products:
Body Composition Monitors for Home Use, InnerScan Monitors, Ironman Monitors, Jenny Craig Scales, Fitness Solution Collections, Scale Plus Body Fat Monitors and with Body Water %, Digital Scales, Digital Lithium Scales, Solar Scales, Analog/Dial Scales, Handheld Health Monitoring Products, Pediatric Scales, Professional Body Composition Analyzer/Scales, Digital Healthcare Scales, Acute and Long-term Care Scales, Veterinary Scales, Food Service/General Purpose Scales, Home Healthcare Products, Mini Scales, Wireless Scales, Segmental Bodyfat Pedometers, Calorie Counting Jumping Rope.
Year Founded:
1946

TASK INDUSTRIES, INC.
PO BOX 420235
PALM COAST, FL 32142
386-246-3439
Fax: 909-629-4967
www.tuffstuff.com
• Sherman Grider, President
info@tuffstuff.com
• Monica Grider, VP
• Tom Bartsch, Publisher
Tom.Bartsch@fwmedia.com
• Scott Fragale, Editor
• Joe Clemens, Associate Editors
• Steve Madson, Advertising Sales
(800) 726-9966
Steve.Madson@fwmedia.com
Products:
Circuit Trainers; Exercisers or Exercise Machines; Free Weight Equipment

TAYLORMADE-ADIDAS GOLF
5545 FERMI COURT
CARLSBAD, CA 92008-7324
760-918-6000
866-530-8624
Fax: 760-918-6008
• Mark King, President / Chief Executive Officer
mark.king@tmag.com
• Sean Toulon, EVP, Product and Brand Creation
sean.toulon@tmag.com
• John Kawaja, EVP, TaylorMade-adidas Golf

john.kawaja@tmag.com
• Brad Barnett, SVP, U.S. Operations
Product:
Golf supplies and equipment.

TC SPORTS
7251 FORD HIGHWAY
TECUMSEH, MI 49286
517-451-5221
800-523-1498
Fax: 517-451-8427
customerservice@tc-sports.com
www.tc-sports.com
• Jill Felbaum, President
Products:
Athletic Equipment

TEAM CALIBER
4606 ROUSH PLACE
CONCORD, NC 28027
704-720-4800
888-332-9700
Fax: 704-720-4905
www.teamcaliber.com
Products:
Toys; Shirts; T-shirts; Hats; Outerwear

TEAM SHOP PREMIUMS
1140 E WASHINGTON STREET
SUITE 206
PHOENIX, AZ 85034
602-635-6400
800-952-5339
Fax: 602-254-1212
info@hdsideas.com
www.hdsideas.com
• Scott Nash, General Partner
scnash@teamshoppremiums.com
• Bob Nanberg, Managing General Partner
(602) 635-6437
Nature of Services:
Team Shop Premiums produces products for staff use, game day giveaways as well as sponsor and sports related gifts.

TEAM SPORTS AMERICA
5790 E SHELBY DRIVE
SUITE 104
MEMPHIS, TN 38141
901-405-8326
888-567-8326
Fax: 901-365-1895
www.teamsportsamerica.com
• David McQuillians, Sales Manager
(901) 365-1779
Products:
Scoreboards: NFL, MLB and Collegiate; Hammocks; Pool Floats; Welcome Mats (18x30); Stepping Stones; Standing Stones; Mini-Standing Stones; Clock Thermometers; Bird Feeders; Bird Houses; Pin Wheels; Copper Lanterns, Umbrellas, Area Rugs.

TEAMLINE
989 W SANDY LAKE ROAD
#200
COPPELL, TX 75019
972-471-0200
800-422-577
Fax: 972-471-0300
customerservice@eteamline.com
www.eteamline.com
• Sue Ann Clark, General Manager
saclark@eteamline.com
• Darinda Howeth
customerservice@eteamline.com

Products:
Team apparel, shoes, equipment, coaches apparel, outwear, accessories and lettering.
Brands:
Nike, Wilson, Mizuno, Easton, McDavid, and others
Clients:
Schools and leagues.

TECNICA USA CORPORATION
19 TECHNOLOGY DRIVE
W LEBANON, NH 3784
603-298-8032
800-258-3897
Fax: 603-298-5790
www.tecnicagroup.com
• Gicancarlo Zanatta, President / Tecnica Group S.P.A.
• John C Stahler, Chief Exeutive Officer / Tecnical USA
Products:
Ski Boots; Outdoor Footwear; Winter Footwear; Travel Footwear; Bags; Socks; Gloves; Apparel; Caps/Hats/Belts

TECNIFIBRE USA
5775 BLUE LAGOON DRIVE
SUITE 110
MIAMI, FL 33126
888-301-7878
Fax: 305-504-8742
info@tecnifibreusa.com
www.tecnifibre.com
• Nicholas Preault, President
(888) 301-7878
• Marco Baron, CEO, North America
(888) 301-7878
mbaron@tecnifibre.com
• Miriam Marquez-Rocha, Office Manager
(888) 301-7878
miriam@tecnifibreusa.com
• Miriam Marquez-Rocha, Office Manager
(786) 380-6353
miriam@tecnifibreusa.com

TEETER HAND UPS/STL INTERNATIONAL, INCORPORATED
9902 162ND STREET
COURT E
PUYALLUP, WA 98375
253-840-5252
800-847-0143
Fax: 253-840-5757
info@teeter-inversion.com
• Roger Teeter, President
rteeter@teeterhangups.com
Products:
Inversion Tables; InversionTable Accessories

TEN SECONDS
429 27TH STREET NW
HICKORY, NC 28601
828-322-2600
800-438-5777
Fax: 828-328-1700
info@tenseconds.com
www.tenseconds.com
• Rob Bell, CEO
• Josh Higgins, VP of Business Development
Products:
Insoles; Shoe Care; Cleats/Spikes; Shoe Laces; Custom Laces/Lanyards; Drymax Sport Socks

TENACIOUS LTD
123 ONIZUKA STREET
SUITE 207
LOS ANGELES, CA 90012
213-617-0449
Fax: 213-617-1252
mail@tenaciousltd.com
www.tenaciousltd.com
• Michiro Toyoshima, Sales
(213) 617-0449
• Yoshinosuke Kurita, Owner
(213) 617-0449
Products:
Headwear Accessories; Skateboard, surf, golf

TENNIS MACHINES, INC.
14520 MANCHESTER ROAD
WINCHESTER, MO 63011
636-394-8811
800-572-1055
Fax: 636-394-3271
jhenry@tennismachines.com
www.tennismachines.com
• Jim Henry, President
jhenry@tennismachines.com
Products:
Stringing Machines; Ball Throwing Machines

TENNIS SURFACES COMPANY
7N730 ROUTE 59
BARTLETT, IL 60103
630-213-1163
Fax: 630-213-1164
tennissurfaces@yahoo.com
www.tennissurfaces.com
• Hank Aldrich, President
• Dudley Pankoke, Truck Division President
(630) 561-2982
• Lesley R Aldrich, Secretary / Treasurer
Products:
Flooring & Boards; Installs artificial turf and dasher boards for indoor soccer fields within the United States; Installs many types of surface coatings for tennis courts.
Year Founded:
1968

TERRAMAR SPORTS WORLDWIDE, LTD.
580 WHITE PLAINS ROAD
SUITE 660
PORT CHESTER, NY 10591
914-934-8000
800-468-7455
Fax: 914-937-0600
customerservice@terramarsports.com
www.terramarsports.com
• Ben Lieberman, President
(914) 934-8000
ben@lamour.com
• Russell Pitman, Vice President
Sales/Marketing
(914) 934-8000
rpitman@terramarsports.com
• Marisa Serrao, Vice President, Credit
(914) 934-8000
mserrao@terramarsports.com
• Barbara Neves, Customer Service
(914) 934-8000
bneves@terramarsports.com
• Nicole Brickman, Customer Service
(914) 934-8000
nbrickman@terramarsports.com
• Bruce Schwartz, Vice President Socks
(914) 934-8000
bschwartz@terramarsports.com

Products:
Sports apparel, including thermal layers, underwear and accessories
Nature of Service:
Importer
Brands:
Terramar, Thermawool, EC2

TERRAPLAS USA RENTALS, LLC
706 WOODLAWN
SUITE 101
KILGORE, TX 75662
903-983-2111
888-972-6837
Fax: 903-983-2324
www.terraplasusa.com
• Sally Beane, Marketing Director
• Michael Beane, Marketing
• Judy Purvis, Marketing
Services:
Turf Protection

TERVIS TUMBLER COMPANY
201 TRIPLE DIAMOND BOULEVARD
N VENICE, FL 34275
941-966-2114
866-886 2537
Fax: 888-876-6887
customercare@tervis.com
www.tervis.com
• Jennifer Bement, Media Marketing Manager
(941) 441-3104
Nature of Service:
Crystal clear insulated drinkware, Licensing opportunities available. Customization of tumblers available.
Year Founded:
1946
Products:
Animal & Wildlife Tumblers; Boating & Marine Tumblers; Clear and Colored Tumblers; Collegiate Tumblers; Garden Splendor Tumblers; Glitter Tumblers; Holiday & Celebration Tumblers; Outdoor Sports Tumblers; Personalized Tumblers; Professional & Service Tumblers; Regional Flair Tumblers; Sports & Leisure Tumblers; Water's Edge Tumblers; Lids & Straws; Ice Buckets
Brands:
Tervis Tumbler®

TEVA BRAND
495-A S FAIRVIEW AVENUE
GOLETA, CA 93117
805-967-0961
800-433-2537
Fax: 805-967-9722
hr@deckers.com
www.deckers.com
• Angel R Martinez, CEO, President & Chairman
ext 507
• Zohar Ziv, Chief Operating Officer
• Thomas A George, Chief Financial Officer
• Graciela Montgomery, Chief Human Resource Officer
Products:
Footwear; Apparel & Accessories

TEXACE CORP.
5405 BANDERA ROAD
SUITE 121
SAN ANTONIO, TX 78238

210-227-7551
800-835-8973
Fax: 210-227-4237
• Jim Blugerman, VP Sales / Marketing
capman@texace.com
Products:
Golf & Fashion Headwear; Premium Signature Cap; Import Base Cap

TEXTILE REVOLUTION
115 PERIMETER CENTER PLACE
SUITE 945
ATLANT, GA 30344
678-990-8002
877-286-7074
Fax: 770-206-2389
Products:
Athletic apparel

TF PUBLISHING
6355 MORENCI TRAIL
INDIANAPOLIS, IN 46268
317-290-1333
888-799-8463
Fax: 317-290-1223
info@tfpublishing.com
www.tfpublishing.com
• Jim Purcell, President
Products:
Sports Calendars

THERMO-SERV/BETRAS
3901 PIPESTONE ROAD
DALLAS, TX 75212
214-631-0307 EXT 7326
800-635-5559
Fax: 214-631-0566
www.thermoserv.com
• Joe Betras, President
(800) 635-5559
jbetras@thermoserv.com
Products:
Sport bottles, tumblers, insulated mugs, coffee mugs, clear sports bottles, stainless steel drinkware and novelty items including custom-molded toppers and cappers
Brands:
Spring Summer Deck Tumblers, John Deere, Monster Mug, Collegiate Items, Jumbo Jackets

THOR-LO, INC.
2210 NEWTON DRIVE
STATESVILLE, NC 28677
888-846-7567
www.thorlo.com
• James L. Throneburg, Chief Executive Officer
• Deb An Lazenby, Product Manager
• Jeff Lawson, Director of Marketing
• Rich Burkley, Managing Director
Products:
Athletic Socks

THOUGHT TECHNOLOGY, LTD.
5250 RUE FERRIER
SUITE 812
MONTR□AL, QC, CANADA H4P 1L3
514-489-8251
800-361-3651
Fax: 514-489-8255
www.thoughttechnology.com
• Helen Mavros, Director, Sales & Marketing
helen@thoughttechnology.com
Nature of Service:
Manufacturer

TIDE-RIDER, INC.
987 WAKEFIELD DRIVE
PO BOX 429
OAKDALE, CA 95361-0429
209-848-4420
800-638-8644
Fax: 209-848-4423
info@tideridersports.com
www.tideridersports.com
• James Smith, Owner/President
(209) 848-4420
info@tideridersports.com
• David Smith, Vice President Marketing
(209) 848-4420
info@tideridersports.com
Year Founded:
1950.
Nature of Service:
U.S. Whistle Distributor of Fox 40, Acme, Windsor, and Spalding Electronic; also Lanyards, Carlton Badminton, Lion Table Tennis Equipment, Scoremaster and Mark V Scorebooks.
Products:
Whistles, lanyards, down counters, whistle tip covers, eyeglass guards, clipboards, scorebooks, shuttlecocks, badminton rackets, table tennis balls, table tennis rackets, and table tennis sets
Products:
Whistles, lanyards, down counters, whistle tip covers, eyeglass guards, clipboards, scorebooks, shuttlecocks, badminton rackets, table tennis balls, table tennis rackets, and table tennis sets
Brands:
Fox 40, Acme, Windsor, Scoremaster, Mark V, Carlton, Lion, Windsor Victor

TIMEX CORPORATION
PO BOX 310
MIDDLEBURY, CT 6762
203-346-5758
800-448-4639
Fax: 203-346-7019
custserv@timex.com
www.timex.com
• Susie Watson, Advertising Director / Public Relations
• Mario Sabatini, Director, Sports Marketing / Sales
• Chris Johnson, Marketing Specialist
• Dan Simoneau, Product Manager, Performance Sports
Products:
Watches, audio, eyewear, thermostats, timer and night lights, weather instruments, pedometers, thermometer, straps, and clock

TINY TOTS SPORTS
7785 SPRING CREEK ROAD
MACUNGIE, PA 18062
610-398-0090
888-299-2880
Fax: 610-398-7831
www.TinyTotSports.com
• John Daddona, Chairman
info@tinytotsports.com
• Dino Daddona, President / Chief Financial Officer
info@tinytotsports.com
• Jack Da Jr, President, Sales & Marketing
info@tinytotsports.com
• Alan Lagarde, Executive Producer / VP, Creative Affair
Products:
Sports videos and books

TIREPATCHEZ
4628 WINWARD COVE LANE
WELLINGTON, FL 33467
561-791-8454
877-728-2439
Fax: 561-791-8789
Products:
Tire patches, tire tattoos and tire studs

TITANIUM SPORTS TECHNOLOGIES
1426 E THIRD AVENUE
KENNEWICK, WA 99337
509-586-6117
800-545-2266
Fax: 509-586-2413
tubing@tilite.com
www.titaniumsports.com
• David S. Lippes, President
• Sandra Gladstone, VP Operations
• Mark Westphal, Director Golf Shaft Sales
Products:
Titanium Mountain and Road Bikes; Titanium Golf Shafts

TITLEIST (COBRA/PINNACLE)
333 BRIDGE STREET
FAIRHAVEN, MA 2719
508-979-2000
800-225-8500
Fax: 508-979-3092
ebizhelp@acushnetgolf.com
www.titleist.com
• Walter R. Uihlein, Chairman / Chief Executive Officer
• Gerald M. Bellis, EVP, Sales and Marketing, Titleist
• William C. Burke Sr, SVP, Chief Financial Officer
Products:
Golf balls, clubs, gloves, shoes, cart bags, travel gear, carry bags, headwear, and other golfing equipment and accessories

TKO SPORTS GROUP, INCORPORATED
4660 PINE TIMBERS
SUITE 198
HOUSTON, TX 77041
713-895-9078
866-856-3488
Fax: 713-895-9078
Inquiries@tkosportsgroup.com
www.tko.com
Products:
Sporting goods and boxing and fitness equipment

TM ATHLETICS
9622 40TH AVENUE SW
TACOMA, WA 98499
253-588-3060
Fax: 253-588-3646
tma@tmathletics.com
www.tmathletics.com
• Maurice Thevenoux, President
Products:
Athletic jackets/sweaters/blankets, and cheerleading supplies

TOMCAT USA
5427 N. NATIONAL DR.
KNOXVILLE, TN 37914
432-694-7070
Fax: 865-673-5818
sales@tomcatusa.com
www.tomcatglobal.com
• John H. James, Chief Executive Officer
• Mitch Clark, President
• Brad Bainhill, Sales Manager
Products:
TOMCAT GLOBAL specializes in the fabrication of aluminum structural components for the entertainmnet and leisure industries, as well as providing related products such as Columbus McKinnon theatrical chain hoists, custom electirc assemblies, lighting products and rigging hardware. TOMCAT USA, TOMCAT Las Vegas, TOMCAT UK, Ltd., TOMCAT Mexico, S.A. de C.V. and Brilliant Stages are subsidiaries of TOMCAT Global Corporation, headquartered in Midland, Texas, USA.

TOMIC GOLF & SKI MFG., INC.
23102 MARIPOSA AVENUE
TORRANCE, CA 90502-2607
310-534-2532
800-678-6642
Fax: 310-539-6010
• Judith Tomic, President
• Jeff Tomic, VP
Products:
Ski poles, paddles ad putter shafts

TOMSED CORPORATION
402 MCKINNEY PARKWAY
LILLINGTON, NC 27546
910-814-3800
800-334-5552
Fax: 910-814-3899
sales@boonedam.us
www.boonedam.us
• Mark Borto, VP, Sales
• Greg Schreiber, National Sales Manager
Products:
Turnstiles, revolving doors, vehicle barriers and entry portals

TONIX CORPORATION
40910 ENCYCLOPEDIA CIRCLE
FREMONT, CA 94538-2470
510-651-8050
800-841-1144
Fax: 510-651-8052
sales@tonixteams.com
www.tonixteams.com
• David T Chen, Owner
sales@tonixteams.com
• Mike Chen, Marketing Director
sales@tonixteams.com
• Chloe Lam, Customer Service Manager
chloe@tonixteams.com
Products:
Team apparel such as sport shirts, warm-up suits, jackets and pullovers
Description:
Supplier of team apparel serving the federal, corporate and athletic industries for over 30 years, Tonix specializes in sports shirts and outerwear.

TOON ART INCORPORATED
581 NORTHLAND BOULEVARD
CINCINNATI, OH 45240
513-851-2357
800-723-2357
Fax: 513-851-2391
www.toonartinc.com
• Greg Akers, President
Products:
Unique, high-value animated products in the sports and entertainment industries

TOP OF THE WORLD CAPS
3001 36TH AVENUE NW
PO BOX 721210
NORMAN, OK 72072
405-360-9856
800-896-8978
Fax: 405-360-0373
info@towcaps.com
www.towcaps.com
• Jasonn Hamby, National Sales Manager
jhamby@towcaps.com
Products:
Sports caps

TOP-COMFO ATHLETIC SOX, INC.
289 GEORGE STREET
LYNCHBURG, VA 24506
804-237-2323
Fax: 804-846-3297
Products:
Athletic Socks

TOP-FLITE COMPANY
425 MEADOW STREET
CHICOPEE, MA 1021
413-536-1200
877-846-9997
Fax: 413-322-2216
www.topflite.com
• Bob Penicka, President/Chief Operating
Officer
• Andrew Isaacman, Vice President
• Andrew Kelleher, VP
Finance/Administration
Products:
Golf balls

TOPPERSCOT LLC
3600 S. YOSEMITE ST.
SUITE 1000
DENVER, CO 80237
303-936-2444
800-334-2518
Fax: 303-936-2778
www.topperscot.com
Products:
Customized Christmas ornaments and
sports ornaments for the NFL, MLB, NHL
and NBA.

TOPPS COMPANY, INC.
ONE WHITEHALL STREET
NEW YORK, NY 10004
212-376-0300
Fax: 212-376-0573
www.topps.com
• Arthur T Shorin, Chairman/Chief Executive
Officer
• Michael A. Brandstaedter, President/Chief
Operating Officer
• Jason K. Thaler, Vice President - Digital
• Douglas P. Kruep, Vice President and
General Manager
• Christopher L. Rodman, Vice President
and Group Managing Director
• Michael J. Drewniak, VP Manufacturing
Products:
Candies, collectibles, baseball cards and
other sports-related trading cards

TORPEDO SPORTS USA, INC.
2401 PGA BOULEVARD
SUITE 190
PALM BEACH GARDENS, FL 33410
561-624-0885
www.torpedosports.com

• Edward Shake, President
• Henry Fong, Chief Executive Officer
• Michael Stanimir, Chief Operating Officer
• Henry Morton, Sales Manager
Products:
Outdoor recreational products for children,
such as toboggans, baby sleds,
snowboards, skateboards, tricycles and
scooters

TOTES ISOTONER, INC.
9655 INTERNATIONAL BOULEVARD
PO BOX 465658
CINCINNATI, OH 45246-5658
513-682-8389
800-762-8712
Fax: 513-682-8606
customerservice@totes.com
www.totes.com
• Douglas Gernert, President / Chief
Executive Officer
customerservice@totes.com
• Donna Deye, Chief Financial Officer
customerservice@totes.com
Products:
Umbrellas, gloves, slippers and rubber
rainboots

TOWN TALK CAP MFG. COMPANY, INC.
6310 CANE RUN ROAD
LOUISVILLE, KY 40258
502-933-7575
800-626-2220
Fax: 502-933-7599
custserv@ttcaps.com
www.ttcaps.com
• Nancy L. Tanner, Office Manager
• Michial D. Vincent, Plant Manager
• Wayne O. M. Joplin, Sr., Owner and CEO
(502) 933-7575
rosec@ttcaps.com
• Joel S Gary, President
joelg@ttcaps.com
• Rose M. Coomes, Vice President
Products:
Headwear for golf tournaments and
promotions
Year Founded:
1919

TOYQUEST
2228 BARRY AVENUE
PO BOX 71292
CLIVE, IA 50325
310-231-7292
800-434-6178
Fax: 310-231-7565
• Brett Bogar, VP Product Development
Products:
Unique, innovative and quality toys and
sporting goods for children.

TR GEAR/PROTONIC
115 PERIMETER CENTER PLACE
SUITE 945
ATLANTA, GA 30344
678-860-3740
Fax: 770-206-2389
• Michael Smoltz, Chief Operating Officer
(678) 990-8002
Products:
Textile Revolution (by ProTonic) is a new
line of patented athletic performance
apparel focusing on blood flow to muscles,
sweat control, and temperature regulation

TRACE ATHLETIC CORPORATION
SEATTLE, WA 98115
888-662-6330
888-662-6330
Fax: 888-662-5453
sales@tr2sports.com
www.tr2sports.com
Products:
Elbow and knee/shin guards and sliding
shorts

TRACKER TRUCKS
3820 OCEANIC DRV
SUITE 311
OCEANSIDE, CA 92056
760-722-1455
800-206-5280
Fax: 760-967-0554
www.trackertrucks.com
Products:
Skateboard trucks

TRACKLITE SYSTEMS
PO BOX 4275
ANDOVER, MA 1810
978-685-9709
800-284-8564
Fax: 978-685-9138
www.tracklite.com
• Arthur H Feinberg
Products:
Synthetic running tracks

**TRAILER CORPORATION OF AMERICA,
INCORPORATED**
601 S 5TH STREET
EASLEY, SC 29640
864-859-9809
800-448-4841
Fax: 864-859-3000
Products:
Auto Utility Trailers

TRANS APPAREL
5000 S OHIO STREET
MICHIGAN CITY, IN 46360
219-879-7341
800-776-7268
Fax: 219-879-0388
www.hartmarx.com
• Homi B Patel, Chairman/CEO
• Thomas Smith, Assistant VP-General
Services
Products:
Branded tailored clothes, trend-right
sportswear and women's apparel

TRANS-LUX SPORTS
1651 N 1000 W
LOGAN, UT 84321
435-753-2224
800-543-7904
Fax: 435-753-2975
• T. J. Nelligan, Consultant
Products:
Scoreboards, Control Systems, Message
Centers, Accessories, Information Displays,
Signage

TRAVELERS CLUB LUGGAGE
5911 FRESCA DRIVE
LA PALMA, CA 90623
714-523-8808
800-368-2582
Fax: 714-523-0188

info@travelersclub.com
www.travelersclub.com
• Peter Yu, President/CEO
Products:
Luggage, Tote Bags, Garment Bags, Duffel Bags, Backpack, Accessories, Radio Collers, Coolers, Specialty Coolers

TREK BICYCLE
801 W MADISON STREET
WATERLOO, WI 53594
920-478-2191
800-473-4743
Fax: 920-478-2774
www.trekbikes.com
• John Burke, President
• Dick Moran, Marketing Director
• John Burke, President
Products:
Manufacturer of bicycles and accessories sold by specialty retailers

TRENDS INTERNATIONAL
5188 W 74TH STREET
INDIANAPOLIS, IN 46268
317-388-1212
866-406-7771
Fax: 317-388-1414
info@trendsinternational.com
www.trendsinternational.com
• Phil St. Jean, President and CEO
• Jeff Loeser, Vice President Licensing
jloeser@trendsinternational.com
• Michelle Kesler, Director Marketing
mkesler@trendsinternational.com
Products:
Manufacturer of licensed and non-licensed posters, calendars and doodle activity kits

TRENWAY TEXTILES, LLC.
FORT PAYNE, AL 35968
256-997-1857
800-251-7504
Fax: 800-441-8138
trenway@trenwaytextiles.com
www.trenwaytextiles.com
• Angie Pritchett, Owner, Production Manager
• Jerome Pritchett, Owner, Accounts Payable/Receivable
• Lucy Long, Administrative Assistant
• Janie Hyder, Administrative Assistant
Products:
Socks for all sports, accessories (Chin strap covers, Custom Logo Wristbands, Headband, Wristbands, Young and Adult Belt, Hockey Socks.
Year Founded:
1977

TRIMAN TELE-GOAL, INC.
415 S FEDERAL HIGHWAY
PO BOX 247
DANIA BEACH, FL 33004
954-920-2727
800-822-6886
Fax: 954-922-0189
• Brian M Berman, Vice President
texacocb2@bellsouth.net
Products:
Strong, light weight and rust resistant aluminum goal post assembly, football goal post pads.
Year Founded:
1969

TRIMOTION
1515 PALISADES DRIVE
SUITE E
PACIFIC PALISADES, CA 900272
310-230-8417
800-874-0035
Fax: 310-230-8418
www.trimotion.com

TRIUS PRODUCTS, LLC.
475 SMITH STREET
MIDDLETOWN, CT 6457
860-632-2020
800-225-9626
Fax: 860-632-1699
• J Ma Thompson, President
Products:
Traps

TROPAR MANUFACTURING COMPANY, INC.
5 VREELAND ROAD
PO BOX 215
FLORHAM PARK, NJ 7932
973-822-2400
Fax: 973-822-2891
tropar@airflyte.com
www.airflyte.com
• Peter V Illaria, President
Products:
Plagues, Wall Clocks, Desk Clocks, Acrylics, pens, gifts and accessories

TROPHY GLOVE COMPANY
122 WASHINGTON AVENUE
ALBIA, IA 52531
641-932-2183
800-323-2928
Fax: 641-932-7430
trophyglove@hotmail.com
• Patricia Nolan, President
• Charles Nolan, Director
• Mike Nolan, Sales
Products:
Baseball Batter-Gloves, Cycling Gloves, Curling Gloves, Football Gloves, Golf Gloves, Gymnastics Hand Protectors, Racquet Sports Gloves, Softball Gloves-Batter, Training & Conditioning Hand Grips, Weight Lifting Gloves, Alpine-Skiing Gloves, Snowboarding

TROPHY WORLD
6400 NW 77TH COURT
MIAMI, FL 33166
305-592-5850
800-526-8652
Fax: 305-592-5854
• Larry Carvez, President
Products:
Trophies, Awards Desk Sets, Medals, Ribbons

TROPHYLAND USA, INC.
7001 W 20 AVENUE
HIALEAH, FL 33014
305-823-4830
800-327-5820
Fax: 305-823-4836
info@trophyland.com
www.trophyland.com
• Paul Fields, President
• Clara Zeinfeld, VP
Products:
Trophy manufacturer offering wholesale trophies, plaques, desk sets, pens,

keychains, ribbons, engraved gifts and awards including corporate awards, athletic, crystal, civic, sports and scholastic awards

TROXEL, LLC
6222 FERRIS SQUARE
SAN DIEGO, CA 92121
858-587-7720
800-288-4280
Fax: 858-587-7733
info@troxelhelmets.com
www.troxelhelmets.com
• Richard Timms, Chairman
• Shay Joaquin, Chief Executive Officer
• Dustin Touchton, Vice President of Marketing
Products:
Provider of ASTM/SEI certified equestrian helmets for competitive, schooling and recreational riding

TROY CORPORATION
2701 N NORMANDY AVENUE
CHICAGO, IL 60707-3605
773-804-9600
800-888-2400
Fax: 773-804-0906
www.troy-corp.com
• Terry Troy, President
troytroycorp@troy-corp.com
Products:
Wholesale manufacturer and distributor of fabrics for the over-the-counter retail market, apparel and craft fabrics for manufacturing, fabric remnants for retail, embroidery and sewing supplies for the monogramming industry and blank activewear for screen printing and for retail.

TRUE FITNESS TECHNOLOGY
865 HOFF ROAD
SAINT LOUIS, MO 63366
800-426-6570
800-426-6570
Fax: 636-272-7148
www.truefitness.com
• Frank Trulaske, Foudner/CEO
• Scott Euler, VP Sales / Marketing
• Stan Gologader, SVP Operations
• Don Mullen, Hospitality Manager
Products:
Gym equipment like treadmills, elliptical trainers, upright and recumbent bikes, multi-station gyms, and TrueStretch

TRUE TEMPER SPORTS, INC.
8275 TOURNAMENT DRIVE
200
MEMPHIS, TN 38125
901-746-2000
800-355-8783
Fax: 901-746-2160
www.truetemper.com
• Scott Hennessy, President / Chief Executive Officer
• Fred Geyer, Chief Financial Officer
• David Hallford, VP Golf Sales
• Scott Hennessy, President and CEO
• Don Brown, Manager of Product Development
Products:
Golf Shafts

TRUEX GOLF
890 WARRINGTON AVENUE
REDWOOD CITY, CA 94063

650-365-3320
800-348-7839
Fax: 650-365-3017
• Don Fernquest, President
Products:
Golf Clubs-Iron or Wood Sets, Putters, Utility-Clubs, Clubheads.

TRUSCO MFG. COMPANY
545 NW 68TH AVENUE
OCALA, FL 34482-8235
352-237-0311
800-327-8859
Fax: 352-237-0346
contact@truscomfg.com
www.truscomfg.com
• Bruce Harris, VP Marketing
Products:
Pavement Marking Equipment & Athletic Field Liners

TUF-WEAR
1001 INDUSTRIAL AVENUE
NORTH PLATTE, NE 69101
308-532-0187
800-445-5210
Fax: 308-532-9133
tufwear@nponline.net
www.tufweardirect.com
• John Gaetano, President
(650) 701-1915
• Linda Williams, Sales Manager
(800) 445-5210
Year Founded:
1931.
Products:
Football - Dial-A-Down. Chain Sets, Field Markers Pylons, Officialss Equipment, Kicking Tee's, Sideline Markers.

TUFF TOE
1442 W COLLINS AVENUE
SUITE G
ORANGE, CA 92867-5443
800-888-0802
800-888-0802
Fax: 714-997-9594
order@tufftoe.com
www.tufftoesports.com
• Ryan Pribble, President
Products:
Tuff Toe Boot Protection (Work Boots, Motorcycle Booots), Tuff Toe Sports(Tuff Toe Pro, Pre Molded Tuff Toe, Tuff Sleeve), Baseball Cleats with Factory Applied Tuff Toe, Softball Cleats with Factory Applied Tuff Toe

TUFLEX RUBBER PRODUCTS
1401 EAST 6TH STREET
TUSCUMBIA, AL 35674
813-870-0390
800-543-0390
Fax: 813-875-2312
sales@tuflex.com
www.tuflex.com
• Fred Franklin, President
• Jerry Pillard, Sales Manager
Products:
Resilient Rubber Flooring

TUNTURI, INC.
VARUSMESTARINTIE 26
PO BOX 60001
AA ALMERE, THE NETHER FIN-20361

-31-546-0050
Fax: -31-546-0059
info@tunturi.com
www.tunturi.com
• Leo Heikkinen, President
info@tunturi.com
• Karen Dixon, VP General Manager
info@tunturi.com
Products:
Treadmills, Cycle ergometers, Recumbent cycles, Exercise cycles, Crosstrainers, Rowers, Stappers, Bicycles and Bicycle accessories

TURFCO MFG., INC.
1655 101ST AVENUE NE
BLAINE, MN 55449-4420
763-785-1000
800-679-8201
Fax: 763-785-0556
sales@turfco.com
www.turfco.com
• George Kinkead, President
sales@turfco.com
• Scott Kinkead, Vice President
sales@turfco.com
• John Kinkead, Chief Executive Officer
sales@turfco.com
• Bob Brophy, Director of Lawn Care Products
Products:
Equipment for Golf & Sports Turf and Lawn maintenance
Description:
Manufacturer of topdressers, seeders, aerators, spreaders, sprayers, edgers and sod cutters.

TURFER SPORTSWEAR
530 WOOD STREET
SUITE B
BRISTOL, RI 2809
800-222-1312
Fax: 401-253-9875
www.turfer.com
• John St Martin, President
sales@turfer.com
• Christine King, VP Marketing
sales@turfer.com
• Fred Morrison, VP Sales
sales@turfer.com
• Jane Shanley, Sales Director
Products:
Windshirts, Polo, Wovens, Jackets, Sweaters, Katahdin Tek Fleece and Accessories

TWIN CITY KNITTING COMPANY, INC.
104 ROCK BARN ROAD NE
CONOVER, NC 28613
828-464-4830
800-438-6884
Fax: 828-465-3209
info@tcksports.com
www.tcksports.com
• Francis B. Davis, President
(828) 464-4830
Products:
Athletic socks, knit hats, wristbands, head bands, women's lacrosse and volleyball uniforms, Kelme soccer uniforms, shoes, balls and bags.
Brands:
Oysox, Racesox, Slog Series, Aware, Krazisox, TCK Women, Grunge, Ulta Grunge, Reacs, Blister Register, Chase

TWIN LABORATORIES, INC.
600 E QUALITY DRIVE
AMERICAN FORK, UT 84003-3302
800-645-5626
Fax: 801-763-0700
product@twinlab.com
www.twinlab.com
• Marc Stover, Director Of Marketing
• Niki Simoneaux, Director of Brand Management
Products:
Nutritional supplements, including a complete line of vitamins, minerals, nutraceuticals, herbs and sports nutrition products

TWINS ENTERPRISES
15 SW PARK
WESTWOOD, MA 02090
800-446-6046
800-446-6046
Fax: 617-585-6231
customorders@47brand.com
www.47brand.com
• Arthur D'Angelo, Owner
info@twinsenterprise.com
• Henry D'Angelo, Owner
info@twinsenterprise.com
• Mark D'Angelo, VP
info@twinsenterprise.com
• David D'Angelo, VP
info@twinsenterprise.com
Products:
Hats, Caps and Visors

TWINS-NY
2171 JERICHO TURNPIKE
SUITE 342
COMMACK, NY 11725-2900
631-858-9184
888-414-4300
Fax: 631-858-9189
rcopp97107@aol.com
Products:
Caps and headwear

TYCA CORPORATION
470 MAIN STREET
CLINTON, MA 1510
978-612-0002
800-522-5387
Fax: 978-612-0003
tyca@tyca.com
www.tyca.com
• Franklin Hardy, President
tyca@tyca.com
• Maryann Castello, Executive Vice President
• Franklin Hardy, President
Products:
Embossed denim totes, jackets, aprons, t-shirts and others
Description:
Tyca is a premier manufacturer of embossed apparel and accessories. USA and Union-made.

TYR SPORT, INC.
15391 SPRINGDALE STREET
HUNTINGTON BEACH, CA 92649
714-897-0799
800-252-7878
Fax: 714-373-0903
www.tyr.com
• Steve Furniss, EVP
• Hans Fassnacht, VP International
• Carlo Bonza, Manager of TYR's European

distribution
- Jared Berger, Product Manager
- Franck Horter, TYR's European General Manager

Products:
Water Sports Accessories, Goggles, Competitive/Performance Swimwear, Triathlon Apparel and Training Equipment

U.S. GAMES, INC.
1901 DIPLOMAT DRIVE
DALLAS, TX 75234
972-484-3484
bmitchell@sportsupplygroup.com
www.sportsupplygroup.com
- Michael J. Blumenfeld, Chief Executive Officer
bmitchell@sportsupplygroup.com
- Terrence M. Babilla, EVP, Chief Operating Officer, General Co
bmitchell@sportsupplygroup.com
- Adam K. Blumenfeld, Chairman and CEO
- Robert Mitchell, Chief Financial Officer
bmitchell@sportsupplygroup.com

Products:
Archery, baseball, softball, basketball, camping, football, tennis and other racquet sports, gymnastics, indoor recration, physical education, soccer, field and floor hockey, lacrosse, track and field, volleybal, weight lifting, fitness equipment and outdoor playground equipment

U.S. REPEATING ARMS COMPANY/WINCHESTER
275 WINCHESTER AVENUE
MORGAN, UT 84050
801-876-2711
Fax: 801-876-3331
webmaster@winchester-guns.com
www.winchesterguns.com
- Bertrand Devillers, Chief Fininacial Officer
webmaster@winchester-guns.com
- Charles Guevremont, Chief Executive Officer
webmaster@winchester-guns.com

Products:
Rifles, shotguns, pistols, and accessories, along with archery and fishing equipment, knives, flashlights, outdoor apparel, footwear, and security safes

U.S. TRAFFIC CORPORATION
2906 CORPORATE WAY
PALMETTO, FL 34221
562-923-9600
800-245-7660
Fax: 562-923-7555
www.peektraffic.com
- Timothy O'Leary, President
sales@ustraffic.net
- Mary Griffin, VP Sales & Marketing
sales@ustraffic.net
- Luis Lopez, Director of Sales

Products:
Electronic traffic controllers, in-ground vehicle sensors, traffic conflict monitors, vehicle and pedestrian signals and power backup systems, electronic variable message signs, directional displays and trailer-mounted arrow panels

U.S.I.A.
1600 RAILROAD AVENUE
PO BOX 1071
ST HELENS, OR 97051

503-366-0212
800-247-8070
Fax: 503-366-0816
www.usia.com
- Lana Johns, Chief Executive Officer
Lana@usia.com
- Kim Johns, President
Kim@usia.com
- Jerry Langan, VP
- Eric Heid, Military Sales & Foreign Military Sales
Eric@usia.com

Products:
Diving Drysuits, Surface Drysuits, Thermalwear and accessories

ULTRA PLAY SYSTEMS, INC.
1675 LOCUST STREET
RED BUD, IL 62278
618-282-8200
800-458-5872
Fax: 618-282-8202
customerservice@uplaytoday.com
www.ultraplay.com
- Philip Clemons, Sales Manager
(618) 282-8200
philip.c@ultraplay.com
- Linda Nagel, Sales
(618) 282-8200

Products:
Basketball - Backstops; Football and Soccer - Goal Posts; Racquet Sports - Tennis Standards; Volleyball - Inserts, Standards

Description:
Manufacturer of outdoor recreational equipment and site amenities

UMBRO U.S.A.
1936 SE CLATSOP STREET
PORTLAND, OR 97202
503-231-8401
800-762-2376
Fax: 503-897-8403
www.umbro.com
- Dave Wray, Sales Manager

Products:
General Sports Activewear, Soccer Bags, Equipment, Balls, Gloves-Goalie, Nets, Referee Uniforms, Sand Soccer Shoes, Socks, Training Gear, Uniforms

UNDER ARMOUR PERFORMANCE APPAREL
1010 SWAN CREEK DRIVE
CURTIS BAY, MD 21226
410-468-2512
888-727-6687
Fax: 410-439-1292
feedback@underarmour.com
www.underarmour.com
- Kevin Plank, President/Founder
feedback@underarmour.com
- Ryan S. Wood, President, International
feedback@underarmour.com

Products:
Diverse sports apparel for men, women and youth

UNIQUE SPORTS PRODUCTS, INC.
840 MCFARLAND PARKWAY
ALPHARETTA, GA 30004
770-442-1977
800-554-3707
Fax: 770-475-2065
sales@uniquesports.us
- Gene Niksich, President/Owner
gene@uniquesports.us

- Gene Niksich, Owner and President
- Mike Niksich, Vice President
mike@uniquesports.us
- Glinda Powers, Customer Service
glinda@uniquesports.us
- Joe Bertolini, Operations Manager
joe@uniquesports.us
- Kevin Niksich, Vice President
kevin@uniquesports.us

Products:
Baseball Eyeblack, Grips, Practice Aids, Rosin Bags, Tape, Key Chains, Eyeglass Holders, Gripping Aids, Shoelaces, Support Products-Joint, Training Aids, Wristbands/Headbands, Golf Accessories, Hot Glove Baseball Accessories, Tennis Tourna Grip, Tennis Court Equipment, Tennis Strings, Balls and other tennis accessories.

Year Founded:
1972

Clients:
National Chain Stores, Sporting Goods Stores.

UNITED SPORTS TECHNOLOGIES/UST
14950 FAA BOULEVARD
SUITE 200
FT WORTH, TX 76155
817-267-2219
800-621-6728
Fax: 817-283-1722
www.ustmamiya.com
- Gene Simpson, Sales / Marketing VP
- Jamie Pipes, Manager of Product
- Shawn Mullin, Tour Manager

Products:
Graphite golf shaft

UNITED STATES PLAYING CARD COMPANY, THE/WPT
300 GAP WAY
ERLANGER, KY 41018
513-396-5700
800-542-7430
800-543-2273
Fax: 866-781-5866
www.usplayingcard.com
- Scott Madding, Director, Global Casino Sales
(859) 815-7518
scottmadding@usplayingcard.com
- Adam McGregor, Vice President Sales - Asia
(853) 6283-351

Products:
Playing Cards and Poker Chips

UNITED TURF INDUSTRIES
123 N PARKRIDGE
WICHITA, KS 67212
316-945-5996
Fax: 316-266-4295
- Lance Pierce, President

Products:
Carpets and Rugs

UNITED TURF, INC.
120 LEONHAUSER LANE
GRANDY, NC 27939
252-457-0591
800-421-7649
Fax: 252-457-0596
- Keith Hall, President

Products:
Grass, Fungicide/Herbicide, Seed Varieties

UNIVERSAL FABRIC STRUCTURES
3115 STATE R
QUAKERTOWN, PA 18969
215-529-9921
800-634-8368
Fax: 215-529-9936
sales@ufsinc.com
www.ufsinc.com
• Dirk Cos, President
(215) 529-9921
dirk@ufsinc.com
• Kirk Klever, Vice President Sales & Project
Management
(800) 634-8368
kirk@ufsinc.com
• Mark Oyer, Business Director
(800) 634-8368
mark@ufsinc.com
• Krista Morris, Customer Service
Officer/Sales Assistant
(800) 634-8368
krista@ufsinc.com
• Mike Belisle, Director/ Sports & Recreation
(267) 347-5450
Products:
Manufacturer of custom and pre-engineered
fabric structures for use in covering
swimming pools, tennis courts, and other
sports fields. UFS creates year-round indoor
sports facilities at a fraction of the cost of
traditional construction and air bubble
structures.

UNIVERSAL GYM EQUIPMENT INC.
769 E. MAIN ST.
VERSAILLES, OH 45380
937-526-9544
800-843-3906
Fax: 662-495-2502
• Steve Sadler, President
info@universalgym.com
• Tom Sadler, VP
• Steve Sadler, President
• John Sadler, Vice President
Products:
Computerized and Manual Exercise Bikes,
Selectorized Weight Training Machines,
Free Weights, Computerized Rowing
Machines, Computerized Stair Machines,
Computerized Treadmills

UNIVERSAL NUTRITION
3 TERMINAL ROAD
NEW BRUNSWICK, NJ 8901
732-545-3130
800-872-0101
Fax: 732-509-0458
info@universalnutrition.com
www.universalnutrition.com
• Clyde Rockoff, President
Products:
Sports Nutrition Supplements, Powders,
Shirts and Bags

UNIVERSAL SPORTS LIGHTING, INC.
2277 OLD ROUTE 66
PO BOX 486
ATLANTA, IL 61723
217-648-5201
800-933-9741
Fax: 517-439-1194
info@qualite.com
• Chuck Lindstrom, President
clindstrom@uslnet.com
Products:
Lighting Fixtures, Mounting Structures, Pole
Options

UPPER DECK COMPANY
5909 SEA OTTER PLACE
CARLSBAD, CA 92010-6621
760-929-6500
800-873-7332
Fax: 760-929-6548
customer_service@upperdeck.com
www.upperdeck.com
• Richard McWilliam, Chief Executive Officer
customer_service@upperdeck.com
• Mary Province, Chief Financial Officer
customer_service@upperdeck.com
• Bill Dully, Chief Operating Officer
customer_service@upperdeck.com
Products:
Sports Cards, Sports Memorabilias, Sports
Die-cast Collectibles, Bobble Heads &
Figurines, Gift Ideas, Gift Certificates,
Display Cases, Poker Chips, Personalized
Cards

USAOPOLY
5607 PALMER WAY
CARLSBAD, CA 92010
760-431-5910
888-876-7659
Fax: 760-431-5880
customersupport@usaopoly.com
www.usaopoly.com
• Maggie Matthews, Vice President
Marketng
(760) 431-5910
maggie@usaopoly.com
• Jeanette Best, Media
(760) 431-5910
jbest@usaopoly.com
• Eric Brendel, Manager Custom Game
Development
(760) 431-5910
ebrendel@usaopoly.com
Products:
Board games and Puzzles

UT GOLF, INC.
4820 JACKSONTOWN ROAD
PO BOX 3008
NEWARK, OH 43056-3008
740-328-4193
800-848-8358
Fax: 800-800-3290
golfworks@golfworks.com
www.golfworks.com
• Dave Stewart, Marketing VP
golfworks@golfworks.com
• Ralph Maltby, Founder
• Britt Lindsey, Vice President Technical
Services
Products:
Heads, Shafts, Grips, Tools

UVEX SPORTS, INC.
110 COMSTOCK PARKWAY
CRANSTON, RI 2921
401-464-8844
888-616-8839
Fax: 401-464-4244
custserv@uvexsports.com
• Carl Helmetag, President
(401) 464-8844
carl@uvexsports.com
• Bruce Campbell, Controller
bruce@uvexsports.com
Products:
Goggles, Winter Helmets, SportGlasses,
Bike Helmets

V-FORMATION\THE NEXED LIFE
99 WOOD AVENUE SOUTH
SUITE 805
ISELIN, NJ 8830
732-321-4040
888-264-5397
Fax: 732-321-4176
www.vformation.com
• Joseph Colonese, President
• Rich Stelnick, Chief Executive Officer
• Theodore Ellenis, Executive VP
• Steve Bogoyevac, General Manager
Products:
Hockey Apparel, Protective Equipment,
Skates, Sticks

VALEO
19275 W CAPITOL DRIVE
SUITE L01
BROOKFIELD, WI 53045
262-314-0070
800-634-2704
Fax: 800-831-9642
valeoinfo@valeoinc.com
www.valeoinc.com
• Chuck Last, National Sales Manager
info@valeoinc.com
Description:
Manufacturer of fitness accessories, lifting
gloves and back support belts.

VALLEY FORGE SPORTS, INC.
533 ABBOTT DRIVE
BROOMALL, PA 19008
610-543-4690
800-220-4834
Fax: 610-328-4582
info@vfgloves.com
• Richard K Greene, President
sales@vfgloves.com
• John E Csaklos, VP
Products:
Golf Gloves, Putters, Umbrellas, Bags

VANGUARD SAILBOATS
300 HIGHPOINT AVENUE
PORTSMOUTH, RI 2871
401-683-0960
800-966-7245
Fax: 401-683-0990
www.teamvanguard.com
• Chip Johns, President
• Jack McVicker, Manufacturing VP
• Amy Larkin, Mktg Svcs Mgr
• Steve Clark, Chairman
Products:
Boats

VARIFLEX INC.
12801 CARMENITA ROAD
SANTA FE SPRINGS, CA 90670
562-484-5100
800-234-9737
Fax: 562-484-5183
www.bravosportscorp.com
• Leonardo L Pais, Chief Executive Officer
Products:
Skates, Skateboards, Scooters, Body
boards, Safety helmets, Athletic protective
equipment, Trampolines and Recreational
canopies

VARSITY BRANDS, INC.
6745 LENOX CENTER COURT
SUITE 300
MEMPHIS, TN 38115

901-387-4306
Fax: 800-792-4337
nlauchaire@varsityspirit.com
www.varsity.com
• Jeffrey G Webb, Vice Chairman / Chief
Executive Officer
• Leonard Toboroff, VP / Director
• John M Nichols, Senior VP / Chief
Financial Officer
• Sheila Noone, VP, Public Relations
(901) 251-5959
snoone@varsityspirit.com
• Marlene Cota, VP, Corporate Alliances
and Business Developm
(901) 387-4306
mcota@varsityspirit.com
• Nicole Lauchaire, VP, Corporate Marketing
& Communications
(901) 251-5903
nlauchaire@varsityspirit.com
• Jackie Martin, Content Manager
(901) 251-5899
jackiemartin@varsityspirit.com
Products:
Cheerleading Uniforms, Dance Team
Uniforms

VECTRA FITNESS CORPORATION
7901 S 190TH STREET
KENT, WA 98032
425-291-9550
800-283-2872
Fax: 425-291-9650
info@vectrafitness.com
www.vectrafitness.com
• Doug Maclean, Founder
info@vectrafitness.com
• Bob Rasmussen, Founder
Products:
Weight Machines

VELVETOP PRODUCTS
1455 NEW YORK AVENUE
HUNTINGTON STATION, NY 11746
631-427-5904
Fax: 631-673-3301
info@velvetop.com
www.velvetop.com
• John B Walsh, President
info@velvetop.com
• Linda Walsh, Secretary / Treasurer
info@velvetop.com
Products:
Pavement products, American stone mix for
athletic field surfaces, field marking paints,
tennic court equipment and resurfacing
material.

VENUS SWIMWEAR
11711 MARCO BEACH DRIVE
JACKSONVILLE, FL 32224
800-648-0411
888-782-2224
Fax: 800-648-0411
email@venus.com
• Daryle Scott, President / Chief Executive
Officer
email@venus.com
Products:
Swimwear and Fashion Apparels

VERMONT ORIGINALS
146 INDUSTRIAL PARK DRIVE
SUITE 4
MORRISVILLE, VT 5661
802-888-6400
800-526-3257

Fax: 802-888-3025
turtle@turtlefur.com
www.vermontoriginals.com
• Margaret Krysiak, President
krysiak@vermontoriginals.com
• Annette Gann, Production Manager
annette@vermontoriginals.com
Products:
Hats, Jackets & Vests, Mittens, Scarves,
Head Scarves, Shoulder Wraps, Baby Hats
& Mittens, Team Logowear

VESPOLI USA, INC.
385 CLINTON AVENUE
NEW HAVEN, CT 6513
203-773-0311
Fax: 203-562-1891
customerservice@vespoli.com
www.vespoli .com
• Mike Vespoli, Chief Executive Officer and
Owner
mvespoli@vespoli.com
• Dave Trond, President
dtrond@vespoli.com
• Mike Vespoli, CEO / Owner
mvespoli@vespoli.com
• David Trond, Vice President of Sales
dtrond@vespoli.com
• Walter Torres, Director or Operation
wtorres@vespoli.com
• Fred Aniballi, Business Office
faniballi@vespoli.com
Products:
Rowing/Crew - Oarlocks, Outriggers,
Shells/Sculls, Shoes

VF BRAND SOLUTIONS
545 MARRIOTT DRIVE
PO BOX 140995
NASHVILLE, TN 37214-0995
866-335-1185
800-733-5271
Fax: 800-877-8329
www.vfbrandsolutions.com
• John Mohman, Marketing Services
Manager
• Angie Wilson, Marketing Services
Coordinator
(615) 565-5358
• Scott Roe, Vice President
• Matthew J. Shatock, Director
Products:
Lee Fleece, Lee Casual, Wrangler Hero

VF CORPORATION
105 CORPORATE CENTER BOULEVARD
PO BOX 21488
GREENSBORO, NC 27408
336-424-6000
877-285-4152
Fax: 336-424-7696
www.vfc.com
• Mackey J McDonald, President/CEO
• George N Derhofer, VP / Chairman
• Robert K Shearer, VP, Finance , Chief
Financial Officer
• Eric W C. Wiseman, Chairman, Chief
Executive Officer & President
• Robert K. Shearer, Senior VP & Chief
Financial Officer
• Scott Baxter, VP
Products:
Jeanswear, Global Intimates, Imagewear,
Outdoor, Sportswear

VIBRA-WHIRL & COMPANY
94 MAIN ST
PO BOX 966
PANHANDLE, TX 79068
806-537-3526
800-255-8722
Fax: 806-537-3442
track_sales@vibrawhirl.com
• Lanny Garner, President
lgarner@vibrawhirl.com
• Sheri Urbanczyk, EVP
surbanczyk@vibrawhirl.com
Products:
Tracks, Turf, Athletic Equipment

VICTORY SPORTS NETS
1805 PIERCE AVENUE
MARINETTE, WI 54143
715-732-2511
800-338-9860
Fax: 715-732-2574
• William Cavill, Sales Manager
Products:
Commercial Fishing Products & Catalog,
Victory Sports Products & Catalog, Craft &
Rosary Twine, Sea King Ultra Fishing Line &
Tip-Up Line, Super Hide Taxidermy Thread,
Custom & Specialty Netting, Seasonal
Specials & Overstock Sales

VIKING ICE, LLC
9450 SW COMMERCE CIRCLE
SUITE 101
WILSONVILLE, OR 97070
503-682-9437
800-698-6036
Fax: 503-682-9098
www.vikingice.com
• Tom Faber, Viking Ice Agent
• Doug McNeill, Viking Ice Agent
Products:
Synthetic Skating Surface

VIKING TECHNOLOGY INC.
2541 STATE ROUTE 250 S.
PO BOX 968
NEW LONDON, OH 44857
419-706-5874
Fax: 419-668-6882
• Leif Ericsson, Owner
lericsson@viking-tech.com
• Cameron Thompson, Founder and
Chairman
(419) 668-8944
mallton@viking-tech.com
Products:
Business Telephone Systems for Sports and
other large facilities.

**VIRCO MANUFACTURING
CORPORATION**
2027 HARPERS WAY
TORRANCE, CA 90501
310-533-0474
800-448-4726
Fax: 800-258-7367
info@virco.com
• Doug Virtue, VP
dougvirtue@virco.com
• Randal Smith, VP Marketing
(800) 448-4726
randalsmith@virco.com
• Don Curran, Recycling, Resource
Recovery and Grounds
(800) 448-4726
doncurran@virco.com
• Bob Roskos, Corporate Copywriter

1219

(800) 448-4726
bobroskos@virco.com
Products:
Portable seating and table products for the public facilities markets

VIRGIL FILMS & ENTERTAINMENT
407 BROOME STREET
#6A
NEW YORK, NY 10013
212-475-2888
646-723-7069
Fax: 212-475-5962
www.virgilfilmsent.com
• Joseph Amodei, President
Joe@virgilfilmsent.com
• Tom O'Hara, CFO
• Kelly O'Brien, Vice President
kelly@virgilfilmsent.com
• James Puleo, Production, Marketing and Design Manager
James@virgilfilmsent.com
Products:
Various specialty sports DVDs and program rights.

VISION FITNESS
1600 LANDMARK DRIVE
PO BOX 280
COTTAGE GROVE, WI 53527
920-648-4090
800-335-4348
Fax: 608-839-8994
www.visionfitness.com
• Christa Walter, Retail Brand Manager
(800) 335-4348
• Ron Carringi, General Manager, Manufacturing Facility
Products:
Treadmills, Elliptical Trainers, Fitness Bikes and Strength Equipment

VITAL/PROMARX
7 NORDEN LANE
HUNTINGTON STATION, NY 11746
972-874-8653
800-777-8482
Fax: 866-326-4478
VitalTeam@Vital-Apparel.com
www.promarx.com
Products:
Women's Team Sports Apparel, Sports Themed Apparel and Matching Accessories in most sports & team colors

VITRONIX PROMOTIONAL GROUP
4680 PARKWAY DRIVE
SUITE 200
MASON, OH 45040
513-398-3695
800 543-4611
Fax: 513-398-7165
customercare@vitronicpromotional.com
www.vitronicpromotional.com
• Steve Hill, General Manager
• Rob Cordes, National Accounts Manager
Products:
Umbrellas, Headwear, Bags & Travel, Business, Crystal, Promotional, Calendar, Camouflage, Golf

VOILE MOUNTAIN EQUIPMENT
2636 S 2700 W
SALT LAKE CITY, UT 84119
801-973-8622
800-670-8622

Fax: 801-973-8918
info@voile-usa.com
www.voile-usa.com
• David Grissom, General Manager
Products:
Core telemark and splitboard equipment

VOLKL SPORT AMERICA CORP
290 PLAINFILED ROAD
W LEBANON, NH 3784
603-298-8282
800-264-4579
Fax: 603-298-8754
www.volkl.com
• Christoph Bronder, President & CEO
Products:
Ski Collection, Performance Ski Wear, Snowboard, Tennis Racquets

VOYAGER EMBLEMS, INC.
PO BOX # 487
LOCKPORT, NY 14095-0487
416-255-3421
800-268-2204
Fax: 416-255-4238
grantr@voyager-emblems.com
www.voyager-emblems.com
• Sally L Grant, President
(800) 268-2204
• Tammy-Lynn Marrelli, Manager Customer Service
(800) 268-2204
Products:
Baseball - Caps; Trophies/Awards - Crests, Emblems, Patches; Talc Twill Appliqu,s

VUARNET
3882 DEL AMO BOULEVARD
SUITE 604
TORRANCE, CA 90503
310-793-5180
800-348-0388
Fax: 310-793-5181
sales@vuarnet.com
www.vuarnetusa.com
• Harold Page, President / Chief Executive Officer
• Angela Torres, Director Business Operations / Administr
Products:
Eyewear - Sunglasses

WAI LANA YOGA
PO BOX 1369
PO BOX 6146
KAILUA, HI 96734
805-986-3557
800-624-9163
888-924-5262
Fax: 805-986-5447
info@wailana.com
www.wailana.com
• Wai Lana, Owner / Founder
• Wai Lana, Founder and President
• Angie Smith, Press / Media
(805) 986-3557
angie@wailana.com
Products:
Yoga DVDs; Yoga Music; Yoga videos; Gift sets, books, aromatherapy candles, incense, t-shirts, eye pillows, women's clothing, hats, clocks & chimes; Yoga equipments - bolsters, blankets, chairs & cushions, yoga balls, mat bags & carriers, yoga & pilates mats, posture props

WALKER & COMPANY
12007 SUNRISE VALLEY DRIVE
SUITE 400
RESTON, VA 20191
703-648-0900
Fax: 703-648-9344
• Christopher W Walker, Founder / President / Chief Executive Of
• Clark Rheinstein, Chief Financial Officer / Leasing Direct
(703) 648-0900
• Chuck Poulson, Property Management and Construction Dir
• Robin Greenstreet, Property Manager
Services:
Developers of Campus-Style Technology Centers

WALL OF FAME WHOLESALE
1501 ZENITH DRIVE
SIOUX CITY, IA 51103
712-202-0501
Fax: 712-293-1500
• Brad Graff, Contact
(712) 202-0501
Products:
Seller of licensed team logo apparel, merchandise, and collectibles for college and pro sports; Selection of fan apparel, headwear, novelties, gifts, home d,cor, accessories, and memorabilia

WARNER/EXCELLTEK
3875 EMBASSY PARKWAY
FRANKLIN PARK, IL 44333
847-455-6730
800-621-1143
Fax: 330-668-7716
• George Warner, Sr, Founder
Products:
Fine wallcoverings and wallpaper products

WARPT INDUSTRIES, INC.
40960 CALIFORNIA OAKS ROAD
SUITE 178
MURRIETA, CA 92563
909-772-6500
Fax: 909-600-2881
www.warpt.com
• Mike Metzger, Founder
• Eric Verkouteren, Webmaster
(909) 600-2771
everkouteren@warpt.com
• Bob Knight, Hosting Service
Products:
Importer of a freestyle-inspired consumer apparel line that is redefining action sports youth culture; T-shirts, Girly T's, Sweatshirts, Hats, Beanies, Jerseys

WASATCH TOURING
702 E 100 S
SALT LAKE CITY, UT 84102
801-359-9361
Fax: 800-766-9729
www.wasatchtouring.com
• Dwight Butler, Founder
store@wasatchtouring.com
• Charles Butler, Founder
store@wasatchtouring.com
Products:
Sports, skiing, hiking, biking, golf, and fishing equipment; Gift card, packs, clothing, car racks, maps, books, DVDs, and snow shoe

WATER SPORTS LLC
407 N. QUENTIN ROAD
SUITE C
PALATINE, IL 60067-4832
847-701-3018
800-283-1683
Fax: 847-991-7189
sales@StreamMachineStore.com
www.streammachinestore.com
Products:
Sports equipment, toys, media storage,
CD/DVD storage cases, TV stand, stream
machines, displays and fitness equipments

WAVE INDUSTRIES
1420 FM 1483
YANTIS, TX 75497
903-383-3573
877-484-5462
Fax: 903-383-3582
sales@wavefishing.com
www.wavefishing.com

WEBSTER WATCH CO., ASSOC.
44 E 32ND STREET
7TH FLOOR
NEW YORK, NY 10016
212-889-3560
800-289-8963
Fax: 212-213-2649
www.avalonwatch.com
• Linda Robbins, President
(800) 289-8963
linda@websterwatch.com
Year Founded:
1927.
Products:
Timing devices, chronographs, digital
stopwatches,fashion, sport, novelty, custom
imprinted, and contemporary watches
Brands:
Bellagio, Avalon, Meridian, Medana, My
Watch, EZC

WEED U.S.A., INC.
5780 HARROW GLEN CT
GALENA, OH 43021
740-548-3881
800-933-3758
Fax: 740-548-3882
info@weedusa.com
www.weedusa.com
• Dennis O'Reilly, VP/ Owner and Operator
Products:
Racquet Sports - Tennis Racquets;
Accessories

WEEKEND EXERCISE COMPANY
6017 RANDOLPH STREET
COMMERCE, CA 90040
858-537-5300
800-666-2127
Fax: 858-537-5400
orderinquiries@marika.com
www.marika.com
• Michael Levinson, President
• Arthur Levinson, Chief Executive Officer
• Carrie Henley, Executive VP and General
Manager
• Marla Echt, Marketing Director
Products:
Gymnastics and Active Apparel; Swimwear
for Water Sports

WELLINGTON LEISURE PRODUCTS
1140 MONTICELLO HIGHWAY
PO BOX 244
MADISON, GA 30650
706-342-1916
800-221-5054
Fax: 706-342-0407
www.wellingtoninc.com
• William Morro, Interim Chief Executive
Officer
• Dan Roberts, EVP
• Marc Emmi, Group VP Sporting Goods
• Harold Tamplin, Sales / National Accounts
VP1
Products:
Water Sports - Flotation Devices, Water
Skis, Water Ski Ropes and Accessories;
Manufacturer of consumer and commercial
rope and webbing, outdoor cushions, cedar
furniture, water sports equipment, Christmas
accessories, crafts, and Tink's hunting
accessories

**WELLS LAMONT SPORTS &
SPECIALTIES**
6640 W TOUHY AVENUE
NILES, IL 60714
847-647-8200
800-323-2830
Fax: 847-470-1026
wligcs@wellslamont.com
www.wellslamont.com
• David W Kennedy, President / Chief
Executive Officer
• Tom Palzer, VP / Chief Financial Officer
• Tim Hartigan, SVP / Retail Operations
General Manager
• William Trainer, Industrial Marketing and
Sales VP
Products:
Manufactures a comprehensive selection of
hand protection including cut resistant, heat
resistant, general purpose, liquid/chemical
resistant, leather gloves and much more

WEST COAST NETTING, INC.
5075 FLIGHTLINE DRIVE
KINGMAN, AZ 86401
928-692-1144
800-854-5741
Fax: 928-692-1501
info@westcoastnetting.com
www.westcoastnetting.com
• Dan Kirkland, President
(928) 692-1144
Dkirkland@westcoastnetting.com
• Jason Joch, Marketing Manager
(928) 692-1144
• Bob Potter, Shop Manager, Production
Bpotter@westcoastnetting.com
• Kim Potter, Purchasing Manager
Kpotter@westcoastnetting.com
Products:
Baseball Cages/Backstops, Basketball Nets,
Field Hockey Nets, Football Goal Nets, Ice
Hockey Stockings, Lacrosse Nets, Racquet
Sports Badminton Equipment, Table Tennis
Equipment, Tennis Court Nets, Soccer Nets,
Timing Devices, Scoreboards, Volleyball
Ball

WEST COAST TURF
42-540 MELANIE PL
PO BOX 4563
PALM DESERT, CA 92211
760-340-7300
888-893-8873

Fax: 760-340-7345
mail@westcoastturf.com
www.westcoastturf.com
• John Foster, President
john.foster@westcoastturf.com
• Joe Foster, VP
joe.foster@westcoastturf.com
• Jeff Cole, Sales VP
jeff.cole@westcoastturf.com
• Danielle Marman, Marketing and PR
Director
danielle@westcoastturf.com
Services:
Services such as custom grown sod,
world-wide shipping and expert installation
of sod, stolons, natural turf

WEST RIDGE DESIGNS
6635 N BALTIMORE AVENUE
241
PORTLAND, OR 97203
503-248-0053
800-548-0053
Fax: 503-274-7685
• Dann Morris, Founder
• Emiko Morris, Founder
Products:
Manufacturing bags and accessories

WESTERN GOLF, INC.
72-105 CORPORATE WAY
PO BOX 970
THOUSAND PALMS, CA 92276
760-343-1050
800-443-4350
Fax: 760-343-2834
info@westerngolf.com
www.westerngolf.com
• Robert Wagner, President
Products:
Golf - Ball Returns, Balls, Clubs-Iron Or
Wood Sets, Clubs-Putters/Utility, Course
Maintenace Equipment, Driving Range,
Nets/Mats, Electric Shoe Cleaner, Flag
Poles, Pull Carts, Tees, Ball Washers,
Range Ball Pickers, Ball Dispensers.

WHAM-O
5903 CHRISTIE AVENUE
EMERYVILLE, CA 94608
888-942-6650
877-944-7501
Fax: 310-286-2350
www.wham-o.com
• Mojde Esfandiari, President
• Richard Knerr, Founder
Products:
Interactive products for all seasons toys,
sporting goods, water and snow tubes,
towables, islands and pool products

WIGWAM MILLS, INC.
3402 CROCKER AVENUE
PO BOX 818
SHEBOYGAN, WI 53081-0818
920-783-1000
800-558-7760
Fax: 920-457-5551
socks@wigwam.com
www.wigwam.com
• Robert E Chesebro Jr, President
socks@wigwam.com
• James Einhauser, Sales / Marketing EVP
socks@wigwam.com
• Jay Kroll, Marketing Director
socks@wigwam.com
• Bob Chesebro, President

• Donna Fischer, Marketing Manager
socks@wigwam.com
Products:
Athletic Socks

WILSON SPORTING GOODS COMPANY
8750 W BRYN MAWR AVENUE
CHICAGO, IL 60631
773-714-6400
800-874-5930
Fax: 773-714-4595
www.wilson.com
• Chris Considine, President
(773) 714-6868
askwilson@wilson.com
• Rick Kerpsack, Interactive Marketing
Director
(773) 714-6441
askwilson@wilson.com
• Tim Clarke, Wilson Golf General Manager
askwilson@wilson.com
Products:
Sports equipment and apparel, Sports
equipment and apparel, including tennis,
football, major and minor league baseball
uniforms

**WILSON TROPHY COMPANY OF
CALIFORNIA**
1724 FRIENZA AVENUE
SACRAMENTO, CA 95815
916-927-9733
800-635-5005
Fax: 916-927-9955
sales@wilsontrophy.com
www.wilsontrophy.com
• Gerald Loomis, President
Gloomis@Wilsontrophy.com
Products:
Sports Memorabilia, Certificates, Custom
Apparel, Custom Medals, Custom Patches,
Custom Pins, Desksets, Laser Acrylic, Laser
Elegance, Little League Baseball, National
Accounts, Oval Relief, Plaques, Resins,
Ribbons & Chenille Pins, Stock Medals,
Time Pieces & Trophies

WINCRAFT INCORPORATED
960 E MARK ST
PO BOX 888
WINONA, MN 55987-0888
800-533-8006
Fax: 507-453-0690
contact@wincraft.com
www.wincraft.com
Description:
Manufacturer of licensed and promotional
products. Established in 1961.

WINDJAMMER INC.
525 N MAIN STREET
BANGOR, PA 18013
610-588-0626
800-441-6958
Fax: 610-588-2046
www.windjammerinc.com
• Anthony J Capozzolo, President / Chief
Executive Officer
windjammer525@netzero.net
• Joseph H Capozzolo, VP
windjammer@epix.net
• John Cannavo, Public Relations Director
Products:
Sportswear such as Sports Bras, Shorts &
Pants; Tees and Tanks; Long Sleeve &
Hanley T-Shirts; Golf Shirts; Athletic-Weight
Crews, Pants, Jams, Pullover Sweatshirts &

Zipper Hooded Jackets; Xtreme T-shirts and
Turtle Neck Sweatshirts; Oxford Jackets;
Nylon Pullover Jackets & Pants; Satin and
Poplin Jackets; and Warm Up Jacket

WINN, INC.
15648 COMPUTER LANE
HUNTINGTON BEACH, CA 92649
714-373-6271
877-854-7601
Fax: 714-379-5463
custsvc@winngrips.com
www.winngrips.com
• Ben Huang, President / Chief Executive
Officer
• Mavis Huang, Import VP / Export Manager
• Mike Coelho, National Sales Manager
• Ben Huang, CEO and Founder
• Jeff Shepherd, Marketing Manager
Products:
Different kinds of Grips

WINNERS CIRCLE SPORTS & GIFTS
1480 HOHOKAM DRIVE
TEMPE, AZ 85281
704-454-4176
800-952-0708
Fax: 704-454-4184
RCCAInfo@lionelnascar.com
www.lionelnascarcollectables.com
• Howard Hitchcock, Vice President and
General Manager
Products:
Sporting goods and apparel

WINTECH RACING
345 WILSON AVENUE
NORWALK, CT 6854
203-866-7223
Fax: 203-866-7224
info@wintechracing.com
www.wintechracing.com
• Howard Winklevoss, Chairman
• Gheorghe Anghel, Operations Manager
Rowing Sponsor:
Official Launch Supplier of United States
Rowing teams.

WINTERLAND PRODUCTIONS
2 BRYANT STREET
SUITE 300
SAN FRANCISCO, CA 94105
415-247-7400
877-687-4277
Fax: 415-247-7407
• Dell Furano, Chief Executive Officer
• Phil Cussen, President / Chief Operating
Officer
• Rick Fish, Artist Relations EVP
rfish@signaturesnet.com
• Django Bayless, New Media Technology /
Artist Relations
dbayless@signaturesnet.com
Products:
General Sports Products - T-shirts

WISSOTA MANUFACTURING COMPANY
865 HIGHWAY 169 N
PLYMOUTH, MN 55441
763-545-1448
Fax: 763-545-1449
www.wissota.com
• William C Schuessler, President
Products:
Ice Skate Sharpener

WITTE GROUP
925 GOLF VIEW DRIVE
FOND DU LAC, WI 54935
920-923-0211
Fax: 920-923-6092
wittegroup@aol.com
• Jack Witte, President
• Mark Witte, Sales Representative
• Mike Witte, Sales Representative
• Carl Harland, Sales Representative
Products:
Baseball - Bases, Batting Helmets,
Plates-Home, Pitcher, Uniforms; Basketball
- Bags-Equipment, Balls-Other, Nets,
Uniforms; Facilities - Field Marking
Equipment; Field Hockey - Uniforms;
Football - Bags-Equipment, Balls-Other,
Helmets, Masks, Practice Equipment

WITTEK GOLF SUPPLY COMPANY
3865 COMMERCIAL AVENUE
NORTHBROOK, IL 60062
847-943-2399
800-869-1800
Fax: 847-412-9591
info@wittekgolf.com
www.wittekgolf.com
• Mike Hilliard, Vice President
• Tom Illies, Plant Manager, Production and
Quality Control
• Pat Wittek, Secretary / Treasurer
info@wittekgolf.com
• Steve Garske, President
info@wittekgolf.com
• Dan Brown, Sales Manager - Sales,
Marketing and Dealer R
Products:
Driving Range Equipment, Golf Course
Accessories, Display Fixtures & Miniature
Golf Supplies

WITZ® SPORT CASES
11282 PYRITES WAY
GOLD RIVER, CA 95670
916-638-0333
800-499-1568
Fax: 916-638-1250
trent@witzprod.com
www.witzprod.com
• Trent Weitz, President/Shareholder
(800) 499-1568
trent@witzprod.com
• Rob Henby, Vice President
(800) 499-1568
rob@witzprod.com
• Chris Cannon, VP of Sales
(800) 499-1568
chris@witzprod.com
Products:
Compact Cases, Contingency Cases,
Electronics Cases, Eyewear Cases, Utility
Cases, Cell Plate Cases, Passport Cases.
Year Founded:
1989

WOLVERINE WORLD WIDE
9341 COURTLAND DRIVE
HB-242
ROCKFORD, MI 49351
616-866-5500
800-789-8586
Fax: 616-866-5500
www.wolverineworldwide.com
• Timothy J O'Donovan, Chairman of the
Board
• Blake W Krueger, President and Chief
Operating Officer

(616) 866-5570
• Stephen L Gulis Jr, EVP, Chief Financial Officer, and Treasu
• Blake W. P Krueger, Chairman of the Board, Chief Executive Office
• R. Paul Guerre, Vice President, General Counsel and Secretary
• Donald T. Grimes, Senior Vice President, Chief Financial Office
• Robin J. Kleinjans-McKee, Vice President, Corporate Planning and Analys
• Pamela L. Linton, Senior Vice President of Global Human Resourc
• Michael Jeppesen, President, Global Operations Group
• James D. Zwiers, Senior Vice President and President, Outdoor
Products:
Athletic Footwear

WOMEN'S GOLF UNLIMITED, INC.
2801 E PLANO PARKWAY
PLANO, TX 75074
973-673-9600
888-894-8465
Fax: 973-227-7018
• Robert L Ross, Chairman / Chief Executive Officer / Co-
• Richard M Maurer, Secretary / Co-Managing Partner
• Douglas A Buffington, President / Chief Operating Officer
Products:
Golf products and accessories

WOMENS GOLFWORKS
PO BOX 3008
NEWARK, OH 43058-3008
740-328-4193
800-848-8358
Fax: 740-323-0311
golfworks@golfworks.com
• Barbara Rathbun, President
Products:
Golf products and accessories such as heads, shafts, grips & tools

WOODS TO WEDGES, INC.
8230 WEHRLE DRIVE
WILLIAMSVILLE, NY 14221
716-632-3021
Fax: 716-633-2693
• Donna Henrich, President
Products:
Golf Clubs-Iron or Wood Sets, Putters, Utility and Custom Clubs

WOOLRICH, INC.
2 MILL STREET
WOOLRICH, PA 17779
877-512-7305
800-966-5372
Fax: 570-769-6234
service@woolrich.com
www.woolrich.com
• Richard Insley, Retail and Marketing SVP
• Michael Collin, President
(207) 612-4253
Products:
Athletic clothes and accessories for men, women and children

WORLD CLASS ATHLETIC SURFACES
817 N BROAD STREET
PO BOX 152
LELAND, MS 38756

662-686-9997
800-748-9649
Fax: 662-686-9977
www.worldclasspaints.com
• David Simmons, President
david@worldclasspaints.com
Year Founded:
1989.
Products:
Full line of athletic field and court accessories, including high-quality marking paints, graphic stencils, tennis court coating materials, and windscreens

WORLD DRYER CORPORATION
5700 MCDERMOTT DRIVE
BERKELEY, IL 60163
708-449-6950
800-323-0701
Fax: 708-449-6958
info@worlddryer.com
www.worlddryer.com
• Tom Vic, President
(708) 949-6950
• Stacey Hefford, Marketing Manager
(708) 949-6950
• Chris Berl, VP of Sales
(708) 949-6950
Products:
Complete line of sanitation products for sports facilities, including warm air hand dryers, both push-button and automatic, automatic soap/lotion/chemical dispensers, hair dryers and employee sensamatic hand wash stations.
Description: AIRMAX HAND DRYER
The AirMax high speed hand dryer dries hands in 15 seconds - half the time of standard warm-air dryers. Delivering a high-volume output of 275 CFM. AirMax operates at the lowest noise level of similar products. AirMax is available in surface mount or ADA-compliant recessed models, both push button and automatic activation. Cover options include cast iron, stainless steel and the newly offered colors of WorldStone, which can also be customized.
Description: MODEL A
The Model A delivers high air velocity to ensure quick hand drying. Other features include trouble free operation, high volume of 200 CFM, a universal type motor (1/10, 7,500 RPM), vandal resistant, and the renowned Word Dryer durability and engineering. Automatic dryer shuts off when hands are removed to conserve energy costs. Push button models are available. Recessed models are ADA compliant.
Description: AIRSTYLE
The Airstyle hair dryers are designed for health clubs, locker rooms and schools. They are safe, efficient and feature a high-powered 80-second push button drying cycle. Available in both surface and recess mounted, Airstyle hair dryers feature a swivel nozzle that can be field converted to the fixed position.
Description: DRY BABY
The DryBaby lines of baby changing stations are durable, easy to clean and built to deliver the World Dryer quality standards. They are designed to be easily maintained while providing a safe changing station. The new vertical changing station provides added space savings. The horizontal ABC-300 HC features plastic laminate inserts to compliment any d,cor.

WORLD FAMOUS TRADING COMPANY LTD.
1478 FAYETTE STREET
EL CAJON, CA 92020
619-448-6563
800-237-0151
800-748-5519
Fax: 619-448-6258
• Terry E Margeson, VP Marketing
Products:
Sporting, Athletic and Recreational Goods and Supplies

WORLD PROMOTIONAL PRODUCTS, INC.
17751 SKY PARK CIRCLE
SUITE F
IRVINE, CA 92614
800-705-7796
Fax: 949-221-0693
• Chris Tyler, Vice President
ctyler@worldpromoproducts.com
Description:
World Promotional Products provides logo and imprinted merchandise - services of which include graphic and creative design, screen print and embroidery.
Clients:
World Promotional Products works with many NBA, MLB, NHL and Fortune 500 companies.
Nature of Services:
Trade Shows; Employee Incentives; Events and Meetings; New Product Launches; Brand Marketing Initiatives; Award Programs; Golf and Charity Events.

WORLD SPORTING GOODS, INC.
PO BOX 579
STAPLETON, AL 36578
251-964-7100
800-633-1270
Fax: 251-964-6310
info@worldsportinggoods.com
www.worldsportinggoods.com
• Danny Forrest, Regional Sales Manager
• Mary Forrest, Marketing Director
Products:
Football Dummies, Practice Equipment, Practice Kick Cages, Sleds, Blockers, Barbells, Exercise Machines, Weight Belts

XL VIDEO, INC.
4025 WELCOME ALL ROAD
SUITE 170 BUILDING F
ATLANTA, GA 30349
404-629-3300
Fax: 404-629-3301
www.xlvideo.com
• John Lewis, Account Executive
(770) 795-7576
jlewis@xlvideo.com
Products:
Video display systems for trade shows, outdoor events, indoor events, concert touring and television shows

XLM CORPORATION
1639 W SHERIDAN AVENUE
OKLAHOMA CITY, OK 73106
405-239-6141
800-223-3207
Fax: 888-561-6737
• Les Hibdon, Owner
Products:
Cycling Products

YARBOROUGH TIME LTD.
14 CLARKE CIRCLE
BETHEL, CT 6801
203-790-7444
800-431-1582
Fax: 203-778-8717
awardsetc@aol.com
• Martin Steinberg, President
• Rebecca Grinnals, Founder and President
Products:
Clocks, Golf Accessories, Lapel Pins,
Medals, Plaques

YARRINGTON MILLS CORPORATION
412 S WARMINSTER ROAD
PO BOX 397
HATBORO, PA 19040
215-674-5125
800-962-3294
Fax: 215-674-0586
Sales@YarringtonMills.com
www.yarringtonmills.com
• James R Yarrington, President / General
Manager
• Benjamin S Yarrington, Sales / Marketing
Manager
Products:
General Sports Products - Fabrics and
Trimmings used to make Award Jackets;
Cheerleading Apparel, Uniforms (Team
Sports), Warm-Up Suits

YEADON FABRIC STRUCTURES LTD.
KERR INDUSTRIAL PARK
RR 3
GUELPH, ONTARIO, CANADA N1H 6H9
519-821-9301
888-493-2366
888-493-2366
Fax: 519-821-9010
www.yeadondomes.com
• Steve Flanagan, President
• Milosh Nadvornik, President
Products:
Manufacturer and installer of air supported
structures for all sports venues

YONEX CORPORATION
20140 S WESTERN AVENUE
TORRANCE, CA 90501
310-793-3800
800-449-6639
Fax: 310-793-3899
support@yonexusa.com
www.yonex.com
• Chitose Renge, EVP Marketing & Sales
• Violet Bernal, Credit
• Jay Tamiya, Customer Service Supervisor
• Minoru Yoneyama, Founding Honorary
Chairman
• Ben Yoneyama, President
Products:
Golf Clubs-Iron or Wood Sets; Racquet
Sports - Badminton and Tennis Racquets

Z COIL PAIN RELIEF FOOTWEAR
6932 4TH STREET NW
ALBUQUERQUE, NM 87107
505-345-2222
800-268-6239
877-628-1586
Fax: 505-345-2224
painfree@zcoil.com
www.zcoil.com
• Alvaro Gallegos, Chairman of the Board
(505) 838-5750
al@zcoil.com

• Andres A Gallegos, Executive VP
(505) 345-2222
andres@zcoil.com
• Thomas C Clausen, Chief Financial Officer
(505) 345-2222
tom@zcoil.com
• Jean-Paul de Jager, PR & Marketing
(505) 345-2222
jeanpaul@zcoil.com
Products:
Pain-relief shoes

ZAMBONI & COMPANY, INC., FRANK J.
15714 COLORADO AVENUE
PARAMOUNT, CA 90723-4211
562-633-0751
Fax: 562-633-9365
sales@zamboni.com
www.zamboni.com
• Richard Zamboni, President
• Frank J Zamboni, EVP
• Doug Peters, Regional Sales Manager
• Wayne Brewer, Operations Manager
Products:
Ice Rink Resurfacing Machines, Ice Rink
Power Edgers, Maintenance Equipment for
Astroturf

ZEBCO
6105 E APACHE
TULSA, OK 74115
918-836-5581
800-588-9030
Fax: 918-836-0154
email.zebco@zebco.com
www.zebco.com
• Ed Bedore, Sales VP
contact.zebco@zebco.com
• Steve Self, Regional Sales Manager
contact.zebco@zebco.com
• Ray Moore, Sales Manager
contact.zebco@zebco.com
Products:
Fishing Accessories, Electric Motors, Reels,
Rods

ZEPHYR GRAF-X INCORPORATED
5443 EARHART ROAD
LOVELAND, CO 80538
970-663-3242
888-282-0994
Fax: 970-663-7695
CustomerService@zhats.com
www.zhats.com
• David Gormley, President
• Wes Gormley, Vice President Product
Development
• Jim Seilbach, Chief Financial Officer
Products:
All Headwear/Athletic Hats
Year Founded:
1993

ZEPPELIN PRODUCTS, INCORPORATED
3178 PEMBROKE ROAD
PEMBROKE PARK, FL 33009
954-989-8808
800-270-1477
Fax: 954-989-8578
Info@zeppro.com
www.zeppro.com
Products:
Leather belts, accessories, knives/money
clips, sandals and pet products

ZERO GLOVES
605 W STONE AVENUE
PO BOX 500
FAIRFIELD, IA 52256-2223
641-472-3191
800-247-3383
Fax: 641-472-3194
www.zerogloves.com
• Nicole Hunt, Vice President
(800) 247-3383
Products:
Skiing-Alpine Accessories, Face Masks,
Glvoes, KnitCaps hats, Skiing-Nordic
Gloves, Snowboard Gloves, Prom-Optional
Gloves, Youth Ski & Work Gloves, Face
Masks, Baseball Caps, Head Bands,
Sweatshirts, Tshirts.
Nature of Service:
Sells gloves to retail and manufacturing
indutries.
Brands:
Zero Gloves & Mittens, FairField Line, Inc;
websites: www.zerogloves.com and
www.fairfieldlineinc.com

ZEROFLEX, INC.
3685 QUAIL ROAD NE
SUITE 200
SAUK RAPIDS, MN 56379
320-251-3080
877-251-3080
Fax: 320-654-1505
• James Donaghue, President
• Sean Donaghue, Sales Director
Products:
Outdoor Posts & Boards, Bike Racks,
Benches, Picnic Tables

ZORREL INTERNATIONAL
13500 15TH STREET
GRANDVIEW, MO 64030-3082
816-765-5212
800-528-8688
Fax: 816-765-3228
info@zorrel.com
www.zorrel.com
• William Gardiner, VP
Products:
T-shirts

Software Manufacturers

AMERICAN WEIGHT AND MEASURES
16501 ZUMAQUE STREET
PO BOX 227
RANCHO SANTA FE, CA 92067
858-204-9699
800-395-4565
Fax: 858-756-0986
• Kenyon C. Clark, President
• Terry Bagley, Sales Manager
Products:
Cutting edge body composition analyzers
Brands:
Body Comp ScaleTM with Ohms Modulation
Logic* Onboard

ARBITRON, INC.
85 BROAD STREET
NEW YORK, NY 10004
410-312-8000
800-864-1224
Fax: 410-312-8607
corporatepressinquiries@nielsen.com
www.nielsen.com

• Amanda Howell, Marketing Services Coordinator
(443) 312-8379
• Trisha Lawson, Sales Assistant
(443) 259-7536
• Mitch Barns, Chief Executive Officer

ATARI INC.
417 5TH AVENUE
FLOOR 7
NEW YORK, NY 10016-2204
212-726-6500
Fax: 212-252-8603
www.atari.com

BOOK4GOLF.COM, INC.
250 FERRAND DRIVE
SUITE 302
TORONTO, ON, CANADA M3C 3G8
416-421-5501
877-662-6654
Fax: 416-429-8457
www.book4golf.com

CONTEMPORARY RESEARCH
4355 EXCEL PKWY
SUITE 600
ADDISON, TX 75001
972-931-2728
888-972-2728
Fax: 972-931-2765
contact@crwww.com
www.contemporaryresearch.com
• Douglas Engstrom, Communications Director
(214) 556-6606
doug@crwww.com
Year Founded:
1993.
Nature of Service:
Designs and creates smart solutions for system integration and HDTV applications.

CRICHLOW DATA SCIENCES
926 E OLEANDER STREET
LAKELAND, FL 33801
863-616-1222
800-678-4535
Fax: 863-616-1219
sales@thegeneralstore.com
www.thegeneralstore.com
• Amanda Rutter, Sales Manager
(800) 678-4535
amanda.rutter@thegeneralstore.com
• Wade Walker, Technical Support Manager
(863) 616-1222
wade@thegeneralstore.com
• Ken Bundy, IT Manager
(863) 616-1222
ken@thegeneralstore.com
Products:
Offers the General Store, an accounting, inventory, POS and management software package for retailers.
Year Founded:
1983

CSI SERVICES/RICS SOFTWARE
4725 MERLE HAY ROAD
SUITE 101
DES MOINES, IA 50322
515-270-8182
800-654-3123
Fax: 515-270-1006
info@ricssoftware.com
• David Becker, Chairman of the Board/CEO

Products:
Developer of RICS. Offers retailers quality computer system.

DARTFISH USA
6505 SHILOH ROAD
SUITE 110-B
ALPHARETTA, GA 30005
404-685-9505
888-655-3850
Fax: 404-685-9130
usa@dartfish.com
www.dartfish.com
• Victor Bergonzoli, President/CEO
victor.bergonzoli@dartfish.com
• Ron Imbriale, Sales VP
usa@dartfish.com
• Mark Matoza, Golf Director
usa@dartfish.com
Products:
Sports electronics, including software programs.

DAXKO
600 UNIVERSITY PARK PLACE
SUITE 500
BIRMINGHAM, AL 35209
205-437-1400
877-729-4786
Fax: 205-437-0225
sales@daxko.com
www.daxko.com
• Tom Patterson, Founder/Chairman
• Anne Randall, Medical Fitness Account Executive
• Barry Thomason, Sales Director
• April Benetallo, Director Marketing/Product Management
• Erie Morring, Medical Fitness Account Executive
Organization
Daxko helps medical fitness centers build healthier communities by driving participation, increasing engagement levels and providing visability into constituents. Only Daxko offers a comprehensive engagement solution consisting of high-quality and customized communication services, best in class consulting and powerful software tools to increase member retention and patient to member conversion. Daxko customers grow 3x faster than centers not partnered with us. Building upon years of knowledge serving 500+ member-based organizations, nobody can touch Daxko's track record for successful project implementation amd amzaing ongoing service.
Sports Organizations served
YMCA's, JCC's, community centers and medical fitness centers.

EA SPORTS
209 REDWOOD SHORES PARKWAY
REDWOOD CITY, CA 94065
650-628-1500
800-959-7331
Fax: 650-628-1323
www.easports.com
• Peter Moore, President EA Sports
pmoore@ea.com
• Carolyn Feinstein
(650) 628-7136
cfeinstein@ea.com
• Brian Movalson, Director of Marketing/EA Sports
• John Riccitello, CEO

• Frank Gibeau, President of EA Labels
• Chris Erb, Vice President of Brand Marketing
• David Tinson, Vice President of Corporate Communications
• Craig Evans, Director of Marketing
• Randy Chase, Senior Product Marketing Manager
Ice Hockey Sponsor:
NHL
Basketball Sponsor:
NBA, WNBA
College Sponsor:
NCAA Basketball, NCAA Football
Football Sponsor:
NFL

ELITE SPORTS ANALYSIS
59 THE BRIDGES
DALGETY BAY, FIFE, SCOTLAND KY11 9XZ
-44-823-937
sales@elitesportsanalysis.com
www.elitesportsanalysis.com
• David Allan, Sales Manager
dallan@elitesportsanalysis.com
Products:
Computer Systems/Software: Athletic Training, Computer Systems/Software: Coaching, Computer Systems/Software: Conditioning, Computer Systems/Software: Fitness Assessment, Computer Systems/Software: Game Statistics, Computer Systems/Software: Management, Computer Systems/Software: Recruiting, Computer Systems/Software: Scouting, Computer Systems/Software: Strength, Fitness Performance Testing: Performance Testing Systems, Mental Training Equipment, Videotaping Systems: Custom Camera Systems, Videotaping Systems: Digital Video Editing Systems, Videotaping Systems: Video Editing Systems, Videotaping Systems: Video Recorders

EMS SOFTWARE, LCC
6465 GREENWOOD PLAZA BLVD
SUITE 600
CENTENNIAL, CO 80111
303-771-0110
800-440-3994
Fax: 303-796-7429
sales@emssoftware.com
www.emssoftware.com
• Dean Evans, President
• Craig Halliday, Chief Executive Officer
• Tim Dillon, Vice President, Sales And Marketing
• Dave Hurley, Executive Sales Director
• Larry Goldman, Director Of Product Marketing
Year Founded & Description:
Founded in 1986, EMS Software produces a room and resource scheduling platform used for sports and meeting venues.

EVENT SOFTWARE
625 N GILBERT ROAD
SUITE 104
GILBERT, AZ 85234
480-517-9990
Fax: 480-517-9994
info@eventsoft.com
www.eventsoft.com

manufacturers/retailers

FITNESS VENTURE GROUP
4554 WEST VILLA THERESA DRIVE
GLENDALE, AZ 85308
602-753-5200
Fax: 602-492-9715
www.moreactive.com
• Don Hoskyns, President
• Don Hoskyns, Managing Partner
• John Domrzalski, Designer

ICONGO.COM
888 7TH AVENUE
10TH FLOOR
NEW YORK, NY 10106
312-265-5010
888-342-9457
Fax: 302-295-4801
sales@hybris.com
www.hybris.com
• Irwin Kramer, Chairman/CEO
• Steven Kramer, VP and Chief Technology Officer
• Joshua Ostrega, VP, Operations
• Robert Rosenbloom, VP, Business Development
Products:
Developer of e-business systems and software

INFINITY PRO SPORTS
405 MITCHELL STREET
BRYAN, TX 77801
979-779-5200
Fax: 979-779-3329
info@infinityprosports.com
www.infinityprosports.com
• Joe Scott, Director of Sales
(979) 779-5024
• Susan Cagle, Head of Accounting
• Uri Geva, CEO
Nature of Services:
Infinity Pro Sports provides technologically advanced web based software and services to the professional and collegiate sports industries including creating and developing web-based solutions, data based marketing software, online gaming, and real time streaming for use in the sports industry.

INFUZER.COM, LLC
1300 S GROVE AVENUE
SUITE 204
BARRINGTON, IL 60010
847-898-9194
Fax: 847-277-0805
sales@infuzer.com
www.infuzer.com
• John Jocke, General Manager
(847) 898-9194
jjocke@infuzer.com
Description:
Infuzer allows fans to download season schedules and off field events into an Outlook, Palm or Lotus Notes calendar and then will update the calendar entries with updates, final scores or event time or date changes.

INTERTICKET, INC.
2 GLENRIDGE DRIVE
BEDFORD, MA 01730
781-275-5724
info@interticket.com
www.interticket.com

MORE ACTIVE
3038 E CACTUS ROAD
PHOENIX, AZ 85032
602-867-1324
Fax: 602-867-3673
www.fitnessventuregroup.com
• Don Hoskyns, President
• Don Hoskyns, Managing Partner
• John Domrzalski, Designer

SNAPSPORTS, INC
2330 CALIFORNIA AVENUE
SALT LAKE CITY, UT 84104
801-746-7555
800-664-3865
Fax: 801-746-7559
info@snapsports.com
www.snapsports.com
• Jorgen Moller, CEO
• Kerry Moller, Chief Operating Officer
• Dan Wollman, Vice President, Sales
dwollman@snapsports.com
• Jeremiah Shapiro, Operations Director
jshapiro@snapsports.com
Description:
The leading manufacturer of suspended modular indoor & outdoor athletic surfacing & components. Used for Residential & Commercial Sports Facilities; as well as customized sports marketing events.

SOUND & VIDEO CREATIONS, INC
2820 AZALEA PLACE
NASHVILLE, TN 37204
615-460-7330
Fax: 615-460-7331
support@clickeffects.com
www.clickeffects.com
• Ed Filmia, Senior Director
Products:
Click Effects Pro-AV, Click Effects Audio, Click Effects Replay

SPONSORSHIP PRO+
1954 AIRPORT ROAD
SUITE 207
ATLANTA, GA 30341
678-720-0700
Fax: 678-720-0704
www.sponsorshippro.com
• Tom Stipes, President
Nature of Services:
SponsorshipPRO+ is an easy-to-use and innovative presentation software tool designed for the sponsorship industry that enables sponsorship sellers to identify, organize, archive and present essential marketing and media files to clients in a dynamic format.
Nature of Services:
SponsorshipPRO+ is an easy-to-use and innovative presentation software tool designed for the sponsorship industry that enables sponsorship sellers to identify, organize, archive and present essential marketing and media files to clients in a dynamic format.

SPORTS SPECIFIC SCIENCES
5574 GOLF POINTE DRIVE
SARASOTA, FL 34243
941-351-7780
Fax: 841-240-2117
www.victortraining.com
• Brad Mayer, President
Products:
Software CD-ROM; SPRI Training

Equipment
Brands:
V.I.C.T.O.R.ia Trim & Tone 1.1;
V.I.C.T.O.R.ia Training Pack; Combination V.I.C.T.O.R.ia Training Pack with V.I.C.T.O.R.ia Trim & Tone Software;
V.I.C.T.O.R. Men's Fat Burner 1.1;
Combination V.I.C.T.O.R. Training Pack with V.I.C.T.O.R. Men's Burner Software;
V.I.C.T.O.R.Men's Muscle Builder 1.1;
V.I.C.T.O.R. Golf 1.1; Combination V.I.C.T.O.R. Training Pack with V.I.C.T.O.R. Men's Golf Software; V.I.C.T.O.R. Baseball 1.1; Combination V.I.C.T.O.R. Training Pack with V.I.C.T.O.R. Men's Baseball Software;
V.I.C.T.O.R. Hockey 1.1; Combination V.I.C.T.O.R. Training Pack with V.I.C.T.O.R. Hockey Software; V.I.C.T.O.R. Soccer 1.1;
Combination V.I.C.

SPORTS STATS INC.
900 N TUCKER BOULEVARD
SAINT LOUIS, MO 63101
314-340-8000
800-22 STATS
800-227-8287
Fax: 847-583-2600

STORIS MANAGEMENT SYSTEMS
400 VALLEY ROAD
SUITE 302
MT ARLINGTON, NJ 7856
973-601-8200
888-478-6747
Fax: 973-601-0078
sales@storis.com
www.storis.com
• Donald J Surdoval, CEO/President
• Donald J. Surdoval, President & Chief Executive Officer
Products:
Management Systems

STRATBRIDGE, INC.
BLANCHARD HOUSE
SUITE 304
249 AYER ROAD
HARVARD, MA 1451
978-772-4647
Fax: 617-977-8630
• Matthew Marolda, Founder/Chief Executive Officer
• Andrew H. Palmer, Strategy & Sales/Marketing
• Thomas L. Doorley, III, Strategy & Growth/Board of Directors
• Anthony J. Marolda, Strategy & Planning/Board of Directors
• Matthew T. Marolda, CEO and Founder
Nature of Services:
StratBridge provides analytic solutions that enable professional sports managers to perform exhaustive diligence research at the touch of a button - StratBridge.net, a platform product, is a Web-native system that seamlessly extracts data from internal and external sources, regardless of format, and then visually renders it in high-resolution plasma displays.

Retailers

24 HOUR FITNESS CENTERS
12647 ACOSTA BOULEVARD
PO BOX 2689
CARLSBAD, CA 92018
925-543-3100
800-224-0240
Fax: 925-543-3200
info@24hourfitness.com
www.24hourfitness.com
• Carl Liebert, III, CEO
info@24hourfitness.com
• Craig Pepin-Donat, Sales and Marketing
EVP
info@24hourfitness.com
Products:
Fitness Accessories, Apparels, Electronics
and Nutritional Products

A&N STORES
6000 RIVER ROAD
SUITE B
RICHMOND, VA 23226
804-226-1324
800-326-1324
Fax: 804-222-4894
info@anstores.com
www.anstores.com
• Mark A Sternheimer, President
(804) 226-1324
info@anstores.com
• Ross Sternheimer, SVP
(804) 226-1324
info@anstores.com
Products:
Athletic Apparel.

**A-ATHLETIC AND MEDICAL SUPPLY
COMPANY**
406 LINK ROAD
HOUSTON, TX 77009
713-861-4777
800-225-9565
Fax: 713-861-7274
www.a-athletic.com
• Ken Mitschke, Sales Specialist Manager
(713) 861-4777
• Mary Dominguez, Finance/Accounts
Receiveable/Accounts Payable
(713) 861-4777
• Ken Mitschke, Sales Specialist/Manager
• Clarence Mitschke, Shipping and
Receiving
Products:
Athletic, medical and industrial supplies

ABERCROMBIE & FITCH CO.
4 LIMITED PARKWAY E
REYNOLDSBURG, OH 43068
614-577-6500
800-666-2595
Fax: 614-283-6710
www.abercrombie.com
• Mike Jeffries, President / Chief Operating
Officer
(614) 577-6500
Products:
Athletic - Rugged Apparel.

ACADEMY SPORTS & OUTDOORS
565 SOUTH MASON ROAD
#419
KATY, TX 77450
281-646-5200
888-922-2336

Fax: 281-646-5000
academy@academy.com
www.academy.com
• David Gochman, Chairman/CEO
academy@academy.com
• Jim Pierce, EVP / Chief Operating Officer
academy@academy.com
• Robert Frennea, Apparel EVP
academy@academy.com
• AJ Blanchard, Hardgoods EVP
academy@academy.com
Products:
Manufacturer of sporting goods.

ACE HARDWARE
2200 KENSINGTON COURT
OAK BROOK, IL 60523-2100
630-990-6600
866-290-5334
Fax: 630-990-6838
affiliates@acehardware.com
www.acehardware.com
• Ray Griffith, President / Chief Executive
Officer
(630) 990-6635
rgriff@acehardware.com
• Rita Kahle, EVP
(630) 990-2693
kahle@acehardware.com
• Art McGivern, SVP / General Counsel &
Secretary
(630) 990-5975
amcgive@acehardware.com
• J. Thomas Glenn, Chairman of the Board
Regional Member Directo
(630) 990-6646
dmyer@acehardware.com
• Ray A. Griffith, President and CEO
• Rita D. Kahle, Executive Vice President
• Jimmy Alexander, Vice President Human
Resources
• William J. Bauman, Vice President Retail
Support
• Lori L. Bossmann, Vice President
Merchandising, Marketing and A
• Ronald J. Knutson, Vice President Finance
Products:
Equipment and tools for Hardware,
Hand/Power Tools, Electrical, Plumbing,
Lawn and Garden, Cleaning Paint Supplies
and Housewares

ACE MAGNETICS.COM
PO BOX 230670
ENCINITAS, CA 92023
760-479-0202
800-599-9098
Fax: 760-942-0050
info@AceMagnetics.com
www.acemagnetics.com
• J. Robert Miktinj, President
info@AceMagnetics.com
Products:
Magnetic bracelets, copper bracelets,
magnetic jewelry worn by famous golfer Mr.
Arnold Palmer. Home of the lightest weight,
most powerful and waterproof patent
pending 'Rally Band.' AceMagnetics
provides a 60 day money back guarantee
and free magnetic bracelet with any $75
Purchase.

ACTION SPORTS COMPANY
12215 E. SKELLY DR.
TULSA, OK 74128
800-580-0307
Fax: 866-282-2444

sales@actionsportscompany.com
actionsportscompany.com
Description:
Batting Cages, Pitching Machines, Field Turf
and Equipment, Putting Greens, Golf Nets
and Mats, Pool Tables, Saunas and Spas,
Uniforms.
Year Founded:
1998

ACTION SPOT SPORTS
3080 MAIN STREET
BUFFALO, NY 14214
716-833-1787
800-249-1077
Fax: 716-8340-6167
info@actionspotsports.com
www.actionspotsports.com
• Miranda Michael, President
Products:
Custom Athletic Apparel For Professional
NHL Hockey & MLB Baseball Teams.

ADVENTURE 16, INC.
4620 ALVARADO CANYON ROAD
SAN DIEGO, CA 92120
619-283-2362 EXT 100
Fax: 619-283-2362
www.adventure16.com
• John D. D. Mead, President
jdmead@adventure16.com
Products:
Outdoor Outfits such as rain gear, whistle,
water bottle, first aid kit, flashlight, map and
compass, emergency blanket,
matches/match container, extra food, signal
mirror, cord, water purification, candle,
sunscreen, knife

ALLIANCE SPORTS GROUP
3025 N. GREAT SOUTHWEST PARKWAY
GRAND PRAIRIE, TX 75050
972-343-1000
800-255-6061
Fax: 972-343-1190
www.alliancesportsgroup.net
• Glenn Bollinger, Chairman / Chief
Executive Officer
• Bob Bollinger, President / Vice Chairman
Products:
Training & Conditioning - Curl Bars,
Dumbbells, Jogging, Mats, Solar Belt/Shorts
& Wraps, Weight Lifting Belts,
Weights-Legs, Ankle.

ALTREC.COM
725 SW UMATILLA AVENUE
SUITE 1000
REDMOND, OR 97756
541-316-2400
800-369-3949
Fax: 800-783-4217
• Mike Morford, Chief Executive Officer
• Tim Shannon, Operations Director
• Mary Fischer, Controller
Products:
Specializes in active adventure sports,
e-commerce and editorial content covering
11 different categories. Jackets, Fleece,
Shirts, Pants, Shoes, Gloves, Long
Underwear, Hats, Socks, Shoes (such as:
Casual Walking, Running Shoes, Trail
Running Shoes, Hiking Boots, Snow Boots,
Ski Boots, Snowboarding Boots, Kids'
Shoes, Sandals, Water Shoes, Sandals),
Gears (such as: Ski, Snowboard,
Snowshoe, Camp & Hike, Climb, Running,

manufacturers/retailers

Paddle, Cycle, Beach, Wakeboarding, Travel, Pet Gear, Gift Ideas

AMAPRO SPORTING GOODS, INC.
242-A ROUTE 109
FARMINGDALE, NY 11735
631-777-1352
800-426-2776
Fax: 631-777-1353
www.amaprosports.com
• Gary Krupsky, President
Products:
Baseball, Basketball, Softball, Volleyball, etc- uniforms, jackets, hats & equipment.
Description:
Retail/Wholesale Selling Team Sports Dealer

AMENIA ARCHERY
5058 NEW YORK 22
AMENIA, NY 12501
845-373-9262
Fax: 845-373-9265
ameniaarchery@yahoo.com
• Anthony Robert, Owner
(845) 373-9262
ameniaarchery@yahoo.com

AMERICAN EAGLE OUTFITTERS
77 HOT METAL STREET
PITTSBURGH, PA 15203
724-776-4857
888-232-4535
Fax: 724-779-5585
custserv@ae.com
www.ae.com
• Roger Markfield, President
• Susan Miller, Merchandising EVP
• Fred Grover, General Merchandise Manager
• Jenny N, Aerie Accessories Manager
• Laurie Z, Senior PR Manager
• Brandon A., Creative Director
• Paul E., Director of Marketing Stratergies
Products:
Men's and Women's apparel, shoes, accessories, belts and flip-flops

AMERICAN SPORTING GOODS COMPANY
2323 MAIN STREET
IRVINE, CA 92614
949-752-6688
800-848-8698
Fax: 949-756-8609
• Margaret Oung, Owner
• Jerry Turner, President
Products:
Outdoor Products - Hiking Boots, Outdoor Crosstraining; Racquet Sports - Shoes; Track & Field/Running - Shoes; Training & Conditioning - Shoes-Aerobic, Shoes-Crosstraining.

ANACONDA SPORTS
85 KATRINE LANE
LAKE KATRINE, NY 12449
845-336-4024
800-327-0074
Fax: 845-336-4593
• Rob Meyer, Internet Services Director
(203) 926-0249
customerservice@anacondasports.com
• Don McGowan, Sales Manager
customerservice@anacondasports.com

Products:
Full Line Sporting Goods, apparels and accessories for baseball, basketball, field hockey, football, soccer, softball, track and field, volleyball, wrestling.

ANC SPORTS ENTERPRISES
2 MANHATTANVILLE ROAD
SUITE 402
PURCHASE, NY 10577
914-696-2100
Fax: 914-696-2101
www.ancsports.com
• Jerome Cifarelli, President & Chief Executive Officer
jcifarelli@ancsports.com
• Daniel Fumai, Executive Vice President, Finance
dfumai@ancsports.com
• Christopher Mascatello, Executive Vice President, Technology Sales
cmascatello@ancsports.com
• Mark J. Stross, Chief Technology Officer
mstross@ancsports.com
Services:
Provides a variety of active signage to sports stadiums, from standard courtside and field-level rotational signage, to backlit rotational signage ranging from ribbon to jumbo sized, and video based LED signage system. Offers teams, facilities, broadcaste

ANY MOUNTAIN, LTD
71 TAMAL VISTA BOULEVARD
CORTE MADERA, CA 94925
415-927-0170
Fax: 415-927-0170
• Bruno Gotzmer, Area Manager
bgotzmer@ssv.net
• Bruno Gotzmer, RegionalManager
• Chi McClean, Sales & Marketing Manager
Products:
Outdoor, ski and snowboard equipment, apparel and accessories.

ATHLETA, LLC
5900 NORTH MEADOWS DRIVE
GROVE CITY, OH 43123
707-769-2610
877-328-4538
Fax: 707-769-2610
info@athleta.com
www.athleta.gap.com
• Scott Kerslake, President / Chief Executive Officer
info@athleta.com
• Tami Anderson, Marketing Director
info@athleta.com
Products:
Sports gears, apparrels and accessories for women.

ATHLETE'S FOOT
3200 WINDY HILL ROAD SE
SUITE 175E
ATLANTA, GA 30339
800-524-6444
888-801-9157
Fax: 770-514-4903
franchise.info@theathletesfoot.com
www.theathletesfoot.com
• Robert J Corliss, President / Chief Executive Officer
franchiseinfo@theathletesfoot.com
• Don Camacho, Chief Financial Officer
franchiseinfo@theathletesfoot.com

• Robert J. Corliss, CEO
franchiseinfo@theathletesfoot.com
Products:
Athletic footwear

ATHLETIC DEALERS OF AMERICA
5423 VILLAGE DRIVE
ROCKLEDGE, FL 32955-6570
321-254-0091 EXT 304
Fax: 321-242-7419
pete@adamember.com
• Peter Schneider, President
(321) 254-0091
pete@adamember.com
Nature of Service:
Buying Group
Year Founded:
1980
Products:
Team Athletic Sporting Goods
Brands:
Adams USA, All Star, ATEC Bison, Brine, Champion Sports, Diamond, Easton, Louieville Slugger, JKP/Jugs, Mikasa, Pro Team, Rawlings, Schutt Sports, Spalding, Tachikara, TC Sports, Under Armour, Wilson.

AUBURN LEATHER COMPANY
125 CALDWELL STREET
PO BOX 338
AUBURN, KY 42206-0338
270-542-4116
800-635-0617
Fax: 270-542-7107
Sales1@auburnleather.com
www.auburnleather.com
• Lisa Howlett, President
sales1@auburnleather.com
• Ida Elliott, VP
sales1@auburnleather.com
• Lisa Howlett, President
Products:
Leather Laces, Leather motorcycle saddlebags, Horse Headstalls, Horse Breaststraps, Reins, Training/Misc. Equipment, Trail Tack, Saddle Accessories, Halters and Leads, Arabian Tack, Saddle Bags, Scabbards, Livestock Equipment, Cowboy Up, Leather
Brands:
Lace & Latigo Leather, Rawhide, Skirting Leather, Strap Leather, Latigo Leather, Harness Leather

AUSTAD'S GOLF STORE'S
8851 E 34TH ST N
WICHITA, KS 67226
316-838-5557
800-444-1234
Fax: 316-838-5557
www.austads.com
• Dave Austad, President
customerservice@austads.com
• Pat Penney, VP / Chief Financial Officer
customerservice@austads.com
• Tim Madden, Sales Officer
Products:
Golf Clubs, Golf Balls, Golf Shoes, Golf Apparel, Gifts for Golfers, Golf Bags & Transport
Brands:
TAYLORMADE RAC OS 2 IRONS (3-PW) - RH STEEL, CALLAWAY '04 BIG BERTHA IRONS (4-10 W) - RH STEEL, TITLEIST VOKEY BLACK NICKEL WEDGE - RH STEEL, TAYLORMADE R580 XD DRIVER -

RH GRAPHITE, CALLAWAY WOMEN'S GAME ENJOYMENT SYSTEM - RH GRAPHITE, TAYLORMADE r7 QUAD 400cc TITANIUM DRIVER - RH GRAPHITE, ODYSSEY WHITE STEEL 2-BALL BLADE PUTTER - RH, ADAMS IDEA A2OS IRON SET (3-4 IW, 5-PW) - RH STEEL, PING G5 460cc TITANIUM DRIVER W/ ALDILA NV65 SHAFT - RH GRAPHITE, CALLAWAY HX TOUR GOLF BALLS, CALLAWAY HX GOLF BALLS, NIKE ONE BLACK GOLF BALL, NIKE MOJO GOLF BALLS 2, PRECEPT PWRDRIVE GOLF BALLS, NIKE ONE PLATINUM GOLF BALL, MAXFLI BLACK MAX GOLF BALLS, TOP

AUSTAD'S GOLF/CATALOG
2801 E 10TH STREET
SIOUX FALLS, SD 57103
316-838-5557
800-444-1234
Fax: 316-838-5557
www.austads.com
• Dave Austad, President
customerservice@austads.com
Products:
Golf Accessories, Golf Apparel, Golf Bags & Transport, Golf Carts, Golf Clubs, Gifts for Golfers, Gift Cards, Golf Gloves, Golf Training Aides, Golf Shoes, Golf Books/Videos
Brands:
ZIVOT STEEL DIVOT TOOL, 6 FOOT POCKET BALL RETRIEVER, TRUNK-IT GOLF GEAR CASE, WIND VENT GOLF UMBRELLA - BLACK/WHITE, GOLFERS WALKING CHAIR, BOXING GLOVE HEADCOVER, FOOTJOY SHOE BAG, NEOPRENE IRON COVERS, ZERO FRICTION GOLF TEE, ARSENAL ULTRALITE STAND BAG, RJ SPORTS WHEELED TRAVEL COVER, SUN MOUNTAIN SPEED CART, RJ SPORTS DELUXE GOLF PULL CART, ARSENAL PREMIUM STAND BAG, SUN MOUNTAIN A-5 STAND BAG, TAYLORMADE TAYLITE 3.5 STAND BAG, TITLEIST X56 3.9 LB STAND BAG, NIKE XTREME SPORT STAND BAG, SUN MOUNTAIN SPEED CART, RJ SPORTS DELUXE GOLF PULL CART, BAG BOY M-310 PULL CART, SUN MOUNTAIN SPEED CART UMBRELLA ATTACHMENT, BAG BOY JUNIOR 3 WHEELED

AUTHENTIC SPORTS INVESTMENTS
28801 US HIGHWAY 19, N
CLEARWATER, FL 33761
727-785-5532
Fax: 727-785-3259
authenticsportsinv@yahoo.com
• Scot Monette, President
• Brad Wells, Executive VP
Description:
Sports Marketing and memorabilia company. Authentic game used and signed memorabilia.
Services Include:
Product Endorsement, Radio/TV Advertisement, Charity/Foundation development, Corporate Player Appearances, Personalized Product Lines, Personal/Client Gifts.

BANKSHOT SPORTS ORGANIZATION
330U N. STONESTREET AVE
SUITE 504
ROCKVILLE, MD 20850
301-309-0260
800-933-0140
Fax: 301-309-0263
bankshotsports@aol.com
www.bankshot.com
• Reeve R. Brenner, Founder/President
bankshotbb@aol.com
• Alan Ray, Technical Director
technical@bankshot.com
• Michelle Worthy, Office Manager
info@bankshot.com
Products:
Permanent Courts, Portable Courts, Bankshot On-A-Roll Trailer Stations, Dunkshot Stations, Bankshot Tennis Stations, Bankshot TriúSport Stations, Player Mats
Brands:
Bank-Around-The-Clock, Bankshot Classic, Junior Classic, Shoot-Around, Six-Pack, Three-Pack, Portable Junior Classic, Portable Shoot-Around, Portable Pro-Pack

BASE MOUNTAIN SPORTS
76 AVONDALE LANE
BEAVER CREEK, CO 81620
970-949-4327
877-255-0159
Fax: 970-949-1691
www.basemountainsports.com
• John M Trtanj, President
Products:
Apparel, Ski/Snowboard
Brands:
Arcteryx, Bogner, Descente, Obermeyer, Killy, Icelandic, Marmot, Oakley, Patagonia, Rossignol, Skea, Tommy Bahama, Atomic, Dalbello, Marker, Volkl, Rossignol, Salomon, Tecnica, Marmot, K2, Burton, Dakine, Liberty, Leki, Armada, Oakley, Grandoe, Swany, Maui Jim, Smith

BASEBALLJUNK.COM
2023 S COOPER
ARLINGTON, TX 76010
817-303-6620
800-850-5007
Fax: 206-666-6508
sportjunk@gmail.com
www.baseballjunk.com
• Gary Leland, Owner / President
sales@sportjunk.com
Products:
Sports apparel, accessories, training aids and equipments
Brands:
DeMarini Diablo 2006 -3, DeMarini Diablo 2005 -5, DeMarini Nitro -3, DeMarini 2006 Vexxum -3, DeMarini 2005 Vexxum -3, DeMarini 2005 Vexxum -5, DeMarini Voodoo, Easton 2005 Stealth Stiff Flex -3, Easton 2006 Havoc -3, Easton 2005 Havoc -3, Easton 2005 Stealth Regular Flex-3, Easton 2006 Stealth Regular Flex-3, Easton 2006 Stealth Stiff Flex-3, Easton Triple 8 - Adult, Easton -3 Triple 7, Louisville Slugger Armor TPX, Louisville Slugger Dynasty Transition -5, Louisville Slugger Dynasty, 2006 Louisville Slugger Air Omaha, 2006 Louisville Slugger Omaha, Miken Freak, Rawlings Liquidmetal Plasma, Worth Asylum -3, Rawlings BGP350 All, Rawlings The

BASS PRO SHOPS
2500 E KEARNEY
SPRINGFIELD, MO 65898
417-873-4383
800-227-7776
Fax: 417-873-4672
www.basspro.com
• John Morris, Founder
• James Hagale, CEO/President
• Stan Lippelman, Vice President Of Marketing
• Larry Whitely, Manager Of Communications and Outdoor Education
• Jenna Kendall, Media Informations Coordinator
Baseball Sponsor:
MLB St Louis Cardinals
Fishing Sponsor:
National Hunting and Fishing Day.
Brands:
Johnny Morris Signature Series Trigger Rods, Qualifier XPSTM Trigger R, Tourney Special Graphite Rods, ExtremeTM XPSTM Woo Dav, ExtremeTM XPSTM Trigger, Browning Fishing Citori Trigger Rods, Browning Fishing SilaFlex Trigger Rods, Bass Pro Shops Johnny Morris Signature Series Spinning Rods, Bass Pro Shops Pro Qualifier XPSTM Spinning, Bass Pro Shops ExtremeTM XPSTM Spinnin, Bass Pro Shops ExtremeTM XPSTM Travel, Bass Pro Shops ExtremeTM XPSTM Woo Dav, Bass Pro Shops Micro LiteTM Graphite Spinning Rod, Browning Fishing Citori Spinning Rods, Browning Fishing SilaFlex Spinning Rods, Bass Pro Shops Tourney Special Premium Graphite Casting, Bass P
Products:
Rods, Reels, Combos, Lures, Rainwear & Footwear, Flies & Kits, Watercraft, Fly Fishing Apparel, Waders & Accessories, Sunglasses, Optics, Black Powder, Shooting Accessories, Decoys & Calls, Treestands, Hunting Videos & Books, Hunting Clothing, Hunting Outerwear, Hunting Boots, Tents, Packs & Bags, Sleeping Bags & Beds, Metal Detectors, Canoes & Kayaks, Paddles & Oars, Canoe & Kayak Accessories, GPS Units, GPS Accessories, Radio & Accessories, Lanterns, Headlamps, Spotlights, Flashlights, Dehydrators, Vacuum Sealers, Kitchen Accesories, Apparel, Footwear.
Sponsor:
Bass Pro Shops Bassmaster Open

BEACON BALLFIELDS
8233 FORSYTHIA ST.
SUITE 120
MIDDLETON, WI 53562
608-824-0068
800-747-5985
Fax: 608-836-0724
info@beaconathletics.com
www.beaconathletics.com
• Jim Myrland, Owner
• Paul Zwaska, Sales Manager
pzwaska@beaconathletics.com
• Benji Brye, Custom Products & Service Specialist
bbrye@beaconathletics.com
• Elizabeth Blum, Custom Products & Service Specialist
eblum@beaconathletics.com
Products:
Field Maintenance & Facilities, Training/Sports Conditioning Equipment, Batting Cages & Accessories, Netting,

Windscreen, Padding, Portable Protective Screens & Backstops, Bases, Pitching, Home Plates, Foul Poles, Turf Protection & Practice Mats, Portable Pitching Mounds, Dugouts & Accessories, Football & Soccer Equipment, Golf Equipment & Accessories
Brands:
Beacon Team Cart, SMART HURDLE #3, SMART HURDLE #4, SMART HURDLE #5, SET OF 4 CROOKED STICKS WITH HANDLE, VOICE BLASTER, BEACON INDOOR TENSIONED SOFTBALL BATTING CAGE 55, BEACON INDOOR TENSIONED BASEBALL BATTING CAGE 70, BEACON DOUBLE BATTING CAGE 55 W/POLES, BEACON DOUBLE BATTING CAGE 70 W/POLES, BEACON DOUBLE BATTING CAGE 55 W/O POLES, BEACON DOUBLE BATTING CAGE 70 W/O POLES, BEACON BATTING CAGE 55 SOFT TOSS NET, BEACON BATTING CAGE 70 SOFT TOSS NET, BEACON INDOOR CAGE 55, 4-FRAME FREESTANDING SOFTBALL CAGE, UNPAINTED, BEACON INDOOR CAGE 55, 4-FRAME FREESTANDING SOFTBALL CAGE, POWDER-COAT PAINT, BEACON 5-FRAME FREESTANDING BASEBALL CAGE UNP

BEALLS ENTERPRISES DEPARTMENT STORES
1806 38TH AVENUE E
BRADENTON, FL 34208
941-747-2355
Fax: 941-746-1171
www.beallsinc.com
• Bob Beall, President / Chief Executive Officer
• Jonny Ortiz, Director of EDI/Merchandise Support
Products:
Misses Apparel, Petite Apparel, Positively Plus Apparel, Juniors Apparel, Lingerie, Jewelry & Watches, Sleepwear, Swimwear, Mens Apparel, Big Mens Apparel, Young Mens Apparel, Sleep & Loungewear, Underwear & Socks, Shoes
Brands:
Adidas, Grasshoppers, ParadiseBay, Aerosoles, Keds, Reebok, BayStudio, KSwiss, Roxy, Bongo, LifeStride, Skechers, CBCollections, Naturalizer, Sperry, Columbia, Nike, SunBay, Converse, NineAndCompany, UnionBay, Dockers, ONeill, EasySpirit, Outlooks, EmmaJames, NewYorkLaundry, AlfredDunner, GloriaVanderbilt, Alia, Haggar, NineAndCompany, Izod, Notations, CaribbeanJoe, JHCollectibles, ParadiseBay, CathyDaniels, Koret, SagHarbor, Lee, Levis, LizClaiborne, Jantzen, ParadiseBay, SuitYourself, SunBay

BEGNI'RS TO PRO'S
STONERIDGE PLAZA
ROCHESTER, NY 14615
585-663-1020
877-663-1020
Fax: 585-663-0058
service@beginrstopros.com
www.beginrstopros.com
• Brad Buckert, Owner
Products:
Balls, Bags, Shoes, Gloves & Supports, Grips, Cleaners, Polishes, Accessories.

BEI GROUP, INC./BASEBALL EXPRESS, INC.
1003 E NAKOMA
SUITE 104
SAN ANTONIO, TX 78216
210-525-9161
800-937-4824
Fax: 210-344-9080
customer.service@baseballexpress.com
• Fred Lummis, Chairman
• Pat Cowles, President
Products:
Baseball Bats, Baseball Gloves, Baseball Footwear, Baseball Accessories, Baseball Apparel, Baseball Bags, Baseball Caps & Visors, Baseball Training Aids, Baseball Uniforms, Baseballs, Batting Gloves, Batting Helmets, Catcher's Gear, Field Equipment, Gifts & Novelty, Sports Medicine
Brands:
LOUISVILLE 06 EXOGRID -3 BAT, LOUISVILLE 06 DYNASTY ADULT -3 BAT, EASTON 06 STEALTH CNT REG FLEX -3 BAT, EASTON 06 STEALTH CNT STIFF FLEX -3 BAT, LOUISVILLE 06 OMAHA ADULT -3 BAT , DEMARINI 06 VEXXUM ADULT -3 BAT, RAWLINGS 06 LIQUIDMETAL PLASMA -3 BAT, LOUISVILLE 06 AIR OMAHA ADULT -3 BAT, DEMARINI 06 VOODOO BASEBALL -3 BAT, MIZUNO 9SPIKE PRO LIMITED LOW 04 BLK/WHT, NIKE 06 AIR HUARACHE 2K4 BLK/WHT/SIL, NIKE 06 SHOX MONSTER METAL BLK/WHT, MIZUNO 05 CHIPPER 9 SPIKE G3 SPIKE, MIZUNO 9 SPIKE VAPOR MID 04 BLK/SIL, MIZUNO 9 SIKE VAPOR LOW 04 BLK/SIL, ADIDAS 05 EXCELSIOR MID METAL BLK/WHT, ADIDAS 05 EXCELSIOR MID METAL BLK/BLK, ADIDAS 05 EXCELSIOR

BELK STORES SERVICES
2801 W TYVOLA ROAD
PO BOX 1099
CHARLOTTE, NC 28201-1099
704-357-1000
866-235-5443
800-669-6550
Fax: 800-633-8141
belk_customer_care@belk.com
www.belk.com
• John R Belk, President/COO
• Mary R Delk, Merchandising & Marketing President
• Thomas M Belk, Chairman and Chief Executive Officer
• H.W. McKay Belk, President

BELLA BAGNO, INC.
5500 W TOUHY AVENUE
SUITE E
SKOKIE, IL 60077
847-673-7328
Fax: 847-673-7338
customerservice@bellabagno.com
www.bellabagno.com
• Cythia Lazarus, President
customerservice@bellabagno.com
• Cynthia Lazarus, Sales & Marketing Officer
customerservice@bellabagno.com
Products:
Sanitary System
Brands:
Bella Bagno hygoletr Sanitary System

BERNEY-KARP, INCORPORATED
3350 E 26TH STREET
VERNON, CA 90058
323-260-7122
800-237-6395
Fax: 323-260-7245
art@ceramic-source.com
www.ceramic-source.com
• Anna Ramos, VP Sales/Marketing
(323) 260-7122
annar@ceramic-source.com
Products:
Ceramics, Acrylics, Bottles, Stainlesswares, Glasswares
Brands:
60-211RB Pink Ribbon, 60-211RB Yellow Ribbon, 60-211GE Nose Mug, 60-331 Hand Grip Mug, 60-211B Light Bulb, 60-211H Hammer, 60-281TU Thumb, 60-278 VB Vertebrae, 60-211I Hammer, 60-211E Paint Brush, 60-211L Wrench, 60-211F Phone, 60-211SC Spine, 60-211CA Caduceus, 60-211ER Ear, 60-211SP Safety Pin, 60-211CM Computer Mouse, 60-211C Cellular, 60-211CW Cow, 60-211EG Eagle, 60-211HH Horse, 60-211BR Bear, 60-211LN Lion, 60-211EL Elephant, 60-281PT Palm Tree, 60-211G Nose, 60-211PB Dow Paw, 60-512 Gas Pump, 62-713-2, 62-625-2, 62-693-3, 62-811-2, 62-632-2, 62-605-3, 62-652-2, 62-689-2, 62-696, 62-694, 62-694-3, 62-709-3, 62-683, 62-708, 62-612-2, 62-

BEST BIKE BUYS
1150 FOOTHILL BOULEVARD
SUITE J
LA CANADA, CA 91001
626-296-6260
webmaster@bestwebbuys.com
www.bestwebbuys.com
• Steve Loyola, President/CEO/Founder
• Audrey Gubler, VP of Market Research
• Sugi Sorensen, VP of Engineering
• David Werntz, Chief Technology Officer
• Steve Loyola, President/CEO/Founder

BI-MART
1680 W. 18TH
EUGENE, OR 97402
541-342-2687
800-456-0681
Fax: 541-342-4241
comments@bimart.com
www.bimart.com
• Marty W Smith, Chairman & Chief Executive Officer
Products:
Photo Products, Housewares, Sporting Goods, Automotive, Hardware, Health & Beauty Products, Toys, Clothing/Shoes, Beer/Food/Wine, Pharmacy Products, Bed & Bath, Baby Goods, Furnitures, Personal Care Appliances, Watches & Clocks, Weather Instruments, Pet Supplies
Brands:
Abu Garcia, Casio, Century, Davidson Ladder, DeLonghi, Dreamer Design, Eagle Electronics, Haier, More Aire, Nikon, Oregon Scientific, Samsung, Schwinn

BICYCLE EXCHANGE, INC.
2034 EISENHOWER AVENUE
SUITE 250
ALEXANDRIA, VA 22314

703-924-5153
888-424-5387
Fax: 703-548-6980
• Jim Bellas, President

BIG 5 SPORTING GOODS
2525 EL SEGUNDO BOULEVARD
EL SEGUNDO, CA 90245
310-536-0611
Fax: 310-297-7585
info@big5sportinggoods.com
www.big5sportinggoods.com
• Steven G Miller, Chairman / President / Chief Executive O
• Gary S Meade, SVP / Secretary / General Counsel
• Richard A Johnson, Store Operations SVP
• Thomas J Schlauch, SVP - Buying
Products:
Provides a full-line brand name sporting goods products including athletic shoes, apparel, team sports equipment, fitness, camping, hunting, fishing, tennis, golf, snowboarding and in-line skating equipment.
Brands:
Adidas, Oasis, Bauer, Body Gloves, Brooks, Yonex, Browning, Bushnell, Coleman, Wilson, Ultra, Converse, Dunlop, Easton, Edelweiss, Everlast, Fila, Titleist, Speedo, Spalding, Shimano, Saucony, RollerBlade, Head, LouisvilleSlugger, Jansport, Hi-Tec, Reebok, Rawlings, Mizuno, Remington, Lifetime, Nike

BIGG'S HYPER SHOPPES
25 WHITNEY DRIVE
SUITE 122
MILFORD, OH 45150
513-248-9300
Fax: 513-248-9731
www.biggshyper.com
• Pierre A Wevers, President
• Paul McHugh, Divisional Merchandise Manager
• Cindy Oplinger, Divisional Merchandise Manager
Products:
Grocery, Clothing, Durable Goods, Auto/Harware, Electronics, Floral, Garden, Movies, Seasonal, Sporting Goods, Stationery, Toys

BIKE LINE
T 117-119 TURNER LN
TURNER SQUARE SHOPPING CENTER
WEST CHESTER, PA 19380
610-436-8984
800-537-2654
Fax: 610-429-4295
www.bikeline.com
• John W Graves, President / Chief Executive Officer
Products:
Premier chain of bicycles and fitness stores. Offers cycling apparel and accessories. Also promotes and suports many rides and local cycling and fitness events.
Brands:
Trek/Nike, Sugoi, and PearlIzumi

BIKEBOARD COMPANY
PO BOX 8597
NEWPORT BEACH, CA 92658
714-568-1300
Fax: 714-568-1304
www.thebikeboard.com

Products:
Manufacturer of Bikeboards, Accessories and Clothing.
Brands:
BikeBoard

BIRKENSTOCK FOOTPRINT SANDALS INC.
8171 REDWOOD BOULEVARD
PO BOX 6140
NOVATO, CA 94945
415-892-4200
800-867-2475
Fax: 415-899-1324
info@birkenstockusa.com
www.birkenstockusa.com
• Margot Fraser, Founder
• Matt Endriss, President / Chief Executive Officer
• Gene Kunde, Chief Operating Officer
• Patrick Hull, Marketing Senior Director
Products:
Footwear, Socks, Shoes, Sandals, Insoles & Arch Supports and Clogs for women, men and kids
Brands:
Birkenstock, J. Garcia, Heidi Klum

BJ'S WHOLESALE CLUB, INC.
1 MERCER ROAD
PO BOX 9601
NATICK, MA 1760
508-651-7400
Fax: 508-651-6114
• Michael T Wedge, President / Chief Executive Officer
• Herbert J Zarkin, Chairman
• Ronald R Dion, Director
• Bert N Mitchell, Director
Products & Services:
A wholesale club chains. Also a marketer of general products like Apparel, Automotive, Baby's Accessories, Computers & Cameras, Gift Cards, Electronics, Groceries & Gourment Foods, Gas & Propane, Household Basics, Jewelry & Gifts, Pets, Office Supplies, Toys. Business Services include: Healthcare Savings Network, Photo Services, Merchant Payment Processing and Service Agreements-BJ's Protection Plus.
Brands:
For Apparel: Jake & Julia, Generation Me, Lanesboro, Taylor Marcs. For Automotive: Exide, ACDelco. For Baby's Accessories: Eddie Bauer, Munchkin, Nuby. For cameras & computers: Brother, Sharp, BUSlink, Sony, Canon, Konica, Kodak, Nikon, Fuji

BLUE DOLPHIN DISTRIBUTORS
221 BLUE JUNIPER BOULEVARD
VENICE, FL 34292
941-484-2229
866-496-7900
Fax: 941-484-2207
Products:
Sporting Goods products such as New York Yankees Talking Bottle Opener, Alabama Crimson Tide Crimson Bottle Holder, Dallas Cowboys Blue Neoprene Bottle Holder, Oklahoma Sooners Musical Bottle Opener, South Carolina Gamecocks Musical Bottle Opener, Florida Gators Musical Bottle Opener, San Francisco 49ers Black Team Logo Neoprene Bottle Coozie, Georgia Bulldogs Red Bottle Holder W/'G'

BLUE RIBBON BLANKETS
120-B MAST STREET
UNIT B
MORGAN HILL, CA 95037
408-779-1997
800-437-6676
Fax: 408-778-5665
www.royalriders.com
Year Founded:
1977.
Products:
Official Riding Blankets for United States Equestrian Federation.

BLUEFLY, INC.
42 W 39TH STREET
9TH FLOOR
NEW YORK, NY 10018
212-944-8000
877-258-3359
Fax: 212-354-3400
flyrep@bluefly.com
www.bluefly.com
• Alan Kane, Chairman of the Board
• Melissa Payner-Gregor, President / Chief Executive Officer
• Patrick C Barry, Chief Financial Officer / Chief Operatin
(212) 944-8000
pat@bluefly.com
• Melissa Payner, President & CEO
Products:
Marketer of brand name designer apparel, bags, footwear and other general sports products.
Brands:
Prada, Vera Wang, Nicole Miller, Gucci, Fendi, Elie Tahari, Giuseppe Zanotti

BOATER'S WORLD
6711 RITZ WAY
BELTSVILLE, MD 20705
877-690-0004
877-999-7489
Fax: 877-552-2244
customerservice@ritzcamera.com
www.boatersworld.com
• Andre Brysha, VP / Chief Marketing Officer
brysha@RitzInteractive.com
Products:
Specializes in fishing tackle, marine electronics, water sports gear and cruising equipment for recreational boaters.

BOB WARD & SONS, INC.
3015 PAXSON STREET
MISSOULA, MT 59801
406-728-3220
800-800-5083
Fax: 406-728-5230
sales@bobwards.com
www.bobwards.com
• Keith Ward, President
• Chad Ward, Operations VP
• Gary Koprivica, General Manager
• Keith Dustrud, Buyer
Products:
Sporting Goods, Men's & Women's Clothing, Footwear, Watches, Apparel & Accessories for Hunting, Fishing and Camping, Gold Accessories, Outerwear.
Brands:
Alpen, Atlas, Atwater Carey Ltd., Belair, BenchMade Knives, Black Diamond, Browning, Brunton, Buck, Caddis, CamelBak, CarryLite, Citizen, Columbia, Columbia River Knife and Tool, Dakota

Watch Co., Dan Bailey, Dunham, DUO Wear, Estwing, Exofficio, Fieldline, Fishpond, Freestyle, Froghair

BOB'S STORES, INC.
160 CORPORATE COURT
MERIDEN, CT 06450
203-235-5775
866-333-2627
Fax: 203-235-6395
www.bobstores.com
• David Farrell, President / Chief Executive Officer
• Ava Hill-Gaunt, DMM Kids VP
Products:
Marketer of brand name footwear, casualwear, workwear, teamwear, activewear and gift cards.
Brands:
Avia, DVS, Lee, Dickies, Reebok, Element, Oakley, Split, Nike, Jansport, Hurley, Dockers, Gandi, Shady, NCAA, Majestic, Marithe Francois Girbaud, Lee Sports, Adidas, Mudd

BON TON STORES, INC.
2801 E MARKET STREET
UNIT 25
YORK, PA 17405
717-757-7660
800-233-7626
Fax: 717-751-319
www.bonton.com
• Tim Grumbacher, Chairman of the Board of Directors
• Byron L Bergren, President / Chief Executive Officer
• James H Baireuther, Vice Chairman, Chief Administrative Offi
• James M Zamberlan, EVP, Stores
Products:
Marketer of Ladies', Men's and Kids' Apparels, Accessories, Fragrances & Cosmetics, Intimate Apparel, Jewelry, Shoes
Brands:
Van Heusen, Geoffrey Beene, Angels, Glo, Levis, Bill Blass, Jeanstar, Goldtoe, Strivectin, Hylexin, Bali, Playtex, Maidenform

BOSCOV'S DEPARTMENT STORES
4500 PERKIOMEN AVENUE
READING, PA 19606
610-779-2000
Fax: 610-370-3495
Joanne.Barker@Boscov.com
www.boscovs.com
• Kenneth Lakin, Director of Operations
(610) 779-2000
klakin@boscovs.com
• Burton Krieger, President
• Barry Goodolf, Buyer, Sports
• Albert Boscov, Chairman, Chief Executive Officer
• Jim Boscov, Vice Chairman of Boscov's Department Store, L
• Sam Flamholz, Co-President, Boscov's Department Store, LLC
• Toni Miller, Senior Executive Vice President, Chief Admini
• Ed McKeaney, Senior Executive Vice President Merchandising
• Russell C. Diehm, Senior Vice President of Finance & Chief Acco
• Jon Holmquist, Senior Vice President, Direct Marketing

Services:
Department store chain.

BOWLERSPARADISE.COM
175 COMMERCE CIRCLE
SUITE A
SACRAMENTO, CA 95815
916-643-9827
888-969-2695
Fax: 916-921-8352
www.bowlersparadise.com
Products:
Bowling Equipment: Balls, Bags, Shoes, Gloves/Supports, Accessories, Cleaners/Polishes, Ball Care Products, Towels, Ball Inserts, Books/Videos, Drilling Service, Apparel, Gifts/Collectibles
Brands:
AMF, Brunswick, Columbia, Ebonite, Elite, Hammer, Morich, PBA, Roto Grip, Storm, Track, NFL Balls, MBL Balls, NCAA Ball, BF World, Circle, Dexter, Halex, Hammer, Linds, Master, Turbo, Neo-Tac, Tenth Frame, Ultimate Bowling

BRANCH BROOK COMPANY
370 ROUTE 36 E
HAZLET, NJ 7730
732-787-6897
Fax: 732-787-0358
customerservice@namcopool.com
• Kevin Ventrice, President
• Raymond Ventrice, VP
Products:
Marketer of Above-Ground Pools, Casual Furniture, Game Center
Brands:
BBC Billiards, Basketball Battle, Kettler

BREEZE SKI RENTAL
2650 S HAVANA
SUITE 205
AURORA, CO 80014
303-232-7547
888-427-3393
Fax: 303-232-7547
info@SkiRentals.com
www.skirentals.com
• Lewis Sapiro, Owner
• Janet Wrightson, Merchandise Manager
• Leigh Wild, Assistant Merchandise Manager
Products:
Sports Packages, Boots, Snowboarding, Snowshoes, Helmets, Skiboards

BRONER, INC.
1750 HARMON ROAD
AUBURN HILLS, MI 48326
800-543-4482
800-521-1318
Fax: 800-276-6375
hats@broner.com
www.broner.com
• David Broner, President
• Robert Broner, VP
Products:
Hats, Caps, Gloves and Accessories
Brands:
Broner

BROOKSTONE COMPANY
ONE INNOVATION WAY
MERRIMACK, NH 3054
866-576-7337
800-846-3000

Fax: 573-581-7361
customerservice@brookstone.com
www.brookstone.com
• Philip W Roizin, Interim President/CEO
• Alexander M Winiecki, Store Operations EVP
• Gregory B Sweeney, General Manager / Direct Marketing VP
• M. Ru Woodard, Merchandising VP
Products:
Retailer of consumer products.

BUILDING #19
140 MAIN ST
RTE 18
WEYMOUTH, MA 2043
781-337-1935
800-225-5061
Fax: 781-749-3691
• William Elovitz, President/CEO
(781) 749-6900
• Jerry Ellis, Chairman
• Paul Slovin, Merchant
Products:
Accessories, Basics and Designer Samples, Domestics, Food, Health & Beauty, Party Goods and Trim a Tree, Furniture and Mattresses, Giftware and Books, Handmade Oriental Rugs, Hardware, Housewares, Office Supplies, Electronics and Back to School, Kids', Men's, and Ladies' Clothing, Luggage and Shoes, Machine Made Oriental Rugs and Broadloom, Sporting Goods, Store and Catalog Stocks, Salvage Goods and Special Projects.
Year Founded:
1964

BUNKER JONES GOLF, INC
9792 EDMONDS WAY
SUITE 406
EDMONDS, WA 98020
425-640-0277
Fax: 425-696-0464
Products:
Online retailer of golf products and services.

BURDINE'S
7 WEST SEVENTH STREET
CINCINNATI, OH 45202
305-577-1500
800-289-6229
Fax: 305-577-2234
www.federated-fds.com
• Terry Lundgren, Chairman/President/CEO
• J. Da Scheiner, Stores Vice Chairman / Director
• Terry J. K Lundgren, Chairman, President and Chief Executive Offic
• Jeffrey Gennette, Chief Merchandising Officer
• Julie Greiner, Chief Merchandise Planning Officer
• Karen M. Hoguet, Chief Financial Officer
• Timothy M. Adams, Chief Private Brand Officer
• Peter Sachse, Chief Stores Officer
• Martine Reardon, Chief Marketing Officer
Products:
Bath Towels & Accessories, Beach Towels, Bed in a Bag, Bedding Basics, Bedding Collections, Blankets & Throws, Down Comforters, Featherbeds & Fiberbeds, Mattress Pads, Pillows, Sheets, Slip Covers, Visco Memory Foam, Window Treatments, Housewares, Women's Apparel and Accessories, Men's Apparel, Kids Apparel,

Shoes, Beauty Products, Jewelry, Watches
Brands:
Calvin Klein, Charter Club, Court of Versailles, DKNY, Hotel Collection, Lauren Ralph Lauren, Lilly Pulitzer, Missoni, Oscar by Oscar de la Renta, Sigrid Olsen, Tommy Bahama, Tommy Hilfiger, Waterford, Denby, Hotel Collection, Jonathan Adler, Kate Spade, Lauren by Ralph Lauren, Lenox, Michael Aram, Mikasa, Nambe, Noritake

BUSYBODY, INC.
11900 COMMUNITY ROAD
SUITE 100
POWAY, CA 92064
562-818-1543
800-466-3348
Fax: 949-258-5744
info@busybody.com
www.busybody.com
• Brian McDermott, President / Chief Executive Officer
• Kenton Va Harten, Chief Financial Officer
• Keith Lynch, Customer Service Director (562) 296-1063
Products:
Ellipticals, Treadmills, Exercise Bikes, Steppers, Rowers, Home Gyms, Home Gym Attachments, Freeweight Equipment, Flexibility Equipment, Fitness Accessories

BUY.COM SPORTS STORE
85 ENTERPRISES
SUITE 100
ALISO VIEJO, CA 92656
949-389-2000
Fax: 949-389-2800
www.rakuten.com
• Scott Blum, Founder/Chairman
• Neel Grover, President / Chief Operating Officer
• Robert Price, Chief Financial Officer
• Roger Andelin, Chief Information Officer
Products:
Sports and fitness apparel and footwear, products for team sports, water sports, winter sports, hiking, hunting, fishing, exercise, running, tennis and golf.
Brands:
Adidas, Wenger, Rawlings, Reebok, Magellan

BWM GLOBAL
3740 HAWTHORNE COURT
WAUKEGEN, IL 60087
847-785-1355
800-831-1117
Fax: 847-785-1712
customerrelations@bmwusa.com
www.bwmglobal.com
• Brad Fish, Division President
• Ronald Kruger, Senior VP
Products:
Apparel, Auto Accessories, Name Badges, Plaques, Trophies, Bags & Totes, Balloon Accessories, Business Accessories, Drink ware, Golf Apparel, Golf Equipment, Headwear, Office Accessories, Barbeque Equipment, Beach Umbrellas, Coach, Duffel Bags, Hartmann, Luggage, Passport Wallets, Travel Kits, Writing Instruments
Brands:
Ashworth, Callaway Golf, Coach, Cutter & Buck, Hartmann, Nike, O'Gio, Titleist, Tommy Hilfiger

C M T SPECIALTY SPORTS
199 ZAN ROAD
PO BOX 6427
CHARLOTTESVILLE, VA 22901
434-975-2704
Fax: 434-975-2845
info@downtownathletic.com
www.downtownathletic.com
• Banks Conner, President
bconner@downtownathletic.com
• Dave Beeler, Sales Staff
dbeeler@downtownathletic.com
• Robert Bell, Sales Staff
rbell@downtownathletic.com
Products:
Hard goods, team uniforms, shoes and cleats, field and gym equipment, awards and promotional items

C4-SPORTS
1137 WOODEDEN DR.
MISSISSAUGA, ON, CANADA L5H 2T7
403-383-1540
800-921-8490
Fax: 410-229-0020
sales@c4sports.ca
www.c4sports.ca
• Gene Sanders, General Manager (703) 287-5974

CABELA'S
ONE CABELA DRIVE
SIDNEY, NE 69160
308-254-6745
800-237-4444
800-237-4444
Fax: 308-254-7345
www.cabelas.com
• Dennis Highby, President / Chief Executive Officer / Di
• Michael Callahan, SVP
• James Cabela, President
• Patrick A. Snyder, Merchandising SVP
• Dave Roehr, Finance VP
• Ralph Castner, VP / Chief Financial Officer
• Steven Krajewski, Real Estate Manager
Products:
Hunting, Fishing and Skiwear

CADAC AMERICA
900 MC FARLAND 400 BOULEVARD
ALPHARETTA, GA 30004
770-569-9736
866-641-2291
Fax: 770-751-9458
• Steven Goldstein, President

CAM COMMERCE SOLUTIONS
17075 NEWHOPE STREET
SUITE A
FOUNTAIN VALLEY, CA 92708
714-338-0200
800-726-3282
Fax: 714-241-9893
www.camcommerce.com
• Geoffrey Knapp, Chairman / Chief Executive Officer / Sec (714) 241-9211
• Paul Ca Jr, Chief Financial Officer / Chief Accounti
• Sherrie Hoffman, Director of Marketing
Products:
Retail STAR Point of Sale POS Software, i.STAR eCommerce Software, Retail ICEr Point of Sale POS Software, CAM32 POS SoftwarE, i.CAM32 eCommerce, MicroBiz

Point of Sale POS Software, X-Charger Credit Card Processing Software

CAMPING WORLD
650 THREE SPRINGS ROAD
BOWLING GREEN, KY 42104
270-781-2718
800-626-3636
Fax: 270-796-8991
info@campingworld.com
www.campingworld.com
• Mark T Gilman, President / Chief Executive Officer
• Jim Bullock, VP
Products:
Vehicle & Product Protection, Club & Member Services, Financial Products & Services

CAMPMOR, INC.
400 CORPORATE DRIVE
PO BOX 680
MAHWAH, NJ 7430
201-825-8300
800-525-4784
Fax: 201-236-3601
customer-service@campmor.com
www.campmor.com
• Daniel Jarashow, President
• Frank Kosco, Merchandising VP
• Anna Chirico, Chief Financial Officer
Products:
Bicycles and Accessories, Binoculars, Books, Camp Furniture and Cots, Camp Tools, Car Racks, Climbing Gear, Clothing by Brand, Clothing for Children, Clothing for Men, Clothing for Women, Compasses and Orienteering, DVDs/CDs/Videos, Electronics and Weather Gadgets, First Aid, Food, Footwear, Gear and Clothing Maintenance, Insect Deterrents, Kitchenware, Knives, Lights and Lanterns, Maps, Packs, Paddlesports, Personal Care, Pets, Portable Toilets and Accessories, Rainwear, Sleds and Snow Tubes, Sleeping Gear, Snowsport Accessories Socks, Stoves, Sunglasses and Eyewear Survival, Swimming & Snorkeling, Tents, The Beach Toys, Travel , Ultra
Brands:
Bellwether, Blackburn Products, Cannondale, Diadora, Lone Peak, Pearl Izumi, Planet Bike, Polar, Profile Design, Topeak, Ambler Mountain, Black Dot, Campmor, Cloudvei, Columbia Sportswear, Convert by Columbia, Duofold, Gordini, Hind, Hot Chillys, Isis, Jansport, Manzella, Marmot, Mountain Hardwear, Moving Comfort, Outdoor Research, Prana, Red Ledge, Russell Athletic, Sara's Prints, Seirus, Smartwool, Sorel, Sportif, Spyder, Terramar, The North Face, Thorlo, Trekmor, Turtle Fur, Wigwam

CANAL JEAN CO.
2236 NOSTRAND AVENUE
BROOKLYN, NY 11210
718-421-7590
Fax: 212-353-2601
• Ira Russack, President
• Neal Levitt, Controller
Products:
General Merchandise

CANNON SPORTS INC.
11614 PENDLETON ST
SUN VALLEY, CA 91352

818-683-1000
800-223-0064
Fax: 818-683-1012
www.cannonsports.com
• Jon Warner, President
(800) 223-0064
• Michael Warner, Director of Strategic
Operations
(800) 223-0064
• Daniel Perez, Sales Manager
(800) 223-0064
Products:
Athletic Field Paint, Baseball/Softball
Equipment, Equipment Storage, Bats,
Batter's Gloves, Catchers Equipment,
Pitching Machines, Radar Guns, Base
Cover, Umpire Gear, Game Clock. Ankle
Braces, Stabilizers, Wraps, Aquatic Therapy
Kickboards, Bags, Bandag
Brands:
AAI, BPI, Cliff Keen, Cosom, Cramer,
Easton, Harvard, Incrediball, Jaypro, Kettler,
Master Lock, Mikasa, Mizuno, Porter, Penn,
Rawlings, Seiko, Spalding, Tachikara,
Whamo, Wilson
Description:
A one stop shop for your physical education
sports equipment needs. Nationwide leader
in wholesale sports equipment supplying our
nation's publicly funded institutions with the
highest quality products, outlasting the
competitiors.
Teams:
Dodgers, Lakers, Angels.
Number of Members:
10
Publications:
Cannon Sports Catalog Volume 24

CARHARTT INC.
5750 MERCURY DRIVE
DEARBORN, MI 48126
313-271-8460
800-833-3118
Fax: 313-271-3455
www.carhartt.com
• Gretchen C Valade, Chairman
• Mark Valade, President / Chief Executive
Officer
• Peter Krause, Chief Financial Officer
• Andrius Viskantas, Public Relations
Manager
Products:
Accessories, Bibs & Coveralls, Flame
Resistant, Footwear, Kids & Youth Apparel,
Outerwear, Jeans & Work Pants, Shirts,
Sweats, Thermal Underwear

CEI
550 PATRICE PLACE
UNIT C
GARDENA, CA 90248
310-630-1690
800-735-0871
Fax: 310-630-1692
feedback@cei-ultrak.com
www.cei-ultrak.com
• Gordon Craig, President
• Merrilee Craig, VP
Products:
Professional Stopwatches, Sport
Stopwatches, Seiko Products, Pedometers,
Timers, Sport Watches, Multi-Sport
Scoreboard, Display Timer, Mechanical
stopwatch, Tally Counter
Brands:
Ultrak, Seiko

CENTURY SPORTING GOODS
1000 CENTURY BOULEVARD
MIDWEST CITY, OK 73110
405-732-2226
800-626-2787
Fax: 800-400-5485
customerservice@centurymartialarts.com
www.centurymartialarts.com
• Sarah Fields
(800) 654-4701
sfields@centuryfitness.com
• Dan Bower, President
• Sara Tsoodle, Marketing Director
• Michael Dillard, CEO & Chairman
Products:
Martial Arts Uniform

CHAMPS SPORTS
311 MANATEE AVENUE W
BRADENTON, FL 34205
941-748-0577
800-991-6813
Fax: 941-741-7189
www.champssports.com
• Ronald R Halls, President / Chief
Executive Officer
• Marla Anderson, Merchandising EVP
• Nick Grayston, Planning / Allocation SVP
• Rubin Hanan, Marketing VP
Products:
Shoes, Clothing, Fan Gear, Equipment,
Accessories
Brands:
Nike, Jordan, adidas, Reebok, Puma, New
Balance, K-Swiss, Timberland, Under
Armour, Majestic, Mizuno, Spalding, Wilson,
Fossil, Ecko, Phat Farm, 3D Sports, ABC
Sports, ABI Accessory, Action Images,
Active Ankle

**CHAPMAN WALTERS INTERCOASTAL
GROUP**
27671 LA PAZ ROAD
LAGUNA NIGUEL, CA 92677
949-448-9940
800-500-8292
Fax: 949-448-7008
cwicbg@aol.com
• Michael Chapman, President
(949) 448-9940
cwicie@aol.com
• Cindi A Walters, VP
(949) 448-9940
redheaddvr@aol.com
Products:
Snorkeling, Diving and Water Sports Gear
and Accessories
Brands:
Body Glove

CHARTER PRODUCTS INC.
111 GATEWAY ROAD
BENSENVILLE, IL 60106-1950
630-616-1927
800-433-9839
Fax: 630-616-0755
www.chartergolf.net
• Thomas A. Krick Sr., President
Products:
Golf Bags for Clubs, Balls, Clubs-Putter,
Clubs-Utility, Gloves, Hats/Caps,
Headcovers, Socks, Tees

CHICAGO GOLF & SPORTS
4400 118TH AVENUE NORTH
SUITE 104
CLEARWATER, FL 33762

727-571-1556
866-571-1556
Fax: 727-571-1357
golfchicago1@yahoo.com
• Tony Liu, President
• Wei-Ming Liu, VP
Products:
Woods, Irons, Putter, Grips, Shafts,
Accessories
Brands:
Chicago Golf, Chicago, Golf Pride, Winn,
Grafalloy

CHICK'S SPORTING GOODS, INC.
1092 NORTHWAY MALL
PITTSBURGH, PA 15237
626-331-8227
877-846-9997
Fax: 626-339-1713
www.dickssportinggoods.com
• James M. Chick, President
• Steve Miller, Chief Financial Officer
• Ed Stack, CEO and Chairman
Products:
Sporting Goods, In-Line Skates, Scooters,
Shoes, Ski Hardware, Softwear/Activewear,
Team Sports, Tennis and Water Sports

CHRISTY SPORTS/SPORTSTALKER
11005 WEST 8TH
SUITE 102
LAKEWOOD, CO 80215
303-323-6143
888-413-6966
Fax: 303-233-5946
estore@christysports.com
www.christysports.com
• Patrick O'Winter, CEO
• Keith Va Velkinburgh, Director
Products:
Ski Gear, Board Gear, Clothing,
Accessories

CITY SPORTS
64 INDUSTRIAL WAY
WILMINGTON, MA 1887
978-988-5100
877-988-2580
Fax: 978-988-5105
www.citysports.com
• Michael R Kennedy, Chief Executive
Officer
(978) 988-5100
mkennedy@citysports.com
• Erik Metzdorf, Buyer
(978) 988-5100
emetzdorf@citysports.com
Products:
Apparel, Footwear and Sporting Equipment
Brands:
Adidas, Nike, Columbia, Patagonia, Moving
Comfore, SportHill, Basics, Puma, Sugoi,
Champion, InSport, Helly Hansen, Speedp,
Brooks, Reebok, Saucony, Converse, Teva,
New Balance, Vans, Timberland, Puma,
Merrell, Salomon, Reef, Mizuno, Mission
Hockey, RollerBlade, Bell, Jansport, Wilson,
Sony, STX, Everlast, Timex, York, Polar,
Speedo, Louisville Slugger.

CLARKS COMPANIES NA
156 OAK STREET
NEWTON UPPER FALLS, MA 2464
617-964-1222
800-211-5461
Fax: 617-243-4210

consumer.services@clarksna.com
www.clarks.com
• Robert Infantino, President
• Steve Katsirubas, Business Systems
Director
Products:
Footwear
Brands:
Clarks England, Bostonian, Indigo, and
Privo

CMS SPORTS
300 S DUNCAN AVENUE
SUITE 218
CLEARWATER, FL 33755
727-441-8450
Fax: 727-441-8439
info@cmssport.com
www.cmssport.com
• Charles Ferrer, President
• John King, Vice President
• Ali Ferrer, Vice President and Treasurer
• Trudy Wise, Manager, Sales and Services

COLLEGE CONCEPTS, LLC.
3350 RIVERWOOD PARKWAY
SUITE 850
ATLANTA, GA 30339
770-859-1420
800-284-4288
Fax: 770-859-1434
webmaster@conceptssport.com
• John C. Staton, President
• Debbie Carlson, EVP
• Rob Manske, Vice President
Products:
Licensed Apparel, Shorts, Sleepwear and
T-shirts
Brands:
Concepts Sport

COLLEGIATE PACIFIC
13950 SENLAC DRIVE
PO BOX 7726
DALLAS, TX 75234
972-243-8100
888-566-8966
Fax: 888-455-3551
• Michael J Blumfield, Chairman / Chief
Executive Officer
• Adam L Blumfield, President
• William Estill, Chief Financial Officer
• Arthur J Coerver, Chief Operating Officer
Products:
Game Tables, Benches & Bleachers,
Scoreboards; Apparel, Equipment and
Accessories of Archery, Badminton,
Baseball & Softball, Basketball, Boxing,
Field Hockey, Football, Gymnastics, Golf,
Racquetball, Scoreboard, Soccer, Tennis,
Soccer, Tennis, Track, Volleyball, Wallyball,
and Outdoor Recreation
Brands:
Adidas, Mark1m Wilson, Spalding,
Diamond, Rawlings, Search, Brine.

COLOR INC.
47 OCTOBER HILL ROAD
HOLLISTON, MA 01746
508-474-2900
Fax: 508-474-2800
www.thecolorstores.com
• Tom Emmons, VP
tom@thecolorstores.com
• Al Shemeklis, President
al@thecolorstores.com
• Tom Emmons, Vice President

Products:
Regional Gift Items, Sports Collectibles,
Imprinted Sportswear and Apparel

CONAN GOLF
470 CLOVERLEAF DRIVE
UNIT B
BALDWIN PARK, CA 91706
626-934-0388
800-964-4899
Fax: 626-934-0377
www.kunnangolf.com
• Gary Zou, Chief Executive Officer
Products:
Sporting Goods, Gold Equipment
Brands:
Echelon Golf, Kunnan Golf, Tech Edge Golf,
Sports Illustrated for Kids Golf

CONVERSE, INC.
ONE HIGH STREET
NORTH ANDOVER, MA 01845-2601
888-792-3307
Fax: 978-983-3503
www.converse.com
• Ellen Garvey, Information Technology
Director
• Jerry Lan, Managing Director, Far East
Operations
• James Stroesser, VP, Sales
• David M Maddocks, Global Marketing VP
Products:
Apparel, Footwear, Sporting Goods and
Equipment
Brands:
Converse, Chuck Taylor, Basketball,
Lifestyle, Jack Purcell, Varvatos

COOPERSBURG SPORTS
120 E STATION AVENUE
COOPERSBURG, PA 18036
610-282-1360
800-227-2891
Fax: 610-282-4611
www.coopersburgsports.com
• Scott Pino, President
(610) 282-1360
spino@coopersburgsports.com
• Steve Bishop, National Sales Manager
sbishop@coopersburgsports.com
• Pat O'Connel, ASI & Custom Manager
poconnell@coopersburgsports.com
• Justin Kotarski, Retail Sales
• Debbie Long, Customer Service
dlong@coopersburgsports.com
• Diane Nace, Artwork/Approvals
dnace@coopersburgsports.com
• Arthene Derr, Accounts Manager
aderr@coopersburgsports.com
Products:
Manufacturers of licensed sports
collectibles.
Brands:
Stackable StarsT

COUCH DISTRIBUTING COMPANY
104 LEE ROAD
PO BOX 50004
WATSONVILLE, CA 95077-5004
831-724-0649
800-542-5555
Fax: 831-724-4293
georgec@couchdistributing.com
www.couchdistributing.com
• Michael Hobby, Vice President - Finance
• Vern Burditt, Vice-President -
Administration

• Steve Vargas, Vice President - Sales
• Gary Jensen, Manager - Delivery
Operations
• Jim Griffin, Fleet Manager
• George W. Couch III, III, President
• Louie Pieracci, Vice President - General
Manager
Auto Sports:
Mazda Raceway Laguna Seca.

COUNTRY CLUB SYSTEMS
500 FAIRPORT ROAD
SUITE 500
FAIRPORT, NY 14450
585-377-6730
800-877-8338
Fax: 585-377-0448
• Don Saleski, President
Products:
General Sports Products - Inventory
management systems for the country club
and golf industry

COVERMASTER, INC.
100 WESTMORE DRIVE
UNIT 11-D
REXDALE, ON, CANADA M9V 5C3
416-745-1811
800-387-5808
Fax: 416-742-6837
info@covermaster.com
www.covermaster.com
• Robert Curry, President
• Gerald Hackett, Regional Sales Director
• Ken Curry, Regional Sales Director
• Bob Curry, President
• Larry Moreland, Regional Sales Director
Products:
Gym Floor Covers, Handling Systems and
Accessories, Divider Curtains, Wall
Padding, Gym Floor Covers, On Desk
Circles, Batting Practice Turf Protection,
Windscreens, Seat Covers, Concert Covers,
Rain Covers
Brands:
Ultima 5000, Universal Plus, Reversible 21,
Classic 2000, Spartan 1000, CoverMate,
CoverClean, PowerMate, Raincover Plus,
Raincover Lite, Raincover SuperLite,
TarpMate, Tarp Machine

CRAZY SHIRTS
99-969 IWAENA STREET
AIEA, HI 96701-3249
800-486-2720
800-771-2720
Fax: 800-486-1276
www.crazyshirts.com
• Mark Hollander, President / Chief
Executive Officer
Products:
T-Shirts; Bottoms, Outerwear, Sportknits,
and Tops for Men, Women, and Kids;
Accessories, Specialty Dye, Club Card, Gift
Certificates

CROWN TROPHY COMPANY
86 NORTH AVENUE
GARWOOD, NJ 7027
908-789-0460
Fax: 908-654-0328
Crown.Trophy@verizon.net
• Dennis Marsh, President
• Leonard Gleckel, Vice President
Products:
Trophies, Medals, Plaques, Ribbons,
Resin/Sculptures, Cups, Glass, Desk

Accessories, Championship Awards, Clocks, Gavels, Pins, Certificates, Badges, Signage, Banners, Bronze Castings, Embedments, Laminations. Trophy Case, Sport Display Cases, Donor Wall, Seasonal Gifts

CYBERSPORTS, INC.
PO BOX 3216
REDMOND, WA 98073-3216
425-882-8889
800-846-3688
Fax: 425-869-9399

DAEWOO INTERNATIONAL CORPORATION
65 CHALLENGER ROAD
RIDGEFIELD PARK, NJ 07660
201-229-4500
Fax: 822-753-9489
beyoon@daewoo.com
www.daewoo.com
• Michael Tae, Assistant Manager
Products:
Racquet Sports - Apparel; Track & Field/Running - Apparel-Run/Jog; Media & Electronics - Appliances, Robot Related Products, IT Related Products, Telecommunications Equipment and Terminals

DARTON ARCHERY
3540 DARTON ROAD
HALE, MI 48739
989-728-4231
Fax: 989-728-2410
www.dartonarchery.com
• Rex Darton, President
• Ted Harpham, Sales Manager
Products:
Darton Accessories/Clothing, GLC Crossbows, GLC Accessories
Brands:
Darton, Great Lakes, Crossbows

DC SPORTS, INC.
18 HUDSON STREET
MECHANICVILLE, NY 12118
518-665-0370
Fax: 518-665-0378
• Bob Brown, President
Products:
Full team dealer of apparel, bags, shoes, balls, baseball, basketball, soccer
Brands:
Adidas, Nike, Reebok, Russell, Don Alleson, Fruit of the Loom

DECATHLON USA SPORTS MEGASTORE
326 BALLARDVALE STREET
WILMINGTON, MA 1887
978-657-0100
Fax: 978-658-4854
www.decathlon-usa.com
• Matthieu Laclercq, Chief Executive Officer
Products:
Sporting Goods Designer and Retailer
Brands:
Tribord, Quechua, Decathlon Cycle, Kalenji

DIAMOND OIL COMPANY
702 SE RACCOON ST.
DES MOINES, IA 50309
515-244-4271
800-422-7563
Fax: 515-244-4273

info@diamondoilco.com
www.lubricants-oil.com
• Chance Jason, Owner
Services:
Fuel Supplier for Iowa Speedway; Turbo Blue; Brad Penn.

DICK'S SPORTING GOODS INC.
1092 NORTHWAY MALL
PITTSBURGH, PA 15237
412-635-9004
877-846-9997
Fax: 412-635-9429
www.dickssportinggoods.com
• Edward W Stack, Chairman / Chief Executive Officer
• William Colomb, President / Chief Operating Officer / Di
• William Newlin, EVP / Chief Administrative Officer
• Ed Stack, CEO and Chairman
Products:
Sporting Goods
Brands:
Adidas, Bowflex, Callaway Golf, Lifetime Basketball, New Balance, Proform Fitness, Reebok, TaylorMade, Under Armour, Concept Shop, Walter Hagen

DILLARD DEPARTMENT STORES
1600 CANTRELL ROAD
LITTLE ROCK, AR 72201
501-376-5200
800-345-5273
Fax: 501-399-7831
questions@dillards.com
www.dillards.com
• Mike Dillard, EVP / Director
• Drue Corbusier, EVP / Director
• Alex Dillard, President / Director
• James I Freeman, SVP / Chief Financial Officer, Director
Products:
Women's apparel, Men's apparel, Children's apparel, Jewelry & Accessories, Cosmetics, Furniture, Gifts, Housewares
Brands:
Adidas, Adrianna Papell, Alain Weiz, Alex Evenings, Allen by Allen B. Schwartz, Aigle, Antigua, Austin Reed, BCBG Max Azria, Bulova, 6 Degrees, Anne Klein, As U Wish, Avenue of the Stars, B. Darlin, Arthur Court, Artimino, Astor Lane, Atlantis, Barbie, Bernhardt, Brookwood, Gallery, Design, Hooker, Italsofa

DIXIE SPORTING GOODS
2400 WESTWOOD AVENUE
RICHMOND, VA 23230
804-353-4943
800-527-7510
Fax: 703-321-7378
www.bsnsports.com
• Ken Caravati, President
• Michael Caravati, Sales / Marketing VP
Products:
Sport Goods
Brands:
Russell Athletic, Rawlings, Nike, Wilson, Easton, Louisville Slugger, Adams, Champion, Don Alleson, Delong, Cliff Keen, AAI, Bison, Asics, Adidas, Worth, Dudley, Twin City, New Era, Gatorade, Douglas, Holloway, Fisher, Gill

INTERNATIONAL SEEDS, INC.
175 W H STREET
PO BOX 229
HALSEY, OR 97348
541-369-2251
800-445-2251
Fax: 541-369-2640
www.dlfis.com
• Brad Jeffreys, Truf/Forage Sales
(541) 369-1837
bradj@intlseed.com
• Steve Johnson, Research Director
(541) 929-3703
stevej@intlseed.com
• Rick Myers, Director Sales / Marketing
(541) 369-1841
rickm@intlseed.com
• Richard Myers, Vice President, Turf & Retail
(541) 368-184
rickm@dlfis.com
• Roeland Kapsenberg, Vice President, Forage
(541) 369-1840
roelandk@dlfis.com
• Claus Ikjaer, General Manager
(541) 369-1813
clausi@dlfis.com
• Alan Muhl, Finanace / Operations Manager
(541) 369-1816
alanm@intlseed.com
• Brad Jeffreys, Turf & Forage Sales
(541) 369-1837
bradj@dlfis.com
• Norm Touhy, National Accounts Manager
(303) 347-9245
normt@dlfis.com
• W. Dan Walters, Seed Production Manager
(541) 369-1827
danw@dlfis.com
Products:
Surfaces: Natural Turf, Golf Turf, Seed, Sand - Domestic and International.
Brands:
C.E.O., Cindy, Cobra, Derby Supreme, Eureka, Gator II, Houndog 5, Longfellow, Major League, P.H.D., Pride, R.2, Regal, Sabre II, Top Hat, Viper

DODD & COMPANY, R.O.
2870 MABRY LANE
PO BOX 191107
ATLANTA, GA 30319-2602
404-869-7661
Fax: 404-869-0632
• Zane Dodd, Chief Executive Officer
• Zane Dodd, President
Products:
Baseball - Base Spikes, Bases, Batting Helmets, Faceguards, Caps, Gloves-Batter, Gloves-Catcher/Fielder/First Base, Glove Oil, Jerseys, Masks, Protective-Catcher/Umpire, Uniforms; Basketball - Uniforms; Football - Arm/Hand Pads, Bags, Equipment, Face Prot

DOLLAR GENERAL CORPORATION
100 MISSION RIDGE
GOODLETTSVILLE, TN 37072-0000
615-855-4000
Fax: 615-855-5252
www.dollargeneral.com
• Richard W Dreiling, Chairman / Chief Executive Officer
• David Tehle, Executive Vice President / Chief Financi

• Kathleen Guion, Division President of Store Operations a
• Beryl Buley, Division President of Merchandising, Mar
Products:
Consumable Basics, Refrigerated Items
Brands:
DG Guarantee, Clover Valley

DOVER SADDLERY, INC
PO BOX 1100
LITTLETON, MA 1460
978-952-8062
800-406-8204
Fax: 978-952-6633
customerservice@doversaddlery.com
www.doversaddlery.com
• Powers David, Founder
• Chesley Chmura, Customer Service Manager
• Patricia Nesto, Buyer
• Laura Derick, Supervisor
• Jim Powers, Founder
Services:
Official mail order catalog company of the United States Equestrian Federation.

DR. JAY'S
7720 KENAMAR COURT
SUITE C
SAN DIEGO, CA 92121-2425
858-634-5595
888-437-5297
Fax: 201-864-1440
service@DrJays.com
www.drjays.com
• Elliott Betesh, President / Apparel
• Raymond Betesh, Buyer / Footwear
Products:
Apparel and Footwear Specialty
Brands:
Adidas, Akademiks, Andrew Stevens, Apple Bottoms, AZZURE, Baby Phat, Basic Essentials, Boutique NYC, Catch A Fire, DKNY Jeans, Ecko Red, Fashion Lab, G-Unit, Girbaud, Graphix Gallery, Guess, Harajuku Lovers, Hustler, JLO, Junk Food, Kenneth Cole, LOT29, New Era, Nike, Pepe Jeans, Prom Shop, Reebok, Request Jeans, Rocawear, Rockers- It's Dangerous, Southpole, T-Star B, The North Face, Timberland, Tommy Girl, Triple 5 Soul, Wanted Shoes, Apple Bottoms,Baby Phat, David & Goliath, Dickies, DKNY Jeans, Dollhouse, Ecko Red, FUBU, Fun Tees, G-Unit, Guess, Hello Kitty, it's happy bunny

DREW PEARSON MARKETING, INC. (DPM)
15006 BELTWAY DRIVE
ADDISON, TX 75001
972-702-8055
800-879-0880
Fax: 972-980-7123
customerservice@drewpearson.com
www.drewpearson.com
• Pearson Drew, Chairman
(952) 939-4900
dpearson@drewpearson.com
Products:
Baseball caps, cold weather headwear and accessories; Silk screening and logo design services

DUCKWALL ALCO STORES, INC.
401 COTTAGE AVENUE
ABILENE, CANADA 67410

785-263-3350
800-976-0542
Fax: 785-263-7531
webmaster@alcostores.com
• Lawrence J Zigerelli, Chief Executive Officer
• James E Schoenbeck, Operations / Advertising SVP
• James E Fennema, Merchandise SVP
• Michael J Gawin, VP / Division Merchandise Manager
Products:
Apparel: Men's, Women's, Kids', Automotive, Candy, Snacks, Food, Crafts, Domestics, Electronics, Video, Audio, Fabrics, Furniture, Gifts, Hardware, Health and Beauty Aids Housewares, Jewelry, Lawn and Garden, Pet Supplies, Seasonal Items, Shoes and Hosiery, Sporting goods, Stationery, Toys

DUNHAM'S ATHLEISURE CORPORATION
5607 NEW KING DRIVE
SUITE #125
TROY, MI 48098
248-674-4991
888-801-9158
Fax: 248-674-4980
www.dunhamssports.com
• Jeff Lynn, President / Chief Executive Officer
• Ken Meehan, EVP / General Merchandise Manager
• Steve Sander, Store Operation EVP
• Marshall Sosne, EVP / Chief Financial Officer
Products:
Sporting Goods
Brands:
Reebok, Adidas, Converse, Nike

DUNLAP CO.
200 BAILEY AVENUE
SUITE 100
FORT WORTH, TX 76107
817-336-4985
Fax: 817-887-1302
• Dale Matthews, SVP / Director, Stores
• Edward Martin, President / Chief Executive Officer
• Reg Martin, Chairman
• Jim Leamy, General Merchandise Manager
Products:
Women's Apparel, Men's Apparel, Children's Apparel, Accessories, Beauty and Fragrance
Brands:
Alfred, Dunner Sag Harbor, Dooney & Bourke, Keds, Van Heusen, Estee Lauder, Bali, Colonial, Candles, Samsonite, Lee Jeans, Gold Toe, Stone, Mountain, Clinique, Haggar, Vanity Fair, Izod, Liz Claiborne, Briggs, Godinger, Cuddlduds, Travel Pro, Dockers, Harve Benard, Wrapper, Lancome, Koret, Fossil, Josephine Chaus, Hanes, Naturalizer, OXO, Malden, Jockey

E & J LAWRENCE CORP/ JIMMY JAZZ
43 HALL STREET
SUITE 7
BROOKLYN, NY 11205
718-596-1414
Fax: 718-596-7288
• Jimmy Khezrie, President / Chief Executive Officer

Products:
Specialty - Apparel/Footwear

EAGLE BUTTON CO.
700-76 BROADWAY
#318
WESTWOOD, NJ 7675
201-652-4063
800-794-6350
Fax: 201-652-2003
info@eaglebutton.com
www.eaglebutton.com
• Arthur Simon, President
Products:
Buttons

EARLY WINTERS
3188 NW ALOCLEK DRIVE
HILLBSBORO, OR 97124
503-614-4600
877-718-7902
800-458-4438
Fax: 503-614-4601
webrep@nortom.com
www.sahalie.blair.com
Products:
Men's Apparel, Women's Apparel, Accessories, Shoes, Gift & Gourmet

EASTBAY, INC.
PO BOX 8066
WAUSAU, WI 54402-8066
715-261-9588
800-826-2205
Fax: 715-261-9550
asktheexperts@eastbay.com
www.eastbay.com
• Ken Hicks, Chairman & CEO
• Dowe Tillema, President/CEO
Products:
Athletic apparel, equipment, and footwear.
Brands:
Nike, Reebok, Adidas and New Balance, Easton, Brute, Phat Farm Baby Phat, Rocawear

EASTERN MOUNTAIN SPORTS, INC.
1 VOSE FARM ROAD
PETERBOROUGH, NH 3458
603-924-9571
888-463-6367
Fax: 603-924-9138
customerservice@ems.com
www.ems.com
• Will Manzer, President and CEO
Year Founded:
1967
Brands:
Black Diamond, CamelBak Hydration Systems, Eagle Creek, EMS, Garmin GPS Units, Gregory Backpacks, Keen Footwear, Kelty, Leatherman Tools, Marmot, Merrell Footwear, Mountain Hardwear, MSR Equipment, Nalgene, Petzl, prAna, Sierra Designs, SmartWool, Teva Footwear, The North Face,Thule Racks, Tubbs Snowshoes
Products:
Gear, Clothing

EB2B COMMERCE, INC.
665 BROADWAY
SUITE 301
NEW YORK, NY 10012
212-477-1700
800-828-3932
Fax: 212-477-6207

info@enabletrading.com
www.easylink.com
• Richard S. Cohan, Chief Executive Officer
• Robert Bacchi, Chief Operating Officer
• Alester Spears, Director, Regional Sales
• Stephen Haber, Director, Client Services
Products & Services:
Supplier portal and enablement services,
Business Transaction Outsourcing Services,
and Professional services
Brands:
TradeGateway, TradeEngine

ECKERD DRUG, INC.
6501 LEGACY DRIVE
PLANO, TX 75024
972-431-1000
800-322-1189
Fax: 972-431-1362
www.jcpenney.com
• Myron E Ullman, III, Chairman/CEO
• Jeff Thompson, VP, Marketing
• Joan M. Gallagher, VP, Public Relations
Products & Services:
Apparel, Footwear, and Accessories for
Men, Women and Kids; Shoes; Jewelry;
Bed & Bath; Window Accessories; Home
Furnishings; Eyewear, Portraits, Gift Cards,
Credit Services
Brands:
JCPenney, St. John's Bay, New Balance,
Nike, Reebok, Converse, Adidas, JCP, Flirt

EDDIE BAUER, INC.
PO BOX 7001
GROVEPORT, OH 43125
425-883-2827
800-426-8020
Fax: 425-755-7696
www.eddiebauer.com
• Fabian Mansson, President and Chief
Executive Officer
• Kathy Boyer, SVP and Chief
Merchandising Officer
• Timothy McLaughlin, SVP and Chief
Financial Officer
• John Ball, Division VP, Menswear
Products:
Men and Women's Apparel, Shoes and
Accessories, Gear
Brands:
EddieBauer, Sueded Terry, Simple, Ruston
Fit-Nano-Tex

EDWIN WATT'S GOLF SHOP, INC.
20 HILL AVENUE
FORT WALTON BEACH, FL 32548
850-362-2005
800-443-4167
Fax: 850-244-5217
service_team@wattsgolf.com
www.edwinwatts.com
• Edwin Watts, President
• Ron Watts, EVP
• John Watson, President/CEO, Golf
Operations
• Robert Anthony, VP, Catalog and Online
• Lynda K. Barr, VP, Chief Financial Officer
• Kerry Kabase, VP, Purchasing and
Inventory
• Sven Kessler, VP, Retail Operations
• Robert Anthony, VP, Marketing and
Advertising
• David DeBra, VP, Merchandise Planning
Products:
Golf Clubs, Bags/Shoes Accessories, Golf
Simulators, Golf Balls, Gift Cards, Gloves,

Training Aids, Apparel
Brands:
Callaway, Titleist, Taylormade, Ping, Nike,
Cleveland, Cobra, Mizuno, Macgregor, Ben
Hogan, Footjoy

EFINGER SPORTING GOODS
513 W UNION AVENUE
PO BOX 2003
BOUND BROOK, NJ 08805
732-356-0604
Fax: 732-805-9860
• Thomas Hoey, President
tomh@efingersports.com
• Murray Greenberg, VP and General
Merchandise Manager
murrayg@efingersports.com
• Patrick Hoey, Store Manager and Buyer
path@efingersports.com
• Evan Greenberg, Vice President
emg@efingersports.com
• Joe Collins, Vice President/Sales Manager
jcyank15@aol.com
Products:
Accessories, Apparel, Base/Softball,
Basketball, Football, Soccer, Running,
Wrestling, Field Hockey, Ice Hockey, Golf,
Hunting, Camping, Fishing, Exercise and
Tennis.
Year Founded:
1907

ELAN-MONARK
81-H BRUNSWICK BOULEVARD
DOLLARD DES ORMEAUX, QC, CANADA
H9B 2J5
514-421-7871
Fax: 514-421-7394
• Bob Orbacz, President
• Rick Sceery, VP, Sales and Marketing
Products:
Snow Sport Equipment
Brands:
Elan, Arter, Dalbello

EREHWON MOUNTAIN OUTFITTER
746 W ALGONQUIN ROAD
ARLINGTON HEIGHTS, IL 60005
847-439-1400
www.erehwon.com
• Martin Stilling, Store Manager
Products:
Clothing for Men, Women and Kids;
Footwear; Hats, Gloves & Underwear;
Novelties; Gear for Climbing, Kayaking,
Snowsports; Travel & Luggages
Brands:
Arc'teryx, Icebreaker, Mountain Hardwear,
Terramar, Cloudveil, Kombi, Patagonia, The
North Face, Columbia Sportswear, Marmot,
Smartwool.

EXPRESS
1 LIMITED PARKWAY
COLUMBUS, OH 43230
614-415-4000
800-477-8844
Fax: 614-415-4200
www.express.com
• Ken Stevens, Chief Executive Officer
(614) 415-4000
• Michael J. Wiess, President & Chief
Executive Officer
Products:
Women's Private-Label Apparel and
Accessories; Menswear

F.A.O. SCHWARZ
767 FIFTH AVENUE
SUITE 601
NEW YORK, NY 10153
212-644-9400
800-876-7867
Fax: 212-308-6094
• Barry Erdos, CEO
• David Niggli, EVP, Merchandising
• Lisa Harnisch, Senior Vice President,
General Merchandising
Products:
Easter & Springtime Gifts, Stuffed Animals,
Dolls & Collectible Dolls, Personalized Gifts,
Arts & Crafts, Electronics, Furniture &
Accessories, Sports Equipment &
Accessories.
Brands:
Patrick & Penelope, American Kennel Club,
Madame Alexander, Robert Tonner, Barbie,
Newborn Nursery.

FACTORY 2-U STORES, INC.
15001 FIGUEROA STREET
GARDENA, CA 90248
858-627-1800
Fax: 858-637-4199
www.factory2-u.com
• Norman G. Plotkin, Chief Executive Officer
and Director
• Robert Wr II, Director
Products:
Operates a chain of off-price retail apparel
and housewares stores.

FAMILY DOLLAR STORES
10401 OLD MONROE ROAD
PO BOX 1017
CHARLOTTE, NC 28201-1017
704-847-6961
Fax: 704-847-0189
info@familydollar.com
www.familydollar.com
• Howard R. Levine, Chairman and Chief
Executive Officer
• R. Ja Kelly, Vice Chairman, Chief
Financial Officer a
• Robert George, EVP and Chief
Merchandising Officer
• Charles S. Gibson Jr, EVP, Supply Chain
Products:
Health & Beauty Aids, Automotive, Food &
Candy; Housewares, Pets, Hardware &
Paint, Home Cleaning Aids, Laundry &
Storage, Picture Frames, Ladies, Socks &
Lingerie; Mens, Boys, Girls and Infants
Apparel and Shoes

FAMOUS FOOTWEAR
7010 MINERAL POINT ROAD
MADISON, WI 53717-1701
608-829-3668
888-869-1053
Fax: 608-827-3353
www.famousfootwear.com
• William A. Dandy, SVP, Retail Sales and
Operations
• George Zelinsky, SVP and General
Merchandising Manager
• J. M. Lang, SVP and Chief Financial
Officer
• James M. Roe, SVP, Real Estate
Products:
Name brand shoes
Brands:
Addidas, Aerosoles, Asics, Avia, Brown
Shoe, Buster Brown, Clarks England,

Columbia, Connie, Dr. Scholl's, Eastland, Eurostep, GBX, Keds, LEI, LifeStride, Luqz, MUDD, Naturalizer, New Balance, Nike, Nunn Bush, Reebok, Rocksport, Skechers, Steve Madden, Timberland, Vans, Westies

FANATICS RETAIL GROUP
5245 COMMONWEALTH AVENUE
JACKSONVILLE, FL 32254
305-348-2000
Fax: 305-348-2963
www.fiusports.com
• Pete Garcia, Athletic Director
(305) 348-0182
pgarcia@fiu.edu
• Alex Duque, Senior Associate AD/CFO
(305) 348-2398
duquea@fiu.edu
• Julie Berg, Senior Associate AD & SWA
(305) 348-2352
bergj@fiu.edu
• Lori-Ann Cox, Senior Associate AD, Advancement
(305) 348-0372
coxla@fiu.edu
• Heath Glick, Chief of Staff
(305) 348-6711
glickh@fiu.edu
• Lucy Prosper, Assistant Director HR/Admin Services
(305) 348-2671
lprospe@fiu.edu
• Derrick Mayfield, Assistant AD, Facilities & Operations
(305) 348-6301
• Pete Garcia, Executive Director, Sports & Entertainment
(305) 348-0182
pgarcia@fiu.edu
Arena Seating Capacity:
5,000
Stadium Seating Capacity:
Football Track (17,000), Baseball (1500), Soccer (1,500), Softball (800).

FANBUZZ.COM
10729 BREN ROAD E
MINNETONKA, MN 55343
952-943-6714
Fax: 952-943-6711
www.fanbuzz.com
• J. Da Wible, VP, Operations
• Scott Killian, President
• Mike Grube, Merchandise Manager
• Brian Wright, Marketing Manager
Products:
Sells licensed apparel to sporting goods industry and customizes individual orders. Also offers e-commerce solutions to teams, leagues, colleges via various content Websites.

FANSEDGE.COM
725 LANDWEHR ROAD
NORTHBROOK, IL 60062
877-965-3955
877-965-3955
Fax: 847-965-2860
www.fansedge.com
• Kevin Bates, Chief Executive Officer
• Brian Neal, Chief Financial Officer and VP, Business
• Pete Hanna, VP, Operations
• Jeff Basso, VP, Technology
Products:
Apparel, Auto Accessories, Autographed Memorabilia, Collectibles, Gift Certificates,

Golf Items and Novelties, Hats, Caps, Visors, Home and Officer, Jewelry, Watches, Accessories, Tailgating/Stadium Gear

FEDERATED DEPARTMENT STORES, INC.
7 W SEVENTH STREET
CINCINNATI, OH 45202
513-579-7000
800-261-5385
Fax: 513-579-7555
www.federated-fds.com
• Terry J. Lundgren, Chairman, Chief Executive Officer, and P
• Karen M. Hoquet, EVP and Chief Financial Officer
• Thomas G. Gody, Vice Chairman
• Thomas L. Cole, Vice Chairman
Products:
General Goods
Brands:
Bloomingdale's and Macy's

FHI, INC./BUSY BODY
11900 COMMUNITY ROAD
SUITE 100
POWAY, CA 92064
562-818-1543
800-466-3348
Fax: 949-258-5744
info@busybody.com
www.busybody.com
• Brian McDermott, President
• Keith Lynch, Customer Service Director
(562) 296-1063
Products:
Ellipticals, Treadmills, Exercise Bikes, Steppers, Rowers, Home Gyms, Home Gym Attachments, Freeweight Equipment, Flexibility Equipment, Fitness Accessories
Brands:
Life Fitness, Precor, Hoist, Parabody, Vision Fitness

FINGERHUT COMPANIES, INC.
6250RIDGEWOOD ROAD
ST CLOUD, MN 56303
952-932-3100
800-208-2500
Fax: 952-936-5441
customerservice@fingerhut.com
www.fingerhut.com
• Theodore Deikel, Chairman and Chief Executive Officer
• Michael Sherman, General Counsel, Secretary and SVP, Busi
• John Buck, EVP
• Andy Johnson, SVP, Marketing
Products:
Home Furnishings, Kitchen and Appliances, Toys and Kids' Stuff, Apparel, Footwear, Personal Care and Luggage, Sporting Goods, Video Games & Entertainment
Brands:
Converse, Reebok, Rocawear, Home Deals

FITNESS COMPANY
ISELIN, NJ 08830
732-548-0970
888-353-6754
Fax: 201-626-3173
• Steve Smith, Chief Executive Officer
(732) 548-0970
Products & Services:
Physical Fitness Facilities

FITNESS SYSTEMS
1700 W 82ND STREET
SUITE 200
MINNEAPOLIS, MN 55431
952-897-5275
800-639-7913
Fax: 952-897-5173
info@hfit.com
www.healthfitness.com
• John Hynes, Buyer
• Bill McMann, Buyer
Products & Services:
Health management and Fitness management

FLAGHOUSE
601 FLAGHOUSE DRIVE
HASBROUCK HEIGHTS, NJ 07604-3116
201-288-7600
800-793-7900
Fax: 800-793-7922
sales@flaghouse.com
www.flaghouse.com
• George Carmel, President
• Keith Gold, Brand Manager
Products:
Sporting Goods, Physical Education, and Recreation.
Year Founded:
1954

FLEET FEET, INC.
406 E MAIN STREET
SUITE 200
CARRBORO, NC 27510
919-942-3102
Fax: 919-932-6176
www.fleetfeetsports.com
• Tom Raynor, Chairman / Chief Executive Officer
• Jeff Phillips, President
• Joey Pointer, Director, Franchise Operations
• Luke Bo Rowe, Vice President
Products:
Footwear, Apparel
Brands:
Saucony, Adidas, Basics, Brooks, Moving Comfort, Mizuno, New Balance, Nike, Insport, Sogoi, Pearl Izumi, Champion, Life is Good, Superfeet, Sporthill

FOLLETT HIGHER EDUCATION GROUP
3 WESBROOK CORPORATE CENTER
SUITE 200
WESTCHESTER, IL 60154
630-279-2330
800-365-5388
Fax: 630-279-2569
• Scott Deaton, EVP, Marketing
(630) 279-2330
• Thomas A. Christopher, President
• Jay Amond, SVP, Chief Financial Officer
• Tom C. Christopher, President and Chief Operating Officer
• Steve Pribyl, Executive Vice President of Retail Operations
• Jay Amond, Senior Vice President and Chief Financial Off
• Doug Thompson, Senior Vice President and Chief Information O
• Gary Shapiro, Senior Vice President of Intellectual Propert
• Audrey Southard, Senior Vice President of Human Resources
• Patrick Usher, Senior Vice President of Sales

manufacturers/retailers

1239

Products:
Books

FOOT LOCKER, INC.
112 W 34TH STREET
NEW YORK, NY 10120
212-720-3700
800-991-6815
Fax: 212-720-4397
www.footlocker-inc.com
• Lauren Peters, Senior VP Strategic Planning
• John D. Morris, Coordinator Sports Marketing
(212) 720-3901
jmorris@footlocker.com
• Robert McHugh, Chief Financial Officer
(212) 720-3948
rmchugh@footlocker.com
• Peter Brown, SVP/CIO/Investor Relations
(212) 720-4254
pbrown@footlocker.com
• Kenneth Hicks, Chairman, President & Chief Executive Officer
Products:
A specialty athletic retailer that operates approximately 3,600 athletic retail stores in 14 countries in North America, Europe and Australia. Operates through its Foot Locker, Lady Foot Locker, Kids Foot Locker and Champs Sports retail stores plus Footaction, Eastboy, Basketball: Women's National Basketball, Association/WNBA, Running: Title - Foot Locker Cross Country Championships

FOOTACTION USA
112 W 34TH STREET
NEW YORK, NY 10120
845-727-6500
800-863-8932
Fax: 845-727-6560
www.footaction.com
• Shawn Neville, President
• Keith Daly, SVP, Footaction
• Steven K. Carnley, VP / Regional Sales Manager
Products:
Footwear, Apparel, Accessories, Fan Gear
Brands:
Nike, Adidas, Jordan, Reebok, Timberland

FRED MEYER STORES, INC.
3800 SE 22ND
PORTLAND, OR 97202
503-232-8844
800-576-4377
Fax: 503-797-5609
kroger.investors@kroger.com
www.fredmeyer.com
• Darrell D. Webb, President
• David Deatherage, VP / Chief Financial Officer
• Lynn Gust, President
• Molly Malone, Senior Vice President and Director
• David Deatherage, Senior Vice President and Chief Financial Off
• Robert Clark, Senior Vice President and Director of the Foo
• Jill McIntosh, Vice President of Human Resources
• Kim Swearinger, Director of Customer Communications and Marke
• Rick Heffner, Senior Director of Store Operations

Products:
General Goods

G GIRL
1004 CROCKER STREET
LOS ANGELES, CA 90021
213-748-2462
Fax: 213-748-2402
Products:
Women's Clothing and Cosmetics

GADZOOKS
4121 INTERNATIONAL PARKWAY
CARROLLTON, TX 75007
972-307-5555
800-966-1355
Fax: 972-662-4290
customerservices@forever21.com
www.gadzooks.com
• Paula Y. Masters, President / Chief Merchandise Officer
• James A. Motley, VP / Chief Financial Officer / Secretary
• George S. Sotirin, VP, Store Operations
Products:
Casual tops, Dressy tops, Basics, Sweaters, Outerwear, Pants, Shorts, Skirts, Dresses, Denim, Accessories, Jewelry

GALYAN'S TRADING COMPANY, INC.
339 METROPOLIS MILE
PLAINFIELD, IN 46168
317-839-4803
877-846-9997
Fax: 317-532-0253
www.galyans.com
• Robert Mang, Chief Executive Officer / Director
• Edwin J. Holman, Pres / Chief Operating Officer
• C. D. Zoba, EVP / General Counsel / Secretary
• Edward Wozniak, SVP / Chief Financial Officer
Products:
Sporting Goods.

GANDER MOUNTAIN COMPANY
180 E FIFTH STREET
SUITE 1300
ST PAUL, MN 55101
252-355-7600
888-542-6337
Fax: 888-477-4040
www.gandermountain.com
• Mark R. Baker, Chief Executive Officer
• Al Dittrich, Chief Operating Officer
• Gary Hauger, EVP
• Jeff Bergmann, VP, Marketing
Products:
Specialty focus on hunting, fishing, and camping, Apparel, Foorwear
Brands:
Columbia Sportswear, Woolrich, Mossy Oak, Pella, Walls, Carhartt, LaCrosse, Rocky, Vasque, Wrangler

GEAR.COM, INC.
6322 S 3000 E
SUITE 100
SALT LAKE CITY, UT 84121
801-947-3100
Fax: 801-944-4629
info@overstock.com
www.gear.com

• Ken Blue, President
• Wayne Wong, Chief Technical Officer
• Dick Holcombe, EVP, Product / Distribution
• Joe Kenny, Chief Financial Officer
Products:
Furniture, Home D,cor, Home Improvement, Housewares, Tools, Jewelry & Watches, Accessories, Recreation & Sport's Collectibles, Sports Gear & Equipment, Audio & Video , Cameras & Optics, Computers & Printers, Home Office Equipment, Telephones, Apparel, Shoes & Access, Books, CDs, Movies & More, Healthcare & Supplies, Gifts & Flowers
Brands:
Dolce & Gabbana, Tahari, Dr Martens, Ralph Lauren, Prada, Betula Birkenstock, Frette, Sony, Movado, Nike

GENE TAYLOR'S SPORTSMEN SUPPLY, INC.
201 W TOMICHI
GUNISSON, CO 81230
970-641-1845
www.genetaylors.com
• Duke O. Taylor, President
• Tony S. Taylor, VP, Buyer
• Marshal F. Taylor, VP Buyer
• Gene Taylor, President / Buyer
Products:
Sporting Goods

GENESCO INC./JOURNEYS
GENESCO PARK 1415 MURFREESBORO ROAD
PO BOX 731
NASHVILLE, TN 37202-0731
615-367-7000
Fax: 615-367-8579
www.genesco.com
• Robert J Dennis, President/Chief Executive
• Robert J. Dennis, EVP and Chief Operating Officer
• James S. Gulmi, SVP, Finance and Chief Financial Officer
• James C. Estepa, SVP, Genesco Retail
Products:
Footwear, Headwear and Accessories
Brands:
Journeys, Journeys Kidz, Johnson & Murphy, Underground Station, Hatworld, Lids, Hat Zone, Cap Factory

GIGA, INC.
2448 INDUSTRIAL PARK DRIVE
MACON, GA 31216
478-788-2448
800-388-2448
Fax: 478-788-4108
online@gigainc.com
www.gigainc.com
• Charlton Veazey, Chief Executive Officer
• Walt Miller, Chief Executive Officer and Buyer
Products:
Freedom Boots, Dessert Steel Toe Boots, Clothing
Brands:
Suede/Camouflage Cordura, Steel Toe, Gore-Tex, BDU Camo Scrubs, and Mobility Folders

GNC CORPORATION
300 6TH AVENUE
PITTSBURGH, PA 15222

412-288-4600
877-463-4700
Fax: 412-288-8379
www.gnc.com

GOLF MART/WORLDWIDE GOLF/ROGER DUNN GOLF
1421 VILLAGE WAY
SANTA ANA, CA 92705
714-558-0074
888-216-5252
Fax: 714-543-6622
www.worldwidegolfshops.com
• Craig McCallister, Chief Executive Officer
• Al Morris, General Manager
Products:
Golf Clubs, Golf Bags, Golf Balls, Golf Gifts, Golf Apparel, Training Aids, Books/Videos, Accessories
Brands:
Callaway, Nike, TaylorMade, Ping, Titleist, Cleveland, Adams, Bite, Acer, Bad Boy, Brush Tee, Paragon, Odessey, Carbite, Champ, hiPPO, Golf Pride, Innova, Kodak, Slazenger, Strata

GOLF USA
4405 N HARRISSON ST
SHAWNEE, OK 74804
405-481-7447
800-488-1107
Fax: 405-481-7409
mail@golfusa.com
www.golfusa.com
• Tom Anthony, Chairman/CEO
• Rck Benson, VP, Franchise Sales and Operations
(405) 751-0015
• Bill Overstreet, VP, Marketing, Sales and Promotions
Products:
Golf Clubs, Golf Bags, Golf Balls, Golf Gifts, Golf Shoes, Golf Apparel, Accessories
Brands:
Titleist, TaylorMade, Nike, Cleveland,TourEdge, FootJoy, Cobra, Pinnacle,MacGregor, Adams, TopFlite

GOLFERS' WAREHOUSE, INC.
75 BRAINARD ROAD
HARTFORD, CT 6114
888-216-5252.
Fax: 860-522-5309
www.golferswarehouse.com
• Jameson Lloyd, Director of Instruction
Products:
Retail Golf Equipment, Clubs, Apparel, Bags & Travel Covers, Carts, Golf Shoes, Golf Accessories, Golf Gifts, Gift Cards
Brands:
Taylor Made, Adidas, Titliest, Foot Joy

GOLFSMITH INTERNATIONAL, INC.
11000 N IH35
AUSTIN, TX 78753
512-821-4050
800-813-6897
Fax: 512-837-1245
www.golfsmith.com
• James D Thompson, President / Chief Executive Officer
• Virginia Bunte, VP / Chief Financial Officer
• Kiprian Miles, VP / Chief Information Officer
• Ginger Bunte, Chief Financial Officer
• Sue E. Gove, President

Products:
Golf and Tennis accessories, balls, clubs, custom club fitting, gifts, gift cards, gloves, grips, Golf Bags & Travel, Home & Office, Outlet, Personalized Gear, Practice and Training, Pre-Owned Clubs, Shoes, Teams and Collegiate, Video & Books
Products:
Golf Clubs, Golf Bags, Golf Balls, Golf Gifts, Golf Shoes, Golf Apparel, Accessories, Custom Club Fitting, Gift Cards, Gloves, Grips, Personalized Gear
Brands:
Callaway, TaylorMade, Cleveland, Cobra, Odyssey, Adidas, Maxfli, Ashworth, Adams, Lynx, MacGregor, Nike, Zevo, Snake Eyes, Golfsmith, Killer Bee, GearForGolf, GiftsForGolf

GREAT OUTDOOR CLOTHING COMPANY
341 SKI WAY
SUITE 201
INCLINE VILLAGE, NV 89451
702-832-9100
800-442-5253
Fax: 800-368-6873
www.greatoutdoorclothing.com
• Stephen Meyers, President
Products:
Outerwear, Technical Jackets, Parkas, Vests, pants and Rainwear
Brands:
Black Ice, SnowLion, Teva, Polartec, Caltech, Helly Hansen, Jansport, Merrell, Alpine Designs, Camelbak and Eagle Creek

GREEN TOP SPORTING GOODS CORPORATION
10150˜LAKERIDGE PARKWAY
ASHLAND, VA 23005
804-550-2188
Fax: 804-550-2693
info@greentophuntfish.com
www.greentophuntfish.com
• Charles G. Thalhimer Jr, President
Products:
Hunting and Fishing Gear; Clothing, Eyewear, Footwear/Waders, Accessories, Lights, Marine Electronics
Brands:
Duck Commander, Echo, Knight & Hale, Lohman, M.A.D, Penn's Woods, Primos, Quaker Boy

GYM SOURCE
40 E 52ND STREET
NEW YORK, NY 10022
212-688-4222
800-496-768123
Fax: 212-750-2886
sales@gymsource.com
www.gymsource.com
• Richard Miller, President & Chief Executive Officer
Products:
Accessories, Bikes, Ellipticals, Steppers, Treadmills, Free Weights, Home Gym
Brands:
Cybex, Tuff Stuff, True, Universal, Hoist, Pro Spot, Schwinn, Diamond Back

H-E-B
PO BOX 839999
SAN ANTONIO, TX 78283-3999
210-938-8357
800 432-3113

Fax: 210-938-8048
www.heb.com
• Cory Basso, Vice President/Advertising
• Charles Butt, Chairman & CEO

HAT WORLD/LIDS CORP.
7555 WOODLAND DRIVE
INDIANAPOLIS, IN 46278
317-334-9428
888-564-4287
Fax: 317-337-1428
contactus@hatworld.com
www.lids.com
• Kenneth J. Kocher, President
• Glenn Campbell, Chief Operating Officer
• Clyde Roenbeck, VP, Field Operations
Products:
Branded Athletic Headwear, Apparel, Accessories
Brands:
Adidas, Kangol, Majestic, New Era, Nike, Reebok, Top of the World, Twins, Zephy r Graf-x

HEALTH FITNESS CORPORATION
1700 WEST 82ND STREET
Suite 200
MINNEAPOLIS, MN 55431
952-831-6830
800-639-7913
Fax: 952-897-5173
jobs@hfit.com
www.healthfitness.com
• K James Ehlen, CEO
• Paul Lotharius, President and Chief Executive Officer
• Brian Gagne, Chief Operations Officer
• Dennis Richling, Chief Medical and Wellness Officer
• Teri Lonergan, Chief Information Officer
• Karen Preusker, Chief Financial Officer
• Mark Totts, Senior Vice President, Product Development
• Sean McManamy, Senior Vice President, Corporate Development
Products & Services:
Offers on-site solutions for corporations, hospitals, communities, and universities in many delivery modes — face to face, Web-based, telephone or mail.

HERB PHILIPSON'S
1899 BLACK RIVER BOULEVARD
ROME, NY 13440
315-336-1302
Fax: 315-337-5840
info@herbphilipsons.com
www.herbphilipsons.com
• Gary Philipson, President
Products:
Apparel, Footwear, Sporting Goods
Brands:
Carhartt, Columbia, Lee, Woolrick, Dickies, Levi's

HIBBETT SPORTING GOODS
2700 MILAN COURT
BIRMINGHAM, AL 35211
205-942-4292
Fax: 205-912-7279
www.hibbett.com
• Michael Newsome, Chairman/Chief Executive Officer
• Joseph Nissan, President/Chief Operations Officer
• Gary A. Smith, VP and Chief Financial Officer

- Jeffry O. Rosenthal, VP Merchandising
- Jeff Rosenthal, President and CEO
Products:
Full Line Sporting Goods
Brands:
New Balance, Easton, Schutt, Fossil, Adidas, K-Swiss, Mizuno, Louisville Slugger, Rawlings

HOIGAARD'S INC.
5425 EXCELSIOR BOULEVARD
SAINT LOUIS PARK, MN 55416
952-929-1351
800-266-8157
Fax: 952-929-2669
info@hoigaards.com
www.hoigaards.com
- Mike White, Buyer
- Bob Soash, Buyer
- Rita Lind, Buyer
- Alex Avedikian, Director, Marketing and Advertising
Products & Services:
Bike Services, Canoe & Kayak Rentals, In-Line Skate Services, Mounting and Other Services, Pack Rentals, Toko Thermo Bag, Snowboard, Tunes

HUDSON TRAIL OUTFITTERS, LTD.
4530 WISCONSON AVE NW
WASHINGTON, DC 20016
202-363-9810
HTO_Customer_Service@hudsontrail.com
- Henry F. Cohan, President
- John Behall, Bike Shop Manager
Products:
Men's and Women's Outerwear, Apparel and Footwear; Watersports Gear, Fly Fishing Gear, Climbing Gear, Cycling Gear, Snowsports Gear, Sleeping Bags, Tents and Shelters
Brands:
Birkenstock, Havana Joe, CW-X, CamelBak Logo, Dansko, Ranger

INTERACTIVECORP/HOME SHOPPING NETWORK
1 HSN DRIVE
SAINT PETERSBURG, FL 33729
212-314-7300
800-933-2887
Fax: 212-314-7379
www.hsn.com
- Bob Diener, President, Hotels.com
- David Litman, Chief Executive Officer, Hotels.com
Products:
Watches, Jewelry, Fashion and Accessories, Beauty, Health and Fitness
Brands:
Absolute, Andrew Lessman, Carolyn Strauss, Diane Gilman, Esteban, Euro-Pro, Gateway, Highgate Manor, Hoover, BFL, Slinky Brand, Maggie Sweet

J. BAKER, INC.
555 TURNPIKE STREET
CANTON, MA 2021
781-821-2500
800-767-0319
Fax: 781-828-3721
info@CasualMale.com
- Jerry Socol, President and Chief Executive Officer
- Brian Eddy, Divisional Merchandise Manager

- Bob Crosby, Buyer
- Mark Fletcher, Buyer
Products:
Shirts, Pants and Jeans, Activewear, Outerwear, Sweaters and Vests, Suit Separates, Sportcoats
Brands:
626 Blue, Calvin Klein, Cutter & Buck, George Foreman, Harbor Bay, Izod, Levi's / Dockers, Nautica, NFL, Polo Jeans Company, Polo Ralph Lauren, Reebok

J.C. PENNEY CORPORATION, INC.
6501 LEGACY DRIVE
PO BOX 8178
MANCHESTER, CT 06040-1463
972-431-1000
800-322-1189
Fax: 972-431-1362
www.jcpenney.com
- Myron E. Ullman III, Chairman and Chief Executive Officer
- Kenneth C. Hicks, President and Chief Merchandising Office
- Robert B. Cavanaugh, EVP and Chief Financial Officer
Products:
Women's, Men's and Kid's Apparel and Sportswear; Jewelry, Window Accessories, Home Furnishings, Housewares, Gifts and Registry
Brands:
St. John's Bay, Arizona, Levi's, Dockers, Delicates, Worthington, a.n.a, Lee

JACOBSON STORES
329 N PARK AVENUE
SUITE 101
WINTER PARK, FL 32789
407-539-2528
- Tammy Giaimo, President
- Beth Aranda, Retail Manager
- Sam June, Creative Director
Products:
Women's Apparel, Women's Shoes and Handbags, Women's Jewelry and Accessories, Men's Apparel.
Brands:
Cole Haan, Sandro Moscoloni

JOHNNY MAC'S SPORTING GOODS
10100 WATSON ROAD
SUNSET HILLS, MO 63127
314-966-5444
800-962-8347
Fax: 314-966-6098
www.johnnymacs.com
- Bob McArthur, President & Chief Executive Officer
- Rick McArthur, Chief Financial Officer
- Bob McArthur, President & CEO
Products:
Sporting Goods, Team Uniforms, Trophies
Brands:
Nike, Under Armour, Rawlings, Easton, Louisville Slugger, Bauer, Reebok, CCM, Mizuno, Russell Athletic, Wilson, Worth, Schutt

JUST FOR FEET
933 MACARTHUR BOULEVARD
MAHWAH, NJ 7430
201-934-2000
Fax: 845-727-6560
www.footstar.com
- Stephen R. Wilson, EVP and Chief Financial Officer

- Jeffrey A. Gordon, President and Chief Executive Officer, J
- J. M. Robinson, Chairman / Chief Executive Officer / Pre
- Joseph C. Caracappa, Chief Information Officer
Products:
Athletic Footwear
Brands:
New Balance, FootStar

JUST SPORTS
3500 S MERIDIAN
SOUTH HILL MALL
PUYALLUP, WA 98373
253-845-7053
Fax: 818-719-9244
www.justsports.net
- Glen Erikson, President
Products:
Sports Retailer, Shoes, Apparel, Accessories

JUSTHERSPORTS.COM
6704 FERRIS ST
BELLAIRE, TX 77401
713-661-7272
888-561-3364
Fax: 713-661-7242
info@justhersports.com
www.sportsforher.com
- Mary Stone, Co-Founder
- Howard Stone, Co-Founder
Products:
Sporting goods and accessories for soccer, softball, basketball, volleyball, cycling, tennis, golf, lacrosse, field hockey, swimming, running, gymnastics, and fitness.
Brands:
Wilson, Spalding, Mikasa, STX, Brine, Champion, Mitre, Tachikara, Penn, Baden, Zoomers, Worth, Barracuda, InSport, Babolat, CamelBak, Bellwether, Reusch, Prince

KERR DRUG INC.
3220 SPRING FOREST ROAD
RALEIGH, NC 27616
919-544-3896
800-494-3053
Fax: 919-544-3796
www.kerrdrug.com
- Anthony Civello, President and Chief Executive Officer
- Richard D. Johnson, EVP and Chief Financial Officer
- William B. Baxley, SVP, Merchandising and Marketing
- Phyllis Patterson
ppatterson@kerrdrug.com
- Diane Eliezer, Director, Marketing
Products & Services:
Health Store

KESSLERS SPORT SHOP, INC.
930 E MAIN STREET
RICHMOND, IN 47374
765-935-2595
800-527-7510
Fax: 765-935-1866
info@kesslersteamsports.com
www.bsnsports.com
- Robert J. Dickman, President
- Jeff Wise, Sales
Products:
Sporting Goods

Brands:
Nike, Adidas, Converse, Reebok

KID'S FOOT LOCKER
112 W 34TH STREET
NEW YORK, NY 10120
212-720-3700
800-991-6684
Fax: 212-720-4397
• Tim Finn, President and Chief Executive Officer
• Rubin Hanan, SVP, Retail Brand Marketing
Products:
Shoes, Clothing, Sports Equipment, Accessories, Fan Gear for Kids.
Brands:
ABC Sports, All Star, American Spirit, Baxter, Colorado, Callaway, Champion, Dickies, Elite Kold, Fubu, Headmaster, Grabber, Glovemate, Adidas, Reebok, Nike

KITTERY TRADING POST
301 US ROUTE ONE
PO BOX 904
KITTERY, ME 03904
603-334-1157
888-587-6246
888-439-9036
Fax: 207-439-8001
info@kitterytradingpost.com
www.kitterytradingpost.com
• Bob Adams, Facilities Director
• David M. Labbe, Chief Financial Officer
• Kevin F. Adams, Treasurer, Archery and Shooting Sports A
• Kim C. Adams, President
Products:
Archery, Camping/Hiking, Fishing, Shooting Sports, Used Guns, Watersports, Wintersports, Footwear, Men's Clothing
Brands:
Columbia Sportswear Company, Carhartt, Woolrich, The North Face, Levis, Under Armour, Exofficio, Mountain Hardwear, Marmot, Ibex, Patagonia, Advanced Elements, Ocean Kayak, Old Town, Ranger, Coleman, Teva, Merrell, Kelty

KLEIN'S ALL SPORT DISTRIBUTORS INC.
14 WETMORE STREET
SUITE 2
NEW YORK MILLS, NY 13417
315-768-8194
Fax: 315-768-1510
• Donald Klein, Chairman
Products:
Sporting and Recreational Goods

KMART CORPORATION
3100 W BIG BEAVER ROAD
TROY, MI 48084
248-463-1000
Fax: 248-463-1454
www.kmart.com
• Aylwin B. Lewis, Chief Executive Officer, Kmart Retail
• William C. Crowley, EVP and Chief Financial Officer
• Dene L. Rogers, EVP, Restructuring and Business Improvem
Products:
Jewelry, Women's and Men's Apparel, Sports Equipment, Baby's Accessories, and other name-brand and private-label items.
Brands:

Jaclyn Smith, Thalia Sodi, Route 66, Joe Boxer, Razor, Schwinn, Martha Stewart

KOHL'S DEPARTMENT STORES
N56 W17000 RIDGEWOOD DRIVE
MENOMONEE FALLS, WI 53051
262-703-7000
855-564-5705
Fax: 262-703-7115
Customer.Service@Kohls.com
www.kohlscorporation.com
• Larry Montgomery, Chairman and Chief Executive Officer
directors@kohls.com
• Kevin Mansell, President
directors@kohls.com
• Arlene Meier, Chief Operating Officer
directors@kohls.com
• Brian Miller, SVP, Corporate Governance
(262) 703-1723
brian.f.miller@kohls.com
• Steven Burd, Lead Director
directors@kohls.com
• Jen Johnson, Director of Public Relations
(262) 703-5241
jen.johnson@kohls.com
• Molly Verette, Senior Public Relations Manager
(262) 703-7008
molly.verette@kohls.com
• Kristen Cunningham, Public Relations Manager
(262) 703-7863
kristen.cunningham@kohls.com
• Tami Kou, Public Relations Manager
(262) 703-7725
tami.kou@kohls.com
Products:
Apparel; Shoes and Accessories for Women, Children and Men; Home Products
Brands:
Carter'sr, Championr, Columbia Sportswear Company, Dockers, Haggar, Healthtex, Jockey, KitchenAid, Krups, Lee, Levi's, Norton McNaughton, Pfaltzgraff, Playtex, Reebok, Vanity Fair.

L.L. BEAN
15 CASCO STREET
FREEPORT, ME 04033-0001
207-552-3028
800-559-0747
Fax: 207-552-3080
preferences@llbean.com
www.llbean.com
• Leon A. Gorman, Chairman
• Chris McCormick, President and Chief Executive Officer
• Mark Fasold, SVP and Chief Financial Officer
• Leon A. Gorman, Chairman of the Board
• Christopher J. McCormick, President and CEO
• Bob Peixotto, SVP, Human Resources
Products:
Outerwear, Footwear, Outdoor Gear and Apparel, Sport Equipment
Brands:
L.L.Bean, Therm-a-Rest, Katahdin, Brown Bear

LADY FOOT LOCKER
120 W 34TH STREET
NEW YORK, NY 10120
715-261-9709
800-991-6686

Fax: 212-720-4397
www.ladyfootlocker.com
• Nick Grayston, President and Chief Executive Officer
Products:
Footwear, Sports Apparel, Accessories, Casualwear and Fan Gear for Women.
Brands:
Ryka, New Balance, Adidas, Converse, Puma, Champion, Saucony, Reebok, Concord, All Star, Colorado, Etonic, ESPN, Ewatch, Franklin, Fox River

LANGHORNE SKI & SPORT
543 LINCOLN HIGHWAY
FAIRLESS HILLS, PA 19030
215-295-4240
800-523-8850
Fax: 215-295-5341
• David M. Constantini, Chief Executive Officer
• Kathy Constantini, Owner and Buyer
Products:
Offers a full line of downhill and Nordic skis and equipment, snowboards, clothing, skateboards, in-line skates, roof racks, services and various summer sport items.

LAS VEGAS GOLF & TENNIS
4711 DEAN MARTIN DRIVE
LAS VEGAS, NV 89169
702-892-9999
www.lvgolf.com
• Steve Puett, President and Chief Executive Officer
• Ted Kallgren, Chief Operating Officer
• Brian Va Duren, VP, Franchise Sales
Products & Services:
Putters, Golf Balls, Golf and Tennis Bags, Golf Apparel, Golf Gifts, Tennis Racquets, Tennis Apparel, Tennis Accessories, Golf and Tennis Shoes, Wedges, Gloves, Outerwear. Services: Custom Club Fitting, Gift Certificates, Lessons and Swing Analysis
Brands:
Adamsn, Brighton, Adidas, Prince, Spalding, Titleist, Cobra, Ashworth, Cross Creek, Wilson, Ping

LAZARUS
4300 ASHFORD DUNWOODY ROAD
ATLANTA, GA 30346
770-396-2800
800-289-6229
Fax: 770-913-5114
www.macys.com
• Andrew P. Pickman, President and Chief Merchandising Office
• Eric Jimenez, Executive Creative Director
Products:
Private-label Apparel, Cosmetics, Jewelry and Housewares
Brands:
Baby Phat Plus, Sketchers, Calvin Klein

LEGENDS SPORTING GOODS
459 KING STREET
LITTLETON, MA 01460
978-339-5222
Fax: 978-264-2922
kevdogsports@aol.com
• William Kahn, President
• Glenn Ferraro, Owner and VP
Products:
Sporting Goods

LEVTRAN ENTERPRISES
7455 NEW RIDGE ROAD
SUITE N
HANOVER, MD 21076
410-850-5900
Fax: 410-494-8707
www.dtlr.com
• Eric Levin, President
• Tony Trantas, VP
• Rick Levin, Co-Founder and Chief
Executive Officer
Products:
Urban apparel, footwear and related
accessories.

LUCY.COM
2701 HARBOR BAY PARKWAY
SUITE 300
ALAMEDA, CA 94502
503-228-2142
877-999-5829
Fax: 503-295-2510
www.lucy.com
• Sue Levin, Co-Founder / Chief Executive
Officer
• Stephen Hochman, Co-Founder / VP
Sales Operations
• Kate Delhagen, VP, Business
Development
• Judith Kempe, Director of Design
Products:
E-tailer: Women's sports retail internet site
and retail store devoted to merging style
with functional sportswear and to meeting
the individual needs of active women of all
ages, sizes, and fitness levels.

MACY'S
151 W 34TH STREET
NEW YORK, NY 10001
212-695-4400
800-264-0069
Fax: 212-494-1057
www.macys.com
• Terry J. Lundgren, Chairman, President &
Chief Executive Officer
Products:
Beauty products, Men's apparel, Women's
Apparel, Shoes, Jewelry, Dinnerware,
Housewares and Kitchen gadgets, Furniture
and Mattresses, Linens, Kitchenware
Brands:
Calvin Klein, Charter Club, Court of
Versailles, DKNY, Hotel Collection, Lauren
Ralph Lauren, Lilly Pulitzer, Missoni, Oscar
by Oscar de la Renta, Sigrid Olsen, Tommy
Bahama, Tommy Hilfiger, Waterford

MACY'S, CALIFORNIA
685 MARKET STREET
SAN FRANCISCO, CA 94105
415-397-3333
Fax: 415-296-4126
www.macys.com
• Terry J. Lundgren, Chairman, President &
Chief Executive Officer
Products:
Beauty products, Men's apparel, Women's
Apparel, Shoes, Jewelry, Dinnerware,
Housewares and Kitchen gadgets, Furniture
and Mattresses, Linens, Kitchenware
Brands:
Calvin Klein, Charter Club, Court of
Versailles, DKNY, Hotel Collection, Lauren
Ralph Lauren, Lilly Pulitzer, Missoni, Oscar
by Oscar de la Renta, Sigrid Olsen, Tommy
Bahama, Tommy Hilfiger, Waterford

MARK'S OUTDOOR SPORTS, INC
1400 MONTGOMERY HIGHWAY
BIRMINGHAM, AL 35216
205-822-2010
877-979-6275
Fax: 205-822-2984
info@marksoutdoors.com
www.marksoutdoors.com
• Mark Whitlock, Owner
(205) 822-2010
mark@marksoutdoor.com
Products:
Fishing & Hunting Accessories, Firearms

MARSHALL'S
1 WORCESTER ROAD
FRAMINGHAM, MA 1701
508-872-2684
888-627-7425
Fax: 508-390-2828
www.marshallsonline.com
• Edmond J. English, President, Chief
Executive Officer, Dire
• Donald G. Campbell, EVP / Finance / CFO
TJX Companies
• Ernie Herrman, EVP / Chief Operating
Officer, Marmaxx G
Products:
Apparel & Accessories: Ladies, Men, Teen,
Kids; shoes, Housewares

MARTIN'S GOLF & TENNIS, INC.
4010 VENTURE DRIVE
DULUTH, GA 30096
888-200-7428
877-272-6030
Fax: 843-272-4772
customerservice@pgatoursuperstore.com
www.pgatoursuperstore.com
• Martin H. Barrier, President
Products:
Sports Equipment and Apparel for Golf and
Tennis.

MAURICE SPORTING GOODS, INC.
1910 TECHNY ROAD
NORTHBROOK, IL 60065
847-715-1500
800-477-3474
Fax: 847-715-1418
CustomerService@maurice.net
www.maurice.net
• Frank Katlin, President
• Bruce Karper, VP / Director Merchandise
Products:
Fishing Tackle, Shooting Sports
Accessories, and other Outdoor Sporting
and Athletic Goods

MAY DEPARTMENT STORES COMPANY
611 OLIVE STREET
SAINT LOUIS, MO 63101
314-342-6300
Fax: 314-342-3064
www.mayco.com

**MAY DEPARTMENT STORES COMPANY,
THE**
611 OLIVE STREET
SAINT LOUIS, MO 63101
314-342-6300
800-223-7440
Fax: 314-342-3064
www.mayco.com
• Eugene S. Kahn, Chairman / Chief
Executive Officer

• John L. Dunham, President / Director
• Thomas D. Fingleton, EVP / Chief
Financial Officer
• Jeffrey S. Califano, SVP, Sportwear
Product Development
Products:
General Goods

MC SPORTS
3070 SHAFFER SE
GRAND RAPIDS, MI 49512
616-942-2600
800-626-1762
Fax: 616-942-2312
www.mcsports.com
• Bruce Ullery, President / Chief Executive
Officer
• Dan Winchester, VP / General Manager
• Joseph Smith, Director of Loss Prevention
(616) 285-1609
jsmith@michsport.com
• Connie Rush, Director of Human
Resources
crush@michsport.com
Products:
Sporting Goods
Brands:
A-Game, A-Tack, A.L.S., B' Warmer, B.S.I.
Products, Camelback, Champion Sports,
Champro, DAC Technologies, Daisy, Corr,
E-Force, Gerber, Halo Sports, Hammer

MCRAE'S, INC.
2801 W TYVOLA ROAD
PO BOX 37201
CHARLOTTE, NC 28217
601-968-6258
866-235-5443
Fax: 601-968-6310
belk_customer_care@belk.com
• Thomas M Belk, Jr, Chairman/CEO
Products:
General Goods

MEGA FITNESS
630 S WICKHAM ROAD, #107
WEST MELBOURNE, FL 32904
321-674-3866
800-925-2772
Fax: 321-694-9914

MEIGRAY GROUP
185 INDUSTRIAL PARKWAY
SUITE C
BRANCHBURG, NJ 8876
908-541-0114
888-463-4472
Fax: 908-541-1123
sales@meigray.com
www.meigray.com
• Barry Meisel, Co-Founder
(908) 541-0114
bmeisel@meigray.com
• Bob Gray, Co-Founder
• Barry Meisel, President
Products:
Jerseys

MEIJER, INC.
2929 WALKER AVENUE, NW
GRAND RAPIDS, MI 49544-9424
616-453-6711
877-363-4537
Fax: 616-791-2572
www.meijer.com

• Larry Zigerelli, SVP, Merchandising
• Paul Boyer, President / Chief Operating Officer
• Doug Meijer, Co-Chairman
• Hendrik G. Meijer, Co-Chairman / Chief Executive Officer

Products:
TVs, VCRs, DVD Players, Audio, Computer Supplies, Photo, Phones, Accessories, Movies, Power Tools, Adhesives, Fasteners, Lighting, Hand Tools, Measurement Tools, Garage, House wares, Kitchenware, Sporting Goods, Toys, Beverages, Specialty Meat and Seafood, Meat and Seafood Sauces, International Cuisine, Gourmet Food Complements, Sweet Delights, Hors d oeuvres

MERCHANT OF TENNIS, INC.
1621 BAYVIEW AVENUE
TORONTO, ON, CANADA M4G 3B5
416-932-2396
888-932-2396
Fax: 416-932-2397
experts@merchantoftennis.com
www.merchantoftennis.com
• Jeff Green, President
• John Ramsbottom, Marketing Manager

Products & Services:
Professional service and the largest selection of racquets, clothing, footwear and accessories.

MERVYN'S
22301 FOOTHILL BOULEVARD
MAILSTOP 2115
HAYWARD, CA 94541
510-727-3000
800-637-8967
Fax: 510-727-2300
• Diane L. Neal, President
• Clay Creasey, Chief Executive Officer
• Maureen W. Kyer, EVP Merchandising
• Lynn Schirmer, EVP / Merchandising Planning

Products:
General Goods

MODELL'S SPORTING GOODS
498 7th AVE
20TH FLOOR
NEW YORK, NY 10018
212-661-4242
800-275-6633
Fax: 212-822-1025
www.modells.com
• William Modell, Chairman
• Mitchell Modell, Chief Financial Officer
• Robert Stevenish, President, Chief Operating Officer
• Lawrence E. Long, Chief Financial Officer

Products:
Sporting Goods, Sporting Apparel, Menswear, Athletic footwear

NATION'S BEST SPORTS
4216 HAHN BOULEVARD
FORT WORTH, TX 76117
817-788-0034
800-379-0155
Fax: 817-788-8542
rmcgill@nbs.com
www.nationsbestsports.com
• Jim Chandley, President
(817) 605-2209
jchandley@nationsbestsports.com
• Angela Mooney, Corporate Secretary

(817) 605-2203
amooney@nationsbestsports.com
• Melissa Offill, Controller
(817) 605-2202
moffill@nationsbestsports.com
• Jim Chandley, President
(817) 605-2209
jchandley@nbs.com
• Bryan Davis, Executive Vice President of Operations
(817) 605-2205
bdavis@nationsbestsports.com
• Steven Baker, Merchandising Vice President
(817) 605-2217
Sbaker@nbs.com
• Dave Nacke, Vice President, Merchandising - Outdoor Divis
(817) 605-2249
dnacke@nbs.com
• Anna VanGoey, Meeting & Exhibit Manager
(817) 605-2214
acorbett@nbs.com
• Julie Cerza, Exhibit Coordinator
(817) 605-2212
jcerza@nbs.com
• Marty Plazo, Divisional Merchandise Manager
(817) 605-2218
mplazo@nbs.com

Products:
National retail buying organization with over 150 members operating more than 1,200 stores

NEVADA BOB'S INTERNATIONAL, INC.
81 BRAINARD ROAD
SUITE 7070
HARTFORD, CT 6114
416-366-2221
800-405-4653
Fax: 416-366-7722
• Kevin R. Baker, President / Chief Executive Officer
(403) 698-8560
• Arnold T. Kondrat, Chairman
(416) 366-2221
• Richard J. Lachcik, Secretary

Products:
Golf Club

Brands:
Adams, Adidas, Armour, Ashworth, Avant, Bag Boy, Bazooka, Ben Hogan, Bennington, Bettinardi, Bite, Bolle, Booklegger, Bushnell, Callaway, Carbite, Cart Caddy, Champ, Cleveland, Club Glove, Cobra, Coppertone, Datrek, Dexter, Dockers, Duck Press, Dunlop, Ecco, Etonic, Fairway, Florsheim, Footjoy, Fore Better Golf, Galaxy Sports, Gean-Edwards, Golden Bear, Golf Achiever, Golf Pride, Great Divide, Greg Norman, GTB, Hi Tec, Hippo, HOG, Izod, Izzo, Kallasy, Sports, Kasco, Kidsklub, La Jolla, Lady Accent, Lady Fairway, Lady Player, Leadbetter, Mac Gregor

NEW YORK GOLF CENTER, INC.
131 W 35TH STREET
NEW YORK, NY 10001
212-564-2255
888-465-7890
Fax: 212-244-6941
contactus@nygolfcenter.com
www.nygolfcenter.com
• Samuel K. Rhee, President
• Jay Shin, Manager Buyer

Products:
Golf Products

NINE WEST GROUP, INC.
1129 WESCHESTER AVENUE
WHITE PLAINS, NY 10604
866-933-9378
800-999-1877
Fax: 914-640-6024
www.ninewest.com
• Rhonda J. Brown, President / Chief Executive Officer
• Wesley R. Card, Chief Financial Officer

Products:
Dress, Sandals, Shoes, Handbags, Jewelry, Wallets, Scarves, Hats

Brands:
Nine West

NORDICTRACK FITNESS STORES
1500 S 1000 W
LOGAN, UT 84321
495-750-5000
877-993-7999
Fax: 435-750-3917
service@iconfitness.com
www.nordictrack.com
• Margie Dupuis, Senior Director, Merchandise
• Sue Benett, Senior Buyer

Products:
Treadmills, Ellipticals, Exercise Bikes, Strength Training, Incline Trainers, Skiers, Steppers, Accessories, Men's Apparel, Women's Apparel, NordicTrack Yoga Elite Kit, iFIT Yoga Health Club Kit, NordicTrack Recovery Premier Kit, Commercial Grade Equipment

Brands:
NordicTrack

NORTH FACE
14450 DOOLITTLE DRIVE
SAN LEANDRO, CA 94577
855-500-8639
888-863-1968
Fax: 510-618-3531
tnf_consumerservices@vfc.com
www.thenorthface.com
• Michael R Egeck, President
• Dan Templin, Chief Financial Officer
• Jody Kalmbach, VP, Marketing
• Steve Rendle, VP Sales, North America
• Aaron Carpenter, Vice President of Marketing

Products:
Men's Apparel, Women's Apparel, Footwear, Accessories, Sleeping Bags, Bags, Sports Gear

ODD JOB TRADING
200 HELEN STREET
S PLAINFIELD, NJ 07080
908-222-1000
888-262-9464
Fax: 908-222-9756
www.dccreatives.com/amazing/
• Stuart Levy, Chief Financial Officer / Chief Executiv

Products:
Offers an amazing range of merchandise such as housewares, electronics, furniture, fashions, cosmetics, cookware, appliances, toys and more, including many name brands.

ODD LOTS/BIG LOTS
300 PHILLIPI ROAD
COLUMBUS, OH 43228-5311
614-278-6800
800-877-1253
Fax: 614-278-6676
talk2us@BigLots.com
www.biglots.com
• Michael J Potter, Chairman / President / Chief Executive O
• Kent Larsson, EVP, Marketing
• Donald Mierzwa, EVP, Store Operations
• Jeffrey Naylor, SVP / Chief Financial Officer
• Norman J. Rankin, General Merchandise Manager
Products:
Consumables, Seasonal Products, Furniture, Housewares, Toys, Gifts

ORVIS COMPANY
1711 BLUE HILLS DRIVE
ROANOKE, VA 24012
540-345-6789
888-235-9763
Fax: 540-343-7053
customerservice@orvis.com
www.orvis.com
• Leigh Perkins, President / Chief Executive Officer
• David Perkins, SVP, Retail & Dealer
• Brian Gowan, VP, Finance
• Raymond G. McCready, President
Products:
Fishing Apparel, Line, Lures, Poles, Reels, Rods, Home Furnishings, Country Gifts

OUTDOOR WORLD, INC.
2720 S RODEO GULCH ROAD
SOQUEL, CA 95073-2026
888-344-9500
888-344-9500
Fax: 831-476-8597
info@theoutdoorworld.com
www.theoutdoorworld.com
• Bob Thomas, Owner
• Chris Thomas, VP, Buyer
chris@theoutdoorworld.com
Products:
Air Guns Backpacking Batteries Beach & Swim Bicycle Accessories Boy Scouts Camping Car Racks Clothing Daypacks Exercise Equipment Fishing Games & Sports Hunting, Camouflage Marine Inflatables Shoes, Boots, Sandals, Cleats Sleeping Bags, Pads Snowboards & Skis Sunglasses & Watches Tents & Canopies

OVERTON'S
111 RED BANKS ROAD
PO BOX 8228
GREENVILLE, NC 27858
252-355-7600
800-334-6541
Fax: 252-355-2923
intl@overtons.com
www.overtons.com
• V. Overton, President
• Herman B. Norris, VP
Products:
Sporting Goods

PAMIDA, INC.
8800 F STREET
OMAHA, NE 68127

402-339-2400
Fax: 402-596-7330
www.shopko.com
• Mike Hopkins, President
• Robert Hafner, SVP, Marketing / Business
• Paul Rothamel, SVP, Store Operations
Products:
Sporting Goods

PARADIES SHOP/PGA TOUR SHOPS
2849 PACES FERRY ROAD
OVERLOOK I, SUITE 400
ATLANTA, GA 30339
404-344-7905
Fax: 404-349-3226
www.theparadiesshops.com
• Gregg Paradies, President
• Dick Dickson, Chairman
• James Paradies, Vice Chairman
• Gregg Paradies, President & Chief Executive Officer
Products:
Apparel, Gifts, Souvenirs, Golf Apparel and Equipment

PARAGON SPORTING GOODS CO. LLC
867 BROADWAY AT 18TH STREET
SUITE 3N
NEW YORK, NY 10003
212-255-8889
800-961-3030
Fax: 212-929-1831
customerservice@paragonsports.com
www.paragonsports.com
• Jerry Blank, Chief Executive Officer
Products:
Sporting Goods & Sports Apparel

PAYLESS SHOESOURCE, INC.
3231 SE 6TH AVENUE
TOPEKA, CANADA 66607
785-233-5171
877-474-6379
Fax: 785-295-6220
www.payless.com
• Duane L Cantrell, President / Director
(785) 295-2013
duane_cantrell@paylessshoesource.com
• Ullrich E Porzig, SVP / Chief Financial Officer / Treasure
• John N Haugh, SVP, Marketing
Products:
Shoes

PEEBLES, INC.
10201 MAIN STREET
HOUSTON, TX 77025
434-447-5200
800-324-3244
Fax: 434-447-5453
• Mike Mooreman, President / Chief Executive Officer
• E. Lail, SVP / Chief Financial Officer / Secretar
• Ronnie W Palmore, SVP / Assistant Secretary
• Marvin H Thomas, Jr., SVP Operations
Products:
General Goods

PERFORMANCE, INC./PERFORMANCE BICYCLE SHOP
PO BOX 2741
CHAPEL HILL, NC 27515
919-933-9113
800-727-2453

Fax: 919-942-5431
www.performancebike.com
• Bob Martin, Chief Executive Officer
Products:
Bicycle & Frames, Men's Clothing, Women's Clothing, Accessories

PETER GLENN SKI & SPORT
2688 NW 29th TERRACE
OAKLAND PARK, FL 33311
954-484-3606
800-818-0946
Fax: 954-739-5724
questions@peterglenn.com
www.peterglenn.com
• Edward J Hamilton, Chairman
Products:
Ski Equipment and Supplies

POWERHOUSE GYMS, INTERNATIONAL
137 SOUTH MAIN
2ND FLOOR
ADRIAN, MI 49221
517-265-5533
Fax: 248-476-4732
customerservice@powerhousegym.com
www.powerhousegym.com
• William K Dabish, President / Co-Founder
customerservice@powerhousegym.com
Products:
gym licensing

PRICE COSTCO WHOLESALE
999 LAKE DRIVE
ISSAQUAH, WA 98027
425-313-8100
800-955-2292
Fax: 425-313-8114
customerservice@costco.com
www.costco.com
• Richard Galanti, EVP / Chief Financial Officer
(425) 313-8203
investor@costco.com
• Bob Nelson, VP / Financial Planning & Investor Relat
(425) 313-8255
investor@costco.com
• Jeff Elliott, Director / Financial Planning & Investor
(425) 313-8264
investor@costco.com
• Muriel Cooper, Community Relations & Administration
(425) 313-6182
MCooper@costco.com
Products:
groceries, candy, appliances, television and media, automotive supplies, tires, toys, hardware, sporting goods, jewelry, watches, cameras, books, housewares, apparel, health and beauty aids, tobacco, furniture, office supplies and office equipment; special food packaging, optical laboratories, meat processing and jewelry distribution

PRO GOLF DISCOUNT
13405 S.E. 30TH STREET
SUITE 1-A
BELLEVUE, WA 98005
425-957-3626
800-394-4653
888-640-4111
Fax: 425-373-3153
service@golfdiscount.com
www.golfdiscount.com

• Randy Silver, President / Buyer
groupsales@progolf.com
• Perry Ponti, General Manager / Buyer
Products:
golf equipment

PRO GOLF OF AMERICA
23399 COMMERCE DRIVE
SUITE B-1
FARMINGTON HILLS, MI 48335
248-994-0553
800-776-4653
Fax: 248-489-9334
• Brian T Donnelly, President / Chief
Operating Officer
(298) 737-0553
bdonnelly@progolfamerica.com
• Kathy Dix, Comptoller
(248) 737-0553
kdix@progolfamerica.com
• Jim Rice, VP Franchise Development
(248) 737-0553
jrice@progolfamerica.com
• Jeff Griffith, Franchise Sales Director
(248) 737-0553
jgriffith@progolfamerica.com
Products:
golf equipment

PRO IMAGE
250 NORTH RED CLIFFS DR.
SUITE 17
ST. GEORGE, UT 84790
435-674-0128
888-477-6326
Fax: 801-296-1319
www.proimage.net
• Dave Riley, President / Chief Executive
Officer
daver@proimage.net
• Ryan Laws, Chief Operating Officer
ryanl@proimage.net
• Dave Riley, President/CEO
daver@proimage.net
• Ryan Laws, Chief Operating Officer
ryanl@proimage.net
• Bill Townsend, VP / General Merchandise
Manager
billt@proimage.net
• Matt MacKay, National Franchise Manager
mattm@proimage.net
Products:
sports fan shop, and one of the greatest
franchising opportunities in the industry

PUSH PEDAL PULL
2306 WEST 41 ST
SIOUX FALLS, SD 57105
605-334-7740
888-861-8978
Fax: 605-336-3328
www.pushpedalpull.com
• Roger D Stewart, President
contact@pushpedalpull.com
• Todd Ibis, Chief Operating Officer
contact@pushpedalpull.com
• Shelley Kramer, Buyer
Products:
treadmills, ellipticals and climbers, home
gyms, exercise bikes, free weights,
accessories, plate loaded, selectorized,
stretching, single-station gyms

QVC NETWORK
1200 WILSON DRIVE AT STUDIO PARK
WEST CHESTER, PA 19380

484-701-1000
888-345-5788
Fax: 484-701-8170
QVCCares@QVC.com
www.qvc.com
• Douglas Briggs, President
• Darlene Daggett, EVP Apparel
• Gregg Bertoni, Fitness Director, Craftsman
Tools
• Mike George, President and CEO
Products:
accessories and shoes, apparel for men and
women, beauty, jewelry, cooking and dining,
gourmet food, home decor and home
improvement, electronics, sports and
fitness, toys, crafts and leisure

R.H. RENY
731 ROUTE 1
NEWCASTLE, ME 4553
207-563-3177
Fax: 207-563-5681
feedback@renys.com
www.renys.com
• John Reny, President
feedback@renys.com
Products:
all kinds of clothing, outerwear by famous
makers, electronics, housewares, lawn and
garden supplies, sheets and towels

RACK ROOM SHOES
8708 JW CLAY BOULEVARD
CHARLOTTE, NC 28262
704-510-0037
Fax: 704-547-8159
www.rackroomshoes.com
• Bob Hartley, President
• Jan Mauldin, Director of Marketing
Products:
shoes, handbags and accessories, dress,
casual, trends, and athletic wear

RAMSEY OUTDOOR STORE
281 ROUTE 10 EAST
PARAMUS TOWN SQUARE, PO BOX 1689
SUCCASUNNA, NJ 07876
201-261-5000
800-699-5874
Fax: 201-261-2742
customerservice@ramseyoutdoor.com
www.ramseyoutdoor.com
• Stuart Levine, President / Owner
customerservice@ramseyoutdoor.com
Products:
fishing, camping, water sports, climbing,
backpacking, hiking, hunting and the
clothing and footwear

RECREATIONAL EQUIPMENT, INC./REI
6750 S 228TH STREET
KENT, WA 98032
253-891-2500
800-426-4840
Fax: 253-891-2523
ip@rei.com
www.rei.com
• Sally Jewell, President / Chief Executive
Officer
publicaffairs@rei.com
• Brad Brown, VP / Information Services
publicaffairs@rei.com
• Brad Johnson, SVP / Chief Financial
Officer / Corporat
publicaffairs@rei.com
• Sally Jewell, President and Chief
Executive Officer

• Matt Hyde, SVP Merchandising
publicaffairs@rei.com
• Bill Baumann, Vice President of
Information Technology
• Rick Bingle, Vice President of Supply
Chain
• Brad Brown, Vice President of
E-Commerce and Direct Sales
• Michelle Clements, Senior Vice President
of Human Resources
• Michael Collins, Vice President of Public
Affairs
Products:
ice axes and climbing equipment, outdoor
gear and clothing

RECWARE BY ACTIVE.COM, INC.
937 ENTERPRISE DRIVE
SACRAMENTO, CA 95825
916-925-9096
888-732-9273
Fax: 916-925-0649
sales@recware.com
• Duane Harlan, Founder/President
• Cyril Juanitas, VP Sales
sales@recware.com

REDDEN MARINE SUPPLY, INC.
1411 ROEDER AVENUE
BELLINGHAM, WA 98225-2916
360-733-0250
800-426-9284
Fax: 360-733-7180
• Ken Brown, Sportnet Sales
gensales@reddeninc.com
• Alan R Chiabai, President
gensales@reddeninc.com
Products:
Retail And Wholesale Commercial Fishing
Gear Marine Related Products Sports
Netting Construction Netting Gloves
Hydraulics

REEBOK INTERNATIONAL LTD.-RETAIL
1895 JW FOSTER BOULEVARD
CANTON, MA 2021
781-401-5000
888-870-1743
Fax: 781-401-7402
www.reebok.com
• Uli Becker, President
• David Baxter, President, Sports Licensed
Division
• Bill Holmes, Human Resources
• Matt O'Toole, Chief Marketing Officer,
Reebok Brand
• John Warren, General Manager, Sports
Licensed Division

RICH'S DEPARTMENT STORES, INC.
223 PERIMETER CENTER PARKWAY
ATLANTA, GA 30346
770-913-4000
Fax: 770-913-5114
• David L Nichols, President / Chief
Operating Officer
• Karen M Hoguet, SVP / Chief Operating
Officer

ROAD RUNNER SPORTS
5549 COPLEY DRIVE
SAN DIEGO, CA 92111
858-636-7652
800-636-3560
Fax: 858-636-7650
www.roadrunnersports.com

• Dave Jewell, Footwear & Accessories Director
Products:
shoes, apparel, accessories, nutrition

ROCKVILLE WASHINGTON GOLF CENTER
N89 W16790 APPLETON AVENUE
SUITE 200
MENOMONEE FALLS, WI 53051
262-255-7600
800-967-5342
Fax: 301-948-7052
brian@golftrips.com
www.washingtongolf.com
• Tim Woodruff, Manager
info@washingtongolf.com
Products:
accessories, apparel, bags, balls, belts, gloves, golf gifts, sandals, polo, outerware, hats, pants

ROGER DUNN GOLF SHOPS
1421 VILLAGE WAY
SANTA ANA, CA 92705
714-558-0074
888-216-5252
Fax: 714-664-0430
santaana@rdgolf.com
www.worldwidegolfshops.com
• Craig A MaCallister, President
• Steve Carfano, Store Manager
Products:
golf equipment

RON JON SURF SHOP OF FLORIDA
4151 NORTH ATLANTIC AVENUE
COCOA BEACH, FL 32931
321-799-8888
888-757-8737
Fax: 321-799-8805
Info@rjss.com
www.ronjonsurfshop.com
• Ed Moritary, President
• Debbie Harvey, Vice President
Products:
Manufacturer and retailer of surfing apparels and equipments

RYNO ATHLETICS
316 S. GLENWOOD ST
TYLER, TX 75702
903-526-4140
888-609-6725
Fax: 800-574-0008
orders@ryno.com
www.ryno.com
• Brandon Steele, President/Chief Executive Officer
• Brandon Steele, President
• Phil Steele, National Sales Manager
Products:
Backpacks and garments bags, baseball bags, premium duffels, specialty sport bags, team/travel duffels.
Year Founded:
1996

SAKS INCORPORATED
12 E 49TH STREET
NEW YORK, NY 10017
212-753-4000
Fax: 205-940-4987
www.saksincorporated.com
• Ronald L Frasch, President/Chief Merchandising Officer

• Stephen I Sadove, Chief Executive Officer
• James A Coggin, President / Chief Administrative Officer
• Stephen E I. Sadove, Chairman and Chief Executive Officer
• Ronald L. Frasch, President and Chief Merchandising Officer
• Douglas Coltharp, EVP / Chief Financial Officer
Products:
Provides a wide assortment of quality fashion apparel, shoes, accessories, cosmetics, and decorative home furnishings

SAM'S CLUB
2101 SE
SIMPLE SAVINGS DRIVE
BENTONVILLE, AR 72716-0745
479-277-7000
888-746-7726
Fax: 479-273-4053
www.samsclub.com
• Brian C Cornell, President / Chief Executive Officer
• Mark D Goodman, EVP, Membership and Marketing
• Greg Johnston, EVP, Operations
Products:
Member-only warehouse club that sells merchandise including appliances and electronics, office supplies, fresh food, clothing, optical and pharmacy services, home furnishings, books, batteries and auto supplies at very low profit margins

SCHEEL'S ALL SPORTS, INC.
3202 13TH AVENUE S
FARGO, ND 58103-3403
701-232-8903
Fax: 701-298-0706
customerservice@scheelssports.com
www.scheelssports.com
• Steve D Scheel, Chief Executive Officer / Chairman
• Chris Skalsky, Corporate Clothing Office Manager
• Dona Ochsner, Store Manager / Partner
• Sherry Senske, Store Manager / Partner
Products:
Retailers of sporting goods and apparel including bikes, footwear, fitness equipment, hunting and fishing gear, bike and exercise machine repairs, raquet stringing, ski equipment maintenance, warranty repairs for shotguns, rifles, handguns

SCHOTTENSTEIN DEPARTMENT STORES
1887 PARSONS AVENUE
COLUMBUS, OH 43207-1933
614-443-0171
Fax: 614-478-2253
• Steve Morgan, Board Chairman
• Jay Schottenstein, Chairman, Chief Executive Officer
• Thomas Ketteler, Chief Operations Officer
Products:
Retailers of clothing goods

SCHUYLKILL VALLEY SPORTS
118 INDUSTRIAL DRIVE
POTTSTOWN, PA 19464
877-711-8100
877-711-8100
Fax: 610-495-8814
customerservice@svsports.com
www.svsports.com

• Jerry Williams, President
(610) 495-8813
• Phil Snyder, Vice President
(610) 495-8813
• Scott Goebel, Vice President
(610) 495-8813
Products:
Retail and wholesale Sporting Goods

SEARS, ROEBUCK & CO.
3333 BEVERLY ROAD
HOFFMAN ESTATES, IL 60179
847-286-2500
800-549-4505
Fax: 847-286-7829
www.sears.com
• Edward S Lampert, Chairman
• Alan J Lacy, Vice Chairman
• Aylwin B Lewis, President / Chief Executive Officer
Products:
Retailers of tools, lawn and garden, home electronics, and automotive repair and maintenance

SERVICE MERCHANDISE COMPANY
PO BOX 810939
SUITE 108
BOCA RATON, FL 33481
561-999-9815
877-643-8165
Fax: 561-999-9817
Info@servicemerchandise.com
www.servicemerchandise.com
• Raymond Zimmerman, Chairman
service@servicemerchandise.com
• Yuyal Moed, Chief Executive Officer
Products:
Retailers of fine jewelry, kitchen and dining, home accents and furniture, watches, electronics, and games and toys

SHARPER IMAGE
1450 BROADWAY
3RD FLOOR
NEW YORK, NY 10018
212-730-0030
877-714-7444
Fax: 212-967-6008
info@sharperimage.com
www.sharperimage.com
• Richard Thalheimer, Chairman / Chief Executive Officer
Richard@sharperimage.com
• Tracey Wan, Vice Chairman / Chief Operating Officer
twan@sharperimage.com
• Bob Thompson, SVP Merchandising
• Craig Traveaux, VP Stores
Products:
retails new, innovative, high-quality proprietary products such as Massage Chairs, Massage & Relaxation, Sound Soothers, Men's Personal Care, Women's Personal Care, Health & Fitness Equipment, Bed & Bath, Electronics & Toys, Personal Care, iPod/MP3, Stereos, DVD, TV & Video, Toys & Games, Robots and Hi-Tech Toys, Cameras & Binoculars, Clocks, Watches, Sports & Recreation, Music CDs, Air Cleaners & Air Purifiers, Office Furnishings, Lamps, Luggage & Travel Accessories, Sports & Recreation, Automotive, Tools & Flashlights, Clocks, Office Electronics, iPod/MP3, MP3 Speakers, ZipConnect, Watches, Safety & Security, Air Cleaners & Air Purifiers, M

SHOE CARNIVAL
7500 E COLUMBIA STREET
EVANSVILLE, IN 47715
812-867-6471
800-430-7463
Fax: 812-867-4261
customerservice@shoecarnival.com
www.shoecarnival.com
• Mark L Lemond, President/Chief Executive
Officer
info@shoecarnival.com
• Clifton Sifford, EVP Merchandise Manager
info@shoecarnival.com
• Timothy T Baker, EVP Store Operations
info@shoecarnival.com
• W. Ke Jackson, SVP / Chief Financial
Officer / Treasure
info@shoecarnival.com
Products:
family footwear

SHOE CITY
12550 WHITTIER BOULEVARD
SUITE 100
WHITTIER, CA 90602
562-698-2400
Fax: 562-696-6767
info@shoecity.com
www.shoecity.com
• Hau-En Ying, Partner
helpme@shoecity.com
Products:
athletic shoes for men, women, juniors and
infants

SHOE SHOW, INC.
2201 TRINITY CHURCH ROAD
CONCORD, NC 28027
704-782-4143
888-557-4637
Fax: 704-782-3411
www.shoeshow.com
• Robert B Tucker, Owner / President
Products:
boots, shoes, sandals

SHOPKO STORES, INC.
700 PILGRIM WAY
PO BOX 19060
GREEN BAY, WI 54307-9060
920-429-2211
800-791-7333
Fax: 920-429-4799
www.shopko.com
• Jack W Eugster, Acting Chief Executive
Officer
OnlineCustomerService@shopko.com
• Brian W Bender, SVP / Chief Financial
Officer / Co-Chief
OnlineCustomerService@shopko.com
• L. Te McDonald, SVP Marketing /
Communications
OnlineCustomerService@shopko.com
• Rodney D Lawrence, SVP Store Marketing
OnlineCustomerService@shopko.com
Products:
general merchandise and retail health
services; men's, women's, children's and
infant's clothing, men's and women's
footwear and jewelry and accessories; home
furnishings, hardware, domestics,
electronics, consumables, health and beauty
aids, automotive and toys

SKI MARKET LTD.
161 QUINCY AVE
QUINCY, MA 2169

617-773-3993
888-876-7433
Fax: 781-890-1811
www.countryski.com
• Robert Ferguson, Chairman
• Andrew Ferguson, President
• Jim Isenberg, Marketing Director
Products:
skis, snowboards, bicycles, DVDs, watches,
skateboards, kayaks

SKI MERCHANDISING CORPORATION
235 CADWELL DRIVE
PO BOX 3929
SPRINGFIELD, MA 1104
413-739-7331
Fax: 413-731-9335
Tgately@sportsshops.com
www.snowsportsmerchandising.com
• Tom Gately, President
tgately@sportsshops.com
• Tom Gately, President
Tgately@sportsshops.com
• Chuck Camerlin, Vice President
Ccamerlin@sportsshops.com
• Carole Tracy, Executive Assistant
Ctracy@sportsshops.com
Products:
ski, snowboard and other snowsport-related
equipment, apparel and accessories

SMACK APPAREL
2310 W STATE STREET
TAMPA, FL 33609
813-250-0627
877-762-2511
Fax: 813-251-4539
www.smackapparel.com

SMITH'S FOOD & DRUG
1550 S REDWOOD ROAD
SALT LAKE CITY, UT 84104
801-974-1400
866-221-4141
Fax: 801-974-1676
kroger.investors@kroger.com
www.smithsfoodanddrug.com
• James Hallsey, President
kroger.investors@kroger.com
• Peter Barth, SVP Human Resources
kroger.investors@kroger.com
• Dave Deatherage, Group VP Chief
Financial Officer Fred Me
kroger.investors@kroger.com
Products:
prescription drug plan, health guide

SNYDER'S DRUG STORES, INC.
14525 HIGHWAY 7
MINNETONKA, MN 55345
952-932-5441
888-443-8481
Fax: 952-936-2512
www.snyderdrug.com
• Gordon D Barker, President / Chief
Executive Officer
privacyofficer@snyderdrug.com
• Williard Wilson, EVP Marketing /
Pharmacy
Products:
health care merchandise, as well as beauty
care items, general merchandise, and
related items and services

SOLAR BLOC HATS
1120 HOLLAND DR
SUITE 9
BOCA RATON, FL 33487-2728
561-994-3001
800-327-5012
Fax: 561-994-3009
cushees@bellsouth.net
www.cushees.com
• Bob Kenny, Founder
cushees@bellsouth.net
Products:
Solarbloc hats and caps, bucket hats, face
saver hats, fishing caps and flap caps
Year Founded:
1977
Description:
Solarbloc hats use materials that have been
tested to provide sun protection and have
been rated atleast 50 upf.
Brands:
Solarbloc; Cushees
Clients:
Golf Shops; Tennis Shops; Beach Shops

SPORT CHALET, INC.
1 SPORT CHALET DRIVE
LA CANADA, CA 91011
818-949-5300
888-801-9162
Fax: 818-790-0087
www.sportchalet.com
• Craig Levra, Chairman/Chief Executive
Officer
• Howard Kaminsky, EVP Finance, Chief
Financial Officer
• Dennis Trausch, EVP Growth and
Development
• Craig Levra, Chairman of the Board, Chief
Executive Office
• Tim Anderson, Executive Vice President,
Retail Operations
• Howard Kaminsky, Executive Vice
President, Finance, Chief Fina
• Tom Tennyson, Executive Vice President
and Chief Merchandis
• Dennis Trausch, Executive Vice President,
Growth and Developm
• Brad Morton, Senior Vice President, Sales
• Ted Jackson, Vice President, Information
Technology and Ch
Products:
Leading operator of full service specialty
sporting goods stores in California, Nevada,
Arizona and Utah. Specializes in gear for
cold-weather as well as warm weather
sports. Stores also sell brand-name shoes,
clothes, and equipment.

SPORTING AUCTION, INC.
37 WILTON ROAD
MILFORD, NH 3055
603-732-0031
800-335-4670
Fax: 603-672-3480
support@sportstop.com
www.sportstop.com
• Paul Dell, Chief Executive Officer
paul@sportstop.com
Products:
Specialty sporting goods retailer with a
focus for Lacrosse, Snowboarding,
Snowshoeing, Field Hockey apparel,
equipments, etc.

SPORTMASTER INTERNATIONAL
700 S JOHNSON DRIVE
MCGREGOR, TX 76657
800-999-9764
800-999-9764
Fax: 254-840-8878
• Clay Young, Director of Operations
(254) 840-0494
• Sharon Cid, EVP
(800) 728-6513
Products:
Tennis grips, string, racquets, novelties, racquet stringing and other equipments

SPORTS ENDEAVORS, INC.
431 US HIGHWAY 70A E
HILLSBOROUGH, NC 27278-9912
919-644-6800
Fax: 919-644-6808
custserv@sportsendeavors.com
www.sportsendeavors.com
• Mike Moylan, President, Chief Executive Officer
president.office@sportsendeavors.com
• Brendan Moylan, Chief Operating Officer
custserv@sportsendeavors.com
• Garrett Putman, VP Online Marketing Internet Marketing D
(919) 644-6800
gputman@sportsendeavors.com
• John Crabhill, Online Properties Creative Director
(919) 644-6800
jcrabill@sportsendeavors.com
Products:
Mail order sporting goods & retail soccer supplies.

SPORTS SPECIALISTS, LTD.
590 FISHERS STATION DRIVE
SUITE 110
VICTOR, NY 14564
585-742-1010
Fax: 585-742-2645
www.sportsspecialistsltd.com
• Stephen R Rogers, President, Chief Executive Officer
(585) 742-1010
• Stephen R. Rogers, President & CEO
(585) 742-1010
• Nancy Toscano, Controller
Services:
Retailer-owned marketing, merchandising and purchasing organization currently active in the specialty ski, snowboard, outdoor and casual furniture industries.

SPORTS WAREHOUSE, INC.
PO BOX 2678
OREGON CITY, OR 97045
503-650-4321
Fax: 503-650-1919
Products:
Sells, buys and trades authentic game used uniforms and equipment

SPORTS, INC.
333 SECOND AVENUE N
LEWISTOWN, MT 59457
406-538-3496
Fax: 800-227-7207
Info@hq.sportsinc.com
www.sportsinc.com
• Nancy Wilson, VP
info@sportsinc.com
• Dave Salvi, Chief Executive Officer

Services:
National member-owned retail buying syndicate, including member stores from all facets of the sporting goods business.

SPORTSMAN'S GUIDE
411 FARWELL AVENUE
PO BOX 239
SOUTH SAINT PAUL, MN 55075-0239
651-451-3030
888-844-0667
800-882-2962
Fax: 800-333-6933
custserv@sportsmansguide.com
www.sportsmansguide.com
• Gary Olen, Chairman
custserv@sportsmansguide.com
• Greg Binkley, President, Chief Executive Officer
custserv@sportsmansguide.com
• John Casler, EVP Merchandising, Marketing and Creativ
custserv@sportsmansguide.com
• Douglas Johnson, VP Marketing
custserv@sportsmansguide.com
Products:
Catalog and internet company which markets value priced outdoor gear and general merchandise, with a special emphasis on outdoor clothing, equipment and footwear. Products include clothing, footwear, hunting and shooting accessories, camping and outdoor recreation equipment, optics, electronics, personal accessory items and a diverse range of additional offerings.

STAGE STORES, INC.
10201 MAIN STREET
HOUSTON, TX 77025
713-667-5601
800-324-3244
800-743-8730
Fax: 713-660-3330
customercomments@stagestores.com
www.stagestoresinc.com
• Andy Hall, President/CEO
• Michael Glazer, President and Chief Executive Officer
Customercomments@stagestores.com
• Steven Lawrence, Chief Merchandising Officer
• Edward Record, Chief Operating Officer
• Oded Shein, Executive Vice President, Chief Financial Off
• Ron Lucas, Executive Vice President, Human Resources
• Steven Hunter, Executive Vice President, Chief Information O
• Richard Stasyszen, Senior Vice President, Finance and Controller
Products:
Brings nationally recognized brand name apparel, accessories, cosmetics and footwear for the entire family to small and mid-size towns and communities. Operates under the Stage, Bealls and Palais Royal and Peebles name.

STERNHEIMER BROS/DBA A&N STORES
6000 RIVER ROAD
SUITE B
RICHMOND, VA 23226
804-226-1325
Fax: 804-222-4894
www.anstores.com
• Mark Sternheimer, President

Products:
Family-owned retail clothing and sportswear store

SUPER SHOE STORES
10365 MOUNT SAVAGE ROAD, NW
CUMBERLAND, MD 21502
301-759-4300
877-704-4106
Fax: 603-386-6126
customercare@supershoes.com
www.supershoes.com
• James Issler, President
customercare@supershoes.com
Products:
Multi-store footwear retailer. Products include different brands of shoes, boots, accessories, handbags, workwear, and nursing apparel. We carry shoes for every person and every activity; from work boots to hunting boots, sandals to slippers.

SYMS
1 SYMS WAY
SECAUCUS, NJ 7094
201-902-9600
800-322-7967
Fax: 201-902-9874
customerservice@syms.com
www.syms.com
• Sy Syms, Chairman
customerservice@syms.com
• Marcy Syms, Chief Executive Officer
customerservice@syms.com
• Ronald Zindman, EVP, General Merchandise Manager
customerservice@syms.com
• Allen Brailsford, EVP Operations
customerservice@syms.com
Products:
Off-price representative for authentic designer and name brand clothes for men and women.

T.J. MAXX
770 COCHITUATE ROAD
FRAMINGHAM, MA 01701
508-390-1000
800-285-6299
Fax: 508-390-2828
www.tjx.com
• Bernard Cammarata, Chairman
• Carol Meryowitz, President
• Edmond English, VP
• Arnold Barron, Chief Operating Officer
• Carol Meyrowitz, Chief Executive Officer
Products:
The largest off-price retailer. Offers brand-name family apparel, giftware, home fashions, women's shoes, accessories and fine jewelry at prices up to 60% below regular department and specialty store prices.

TEAM ATHLETIC GOODS/TAG, INC.
3 SHARPIE WAY
SHELBYVILLE, TN 37160
615-410-4390
888-796-0734
Fax: 615-410-4388
info@tagsportswear.com
tagsportswear.com
• Philip Rosati, President/Chief Executive Officer
• Darcy Kinder, V.P./Director of Operations
• Robin Catiller, Office Manager/Single Billing

• Tim Loudermilk, Product Manager/Research & Development
• Carrie Bretz, Executive Assistant/Marketing
Year Founded:
1979
Description:
Manufacturer of team sporting goods, equipment and clothing.

TGM FITNESS, INC.
183 S. MAIN ST.
MOUNT CLEMENS, MI 48043
586-775-2760
888-892-784
Fax: 586-741-0052
service@tgmskateboards.com
www.tgmskateboards.com
• Mary Bonten, President, Buyer
• Charles L Bonten, Buyer
Products:
Fitness equipment and apparel

THE FEMALE ATHLETE, INC.
601 PACKARD COURT
SAFETY HARBOR, FL 34695
800-586-7738
Fax: 800-456-1223
• Mary Tenety, Co-Founder, President
mail@sweetandpowerful.com
• Lori Schmid, Co-Founder, VP
mail@sweetandpowerful.com
Products:
Sportswear and teen clothing store made especially for girls

THE WALKING COMPANY
519 LINCOLN COUNTY PARKWAY
LINCOLNTON, NC 28092
818-709-2200
800-642-9265
Fax: 818-709-2210
www.thewalkingcompany.com
• Greg Milne, Chief Executive Officer
Products:
Provides the most technically-advanced comfort footwear available

TOMMY HILFIGER
601 W 26TH STREET
NEW YORK, NY 10001
212-549-6000
888-866-6948
tommyhelp@tommy.com
www.tommy.com
• Thomas J. Hilfiger, Founder/Principal Designer
• Daniel F. Grieder, CEO
• Ludo Omnisk, Chief Operating Officer
• Avery Baker, Chief Marketing Operator
• Gary Shienbaum, CEO North America
• Tommy Hilfiger, Designer & Visionary
• Quentin Walsh, SVP/Corporate Controller
Description:
Designs, sources and markets men's and women's sportswear.

TOP 100 BASKETBALL RECRUITING SHOWCASE
511 E KING STREET
BOONE, NC 28607
828-264-9547
828-264-9547
Fax: 828-264-0065
www.gamewornuniforms.com
• Wayne Otto, Executive Director

Products:
Team Pins, Balls/Accessories, Misc. Items, Baseball Helmets, Bench Towels, College Items, Football Helmets, Football Jerseys, Compression Shorts, NBA Armbands, NBA Bath Robes, NBA Game Balls, NBA Autographed Game Balls, NBA Game Jerseys, NBA Game Shoes, NBA Game Shorts, NBA Practice Items, NBA Shooting Shirts, NBA Socks, NBA Warm Up Jacket, NBA Warm Up Pants, MLB Baseball Pants, MLB BP Jerseys, MLB Game Bats, MLB Game Jackets, MLB Pull Over Jacket, MLB Game Jerseys, MLB Player Caps, NHL Hockey Gloves, NHL Hockey Jerseys, NHL Hockey Pants, NHL Hockey Skates, NHL Hockey Sticks, Hockey Pucks, Locker Name Plate, Replica Stadiums, Equipment/Travel

TRI-STATE DISTRIBUTOR
1104 PULLMAN ROAD
MOSCOW, ID 83843
208-882-4555
887-878-2835
Fax: 208-882-8427
jpower@t-state.com
www.t-state.com
• L. Connelly, President
Products:
Clothes, shoes and sports equipment.

TRIPLE S SPORTING SUPPLIES, INC.
325 CREEKSIDE DRIVE
AMHERST, NY 14228
716-691-3777
800-942-3777
Fax: 716-691-4305
triple-s@att.com
www.triplessportingsupplies.com
• Dave Sheffield, President
(716) 691-3777
• Gary Sheffield, Vice President
(716) 691-3777
Products:
Fishing Tackle, HUnting Supplies and Footwear
Nature of Service:
Wholesale Distributor Spotring Supplies
Brands:
Purefishing, Zebco, Shakespeare, Doiwa, Shimano, Eagle Claw, Optronics, Wildlife Research Stearns, Hodgman, Minnkota, Normark Challenger, Pradco, Cannon Downriggers Mepps, Mr Twister, Zoom Eyewear and more
Year Founded:
1969

TURNER'S OUTDOORSMAN
11738 SAN MARIN STREET
SUITE A
RANCHO CUCAMONGA, CA 91730
909-923-3009
Fax: 909-923-3022
www.turners.com
• Shirley Andrews, Owner
• Don Small, President / Chief Executive Officer
• Bob Hostetter, Match Director
• Rob Zubak, Director of Sales
robzubak@turners.com
Products:
Spinfisher Metal Series, Cherrywood Rods, Sweep Fire, Pink Fluorocarbon, Hooks, AL391 - Urika Sporting, G22 Semi-Auto .22IR, 870 Special Purpose Shotgun,

SIGMA9MM OR 40 S&W , Deckboot and more.

U.S. CAVALRY, INC
2855 CENTENNIAL AVENUE
RADCLIFF, KY 40160-9000
270-351-1164
800-777-7172
Fax: 270-352-0266
service@uscav.com
www.uscav.com
• Randall Acton, President
Products:
ACU, Bags and Luggage, Clothing, Electronics, Eyewear, Field Equipment, Footwear, Gifts and Novelty, Headwear, Insignia, Knives, Optics, Tools and Watches. Men US Air Force Stealth Pilot Watches, Tactical Full T-Shirt, Waterproof Boots, Desert Mil Spec Boots, Flashlight, Army Combat Uniform (ACU) Shirt, Army Combat Uniform (ACU) Trousers, Com-Tac Headset, 2nd Generation Universal Parka and more.

U.S. FACTORY OUTLETS, INC.
7 PENN PLAZA
NEW YORK, NY 10001
212-563-3650
Fax: 212-967-9872
• Frederic K Raiff, President / Chief Executive Officer
• Frederic K. Raiff, Owner
• Michael Metrose, VP / General Merchandise Manager
Products:
60 percent apparel and 40 percent hard goods and domestics.

UP AGAINST THE WALL
1420 WISCONSIN AVENUE NW
WASHINGTON, DC 20007
202-337-6610
Fax: 202-333-1246
www.upagainstthewall.com
• Charles Rendelman, President
Number/Location of Stores:
16. DC, MD, VA.

VALUE CITY DEPARTMENT STORES
3241 WESTERVILLE ROAD
COLUMBUS, OH 43224
614-471-4722
Fax: 614-478-2253
websupport@vcf.com
www.valuecity.com
• Jay L Schottenstein, Chairman
• John C. Rossler, President / Chief Executive Officer
• Charles Rath, EVP, Chief Marketing Officer
Products:
Men's, ladies and kids shoes.

VANS, INC.
6550 KATELLA AVE
CYPRESS, CA
855-909-8267
800-826-7800
Fax: 562-565-8406
vanscustserv@vfc.com
www.vans.com
• Walter E Schoenfeld, Chairman
• Gary H. Schoenfeld, President & Chief Executive Officer
• Scott J Blechman, VP & Chief Financial

Officer
• Craig E Gosselin, SVP, Secretary & General Counsel
Products:
CUSTOM SHOES - Full Collection; MENS SHOES - Classics, Band Classics, Core Skate, Skate Performance, Sandals; WOMENS SHOES - Classics, Fashion, Active, Sandals; BOYS SHOES - Classics, Band Classics, Core Skate, MISSYS SHOES - Full Collection; TODDLERS SHOES - Full Collection; INFANTS SHOES - Full Collection; MENS APPAREL - Tops, Tees, Pants; WOMENS APPAREL - Fashion Tops, Tees, Bottoms and Skirts; ACCESSORIES - Full Collection.

VARIETY WHOLESALERS
PO BOX 947
HENDERSON, NC 27536
252-430-2600
Fax: 919-790-5349
info@vwstores.com
www.vwstores.com
• Frances Winslow, VP Human Resources (252) 430-2491
• Art Pope, Vice Chairman, President, and Chief Fina
apope@vwstores.com
• Frances Winslow, Vice President of Human Resources
(252) 430-2041
fwinslow@vwstores.com
• Phil Pope Sr., Vice President / Real Estate
(252) 430-2618
ppope@vwstores.com
• Todd Hope, Dispatcher
(252) 430-2196
jhope@vwstores.com
• Terry Ellenwood, Director of Transportation
(252) 430-2143
terrye@vwstores.com
• Wayne Stainback, Regional Director of Leasing
(252) 430-2609
wstainback@vwstores.com
• Ken Dickerson, Director of Maintenance Services
(252) 430-2845
kend@vwstores.com
• Tim Hedgepeth, Inbound Logistics Manager
(252) 430-2464
thedgepeth@vwstores.com
Products:
Assortment of retail merchandise including both hardlines (toys, health and beauty aids, housewares, furniture, sporting goods, snacks, etc.) and softlines (clothing, accessories, jewelry, etc.).

VENATOR GROUP, INC.
112 W 34TH STREET
NEW YORK, NY 10120
212-720-3700
800-991-6815
www.footlocker-inc.com
• Matthew D Serra, Chairman of the Board, President and Chi
• Christopher A. Sinclair, Executive Chairman of the Board, Scanden
• Purdy Crawford, Corporate Director
• Bruce L. Gi Hartman, Executive Vice President and Chief Financial
• Lauren B. Peters, Senior Vice President - Strategic Planning

• John A. Maurer, Vice President, Treasurer and Investor Relati
Products:
Sports apparel

VIM
164-01 JAMAICA AVENUE
JAMAICA, NY 11432
718-297-3227
888-584-6669
Fax: 718-387-7084
customerservice@vim.com
www.vim.com
• Joseph Joseph, President
• Joseph Renate, Buyer
• Kathy Tema, Buyer
• Vicki Patel, Buyer

W.H. SMITH
3200 WINDY HILL ROAD
1500 W TOWER
ATLANTA, GA 30339
404-952-0705
800-795-0705
Fax: 404-951-1352
www.whsmith.co.uk
• Sara Hinckley, Buyer

WAL-MART STORES, INC.
702 SW 8TH STREET
BENTONVILLE, AR 72716-8611
479-273-4000
800-925-6278
Fax: 479-273-4053
www.walmartstores.com
• Robson S Walton, Chairman
• Lee H. Scott, Jr, President and Chief Executive Officer
• David D Glass, Executive Committee Chairman of the Boar
• Eduardo W Castro-Wright, Vice Chairman
• Michael T. Duke, President and Chief Executive Officer
• M. Susan Chambers, Executive Vice President, People Division
• Leslie A. Dach, Executive Vice President, Corporate Affairs
• Brian C. Cornell, Executive VP, President and CEO, Sam's Club
• Charles M. Holley, Jr., Executive Vice President and Chief Financial
• Jeffrey J. Gearhart, Executive Vice President, General Counsel and
Products:
Electronics (MP3 Players, Portable DVD Players, laptops, cell phones, desktops, and more); Toys (bikes, scooters chairs & sofas, play tents & slumber bags, dolls and more); sports & Fitness (treadmills, home gyms, ab equipment, ellipticals and more); Apparel (Women's Piped Stretch Jacket, Faded Glory - Men's Denim Shirt, accessories and more); Pharmacy (Blood Pressure Monitors, Bathroom Safety, Mobility Aids, Contact Lenses, Exercise Equipment) and more.

WALGREEN COMPANY
200 WILMOT ROAD
DEERFIELD, IL 60015
877-250-5823
800-925-4733
Fax: 847-914-2804
investor.relations@walgreens.com
www.walgreen.com
• Gregory D Wasson, President/CEO
• Jeffrey A. Rein, President and Chief Operation Officer

• George J Riedl, Marketing EVP
• Trent E Taylor, Chief Information Officer, EVP
Services:
-Pharmacy Network, Claims Processing, Implementation and Transition, Formulary Management, Comprehensive Reporting, Online Access, Clinical Services, Advantage90T and Consumer Choice Pharmacy (CCP). -Dual Verification, Full-order Imaging, Intercom Plusr and Pharmacist Supervision. -Respiratory Services, Home Infusion Therapies and Home Medical Equipment (HME). -Cost-containment Solutions, Walgreen Advantage, Health Management, Benefit Coordination and Account Management.

WASHINGTON GOLF CENTER
N89 W16790 APPLETON AVENUE
SUITE 200
MENOMONEE FALLS, WI 53051
262-255-7600
800-967-5342
Fax: 301-948-7052
brian@golftrips.com
www.washingtongolf.com
• Chong Su Chay, Chairman
(703) 979-7888
info@washingtongolf.com
• Randy Ramsey, VP
info@washingtongolf.com
Products:
Clubs (Adams 460 Dual , Adams RPM 430Q, Bridgestone J33R, Callaway Big Bertha 454, Callaway FT-3 Fusion Drivers, Callaway Women's X 460 and more); Bags (Carry/Stand, Cart, Push/Pull Carts, Travel, Women's bag, Accessories); Shoes (Men's, Women's, Juniors, Socks, Sandals and Accessories); Balls (Bridgestone B330, Bridgestone B330-S, Callaway Big Bertha Balls, Callaway HX Hot Balls, Callaway HX Tour 56 Balls, Callaway HX Tour Balls); Apparel (Men's, Women's, Juniors, Gloves, Accessories and Visors); and Accessories (Golf Gift, Tools, Books/Videos, Practice Aids, Gloves and Golf Grips).

WAVE RIDING VEHICLES
1900 CYPRESS AVENUE
VIRGINIA BEACH, VA 23451
757-422-8823
Fax: 757-428-6328
www.waveridingvehicles.com
• Leslie G Shaw, Jr, President
Products:
Tees (Bond Girl, Electro Tourist, North Shore), hoods (Buckshot, Dali Lama, Formation), mens (Shooter Jacket, Snow Summit, Paolo), chicas (Rastar, Ribbed, Birdie), youth, lids (Cult Flexfit, EOP 2 Flexfit, Low Pro Flexfit) and stuff (3/2 Wetsuit, 4/3 Wetsuit, Non-fade Rack Pads).

WEST MARINE, INC.
PO BOX 50070
WATSONVILLE, CA 95077-0070
831-728-2700
800-262-8464
Fax: 831-761-4421
wmCustomerService@westmarine.com
www.westmarine.com
• Geoff Eisenberg, President/Chief Executive Officer
• Eric Nelson, SVP / Chief Financial Officer
• Geoff Eisenberg, CEO and President

Products:
Anchor & Docking, Boats & Motors, Books & Videos, Cabinet & Deck Hardware, Clothing, Cordage, Electrical, Electronics, Engine Systems, Fasteners, Fishing, Interior, Cabin & Galley, Navigation, Paint & Maintenance, Plumbingm, Safety, Sailboat, Seating & Covers, Trailers & Parts, Ventilation and Watersports.

WHOLESALE SPORTS OUTDOOR OUTFITTERS
25 HERITAGE MEADOWS WAY SE
CALGARY, AB, CANADA T2H 0A7
253-835-4100
800-696-0253
Fax: 403-253-5518
• Norm P. Daniels, Chairman, Pres, Chief Executive Officer

• Phil Pepin, VP / Chief Financial Officer
• Ed Ariniello, VP, Operations
• Ron J. Menconi, VP / Merchandising / Marketing
Services:
Rentals, Bike Services, Tech Services, Guide Services

YORK BARBELL COMPANY
3300 BOARD ROAD
YORK, PA 17406
717-767-6481
800-358-9675
Fax: 717-764-0044
www.yorkbarbell.com
• Tim Bonitz, Marketing and Sales
Products:
Commercial Weight Equipment Quad-Grip Olympic Plates, Solid Rubber Training Bumpers, Olympic Iron Training Plates, Elite Competition Bumper Sets and Plates, USA-Made Elite Competition Olympic Bars, USA-Made Competition/Training Bars, Machine Attachment Bars, PRO-HEX Dumbbells, Rubber Hex Dumbbells, Iron or Rubber Gym-Style Dumbbells, Fixed Curl and Straight Barbells, Neo-Hex Neoprene Fitbells, Vinyl Fitbells and Racks, 2-Sided A-Frame Rack AF-6 (69002), 2-Sided Vertical Dumbbell Rack V-2-8 (69001), 2-Tier Dumbbell Racks with Saddle 2T-SDR-10 (69030), Single-Sided Weight Tree SSWT (69042), 40 lb. Aerobic Weight Set AWS-40 (10164) and 40 lb.

9

events, meetings & trade shows

events/meetings/shows

TBA, 2021
AAU NATIONAL CONVENTION
AMATEUR ATHLETIC UNION
Phone: 407-934-7200
Fax: 407-934-7242
www.aausports.org

TBA, 2021
ARNOLD SPORTS FESTIVAL
ARNOLD SPORTS FESTIVAL
Phone: 614-431-2600
Fax: 614-431-3492
www.arnoldsportsfestival.com

TBA, 2021
AXS FACILITIES & FRANCHISES AND
TICKETING SYMPOSIUM
STREET & SMITH'S SPORTS
BUSINESS JOURNAL
Phone: 704-973-1500
www.sportsbusinessdaily.com

TBA, 2021
IDEA WORLD CONVENTION
Anaheim, CA
IDEA HEALTH & FITNESS
ASSOCIATION
Phone: 858-535-8979
Fax: 619-344-0380
contact@ideafit.com
www.ideafit.com

TBA, 2021
IEG CONFERENCE
IEG
Phone: 312-944-1727
ieg@sponsorship.com
www.sponsorship.com

TBA, 2021
SHOT SHOW
Las Vegas, NV
Sands Expo & Convention Center
NATIONAL SHOOTING SPORTS
FOUNDATION
Phone: 203-426-1320
Fax: 203-426-1087
shotshow.com

TBA, 2021
USAG NATIONAL CONGRESS &
TRADE SHOW
St. Louis, MO
USA GYMNASTICS
Phone: 317-237-5050
Fax: 317-237-5069
membership@usagym.org
usagym.org

Jan TBA, 2021
THE SUPERNATIONALS CUSTOM
AUTO SHOW
Albuquerque, NM
Lujan Complex, Expo New Mexico
SUPERNATIONALS
Phone: 505-332-9222
www.thesupernationals.com

Jan 6 - Jan 8, 2021
NSCA COACHES CONFERENCE
New Orleans, LA
NATIONAL STRENGTH &
CONDITIONING ASSOCIATION
Phone: 800-815-6826
Fax: 719-632-6367
conferences@nsca.com
www.nsca.com

Jan 6 - Mar 19, 2021
SIA OUTDOOR + SNOWSHOW
SNOWSPORTS INDUSTRIES AMERICA
Phone: 435-657-5140

Fax: 435-659-3434
info@snowsports.org
snowsports.org

Jan 7 - Jan 10, 2021
ABCA CONVENTION
Washington, DC
AMERICAN BASEBALL COACHES
ASSOCIATION
Phone: 336-821-3140
Fax: 336-886-0000
www.abca.org

Jan 10 - Jan 12, 2021
AFCA NATIONAL CONVENTION
Nashville, TN
AMERICAN FOOTBALL COACHES
ASSOCIATION
Phone: 254-754-9900
Fax: 254-754-7373
info@afca.com
www.afca.com

Jan 11 - Jan 15, 2021
ATA TRADE SHOW
ARCHERY TRADE ASSOCIATION
Phone: 507-233-8130
Fax: 507-233-8140
www.archerytrade.org

Jan 11 - Jan 15, 2021
NSCAA CONVENTION
Baltimore, MD
NATIONAL SOCCER COACHES
ASSOCIATION OF AMERICA
Phone: 816-471-1941
Fax: 816-474-7408
unitedsoccercoaches.org

Jan 12 - Jan 16, 2021
CHICAGO BOAT, RV & STRICTLY
SAIL SHOW
Chicago, IL
McCormick Place
NATIONAL MARINE MANUFACTURERS
ASSOCIATION
Phone: 312-946-6200
Fax: 312-946-0401
www.nmma.org

Jan 12 - Jan 13, 2021
STMA CONFERENCE & EXHIBITION
SPORTS TURF MANAGERS
ASSOCIATION
Phone: 800-323-3875
Fax: 785-843-2977
stma.org

Jan 15 - Jan 17, 2021
GREAT ROCKIES SPORTSHOW
Billings, MT
Metra Park ExpoCenter
GREAT ROCKIES SPORTSHOW
Phone: 406-580-3907
Fax: 406-388-6277
www.greatrockiesshow.com

Jan 20 - Jan 23, 2021
SACRAMENTO INTERNATIONAL
SPORTSMEN'S EXPO
Sacramento, CA
Cal Expo, State Fairgrounds
INTERNATIONAL SPORTSMEN'S
EXPOSITIONS
Phone: 800-545-6100
Fax: 360-693-3352
International Ph: 360-693-3700
www.sportsexpos.com

Jan 29 - Jan 31, 2021
RED RIVER VALLEY BOAT & MARINE
PRODUCTS SHOW
Fargo, ND
Fargodome
CENAIKO PRODUCTIONS
Phone: 763-755-8111
Fax: 763-755-8124
www.cenaiko.com

Feb TBA, 2021
SOARING SOCIETY OF AMERICA
CONVENTION
SOARING SOCIETY OF AMERICA
Phone: 575-392-1177
Fax: 575-392-8154
www.ssa.org

Feb TBA, 2021
ST. LOUIS GOLF EXPO
St. Charles, MO
St. Charles Convention Center
VARSITY COMMUNICATIONS
Phone: 888-367-6420
Fax: 425-412-7082
www.varsitycommunications.com

Feb 15 - Feb 17, 2021
ASBA WINTER MEETING
AMERICAN SPORTS BUILDERS
ASSOCIATION
Phone: 410-730-9595
Fax: 410-730-8833
info@sportsbuilders.org
www.sportsbuilders.org

Feb 22 - Feb 24, 2021
LAS VEGAS WORLD AMATEUR
Las Vegas, NV
CASCADIA EVENTS
Phone: 206-659-5703
john@cascadiaevents.com
cascadiaevents.com

Feb 23 - Feb 25, 2021
NIRSA ANNUAL CONFERENCE &
RECREATIONAL SPORTS EX PO
Phoenix, AZ
Phoenix Convention Center
NATIONAL INTRAMURAL RECREATION
SPORTS ASSOCIATION
Phone: 541-766-8211
Fax: 541-766-8284
nirsa@nirsa.org
nirsa.net

Feb 26 - Feb 28, 2021
VANCOUVER GOLF EXPO
Vancouver, Canada
Pacific National Exhibition
NATIONAL GOLF COURSE OWNERS
ASSOCIATION CANADA
Phone: 613-226-3616
Fax: 613-226-4148
ngcoa@ngcoa.ca
www.ngcoa.ca

Mar 4 - Mar 7, 2021
RED RIVER VALLEY SPORTSMEN'S
SHOW
Fargo, ND
Fargodome
CENAIKO PRODUCTIONS
Phone: 763-755-8111
Fax: 763-755-8124
www.cenaiko.com

Mar 8 - Mar 14, 2021
OTTAWA-GATINEAU GOLF EXPO
Ottawa, Canada

EY Centre
NATIONAL GOLF COURSE OWNERS
ASSOCIATION CANADA
Phone: 613-226-3616
Fax: 613-226-4148
ngcoa@ngcoa.ca
www.ngcoa.ca

Mar 10, 2021
TRAPS INSTITUTE & EXPO
TEXAS RECREATION & PARK SOCIETY
Phone: 512-267-5550
Fax: 512-267-5557
traps@traps.org
www.traps.org

Mar 11 - Mar 14, 2021
SIOUX EMPIRE SPORTSMEN'S
BOAT, CAMPING & VACATIO N SHOW
Sioux Falls, SD
Sioux Falls Arena & Convention Center
CENAIKO PRODUCTIONS
Phone: 763-755-8111
Fax: 763-755-8124
www.cenaiko.com

Mar 15 - Mar 21, 2021
MONTREAL GOLF EXPO
Montreal, Canada
Place Sports Experts
NATIONAL GOLF COURSE OWNERS
ASSOCIATION CANADA
Phone: 613-226-3616
Fax: 613-226-4148
ngcoa@ngcoa.ca
www.ngcoa.ca

Mar 15 - Mar 21, 2021
QUEBEC GOLF EXPO
L,vis, Canada
Centre des congrŠs
NATIONAL GOLF COURSE OWNERS
ASSOCIATION CANADA
Phone: 613-226-3616
Fax: 613-226-4148
ngcoa@ngcoa.ca
www.ngcoa.ca

Mar 17 - Mar 20, 2021
SALT LAKE CITY INTERNATIONAL
SPORTSMEN'S EXPO
Salt Lake City, UT
Mountain America Expo Center
INTERNATIONAL SPORTSMEN'S
EXPOSITIONS
Phone: 800-545-6100
Fax: 360-693-3352
International Ph: 360-693-3700
www.sportsexpos.com

Mar 19 - Mar 20, 2021
IHRSA FITNESS BRASIL LATIN
AMERICAN CONFERENCE & TRADE
SHOW
Sao Paulo, Brazil
INTERNATIONAL HEALTH, RACQUET &
SPORTSCLUB ASSOCIATION
Phone: 800-228-4772
Fax: 617-951-0056
info@ihrsa.org
www.ihrsa.org

Mar 24 - Mar 28, 2021
PACIFIC NORTHWEST
SPORTSMEN'S SHOW
Portland, OR
Portland Expo Center
O'LOUGHLIN TRADE SHOWS
Phone: 503-246-8291
Fax: 503-246-1066

info@otshows.com
www.thesportshows.com

Mar 24 - Jan 28, 2021
PORTLAND BOAT SHOW
Portland, OR
Portland Expo Center
O'LOUGHLIN TRADE SHOWS
Phone: 503-246-8291
Fax: 503-246-1066
info@otshows.com
www.thesportshows.com

Mar 24 - Mar 27, 2021
SCOTTSDALE INTERNATIONAL
SPORTSMEN'S EXPO
Scottsdale, AZ
WestWorld of Scottsdale
INTERNATIONAL SPORTSMEN'S
EXPOSITIONS
Phone: 800-545-6100
Fax: 360-693-3352
International Ph: 360-693-3700
www.sportsexpos.com

Mar 31 - Apr 1, 2021
WBCA CONVENTION
WOMEN'S BASKETBALL COACHES
ASSOCIATION
Phone: 770-279-8027
Fax: 770-279-8473
membership@wbca.org
www.wbca.org

Apr 7 - Apr 11, 2021
ACSM'S HEALTH & FITNESS SUMMIT
& EXPOSITION
AMERICAN COLLEGE OF SPORTS
MEDICINE
Phone: 317-637-9200
Fax: 317-634-7817
www.acsm.org

Apr 8, 2021
ORANGE BOWL FAMILY FUN AND FIT
DAY
Fort Lauderdale, FL
Orange Bowl Field
CAPITAL ONE ORANGE BOWL
Phone: 305-341-4700
Fax: 305-341-4771
tickets@orangebowl.org
www.orangebowl.org

Apr 13 - Apr 16, 2021
MPRA CONFERENCE & EXPO
Columbia, MO
Holiday Inn Executive Center
MISSOURI PARK & RECREATION
ASSOCIATION
Phone: 573-636-3828
Fax: 573-635-7988
info@mopark.org
www.mopark.org

Apr 13 - Apr 17, 2021
SHAPE AMERICA NATIONAL
CONVENTION & EXPO
Salt Lake City, UT
SHAPE AMERICA
Phone: 800-213-7193
Fax: 703-476-9527

Apr 24 - Apr 25, 2021
HOGEYE MARATHON & RELAYS
Springdale, AR
HOGEYE MARATHON
Phone: 479-445-9251
Fax: 479-575-5778
info@hogeyemarathon.com
www.hogeyemarathon.com

May 5 - May 9, 2021
CINCINNATI AUTO EXPO
Cincinnati, OH
Duke Energy Convention Center
DUKE ENERGY CONVENTION CENTER
Phone: 513-326-7100
info@cincinnatiautoexpo.com
cincinnatiautoexpo.com

May 5 - May 8, 2021
INTERNATIONAL AQUATIC FITNESS
CONFERENCE
Daytona Beach, FL
AQUATIC EXERCISE ASSOCIATION
Phone: 941-486-8600
aeawave.org

May 15 - May 16, 2021
CLEVELAND MARATHON HEALTH &
FITNESS EXPO
Cleveland, OH
CLEVELAND MARATHON
Phone: 800-467-3826
Fax: 216-378-0143
www.clevelandmarathon.com

May 19 - May 20, 2021
NATIONAL SPORTS FORUM
Atlanta, GA
NATIONAL SPORTS FORUM
Phone: 800-232-3133
Fax: 619-469-4007
info@sports-forum.com
www.sports-forum.com

Jun 3 - Jun 5, 2021
NASSM CONFERENCE
NORTH AMERICAN SOCIETY FOR
SPORT MANAGEMENT
Phone: 724-482-6277
conference@nassm.org
www.nassm.com

Jun 6 - Jun 10, 2021
AEMA CONVENTION
Atlanta, GA
Marriott Marquis
ATHLETIC EQUIPMENT MANAGERS
ASSOCIATION
Phone: 217-678-1004
Fax: 217-678-1005
equipmentmanagers.org

Jun 7 - Jun 10, 2021
COSIDA CONVENTION
COLLEGE SPORTS INFORMATION
DIRECTORS OF AMERICA
willroleson@cosida.com
www.cosida.com

Jun 9 - Jun 10, 2021
USA HOCKEY ANNUAL CONGRESS
Denver, CO
Denver Marriott Tech Center
USA HOCKEY
Phone: 719-576-8724
Fax: 719-538-1160
usah@usahockey.org
www.usahockey.com

Jun 15 - Jun 17, 2021
MPI WORLD EDUCATION CONGRESS
Las Vegas, NV
MEETING PROFESSIONALS
INTERNATIONAL
Phone: 972-702-3000
Fax: 972-702-3065
www.mpiweb.org

Jun 15 - Jun 17, 2021
ROCKY MOUNTAIN OUTDOOR SHOW
TBA
WESTERN WINTER SPORTS REP
ASSOCIATION
Phone: 303-532-4002
Fax: 866-929-4572
info@wwsra.com
www.wwsra.com

Jun 22 - Jun 24, 2021
NORTHWEST SUMMER SHOW
TBA
WESTERN WINTER SPORTS REP
ASSOCIATION
Phone: 303-532-4002
Fax: 866-929-4572
info@wwsra.com
www.wwsra.com

Jun 25 - Jun 27, 2021
TAMPA BOAT SHOW
Tampa, FL
Florida State Fairgrounds
TAMPA BAY EXPOS
Phone: 727-893-8523
dlabell@tampabay.com
www.tampabay.com/expos

Jun 27 - Jun 30, 2021
ANA ADVERTISING FINANCIAL
MANAGEMENT CONFERENCE
ASSOCIATION OF NATIONAL
ADVERTISERS
Phone: 212-697-5950
Fax: 212-687-7310
www.ana.net

Jul 7 - Jul 10, 2021
NSCA NATIONAL CONFERENCE &
EXHIBITION
Las Vegas, NV
NATIONAL STRENGTH &
CONDITIONING ASSOCIATION
Phone: 800-815-6826
Fax: 719-632-6367
conferences@nsca.com
www.nsca.com

Jul 20 - Jul 22, 2021
APPA ANNUAL MEETING &
EXHIBITION
Fort Worth, TX
ASSOCIATION OF HIGHER
EDUCATION FACILITIES OFFICERS
Phone: 703-684-1446
Fax: 703-549-2772
www.appa.org

Jul 27 - Jul 28, 2021
NACDA CONVENTION
NATIONAL ASSOCIATION OF
COLLEGIATE DIRECTORS OF
ATHLETICS
Phone: 440-892-4000
Fax: 440-892-4007
www.nacda.com

Jul 28 - Jul 30, 2021
BILLIARD & HOME LEISURE EXPO
Las Vegas, NV
South Point Hotel and Convention
Center
BILLIARD CONGRESS OF AMERICA
Phone: 303-243-5070
www.bca-pool.com

Jul 28 - Jul 30, 2021
NATIONAL WELLNESS
CONFERENCE
Cincinnati, oH

NATIONAL WELLNESS INSTITUTE
Phone: 715-342-2969
Fax: 715-342-2979
nwc@nationalwellness.org
www.nationalwellness.org

Aug TBA, 2021
CASCADIA SHOOTOUT
CASCADIA EVENTS
Phone: 206-659-5703
john@cascadiaevents.com
cascadiaevents.com

Aug 2 - Aug 5, 2021
IAVM VENUECONNECT ANNUAL
CONFERENCE & TRADE SHOW
Atlanta, GA
Georgia World Congress Center
INTERNATIONAL ASSOCIATION OF
VENUE MANAGERS
Phone: 972-906-7441
Fax: 972-906-7418
www.iavm.org

Aug 3 - Aug 5, 2021
SPORTS OFFICIATING SUMMIT
NATIONAL ASSOCIATION OF SPORTS
OFFICIALS
Phone: 262-632-5448
Fax: 262-632-5460
www.naso.org

Aug 10 - Aug 12, 2021
OUTDOOR RETAILER SUMMER
MARKET
Denver, CO
EMERALD EXPOSITIONS
Phone: 949-226-5700
info@emeraldexpo.com
www.emeraldexpositions.com

Aug 13 - Aug 25, 2021
PERRY BUCKARAMA
Perry, GA
Georgia National Fairgrounds
GEORGIA WILDLIFE FEDERATION
Phone: 770-787-7887
Fax: 770-787-9229
info@gwf.org
www.gwf.org

Sept 15 - Sept 19, 2021
TWIF WORLD OUTDOOR
CHAMPIONSHIP
Getxo, Basque Country
TUG OF WAR INTERNATIONAL
FEDERATION
Phone: 608-879-2869
twif@t6b.com
www.tugofwar-twif.org

Sept 20 - Sept 22, 2021
IHRSA INTERNATIONAL
CONVENTION & TRADE SHOW
Los Angeles, CA
INTERNATIONAL HEALTH, RACQUET &
SPORTSCLUB ASSOCIATION
Phone: 800-228-4772
Fax: 617-951-0056
info@ihrsa.org
www.ihrsa.org

Sept 21 - Sept 26, 2021
2021 UNITED STATES AQUATIC
SPORTS CONVENTION
Atlanta, GA
Hyatt Regency
UNITED STATES AQUATIC SPORTS
www.usaquaticsports.org

Sept 21 - Sept 23, 2021
NRPA CONFERENCE
Orlando, FL
Orange County Convention Center
NATIONAL RECREATION & PARK
ASSOCIATION
Phone: 800-626-6772
customerservice@nrpa.org
www.nrpa.org

Sept 23 - Sept 26, 2021
NORWALK BOAT SHOW
Norwalk, CT
Norwalk Cove Marina
NATIONAL MARINE MANUFACTURERS
ASSOCIATION
Phone: 312-946-6200
Fax: 312-946-0401
www.nmma.org

Sept 24 - Sept 26, 2021
INDIANAPOLIS FALL BOAT & RV
SHOW
Indianapolis, IN
RENFRO PRODUCTIONS
Phone: 877-892-1723
Fax: 765-641-7756
info@renfroproductions.com
renfroproductions.com

Sept 27 - Sept 30, 2021
TEAMS '20 CONFERENCE & EXPO
Atlantic City, NJ
shapehealthhalf.com

Sept 29 - Oct 1, 2021
2021 CPRA CONFERENCE & TRADE
SHOW
Snowmass Village, CO
COLORADO PARKS & RECREATION
ASSOCIATION
Phone: 303-231-0943
Fax: 303-237-9750
cpra@cpra-web.org
www.cpra-web.org

Oct TBA, 2021
ICAA CONFERENCE & TRADE SHOW
INTERNATIONAL COUNCIL ON ACTIVE
AGING
Phone: 604-734-4466
Fax: 604-708-4464
info@icaa.cc
www.icaa.cc

Oct 1 - Oct 3, 2021
MEDTRONIC TWIN CITIES
MARATHON
Minneapolis, MN
TWIN CITIES IN MOTION
Phone: 651-289-7700
Fax: 651-289-7720
info@tcmevents.org
www.tcmevents.org

Oct 1 - Oct 3, 2021
MIDWEST MANIA FITNESS PRO
CONVENTION
Chicago, IL
SCW FITNESS EDUCATION
Phone: 847-562-4020
Fax: 847-562-4080
registration@scwfit.com
scwfit.com

Oct 2 - Oct 5, 2021
CSCM NATIONAL CONFERENCE
Montreal, Canada
CANADIAN SOCIETY OF CLUB
MANAGERS
Phone: 416-979-0640

events/meetings/shows

Fax: 416-979-1144
national@cscm.org
www.cscm.org

Oct 5 - Oct 8, 2021
ANA MASTERS OF MARKETING
CONFERENCE
ASSOCIATION OF NATIONAL
ADVERTISERS
Phone: 212-697-5950
Fax: 212-687-7310
www.ana.net

Oct 11 - Oct 16, 2021
AKA ANNUAL CONVENTION
Ocean City, MD
Princess Royale Oceanfront Resort
AMERICAN KITEFLIERS ASSOCIATION
Phone: 609-755-5483
kite.org

Oct 13 - Oct 14, 2021
RADIO SHOW
Nashville, TN
NATIONAL ASSOCIATION OF
BROADCASTERS
Phone: 202-595-2052
nab@nab.org
www.nab.org

Oct 25 - Oct 29, 2021
SPORTSETA SYMPOSIUM
Birmingham, AL
SPORTS EVENTS AND TOURISM
ASSOCIATION
Phone: 513-281-3888
Fax: 513-281-1765
info@sportseta.org
www.sportseta.org

Oct 26 - Oct 29, 2021
FSB INTERNATIONAL TRADE FAIR
FOR AMENITY AREAS, SPORTS &
POOL FACILITIES
Cologne, Germany
KOELNMESSE
International Ph: +49 1806 603 500
fsb@visitor.koelnmesse.de
www.fsb-cologne.com

Oct 27 - Oct 30, 2021
ATHLETIC BUSINESS SHOW
San Antonio, TX
ATHLETIC BUSINESS
Phone: 608-249-0186
www.athleticbusiness.com

Oct 27 - Oct 29, 2021
MFA ANNUAL CONFERENCE
San Antonio, TX
MEDICAL FITNESS ASSOCIATION
Phone: 910-420-8610
Fax: 910-420-8733
www.medicalfitness.org

Nov TBA, 2021
SOCCEREX USA CONVENTION
SOCCEREX
International Ph: +44 208 742 7100
enquiry@soccerex.com
www.soccerex.com

Nov 2 - Nov 4, 2021
SIBEC EUROPE
Sardinia, Italy
Forte Village Resort
QUESTEX-MCLEAN EVENTS
Phone: 617-219-8300
info@questex.com
hbs.questex.com

Nov 5 - Nov 7, 2021
DALLAS MANIA FITNESS PRO
CONVENTION
Dallas, TX
SCW FITNESS EDUCATION
Phone: 847-562-4020
Fax: 847-562-4080
registration@scwfit.com
scwfit.com

Nov 10 - Nov 13, 2021
PILATES METHOD ALLIANCE
CONFERENCE
Tacoma, WA
PILATES METHOD ALLIANCE
Phone: 305-573-4946
Fax: 305-573-4461
info@pilatesmethodalliance.org
www.pilatesmethodalliance.org

Dec 4, 2021
ST. JUDE MARATHON EXPO
Memphis, TN
ST. JUDE MARATHON
Phone: 901-578-1555
Fax: 901-578-6696
marathon@stjude.org
www.stjudemarathon.org

Dec 10 - Dec 12, 2021
BOSTON MANIA FITNESS PRO
CONVENTION
Boston, MA
SCW FITNESS EDUCATION
Phone: 847-562-4020
Fax: 847-562-4080
registration@scwfit.com
scwfit.com

TBA, 2022
ATLANTIC CANADA GOLF EXPO
Halifax, Canada
Cunard Cemtre
NATIONAL GOLF COURSE OWNERS
ASSOCIATION CANADA
Phone: 613-226-3616
Fax: 613-226-4148
ngcoa@ngcoa.ca
www.ngcoa.ca

TBA, 2022
CAA WORLD CONGRESS OF
SPORTS
STREET & SMITH'S SPORTS
BUSINESS JOURNAL
Phone: 704-973-1500
www.sportsbusinessdaily.com

TBA, 2022
FISHARAMA/TURKEYRAMA
Perry, GA
GEORGIA WILDLIFE FEDERATION
Phone: 770-787-7887
Fax: 770-787-9229
info@gwf.org
www.gwf.org

TBA, 2022
IHRSA EUROPEAN CONGRESS
INTERNATIONAL HEALTH, RACQUET &
SPORTSCLUB ASSOCIATION
Phone: 800-228-4772
Fax: 617-951-0056
info@ihrsa.org
www.ihrsa.org

TBA, 2022
PITTSBURGH GOLF AND TRAVEL
SHOW
Pittsburgh, PA
Monroeville Convention Center

NORTH COAST GOLF SHOWS
Phone: 561-320-9782
Fax: 561-320-9783
northcoastgolfandtravelshows.com

TBA, 2022
PORTLAND GOLF SHOW
Portland, OR
Oregon Convention Center
VARSITY COMMUNICATIONS
Phone: 888-367-6420
Fax: 425-412-7082
www.varsitycommunications.com

TBA, 2022
THE FLY FISHING SHOW -
COLORADO
Denver, CO
Denver Mart
FLY FISHING SHOW
Phone: 814-443-3638
Fax: 814-443-3943
info@flyfishingshow.com
www.flyfishingshow.com

TBA, 2022
WINNIPEG GOLF EXPO
Winnipeg, Canada
Red River Exhibition Place
NATIONAL GOLF COURSE OWNERS
ASSOCIATION CANADA
Phone: 613-226-3616
Fax: 613-226-4148
ngcoa@ngcoa.ca
www.ngcoa.ca

Jan TBA, 2022
CINCINNATI GOLF SHOW
Cincinnati, OH
Duke Energy Convention Center
HART PRODUCTIONS
Phone: 877-704-8190
Fax: 513-797-1013
hartproductions.com

Jan TBA, 2022
COLUMBUS GOLF SHOW
Columbus, OH
Ohio Expo Center
NORTH COAST GOLF SHOWS
Phone: 561-320-9782
Fax: 561-320-9783
northcoastgolfandtravelshows.com

Jan TBA, 2021
MINNESOTA SPORTSMEN'S SHOW
St. Paul, MN
St. Paul RiverCentre
CENAIKO PRODUCTIONS
Phone: 763-755-8111
Fax: 763-755-8124
www.cenaiko.com

Jan TBA, 2022
NASHVILLE BOAT & SPORTSHOW
Nashville, TN
Music City Center
NATIONAL MARINE MANUFACTURERS
ASSOCIATION
Phone: 312-946-6200
Fax: 312-946-0401
www.nmma.org

Jan TBA, 2022
NCAA CONVENTION
NATIONAL COLLEGIATE ATHLETIC
ASSOCIATION
Phone: 317-917-6222
Fax: 317-917-6888
www.ncaa.org

Jan TBA, 2022
NEBRASKA GOLF SHOW
Omaha, NB
CHi Health Center Omaha
VARSITY COMMUNICATIONS
Phone: 888-367-6420
Fax: 425-412-7082
www.varsitycommunications.com

Jan TBA, 2022
NEW YORK BOAT SHOW
New York, NY
Jacob Javits Convention Center
NATIONAL MARINE MANUFACTURERS
ASSOCIATION
Phone: 312-946-6200
Fax: 312-946-0401
www.nmma.org

Jan TBA, 2022
STRICTLY SAIL CHICAGO
Chicago, IL
McCormick Place
NATIONAL MARINE MANUFACTURERS
ASSOCIATION
Phone: 312-946-6200
Fax: 312-946-0401
www.nmma.org

Jan 6 - Jan 9, 2022
ABCA CONVENTION
Chicago, IL
AMERICAN BASEBALL COACHES
ASSOCIATION
Phone: 336-821-3140
Fax: 336-886-0000
www.abca.org

Jan 6 - Jan 9, 2021
DENVER INTERNATIONAL
SPORTSMEN'S EXPO
Denver, CO
Colorado Convention Center
INTERNATIONAL SPORTSMEN'S
EXPOSITIONS
Phone: 800-545-6100
Fax: 360-693-3352
International Ph: 360-693-3700
www.sportsexpos.com

Jan 14 - Jan 16, 2022
CINCINNATI TRAVEL, SPORTS &
BOAT SHOW
Cincinnati, OH
Duke Energy Convention Center
HART PRODUCTIONS
Phone: 877-704-8190
Fax: 513-797-1013
hartproductions.com

Jan 14 - Feb 15, 2022
SOUTHWESTERN EXPO AND
LIVESTOCK SHOW
Fort Worth, TX
PROFESSIONAL RODEO COWBOY
ASSOCIATION
Phone: 719-593-8840
Fax: 719-548-4876
prorodeor@prorodeo.com
www.prorodeo.com

Jan 17 - Jan 20, 2022
INTIX ANNUAL CONFERENCE
Orland, FL
INTERNATIONAL TICKETING
ASSOCIATION
Phone: 212-629-4036
Fax: 212-629-8532
info@intix.org
www.intix.org

Jan 20 - Jan 23, 2022
MINNEAPOLIS BOAT SHOW
Minneapolis, MN
Minneapolis Convention Center
NATIONAL MARINE MANUFACTURERS
ASSOCIATION
Phone: 312-946-6200
Fax: 312-946-0401
www.nmma.org

Jan 21 - Jan 23, 2022
THE FLY FISHING SHOW -
MASSACHUSETTS
Marlborough, MA
Royal Plaza
FLY FISHING SHOW
Phone: 814-443-3638
Fax: 814-443-3943
info@flyfishingshow.com
www.flyfishingshow.com

Jan 24 - Jan 26, 2022
GOLF BUSINESS CONFERENCE
Orlando, FL
NATIONAL GOLF COURSE OWNERS
ASSOCIATION
Phone: 800-933-4262
Fax: 843-881-9958
ndownie@ngcoa.org
ngcoa.org

Jan 25 - Jan 28, 2022
PGA FASHION & DEMO EXPERIENCE
Orlando, FL
PGA FASHION & DEMO EXPERIENCE
Phone: 203-840-5628
Fax: 203-840-9628
inquiry@pga.reedexpo.com
www.pgalasvegas.com

Jan 26 - Jan 30, 2022
LOUISVILLE BOAT, RV &
SPORTSHOW
Louisville, KY
Kentucky Exposition Center
NATIONAL MARINE MANUFACTURERS
ASSOCIATION
Phone: 312-946-6200
Fax: 312-946-0401
www.nmma.org

Jan 26 - Jan 28, 2022
OUTDOOR RETAILER SNOW SHOW
Denver, CO
EMERALD EXPOSITIONS
Phone: 949-226-5700
info@emeraldexpo.com
www.emeraldexpositions.com

Jan 26 - Jan 30, 2022
WASHINGTON SPORTSMEN'S SHOW
Puyallup, WA
Washington State Fair Events Center
O'LOUGHLIN TRADE SHOWS
Phone: 503-246-8291
Fax: 503-246-1066
info@otshows.com
www.thesportshows.com

Jan 27 - Jan 30, 2022
CHICAGOLAND FISHING, TRAVEL &
OUTDOOR EXPO
Schaumburg, IL
Schaumburg Convention Center
EASTERN FISHING & OUTDOOR
EXPOSITION
Phone: 603-431-4315
Fax: 603-431-1971
info@sportshows.com
www.sportshows.com

Jan 28 - Jan 30, 2022
THE FLY FISHING SHOW - NEW
JERSEY
Somerset, NJ
Garden State Convention Center
FLY FISHING SHOW
Phone: 814-443-3638
Fax: 814-443-3943
info@flyfishingshow.com
www.flyfishingshow.com

Feb TBA, 2022
CLEVELAND GOLF SHOW
Cleveland, OH
I-X Center
NORTH COAST GOLF SHOWS
Phone: 561-320-9782
Fax: 561-320-9783
northcoastgolfandtravelshows.com

Feb TBA, 2022
PHILADELPHIA GOLF SHOW
Philadelphia, PA
Greater Philadelphia Expo Center
NORTH COAST GOLF SHOWS
Phone: 561-320-9782
Fax: 561-320-9783
northcoastgolfandtravelshows.com

Feb TBA, 2022
STRICTLY SAIL MIAMI
Miami, FL
Miamarina at Bayside Marketplace
NATIONAL MARINE MANUFACTURERS
ASSOCIATION
Phone: 312-946-6200
Fax: 312-946-0401
www.nmma.org

Feb TBA, 2022
THE FLY FISHING SHOW -
WASHINGTON
Lynwood, WA
Lynwood Convention Center
FLY FISHING SHOW
Phone: 814-443-3638
Fax: 814-443-3943
info@flyfishingshow.com
www.flyfishingshow.com

Feb TBA, 2022
WASHINGTON GOLF SHOW
Chantilly, VA
Dulles Expo Center
NORTH COAST GOLF SHOWS
Phone: 561-320-9782
Fax: 561-320-9783
northcoastgolfandtravelshows.com

Feb 4 - Feb 6, 2022
ST. CLOUD SPORTSMEN'S SHOW
St. Cloud, MN
St. Cloud River's Edge Convention
Center
CENAIKO PRODUCTIONS
Phone: 763-755-8111
Fax: 763-755-8124
www.cenaiko.com

Feb 4 - Feb 5, 2022
THE FLY FISHING SHOW - GEORGIA
Atlanta, GA
Infinite Energy Center
FLY FISHING SHOW
Phone: 814-443-3638
Fax: 814-443-3943
info@flyfishingshow.com
www.flyfishingshow.com

events/meetings/shows

Feb 5 - Feb 10, 2022
GOLF INDUSTRY SHOW &
EDUCATION CONFERENCE
San Diego, CA
GOLF COURSE SUPERINTENDENTS
ASSOCIATION OF AMERICA
Phone: 800-472-7878
Fax: 785-832-3643
mbrhelp@gcsaa.org
www.gcsaa.org

Feb 16 - Feb 20, 2022
MIAMI INTERNATIONAL BOAT SHOW
Miami, FL
Miami Marine Stadium Park & Basin
NATIONAL MARINE MANUFACTURERS
ASSOCIATION
Phone: 312-946-6200
Fax: 312-946-0401
www.nmma.org

Feb 18 - Feb 20, 2022
ALLEGHENY SPORT, TRAVEL &
OUTDOOR SHOW
Monroeville, PA
Monroeville Convention Center
EXPOSITIONS INC.
Phone: 216-529-1300
Fax: 216-529-0311
showinfo@expoinc.com
expoinc.com

Feb 18 - Feb 27, 2022
INDIANA MOTORCYCLE EXPO
Indianapolis, IN
Indiana State Fairgrounds
RENFRO PRODUCTIONS
Phone: 877-892-1723
Fax: 765-641-7756
info@renfroproductions.com
renfroproductions.com

Feb 18 - Feb 27, 2022
INDIANAPOLIS BOAT, SPORT &
TRAVEL SHOW
Indianapolis, IN
Indiana State Fairgrounds
RENFRO PRODUCTIONS
Phone: 877-892-1723
Fax: 765-641-7756
info@renfroproductions.com
renfroproductions.com

Feb 24 - Feb 27, 2022
INDIANA DEER, TURKEY &
WATERFOWL EXPOSITION
Indianapolis, IN
Indiana State Fairgrounds
RENFRO PRODUCTIONS
Phone: 877-892-1723
Fax: 765-641-7756
info@renfroproductions.com
renfroproductions.com

Feb 25 - Feb 27, 2022
DC MANIA FITNESS PRO
CONVENTION
Herndon, VA
SCW FITNESS EDUCATION
Phone: 847-562-4020
Fax: 847-562-4080
registration@scwfit.com
scwfit.com

Feb 25 - Feb 27, 2022
THE FLY FISHING SHOW -
CALIFORNIA
Pleasanton, CA
Alameda County Fairgrounds

FLY FISHING SHOW
Phone: 814-443-3638
Fax: 814-443-3943
info@flyfishingshow.com
www.flyfishingshow.com

Feb 25 - Feb 27, 2022
THE OUTDOOR ADVENTURE SHOW -
TORONTO
Toronto, Canada
The International Centre
NATIONAL EVENT MANAGEMENT INC.
Phone: 800-891-4859
Fax: 905-477-7872
info@nationalevent.com
www.nationalevent.com

Mar TBA, 2022
LET'S PLAY HOCKEY EXPO
St. Paul, MN
RiverCentre
LET'S PLAY HOCKEY
Phone: 320-333-3279
letsplay@letsplayhockey.com
www.letsplayhockey.com

Mar TBA, 2022
LOUISIANA SPORTSMAN SHOW &
FESTIVAL
Gonzales, LA
Lamar-Dixon Expo Center
LOUISIANA SPORTSMAN SHOW
Phone: 985-758-7217
Fax: 985-758-7000
jackf@lasmag.com
www.louisianasportsmanshow.com

Mar TBA, 2022
NORTHEAST FISHING & HUNTING
SHOW
Hartford, CT
Connecticut Convention Center
NORTH EAST EXPOS, INC.
Phone: 860-844-8461
kristie@northeastexpos.com
www.northeastexpos.com

Mar 3 - Mar 6, 2022
WORLD FISHING & OUTDOOR
EXPOSITION
Suffern, NY
Rockland Community College Field
House
EASTERN FISHING & OUTDOOR
EXPOSITION
Phone: 603-431-4315
Fax: 603-431-1971
info@sportshows.com
www.sportshows.com

Mar 5 - Mar 6, 2022
THE FLY FISHING SHOW -
PENNSYLVANIA
Lancaster, PA
Lancaster County Convention Center
FLY FISHING SHOW
Phone: 814-443-3638
Fax: 814-443-3943
info@flyfishingshow.com
www.flyfishingshow.com

Mar 5 - Mar 6, 2022
THE OUTDOOR ADVENTURE SHOW -
VANCOUVER
Vancouver, Canada
Vancouver Convention Center
NATIONAL EVENT MANAGEMENT INC.
Phone: 800-891-4859
Fax: 905-477-7872
info@nationalevent.com
www.nationalevent.com

Mar 10 - Mar 13, 2022
CENTRAL OREGON SPORTMEN'S
SHOW
Redmond, OR
Deschutes County Fair & Expo Center
O'LOUGHLIN TRADE SHOWS
Phone: 503-246-8291
Fax: 503-246-1066
info@otshows.com
www.thesportshows.com

Mar 11 - Mar 12, 2022
JAPAN GOLF FAIR
Yokohama, Japan
Pacifico Yokohama
JAPAN GOLF FAIR
International Ph: 011-81-3-3468-4378
International Fax: 011-81-3-3437-8401
info@japangolffair.com
www.japangolffair.com

Mar 18 - Mar 20, 2022
CALIFORNIA MANIA FITNESS PRO
CONVENTION
Burlingham, CA
SCW FITNESS EDUCATION
Phone: 847-562-4020
Fax: 847-562-4080
registration@scwfit.com
scwfit.com

Mar 18 - Mar 20, 2022
SALTWATER FISHING EXPO
Edison, NJ
New Jersey Convention & Expo Center
EASTERN FISHING & OUTDOOR
EXPOSITION
Phone: 603-431-4315
Fax: 603-431-1971
info@sportshows.com
www.sportshows.com

Mar 19 - Mar 20, 2022
THE OUTDOOR ADVENTURE SHOW -
CALGARY
Calgary, Canada
Stampede Park
NATIONAL EVENT MANAGEMENT INC.
Phone: 800-891-4859
Fax: 905-477-7872
info@nationalevent.com
www.nationalevent.com

Mar 26 - Mar 27, 2022
THE OUTDOOR ADVENTURE SHOW -
MONTREAL
Montreal, Canada
Palais des CongrŠs
NATIONAL EVENT MANAGEMENT INC.
Phone: 800-891-4859
Fax: 905-477-7872
info@nationalevent.com
www.nationalevent.com

May TBA, 2022
INTERSPORT BRAND ENGAGEMENT
SUMMIT
Chicago, IL
Renaissance Chicago Downtown
STREET & SMITH'S SPORTS
BUSINESS JOURNAL
Phone: 704-973-1500
www.sportsbusinessdaily.com

May 20 - May 22, 2022
FLORIDA MANIA FITNESS PRO
CONVENTION
Orlando, FL
SCW FITNESS EDUCATION
Phone: 847-562-4020

Fax: 847-562-4080
registration@scwfit.com
scwfit.com

Jul 22 - Jul 24, 2022
ATLANTA MANIA FITNESS PRO
CONVENTION
Atlanta, GA
SCW FITNESS EDUCATION
Phone: 847-562-4020
Fax: 847-562-4080
registration@scwfit.com
scwfit.com

Nov TBA, 2022
GOLF BUSINESS CANADA
CONFERENCE & TRADE SHOW
Niagara Falls, Canada
NATIONAL GOLF COURSE OWNERS
ASSOCIATION CANADA
Phone: 613-226-3616
Fax: 613-226-4148
ngcoa@ngcoa.ca
www.ngcoa.ca

events/meetings/shows

events/meetings/shows

events/meetings/shows

TBA, 2021
AAU INTERNATIONAL BASEBALL
CHAMPIONSHIPS
AMATEUR ATHLETIC UNION
Phone: 407-934-7200
Fax: 407-934-7242
www.aausports.org

TBA, 2021
AAU JUDO NATIONAL
CHAMPIONSHIP
AMATEUR ATHLETIC UNION
Phone: 407-934-7200
Fax: 407-934-7242
www.aausports.org

TBA, 2021
AAU NATIONAL BADMINTON
CHAMPIONSHIPS
AMATEUR ATHLETIC UNION
Phone: 407-934-7200
Fax: 407-934-7242
www.aausports.org

TBA, 2021
ARNOLD AMATEUR NPC
CHAMPIONSHIPS
Columbus, OH
ARNOLD SPORTS FESTIVAL
Phone: 614-431-2600
Fax: 614-431-3492
www.arnoldsportsfestival.com

TBA, 2021
ARNOLD CLASSIC
Columbus, OH
Columbus Convention Center
ARNOLD SPORTS FESTIVAL
Phone: 614-431-2600
Fax: 614-431-3492
www.arnoldsportsfestival.com

TBA 2021
BALTIC OPEN
WTA
Phone: 727-895-5000
Fax: 727-894-1982
feedback@wtatennis.com
www.wtatennis.com

TBA 2021
BASEBALL CANADA CUP
CHAMPIONSHIPS
TBA
BASEBALL CANADA
Phone: 613-748-5606
Fax: 613-748-5767
info@baseball.ca
www.baseball.ca

TBA, 2021
BIG-D TEXAS MARATHON
Dallas, TX
Cotton Bowl, Fair Park
BIG-D TEXAS MARATHON

TBA, 2021
BIKINI INTERNATIONAL
COMPETITION
Columbus, OH
Columbus Convention Center
ARNOLD SPORTS FESTIVAL
Phone: 614-431-2600
Fax: 614-431-3492
www.arnoldsportsfestival.com

TBA, 2021
BNP PARIBAS OPEN
Indian Wells, CA
WTA
Phone: 727-895-5000

Fax: 727-894-1982
feedback@wtatennis.com
www.wtatennis.com

TBA, 2021
BOBSLED EUROPEAN CUP
USA BOBSLED & SKELETON
FEDERATION
Phone: 518-523-1842
Fax: 518-523-9491
www.teamusa.org/USA-Bobsled-Skeleton
-Federation

TBA, 2021
BOBSLED NORTH AMERICAN CUP
USA BOBSLED & SKELETON
FEDERATION
Phone: 518-523-1842
Fax: 518-523-9491
www.teamusa.org/USA-Bobsled-Skeleton
-Federation

TBA, 2021
CALGARY NATIONAL BANK ATP
CHALLENGER 90
Calgary, Canada
TENNIS CANADA
Phone: 416-665-9777
Fax: 416-665-9017
info@tenniscanada.com
www.tenniscanada.com

TBA, 2021
DRUMMONDVILLE NATIONAL BANK
ATP CHALLENGER 80
Drummondville, Canada
TENNIS CANADA
Phone: 416-665-9777
Fax: 416-665-9017
info@tenniscanada.com
www.tenniscanada.com

TBA, 2021
ELITE MEN'S WORLD
CHAMPIONSHIPS
USA BOXING
Phone: 719-866-2323
www.teamusa.org/USA-Boxing

TBA, 2021
ELITE WOMEN'S WORLD
CHAMPIONSHIPS
USA BOXING
Phone: 719-866-2323
www.teamusa.org/USA-Boxing

TBA, 2021
EMIL JECHEV YOUTH MEMORIAL
TOURNAMENT
USA BOXING
Phone: 719-866-2323
www.teamusa.org/USA-Boxing

TBA, 2021
FIGURE INTERNATIONAL
Columbus, OH
Columbus Convention Center
ARNOLD SPORTS FESTIVAL
Phone: 614-431-2600
Fax: 614-431-3492
www.arnoldsportsfestival.com

TBA, 2021
FINA DIVING WORLD SERIES
MONTREAL
USA DIVING
Phone: 317-237-5252
Fax: 317-237-5257
Dan.Laak@usadiving.org
www.teamusa.org/USA-Diving

TBA, 2021
FINA GRAND PRIX MADRID
Madrid, Spain
USA DIVING
Phone: 317-237-5252
Fax: 317-237-5257
Dan.Laak@usadiving.org
www.teamusa.org/USA-Diving

TBA, 2021
FINA GRAND PRIX ROSTOCK
Madrid, Spain
USA DIVING
Phone: 317-237-5252
Fax: 317-237-5257
Dan.Laak@usadiving.org
www.teamusa.org/USA-Diving

TBA, 2021
FITNESS INTERNATIONAL
COMPETITION
Columbus, OH
Columbus Convention Center
ARNOLD SPORTS FESTIVAL
Phone: 614-431-2600
Fax: 614-431-3492
www.arnoldsportsfestival.com

TBA, 2021
GOLF CROQUET WORLD
CHAMPIONSHIP
US CROQUET ASSOCIATION
Phone: 561-478-0760
Fax: 561-686-5507
usca@msn.com
www.croquetamerica.com

TBA, 2021
NCAA DIVISION II FOOTBALL FINALS
McKinney, TX
McKinney ISD Stadium
NATIONAL COLLEGIATE ATHLETIC
ASSOCIATION
Phone: 317-917-6222
Fax: 317-917-6888
www.ncaa.org

TBA, 2021
NCAA DIVISION II MEN'S SOCCER
FINALS
NATIONAL COLLEGIATE ATHLETIC
ASSOCIATION
Phone: 317-917-6222
Fax: 317-917-6888
www.ncaa.org

TBA, 2021
NCAA DIVISION II MEN'S/WOMEN'S
CROSS COUNTRY FIN ALS
NATIONAL COLLEGIATE ATHLETIC
ASSOCIATION
Phone: 317-917-6222
Fax: 317-917-6888
www.ncaa.org

TBA, 2021
NCAA DIVISION II WOMEN'S
VOLLEYBALL FINALS
NATIONAL COLLEGIATE ATHLETIC
ASSOCIATION
Phone: 317-917-6222
Fax: 317-917-6888
www.ncaa.org

TBA, 2021
NCAA DIVISION III FOOTBALL FINALS
NATIONAL COLLEGIATE ATHLETIC
ASSOCIATION
Phone: 317-917-6222

events/meetings/shows

1275

Fax: 317-917-6888
www.ncaa.org

TBA, 2021
NCAA DIVISION III MEN'S
BASKETBALL FINALS
NATIONAL COLLEGIATE ATHLETIC
ASSOCIATION
Phone: 317-917-6222
Fax: 317-917-6888
www.ncaa.org

TBA, 2021
NCAA DIVISION III MEN'S ICE
HOCKEY FINALS
NATIONAL COLLEGIATE ATHLETIC
ASSOCIATION
Phone: 317-917-6222
Fax: 317-917-6888
www.ncaa.org

TBA, 2021
NCAA DIVISION III MEN'S SOCCER
FINALS
NATIONAL COLLEGIATE ATHLETIC
ASSOCIATION
Phone: 317-917-6222
Fax: 317-917-6888
www.ncaa.org

TBA, 2021
NCAA DIVISION III MEN'S
WRESTLING FINALS
NATIONAL COLLEGIATE ATHLETIC
ASSOCIATION
Phone: 317-917-6222
Fax: 317-917-6888
www.ncaa.org

TBA, 2021
NCAA DIVISION III MEN'S/WOMEN'S
CROSS COUNTRY FI NALS
NATIONAL COLLEGIATE ATHLETIC
ASSOCIATION
Phone: 317-917-6222
Fax: 317-917-6888
www.ncaa.org

TBA, 2021
NCAA DIVISION III MEN'S/WOMEN'S
SWIMMING & DIVIN G FINALS
NATIONAL COLLEGIATE ATHLETIC
ASSOCIATION
Phone: 317-917-6222
Fax: 317-917-6888
www.ncaa.org

TBA, 2021
NCAA DIVISION III MEN'S/WOMEN'S
TRACK, INDOOR FI NALS
NATIONAL COLLEGIATE ATHLETIC
ASSOCIATION
Phone: 317-917-6222
Fax: 317-917-6888
www.ncaa.org

TBA, 2021
NCAA DIVISION III WOMEN'S
BASKETBALL FINALS
NATIONAL COLLEGIATE ATHLETIC
ASSOCIATION
Phone: 317-917-6222
Fax: 317-917-6888
www.ncaa.org

TBA, 2021
NCAA DIVISION III WOMEN'S ICE
HOCKEY CHAMPIONSHI PS
NATIONAL COLLEGIATE ATHLETIC
ASSOCIATION
Phone: 317-917-6222

Fax: 317-917-6888
www.ncaa.org

TBA, 2021
NCAA DIVISION III WOMEN'S
SOCCER FINALS
NATIONAL COLLEGIATE ATHLETIC
ASSOCIATION
Phone: 317-917-6222
Fax: 317-917-6888
www.ncaa.org

TBA, 2021
NCAA DIVISION III WOMEN'S
VOLLEYBALL FINALS
NATIONAL COLLEGIATE ATHLETIC
ASSOCIATION
Phone: 317-917-6222
Fax: 317-917-6888
www.ncaa.org

TBA, 2021
NCAA NATIONAL COLLEGIATE
MEN'S GYMNASTICS FINALS
NATIONAL COLLEGIATE ATHLETIC
ASSOCIATION
Phone: 317-917-6222
Fax: 317-917-6888
www.ncaa.org

TBA, 2021
NCAA NATIONAL COLLEGIATE
MEN'S VOLLEYBALL SEMI-F INAL &
FINAL ROUNDS
NATIONAL COLLEGIATE ATHLETIC
ASSOCIATION
Phone: 317-917-6222
Fax: 317-917-6888
www.ncaa.org

TBA, 2021
NCAA NATIONAL COLLEGIATE
MEN'S WATER POLO FINALS
NATIONAL COLLEGIATE ATHLETIC
ASSOCIATION
Phone: 317-917-6222
Fax: 317-917-6888
www.ncaa.org

TBA, 2021
NMRA INTERNATIONAL
CHAMPIONSHIPS
USA RACQUETBALL
Phone: 719-635-5396
Fax: 719-635-0685
mwedel@usaracquetball.com
www.teamusa.org/USA-Racquetball

TBA, 2021
ORACLE CHALLENGER SERIES
Newport Beach, CA
WTA
Phone: 727-895-5000
Fax: 727-894-1982
feedback@wtatennis.com
www.wtatennis.com

TBA, 2021
ORACLE CHALLENGER SERIES
Indian Wells, CA
WTA
Phone: 727-895-5000
Fax: 727-894-1982
feedback@wtatennis.com
www.wtatennis.com

TBA, 2021
ORACLE CHALLENGER SERIES
New Haven, CT
WTA
Phone: 727-895-5000
Fax: 727-894-1982

feedback@wtatennis.com
www.wtatennis.com

TBA, 2021
ORACLE CHALLENGER SERIES
Houston, TX
WTA
Phone: 727-895-5000
Fax: 727-894-1982
feedback@wtatennis.com
www.wtatennis.com

TBA, 2021
RACE GUN NATIONALS
US PRACTICAL SHOOTING
ASSOCIATION
Phone: 360-855-2245
Fax: 360-855-0380
office@uspsa.org
www.uspsa.org

TBA, 2021
REVOLVER/L10 NATIONALS
Talladega, AL
US PRACTICAL SHOOTING
ASSOCIATION
Phone: 360-855-2245
Fax: 360-855-0380
office@uspsa.org
www.uspsa.org

TBA, 2021
SHENZHEN OPEN
Shenzhen, China
WTA
Phone: 727-895-5000
Fax: 727-894-1982
feedback@wtatennis.com
www.wtatennis.com

TBA, 2021
SILHOUETTE NATIONAL
CHAMPIONSHIPS - BLACK POWDER
RIFLE SCOPE
NATIONAL RIFLE ASSOCIATION -
COMPETITIVE SHOOTING DIVISION
Phone: 703-267-1465
competitions.nra.org

TBA, 2021
SILHOUETTE NATIONAL
CHAMPIONSHIPS - HIGH POWER
RIFLE
NATIONAL RIFLE ASSOCIATION -
COMPETITIVE SHOOTING DIVISION
Phone: 703-267-1465
competitions.nra.org

TBA, 2021
SILHOUETTE NATIONAL
CHAMPIONSHIPS - LEVER ACTION
RIFLE
NATIONAL RIFLE ASSOCIATION -
COMPETITIVE SHOOTING DIVISION
Phone: 703-267-1465
competitions.nra.org

TBA, 2021
SILHOUETTE NATIONAL
CHAMPIONSHIPS - SMALLBORE
RIFLE
Ridgway, PA
NATIONAL RIFLE ASSOCIATION -
COMPETITIVE SHOOTING DIVISION
Phone: 703-267-1465
competitions.nra.org

TBA, 2021
SPRING MASTERS NATIONAL
CHAMPIONSHIPS
USA DIVING
Phone: 317-237-5252

Fax: 317-237-5257
Dan.Laak@usadiving.org
www.teamusa.org/USA-Diving

TBA, 2021
STIHL TIMBERSPORTS CANADIAN
CHAMPIONSHIP
STIHL TIMBERSPORTS
www.stihlusa.com/stihl-timbersports

TBA, 2021
STIHL TIMBERSPORTS CHAMPIONS
TROPHY
STIHL TIMBERSPORTS
www.stihlusa.com/stihl-timbersports

TBA, 2021
STIHL TIMBERSPORTS WORLD
CHAMPIONSHIP
STIHL TIMBERSPORTS
www.stihlusa.com/stihl-timbersports

TBA, 2021
SUMMER MASTERS NATIONAL
CHAMPIONSHIPS
Mission Viejo, CA
USA DIVING
Phone: 317-237-5252
Fax: 317-237-5257
Dan.Laak@usadiving.org
www.teamusa.org/USA-Diving

TBA, 2021
THE WORLD GAMES
Birmingham, AL
THE WORLD GAMES
www.theworldgames.org

TBA, 2021
U19 WORLD CUP
INTERNATIONAL KORFBALL
FEDERATION
International Ph: 011-31-343-499655
International Fax: 011-31-343-499650
office@ikf.org
www.ikf.org

TBA, 2021
US FATHER-SON &
MOTHER-DAUGHTER SQUASH
DOUBLES C HAMPIONSHIPS
UNITED STATES SQUASH RACQUETS
ASSOCIATION
Phone: 212-268-4090
Fax: 212-268-4091
office@ussquash.com
www.ussquash.com

TBA, 2021
US REVOLUTION TOUR
TBA
U.S. SKI AND SNOWBOARD
ASSOCIATION
Phone: 435-649-9090
Fax: 435-649-3613
membership@usskiandsnowboard.org
usskiandsnowboard.org

TBA, 2021
USA BROOMBALL NATIONAL
CHAMPIONSHIPS
USA BROOMBALL
contact@usbabroomball.org
usbabroomball.org

TBA, 2021
USA RACQUETBALL NATIONAL
DOUBLES CHAMPIONSHIPS
USA RACQUETBALL
Phone: 719-635-5396
Fax: 719-635-0685

mwedel@usaracquetball.com
www.teamusa.org/USA-Racquetball

TBA, 2021
USA RACQUETBALL NATIONAL HIGH
SCHOOL CHAMPIONSHI PS
USA RACQUETBALL
Phone: 719-635-5396
Fax: 719-635-0685
mwedel@usaracquetball.com
www.teamusa.org/USA-Racquetball

TBA, 2021
USA RACQUETBALL NATIONAL
INTERCOLLEGIATE CHAMPIO
NSHIPS
USA RACQUETBALL
Phone: 719-635-5396
Fax: 719-635-0685
mwedel@usaracquetball.com
www.teamusa.org/USA-Racquetball

TBA, 2021
USA RACQUETBALL NATIONAL
JUNIOR CHAMPIONSHIPS
USA RACQUETBALL
Phone: 719-635-5396
Fax: 719-635-0685
mwedel@usaracquetball.com
www.teamusa.org/USA-Racquetball

TBA, 2021
USA RACQUETBALL NATIONAL
SINGLES CHAMPIONSHIPS
USA RACQUETBALL
Phone: 719-635-5396
Fax: 719-635-0685
mwedel@usaracquetball.com
www.teamusa.org/USA-Racquetball

TBA, 2021
USCA COLLEGIATE CHAMPIONSHIP
US CROQUET ASSOCIATION
Phone: 561-478-0760
Fax: 561-686-5507
usca@msn.com
www.croquetamerica.com

TBA, 2021
USCA MID-ATLANTIC REGIONAL
CHAMPIONSHIP
US CROQUET ASSOCIATION
Phone: 561-478-0760
Fax: 561-686-5507
usca@msn.com
www.croquetamerica.com

Jan TBA, 2021
NATIONAL CAPITAL DC OPEN
USA BADMINTON
Phone: 714-765-2952
usab@usabadminton.org
www.usabadminton.org

Jan 1, 2021
CHICK-FIL-A PEACH BOWL
Atlanta, GA
Mercedes-Benz Stadium
CHICK-FIL-A PEACH BOWL
Phone: 404-586-8500
Fax: 404-586-8508
tickets@cfabowl.com
www.chick-fil-apeachbowl.com

Jan 2 - Jan 3, 2021
AAU WINTER YOUTH NATIONALS
AMATEUR ATHLETIC UNION
Phone: 407-934-7200
Fax: 407-934-7242
www.aausports.org

Jan 2, 2021
FIESTA BOWL
Glendale, AZ
State Farm Stadium
FIESTA BOWL
Phone: 480-350-0900
Fax: 480-350-0915
prdept@fiestabowl.org
www.fiestabowl.org

Jan 2, 2021
PAPAGO 6 MTB RACE
Tempe, AZ
BLUEWOLF EVENTS

Jan 2, 2021
TAXSLAYER GATOR BOWL
Jacksonville, FL
Tiaa Bank Field
TAXSLAYER GATOR BOWL
Phone: 904-798-1700
Fax: 904-632-2080
tickets@taxslayerbowl.com
www.taxslayergatorbowl.com

Jan 4 - Jan 6, 2021
FLORIDA NON-WALKING SINGLES
Lakeland, FL
NATIONAL SHUFFLEBOARD
ASSOCIATION
usansa.weebly.com

Jan 6 - Jan 10, 2021
SENTRY TOURNAMENT OF
CHAMPIONS
Kapalua, HI
Plantation Course at Kapalua
PGA TOUR
Phone: 904-285-3700
www.pgatour.com

Jan 7 - Jan 10, 2021
2021 OK TIRE & BKT TIRES GROUP
CONTINENTAL CUP
Oakville, Canada
Sixteen Mile Sports Complex
CURLING CANADA
Phone: 613-834-2076
Fax: 613-834-0716
championships@curling.ca
www.curling.ca

Jan 7 - Jan 13, 2021
DELRAY BEACH OPEN
Delray Beach, FL
ATP TOUR 250
www.atptour.com

Jan 8 - Jan 10, 2021
2021 470 NORTH AMERICAN
CHAMPIONSHIPS
Miami, FL
Coconut Grove Sailing Club
WORLD SAILING
International Ph: 44 (0)20 3940 4888
www.sailing.org

Jan 11 - Jan 21, 2021
US FIGURE SKATING
CHAMPIONSHIPS
Las Vegas, NV
Orleans Arena
U.S. FIGURE SKATING
Phone: 719-635-5200
Fax: 719-635-9548
info@usfigureskating.org
www.usfigureskating.org

events/meetings/shows

Jan 14 - Jan 17, 2021
SONY OPEN IN HAWAII
Honolulu, HI
Waialae Country Club
PGA TOUR
Phone: 904-285-3700
www.pgatour.com

Jan 16, 2021
WOMEN'S 50+ NATIONALS
Philadelphia, PA
AMERICAN PLATFORM TENNIS
ASSOCIATION
Phone: 888-744-9490
apta@platformtennis.org
www.platformtennis.org

Jan 18 - Feb 18, 2021
CANADIAN YOUTH LONG TRACK
CHAMPIONSHIPS
SPEED SKATING CANADA
Phone: 613-260-3669
Fax: 613-260-3660
ssc@speedskating.ca
www.speedskating.ca

Jan 21 - Jan 24, 2021
ABU DHABI HSBC CHAMPIONSHIP
United Arab Emirates
Abu Dhabi Golf Club
PGA EUROPEAN TOUR
International Ph: 44-0-1344-840400
International Fax: 44-0-1344-840500
www.europeantour.com

Jan 21 - Jan 24, 2021
BALTIMORE BOAT SHOW
Baltimore, MD
Baltimore Convention Center
NATIONAL MARINE MANUFACTURERS
ASSOCIATION
Phone: 312-946-6200
Fax: 312-946-0401
www.nmma.org

Jan 21 - Jan 31, 2021
FISU WINTER UNIVERSIADE
Lucerne, Switzerland
FEDERATION INTERNATIONALE DU
SPORT UNIVERSIADE
International Ph: 41-0-216130810
International Fax: 41-0-216015612
fisu@fisu.net
www.fisu.net

Jan 21 - Jan 23, 2021
MITSUBISHI ELECTRIC
CHAMPIONSHIP AT HUALALAI
Ka'upulehu-Kona, HI
Hualalai Golf Course
PGA CHAMPIONS TOUR
Phone: 904-285-3700
www.pgatour.com/champions

Jan 25 - Jan 27, 2021
FLORIDA DOUBLES
Trailer Estates, FL
NATIONAL SHUFFLEBOARD
ASSOCIATION
usansa.weebly.com

Jan 28 - Jan 31, 2021
OMEGA DUBAI DESERT CLASSIC
Dubai, United Arab Emirates
Emirates Golf Club
PGA EUROPEAN TOUR
International Ph: 44-0-1344-840400
International Fax: 44-0-1344-840500
www.europeantour.com

Jan 30 - Jan 31, 2021
NFAA SOUTHERN INDOOR
SECTIONALS
NATIONAL FIELD ARCHERY
ASSOCIATION
Phone: 605-260-9279
info@nfaausa.com
www.nfaausa.com

Feb TBA, 2021
CALGARY WORLD CUP
Calgary, Canada
USA BOBSLED & SKELETON
FEDERATION
Phone: 518-523-1842
Fax: 518-523-9491
www.teamusa.org/USA-Bobsled-Skeleton
-Federation

Feb TBA, 2021
USHA NATIONAL COLLEGIATE
CHAMPIONSHIPS
UNITED STATES HANDBALL
ASSOCIATION
Phone: 520-795-0434
Fax: 520-795-0465
handball@ushandball.org
www.ushandball.org

Feb 1 - Feb 27, 2021
ADELAIDE INTERNATIONAL
Adelaide, Australia
WTA
Phone: 727-895-5000
Fax: 727-894-1982
feedback@wtatennis.com
www.wtatennis.com

Feb 2 - Feb 13, 2021
SPECIAL OLYMPICS WORLD WINTER
GAMES
TBA
SPECIAL OLYMPICS
Phone: 202-628-3630
Fax: 202-824-0200
cweir@specialolympics.org
www.specialolympics.org

Feb 4 - Feb 7, 2021
SAUDI INTERNATIONAL
King Abdullah Economic City, Saudi
Arabia
Royal Greens Golf & Country Club
PGA EUROPEAN TOUR
International Ph: 44-0-1344-840400
International Fax: 44-0-1344-840500
www.europeantour.com

Feb 4 - Feb 7, 2021
WASTE MANAGEMENT PHOENIX
OPEN
Scottsdale, AZ
TPC Scottsdale
PGA TOUR
Phone: 904-285-3700
www.pgatour.com

Feb 6 - Feb 9, 2021
ISPS HANDA VIC OPEN
Victoria, Australia
13th Beach Golf Links
LPGA TOUR
Phone: 386-274-6200
Fax: 386-274-1099
www.lpga.com

Feb 8 - Feb 21, 2021
AUSTRALIAN OPEN
Melbourne, Australia

TENNIS AUSTRALIA
International Ph: +61-3-9914-4677
www.tennis.com.au

Feb 8 - Feb 14, 2021
THAILAND OPEN
Hua Hin, Thailand
WTA
Phone: 727-895-5000
Fax: 727-894-1982
feedback@wtatennis.com
www.wtatennis.com

Feb 9, 2021
BUSCH CLASH
Daytona Beach, FL
Daytona International Speedway
NASCAR CUP SERIES
www.nascar.com

Feb 11 - Feb 14, 2021
AT&T PEBBLE BEACH NATIONAL
PRO-AM
Pebble Beach, CA
Pebble Beach Golf Links
PGA TOUR
Phone: 904-285-3700
www.pgatour.com

Feb 11 - Feb 14, 2021
BASSMASTER ELITE SERIES - ST.
JOHNS RIVER
Palatka, FL
St. Johns River
BASS ANGLERS SPORTSMAN
SOCIETY
Phone: 877-227-7872
bassmaster@emailcustomerservice.com
www.bassmaster.com

Feb 11, 2021
BLUEGREEN VACATIONS DUEL
DAYTONA 1&2
Daytona Beach, FL
Daytona International Speedway
NASCAR CUP SERIES
www.nascar.com

Feb 11 - Feb 16, 2021
ISPS HANDA WOMEN'S AUSTRALIAN
OPEN
Seaton, Australia
Royal Adelaide Golf Club
LPGA TOUR
Phone: 386-274-6200
Fax: 386-274-1099
www.lpga.com

Feb 11 - Feb 17, 2021
MAG CANADIAN GYMNASTIC
CHAMPIONSHIPS
GYMNASTICS CANADA GYMNASTIQUE
Phone: 613-748-5637
Fax: 613-748-5691
info@gymcan.org
www.gymcan.org

Feb 12 - Feb 14, 2021
NFAA RUSHMORE RUMBLE
Yankton, SD
Easton Yankton Archery Center
NATIONAL FIELD ARCHERY
ASSOCIATION
Phone: 605-260-9279
info@nfaausa.com
www.nfaausa.com

Feb 13, 2021
SAN MIGUEL BUZZ MARATHON
San Miguel, CA

Camp Roberts Army National Guard
Reservation
SAN MIGUEL BUZZ MARATHON
Phone: 805-467-3216
Fax: 805-467-3410
www.buzzmarathon.org

Feb 14, 2021
DAYTONA 500
Daytona Beach, FL
Daytona International Speedway
NASCAR CUP SERIES
www.nascar.com

Feb 15, 2021
NEXTERA ENERGY 250
Daytona Beach, FL
Daytona International Speedway
NASCAR CAMPING WORLD TRUCK
SERIES
Phone: 800-630-0535
www.nascar.com

Feb 18 - Feb 21, 2021
GENESIS INVITATIONAL
Pacific Palisades, CA
Riviera Country Club
PGA TOUR
Phone: 904-285-3700
www.pgatour.com

Feb 18 - Feb 21, 2021
LECOM SUNCOAST CLASSIC
Lakewood Ranch, FL
Lakewood National Golf Club
PGA KORN FERRY TOUR
Phone: 904-285-3700
Fax: 904-285-7913
www.pgatour.com

Feb 19 - Feb 20, 2021
PASCO COUNTY FAIR
CHAMPIONSHIP RODEO
Dade City, FL
PROFESSIONAL RODEO COWBOY
ASSOCIATION
Phone: 719-593-8840
Fax: 719-548-4876
prorodeor@prorodeo.com
www.prorodeo.com

Feb 20 - Feb 21, 2021
NFAA MIDWEST INDOOR
SECTIONALS
NATIONAL FIELD ARCHERY
ASSOCIATION
Phone: 605-260-9279
info@nfaausa.com
www.nfaausa.com

Feb 22 - Mar 28, 2021
CANADIAN YOUTH SHORT TRACK
CHAMPIONSHIPS
SPEED SKATING CANADA
Phone: 613-260-3669
Fax: 613-260-3660
ssc@speedskating.ca
www.speedskating.ca

Feb 25, 2021
AKC POINTING BREED GUN DOG
CHAMPIONSHIP
Sonoita, AZ
Empire Ranch
AMERICAN KENNEL CLUB
Phone: 919-233-9767
Fax: 919-816-4246
info@akc.org
www.akc.org

Feb 25, 2021
AKC POINTING BREED WALKING
GUN DOG CHAMPIONSHIP
Sonoita, AZ
Empire Ranch
AMERICAN KENNEL CLUB
Phone: 919-233-9767
Fax: 919-816-4246
info@akc.org
www.akc.org

Feb 25 - Feb 28, 2021
BASSMASTER ELITE SERIES -
TENNESSEE RIVER
Knoxville, TN
Tennessee River
BASS ANGLERS SPORTSMAN
SOCIETY
Phone: 877-227-7872
bassmaster@emailcustomerservice.com
www.bassmaster.com

Feb 25 - Feb 28, 2021
HOYT ARCHERY ALABAMA PRO/AM
Foley, AL
Graham Creek Nature Preserve
ARCHERY SHOOTERS ASSOCIATION
Phone: 770-795-0232
Fax: 770-795-0953
info@asaarchery.com
www.asaarchery.com

Feb 25 - Feb 28, 2021
PUERTO RICO OPEN
Rio Grande, Puerto Rico
Coco Beach Golf & Country Club
PGA TOUR
Phone: 904-285-3700
www.pgatour.com

Feb 25 - Feb 28, 2021
WGC MEXICO CHAMPIONSHIP
Mexico City, Mexico
Club de Golf Chapultepec
PGA TOUR
Phone: 904-285-3700
www.pgatour.com

Feb 26 - Feb 28, 2021
COLOGUARD CLASSIC
Tucson, AZ
Omni Tucson National
PGA CHAMPIONS TOUR
Phone: 904-285-3700
www.pgatour.com/champions

Feb 26 - Feb 28, 2021
MEN'S 45+/55+/65+ NATIONALS
Wilmington, DE
AMERICAN PLATFORM TENNIS
ASSOCIATION
Phone: 888-744-9490
apta@platformtennis.org
www.platformtennis.org

Feb 26, 2021
NASTIA LIUKIN CUP
Milwaukee, WN
Fiserv Forum
USA GYMNASTICS
Phone: 317-237-5050
Fax: 317-237-5069
membership@usagym.org
usagym.org

Feb 27 - Feb 28, 2021
NFAA GREAT LAKES INDOOR
SECTIONALS
NATIONAL FIELD ARCHERY
ASSOCIATION

Phone: 605-260-9279
info@nfaausa.com
www.nfaausa.com

Feb 27 - Mar 7, 2021
NFAA SOUTHEAST INDOOR
SECTIONALS
NATIONAL FIELD ARCHERY
ASSOCIATION
Phone: 605-260-9279
info@nfaausa.com
www.nfaausa.com

Feb 28, 2021
DIXIE VODKA 400
Homestead, FL
Homestead-Miami Speedway
NASCAR CUP SERIES
www.nascar.com

Feb 28, 2021
WOMEN'S 60+ NATIONALS
Wilmington, DE
AMERICAN PLATFORM TENNIS
ASSOCIATION
Phone: 888-744-9490
apta@platformtennis.org
www.platformtennis.org

Mar TBA, 2021
COLOMBIAN SPEEDSKATING
CHAMPIONSHIPS
Colorado Springs, CO
US SPEEDSKATING
Phone: 801-417-5360
Fax: 801-417-5361
www.teamusa.org/us-speedskating

Mar TBA, 2021
ELITE BMX NATIONAL
CHAMPIONSHIPS
Houston, TX
USA CYCLING
Phone: 719-434-4200
Fax: 719-434-4300
help@usacycling.org
www.usacycling.org

Mar TBA, 2021
FASTENAL PARALLEL 45 FIS CROSS
COUNTRY WORLD CUP
Minneapolis, MN
U.S. SKI AND SNOWBOARD
ASSOCIATION
Phone: 435-649-9090
Fax: 435-649-3613
membership@usskiandsnowboard.org
usskiandsnowboard.org

Mar TBA, 2021
HARBOUR POINTE OPEN LOCAL
CHAMPIONSHIP
Mukilteo, WA
USA BADMINTON
Phone: 714-765-2952
usab@usabadminton.org
www.usabadminton.org

Mar TBA, 2021
OMAEZAKI CUP
Omaezaki City, Shizuoka, Japan
Omaezaki Long Beach
INTERNATIONAL WINDSURFING TOUR
internationalwindsurfingtour.com

Mar TBA, 2021
USA BOXING MASTER'S NATIONAL
CHAMPIONSHIPS
Reno, NV

USA BOXING
Phone: 719-866-2323
www.teamusa.org/USA-Boxing

Mar TBA, 2021
USHA MASTERS SINGLES
INVITATIONAL
UNITED STATES HANDBALL
ASSOCIATION
Phone: 520-795-0434
Fax: 520-795-0465
handball@ushandball.org
www.ushandball.org

Mar TBA, 2021
WESTERN QUALIFIER
Reno, NV
USA BOXING
Phone: 719-866-2323
www.teamusa.org/USA-Boxing

Mar 1 - Mar 7, 2021
OPEN 6EM SENS - METROPOLE DE
LYON, FRANCE
Lyon, France
WTA
Phone: 727-895-5000
Fax: 727-894-1982
feedback@wtatennis.com
www.wtatennis.com

Mar 1 - Mar 3, 2021
PARA WORLD CHAMPIONSHIPS
La Plagne, France
USA BOBSLED & SKELETON
FEDERATION
Phone: 518-523-1842
Fax: 518-523-9491
www.teamusa.org/USA-Bobsled-Skeleton
-Federation

Mar 1 - Mar 6, 2021
QATAR TOTAL OPEN
Doha, Qatar
WTA
Phone: 727-895-5000
Fax: 727-894-1982
feedback@wtatennis.com
www.wtatennis.com

Mar 2 - Mar 11, 2021
FIS JUNIOR WORLD CHAMPIONSHIP
Narvik, Norway
FIS SKIING CHAMPIONSHIPS
International Ph: 44-33-244-6161
International Fax: 44-33-244-6171
mail@fisski.ch
www.fis-ski.com

Mar 4 - Mar 6, 2021
BASSMASTER OPENS CENTRAL
OPEN - HARRIS CHAIN OF LAKES
Leesburg, FL
Harris Chain of Lakes
BASS ANGLERS SPORTSMAN
SOCIETY
Phone: 877-227-7872
bassmaster@emailcustomerservice.com
www.bassmaster.com

Mar 4 - Mar 7, 2021
OMAN OPEN
Muscat, Oman
Al Mouj Golf
PGA EUROPEAN TOUR
International Ph: 44-0-1344-840400
International Fax: 44-0-1344-840500
www.europeantour.com

Mar 5 - Mar 7, 2021
EASTERN ADULT SECTIONAL
CHAMPIONSHIPS
Ardmore, PA
U.S. FIGURE SKATING
Phone: 719-635-5200
Fax: 719-635-9548
info@usfigureskating.org
www.usfigureskating.org

Mar 5 - Mar 7, 2021
NFAA MIDATLANTIC INDOOR
SECTIONALS
NATIONAL FIELD ARCHERY
ASSOCIATION
Phone: 605-260-9279
info@nfaausa.com
www.nfaausa.com

Mar 5 - Mar 7, 2021
PACIFIC COAST ADULT SECTIONAL
CHAMPIONSHIPS
Las Vegas, NV
U.S. FIGURE SKATING
Phone: 719-635-5200
Fax: 719-635-9548
info@usfigureskating.org
www.usfigureskating.org

Mar 5 - Mar 14, 2021
TIM HORTONS BRIER
Calgary, Canada
Winsport Arena
CURLING CANADA
Phone: 613-834-2076
Fax: 613-834-0716
championships@curling.ca
www.curling.ca

Mar 6 - Mar 7, 2021
AAU VOLLEYBALL CLASSIC
Orlando, FL
AMATEUR ATHLETIC UNION
Phone: 407-934-7200
Fax: 407-934-7242
www.aausports.org

Mar 6 - Mar 20, 2021
DUBAI DUTY FREE TENNIS
CHAMPIONSHIPS
Dubai, United Arab Emirates
Dubai Duty Free Tennis Stadium
ATP WORLD TOUR 500
www.atpworldtour.com

Mar 6 - Mar 20, 2021
DUBAI DUTY FREE TENNIS
CHAMPIONSHIPS
Dubai, UAE
WTA
Phone: 727-895-5000
Fax: 727-894-1982
feedback@wtatennis.com
www.wtatennis.com

Mar 6 - Mar 13, 2021
WORLD WHEELCHAIR
CHAMPIONSHIP
Beijing, China
USA CURLING
Phone: 715-344-1199
Fax: 715-344-2279
info@usacurl.org
www.teamusa.org/USA-Curling

Mar 7, 2021
CRASH-B SPRINTS WORLD INDOOR
ROWING CHAMPIONSHIP
Boston, MA

Boston University Track and Tennis
Center
CRASH-B SPRINTS
office@crash-b.org
www.crash-b.org

Mar 7, 2021
PENNZOIL 400
Las Vegas, NV
Las Vegas Motor Speedway
NASCAR CUP SERIES
www.nascar.com

Mar 8 - Mar 13, 2021
ABIERTO ZAPOPAN 2021
Zapopan, Mexico
WTA
Phone: 727-895-5000
Fax: 727-894-1982
feedback@wtatennis.com
www.wtatennis.com

Mar 9, 2021
DAYTONA ATV SUPERCROSS
Daytona, FL
Daytona International Speedway
AMA PRO RACING
Phone: 386-492-1014
Fax: 386-274-2335
communications@amaproracing.com
www.amaproracing.com

Mar 10 - Mar 14, 2021
COMMERCIAL BANK QATAR
MASTERS
Doha, Quatar
Education City Golf Club
PGA EUROPEAN TOUR
International Ph: 44-0-1344-840400
International Fax: 44-0-1344-840500
www.europeantour.com

Mar 11 - Mar 14, 2021
AMALIE MOTOR OIL NHRA
GATORNATIONALS
Gainesville, FL
Gainesville Raceway
NATIONAL HOT ROD ASSOCIATION
Phone: 626-914-4761
Fax: 626-963-5360
nhra@nhra.com
www.nhra.com

Mar 11 - Mar 14, 2021
ARCADIA ALL-FLORIDA
CHAMPIONSHIP RODEO
Arcadia, FL
PROFESSIONAL RODEO COWBOY
ASSOCIATION
Phone: 719-593-8840
Fax: 719-548-4876
prorodeor@prorodeo.com
www.prorodeo.com

Mar 11 - Mar 21, 2021
ATP TOUR MASTERS 1000 - BNP
PARIBAS OPEN
Indian Wells, CA
ATP TOUR MASTERS 1000
www.atptour.com

Mar 11 - Mar 13, 2021
NCAA DIVISION I MEN'S/WOMEN'S
TRACK, INDOOR FINA LS
Fayetteville, AR
Randal Tyson Center
NATIONAL COLLEGIATE ATHLETIC
ASSOCIATION
Phone: 317-917-6222
Fax: 317-917-6888
www.ncaa.org

Mar 11 - Mar 13, 2021
NCAA DIVISION II MEN'S/WOMEN'S
TRACK, INDOOR FIN ALS
Birmingham, AL
Birmingham CrossPlex
NATIONAL COLLEGIATE ATHLETIC
ASSOCIATION
Phone: 317-917-6222
Fax: 317-917-6888
www.ncaa.org

Mar 11 - Mar 14, 2021
THE PLAYERS CHAMPIONSHIP
Ponte Vedra Beach, FL
TPC Sawgrass
PGA TOUR
Phone: 904-285-3700
www.pgatour.com

Mar 12 - Mar 14, 2021
AAU INDOOR TRACK & FIELD
NATIONAL CHAMPIONSHIP
Landover, MD
PG Sports and Learning Center
AMATEUR ATHLETIC UNION
Phone: 407-934-7200
Fax: 407-934-7242
www.aausports.org

Mar 12 - Mar 14, 2021
MIDWESTERN ADULT SECTIONAL
CHAMPIONSHIPS
Fort Wayne, IN
U.S. FIGURE SKATING
Phone: 719-635-5200
Fax: 719-635-9548
info@usfigureskating.org
www.usfigureskating.org

Mar 12 - Mar 13, 2021
NCAA DIVISION II WRESTLING
FINALS
St. Louis, MO
America's Center Convention Complex
NATIONAL COLLEGIATE ATHLETIC
ASSOCIATION
Phone: 317-917-6222
Fax: 317-917-6888
www.ncaa.org

Mar 12 - Mar Mar 14, 2021
NFAA NEW ENGLAND INDOOR
SECTIONALS
NATIONAL FIELD ARCHERY
ASSOCIATION
Phone: 605-260-9279
info@nfaausa.com
www.nfaausa.com

Mar 12 - Apr 12, 2021
THE VEGAS SHOOT-WORLD
ARCHERY FESTIVAL
Las Vegas, NV
NATIONAL FIELD ARCHERY
ASSOCIATION
Phone: 605-260-9279
info@nfaausa.com
www.nfaausa.com

Mar 12 - Mar 13, 2021
VOLUSIA HALF-MILE I & II
Barberville, FL
Volusia Speedway Park
AMA PRO RACING
Phone: 386-492-1014
Fax: 386-274-2335
communications@amaproracing.com
www.amaproracing.com

Mar 13 - Mar 27, 2021
BAYOU CITY CLASSIC
Houston, TX
HOUSTON AREA ROAD RUNNERS
ASSOCIATION
www.bayoucityclassic.org

Mar 13, 2021
BEL MONTE ENDURANCE RACES
Blue Ridge Mouuntains, VA
BAD TO THE BONE
Phone: 434-218-0402
francesca@badtothebone.biz
badtothebone.biz

Mar 14, 2021
BIG ISLAND MARATHON
Hilo, HI
BIG ISLAND INTERNATIONAL
MARATHON
Phone: 808-969-7400
www.hilomarathon.org

Mar 14, 2021
INSTACART 500
Phoenix, AZ
Phoenix Raceway
NASCAR CUP SERIES
www.nascar.com

Mar 14 - Mar 17, 2021
NRA INTERCOLLEGIATE PISTOL
CHAMPIONSHIPS
Ft. Benning, GA
NATIONAL RIFLE ASSOCIATION -
COMPETITIVE SHOOTING DIVISION
Phone: 703-267-1465
competitions.nra.org

Mar 12 - Mar 15, 2021
ABIERTO GNP SEGUROS
Monterrey, Mexico
WTA
Phone: 727-895-5000
Fax: 727-894-1982
feedback@wtatennis.com
www.wtatennis.com

Mar 15 - Mar 20, 2021
ABIERTO MEXICANO
Acapulco, Gro, Mexico
Princess Mundo Imperial
ATP WORLD TOUR 500
www.atpworldtour.com

Mar 15 - Mar 20, 2021
ABIERTO MEXICANO TELCEL
PRESENTADO POR HSBC
Acapulco, Mexico
WTA
Phone: 727-895-5000
Fax: 727-894-1982
feedback@wtatennis.com
www.wtatennis.com

Mar 15, 2021
NCAA DIVISION I MEN'S CROSS
COUNTRY FINALS
Stillwater, OK
OSU Cross Country Course
NATIONAL COLLEGIATE ATHLETIC
ASSOCIATION
Phone: 317-917-6222
Fax: 317-917-6888
www.ncaa.org

Mar 15 - Mar 21, 2021
ST. PETERSBURG LADIES TROPHY
St. Petersburg, Russia
WTA
Phone: 727-895-5000

Fax: 727-894-1982
feedback@wtatennis.com
www.wtatennis.com

Mar 17 - Mar 20, 2021
NCAA DIVISION I WOMEN'S
SWIMMING & DIVING FINALS
Greensboro, NC
Greensboro Aquatic Center
NATIONAL COLLEGIATE ATHLETIC
ASSOCIATION
Phone: 317-917-6222
Fax: 317-917-6888
www.ncaa.org

Mar 17 - Mar 20, 2021
NCAA DIVISION II MEN/WOMEN'S
SWIMMING & DIVING F INALS
Birmingham, AL
Birmingham CrossPlex
NATIONAL COLLEGIATE ATHLETIC
ASSOCIATION
Phone: 317-917-6222
Fax: 317-917-6888
www.ncaa.org

Mar 17 - Mar 24, 2021
RG CANADIAN GYMNASTIC
CHAMPIONSHIPS
GYMNASTICS CANADA GYMNASTIQUE
Phone: 613-748-5637
Fax: 613-748-5691
info@gymcan.org
www.gymcan.org

Mar 18 - Mar 21, 2021
BASSMASTER ELITE SERIES -
PICKWICK LAKE
Florence, AL
Pickwick Lake
BASS ANGLERS SPORTSMAN
SOCIETY
Phone: 877-227-7872
bassmaster@emailcustomerservice.com
www.bassmaster.com

Mar 18 - Mar 21, 2021
CHITIMACHA LOUISIANA OPEN
Broussard, Louisiana
Le Triomphe Country Club
PGA KORN FERRY TOUR
Phone: 904-285-3700
Fax: 904-285-7913
www.pgatour.com

Mar 18 - Mar 21, 2021
KENYA OPEN
Nairobi, Kenya
Karen Country Club
PGA EUROPEAN TOUR
International Ph: 44-0-1344-840400
International Fax: 44-0-1344-840500
www.europeantour.com

Mar 18 - Mar 25, 2021
MIXED DOUBLES CHAMPIONSHIP
Calgary, Canada
Winsport Arena
CURLING CANADA
Phone: 613-834-2076
Fax: 613-834-0716
championships@curling.ca
www.curling.ca

Mar 18 - Mar 20, 2021
NCAA DIVISION I WRESTLING
FINALS
St. Louis, MO
Enterprise Center
NATIONAL COLLEGIATE ATHLETIC
ASSOCIATION

events/meetings/shows

Phone: 317-917-6222
Fax: 317-917-6888
www.ncaa.org

Mar 18 - Mar 21, 2021
THE HONDA CLASSIC
Palm Beach Gardens, FL
PGA National Champion Course
PGA TOUR
Phone: 904-285-3700
www.pgatour.com

Mar 19 - Mar 20, 2021
AAU FOLKSTYLE WORLD
CHAMPIONSHIP
Spearfish, SD
AMATEUR ATHLETIC UNION
Phone: 407-934-7200
Fax: 407-934-7242
www.aausports.org

Mar 19 - Mar 20, 2021
AAU SPRING YOUTH NATIONALS
Kingsport, TX
TNT Sportplex
AMATEUR ATHLETIC UNION
Phone: 407-934-7200
Fax: 407-934-7242
www.aausports.org

Mar 19 - Mar 21, 2021
NFAA INDOOR NATIONAL
CHAMPIONSHIPS
NATIONAL FIELD ARCHERY
ASSOCIATION
Phone: 605-260-9279
info@nfaausa.com
www.nfaausa.com

Mar 19 - Mar 21, 2021
YUENGLING SHAMROCK MARATHON
Virginia Beach, VA
SHAMROCK MARATHON
Phone: 757-412-1056
Fax: 757-412-1058
info@shamrockmarathon.com
www.shamrockmarathon.com

Mar 20, 2021
FR8AUCTIONS 200
Hampton, GA
Atlanta Motor Speedway
NASCAR CAMPING WORLD TRUCK
SERIES
Phone: 800-630-0535
www.nascar.com

Mar 20 - Mar 22, 2021
NRA INTERCOLLEGIATE RIFLE CLUB
CHAMPIONSHIPS
Ft. Benning, GA
NATIONAL RIFLE ASSOCIATION -
COMPETITIVE SHOOTING DIVISION
Phone: 703-267-1465
competitions.nra.org

Mar 20 - Jun 30, 2021
SUNSHINE STATE GAMES
Various
SUNSHINE STATE GAMES
Phone: 850-577-7200
info@playinflorida.com
playinflorida.com

Mar 21, 2021
FOLDS OF HONOR QUIKTRIP 500
Hampton, GA
Atlanta Motor Speedway
NASCAR CUP SERIES
www.nascar.com

Mar 22 - Mar 28, 2021
FIGURE SKATING WORLD
CHAMPIONSHIPS
Stockholm, Sweden
U.S. FIGURE SKATING
Phone: 719-635-5200
Fax: 719-635-9548
info@usfigureskating.org
www.usfigureskating.org

Mar 22 - Apr 4, 2021
MIAMI OPEN PRESENTED BY ITAU
Miami, FL
WTA
Phone: 727-895-5000
Fax: 727-894-1982
feedback@wtatennis.com
www.wtatennis.com

Mar 22 - Mar 28, 2021
SAVANNAH GOLF CHAMPIONSHIP
Savannah, GA
Deer Creek Golf Club
PGA KORN FERRY TOUR
Phone: 904-285-3700
Fax: 904-285-7913
www.pgatour.com

Mar 23 - Mar 26, 2021
NCAA DIVISION II WOMEN'S
BASKETBALL FINALS
Columbus, OH
Greater Columbus Convention
NATIONAL COLLEGIATE ATHLETIC
ASSOCIATION
Phone: 317-917-6222
Fax: 317-917-6888
www.ncaa.org

Mar 24, 2021
ALL STAR CHAMPIONSHIPS
Anaheim, CA
Anaheim Convention Center
UNITED SPIRIT ASSOCIATION
Phone: 800-886-4872
Fax: 866-761-9365
info@usacamps.com
usa.varsity.com

Mar 24 - Apr 4, 2021
ATP TOUR MASTERS 1000 - MIAMI
OPEN
Miami, FL
ATP TOUR MASTERS 1000
www.atptour.com

Mar 24 - Mar 27, 2021
NCAA DIVISION I MEN'S SWIMMING &
DIVING FINALS
Greensboro, NC
Greensboro Aquatic Center
NATIONAL COLLEGIATE ATHLETIC
ASSOCIATION
Phone: 317-917-6222
Fax: 317-917-6888
www.ncaa.org

Mar 24 - Mar 27, 2021
NCAA DIVISION II MEN'S
BASKETBALL FINALS
Evansville, IN
Ford Center
NATIONAL COLLEGIATE ATHLETIC
ASSOCIATION
Phone: 317-917-6222
Fax: 317-917-6888
www.ncaa.org

Mar 24 - Mar 28, 2021
NORTH AMERICAN & US BIATHLON
CHAMPIONSHIPS
West Yellowstone, MT
UNITED STATES BIATHLON
ASSOCIATION
Phone: 207-688-6500
Fax: 207-688-6505
info@usbiathlon.org
www.usbiathlon.org

Mar 24 - Mar 28, 2021
WGC-DELL TECHNOLOGIES MATCH
PLAY
Austin, TX
Austin Country Club
PGA TOUR
Phone: 904-285-3700
www.pgatour.com

Mar 25 - Mar 28, 2021
KIA CLASSIC
Carlsbad, CA
Aviara Golf Club
LPGA TOUR
Phone: 386-274-6200
Fax: 386-274-1099
www.lpga.com

Mar 25 - Mar 31, 2021
WAG CANADIAN GYMNASTIC
CHAMPIONSHIPS
GYMNASTICS CANADA GYMNASTIQUE
Phone: 613-748-5637
Fax: 613-748-5691
info@gymcan.org
www.gymcan.org

Mar 26 - Mar 28, 2021
AKC NATIONAL AGILITY
CHAMPIONSHIPS
Tulsa, OK
Tulsa Expo Centre
AMERICAN KENNEL CLUB
Phone: 919-233-9767
Fax: 919-816-4246
info@akc.org
www.akc.org

Mar 26 - Mar 28, 2021
MIXED NATIONALS
Rye, NY
AMERICAN PLATFORM TENNIS
ASSOCIATION
Phone: 888-744-9490
apta@platformtennis.org
www.platformtennis.org

Mar 26 - Mar 27, 2021
USA GYMNASTICS MEN'S
COLLEGIATE CHAMPIONSHIPS
Springfield, MA
USA GYMNASTICS
Phone: 317-237-5050
Fax: 317-237-5069
membership@usagym.org
usagym.org

Mar 27, 2021
GOLDEN GATE HEADLANDS
MARATHON, HALF MARATHON & 10K
Sausalito, CA
Fort Barry, Golden Gate National
Recreation Area
ENVIRO-SPORTS
Phone: 415-868-1829
info@envirosports.com
envirosports.com

Mar 27 - Apr 17, 2021
STATE GAMES OF MISSISSIPPI
Meridian, MS
STATE GAMES OF MISSISSIPPI
Phone: 601-482-0205
info@stategamesofms.org
www.stategamesofms.org

Mar 28, 2021
AUSTRALASIAN CHAMPIONSHIPS
Sydney, Australia
INTERNATIONAL FEDERATION OF
BODY BUILDING & FITNESS
International Ph: 34-91-535-28-19
contact@ifbb.com
www.ifbb.com

Mar 28, 2021
FOOD CITY DIRT RACE
Bristol, TN
Bristol Motor Speedway
NASCAR CUP SERIES
www.nascar.com

Mar 29 - Apr 4, 2021
VALERO TEXAS OPEN
San Antonio, TX
TPC San Antonio
PGA TOUR
Phone: 904-285-3700
www.pgatour.com

Apr TBA, 2021
BILLIE JEAN KING CUP
Switzerland
TENNIS CANADA
Phone: 416-665-9777
Fax: 416-665-9017
info@tenniscanada.com
www.tenniscanada.com

Apr TBA, 2021
COLLEGIATE BMX NATIONAL
CHAMPIONSHIPS
TBA
USA CYCLING
Phone: 719-434-4200
Fax: 719-434-4300
help@usacycling.org
www.usacycling.org

Apr TBA, 2021
DAVIS CUP QUARTERFINALS
INTERNATIONAL TENNIS FEDERATION
International Ph: +44 (0)20 88786464
International Fax: +44 (0)20 88787799
communications@itftennis.com
www.itftennis.com

Apr TBA, 2021
TOPOCALMA INFERNAL
Topocalma, Chile
INTERNATIONAL WINDSURFING TOUR
internationalwindsurfingtour.com

Apr 1 - Apr 4, 2021
ANA INSPIRATION
Rancho Mirage, CA
Mission Hills Country Club
LPGA TOUR
Phone: 386-274-6200
Fax: 386-274-1099
www.lpga.com

Apr 1 - Apr 3, 2021
BASSMASTER OPENS CENTRAL
OPEN - LEWIS SMITH LAKE
Jasper, AL
Lewis Smith Lake
BASS ANGLERS SPORTSMAN
SOCIETY

Phone: 877-227-7872
bassmaster@emailcustomerservice.com
www.bassmaster.com

Apr 1- Apr 30, 2021
MAUI MARATHON
Maui, HI
MAUI MARATHON
Phone: 808-222-2484
mauimarathonexpor@gmail.com
www.mauimarathon.com

Apr 2 - Apr 4, 2021
NCAA DIVISION I WOMEN'S
BASKETBALL FINALS
San Antonio, TX
Alamodome
NATIONAL COLLEGIATE ATHLETIC
ASSOCIATION
Phone: 317-917-6222
Fax: 317-917-6888
www.ncaa.org

Apr 2 - Apr 5, 2021
SIBERIAN POWER SHOW
Krasnoyarsk, Russia
INTERNATIONAL FEDERATION OF
BODY BUILDING & FITNESS
International Ph: 34-91-535-28-19
contact@ifbb.com
www.ifbb.com

Apr 2 - Apr 11, 2021
WORLD MEN'S CHAMPIONSHIP
Calgary, Canada
USA CURLING
Phone: 715-344-1199
Fax: 715-344-2279
info@usacurl.org
www.teamusa.org/USA-Curling

Apr 3, 2021
ANDREW JACKSON MARATHON
Jackson, TN
ANDREW JACKSON MARATHON
danny@crossett.com

Apr 3 - Apr 5, 2021
NCAA DIVISION I MEN'S
BASKETBALL FINALS
Indianapolis, IN
Lucas Oil Stadium
NATIONAL COLLEGIATE ATHLETIC
ASSOCIATION
Phone: 317-917-6222
Fax: 317-917-6888
www.ncaa.org

Apr 3, 2021
ROCKIN K TRAIL MARATHON
Ellsworth, KS
Kanapolis State Park
KANSAS ULTRARUNNERS' SOCIETY
www.ksultrarunners.org

Apr 3 - Apr 11, 2021
VOLVO CAR OPEN
Charleston, SC
WTA
Phone: 727-895-5000
Fax: 727-894-1982
feedback@wtatennis.com
www.wtatennis.com

Apr 3 - Apr 11, 2021
WORLD MEN'S CURLING
CHAMPIONSHIP
Calgary, Canada
CURLING CANADA
Phone: 613-834-2076
Fax: 613-834-0716

championships@curling.ca
www.curling.ca

Apr 4, 2021
ANNUAL REZ RUN 5K+
St. Louis, MO
FIRST BAPTIST CHURCH OF
CRESTWOOD
Phone: 314-843-1130
fbccrestwood@gmail.com

Apr 5 - Apr 11, 2021
COPA COLSANITAS
Bogota, Colombia
WTA
Phone: 727-895-5000
Fax: 727-894-1982
feedback@wtatennis.com
www.wtatennis.com

Apr 5 - Apr 11, 2021
MASTERS TOURNAMENT
Augusta, GA
Augusta National Golf Club
PGA TOUR
Phone: 904-285-3700
www.pgatour.com

Apr 8 - Apr 11, 2021
BASSMASTER ELITE SERIES -
SABINE RIVER
Orange, TX
Sabine River
BASS ANGLERS SPORTSMAN
SOCIETY
Phone: 877-227-7872
bassmaster@emailcustomerservice.com
www.bassmaster.com

Apr 8 - Apr 10, 2021
NCAA DIVISION I MEN'S ICE HOCKEY
FINALS
Pittsburg, PA
PPG Paints Arena
NATIONAL COLLEGIATE ATHLETIC
ASSOCIATION
Phone: 317-917-6222
Fax: 317-917-6888
www.ncaa.org

Apr 8 - Apr 11, 2021
TYR PRO SWIM SERIES MISSION
VIEJO
Mission Viejo, CA
USA SWIMMING
Phone: 719-866-4578
Fax: 719-866-4049
imclemore@usaswimming.org
www.usaswimming.org

Apr 9 - Apr 11, 2021
AAU DRUG FREE NORTH AMERICAN
BODYBUILDING & FITN ESS
CHAMPIONSHIPS
Laughlin, NV
Harrah's Resort Hotel Casino
AMATEUR ATHLETIC UNION
Phone: 407-934-7200
Fax: 407-934-7242
www.aausports.org

Apr 9 - Apr 11, 2021
LUCAS OIL NHRA
WINTERNATIONALS
Pomona, CA
Auto Club Raceway at Pomona
NATIONAL HOT ROD ASSOCIATION
Phone: 626-914-4761
Fax: 626-963-5360
nhra@nhra.com
www.nhra.com

events/meetings/shows

Apr 10, 2021
AAU ORCHARD POWERLIFTING
MEET
Orchard, NE
AMATEUR ATHLETIC UNION
Phone: 407-934-7200
Fax: 407-934-7242
www.aausports.org

Apr 10, 2021
CHARLOTTESVILLE MARATHON
Charlottesville, VA
BAD TO THE BONE
Phone: 434-218-0402
francesca@badtothebone.biz
badtothebone.biz

Apr 10 - Apr 11, 2021
GO ST. LOUIS MARATHON
St. Louis, MO
SPIRIT OF ST. LOUIS MARATHON
Phone: 314-727-0800
Fax: 314-727-0893
info@gostlouis.org
www.gostlouis.org

Apr 10, 2021
HALF MARATHON UNPLUGGED
Burlington, VT
RUN VERMONT
Phone: 802-863-8412
info@runvermont.org
www.runvermont.org

Apr 10 - Apr 25, 2021
SALT LAKE CITY MARATHON
Salt Lake City, UT
LIFE TIME FITNESS
ltfmedia@lifetimefitness.com
www.eventsbylifetime.com

Apr 10 - Apr 11, 2021
THREE PALMS
Conroe, TX
Three Palms Action Sports Park
AMA PRO RACING
Phone: 386-492-1014
Fax: 386-274-2335
communications@amaproracing.com
www.amaproracing.com

Apr 10 - Apr 11, 2021
USA GYMNASTICS WOMEN'S
COLLEGIATE CHAMPIONSHIPS
Cape Girardeau, MO
USA GYMNASTICS
Phone: 317-237-5050
Fax: 317-237-5069
membership@usagym.org
usagym.org

Apr 11 - Apr 18, 2021
ATP TOUR MASTERS 1000 -
MONTE-CARLO ROLEX MASTERS
Monte Carlo, Monaco
ATP TOUR MASTERS 1000
www.atptour.com

Apr 11 - Apr 17, 2021
LOTTE CHAMPIONSHIP
Kapolei, Oahu, Hawaii
Ko Olina Golf Club
LPGA TOUR
Phone: 386-274-6200
Fax: 386-274-1099
www.lpga.com

Apr 11, 2021
OHIO RIVER ROAD RUNNERS
MARATHON & HALF MARATHON
Xenia, OH

OHIO RIVER ROAD RUNNERS CLUB
www.orrrc.org

Apr 12 - Apr 18, 2021
2021 KUNMING OPEN
Anning, China
WTA
Phone: 727-895-5000
Fax: 727-894-1982
feedback@wtatennis.com
www.wtatennis.com

Apr 12 - Apr 18, 2021
RBC HERITAGE
Hilton Head, SC
Harbour Town Golf Links
PGA TOUR
Phone: 904-285-3700
www.pgatour.com

Apr 13, 2021
CLAY SHOOT FOR CONSERVATION
Mansfield, GA
Burge Plantation
GEORGIA WILDLIFE FEDERATION
Phone: 770-787-7887
Fax: 770-787-9229
info@gwf.org
www.gwf.org

Apr 14 - Apr 18, 2021
TG CANADIAN GYMNASTIC
CHAMPIONSHIPS
GYMNASTICS CANADA GYMNASTIQUE
Phone: 613-748-5637
Fax: 613-748-5691
info@gymcan.org
www.gymcan.org

Apr 14 - Apr 17, 2021
US ADULT FIGURE SKATING
CHAMPIONSHIPS
Fairport, NY
Rochester Ice Center
U.S. FIGURE SKATING
Phone: 719-635-5200
Fax: 719-635-9548
info@usfigureskating.org
www.usfigureskating.org

Apr 15 - 18, 2021
ADULT MEN'S NATIONAL
CHAMPIONSHIPS
Tampa, FL
Adventhealth Center Ice
USA HOCKEY
Phone: 719-576-8724
Fax: 719-538-1160
usah@usahockey.org
www.usahockey.com

Apr 15 - Apr 17, 2021
BASSMASTER OPENS CENTRAL
OPEN - DOUGLAS LAKE
Dandridge, TN
Douglas Lake
BASS ANGLERS SPORTSMAN
SOCIETY
Phone: 877-227-7872
bassmaster@emailcustomerservice.com
www.bassmaster.com

Apr 16 - Apr 18, 2021
CHUBB CLASSIC
Naples, FL
Tiburon Golf Club
PGA CHAMPIONS TOUR
Phone: 904-285-3700
www.pgatour.com/champions

Apr 16 - Apr 18, 2021
DENSO SPARK PLUGS NHRA
FOUR-WIDE NATIONALS
Las Vegas, NV
The Strip at Las Vegas Motor Speedway
NATIONAL HOT ROD ASSOCIATION
Phone: 626-914-4761
Fax: 626-963-5360
nhra@nhra.com
www.nhra.com

Apr 16, 2021
DIVISION I & PARAFENCING
NATIONAL CHAMPIONSHIPS
Fort Worth, TX
Forth Worth Convention Center
USA FENCING
Phone: 719-866-4511
Fax: 719-632-5737
information@usfencing.org
www.usfencing.org

Apr 16 - Apr 17, 2021
NCAA NATIONAL COLLEGIATE
WOMEN'S GYMNASTICS FINA LS
Fort Worth, TX
Dickies Arena
NATIONAL COLLEGIATE ATHLETIC
ASSOCIATION
Phone: 317-917-6222
Fax: 317-917-6888
www.ncaa.org

Apr 16 - Apr 18, 2021
OPEN WATER NATIONALS &
JUNIORS
Fort Myers, FL
USA SWIMMING
Phone: 719-866-4578
Fax: 719-866-4049
imclemore@usaswimming.org
www.usaswimming.org

Apr 17, 2021
GRANDMA'S MARATHON
Duluth, MN
Two Harbors To Duluth
GRANDMA'S MARATHON
Phone: 218-727-0947
grandmas@grandmasmarathon.com
www.grandmasmarathon.com

Apr 17, 2021
NATIONAL COLLEGIATE
TAEKWONDO CHAMPIONSHIPS
NATIONAL COLLEGIATE TAEKWONDO
ASSOCIATION
ncta-usa.com

Apr 17, 2021
TOYOTACARE 250
Richmond, VA
Richmond Raceway
NASCAR CAMPING WORLD TRUCK
SERIES
Phone: 800-630-0535
www.nascar.com

Apr 18 - Apr 23, 2021
FINA DIVING WORLD CUP
Tokyo, Japan
USA DIVING
Phone: 317-237-5252
Fax: 317-237-5257
Dan.Laak@usadiving.org
www.teamusa.org/USA-Diving

Apr 18, 2021
HONDA GRAND PRIX OF ALABAMA
Birmingham, AL

Barber Motorsports Park
NTT INDYCAR SERIES
Phone: 317-492-6526
indycar@indycar.com
www.indycar.com

Apr 18, 2021
SHAPE WOMEN'S HALF MARATHON
New York, NY
Central Park

Apr 18, 2021
TOYOTA OWNERS 400
Richmond, VA
Richmond Raceway
NASCAR CUP SERIES
www.nascar.com

Apr 19 - Apr 25, 2021
ISTANBUL OPEN
Istanbul, Turkey
WTA
Phone: 727-895-5000
Fax: 727-894-1982
feedback@wtatennis.com
www.wtatennis.com

Apr 19 - Apr 23, 2021
NGA SPRING MEET
Abilene, KS
NATIONAL GREYHOUND
ASSOCIATION
Phone: 785-263-4660
Fax: 785-263-4689
nga@ngagreyhounds.com
www.ngagreyhounds.com

Apr 19 - Apr 25, 2021
PORSCHE TENNIS GRAND PRIX
Stuttgart, Germany
WTA
Phone: 727-895-5000
Fax: 727-894-1982
feedback@wtatennis.com
www.wtatennis.com

Apr 19 - Apr 25, 2021
ZURICH CLASSIC OF NEW ORLEANS
Avondale, LA
TPC Louisiana
PGA TOUR
Phone: 904-285-3700
www.pgatour.com

Apr 21 - Apr 24, 2021
2022 SPEEDO EASTERN CANADIAN
CHAMPIONSHIPS
SWIMMING CANADA
Phone: 613-260-1348
Fax: 613-260-0804
natloffice@swimming.ca
www.swimming.ca

Apr 21 - Apr 24, 2021
2022 SPEEDO WESTERN CANADIAN
CHAMPIONSHIPS
SWIMMING CANADA
Phone: 613-260-1348
Fax: 613-260-0804
natloffice@swimming.ca
www.swimming.ca

Apr 21 - Apr 24, 2021
HUGEL-AIR PREMIA LA OPEN
Los Angeles, CA
Wilshire Country Club
LPGA TOUR
Phone: 386-274-6200
Fax: 386-274-1099
www.lpga.com

Apr 22 - Apr 25, 2021
ADULT WOMEN'S NATIONAL
CHAMPIONSHIPS
Tampa, FL
Adventhealth Center Ice
USA HOCKEY
Phone: 719-576-8724
Fax: 719-538-1160
usah@usahockey.org
www.usahockey.com

Apr 22 - Apr 25, 2021
BASSMASTER ELITE SERIES - LAKE
FORK
Quitman, TX
Lake Fork
BASS ANGLERS SPORTSMAN
SOCIETY
Phone: 877-227-7872
bassmaster@emailcustomerservice.com
www.bassmaster.com

Apr 22 - Apr 24, 2021
BIG SUR INTERNATIONAL
MARATHON
Carmel, CA
BIG SUR MARATHON FOUNDATION
Phone: 831-625-6226
Fax: 831-625-2119
info@bsim.org
www.bsim.org

Apr 22 - Apr 25, 2021
EASTON SOUTHWEST SHOOT OUT
Paris, TX
Love Civic Center
ARCHERY SHOOTERS ASSOCIATION
Phone: 770-795-0232
Fax: 770-795-0953
info@asaarchery.com
www.asaarchery.com

Apr 22, 2021
KENTUCKY DERBY FESTIVAL
MARATHON
Louisville, KY
KENTUCKY DERBY FESTIVAL
Phone: 800-928-3378
Fax: 502-589-4674
minimarathon@kdf.org
www.derbyfestivalmarathon.com

Apr 22 - Apr 25, 2021
LAND ROVER KENTUCKY
THREE-DAY EVENT
Lexington, KY
Kentucky Horse Park
US EQUESTRIAN FEDERATION
Phone: 859-258-2472
Fax: 859-231-6662
www.usef.org

Apr 22 - Apr 24, 2021
NCAA DIVISION I WOMEN'S
VOLLEYBALL FINALS
Omaha, NE
CHI Health Center Omaha
NATIONAL COLLEGIATE ATHLETIC
ASSOCIATION
Phone: 317-917-6222
Fax: 317-917-6888
www.ncaa.org

Apr 23 - Apr 24, 2021
NCAA DIVISION III MEN'S
VOLLEYBALL FINALS
TBA
NATIONAL COLLEGIATE ATHLETIC
ASSOCIATION
Phone: 317-917-6222

Fax: 317-917-6888
www.ncaa.org

Apr 23 - Apr 24, 2021
SWING THOUGHT NATIONAL PRO
SERIES - BRUNSWICK CO UNTRY
CLUB
Brunswick, GA
Brunswick Country Club
SWING THOUGHT TOURNAMENTS
Phone: 800-992-8748
info@swingthought.com
www.swingthought.com

Apr 23 - Apr 24, 2021
SWING THOUGHT NATIONAL PRO
SERIES - SANCTUARY GO LF CLUB
Waverly, GA
Sanctuary Golf Club
SWING THOUGHT TOURNAMENTS
Phone: 800-992-8748
info@swingthought.com
www.swingthought.com

Apr 24 - May 1, 2021
KENTUCKY DERBY
Louisville, KY
Churchill Downs
CHURCHILL DOWNS
Phone: 502-636-4400
customerservice@kyderby.com
www.churchilldowns.com

Apr 24, 2021
PINE LINE MARATHON
Medford, WI
Medford City Park
PINE LINE TRAIL MARATHON
Phone: 715-748-4729

Apr 24 - Apr 28, 2021
US WOMEN'S AMATEUR FOUR-BALL
Carrollton, TX
Maridoe Golf Club
U.S. GOLF ASSOCIATION
Phone: 908-234-2300
Fax: 908-234-9687
www.usga.org

Apr 25, 2021
BOULDERTHON
Boulder, CO
RUN BOULDER EVENTS
Phone: 303-517-7046
www.runboulderevents.com

Apr 25, 2021
DELAWARE MARATHON RUNNING
FESTIVAL
Wilmington, DE
Tubman Garrett Riverfront Park
CORRIGAN SPORTS ENTERPRISES
Phone: 410-605-9381
Fax: 410-605-9389
customerservice@corrigansports.com
www.corrigansports.com

Apr 25, 2021
FIRESTONE GRAND PRIX OF ST.
PETERSBURG
St. Petersburg, FL
Streets of St. Petersburg
NTT INDYCAR SERIES
Phone: 317-492-6526
indycar@indycar.com
www.indycar.com

Apr 25, 2021
GEICO 500
Talladega, AL
Talladega Superspeedway

events/meetings/shows

NASCAR CUP SERIES
www.nascar.com

Apr 25, 2021
MERCY HEALTH GLASS CITY
MARATHON
Toledo, OH
TOLEDO ROAD RUNNERS CLUB
Phone: 419-340-1815
info@glasscitymarathon.org
glasscitymarathon.org

Apr 26 - May 2, 2021
INSPERITY INVITATIONAL
The Woodlands, TX
The Woodlands Country Club
PGA CHAMPIONS TOUR
Phone: 904-285-3700
www.pgatour.com/champions

Apr 26 - May 2, 2021
VALSPAR CHAMPIONSHIP
Palm Harbor, FL
Innisbrook Resort Copperhead
PGA TOUR
Phone: 904-285-3700
www.pgatour.com

Apr 27 - Apr 28, 2021
SHIPROCK MARATHON
Shiprock, NM
FOUR CORNERS FITNESS &
WELLNESS ASSOCIATION
Phone: 435-233-8068
info@shiprockmarathon.com
www.shiprockmarathon.com

Apr 29 - May 1, 2021
BASSMASTER OPENS CENTRAL
OPEN - PICKWICK LAKE
Counce, TN
Pickwick Lake
BASS ANGLERS SPORTSMAN
SOCIETY
Phone: 877-227-7872
bassmaster@emailcustomerservice.com
www.bassmaster.com

Apr 29 - May 2, 2021
HSBC WOMEN'S WORLD
CHAMPIONSHIP
Singapore
Sentosa Golf Club
LPGA TOUR
Phone: 386-274-6200
Fax: 386-274-1099
www.lpga.com

Apr 29 - May 2, 2021
PORTUGAL MASTERS
Vilamoura, Portugal
Dom Pedro Victoria Golf Course
PGA EUROPEAN TOUR
International Ph: 44-0-1344-840400
International Fax: 44-0-1344-840500
www.europeantour.com

Apr 29 - May 2, 2021
TYR 18 & UNDER SPRING CUP
USA SWIMMING
Phone: 719-866-4578
Fax: 719-866-4049
imclemore@usaswimming.org
www.usaswimming.org

Apr 29 - Apr 30, 2021
WALLEYE
TOUR-CHAMBERLAIN-OACOMA
Chamberlain-Oacoma, SD
Lake Francis Case

NATIONAL WALLEYE TOUR
Phone: 612-424-0708
Fax: 866-727-2809
www.nationalwalleyetour.com

Apr 30 - May 1, 2021
DANCE NATIONALS
Anaheim, CA
Anaheim Convention Center
UNITED SPIRIT ASSOCIATION
Phone: 800-886-4872
Fax: 866-761-9365
info@usacamps.com
usa.varsity.com

Apr 30 - May 2, 2021
HIGH SCHOOL SPIRIT NATIONALS
Anaheim, CA
Anaheim Convention Center
UNITED SPIRIT ASSOCIATION
Phone: 800-886-4872
Fax: 866-761-9365
info@usacamps.com
usa.varsity.com

Apr 30 - May 2, 2021
KISSIMMEE OPEN
Kissimmee, FL
NATIONAL X BALL LEAGUE
camille@nxlpaintball.com
nxlpaintball.com

Apr 30 - May 9, 2021
MUTUA MADRID OPEN
Madrid, Spain
WTA
Phone: 727-895-5000
Fax: 727-894-1982
feedback@wtatennis.com
www.wtatennis.com

Apr 30 - May 2, 2021
NFAA MARKED 3-D NATIONAL
CHAMPIONSHIP
NATIONAL FIELD ARCHERY
ASSOCIATION
Phone: 605-260-9279
info@nfaausa.com
www.nfaausa.com

Apr 30 - May 2, 2021
NHRA SOUTHERN NATIONALS
Commerce, GA
Atlanta Dragway
NATIONAL HOT ROD ASSOCIATION
Phone: 626-914-4761
Fax: 626-963-5360
nhra@nhra.com
www.nhra.com

Apr 30, 2021
SINGLE STACK NATIONALS
Brooklyn, MI
Brooklyn Sportsman's Club
US PRACTICAL SHOOTING
ASSOCIATION
Phone: 360-855-2245
Fax: 360-855-0380
office@uspsa.org
www.uspsa.org

Apr 30 - May 2, 2021
USA BMX DIXIELAND NATIONALS
Powder Springs, GA
USA BMX
Phone: 480-961-1903
Fax: 480-961-1842
www.usabmx.com

Apr 30 - May 9, 2021
WORLD WOMEN'S CHAMPIONSHIP
Calrgary, Canada

USA CURLING
Phone: 715-344-1199
Fax: 715-344-2279
info@usacurl.org
www.teamusa.org/USA-Curling

Apr 30 - May 9, 2021
WORLD WOMEN'S CURLING
CHAMPIONSHIPS
Calgary, Canada
Markin McPhail Centre
CURLING CANADA
Phone: 613-834-2076
Fax: 613-834-0716
championships@curling.ca
www.curling.ca

May TBA, 2021
MIXED DOUBLES NATIONAL
CHAMPIONSHIP
Bemidji, MN
USA CURLING
Phone: 715-344-1199
Fax: 715-344-2279
info@usacurl.org
www.teamusa.org/USA-Curling

May TBA, 2021
PACASMAYO CLASSIC
Pacasmayo, Peru
INTERNATIONAL WINDSURFING TOUR
internationalwindsurfingtour.com

May TBA, 2021
THE STEEL CHALLENGE WORLD
SPEED SHOOTING CHAMPIO NSHIP
Talladega, AL
US PRACTICAL SHOOTING
ASSOCIATION
Phone: 360-855-2245
Fax: 360-855-0380
office@uspsa.org
www.uspsa.org

May TBA, 2021
YONEX BOSTON OPEN
Cambridge, MA
USA BADMINTON
Phone: 714-765-2952
usab@usabadminton.org
www.usabadminton.org

May 1, 2021
ATLANTA SUPER TT
Atlanta, GA
Atlanta Motor Speedway
AMA PRO RACING
Phone: 386-492-1014
Fax: 386-274-2335
communications@amaproracing.com
www.amaproracing.com

May 1, 2021
ULTRA RACE OF CHAMPIONS
Blue Ridge Mountains, VA
BAD TO THE BONE
Phone: 434-218-0402
francesca@badtothebone.biz
badtothebone.biz

May 1 - May 2, 2021
DIAMOND CUP MALTA
Malta
INTERNATIONAL FEDERATION OF
BODY BUILDING & FITNESS
International Ph: 34-91-535-28-19
contact@ifbb.com
www.ifbb.com

May 1, 2021
EISENHOWER MARATHON
Abilene, TX

Chisholm Trail
EISENHOWER MARATHON
Phone: 785-263-3474
scathey79@yahoo.com
eisenhowermarathon.net

May 1 - May 2, 2021
FREDERICK RUNNING FESTIVAL
Frederick, MD
Frederick Fair Grounds
CORRIGAN SPORTS ENTERPRISES
Phone: 410-605-9381
Fax: 410-605-9389
customerservice@corrigansports.com
www.corrigansports.com

May 1, 2021
GENESYS 300
Fort Worth, TX
Texas Motor Speedway
NTT INDYCAR SERIES
Phone: 317-492-6526
indycar@indycar.com
www.indycar.com

May 2, 2021
AAU CHEERLEADING NATIONAL
CHAMPIONSHIP
Glen Carbon, IL
The Sports Academy
AMATEUR ATHLETIC UNION
Phone: 407-934-7200
Fax: 407-934-7242
www.aausports.org

May 2 - May 9, 2021
ATP TOUR MASTERS 1000 - MUTUA
MADRID OPEN
Madrid, Spain
ATP TOUR MASTERS 1000
www.atptour.com

May 2, 2021
LINCOLN MARATHON
Lincoln, NE
LINCOLN TRACK CLUB
Phone: 402-435-3504
www.lincolnmarathon.org

May 2, 2021
NASCAR CUP SERIES RACE AT
KANSAS
Kansas City, KS
Kansas Speedway
NASCAR CUP SERIES
www.nascar.com

May 2, 2021
USA JUNIOR NATIONALS
Anaheim, CA
Anaheim Convention Center
UNITED SPIRIT ASSOCIATION
Phone: 800-886-4872
Fax: 866-761-9365
info@usacamps.com
usa.varsity.com

May 2, 2021
XPEL 375
Fort Worth, TX
Texas Motor Speedway
NTT INDYCAR SERIES
Phone: 317-492-6526
indycar@indycar.com
www.indycar.com

May 3 - May 4 2021
FLORIDA DOUBLES
Lakeland, FL

NATIONAL SHUFFLEBOARD
ASSOCIATION
usansa.weebly.com

May 3 - May 9, 2021
WELLS FARGO CHAMPIONSHIP
Charlotte, NC
Quail Hollow Club
PGA TOUR
Phone: 904-285-3700
www.pgatour.com

May 5 - May 9, 2021
REGIONS TRADITION
Birmingham, AL
Greystone Golf & Country Club
PGA CHAMPIONS TOUR
Phone: 904-285-3700
www.pgatour.com/champions

May 6, 2021
AMA PRO HILLCLIMB
Scottsburg, IN
High Fly MX Park 2.0
AMA PRO RACING
Phone: 386-492-1014
Fax: 386-274-2335
communications@amaproracing.com
www.amaproracing.com

May 6 - May 9, 2021
BASSMASTER ELITE SERIES -
NEELY HENRY LAKE
Gadsden, AL
Neelt Henry Lake
BASS ANGLERS SPORTSMAN
SOCIETY
Phone: 877-227-7872
bassmaster@emailcustomerservice.com
www.bassmaster.com

May 6 - May 9, 2021
HONDA LPGA THAILAND
Chonburi, Thailand
Siam Country Club
LPGA TOUR
Phone: 386-274-6200
Fax: 386-274-1099
www.lpga.com

May 6 - May 8, 2021
NEXTGEN PACIFIC CHAMPIONSHIP
TBA, BC, Canada
ROYAL CANADIAN GOLF
ASSOCIATION
Phone: 905-849-9700
Fax: 905-845-7040
info@golfcanada.ca
www.golfcanada.ca

May 6 - May 9, 2021
OPEN DE FRANCE
Guyancourt, France
Le Golf National
PGA EUROPEAN TOUR
International Ph: 44-0-1344-840400
International Fax: 44-0-1344-840500
www.europeantour.com

May 6 - May 9, 2021
SIMMONS BANK OPEN FOR THE
SNEDEKER FOUNDATION
Nashville, TN
Nashville Golf & Athletic Club
PGA KORN FERRY TOUR
Phone: 904-285-3700
Fax: 904-285-7913
www.pgatour.com

May 7 - May 9, 2021
COLLEGIATE ROAD NATIONAL
CHAMPIONSHIPS
Augusta, GA
USA CYCLING
Phone: 719-434-4200
Fax: 719-434-4300
help@usacycling.org
www.usacycling.org

May 7 - May 9, 2021
RIEGLER & PARTNER AUSTRIAN
LEGENDS
Frohnleiten, Austria
Golfclub Murhof
PGA EUROPEAN STAYSURE TOUR
International Ph: 44-0-1344-840400
International Fax: 44-0-1344-840500
www.europeantour.com/staysure-tour

May 7 - May 9, 2021
TIGER CLASSIC - DIAMOND CUP
ROMANIA
Bucharest, Romania
INTERNATIONAL FEDERATION OF
BODY BUILDING & FITNESS
International Ph: 34-91-535-28-19
contact@ifbb.com
www.ifbb.com

May 7 - May 9, 2021
USA BMX SILVER DOLLAR
NAITONALS
Las Vegas, NV
USA BMX
Phone: 480-961-1903
Fax: 480-961-1842
www.usabmx.com

May 7 - May 9, 2021
USA GYMNASTICS LEVEL 9
EASTERN CHAMPIONSHIPS
College Park, GA
Georgia International Convention Center
USA GYMNASTICS
Phone: 317-237-5050
Fax: 317-237-5069
membership@usagym.org
usagym.org

May 7 - May 9, 2021
USA GYMNASTICS LEVEL 9
WESTERN CHAMPIONSHIPS
Coralville, IA
Xtream Arena
USA GYMNASTICS
Phone: 317-237-5050
Fax: 317-237-5069
membership@usagym.org
usagym.org

May 8 - May 9, 2021
HARMONY GENEVA MARATHON FOR
UNICEF
Lake Geneva, WI
OC SPORT
www.ocsport.com

May 8 - May 9, 2021
WORLD FIT MODEL CUP
Riga, Latvia
INTERNATIONAL FEDERATION OF
BODY BUILDING & FITNESS
International Ph: 34-91-535-28-19
contact@ifbb.com
www.ifbb.com

May 9 - May 16, 2021
ATP TOUR MASTERS 1000 -
INTERNAZIONALI BNL D'ITA LIA
Rome, Italy
ATP TOUR MASTERS 1000
www.atptour.com

May 9 - May 16, 2021
INTERNAZIONALI BNL D'ITALIA
Rome, Italy
WTA
Phone: 727-895-5000
Fax: 727-894-1982
feedback@wtatennis.com
www.wtatennis.com

May 10 - May 16, 2021
AT&T BYRON NELSON
CHAMPIONSHIP
McKinney, TX
TPC Craig Ranch
PGA TOUR
Phone: 904-285-3700
www.pgatour.com

May 10 - May 16, 2021
VISIT KNOXVILLE OPEN
Knoxville, TN
Holston Hills Country Club
PGA KORN FERRY TOUR
Phone: 904-285-3700
Fax: 904-285-7913
www.pgatour.com

May 11 - May 15, 2021
NCAA DIVISION II WOMEN'S GOLF
FINALS
Detroit, MI
TPC Michigan
NATIONAL COLLEGIATE ATHLETIC
ASSOCIATION
Phone: 317-917-6222
Fax: 317-917-6888
www.ncaa.org

May 11 - May 14, 2021
NCAA DIVISION III MEN'S GOLF
FINALS
Wheeling, WV
Oglebay Resort & Conference Center
NATIONAL COLLEGIATE ATHLETIC
ASSOCIATION
Phone: 317-917-6222
Fax: 317-917-6888
www.ncaa.org

May 11 - May 14, 2021
NCAA DIVISION III WOMEN'S GOLF
FINALS
Lansing, MI
Forest Akers
NATIONAL COLLEGIATE ATHLETIC
ASSOCIATION
Phone: 317-917-6222
Fax: 317-917-6888
www.ncaa.org

May 12 - May 15, 2021
BETFRED BRITISH MASTERS
Newcastle-upon-Tyne, England
Close House Golf Course
PGA EUROPEAN TOUR
International Ph: 44-0-1344-840400
International Fax: 44-0-1344-840500
www.europeantour.com

May 12 - May 15, 2021
TYR PRO SWIM SERIES
INDIANAPOLIS
Indianapolis, IN

USA SWIMMING
Phone: 719-866-4578
Fax: 719-866-4049
imclemore@usaswimming.org
www.usaswimming.org

May 13 - May 15, 2021
2021 ICF PARACANOE WORLD CUP
Szeged, Hungary
INTERNATIONAL CANOE FEDERATION
International Ph: 41 (0)21 612 0290
info@canoeicf.com
www.canoeicf.com

May 13 - May 16, 2021
CANADA CUP GRAND PRIX
Toronto, Canada
DIVING CANADA
Phone: 613-736-5238
Fax: 613-736-0409
cada@diving.ca
www.diving.ca

May 13 - May 17, 2021
EUROPEAN CHAMPIONSHIPS
Santa Susana, Spain
INTERNATIONAL FEDERATION OF
BODY BUILDING & FITNESS
International Ph: 34-91-535-28-19
contact@ifbb.com
www.ifbb.com

May 13 - May 17, 2021
NCAA DIVISION I MEN'S SOCCER
FINALS
Cary, NC
WakeMed Soccer Park
NATIONAL COLLEGIATE ATHLETIC
ASSOCIATION
Phone: 317-917-6222
Fax: 317-917-6888
www.ncaa.org

May 14 - May 16, 2021
2021 ICF CANOE SPRINT WORLD
CUP 1
Szeged, Hungary
INTERNATIONAL CANOE FEDERATION
International Ph: 41 (0)21 612 0290
info@canoeicf.com
www.canoeicf.com

May 14 - May 16, 2021
ARNOLD CLASSIC AFRICA
Johannesburg, South Africa
INTERNATIONAL FEDERATION OF
BODY BUILDING & FITNESS
International Ph: 34-91-535-28-19
contact@ifbb.com
www.ifbb.com

May 14 - May 15, 2021
FRIVOLTEN CUP
Herrljunga, Sweden
GK FRIVOLTEN
frivolten.com

May 14 - May 16, 2021
MITSUBISHI ELECTRIC CLASSIC
Duluth, GA
TPC Sugarloaf
PGA CHAMPIONS TOUR
Phone: 904-285-3700
www.pgatour.com/champions

May 14 - May 15, 2021
PREAKNESS STAKES
Baltimore, MD
Pimlico Race Course
PIMLICO RACE COURSE
Phone: 410-542-9400

info@marylandracing.com
www.marylandracing.com

May 15, 2021
BROOKINGS MARATHON
Brookings, SD
BROOKINGS MARATHON
run@brookingsmarathon.com
www.brookingsmarathon.com

May 15 - May 16, 2021
CAPITAL CITY MARATHON
Olympia, WA
CAPITAL CITY MARATHON
racedirector@ccmaboard.org
www.capitalcitymarathon.org

May 15 - May 16, 2021
CELLCOM GREEN BAY MARATHON
Green Bay, WI
CELLCOM GREEN BAY MARATHON
Phone: 920-432-6272
info@cellcomgreenbaymarathon.com
www.cellcomgreenbaymarathon.com

May 15, 2021
GMR GRAND PRIX
Indianapolis, IN
Indianapolis Motor Speedway
NTT INDYCAR SERIES
Phone: 317-492-6526
indycar@indycar.com
www.indycar.com

May 15 - May 16, 2021
HIGH POINT
Mount Morris, PA
High Point Raceway
AMA PRO RACING
Phone: 386-492-1014
Fax: 386-274-2335
communications@amaproracing.com
www.amaproracing.com

May 15 - May 22, 2021
INTERNATIONAUX DE STRASBOURG
Strasbourg, France
WTA
Phone: 727-895-5000
Fax: 727-894-1982
feedback@wtatennis.com
www.wtatennis.com

Mar 15, 2021
NAPA VALLEY TRAIL MARATHON,
HALF MARATHON & 10K
Calistoga, CA
Bothe-Napa State Park
ENVIRO-SPORTS
Phone: 415-868-1829
info@envirosports.com
envirosports.com

May 15, 2021
NASCAR CUP SERIES RACE AT
DOVER
Dover, DE
Dover International Speedway
NASCAR CUP SERIES
www.nascar.com

May 15 - May 16, 2021
NCWSA ALL-STARS
Jacksonville, IL
JAWS Water Ski Lake
NATIONAL COLLEGIATE WATER SKI
ASSOCIATION
www.thencwsa.com

May 15, 2021
OGDEN MARATHON
Odgen, UT
GOAL FOUNDATION
Phone: 801-399-1773
Fax: 248-654-0797
info@goalfoundation.com
www.ogdenmarathon.com

May 16, 2021
DRYDENE 400
Dover, DE
Dover International Speedway
NASCAR CUP SERIES
www.nascar.com

May 16 - May 22, 2021
GRAND PRIX DE SAR LA PRINCESSE
LALLA MERYEM
Rabat, Morocco
WTA
Phone: 727-895-5000
Fax: 727-894-1982
feedback@wtatennis.com
www.wtatennis.com

May 16, 2021
NCAA DIVISION I FOOTBALL FINALS
Frisco, TX
Toyota Stadium
NATIONAL COLLEGIATE ATHLETIC
ASSOCIATION
Phone: 317-917-6222
Fax: 317-917-6888
www.ncaa.org

May 16, 2021
SUGARLOAF MARATHON & 15K
Carrabassett Valley, ME
SUGARLOAF MARATHON
Phone: 207-237-2000
Fax: 207-237-3768
info@sugarloaf.com
www.sugarloaf.com

May 16 - May 23, 2021
WORLD MIXED DOUBLES & WORLD
SENIOR CHAMPIONSHIPS
TBA
USA CURLING
Phone: 715-344-1199
Fax: 715-344-2279
info@usacurl.org
www.teamusa.org/USA-Curling

May 17 - May 23, 2021
KANSAS CITY GOLF CLASSIC
Kansas City, KS
Blue Hills Country Club
PGA KORN FERRY TOUR
Phone: 904-285-3700
Fax: 904-285-7913
www.pgatour.com

May 17 - May 21, 2021
NCAA DIVISION II MEN'S GOLF
FINALS
Palm Beach Gardens, FL
PGA National Resort
NATIONAL COLLEGIATE ATHLETIC
ASSOCIATION
Phone: 317-917-6222
Fax: 317-917-6888
www.ncaa.org

May 17 - May 23, 2021
PGA CHAMPIONSHIP
San Francisco, CA
TPC Harding Park

PGA TOUR
Phone: 904-285-3700
www.pgatour.com

May 17 - Jun 6, 2021
ROLAND GARROS
Paris, France
Stade Roland Garros
FRENCH TENNIS FEDERATION
www.fft.fr

May 18 - May 22, 2021
NCAA DIVISION II MEN'S/WOMEN'S
TENNIS FINALS
Surprise, AZ
Surprise Tennis & Racquet Complex
NATIONAL COLLEGIATE ATHLETIC
ASSOCIATION
Phone: 317-917-6222
Fax: 317-917-6888
www.ncaa.org

May 19 - May 20, 2021
SWING THOUGHT NATIONAL PRO
SERIES - THE CLUB AT LA COSTA
San Diego, CA
The Club At La Costa
SWING THOUGHT TOURNAMENTS
Phone: 800-992-8748
info@swingthought.com
www.swingthought.com

May 20 - May 29, 2021
NCAA DIVISION I MEN'S/WOMEN'S
TENNIS FINALS
Orlando, FL
USTA National Campus
NATIONAL COLLEGIATE ATHLETIC
ASSOCIATION
Phone: 317-917-6222
Fax: 317-917-6888
www.ncaa.org

May 20 - May 23, 2021
PURE SILK CHAMPIONSHIP
Williamsburg, VA
Kingsmill Resort
LPGA TOUR
Phone: 386-274-6200
Fax: 386-274-1099
www.lpga.com

May 20 - May 30, 2021
YMBL CHAMPIONSHIP RODEO
Beaumont, TX
PROFESSIONAL RODEO COWBOY
ASSOCIATION
Phone: 719-593-8840
Fax: 719-548-4876
prorodeor@prorodeo.com
www.prorodeo.com

May 21 - May 23, 2021
2021 ICF CANOE SPRINT WORLD
CUP 2
Barnaul, Russia
INTERNATIONAL CANOE FEDERATION
International Ph: 41 (0)21 612 0290
info@canoeicf.com
www.canoeicf.com

May 21 - May 24, 2021
CANADIAN JUNIOR CLOSED
CHAMPIONSHIPS
Ottawa, Canada
SQUASH CANADA
Phone: 613-228-7724
Fax: 613-228-7232
info@squash.ca
www.squash.ca

May 21 - May 23, 2021
NCAA DIVISION II WOMEN'S
LACROSSE FESTIVAL
Salem, VA
Kerr Stadium
NATIONAL COLLEGIATE ATHLETIC
ASSOCIATION
Phone: 317-917-6222
Fax: 317-917-6888
www.ncaa.org

May 21 - May 23, 2021
OPEN BALKAN CUP
Knjazevac, Serbia
INTERNATIONAL FEDERATION OF
BODY BUILDING & FITNESS
International Ph: 34-91-535-28-19
contact@ifbb.com
www.ifbb.com

May 22 - May 28, 2021
2021 FINN WORLD MASTERS
Medemblik, Netherlands
WORLD SAILING
International Ph: 44 (0)20 3940 4888
www.sailing.org

May 22 - May 24, 2021
2021 ICF WILDWATER CANOEING
WORLD CUP
Treignac, France
INTERNATIONAL CANOE FEDERATION
International Ph: 41 (0)21 612 0290
info@canoeicf.com
www.canoeicf.com

May 22 - May 23, 2021
NCAA DIVISION III WOMEN'S
LACROSSE FINALS
Salem, VA
Kerr Stadium
NATIONAL COLLEGIATE ATHLETIC
ASSOCIATION
Phone: 317-917-6222
Fax: 317-917-6888
www.ncaa.org

May 22, 2021
TEXAS HALF-MILE
Fort Worth, TX
Texas Motor Speedway
AMA PRO RACING
Phone: 386-492-1014
Fax: 386-274-2335
communications@amaproracing.com
www.amaproracing.com

May 22 - May 26, 2021
US AMATEUR FOUR-BALL
DuPont, WA
The Home Course
U.S. GOLF ASSOCIATION
Phone: 908-234-2300
Fax: 908-234-9687
www.usga.org

May 23 - Jun 6, 2021
CHAMPIONNATS INTERNATIONAUX
DE FRANCE
Paris, France
WTA
Phone: 727-895-5000
Fax: 727-894-1982
feedback@wtatennis.com
www.wtatennis.com

May 24 - May 29, 2021
EUROPEAN CHAMPIONSHIPS
Split, Croatia
Sailing Club Mornar

INTERNATIONAL STAR CLASS YACHT
ASSOCIATION
Phone: 619-222-0252
Fax: 619-222-0528
office@starclass.org
www.starclass.org

May 24 - May 26, 2021
NCAA DIVISION I WOMEN'S GOLF
FINALS
Scottsdale, AZ
Grayhawk Golf Club
NATIONAL COLLEGIATE ATHLETIC
ASSOCIATION
Phone: 317-917-6222
Fax: 317-917-6888
www.ncaa.org

May 24 - May 30, 2021
NCAA DIVISION III MEN'S/WOMEN'S
TENNIS FINALS
Claremont, CA
Biszantz Family Tennis Center
NATIONAL COLLEGIATE ATHLETIC
ASSOCIATION
Phone: 317-917-6222
Fax: 317-917-6888
www.ncaa.org

May 27 - May 30, 2021
CHARLES SCHWAB CHALLENGE
Fort Worth, TX
Colonial Country Club
PGA TOUR
Phone: 904-285-3700
www.pgatour.com

May 27 - May 30, 2021
EVAN SCHOLARS INVITATIONAL
Glenview, IL
The Glen Club
PGA KORN FERRY TOUR
Phone: 904-285-3700
Fax: 904-285-7913
www.pgatour.com

May 27 - May 30, 2021
KITCHENAID SENIOR PGA
CHAMPIONSHIP
Tulsa, OK
Southern Hills Country Club
PGA CHAMPIONS TOUR
Phone: 904-285-3700
www.pgatour.com/champions

May 27 - May 29, 2021
NCAA DIVISION II MEN'S/WOMEN'S
TRACK, OUTDOOR FI NALS
Alldendale, MI
GVSU South Complex
NATIONAL COLLEGIATE ATHLETIC
ASSOCIATION
Phone: 317-917-6222
Fax: 317-917-6888
www.ncaa.org

May 27 - May 31, 2021
NCAA DIVISION II SOFTBALL FINALS
Denver, CO
The Regency Athletic Complex
NATIONAL COLLEGIATE ATHLETIC
ASSOCIATION
Phone: 317-917-6222
Fax: 317-917-6888
www.ncaa.org

May 27 - May 29, 2021
NCAA DIVISION III MEN'S/WOMEN'S
TRACK, OUTDOOR F INALS
TBA

NATIONAL COLLEGIATE ATHLETIC
ASSOCIATION
Phone: 317-917-6222
Fax: 317-917-6888
www.ncaa.org

May 27 - Jun 1, 2021
NCAA DIVISION III SOFTBALL FINALS
Salem, VA
Moyer Park
NATIONAL COLLEGIATE ATHLETIC
ASSOCIATION
Phone: 317-917-6222
Fax: 317-917-6888
www.ncaa.org

May 27 - May 28, 2021
WALLEYE TOUR-STURGEON BAY
Sturgeon Bay, WI
NATIONAL WALLEYE TOUR
Phone: 612-424-0708
Fax: 866-727-2809
www.nationalwalleyetour.com

May 28, 2021
ASICS UWW CADET & UNIVERSITY
NATIONALS
UNITED WORLD WRESTLING
International Ph: +41 21 312 84 26
info@unitedworldwrestling.org
unitedworldwrestling.org

May 28 - May 30, 2021
DIAMOND CUP FRANCE
Divonne, France
INTERNATIONAL FEDERATION OF
BODY BUILDING & FITNESS
International Ph: 34-91-535-28-19
contact@ifbb.com
www.ifbb.com

May 28 - May 30, 2021
MASTERS WATER SKI &
WAKEBOARD TOURNAMENT
Pine Mountain, GA
Callaway Gardens
NAUTIQUE EVENTS
Phone: 407-855-4141
Fax: 407-851-7844
masters@nautique.com
www.masterswaterski.com

May 28 - Jun 2, 2021
NCAA DIVISION I MEN'S GOLF
FINALS
Scottsdale, AZ
Grayhawk Gold Club
NATIONAL COLLEGIATE ATHLETIC
ASSOCIATION
Phone: 317-917-6222
Fax: 317-917-6888
www.ncaa.org

May 28 - May 30, 2021
NCAA DIVISION I ROWING FINALS
Sarasota, FL
Nathan Benderson Park
NATIONAL COLLEGIATE ATHLETIC
ASSOCIATION
Phone: 317-917-6222
Fax: 317-917-6888
www.ncaa.org

May 28 - May 30, 2021
NCAA DIVISION I WOMEN'S
LACROSSE FINALS
Towson, MD
Johnny Unitas Stadium
NATIONAL COLLEGIATE ATHLETIC
ASSOCIATION
Phone: 317-917-6222

Fax: 317-917-6888
www.ncaa.org

May 28 - May 30, 2021
NCAA DIVISION II ROWING FINALS
Sarasota, FL
Nathan Benderson Park
NATIONAL COLLEGIATE ATHLETIC
ASSOCIATION
Phone: 317-917-6222
Fax: 317-917-6888
www.ncaa.org

May 28 - May 29, 2021
NCAA DIVISION III ROWING FINALS
Sarasota, FL
Nathan Benderson Park
NATIONAL COLLEGIATE ATHLETIC
ASSOCIATION
Phone: 317-917-6222
Fax: 317-917-6888
www.ncaa.org

May 28 - May 30, 2021
NEXTGEN ONTARIO CHAMPIONSHIP
Port Elgin, Canada
Saugeen Gold Club
ROYAL CANADIAN GOLF
ASSOCIATION
Phone: 905-849-9700
Fax: 905-845-7040
info@golfcanada.ca
www.golfcanada.ca

May 28 - Oct 10, 2021
NHRA LUCAS OIL DRAG RACING
SERIES
Various
NATIONAL HOT ROD ASSOCIATION
Phone: 626-914-4761
Fax: 626-963-5360
nhra@nhra.com
www.nhra.com

May 28, 2021
NORTH CAROLINA EDUCATION
LOTTERY 200
Concord, NC
Charlotte Motor Speedway
NASCAR CAMPING WORLD TRUCK
SERIES
Phone: 800-630-0535
www.nascar.com

May 28 - Jun 2, 2021
OPEN NATIONAL CHAMPIONSHIPS
Columbus, OH
USA VOLLEYBALL
Phone: 719-228-6800
Fax: 719-228-6899
postmaster@usav.org
www.teamusa.org/USA-Volleyball

May 29 - May 30, 2021
AONIA PASS
Washington, GA
Aonia Pass MX
AMA PRO RACING
Phone: 386-492-1014
Fax: 386-274-2335
communications@amaproracing.com
www.amaproracing.com

May 29, 2021
BAYSHORE MARATHON
Traverse City, MI
TRAVERSE CITY TRACK CLUB
Phone: 231-941-8118
www.bayshoremarathon.org

May 29 - May 31, 2021
BOLDERBOULDER 10K
Boulder, CO
BOLDER BOULDER
Phone: 303-444-7223
Fax: 303-447-9177
race@bolderboulder.com
bb10k.bolderboulder.com

May 29 - May 30, 2021
BUFFALO MARATHON
Buffalo, NY
BUFFALO MARATHON
information@buffalomarathon.com
www.buffalomarathon.com

May 29, 2021
CHICAGO HALF-MILE
Joliet, IL
Route 66 Speedway
AMA PRO RACING
Phone: 386-492-1014
Fax: 386-274-2335
communications@amaproracing.com
www.amaproracing.com

May 29 - May 30, 2021
CROSSROADS CANADA CUP
Mont Tremblant, QC
CANADIAN CYCLING ASSOCIATION
Phone: 613-248-1353
Fax: 613-248-9311
general@cyclingcanada.ca
www.cyclingcanada.ca

May 29, 2021
FOX RACEWAY NATIONAL
Pala, CA
Fox Raceway
AMA PRO RACING
Phone: 386-492-1014
Fax: 386-274-2335
communications@amaproracing.com
www.amaproracing.com

May 29 - May 31, 2021
NCAA DIVISION I MEN'S LACROSSE
FINALS
East Hartford, CT
Pratt and Whitney Stadium
NATIONAL COLLEGIATE ATHLETIC
ASSOCIATION
Phone: 317-917-6222
Fax: 317-917-6888
www.ncaa.org

May 29, 2021
TRENT/WALDRON GLACIER HALF
MARATHON
Anchorage, AK
Westchester Lagoon
ANCHORAGE RUNNING CLUB
Phone: 907-258-4964
info@anchoragerunningclub.org
www.anchoragerunningclub.org

May 29, 2021
VIRGINIA WINE COUNTRY HALF
MARATHON
Leesburg, VA
BAD TO THE BONE
Phone: 434-218-0402
francesca@badtothebone.biz
badtothebone.biz

May 30, 2021
COCA-COLA 600
Concord, NC
Charlotte Motor Speedway

NASCAR CUP SERIES
www.nascar.com

May 30, 2021
COEUR D'ALENE MARATHON
Coeur d'Alene, ID
COEUR D'ALENE MARATHON
runsignup.com/Race/ID/CoeurDAlene/nsplit

May 30, 2021
INDIANAPOLIS 500
Indianapolis, IN
Indianapolis Motor Speedway
NTT INDYCAR SERIES
Phone: 317-492-6526
indycar@indycar.com
www.indycar.com

May 30, 2021
NCAA DIVISION II MEN'S LACROSSE
FINALS
East Hartford, CT
Pratt and Whitney Stadium
NATIONAL COLLEGIATE ATHLETIC
ASSOCIATION
Phone: 317-917-6222
Fax: 317-917-6888
www.ncaa.org

May 30, 2021
NCAA DIVISION III MEN'S LACROSSE
FINALS
East Hartford, CT
Pratt and Whitney Stadium
NATIONAL COLLEGIATE ATHLETIC
ASSOCIATION
Phone: 317-917-6222
Fax: 317-917-6888
www.ncaa.org

May 30, 2021
WYOMING MARATHON
Cheyenne, WY
CHEYENNE TRACK CLUB
Phone: 307-778-7866
Fax: 307-778-7876
fotrockies@bresnan.net
wyomingmarathonraces.weebly.com

May 31 - Jun 6, 2021
CROATIA BOL OPEN
Bol, Croatia
WTA
Phone: 727-895-5000
Fax: 727-894-1982
feedback@wtatennis.com
www.wtatennis.com

May 31, 2021
LIFE TIME TRI/CAP TEX
Austin, TX
LIFE TIME FITNESS
ltfmedia@lifetimefitness.com
www.eventsbylifetime.com

May 31 - Jun 6, 2021
THE MEMORIAL TOURNAMENT
Dublin, OH
Muirfield Village Golf Club
PGA TOUR
Phone: 904-285-3700
www.pgatour.com

Jun TBA, 2021
NATIONAL THREE POSITION AIR
RIFLE CHAMPIONSHIPS SPORTER
NATIONAL RIFLE ASSOCIATION -
COMPETITIVE SHOOTING DIVISION
Phone: 703-267-1465
competitions.nra.org

Jun TBA, 2021
NATURAL CHI-TOWN SHOWDOWN
OPEN
NATIONAL AMATEUR BODYBUILDERS
ASSOCIATION
info@nabbausa.com
www.nabba.com

Jun TBA, 2021
PISTOL RIVER WAVE BASH
Pistol River, OR
INTERNATIONAL WINDSURFING TOUR
internationalwindsurfingtour.com

Jun TBA, 2021
POWERADE STATE GAMES OF
NORTH CAROLINA
NORTH CAROLINA AMATEUR SPORTS
Phone: 919-361-1133
Fax: 919-361-2559
ncas@ncsports.org
www.ncsports.org

Jun TBA, 2021
USHA NATIONAL FOUR-WALL
CHAMPIONSHIPS
UNITED STATES HANDBALL
ASSOCIATION
Phone: 520-795-0434
Fax: 520-795-0465
handball@ushandball.org
www.ushandball.org

Jun 1 - Jun 4, 2021
CANADIAN UNIVERSITY & COLLEGE
CHAMPIONSHIP
TBA
TBA
ROYAL CANADIAN GOLF
ASSOCIATION
Phone: 905-849-9700
Fax: 905-845-7040
info@golfcanada.ca
www.golfcanada.ca

Jun 1 - Jun 6, 2021
PRINCIPAL CHARITY CLASSIC
Des Moines, IA
Wakonda Club
PGA CHAMPIONS TOUR
Phone: 904-285-3700
www.pgatour.com/champions

Jun 2 - Jun 3, 2021
SWING THOUGHT NATIONAL PRO
SERIES - BELMONT LAKE S GOLF
CLUB
Rocky Mount, NC
Belmont Lake Golf Club
SWING THOUGHT TOURNAMENTS
Phone: 800-992-8748
info@swingthought.com
www.swingthought.com

Jun 3 - Jun 9, 2021
NCAA DIVISION I SOFTBALL FINALS
Oklahoma City, OK
USA Softball Hall of Fame Stadium
NATIONAL COLLEGIATE ATHLETIC
ASSOCIATION
Phone: 317-917-6222
Fax: 317-917-6888
www.ncaa.org

Jun 3 - Jun 9, 2021
NCAA DIVISION III BASEBALL FINALS
Cedar Rapids, IA
Perfect Game Field at Veterans
Memorial Stadium

NATIONAL COLLEGIATE ATHLETIC
ASSOCIATION
Phone: 317-917-6222
Fax: 317-917-6888
www.ncaa.org

Jun 3 - Jun 6, 2021
PORSCHE EUROPEAN OPEN
Hamburg, Germany
Green Eagle Golf Courses
PGA EUROPEAN TOUR
International Ph: 44-0-1344-840400
International Fax: 44-0-1344-840500
www.europeantour.com

Jun 3 - Jun 6, 2021
THE REX HOSPITAL OPEN
Raleigh, NC
The Country Club at Wakefield
Plantation
PGA KORN FERRY TOUR
Phone: 904-285-3700
Fax: 904-285-7913
www.pgatour.com

Jun 3 - Jun 6, 2021
TRU BALL & BLACK EAGLE PRO/AM
London, KY
ARCHERY SHOOTERS ASSOCIATION
Phone: 770-795-0232
Fax: 770-795-0953
info@asaarchery.com
www.asaarchery.com

Jun 3 - Jun 6, 2021
US WOMEN'S OPEN
San Francisco, CA
The Olympic Club
U.S. GOLF ASSOCIATION
Phone: 908-234-2300
Fax: 908-234-9687
www.usga.org

Jun 3 - Jun 6, 2021
US WOMEN'S OPEN
Houston, TX
Champions Golf Course
LPGA TOUR
Phone: 386-274-6200
Fax: 386-274-1099
www.lpga.com

Jun 4 - Jun 5, 2021
BAIE ST PAUL CANADA CUP
Baie St. Paul, Canada
CANADIAN CYCLING ASSOCIATION
Phone: 613-248-1353
Fax: 613-248-9311
general@cyclingcanada.ca
www.cyclingcanada.ca

Jun 4 - Jun 6, 2021
NEXTGEN WESTERN
CHAMPIONSHIP
TBA, AB, Canada
ROYAL CANADIAN GOLF
ASSOCIATION
Phone: 905-849-9700
Fax: 905-845-7040
info@golfcanada.ca
www.golfcanada.ca

Jun 4 - Jun 6, 2021
VIRGINIA NHRA NATIONALS
North Dinwiddie, VA
Virginia Motorsports Park
NATIONAL HOT ROD ASSOCIATION
Phone: 626-914-4761
Fax: 626-963-5360
nhra@nhra.com
www.nhra.com

Jun 5, 2021
ALCATRAZ SHARKFEST SWIM
San Francisco, CA
Alcatraz Island
ENVIRO-SPORTS
Phone: 415-868-1829
info@envirosports.com
envirosports.com

Jun 5 - Jun 13, 2021
AMERICAN FAMILY INSURANCE
CHAMPIONSHIP
Madison, WI
University Ridge Golf Club
PGA CHAMPIONS TOUR
Phone: 904-285-3700
www.pgatour.com/champions

Jun 5 - Jun 7, 2021
DEADWOOD-MICKELSON TRAIL
MARATHON
Deadwood, SD
DEADWOOD-MICKELSON TRAIL
MARATHON
Phone: 605-390-6137
www.deadwoodmickelsontrailmarathon.com

Jun 5 - Jun 7, 2021
FIT MODEL WORLD CUP
Riga, Latvia
INTERNATIONAL FEDERATION OF
BODY BUILDING & FITNESS
International Ph: 34-91-535-28-19
contact@ifbb.com
www.ifbb.com

Jun 5 - Jun 13, 2021
LIBEMA OPEN
's-Hertogenbosch, Netherlands
WTA
Phone: 727-895-5000
Fax: 727-894-1982
feedback@wtatennis.com
www.wtatennis.com

Jun 5 - Jun 6, 2021
MULTI-GUN NATIONALS
US PRACTICAL SHOOTING
ASSOCIATION
Phone: 360-855-2245
Fax: 360-855-0380
office@uspsa.org
www.uspsa.org

Jun 5 - Jun 12, 2021
NCAA DIVISION II BASEBALL FINALS
Cary, NC
USA Baseball Training Complex
NATIONAL COLLEGIATE ATHLETIC
ASSOCIATION
Phone: 317-917-6222
Fax: 317-917-6888
www.ncaa.org

Jun 5, 2021
NEWPORT MARATHON
Newport, OR
NEWPORT MARATHON
Phone: 541-265-3446
run@newportmarathon.org
www.newportmarathon.org

Jun 5 - Jun 13, 2021
NOTTINGHAM OPEN
Nottingham, Great Britain
Nottingham Tennis Centre
WTA
Phone: 727-895-5000
Fax: 727-894-1982

feedback@wtatennis.com
www.wtatennis.com

Jun 5 - Jun 6, 2021
PCC NATIONALS
US PRACTICAL SHOOTING
ASSOCIATION
Phone: 360-855-2245
Fax: 360-855-0380
office@uspsa.org
www.uspsa.org

Jun 5, 2021
THUNDER VALLEY NATIONAL
Lakewood, CO
Thunder Valley Motocross Park
AMA PRO RACING
Phone: 386-492-1014
Fax: 386-274-2335
communications@amaproracing.com
www.amaproracing.com

Jun 6, 2021
AMA PRO HILLCLIMB
Spring Grove, PA
White Rose Motorcycle Club
AMA PRO RACING
Phone: 386-492-1014
Fax: 386-274-2335
communications@amaproracing.com
www.amaproracing.com

Jun 6, 2021
STEAMBOAT MARATHON
Steamboat Springs, CO
STEAMBOAT MARATHON
Phone: 970-879-0880
Fax: 970-879-3550
marathon@steamboatchamber.com
www.steamboatchamber.com

Jun 6, 2021
TOYOTA-SAVE MART 350
Sonoma, CA
Sonoma Raceway
NASCAR CUP SERIES
www.nascar.com

Jun 7 - Jun 13, 2021
FIBA AMERICAS U16 CHAMPIONSHIP
FOR MEN
TBA
USA BASKETBALL
Phone: 719-590-4800
Fax: 719-590-4811
fanmail@usabasketball.com
www.usab.com

Jun 7 - Jun 8, 2021
OHIO MIXED DOUBLES
Akron, OH
NATIONAL SHUFFLEBOARD
ASSOCIATION
usansa.weebly.com

Jun 9 - Jun 12, 2021
NCAA DIVISION I MEN'S/WOMEN'S
TRACK, OUTDOOR FIN ALS
Eugene, OR
Hayward Field
NATIONAL COLLEGIATE ATHLETIC
ASSOCIATION
Phone: 317-917-6222
Fax: 317-917-6888
www.ncaa.org

Jun 10 - Jun 13, 2021
BMW CHARITY PRO-AM
Greer, SC
Thornblade Club

PGA KORN FERRY TOUR
Phone: 904-285-3700
Fax: 904-285-7913
www.pgatour.com

Jun 10 - Jun 13, 2021
LPGA MEDIHEAL CHAMPIONSHIP
Daly City, CA
Lake Merced Golf Club
LPGA TOUR
Phone: 386-274-6200
Fax: 386-274-1099
www.lpga.com

Jun 10 - Jun 13, 2021
SCANDINAVIAN INVITATION
Gothenburg, Sweden
Hills Golf & Sports Club
PGA EUROPEAN TOUR
International Ph: 44-0-1344-840400
International Fax: 44-0-1344-840500
www.europeantour.com

Jun 10 - Jun 13, 2021
SUMMER SENIOR NATIONAL
CHAMPIONSHIPS
Toronto, Canada
DIVING CANADA
Phone: 613-736-5238
Fax: 613-736-0409
cada@diving.ca
www.diving.ca

Jun 10 - Jun 16, 2021
TEAM DART CHAMPIONSHIPS
Las Vegas, NV
Westgate Las Vegas Resort & Casino
NATIONAL DART ASSOCIATION
Phone: 800-808-9884
Fax: 708-226-1310
info@ndadarts.com
www.ndadarts.com

Jun 11 - Jun 13, 2021
ALABAMA STATE GAMES
Birmingham, AL
ASF FOUNDATION
Phone: 800-467-0422
Fax: 334-280-0988
support@asffoundation.org
www.asffoundation.org

Jun 11 - Jun 13, 2021
BASSMASTER CLASSIC
Fort Worth, TX
Lake Ray Roberts
BASS ANGLERS SPORTSMAN
SOCIETY
Phone: 877-227-7872
bassmaster@emailcustomerservice.com
www.bassmaster.com

Jun 11 - Jun 13, 2021
DIAMOND CUP LUXEMBOURG
Mondorf-Les-Bains, Luxembourg
INTERNATIONAL FEDERATION OF
BODY BUILDING & FITNESS
International Ph: 34-91-535-28-19
contact@ifbb.com
www.ifbb.com

Jun 11 - Jun 13, 2021
NEXTGEN PRAIRIE CHAMPIONSHIP
Ste. Anne, Canada
Quarry Oaks Golf Course
ROYAL CANADIAN GOLF
ASSOCIATION
Phone: 905-849-9700
Fax: 905-845-7040
info@golfcanada.ca
www.golfcanada.ca

Jun 4 - Jun 6, 2021
NHRA NEW ENGLAND NATIONALS
Epping, NH
New England Dragway
NATIONAL HOT ROD ASSOCIATION
Phone: 626-914-4761
Fax: 626-963-5360
nhra@nhra.com
www.nhra.com

Jun 11 - Jun 13, 2021
WORLD CHILDREN CHAMPIONSHIPS
Cacak, Serbia
INTERNATIONAL FEDERATION OF
BODY BUILDING & FITNESS
International Ph: 34-91-535-28-19
contact@ifbb.com
www.ifbb.com

Jun 12 - Jun 13, 2021
BALKAN CHAMPIONSHIPS
Drobeta, Turnu Severin, Romania
INTERNATIONAL FEDERATION OF
BODY BUILDING & FITNESS
International Ph: 34-91-535-28-19
contact@ifbb.com
www.ifbb.com

Jun 12 - Jun 13, 2021
CHEVROLET DUAL IN DETROIT 1&2
Detroit, MI
The Raceway at Belle Isle Park
NTT INDYCAR SERIES
Phone: 317-492-6526
indycar@indycar.com
www.indycar.com

Jun 12, 2021
HATFIELD-MCCOY MARATHON
Williamson, WV
HATFIELD-MCCOY MARATHON

Jun 12, 2021
NASCAR CAMPING WORLD TRUCK
SERIES RACE AT TEXAS
Fort Worth, TX
Texas Motor Speedway
NASCAR CAMPING WORLD TRUCK
SERIES
Phone: 800-630-0535
www.nascar.com

Jun 12, 2021
ROMANCING THE ISLAND HALF
MARATHON & 10K
Tiburon, CA
Angel Island State Park
ENVIRO-SPORTS
Phone: 415-868-1829
info@envirosports.com
envirosports.com

Jun 12, 2021
SPEEDYCASH.COM 200
Fort Worth, TX
Texas Motor Speedway
NASCAR CAMPING WORLD TRUCK
SERIES
Phone: 800-630-0535
www.nascar.com

Jun 13, 2021
AMA PRO HILLCLIMB
Freemansburg, PA
Bushkill Valley Motorcycle Club
AMA PRO RACING
Phone: 386-492-1014
Fax: 386-274-2335
communications@amaproracing.com
www.amaproracing.com

Jun 13, 2021
NASCAR ALL-STAR OPEN
Concord, NC
Charlotte Motor Speedway
NASCAR CUP SERIES
www.nascar.com

Jun 13, 2021
NASCAR ALL-STAR RACE
Concord, NC
Charlotte Motor Speedway
NASCAR CUP SERIES
www.nascar.com

Jun 14 - Jun 20, 2021
BIRMINGHAM CLASSIC
Birmingham, Great Britain
WTA
Phone: 727-895-5000
Fax: 727-894-1982
feedback@wtatennis.com
www.wtatennis.com

Jun 14 - Jun 18, 2021
US NATIONAL RACING TOUR
Various
US WINDSURFING ASSOCIATION
Phone: 877-386-8708
info@uswindsurfing.org
uswindsurfing.org

Jun 14 - Jun 20, 2021
WICHITA OPEN
Wichita, KS
Crestview Country Club
PGA KORN FERRY TOUR
Phone: 904-285-3700
Fax: 904-285-7913
www.pgatour.com

Jun 15 - Jun 19, 2021
CANADIAN MEN'S TEAM
CHAMPIONSHIP
Niagara-On-The-Lake, Canada
The Club at White Oaks
SQUASH CANADA
Phone: 613-228-7724
Fax: 613-228-7232
info@squash.ca
www.squash.ca

Jun 15 - Jun 19, 2021
CANADIAN WOMEN'S TEAM
CHAMPIONSHIP
Niagara-On-The-Lake, Canada
The Club at White Oaks
SQUASH CANADA
Phone: 613-228-7724
Fax: 613-228-7232
info@squash.ca
www.squash.ca

Jun 16 - Jun 20, 2021
CANADIAN SQUASH
CHAMPIONSHIPS
Niagara-On-The-Lake, Canada
The Club at White Oaks
SQUASH CANADA
Phone: 613-228-7724
Fax: 613-228-7232
info@squash.ca
www.squash.ca

Jun 16 - Jun 17, 2021
SWING THOUGHT NATIONAL PRO
SERIES - RANCHO BERNA RDO INN
San Diego, CA
Rancho Bernardo Inn
SWING THOUGHT TOURNAMENTS
Phone: 800-992-8748

info@swingthought.com
www.swingthought.com

Jun 17 - Jun 29, 2021
AAU JUNIOR NATIONAL VOLLEYBALL
CHAMPIONSHIPS
Orlando, FL
ESPN Wide World of Sports
AMATEUR ATHLETIC UNION
Phone: 407-934-7200
Fax: 407-934-7242
www.aausports.org

Jun 17 - Jun 20, 2021
FARMFOODS EUROPEAN LEGENDS
LINKS CHAMPIONSHIP
Padstow, England
Trevose Golf & Country Club
PGA EUROPEAN STAYSURE TOUR
International Ph: 44-0-1344-840400
International Fax: 44-0-1344-840500
www.europeantour.com/staysure-tour

Jun 17 - Jun 20, 2021
MEIJER LPGA CLASSIC FOR SIMPLY
GIVE
Grand Rapids, MI
Blythefield Country Club
LPGA TOUR
Phone: 386-274-6200
Fax: 386-274-1099
www.lpga.com

Jun 17 - Jun 20, 2021
US OPEN
San Diego, CA
Torrey Pines Golf Course
U.S. GOLF ASSOCIATION
Phone: 908-234-2300
Fax: 908-234-9687
www.usga.org

Jun 18 - Jun 29, 2021
AAU BOYS' & GIRLS' VOLLEYBALL
NATIONAL CHAMPIONS HIPS
Orlando, FL
Orlando Sports Center
AMATEUR ATHLETIC UNION
Phone: 407-934-7200
Fax: 407-934-7242
www.aausports.org

Jun 18 - Jun 20, 2021
CANMORE CANADA CUP
Canmore, Canada
CANADIAN CYCLING ASSOCIATION
Phone: 613-248-1353
Fax: 613-248-9311
general@cyclingcanada.ca
www.cyclingcanada.ca

Jun 18 - Jun 20, 2021
DIAMOND CUP OSTRAVA
Ostrava, Czech Republic
INTERNATIONAL FEDERATION OF
BODY BUILDING & FITNESS
International Ph: 34-91-535-28-19
contact@ifbb.com
www.ifbb.com

Jun 18 - Jun 19, 2021
OKLAHOMA CITY MILE I & II
Oklahoma City, OK
Remington Park
AMA PRO RACING
Phone: 386-492-1014
Fax: 386-274-2335
communications@amaproracing.com
www.amaproracing.com

Jun 18 - Jun 20, 2021
US SINGLEHANDED
CHAMPIONSHIPS
Norfolk, VA
Big Blue Sailing Academy
US SAILING
Phone: 401-683-0800
Fax: 401-683-0840
info@ussailing.org
www.ussailing.org

Jun 18 - Jun 20, 2021
USA BMX MIDWEST NATIONALS
Rockford, IL
USA BMX
Phone: 480-961-1903
Fax: 480-961-1842
www.usabmx.com

Jun 19, 2021
HIGH POINT NATIONAL
Mount Morris, PA
High Point Raceway
AMA PRO RACING
Phone: 386-492-1014
Fax: 386-274-2335
communications@amaproracing.com
www.amaproracing.com

Jun 19, 2021
LEADVILLE TRAIL MARATHON &
HEAVY HALF
Leadville, CO
LEADVILLE TRAIL MARATHON
leadville@ltevents.zendesk.com
www.leadvilleraceseries.com

Jun 19, 2021
MAYOR'S MARATHON
Anchorage, AK
UAA ATHLETICS DEPARTMENT
track@uaa.alaska.edu
www.mayorsmarathon.com

Jun 19 - Jun 30, 2021
NCAA DIVISION I BASEBALL FINALS
Omaha, NE
TD Ameritrade Park Omaha
NATIONAL COLLEGIATE ATHLETIC
ASSOCIATION
Phone: 317-917-6222
Fax: 317-917-6888
www.ncaa.org

Jun 19 - Jun 20, 2021
PANORAMA CANADA CUP
Panorama, Canada
CANADIAN CYCLING ASSOCIATION
Phone: 613-248-1353
Fax: 613-248-9311
general@cyclingcanada.ca
www.cyclingcanada.ca

Jun 19 - Jun 20, 2021
SUNSET RIDGE
Walnut, IL
Sunset Ridge MX
AMA PRO RACING
Phone: 386-492-1014
Fax: 386-274-2335
communications@amaproracing.com
www.amaproracing.com

Aug 20, 2021
ALCATRAZ XL ESCAPE FROM THE
ROCK DUATHLON
San Francisco, CA
Alcatraz Island
ENVIRO-SPORTS
Phone: 415-868-1829

info@envirosports.com
envirosports.com

Jun 20 - Jun 26, 2021
BAD HOMBURG OPEN
Bad Homburg, Germany
WTA
Phone: 727-895-5000
Fax: 727-894-1982
feedback@wtatennis.com
www.wtatennis.com

Jun 20, 2021
ESTES PARK MARATHON
Estes Park, CO
ESTES PARK MARATHON
Phone: 970-586-8189
belle@epmarathon.org
www.epmarathon.org

Jun 20 - Jun 27, 2021
FIBA AMERICAS U16 CHAMPIONSHIP
FOR WOMEN
TBA
USA BASKETBALL
Phone: 719-590-4800
Fax: 719-590-4811
fanmail@usabasketball.com
www.usab.com

Jun 20, 2021
REV GROUP GRAND PRIX AT ROAD
AMERICA
Elkhart Lake, WI
Road America
NTT INDYCAR SERIES
Phone: 317-492-6526
indycar@indycar.com
www.indycar.com

Jun 20, 2021
SAN JUAN ISLAND MARATHON
Friday Harbor, WA
LAKEDALE RESORT
Phone: 800-617-2267
www.lakedale.com

Jun 6, 2021
CASPER WYOMING MARATHON
Casper, WY
CASPER WYOMING MARATHON
Phone: 307-577-4974
www.runwyoming.com

Jun 21 - Jun 27, 2021
EASTBOURNE INTERNATIONAL
Eastbourne, Great Britain
WTA
Phone: 727-895-5000
Fax: 727-894-1982
feedback@wtatennis.com
www.wtatennis.com

Jun 22 - Jun 27, 2021
KPMG WOMEN'S PGA
CHAMPIONSHIP
Newton Square, PA
Aronimink Golf Club
LPGA TOUR
Phone: 386-274-6200
Fax: 386-274-1099
www.lpga.com

Jun 22 - Jun 27, 2021
USA GYMNASTICS CHAMPIONSHIPS
St. Louis, MO
America's Center Convention Complex
& The Dome
USA GYMNASTICS
Phone: 317-237-5050
Fax: 317-237-5069

membership@usagym.org
usagym.org

Jun 23 - Jun 27, 2021
BMW INTERNATIONAL OPEN
Munich, Germany
Golf Club Munich Eichenried
PGA EUROPEAN TOUR
International Ph: 44-0-1344-840400
International Fax: 44-0-1344-840500
www.europeantour.com

Jun 23 - Jun 27, 2021
BRIDGESTONE SENIOR PLAYERS
CHAMPIONSHIP
Akron, OH
Firestone Country Club
PGA CHAMPIONS TOUR
Phone: 904-285-3700
www.pgatour.com/champions

Jun 23 - Jun 27, 2021
MATHEWS PRO/AM
Metropolis, IL
ARCHERY SHOOTERS ASSOCIATION
Phone: 770-795-0232
Fax: 770-795-0953
info@asaarchery.com
www.asaarchery.com

Jun 24 - Jun 27, 2021
AMATEUR ROAD NATIONAL
CHAMPIONSHIPS
Clay County, FL
USA CYCLING
Phone: 719-434-4200
Fax: 719-434-4300
help@usacycling.org
www.usacycling.org

Jun 24 - Jun 27, 2021
SUMMIT RACING EQUIPMENT NHRA
NATIONALS
Norwalk, OH
Summit Racing Equipment Motorsports
Park
NATIONAL HOT ROD ASSOCIATION
Phone: 626-914-4761
Fax: 626-963-5360
nhra@nhra.com
www.nhra.com

Jun 24 - Jun 27, 2021
TRAVELERS CHAMPIONSHIP
Cromwell, CT
TPC River Highlands
PGA TOUR
Phone: 904-285-3700
www.pgatour.com

Jun 24 - Jun 25, 2021
WALLEYE TOUR-HURON
Huron, OH
Lake Erie
NATIONAL WALLEYE TOUR
Phone: 612-424-0708
Fax: 866-727-2809
www.nationalwalleyetour.com

Jun 25 - Jun 28, 2021
AAU 5TH GRADE DI, DII & DIII GIRLS'
BASKETBALL C HAMPIONSHIPS
West Chester, OH
AMATEUR ATHLETIC UNION
Phone: 407-934-7200
Fax: 407-934-7242
www.aausports.org

Jun 25 - Jun 28, 2021
AAU 6TH GRADE DI, DII & DIII GIRLS'
BASKETBALL C HAMPIONSHIPS
West Chester, OH
AMATEUR ATHLETIC UNION
Phone: 407-934-7200
Fax: 407-934-7242
www.aausports.org

Jun 25 - Jun 28, 2021
AAU 7TH GRADE DI, DII & DIII GIRLS'
BASKETBALL C HAMPIONSHIPS
West Chester, OH
AMATEUR ATHLETIC UNION
Phone: 407-934-7200
Fax: 407-934-7242
www.aausports.org

Jun 25, 2021
CHICAGOLAND 225
Joliet, IL
Chicagoland Speedway
NASCAR CAMPING WORLD TRUCK
SERIES
Phone: 800-630-0535
www.nascar.com

Jun 25 - Jun 27, 2021
PHILADELPHIA OPEN
Philadelphia, PA
NATIONAL X BALL LEAGUE
camille@nxlpaintball.com
nxlpaintball.com

Jun 26 - Jun 27, 2021
GEORGIA GRAND PRIX
Tbilisi, Georgia
INTERNATIONAL FEDERATION OF
BODY BUILDING & FITNESS
International Ph: 34-91-535-28-19
contact@ifbb.com
www.ifbb.com

Jun 26 - Jul 5, 2021
GIRLS' JUNIOR NATIONAL
CHAMPIONSHIP
Dallas, TX
USA VOLLEYBALL
Phone: 719-228-6800
Fax: 719-228-6899
postmaster@usav.org
www.teamusa.org/USA-Volleyball

Jun 26 - Jun 27, 2021
JUNIOR U.S. OPEN WATER SKI
CHAMPIONSHIPS
Martindale, TX
USA WATER SKI
Phone: 863-324-4341
Fax: 863-325-8259
www.usawaterski.org

Jun 26, 2021
LIMA HALF-MILE
Lima, OH
Allen County Fairgrounds
AMA PRO RACING
Phone: 386-492-1014
Fax: 386-274-2335
communications@amaproracing.com
www.amaproracing.com

Jun 26, 2021
NASCAR CUP SERIES RACE AT
POCONO 1
Long Pond, PA
Pocono Raceway
NASCAR CUP SERIES
www.nascar.com

Jun 26, 2021
SOUTHWICK NATIONAL
Southwick, MA
The Wick 338
AMA PRO RACING
Phone: 386-492-1014
Fax: 386-274-2335
communications@amaproracing.com
www.amaproracing.com

Jun 26 - Jul 18, 2021
TOUR DE FRANCE
Paris, France
AMAURY SPORT ORGANIZATION
International Ph: 33-1-41-33-14-00
contact@aso.fr
www.aso.fr

Jun 26 - Jun 27, 2021
WHISTLER CANADA CUP
Whistler, Canada
CANADIAN CYCLING ASSOCIATION
Phone: 613-248-1353
Fax: 613-248-9311
general@cyclingcanada.ca
www.cyclingcanada.ca

Jun 27, 2021
NASCAR CUP SERIES RACE AT
POCONO 2
Long Pond, PA
Pocono Raceway
NASCAR CUP SERIES
www.nascar.com

Jun 28 - Jul 4, 2021
ANNUAL WORLD'S OLDEST
CONTINUOUS RODEO
Prescott, AZ
PROFESSIONAL RODEO COWBOY
ASSOCIATION
Phone: 719-593-8840
Fax: 719-548-4876
prorodeor@prorodeo.com
www.prorodeo.com

Jun 28 - Jul 4, 2021
DICK'S SPORTING GOODS OPEN
Endicott, NY
En-Joie Golf Club
PGA CHAMPIONS TOUR
Phone: 904-285-3700
www.pgatour.com/champions

Jun 28 - Jul 4, 2021
FITNESS SPORTS GAMES
Santa Susanna, Spain
INTERNATIONAL FEDERATION OF
BODY BUILDING & FITNESS
International Ph: 34-91-535-28-19
contact@ifbb.com
www.ifbb.com

Jun 28 - Jun 30, 2021
NEXTGEN QUEBEC CHAMPIONSHIP
Hemmingford, Canada
Club de Golf de Hemmingford
ROYAL CANADIAN GOLF
ASSOCIATION
Phone: 905-849-9700
Fax: 905-845-7040
info@golfcanada.ca
www.golfcanada.ca

Jun 28 - Jul 11, 2021
THE CHAMPIONSHIPS
Wimbledon, Great Britain
WTA
Phone: 727-895-5000
Fax: 727-894-1982

events/meetings/shows

feedback@wtatennis.com
www.wtatennis.com

Jun 28 - Jul 11, 2021
WIMBLEDON
London, United Kingdom
THE ALL ENGLAND LAWN TENNIS
CLUB
International Ph: +44 (0)20 89441066
International Fax: +44 (0)20 89478752
www.wimbledon.com

Jun 29 - Jul 3, 2021
AAU KARATE NATIONAL
CHAMPIONSHIPS
Greensville, SC
Bon Secours Wellness Arena
AMATEUR ATHLETIC UNION
Phone: 407-934-7200
Fax: 407-934-7242
www.aausports.org

Jun 30 - Jul 7, 2021
BOYS' JUNIOR NATIONAL
CHAMPIONSHIP
Reno, NV
USA VOLLEYBALL
Phone: 719-228-6800
Fax: 719-228-6899
postmaster@usav.org
www.teamusa.org/USA-Volleyball

Jul TBA, 2021
AAU GIRLS' BASKETBALL
INTERNATIONAL CHAMPIONSHIP S
Orlando, FL
AMATEUR ATHLETIC UNION
Phone: 407-934-7200
Fax: 407-934-7242
www.aausports.org

Jul TBA, 2021
AAU NATIONAL BASEBALL
CHAMPIONSHIP VIRGINIA
Virginia Beach, VA
AMATEUR ATHLETIC UNION
Phone: 407-934-7200
Fax: 407-934-7242
www.aausports.org

Jul TBA, 2021
JUNIOR BEACH TOUR NATIONAL
CHAMPIONSHIPS
Huntington Beach, CA
USA VOLLEYBALL
Phone: 719-228-6800
Fax: 719-228-6899
postmaster@usav.org
www.teamusa.org/USA-Volleyball

Jul TBA, 2021
JUNIOR NATIONAL CHAMPIONSHIPS
Frisco, TX
USA BADMINTON
Phone: 714-765-2952
usab@usabadminton.org
www.usabadminton.org

Jul TBA, 2021
NATIONAL THREE POSITION AIR
RIFLE CHAMPIONSHIP P RECISION
NATIONAL RIFLE ASSOCIATION -
COMPETITIVE SHOOTING DIVISION
Phone: 703-267-1465
competitions.nra.org

Jul TBA, 2021
USA SOFTBALL INTERNATIONAL
CUP
USA SOFTBALL
Phone: 405-424-5266

info@softball.org
www.usasoftball.com

Jul 1 - Jul 4, 2021
AAU 13 & UNDER DI & DII BOYS'
BASKETBALL WORLD C
HAMPIONSHIPS
Greensboro, NC
AMATEUR ATHLETIC UNION
Phone: 407-934-7200
Fax: 407-934-7242
www.aausports.org

Jul 1 - Jul 4, 2021
AAU 14U & 15U/9TH EAST COAST DIII
BOYS' BASKETBA LL
CHAMPIONSHIPS
Hampton, VA
AMATEUR ATHLETIC UNION
Phone: 407-934-7200
Fax: 407-934-7242
www.aausports.org

Jul 1 - Jul 4, 2021
AAU 15U/9TH GRADE DI & DII BOYS'
BASKETBALL WORL D
CHAMPIONSHIPS
Orlando, FL
AMATEUR ATHLETIC UNION
Phone: 407-934-7200
Fax: 407-934-7242
www.aausports.org

Jul 1 - Jul 4, 2021
AAU 16U/10TH GRADE & 17U/11TH
GRADE EAST COAST D III BOYS'
BASKETBALL CHAMPIONSHIPS
Hampton, VA
AMATEUR ATHLETIC UNION
Phone: 407-934-7200
Fax: 407-934-7242
www.aausports.org

Jul 1 - Jul 4, 2021
AAU 7TH GRADE DI & DII BOYS'
BASKETBALL WORLD CH
AMPIONSHIPS
Greensboro, NC
AMATEUR ATHLETIC UNION
Phone: 407-934-7200
Fax: 407-934-7242
www.aausports.org

Jul 1 - Jul 4, 2021
AAU WEST COAST TRACK & FIELD
NATIONAL CHAMPIONSH IP
Reno, NV
AMATEUR ATHLETIC UNION
Phone: 407-934-7200
Fax: 407-934-7242
www.aausports.org

Jul 1 - Jul 4, 2021
DUBAI DUTY FREE IRISH OPEN
Thomastown, Co Kilkenny, Ireland
Mount Juliet Estate
PGA EUROPEAN TOUR
International Ph: 44-0-1344-840400
International Fax: 44-0-1344-840500
www.europeantour.com

Jul 1 - Jul 7, 2021
ELITE TRACK NATIONAL
CHAMPIONSHIPS
Carson, CA
USA CYCLING
Phone: 719-434-4200
Fax: 719-434-4300
help@usacycling.org
www.usacycling.org

Jul 1 - Jul 7, 2021
PARA-CYCLING TRACK NATIONAL
CHAMPIONSHIPS
Carson, CA
USA CYCLING
Phone: 719-434-4200
Fax: 719-434-4300
help@usacycling.org
www.usacycling.org

Jul 1 - Jul 4, 2021
SPEEDO JUNIOR ELITE NATIONAL
CHAMPIONSHIPS
Winnipeg, Canada
DIVING CANADA
Phone: 613-736-5238
Fax: 613-736-0409
cada@diving.ca
www.diving.ca

Jul 1 - Jul 3, 2021
US OPEN - MARTIAL ARTS
CHAMPIONSHIPS
Orlando, FL
USA OPEN KARATE
usopen-karate.com

Jul 1 - Jul 4, 2021
VOLUNTEERS OF AMERICA CLASSIC
The Colony, TX
Old American Golf Club
LPGA TOUR
Phone: 386-274-6200
Fax: 386-274-1099
www.lpga.com

Jul 2 - Jul 5, 2021
AAU 7U, 8U & 2ND GRADE BOYS'
BASKETBALL WORLD CH
AMPIONSHIPS
Westminster, MD
AMATEUR ATHLETIC UNION
Phone: 407-934-7200
Fax: 407-934-7242
www.aausports.org

Jul 2 - Jul 4, 2021
HOME OF CHAMPIONS RODEO
Red Lodge, MT
PROFESSIONAL RODEO COWBOY
ASSOCIATION
Phone: 719-593-8840
Fax: 719-548-4876
prorodeor@prorodeo.com
www.prorodeo.com

Jul 2 - Jul 4, 2021
USA BMX STARS & STRIPES
NATIONALS
Pittsburgh, PA
USA BMX
Phone: 480-961-1903
Fax: 480-961-1842
www.usabmx.com

July 3 - July 5, 2021
2021 ICF CANOE OCEAN RACING
WORLD CUP
Lanzarote, Spain
INTERNATIONAL CANOE FEDERATION
International Ph: 41 (0)21 612 0290
info@canoeicf.com
www.canoeicf.com

Jul 3 - Jul 6, 2021
AAU 11 & UNDER DI, DII & DIII BOYS'
BASKETBALL W ORLD
CHAMPIONSHIPS
Orlando, FL

AMATEUR ATHLETIC UNION
Phone: 407-934-7200
Fax: 407-934-7242
www.aausports.org

Jul 3 - Jul 6, 2021
AAU 2ND & 3RD GRADE GIRLS'
BASKETBALL CHAMPIONSH IPS
Orlando, FL
AMATEUR ATHLETIC UNION
Phone: 407-934-7200
Fax: 407-934-7242
www.aausports.org

Jul 3 - Jul 6, 2021
AAU 3RD GRADE DI & DII BOYS'
BASKETBALL WORLD CH
AMPIONSHIPS
Orlando, FL
AMATEUR ATHLETIC UNION
Phone: 407-934-7200
Fax: 407-934-7242
www.aausports.org

Jul 3 - Jul 6, 2021
AAU 4TH GRADE DI, DII & DIII GIRLS'
BASKETBALL C HAMPIONSHIPS
Orlando, FL
AMATEUR ATHLETIC UNION
Phone: 407-934-7200
Fax: 407-934-7242
www.aausports.org

Jul 3 - Jul 6, 2021
AAU 5TH GRADE DI & DII BOYS'
BASKETBALL WORLD CH
AMPIONSHIPS
Orlando, FL
AMATEUR ATHLETIC UNION
Phone: 407-934-7200
Fax: 407-934-7242
www.aausports.org

Jul 3 - Jul 6, 2021
AAU 9 & UNDER DI & DII BOYS'
BASKETBALL WORLD CH
AMPIONSHIPS
Orlando, FL
AMATEUR ATHLETIC UNION
Phone: 407-934-7200
Fax: 407-934-7242
www.aausports.org

Jul 3 - Jul 4, 2021
CLASSIC PHYSIQUE OF AMERICA
Quito, Ecuador
INTERNATIONAL FEDERATION OF
BODY BUILDING & FITNESS
International Ph: 34-91-535-28-19
contact@ifbb.com
www.ifbb.com

Jul 3 - Jul 11, 2021
FIBA U19 WORLD CUP FOR MEN
Daugavpils and Riga, Latvia
USA BASKETBALL
Phone: 719-590-4800
Fax: 719-590-4811
fanmail@usabasketball.com
www.usab.com

Jul 3 - Jul 9, 2021
J80 WORLD CHAMPIONSHIP
Rungsted, Copenhagen
WORLD SAILING
International Ph: 44 (0)20 3940 4888
www.sailing.org

Jul 3 - Jul 4, 2021
PLEASURE VALLEY
Seward, PA

Pleasure Valley Raceway
AMA PRO RACING
Phone: 386-492-1014
Fax: 386-274-2335
communications@amaproracing.com
www.amaproracing.com

Jul 3, 2021
REDBUD NATIONAL
Buchanan, MI
RedBux MX
AMA PRO RACING
Phone: 386-492-1014
Fax: 386-274-2335
communications@amaproracing.com
www.amaproracing.com

Jul 3 - Jul 6, 2021
USA FENCING NATIONAL
CHAMPIONSHIPS
Philadelphia, PA
USA FENCING
Phone: 719-866-4511
Fax: 719-632-5737
information@usfencing.org
www.usfencing.org

Jul 4 - Jul 10, 2021
AAU TAEKWONDO NATIONAL
CHAMPIONSHIPS
Las Vegas, NV
MGM Grand Hotel & Resort
AMATEUR ATHLETIC UNION
Phone: 407-934-7200
Fax: 407-934-7242
www.aausports.org

Jul 4, 2021
HONDA INDY 200 AT MID-OHIO
Lexington, OH
Mid-Ohio Sports Car Course
NTT INDYCAR SERIES
Phone: 317-492-6526
indycar@indycar.com
www.indycar.com

Jul 5 - Jul 11, 2021
AAU NATIONAL BASEBALL
CHAMPIONSHIP LOUISIANA
Sterlington, LA
Sterlington Sports Complex
AMATEUR ATHLETIC UNION
Phone: 407-934-7200
Fax: 407-934-7242
www.aausports.org

Jul 5 - Jul 11, 2021
JOHN DEERE CLASSIC
Silvis, IL
TPC Deere Run
PGA TOUR
Phone: 904-285-3700
www.pgatour.com

Jul 5 - Jul 18, 2021
NORDEA OPEN
Bastad, Sweden
WTA
Phone: 727-895-5000
Fax: 727-894-1982
feedback@wtatennis.com
www.wtatennis.com

Jul 7 - Jul 11, 2021
AAU 10 & UNDER DI & DII BOYS'
BASKETBALL WORLD C
HAMPIONSHIPS
Clarksville, TN
AMATEUR ATHLETIC UNION
Phone: 407-934-7200

Fax: 407-934-7242
www.aausports.org

Jul 7 - Jul 11, 2021
AAU 4TH GRADE DI & DII BOYS'
BASKETBALL WORLD CH
AMPIONSHIPS
Hampton Roads, VA
AMATEUR ATHLETIC UNION
Phone: 407-934-7200
Fax: 407-934-7242
www.aausports.org

Jul 7 - Jul 9, 2021
AAU SOUTHEAST DIII BOYS'
BASKETBALL CHAMPIONSHIP S
Orlando, FL
AMATEUR ATHLETIC UNION
Phone: 407-934-7200
Fax: 407-934-7242
www.aausports.org

Jul 7 - Jul 17, 2021
NATIONAL JUNIOR OLYMPICS
Lubbock, TX
USA BOXING
Phone: 719-866-2323
www.teamusa.org/USA-Boxing

Jul 8 - Jul 9, 2021
AAU TRACK & FIELD PRIMARY
NATIONAL CHAMPIONSHIPS
Orlando, FL
AMATEUR ATHLETIC UNION
Phone: 407-934-7200
Fax: 407-934-7242
www.aausports.org

Jul 8 - Jul 11, 2021
ABERDEEN STANDARD
INVESTMENTS SCOTTISH OPEN
North Berwick, Scotland, UK
The Renaissance Club
PGA EUROPEAN TOUR
International Ph: 44-0-1344-840400
International Fax: 44-0-1344-840500
www.europeantour.com

Jul 8 - Jul 11, 2021
BASSMASTER ELITE SERIES - LAKE
CHAMPLAIN
Plattsburgh, NY
Lake Champlain
BASS ANGLERS SPORTSMAN
SOCIETY
Phone: 877-227-7872
bassmaster@emailcustomerservice.com
www.bassmaster.com

Jul 8 - Jul 12, 2021
GRANDFATHER MOUNTAIN
HIGHLAND GAMES
Linville, NC
GRANDFATHER MOUNTAIN HIGHLAND
GAMES
Phone: 828-733-1333
Fax: 828-733-0092
weaverjt@appstate.edu
www.gmhg.org

Jul 8 - Jul 11, 2021
MARATHON LPGA CLASSIC
Sylvania, OH
Highland Meadows Golf Club
LPGA TOUR
Phone: 386-274-6200
Fax: 386-274-1099
www.lpga.com

Jul 8 - Jul 11, 2021
TPC COLORADO CHAMPIONSHIP AT
HERON LAKES
Berthoud, CO
TPC Colorado
PGA KORN FERRY TOUR
Phone: 904-285-3700
Fax: 904-285-7913
www.pgatour.com

Jul 8 - Jul 11, 2021
US SENIOR OPEN CHAMPIONSHIP
Omaha, NB
Omaha Country Club
PGA CHAMPIONS TOUR
Phone: 904-285-3700
www.pgatour.com/champions

Jul 8 - Jul 11, 2021
US SENIOR OPEN CHAMPIONSHIP
Omaha, NB
Omaha Country Club
PGA EUROPEAN STAYSURE TOUR
International Ph: 44-0-1344-840400
International Fax: 44-0-1344-840500
www.europeantour.com/staysure-tour

Jul 9, 2021
AKC RALLY NATIONAL
CHAMPIONSHIP
Wilmington, OH
AMERICAN KENNEL CLUB
Phone: 919-233-9767
Fax: 919-816-4246
info@akc.org
www.akc.org

Jul 9 - Jul 18, 2021
MOUNTAIN BIKE NATIONAL
CHAMPIONSHIPS
Winter Park, CO
USA CYCLING
Phone: 719-434-4200
Fax: 719-434-4300
help@usacycling.org
www.usacycling.org

Jul 9 - Jul 18, 2021
NARCH FINALS
Irvine, CA
The Rinks, Irvine Inline
NORTH AMERICAN ROLLER HOCKEY
CHAMPIONSHIPS
Phone: 760-889-6909
daryn@narch.com
www.narch.com

Jul 9, 2021
NASCAR CAMPING WORLD TRUCK
SERIES RACE AT KNOXVI LLE
Knoxville, IA
Knoxville Raceway
NASCAR CAMPING WORLD TRUCK
SERIES
Phone: 800-630-0535
www.nascar.com

Jul 9 - Jul 11, 2021
SWISS SENIORS OPEN
Bad Ragaz, Switzerland
PGA EUROPEAN STAYSURE TOUR
International Ph: 44-0-1344-840400
International Fax: 44-0-1344-840500
www.europeantour.com/staysure-tour

Jul 7 - Aug 2, 2021
USA ROLLER SPORTS NATIONAL
CHAMPIONSHIPS
Cedar Rapids, IA

USA ROLLER SPORTS
Phone: 402-483-7551
Fax: 402-483-1465
www.teamusa.org/USA-Roller-Sports

Jul 10 - Jul 17, 2021
AAU TRACK & FIELD CLUB
CHAMPIONSHIPS
Kissimmee, FL
AMATEUR ATHLETIC UNION
Phone: 407-934-7200
Fax: 407-934-7242
www.aausports.org

Jul 10 - Jul 11, 2021
AKC NATIONAL OBEDIENCE
CHAMPIONSHIP
Wilmington, OH
AMERICAN KENNEL CLUB
Phone: 919-233-9767
Fax: 919-816-4246
info@akc.org
www.akc.org

Jul 10, 2021
GRANDFATHER MOUNTAIN
MARATHON
Boone, NC
GRANDFATHER MOUNTAIN HIGHLAND
GAMES
Phone: 828-733-1333
Fax: 828-733-0092
weaverjt@appstate.edu
www.gmhg.org

Jul 10 - Jul 18, 2021
LADIES OPEN LAUSANNE
Lausanne, Switzerland
WTA
Phone: 727-895-5000
Fax: 727-894-1982
feedback@wtatennis.com
www.wtatennis.com

Jul 10, 2021
LADY LIBERTY SHARKFEST SWIM
Jersey City, NJ
Liberty State Park
ENVIRO-SPORTS
Phone: 415-868-1829
info@envirosports.com
envirosports.com

Jul 11, 2021
HONDA INDY TORONTO
Toronto, Canada
Streets of Toronto
NTT INDYCAR SERIES
Phone: 317-492-6526
indycar@indycar.com
www.indycar.com

Jul 11, 2021
PANASONIC NEW YORK CITY
TRIATHLON
New York, NY
LIFE TIME FITNESS
ltfmedia@lifetimefitness.com
www.eventsbylifetime.com

Jul 11, 2021
QUAKER STATE 400
Sparta, KY
Kentucky Speedway
NASCAR CUP SERIES
www.nascar.com

Jul 11 - Jul 18, 2021
THE OPEN CHAMPIONSHIP
Sandwich, Kent, England
Royal St. George's Golf Course

PGA TOUR
Phone: 904-285-3700
www.pgatour.com

Jul 12 - Jul 15, 2021
AAU 12 & UNDER DI & DII BOYS'
BASKETBALL WORLD C
HAMPIONSHIPS
Hampton, VA
AMATEUR ATHLETIC UNION
Phone: 407-934-7200
Fax: 407-934-7242
www.aausports.org

Jul 12 - Jul 18, 2021
J&T BANKA PRAGUE OPEN
Prague, Czech Republic
WTA
Phone: 727-895-5000
Fax: 727-894-1982
feedback@wtatennis.com
www.wtatennis.com

Jul 12 - Jul 17, 2021
US GIRLS' JUNIOR
Chevy Chase, MD
columbia country club
U.S. GOLF ASSOCIATION
Phone: 908-234-2300
Fax: 908-234-9687
www.usga.org

Jul 13 - Jul 16, 2021
AAU 16U/10TH GRADE DI & DII BOYS'
BASKETBALL WOR LD
CHAMPIONSHIPS
Orlando, FL
AMATEUR ATHLETIC UNION
Phone: 407-934-7200
Fax: 407-934-7242
www.aausports.org

Jul 13 - Jul 16, 2021
AAU 17U/11TH GRADE DI & DII BOYS'
BASKETBALL WOR LD
CHAMPIONSHIPS
Orlando, FL
AMATEUR ATHLETIC UNION
Phone: 407-934-7200
Fax: 407-934-7242
www.aausports.org

Jul 13 - Jul 16, 2021
AAU 20 & UNDER BOYS'
BASKETBALL WORLD CHAMPIONSH
IPS
Orlando, FL
AMATEUR ATHLETIC UNION
Phone: 407-934-7200
Fax: 407-934-7242
www.aausports.org

Jul 13 - Jul 15, 2021
NEXTGEN ATLANTIC CHAMPIONSHIP
Cardigan, Canada
Dundarave Golf Course
ROYAL CANADIAN GOLF
ASSOCIATION
Phone: 905-849-9700
Fax: 905-845-7040
info@golfcanada.ca
www.golfcanada.ca

Jul 13 - Jul 14, 2021
US LACROSSE NATIONALS
Frederica, DE
US LACROSSE
Phone: 410-235-6882
Fax: 410-366-6735
info@uslacrosse.org
www.uslacrosse.org

Jul 14 - Jul 17, 2021
DOW GREAT LAKES BAY
INVITATIONAL
Midland, MI
Midland Country Club
LPGA TOUR
Phone: 386-274-6200
Fax: 386-274-1099
www.lpga.com

Jul 15 - Jul 18, 2021
2021 ICF JUNIOR & U23 CANOE
SPRINT WORLD CHAMPIO NSHIPS
Montemor-O-Velho, Portugal
INTERNATIONAL CANOE FEDERATION
International Ph: 41 (0)21 612 0290
info@canoeicf.com
www.canoeicf.com

Jul 15 - Jul 18, 2021
AAU 6TH GRADE DI & DII BOYS'
BASKETBALL WORLD CH
AMPIONSHIPS
Hampton, VA
AMATEUR ATHLETIC UNION
Phone: 407-934-7200
Fax: 407-934-7242
www.aausports.org

Jul 15 - Jul 18, 2021
AAU WEST COAST BOYS'
BASKETBALL CHAMPIONSHIPS
Las Vegas, NV
AMATEUR ATHLETIC UNION
Phone: 407-934-7200
Fax: 407-934-7242
www.aausports.org

Jul 15 - Jul 18, 2021
BASSMASTER ELITE SERIES - ST.
LAWRENCE RIVER
Waddington, NY
St. Lawrence River
BASS ANGLERS SPORTSMAN
SOCIETY
Phone: 877-227-7872
bassmaster@emailcustomerservice.com
www.bassmaster.com

Jul 15 - Jul 18, 2021
LINCOLN LAND CHAMPIONSHIP
Springfield, IL
Panther Creek Country Club
PGA KORN FERRY TOUR
Phone: 904-285-3700
Fax: 904-285-7913
www.pgatour.com

Jul 15 - Jul 18, 2021
WISCONSIN STATE WATER SKI
SHOW CHAMPIONSHIPS
Wisconsin Rapids, WI
South Wood County Park, Lake
Wazeecha - Red Beach
WISCONSIN RAPIDS AQUA SKIERS
Phone: 715-323-1577
www.aquaskiers.org

Jul 16 - Jul 18, 2021
DODGE MILE-HIGH NHRA
NATIONALS
Morrison, CO
Bandimere Speedway
NATIONAL HOT ROD ASSOCIATION
Phone: 626-914-4761
Fax: 626-963-5360
nhra@nhra.com
www.nhra.com

Jul 16 - Jul 18, 2021
FLORIDA GRAND PRIX
Boca Ratçn, FL
INTERNATIONAL FEDERATION OF
BODY BUILDING & FITNESS
International Ph: 34-91-535-28-19
contact@ifbb.com
www.ifbb.com

Jul 16, 2021
US MARINE CORPS US OPEN
Las Vegas, NV
USA WRESTLING
Phone: 719-598-8181
Fax: 719-598-9440
www.teamusa.org/USA-Wrestling

Jul 17 - Jul 20, 2021
AAU 14 & UNDER DI & DII BOYS'
BASKETBALL WORLD C
HAMPIONSHIPS
Orlando, FL
AMATEUR ATHLETIC UNION
Phone: 407-934-7200
Fax: 407-934-7242
www.aausports.org

Jul 17 - Jul 20, 2021
AAU 8TH GRADE DI & DII BOYS'
BASKETBALL WORLD CH
AMPIONSHIPS
Orlando, FL
AMATEUR ATHLETIC UNION
Phone: 407-934-7200
Fax: 407-934-7242
www.aausports.org

Jul 17 - Jul 20, 2021
AAU BOYS' BASKETBALL
INTERNATIONAL CHAMPIONSHIPS
Orlando, FL
AMATEUR ATHLETIC UNION
Phone: 407-934-7200
Fax: 407-934-7242
www.aausports.org

Jul 17, 2021
DUQUOIN MILE
DuQuoin, IL
DuQuoin State Fairgrounds
AMA PRO RACING
Phone: 386-492-1014
Fax: 386-274-2335
communications@amaproracing.com
www.amaproracing.com

Jul 17, 2021
SPRING CREEK NATIONAL
Millville, MN
Spring Creek MX Park
AMA PRO RACING
Phone: 386-492-1014
Fax: 386-274-2335
communications@amaproracing.com
www.amaproracing.com

Jul 17 - Jul 18, 2021
UNADILLA
New Berlin, NY
Unadilla MX
AMA PRO RACING
Phone: 386-492-1014
Fax: 386-274-2335
communications@amaproracing.com
www.amaproracing.com

Jul 17 - Jul 20, 2021
USA WATER POLO NATIONAL
JUNIOR OLYMPICS - SESS 1
USA WATER POLO
Phone: 714-500-5445
Fax: 714-960-2431
www.usawaterpolo.org

Jul 18 - Jul 21, 2021
AAU 10U & 11U EAST COAST DIII
BOYS' BASKETBALL C
HAMPIONSHIPS
Hampton, VA
AMATEUR ATHLETIC UNION
Phone: 407-934-7200
Fax: 407-934-7242
www.aausports.org

Jul 18 - Jul 21, 2021
AAU 12U & 13U EAST COAST DIII
BOYS' BASKETBALL C
HAMPIONSHIPS
Hampton, VA
AMATEUR ATHLETIC UNION
Phone: 407-934-7200
Fax: 407-934-7242
www.aausports.org

Jul 18, 2021
FOXWOODS RESORT CASINO 301
Loudon, NH
New Hampshire Motor Speedway
NASCAR CUP SERIES
www.nascar.com

Jul 18 - Jul 24, 2021
GIRLS 18 AND UNDER GOLD
NATIONAL CHAMPIONSHIP
Salem, VA
USA SOFTBALL
Phone: 405-424-5266
Fax: 405-424-3855
rcress@softball.org
www.teamusa.org/USA-Softball

Jul 18, 2021
MYSTIC SHARKFEST SWIM
Mystic, CT
Mystic Harbor
ENVIRO-SPORTS
Phone: 415-868-1829
info@envirosports.com
envirosports.com

Jul 19 - Jul 25, 2021
30 PALERMO LADIES OPEN
Palermo, Italy
WTA
Phone: 727-895-5000
Fax: 727-894-1982
feedback@wtatennis.com
www.wtatennis.com

Jul 19 - Jul 21, 2021
OHIO SINGLES
WALKING/NON-WALKING
Lakeside, OH
NATIONAL SHUFFLEBOARD
ASSOCIATION
usansa.weebly.com

Jul 19 - Jul 24, 2021
US JUNIOR AMATEUR
Village of Pinehurst, NC
The Country Club of North Carolina
U.S. GOLF ASSOCIATION
Phone: 908-234-2300
Fax: 908-234-9687
www.usga.org

Jul 20 - Jul 22, 2021
AAU 10TH GRADE DI & DII GIRLS'
BASKETBALL NCAA W ORLD
CHAMPIONSHIPS
Minneapolis, MN
AMATEUR ATHLETIC UNION
Phone: 407-934-7200
Fax: 407-934-7242
www.aausports.org

Jul 20 - Jul 22, 2021
AAU 11TH GRADE DI & DII GIRLS'
BASKETBALL NCAA W ORLD
CHAMPIONSHIPS
Minneapolis, MN
AMATEUR ATHLETIC UNION
Phone: 407-934-7200
Fax: 407-934-7242
www.aausports.org

Jul 20 - Jul 22, 2021
AAU 9TH GRADE DI & DII GIRLS'
BASKETBALL NCAA WO RLD
CHAMPIONSHIPS
Minneapolis, MN
AMATEUR ATHLETIC UNION
Phone: 407-934-7200
Fax: 407-934-7242
www.aausports.org

Jul 20 - Jul 23, 2021
CANADIAN WOMEN'S AMATEUR
CHAMPIONSHIP
Ile Bizard, Canada
Royal Montreal Golf Club
ROYAL CANADIAN GOLF
ASSOCIATION
Phone: 905-849-9700
Fax: 905-845-7040
info@golfcanada.ca
www.golfcanada.ca

Jul 21 - Jul 25, 2021
AAU GIRLS' JUNIOR NATIONAL
BEACH VOLLEYBALL CHAM
PIONSHIP
Hermosa Beach, CA
AMATEUR ATHLETIC UNION
Phone: 407-934-7200
Fax: 407-934-7242
www.aausports.org

Jul 21, 2021
OHIO JUNIOR SINGLES 15 & UNDER
Lakeside, OH
NATIONAL SHUFFLEBOARD
ASSOCIATION
usansa.weebly.com

Jul 22 - Jul 25, 2021
3M OPEN
Blaine, MN
TPC Twin Cities
PGA TOUR
Phone: 904-285-3700
www.pgatour.com

Jul 22 - Jul 25, 2021
AAU 8TH GRADE DI, DII & DIII GIRLS'
BASKETBALL C HAMPIONSHIPS
Hampton, VA
AMATEUR ATHLETIC UNION
Phone: 407-934-7200
Fax: 407-934-7242
www.aausports.org

Jul 22 - Jul 23, 2021
OHIO DOUBLES
Lakeside, OH
NATIONAL SHUFFLEBOARD
ASSOCIATION
usansa.weebly.com

Jul 22 - Jul 25, 2021
PRICE CUTTER CHARITY
CHAMPIONSHIP
Springfield, MO
Highland Springs Country Club
PGA KORN FERRY TOUR
Phone: 904-285-3700
Fax: 904-285-7913
www.pgatour.com

Jul 22 - Jul 25, 2021
THE AMUNDI EVIAN CHAMPIONSHIP
Evian-les-Bains, France
Evian Resort Golf Club
LPGA TOUR
Phone: 386-274-6200
Fax: 386-274-1099
www.lpga.com

Jul 22 - Jul 25, 2021
THE SENIOR OPEN CHAMPIONSHIP
Berkshire, England
Sunningdale Golf Club
PGA CHAMPIONS TOUR
Phone: 904-285-3700
www.pgatour.com/champions

Jul 22 - Jul 25, 2021
USA WATER POLO NATIONAL
JUNIOR OLYMPICS - SESS 2
USA WATER POLO
Phone: 714-500-5445
Fax: 714-960-2431
www.usawaterpolo.org

Jul 23, 2021
JUNEAU MARATHON & HALF
MARATHON
Juneau, AK
JUNEAU TRAIL & ROAD RUNNERS
houstonlaws@yahoo.com
juneauserr.wixsite.com/serr/marathon

Jul 23 - Jul 25, 2021
NHRA SONOMA NATIONALS
Sonoma, CA
Sonoma Raceway
NATIONAL HOT ROD ASSOCIATION
Phone: 626-914-4761
Fax: 626-963-5360
nhra@nhra.com
www.nhra.com

Jul 23 - Jul 25, 2021
USA BMX MIDAMERICA NATIONALS
Raytown, MO
USA BMX
Phone: 480-961-1903
Fax: 480-961-1842
www.usabmx.com

Jul 23 - Aug 8, 2021
XXXII OLYMPIC SUMMER GAMES
Tokyo, Japan
INTERNATIONAL OLYMPIC
COMMITTEE
International Ph: 41-21-621-61-11
International Fax: 41-21-621-62-16
www.olympic.org

Jul 24, 2021
PORT ROYAL HALF-MILE
Port Royal, PA
Port Royal Speedway
AMA PRO RACING
Phone: 386-492-1014
Fax: 386-274-2335

communications@amaproracing.com
www.amaproracing.com

Jul 24 - Jul 25, 2021
SF CLASSIC & UN CHALLENGE
San Francisco, CA
St. Francis Yacht Club
ST. FRANCIS YACHT CLUB
Phone: 415-563-6363
Fax: 415-563-8670
frontdesk@stfyc.com
www.stfyc.com

Jul 24, 2021
WASHOUGAL NATIONAL
Washougal, WA
Washougal MX Park
AMA PRO RACING
Phone: 386-492-1014
Fax: 386-274-2335
communications@amaproracing.com
www.amaproracing.com

Jul 26 - Aug 2, 2021
2021 CANADIAN JUNIOR
CHAMPIONSHIPS
Calgary, Canada
Repsol Centre
SWIMMING CANADA
Phone: 613-260-1348
Fax: 613-260-0804
natloffice@swimming.ca
www.swimming.ca

Jul 26 - Jul 29, 2021
CANADIAN JUNIOR GIRLS
CHAMPIONSHIP
Sainte-Marie, Canada
Club de golf de Sainte-Marie
ROYAL CANADIAN GOLF
ASSOCIATION
Phone: 905-849-9700
Fax: 905-845-7040
info@golfcanada.ca
www.golfcanada.ca

Jul 26 - Jul 31, 2021
ISI WORLD RECREATIONAL TEAM
CHAMPIONSHIPS
Minneapolis, MN
NSC Super Rink
ICE SKATING INSTITUTE
Phone: 972-735-8800
Fax: 972-735-8815
events@skateisi.org
www.skateisi.org

Jul 28 - Aug 7, 2021
AAU JUNIOR OLYMPIC GAMES
Houston, TX
AMATEUR ATHLETIC UNION
Phone: 407-934-7200
Fax: 407-934-7242
www.aausports.org

Jul 29 - Aug 3, 2021
US DIVING JUNIOR NATIONAL
CHAMPIONSHIPS
Indianapolis, IN
USA DIVING
Phone: 317-237-5252
Fax: 317-237-5257
Dan.Laak@usadiving.org
www.teamusa.org/USA-Diving

Jul 30 - Aug 1, 2021
AAU KARATE JUNIOR OLYMPIC
GAMES
Houston, TX
George R. Brown Convention Center

AMATEUR ATHLETIC UNION
Phone: 407-934-7200
Fax: 407-934-7242
www.aausports.org

Jul 30 - Aug 1, 2021
NHRA NORTHWEST NATIONALS
Kent, WA
Pacific Raceways
NATIONAL HOT ROD ASSOCIATION
Phone: 626-914-4761
Fax: 626-963-5360
nhra@nhra.com
www.nhra.com

Jul 30 - Aug 1, 2021
USA BMX GREAT SALT LAKE
NATIONALS
West Jordan, UT
USA BMX
Phone: 480-961-1903
Fax: 480-961-1842
www.usabmx.com

Jul 30 - Jul 31, 2021
WORLD BEACH KORKBALL
CHAMPIONSHIP
TBA
INTERNATIONAL KORFBALL
FEDERATION
International Ph: 011-31-343-499655
International Fax: 011-31-343-499650
office@ikf.org
www.ikf.org

Jul 31 - Aug 1, 2021
AAU DRUG FREE INTERNATIONAL
BODYBUILDING & FITNE SS
CHAMPIONSHIPS
Las Vegas, NV
Rio Hotel
AMATEUR ATHLETIC UNION
Phone: 407-934-7200
Fax: 407-934-7242
www.aausports.org

Jul 31 - Aug 1, 2021
AAU DRUG FREE INTERNATIONAL
POWERLIFTING, WEIGHT LIFTING &
FEATS OF STRENGTH
CHAMPIONSHIPS
Las Vegas, NV
Rio Hotel
AMATEUR ATHLETIC UNION
Phone: 407-934-7200
Fax: 407-934-7242
www.aausports.org

Jul 31 - Aug 8, 2021
CITI OPEN
Washington, DC
WTA
Phone: 727-895-5000
Fax: 727-894-1982
feedback@wtatennis.com
www.wtatennis.com

Jul 31 - Aug 1, 2021
REDBUD
Buchanan, MI
RedBud MX
AMA PRO RACING
Phone: 386-492-1014
Fax: 386-274-2335
communications@amaproracing.com
www.amaproracing.com

Aug TBA, 2021
BLUEGRASS STATE GAMES
Lexington, KY

BLUEGRASS STATE GAMES
Phone: 859-286-5158
Fax: 859-286-5158
info@bgsg.org
www.bgsg.org

Aug TBA, 2021
JUNIOR INTERNATIONAL
BADMINTON CHAMPIONSHIPS
Bulgaria
USA BADMINTON
Phone: 714-765-2952
usab@usabadminton.org
www.usabadminton.org

Aug TBA, 2021
MASTERS ROAD NATIONAL
CHAMPIONSHIPS
Cedar City, UT
USA CYCLING
Phone: 719-434-4200
Fax: 719-434-4300
help@usacycling.org
www.usacycling.org

Aug TBA, 2021
SHOT CLOCK CHALLENGE
TBA
PGA EUROPEAN TOUR
International Ph: 44-0-1344-840400
International Fax: 44-0-1344-840500
www.europeantour.com

Aug 2 - Aug 5, 2021
CANADIAN MEN'S AMATEUR
CHAMPIONSHIP
Laval, Canada
Club de Golf de Laval-Sur-Le-Lac
ROYAL CANADIAN GOLF
ASSOCIATION
Phone: 905-849-9700
Fax: 905-845-7040
info@golfcanada.ca
www.golfcanada.ca

Aug 2 - Aug 8, 2021
FEDEX ST. JUDE INVITATIONAL
Memphis, TN
TPC Southwind
PGA TOUR
Phone: 904-285-3700
www.pgatour.com

Aug 2 - Aug 8, 2021
MUBADALA SILICON VALLEY
San Jose, CA
WTA
Phone: 727-895-5000
Fax: 727-894-1982
feedback@wtatennis.com
www.wtatennis.com

Aug 2 - Aug 12, 2021
NORTH AMERICAN CHAMPIONSHIPS
Lake Tahoe, CA
US ORIENTEERING
Phone: 215-482-9479
contact@orienteeringusa.org
orienteeringusa.org

Aug 2 - Aug 8, 2021
US WOMEN'S AMATEUR
Rye, NY
Westchester Country Club
U.S. GOLF ASSOCIATION
Phone: 908-234-2300
Fax: 908-234-9687
www.usga.org

Aug 2 - Aug 8, 2021
UTAH CHAMPIONSHIP
Farmington, UT
Oakridge Country Club
PGA KORN FERRY TOUR
Phone: 904-285-3700
Fax: 904-285-7913
www.pgatour.com

Aug 2 - Aug 8, 2021
WGC-FEDEX ST. JUDE INVITATIONAL
Memphis, TN
TPC Southwind
PGA TOUR
Phone: 904-285-3700
www.pgatour.com

Aug 4 - Aug 7, 2021
BAREFOOT NATIONAL
CHAMPIONSHIPS
Conroe, TX
USA WATER SKI
Phone: 863-324-4341
Fax: 863-325-8259
www.usawaterski.org

Aug 6 - Aug 8, 2021
CYCLE NORTH CAROLINA
MOUNTAIN RIDE
Forest City, NC
NORTH CAROLINA AMATEUR SPORTS
Phone: 919-361-1133
Fax: 919-361-2559
ncas@ncsports.org
www.ncsports.org

Aug 6 - Aug 15, 2021
ROGERS CUP PRESENTED BY
NATIONAL BANK
Montreal, Canada
WTA
Phone: 727-895-5000
Fax: 727-894-1982
feedback@wtatennis.com
www.wtatennis.com

Aug 7 - Aug 8, 2021
AAU BOYS' JUNIOR NATIONAL
BEACH VOLLEYBALL CHAMP
IONSHIP
AMATEUR ATHLETIC UNION
Phone: 407-934-7200
Fax: 407-934-7242
www.aausports.org

Aug 7 - Aug 8, 2021
DIVISION 2 SHOW SKI NATIONAL
CHAMPIONSHIPS
Shawano, WI
USA WATER SKI
Phone: 863-324-4341
Fax: 863-325-8259
www.usawaterski.org

Aug 7 - Aug 15, 2021
FIBA U19 WORLD CUP FOR WOMEN
Debrecent, Hungary
USA BASKETBALL
Phone: 719-590-4800
Fax: 719-590-4811
fanmail@usabasketball.com
www.usab.com

Aug 7 - Aug 14, 2021
LASER 4.7 YOUTH WORLD
CHAMPIONSHIPS
Dun Laoghaire, Ireland
WORLD SAILING
International Ph: 44 (0)20 3940 4888
www.sailing.org

events/meetings/shows

1301

Aug 8, 2021
GO BOWLING AT THE GLEN
Watkins Glen, NY
Watkins Glen International
NASCAR CUP SERIES
www.nascar.com

Aug 8 - Aug 14, 2021
GOODE U.S. WATER SKI NATIONAL
CHAMPIONSHIPS
Wilmington, IL
USA WATER SKI
Phone: 863-324-4341
Fax: 863-325-8259
www.usawaterski.org

Aug 8, 2021
LAKE TAHOE SHARKFEST SWIM
Incline Village, NV
Sand Harbour State Park
ENVIRO-SPORTS
Phone: 415-868-1829
info@envirosports.com
envirosports.com

Aug 8, 2021
MUSIC CITY GRAND PRIX
Nashville, TN
Streets of Nashville
NTT INDYCAR SERIES
Phone: 317-492-6526
indycar@indycar.com
www.indycar.com

Aug 9 - Aug 15, 2021
ATP TOUR MASTERS 1000 - ROGERS
CUP
Toronto, Canada
ATP TOUR MASTERS 1000
www.atptour.com

Aug 9 - Aug 12, 2021
CANADIAN JUNIOR BOYS
CHAMPIONSHIP
Sainte-Julie, Canada
Vall,e du Richelieu
ROYAL CANADIAN GOLF
ASSOCIATION
Phone: 905-849-9700
Fax: 905-845-7040
info@golfcanada.ca
www.golfcanada.ca

Aug 9 - Aug 15, 2021
PINNACLE BANK CHAMPIONSHIP
Omaha, NE
The Club at Indian Creek
PGA KORN FERRY TOUR
Phone: 904-285-3700
Fax: 904-285-7913
www.pgatour.com

Aug 9 - Aug 15, 2021
US AMATEUR
Oakmont, PA
Oakmont Country Club
U.S. GOLF ASSOCIATION
Phone: 908-234-2300
Fax: 908-234-9687
www.usga.org

Aug 10 - Aug 15, 2021
WYNDHAM CHAMPIONSHIP
Greensboro, NC
Sedgefield Country Club
PGA TOUR
Phone: 904-285-3700
www.pgatour.com

Aug 11 - Aug 15, 2021
SHAW CHARITY CLASSIC
Calgary, AB
Canyon Meadows Golf & Country Club
PGA CHAMPIONS TOUR
Phone: 904-285-3700
www.pgatour.com/champions

Aug 12 - Aug 15, 2021
2021 ICF DRAGON BOAT CLUB
CREW WORLD CHAMPIONSHI PS
Poznan, Poland
INTERNATIONAL CANOE FEDERATION
International Ph: 41 (0)21 612 0290
info@canoeicf.com
www.canoeicf.com

Aug 12 - Aug 15, 2021
LADIES SCOTTISH OPEN
North Berwick, Scotland
Renaissance Club
LPGA TOUR
Phone: 386-274-6200
Fax: 386-274-1099
www.lpga.com

Aug 13 - Aug 15, 2021
CENTRAL AMERICAN & CARIBBEAN
CHAMPIONSHIPS
Salvador
INTERNATIONAL FEDERATION OF
BODY BUILDING & FITNESS
International Ph: 34-91-535-28-19
contact@ifbb.com
www.ifbb.com

Aug 13 - Aug 15, 2021
DIVISION 1 SHOW SKI NATIONAL
CHAMPIONSHIPS
Janesville, WI
USA WATER SKI
Phone: 863-324-4341
Fax: 863-325-8259
www.usawaterski.org

Aug 13 - Aug 15, 2021
MENARDS NHRA PETARMOR
NATIONALS
Topeka, KS
Heartland Motorsports Park
NATIONAL HOT ROD ASSOCIATION
Phone: 626-914-4761
Fax: 626-963-5360
nhra@nhra.com
www.nhra.com

Aug 14 - Aug 15, 2021
LORETTA LYNN RANCH
Hurricane Mills, TN
Loretta Lynn Ranch
AMA PRO RACING
Phone: 386-492-1014
Fax: 386-274-2335
communications@amaproracing.com
www.amaproracing.com

Aug 14, 2021
NEW YORK SHORT TRACK
Weedsport, NY
Weedsport Speedway
AMA PRO RACING
Phone: 386-492-1014
Fax: 386-274-2335
communications@amaproracing.com
www.amaproracing.com

Aug 14, 2021
UNADILLA NATIONAL
New Berlin, NY
Unadilla MX

AMA PRO RACING
Phone: 386-492-1014
Fax: 386-274-2335
communications@amaproracing.com
www.amaproracing.com

Aug 14 - Aug 21, 2021
USA BMX WORLD CHAMPIONSHIPS
Papendal-Arnhem, Netherlands
USA BMX
Phone: 480-961-1903
Fax: 480-961-1842
www.usabmx.com

Aug 14 - Aug 22, 2021
WESTERN & SOUTHERN OPEN
Cincinnati, OH
WTA
Phone: 727-895-5000
Fax: 727-894-1982
feedback@wtatennis.com
www.wtatennis.com

Aug 15 - Aug 22, 2021
ATP TOUR MASTERS 1000 -
WESTERN & SOUTHERN OPEN
Cincinnati, OH
ATP TOUR MASTERS 1000
www.atptour.com

Aug 15, 2021
BIG MACHINE VODKA BRICKYARD
400
Indianapolis, IN
Indianapolis Motor Speedway
NASCAR CUP SERIES
www.nascar.com

Aug 16 - Aug 22, 2021
BOEING CLASSIC
Snoqualmie, WA
The Club at Snoqualmie Ridge
PGA CHAMPIONS TOUR
Phone: 904-285-3700
www.pgatour.com/champions

Aug 16 - Aug 22, 2021
THE NORTHERN TRUST
Jersey City, NJ
Liberty National Golf Club
PGA TOUR
Phone: 904-285-3700
www.pgatour.com

Aug 17 - Aug 22, 2021
WORLD TRIATHLON CHAMPIONSHIP
FINALS
Edmonton, Canada
WORLD TRIATHLON
International Ph: +41 21 614 60 30
International Fax: +41 21 614 60 39
www.triathlon.org

Aug 18 - Aug 29, 2021
FISU SUMMER WORLD UNIVERSITY
GAMES
Chengdu, China
FEDERATION INTERNATIONALE DU
SPORT UNIVERSIADE
International Ph: 41-0-216130810
International Fax: 41-0-216015612
fisu@fisu.net
www.fisu.net

Aug 18 - Aug 22, 2021
LUCAS OIL NHRA NATIONALS
Brainerd, MN
Brainerd International Raceway
NATIONAL HOT ROD ASSOCIATION
Phone: 626-914-4761
Fax: 626-963-5360

nhra@nhra.com
www.nhra.com

Auh 18 - Aug 21, 2021
STAR NORTH AMERICAN
CHAMPIONSHIPS
Newport, CA
Newport Harbor Yacht Club
INTERNATIONAL STAR CLASS YACHT
ASSOCIATION
Phone: 619-222-0252
Fax: 619-222-0528
office@starclass.org
www.starclass.org

Aug 19- Aug 22, 2021
2021 ICF JUNIOR & U23 CANOE
SLALOM WORLD CHAMPIO NSHIPS
Solkan, Slovenia
INTERNATIONAL CANOE FEDERATION
International Ph: 41 (0)21 612 0290
info@canoeicf.com
www.canoeicf.com

Aug 19 - Aug 22, 2021
AIG WOMEN'S BRITISH OPEN
Troon, Scotland
Royal Troon Golf Club
LPGA TOUR
Phone: 386-274-6200
Fax: 386-274-1099
www.lpga.com

Aug 19 - Aug 22, 2021
ALBERTSONS BOISE OPEN
Boise, ID
Hillcrest Country Club
PGA KORN FERRY TOUR
Phone: 904-285-3700
Fax: 904-285-7913
www.pgatour.com

Aug 19 - Aug 22, 2021
US WOMEN'S MATCH RACING
CHAMPIONSHIP
San Diego, CA
San Diego Yacht Club
US SAILING
Phone: 401-683-0800
Fax: 401-683-0840
info@ussailing.org
www.ussailing.org

Aug 20 - Aug 21, 2021
EXTREME EVENTS MINNESOTA
CHAMPIONSHIP RODEO
Waconia, MN
PROFESSIONAL RODEO COWBOY
ASSOCIATION
Phone: 719-593-8840
Fax: 719-548-4876
prorodeor@prorodeo.com
www.prorodeo.com

Aug 20 - Aug 22, 2021
WOMEN'S OPEN SLOW PITCH
NATIONAL CHAMPIONSHIP
Henderson, TN
USA SOFTBALL
Phone: 405-424-5266
Fax: 405-424-3855
rcress@softball.org
www.teamusa.org/USA-Softball

Aug 20, 2021
WWT RACEWAY 200
Madison, IL
World Wide Technology Raceway at
Gateway
NASCAR CAMPING WORLD TRUCK
SERIES

Phone: 800-630-0535
www.nascar.com

Aug 21, 2021
BOMMARITO AUTOMOTIVE GROUP
500
Madison, IL
Gateway Motorsports Park
NTT INDYCAR SERIES
Phone: 317-492-6526
indycar@indycar.com
www.indycar.com

Aug 21, 2021
BUDDS CREEK NATIONAL
Mechanicsville, MD
Budds Creek Raceway
AMA PRO RACING
Phone: 386-492-1014
Fax: 386-274-2335
communications@amaproracing.com
www.amaproracing.com

Aug 21 - Aug 22, 2021
JUNIOR WATER SKI WORLD
CHAMPIONSHIPS
Santa Rosa Beach, FL
Pickos Waterski and Wakeboard School
INTERNATIONAL WATERSKI &
WAKEBOARD FEDERATION
iwwf@iwwfed.com
www.iwsf.com

Aug 21, 2021
PEORIA TT
Peoria, IL
Peoria Motorcycle Club
AMA PRO RACING
Phone: 386-492-1014
Fax: 386-274-2335
communications@amaproracing.com
www.amaproracing.com

Aug 21 Aug 22, 2021
PIKES PEAK MARATHON
Colorado Springs, CO
PIKES PEAK MARATHON
Phone: 719-473-2625
info@pikespeakmarathon.org
www.pikespeakmarathon.org

Aug 21, 2021
PREFONTAINE CLASSIC
Eugene, OR
Hayward Field
OREGON TRACK CLUB
Phone: 541-343-7247
meetingdirector@preclassic.com
www.runnerspace.com/PreClassic

Aug 22, 2021
FIREKEEPERS CASINO 400
Brooklyn, MI
Michigan International Speedway
NASCAR CUP SERIES
www.nascar.com

Aug 23 - Aug 29, 2021
CP CANADIAN WOMEN'S OPEN
Vancouver, Canada
Shaughnessy Golf & Country Club
LPGA TOUR
Phone: 386-274-6200
Fax: 386-274-1099
www.lpga.com

Aug 23 - Sept 4, 2021
INLINE HOCKEY WORLD
CHAMPIONSHIP
Colombia

USA ROLLER SPORTS
Phone: 402-483-7551
Fax: 402-483-1465
www.teamusa.org/USA-Roller-Sports

Aug 23 - Sept 2, 2021
TAHITI PRO TEAHUPO'O
Teahupo'o, Tahiti
WORLD SURF LEAGUE
International Ph: +1-310-450-1212
asp@aspworldtour.com
www.worldsurfleague.com

Aug 24 - Aug 27, 2021
CANADIAN MEN'S MID-AMATEUR
CHAMPIONSHIP
Fort McMurray, Canada
Fort McMurray Golf Club
ROYAL CANADIAN GOLF
ASSOCIATION
Phone: 905-849-9700
Fax: 905-845-7040
info@golfcanada.ca
www.golfcanada.ca

Aug 24 - Aug 29, 2021
US DRESSAGE FESTIVAL OF
CHAMPIONS
Wayne, IL
Lamplight Equestrian Center
US EQUESTRIAN FEDERATION
Phone: 859-258-2472
Fax: 859-231-6662
www.usef.org

Aug 24 - Aug 29, 2021
US PARA SAILING CHAMPIONSHIP
Newport, RI
Sail Newport
WORLD SAILING
International Ph: 44 (0)20 3940 4888
www.sailing.org

Aug 24 - Aug 29, 2021
US PARA SAILING CHAMPIONSHIP
Newport, RI
Sail Newport
US SAILING
Phone: 401-683-0800
Fax: 401-683-0840
info@ussailing.org
www.ussailing.org

Aug 26 - Aug 29, 2021
ASA CLASSIC
Russell County, AL
ARCHERY SHOOTERS ASSOCIATION
Phone: 770-795-0232
Fax: 770-795-0953
info@asaarchery.com
www.asaarchery.com

Aug 26 - Aug 29, 2021
BMW CHAMPIONSHIP
Owings Mills, MD
Caves Valley Golf Club
PGA TOUR
Phone: 904-285-3700
www.pgatour.com

Aug 26 - Aug 28, 2021
CURTIS CUP
Wales, United Kingdom
U.S. GOLF ASSOCIATION
Phone: 908-234-2300
Fax: 908-234-9687
www.usga.org

Aug 26 - Aug 30, 2021
ELITE ARCHERY PRO/AM
Russel County, AL

ARCHERY SHOOTERS ASSOCIATION
Phone: 770-795-0232
Fax: 770-795-0953
info@asaarchery.com
www.asaarchery.com

Aug 26 - Aug 29, 2021
NATIONWIDE CHILDREN'S HOSPITAL
CHAMPIONSHIP
Columbus, OH
The OSU Golf Club
PGA KORN FERRY TOUR
Phone: 904-285-3700
Fax: 904-285-7913
www.pgatour.com

Aug 26 - Aug 28, 2021
OMEGA EUROPEAN MASTERS
Crans Montana, Switzerland
Cras-sur-Sierre Golf Club
PGA EUROPEAN TOUR
International Ph: 44-0-1344-840400
International Fax: 44-0-1344-840500
www.europeantour.com

Aug 27 - Aug 29, 2021
THE ALLY CHALLENGE
Grand Blanc, MI
Warwick Hills Golf & Country Club
PGA CHAMPIONS TOUR
Phone: 904-285-3700
www.pgatour.com/champions

Aug 28, 2021
AMA PRO HILLCLIMB
Scottsburg, IN
High Fly MX Park 2.0 II
AMA PRO RACING
Phone: 386-492-1014
Fax: 386-274-2335
communications@amaproracing.com
www.amaproracing.com

Aug 28, 2021
ANGEL ISLAND HALF MARATHON &
10K
Tiburon, CA
Angel Island State Park
ENVIRO-SPORTS
Phone: 415-868-1829
info@envirosports.com
envirosports.com

Aug 28, 2021
CHICAGO TRIATHLON SUPERSPRINT
Chicago, IL
LIFE TIME FITNESS
ltfmedia@lifetimefitness.com
www.eventsbylifetime.com

Aug 28, 2021
COKE ZERO SUGAR 400
Daytona Beach, FL
Daytona International Speedway
NASCAR CUP SERIES
www.nascar.com

Aug 28, 2021
IRONMAN NATIONAL
Crawfordsville, IN
Ironman Raceway
AMA PRO RACING
Phone: 386-492-1014
Fax: 386-274-2335
communications@amaproracing.com
www.amaproracing.com

Aug 28, 2021
LIFE TIME KIDS TRI - CHICAGO
Chicago, IL

LIFE TIME FITNESS
ltfmedia@lifetimefitness.com
www.eventsbylifetime.com

Aug 28 - Aug 29, 2021
TRANSAMERICA CHICAGO
TRIATHLON
Chicago, IL
LIFE TIME FITNESS
ltfmedia@lifetimefitness.com
www.eventsbylifetime.com

Aug 28 - Sept 2, 2021
US SENIOR AMATEUR
Gosse Pointe Farms, MI
Country Club of Detroit
U.S. GOLF ASSOCIATION
Phone: 908-234-2300
Fax: 908-234-9687
www.usga.org

Aug 30 - Sept 12, 2021
2021 US OPEN TENNIS
CHAMPIONSHIPS
Flushing Meadows, NY
WTA
Phone: 727-895-5000
Fax: 727-894-1982
feedback@wtatennis.com
www.wtatennis.com

Aug 30 - Sept 12, 2021
US OPEN
UNITED STATES TENNIS
ASSOCIATION
Phone: 914-696-7000
www.usta.com

Aug 31 - Sept 6, 2021
2021 SOLHEIM CUP
Toledo, OH
Inverness Golf Club
LPGA TOUR
Phone: 386-274-6200
Fax: 386-274-1099
www.lpga.com

Aug 31 - Sept 2, 2021
CANADIAN WOMEN'S MID-AMATEUR
& SENIOR CHAMPIONSH IP
Bromont, Canada
Golf Chateau-Bromont
ROYAL CANADIAN GOLF
ASSOCIATION
Phone: 905-849-9700
Fax: 905-845-7040
info@golfcanada.ca
www.golfcanada.ca

Sept TBA, 2021
DAVIS CUP SEMIFINALS
INTERNATIONAL TENNIS FEDERATION
International Ph: +44 (0)20 88786464
International Fax: +44 (0)20 88787799
communications@itftennis.com
www.itftennis.com

Sept TBA, 2021
GUANGZHOU INTERNATIONAL
WOMEN'S OPEN
Guangzhou, China
WTA
Phone: 727-895-5000
Fax: 727-894-1982
feedback@wtatennis.com
www.wtatennis.com

Sept TBA, 2021
HANA-CUPID JAPAN WOMEN'S OPEN
Hiroshima, Japan
WTA
Phone: 727-895-5000

Fax: 727-894-1982
feedback@wtatennis.com
www.wtatennis.com

Sept TBA, 2021
JIANGXI OPEN
Nanchang, China
WTA
Phone: 727-895-5000
Fax: 727-894-1982
feedback@wtatennis.com
www.wtatennis.com

Sept TBA, 2021
KEB HANA BANK KOREA OPEN
Seoul, Korea
WTA
Phone: 727-895-5000
Fax: 727-894-1982
feedback@wtatennis.com
www.wtatennis.com

Sept TBA, 2021
MARATHON MOUNTAIN BIKE
NATIONAL CHAMPIONSHIPS
Palo Duro, TX
USA CYCLING
Phone: 719-434-4200
Fax: 719-434-4300
help@usacycling.org
www.usacycling.org

Sept TBA, 2021
NATIONAL POLICE SHOOTING
CHAMPIONSHIPS
NATIONAL RIFLE ASSOCIATION -
COMPETITIVE SHOOTING DIVISION
Phone: 703-267-1465
competitions.nra.org

Sept TBA, 2021
TASHKENT OPEN
Tashkent, Uzbekistan
WTA
Phone: 727-895-5000
Fax: 727-894-1982
feedback@wtatennis.com
www.wtatennis.com

Sept TBA, 2021
TORAY PAN PACIFIC OPEN
Tokyo, Japan
WTA
Phone: 727-895-5000
Fax: 727-894-1982
feedback@wtatennis.com
www.wtatennis.com

Sept TBA, 2021
USHA NATIONAL THREE-WALL
CHAMPIONSHIPS
UNITED STATES HANDBALL
ASSOCIATION
Phone: 520-795-0434
Fax: 520-795-0465
handball@ushandball.org
www.ushandball.org

Sept 1 - Sept 5, 2021
DODGE NHRA NATIONALS
Las Vegas, NV
Las Vegas Motor Speedway
NATIONAL HOT ROD ASSOCIATION
Phone: 626-914-4761
Fax: 626-963-5360
nhra@nhra.com
www.nhra.com

Sept 1 - Sept 5, 2021
NHRA U.S. NATIONALS
Indianapolis, IN
Lucas Oil Raceway

NATIONAL HOT ROD ASSOCIATION
Phone: 626-914-4761
Fax: 626-963-5360
nhra@nhra.com
www.nhra.com

Sept 1 - Sept 5, 2021
USCA NATIONAL GOLF CROQUET
CHAMPIONSHIP
Hartfield, VA
Chesapeake Bay Croquet Club
US CROQUET ASSOCIATION
Phone: 561-478-0760
Fax: 561-686-5507
usca@msn.com
www.croquetamerica.com

Sept 2 - Sept 5, 2021
ITALIAN OPEN
TBA, Italy
PGA EUROPEAN TOUR
International Ph: 44-0-1344-840400
International Fax: 44-0-1344-840500
www.europeantour.com

Sept 2 - Sept 5, 2021
KORN FERRY TOUR CHAMPIONSHIP
Newburgh, IN
Victoria National Golf Club
PGA KORN FERRY TOUR
Phone: 904-285-3700
Fax: 904-285-7913
www.pgatour.com

Sept 2 - Sept 5, 2021
THE TOUR CHAMPIONSHIP
Atlanta, GA
East Lake Golf Club
PGA TOUR
Phone: 904-285-3700
www.pgatour.com

Sept 3 - Sept 4, 2021
INTERNATIONAL GRAND PRIX
MALTA
Malta
INTERNATIONAL FEDERATION OF
BODY BUILDING & FITNESS
International Ph: 34-91-535-28-19
contact@ifbb.com
www.ifbb.com

Sept 3 - Sept 5, 2021
MISTER & MISS UNIVERSO
Asuncion, Paraguay
INTERNATIONAL FEDERATION OF
BODY BUILDING & FITNESS
International Ph: 34-91-535-28-19
contact@ifbb.com
www.ifbb.com

Sept 4 - Sept 5, 2021
BRIARCLIFF
Nashport, OH
Briarcliff MX
AMA PRO RACING
Phone: 386-492-1014
Fax: 386-274-2335
communications@amaproracing.com
www.amaproracing.com

Sept 4 - Sept 11, 2021
INLINE SPEED SKATING WORLD
CHAMPIONSHIP
Colombia
USA ROLLER SPORTS
Phone: 402-483-7551
Fax: 402-483-1465
www.teamusa.org/USA-Roller-Sports

Sept 4 - Sept 5, 2021
NORDIC FITNESS EXPO
Turku, Finland
INTERNATIONAL FEDERATION OF
BODY BUILDING & FITNESS
International Ph: 34-91-535-28-19
contact@ifbb.com
www.ifbb.com

Sept 4, 2021
PALA NATIONAL/FOX RACEWAY
NATIONAL
Pala, CA
Fox Raceway
AMA PRO RACING
Phone: 386-492-1014
Fax: 386-274-2335
communications@amaproracing.com
www.amaproracing.com

Sept 5, 2021
POCATELLO MARATHON
Pocatello, ID
POCATELLO MARATHON
Phone: 208-233-4754
pocatellorun@gmail.com
www.pocatellomarathon.com

Sept 4, 2021
SPRINGFIELD MILE I
Springfield, IL
Illinois State Fairgrounds
AMA PRO RACING
Phone: 386-492-1014
Fax: 386-274-2335
communications@amaproracing.com
www.amaproracing.com

Sept 4 - Sept 11, 2021
STAR WORLD CHAMPIONSHIP
Kiellinie, Germany
Kieler Yacht Club
INTERNATIONAL STAR CLASS YACHT
ASSOCIATION
Phone: 619-222-0252
Fax: 619-222-0528
office@starclass.org
www.starclass.org

Sept 5, 2021
CHEVROLET SILVERADO 250
Bowmanville, Canada
Canadian Tire Motorsport Park
NASCAR CAMPING WORLD TRUCK
SERIES
Phone: 800-630-0535
www.nascar.com

Sept 5, 2021
SOUTHERN 500
Darlington, SC
Darlington Raceway
NASCAR CUP SERIES
www.nascar.com

Sept 5, 2021
SPRINGFIELD MILE II
Springfield, IL
Illinois State Fairgrounds
AMA PRO RACING
Phone: 386-492-1014
Fax: 386-274-2335
communications@amaproracing.com
www.amaproracing.com

Sept 6 - Sept 12, 2021
ASCENSION CHARITY CLASSIC
St. Louis, MO
Norwood Hills Country Club

PGA CHAMPIONS TOUR
Phone: 904-285-3700
www.pgatour.com/champions

Sept 7 - Sept 10, 2021
CANADIAN MEN'S SENIOR
CHAMPIONSHIP
New Minas, Canada
Ken-Wo Country Club
ROYAL CANADIAN GOLF
ASSOCIATION
Phone: 905-849-9700
Fax: 905-845-7040
info@golfcanada.ca
www.golfcanada.ca

Sept 9 - Sept 12, 2021
BMW PGA CHAMPIONSHIP
Surrey, England
Wentworth Club
PGA EUROPEAN TOUR
International Ph: 44-0-1344-840400
International Fax: 44-0-1344-840500
www.europeantour.com

Sept 9 - Sept 11, 2021
COLLEGIATE TRACK NATIONAL
CHAMPIONSHIPS
Indianapolis, IN
USA CYCLING
Phone: 719-434-4200
Fax: 719-434-4300
help@usacycling.org
www.usacycling.org

Sept 9 - Sept 19, 2021
MEN'S JUNIOR PAN AM GAMES
Cali, Colombia
USA GYMNASTICS
Phone: 317-237-5050
Fax: 317-237-5069
membership@usagym.org
usagym.org

Sept 9 - Sept 12, 2021
MOPAR EXPRESS LANE NHRA
NATIONALS
Mohnton, PA
Maple Grove Raceway
NATIONAL HOT ROD ASSOCIATION
Phone: 626-914-4761
Fax: 626-963-5360
nhra@nhra.com
www.nhra.com

Sept 9, 2021
NORTH CAROLINA DOUBLES
Hendersonville, NC
NATIONAL SHUFFLEBOARD
ASSOCIATION
usansa.weebly.com

Sept 10 - Sept 12, 2021
EUROPEAN CUP
Sibiu, Romania
INTERNATIONAL FEDERATION OF
BODY BUILDING & FITNESS
International Ph: 34-91-535-28-19
contact@ifbb.com
www.ifbb.com

Sept 10 - Sept 12, 2021
EUROPEAN FIT MODEL
CHAMPIONSHIPS
Latvia
INTERNATIONAL FEDERATION OF
BODY BUILDING & FITNESS
International Ph: 34-91-535-28-19
contact@ifbb.com
www.ifbb.com

Sept 10 - Sept 12, 2021
FIT MODEL INTERCONTINENTAL
Riga, Latvia
INTERNATIONAL FEDERATION OF
BODY BUILDING & FITNESS
International Ph: 34-91-535-28-19
contact@ifbb.com
www.ifbb.com

Sept 10 - Sept 15, 2021
US SENIOR WOMEN'S AMATEUR
Point Clear, AL
The Lakewood Club
U.S. GOLF ASSOCIATION
Phone: 908-234-2300
Fax: 908-234-9687
www.usga.org

Sept 11, 2021
FEDERATED AUTO PARTS 400
Richmond, VA
Richmond International Raceway
NASCAR CUP SERIES
www.nascar.com

Sept 11, 2021
GOLDEN GATE SHARKFEST SWIM
Sausalito, CA
Under the Golden Gate Bridge
ENVIRO-SPORTS
Phone: 415-868-1829
info@envirosports.com
envirosports.com

Sept 11, 2021
HANGTOWN MOTOCROSS CLASSIC
Rancho Cordova, CA
Prairie City OHV Park
AMA PRO RACING
Phone: 386-492-1014
Fax: 386-274-2335
communications@amaproracing.com
www.amaproracing.com

Sept 11 - Sept 12, 2021
MED CITY MARATHON
Rochester, MN
MED CITY MARATHON
Phone: 507-254-2703
Fax: 507-288-8058
medcityevents@outlook.com
www.medcitymarathon.com

Sept 11, 2021
PARK CITY HALF MARATHON
Park City, UT
UTAH ROAD RUNNERS
events@saltlakerunningco.com
pctrailseries.com

Sept 11, 2021
US OPEN WATER SKI RACING
NATIONAL CHAMPIONSHIPS
TBA
NATIONAL WATER SKI RACING
ASSOCIATION
www.nwsra.net

Sept 12, 2021
GRAND PRIX OF PORTLAND
Portland, OR
Portland International Raceway
NTT INDYCAR SERIES
Phone: 317-492-6526
indycar@indycar.com
www.indycar.com

Sept 12, 2021
WHIDBEY ISLAND MARATHON AND
HALF MARATHON
Oak Harbor, WA
WHIDBEY ISLAND MARATHON & HALF
MARATHON
Phone: 360-279-4500
runwhidbey@oakharbor.org
runwhidbey.com

Sept 13, 2021
NORTH CAROLINA SINGLES
Hendersonville, NC
NATIONAL SHUFFLEBOARD
ASSOCIATION
usansa.weebly.com

Sept 13 - Sept 19, 2021
SANFORD INTERNATIONAL
Sioux Falls, SD
Minnehaha Country Club
PGA CHAMPIONS TOUR
Phone: 904-285-3700
www.pgatour.com/champions

Sept 13 - Sept 19, 2021
ZHENGZHOU OPEN
Zhengzhou, China
WTA
Phone: 727-895-5000
Fax: 727-894-1982
feedback@wtatennis.com
www.wtatennis.com

Sept 14 - Sept 19, 2021
MASTERS TRACK NATIONAL
CHAMPIONSHIPS
Breinigsville, PA
USA CYCLING
Phone: 719-434-4200
Fax: 719-434-4300
help@usacycling.org
www.usacycling.org

Sept 16 - Sept 19, 2021
CAMBIA PORTLAND CLASSIC
Portland, OR
Columbia Edgewater Country Club
LPGA TOUR
Phone: 386-274-6200
Fax: 386-274-1099
www.lpga.com

Sept 16 - Sept 19, 2021
KLM OPEN
Cromvoirt, The Netherlands
Bernardus Golf
PGA EUROPEAN TOUR
International Ph: 44-0-1344-840400
International Fax: 44-0-1344-840500
www.europeantour.com

Sept 16, 2021
NORTH CAROLINA MIXED DOUBLES
Hendersonville, NC
NATIONAL SHUFFLEBOARD
ASSOCIATION
usansa.weebly.com

Sept 16, 2021
UNOH 200
Bristol, TN
Bristol Motor Speedway
NASCAR CAMPING WORLD TRUCK
SERIES
Phone: 800-630-0535
www.nascar.com

Sept 17 - Sept 25, 2021
2021 DONGFENG MOTOR WUHAN
OPEN
Wuhan, China
WTA
Phone: 727-895-5000
Fax: 727-894-1982
feedback@wtatennis.com
www.wtatennis.com

Sept 17 - Sept 19, 2021
AAA INSURANCE NHRA MIDWEST
NATIONALS
Madison, IL
World Wide Technology Raceway
NATIONAL HOT ROD ASSOCIATION
Phone: 626-914-4761
Fax: 626-963-5360
nhra@nhra.com
www.nhra.com

Sept 17 - Sept 18, 2021
ARNOLD CLASSIC EUROPE
Sevilla, Spain
INTERNATIONAL FEDERATION OF
BODY BUILDING & FITNESS
International Ph: 34-91-535-28-19
contact@ifbb.com
www.ifbb.com

Sept 17 - Sept 20, 2021
ARNOLD SPORTS FESTIVAL
EUROPE
Sevilla, Spain
INTERNATIONAL FEDERATION OF
BODY BUILDING & FITNESS
International Ph: 34-91-535-28-19
contact@ifbb.com
www.ifbb.com

Spet 17 - Sept 19, 2021
CHICAGO OPEN
Chicago, IL
NATIONAL X BALL LEAGUE
camille@nxlpaintball.com
nxlpaintball.com

Sept 17 - Sept 19, 2021
COMMUNITY FIRST FOX CITIES
MARATHON
Appleton, WI
COMMUNITY FIRST FOX CITIES
MARATHON
Phone: 877-230-7223
Fax: 920-830-0921
info@foxcitiesmarathon.org
www.foxcitiesmarathon.org

Sept 17 - Sept 19, 2021
LONG ISLAND MARATHON FESTIVAL
East Meadow, NY
LONG ISLAND MARATHON
raceawesome@raceawesome.com

Sept 17 - Sept 19, 2021
NHRA CAROLINA NATIONALS
Concord, NC
zMax Dragway
NATIONAL HOT ROD ASSOCIATION
Phone: 626-914-4761
Fax: 626-963-5360
nhra@nhra.com
www.nhra.com

Sept 17 - Sept 18, 2021
TBA MILE
TBA
AMA PRO RACING
Phone: 386-492-1014
Fax: 386-274-2335

communications@amaproracing.com
www.amaproracing.com

Sept 17 - Sept 19, 2021
US CHAMPIONSHIP OF CHAMPIONS
TBA
US SAILING
Phone: 401-683-0800
Fax: 401-683-0840
info@ussailing.org
www.ussailing.org

Sept 18, 2021
AIR FORCE MARATHON
Riverside, OH
National Museum of the U.S. Air Force
USAF MARATHON
Phone: 800-467-1823
Fax: 937-656-1000
usaf.marathon@us.af.mil
www.usafmarathon.com

Sept 18, 2021
AMA PRO HILLCLIMB
Spring Grove, PA
White Rose Motorcycle Club II
AMA PRO RACING
Phone: 386-492-1014
Fax: 386-274-2335
communications@amaproracing.com
www.amaproracing.com

Sept 18, 2021
BASS PRO SHOPS NRA NIGHT RACE
Bristol, TN
Bristol Motor Speedway
NASCAR CUP SERIES
www.nascar.com

Sept 18, 2021
LOGAN CITY MARATHON
Logan, UT
LOGAN CITY MARATHON
www.logandowntown.org

Sept 18 - Sept 19, 2021
SAN FRANCISCO MARATHON
San Francisco, CA
SAN FRANCISCO MARATHON
Phone: 888-958-6668
customersupport@thesfmarathon.com
www.thesfmarathon.com

Sept 19, 2021
AVENUE OF THE GIANTS
MARATHON
Eureka, CA
THE AVE
Phone: 707-822-1861
ctimek@aol.com
www.theave.org

Sept 19, 2021
FIRESTONE GRAND PRIX OF
MONTEREY
Monterey, CA
WeatherTech Raceway Laguna Seca
NTT INDYCAR SERIES
Phone: 317-492-6526
indycar@indycar.com
www.indycar.com

Sept 19, 2021
OMAHA MARATHON
Omaha, NE
OMAHA MARATHON
Phone: 845-247-7275
info@hitsendurance.com
www.omahamarathon.com

Sept 20 - Sept 26, 2021
PURE INSURANCE CHAMPIONSHIP
Monterey Peninsula, CA
Pebble Beach Golf Links
PGA CHAMPIONS TOUR
Phone: 904-285-3700
www.pgatour.com/champions

Sept 20 - Sept 26, 2021
WALMART NW ARKANSAS
CHAMPIONSHIP
Rogers, AR
Pinnacle Country Club
LPGA TOUR
Phone: 386-274-6200
Fax: 386-274-1099
www.lpga.com

Sept 22 - Sept 24, 2021
WALLEYE TOUR CHAMPIONSHIP
Otter Tail Lake, MD
NATIONAL WALLEYE TOUR
Phone: 612-424-0708
Fax: 866-727-2809
www.nationalwalleyetour.com

Sept 23 - Sept 26, 2021
ROXY JUNIOR PRO
France
WORLD SURF LEAGUE
International Ph: +1-310-450-1212
asp@aspworldtour.com
www.worldsurfleague.com

Sept 24 - Sept 25, 2021
DIAMOND CUP PRAGUE
Czech Republic
INTERNATIONAL FEDERATION OF
BODY BUILDING & FITNESS
International Ph: 34-91-535-28-19
contact@ifbb.com
www.ifbb.com

Sept 24, 2021
NASCAR CAMPING WORLD TRUCK
SERIES PLAYOFF RACE AT LAS
VEGAS
Las Vegas, NV
Las Vegas Motor Speedway
NASCAR CAMPING WORLD TRUCK
SERIES
Phone: 800-630-0535
www.nascar.com

Sept 24 - Sept 26, 2021
RYDER CUP
Haven, WI
Whistling Straits Golf Course
PGA EUROPEAN TOUR
International Ph: 44-0-1344-840400
International Fax: 44-0-1344-840500
www.europeantour.com

Sept 24 - Sept 26, 2021
US OFFSHORE CHAMPIONSHIP
Annapolis, MD
Naval Academy Sailing Squadron
US SAILING
Phone: 401-683-0800
Fax: 401-683-0840
info@ussailing.org
www.ussailing.org

Sept 24 - Sept 26, 2021
US TEAM RACING CHAMPIONSHIP
Bristol, RI
Bristol Yacht Club
US SAILING
Phone: 401-683-0800
Fax: 401-683-0840

info@ussailing.org
www.ussailing.org

Sept 24, 2021
WORLD OF WESTGATE 200
Las Vegas, NV
Las Vegas Motor Speedway
NASCAR CAMPING WORLD TRUCK
SERIES
Phone: 800-630-0535
www.nascar.com

Sept 25, 2021
FIRSTENERGY AKRON MARATHON,
HALF MARATHON & TEAM RELAY
Akron, OH
ROAD RUNNER AKRON MARATHON
Phone: 330-434-2786
Fax: 330-434-0738
info@akronmarathon.org
www.akronmarathon.org

Sept 25, 2021
SUNBURST MARATHON
South Bend, IN
BEACON HEALTH SYSTEM
Phone: 574-647-1000

Sept 25 - Sept 30, 2021
US MID-AMATEUR
Siasconset, MA
Sankaty Head Golf Club
U.S. GOLF ASSOCIATION
Phone: 908-234-2300
Fax: 908-234-9687
www.usga.org

Sept 25 - Sept 30, 2021
US WOMEN'S MID-AMATEUR
Bluffton, SC
Berkeley Hall Club
U.S. GOLF ASSOCIATION
Phone: 908-234-2300
Fax: 908-234-9687
www.usga.org

Sept 26, 2021
ACURA GRAND PRIX OF LONG
BEACH
Long Beach, CA
Streets of Long Beach
NTT INDYCAR SERIES
Phone: 317-492-6526
indycar@indycar.com
www.indycar.com

Sept 26, 2021
AMA PRO HILLCLIMB
Freemansburg, PA
Freemansburg Ii
AMA PRO RACING
Phone: 386-492-1014
Fax: 386-274-2335
communications@amaproracing.com
www.amaproracing.com

Sept 26, 2021
SOUTH POINT 400
Las Vegas, NV
Las Vegas Motor Speedway
NASCAR CUP SERIES
www.nascar.com

Sept 27 - Oct 3, 2021
QUICKSILVER PRO
France
WORLD SURF LEAGUE
International Ph: +1-310-450-1212
asp@aspworldtour.com
www.worldsurfleague.com

events/meetings/shows

Sept 30 - Oct 3, 2021
2021 ICF CANOE MARATHON WORLD
CHAMPIONSHIP
Bascov, Romania
INTERNATIONAL CANOE FEDERATION
International Ph: 41 (0)21 612 0290
info@canoeicf.com
www.canoeicf.com

Oct TBA, 2021
ALOHA CLASSIC
INTERNATIONAL WINDSURFING TOUR
internationalwindsurfingtour.com

Oct TBA, 2021
BGL BNP PARIBAS LUXEMBOURG
OPEN
Luxembourg
WTA
Phone: 727-895-5000
Fax: 727-894-1982
feedback@wtatennis.com
www.wtatennis.com

Oct TBA, 2021
COLUMBUS MARATHON
Columbus, OH
Downtown Columbus
COLUMBUS MARATHON
Phone: 614-421-7866
Fax: 614-263-3518
info@columbusmarathon.com
www.columbusmarathon.com

Oct TBA, 2021
FACTORY GUN NATIONALS
Frostproof, FL
US PRACTICAL SHOOTING
ASSOCIATION
Phone: 360-855-2245
Fax: 360-855-0380
office@uspsa.org
www.uspsa.org

Oct TBA, 2021
FALL CLASSIC HALF MARATHON &
10K
Vancouver, Canada
BAD TO THE BONE
Phone: 434-218-0402
francesca@badtothebone.biz
badtothebone.biz

Oct TBA, 2021
HENGQIN LIFE WTA ELITE TROPHY
ZHUHAI 2020
Zhuhai, China
WTA
Phone: 727-895-5000
Fax: 727-894-1982
feedback@wtatennis.com
www.wtatennis.com

Oct TBA, 2021
PRUDENTIAL HONG KONG TENNIS
OPEN
Hong Kong, China
WTA
Phone: 727-895-5000
Fax: 727-894-1982
feedback@wtatennis.com
www.wtatennis.com

Oct TBA, 2021
SHRINERS HOSPITAL FOR
CHILDREN OPEN
Las Vegas, NV
TPC Summerlin

PGA TOUR
Phone: 904-285-3700
www.pgatour.com

Oct TBA, 2021
TAIPEI OEC OPEN
Taipei, Chinese Taipei
WTA
Phone: 727-895-5000
Fax: 727-894-1982
feedback@wtatennis.com
www.wtatennis.com

Oct TBA, 2021
TIANJIN OPEN
Tianjin, China
WTA
Phone: 727-895-5000
Fax: 727-894-1982
feedback@wtatennis.com
www.wtatennis.com

Oct TBA, 2021
TOYOTA NATIONAL
CHAMPIONSHIPS U15 CUP
TBA, Canada
CANADIAN SOCCER ASSOCIATION
Phone: 613-237-7678
Fax: 613-237-1516
info@soccercan.ca
www.canadasoccer.com

Oct TBA, 2021
TOYOTA NATIONAL
CHAMPIONSHIPS U17 CUP
TBA, Canada
CANADIAN SOCCER ASSOCIATION
Phone: 613-237-7678
Fax: 613-237-1516
info@soccercan.ca
www.canadasoccer.com

Oct TBA, 2021
WALTER CHILDS MARATHON
Springfield, MA
GREATER SPRINGFIELD HARRIERS
Phone: 413-734-0955
fastfeetinc@comcast.net
www.harriers.org

Oct TBA, 2021
WORLD ROLLER GAMES
Argentina
USA ROLLER SPORTS
Phone: 402-483-7551
Fax: 402-483-1465
www.teamusa.org/USA-Roller-Sports

Oct 1 - Oct 3, 2021
AAU DRUG FREE WORLD
BODYBUILDING & FITNESS CHAMP
IONSHIPS
Laughlin, NV
Harrah's Resort Hotel Casino
AMATEUR ATHLETIC UNION
Phone: 407-934-7200
Fax: 407-934-7242
www.aausports.org

Oct 1 - Oct 3, 2021
AAU DRUG FREE WORLD
POWERLIFTING, WEIGHTLIFTING,
FOS & MAS CHAMPIONSHIPS
Laughlin, NV
Harrah's Resort Hotel Casino
AMATEUR ATHLETIC UNION
Phone: 407-934-7200
Fax: 407-934-7242
www.aausports.org

Oct 1 - Oct 3, 2021
MISTER UNIVERSE PRO & RAFAEL
VERA CLASSIC PRO QU ALIFIERS
Marbella, Spain
INTERNATIONAL FEDERATION OF
BODY BUILDING & FITNESS
International Ph: 34-91-535-28-19
contact@ifbb.com
www.ifbb.com

Oct 1 - Oct 3, 2021
SHOPRITE LPGA CLASSIC
Galloway, NJ
Seaview
LPGA TOUR
Phone: 386-274-6200
Fax: 386-274-1099
www.lpga.com

Oct 1 - Oct 3, 2021
US MATCH RACING CHAMPIONSHIP
Long Beach, CA
Long Beach Yacht Club
US SAILING
Phone: 401-683-0800
Fax: 401-683-0840
info@ussailing.org
www.ussailing.org

Oct 2, 2021
BIG SUR TRAIL MARATHON, HALF
MARATHON & 5 MILE
Big Sur, CA
Andrew Molera State Park
ENVIRO-SPORTS
Phone: 415-868-1829
info@envirosports.com
envirosports.com

Oct 2 - Oct 9, 2021
CYCLE NORTH CAROLINA
MOUNTAINS TO COAST
Sparta, NC
NORTH CAROLINA AMATEUR SPORTS
Phone: 919-361-1133
Fax: 919-361-2559
ncas@ncsports.org
www.ncsports.org

Oct 2, 2021
NASCAR CAMPING WORLD TRUCK
PLAYOFF RACE AT TALLADEGA
Talladega, AL
Talladega Superspeedway
NASCAR CAMPING WORLD TRUCK
SERIES
Phone: 800-630-0535
www.nascar.com

Oct 2 - Oct 3, 2021
OKLAHOMA CITY MEMORIAL
MARATHON
Oklahoma City, OK
OKLAHOMA CITY MARATHON
Phone: 405-525-4242
Fax: 405-521-9907
help@okcmarathon.com
www.okcmarathon.com

Oct 2, 2021
ST. GEORGE MARATHON
St. George, UT
ST. GEORGE MARATHON
Phone: 435-627-4500
Fax: 435-627-4509
marathon@sgcity.org
www.stgeorgemarathon.com

Oct 3 - Oct 10, 2021
CHINA OPEN
Beijing, China
WTA
Phone: 727-895-5000
Fax: 727-894-1982
feedback@wtatennis.com
www.wtatennis.com

Oct 3 - Oct 6, 2021
LEGENDS CUP
Mallorca, Spain
Palma Sport & Tennis Club
ATP CHAMPIONS TOUR
www.atpchampionstour.com

Oct 3, 2021
MAINE MARATHON
Portland, ME
THE MAINE MARATHON
Phone: 207-749-9160
racedirector@mainemarathon.com
www.mainemarathon.com

Oct 3, 2021
MILWAUKEE LAKEFRONT
MARATHON
Milwaukee, WI
BADGERLAND STRIDERS
Phone: 414-688-7561
milwaukeelakefrontmarathon@gmail.com
www.milwaukeelakefrontmarathon.org

Oct 4 - Oct 10, 2021
FOUNDERS CUP
West Caldwell, NJ
Mountain Ridge Country Club
LPGA TOUR
Phone: 386-274-6200
Fax: 386-274-1099
www.lpga.com

Oct 5 - Oct 7, 2021
USCA NATIONAL AMERICAN RULES
CHAMPIONSHIP
West Palm Beach, FL
National Croquet Center
US CROQUET ASSOCIATION
Phone: 561-478-0760
Fax: 561-686-5507
usca@msn.com
www.croquetamerica.com

Oct 6 - Oct 10, 2021
2021 UNITEDHEALTHCARE US OPEN
RACQUETBALL CHAMPI ONSHIPS
Minneapolis, MN
USA RACQUETBALL
Phone: 719-635-5396
Fax: 719-635-0685
mwedel@usaracquetball.com
www.teamusa.org/USA-Racquetball

Oct 7 - Oct 10, 2021
AAA TEXAS NHRA FALL NATIONALS
Ennis, TX
Texas Motorplex
NATIONAL HOT ROD ASSOCIATION
Phone: 626-914-4761
Fax: 626-963-5360
nhra@nhra.com
www.nhra.com

Oct 7 - Oct 10, 2021
MUTUACTIVOS OPEN DE ESPANA
Madrid, Spain
Club de Campo Villa de Madrid
PGA EUROPEAN TOUR
International Ph: 44-0-1344-840400

International Fax: 44-0-1344-840500
www.europeantour.com

Oct 7 - Oct 11, 2021
SOUTH AMERICAN CHAMPIONSHIPS
Buenos Aires, Argentina
INTERNATIONAL FEDERATION OF
BODY BUILDING & FITNESS
International Ph: 34-91-535-28-19
contact@ifbb.com
www.ifbb.com

Oct 8, 2021
CHARLOTTE HALF-MILE
Charlotte, NC
Charlotte Motor Speedway
AMA PRO RACING
Phone: 386-492-1014
Fax: 386-274-2335
communications@amaproracing.com
www.amaproracing.com

Oct 8 - Oct 9, 2021
FITNESS MANIA CLASSIC V
Kladno, Czech Republic
INTERNATIONAL FEDERATION OF
BODY BUILDING & FITNESS
International Ph: 34-91-535-28-19
contact@ifbb.com
www.ifbb.com

Oct 8 - Oct 10, 2021
HEARTLAND 100 SPIRIT OF THE
PRAIRIE RACE
Cassoday, KS
KANSAS ULTRARUNNERS' SOCIETY
www.ksultrarunners.org

Oct 8 - Oct 9, 2021
INTERNATIONAL BELLUX CUP
LUXEMBOURG
Munsbach, Luxembourg
INTERNATIONAL FEDERATION OF
BODY BUILDING & FITNESS
International Ph: 34-91-535-28-19
contact@ifbb.com
www.ifbb.com

Oct 8 - Oct 10, 2021
ISI ADULT CHAMPIONSHIPS
Las Vegas, NV
Las Vegas Ice Center
ICE SKATING INSTITUTE
Phone: 972-735-8800
Fax: 972-735-8815
events@skateisi.org
www.skateisi.org

Oct 8 - Oct 11, 2021
US YOUTH SAILING CHAMPIONSHIP
Arapahoe, NC
Camp Sea Gull
WORLD SAILING
International Ph: 44 (0)20 3940 4888
www.sailing.org

Oct 9, 2021
BALTIMORE RUNNING FESTIVAL
Baltimore, MD
BALTIMORE MARATHON
Phone: 410-605-9381
Fax: 410-605-9389
customerservice@corrigansports.com
www.thebaltimoremarathon.com

Oct 9, 2021
EVERSOURCE HARTFORD
MARATHON
Hartford, CT
Bushnell Park

HARTFORD MARATHON FOUNDATION
Phone: 860-652-8866
Fax: 860-652-8145
info@hartfordmarathon.com
www.hartfordmarathon.com

Oct 9 - Oct 10, 2021
JETBLUE LONG BEACH MARATHON
& HALF MARATHON
Long Beach, CA
MOTIV RUNNING
lbinfo@motivsports.com
www.motivrunning.com

Oct 9, 2021
YMCA WHISKEY ROW MARATHON
Prescott, AZ
PRESCOTT YMCA
Phone: 928-445-7221
Fax: 928-445-5135
wrm@prescottymca.org
www.whiskeyrowmarathon.com

Oct 10 - Oct 17, 2021
2021 LASER RADIAL MEN'S WORLD
CHAMPIONSHIP
Shoreacres, TX
WORLD SAILING
International Ph: 44 (0)20 3940 4888
www.sailing.org

Oct 10, 2021
AMA PRO HILLCLIMB
Oregonia, OH
Dayton MC Club/Devil's Staircase
AMA PRO RACING
Phone: 386-492-1014
Fax: 386-274-2335
communications@amaproracing.com
www.amaproracing.com

Oct 10 - Oct 17, 2021
ATP TOUR MASTERS 1000 -
SHANGHAI ROLEX MASTERS
Shanghai, China
ATP TOUR MASTERS 1000
www.atptour.com

Oct 10, 2021
BANK OF AMERICA CHICAGO
MARATHON
Chicago, IL
BANK OF AMERICA CHICAGO
MARATHON
Phone: 312-904-9800
Fax: 312-904-6521
office@chicagomarathon.com
www.chicagomarathon.com

Oct 10, 2021
BANK OF AMERICA ROVAL 400
Concord, NC
Charlotte Motor Speedway
NASCAR CUP SERIES
www.nascar.com

Oct 10, 2021
SAN DIEGO SHARKFEST SWIM
San Diego, CA
San Diego Harbor
ENVIRO-SPORTS
Phone: 415-868-1829
info@envirosports.com
envirosports.com

Oct 10, 2021
STEAMTOWN MARATHON
Scranton, PA
STEAMTOWN MARATHON
Phone: 570-342-0427
Fax: 570-342-0422

events/meetings/shows

1309

racecommittee@hotmail.com
www.steamtownmarathon.com

Oct 10, 2021
TOWPATH MARATHON
Boston, OH
Cuyahoga Valley National Park
OHIO CANAL CORRIDOR
Phone: 216-520-1825
Fax: 216-520-1833
www.towpathtrilogy.com

Oct 10 - Oct 17, 2021
UPPER AUSTRIA LADIES LINZ
Linz, Austria
WTA
Phone: 727-895-5000
Fax: 727-894-1982
feedback@wtatennis.com
www.wtatennis.com

Oct 11, 2021
BOSTON MARATHON
Boston, MA
BOSTON ATHLETIC ASSOCIATION
Phone: 617-236-1652
Fax: 617-236-4505
info@baa.org
www.baa.org

Oct 11, 2021
CITY OF TREES MARATHON
Boise, ID
Park Center Park
CITY OF TREES RACING
ASSOCIATION
jeff@bluecirclesports.com
www.cityoftreesmarathon.com

Oct 14 - Oct 17, 2021
BUICK LPGA SHANGHAI
Shanghai, China
Qizhong Garden Golf Club
LPGA TOUR
Phone: 386-274-6200
Fax: 386-274-1099
www.lpga.com

Oct 14 - Oct 17, 2021
COLLEGIATE MOUNTAIN BIKE
NATIONAL CHAMPIONSHIPS
Durango, CO
Purgatory Resort
USA CYCLING
Phone: 719-434-4200
Fax: 719-434-4300
help@usacycling.org
www.usacycling.org

Oct 14 - Oct 15, 2021
DUBAI MUSCLE BEACH & FEMALE
FITNESS WORLD CUP
Dubai, United Arab Emirates
INTERNATIONAL FEDERATION OF
BODY BUILDING & FITNESS
International Ph: 34-91-535-28-19
contact@ifbb.com
www.ifbb.com

Oct 15 - Oct 17, 2021
DIAMOND CUP SKOPJE
Skopje, Republic of North Macedonia
INTERNATIONAL FEDERATION OF
BODY BUILDING & FITNESS
International Ph: 34-91-535-28-19
contact@ifbb.com
www.ifbb.com

Oct 15 - Oct 16, 2021
NORTH AMERICAN NATIONAL
CHAMPIONSHIPS
Salem, VA
Salem Civic Center
AMERICAN STRONGMAN
CORPORATION
Phone: 314-565-5970
americanstrongmancorporation@gmail.com
strongmancorporation.com

Oct 15 - Oct 17, 2021
SAS CHAMPIONSHIP
Cary, NC
Prestonwood Country Club
PGA CHAMPIONS TOUR
Phone: 904-285-3700
www.pgatour.com/champions

Oct 16 - Oct 17, 2021
DES MOINES MARATHON
Des Moines, IA
DES MOINES MARATHON
HEADQUARTERS
Phone: 515-288-2692
Fax: 515-255-9051
info@desmoinesmarathon.com
www.desmoinesmarathon.com

Oct 16 - Oct 18, 2021
DIAMOND CUP TUNISIA & MAGHREB
ARAB CHAMPIONSHIPS
Tunis, Tunisia
INTERNATIONAL FEDERATION OF
BODY BUILDING & FITNESS
International Ph: 34-91-535-28-19
contact@ifbb.com
www.ifbb.com

Oct 16 - Oct 17, 2021
INTERNATIONAL AUSTRIAN
CHAMPIONSHIOPS
Wels, Austria
INTERNATIONAL FEDERATION OF
BODY BUILDING & FITNESS
International Ph: 34-91-535-28-19
contact@ifbb.com
www.ifbb.com

Oct 16 - Oct 17, 2021
NEW JERSEY MARATHON
Oceanport, NJ
LIFE TIME FITNESS
ltfmedia@lifetimefitness.com
www.eventsbylifetime.com

Oct 17, 2021
AUTOTRADER ECHOPARK
AUTOMOTIVE 500
Fort Worth, TX
Texas Motor Speedway
NASCAR CUP SERIES
www.nascar.com

Oct 17, 2021
GREEN MOUNTAIN MARATHON &
HALF MARATHON
South Hero, VT
Lake Champlian
GREEN MOUNTAIN ATHLETIC
ASSOCIATION
Phone: 802-373-4762
info@gmaa.net
www.gmaa.net

Oct 17, 2021
METRO HEALTH GRAND RAPIDS
MARATHON
Grand Rapids, MI

GRAND RAPIDS MARATHON
Phone: 616-293-3145
rungrmarathon@gmail.com
www.grandrapidsmarathon.com

Oct 17, 2021
MOUNT DESERT ISLAND MARATHON
& HALF MARATHON
Bar Harbor, ME
CROW ATHLETICS
www.crowathletics.com

Oct 18 - Oct 24, 2021
VTB KREMLIN CUP
Moscow, Russia
WTA
Phone: 727-895-5000
Fax: 727-894-1982
feedback@wtatennis.com
www.wtatennis.com

Oct 21 - Oct 24, 2021
BMW LADIES CHAMPIONSHIP
Busan, South Korea
LPGA International Busan
LPGA TOUR
Phone: 386-274-6200
Fax: 386-274-1099
www.lpga.com

Oct 21 - Oct 23, 2021
COLLEGIATE WATER SKI NATIONAL
CHAMPIONSHIPS
NATIONAL COLLEGIATE WATER SKI
ASSOCIATION
www.thencwsa.com

Oct 21 - Oct 24, 2021
TROPHEE HASSAN II
Rabat, Morocco
Royal Golf Dar Es Salam
PGA EUROPEAN TOUR
International Ph: 44-0-1344-840400
International Fax: 44-0-1344-840500
www.europeantour.com

Oct 22 - Oct 24, 2021
DOMINION ENERGY CHARITY
CLASSIC
Richmond, VA
The Country Club of Virginia
PGA CHAMPIONS TOUR
Phone: 904-285-3700
www.pgatour.com/champions

Oct 22 - Oct 23, 2021
GRAND PRIX PHILIPPINES
Manila, Philippines
INTERNATIONAL FEDERATION OF
BODY BUILDING & FITNESS
International Ph: 34-91-535-28-19
contact@ifbb.com
www.ifbb.com

Oct 22 - Oct 24, 2021
US ADULT SAILING CHAMPIONSHIP
Kemah, TX
Texas Corinthian Yacht Club
US SAILING
Phone: 401-683-0800
Fax: 401-683-0840
info@ussailing.org
www.ussailing.org

Oct 23 - Oct 24, 2021
DIAMOND CUP BELGIUM
Mons, Belgium
INTERNATIONAL FEDERATION OF
BODY BUILDING & FITNESS
International Ph: 34-91-535-28-19

contact@ifbb.com
www.ifbb.com

Oct 23, 2021
MARATHON 2 MARATHON
Marathon, TX
MARATHON TO MARATHON
www.marathon2marathon.com

Oct 23, 2021
NAPA WINE COUNTRY MARATHON,
HALF MARATHON & 10K
Calistoga, CA
Silverado Trail
ENVIRO-SPORTS
Phone: 415-868-1829
info@envirosports.com
envirosports.com

Oct 23 - Oct 24, 2021
ROCK 'N' ROLL MARATHON
San Diego, CA
ROCK 'N' ROLL MARATHON SERIES
Phone: 858-450-6510
Fax: 858-450-6905
leads@competitorgroup.com
www.runrocknroll.com

Oct 24, 2021
COLORADO MARATHON
Fort Collins, CO
COLORADO MARATHON
logan@thecoloradomarathon.com
comarathon.com

Oct 24, 2021
HOLLYWOOD CASINO 400
Kansas City, KS
Kansas Speedway
NASCAR CUP SERIES
www.nascar.com

Oct 24, 2021
VERMONT CITY MARATHON
Burlington, VT
RUN VERMONT
Phone: 802-863-8412
info@runvermont.org
www.runvermont.org

Oct 25 - Oct 230, 2021
EUROPA CUP
TBA
INTERNATIONAL KORFBALL
FEDERATION
International Ph: 011-31-343-499655
International Fax: 011-31-343-499650
office@ikf.org
www.ikf.org

Oct 28, 2021
AAU DRUG FREE UNIVERSE
BODYBUILDING & FITNESS CH
AMPIONSHIPS
Las Vegas, NV
Plaza Hotel
AMATEUR ATHLETIC UNION
Phone: 407-934-7200
Fax: 407-934-7242
www.aausports.org

Oct 28 - Oct 31, 2021
HERO INDIAN OPEN
TBC
TBC
PGA EUROPEAN TOUR
International Ph: 44-0-1344-840400
International Fax: 44-0-1344-840500
www.europeantour.com

Oct 28 - Oct 31, 2021
TAIWAN SWINGING SKIRTS LPGA
New Taipei City, Chinese Taipei
Miramar Golf Country Club
LPGA TOUR
Phone: 386-274-6200
Fax: 386-274-1099
www.lpga.com

Oct 28 - Oct 31, 2021
WGC - HSBC CHAMPIONS
Shanghai, China
Sheshan International Golf Club
PGA EUROPEAN TOUR
International Ph: 44-0-1344-840400
International Fax: 44-0-1344-840500
www.europeantour.com

Oct 29 - Oct 31, 2021
ARNOLD SOUTH AMERICA
ARNOLD SPORTS FESTIVAL
Phone: 614-431-2600
Fax: 614-431-3492
www.arnoldsportsfestival.com

Oct 29 - Oct 31, 2021
DIAMOND CUP SERBIA
Cacak, Serbia
INTERNATIONAL FEDERATION OF
BODY BUILDING & FITNESS
International Ph: 34-91-535-28-19
contact@ifbb.com
www.ifbb.com

Oct 29 - Oct 31, 2021
PEPA GRAND PRIX
Opava, Czech Republic
INTERNATIONAL FEDERATION OF
BODY BUILDING & FITNESS
International Ph: 34-91-535-28-19
contact@ifbb.com
www.ifbb.com

Oct 30 - Oct 31, 2021
CAPE COD MARATHON
Falmouth, MA
CAPE COD MARATHON
Phone: 508-540-6959
Fax: 508-548-0617
info@capecodmarathon.com
www.capecodmarathon.com

Oct 30, 2021
NASCAR CAMPING WORLD TRUCK
SERIES AT MARTINSVILLE
Martinsville, VA
Martinsville Speedway
NASCAR CAMPING WORLD TRUCK
SERIES
Phone: 800-630-0535
www.nascar.com

Oct 30, 2021
NASCAR CUP SERIES PLAYOFF
RACE AT MARTINSVILLE
Martinsville, VA
Martinsville Speedway
NASCAR CUP SERIES
www.nascar.com

Oct 31, 2021
CINCINNATI FLYING PIG MARATHON
Cincinnati, OH
CINCINNATI FLYING PIG MARATHON
Phone: 513-721-7447
info@flyingpigmarathon.com
www.flyingpigmarathon.com

Oct 31, 2021
MARINE CORPS MARATHON
Arlington, VA

MARINE CORPS MARATHON
Phone: 800-786-8762
Fax: 703-784-2265
mcm.info@usmc.mil
www.marinemarathon.com

Nov TBA, 2021
MAYAKOBA GOLF CLASSIC
Mexico
PGA TOUR
Phone: 904-285-3700
www.pgatour.com

Nov TBA, 2021
MONTEREY BAY HALF MARATHON
Monterey, CA
BIG SUR MARATHON FOUNDATION
Phone: 831-625-6226
Fax: 831-625-2119
info@bsim.org
www.bsim.org

Nov TBA, 2021
SANTA CLARITA MARATHON
Santa Clarita, CA
SANTA CLARITA MARATHON
Phone: 661-250-3787
Fax: 661-255-1966
marathon@santa-clarita.com
www.scmarathon.org

Nov TBA, 2021
SHISEIDO WTA FINALS SHENZHEN
Shenzhen, China
WTA
Phone: 727-895-5000
Fax: 727-894-1982
feedback@wtatennis.com
www.wtatennis.com

Nov TBA, 2021
TURKEY TROT MIAMI
Miami, FL
LIFE TIME FITNESS
ltfmedia@lifetimefitness.com
www.eventsbylifetime.com

Nov TBA, 2021
USA BMX GRANDS RACE OF
CHAMPIONS
Nov TBA, 2021
USA BMX
Phone: 480-961-1903
Fax: 480-961-1842
www.usabmx.com

Nov 1 - Nov 5, 2021
US MULTIHULL CHAMPIONSHIP
Corpus Christi, TX
Corpus Christi Yacht Club
US SAILING
Phone: 401-683-0800
Fax: 401-683-0840
info@ussailing.org
www.ussailing.org

Nov 3 - Nov 7, 2021
WORLD MEN'S CHAMPIONSHIPS &
CONGRESS
TBA
INTERNATIONAL FEDERATION OF
BODY BUILDING & FITNESS
International Ph: 34-91-535-28-19
contact@ifbb.com
www.ifbb.com

Nov 4 - Nov 7, 2021
TOTO JAPAN CLASSIC
Shiga, Japan
Seta Golf Course
LPGA TOUR
Phone: 386-274-6200

Fax: 386-274-1099
www.lpga.com

Nov 4 - Nov 7, 2021
VOLVO CHINA OPEN
Shenzhen, China
Genzon Golf Course
PGA EUROPEAN TOUR
International Ph: 44-0-1344-840400
International Fax: 44-0-1344-840500
www.europeantour.com

Nov 5 - Nov 7, 2021
BOCA RATON CHAMPIONSHIP
Boca Raton, FL
The Old Course at Broken Sound
PGA CHAMPIONS TOUR
Phone: 904-285-3700
www.pgatour.com/champions

Nov 5 - Nov 7, 2021
CYCLE NORTH CAROLINA COASTAL
RIDE
Oriental, NC
NORTH CAROLINA AMATEUR SPORTS
Phone: 919-361-1133
Fax: 919-361-2559
ncas@ncsports.org
www.ncsports.org

Nov 5, 2021
LUCAS OIL 150
Avondale, AZ
Phoenix Raceway
NASCAR CAMPING WORLD TRUCK
SERIES
Phone: 800-630-0535
www.nascar.com

Nov 5 - Nov 7, 2021
SENIOR ITALIAN OPEN
TBA, Italy
PGA EUROPEAN STAYSURE TOUR
International Ph: 44-0-1344-840400
International Fax: 44-0-1344-840500
www.europeantour.com/staysure-tour

Nov 6, 2021
INDIANAPOLIS MARATHON & HALF
MARATHON
Indianapolis, IN
INDIANAPOLIS MARATHON CORP
Phone: 317-454-8519
nfo@beyondmonumental.org
www.monumentalmarathon.com

Nov 6, 2021
OLATHE KS MARATHON
Olathe, KS
OLATHE CHAMBER OF COMMERCE
Phone: 913-764-1050
Fax: 913-782-4636
marathon@olathe.org
www.olathemarathon.com

Nov 7, 2021
LOS ANGELES MARATHON
Los Angeles, CA
CONQUR ENDURANCE GROUP
Phone: 213-542-3000
info@goconqur.com
goconqur.com

Nov 7, 2021
NASCAR CUP SERIES
CHAMPIONSHIP
Phoenix, AZ
Phoenix Raceway
NASCAR CUP SERIES
www.nascar.com

Nov 7, 2021
TCS NEW YORK CITY MARATHON
New York, NY
NEW YORK ROAD RUNNERS
Phone: 855-569-6977
marathonmailer@nyrr.org
www.tcsnycmarathon.org

Nov 10 - Nov 14, 2021
MISS & MISTER AMERICA
Quito, Ecuador
INTERNATIONAL FEDERATION OF
BODY BUILDING & FITNESS
International Ph: 34-91-535-28-19
contact@ifbb.com
www.ifbb.com

Nov 11 - Nov 14, 2021
AUTO CLUB NHRA FINALS
Pomona, CA
Auto Club Raceway at Pomona
NATIONAL HOT ROD ASSOCIATION
Phone: 626-914-4761
Fax: 626-963-5360
nhra@nhra.com
www.nhra.com

Nov 11 - Nov 14, 2021
CHARLES SCHWAB CUP
CHAMPIONSHIP
Phoenix, AZ
Phoenix Country Club
PGA CHAMPIONS TOUR
Phone: 904-285-3700
www.pgatour.com/champions

Nov 11 - Nov 14, 2021
NXL WORLD CUP
Kissimmee, FL
NATIONAL X BALL LEAGUE
camille@nxlpaintball.com
nxlpaintball.com

Nov 13 - Nov 14, 2021
MALIBU INTERNATIONAL HALF
MARATHON & 5K
Malibu, CA
MALIBU INTERNATIONAL MARATHON
Phone: 310-745-8231
info@malibumarathon.com
www.malibumarathon.com

Nov 13, 2021
RICHMOND MARATHON
Richmond, VA
RICHMOND MARATHON
Phone: 804-285-9495
Fax: 804-285-3132
marathon@sportsbackers.org
www.richmondmarathon.com

Nov 14, 2021
ATHENS MARATHON
Athens, Greece
ATHENS MARATHON COMMITTEE
Phone: 740-594-3825
Fax: 740-594-2525
athensohiomarathon@gmail.com
www.athensmarathon.com

Nov 14, 2021
MADISON MARATHON FULL & HALF
Madison, WI
MADISON FESTIVALS
Phone: 608-276-9797
Fax: 608-226-9550
events@madisonfestivals.com
www.madisonfestivals.com

Nov 15 - Nov 21, 2021
RSM CLASSIC
Sea Island, GA
Sea Island Golf Club
PGA TOUR
Phone: 904-285-3700
www.pgatour.com

Nov 18 - Nov 21, 2021
CME GROUP TOUR CHAMPIONSHIP
Naples, FL
Tiburon Golf Club
LPGA TOUR
Phone: 386-274-6200
Fax: 386-274-1099
www.lpga.com

Nov 18 - Nov 21, 2021
DP WORLD TOUR CHAMPIONSHIP
DUBAI
Dubai, United Arab Emirates
Jumeirah Golf Estates
PGA EUROPEAN TOUR
International Ph: 44-0-1344-840400
International Fax: 44-0-1344-840500
www.europeantour.com

Nov 19 - Nov 21, 2021
DIAMOND CUP CANCUN
Cancun, Mexico
INTERNATIONAL FEDERATION OF
BODY BUILDING & FITNESS
International Ph: 34-91-535-28-19
contact@ifbb.com
www.ifbb.com

Nov 19 - Nov 21, 2021
DIAMOND CUP ROME
Rome, Italy
INTERNATIONAL FEDERATION OF
BODY BUILDING & FITNESS
International Ph: 34-91-535-28-19
contact@ifbb.com
www.ifbb.com

Nov 20 - Nov 21, 2021
LITTLE ROCK MARATHON
Little Rock, AR
LITTLE ROCK MARATHON
Phone: 501-371-4639
glamm@littlerock.gov
www.littlerockmarathon.com

Nov 20 - Nov 21, 2021
PHILADELPHIA MARATHON
Philadelphia, PA
PHILADELPHIA MARATHON
Phone: 215-683-2122
Fax: 215-683-2099
info@philadelphiamarathon.com
philadelphiamarathon.com

Nov 21, 2021
CFL GREY CUP
TBA, Canada
CANADIAN FOOTBALL LEAGUE
Phone: 416-322-9650
Fax: 416-322-9651
www.cfl.ca

Nov 22 - Nov 28, 2021
CABLE WAKEBOARD WORLD
CHAMPIONSHIPS
Pathum Thani, Thailand
INTERNATIONAL WATERSKI &
WAKEBOARD FEDERATION
iwwf@iwwfed.com
www.iwsf.com

Nov 25 - Nov 28, 2021
CHAMPIONS TENNIS
London, United Kingdom
Royal Albert Hall
ATP CHAMPIONS TOUR
www.atpchampionstour.com

Nov 25 - Dec 5, 2021
DAVIS CUP FINAL
Madrid, Spain
La Caja Magica
INTERNATIONAL TENNIS FEDERATION
International Ph: +44 (0)20 88786464
International Fax: +44 (0)20 88787799
communications@itftennis.com
www.itftennis.com

Nov 26, 2021
LIFETIME TURKEY DAY 5K
Chicago, IL
LIFE TIME FITNESS
ltfmedia@lifetimefitness.com
www.eventsbylifetime.com

Nov 26 - Nov 28, 2021
WORLD FITNESS CHAMPIONSHIPS
Perpignan, France
INTERNATIONAL FEDERATION OF
BODY BUILDING & FITNESS
International Ph: 34-91-535-28-19
contact@ifbb.com
www.ifbb.com

Nov 26 - Nov 28, 2021
WORLD MASTER CHAMPIONSHIPS
Perpignan, France
INTERNATIONAL FEDERATION OF
BODY BUILDING & FITNESS
International Ph: 34-91-535-28-19
contact@ifbb.com
www.ifbb.com

Nov 28, 2021
AMICA INSURANCE SEATTLE
MARATHON
Seattle, WA
Seattle Center
SEATTLE MARATHON ASSOCIATION
Phone: 206-729-3660
info@seattlemarathon.org
www.seattlemarathon.org

Dec TBA, 2021
AUTOZONE LIBERTY BOWL
Memphis, TN
Liberty Bowl Memorial Stadium
AUTOZONE LIBERTY BOWL
Phone: 901-795-7700
Fax: 901-795-7826
hgraeter@libertybowl.org
www.libertybowl.org

Dec TBA, 2021
BELK BOWL
Charlotte, NC
Bank of America Stadium
BELK BOWL
Phone: 704-644-4047
Info@CharlotteSports.org
www.belkbowl.com

Dec TBA, 2021
BILLABONG PIPE MASTERS
Oahu, Hawaii
Banzai Pipeline
WORLD SURF LEAGUE
International Ph: +1-310-450-1212
asp@aspworldtour.com
www.worldsurfleague.com

Dec TBA, 2021
BRISBANE INTERNATIONAL
Brisbane, Australia
ATP TOUR 250
www.atptour.com

Dec TBA, 2021
CYCLOCROSS NATIONAL
CHAMPIONSHIPS
Dupage County, IL
USA CYCLING
Phone: 719-434-4200
Fax: 719-434-4300
help@usacycling.org
www.usacycling.org

Dec TBA, 2021
INDEPENDENCE BOWL
Shreveport, LA
Independence Stadium
INDEPENDENCE BOWL FOUNDATION
Phone: 318-221-0712
Fax: 318-221-7366
independencebowl.org

Dec TBA, 2021
LENDING TREE BOWL
Mobile, AL
Ladd-Peebles Stadium
LENDING TREE BOWL
Phone: 251-635-0011
contact@mabowl.com
lendingtreebowl.com

Dec TBA, 2021
NEW ORLEANS BOWL
New Orleans, LA
Mercedes-Benz Superdome
NEW ORLEANS BOWL
Phone: 504-525-5678
Fax: 504-529-1622
www.neworleansbowl.org

Dec TBA, 2021
OPEN BLS DE LIMOGES
Limoges, France
WTA
Phone: 727-895-5000
Fax: 727-894-1982
feedback@wtatennis.com
www.wtatennis.com

Dec TBA, 2021
PNC FATHER SON CHALLENGE
Orlando, FL
Ritz-Carlton Golf Club
PGA CHAMPIONS TOUR
Phone: 904-285-3700
www.pgatour.com/champions

Dec TBA, 2021
REDBOX BOWL
Santa Clara, CA
Levi's Stadium
SAN FRANCISCO BOWL GAME
ASSOCIATION
www.redboxbowl2021.com

Dec TBA, 2021
SOFI HAWAII BOWL
Honolulu, HI
Aloha Stadium
SOFI HAWAII BOWL
www.thehawaiibowl.com

Dec TBA, 2021
SOUTH AFRICAN OPEN
Sun City, South Africa
Gary Player Country Club

PGA EUROPEAN TOUR
International Ph: 44-0-1344-840400
International Fax: 44-0-1344-840500
www.europeantour.com

Dec TBA, 2021
SPEEDO WINTER JR.
CHAMPIONSHIPS
TBA
USA SWIMMING
Phone: 719-866-4578
Fax: 719-866-4049
imclemore@usaswimming.org
www.usaswimming.org

Dec TBA, 2021
TRANSPERFECT MUSIC CITY BOWL
Nashville, TN
Nissan Stadium
TRANSPERFECT MORTGAGE MUSIC
CITY BOWL
Phone: 615-743-3130
www.musiccitybowl.com

Dec TBA, 2021
VALERO ALAMO BOWL
San Antonio, TX
The Alamodome
SAN ANTONIO BOWL ASSOCIATION
Phone: 210-226-2695
Fax: 210-704-6399
info@alamobowl.com
www.alamobowl.com

Dec 3 - Dec 5, 2021
ISI HOLIDAY CHALLENGE
Simi Valley, CA
Iceoplex Simi Valley
ICE SKATING INSTITUTE
Phone: 972-735-8800
Fax: 972-735-8815
events@skateisi.org
www.skateisi.org

Dec 3 - Dec 5, 2021
WORLD JUNIOR CHAMPIONSHIPS
TBA
INTERNATIONAL FEDERATION OF
BODY BUILDING & FITNESS
International Ph: 34-91-535-28-19
contact@ifbb.com
www.ifbb.com

Dec 4, 2021
DEATH VALLEY TRAIL MARATHON &
HALF MARATHON
Death Valley, CA
Titus Canyon
ENVIRO-SPORTS
Phone: 415-868-1829
info@envirosports.com
envirosports.com

Dec 4 - Dec 5, 2021
MERCOSUR CUP
Mendoza, Argentina
INTERNATIONAL FEDERATION OF
BODY BUILDING & FITNESS
International Ph: 34-91-535-28-19
contact@ifbb.com
www.ifbb.com

Dec 4, 2021
ST. JUDE MARATHON
Memphis, TN
ST. JUDE MARATHON
Phone: 901-578-1555
Fax: 901-578-6696
marathon@stjude.org
www.stjudemarathon.org

events/meetings/shows

1313

Dec 10 - Dec 12, 2021
BMW DALLAS MARATHON
Dallas, TX
Dallas City Hall Plaza
DWRM
Phone: 214-800-2087
www.rundallas.com

Dec 10 - Dec 12, 2021
USCA NATIONAL CROQUET CLUB
DOUBLES CHAMPIONSHIP
West Palm Beach, FL
National Croquet Center
US CROQUET ASSOCIATION
Phone: 561-478-0760
Fax: 561-686-5507
usca@msn.com
www.croquetamerica.com

Dec 11, 2021
HARK THE HERALD ANGELS HALF
MARATHON & 10K
Tiburon, CA
Angel Island State Park
ENVIRO-SPORTS
Phone: 415-868-1829
info@envirosports.com
envirosports.com

Dec 31, 2021
GOODYEAR COTTON BOWL
CLASSIC
Arlington, TX
AT&T Stadium
GOODYEAR COTTON BOWL CLASSIC
Phone: 817-892-4800
Fax: 817-892-4810
cso@attcottonbowl.com
www.cottonbowl.com

Dec 31, 2021
TONY THE TIGER SUN BOWL
El Paso, TX
Sun Bowl Stadium
SUN BOWL ASSOCIATION
Phone: 915-533-4416
Fax: 915-533-0661
bolivas@sunbowl.org
www.sunbowl.org

TBA, 2022
AAU AMERICAN CHAMPIONSHIPS
AMATEUR ATHLETIC UNION
Phone: 407-934-7200
Fax: 407-934-7242
www.aausports.org

TBA, 2022
AAU BOY'S VOLLEYBALL WINTER
NATIONALS
AMATEUR ATHLETIC UNION
Phone: 407-934-7200
Fax: 407-934-7242
www.aausports.org

TBA, 2022
AKC NATIONAL CHAMPIONSHIP
AMERICAN KENNEL CLUB
Phone: 919-233-9767
Fax: 919-816-4246
info@akc.org
www.akc.org

TBA, 2022
AKC OBEDIENCE CLASSIC
AMERICAN KENNEL CLUB
Phone: 919-233-9767
Fax: 919-816-4246
info@akc.org
www.akc.org

TBA, 2022
ARNOLD PALMER INVITATIONAL
PGA TOUR
Phone: 904-285-3700
www.pgatour.com

TBA, 2022
ASB CLASSIC 2022
WTA
Phone: 727-895-5000
Fax: 727-894-1982
feedback@wtatennis.com
www.wtatennis.com

TBA, 2022
BEACH & BELT WRESTLING
NATIONAL CHAMPIONSHIPS
Carolina Beach, NC
USA WRESTLING
Phone: 719-598-8181
Fax: 719-598-9440
www.teamusa.org/USA-Wrestling

TBA, 2022
CANADIAN CHAMPIONSHIP
TBA, Canada
CANADIAN SOCCER ASSOCIATION
Phone: 613-237-7678
Fax: 613-237-1516
info@soccercan.ca
www.canadasoccer.com

TBA, 2022
CANADIAN SWIMMING
CHAMPIONSHIPS
SWIMMING CANADA
Phone: 613-260-1348
Fax: 613-260-0804
natloffice@swimming.ca
www.swimming.ca

TBA, 2022
CANADIAN WHEELCHAIR CURLING
CHAMPIONSHIP
CURLING CANADA
Phone: 613-834-2076
Fax: 613-834-0716
championships@curling.ca
www.curling.ca

TBA, 2022
CLUB NATIONAL CHAMPIONSHIPS
Laurel, MD
USA CURLING
Phone: 715-344-1199
Fax: 715-344-2279
info@usacurl.org
www.teamusa.org/USA-Curling

TBA, 2022
COLLEGIATE CLUB NATIONAL
CHAMPIONSHIPS
TBA
USA TRIATHLON
Phone: 719-955-2807
info@usatriathlon.org
www.teamusa.org/usa-triathlon

TBA, 2022
COUNTRY CLUB DE BOGOTA
CHAMPIONSHIP
Bogota, Colombia
Country Club de Bogota-Lagos
PGA KORN FERRY TOUR
Phone: 904-285-3700
Fax: 904-285-7913
www.pgatour.com

TBA 2022
EASTERN HEMISPHERE
CHAMPIONSHIP
TBA
INTERNATIONAL STAR CLASS YACHT
ASSOCIATION
Phone: 619-222-0252
Fax: 619-222-0528
office@starclass.org
www.starclass.org

TBA, 2022
FARMERS INSURANCE OPEN
PGA TOUR
Phone: 904-285-3700
www.pgatour.com

TBA, 2022
GEEBEE TOURNAMENT
TBA
USA BOXING
Phone: 719-866-2323
www.teamusa.org/USA-Boxing

TBA, 2022
HOAG CLASSIC
PGA CHAMPIONS TOUR
Phone: 904-285-3700
www.pgatour.com/champions

TBA, 2022
JUNIOR WORLD CHAMPIONSHIP
INTERNATIONAL STAR CLASS YACHT
ASSOCIATION
Phone: 619-222-0252
Fax: 619-222-0528
office@starclass.org
www.starclass.org

TBA, 2022
MASTERCARD JAPAN
CHAMPIONSHIP
Narita-shi, Chiba, Japan
Narita Golf Club - Accordia Golf
PGA CHAMPIONS TOUR
Phone: 904-285-3700
www.pgatour.com/champions

TBA, 2022
MELGES 24 WORLD CHAMPIONSHIP
WORLD SAILING
International Ph: 44 (0)20 3940 4888
www.sailing.org

TBA, 2022
MEN'S & WOMEN'S NATIONALS &
PRESIDENT'S CUP
Darien, CT
AMERICAN PLATFORM TENNIS
ASSOCIATION
Phone: 888-744-9490
apta@platformtennis.org
www.platformtennis.org

TBA, 2022
MID-ATLANTIC BODYBUILDING
CHAMPIONSHIPS
NATIONAL AMATEUR BODYBUILDERS
ASSOCIATION
info@nabbausa.com
www.nabba.com

TBA, 2022
NCAA NATIONAL COLLEGIATE
WOMEN'S WATER POLO FINA LS
NATIONAL COLLEGIATE ATHLETIC
ASSOCIATION
Phone: 317-917-6222
Fax: 317-917-6888
www.ncaa.org

TBA, 2022
NIKE HOOP SUMMIT
Portland, OR
Moda Center
USA BASKETBALL
Phone: 719-590-4800
Fax: 719-590-4811
fanmail@usabasketball.com
www.usab.com

TBA, 2022
OSLO GRAND PRIX
Oslo, Norway
INTERNATIONAL FEDERATION OF
BODY BUILDING & FITNESS
International Ph: 34-91-535-28-19
contact@ifbb.com
www.ifbb.com

TBA, 2022
RAPISCAN SYSTEMS CLASSIC
Biloxi, MS
Fallen Oak
PGA CHAMPIONS TOUR
Phone: 904-285-3700
www.pgatour.com/champions

TBA, 2022
RIP CURL PRO BELLS BEACH
Bells Beach, Victoria, Australia
WORLD SURF LEAGUE
International Ph: +1-310-450-1212
asp@aspworldtour.com
www.worldsurfleague.com

TBA, 2022
SUPERTOUR FINALS
Vernon, Canada
Sovereign Lake Nordic Center
U.S. SKI AND SNOWBOARD
ASSOCIATION
Phone: 435-649-9090
Fax: 435-649-3613
membership@usskiandsnowboard.org
usskiandsnowboard.org

TBA, 2022
TEXAS NON-WALKING SINGLES
San Benito, TX
NATIONAL SHUFFLEBOARD
ASSOCIATION
usansa.weebly.com

TBA, 2022
TRIGIRL SUPER SPRINT TRIATHLON
& DUATHLON
Houston, TX
Alexander Deussen Park
TRIGIRL SPORTS
Phone: 832-423-4236
www.trigirlsports.com

TBA, 2022
US JUNIOR BRONZE
CHAMPIONSHIPS
UNITED STATES SQUASH RACQUETS
ASSOCIATION
Phone: 212-268-4090
Fax: 212-268-4091
office@ussquash.com
www.ussquash.com

TBA, 2022
US JUNIOR DOUBLES SQUASH
CHAMPIONSHIPS
UNITED STATES SQUASH RACQUETS
ASSOCIATION
Phone: 212-268-4090
Fax: 212-268-4091
office@ussquash.com
www.ussquash.com

TBA, 2022
US JUNIOR SILVER CHAMPIONSHIPS
UNITED STATES SQUASH RACQUETS
ASSOCIATION
Phone: 212-268-4090
Fax: 212-268-4091
office@ussquash.com
www.ussquash.com

TBA, 2022
US JUNIOR WOMEN'S
SINGLEHANDED CHAMPIONSHIP
WORLD SAILING
International Ph: 44 (0)20 3940 4888
www.sailing.org

TBA, 2022
US LACROSSE WOMEN'S
COLLEGIATE NATIONAL CHAMPION
SHPS
US LACROSSE
Phone: 410-235-6882
Fax: 410-366-6735
info@uslacrosse.org
www.uslacrosse.org

TBA, 2022
US LACROSSE WOMEN'S DIVISION
NATIONAL TOURNAMENT
US LACROSSE
Phone: 410-235-6882
Fax: 410-366-6735
info@uslacrosse.org
www.uslacrosse.org

TBA, 2022
US MIXED DOUBLES & HARDBALL
SINGLES CHAMPIONSHIP S
UNITED STATES SQUASH RACQUETS
ASSOCIATION
Phone: 212-268-4090
Fax: 212-268-4091
office@ussquash.com
www.ussquash.com

TBA, 2022
US NATIONAL SQUASH
CHAMPIONSHIPS
UNITED STATES SQUASH RACQUETS
ASSOCIATION
Phone: 212-268-4090
Fax: 212-268-4091
office@ussquash.com
www.ussquash.com

TBA, 2022
US OPEN BASKETBALL
CHAMPIONSHIPS
Westfield, IN
USA BASKETBALL
Phone: 719-590-4800
Fax: 719-590-4811
fanmail@usabasketball.com
www.usab.com

TBA, 2022
USA BMX GREAT NORTHWEST
NATIONALS
Redmond, OR
USA BMX
Phone: 480-961-1903
Fax: 480-961-1842
www.usabmx.com

TBA, 2022
USA TAEKWONDO NATIONAL
CHAMPIONSHIPS
USA TAEKWONDO
Phone: 719-866-4632
Fax: 719-866-4642
www.teamusa.org/usa-taekwondo

TBA, 2022
USA ULTIMATE BEACH
CHAMPIONSHIPS
Virginia Beach, VA
USA ULTIMATE
Phone: 800-872-4384
Fax: 719-219-8322
info@usaultimate.org
www.usaultimate.org

TBA, 2022
USA ULTIMATE D-I COLLEGE
CHAMPIONSHIPS
USA ULTIMATE
Phone: 800-872-4384
Fax: 719-219-8322
info@usaultimate.org
www.usaultimate.org

TBA, 2022
USA ULTIMATE D-III COLLEGE
CHAMPIONSHIPS
USA ULTIMATE
Phone: 800-872-4384
Fax: 719-219-8322
info@usaultimate.org
www.usaultimate.org

TBA, 2022
USA ULTIMATE MASTERS
CHAMPIONSHIPS
USA ULTIMATE
Phone: 800-872-4384
Fax: 719-219-8322
info@usaultimate.org
www.usaultimate.org

TBA, 2022
WESTERN HEMISPHERE
CHAMPIONSHIPS
TBA
INTERNATIONAL STAR CLASS YACHT
ASSOCIATION
Phone: 619-222-0252
Fax: 619-222-0528
office@starclass.org
www.starclass.org

TBA, 2022
WORLD ALLROUND
CHAMPIONSHIPS
Hamar, Norway
Vikingskipet
US SPEEDSKATING
Phone: 801-417-5360
Fax: 801-417-5361
www.teamusa.org/us-speedskating

TBA, 2022
X GAMES MINNEAPOLIS
Minneapolis, MN
ESPN
xgames.espn.com/xgames

TBA, 2022
YOUTH SUMMER OLYMPIC GAMES
Dakar, Senegal
INTERNATIONAL OLYMPIC
COMMITTEE
International Ph: 41-21-621-61-11
International Fax: 41-21-621-62-16
www.olympic.org

Jan TBA, 2022
ASB CLASSIC (M)
Auckland, New Zealand
ATP TOUR 250
www.atptour.com

Jan TBA, 2022
BRISBANE INTERNATIONAL
Brisbane, Australia
WTA
Phone: 727-895-5000
Fax: 727-894-1982
feedback@wtatennis.com
www.wtatennis.com

Jan TBA, 2022
CANADIAN JUNIOR CHAMPIONSHIPS
TBA
CURLING CANADA
Phone: 613-834-2076
Fax: 613-834-0716
championships@curling.ca
www.curling.ca

Jan TBA, 2022
CANADIAN JUNIOR LONG TRACK
CHAMPIONSHIPS
TBA
SPEED SKATING CANADA
Phone: 613-260-3669
Fax: 613-260-3660
ssc@speedskating.ca
www.speedskating.ca

Jan TBA, 2022
EAST WEST SHRINE BOWL
St. Petersburg, FL
Tropicana Field
EAST WEST SHRINE GAME
Phone: 813-281-8686
Fax: 813-281-8687
eastwestshrinegame@shrinenet.org
www.shrinegame.com

Jan TBA, 2022
FAMOUS IDAHO POTATO BOWL
FAMOUS IDAHO POTATO BOWL
Phone: 208-424-1011
Fax: 208-424-1121
www.famousidahopotatobowl.com

Jan TBA, 2022
HOBART INTERNATIONAL
Hobart, Australia
WTA
Phone: 727-895-5000
Fax: 727-894-1982
feedback@wtatennis.com
www.wtatennis.com

Jan TBA, 2022
LATIN AMERICA AMATEUR
U.S. GOLF ASSOCIATION
Phone: 908-234-2300
Fax: 908-234-9687
www.usga.org

Jan TBA, 2022
MOROCCO CHAMPIONS
Marrakech, Marocco
Samanah Golf Club
PGA CHAMPIONS TOUR
Phone: 904-285-3700
www.pgatour.com/champions

Jan TBA, 2022
NFL PRO BOWL
TBA
NATIONAL FOOTBALL LEAGUE
Phone: 212-450-2000
www.nfl.com

Jan TBA, 2022
PANAMA CHAMPIONSHIP
Panama City, Panama
Panama Golf Club

PGA KORN FERRY TOUR
Phone: 904-285-3700
Fax: 904-285-7913
www.pgatour.com

Jan TBA, 2022
US SHORT TRACK CHAMPIONSHIPS
& JUNIOR CHAMPIONSH IPS
Kearns, UT
US SPEEDSKATING
Phone: 801-417-5360
Fax: 801-417-5361
www.teamusa.org/us-speedskating

Jan TBA, 2022
X GAMES ASPEN
Aspen, CO
ESPN
xgames.espn.com/xgames

Jan 1, 2022
ALLSTATE SUGAR BOWL
New Orleans, LA
Mercedes-Benz Superdome
ALLSTATE SUGAR BOWL
Phone: 504-828-2440
Fax: 504-828-2441
info@sugarbowl.org
www.allstatesugarbowl.org

Jan 1, 2022
OUTBACK BOWL
Tampa, FL
Raymond James Stadium
OUTBACK BOWL
Phone: 813-874-2695
Fax: 813-873-1959
info@outbackbowl.com
www.outbackbowl.com

Jan 1, 2022
ROSE BOWL GAME
Pasadena, CA
Rose Bowl Stadium
PASADENA TOURNAMENT OF ROSES
ASSOCIATION
Phone: 626-449-4100
www.tournamentofroses.com

Jan 14 - Jan 16, 2022
USCA NATIONAL CROQUET CLUB
SINGLES CHAMPIONSHIP
West Palm Beach, FL
National Croquet Center
US CROQUET ASSOCIATION
Phone: 561-478-0760
Fax: 561-686-5507
usca@msn.com
www.croquetamerica.com

Jan 28 - Feb 6, 2022
SCOTTIES TOURNAMENT OF
HEARTS
Thunder Bay, Canada
Fort Williams Gardens
CURLING CANADA
Phone: 613-834-2076
Fax: 613-834-0716
championships@curling.ca
www.curling.ca

Jan 29, 2022
SENIOR BOWL
Mobile, AL
Ladd-Peebles Stadium
SENIOR BOWL
Phone: 251-438-2276
Fax: 251-432-0409
srbowl@seniorbowl.com
www.seniorbowl.com

Feb TBA, 2022
ARIZONA NON-WALKING SINGLES
Mesa Spirit, AZ
NATIONAL SHUFFLEBOARD
ASSOCIATION
usansa.weebly.com

Feb TBA, 2022
CANADA MASTERS SPRINT
CHAMPIONSHIPS
Shelton, CT
US SPEEDSKATING
Phone: 801-417-5360
Fax: 801-417-5361
www.teamusa.org/us-speedskating

Feb TBA, 2022
DAVE FREEMAN JUNIOR OPEN
LOCAL CHAMPIONSHIPS
San Diego, CA
USA BADMINTON
Phone: 714-765-2952
usab@usabadminton.org
www.usabadminton.org

Feb TBA, 2022
DAVE FREEMAN OPEN
San Diego, CA
USA BADMINTON
Phone: 714-765-2952
usab@usabadminton.org
www.usabadminton.org

Feb TBA, 2022
EGRET OPEN LOCAL
CHAMPIONSHIP
Schaumburg, IL
USA BADMINTON
Phone: 714-765-2952
usab@usabadminton.org
www.usabadminton.org

Feb TBA, 2022
MEN'S 50+/60+/70+ NATIONALS
Greenville, DE
AMERICAN PLATFORM TENNIS
ASSOCIATION
Phone: 888-744-9490
apta@platformtennis.org
www.platformtennis.org

Feb TBA, 2022
NHRA ARIZONA NATIONALS
Chandler, AZ
Wild Horse Pass Motorsports Park
NATIONAL HOT ROD ASSOCIATION
Phone: 626-914-4761
Fax: 626-963-5360
nhra@nhra.com
www.nhra.com

Feb TBA, 2022
SUPER BOWL LVI
Inglewood, CA
SoFi Stadium
NATIONAL FOOTBALL LEAGUE
Phone: 212-450-2000
www.nfl.com

Feb TBA, 2022
US SYNCHRONIZED SKATING
CHAMPIONSHIPS
U.S. FIGURE SKATING
Phone: 719-635-5200
Fax: 719-635-9548
info@usfigureskating.org
www.usfigureskating.org

Feb TBA, 2022
USA COLLEGIATE CHAMPIONSHIPS
Anaheim, CA

Anaheim Convention Center
UNITED SPIRIT ASSOCIATION
Phone: 800-886-4872
Fax: 866-761-9365
info@usacamps.com
usa.varsity.com

Feb TBA, 2022
WOMEN'S WORLD CHAMPIONSHIPS
AMERICAN BANDY ASSOCIATION
www.usabandy.com

Feb TBA, 2022
WORLD JUNIOR CURLING
CHAMPIONSHIPS
TBA
USA CURLING
Phone: 715-344-1199
Fax: 715-344-2279
info@usacurl.org
www.teamusa.org/USA-Curling

Feb TBA, 2022
WORLD SPRINT CHAMPIONSHIPS
US SPEEDSKATING
Phone: 801-417-5360
Fax: 801-417-5361
www.teamusa.org/us-speedskating

Feb 4 - Feb 20, 2022
XXIIII OLYMPIC WINTER GAMES
Beijing, China
INTERNATIONAL OLYMPIC
COMMITTEE
International Ph: 41-21-621-61-11
International Fax: 41-21-621-62-16
www.olympic.org

Feb 6, 2022
MIAMI MARATHON & HALF
MARATHON
Miami, FL
LIFE TIME FITNESS
ltfmedia@lifetimefitness.com
www.eventsbylifetime.com

Feb 10 - Feb 13, 2021
LABATT BLUE USA POND HOCKEY
NATIONAL CHAMPIONSHI PS
Eagle River, WI
Dollar Lake
USA HOCKEY
Phone: 719-576-8724
Fax: 719-538-1160
usah@usahockey.org
www.usahockey.com

Feb 11 - Feb 20, 2022
DELRAY BEACH OPEN
Delray Beach, FL
The Delray Beach Stadium & Tennis
Centre
ATP CHAMPIONS TOUR
www.atpchampionstour.com

Feb 11 - Feb 13, 2021
MERCEDES-BENZ MARATHON
Birmingham, AL
Boutwell Auditorium
BIRMINGHAM MARATHON, INC.
Phone: 205-870-7771
Fax: 205-870-7729
info@mercedesmarathon.com
www.mercedesmarathon.com

Feb 18 - Feb 20, 2022
ISI WINTER CLASSIC
San Jose, CA
ICE SKATING INSTITUTE
Phone: 972-735-8800
Fax: 972-735-8815

events@skateisi.org
www.skateisi.org

Mar TBA, 2022
AIR NATION FREESTYLE NATIONALS
Calgary, Canada
Winsport Canada Olympic Park
CANADA SNOWBOARD
Fax: 604-568-1639
info@canadasnowboard.ca
www.canadasnowboard.ca

Mar TBA, 2022
AMERICAN CUP
TBA
INTERNATIONAL GYMNASTICS
FEDERATION
International Ph: +41-21-321-55-10
info@fig-gymnastics.org
www.gymnastics.sport

Mar TBA, 2022
AUTO CLUB 400
Fontana, CA
Auto Club Speedway
NASCAR CUP SERIES
www.nascar.com

Mar TBA, 2022
CALIFORNIA ANY DOUBLES
Hemet, CA
NATIONAL SHUFFLEBOARD
ASSOCIATION
usansa.weebly.com

Mar TBA, 2022
CANADIAN YOUTH CHALLENGE
CHAMPIONSHIP
Winnipeg, Canada
CANADIAN 5 PIN BOWLERS
ASSOCIATION
Phone: 613-744-5090
Fax: 613-744-2217
sheila.c5pba@gmail.com
www.c5pba.ca

Mar TBA, 2022
CCAA MEN'S NATIONAL
BASKETBALL CHAMPIONSHIP
Toronto, Canada
Humber College
CANADA BASKETBALL
Phone: 416-614-8037
Fax: 416-614-9570
info@basketball.ca
www.basketball.ca

Mar TBA, 2022
CCAA WOMEN'S NATIONAL
BASKETBALL CHAMPIONSHIP
Vancouver, Canada
Vancouver Island University
CANADA BASKETBALL
Phone: 416-614-8037
Fax: 416-614-9570
info@basketball.ca
www.basketball.ca

Mar TBA, 2022
CIS WOMEN'S BASKETBALL
CHAMPIONSHIP
Toronto, Canada
Ryerson University
CANADA BASKETBALL
Phone: 416-614-8037
Fax: 416-614-9570
info@basketball.ca
www.basketball.ca

Mar TBA, 2022
COLLEGE NATIONAL
CHAMPIONSHIP
Fargo, ND
USA CURLING
Phone: 715-344-1199
Fax: 715-344-2279
info@usacurl.org
www.teamusa.org/USA-Curling

Mar TBA, 2022
ELITE NATIONAL CHAMPIONSHIPS
TBA
USA TRIATHLON
Phone: 719-955-2807
info@usatriathlon.org
www.teamusa.org/usa-triathlon

Mar TBA, 2022
FREESTYLE AERIALS NATIONAL
CHAMPIONSHIPS
U.S. SKI AND SNOWBOARD
ASSOCIATION
Phone: 435-649-9090
Fax: 435-649-3613
membership@usskiandsnowboard.org
usskiandsnowboard.org

Mar TBA, 2022
IWWF WORLD SKI SHOW
TOURNAMENT
TBA
INTERNATIONAL WATERSKI &
WAKEBOARD FEDERATION
iwwf@iwwfed.com
www.iwsf.com

Mar TBA, 2022
MEN'S 145+ NATIONALS
Scarsdale, NY
AMERICAN PLATFORM TENNIS
ASSOCIATION
Phone: 888-744-9490
apta@platformtennis.org
www.platformtennis.org

Mar TBA, 2022
NATIONAL COLLEGIATE MIXED
RIFLE FINALS
Lexington, KY
Memorial Coliseum
NATIONAL COLLEGIATE ATHLETIC
ASSOCIATION
Phone: 317-917-6222
Fax: 317-917-6888
www.ncaa.org

Mar TBA 2022
SENIOR NATIONAL CHAMPIONSHIPS
Fairbanks, AK
USA CURLING
Phone: 715-344-1199
Fax: 715-344-2279
info@usacurl.org
www.teamusa.org/USA-Curling

Mar TBA, 2022
SPEED NATION ALPINE NATIONALS
Blue Mountains, Canada
Blue Mountain Resort
CANADA SNOWBOARD
Fax: 604-568-1639
info@canadasnowboard.ca
www.canadasnowboard.ca

Mar TBA, 2022
SPEED NATION SBX NATIONALS
Kelowna, Canada
Big White Ski Resort

events/meetings/shows

1317

CANADA SNOWBOARD
Fax: 604-568-1639
info@canadasnowboard.ca
www.canadasnowboard.ca

Mar TBA, 2022
US LONG TRACK AMCUP FINAL &
MASTERS CHAMPIONSHIP S
Kearns, UT
US SPEEDSKATING
Phone: 801-417-5360
Fax: 801-417-5361
www.teamusa.org/us-speedskating

Mar TBA, 2022
WORLD SHORT TRACK
CHAMPIONSHIPS
US SPEEDSKATING
Phone: 801-417-5360
Fax: 801-417-5361
www.teamusa.org/us-speedskating

Mar 19, 2022
SWEDEN GRAND PRIX
Malmo, Sweden
INTERNATIONAL FEDERATION OF
BODY BUILDING & FITNESS
International Ph: 34-91-535-28-19
contact@ifbb.com
www.ifbb.com

Apr TBA, 2022
CANADIAN MIXED DOUBLES
CHAMPIONSHIPS
TBA
SQUASH CANADA
Phone: 613-228-7724
Fax: 613-228-7232
info@squash.ca
www.squash.ca

Apr TBA, 2022
D1 ELITE NATIONAL CHAMPIONSHIP
USA RUGBY
Phone: 303-539-0300
Fax: 303-539-0311
membership@usa.rugby
www.usa.rugby

Apr TBA, 2022
DRAKE RELAYS
Des Moines, IA
Drake Stadium, Drake University
DRAKE RELAYS
Phone: 515-271-2889
Fax: 515-271-4189
www.godrakebulldogs.com

Apr TBA, 2022
FUTSAL CANADIAN CHAMPIONSHIP
TBA, Canada
CANADIAN SOCCER ASSOCIATION
Phone: 613-237-7678
Fax: 613-237-1516
info@soccercan.ca
www.canadasoccer.com

Apr TBA, 2022
INTER PROVINCIAL CHAMPIONSHIP
Kelowna, Canada
CANADIAN 5 PIN BOWLERS
ASSOCIATION
Phone: 613-744-5090
Fax: 613-744-2217
sheila.c5pba@gmail.com
www.c5pba.ca

Apr TBA, 2022
MAYBANK CHAMPIONSHIP
MALAYSIA
Kuala Lumpur, Malaysia
Saujana Golf & Country Club

PGA EUROPEAN TOUR
International Ph: 44-0-1344-840400
International Fax: 44-0-1344-840500
www.europeantour.com

Apr TBA, 2022
PENN RELAYS
University of Pennsylvania
Franklin Field
UNIVERSITY OF PENNSYLVANIA
Phone: 215-898-6145
pennrela@pobox.upenn.edu
www.thepennrelays.com

Apr TBA, 2022
VLTBC ITF INDOOR MASTERS
CHAMPIONSHIPS
INTERNATIONAL TENNIS FEDERATION
International Ph: +44 (0)20 88786464
International Fax: +44 (0)20 88787799
communications@itftennis.com
www.itftennis.com

Apr TBA, 2022
YAKIMA RIVER CANYON MARATHON
Ellensburg - Selah, WA
HARD CORE RUNNER'S CLUB
Phone: 425-226-1518

Apr 1, 2022
CANADIAN TRACK CYCLING
CHAMPIONSHIPS
TBA
CANADIAN CYCLING ASSOCIATION
Phone: 613-248-1353
Fax: 613-248-9311
general@cyclingcanada.ca
www.cyclingcanada.ca

Apr 3, 2022
NORTH POLE MARATHON
Arctic Ocean, NT
Geographic North Pole
POLAR RUNNING ADVENTURES
International Ph: 011 353 91 443 408
International Fax: 011 353 91 443 408
rd@npmarathon.com
www.npmarathon.com

Apr 24, 2022
MT. TAM WILD BOAR HALF
MARATHON & 10K
Mill Valley, CA
Mt. Tamalpais State Park
ENVIRO-SPORTS
Phone: 415-868-1829
info@envirosports.com
envirosports.com

May TBA, 2022
CAN / AM VETERANS CUP
Markham, Toronto
Vango Toronto Fencing Centre
CANADIAN FENCING FEDERATION
Phone: 647-476-2401
Fax: 647-476-2402
cff@fencing.ca
www.fencing.ca

May TBA, 2022
CANADIAN GYMNASTICS
CHAMPIONSHIPS
TBA, Canada
GYMNASTICS CANADA GYMNASTIQUE
Phone: 613-748-5637
Fax: 613-748-5691
info@gymcan.org
www.gymcan.org

May TBA, 2022
CANADIAN NATIONAL HANDBALL
CHAMPIONSHIPS
CANADIAN HANDBALL
www.canadianhandball.com

May TBA, 2022
CARDEROCK RUNNING FESTIVAL
Carderock, MD
MARATHON CHARITY COOPERATION
www.mc-coop.org

May TBA, 2022
COLD WATER CLASSIC
Aurora, CO
Cherry Creek State Park
ROCKY MOUNTAIN WINDSURFING
ASSOC.
rmwa.org

May TBA, 2022
COLLEGE 7S NATIONAL
CHAMPIONSHIPS
USA RUGBY
Phone: 303-539-0300
Fax: 303-539-0311
membership@usa.rugby
www.usa.rugby

May TBA, 2022
D1A NATIONAL CHAMPIONSHIP
USA RUGBY
Phone: 303-539-0300
Fax: 303-539-0311
membership@usa.rugby
www.usa.rugby

May TBA, 2022
SPRING COLLEGE CHAMPIONSHIPS
USA RUGBY
Phone: 303-539-0300
Fax: 303-539-0311
membership@usa.rugby
www.usa.rugby

May TBA, 2022
WET/KASHY FINS SPRING REGATTA
WINDSURFING ENTHUSIASTS OF
TIDEWATER, INC.
sailwet1@gmail.com
www.sailwet.com

May 8, 2022
MUIR WOODS MARATHON, HALF
MARATHON & 7 MILE
Stinson Beach, CA
Stinson Beach Park
ENVIRO-SPORTS
Phone: 415-868-1829
info@envirosports.com
envirosports.com

May 13 - May 29, 2022
FINA WORLD AQUATIC
CHAMPIONSHIPS
TBA
USA SWIMMING
Phone: 719-866-4578
Fax: 719-866-4049
imclemore@usaswimming.org
www.usaswimming.org

May 21 - May 22, 2022
RITE AID CLEVELAND MARATHON
Cleveland, OH
CLEVELAND MARATHON
Phone: 800-467-3826
Fax: 216-378-0143
www.clevelandmarathon.com

May 31 - Jun 9, 2022
MASTERS WORLD CHAMPIONSHIPS
Island of Kyushu, Japan
USA DIVING
Phone: 317-237-5252
Fax: 317-237-5257
Dan.Laak@usadiving.org
www.teamusa.org/USA-Diving

Jun TBA, 2022
CANADIAN OPEN CHAMPIONSHIP
St. John's, Canada
CANADIAN 5 PIN BOWLERS
ASSOCIATION
Phone: 613-744-5090
Fax: 613-744-2217
sheila.c5pba@gmail.com
www.c5pba.ca

Jun TBA, 2022
CANADIAN TRIATHLON
CHAMPIONSHIPS
TBA
TRIATHLON CANADA
Phone: 250-412-1795
Fax: 250-412-1794
info@triathloncanada.com
www.triathloncanada.com

Jun TBA, 2022
CLUB CHAMPIONSHIPS
USA RUGBY
Phone: 303-539-0300
Fax: 303-539-0311
membership@usa.rugby
www.usa.rugby

Jun TBA, 2022
INNISFAIL PRO RODEO
Innisfail Alberta, Canada
Daines Ranch
PROFESSIONAL RODEO COWBOY
ASSOCIATION
Phone: 719-593-8840
Fax: 719-548-4876
prorodeor@prorodeo.com
www.prorodeo.com

Jun TBA, 2022
LARRY H MILLER UTAH SUMMER
GAMES
Cedar City, UT
Southern Utah University
UTAH SUMMER GAMES
Phone: 435-865-8421
Fax: 435-865-8548

Jun TBA, 2022
NHRA THUNDER VALLEY NATIONALS
Bristol, TN
Bristol Dragway
NATIONAL HOT ROD ASSOCIATION
Phone: 626-914-4761
Fax: 626-963-5360
nhra@nhra.com
www.nhra.com

Jun TBA, 2022
RBC CANADIAN OPEN
TBA
ROYAL CANADIAN GOLF
ASSOCIATION
Phone: 905-849-9700
Fax: 905-845-7040
info@golfcanada.ca
www.golfcanada.ca

Jun TBA, 2022
US SPEEDSKATING CONGRESS
US SPEEDSKATING
Phone: 801-417-5360

Fax: 801-417-5361
www.teamusa.org/us-speedskating

Jun 5 - Jun 10, 2022
SPECIAL OLYMPICS USA NATIONAL
GAMES
Orlando, FL
SPECIAL OLYMPICS
Phone: 202-628-3630
Fax: 202-824-0200
cweir@specialolympics.org
www.specialolympics.org

Jun 19, 2022
RUN IN THE NAME OF LOVE
Carmel, CA
BIG SUR MARATHON FOUNDATION
Phone: 831-625-6226
Fax: 831-625-2119
info@bsim.org
www.bsim.org

Jun 25 - Jun 26, 2022
KONA MARATHON & KONA HALF
MARATHON
Keauhou-Kona, HI
Waikoloa Beach Resort
KONA MARATHON
Phone: 808-967-8285
raceinfo@konamarathon.com
www.konamarathon.com

Jul TBA, 2022
AAU DIVING NATIONAL
CHAMPIONSHIP
San Antonio, TX
Northside ISD Swim Center
AMATEUR ATHLETIC UNION
Phone: 407-934-7200
Fax: 407-934-7242
www.aausports.org

Jul TBA, 2022
CLUB NATIONAL CHAMPIONSHIPS
TBA
USA TRIATHLON
Phone: 719-955-2807
info@usatriathlon.org
www.teamusa.org/usa-triathlon

Jul TBA, 2022
LIQUI MOLY OPEN KARLSRUHE
Karlsruhe, Germany
WTA
Phone: 727-895-5000
Fax: 727-894-1982
feedback@wtatennis.com
www.wtatennis.com

Jul TBA, 2022
OUTDOOR FIELD NATIONAL
CHAMPIONSHIPS
NATIONAL FIELD ARCHERY
ASSOCIATION
Phone: 605-260-9279
info@nfaausa.com
www.nfaausa.com

Jul TBA, 2022
ROUTE 66 NHRA NATIONALS
Elwood, IL
Route 66 Raceway
NATIONAL HOT ROD ASSOCIATION
Phone: 626-914-4761
Fax: 626-963-5360
nhra@nhra.com
www.nhra.com

Jul TBA, 2022
US JUNIOR WOMEN'S
DOUBLEHANDED CHAMPIONSHIP
Oklahoma City, OK
Oklahoma City Boat Club
US SAILING
Phone: 401-683-0800
Fax: 401-683-0840
info@ussailing.org
www.ussailing.org

Jul 7 - Jul 17, 2022
WORLD GAMES KORFBALL
TBA
INTERNATIONAL KORFBALL
FEDERATION
International Ph: 011-31-343-499655
International Fax: 011-31-343-499650
office@ikf.org
www.ikf.org

Aug TBA, 2022
7S NATIONAL CHAMPIONSHIPS
USA RUGBY
Phone: 303-539-0300
Fax: 303-539-0311
membership@usa.rugby
www.usa.rugby

Aug TBA, 2022
CANADA BASKETBALL 15U/17U
MEN'S NATIONAL CHAMPIO NSHIPS
CANADA BASKETBALL
Phone: 416-614-8037
Fax: 416-614-9570
info@basketball.ca
www.basketball.ca

Aug TBA, 2022
CANADA BASKETBALL 15U/17U
WOMEN'S NATIONAL CHAMP
IONSHIPS
CANADA BASKETBALL
Phone: 416-614-8037
Fax: 416-614-9570
info@basketball.ca
www.basketball.ca

Aug 25 - Aug 28, 2022
WOMEN'S WORLD AMATEUR TEAM
France
Le Golf National
INTERNATIONAL GOLF FEDERATION
International Ph: +41 21 623 12 12
International Fax: +41 +41 216 01 64
info@lgfmail.org
www.igfgolf.org

Aug 25 - Aug 28, 2022
WORLD AMATEUR TEAM
France
Le Golf National
INTERNATIONAL GOLF FEDERATION
International Ph: +41 21 623 12 12
International Fax: +41 +41 216 01 64
info@lgfmail.org
www.igfgolf.org

Sept TBA, 2022
AMERICAN DISCOVERY TRAIL
MARATHON
Colorado Springs, CO
PIKES PEAK ROAD RUNNERS
runadtmarathon@yahoo.com
www.adtmarathon.com

Sept 19 - Sept 25, 2022
PRESIDENT'S CUP
Charlotte, NC
Quail Hollow Club

PGA TOUR
Phone: 904-285-3700
www.pgatour.com

Nov TBA, 2022
TURKISH AIRLINES OPEN
TBA, Turkey
PGA EUROPEAN TOUR
International Ph: 44-0-1344-840400
International Fax: 44-0-1344-840500
www.europeantour.com

Dec TBA, 2022
HERO WORLD CHALLENGE
PGA TOUR
Phone: 904-285-3700
www.pgatour.com

Dec TBA, 2022
HONMA HONG KONG OPEN
Fanling, Hong Kong
Hong Kong Golf Club
PGA EUROPEAN TOUR
International Ph: 44-0-1344-840400
International Fax: 44-0-1344-840500
www.europeantour.com

Apr TBA, 2023
ISI SYNCHRONIZED
CHAMPIONSHIPS
ICE SKATING INSTITUTE
Phone: 972-735-8800

Fax: 972-735-8815
events@skateisi.org
www.skateisi.org

Jun 16 - Jun 25, 2023
SPECIAL OLYMPICS WORLD
SUMMER GAMES
Berlin, Germany
SPECIAL OLYMPICS
Phone: 202-628-3630
Fax: 202-824-0200
cweir@specialolympics.org
www.specialolympics.org

Aug 25 - Sept 10, 2023
FIBA BASKETBALL WORLD CUP
Indonesia, Japan & Philippines
USA BASKETBALL
Phone: 719-590-4800
Fax: 719-590-4811
fanmail@usabasketball.com
www.usab.com

Jan 19 - Feb 2, 2024
YOUTH WINTER OLYMPIC GAMES
Gangwon, South Korea
INTERNATIONAL OLYMPIC
COMMITTEE
International Ph: 41-21-621-61-11
International Fax: 41-21-621-62-16
www.olympic.org

All Sports

Jul 28 - Aug 7, 2021
AAU JUNIOR OLYMPIC GAMES
Houston, TX
AMATEUR ATHLETIC UNION
Phone: 407-934-7200
Fax: 407-934-7242
www.aausports.org

Aug 18 - Aug 29, 2021
FISU SUMMER WORLD UNIVERSITY
GAMES
Chengdu, China
FEDERATION INTERNATIONALE DU
SPORT UNIVERSIADE
International Ph: 41-0-216130810
International Fax: 41-0-216015612
fisu@fisu.net
www.fisu.net

Jan 21 - Jan 31, 2021
FISU WINTER UNIVERSIADE
Lucerne, Switzerland
FEDERATION INTERNATIONALE DU
SPORT UNIVERSIADE
International Ph: 41-0-216130810
International Fax: 41-0-216015612
fisu@fisu.net
www.fisu.net

Feb 4 - Feb 20, 2022
XXIIII OLYMPIC WINTER GAMES
Beijing, China
INTERNATIONAL OLYMPIC
COMMITTEE
International Ph: 41-21-621-61-11
International Fax: 41-21-621-62-16
www.olympic.org

Jul 23 - Aug 8, 2021
XXXII OLYMPIC SUMMER GAMES
Tokyo, Japan
INTERNATIONAL OLYMPIC
COMMITTEE
International Ph: 41-21-621-61-11
International Fax: 41-21-621-62-16
www.olympic.org

TBA, 2022
YOUTH SUMMER OLYMPIC GAMES
Dakar, Senegal
INTERNATIONAL OLYMPIC
COMMITTEE
International Ph: 41-21-621-61-11
International Fax: 41-21-621-62-16
www.olympic.org

Jan 19 - Feb 2, 2024
YOUTH WINTER OLYMPIC GAMES
Gangwon, South Korea
INTERNATIONAL OLYMPIC
COMMITTEE
International Ph: 41-21-621-61-11
International Fax: 41-21-621-62-16
www.olympic.org

Archery

Aug 26 - Aug 29, 2021
ASA CLASSIC
Russell County, AL
ARCHERY SHOOTERS ASSOCIATION
Phone: 770-795-0232
Fax: 770-795-0953
info@asaarchery.com
www.asaarchery.com

Apr 22 - Apr 25, 2021
EASTON SOUTHWEST SHOOT OUT
Paris, TX
Love Civic Center
ARCHERY SHOOTERS ASSOCIATION
Phone: 770-795-0232
Fax: 770-795-0953
info@asaarchery.com
www.asaarchery.com

Aug 26 - Aug 30, 2021
ELITE ARCHERY PRO/AM
Russel County, AL
ARCHERY SHOOTERS ASSOCIATION
Phone: 770-795-0232
Fax: 770-795-0953
info@asaarchery.com
www.asaarchery.com

Feb 25 - Feb 28, 2021
HOYT ARCHERY ALABAMA PRO/AM
Foley, AL
Graham Creek Nature Preserve
ARCHERY SHOOTERS ASSOCIATION
Phone: 770-795-0232
Fax: 770-795-0953
info@asaarchery.com
www.asaarchery.com

Jun 23 - Jun 27, 2021
MATHEWS PRO/AM
Metropolis, IL
ARCHERY SHOOTERS ASSOCIATION
Phone: 770-795-0232
Fax: 770-795-0953
info@asaarchery.com
www.asaarchery.com

Feb 27 - Feb 28, 2021
NFAA GREAT LAKES INDOOR
SECTIONALS
NATIONAL FIELD ARCHERY
ASSOCIATION
Phone: 605-260-9279
info@nfaausa.com
www.nfaausa.com

Mar 19 - Mar 21, 2021
NFAA INDOOR NATIONAL
CHAMPIONSHIPS
NATIONAL FIELD ARCHERY
ASSOCIATION
Phone: 605-260-9279
info@nfaausa.com
www.nfaausa.com

Apr 30 - May 2, 2021
NFAA MARKED 3-D NATIONAL
CHAMPIONSHIP
NATIONAL FIELD ARCHERY
ASSOCIATION
Phone: 605-260-9279
info@nfaausa.com
www.nfaausa.com

Mar 5 - Mar 7, 2021
NFAA MIDATLANTIC INDOOR
SECTIONALS
NATIONAL FIELD ARCHERY
ASSOCIATION
Phone: 605-260-9279
info@nfaausa.com
www.nfaausa.com

Feb 20 - Feb 21, 2021
NFAA MIDWEST INDOOR
SECTIONALS
NATIONAL FIELD ARCHERY
ASSOCIATION
Phone: 605-260-9279

info@nfaausa.com
www.nfaausa.com

Mar 12 - Mar Mar 14, 2021
NFAA NEW ENGLAND INDOOR
SECTIONALS
NATIONAL FIELD ARCHERY
ASSOCIATION
Phone: 605-260-9279
info@nfaausa.com
www.nfaausa.com

Feb 12 - Feb 14, 2021
NFAA RUSHMORE RUMBLE
Yankton, SD
Easton Yankton Archery Center
NATIONAL FIELD ARCHERY
ASSOCIATION
Phone: 605-260-9279
info@nfaausa.com
www.nfaausa.com

Feb 27 - Mar 7, 2021
NFAA SOUTHEAST INDOOR
SECTIONALS
NATIONAL FIELD ARCHERY
ASSOCIATION
Phone: 605-260-9279
info@nfaausa.com
www.nfaausa.com

Jan 30 - Jan 31, 2021
NFAA SOUTHERN INDOOR
SECTIONALS
NATIONAL FIELD ARCHERY
ASSOCIATION
Phone: 605-260-9279
info@nfaausa.com
www.nfaausa.com

Jul TBA, 2022
OUTDOOR FIELD NATIONAL
CHAMPIONSHIPS
NATIONAL FIELD ARCHERY
ASSOCIATION
Phone: 605-260-9279
info@nfaausa.com
www.nfaausa.com

Mar 12 - Apr 12, 2021
THE VEGAS SHOOT-WORLD
ARCHERY FESTIVAL
Las Vegas, NV
NATIONAL FIELD ARCHERY
ASSOCIATION
Phone: 605-260-9279
info@nfaausa.com
www.nfaausa.com

Jun 3 - Jun 6, 2021
TRU BALL & BLACK EAGLE PRO/AM
London, KY
ARCHERY SHOOTERS ASSOCIATION
Phone: 770-795-0232
Fax: 770-795-0953
info@asaarchery.com
www.asaarchery.com

Auto Racing

Oct 17, 2021
AUTOTRADER ECHOPARK
AUTOMOTIVE 500
Fort Worth, TX
Texas Motor Speedway
NASCAR CUP SERIES
www.nascar.com

Feb 11, 2021
BLUEGREEN VACATIONS DUEL
DAYTONA 1&2
Daytona Beach, FL
Daytona International Speedway
NASCAR CUP SERIES
www.nascar.com

Feb 9, 2021
BUSCH CLASH
Daytona Beach, FL
Daytona International Speedway
NASCAR CUP SERIES
www.nascar.com

Mar 21, 2021
FOLDS OF HONOR QUIKTRIP 500
Hampton, GA
Atlanta Motor Speedway
NASCAR CUP SERIES
www.nascar.com

Apr 25, 2021
GEICO 500
Talladega, AL
Talladega Superspeedway
NASCAR CUP SERIES
www.nascar.com

Oct 30, 2021
NASCAR CUP SERIES PLAYOFF
RACE AT MARTINSVILLE
Martinsville, VA
Martinsville Speedway
NASCAR CUP SERIES
www.nascar.com

Jul 11, 2021
QUAKER STATE 400
Sparta, KY
Kentucky Speedway
NASCAR CUP SERIES
www.nascar.com

Sept 17 - Sept 19, 2021
AAA INSURANCE NHRA MIDWEST
NATIONALS
Madison, IL
World Wide Technology Raceway
NATIONAL HOT ROD ASSOCIATION
Phone: 626-914-4761
Fax: 626-963-5360
nhra@nhra.com
www.nhra.com

Oct 7 - Oct 10, 2021
AAA TEXAS NHRA FALL NATIONALS
Ennis, TX
Texas Motorplex
NATIONAL HOT ROD ASSOCIATION
Phone: 626-914-4761
Fax: 626-963-5360
nhra@nhra.com
www.nhra.com

Sept 26, 2021
ACURA GRAND PRIX OF LONG
BEACH
Long Beach, CA
Streets of Long Beach
NTT INDYCAR SERIES
Phone: 317-492-6526
indycar@indycar.com
www.indycar.com

Mar 11 - Mar 14, 2021
AMALIE MOTOR OIL NHRA
GATORNATIONALS
Gainesville, FL
Gainesville Raceway

NATIONAL HOT ROD ASSOCIATION
Phone: 626-914-4761
Fax: 626-963-5360
nhra@nhra.com
www.nhra.com

Mar TBA, 2022
AUTO CLUB 400
Fontana, CA
Auto Club Speedway
NASCAR CUP SERIES
www.nascar.com

Nov 11 - Nov 14, 2021
AUTO CLUB NHRA FINALS
Pomona, CA
Auto Club Raceway at Pomona
NATIONAL HOT ROD ASSOCIATION
Phone: 626-914-4761
Fax: 626-963-5360
nhra@nhra.com
www.nhra.com

Oct 10, 2021
BANK OF AMERICA ROVAL 400
Concord, NC
Charlotte Motor Speedway
NASCAR CUP SERIES
www.nascar.com

Sept 18, 2021
BASS PRO SHOPS NRA NIGHT RACE
Bristol, TN
Bristol Motor Speedway
NASCAR CUP SERIES
www.nascar.com

Aug 15, 2021
BIG MACHINE VODKA BRICKYARD
400
Indianapolis, IN
Indianapolis Motor Speedway
NASCAR CUP SERIES
www.nascar.com

Aug 21, 2021
BOMMARITO AUTOMOTIVE GROUP
500
Madison, IL
Gateway Motorsports Park
NTT INDYCAR SERIES
Phone: 317-492-6526
indycar@indycar.com
www.indycar.com

Jun 12 - Jun 13, 2021
CHEVROLET DUAL IN DETROIT 1&2
Detroit, MI
The Raceway at Belle Isle Park
NTT INDYCAR SERIES
Phone: 317-492-6526
indycar@indycar.com
www.indycar.com

Sept 5, 2021
CHEVROLET SILVERADO 250
Bowmanville, Canada
Canadian Tire Motorsport Park
NASCAR CAMPING WORLD TRUCK
SERIES
Phone: 800-630-0535
www.nascar.com

Jun 25, 2021
CHICAGOLAND 225
Joliet, IL
Chicagoland Speedway
NASCAR CAMPING WORLD TRUCK
SERIES
Phone: 800-630-0535
www.nascar.com

May 30, 2021
COCA-COLA 600
Concord, NC
Charlotte Motor Speedway
NASCAR CUP SERIES
www.nascar.com

Aug 28, 2021
COKE ZERO SUGAR 400
Daytona Beach, FL
Daytona International Speedway
NASCAR CUP SERIES
www.nascar.com

Feb 14, 2021
DAYTONA 500
Daytona Beach, FL
Daytona International Speedway
NASCAR CUP SERIES
www.nascar.com

Apr 16 - Apr 18, 2021
DENSO SPARK PLUGS NHRA
FOUR-WIDE NATIONALS
Las Vegas, NV
The Strip at Las Vegas Motor Speedway
NATIONAL HOT ROD ASSOCIATION
Phone: 626-914-4761
Fax: 626-963-5360
nhra@nhra.com
www.nhra.com

Feb 28, 2021
DIXIE VODKA 400
Homestead, FL
Homestead-Miami Speedway
NASCAR CUP SERIES
www.nascar.com

Jul 16 - Jul 18, 2021
DODGE MILE-HIGH NHRA
NATIONALS
Morrison, CO
Bandimere Speedway
NATIONAL HOT ROD ASSOCIATION
Phone: 626-914-4761
Fax: 626-963-5360
nhra@nhra.com
www.nhra.com

Sept 1 - Sept 5, 2021
DODGE NHRA NATIONALS
Las Vegas, NV
Las Vegas Motor Speedway
NATIONAL HOT ROD ASSOCIATION
Phone: 626-914-4761
Fax: 626-963-5360
nhra@nhra.com
www.nhra.com

May 16, 2021
DRYDENE 400
Dover, DE
Dover International Speedway
NASCAR CUP SERIES
www.nascar.com

Sept 11, 2021
FEDERATED AUTO PARTS 400
Richmond, VA
Richmond International Raceway
NASCAR CUP SERIES
www.nascar.com

Aug 22, 2021
FIREKEEPERS CASINO 400
Brooklyn, MI
Michigan International Speedway
NASCAR CUP SERIES
www.nascar.com

Sept 19, 2021
FIRESTONE GRAND PRIX OF
MONTEREY
Monterey, CA
WeatherTech Raceway Laguna Seca
NTT INDYCAR SERIES
Phone: 317-492-6526
indycar@indycar.com
www.indycar.com

Apr 25, 2021
FIRESTONE GRAND PRIX OF ST.
PETERSBURG
St. Petersburg, FL
Streets of St. Petersburg
NTT INDYCAR SERIES
Phone: 317-492-6526
indycar@indycar.com
www.indycar.com

Mar 28, 2021
FOOD CITY DIRT RACE
Bristol, TN
Bristol Motor Speedway
NASCAR CUP SERIES
www.nascar.com

Jul 18, 2021
FOXWOODS RESORT CASINO 301
Loudon, NH
New Hampshire Motor Speedway
NASCAR CUP SERIES
www.nascar.com

Mar 20, 2021
FR8AUCTIONS 200
Hampton, GA
Atlanta Motor Speedway
NASCAR CAMPING WORLD TRUCK
SERIES
Phone: 800-630-0535
www.nascar.com

May 1, 2021
GENESYS 300
Fort Worth, TX
Texas Motor Speedway
NTT INDYCAR SERIES
Phone: 317-492-6526
indycar@indycar.com
www.indycar.com

May 15, 2021
GMR GRAND PRIX
Indianapolis, IN
Indianapolis Motor Speedway
NTT INDYCAR SERIES
Phone: 317-492-6526
indycar@indycar.com
www.indycar.com

Aug 8, 2021
GO BOWLING AT THE GLEN
Watkins Glen, NY
Watkins Glen International
NASCAR CUP SERIES
www.nascar.com

Sept 12, 2021
GRAND PRIX OF PORTLAND
Portland, OR
Portland International Raceway
NTT INDYCAR SERIES
Phone: 317-492-6526
indycar@indycar.com
www.indycar.com

Oct 24, 2021
HOLLYWOOD CASINO 400
Kansas City, KS

Kansas Speedway
NASCAR CUP SERIES
www.nascar.com

Apr 18, 2021
HONDA GRAND PRIX OF ALABAMA
Birmingham, AL
Barber Motorsports Park
NTT INDYCAR SERIES
Phone: 317-492-6526
indycar@indycar.com
www.indycar.com

Jul 4, 2021
HONDA INDY 200 AT MID-OHIO
Lexington, OH
Mid-Ohio Sports Car Course
NTT INDYCAR SERIES
Phone: 317-492-6526
indycar@indycar.com
www.indycar.com

Jul 11, 2021
HONDA INDY TORONTO
Toronto, Canada
Streets of Toronto
NTT INDYCAR SERIES
Phone: 317-492-6526
indycar@indycar.com
www.indycar.com

May 30, 2021
INDIANAPOLIS 500
Indianapolis, IN
Indianapolis Motor Speedway
NTT INDYCAR SERIES
Phone: 317-492-6526
indycar@indycar.com
www.indycar.com

Mar 14, 2021
INSTACART 500
Phoenix, AZ
Phoenix Raceway
NASCAR CUP SERIES
www.nascar.com

Nov 5, 2021
LUCAS OIL 150
Avondale, AZ
Phoenix Raceway
NASCAR CAMPING WORLD TRUCK
SERIES
Phone: 800-630-0535
www.nascar.com

Aug 18 - Aug 22, 2021
LUCAS OIL NHRA NATIONALS
Brainerd, MN
Brainerd International Raceway
NATIONAL HOT ROD ASSOCIATION
Phone: 626-914-4761
Fax: 626-963-5360
nhra@nhra.com
www.nhra.com

Apr 9 - Apr 11, 2021
LUCAS OIL NHRA
WINTERNATIONALS
Pomona, CA
Auto Club Raceway at Pomona
NATIONAL HOT ROD ASSOCIATION
Phone: 626-914-4761
Fax: 626-963-5360
nhra@nhra.com
www.nhra.com

Aug 13 - Aug 15, 2021
MENARDS NHRA PETARMOR
NATIONALS
Topeka, KS

Heartland Motorsports Park
NATIONAL HOT ROD ASSOCIATION
Phone: 626-914-4761
Fax: 626-963-5360
nhra@nhra.com
www.nhra.com

Sept 9 - Sept 12, 2021
MOPAR EXPRESS LANE NHRA
NATIONALS
Mohnton, PA
Maple Grove Raceway
NATIONAL HOT ROD ASSOCIATION
Phone: 626-914-4761
Fax: 626-963-5360
nhra@nhra.com
www.nhra.com

Aug 8, 2021
MUSIC CITY GRAND PRIX
Nashville, TN
Streets of Nashville
NTT INDYCAR SERIES
Phone: 317-492-6526
indycar@indycar.com
www.indycar.com

Jun 13, 2021
NASCAR ALL-STAR OPEN
Concord, NC
Charlotte Motor Speedway
NASCAR CUP SERIES
www.nascar.com

Jun 13, 2021
NASCAR ALL-STAR RACE
Concord, NC
Charlotte Motor Speedway
NASCAR CUP SERIES
www.nascar.com

Oct 2, 2021
NASCAR CAMPING WORLD TRUCK
PLAYOFF RACE AT TALLADEGA
Talladega, AL
Talladega Superspeedway
NASCAR CAMPING WORLD TRUCK
SERIES
Phone: 800-630-0535
www.nascar.com

Oct 30, 2021
NASCAR CAMPING WORLD TRUCK
SERIES AT MARTINSVILLE
Martinsville, VA
Martinsville Speedway
NASCAR CAMPING WORLD TRUCK
SERIES
Phone: 800-630-0535
www.nascar.com

Sept 24, 2021
NASCAR CAMPING WORLD TRUCK
SERIES PLAYOFF RACE AT LAS
VEGAS
Las Vegas, NV
Las Vegas Motor Speedway
NASCAR CAMPING WORLD TRUCK
SERIES
Phone: 800-630-0535
www.nascar.com

Jul 9, 2021
NASCAR CAMPING WORLD TRUCK
SERIES RACE AT KNOXVILLE
Knoxville, IA
Knoxville Raceway
NASCAR CAMPING WORLD TRUCK
SERIES
Phone: 800-630-0535
www.nascar.com

events/meetings/shows

1323

Jun 12, 2021
NASCAR CAMPING WORLD TRUCK
SERIES RACE AT TEXAS
Fort Worth, TX
Texas Motor Speedway
NASCAR CAMPING WORLD TRUCK
SERIES
Phone: 800-630-0535
www.nascar.com

Nov 7, 2021
NASCAR CUP SERIES
CHAMPIONSHIP
Phoenix, AZ
Phoenix Raceway
NASCAR CUP SERIES
www.nascar.com

May 15, 2021
NASCAR CUP SERIES RACE AT
DOVER
Dover, DE
Dover International Speedway
NASCAR CUP SERIES
www.nascar.com

May 2, 2021
NASCAR CUP SERIES RACE AT
KANSAS
Kansas City, KS
Kansas Speedway
NASCAR CUP SERIES
www.nascar.com

Jun 26, 2021
NASCAR CUP SERIES RACE AT
POCONO 1
Long Pond, PA
Pocono Raceway
NASCAR CUP SERIES
www.nascar.com

Jun 27, 2021
NASCAR CUP SERIES RACE AT
POCONO 2
Long Pond, PA
Pocono Raceway
NASCAR CUP SERIES
www.nascar.com

Feb 15, 2021
NEXTERA ENERGY 250
Daytona Beach, FL
Daytona International Speedway
NASCAR CAMPING WORLD TRUCK
SERIES
Phone: 800-630-0535
www.nascar.com

Feb TBA, 2022
NHRA ARIZONA NATIONALS
Chandler, AZ
Wild Horse Pass Motorsports Park
NATIONAL HOT ROD ASSOCIATION
Phone: 626-914-4761
Fax: 626-963-5360
nhra@nhra.com
www.nhra.com

Sept 17 - Sept 19, 2021
NHRA CAROLINA NATIONALS
Concord, NC
zMax Dragway
NATIONAL HOT ROD ASSOCIATION
Phone: 626-914-4761
Fax: 626-963-5360
nhra@nhra.com
www.nhra.com

May 28 - Oct 10, 2021
NHRA LUCAS OIL DRAG RACING
SERIES
Various
NATIONAL HOT ROD ASSOCIATION
Phone: 626-914-4761
Fax: 626-963-5360
nhra@nhra.com
www.nhra.com

Jun 4 - Jun 6, 2021
NHRA NEW ENGLAND NATIONALS
Epping, NH
New England Dragway
NATIONAL HOT ROD ASSOCIATION
Phone: 626-914-4761
Fax: 626-963-5360
nhra@nhra.com
www.nhra.com

Jul 30 - Aug 1, 2021
NHRA NORTHWEST NATIONALS
Kent, WA
Pacific Raceways
NATIONAL HOT ROD ASSOCIATION
Phone: 626-914-4761
Fax: 626-963-5360
nhra@nhra.com
www.nhra.com

Jul 23 - Jul 25, 2021
NHRA SONOMA NATIONALS
Sonoma, CA
Sonoma Raceway
NATIONAL HOT ROD ASSOCIATION
Phone: 626-914-4761
Fax: 626-963-5360
nhra@nhra.com
www.nhra.com

Apr 30 - May 2, 2021
NHRA SOUTHERN NATIONALS
Commerce, GA
Atlanta Dragway
NATIONAL HOT ROD ASSOCIATION
Phone: 626-914-4761
Fax: 626-963-5360
nhra@nhra.com
www.nhra.com

Jun TBA, 2022
NHRA THUNDER VALLEY NATIONALS
Bristol, TN
Bristol Dragway
NATIONAL HOT ROD ASSOCIATION
Phone: 626-914-4761
Fax: 626-963-5360
nhra@nhra.com
www.nhra.com

Sept 1 - Sept 5, 2021
NHRA U.S. NATIONALS
Indianapolis, IN
Lucas Oil Raceway
NATIONAL HOT ROD ASSOCIATION
Phone: 626-914-4761
Fax: 626-963-5360
nhra@nhra.com
www.nhra.com

May 28, 2021
NORTH CAROLINA EDUCATION
LOTTERY 200
Concord, NC
Charlotte Motor Speedway
NASCAR CAMPING WORLD TRUCK
SERIES
Phone: 800-630-0535
www.nascar.com

Mar 7, 2021
PENNZOIL 400
Las Vegas, NV
Las Vegas Motor Speedway
NASCAR CUP SERIES
www.nascar.com

Jun 20, 2021
REV GROUP GRAND PRIX AT ROAD
AMERICA
Elkhart Lake, WI
Road America
NTT INDYCAR SERIES
Phone: 317-492-6526
indycar@indycar.com
www.indycar.com

Jul TBA, 2022
ROUTE 66 NHRA NATIONALS
Elwood, IL
Route 66 Raceway
NATIONAL HOT ROD ASSOCIATION
Phone: 626-914-4761
Fax: 626-963-5360
nhra@nhra.com
www.nhra.com

Sept 26, 2021
SOUTH POINT 400
Las Vegas, NV
Las Vegas Motor Speedway
NASCAR CUP SERIES
www.nascar.com

Sept 5, 2021
SOUTHERN 500
Darlington, SC
Darlington Raceway
NASCAR CUP SERIES
www.nascar.com

Jun 12, 2021
SPEEDYCASH.COM 200
Fort Worth, TX
Texas Motor Speedway
NASCAR CAMPING WORLD TRUCK
SERIES
Phone: 800-630-0535
www.nascar.com

Jun 24 - Jun 27, 2021
SUMMIT RACING EQUIPMENT NHRA
NATIONALS
Norwalk, OH
Summit Racing Equipment Motorsports
Park
NATIONAL HOT ROD ASSOCIATION
Phone: 626-914-4761
Fax: 626-963-5360
nhra@nhra.com
www.nhra.com

Apr 18, 2021
TOYOTA OWNERS 400
Richmond, VA
Richmond Raceway
NASCAR CUP SERIES
www.nascar.com

Jun 6, 2021
TOYOTA-SAVE MART 350
Sonoma, CA
Sonoma Raceway
NASCAR CUP SERIES
www.nascar.com

Apr 17, 2021
TOYOTACARE 250
Richmond, VA
Richmond Raceway

NASCAR CAMPING WORLD TRUCK
SERIES
Phone: 800-630-0535
www.nascar.com

Sept 16, 2021
UNOH 200
Bristol, TN
Bristol Motor Speedway
NASCAR CAMPING WORLD TRUCK
SERIES
Phone: 800-630-0535
www.nascar.com

Jun 4 - Jun 6, 2021
VIRGINIA NHRA NATIONALS
North Dinwiddie, VA
Virginia Motorsports Park
NATIONAL HOT ROD ASSOCIATION
Phone: 626-914-4761
Fax: 626-963-5360
nhra@nhra.com
www.nhra.com

Sept 24, 2021
WORLD OF WESTGATE 200
Las Vegas, NV
Las Vegas Motor Speedway
NASCAR CAMPING WORLD TRUCK
SERIES
Phone: 800-630-0535
www.nascar.com

Aug 20, 2021
WWT RACEWAY 200
Madison, IL
World Wide Technology Raceway at
Gateway
NASCAR CAMPING WORLD TRUCK
SERIES
Phone: 800-630-0535
www.nascar.com

May 2, 2021
XPEL 375
Fort Worth, TX
Texas Motor Speedway
NTT INDYCAR SERIES
Phone: 317-492-6526
indycar@indycar.com
www.indycar.com

Badminton

TBA, 2021
AAU NATIONAL BADMINTON
CHAMPIONSHIPS
AMATEUR ATHLETIC UNION
Phone: 407-934-7200
Fax: 407-934-7242
www.aausports.org

Feb TBA, 2022
DAVE FREEMAN JUNIOR OPEN
LOCAL CHAMPIONSHIPS
San Diego, CA
USA BADMINTON
Phone: 714-765-2952
usab@usabadminton.org
www.usabadminton.org

Feb TBA, 2022
DAVE FREEMAN OPEN
San Diego, CA
USA BADMINTON
Phone: 714-765-2952
usab@usabadminton.org
www.usabadminton.org

Feb TBA, 2022
EGRET OPEN LOCAL
CHAMPIONSHIP
Schaumburg, IL
USA BADMINTON
Phone: 714-765-2952
usab@usabadminton.org
www.usabadminton.org

Mar TBA, 2021
HARBOUR POINTE OPEN LOCAL
CHAMPIONSHIP
Mukilteo, WA
USA BADMINTON
Phone: 714-765-2952
usab@usabadminton.org
www.usabadminton.org

Aug TBA, 2021
JUNIOR INTERNATIONAL
BADMINTON CHAMPIONSHIPS
Bulgaria
USA BADMINTON
Phone: 714-765-2952
usab@usabadminton.org
www.usabadminton.org

Jul TBA, 2021
JUNIOR NATIONAL CHAMPIONSHIPS
Frisco, TX
USA BADMINTON
Phone: 714-765-2952
usab@usabadminton.org
www.usabadminton.org

Jan TBA, 2021
NATIONAL CAPITAL DC OPEN
USA BADMINTON
Phone: 714-765-2952
usab@usabadminton.org
www.usabadminton.org

May TBA, 2021
YONEX BOSTON OPEN
Cambridge, MA
USA BADMINTON
Phone: 714-765-2952
usab@usabadminton.org
www.usabadminton.org

Bandy

Feb TBA, 2022
WOMEN'S WORLD CHAMPIONSHIPS
AMERICAN BANDY ASSOCIATION
www.usabandy.com

Baseball

TBA, 2021
AAU INTERNATIONAL BASEBALL
CHAMPIONSHIPS
AMATEUR ATHLETIC UNION
Phone: 407-934-7200
Fax: 407-934-7242
www.aausports.org

Jul 5 - Jul 11, 2021
AAU NATIONAL BASEBALL
CHAMPIONSHIP LOUISIANA
Sterlington, LA
Sterlington Sports Complex
AMATEUR ATHLETIC UNION
Phone: 407-934-7200
Fax: 407-934-7242
www.aausports.org

Jul TBA, 2021
AAU NATIONAL BASEBALL
CHAMPIONSHIP VIRGINIA
Virginia Beach, VA
AMATEUR ATHLETIC UNION
Phone: 407-934-7200
Fax: 407-934-7242
www.aausports.org

TBA 2021
BASEBALL CANADA CUP
CHAMPIONSHIPS
TBA
BASEBALL CANADA
Phone: 613-748-5606
Fax: 613-748-5767
info@baseball.ca
www.baseball.ca

Jun 19 - Jun 30, 2021
NCAA DIVISION I BASEBALL FINALS
Omaha, NE
TD Ameritrade Park Omaha
NATIONAL COLLEGIATE ATHLETIC
ASSOCIATION
Phone: 317-917-6222
Fax: 317-917-6888
www.ncaa.org

Jun 5 - Jun 12, 2021
NCAA DIVISION II BASEBALL FINALS
Cary, NC
USA Baseball Training Complex
NATIONAL COLLEGIATE ATHLETIC
ASSOCIATION
Phone: 317-917-6222
Fax: 317-917-6888
www.ncaa.org

Jun 3 - Jun 9, 2021
NCAA DIVISION III BASEBALL FINALS
Cedar Rapids, IA
Perfect Game Field at Veterans
Memorial Stadium
NATIONAL COLLEGIATE ATHLETIC
ASSOCIATION
Phone: 317-917-6222
Fax: 317-917-6888
www.ncaa.org

Basketball

Jul 7 - Jul 11, 2021
AAU 10 & UNDER DI & DII BOYS'
BASKETBALL WORLD C
HAMPIONSHIPS
Clarksville, TN
AMATEUR ATHLETIC UNION
Phone: 407-934-7200
Fax: 407-934-7242
www.aausports.org

Jul 20 - Jul 22, 2021
AAU 10TH GRADE DI & DII GIRLS'
BASKETBALL NCAA W ORLD
CHAMPIONSHIPS
Minneapolis, MN
AMATEUR ATHLETIC UNION
Phone: 407-934-7200
Fax: 407-934-7242
www.aausports.org

Jul 18 - Jul 21, 2021
AAU 10U & 11U EAST COAST DIII
BOYS' BASKETBALL C
HAMPIONSHIPS
Hampton, VA
AMATEUR ATHLETIC UNION
Phone: 407-934-7200

Fax: 407-934-7242
www.aausports.org

Jul 3 - Jul 6, 2021
AAU 11 & UNDER DI, DII & DIII BOYS'
BASKETBALL W ORLD
CHAMPIONSHIPS
Orlando, FL
AMATEUR ATHLETIC UNION
Phone: 407-934-7200
Fax: 407-934-7242
www.aausports.org

Jul 20 - Jul 22, 2021
AAU 11TH GRADE DI & DII GIRLS'
BASKETBALL NCAA W ORLD
CHAMPIONSHIPS
Minneapolis, MN
AMATEUR ATHLETIC UNION
Phone: 407-934-7200
Fax: 407-934-7242
www.aausports.org

Jul 12 - Jul 15, 2021
AAU 12 & UNDER DI & DII BOYS'
BASKETBALL WORLD C
HAMPIONSHIPS
Hampton, VA
AMATEUR ATHLETIC UNION
Phone: 407-934-7200
Fax: 407-934-7242
www.aausports.org

Jul 18 - Jul 21, 2021
AAU 12U & 13U EAST COAST DIII
BOYS' BASKETBALL C
HAMPIONSHIPS
Hampton, VA
AMATEUR ATHLETIC UNION
Phone: 407-934-7200
Fax: 407-934-7242
www.aausports.org

Jul 1 - Jul 4, 2021
AAU 13 & UNDER DI & DII BOYS'
BASKETBALL WORLD C
HAMPIONSHIPS
Greensboro, NC
AMATEUR ATHLETIC UNION
Phone: 407-934-7200
Fax: 407-934-7242
www.aausports.org

Jul 17 - Jul 20, 2021
AAU 14 & UNDER DI & DII BOYS'
BASKETBALL WORLD C
HAMPIONSHIPS
Orlando, FL
AMATEUR ATHLETIC UNION
Phone: 407-934-7200
Fax: 407-934-7242
www.aausports.org

Jul 1 - Jul 4, 2021
AAU 14U & 15U/9TH EAST COAST DIII
BOYS' BASKETBA LL
CHAMPIONSHIPS
Hampton, VA
AMATEUR ATHLETIC UNION
Phone: 407-934-7200
Fax: 407-934-7242
www.aausports.org

Jul 1 - Jul 4, 2021
AAU 15U/9TH GRADE DI & DII BOYS'
BASKETBALL WORL D
CHAMPIONSHIPS
Orlando, FL
AMATEUR ATHLETIC UNION
Phone: 407-934-7200

Fax: 407-934-7242
www.aausports.org

Jul 1 - Jul 4, 2021
AAU 16U/10TH GRADE & 17U/11TH
GRADE EAST COAST D III BOYS'
BASKETBALL CHAMPIONSHIPS
Hampton, VA
AMATEUR ATHLETIC UNION
Phone: 407-934-7200
Fax: 407-934-7242
www.aausports.org

Jul 13 - Jul 16, 2021
AAU 16U/10TH GRADE DI & DII BOYS'
BASKETBALL WOR LD
CHAMPIONSHIPS
Orlando, FL
AMATEUR ATHLETIC UNION
Phone: 407-934-7200
Fax: 407-934-7242
www.aausports.org

Jul 13 - Jul 16, 2021
AAU 17U/11TH GRADE DI & DII BOYS'
BASKETBALL WOR LD
CHAMPIONSHIPS
Orlando, FL
AMATEUR ATHLETIC UNION
Phone: 407-934-7200
Fax: 407-934-7242
www.aausports.org

Jul 13 - Jul 16, 2021
AAU 20 & UNDER BOYS'
BASKETBALL WORLD CHAMPIONSH
IPS
Orlando, FL
AMATEUR ATHLETIC UNION
Phone: 407-934-7200
Fax: 407-934-7242
www.aausports.org

Jul 3 - Jul 6, 2021
AAU 2ND & 3RD GRADE GIRLS'
BASKETBALL CHAMPIONSH IPS
Orlando, FL
AMATEUR ATHLETIC UNION
Phone: 407-934-7200
Fax: 407-934-7242
www.aausports.org

Jul 3 - Jul 6, 2021
AAU 3RD GRADE DI & DII BOYS'
BASKETBALL WORLD CH
AMPIONSHIPS
Orlando, FL
AMATEUR ATHLETIC UNION
Phone: 407-934-7200
Fax: 407-934-7242
www.aausports.org

Jul 7 - Jul 11, 2021
AAU 4TH GRADE DI & DII BOYS'
BASKETBALL WORLD CH
AMPIONSHIPS
Hampton Roads, VA
AMATEUR ATHLETIC UNION
Phone: 407-934-7200
Fax: 407-934-7242
www.aausports.org

Jul 3 - Jul 6, 2021
AAU 4TH GRADE DI, DII & DIII GIRLS'
BASKETBALL C HAMPIONSHIPS
Orlando, FL
AMATEUR ATHLETIC UNION
Phone: 407-934-7200
Fax: 407-934-7242
www.aausports.org

Jul 3 - Jul 6, 2021
AAU 5TH GRADE DI & DII BOYS'
BASKETBALL WORLD CH
AMPIONSHIPS
Orlando, FL
AMATEUR ATHLETIC UNION
Phone: 407-934-7200
Fax: 407-934-7242
www.aausports.org

Jun 25 - Jun 28, 2021
AAU 5TH GRADE DI, DII & DIII GIRLS'
BASKETBALL C HAMPIONSHIPS
West Chester, OH
AMATEUR ATHLETIC UNION
Phone: 407-934-7200
Fax: 407-934-7242
www.aausports.org

Jul 15 - Jul 18, 2021
AAU 6TH GRADE DI & DII BOYS'
BASKETBALL WORLD CH
AMPIONSHIPS
Hampton, VA
AMATEUR ATHLETIC UNION
Phone: 407-934-7200
Fax: 407-934-7242
www.aausports.org

Jun 25 - Jun 28, 2021
AAU 6TH GRADE DI, DII & DIII GIRLS'
BASKETBALL C HAMPIONSHIPS
West Chester, OH
AMATEUR ATHLETIC UNION
Phone: 407-934-7200
Fax: 407-934-7242
www.aausports.org

Jul 1 - Jul 4, 2021
AAU 7TH GRADE DI & DII BOYS'
BASKETBALL WORLD CH
AMPIONSHIPS
Greensboro, NC
AMATEUR ATHLETIC UNION
Phone: 407-934-7200
Fax: 407-934-7242
www.aausports.org

Jun 25 - Jun 28, 2021
AAU 7TH GRADE DI, DII & DIII GIRLS'
BASKETBALL C HAMPIONSHIPS
West Chester, OH
AMATEUR ATHLETIC UNION
Phone: 407-934-7200
Fax: 407-934-7242
www.aausports.org

Jul 2 - Jul 5, 2021
AAU 7U, 8U & 2ND GRADE BOYS'
BASKETBALL WORLD CH
AMPIONSHIPS
Westminster, MD
AMATEUR ATHLETIC UNION
Phone: 407-934-7200
Fax: 407-934-7242
www.aausports.org

Jul 17 - Jul 20, 2021
AAU 8TH GRADE DI & DII BOYS'
BASKETBALL WORLD CH
AMPIONSHIPS
Orlando, FL
AMATEUR ATHLETIC UNION
Phone: 407-934-7200
Fax: 407-934-7242
www.aausports.org

Jul 22 - Jul 25, 2021
AAU 8TH GRADE DI, DII & DIII GIRLS'
BASKETBALL C HAMPIONSHIPS
Hampton, VA
AMATEUR ATHLETIC UNION
Phone: 407-934-7200
Fax: 407-934-7242
www.aausports.org

Jul 3 - Jul 6, 2021
AAU 9 & UNDER DI & DII BOYS'
BASKETBALL WORLD CH
AMPIONSHIPS
Orlando, FL
AMATEUR ATHLETIC UNION
Phone: 407-934-7200
Fax: 407-934-7242
www.aausports.org

Jul 20 - Jul 22, 2021
AAU 9TH GRADE DI & DII GIRLS'
BASKETBALL NCAA WO RLD
CHAMPIONSHIPS
Minneapolis, MN
AMATEUR ATHLETIC UNION
Phone: 407-934-7200
Fax: 407-934-7242
www.aausports.org

Jul 17 - Jul 20, 2021
AAU BOYS' BASKETBALL
INTERNATIONAL CHAMPIONSHIPS
Orlando, FL
AMATEUR ATHLETIC UNION
Phone: 407-934-7200
Fax: 407-934-7242
www.aausports.org

Jul TBA, 2021
AAU GIRLS' BASKETBALL
INTERNATIONAL CHAMPIONSHIP S
Orlando, FL
AMATEUR ATHLETIC UNION
Phone: 407-934-7200
Fax: 407-934-7242
www.aausports.org

Jul 7 - Jul 9, 2021
AAU SOUTHEAST DIII BOYS'
BASKETBALL CHAMPIONSHIP S
Orlando, FL
AMATEUR ATHLETIC UNION
Phone: 407-934-7200
Fax: 407-934-7242
www.aausports.org

Jul 15 - Jul 18, 2021
AAU WEST COAST BOYS'
BASKETBALL CHAMPIONSHIPS
Las Vegas, NV
AMATEUR ATHLETIC UNION
Phone: 407-934-7200
Fax: 407-934-7242
www.aausports.org

Aug TBA, 2022
CANADA BASKETBALL 15U/17U
MEN'S NATIONAL CHAMPIO NSHIPS
CANADA BASKETBALL
Phone: 416-614-8037
Fax: 416-614-9570
info@basketball.ca
www.basketball.ca

Aug TBA, 2022
CANADA BASKETBALL 15U/17U
WOMEN'S NATIONAL CHAMP
IONSHIPS
CANADA BASKETBALL
Phone: 416-614-8037

Fax: 416-614-9570
info@basketball.ca
www.basketball.ca

Mar TBA, 2022
CCAA MEN'S NATIONAL
BASKETBALL CHAMPIONSHIP
Toronto, Canada
Humber College
CANADA BASKETBALL
Phone: 416-614-8037
Fax: 416-614-9570
info@basketball.ca
www.basketball.ca

Mar TBA, 2022
CCAA WOMEN'S NATIONAL
BASKETBALL CHAMPIONSHIP
Vancouver, Canada
Vancouver Island University
CANADA BASKETBALL
Phone: 416-614-8037
Fax: 416-614-9570
info@basketball.ca
www.basketball.ca

Mar TBA, 2022
CIS WOMEN'S BASKETBALL
CHAMPIONSHIP
Toronto, Canada
Ryerson University
CANADA BASKETBALL
Phone: 416-614-8037
Fax: 416-614-9570
info@basketball.ca
www.basketball.ca

Jun 7 - Jun 13, 2021
FIBA AMERICAS U16 CHAMPIONSHIP
FOR MEN
TBA
USA BASKETBALL
Phone: 719-590-4800
Fax: 719-590-4811
fanmail@usabasketball.com
www.usab.com

Jun 20 - Jun 27, 2021
FIBA AMERICAS U16 CHAMPIONSHIP
FOR WOMEN
TBA
USA BASKETBALL
Phone: 719-590-4800
Fax: 719-590-4811
fanmail@usabasketball.com
www.usab.com

Aug 25 - Sept 10, 2023
FIBA BASKETBALL WORLD CUP
Indonesia, Japan & Philippines
USA BASKETBALL
Phone: 719-590-4800
Fax: 719-590-4811
fanmail@usabasketball.com
www.usab.com

Jul 3 - Jul 11, 2021
FIBA U19 WORLD CUP FOR MEN
Daugavpils and Riga, Latvia
USA BASKETBALL
Phone: 719-590-4800
Fax: 719-590-4811
fanmail@usabasketball.com
www.usab.com

Aug 7 - Aug 15, 2021
FIBA U19 WORLD CUP FOR WOMEN
Debrecent, Hungary
USA BASKETBALL
Phone: 719-590-4800
Fax: 719-590-4811

fanmail@usabasketball.com
www.usab.com

Apr 3 - Apr 5, 2021
NCAA DIVISION I MEN'S
BASKETBALL FINALS
Indianapolis, IN
Lucas Oil Stadium
NATIONAL COLLEGIATE ATHLETIC
ASSOCIATION
Phone: 317-917-6222
Fax: 317-917-6888
www.ncaa.org

Apr 2 - Apr 4, 2021
NCAA DIVISION I WOMEN'S
BASKETBALL FINALS
San Antonio, TX
Alamodome
NATIONAL COLLEGIATE ATHLETIC
ASSOCIATION
Phone: 317-917-6222
Fax: 317-917-6888
www.ncaa.org

Mar 24 - Mar 27, 2021
NCAA DIVISION II MEN'S
BASKETBALL FINALS
Evansville, IN
Ford Center
NATIONAL COLLEGIATE ATHLETIC
ASSOCIATION
Phone: 317-917-6222
Fax: 317-917-6888
www.ncaa.org

Mar 23 - Mar 26, 2021
NCAA DIVISION II WOMEN'S
BASKETBALL FINALS
Columbus, OH
Greater Columbus Convention
NATIONAL COLLEGIATE ATHLETIC
ASSOCIATION
Phone: 317-917-6222
Fax: 317-917-6888
www.ncaa.org

TBA, 2021
NCAA DIVISION III MEN'S
BASKETBALL FINALS
NATIONAL COLLEGIATE ATHLETIC
ASSOCIATION
Phone: 317-917-6222
Fax: 317-917-6888
www.ncaa.org

TBA, 2021
NCAA DIVISION III WOMEN'S
BASKETBALL FINALS
NATIONAL COLLEGIATE ATHLETIC
ASSOCIATION
Phone: 317-917-6222
Fax: 317-917-6888
www.ncaa.org

TBA, 2022
NIKE HOOP SUMMIT
Portland, OR
Moda Center
USA BASKETBALL
Phone: 719-590-4800
Fax: 719-590-4811
fanmail@usabasketball.com
www.usab.com

TBA, 2022
US OPEN BASKETBALL
CHAMPIONSHIPS
Westfield, IN
USA BASKETBALL
Phone: 719-590-4800

Fax: 719-590-4811
fanmail@usabasketball.com
www.usab.com

Biathlon

Mar 24 - Mar 28, 2021
NORTH AMERICAN & US BIATHLON
CHAMPIONSHIPS
West Yellowstone, MT
UNITED STATES BIATHLON
ASSOCIATION
Phone: 207-688-6500
Fax: 207-688-6505
info@usbiathlon.org
www.usbiathlon.org

Bobsledding

TBA, 2021
BOBSLED EUROPEAN CUP
USA BOBSLED & SKELETON
FEDERATION
Phone: 518-523-1842
Fax: 518-523-9491
www.teamusa.org/USA-Bobsled-Skeleton
-Federation

TBA, 2021
BOBSLED NORTH AMERICAN CUP
USA BOBSLED & SKELETON
FEDERATION
Phone: 518-523-1842
Fax: 518-523-9491
www.teamusa.org/USA-Bobsled-Skeleton
-Federation

Feb TBA, 2021
CALGARY WORLD CUP
Calgary, Canada
USA BOBSLED & SKELETON
FEDERATION
Phone: 518-523-1842
Fax: 518-523-9491
www.teamusa.org/USA-Bobsled-Skeleton
-Federation

Mar 1 - Mar 3, 2021
PARA WORLD CHAMPIONSHIPS
La Plagne, France
USA BOBSLED & SKELETON
FEDERATION
Phone: 518-523-1842
Fax: 518-523-9491
www.teamusa.org/USA-Bobsled-Skeleton
-Federation

Body Building

TBA, 2022
AAU AMERICAN CHAMPIONSHIPS
AMATEUR ATHLETIC UNION
Phone: 407-934-7200
Fax: 407-934-7242
www.aausports.org

TBA, 2021
ARNOLD CLASSIC
Columbus, OH
Columbus Convention Center
ARNOLD SPORTS FESTIVAL
Phone: 614-431-2600
Fax: 614-431-3492
www.arnoldsportsfestival.com

May 14 - May 16, 2021
ARNOLD CLASSIC AFRICA
Johannesburg, South Africa

INTERNATIONAL FEDERATION OF
BODY BUILDING & FITNESS
International Ph: 34-91-535-28-19
contact@ifbb.com
www.ifbb.com

Sept 17 - Sept 18, 2021
ARNOLD CLASSIC EUROPE
Sevilla, Spain
INTERNATIONAL FEDERATION OF
BODY BUILDING & FITNESS
International Ph: 34-91-535-28-19
contact@ifbb.com
www.ifbb.com

Oct 29 - Oct 31, 2021
ARNOLD SOUTH AMERICA
ARNOLD SPORTS FESTIVAL
Phone: 614-431-2600
Fax: 614-431-3492
www.arnoldsportsfestival.com

Sept 17 - Sept 20, 2021
ARNOLD SPORTS FESTIVAL
EUROPE
Sevilla, Spain
INTERNATIONAL FEDERATION OF
BODY BUILDING & FITNESS
International Ph: 34-91-535-28-19
contact@ifbb.com
www.ifbb.com

Mar 28, 2021
AUSTRALASIAN CHAMPIONSHIPS
Sydney, Australia
INTERNATIONAL FEDERATION OF
BODY BUILDING & FITNESS
International Ph: 34-91-535-28-19
contact@ifbb.com
www.ifbb.com

Jun 12 - Jun 13, 2021
BALKAN CHAMPIONSHIPS
Drobeta, Turnu Severin, Romania
INTERNATIONAL FEDERATION OF
BODY BUILDING & FITNESS
International Ph: 34-91-535-28-19
contact@ifbb.com
www.ifbb.com

TBA, 2021
BIKINI INTERNATIONAL
COMPETITION
Columbus, OH
Columbus Convention Center
ARNOLD SPORTS FESTIVAL
Phone: 614-431-2600
Fax: 614-431-3492
www.arnoldsportsfestival.com

Aug 13 - Aug 15, 2021
CENTRAL AMERICAN & CARIBBEAN
CHAMPIONSHIPS
Salvador
INTERNATIONAL FEDERATION OF
BODY BUILDING & FITNESS
International Ph: 34-91-535-28-19
contact@ifbb.com
www.ifbb.com

Jul 3 - Jul 4, 2021
CLASSIC PHYSIQUE OF AMERICA
Quito, Ecuador
INTERNATIONAL FEDERATION OF
BODY BUILDING & FITNESS
International Ph: 34-91-535-28-19
contact@ifbb.com
www.ifbb.com

Oct 23 - Oct 24, 2021
DIAMOND CUP BELGIUM
Mons, Belgium

INTERNATIONAL FEDERATION OF
BODY BUILDING & FITNESS
International Ph: 34-91-535-28-19
contact@ifbb.com
www.ifbb.com

Nov 19 - Nov 21, 2021
DIAMOND CUP CANCUN
Cancun, Mexico
INTERNATIONAL FEDERATION OF
BODY BUILDING & FITNESS
International Ph: 34-91-535-28-19
contact@ifbb.com
www.ifbb.com

May 28 - May 30, 2021
DIAMOND CUP FRANCE
Divonne, France
INTERNATIONAL FEDERATION OF
BODY BUILDING & FITNESS
International Ph: 34-91-535-28-19
contact@ifbb.com
www.ifbb.com

Jun 11 - Jun 13, 2021
DIAMOND CUP LUXEMBOURG
Mondorf-Les-Bains, Luxembourg
INTERNATIONAL FEDERATION OF
BODY BUILDING & FITNESS
International Ph: 34-91-535-28-19
contact@ifbb.com
www.ifbb.com

May 1 - May 2, 2021
DIAMOND CUP MALTA
Malta
INTERNATIONAL FEDERATION OF
BODY BUILDING & FITNESS
International Ph: 34-91-535-28-19
contact@ifbb.com
www.ifbb.com

Jun 18 - Jun 20, 2021
DIAMOND CUP OSTRAVA
Ostrava, Czech Republic
INTERNATIONAL FEDERATION OF
BODY BUILDING & FITNESS
International Ph: 34-91-535-28-19
contact@ifbb.com
www.ifbb.com

Sept 24 - Sept 25, 2021
DIAMOND CUP PRAGUE
Czech Republic
INTERNATIONAL FEDERATION OF
BODY BUILDING & FITNESS
International Ph: 34-91-535-28-19
contact@ifbb.com
www.ifbb.com

Nov 19 - Nov 21, 2021
DIAMOND CUP ROME
Rome, Italy
INTERNATIONAL FEDERATION OF
BODY BUILDING & FITNESS
International Ph: 34-91-535-28-19
contact@ifbb.com
www.ifbb.com

Oct 29 - Oct 31, 2021
DIAMOND CUP SERBIA
Cacak, Serbia
INTERNATIONAL FEDERATION OF
BODY BUILDING & FITNESS
International Ph: 34-91-535-28-19
contact@ifbb.com
www.ifbb.com

Oct 15 - Oct 17, 2021
DIAMOND CUP SKOPJE
Skopje, Republic of North Macedonia

INTERNATIONAL FEDERATION OF
BODY BUILDING & FITNESS
International Ph: 34-91-535-28-19
contact@ifbb.com
www.ifbb.com

Oct 16 - Oct 18, 2021
DIAMOND CUP TUNISIA & MAGHREB
ARAB CHAMPIONSHIPS
Tunis, Tunisia
INTERNATIONAL FEDERATION OF
BODY BUILDING & FITNESS
International Ph: 34-91-535-28-19
contact@ifbb.com
www.ifbb.com

Oct 14 - Oct 15, 2021
DUBAI MUSCLE BEACH & FEMALE
FITNESS WORLD CUP
Dubai, United Arab Emirates
INTERNATIONAL FEDERATION OF
BODY BUILDING & FITNESS
International Ph: 34-91-535-28-19
contact@ifbb.com
www.ifbb.com

May 13 - May 17, 2021
EUROPEAN CHAMPIONSHIPS
Santa Susana, Spain
INTERNATIONAL FEDERATION OF
BODY BUILDING & FITNESS
International Ph: 34-91-535-28-19
contact@ifbb.com
www.ifbb.com

Sept 10 - Sept 12, 2021
EUROPEAN CUP
Sibiu, Romania
INTERNATIONAL FEDERATION OF
BODY BUILDING & FITNESS
International Ph: 34-91-535-28-19
contact@ifbb.com
www.ifbb.com

Sept 10 - Sept 12, 2021
EUROPEAN FIT MODEL
CHAMPIONSHIPS
Latvia
INTERNATIONAL FEDERATION OF
BODY BUILDING & FITNESS
International Ph: 34-91-535-28-19
contact@ifbb.com
www.ifbb.com

TBA, 2021
FIGURE INTERNATIONAL
Columbus, OH
Columbus Convention Center
ARNOLD SPORTS FESTIVAL
Phone: 614-431-2600
Fax: 614-431-3492
www.arnoldsportsfestival.com

Sept 10 - Sept 12, 2021
FIT MODEL INTERCONTINENTAL
Riga, Latvia
INTERNATIONAL FEDERATION OF
BODY BUILDING & FITNESS
International Ph: 34-91-535-28-19
contact@ifbb.com
www.ifbb.com

Jun 5 - Jun 7, 2021
FIT MODEL WORLD CUP
Riga, Latvia
INTERNATIONAL FEDERATION OF
BODY BUILDING & FITNESS
International Ph: 34-91-535-28-19
contact@ifbb.com
www.ifbb.com

TBA, 2021
FITNESS INTERNATIONAL
COMPETITION
Columbus, OH
Columbus Convention Center
ARNOLD SPORTS FESTIVAL
Phone: 614-431-2600
Fax: 614-431-3492
www.arnoldsportsfestival.com

Oct 8 - Oct 9, 2021
FITNESS MANIA CLASSIC V
Kladno, Czech Republic
INTERNATIONAL FEDERATION OF
BODY BUILDING & FITNESS
International Ph: 34-91-535-28-19
contact@ifbb.com
www.ifbb.com

Jun 28 - Jul 4, 2021
FITNESS SPORTS GAMES
Santa Susanna, Spain
INTERNATIONAL FEDERATION OF
BODY BUILDING & FITNESS
International Ph: 34-91-535-28-19
contact@ifbb.com
www.ifbb.com

Jul 16 - Jul 18, 2021
FLORIDA GRAND PRIX
Boca Ratón, FL
INTERNATIONAL FEDERATION OF
BODY BUILDING & FITNESS
International Ph: 34-91-535-28-19
contact@ifbb.com
www.ifbb.com

Jun 26 - Jun 27, 2021
GEORGIA GRAND PRIX
Tbilisi, Georgia
INTERNATIONAL FEDERATION OF
BODY BUILDING & FITNESS
International Ph: 34-91-535-28-19
contact@ifbb.com
www.ifbb.com

Oct 22 - Oct 23, 2021
GRAND PRIX PHILIPPINES
Manila, Philippines
INTERNATIONAL FEDERATION OF
BODY BUILDING & FITNESS
International Ph: 34-91-535-28-19
contact@ifbb.com
www.ifbb.com

Oct 16 - Oct 17, 2021
INTERNATIONAL AUSTRIAN
CHAMPIONSHIOPS
Wels, Austria
INTERNATIONAL FEDERATION OF
BODY BUILDING & FITNESS
International Ph: 34-91-535-28-19
contact@ifbb.com
www.ifbb.com

Oct 8 - Oct 9, 2021
INTERNATIONAL BELLUX CUP
LUXEMBOURG
Munsbach, Luxembourg
INTERNATIONAL FEDERATION OF
BODY BUILDING & FITNESS
International Ph: 34-91-535-28-19
contact@ifbb.com
www.ifbb.com

Sept 3 - Sept 4, 2021
INTERNATIONAL GRAND PRIX
MALTA
Malta
INTERNATIONAL FEDERATION OF
BODY BUILDING & FITNESS

International Ph: 34-91-535-28-19
contact@ifbb.com
www.ifbb.com

Dec 4 - Dec 5, 2021
MERCOSUR CUP
Mendoza, Argentina
INTERNATIONAL FEDERATION OF
BODY BUILDING & FITNESS
International Ph: 34-91-535-28-19
contact@ifbb.com
www.ifbb.com

TBA, 2022
MID-ATLANTIC BODYBUILDING
CHAMPIONSHIPS
NATIONAL AMATEUR BODYBUILDERS
ASSOCIATION
info@nabbausa.com
www.nabba.com

Nov 10 - Nov 14, 2021
MISS & MISTER AMERICA
Quito, Ecuador
INTERNATIONAL FEDERATION OF
BODY BUILDING & FITNESS
International Ph: 34-91-535-28-19
contact@ifbb.com
www.ifbb.com

Sept 3 - Sept 5, 2021
MISTER & MISS UNIVERSO
Asuncion, Paraguay
INTERNATIONAL FEDERATION OF
BODY BUILDING & FITNESS
International Ph: 34-91-535-28-19
contact@ifbb.com
www.ifbb.com

Oct 1 - Oct 3, 2021
MISTER UNIVERSE PRO & RAFAEL
VERA CLASSIC PRO QU ALIFIERS
Marbella, Spain
INTERNATIONAL FEDERATION OF
BODY BUILDING & FITNESS
International Ph: 34-91-535-28-19
contact@ifbb.com
www.ifbb.com

Jun TBA, 2021
NATURAL CHI-TOWN SHOWDOWN
OPEN
NATIONAL AMATEUR BODYBUILDERS
ASSOCIATION
info@nabbausa.com
www.nabba.com

Sept 4 - Sept 5, 2021
NORDIC FITNESS EXPO
Turku, Finland
INTERNATIONAL FEDERATION OF
BODY BUILDING & FITNESS
International Ph: 34-91-535-28-19
contact@ifbb.com
www.ifbb.com

May 21 - May 23, 2021
OPEN BALKAN CUP
Knjazevac, Serbia
INTERNATIONAL FEDERATION OF
BODY BUILDING & FITNESS
International Ph: 34-91-535-28-19
contact@ifbb.com
www.ifbb.com

TBA, 2022
OSLO GRAND PRIX
Oslo, Norway
INTERNATIONAL FEDERATION OF
BODY BUILDING & FITNESS
International Ph: 34-91-535-28-19

events/meetings/shows

contact@ifbb.com
www.ifbb.com

Oct 29 - Oct 31, 2021
PEPA GRAND PRIX
Opava, Czech Republic
INTERNATIONAL FEDERATION OF
BODY BUILDING & FITNESS
International Ph: 34-91-535-28-19
contact@ifbb.com
www.ifbb.com

Apr 2 - Apr 5, 2021
SIBERIAN POWER SHOW
Krasnoyarsk, Russia
INTERNATIONAL FEDERATION OF
BODY BUILDING & FITNESS
International Ph: 34-91-535-28-19
contact@ifbb.com
www.ifbb.com

Oct 7 - Oct 11, 2021
SOUTH AMERICAN CHAMPIONSHIPS
Buenos Aires, Argentina
INTERNATIONAL FEDERATION OF
BODY BUILDING & FITNESS
International Ph: 34-91-535-28-19
contact@ifbb.com
www.ifbb.com

Mar 19, 2022
SWEDEN GRAND PRIX
Malmo, Sweden
INTERNATIONAL FEDERATION OF
BODY BUILDING & FITNESS
International Ph: 34-91-535-28-19
contact@ifbb.com
www.ifbb.com

May 7 - May 9, 2021
TIGER CLASSIC - DIAMOND CUP
ROMANIA
Bucharest, Romania
INTERNATIONAL FEDERATION OF
BODY BUILDING & FITNESS
International Ph: 34-91-535-28-19
contact@ifbb.com
www.ifbb.com

Jun 11 - Jun 13, 2021
WORLD CHILDREN CHAMPIONSHIPS
Cacak, Serbia
INTERNATIONAL FEDERATION OF
BODY BUILDING & FITNESS
International Ph: 34-91-535-28-19
contact@ifbb.com
www.ifbb.com

May 8 - May 9, 2021
WORLD FIT MODEL CUP
Riga, Latvia
INTERNATIONAL FEDERATION OF
BODY BUILDING & FITNESS
International Ph: 34-91-535-28-19
contact@ifbb.com
www.ifbb.com

Nov 26 - Nov 28, 2021
WORLD FITNESS CHAMPIONSHIPS
Perpignan, France
INTERNATIONAL FEDERATION OF
BODY BUILDING & FITNESS
International Ph: 34-91-535-28-19
contact@ifbb.com
www.ifbb.com

Dec 3 - Dec 5, 2021
WORLD JUNIOR CHAMPIONSHIPS
TBA
INTERNATIONAL FEDERATION OF
BODY BUILDING & FITNESS
International Ph: 34-91-535-28-19

contact@ifbb.com
www.ifbb.com

Nov 26 - Nov 28, 2021
WORLD MASTER CHAMPIONSHIPS
Perpignan, France
INTERNATIONAL FEDERATION OF
BODY BUILDING & FITNESS
International Ph: 34-91-535-28-19
contact@ifbb.com
www.ifbb.com

Nov 3 - Nov 7, 2021
WORLD MEN'S CHAMPIONSHIPS &
CONGRESS
TBA
INTERNATIONAL FEDERATION OF
BODY BUILDING & FITNESS
International Ph: 34-91-535-28-19
contact@ifbb.com
www.ifbb.com

Bowling

Jun TBA, 2022
CANADIAN OPEN CHAMPIONSHIP
St. John's, Canada
CANADIAN 5 PIN BOWLERS
ASSOCIATION
Phone: 613-744-5090
Fax: 613-744-2217
sheila.c5pba@gmail.com
www.c5pba.ca

Mar TBA, 2022
CANADIAN YOUTH CHALLENGE
CHAMPIONSHIP
Winnipeg, Canada
CANADIAN 5 PIN BOWLERS
ASSOCIATION
Phone: 613-744-5090
Fax: 613-744-2217
sheila.c5pba@gmail.com
www.c5pba.ca

Apr TBA, 2022
INTER PROVINCIAL CHAMPIONSHIP
Kelowna, Canada
CANADIAN 5 PIN BOWLERS
ASSOCIATION
Phone: 613-744-5090
Fax: 613-744-2217
sheila.c5pba@gmail.com
www.c5pba.ca

Boxing

TBA, 2021
ELITE MEN'S WORLD
CHAMPIONSHIPS
USA BOXING
Phone: 719-866-2323
www.teamusa.org/USA-Boxing

TBA, 2021
ELITE WOMEN'S WORLD
CHAMPIONSHIPS
USA BOXING
Phone: 719-866-2323
www.teamusa.org/USA-Boxing

TBA, 2021
EMIL JECHEV YOUTH MEMORIAL
TOURNAMENT
USA BOXING
Phone: 719-866-2323
www.teamusa.org/USA-Boxing

TBA, 2022
GEEBEE TOURNAMENT
TBA
USA BOXING
Phone: 719-866-2323
www.teamusa.org/USA-Boxing

Jul 7 - Jul 17, 2021
NATIONAL JUNIOR OLYMPICS
Lubbock, TX
USA BOXING
Phone: 719-866-2323
www.teamusa.org/USA-Boxing

Mar TBA, 2021
USA BOXING MASTER'S NATIONAL
CHAMPIONSHIPS
Reno, NV
USA BOXING
Phone: 719-866-2323
www.teamusa.org/USA-Boxing

Mar TBA, 2021
WESTERN QUALIFIER
Reno, NV
USA BOXING
Phone: 719-866-2323
www.teamusa.org/USA-Boxing

Broomball

TBA, 2021
USA BROOMBALL NATIONAL
CHAMPIONSHIPS
USA BROOMBALL
contact@usbabroomball.org
usbabroomball.org

Canoeing & Kayaking

Sept 30 - Oct 3, 2021
2021 ICF CANOE MARATHON WORLD
CHAMPIONSHIP
Bascov, Romania
INTERNATIONAL CANOE FEDERATION
International Ph: 41 (0)21 612 0290
info@canoeicf.com
www.canoeicf.com

July 3 - July 5, 2021
2021 ICF CANOE OCEAN RACING
WORLD CUP
Lanzarote, Spain
INTERNATIONAL CANOE FEDERATION
International Ph: 41 (0)21 612 0290
info@canoeicf.com
www.canoeicf.com

May 14 - May 16, 2021
2021 ICF CANOE SPRINT WORLD
CUP 1
Szeged, Hungary
INTERNATIONAL CANOE FEDERATION
International Ph: 41 (0)21 612 0290
info@canoeicf.com
www.canoeicf.com

May 21 - May 23, 2021
2021 ICF CANOE SPRINT WORLD
CUP 2
Barnaul, Russia
INTERNATIONAL CANOE FEDERATION
International Ph: 41 (0)21 612 0290
info@canoeicf.com
www.canoeicf.com

Aug 12 - Aug 15, 2021
2021 ICF DRAGON BOAT CLUB
CREW WORLD CHAMPIONSHI PS
Poznan, Poland
INTERNATIONAL CANOE FEDERATION
International Ph: 41 (0)21 612 0290
info@canoeicf.com
www.canoeicf.com

Aug 19- Aug 22, 2021
2021 ICF JUNIOR & U23 CANOE
SLALOM WORLD CHAMPIO NSHIPS
Solkan, Slovenia
INTERNATIONAL CANOE FEDERATION
International Ph: 41 (0)21 612 0290
info@canoeicf.com
www.canoeicf.com

Jul 15 - Jul 18, 2021
2021 ICF JUNIOR & U23 CANOE
SPRINT WORLD CHAMPIO NSHIPS
Montemor-O-Velho, Portugal
INTERNATIONAL CANOE FEDERATION
International Ph: 41 (0)21 612 0290
info@canoeicf.com
www.canoeicf.com

May 13 - May 15, 2021
2021 ICF PARACANOE WORLD CUP
Szeged, Hungary
INTERNATIONAL CANOE FEDERATION
International Ph: 41 (0)21 612 0290
info@canoeicf.com
www.canoeicf.com

May 22 - May 24, 2021
2021 ICF WILDWATER CANOEING
WORLD CUP
Treignac, France
INTERNATIONAL CANOE FEDERATION
International Ph: 41 (0)21 612 0290
info@canoeicf.com
www.canoeicf.com

Cheerleading

May 2, 2021
AAU CHEERLEADING NATIONAL
CHAMPIONSHIP
Glen Carbon, IL
The Sports Academy
AMATEUR ATHLETIC UNION
Phone: 407-934-7200
Fax: 407-934-7242
www.aausports.org

Mar 24, 2021
ALL STAR CHAMPIONSHIPS
Anaheim, CA
Anaheim Convention Center
UNITED SPIRIT ASSOCIATION
Phone: 800-886-4872
Fax: 866-761-9365
info@usacamps.com
usa.varsity.com

Apr 30 - May 1, 2021
DANCE NATIONALS
Anaheim, CA
Anaheim Convention Center
UNITED SPIRIT ASSOCIATION
Phone: 800-886-4872
Fax: 866-761-9365
info@usacamps.com
usa.varsity.com

Apr 30 - May 2, 2021
HIGH SCHOOL SPIRIT NATIONALS
Anaheim, CA

Anaheim Convention Center
UNITED SPIRIT ASSOCIATION
Phone: 800-886-4872
Fax: 866-761-9365
info@usacamps.com
usa.varsity.com

Feb TBA, 2022
USA COLLEGIATE CHAMPIONSHIPS
Anaheim, CA
Anaheim Convention Center
UNITED SPIRIT ASSOCIATION
Phone: 800-886-4872
Fax: 866-761-9365
info@usacamps.com
usa.varsity.com

May 2, 2021
USA JUNIOR NATIONALS
Anaheim, CA
Anaheim Convention Center
UNITED SPIRIT ASSOCIATION
Phone: 800-886-4872
Fax: 866-761-9365
info@usacamps.com
usa.varsity.com

Croquet

TBA, 2021
GOLF CROQUET WORLD
CHAMPIONSHIP
US CROQUET ASSOCIATION
Phone: 561-478-0760
Fax: 561-686-5507
usca@msn.com
www.croquetamerica.com

TBA, 2021
USCA COLLEGIATE CHAMPIONSHIP
US CROQUET ASSOCIATION
Phone: 561-478-0760
Fax: 561-686-5507
usca@msn.com
www.croquetamerica.com

TBA, 2021
USCA MID-ATLANTIC REGIONAL
CHAMPIONSHIP
US CROQUET ASSOCIATION
Phone: 561-478-0760
Fax: 561-686-5507
usca@msn.com
www.croquetamerica.com

Oct 5 - Oct 7, 2021
USCA NATIONAL AMERICAN RULES
CHAMPIONSHIP
West Palm Beach, FL
National Croquet Center
US CROQUET ASSOCIATION
Phone: 561-478-0760
Fax: 561-686-5507
usca@msn.com
www.croquetamerica.com

Dec 10 - Dec 12, 2021
USCA NATIONAL CROQUET CLUB
DOUBLES CHAMPIONSHIP
West Palm Beach, FL
National Croquet Center
US CROQUET ASSOCIATION
Phone: 561-478-0760
Fax: 561-686-5507
usca@msn.com
www.croquetamerica.com

Jan 14 - Jan 16, 2022
USCA NATIONAL CROQUET CLUB
SINGLES CHAMPIONSHIP
West Palm Beach, FL
National Croquet Center
US CROQUET ASSOCIATION
Phone: 561-478-0760
Fax: 561-686-5507
usca@msn.com
www.croquetamerica.com

Sept 1 - Sept 5, 2021
USCA NATIONAL GOLF CROQUET
CHAMPIONSHIP
Hartfield, VA
Chesapeake Bay Croquet Club
US CROQUET ASSOCIATION
Phone: 561-478-0760
Fax: 561-686-5507
usca@msn.com
www.croquetamerica.com

Cross Country

Mar 15, 2021
NCAA DIVISION I MEN'S CROSS
COUNTRY FINALS
Stillwater, OK
OSU Cross Country Course
NATIONAL COLLEGIATE ATHLETIC
ASSOCIATION
Phone: 317-917-6222
Fax: 317-917-6888
www.ncaa.org

TBA, 2021
NCAA DIVISION II MEN'S/WOMEN'S
CROSS COUNTRY FIN ALS
NATIONAL COLLEGIATE ATHLETIC
ASSOCIATION
Phone: 317-917-6222
Fax: 317-917-6888
www.ncaa.org

TBA, 2021
NCAA DIVISION III MEN'S/WOMEN'S
CROSS COUNTRY FI NALS
NATIONAL COLLEGIATE ATHLETIC
ASSOCIATION
Phone: 317-917-6222
Fax: 317-917-6888
www.ncaa.org

Curling

Jan 7 - Jan 10, 2021
2021 OK TIRE & BKT TIRES GROUP
CONTINENTAL CUP
Oakville, Canada
Sixteen Mile Sports Complex
CURLING CANADA
Phone: 613-834-2076
Fax: 613-834-0716
championships@curling.ca
www.curling.ca

Jan TBA, 2022
CANADIAN JUNIOR CHAMPIONSHIPS
TBA
CURLING CANADA
Phone: 613-834-2076
Fax: 613-834-0716
championships@curling.ca
www.curling.ca

events/meetings/shows

TBA, 2022
CANADIAN WHEELCHAIR CURLING
CHAMPIONSHIP
CURLING CANADA
Phone: 613-834-2076
Fax: 613-834-0716
championships@curling.ca
www.curling.ca

Apr 3 - Apr 11, 2021
WORLD MEN'S CURLING
CHAMPIONSHIP
Calgary, Canada
CURLING CANADA
Phone: 613-834-2076
Fax: 613-834-0716
championships@curling.ca
www.curling.ca

Apr 30 - May 9, 2021
WORLD WOMEN'S CURLING
CHAMPIONSHIPS
Calgary, Canada
Markin McPhail Centre
CURLING CANADA
Phone: 613-834-2076
Fax: 613-834-0716
championships@curling.ca
www.curling.ca

TBA, 2022
CLUB NATIONAL CHAMPIONSHIPS
Laurel, MD
USA CURLING
Phone: 715-344-1199
Fax: 715-344-2279
info@usacurl.org
www.teamusa.org/USA-Curling

Mar TBA, 2022
COLLEGE NATIONAL
CHAMPIONSHIP
Fargo, ND
USA CURLING
Phone: 715-344-1199
Fax: 715-344-2279
info@usacurl.org
www.teamusa.org/USA-Curling

Mar 18 - Mar 25, 2021
MIXED DOUBLES CHAMPIONSHIP
Calgary, Canada
Winsport Arena
CURLING CANADA
Phone: 613-834-2076
Fax: 613-834-0716
championships@curling.ca
www.curling.ca

May TBA, 2021
MIXED DOUBLES NATIONAL
CHAMPIONSHIP
Bemidji, MN
USA CURLING
Phone: 715-344-1199
Fax: 715-344-2279
info@usacurl.org
www.teamusa.org/USA-Curling

Jan 28 - Feb 6, 2022
SCOTTIES TOURNAMENT OF
HEARTS
Thunder Bay, Canada
Fort Williams Gardens
CURLING CANADA
Phone: 613-834-2076
Fax: 613-834-0716
championships@curling.ca
www.curling.ca

Mar TBA 2022
SENIOR NATIONAL CHAMPIONSHIPS
Fairbanks, AK
USA CURLING
Phone: 715-344-1199
Fax: 715-344-2279
info@usacurl.org
www.teamusa.org/USA-Curling

Mar 5 - Mar 14, 2021
TIM HORTONS BRIER
Calgary, Canada
Winsport Arena
CURLING CANADA
Phone: 613-834-2076
Fax: 613-834-0716
championships@curling.ca
www.curling.ca

Feb TBA, 2022
WORLD JUNIOR CURLING
CHAMPIONSHIPS
TBA
USA CURLING
Phone: 715-344-1199
Fax: 715-344-2279
info@usacurl.org
www.teamusa.org/USA-Curling

Apr 2 - Apr 11, 2021
WORLD MEN'S CHAMPIONSHIP
Calgary, Canada
USA CURLING
Phone: 715-344-1199
Fax: 715-344-2279
info@usacurl.org
www.teamusa.org/USA-Curling

May 16 - May 23, 2021
WORLD MIXED DOUBLES & WORLD
SENIOR CHAMPIONSHIPS
TBA
USA CURLING
Phone: 715-344-1199
Fax: 715-344-2279
info@usacurl.org
www.teamusa.org/USA-Curling

Mar 6 - Mar 13, 2021
WORLD WHEELCHAIR
CHAMPIONSHIP
Beijing, China
USA CURLING
Phone: 715-344-1199
Fax: 715-344-2279
info@usacurl.org
www.teamusa.org/USA-Curling

Apr 30 - May 9, 2021
WORLD WOMEN'S CHAMPIONSHIP
Calrgary, Canada
USA CURLING
Phone: 715-344-1199
Fax: 715-344-2279
info@usacurl.org
www.teamusa.org/USA-Curling

Cycling

Jun 24 - Jun 27, 2021
AMATEUR ROAD NATIONAL
CHAMPIONSHIPS
Clay County, FL
USA CYCLING
Phone: 719-434-4200
Fax: 719-434-4300
help@usacycling.org
www.usacycling.org

Jun 4 - Jun 5, 2021
BAIE ST PAUL CANADA CUP
Baie St. Paul, Canada
CANADIAN CYCLING ASSOCIATION
Phone: 613-248-1353
Fax: 613-248-9311
general@cyclingcanada.ca
www.cyclingcanada.ca

Apr 1, 2022
CANADIAN TRACK CYCLING
CHAMPIONSHIPS
TBA
CANADIAN CYCLING ASSOCIATION
Phone: 613-248-1353
Fax: 613-248-9311
general@cyclingcanada.ca
www.cyclingcanada.ca

Jun 18 - Jun 20, 2021
CANMORE CANADA CUP
Canmore, Canada
CANADIAN CYCLING ASSOCIATION
Phone: 613-248-1353
Fax: 613-248-9311
general@cyclingcanada.ca
www.cyclingcanada.ca

Apr TBA, 2021
COLLEGIATE BMX NATIONAL
CHAMPIONSHIPS
TBA
USA CYCLING
Phone: 719-434-4200
Fax: 719-434-4300
help@usacycling.org
www.usacycling.org

Oct 14 - Oct 17, 2021
COLLEGIATE MOUNTAIN BIKE
NATIONAL CHAMPIONSHIPS
Durango, CO
Purgatory Resort
USA CYCLING
Phone: 719-434-4200
Fax: 719-434-4300
help@usacycling.org
www.usacycling.org

May 7 - May 9, 2021
COLLEGIATE ROAD NATIONAL
CHAMPIONSHIPS
Augusta, GA
USA CYCLING
Phone: 719-434-4200
Fax: 719-434-4300
help@usacycling.org
www.usacycling.org

Sept 9 - Sept 11, 2021
COLLEGIATE TRACK NATIONAL
CHAMPIONSHIPS
Indianapolis, IN
USA CYCLING
Phone: 719-434-4200
Fax: 719-434-4300
help@usacycling.org
www.usacycling.org

May 29 - May 30, 2021
CROSSROADS CANADA CUP
Mont Tremblant, QC
CANADIAN CYCLING ASSOCIATION
Phone: 613-248-1353
Fax: 613-248-9311
general@cyclingcanada.ca
www.cyclingcanada.ca

Dec TBA, 2021
CYCLOCROSS NATIONAL
CHAMPIONSHIPS
Dupage County, IL
USA CYCLING
Phone: 719-434-4200
Fax: 719-434-4300
help@usacycling.org
www.usacycling.org

Mar TBA, 2021
ELITE BMX NATIONAL
CHAMPIONSHIPS
Houston, TX
USA CYCLING
Phone: 719-434-4200
Fax: 719-434-4300
help@usacycling.org
www.usacycling.org

Jul 1 - Jul 7, 2021
ELITE TRACK NATIONAL
CHAMPIONSHIPS
Carson, CA
USA CYCLING
Phone: 719-434-4200
Fax: 719-434-4300
help@usacycling.org
www.usacycling.org

Sept TBA, 2021
MARATHON MOUNTAIN BIKE
NATIONAL CHAMPIONSHIPS
Palo Duro, TX
USA CYCLING
Phone: 719-434-4200
Fax: 719-434-4300
help@usacycling.org
www.usacycling.org

Aug TBA, 2021
MASTERS ROAD NATIONAL
CHAMPIONSHIPS
Cedar City, UT
USA CYCLING
Phone: 719-434-4200
Fax: 719-434-4300
help@usacycling.org
www.usacycling.org

Sept 14 - Sept 19, 2021
MASTERS TRACK NATIONAL
CHAMPIONSHIPS
Breinigsville, PA
USA CYCLING
Phone: 719-434-4200
Fax: 719-434-4300
help@usacycling.org
www.usacycling.org

Jul 9 - Jul 18, 2021
MOUNTAIN BIKE NATIONAL
CHAMPIONSHIPS
Winter Park, CO
USA CYCLING
Phone: 719-434-4200
Fax: 719-434-4300
help@usacycling.org
www.usacycling.org

Jun 19 - Jun 20, 2021
PANORAMA CANADA CUP
Panorama, Canada
CANADIAN CYCLING ASSOCIATION
Phone: 613-248-1353
Fax: 613-248-9311
general@cyclingcanada.ca
www.cyclingcanada.ca

Jul 1 - Jul 7, 2021
PARA-CYCLING TRACK NATIONAL
CHAMPIONSHIPS
Carson, CA
USA CYCLING
Phone: 719-434-4200
Fax: 719-434-4300
help@usacycling.org
www.usacycling.org

Jun 26 - Jul 18, 2021
TOUR DE FRANCE
Paris, France
AMAURY SPORT ORGANIZATION
International Ph: 33-1-41-33-14-00
contact@aso.fr
www.aso.fr

Apr 30 - May 2, 2021
USA BMX DIXIELAND NATIONALS
Powder Springs, GA
USA BMX
Phone: 480-961-1903
Fax: 480-961-1842
www.usabmx.com

Nov TBA, 2021
USA BMX GRANDS RACE OF
CHAMPIONS
TBA
USA BMX
Phone: 480-961-1903
Fax: 480-961-1842
www.usabmx.com

TBA, 2022
USA BMX GREAT NORTHWEST
NATIONALS
Redmond, OR
USA BMX
Phone: 480-961-1903
Fax: 480-961-1842
www.usabmx.com

Jul 30 - Aug 1, 2021
USA BMX GREAT SALT LAKE
NATIONALS
West Jordan, UT
USA BMX
Phone: 480-961-1903
Fax: 480-961-1842
www.usabmx.com

Jul 23 - Jul 25, 2021
USA BMX MIDAMERICA NATIONALS
Raytown, MO
USA BMX
Phone: 480-961-1903
Fax: 480-961-1842
www.usabmx.com

Jun 18 - Jun 20, 2021
USA BMX MIDWEST NATIONALS
Rockford, IL
USA BMX
Phone: 480-961-1903
Fax: 480-961-1842
www.usabmx.com

May 7 - May 9, 2021
USA BMX SILVER DOLLAR
NAITONALS
Las Vegas, NV
USA BMX
Phone: 480-961-1903
Fax: 480-961-1842
www.usabmx.com

Jul 2 - Jul 4, 2021
USA BMX STARS & STRIPES
NATIONALS
Pittsburgh, PA
USA BMX
Phone: 480-961-1903
Fax: 480-961-1842
www.usabmx.com

Aug 14 - Aug 21, 2021
USA BMX WORLD CHAMPIONSHIPS
Papendal-Arnhem, Netherlands
USA BMX
Phone: 480-961-1903
Fax: 480-961-1842
www.usabmx.com

Jun 26 - Jun 27, 2021
WHISTLER CANADA CUP
Whistler, Canada
CANADIAN CYCLING ASSOCIATION
Phone: 613-248-1353
Fax: 613-248-9311
general@cyclingcanada.ca
www.cyclingcanada.ca

Darts

Jun 10 - Jun 16, 2021
TEAM DART CHAMPIONSHIPS
Las Vegas, NV
Westgate Las Vegas Resort & Casino
NATIONAL DART ASSOCIATION
Phone: 800-808-9884
Fax: 708-226-1310
info@ndadarts.com
www.ndadarts.com

Diving

Jul TBA, 2022
AAU DIVING NATIONAL
CHAMPIONSHIP
San Antonio, TX
Northside ISD Swim Center
AMATEUR ATHLETIC UNION
Phone: 407-934-7200
Fax: 407-934-7242
www.aausports.org

May 13 - May 16, 2021
CANADA CUP GRAND PRIX
Toronto, Canada
DIVING CANADA
Phone: 613-736-5238
Fax: 613-736-0409
cada@diving.ca
www.diving.ca

Apr 18 - Apr 23, 2021
FINA DIVING WORLD CUP
Tokyo, Japan
USA DIVING
Phone: 317-237-5252
Fax: 317-237-5257
Dan.Laak@usadiving.org
www.teamusa.org/USA-Diving

TBA, 2021
FINA DIVING WORLD SERIES
MONTREAL
USA DIVING
Phone: 317-237-5252
Fax: 317-237-5257
Dan.Laak@usadiving.org
www.teamusa.org/USA-Diving

events/meetings/shows

TBA, 2021
FINA GRAND PRIX MADRID
Madrid, Spain
USA DIVING
Phone: 317-237-5252
Fax: 317-237-5257
Dan.Laak@usadiving.org
www.teamusa.org/USA-Diving

TBA, 2021
FINA GRAND PRIX ROSTOCK
Madrid, Spain
USA DIVING
Phone: 317-237-5252
Fax: 317-237-5257
Dan.Laak@usadiving.org
www.teamusa.org/USA-Diving

May 31 - Jun 9, 2022
MASTERS WORLD CHAMPIONSHIPS
Island of Kyushu, Japan
USA DIVING
Phone: 317-237-5252
Fax: 317-237-5257
Dan.Laak@usadiving.org
www.teamusa.org/USA-Diving

Jul 1 - Jul 4, 2021
SPEEDO JUNIOR ELITE NATIONAL
CHAMPIONSHIPS
Winnipeg, Canada
DIVING CANADA
Phone: 613-736-5238
Fax: 613-736-0409
cada@diving.ca
www.diving.ca

TBA, 2021
SPRING MASTERS NATIONAL
CHAMPIONSHIPS
USA DIVING
Phone: 317-237-5252
Fax: 317-237-5257
Dan.Laak@usadiving.org
www.teamusa.org/USA-Diving

TBA, 2021
SUMMER MASTERS NATIONAL
CHAMPIONSHIPS
Mission Viejo, CA
USA DIVING
Phone: 317-237-5252
Fax: 317-237-5257
Dan.Laak@usadiving.org
www.teamusa.org/USA-Diving

Jun 10 - Jun 13, 2021
SUMMER SENIOR NATIONAL
CHAMPIONSHIPS
Toronto, Canada
DIVING CANADA
Phone: 613-736-5238
Fax: 613-736-0409
cada@diving.ca
www.diving.ca

Jul 29 - Aug 3, 2021
US DIVING JUNIOR NATIONAL
CHAMPIONSHIPS
Indianapolis, IN
USA DIVING
Phone: 317-237-5252
Fax: 317-237-5257
Dan.Laak@usadiving.org
www.teamusa.org/USA-Diving

Dog Showing

Mar 26 - Mar 28, 2021
AKC NATIONAL AGILITY
CHAMPIONSHIPS
Tulsa, OK
Tulsa Expo Centre
AMERICAN KENNEL CLUB
Phone: 919-233-9767
Fax: 919-816-4246
info@akc.org
www.akc.org

TBA, 2022
AKC NATIONAL CHAMPIONSHIP
AMERICAN KENNEL CLUB
Phone: 919-233-9767
Fax: 919-816-4246
info@akc.org
www.akc.org

Jul 10 - Jul 11, 2021
AKC NATIONAL OBEDIENCE
CHAMPIONSHIP
Wilmington, OH
AMERICAN KENNEL CLUB
Phone: 919-233-9767
Fax: 919-816-4246
info@akc.org
www.akc.org

TBA, 2022
AKC OBEDIENCE CLASSIC
AMERICAN KENNEL CLUB
Phone: 919-233-9767
Fax: 919-816-4246
info@akc.org
www.akc.org

Feb 25, 2021
AKC POINTING BREED GUN DOG
CHAMPIONSHIP
Sonoita, AZ
Empire Ranch
AMERICAN KENNEL CLUB
Phone: 919-233-9767
Fax: 919-816-4246
info@akc.org
www.akc.org

Feb 25, 2021
AKC POINTING BREED WALKING
GUN DOG CHAMPIONSHIP
Sonoita, AZ
Empire Ranch
AMERICAN KENNEL CLUB
Phone: 919-233-9767
Fax: 919-816-4246
info@akc.org
www.akc.org

Jul 9, 2021
AKC RALLY NATIONAL
CHAMPIONSHIP
Wilmington, OH
AMERICAN KENNEL CLUB
Phone: 919-233-9767
Fax: 919-816-4246
info@akc.org
www.akc.org

Equestrian

Apr 22 - Apr 25, 2021
LAND ROVER KENTUCKY
THREE-DAY EVENT
Lexington, KY

Kentucky Horse Park
US EQUESTRIAN FEDERATION
Phone: 859-258-2472
Fax: 859-231-6662
www.usef.org

Aug 24 - Aug 29, 2021
US DRESSAGE FESTIVAL OF
CHAMPIONS
Wayne, IL
Lamplight Equestrian Center
US EQUESTRIAN FEDERATION
Phone: 859-258-2472
Fax: 859-231-6662
www.usef.org

Fencing

May TBA, 2022
CAN / AM VETERANS CUP
Markham, Toronto
Vango Toronto Fencing Centre
CANADIAN FENCING FEDERATION
Phone: 647-476-2401
Fax: 647-476-2402
cff@fencing.ca
www.fencing.ca

Apr 16, 2021
DIVISION I & PARAFENCING
NATIONAL CHAMPIONSHIPS
Fort Worth, TX
Forth Worth Convention Center
USA FENCING
Phone: 719-866-4511
Fax: 719-632-5737
information@usfencing.org
www.usfencing.org

Jul 3 - Jul 6, 2021
USA FENCING NATIONAL
CHAMPIONSHIPS
Philadelphia, PA
USA FENCING
Phone: 719-866-4511
Fax: 719-632-5737
information@usfencing.org
www.usfencing.org

Figure Skating

Mar 5 - Mar 7, 2021
EASTERN ADULT SECTIONAL
CHAMPIONSHIPS
Ardmore, PA
U.S. FIGURE SKATING
Phone: 719-635-5200
Fax: 719-635-9548
info@usfigureskating.org
www.usfigureskating.org

Mar 22 - Mar 28, 2021
FIGURE SKATING WORLD
CHAMPIONSHIPS
Stockholm, Sweden
U.S. FIGURE SKATING
Phone: 719-635-5200
Fax: 719-635-9548
info@usfigureskating.org
www.usfigureskating.org

Mar 12 - Mar 14, 2021
MIDWESTERN ADULT SECTIONAL
CHAMPIONSHIPS
Fort Wayne, IN
U.S. FIGURE SKATING
Phone: 719-635-5200
Fax: 719-635-9548

info@usfigureskating.org
www.usfigureskating.org

Mar 5 - Mar 7, 2021
PACIFIC COAST ADULT SECTIONAL
CHAMPIONSHIPS
Las Vegas, NV
U.S. FIGURE SKATING
Phone: 719-635-5200
Fax: 719-635-9548
info@usfigureskating.org
www.usfigureskating.org

Apr 14 - Apr 17, 2021
US ADULT FIGURE SKATING
CHAMPIONSHIPS
Fairport, NY
Rochester Ice Center
U.S. FIGURE SKATING
Phone: 719-635-5200
Fax: 719-635-9548
info@usfigureskating.org
www.usfigureskating.org

Jan 11 - Jan 21, 2021
US FIGURE SKATING
CHAMPIONSHIPS
Las Vegas, NV
Orleans Arena
U.S. FIGURE SKATING
Phone: 719-635-5200
Fax: 719-635-9548
info@usfigureskating.org
www.usfigureskating.org

Feb TBA, 2022
US SYNCHRONIZED SKATING
CHAMPIONSHIPS
U.S. FIGURE SKATING
Phone: 719-635-5200
Fax: 719-635-9548
info@usfigureskating.org
www.usfigureskating.org

Fishing

Jun 11 - Jun 13, 2021
BASSMASTER CLASSIC
Fort Worth, TX
Lake Ray Roberts
BASS ANGLERS SPORTSMAN
SOCIETY
Phone: 877-227-7872
bassmaster@emailcustomerservice.com
www.bassmaster.com

Jul 8 - Jul 11, 2021
BASSMASTER ELITE SERIES - LAKE
CHAMPLAIN
Plattsburgh, NY
Lake Champlain
BASS ANGLERS SPORTSMAN
SOCIETY
Phone: 877-227-7872
bassmaster@emailcustomerservice.com
www.bassmaster.com

Apr 22 - Apr 25, 2021
BASSMASTER ELITE SERIES - LAKE
FORK
Quitman, TX
Lake Fork
BASS ANGLERS SPORTSMAN
SOCIETY
Phone: 877-227-7872
bassmaster@emailcustomerservice.com
www.bassmaster.com

May 6 - May 9, 2021
BASSMASTER ELITE SERIES -
NEELY HENRY LAKE
Gadsden, AL
Neelt Henry Lake
BASS ANGLERS SPORTSMAN
SOCIETY
Phone: 877-227-7872
bassmaster@emailcustomerservice.com
www.bassmaster.com

Mar 18 - Mar 21, 2021
BASSMASTER ELITE SERIES -
PICKWICK LAKE
Florence, AL
Pickwick Lake
BASS ANGLERS SPORTSMAN
SOCIETY
Phone: 877-227-7872
bassmaster@emailcustomerservice.com
www.bassmaster.com

Apr 8 - Apr 11, 2021
BASSMASTER ELITE SERIES -
SABINE RIVER
Orange, TX
Sabine River
BASS ANGLERS SPORTSMAN
SOCIETY
Phone: 877-227-7872
bassmaster@emailcustomerservice.com
www.bassmaster.com

Feb 11 - Feb 14, 2021
BASSMASTER ELITE SERIES - ST.
JOHNS RIVER
Palatka, FL
St. Johns River
BASS ANGLERS SPORTSMAN
SOCIETY
Phone: 877-227-7872
bassmaster@emailcustomerservice.com
www.bassmaster.com

Jul 15 - Jul 18, 2021
BASSMASTER ELITE SERIES - ST.
LAWRENCE RIVER
Waddington, NY
St. Lawrence River
BASS ANGLERS SPORTSMAN
SOCIETY
Phone: 877-227-7872
bassmaster@emailcustomerservice.com
www.bassmaster.com

Feb 25 - Feb 28, 2021
BASSMASTER ELITE SERIES -
TENNESSEE RIVER
Knoxville, TN
Tennessee River
BASS ANGLERS SPORTSMAN
SOCIETY
Phone: 877-227-7872
bassmaster@emailcustomerservice.com
www.bassmaster.com

Apr 15 - Apr 17, 2021
BASSMASTER OPENS CENTRAL
OPEN - DOUGLAS LAKE
Dandridge, TN
Douglas Lake
BASS ANGLERS SPORTSMAN
SOCIETY
Phone: 877-227-7872
bassmaster@emailcustomerservice.com
www.bassmaster.com

Mar 4 - Mar 6, 2021
BASSMASTER OPENS CENTRAL
OPEN - HARRIS CHAIN OF LAKES
Leesburg, FL
Harris Chain of Lakes
BASS ANGLERS SPORTSMAN
SOCIETY
Phone: 877-227-7872
bassmaster@emailcustomerservice.com
www.bassmaster.com

Apr 1 - Apr 3, 2021
BASSMASTER OPENS CENTRAL
OPEN - LEWIS SMITH LAKE
Jasper, AL
Lewis Smith Lake
BASS ANGLERS SPORTSMAN
SOCIETY
Phone: 877-227-7872
bassmaster@emailcustomerservice.com
www.bassmaster.com

Apr 29 - May 1, 2021
BASSMASTER OPENS CENTRAL
OPEN - PICKWICK LAKE
Counce, TN
Pickwick Lake
BASS ANGLERS SPORTSMAN
SOCIETY
Phone: 877-227-7872
bassmaster@emailcustomerservice.com
www.bassmaster.com

Sept 22 - Sept 24, 2021
WALLEYE TOUR CHAMPIONSHIP
Otter Tail Lake, MD
NATIONAL WALLEYE TOUR
Phone: 612-424-0708
Fax: 866-727-2809
www.nationalwalleyetour.com

Apr 29 - Apr 30, 2021
WALLEYE
TOUR-CHAMBERLAIN-OACOMA
Chamberlain-Oacoma, SD
Lake Francis Case
NATIONAL WALLEYE TOUR
Phone: 612-424-0708
Fax: 866-727-2809
www.nationalwalleyetour.com

Jun 24 - Jun 25, 2021
WALLEYE TOUR-HURON
Huron, OH
Lake Erie
NATIONAL WALLEYE TOUR
Phone: 612-424-0708
Fax: 866-727-2809
www.nationalwalleyetour.com

May 27 - May 28, 2021
WALLEYE TOUR-STURGEON BAY
Sturgeon Bay, WI
NATIONAL WALLEYE TOUR
Phone: 612-424-0708
Fax: 866-727-2809
www.nationalwalleyetour.com

Football

Jan 1, 2022
ALLSTATE SUGAR BOWL
New Orleans, LA
Mercedes-Benz Superdome
ALLSTATE SUGAR BOWL
Phone: 504-828-2440
Fax: 504-828-2441
info@sugarbowl.org
www.allstatesugarbowl.org

Dec TBA, 2021
AUTOZONE LIBERTY BOWL
Memphis, TN
Liberty Bowl Memorial Stadium
AUTOZONE LIBERTY BOWL
Phone: 901-795-7700
Fax: 901-795-7826
hgraeter@libertybowl.org
www.libertybowl.org

Dec TBA, 2021
BELK BOWL
Charlotte, NC
Bank of America Stadium
BELK BOWL
Phone: 704-644-4047
Info@CharlotteSports.org
www.belkbowl.com

Nov 21, 2021
CFL GREY CUP
TBA, Canada
CANADIAN FOOTBALL LEAGUE
Phone: 416-322-9650
Fax: 416-322-9651
www.cfl.ca

Jan 1, 2021
CHICK-FIL-A PEACH BOWL
Atlanta, GA
Mercedes-Benz Stadium
CHICK-FIL-A PEACH BOWL
Phone: 404-586-8500
Fax: 404-586-8508
tickets@cfabowl.com
www.chick-fil-apeachbowl.com

Jan TBA, 2022
FAMOUS IDAHO POTATO BOWL
FAMOUS IDAHO POTATO BOWL
Phone: 208-424-1011
Fax: 208-424-1121
www.famousidahopotatobowl.com

Jan 2, 2021
FIESTA BOWL
Glendale, AZ
State Farm Stadium
FIESTA BOWL
Phone: 480-350-0900
Fax: 480-350-0915
prdept@fiestabowl.org
www.fiestabowl.org

Dec 31, 2021
GOODYEAR COTTON BOWL
CLASSIC
Arlington, TX
AT&T Stadium
GOODYEAR COTTON BOWL CLASSIC
Phone: 817-892-4800
Fax: 817-892-4810
cso@attcottonbowl.com
www.cottonbowl.com

Dec TBA, 2021
INDEPENDENCE BOWL
Shreveport, LA
Independence Stadium
INDEPENDENCE BOWL FOUNDATION
Phone: 318-221-0712
Fax: 318-221-7366
independencebowl.org

Dec TBA, 2021
LENDING TREE BOWL
Mobile, AL
Ladd-Peebles Stadium
LENDING TREE BOWL
Phone: 251-635-0011

contact@mabowl.com
lendingtreebowl.com

May 16, 2021
NCAA DIVISION I FOOTBALL FINALS
Frisco, TX
Toyota Stadium
NATIONAL COLLEGIATE ATHLETIC
ASSOCIATION
Phone: 317-917-6222
Fax: 317-917-6888
www.ncaa.org

TBA, 2021
NCAA DIVISION II FOOTBALL FINALS
McKinney, TX
McKinney ISD Stadium
NATIONAL COLLEGIATE ATHLETIC
ASSOCIATION
Phone: 317-917-6222
Fax: 317-917-6888
www.ncaa.org

TBA, 2021
NCAA DIVISION III FOOTBALL FINALS
NATIONAL COLLEGIATE ATHLETIC
ASSOCIATION
Phone: 317-917-6222
Fax: 317-917-6888
www.ncaa.org

Dec TBA, 2021
NEW ORLEANS BOWL
New Orleans, LA
Mercedes-Benz Superdome
NEW ORLEANS BOWL
Phone: 504-525-5678
Fax: 504-529-1622
www.neworleansbowl.org

Jan TBA, 2022
NFL PRO BOWL
TBA
NATIONAL FOOTBALL LEAGUE
Phone: 212-450-2000
www.nfl.com

Jan 1, 2022
OUTBACK BOWL
Tampa, FL
Raymond James Stadium
OUTBACK BOWL
Phone: 813-874-2695
Fax: 813-873-1959
info@outbackbowl.com
www.outbackbowl.com

Dec TBA, 2021
REDBOX BOWL
Santa Clara, CA
Levi's Stadium
SAN FRANCISCO BOWL GAME
ASSOCIATION
www.redboxbowl2021.com

Jan 1, 2022
ROSE BOWL GAME
Pasadena, CA
Rose Bowl Stadium
PASADENA TOURNAMENT OF ROSES
ASSOCIATION
Phone: 626-449-4100
www.tournamentofroses.com

Jan 29, 2022
SENIOR BOWL
Mobile, AL
Ladd-Peebles Stadium
SENIOR BOWL
Phone: 251-438-2276
Fax: 251-432-0409

srbowl@seniorbowl.com
www.seniorbowl.com

Dec TBA, 2021
SOFI HAWAII BOWL
Honolulu, HI
Aloha Stadium
SOFI HAWAII BOWL
www.thehawaiibowl.com

Feb TBA, 2022
SUPER BOWL LVI
Inglewood, CA
SoFi Stadium
NATIONAL FOOTBALL LEAGUE
Phone: 212-450-2000
www.nfl.com

Jan 2, 2021
TAXSLAYER GATOR BOWL
Jacksonville, FL
Tiaa Bank Field
TAXSLAYER GATOR BOWL
Phone: 904-798-1700
Fax: 904-632-2080
tickets@taxslayerbowl.com
www.taxslayergatorbowl.com

Dec 31, 2021
TONY THE TIGER SUN BOWL
El Paso, TX
Sun Bowl Stadium
SUN BOWL ASSOCIATION
Phone: 915-533-4416
Fax: 915-533-0661
bolivas@sunbowl.org
www.sunbowl.org

Dec TBA, 2021
TRANSPERFECT MUSIC CITY BOWL
Nashville, TN
Nissan Stadium
TRANSPERFECT MORTGAGE MUSIC
CITY BOWL
Phone: 615-743-3130
www.musiccitybowl.com

Dec TBA, 2021
VALERO ALAMO BOWL
San Antonio, TX
The Alamodome
SAN ANTONIO BOWL ASSOCIATION
Phone: 210-226-2695
Fax: 210-704-6399
info@alamobowl.com
www.alamobowl.com

Frisbee

TBA, 2022
USA ULTIMATE BEACH
CHAMPIONSHIPS
Virginia Beach, VA
USA ULTIMATE
Phone: 800-872-4384
Fax: 719-219-8322
info@usaultimate.org
www.usaultimate.org

TBA, 2022
USA ULTIMATE D-I COLLEGE
CHAMPIONSHIPS
USA ULTIMATE
Phone: 800-872-4384
Fax: 719-219-8322
info@usaultimate.org
www.usaultimate.org

TBA, 2022
USA ULTIMATE D-III COLLEGE
CHAMPIONSHIPS
USA ULTIMATE
Phone: 800-872-4384
Fax: 719-219-8322
info@usaultimate.org
www.usaultimate.org

TBA, 2022
USA ULTIMATE MASTERS
CHAMPIONSHIPS
USA ULTIMATE
Phone: 800-872-4384
Fax: 719-219-8322
info@usaultimate.org
www.usaultimate.org

State & World Games

Jun 11 - Jun 13, 2021
ALABAMA STATE GAMES
Birmingham, AL
ASF FOUNDATION
Phone: 800-467-0422
Fax: 334-280-0988
support@asffoundation.org
www.asffoundation.org

Aug TBA, 2021
BLUEGRASS STATE GAMES
Lexington, KY
BLUEGRASS STATE GAMES
Phone: 859-286-5158
Fax: 859-286-5158
info@bgsg.org
www.bgsg.org

Nov 5 - Nov 7, 2021
CYCLE NORTH CAROLINA COASTAL
RIDE
Oriental, NC
NORTH CAROLINA AMATEUR SPORTS
Phone: 919-361-1133
Fax: 919-361-2559
ncas@ncsports.org
www.ncsports.org

Aug 6 - Aug 8, 2021
CYCLE NORTH CAROLINA
MOUNTAIN RIDE
Forest City, NC
NORTH CAROLINA AMATEUR SPORTS
Phone: 919-361-1133
Fax: 919-361-2559
ncas@ncsports.org
www.ncsports.org

Oct 2 - Oct 9, 2021
CYCLE NORTH CAROLINA
MOUNTAINS TO COAST
Sparta, NC
NORTH CAROLINA AMATEUR SPORTS
Phone: 919-361-1133
Fax: 919-361-2559
ncas@ncsports.org
www.ncsports.org

Jan TBA, 2022
EAST WEST SHRINE BOWL
St. Petersburg, FL
Tropicana Field
EAST WEST SHRINE GAME
Phone: 813-281-8686
Fax: 813-281-8687
eastwestshrinegame@shrinenet.org
www.shrinegame.com

Jun TBA, 2022
LARRY H MILLER UTAH SUMMER
GAMES
Cedar City, UT
Southern Utah University
UTAH SUMMER GAMES
Phone: 435-865-8421
Fax: 435-865-8548

Jun TBA, 2021
POWERADE STATE GAMES OF
NORTH CAROLINA
NORTH CAROLINA AMATEUR SPORTS
Phone: 919-361-1133
Fax: 919-361-2559
ncas@ncsports.org
www.ncsports.org

Jun 5 - Jun 10, 2022
SPECIAL OLYMPICS USA NATIONAL
GAMES
Orlando, FL
SPECIAL OLYMPICS
Phone: 202-628-3630
Fax: 202-824-0200
cweir@specialolympics.org
www.specialolympics.org

Jun 16 - Jun 25, 2023
SPECIAL OLYMPICS WORLD
SUMMER GAMES
Berlin, Germany
SPECIAL OLYMPICS
Phone: 202-628-3630
Fax: 202-824-0200
cweir@specialolympics.org
www.specialolympics.org

Feb 2 - Feb 13, 2021
SPECIAL OLYMPICS WORLD WINTER
GAMES
TBA
SPECIAL OLYMPICS
Phone: 202-628-3630
Fax: 202-824-0200
cweir@specialolympics.org
www.specialolympics.org

Mar 27 - Apr 17, 2021
STATE GAMES OF MISSISSIPPI
Meridian, MS
STATE GAMES OF MISSISSIPPI
Phone: 601-482-0205
info@stategamesofms.org
www.stategamesofms.org

Mar 20 - Jun 30, 2021
SUNSHINE STATE GAMES
Various
SUNSHINE STATE GAMES
Phone: 850-577-7200
info@playinflorida.com
playinflorida.com

Golf

Jul 22 - Jul 25, 2021
3M OPEN
Blaine, MN
TPC Twin Cities
PGA TOUR
Phone: 904-285-3700
www.pgatour.com

Jul 26 - Jul 29, 2021
CANADIAN JUNIOR GIRLS
CHAMPIONSHIP
Sainte-Marie, Canada
Club de golf de Sainte-Marie

ROYAL CANADIAN GOLF
ASSOCIATION
Phone: 905-849-9700
Fax: 905-845-7040
info@golfcanada.ca
www.golfcanada.ca

Jun 1 - Jun 4, 2021
CANADIAN UNIVERSITY & COLLEGE
CHAMPIONSHIP
TBA
TBA
ROYAL CANADIAN GOLF
ASSOCIATION
Phone: 905-849-9700
Fax: 905-845-7040
info@golfcanada.ca
www.golfcanada.ca

Jul 20 - Jul 23, 2021
CANADIAN WOMEN'S AMATEUR
CHAMPIONSHIP
Ile Bizard, Canada
Royal Montreal Golf Club
ROYAL CANADIAN GOLF
ASSOCIATION
Phone: 905-849-9700
Fax: 905-845-7040
info@golfcanada.ca
www.golfcanada.ca

Aug 31 - Sept 2, 2021
CANADIAN WOMEN'S MID-AMATEUR
& SENIOR CHAMPIONSH IP
Bromont, Canada
Golf Chateau-Bromont
ROYAL CANADIAN GOLF
ASSOCIATION
Phone: 905-849-9700
Fax: 905-845-7040
info@golfcanada.ca
www.golfcanada.ca

Dec TBA, 2022
HERO WORLD CHALLENGE
PGA TOUR
Phone: 904-285-3700
www.pgatour.com

May 17 - May 23, 2021
KANSAS CITY GOLF CLASSIC
Kansas City, KS
Blue Hills Country Club
PGA KORN FERRY TOUR
Phone: 904-285-3700
Fax: 904-285-7913
www.pgatour.com

Jul 13 - Jul 15, 2021
NEXTGEN ATLANTIC CHAMPIONSHIP
Cardigan, Canada
Dundarave Golf Course
ROYAL CANADIAN GOLF
ASSOCIATION
Phone: 905-849-9700
Fax: 905-845-7040
info@golfcanada.ca
www.golfcanada.ca

May 28 - May 30, 2021
NEXTGEN ONTARIO CHAMPIONSHIP
Port Elgin, Canada
Saugeen Gold Club
ROYAL CANADIAN GOLF
ASSOCIATION
Phone: 905-849-9700
Fax: 905-845-7040
info@golfcanada.ca
www.golfcanada.ca

May 6 - May 8, 2021
NEXTGEN PACIFIC CHAMPIONSHIP
TBA, BC, Canada
ROYAL CANADIAN GOLF
ASSOCIATION
Phone: 905-849-9700
Fax: 905-845-7040
info@golfcanada.ca
www.golfcanada.ca

Jun 11 - Jun 13, 2021
NEXTGEN PRAIRIE CHAMPIONSHIP
Ste. Anne, Canada
Quarry Oaks Golf Course
ROYAL CANADIAN GOLF
ASSOCIATION
Phone: 905-849-9700
Fax: 905-845-7040
info@golfcanada.ca
www.golfcanada.ca

Jun 28 - Jun 30, 2021
NEXTGEN QUEBEC CHAMPIONSHIP
Hemmingford, Canada
Club de Golf de Hemmingford
ROYAL CANADIAN GOLF
ASSOCIATION
Phone: 905-849-9700
Fax: 905-845-7040
info@golfcanada.ca
www.golfcanada.ca

Jun 4 - Jun 6, 2021
NEXTGEN WESTERN
CHAMPIONSHIP
TBA, AB, Canada
ROYAL CANADIAN GOLF
ASSOCIATION
Phone: 905-849-9700
Fax: 905-845-7040
info@golfcanada.ca
www.golfcanada.ca

Sept 19 - Sept 25, 2022
PRESIDENT'S CUP
Charlotte, NC
Quail Hollow Club
PGA TOUR
Phone: 904-285-3700
www.pgatour.com

Jun TBA, 2022
RBC CANADIAN OPEN
TBA
ROYAL CANADIAN GOLF
ASSOCIATION
Phone: 905-849-9700
Fax: 905-845-7040
info@golfcanada.ca
www.golfcanada.ca

Nov 15 - Nov 21, 2021
RSM CLASSIC
Sea Island, GA
Sea Island Golf Club
PGA TOUR
Phone: 904-285-3700
www.pgatour.com

May 10 - May 16, 2021
VISIT KNOXVILLE OPEN
Knoxville, TN
Holston Hills Country Club
PGA KORN FERRY TOUR
Phone: 904-285-3700
Fax: 904-285-7913
www.pgatour.com

Feb 4 - Feb 7, 2021
WASTE MANAGEMENT PHOENIX
OPEN
Scottsdale, AZ
TPC Scottsdale
PGA TOUR
Phone: 904-285-3700
www.pgatour.com

May 3 - May 9, 2021
WELLS FARGO CHAMPIONSHIP
Charlotte, NC
Quail Hollow Club
PGA TOUR
Phone: 904-285-3700
www.pgatour.com

Aug 31 - Sept 6, 2021
2021 SOLHEIM CUP
Toledo, OH
Inverness Golf Club
LPGA TOUR
Phone: 386-274-6200
Fax: 386-274-1099
www.lpga.com

Jul 8 - Jul 11, 2021
ABERDEEN STANDARD
INVESTMENTS SCOTTISH OPEN
North Berwick, Scotland, UK
The Renaissance Club
PGA EUROPEAN TOUR
International Ph: 44-0-1344-840400
International Fax: 44-0-1344-840500
www.europeantour.com

Jan 21 - Jan 24, 2021
ABU DHABI HSBC CHAMPIONSHIP
United Arab Emirates
Abu Dhabi Golf Club
PGA EUROPEAN TOUR
International Ph: 44-0-1344-840400
International Fax: 44-0-1344-840500
www.europeantour.com

Aug 19 - Aug 22, 2021
AIG WOMEN'S BRITISH OPEN
Troon, Scotland
Royal Troon Golf Club
LPGA TOUR
Phone: 386-274-6200
Fax: 386-274-1099
www.lpga.com

Aug 19 - Aug 22, 2021
ALBERTSONS BOISE OPEN
Boise, ID
Hillcrest Country Club
PGA KORN FERRY TOUR
Phone: 904-285-3700
Fax: 904-285-7913
www.pgatour.com

Jun 5 - Jun 13, 2021
AMERICAN FAMILY INSURANCE
CHAMPIONSHIP
Madison, WI
University Ridge Golf Club
PGA CHAMPIONS TOUR
Phone: 904-285-3700
www.pgatour.com/champions

Apr 1 - Apr 4, 2021
ANA INSPIRATION
Rancho Mirage, CA
Mission Hills Country Club
LPGA TOUR
Phone: 386-274-6200
Fax: 386-274-1099
www.lpga.com

TBA, 2022
ARNOLD PALMER INVITATIONAL
PGA TOUR
Phone: 904-285-3700
www.pgatour.com

Sept 6 - Sept 12, 2021
ASCENSION CHARITY CLASSIC
St. Louis, MO
Norwood Hills Country Club
PGA CHAMPIONS TOUR
Phone: 904-285-3700
www.pgatour.com/champions

May 10 - May 16, 2021
AT&T BYRON NELSON
CHAMPIONSHIP
McKinney, TX
TPC Craig Ranch
PGA TOUR
Phone: 904-285-3700
www.pgatour.com

Feb 11 - Feb 14, 2021
AT&T PEBBLE BEACH NATIONAL
PRO-AM
Pebble Beach, CA
Pebble Beach Golf Links
PGA TOUR
Phone: 904-285-3700
www.pgatour.com

May 12 - May 15, 2021
BETFRED BRITISH MASTERS
Newcastle-upon-Tyne, England
Close House Golf Course
PGA EUROPEAN TOUR
International Ph: 44-0-1344-840400
International Fax: 44-0-1344-840500
www.europeantour.com

Aug 26 - Aug 29, 2021
BMW CHAMPIONSHIP
Owings Mills, MD
Caves Valley Golf Club
PGA TOUR
Phone: 904-285-3700
www.pgatour.com

Jun 10 - Jun 13, 2021
BMW CHARITY PRO-AM
Greer, SC
Thornblade Club
PGA KORN FERRY TOUR
Phone: 904-285-3700
Fax: 904-285-7913
www.pgatour.com

Jun 23 - Jun 27, 2021
BMW INTERNATIONAL OPEN
Munich, Germany
Golf Club München Eichenried
PGA EUROPEAN TOUR
International Ph: 44-0-1344-840400
International Fax: 44-0-1344-840500
www.europeantour.com

Oct 21 - Oct 24, 2021
BMW LADIES CHAMPIONSHIP
Busan, South Korea
LPGA International Busan
LPGA TOUR
Phone: 386-274-6200
Fax: 386-274-1099
www.lpga.com

Sept 9 - Sept 12, 2021
BMW PGA CHAMPIONSHIP
Surrey, England
Wentworth Club

PGA EUROPEAN TOUR
International Ph: 44-0-1344-840400
International Fax: 44-0-1344-840500
www.europeantour.com

Nov 5 - Nov 7, 2021
BOCA RATON CHAMPIONSHIP
Boca Raton, FL
The Old Course at Broken Sound
PGA CHAMPIONS TOUR
Phone: 904-285-3700
www.pgatour.com/champions

Aug 16 - Aug 22, 2021
BOEING CLASSIC
Snoqualmie, WA
The Club at Snoqualmie Ridge
PGA CHAMPIONS TOUR
Phone: 904-285-3700
www.pgatour.com/champions

Jun 23 - Jun 27, 2021
BRIDGESTONE SENIOR PLAYERS
CHAMPIONSHIP
Akron, OH
Firestone Country Club
PGA CHAMPIONS TOUR
Phone: 904-285-3700
www.pgatour.com/champions

Oct 14 - Oct 17, 2021
BUICK LPGA SHANGHAI
Shanghai, China
Qizhong Garden Golf Club
LPGA TOUR
Phone: 386-274-6200
Fax: 386-274-1099
www.lpga.com

Sept 16 - Sept 19, 2021
CAMBIA PORTLAND CLASSIC
Portland, OR
Columbia Edgewater Country Club
LPGA TOUR
Phone: 386-274-6200
Fax: 386-274-1099
www.lpga.com

Aug 9 - Aug 12, 2021
CANADIAN JUNIOR BOYS
CHAMPIONSHIP
Sainte-Julie, Canada
Vall,e du Richelieu
ROYAL CANADIAN GOLF
ASSOCIATION
Phone: 905-849-9700
Fax: 905-845-7040
info@golfcanada.ca
www.golfcanada.ca

Aug 2 - Aug 5, 2021
CANADIAN MEN'S AMATEUR
CHAMPIONSHIP
Laval, Canada
Club de Golf de Laval-Sur-Le-Lac
ROYAL CANADIAN GOLF
ASSOCIATION
Phone: 905-849-9700
Fax: 905-845-7040
info@golfcanada.ca
www.golfcanada.ca

Aug 24 - Aug 27, 2021
CANADIAN MEN'S MID-AMATEUR
CHAMPIONSHIP
Fort McMurray, Canada
Fort McMurray Golf Club
ROYAL CANADIAN GOLF
ASSOCIATION
Phone: 905-849-9700
Fax: 905-845-7040

info@golfcanada.ca
www.golfcanada.ca

Sept 7 - Sept 10, 2021
CANADIAN MEN'S SENIOR
CHAMPIONSHIP
New Minas, Canada
Ken-Wo Country Club
ROYAL CANADIAN GOLF
ASSOCIATION
Phone: 905-849-9700
Fax: 905-845-7040
info@golfcanada.ca
www.golfcanada.ca

May 27 - May 30, 2021
CHARLES SCHWAB CHALLENGE
Fort Worth, TX
Colonial Country Club
PGA TOUR
Phone: 904-285-3700
www.pgatour.com

Nov 11 - Nov 14, 2021
CHARLES SCHWAB CUP
CHAMPIONSHIP
Phoenix, AZ
Phoenix Country Club
PGA CHAMPIONS TOUR
Phone: 904-285-3700
www.pgatour.com/champions

Mar 18 - Mar 21, 2021
CHITIMACHA LOUISIANA OPEN
Broussard, Louisiana
Le Triomphe Country Club
PGA KORN FERRY TOUR
Phone: 904-285-3700
Fax: 904-285-7913
www.pgatour.com

Apr 16 - Apr 18, 2021
CHUBB CLASSIC
Naples, FL
Tiburon Golf Club
PGA CHAMPIONS TOUR
Phone: 904-285-3700
www.pgatour.com/champions

Nov 18 - Nov 21, 2021
CME GROUP TOUR CHAMPIONSHIP
Naples, FL
Tiburon Golf Club
LPGA TOUR
Phone: 386-274-6200
Fax: 386-274-1099
www.lpga.com

Feb 26 - Feb 28, 2021
COLOGUARD CLASSIC
Tucson, AZ
Omni Tucson National
PGA CHAMPIONS TOUR
Phone: 904-285-3700
www.pgatour.com/champions

Mar 10 - Mar 14, 2021
COMMERCIAL BANK QATAR
MASTERS
Doha, Quatar
Education City Golf Club
PGA EUROPEAN TOUR
International Ph: 44-0-1344-840400
International Fax: 44-0-1344-840500
www.europeantour.com

TBA, 2022
COUNTRY CLUB DE BOGOTA
CHAMPIONSHIP
Bogota, Colombia
Country Club de Bogota-Lagos

PGA KORN FERRY TOUR
Phone: 904-285-3700
Fax: 904-285-7913
www.pgatour.com

Aug 23 - Aug 29, 2021
CP CANADIAN WOMEN'S OPEN
Vancouver, Canada
Shaughnessy Golf & Country Club
LPGA TOUR
Phone: 386-274-6200
Fax: 386-274-1099
www.lpga.com

Aug 26 - Aug 28, 2021
CURTIS CUP
Wales, United Kingdom
U.S. GOLF ASSOCIATION
Phone: 908-234-2300
Fax: 908-234-9687
www.usga.org

Jun 28 - Jul 4, 2021
DICK'S SPORTING GOODS OPEN
Endicott, NY
En-Joie Golf Club
PGA CHAMPIONS TOUR
Phone: 904-285-3700
www.pgatour.com/champions

Oct 22 - Oct 24, 2021
DOMINION ENERGY CHARITY
CLASSIC
Richmond, VA
The Country Club of Virginia
PGA CHAMPIONS TOUR
Phone: 904-285-3700
www.pgatour.com/champions

Jul 14 - Jul 17, 2021
DOW GREAT LAKES BAY
INVITATIONAL
Midland, MI
Midland Country Club
LPGA TOUR
Phone: 386-274-6200
Fax: 386-274-1099
www.lpga.com

Nov 18 - Nov 21, 2021
DP WORLD TOUR CHAMPIONSHIP
DUBAI
Dubai, United Arab Emirates
Jumeirah Golf Estates
PGA EUROPEAN TOUR
International Ph: 44-0-1344-840400
International Fax: 44-0-1344-840500
www.europeantour.com

Jul 1 - Jul 4, 2021
DUBAI DUTY FREE IRISH OPEN
Thomastown, Co Kilkenny, Ireland
Mount Juliet Estate
PGA EUROPEAN TOUR
International Ph: 44-0-1344-840400
International Fax: 44-0-1344-840500
www.europeantour.com

May 27 - May 30, 2021
EVAN SCHOLARS INVITATIONAL
Glenview, IL
The Glen Club
PGA KORN FERRY TOUR
Phone: 904-285-3700
Fax: 904-285-7913
www.pgatour.com

events/meetings/shows

TBA, 2022
FARMERS INSURANCE OPEN
PGA TOUR
Phone: 904-285-3700
www.pgatour.com

Jun 17 - Jun 20, 2021
FARMFOODS EUROPEAN LEGENDS
LINKS CHAMPIONSHIP
Padstow, England
Trevose Golf & Country Club
PGA EUROPEAN STAYSURE TOUR
International Ph: 44-0-1344-840400
International Fax: 44-0-1344-840500
www.europeantour.com/staysure-tour

Aug 2 - Aug 8, 2021
FEDEX ST. JUDE INVITATIONAL
Memphis, TN
TPC Southwind
PGA TOUR
Phone: 904-285-3700
www.pgatour.com

Oct 4 - Oct 10, 2021
FOUNDERS CUP
West Caldwell, NJ
Mountain Ridge Country Club
LPGA TOUR
Phone: 386-274-6200
Fax: 386-274-1099
www.lpga.com

Feb 18 - Feb 21, 2021
GENESIS INVITATIONAL
Pacific Palisades, CA
Riviera Country Club
PGA TOUR
Phone: 904-285-3700
www.pgatour.com

Oct 28 - Oct 31, 2021
HERO INDIAN OPEN
TBC
TBC
PGA EUROPEAN TOUR
International Ph: 44-0-1344-840400
International Fax: 44-0-1344-840500
www.europeantour.com

TBA, 2022
HOAG CLASSIC
PGA CHAMPIONS TOUR
Phone: 904-285-3700
www.pgatour.com/champions

May 6 - May 9, 2021
HONDA LPGA THAILAND
Chonburi, Thailand
Siam Country Club
LPGA TOUR
Phone: 386-274-6200
Fax: 386-274-1099
www.lpga.com

Dec TBA, 2022
HONMA HONG KONG OPEN
Fanling, Hong Kong
Hong Kong Golf Club
PGA EUROPEAN TOUR
International Ph: 44-0-1344-840400
International Fax: 44-0-1344-840500
www.europeantour.com

Apr 29 - May 2, 2021
HSBC WOMEN'S WORLD
CHAMPIONSHIP
Singapore
Sentosa Golf Club

LPGA TOUR
Phone: 386-274-6200
Fax: 386-274-1099
www.lpga.com

Apr 21 - Apr 24, 2021
HUGEL-AIR PREMIA LA OPEN
Los Angeles, CA
Wilshire Country Club
LPGA TOUR
Phone: 386-274-6200
Fax: 386-274-1099
www.lpga.com

Apr 26 - May 2, 2021
INSPERITY INVITATIONAL
The Woodlands, TX
The Woodlands Country Club
PGA CHAMPIONS TOUR
Phone: 904-285-3700
www.pgatour.com/champions

Feb 6 - Feb 9, 2021
ISPS HANDA VIC OPEN
Victoria, Australia
13th Beach Golf Links
LPGA TOUR
Phone: 386-274-6200
Fax: 386-274-1099
www.lpga.com

Feb 11 - Feb 16, 2021
ISPS HANDA WOMEN'S AUSTRALIAN
OPEN
Seaton, Australia
Royal Adelaide Golf Club
LPGA TOUR
Phone: 386-274-6200
Fax: 386-274-1099
www.lpga.com

Sept 2 - Sept 5, 2021
ITALIAN OPEN
TBA, Italy
PGA EUROPEAN TOUR
International Ph: 44-0-1344-840400
International Fax: 44-0-1344-840500
www.europeantour.com

Jul 5 - Jul 11, 2021
JOHN DEERE CLASSIC
Silvis, IL
TPC Deere Run
PGA TOUR
Phone: 904-285-3700
www.pgatour.com

Mar 18 - Mar 21, 2021
KENYA OPEN
Nairobi, Kenya
Karen Country Club
PGA EUROPEAN TOUR
International Ph: 44-0-1344-840400
International Fax: 44-0-1344-840500
www.europeantour.com

Mar 25 - Mar 28, 2021
KIA CLASSIC
Carlsbad, CA
Aviara Golf Club
LPGA TOUR
Phone: 386-274-6200
Fax: 386-274-1099
www.lpga.com

May 27 - May 30, 2021
KITCHENAID SENIOR PGA
CHAMPIONSHIP
Tulsa, OK
Southern Hills Country Club

PGA CHAMPIONS TOUR
Phone: 904-285-3700
www.pgatour.com/champions

Sept 16 - Sept 19, 2021
KLM OPEN
Cromvoirt, The Netherlands
Bernardus Golf
PGA EUROPEAN TOUR
International Ph: 44-0-1344-840400
International Fax: 44-0-1344-840500
www.europeantour.com

Sept 2 - Sept 5, 2021
KORN FERRY TOUR CHAMPIONSHIP
Newburgh, IN
Victoria National Golf Club
PGA KORN FERRY TOUR
Phone: 904-285-3700
Fax: 904-285-7913
www.pgatour.com

Jun 22 - Jun 27, 2021
KPMG WOMEN'S PGA
CHAMPIONSHIP
Newton Square, PA
Aronimink Golf Club
LPGA TOUR
Phone: 386-274-6200
Fax: 386-274-1099
www.lpga.com

Aug 12 - Aug 15, 2021
LADIES SCOTTISH OPEN
North Berwick, Scotland
Renaissance Club
LPGA TOUR
Phone: 386-274-6200
Fax: 386-274-1099
www.lpga.com

Jan TBA, 2022
LATIN AMERICA AMATEUR
U.S. GOLF ASSOCIATION
Phone: 908-234-2300
Fax: 908-234-9687
www.usga.org

Feb 18 - Feb 21, 2021
LECOM SUNCOAST CLASSIC
Lakewood Ranch, FL
Lakewood National Golf Club
PGA KORN FERRY TOUR
Phone: 904-285-3700
Fax: 904-285-7913
www.pgatour.com

Jul 15 - Jul 18, 2021
LINCOLN LAND CHAMPIONSHIP
Springfield, IL
Panther Creek Country Club
PGA KORN FERRY TOUR
Phone: 904-285-3700
Fax: 904-285-7913
www.pgatour.com

Apr 11 - Apr 17, 2021
LOTTE CHAMPIONSHIP
Kapolei, Oahu, Hawaii
Ko Olina Golf Club
LPGA TOUR
Phone: 386-274-6200
Fax: 386-274-1099
www.lpga.com

Jun 10 - Jun 13, 2021
LPGA MEDIHEAL CHAMPIONSHIP
Daly City, CA
Lake Merced Golf Club
LPGA TOUR
Phone: 386-274-6200

Fax: 386-274-1099
www.lpga.com

Jul 8 - Jul 11, 2021
MARATHON LPGA CLASSIC
Sylvania, OH
Highland Meadows Golf Club
LPGA TOUR
Phone: 386-274-6200
Fax: 386-274-1099
www.lpga.com

TBA, 2022
MASTERCARD JAPAN
CHAMPIONSHIP
Narita-shi, Chiba, Japan
Narita Golf Club - Accordia Golf
PGA CHAMPIONS TOUR
Phone: 904-285-3700
www.pgatour.com/champions

Apr 5 - Apr 11, 2021
MASTERS TOURNAMENT
Augusta, GA
Augusta National Golf Club
PGA TOUR
Phone: 904-285-3700
www.pgatour.com

Nov TBA, 2021
MAYAKOBA GOLF CLASSIC
Mexico
PGA TOUR
Phone: 904-285-3700
www.pgatour.com

Apr TBA, 2022
MAYBANK CHAMPIONSHIP
MALAYSIA
Kuala Lumpur, Malaysia
Saujana Golf & Country Club
PGA EUROPEAN TOUR
International Ph: 44-0-1344-840400
International Fax: 44-0-1344-840500
www.europeantour.com

Jun 17 - Jun 20, 2021
MEIJER LPGA CLASSIC FOR SIMPLY
GIVE
Grand Rapids, MI
Blythefield Country Club
LPGA TOUR
Phone: 386-274-6200
Fax: 386-274-1099
www.lpga.com

Jan 21 - Jan 23, 2021
MITSUBISHI ELECTRIC
CHAMPIONSHIP AT HUALALAI
Ka'upulehu-Kona, HI
Hualalai Golf Course
PGA CHAMPIONS TOUR
Phone: 904-285-3700
www.pgatour.com/champions

May 14 - May 16, 2021
MITSUBISHI ELECTRIC CLASSIC
Duluth, GA
TPC Sugarloaf
PGA CHAMPIONS TOUR
Phone: 904-285-3700
www.pgatour.com/champions

Jan TBA, 2022
MOROCCO CHAMPIONS
Marrakech, Marocco
Samanah Golf Club
PGA CHAMPIONS TOUR
Phone: 904-285-3700
www.pgatour.com/champions

Oct 7 - Oct 10, 2021
MUTUACTIVOS OPEN DE ESPANA
Madrid, Spain
Club de Campo Villa de Madrid
PGA EUROPEAN TOUR
International Ph: 44-0-1344-840400
International Fax: 44-0-1344-840500
www.europeantour.com

Aug 26 - Aug 29, 2021
NATIONWIDE CHILDREN'S HOSPITAL
CHAMPIONSHIP
Columbus, OH
The OSU Golf Club
PGA KORN FERRY TOUR
Phone: 904-285-3700
Fax: 904-285-7913
www.pgatour.com

May 28 - Jun 2, 2021
NCAA DIVISION I MEN'S GOLF
FINALS
Scottsdale, AZ
Grayhawk Gold Club
NATIONAL COLLEGIATE ATHLETIC
ASSOCIATION
Phone: 317-917-6222
Fax: 317-917-6888
www.ncaa.org

May 24 - May 26, 2021
NCAA DIVISION I WOMEN'S GOLF
FINALS
Scottsdale, AZ
Grayhawk Gold Club
NATIONAL COLLEGIATE ATHLETIC
ASSOCIATION
Phone: 317-917-6222
Fax: 317-917-6888
www.ncaa.org

May 17 - May 21, 2021
NCAA DIVISION II MEN'S GOLF
FINALS
Palm Beach Gardens, FL
PGA National Resort
NATIONAL COLLEGIATE ATHLETIC
ASSOCIATION
Phone: 317-917-6222
Fax: 317-917-6888
www.ncaa.org

May 11 - May 15, 2021
NCAA DIVISION II WOMEN'S GOLF
FINALS
Detroit, MI
TPC Michigan
NATIONAL COLLEGIATE ATHLETIC
ASSOCIATION
Phone: 317-917-6222
Fax: 317-917-6888
www.ncaa.org

May 11 - May 14, 2021
NCAA DIVISION III MEN'S GOLF
FINALS
Wheeling, WV
Oglebay Resort & Conference Center
NATIONAL COLLEGIATE ATHLETIC
ASSOCIATION
Phone: 317-917-6222
Fax: 317-917-6888
www.ncaa.org

May 11 - May 14, 2021
NCAA DIVISION III WOMEN'S GOLF
FINALS
Lansing, MI
Forest Akers

NATIONAL COLLEGIATE ATHLETIC
ASSOCIATION
Phone: 317-917-6222
Fax: 317-917-6888
www.ncaa.org

Mar 4 - Mar 7, 2021
OMAN OPEN
Muscat, Oman
Al Mouj Golf
PGA EUROPEAN TOUR
International Ph: 44-0-1344-840400
International Fax: 44-0-1344-840500
www.europeantour.com

Jan 28 - Jan 31, 2021
OMEGA DUBAI DESERT CLASSIC
Dubai, United Arab Emirates
Emirates Golf Club
PGA EUROPEAN TOUR
International Ph: 44-0-1344-840400
International Fax: 44-0-1344-840500
www.europeantour.com

Aug 26 - Aug 28, 2021
OMEGA EUROPEAN MASTERS
Crans Montana, Switzerland
Cras-sur-Sierre Golf Club
PGA EUROPEAN TOUR
International Ph: 44-0-1344-840400
International Fax: 44-0-1344-840500
www.europeantour.com

May 6 - May 9, 2021
OPEN DE FRANCE
Guyancourt, France
Le Golf National
PGA EUROPEAN TOUR
International Ph: 44-0-1344-840400
International Fax: 44-0-1344-840500
www.europeantour.com

Jan TBA, 2022
PANAMA CHAMPIONSHIP
Panama City, Panama
Panama Golf Club
PGA KORN FERRY TOUR
Phone: 904-285-3700
Fax: 904-285-7913
www.pgatour.com

May 17 - May 23, 2021
PGA CHAMPIONSHIP
San Francisco, CA
TPC Harding Park
PGA TOUR
Phone: 904-285-3700
www.pgatour.com

Aug 9 - Aug 15, 2021
PINNACLE BANK CHAMPIONSHIP
Omaha, NE
The Club at Indian Creek
PGA KORN FERRY TOUR
Phone: 904-285-3700
Fax: 904-285-7913
www.pgatour.com

Dec TBA, 2021
PNC FATHER SON CHALLENGE
Orlando, FL
Ritz-Carlton Golf Club
PGA CHAMPIONS TOUR
Phone: 904-285-3700
www.pgatour.com/champions

Jun 3 - Jun 6, 2021
PORSCHE EUROPEAN OPEN
Hamburg, Germany
Green Eagle Golf Courses

events/meetings/shows

1341

PGA EUROPEAN TOUR
International Ph: 44-0-1344-840400
International Fax: 44-0-1344-840500
www.europeantour.com

Apr 29 - May 2, 2021
PORTUGAL MASTERS
Vilamoura, Portugal
Dom Pedro Victoria Golf Course
PGA EUROPEAN TOUR
International Ph: 44-0-1344-840400
International Fax: 44-0-1344-840500
www.europeantour.com

Jul 22 - Jul 25, 2021
PRICE CUTTER CHARITY
CHAMPIONSHIP
Springfield, MO
Highland Springs Country Club
PGA KORN FERRY TOUR
Phone: 904-285-3700
Fax: 904-285-7913
www.pgatour.com

Jun 1 - Jun 6, 2021
PRINCIPAL CHARITY CLASSIC
Des Moines, IA
Wakonda Club
PGA CHAMPIONS TOUR
Phone: 904-285-3700
www.pgatour.com/champions

Feb 25 - Feb 28, 2021
PUERTO RICO OPEN
Rio Grande, Puerto Rico
Coco Beach Golf & Country Club
PGA TOUR
Phone: 904-285-3700
www.pgatour.com

Sept 20 - Sept 26, 2021
PURE INSURANCE CHAMPIONSHIP
Monterey Peninsula, CA
Pebble Beach Golf Links
PGA CHAMPIONS TOUR
Phone: 904-285-3700
www.pgatour.com/champions

May 20 - May 23, 2021
PURE SILK CHAMPIONSHIP
Williamsburg, VA
Kingsmill Resort
LPGA TOUR
Phone: 386-274-6200
Fax: 386-274-1099
www.lpga.com

TBA, 2022
RAPISCAN SYSTEMS CLASSIC
Biloxi, MS
Fallen Oak
PGA CHAMPIONS TOUR
Phone: 904-285-3700
www.pgatour.com/champions

Apr 12 - Apr 18, 2021
RBC HERITAGE
Hilton Head, SC
Harbour Town Golf Links
PGA TOUR
Phone: 904-285-3700
www.pgatour.com

May 5 - May 9, 2021
REGIONS TRADITION
Birmingham, AL
Greystone Golf & Country Club
PGA CHAMPIONS TOUR
Phone: 904-285-3700
www.pgatour.com/champions

May 7 - May 9, 2021
RIEGLER & PARTNER AUSTRIAN
LEGENDS
Frohnleiten, Austria
Golfclub Murhof
PGA EUROPEAN STAYSURE TOUR
International Ph: 44-0-1344-840400
International Fax: 44-0-1344-840500
www.europeantour.com/staysure-tour

Sept 24 - Sept 26, 2021
RYDER CUP
Haven, WI
Whistling Straits Golf Course
PGA EUROPEAN TOUR
International Ph: 44-0-1344-840400
International Fax: 44-0-1344-840500
www.europeantour.com

Sept 13 - Sept 19, 2021
SANFORD INTERNATIONAL
Sioux Falls, SD
Minnehaha Country Club
PGA CHAMPIONS TOUR
Phone: 904-285-3700
www.pgatour.com/champions

Oct 15 - Oct 17, 2021
SAS CHAMPIONSHIP
Cary, NC
Prestonwood Country Club
PGA CHAMPIONS TOUR
Phone: 904-285-3700
www.pgatour.com/champions

Feb 4 - Feb 7, 2021
SAUDI INTERNATIONAL
King Abdullah Economic City, Saudi
Arabia
Royal Greens Golf & Country Club
PGA EUROPEAN TOUR
International Ph: 44-0-1344-840400
International Fax: 44-0-1344-840500
www.europeantour.com

Mar 22 - Mar 28, 2021
SAVANNAH GOLF CHAMPIONSHIP
Savannah, GA
Deer Creek Golf Club
PGA KORN FERRY TOUR
Phone: 904-285-3700
Fax: 904-285-7913
www.pgatour.com

Jun 10 - Jun 13, 2021
SCANDINAVIAN INVITATION
Gothenburg, Sweden
Hills Golf & Sports Club
PGA EUROPEAN TOUR
International Ph: 44-0-1344-840400
International Fax: 44-0-1344-840500
www.europeantour.com

Nov 5 - Nov 7, 2021
SENIOR ITALIAN OPEN
TBA, Italy
PGA EUROPEAN STAYSURE TOUR
International Ph: 44-0-1344-840400
International Fax: 44-0-1344-840500
www.europeantour.com/staysure-tour

Jan 6 - Jan 10, 2021
SENTRY TOURNAMENT OF
CHAMPIONS
Kapalua, HI
Plantation Course at Kapalua
PGA TOUR
Phone: 904-285-3700
www.pgatour.com

Aug 11 - Aug 15, 2021
SHAW CHARITY CLASSIC
Calgary, AB
Canyon Meadows Golf & Country Club
PGA CHAMPIONS TOUR
Phone: 904-285-3700
www.pgatour.com/champions

Oct 1 - Oct 3, 2021
SHOPRITE LPGA CLASSIC
Galloway, NJ
Seaview
LPGA TOUR
Phone: 386-274-6200
Fax: 386-274-1099
www.lpga.com

Aug TBA, 2021
SHOT CLOCK CHALLENGE
TBA
PGA EUROPEAN TOUR
International Ph: 44-0-1344-840400
International Fax: 44-0-1344-840500
www.europeantour.com

Oct TBA, 2021
SHRINERS HOSPITAL FOR
CHILDREN OPEN
Las Vegas, NV
TPC Summerlin
PGA TOUR
Phone: 904-285-3700
www.pgatour.com

May 6 - May 9, 2021
SIMMONS BANK OPEN FOR THE
SNEDEKER FOUNDATION
Nashville, TN
Nashville Golf & Athletic Club
PGA KORN FERRY TOUR
Phone: 904-285-3700
Fax: 904-285-7913
www.pgatour.com

Jan 14 - Jan 17, 2021
SONY OPEN IN HAWAII
Honolulu, HI
Waialae Country Club
PGA TOUR
Phone: 904-285-3700
www.pgatour.com

Dec TBA, 2021
SOUTH AFRICAN OPEN
Sun City, South Africa
Gary Player Country Club
PGA EUROPEAN TOUR
International Ph: 44-0-1344-840400
International Fax: 44-0-1344-840500
www.europeantour.com

Jun 2 - Jun 3, 2021
SWING THOUGHT NATIONAL PRO
SERIES - BELMONT LAKE S GOLF
CLUB
Rocky Mount, NC
Belmont Lake Golf Club
SWING THOUGHT TOURNAMENTS
Phone: 800-992-8748
info@swingthought.com
www.swingthought.com

Apr 23 - Apr 24, 2021
SWING THOUGHT NATIONAL PRO
SERIES - BRUNSWICK CO UNTRY
CLUB
Brunswick, GA
Brunswick Country Club
SWING THOUGHT TOURNAMENTS
Phone: 800-992-8748

info@swingthought.com
www.swingthought.com

Jun 16 - Jun 17, 2021
SWING THOUGHT NATIONAL PRO
SERIES - RANCHO BERNA RDO INN
San Diego, CA
Rancho Bernardo Inn
SWING THOUGHT TOURNAMENTS
Phone: 800-992-8748
info@swingthought.com
www.swingthought.com

Apr 23 - Apr 24, 2021
SWING THOUGHT NATIONAL PRO
SERIES - SANCTUARY GO LF CLUB
Waverly, GA
Sanctuary Golf Club
SWING THOUGHT TOURNAMENTS
Phone: 800-992-8748
info@swingthought.com
www.swingthought.com

May 19 - May 20, 2021
SWING THOUGHT NATIONAL PRO
SERIES - THE CLUB AT LA COSTA
San Diego, CA
The Club At La Costa
SWING THOUGHT TOURNAMENTS
Phone: 800-992-8748
info@swingthought.com
www.swingthought.com

Jul 9 - Jul 11, 2021
SWISS SENIORS OPEN
Bad Ragaz, Switzerland
PGA EUROPEAN STAYSURE TOUR
International Ph: 44-0-1344-840400
International Fax: 44-0-1344-840500
www.europeantour.com/staysure-tour

Oct 28 - Oct 31, 2021
TAIWAN SWINGING SKIRTS LPGA
New Taipei City, Chinese Taipei
Miramar Golf Country Club
LPGA TOUR
Phone: 386-274-6200
Fax: 386-274-1099
www.lpga.com

Aug 27 - Aug 29, 2021
THE ALLY CHALLENGE
Grand Blanc, MI
Warwick Hills Golf & Country Club
PGA CHAMPIONS TOUR
Phone: 904-285-3700
www.pgatour.com/champions

Jul 22 - Jul 25, 2021
THE AMUNDI EVIAN CHAMPIONSHIP
Evian-les-Bains, France
Evian Resort Golf Club
LPGA TOUR
Phone: 386-274-6200
Fax: 386-274-1099
www.lpga.com

Mar 18 - Mar 21, 2021
THE HONDA CLASSIC
Palm Beach Gardens, FL
PGA National Champion Course
PGA TOUR
Phone: 904-285-3700
www.pgatour.com

May 31 - Jun 6, 2021
THE MEMORIAL TOURNAMENT
Dublin, OH
Muirfield Village Golf Club

PGA TOUR
Phone: 904-285-3700
www.pgatour.com

Aug 16 - Aug 22, 2021
THE NORTHERN TRUST
Jersey City, NJ
Liberty National Golf Club
PGA TOUR
Phone: 904-285-3700
www.pgatour.com

Jul 11 - Jul 18, 2021
THE OPEN CHAMPIONSHIP
Sandwich, Kent, England
Royal St. George's Golf Course
PGA TOUR
Phone: 904-285-3700
www.pgatour.com

Mar 11 - Mar 14, 2021
THE PLAYERS CHAMPIONSHIP
Ponte Vedra Beach, FL
TPC Sawgrass
PGA TOUR
Phone: 904-285-3700
www.pgatour.com

Jun 3 - Jun 6, 2021
THE REX HOSPITAL OPEN
Raleigh, NC
The Country Club at Wakefield
Plantation
PGA KORN FERRY TOUR
Phone: 904-285-3700
Fax: 904-285-7913
www.pgatour.com

Jul 22 - Jul 25, 2021
THE SENIOR OPEN CHAMPIONSHIP
Berkshire, England
Sunningdale Golf Club
PGA CHAMPIONS TOUR
Phone: 904-285-3700
www.pgatour.com/champions

Sept 2 - Sept 5, 2021
THE TOUR CHAMPIONSHIP
Atlanta, GA
East Lake Golf Club
PGA TOUR
Phone: 904-285-3700
www.pgatour.com

Nov 4 - Nov 7, 2021
TOTO JAPAN CLASSIC
Shiga, Japan
Seta Golf Course
LPGA TOUR
Phone: 386-274-6200
Fax: 386-274-1099
www.lpga.com

Jul 8 - Jul 11, 2021
TPC COLORADO CHAMPIONSHIP AT
HERON LAKES
Berthoud, CO
TPC Colorado
PGA KORN FERRY TOUR
Phone: 904-285-3700
Fax: 904-285-7913
www.pgatour.com

Jun 24 - Jun 27, 2021
TRAVELERS CHAMPIONSHIP
Cromwell, CT
TPC River Highlands
PGA TOUR
Phone: 904-285-3700
www.pgatour.com

Oct 21 - Oct 24, 2021
TROPHEE HASSAN II
Rabat, Morocco
Royal Golf Dar Es Salam
PGA EUROPEAN TOUR
International Ph: 44-0-1344-840400
International Fax: 44-0-1344-840500
www.europeantour.com

Nov TBA, 2022
TURKISH AIRLINES OPEN
TBA, Turkey
PGA EUROPEAN TOUR
International Ph: 44-0-1344-840400
International Fax: 44-0-1344-840500
www.europeantour.com

Aug 9 - Aug 15, 2021
US AMATEUR
Oakmont, PA
Oakmont Country Club
U.S. GOLF ASSOCIATION
Phone: 908-234-2300
Fax: 908-234-9687
www.usga.org

May 22 - May 26, 2021
US AMATEUR FOUR-BALL
DuPont, WA
The Home Course
U.S. GOLF ASSOCIATION
Phone: 908-234-2300
Fax: 908-234-9687
www.usga.org

Jul 12 - Jul 17, 2021
US GIRLS' JUNIOR
Chevy Chase, MD
columbia country club
U.S. GOLF ASSOCIATION
Phone: 908-234-2300
Fax: 908-234-9687
www.usga.org

Jul 19 - Jul 24, 2021
US JUNIOR AMATEUR
Village of Pinehurst, NC
The Country Club of North Carolina
U.S. GOLF ASSOCIATION
Phone: 908-234-2300
Fax: 908-234-9687
www.usga.org

Sept 25 - Sept 30, 2021
US MID-AMATEUR
Siasconset, MA
Sankaty Head Golf Club
U.S. GOLF ASSOCIATION
Phone: 908-234-2300
Fax: 908-234-9687
www.usga.org

Jun 17 - Jun 20, 2021
US OPEN
San Diego, CA
Torrey Pines Golf Course
U.S. GOLF ASSOCIATION
Phone: 908-234-2300
Fax: 908-234-9687
www.usga.org

Aug 28 - Sept 2, 2021
US SENIOR AMATEUR
Gosse Pointe Farms, MI
Country Club of Detroit
U.S. GOLF ASSOCIATION
Phone: 908-234-2300
Fax: 908-234-9687
www.usga.org

events/meetings/shows

Jul 8 - Jul 11, 2021
US SENIOR OPEN CHAMPIONSHIP
Omaha, NB
Omaha Country Club
PGA CHAMPIONS TOUR
Phone: 904-285-3700
www.pgatour.com/champions

Jul 8 - Jul 11, 2021
US SENIOR OPEN CHAMPIONSHIP
Omaha, NB
Omaha Country Club
PGA EUROPEAN STAYSURE TOUR
International Ph: 44-0-1344-840400
International Fax: 44-0-1344-840500
www.europeantour.com/staysure-tour

Sept 10 - Sept 15, 2021
US SENIOR WOMEN'S AMATEUR
Point Clear, AL
The Lakewood Club
U.S. GOLF ASSOCIATION
Phone: 908-234-2300
Fax: 908-234-9687
www.usga.org

Aug 2 - Aug 8, 2021
US WOMEN'S AMATEUR
Rye, NY
Westchester Country Club
U.S. GOLF ASSOCIATION
Phone: 908-234-2300
Fax: 908-234-9687
www.usga.org

Apr 24 - Apr 28, 2021
US WOMEN'S AMATEUR FOUR-BALL
Carrollton, TX
Maridoe Golf Club
U.S. GOLF ASSOCIATION
Phone: 908-234-2300
Fax: 908-234-9687
www.usga.org

Sept 25 - Sept 30, 2021
US WOMEN'S MID-AMATEUR
Bluffton, SC
Berkeley Hall Club
U.S. GOLF ASSOCIATION
Phone: 908-234-2300
Fax: 908-234-9687
www.usga.org

Jun 3 - Jun 6, 2021
US WOMEN'S OPEN
San Francisco, CA
The Olympic Club
U.S. GOLF ASSOCIATION
Phone: 908-234-2300
Fax: 908-234-9687
www.usga.org

Jun 3 - Jun 6, 2021
US WOMEN'S OPEN
Houston, TX
Champions Golf Course
LPGA TOUR
Phone: 386-274-6200
Fax: 386-274-1099
www.lpga.com

Aug 2 - Aug 8, 2021
UTAH CHAMPIONSHIP
Farmington, UT
Oakridge Country Club
PGA KORN FERRY TOUR
Phone: 904-285-3700
Fax: 904-285-7913
www.pgatour.com

Mar 29 - Apr 4, 2021
VALERO TEXAS OPEN
San Antonio, TX
TPC San Antonio
PGA TOUR
Phone: 904-285-3700
www.pgatour.com

Apr 26 - May 2, 2021
VALSPAR CHAMPIONSHIP
Palm Harbor, FL
Innisbrook Resort Copperhead
PGA TOUR
Phone: 904-285-3700
www.pgatour.com

Jul 1 - Jul 4, 2021
VOLUNTEERS OF AMERICA CLASSIC
The Colony, TX
Old American Golf Club
LPGA TOUR
Phone: 386-274-6200
Fax: 386-274-1099
www.lpga.com

Nov 4 - Nov 7, 2021
VOLVO CHINA OPEN
Shenzhen, China
Genzon Golf Course
PGA EUROPEAN TOUR
International Ph: 44-0-1344-840400
International Fax: 44-0-1344-840500
www.europeantour.com

Sept 20 - Sept 26, 2021
WALMART NW ARKANSAS
CHAMPIONSHIP
Rogers, AR
Pinnacle Country Club
LPGA TOUR
Phone: 386-274-6200
Fax: 386-274-1099
www.lpga.com

Oct 28 - Oct 31, 2021
WGC - HSBC CHAMPIONS
Shanghai, China
Sheshan International Golf Club
PGA EUROPEAN TOUR
International Ph: 44-0-1344-840400
International Fax: 44-0-1344-840500
www.europeantour.com

Feb 25 - Feb 28, 2021
WGC MEXICO CHAMPIONSHIP
Mexico City, Mexico
Club de Golf Chapultepec
PGA TOUR
Phone: 904-285-3700
www.pgatour.com

Mar 24 - Mar 28, 2021
WGC-DELL TECHNOLOGIES MATCH
PLAY
Austin, TX
Austin Country Club
PGA TOUR
Phone: 904-285-3700
www.pgatour.com

Aug 2 - Aug 8, 2021
WGC-FEDEX ST. JUDE INVITATIONAL
Memphis, TN
TPC Southwind
PGA TOUR
Phone: 904-285-3700
www.pgatour.com

Jun 14 - Jun 20, 2021
WICHITA OPEN
Wichita, KS
Crestview Country Club
PGA KORN FERRY TOUR
Phone: 904-285-3700
Fax: 904-285-7913
www.pgatour.com

Aug 25 - Aug 28, 2022
WOMEN'S WORLD AMATEUR TEAM
France
Le Golf National
INTERNATIONAL GOLF FEDERATION
International Ph: +41 21 623 12 12
International Fax: +41 +41 216 01 64
info@lgfmail.org
www.igfgolf.org

Aug 25 - Aug 28, 2022
WORLD AMATEUR TEAM
France
Le Golf National
INTERNATIONAL GOLF FEDERATION
International Ph: +41 21 623 12 12
International Fax: +41 +41 216 01 64
info@lgfmail.org
www.igfgolf.org

Aug 10 - Aug 15, 2021
WYNDHAM CHAMPIONSHIP
Greensboro, NC
Sedgefield Country Club
PGA TOUR
Phone: 904-285-3700
www.pgatour.com

Apr 19 - Apr 25, 2021
ZURICH CLASSIC OF NEW ORLEANS
Avondale, LA
TPC Louisiana
PGA TOUR
Phone: 904-285-3700
www.pgatour.com

Greyhound Racing

Apr 19 - Apr 23, 2021
NGA SPRING MEET
Abilene, KS
NATIONAL GREYHOUND
ASSOCIATION
Phone: 785-263-4660
Fax: 785-263-4689
nga@ngagreyhounds.com
www.ngagreyhounds.com

Gymnastics

Mar TBA, 2022
AMERICAN CUP
TBA
INTERNATIONAL GYMNASTICS
FEDERATION
International Ph: +41-21-321-55-10
info@fig-gymnastics.org
www.gymnastics.sport

May TBA, 2022
CANADIAN GYMNASTICS
CHAMPIONSHIPS
TBA, Canada
GYMNASTICS CANADA GYMNASTIQUE
Phone: 613-748-5637
Fax: 613-748-5691
info@gymcan.org
www.gymcan.org

May 14 - May 15, 2021
FRIVOLTEN CUP
Herrljunga, Sweden
GK FRIVOLTEN
frivolten.com

Feb 11 - Feb 17, 2021
MAG CANADIAN GYMNASTIC
CHAMPIONSHIPS
GYMNASTICS CANADA GYMNASTIQUE
Phone: 613-748-5637
Fax: 613-748-5691
info@gymcan.org
www.gymcan.org

Sept 9 - Sept 19, 2021
MEN'S JUNIOR PAN AM GAMES
Cali, Colombia
USA GYMNASTICS
Phone: 317-237-5050
Fax: 317-237-5069
membership@usagym.org
usagym.org

Feb 26, 2021
NASTIA LIUKIN CUP
Milwaukee, WN
Fiserv Forum
USA GYMNASTICS
Phone: 317-237-5050
Fax: 317-237-5069
membership@usagym.org
usagym.org

TBA, 2021
NCAA NATIONAL COLLEGIATE
MEN'S GYMNASTICS FINALS
NATIONAL COLLEGIATE ATHLETIC
ASSOCIATION
Phone: 317-917-6222
Fax: 317-917-6888
www.ncaa.org

Apr 16 - Apr 17, 2021
NCAA NATIONAL COLLEGIATE
WOMEN'S GYMNASTICS FINA LS
Fort Worth, TX
Dickies Arena
NATIONAL COLLEGIATE ATHLETIC
ASSOCIATION
Phone: 317-917-6222
Fax: 317-917-6888
www.ncaa.org

Mar 17 - Mar 24, 2021
RG CANADIAN GYMNASTIC
CHAMPIONSHIPS
GYMNASTICS CANADA GYMNASTIQUE
Phone: 613-748-5637
Fax: 613-748-5691
info@gymcan.org
www.gymcan.org

Apr 14 - Apr 18, 2021
TG CANADIAN GYMNASTIC
CHAMPIONSHIPS
GYMNASTICS CANADA GYMNASTIQUE
Phone: 613-748-5637
Fax: 613-748-5691
info@gymcan.org
www.gymcan.org

Jun 22 - Jun 27, 2021
USA GYMNASTICS CHAMPIONSHIPS
St. Louis, MO
America's Center Convention Complex
& The Dome
USA GYMNASTICS
Phone: 317-237-5050
Fax: 317-237-5069

membership@usagym.org
usagym.org

May 7 - May 9, 2021
USA GYMNASTICS LEVEL 9
EASTERN CHAMPIONSHIPS
College Park, GA
Georgia International Convention Center
USA GYMNASTICS
Phone: 317-237-5050
Fax: 317-237-5069
membership@usagym.org
usagym.org

May 7 - May 9, 2021
USA GYMNASTICS LEVEL 9
WESTERN CHAMPIONSHIPS
Coralville, IA
Xtream Arena
USA GYMNASTICS
Phone: 317-237-5050
Fax: 317-237-5069
membership@usagym.org
usagym.org

Mar 26 - Mar 27, 2021
USA GYMNASTICS MEN'S
COLLEGIATE CHAMPIONSHIPS
Springfield, MA
USA GYMNASTICS
Phone: 317-237-5050
Fax: 317-237-5069
membership@usagym.org
usagym.org

Apr 10 - Apr 11, 2021
USA GYMNASTICS WOMEN'S
COLLEGIATE CHAMPIONSHIPS
Cape Girardeau, MO
USA GYMNASTICS
Phone: 317-237-5050
Fax: 317-237-5069
membership@usagym.org
usagym.org

Mar 25 - Mar 31, 2021
WAG CANADIAN GYMNASTIC
CHAMPIONSHIPS
GYMNASTICS CANADA GYMNASTIQUE
Phone: 613-748-5637
Fax: 613-748-5691
info@gymcan.org
www.gymcan.org

Handball

May TBA, 2022
CANADIAN NATIONAL HANDBALL
CHAMPIONSHIPS
CANADIAN HANDBALL
www.canadianhandball.com

Mar TBA, 2021
USHA MASTERS SINGLES
INVITATIONAL
UNITED STATES HANDBALL
ASSOCIATION
Phone: 520-795-0434
Fax: 520-795-0465
handball@ushandball.org
www.ushandball.org

Feb TBA, 2021
USHA NATIONAL COLLEGIATE
CHAMPIONSHIPS
UNITED STATES HANDBALL
ASSOCIATION
Phone: 520-795-0434
Fax: 520-795-0465

handball@ushandball.org
www.ushandball.org

Jun TBA, 2021
USHA NATIONAL FOUR-WALL
CHAMPIONSHIPS
UNITED STATES HANDBALL
ASSOCIATION
Phone: 520-795-0434
Fax: 520-795-0465
handball@ushandball.org
www.ushandball.org

Sept TBA, 2021
USHA NATIONAL THREE-WALL
CHAMPIONSHIPS
UNITED STATES HANDBALL
ASSOCIATION
Phone: 520-795-0434
Fax: 520-795-0465
handball@ushandball.org
www.ushandball.org

Horse Racing

Apr 24 - May 1, 2021
KENTUCKY DERBY
Louisville, KY
Churchill Downs
CHURCHILL DOWNS
Phone: 502-636-4400
customerservice@kyderby.com
www.churchilldowns.com

May 14 - May 15, 2021
PREAKNESS STAKES
Baltimore, MD
Pimlico Race Course
PIMLICO RACE COURSE
Phone: 410-542-9400
info@marylandracing.com
www.marylandracing.com

Ice Hockey

Apr 15 - 18, 2021
ADULT MEN'S NATIONAL
CHAMPIONSHIPS
Tampa, FL
Adventhealth Center Ice
USA HOCKEY
Phone: 719-576-8724
Fax: 719-538-1160
usah@usahockey.org
www.usahockey.com

Apr 22 - Apr 25, 2021
ADULT WOMEN'S NATIONAL
CHAMPIONSHIPS
Tampa, FL
Adventhealth Center Ice
USA HOCKEY
Phone: 719-576-8724
Fax: 719-538-1160
usah@usahockey.org
www.usahockey.com

Feb 10 - Feb 13, 2021
LABATT BLUE USA POND HOCKEY
NATIONAL CHAMPIONSHI PS
Eagle River, WI
Dollar Lake
USA HOCKEY
Phone: 719-576-8724
Fax: 719-538-1160
usah@usahockey.org
www.usahockey.com

events/meetings/shows

Apr 8 - Apr 10, 2021
NCAA DIVISION I MEN'S ICE HOCKEY
FINALS
Pittsburg, PA
PPG Paints Arena
NATIONAL COLLEGIATE ATHLETIC
ASSOCIATION
Phone: 317-917-6222
Fax: 317-917-6888
www.ncaa.org

TBA, 2021
NCAA DIVISION III MEN'S ICE
HOCKEY FINALS
NATIONAL COLLEGIATE ATHLETIC
ASSOCIATION
Phone: 317-917-6222
Fax: 317-917-6888
www.ncaa.org

TBA, 2021
NCAA DIVISION III WOMEN'S ICE
HOCKEY CHAMPIONSHI PS
NATIONAL COLLEGIATE ATHLETIC
ASSOCIATION
Phone: 317-917-6222
Fax: 317-917-6888
www.ncaa.org

Ice Skating

Oct 8 - Oct 10, 2021
ISI ADULT CHAMPIONSHIPS
Las Vegas, NV
Las Vegas Ice Center
ICE SKATING INSTITUTE
Phone: 972-735-8800
Fax: 972-735-8815
events@skateisi.org
www.skateisi.org

Dec 3 - Dec 5, 2021
ISI HOLIDAY CHALLENGE
Simi Valley, CA
Iceoplex Simi Valley
ICE SKATING INSTITUTE
Phone: 972-735-8800
Fax: 972-735-8815
events@skateisi.org
www.skateisi.org

Apr TBA, 2023
ISI SYNCHRONIZED
CHAMPIONSHIPS
ICE SKATING INSTITUTE
Phone: 972-735-8800
Fax: 972-735-8815
events@skateisi.org
www.skateisi.org

Feb 18 - Feb 20, 2022
ISI WINTER CLASSIC
San Jose, CA
ICE SKATING INSTITUTE
Phone: 972-735-8800
Fax: 972-735-8815
events@skateisi.org
www.skateisi.org

Jul 26 - Jul 31, 2021
ISI WORLD RECREATIONAL TEAM
CHAMPIONSHIPS
Minneapolis, MN
NSC Super Rink
ICE SKATING INSTITUTE
Phone: 972-735-8800
Fax: 972-735-8815
events@skateisi.org
www.skateisi.org

Korfball

Oct 25 - Oct 230, 2021
EUROPA CUP
TBA
INTERNATIONAL KORFBALL
FEDERATION
International Ph: 011-31-343-499655
International Fax: 011-31-343-499650
office@ikf.org
www.ikf.org

TBA, 2021
U19 WORLD CUP
INTERNATIONAL KORFBALL
FEDERATION
International Ph: 011-31-343-499655
International Fax: 011-31-343-499650
office@ikf.org
www.ikf.org

Jul 30 - Jul 31, 2021
WORLD BEACH KORKBALL
CHAMPIONSHIP
TBA
INTERNATIONAL KORFBALL
FEDERATION
International Ph: 011-31-343-499655
International Fax: 011-31-343-499650
office@ikf.org
www.ikf.org

Jul 7 - Jul 17, 2022
WORLD GAMES KORFBALL
TBA
INTERNATIONAL KORFBALL
FEDERATION
International Ph: 011-31-343-499655
International Fax: 011-31-343-499650
office@ikf.org
www.ikf.org

Lacrosse

May 29 - May 31, 2021
NCAA DIVISION I MEN'S LACROSSE
FINALS
East Hartford, CT
Pratt and Whitney Stadium
NATIONAL COLLEGIATE ATHLETIC
ASSOCIATION
Phone: 317-917-6222
Fax: 317-917-6888
www.ncaa.org

May 28 - May 30, 2021
NCAA DIVISION I WOMEN'S
LACROSSE FINALS
Towson, MD
Johnny Unitas Stadium
NATIONAL COLLEGIATE ATHLETIC
ASSOCIATION
Phone: 317-917-6222
Fax: 317-917-6888
www.ncaa.org

May 30, 2021
NCAA DIVISION II MEN'S LACROSSE
FINALS
East Hartford, CT
Pratt and Whitney Stadium
NATIONAL COLLEGIATE ATHLETIC
ASSOCIATION
Phone: 317-917-6222
Fax: 317-917-6888
www.ncaa.org

May 21 - May 23, 2021
NCAA DIVISION II WOMEN'S
LACROSSE FESTIVAL
Salem, VA
Kerr Stadium
NATIONAL COLLEGIATE ATHLETIC
ASSOCIATION
Phone: 317-917-6222
Fax: 317-917-6888
www.ncaa.org

May 30, 2021
NCAA DIVISION III MEN'S LACROSSE
FINALS
East Hartford, CT
Pratt and Whitney Stadium
NATIONAL COLLEGIATE ATHLETIC
ASSOCIATION
Phone: 317-917-6222
Fax: 317-917-6888
www.ncaa.org

May 22 - May 23, 2021
NCAA DIVISION III WOMEN'S
LACROSSE FINALS
Salem, VA
Kerr Stadium
NATIONAL COLLEGIATE ATHLETIC
ASSOCIATION
Phone: 317-917-6222
Fax: 317-917-6888
www.ncaa.org

Jul 13 - Jul 14, 2021
US LACROSSE NATIONALS
Frederica, DE
US LACROSSE
Phone: 410-235-6882
Fax: 410-366-6735
info@uslacrosse.org
www.uslacrosse.org

TBA, 2022
US LACROSSE WOMEN'S
COLLEGIATE NATIONAL CHAMPION
SHPS
US LACROSSE
Phone: 410-235-6882
Fax: 410-366-6735
info@uslacrosse.org
www.uslacrosse.org

TBA, 2022
US LACROSSE WOMEN'S DIVISION
NATIONAL TOURNAMENT
US LACROSSE
Phone: 410-235-6882
Fax: 410-366-6735
info@uslacrosse.org
www.uslacrosse.org

Martial Arts

TBA, 2021
AAU JUDO NATIONAL
CHAMPIONSHIP
AMATEUR ATHLETIC UNION
Phone: 407-934-7200
Fax: 407-934-7242
www.aausports.org

Jul 30 - Aug 1, 2021
AAU KARATE JUNIOR OLYMPIC
GAMES
Houston, TX
George R. Brown Convention Center
AMATEUR ATHLETIC UNION
Phone: 407-934-7200

Fax: 407-934-7242
www.aausports.org

Jun 29 - Jul 3, 2021
AAU KARATE NATIONAL
CHAMPIONSHIPS
Greensville, SC
Bon Secours Wellness Arena
AMATEUR ATHLETIC UNION
Phone: 407-934-7200
Fax: 407-934-7242
www.aausports.org

TBA, 2021
ARNOLD AMATEUR NPC
CHAMPIONSHIPS
Columbus, OH
ARNOLD SPORTS FESTIVAL
Phone: 614-431-2600
Fax: 614-431-3492
www.arnoldsportsfestival.com

Jul 1 - Jul 3, 2021
US OPEN - MARTIAL ARTS
CHAMPIONSHIPS
Orlando, FL
USA OPEN KARATE
usopen-karate.com

Motorcycle Racing

May 6, 2021
AMA PRO HILLCLIMB
Scottsburg, IN
High Fly MX Park 2.0
AMA PRO RACING
Phone: 386-492-1014
Fax: 386-274-2335
communications@amaproracing.com
www.amaproracing.com

Jun 6, 2021
AMA PRO HILLCLIMB
Spring Grove, PA
White Rose Motorcycle Club
AMA PRO RACING
Phone: 386-492-1014
Fax: 386-274-2335
communications@amaproracing.com
www.amaproracing.com

Jun 13, 2021
AMA PRO HILLCLIMB
Freemansburg, PA
Bushkill Valley Motorcycle Club
AMA PRO RACING
Phone: 386-492-1014
Fax: 386-274-2335
communications@amaproracing.com
www.amaproracing.com

Aug 28, 2021
AMA PRO HILLCLIMB
Scottsburg, IN
High Fly MX Park 2.0 II
AMA PRO RACING
Phone: 386-492-1014
Fax: 386-274-2335
communications@amaproracing.com
www.amaproracing.com

Sept 18, 2021
AMA PRO HILLCLIMB
Spring Grove, PA
White Rose Motorcycle Club II
AMA PRO RACING
Phone: 386-492-1014
Fax: 386-274-2335
communications@amaproracing.com
www.amaproracing.com

Sept 26, 2021
AMA PRO HILLCLIMB
Freemansburg, PA
Freemansburg Ii
AMA PRO RACING
Phone: 386-492-1014
Fax: 386-274-2335
communications@amaproracing.com
www.amaproracing.com

Oct 10, 2021
AMA PRO HILLCLIMB
Oregonia, OH
Dayton MC Club/Devil's Staircase
AMA PRO RACING
Phone: 386-492-1014
Fax: 386-274-2335
communications@amaproracing.com
www.amaproracing.com

May 29 - May 30, 2021
AONIA PASS
Washington, GA
Aonia Pass MX
AMA PRO RACING
Phone: 386-492-1014
Fax: 386-274-2335
communications@amaproracing.com
www.amaproracing.com

May 1, 2021
ATLANTA SUPER TT
Atlanta, GA
Atlanta Motor Speedway
AMA PRO RACING
Phone: 386-492-1014
Fax: 386-274-2335
communications@amaproracing.com
www.amaproracing.com

Sept 4 - Sept 5, 2021
BRIARCLIFF
Nashport, OH
Briarcliff MX
AMA PRO RACING
Phone: 386-492-1014
Fax: 386-274-2335
communications@amaproracing.com
www.amaproracing.com

Aug 21, 2021
BUDDS CREEK NATIONAL
Mechanicsville, MD
Budds Creek Raceway
AMA PRO RACING
Phone: 386-492-1014
Fax: 386-274-2335
communications@amaproracing.com
www.amaproracing.com

Oct 8, 2021
CHARLOTTE HALF-MILE
Charlotte, NC
Charlotte Motor Speedway
AMA PRO RACING
Phone: 386-492-1014
Fax: 386-274-2335
communications@amaproracing.com
www.amaproracing.com

May 29, 2021
CHICAGO HALF-MILE
Joliet, IL
Route 66 Speedway
AMA PRO RACING
Phone: 386-492-1014
Fax: 386-274-2335
communications@amaproracing.com
www.amaproracing.com

Mar 9, 2021
DAYTONA ATV SUPERCROSS
Daytona, FL
Daytona International Speedway
AMA PRO RACING
Phone: 386-492-1014
Fax: 386-274-2335
communications@amaproracing.com
www.amaproracing.com

Jul 17, 2021
DUQUOIN MILE
DuQuoin, IL
DuQuoin State Fairgrounds
AMA PRO RACING
Phone: 386-492-1014
Fax: 386-274-2335
communications@amaproracing.com
www.amaproracing.com

May 29, 2021
FOX RACEWAY NATIONAL
Pala, CA
Fox Raceway
AMA PRO RACING
Phone: 386-492-1014
Fax: 386-274-2335
communications@amaproracing.com
www.amaproracing.com

Sept 11, 2021
HANGTOWN MOTOCROSS CLASSIC
Rancho Cordova, CA
Prairie City OHV Park
AMA PRO RACING
Phone: 386-492-1014
Fax: 386-274-2335
communications@amaproracing.com
www.amaproracing.com

May 15 - May 16, 2021
HIGH POINT
Mount Morris, PA
High Point Raceway
AMA PRO RACING
Phone: 386-492-1014
Fax: 386-274-2335
communications@amaproracing.com
www.amaproracing.com

Jun 19, 2021
HIGH POINT NATIONAL
Mount Morris, PA
High Point Raceway
AMA PRO RACING
Phone: 386-492-1014
Fax: 386-274-2335
communications@amaproracing.com
www.amaproracing.com

Aug 28, 2021
IRONMAN NATIONAL
Crawfordsville, IN
Ironman Raceway
AMA PRO RACING
Phone: 386-492-1014
Fax: 386-274-2335
communications@amaproracing.com
www.amaproracing.com

Jun 26, 2021
LIMA HALF-MILE
Lima, OH
Allen County Fairgrounds
AMA PRO RACING
Phone: 386-492-1014
Fax: 386-274-2335
communications@amaproracing.com
www.amaproracing.com

Aug 14 - Aug 15, 2021
LORETTA LYNN RANCH
Hurricane Mills, TN
Loretta Lynn Ranch
AMA PRO RACING
Phone: 386-492-1014
Fax: 386-274-2335
communications@amaproracing.com
www.amaproracing.com

Aug 14, 2021
NEW YORK SHORT TRACK
Weedsport, NY
Weedsport Speedway
AMA PRO RACING
Phone: 386-492-1014
Fax: 386-274-2335
communications@amaproracing.com
www.amaproracing.com

Jun 18 - Jun 19, 2021
OKLAHOMA CITY MILE I & II
Oklahoma City, OK
Remington Park
AMA PRO RACING
Phone: 386-492-1014
Fax: 386-274-2335
communications@amaproracing.com
www.amaproracing.com

Sept 4, 2021
PALA NATIONAL/FOX RACEWAY
NATIONAL
Pala, CA
Fox Raceway
AMA PRO RACING
Phone: 386-492-1014
Fax: 386-274-2335
communications@amaproracing.com
www.amaproracing.com

Aug 21, 2021
PEORIA TT
Peoria, IL
Peoria Motorcycle Club
AMA PRO RACING
Phone: 386-492-1014
Fax: 386-274-2335
communications@amaproracing.com
www.amaproracing.com

Jul 3 - Jul 4, 2021
PLEASURE VALLEY
Seward, PA
Pleasure Valley Raceway
AMA PRO RACING
Phone: 386-492-1014
Fax: 386-274-2335
communications@amaproracing.com
www.amaproracing.com

Jul 24, 2021
PORT ROYAL HALF-MILE
Port Royal, PA
Port Royal Speedway
AMA PRO RACING
Phone: 386-492-1014
Fax: 386-274-2335
communications@amaproracing.com
www.amaproracing.com

Jul 31 - Aug 1, 2021
REDBUD
Buchanan, MI
RedBud MX
AMA PRO RACING
Phone: 386-492-1014
Fax: 386-274-2335
communications@amaproracing.com
www.amaproracing.com

Jul 3, 2021
REDBUD NATIONAL
Buchanan, MI
RedBux MX
AMA PRO RACING
Phone: 386-492-1014
Fax: 386-274-2335
communications@amaproracing.com
www.amaproracing.com

Jun 26, 2021
SOUTHWICK NATIONAL
Southwick, MA
The Wick 338
AMA PRO RACING
Phone: 386-492-1014
Fax: 386-274-2335
communications@amaproracing.com
www.amaproracing.com

Jul 17, 2021
SPRING CREEK NATIONAL
Millville, MN
Spring Creek MX Park
AMA PRO RACING
Phone: 386-492-1014
Fax: 386-274-2335
communications@amaproracing.com
www.amaproracing.com

Sept 4, 2021
SPRINGFIELD MILE I
Springfield, IL
Illinois State Fairgrounds
AMA PRO RACING
Phone: 386-492-1014
Fax: 386-274-2335
communications@amaproracing.com
www.amaproracing.com

Sept 5, 2021
SPRINGFIELD MILE II
Springfield, IL
Illinois State Fairgrounds
AMA PRO RACING
Phone: 386-492-1014
Fax: 386-274-2335
communications@amaproracing.com
www.amaproracing.com

Jun 19 - Jun 20, 2021
SUNSET RIDGE
Walnut, IL
Sunset Ridge MX
AMA PRO RACING
Phone: 386-492-1014
Fax: 386-274-2335
communications@amaproracing.com
www.amaproracing.com

Sept 17 - Sept 18, 2021
TBA MILE
TBA
AMA PRO RACING
Phone: 386-492-1014
Fax: 386-274-2335
communications@amaproracing.com
www.amaproracing.com

May 22, 2021
TEXAS HALF-MILE
Fort Worth, TX
Texas Motor Speedway
AMA PRO RACING
Phone: 386-492-1014
Fax: 386-274-2335
communications@amaproracing.com
www.amaproracing.com

Apr 10 - Apr 11, 2021
THREE PALMS
Conroe, TX
Three Palms Action Sports Park
AMA PRO RACING
Phone: 386-492-1014
Fax: 386-274-2335
communications@amaproracing.com
www.amaproracing.com

Jun 5, 2021
THUNDER VALLEY NATIONAL
Lakewood, CO
Thunder Valley Motocross Park
AMA PRO RACING
Phone: 386-492-1014
Fax: 386-274-2335
communications@amaproracing.com
www.amaproracing.com

Jul 17 - Jul 18, 2021
UNADILLA
New Berlin, NY
Unadilla MX
AMA PRO RACING
Phone: 386-492-1014
Fax: 386-274-2335
communications@amaproracing.com
www.amaproracing.com

Aug 14, 2021
UNADILLA NATIONAL
New Berlin, NY
Unadilla MX
AMA PRO RACING
Phone: 386-492-1014
Fax: 386-274-2335
communications@amaproracing.com
www.amaproracing.com

Mar 12 - Mar 13, 2021
VOLUSIA HALF-MILE I & II
Barberville, FL
Volusia Speedway Park
AMA PRO RACING
Phone: 386-492-1014
Fax: 386-274-2335
communications@amaproracing.com
www.amaproracing.com

Jul 24, 2021
WASHOUGAL NATIONAL
Washougal, WA
Washougal MX Park
AMA PRO RACING
Phone: 386-492-1014
Fax: 386-274-2335
communications@amaproracing.com
www.amaproracing.com

Orienteering

Aug 2 - Aug 12, 2021
NORTH AMERICAN CHAMPIONSHIPS
Lake Tahoe, CA
US ORIENTEERING
Phone: 215-482-9479
contact@orienteeringusa.org
orienteeringusa.org

Paintball

Sept 17 - Sept 19, 2021
CHICAGO OPEN
Chicago, IL

NATIONAL X BALL LEAGUE
camille@nxlpaintball.com
nxlpaintball.com

Apr 30 - May 2, 2021
KISSIMMEE OPEN
Kissimmee, FL
NATIONAL X BALL LEAGUE
camille@nxlpaintball.com
nxlpaintball.com

Nov 11 - Nov 14, 2021
NXL WORLD CUP
Kissimmee, FL
NATIONAL X BALL LEAGUE
camille@nxlpaintball.com
nxlpaintball.com

Jun 25 - Jun 27, 2021
PHILADELPHIA OPEN
Philadelphia, PA
NATIONAL X BALL LEAGUE
camille@nxlpaintball.com
nxlpaintball.com

Platform Tennis

TBA, 2022
MEN'S & WOMEN'S NATIONALS &
PRESIDENT'S CUP
Darien, CT
AMERICAN PLATFORM TENNIS
ASSOCIATION
Phone: 888-744-9490
apta@platformtennis.org
www.platformtennis.org

Mar TBA, 2022
MEN'S 145+ NATIONALS
Scarsdale, NY
AMERICAN PLATFORM TENNIS
ASSOCIATION
Phone: 888-744-9490
apta@platformtennis.org
www.platformtennis.org

Feb 26 - Feb 28, 2021
MEN'S 45+/55+/65+ NATIONALS
Wilmington, DE
AMERICAN PLATFORM TENNIS
ASSOCIATION
Phone: 888-744-9490
apta@platformtennis.org
www.platformtennis.org

Feb TBA, 2022
MEN'S 50+/60+/70+ NATIONALS
Greenville, DE
AMERICAN PLATFORM TENNIS
ASSOCIATION
Phone: 888-744-9490
apta@platformtennis.org
www.platformtennis.org

Mar 26 - Mar 28, 2021
MIXED NATIONALS
Rye, NY
AMERICAN PLATFORM TENNIS
ASSOCIATION
Phone: 888-744-9490
apta@platformtennis.org
www.platformtennis.org

Jan 16, 2021
WOMEN'S 50+ NATIONALS
Philadelphia, PA
AMERICAN PLATFORM TENNIS
ASSOCIATION
Phone: 888-744-9490

apta@platformtennis.org
www.platformtennis.org

Feb 28, 2021
WOMEN'S 60+ NATIONALS
Wilmington, DE
AMERICAN PLATFORM TENNIS
ASSOCIATION
Phone: 888-744-9490
apta@platformtennis.org
www.platformtennis.org

Racquetball

Oct 6 - Oct 10, 2021
2021 UNITEDHEALTHCARE US OPEN
RACQUETBALL CHAMPI ONSHIPS
Minneapolis, MN
USA RACQUETBALL
Phone: 719-635-5396
Fax: 719-635-0685
mwedel@usaracquetball.com
www.teamusa.org/USA-Racquetball

TBA, 2021
NMRA INTERNATIONAL
CHAMPIONSHIPS
USA RACQUETBALL
Phone: 719-635-5396
Fax: 719-635-0685
mwedel@usaracquetball.com
www.teamusa.org/USA-Racquetball

TBA, 2021
USA RACQUETBALL NATIONAL
DOUBLES CHAMPIONSHIPS
USA RACQUETBALL
Phone: 719-635-5396
Fax: 719-635-0685
mwedel@usaracquetball.com
www.teamusa.org/USA-Racquetball

TBA, 2021
USA RACQUETBALL NATIONAL HIGH
SCHOOL CHAMPIONSHI PS
USA RACQUETBALL
Phone: 719-635-5396
Fax: 719-635-0685
mwedel@usaracquetball.com
www.teamusa.org/USA-Racquetball

TBA, 2021
USA RACQUETBALL NATIONAL
INTERCOLLEGIATE CHAMPIO
NSHIPS
USA RACQUETBALL
Phone: 719-635-5396
Fax: 719-635-0685
mwedel@usaracquetball.com
www.teamusa.org/USA-Racquetball

TBA, 2021
USA RACQUETBALL NATIONAL
JUNIOR CHAMPIONSHIPS
USA RACQUETBALL
Phone: 719-635-5396
Fax: 719-635-0685
mwedel@usaracquetball.com
www.teamusa.org/USA-Racquetball

TBA, 2021
USA RACQUETBALL NATIONAL
SINGLES CHAMPIONSHIPS
USA RACQUETBALL
Phone: 719-635-5396
Fax: 719-635-0685
mwedel@usaracquetball.com
www.teamusa.org/USA-Racquetball

Rodeo

Jun 28 - Jul 4, 2021
ANNUAL WORLD'S OLDEST
CONTINUOUS RODEO
Prescott, AZ
PROFESSIONAL RODEO COWBOY
ASSOCIATION
Phone: 719-593-8840
Fax: 719-548-4876
prorodeor@prorodeo.com
www.prorodeo.com

Mar 11 - Mar 14, 2021
ARCADIA ALL-FLORIDA
CHAMPIONSHIP RODEO
Arcadia, FL
PROFESSIONAL RODEO COWBOY
ASSOCIATION
Phone: 719-593-8840
Fax: 719-548-4876
prorodeor@prorodeo.com
www.prorodeo.com

Aug 20 - Aug 21, 2021
EXTREME EVENTS MINNESOTA
CHAMPIONSHIP RODEO
Waconia, MN
PROFESSIONAL RODEO COWBOY
ASSOCIATION
Phone: 719-593-8840
Fax: 719-548-4876
prorodeor@prorodeo.com
www.prorodeo.com

Jul 2 - Jul 4, 2021
HOME OF CHAMPIONS RODEO
Red Lodge, MT
PROFESSIONAL RODEO COWBOY
ASSOCIATION
Phone: 719-593-8840
Fax: 719-548-4876
prorodeor@prorodeo.com
www.prorodeo.com

Jun TBA, 2022
INNISFAIL PRO RODEO
Innisfail Alberta, Canada
Daines Ranch
PROFESSIONAL RODEO COWBOY
ASSOCIATION
Phone: 719-593-8840
Fax: 719-548-4876
prorodeor@prorodeo.com
www.prorodeo.com

Feb 19 - Feb 20, 2021
PASCO COUNTY FAIR
CHAMPIONSHIP RODEO
Dade City, FL
PROFESSIONAL RODEO COWBOY
ASSOCIATION
Phone: 719-593-8840
Fax: 719-548-4876
prorodeor@prorodeo.com
www.prorodeo.com

May 20 - May 30, 2021
YMBL CHAMPIONSHIP RODEO
Beaumont, TX
PROFESSIONAL RODEO COWBOY
ASSOCIATION
Phone: 719-593-8840
Fax: 719-548-4876
prorodeor@prorodeo.com
www.prorodeo.com

events/meetings/shows

Roller Sports

Aug 23 - Sept 4, 2021
INLINE HOCKEY WORLD
CHAMPIONSHIP
Colombia
USA ROLLER SPORTS
Phone: 402-483-7551
Fax: 402-483-1465
www.teamusa.org/USA-Roller-Sports

Sept 4 - Sept 11, 2021
INLINE SPEED SKATING WORLD
CHAMPIONSHIP
Colombia
USA ROLLER SPORTS
Phone: 402-483-7551
Fax: 402-483-1465
www.teamusa.org/USA-Roller-Sports

Jul 9 - Jul 18, 2021
NARCH FINALS
Irvine, CA
The Rinks, Irvine Inline
NORTH AMERICAN ROLLER HOCKEY
CHAMPIONSHIPS
Phone: 760-889-6909
daryn@narch.com
www.narch.com

Jul 7 - Aug 2, 2021
USA ROLLER SPORTS NATIONAL
CHAMPIONSHIPS
Cedar Rapids, IA
USA ROLLER SPORTS
Phone: 402-483-7551
Fax: 402-483-1465
www.teamusa.org/USA-Roller-Sports

Oct TBA, 2021
WORLD ROLLER GAMES
Argentina
USA ROLLER SPORTS
Phone: 402-483-7551
Fax: 402-483-1465
www.teamusa.org/USA-Roller-Sports

Rowing/Crew

Mar 7, 2021
CRASH-B SPRINTS WORLD INDOOR
ROWING CHAMPIONSHIP
Boston, MA
Boston University Track and Tennis
Center
CRASH-B SPRINTS
office@crash-b.org
www.crash-b.org

May 28 - May 30, 2021
NCAA DIVISION I ROWING FINALS
Sarasota, FL
Nathan Benderson Park
NATIONAL COLLEGIATE ATHLETIC
ASSOCIATION
Phone: 317-917-6222
Fax: 317-917-6888
www.ncaa.org

May 28 - May 30, 2021
NCAA DIVISION II ROWING FINALS
Sarasota, FL
Nathan Benderson Park
NATIONAL COLLEGIATE ATHLETIC
ASSOCIATION
Phone: 317-917-6222
Fax: 317-917-6888
www.ncaa.org

May 28 - May 29, 2021
NCAA DIVISION III ROWING FINALS
Sarasota, FL
Nathan Benderson Park
NATIONAL COLLEGIATE ATHLETIC
ASSOCIATION
Phone: 317-917-6222
Fax: 317-917-6888
www.ncaa.org

Rugby

Aug TBA, 2022
7S NATIONAL CHAMPIONSHIPS
USA RUGBY
Phone: 303-539-0300
Fax: 303-539-0311
membership@usa.rugby
www.usa.rugby

Jun TBA, 2022
CLUB CHAMPIONSHIPS
USA RUGBY
Phone: 303-539-0300
Fax: 303-539-0311
membership@usa.rugby
www.usa.rugby

May TBA, 2022
COLLEGE 7S NATIONAL
CHAMPIONSHIPS
USA RUGBY
Phone: 303-539-0300
Fax: 303-539-0311
membership@usa.rugby
www.usa.rugby

Apr TBA, 2022
D1 ELITE NATIONAL CHAMPIONSHIP
USA RUGBY
Phone: 303-539-0300
Fax: 303-539-0311
membership@usa.rugby
www.usa.rugby

May TBA, 2022
D1A NATIONAL CHAMPIONSHIP
USA RUGBY
Phone: 303-539-0300
Fax: 303-539-0311
membership@usa.rugby
www.usa.rugby

May TBA, 2022
SPRING COLLEGE CHAMPIONSHIPS
USA RUGBY
Phone: 303-539-0300
Fax: 303-539-0311
membership@usa.rugby
www.usa.rugby

Running

Sept 18, 2021
AIR FORCE MARATHON
Riverside, OH
National Museum of the U.S. Air Force
USAF MARATHON
Phone: 800-467-1823
Fax: 937-656-1000
usaf.marathon@us.af.mil
www.usafmarathon.com

Aug 20, 2021
ALCATRAZ XL ESCAPE FROM THE
ROCK DUATHLON
San Francisco, CA
Alcatraz Island

ENVIRO-SPORTS
Phone: 415-868-1829
info@envirosports.com
envirosports.com

Sept TBA, 2022
AMERICAN DISCOVERY TRAIL
MARATHON
Colorado Springs, CO
PIKES PEAK ROAD RUNNERS
runadtmarathon@yahoo.com
www.adtmarathon.com

Nov 28, 2021
AMICA INSURANCE SEATTLE
MARATHON
Seattle, WA
Seattle Center
SEATTLE MARATHON ASSOCIATION
Phone: 206-729-3660
info@seattlemarathon.org
www.seattlemarathon.org

Apr 3, 2021
ANDREW JACKSON MARATHON
Jackson, TN
ANDREW JACKSON MARATHON
danny@crossett.com

Aug 28, 2021
ANGEL ISLAND HALF MARATHON &
10K
Tiburon, CA
Angel Island State Park
ENVIRO-SPORTS
Phone: 415-868-1829
info@envirosports.com
envirosports.com

Apr 4, 2021
ANNUAL REZ RUN 5K+
St. Louis, MO
FIRST BAPTIST CHURCH OF
CRESTWOOD
Phone: 314-843-1130
fbccrestwood@gmail.com

Nov 14, 2021
ATHENS MARATHON
Athens, Greece
ATHENS MARATHON COMMITTEE
Phone: 740-594-3825
Fax: 740-594-2525
athensohiomarathon@gmail.com
www.athensmarathon.com

Sept 19, 2021
AVENUE OF THE GIANTS
MARATHON
Eureka, CA
THE AVE
Phone: 707-822-1861
ctimek@aol.com
www.theave.org

Oct 9, 2021
BALTIMORE RUNNING FESTIVAL
Baltimore, MD
BALTIMORE MARATHON
Phone: 410-605-9381
Fax: 410-605-9389
customerservice@corrigansports.com
www.thebaltimoremarathon.com

Oct 10, 2021
BANK OF AMERICA CHICAGO
MARATHON
Chicago, IL
BANK OF AMERICA CHICAGO
MARATHON
Phone: 312-904-9800

Fax: 312-904-6521
office@chicagomarathon.com
www.chicagomarathon.com

Mar 13 - Mar 27, 2021
BAYOU CITY CLASSIC
Houston, TX
HOUSTON AREA ROAD RUNNERS
ASSOCIATION
www.bayoucityclassic.org

May 29, 2021
BAYSHORE MARATHON
Traverse City, MI
TRAVERSE CITY TRACK CLUB
Phone: 231-941-8118
www.bayshoremarathon.org

Mar 13, 2021
BEL MONTE ENDURANCE RACES
Blue Ridge Mouuntains, VA
BAD TO THE BONE
Phone: 434-218-0402
francesca@badtothebone.biz
badtothebone.biz

Mar 14, 2021
BIG ISLAND MARATHON
Hilo, HI
BIG ISLAND INTERNATIONAL
MARATHON
Phone: 808-969-7400
www.hilomarathon.org

Apr 22 - Apr 24, 2021
BIG SUR INTERNATIONAL
MARATHON
Carmel, CA
BIG SUR MARATHON FOUNDATION
Phone: 831-625-6226
Fax: 831-625-2119
info@bsim.org
www.bsim.org

Oct 2, 2021
BIG SUR TRAIL MARATHON, HALF
MARATHON & 5 MILE
Big Sur, CA
Andrew Molera State Park
ENVIRO-SPORTS
Phone: 415-868-1829
info@envirosports.com
envirosports.com

TBA, 2021
BIG-D TEXAS MARATHON
Dallas, TX
Cotton Bowl, Fair Park
BIG-D TEXAS MARATHON

Dec 10 - Dec 12, 2021
BMW DALLAS MARATHON
Dallas, TX
Dallas City Hall Plaza
DWRM
Phone: 214-800-2087
www.rundallas.com

May 29 - May 31, 2021
BOLDERBOULDER 10K
Boulder, CO
BOLDER BOULDER
Phone: 303-444-7223
Fax: 303-447-9177
race@bolderboulder.com
bb10k.bolderboulder.com

Oct 11, 2021
BOSTON MARATHON
Boston, MA
BOSTON ATHLETIC ASSOCIATION
Phone: 617-236-1652

Fax: 617-236-4505
info@baa.org
www.baa.org

Apr 25, 2021
BOULDERTHON
Boulder, CO
RUN BOULDER EVENTS
Phone: 303-517-7046
www.runboulderevents.com

May 15, 2021
BROOKINGS MARATHON
Brookings, SD
BROOKINGS MARATHON
run@brookingsmarathon.com
www.brookingsmarathon.com

May 29 - May 30, 2021
BUFFALO MARATHON
Buffalo, NY
BUFFALO MARATHON
information@buffalomarathon.com
www.buffalomarathon.com

Oct 30 - Oct 31, 2021
CAPE COD MARATHON
Falmouth, MA
CAPE COD MARATHON
Phone: 508-540-6959
Fax: 508-548-0617
info@capecodmarathon.com
www.capecodmarathon.com

May 15 - May 16, 2021
CAPITAL CITY MARATHON
Olympia, WA
CAPITAL CITY MARATHON
racedirector@ccmaboard.org
www.capitalcitymarathon.org

May TBA, 2022
CARDEROCK RUNNING FESTIVAL
Carderock, MD
MARATHON CHARITY COOPERATION
www.mc-coop.org

Jun 6, 2021
CASPER WYOMING MARATHON
Casper, WY
CASPER WYOMING MARATHON
Phone: 307-577-4974
www.runwyoming.com

May 15 - May 16, 2021
CELLCOM GREEN BAY MARATHON
Green Bay, WI
CELLCOM GREEN BAY MARATHON
Phone: 920-432-6272
info@cellcomgreenbaymarathon.com
www.cellcomgreenbaymarathon.com

Apr 10, 2021
CHARLOTTESVILLE MARATHON
Charlottesville, VA
BAD TO THE BONE
Phone: 434-218-0402
francesca@badtothebone.biz
badtothebone.biz

Oct 31, 2021
CINCINNATI FLYING PIG MARATHON
Cincinnati, OH
CINCINNATI FLYING PIG MARATHON
Phone: 513-721-7447
info@flyingpigmarathon.com
www.flyingpigmarathon.com

Oct 11, 2021
CITY OF TREES MARATHON
Boise, ID
Park Center Park

CITY OF TREES RACING
ASSOCIATION
jeff@bluecirclesports.com
www.cityoftreesmarathon.com

May 30, 2021
COEUR D'ALENE MARATHON
Coeur d'Alene, ID
COEUR D'ALENE MARATHON
runsignup.com/Race/ID/CoeurDAlene/nsp
lit

Oct 24, 2021
COLORADO MARATHON
Fort Collins, CO
COLORADO MARATHON
logan@thecoloradomarathon.com
comarathon.com

Oct TBA, 2021
COLUMBUS MARATHON
Columbus, OH
Downtown Columbus
COLUMBUS MARATHON
Phone: 614-421-7866
Fax: 614-263-3518
info@columbusmarathon.com
www.columbusmarathon.com

Sept 17 - Sept 19, 2021
COMMUNITY FIRST FOX CITIES
MARATHON
Appleton, WI
COMMUNITY FIRST FOX CITIES
MARATHON
Phone: 877-230-7223
Fax: 920-830-0921
info@foxcitiesmarathon.org
www.foxcitiesmarathon.org

Jun 5 - Jun 7, 2021
DEADWOOD-MICKELSON TRAIL
MARATHON
Deadwood, SD
DEADWOOD-MICKELSON TRAIL
MARATHON
Phone: 605-390-6137
www.deadwoodmickelsontrailmarathon.co
m

Apr 25, 2021
DELAWARE MARATHON RUNNING
FESTIVAL
Wilmington, DE
Tubman Garrett Riverfront Park
CORRIGAN SPORTS ENTERPRISES
Phone: 410-605-9381
Fax: 410-605-9389
customerservice@corrigansports.com
www.corrigansports.com

Oct 16 - Oct 17, 2021
DES MOINES MARATHON
Des Moines, IA
DES MOINES MARATHON
HEADQUARTERS
Phone: 515-288-2692
Fax: 515-255-9051
info@desmoinesmarathon.com
www.desmoinesmarathon.com

Apr TBA, 2022
DRAKE RELAYS
Des Moines, IA
Drake Stadium, Drake University
DRAKE RELAYS
Phone: 515-271-2889
Fax: 515-271-4189
www.godrakebulldogs.com

events/meetings/shows

May 1, 2021
EISENHOWER MARATHON
Abilene, TX
Chisholm Trail
EISENHOWER MARATHON
Phone: 785-263-3474
scathey79@yahoo.com
eisenhowermarathon.net

Jun 20, 2021
ESTES PARK MARATHON
Estes Park, CO
ESTES PARK MARATHON
Phone: 970-586-8189
belle@epmarathon.org
www.epmarathon.org

Oct 9, 2021
EVERSOURCE HARTFORD
MARATHON
Hartford, CT
Bushnell Park
HARTFORD MARATHON FOUNDATION
Phone: 860-652-8866
Fax: 860-652-8145
info@hartfordmarathon.com
www.hartfordmarathon.com

Oct TBA, 2021
FALL CLASSIC HALF MARATHON &
10K
Vancouver, Canada
BAD TO THE BONE
Phone: 434-218-0402
francesca@badtothebone.biz
badtothebone.biz

Sept 25, 2021
FIRSTENERGY AKRON MARATHON,
HALF MARATHON & TEAM RELAY
Akron, OH
ROAD RUNNER AKRON MARATHON
Phone: 330-434-2786
Fax: 330-434-0738
info@akronmarathon.org
www.akronmarathon.org

May 1 - May 2, 2021
FREDERICK RUNNING FESTIVAL
Frederick, MD
Frederick Fair Grounds
CORRIGAN SPORTS ENTERPRISES
Phone: 410-605-9381
Fax: 410-605-9389
customerservice@corrigansports.com
www.corrigansports.com

Apr 10 - Apr 11, 2021
GO ST. LOUIS MARATHON
St. Louis, MO
SPIRIT OF ST. LOUIS MARATHON
Phone: 314-727-0800
Fax: 314-727-0893
info@gostlouis.org
www.gostlouis.org

Mar 27, 2021
GOLDEN GATE HEADLANDS
MARATHON, HALF MARATHON & 10K
Sausalito, CA
Fort Barry, Golden Gate National
Recreation Area
ENVIRO-SPORTS
Phone: 415-868-1829
info@envirosports.com
envirosports.com

Jul 8 - Jul 12, 2021
GRANDFATHER MOUNTAIN
HIGHLAND GAMES
Linville, NC
GRANDFATHER MOUNTAIN HIGHLAND
GAMES
Phone: 828-733-1333
Fax: 828-733-0092
weaverjt@appstate.edu
www.gmhg.org

Jul 10, 2021
GRANDFATHER MOUNTAIN
MARATHON
Boone, NC
GRANDFATHER MOUNTAIN HIGHLAND
GAMES
Phone: 828-733-1333
Fax: 828-733-0092
weaverjt@appstate.edu
www.gmhg.org

Apr 17, 2021
GRANDMA'S MARATHON
Duluth, MN
Two Harbors To Duluth
GRANDMA'S MARATHON
Phone: 218-727-0947
grandmas@grandmasmarathon.com
www.grandmasmarathon.com

Oct 17, 2021
GREEN MOUNTAIN MARATHON &
HALF MARATHON
South Hero, VT
Lake Champlian
GREEN MOUNTAIN ATHLETIC
ASSOCIATION
Phone: 802-373-4762
info@gmaa.net
www.gmaa.net

Apr 10, 2021
HALF MARATHON UNPLUGGED
Burlington, VT
RUN VERMONT
Phone: 802-863-8412
info@runvermont.org
www.runvermont.org

May 8 - May 9, 2021
HARMONY GENEVA MARATHON FOR
UNICEF
Lake Geneva, WI
OC SPORT
www.ocsport.com

Jun 12, 2021
HATFIELD-MCCOY MARATHON
Williamson, WV
HATFIELD-MCCOY MARATHON

Oct 8 - Oct 10, 2021
HEARTLAND 100 SPIRIT OF THE
PRAIRIE RACE
Cassoday, KS
KANSAS ULTRARUNNERS' SOCIETY
www.ksultrarunners.org

Nov 6, 2021
INDIANAPOLIS MARATHON & HALF
MARATHON
Indianapolis, IN
INDIANAPOLIS MARATHON CORP
Phone: 317-454-8519
nfo@beyondmonumental.org
www.monumentalmarathon.com

Oct 9 - Oct 10, 2021
JETBLUE LONG BEACH MARATHON
& HALF MARATHON
Long Beach, CA
MOTIV RUNNING
lbinfo@motivsports.com
www.motivrunning.com

Jul 23, 2021
JUNEAU MARATHON & HALF
MARATHON
Juneau, AK
JUNEAU TRAIL & ROAD RUNNERS
houstonlaws@yahoo.com
juneauserr.wixsite.com/serr/marathon

Apr 22, 2021
KENTUCKY DERBY FESTIVAL
MARATHON
Louisville, KY
KENTUCKY DERBY FESTIVAL
Phone: 800-928-3378
Fax: 502-589-4674
minimarathon@kdf.org
www.derbyfestivalmarathon.com

Jun 25 - Jun 26, 2022
KONA MARATHON & KONA HALF
MARATHON
Keauhou-Kona, HI
Waikoloa Beach Resort
KONA MARATHON
Phone: 808-967-8285
raceinfo@konamarathon.com
www.konamarathon.com

Jun 19, 2021
LEADVILLE TRAIL MARATHON &
HEAVY HALF
Leadville, CO
LEADVILLE TRAIL MARATHON
leadville@ltevents.zendesk.com
www.leadvilleraceseries.com

Nov 26, 2021
LIFETIME TURKEY DAY 5K
Chicago, IL
LIFE TIME FITNESS
ltfmedia@lifetimefitness.com
www.eventsbylifetime.com

May 2, 2021
LINCOLN MARATHON
Lincoln, NE
LINCOLN TRACK CLUB
Phone: 402-435-3504
www.lincolnmarathon.org

Nov 20 - Nov 21, 2021
LITTLE ROCK MARATHON
Little Rock, AR
LITTLE ROCK MARATHON
Phone: 501-371-4639
glamm@littlerock.gov
www.littlerockmarathon.com

Sept 18, 2021
LOGAN CITY MARATHON
Logan, UT
LOGAN CITY MARATHON
www.logandowntown.org

Sept 17 - Sept 19, 2021
LONG ISLAND MARATHON FESTIVAL
East Meadow, NY
LONG ISLAND MARATHON
raceawesome@raceawesome.com

Nov 7, 2021
LOS ANGELES MARATHON
Los Angeles, CA

CONQUR ENDURANCE GROUP
Phone: 213-542-3000
info@goconqur.com
goconqur.com

Nov 14, 2021
MADISON MARATHON FULL & HALF
Madison, WI
MADISON FESTIVALS
Phone: 608-276-9797
Fax: 608-226-9550
events@madisonfestivals.com
www.madisonfestivals.com

Oct 3, 2021
MAINE MARATHON
Portland, ME
THE MAINE MARATHON
Phone: 207-749-9160
racedirector@mainemarathon.com
www.mainemarathon.com

Nov 13 - Nov 14, 2021
MALIBU INTERNATIONAL HALF
MARATHON & 5K
Malibu, CA
MALIBU INTERNATIONAL MARATHON
Phone: 310-745-8231
info@malibumarathon.com
www.malibumarathon.com

Oct 23, 2021
MARATHON 2 MARATHON
Marathon, TX
MARATHON TO MARATHON
www.marathon2marathon.com

Oct 31, 2021
MARINE CORPS MARATHON
Arlington, VA
MARINE CORPS MARATHON
Phone: 800-786-8762
Fax: 703-784-2265
mcm.info@usmc.mil
www.marinemarathon.com

Apr 1- Apr 30, 2021
MAUI MARATHON
Maui, HI
MAUI MARATHON
Phone: 808-222-2484
mauimarathonexpor@gmail.com
www.mauimarathon.com

Jun 19, 2021
MAYOR'S MARATHON
Anchorage, AK
UAA ATHLETICS DEPARTMENT
track@uaa.alaska.edu
www.mayorsmarathon.com

Sept 11 - Sept 12, 2021
MED CITY MARATHON
Rochester, MN
MED CITY MARATHON
Phone: 507-254-2703
Fax: 507-288-8058
medcityevents@outlook.com
www.medcitymarathon.com

Feb 11 - Feb 13, 2021
MERCEDES-BENZ MARATHON
Birmingham, AL
Boutwell Auditorium
BIRMINGHAM MARATHON, INC.
Phone: 205-870-7771
Fax: 205-870-7729
info@mercedesmarathon.com
www.mercedesmarathon.com

Apr 25, 2021
MERCY HEALTH GLASS CITY
MARATHON
Toledo, OH
TOLEDO ROAD RUNNERS CLUB
Phone: 419-340-1815
info@glasscitymarathon.org
glasscitymarathon.org

Oct 17, 2021
METRO HEALTH GRAND RAPIDS
MARATHON
Grand Rapids, MI
GRAND RAPIDS MARATHON
Phone: 616-293-3145
rungrmarathon@gmail.com
www.grandrapidsmarathon.com

Feb 6, 2022
MIAMI MARATHON & HALF
MARATHON
Miami, FL
LIFE TIME FITNESS
ltfmedia@lifetimefitness.com
www.eventsbylifetime.com

Oct 3, 2021
MILWAUKEE LAKEFRONT
MARATHON
Milwaukee, WI
BADGERLAND STRIDERS
Phone: 414-688-7561
milwaukeelakefrontmarathon@gmail.com
www.milwaukeelakefrontmarathon.org

Nov TBA, 2021
MONTEREY BAY HALF MARATHON
Monterey, CA
BIG SUR MARATHON FOUNDATION
Phone: 831-625-6226
Fax: 831-625-2119
info@bsim.org
www.bsim.org

Oct 17, 2021
MOUNT DESERT ISLAND MARATHON
& HALF MARATHON
Bar Harbor, ME
CROW ATHLETICS
www.crowathletics.com

Apr 24, 2022
MT. TAM WILD BOAR HALF
MARATHON & 10K
Mill Valley, CA
Mt. Tamalpais State Park
ENVIRO-SPORTS
Phone: 415-868-1829
info@envirosports.com
envirosports.com

May 8, 2022
MUIR WOODS MARATHON, HALF
MARATHON & 7 MILE
Stinson Beach, CA
Stinson Beach Park
ENVIRO-SPORTS
Phone: 415-868-1829
info@envirosports.com
envirosports.com

Mar 15, 2021
NAPA VALLEY TRAIL MARATHON,
HALF MARATHON & 10K
Calistoga, CA
Bothe-Napa State Park
ENVIRO-SPORTS
Phone: 415-868-1829
info@envirosports.com
envirosports.com

Oct 23, 2021
NAPA WINE COUNTRY MARATHON,
HALF MARATHON & 10K
Calistoga, CA
Silverado Trail
ENVIRO-SPORTS
Phone: 415-868-1829
info@envirosports.com
envirosports.com

Oct 16 - Oct 17, 2021
NEW JERSEY MARATHON
Oceanport, NJ
LIFE TIME FITNESS
ltfmedia@lifetimefitness.com
www.eventsbylifetime.com

Jun 5, 2021
NEWPORT MARATHON
Newport, OR
NEWPORT MARATHON
Phone: 541-265-3446
run@newportmarathon.org
www.newportmarathon.org

Apr 3, 2022
NORTH POLE MARATHON
Arctic Ocean, NT
Geographic North Pole
POLAR RUNNING ADVENTURES
International Ph: 011 353 91 443 408
International Fax: 011 353 91 443 408
rd@npmarathon.com
www.npmarathon.com

May 15, 2021
OGDEN MARATHON
Odgen, UT
GOAL FOUNDATION
Phone: 801-399-1773
Fax: 248-654-0797
info@goalfoundation.com
www.ogdenmarathon.com

Apr 11, 2021
OHIO RIVER ROAD RUNNERS
MARATHON & HALF MARATHON
Xenia, OH
OHIO RIVER ROAD RUNNERS CLUB
www.orrrc.org

Oct 2 - Oct 3, 2021
OKLAHOMA CITY MEMORIAL
MARATHON
Oklahoma City, OK
OKLAHOMA CITY MARATHON
Phone: 405-525-4242
Fax: 405-521-9907
help@okcmarathon.com
www.okcmarathon.com

Nov 6, 2021
OLATHE KS MARATHON
Olathe, KS
OLATHE CHAMBER OF COMMERCE
Phone: 913-764-1050
Fax: 913-782-4636
marathon@olathe.org
www.olathemarathon.com

Sept 19, 2021
OMAHA MARATHON
Omaha, NE
OMAHA MARATHON
Phone: 845-247-7275
info@hitsendurance.com
www.omahamarathon.com

Sept 11, 2021
PARK CITY HALF MARATHON
Park City, UT

events/meetings/shows

UTAH ROAD RUNNERS
events@saltlakerunningco.com
pctrailseries.com

Apr TBA, 2022
PENN RELAYS
University of Pennsylvania
Franklin Field
UNIVERSITY OF PENNSYLVANIA
Phone: 215-898-6145
pennrela@pobox.upenn.edu
www.thepennrelays.com

Nov 20 - Nov 21, 2021
PHILADELPHIA MARATHON
Philadelphia, PA
PHILADELPHIA MARATHON
Phone: 215-683-2122
Fax: 215-683-2099
info@philadelphiamarathon.com
philadelphiamarathon.com

Aug 21 Aug 22, 2021
PIKES PEAK MARATHON
Colorado Springs, CO
PIKES PEAK MARATHON
Phone: 719-473-2625
info@pikespeakmarathon.org
www.pikespeakmarathon.org

Apr 24, 2021
PINE LINE MARATHON
Medford, WI
Medford City Park
PINE LINE TRAIL MARATHON
Phone: 715-748-4729

Sept 5, 2021
POCATELLO MARATHON
Pocatello, ID
POCATELLO MARATHON
Phone: 208-233-4754
pocatellorun@gmail.com
www.pocatellomarathon.com

Nov 13, 2021
RICHMOND MARATHON
Richmond, VA
RICHMOND MARATHON
Phone: 804-285-9495
Fax: 804-285-3132
marathon@sportsbackers.org
www.richmondmarathon.com

May 21 - May 22, 2022
RITE AID CLEVELAND MARATHON
Cleveland, OH
CLEVELAND MARATHON
Phone: 800-467-3826
Fax: 216-378-0143
www.clevelandmarathon.com

Oct 23 - Oct 24, 2021
ROCK 'N' ROLL MARATHON
San Diego, CA
ROCK 'N' ROLL MARATHON SERIES
Phone: 858-450-6510
Fax: 858-450-6905
leads@competitorgroup.com
www.runrocknroll.com

Apr 3, 2021
ROCKIN K TRAIL MARATHON
Ellsworth, KS
Kanapolis State Park
KANSAS ULTRARUNNERS' SOCIETY
www.ksultrarunners.org

Jun 19, 2022
RUN IN THE NAME OF LOVE
Carmel, CA

BIG SUR MARATHON FOUNDATION
Phone: 831-625-6226
Fax: 831-625-2119
info@bsim.org
www.bsim.org

Apr 10 - Apr 25, 2021
SALT LAKE CITY MARATHON
Salt Lake City, UT
LIFE TIME FITNESS
ltfmedia@lifetimefitness.com
www.eventsbylifetime.com

Sept 18 - Sept 19, 2021
SAN FRANCISCO MARATHON
San Francisco, CA
SAN FRANCISCO MARATHON
Phone: 888-958-6668
customersupport@thesfmarathon.com
www.thesfmarathon.com

Jun 20, 2021
SAN JUAN ISLAND MARATHON
Friday Harbor, WA
LAKEDALE RESORT
Phone: 800-617-2267
www.lakedale.com

Feb 13, 2021
SAN MIGUEL BUZZ MARATHON
San Miguel, CA
Camp Roberts Army National Guard
Reservation
SAN MIGUEL BUZZ MARATHON
Phone: 805-467-3216
Fax: 805-467-3410
www.buzzmarathon.org

Nov TBA, 2021
SANTA CLARITA MARATHON
Santa Clarita, CA
SANTA CLARITA MARATHON
Phone: 661-250-3787
Fax: 661-255-1966
marathon@santa-clarita.com
www.scmarathon.org

Apr 18, 2021
SHAPE WOMEN'S HALF MARATHON
New York, NY
Central Park

Apr 27 - Apr 28, 2021
SHIPROCK MARATHON
Shiprock, NM
FOUR CORNERS FITNESS &
WELLNESS ASSOCIATION
Phone: 435-233-8068
info@shiprockmarathon.com
www.shiprockmarathon.com

Oct 2, 2021
ST. GEORGE MARATHON
St. George, UT
ST. GEORGE MARATHON
Phone: 435-627-4500
Fax: 435-627-4509
marathon@sgcity.org
www.stgeorgemarathon.com

Dec 4, 2021
ST. JUDE MARATHON
Memphis, TN
ST. JUDE MARATHON
Phone: 901-578-1555
Fax: 901-578-6696
marathon@stjude.org
www.stjudemarathon.org

Jun 6, 2021
STEAMBOAT MARATHON
Steamboat Springs, CO

STEAMBOAT MARATHON
Phone: 970-879-0880
Fax: 970-879-3550
marathon@steamboatchamber.com
www.steamboatchamber.com

Oct 10, 2021
STEAMTOWN MARATHON
Scranton, PA
STEAMTOWN MARATHON
Phone: 570-342-0427
Fax: 570-342-0422
racecommittee@hotmail.com
www.steamtownmarathon.com

May 16, 2021
SUGARLOAF MARATHON & 15K
Carrabassett Valley, ME
SUGARLOAF MARATHON
Phone: 207-237-2000
Fax: 207-237-3768
info@sugarloaf.com
www.sugarloaf.com

Sept 25, 2021
SUNBURST MARATHON
South Bend, IN
BEACON HEALTH SYSTEM
Phone: 574-647-1000

Nov 7, 2021
TCS NEW YORK CITY MARATHON
New York, NY
NEW YORK ROAD RUNNERS
Phone: 855-569-6977
marathonmailer@nyrr.org
www.tcsnycmarathon.org

Oct 10, 2021
TOWPATH MARATHON
Boston, OH
Cuyahoga Valley National Park
OHIO CANAL CORRIDOR
Phone: 216-520-1825
Fax: 216-520-1833
www.towpathtrilogy.com

May 29, 2021
TRENT/WALDRON GLACIER HALF
MARATHON
Anchorage, AK
Westchester Lagoon
ANCHORAGE RUNNING CLUB
Phone: 907-258-4964
info@anchoragerunningclub.org
www.anchoragerunningclub.org

Nov TBA, 2021
TURKEY TROT MIAMI
Miami, FL
LIFE TIME FITNESS
ltfmedia@lifetimefitness.com
www.eventsbylifetime.com

May 1, 2021
ULTRA RACE OF CHAMPIONS
Blue Ridge Mouuntains, VA
BAD TO THE BONE
Phone: 434-218-0402
francesca@badtothebone.biz
badtothebone.biz

Oct 24, 2021
VERMONT CITY MARATHON
Burlington, VT
RUN VERMONT
Phone: 802-863-8412
info@runvermont.org
www.runvermont.org

May 29, 2021
VIRGINIA WINE COUNTRY HALF
MARATHON
Leesburg, VA
BAD TO THE BONE
Phone: 434-218-0402
francesca@badtothebone.biz
badtothebone.biz

Oct TBA, 2021
WALTER CHILDS MARATHON
Springfield, MA
GREATER SPRINGFIELD HARRIERS
Phone: 413-734-0955
fastfeetinc@comcast.net
www.harriers.org

Sept 12, 2021
WHIDBEY ISLAND MARATHON AND
HALF MARATHON
Oak Harbor, WA
WHIDBEY ISLAND MARATHON & HALF
MARATHON
Phone: 360-279-4500
runwhidbey@oakharbor.org
runwhidbey.com

May 30, 2021
WYOMING MARATHON
Cheyenne, WY
CHEYENNE TRACK CLUB
Phone: 307-778-7866
Fax: 307-778-7876
fotrockies@bresnan.net
wyomingmarathonraces.weebly.com

Apr TBA, 2022
YAKIMA RIVER CANYON MARATHON
Ellensburg - Selah, WA
HARD CORE RUNNER'S CLUB
Phone: 425-226-1518

Oct 9, 2021
YMCA WHISKEY ROW MARATHON
Prescott, AZ
PRESCOTT YMCA
Phone: 928-445-7221
Fax: 928-445-5135
wrm@prescottymca.org
www.whiskeyrowmarathon.com

Mar 19 - Mar 21, 2021
YUENGLING SHAMROCK MARATHON
Virginia Beach, VA
SHAMROCK MARATHON
Phone: 757-412-1056
Fax: 757-412-1058
info@shamrockmarathon.com
www.shamrockmarathon.com

Sailing

Jan 8 - Jan 10, 2021
2021 470 NORTH AMERICAN
CHAMPIONSHIPS
Miami, FL
Coconut Grove Sailing Club
WORLD SAILING
International Ph: 44 (0)20 3940 4888
www.sailing.org

May 22 - May 28, 2021
2021 FINN WORLD MASTERS
Medemblik, Netherlands
WORLD SAILING
International Ph: 44 (0)20 3940 4888
www.sailing.org

Oct 10 - Oct 17, 2021
2021 LASER RADIAL MEN'S WORLD
CHAMPIONSHIP
Shoreacres, TX
WORLD SAILING
International Ph: 44 (0)20 3940 4888
www.sailing.org

Jan 21 - Jan 24, 2021
BALTIMORE BOAT SHOW
Baltimore, MD
Baltimore Convention Center
NATIONAL MARINE MANUFACTURERS
ASSOCIATION
Phone: 312-946-6200
Fax: 312-946-0401
www.nmma.org

TBA 2022
EASTERN HEMISPHERE
CHAMPIONSHIP
TBA
INTERNATIONAL STAR CLASS YACHT
ASSOCIATION
Phone: 619-222-0252
Fax: 619-222-0528
office@starclass.org
www.starclass.org

May 24 - May 29, 2021
EUROPEAN CHAMPIONSHIPS
Split, Croatia
Sailing Club Mornar
INTERNATIONAL STAR CLASS YACHT
ASSOCIATION
Phone: 619-222-0252
Fax: 619-222-0528
office@starclass.org
www.starclass.org

Jul 3 - Jul 9, 2021
J80 WORLD CHAMPIONSHIP
Rungsted, Copenhagen
WORLD SAILING
International Ph: 44 (0)20 3940 4888
www.sailing.org

TBA, 2022
JUNIOR WORLD CHAMPIONSHIP
INTERNATIONAL STAR CLASS YACHT
ASSOCIATION
Phone: 619-222-0252
Fax: 619-222-0528
office@starclass.org
www.starclass.org

Aug 7 - Aug 14, 2021
LASER 4.7 YOUTH WORLD
CHAMPIONSHIPS
Dun Laoghaire, Ireland
WORLD SAILING
International Ph: 44 (0)20 3940 4888
www.sailing.org

TBA, 2022
MELGES 24 WORLD CHAMPIONSHIP
WORLD SAILING
International Ph: 44 (0)20 3940 4888
www.sailing.org

Auh 18 - Aug 21, 2021
STAR NORTH AMERICAN
CHAMPIONSHIPS
Newport, CA
Newport Harbor Yacht Club
INTERNATIONAL STAR CLASS YACHT
ASSOCIATION
Phone: 619-222-0252
Fax: 619-222-0528
office@starclass.org
www.starclass.org

Sept 4 - Sept 11, 2021
STAR WORLD CHAMPIONSHIP
Kiellinie, Germany
Kieler Yacht Club
INTERNATIONAL STAR CLASS YACHT
ASSOCIATION
Phone: 619-222-0252
Fax: 619-222-0528
office@starclass.org
www.starclass.org

Oct 22 - Oct 24, 2021
US ADULT SAILING CHAMPIONSHIP
Kemah, TX
Texas Corinthian Yacht Club
US SAILING
Phone: 401-683-0800
Fax: 401-683-0840
info@ussailing.org
www.ussailing.org

Sept 17 - Sept 19, 2021
US CHAMPIONSHIP OF CHAMPIONS
TBA
US SAILING
Phone: 401-683-0800
Fax: 401-683-0840
info@ussailing.org
www.ussailing.org

Jul TBA, 2022
US JUNIOR WOMEN'S
DOUBLEHANDED CHAMPIONSHIP
Oklahoma City, OK
Oklahoma City Boat Club
US SAILING
Phone: 401-683-0800
Fax: 401-683-0840
info@ussailing.org
www.ussailing.org

TBA, 2022
US JUNIOR WOMEN'S
SINGLEHANDED CHAMPIONSHIP
WORLD SAILING
International Ph: 44 (0)20 3940 4888
www.sailing.org

Oct 1 - Oct 3, 2021
US MATCH RACING CHAMPIONSHIP
Long Beach, CA
Long Beach Yacht Club
US SAILING
Phone: 401-683-0800
Fax: 401-683-0840
info@ussailing.org
www.ussailing.org

Nov 1 - Nov 5, 2021
US MULTIHULL CHAMPIONSHIP
Corpus Christi, TX
Corpus Christi Yacht Club
US SAILING
Phone: 401-683-0800
Fax: 401-683-0840
info@ussailing.org
www.ussailing.org

Sept 24 - Sept 26, 2021
US OFFSHORE CHAMPIONSHIP
Annapolis, MD
Naval Academy Sailing Squadron
US SAILING
Phone: 401-683-0800
Fax: 401-683-0840
info@ussailing.org
www.ussailing.org

events/meetings/shows

Aug 24 - Aug 29, 2021
US PARA SAILING CHAMPIONSHIP
Newport, RI
Sail Newport
WORLD SAILING
International Ph: 44 (0)20 3940 4888
www.sailing.org

Aug 24 - Aug 29, 2021
US PARA SAILING CHAMPIONSHIP
Newport, RI
Sail Newport
US SAILING
Phone: 401-683-0800
Fax: 401-683-0840
info@ussailing.org
www.ussailing.org

Jun 18 - Jun 20, 2021
US SINGLEHANDED
CHAMPIONSHIPS
Norfolk, VA
Big Blue Sailing Academy
US SAILING
Phone: 401-683-0800
Fax: 401-683-0840
info@ussailing.org
www.ussailing.org

Sept 24 - Sept 26, 2021
US TEAM RACING CHAMPIONSHIP
Bristol, RI
Bristol Yacht Club
US SAILING
Phone: 401-683-0800
Fax: 401-683-0840
info@ussailing.org
www.ussailing.org

Aug 19 - Aug 22, 2021
US WOMEN'S MATCH RACING
CHAMPIONSHIP
San Diego, CA
San Diego Yacht Club
US SAILING
Phone: 401-683-0800
Fax: 401-683-0840
info@ussailing.org
www.ussailing.org

Oct 8 - Oct 11, 2021
US YOUTH SAILING CHAMPIONSHIP
Arapahoe, NC
Camp Sea Gull
WORLD SAILING
International Ph: 44 (0)20 3940 4888
www.sailing.org

TBA, 2022
WESTERN HEMISPHERE
CHAMPIONSHIPS
TBA
INTERNATIONAL STAR CLASS YACHT
ASSOCIATION
Phone: 619-222-0252
Fax: 619-222-0528
office@starclass.org
www.starclass.org

Shooting/Hunting

Apr 13, 2021
CLAY SHOOT FOR CONSERVATION
Mansfield, GA
Burge Plantation
GEORGIA WILDLIFE FEDERATION
Phone: 770-787-7887
Fax: 770-787-9229

info@gwf.org
www.gwf.org

Oct TBA, 2021
FACTORY GUN NATIONALS
Frostproof, FL
US PRACTICAL SHOOTING
ASSOCIATION
Phone: 360-855-2245
Fax: 360-855-0380
office@uspsa.org
www.uspsa.org

Jun 5 - Jun 6, 2021
MULTI-GUN NATIONALS
US PRACTICAL SHOOTING
ASSOCIATION
Phone: 360-855-2245
Fax: 360-855-0380
office@uspsa.org
www.uspsa.org

Mar TBA, 2022
NATIONAL COLLEGIATE MIXED
RIFLE FINALS
Lexington, KY
Memorial Coliseum
NATIONAL COLLEGIATE ATHLETIC
ASSOCIATION
Phone: 317-917-6222
Fax: 317-917-6888
www.ncaa.org

Sept TBA, 2021
NATIONAL POLICE SHOOTING
CHAMPIONSHIPS
NATIONAL RIFLE ASSOCIATION -
COMPETITIVE SHOOTING DIVISION
Phone: 703-267-1465
competitions.nra.org

Jul TBA, 2021
NATIONAL THREE POSITION AIR
RIFLE CHAMPIONSHIP P RECISION
NATIONAL RIFLE ASSOCIATION -
COMPETITIVE SHOOTING DIVISION
Phone: 703-267-1465
competitions.nra.org

Jun TBA, 2021
NATIONAL THREE POSITION AIR
RIFLE CHAMPIONSHIPS SPORTER
NATIONAL RIFLE ASSOCIATION -
COMPETITIVE SHOOTING DIVISION
Phone: 703-267-1465
competitions.nra.org

Mar 14 - Mar 17, 2021
NRA INTERCOLLEGIATE PISTOL
CHAMPIONSHIPS
Ft. Benning, GA
NATIONAL RIFLE ASSOCIATION -
COMPETITIVE SHOOTING DIVISION
Phone: 703-267-1465
competitions.nra.org

Mar 20 - Mar 22, 2021
NRA INTERCOLLEGIATE RIFLE CLUB
CHAMPIONSHIPS
Ft. Benning, GA
NATIONAL RIFLE ASSOCIATION -
COMPETITIVE SHOOTING DIVISION
Phone: 703-267-1465
competitions.nra.org

Jun 5 - Jun 6, 2021
PCC NATIONALS
US PRACTICAL SHOOTING
ASSOCIATION
Phone: 360-855-2245
Fax: 360-855-0380

office@uspsa.org
www.uspsa.org

TBA, 2021
RACE GUN NATIONALS
US PRACTICAL SHOOTING
ASSOCIATION
Phone: 360-855-2245
Fax: 360-855-0380
office@uspsa.org
www.uspsa.org

TBA, 2021
REVOLVER/L10 NATIONALS
Talladega, AL
US PRACTICAL SHOOTING
ASSOCIATION
Phone: 360-855-2245
Fax: 360-855-0380
office@uspsa.org
www.uspsa.org

TBA, 2021
SILHOUETTE NATIONAL
CHAMPIONSHIPS - BLACK POWDER
RIFLE SCOPE
NATIONAL RIFLE ASSOCIATION -
COMPETITIVE SHOOTING DIVISION
Phone: 703-267-1465
competitions.nra.org

TBA, 2021
SILHOUETTE NATIONAL
CHAMPIONSHIPS - HIGH POWER
RIFLE
NATIONAL RIFLE ASSOCIATION -
COMPETITIVE SHOOTING DIVISION
Phone: 703-267-1465
competitions.nra.org

TBA, 2021
SILHOUETTE NATIONAL
CHAMPIONSHIPS - LEVER ACTION
RIFLE
NATIONAL RIFLE ASSOCIATION -
COMPETITIVE SHOOTING DIVISION
Phone: 703-267-1465
competitions.nra.org

TBA, 2021
SILHOUETTE NATIONAL
CHAMPIONSHIPS - SMALLBORE
RIFLE
Ridgway, PA
NATIONAL RIFLE ASSOCIATION -
COMPETITIVE SHOOTING DIVISION
Phone: 703-267-1465
competitions.nra.org

Apr 30, 2021
SINGLE STACK NATIONALS
Brooklyn, MI
Brooklyn Sportsman's Club
US PRACTICAL SHOOTING
ASSOCIATION
Phone: 360-855-2245
Fax: 360-855-0380
office@uspsa.org
www.uspsa.org

May TBA, 2021
THE STEEL CHALLENGE WORLD
SPEED SHOOTING CHAMPIO NSHIP
Talladega, AL
US PRACTICAL SHOOTING
ASSOCIATION
Phone: 360-855-2245
Fax: 360-855-0380
office@uspsa.org
www.uspsa.org

Shuffleboard

Feb TBA, 2022
ARIZONA NON-WALKING SINGLES
Mesa Spirit, AZ
NATIONAL SHUFFLEBOARD
ASSOCIATION
usansa.weebly.com

Mar TBA, 2022
CALIFORNIA ANY DOUBLES
Hemet, CA
NATIONAL SHUFFLEBOARD
ASSOCIATION
usansa.weebly.com

Jan 25 - Jan 27, 2021
FLORIDA DOUBLES
Trailer Estates, FL
NATIONAL SHUFFLEBOARD
ASSOCIATION
usansa.weebly.com

May 3 - May 4 2021
FLORIDA DOUBLES
Lakeland, FL
NATIONAL SHUFFLEBOARD
ASSOCIATION
usansa.weebly.com

Jan 4 - Jan 6, 2021
FLORIDA NON-WALKING SINGLES
Lakeland, FL
NATIONAL SHUFFLEBOARD
ASSOCIATION
usansa.weebly.com

Sept 9, 2021
NORTH CAROLINA DOUBLES
Hendersonville, NC
NATIONAL SHUFFLEBOARD
ASSOCIATION
usansa.weebly.com

Sept 16, 2021
NORTH CAROLINA MIXED DOUBLES
Hendersonville, NC
NATIONAL SHUFFLEBOARD
ASSOCIATION
usansa.weebly.com

Sept 13, 2021
NORTH CAROLINA SINGLES
Hendersonville, NC
NATIONAL SHUFFLEBOARD
ASSOCIATION
usansa.weebly.com

Jul 22 - Jul 23, 2021
OHIO DOUBLES
Lakeside, OH
NATIONAL SHUFFLEBOARD
ASSOCIATION
usansa.weebly.com

Jul 21, 2021
OHIO JUNIOR SINGLES 15 & UNDER
Lakeside, OH
NATIONAL SHUFFLEBOARD
ASSOCIATION
usansa.weebly.com

Jun 7 - Jun 8, 2021
OHIO MIXED DOUBLES
Akron, OH
NATIONAL SHUFFLEBOARD
ASSOCIATION
usansa.weebly.com

Jul 19 - Jul 21, 2021
OHIO SINGLES
WALKING/NON-WALKING
Lakeside, OH
NATIONAL SHUFFLEBOARD
ASSOCIATION
usansa.weebly.com

TBA, 2022
TEXAS NON-WALKING SINGLES
San Benito, TX
NATIONAL SHUFFLEBOARD
ASSOCIATION
usansa.weebly.com

Skiing

Mar TBA, 2021
FASTENAL PARALLEL 45 FIS CROSS
COUNTRY WORLD CUP
Minneapolis, MN
U.S. SKI AND SNOWBOARD
ASSOCIATION
Phone: 435-649-9090
Fax: 435-649-3613
membership@usskiandsnowboard.org
usskiandsnowboard.org

Mar 2 - Mar 11, 2021
FIS JUNIOR WORLD CHAMPIONSHIP
Narvik, Norway
FIS SKIING CHAMPIONSHIPS
International Ph: 44-33-244-6161
International Fax: 44-33-244-6171
mail@fisski.ch
www.fis-ski.com

Mar TBA, 2022
FREESTYLE AERIALS NATIONAL
CHAMPIONSHIPS
U.S. SKI AND SNOWBOARD
ASSOCIATION
Phone: 435-649-9090
Fax: 435-649-3613
membership@usskiandsnowboard.org
usskiandsnowboard.org

TBA, 2022
SUPERTOUR FINALS
Vernon, Canada
Sovereign Lake Nordic Center
U.S. SKI AND SNOWBOARD
ASSOCIATION
Phone: 435-649-9090
Fax: 435-649-3613
membership@usskiandsnowboard.org
usskiandsnowboard.org

TBA, 2021
US REVOLUTION TOUR
TBA
U.S. SKI AND SNOWBOARD
ASSOCIATION
Phone: 435-649-9090
Fax: 435-649-3613
membership@usskiandsnowboard.org
usskiandsnowboard.org

Snowboarding

Mar TBA, 2022
AIR NATION FREESTYLE NATIONALS
Calgary, Canada
Winsport Canada Olympic Park
CANADA SNOWBOARD
Fax: 604-568-1639

info@canadasnowboard.ca
www.canadasnowboard.ca

Mar TBA, 2022
SPEED NATION ALPINE NATIONALS
Blue Mountains, Canada
Blue Mountain Resort
CANADA SNOWBOARD
Fax: 604-568-1639
info@canadasnowboard.ca
www.canadasnowboard.ca

Mar TBA, 2022
SPEED NATION SBX NATIONALS
Kelowna, Canada
Big White Ski Resort
CANADA SNOWBOARD
Fax: 604-568-1639
info@canadasnowboard.ca
www.canadasnowboard.ca

Jan TBA, 2022
X GAMES ASPEN
Aspen, CO
ESPN
xgames.espn.com/xgames

TBA, 2022
X GAMES MINNEAPOLIS
Minneapolis, MN
ESPN
xgames.espn.com/xgames

Soccer

TBA, 2022
CANADIAN CHAMPIONSHIP
TBA, Canada
CANADIAN SOCCER ASSOCIATION
Phone: 613-237-7678
Fax: 613-237-1516
info@soccercan.ca
www.canadasoccer.com

Apr TBA, 2022
FUTSAL CANADIAN CHAMPIONSHIP
TBA, Canada
CANADIAN SOCCER ASSOCIATION
Phone: 613-237-7678
Fax: 613-237-1516
info@soccercan.ca
www.canadasoccer.com

May 13 - May 17, 2021
NCAA DIVISION I MEN'S SOCCER
FINALS
Cary, NC
WakeMed Soccer Park
NATIONAL COLLEGIATE ATHLETIC
ASSOCIATION
Phone: 317-917-6222
Fax: 317-917-6888
www.ncaa.org

TBA, 2021
NCAA DIVISION II MEN'S SOCCER
FINALS
NATIONAL COLLEGIATE ATHLETIC
ASSOCIATION
Phone: 317-917-6222
Fax: 317-917-6888
www.ncaa.org

TBA, 2021
NCAA DIVISION III MEN'S SOCCER
FINALS
NATIONAL COLLEGIATE ATHLETIC
ASSOCIATION
Phone: 317-917-6222

Fax: 317-917-6888
www.ncaa.org

TBA, 2021
NCAA DIVISION III WOMEN'S
SOCCER FINALS
NATIONAL COLLEGIATE ATHLETIC
ASSOCIATION
Phone: 317-917-6222
Fax: 317-917-6888
www.ncaa.org

Oct TBA, 2021
TOYOTA NATIONAL
CHAMPIONSHIPS U15 CUP
TBA, Canada
CANADIAN SOCCER ASSOCIATION
Phone: 613-237-7678
Fax: 613-237-1516
info@soccercan.ca
www.canadasoccer.com

Oct TBA, 2021
TOYOTA NATIONAL
CHAMPIONSHIPS U17 CUP
TBA, Canada
CANADIAN SOCCER ASSOCIATION
Phone: 613-237-7678
Fax: 613-237-1516
info@soccercan.ca
www.canadasoccer.com

Softball

Jul 18 - Jul 24, 2021
GIRLS 18 AND UNDER GOLD
NATIONAL CHAMPIONSHIP
Salem, VA
USA SOFTBALL
Phone: 405-424-5266
Fax: 405-424-3855
rcress@softball.org
www.teamusa.org/USA-Softball

Jun 3 - Jun 9, 2021
NCAA DIVISION I SOFTBALL FINALS
Oklahoma City, OK
USA Softball Hall of Fame Stadium
NATIONAL COLLEGIATE ATHLETIC
ASSOCIATION
Phone: 317-917-6222
Fax: 317-917-6888
www.ncaa.org

May 27 - May 31, 2021
NCAA DIVISION II SOFTBALL FINALS
Denver, CO
The Regency Athletic Complex
NATIONAL COLLEGIATE ATHLETIC
ASSOCIATION
Phone: 317-917-6222
Fax: 317-917-6888
www.ncaa.org

May 27 - Jun 1, 2021
NCAA DIVISION III SOFTBALL FINALS
Salem, VA
Moyer Park
NATIONAL COLLEGIATE ATHLETIC
ASSOCIATION
Phone: 317-917-6222
Fax: 317-917-6888
www.ncaa.org

Jul TBA, 2021
USA SOFTBALL INTERNATIONAL
CUP
USA SOFTBALL
Phone: 405-424-5266

info@softball.org
www.usasoftball.com

Aug 20 - Aug 22, 2021
WOMEN'S OPEN SLOW PITCH
NATIONAL CHAMPIONSHIP
Henderson, TN
USA SOFTBALL
Phone: 405-424-5266
Fax: 405-424-3855
rcress@softball.org
www.teamusa.org/USA-Softball

Speedskating

Feb TBA, 2022
CANADA MASTERS SPRINT
CHAMPIONSHIPS
Shelton, CT
US SPEEDSKATING
Phone: 801-417-5360
Fax: 801-417-5361
www.teamusa.org/us-speedskating

Jan TBA, 2022
CANADIAN JUNIOR LONG TRACK
CHAMPIONSHIPS
TBA
SPEED SKATING CANADA
Phone: 613-260-3669
Fax: 613-260-3660
ssc@speedskating.ca
www.speedskating.ca

Jan 18 - Feb 18, 2021
CANADIAN YOUTH LONG TRACK
CHAMPIONSHIPS
SPEED SKATING CANADA
Phone: 613-260-3669
Fax: 613-260-3660
ssc@speedskating.ca
www.speedskating.ca

Feb 22 - Mar 28, 2021
CANADIAN YOUTH SHORT TRACK
CHAMPIONSHIPS
SPEED SKATING CANADA
Phone: 613-260-3669
Fax: 613-260-3660
ssc@speedskating.ca
www.speedskating.ca

Mar TBA, 2021
COLOMBIAN SPEEDSKATING
CHAMPIONSHIPS
Colorado Springs, CO
US SPEEDSKATING
Phone: 801-417-5360
Fax: 801-417-5361
www.teamusa.org/us-speedskating

Mar TBA, 2022
US LONG TRACK AMCUP FINAL &
MASTERS CHAMPIONSHIP S
Kearns, UT
US SPEEDSKATING
Phone: 801-417-5360
Fax: 801-417-5361
www.teamusa.org/us-speedskating

Jan TBA, 2022
US SHORT TRACK CHAMPIONSHIPS
& JUNIOR CHAMPIONSH IPS
Kearns, UT
US SPEEDSKATING
Phone: 801-417-5360
Fax: 801-417-5361
www.teamusa.org/us-speedskating

Jun TBA, 2022
US SPEEDSKATING CONGRESS
US SPEEDSKATING
Phone: 801-417-5360
Fax: 801-417-5361
www.teamusa.org/us-speedskating

TBA, 2022
WORLD ALLROUND
CHAMPIONSHIPS
Hamar, Norway
Vikingskipet
US SPEEDSKATING
Phone: 801-417-5360
Fax: 801-417-5361
www.teamusa.org/us-speedskating

Mar TBA, 2022
WORLD SHORT TRACK
CHAMPIONSHIPS
US SPEEDSKATING
Phone: 801-417-5360
Fax: 801-417-5361
www.teamusa.org/us-speedskating

Feb TBA, 2022
WORLD SPRINT CHAMPIONSHIPS
US SPEEDSKATING
Phone: 801-417-5360
Fax: 801-417-5361
www.teamusa.org/us-speedskating

Squash

May 21 - May 24, 2021
CANADIAN JUNIOR CLOSED
CHAMPIONSHIPS
Ottawa, Canada
SQUASH CANADA
Phone: 613-228-7724
Fax: 613-228-7232
info@squash.ca
www.squash.ca

Jun 15 - Jun 19, 2021
CANADIAN MEN'S TEAM
CHAMPIONSHIP
Niagara-On-The-Lake, Canada
The Club at White Oaks
SQUASH CANADA
Phone: 613-228-7724
Fax: 613-228-7232
info@squash.ca
www.squash.ca

Apr TBA, 2022
CANADIAN MIXED DOUBLES
CHAMPIONSHIPS
TBA
SQUASH CANADA
Phone: 613-228-7724
Fax: 613-228-7232
info@squash.ca
www.squash.ca

Jun 16 - Jun 20, 2021
CANADIAN SQUASH
CHAMPIONSHIPS
Niagara-On-The-Lake, Canada
The Club at White Oaks
SQUASH CANADA
Phone: 613-228-7724
Fax: 613-228-7232
info@squash.ca
www.squash.ca

Jun 15 - Jun 19, 2021
CANADIAN WOMEN'S TEAM
CHAMPIONSHIP
Niagara-On-The-Lake, Canada
The Club at White Oaks
SQUASH CANADA
Phone: 613-228-7724
Fax: 613-228-7232
info@squash.ca
www.squash.ca

TBA, 2021
US FATHER-SON &
MOTHER-DAUGHTER SQUASH
DOUBLES C HAMPIONSHIPS
UNITED STATES SQUASH RACQUETS
ASSOCIATION
Phone: 212-268-4090
Fax: 212-268-4091
office@ussquash.com
www.ussquash.com

TBA, 2022
US JUNIOR BRONZE
CHAMPIONSHIPS
UNITED STATES SQUASH RACQUETS
ASSOCIATION
Phone: 212-268-4090
Fax: 212-268-4091
office@ussquash.com
www.ussquash.com

TBA, 2022
US JUNIOR DOUBLES SQUASH
CHAMPIONSHIPS
UNITED STATES SQUASH RACQUETS
ASSOCIATION
Phone: 212-268-4090
Fax: 212-268-4091
office@ussquash.com
www.ussquash.com

TBA, 2022
US JUNIOR SILVER CHAMPIONSHIPS
UNITED STATES SQUASH RACQUETS
ASSOCIATION
Phone: 212-268-4090
Fax: 212-268-4091
office@ussquash.com
www.ussquash.com

TBA, 2022
US MIXED DOUBLES & HARDBALL
SINGLES CHAMPIONSHIP S
UNITED STATES SQUASH RACQUETS
ASSOCIATION
Phone: 212-268-4090
Fax: 212-268-4091
office@ussquash.com
www.ussquash.com

TBA, 2022
US NATIONAL SQUASH
CHAMPIONSHIPS
UNITED STATES SQUASH RACQUETS
ASSOCIATION
Phone: 212-268-4090
Fax: 212-268-4091
office@ussquash.com
www.ussquash.com

Surfing

Dec TBA, 2021
BILLABONG PIPE MASTERS
Oahu, Hawaii
Banzai Pipeline
WORLD SURF LEAGUE
International Ph: +1-310-450-1212

asp@aspworldtour.com
www.worldsurfleague.com

Sept 27 - Oct 3, 2021
QUICKSILVER PRO
France
WORLD SURF LEAGUE
International Ph: +1-310-450-1212
asp@aspworldtour.com
www.worldsurfleague.com

TBA, 2022
RIP CURL PRO BELLS BEACH
Bells Beach, Victoria, Australia
WORLD SURF LEAGUE
International Ph: +1-310-450-1212
asp@aspworldtour.com
www.worldsurfleague.com

Sept 23 - Sept 26, 2021
ROXY JUNIOR PRO
France
WORLD SURF LEAGUE
International Ph: +1-310-450-1212
asp@aspworldtour.com
www.worldsurfleague.com

Aug 23 - Sept 2, 2021
TAHITI PRO TEAHUPO'O
Teahupo'o, Tahiti
WORLD SURF LEAGUE
International Ph: +1-310-450-1212
asp@aspworldtour.com
www.worldsurfleague.com

Swimming

Jul 26 - Aug 2, 2021
2021 CANADIAN JUNIOR
CHAMPIONSHIPS
Calgary, Canada
Repsol Centre
SWIMMING CANADA
Phone: 613-260-1348
Fax: 613-260-0804
natloffice@swimming.ca
www.swimming.ca

Apr 21 - Apr 24, 2021
2022 SPEEDO EASTERN CANADIAN
CHAMPIONSHIPS
SWIMMING CANADA
Phone: 613-260-1348
Fax: 613-260-0804
natloffice@swimming.ca
www.swimming.ca

Apr 21 - Apr 24, 2021
2022 SPEEDO WESTERN CANADIAN
CHAMPIONSHIPS
SWIMMING CANADA
Phone: 613-260-1348
Fax: 613-260-0804
natloffice@swimming.ca
www.swimming.ca

Jun 5, 2021
ALCATRAZ SHARKFEST SWIM
San Francisco, CA
Alcatraz Island
ENVIRO-SPORTS
Phone: 415-868-1829
info@envirosports.com
envirosports.com

TBA, 2022
CANADIAN SWIMMING
CHAMPIONSHIPS
SWIMMING CANADA
Phone: 613-260-1348

Fax: 613-260-0804
natloffice@swimming.ca
www.swimming.ca

May 13 - May 29, 2022
FINA WORLD AQUATIC
CHAMPIONSHIPS
TBA
USA SWIMMING
Phone: 719-866-4578
Fax: 719-866-4049
imclemore@usaswimming.org
www.usaswimming.org

Sept 11, 2021
GOLDEN GATE SHARKFEST SWIM
Sausalito, CA
Under the Golden Gate Bridge
ENVIRO-SPORTS
Phone: 415-868-1829
info@envirosports.com
envirosports.com

Dec 11, 2021
HARK THE HERALD ANGELS HALF
MARATHON & 10K
Tiburon, CA
Angel Island State Park
ENVIRO-SPORTS
Phone: 415-868-1829
info@envirosports.com
envirosports.com

Jul 10, 2021
LADY LIBERTY SHARKFEST SWIM
Jersey City, NJ
Liberty State Park
ENVIRO-SPORTS
Phone: 415-868-1829
info@envirosports.com
envirosports.com

Aug 8, 2021
LAKE TAHOE SHARKFEST SWIM
Incline Village, NV
Sand Harbour State Park
ENVIRO-SPORTS
Phone: 415-868-1829
info@envirosports.com
envirosports.com

Jul 18, 2021
MYSTIC SHARKFEST SWIM
Mystic, CT
Mystic Harbor
ENVIRO-SPORTS
Phone: 415-868-1829
info@envirosports.com
envirosports.com

Mar 24 - Mar 27, 2021
NCAA DIVISION I MEN'S SWIMMING &
DIVING FINALS
Greensboro, NC
Greensboro Aquatic Center
NATIONAL COLLEGIATE ATHLETIC
ASSOCIATION
Phone: 317-917-6222
Fax: 317-917-6888
www.ncaa.org

Mar 17 - Mar 20, 2021
NCAA DIVISION I WOMEN'S
SWIMMING & DIVING FINALS
Greensboro, NC
Greensboro Aquatic Center
NATIONAL COLLEGIATE ATHLETIC
ASSOCIATION
Phone: 317-917-6222
Fax: 317-917-6888
www.ncaa.org

Mar 17 - Mar 20, 2021
NCAA DIVISION II MEN/WOMEN'S
SWIMMING & DIVING F INALS
Birmingham, AL
Birmingham CrossPlex
NATIONAL COLLEGIATE ATHLETIC
ASSOCIATION
Phone: 317-917-6222
Fax: 317-917-6888
www.ncaa.org

TBA, 2021
NCAA DIVISION III MEN'S/WOMEN'S
SWIMMING & DIVIN G FINALS
NATIONAL COLLEGIATE ATHLETIC
ASSOCIATION
Phone: 317-917-6222
Fax: 317-917-6888
www.ncaa.org

Apr 16 - Apr 18, 2021
OPEN WATER NATIONALS &
JUNIORS
Fort Myers, FL
USA SWIMMING
Phone: 719-866-4578
Fax: 719-866-4049
imclemore@usaswimming.org
www.usaswimming.org

Jun 12, 2021
ROMANCING THE ISLAND HALF
MARATHON & 10K
Tiburon, CA
Angel Island State Park
ENVIRO-SPORTS
Phone: 415-868-1829
info@envirosports.com
envirosports.com

Oct 10, 2021
SAN DIEGO SHARKFEST SWIM
San Diego, CA
San Diego Harbor
ENVIRO-SPORTS
Phone: 415-868-1829
info@envirosports.com
envirosports.com

Dec TBA, 2021
SPEEDO WINTER JR.
CHAMPIONSHIPS
TBA
USA SWIMMING
Phone: 719-866-4578
Fax: 719-866-4049
imclemore@usaswimming.org
www.usaswimming.org

Apr 29 - May 2, 2021
TYR 18 & UNDER SPRING CUP
USA SWIMMING
Phone: 719-866-4578
Fax: 719-866-4049
imclemore@usaswimming.org
www.usaswimming.org

May 12 - May 15, 2021
TYR PRO SWIM SERIES
INDIANAPOLIS
Indianapolis, IN
USA SWIMMING
Phone: 719-866-4578
Fax: 719-866-4049
imclemore@usaswimming.org
www.usaswimming.org

Apr 8 - Apr 11, 2021
TYR PRO SWIM SERIES MISSION
VIEJO
Mission Viejo, CA
USA SWIMMING
Phone: 719-866-4578
Fax: 719-866-4049
imclemore@usaswimming.org
www.usaswimming.org

Taekwondo

Jul 4 - Jul 10, 2021
AAU TAEKWONDO NATIONAL
CHAMPIONSHIPS
Las Vegas, NV
MGM Grand Hotel & Resort
AMATEUR ATHLETIC UNION
Phone: 407-934-7200
Fax: 407-934-7242
www.aausports.org

Apr 17, 2021
NATIONAL COLLEGIATE
TAEKWONDO CHAMPIONSHIPS
NATIONAL COLLEGIATE TAEKWONDO
ASSOCIATION
ncta-usa.com

TBA, 2022
USA TAEKWONDO NATIONAL
CHAMPIONSHIPS
USA TAEKWONDO
Phone: 719-866-4632
Fax: 719-866-4642
www.teamusa.org/usa-taekwondo

Tennis

Sept 17 - Sept 25, 2021
2021 DONGFENG MOTOR WUHAN
OPEN
Wuhan, China
WTA
Phone: 727-895-5000
Fax: 727-894-1982
feedback@wtatennis.com
www.wtatennis.com

Apr 12 - Apr 18, 2021
2021 KUNMING OPEN
Anning, China
WTA
Phone: 727-895-5000
Fax: 727-894-1982
feedback@wtatennis.com
www.wtatennis.com

Aug 30 - Sept 12, 2021
2021 US OPEN TENNIS
CHAMPIONSHIPS
Flushing Meadows, NY
WTA
Phone: 727-895-5000
Fax: 727-894-1982
feedback@wtatennis.com
www.wtatennis.com

Jul 19 - Jul 25, 2021
30 PALERMO LADIES OPEN
Palermo, Italy
WTA
Phone: 727-895-5000
Fax: 727-894-1982
feedback@wtatennis.com
www.wtatennis.com

Mar 12 - Mar 15, 2021
ABIERTO GNP SEGUROS
Monterrey, Mexico
WTA
Phone: 727-895-5000
Fax: 727-894-1982
feedback@wtatennis.com
www.wtatennis.com

Mar 15 - Mar 20, 2021
ABIERTO MEXICANO
Acapulco, Gro, Mexico
Princess Mundo Imperial
ATP WORLD TOUR 500
www.atpworldtour.com

Mar 15 - Mar 20, 2021
ABIERTO MEXICANO TELCEL
PRESENTADO POR HSBC
Acapulco, Mexico
WTA
Phone: 727-895-5000
Fax: 727-894-1982
feedback@wtatennis.com
www.wtatennis.com

Mar 8 - Mar 13, 2021
ABIERTO ZAPOPAN 2021
Zapopan, Mexico
WTA
Phone: 727-895-5000
Fax: 727-894-1982
feedback@wtatennis.com
www.wtatennis.com

Feb 1 - Feb 27, 2021
ADELAIDE INTERNATIONAL
Adelaide, Australia
WTA
Phone: 727-895-5000
Fax: 727-894-1982
feedback@wtatennis.com
www.wtatennis.com

Jan TBA, 2022
ASB CLASSIC (M)
Auckland, New Zealand
ATP TOUR 250
www.atptour.com

TBA, 2022
ASB CLASSIC 2022
WTA
Phone: 727-895-5000
Fax: 727-894-1982
feedback@wtatennis.com
www.wtatennis.com

Mar 11 - Mar 21, 2021
ATP TOUR MASTERS 1000 - BNP
PARIBAS OPEN
Indian Wells, CA
ATP TOUR MASTERS 1000
www.atptour.com

May 9 - May 16, 2021
ATP TOUR MASTERS 1000 -
INTERNAZIONALI BNL D'ITA LIA
Rome, Italy
ATP TOUR MASTERS 1000
www.atptour.com

Mar 24 - Apr 4, 2021
ATP TOUR MASTERS 1000 - MIAMI
OPEN
Miami, FL
ATP TOUR MASTERS 1000
www.atptour.com

Apr 11 - Apr 18, 2021
ATP TOUR MASTERS 1000 -
MONTE-CARLO ROLEX MASTERS
Monte Carlo, Monaco
ATP TOUR MASTERS 1000
www.atptour.com

May 2 - May 9, 2021
ATP TOUR MASTERS 1000 - MUTUA
MADRID OPEN
Madrid, Spain
ATP TOUR MASTERS 1000
www.atptour.com

Aug 9 - Aug 15, 2021
ATP TOUR MASTERS 1000 - ROGERS
CUP
Toronto, Canada
ATP TOUR MASTERS 1000
www.atptour.com

Oct 10 - Oct 17, 2021
ATP TOUR MASTERS 1000 -
SHANGHAI ROLEX MASTERS
Shanghai, China
ATP TOUR MASTERS 1000
www.atptour.com

Aug 15 - Aug 22, 2021
ATP TOUR MASTERS 1000 -
WESTERN & SOUTHERN OPEN
Cincinnati, OH
ATP TOUR MASTERS 1000
www.atptour.com

Feb 8 - Feb 21, 2021
AUSTRALIAN OPEN
Melbourne, Australia
TENNIS AUSTRALIA
International Ph: +61-3-9914-4677
www.tennis.com.au

Jun 20 - Jun 26, 2021
BAD HOMBURG OPEN
Bad Homburg, Germany
WTA
Phone: 727-895-5000
Fax: 727-894-1982
feedback@wtatennis.com
www.wtatennis.com

TBA 2021
BALTIC OPEN
WTA
Phone: 727-895-5000
Fax: 727-894-1982
feedback@wtatennis.com
www.wtatennis.com

Oct TBA, 2021
BGL BNP PARIBAS LUXEMBOURG
OPEN
Luxembourg
WTA
Phone: 727-895-5000
Fax: 727-894-1982
feedback@wtatennis.com
www.wtatennis.com

Apr TBA, 2021
BILLIE JEAN KING CUP
Switzerland
TENNIS CANADA
Phone: 416-665-9777
Fax: 416-665-9017
info@tenniscanada.com
www.tenniscanada.com

Jun 14 - Jun 20, 2021
BIRMINGHAM CLASSIC
Birmingham, Great Britain

WTA
Phone: 727-895-5000
Fax: 727-894-1982
feedback@wtatennis.com
www.wtatennis.com

TBA, 2021
BNP PARIBAS OPEN
Indian Wells, CA
WTA
Phone: 727-895-5000
Fax: 727-894-1982
feedback@wtatennis.com
www.wtatennis.com

Dec TBA, 2021
BRISBANE INTERNATIONAL
Brisbane, Australia
ATP TOUR 250
www.atptour.com

Jan TBA, 2022
BRISBANE INTERNATIONAL
Brisbane, Australia
WTA
Phone: 727-895-5000
Fax: 727-894-1982
feedback@wtatennis.com
www.wtatennis.com

TBA, 2021
CALGARY NATIONAL BANK ATP
CHALLENGER 90
Calgary, Canada
TENNIS CANADA
Phone: 416-665-9777
Fax: 416-665-9017
info@tenniscanada.com
www.tenniscanada.com

May 23 - Jun 6, 2021
CHAMPIONNATS INTERNATIONAUX
DE FRANCE
Paris, France
WTA
Phone: 727-895-5000
Fax: 727-894-1982
feedback@wtatennis.com
www.wtatennis.com

Nov 25 - Nov 28, 2021
CHAMPIONS TENNIS
London, United Kingdom
Royal Albert Hall
ATP CHAMPIONS TOUR
www.atpchampionstour.com

Oct 3 - Oct 10, 2021
CHINA OPEN
Beijing, China
WTA
Phone: 727-895-5000
Fax: 727-894-1982
feedback@wtatennis.com
www.wtatennis.com

Jul 31 - Aug 8, 2021
CITI OPEN
Washington, DC
WTA
Phone: 727-895-5000
Fax: 727-894-1982
feedback@wtatennis.com
www.wtatennis.com

Apr 5 - Apr 11, 2021
COPA COLSANITAS
Bogota, Colombia
WTA
Phone: 727-895-5000
Fax: 727-894-1982

feedback@wtatennis.com
www.wtatennis.com

May 31 - Jun 6, 2021
CROATIA BOL OPEN
Bol, Croatia
WTA
Phone: 727-895-5000
Fax: 727-894-1982
feedback@wtatennis.com
www.wtatennis.com

Nov 25 - Dec 5, 2021
DAVIS CUP FINAL
Madrid, Spain
La Caja Magica
INTERNATIONAL TENNIS FEDERATION
International Ph: +44 (0)20 88786464
International Fax: +44 (0)20 88787799
communications@itftennis.com
www.itftennis.com

Apr TBA, 2021
DAVIS CUP QUARTERFINALS
INTERNATIONAL TENNIS FEDERATION
International Ph: +44 (0)20 88786464
International Fax: +44 (0)20 88787799
communications@itftennis.com
www.itftennis.com

Sept TBA, 2021
DAVIS CUP SEMIFINALS
INTERNATIONAL TENNIS FEDERATION
International Ph: +44 (0)20 88786464
International Fax: +44 (0)20 88787799
communications@itftennis.com
www.itftennis.com

Feb 11 - Feb 20, 2022
DELRAY BEACH OPEN
Delray Beach, FL
The Delray Beach Stadium & Tennis
Centre
ATP CHAMPIONS TOUR
www.atpchampionstour.com

Jan 7 - Jan 13, 2021
DELRAY BEACH OPEN
Delray Beach, FL
ATP TOUR 250
www.atptour.com

TBA, 2021
DRUMMONDVILLE NATIONAL BANK
ATP CHALLENGER 80
Drummondville, Canada
TENNIS CANADA
Phone: 416-665-9777
Fax: 416-665-9017
info@tenniscanada.com
www.tenniscanada.com

Mar 6 - Mar 20, 2021
DUBAI DUTY FREE TENNIS
CHAMPIONSHIPS
Dubai, United Arab Emirates
Dubai Duty Free Tennis Stadium
ATP WORLD TOUR 500
www.atpworldtour.com

Mar 6 - Mar 20, 2021
DUBAI DUTY FREE TENNIS
CHAMPIONSHIPS
Dubai, UAE
WTA
Phone: 727-895-5000
Fax: 727-894-1982
feedback@wtatennis.com
www.wtatennis.com

events/meetings/shows

Jun 21 - Jun 27, 2021
EASTBOURNE INTERNATIONAL
Eastbourne, Great Britain
WTA
Phone: 727-895-5000
Fax: 727-894-1982
feedback@wtatennis.com
www.wtatennis.com

May 16 - May 22, 2021
GRAND PRIX DE SAR LA PRINCESSE
LALLA MERYEM
Rabat, Morocco
WTA
Phone: 727-895-5000
Fax: 727-894-1982
feedback@wtatennis.com
www.wtatennis.com

Sept TBA, 2021
GUANGZHOU INTERNATIONAL
WOMEN'S OPEN
Guangzhou, China
WTA
Phone: 727-895-5000
Fax: 727-894-1982
feedback@wtatennis.com
www.wtatennis.com

Sept TBA, 2021
HANA-CUPID JAPAN WOMEN'S OPEN
Hiroshima, Japan
WTA
Phone: 727-895-5000
Fax: 727-894-1982
feedback@wtatennis.com
www.wtatennis.com

Oct TBA, 2021
HENGQIN LIFE WTA ELITE TROPHY
ZHUHAI 2020
Zhuhai, China
WTA
Phone: 727-895-5000
Fax: 727-894-1982
feedback@wtatennis.com
www.wtatennis.com

Jan TBA, 2022
HOBART INTERNATIONAL
Hobart, Australia
WTA
Phone: 727-895-5000
Fax: 727-894-1982
feedback@wtatennis.com
www.wtatennis.com

May 15 - May 22, 2021
INTERNATIONAUX DE STRASBOURG
Strasbourg, France
WTA
Phone: 727-895-5000
Fax: 727-894-1982
feedback@wtatennis.com
www.wtatennis.com

May 9 - May 16, 2021
INTERNAZIONALI BNL D'ITALIA
Rome, Italy
WTA
Phone: 727-895-5000
Fax: 727-894-1982
feedback@wtatennis.com
www.wtatennis.com

Apr 19 - Apr 25, 2021
ISTANBUL OPEN
Istanbul, Turkey
WTA
Phone: 727-895-5000
Fax: 727-894-1982

feedback@wtatennis.com
www.wtatennis.com

Jul 12 - Jul 18, 2021
J&T BANKA PRAGUE OPEN
Prague, Czech Republic
WTA
Phone: 727-895-5000
Fax: 727-894-1982
feedback@wtatennis.com
www.wtatennis.com

Sept TBA, 2021
JIANGXI OPEN
Nanchang, China
WTA
Phone: 727-895-5000
Fax: 727-894-1982
feedback@wtatennis.com
www.wtatennis.com

Sept TBA, 2021
KEB HANA BANK KOREA OPEN
Seoul, Korea
WTA
Phone: 727-895-5000
Fax: 727-894-1982
feedback@wtatennis.com
www.wtatennis.com

Jul 10 - Jul 18, 2021
LADIES OPEN LAUSANNE
Lausanne, Switzerland
WTA
Phone: 727-895-5000
Fax: 727-894-1982
feedback@wtatennis.com
www.wtatennis.com

Oct 3 - Oct 6, 2021
LEGENDS CUP
Mallorca, Spain
Palma Sport & Tennis Club
ATP CHAMPIONS TOUR
www.atpchampionstour.com

Jun 5 - Jun 13, 2021
LIBEMA OPEN
's-Hertogenbosch, Netherlands
WTA
Phone: 727-895-5000
Fax: 727-894-1982
feedback@wtatennis.com
www.wtatennis.com

Jul TBA, 2022
LIQUI MOLY OPEN KARLSRUHE
Karlsruhe, Germany
WTA
Phone: 727-895-5000
Fax: 727-894-1982
feedback@wtatennis.com
www.wtatennis.com

Mar 22 - Apr 4, 2021
MIAMI OPEN PRESENTED BY ITAU
Miami, FL
WTA
Phone: 727-895-5000
Fax: 727-894-1982
feedback@wtatennis.com
www.wtatennis.com

Aug 2 - Aug 8, 2021
MUBADALA SILICON VALLEY
San Jose, CA
WTA
Phone: 727-895-5000
Fax: 727-894-1982
feedback@wtatennis.com
www.wtatennis.com

Apr 30 - May 9, 2021
MUTUA MADRID OPEN
Madrid, Spain
WTA
Phone: 727-895-5000
Fax: 727-894-1982
feedback@wtatennis.com
www.wtatennis.com

May 20 - May 29, 2021
NCAA DIVISION I MEN'S/WOMEN'S
TENNIS FINALS
Orlando, FL
USTA National Campus
NATIONAL COLLEGIATE ATHLETIC
ASSOCIATION
Phone: 317-917-6222
Fax: 317-917-6888
www.ncaa.org

May 18 - May 22, 2021
NCAA DIVISION II MEN'S/WOMEN'S
TENNIS FINALS
Surprise, AZ
Surprise Tennis & Racquet Complex
NATIONAL COLLEGIATE ATHLETIC
ASSOCIATION
Phone: 317-917-6222
Fax: 317-917-6888
www.ncaa.org

May 24 - May 30, 2021
NCAA DIVISION III MEN'S/WOMEN'S
TENNIS FINALS
Claremont, CA
Biszantz Family Tennis Center
NATIONAL COLLEGIATE ATHLETIC
ASSOCIATION
Phone: 317-917-6222
Fax: 317-917-6888
www.ncaa.org

Jul 5 - Jul 18, 2021
NORDEA OPEN
Bastad, Sweden
WTA
Phone: 727-895-5000
Fax: 727-894-1982
feedback@wtatennis.com
www.wtatennis.com

Jun 5 - Jun 13, 2021
NOTTINGHAM OPEN
Nottingham, Great Britain
Nottingham Tennis Centre
WTA
Phone: 727-895-5000
Fax: 727-894-1982
feedback@wtatennis.com
www.wtatennis.com

Mar 1 - Mar 7, 2021
OPEN 6EM SENS - METROPOLE DE
LYON, FRANCE
Lyon, France
WTA
Phone: 727-895-5000
Fax: 727-894-1982
feedback@wtatennis.com
www.wtatennis.com

Dec TBA, 2021
OPEN BLS DE LIMOGES
Limoges, France
WTA
Phone: 727-895-5000
Fax: 727-894-1982
feedback@wtatennis.com
www.wtatennis.com

TBA, 2021
ORACLE CHALLENGER SERIES
Newport Beach, CA
WTA
Phone: 727-895-5000
Fax: 727-894-1982
feedback@wtatennis.com
www.wtatennis.com

TBA, 2021
ORACLE CHALLENGER SERIES
Indian Wells, CA
WTA
Phone: 727-895-5000
Fax: 727-894-1982
feedback@wtatennis.com
www.wtatennis.com

TBA, 2021
ORACLE CHALLENGER SERIES
New Haven, CT
WTA
Phone: 727-895-5000
Fax: 727-894-1982
feedback@wtatennis.com
www.wtatennis.com

TBA, 2021
ORACLE CHALLENGER SERIES
Houston, TX
WTA
Phone: 727-895-5000
Fax: 727-894-1982
feedback@wtatennis.com
www.wtatennis.com

Apr 19 - Apr 25, 2021
PORSCHE TENNIS GRAND PRIX
Stuttgart, Germany
WTA
Phone: 727-895-5000
Fax: 727-894-1982
feedback@wtatennis.com
www.wtatennis.com

Oct TBA, 2021
PRUDENTIAL HONG KONG TENNIS
OPEN
Hong Kong, China
WTA
Phone: 727-895-5000
Fax: 727-894-1982
feedback@wtatennis.com
www.wtatennis.com

Mar 1 - Mar 6, 2021
QATAR TOTAL OPEN
Doha, Qatar
WTA
Phone: 727-895-5000
Fax: 727-894-1982
feedback@wtatennis.com
www.wtatennis.com

Aug 6 - Aug 15, 2021
ROGERS CUP PRESENTED BY
NATIONAL BANK
Montreal, Canada
WTA
Phone: 727-895-5000
Fax: 727-894-1982
feedback@wtatennis.com
www.wtatennis.com

May 17 - Jun 6, 2021
ROLAND GARROS
Paris, France
Stade Roland Garros
FRENCH TENNIS FEDERATION
www.fft.fr

TBA, 2021
SHENZHEN OPEN
Shenzhen, China
WTA
Phone: 727-895-5000
Fax: 727-894-1982
feedback@wtatennis.com
www.wtatennis.com

Nov TBA, 2021
SHISEIDO WTA FINALS SHENZHEN
Shenzhen, China
WTA
Phone: 727-895-5000
Fax: 727-894-1982
feedback@wtatennis.com
www.wtatennis.com

Mar 15 - Mar 21, 2021
ST. PETERSBURG LADIES TROPHY
St. Petersburg, Russia
WTA
Phone: 727-895-5000
Fax: 727-894-1982
feedback@wtatennis.com
www.wtatennis.com

Oct TBA, 2021
TAIPEI OEC OPEN
Taipei, Chinese Taipei
WTA
Phone: 727-895-5000
Fax: 727-894-1982
feedback@wtatennis.com
www.wtatennis.com

Sept TBA, 2021
TASHKENT OPEN
Tashkent, Uzbekistan
WTA
Phone: 727-895-5000
Fax: 727-894-1982
feedback@wtatennis.com
www.wtatennis.com

Feb 8 - Feb 14, 2021
THAILAND OPEN
Hua Hin, Thailand
WTA
Phone: 727-895-5000
Fax: 727-894-1982
feedback@wtatennis.com
www.wtatennis.com

Jun 28 - Jul 11, 2021
THE CHAMPIONSHIPS
Wimbledon, Great Britain
WTA
Phone: 727-895-5000
Fax: 727-894-1982
feedback@wtatennis.com
www.wtatennis.com

Oct TBA, 2021
TIANJIN OPEN
Tianjin, China
WTA
Phone: 727-895-5000
Fax: 727-894-1982
feedback@wtatennis.com
www.wtatennis.com

Sept TBA, 2021
TORAY PAN PACIFIC OPEN
Tokyo, Japan
WTA
Phone: 727-895-5000
Fax: 727-894-1982
feedback@wtatennis.com
www.wtatennis.com

Oct 10 - Oct 17, 2021
UPPER AUSTRIA LADIES LINZ
Linz, Austria
WTA
Phone: 727-895-5000
Fax: 727-894-1982
feedback@wtatennis.com
www.wtatennis.com

Aug 30 - Sept 12, 2021
US OPEN
UNITED STATES TENNIS
ASSOCIATION
Phone: 914-696-7000
www.usta.com

Apr TBA, 2022
VLTBC ITF INDOOR MASTERS
CHAMPIONSHIPS
INTERNATIONAL TENNIS FEDERATION
International Ph: +44 (0)20 88786464
International Fax: +44 (0)20 88787799
communications@itftennis.com
www.itftennis.com

Apr 3 - Apr 11, 2021
VOLVO CAR OPEN
Charleston, SC
WTA
Phone: 727-895-5000
Fax: 727-894-1982
feedback@wtatennis.com
www.wtatennis.com

Oct 18 - Oct 24, 2021
VTB KREMLIN CUP
Moscow, Russia
WTA
Phone: 727-895-5000
Fax: 727-894-1982
feedback@wtatennis.com
www.wtatennis.com

Aug 14 - Aug 22, 2021
WESTERN & SOUTHERN OPEN
Cincinnati, OH
WTA
Phone: 727-895-5000
Fax: 727-894-1982
feedback@wtatennis.com
www.wtatennis.com

Jun 28 - Jul 11, 2021
WIMBLEDON
London, United Kingdom
THE ALL ENGLAND LAWN TENNIS
CLUB
International Ph: +44 (0)20 89441066
International Fax: +44 (0)20 89478752
www.wimbledon.com

Sept 13 - Sept 19, 2021
ZHENGZHOU OPEN
Zhengzhou, China
WTA
Phone: 727-895-5000
Fax: 727-894-1982
feedback@wtatennis.com
www.wtatennis.com

Timbersports

TBA, 2021
STIHL TIMBERSPORTS CANADIAN
CHAMPIONSHIP
STIHL TIMBERSPORTS
www.stihlusa.com/stihl-timbersports

events/meetings/shows

TBA, 2021
STIHL TIMBERSPORTS CHAMPIONS
TROPHY
STIHL TIMBERSPORTS
www.stihlusa.com/stihl-timbersports

TBA, 2021
STIHL TIMBERSPORTS WORLD
CHAMPIONSHIP
STIHL TIMBERSPORTS
www.stihlusa.com/stihl-timbersports

Track & Field

Mar 12 - Mar 14, 2021
AAU INDOOR TRACK & FIELD
NATIONAL CHAMPIONSHIP
Landover, MD
PG Sports and Learning Center
AMATEUR ATHLETIC UNION
Phone: 407-934-7200
Fax: 407-934-7242
www.aausports.org

Jul 10 - Jul 17, 2021
AAU TRACK & FIELD CLUB
CHAMPIONSHIPS
Kissimmee, FL
AMATEUR ATHLETIC UNION
Phone: 407-934-7200
Fax: 407-934-7242
www.aausports.org

Jul 8 - Jul 9, 2021
AAU TRACK & FIELD PRIMARY
NATIONAL CHAMPIONSHIPS
Orlando, FL
AMATEUR ATHLETIC UNION
Phone: 407-934-7200
Fax: 407-934-7242
www.aausports.org

Jul 1 - Jul 4, 2021
AAU WEST COAST TRACK & FIELD
NATIONAL CHAMPIONSH IP
Reno, NV
AMATEUR ATHLETIC UNION
Phone: 407-934-7200
Fax: 407-934-7242
www.aausports.org

Mar 11 - Mar 13, 2021
NCAA DIVISION I MEN'S/WOMEN'S
TRACK, INDOOR FINA LS
Fayetteville, AR
Randal Tyson Center
NATIONAL COLLEGIATE ATHLETIC
ASSOCIATION
Phone: 317-917-6222
Fax: 317-917-6888
www.ncaa.org

Jun 9 - Jun 12, 2021
NCAA DIVISION I MEN'S/WOMEN'S
TRACK, OUTDOOR FIN ALS
Eugene, OR
Hayward Field
NATIONAL COLLEGIATE ATHLETIC
ASSOCIATION
Phone: 317-917-6222
Fax: 317-917-6888
www.ncaa.org

Mar 11 - Mar 13, 2021
NCAA DIVISION II MEN'S/WOMEN'S
TRACK, INDOOR FIN ALS
Birmingham, AL
Birmingham CrossPlex

NATIONAL COLLEGIATE ATHLETIC
ASSOCIATION
Phone: 317-917-6222
Fax: 317-917-6888
www.ncaa.org

May 27 - May 29, 2021
NCAA DIVISION II MEN'S/WOMEN'S
TRACK, OUTDOOR FI NALS
Alldendale, MI
GVSU South Complex
NATIONAL COLLEGIATE ATHLETIC
ASSOCIATION
Phone: 317-917-6222
Fax: 317-917-6888
www.ncaa.org

TBA, 2021
NCAA DIVISION III MEN'S/WOMEN'S
TRACK, INDOOR FI NALS
NATIONAL COLLEGIATE ATHLETIC
ASSOCIATION
Phone: 317-917-6222
Fax: 317-917-6888
www.ncaa.org

May 27 - May 29, 2021
NCAA DIVISION III MEN'S/WOMEN'S
TRACK, OUTDOOR F INALS
TBA
NATIONAL COLLEGIATE ATHLETIC
ASSOCIATION
Phone: 317-917-6222
Fax: 317-917-6888
www.ncaa.org

Aug 21, 2021
PREFONTAINE CLASSIC
Eugene, OR
Hayward Field
OREGON TRACK CLUB
Phone: 541-343-7247
meetingdirector@preclassic.com
www.runnerspace.com/PreClassic

Triathlon

Jan 2, 2021
PAPAGO 6 MTB RACE
Tempe, AZ
BLUEWOLF EVENTS

Mar TBA, 2022
ELITE NATIONAL CHAMPIONSHIPS
TBA
USA TRIATHLON
Phone: 719-955-2807
info@usatriathlon.org
www.teamusa.org/usa-triathlon

Aug 17 - Aug 22, 2021
WORLD TRIATHLON CHAMPIONSHIP
FINALS
Edmonton, Canada
WORLD TRIATHLON
International Ph: +41 21 614 60 30
International Fax: +41 21 614 60 39
www.triathlon.org

Jun TBA, 2022
CANADIAN TRIATHLON
CHAMPIONSHIPS
TBA
TRIATHLON CANADA
Phone: 250-412-1795
Fax: 250-412-1794
info@triathloncanada.com
www.triathloncanada.com

Aug 28, 2021
CHICAGO TRIATHLON SUPERSPRINT
Chicago, IL
LIFE TIME FITNESS
ltfmedia@lifetimefitness.com
www.eventsbylifetime.com

Jul TBA, 2022
CLUB NATIONAL CHAMPIONSHIPS
TBA
USA TRIATHLON
Phone: 719-955-2807
info@usatriathlon.org
www.teamusa.org/usa-triathlon

TBA, 2022
COLLEGIATE CLUB NATIONAL
CHAMPIONSHIPS
TBA
USA TRIATHLON
Phone: 719-955-2807
info@usatriathlon.org
www.teamusa.org/usa-triathlon

Dec 4, 2021
DEATH VALLEY TRAIL MARATHON &
HALF MARATHON
Death Valley, CA
Titus Canyon
ENVIRO-SPORTS
Phone: 415-868-1829
info@envirosports.com
envirosports.com

Aug 28, 2021
LIFE TIME KIDS TRI - CHICAGO
Chicago, IL
LIFE TIME FITNESS
ltfmedia@lifetimefitness.com
www.eventsbylifetime.com

May 31, 2021
LIFE TIME TRI/CAP TEX
Austin, TX
LIFE TIME FITNESS
ltfmedia@lifetimefitness.com
www.eventsbylifetime.com

Jul 11, 2021
PANASONIC NEW YORK CITY
TRIATHLON
New York, NY
LIFE TIME FITNESS
ltfmedia@lifetimefitness.com
www.eventsbylifetime.com

Aug 28 - Aug 29, 2021
TRANSAMERICA CHICAGO
TRIATHLON
Chicago, IL
LIFE TIME FITNESS
ltfmedia@lifetimefitness.com
www.eventsbylifetime.com

TBA, 2022
TRIGIRL SUPER SPRINT TRIATHLON
& DUATHLON
Houston, TX
Alexander Deussen Park
TRIGIRL SPORTS
Phone: 832-423-4236
www.trigirlsports.com

Volleyball

TBA, 2022
AAU BOY'S VOLLEYBALL WINTER
NATIONALS
AMATEUR ATHLETIC UNION
Phone: 407-934-7200
Fax: 407-934-7242
www.aausports.org

Jun 18 - Jun 29, 2021
AAU BOYS' & GIRLS' VOLLEYBALL
NATIONAL CHAMPIONS HIPS
Orlando, FL
Orlando Sports Center
AMATEUR ATHLETIC UNION
Phone: 407-934-7200
Fax: 407-934-7242
www.aausports.org

Aug 7 - Aug 8, 2021
AAU BOYS' JUNIOR NATIONAL
BEACH VOLLEYBALL CHAMP
IONSHIP
AMATEUR ATHLETIC UNION
Phone: 407-934-7200
Fax: 407-934-7242
www.aausports.org

Jul 21 - Jul 25, 2021
AAU GIRLS' JUNIOR NATIONAL
BEACH VOLLEYBALL CHAM
PIONSHIP
Hermosa Beach, CA
AMATEUR ATHLETIC UNION
Phone: 407-934-7200
Fax: 407-934-7242
www.aausports.org

Jun 17 - Jun 29, 2021
AAU JUNIOR NATIONAL VOLLEYBALL
CHAMPIONSHIPS
Orlando, FL
ESPN Wide World of Sports
AMATEUR ATHLETIC UNION
Phone: 407-934-7200
Fax: 407-934-7242
www.aausports.org

Mar 6 - Mar 7, 2021
AAU VOLLEYBALL CLASSIC
Orlando, FL
AMATEUR ATHLETIC UNION
Phone: 407-934-7200
Fax: 407-934-7242
www.aausports.org

Jun 30 - Jul 7, 2021
BOYS' JUNIOR NATIONAL
CHAMPIONSHIP
Reno, NV
USA VOLLEYBALL
Phone: 719-228-6800
Fax: 719-228-6899
postmaster@usav.org
www.teamusa.org/USA-Volleyball

Jun 26 - Jul 5, 2021
GIRLS' JUNIOR NATIONAL
CHAMPIONSHIP
Dallas, TX
USA VOLLEYBALL
Phone: 719-228-6800
Fax: 719-228-6899
postmaster@usav.org
www.teamusa.org/USA-Volleyball

Jul TBA, 2021
JUNIOR BEACH TOUR NATIONAL
CHAMPIONSHIPS
Huntington Beach, CA

USA VOLLEYBALL
Phone: 719-228-6800
Fax: 719-228-6899
postmaster@usav.org
www.teamusa.org/USA-Volleyball

Apr 22 - Apr 24, 2021
NCAA DIVISION I WOMEN'S
VOLLEYBALL FINALS
Omaha, NE
CHI Health Center Omaha
NATIONAL COLLEGIATE ATHLETIC
ASSOCIATION
Phone: 317-917-6222
Fax: 317-917-6888
www.ncaa.org

TBA, 2021
NCAA DIVISION II WOMEN'S
VOLLEYBALL FINALS
NATIONAL COLLEGIATE ATHLETIC
ASSOCIATION
Phone: 317-917-6222
Fax: 317-917-6888
www.ncaa.org

Apr 23 - Apr 24, 2021
NCAA DIVISION III MEN'S
VOLLEYBALL FINALS
TBA
NATIONAL COLLEGIATE ATHLETIC
ASSOCIATION
Phone: 317-917-6222
Fax: 317-917-6888
www.ncaa.org

TBA, 2021
NCAA DIVISION III WOMEN'S
VOLLEYBALL FINALS
NATIONAL COLLEGIATE ATHLETIC
ASSOCIATION
Phone: 317-917-6222
Fax: 317-917-6888
www.ncaa.org

TBA, 2021
NCAA NATIONAL COLLEGIATE
MEN'S VOLLEYBALL SEMI-F INAL &
FINAL ROUNDS
NATIONAL COLLEGIATE ATHLETIC
ASSOCIATION
Phone: 317-917-6222
Fax: 317-917-6888
www.ncaa.org

May 28 - Jun 2, 2021
OPEN NATIONAL CHAMPIONSHIPS
Columbus, OH
USA VOLLEYBALL
Phone: 719-228-6800
Fax: 719-228-6899
postmaster@usav.org
www.teamusa.org/USA-Volleyball

Water Polo

Jul 17 - Jul 20, 2021
USA WATER POLO NATIONAL
JUNIOR OLYMPICS - SESS 1
USA WATER POLO
Phone: 714-500-5445
Fax: 714-960-2431
www.usawaterpolo.org

Jul 22 - Jul 25, 2021
USA WATER POLO NATIONAL
JUNIOR OLYMPICS - SESS 2
USA WATER POLO
Phone: 714-500-5445

Fax: 714-960-2431
www.usawaterpolo.org

TBA, 2021
NCAA NATIONAL COLLEGIATE
MEN'S WATER POLO FINALS
NATIONAL COLLEGIATE ATHLETIC
ASSOCIATION
Phone: 317-917-6222
Fax: 317-917-6888
www.ncaa.org

TBA, 2022
NCAA NATIONAL COLLEGIATE
WOMEN'S WATER POLO FINA LS
NATIONAL COLLEGIATE ATHLETIC
ASSOCIATION
Phone: 317-917-6222
Fax: 317-917-6888
www.ncaa.org

Water Skiing

Aug 4 - Aug 7, 2021
BAREFOOT NATIONAL
CHAMPIONSHIPS
Conroe, TX
USA WATER SKI
Phone: 863-324-4341
Fax: 863-325-8259
www.usawaterski.org

Nov 22 - Nov 28, 2021
CABLE WAKEBOARD WORLD
CHAMPIONSHIPS
Pathum Thani, Thailand
INTERNATIONAL WATERSKI &
WAKEBOARD FEDERATION
iwwf@iwwfed.com
www.iwsf.com

Oct 21 - Oct 23, 2021
COLLEGIATE WATER SKI NATIONAL
CHAMPIONSHIPS
NATIONAL COLLEGIATE WATER SKI
ASSOCIATION
www.thencwsa.com

Aug 13 - Aug 15, 2021
DIVISION 1 SHOW SKI NATIONAL
CHAMPIONSHIPS
Janesville, WI
USA WATER SKI
Phone: 863-324-4341
Fax: 863-325-8259
www.usawaterski.org

Aug 7 - Aug 8, 2021
DIVISION 2 SHOW SKI NATIONAL
CHAMPIONSHIPS
Shawano, WI
USA WATER SKI
Phone: 863-324-4341
Fax: 863-325-8259
www.usawaterski.org

Aug 8 - Aug 14, 2021
GOODE U.S. WATER SKI NATIONAL
CHAMPIONSHIPS
Wilmington, IL
USA WATER SKI
Phone: 863-324-4341
Fax: 863-325-8259
www.usawaterski.org

Mar TBA, 2022
IWWF WORLD SKI SHOW
TOURNAMENT
TBA

events/meetings/shows

INTERNATIONAL WATERSKI &
WAKEBOARD FEDERATION
iwwf@iwwfed.com
www.iwsf.com

Jun 26 - Jun 27, 2021
JUNIOR U.S. OPEN WATER SKI
CHAMPIONSHIPS
Martindale, TX
USA WATER SKI
Phone: 863-324-4341
Fax: 863-325-8259
www.usawaterski.org

Aug 21 - Aug 22, 2021
JUNIOR WATER SKI WORLD
CHAMPIONSHIPS
Santa Rosa Beach, FL
Pickos Waterski and Wakeboard School
INTERNATIONAL WATERSKI &
WAKEBOARD FEDERATION
iwwf@iwwfed.com
www.iwsf.com

May 28 - May 30, 2021
MASTERS WATER SKI &
WAKEBOARD TOURNAMENT
Pine Mountain, GA
Callaway Gardens
NAUTIQUE EVENTS
Phone: 407-855-4141
Fax: 407-851-7844
masters@nautique.com
www.masterswaterski.com

May 15 - May 16, 2021
NCWSA ALL-STARS
Jacksonville, IL
JAWS Water Ski Lake
NATIONAL COLLEGIATE WATER SKI
ASSOCIATION
www.thencwsa.com

TBA, 2021
THE WORLD GAMES
Birmingham, AL
THE WORLD GAMES
www.theworldgames.org

Sept 11, 2021
US OPEN WATER SKI RACING
NATIONAL CHAMPIONSHIPS
TBA
NATIONAL WATER SKI RACING
ASSOCIATION
www.nwsra.net

Jul 15 - Jul 18, 2021
WISCONSIN STATE WATER SKI
SHOW CHAMPIONSHIPS
Wisconsin Rapids, WI
South Wood County Park, Lake
Wazeecha - Red Beach
WISCONSIN RAPIDS AQUA SKIERS
Phone: 715-323-1577
www.aquaskiers.org

Weightlifting

Jul 31 - Aug 1, 2021
AAU DRUG FREE INTERNATIONAL
BODYBUILDING & FITNE SS
CHAMPIONSHIPS
Las Vegas, NV
Rio Hotel
AMATEUR ATHLETIC UNION
Phone: 407-934-7200
Fax: 407-934-7242
www.aausports.org

Jul 31 - Aug 1, 2021
AAU DRUG FREE INTERNATIONAL
POWERLIFTING, WEIGHT LIFTING &
FEATS OF STRENGTH
CHAMPIONSHIPS
Las Vegas, NV
Rio Hotel
AMATEUR ATHLETIC UNION
Phone: 407-934-7200
Fax: 407-934-7242
www.aausports.org

Apr 9 - Apr 11, 2021
AAU DRUG FREE NORTH AMERICAN
BODYBUILDING & FITN ESS
CHAMPIONSHIPS
Laughlin, NV
Harrah's Resort Hotel Casino
AMATEUR ATHLETIC UNION
Phone: 407-934-7200
Fax: 407-934-7242
www.aausports.org

Oct 28, 2021
AAU DRUG FREE UNIVERSE
BODYBUILDING & FITNESS CH
AMPIONSHIPS
Las Vegas, NV
Plaza Hotel
AMATEUR ATHLETIC UNION
Phone: 407-934-7200
Fax: 407-934-7242
www.aausports.org

Oct 1 - Oct 3, 2021
AAU DRUG FREE WORLD
BODYBUILDING & FITNESS CHAMP
IONSHIPS
Laughlin, NV
Harrah's Resort Hotel Casino
AMATEUR ATHLETIC UNION
Phone: 407-934-7200
Fax: 407-934-7242
www.aausports.org

Oct 1 - Oct 3, 2021
AAU DRUG FREE WORLD
POWERLIFTING, WEIGHTLIFTING,
FOS & MAS CHAMPIONSHIPS
Laughlin, NV
Harrah's Resort Hotel Casino
AMATEUR ATHLETIC UNION
Phone: 407-934-7200
Fax: 407-934-7242
www.aausports.org

Apr 10, 2021
AAU ORCHARD POWERLIFTING
MEET
Orchard, NE
AMATEUR ATHLETIC UNION
Phone: 407-934-7200
Fax: 407-934-7242
www.aausports.org

Oct 15 - Oct 16, 2021
NORTH AMERICAN NATIONAL
CHAMPIONSHIPS
Salem, VA
Salem Civic Center
AMERICAN STRONGMAN
CORPORATION
Phone: 314-565-5970
americanstrongmancorporation@gmail.com
strongmancorporation.com

Windsurfing

Oct TBA, 2021
ALOHA CLASSIC
INTERNATIONAL WINDSURFING TOUR
internationalwindsurfingtour.com

May TBA, 2022
COLD WATER CLASSIC
Aurora, CO
Cherry Creek State Park
ROCKY MOUNTAIN WINDSURFING
ASSOC.
rmwa.org

Mar TBA, 2021
OMAEZAKI CUP
Omaezaki City, Shizuoka, Japan
Omaezaki Long Beach
INTERNATIONAL WINDSURFING TOUR
internationalwindsurfingtour.com

May TBA, 2021
PACASMAYO CLASSIC
Pacasmayo, Peru
INTERNATIONAL WINDSURFING TOUR
internationalwindsurfingtour.com

Jun TBA, 2021
PISTOL RIVER WAVE BASH
Pistol River, OR
INTERNATIONAL WINDSURFING TOUR
internationalwindsurfingtour.com

Jul 24 - Jul 25, 2021
SF CLASSIC & UN CHALLENGE
San Francisco, CA
St. Francis Yacht Club
ST. FRANCIS YACHT CLUB
Phone: 415-563-6363
Fax: 415-563-8670
frontdesk@stfyc.com
www.stfyc.com

Apr TBA, 2021
TOPOCALMA INFERNAL
Topocalma, Chile
INTERNATIONAL WINDSURFING TOUR
internationalwindsurfingtour.com

Jun 14 - Jun 18, 2021
US NATIONAL RACING TOUR
Various
US WINDSURFING ASSOCIATION
Phone: 877-386-8708
info@uswindsurfing.org
uswindsurfing.org

May TBA, 2022
WET/KASHY FINS SPRING REGATTA
WINDSURFING ENTHUSIASTS OF
TIDEWATER, INC.
sailwet1@gmail.com
www.sailwet.com

Wrestling

May 28, 2021
ASICS UWW CADET & UNIVERSITY
NATIONALS
UNITED WORLD WRESTLING
International Ph: +41 21 312 84 26
info@unitedworldwrestling.org
unitedworldwrestling.org

Mar 19 - Mar 20, 2021
AAU FOLKSTYLE WORLD
CHAMPIONSHIP
Spearfish, SD

AMATEUR ATHLETIC UNION
Phone: 407-934-7200
Fax: 407-934-7242
www.aausports.org

Mar 19 - Mar 20, 2021
AAU SPRING YOUTH NATIONALS
Kingsport, TX
TNT Sportplex
AMATEUR ATHLETIC UNION
Phone: 407-934-7200
Fax: 407-934-7242
www.aausports.org

Jan 2 - Jan 3, 2021
AAU WINTER YOUTH NATIONALS
AMATEUR ATHLETIC UNION
Phone: 407-934-7200
Fax: 407-934-7242
www.aausports.org

TBA, 2022
BEACH & BELT WRESTLING
NATIONAL CHAMPIONSHIPS
Carolina Beach, NC
USA WRESTLING
Phone: 719-598-8181

Fax: 719-598-9440
www.teamusa.org/USA-Wrestling

Mar 18 - Mar 20, 2021
NCAA DIVISION I WRESTLING
FINALS
St. Louis, MO
Enterprise Center
NATIONAL COLLEGIATE ATHLETIC
ASSOCIATION
Phone: 317-917-6222
Fax: 317-917-6888
www.ncaa.org

Mar 12 - Mar 13, 2021
NCAA DIVISION II WRESTLING
FINALS
St. Louis, MO
America's Center Convention Complex
NATIONAL COLLEGIATE ATHLETIC
ASSOCIATION
Phone: 317-917-6222
Fax: 317-917-6888
www.ncaa.org

TBA, 2021
NCAA DIVISION III MEN'S
WRESTLING FINALS
NATIONAL COLLEGIATE ATHLETIC
ASSOCIATION
Phone: 317-917-6222
Fax: 317-917-6888
www.ncaa.org

Jul 16, 2021
US MARINE CORPS US OPEN
Las Vegas, NV
USA WRESTLING
Phone: 719-598-8181
Fax: 719-598-9440
www.teamusa.org/USA-Wrestling

10
indexes

A

A A. Brosso, Robert President
BROSSO, WILHELM & MCWILLIAMS, INC., 1060

A L Gaudreau, William President
GAUDREAU, INC. ARCHITECTS/PLANNERS/ENGINEERS, 1067

A Paniagua Jr., Ralph President & CEO
R. PANIAGUA, INC., 813

A'Costa, Peter National Sales Manager
PRECISION COMPOSITES, 1187

A., Brandon Creative Director
AMERICAN EAGLE OUTFITTERS, 1228

A. A Castiglia, Dennis Partner, Investment Management
LUMSDEN & MCCORMICK, LLP, 850

A. A Davis, Jeremy Associate Attorney
COHN, WILLIAM A., 882

A. A Durost, Richard Executive Director
MAINE PRINCIPAL'S ASSOCIATION, 198

A. A. Kanai, Mark Member
KANAI, MARK A., 896

A. A. Shneider, Jeffrey Principal Emeritus
CSHQA ARCHITECTS/ENGINEERS/PLANNERS, 1063

A. A. Zinn, Harry Attorney
BATE, PETERSON, DEACON, ZINN & YOUNG, LLP, 873

A. Beesley III, Wilford Lawyer
PRINCE YEATES, 910

A. D. Baker, Richard Chairman
OCEAN PACIFIC APPAREL CORPORATION, 1181

A. De Francis, Joseph VP - Treasurer
TRIPLE CROWN PRODUCTIONS, 823

A. E. Barbour, John CEO & Chairman of the Board
GURWIN, DAVID A., 845

A. H. Murray, Vincent Attorney
MURRAY & MURRAY, 907

A. Hillerich IV, John President / Chief Executive Officer
LOUISVILLE SLUGGER, 1155, 1168

A. Jack Hillerich III, John Chairman of the Board
LOUISVILLE SLUGGER, 1168

A. Krick Sr., Thomas President
CHARTER PRODUCTS INC., 1234

A. M Bevan, Lee Local Office Administrator
DAVIS & KUELTHAU, S.C., 884

A. Mc Grath, Richard President
RIGHT GARD CORPORATION, 1193

A. Murray Jr, Vincent Founding Member
MURRAY & MURRAY, 907

A. P. Salminen, Judith Director of Human Resources
FOSTER, SWIFT, COLLINS & SMITH, P.C., 890

A. R Lombardi, Robert Execuitve Director
PENNSYLVANIA INTERSCHOLASTIC ATHLETIC ASSOCIATION, 200

A. R. Arestides, Alexander Associate
WATTS, STEVEN R., 924

A. Sims Jr, James President/Principal
SIMS, JR. JAMES A., 864

A. Van Deuren, Richard Chairman
REINHART, BOERNER, VAN DEUREN S.C., 911

A. Van Wert, Ronald Member
ETTER, MCMAHON, LAMBERSON & CLARY, P.C.A., 888

A. W. Walden, James Founder
WALDON, GROUP THE, 868

A. W. Whitman, Robert Chairman
FRANKLIN COVEY, 791

A.Gossen, Paul Principal
GEIGER ENGINEERS, 1067

APR, Jesse Director, International Public Relations
LAS VEGAS CONVENTION & VISITOR'S AUTHORITY, 990

APR, Lee Communications Manager
LEE ISLAND COAST VISITOR & CONVENTION BUREAU, 237

APR, Vince Vice President of Public Affairs
LAS VEGAS CONVENTION & VISITOR'S AUTHORITY, 990

ATC, Bill Head Athletic Trainer/Equipment Manager
UNITED STATES HOCKEY LEAGUE, 137

ATC, Colin Team Trainer
UNITED STATES HOCKEY LEAGUE, 136

ATC, L.A.T., Corey Athletic Trainer/Equipment Manager/Stren
UNITED STATES HOCKEY LEAGUE, 137

ATC/L, Wayne Athletic Trainer
WESTERN HOCKEY LEAGUE, 138

Aaberg, Brad Officials Coordinator
NORTH COUNTRY REGION/USA VOLLEYBALL, 210

Aamodt, Dave General Manager
KIT, 627

Aamodt, Jason Assistant Dean of Online Legal Education
THE UNIVERSITY OF TULSA COLLEGE OF LAW, 921

Aamodt, Norman President/Chief Executive Officer
EVENT STRATEGY GROUP, 790

Aanenson, Bill General Sales Manager
KOMO 1000 AM RADIO, 632

Aanenson, Steve President
OLD DUTCH FOODS, 739

Aanonsen, Aaron Senior Associate Director of Athletics
LAKELAND COLLEGE ATHLETICS, 391

Aaron, Arnold Assistant Football Coach
NJCAA REGION VI WOMEN'S, 285

Aaron, Candice Chair
LANCE ARMSTRONG FOUNDATION, 190

Aaron, Cheryl Director of Athletics
WENTWORTH INSTITUTE OF TECHNOLOGY ATHLETICS(WIT), 407

Aaron, Matthew President & CEO
SPECIAL OLYMPICS PENNSYLVANIA, 195

Aaron, Rick Sports Director
KSTU-TV, 703

Aaron, Sammy Vice Chairman
G III SPORTS, 1146

Aaron, Thomas Chair/Director
WEBBER INTERNATIONAL UNIVERSITY, 439

Aarons, Jared Sports Anchor
KGAN-TV, 698

Abalan, Mark Associate Head Coach
UNITED STATES HOCKEY LEAGUE, 137

Abaray, Christyn Director of Athletics
LAWRENCE UNIVERSITY ATHLETICS, 392

Abarca, Carlos Lawyer
SCHUTTS & BOWEN, 914

Abare, Terri Partner
LAMPLEY, NATHANIEL, 898

Abare, TerriReyering Partner
LAMPLEY, NATHANIEL, 898

Abascal, Manuel Partner
SAUER, JR., RUSSELL F., 914

Abatemarco, Tracy Partner
WILSON, ELSER, MOSKOWITZ ET AL, 925

Abbinanti, Sandy Commissioner/CEO
GREAT LAKES REGION/USA VOLLEYBALL, 209

Abbot, Jeff Executive Director
TENNESSEE PGA SECTIONAL OFFICE, 107

Abbott, C. Owner/Governor
ONTARIO HOCKEY LEAGUE, 134

Abbott, Carter WG Committee Chair
US LACROSSE, 141

Abbott, Chad Program Director
KFXN-AM, 625

Abbott, Darren President
AMERICAN HOCKEY LEAGUE/AHL, 127

Abbott, Don National Sales Manager
AEROBIE, INC, 556, 1104

Abbott, Duane Western Sales Manager
BODY SOLID, INC., 1118

Abbott, Eddie Operations Manager
VIKING HALL CIVIC CENTER, 1025

Abbott, Gary Special Projects/Communications Director
USA WRESTLING, 211

Abbott, Jim Director of Athletics
OKLAHOMA CITY UNIVERSITY ATHLETICS, 316

Abbott, Kevin Partner
REED SMITH, 911

Abbott, Kevin Operations Manager
VAN ANDEL ARENA, 1024

Abbott, Mark President/Deputy Commissioner
MAJOR LEAGUE SOCCER, 157

Abbott, Michael Partner
ADKINS, M. DOUGLAS, 870

Abbott, Mike Chief Financial Officer
BURTON SNOWBOARDS, 1122

Abbott, Neil Founder/Partner
ABBOTT MANAGEMENT GROUP, 832

Abbott, Rick Acting General Manager
USL CHAMPIONSHIP, 158

Abbott, Scott Executive Director
SACRAMENTO RUNNING ASSOCIATION, 148

Abbott, Tom Chief Executive Officer
PRECISE INTERNATIONAL, 1187

Abboud, Jannet Special Counsel
PIPER RUDNICK LLP, 1071

Abdelfattah, Mahmoud Head Coach
NATIONAL BASKETBALL ASSOCIATION DEVELOPMENT LEAGUE, 60

Abdo, Amy Director
FENNEMORE CRAIG, A PROFESSIONAL CORPORATION, 889

Abdou, Mark Head General Counsel
PARK LANE - INVESTMENT BANKING SERVICES, 777

Abdourazakou, Yann Assistant Professor
CANISIUS COLLEGE - SCHOOL OF EDUCATION & HUMAN SERVICES, 414

Abdur-Rahim, Shareef President
NATIONAL BASKETBALL ASSOCIATION DEVELOPMENT LEAGUE, 59

Abdur-Rahkman, Dawud Coordinator of Diversity
MUHLENBERG COLLEGE ATHLETICS, 396

Abdur-Rahman, Kevin Director of Athletics
CITY COLLEGE OF NEW YORK ATHLETICS, 382

Abeel, Timothy Partner
RAWLE LAW OFFICES, 910

Abeita, April Licensing Administrator
NEW MEXICO RACING COMMISSION, 81

Abel, Bill Contact
INDY PRO 2000, 22

Abel, Cabrelle Associate, Seattle
PRESTON, GATES & ELLIS, 910

Abel, Jim Chairman
HAYMARKET PARK, 978

Abel, Liz Assistant Athletic Director/Sports Infor
JON M. HUNTSMAN CENTER, 986

Abeles, Dan Member
ECKERT SEAMANS, 887

Abeles, Jerrold Partner
MCSHERRY, JR., WILLIAM J., 852

Abell, Gene Sports Editor
LEXINGTON HERALD-LEADER, 506

Abello, Paola Associate
GREENBERG TRAURIG, LLP, 892

Abendroth, Thomas Partner
SCHIFF HARDIN LLP, 862

Abendroth, Tom Vice President
ACTION FLOOR SYSTEMS, LLC, 1102

Abercrombie, Bill President
ONTARIO HOCKEY LEAGUE, 134

Abercrombie, Jr., Jr., W. Attorney
MCKENZIE, W. SHELBY, 904

Aberg, Cissy Sports Marketing Manager
PLANO CONVENTION & VISITORS BUREAU, 242

Abernathy, Joe Vice President, Stadium Operations
BUSCH STADIUM, 962

Abernethy, Ted Undergraduate Program Coordinator
ST. THOMAS UNIVERSITY, 436

Abes, Alan Partner
COMODECA, JAMES A., 883

Abes, Edward Partner
ABES & BAUMANN, 870

Abhraham, David VP
GAGLIARDI INSURANCE SERVICES, 776

Abida, Maurad Practice Group Head
PIPER RUDNICK LLP, 1071

Abney, David Chief Executive Officer
UNITED PARCEL SERVICE OF AMERICA, INC./UPS, 743

Abney, Jordan Executive Director
BC SCHOOL SPORTS, 197

Abney, Robertha Associate Professor
SLIPPERY ROCK UNIVERSITY, 435

Abode, Joe PPA Commisioner
PROFESSIONAL PUTTERS ASSOCIATION, 108

Aboid, Joe PPA Commissioner
PROFESSIONAL PUTTERS ASSOCIATION, 108

Abott, Jim Speaker
NATIONWIDE SPEAKERS BUREAU, 854

Abraham, Dennis Director, Pro Scouting
NATIONAL FOOTBALL LEAGUE/NFL, 96

Abraham, Dirk News/Sports Director
KDOM-FM, 622

Abraham, Jay EVP
RHINO SPORTS, 1193

Abraham, Lynne Partner
EGAN, ROBERT T., 887

Abraham, Magid President/Chief Executive
Officer/Co-Fou
COMSCORE MEDIA METRIX, 787

Abraham, Nathan Assistant Director of Turf &
Grounds
CARTER FINLEY STADIUM, 963

Abraham, Scott Sports Anchor
KHAS-TV, 698

Abraham, Thomas Owner
PADDLE TRAMPS MFG. COMPANY, 1183

Abraham, Trisonya Director of Basketball
SPORTS MANAGEMENT WORLDWIDE, 819

Abramowitz, Mitchell President/Owner
MITCHEL ABRAMOWITZ, A.I.A., 1071

Abramowski, Tammy Traffic Director
WQSN AM 1660, 670

Abrams, David Executive Director/Sports
Financing
FLORIDA ATLANTIC UNIVERSITY COLLEGE
OF BUSINESS, 420

Abrams, Harvey President
INTERNATIONAL INSTITUTE FOR SPORT
HISTORY, 252

Abrams, Jim Director, College Scouting
NATIONAL FOOTBALL LEAGUE/NFL, 96

Abrams, John Facilities/Operations Manager
PETERSEN EVENTS CENTER, 1001

Abrams, Kevin VP, Football Operations
NATIONAL FOOTBALL LEAGUE/NFL, 96

Abrams, Nicola Vice President
HARNESS HORSE YOUTH FOUNDATION, 76

Abrams, Norman Partner
PIPER RUDNICK LLP, 1071

Abramson, Bill Sports Editor
ENTERPRISE, 489

Abramson, Mike Assistant General Manager
EASTERN LEAGUE, 38

Abramson, Paul Vice President of National
Accounts
PROFESSIONAL SPORTS PUBLICATIONS, 583

Abreu, Stephen Associate
PIPER RUDNICK LLP, 1071

Abromaitis, Jim Director of Athletics
ALBERTUS MAGNUS COLLEGE ATHLETICS, 377

Abruzzo, Joe Head Athletic Trainer
STATEN ISLAND ATHLETICS, COLLEGE OF
(CSI), 404

Abud, Marcelo President, Labatt Canada
BUDWEISER CANADA, 734

Accardi, Jonathan Assistant Athletics Director
KEUKA COLLEGE ATHLETICS, 391

Acee, Kevin Sports Reporter
SAN DIEGO UNION-TRIBUNE, 532

Acevedo, Ramon Past President
WORLD BOXING ORGANIZATION, 67

Aceves, William Law Professor/Director,
International Le
CALIFORNIA WESTERN SCHOOL OF LAW, 880

Achenbach, James Associate Editor
GOLFWEEK, 568

Achey, Jeff Managing Editor
CLIMBING, 560

Achilles, Jennifer Associate
REED SMITH LLP, 911

Ackelson, Mike Anchor
WFMJ-TV, 710

Acker, Ann Partner
CHAPMAN & CUTLER, 881

Acker, Beth Execuitve Assistant
PROTECT MANAGEMENT CORP., 859

Acker, Brian Sports Information Director
ROCKFORD COLLEGE ATHLETICS, 400

Acker, Joe Director of Athletic Media Relations
LAWRENCE UNIVERSITY ATHLETICS, 392

Ackerman, Robert Faculty Athletics
Representative
WAYNE STATE UNIVERSITY, 439

Ackerman, Val Commissioner
BIG EAST CONFERENCE, 281, 290

Ackerman, Wystan Partner
DANIELS, ERIC D., 884

Ackermann, Kristina Associate Editor
TRANSWORLD BUSINESS, 558, 595

Acklin, Russell Sport Information Director
FISK UNIVERSITY ATHLETICS, 386

Ackourey, Peter Shareholder
BUCHANAN INGERSOLL ROONEY PC, 878

Acoleyen, Jan Chief Human Resources Officer
BARCO MEDIA, 1114

Acosta, Janis Partner
MCCAREINS, R. MARK, 903

Acosta, Rafael Chief Executive
WOIZ-AM, 667

Acosta, Tina International Travel Consultant
ANTHONY TRAVEL, INC., 935

Acosta, Tony Sports Copy Editor
RECORD (CA), 527

Acquarulo, JoAnn Assistant Athletic Director for
Operatio
TRINITY COLLEGE ATHLETICS, 406

Acton, Randall President
U.S. CAVALRY, INC, 1251

Adachi, Joe President & CEO
CANON U.S.A., 1123

Adachi, Themy Director of Athletics
MILLS COLLEGE ATHLETICS, 395

Adair, Will Associate Commissioner
PENNSYLVANIA STATE ATHLETIC
CONFERENCE, 301

Adam, Jakub Partner
PIPER RUDNICK LLP, 1071

Adama, James Partner
ADKINS, M. DOUGLAS, 870

Adamany, Katherine Associate
JOHNSON & BELL, 896

Adamle, Mark President, Sales
INTERSPORT, INC., 606

Adams, Alan Contributing Writer
RINKSIDE, 584

Adams, Alfred Lawyer
WOMBLE, CARLYLE, SANDRIDGE & RICE,
PLLC, 926

Adams, Allen President
UNITED STATES YOUTH VOLLEYBALL
LEAGUE, 176

Adams, Alvan VP Facility Manager
US AIRWAYS CENTER, 1023

Adams, B.J. Associate Coach
ONTARIO HOCKEY LEAGUE, 133

Adams, Barney Chairman of the Board
ADAMS GOLF GP CORPORATION, 1103

Adams, Benjamin Member
DANIELS, ERIC D., 884

Adams, Bob Facilities Director
KITTERY TRADING POST, 1243

Adams, Brett Director of Athletics
STEVENSON UNIVERSITY, 405, 1041

Adams, Bruce Partner
RICE & RICE, 861

Adams, Charlie Sports Director
WSBT-TV, 717

Adams, Craig Vice President of Game Day
Operations
DEVAULT MEMORIAL STADIUM, 854, 970

Adams, Dan Advertising Vice President
TUCSON CITIZEN, 546

Adams, Darrel News Director
WBBH - NBC 2, 707

Adams, Dave EVP
SEATTLE SYSTEMS/LENOX HILL BRACE
COMPANY, 1198

Adams, Don Chief Executive Officer
SAIL CANADA, 178

Adams, Emily Administrative Assistant Sr.
IDAHO, UNIVERSITY OF, 423

Adams, Gary Lawyer
PELLETTIERI RABSTEIN AND ALTMAN, 908

Adams, Gerald Co-Founder and group Director
VISION SPORTS & ENTERTAINMENT
PARTNERS, 825

Adams, Gray Attorney
PELLETTIERI RABSTEIN AND ALTMAN, 908

Adams, Greg Partner
SMITH, PAYTON, 917

Adams, Greg Partner
TARSHES, DAVID C., 920

Adams, Gregory Associate
FENNEMORE CRAIG, A PROFESSIONAL
CORPORATION, 889

Adams, Grethe President
SOUTHERN UMBRELLA COMPANY, INC./DBA
SOUTHERN PLUS, 1203

Adams, Hank Chief Executive Officer
SPORTVISION, 608

Adams, Jackie Director, Marketing Promotions
TURNER SPORTS, INC., 685

Adams, Jameson Associate Athletic Director
ST. EDWARDS UNIVERSITY ATHLETICS, 372

Adams, Jamie Assistant Athletic Director,
Marketing &
UNIVERSITY OF NORTH TEXAS-COLISEUM,
1022

Adams, Jason Assistant General
Manager/Ticketing
FLORIDA STATE LEAGUE, 39

Adams, Jean Lawyer
WOMBLE, CARLYLE, SANDRIDGE & RICE,
PLLC, 926

Adams, Jennifer Associate
ECKERT SEAMANS, 887

Adams, Jennifer Partner
GOLDSMITH, JAMES A., 891

Adams, Jessica Vice President Of Operations
EAST COAST HOCKEY LEAGUE/ECHL, 130

Adams, Joe Sports Director
WOPP-AM, 667

Adams, John Director, University Marketing
JOHN F. SAVAGE HALL, 503, 985

Adams, John Counsel
SCHIFF HARDIN LLP, 862

Adams, Josh Sports Producer
WNCN-TV, 585, 715

Adams, Katrina Vice President
INTERNATIONAL TENNIS FEDERATION, 171

Adams, Kevin General Manager
AMERICAN HOCKEY LEAGUE/AHL, 128

Adams, Kevin Treasurer, Archery and Shooting
Sports A
KITTERY TRADING POST, 1243

Adams, Kevyn General Manager
NATIONAL HOCKEY LEAGUE/NHL, 123

Adams, Kim President
KITTERY TRADING POST, 1243

Adams, Lynne Attorney
OSBORN MALEDON, P.A., 908

Adams, Mark Marketing
DODGER INDUSTRIES INC., 1135

Adams, Mary Lawyer
WOMBLE, CARLYLE, SANDRIDGE & RICE,
PLLC, 926

Adams, Michael UGA President
SANFORD STADIUM, 1009

Adams, Michelle Law Professor
BERSHAD, LAWRENCE, 875

Adams, Mike Treasurer
SNOWSPORTS INDUSTRIES AMERICA, 153

Adams, Nathan Overnight DJ/Sports Anchor
WBXX-FM, 647

Adams, Nick Chief Marketing Officer
USA/BMX, THE AMERICAN BICYCLE
ASSOCIATION, 71

Adams, Payton Coordinator of Athletic Operations
WILLIAM R. JOHNSON COLISEUM, 1028

Adams, Peg Treasurer
GEORGIA AAU ASSOCIATION, 212

Adams, Peter President
MATCH POINT, 1171

Adams, Reid Lawyer
WOMBLE, CARLYLE, SANDRIDGE & RICE,
PLLC, 926

Adams, Robert
WILSON, ELSER, MOSKOWITZ ET AL, 925

Adams, Russell Sports Writer
WALL STREET JOURNAL, 550

Adams, Sam Sports Reporter
KEZI-TV, 94, 530, 621, 697

Alexander, Julie Athletic Trainer
EASTERN CONNECTICUT STATE
UNIVERSITY (ECSU) ATHLETICS, 384
Alexander, Keith Assistant Executive Director
LOUISIANA HS ATHLETIC ASSOCIATION, 198
Alexander, Kevin Operations Manager
LIBERTY BOWL MEMORIAL STADIUM, 991
Alexander, Lori Senior Associate AD, Internal
Operations
VANDERBILT UNIVERSITY ATHLETICS, 348
Alexander, Marty Advertising Manager
HUNTINGTON HERALD-PRESS, 498
Alexander, Mary Advertising Director
ELKHART TRUTH, 489
Alexander, Mary Attorney
ALEXANDER & ASSOCIATES, P.C. MARY, 871
Alexander, Mike Director
BADMINTON CANADA, 25
Alexander, Paul Sports Anchor
THE FRED HONSBERGER SHOW, 613
Alexander, Ted Sports Director
WTKR-TV, 718
Alfond, Theodore EVP
DEXTER SHOE COMPANY, 1134
Alfonso, Shylah Partner
PERKINS COIE LAW FIRM, 909
Alford, Linda Administrative Coordinator
UNIVERSITY CENTER, 1015, 1021
Alford, Parrish Collegiate Sports Reporter
NORTHEAST MISSISSIPPI DAILY JOURNAL,
518
Alford, Steve Head Coach, Men's Basketball
PAULEY PAVILION, 1000
Algeri, Mark VP of Sales
HDS PROMOTIONAL MARKETING, 795
Algeri, Steve Sports Editor
DAILY TIMES CHRONICLE, 483
Alguacil, Jose Manager
PACIFIC COAST LEAGUE OF
PROFESSIONAL BASEBALL CLUBS, 39, 49
Ali, Laila President
WOMEN'S SPORTS FOUNDATION, 224
Ali, Yaser Attorney
OSBORN MALEDON, P.A., 908
Aliaga, Oscar ProgramDirector
LOUISVILLE, UNIVERSITY OF, 426
Aliano, Chris Director of Athletic Communications
MERRIMACK COLLEGE ATHLETICS(MC), 364
Alioto, Mario Executive VP, Business Operations
NATIONAL LEAGUE OF PROFESSIONAL
BASEBALL CLUBS, THE, 32
Alladin, Chad Head Athletic Trainer
CARLETON COLLEGE ATHLETICS, 380
Allain, J.M. President & CEO
FAIR-PLAY SCOREBOARDS, 1142
Allaire, Benoit Assistant Coach & Goaltending
Coach
NATIONAL HOCKEY LEAGUE/NHL, 125
Allan, David Sales Manager
ELITE SPORTS ANALYSIS, 1225
Allan, Lance Sports Anchor
WTMJ-TV, 718
Allan, Paul Associate Athletic Director
MINNESOTA STATE UNVERSITY - MANKATO
ATHLETICS (MSUM), 365
Allbee, Dannon Associate
PERKINS COIE LAW FIRM, 909
Allbright, Kathy President, Director at Large
VERMONT STATE WOMEN'S GOLF
ASSOCIATION, 116
Allbright, Rooney President
NJCAA REGION XIV WOMEN'S, 286
Allbritton, Mike President / Chief Operating
Officer
COLUMBIA 300, INC., 1128
Alldredge, Annita Finance Director
UNITED STATES SPORTS ACADEMY, 438,
596
Allee, Bill Sports Editor
DISPATCH (IL), 487
Allee, John Sports Reporter
WSAW-TV, 717
Allee-Walsh, Brian Sports Writer
TIMES-PICAYUNE, 545
Allen, A. Shareholder
IBACH, JOHN R., 894
Allen, Ben Vice President
WESTERN SUBURBS RUGBY FOOTBALL
CLUB, 148

Allen, Bill Vice President/CFO
PRO FOOTBALL HALL OF FAME, 256
Allen, Blake Assistant Athletics Director
SOUTHEASTERN OKLAHOMA STATE
UNIVERSITY ATHLETICS, 371
Allen, Bob Weekday Sports Director
KTRK-TV, 627, 703
Allen, C. President and Chief Executive Officer
SPORTING NEWS, 590
Allen, Charles Director of ASG Logistics
AMATEUR SPORTS GROUP, INC., 833
Allen, Charlie President
FIREBIRD INTERNATIONAL RACEWAY, 1034
Allen, Charlotte Marketing/Public Relations Man
DALLAS CONVENTION CENTER, 230
Allen, Chris President, COO
SOUTHERN LEAGUE OF PROFESSIONAL
BASEBALL CLUBS, 53
Allen, Clint Partner
EGAN, ROBERT T., 887
Allen, Dave Vice President of Sales and
Marketing
CALIFORNIA SPEEDWAY, 508, 567, 1031
Allen, Dede Assoc. Athletic Director (Compliance
& A
UAA SPORTS ARENA, 1021
Allen, Donna Vice President of Sales & Marketing
NORFOLK CONVENTION & VISITORS
BUREAU, 240
Allen, Eddy General Manager
WDOR-FM, 650
Allen, Frank Partner
EGAN, ROBERT T., 887
Allen, Gayla Executive Assistant
SOUTHLAND PARK, 1057
Allen, Heath Sports Reporter
NORTHWEST ARKANSAS TIMES, 518
Allen, Herb Department Editor
FLORIDA SPORTSMAN, 565
Allen, Jeff Board Member
DELAWARE STATE GOLF ASSOCIATION, 110
Allen, Jeffery COO and CFO
ROSE BOWL HALL OF FAME, 256
Allen, Jeffrey Senior Counsel
EVANS, ESQ., THOMAS S., 888
Allen, Jennifer Associate
MCSHERRY, JR., WILLIAM J., 852
Allen, Jody Chair
NATIONAL FOOTBALL LEAGUE/NFL, 58, 97
Allen, Joe Associate
PHILLIPS & AKERS PC, 909
Allen, John Member (Partner)
EVANS, ESQ., THOMAS S., 888
Allen, Justin Sports Anchor/Reporter
WTSP-TV, 719
Allen, Karen Assistant Athletic Director
SHORTER UNIVERSITY ATHLETICS, 370
Allen, Kevin Ice Hockey Columnist
USA TODAY, 89, 548
Allen, Kevin Member
ECKERT SEAMANS, 887
Allen, Laura Editor
HUNTER & SPORT HORSE, 570
Allen, Lisa Publisher
HUNTER & SPORT HORSE, 570
Allen, Lonny Athletic Director
TIFFIN UNIVERSITY ATHLETICS, 373
Allen, Maggie President Elect
MAINE PRINCIPAL'S ASSOCIATION, 198
Allen, Mark Head Athletic Trainer
WESTERN CONNECTICUT STATE
UNIVERSITY ATHLETICS, 408, 808
Allen, Marty Sports Producer
THE MIKE TRIVISONNO SHOW, 194, 614
Allen, Matthew President / Chief Merchandising
Officer
ICON HEALTH & FITNESS, INC., 1157
Allen, Michael Development Director
THE ACCESS FUND, 69
Allen, Nate Sports Reporter
TULSA WORLD, 547
Allen, P.Blake Partner
DUANE MORRIS LLP, 886
Allen, Patrick Lawyer
WOMBLE, CARLYLE, SANDRIDGE & RICE,
PLLC, 926
Allen, Paul General Manager
TEXAS BASEBALL LEAGUE, 53

Allen, Paul Chairman
FIRST AND GOAL, INC., 1074
Allen, Percy Sports Reporter
SEATTLE TIMES, 534
Allen, Richard Multimedia & IT Manager
COLLEGE FOOTBALL HALL OF FAME, 250
Allen, Robert Principal
BSA ARCHITECTS, 1061
Allen, Rusty Vice President of Athletics
TABOR COLLEGE ATHLETICS, 320
Allen, Scott Assistant Coach
AMERICAN HOCKEY LEAGUE/AHL, 127
Allen, Stephen Member
STITES & HARBISON, 866
Allen, Stu Svp Business Services
ACTIVE INTERNATIONAL, 774
Allen, Sylvia Founder
ALLEN CONSULTING, INC., 780
Allen, Thomas Attorney
WYRICK, ROBBINS, YATES & PONTON, L.L.P,
927
Allen, Tim Sr. Associate Commissioner
BIG 12 CONFERENCE, 290
Allen, Traer General Manager
FLORIDA STATE LEAGUE, 40
Allen, Valerie Head Athletic Trainer
VIRGINIA UNION UNIVERSITY
ATHLETICS(VUU), 375
Allen, Wilbur Finance Manager
CANTON MEMORIAL CIVIC CENTER, 963
Allen, Zach Head Athletic Trainer
MILLIGAN COLLEGE ATHLETICS, 315
Allen, Zachary Director
CROWE & DUNLEVY, 839
Allender, Billie Advertising Manager
MOUNT PLEASANT NEWS, 512
Aller, Jim Assistant Athletic Director
EASTERN NAZARENE COLLEGE(ENC)
ATHLETICS, 385
Allera, Edward Board of Director
GURWIN, DAVID A., 845
Alles, Dave Sports Director/Anchor
KSBY-TV, 702
Alley, Gene Associate Athletic Director
BECKER COLLEGE, 379
Allgeier, Hank Senior Graphic Tech
METRO SIGNS ADVERTISING, INC., 1173
Allgeier, Patrick Assistant Athletic Director
MILLIKIN UNIVERSITY ATHLETICS, 395
Allgeier, Tammy National Sales Manager
TANDEM SPORT, 1210
Allhands, Gina Vice President, Chief Financial
Officer
SAN MATEO COUNTY/SILICON VALLEY
CONVENTION & VISITORS BUREAU, 244
Allie, Zachary Associate
WINSTEAD ATTORNEYS, 926
Allina, Mike President
BC SCHOOL SPORTS, 197
Allison, Ian Chief Operating Officer
CANADIAN PREMIER LEAGUE, 156
Allison, James Technical Chief
FORMULA 1, 20
Allison, Mike Treasurer
LAKE COUNTY, ILLINOIS - CONVENTION &
VISITORS BUREAU, 236
Allison, Randy Vice President
UNITED STATES PARACHUTE
ASSOCIATION, 14
Allison, Robert EVP Special Facilities
SRI SPORTS, INC., 1206
Allison, Ryan Sports Director
WKBN-TV, 713
Allison, Todd Associate
FENNEMORE CRAIG, A PROFESSIONAL
CORPORATION, 889
Allman, Eric Director of Stadium Operations
STATE MUTUAL STADIUM, 1014
Allman, Robert Attorney
ALLMAN & MITZNER, LLC, 871
Allnoch, Allen Features Editor
LINKS MAGAZINE-THE BEST OF GOLF, 574
Allo, Keith Executive Producer
P.A.S.S. SPORTS, 608
Allocco, Frank Executive Sr. Associate AD,
External Rel
SAN FRANCISCO ATHLETICS, UNIVERSITY
OF, 343

Executive Index

Anderson, Rod Partner
HOLLAND & KNIGHT, 893
Anderson, Ron Director of Financial Aid
ASBURY COLLEGE ATHLETICS, 306
Anderson, S. Executive Director
MCKENNA, LONG & ALDRIDGE, LLP, 904
Anderson, Sandra Finance Director
IOWA HS ATHLETIC ASSOCIATION, 198
Anderson, Sandra Partner
VORYS, SATER, SEYMOUR & PEASE, 923
Anderson, Scott General Manager
KSKI-FM, 534, 636
Anderson, Scyld Attorney
ISAAC, BRANT, LEDMAN & TEETOR, 895
Anderson, Shawn Product Supervisor
EXIBITION PARK - LETHBRIDGE, 1047
Anderson, Shelly Reporter
PITTSBURGH POST-GAZETTE, 524
Anderson, Shrine Principal
ELLENZWEIG ASSOCIATES, INC., 1064
Anderson, Stanice Owner
ANDERSON & TUCKER, 871
Anderson, Steve EVP, News, Talent, and Content
Operation
ESPN TELEVISION, 611, 615, 681
Anderson, Tami Marketing Director
ATHLETA, LLC, 1228
Anderson, Tim Executive Vice President, Retail
Operati
SPORT CHALET, INC., 1249
Anderson, Todd Director of Communications
UNIVERSITY OF NORTH CAROLINA
PEMBROKE ATHLETICS(UNCP), 367
Anderson, Tom Director Of Athletics
NJCAA REGION IX WOMEN'S, 258, 285, 1041
Anderson, Trent Director, Building Operations
SCOTIABANK SADDLEDOME, 1010
Anderson, Wally Vice President of Baseball
Operations
PECOS LEAGUE (INDEPENDENT LEAGUE),
50
Anderson, Wayne Marketing
PW ATHLETIC COMPANY, INC., 1190
Anderson, Wes Sports Director
WGRE-FM, 655
Anderson, Wesley Health Care Attourney
REINHART, BOERNER, VAN DEUREN S.C.,
911
Anderson, Woody Sports Reporter (College)
HARTFORD COURANT, 495
Anderson, Zellina Ticket Office Manager
WJ HALE STADIUM, 1029
Anderson, Jr, Charles Finance and
Administration Chair
MIZELL, CATHERINE, 906
Anderson-Ray, Ben Chief Executive Officer
NEW HERMES INC., 1179
Andlauer, Michael Owner
ONTARIO HOCKEY LEAGUE, 133
Ando, Bill Senior Editor
SOUTHERN BOATING MAGAZINE, 575, 588
Andorka, Frank Managing Editor
GOLFDOM, 567
Andracchi, Frank Chairman
SPECIAL OLYMPICS MARYLAND, 193
Andracchio, Gianni Account Executive
BMORE SPORTS, 1118
Andrade, Frank Publisher
LA OFERTA NEWSPAPER, 503
Andrade, Lydia Faculty Athletic Representative
UNIVERSITY OF THE INCARNATE WORD
ATHLETICS, 361
Andrade-Morioka, Angie President/Regional
Commissioner
MOKU O KEAWE REGIONAL
COMMISSIONER/USA VOLLEYBALL, 210
Andrassy, AJ National Sports Forum (NSF)
Competition
OHIO UNIVERSITY, 433
Andre, Scott Sports Lawyer
LAURIA TOKUNGA GATES & LINN, LLP, 899
Andreeta, Mike Director of Competiton
PLACERVILLE SPEEDWAY, 1040
Andrejko, J.P. Assistant Director of Intercollegiate
At
KING'S COLLEGE ATHLETICS, 391
Andreoff, Christopher Member
JAFFE, RAITT, HEUER & WEISS, PC, 895

Andreoli, Ron Simulcast Coordinator
LES BOIS PARK, 1050
Andreozzi, Mark Fitness Coordinator, Club Sports
Directo
ROGER WILLIAMS UNIVERSITY ATHLETICS,
401
Andreson, Barry Maintenance Mechanic II
NJCAA REGION III MEN'S, 284
Andreson, Charlotte ASSISTANT TO THE
PRESIDENT AND CEO
RENO-SPARKS CONVENTION AUTHORITY,
243
Andreson, Stephen President, S.H.A. Enterprises
NEWPORT SPORTS MUSEUM, 256
Andretti, Michael CEO/Chair
INDYCAR, 21, 22
Andrew, Aguilar Assistant General Manager
SMITH-WILLIS STADIUM, 1012
Andrew, Jim Chief Strategy & Innovation Officer
PHILIPS LIGHTING COMPANY, 1185
Andrew, Marcia Partner
TAFT, STETTINIUS & HOLLISTER, 867
Andrew, Mary Chair/Commissioner
FLORIDA REGIONAL COMMISSIONER/USA
VOLLEYBALL, 209
Andrew, Michael Chairman
KPMG CONVENTION, SPORTS &
ENTERTAINMENT PRACTICE, 766
Andrew, Troy Executive Director/CEO
WASHINGTON STATE GOLF ASSOCIATION,
116
Andrew An Rodrigues, M. President
ARCHITECTS DELAWIE WILKES RODRIGUES
BARKER, 1059
Andrews, Art News Director
WPEN-AM, 668
Andrews, Brad Senior Director, Hockey &
Business Opera
AMERICAN HOCKEY LEAGUE/AHL, 127
Andrews, Carley Partner
PRESTON, GATES & ELLIS, 910
Andrews, Damon Sports Director
KTLA-TV, 687, 703
Andrews, David Chair
AMERICAN HOCKEY LEAGUE/AHL, 126
Andrews, David Attorney
HERSHNER, HUNTER, ANDREWS, NEILL &
SMITH L,L,P., 893
Andrews, Don President
QUICK TICK INTERNATIONAL, INC., 942
Andrews, Greg VP of Business Operations
GLOBAL SPORTS PRODUCTIONS, 601
Andrews, Jerald President/Executive Director
MISSOURI SPORTS HALL OF FAME, 253
Andrews, Jim Senior Vice President, Content
Strategy
IEG, LLC, 570, 796
Andrews, John Vice President Marketing
SOF SOLE, 1201
Andrews, Johnny Vice President/General
Manager
WWL, 678
Andrews, Ken Executive Director
MIDDLE ATLANTIC STATES COLLEGIATE
ATHLETIC CORPORATION, 297
Andrews, Lisa Assistant President
QUICK TICK INTERNATIONAL, INC., 942
Andrews, Michelle Orthopaedic Surgeon
CINCINNATI SPORTSMEDICINE &
ORTHOPAEDIC CENTER, 929
Andrews, Phil Chief Executive Officer/General
Secretar
USA WEIGHTLIFTING, 211, 597
Andrews, Scott President
EL MIRAGE DRY LAKE, 1042
Andrews, Shirley Owner
TURNER'S OUTDOORSMAN, 1251
Andrews, Skip Program Director
WHAN-AM, 655
Andrews, Thomas Shareholder
JOHNSON & BELL, 896
Andriatch, Mike Sports Information Director
SPECIAL OLYMPICS STADIUM, 1013
Andriola, James Partner
REED SMITH LLP, 911
Andrus, James Partner
PRESTON, GATES & ELLIS, 910

Andrus, Jim Assoc. Commissioner
Business/Finance
MOUNTAIN WEST CONFERENCE, 298
Andrusyszyn, Adam Assistant Director, Facilities
& Ops.
COLLEGE OF WILLIAM & MARY, 967
Anesh, Mark Partner
WILSON, ELSER, MOSKOWITZ ET AL, 925
Anez, Scott Sports Director
WDBO-AM, 649
Anfang, Jill Assistant Director
ROSEVILLE PARKS AND RECREATION, 243
Angarola, Joann Shareholder
JOHNSON & BELL, 896
Angel, Margaret Shareholder
BUCHANAN INGERSOLL ROONEY PC, 878
Angel, Miguel Head Coach
CANADIAN PREMIER LEAGUE, 156
Angel, Rex President
LYNCHBURG CITY STADIUM, 993
Angel, Seth EVP & General Manager
ROYAL PURPLE RACEWAY, 1041
Angelico, Paul Secretary-Treasurer
COLORADO HS ACTIVITIES ASSOCIATION,
197
Angelillo, Greg Sports Reporter
WZBN-TV, 721
Angeline, Dave News Director
WJVS-FM, 660
Angelis, Theodore Partner
PRESTON, GATES & ELLIS, 910
Angell, Bill Supritenent
NEBRASKA STATE FAIR, 1051
Angelo, Arlene Partner
WEBB, WILLIAM Y., 924
Angelo, Dan Sports Editor
SANDUSKY REGISTER, 533
Angelos, Craig Deputy Director of Athletics
TEMPLE UNIVERSITY ATHLETICS, 346, 1004
Angelos, John Chair/Chief Executive Officer
AMERICAN LEAGUE OF PROFESSIONAL
BASEBALL CLUBS, THE, 29
Angelos, Louis Managing Partner
USL LEAGUE TWO, 160
Angelos, Peter Ownership Representative
AMERICAN LEAGUE OF PROFESSIONAL
BASEBALL CLUBS, THE, 29
Angelos, Peter Chief Executive Officer
ED SMITH STADIUM/SPORTS COMPLEX, 972
Anger, Greg Marketing Director
IRWIN SPORTS, 1159
Anger, Kimberly Advertising Director
LODI NEWS-SENTINEL, 506
Anghel, Gheorghe Operations Manager
WINTECH RACING, 1222
Angilly, Paul Sports Editor
BRISTOL PRESS, 469
Angioli, Carmine Sports Editor
STATEN ISLAND ADVANCE, 540
Angle, Martin Non-Executive Chairman
N.E.C. ARENA BIRMINGHAM, 997
Anglin, Ruth Fair Activities Manager
YAKIMA VALLEY SUNDOME, 1030
Angott, Chris Secretary
GOLF ASSOCIATION OF MICHIGAN, 110
Angotti, Vince Sports Management Program
Coordinator
TOWSON STATE UNIVERSITY, 438
Angulo, Oscar Sports Producer
WFTS-TV, 686, 711
Angus, Nancy Executive Director
MARIO LEMIEUX FOUNDATION, 190
Angyan, James Paralegal
MILLER CANFIELD SPORTS, 853
Anhaeuser, Mike Head Coach/General Manager
USL CHAMPIONSHIP, 158
Anholt, Peter General Manager
WESTERN HOCKEY LEAGUE, 138
Aniballi, Fred Business Office
VESPOLI USA, INC., 1219
Ankenbrand, Larry Professor
EASTERN ILLINOIS UNIVERSITY, 419
Ankeny, Kevin General Manager
WGFR-FM, 654
Ann Bo Bolick, Mary Lecturer
APPALACHIAN STATE UNIVERSITY, 412
Ann Kempf Townsley, Bett Womens Soccer
Head Coach
WEST CHESTER UNIVERSITY, 439

1442

executive index

B

B McKnight Jr, Robert Chairman / Chief
Executive Officer
QUIKSILVER, 1190

B., Pat Office Assistant
SPORTS HEALTH, 1205

B. B Demyanick, Dale Partner, Tax Planning
LUMSDEN & MCCORMICK, LLP, 850

B. B Rimington, David President
BOOMER ESIASON FOUNDATION, 189

B. B. Cipolletti, George President & CEO
OMNI BODYWORK, 1182

B. C Brosnick, Richard VP and Shareholder
FELDMAN, OSCAR, 842

B. Craven III, James
CRAVEN, JAMES B., III, 839

B. Hunt Jr, James Partner
CLINARD, KEITH ASHFORD, 882

B. McKnight Jr., Robert Executive Chairman
QUIKSILVER, 1190

B. P. Kupelian, Peter Attorney
KUPELIAN, ORMOND & MAGY, 898

B. R. Schaumann, Neils Dean
CALIFORNIA WESTERN SCHOOL OF LAW,
880

B. W. Brosnick, Richard VP/Shareholder
BUTZEL LONG, A PROFESSIONAL
CORPORATION, 880

B.S., Roy Advising Database Analyst
SAM BOYD STADIUM, 1009

Baalke, Trent General Manager
NATIONAL FOOTBALL LEAGUE/NFL, 96

Baba, Jim Executive Director
BASEBALL CANADA, 26

Babb, Diana Senior Editor
COMPETITOR, 560, 561

Babb, James Editor
GRAY'S SPORTING JOURNAL, 568

Babb, Kathy Account Manager
TOOLBOX STUDIOS, 823

Babbage, Dawn Associate Professor
NJCAA REGION III MEN'S, 284

Babbitt, Alan Sports Information Director
HOPE COLLEGE ATHLETICS, 389, 497

Babbitt, Bob Publisher
COMPETITOR, 560, 561

Babby, Ken Owner/CEO
SOUTHERN LEAGUE OF PROFESSIONAL
BASEBALL CLUBS, 38, 52, 963

Babcock, Nick Sports Editor
WENATCHEE WORLD, 551

Babcock, Shannon Management Director
361o EXPERIENTIAL, 779

Babcock, Whit Director of Athletics
VIRGINIA TECH ATHLETICS, 349, 964

Babiarz, Lou Sports Editor
BISMARCK TRIBUNE, 467

Babich, Eileen Operations Assistant
CENTRAL FLORIDA SPORTS COMMISSION,
228

Babich, Leslie Attorney
CASHATT, BRENT A., 881

Babich, Todd Attorney
CASHATT, BRENT A., 881

Babilla, Terrence EVP, Chief Operating Officer,
General Co
U.S. GAMES, INC., 1217

Babineau, Jeff Deputy Editor
GOLFWEEK, 568

Babisak, Jennifer Sales Support
SPORTS TRAVEL, INC., 937

Babnik, Ray Head Athletic Trainer
GREENSBORO COLLEGE ATHLETICS, 387

Bacchi, Robert Chief Operating Officer
EB2B COMMERCE, INC., 1237

Bach, Daniel General Manager
TURFWAY PARK, 1054

Bach, Greg Editor/Communication Director
YOUTH SPORTS JOURNAL, 265, 600

Bach, Jim Associate AD, Business Operations
KANSAS STATE UNIVERSITY ATHLETICS,
333

Bach, Peder President
JIFFY LINE STRIPERS, 1160

Bach, Robert Chairman Emeritus
BOYS & GIRLS CLUBS OF AMERICA, 264

Bach, Ryan Goaltending Coach
AMERICAN HOCKEY LEAGUE/AHL, 127

Bacha, Eugene Chairman Sport & Leisure Studies
JERSEY CITY STATE COLLEGE, 424

Bachelart, Eric President/CEO
IMSA PROTOTYPE CHALLENGE, 21

Bachman, Dan President
NATIONAL GYMNASTICS JUDGES
ASSOCIATION, INC., 120

Bachman, Dennis Director
KANSAS RACING AND GAMING
COMMISSION, 80

Bachman, Rachel Sports Reporter
OREGONIAN, 520

Bachman, Richard Goaltending Coach
AMERICAN HOCKEY LEAGUE/AHL, 127

Bachman, William Chief Operating Officer
BINGHAM MCCUTCHEN LLP, 875

Bachrach, Joshua Partner
RAWLE LAW OFFICES, 910

Bachrach, Ric Chief Executive Officer
CELEBRITY FOCUS, INC., 785

Bachs, Pam Advertising Manager
KDSJ-AM, 622

Bacigal, Margaret Professor/Administrative
Director
SHEPHERD, JR., ROBERT E., 915

Bacigal, Ronald Professor
SHEPHERD, JR., ROBERT E., 915

Bacigalupi, Bill Advertising Sales
KGO-TV, 698

Back, Billy Head Coach
SPOKANE SHOCK, 94

Back, Brad Senior Vice President Group
Management D
361o EXPERIENTIAL, 779

Backman, Wally Manager
PACIFIC COAST LEAGUE OF
PROFESSIONAL BASEBALL CLUBS, 49

Backs, Jason EVP/Chief Operations Officer
WORK IN SPORTS, 757

Backstrom, Ralph Founder
AMERICAN HOCKEY LEAGUE/AHL, 127

Backus, Amy Director of Athletics
CASE WESTERN RESERVE UNIVERSITY
ATHLETICS, 381, 982

Backus, Bob Director of Athletics
STATE UNIVERSITY OF NEW YORK AT
DELHI ATHLETICS, 320

Bacon, Chris Director of Fan Entertainment
DUNN FIELD, 971

Bacon, Scott Sports Director
WOBN-FM, 667

Bacot, Jack Editor-in-Chief
GOLF PRODUCT NEWS, 567

Badain, Marc President
NATIONAL FOOTBALL LEAGUE/NFL, 96

Baddeley, Aaron Representative Player
PRO SPORT MANAGEMENT, 858

Baddour, Dick Athletic Director
KENAN MEMORIAL STADIUM, 987

Badell, Jason CFO/Commissioner
INTERMOUNTAIN VOLLEYBALL
ASSOCIATION, 210

Baden, Colin CEO
OAKLEY, INC., 1181

Bader, Jerry News Director
WIXX-FM, 658

Bader, Micah Sports Editor
ALBERT LEA TRIBUNE, 461

Badescu, Eduardo Head Coach
USL LEAGUE TWO, 164

Badgett, Cameron Director of Ticket Operations
CHENEY STADIUM, 965

Badgley, Bonnie Director of Finance
INTERNATIONAL LEAGUE, 42

Badich, Yasmeen Director, Marketing
AMERICAN HOCKEY LEAGUE/AHL, 127

Badkar, Dinesh Associate
IRVING, PAUL H., 895

Badylak, Ken Sports Information Director
SAINT JOSEPH'S COLLEGE ATHLETICS, 370

Badzinski, Joel Sports Reporter
LA CROSSE TRIBUNE, 503

Baechtold, James Lawyer
SHUMATE, FLAHERTY & EUBANKS &
BAECHTOLD, P.S.C., 916

Baedeker, Rick Executive Director
CALIFORNIA HORSE RACING BOARD, 80

Baehman, Beau Sports Director
KMIZ-TV, 700

Baehnan, Beau Sports Director
KMIZ-TV, 700

Baer, Herb President
POLAR ELECTRO INC., 1186

Baer, Joshua Chief Technology Consultant
SPORTS MEDIA CHALLENGE, 831, 940

Baer, Laurence President/CEO
NATIONAL LEAGUE OF PROFESSIONAL
BASEBALL CLUBS, THE, 32

Baer, Tracy Attorney
WEBER & BAER, LLP, 924

Baer, Tracy Member
WEBER & BAER, LLP, 924

Bagala, Rich Sports Producer
WWOR-TV, 720

Bagby, Glen Partner
DINSMORE, 885

Bagby, Marty Sports Director
WTCO-AM, 675

Bagby, Thomas President
CARDWELL, VICTOR, 880

Bageorgos, Megan Head Athletic Trainer
RAMAPO COLLEGE OF NEW JERSEY
ATHLETICS, 399

Baggett, Dudley Landscaping Director
JS DORTON ARENA, 986

Baggett, W. Chairman Emeritus/Shareholder
HICKS, JERRY, 893

Baggot, Andy College Sports Reporter
WISCONSIN STATE JOURNAL, 552

Baggott, Dave President
PIONEER BASEBALL LEAGUE, 51, 992

Baggott, Iann Chair
FIELD HOCKEY CANADA, 120

Bagley, Jim Associate
RUSSELL REYNOLDS ASSOCIATES, INC.,
756

Bagley, Joanne Senior Staff Specialist
ROCHESTER INSTITUTE OF TECHNOLOGY
ATHLETICS, 400

Bagley, Keith News Director
WBFD-AM, 644, 645

Bagley, Terry Sales Manager
AMERICAN WEIGHT AND MEASURES, 1224

Bahou, Tony Sports Anchor
WAPT-TV, 707

Bahr, C.J. Director of Stadium Operations
FIRST AMERICAN BANK BALLPARK, 974

Bahr, Jeff Director of Manufacturing
FIBERESIN INDUSTRIES, INC., 1142

Bahrami, Ray Senior Vice President, Sales
FOX SPORTS NETWORKS/FOX SPORTS
NET, 683

Baibak, John News Director
WNNZ-AM, 657, 666

Baier, Russell Vice President
CARDIOSPORT, 1124

Bailes, Gord Sales VP
GARMONT USA, INC., 1147

Bailey, Allan General Manager
NORTHWEST BASEBALL LEAGUE, 48

Bailey, Bill News Director
KGBR-FM, 625

Bailey, Braydon Chief Executive Officer
HAMMAKA, 1152

Bailey, Buddy Manager
SOUTHERN LEAGUE OF PROFESSIONAL
BASEBALL CLUBS, 53

Bailey, Chris General Manager
WAUD-AM, 644

Bailey, Chuck Director, Communications
EAST COAST HOCKEY LEAGUE/ECHL, 129

Bailey, Connie Sales Contact
SPORTSPRINT, 1206

Bailey, Dan Merchandise Manager
CAROLINA LEAGUE, 37

Bailey, David Executive Director
BAIZLEY, DONALD, 872

Bailey, Debbie Customer Service, Athletic Fields
COLBOND, INC., 1128

Bailey, Doug President
NEWTEX USA, 1179

Bailey, Duane Deputy AD/CFO
LOUISIANA AT LAFAYETTE ATHLETICS,
UNIVERSITY OF, 334

Bailey, Greg Sports Director
WCNC-TV, 699, 709

Bailey, Ian Executive Vice President & General
Manag

Baldwin, Eileen Member
DANIELS, ERIC D., 884
Baldwin, Keith Partner
SMITH, PAYTON, 917
Baldwin, Larry Executive Manager
NAPLES-FORT MYERS GREYHOUND TRACK, 1056
Baldwin, Martha Head Athletic Trainer
CONCORDIA UNIVERSITY AT AUSTIN ATHLETICS, 383
Baldwin, Mike Sports Writer
OKLAHOMAN, 471, 519
Baldwin, Sam Sports Information Coordinator
UNIVERSITY OF ALABAMA IN HUNTSVILLE ATHLETICS, 374
Baldwin, Sue Interim President
METRO DENVER SPORTS COMMISSION, 239
Baldwin, Susan Consultant
SPENCER STUART, 756
Baldwin, Tim Head Golf Coach/Assistant AD for Special
UNIVERSITY CENTER, 1015, 1021
Baldwin, Timothy Co-Director
INDIANA UNIVERSITY, 423
Baldwin, Tyson Assoc. AD for External Operations
ARKANSAS LITTLE ROCK ATHLETICS, UNIVERSITY OF, 323
Balentine, Ian Advertising Manager
MOUNTAIN DEMOCRAT, 512
Bales, Jennifer Director Of Sales
LAS CRUCES CONVENTION & VISITORS BUREAU, 237
Bales, Mike Assistant Coach
NATIONAL HOCKEY LEAGUE/NHL, 123
Bales, Stacey Firm Administrator
BARRETT, WILLIAM A., 873
Balfe, Joseph Sales Administration Manager
ENDURA RUBBER FLOORING, 1139
Balginy, John News Director
KUPI-AM, 637
Balistreri, Joseph Real Estate/Banking & Finance Attourney
REINHART, BOERNER, VAN DEUREN S.C., 911
Baliva, Nathan Director of Media & Baseball Operations
MIDWEST LEAGUE, 45
Balke, Ben President
ETCHASOFT, INC., 1140
Balkin, Fred Principal
STEIN, SPERLING, BENNETT, DE JONG, DRISCOLL & GREENFEIG, P.C., 918
Balkin, Fred Principal
STEIN, SPERLING, BENNETT, DE JONG, DRISCOLL & GREENFEIG, P.C., 918
Ball, David Principal
FRANK, MONTE E., 890
Ball, Heather Director of events
ROSS, STEPHEN F., 913
Ball, John Division VP, Menswear
EDDIE BAUER, INC., 1238
Ball, Joshua Sports Editor
WILLIAMSON DAILY NEWS, 552
Ball, Kevin Director of Editorial Content & Copy Chi
OUTSIDE THE LINES, 688
Ball, Russ Executive VP/Director, Football Operatio
NATIONAL FOOTBALL LEAGUE/NFL, 95
Ball, Terrie Accounting and Payroll Manager
PHOENIX INTERNATIONAL RACEWAY, 1040
Ballantyne, Stuart Senior VP, Operations
NATIONAL HOCKEY LEAGUE/NHL, 124
Ballantyne, Todd Marketing Manager
KYW-TV, 706
Ballard, Brady General Manager
JACKIE ROBINSON BALLPARK, 983
Ballard, Brett Play-By-Play
WOPP-AM, 667
Ballard, Chris General Manager
NATIONAL FOOTBALL LEAGUE/NFL, 95, 591
Ballard, Dave President
GEORGIA STATE GOLF ASSOCIATION, 100
Ballard, Kenneth President & Founding Partner
BALLARD KING & ASSOCIATES, 1059
Ballard, Michael Sports Information Director
RUTGERS UNIVERSITY-CAMDEN ATHLETICS, 401

Ballard, Steve Sports Reporter
INDIANAPOLIS STAR, 499
Ballas, Jackie Director, Operations
SANDOWN PARK, 1053
Ballein, John Executive Associate AD
VIRGINIA TECH ATHLETICS, 349
Baller, Ann Associate Director of Athletic Facilitie
HOFSTRA UNIVERSITY STADIUM & ARENA, 979
Ballinger, Taylor Special Events Director
SPECIAL OLYMPICS KENTUCKY, 193
Ballmer, Steve Chairman
NATIONAL BASKETBALL ASSOCIATION/NBA, 57
Ballou, Bill Sports Reporter
TELEGRAM & GAZETTE, 542
Ballou, John Sports Writer
GARDNER NEWS, 493
Ballou, Rick Host
THE RICK BALLOU SHOW, 617
Ballou, Ty President
PLB SPORTS, 810
Balls, R. Partner
DURANTE, CHARLES J., 886
Balma, Larry Founder
CLIMAX MANUFACTURES, 1127
Balogh, Robert Vice President
INTERNATIONAL BOXING ORGANIZATION, 67
Bals, Nancy Associate Athletics Director
WESTFIELD STATE COLLEGE ATHLETICS (WSC), 408
Balsamo, Joe President
USL LEAGUE TWO, 161
Baltimore, Bryon Lawyer
BALTIMORE, BRYON, 872
Baltz, Tracy Marketing Director
BADGER STATE GAMES, 249, 259
Baltzell, Amy President-Elect
ASSOCIATION FOR APPLIED SPORT PSYCHOLOGY/AAASP, 216
Balvich, John General Manager
WIBN-FM, 657
Balwin, Bruce President
SOUTHERN LEAGUE OF PROFESSIONAL BASEBALL CLUBS, 53
Balz, Davis Associate
GUNSTER, YOAKLEY & STEWART, P.C., 845
Balzer, Barb Travel Counselor
BISMARCK-MANDAN CONVENTION & VISITORS BUREAU, 227
Balzer, Paula CEO
TBA ENTERTAINMENT CORPORATION, 821
Balzola, Inaki International Director
PROFESSIONAL TENNIS REGISTRY, 172
Bamber, Simon President
KAPPA USA, 1162
Bamberger, Greg Director of Athletics
KUTZTOWN UNIVERSITY ATHLETICS (KU ATHLETICS), 362
Bamberger, Michael Sports Senior Writer
SPORTS ILLUSTRATED, 591
Bamford, David National Sports Forum (NSF) Competition
OHIO UNIVERSITY, 433
Bamford, John Advertising Manager
TIMES RECORD, 544
Bamford, Ryan Director of Athletics
UMASS AMHERST ATHLETICS, 348
Bammert, Carl Assistant Athletic Director
NORTHERN MICHIGAN UNIVERSITY (NMU), 367, 958, 1016
Bamonti, Mike Senior Associate AD, Advancement
ILLINOIS AT CHICAGO ATHLETICS, UNVIERSITY OF, 332
Banasky, Ed Vice President
FITNESS MASTER INC, 1144
Bandimere, III, John Executive Vice President, General Manage
BANDIMERE SPEEDWAY, 1031
Bandimere, Jr., John President
BANDIMERE SPEEDWAY, 1031
Bandy, Shirley President
VA MEMORIAL STADIUM, 1024
Baney, Matt Sports Editor
LEWISTON MORNING TRIBUNE, 505
Banford, Beatrice Associate AD/SWA
MARSHALL UNIVERSITY ATHLETICS, 336

Bang, Dave Owner
PW ATHLETIC COMPANY, INC., 1190
Bang, Jens CEO
CONE COMMUNICATIONS, 760
Banga, Ajay President and CEO
MASTERCARD, 738
Bangs, Kathleen Staff Writer
INTERNATIONAL FIGURE SKATING, 571
Baniel, Paul VP, Finance & Administration
NATIONAL FOOTBALL LEAGUE/NFL, 95
Banka, Dennis Station Owner
WUCZ-FM, 677
Banker, Laurey Director of Product Management
JOHNSONITE, 1161
Banks, Carray Faculty Athletics Representative
NORFOLK STATE UNIVERSITY ATHLETICS(NSU), 366
Banks, Jeremy Editor
KANSAS CITY KANSAN, 502
Banks, Jimmy Director of Intramurals
MILWAUKEE SCHOOL OF ENGINEERING ATHLETICS (MSOE), 395
Banks, Kevin Vice President for Student Affairs
HUGHES STADIUM (MD), 980
Banks, Lacy Sports Reporter
CHICAGO SUN-TIMES, 472
Banks, Omar Exec. Assoc. AD
VIRGINIA TECH ATHLETICS, 281, 325, 349, 996
Banks, Roman Director Of Athletics
SOUTHERN UNIVERSITY ATHLETICS, 345
Banks, Esq., Chiquita
BLACK ENTERTAINMENT & SPORTS LAWYERS ASSOCIATION INC, 216
Bankston, Michael Vice Chair
FUTURE FOR KIDS, 843
Bankston, Tony Assistant Athletic Director
ILLINOIS WESLEYAN UNIVERSITY ATHLETICS, 390
Banner, Jr., Robert Publisher
CHRONICLE OF THE HORSE, 560
Bannerman, George Sales
BANNERMAN LTD., 1114
Bannerman, Ron Sales
BANNERMAN LTD., 1114
Bannick, Karen Office Manager
KENTUCKY SPEEDWAY, 1036
Banning, Chuck Sports Editor
DAY, 484
Banning, David President
CONTINENTAL SPORTS SUPPLY, INC., 1129
Banning, Troy Sports Editor
DAILY FREEMAN-JOURNAL, 478
Banning-Wright, Ann Chief Strategy Officer
SH GROUP, 1071
Bannon, Gemma Exec. Asst. to the President & CEO, Offi
GRAND PRIX ASSOCIATION OF LONG BEACH, 16
Bannon, Jeffrey Director of Marketing
THE WINNIPED BLUE BOMBERS, 1018
Bannon, Martin Director, Marketing
GRAND PRIX ASSOCIATION OF LONG BEACH, 16
Bannon, Thomas VP, Communications
HOOSIER PARK, 1049
Bannon, Tim Deputy Sports Editor
CHICAGO TRIBUNE SPORTS, 472, 721
Banowetz, Jeff Editor
TWIN CITIES SPORTS, 579, 584, 596
Banse, Troy Head Athletic Trainer
GUSTAVUS ADOLPHUS COLLEGE ATHLETICS, 388
Baptise, Brian Director of Athletics
LA SALLE UNIVERSITY ATHLETICS, 334
Baptist, Bob Sports Reporter
COLUMBUS DISPATCH, 474
Barajas, Andrew Sales Executive & Trade Show Manager
CHAMPION BALL COMPANY, 1125
Barajas, Rod Manager
TEXAS BASEBALL LEAGUE, 34, 54
Barakat, Christine Assignments Editor
EQUUS, 563
Barakat, Rick Vice President
INTERNATIONAL SPORTS PROPERTIES, INC., 798

executive index

Bartelstein, Mark CEO & Founder
PRIORITY SPORTS & ENTERTAINMENT, 857, 858

Bartelt, Gail Corporate Hospitality/Rentals
ROAD AMERICA, 1041

Bartelt, Jason Director of Athletics
MARIAN COLLEGE OF FOND DU LAC ATHLETICS, 393

Bartenstein, Kurt Advertising Manager
LEADER, 505

Barter, Meghan Associate Athletic Director
UNIVERSITY OF WEST FLORIDA ATHLETICS (UWF), 375

Bartfeld, Arnold Partner
REED SMITH LLP, 911

Barth, Bradley Associate Attorney/Notary Public
BARTH, BERUS & CALDERON, LLP, 873

Barth, Bud Sports Reporter
TELEGRAM & GAZETTE, 542

Barth, David Advertising Manager
NEWS-HERALD (PORT CLINTON), 516

Barth, Harry Founding Member/Senior Partner
BARTH, BERUS & CALDERON, LLP, 873

Barth, Kurt Assistant Athletic Director
EUREKA COLLEGE (EC) ATHLETICS, 386

Barth, Pete Sports Editor
SHEBOYGAN PRESS, 496, 535

Barth, Peter SVP Human Resources
SMITH'S FOOD & DRUG, 1249

Bartholomew, Dave President / Chief Executive Officer
MOUNTAIN SAFETY RESEARCH, 1176

Bartholomew, Jeffrey Shareholder
ROBINSON, WATERS & E'DORISIO, 912

Barthuly, Lourra Athletic Director
NORTHWEST COLLEGE ATHLETICS, 316

Bartik, Kelli Sports Reporter/Anchor
WCCB-TV, 708

Bartko, Jim Director of Athletics
BULLDOGS STADIUM, 961

Bartle, Scott President
OUTSIDE THE BOX MARKETING, INC, 855

Bartlett, Charlie Sports Reporter/Anchor
KAUZ-TV, 695

Bartlett, Dan Founder/Owner
SPLITSEASONTICKETS, LLC, 942

Bartlett, Heather Director of Concessions & Merchandise
NEW YORK-PENNSYLVANIA LEAGUE, 47, 1018

Bartlett, Jeff Sports Writer
TIMES-MAIL, 545

Bartlett, John Director of Athletic Facilities
WESTERN OREGON UNIVERSITY ATHLETICS (WOU), 376

Bartlett, Jonathan Senior Director of The First Tee of WV
WEST VIRGINIA GOLF ASSOCIATION, 116

Bartlett, Michele Director, Development
MACDONALD, JAMES, 901

Bartley, Ginger Treasurer
COLORADO HILL CLIMB ASSOCIATION, 84

Bartling, Monica Advertising Director
WICHITA FALLS TIMES RECORD NEWS, 552

Bartold, Steve IC4A Administrator
INTERCOLLEGIATE ASSOCIATION OF AMATEUR ATHLETES OF AMERICA/IC4A, 175

Bartolotta, Steven Assistant Sports Information Director
UNIVERSITY OF NORTH TEXAS-COLISEUM, 1022

Bartolotta, Vincent Partner
THORSNES, BARTOLOTTA & MCGUIRE, 922

Barton, April Director for Academic Computing
TAGGART, WALTER J., 867

Barton, April Assistant Dean, Academic Computing
TAGGART, WALTER J., 867

Barton, Derek News Director
KZEW-FM, 640

Barton, Jeff Director of Development, College of Phar
JOHN F. SAVAGE HALL, 985

Barton, Ken Vice President, Industrial Sales and Man
ECLECTIC PRODUCTS, INC., 1138

Barton, Michael EVP/Chief Administrative Officer
CONSOLIDATED GRAPHICS, 787

Barton, Richard President
NATIONAL INTERSCHOLASTIC ATHLETIC ADMINISTRATORS ASSOCIATION/NIAA, 201

Bartosik, Norbert CEO & General Manager
CALEXPO, 1032

Bartosik, Norbert General Manager
CALIFORNIA EXPOSITION & STATE FAIR, 1046

Bartoszewicz, Joseph Attorney
MEYER, UNKOVIC & SCOTT, LLP, 905

Bartow, Brian Director, Communications
NATIONAL LEAGUE OF PROFESSIONAL BASEBALL CLUBS, THE, 33

Bartowski, Steve Director of Tournaments
NEW JERSEY PGA SECTION, 106

Bartsch, Tom Publisher
TASK INDUSTRIES, INC., 1211

Bartscher, Larry Advertising Director
NORFOLK DAILY NEWS, 517

Baruck, Glenn President
LEO'S DANCEWEAR, INC., 1166

Barudin, Roy EVP Brand Development
CHAMPIONSHIP GROUP, INC., 837

Barzilai, Peter Baseball Assignment Editor
USA TODAY, 548

Basche, Bob Chairman
MILLSPORT, LLC, 804

Baseball, Ryan-Sanders Owners
PACIFIC COAST LEAGUE OF PROFESSIONAL BASEBALL CLUBS, 49

Basgall, Frank Attorney
THOMAS S. BUSCH, 921

Bash, Susan Sales Manager
NORMAN CONVENTION & VISITORS BUREAU, 241

Bashaw, Nathan Sports Information Director
WESTFIELD STATE COLLEGE ATHLETICS (WSC), 408

Bashian, Alison Marketing Manager
EMPLOYEE SERVICES MANAGEMENT, 562

Bashore, Cody Sports Editor
ARIZONA DAILY SUN, 463

Basil, Jon Director of Ticket Sales
DUTCHESS STADIUM, 971

Basil, Meredith Associate Athletics Director/SWA
CAL STATE FULLERTON ATHLETICS, 325

Basile, Katherine Partner
DURANTE, CHARLES J., 886

Basile, Mike Director, Hockey Operations
FEDERAL HOCKEY LEAGUE, 173

Baskerville, Wayne Associate Commissioner
BIG TEN ATHLETIC CONFERENCE, 290

Baskin, Andy Sports Director
WEWS-TV, 710

Basnett, Doug Secretary
SPECIAL OLYMPICS NEW HAMPSHIRE, 194

Bason, LaKyva Assistant Athletic Director
WILEY COLLEGE ATHLETICS, 322

Basovsky, Justin Coordinator of Volleyball Officials
COLLEGE CONFERENCE OF ILLINOIS AND WISCONSIN, 292

Bass, Betty Advertising Manager
GOLF RANGE TIMES, 567

Bass, George Partner
AAI SPORTS INC. & AAI INTERNATIONAL, INC., 832

Bass, Holly CEO
COBB TRAVEL & TOURISM, 229

Bass, Holly Chief Executive Officer
COBB TRAVEL & TOURISM, 229

Bass, James Assistant Professor
TENNESSEE STATE UNIVERSITY, 437

Bass, Jimmy Director of Athletics
NORTH CAROLINA WILMINGTON ATHLETICS, UNIVERSITY OF, 339

Bass, John Announcer
MERCED FAIRGROUNDS SPEEDWAY, 1038

Bass, Jordan Coordinator, Lifetime Activities Program
FLORIDA STATE UNIVERSITY, 420

Bass, Kennie Sports Reporter
WCHS-TV, 708

Bass, Martha Associate Professor of Health and Exerci
MISSISSIPPI, UNIVERSITY OF, 430

Bass, Mike Sports Editor
SAINT PAUL PIONEER PRESS, 531

Bass, Nicholas Chief Operating Officer
ALPINE CANADA, 151

Bass, Rob Project Architect
ALBANESE/BROOKS/ASSOCIATES P.C., 1058

Bass, Sherman General Manager
AMARILLO CIVIC CENTER COMPLEX, 954

Bass, Jr., George Chief Executive Officer/President
AAI SPORTS INC. & AAI INTERNATIONAL, INC., 832

Bassett, David Professor
TENNESSEE, KNOXVILLE, UNIVERSITY OF, 437

Bassett, Graham Director of Doubles and Professional Squ
U.S. SQUASH, 169

Bassett, Matthew Director of Athletics
LE MOYNE COLLEGE ATHLETICS, 362

Bassett, Susan Director of Intercollegiate Athletics
ITHACA COLLEGE ATHLETICS, 390

Bassetti, John High School ; Prep Sports Staff Writer
VINDICATOR, 549

Basso, Cory Vice President/Advertising
H-E-B, 1241

Basso, Jeff VP, Technology
FANSEDGE.COM, 1239

Bastable, Alan Senior Associate Editor
GOLF MAGAZINE, 567

Basterfield, Erin General Manager
NATIONAL BASKETBALL LEAGUE OF CANADA, 59

Bastian, Ed Chief Executive Officer
DELTA AIR LINES, 735

Batarla, Rob Executive Vice President
AMERICAN PHYSICAL THERAPY ASSOCIATION, 84

Batchelor, George Sales / Marketing Director
PROTEAM BY HAUSMANN, 1189

Batchelor, Kassie Senior Associate AD, Compliance/SWA
WISCONSIN GREEN BAY ATHLETICS, UNIVERSITY OF, 350

Batcher, Stephen Sports Information Director
MINNESOTA-MORRIS ATHLETICS, UNIVERSITY OF (UMM), 395

Bate, David Attorney
BATE, PETERSON, DEACON, ZINN & YOUNG, LLP, 873

Batech, Chris
HOLIDAY RACEWAY, 1035

Bateman, David Partner
PRESTON, GATES & ELLIS, 910

Bates, Brad Director of Athletics
SILVIO O. CONTE FORUM, 1011

Bates, Cathy Chief Information Officer
COLE, DAYTON T., 882

Bates, Dennis Assoc. AD, Finance
SIENA COLLEGE ATHLETICS, 344

Bates, Joe Sports Reporter
JOURNAL STAR, 501

Bates, Kevin Chief Executive Officer
FANSEDGE.COM, 1239

Bates, Sam Owner
NORTH ALABAMA SPEEDWAY, 1039

Bates, Win Sports Writer
ENTERPRISE, 489

Batey, Alan EVP and President, North America
GENERAL MOTORS, 736

Bathey, Jim VP, Ticket Sales
NATIONAL LEAGUE OF PROFESSIONAL BASEBALL CLUBS, THE, 32

Batista-Salas, Luis Founder/Chairman of the Championship Com
WORLD BOXING ORGANIZATION, 67

Batiste, Fred Sports Reporter
DAILY STAR, 483

Batley, James Senior Associate AD, Development
LOYOLA MARYMOUNT UNIVERSITY, 335

Batra, Narinder President
INTERNATIONAL HOCKEY FEDERATION (FIH), 203

Battaglia, Robert President
RACING REFLECTIONS INC, 1191

Battaglia, S. Attorney
EVANS, ESQ., THOMAS S., 888

executive index

Beall, Robert President & Chief Executive Officer
SHIRK STADIUM, 1011
Beall, William Partner
BEALL & BURKHARDT, 874
Beam, Alan Art Director
PRO-LINE CAP COMPANY, 1188
Beam, Dwayne Deputy Athletic Director
COASTAL CAROLINA UNIVERSITY
ATHLETICS, 326
Beamon, Ed CEO
VELOCITY SPORTS & ENTERTAINMENT, 773
Beams, Jason Track Promoter
HOLIDAY RACEWAY, 1035
Beams, Jonathan
HOLIDAY RACEWAY, 1035
Bean, Al Director of Athletics
SOUTHERN MAINE ATHLETICS, UNIVERSITY
OF, 402
Bean, Carla Advertising Manager
WEST PLAINS DAILY QUILL, 551
Bean, Frank Executive Director
AMERICAN ARMSPORT ASSOCIATION, 15
Bean, John Governor and President
NATIONAL LACROSSE LEAGUE, 123, 138,
141
Bean, Karen Executive Director
AMERICAN ARMSPORT ASSOCIATION, 15
Bean, Matt Managing Editor
SI.COM, 722
Beane, Billy Executive VP, Baseball Operations
AMERICAN LEAGUE OF PROFESSIONAL
BASEBALL CLUBS, THE, 30
Beane, Brandon General Manager
NATIONAL FOOTBALL LEAGUE/NFL, 95
Beane, Michael Marketing
TERRAPLAS USA RENTALS, LLC, 1212
Beane, Pat Sports Editor
HERALD-TIMES, 497
Beane, Sally Marketing Director
TERRAPLAS USA RENTALS, LLC, 1212
Beanon, David Chairman
DUNLOP/MAXFLI/SLAZENGER GROUP
AMERICAS, 1136
Beans, Frank Partner
THE COLLABORATIVE, INC., 1062
Bear, Bruce President/Chief Executive Officer
BEAR ENTHUSIAST MARKETING GROUP,
783
Bear, Jason Senior Account Executive
BEAR ENTHUSIAST MARKETING GROUP,
783
Bear, Roger Chairman
KEYSTONE MARKETING, INC., 800
Beard, Randy Executive Sports Editor
TALLAHASSEE DEMOCRAT, 541
Beard, Rick Director of Athletics
LEBANON VALLEY COLLEGE ATHLETICS
(LVC), 392
Beard, Rod Sports Producer
DETROIT NEWS, 486
Bearden, Richard Partner
IMPACT MANAGEMENT GROUP, INC., 797
Beardow, Warren
GOLF-ART.COM, INC., 1150
Bearse, Stacy Publisher
HORSE, 557, 569
Beaschler, Ron Coordinator
OHIO NORTHERN UNIVERSITY, 432
Beasley, Ashlyn Director for Game Operations
ILLINOIS AT SPRINGFIELD ATHLETICS,
UNIVERSITY OF, 361
Beasley, Bradley Attorney
BOESCHE MCDERMOTT LLP, 876
Beasley, Chris Marketing Director
BLUE BOOK OF COLLEGE ATHLETICS, 600
Beasley, David Assistand Athletics Director
BERRY COLLEGE ATHLETICS, 306
Beasley, Frank Director of Athletics
FLORIDA HIGH SCHOOL ATHLETIC
ASSOCIATION, 197
Beasley, Larry President / Chief Operating Officer
FN THOMPSON COMPANY, 1144
Beasley, Leah Associate A.D./Marketing and
Game Manage
THOMAS ASSEMBLY CENTER, 984, 1018
Beasley, Rogers VP of racing
KEENELAND ASSOCIATION, INC, 1050
Beasley, W.B. Director, Racing
KEENELAND ASSOCIATION, INC, 1050

Beasley, Jr., Chris Marketing Director
NATIONAL DIRECTORY OF HIGH SCHOOL
COACHES, 602
Beasock, Ray Sports Copy Editor
LEDGER, 505
Beason, Kim Professor of Park & Recreation
Managemen
MISSISSIPPI, UNIVERSITY OF, 430
Beaton, Barbara Sales Direcor
RELIANT ASTRODOME COMPLEX, 1005
Beaton, Kelly Sports Writer
WATERLOO-CEDAR FALLS COURIER, 550
Beattie, Andrew Director Of Recreation &
Athletics
EVERGREEN STATE UNIVERSITY
ATHLETICS, 311
Beattie, Chad Director of Athletic Communications
LYNN UNIVERSITY ATHLETICS, 363
Beattie, Kevin Associate Athletic Director for
Communic
RENSSELAER POLYTECHNIC INSTITUTE
ATHLETICS, 400
Beattie, Terry Associate Athletic Director
WEST CHESTER UNIVERSITY
ATHLETICS(WCU), 375, 973
Beatty, Amy Concessions & Facilities
LEGION STADIUM COMPLEX, 991
Beatty, Bryan Assistant Athletic Director,
Compliance
DRURY UNIVERSITY (DU) ATHLETICS, 357
Beatty, Marion Lawyer
MILLER, PEARSON, GLOE, BURNS, BEATTY
& PARRISH, P.L.C., 905
Beatty, Stephen Athletics Operations Assistant
DAEMEN COLLEGE ATHLETICS, 356
Beatty, William Shareholder
JOHNSON & BELL, 896
Beaty, David Head Coach, Football
MEMORIAL STADIUM (KANSAS), 995
Beaty, Leslie Athletic Trainer
SCIENCE AND ARTS OF OKLAHOMA
ATHLETICS, UNIVERSITY OF, 316, 318
Beauchamp, Jeff Vice President/Station Manager
WBAL RADIO, 644
Beaudoin, Jamie Associate Athletics Director
MAINE AT FARMINGTON ATHLETICS,
UNIVERSITY OF, 393
Beaudry, Francois President
QUEBEC MAJOR JUNIOR HOCKEY LEAGUE,
135
Beaudry, Matt Director of Athletics & Recreation
MICHIGAN-DEARBORN ATHLETICS,
UNIVERSITY OF, 314
Beaulieu, Charlie Secretary
GOLF CANADA, 100
Beauregard, Kathy Director of Athletics
WESTERN MICHIGAN UNIVERSITY
ATHLETICS, 349
Beausoleil, Serge General Manager & Head
Coach
QUEBEC MAJOR JUNIOR HOCKEY LEAGUE,
135
Beautyman, Michael Chairperson
BEAUTYMAN ASSOCIATES, P.C., 874
Beaver, Don President
SOUTH ATLANTIC LEAGUE, 52
Beaver, Donald Owner/President
PACIFIC COAST LEAGUE OF
PROFESSIONAL BASEBALL CLUBS, 49
Beaver, Jerry General Manager
KBYR - TALK 700, 621
Becerril, Jaime Sports Anchor
KWEX-TV, 705
Bechac, Andrew Senior Associate AD, Internal
Ops.
SOUTHEASTERN LOUISIANA UNIVERSITY
ATHLETICS, 344, 1015, 1021
Bechae, Andrew Facility Director
STRAWBERRY STADIUM, 1015
Bechard, Jerome Head Coach
FEDERAL HOCKEY LEAGUE, 131
Becher, Jonathan President
AMERICAN HOCKEY LEAGUE/AHL, 125, 128
Becher, Scott President
SPORTS & SPONSORSHIPS, INC., 864
Becherer, Matthew Track President
HOMESTEAD-MIAMI SPEEDWAY, LLC, 765,
1035

Bechet, Leon Partner
MILLING BENSON WOODWARD, L.L.P., 905
Bechta, Jack Owner
BECHTA, JACK D./JB SPORTS, 835
Bechtel, Mark Senior Editor
SPORTS ILLUSTRATED, 591
Bechtol, Dennis Chair/Director
NORTHWOOD UNIVERSITY FLORIDA
CAMPUS, 432
Bechtold, Camie Senior Associate AD,
Administration
MONTANA STATE UNIVERSITY ATHLETICS,
337
Beck, Alex General Manager
KAUR-FM, 619
Beck, Bill Sports Editor
TRUTH, 489, 546
Beck, Brain Assistant Executive Director;
Compliance
NATIONAL JUNIOR COLLEGE ATHLETIC
ASSOCIATION/NJCAA, 283
Beck, Bruce Weekend Sports Anchor
WNBC-TV, 715
Beck, Cherie Corporate secretary, associate legal
cou
THOMAS M. COOLEY LAW SCHOOL, 921
Beck, Craig Sports Writer
CALEDONIAN RECORD, 470
Beck, Fred Chief Financial Officer
ICON HEALTH & FITNESS, INC., 1157
Beck, Gary Treasurer
VIRGINIA STATE GOLF ASSOCIATION, 116
Beck, Gary Co-Founder / Director
H.S.T. INC., 1152
Beck, Howard Sports Reporter
NEW YORK TIMES, 514
Beck, Jeremy Management Assistant
IDAHO STATE POLICE, 80
Beck, Lynette Marketing Director
BERNIER, CARR & ASSOCIATES, 1060
Beck, Michael Partner
REICH, ROBERT S., 911
Beck, Michelle Asst. Commissioner For External
Relation
NORTHERN SUN INTERCOLLEGIATE
CONFERENCE, 300
Beck, Randy Co-Founder / Chief Executive Officer
H.S.T. INC., 1152
Beck, Richard Partner
FOSTER, DON, 890
Beck, Scott President/CEO
SALT LAKE CONVENTION & VISITORS
BUREAU, 244
Beck, Steve President/CEO
MILITARY BOWL, 92
Beckenbach, Pete Regional Sales Director
HACHETTE FILIPACCHI MEDIA, 568
Becker, Aaron Athletics Facilities Coordinator
COLLEGE OF NEW JERSEY ATHLETICS
(TCNJ), 382
Becker, Alan Founding Shareholder
BECKER & POLIAKOFF, P.A., 874
Becker, Ben Sports Director
WPTV-TV, 686, 716
Becker, Carol Advertising Director
ITHACA JOURNAL, 500
Becker, David Chairman of the Board/CEO
CSI SERVICES/RICS SOFTWARE, 1225
Becker, Dennis President/CEO
MOBIVITY, 766, 804
Becker, Joe Sports Anchor
KGW-TV, 698
Becker, Jon Sports Editor
DAILY REVIEW (CA), 482
Becker, Keri Athletic Director
GRAND VALLEY STATE UNIVERSITY
ATHLETICS, 360
Becker, Mark Director of Sports Information
CALIFORNIA INSTITUTE OF TECHNOLOGY
ATHLETICS, 380
Becker, Maureen Executive Director
INTERNATIONAL POLICE MOUNTAIN BIKE
ASSOCIATION (IPMBA), 70
Becker, Mike Director of Tickets
EASTERN LEAGUE, 39, 974
Becker, Noah Director of Athletic Communications
FROSTBURG STATE UNIVERSITY
ATHLETICS (FSU), 386

Becker, Paul Senior Associate
NBBJ, 1071
Becker, Rich Sports Director
WXXA-TV, 721
Becker, Robert Sports Editor
GRAND RAPIDS PRESS, 494
Becker, Tim Sports Director
KPTV-TV, 702
Becker, Timothy Lawyer
ZIMMERMAN REED, P.L.LP., 928
Becker, Uli President
REEBOK APPAREL GROUP, 1192
Becker, Uli President
REEBOK INTERNATIONAL LTD.-RETAIL, 1247
Becker, William Attorney
BECKER, WILLIAM F.X., 874
Beckerman, Dan President & CEO
MAJOR LEAGUE SOCCER, 124, 157
Becket, Welton Founder
AECOM, 1058
Beckett, James Owner
VINTAGE BECKETT SPORTS
COLLECTIBLES, 597
Beckett, Keith Director of Athletics
WOOSTER ATHLETICS, THE COLLEGE OF,
410
Beckett, Lisa Associate Director of Athletics
POMONA-PITZER COLLEGES ATHLETICS,
399
Beckett, Thomas Director of Athletics
YALE BOWL, 982, 1030
Beckham, David Owner/President
MAJOR LEAGUE SOCCER, 157
Beckham, Paul Chairman
HOPE-BECKHAM, INC., 796
Beckhardt, Charles Sports Director
WTTR-AM, 677
Beckley, Jean Advertising Manager
CHRONICLE (CT), 472
Beckman, Mark Executive Director
MONTANA HS ASSOCIATION, 199
Beckman, Sherry Volunteer Committee,Chair
USTA FLORIDA, 173
Beckner, Allen Producer
FOX 59 OVERTIME, 687
Beckner, Lisa Office Manager
VIKING HALL CIVIC CENTER, 1025
Beckwith, Robert Vice President, Finance
CROSMAN CORPORATION, 1131
Beczynski, Ron Facilities Director
JOHN F. SAVAGE HALL, 985
Beddow, Rick Chief Operating Officer
SPECIAL OLYMPICS FLORIDA, 192
Bedell, Daniel Associate
JOHNSON & BELL, 896
Bedell, Tom Owner
PURE FISHING, 1189
Bedier, Kim Director
TACOMA DOME, 1016
Bedingfield, Cindy CEO
REDWOOD ACRES FAIRGROUNDS, 1041
Bedinghaus, Bob Director, Business
Development
NATIONAL FOOTBALL LEAGUE/NFL, 95
Beditz, PhD, Joseph President & Chief Executive
Officer
NATIONAL GOLF FOUNDATION, 103
Bednar, Jared Head Coach
NATIONAL HOCKEY LEAGUE/NHL, 123
Bednarova, Zuzana Business Development
BUSINESS LAW VENTURES, 879
Bednarowski, John Sports Editor
MARIETTA DAILY JOURNAL, 508
Bednarsh, Joe Athletic Director
YESHIVA UNIVERSITY ATHLETICS, 410
Bednarz, Rick VP, Sales
ONFIELD APPAREL GROUP, LLC
HEADWARE DIVISION, 1182
Bedore, Ed Sales VP
ZEBCO, 1224
Bedore, Gary Sports Assistant Editor
JOURNAL-WORLD, 502
Bedoya, Bonnie Assistant to the Athletic Director
CHAMINADE UNIVERSITY ATHLETICS, 355
Bedway, Nick Sports Editor
WHEELING NEWS-REGISTER, 551
Bee, Mark Advertising Director
SALISBURY POST, 532

Beebe, Dick Publisher
MARC TIMES RACING NEWS, 575
Beebe, Phil Sports Editor
STAR PRESS, 539
Beech, Joseph Partner
SCHOENI, K. ROGER, 914
Beecher, Jim Publisher/Editor
JUNIOR BASEBALL, 573
Beek, Paul
KWNO-FM, 639
Beekman, Bill Athletics Director
MICHIGAN STATE UNIVERSITY ATHLETICS,
337
Beekman, Kim Managing Editor
SKI MAGAZINE, 586
Beelby, Rick Director
HOWARD PAYNE UNIVERSITY, 423
Beeler, Dave Sales Staff
C M T SPECIALTY SPORTS, 1233
Beeman, Derek VP, Ticket Sales & Business
Insights
NATIONAL FOOTBALL LEAGUE/NFL, 95
Beeman, Timothy Chairman/Chief Executive
Officer
MIRAMAR EVENTS, 766
Beene, Charles Editor
VERMONT SOCCER ASSOCIATION NEWS,
577, 579, 580, 588, 593, 595, 597
Beene, Darrin Sports Writer
NEWS TRIBUNE, 516
Beers, Butch Program Coordinator
SPECIAL OLYMPICS NEW HAMPSHIRE, 194
Beesley, Wilford Lawyer
PRINCE YEATES, 910
Beffa, Bruce Senior Producer
CAPPY PRODUCTIONS INC., 604
Beffa, Nancy Vice President/Executive Vice
President
CAPPY PRODUCTIONS INC., 604
Beffert, Brad Head Athletic Trainer
GREAT FALLS ATHLETICS, UNIVERSITY OF,
311
Begay, Chip Sports Director
KIPA-AM, 627
Begdan, Pamela Manager
SALAUN SPORTS, INC., HENRI, 1196
Begeron, Kate Treasurer
WORLD FLYING DISC FEDERATION, 98
Beggins, Mary President
CELEBRITY MARKETING GROUP, 837
Begley, Stephanie Head Athletic Trainer
METROPOLITAN STATE UNIVERSITY OF
DENVER ATHLETICS, 364
Begly, Brain National Resource Manager
SOCCER ASSOCIATION FOR YOUTH, 266
Behall, John Bike Shop Manager
HUDSON TRAIL OUTFITTERS, LTD., 1242
Behan, Mike Secretary
NORTHEASTERN NEW YORK PGA
SECTIONAL OFFICE, 106
Behan, Theresa Head Athletic Trainer
THOMAS MORE COLLEGE ATHLETICS, 405
Behanian, Bob Sports Reporter
WCSC-TV, 709
Behar, Doug Senior VP, Stadium Operations
AMERICAN LEAGUE OF PROFESSIONAL
BASEBALL CLUBS, THE, 30
Behler, Judy Advertising Manager
LIVING ABOARD MAGAZINE, 574
Behlman, Debbie Director Marketing
ATHENA GOLF, 1111
Behm, Maria Senior Associate AD, Business
Affairs
LOYOLA MARYMOUNT UNIVERSITY, 335
Behnke, Kerry Administrative Support Asstistant
FLORIDA STATE UNIVERSITY, 420
Behnke, Lori Academic Secretary
LORAS COLLEGE, 426
Behrens, Jeanette Operations Assistant
CLARDY, DON S., 882
Behymer, Mike Business Development
COSTANTE GROUP SPORTS & EVENT
MARKETING, LLC, 761
Beideman, Don Sports Reporter
PHILADELPHIA INQUIRER, 523
Beidner, Michelle Co-Founder
MiCa SPORTS, 756
Beiersdorf, Oliver Partner
REED SMITH LLP, 911

Beighley, Mark Sports Director
KDLR-AM, 622
Beightol, Scott Partner
TREBATOSKI, CHRIS J., 922
Beil, Larry Sports Anchor
KGO-TV, 698
Beiler, Benjamin President and CEO
PUTTERMAN ATHLETICS, 1190
Beilke, Jim Publisher
SNOWTECH MAGAZINE, 587
Beilke, Kevin Managing Editor
SNOWTECH MAGAZINE, 587
Bein, Barbara Finance Administrator
DANVILLE AREA CONVENTION & VISITOR
BUREAU, 230
Beirne, Sean Vice Chair
COLORADO RACING COMMISSION, 80, 118
Beisker, Betty Human Resources VP
VENUEWORKS, 1075
Beitler, Paul Sports Editor
NEWS-BANNER, 516
Beito, Howard Assistant Coach
NORTH AMERICAN HOCKEY LEAGUE, 132
Beitz, Joseph Sports Information Director
SALEM STATE COLLEGE ATHLETICS, 402
Beitzel, Ben Sports Reporter
GWINNETT DAILY POST, 495
Bekelja, Joseph Partner
MARGOLIS EDELSTEIN, 902
Belanger, France Executive VP & Chief
Commercial Officer
NATIONAL HOCKEY LEAGUE/NHL, 124
Belardinelli, Valerie Media/Public Relations
AGGRESSIVE SKATERS ASSOCIATION, 139
Belber, Bob General Manager
TIMES UNION CENTER, 1019
Belbin, Ken Sports Information Director
DANIEL WEBSTER COLLEGE ATHLETICS
(DWC), 383
Belchic, Layne Vice President
MOFFETT PRODUCTIONS, INC., 607
Belden, Molly Associate Commissioner For
Compliance
NORTHEAST-10 CONFERENCE, 299
Belding, Dave VP, Technical Operations
MITSUBISHI DIAMOND VISION, 1174
Belew, Bart Assistant Athletics Director for Athleti
SKYHAWK STADIUM, 1012
Belfrage, Greg News Director
KWSN-AM, 623, 639
Belichick, Bill Head Coach
NATIONAL FOOTBALL LEAGUE/NFL, 96
Belinfante, Geoff Senior Vice President/Executive
Producer
SPORTS NEWSATELLITE, 694
Belinfante, Geoffrey Senior VP/Executive
Producer
THE PHOENIX COMUNICATIONS GROUP,
INC., 609
Belisle, Merritt Chairman
HIGH END SYSTEMS, INC, 1155
Belisle, Mike Director/ Sports & Recreation
UNIVERSAL FABRIC STRUCTURES, 1218
Belk, H.W. President
BELK STORES SERVICES, 1230
Belk, John President/COO
BELK STORES SERVICES, 1230
Belk, Thomas Chairman and Chief Executive
Officer
BELK STORES SERVICES, 1230
Belk, Jr, Thomas Chairman/CEO
MCRAE'S, INC., 1244
Bell, Bob Chief Executive Officer
HICKORY BRANDS, INC., 1154
Bell, Chris Vice President, Software Engineering
UNGERBOECK SYSTEMS, INC., 63, 224
Bell, Cindy EVP Meeting Services
PGI, INC., 809
Bell, Daniel Game Presentation Manager
AMERICAN HOCKEY LEAGUE/AHL, 128
Bell, Daniel Senior Vice President, Hotels &
Leisure
TANGENT ASSOCIATES, INC., 1077
Bell, Dee Marketing Manager
ANTHONY TRAVEL, INC., 935
Bell, Dwight President
USA LUGE, 142, 207
Bell, Gregg Sports Senior Writer
SACRAMENTO BEE, 530

Best, Tom General Manager
WRIC TV-8, 717
Beste, Alan Executive Director
IOWA HS ATHLETIC ASSOCIATION, 198
Bestrom, Craig Senior Editor
GOLF DIGEST, 566
Betbeze, J. Partner
MILLING BENSON WOODWARD, L.L.P., 905
Betchkal, Janice Chief Financial Officer
RELIABLE OF MILWAUKEE, 1192
Betesh, Elliott President / Apparel
DR. JAY'S, 1237
Betesh, Raymond Buyer / Footwear
DR. JAY'S, 1237
Beth, DeBauche Commissioner
OHIO VALLEY CONFERENCE, 300
Bethill, Charles Partner
THACHER PROFFITT & WOOD, 921
Bethke, Jack District Govenor
CONNECTICUT AAU ASSOCIATION, 212
Betit, Paul Sports Reporter
PORTLAND PRESS HERALD, MAINE SUNDAY
TELEGRAM, 525
Betker, Brad Sports Copy Editor
DETROIT FREE PRESS, 486
Betow, Gary Partner
CONNER & WINTERS, P.L.L.C., 883
Betras, Joe President
THERMO-SERV/BETRAS, 1212
Betres, Missy Senior Manager, ESPN Events
BIRMINGHAM BOWL, 90
Bettencourt, Andrew Sports Reporter
VISALIA TIMES-DELTA, 549
Bettilyon, Erika Office Manager
FLORIDA STATE UNIVERSITY, 420
Bettle, Jeremy Director of High Performance
NATIONAL HOCKEY LEAGUE/NHL, 122
Bettman, Gary Commissioner
NATIONAL HOCKEY LEAGUE/NHL, 122
Betts, Glenn Building Operations
CAMP RANDALL STADIUM, 963
Betz, Bill Sports Director
KMFY-FM, 630
Beuhring, Laura Director of Golf
RAYMOND JAMES STADIUM, 1004
Bevacqua, Peter Chief Executive Officer
PGA OF AMERICA/PROFESSIONAL
GOLFERS' ASSOCIATION OF AMERICA, 103
Bevans, Michael Executive Editor
SPORTS ILLUSTRATED, 591
Bevard, Darren Principal
COUNSILMAN-HUNSAKER, 1062
Beverage, Morris President
NJCAA REGION XII MEN'S, 286
Bevere, Kelly Director of Compliance
MIDDLEBURY COLLEGE ATHLETICS (MCA),
395
Beveridge, Janell Commissioner
NEBRASKA STATE RACING COMMISSION, 81
Beverly, Sharon Executive Director of Athletics
COLLEGE OF NEW JERSEY ATHLETICS
(TCNJ), 382
Bevevino, D.J. Interim Associate Athletic Director
CLARION UNIVERSITY OF PENNSYLVANIA
ATHLETICS, 355
Bevilacqua, Mark Director of Youth Rugby
WESTERN SUBURBS RUGBY FOOTBALL
CLUB, 148
Bevillard, Caroline Senior Associate AD,
Administration/SWA
EAST CAROLINA UNIVERSITY ATHLETICS,
328
Bey, Gwen Chief Administrative Officer
KENYON & KENYON (DC OFFICE), 897
Beyer, Dave Sports Information Director
MCMURRY UNIVERSITY ATHLETICS, 395
Beyer, James Partner
WATTS, STEVEN R., 924
Beyer, Theresa Director of Marketing
WFAN SPORTS RADIO, 652
Beyers, Maureen Attorney
OSBORN MALEDON, P.A., 908
Beyette, Bob News Director
970 WATH, 611
Beyor, Pamela Chairperson
BERNIER, CARR & ASSOCIATES, 1060
Beyrer, Brian Senior Associate AD,
Communications
IONA COLLEGE ATHLETICS, 332

Bezbatchenko, Tim President/General Manager
MAJOR LEAGUE SOCCER, 157
Bhatia, Sanjeev Orthopaedic Surgeon
CINCINNATI SPORTSMEDICINE &
ORTHOPAEDIC CENTER, 929
Bhatti, Usman Principal - PMK International
PELTON MARSH KINSELLA, 830
Bhender, Lisa Office Coordinator
CHICAGOLAND SPEEDWAY, 1033
Biagi, Fred Co-Owner
NASCAR XFINITY SERIES, 24
Biagi, Greg Co-Owner
NASCAR XFINITY SERIES, 24
Bialas, Dave Team Manager
FLORIDA STATE LEAGUE, 40
Bialas, Michael Assistant Sports Editor
ROCKY MOUNTAIN NEWS, 530
Bialek, Joe Director of Sales
EASTERN LEAGUE, 39
Bialka, Mike Sports Editor
BRAINERD DAILY DISPATCH, 468
Biancamano, David Senior Associate AD,
Development
UMASS AMHERST ATHLETICS, 348
Bianchi, Mandy Account Manager
EXTRAORDINARY EVENTS, 763
Bianchi, Mike Sports Senior Columnist
ORLANDO SENTINEL, 520
Bianco, Frank President
INTERNATIONAL MICROTECH, INC., 1159
Biasca, Meredith
REDWOOD ACRES FAIRGROUNDS, 1041
Bibb, Greg President/CEO
WOMEN'S NATIONAL BASKETBALL
ASSOCIATION, 61
Bibb, Missy Secretary
LADIES BIRMINGHAM GOLF ASSOCIATION,
111
Bibeau, Ron Secretary
NEW ENGLAND PGA SECTIONAL OFFICE,
105
Bibishkov, Krum Head Coach
CANADIAN SOCCER LEAGUE, 156
Biche-Labbe, Deb Associate Athletic Director
THOMAS COLLEGE ATHLETICS, 405
Bick, Joe President, Founder
PRO STAR MANAGEMENT, INC., 858
Bickel, Stu Assistant General Manager/Head
Coach
NORTH AMERICAN HOCKEY LEAGUE, 132
Bickerton, Rachael 2nd Vice President
INTERNATIONAL COLLEGIATE LICENSING
ASSOCIATION/ICLA, 282
Bickford, Brian Treasurer
MAINE STATE GOLF ASSOCIATION, 111
Bickford, Gaven General Manager/Director,
Scouting
NORTH AMERICAN HOCKEY LEAGUE, 132
Bickford, Jim President
AMERICAN DREAMS, 781
Bickford, Meredith Associate Director of Athletics
SOUTHERN MAINE ATHLETICS, UNIVERSITY
OF, 402
Bickham, John President and COO
CHARTER COMMUNICATIONS, 735
Bickhart, Terry Sports Editor
READING EAGLE, 527
Bickley, Dan Sports Columnist
ARIZONA REPUBLIC, 463
Bickmeier, Dennis President
RICHMOND INTERNATIONAL RACEWAY,
1041
Biddinger, Allen Facilities/Events Manager
STABLER ARENA, 1014
Biddix, Patrick General Manager
MELBOURNE GREYHOUND PARK & CLUB 52
POKER, 1056
Biddle, Carrie Vice President of Sales
MAGNETSTREET, 1169
Biddle, David Sports Editor
MADISON PRESS, 508
Biddle, Joe Sports Columnist
TENNESSEAN, 542
Biderman, Paul Director - Institute of Public Law
MATHEWSON, ALFRED D., 903
Bidges, Stacey National Sales Manager
RIGHT GARD CORPORATION, 1193

Bidlack, Steve Marketing And Communications
Manager
MID-OHIO SPORTS CAR COURSE, 1038
Bidwill, Michael Owner
NATIONAL FOOTBALL LEAGUE/NFL, 94
Bie, Tom Editor
POWDER, 582
Biehl, Mike Director, College Scouting
NATIONAL FOOTBALL LEAGUE/NFL, 97
Bielak, Michael Director of Athletic
Communications
STATE UNIVERSITY OF NEW YORK
COLLEGE AT OSWEGO(SUNY), 404
Bielec, Patrick Director of Ballpark Operations
C.O. BROWN STADIUM, 962
Bien, Ken Immediate Past President
SOUTHERN CALIFORNIA GOLF
ASSOCIATION, 115
Bienvenu, Lionel Sports Anchor
KMGH-TV, 699
Bieri, Chris Sports Editor
MINOT DAILY NEWS, 511
Bieri, Jeanie Director, Marketing
MUSCO SPORTS-LIGHTING, 1176
Biering, Raymond Partner
ADAMSKI MOROSKI MADDEN & GREEN LLP,
870
Bierley, Craig GMC Advertising and Sales
Promotion Dire
GAME TIME, INC., 1146
Bierly, Angie Advertising Manager
PARIS DAILY BEACON NEWS, 522
Biertempfel, Rob Sports Writer
PITTSBURGH TRIBUNE-REVIEW, 524
Bierwirth, Chandra Associate AD, Compliance
GEORGE WASHINGTON UNIVERSITY
ATHLETICS, 330
Bigby, Tom Station Manager/Pro General
Manager
WIP SPORTSRADIO 610, 658
Bigelow, Bill Sports Editor
BULLETIN, 469
Bigelow, Chandler CFO
SENNET, CHARLES J., 863
Bigelow, Chris President
BIGELOW COMPANIES, THE, 1073, 1076
Bigelow, Doug Vice Presidnet
E&D SPECIALTY STANDS INC., 1137
Bigelow, Kelli Executive Assistant, President
SPECIAL OLYMPICS CONNECTICUT, 192
Biggane, Brian Sports Reporter
PALM BEACH POST, 521
Biggar, Lynn EVP/Chief Marketing &
Communications Off
VISA USA, 743
Biggerstaff, Randy Director of Athletic Training
LINDENWOOD UNIVERSITY ATHLETICS, 363
Biggerstaff, Tim Program Director
WCSL-AM, 649
Biggs, Craig Associate Athletics Director
LT SMITH STADIUM, 970, 993
Biggs, Jessie Assistant Athletic Director
INDIANA INSTITUTE OF TECHNOLOGY
ATHLETICS, 312
Biggs, Jimmy Food and Beverage Manager
KELLOGG ARENA, 245, 987
Bigland, Reid Head of U.S. Sales
FCA US, LLC, 736
Bihler, Gene Vice President
INTERNATIONAL BOWHUNTING
ORGANIZATION, 14
Bihr, Katherine Vice President,
Programs/Education
TIGER WOODS FOUNDATION, 191
Biilik, Steven Chairman
MOUNTAINEER CASINO, RACE TRACK &
RESORT, 1051
Bikoff, Ken Editor
INSIDE INDIANA, 570
Bikowski, Emily Women's Lacrosse Head Coach
NEWBERRY COLLEGE, 431
Bilas, Jay Analyst
COLLEGE GAMEDAY, 615
Bilas, Jim Marketing Director
DIVERSA PRODUCTS GROUP, 1110, 1135
Bilello, Brian President
MAJOR LEAGUE SOCCER, 157

executive index

WEST VIRGINIA UNIVERSITY/WVU
COLISEUM, 1027
Borman, Matthew Deputy AD, Development
GEORGIA ATHLETICS, UNIVERSITY OF, 330
Borman, Scott President
AMPROS TROPHIES, 1109
Born, David Guest Service Director
SAVVIS CENTER, 1010
Born, Marco Director of Athletics
LAMAR UNIVERSITY ATHLETICS, 334
Born, Mike Director of NBA Scouting
KAUFFMAN SPORTS MANAGEMENT GROUP, 849
Born, Peter President
BOGNER, 1119
Bornstein, Steve Media EVP
BERTHELSEN, RICHARD, 835
Boroomand, Farah Chief Financial Officer
AMF BOWLING WORLDWIDE, 1108
Borrego, James Head Coach
NATIONAL BASKETBALL ASSOCIATION/NBA, 56
Borrego, Rene President/CEO
NATIONAL BASKETBALL ASSOCIATION
DEVELOPMENT LEAGUE, 60
Borrelli, Tom Sports Writer
BUFFALO NEWS, 469
Borreson, Candy Marketing SVP
KEYSTONE MARKETING, INC., 800
Borrie, Stuart Director of Operations
BADMINTON WORLD FEDERATION, 25
Borris, Jeff General Counsel
BEVERLY HILLS SPORTS COUNCIL, 835, 875
Borst, Nichole Head Athletic Trainer
MONTANA STATE UNIVERSITY-NORTHERN
ATHLETICS, 315
Borsuk, Marie Business Manager
WORLD KARTING ASSOCIATION, 19
Bortner, Jan Assistant Athletic Director
BEAVER STADIUM, 957
Borto, Mark VP, Sales
TOMSED CORPORATION, 1213
Borton, John Editor
WOLVERINE, 599
Bortscheller, Sara Athletic Trainer
MOUNT MARTY COLLEGE ATHLETICS, 315
Bos, Matt Sports Information Director
NORTHWESTERN COLLEGE (IA) ATHLETICS, 316
Bosalavage, Wendy President
AMERICAN LEISURE CORPORATION, 1058
Bosch, Joseph Executive Vice President/Chief
HR Office
DIRECTV, INC., 693
Bosch, Manel CEO Worldwide Operations
INTERPERFORMANCES, INC., 848
Bosco, Lew Director Horner Study Center
HORNER FLOORING COMPANY, 1156
Bosco, Mary Partner
PATTON BOGGS, 908
Boscolo, Benjamin Attorney
CHASEN & BOSCOLO CHARTERED, 881
Boscov, Albert Chairman, Chief Executive Officer
BOSCOV'S DEPARTMENT STORES, 1232
Boscov, Jim Vice Chairman of Boscov's
Department Sto
BOSCOV'S DEPARTMENT STORES, 1232
Bosh, Jon Head Athletics Trainer
WHITWORTH COLLEGE ATHLETICS, 409
Boshers, Connie Director of Administration
NASHVILLE SUPERSPEEDWAY, 1039
Bosiwick, Larry General Manager/Owner
WRMS-FM, 672
Boskey, Craig Senior VP Finance
NATIONAL MARINE MANUFACTURERS
ASSOCIATION, 64
Bossard, Roger Head Groundskeeper
AMERICAN LEAGUE OF PROFESSIONAL
BASEBALL CLUBS, THE, 29
Bossell, Candace Head Coach, Women's
Lacrosse
MCCARTHY STADIUM, 994
Bossmann, Lori Vice President Merchandising,
Marketing
ACE HARDWARE, 1227
Bosso, Sarah Assistant General Manager
CALIFORNIA LEAGUE (A-LEVEL), 36, 978
Bostic, Kyle Sports Editor
NEW YORK DAILY CHALLENGE, 514

Bostic, Renee Director of Athletics
MEDGAR EVERS COLLEGE ATHLETICS
(MEC), 395
Bostock, Roy Co-Owner
SOUTH ATLANTIC LEAGUE, 51
Boston, Wallace President & Chief Executive
Officer
AMERICAN MILITARY UNIVERSITY, 411
Bostwick, Kyle Vice President
NEW YORK-PENNSYLVANIA LEAGUE, 47, 1025
Boswell, Jackie Assistant Athletics Director
STEVENSON UNIVERSITY, 405
Boswell, Robert President
SUN SHADER INTERNATIONAL,
INC./WASHINGTON SQUARE GARDEN, INC., 1209
Botelho, Dave Head Athletic Trainer
NORWICH UNIVERSITY ATHLETICS, 398
Bothof, Ken Director of Athletics
NORTHERN KENTUCKY UNIVERSITY
ATHLETICS, 340
Botkin, Brad Sports Writer
TIMES-STANDARD, 545
Bott, Jason Producer
PRIME TIME PADRES, 688, 690, 692
Bottelo, Nancy President/CEO
SPECIAL OLYMPICS HAWAII, 192
Bottke, Warren President
SOUTH FLORIDA PGA, 114
Botts, Jeff Program Director
KANE-AM, 619
Bouchard, Gilles Assistant Coach
AMERICAN HOCKEY LEAGUE/AHL, 128
Bouchard, Jo‰l Head Coach
AMERICAN HOCKEY LEAGUE/AHL, 127
Bouchard, Rick President
NORTH AMERICAN HOCKEY LEAGUE, 132
Bouchard-Hall, Derek President/Chief Operating
Officer
USA CYCLING, 71, 72, 206
Boucher, Eric President
QUEBEC MAJOR JUNIOR HOCKEY LEAGUE, 135
Boucher, Mathieu Director, Performance
Development
CYCLING CANADA, 70
Boucher, Philippe General Manager
QUEBEC MAJOR JUNIOR HOCKEY LEAGUE, 135
Boucher, Robert Dean of Human Kinetics
WINDSOR, UNIVERSITY OF, 440
Boucher, Sebastian Manager
FRONTIER LEAGUE, 41
Bouchez, Richard Promotions Manager
KOAA-TV, 700
Bouck, Craig President, CEO
BARKER RINKER SEACAT ARCHITECTURE, 1059
Bouclet, Philippe Vice President
WORLD ARCHERY FEDERATION, 15
Bouda, Michael Manager
JEDC SPORTS AND ENTERTAINMENT
DIVISION/JACKSONVILLE FLORIDA, 235
Boudreau, Ben Assistant Coach
EAST COAST HOCKEY LEAGUE/ECHL, 129, 130
Boudreau, Monica Account Manager
RIDEAU CARLETON RACEWAY, 1053
Boudreaux, Robert Executive Vice President
UNITED STATES SPECIALTY SPORTS
ASSOCATION, 168
Boudriex, Sou Advertising Sales
WBUK-FM, 646
Bough, Deborah Computer & Information
Systems Manager
GREATER LANSING CONVENTION &
VISITORS BUREAU, 233
Boughner, Bob Head Coach
NATIONAL HOCKEY LEAGUE/NHL, 125
Bouko, Darren Manager Business Development
HOCKEY HALL OF FAME AND MUSEUM, 251
Boulay, Pat President
SHOOTING FEDERATION OF CANADA, 150
Boulerice, Pierre Vice President
RESEAU DU SPORTETUDIANT DU QUEBEC, 201
Boulton, Frank Principal Owner
ATLANTIC LEAGUE, 35, 956, 958

Bouma, Glenn Athletics Director
DORDT COLLEGE ATHLETICS, 310
Bounds, Martin VP Business Development
STREET & SMITH'S SPORTSBUSINESS
JOURNAL, 593
Bounsall, Phil Treasurer
SPECIAL OLYMPICS INDIANA, 193
Bourg, Michelle Co-Editor & Features Writer
WINGFOOT, 599
Bourgeois, Beth Director, Communications
U.S. OLYMPIC COMMITTEE BROADCASTING
DIVISION, 609
Bourgeois, Pat President/CEO
SPECIAL OLYMPICS LOUISIANA, 193
Bourgerie, Alexia Principal
STEIN, SPERLING, BENNETT, DE JONG,
DRISCOLL & GREENFEIG, P.C., 918
Bouris, Greg Director Communications
MAJOR LEAGUE BASEBALL PLAYERS
ASSOCIATION, 850
Bourke, Kevin Chief Creations Officer
IOWA GAMES, 261
Bourne, David Special Reports Editor
SPORTS BUSINESS JOURNAL, 590
Bourne, Jeff Director of Athletics
JAMES MADISON UNIVERSITY ATHLETICS, 333
Bourne, Jenny Faculty Athletic Representative
CARLETON COLLEGE ATHLETICS, 380
Bourne, Richard President
ASICS AMERICA CORPORATION, 1111
Bourque, Peter Assistant Athletic Director
CATAWBA COLLEGE ATHLETICS, 354
Bourquin, Bruce Sports Reporter
SIERRA VISTA HERALD, 535
Bourrie, Eric Sales Representative
H E HODGE COMPANY, 1151
Bousfield, Jeff Associate
GLASS ARCHITECTS, 1067
Bouska, Dan Equipment Manager
UNITED STATES HOCKEY LEAGUE, 137
Boutcher, David Chair of Business & Finance
Department
REED SMITH, 911
Boutillier, Carol Office Administrator
LAYMAN, MICHAEL L., 899
Boutin, Stephen Founder
BOUTIN, DENTINO, GIBSON, DI GUISTO,
HODELL, INC., 876
Bouvier, Arthur Director of Stadium Operations
G. RICHARD PFITZNER STADIUM, 975
Bouyea, Brien Communications coordinator
NATIONAL MUSEUM OF RACING HALL OF
FAME, 255
Bouza, David President
STRENGTH SYSTEMS, INC., 1208
Bouza, Kevin Marketing / Operations VP
STRENGTH SYSTEMS, INC., 1208
Bouzidi, Karim Executive Director
INTERNATIONAL BOXING ASSOCIATION
(AIBA), 67
Bove, Jeffrey Partner
DURANTE, CHARLES J., 886
Bovee, Jerry Deputy AD, External Affairs
UTAH STATE UNIVERSITY ATHLETICS, 348, 969
Bowden, Paul Associate AD, Student-Athlete
Support Se
HOWARD UNIVERSITY ATHLETICS, 332
Bowden, Todd Director of Athletic Training
JOHN BROWN UNIVERSITY ATHLETICS, 313
Bowditch, Fred Manager
CROAKIES, 1131
Bowdon, James Coordinating Producer
ESPN, 690
Bowen, Barbara Advertising Manager
WBKB-TV, 708
Bowen, Crystal Director of Ticket Operations
MIDWEST LEAGUE, 44
Bowen, David Senior Consultant
ACENTECH INC., 828
Bowen, Kevin Head Of Referees
USA BANDY, 25
Bowen, Les Professional Football Reporter
PHILADELPHIA DAILY NEWS, 523
Bowen, Shane Sports Editor
SUN NEWS, 541
Bowen, Tom Vice Chancellor for Intercollegiate
Athl

ARKANSAS STATE UNIVERSITY ATHLETICS, 323

Bowens, Daniel Executive Creative Director
DRAFTWORLDWIDE, 789

Bowens, Frank Manager, Ballpark Operations
NATIONAL LEAGUE OF PROFESSIONAL BASEBALL CLUBS, THE, 32

Bower, Curtis Vice Chairman Of The Board
PARSONS, 1071

Bower, Dan President
CENTURY SPORTING GOODS, 1234

Bower, Jeff Senior VP, Basketball Operations
NATIONAL BASKETBALL ASSOCIATION/NBA, 58

Bower, Shannon Publisher
GOLF GEORGIA, 566

Bowers, Chris Event Manager
PK PARK, 1002

Bowers, Helen General Manager
CUSTOM SPORTSWEAR CORP/DBA SPORTSWEAR UNLIMITED, 1132

Bowers, J. Chief Executive Officer
AMERICAN PHYSICAL THERAPY ASSOCIATION, 929

Bowers, Jeff Associate Director of Athletics
VIRGINIA WESLEYAN COLLEGE ATHLETICS(VWC), 407

Bowers, Katie Head Athletic Trainer
ILLINOIS AT SPRINGFIELD ATHLETICS, UNIVERSITY OF, 361

Bowers, Kirstie Senior Associate Director of Athletics/S
BOSTON UNIVERSITY ATHLETICS, 324

Bowers, Michael Chief Executive Officer
AMERICAN PHYSICAL THERAPY ASSOCIATION, 84

Bowers, Pete Station Manager
WBFH RADIO, 614

Bowers, Rachel Sports Editor
ATHENS BANNER-HERALD, 464

Bowers, Thomas Co-Director
INDIANA UNIVERSITY, 423

Bowie, Chris Sports Editor
BOONVILLE DAILY NEWS, 467

Bowie, Glenn Chair
WATER SKI & WAKEBOARD CANADA, 177

Bowie, Nikki Secretary
U.S. LIFESAVING ASSOCIATION, 170

Bowker, Jennie Head Athletic Trainer
HOOD COLLEGE ATHLETICS, 389

Bowlen, Pat Owner
NATIONAL FOOTBALL LEAGUE/NFL, 95

Bowler, Bill GM & VP, Hockey Operations
ONTARIO HOCKEY LEAGUE, 134

Bowler, Heather Senior Vice President, Communications
WOMEN'S TENNIS ASSOCIATION TOUR, 174

Bowles, Crandall Chairman of Public Responsibilty Committ
JPMORGAN CHASE BANK, N.A., 776

Bowles, David Maintainence Supervisor
REYNOLDS COLISEUM, 1005

Bowles, Donald Owner
WRAC-FM, 670

Bowles, Erskine President
BUNTING, ELIZABETH C., 879

Bowles, Ryan Athletic Director
ST. OLAF COLLEGE ATHLETICS, 403

Bowley, Tanya Marketing Director
TD WATERHOUSE CENTRE, 1017

Bowling, James Carter-Finley Stadium Facilities
CARTER FINLEY STADIUM, 963

Bowling, Joe News Director
KDEX-AM, 622

Bowlsby, Bob Commissioner
BIG 12 CONFERENCE, 290

Bowman, Becky Director of Compliance
SOUTHERN WESLEYAN UNIVERSITY ATHLETICS, 372

Bowman, Bill Sports Editor
DAILY ITEM (PA), 479

Bowman, Dale Sports Writer (Outdoors)
CHICAGO SUN-TIMES, 472

Bowman, Don Sports Reporter
FORT WORTH STAR-TELEGRAM, 491

Bowman, Jack Direcotr Of Business Development
BEAR ARCHERY, 1115

Bowman, James Advertising Manager
WAVT-FM, 644

Bowman, Kris Executive Director
U.S. POLO ASSOCIATION, 79, 145

Bowman, Larry Senior Director Stadium Operations & Sec
TURNER FIELD, 1020

Bowman, Marcus Assistant Athletic Director for Administ
PETERSON EVENTS CENTER, 1001

Bowman, Matt Executive VP & Chief Revenue Officer
NATIONAL HOCKEY LEAGUE/NHL, 123

Bowman, Phil High School Sports Reporter
POST AND COURIER, 525

Bowman, Raymond Head Athletic Trainer
MINNESOTA-MORRIS ATHLETICS, UNIVERSITY OF (UMM), 395

Bowman, Reyn President
DURHAM CONVENTION & VISITORS BUREAU, 231

Bowman, Stan President, Hockey Operations/General Man
NATIONAL HOCKEY LEAGUE/NHL, 123

Bowman, Tad Venue Director
DENVER COLISEUM, 969

Bowman, Tommy Sports Reporter
WINSTON-SALEM JOURNAL, 552

Bowman, William Sports Editor
DANVILLE NEWS, 484

Bown, Tanner Director Of Competition
SOUTHERN NEVADA GOLF ASSOCIATION, 115

Bownes, Kim Interim Athletic Director
PLYMOUTH STATE UNIVERSITY ATHLETICS, 399

Bowness, Rick Head Coach
NATIONAL HOCKEY LEAGUE/NHL, 123

Bowser, Bruce President/CEO
AMJ CAMPBELL, 934

Bowser, Bruce President/Chief Executive Officer
AMJ CAMPBELL, 934

Bowser, Clake Operator
AUTO CLUB FAMOSO, 1031

Bowsher, Nick Associate Athletic Director
MONTANA TECH ATHLETICS, 315

Bowyer, Jeff National Sales Manager
BRUTE WRESTLING, 1103, 1121

Box, Collin Executive Director
USL LEAGUE TWO, 162

Box, Mike Chairman
NJCAA REGION V MEN'S, 285

Box, Paul Program Director
KBEL-AM, 620

Boyages, Rick Associate Commissioner, Men's Basketball
BIG TEN ATHLETIC CONFERENCE, 290

Boyan, Todd Vice President/General Manager, Sun Life
SUN LIFE STADIUM, 1016

Boyce, David Sports Reporter
KANSAS CITY STAR, 502

Boychuk, Conrad Senior Director, Recreation and Venue De
CEI ARCHITECTURE, 1061

Boyd, Ahmad Associate AD, Academics/Student Services
CHICAGO STATE UNIVERSITY ATHLETICS, 326

Boyd, C. Advertising Manager
M.B.I. PRODUCTS CO., INC., 830

Boyd, Craig Head Athletic Trainer
MOREHOUSE COLLEGE ATHLETICS, 366

Boyd, Dave Program Director
KITO-FM, 627

Boyd, David Event Manager
COLUMBUS, GA SPORTS & EVENTS COUNCIL, 229

Boyd, Donny At-Large director
SPECIAL OLYMPICS MARYLAND, 193

Boyd, Gary EVP/Chief Development Officer
PARSONS, 1071

Boyd, James General Manager
ONTARIO HOCKEY LEAGUE, 134

Boyd, Jean Deputy Athletics Director
ARIZONA STATE UNIVERSITY ATHLETICS, 323

Boyd, Joel Source Editor, Sports
CHICAGO TRIBUNE SPORTS, 721

Boyd, Leona Advertising Manager
KITO-AM, 627

Boyd, Luke Sports Reporter
CUSHING DAILY CITIZEN, 477

Boyd, Lynn Director of Handicapping
CHICAGO DISTRICT GOLF ASSOCIATION, 109

Boyd, Malik Director, Pro Personnel
NATIONAL FOOTBALL LEAGUE/NFL, 95

Boyd, Michelle Head Athletic Trainer
TRUMAN STATE UNIVERSITY ATHLETICS, 374

Boyd, Rick Director, Hockey Operations/General Mana
NORTH AMERICAN HOCKEY LEAGUE, 132

Boyd, William Chief Financial Officer
SPARTA GROUP MEDIA/COACHES, INC., 864

Boyd, Jr., W. Shareholder
CLARDY, DON S., 882

Boyd-Bradley, Leslie Vice President Business Development
BODY WISE INTERNATIONAL, 1119

Boyden, Lindsay Assistant AD (Marketing)
LT SMITH STADIUM, 993

Boyer, Bill Operations Manager
KGFW-AM, 625

Boyer, Chris Deputy Athletic Director, External Ops.
CARTER FINLEY STADIUM, 963

Boyer, Georges Co Owner
SKEA, LTD., 1200

Boyer, Jocelyn Owner / Fashion Coordinator
SKEA, LTD., 1200

Boyer, Kathy SVP and Chief Merchandising Officer
EDDIE BAUER, INC., 1238

Boyer, Leroy Sports Editor
REPUBLICAN & HERALD, 529

Boyer, Mary Sports Reporter
PLAIN DEALER, 524

Boyer, Paul President / Chief Operating Officer
MEIJER, INC., 1244

Boyer-Irwin, Diane President
SKEA, LTD., 1200

Boyes, Jerry Director of Athletics
BUFFALO STATE COLLEGE ATHLETICS, 380

Boyette, John Sports Editor
AUGUSTA CHRONICLE, 464

Boykin, Mike EVP Sports
GMR MARKETING, 764

Boylan, Rick President
GOLF COURSE BUILDERS ASSOCIATION OF AMERICA, 100

Boyle, Gertrude Chairwoman
COLUMBIA SPORTSWEAR COMPANY, 1128

Boyle, Joan Secretary
SOUTH JERSEY GOLF ASSOCIATION, 114

Boyle, Mary Associate AD, Business Operations/CFO
OHIO UNIVERSITY ATHLETICS, 340

Boyle, Timothy President & Chief Executive Officer
COLUMBIA SPORTSWEAR COMPANY, 1128

Boyles, Dana Advertising Manager
DUNCAN BANNER, 487

Boyles, Kristy Operations and Community Relations
MAJOR LEAGUE LACROSSE, 141

Boyles, Mike Associate Director
CALGARY ATHLETICS, UNIVERSITY OF, 307

Boymer, Jack Sports Information Director
ST. JOSEPH ATHLETICS, COLLEGE OF, 320

Boyre, Jean-Louis President
BABOLAT VS NORTH AMERICA, INC., 1113

Bozarth, Tina Operations Manager
RACEAMERICA, INC., 1190

Bozek, Jen Senior Associate Director of Athletics
ELMIRA COLLEGE ATHLETICS, 385

Bozich, Mike Ass. Director of Operations
HAZEL PARK HARNESS RACEWAY (HPHR), 1049

Bozich, Richard Sports Columnist
COURIER-JOURNAL, 476

Bozzuto, Barbara Partner
LOWENSTEIN EVENT MARKETING GROUP, 802

Bozzuto, Bob Field Manager
FRONTIER LEAGUE, 42

Branton, Tim Outside Sales
ELECTRO-MECH SCOREBOARD COMPANY, 1138
Braojos, Jose Director Ticket Sales
DISCOVER ORANGE BOWL, 92
Brasel, Jeff Sports Editor
HARRISON DAILY TIMES, 495
Brasfield, Carrie Merchandising Director
SMITH-WILLS STADIUM, 1012
Brashear, Rich Vice President
NORTHERN NEVADA GOLF ASSOCIATION, 113
Brasington, Brittany Assistant Athletic Director
CONCORDIA UNIVERSITY IRVINE ATHLETICS, 356
Brassard, Drew Chief Information Officer
BRAVO SPORTS, 1120
Brassfield, Tim Executive Director
OKLAHOMA CITY ALL SPORTS ASSOCIATION, 241
Brassfield, Tim Executive Director
SOONER STATE GAMES, 262
Braswell, Tommy Outdoors Writer
POST AND COURIER, 525
Bratkovich, Megan Assistant Director of Athletics
CALDWELL UNIVERSITY ATHLETICS, 353
Bratman, Rick CEO
AGGRESSIVE SKATERS ASSOCIATION, 139
Bratton, Kelly Associate Athletic Director
MARTIN METHODIST COLLEGE ATHLETICS, 314
Bratz, Mike Director of Player Personnel
KAUFFMAN SPORTS MANAGEMENT GROUP, 849
Brauer, Tim Vice-Chairperson
SPECIAL OLYMPICS HAWAII, 192
Brauks, Craig General Manager
LAM LIGHTING SYSTEMS, 1165
Braun, Amanda Director of Athletics
WISCONSIN MILWAUKEE ATHLETICS, UNIVERSITY OF, 350
Braun, Steve Vice President
GOLF ASSOCIATION OF MICHIGAN, 110
Brausch, Jeff President/Chief Executive Officer
HIGHLINE SPORTS & ENTERTAINMENT, 765
Brausch, Kelli Controller
HIGHLINE SPORTS & ENTERTAINMENT, 765
Braverman, Erik SVP, Marketing, Communications & Broadca
NATIONAL LEAGUE OF PROFESSIONAL BASEBALL CLUBS, THE, 32
Brawley, Nancy Director, National Officials Program
DIVING PLONGEON CANADA, 73
Brawley, Sally Vice President
WENATCHEE VALLEY SPORTS COUNCIL, 249
Brawley, Steve Advertising Manager
VELO NEWS, 597
Brawner, Brian Sports Director
WWIS-AM, 678
Bray, Augustus Governor
SOUTH TEXAS AAU ASSOCIATION, 214
Bray, Carolyn Sports Information Director
SAINT MARY ATHLETICS, COLLEGE OF, 318
Bray, Christian Director of Compliance
YALE BOWL, 1030
Bray, Jeff Associate Athletics Director
KEUKA COLLEGE ATHLETICS, 391
Bray, Kacie Director of Marketing
WASHINGTON STATE GOLF ASSOCIATION, 116
Bray, Sarah Editorial Assistant
WOODENBOAT, 599
Bray, Tim Communications Director
KENTUCKY SPEEDWAY, 1036
Brayer, Lori Marketing Director
WGN-AM, 655
Braza, James Shareholder
DAVIS & KUELTHAU, S.C., 884
Braza, Mary Partner/Practice Chair
FOLEY & LARDNER, 889
Braziel, Willie Governor
MINNESOTA AAU ASSOCIATION, 213
Brazier, Bob General Manager
MOBILE CIVIC CENTER, 996
Brazil, Aine Managing Principal
THORNTON-TOMASETTI ENGINEERS, 1072

Brazil, Brodie Sports Reporter
KICU-TV, 698
Brazil, Cheryl Assistant Director of Athletics
LAKE FOREST COLLEGE ATHLETICS, 391
Brazil, Danielle Director Marketing
FAMOUS POTATO IDAHO BOWL, 91
Brazill, Jim Senior Associate AD
SAINT FRANCIS UNIVERSITY ATHLETICS, 343
Brazo, Dan Facility Manager, Notre Dame Stadium
NOTRE DAME STADIUM, 998
Brazzle, Ken Sports
TUCSON CITIZEN, 546
Bream, Scott VP, Player Personnel
AMERICAN LEAGUE OF PROFESSIONAL BASEBALL CLUBS, THE, 30
Breault, Renee Head Athletic Trainer
ST. MICHAEL'S COLLEGE ATHLETICS(SMC), 372
Breaux, Gerald Executive Director
LAFAYETTE CONVENTION & VISITORS BUREAU, 236
Breaux, Phil Attorney
BREAUX, PAUL P., 877
Brecher, Howard Partner/Tort Defense Division Head
WEINER LESNIAK LLP, 869
Breckenridge, Mike Program Director
WQKT-FM, 661, 670
Breckenridge, Ryanne Head Athletic Trainer
UNIVERSITY OF WISCONSIN-PLATTEVILLE (UWP), 410, 1001
Breckner, Scott Director
JACK BRESLIN STUDENT EVENTS CENTER, 983
Breczinski, Erin Athletic Tickets Manager
STANLEY J MARSHALL HPER CENTER, 1014
Bredre, Melvin Partner
LAMPLEY, NATHANIEL, 898
Breecker, Spencer Partner
KAUFFMAN SPORTS MANAGEMENT GROUP, 849
Breed, Giff Managing Director Golf/Outdoors
OCTAGON SPORTS, 807, 854
Breed, Thomas Partner
WOOD & LAMPING LLP, 926
Breeden, Tiffany Billing & Collections Manager
CLARDY, DON S., 882
Breeding, James Vice President of Business Operations
LOUISVILLE SLUGGER FIELD, 992
Breen, Dave President/CEO
SPECIAL OLYMPICS ILLINOIS, 193
Breen, Jim President
AIR SHOW NETWORK, 13
Breen, Jim President/Founder
UMBRELLA ENTERTAINMENT GROUP, 824
Breen, Joel Digital Account Director
ALLOY MARKETING & PROMOTION, 781
Breer, Jeff Reporter
SOUTHEAST MISSOURIAN, 536
Brehm, George VP Sales and Marketing
B & G EQUIPMENT COMPANY, 1112
Brehm, Mike Ice Hockey Assignment Editor
USA TODAY, 548
Breier, Eric Assistant Sports Editor
NORTH COUNTY TIMES, 518
Breiner, Nathan Director of Stadium Operations
HANK AARON STADIUM, 977
Breitborde, Harriet Creative Director
BOARDWALK, 784
Breithaupt, Charles Executive Director
TEXAS UNIVERSITY INTERSCHOLASTIC LEAGUE, 200
Brekke, Steve Associate Athletic Director, Development
UNIVERSITY OF NORTH DAKOTA (UND), 367, 981
Bremel, Tim Promotions Director
WJVL-FM, 648, 660
Bremner, Dan Head Coach/General Manager
SOUTHERN PROFESSIONAL HOCKEY LEAGUE, 136
Brendel, Eric Manager Custom Game Development
USAOPOLY, 1218

Breneisen, Ken
SACRAMENTO RACEWAY PARK (DRAGSTRIP/MX), 1041
Brener, Gabriel Controlling Owner
MAJOR LEAGUE SOCCER, 157
Breniman, Aaron Director of Marketing & Communications
OREGON GOLF ASSOCIATION, 114
Brenn, Dave Executive Director, Competition
IMCA, 16
Brennan, Christine Sports Columnist
USA TODAY, 548
Brennan, Don Sports Director
WWSB-TV, 720
Brennan, Jimmy Head Coach/Technical Director
CANADIAN PREMIER LEAGUE, 156
Brennan, Kyle Deputy AD, Internal Operations
UTAH ATHLETICS, UNIVERSITY OF, 332, 348
Brennan, Mary Assistant Secretary
SCOTT, DAVID R., 915
Brennan, Rob Weekend Sports Anchor
WMGM-TV, 715
Brennan, Staci Associate Director of Athletics
HOOD COLLEGE ATHLETICS, 389
Brennan, Tim Sports Information Director
SALISBURY UNIVERSITY ATHLETICS, 402
Brennan, Tom Director of Athletics
GOLDEY BEACOM COLLEGE ATHLETICS, 360
Brennan, William President & CEO
FORSYTHE & ASSOCIATES, INC., 935
Brennecke, Robert Assistant Commissioner
SUNSHINE STATE CONFERENCE, 295, 304
Brenneman, Terry Treasurer
INTERNATIONAL BOWLING MUSEUM AND HALL OF FAME, 252
Brenner, Anita Deputy Director of Athletics/SWA
CORNELL UNIVERSITY ATHLETICS, 327
Brenner, Anne Director of Sponsorships
TRI-CITIES STADIUM, 1019
Brenner, Hillary Marketing Coordinator
TACOMA DOME, 1016
Brenner, Jack Clubhouse Manager
TRADITION FIELD SPORTS COMPLEX, 1019
Brenner, Reeve Founder/President
BANKSHOT SPORTS ORGANIZATION, 1229
Brenner, Rich Producer
RICH BRENNER'S SPORTS SUNDAY, 688
Brenner, Rick President/General Manager
EASTERN LEAGUE, 38

Brents, Phillip Sports Editor
STAR NEWS, 538
Bresee, Matt President
NATIONAL BASKETBALL ASSOCIATION DEVELOPMENT LEAGUE, 59
Breseman, Brian Senior Director, Broadcasting, Programs
NATIONAL HOCKEY LEAGUE/NHL, 125
Breslauer, Ken Communications Director/Track Historian
SEBRING INTERNATIONAL RACEWAY, 1042
Breslin, Robin President
BRESLIN, RIDYARD, FADERO ARCHITECTS, 1060
Breslin, Ted Vice President & CFO
CONVENTURES, INC., 761
Bresnahan, Mike Professional Basketball Staff Writer
LOS ANGELES TIMES, 507
Bresnahan, Tammy Director Of Academic Programs
DAN MARINO FOUNDATION, 189
Breton, Marcos Sports Senior Writer
SACRAMENTO BEE, 530
Brett, Bobby President & Owner
WESTERN HOCKEY LEAGUE, 48, 139
Brett, Chris Weekend Sports Anchor
WTAP-TV, 718
Brett, George VP, Baseball Operations
AMERICAN LEAGUE OF PROFESSIONAL BASEBALL CLUBS, THE, 30
Brett, Jen Managing Editor
BLUE WATER SAILING, 557
Brett, Natalie National Team Manager
CANOEKAYAK CANADA, 68
Bretz, Carrie Executive Assistant/Marketing
TEAM ATHLETIC GOODS/TAG, INC., 1250

Breunig, Mary Sales and Promotions Manager - Midwest
GNC CORPORATION, 1148
Brewer, Beth Publisher
EVENING TIMES (NY), 490
Brewer, Bobby Vice President
PREMIER MANAGEMENT GROUP, 857
Brewer, Chip Chairman
NATIONAL GOLF FOUNDATION, 103
Brewer, Christi Instructor in Exercise Science Health, E
MISSISSIPPI, UNIVERSITY OF, 430
Brewer, Conant President
BREWER'S LEDGE, INC., 1120
Brewer, Dave Manager, Operations
MAJOR LEAGUE LACROSSE, 141
Brewer, Jeff Vice President
BREWER'S LEDGE, INC., 1120
Brewer, Valerie Entairtainment Assistant
NEBRASKA STATE FAIR, 1051
Brewer, Wayne Operations Manager
ZAMBONI & COMPANY, INC., FRANK J., 1224
Brewer, William Attorney
HERSHNER, HUNTER, ANDREWS, NEILL & SMITH L,L,P., 893
Brewington, Yogi Ticket & Corporate Sales Executive
CAROLINA LEAGUE, 37
Brewster, Louis Sports Editor
SAN BERNARDINO SUN, 499, 532
Brewton-Dufur, Jennie Art Director
INTERBIKE, 765
Brex, Joe Business Manager
SYDNEY ENTERTAINMENT CENTRE, 1016
Breyer, Kris Vice President, Central Region
AMERICAN MORGAN HORSE ASSOCIATION, 74
Breyfogle, Art Sports Sales Manager
SPORTSRADIO 1460 KENO, 642
Breymeyer, Tami 3rd Vice President and Secretary
INTERNATIONAL COLLEGIATE LICENSING ASSOCIATION/ICLA, 282
Brezner, Melissa Promotion Manager
KTRH-AM, 637
Brian, Eric Athletic Academic Coordinator
INDIANA UNIVERSITY SOUTHEAST ATHLETICS, 312
Brian, Shallcross General Manager
PRINCE GEORGE'S STADIUM, 1002
Brick, Adam Senior Associate Athletic Director Legal
BRICK, ADAM, 877
Bricker, Charles Sports Columnist
SOUTH FLORIDA SUN-SENTINEL, 536
Bricker, Josh Sports & Events Sales Manager
DUBLIN CONVENTION & VISITOR BUREAU, 231
Brickett, Scott Assistant Athletic Director, Sports Medi
TAMPA ATHLETICS, UNIVERSITY OF, 373
Brickey, James Attorney
BRICKEY JAMES N. L.C., 877
Brickley, John Sports Director
WSOU-FM, 674
Brickman, Nicole Customer Service
TERRAMAR SPORTS WORLDWIDE, LTD., 1212
Brickman, Stefanie Communications Manager
NORMAN CONVENTION & VISITORS BUREAU, 241
Bridgemann, Johnny Vice President
TENNESSEE PGA SECTIONAL OFFICE, 107
Bridger, John Executive Director
THUNDERBIRDS, THE, 246
Bridges, Eddie Program Director
WFGN-AM, 653
Bridges, Harold Attorney
BRIDGES, HAROLD A., 877
Bridges, Melanie Secretary
ARIZONA WOMEN'S GOLF ASSOCIATION, 109
Bridges, Pat Editor
SNOWBOARDER MAGAZINE, 516, 587
Bridges, CRDE, Robyn Communication Director
AUBURN/OPELIKA CONVENTION & VISITORS BUREAU, 226

Bridich, Jeff Executive VP/General Manager
NATIONAL LEAGUE OF PROFESSIONAL BASEBALL CLUBS, THE, 31
Bridich, Jeff Sr. Vice President & General Manager
COORS FIELD, 968
Brielmaier, Bret Head Coach
NATIONAL BASKETBALL ASSOCIATION DEVELOPMENT LEAGUE, 59
Brien, Kelly Administrative Assistant
NEBRASKA STATE FAIR, 1051
Brien, Kirk VP and General Manager
EXHIBIT ENTERPRISES, 791
Brien, Patrick President University
KIMBROUGH MEMORIAL STADIUM, 988
Briere, Danny President & General Manager
EAST COAST HOCKEY LEAGUE/ECHL, 130
Briere, Robert Advertising Director
MIDDLETOWN PRESS, 510
Briere, Steve Goaltending Coach
NATIONAL HOCKEY LEAGUE/NHL, 125
Brigandi, Ben Sports Editor
WILLIAMSPORT SUN-GAZETTE, 552
Briggemann, Brent Sports Writer
ST. JOSEPH NEWS-PRESS, 538
Briggs, Ben Vice President Club Relations
CONNECTICUT STATE GOLF ASSOCIATION, 109
Briggs, Bill Sports Writer
DENVER POST, 485
Briggs, Douglas President
QVC NETWORK, 1247
Briggs, Elizabeth Assistant Athletic Director, Premium Sea
COMMONWEALTH STADIUM (KENTUCKY), 967
Briggs, Jerry Assistant Sports Editor
SAN ANTONIO EXPRESS-NEWS, 532
Briggs, Mark Head Coach
USL CHAMPIONSHIP, 159
Briggs, Matt Circulation/Fulfillment Specialist
TEXAS FOOTBALL, 594
Briggs, Michael Promotions Director
KNZR-AM, 632
Briggs, Randy President
FLORIDA STATE GOLF ASSOCIATION, 110
Briggs, Ryan Sports Information Director
GROVE CITY COLLEGE ATHLETICS, 387
Briggs, William Adjunct Professor of Law
BRIGGS, BUCK, 877
Bright, George Associate Director Of Athletics
LAFAYETE COLLEGE, 989
Bright, James Shareholder
WATSON, RICHARD, 923
Bright, Julie Sr. Assoc. AD/Administration
JACK TRICE STADIUM, 982, 983
Bright, Katie Assistant Commissioner
SOUTHERN STATES ATHLETIC CONFERENCE, 303
Brighum, G. Legal Assisatant
DEUTCH, ALLAN H, 885
Brigl, Thom Owner/Chief Executive Officer
NORTH AMERICAN HOCKEY LEAGUE, 132
Briglia, Joseph Vice President of Development
VENUWORKS, 1075, 1076
Brignall, Alan Sports Editor
FINGER LAKES TIMES, 491
Brim, Cadena General Manager
WOMEN'S FOOTBALL ALLIANCE / WFA, 98
Brimecombe, Michelle Assistant Professor & Program Director,
CAZENOVIA COLLEGE, 415
Brind'Amour, Rod Head Coach
NATIONAL HOCKEY LEAGUE/NHL, 123
Brindle, Shelley EVP, Domestic Network Distribution
HBO SPORTS, 683
Brine, Bill Founder
SPORT HELMETS, INC., 1204
Briner, Sean Director of Athletic Development
CALIFORNIA STATE UNIVERSITY - SAN MARCOS ATHLETICS, 308
Bringger, Ryan VP, Ticket Sales & Services
NATIONAL LEAGUE OF PROFESSIONAL BASEBALL CLUBS, THE, 33
Brink, Kim Vice President
NASCAR, 694
Brink, Steven Chief Financial Officer
QUIKSILVER, 1190

Brinker, Adam Assistant Athletics Director, Facilities
UNION COLLEGE (NY) ATHLETICS, 406
Brinker, Jennifer Senior Director of Advertising
GNC CORPORATION, 1148
Brinkley, Robbie Assistant to the Director of Athletics
ROBINS STADIUM, 1006
Brinks, Mark Sports Writer
KTLA-TV, 703
Brinson, Van President & CEO
WORLD T.E.A.M. SPORTS, 225
Brinton, Steve Treasurer
UTAH GOLF ASSOCIATION, 115
Brisack, Al Director of Athletics
EDGEWOOD COLLEGE ATHLETICS, 385
Brisbin, Corey Western States Sales/Technical Manager
NGI SPORTS, 1179
Brisbin, Ryan Sports Information Director
SCHREINER UNIVERSITY ATHLETICS, 318
Briscoe, Chad Director of Athletics
GRACE COLLEGE ATHLETICS, 311
BriseBois, Julien VP & General Manager/Alternate Governor
NATIONAL HOCKEY LEAGUE/NHL, 125
Briseno, Phillip Sales Manager
RACEAMERICA, INC., 1190
Brisevac, Vojislav Manager
CANADIAN SOCCER LEAGUE, 156
Brito, Nestor Director of Operations
MEXICAN LEAGUE A.C. (AAA LEVEL), 43
Britt, Elisa Executive Secretary
JOHNSON CITY CONVENTION & VISITORS BUREAU, 235
Britt, Glenda Director of Finance
JOHNSON CITY CONVENTION & VISITORS BUREAU, 235
Britt, Kenneth Executive Director
TAULBEE, GEORGE M., 920
Brittain, Ray Vice President
YOUTH BOWL CANADA, 66, 67
Britten, Elizabeth Associate Editor
POWER & MOTORYACHT, 582
Britten, Paul President
BRITTEN MEDIA, 759
Britten, Tom President
BRITTEN-MEDIA, 1120
Britton, Dan Executive Vice President - International
FELLOWSHIP OF CHRISTIAN ATHLETES, 218
Britton, Keith Producer
SPORTS RADIO 97.1 THE FAN, 641
Britton, Kirsten Senior Associate AD, Administration/SWA
UMASS AMHERST ATHLETICS, 348
Britton, Todd President
YOUTH BOWL CANADA, 66, 67
Britton-Baeza, Della President/CEO
JACKIE ROBINSON FOUNDATION, 189
Britz, Patrick Commissioner
SOUTH ATLANTIC CONFERENCE, 302
Brivio, David Team Chief
FORMULA 1, 20
Brizzle, Lorna Bookkeeper/Membership Services
NATIONAL JUNIOR COLLEGE ATHLETIC ASSOCIATION/NJCAA, 283
Brne, Terri Senior Associate AD/SWA
NORTH CAROLINA ASHEVILLE ATHLETICS, UNIVERSITY OF, 339
Broadbent, Dave Chief Financial Officer
BUSHNELL SPORT OPTICS, 1122
Broadhead, Matt Head Coach
USL LEAGUE TWO, 162
Broadway, Julie Executive Director
AMERICAN MORGAN HORSE ASSOCIATION, 74
Broadway, Larry Director of Minor League Operations
PNC PARK, 1002
Brobst, Jennifer Clinical Supervising Lawyer
SMITH, CHARLES EDISON, 917
Brocato, Ron Sports Editor
CLARION HERALD, 473
Brocious, Heather Sports Information Director
WILLIAM PATERSON UNIVERSITY OF NEW JERSEY ATHLETICS, 409

executive index

STEPHEN F. AUSTIN STATE UNIVERSITY
ATHLETICS, 345
Bryant, Cedric Chief Science Officer
AMERICAN COUNCIL ON EXERCISE, 83
Bryant, Clint Director of Athletics
AUGUSTA STATE UNIVERSITY ATHLETICS,
352
Bryant, Cynthia Director
CALEXPO, 1032
Bryant, Geoff President
UNITED STATES GOLF TEACHERS
FEDERATION, 117
Bryant, Jennifer Editor
USDF CONNECTION, 597
Bryant, John Commissioner
PUGET SOUND REGIONAL
COMMISSIONER/USA VOLLEYBALL, 210
Bryant, Keith Chief Executive Officer
USA JUDO, 207
Bryant, Larry Governor
ARKANSAS AAU ASSOCIATION, 212
Bryant, Leroy Sports Editor
INDIANA HERALD, 499
Bryant, Mark Director of Multimedia Development
BIG SOUTH CONFERENCE, 290
Bryant, Philip Commissioner
GULF COAST REGIONAL
COMMISSIONER/USA VOLLEYBALL, 209
Bryant, Richard President
INDIANA FOOTBALL HALL OF FAME, 251
Bryant, Rick VP
SUNFLOWER STATE GAMES, 263
Bryant, Rusty Executive Director & General
Manager
USL LEAGUE TWO, 162
Bryant, Sam Vice President
UNITED STATES GOLF TEACHERS
FEDERATION, 117
Bryant, Stanley President
GEAR PRO-TEC, 1147
Bryant, Steve President, Majority Owner
CAROLINA LEAGUE, 37, 815
Bryant, Tom President
STAIRMASTER HEALTH AND FITNESS
PRODUCTS, 1207
Bryce, Charles Sports Editor
SAN ANGELO STANDARD TIMES, 532
Bryce, Lisa Business Manager
KGSO 1410 SPORTS RADIO, 612
Brycz, Kimberly SVP, Global Human Resources
GENERAL MOTORS, 736
Brye, Benji Custom Products & Service Specialist
BEACON ATHLETICS, 1229
Brylin, Sergei Assistant Coach
AMERICAN HOCKEY LEAGUE/AHL, 126
Bryne, Richard Chief Executive Officer
SPEEDPLAY, INC., 1203
Brysha, Andre VP / Chief Marketing Officer
BOATER'S WORLD, 1231
Brzezinski, Rob Executive VP, Football
Operations
NATIONAL FOOTBALL LEAGUE/NFL, 96
Brzostowski, Sammy Ticket Office Manager
VETERANS MEMORIAL STADIUM (CEDAR
RAPIDS), 1025
Bubach, Brian Associate Director
NORTH DAKOTA HS ACTIVITIES
ASSOCIATION, 199
Bubb, Paul Administration - Associate AD -
External
ROY STEWART STADIUM, 1003, 1008
Bubb, Sean Executive Director/Head Coach
USL LEAGUE TWO, 161
Bubolz, Kerry President, COO & Alternate
Governor
NATIONAL HOCKEY LEAGUE/NHL, 126
Buccelli, Tod Marketing/Promotion Director
WIAT - CBS 42, 712
Bucci, Dan General Manager
LINCOLN PARK, 1056
Bucci, Steve Sports Reporter
KYW-TV, 706
Bucciarelli, Brain Vice President
ASSOCIATION OF LUXURY SUITE
DIRECTORS, 216
Buccilli, Tony Director of Team Operations
NATIONAL PRO FASTPITCH, 168
Bucek, Michael VP, Marketing & Business
Development

AMERICAN LEAGUE OF PROFESSIONAL
BASEBALL CLUBS, THE, 30
Buchalter, Carol Chairman
PARKER LABORATORIES, INC., 1183
Buchalter, Neal President
PARKER LABORATORIES, INC., 1183
Buchan, Jim Sports Editor
WALLA WALLA UNION-BULLETIN, 550
Buchan, Mary Assoc. Athletics Director/Fiscal
Operati
WAYNE STATE UNIVERSITY, 439
Buchan, Ryan Sports Editor
DODGE CITY DAILY GLOBE, 487
Buchan, Stephem Associate Program Director /
Adjunct Pro
LONG BEACH STATE UNIVERSITY, 426
Buchanan, Chad General Manager
NATIONAL BASKETBALL ASSOCIATION/NBA,
57
Buchanan, Eugene Publisher
PADDLER, 581
Buchanan, Ginger Promotions Director
KBEE-FM, 620
Buchanan, Kathy Director Of Computer Services
U.S. PROFESSIONAL TENNIS ASSOCIATION,
172
Buchanan, Megan Associate Athletic Director
SKIDMORE COLLEGE ATHLETICS, 402
Buchanan, Metthew Principal
FLEWELLING & MOODY, 1066
Buchanan, Michael Sports Anchor
WTRP-AM, 676
Buchanan, Mike News Director
KBIZ-AM, 620
Buchanan, Rusty
FLORIDA'S SPACE COAST OFFICE OF
TOURISM, 232
Buchanan, Sally Program Director
WPRZ-AM, 669
Buchanan, Sharon National Sales Manager
WMAQ TV CHICAGO, 715
Buchanan, Teresa Purchasing Executive
KING LOUIE INTERNATIONAL, INC., 1163
Buchanan, Thomas President
BAKER, DAVID L., 872
Buchanan, Zack Sports Editor
DAILY NEWS (WA), 480
Buchberger, Kelly Head Coach
WESTERN HOCKEY LEAGUE, 139
Buche, Time President and CEO
MOTORCYCLE SAFETY FOUNDATION, 144
Bucher, Christine Senior Editor
BICYCLING, 557
Bucher, Ric Senior Writer
ESPN THE MAGAZINE, 563
Buchko, Garth President and Chief Executive
Officer
THE WINNIPED BLUE BOMBERS, 1018
Buchman, Bruce Treasurer
SUN COUNTRY AMATEUR GOLF
ASSOCIATION, 115
Buchner, Mary Assistant To The VP For Athletics
COKER COLLEGE ATHLETICS, 356
Bucholz, Seymour Of Counsel
GARVEY, SCHUBERT & BARER, 891
Buck, C CEO
BUCK KNIVES, INC., 1121
Buck, Charles President
BUCK KNIVES, INC., 1121
Buck, Charles Chairman / Chief Executive Officer
BUCK KNIVES, INC., 1121
Buck, David Assistant Athletic Director
UNIVERSITY OF FINDLAY (UF) ATHLETICS,
32, 359
Buck, Fred Partner
RAWLE LAW OFFICES, 910
Buck, John EVP
FINGERHUT COMPANIES, INC., 1239
Buck, Kelcey Sports Information Director
WASHINGTON UNIVERSITY ATHLETICS, 407
Buck, Michele President & CEO
THE HERSHEY CO., 742
Buck, Ray Sports Columnist
FORT WORTH STAR-TELEGRAM, 491
Buck, Rogers General Manager
HUNTSVILLE STARS, 981
Buckert, Brad Owner
BEGNI'RS TO PRO'S, 1230

Buckingham, Bill Director Of Member Services
U.S. SQUASH, 169
Buckingham, Jackie Chief Executive Officer
SYNCHRO CANADA, 170
Buckle, Alan Deputy Chairman
KPMG CONVENTION, SPORTS &
ENTERTAINMENT PRACTICE, 766
Buckles, Nick Group Chief Executive
WACKENHUT SPORTS SECURITY, 774
Buckley, Bredan Booking & Scheduling Director
VALUE CITY ARENA/JEROME
SCHOTTENSTEIN CENTER, 1024
Buckley, Clint Sports Reporter
TYLER MORNING TELEGRAPH, 547
Buckley, Donald EVP, Program Marketing, Digital
Services
SHOWTIME SPORTS, 686
Buckley, George Chairman / Chief Executive
Officer
BRUNSWICK CORPORATION, 1121
Buckley, Mike Goaltending Coach
NATIONAL HOCKEY LEAGUE/NHL, 125
Buckley, Nick General Sports
BATTLE CREEK ENQUIRER, 465
Buckley, Sheila Publisher
SPORTS ILLUSTRATED, 591
Buckley, Steve Sports Columnist
BOSTON HERALD, 468
Buckley, Tim Sports Writer
DESERET MORNING NEWS, 485
Bucklin-Webber, Shari Men's and Women's
Tennis Head Coach
MILLERVILLE UNIVERSITY, 429
Buckman, Franki Vice President
FIREBIRD INTERNATIONAL RACEWAY, 1034
Buckner, Jack CEO
BRITISH TRIATHLON ASSOCIATION, 175
Buckner, Wanda Advertising Manager
SAMPSON INDEPENDENT, 532
Buczkowski, Michael Vice President/General
Manager
INTERNATIONAL LEAGUE, 42, 966
Buczkowski, Terrance Vice President Marketing
& Business Deve
AMERICAN HOCKEY LEAGUE/AHL, 126
Budd, Sarah Director, Ticket Operations &
Community
NEW YORK-PENNSYLVANIA LEAGUE, 48,
957
Budd, TJ Sports Information Director
PALM BEACH ATLANTIC UNIVERSITY
ATHLETICS(PBA), 368
Buddie, Mike Director of Athletics
U.S. MILITARY ACADEMY ATHLETICS, 347
Buddle, Edson Head Coach
USL LEAGUE TWO, 163
Budenholzer, Mike Head Coach
NATIONAL BASKETBALL ASSOCIATION/NBA,
57
Budig, Dr. Co-Owner
JOSEPH P. RILEY, JR PARK, 986
Budine, Marc Interactive/Online Sales Manager
SPORTS TALK/THE TICKET, 613
Budman, Michael Co-Founder
ROOTS APPAREL, 1194
Budz, Tracey Public Relations
LIFE PRIORITY, INC., 1166
Buechele, Mark General Manager
ABC FLAG MANUFACTURING CO., 1100
Buehler, Gary Treasurer
NATIONAL HORSESHOE PITCHERS
ASSOCIATION, 139
Buehler, Jana Academic Learning Specialist
WAGNER FIELD/KSU, 1026
Buehner, Jim Owner
EXCLUSIVELY EXPO, INC., 1141
Buehner, Marie Marketing Manager
EXCLUSIVELY EXPO, INC., 1141
Buelow, Bob Sales / Marketing Director
SETCOM CORPORATION, 1198
Buendorf, Larry Chief Security Officer
HAMAKAWA, CURT L., 846
Bueno, Luis Sports Columnist
PRESS-ENTERPRISE (CA), 526
Buerger, Mark Communications Director
SPECIAL OLYMPICS KENTUCKY, 193
Buetel, Barry Sports Director
WTEV-TV, 718

Caputo, Brian General Manager
MULLINS CENTER, 996

Caputo, Chris Sports Information Director
UNIVERSITY OF PITTSBURGH AT
JOHNSTOWN ATHLETICS, 369

Caputo, Pat Sports Columnist
OAKLAND PRESS, 518

Caputo, Tony Assistant Athletic Director
SOUTHERN VIRGINIA UNIVERSITY
ATHLETICS, 403

Carabello, MaryLyn Associate
GARVEY, SCHUBERT & BARER, 891

Caracappa, Joseph Chief Information Officer
JUST FOR FEET, 1242

Caraker, Mike Chief Information Officer
FGM ARCHITECTS & ENGINEERS, 1066

Caravati, Ken President
DIXIE SPORTING GOODS, 1236

Caravati, Michael Sales / Marketing VP
DIXIE SPORTING GOODS, 1236

Caraviello, David Sports Reporter
POST AND COURIER, 525

Carbajal, Brooke Director of Sports Information
COLORADO CHRISTIAN UNIVERSITY
ATHLETICS (CCU), 356

Carbery, Spencer Head Coach
AMERICAN HOCKEY LEAGUE/AHL, 127

Carboneau, Jim MG Committee Chair
US LACROSSE, 141

Carbonell, Anna Vice President
WNBC-TV, 715

Carbonell, John Founder
SUPER BOAT INTERNATIONAL, 65

Carchidi, Sam Sports Reporter
PHILADELPHIA INQUIRER, 523

Card, Steven Director of Athletics
WESTERN WASHINGTON UNIVERSITY
ATHLETICS (WWU), 376

Card, Wesley Chief Financial Officer
NINE WEST GROUP, INC., 1245

Carden, Barbara Program Director
27 SPORTS SPECTRUM, 686

Carden, Sandy Retail Advertising Manager
TALLADEGA DAILY HOME, 541

Cardenas, Jose Chairman and Partner
CLARKE, ALLEN R., 837

Carder, Rory Managing Director, Principal
THE DAVIS EXPERIENCE, 1072

Cardile, Enrico Technical Chief
FORMULA 1, 20

Cardinal, Glenn General Manager
WRNX-FM, 672

Cardon, Mark Weekend Sports Editor
SARASOTA HERALD-TRIBUNE, 533

Cardoza, Nancy Vice president
INTERNATIONAL TENNIS HALL OF FAME
AND MUSEUM, 253

Cardwell, Derek Host
LET'S TALK RACING, 612

Cardwell, Victor Principal
CARDWELL, VICTOR, 880

Care, James Promotions Producer
WHOI-TV, 712

Caren, Gregg Sr.VP
SMG, 769, 1075

Carey, Chet Assistant General Manager/Sales
Marketin
SMITH-WILLS STADIUM, 1012

Carey, David Account Executive
PERFECT CURVE, INC., 1184

Carey, Don Owner
DON CAREY & ASSOCIATES, 1064

Carey, Harveycutter Director of Civic Facilities
SALEM CIVIC CENTER, 1009

Carey, Jack Sports Writer
USA TODAY, 548

Carey, Len Senior Vice President/Facilities
PAXRACING, 1052

Carey, Michael President
SPORTS PERSONALITIES, INC., 865

Carey, Mike President
SEIRUS SPORTS ACCESSORIES, 1198

Carey, Tim President
CHICAGOLAND SPEEDWAY, 1033

Carey, Tim President & General Manager
HAWTHORNE RACE COURSE, 1049

Carey, Wayne Vice President
DELAWARE STATE GOLF ASSOCIATION, 110

Carey, Wendy VP
SEIRUS SPORTS ACCESSORIES, 1198

Carfagna, Peter Chairman, Secretary/Treasurer
CLASSIC PARK, 966

Carfano, Steve Store Manager
ROGER DUNN GOLF SHOPS, 1248

Carfora, Joseph VP Of Sales
NIKON SPORTS & RECREATIONAL OPTICS,
1179

Cargnan, Travis Athletic Director
MAINE AT MACHIAS ATHLETICS,
UNIVERSITY OF, 314

Carideo, Chris Assistant Athletic Director
WIDENER UNIVERSITY ATHLETICS, 409

Cariello, Vince President
FREEMAN PRODUCTS, INC., 1145

Carifo, Edward Sports Editor
MARSHALL NEWS MESSENGER, 508

Caris, Bruce Sales Manager
EIGER SPORTSWEAR, INC., 1138

Carkner, Matt Assistant Coach
AMERICAN HOCKEY LEAGUE/AHL, 126

Carl, Lance Associate AD
COLORADO ATHLETICS, UNIVERSITY OF,
326

Carl, Peggy Director of Athletics & Recreation
SALEM STATE COLLEGE ATHLETICS, 402

Carle, Jack Sports Editor
SENTINEL-TRIBUNE, 535

Carley, Cole President/CEO
FARGO-MOORHEAD CONVENTION &
VISITOR BUREAU, 232

Carlile, Rob Sports Director
WZCT-AM, 680

Carlin, Dan Vice President, Programming &
Research
FOX SPORTS NETWORKS/FOX SPORTS
NET, 683

Carlin, Linda Treasurer
SISKAYOU MOTOR SPEEDWAY, 1042

Carlin, Rob Sports Anchor
WVTM-TV, 720

Carlin, Trevor Founder
INDYCAR, 22

Carling, Scott Advertising Manager
EQUESTRIAN, 75, 563

Carlisle, Chris Senior Vice President, Marketing
FX NETWORKS, LLC, 683

Carlisle, Doug News Director
WMFD-AM, 664

Carlisle, Jim Sports Writer
VENTURA COUNTY STAR, 549

Carlisle, Rick Head Coach
NATIONAL BASKETBALL ASSOCIATION/NBA,
57

Carlo, Louis Director, Operations
NORTHVILLE DOWNS, 1051

Carlo, Theresa CFO
WHEELSTV, 685

Carlock, Lisa Finance & Operations Director
USA BOBSLED & SKELETON, 65, 206

Carlomagno, Matthew Vice President, Human
Resources
INTERNATIONAL SPORTS PROPERTIES,
INC., 798

Carlsen, Tony Secretary/Treasurer
CANADIAN SOCIETY FOR PSYCHOMOTOR
LEARNING & SPORT PSYCHOLOGY, 217

Carlson, Andrew Head Athletic Trainer
JUDSON UNIVERSITY, 313

Carlson, Bob President/Founder
ARBOR, 516, 1109

Carlson, Brent Marketing / Sales Director
SEATTLE BIKE SUPPLY, 1198

Carlson, Charle Sports Editor
RENO GAZETTE-JOURNAL, 528

Carlson, Cheryl Director of Finance and Human
Resources
MIDWEST LEAGUE, 46, 1014

Carlson, Debbie EVP
COLLEGE CONCEPTS, LLC., 1235

Carlson, Donald Attorney
CRIVELLO, CARLSON, MENTKOWSKI S.C.,
884

Carlson, Geri Vice President
JIFFY LINE STRIPERS, 1160

Carlson, Jenni Sports Columnist
OKLAHOMAN, 519

Carlson, Jennie Executive Vice President
YMCA USA, 86

Carlson, Jill Sports Anchor
WFLD-TV, 710

Carlson, Linda Classified Manager
DAILY SENTINEL (NY), 482

Carlson, Mark President/Head Coach/General
Manager
UNITED STATES HOCKEY LEAGUE, 136

Carlson, Matt President & Chief Executive Officer
NATIONAL SPORTING GOODS ASSOCIATION
(NSGA), 222, 283, 805

Carlson, Paula Chair, Presidents Council
IOWA INTERCOLLEGIATE ATHLETIC
CONFERENCE, 295

Carlson, Peter Promotions Manager
WCIA-TV, 708

Carlson, Richard Founder
AMERICAN WHEELCHAIR BOWLING
ASSOCIATION, 65

Carlson, Richard Attorney
HUNEGS, STONE, LENEAVE, KYAS &
THORNTON, P.A., 894

Carlson, Robert General Manager/Public
Relations
PORSCHE CARS NORTH AMERICA, 1186

Carlson, W. Executive Vice President, Operations
DISH NETWORK, 694

Carlson, Zac Operations Coordinator
ROCHESTER AMATEUR SPORTS
COMMISSION, 243

Carlsson, Bo Scientific Committee
EUROPEAN ASSOCIATION FOR SPORT
MANAGEMENT, THE, 218

Carlton, Chuck Sports Reporter
DALLAS MORNING NEWS, 483

Carlton, Dawn
SKI SKOOT INC, 1200

Carlton, Dean President
BALLOON FEDERATION OF AMERICA, 13

Carlton, Jeff Sports Reporter
GREENSBORO NEWS & RECORD, 494

Carlton, Kristen Editor
PRICE MEDIA, 582

Carlton, M. Head Athletic Trainer
HANOVER COLLEGE ATHLETICS, 388

Carlton, Michelle Commissioner
KEYSTONE REGIONAL COMMISSIONER/USA
VOLLEYBALL, 210

Carlucci, Carl Chief Financial Officer/President
RED MC EWEN BASEBALL FIELD, 1004

Carmack, Bryan Executive Board
WESTERN COLORADO DRAGWAY, 1044

Carmack, Lesa Booking Coordinator
ARKANSAS STATE UNIVERSITY
CONVOCATION CENTER, 955

Carmann, Kami Sports Reporter
WTVF-TV, 719

Carmel, George President
FLAGHOUSE, 1239

Carmichael, Chris Vice President, Ticket
Operations
EAST COAST HOCKEY LEAGUE/ECHL, 130

Carmichael, Don General Manager
WBAY - WBAY-TV 2, 707

Carmichael, Jason Director of Athletics
CALIFORNIA STATE UNIVERSITY-EAST BAY
ATHLETICS, 353

Carmichael, Kim Chief Of Staff
TEXAS UNIVERSITY INTERSCHOLASTIC
LEAGUE, 200

Carmichael, Rob Head Athletic Trainer
CULVER-STOCKTON COLLEGE ATHLETICS,
309

Carmody, Stephen Attorney
BRUNINI, GRANTHAM GROWE & HEWES,
P.L.L.C., 878

Carnahan, Scott Athletic Director
LINFIELD COLLEGE ATHLETICS, 392

Carnathan, Edward Sports Sales
LAS CRUCES CONVENTION & VISITORS
BUREAU, 237

Carneiro, Yolanda VP,Sales Development
CAREY WORLDWIDE CHAUFFERED
SERVICES, 935

Carnell, Doug EVP of Operations
SPL INTEGRATED SOLUTIONS, 831

executive index

Coe, Tricia Assistant General Manager
FEDERAL HOCKEY LEAGUE, 131

Coelho, Mike National Sales Manager
WINN, INC., 1222

Coen, Bill Head Coach, Men's Basketball
MATTHEWS ARENA, 994

Coen, Scott Sports Director
WGGB-TV, 711

Coenen, Doug Principal/Managing Directo
WALTER P MOORE, 1073

Coerver, Arthur Chief Operating Officer
COLLEGIATE PACIFIC, 1235

Coetzee, Denton Chief Executive Officer &
President
EASY RACERS, 1138

Coffell, Ryan Controller
KING PAR CORPORATION, 1163

Coffey, Dick President
OLYMPIA SPORTS, 1182

Coffey, Kristina Business Office
PLACERVILLE SPEEDWAY, 1040

Coffey, Lisa Sports Reporter
LEDGER, 505

Coffey, Randon Director of Marketing
MISSOURI SOUTHERN STATE UNIVERSITY
ATHLETICS, 365

Coffey, Theresa Finance Manager
ATLANTIC LEAGUE, 36

Coffin, Jay Staff Writer
GOLFWEEK, 568

Coffler, Ryan Controller
ORLIMAR GOLF COMPANY, 1183

Coffman, Mark Security Supervisor
SOLANO COUNTY FAIRGROUNDS, 1053

Coffman, Tom Deputy AD, Development
DUKE UNIVERSITY ATHLETICS, 328

Cofield, Remy General Manager
NATIONAL BASKETBALL ASSOCIATION
DEVELOPMENT LEAGUE, 60

Cogan, Karen Associate Editor/Clinical
Counseling
JOURNAL OF APPLIED SPORT
PSYCHOLOGY, 572

Cogen, Jeff Marketing EVP
TEXAS RANGERS BASEBALL CLUB, 1017

Coggeshall, Tim VP of Sales
BOWLINGSHIRT.COM, 1119

Coggin, James President / Chief Administrative
Officer
SAKS INCORPORATED, 1248

Cogley, Mark General Management
BUTLER HEAVY STRUCTURES, 1061

Cohan, Henry President
HUDSON TRAIL OUTFITTERS, LTD., 1242

Cohan, Richard Chief Executive Officer
EB2B COMMERCE, INC., 1237

Cohea, Danielle Associate AD, Compliance
CLEVELAND STATE UNIVERSITY
ATHLETICS, 326

Cohen, Andrew Chief Executive Officer
A TEAM, 562, 592, 779

Cohen, Ariel Assistant Marketing Director
WCLH-FM, 648

Cohen, Arthur Principal
ARCHITECTURAL RESOURCES CAMBRIDGE
INC., 1059

Cohen, Bob President/Chief Executive Officer
SCARBOROUGH SPORTS MARKETING, 637,
666, 815

Cohen, Brad Director of Athletics
LONG ISLAND UNIVERSITY, C.W. POST
ATHLETICS, 363

Cohen, Bruce Vice President, Sales/Marketing
IRWIN SEATING COMPANY, 1159

Cohen, Bryan Special Projects Coordinator
HAMPTON CLASSIC HORSE SHOW, 76

Cohen, Cheryl Vice President/Executive Producer
PLATINUM ENTERTAINMENT PARTNERS II,
608

Cohen, Cindy Associate Athletic Director
WILLIAM PATERSON UNIVERSITY OF NEW
JERSEY ATHLETICS, 409

Cohen, David Sr. EVP and Chief Diversity Officer
COMCAST CORPORATION, 735

Cohen, Doug Assistant General Manager
BETHPAGE BALLPARK, 958

Cohen, Evan Program Director
WTLX-FM, 676

Cohen, Ilene Athletic Director
NJCAA REGION XIX WOMEN'S, 287

Cohen, Irwin Commissioner
NEW ENGLAND INTERCOLLEGIATE
AMATEUR ATHLETIC ASSOCIATION, 284

Cohen, Jack Publisher
COLLEGE & PRO FOOTBALL NEWSWEEKLY,
537, 561

Cohen, Jeff Director of Merchandising
NEW YORK-PENNSYLVANIA LEAGUE, 47,
991

Cohen, Jennifer Director of Athletics
WASHINGTON ATHLETICS, UNIVERSITY OF,
349, 978

Cohen, Jerry Founder
EBBETS FIELD FLANNELS, 1026, 1138

Cohen, Jim EVP,Mergers and Acquisition
CONSOLIDATED GRAPHICS, 787

Cohen, John Director of Athletics
MISSISSIPPI STATE UNIVERSITY
ATHLETICS, 227, 337

Cohen, Joshua Manager
BARRETT SPORTS GROUP, 783

Cohen, Kathryn General Manager
FOX SPORTS PRIME TICKET, 682, 683

Cohen, Ken Editor
GOLF TRAVELER, 567

Cohen, Kenneth Partner
RAGSDALE, RICHARD A., 910

Cohen, Kevin Sports Director
WCOS, 648

Cohen, Laura Web Editor
GATOR BAIT, 566

Cohen, Lee President
USL LEAGUE TWO, 160, 163

Cohen, Lee Head Athletic Trainer
SPECIAL OLYMPICS STADIUM, 1013

Cohen, Louis Partner
PIPER MARBURY RUDNICK & WOLFE, 909

Cohen, Mark Partner
MARGOLIS EDELSTEIN, 902

Cohen, Marty General Manager/Editor
GATOR BAIT, 566

Cohen, Mitch Strategic Execution Leader
PRICEWATERHOUSECOOPERS, 768

Cohen, Neil Managing Editor
SPORTS ILLUSTRATED FOR KIDS, 591

Cohen, Rachel Sports Reporter
DALLAS MORNING NEWS, 483

Cohen, Renee Marketing Manager
PAC-10 PROPERTIES, 808

Cohen, Richard President
WALDON, GROUP THE, 868

Cohen, Robert Partner
COHEN, ROBERT M., 882

Cohen, Robert Founder
COHEN, ROBERT M., 882

Cohen, Rod Sports Producer
KTTV-TV, 696, 703

Cohen, Sanford Host
LET'S TALK SPORTS, 612

Cohen, Steve Vice President
NEW YORK-PENNSYLVANIA LEAGUE, 32, 47

Cohen, Tim Treasurer
CALIFORNIA THOROUGHBRED BREEDERS
ASSOCIATION, 75

Cohen, Walter Attorney
OBERMAYER, REBMANN, MAXWELL &
HIPPEL, LLP, 907

Cohn, Bob Sports Writer
WASHINGTON TIMES, 550

Cohn, David Director Of Member Services &
Communicat
WISCONSIN STATE GOLF ASSOCIATION,
116

Cohn, Gerald Chief Executive Officer
GEORGIA BOOT, 1148

Cohn, Justin Sports Reporter
JOURNAL GAZETTE, 501

Cohn, Linda Anchor
ESPN, 690

Cohn, Lowell Sports Reporter
PRESS DEMOCRAT, 526

Cohn, William Principal Attorney
COHN, WILLIAM A., 882

Coia, Sonja Operating Manager VP
ELBY GIFTS, 1138

Coiner, Skip Art Director
SAND SPORTS, 585

Coito, Wayne Multimedia Specialist
PACIFIC WEST CONFERENCE, 301

Colarossi, Robert Publisher
USA GYMNASTICS, 596

Colbert, Cary Sup. Of Ops & Sales Fulfillment
NEW MEXICO BOWL, 92

Colbert, Kelly Assistant Athletic Director
STATE UNIVERSITY OF NEW YORK
INSTITUTE OF TECHNOLOGY
ATHLETICS(SU, 404

Colbert, Kevin VP/General Manager
NATIONAL FOOTBALL LEAGUE/NFL, 97, 978

Colboch, Craig General Manager
WIBW AM 580 RADIO, 657

Colbrese, Mike Executive Director
WASHINGTON INTERSCHOLASTIC
ACTIVITIES ASSOCIATION, 200

Colburn, Bob VP / General Manager
BAUER NIKE HOCKEY, INC., 1115

Colburn, David Provost & Vice President
Academic Affair
FLORIDA, UNIVERSITY OF, 421

Colby, Joan Editor/Advertising Manager
ILLINOIS RACING NEWS, 570

Colby, Susan VP Guest Services
NEW HAMPSHIRE MOTOR SPEEDWAY, 1039

Cole, Bill College Sports Reporter
WINSTON-SALEM JOURNAL, 552

Cole, Carleton Sports Producer
KHOU-TV, 698

Cole, Cheryl Senior Woman Administrator
STATE UNIVERSITY OF NEW YORK
COLLEGE AT PLATTSBURGH
ATHLETICS(SUN, 404

Cole, Darlene Venue Manager
VIKING HALL CIVIC CENTER, 1025

Cole, Dayton University Attorney
COLE, DAYTON T., 882

Cole, Jack Director of Athletics
MESSIAH COLLEGE ATHLETICS, 395, 428

Cole, Jason Sports Writer
MIAMI HERALD, 510

Cole, Jeff Sales VP
WEST COAST TURF, 1221

Cole, Jim Director of Athletics
MERCER UNIVERSITY ATHLETICS, 336

Cole, John President
JEBCO, 1160

Cole, Justin General Manager
TEXAS BASEBALL LEAGUE, 53

Cole, Kelly Head Coach, Women's Basketball
MATTHEWS ARENA, 994

Cole, Kim Assistant Director
NEW JERSEY STATE INTERSCHOLASTIC
ATHLETIC ASSOCIATION, 199

Cole, Lady President
ALLEN UNIVERSITY ATHLETICS, 305

Cole, Michael EVP and COO
KIA MOTORS AMERICA, 737

Cole, Ozzie Racing Secretary
ROCKINGHAM PARK, 1053

Cole, Pam Administrative Assistant
WILLIAM R. JOHNSON COLISEUM, 1028

Cole, Ray President
WOI-TV, 716

Cole, Rod Director for Athletic Performance
TARLETON STATE UNIVERSITY ATHLETICS,
373

Cole, Roz President
PPI MARKETING, 857

Cole, Stan Assoc. AD, Communications
CAMPBELL UNIVERSITY ATHLETICS, 325

Cole, Steve Associate Athletics Director, Internal
A
WILLIAM & MARY HALL, 1026, 1028

Cole, Thomas Vice Chairman
FEDERATED DEPARTMENT STORES, INC.,
1239

Cole, Victor General Manager
LOUISVILLE XTREME, 94

Coleman, Andrew Assistant Professor
LIBERTY UNIVERSITY, 425

Coleman, Bill Owner/News Director
KOKB-AM, 632

Coleman, Chris Chair
DES MOINES AREA SPORTS COMMISSION,
230

executive index

Consolo, Kristen MPS Sports Industry Management Program M
GEORGETOWN UNIVERSITY, 421

Constance, Dale Sports Editor
SELMA TIMES-JOURNAL, 489, 534

Constantini, David Chief Executive Officer
LANGHORNE SKI & SPORT, 1243

Constantini, Kathy Owner and Buyer
LANGHORNE SKI & SPORT, 1243

Constantino, Charles Sports News Assistant
ARIZONA DAILY STAR, 463

Constantino, Jennifer NCAA Compliance Officer
LAKE SUPERIOR STATE UNIVERSITY ATHLETICS (LSSU), 362

Conta, Jeffrey Attorney
CROAK, FRANCIS R., 883, 884

Conte, Chris Athletic Director
TEXAS AT AUSTIN ATHLETICS, UNIVERSITY OF, 346, 972

Conte, James Attorney
MCDONALD, SNYDER & WILLIAMS P.C., 903

Contento, Duane Senior Vice President
AD ART SIGN COMPANY, 1103

Conti, Melissa Asst. Commissioner of Championships
COLONIAL ATHLETIC ASSOCIATION, 293

Contorno, Ron President
FULL HOUSE SPORTS MARKETING, 792

Contos, Becky Sales and marketing manager
NATIONAL AUTOMOBILE MUSEUM, 254

Contos, Persefone Sports Anchor
WVIT-TV, 720

Contreras, Anthony Manager
NORTHWEST BASEBALL LEAGUE, 35, 48

Contreras, John Editor
LAMAR DAILY NEWS, 504

Contreras, Veronica Sports Anchor
WNJU-TV, 715

Contreras, Victor Assistant Sports Editor
SACRAMENTO BEE, 530

Converse, Dave Director of Engineering
EXMARK MANUFACTURING, 1141

Converset, Don Assistant Sports Editor
NEWS-SENTINEL, 517

Conville, Kirk President
BAGGO, 1113

Conway, Chip Senior VP, Operations
NATIONAL FOOTBALL LEAGUE/NFL, 95

Conway, Geogory Partner
LIEBMANN, CONWAY, OLEJNICZAK & JERRY, 900

Conway, Gregory Attorney
LIEBMANN, CONWAY, OLEJNICZAK & JERRY, 900

Conway, John VP Sales/Administration
NATIONAL TICKET COMPANY, 941

Conway, Kevin Sports Information Director
MILWAUKEE SCHOOL OF ENGINEERING ATHLETICS (MSOE), 395

Conway, Matt Vice President
CRAMER PRODUCTS, INC., 954, 1130

Conway, Michael Financial Planner/Principal
CONWAY, MICHAEL W., 838

Conway, Vince Weekend Sports Anchor/Reporter
WTVO-TV, 719

Conwell, Dean Executive Director
BEAUMONT CONVENTION & VISITORS BUREAU, 227

Coode, Robert Partner
SKODA, MINOTTI & CO., 916

Cook, Alice Sports Reporter
WBZ-TV, 708

Cook, Anne Director, Club Operations
INSIGHT SPORTS MANAGEMENT CO, LLC, 797

Cook, Anthony Sports Editor
PARSONS SUN, 522

Cook, Bill Director of Public Relations
SAMUEL J. PLUMERI FIELD AT MERCER COUNTY WATERFRONT PARK, 809, 1009

Cook, Brad Founder
SPORTSPILOT, INC., 723

Cook, Brian Chief Executive Officer
STAIRMASTER HEALTH AND FITNESS PRODUCTS, 1207

Cook, Bruce Crew Chief
NASCAR GANDER OUTDOORS TRUCK SERIES, 23

Cook, Chad Associate Commissioner Marketing
BIG SOUTH CONFERENCE, 290

Cook, Dave Sports Producer
WFLA-TV, 710

Cook, Don Director Racing
THE DOWNS RACETRACK & CASINO AT ALBUQUERQUE, 1054

Cook, Doug Chairman of the Board
COUNSILMAN-HUNSAKER, 1062

Cook, Greg Principal
HOLABIRD & ROOT, 1070

Cook, Jack Principal
FENTRESS ARCHITECTS, 1065

Cook, Jeff Director of Ticket Operations
FLORIDA STATE LEAGUE, 39

Cook, Jeffrey Firm Administrator
HERSHNER, HUNTER, ANDREWS, NEILL & SMITH L,L,P., 893

Cook, Jennifer Facility Marketing/Ticket Sales Manager
HULMAN CENTER, 981

Cook, Jerry President
OVERLAND PARK CONVENTION & VISITORS BUREAU, 241, 262

Cook, Jill Senior Woman Administrator
WESTERN CONNECTICUT STATE UNIVERSITY ATHLETICS, 408

Cook, John President
ARC ICESPORTS & ENTERTAINMENT, 1059

Cook, Kelly President
STRIVERS GROUP, 866

Cook, Mary Corporate Dept Manager
HARMON TRAVEL SERVICE, 936

Cook, Mollie Sales/Service Representative
BLIMP WORKS, INC., 784

Cook, Pam News Director
WHBC-FM, 656

Cook, Peter Advertising Director
HICKORY DAILY RECORD, 497

Cook, R. President
AMERICAN OSTEOPATHIC ACADEMY OF SPORTS MEDICINE, 929

Cook, Richard Vice Chair
LOS ANGELES SPORTS COUNCIL, 238

Cook, Robert Chief Financial Officer
NICKLAUS GOLF EQUIPMENT COMPANY, L.C., 1179

Cook, Robin Officer at Large
ARIZONA WOMEN'S GOLF ASSOCIATION, 109

Cook, Ron Sports Columnist
PITTSBURGH POST-GAZETTE, 524

Cook, Scott President
AMERICAN OSTEOPATHIC ACADEMY OF SPORTS MEDICINE, 84

Cook, Shelby Online Service Coordinator
EQUIBASE COMPANY, 938

Cook, Steve National AV Consultant Manager
DRAPER INC., 382, 1135

Cook, Tim Athletics Director
LIFE PACIFIC COLLEGE ATHLETICS, 362

Cook, Vincent Sports Editor
FINE PRINT NEWS, 491

Cooke, Diane President / Chief Executive Officer
SEATING SERVICES INCORPORATED, 1198

Cooke, Dick Associate AD
DAVIDSON COLLEGE ATHLETICS, 327

Cooke, Jeanie Executive Director
DANVILLE AREA CONVENTION & VISITOR BUREAU, 230

Cooke, Nate Head Athletic Trainer
YORK COLLEGE (PENNSYLVANIA) ATHLETICS, 411

Cooke, Nick Coordinator of Sports Medicine
HOBART COLLEGE ATHLETICS, 389

Cooke, Timothy Sales & Marketing VP
SEATING SERVICES INCORPORATED, 1198

Cooke, Jr., Frederick Attorney
RUBIN, ERIC M., 913

Cooker, Crocker Director of Athletics
CONNECTICUT COLLEGE ATHLETICS, 383

Cooksey, Tom Vice President
KENTUCKY GOLF ASSOCIATION, 105, 111

Cookson, Brian President
UNION CYCLISTE INTERNATIONALE (UCI), 71, 203

Cookson, Victoria General Manager
HOLMAN STADIUM, 979

Cooley, Archie Football Coach
PAUL QUINN COLLEGE ATHLETICS, 317

Coombs, Joe Head Coach/General Manager
NORTH AMERICAN HOCKEY LEAGUE, 132

Coome, Freya Head Coach
NATIONAL WOMEN'S SOCCER LEAGUE, 158

Coomer, Cathy General Manager
KRSC-FM, 634

Coomes, Rose Vice President
TOWN TALK CAP MFG. COMPANY, INC., 1214

Coon, Robert Director of Media Relations & Marketing
MIDWEST LEAGUE, 44

Coon, Timothy
WILSON, ELSER, MOSKOWITZ ET AL, 925

Coonan, Dan President/CEO
EASTERN COLLEGE ATHLETIC CONFERENCE/ECAC, 293

Coonce, Perry Director of Operations
USA BROOMBALL, 68

Coonelly, Frank President
PNC PARK, 1002

Cooney, Bob Sports Reporter
PHILADELPHIA DAILY NEWS, 523

Cooney, Frank President
SPORTS XCHANGE, THE, 722

Cooney, Kevin Sports Writer
BUCKS COUNTY COURIER TIMES, 469

Cooney, Michael Men's Basketball Coach
UNIVERSITY OF WEST GEORGIA DEPARTMENT OF INTERCOLLEGIATE ATHLETIC, 373

Coons, Gex Chief Executive Officer
GEXCO ENTERPRISES, 1148

Cooper, Allison Director of Marketing
METROPOLITAN TUCSON CONVENTION & VISITORS BUREAU, 239

Cooper, Brian Chairman
CANADA BASKETBALL, 54

Cooper, Bruce Weekend Sports Reporter
KPNX-TV, 701

Cooper, Cathy Partner, Production And Content
AURA360 VENTURES, 782

Cooper, Charles Sales Manager
PRO SPECIALTIES GROUP, 1188

Cooper, Dave Vice President Saless
NATIONAL MOBILE TELEVISION PRODUCTIONS, INC., 607

Cooper, David Assistant Sports Editor
FRESNO BEE, 492

Cooper, Denise President
SAN DIEGO HALL OF CHAMPIONS SPORTS MUSEUM, THE, 257

Cooper, Dennis Chairman
MARKETING EVENT PARTNERS, 766

Cooper, Donna Account Executive
KWES-TV, 705

Cooper, Dwaine Assoc Executive Director Finance/Adminis
USA WRESTLING, 211

Cooper, Elizabeth Co-Founder
JHG TOWNSEND, 799, 830

Cooper, Joel Founder
GOTCHA INTERNATIONAL, 1150

Cooper, John Head Coach, Men's Basketball
MILLETT HALL, 249, 635, 995

Cooper, Jon Head Coach
NATIONAL HOCKEY LEAGUE/NHL, 125

Cooper, Joseph Member
COOPER & COOPER LLD, 838

Cooper, Kory Goaltending Development Coach
AMERICAN HOCKEY LEAGUE/AHL, 126

Cooper, Lonnie CEO
CAREER SPORTS & ENTERTAINMENT, 836

Cooper, Mike Co-Owner & President
NORTH AMERICAN HOCKEY LEAGUE, 131, 620

Cooper, Molly Director Of Tournament & Member Programs
PACIFIC NORTHWEST PGA SECTIONAL OFFICE, 106

Cooper, Muriel Community Relations & Administration
PRICE COSTCO WHOLESALE, 1246

Cooper, Paul President
MARKETING EVENT PARTNERS, 766

Cooper, Richard Partner
WILLIAMS & CONNOLLY, 869

Executive Index

Cooper, Rick Athletics Director
WAYLAND BAPTIST UNIVERSITY ATHLETICS, 322

Cooper, Robin 1st Vice President
INTERNATIONAL COLLEGIATE LICENSING ASSOCIATION/ICLA, 282

Cooper, Scott Owner / President
COOPSPORT INTERNATIONAL LP, 1130

Cooper, Thomas Interim Stadium Manager
VETERANS MEMORIAL STADIUM, 1025

Cooper, Tim Sports Reporter
ARKANSAS DEMOCRAT-GAZETTE, 463

Cooper, Tom Event Manager
MISSISSIPPI VETERANS MEMORIAL STADIUM, 995

Coore, Bill Partner
COORE AND CRENSHAW, 0

Coover, Michael Producer
WE ARE THERE SATURDAY, 617

Copacia, Ryan Manager
GENERAL SPORTS TURF SYSTEMS, 755

Cope, George President & CEO, BCE and Bell Canada
BELL CANADA, 734

Cope, Melody Vice President for Athletics
DOWLING COLLEGE (DC) ATHLETICS, 357

Copeland, Ann Vice President
COPELAND COMPANY, INC., HAL, 787

Copeland, Harry President
COPELAND COMPANY, INC., HAL, 787

Copeland, Jack Managing Editor
NCAA NEWS, 578

Copeland, Melanie Administration Assistant
PLANO CONVENTION & VISITORS BUREAU, 242

Coplin, Eric Director of Athletics Communications
SOUTHERN NEW HAMPSHIRE UNIVERSITY ATHLETICS, 372

Copple, Barry Operations Manager
ERIE INSURANCE ARENA, 972

Coppo, Matt Director, Ticket Operations
AMERICAN LEAGUE OF PROFESSIONAL BASEBALL CLUBS, THE, 29

Coppock, Chet Host
CHET COPPOCK, 615

Coppola, Frank Sports Editor
PORTSMOUTH HERALD, 525

Coppola, Rich Sports Director
WTIC-TV, 718

Copps, Kenny Ticket Manager
ANDY KERR STADIUM, 954

Coppus, Troy Instructor
EVANSVILLE, UNIVERSITY OF, 420

Corales, Alan General Manager
WKVM-AM, 661

Corbat, Michael Chief Executive Officer, Citigroup
CITIGROUP, INC., 735

Corbet, Peter Co-Chief Executive Officer
TEAMWORKS CENTERS, 1017

Corbett, Bruce Attorney
CORBETT & STEELMAN, 884

Corbett, Christi Promotion Manager
KDLH-TV, 697

Corbett, David Founder and Senior Consultant
NEW DIRECTIONS, 936

Corbett, James President & CEO, Canadian Outback Advent
LEADING BRANDS, 555, 1165

Corbett, John Chief Executive Officer
SPECIAL OLYMPICS WEST VIRGINIA, 196

Corbett, Neil Sports Editor
CITIZENS' VOICE, 473

Corbin, Dan General Manager
RIVERFRONT STADIUM, 1006

Corbin, Herbert Founding Partner
KCSA PUBLIC RELATIONS WORLDWIDE, 800

Corbin, Jeffrey Managing Partner/Chief Executive Officer
KCSA PUBLIC RELATIONS WORLDWIDE, 800

Corbin, Laura Chairwoman, Publicity Manager
SPARTANBURG CONVENTION & VISITORS BUREAU, 244

Corbusier, Drue EVP / Director
DILLARD DEPARTMENT STORES, 1236

Corby, John Host
THE JOHN CORBY SHOW, 614

Corcoran, Chris Vice President/Affiliate Management
WESTWOODONE, 611

Corcoran, Chuck Entertainment VP
GEM GROUP, 844

Corcoran, Jack Sports Reporter
TALLAHASSEE DEMOCRAT, 541

Corcoran, Nicole Executive Associate AD/SWA
KANSAS UNIVERSITY ATHLETICS, 333

Cordaro, John Assistant Executive Director for Ticketi
INDEPENDENCE STADIUM, 982

Cordaro, Martie President
USL LEAGUE ONE, 49, 160, 1007

Cordasco, Nicholas Talent representation
PRINCE MARKETING GROUP, 811, 857

Cordell, Bethany Senior Associate AD, Annual Giving
MONTANA STATE UNIVERSITY ATHLETICS, 337

Cordell, Carten Sports Editor
ROSWELL NEIGHBOR, 530

Cordell, De Sales and Marketing VP / ACC Properties
RAYCOM SPORTS, 813

Cordell, Leigha Event Sales Coordinator
LAWRENCE JOEL VETERANS MEMORIAL COLISEUM, 990

Cordell, Martha Assistant Dean for Student Compliance an
THE UNIVERSITY OF TULSA COLLEGE OF LAW, 921

Cordella, Rick Senior VP & General Manager, Digital Med
ROTOWORLD, 722

Cordero, Dave Director of Communications
WORLD GOLF VILLAGE, 118

Cordes, Rob National Accounts Manager
VITRONIX PROMOTIONAL GROUP, 1220

Cordick, Denis VP, Marketing
AMJ CAMPBELL, 934

Cordill, Brian Director of Event Operations
BRAMLAGE COLISEUM, 960

Cordingley, Troy Head Coach
NATIONAL LACROSSE LEAGUE, 141

Cordischi, Scott Sports Director
WPRO, 669

Cordova, Art Director, Accounting & Finance
HOMESTEAD-MIAMI SPEEDWAY, LLC, 1035

Core-Drevecky, Leslie President, PGA
COLORADO SECTION PGA, 99

Corelis, Jim AVP, Applications
STATS LLC, 939

Corey, Bill Sports Editor
PROVIDENCE JOURNAL, 527

Corey, Mark Principal
FLAD ARCHITECTS, 1066

Corey, Mike Chief Steward
REMINGTON PARK, 1052

Corey, Steven Attorney
BLANC, DAVID, 876

Corhern, Thomas Sports Writer
HERALD-CITIZEN, 496

Corino, Mark President elect, 1st VP
EASTERN ASSOCIATION OF ROWING COLLEGES, 147

Corino, Mark Director of Athletics
CALDWELL UNIVERSITY ATHLETICS, 353

Corkran, Steve Sports Reporter (NFL)
CONTRA COSTA TIMES, 475

Corl, Chris General Manager
U.S. CELLULAR CENTER, 1020

Corley, Kelly Vice President Finance
LANCE ARMSTRONG FOUNDATION, 190

Corley, Scott Director of Athletics
BELMONT UNIVERSITY ATHLETICS, 324

Corliss, Robert President / Chief Executive Officer
ATHLETE'S FOOT, 1228

Corliss, Robert CEO
ATHLETE'S FOOT, 1228

Cormier, Gilles Executive Director
QUEBEC MAJOR JUNIOR HOCKEY LEAGUE, 134

Cormier, Mary 1st Vice President
NEW HAMPSHIRE WOMEN'S GOLF ASSOCIATION, 113

Corn, Mike Assistant Director
U.S. TRACK & FIELD AND CROSS COUNTRY COACHES ASSOCIATION, 175

Cornacchione, Matt Director of Athletic Facilities
NYACK COLLEGE ATHLETICS, 368

Cornelis, Thom Sports Director
KWQC-TV, 705

Cornelison, Edna Promoter
NEA SPEEDWAY, 1039

Cornelison, Hugh Promoter
NEA SPEEDWAY, 1039

Cornelius, Judy Promotions Manager
WHNT-TV, 712

Cornelius, Steve Sports Editor
COMMONWEALTH-JOURNAL, 475

Cornell, Brian Chairman and CEO
TARGET STORES, 742

Cornell, Brian President / Chief Executive Officer
SAM'S CLUB, 1248

Cornell, Brian Executive VP, President and CEO, Sam's C
WAL-MART STORES, INC., 1252

Cornell, Robert Director
STARR RINK, 1014

Cornetta, Louise Senior Coordinating Producer
WEEKEND GAMENIGHT, 615, 617

Cornilles, Robert Founder/CEO
GAME FACE, INC., 755

Cornish, Brett Marketing/Sales Director
I WIRELESS CENTER, 981

Cornwall, Danielle Assistant Director Of Educational Progra
JACKIE ROBINSON FOUNDATION, 189

Cornwall, Josh Sports Information Director
GORDON COLLEGE ATHLETICS, 387

Cornwell, Bill News Director
WKEE-FM, 660

Cornwell, Brittany Graduate Assistant, Events and Conferenc
ROSE BASKETBALL ARENA, 987, 1007

Cornwell, Jennifer Marketing Director
ROOTS APPAREL, 1194

Cornwell, Lisa Weekend Sports Anchor/Reporter
WCPO-TV, 709

Cornwell, Scott Director Of Operations
UNIVERSITY HALL, 1000, 1021

Cornwell, Steve Executive Vice President Operations
HOST COMMUNICATIONS, INC., 796

Cornwell, Tanya Ticket Manager
ROBINS CENTER, 1006

Coro, Paul Sports/NBA Reporter
ARIZONA REPUBLIC, 463

Corpos, Mike Sports Writer
DAILY REPUBLIC, 482

Corpuz, Rey Marketing Director
MCDAVID, 1172

Corr, David EVP / Executive Creative Director
PUBLICIS NEW YORK, 812

Corrada, Santiago President/Chief Executive Officer
TAMPA CONVENTION & VISITORS BUREAU, 246

Corrao, Robert Chairman/Chief Executive Officer
SPORTS IMPACT, INC., 584, 865

Corredor, Nestor Manager
ARIZONA LEAGUE (ROOKIE), 34

Correia, Celso President
USL LEAGUE TWO, 163

Corrigan, Boo Director of Athletics
NORTH CAROLINA STATE UNIVERSITY ATHLETICS, 339, 965, 995

Corriveau, Dave Sports Reporter
VALLEY NEWS, 548

Corry, Stacey Director of Athletic Communications
STATE UNIVERSITY OF NEW YORK COLLEGE AT BROCKPORT ATHLETICS (SUNY, 404

Corsano, Anthony CEO
ANVIL KNITWEAR INC., 1109

Corsi, Fred Operations VP
SAVVIS CENTER, 1010

Corsi, Jim Goaltending Development Coach
AMERICAN HOCKEY LEAGUE/AHL, 127

Corso, Cliff Managing Director
MBIA INSURANCE CORPORATION, 777

Corsoe, Frank Sports Editor
BLADE, 467

Corullo, Dan Secretary
ACTION FLOOR SYSTEMS, LLC, 1102

Corum, Debbie Athletic Director
SOUTHERN UTAH UNIVERSITY ATHLETICS, 345

executive index

Dam, Gary Director of Corporate Relations
DETROIT BOWL (QUICK LANE BOWL), 91

Dam, Jim VP, Ticket Sales & Service
NATIONAL FOOTBALL LEAGUE/NFL, 95

Dambach, Jason Executive Vice President,
General Manage
TEXAS BASEBALL LEAGUE, 47, 53, 971

Dame, Benjamin Complex Director
LAWRENCE JOEL VETERANS MEMORIAL
COLISEUM, 990

Dame, Benjamin Director, Public Assembly
Facilities
LAWRENCE JOEL VETERANS MEMORIAL
COLISEUM, 990

Dameron, Kim Head Coach, Football
O'BRIEN FIELD, 998

Dames, Rory Head Coach
NATIONAL WOMEN'S SOCCER LEAGUE, 158

Damin, Marty Vice President/Sales Sports
WESTWOODONE, 610, 611

Dammrich, Thomas President
NATIONAL MARINE MANUFACTURERS
ASSOCIATION, 64

Damon, Beck Member, Ardc Committee
AMAROO PARK, 1031

Damon, George Senior Associate
HENDERSON ENGINEERS INC., 829

Damon, Jud Director of Athletics
FLAGLER COLLEGE ATHLETICS, 359

Damon, Robert CFO
KATZ MEDIA CORPORATION, 800, 849

Damphousse, Kelly Associate Dean
OKLAHOMA, UNIVERSITY OF, 433

Damron, Ron Associate Athletic Director/Facility
Ope
JONES AT&T STADIUM, 986

Danahey, Joe Assistant AD For Sports
Information
CONCORDIA UNIVERSITY (OR) ATHLETICS,
356

Danals, Brandt Athletics Director
SILVER LAKE COLLEGE ATHLETICS, 344

Danburg, Curtis VP, Communications &
Community Impact
AMERICAN LEAGUE OF PROFESSIONAL
BASEBALL CLUBS, THE, 29

Dance, Reggie Contact
PRINCE MARKETING GROUP, 811, 857

Danch, Michael Associate Athletics Director
(Facilities
JOYCE ATHLETIC & CONVOCATION
CENTER, 883, 986

Dandes, Jon Treasurer
NEW YORK-PENNSYLVANIA LEAGUE (A
LEVEL), 46

Dandes, Jonathan President, Rich Baseball
Operations
INTERNATIONAL LEAGUE, 42, 966

Dandy, William SVP, Retail Sales and Operations
FAMOUS FOOTWEAR, 1238

Dane, Chris Head Athletic Trainer
WEST TEXAS A&M UNIVERSITY ATHLETICS
(WTAMU), 376

Dane, Phil Athletic Director
SKYHAWK STADIUM, 1012

Danell, Sheree Administrative Assistant to
Athletics
MARTIN LUTHER COLLEGE ATHLETICS, 314

Danforth, Austin Sports Reporter
BENNINGTON BANNER, 466

Dangerfield, Phil Vice President, Football
Operations
FIRST ENERGY STADIUM, 974

Danheiser, Dennis Sports Assistant Editor
BUFFALO NEWS, 469

Daniel, James Director
KITE TRADE ASSOCIATION INTERNATIONAL,
140

Daniel, Lee Executive Director
TALLAHASSEE SPORTS COUNCIL, 246

Daniel, Martin Director of Athletic Training
KENTUCKY WESLEYAN COLLEGE
ATHLETICS, 361

Daniel, Matt Head Athletic Trainer
NORTH GEORGIA COLLEGE & STATE
UNIVERSITY ATHLETICS, 367

Daniel, Rich Owner/President
WOMEN'S FOOTBALL ALLIANCE / WFA, 97

Daniel, Tami Office Coordinator
TRAPSHOOTING HALL OF FAME AND
MUSEUM, 257

Daniel, Tim Director of Athletics
DICKINSON STATE UNIVERSITY ATHLETICS,
257, 310

Daniel, Willie Director
GRAMBLING STATE UNIVERSITY, 422

Daniels, Amanda VP
IGNITION, INC., 796

Daniels, Chuck President
OOLTEWAH MANUFACTURING COMPANY,
1182

Daniels, Darrell News Director
WBES-AM, 645

Daniels, Donna Executive VP & Prudential Center
GM
NATIONAL HOCKEY LEAGUE/NHL, 124

Daniels, Doug Sports Editor
DU QUOIN EVENING CALL, 487

Daniels, Eddie Sports Reporter
TAMPA TRIBUNE, 541

Daniels, Janie Classified Manager
REGISTER NEWS, 528

Daniels, Jeff Assistant Coach
NATIONAL HOCKEY LEAGUE/NHL, 123

Daniels, John Athletic Photographer
LIVINGSTONE COLLEGE, 426

Daniels, Jon President, Baseball Operations
AMERICAN LEAGUE OF PROFESSIONAL
BASEBALL CLUBS, THE, 31

Daniels, Kelly Director of Accounting
MICHIGAN INTERNATIONAL SPEEDWAY
(MIS), 1038

Daniels, Lenny Executive Vice President/Chief
Operating
TURNER SPORTS, INC., 685

Daniels, Leroy NFLPA Certified Contract
Advisor/Agent
TOP NOTCH SPORTS MANAGEMENT, 868

Daniels, Mark Sports Director
WNFL 1140-AM, 549, 665

Daniels, Mike Assistant Commissioner Marketing
BIG WEST CONFERENCE, 291

Daniels, Norm Chairman, Pres, Chief Executive
Officer
WHOLESALE SPORTS OUTDOOR
OUTFITTERS, 1253

Daniels, Rob Sports Reporter
GREENSBORO NEWS & RECORD, 494

Daniels, Sean Properties VP
PRORODEO SPORTS NEWS, 583

Daniels, Terry Maintainace Supritendent
SOUTH BOSTON SPEEDWAY, 1042

Daniels, Tiffany Senior Associate Athletics
Director, Ext
GEORGIA STATE UNIVERSITY, 421

Daniels, Tommy Vice President Of Broadcasting
& Media R
EAST COAST HOCKEY LEAGUE/ECHL, 129

Daniels, Toni Director of Sales
WINGS EVENT CENTER, 1028

Daniels, Vicki News Director
KTRS-FM, 637

Danielson, Brent Chairman of the Board
THOMAS M. COOLEY LAW SCHOOL, 921

Danielson, Karl Architect
DAHLIN GROUP ARCHITECTS PLANNERS,
1063

Danielsson, Magnus Intl VP
FELD MOTOR SPORTS, 16

Danison, Chris Crew Chief
IMSA WEATHERTECH SPORTSCAR
CHAMPIONSHIP, 21

Danley, Stacy Director of Athletics
SOUTH CAROLINA STATE UNIVERSITY
ATHLETICS, 344

Dann, Danny VP, Marketing & Advertising
NATIONAL LEAGUE OF PROFESSIONAL
BASEBALL CLUBS, THE, 32

Dann, Michael Sports Editor
DAILY REGISTER, 482

Dannelly, Jess Associate AD, Community
Outreach
COASTAL CAROLINA UNIVERSITY
ATHLETICS, 326

Dannen, Troy Director of Athletics
TULANE UNIVERSITY ATHLETICS, 347

Danner, Dee Director, Ticketing
EAST COAST HOCKEY LEAGUE/ECHL, 130

Danner, Mark Director
JEFFERSON COUNTY FAIRGROUNDS (JCF),
1050

Dannhauser, Stephen Chairman
WEIL, GOTSHAL & MANGES, 924

Dannheim, Callye Game Operations
TEXAS BOWL, 93

Danos, Jon Exec. Director of Athletics
NEW HAMPSHIRE ATHLETICS, UNIVERSITY
OF, 35, 338, 968

Dant, Steve General Manager
WB 32, 707

Dantuono, Doug Vice President
TOLEDO DISTRICT GOLF ASSOCIATION, 115

Danz, Tom Sports Editor
SOUTHWEST NEWS-HERALD, 473, 537

Danzer, Paul Sports Writer
COLUMBIAN, 474

Danziger, Rona Program Director
WDFN - 1130 AM THE FAN, 650

Daoust, Pascal General Manager
QUEBEC MAJOR JUNIOR HOCKEY LEAGUE,
135

Daoust, Pierre Vice President, Administration
QUEBEC MAJOR JUNIOR HOCKEY LEAGUE,
134

Dapp, Scott Interim Director of Athletics
MORAVIAN COLLEGE ATHLETICS, 396

Dapper, Katelyn Executive Office Coordinator
U.S. SPORTS ACROBATICS/USSA, 120

Darak, Sr., Dennis Executive Director/CEO
TRI-STATE PGA SECTIONAL OFFICE, 107

Darbar, Kethan Sports Information Coordinator
EMMANUEL COLLEGE (EC) ATHLETICS, 358

Darby, Brian Operations Supervisor
RENSSELAER POLYTECHNIC
INSTITUTE/HOUSTON FIELD, 1005

Darby, David Sports Editor
DETROIT FREE PRESS, 486

Darby, Jeff Senior Associate AD, Communications
TEXAS AT EL PASO ATHLETICS,
UNIVERSITY OF, 346

Darche, Mathieu Director, Hockey Operations
NATIONAL HOCKEY LEAGUE/NHL, 125

Dare, Chad Sports Editor
COMMERCIAL NEWS, 475

Dare, John Managing Director Structured Finance
a
MBIA INSURANCE CORPORATION, 777

Darger, Liz Sr. Associate AD/SWA
BRIGHAM YOUNG UNIVERSITY ATHLETICS,
324

Dark, Lisa Associate Head Coach, Women's
Basketball
MOODY COLISEUM, 996

Darke, Dennis Asst. AD, Facilities & Operations
INDIANA STATE UNIVERSITY ATHLETICS,
332

Darling, David Program Director
KSKY-AM, 636

Darling, Jenny Chief Financial Officer
NATIONAL HOCKEY LEAGUE/NHL, 125

Darling, Jim Chair
BELLINGHAM/WHATCOM CHAMBER OF
COMMERCE, 227

Darling, Joshua Sports Information Director
CLAYTON COLLEGE & STATE UNIVERSITY
ATHLETICS, 356

Darling, Karen Administrative
Assistant/Webmaster
THOROUGHBRED RACING ASSOCIATIONS,
78

Darling, Sue Head Coach, Women's Basketball
J. LAWRENCE WALKUP SKYDOME, 983

Darne, Richard Database Administrator
ADVENTURE CYCLING ASSOCIATION, 70

Darnell, Denny Secretary
MOTORSPORTS MUSEUM AND HALL OF
FAME OF AMERICA, 254

Darnell, Gary Associate Executive Director
AMERICAN FOOTBALL COACHES
ASSOCIATION, 88

Darren, Richie Director of Athletics
WEBBER INTERNATIONAL UNIVERSITY
ATHLETICS, 322

Darrington, Susan Exececutive VP, Rogers Place
ROGERS PLACE, 1007

Darton, Rex President
DARTON ARCHERY, 1236
Darwish, Daniel President
CORPORATE AMERICA AVIATION, INC., 935
Daschel, Nick Sports Columnist
COLUMBIAN, 474
Daski, Robert Sports Reporter
POTOMAC NEWS, 508, 526
Datcher, Dwight Director of Athletics
WHEELOCK COLLEGE ATHLETICS, 408
Dater, Adrian Sports Writer
DENVER POST, 485
Dau, Mark President
HUNTERDON GROUP, INC., 606
Daubach, Joe Special Events Director
SUN BOWL, 93
Dauber, Julie Sales Representative
PRO BOUND SPORTS, 1188
Dauer, Jim partner
DAUER HASWELL ARCHITECTS, 1063
Dauer, Jr., Robert Attorney
MEYER, UNKOVIC & SCOTT, LLP, 905
Daugherity, Dan Advertising Manager/Sports Director
WPXN-FM, 669
Daugherty, Andrew Executive Vice President
PACIFIC COAST LEAGUE OF PROFESSIONAL BASEBALL CLUBS, 49
Daugherty, Barbara Director of Business Operations
SAN BERNARDINO AREA CONVENTION & VISITORS BUREAU, 244
Daugherty, Brad Owner
NASCAR CUP SERIES, 23
Daugherty, Kyle Director of Business Development
PACIFIC COAST LEAGUE OF PROFESSIONAL BASEBALL CLUBS, 49
Daugherty, Paul Sports Columnist
CINCINNATI ENQUIRER, 472
Daugherty, Robyn Director of Athletics
JOHN BROWN UNIVERSITY ATHLETICS, 313
Daugherty, Steve Sports Director
WNUS-FM, 666
Daum, Nathalie Marketing Director
DEWALD, SCOTT D., 885
Daum, Shana SVP, Community Relations & Public Affair
NATIONAL LEAGUE OF PROFESSIONAL BASEBALL CLUBS, THE, 32
Davakos, Harry Director
CITADEL, THE, 415
Davalillo, Marco Manager
MEXICAN LEAGUE A.C., 44
Davenport, Ann Regional Commissioner
SOUTHERN CALIFORNIA REGIONAL COMMISSIONER/USA VOLLEYBALL, 211
Davenport, Dawn Weekend Sports Anchor ; Reporter
WRIC-TV, 717
Davenport, Denny Foundation Consultant
CHICAGO DISTRICT GOLF ASSOCIATION, 109
Davenport, Griff AIA Managing Principal
DLR GROUP, 1064
Davenport, Jennifer Chief Marketing Officer
NATIONAL FOOTBALL LEAGUE/NFL, 95
Davenport, Jennifer Director of Marketing
CHERNESKY, RICHARD, 881
Davenport, Mike Head Coach
NATIONAL PRO FASTPITCH, 168
Davenport, Mo SVP and General Manager
HILL & SCHLERETH, 615
Davenport, Rob Advertising Manager
SENTINEL-TRIBUNE, 535
Davenport, Robert Director of Athletics
OKLAHOMA BAPTIST UNIVERSITY ATHLETICS, 368
Davenport, Shannon Office Manager
SOUTHERN CALIFORNIA REGIONAL COMMISSIONER/USA VOLLEYBALL, 211
Davenport, Suya Executive Director
LEE ISLAND COAST VISITOR & CONVENTION BUREAU, 237
Daves, Art Vice President Operations/New Business
CARSON EVENTS INTERNATIONAL, INC., 760
Daves, Jim Facilities Manager
HUSKY STADIUM, 981

Davey, Kevin President
RADIUS GROUP, INC., 813
Davey, Simon Executive Director/General Manager
USL LEAGUE TWO, 163
David, Culley Head Coach
NATIONAL FOOTBALL LEAGUE/NFL, 95
David, John Founder/President
MULTICULTURAL GOLF ASSOCIATION OF AMERICA, 71, 102
David, Mike Executive Director
INDIANA GOLF ASSOCIATION, 105, 110
David, Oliver Head Coach
UNITED STATES HOCKEY LEAGUE, 136
David, Paul Co-Founder/Executive Vice President
MULTICULTURAL GOLF ASSOCIATION OF AMERICA, 102
David, Powers Founder
DOVER SADDLERY, INC, 1237
David, Ross Director
SHOW ME CENTER, 1011
Davidoff, Ken Sports Writer
NEWSDAY, 517
Davidowitz, Robert Group Publisher
MOUNTAIN BIKE, 577
Davidson, Art Sports Editor
MILFORD DAILY NEWS, 510
Davidson, Bill Chief Financial Officer
EAST COAST HOCKEY LEAGUE/ECHL, 129
Davidson, Bob Sports Editor
SALINA JOURNAL, 531
Davidson, Diana Editor
SADDLE HORSE REPORT, 585
Davidson, Garry General Manager
WESTERN HOCKEY LEAGUE, 138
Davidson, Greg Web Developer
SOLE CUSTOM FOOTBEDS, 1202
Davidson, Jeremy Manager Marketing/Communications
SPECIAL OLYMPICS ILLINOIS, 193
Davidson, Joe Sports Senior Writer
SACRAMENTO BEE, 530
Davidson, John President
NATIONAL HOCKEY LEAGUE/NHL, 125
Davidson, Keith Director of Athletics
MARYLAND EASTERN SHORE ATHLETICS, UNIVERSITY OF, 336
Davidson, Matt Advertising Manager
IDAHO PRESS-TRIBUNE, 498
Davidson, Nick Athletic Director
AQUINAS COLLEGE ATHLETICS, 305
Davidson, Randal Sports Director
WBLJ-AM, 646
Davidson, Ron Advertising Director
MONTGOMERY ADVERTISER, 511
Davidson, Scott Manager
SOCCER SPORT SUPPLY CO., INC., 667, 1201
Davidson, Wendy Secretary
WESTERN AUSTRALIA BLIND GOLF ASSOCIATION, 117
Davie, Keith Athletic Director
NYACK COLLEGE ATHLETICS, 368
Davies, Colleen Global Head of Legal Personnel
REED SMITH, 911
Davies, Dan Senior Associate AD, Internal Operations
MONTANA STATE UNIVERSITY ATHLETICS, 337
Davies, Dave Sports Editor
CHICO ENTERPRISE-RECORD, 472
Davies, Fran Director of Communications & Marketing
CATHOLIC YOUTH ORGANIZATION (CYO), 264
Davies, Jeffrey Chief of Staff
BUNTING, ELIZABETH C., 879
Davies, Jordan Adjunct Professor
LIBERTY UNIVERSITY, 425
Davies, Mike Director of Global Communications
PRICEWATERHOUSECOOPERS, 768
Davies-Gooch, Callie Stakes Manager
HAMBLETONIAN SOCIETY, 75
Davila, Catherine Head Coach
WOMEN'S PREMIER SOCCER LEAGUE, 165
Davila, Iteace Accounts Receivable
FANMATS LLC, 1142
Davin, Katie Dept. Chairperson/Associate Professor

JOHNSON & WALES UNIVERSITY SPORTS/ENTERTAINMENT & EVENT MANAGEMEN, 424
Davis, Adam Chief Commercial Officer
NATIONAL HOCKEY LEAGUE/NHL, 124
Davis, Adrian Chief Attourney Development Officer
SAUER, JR., RUSSELL F., 914
Davis, Alan Editor
MOUNTAIN BIKING, 577
Davis, Alicia EVP, Global Manufacturing
GENERAL MOTORS, 736
Davis, Andrew Radio Program Director
SNOCOUNTRY MOUNTAIN REPORTS, 641
Davis, Ann Director
LADD PEEBLES STADIUM, 989
Davis, Barker College Sports Reporter
WASHINGTON TIMES, 550
Davis, Bear VP, Head Coach
MAJOR LEAGUE LACROSSE, 141
Davis, Becky Executive Assistant
SCOTT STADIUM, 1010
Davis, Brad Associate Athletic Director
MERRIMACK COLLEGE ATHLETICS(MC), 364
Davis, Brandon Head Athletic Trainer
HAMPDEN-SYDNEY COLLEGE (HSC) ATHLETICS, 388
Davis, Brian Sports Reporter
DALLAS MORNING NEWS, 107, 483
Davis, Brittany Assistant Athletic Trainer
SAINT MARY'S UNIVERSITY (TX) ATHLETICS, 318
Davis, Bryan Executive Vice President of Operations
NATION'S BEST SPORTS, 480, 1202, 1245
Davis, Claudine Facility Sales Director
JS DORTON ARENA, 986
Davis, Dan Director of Athletic Training
BOWDOIN COLLEGE ATHLETICS, 379
Davis, Danny H.S. Sports Reporter
AUSTIN AMERICAN-STATESMAN, 464
Davis, Dave Sports Wire Editor
DAY, 484
Davis, David Director/Shareholder
DAVIS & WILKERSON, 885
Davis, Dennis President
SEALFLEX INDUSTRIES, INC., 1197
Davis, Don General Manager
WGAB, 654
Davis, Donald Partner
MARGOLIS EDELSTEIN, 902
Davis, Donn Director At Large
USTA FLORIDA, 173
Davis, Eddie Interim President
KYLE FIELD, 988
Davis, Eddy Director
UNIVISION TELEVISION NETWORK, 685
Davis, Ellen Secretary
GOLF COURSE BUILDERS ASSOCIATION OF AMERICA, 100
Davis, Fern Director of Sales & Business Development
ROYAL PURPLE RACEWAY, 1041
Davis, Francis President
TWIN CITY KNITTING COMPANY, INC., 1216
Davis, Gary Partner
WOOD & LAMPING LLP, 926
Davis, Gerald Sports Assistant Editor
STATE, 539
Davis, Greg Simulcasting
THISTLEDOWN RACINO, 962, 1054
Davis, Howard Founder
DAVIS, HOWARD E. (BEN), 840
Davis, JJ Sports Director
KPTM-TV, 702
Davis, Jack Event Supervisor
SHOW ME CENTER, 1011
Davis, Jaclyn Senior Women's Administrator
SUFFOLK UNIVERSITY ATHLETICS, 405
Davis, James Chairman and Chief Executive Officer
NEW BALANCE ATHLETIC SHOE, INC., 1178
Davis, Jamie CEO
USA VOLLEYBALL, 208
Davis, Jason Sports Editor
MOUNTAIN PRESS, 513
Davis, Jeannine Office Manager
UTAH SUMMER GAMES, 263

Dimon, Jamie Chairman/Executive Committee
JPMORGAN CHASE BANK, N.A., 776
Dimond, Mike Executive Vice President
AMERICAN AMATEUR BASEBALL
CONGRESS, 25
Dimperio, Leda Systems Administrator
BIRMINGHAM RACING COMMISSION, 79
Dinardo, Dominick Sports Editor
MEADVILLE TRIBUNE, 509
Dinauer, Jake Head Athletic Trainer
CARTHAGE COLLEGE ATHLETICS, 381
Dineen, Gord Assistant Coach
AMERICAN HOCKEY LEAGUE/AHL, 128
Dineen, Kevin Head Coach
AMERICAN HOCKEY LEAGUE/AHL, 128
Ding, Kevin Sports Reporter
ORANGE COUNTY REGISTER, 520
Dingman, Sharon Volleyball Head Coach
IOWA, UNIVERSITY OF, 424
Dinihanian, Janet Athletics Administrative
Specialist
UNIVERSITY OF NEW HAVEN(UNH), 366
Dinkelman, Brian Hitting Coach
MIDWEST LEAGUE, 45
Dinote, Steven Armed Forces Sports Secretariat
U.S. ARMED FORCES SPORTS, 201
Dinsdale, Mike Treasurer
WORLD KARATE FEDERATION, 143
Dinsmore, Katie Sales Manager
HATCHERS MANUFACTURING INC., 1153
Dinsmore PC, LLO, Richard Attorney
HUNEGS, STONE, LENEAVE, KYAS &
THORNTON, P.A., 894
Dinwiddie, Peter Executive VP, Basketball
Operations
NATIONAL BASKETBALL ASSOCIATION/NBA,
58
Dinwiddie, Ryan Head Coach
CANADIAN FOOTBALL LEAGUE/CFL, 94
Dio, Susan Chairman and President, BP America
BP AMERICA, 734
Dion, Ronald Director
BJ'S WHOLESALE CLUB, INC., 1231
Diorka, Michael Associate AD, Facility
Management
FRANKLIN FIELD, 975
Dipietro, Robert EVP
PIMLICO RACE COURSE, 1052
Dipoto, Jerry Executive VP/General Manager
AMERICAN LEAGUE OF PROFESSIONAL
BASEBALL CLUBS, THE, 30
Dirienzo, Joseph Sales/Marketing Director
JENNERSTOWN SPEEDWAY, 1036
Dirks, Nicole Advertising Director
DODGE CITY DAILY GLOBE, 487
Dirocco, Michael Sports Writer
FLORIDA TIMES-UNION, 491
Disandro, Bill General Manager/Bay State
TEAMWORKS CENTERS, 1017
Discepolo, John Sports Anchor/Reporter
WCBS-TV, 708
Discepolo, Michaelanne EVP, Human Resources
PRIMEDIA, 768
Discipio, Tom Sales
SURFACE AMERICA, 1209
Disciullo, John Promotion Director
WKBW-TV, 713
Disney, Kyle Stadium Operations Coordinator
COMMUNITYAMERICA BALLPARK, 967
Dissette, Tom VP, Corporate Sales and Services
MAJOR LEAGUE LACROSSE, 141
Dissinger, Donald Senior Vice President
EWING COLE CHERRY BROTT, 1065
Disson, Stephen Director of Events
DISSON SKATING, 788
Distefano, Benny Hitting Coach
TRADITION FIELD SPORTS COMPLEX, 1019
Distelhorst, Mike Advertising Director
GREELEY TRIBUNE, 494
Ditmore, Justin Sports Director
WSLS-TV, 718
Ditrinco, Greg Executive Editor
SKI MAGAZINE, 586
Dittman, Jeff Athletic Director
DAKOTA STATE UNIVERSITY ATHLETICS,
310
Dittmer, II, E. Attorney
TALLEY, ANTHONY, HUGHES & KNIGHT
L.L.C., 920

Dittrich, Al Chief Operating Officer
GANDER MOUNTAIN COMPANY, 1240
Ditzler, Christen SWA/Head Women's Basketball
Coach
LYCOMING COLLEGE ATHLETICS, 392
Diuguid, Todd Associate Athletic Director
CHARLESTON ATHLETICS, UNIVERSITY OF,
355
Diulus, Gregory Attorney
CINDRICH & COMPANY, 881
Diver, Raychel Director of Internal Operations
BREVARD COLLEGE ATHLETICS, 307
Dix, Brian A-8 Director
MIDDLE ATLANTIC PGA, 105
Dix, Kathy Comptroller
PRO GOLF OF AMERICA, 1247
Dixon, Ann Secretary
WOMEN'S GOLF ASSOCIATION OF
BALTIMORE, 118
Dixon, Bill Vice President of Operations
PRECOR, INC., 1187
Dixon, Bob Sports Director
WRIL-FM, 671
Dixon, Bruce Chief Executive Officer
HIND, INC., 1155
Dixon, David Head Coach
USL LEAGUE TWO, 160, 1067
Dixon, Fred National Sales Manager
GILL ATHLETICS, 1148
Dixon, Jean News Director
WTRN-AM, 676
Dixon, Karen VP General Manager
TUNTURI, INC., 1216
Dixon, Latoya Promotions Director
WERQ-FM, 652
Dixon, Mark President & Owner
ADOLFSON & PERTSON, INC., 1058
Dixon, Mike Director, Minor League Operations &
Alt.
AMERICAN HOCKEY LEAGUE/AHL, 82, 128
Dixon, Oscar Sports Editor
USA TODAY, 548
Doak, Tom Principal / Founder
RENAISSANCE GOLF DESIGN, INC., 1192
Doan, Shane Chief Hockey Development Officer
NATIONAL HOCKEY LEAGUE/NHL, 122
Doane, Vic Sports Director
KLGA-FM, 629
Dobbin, Jeff Assistant Director of Athletic
Communica
NORWICH UNIVERSITY ATHLETICS, 398
Dobbs, Jan Executive Administrator
CLIFF KEEN ATHLETIC INC., 1127
Dobbs, Kathryn Senior VP & Chief Marketing
Officer
NATIONAL HOCKEY LEAGUE/NHL, 123
Dobek, Betty Classified Manager
NEWS JOURNAL (DE), 515
Dobek, Marty Marketing and Communication
DETROIT METRO SPORTS COMMISSION,
231
Dobie, Michael Sports Reporter
NEWSDAY, 517
Dobin, Allison Director of Marketing
USF SUN DOME, 1023
Dobina, Donald President
MPC PROMOTIONS, 1176
Dobmeier, Jim President & Founder
A-TURF, 1099, 1209
Dobnikar, Karen Human Resource Manager
BIRMINGHAM, GREATER CONVENTION &
VISITORS BUREAU, 227, 259
Dobson, Abigail BOD
LUNDY'S SPECIAL EVENTS, 1074, 1077
Dobson, Michael Promotions Director
WSB-AM, 673
Doby, Don President/Media Relations
IMAGE MARKETING, 797
Dobyns, Jassen Head Athletic Trainer
URBANA UNIVERSITY ATHLETICS, 321
Dochterman, Cliff Director of Athletics
UNIVERSITY OF CALIFORNIA SANTA CRUZ
ATHLETICS, 308, 380
Dochterman, Scott Sports Editor
ST. JOSEPH NEWS-PRESS, 538
Dockery, Steve Golf Course Superintendent
METHODIST COLLEGE PROFESSIONAL
GOLF MANAGEMENT PROGRAM, 102

Dockery, Wade Tournament Director
DIXIE PGA SECTIONAL OFFICE, 104
Dockter, Allen Football Officials Supervisor
DAKOTA-10 ATHLETIC CONFERENCE, 293
Docktor, Chad Director, Junior Tennis
USTA MIDWEST, 173
Dodd, Bobby President
AMATEUR ATHLETIC UNION KARATE
PROGRAM, 142
Dodd, K. Attorney
MILLER, KAGAN RODRIGUEZ AND SILVER,
P.A., 905
Dodd, Regan Assistant Professor of Health
MISSOURI WESTERN STATE COLLEGE, 430
Dodd, Thomas Director of Aquatics
CALIFORNIA LUTHERAN UNIVERSITY
ATHLETICS / CLU SPORTS, 380
Dodd, Zane President
DODD & COMPANY, R.O., 1236
Dodderidge, John Sports Information Director
ROCKHURST UNIVERSITY ATHLETICS, 369
Dodds, Darrell Editor
HORSE & RIDER, 569
Dodds, Julie Director of Convention Sales
VISIT ANCHORAGE, 248
Doden, Eric General Manager
MASTER SPORTS, 1171
Doden, Jim Coordinator of Baseball Umpires
WISCONSIN INTERCOLLEGIATE ATHLETIC
CONFERENCE, 305
Dodge, Dean Sales Manager/Audio Division
DAKTRONICS, INC., 1133
Dodge, Jeff General Manager, Food & Beverage
FRONTIER FIELD, 975
Dodge, R. EVP, General Counsel & Secretary
DISH NETWORK, 694
Dodges, Jeff Director of Communications
UNIVERSITY OF NORTH ALABAMA
ATHLETICS(UNA), 367
Dodorico, Paul Vice President
AMERICAN THREE QUARTER MIDGET
RACING ASSOCIATION, 16
Dodson, Randy Publisher
FAIRWAYS, 564
Doepel, Robert President
CHICAGO SCENIC STUDIO, 1062
Doerfler, Doug Chief Financial Officer
STINSON MORRISON HECKER LLP, 918
Doerksen, Richard VP, Hockey
WESTERN HOCKEY LEAGUE, 138
Doerner, Bill Station Manager
KSIX-AM, 635
Doggett, Jana Deputy Athletics Director, External
Oper
DEE GLEN SMITH SPECTRUM, 969
Doherty, Justin Senior Associate Athletic Director
WISCONSIN-MADISON FIELDHOUSE, 1029
Doherty, Karen Facilities Coordinator
GREYHOUND STADIUM, 977
Doherty, Marian Manager
LEGION STADIUM COMPLEX, 991
Doherty, Robert President
SPECIAL OLYMPICS CONNECTICUT, 192
Doherty, Susan Executive Assistant
TEXAS UNIVERSITY INTERSCHOLASTIC
LEAGUE, 200
Doherty, Tim Hitting Coach
INTERNATIONAL LEAGUE, 43
Dohetry, Bob Vice President
NEW HAMPSHIRE SNOWMOBILE
ASSOCIATION, 154
Dohlman, Amber Co-Sports Information Director
UNIVERSITY OF WISCONSIN - RIVER FALLS
ATHLETICS (UW-RIVER FALLS), 410
Dohren, Tamara Promotional Coordinator
CORUS RADIO, 610
Dohrmann, George Staff Writer
SPORTS ILLUSTRATED, 591
Dolan, Bernie Executive Director
WEST VIRGINIA SECONDARY SCHOOL
ACTIVITIES COMMISSION, 201
Dolan, James Owner/Chairman
NATIONAL BASKETBALL ASSOCIATION/NBA,
58
Dolan, John Chief Operating Officer
RELAY SPORTS AND ENTERTAINMENT
MARKETING, 814

Doyle, Kevin President, Sales & Distributor
Operation
MILLERCOORS, 738
Doyle, Matt Sports Writer
TULSA WORLD, 547
Doyle, Mike Vice President/Architect
COMMUNICATION ARTS INCORPORATED,
1062
Doyle, Patrick Executive Vice President/Chief
Financial
DIRECTV, INC., 693
Doyle, Paul Sports Reporter (Baseball)
HARTFORD COURANT, 495
Doyle, Richard President
COMFORT LINE PRODUCTS, 1128
Doyle, Jr, Daniel Founder/Executive Director
INSTITUTE FOR INTERNATIONAL SPORT,
218
Dozier, Missye Sports Director
MISSISSIPPI, STATE GAMES OF, 261
Dozier, Tom Sports Editor
PROGRESS-INDEX, 527
Drachkovitch, Rasha Founder
44 BLUE PRODUCTIONS, INC., 603
Draft, Howard Executive Chairman
DRAFTWORLDWIDE, 789
Dragan, Stephanie Assistant Athletics Director
FRANKLIN PIERCE UNIVERSITY ATHLETICS,
359
Drager, Ron President & Chief Executive Officer
ARCA RACING SERIES, 16
Dragone, Christopher Director
NATIONAL MUSEUM OF RACING HALL OF
FAME, 255
Draine, Michael Sports Agent
INTRASPORT MANAGEMENT GROUP, 848
Drake, Alan News/Sports Director
WIRY-AM, 658
Drake, Ducky News Director ; Sports Director
WIRY-AM, 658
Drapcho, Gary Sports Director
WSEE-TV, 717
Drape, Joe Sports Reporter
NEW YORK TIMES, 514
Draper, Kris Director, Amateur Scouting
NATIONAL HOCKEY LEAGUE/NHL, 123
Draper, Laurie Member Services & Program
Director
ROCKY MOUNTAIN PGA SECTIONAL
OFFICE, 106
Drass, Mike Executive Director of Athletics
WESLEY COLLEGE ATHLETICS, 407
Drayer, Matt General Manager
RUSSELL E. DIETHRICK JR. PARK, 1008
Drayer, Matthew General Manager
NEW YORK-PENNSYLVANIA LEAGUE, 47
Dreher, James VP General Manager
DURHAM BOAT COMPANY, 1136
Dreher, Josh Head Athletic Trainer
ADAMS STATE UNIVERSITY ATHLETICS, 351
Dreiling, Dave Owner
GTM SPORTSWEAR, 1151
Dreiling, Richard Chairman / Chief Executive
Officer
DOLLAR GENERAL CORPORATION, 1236
Dreissigacker, Richard President
CONCEPT II, INC., 1129
Dreistadt, Michele Director of Intramurals
MOUNT ST. MARY COLLEGE ATHLETICS,
396
Dressel, Jim Editor
BOWLERS JOURNAL INTERNATIONAL, 558
Dreves, Mike Interim Department Chair
GROVE CITY COLLEGE ATHLETICS, 387
Drew, Chelsea Legal Assistant
BECKER, WILLIAM F.X., 874
Drew, Homer Associate Director of Athletics
VALPARAISO UNIVERSITY, 439
Drew, Jay Sports Reporter
SALT LAKE TRIBUNE, 532
Drew, Loyda Project Manager
MOBIVITY, 766, 804
Drew, Pearson Chairman
DREW PEARSON MARKETING, INC. (DPM),
1237
Drew, Tyson Associate AD, Facility
Operations/Event
WAR MEMORIAL STADIUM (WY), 1026

Drewes, Doug Executive Vice President
OVATION FOOD SERVICES LP, 1077
Drewniak, Michael VP Manufacturing
TOPPS COMPANY, INC., 1214
Drews, David EVP/Chief Financial Officer
GEORGE P. JOHNSON COMPANY, 793
Drickey, Steven General Counsel
LIFE FITNESS, INC., 1166
Drie-Andrzjewski, Linda Director of Athletics
WILMINGTON UNIVERSITY ATHLETICS
(DELAWARE), 376
Driedger, Andrea Director, Finance
CANADA BASKETBALL, 54
Driessen, Christine EVP & CFO
OUTSIDE THE LINES, 681, 688
Driffill, Tom Human Resource Manager
HOYT USA, 1156
Driggers, Chris Director, Pro Scouting
NATIONAL FOOTBALL LEAGUE/NFL, 96
Driggers, Justin Sports Writer
MORNING NEWS (SC), 500, 512
Drigotas, John Group Sales Director
TOP OF THE THIRD, 1019
Drimmer, Lillian Associate Professor of
Management
TIFFIN UNIVERSITY, 437
Drinen, Doug Football Operations
SPORTS REFERENCE, THE, 939
Dring, Scott Executive Director
DUBLIN CONVENTION & VISITOR BUREAU,
231
Drinkill, Dave General Manager
ONTARIO HOCKEY LEAGUE, 134
Driscoll, David Principal
STEIN, SPERLING, BENNETT, DE JONG,
DRISCOLL & GREENFEIG, P.C., 918
Driscoll, Dennis Director of Athletic
Communications
MARIAN COLLEGE OF FOND DU LAC
ATHLETICS, 333, 393
Driscoll, Dill Founder
IGNITION, INC., 796
Driscoll, Elaine Director of Communications
MASSACHUSETTS GAMING COMMISSION,
81
Driscoll, Jenny Assistant Editor
SKATING, 586
Driscoll, Lori Advertising Director
TIMES HERALD (MI), 544
Driscoll, Mark Founder
IGNITION, INC., 796
Driscoll, Mike Treasurer-South West Region
U.S. HANDBALL ASSOCIATION, 120
Driscoll, Sean Director, Ticket Sales & Services
EAST COAST HOCKEY LEAGUE/ECHL, 129
Driscoll, Susan Founder
IGNITION, INC., 796
Driscoll, Terry Athletics Director
WILLIAM & MARY HALL, 967, 1026, 1028
Driscoll, Timothy President / Chief Executive
Officer
ALUMINUM ATHLETIC EQUIPMENT
COMPANY (AAE), 1107
Driscoll, Tony Exec. Dir., Marketing,
Communications &
USA HOCKEY, 122
Driscoll, Jr., Robert Athletic Director
PROVIDENCE COLLEGE ATHLETICS, 342
Driskell, Lavon Athletic Director
BLUE MOUNTAIN COLLEGE ATHLETICS, 307
Driskill, Dustin Director of Sports Medicine
LUBBOCK CHRISTIAN UNIVERSITY
ATHLETICS, 313
Driver, Brian Program Director
WNKT-FM, 665
Driver, Kristi Sports Manager
NORTH CAROLINA SPORTS DEVELOPMENT
OFFICE, 241
Droddy, J.D. League Adjudicator
PECOS LEAGUE, 50
Droge, Brandon Sports Information Director
AVILA UNIVERSITY ATHLETICS, 306
Drohan, Kate 2nd VP
NATIONAL FASTPITCH COACHES
ASSOCIATION/NFCA, 167
Drolet, Denis President / Chief Executive Officer
IN GLAS COMPANY, 1158
Drucker, Jason Sales
FABRICATION ENTERPRISES, 1142

Druckman, Lauren Sales Manager
GULBENKIAN SWIM, INC., 1151
Druenen, Sid Director of Soccer & Head Coach
USL LEAGUE TWO, 161
Druiz, Fae Vice President
BULOVA WATCH COMPANY, 1122
Drummey, Maureen Sports Assistant Editor
SKI MAGAZINE, 586
Drummond, Kristen Associate AD,
Compliance/SWA
MARYLAND EASTERN SHORE ATHLETICS,
UNIVERSITY OF, 336
Drummond, Troy Associate Director of Athletics,
Operati
BROWNWOOD COLISEUM, 961
Drumond, Moises Head Coach
WOMEN'S PREMIER SOCCER LEAGUE, 164
Drury, Chris General Manager, Wolfpack
AMERICAN HOCKEY LEAGUE/AHL, 125, 127
Dryden, Deidra Associate Athletic Director
SOUTHERN VIRGINIA UNIVERSITY
ATHLETICS, 403
DuBoi, Cari Secretary
NATIONAL ASSOCIATION OF COLLEGIATE
GYMNASTICS COACHES - WOMEN, 119
DuBois, Brent Athletic Trainer
UNITED STATES HOCKEY LEAGUE, 137
DuBois, Kimberly National Sales Manager
HEART RATE, INC., 1154
DuBrueler, Justin Sr.Director Accounting
RICHMOND INTERNATIONAL RACEWAY,
1041
DuBuis, Carolyn Human Resources Director
BETA DESIGN GROUP, INC., 1060
DuPree, David Sports Reporter
USA TODAY, 548
DuPuis, Carol Director of Sales and Marketing
SEAGATE CENTRE, 1010
DuPuy, Robert President/Chief Operating Officer
MAJOR LEAGUE BASEBALL PROPERTIES,
901
DuTeau, Randy Event Manager
AUGUSTA SPORTS COUNCIL, GREATER, 226
DuVivier, Lynne President
CREATIVE FACTOR, INC., 761
Duarte, Miguel Chief of Staff
AMERICAN LEAGUE OF PROFESSIONAL
BASEBALL CLUBS, THE, 30
Dubas, Kyle General Manager
NATIONAL HOCKEY LEAGUE/NHL, 125
Dubb, Michael Principal
AQUEDUCT, 1051
Dube, Nigel Assistant Coach
NORTH AMERICAN HOCKEY LEAGUE, 132
Dube, Philippe President and Chief Executive
Officer
CCM HOCKEY, 1125
Dubicki, Stan Goaltending Coach
AMERICAN HOCKEY LEAGUE/AHL, 126
Dubiel, Robert President
COBRA PUMA GOLF, 1127
Dubin, Dave Circulation Director
ATHLETIC MANAGEMENT, 555
Dubin, Stephen Partner
YEE & DUBIN LLP, 869
Dubinsky, Brandon Negotiating Committee
NHLPA: NATIONAL HOCKEY LEAGUE
PLAYERS' ASSOCIATION, 854
Dubois, Eric Assistant Coach
AMERICAN HOCKEY LEAGUE/AHL, 127
Dubois, Troy Sales/Marketing
CABANA BANNERS, 1123
Dubose, Antoinette 1st Lt. Governor/Office
Manager
MARYLAND AAU ASSOCIATION, 213
Dubow, Brad General Manager
KROD, 634
Dubra, Charles Interim Director of Athletics
HUSTON-TILLOTSON COLLEGE ATHLETICS,
312
Dubrasich, Paul Senior Counsel
CAMPBELL, ROBERT G., 880
Ducey, Marjie State College Sports Writer
OMAHA WORLD-HERALD, 519
Ducharme, Dominique Interim Head Coach
NATIONAL HOCKEY LEAGUE/NHL, 124
Ducharme, Edward Sports Agent
PROFESSIONAL SPORTS MANAGEMENT
GROUP, 859

Elsberry, Chris Sports Columnist
CONNECTICUT POST, 475

Else, Katie Marketing Director
PANASTADIA INTERNATIONAL, 581

Elsinga, Paul Chief Financial Officer
OCEANIC USA, 1181

Elson, Chris Marketing Director
HARRISON SPORTS, INC., 1153

Elswick, Mike Sports Editor
TRIBUNE-DEMOCRAT, 546

Elvin, Bruce Assistant Dean, Career Services
WEISTART, JOHN C., 925

Elway, John President, Football Operations
NATIONAL FOOTBALL LEAGUE/NFL, 95

Elwell, Tom Chief Executive Officer
ETONIC, 1140

Elwood, Charlie Deputy Director of Athletics
FORDHAM UNIVERSITY ATHLETICS, 330

Ely, Erich Associate Athletics Director, Facilities
BAKER ATHLETICS COMPLEX, 956

Ely, Evan Manager, Sports Marketing
NYC & COMPANY, 241

Ely, Herb Attoney
ELY, BETTINI, ULMAN & ROSENBLATT, 888

Ely, Herbert Attorney
ELY, BETTINI, ULMAN & ROSENBLATT, 888

Ely, James Vice President Sales & Marketing
BERRY & HOMER, 783

Elzinga, Heidi Assistant To President
VAIL VALLEY FOUNDATION, 773

Elzner, Danny Sports Director
KETK-TV, 697

Emanuelli, Todd Sports Director
WMCR-FM, 664

Embler, Jonathan Vice President, Sports
Programs
SPECIAL OLYMPICS UTAH, 195

Embree, Chuck Sports Editor
MOBERLY MONITOR-INDEX & DEMOCRAT,
511

Embree, John Chief Executive Officer
U.S. PROFESSIONAL TENNIS ASSOCIATION,
172

Embrey, Tom Director of Events & Guest Services
BB&T CENTER, 957

Emendorfer, Mike Interim Athletic Director
UNIVERSITY OF WISCONSIN-PLATTEVILLE
(UWP), 410

Emenhiser, Noel Assistant Athletic Director
MADONNA UNIVERSITY ATHLETICS, 314

Emeno, Jr., Martin Director Operations
GOLF ASSOCIATION OF PHILADELPHIA, 110

Emerich, Scott Sports Director
WXOW-TV, 721

Emerick, William Partner
EMERICK, WILLIAM E., 888

Emerline, Angie Vice President, Human
Resources
CAPITOL SPORTS NETWORK, 693

Emerson, Beverly Account Manager
NCR, 1177

Emerson, Keira Vice President, Strategy &
Business Inte
NATIONAL HOCKEY LEAGUE/NHL, 125

Emerson, Ramona Managing Partner, Seattle
PRESTON, GATES & ELLIS, 910

Emerson, Ryan Director of Athletics for Sports
Informa
COLBY-SAWYER COLLEGE ATHLETICS, 382

Emery, Mark Senior Associate
BURGOYNE, ROBERT A., 879

Emery, William President
FOCUS GOLF SYSTEMS, INC., 1145

Emigh, Kay Head Athletic Trainer
GROVE CITY COLLEGE ATHLETICS, 387

Emini, Edita National Team Sales Manager
ADOLPH KIEFER & ASSOCIATES, 1103

Eminian, Dave Sports Reporter
JOURNAL STAR, 501

Emke, Ben Head Athletic Trainer
ROCHESTER INSTITUTE OF TECHNOLOGY
ATHLETICS, 400

Emmanuel Bello Rustrian, Juan COO
MEXICAN LEAGUE A.C., 44

Emmert, Mark President
NATIONAL COLLEGIATE ATHLETIC
ASSOCIATION/NCAA, 55, 283

Emmert, Scott Vice President, Communications
NATIONAL HOCKEY LEAGUE/NHL, 125

Emmett, Jay Board of Directors
4LICENSING CORPORATION, 779

Emmett, Steve Skating & Skills Coach
NORTH AMERICAN HOCKEY LEAGUE, 132

Emmi, Marc Group VP Sporting Goods
WELLINGTON LEISURE PRODUCTS, 1221

Emmons, Charity Marketing Manager
SCHWINN CYCLING & FITNESS, 1197

Emmons, Donald Sports Writer
BLADE, 467

Emmons, Jim Associate Publisher
WAKE BOARDING MAGAZINE, 598

Emmons, Mark Sports Columnist
SAN JOSE MERCURY NEWS, 533

Emmons, Tom Vice President
COLOR INC., 1235

Emrick, Chris Athletic Trainer
EAST COAST HOCKEY LEAGUE/ECHL, 129

Emrick, Rae Head Athletic Trainer
WEST VIRGINIA WESLEYAN ATHLETICS
(WVWC), 376

Endicott, Becky Senior Associate AD/SWA
WICHITA STATE UNIVERSITY ATHLETICS,
349

Endress, Dave Director of Business Development
ROSENBLATT STADIUM, 1007

Endriss, Matt President / Chief Executive Officer
BIRKENSTOCK FOOTPRINT SANDALS INC.,
1231

Eng, Patrick Partner
ENG & WOODS, 888

Engberg, David General Manager
KLZZ-FM, 630

Engel, Chris Sports Director
WPDM-AM/WSNN-FM, 668

Engel, Donald Attorney
FOX & SPILLANE, LLP, 890

Engel, Jennifer Sports Reporter
FORT WORTH STAR-TELEGRAM, 491

Engel, Joanna Director of Athletic Training
Services
UNIVERSITY OF LA VERNE ATHLETICS, 391

Engel, Mac Sports Reporter (Rangers)
FORT WORTH STAR-TELEGRAM, 491

Engelbert, Cathy Commissioner
WOMEN'S NATIONAL BASKETBALL
ASSOCIATION, 60

Engelbrecht, Eileen VP
ROBOT FACTORY, 1194

Engelbrecht, G. Treasurer
METROPOLITAN AMATEUR GOLF
ASSOCIATION, 112

Engelbrecht, Skip President
ROBOT FACTORY, 1194

Engelenhoven, Deb Advertising Manager
OSKALOOSA HERALD, 520

Engelhard, Hadley President
ENTER SPORTS MANAGEMENT, 841

Engelhardt, Erin Assistant Athletic Director
SEATTLE UNIVERSITY ATHLETICS, 318

Engelhardt, John Director, Public Relations
BELTERRA PARK, 1045

Engelsman, Lindsey Athletics Brand Manager
HOPE COLLEGE ATHLETICS, 389

Engemann, Eric Indoor Sports Coordinator
BATON ROUGE AREA SPORTS
FOUNDATION, 226

Engen, Lloyd Sports Editor
VALLEY COURIER, 548

Engh, Brent Sports Reporter
CAPITAL TIMES, 470

Engh, Fred President/Chief Executive Officer
YOUTH SPORTS JOURNAL, 265, 600

Engh, Fred Founder/CEO
YOUTH DEVELOPMENT/A DIVISION OF THE
NATIONAL ALLIANCE FOR YOUTH S, 265

Engh, John COO
YOUTH DEVELOPMENT/A DIVISION OF THE
NATIONAL ALLIANCE FOR YOUTH S, 265

Engilis, Amy Head Athletic Trainer
WARNER PACIFIC COLLEGE ATHLETICS,
321

Engl, Paul Sponsorship Director
ROSE BOWL STADIUM, 1007

Engle, Bryan Assistant Athletic Director
CALIFORNIA BAPTIST UNIVERSITY
ATHLETICS, 308

Englert, James Industry Liaison
INTERNATIONAL POLICE MOUNTAIN BIKE
ASSOCIATION (IPMBA), 70

Englett, Mickey Athletic Director
NJCAA REGION VIII WOMEN'S, 286

English, Antonya Sports Writer
ST. PETERSBURG TIMES, 538

English, Chris Owner and President
CAMPANELLI STADIUM, 963

English, Claude Director of Athletics
PARK UNIVERSITY PIRATE ATHLETICS, 317

English, Edmond President, Chief Executive
Officer, Dire
MARSHALL'S, 1244

English, Edmond VP
T.J. MAXX, 1250

English, Liz Marketing Director
BETA DESIGN GROUP, INC., 1060

English, Ryan Assistant General Manager
CALIFORNIA LEAGUE (A-LEVEL), 36

Engstorm, Peter Legal Counsel
BAKER & MCKENZIE, 872

Engstrom, Douglas Communications Director
CONTEMPORARY RESEARCH, 1225

Enke, Jordan Director of Facilities
MAPFRE STADIUM, 993

Enna, Patty Controller
SPEED SKATELUBE, 1203

Ennis, Nick Director, Baseball Operations
NATIONAL LEAGUE OF PROFESSIONAL
BASEBALL CLUBS, THE, 32

Ennis, Patrick Director of Stadium Operations
CAROLINA LEAGUE, 37

Ennist, Diane Sr.VP ,General Counsel
CAREY WORLDWIDE CHAUFFERED
SERVICES, 935

Enoch, Nicholas Partner
LUBIN & ENOCH, P.C., 901

Enos, Ben Sports Reporter
ALAMEDA JOURNAL, 461

Enrietto, John Sports Editor
BUTLER EAGLE, 470

Enriquez, Ray Project Engineer
SMITH, FAUSE, MCDONALD, INC., 831

Enriquez, Raymundo Partner
BAKER & MCKENZIE, 872

Ensley, Debbie Advertising Manager
OWATONNA PEOPLE'S PRESS, 521

Enslinger, Dustin Head Athletic Trainer
EMPORIA STATE UNIVERSITY (ESU)
ATHLETICS, 358

Ensor, Richard Commissioner
METRO ATLANTIC ATHLETIC CONFERENCE,
296

Ensor, Tony President/General Manager
PACIFIC COAST LEAGUE OF
PROFESSIONAL BASEBALL CLUBS, 48

Ensrud, Jason Head Athletic Trainer
NEBRASKA WESLEYAN UNIVERSITY
ATHLETICS, 396

Entelisano, Joe Advertising Manager
DAILY SENTINEL (NY), 482

Entrup, Matt Sports Editor
EAST OREGONIAN, 488

Entwhistle, Darren President & CEO
TELUS CORPORATION, 742

Enwright, Sherri Classified Manager
CLINTON HERALD, 473

Enzler, Jerry Executive Director
NATIONAL MISSISSIPPI RIVER MUSEUM &
AQUARIUM, 255

Eom, Young President & CEO, Samsung
Electronics Ame
SAMSUNG ELECTRONICS NA, 740

Epner, Paul Chief Executive Officer/President
HANG TEN INTERNATIONAL LICENSING
CALIFORNIA CORPORATION, 795

Epp, Tyler Executive VP, Business Operations
NATIONAL FOOTBALL LEAGUE/NFL, 96

Epperson, John Special Counsel
HARRIS, ALAN E., 892

Epperson, Richard Athletic Director
HAMPDEN-SYDNEY COLLEGE (HSC)
ATHLETICS, 388

Eppler, Billy General Manager
ANGELS STADIUM OF ANAHEIM, 955

Eppley, Donnie Associate Executive Director
INTERNATIONAL ASSOCIATION OF

F

FNP, Mike Team Medical Provider
FEDERAL HOCKEY LEAGUE, 131

Faass, Judy CEO
FAASST MOTORSPORTS INC., 1034

Faber, David Assistant Athletics Director of Operatio
CAJUN FIELD STADIUM, 962

Faber, Jim Senior Associate
WRIGHTSON, JOHNSON, HADDON & WILLIAMS, INC., 832

Faber, Tom Viking Ice Agent
VIKING ICE, LLC, 1219

Fabian, Dan Senior Director, Baseball Operations
AMERICAN LEAGUE OF PROFESSIONAL BASEBALL CLUBS, THE, 29

Fabianich, Danelle Senior Associate AD, Aministration/SWA
TENNESSEE MARTIN ATHLETICS, UNIVERSITY OF, 346, 1012

Fabrizio, Tony Auto Racing Reporter
TAMPA TRIBUNE, 541

Fabry, John President / Chief Executive Officer
SARANAC GLOVE COMPANY, 1196

Facer, Dirk Sports Writer
DESERET MORNING NEWS, 485

Facinoli, David Sports Editor
SUN-GAZETTE, 541

Facione, Steve SVP
OLYMPIA ENTERTAINMENT, INC., 807

Fagan, Howard Director, Marketing
HAWTHORNE RACE COURSE, 1049

Fagan, Kerri Assoc. Commissioner For Sports Admin
NORTHEAST-10 CONFERENCE, 299

Fagan, Mike Promotion Manager/Sports Director
WDHC-FM, 649, 650

Fagerli, Al Sports Director
WJVL-FM, 648, 660

Fagerstrom, Scott Sports Editor
AKRON BEACON JOURNAL, 461

Fahey, Art Director
LA CROSSE CENTER, 989

Fahey, Brendan Deputy AD
WAGNER COLLEGE ATHLETICS, 349

Fahey, Chris Director Of Corporate Sponsorships
CALIFORNIA INTERSCHOLASTIC FEDERATION, 197

Fahleson, Genger Executive Director
IDAHO GOLF ASSOCIATION, 110

Fahsbender, Justin Vice President, Ticket Sales
AMERICAN HOCKEY LEAGUE/AHL, 126

Failor, Ben News Director
WYNT-FM, 665, 679

Fain, Dick Sports Director
SPORTS RADIO KJR, 612

Fair, Tim Assistant Director of Operatinos
CALIHAN HALL, 962

Fairbairn, John Director of Human Resources
THORNTON-TOMASETTI ENGINEERS, 1072

Fairbairn, Robert Senior Managing Director
BLACKROCK, 775

Fairbank, Dave College Sports Reporter
DAILY PRESS (VA), 481

Fairbanks, Heather Sports Information Director
PRINCIPIA COLLEGE ATHLETICS, 399

Fairchild, Grant Director of Athletic Training
MARTIN METHODIST COLLEGE ATHLETICS, 314

Fairfield, Bill President/CEO
INFOUSA, 797

Fairhurst, David Exec. VP and Chief People Officer
MCDONALD'S CORPORATION, 738

Fairweather, Bill Producer
NFL PRIMETIME, 692

Fairweather, Kelly Chief Executive Officer
FIELD HOCKEY, FEDERATION INTERNATIONALE DE HOCKEY (FIH), 121

Fairweather, Simon CCO
EXHIBIT ENTERPRISES, 791

Faison, Brian Athletics Director
UNIVERSITY OF NORTH DAKOTA (UND), 335, 367

Faivre, Chris Director of Marketing and Communications
LAS CRUCES CONVENTION & VISITORS BUREAU, 237

Fajerski, Deborah Secretary
KEYSTONE REGIONAL COMMISSIONER/USA VOLLEYBALL, 210

Falato, Michael SVP of Sales & Business Development
MOBIVITY, 766, 804

Falco, Dina Sports Director
WFSB-TV, 711

Falco, Randel President/Chief Executive Officer/Direct
GALAVISION, 683

Falcon, W. Attorney
CHASEN & BOSCOLO CHARTERED, 881

Faldon, Scott Sports Editor
SOUTHWEST TIMES RECORD, 537

Falender, Andrew President
AEF EMBLEMS, 1104

Fales, Andy Weekend Sports Anchor
KMBC-TV, 699

Fales, Dan Editor-at-Large
MOTOR BOATING, 577

Falk, Bill Founder
M-F ATHLETIC COMPANY, 1169

Falk, Chad Executive Director
MANITOBA HS ATHLETIC ASSOCIATION, 198

Falk, David Chairman and Chief Executive Officer
SFX SPORTS GROUP, 863

Falk, David Chairman and Chief Executive Officer
SFX SPORTS GROUP, INC., 863

Falk, Eric VP, Administrative
M-F ATHLETIC COMPANY, 1169

Falk, Rich Associate Commissioner
BIG TEN ATHLETIC CONFERENCE, 835

Falk, Sandy Advertising Director
WAUSAU DAILY HERALD, 551

Falk, Thomas Vice Chairman
BOYS & GIRLS CLUBS OF AMERICA, 264

Falk-Day, Tamie Director of Athletics
UNIVERSITY OF WISCONSIN-PARKSIDE ATHLETICS (UW-P), 377

Falkenhagen, Kim Director of Athletics
NORTHLAND COLLEGE ATHLETICS, 397

Falkner, Jeff Athletics Director
CALIFORNIA STATE UNIVERSITY-DOMINGUEZ HILLS ATHLETICS, 353

Falks, Dee Federation Director
ARCHERY SHOOTERS ASSOCIATION, 14

Fall, Elliot General Manager
USL CHAMPIONSHIP, 158, 159

Fall, Josh Team Manager
NATIONAL BASKETBALL LEAGUE OF CANADA, 59

Fallacaro, Anthony Director of Athletics
SOUTHERN NEW HAMPSHIRE UNIVERSITY ATHLETICS, 345, 372

Fallen, Wendy Associate Commissioner, Championships
BIG TEN ATHLETIC CONFERENCE, 290, 835

Faller, Mark Sports Editor/Director of Sports Center
ARIZONA REPUBLIC, 463

Fallon, Steve Executive Director
TEXAS SPORTS HALL OF FAME & MUSEUM, 257

Fallon, Tom Program Director
WEEX-AM, 651

Falls, Kelly Director of Sales & Marketing
CANADIAN SPORTING GOODS ASSOCIATION, 217

Faltinek, James President/Chief Executive Officer
NSGA BUYING GUIDE, 602

Falvo, Toni Dir Research Marketing and Press
WMAQ TV CHICAGO, 715

Famis, Jeff Media Contact
ST. PETERSBERG BOWL, 93

Famularo, Joshua Equipment Manager
UNITED STATES HOCKEY LEAGUE, 137

Fandel, Brad Director of Sales
DOUGLAS INDUSTRIES, INC., 1135

Fanelli, Steve VP, Sales & Business Operations
AMERICAN LEAGUE OF PROFESSIONAL BASEBALL CLUBS, THE, 30

Faneuil, Robert Attorney
FANEUIL, ROBERT A., 889

Fang, Shiny Secretary
UNION INTERNATIONALE DE PENTATHLON MODERNE (UIPM), 144, 203

Fangio, Vic Head Coach
NATIONAL FOOTBALL LEAGUE/NFL, 95

Fanjul, Oscar Director
MARSH & MCLENNAN, 777

Fankhauser, Thomas Treasurer
AMERICAN CUESPORTS ALLIANCE, 61

Fannin, Mike Managing Editor/Sports and Features
KANSAS CITY STAR, 502

Fanning, Moira Director Of Publicity
HAMBLETONIAN SOCIETY, 75

Fant, Sam BOD
SAN JOAQUIN COUNTY FAIR, 1053

Fanta, Jay Operations Assistant
ROCHESTER AMATEUR SPORTS COMMISSION, 243

Fantino, John Sports Editor
BURLINGTON FREE PRESS, 470

Faour, Fred Sports Editor
HOUSTON CHRONICLE, 498

Farago, Judit Chief Executive Officer
INTERNATIONAL TABLE TENNIS FEDERATION (ITTF), 203

Farago, Steve VP of Baseball Operations & Special Even
SOUTH ATLANTIC LEAGUE, 52

Farah, Roger President / Chief Operating Officer
POLO BY RALPH LAUREN, 1186

Farber, Michael Senior Writer
SPORTS ILLUSTRATED, 591

Farber, Neil Vice President
PROFESSIONAL SPORTS PUBLICATIONS, 583

Fargo, Tom Sports Editor
DAILY NEWS TRANSCRIPT, 481

Faria, Steve Promoter
THUNDERBOWL RACEWAY, 1044

Farias, Gabe Sports Editor
SOUTHSIDE REPORTER, 537

Faribault, John Program Coordinator
BAYLOR UNIVERSITY, 413

Farina, John Sports Information Director
EMORY UNIVERSITY ATHLETICS, 385

Farina, William Vice President Advertising Sales
COX COMMUNICATIONS, 605

Farinella, Mark Sports Reporter
SUN CHRONICLE, 541

Farkas, Mike President/Owner
ONLINE SPORTS, 722

Farkas, Uri Deputy AD
NORTHERN ARIZONA UNIVERSITY ATHLETICS, 340

Farlenza, Jim VP/Executive Director Sports Division
THE SPORT SUMMIT SPORTS BUSINESS DIRECTORY, 603

Farley, Jerry President
HACKLER, KENNETH P., 846

Farley, Matthew Counsel
DRINKER BIDDLE, 886

Farley, Ryan Secretary
SOUTHERN ILLINOIS GOLF ASSOCIATION, 115

Farley, William CEO
BODY WISE INTERNATIONAL, 1119

Farmer, Brad Marketing Director
ARBOR, 1109

Farmer, Joanne Rules Director
WOMEN'S SOUTHERN CALIFORNIA GOLF ASSOCIATION, 117

Farmer, Malcolm President/General Manager
NATIONAL BASKETBALL ASSOCIATION DEVELOPMENT LEAGUE, 60

Farmer, Paul Sports Editor
DAILY REPUBLIC, 482

Farmer, Sam Sports Reporter (National)
LOS ANGELES TIMES, 507

Farmer, Scott Director of Athletics
CAJUN FIELD STADIUM, 962

Farnham, Jane Production Director
SAILING MAGAZINE, 585

Farnham, Sheralyn Analyst Executive
BAKER, DAVID L., 872

Farnsworth, Bob President
GAME TIME, INC., 1146

Farnsworth, Clare Sports Reporter
SEATTLE POST-INTELLIGENCER, 534

Farnsworth, Jane Director Marketing
INTERNATIONAL SPORTS TIMING, 1159

Fine, Mike Sports Reporter
PATRIOT LEDGER, 522
Fine, Neil President
NEIL ENTERPRISES, 563, 1178
Fineran, John Sports Editor
CHARLOTTE SUN HERALD, 471
Finger, Mike Sports Columnist (College)
SAN ANTONIO EXPRESS-NEWS, 532
Fingleton, Thomas EVP / Chief Financial Officer
MAY DEPARTMENT STORES COMPANY,
THE, 1244
Fink, Janet Sport Management Program
Coord/Prof.
OHIO STATE UNIVERSITY, 432
Fink, Laurence Chairman and Chief Executive
Officer
BLACKROCK, 775
Fink, Laurence Chairman/Chief Executive Officer
BLACKROCK, 775
Fink, Mark Of Counsel
MONTGOMERY, MCCRACKEN, WALKER &
RHODAS, LLP, 906
Fink, Ray Director of Athletic Media Relations
OKLAHOMA BAPTIST UNIVERSITY
ATHLETICS, 368
Fink, Shaney Director of Athletics
SEATTLE UNIVERSITY ATHLETICS, 318
Fink, Shannon Group Sales
BELTERRA PARK, 1045
Finkel, Brian Creative Director
HORROW, RICK, 846
Finkelmeier, Louis Attorney at Law
FINKELMEIER LAW FIRM, 889
Finkelmeyer, Todd Sports Reporter
CAPITAL TIMES, 470
Finkle, Thomas Chief Client Services Officer
GFK CUSTOM RESEARCH NORTH AMERICA,
793
Finkmore, Richard Law Professor/Director, Louis
M. Brown P
CALIFORNIA WESTERN SCHOOL OF LAW,
880
Finks, Frederick President
ASHLAND UNIVERSITY, 412
Finlay, Thomas CEO
USL LEAGUE TWO, 160
Finley, Bill Director of Finance
NATIONAL SKI PATROL, 152
Finley, David VP, Scouting
NATIONAL LEAGUE OF PROFESSIONAL
BASEBALL CLUBS, THE, 32
Finley, Jimmy Sports Information Director
LA ROCHE COLLEGE ATHLETICS (LRC), 391
Finley, Joe Owner
INTERNATIONAL LEAGUE, 42
Finley, John Athletic Trainer
EAST COAST HOCKEY LEAGUE/ECHL, 130
Finley, Maureen Director of Finance
SOUTHLAND PARK, 1057
Finley, Ryan Sports Editor
ARIZONA DAILY STAR, 463
Finn, Chad Sports Media Columnist
BOSTON GLOBE, 468
Finn, Courtney Athletic Operations Assistant
BENTLEY UNIVERSITY ATHLETICS, 352
Finn, David Chairman
RUDER/FINN SPORTS, INC., 815, 861
Finn, Frank VP/Editor-in-Chief
SPORTING GOODS & ACTIVEWEAR BUYERS
DIRECTORY, 602, 603
Finn, Jackie Manager, Social Media and
Marketing Oper
BIG EAST CONFERENCE, 290
Finn, John News Director
WILQ-FM, 647, 658
Finn, Mike Associate Commissioner/Football
Communic
ATLANTIC COAST CONFERENCE, 289
Finn, Ryan Managing Director Championships
TEXAS GOLF ASSOCIATION, 115
Finn, Steve Assistant Executive Director
GATEWAY PGA SECTIONAL OFFICE, 104
Finn, Tim President and Chief Executive Officer
KID'S FOOT LOCKER, 1243
Finn, Tommy Vice President, Corporate
Partnerships
PPI MARKETING, 857
Finnegan, Eric VP
BASS IND INCORPORATED, 1115

Finnegan, Kathleen Associate Director of
Athletics
RAMAPO COLLEGE OF NEW JERSEY
ATHLETICS, 399
Finnegan, Keith Director of Operations &
Personnel
AMATEUR SPORTS GROUP, INC., 833
Finnegan, Robert Engineering VP
BARRECRAFTERS, 1114
Finnegan, Jennifer Accounting Coordinator
TAMPA CONVENTION & VISITORS BUREAU,
246
Finnell, Hunter Sports Director
KION-TV, 699
Finney, Peter Sports Columnist
TIMES-PICAYUNE, 545
Finney, Sarah Athletics Communications Director
SEATTLE UNIVERSITY ATHLETICS, 318
Finney, Jr., Peter Contributing Editor
GOLF PRODUCT NEWS, 567
Finnoff, Jonathan Medical Director
MAYO CLINIC SPORTS MEDICINE, 931
Finocchio, Dave Founder, VP of Content
BLEACHER REPORT, 721
Finucane, Anne Vice Chairman
BANK OF AMERICA CORPORATION, 733
Finz, Noah Sports Director
WTNH-TV, 719
Fioranelli, Jesse General Manager
MAJOR LEAGUE SOCCER, 158
Fiore, David President / Chief Executive Officer
BALFOUR CO., 1113
Fiore, Fernando Host
REPUBLICA DEPORTIVA, 692
Fiore, Jennifer Associate
ALEXANDER & ASSOCIATES, P.C. MARY, 871
Fiore, Melanie Director of Business
PACIFIC COAST LEAGUE OF
PROFESSIONAL BASEBALL CLUBS (AAA
LEVEL), 48
Fiorini, Jeff General Manager
EATON GOLF PRIDE, 1138
Fiorito, Matt Sports Writer (Bowling)
DETROIT FREE PRESS, 486
Fipps, Paul Chief Digital Officer
UNDER ARMOUR, 742
Fireman, Paul Chairman / Chief Executive Officer
ROCKPORT COMPANY, 1194
Fireman, Simon Chairman
AQUA LEISURE IND., INC., 1109
Firestone, Dan Assistant Sports Editor
BLADE, 467
Firova, Dan Manager
MEXICAN LEAGUE A.C., 44
Fisch, Pete Associate AD, Venue Management
WAKE FOREST BASEBALL PARK, 1026
Fisch, Zack Director, Communications &
Broadcasting
EAST COAST HOCKEY LEAGUE/ECHL, 127,
130
Fischbach, Bruce Secretary
NATIONAL WHEELCHAIR BASKETBALL
ASSOCIATION, 55
Fischer, Donna Marketing Manager
WIGWAM MILLS, INC., 1221
Fischer, Josh VP Marketing / Marketing Director
LOUISVILLE GOLF, 1168
Fischer, Kellie Executive VP/Chief Financial
Officer
AMERICAN LEAGUE OF PROFESSIONAL
BASEBALL CLUBS, THE, 31
Fischer, Larry VP, Sales
LOUISVILLE GOLF, 1168
Fischer, Louanne Director of Sales
GRAND SLAM SPORTS MARKETING, 794
Fischer, Mary Controller
ALTREC.COM, 1227
Fischer, Michael VP, Player Personnel
WOMEN'S NATIONAL BASKETBALL
ASSOCIATION, 61
Fischer, Rick News Director
KMEM-FM, 630
Fischer, Todd Account Supervisor
GMR MARKETING, 764
Fischler, Shirley Contributing Writer
RINKSIDE, 584
Fischler, Stan Contributing Editor
RINKSIDE, 584

Fish, Betty Promotions Manager
WHTM-TV, 712
Fish, Brad Division President
BWM GLOBAL, 1233
Fish, Randy Editor
DRAG RACER MAGAZINE, 562
Fish, Rick Artist Relations EVP
WINTERLAND PRODUCTIONS, 816, 1222
Fish, Shiela Assistant Director
SPRINGFIELD AREA SPORTS COMMISSION,
245
Fish, Stephanie General Manager
ZOOPERSTARS!, 783, 827
Fishbein, Jonathan President
VIDEO SPORTS, INC., 609
Fishburne, Keith President/CEO
SPECIAL OLYMPICS NORTH CAROLINA, 194
Fisher, Adam Director Of Operations & Facility
MID-OHIO SPORTS CAR COURSE, 1038
Fisher, Amanda Executive Director
SOUTHERN OHIO PGA SECTIONAL OFFICE,
107
Fisher, Annie Programs Director
UTAH PGA SECTIONAL OFFICE, 107
Fisher, Bob Principal
GREENWAY GROUP, THE, 629, 640, 1067
Fisher, Bryan Director of Athletic Relations
JOHN E. TUCKER COLISEUM, 985
Fisher, Bud Associate AD/Head Coach of Nordic
Skiing
WILLIAMS COLLEGE ATHLETICS, 1028
Fisher, Dennis Sports Editor
LANCASTER NEW ERA, 504
Fisher, Derek Head Coach/General Manager
WOMEN'S NATIONAL BASKETBALL
ASSOCIATION, 61
Fisher, Diana Director, Group Sales & Community
Relati
UNITED STATES HOCKEY LEAGUE, 137
Fisher, Drew Senior Vice President, Information
CLEAR CHANNEL ENTERTAINMENT, INC.,
695
Fisher, Jamie Womens Basketball Assistant
Coach
NJCAA REGION II WOMEN'S, 284
Fisher, Jeffrey Principal
FFKR ARCHITECTS, 1065
Fisher, Jocelyn Senior Associate Director of
Athletics
USF SOCCER STADIUM, 1023
Fisher, John Managing Partner/Board Member
MAJOR LEAGUE SOCCER, 30, 31, 158
Fisher, John Chief Executive Officer/Chairman
SAUCONY, 1197
Fisher, Julene Assistant Director of Athletics
MANHATTANVILLE COLLEGE ATHLETICS,
393
Fisher, Kyle Athletic Trainer
MAINE AT FORT KENT ATHLETICS,
UNIVERSITY OF, 314, 1007
Fisher, Larry Executive Director
INTERNATIONAL SOFTBALL CONGRESS, 166
Fisher, Lawrence Chief Legal Officer/Secretary
FLUOR CORPORATION, 1066
Fisher, Linda Special Event Manager
HIAWATHA HORSE PARK &
ENTERTAINMENT CENTRE, 1049
Fisher, Mark Sports Information Director
CARNEGIE MELLON UNIVERSITY
ATHLETICS, 357, 381
Fisher, Matt News/Sports Director
KKIA-FM, 628
Fisher, Patrick Executive Director
NUTMEG STATE GAMES, 262
Fisher, Peter Senior Managing Director
BLACKROCK, 775
Fisher, Rev. President
SIMMONS FIELD, 1011
Fisher, Ryan Assistant director of operations
LISTON B. RAMSEY REGIONAL ACTIVITY
CENTER, 992
Fisher, Sam President-Tract Division
U.S. TENNIS COURT & TRACK BUILDERS
ASSOCIATION, 1072
Fisher, Sara Advertising Manager
PAULS VALLEY DAILY DEMOCRAT, 522
Fisher, Scott President/Owner
BLIMPWORKS, 784

Fisher, Steve Advertising Director
TELEGRAPH HERALD, 542
Fisher, Terri Advertising Manager
DU QUOIN EVENING CALL, 487
Fishman, Aubrey Marketing Director
STREET CHARACTERS, INC., 820
Fisk, Erin Director of Ticketing
HOLT ARENA, 979
Fisk, Jerry Assistant Athletic Director of Event
ELMIRA COLLEGE ATHLETICS, 385
Fiskum, Stephen Principal
HAMMEL, GREEN AND ABRAHAMSON INC.,
1068
Fiss, Charlie News Director
KDXL-FM, 90, 623
Fitch, Jerome Athletic Director
CLAFLIN UNIVERSITY ATHLETICS, 355
Fite, Skip Head Baseball Coach
UNIVERSITY OF WEST GEORGIA
DEPARTMENT OF INTERCOLLEGIATE
ATHLETIC, 373
Fitterer, Scott General Manager
NATIONAL FOOTBALL LEAGUE/NFL, 95
Fitz-Gerald, Sarah Vice President
WORLD SQUASH FEDERATION/WSF, 169
FitzSimons, Ryan Founder/Chief Executive
Officer
GIGUNDA GROUP, 793
Fitzenreider, Nick VP, Operations & Security
PACIFIC COAST LEAGUE OF
PROFESSIONAL BASEBALL CLUBS, 49, 964
Fitzgerald, Carol Customer Service
Representative
ACCUFITNESS, LLC, 1101
Fitzgerald, Courtney Public Relations Manager -
Leisure
LAS VEGAS CONVENTION & VISITOR'S
AUTHORITY, 990
Fitzgerald, Jeff News Director
WLIO-TV, 714
Fitzgerald, John President
SPORTSPLEX OPERATORS AND
DEVELOPERS ASSOCIATION/SODA, 223
Fitzgerald, Martha Director of Communications
BRIGGS, BUCK, 877
Fitzgerald, Michael Managing Director
AMBAC ASSURANCE CORPORATION, 775
Fitzgerald, Pat Head Coach, Football
RYAN FIELD, 1009
Fitzgerald, Ryan Event Manager
CFE ARENA, 964
Fitzgerald, Scott Sports Editor
SOUTHWEST COUNTY JOURNAL, 536, 537
Fitzgerald, Susan Publisher
INTERNATIONAL FIGURE SKATING, 571
Fitzgerald, Thomas Sports Reporter
SAN FRANCISCO CHRONICLE, 532
Fitzgerald, Tim President
WESTERN PENNSYLVANIA GOLF
ASSOCIATION, 116
Fitzgerald, Tom Executive VP & General Manager
NATIONAL HOCKEY LEAGUE/NHL, 115, 124
Fitzmaurice, Sean Coordinator of Facilities
ITHACA COLLEGE ATHLETICS, 390
Fitzpatrick, Chris Associate Director of
Braodcasting
NCAA, 607
Fitzpatrick, Frank Sports Reporter
PHILADELPHIA INQUIRER, 523
Fitzpatrick, Kevin Sports Agent
FIRST STRING MANAGEMENT, 842
Fitzpatrick, Tim Director of Athletics
UNITED STATES COAST GUARD ACADEMY
ATHLETICS, 406, 936
Fitzpatrick-Navarro, Tara Executive Director
USTA MID-ATLANTIC, 173
Fitzsimons, Jerry Executive Director
VOLLEYBALL HALL OF FAME INC., 258
Flading, John President and CEO
SWING AWAY SPORTS PRODUCTS, INC.,
1210
Fladung, Thom Editor/Vice President
SAINT PAUL PIONEER PRESS, 531
Flagg, Niel President
SPORTS POSTER WAREHOUSE, 1205
Flagg, Rick News Director
WNLS, 641, 666
Flaherty, Bill Director of Sales
1510 THE ZONE, 618

Flaherty, Christopher Chief Business
Development Officer
CHERNESKY, RICHARD, 881
Flaherty, Joseph Director
LEHIGH CARBON COMMUNITY COLLEGE,
425
Flaherty, Lee Chief Executive Officer
FLAIR COMMUNICATIONS, 791
Flaherty, Rebecca General Manager
MAXIMUM SPORTS MANAGEMENT, 852
Flaherty, Rob Senior Partner, CEO
KETCHUM NEW YORK, 800
Flajole, Brian Golf & Business Development VP
RAYCOM SPORTS, 813
Flakus, Zach Deputy Director of Athletics
NORTHERN STATE UNIVERSITY(NSU), 367
Flamholz, Sam Co-President, Boscov's
Department Store,
BOSCOV'S DEPARTMENT STORES, 1232
Flamini, Stephanie Assistant Athletics Director
GUILFORD COLLEGE ATHLETICS, 387
Flaminio, Joann President
BOSTON ATHLETIC ASSOCIATION, 148
Flanagan, Debbie President
CANADIAN SPORT PARACHUTING
ASSOCIATION, 13
Flanagan, Ian Treasurer
CANADIAN SPORT PARACHUTING
ASSOCIATION, 13
Flanagan, Jeffrey Sports Reporter
KANSAS CITY STAR, 502
Flanagan, Kelly Editor
SPORT JOURNAL, 589
Flanagan, Kelly Assistant Editor
SPORTS JOURNAL, 591
Flanagan, Lori Director of Athletics
UNIVERSITY OF MISSOURI-ST. LOUIS
ATHLETICS(UMSL), 374
Flanagan, Mike Assistant Coach
EAST COAST HOCKEY LEAGUE/ECHL, 129
Flanagan, Olivia Secretary/Treasurer
GEORGIA STATE GOLF ASSOCIATION, 100
Flanagan, Steve President
YEADON FABRIC STRUCTURES LTD., 1224
Flanders, Scott CEO
PLAYBOY ENTERTAINMENT GROUP, 856
Flanigan, John Partner
HAILE, SHAW & PFAFFENBERGER, P.A., 892
Flanik, Gregory CIO
BALDWIN-WALLACE COLLEGE - LOU
HIGGINS CENTER, 412
Flannagan, Tom Sports Columnist
STATEN ISLAND ADVANCE, 540
Flannelly, Shawn Manager - Business
Develpoment
16W MARKETING, LLC, 778
Flannery, Bob General Manager
NORTHWEST BASEBALL LEAGUE, 48
Flannery, Chris COO
NEW YORK-PENNSYLVANIA LEAGUE, 46,
1194
Flannery, Tim Host
PRIME TIME PADRES, 692
Flateau, Rick Head Athletic Trainer
CLARK ATLANTA UNIVERSITY ATHLETICS,
355
Flathers, Chuck Vice President Of Sales
OCEANTIS SPORTS, 1181
Flatin, Jean-Christophe President, Innovation,
Science and Techn
MARS NORTH AMERICA, 738
Flato-Dominy, Wyndy Director, Operations
WOMEN'S FOOTBALL ALLIANCE / WFA, 97
Flatt, Taylor Sports Information Director
UNIVERSITY OF ALABAMA IN HUNTSVILLE
ATHLETICS, 374
Flavin, Jim VP, Business Development
PACIFIC COAST LEAGUE OF
PROFESSIONAL BASEBALL CLUBS, 50
Flay, Bobby Team
AQUEDUCT, 1051
Fleaming, Ian Acting Raceway Manager
WESTERN FAIR ENTERTAINMENT CENTRE,
1055
Fleder, Rob Sports Executive Editor
SPORTS ILLUSTRATED, 591
Fleenor, David Contributor
SOCCER365.COM, 722

Fleet, Bill Co-Chairman
ROME SPORTS HALL OF FAME & MUSEUM,
256
Fleetwood, Debi Ice Programs Coordinator
NORTH AMERICAN HOCKEY LEAGUE, 133
Flegel, Steve Sports Information Director
WHITWORTH COLLEGE ATHLETICS, 409
Fleischer, Mark Program/Sports Director
WDSM-AM, 650
Fleischer, Russell Director
ADAMS GOLF GP CORPORATION, 1103
Fleischman, Bill Assistant Sports Editor
PHILADELPHIA DAILY NEWS, 523
Fleischman, Robert Professor/Sport
Management Program Coord
EAST STROUDSBURG UNIVERSITY OF, 419
Fleishman, Bill President
CONE COMMUNICATIONS, 760
Fleishman, Charles Chief Marketing Officer
SRI SPORTS, INC., 1206
Fleming, Bob Lawyer
REDWINE, THOMAS R., 911
Fleming, David Senior Writer
ESPN THE MAGAZINE, 563
Fleming, Edward Partner
MCDONALD, FLEMING, MOORHEAD &
FERGUSON, GREEN & SMITH, 903
Fleming, Gary President
ALPINA SPORTS CORPORATION, 1106
Fleming, Gloria Advertising Manager
WEST HAWAII TODAY, 551
Fleming, Jack President
JUMPIN' JACK SPORTS, 799
Fleming, Jason Assistant Comptroller
OHIO HS ATHLETIC ASSOCIATION, 199
Fleming, Jeffrey Associate Publisher
SEA MAGAZINE, 558, 585
Fleming, Kevin Director, Sales
ATLANTIC LEAGUE, 35
Fleming, Kiley Box Office Manager
WRIGHT STATE UNIVERSITY NUTTER
CENTER, 1029
Fleming, Leslie Secretary
ANCHORAGE WOMEN'S GOLF
ASSOCIATION, 108
Flesher, Bill Executive Vice President
WINNERCOMM, INC., 610
Flessas, Costas Head Coach
WOMEN'S PREMIER SOCCER LEAGUE, 164
Fletcher, Allan Chief Executive Officer
ASHWORTH, INC., 1110
Fletcher, Carol Sports Management Assistant
Professor
ST. JOHN'S UNIVERSITY, 74, 436
Fletcher, Chuck President, Hockey
Operations/GM/Alternat
NATIONAL HOCKEY LEAGUE/NHL, 125
Fletcher, Davey Marketing/Sales
TEXAS BOWL, 93
Fletcher, Jeff Ticket Manager
STATE MUTUAL STADIUM, 526, 1014
Fletcher, Katy Brand Manager
RAZOR USA LLC, 1192
Fletcher, Mark Buyer
J. BAKER, INC., 1242
Fletcher, Richard Deputy Director of Athletics
MOREHEAD STATE UNIVERSITY ATHLETICS,
338
Fleury, Kristen Assistant Athletic Director
DICKINSON STATE UNIVERSITY ATHLETICS,
310
Flickema, Thomas President
DAKOTA-10 ATHLETIC CONFERENCE, 293
Flicker, Michael Director of Athletic Training
LENOIR-RHYNE UNIVERSITY ATHLETICS,
362
Flickinger, Grace Faculty Athletic Representative
GULF COAST ATHLETIC CONFERENCE, 294
Flink, Edward Sports Writer
NEWS-TIMES, 517
Flint, Dana Faculty Athletics Representative
LINCOLN UNIVERSITY ATHLETICS, 363
Flint, Dave Head Coach, Women's Hockey
MATTHEWS ARENA, 994
Flipovich, Tim Arena Supervisor
VALUE CITY ARENA/JEROME
SCHOTTENSTEIN CENTER, 1024

Flippo, Hilliari Development & Public Relations Assistant
NJCAA REGION XVII MEN'S, 287

Flock, John Associate
BRADLEY & GMELICH, 877

Flolid, Seth General Manager
MIDWEST LEAGUE, 44

Flood, Bill President
CONNECTICUT PGA SECTIONAL OFFICE, 104

Flood, T.J. President
SPORT CHEK, 741

Flora, Calabrese Associate Principal
WISS, JANNEY, ELSTNER ASSOCIATES, INC./WJE, 1073

Florence, Amber Chief Financial Officer
NATIONAL THOROUGHBRED RACING, 77

Flores, Adolfo Treasurer
WORLD BOXING ORGANIZATION, 67

Flores, Brian Head Coach
NATIONAL FOOTBALL LEAGUE/NFL, 96

Flores, David Sports Columnist
SAN ANTONIO EXPRESS-NEWS, 532

Flores, Luis General Manager
MEXICAN LEAGUE A.C., 44

Flores, Ray Product Manager
EMPIRE SPORTS/SISCO SPORTS, 1139

Flores, Vennessa CSR
KOLDER INC, 1163

Florio, Terri Executive Director
MALIVAI WASHINGTON KIDS FOUNDATION, 173, 190

Florkiewicz, Bryan Director, Game Operations
EAST COAST HOCKEY LEAGUE/ECHL, 129

Flower, Patrick Director of Ticket Sales
EASTERN LEAGUE, 39

Flowers, Courtney Assistant Professor
UNIVERSITY OF WEST GEORGIA, 438

Flowers, David Director
FOX SPORTS INTERNATIONAL, 682

Flowers, Jennifer Commissioner (Women's)
WESTERN COLLEGIATE HOCKEY ASSOCIATION, 122

Flowers, Paul President
LIFELINE INTERNATIONAL, INC., 1166

Floyd, Blair General Manager
SOUTHERN PROFESSIONAL HOCKEY LEAGUE, 136

Floyd, Chad Head Athletic Trainer
UNIVERSITY OF THE OZARKS ATHLETICS, 398

Floyd, Harry Athletic Secretary
JAYNE STADIUM, 953, 984

Floyd, Jeff Promotions Manager
WOLO-TV, 716

Floyd, Lincoln Director of development
PIKES PEAK INTERNATIONAL RACEWAY, 256

Floyd, Mark Vice Chair, Labor & Employment Practice
THOMPSON HINE, 867

Floyd, R.T. Director of Athletic Training & Sports M
WEST ALABAMA ATHLETICS, UNIVERSITY OF, 375

Fluhr, Jeff Co-Founder and Chief Executive Officer
STUBHUB, 942

Fluke, Steve Associate Athletics Director for Complia
OKLAHOMA BAPTIST UNIVERSITY ATHLETICS, 368

Flutie, Laurie Vice President/Co-Founder
DOUG FLUTIE, JR. FOUNDATION FOR AUTISM, 189

Fluty, Lisa Chief Information Officer
HOST COMMUNICATIONS, INC., 796

Fly, William Staff
FLY, WILLIAM L., 889

Flynn, Betty Executive Director
THOROUGHBRED CLUB OF AMERICA, 77

Flynn, Dennis Governor
CANADA'S SPORTS HALL OF FAME, 250

Flynn, John President
STROMGREN SUPPORTS, INC., 81, 1208

Flynn, Josh Assistant General Manager
NATIONAL HOCKEY LEAGUE/NHL, 123

Flynn, Kevin EVP
KIKU OBATA & COMPANY, 801

Flynn, Liz Director of Marketing
UNIVERSITY HALL, 1021

Flynn, Margo VP Marketing
TAMPA BAY DOWNS, 1054

Flynn, Mike Sports Information Director
KIDD BREWER STADIUM, 988

Flynn, Patrick Sports Writer
NORTHWEST FLORIDA DAILY NEWS, 518

Flynn, Robin Senior Consultant
KAGAN WORLD MEDIA, 575, 799

Flynn, Tim Assistant Athletics Director
COLORADO SCHOOL OF MINES ATHLETICS (CSM), 121, 297, 356

Flynn, Timothy Chairman Kpmg International
KPMG CONVENTION, SPORTS & ENTERTAINMENT PRACTICE, 766

Fogarty, Jamie Senior Associate AD/SWA
IONA COLLEGE ATHLETICS, 332

Fogarty, Timothy President
CENTURY SPORTS, INC., 1125

Fogel, Ken Executive Vice-President
APPALACHIAN POWER PARK, 955

Fogelgaren, Eric Partner
FOGELGAREN, FORMAN & BERGMAN, 889

Fogle, Karen Association & Corporate Sales Manager
PLANO CONVENTION & VISITORS BUREAU, 242

Foguth, Carter Head Coach
NORTH AMERICAN HOCKEY LEAGUE, 132

Fojtasek, Lori Assistant Executive Director/Sales
IRVING CONVENTION & VISITORS BUREAU, 235

Folan, Amy Executive Senior Associate AD
TEXAS AT AUSTIN ATHLETICS, UNIVERSITY OF, 325, 346

Folan, Tim Senior Associate AD, Development
PENNSYLVANIA ATHLETICS, UNIVERSITY OF, 341

Foland, Penny Head Athletic Trainer
NYACK COLLEGE ATHLETICS, 368

Folda, Joe Director of Athletics
UNIVERSITY OF SOUTHERN COLORADO ATHLETICS, 371

Foldesy, Jody Sports Reporter
WASHINGTON TIMES, 550

Foley, Bill Chair, CEO & Governor
NATIONAL HOCKEY LEAGUE/NHL, 126

Foley, Christopher Chief Financial Officer
NEIGHBORHOOD BOX OFFICE, 941

Foley, David Executive Director
AMERICAN ASSOCIATION OF EQUINE PRACTITIONERS, 73

Foley, Joe Senior Associate AD, Advancement
PENN STATE UNIVERSITY ATHLETICS, 341

Foley, Kevin President
POSITION SPORTS MARKETING, 857

Foley, Mark Secretary
MINNESOTA PGA SECTIONAL OFFICE, 105

Foley, Marshall Associate Athletic Director
OAKLAND UNIVERSITY ATHLETICS(OU), 340, 368

Foley, Martha News Director
WXLU-FM, 674, 679

Foley, Mike President
US PRACTICAL SHOOTING ASSOCIATION (USPSA), 150

Foley, Robert Chief Business Officer
NATIONAL HOCKEY LEAGUE/NHL, 126

Foley, Solomon Treasurer
ROCKFORD AREA CONVENTION & VISITORS BUREAU, 243

Foley, Wilma Mutuels
THUNDER RIDGE RACING AND ENTERTAINMENT COMPLEX, 1054

Folger, Lee President
BASEBALL AMERICA, 556

Folk, Jim VP, Ballpark Improvements
AMERICAN LEAGUE OF PROFESSIONAL BASEBALL CLUBS, THE, 29

Folks, Lonnie Director of Athletics and Recreation
RICHARD STOCKTON COLLEGE OF NJ ATHLETICS, 400

Follansbee, Dave Assistant Food and Beverage Supervisor
LA CROSSE CENTER, 989

Follett, Shannon Administration and Operations Manager
FLORIDA STATE LEAGUE, 40

Follette, Laurie Chief Executive Officer
SPECIAL OLYMPICS IDAHO, 192

Followill, Mark Sports Director
KTCK/THE TICKET, 636

Folser, David Sports Editor
SOUTHWEST DAILY NEWS, 537

Folsom, Kim Executive Assistant
USA HOCKEY, 122, 207

Folts, Perry President
POHLMAN FIELD, 1002

Foltz, Bill President & COO
NATIONAL HOCKEY LEAGUE/NHL, 122

Foltz, Marisa Head Athletic Trainer
EVANGEL UNIVERSITY ATHLETICS, 311

Folz, Ceil President
VAIL VALLEY FOUNDATION, 773

Fonde, Tim Sports Editor
TIMES HERALD (PA), 544

Fondulas, Peter EVP
TAYLOR RESEARCH & CONSULTING GROUP, INC., 821

Fonfa, Andrew Chief Executive Officer
PLATINUM ENTERTAINMENT PARTNERS II, 608

Fonfara, Joseph Attorney
HASLER, FONFARA AND MAXWELL, LLP, 892

Fonfara, Pete Director, Finance
NATIONAL FOOTBALL LEAGUE/NFL, 97

Fong, David Sports Editor
TROY DAILY NEWS, 546

Fong, Henry Chief Executive Officer
TORPEDO SPORTS USA, INC., 1214

Fons, Randall Managing Partner
MORRISON & FOERSTER LLP, 906

Fonseca, Jonathan President
WOMEN'S PREMIER SOCCER LEAGUE, 166

Fontaine, David Director of Athletics
UTICA COLLEGE ATHLETICS(UC), 406

Fontaine, Jacques President
WORLD SQUASH FEDERATION/WSF, 169

Fontaine, Kathie Customer Relation Director
ALL STAR SPORTING GOODS, 1105

Fontaine, Laurn Customer Service Representative
SUPERIOR FLOOR COMPANY, INC., 1099, 1209

Fontaine, Paul President
HARNESS TRACKS OF AMERICA, 76

Fontana, Richard Attorney
BERMAN, HOWARD E., 874

Fontana, Scott Sports Writer
AM NEW YORK, 462

Fontenot, Terry General Manager
NATIONAL FOOTBALL LEAGUE/NFL, 95

Fontes, Katie Coordinator Sponsor Services
CALIFORNIA MEMORIAL STADIUM, 962

Fontes, Marty Race Director
BEST BET, 1055

Fonzi, Joe Weekend Sports Anchor
KTVU-TV, 689, 704

Foote, Kevin Sports Editor
THE ADVERTISER, 543

Foote, Russell Advertising Manager
EVENING SUN (NY), 490

Footz, Nona Board Member
EXECUTIVE WOMEN'S GOLF ASSOCIATION, 99

Forbes, Chris Associate Deputy Minister
AGRICULTURE AND AGRI-FOOD CANADA, 79

Forbes, David Sports Editor
SOUTHBRIDGE EVENING NEWS, 536

Forbes, Gavin Tournament Representative
ATP WORLD TOUR, 171

Forbes, Jerry Sports Information Director
BRESCIA COLLEGE ATHLETICS, 307

Forbes, Mark Treasurer
U.S. HANG GLIDING AND PARAGLIDING ASSOCIATION, 14

Forbis, Barry Sports Editor
ROCKY MOUNTAIN NEWS, 472, 530

Force, Katie Promotions & Community Relations Coordin
ATLANTIC LEAGUE, 35

Force, Pete VP-Business Development
SPORTS LOOP, 865

Ford, Alan Sports Editor
SHELBY STAR, 535

Ford, Anthony General Manager
A.J. MCCLUNG MEMORIAL STADIUM, 953

Ford, Ben Sports Writer
ELKHART TRUTH, 489
Ford, Beverly Promotions Director
WXVT-TV, 721
Ford, Blanche Administrative Assisstant
LIVINGSTONE COLLEGE, 426
Ford, Bob Director, Business Development
ATLANTIC LEAGUE, 35, 523
Ford, Brett Sports Information Director
WESLEY COLLEGE ATHLETICS, 407
Ford, Caden Sports Information Director
STERLING COLLEGE ATHLETICS, 320
Ford, Carl Sports Director
WRNA-AM, 672
Ford, Charles Managing Editor
BOSTON HANNAH INTERNATIONAL, 558
Ford, Cindy General Manager
WGET, 654
Ford, Duane President
NORTH AMERICAN BOXING FEDERATION,
67
Ford, Eileen Executive Director
COWBOY STATE GAMES, 260
Ford, Graham President
LIFE SAVING/UTILITARIAN SPORTS,
FEDERATION INTERNATIONALE DE, 170
Ford, Ken Assistant Treasurer
AMERICAN MOTORCYCLIST ASSOCIATION,
143
Ford, Kirsten Assistant Commissioner
ROCKY MOUNTAIN ATHLETIC
CONFERENCE, 302
Ford, Mark Executive Director
PROFESSIONAL FOOTBALL RESEARCHERS
ASSOCIATION, 90
Ford, Michael Sr. University Counsel for Tax,
Corporat
BERNARD, PAMELA J., 874
Ford, Milt Sales/Marketing Director
MESA CONVENTION & VISITORS BUREAU,
239
Ford, Robert Partner
THOMPSON HINE, 867
Ford, Scott Assistant Coach
AMERICAN HOCKEY LEAGUE/AHL, 127
Ford, Stephanie Marketing Director
CONNECTICUT INTERSCHOLASTIC
ATHLETIC CONFERENCE, 197
Ford, Steve Sports Reporter
EVANSVILLE COURIER & PRESS, 490
Ford, Tom Dept. Chairperson
COLUMBUS STATE UNIVERSITY, 417
Ford, Jr., William Executive Chairman
FORD MOTOR COMPANY, 736
Ford-Kee, Dianthia Director of Athletics
MISSISSIPPI VALLEY STATE UNIVERSITY
ATHLETICS, 337, 993, 1005
Forde, Kevin Director of Athletics
WHEELING JESUIT UNIVERSITY ATHLETICS
(WJU), 376
Foreman, Bobby Baseball Assistant Coach
NJCAA REGION II WOMEN'S, 284
Foreman, David Vice President
FOREMAN ARCHITECTS ENGINEERS INC.,
1066
Foreman, Hank Associate Vice Chancellor for
University
COLE, DAYTON T., 882
Foreman, Michael VP, Government and
International Sales
POINT BLANK SOLUTIONS, 1186
Foreman, Phillip CEO and President
FOREMAN ARCHITECTS ENGINEERS INC.,
1066
Foreman, Tim Facility Manager
EASTERN LEAGUE, 38, 974
Forester, David Director of Event Operations
OKLAHOMA CITY ALL SPORTS
ASSOCIATION, 241
Forester, Thomas Sports Anchor
WOFL-TV, 715
Forestier, Tom Managing Shareholder
WINSTEAD ATTORNEYS, 926
Forge, Bil General Manager
WESTERN HOCKEY LEAGUE, 138
Forgues, Brittany Associate
ABBOTT MANAGEMENT GROUP, 832

Forgus, Karen Senior VP, Business Operations
NATIONAL LEAGUE OF PROFESSIONAL
BASEBALL CLUBS, THE, 31
Forgy, John General Counsel
KENTUCKY HORSE RACING COMMISSION,
80
Forlenzo, Jay Vice President
FAIRTRON, 1142
Forma, Jared General Manager
FLORIDA STATE LEAGUE, 39, 987
Forman, Jonathan Partner
FOGELGAREN, FORMAN & BERGMAN, 889
Forman, Sarah Community Coordinator
NEW ORLEANS METROPOLITAN
CONVENTION & VISITORS BUREAU, 240
Forman, Sean Owner
SPORTS REFERENCE, THE, 939
Fornabaio, Michael Sports Reporter
CONNECTICUT POST, 475
Fornaciari, Sara Event Director
SPORTS PLUS, 770
Fornataro, Mike Sales/Marketing Manager
NATIONAL TRAIL RACEWAY, 1039
Forner, Tracy Anchor
FOX 59 OVERTIME, 687
Forrest, Andrew General Manager, Business
Operations
USL CHAMPIONSHIP, 159
Forrest, Danny Regional Sales Manager
WORLD SPORTING GOODS, INC., 1223
Forrest, Harland General Sales Manager
KELA, 623
Forrest, J.D. Head Coach
AMERICAN HOCKEY LEAGUE/AHL, 129
Forrest, Jim Program Director
WQXX-FM, 670
Forrest, Mary Marketing Director
WORLD SPORTING GOODS, INC., 1223
Forrester, Kimberly Publications
Manager/Managing Editor
U.S. PROFESSIONAL TENNIS ASSOCIATION,
172
Forrester, Rosslyn Sales
GORILLA MARKETING, INC., 794
Forsee, Gary President
ARNET, WILLIAM F., 871
Forsman, Carrie Director of Facilities
WELSH RYAN ARENA, 1027
Forsman, Michael Attorney
BOESCHE MCDERMOTT LLP, 876
Forst, David General Manager
AMERICAN LEAGUE OF PROFESSIONAL
BASEBALL CLUBS, THE, 30
Forster, Jeff President
NATIONWIDE SPORTS, INC., 940
Forster, Vicki President
BVT PRODUCTS, LLC, 1122
Forster-Holt, Nancy Owner
SHAW & TENNEY, 1199
Forstmann, Theodore Chairman/CEO
IMG LOS ANGELES/IMG X SPORTS, 847
Forstmann, Theodore Chairman/CEO
SCHOEPPLER, KURT J., 862
Forsyth, Jim News Director
TICKET760 KTKR, 642
Forsythe, John General Manager
WNJC-AM, 665
Forsythe, Lee Assistant Athletic Director,
Facilities
DIDDLE ARENA, 970
Forsythe, Richard Chairman
FORSYTHE & ASSOCIATES, INC., 935
Fort, Tom President
DELAWARE SPORTS MUSEUM AND HALL OF
FAME, 250
Forte, Kevin Group Sales Coordinator
JERRY UHT PARK, 984
Forthofer, Bill Station Manager
WLKR-AM, 662
Fortier, Jason Head Coach/General Manager
NORTH AMERICAN HOCKEY LEAGUE, 133
Fortier, □tienne Administrative Director
QUEBEC MAJOR JUNIOR HOCKEY LEAGUE,
134
Fortin, Bryant Director of Junior Golf
ARKANSAS STATE GOLF ASSOCIATION, 109
Fortini, Nick Director of Sports Information
SAN DIEGO CHRISTIAN COLLEGE
ATHLETICS, 318

Fortna, Jeffery State Treasurer
PENNSYLVANIA SPORTS HALL OF FAME,
256
Fortner, Jenny Chair
SPECIAL OLYMPICS ILLINOIS, 193
Fortosis, Bob Director of Athletics
ECKERD COLLEGE ATHLETICS, 357
Fortson, Tomas Vice President/Men's
COLLEGE SQUASH ASSOCIATION/MENS &
WOMEN'S INTERCOLLEGIATE COMPETI, 168
Fortuna, Bob High School Sports Writer
PLAIN DEALER, 524
Fortuna, Robert Sales
CARROM COMPANY, 1124
Fortuna, Ted Officer
CANADIAN SAFE BOATING COUNCIL, 64
Fortune, Matt Associate AD, Facilities
DELAWARE STATE UNIVERSITY ATHLETICS,
327
Fortus, Bob Sports Columnist (Horse Racing)
TIMES-PICAYUNE, 545
Fosko, Joey Sports Reporter
PADUCAH SUN, 521
Foss, Eric President
ARAMARK CORPORATION, 782, 1073, 1076
Fossberg, Brad Sports Director
KMMJ, 630
Fosse, Pam Director
JAMESTOWN CIVIC CENTER, 984
Fossum, Jim Sports Editor
LAS VEGAS REVIEW-JOURNAL, 504
Foster, Alan Athletics Director
BACONE COLLEGE ATHLETICS, 306
Foster, Andrew Associate AD, Operations &
Facilities
LAFAYETTE COLLEGE ATHLETICS, 334
Foster, Andy Sports Director/Music
WOHS, 649, 655, 667
Foster, Bob Head Athletic Trainer
MONMOUTH COLLEGE ATHLETICS, 396
Foster, Brenda Classified Manager
WASHINGTON DAILY NEWS, 550
Foster, Brent Sports Editor
DAILY GUIDE, 479
Foster, Brian Director of Marketing &
Communications
ARIZONA GOLF ASSOCIATION, 108
Foster, Bruce Executive VP/CFO
4LICENSING CORPORATION, 779
Foster, Cameron President
FOSTER & EASLEY SPORTS MANAGEMENT
GROUP, 842
Foster, Chris Sports Reporter (Kings)
LOS ANGELES TIMES, 507
Foster, Cindy Executive Assistant CVB
JOHNSON CITY CONVENTION & VISITORS
BUREAU, 235
Foster, Courtney VP
FOSTER & EASLEY SPORTS MANAGEMENT
GROUP, 842
Foster, Craig President, Operations
QUEBEC MAJOR JUNIOR HOCKEY LEAGUE,
135, 860
Foster, David Editor-in-Chief
GRAY'S SPORTING JOURNAL, 568
Foster, Deana President
WOMEN ON WHEELS MOTORCYCLE
ASSOCIATION, 144
Foster, Don Sports Editor
STARKVILLE DAILY NEWS, 539
Foster, Don Partner
FOSTER, DON, 890
Foster, Fred Sales Service
ALL AMERICAN SCOREBOARDS, 1105
Foster, Joe VP
WEST COAST TURF, 1221
Foster, John President
WEST COAST TURF, 1221
Foster, Laurence Editor In Chief
RACER, 583
Foster, Lisa Director of Finance
THE CROWN COMPLEX, 1018
Foster, Mark National Sales Manager
MITSUBISHI DIAMOND VISION, 547, 1174
Foster, Paul Owner/Chairman
PACIFIC COAST LEAGUE OF
PROFESSIONAL BASEBALL CLUBS, 48

French, Doug CFO
TELUS CORPORATION, 742

French, Jamison Head Athletic Trainer
OHIO DOMINICAN UNIVERSITY ATHLETICS,
316

French, Kim Editor
HOOF BEATS, 569

French, Mark Head Coach
EAST COAST HOCKEY LEAGUE/ECHL, 130

French, Ron Sports Reporter
DETROIT NEWS, 486

Frennea, Robert Apparel EVP
ACADEMY SPORTS & OUTDOORS, 1227

Frens, Meg Athletic Training Program Director
HOPE COLLEGE ATHLETICS, 389

Frentress, Curt President and Principal-in-Charge
of Des
FENTRESS ARCHITECTS, 1065

Frenz, Michael Executive Director
MD STADIUM AUTHORITY, 852

Frerichs, Richard Principal
FFKR ARCHITECTS, 1065

Frese, Eric Head Baseball Coach
PIONEER FIELD, 1001

Frese, William Secretary
NEW JERSEY STATE GOLF ASSOCIATION,
113

Fresher, Michael General Manager
RENTSCHLER FIELD, 1005

Freud, Chris Sports Editor
VAIL DAILY, 548

Freund, Conrad Chief Operating Officer
LA84 FOUNDATION, 253

Freund, Peter Co-Owner
JOSEPH P. RILEY, JR PARK, 986

Frevola, Jim Senior VP & Chief Sales Officer
NATIONAL HOCKEY LEAGUE/NHL, 126

Frey, Audrey Finance & Administration Manager
SYNCHRO CANADA, 170

Frey, Chris Facilities, Operations Manager
FARREL STADIUM, 973

Friar, Erin Sports News Editor
WALL STREET JOURNAL, 550

Friberg, Emil President
FRIBERG ASSOCIATES INC., 1067

Friberg, Emil Chairman of the Board
FRIBERG ASSOCIATES INC., 1067

Frick, Kenneth VP/Chief Financial Officer
CENTERPLATE, 1074, 1076

Frickman, David Sports Editor
INPLAY, 570

Fridman, Arkady Inside Sales Manager
INTERNATIONAL AUDARENA GUIDE, 601

Fried, Barry Director of Athletics
VITERBO ATHLETICS UNIVERSITY, 321

Fried, Gil Professor/Chair
NEW HAVEN, UNIVERSITY OF, 431

Fried, Jeffrey President
FRIED & COMPANY, P.C., 843

Fried, Kenny Executive Vice President
BROTMAN WINTER FRIED
COMMUNICATIONS, INC., 759

Friedberg, James
ISRAEL, FRIEDBERG & KORBATOV L.L.P.,
895

Friedland, Laura VP
HARPER INDUSTRIES INC, 1153

Friedland, Lloyd Attorney
LIBRETT, FRIEDLAND & LIEBERMAN, 856,
900

Friedland, Robert Head Coach
USL LEAGUE TWO, 161

Friedland, Thomas President
HARPER INDUSTRIES INC, 1153

Friedlander, Andy Sports Reporter
FORT WORTH STAR-TELEGRAM, 491

Friedlander, Brett Contributing Writer
RINKSIDE, 584

Friedlander, Joshua Chief Human Resources
Officer
SAUER, JR., RUSSELL F., 914

Friedman, Andrew President, Baseball
Operations
NATIONAL LEAGUE OF PROFESSIONAL
BASEBALL CLUBS, THE, 32

Friedman, Bob President
DIVOTS SPORTSWEAR COMPANY, INC.,
1135

Friedman, Dick Senior Editor
SPORTS ILLUSTRATED, 591

Friedman, Gary Director of Athletics
REDBIRD ARENA, 1004

Friedman, Henry SVP Sales
EASTPAK CORPORATION, 1138

Friedman, Michael Founder and President
MASTER HOME PRODUCTS, 1171

Friedman, Mike Sports Director
KFDM-TV, 697

Friedman, Tedd Attorney
KATZ, TELLER, BRANT & HILD, 897

Friedman, Vicki Sports Writer
VIRGINIAN-PILOT, 549

Friedrich, Joe Coordinator of Sports Medicine
GEORGIAN COURT COLLEGE ATHLETICS,
360

Friedrichs, Wade Marketing
SPEED SKATELUBE, 1203

Friedrichs, Wades Marketing
SPEED SKATELUBE, 1203

Friedson, Richard Treasurer
MULTICULTURAL GOLF ASSOCIATION OF
AMERICA, 102

Friello, Mike Governor
ADIRONDACK AAU ASSOCIATION, 212

Friend, Amy Public Relations Director
PIONEER NEW MEDIA TECHNOLOGIES,
INC., 1185

Friend, John Athletics Consultant
PURDUE UNIVERSITY CALUMET ATHLETICS,
317

Friend, Rob CEO
CANADIAN PREMIER LEAGUE, 156

Friend, Tom Senior Writer
ESPN THE MAGAZINE, 563

Friesen, Rudy GM
EXIBITION PARK - LETHBRIDGE, 1047

Friesen, Stewart Co-Owner
NASCAR GANDER OUTDOORS TRUCK
SERIES, 23

Frieze, Irene Professor
HOLMES, RICH, 894

Friisdahl, Michael President/CEO, Maple Leaf
Sports & Enter
SCOTIABANK ARENA, 958, 1010

Frijia, Mark General Manager
NATIONAL BASKETBALL LEAGUE OF
CANADA, 59

Frijia, Vito Owner
NATIONAL BASKETBALL LEAGUE OF
CANADA, 59

Frimmel, Gabe Advertising Manager
PAINTBALL MAGAZINE, 553, 581

Frisbee, Shane Marketing Committee Chair
JACKSONVILLE AND THE BEACHES
CONVENTION AND VISITORS BUREAU, 235

Frisbey, Jinni Senior Associate AD/SWA
SOUTH ALABAMA ATHLETICS, UNIVERSITY
OF, 344

Frisch, Diane General Manager
ESPN 1490 THE FAN, 618

Frisk, Robert Assistant Managing Editor/Sports
DAILY HERALD (IL), 479

Fritch, Herbert Chair, Governor & Owner
NATIONAL HOCKEY LEAGUE/NHL, 124

Fritz, Bob Manager
PECOS LEAGUE, 50

Fritz, Carl Marketing Manager
SENECA SPORTS INC., 1198

Fritz, Douglas President
RICHMOND INTERNATIONAL RACEWAY,
1041

Fritz, Owen Sales VP
AMERICAN SEATING, 1108

Fritz, Richard Director of Events
STABLER ARENA, 1014

Fritz, Robbie Director of Instruction, PGA Certified
METHODIST COLLEGE PROFESSIONAL
GOLF MANAGEMENT PROGRAM, 102

Fritz, Ron Sports Editor
SUN (MD), 465, 515, 541

Fritz, Steve Athletic Director
ST. THOMAS UNIVERSITY ATHLETICS, 403

Fritze, Greg Vice President
KANSAS SPEEDWAY, 1036

Frizzel, Ron General Manager
WVMJ-FM, 678

Froehle, Paul VP, Ticket Operations
AMERICAN LEAGUE OF PROFESSIONAL
BASEBALL CLUBS, THE, 30

Froehlich, Bob Owner & Board of Directors
MIDWEST LEAGUE, 45

Froehlich, Cheryl Owner & Board of Directors
MIDWEST LEAGUE, 45

Froehlich, Ron President
INTERNATIONAL WORLD GAMES
ASSOCIATION/IWGA, 261

Froelich, Cezar Partner
SHEFSKY, LLOYD E., 915

Froendt, Bruce Commissioner
NATIONAL WHEELCHAIR SOFTBALL
ASSOCIATION, 167

Froggatt, Matthew Chief development Officer
TNS SPORT - NORTH AMERICA, 823

Fromer, Todd Managing Partner/Investor
Relations
KCSA PUBLIC RELATIONS WORLDWIDE, 800

Fromm, Ronald Chairman and Chief Executive
Officer
NATURAL SPORT, 1177

Frosch, Melanie Vice President, Sports and
Competition
SPECIAL OLYMPICS SOUTH DAKOTA, 195

Frost, Allen Mizzou Sports Park Facils. Mgr. -
Memori
FAUROT FIELD AT MEMORIAL STADIUM, 973

Frost, Andy Vice President
ST. LOUIS DISTRICT GOLF ASSOCIATION,
115

Frost, Brad Head Coach, Women's Hockey
MARIUCCI ARENA, 993

Frost, Mike General Manager
GREENSBORO COLISEUM COMPLEX, 977

Frost, Ray Assistant Manager for Operations
JS DORTON ARENA, 986

Frost, Rob Athletic Trainer/Equipment Manager
UNITED STATES HOCKEY LEAGUE, 137

Frost, Rufus Managing Director
AURA360 VENTURES, 782

Frost, Ryan Assistant Athletic Director
SPRING ARBOR COLLEGE ATHLETICS, 319

Frost, Shelley President/CEO
PACIFIC COLISEUM, 999

Frost, Steve Sports Information Coordinator
SIMON FRASER UNIVERSITY ATHLETICS,
371

Frost, Timothy President
FROST MOTORSPORTS, LLC., 16

Frostner, Manfred Contact
THINK TANK COMMUNICATIONS, 772

Frostrom, Karen Partner
THORSNES, BARTOLOTTA & MCGUIRE, 922

Frugoli, William Auditor
MARSHFIELD FAIR, 1050

Fry, Chris Managing Director of Corporate
CANADIAN PROFESSIONAL GOLFERS'
ASSOCIATION, 99

Fry, Doug President
WISCONSIN STATE GOLF ASSOCIATION,
116

Fry, Helen Business Operations Director
WORLD SAILING, 204

Fry, Kindra Director of Sales-Sports &
Conventions
BRYAN-COLLEGE STATION CONVENTION &
VISITORS BUREAU, SPORTS DEPT, 259

Fry, Mike Maintenance Manager
MEMPHIS MOTORSPORTS PARK (MMP),
1037

Fry, Nathan Senior Associate AD
HARVARD UNIVERSITY ATHLETICS, 331

Fry, Pat Technical Chief
FORMULA 1, 20

Frye, Darrell Finance and Administration VP
HARRISS & COVINGTON INC., 1153

Frye, Jay President
INDYCAR, 22

Frye, Whitney Associate Commissioner
NORTH CAROLINA HS ATHLETIC
ASSOCIATION, 199

Fryer, Steve Sports Reporter
ORANGE COUNTY REGISTER, 520

Fryling, Mike General Manager
TED CONSTANT CONVOCATION CENTER,
1017

Ganoe, Chris Operations Manager
CALIFORNIA LEAGUE (A-LEVEL), 36
Gansey, Mike General Manager
NATIONAL BASKETBALL ASSOCIATION
DEVELOPMENT LEAGUE, 59
Ganter, Fran Associate Athletic Director for
Football
BEAVER STADIUM, 957
Gantt, Dave Vice President Of Athletics
GREAT FALLS ATHLETICS, UNIVERSITY OF,
311
Gantt, Edgar Associate Commissioner
SOUTHWESTERN ATHLETIC CONFERENCE,
303
Ganucheau, Renee President
EVENT SPECIALIST OF NEW ORLEANS, 682
Ganz, Bo Products/Director
BO GANZ PRODUCTIONS, 604
Gapinski, Brian Editor
MIDWEST RACING NEWS, 576
Gappens, Jerry EVP/General Manager
NEW HAMPSHIRE MOTOR SPEEDWAY, 1033,
1039
Garafano, Nicole Events Director
TAGGART, WALTER J., 867
Garamella, Michael Executive Director
GARDEN STATE GAMES, 260
Garant, Trey Associate Manager
YOST ICE ARENA, 1030
Garay, Christina Building Supervisor
UTEP SPECIAL EVENTS, 1024
Garbalosa, Rudy Baseball Head Coach
LYNN UNIVERSITY, 427
Garber, Carol President
AMERICAN COLLEGE OF SPORTS
MEDICINE, 83
Garber, Don Commissioner
MAJOR LEAGUE SOCCER, 157
Garber, Jan Programs Manager
GOLF ASSOCIATION OF PHILADELPHIA, 110
Garber, Natasha Senior Editor
SPECIAL EVENTS MAGAZINE, 589
Garber, Richard Owner
ONTARIO HOCKEY LEAGUE, 134
Garbett, Mike Sports Copy Editor
TAMPA TRIBUNE, 541
Garcia, Al Vice President of Operations
HOMESTEAD-MIAMI SPEEDWAY, LLC, 1035
Garcia, Albert VP/Operations
HOMESTEAD-MIAMI SPEEDWAY, LLC, 1035
Garcia, Arthur Sports Writer (College)
FORT WORTH STAR-TELEGRAM, 491
Garcia, Danny Director Tournament Operations
RICHLIN GROUP, 769
Garcia, Debbie Executive Senior Associate
AD/SWA
TEXAS AT ARLINGTON ATHLETICS,
UNIVERSITY OF, 346
Garcia, Dinora Executive Assistant
SOUTH PADRE ISLAND CONVENTION &
VISITORS BUREAU, 244
Garcia, Erick Head Coach
WOMEN'S PREMIER SOCCER LEAGUE, 165
Garcia, Irma Director of Athletics
ST. FRANCIS COLLEGE ATHLETICS (SFC),
372
Garcia, Jaime Athletic Trainer
EAST COAST HOCKEY LEAGUE/ECHL, 129
Garcia, Jose President
MEXICAN LEAGUE A.C., 44
Garcia, Kim Director of Events
DISCOVER ORANGE BOWL, 92
Garcia, Marta Sports Editor
MUNDO HISPANICO, 513
Garcia, Patricia Sports Editor
MINIONDAS, 511
Garcia, Paul Sports Anchor/Reporter
WKOW-TV, 714
Garcia, Pete Executive Director of Sports &
Entertain
FLORIDA INTERNATIONAL UNIVERSITY
ATHLETICS, 329, 1239
Garcia, Phillip General Manager
USL LEAGUE TWO, 161
Garcia, Ralph Chief Operations Officer
5TH AND OCEAN CLOTHING, 1099
Garcia, Rick Sports Director
KTTV-TV, 696, 703

Garcia, Stephen Sports Reporter
ALICE ECHO NEWS, 462
Gard, Jeff Head Men's Basketball Coach
PIONEER FIELD, 1001
Garden, Noah Chief Revenue Officer
NATIONAL LEAGUE OF PROFESSIONAL
BASEBALL CLUBS, THE, 31
Gardener, Laura General Manager
THOROUGHBRED CLUB OF AMERICA, 77
Gardiner, Andy Sports Writer
USA TODAY, 548
Gardiner, William VP
ZORREL INTERNATIONAL, 1224
Gardner, Billy Manager
INTERNATIONAL LEAGUE, 43
Gardner, Bob Executive Director
NATIONAL FEDERATION OF STATE HIGH
SCHOOL ASSOCIATIONS, 196
Gardner, Brian VP
HO SPORTS INC., 97, 1155
Gardner, Carrie Associate Director of Athletics
CHRISTOPHER NEWPORT UNIVERSITY
ATHLETICS, 382
Gardner, Chene Chief Financial Officer
SPORTSNUTS, INC., 723
Gardner, Cheryl Athletic Department Secretary
LOCK HAVEN UNIVERSITY ATHLETICS
(LHU), 363
Gardner, Chris Marketing Director
WPRO, 669
Gardner, Dallas Board Chairman
NATIONAL HOT ROD ASSOCIATION, 1039
Gardner, Dave President & CEO
HONDA CANADA INC., 737
Gardner, Eric General Manager of Operations
CAROLINA LEAGUE, 37
Gardner, Megan Marketing Opportunities
BLALOCK COMPANY, JANE, 759
Gardner, P. Owner
KGPQ-FM, 625
Gardner, Paul Sports Reporter
NEW YORK SUN, 514
Gardner, Scott President
INTERNATIONAL HOT ROD ASSOCIATION,
17
Gardner, Susan Counsel
ARNET, WILLIAM F., 871
Gardner, Tanner Senior Associate AD/COO
RICE UNIVERSITY ATHLETICS, 342
Gardner, Tim Sales Manager
BRUTE GROUP, 712, 1121
Gardula, Peter Senior Associate Director of
Athletics
ASSUMPTION COLLEGE ATHLETICS, 352
Garelick, Amy Head Coach
WOMEN'S PREMIER SOCCER LEAGUE, 164
Garey, Rix Advertising Manager
KFDM-TV, 697
Garfield, Dana Director of Athletics
MITCHELL COLLEGE ATHLETICS, 396
Garfield, Frederick Partner
SPAIN & GILLON, LLC, 864
Garfield, Jay Head Athletic Trainer
NOTRE DAME COLLEGE ATHLETICS, 367
Garfinkel, Tom President/CEO
NATIONAL FOOTBALL LEAGUE/NFL, 96, 1016
Gargalianos, Peter Director, Field Operations
TRAKUS, INC., 940
Gargano, Jeri VP,Managing Director
ASAP SPORTS, 828
Gargiulo, Tina Event Marketing Director
NATIONAL MEDIA GROUP, INC., 805
Garibaldi, Ph.D., Antoine President
GOLDMAN, LEE, 891
Garin, Michael VP, Hospitality
CANTERBURY PARK, 1046
Garland, Bruce SVP/Racing Operations
MEADOWLANDS/NEW JERSEY SPORTS &
EXPOSITION AUTHORITY, 1074
Garland, Chad Assistant Director, Events and
Conferenc
ROSE BASKETBALL ARENA, 987, 1007
Garland, Craig Sales Manager
GEORGIA MARBLE COMPANY, 1148
Garley, Rosemary Manager
NEW MEXICO RACING COMMISSION, 81
Garlits, Don Chief Executive Officer
DON GARLITS MUSEUM OF DRAG RACING
AND INTERNATIONAL DRAG RACING H, 251

Garlock, Pete Director Of Sales
ELGIN AREA CONVENTION & VISITORS
BUREAU, 231
Garner, Andrew Sports Editor
ANDALUSIA STAR NEWS, 462
Garner, Chad Sports Editor
SENTINEL AND ENTERPRISE, 534
Garner, Darrin Manager
ARIZONA LEAGUE (ROOKIE), 35
Garner, David Chairman
NJCAA REGION XXIII WOMEN'S, 288
Garner, Gary Advertising Manager
TEMPLE DAILY TELEGRAM, 542
Garner, Lanny President
VIBRA-WHIRL & COMPANY, 1219
Garner, Mitchell President
ROAD RUNNERS CLUB OF AMERICA, 148
Garner, Sean Strength & Conditioning Coach
EAST COAST HOCKEY LEAGUE/ECHL, 130
Garnes, Michael President
NEXT LEVEL EXECUTIVE SEARCH, 756
Garnes, Michael Founder/President
NEXT LEVEL SPORTS, INC., 806
Garnhum, Shawnna Sales
SAINT JOHN DESTINATION MANAGEMENT
INC, 243
Garofalo, Robb Sports Information Director
PRESENTATION COLLEGE ATHLETICS, 317,
716
Garrard, Michael Sports Information
OREGON INSTITUTE OF TECHNOLOGY
ATHLETICS, 316
Garraway, Jay Finance/Administration Director
MOBILE BAY CONVENTION & VISITORS
BUREAU, 240
Garretson, Jeff General Manager
YAKIMA COUNTY STADIUM, 1030
Garrett, Brad Assistant Executive Director
OREGON SCHOOL ACTIVITIES
ASSOCIATION, 200
Garrett, Daniel Assistant Director of
Intercollegiate At
CALIFORNIA STATE UNIVERSITY-LOS
ANGELES ATHLETICS, 354
Garrett, Dr. Senior Associate AD/Sport Admin.
and Sup
RICE STADIUM, 1005
Garrett, Greg Sports Host
WSHW-FM, 673
Garrett, Jim Advertising Manager
LAWTON CONSTITUTION, 228, 505
Garrett, Kevin Director of Athletics
CONCORD UNIVERSITY ATHLETICS, 356
Garrett, Mary Director Marketing/Communications
NORFOLK CONVENTION & VISITORS
BUREAU, 240
Garrett, Matt Sport Management Coordinator
LORAS COLLEGE, 426
Garrett, Norb Editorial Director
TENNIS, 594
Garrett, Salina Financial Analyst
KNOXVILLE CIVIC AUDITORIUM/COLISEUM,
988
Garrett, Scott Director of Athletics
CLEVELAND STATE UNIVERSITY
ATHLETICS, 326, 555, 958
Garrett, Todd Director of Athletics
MIDAMERICA NAZARENE UNIVERSITY
ATHLETICS, 315
Garrettt, Scott President, Advertising Sales
ATHLON SPORTS COMMUNICATIONS, 555
Garrick, Kelly Director of Sports and Competition
SPECIAL OLYMPICS SOUTH CAROLINA, 195
Garriett, Robbie Coordinator of Administrative
Services
QUEENS UNIVERSITY OF CHARLOTTE, 369
Garrigan, Mike anchor
WIFR-TV, 712
Garrigus, R.L. News Director
KICE-AM, 626
Garrioch, Bruce Contributing Writer
RINKSIDE, 584
Garrison, Carri Association Director
WESTERN WINTER SPORTS
REPRESENTATIVES ASSOCIATION, 224
Garrison, David Chairman/Chief Executive Officer
VERESTAR, 695
Garrison, Jay Sports Director
WHBU-AM, 656

Gilmore, Louis Director of Business Developmetn
RICHMOND INTERNATIONAL RACEWAY,
1041

Gilmore, Steward Director
SOUTHERN ILLINOIS GOLF ASSOCIATION,
115

Gilner, Brian Operations Manager
BB&T CENTER, 957

Gilpin, James Head Coach
USL LEAGUE TWO, 161

Gilroy, Maureen Marketing Director
IEG SPONSORSHIP SOURCEBOOK, 601

Gilson, Rick Vice-Presdient
ALBERTA SCHOOLS' ATHLETIC
ASSOCIATION, 197

Gilula, Jonathan Executive VP/COO
AMERICAN LEAGUE OF PROFESSIONAL
BASEBALL CLUBS, THE, 29

Gimblette, Peter Marketing Manager
WOFX-AM, 667

Gimelstob, Justin Player Representative
ATP WORLD TOUR, 171

Gines, D. Vice President of Intercollegiate Athlet
TEXAS A&M UNIVERSITY-KINGSVILLE
ATHLETICS, 373

Gines, Scott Director of Athletics
DELAWARE STATE UNIVERSITY ATHLETICS,
327, 417

Gingerich, Amanda Junior Golf Director
WESTERN NEW YORK PGA SECTION
OFFICE, 107

Gingras, Gerard Athletic Trainer
NJCAA REGION III WOMEN'S, 285

Gingrich, Laura Associate Athletic Director
ALVERNIA UNIVERSITY
ATHLETICS-READING, 377

Ginn, Jeff Head Coach
WOMEN'S PREMIER SOCCER LEAGUE, 166

Ginn, Leighton Sports Reporter
DESERT SUN, 486

Ginnane, Dawn Advertising Director
ST. AUGUSTINE RECORD, 538

Ginolfi, Frank Chief Financial Officer
GENERAL SPORTCRAFT COMPANY, LTD.,
1147

Ginsberg, Adam Advertising Manager
MUSCULAR DEVELOPMENT, 577

Ginter, William Chairman of the Board
ALL-AMERICAN SOAP BOX DERBY, 264

Ginty, Maureen Executive VP
SMG, 769, 1075

Gioglio, Tom Director of Athletics
LOCK HAVEN UNIVERSITY ATHLETICS
(LHU), 363

Gioia, Horace Attorney
SULLIVAN OLIVARIO & GIOIA LLP, 919

Giombetti, Gary Sports Editor
HIBBING DAILY TRIBUNE, 497

Gionfriddo, Michael VP
QUABAUG CORPORATION, 1190

Giordano, P. Managing Editor
GOLD SHEET, 566

Giordano, Paul Communications Manager
METROPOLITAN PROFESSIONAL GOLFERS
ASSOCIATION, 105

Giorgio, Michael Co-Owner, Agent
NATIONAL SPORTS MANAGEMENT INC., 854

Giorgio, Tony Marketing Specialist
NATIONAL SPORTS MANAGEMENT INC., 854

Giorno, John President
STERLING TROPHIES, INC., 1208

Giotto, Thomas Executive Shareholder
GURWIN, DAVID A., 845

Giovanis, Ted Owner
IMSA MICHELIN PILOT CHALLENGE, 20

Gipson, Lynn Executive Director
AMATEUR TRAPSHOOTING ASSOCIATION,
149

Giraldo, Rene Host
BOXEO TELEMUNDO, 690

Giraldo, Sebastian Head Coach
USL LEAGUE TWO, 161

Girard, Gary Operations Director
MILWAUKEE MILE, 1038

Girardin, Steve President and CEO
BLUE BIRD CORPORATION, 935

Giraud, Jose General Manager
WUPR-AM, 677

Girdwood, Anna Director of Compliance
LINDENWOOD UNIVERSITY ATHLETICS, 363

Girdy, Harvey CEO
INTERNATIONAL SEAWAY TRADING
CORPORATION, 1159

Girod, Doug Executive Vice Chancellor
POTTORFF, JAMES P. JR., 909

Girolamo, Carol Assistant Athletic Director
DELAWARE VALLEY COLLEGE(DVC)
ATHLETICS, 384

Girouard, Eric Director, Stadium Operations
STADE SAPUTO, 1014

Giroux, Avery Box Office Manager
GLENS FALLS CIVIC CENTER, 977

Girsch, Mike VP/General Manager
NATIONAL LEAGUE OF PROFESSIONAL
BASEBALL CLUBS, THE, 33

Girvan, Joe Sports Director
WCJB-TV, 709

Gisclair, Jerry Owner
KLEB-AM, 629

Gisel, Brian Ultimate Committee Chair
WORLD FLYING DISC FEDERATION, 98

Gisel, Jr., William Vice President/Secretary
INTERNATIONAL LEAGUE, 42

Gissune, Neille Sports Director
WENY-TV, 710

Gitcheva, Sashka Program Coordinator
BRITISH COLUMBIA RHYTHMIC SPORTIVE
GYMNASTICS FEDERATION, 119

Gitelman, Ellen President
AMERICAN GRAPHITI, 758

Gittel, Tim Vice President - Business Operations
TRI-CITIES STADIUM, 1019

Giudice, Michael Sr .M.D
AQUEDUCT, 1051

Giudicessi, Michael Corporate Secretary
PACIFIC COAST LEAGUE OF
PROFESSIONAL BASEBALL CLUBS, 49, 1010

Giugliano, Rick Director, Marketing & Events
NATIONAL FOOTBALL LEAGUE/NFL, 97

Giulio, Kelly-Ann Director of Sports Information
DOMINICAN COLLEGE (DC) ATHLETICS, 357

Giunta, Joe Director of Athletics
DICKINSON COLLEGE(DC) ATHLETICS, 384

Giusto, Stephen Executive Vice President/Chief
Financial
KORN/FERRY INTERNATIONAL, 756

Give, Rich Sports Editor
HANFORD SENTINEL, 495

Givens, Jim Associate Athletic Director
UNIVERSITY OF FINDLAY (UF) ATHLETICS,
359

Giza, Anna Promotion Manager
WWLP-TV, 720

Gladchuk, Chet Director of Athletics
U.S. NAVAL ACADEMY ATHLETICS, 347, 997

Gladchuk, John Senior Associate AD, External
Affairs
NEVADA AT LAS VEGAS ATHLETICS,
UNIVERSITY OF, 338

Gladden, Robert Vice President
MOTORCYCLE SAFETY FOUNDATION, 144

Gladstone, James Director, Scouting Strategy
NATIONAL FOOTBALL LEAGUE/NFL, 96

Gladstone, Sandra VP Operations
TITANIUM SPORTS TECHNOLOGIES, 1213

Gladstone, William President, Principal Owner
NEW YORK-PENNSYLVANIA LEAGUE, 47,
986

Glanton, Val Senior Event Manager
JACKSONVILLE VETERANS MEMORIAL
ARENA, 983

Glas, Rich Athletic Director
CONCORDIA COLLEGE (MN) ATHLETICS, 383

Glasco, Misty Marketing & Events Specialist
BAKERSFIELD CONVENTION & VISITORS
BUREAU, GREATER, 226

Glaser, Charles 2nd Vice President
AMERICAN BLIND BOWLING ASSOCIATION,
65

Glaser, Daniel Director
MARSH & MCLENNAN, 777

Glaser, Mark Sr. Vice President, Operations
CONTEMPORARY SERVICES
CORPORATION, 774

Glaser, Mark Shareholder
GREENBERG TRAURIG, LLP, 892

Glaser, Scott Senior Associate Director of
Athletics/F
USF SOCCER STADIUM, 1004, 1023

Glasgow, Dennis Program Director
SPORTS RADIO 1080 THE FAN/KFXX, 641

Glasgow, Travis Senior Associate AD
KENNESAW STATE UNIVERSITY ATHLETICS,
333

Glasier, Bruce Sports Director
WCSH-TV, 709

Glass, Anne Human Resources Director
GLASS ARCHITECTS, 1067

Glass, Dan Director Stadium Operations
KAUFFMAN STADIUM, 987

Glass, David Executive Committee Chairman of
the Boar
WAL-MART STORES, INC., 1252

Glass, Eric Head Coach
NATIONAL BASKETBALL ASSOCIATION
DEVELOPMENT LEAGUE, 60, 1067

Glass, Fred Vice President & Director of Athletics
MEMORIAL STADIUM (INDIANA), 995

Glass, Jim Promotions Director
WFAA-TV, 710

Glass, Robert News Director
WFFC-FM, 653

Glass, Stephen Head Coach
USL CHAMPIONSHIP, 158

Glasscox, Austin Director of Fan Development
GRAYSON STADIUM, 977

Glassman, Michael Sales / Marketing VP
SPORTS SUPPLY GROUP, 1205

Glassman, Stuart EVP
WOLF GROUP-OH, 826

Glatczak, Adam Sports Information Director
LAKELAND COLLEGE ATHLETICS, 304, 391

Glauber, Bob Sports Columnist (NFL)
NEWSDAY, 517

Glauberman, Nancy Senior Vice President,
Business Developm
SHOWTIME SPORTS, 686

Glavin, Tony Owner/President/Head Coach
USL LEAGUE TWO, 163

Glavine, Mike Head Coach, Baseball
PARSONS FIELD/FRIEDMAN DIAMOND, 999

Glazer, Bryan Owner/Chairman
NATIONAL FOOTBALL LEAGUE/NFL, 97

Glazer, Michael President and Chief Executive
Officer
STAGE STORES, INC., 1250

Glazer, Steven Of Counsel
RUBENSTEIN, MARK A., 913

Gleason, Brian Administrative Assistant
GOLDEN STATE ATHLETIC CONFERENCE,
294

Gleason, Bucky Sports Writer
BUFFALO NEWS, 469

Gleason, Cheryl Assistant Executive Director
KANSAS STATE HS ACTIVITIES
ASSOCIATION, 198

Gleason, Dan Contributing Editor
GOLF PRODUCT NEWS, 567

Gleason, John Manager of Field Services
MATEFLEX-MELE CORPORATION, 1171

Gleason, Josh Athletic Director
GOSHEN COLLEGE ATHLETICS, 311

Gleason, Kevin Sports Columnist
TIMES HERALD RECORD, 544

Gleason, Mike Advertising Manager
CINCINNATI POST, 473

Gleason, Sean Chief Executive Officer
PROFESSIONAL BULL RIDERS (PBR), 146

Gleason, Tim Commissioner
OHIO ATHLETIC CONFERENCE, 300

Glebe, Dustin Coordinator
RIEDELL SHOES, INC., 1193

Gleckel, Leonard Vice President
CROWN TROPHY COMPANY, 1235

Gledhill, Judy Accounts Receivable
LAFAYETTE INSTRUMENT COMPANY, 1165

Gleiser, Paul Owner
KEES-AM, 623

Gleisner, Don President
ALL AMERICAN SPORTS CORP/RIDDELL ALL
AMERICAN, 1105

Glendinning, Stewart CEO
DENVER, UNIVERSITY OF, 418

Glenn, Bob President
ATHENS STATE COLLEGE ATHLETICS, 306

AMERICAN LEAGUE OF PROFESSIONAL
BASEBALL CLUBS, THE, 30
Goldberg, Mark Publisher
TRAINING AND CONDITIONING, 555, 561, 595
Goldberg, Michael Chief Executive Officer
NATIONAL MEDIA GROUP, INC., 805
Goldberg, Stan Sports Editor
FREDERICK NEWS-POST, 492
Goldberg, Steve Sports Producer
WBBM-TV, 708
Goldblatt, Dan President
FIRST SERVICE, 1143
Golden, Andrew Advertising Manager
SPEEDHORSE-THE RACING REPORT, 589
Golden, Brian Sports Writer
ANTELOPE VALLEY PRESS, 463
Golden, Connie Publisher
SPEEDHORSE-THE RACING REPORT, 589
Golden, Matt Managing Partner
REESE SPORTS, 814
Golden, Patricia VP/Dir Sls
WMAQ TV CHICAGO, 715
Golden, Peter
IMS SPORTS, 847
Golden, Todd Sports Editor
TRIBUNE-STAR, 546
Goldfarb, Evan EVP, Media Services
SIMMONS MARKET RESEARCH
BUREAU/SMRB, 816
Goldfarb, Jeffrey Director of Strategic Planning
G III SPORTS, 1146
Goldfarb, Morris Chief Executive Officer /
Chairman
G III SPORTS, 1146
Goldie, Leigh President
CANADIAN COLLEGIATE ATHLETIC
ASSOCIATION, 281
Golding, Peter Deputy President
BADMINTON PAN AM, 25
Goldklang, Jeff President
NEW YORK-PENNSYLVANIA LEAGUE, 47,
971
Goldklang, Marv Principal Owner
FLORIDA STATE LEAGUE, 40
Goldklang, Marvin Chairman
SOUTH ATLANTIC LEAGUE, 51, 986
Goldman, Andrew President & Alternate
Governor
UNITED STATES HOCKEY LEAGUE, 137
Goldman, Christie Business Development
Executive
CLARK ENTERPRISES, 1062
Goldman, Harvery President/Chief Operating
Officer
SH GROUP, 1071
Goldman, Larry Director Of Product Marketing
EMS SOFTWARE, LCC, 1225
Goldman, Lee Law Professor
GOLDMAN, LEE, 891
Goldman, Mark Chairman
EASTPAK CORPORATION, 1138
Goldman, Richard Executive Director
ST. AUGUSTINE, PONTE VEDRA & THE
BEACHES VISITORS & CONVENTION BU, 245
Goldman, Ron Executive Director
ST. AUGUSTINE, PONTE VEDRA & THE
BEACHES VISITORS & CONVENTION BU, 245
Goldman, Shari Marketing Assistant
BOSE CORPORATION, 828
Goldman, Stuart Sports Editor
EMPORIA GAZETTE, 489
Goldmeier, Allen President
RAND INTERNATIONAL, 1191
Goldmeier, Steven VP
RAND INTERNATIONAL, 1191
Goldner, Lindsay Director, Communications &
Marketing
NATIONAL WOMEN'S SOCCER LEAGUE, 158
Goldner, Lisa Co-Chair Environmental Law
BOSE MCKINNEY & EVANS LLP, 876
Goldscher, Eric Client Services Director
AQUARIUS SPORTS AND ENTERTAINMENT,
781
Goldscher, Jeff Executive VP, Marketing &
Creative
AQUARIUS SPORTS AND ENTERTAINMENT,
781
Goldsen, Bruce Owner
WIBM-AM, 657

Goldsmith, Nicholas Senior Principal
FTL DESIGN ENGINEERING STUDIO, 1067
Goldsmith, Sammy Accounts Payable
SPIKE TV, 685
Goldstein, David COO
CANADIAN FOOTBALL LEAGUE/CFL, 93
Goldstein, Eric Sports Editor
BRIDGETON NEWS, 468
Goldstein, Jay Editor
MARYLAND SOCCER NEWS, 575
Goldstein, Kevin Special Asst. General Manager,
Player Pe
AMERICAN LEAGUE OF PROFESSIONAL
BASEBALL CLUBS, THE, 30
Goldstein, Roger Principal
GOODY CLANCY, 1067
Goldstein, Steven President
CADAC AMERICA, 1233
Goldsticker, Julie Editor
BOXING USA, 559
Goldston, Maile Receptionist
USA/BMX, THE AMERICAN BICYCLE
ASSOCIATION, 71
Golebie, Katherine Assistant Director of Athletics
LA ROCHE COLLEGE ATHLETICS (LRC), 391
Golic, Mike Sports Host
KMVP-AM, 615, 631
Golisch, Paul Dean of Information Technology
NJCAA REGION I MEN'S, 284
Goll, Scott Editor
SPORTSWIRE/BUSINESS WIRE, 723
Gollnick, Scott VP Sales/Marketing
OT SPORTS, 1183
Golner, Ken Director for Communications
CURRY COLLEGE ATHLETICS, 383
Gologader, Stan SVP Operations
TRUE FITNESS TECHNOLOGY, 1215
Goltermann, Chris VP
ST. LOUIS BRAID COMPANY, 1206
Goltermann, Thomas President
ST. LOUIS BRAID COMPANY, 1206
Golub, Mike SVP-Marketing and Business
Operations
JEANNIE BAUMGARTNER, 896
Gombau, Josep Head Coach & Sporting Director
USL CHAMPIONSHIP, 159
Gomes, Charles Director of Athletics
STATEN ISLAND ATHLETICS, COLLEGE OF
(CSI), 404
Gomes, Joe Director of Communications
ACUSHNET COMPANY, 1102
Gomez, David HPER Instructor
ALCORN STATE UNIVERSITY, 411
Gomez, Glen News Director
KJIN-AM, 627
Gomez, Marcelo Executive Vice President
INTERNATIONAL RACQUETBALL
FEDERATION (IRF), 145
Gomez, Mark Sports Reporter
SAN JOSE MERCURY NEWS, 533
Gomez, Rick EVP, Chief Marketing Officer
TARGET STORES, 742
Gomez, Yvonne Advertising Director
DAILY TIMES (NM), 483
Gomont, Christine Accounting
SHOWPROCO, LLC, 769
Gompertz, Mark SVP Video Services
POWER IMAGES, 810
Gomric, Steve General Manager
FRONTIER LEAGUE, 41, 976
Gondek, Chris Director of Athletic
Communications
HARTWICK COLLEGE ATHLETICS, 388
Gonnella, Nick Sports Editor
GREENSBURG DAILY NEWS, 494
Gonsalves, Gregg Chairman
JACKIE ROBINSON FOUNDATION, 189
Gonyea, Greg Customer Sales Manager
ALPHA RACQUET SPORTS, 1106
Gonzales, Frank Manager
NORTHWEST BASEBALL LEAGUE, 48
Gonzales, Mark Sports Reporter
CHICAGO TRIBUNE, 472
Gonzalez, David Director of Sports Medicine
LEHMAN COLLEGE ATHLETICS, 392
Gonzalez, Dianne Busines Manager/Florida
Operations
JACK RUSSELL MEMORIAL STADIUM, 983

Gonzalez, Dr. The Provost
COLE, DAYTON T., 882
Gonzalez, Drew Vice President
CAPE FEAR RUGBY FOOTBALL CLUB, 147
Gonzalez, Elysa Svp Marketing
ACTIVE INTERNATIONAL, 774
Gonzalez, Isabel Administrative Coordinator
CAL STATE UNIVERSITY - BAKERSFIELD,
SCHOOL OF BUSINESS AND PUBLIC, 414
Gonzalez, Jimmy Team Manager
MIDWEST LEAGUE, 46
Gonzalez, Junior Head Coach
USL CHAMPIONSHIP, 159
Gonzalez, Lori Provost & Executive Vice
Chancellor
COLE, DAYTON T., 882
Gonzalez, Luichi Head Coach
MAJOR LEAGUE SOCCER, 157
Gonzalez, Mark Sales Manager
ALPHA RACQUET SPORTS, 1106
Gonzalez, Mercedes CFO
FTL DESIGN ENGINEERING STUDIO, 1067
Gonzalez, Michelle Administrative Assistant
CORPUS CHRISTI GREYHOUND RACE
TRACK, 1055
Gonzalez, Oscar Sports Editor
MONITOR, 511
Gonzalez, Ralph Vice President
SOUTH JERSEY GOLF ASSOCIATION, 114
Gonzalez, Trina Executive Assistant to General
Manager
SOLANO COUNTY FAIRGROUNDS, 1053
Gonzalez, Victor Manager, Florida Operations
AMERICAN LEAGUE OF PROFESSIONAL
BASEBALL CLUBS, THE, 30
Gooby, Trevor Senior Director of Florida
Operations
FLORIDA STATE LEAGUE, 30, 39
Gooch, David VP
POWERS EMBROIDERY/ CHENILLE, INC.,
USA, 1187
Good, Dan VP, Business Development
NATIONAL LEAGUE OF PROFESSIONAL
BASEBALL CLUBS, THE, 33
Good, David Sports Editor
BERWYN-CICERO-STICKNEY-FOREST VIEW
LIFE, 467
Good, Julie Secretary
AMERICAN MINIATURE HORSE
ASSOCIATION, 74
Good, Stephen Managing Partner
ADKINS, M. DOUGLAS, 870
Goodale, Brad Director of Group Sales
LYNCHBURG CITY STADIUM, 993
Goodall, Bryan Assistant Athletics Director, Ticket
Ope
HANCOCK STADIUM, 977
Goodall, Cricket Executive Director
MARYLAND MILLION, 77
Goodboe, Dr. Vp Human Resources/Corporate
Learning Of
WACKENHUT SPORTS SECURITY, 774
Goodbread, Bill National Sales Manager
ALTUS ATHLETIC MFG. COMPANY, 1106
Goode, Cindy News Director
KDBS-AM, 622
Goode, David President
GOODE SKI TECHNOLOGIES, 1150
Goode, Nancy Vice President ofFinance &
Administrati
DES MOINES CONVENTION & VISITORS
BUREAU, GREATER, 230
Goode, Scott Assistant Athletic Director, Sports
Info
HARDING UNIVERSITY ATHLETICS, 360
Goodell, Chris General Manager
COPELAND PARK, 968
Goodell, Roger EVP/Chief Operating Officer
NFL BUSINESS VENTURES, 89, 94, 807
Goodenough, Kathy On Air Presentation
Manager
FOX SPORTS NET ARIZONA, 682
Gooding, Carl Station Manager
WDOG-FM, 650
Goodman, Andrew Owner
GARVEY, SCHUBERT & BARER, 891
Goodman, Douglas President
BIOLIFE, LLC, 1117

executive index

Hafner, Robert SVP, Marketing / Business
PAMIDA, INC., 1246
Haft, Chris Sports Reporter
SAN JOSE MERCURY NEWS, 533
Hagale, James CEO/President
BASS PRO SHOPS, 1115, 1229
Hagan, Chris Sports Broadcaster
FOX 59 OVERTIME, 687
Hagan, Jeff Chief Operating Officer
AMERICAN HOCKEY LEAGUE/AHL, 128
Hagan, Rob Senior Associate AD, Student-Athlete
Wel
VILLANOVA UNIVERSITY ATHLETICS, 348
Hagel, Scott Senior VP, Marketing &
Communications
NATIONAL FOOTBALL LEAGUE/NFL, 95
Hagen, Brian Associate General Manager
NATIONAL BASKETBALL ASSOCIATION/NBA,
56, 619
Hagen, Dan Head Athletic Trainer
ST. OLAF COLLEGE ATHLETICS, 403
Hagen, Erin Assoc. AD, Admin. & Strategic
Inits./SWA
LIBERTY UNIVERSITY ATHLETICS, 334
Hagen, Mike Asst. Commissioner for Compliance
ATLANTIC SUN CONFERENCE, 289
Hagen, Paul National Baseball Reporter
PHILADELPHIA DAILY NEWS, 523
Hager, Brent Associate Commissioner for
External Oper
WEST VIRGINIA INTERCOLLEGIATE
ATHLETIC CONFERENCE, 305
Hager, Cyndi Administrative Assistant
NORTH AMERICAN HOCKEY LEAGUE, 131
Hager, Michael Vice President for Administration
& Fina
UNI-DOME, 1021
Hager, Tom Associate Athletics Director
UNIVERSITY OF JAMESTOWN ATHLETICS,
321
Hagerman, Scott Sports Editor
OWENSBORO MESSENGER-INQUIRER, 521
Hagerty, Ed Editor
RUGBY, 585
Hagerty, Edward Publisher
RUGBY, 585
Hages, Roger Retail Advertising Manager
MACOMB DAILY, 507
Hagg, Janice Administrative Assistant
NATIONAL TRAIL RACEWAY, 1039
Haggerty, David President
PENN RACQUET SPORTS, 171, 203, 1184
Haglof, Jon Sports Editor
MIDDLEBORO GAZETTE, 510
Hagstrom, Chris Director of Creative Services
and Promot
MIDWEST LEAGUE, 46
Hague, Des President and Chief Executive Officer
CENTERPLATE, 1074, 1076
Hague, Jim Sports Reporter
STAR-LEDGER, 539
Hahn, Aaron Vice President, Assistant GM
MIDWEST LEAGUE, 46, 975
Hahn, Chris President/CEO
SPECIAL OLYMPICS KANSAS, 193
Hahn, Cindy Director of Compliance
OHIO DOMINICAN UNIVERSITY ATHLETICS,
316
Hahn, Ernie General Manager
VALLEY VIEW CASINO CENTER, 1024
Hahn, Kevin Executive Vice President of
Sales/Market
PROFESSIONAL SPORTS PUBLICATIONS,
583
Hahn, Rich Operations Director
BOOMER ESIASON FOUNDATION, 189
Hahn, Rick Senior VP/General Manager
AMERICAN LEAGUE OF PROFESSIONAL
BASEBALL CLUBS, THE, 29
Hahn, Sandy President
PERFECTION EQUIPMENT, INC., 1077
Hahs, Chris Sales Executive
SUCCESS PROMOTIONS, 821
Haider, Colleen Secretary
YOUTH BOWL CANADA, 67
Haidet, Doug Sports Editor
ASHLAND TIMES-GAZETTE, 464
Haile, Jr., Robert Lawyer
HAILE, SHAW & PFAFFENBERGER, P.A., 892

Hailey, Terry News Director
WTPR-AM, 643, 652, 676
Haines, Andy Manager
PACIFIC COAST LEAGUE OF
PROFESSIONAL BASEBALL CLUBS, 49
Haines, Dana Head Athletic Trainer
LIFE PACIFIC COLLEGE ATHLETICS, 362
Haines, Johny Vice-Chairman
NFL ALUMNI ASSOCIATION, 89
Haines, Ken President & CEO
RAYCOM SPORTS, 813
Haines, Kyle Director, Player Development
NATIONAL LEAGUE OF PROFESSIONAL
BASEBALL CLUBS, THE, 32
Haines, Sylvia Secretary-Treasurer
HAMPTON ROADS SPORTS COMMISSION,
234
Hains, Art Sports Director
KWTO-FM, 639
Hairopoulos, Kate Sports Reporter
DALLAS MORNING NEWS, 483
Hairston, Carl Associate AD, External Affairs
NORTH CAROLINA A&T STATE UNIVERSITY
ATHLETICS, 339
Haisten, Bill Sports Reporter
TULSA WORLD, 547
Hajdu, Amanda Director of Academic Services
UNIVERSITY OF NORTH DAKOTA (UND), 367
Hajdu, Jayson Director of Media Relations
UNIVERSITY OF NORTH DAKOTA (UND), 367
Hajdu, Zsolt Head Athletics Trainer
STATE UNIVERSITY OF NEW YORK
COLLEGE AT OLD WESTBURY
ATHLETICS(SU, 404
Hajt, Chris Assistant Coach
AMERICAN HOCKEY LEAGUE/AHL, 127
Haken, Matt Director of Sports Marketing
FOX CITIES CONVENTION AND VISITORS
BUREAU, 232
Haker, Catherine Director of Athletics
COLLEGE OF SAINT ROSE ATHLETICS, 370
Hakim, Allen Publisher
AMERICAN TURF MONTHLY, 555
Hakins, Dave Executive Director
VERMONT SPORTS & EVENTS COUNCIL, 248
Haklin, Joe Director Of Athletics
INTERCOLLEGIATE OFFICIATING
ASSOCIATION, 281
Haklin, Joseph Director of Athletics
WABASH COLLEGE ATHLETICS, 407
Halbert, Jay Chief Financial Officer/General
Counsel
VENUE 1, 832
Halbleib, Greg Sports Director
WJBC, 659
Hald, Patrick President/COO
NORDICTRACK, 1180
Halden, Chris League Commissioner
USA BANDY, 25
Hale, Alan Operations Manager/R&D
PERFECTION EQUIPMENT, INC., 1077
Hale, Brian ESPN Manager
WCCW-AM, 647
Hale, George Program/Sports Director
WABI-AM, 642
Hale, Mark Sports Reporter
NEW YORK POST, 514
Hale, Michael Sports Director
WSYY-AM, 675
Hale, Paula President & CEO
USTA SOUTHERN, 173
Hale, Steve President/CEO
SENIOR BOWL, 93
Hale, Terri Advertising Director
BLUEFIELD DAILY TELEGRAPH, 467
Hale Boggs , Jr., Thomas Chairman
PATTON BOGGS, 908
Halem, Dan Chief Legal Officer & Deputy
Commissione
NATIONAL LEAGUE OF PROFESSIONAL
BASEBALL CLUBS, THE, 27, 29, 31
Hales, Ben Senior VP/Chief Operating Officer
NATIONAL FOOTBALL LEAGUE/NFL, 96
Haleski, Joe General Partner/Chairman/Governor
EAST COAST HOCKEY LEAGUE/ECHL, 130
Haley, Ellen Public Relations
MAIN EVENTS, 806, 850
Haley, Mary Managing Editor
MUSHING MAGAZINE, 578

Haley, Robert President / Director
SPORT HALEY INC., 1204
Haley, Taitano Associate AD, External
Relations/SWA
NORTHWESTERN STATE UNIVERSITY OF
LOUISIANA ATHLETICS, 340
Halferty, Liam Director of Athletics
Communications
CENTRE COLLEGE ATHLETICS, 381
Halfpenny, Laura Executive Director
GEORGIA SOCCER, 154
Haliburton, Ronnie Associate Athletic Director
TIGER STADIUM, 954, 1019
Halkett, Ryan Senior VP, Game Presentation
NATIONAL HOCKEY LEAGUE/NHL, 124
Hall, Andy President/CEO
STAGE STORES, INC., 1250
Hall, Ann VP Humann resources& Administration
DEL MAR THOROUGHBRED CLUB, 1046
Hall, April Volleyball Head Coach
WESTERN ILLINOIS UNIVERSITY, 440
Hall, Becky Director of Athletics
OGLETHORPE UNIVERSITY ATHLETICS, 398
Hall, Bill Secretary
USA HOCKEY, 207
Hall, Caitlin Athletic Trainer
NATIONAL PRO FASTPITCH, 168
Hall, Carl Director of Arena Management
RUPP ARENA, 1008
Hall, Chuck Advertising/General Manager
WLRT-AM, 663
Hall, Courtney Associate AD, Business
Administration
CHARLESTON SOUTHERN UNIVERSITY
ATHLETICS, 325
Hall, Dana Senior Associate Director of Athletics
MARY WASHINGTON UNIVERSITY
ATHLETICS, 394
Hall, Danielle Assistant Athletics Director for
Operati
CROWN COLLEGE ATHLETICS, 309
Hall, Dave Sports Anchor
KVVU-TV, 705
Hall, David Senior Associate AD, Compliance
FRESNO STATE ATHLETICS, 330
Hall, David Vice President
ADP LEMCO, INC., 1103
Hall, Dennis Sports Assistant Editor
DALLAS MORNING NEWS, 483
Hall, Derrick CEO/President
NATIONAL LEAGUE OF PROFESSIONAL
BASEBALL CLUBS, THE, 31
Hall, Donna Senior Vice President Marketing &
Client
COX MEDIA GROUP, 610
Hall, Dwight Director of Baseball Operations
PACIFIC COAST LEAGUE OF
PROFESSIONAL BASEBALL CLUBS (AAA
LEVEL), 48
Hall, Elizabeth Manager of Sales & Events
WORLD GOLF VILLAGE, 118
Hall, Floyd Owner and Chairman
FRONTIER LEAGUE, 41, 1030
Hall, Grant Host
SPORTS LINE LIVE, 688
Hall, Gwen Sr Vice President, Academic
Operations O
AMERICAN MILITARY UNIVERSITY, 411
Hall, Jamie Assistant AD, Academic Services
NORTHEASTERN STATE UNIVERSITY
ATHLETICS, 340
Hall, Jay Senior Director of Business Affairs
NATIONAL SENIOR GAMES ASSOCIATION,
221
Hall, Jerry Partner
BROWN, HALL, SHORE & MCKINLEY LLP,
877
Hall, Jim Director of Athletics & Recreation
SPRING HILL COLLEGE ATHLETICS, 129, 319
Hall, Jon Director of Athletics
UNIVERSITY OF SOUTHERN INDIANA
ATHLETICS, 371
Hall, Julie Assistant Athletic Director
ELMHURST COLLEGE ATHLETICS, 385
Hall, Keith President
UNITED TURF, INC., 1037, 1217
Hall, Kevin Women's Basketball Coach
OCCIDENTAL COLLEGE ATHLETICS, 373,
398, 698

Hammann, Gregg President and Chief Executive Officer
NAUTILUS HPS, INC., 1177

Hammaren, Greg Vice President/General Manager
FOX SPORTS NET DETROIT, 682

Hammeke, Curtis Athletic Director
FORT HAYS STATE UNIVERSITY ATHLETICS (FHSU), 359

Hammel, Bruce Sports Copy Editor
SAN JOSE MERCURY NEWS, 533

Hammel, Dave Principal
BARKER RINKER SEACAT ARCHITECTURE, 1059

Hammel, Steve Vice President/GM, WRAL-TV
CAPITOL SPORTS NETWORK, 693

Hammel, Teri Director of Sales & Finance
DECATUR AREA CONVENTION & VISITORS BUREAU, 230

Hammer, Alison Assistant Director of Athletics, Sports
UNIVERSITY OF DISTRICT OF COLUMBIA ATHLETICS, 357

Hammer, Bonnie Chairman
USA NETWORK, 685

Hammer, Dick Sports Director
WEST-AM, 652

Hammer, Kelly Program Director
KBER-FM, 620

Hammer, Lee Program Director
KNBR RADIO, 631

Hammer, Matt Athletic Director/Men's Basketball Coach
NJCAA REGION IX MEN'S, 285

Hammerstrom, Art Account Executive
MURPHY & ORR EXHIBITS, 804

Hammes, Dan Deputy Commissioner
IOWA INTERCOLLEGIATE ATHLETIC CONFERENCE, 295

Hammill, Ryan Sports Reporter
ORANGE COUNTY REGISTER, 520

Hammock, David General Manager
KMUN-FM, 631

Hammock, Robby Manager
SOUTHERN LEAGUE OF PROFESSIONAL BASEBALL CLUBS, 53

Hammock, Will Sports Editor
GWINNETT DAILY POST, 495

Hammond, Curt Vice President
PACIFIC NORTHWEST SKI ASSOCIATION, 152

Hammond, Emmett Vice President/Secretary/Treasurer
PACIFIC COAST LEAGUE OF PROFESSIONAL BASEBALL CLUBS, 48

Hammond, Eric Sports Copy Editor
BISMARCK TRIBUNE, 467

Hammond, Evan Editorial Director
BLOODHORSE MAGAZINE, 75

Hammond, Harvey Executive Chairman
HNTB CORP., 1070

Hammond, Jeff Athletics Director
PETE TAYLOR BASEBALL PARK, 1000

Hammond, John General Manager
NATIONAL BASKETBALL ASSOCIATION/NBA, 58, 849

Hammond, Matt Sports Editor
BELLEFONTAINE EXAMINER, 466

Hammond, Paul Assistant Athletic Director/Facilities O
JAMES A. RHODES ARENA, 983

Hammond, Phyllis VP Public Relations
DALLAS CONVENTION & VISITORS BUREAU, 230

Hammond, Robert Sports Editor
LARAMIE DAILY BOOMERANG, 504

Hammond, Seth Vice President
WESTERN RACING ASSOCIATION, 19

Hammond, Tiffany Head Athletic Trainer
INDIANA UNIVERSITY SOUTHEAST ATHLETICS, 312

Hammond, Troy President
NORTH CENTRAL COLLEGE ATHLETICS, 397

Hammond-Graf, Jessica Deputy AD/SWA
MARYLAND-BALTIMORE COUNTY ATHLETICS, UNIVERSITY OF, 336

Hammons, Randy Sports Editor
LAUREL LEADER-CALL, 505

Hamp, Sheila Owner/Chair
NATIONAL FOOTBALL LEAGUE/NFL, 95

Hampel, Phil Independent Director
UNITED STATES SOO BAHK DO FEDERATION, 143

Hampson, Joe VP Sports & Community Outreach
SPECIAL OLYMPICS WASHINGTON, 195

Hampton, Alvin Sales/Marketing Director
LOUISVILLE METRO HALL, 992

Hampton, Danny News Director
KXKX-FM, 635, 639

Hampton, Herlecia General Manager
GREENETRACK INC., 1056

Hampton, Nate Assistant Director
MICHIGAN HS ATHLETIC ASSOCIATION, 198

Hampton, Rickey Sports Columnist
FLINT JOURNAL, 491

Hampton, Rusty Sports Editor
CLARION-LEDGER, 473

Hampton, Stephanie Director of Operations
NATIONAL MOBILE TELEVISION PRODUCTIONS, INC., 607

Hamre, John 2nd Vice President
NATIONAL WHEELCHAIR SOFTBALL ASSOCIATION, 167

Hamrick, John President
WOMEN'S PREMIER SOCCER LEAGUE, 164

Hamrick, Kyle Producer and Video Specialist
COSTANTE GROUP SPORTS & EVENT MARKETING, LLC, 761

Hamrick, Liz Event Coordinator
PENSACOLA SPORTS ASSOCIATION, 242

Hamrick, Mike Dept. Chairperson
MEMPHIS, UNIVERSITY OF, 336, 428, 962, 984

Hamzy, Donnia Office Manager
LIME ROCK PARK, 1037

Han, Bernie EVP/Chief Operating Officer
DISH NETWORK, 694

Hana, James Sports Director
WRDL-FM, 671

Hanagriff, Charles Sports Director
WIBR, 657

Hanan, Rubin SVP, Retail Brand Marketing
KID'S FOOT LOCKER, 1234, 1243

Hanberry, Dwayne Sports Information Director
SOUTHERN COLLEGIATE ATHLETIC CONFERENCE, 302

Hancock, Jayne President/CEO
JHG TOWNSEND, 799

Hancock, Jennifer Editor
AMERICAN QUARTER HORSE RACING JOURNAL, 554

Hancock, Jeremy Head Athletic Trainer
ASHLAND UNIVERSITY ATHLETICS, 352

Hancock, Jody Retail Sales Manager
KOLDER INC., 1163

Hancock, Katrina Sports Anchor
WDIV-TV, 709

Hancock, Kendra Director for Student-Athlete Support
CAMPBELL UNIVERSITY ATHLETICS, 325

Hancock, Mike Vice President, Business Development
NOBIS WORKS CENTER, 190

Hancocks, Matthew Group Director
VISION SPORTS & ENTERTAINMENT PARTNERS, 825

Hand, Deanna Associate Director of Athletics
HOUGHTON COLLEGE ATHLETICS, 389

Handel, Jeremy Senior Manager, Public Affairs
LAS VEGAS CONVENTION & VISITOR'S AUTHORITY, 990

Handel, Ray Promotions Director
WKXW-FM, 662

Handel, Ted Senior Counsel
CAMPBELL, ROBERT G., 880

Handelman, Mike Chief Sales Officer
HNTB CORP., 1070

Handerland, Karina Senior Associate AD
PORTLAND ATHLETICS, UNIVERSITY OF, 341

Handley, Brian Sports Assistant Editor
DETROIT NEWS, 486

Handy, Alan Track Manager
PLACERVILLE SPEEDWAY, 1040

Handy, Sherry Program Director
WWAG-FM, 678

Hanes, Jason Sports Information Director
REINHARDT UNIVERSITY ATHLETICS, 317

Hanes-Romano, Katie Head Athletic Trainer
JOHNSON C. SMITH UNIVERSITY ATHLETICS, 361

Hanessian, Jack General Manager
BELTERRA PARK, 1045

Haney, Dave Sports Director
WKDE-FM, 660

Haney, Jeff Sports Columnist
LAS VEGAS SUN, 505

Haney, Kelley Assistant Director Of Athletics
VIRGINIA HS LEAGUE, 200

Hanish, Jan Assistant Vice President for Administrat
UNI-DOME, 1021

Hankin, David Chief Executive Officer
AMF BOWLING WORLDWIDE, 1108

Hankin, Ira Production Director
SPORTS BYLINE USA, 608

Hankin, Steve Chief Executive Officer
SENTIENT, 936

Hankins, Dona Sports Night Editor
ST. PETERSBURG TIMES, 538

Hankins, Jamie 2nd Vice President
WALKING HORSE TRAINER'S ASSOCIATION, 79

Hankins, Kim First Vice President
HARNESS HORSEMEN INTERNATIONAL, 76

Hankins, Patsy Women's Chairman
INTERNATIONAL GOLF FEDERATION, 101

Hankins, Tom Head Coach
NATIONAL BASKETBALL ASSOCIATION DEVELOPMENT LEAGUE, 59

Hankle, James
SHERRARD, GERMAN & KELLY, 915

Hankosky, Scott Chief Executive Officer
HEALTHANDWELLNESSJOBS.COM, 755

Hanks, Fiona Head Athletic Trainer
UNIVERSITY OF FINDLAY (UF) ATHLETICS, 359

Hanks, Roy Sales
SKILLBUILDERS, INC., 1200

Hanley, Bill President
TEXAS GOLF ASSOCIATION, 115

Hanley, Brian Sports Writer (Hockey)
CHICAGO SUN-TIMES, 472

Hanline, Brian Sr. VP Anf Chief Medical Officer
NATIONAL COLLEGIATE ATHLETIC ASSOCIATION/NCAA, 283

Hanlon, Pat Senior VP, Communications
NATIONAL FOOTBALL LEAGUE/NFL, 96

Hanna, Al Sports Director
KCMC, 621

Hanna, Gary Head Athletic Trainer
EDINBORO UNIVERSITY OF PENNSYLVANIA ATHLETICS, 358

Hanna, John Advertising Manager/Publisher
NET NEWS, 172, 579

Hanna, Mike Director of Athletics
HOBART COLLEGE ATHLETICS, 389

Hanna, Pete VP, Operations
FANSEDGE.COM, 1239

Hannah, Chris Director of Facilities and Game Ops.
BOBCAT STADIUM TEXAS STATE, 959

Hanneke, Dan Executive Director
LAS VEGAS BOWL, 91

Hannell, Nancy Advertising Director
DAVIS ENTERPRISE, 484

Hanners, Chris Owner
VA MEMORIAL STADIUM, 1024

Hannes, Ted Vice President/Fundraising Chair
DWARF ATHLETIC ASSOCIATION OF AMERICA, 218

Hannes, V. Sports Host
WMAQ-TV, 715

Hannon, Bob Sports Director
WYTV-TV, 721

Hannon, Dick Advertising Manager
WPIG-FM, 656, 668

Hannon, Jim Director, Public Relations
MAYWOOD PARK, 1050

Hannon, Laura Director, Comcast SportsNet New England
COMCAST SPORTSNET NEW ENGLAND, 681

Hannon, Mark General Manager
WBCN-FM, 645

Harty, John VP, Marketing
CANTERBURY PARK, 1046
Harty, Maureen Athletic Director
NORTHWESTERN UNIVERSITY, 432
Hartzler, Murray Athletics Director
FRANCIS MARION UNIVERSITY ATHLETICS
(FMU), 359
Harutunian, Alfred Chief Financial Officer
SAUER, JR., RUSSELL F., 914
Harvet, Mark Treasurer
AMERICAN WATER SKI EDUCATIONAL
FOUNDATION/WATER SKI HALL OF FAME/,
250
Harvey, Ben Executive Producer
VIP COVERAGE, LLC, 685
Harvey, Bob President
GOLD CREST ENGRAVING, 1149
Harvey, Buck Sports Columnist
SAN ANTONIO EXPRESS-NEWS, 532
Harvey, Carolyn General Manager
BIRMINGHAM INTERNATIONAL RACEWAY,
1032
Harvey, Craig Sports Editor
OBSERVER (NY), 519
Harvey, Debbie Vice President
RON JON SURF SHOP OF FLORIDA, 1248
Harvey, Donna 2nd Vice President
NEW HAMPSHIRE WOMEN'S GOLF
ASSOCIATION, 113
Harvey, Elaine Assistant Athletics Director for
Communi
JOHNSON STATE COLLEGE ATHLETICS, 390
Harvey, Erin Assistant Athletic Director
WILMINGTON UNIVERSITY ATHLETICS
(DELAWARE), 376
Harvey, Gary
CRADDOCK-CUNNINGHAM ARCHITECTURAL
PARTNERS, 1063
Harvey, Gerald Vice Chair
SCOTT, DAVID R., 915
Harvey, James Team Manager
MAINE AT FORT KENT ATHLETICS,
UNIVERSITY OF, 314, 849
Harvey, Jeff Director of Sales
INTERNATIONAL MICRO SYSTEMS, INC.,
941, 1074, 1077
Harvey, Joi Senior Administrative Assistant
OUTDOOR LIFE, 580
Harvey, Kyle Corporate Marketing Manager
C.O. BROWN STADIUM, 962
Harvey, Mike Athletic Director
WINDSOR ATHLETICS, UNIVERSITY OF, 322
Harvey, Nancy Vice President
ARABIAN HORSE ASSOCIATION, 75
Harvey, Nick Ticket Manager
QUAD CITIES RIVER BANDITS, 1003
Harvey, Pete Director of Sport Development
BUFFALO NIAGARA SPORTS COMMISSION,
227
Harvey, Terasa Advertising Director
DAILY CITIZEN, 478
Harvey, William President of Hampton University
HAMPTON UNIVERSITY, 422
Harveycutter, R. Civic Facilities Director
OLD DOMINION ATHLETIC CONFERENCE,
300
Harvin, Katherine Marketing Director
KPRC-TV, 701
Harwell, Mark President
VINTAGE BECKETT SPORTS
COLLECTIBLES, 597
Harwood, Michael Advertising Director
ENTERPRISE, 489
Harwood, Tim Director, Broadcasting & Media
Relations
UNITED STATES HOCKEY LEAGUE, 137
Harzinski, Terry Executive Director
BISMARCK-MANDAN CONVENTION &
VISITORS BUREAU, 227
Hasan, Samer Orthopaedic Surgeon
CINCINNATI SPORTSMEDICINE &
ORTHOPAEDIC CENTER, 929
Hascall, Carl President
HASCALL SPORTSWEAR, INC., 1153
Hascall, Linda VP
HASCALL SPORTSWEAR, INC., 1153
Hascher, Jane Editor
LOG, 574

Hascup, David President
AMERICAN DARTS ORGANIZATION, 72
Hase, Jason Secretary
NORTHERN TEXAS PGA SECTIONAL
OFFICE, 106
Haselman, Bill Manager
CALIFORNIA LEAGUE (A-LEVEL), 36
Hasen, Mike Head Coach
NATIONAL LACROSSE LEAGUE, 142
Hash, DeDe VP Security /Asset Management
BRISTOL MOTOR SPEEDWAY & DRAGWAY,
1032
Hashim, Sharief Interim Director of Athletics
SOUTHERN VERMONT COLLEGE
ATHLETICS, 403
Hashiro, Kevin Sports Information Director
CHAMINADE UNIVERSITY ATHLETICS, 355
Haskin, Dave Associate Athletic Director, External
Af
DRAKE STADIUM, 971
Haskins, Rick Vice President of Marketing
FX NETWORKS, LLC, 683
Haskovec, Jarrett Member
LUBIN & ENOCH, P.C., 901
Haslam, Bill Chair
MIZELL, CATHERINE, 906
Haslam, Kent Director of Athletics
MONTANA ATHLETICS, UNIVERSITY OF, 337
Hasler, Timothy Attorney
HASLER, FONFARA AND MAXWELL, LLP, 892
Hass, Amy Associate Vice President and Deputy
Gene
BERNARD, PAMELA J., 874
Hass, Bill Sports Writer
GREENSBORO NEWS & RECORD, 494
Hassan, Fred Chairman
BAUSCH & LOMB, 1115
Hassan, John Sports Senior Editor
ESPN THE MAGAZINE, 563
Hassan, Nazmul Director (Bangladesh)
INTERNATIONAL CRICKET COUNCIL, 69
Hassard, Geoffrey Sports Information Director
STATE UNIVERSITY OF NEW YORK
COLLEGE AT ONEONTA ATHLETICS(SUNY),
404
Hasse, John Ass.Director
KIMBROUGH MEMORIAL STADIUM, 988
Hassel, Chris Sports Reporter/Anchor
WHO-TV, 712
Hasseltine, Terry Executive Director
MARYLAND SPORTS, 238
Hassett, Chris VP Communications
JHG TOWNSEND, 830
Hassett, Joe Sports Director
KHBT-FM, 626
Hassett, Tim Vice President of Stadium
Operations
ARROWHEAD STADIUM, 955
Hassinger, Scott Sports Reporter
THREE RIVERS COMMERCIAL-NEWS, 543
Hasson, Devin Sports Editor
MESQUITE NEWS, 509
Hastings, Calvin General Manager/Sales
WOHS, 649, 655, 667
Hastings, Chris VP
SPORT & SOCIAL CLUBS OF THE U.S., 818
Hastings, Greg Promotions
WGH-AM THE SCORE, 655
Hastings, Kent PRESIDENT
DELAWARE COUNTY FAIR, 1046
Hastings, Mark Advertising Manager
IOLA REGISTER, 500
Hastings, Scott Host
SPORTS ZOO, 613
Hastings, Terresa Office Manager
WOHS, 649, 655, 667
Hastings, Tom Deputy Athletics Director
UC SANTA BARBARA ATHLETICS, 348, 937
Hasty, Taylor Athletic Director
BRYAN COLLEGE ATHLETICS, 307
Haswell, Brad RA
DAUER HASWELL ARCHITECTS, 1063
Haszard, Sharon VP
EXECUTIVE RESTROOM TRAILERS, 1077
Haszard, Tim President
EXECUTIVE RESTROOM TRAILERS, 1077
Hatano, Yoshiro Partner
ACCUSPLIT, 1101

Hatch, Julie Assistant General Manager
PIONEER BASEBALL LEAGUE, 51, 960
Hatch, Ric North American Sales Director
PATAGONIA, 1184
Hatchell, Steven President and CEO
NATIONAL FOOTBALL FOUNDATION AND
COLLEGE HALL OF FAME, INC., THE, 250,
254
Hatcher, Derian Head Coach
ONTARIO HOCKEY LEAGUE, 134
Hatcher, Karen Exec. Sr. Assoc. AD, External
Relations
CINCINNATI ATHLETICS, UNIVERSITY OF,
326
Hatcher, Rick President/Executive Director
LEXINGTON AREA SPORTS AUTHORITY, 237
Hater, Mike President/General Manger
LUCKY'S CARD ROOM, 1056
Hatfield, Amy Director of Content Marketing
ARCHERY TRADE ASSOCIATION, 14
Hatfield, Dottie Classified Manager
LOGAN BANNER, 506
Hatfield, Lorena Marketing Resources Manager
K & K INSURANCE GROUP, 776
Hatfield, Sandy Director of Athletics
DRAKE STADIUM, 971
Hatfield, Susan Marketing Director
SCA PROMOTIONS, INC., 815
Hatfield, Tanya Promotions Director
KABZ-FM, 619

Hathaway, George Facilities Manager
SARATOGA RACETRACK, 1053
Hathaway, Harry Counsel
FULBRIGHT & JAWORSKI .L.L.P., 890
Hathaway, Irene Resident Director
MILLER CANFIELD SPORTS, 853
Hathaway, Jennifer Director of Communications
HUMBERT HUMPHREY METRODOME, 980
Hathaway, Leslie Director of Operations
FX NETWORKS, LLC, 683
Hathcock, Chuck Sports Editor
DAILY SENTINEL STAR, 482
Hathcock, Mike Sports Director
WGAD-AM, 654
Hathorn, Jan Athletic Director
WASHINGTON AND LEE UNIVERSITY
ATHLETICS, 407
Hathway, Bob Director of Strategic Development
NATIONAL LACROSSE LEAGUE, 142
Hathway, Chase Assistant General Manager
TED CONSTANT CONVOCATION CENTER,
1017
Hatley, Trip Advertising Manager
ROME NEWS-TRIBUNE, 530
Hatten, Justin Sports Editor
OLNEY DAILY MAIL, 519
Hatten, William Intramurals and Facilities
Coordinator
CAPITAL CITY STADIUM, 963
Hatter, Bill President
NATIONAL DARTS FEDERATION OF
CANADA, 72
Hattersley, Gavin CEO, MillerCoors
MOLSONCOORS, 738
Hatting, Carolyn Advertising Manager
EMPORIA GAZETTE, 489
Hattori, Shigeaki Owner
NASCAR GANDER OUTDOORS TRUCK
SERIES, 23
Hauck, Sheri First Vice President
WOMEN'S SOUTHERN CALIFORNIA GOLF
ASSOCIATION, 117
Hauenstein, Eric General Manager
KFNZ, 624
Hauenstein, Glen President
DELTA AIR LINES, 735
Hauer, Patrick Tournament Operations Associate
INTERNATIONAL JUNIOR GOLF TOUR/IJGT,
101
Haufe, Bill Sports Editor
STAR-DEMOCRAT, 539
Hauff, Caitlyn Co-Editor
JOURNAL OF SPORT BEHAVIOR, 572
Haug, Curtis VP, General Manager
MIDWEST LEAGUE, 45
Haugen, Erik Director of Program Development &
Acquis

NEW ENGLAND SPORTS NETWORK/NESN, 684

Hauger, Gary EVP
GANDER MOUNTAIN COMPANY, 1240

Haugh, John SVP, Marketing
PAYLESS SHOESOURCE, INC., 1246

Haught, Steve Accounting Manager
PETERSEN EVENTS CENTER, 1001

Haun, Randy Information System
COBBLESTONES ACTIVEWEAR, 1127

Haun, Ed.D., John Executive Director
VIRGINIA HS LEAGUE, 200

Haupt, Chris Chief Technology Officer
ONLINE SPORTS, 722

Haur, John Director of Marketing
ATHLETIC RESOURCE MANAGEMENT, INC., 834

Haus, William Attorney/Partner
HAUS & ROMAN, LLP, 892

Hauscarriague, John Senior Associate AD, Finance
UC IRVINE ATHLETICS, 348

Hausen, Dave President
DUNBROOKE, 1136

Hauser, Anthony Concessions Manager
PICO RIVERA SPORTS ARENA, 1001

Hauser, Dan Athletic Director
HIGH POINT UNIVERSITY ATHLETICS, 331

Hauser, Deb Associate Director
WISCONSIN INTERSCHOLASTIC ATHLETIC ASSOCIATION, 201

Hauser, Jeff Chief Executive Officer
CHALLENGE ASPEN, 217

Hauser, Konan Advertising Director
VISALIA TIMES-DELTA, 549

Hauser, Lee Advertising Manager
WBLA-AM, 646

Hauser, Ralph Manager
PICO RIVERA SPORTS ARENA, 1001

Hauser, Rick Senior Vice President/Account Director
BEAR ENTHUSIAST MARKETING GROUP, 783

Hausmann, Steve President
MONROE COUNTY SPORTS COMMISSION, 240

Haute, Dan Team Manager
USA CYCLING, 72

Havard, Donald Fiscal Officer
OHIO STATE UNIVERSITY, 432

Havard, Ian Publisher
RACER, 583

Havaris, Eva Chief Executive Officer
EQUINE CANADA, 75

Havenick, Fred President and Chief Executive Officer
FLAGLER DOG TRACK, 1055

Haverick, David President
CHICAGO DISTRICT GOLF ASSOCIATION, 109

Haverlock, Kevin Business Dept. Chairperson
TOMPKINS CORTLAND COMMUNITY COLLEGE, 438

Haversat, Jeffrey General Partner
PIONEER INDUSTRIES, INC., 1185

Hawes, Don Sports Director
WVTM-TV, 720

Hawes, Steve Advertising Manager
HERALD (WA), 496

Hawk, Andy Associate Publisher
SKI RACING, 586

Hawk, Donald Chief Racing Development Officer
SPEEDWAY MOTORSPORTS, INC., 18, 1075

Hawk, Joe Sports Editor
LAS VEGAS REVIEW-JOURNAL, 504

Hawk, Tony President
TONY HAWK FOUNDATION, 191

Hawke, Nancie Counsel
ARNET, WILLIAM F., 871

Hawke, Randy Program Director
WJJO-FM, 659

Hawke, Sandra Marketing Director
METRAPARK, 1051

Hawkins, Billy Sport Studies Program Coordinator
GEORGIA, UNIVERSITY OF, 422

Hawkins, Dennis Associate AD, Finance & Administration

DELAWARE STATE UNIVERSITY ATHLETICS, 327

Hawkins, Drew National Sales Manager
BLUE BIRD CORPORATION, 935

Hawkins, Gary Deputy Sports Editor & Columnist
KENNEBEC JOURNAL, 502

Hawkins, H President/Chief Executive Officer
HKS INC, 1069

Hawkins, Jack President
PROPET USA INC., 1189

Hawkins, Jason General Manager
USL CHAMPIONSHIP, 159

Hawkins, Jonathan Sr administrative director
LAMPART, ABE, 898

Hawkins, Kelly Promotion Director
KKLZ-FM, 628

Hawkins, Kenny Sports Director
WJHL-TV, 713

Hawkins, Larry General Manager
SOUTH ATLANTIC LEAGUE, 51, 994

Hawkins, Matt Sports Marketing Manager
BLOOMINGTON-NORMAL AREA SPORTS COMMISSION, 227

Hawkins, Ralph Chairman and CEO
HKS INC, 1069

Hawkins, Richard Executive Director
USA ROLLER SPORTS, 146

Hawkins, Scott Chairperson/Assistant Professor
LIBERTY UNIVERSITY, 425

Hawkins, Tim Chief Customer Officer & Chief Marketing
NAUTILUS HPS, INC., 1177

Hawks, Cliff General Manager
NASHVILLE SUPERSPEEDWAY, 1039

Hawks, Travis Director of Ticketing & Stadium Operatio
PIONEER BASEBALL LEAGUE, 50

Hawley, Chad Associate Commissioner, Compliance
BIG TEN ATHLETIC CONFERENCE, 290

Hawley, Glenda Advertising Director
RUTLAND HERALD, 530

Hawley, Mardele Administrative Support Coordinator
BALDWIN-WALLACE COLLEGE - LOU HIGGINS CENTER, 412

Hawman, Paul Race Secretary
DRESDEN RACEWAY, 1046

Haworth, Don Director of Sports Medicine
FARMINGDALE STATE UNIVERSITY (FSU) ATHLETICS, 386

Haworth, Jim Chairman
PROFESSIONAL BULL RIDERS (PBR), 146

Haxton, Alison Event Coordinator
NEW MEXICO STATE FAIR, 1051

Haxton, Geoff News Director
KXLS-FM, 639

Hay, Bill Chairman/Chief Executive Officer
HOCKEY HALL OF FAME AND MUSEUM, 251

Hay, Jon Head Athletic Trainer
LOUISIANA COLLEGE ATHLETICS, 392

Hay, Paul Vice President of Advertising
JUNEAU EMPIRE, 502

Hayashi, Shusaku Head Athletic Trainer
MCMURRY UNIVERSITY ATHLETICS, 395

Haycox, Richard Advertising Manager
HOPE STAR, 498

Hayden, Bobby Sports Director
KMGH-TV, 699

Hayden, Chris Director of Operations
BRICK BREEDEN FIELDHOUSE, 960

Hayden, Shanda Associate Director, Academic and Career
UNIVERSITY OF KANSAS, 1022

Hayden, Zern 1st VP
LAKE COUNTY FAIR, 1050

Haydon, John Sports Reporter
WASHINGTON TIMES, 550

Hayes, Ben President
NEW YORK-PENNSYLVANIA LEAGUE (A LEVEL), 46

Hayes, Ben Director of Food and Beverage
STANLEY COVELESKI REGIONAL STADIUM, 1014

Hayes, Bill President and CEO
SAFWAY SERVICES, LLC, 250, 1196

Hayes, Brian Treasurer
CANADIAN TEAM HANDBALL FEDERATION, 120

Hayes, Chris Production Editor
ORLANDO SENTINEL, 520

Hayes, Garet Vice President
HOPE-BECKHAM, INC., 796

Hayes, Jack Director of Athletics
BROWN STADIUM, 961

Hayes, Jimmy Chairman
AUTOTRADER.COM, INC, 681

Hayes, Keith Principal
BARKER RINKER SEACAT ARCHITECTURE, 1059

Hayes, LaNorris Grounds and Maintenance Staff
BRAGG MEMORIAL STADIUM, 960

Hayes, Laurie League Administrator
NEW YORK-PENNSYLVANIA LEAGUE (A LEVEL), 46

Hayes, Marcus Sports Writer
PHILADELPHIA DAILY NEWS, 523

Hayes, Nancy Operation Officer
DANIELS, ERIC D., 884

Hayes, Pete Sports Editor
TELEGRAPH (IL), 542

Hayes, Robert Senior Associate
BRESLIN, RIDYARD, FADERO ARCHITECTS, 1060

Hayes, Ted Chief Executive Officer, President
STATE OF KANSAS SPORTS HALL OF FAME, 257

Hayes, William Director of Athletics
WINSTON-SALEM STATE UNIVERSITY, 441

Haynes, Brad Assistant Athletic Director
FORT HAYS STATE UNIVERSITY ATHLETICS (FHSU), 359

Haynes, Joe Advertising Manager
KCTI-AM, 622

Haynes, Kanett Athletics Business Manager
SOUTH CAROLINA-SPARTANBURG ATHLETICS, UNIVERSITY OF, 371

Haynes, Michael Chief Financial Officer
SPECIALIZED BICYCLE COMPONENTS, INC., 1203

Haynes, Roger Director of Athletics
MONMOUTH COLLEGE ATHLETICS, 396

Haynes, Sheila President
MISSISSIPPI WOMEN'S GOLF ASSOCIATION, 112

Haynes, Trevor President & CEO
SUBWAY RESTAURANTS, 741

Hays, Kim Advertising Director
WINCHESTER SUN, 552

Hays, Sharon Office Manager
FOUR STATES FAIR & RODEO, 1048

Hayward, Len Sports Editor
MIDLAND REPORTER-TELEGRAM, 510

Hayward, Wally Chief Executive Officer
RELAY SPORTS AND ENTERTAINMENT MARKETING, 814

Haywood, Jerry Faculty Athletic Representative
FORT VALLEY STATE UNIVERSITY ATHLETICS (FVSU), 359

Hazel, Donna Managing Editor
BOWLING WORLD, 559

Hazeltine, Rick Sports Assistant Editor
DAILY NEWS (CA), 480

Hazelton, Rich Editor
48 DEGREES NORTH, 553

Hazen, Mike Executive VP/General Manager
NATIONAL LEAGUE OF PROFESSIONAL BASEBALL CLUBS, THE, 31, 973

Hazlett, Carl Attorney/Partner
HAZLETT, WILKES & BAYHAM, 893

Hazman, David Sales Manager
CELLO PROFESSIONAL PRODUCTS, 1125

Heacock, Lesa Advertising Manager
KENTON TIMES, 503

Head, Daniel Athletic Director
NJCAA REGION XXII WOMEN'S, 288

Head, Jerad Team Manager
NEW YORK-PENNSYLVANIA LEAGUE, 46

Head, Stacy President
SAPIR, EDDIE L., THE HONORABLE, 913

Head, Steve Executive Vice President Sales
SOF SOLE, 1201

Head, Jr., Albon Managing Partner
JACKSON WALKER LLP, 848

Headley, Richard Sports Editor
HOLDREGE DAILY CITIZEN, 497

Headrick, Melba Advertising Manager
KSMO-AM, 636

executive index

Huckstep, M. Chairman/Executive Committee
ADAMS & REESE, 870

Huda, Jess Assistant Director of Athletics
CABRINI COLLEGE ATHLETICS, 380

Hudgins, Richard Advertising Manager
SADDLE HORSE REPORT, 585

Hudgins, Richard Advertising Manager
VOICE OF THE TENNESSEE WALKING
HORSE MAGAZINE, 597

Hudnall, Hugh Director of
Marketing/Advertising/Market
TRIBUNE-DEMOCRAT, 546

Hudson, Andrea Volleyball Head Coach
LEE UNIVERSITY ATHLETICS, 362

Hudson, Arlene Advertising Manager
SANTA CRUZ SENTINEL, 533

Hudson, Becky Secretary/Treasurer
ARIZONA REGIONAL COMMISSIONER/USA
VOLLEYBALL, 209

Hudson, Ben Publisher
SOUTHWEST HORSE TRACK, 588

Hudson, Bob Sports Editor
SPECTRUM, 537

Hudson, Carolyn Recording Secretary
MARYLAND STATE GOLF ASSOCIATION -
WOMEN'S DIVISION, 111

Hudson, Clarence Executive Director
IOWA GAMES, 261

Hudson, Emanuel Track & Field/Football/Tennis,
Attorney
HS INTERNATIONAL, 846

Hudson, Gene Advertising Manager
DAILY SOUTHERNER, 482

Hudson, Hugh Sales Manager
HUDSON BOAT WORKS INC., 1156

Hudson, Joe General Manager
CALIFORNIA LEAGUE (A-LEVEL), 36

Hudson, Karen Vice Chairman
SPECIAL OLYMPICS NEW MEXICO, 194

Hudson, Kathleen Controller
FRONTIER LEAGUE, 41

Hudson, Katy Coord Financial Services
BAKER, DAVID L., 872

Hudson, Lise Director of Sales
THE ZONE SPORTS RADIO 1300 AM, 642

Hudson, Mark President
OKLAHOMA SECONDARY SCHOOL
ACTIVITIES ASSOCIATION, 200

Hudson, Mike General Manager
KWIK, 638

Hudson, Randy Director Of Design
HAYES LARGE ARCHITECTS, 1068

Hudson, Stuart National Sales Manager
ELLESSE U.S.A., INC., 1139

Hudson, Tom Sports Director
KREM-TV, 702

Hue, Laura Associate AD, Compliance
INDIANA UNIVERSITY-PURDUE UNIVERSITY
INDIANAPOLIS, 332

Huebel, Kerri Assistant Athletic Director
MARIAN COLLEGE OF FOND DU LAC
ATHLETICS, 393

Huebner, Brett Associate Director of Athletics /
CFO
RED MC EWEN BASEBALL FIELD, 1004

Huebner, Joe Director of Business Development
CARLSON DESIGN/CONSTRUCT CORP.,
1061

Huebner, Vic Treasurer
U.S. CURLING ASSOCIATION, 70

Huelfing, Tim General Manager
WYXY-FM, 680

Hueregue, Paul Design Director
SQUASH MAGAZINE, 592

Huerta, Terry Human Resource & Payroll
Manager
SEAGATE CENTRE, 1010

Huey, J.D. Vice President/General Manager
WIAT - CBS 42, 712

Huff, Bill Sports Director
WBAG-AM, 644

Huff, Cliff Senior Associate Athletics Director
CLARK ATLANTA UNIVERSITY ATHLETICS,
355

Huff, Danielle Vice President/Owner
C & H BASEBALL, 1122

Huff, Kyle Head Athletic Trainer
HUNTINGDON COLLEGE ATHLETICS, 389

Huff, Laura Director of Marketing
LISTON B. RAMSEY REGIONAL ACTIVITY
CENTER, 992

Huff, Megan Sports Sales Manager
SOUTH BEND/MISHAWAKA CONVENTION &
VISITORS BUREAU, 263

Huff, Rob President
C & H BASEBALL, 1122

Huff, Samantha Program & Planning Manager
GOLF COURSE BUILDERS ASSOCIATION OF
AMERICA, 100

Huff, Stephanie Hr and Contract Services
Manager
SPOKANE VETERANS MEMORIAL ARENA,
1013

Huff, Will Deputy Director of Athletics, Operations
TOWSON STATE UNIVERSITY ATHLETICS,
347

Huffman, Aaron Athletic Director
WEST LIBERTY UNIVERSITY ATHLETICS, 375

Huffman, Jamie Assistant General
Manager/Director, Scou
UNITED STATES HOCKEY LEAGUE, 137

Huffman, Kerry Assistant Coach
AMERICAN HOCKEY LEAGUE/AHL, 127

Huffman, Kris Assistant Athletics Director
DE PAUW UNIVERSITY ATHLETICS, 384

Huffman, Rick Director of Sales & Marketing
SIOUX FALLS ARENA, 1011

Hufnagel, John President/General Manager
CANADIAN FOOTBALL LEAGUE/CFL, 93

Huftalen, Steve AVP of Corporate Development &
Special E
SPECIAL OLYMPICS MASSACHUSETTS, 193

Hugdaln, Geroge Secretary
US LACROSSE, 141

Huge, Samantha Athletics Director
WILLIAM & MARY ATHLETICS, COLLEGE OF,
350

Huge, Thom News Director
KZMQ-AM, 640

Hugelmeyer, Frank President
OUTDOOR INDUSTRY ASSOCIATION, 222

Huggins, Billy Vice President
WPDE-TV, 716

Huggins, Jeff Senior Vice President
YESAWICH, PEPPERDINE, BROWNE &
RUSSELL, 827

Huggins, Malcolm Assistant Director of Athletics
STATE UNIVERSITY OF NEW YORK
COLLEGE AT OSWEGO(SUNY), 404

Hugh, Leslie Parks/Recreation Director
LAKEVIEW ARENA, 990

Hughes, Brian News Director
WARM-AM, 612, 644

Hughes, Dan Head Coach
WOMEN'S NATIONAL BASKETBALL
ASSOCIATION, 61, 668

Hughes, David Sports Reporter
TRIBUNE-STAR, 546

Hughes, Donald Senior VP / Chief Financial
Officer
LANDS' END, INC., 1165

Hughes, Edward VP Marketing
DUNLOP/MAXFLI/SLAZENGER GROUP
AMERICAS, 1136

Hughes, Ellen Ticket Manager
SUN BOWL, 93

Hughes, G. President
CAROLINAS GOLF ASSOCIATION, 109

Hughes, Jack Executive Director
GAINESVILLE SPORTS COMMISSION, 232

Hughes, Jami Assistant Athletic Director-Daily
Operat
HOLY FAMILY COLLEGE ATHLETICS, 361

Hughes, Janine Managing Editor
GOLF FOR WOMEN, 566

Hughes, Jerry Athletics Director
CENTRAL MISSOURI STATE UNIVERSITY
ATHLETICS, 354, 1025

Hughes, Joe Sports Director
KIVI-TV, 699

Hughes, John Commissioner/Executive Director
WESTERN EMPIRE, 211

Hughes, John Sports Information Director
LA GRANGE COLLEGE ATHLETICS, 391, 599

Hughes, Kevin President
NORTHEASTERN NEW YORK PGA
SECTIONAL OFFICE, 106

Hughes, Kit Senior Associate AD
BOWLING GREEN STATE UNIVERSITY
ATHLETICS, 324

Hughes, Lee Sports Director
KMA-AM, 630

Hughes, Lindsey Assistant Athletic Director
COLUMBIA COLLEGE OF S. CAROLINA
ATHLETICS, 309

Hughes, Lisa Vice President, Human Resources
& Admini
NOBIS WORKS CENTER, 190

Hughes, Mark Assistant General Manager
NATIONAL BASKETBALL ASSOCIATION/NBA,
57

Hughes, Merrill Treasurer
UNITED STATES BILLIARD ASSOCIATION, 63

Hughes, Michael Chief Executive Officer
NATIONAL GOLF COURSE OWNERS
ASSOCIATION, 102

Hughes, Michelle Promotions Manager
KKTV-TV, 699

Hughes, Paul Attorney
PIERCE & HUGHES P.C., 909

Hughes, Paul Lawyer
TALLEY, ANTHONY, HUGHES & KNIGHT
L.L.C., 920

Hughes, Rob Sports Reporter
INTERNATIONAL HERALD TRIBUNE, 500

Hughes, Rusty Project Coordinator
SOUTHERN BLEACHER COMPANY, INC.,
1202

Hughes, Scott Project Manager
COMPASS COLLECTIVE, 760

Hughes, Theresa Racing Secretary
LUCKY'S CARD ROOM, 1056

Hughes, Tim Director of Facilities
VICTORY FIELD, 1025

Hughes, Tom Vice President
HOPE-BECKHAM, INC., 796

Hughey, Dan SVP National Sales
COLONIAL LIFE & ACCIDENT INSURANCE
COMPANY, 787

Hughson, Kendall Asst. GM/Dir of Stadium
Operations
RIVERFRONT STADIUM, 1006

Huguenard, Lee Classified Manager
CITIZEN TRIBUNE, 473

Huhn, Kevin Deputy Sports Editor
ROCKY MOUNTAIN NEWS, 530

Huisman, Tom Director Operations &
Development
CANADIAN INTERUNIVERSITY SPORT, 281

Huisman, Travis CFO
MCNETT CORPORATION, 1172

Huitrado, Dean Advertising Director
THRASHER SKATEBOARD MAGAZINE, 595

Huizenga, Rob Assistant Athletics Director
SAINT XAVIER UNIVERSITY ATHLETICS, 318

Hula, Ed Founder
AROUND THE RINGS, 610

Hula, Sheila Publisher
AROUND THE RINGS, 610

Hull, Allison Faculty Athletic Representative
WEST VIRGINIA WESLEYAN ATHLETICS
(WVWC), 376

Hull, Angie Associate AD, Academic Service
KENT STATE UNIVERSITY ATHLETICS, 333

Hull, Carrie Executive Director, Maryland Horse
Counc
EQUIERY, 563

Hull, Edward President
LINCOLN FINANCIAL MEDIA, 606

Hull, Justin Talk Host
WHBY-AM, 656

Hull, Mike Managing Director
INDYCAR, 22

Hull, Patrick Marketing Senior Director
BIRKENSTOCK FOOTPRINT SANDALS INC.,
1231

Hull, Robin Business Manager
PHILIP B. ELFSTROM STADIUM, 1001

Hulne, Rocky Sports Editor
AUSTIN DAILY HERALD, 464

Hulse, Gil Sports Assistant Editor
SPOKESMAN-REVIEW, 537

Hulsey, Emily Handicap/Website Coordinator
MONTANA STATE GOLF ASSOCIATION, 112

executive index

J

Johannes, Robert Partner
TREBATOSKI, CHRIS J., 922
Johannesen, Kirk Sports Editor
REPUBLIC, 529
Johanningmeier, Tom Sports Deputy Editor
FORT WORTH STAR-TELEGRAM, 491
Johansen, Ashlie General Manager
KWCR-FM, 638
Johansen, Brad Sports Anchor
WKRC-TV, 714
Johansen, Jon Publisher
MAINE COASTAL NEWS, 575
Johansen, Robert President
SKB SHOTGUNS, 1200
Johansson, Andreas Owner
FEDERAL HOCKEY LEAGUE, 131
Johansson, Robin Owner
FEDERAL HOCKEY LEAGUE, 131
John, Allen Sports Columnist
WALL STREET JOURNAL, 550
John, Bernie Assistant Coach
EAST COAST HOCKEY LEAGUE/ECHL, 129
John, Bill President
BOAST, INC., 1118
John, Linda Executive Director
VISIT EAU CLAIRE, 248
John, Micheal Vice Chair
DENVER, UNIVERSITY OF, 418
John, Nader Assistant GM/Business Manager
DAMASCHKE FIELD, 969
John, Ronald Director of Athletics
YORK COLLEGE (CUNY) ATHLETICS, 411
John, Stephen General Manager
CAMBRIA COUNTY WAR MEMORIAL, 962
John, Timberlake General Manager
JACK RUSSELL MEMORIAL STADIUM, 983
John & Cori Kirkpatrick, Dr. Executive Directors
AMERICAN MEDICAL TENNIS ASSOCIATION,
171
Johns, Chip President
VANGUARD SAILBOATS, 1218
Johns, Hank VP
GRAPHITE MASTER, 1151
Johns, Jerry EVP / Chief Operating Officer
SAFWAY SERVICES, LLC, 1196
Johns, Kim President
U.S.I.A., 991, 1217
Johns, Lana Chief Executive Officer
U.S.I.A., 1217
Johns, Michael Manager
FLORIDA STATE LEAGUE, 39
Johnson, Aaron Assistant General Manager, Dir.
of Food/
CAROLINA LEAGUE, 37, 975
Johnson, Allen Executive Director
TD WATERHOUSE CENTRE, 532, 999, 1017
Johnson, Andy SVP, Marketing
FINGERHUT COMPANIES, INC., 1239
Johnson, Arthur Executive Senior Associate AD
TEXAS AT AUSTIN ATHLETICS, UNIVERSITY
OF, 346
Johnson, Betty Inside Sales, Representative
Quotations,
MILLERBERND MANUFACTURING
COMPANY, 1174
Johnson, Bill Executive Vice President
PROFILES SPORTS, INC., 644, 859
Johnson, Bob Purchasing Manager
HUNTER MANUFACTURING GROUP INC,
200, 214, 1157
Johnson, Brad SVP / Chief Financial Officer /
Corporat
RECREATIONAL EQUIPMENT, INC./REI, 1247
Johnson, Brandon Director of Intramurals
POMONA-PITZER COLLEGES ATHLETICS,
399
Johnson, Brett Editor
USROWING, 147, 597
Johnson, Brittney Associate AD, Compliance
PRAIRIE VIEW A&M UNIVERSITY
ATHLETICS, 342
Johnson, Britton Assistant Professor of Physical
Educatio
MISSOURI WESTERN STATE COLLEGE, 430
Johnson, Bryce Sports Director
WASU-FM, 644
Johnson, C.J. VP - Ticket Sales
CAROLINA LEAGUE, 38

Johnson, Cavell Head Coach
NATIONAL BASKETBALL LEAGUE OF
CANADA, 59
Johnson, Charinus Chief Operating Officer
DAN MARINO FOUNDATION, 189
Johnson, Charlene Director of Athletics
SOUTH CAROLINA STATE UNIVERSITY, 1013
Johnson, Charley President and CEO
FARGO-MOORHEAD CONVENTION &
VISITOR BUREAU, 232
Johnson, Chas Sports Information Director
NORTHLAND COLLEGE ATHLETICS, 397
Johnson, Chris Marketing Specialist
TIMEX CORPORATION, 116, 1213
Johnson, Christina Sr. Director,
Digital/Media/Game Operati
EAST COAST HOCKEY LEAGUE/ECHL, 129
Johnson, Christopher Vice Chair/CEO
NATIONAL FOOTBALL LEAGUE/NFL, 96, 1017
Johnson, Chuck General Manager
PACIFIC COAST LEAGUE OF
PROFESSIONAL BASEBALL CLUBS, 49
Johnson, Connor Head Coach
NATIONAL BASKETBALL ASSOCIATION
DEVELOPMENT LEAGUE, 59
Johnson, Curt President/General Manager
USL LEAGUE TWO, 158, 162
Johnson, Dale News Director
KRKR-FM, 624, 634
Johnson, Dan Program Manager
K & K INSURANCE GROUP, 485, 776
Johnson, Daniel Chief Operating Partner
CHAPMAN & CUTLER, 881
Johnson, Danita President, Business Operations
MAJOR LEAGUE SOCCER, 157
Johnson, Darci Director of Human Resources
MIDDLEBERG RIDDLE GROUP, 905
Johnson, Darren Director of Sales
CAROLINA LEAGUE, 37, 993
Johnson, Dave CFO
MORETZ SPORTS, 43, 481, 676, 1054, 1175
Johnson, Davey Senior Advisor, Baseball
VANTAGE SPORTS MANAGEMENT, 868
Johnson, David President
NORTH SPORTS, INC., 150, 207, 409, 785,
876, 1161, 1180
Johnson, Dean Associate Director of Athletics
CALDWELL UNIVERSITY ATHLETICS, 353,
628, 637
Johnson, Dee Membership Director
MISSOURI WOMEN'S GOLF ASSOCIATION,
112
Johnson, Dennis Sport Sciences Assoc.
Prof./Asst. Dean
WINGATE UNIVERSITY, 440
Johnson, Deron Senior Advisor, Scouting
AMERICAN LEAGUE OF PROFESSIONAL
BASEBALL CLUBS, THE, 30
Johnson, Derrick Athletic Director
ELIZABETH CITY STATE UNIVERSITY (ECSU)
ATHLETICS, 358
Johnson, Don News Director
WKYR-FM, 662
Johnson, Doug Publisher
LETS PLAY SOFTBALL, 574
Johnson, Douglas VP Marketing
SPORTSMAN'S GUIDE, 1250
Johnson, DuWayne President
PREMIERE MANAGEMENT, 857
Johnson, Dwight Assistant General
Manager/Director of Op
RICHMOND COLISEUM, 821, 1000, 1005
Johnson, Earvin Chairman
MAGIC JOHNSON FOUNDATION, 190
Johnson, Ed Assistant Sports Editor
ALBUQUERQUE JOURNAL, 461
Johnson, Edward Board of Director
EASTERN ATHLETIC SERVICES, 840
Johnson, Elizabeth Secretary
PARACHUTE INDUSTRY ASSOCIATION, 13
Johnson, Eric Sports Director
KOMO-TV, 526, 701
Johnson, Ernie SVP / Chief Financial Officer
CUTTER AND BUCK, INC., 1132
Johnson, Felicia Associate Athletic Director
VIRGINIA UNION UNIVERSITY
ATHLETICS(VUU), 375

Johnson, Frank Interim Athletic Director
WARNER PACIFIC COLLEGE ATHLETICS,
321
Johnson, Garrit Art Director
FAIRWAYS, 564
Johnson, Gary Principal
CAMBRIDGE SEVEN ASSOCIATES INC., 1061
Johnson, George Senior Vice President
RAYCOM SPORTS, 713, 813
Johnson, Glen Secretary General
TUG OF WAR FEDERATION, 175
Johnson, Glen Attorney/Partner
CLAYBORNE, COURTNEY, 882
Johnson, Glenn Vice President, Information
Technology
NATIONAL HOCKEY LEAGUE/NHL, 123
Johnson, Greg Promotions Manager
WPBN-TV, 507, 716
Johnson, Harold Sports Reporter
WSOC-TV, 718
Johnson, Heidi Director of Media Relations &
Promotions
WEEDE ARENA, 1027
Johnson, Helena Sports Director
WCFM-FM, 648
Johnson, J.W. Owner/Executive VP
NATIONAL FOOTBALL LEAGUE/NFL, 95
Johnson, Jack Chief Advocacy Officer
DESTINATION MARKETING ASSOCIATION
INTERNATIONAL, 218
Johnson, James Sports Reporter
DEMOCRAT AND CHRONICLE, 485
Johnson, Jamie Associate AD, Compliance
CHICAGO STATE UNIVERSITY ATHLETICS,
326
Johnson, Janet Advertising Manager
HOLLAND SENTINEL, 497
Johnson, Janette Marketing/Promotion Director
WDEL-AM, 649
Johnson, Jason Managing Editor
POWERBOAT, 582
Johnson, Jay Head Athletic Trainer
FLORIDA INSTITUTE OF TECHNOLOGY
ATHLETICS (FIT), 359
Johnson, Jean-Michel Director of Indexing
Services
SPORT INFORMATION RESOURCE
CENTER/SIRC, 603
Johnson, Jeff Vice President Sales
ALL STAR SPORTING GOODS, 107, 1105
Johnson, Jeff Executive Director
MINNEAPOLIS CONVENTION & VISITORS
ASSOCIATION, GREATER, 239
Johnson, Jen Director of Public Relations
KOHL'S DEPARTMENT STORES, 1243
Johnson, Jennifer Director of Marketing and
Community Rela
MIDWEST LEAGUE, 45
Johnson, Jeremiah President
MIDWEST RUGBY FOOTBALL UNION, 147
Johnson, Jill Station Sales Manager
KVOL AM/FM, 638
Johnson, Jim Athletic Director
PITTSBURG STATE UNIVERSITY ATHLETICS,
369, 656, 963, 1027
Johnson, John Chief Operations Officer
RELIABLE OF MILWAUKEE, 97, 338, 1192
Johnson, John Communications Director
MICHIGAN HS ATHLETIC ASSOCIATION, 198
Johnson, Jon Sports Editor
DOTHAN EAGLE, 487
Johnson, Julia Director, Sales
AMERICAN HOCKEY LEAGUE/AHL, 128
Johnson, Julie Athletic Director
RIPON COLLEGE ATHLETICS, 400
Johnson, K.C. Sports Writer
CHICAGO TRIBUNE, 472
Johnson, Kathy VP Sales/Marketing
FITNESS EM, LLC, 1143
Johnson, Kelly Vice Chair/Treasurer
SPECIAL OLYMPICS SOUTHERN
CALIFORNIA, 195
Johnson, Ken News Director
KOKC-AM, 632
Johnson, Kent Assoc. Dir for Event Operations
KIMBROUGH MEMORIAL STADIUM, 988
Johnson, Kerry Advertising Manager
KOVC-AM, 632

Kalafer, Josh Vice Chairman
ATLANTIC LEAGUE, 35

Kalafer, Steve Chairman
ATLANTIC LEAGUE, 35

Kalahar, Gary Sports Reporter
JACKSON CITIZEN PATRIOT, 500

Kalb, Jerry Assistant General Manager
SCIOTO DOWNS, 1053

Kalb, Steven Program Director
KEOL-FM, 623

Kaler, Bill Assistant Athletics Director/Compliance
SKYHAWK ARENA, 1012

Kales, Jeannette Classified Manager
SKAGIT VALLEY HERALD, 535

Kalil, Fred Sports Director
WXIA-TV, 721

Kalin, Nathan Secretary
NEBRASKA PGA SECTIONAL OFFICE, 105

Kalina, Dennis Deputy Director of Athletics
BINGHAMTON UNIVERSITY, 324

Kalis, Christopher Lawyer
KALIS, CHRISTOPHER A., 896

Kalis, Rudy Sports Director
WSMV-TV, 718

Kalish, Joe Sales
GORILLA MARKETING, INC., 794

Kallander, Kyle Commissioner
BIG SOUTH CONFERENCE, 290

Kallay, Mike Publisher
STREET & SMITH'S SPORTS GEAR, 593

Kallechy, Jesse Assistant Coach/Director, Hockey
Operati
SOUTHERN PROFESSIONAL HOCKEY
LEAGUE, 136

Kallgren, Ted Chief Operating Officer
LAS VEGAS GOLF & TENNIS, 1243

Kalm, Kent Dept. Acting Chairperson
MINNESOTA STATE UNIVERSITY-MANKATO,
429

Kalm, Richard Executive Director
MICHIGAN GAMING CONTROL BOARD, 81

Kalmansohn, Mark
MCPHERSON & KALMANSOHN, 904

Kalmbach, Jody VP, Marketing
NORTH FACE, 1180, 1245

Kalna, Terry Chief Revenue Officer
NATIONAL HOCKEY LEAGUE/NHL, 125

Kalter, Craig Marketing VP
HANG TEN INTERNATIONAL LICENSING
CALIFORNIA CORPORATION, 1130

Kaluza, Rick Senior Associate AD, Finance &
Business
PENN STATE UNIVERSITY ATHLETICS, 341

Kamada, Bruce Director of Sales/Sponsorship
Developmen
BANDIMERE SPEEDWAY, 1031

Kameisha, John Senior Vice President
EASTERN LEAGUE, 39

Kamiel, Jerald President
GARAN, INC., 1147

Kaminski, Paul General Manager
MOTOR SPORTS RADIO, 607

Kaminsky, Howard Executive Vice President,
Finance, Chief
SPORT CHALET, INC., 1249

Kamiyama, Mark Sales and Marketing SVP
OMNICO GROUP, 942

Kamler, Brian Head Coach
USL LEAGUE TWO, 161

Kamradt, Cindy Stadium Planning & Special
Projects Dire
YANKEE STADIUM, 1030

Kamstra, Garrett President/CEO
GAME MASTER ATHLETIC COMPANY, 1146

Kanaby, Bob Publisher
INTERSCHOLASTIC ATHLETIC
ADMINISTRATION, 571

Kanady, Robert Executive Director
NFHS NEWS, 579

Kanaley, Michael Vice Chairman/Secretary
NEGRO LEAGUES BASEBALL MUSEUM, 255

Kandarian, Steven Chairman, President and CEO
METLIFE, 738

Kandt, Rob News Editor
LEXINGTON HERALD-LEADER, 506

Kane, Alan Chairman of the Board
BLUEFLY, INC., 1231

Kane, Brent Marketing Director
PENN FISHING TACKLE COMPANY, 1184

Kane, Brittany Senior Associate Director of
Athletics
BOSTON UNIVERSITY ATHLETICS, 324

Kane, Chris Sports Director
WAGT-TV, 707

Kane, Dave Sports Writer
STATE JOURNAL-REGISTER, 540

Kane, Jason Sales Manager
EAST COAST HOCKEY LEAGUE/ECHL, 130

Kane, Jennifer Chair/Director
NORTH FLORIDA UNIVERSITY OF, 432

Kane, John Senior Associate Athletic Director
SILVIO O. CONTE FORUM, 1011

Kane, Joseph President
NEW HAMPSHIRE GOLF ASSOCIATION, 113

Kane, Kenny Media &Communications Senior
Director
DAYTONA INTERNATIONAL SPEEDWAY,
1033

Kane, Laurel Associate Athletic Director
CLARKSON UNIVERSITY ATHLETICS, 382

Kane, Liz Sports Editor
MOUNTAIN DEMOCRAT, 512

Kane, Margery Journal Managing Editor
INTERNATIONAL JOURNAL OF ATHLETIC
THERAPY AND TRAINING, 571

Kane, Mary Director/Professor
MINNESOTA, UNIVERSITY OF, 429

Kane, Rachel Development & Marketing Director
EXECUTIVE DIVERSIONS, 1141

Kane, Susan Assistant Athletic Director
NORTH CENTRAL COLLEGE ATHLETICS, 397

Kaneps, Andris President
AMERICAN COLLEGE OF VETERINARY
SPORTS MEDICINE AND REHABILITATION,
928

Kaneshiro, Stacy Sports Reporter
HONOLULU ADVERTISER, 497

Kaneuji, Mac Director, Development
INTERNATIONAL FEDERATION OF
AMERICAN FOOTBALL, 89

Kang, Cathay President
ADER SPORTING GOODS INC., 1103

Kanies, Barbara National Sales Manager
LEO'S DANCEWEAR, INC., 1166

Kanigowski, Karen Manager
FOX SPORTS NET DETROIT, 608, 682

Kannenberg, Mark Vice President
WISCONSIN STATE GOLF ASSOCIATION,
116

Kanters, Michael Chair/Director
NORTH CAROLINA STATE UNIVERSITY, 431

Kantowski, Ron Sports Columnist
LAS VEGAS SUN, 505

Kantrovitz, Dan VP, Scouting
NATIONAL LEAGUE OF PROFESSIONAL
BASEBALL CLUBS, THE, 31

Kantrowitz, Marc Managing Director
PHS, LTD., 856

Kanupp, Alan Race Director
HICKORY MOTOR SPEEDWAY, 1035

Kapadia, Sheil Sports Editor
PHILADELPHIA INQUIRER, 518, 523

Kapanke, Ben Assistant General Manager
COPELAND PARK, 968

Kapanke, Dan Owner
COPELAND PARK, 968

Kapanke, Elizabeth Director of Merchandising
COPELAND PARK, 968

Kapanke, Ernie Vice President
EVENTIVE MARKETING, 762

Kapiioho, Charlee Communications Manager
ALOHA PGA SECTIONAL OFFICE, 104

Kapitan, Colin Officials Coordinator
NORTH CENTRAL INTERCOLLEGIATE
ATHLETIC CONFERENCE, 299

Kapito, Robert President
BLACKROCK, 775

Kaplan, Cliff President, Advertising and
Sponsorship S
DORNA USA, LLC, 789

Kaplan, Dean Managing Director
PUBLIC FINANCIAL MANAGEMENT, 777

Kaplan, Doug President/Publisher
WINDY CITY SPORTS, 575, 576, 579, 596,
599, 825

Kaplan, Felice Managing Editor
T & L GOLF, 594

Kaplan, Gary
KAPLAN, GARY L., 896

Kaplan, Geoff Secretary
PROFESSIONAL FOOTBALL ATHLETIC
TRAINERS SOCIETY, 89

Kaplan, Harold Chairman/Partner
DRINKER BIDDLE, 886

Kaplan, Jed Managing Partner
NATIONAL BASKETBALL ASSOCIATION
DEVELOPMENT LEAGUE, 59

Kaplan, Joshua Associate AD, Facilities
Operations & Ev
MARYLAND STADIUM, 994

Kaplan, Keith Partner
FOSTER, DON, 890

Kaplan, Lenny Director of Athletics
NEW JERSEY INSTITUTE OF
TECHNOLOGY(NJIT), 397

Kaplan, Malinda Program Director
LIFELONG FITNESS ALLIANCE, 85

Kaplowitz, Steve Sports Director
KROD, 634

Kapp, Keith Vice President
MAUPIN, TAYLOR, P.A., 851

Kappner, Johanna Chief Financial Officer
NATIONAL FOOTBALL LEAGUE/NFL, 95

Kapral, Robert Sports Editor
TIMES-LEADER, 544

Kapsenberg, Roeland Vice President, Forage
DLF INTERNATIONAL SEEDS, 1236

Kaptzan, Alex Vice President of Convention Sales
and S
TAMPA CONVENTION & VISITORS BUREAU,
246

Kapur, Amit CEO and Co Founder
GRAVITY TELEVISION & SPORTS
MARKETING, 606, 794

Karahuta, Craig VP, Football & Cheer Operations
AMERICAN YOUTH FOOTBALL, 89

Karakawa, Masayuki President/Chief Technology
Officer
CORPORATION FOR LASER OPTICS
RESEARCH, 1130

Karam, Paula Treasurer
LOUISIANA WOMEN'S GOLF ASSOCIATION,
111

Karant, Nicholas Vice President
BODY WRAPPERS/ANGELO LUZIO, 1119

Karayiannis, Jimmy Senior Associate AD,
External Operations
SOUTHERN ILLINOIS UNIVERSITY
ATHLETICS, 344

Karbo, Keith Marketing Director
MICHIGAN INTERNATIONAL SPEEDWAY
(MIS), 1038

Karcher, Chad Athletic Trainer
YORK COLLEGE (NE) ATHLETICS, 322

Karegeannes, Nick General Manager
RUDIG TROPHIES, 1195

Karen, Lackey Owner
CAPITOL SPEEDWAY, 1032

Karger, Mardy News Director
KBUN-AM, 620

Karis-Madigan, Susan General Manager
XTRA SPORTS 910, 680

Karkos, Norm Sports Director
WMTW-TV, 689, 715

Karl, Coby Head Coach
NATIONAL BASKETBALL ASSOCIATION
DEVELOPMENT LEAGUE, 60

Karlgaard, Joe Director of Athletics
RICE UNIVERSITY ATHLETICS, 342

Karlin, Terry VP Team Sales
STROMGREN SUPPORTS, INC., 1208

Karlis, Jack Sports Editor
TONAWANDA NEWS, 545

Karlitz, Herb President
KARLITZ & CO., 799

Karlovec, Bob Sports Director
WKNR SPORTS RADIO, 661

Karmitz, Ronald VP
AD MFG. COMPANY, 1103

Karner, Gary Commissioner
WISCONSIN INTERCOLLEGIATE ATHLETIC
CONFERENCE, 305

Karnick, Patrick Treasurer
GOLF COURSE BUILDERS ASSOCIATION OF
AMERICA, 100

Karnisovas, Arturas Executive VP, Basketball Operations
NATIONAL BASKETBALL ASSOCIATION/NBA, 56

Karns, Monty Sr. Associate Athletic Director, Facilit
BOONE PICKENS STADIUM, 959

Karon, Michael National President
AMERICAN YOUTH SOCCER ORGANIZATION, 154

Karp, Louis Partner
WEINER LESNIAK LLP, 869

Karpa, Dave Assistant Coach
ONTARIO HOCKEY LEAGUE, 133

Karper, Bruce VP / Director Merchandise
MAURICE SPORTING GOODS, INC., 1244

Karpf, Jennifer Founder/President
NATIONAL SPORTS MARKETING NETWORK, 221

Karpowich, Michael Director, Corporate Partnerships
AMERICAN HOCKEY LEAGUE/AHL, 126

Karr, Forrest Director of Athletics
NORTHERN MICHIGAN UNIVERSITY (NMU), 204, 367, 958, 1016

Karras, Stath President & CEO
BURNHAM REAL ESTATE SERVICES, 1061

Karrs, John Sports Information Director
LENOIR-RHYNE UNIVERSITY ATHLETICS, 362

Karsenti, Michel Publisher
YACHTS INTERNATIONAL, 600

Karsner, Mark Attorney
KARSNER & MEEHAN P.C., 897

Kartchner, Ryan Vice President
UTAH PGA SECTIONAL OFFICE, 107

Kartiganer, Ira President
IRA K. MEDALS & AWARDS INC., 1159

Karvonen, Lori Trainer
NORTH AMERICAN HOCKEY LEAGUE, 132

Kasachkoff, Sharon Director Operations
JACKSON WALKER LLP, 848

Kaser, Hope Vice President Operations
CONCESSION SOLUTIONS, INC., 1076

Kasey, Dennis Sports Director
WHMB-TV, 712

Kashow, Carol Director of Athletics
JOHN JAY COLLEGE OF CRIMINAL JUSTICE ATHLETICS, 390

Kasl, Scott New Owner
PRAIRIE GOLF, 108

Kasle, Eden News Director
WTBU-AM, 675

Kaspar, Bern Chief Executive Officer
WSHW-FM, 673

Kasper, Dave General Manager/VP, Soccer Operations
MAJOR LEAGUE SOCCER, 157

Kasper, Jon Asst. Commissioner of Media Relations
BIG SKY CONFERENCE, 290

Kasper, Susan Public Relations Liaison
ECA WORLD FITNESS ALLIANCE, 84

Kass, Steve Founder/Chief Executive Officer
AMERICAN LEISURE CORPORATION, 1058

Kassan, Michael Founder
MEDIALINK WORLDWIDE, 607

Kassel, Tim SVP Administration
CHAMPIONS WORLD, 786

Kastein, Mark Station Manager
WMBE-AM AND WCLB, 663

Kasten, Jack Director of Group Sales & Operations
NEW YORK-PENNSYLVANIA LEAGUE, 47

Kasten, Lenny National Team Manager
USA BOBSLED & SKELETON, 65, 206

Kasten, Stan CEO/President
NATIONAL LEAGUE OF PROFESSIONAL BASEBALL CLUBS, THE, 32

Kasten, Todd Partner
DIRECTION, 788

Kasubinski, Kevin Manager Of Club Services & IT
FLORIDA STATE GOLF ASSOCIATION, 110

Kaszeta, Jessica Box Office/Ticket Manager
JOSEPH L. BRUNO STADIUM, 986

Katalinas, Sue President
QUICKEN LOANS ARENA, 1003

Katehi, P.B Chancellor
TOOMEY FIELD, 1019

Kates, Beth Athletic Trainer/Outreach Coordinator
NATIONAL CENTER FOR SPORTS SAFETY, 265

Kathary, Greg Producer
FOX 59 OVERTIME, 687

Kathmann, Jo President/CEO
TOURISM BUREAU ILLINOISOUTH, 246

Katker, John National Sales Manager
FREESTYLE USA, 1145

Katler, Stacy Senior State Veterinarian
OREGON RACING COMMISSION, 82

Katlin, Frank President
MAURICE SPORTING GOODS, INC., 1244

Kato, Ryozo Chairman of the Board of Directors
JAPANESE BASEBALL HALL OF FAME AND MUSEUM, 253

Kato, Yasuji Partner
ACCUSPLIT, 1101

Katrnak, Helen VP
SOLAR TAN THRU SUITS, 1202

Katsirubas, Steve Business Systems Director
CLARKS COMPANIES NA, 1234

Katz, Cindy Talent Producer
GLOBAL SPORTS & ENTERTAINMENT, 793

Katz, Daryl Owner & Governor
NATIONAL HOCKEY LEAGUE/NHL, 124

Katz, Daryl Owner
AMERICAN HOCKEY LEAGUE/AHL, 126

Katz, Howard Chief Operating Officer
NFL FILMS, 607

Katz, John President
SOUTH ATLANTIC LEAGUE, 51

Katz, Marc Sports Reporter
DAYTON DAILY NEWS, 484

Katz, Morton. Founder
HERMAN, HERMAN, KATZ & COTLAR, L.L.P., 893

Katz, Paul Sales and Promotions Manager - Western
GNC CORPORATION, 1148

Katz, Reuven Lawyer
KATZ, TELLER, BRANT & HILD, 897

Katz, Sam President, Winnipeg Goldeyes
SHAW PARK, 1011

Katz, Saul President
CITI FIELD, 966

Katz, William Chief Marketing Officer
JERSEY NAPS, 1160

Katzman, David Vice Chairman
QUICKEN LOANS ARENA, 1003

Kaufer, Lillian Paralegal
LAW OFFICE OF WILLIAM D HOCHBERG, 899

Kauffman, Larry Vice President of Finance
KAUFFMAN SPORTS MANAGEMENT GROUP, 849

Kauffman, Peg Associate Director of Athletics
MILLERSVILLE UNIVERSITY ATHLETICS, 365

Kauffman, Rob Co-Owner
INDYCAR, 22

Kauffman, Steve Founder and President
KAUFFMAN SPORTS MANAGEMENT GROUP, 849

Kauffman, Yvonne Director of Atletic Advancement
ELIZABETHTOWN COLLEGE ATHLETICS, 385

Kaufman, Abby Athletic Trainer
NORTHLAND COLLEGE ATHLETICS, 397

Kaufman, Dalton General Manager & Coach
WOMEN'S PREMIER SOCCER LEAGUE, 164

Kaufman, Ira Sports Reporter
TAMPA TRIBUNE, 541

Kaufman, Jenneen Vice President/CFO
LP FIELD, 992

Kaufman, Kathy Advertising Manager
NEBRASKA CITY NEWS-PRESS, 513

Kaufman, Mark President
ATHLETICO PHYSICAL THERAPY, 929

Kaufmann, Josh Sports Editor
ST. ALBANS MESSENGER, 538

Kaufmann, Martin Assistant Editor
GOLFWEEK, 568

Kaul, Alice Treasurer
KANSAS WOMEN'S GOLF ASSOCIATION, 111

Kaul, Anil President
BADMINTON CANADA, 25

Kaulig, Matt Owner
NASCAR XFINITY SERIES, 24

Kaurala, Michael Operations Manager
UNITED STATES OLYMPIC EDUCATION CENTER, 224

Kaurala, Mike Operations Manager
U.S. OLYMPIC TRAINING SITE, 204

Kauth, Bill Head Athletic Trainer
ILLINOIS WESLEYAN UNIVERSITY ATHLETICS, 390

Kautz, John Production Manager
FOX SPORTS OHIO, 683

Kaval, David President
AMERICAN LEAGUE OF PROFESSIONAL BASEBALL CLUBS, THE, 30

Kavanagh, Jerry New York Bureau Chief
STREET & SMITH'S SPORTSBUSINESS JOURNAL, 593

Kavanagh, Ken Director of Athletics
FLORIDA GULF COAST UNIVERSITY ATHLETICS (FGCU), 359

Kavanaugh, Jen Senior VP, Media & Marketing
NATIONAL FOOTBALL LEAGUE/NFL, 96

Kawaja, John EVP, TaylorMade-adidas Golf
TAYLORMADE-ADIDAS GOLF, 1211

Kawakami, Tim Sports Columnist
SAN JOSE MERCURY NEWS, 533

Kawasaki, Curtis Controller
JKP SPORTS, 1160

Kay, Brady Editor
PONTOON & DECK BOAT, 582

Kay, Cathy General Manager/Controller
MASTER INDUSTRIES WORLDWIDE, LLC, 116, 1171

Kay, David Assistant General Manager
GARY SOUTH SHORE RAILCATS, 976

Kay, Liz Promotions Director
SPORTS RADIO 1080 THE FAN/KFXX, 641

Kay, Steve Treasurer
WASHINGTON STATE GOLF ASSOCIATION, 116

Kay, Steven Attorney
KAY & MERKLE, 897

Kaye, Gordon CEO
USA TABLE TENNIS, 171, 208

Kayser, Tom President/Treasurer
TEXAS BASEBALL LEAGUE (AA LEVEL), 53

Kazarian, Dan Promoter
PERRIS AUTO SPEEDWAY, 1040

Kazazian, Harry CEO
EXXEL OUTDOORS, 1141

Kazmiercak, DJ Senior Vice President, Sales & Marketing
PRESS PASS INC, 1187

Kealty, Jeff Assisant GM & Director, Scouting
NATIONAL HOCKEY LEAGUE/NHL, 124

Keane, Colin Lacrosse Operations Manager
MAJOR LEAGUE LACROSSE, 141

Keane, Patrick Executive Shareholder
GURWIN, DAVID A., 845

Keaney, Mark Sponsorship Sales
BLALOCK COMPANY, JANE, 759

Kearney, Andrew Associate AD, Compliance & Admin.
NICHOLLS STATE UNIVERSITY ATHLETICS, 339

Keathley, Hank Sports Columnist
TIMES-REPORTER, 545

Keating, Dan General Manager/Sports Director
KMSR-AM, 630, 631

Keating, Joyce Office Manager
FURMAN, INC., ANTHONY M., 792

Keating, Mary Owner/Sales Manager
KMSR-AM, 630, 631

Keating, Michael Regional Sales Manager
SOLE CHOICE, INC., 1202

Keating, Sonja SVP, General Counsel
UNITED STATES EQUESTRIAN FEDERATION, 78

Keating, Steven President & Chief Executive Officer
SOLE CHOICE, INC., 1202

Keaton, Lottie Treasurer
ARKANSAS AAU ASSOCIATION, 212

Keck, Al Sports Director
WFTS-TV, 686, 711

Keddie, Alex Senior Associate AD, Compliance
EAST CAROLINA UNIVERSITY ATHLETICS, 328

Kohl, Lacey Operations
CARRIER DOME, 963

Kohler, Matthew President
NASCAR CUP SERIES, 23

Kohler, Maxie Educational Psychology and Research
UNIVERSITY OF ALABAMA - COLLEGE OF EDUCATION/ HUMAN ENVIRONMENTAL, 438

Kohler, Michael CEO
NASCAR CUP SERIES, 23

Kohler, Shaneen Editor
HORSE NEWS, 569

Kohls, Jerry Director of racing
PORTLAND MEADOWS, 1052

Kohls, Kyle Assistant General Manager
JOE FABER FIELD, 984

Kohn, Selina Director of Athletics
PAINE COLLEGE, 368

Kohon, Mike Sports Writer
GRAND HAVEN TRIBUNE, 493

Kohrs, Dave Assistant Director for Facilities
UNI-DOME, 1021

Kohs, Cheryl Vice President Event Management
PCGCAMPBELL, 809

Kohs, Patrick Sports Director
KCHS-AM, 621

Kohuth, Barbara VP
GOLF SOLUTIONS WORLDWIDE, 1149

Kohuth, Frank President
GOLF SOLUTIONS WORLDWIDE, 1149

Koita, Dorah Secretary General
INTERNATIONAL MILITARY SPORTS COUNCIL, 201

Kojima, Tad Chairman
DAIWA CORPORATION, 1133

Kokoletsos, Bill President
STRONGWALL SYSTEMS INC., 1208

Kokoskie, Douglas Senior Associate AD for Facilites/Events
RUTGERS ATHLETIC CENTER, 1008

Kolacek, Erin Athletic Trainer
MIDDLE ATLANTIC STATES COLLEGIATE ATHLETIC CORPORATION, 297

Kolanski, Kevin Advertising Manager
TIMES-LEADER, 544

Kolasinski, Matt Associate General Manager
GILL COLISEUM, 976

Kolb, Amanda Tournament Administration
TRANS-MISSISSIPPI GOLF ASSOCIATION, 115

Kolb, David Publisher
HOCKEY BLACK BOOK, 601

Kolb, Jonathan General Manager
WOMEN'S NATIONAL BASKETBALL ASSOCIATION, 61

Kolbe, Tom Assistant Athletic Director, Communicati
TAMPA ATHLETICS, UNIVERSITY OF, 373

Kolber, Suzy Reporter
NFL 2NIGHT, 690, 692

Kolek, Craig Associate Athletic Director
RIVIER UNIVERSITY ATHLETICS, 400

Kolins, Jennifer Men's Tennis Head Coach
WESTERN NEW ENGLAND COLLEGE, 440

Kollar, Ron Sports Editor
STANDARD-SPEAKER, 538

Kollars, Brian Sports Section Editor
DAYTON DAILY NEWS, 484

Kolodziey, Greg General Manager
USL LEAGUE TWO, 163

Kolzig, Olaf Ownership Partner
WESTERN HOCKEY LEAGUE, 139

Komito, Jason Marketing/Promotion Manager
KFNS-AM, 624

Komoroski, Len CEO
NATIONAL BASKETBALL ASSOCIATION/NBA, 56, 1003

Komowroski, Brian Alternate Governor
EAST COAST HOCKEY LEAGUE/ECHL, 130

Kompon, Jaime Associate Coach
NATIONAL HOCKEY LEAGUE/NHL, 126

Koncel, Jerry Editor
MARINA DOCK AGE, 558, 575

Kondrat, Arnold Chairman
NEVADA BOB'S INTERNATIONAL, INC., 1245

Konicki, Darryl Sports Information Director
ARCADIA UNIVERSITY ATHLETICS DEPARTMENT-GLENSIDE, 378

Kono, Yasuyki President
TAIYO BIRDAIR CORPORATION, 1210

Konopasek, Richard Finance VP / Chief Financial Officer
BUCK KNIVES, INC., 1121

Konradi, Mark Sports Assistant Editor
DALLAS MORNING NEWS, 483

Konradi, Michael VP External Affairs
COTTON BOWL CLASSIC, 90

Konriff, Doug National Sales Manager
HOLOUBEK, INC., 1156

Konya, Jeff Director of Athletics
OAKLAND UNIVERSITY ATHLETICS(OU), 340, 368

Konyesni, Matt Communications and Tournament Manager
NORTHERN OHIO GOLF ASSOCIATION, 103

Koo, Yunjoo HHP Coordinator
MARYLAND, UNIVERSITY OF, 427

Koonce, Charles Associate Director/Internship Director
METHODIST COLLEGE PROFESSIONAL GOLF MANAGEMENT PROGRAM, 102

Koonce, Edie Administrator
MIDDLEBERG RIDDLE GROUP, 905

Koonin, Steve CEO
NATIONAL BASKETBALL ASSOCIATION/NBA, 56

Koonz, Brian Sports Reporter
NEWS-TIMES, 517

Koopmann, Bob Assistant Athletic Director
ROCKFORD COLLEGE ATHLETICS, 400

Kooy, Timothy
GEIGER & KEEN LLP, 891

Kopas, Matt Vice President of Ticketing
ATLANTIC LEAGUE, 35

Kopcsak, Michael Partner
GOWEN, GEORGE W., 891

Kopelke, Paul News Director
WNST-AM, 666

Kopp, Brian Vice President, Strategic Planning
STATS LLC, 939

Kopp, Mara President
COW PALACE, 968

Kopp, Terry Director of Sales
BOISE CONVENTION & VISITORS BUREAU, 227

Koppelman, Baker Senior VP, Ticket Sales & Operations
NATIONAL FOOTBALL LEAGUE/NFL, 95

Koppelman, Lilli Event Director
ECA WORLD FITNESS ALLIANCE, 84

Koprivica, Gary General Manager
BOB WARD & SONS, INC., 1231

Kopsa, Cory Advertising Manager/News & Sports Direct
KRFS-AM, 634

Kopsea, Matt Sports Reporter
SOUTH BEND TRIBUNE, 536

Kor, Alex President
AMERICAN ACADEMY OF PODIATRIC SPORTS MEDICINE, 83

Koranda, Stephen Executive Director
NORMAN CONVENTION & VISITORS BUREAU, 241

Korando, Russell Sports Editor
ST. CHARLES JOURNAL, 538

Korba, Andrew Director of Sports Information
HIRAM COLLEGE ATHLETICS, 389

Korba, Tati Assistant Athletic Director
GOUCHER COLLEGE ATHLETICS, 387

Korbatov, Igor
ISRAEL, FRIEDBERG & KORBATOV L.L.P., 895

Korbyl, Richard President
AWARDS AND PERSONALIZATION ASSOCIATION, 216

Korch, Jody Sports Editor
EAGLE HERALD, 487

Korch, William News Director
WEDO-AM, 651

Kordes, Ron President
PIONEER REGIONAL COMMISSIONER/USA VOLLEYBALL, 210

Koreen, Nancy Managing Editor
PARACHUTIST, 581

Korff, John President
KORFF ENTERPRISES, 766

Korff, William Sports Reporter
BANNER-NEWS, 465

Korman, Howard CEO
BEST BET, 1055

Korn, Alison Manager, Media Relations & Communication
CANADIAN PARALYMPIC COMMITTEE, 191

Korn, Corinne Office Manager
INTERNATIONAL ASSOCIATION OF GOLF TOUR OPERATORS, 101

Korn, Leonard Vice President
INTERNATIONAL LEAGUE, 43

Kornachuk, Shanna Senior Associate AD, Compliance & Studen
QUINNIPIAC UNIVERSITY ATHLETICS, 342

Kornacki, Karen Sports Reporter
KMBC-TV, 699

Kornberg, Howard Sole Practitioner
KORNBURG, HOWARD CRAIG, 898

Kornblut, Phil Host
SPORTS TALK, 616

Kornder, Nick Asst. Commissioner For Media Relations
NORTHERN SUN INTERCOLLEGIATE CONFERENCE, 300

Kornegay, Tim Executive VP & CFO
AMERICAN LEAGUE OF PROFESSIONAL BASEBALL CLUBS, THE, 30

Kort, Shari Advertising Manager
GEORGIA MARBLE COMPANY, 1148

Korte, Steve Sports Reporter
BELLEVILLE NEWS-DEMOCRAT, 466

Kortekaas, Sally Classified Manager
HERALD (WA), 496

Korth, Joanne NFL, Bucs, NHL/Lightning
TAMPA TRIBUNE, 541

Korth, Todd Editor
PACKER REPORT, 581

Korzeniewski, Keri President
KESN-FM, 623

Kosco, Frank Merchandising VP
CAMPMOR, INC., 1233

Koscs, Matt Head Athletic Trainer
NEW JERSEY INSTITUTE OF TECHNOLOGY(NJIT), 397

Kosel, Warren Senior Director, Public Relations
AMERICAN HOCKEY LEAGUE/AHL, 128

Koser, Kathy Department Chairperson
CALIFORNIA STATE UNIVERSITY-FULLERTON, 414

Kosiba, Cassie Associate AD, Internal Ops./SWA
SOUTH DAKOTA SCHOOL OF MINES & TECHNOLOGY ATHLETICS, 344

Kosin, Phil Publisher
CHICAGOLAND GOLF, 560

Koski, John Vice President
WHBQ-TV, 711

Koson, Mark Stadium Manager
UNM ARENA, 1023

Kosseff, Alex Executive Director
AMERICAN MOUNTAIN GUIDES ASSOCIATION, 69

Kost, Jacqueline Legal Personnel Director
BAKER & DANIELS, 872

Kostecka, Norma Advertising Director
NAPA VALLEY REGISTER, 513

Kosten, Herb Finance VP
LITTLE MISS TENNIS/TV SPORTS, 1167

Kosten, Marilyn Founder/President
LITTLE MISS TENNIS/TV SPORTS, 1167

Kosth, Dan Chief Executive Officer
SPORTS MEDIA, INC., 1205

Kostur, Pat
WFRM-AM, 653

Kosub, LeAnna Assistant Sports Editor
SAN ANTONIO EXPRESS-NEWS, 532

Koszewski, Bill Chief Technology Officer & Interim CEO
PROGEAR, INC., 1189

Kotarba, Richard Partner
MEYER, UNKOVIC & SCOTT, LLP, 905

Kotarski, Justin Retail Sales
COOPERSBURG SPORTS, 1235

Kotcher, Ray Senior Partner & Chairman
KETCHUM NEW YORK, 800

Kotchik, Jim SVP/Chief Financial Officer
ROSE QUARTER BOX OFFICE, 1007

Kotelly, Mary Human Resources Executive
PORTER ATHLETIC EQUIPMENT COMPANY,
1186

Kothe, Paula Advertising Director
FAIRBANKS DAILY NEWS-MINER, 490

Kotlarek, Neal Editor
PAR EXCELLANCE MAGAZINE, 581

Kotrappa, Vijay Programs/General Information
AMERICA'S SCHOOLS PROGRAM, 775

Kotsonis, Nick Attorney
CRIVELLO, CARLSON, MENTKOWSKI S.C.,
884

Kotyk, Brenden Manager, Hockey Operations &
Assistant C
EAST COAST HOCKEY LEAGUE/ECHL, 130

Kou, Tami Public Relations Manager
KOHL'S DEPARTMENT STORES, 1243

Koudelka, Steve Assistant Athletic Director
LYNCHBURG COLLEGE ATHLETICS, 392

Koukis, Natalie Men's and Women's
Swimming/Diving Head C
WITTENBERG UNIVERSITY, 441

Kouleyan, Armen President
EXXEL OUTDOORS, 1141

Kousouris, Lou Senior VP. Business
Development
AMERICAN LEAGUE OF PROFESSIONAL
BASEBALL CLUBS, THE, 29

Koutsothanasis, Argy Contributing Writer
GOLF FOR WOMEN, 566

Kouvaris, Sam Sports Director
WJXT-TV, 713

Kovac, Joan Chairperson
BERGERON RODEO GROUNDS AND
ENTERTAINMENT CENTER, 1045

Kovach, Brad Senior Associate Editor
MOTOR BOATING, 577

Kovach, Eva Athletic Department Coordinator
CONNECTICUT COLLEGE ATHLETICS, 383

Kovak, Mike Sports Reporter
OBSERVER-REPORTER, 519

Kovash, Ken VP, Player Personnel
NATIONAL FOOTBALL LEAGUE/NFL, 95

Koveleski, Oscar Founder/Designer
AUTO SPORTS MARKETING GROUP, 758,
782

Kowachek, Ed President
SUN MOUNTAIN SPORTS, 1209

Kowalczyk, Paul Director of Athletics
HUGHES STADIUM (CO), 980

Kowalski, Terry Promotions Director
WTEN-TV, 718

Kowalski, Will Golf, Bowling, General Sports
BATTLE CREEK ENQUIRER, 465

Kowalsky, Rick Assistant Coach
NATIONAL HOCKEY LEAGUE/NHL, 124

Kowel, Barb Director Of Professional
Development
COLLEGE SPORTS INFORMATION
DIRECTORS OF AMERICA/COSIDA, 281

Koyama, Monica New Media Director
FX NETWORKS, LLC, 683

Kozak, Stefan Chief Executive Officer
RED BULL NORTH AMERICA, 740

Kozil, Cindy Vice President
NJCAA REGION XXI WOMEN'S, 288

Kozinn, Jared Director of Business Development
FORD FIELD, 974

Kozlevcar, Sandra General Manager
WFIN RADIO, 653

Kozlowski, Ginny Executive Director
VISIT NEW HAVEN, 248

Kozlowski, Virginia Director
VISIT NEW HAVEN, 248

Kozminski, Whendy Sports Editor
RECORD-ARGUS, 528

Kozole, Kelly Senior VP, Business Development
NATIONAL FOOTBALL LEAGUE/NFL, 95

Kppinski, Kenny Head Groundskeeper
LINDQUIST FIELD, 992

Kraak, Robert President
RODER USA, INC., 1075

Krabach, Sean Director of Event Operations
DETROIT METRO SPORTS COMMISSION,
231

Kraemer, Jayne Asst General Manager / Events
RUSHMORE PLAZA CIVIC CENTER, 1008

Kraft, Harvey Marketing Director
KAGAN WORLD MEDIA, 799

Kraft, Jonathan President
NATIONAL FOOTBALL LEAGUE/NFL, 96

Kraft, Justin Assistant Professor of Physical
Educatio
MISSOURI WESTERN STATE COLLEGE, 430

Kraft, Pat Director of Athletics
BOSTON COLLEGE ATHLETICS, 324

Kraft, Pat Executive Director, Citywide Sales
PHILADELPHIA SPORTS CONGRESS, 242

Kraft, Patrick Director of Athletics
TEMPLE UNIVERSITY ATHLETICS, 346

Kraft, Robert Chairman/CEO
NATIONAL FOOTBALL LEAGUE/NFL, 96

Kraft, Robert Partner
LEVINSON, FRIEDMAN, P.S., 899

Krafthofer, Mike News Director
WARK-AM, 643

Krafthofer, Shaun Assistant Facility
Director/Evening Supe
UNIVERSITY OF HARTFORD SPORTS
CENTER, 1022

Kraftick, Chris Athletic Director
CUMBERLAND COLLEGE ATHLETICS, 309

Krage, Joe Chief Financial Officer
MIKEN SPORTS, 1173

Kragthorpe, Kurt Sports Writer
SALT LAKE TRIBUNE, 532

Krahn, Rebecca Mutuel Manager and Assistant
General Man
GENEVA LAKES GREYHOUND TRACK, 1056

Krajewski, Steven Real Estate Manager
CABELA'S, 1123, 1233

Krakora, Kevin Executive VP/CFO
DIEBOLD INCORPORATED, 1135

Kral, Darcy Managing Director of Membership &
Suppor
CANADIAN PROFESSIONAL GOLFERS'
ASSOCIATION, 99

Krall, Nick VP & General Manager
NATIONAL LEAGUE OF PROFESSIONAL
BASEBALL CLUBS, THE, 31

Kram, Jon President
UNITED STATES HOCKEY LEAGUE, 136

Kramarck, Steve Program Director
WKHS-FM, 660

Kramer, Ed General Manager
WPDR RADIO, 640, 668

Kramer, Irwin Chairman/CEO
ICONGO.COM, 1226

Kramer, Jack President
JACKSTER COMPANY, 1159

Kramer, Jill Women's Volleyball Head Coach
WEST VIRGINIA UNIVERSITY, 439

Kramer, Kent President
PROFESSIONAL SPORTS MARKETING, INC.,
811, 859

Kramer, Kristine Commissioner
IOWA RACING & GAMING COMMISSION, 80

Kramer, Kurt VP
PROFESSIONAL SPORTS MARKETING, INC.,
811, 859

Kramer, Kyle Founder
SPORTS LINK, INC., 865

Kramer, Matt Director Public Relations
CAREER SPORTS & ENTERTAINMENT, 836

Kramer, Michaela Publications Editor
NATIONAL TRACTOR PULLERS
ASSOCIATION, 18

Kramer, Richard Chairman, CEO and President
GOODYEAR TIRE & RUBBER CO., THE, 736

Kramer, Rob President
INTERNATIONAL GAME FISH ASSOCIATION,
88

Kramer, Shelley Buyer
PUSH PEDAL PULL, 1247

Kramer, Steven VP and Chief Technology Officer
ICONGO.COM, 1226

Kramer, Ted Publisher
OBSERVER (OR), 519

Kramig, Tom President/CEO
FRONTIER LEAGUE, 41

Kramme, Keith Director of Retention
MIDLAND UNIVERSITY, 315

Kranjc, Chris Assistant Athletic Director
HASTINGS COLLEGE ATHLETICS, 312

Kranjcec, Mark Retail Advertising Director
DAILY CAMERA, 478

Krantz, Bryan President
FAIR GROUNDS CORPORATION, 1047

Krantz, Drew Marketing Associate
FITNESS INFORMATION TECHNOLOGY, 564

Kraska, Kyle Sports Director/Anchor
KFMB-TV, 697

Krath, Joe Vice President/Creative Director
MOFFETT PRODUCTIONS, INC., 607

Kratish, Esther Treasurer
KRYPTONICS U.S.A., 1164

Kratish, Samuel President
KRYPTONICS U.S.A., 1164

Kratz, Janelle Head Athletic Trainer
REDLANDS ATHLETICS, UNIVERSITY OF,
400

Kratzer, Jarrett Associate AD, Operations
HARTFORD ATHLETICS, UNIVERSITY OF,
331

Krause, Bob Athletics Director
WAGNER FIELD/KSU, 1026

Krause, David Attorney
ROLLINS, RON, 912

Krause, Earl Asst Editor
AREA AUTO RACING NEWS, 555

Krause, Hans President
RAE CROWTHER COMPANY, 1191

Krause, Peter Chief Financial Officer
CARHARTT INC., 1234

Krause, Steve Sports Editor
DAILY ITEM (MA), 479

Krauss, Mark President
AMERICAN CORD & WEBBING COMPANY,
INC., 1107

Kravitz, Bob Sports Columnist
INDIANAPOLIS STAR, 499

Krawitz, Natalie Finance and Administration VP
ARNET, WILLIAM F., 871

Krebs, Becky President
NJCAA REGION XIV MEN'S, 286

Krebs, Paul Vice-President, Athletics
UNM ARENA, 1023

Kreeft, Andrew Partner
ROSENTHAL, ROBERT E., 912

Kreibich, Josh General Manager
NATIONAL BASKETBALL ASSOCIATION
DEVELOPMENT LEAGUE, 60

Kreidler, Mark Sports Columnist
SACRAMENTO BEE, 530

Kreidler, Phil College Scouting Coordinator
NATIONAL FOOTBALL LEAGUE/NFL, 97

Kreidt, Tim Head Athletic Trainer
DICKINSON STATE UNIVERSITY ATHLETICS,
310

Kreig, Richard Lawyer
LEWIS, KING, KRIEG & WALDROP, P.C., 900

Kreigbaum, Joe Local Sales/Dealer Support
RHINO SPORTS, 1193

Kreis, Jason Head Coach
USL LEAGUE ONE, 160

Kreisen, John Contributing Writer
RINKSIDE, 584

Kreiter, Keith Founder/CEO
EDGE SPORTS INTERNATIONAL, INC., 840

Krejcarek, Bob Sports Director
WLDY-AM, 662

Krejci, Bill Athletic Director
NJCAA REGION XI WOMEN'S, 286

Krell, Marnie Marketing & Communications
Coordinator
CANADA'S SPORTS HALL OF FAME, 250

Kremchek, Timothy Medical Director
NATIONAL LEAGUE OF PROFESSIONAL
BASEBALL CLUBS, THE, 31

Kremer, Andrea Reporter
NFL 2NIGHT, 692

Kremer, Joe Vice President, General Manager
CAROLINA LEAGUE, 37

Kremer, Ron Sports Writer
HERALD-NEWS, 496

Krenicki, Aimee Head Athletic Trainer
MITCHELL COLLEGE ATHLETICS, 396

Krenke, Brian President
KI, 1163

Krenzer, Paul Director of Ticket Operations
FLORIDA STATE LEAGUE, 39

Krepto, Laurie Associate
MONTGOMERY, MCCRACKEN, WALKER &
RHODAS, LLP, 906

Kresky, Pete Director of Corporate Sales and
Sponsors

Kuhn, John Director of Business Development
FLORIDA STATE LEAGUE, 40, 1011, 1019
Kuhn, Maddie Sports Reporter
HUGO DAILY NEWS, 498
Kuhn, Rick Vice President
NORTH DAKOTA GOLF ASSOCIATION, 113
Kuhnel, Doug Senior Vice President
VENUWORKS, 1075, 1076
Kuhns, Mike Sports Editor
POCONO RECORD, 524
Kuhnt, Bernhard President & CEO
BMW OF NORTH AMERICA, LLC, 734
Kukla, Ryan Director of Ticket Operations
SCHAUMBURG BOOMERS STADIUM, 1010
Kuklinski, Dan Director of Athletic
Communications
CARDINAL STRITCH UNIVERSITY
ATHLETICS, 308
Kulczycki, Bill Sales Director
PATAGONIA, 1184
Kulczyk, Katherine Media Contact
NEW ERA CAP, CO, 1178
Kulesza, J. Vice-President
NJCAA REGION XXI WOMEN'S, 288
Kulfan, Ted Sports Reporter
DETROIT NEWS, 486
Kulina, Robert VP/General Manager
MONMOUTH PARK, 1051
Kulish, Rob Director of Athletic Communications
RUTGERS UNIVERSITY-NEWARK
ATHLETICS, 401
Kulkarni, Arun President
KOOLATRON, 1164
Kull, Ed Director of Intercollegiate Athletics
FORDHAM UNIVERSITY ATHLETICS, 330
Kull, Scott Deputy AD, External Operations
UTAH ATHLETICS, UNIVERSITY OF, 348
Kulland, Jake Sports Director
KNDK-FM, 631
Kullenberg, David Tournmant Official, PGA
CAROLINAS PGA SECTION, 104
Kulp, Kevin President
EASTERN LEAGUE, 38
Kumar, Rajni Manager
FAIRMOUNT PARK RACETRACK, 1047
Kummola, Kalervo Vice President (FIN)
INTERNATIONAL ICE HOCKEY FEDERATION
(IIHF), 122
Kump, Joan Promotions Director
WJPZ-FM, 659
Kunde, Gene Chief Operating Officer
BIRKENSTOCK FOOTPRINT SANDALS INC.,
1231
Kunsey, Steve Director, Business Development
AMERICAN HOCKEY LEAGUE/AHL, 128
Kuntz, Daniel Athletic Director
CALIFORNIA LUTHERAN UNIVERSITY
ATHLETICS / CLU SPORTS, 380
Kunz, Mark Sports Director
WBKB-TV, 708
Kupchak, Mitch General Manager/President,
Basketball Op
NATIONAL BASKETBALL ASSOCIATION/NBA,
56
Kupelian, Peter Lawyer
KUPELIAN, ORMOND & MAGY, 898
Kupen, Marcel President
MARCEL V. KUPER, CPA/PFS, CFE, 776
Kuper, Melissa Assistant GM
ROGER DEAN STADIUM, 1006
Kuperstein, Adam Sports Anchor/Reporter
WTVJ-TV, 719
Kupper, Mike Senior Assistant Sports Editor
LOS ANGELES TIMES, 507
Kupperman, Louis Partner
OBERMAYER, REBMANN, MAXWELL &
HIPPEL, LLP, 907
Kuppig, Vince Sports Editor
HASTINGS TRIBUNE, 495
Kura, Michael
POITINGER REDMOND LYONS KURA &
WALKER, 856
Kuri, Carlos President
CEO MANUFACTURERS, 1125
Kurita, Yoshinosuke Owner
TENACIOUS LTD, 1212
Kurkjian, Adam Sports Writer
DAILY NEWS TRANSCRIPT, 481

Kurkowski, Cindy President
BADGE-A-MINIT LTD., 1113
Kurkowski, Sue Director, Facility Operations
STATE UNIVERSITY OF NEW YORK, 1015
Kurn, Werner Secretary
DIVING EQUIPMENT & MARKETING
ASSOCIATION, 73
Kurpius, David Associate Vice Chancellor for
Enrollment
TIGER STADIUM, 1019
Kurtenbach, Aelred Chairman
DAKTRONICS, INC., 1133
Kurtenbach, Frank Vice President Sales
DAKTRONICS, INC., 1133
Kurtin, Anthony Associate Director of Athletics
ST. FRANCIS COLLEGE ATHLETICS (SFC),
372
Kurtz, Amanda Senior Associate AD/SWA
PEPPERDINE UNIVERSITY ATHLETICS, 341
Kurtz, Glory Editor
WOMEN'S PRO RODEO NEWS, 556, 583, 599
Kurtz, Jason Sports Director
WZVN-TV, 721
Kurtz, Jesse Weekend Sports Anchor
KKTV-TV, 699
Kurtz, Nolan Executive Director/Practice
Operations
BUCHANAN INGERSOLL ROONEY PC, 845,
878
Kurtz, Norman Chairman
WSP, 1073
Kurtzner, Bob Strength & Conditioning
Coordinator
SOUTHERN VERMONT COLLEGE
ATHLETICS, 403
Kurvers, Peter Honorary President
MINNESOTA PGA SECTIONAL OFFICE, 105
Kurvers, Tom General Manager & Alternate
Governor
AMERICAN HOCKEY LEAGUE/AHL, 124, 127
Kurz, Jason Sports Director
WZVN-TV, 721
Kush, Ken Sports Editor/Writer
YORK NEWS-TIMES, 553
Kushner, Jeff Marketing Director
ABSOLUTE FITNESS, INC, 1100
Kushner, Scott Chief Operating Officer
IN STORE SPORTS NETWORK, 684
Kusinski, Peggy Sports Reporter
WMAQ-TV, 715
Kusinuk, Michael Sports Marketing Director
LEHIGH VALLEY SPORTS COMMISSION, 237
Kuster, Tom Associate AD, Sports Performance
JAMES MADISON UNIVERSITY ATHLETICS,
333
Kutches, Alex Secretary
THE ACCESS FUND, 69
Kutler, Ken Intercollegiate Athletics Director
ITHACA COLLEGE ATHLETICS, 982
Kuttner, Peter President
CAMBRIDGE SEVEN ASSOCIATES INC., 1061
Kuwada, Robert Sports Reporter (UCLA)
ORANGE COUNTY REGISTER, 520
Kuykendall, Charles SVP/Principal
BMK ARCHITECTS, 1060
Kuykendall, Steve Crew Chief
NASCAR GANDER OUTDOORS TRUCK
SERIES, 23
Kuzcka, Kathy Circulation
AROUND THE RINGS, 610
Kuzmick, Thomas Partner
RAWLE LAW OFFICES, 910
Kuznar, Christine Senior Associate AD,
Academics/SWA
INDIANA UNIVERSITY-PURDUE UNIVERSITY
FORT WAYNE, 332
Kvas, William Attorney
HUNEGS, STONE, LENEAVE, KYAS &
THORNTON, P.A., 894
Kvederis, Brad Sports Writer
VALLEJO TIMES-HERALD, 548
Kvinlaug, Steve Sales VP
ALPINA SPORTS CORPORATION, 1106
Kwapis, John Chief Operating Officer
BLUE BIRD CORPORATION, 935
Kwasney, Ben Sports Copy Editor
VENTURA COUNTY STAR, 549
Kyer, Maureen EVP Merchandising
MERVYN'S, 1245

Kyle, Tim Athletic Director
SPECTRUM CORPORATION, 1203
Kyler, Jake Copy Editor
STREET & SMITH'S SPORTSBUSINESS
JOURNAL, 593
Kyles, Charles Member
STUART LAW FIRM, P.L.L.C, 919
Kyrias, Alex Director, Communications & Sales
NORTH AMERICAN HOCKEY LEAGUE, 131
Kysela, Chris Sales
M.B.I. PRODUCTS CO., INC., 830

L

L Gebhart, Esq, Patrick Assistant Executive
Director
PENNSYLVANIA INTERSCHOLASTIC
ATHLETIC ASSOCIATION, 200
L Gulis Jr, Stephen EVP, Chief Financial Officer,
and Treasu
WOLVERINE WORLD WIDE, 1222
L J. Harper, Scott Attorney
BROWN, HALL, SHORE & MCKINLEY LLP,
877
L Jo Belle, John President
KINSEY ASSOCIATES, 1070
L L. Boeckmann, Alan Chairman/Chief Executive
Officer
FLUOR CORPORATION, 1066
L Werbell IV, Mitchell President
BRIGADE QM, 1120
L. A. Sellers, Jeffery Attorney
STOREY, MOYES, 918
L. D Allain, Jean-Marc President & Chief
Executive Officer
FAIRTRON, 1142
L. Gi Hartman, Bruce Executive Vice President
and Chief Finan
VENATOR GROUP, INC., 1252
L. Howson Jr, Arthur Shareholder
CLARDY, DON S., 882
L. Jo Katz, Brian President
PINNACLE ENTERPRISES, INC., 856
L. M. Layman, Michael Attorney
LAYMAN, MICHAEL L., 899
L. M. Sanett, Stephen Vice-Chairman, President
and Interim Chi
STURM, RUGER & COMPANY, INC., 1208
L. Tanner Jr, James Partner
WILLIAMS & CONNOLLY, 869
LaBarbera, Mark Director of Athletics
VALPARAISO UNIVERSITY, 348, 439
LaBelle, Kurt Sports Anchor
KHQA-TV, 698
LaBianco, Jaime Executive Secretary
WILLIAM & MARY HALL, 1026, 1028
LaBoy, Drew Director of Ticket Sales/Operations
ATLANTIC LEAGUE, 35, 956
LaBrake, Randy Associate Director of Athletics
ST. LAWRENCE UNIVERSITY ATHLETICS,
403
LaBrie, Brad Sports Editor
PENINSULA DAILY NEWS, 522
LaBroad, Michael Chief Marketing Officer
RFDTV, 694
LaBue, Joe VP, Ticket Sales & Services
NATIONAL FOOTBALL LEAGUE/NFL, 95
LaChica, Angela Vice President
SAN DIEGO HALL OF CHAMPIONS SPORTS
MUSEUM, THE, 257
LaComfora, Peggy Promotions Manager
KYTV-TV, 706
LaCroix, Norman Chief Financial Officer
QUINN, JAMES W., 910
LaFleur, Matt Head Coach
NATIONAL FOOTBALL LEAGUE/NFL, 95
LaFollette, Drew Director of Promotions &
Marketing
MIDWEST LEAGUE, 45
LaForest, Leonardo President
MARSHFIELD FAIR, 1050
LaFoy, Cheryl Director of Event Operations
BOBBY DODD STADIUM AT HISTORIC
GRANT FIELD, 959
LaGamma, Sean Managing Director
TIMELINE VIDEO, 609
LaGesse, Bobby Sports Editor
DAILY TRIBUNE (IA), 483

NEW ENGLAND ATHLETICS, UNIVERSITY OF, 397

Leighton, Tim Sports Reporter (High School)
SAINT PAUL PIONEER PRESS, 531

Leiker, Allen Sports Assistant Editor
LAS VEGAS REVIEW-JOURNAL, 504

Leimgruber, Jennifer Senior Vice President of Programming
PREMIERE RADIO NETWORKS, 611

Leinen, John Vice President of Convention & Tour
RENO-SPARKS CONVENTION AUTHORITY, 243

Leip, Tom Business Operations
NORTHWEST BASEBALL LEAGUE, 48

Leipold, Craig Owner & Governor
NATIONAL HOCKEY LEAGUE/NHL, 124

Leisering, David Interim Director of Sports Information
BLOOMSBURG UNIVERSITY ATHLETICS, 353

Leishman, Nadine Sports Communications Coordinator
PARK UNIVERSITY PIRATE ATHLETICS, 317

Leisner, Jeanne Treasurer
SOUTH JERSEY GOLF ASSOCIATION, 114

Leistner, Klaus Vice President, Finance
INTERNATIONAL BIATHLON UNION (IBU), 61, 202

Leitao, Alex Chief Executive Officer
NATIONAL WOMEN'S SOCCER LEAGUE, 158

Leiter, Alex President / Chief Executive Officer
5TH AND OCEAN CLOTHING, 1099

Leiter, Luis Vice President
5TH AND OCEAN CLOTHING, 1099

Leitner, Elaine President
KITE TRADE ASSOCIATION INTERNATIONAL, 140

Leitner, Jim Sports Editor
TELEGRAPH HERALD, 542

LeitÆo, Alex CEO
MAJOR LEAGUE SOCCER, 157

Leiweke, Tim President & CEO,AEG
STAPLES CENTER/ANSCHUTZ ENTERTAINMENT GROUP, 1014

Leiweke, Tod Owner & CEO
NATIONAL HOCKEY LEAGUE/NHL, 125

Lekhtman, Gregory President
BIOSIG INSTRUMENTS, INC., 1117

Leland, Carl Vice President
NATIONAL ASSOCIATION OF COLLEGIATE GYMNASTICS COACHES - WOMEN, 119

Leland, Gary Owner / President
BASEBALLJUNK.COM, 1229

Leloudis, George Executive Director
CARDWELL, VICTOR, 880

Lemak, Lawrence Founder
NATIONAL CENTER FOR SPORTS SAFETY, 931

Lemak, Matthew Chairman
NATIONAL CENTER FOR SPORTS SAFETY, 265

Lemak, Matthew Chief Executive Officer
LEMAK SPORTS MEDICINE & ORTHOPEDICS, 930

Lemay, Christina Associate Director
ESPN TELEVISION, 681

Lembo, Elaine Managing Editor
CRUISING WORLD, 561

Lemerand, Eric IRM Operations Manager
ELLIS PARK, 1047

Lemieux, Jason Recreational Sales & Marketing
NOLIMITZ, 1180

Lemieux, Mario Co-Owner & Chair
NATIONAL HOCKEY LEAGUE/NHL, 125, 190

Lemm, Erica Senior Woman Administrator
YESHIVA UNIVERSITY ATHLETICS, 410

Lemon, Brian VP, Lacrosse Operations
NATIONAL LACROSSE LEAGUE, 141

Lemon, Chet Director
FLORIDA AAU ASSOCIATION, 212

Lemon, Jennifer Advertising Director
PRESS-TELEGRAM, 527

Lemon, John Director, System Implementation and Cus
TICKET TO GO, LLC, 943

Lemond, Mark President/Chief Executive Officer
SHOE CARNIVAL, 1249

Lemons, Bruce President
FORESITE DESIGN, INC., 1066

Lemons, David Principal
COOKE DOUGLASS FARR LEMONS/LTD., 1062

Lemons, David Principal
COOKE DOUGLASS FARR LEMONS/LTD., 1062

Lemox, Cheryl Senior Vice President, Marketing & Promo
INTEGRATED SPORTS MARKETING, 685

Lempke, Roger VP
NEBRASKA SPORTS COUNCIL, 262

Len, Robert Partner
WOLF GROUP-NY, 826

Lenarz, Josh Assistant Athletics Director
TRINITY CHRISTIAN COLLEGE ATHLETICS, 321

Lenfest, Richard Athletics Director
WESTFIELD STATE COLLEGE ATHLETICS (WSC), 408

Lengerich, Ryan Director of Sports Information
MOUNT ST. JOSEPH ATHLETICS, COLLEGE OF, 396

Lenggenhager, Marilyn Treasurer
ARKANSAS WOMEN'S GOLF ASSOCIATION, 109

Lenich, Mike Treasurer
U.S. HOCKEY HALL OF FAME, 257

Lennon, Dale Director of Athletics
MARY ATHLETICS, UNIVERSITY OF, 336

Lennon, Dave Sports Reporter (Yankees)
NEWSDAY, 517

Lennon, Elizabeth Sports Life coach
PATTERSON SPORTS VENTURES, 808

Lennox, Dave President/CEO
SPECIAL OLYMPICS WASHINGTON, 195

Lennox, William University President
SAINT LEO UNIVERSITY, 370

Lenstrom, Jay Chief Marketing Officer
GMR MARKETING, 764

Lenth, Teri Corporate Sponsorships Director
BIG TEN ATHLETIC CONFERENCE, 290

Lentz, Ben Director, Ticket Operations
NATIONAL FOOTBALL LEAGUE/NFL, 97

Lentz, Heather Promotions Director
KSDR-AM, 635

Lentz, Jim CEO
TOYOTA MOTOR SALES, U.S.A., 742

Lentz, Mike Director, Ticket Operations
AMERICAN LEAGUE OF PROFESSIONAL BASEBALL CLUBS, THE, 31

Lenz, Darrin Service Manager
AUTOMATED BATTING CAGES CORPORATION, 1112

Lenz, John Sports Editor
DAILY STAR, 483

Lenz, Mark Group SVP/Chief Financial Officer
SHOR, ALAN P., 916

Lenz, Melanie Chief Development Officer
AMERICAN LEAGUE OF PROFESSIONAL BASEBALL CLUBS, THE, 30

Leo, Don Sports Director
WJOX-AM SPORTS RADIO, 659

Leon, Lee Director of Athletics
ABILENE CHRISTIAN UNIVERSITY ATHLETICS, 334, 350, 1023

Leon, Rene Program Director
KZNM-FM, 640

Leon, Rennie Director of Marketing Development
SMOKIES PARK, 1012

Leonard, Amy Director of Development for Athletics
CALIFORNIA BAPTIST UNIVERSITY ATHLETICS, 308

Leonard, Bruce Classified Manager
STANDARD-SPEAKER, 538

Leonard, John Executive Director
AMERICAN SWIMMING COACHES ASSOCIATION, 170

Leonard, Kelly General Manager
KRAN, 633

Leonard, Leanne Secretary
WOMEN'S METROPOLITAN GOLF ASSOCIATION, 117

Leonard, Ran Chairman
OKLAHOMA HORSE RACING COMMISSION, 82

Leonard, Scott CEO
A.D.D. MARKETING AND ADVERTISING, 779

Leonard, Sean Svp/CFO
AMBAC ASSURANCE CORPORATION, 775

Leonard, Tim Director of Athletics
TOWSON STATE UNIVERSITY ATHLETICS, 347

Leonard, Tod Sports Reporter
SAN DIEGO UNION-TRIBUNE, 532

Leonardi, Dave Publisher
SKIER NEWS, 586

Leone, Charles Operations Division Manager
ORLANDO CITRUS BOWL, 999

Leonis, Ted Founder/Chairman/Majoriy Owner/CEO
VERIZON CENTER, 1024

Leonsis, Ted Founder, Chair, Principal Partner & CEO
NATIONAL HOCKEY LEAGUE/NHL, 58, 126

Lepine, Gilles Director, Performance and Team Support
BRITISH COLUMBIA ATHLETICS, UNIVERSITY OF, 307

Lepkowski, Craig Secretary
INTERNATIONAL POLICE MOUNTAIN BIKE ASSOCIATION (IPMBA), 70

Lepore, Marianne Office Administrator
GARDEN EMPIRE VOLLEYBALL ASSOCIATION, 209

Lepping, Rich Chairman of the Board
U.S. CURLING ASSOCIATION, 70

Lerch, E. Senior Vice President
L. ROBERT KIMBALL & ASSOCIATES, 1070

Lerch, Wayne Principal
ERICKSON MCGOVERN, 1065

Lerette, Lindsay Sales and Marketing Manager
KELLOGG ARENA, 245, 987

Lerick, Tom General Manager / Construction
H&B SPECIALIZED PRODUCTS, 1151

Lerman, Steve Director, Sales and Marketing
LYCIAN STAGE LIGHTING, 1169

Lermond, David Deputy Executive Secretary
VIRGINIA RACING COMMISSION, 83

Lerner, Mark Managing Principal Owner
NATIONAL LEAGUE OF PROFESSIONAL BASEBALL CLUBS, THE, 33

Lerner, Stephen Partner
SQUIRE, SANDERS & DEMPSEY, LLP, 917

Lerner, Theodore Founding Principal Owner
NATIONAL LEAGUE OF PROFESSIONAL BASEBALL CLUBS, THE, 33, 997

Les, Wally GHIN Regional Manager-SE Florida
FLORIDA STATE GOLF ASSOCIATION, 110

Lesako, Mark Head Athletic Trainer
WASHINGTON & JEFFERSON COLLEGE ATHLETICS (W&J), 407

Lesar, Al Sports Assistant Editor
SOUTH BEND TRIBUNE, 536

Leschper, Lee Advertising Manager
JUNEAU EMPIRE, 502

Lese, Jon Treasurer
FAIRFIELD COUNTY SPORTS COMMISSION, 232

Lesesne, Troy Head Coach
USL LEAGUE TWO, 159, 162

Lesher, Wayne President
AMERICAN RACING DRIVERS CLUB INC./ARDC, 16

Leske, Lucy Vice-Chairman
NJCAA REGION XXI MEN'S, 288

Lesley, Campbell Publicity Director
WHEELING ISLAND GAMING, INC., 1057

Leslie, Bryan Director, Building Operations
COCA-COLA COLISEUM, 966

Leslie, Jack Chairman
WEBER SHANDWICK WORLDWIDE, 825

Leslie, Mike Head Coach
NATIONAL BASKETBALL LEAGUE OF CANADA, 59

Lesmerises, Doug Sports Reporter
NEWS JOURNAL (DE), 88, 515

Lesniak, Raymond Senior Partner/Corporate Law Department
WEINER LESNIAK LLP, 869

Lesnick, David Sports Editor
DAILY INTER LAKE, 479

Lesnik, Josh President
KEMPERLESNIK, 101

Lessard, Jeff Executive Vice President
FOX RIVER MILLS, INC., 1145

executive index

Mancuso, Bob Chairman
GREATER OMAHA SPORTS COMMITTEE, 233

Mandalinski, Sarah Marketing Director
US CELLULAR CENTER, 1023

Mandel, Eric Sports Reporter
DAILY BREEZE, 477

Mandel, Irwin SVP, Financial & Legal
MANDEL, IRWIN, 902

Mandelaro, James Sports Writer
DEMOCRAT AND CHRONICLE, 485

Mandell, Bruce Chairman
USL CHAMPIONSHIP, 159

Mandery, Sharon Event Services Director
PERSHING CENTER, 1000

Mandeville, Karen Administrative Assistant
WEST VIRGINIA INTERCOLLEGIATE
ATHLETIC CONFERENCE, 305

Mandeville, Lou Sports Director
WOON-AM, 667

Mandraccia, Jenna Attoney
ELY, BETTINI, ULMAN & ROSENBLATT, 888

Mandrick, Fred Owner/Founder
A.V. CONCEPTS, 827

Manemeit, Craig Associate
LICARI & WALSH, L.L.C., 900

Maner, Sue Executive Vice President
SPECIAL OLYMPICS SOUTH CAROLINA, 195

Maneri, Lauren Program Specialist
SPECIAL OLYMPICS NEW YORK, 194

Manetta, Edward Commissioner
NEW YORK COLLEGIATE ATHLETIC
CONFERENCE, 299

Maney, Tom Senior Vice President Advertising
Sales
FOX SPORTS NETWORKS/FOX SPORTS
NET, 683

Manfred, Rob Executive Vice President,
Economics & Le
KAUFFMAN STADIUM, 27, 29, 31, 987

Mang, Robert Chief Executive Officer / Director
GALYAN'S TRADING COMPANY, INC., 1240

Mangan, Chris Sports Editor
CAPITAL JOURNAL, 470

Mangan, John Program Director
KVTI-FM, 638

Mangan, Tony News Director
KLXS-FM, 629

Manganello, Ed Chairman
OLYMPIA SPORTS, 1182

Mangano, Edward Ex Officio
NASSAU COUNTY SPORTS COMMISSION, 240

Mangano, Mary Membership Coordinator
ICE SKATING INSTITUTE, 86

Mangas, Mike Sports Director
KRCR-TV, 702

Mange, Tela Vice President Communications
SPECIAL OLYMPICS TEXAS, 195

Mangels, Tonya Marketing/Sales Director
KAUFFMAN STADIUM, 987

Manget, Daniel Sports Information Director
MILLIGAN COLLEGE ATHLETICS, 315

Mangini, Ron SVP
JACQUES MORET, 1159

Mangione, Fred Chief Operating Officer
BARCLAYS CENTER, 956

Manglesdorf, Liz ISI National Skating Programs
Coordinato
ICE SKATING INSTITUTE, 86

Mango, James Chief Operating Officer
PIMLICO RACE COURSE, 1052

Mangrum, Will Senior Vice President
BRAILSFORD & DUNLAVEY, 1060

Mangum, A. Editor
WESTERN HORSEMAN, 598

Manheimer, Micki Sports Information Associate
WHITTIER FIELD, 1027

Manhing, Don President
NJCAA REGION IV WOMEN'S, 285

Manhufe, Paul Advertising Manager
SIERRA VISTA HERALD, 535

Maniates, Cindy Costume Artist
AARDVARK MASCOTS, 1100

Manickam, Shanta Manager of Marketing and
Digital Service
AMERICAN URBAN RADIO NETWORKS, 610

Manion, Kirt Sports Editor
NEBRASKA CITY NEWS-PRESS, 513

Manion, Laura Business Development
GROUP II COMMUNICATIONS, 845

Mankin, Robert Senior Associate
NBBJ, 1071

Manley, Dirk Director, New Business
Development
EAST COAST HOCKEY LEAGUE/ECHL, 129

Manley, Greg Vice President
PACIFIC NORTHWEST PGA SECTIONAL
OFFICE, 106

Manley, Len Sales
KART MARKETING INTERNATIONAL, INC,
573, 800

Manley, Michael CEO
FCA US, LLC, 736

Mann, Aaron Communications and Media
USA CANOE/KAYAK, 68, 206

Mann, Brian Senior Associate AD
UC BERKELEY ATHLETICS, 347

Mann, Harold News/Sports Director
KLVI-AM 560, 629

Mann, Jennifer Reporter -Advertising, Marketing,
Public
KANSAS CITY STAR, 502

Mann, Marie President
BRIGHT SITES, INC, 1120

Mann, Michael Sales Manager
CHET COPPOCK, 615

Mann, Mitch Associate AD, External Operations
FALCON STADIUM, 973

Mann, Randy Vice President for Athletics
MARY HARDIN-BAYLOR ATHLETICS(UMHB),
394

Mann, Robert Chief Executive Officer
BRIGHT SITES, INC, 1120

Mann, Troy Head Coach
AMERICAN HOCKEY LEAGUE/AHL, 126

Mann, Victor Head Coach
CEDAR RAPIDS RIVER KINGS, 94

Manning, Archie Chairman
NATIONAL FOOTBALL FOUNDATION AND
COLLEGE HALL OF FAME, INC., THE, 250,
254

Manning, Bill President
USL LEAGUE ONE, 94, 158, 160

Manning, D. Marketing Director
CELEBRITY SUPPLIERS OF LAS VEGAS, 837

Manning, Jeff Advertising Reporter
OREGONIAN, 520

Manning, Jonathan Sports Editor
SOUTHWEST DAILY NEWS, 537

Manning, Joshua Editor
FLORIDA HORSEMEN, 565

Manning, Julie Deputy Athletics Director/SWA
MINNESOTA ATHLETICS, UNIVERSITY OF,
337

Manning, Lisa Senior VP, Marketing
NATIONAL FOOTBALL LEAGUE/NFL, 94

Manning, Marcus Director of Athletics
MARYVILLE UNIVERSITY ATHLETICS, 364

Manning, Michael Partner
STINSON MORRISON HECKER LLP, 918

Manning, Michelle Senior Woman Administrator
ITHACA COLLEGE ATHLETICS, 390

Manning, Steven Partner
MANNING, MARDER, KASS, ELLROD, &
RAMIREZ, 902

Manning, Tom Director, Marketing/Sales/Public
Relatio
PRAIRIE MEADOWS RACETRACK AND
CASINO, INC, 1052

Mannino, Brian Director of Baseball Operations
VA MEMORIAL STADIUM, 1024

Mannino, Peter Head Coach
UNITED STATES HOCKEY LEAGUE, 136

Mannion, Dennis President & CEO
PALACE OF AUBURN HILLS, THE, 222, 855,
999

Mannix, Dan President/CEO
LEADDOG MARKETING GROUP, 801

Manns, Kevin Director of Athletics for Media
Relation
WINSTON-SALEM STATE UNIVERSITY
ATHLETICS, 377

Mano, Barry Publisher
REFEREE MAGAZINE, 220, 584

Manoloff, Dennis Sports Writer
PLAIN DEALER, 524

Manos, Mike Program Director
KADA-AM, 619

Mansell, John Senior Analyst/Consultant
KAGAN WORLD MEDIA, 575, 799

Mansell, Kevin President
KOHL'S DEPARTMENT STORES, 1243

Mansfield, Christina Vice President Human
Resources
GARDA WORLD, 774

Mansfield, David President
CORSAIR DISPLAY SYSTEMS, INC., 1130

Mansfield, Eileen Managing Editor
POWER & MOTORYACHT, 582

Mansfield, Gregg Editor
POWERBOAT, 582

Mansfield, Jim Executive Director
MUNCIE SPORTS COMMISSION INC, 240

Mansfield, Timothy Principal
CAMBRIDGE SEVEN ASSOCIATES INC., 1061

Manske, Rob Vice President
COLLEGE CONCEPTS, LLC., 1235

Mansolino, Tony Hitting Coach
EASTERN LEAGUE, 38

Manson, Dan Treasurer
MONROE COUNTY SPORTS COMMISSION,
240

Manson, Dave Assistant Coach
AMERICAN HOCKEY LEAGUE/AHL, 126

Mansouri, Ali Owner
USL LEAGUE TWO, 162

Mansson, Fabian President and Chief Executive
Officer
EDDIE BAUER, INC., 1238

Mansueto, Joe Owner/Chairman
MAJOR LEAGUE SOCCER, 157

Mansur, Linda Editor/Publisher
REVENUES FROM SPORTS VENUES, 602

Mansusi, Thomas General Sales Manager
WFAN SPORTS RADIO, 652

Manthei, Farrah Deputy AD/SWA
ILLINOIS AT CHICAGO ATHLETICS,
UNVIERSITY OF, 332

Mantz, Sheila Advertising Manager
VICKSBURG POST, 549

Manuel, John Co-Editor in Chief
BASEBALL AMERICA, 556

Manuel, Ryan VP - Baseball Operations
CAROLINA LEAGUE, 38

Manuel, Warde Director of Athletics
MICHIGAN ATHLETICS, UNIVERSITY OF, 336,
995

Manzano, Rinny Vice President
STELLARTV-SPORTS, 609

Manzello, Nick Sports Columnist
TELEGRAM & GAZETTE, 542

Manzer, Will President and CEO
EASTERN MOUNTAIN SPORTS, INC., 1237

Manzi, John Director, Public Relations
MONTICELLO RACEWAY, 1051

Manzione, AmySue Operations Coordinator
GEORGE M. STEINBRENNER FIELD, 976

Manzo, Barbara Vice president
USTA FLORIDA, 173

Maples, Steve Executive Director
VON BRAUN CENTER, 1026

Maquire, Mick Assistant Athletic Director
CLARKSON UNIVERSITY ATHLETICS, 382

Mara, Chris Senior VP, Player Personnel
NATIONAL FOOTBALL LEAGUE/NFL, 96

Mara, Dan Internal Operations
CENTRAL ATLANTIC COLLEGIATE
CONFERENCE, 291

Mara, John President/CEO
NATIONAL FOOTBALL LEAGUE/NFL, 96

Marakhovski, Roman Assistant/Video Coach
EAST COAST HOCKEY LEAGUE/ECHL, 129

Marano, Brandon General Manager
LAKEWOOD BLUECLAWS, 990

Marca, Gian-Michele Partner
COOLEY, GODWARD, LLP, 883

Marcel, Andre Program Director
WDKX-FM, 650

Marcelo, Cassandra Marketing and Box Office
Coordinator
U.S. CELLULAR CENTER, 1020

March, Cody Director of Operations
COLUMBIA EMPIRE REGIONAL
COMMISSIONER/USA VOLLEYBALL, 209

Marquardt, Jon Group Sales Manager
UNITED STATES HOCKEY LEAGUE, 137
Marquez, Paty Project Architect
ALBANESE/BROOKS/ASSOCIATES P.C., 1058
Marquez, Sally Executive Director
NEW MEXICO ACTIVITIES ASSOCIATION, 199
Marquez-Rocha, Miriam Office Manager
TECNIFIBRE USA, 1211
Marquis, Trent Chairman
YAKIMA VALLEY SUNDOME, 1030
Marr, Greg Editor-in-Chief
SILENT SPORTS, 586
Marran, Dave Sports Editor
KENOSHA NEWS, 502
Marrapese-Burrell, Nancy Sports Reporter
BOSTON GLOBE, 468
Marrelli, Tammy-Lynn Manager Customer Service
VOYAGER CUSTOM PRODUCTS, 1220
Marrello, John General Manager
USL LEAGUE TWO, 163
Marrero, Eli Manager
FLORIDA STATE LEAGUE, 39
Marrochello, Drew Director of Athletics
BOSTON UNIVERSITY ATHLETICS, 324, 997
Marrone, Phillip Member
MARRONE, ROBINSON, FREDERICK & FOSTER, 902
Mars, Jacqueline Vice Chairman
NATIONAL SPORTING LIBRARY, THE, 255
Mars-Proietti, Laura Editorial Director
SPORTS MARKET PLACE DIRECTORY, 603
Marsack, Gary Attorney
LINDNER & MARSACK, S.C., 900
Marschalek, Jim Vice President
ADVANCED DESIGN CONCEPTS, 1104
Marsee, Mike Sports Writer
ADVOCATE-MESSENGER, 461
Marsh, Chris Category Manager
LESCO, INC., 15, 1166
Marsh, Dave Athletic Director
NORTHWOOD UNIVERSITY, 367
Marsh, David VP
PELTON MARSH KINSELLA, 830
Marsh, Dennis President
CROWN TROPHY COMPANY, 1235
Marsh, Jim Advertising Manager
CANOE & KAYAK MAGAZINE, 559
Marsh, John President
S.L. OUTERBANKS LLC, 1196
Marsh, Mike Principal
DAVIS DESIGN, 1063
Marshall, Bryan Director for Sports Information
MILLIKIN UNIVERSITY ATHLETICS, 395
Marshall, Chris Director, Corporate Sales & Partnerships
PIONEER BASEBALL LEAGUE, 50, 958
Marshall, Clint News Director
WDPN-AM, 650
Marshall, Darlene Executive Director of Elementary Educati
TRINITY MOTHER FRANCES ROSE STADIUM, 1020
Marshall, Debra Vice President, Marketing
HEALTH FITNESS CORPORATION, 1068
Marshall, Douglas Attorney
KAY & MERKLE, 897
Marshall, Ian Vice President
CONNECTICUT PGA SECTIONAL OFFICE, 104
Marshall, Jim Vice President
WYOMING STATE GOLF ASSOCIATION, 117
Marshall, John General Manager/Vice President
CALDER CASINO & RACE COURSE, 1046
Marshall, Kathy Operations
PENDLETON CONVENTION CENTER, 1000
Marshall, Ken Director Operations
HAZEL PARK HARNESS RACEWAY (HPHR), 1049
Marshall, Lance Assistant Director of Athletics
FRANKLIN COLLEGE ATHLETICS (FC), 386
Marshall, Larry Director of Athletics
WAYNESBURG COLLEGE ATHLETICS, 407
Marshall, Patti Marketing Director
WBOB-AM 1160 SPORTS RADIO, 646
Marshall, Sharon General Counsel
ACTIVE INTERNATIONAL, 774

Marshall, Tonja Sports Program Manager
CANTON/STARK COUNTY CONVENTION & VISITORS BUREAU, 259
Marso, John Co-Owner
RIVERFRONT STADIUM, 1006
Marson, Eric Editor
LA GOLF MAGAZINE, 573
Marson, Jo Faculty Athletics Representative
VITERBO ATHLETICS UNIVERSITY, 321
Martel, Peter Vice President
NJCAA REGION XXI WOMEN'S, 288
Martella, Rob Director of Operations
U.S. YOUTH SOCCER ASSOCIATION, 266
Marten, Steve General Manager
WBIG-AM, 646
Martens, Rainer Publisher
SPORT HISTORY REVIEW, 215, 571, 589
Martens, Steve President
INTERNATIONAL HANDGUN METALLIC SILHOUETTE ASSOCIATION, 149
Martensen, Finn Attorney at law
SELECT SPORT AMERICA, 1198
Marth, Ben Sports Reporter
WGEM-TV, 711
Martha, Morales Vice President
ASSOCIATION OF INTERNATIONAL MARATHONS AND DISTANCE RACES, 148
Martin, Adam Director of Facilities and Operations
CONVOCATION CENTER: EMU, 967
Martin, Becky Assistant Director of Athletics
MCDANIEL COLLEGE ATHLETICS, 394
Martin, Bob Chief Executive Officer
PERFORMANCE, INC./PERFORMANCE BICYCLE SHOP, 1246
Martin, Bobby Director of Athletics
SOUTHERN NAZARENE UNIVERSITY ATHLETICS, 371
Martin, Bowie President
MARTIN-KILPATRICK, 1170
Martin, Brandon Director of Athletics
MISSOURI-KANSAS CITY ATHLETICS, UNIVERSITY OF, 337
Martin, Bridget Senior Associate AD, Compliance/SWA
MCNEESE STATE UNIVERSITY ATHLETICS, 336
Martin, Bud Senior Vice President, SFX Sports
SFX SPORTS GROUP, 863
Martin, Cathy News Director
WLER-FM, 662
Martin, Chris Assistant Athletics Director
SOUTHWEST BAPTIST UNIVERSITY ATHLETICS, 292, 372
Martin, Craig Managing Partner
MORRISON & FOERSTER LLP, 906
Martin, Dan Director of Facilities and Operations
MASSACHUSETTS INSTITUTE OF TECHNOLOGY (MIT), 394, 514
Martin, Darrick Head Caoch
NATIONAL BASKETBALL ASSOCIATION DEVELOPMENT LEAGUE, 60
Martin, Dave President, Gable
MARTIN STONE QUARRIES, 402, 1170
Martin, David Vice President, Business Development
U/S SPORTS ADVISORS, 430, 764, 868
Martin, Dennis VP Sales
WQSN AM 1660, 670
Martin, Derek President
CANADIAN PREMIER LEAGUE, 156, 477
Martin, Don Principal
MARTIN SPORTS, INC., 689, 1170
Martin, Doug COO
COLORADO SPRINGS SPORTS CORPORATION, 229
Martin, Drew Executive Senior Associate AD, External
TEXAS AT AUSTIN ATHLETICS, UNIVERSITY OF, 346
Martin, Edmund Board Chairman
ACKERMAN MCQUEEN ADVERTISING, 1058
Martin, Edward President
ASSOCIATION OF RACING COMMISSIONERS INTERNATIONAL, 82, 118
Martin, Edward President / Chief Executive Officer
DUNLAP CO., 1237
Martin, Elizabeth General Manager
CALIFORNIA LEAGUE (A-LEVEL), 36, 1009

Martin, Emily Special Events Manager
WAR MEMORIAL STADIUM, 1026
Martin, Gary Sports Editor
FORT BEND HERALD & TEAXS COASTER, 491
Martin, Gay Sales Coordinator
STANLY HEADWEAR, 1207
Martin, Glenn President
MARTIN STONE QUARRIES, 1170
Martin, Greg Treasurer
AMERICAN SOCIETY OF GOLF COURSE ARCHITECTS, 98
Martin, Hannah Athletics Administrative Assistant
KANSAS WESLEYAN UNIVERSITY ATHLETICS, 313
Martin, Harold Sports Copy Editor
OWENSBORO MESSENGER-INQUIRER, 521
Martin, Harry Partner
STEAMBOAT SKI & BIKE KARE INC., 1208
Martin, Ian Program Director
KNML - ALBUQUERQUE, 631
Martin, J. VP / Head Designer
FUBU THE COLLECTION, 1146
Martin, Jackie Content Manager
VARSITY BRANDS, INC., 1218
Martin, James Senior Editor
TENNIS, 594
Martin, Jamie EVP Racing
MOHAWK RACETRACK, 1051
Martin, Janet President
COMMUNICATION ARTS INCORPORATED, 1062
Martin, Jean Advertising Manager
WKVG-AM, 661
Martin, Jeff Creative Services Director
CHAMPIONSHIP GROUP, INC., 218, 837
Martin, Jenny Account Director
THE KING PARTNERSHIP, 822
Martin, Jessica Director of Marketing
ESPN TELEVISION, 681
Martin, Joe Treasurer
FEDERATION OF PETANQUE USA, 144
Martin, John President
TURFER SPORTSWEAR, 1216
Martin, Jon Assistant Commissioner
NORTH CENTRAL INTERCOLLEGIATE ATHLETIC CONFERENCE, 299
Martin, Josh Sports Editor
GETTYSBURG TIMES, 493
Martin, Juanita Assistant to the President
ATLANTA MOTOR SPEEDWAY, 1031
Martin, Keith Athletic Director
NJCAA REGION III MEN'S, 284
Martin, Kirby Director Of Competitions
GOLF ASSOCIATION OF PHILADELPHIA, 110
Martin, LeAnn Vice President
U.S. HANDBALL ASSOCIATION, 120
Martin, Leon Owner
NATIONAL BASKETBALL LEAGUE OF CANADA, 59
Martin, Lonnie El Mirage Maintenance Club Liaison
EL MIRAGE DRY LAKE, 1042
Martin, Mark Chief Operating Officer
MARMOT MOUNTAIN LTD., 708, 1170
Martin, Mary Vice President
NATIONAL ASSOCIATION OF WOMEN'S GYMNASTICS JUDGES, 119
Martin, Matt Vice President Market Manager
TICKET760 KTKR, 642
Martin, Maurice Agent
BLACKSTAR SPORTS MANAGEMENT, INC., 836
Martin, Mike Sr. Vice President Of Sales & Service
EAST COAST HOCKEY LEAGUE/ECHL, 129
Martin, Nanett President
SAN JOAQUIN COUNTY FAIR, 1053
Martin, Preston Governor
POTOMAC VALLEY AAU ASSOCIATION, 214
Martin, Reg Chairman
DUNLAP CO., 1237
Martin, Ren, General Manager
FRONTIER LEAGUE, 42
Martin, Rhonda Athletics Office Manager
MOUNT MERCY COLLEGE ATHLETICS, 316, 633
Martin, Rod VP
MARTIN STONE QUARRIES, 1170

executive index

Executive Index

Michael, Vollmer Vice Chair
CANADIAN SAFE BOATING COUNCIL, 64

Michaelian, Jim President/CEO
GRAND PRIX ASSOCIATION OF LONG
BEACH, 16

Michaelis, Vicki (703)570-8777
USA TODAY, 548

Michaels, Andrea President of Extraordinary
Events
EXTRAORDINARY EVENTS, 763

Michaels, Bob Sports Director
WELM-AM, 652

Michaels, Brendan Operations Manager
WKAN AM 1320, 660

Michaels, Carrie Associate Director of Athletics
SHIPPENSBURG UNIVERSITY OF
PENNSYLVANIA ATHLETICS, 370

Michaels, Chad Sports Director
WDOR-FM, 650

Michaels, Dan Program Director
WBIZ-AM SPORTS RADIO, 646

Michaels, Elaine President
SAN DIEGO COUNTY WOMEN'S GOLF
ASSOCIATION, 114

Michaels, Jeff Director of Athletics
SHIPPENSBURG UNIVERSITY OF
PENNSYLVANIA ATHLETICS, 370

Michaels, Jon EVP Operations
EXTRAORDINARY EVENTS, 763

Michaels, Scott General Manager
PETERSEN EVENTS CENTER, 1001

Michalec, Matt Director of Sports
Communications
NORFOLK STATE UNIVERSITY
ATHLETICS(NSU), 366

Michalik, Bettiann Sports Information Director
FITCHBURG STATE COLLEGE (FSC)
ATHLETICS, 386

Micham, Ray Architect/Partner
THE COLLABORATIVE, INC., 1062

Michaud, Marcel Customer Service Associate
BLADEMASTER, 1118

Michaud, Nancy Senior VP, General Counsel -
Secretary
HUFFY BICYCLE COMPANY, 1157

Michaud, Nancy SVP, General Counsel /
Secretary
ROYCE UNION BICYCLE COMPANY, INC.,
1195

Michaux, Scott Sports Columnist
AUGUSTA CHRONICLE, 464

Michele, Dennis President
AMERICAN VOLKSSPORT
ASSOCIATION/AVA, 216

Micheletto, John Head Coach, Ice Hockey
MULLINS CENTER, 996

Michelle A. Haggar, Dr. MD
HAGGAR CORPORATION, 1152

Michelotti, Brian Assistant Director
MONTANA HS ASSOCIATION, 199

Michiaels, Jeramy Associate Director of
Broadcasting
NCAA, 607

Michlig, Keith Assistant Athletic Director for
Sports I
GEORGIA SOUTHWESTERN STATE
UNIVERSITY ATHLETICS, 360

Middlebrook, Chris President
USA BANDY, 25

Middleburg, Ira Managing Partner
MIDDLEBERG RIDDLE GROUP, 905

Middleton, Donnie Sports Director
KMEM-FM, 630

Middleton, John Managing Partner
NATIONAL LEAGUE OF PROFESSIONAL
BASEBALL CLUBS, 32

Middleton, Kisha Athletic Business Manager
LINCOLN UNIVERSITY ATHLETICS, 363

Middleton, Michelle Administrative and Finance
EXPLORE FAIRBANKS, 231

Middleton, Rand Sports Reporter
WEST CENTRAL TRIBUNE, 551

Midkiff, Patty Controller
NATIONAL SPORTS AGENCY, 853

Midland, Greg Associate Editor
GOLF MAGAZINE, 567

Miech, Rob Sports Reporter
LAS VEGAS SUN, 505

Miedema, Laurence Sports Reporter
SAN JOSE MERCURY NEWS, 533

Mientkiewicz, Doug Manager
SOUTHERN LEAGUE OF PROFESSIONAL
BASEBALL CLUBS, 52, 992

Miers, Don Florida Operations Director
JOKER MARCHANT STADIUM, 986

Mierzwa, Donald EVP, Store Operations
ODD LOTS/BIG LOTS, 1246

Mietus, Jeff President
WESTERN NEW YORK PGA SECTION
OFFICE, 107

Migala, Dan Executive Editor
TEAM MARKETING REPORT, 576, 594

Migala, Katie Customer Service
MIGALA REPORT, 576

Miglarese, John Head Coach
USL LEAGUE TWO, 163

Miglia, Dave Operations Manager
CARSON EVENTS INTERNATIONAL, INC., 760

Migliano, Kristen Director of Athletics
LYNN UNIVERSITY, 427

Migra, Bob Sports Writer
PLAIN DEALER, 524

Miguel-Minford, Dawne Advertising Manager
MAUI NEWS, 509

Mike, Vickee Advertising Manager
EVENING TIMES (PA), 490

Mike, Woleben President
PHILIP B. ELFSTROM STADIUM, 1001

Mikel, Seth Assistant Athletics Director for
Communic
TAYLOR UNIVERSITY ATHLETICS, 320

Mikesch, Pat Head Coach/General Manager
UNITED STATES HOCKEY LEAGUE, 137

Miketinac, Chuck Host
MAXIMUM SPORTS, 687

Mikkelson, Chastity Secretary
JAMESTOWN CIVIC CENTER, 984

Mikkelson, Ryan Sports Information Director
UNIVERSITY OF JAMESTOWN ATHLETICS,
321

Miklasz, Bernie Sports Columnist
SAINT LOUIS POST-DISPATCH, 531

Mikler, Kip Editor
VELO NEWS, 597

Mikoshiba, Toshiaki Chairman & CEO, American
Honda Motor Co.
AMERICAN HONDA MOTOR CO., 733

Miktinj, J. President
ACE MAGNETICS.COM, 1227

Mikulik, Joe Manager
TEXAS BASEBALL LEAGUE, 53

Miladi, Alex Refree Director
UNITED STATES SOO BAHK DO
FEDERATION, 143

Milam, Brian Sports Director
WYMT-TV, 721

Milani, Jerry Assoc. Commissioner Media
Relations
NEW YORK COLLEGIATE ATHLETIC
CONFERENCE, 299

Milani, Mo Treasurer
GREENSBORO SPORTS COMMISSION, 233

Milano, Filippo Coach
WOMEN'S PREMIER SOCCER LEAGUE, 164

Milanovich, Jasmina Corporate Secretary &
Director
ALCOHOL AND GAMING COMMISSION OF
ONTARIO, 79

Miles, Brent President
NORTHWEST BASEBALL LEAGUE, 36, 48,
992, 1019

Miles, David Assistant Director- Booking
LAVELL EDWARDS STADIUM, 990

Miles, Dwight Director, Sales & Marketing
EATON GOLF PRIDE, 1138

Miles, Gary Sports Deputy Editor
PHILADELPHIA INQUIRER, 523

Miles, Kathleen Chief Financial Officer
FGM ARCHITECTS & ENGINEERS, 1066

Miles, Kiprian VP / Chief Information Officer
GOLFSMITH INTERNATIONAL, INC., 1150,
1241

Miles, Mark CEO
INDYCAR, 22

Miles, Mark Vice President of Business
Operations/Sa
WESTERN HOCKEY LEAGUE, 139

Miles, Patrick Advertising Manager
REFEREE MAGAZINE, 584

Miles-Ralston, Cathy Editor
CHICAGO DISTRICT GOLFER, 560

Miley, Josh Head Athletic Trainer
HANNIBAL-LA GRANGE COLLEGE
ATHLETICS, 311

Milholm, Joelle Sports Reporter
LODI NEWS-SENTINEL, 506

Milian, Jorge Sports Reporter
PALM BEACH POST, 521

Milios, Andrew VP, Ticket Sales
CHUKCHANSI PARK, 965

Miliotis, Dino Owner
D.P.M. ENTERPRISES, 1132

Milkman, Velvet Administration - Senior Woman
Administra
ROY STEWART STADIUM, 1008

Milkovic, Mile Manager
CANADIAN SOCCER LEAGUE, 156

Mill, Brandon Director
FOCUS GOLF SYSTEMS, INC., 1145

Millar, Alan General Manager
WESTERN HOCKEY LEAGUE, 138

Millar, Matt Goaltending Development Coach
AMERICAN HOCKEY LEAGUE/AHL, 127

Millen, Corey Head Coach/General Manager
NORTH AMERICAN HOCKEY LEAGUE, 133

Millen, Michael Secretary
VIRGINIA STATE GOLF ASSOCIATION, 116

Millen, Pat President, Chief Executive Officer
INTEGRITY SPORTS MARKETING, MEDIA &
MANAGEMENT, 797

Millen, Rod President/Chief Executive Officer
RHYS MILLEN RACING, 18

Miller, Alex National Competition Director
SPORTSCAR VINTAGE RACING
ASSOCIATION, 18

Miller, Alison Chief Development Officer
SPECIAL OLYMPICS MICHIGAN, 193

Miller, Allyn President
FLAIR COMMUNICATIONS, 791

Miller, Amy Corporate Press Contact
PRIORITY HEALTH, 72

Miller, Aon President
TENNESSEE GOLF ASSOCIATION/TGA, 115

Miller, Arthur President
DRYBRANCH, INC./SPORT DESIGN, 1136

Miller, B.J. Assistant General Manager
PIONEER BASEBALL LEAGUE, 50

Miller, Becky Promotions Director
KWNB-TV, 705

Miller, Beth Sr. Associate Athletic Director/Senior
W
KENAN MEMORIAL STADIUM, 987

Miller, Bethany Director of Athletics
BIOLA UNIVERSITY ATHLETICS, 307

Miller, Bill Director of Athletics
TEXAS LUTHERAN UNIVERSITY ATHLETICS,
405

Miller, Bob Sports Editor
TYRONE DAILY HERALD, 547

Miller, Brian SVP, Corporate Governance
KOHL'S DEPARTMENT STORES, 389, 395,
1243

Miller, Brooks Assistant Athletic Director
TRINE UNIVERSITY ATHLETICS, 321

Miller, Bryce Executive Sports Editor
DES MOINES REGISTER, 485

Miller, Buddy Advertising Manager
WAGT-TV, 707

Miller, Carolyn Sales & Product Information
ADVANCED CUTTING SYSTEMS, INC., 1103

Miller, Casey Membership Manager
U.S. TAEKWONDO UNION, 143

Miller, Catherine Owner & Director
MILLER & ASSOCIATES, CATHERINE, 766

Miller, Chance Senior Deputy AD
SOUTH CAROLINA ATHLETICS, UNIVERSITY
OF, 344

Miller, Charlie Managing Editor
ATHLON SPORTS COMMUNICATIONS, 555

Miller, Chris Head Athletic Trainer
LINDSEY WILSON COLLEGE ATHLETICS, 97,
114, 313, 538, 653, 710

Miller, Cliff Asst. AD, Development
CHARLESTON SOUTHERN UNIVERSITY
ATHLETICS, 325

Monchaux, Jan Technical Chief
FORMULA 1, 19

Mondale, Ted CEO/Executive Director
HUMBERT HUMPHREY METRODOME, 980

Mondillo, Keith Director of Athletics
GWYNEDD MERCY COLLEGE ATHLETICS,
388

Mondora, Kelly Operations Director
HAAS-JORDAN COMPANY, 1152

Mondou, Martin General Manager
QUEBEC MAJOR JUNIOR HOCKEY LEAGUE,
135

Monette, Scot President
AUTHENTIC SPORTS INVESTMENTS, 1229

Monfore, Robert
MONFORE GROUP, INC, 853

Monfort, Charles Owner/General Partner
NATIONAL LEAGUE OF PROFESSIONAL
BASEBALL CLUBS, THE, 31

Monfort, Richard Owner/Chairman/CEO
NATIONAL LEAGUE OF PROFESSIONAL
BASEBALL CLUBS, THE, 31, 968

Monfrey, Pat Publisher
HEALTH & FITNESS MAGAZINE, 569

Mong, Harry Regional Sports Director
SPECIAL OLYMPICS NEVADA, 194

Mongell, Mike President
GEORGIA PGA SECTIONAL OFFICE, 104

Mongello, Kara Office Administrator
AMERICAN HORSE COUNCIL, 73

Moniaci, Steve Director of Athletics
HOUSTON BAPTIST UNIVERSITY
ATHLETICS, 312

Moninghoff, Mick Sports Director
WQAD-TV, 717

Monke, Dustin Sports Editor
DICKINSON PRESS, 487

Monken, Jeff Head Coach, Football
MICHIE STADIUM, 995

Monkiewicz, Diane Interim Assistant Director of
Athletics
MANSFIELD UNIVERSITY ATHLETICS, 363

Monkres, Kim Assistant Director
UTAH HIGH SCHOOL ACTIVITIES
ASSOCIATION, 200

Monnens, Ryan Director, Professional Scouting
NATIONAL FOOTBALL LEAGUE/NFL, 96

Monnin, Mary Sports Writer
BUFFALO NEWS, 469

Monopli, Joy Advertising Director
NEWS & ADVANCE, 515

Monroe, Mark Sports Writer
BLADE, 467

Monroe, Melanie Head Athletic Trainer
TRINITY CHRISTIAN COLLEGE ATHLETICS,
321

Monroe, Mike NBA Sports Writer
SAN ANTONIO EXPRESS-NEWS, 532

Monsky, Robin President
ROUND ROBIN SPORTS, 815

Monson, Doug Director of Athletic
Communications
STONEHILL COLLEGE ATHLETICS, 373

Monson, Gordon Sports Columnist
SALT LAKE TRIBUNE, 532

Montag, Thomas Chief Operating Officer
BANK OF AMERICA CORPORATION, 733

Montagna, Deanna Director Of Office Operations
& Students
ALASKA SCHOOL ACTIVITIES ASSOCIATION,
197

Montague, Jeff Undergraduate Coordinator/Asst.
Dean
TEMPLE UNIVERSITY, 437

Montague, Krista Athletic Director
MONTANA STATE UNIVERSITY BILLINGS
ATHLETICS, 366

Montana, Todd Assistant Director of Athletics
LASELL COLLEGE ATHLETICS, 392

Montanez, Roberto President
PARACHUTE INDUSTRY ASSOCIATION, 13

Montecalvo, Ed Contractor Services
LEE TENNIS PRODUCTS, 1165

Montesi, Robert Marketing Director
WFSB-TV, 711

Monteson, Patricia Principal
HEALTH FITNESS DYNAMICS, INC., 1069

Monteson, Patty Founder & Co-Owner
HEALTH FITNESS DYNAMICS, INC., 1069

Montez, Mario Sports Director
KUVN-TV, 704

Montgomery, Annalece Marketing Coordinator
USA WATER POLO, INC., 211

Montgomery, Daron Director of Athletics
SAINT ANSELM COLLEGE ATHLETICS, 370

Montgomery, David General Partner
FLORIDA STATE LEAGUE, 39, 966

Montgomery, Eric Director of Sports info. /
Marketing
HEART OF AMERICA ATHLETIC
CONFERENCE, 295, 511

Montgomery, Gary Host
SPORTS PAGE, 688

Montgomery, Graciela Chief Human Resource
Officer
TEVA BRAND, 1134, 1212

Montgomery, Janet Associate Athletic Director
WEST ALABAMA ATHLETICS, UNIVERSITY
OF, 375

Montgomery, Kevin HPER Instructor
ALCORN STATE UNIVERSITY, 411

Montgomery, Kyle Head Athletic Trainer
NJCAA REGION VI WOMEN'S, 285

Montgomery, Larry Chairman and Chief
Executive Officer
KOHL'S DEPARTMENT STORES, 1243

Montgomery, Mike Sports Director
WSAL-AM, 672

Montgomery, Paige Circulation Director
STREET & SMITH'S SPORTSBUSINESS
JOURNAL, 593

Montgomery, Scott Marketing VP
CANNONDALE BICYCLE CORPORATION,
1123

Montgomery, Seth Asst. AD,
Communications/Public Relation
CHARLESTON SOUTHERN UNIVERSITY
ATHLETICS, 325

Montgomery, Steve Marketing Sales Manager
RUSHMORE PLAZA CIVIC CENTER, 1008

Montigny, Michael Treasurer
RHODE ISLAND GOLF ASSOCIATION, 114

Montinieri, Josh Executive Director, Tickets
EASTERN LEAGUE, 38

Montmollin, Phil Public Relations
HOMESTEAD MOTORSPORTS COMPLEX,
1035

Montolio, Robert Sales Manager / Slumber Bags
& Tents
SENECA SPORTS INC., 1198

Montopoli, Peter General Secretary
CANADA SOCCER, 154

Montoya, Dave Mutuel Manager
PUEBLO GREYHOUND PARK, 1057

Montoya, Jorge Advertising Manager
KTXS-TV, 704

Montri, Ron Sports Editor
MONROE EVENING NEWS, 511

Monty, Mark Director of Athletics Department
LAWRENCE A. WIEN STADIUM, 990

Monzon, Ana Customer Service
HANCO-M. HANDELSMAN COMPANY, 1152

Moodey, Jon CEO
USL LEAGUE TWO, 160

Moody, Darrell Sports Reporter
NEVADA APPEAL, 513

Moody, Keegan Ticket Operations
CAROLINA LEAGUE, 37

Moody, Roger Deputy Director Sports
BSKYB, 617

Moody, Sam Director of Operations
CASSEMCO, INC., 1124

Moody, Walt Sports Editor
CENTRE DAILY TIMES, 471

Moon, Bob Sales Manager
BLADEMASTER, 1118

Moon, Danielle Sales & Marketing Coordinator
MINNEAPOLIS METRO NORTH CONVENTION
& VISITORS BUREAU, 239

Moon, Ingrid President/Chief Executive Officer
PACIFIC SPORTFEST, 767

Moon, Je Of Counsel
GARVEY, SCHUBERT & BARER, 891

Moon, Jordan Associate Editor
SPORT JOURNAL, 589

Moon, Josh Director of Athletics
NORTHERN STATE UNIVERSITY(NSU), 367

Moon, Leroy Advertising Manager
WSMG-AM, 674

Moon, Sam Sales Consultant
FIBEROPTIC LIGHTING INC., 1143

Mooney, Andrew Chief Executive Officer &
President
QUIKSILVER, 1190

Mooney, Angela Corporate Secretary
NATION'S BEST SPORTS, 1245

Mooney, Erin Director of Communications
NATIONAL SPORTS FORUM, 805

Mooney, Jeff Owner
CALIFORNIA LEAGUE (A-LEVEL), 36

Mooney, John President, Racing Services
LAUREL PARK, 1050

Mooney, Kevin News Director
KNEB-FM, 631

Mooney, Laura Director of Athletics
MASSACHUSETTS COLLEGE OF LIBERAL
ARTS ATHLETICS(MCLA), 394

Mooney, Mike Director of Athletics
STATE UNIVERSITY OF NEW YORK
COLLEGE AT GENESEO ATHLETICS (SUNY),
404

Mooney, Pat Volleyball Head Coach
NJCAA REGION I WOMEN'S, 284

Mooney, Starr Promoter
BATESVILLE MOTOR SPEEDWAY, 1032

Mooney, Tim Associate AD for External
Operations
IDAHO, UNIVERSITY OF, 332, 423

Mooneyham, Mike Sports Columnist
POST AND COURIER, 525

Mooradian, Jody Senior Associate Athletics
Director - SW
SILVIO O. CONTE FORUM, 402, 1011

Moore, A.A. Assistant Sports Information Director
GULF SOUTH CONFERENCE, 294

Moore, Alice Director of Human Resources
DAN MARINO FOUNDATION, 189

Moore, Austin Sports Assistant Editor
TALLADEGA DAILY HOME, 541

Moore, Ben Pitching Coach
FRONTIER LEAGUE, 42

Moore, Bill Manager
PECOS LEAGUE, 50, 113

Moore, Billy Track Supritendent
MARTINSVILLE SPEEDWAY, 1037

Moore, Bob Director for Kinesiology, Sport And
Recr
HARDIN-SIMMONS UNIVERSITY, 422

Moore, Brian Director of Marketing
FINGER LAKES GAMING & RACETRACK,
1047

Moore, Butch The Dispatch Printing Company
GREATER COLUMBUS SPORTS
COMMISSION, 233

Moore, Carlitta Director of Sports Medicine
FAYETTEVILLE STATE UNIVERSITY (FSU)
ATHLETICS, 358

Moore, Carrie Director of Physical Education
MASSACHUSETTS INSTITUTE OF
TECHNOLOGY (MIT), 394

Moore, Charles Executive Director
WYOMING PARI-MUTUEL COMMISSION, 83

Moore, Colin Executive Editor
OUTDOOR LIFE, 580

Moore, Dan National Sales Manager -Corporate
Divisi
SLAZENGER GOLF PRODUCTS CO, 1201

Moore, Danta Match Secretary
WESTERN SUBURBS RUGBY FOOTBALL
CLUB, 148

Moore, Darin Head Athletic Trainer
MISSOURI SOUTHERN STATE UNIVERSITY
ATHLETICS, 365

Moore, Dayton Senior VP, Baseball
Operations/General M
AMERICAN LEAGUE OF PROFESSIONAL
BASEBALL CLUBS, THE, 30

Moore, Deirdre Associate AD/SWA
LONG ISLAND UNIVERSITY BROOKLYN
ATHLETICS, 334

Moore, Donald President/General Manager
SOUTH ATLANTIC LEAGUE, 51

Moore, Doug Advertising Manager
PORTERVILLE RECORDER, 83, 525

Moore, Eric Managing Editor
ONNIDAN GROUP, THE, 939

Morgan, John President
JFM SPORTS, INC., 606
Morgan, Kelsey
PREMIER MANAGEMENT GROUP, 857
Morgan, Kiera News Director
KNPT-AM, 632
Morgan, Linda Executive Director
YUMA CONVENTION & VISITORS BUREAU,
249
Morgan, Marlon Sports Writer
COMMERCIAL APPEAL, 474
Morgan, Max Sports Anchor
KDFW-TV, 696
Morgan, Michelle Associate Athletic Director
ST. THOMAS UNIVERSITY ATHLETICS, 403
Morgan, R President
AMERICAN SOUTHWEST CONFERENCE, 289
Morgan, Rich Chair
US LACROSSE, 141
Morgan, Robin Customer Service / Credit
Manager
ALL STAR FOWNES, 1105
Morgan, Stanley President
MID-SOUTH SPORTS MANAGEMENT, 852
Morgan, Steve Board Chairman
SCHOTTENSTEIN DEPARTMENT STORES,
1248
Morgan, Sue Editor
LATITUDES & ATTITUDES, 573
Morgan, Tom Sports Director
WQTM, 653, 670
Morgan, Travis Chief Executive Officer
UNITED STATES HOCKEY LEAGUE, 137
Morgan, Wally Operations/EDI/Shipping
FREMONT DIE CONSUMER PRODUCTS INC,
1145
Morgen, David President
HAR-TRU, 1153
Morgenstein, Evan President/Chief Executive
Officer
PREMIER MANAGEMENT GROUP, 857
Morgenstern, George Publisher
ROCHESTER GOLF WEEK, 584
Morgigno, Dennis Station Manager
PRIME TIME PADRES, 690, 692
Moriarty, Michele Registrar/Office Manager
FLORIDA REGIONAL COMMISSIONER/USA
VOLLEYBALL, 209
Moriarty, William Lawyer
SASSOON & CYMROT LLP, 913
Morici, Antonio Senior VP, Ticket Sales
NATIONAL LEAGUE OF PROFESSIONAL
BASEBALL CLUBS, THE, 32
Morii, Keiko Director Of Marketing And Public
Relatio
KASCO CORPORATION OF AMERICA, 1162
Morikis, John President & CEO
SHERWIN-WILLIAMS CO., 741
Morin, Don General Manager
KALE-AM, 619
Morin, Travis Assistant Coach
AMERICAN HOCKEY LEAGUE/AHL, 128
Morisco, Joseph President / Chief Executive
Officer
DELTA GOLF COMPANY, 1134
Moritary, Ed President
RON JON SURF SHOP OF FLORIDA, 1248
Morith, Brianne Head Athletic Trainer
ST. ANDREWS PRESBYTERIAN
ATHLETICS(SAPC), 319
Moritz, Amy Sports Writer
BUFFALO NEWS, 469
Morkovsky, Wayne Editor
TEXAS GOLFER MAGAZINE, 594
Morley, Cindy Sports Reporter
TODAY IN PEACHTREE CITY, 545
Morley, Jim President
IGLOO PRODUCTS CORPORATION, 1157
Morley, Mark Vice President
PROSPORTS MVP, 812
Morman, Russ Manager
CALIFORNIA LEAGUE (A-LEVEL), 36
Morneau, Conrad VP Technical
INTERNATIONAL FEDERATION OF
BROOMBALL ASSOCIATIONS, 68
Mornet, Daniel VP
ROSSIGNOL SKI COMPANY, INC., 1194
Morning, Chuck Registrar
WISCONSIN AAU DISTRICT, 215

Moroney, William Chief Executive Officer
US EQUESTRIAN FEDERATION, 205
Moroski, Martin Partner/Co-Founder
ADAMSKI MOROSKI MADDEN & GREEN LLP,
870
Morreale, Nick Secretary/Treasurer
BUFFALO DISTRICT GOLF ASSOCIATION,
109
Morrell, Amber Cheerleading Head Coach
NEWBERRY COLLEGE, 431
Morrell, Caryl President
WENATCHEE VALLEY SPORTS COUNCIL,
249
Morrell, Chuck Head Coach/Athletic Director
MONTANA TECH ATHLETICS, 315
Morrell, Kevin Producer
FOX SPORTS SUNDAY, 687
Morrell, Lynn Dept. Chairperson
MARIAN COLLEGE, 427
Morrell, Stephanie General Manager
JOE MARTIN FIELD, 985

Morrice, Peter Executive Editor
GOLF MAGAZINE, 567
Morrill, Geary Chief Engineer
WQSN AM 1660, 670
Morring, Erie Medical Fitness Account Executive
DAXKO, 1225
Morris, Al General Manager
GOLF MART/WORLDWIDE GOLF/ROGER
DUNN GOLF, 1241
Morris, Brad Director, Business Operations
INTERNATIONAL LEAGUE, 42, 473
Morris, Brent Advertising Director
MANASSAS JOURNAL MESSENGER, 508
Morris, Chris Sports Editor
NEWS & ADVANCE, 515
Morris, Christopher Management Committee
Member
BASSFORD, LOCKHART, TRUESDELL &
BRIGGS, P.A., 873
Morris, Dann Founder
WEST RIDGE DESIGNS, 1221
Morris, Emiko Founder
WEST RIDGE DESIGNS, 1221
Morris, Greg Secretary
PACIFIC NORTHWEST PGA SECTIONAL
OFFICE, 106
Morris, J.B. Senior Editor
ESPN THE MAGAZINE, 563
Morris, Jamie Station Manager
WRHU-FM, 671
Morris, Jason Regional Manager Mid Market
Solutions
INFOUSA, 797
Morris, Jennifer Shipping & Accounting
GOALSETTER SYSTEMS, INC., 1149
Morris, Jenny Office Assistant
SOUTH BOSTON SPEEDWAY, 1042
Morris, Jim Vice Chairman
NATIONAL BASKETBALL ASSOCIATION/NBA,
57
Morris, John Founder
BASS PRO SHOPS, 1115, 1229
Morris, John Coordinator Sports Marketing
FOOT LOCKER, INC., 1240
Morris, Justin Assistant Athletic Director
STERLING COLLEGE ATHLETICS, 320
Morris, Krista Customer Service Officer/Sales
Assistant
UNIVERSAL FABRIC STRUCTURES, 1218
Morris, Mario Deputy AD, Business Operations
NOTRE DAME ATHLETICS, UNIVERSITY OF,
340, 1029
Morris, Muffin Head Athletic Trainer
WAYNE STATE COLLEGE, 375
Morris, Nick Sports Information Director
OKLAHOMA WESLEYAN UNIVERSITY
ATHLETICS, 316
Morris, Noreen Commissioner
NORTHEAST CONFERENCE, 299
Morris, Pancho Sports Writer
NEW MEXICAN, 514
Morris, Racheal Associate Athletic Director
UNIVERSITY OF SOUTHERN COLORADO
ATHLETICS, 371
Morris, Robert Founder / VP
PINNACLE ENTERPRISES, INC., 856

Morris, Ron Sports Columnist
STATE, 539
Morris, Sid President/Chief Executive Officer
NASCAR COUNTRY, 607
Morris, Stuart Director, Field Operations
SMOKIES PARK, 1012
Morris, Ted Executive Director
US SPEEDSKATING, 168, 205
Morris, Tom Advertising Manager
TULSA WORLD, 547
Morris, William Publisher
GRAY'S SPORTING JOURNAL, 568
Morrison, Brian Associate Director of
Athletics/Major Gi
PETE TAYLOR BASEBALL PARK, 1000
Morrison, Dave Director, Player Personnel
NATIONAL HOCKEY LEAGUE/NHL, 125, 528
Morrison, Fred VP Sales
TURFER SPORTSWEAR, 1216
Morrison, Jenni Assistant to the Athletic Director
CALIFORNIA UNIVERSITY OF
PENNSYLVANIA ATHLETICS, 354
Morrison, Jim Editor
NATIONAL HAWKEYE RACING NEWS, 578
Morrison, John Sports Management Associate
SPORTS LOOP, 865
Morrison, Mark Assistant Coach
NATIONAL HOCKEY LEAGUE/NHL, 122
Morrison, Mikie Director of Operations
APPALACHIAN LEAGUE, 33, 961
Morrison, Nicole Executive Director
DETLEF SCHREMPF FOUNDATION, 189
Morrison, Randall President
CANADIAN BILLIARDS & SNOOKER
ASSOCIATION, 62
Morrison, Rob Director of Facilities
J. LAWRENCE WALKUP SKYDOME, 983
Morrison, Scott Head Coach
NATIONAL BASKETBALL ASSOCIATION
DEVELOPMENT LEAGUE, 60
Morrison, Sid Vice Chairman
YAKIMA VALLEY SUNDOME, 1030
Morrison, Sil Classified Manager
STAR-DEMOCRAT, 539
Morrison, Tommy President
GEORGIA BOOT, 1148
Morrison-Archer, Courtney Assistant
Commissioner of Media Relation
CONFERENCE USA, 293
Morrissey, John Racing Secretary
SUFFOLK DOWNS, 1054
Morrissey, Mary President
WOMEN'S GOLF ASSOCIATION OF
WESTERN PENNSYLVANIA, 117
Morrissey, Matt Marketing & Vendor Operations
STADIUM JUMPING, INC., 77
Morrissey, Michael President
STADIUM JUMPING, INC., 77
Morro, William Interim Chief Executive Officer
WELLINGTON LEISURE PRODUCTS, 1221
Morrocco, Jaime Director,Technology ,Quality
Control and
ASAP SPORTS, 828
Morrow, Crystal Administration - Assistant to the
Athlet
ROY STEWART STADIUM, 1008
Morrow, Don Editor
SPORT HISTORY REVIEW, 589
Morrow, Elizabeth Box Office Manager
KNOXVILLE CIVIC AUDITORIUM/COLISEUM,
988
Morrow, Jeff Executive Director, Player Personnel
NATIONAL FOOTBALL LEAGUE/NFL, 95, 546
Morrow, Lisa Vice President
LAFAYETTE-WEST LAFAYETTE
CONVENTION & VISITORS BUREAU, 236
Morse, Brandon Promoter
PLAZA PARK RACEWAY, 1040
Morse, Brian Immediate Past President
NORTHERN CALIFORNIA GOLF
ASSOCIATION, 113
Morse, Mike VP, Western & International Sales
CALIFONE INTERNATIONAL, INC., 828
Morse, Tim Sports Reporter
ALBANY HERALD, 461
Mort, Kristin Senior Assciate Director Of Athletics
Fo
MESA STATE COLLEGE ATHLETICS(MSC),
364

Mroz, Greg Director of Broadcasting & Media
Relatio
MIDWEST LEAGUE, 45
Mrozek, Donald Chairman
HINSHAW & CULBERSON LLP, 846
Mrozek, Donald Chairman
VAINISI, JEROME R., 846, 922
Mucher, Jason Director of Compliance and
Communication
HOUGHTON COLLEGE ATHLETICS, 389
Muchmore, Clyde Chairman Appellate Practice
CROWE & DUNLEVY, 839
Mudd, Michael Director of Athletics
WORCESTER STATE UNIVERSITY
ATHLETICS, 410
Mudd, Ray Events Manager
THUNDERHILL RACEWAY PARK, 1044
Muder, Craig Directoro of Communications
NATIONAL BASEBALL HALL OF FAME AND
MUSEUM, 254
Mueller, Brett President
MUELLER SPORTS MEDICINE, INC., 1176
Mueller, Curt Chief Executive Officer
MUELLER SPORTS MEDICINE, INC., 1176
Mueller, Doris Chairman
GREATER AUSTIN SPORTS ASSOCIATION,
233
Mueller, E.C. Racetrack Manager
PORTLAND INTERNATIONAL RACEWAY,
1040
Mueller, Ed Sales
WMBE-AM AND WCLB, 663
Mueller, Frederick Sport Administration Professor
NORTH CAROLINA, UNIVERSITY OF, 431
Mueller, Jeannette Chief Financial Officer
RELAY SPORTS AND ENTERTAINMENT
MARKETING, 814
Mueller, Jeff VP
MUELLER SPORTS MEDICINE, INC., 1176
Mueller, Tim General Manager
SOUTH ATLANTIC LEAGUE, 52, 955
Mugford, Angus President
ASSOCIATION FOR APPLIED SPORT
PSYCHOLOGY/AAASP, 216
Muhl, Alan Finanace / Operations Manager
DLF INTERNATIONAL SEEDS, 1236
Muhlfelder, James President / Chief Executive
Officer
DEBEER LACROSSE, 1134
Muir, Bernard Director of Athletics
STANFORD UNIVERSITY ATHLETICS, 345
Muir, Norman Associate Professor, and Dean,
Undergrad
MEDAILLE COLLEGE, 428
Mukhamedolla, Agzamov VP Asia
WORLD ARMWRESTLING FEDERATION, 15
Mulay, Rene Editor
EMPLOYEE SERVICES MANAGEMENT, 562
Mulcahy, Charles Partner
WYNN & WYNN, P.C., 927
Mulcahy, Michael President/Chief Executive
Officer
FAIRTRON, 1142
Mulcahy, Robert Athletic Director
LOUIS BROWN ALTHETIC CENTER, 992
Mulch, Lori Assistant General Manager
KANSAS STATE FAIR (KSF), 1050
Muldoon, Barb Treasurer
NEBRASKA WOMEN'S AMATEUR GOLF
ASSOCIATION, 113
Muldoon, James Asst. Commissioner of Public
Relations
PACIFIC-10 CONFERENCE, 301
Muldoon, Liz Second VP
QUINTE EX FALL FAIR, 1052
Muldoon, Mike Sports Writer
EAGLE-TRIBUNE, 488
Mule, Marty Sports Writer
TIMES-PICAYUNE, 545
Mulford, Joe Senior Associate AD
UC BERKELEY ATHLETICS, 347
Mulhausen, Dan VP, Business Operations &
Marketing Comm
WESTERN HOCKEY LEAGUE, 139
Mulhern, Tom Sports Reporter
WISCONSIN STATE JOURNAL, 552
Mulholland, Thad Partner
ENG & WOODS, 888

Mullany, Joe President
DMC ORTHOPAEDICS & SPORTS MEDICINE,
930
Mullen, Bryan Sports Writer
TENNESSEAN, 542
Mullen, Don Hospitality Manager
TRUE FITNESS TECHNOLOGY, 1215
Mullen, Jim Assistant Director of Athletics
ASSUMPTION COLLEGE ATHLETICS, 352
Mullen, Mike Athletics Senior Editor/Sports
Director
WBUK-FM, 646
Mullen, Scott Executive Director
I WIRELESS CENTER, 981
Mullens, Rob Athletic Director
OREGON ATHLETICS, UNIVERSITY OF, 341,
956, 994
Muller, Angela Associate Director Of Athletics
CONCORDIA UNIVERSITY (NE) ATHLETICS,
309
Muller, Jim Associate Director
WAGNER FIELD/KSU, 960, 1026
Muller, Joe Athletic Director
CENTRAL OKLAHOMA ATHLETICS,
UNIVERSITY OF, 354
Muller, Kira Director of Advertising Sales
LACROSSE MAGAZINE, 573
Muller, Matthias President
PORSCHE CARS NORTH AMERICA, 1186
Muller, Todd Club Coordinator
USA CYCLING, 72
Mullholland, Chris Producer
FIRST 4 SPORTS - SATURDAY, 687
Mulligan, John EVP, Chief Operating Officer
TARGET STORES, 742
Mulligan, Mike Sports Columnist
CHICAGO SUN-TIMES, 472
Mulliken, Ron Advertising Director
GOLF MAGAZINE, 567
Mullikin, Jeff Assistant Athletic Director
TOCCOA FALLS COLLEGE ATHLETICS, 373
Mullin, Jennifer Marketing & Public Relations
Assistant
NORFOLK CONVENTION & VISITORS
BUREAU, 240
Mullin, Jim President
FOOTBALL CANADA, 88
Mullin, Mark Director of Athletics
MISSOURI-ROLLA ATHLETICS, UNIVERSITY
OF (UMR), 365
Mullin, Michelle Sales Vice President
METRO SPORTS NY, 575
Mullin, Paul Sponsorship Services Manager
NEW YORK-PENNSYLVANIA LEAGUE, 46,
973
Mullin, Shawn Tour Manager
UNITED SPORTS TECHNOLOGIES/UST, 1217
Mullins, Carl Publisher
QUARTER HORSE NEWS, 77, 556, 583
Mullins, Craig Chairman of the Board
BROWNING DAY MULLINS DIERDORF
ARCHITECTS, 1060
Mullins, Dave Account Executive
GMR MARKETING, 764
Mullins, Jim Assistant Director of Athletics
UMASS DARTMOUTH ATHLETIC
DEPARTMENT, 394
Mullins, Steve Director of Athletics
ARKANSAS TECH UNIVERSITY ATHLETICS,
351, 961, 985
Mullins, Susan Vice President
WYTI-AM/FM, 679
Mullins, Tabatha Executive Director
PRINCE WILLIAM COUNTY/MANASSAS
CONVENTION & VISITORS BUREAU, 242
Mullison, Dave Manager
Marketing/Communications
ATLANTA MOTOR SPEEDWAY, 1031
Mullon, Bill Director of Sports Marketing
WQAM 560 SPORTS RADIO, 669
Mullowney, Rob Chief Operating Officer
AMERICAN HOCKEY LEAGUE/AHL, 126
Mulloy, Mark Sports Information/Media Relations
MID-SOUTH CONFERENCE, 297
Mulock, Micah Sports Information Director
LIFE PACIFIC COLLEGE ATHLETICS, 362
Mulrenin, Patrick Director
ACKERMAN, VALERIE B., 870

Mulrooney, Pat Program Director/Sports
WRTK, 672
Mulroy, Paola VP Finance
SOCCER MARKETING & PROMOTIONS, INC.,
769
Mulroy, Thomas Founder/President
SOCCER MARKETING & PROMOTIONS, INC.,
769
Mulryan, Matt Sales Manager
DACOR SPORT, 1132, 1133
Multer, Mark Sports Editor
WAUSAU DAILY HERALD, 551
Mulvaney, Todd President
PLASTIMAYD CORPORATION, 1185
Munday, Trevor Managing Director
DESTINET LIMITED, 941
Mundell, Don Head Athletic Trainer
WESTERN STATE COLLEGE ATHLETICS
(WSC), 376
Mundle, Michelle Athletic Department Secretary
HANNIBAL-LA GRANGE COLLEGE
ATHLETICS, 311
Mundy, Megan Athletic Business and Operations
Coordin
KING'S COLLEGE ATHLETICS, 391
Mungham, Tom Chief Operating Officer
ALCOHOL AND GAMING COMMISSION OF
ONTARIO, 79
Mungo, Leonard Regional Field Director
MUNGO AND ASSOCIATES, P.C., 906
Munjoy, Ken Advertising Director
DAILY JOURNAL (IL), 480
Munk, Josh Associate Director of Football
Operation
BIG TEN ATHLETIC CONFERENCE, 290
Munn, Jeff Chief Operating Officer
HARLEM GLOBETROTTERS, 56
Munn, Scott Sports Assistant Editor
OKLAHOMAN, 519
Munoz, Carlos Sports Reporter
KTMD-TV, 703
Munoz, Daniel Editor
LA PRENSA SAN DIEGO, 504
Munoz, Mike Head Coach
USL LEAGUE ONE, 160
Munoz, Oscar Chief Executive Officer
UNITED CONTINENTAL HOLDINGS, 742
Munoz, SJ Sports Editor/Writer
YORK NEWS-TIMES, 553
Munroe, Mark Commissioner
OHIO STATE RACING COMMISSION, 82
Munroe, Morgan Compliance Officer
ALBERTA SCHOOLS' ATHLETIC
ASSOCIATION, 197
Munroe, Tim VP Business Development
CONE COMMUNICATIONS, 760
Munsell, Joe General Manager
KXMO-FM, 639
Munson, Larry Sports Host
WSB-AM, 673
Munson, William Operations VP
RALPH WILSON STADIUM, 1003
Munt, Glada Director of Intercollegiate Athletics
SOUTHWESTERN UNIVERSITY ATHLETICS,
403
Murakami, Michael Principal
MURAKAMI/NELSON, 1071
Murase, Etsuko Chief Financial Officer/Chief
Operations
BOOMER ESIASON FOUNDATION, 189
Murat, Caroline Finance Manager
WORLD ARCHERY FEDERATION, 15
Muratore, Horacio President
INTERNATIONAL BASKETBALL FEDERATION
(FIBA), 202
Murdoch, Courtney Owner & Manager
WOMEN'S PREMIER SOCCER LEAGUE, 166
Murdoch, James Chariman/Chief Executive
Officer
STAR GROUP LIMITED, 694
Murdoch, Paul President
U.S. HANG GLIDING AND PARAGLIDING
ASSOCIATION, 14
Murdock, Allison Deputy Managing Partner
STINSON MORRISON HECKER LLP, 918
Murdock, James Founder/President
ENDLESS POOLS, INC., 1139
Murdock, Justin Sports Writer
ENQUIRER-JOURNAL, 489

Murdock, Kevin Head Coach
NORTH AMERICAN HOCKEY LEAGUE, 132
Murdock, Mark Sports Editor
THE STAR, 543
Murdy, Wayne Chair
DENVER, UNIVERSITY OF, 418
Murillo, Ken Team Owner
IMSA MICHELIN PILOT CHALLENGE, 20
Murnane, Jim Associate Athletic Director
UTICA COLLEGE ATHLETICS(UC), 406
Muroski, Liz Director of Media and Promotions
CAROLINAS PGA SECTION, 104
Murphy, Brad Executive Director
ADAMS CENTER, 953
Murphy, Brian Head Athletic Trainer
LA SIERRA UNIVERSITY ATHLETICS, 313,
539
Murphy, Brian Publisher/Editor
SPORTS MARKETING LETTER COMPANY,
591
Murphy, Brian
BRIAN J. MURPHY CONSULTANT, 785
Murphy, Chad Executive Director
UNITED STATES BOWLING CONGRESS, 66
Murphy, Chetara Assistant Director of Athletics
MEDGAR EVERS COLLEGE ATHLETICS
(MEC), 395
Murphy, Chris President
NATIONAL BASKETBALL ASSOCIATION
DEVELOPMENT LEAGUE, 60, 656
Murphy, Dan Sports Director
WTEN-TV, 718
Murphy, Daniel Chairman
GATOR BOWL, 91
Murphy, Darren Senior Director, Finance &
Operations
AMERICAN HOCKEY LEAGUE/AHL, 126
Murphy, Dawn Finance and Administrative
Director
EXPLORE FAIRBANKS, 231
Murphy, Dennis Commissioner
NATIONAL JUNIOR BASKETBALL, 55
Murphy, Diana Vice President
U.S. GOLF ASSOCIATION/USGA, 108
Murphy, Eric Weekend Sports Anchor
WOI-TV, 716
Murphy, Erich Sports Editor
DAILY LEADER (IL), 480
Murphy, Gord Associate Head Coach
AMERICAN HOCKEY LEAGUE/AHL, 127
Murphy, Jack Head Coach, Men's Basketball
J. LAWRENCE WALKUP SKYDOME, 983
Murphy, James President/General Manager
ATLANTIC CITY RACE COURSE, 1045
Murphy, Jason Facilities Director
UNIVERSITY OF WISCONSIN-LA CROSSE,
409, 995
Murphy, Jerome Sports Reporter
ARGUS-PRESS, 463
Murphy, Jim Sports Editor
JUICE SOUND, SURF SKATE MAGAZINE, 573
Murphy, Joe Sports Writer
EAGLE-TRIBUNE, 488
Murphy, John Assistant Sports Information
Director
MAYVILLE STATE UNIVERSITY ATHLETICS,
314, 713, 1059
Murphy, John SVP/Controller/Chief Accounting
Officer
DIRECTV, INC., 693
Murphy, Karen Chief Financial Officer
NATIONAL FOOTBALL LEAGUE/NFL, 95
Murphy, Katie Sales & Event Coordinator
UNITED STATES HOCKEY LEAGUE, 137
Murphy, Keith Sports Director
WHO-TV, 712
Murphy, Kelly Host Appearances
YAHOO! SPORTS RADIO, 611
Murphy, Kevin Team/Sports Construction Sales
AMERICAN ATHLETIC INC., 141, 1107
Murphy, Leslie Executive Director
NATIONAL DART ASSOCIATION, 72
Murphy, Malia Head Athletic Trainer
BLACKBURN COLLEGE ATHLETICS, 379
Murphy, Mark President/CEO
NATIONAL FOOTBALL LEAGUE/NFL, 95, 468
Murphy, Mark President
LAMBEAU FIELD, 990

Murphy, Matt Manager of Athletic Operations
NOTRE DAME COLLEGE ATHLETICS, 367,
615
Murphy, Matthew Editor
WOODENBOAT, 599
Murphy, Megan Event and Group Manager
SAM LYNN BALLPARK, 1009
Murphy, Michael Editor
BALLOON LIFE, 556
Murphy, Mike Sports Host
WJPF-AM, 659
Murphy, Nancy Vice President Sales
LAS VEGAS CONVENTION & VISITORS
AUTHORITY, 116, 237
Murphy, Nicola Director Marketing, Athlete &
Property M
OCTAGON ATHLETES & PERSONALITIES
DIVISION, 854
Murphy, Patrick President, Business Operations
NATIONAL HOCKEY LEAGUE/NHL, 104, 122,
861
Murphy, Paul Associate Director of Athletics
GWYNEDD MERCY COLLEGE ATHLETICS,
388
Murphy, R. Vice President Network Operations
GOLF CHANNEL, THE, 605, 695
Murphy, Ric President/Chief Executive Officer
USADATA.COM, 824
Murphy, Rick General Manager
JOSEPH L. BRUNO STADIUM, 986
Murphy, Rita Vice Chairman of Captains Charities
CLASSIC PARK, 966
Murphy, Robert President
MIDWEST LEAGUE, 45, 974
Murphy, Sean Assistant Managing Editor - Sports
VICKSBURG POST, 55, 549
Murphy, Steve President
ALOHA PGA SECTIONAL OFFICE, 104
Murphy, Tim P.E., Associate & Project Manager
PAIGE DESIGN GROUP, 561, 762, 1071
Murphy, Tom General Manager
GEORGE J. SHERMAN FAMILY-SPORTS
COMPLEX, 976
Murphy, Traci Associate Athletic Director
CANISIUS COLLEGE - SCHOOL OF
EDUCATION & HUMAN SERVICES, 414
Murpy, John Manager/Curator
SPORTS IMMORTALS, 257
Murraine, Clair Sports Reporter
TALLAHASSEE DEMOCRAT, 541
Murray, Annette Public Information Director
NJCAA REGION IX MEN'S, 285
Murray, Ben Creative Specialist
SOUTH BEND/MISHAWAKA CONVENTION &
VISITORS BUREAU, 263
Murray, Bill Director of Fun
JOSEPH P. RILEY, JR PARK, 986
Murray, Bob President, Hockey Operations
AMERICAN HOCKEY LEAGUE/AHL, 122, 128
Murray, Bruce VP Standardbred Racing
MOHAWK RACETRACK, 1051
Murray, Carol Executive Assistant to the
President
NJCAA REGION XV WOMEN'S, 287
Murray, Chris Sports Editor
PHILADELPHIA TRIBUNE, 523
Murray, Douglas Negotiating Committee:
NHLPA: NATIONAL HOCKEY LEAGUE
PLAYERS' ASSOCIATION, 854
Murray, James Principal/Director
CSHQA
ARCHITECTS/ENGINEERS/PLANNERS, 1063
Murray, Jane Director of Services
THOROUGHBRED RACING ASSOCIATIONS,
78
Murray, John Attorney
LINDNER & MARSACK, S.C., 900
Murray, Kristen Incoming Vice Chair
US LACROSSE, 141
Murray, LaKitha Senior Associate Director of
Athletics
COLLEGE OF NEW JERSEY ATHLETICS
(TCNJ), 382
Murray, Lisa Executive Vice President & Chief
Marketi
OCTAGON SPORTS, 807, 842, 854
Murray, Marty General Manager/Head Coach
UNITED STATES HOCKEY LEAGUE, 137

Murray, Melanie Advertising Manager
VALLEY NEWS DISPATCH, 548
Murray, Michael Executive VP, Hockey
Operations
AMERICAN HOCKEY LEAGUE/AHL, 126
Murray, Mike President/General Manager
SOUTHERN PROFESSIONAL HOCKEY
LEAGUE, 136
Murray, Natalie Vice President, Regional Sales
Manager
FOX SPORTS NETWORKS/FOX SPORTS
NET, 683
Murray, Neil News Director
WGMA-AM, 655
Murray, Patrick News Director
WZLX-FM, 680
Murray, Rob Head Coach/Director, Hockey
Operations
EAST COAST HOCKEY LEAGUE/ECHL, 130
Murray, Scott Goaltending Coach
NATIONAL HOCKEY LEAGUE/NHL, 126, 706
Murray, Sherrie Administrative Assistant & Office
Manage
CHARLES M. MURPHY ATHLETIC CENTER,
965
Murray, Steve Commissioner
PENNSYLVANIA STATE ATHLETIC
CONFERENCE, 301
Murray, Tim Director of Athletics
MARIST COLLEGE ATHLETICS, 335
Murray-MacDonell, Sandra Executive Director
CANADIAN COLLEGIATE ATHLETIC
ASSOCIATION, 281
Murrell, Tony Controller
METROPOLITAN PROFESSIONAL GOLFERS
ASSOCIATION, 105
Murrey, Bob President, Owner
USA COACHES CLINICS, INC., 824
Murrey, Daniel Chief Executive Officer
ORTHOCAROLINA, 932
Murrey, Patrick President
MURREY INTERNATIONAL, 1176
Murrietta, Jeannette Booking Manager
DENVER COLISEUM, 969
Murry, Saye Advertising Manager
OWENSBORO MESSENGER-INQUIRER, 521
Murstein, Andrew Co-Owner
NASCAR CUP SERIES, 23
Murtha, Francis President
PROFESSIONAL SPORTS CONSULTANTS,
INC., 859
Murtha, Matthew VP, Stadium/Structures
PROFESSIONAL SPORTS CONSULTANTS,
INC., 859
Murtland, Carol Purchasing Manager
KOOLATRON, 1164
Murumets, Kelly President & Chief Executive
Officer
TENNIS CANADA, 172
Murzynski, Terrence Owner
SPORTSVISIONS, 771
Musa, Scott Athletic Communications Director
SHENANDOAH UNIVERSITY ATHLETICS, 402
Musallam, Husain Vice President
FEDERATION INTERNATIONALE DE
NATATION (FINA), 73, 202
Muscari, David Vice President
WFAA-TV, 710
Muscutt, Scott General Manager
NORTH AMERICAN HOCKEY LEAGUE, 133
Muse, Bill Athletic Director
NJCAA REGION II WOMEN'S, 284
Muse, Dan Under-18 Team Head Coach
UNITED STATES HOCKEY LEAGUE, 137
Muse, Micheal. Architect/Partner
THE COLLABORATIVE, INC., 1062
Muse, Scott President
HUBBELL LIGHTING, INC., 1156
Musgjerd, Jean Women's Athletic Director
NJCAA REGION XIII WOMEN'S, 286
Musgrave, Chuck Principal, CFO
BARKER RINKER SEACAT ARCHITECTURE,
1059
Musgrove, Peter Facilities/Operations Manager
GREAT CANADIAN GAMING CORPORATION,
1048
Mushel, Jessica Assistant Director of Athletics
MOUNT ST. MARY COLLEGE ATHLETICS,
396

Mushinski, Ian Head Athletic Trainer
WINSTON-SALEM STATE UNIVERSITY
ATHLETICS, 377
Mushnick, Phil Sports Columnist
NEW YORK POST, 514
Music, Lyn Facilities/Events Management Director
SUN DEVIL STADIUM, 1015
Musick, Ashley Head Athletic Trainer
CALIFORNIA STATE
UNIVERSITY-DOMINGUEZ HILLS ATHLETICS,
353
Musil, Matt Sports Reporter
KHOU-TV, 698
Muskewitz, Al Golf and JSU Teams Writer
ANNISTON STAR, 462
Muskovich, John Chief Executive Officer /
President
ROYCE UNION BICYCLE COMPANY, INC.,
1157, 1195
Mussellam, Geoff Communications Manager
HASTINGS RACECOURSE, 1049
Musselman, Gary Executive Director
KANSAS STATE HS ACTIVITIES
ASSOCIATION, 196, 198
Musselwhite, Susan Assistant Athletic Director
MISSISSIPPI COLLEGE ATHLETICS (MC), 365
Musso, Mark President/CEO
SPECIAL OLYMPICS MISSOURI, 193
Musson, Renne Associate Director
STEPHEN C O'CONNELL CENTER, 1015
Must, Gary General Manager
DELAWARE COUNTY FAIR, 1046
Muston, Jen Assistant Director of Athletics
YORK COLLEGE (PENNSYLVANIA)
ATHLETICS, 411
Mutombo, Patrick Head Coach
NATIONAL BASKETBALL ASSOCIATION
DEVELOPMENT LEAGUE, 60
Mutti, Raj Marketing Manager
HASTINGS RACECOURSE, 1049
Mutz, Sam National Football Commissioner
POP WARNER LITTLE SCHOLARS, 89
Muus, Charlie Director of Maintenance &
Operations
RALPH ENGELSTAD ARENA, 1003
Muzzi, Luiz Executive VP, Soccer Operations
MAJOR LEAGUE SOCCER, 157
Myatt, Michael Director of Corporate Relations
INTERNATIONAL GAME FISH ASSOCIATION,
88
Mycoskie, Chris Sports Director
KTVE-TV, 704
Myer, Brad Sports Director
WNSV-FM, 666
Myer, Marissa Chief Executive Officer, President,
Dire
YAHOO! SPORTS, 723
Myer, Mike Executive Editor
INTELLIGENCER, 499
Myers, Andre Aquatics Director
UNIVERSITY OF DISTRICT OF COLUMBIA
ATHLETICS, 357
Myers, Bob General Manager
NATIONAL BASKETBALL ASSOCIATION/NBA,
57
Myers, Chad Vice President/Treasurer
MIDWEST PGA SECTIONAL OFFICE, 105
Myers, Charlene Domestic Customer Service
AEROBIE, INC, 1104
Myers, Chris Sports Information Director
WHEELING JESUIT UNIVERSITY ATHLETICS
(WJU), 376
Myers, Deana Analyst
MEDIA SPORTS BUSINESS, 575
Myers, Gene Sports Editor
DETROIT FREE PRESS, 486
Myers, Gerald Director of Athletics
JONES SBC STADIUM, 986
Myers, Harriette Treasurer
MISSOURI WOMEN'S GOLF ASSOCIATION,
112
Myers, Harry News Director
WBAG-AM, 644
Myers, Julie Director of Communications
U.S. PROFESSIONAL TENNIS ASSOCIATION,
172
Myers, Mary Assistant Executive Director
SSLASPA DBA SPORT & RECREATION LAW
ASSOCIATION, 223

Myers, Nancy Ticket Assistant
MINNESOTA STATE HS LEAGUE, 199
Myers, Richard Vice President, Turf & Retail
DLF INTERNATIONAL SEEDS, 1236
Myers, Rick Director Sales / Marketing
DLF INTERNATIONAL SEEDS, 461, 1236
Myers, Robert Dept. Dean
PALM BEACH ATLANTIC UNIVERSITY, 433
Myers, Rod Host
SPORTS CORNER, 693
Myers, Ron Director of Florida Operations
FLORIDA STATE LEAGUE, 39, 40
Myers, Tom Associate Athletic Director/Facilities
WEEDE ARENA, 963, 1027
Myerson, Bob President
K & S PROMOTIONS, 799
Myerson, Joe Senior Editor
OFFSHORE, 580
Myford, Greg Associate Athletic Director of
Business
BEAVER STADIUM, 957
Myhre, Rich Sports Reporter
HERALD (WA), 496
Mykins, Bill Vice president
BRAILSFORD & DUNLAVEY, 1060
Myler, Cameron Associate
FRANKFURT, KURNIT, KLEIN & SELZ, P.C.,
890
Mylett, Bill Sales Manager
MONDO AMERICA, INC., 1174
Mylor, Pam Service Coordinator
KENTUCKY SPEEDWAY, 1036
Mylor, Terry Operations
SAN JOSE MUNICIPAL STADIUM, 1009
Mylymok, Clint Head Coach/General Manager
NORTH AMERICAN HOCKEY LEAGUE, 132
Myrland, Jim Owner
BEACON ATHLETICS, 1229
Myrold, Chris Director
BURWASH INTERNATIONAL, PETER, 759
Myron, Dennis Ticket Operations Director
ST JOHN'S UNIVERSITY, 1013

N

N, Jenny Aerie Accessories Manager
AMERICAN EAGLE OUTFITTERS, 1228
N Funkhouser Jr, Richard President
HT TENNIS, 1156
N. Feist III, Howard Chief Financial Officer /
Finance VP
ABI TAPE PRODUCTS, 1100
N. H. Boeder, Jeremy Attorney
TRIBLER, ORPETT & CRONE, 922
N. N Mertz, Melissa Associate Executive Director
PENNSYLVANIA INTERSCHOLASTIC
ATHLETIC ASSOCIATION, 200
N. W. Adams, Diana President and Chief
Executive Officer
AMBAC ASSURANCE CORPORATION, 775
N/A, Derrick Editor
SPORTS EYE, 537
Naamani, Jadd Program Director
WMLN-FM, 664
Naatz, Duey Athletic Director
UNIVERSITY OF WISCONSIN - STOUT
ATHLETICS (UW-STOUT), 410
Nabokov, Evgeni Goaltending Coach
NATIONAL HOCKEY LEAGUE/NHL, 125
Nabozny, Heather Head Groundskeeper
COMERICA PARK, 967
Nace, Diane Artwork/Approvals
COOPERSBURG SPORTS, 1235
Nace, Kelly Event Director
TAP, LLC, 62
Nacewicz, Steve President
CENTRAL NEW YORK PGA SECTIONAL
OFFICE, 104
Nachand, Jean Vice President, Competition
WOMEN'S TENNIS ASSOCIATION TOUR, 174
Nacke, Dave Vice President, Merchandising -
Outdoor
NATION'S BEST SPORTS, 1245
Nackman, Neal Chief Financial Officer
G III SPORTS, 1146
Naddelman, Rob President
BASEBALL FACTORY, 26
Nadeau, Brad Director of Athletic
Communications

MIDDLEBURY COLLEGE ATHLETICS (MCA),
395
Nadeau, Donny Sports Information Director
SAINT MARY'S UNIVERSITY (MN)
ATHLETICS, 401
Nadel, Roger VP/General Manager
KMPC-AM, 630
Nadella, Satya Chief Executive Officer
MICROSOFT CORPORATION, 738
Nader, Tom Sports Editor
RECORD-COURIER, 477, 528
Nading, Lance President
U.S. JUDO, INC/USA JUDO, 143
Nadolski, Jaynee Asst.
Commissioner/Championships Info
BIG SKY CONFERENCE, 290
Nadorf, Wayne Sales Assistant VP / Director
EVERLAST WORLDWIDE, INC., 1140
Nadvornik, Milosh President
YEADON FABRIC STRUCTURES LTD., 1224
Nafe, Rick Operations/Facilities VP
TROPICANA FIELD, 1020
Naff, Abe Director of Athletics
FERRUM COLLEGE ATHLETICS, 386
Nagamura, Paulo Head Coach
USL CHAMPIONSHIP, 159
Nagao, Danielle Vice President of Financial
Operations
TICKETS.COM, 943
Nagel, Linda Sales
ULTRA PLAY SYSTEMS, INC., 1217
Nagel, Mark Chairman
SAN JOSE STATE UNIVERSITY, 421, 434
Naggar, Sara Communications Director
BIG EAST CONFERENCE, 290
Nagle, Andrew EVP
A-B EMBLEM, 1099
Nagle, Patrick Executive Director
ALLSTATE ARENA, 954
Nagy, Chris Sports Editor
NEWS-ITEM, 516
Nagy, Matt Head Coach
NATIONAL FOOTBALL LEAGUE/NFL, 95
Nahas, Jim VP / Assistant General Manager
SEC TAYLOR STADIUM, 1010
Nahigian, Matt Program Director
WAIT-AM, 611, 617, 643
Nahon, Paul General Manager
MYLAN WORLD TEAM TENNIS, 174
Naidoo, Urvasi CEO
NETBALL ASSOCIATIONS, INTERNATIONAL
FEDERATION OF, 144
Naifeh, Larry Executive Associate AD
OKLAHOMA ATHLETICS, UNIVERSITY OF,
341
Naik, Sudhir Deputy Director
NEW HAMPSHIRE RACING AND
CHARITABLE GAMING COMMISSION, 81, 119
Nairn, Rich Exec. Vice President,
Communications & B
NATIONAL HOCKEY LEAGUE/NHL, 122
Nakaahiki, Nina Secretary
SPECIAL OLYMPICS HAWAII, 192
Nakama, Wes High School Sports Reporter
HONOLULU ADVERTISER, 497
Nalchajian-Cohen, Debbie
Communications/Media Relations
BIG FRESNO FAIR (BFF), 1045
Namm, Keith Sports Reporter
POST AND COURIER, 525
Nanberg, Bob Managing General Partner
TEAM SHOP PREMIUMS, 1211
Nance, Carolyn HPER Complex Facilities
Manager
GOLDEN LION STADIUM, 977
Nance, Frederick Managing Partner
SQUIRE, SANDERS & DEMPSEY, LLP, 917
Nance, Jack Executive Director
CAROLINAS GOLF ASSOCIATION, 109
Nance, Martin Executive VP/Chief Marketing
Officer
NATIONAL FOOTBALL LEAGUE/NFL, 96
Nance, Stanford Senior Associate Director of
Athletics
EMERSON COLLEGE ATHLETICS, 385
Nangle, Shelly Executive VP & COO
SPECIAL OLYMPICS NEW YORK, 194
Nanney, David Head Groundskeeper
JOE O'BRIEN FIELD, 985

executive index

Painter, Travis Assistant General Manager, Baseball Opera
MIDWEST LEAGUE, 46, 996

Pais, Charles Treasurer
CRICKET CANADA, 69

Pais, Leonardo Chief Executive Officer
BRAVO SPORTS, 1120

Pais, Leonardo Chief Executive Officer
VARIFLEX INC., 1218

Paisley, Doug President/Governor
WESTERN HOCKEY LEAGUE, 138

Paisley, Joe Sports Editor
TIMES-NEWS, 545

Paiva, Joni President
NISSAN CANADA, 739

Palace, Leslie Advertising Sales Manager
TOPEKA CAPITAL-JOURNAL, 545

Paladino, Brent Director, Competitions & Communications
CONNECTICUT STATE GOLF ASSOCIATION, 109

Palafox, Luis Assistant Director
PRO-AM BEACH SOCCER, 155

Palan, Robert President
KING LOUIE INTERNATIONAL, INC., 1163

Palango, Dan Agent
M.D. GILLIS & ASSOCIATES LTD., 850

Palaszewski, Madeline Promotion Director
KSBY-TV, 702

Palazzari, Doug Executive Director
U.S. HOCKEY HALL OF FAME, 257

Palches, Stefan Secretary
MIDWEST RUGBY FOOTBALL UNION, 147

Palcic, Amy VP, Football Communications
NATIONAL FOOTBALL LEAGUE/NFL, 93, 96

Palenchar, Dave Chairman Emeritus
STATE GAMES OF AMERICA, 263

Palermo, Giorgio Player Representative
ATP WORLD TOUR, 171

Palermo, Jessica Director, Championships
BIG TEN ATHLETIC CONFERENCE, 290

Palermo, Philip Director of Operations
FINGER LAKES GAMING & RACETRACK, 1047

Paley, Tom Secretary
UNITED STATES BILLIARD ASSOCIATION, 63

Paliafito, Jim Senior Director, Player Evaluation
NATIONAL HOCKEY LEAGUE/NHL, 125

Palin, Chris Vice President of Sales & Marketing
EAST COAST HOCKEY LEAGUE/ECHL, 129

Palis, Terry President
CORPORATE COMMUNICATIONS, INC., 761

Palisi, Mike Executive Vice President
NELLIGAN SPORTS MARKETING, INC., 806

Palivec, Donna Department Chair
BEMIDJI STATE UNIVERSITY, 413

Palko, Andy Head Athletic Trainer
WAYNESBURG COLLEGE ATHLETICS, 407

Palladino, Jeff Director of Group Sales & Ticket Operati
YOGI BERRA STADIUM, 1030

Pallerino, Michael Editor
SPORTS EDGE MAGAZINE, 590, 591

Pallister, Jane Assoc. Athletic Director (Internal Affai
UAA SPORTS ARENA, 1021

Palm, Matt Athletic Director
HEIDELBERG UNIVERSITY ATHLETICS, 388

Palm-Porter, Andrea Advertising Director
VAIL DAILY, 548

Palma, Tony President
EASTON SPORTS, INC., 1137

Palmaz, Martin Executive Director
U.S. HANG GLIDING AND PARAGLIDING ASSOCIATION, 14

Palmer, Andrew Strategy & Sales/Marketing
STRATBRIDGE, INC., 820, 939, 1226

Palmer, Betty Assoc. AD, Academics
CHARLESTON SOUTHERN UNIVERSITY ATHLETICS, 325

Palmer, Brad Sports Reporter
WLS-TV, 714

Palmer, Dan Sports Director
WDOE-AM/FM, 650

Palmer, Dave President
970 WATH, 611

Palmer, Debora Advertising Manager
KSNF-TV, 703

Palmer, Dedra Associate AD/SWA
NIAGARA UNIVERSITY ATHLETICS, 339

Palmer, Eden Athletic Trainer
HOUGHTON COLLEGE ATHLETICS, 389

Palmer, Emily Interscholastic/Club Development Directo
USA CYCLING, 206

Palmer, Gary President / CEO
PRAIRIE MEADOWS RACETRACK AND CASINO, INC, 1052

Palmer, Gib President
VIRGINIA STATE GOLF ASSOCIATION, 116

Palmer, Joe Goaltending & Video Coach
AMERICAN HOCKEY LEAGUE/AHL, 128

Palmer, Lance Partner
LEVINSON, FRIEDMAN, P.S., 899

Palmer, Lisa General Manager/Sales
ADLINK, 780

Palmer, Lorene President
JUNEAU CONVENTION & VISITORS BUREAU, 235

Palmer, Ray Executive Director
PENSACOLA SPORTS ASSOCIATION, 242

Palmer, Steve Chair
SPECIAL OLYMPICS IOWA, 193

Palmer, Tod Sports Editor
OLATHE NEWS, 519

Palmer, Tom Sports Director
KBCR-AM, 620

Palmerini, John Law Clerk
THOMAS PILACEK & ASSOCIATES, 921

Palmero, Nestor VP
OCEANIC USA, 1181

Palmore, Ronnie SVP / Assistant Secretary
PEEBLES, INC., 1246

Palmquist, Joe Sports Editor
SPOKESMAN-REVIEW, 537

Palokangas, Brian Advertising Director
HIBBING DAILY TRIBUNE, 497

Palombo, Tom Director of Athletics
GUILFORD COLLEGE ATHLETICS, 387

Paluch, Dan News Director
MARSHALL RADIO, 641

Paluseo, Jeff Strength & Conditioning Coach
NORTH AMERICAN HOCKEY LEAGUE, 132

Paluszak, Michael General Manager
SOLANO COUNTY FAIRGROUNDS, 1053

Palzer, Tom VP / Chief Financial Officer
WELLS LAMONT SPORTS & SPECIALTIES, 1221

Pampado, Fabio Principal
INDY PRO 2000, 22

Panaccio, Tim Sports Writer
PHILADELPHIA INQUIRER, 523

Panarese St. Clair, Lauren Marketing Director
AURA360 VENTURES, 782

Pandiscia, Carol Senior Vice President Of Technology, Bus
ESPN TELEVISION, 681

Pandolfo, Jay Assistant Coach
NATIONAL HOCKEY LEAGUE/NHL, 123

Pandrok, Fred Marketing Director
KDUS-AM 1060 SPORTS, 623

Paniagua, Joseph Vice President
KING PANIAGUA, 573

Paniagua, Ralph President
R. PANIAGUA, INC., 813

Panic, Radivoj Head Coach
CANADIAN SOCCER LEAGUE, 156

Pankoke, Dudley Truck Division President
TENNIS SURFACES COMPANY, 1212

Pankow, Kae Vice President, Sales
ONTARIO HOCKEY LEAGUE, 134

Pankow, Mike Sports Information Director
MAINE AT PRESQUE ISLE ATHLETICS, UNIVERSITY OF, 393

Pankratz, Joe Owner
NORTH AMERICAN HOCKEY LEAGUE, 132

Pannell, Eric Assistant Director of Sports Information
DRURY UNIVERSITY (DU) ATHLETICS, 357

Panno, Jon Product Manager
EKTELON, 1138

Pannone, Ryan Head Coach
NATIONAL BASKETBALL ASSOCIATION DEVELOPMENT LEAGUE, 59

Panozzo, Mike Publisher
BOWLERS JOURNAL INTERNATIONAL, 557, 558

Pantages, Lisa Senior VP/Chief Financial Officer
NATIONAL LEAGUE OF PROFESSIONAL BASEBALL CLUBS, THE, 32

Panter, Chris Sports Information Director
GWYNEDD MERCY COLLEGE ATHLETICS, 388

Pantera, Matthew Chair/Director
SPRINGFIELD COLLEGE, 436

Panzenhagen, Tom (313)222-6730
DETROIT FREE PRESS, 486

Paolantonio, Sal Reporter
NFL 2NIGHT, 692

Paoletti, Dennis Principal
SHEN MILSON & WILKE, 1072

Paoletti, Tracy Vice President
SPORTING GOODS AGENTS ASSOCIATION (SGAA), 288

Paoli, David Member
PAOLI & SHEA, P.C., 855

Paoli, Grace Marketing Communications Manager
COMMUNITY PROFESSIONAL LOUDSPEAKERS, 829

Paoli, Juliana Chief Marketing Officer
CALIFORNIA LEAGUE (A-LEVEL), 36

Paolini, Mike Head Coach
WOMEN'S PREMIER SOCCER LEAGUE, 166

Paolisso, Paul President
PAOLISSO & ASSOCIATES, INC., 808

Papadakis, Alec CEO
USL LEAGUE TWO, 158, 160

Paparesta, Nick Head Athletic Trainer
AMERICAN LEAGUE OF PROFESSIONAL BASEBALL CLUBS, THE, 30

Papazian, Jerry Managing Director
FOUNTAINHEAD ASSOCIATES, 1066

Pape, Andrew Classified Manager
REPUBLICAN-AMERICAN, 529

Pape, David Sports Information Director
CARLETON COLLEGE ATHLETICS, 380

Pape, Mike Secretary
IOWA GOLF ASSOCIATION, 111

Papendick, John Sports Editor
ABERDEEN AMERICAN NEWS, 461

Papichs, Mark Director of Athletics
UNIVERSITY OF THE INCARNATE WORD ATHLETICS, 361

Papierniak, Bill General Manager
JACKIE ROBINSON BALLPARK, 983

Papineau, Rob Vice President & General Manager
ONTARIO HOCKEY LEAGUE, 134

Pappalardo, Joe Director of Merchandising
EASTERN LEAGUE, 39, 1009

Pappas, Arthur Chairman
MASSACHUSETTS AMATEUR SPORTS FOUNDATION, 261

Pappas, Rallis President
INFORMATION & DISPLAY SYSTEMS, INC., 830

Pappas, Tom Attorney
BURELSON, PATE & GIBSON, L.L.P., 879

Paquet, Martin Director, Operations
QUEBEC MAJOR JUNIOR HOCKEY LEAGUE, 135

Paquet, Jackie Associate Athletics Director
INDIANAPOLIS ATHLETICS, UNIVERSITY OF, 361

Paquette, John Associate Commissioner, Sports Media Rel
BIG EAST CONFERENCE, 290

Paquette, Mark Sr. Assoc. AD, Facilities & Stadium Mana
COLORADO STATE UNIVERSITY ATHLETICS, 326

Paquin, Steve Second Vice President
INDIANA GOLF ASSOCIATION, 110

Parada, Trini Promotions Assistant
KVIA-TV, 705

Paradero, Adela Promotions Director
KDF-TV, 696

Paradies, Gregg President & Chief Executive Officer
PARADIES SHOP/PGA TOUR SHOPS, 1246

Paradies, James Vice Chairman
PARADIES SHOP/PGA TOUR SHOPS, 1246

Parage, Gaston President
INTERNATIONAL POWERLIFTING FEDERATION, 177

Price, Marsha Administrative Assistant
HUGHES STADIUM (MD), 980
Price, Mike Advertising Director
EL PASO TIMES, 489
Price, Robert Chief Financial Officer
BUY.COM SPORTS STORE, 1233
Price, Susan Managing Editor
SLAM, 587
Price, Terry Sports Reporter (Boxing)
HARTFORD COURANT, 495
Price, Tic Head Coach, Men's Basketball
MONTAGNE CENTER, 996
Price, Tim Sports Reporter (Horse Racing)
FORT WORTH STAR-TELEGRAM, 491
Price, Tom Assistant Athletic Director
BLUEFIELD COLLEGE ATHLETICS, 307, 353
Price, Tyler Assistant Director of Athletics,
Communi
BAKER UNIVERSITY ATHLETICS, 306
Price, Videl Director of Compliance
MEDGAR EVERS COLLEGE ATHLETICS
(MEC), 395
Prichard, Louis Secretary-Treasurer
THOROUGHBRED CLUB OF AMERICA, 77
Prichett, Scott Director Of Marketing
SPORTS TALK/THE TICKET, 613
Prickett, Jared Governor
KENTUCKY AAU ASSOCIATION, 212
Prickett, Ryan Sports Information Director
FORT HAYS STATE UNIVERSITY ATHLETICS
(FHSU), 359
Priddy, Tommy Sports Editor
PARIS POST-INTELLIGENCER, 522
Pridemore, Will Associate AD, Student Athlete
Services
WEBER STATE UNIVERSITY ATHLETICS, 349
Pridham, Brandon Assistant General Manager
NATIONAL HOCKEY LEAGUE/NHL, 125
Pries, Lonnie Director of Athletics
CONCORDIA UNIVERSITY (MI) ATHLETICS,
309
Prieskorn-Thomas, Gina Owner
DUKE CITY GLADIATORS, 94
Priest, Andy Assistant Executive Director
CAROLINAS GOLF ASSOCIATION, 109
Priest, Mike President & Alternate Governor
NATIONAL HOCKEY LEAGUE/NHL, 123
Priest, Ross Sports Editor
YUMA DAILY SUN, 553
Priest, Tiffany Director of Women's Golf and
Membership
CAROLINAS GOLF ASSOCIATION, 109
Priester, Melissa Director of Client Service
GENERAL SPORTS TURF SYSTEMS, 844
Priestner, Colin General Manager/President
WESTERN HOCKEY LEAGUE, 138
Priestner, Mike Owner/Governor
WESTERN HOCKEY LEAGUE, 138
Priluker, Louis Secretary
IBF/USBA, 67
Primeau, Keith President, Hockey Operations
UNITED STATES HOCKEY LEAGUE, 137
Primerano, Lauren President
USA TRACK & FIELD - NEW YORK, 175
Prince, Catherine Sports Information Director
CITY COLLEGE OF NEW YORK ATHLETICS,
382
Prince, Chandler Manager, Business
Development
BUTLER BOWL, 962
Prince, Daren President and CEO
PRINCE MARKETING GROUP, 811, 857
Prince, Darren President/CEO
PRINCE MARKETING GROUP, 811, 857
Prince, Jay Publisher
SQUASH MAGAZINE, 592
Prince, Jeff Chair
USA SHOOTING, 207
Prince, Linda Advertising Manager
CARMI TIMES, 470
Prince, Mollie Marketing Manager
PELTON MARSH KINSELLA, 830
Prince, Patrick Sports Assistant Editor
TULSA WORLD, 547
Prince, Paul Editorial
NSGA RETAIL FOCUS, 580
Prince, Paul Advertising Manager
NSGA RETAIL FOCUS, 580

Prince, Paul Vice President/Business
Development
NSGA BUYING GUIDE, 602
Prince, Skip Senior Advisor
UNITED STATES HOCKEY LEAGUE, 136
Prince, Tom Manager
EASTERN LEAGUE, 38
Principe, Gerald Partner
HAILE, SHAW & PFAFFENBERGER, P.A., 892
Principe, Pat Sports Director ; Anchor
WGAL-TV, 711
Prine, Karla Secretary, Marketing and
Communications
IRVING CONVENTION & VISITORS BUREAU,
235
Pringle, Mickey President
SOUTH CAROLINA HIGH SCHOOL LEAGUE,
200
Print, John Director of Soccer
SPORTS MANAGEMENT WORLDWIDE, 819
Prinz, Laurie Editor
EQUUS, 563
Prioletti, Steve Tournament Manager
WESTERN GOLF ASSOCIATION/EVANS
SCHOLARS FOUNDATION, 116
Pristash, Bob Associate AD, Media Relations
EVANSVILLE ATHLETICS, UNIVERSITY OF,
329
Pritchard, Bob President
FISHER ATHLETIC EQUIPMENT, INC., 1143
Pritchard, Brian VP
FISHER ATHLETIC EQUIPMENT, INC., 1143
Pritchard, Griffin Sports Writer
SELMA TIMES-JOURNAL, 534
Pritchard, Jay Marketing Director
SUN BOWL, 93
Pritchard, Julie Director, Marketing
BLUFFS RUN, 1055
Pritchard, Kevin President, Basketball Operations
NATIONAL BASKETBALL ASSOCIATION/NBA,
57, 956
Pritchard, Phil Vice President, Resource Centre
and Cura
HOCKEY HALL OF FAME AND MUSEUM, 251
Pritchard, Robert Chief Executive Officer
MARKETFORCE ONE, INC., 851
Pritchard, Robert President
FISHER ATHLETIC EQUIPMENT, INC., 1143
Pritchett, Angie Owner, Production Manager
TRENWAY, LLC, 1215
Pritchett, Darin Host/Producer
WEEKDAY SPORTSBEAT, 614
Pritchett, Jerome Owner, Accounts
Payable/Receivable
TRENWAY, LLC, 1215
Pritchett, Jon President / Chief Executive Officer
GENERAL SPORTS VENUE ASTROTURF,
1147
Pritchett, Michael Assistant Athletics Director,
Facilities
WILLIAM & MARY HALL, 967, 1026, 1028
Pritts, Ron Sports Editor
DAILY AMERICAN, 477
Pritz, Thom Advertising Manager
WPBN-TV, 716
Prochazka, Zuzana Board of Directors
BOATING WRITERS INTERNATIONAL, 64
Procops, Christine Senior VP/Chief Financial
Officer
NATIONAL FOOTBALL LEAGUE/NFL, 96
Procos, Mark Vice President
PARACHUTE INDUSTRY ASSOCIATION, 13
Procter, Kevin Sports Reporter
TENNESSEAN, 542
Proctor, Josh Chief Financial Officer
NATIONAL BASKETBALL ASSOCIATION/NBA,
57
Proctor, Justin Marketing Director
C.H. GUERNSEY & CO., 1061
Proctor, Martha Coordinator of Internal
Operations
NORTH CAROLINA WESLEYAN COLLEGE
ATHLETICS, 397
Proctor, Stephen Chairman
SPORTS MARKETING SURVEYS USA, 819
Proffitt, Beth Advertising Director
COMMERCIAL DISPATCH, 475
Proffitt, Rob General Manager
NORTH AMERICAN HOCKEY LEAGUE, 132

Prohinsie, Tim Athletic Trainer
NJCAA REGION XV MEN'S, 287
Prosper, Lucy Assistant Director HR/Admin
Services
FANATICS RETAIL GROUP, 1239
Prosser, Angie Director Special Events
CITY OF GREENVILLE - SPECIAL EVENTS,
229
Prosser, Linda Pari-Mutuel Manager
GREAT CANADIAN GAMING CORPORATION,
1048
Proteau, Greg Executive Director, Secretary and
Treasu
BOATING WRITERS INTERNATIONAL, 64
Protzman, Chris General Manager
WQBB-AM, 669
Proud, Aubrey Business Development
WORLD GOLF HOSPITALITY, 773
Provencher, Kevin Sports Writer
UNION LEADER, 547
Provenza, Frank Marketing Director
PUEBLO GREYHOUND PARK, 1057
Provenzano, Corey Private Military Contractor
Sales, OEM B
POINT BLANK SOLUTIONS, 1186
Providenti, Donna COO
LEADDOG MARKETING GROUP, 801
Province, Mary Chief Financial Officer
UPPER DECK COMPANY, 1218
Province, Nancy Department Secretary
WASHBURN UNIVERSITY OF TOPEKA, 439
Pruchnicki, Susan Principal
BOND ARCHITECTS, 1060
Prud'homme, Sylvain President and CEO,
Canada
LOWE'S, 738
Pruent, Debra Chief Operations Officer
GFK CUSTOM RESEARCH NORTH AMERICA,
793
Pruett, Adam Director of Recreational Sports
CLAREMONT-MUDD-SCRIPPS COLLEGES
ATHLETICS, 382
Pruett, Carl Advertising Sales
WEKS-FM, 651
Pruis, Marco Head Coach
USL LEAGUE TWO, 161
Pruitt, Andy Sports Reporter
WCSC-TV, 709
Pruitt, Laura Director of Athletics
MOUNT ST. VINCENT ATHLETICS, COLLEGE
OF, 396
Pruyn, Christie Executive Director
INTERNATIONAL LIVE EVENTS
ASSOCIATION, 219
Pryce, Tegan Venue Services Manager
SYDNEY ENTERTAINMENT CENTRE, 1016
Pryde, Susan Human Resources Director
IRWIN SPORTS, 1159
Pryer, Don Director, Stadium Operations
ATLANTIC LEAGUE, 35
Pryor, David Assistant Athletic Director, Sports
Medi
DELTA STATE UNIVERSITY (DSU)
ATHLETICS, 357
Pryor, Glen Chief Financial Administrator (Dallas)
WINSTEAD ATTORNEYS, 926
Pryor, Greg President
LIFE PRIORITY, INC., 1166
Pryor, Joanna Athletic Director
NEWMAN UNIVERSITY ATHLETICS, 339
Pryor, Michelle Marketing Director
LIFE PRIORITY, INC., 1166
Pryson, Mike Sports Reporter
JACKSON CITIZEN PATRIOT, 500
Publicover, Mark Product Safety Inventor/CEO
JUMPSPORT, 1161
Puccini, Robert Chairman President, Mizuno USA
THE SPORTS & FITNESS INDUSTRY
ASSOCIATION (SFIA), 822
Pucher, Frank Senior Associate AD, External
Relations
FRESNO STATE ATHLETICS, 330
Puchyr, T.J. Co-Owner
NASCAR CUP SERIES, 23
Pucino, Scott Executive Vice President, Baseball
CSMG INTERNATIONAL, LTD, 788
Puck, Amanda Director Business
Development/Public Rel
XA, THE EXPERIENTIAL AGENCY, 827

Puddester, Frederick Chairman
MD STADIUM AUTHORITY, 852
Puderbach, Brendan Contact
INDY PRO 2000, 22
Puett, Steve President and Chief Executive
Officer
LAS VEGAS GOLF & TENNIS, 1243
Pugh, Chuck Executive VP Sales & Marketing
CHEER KIDS, 1126
Pugh, Dave General Manager
WDFN - 1130 AM THE FAN, 650
Pugh, Douglas Partner
ENG & WOODS, 888
Pugliese, Nick (813)259-7854
TAMPA TRIBUNE, 541
Puglise, Joe Market Manager
KOY-AM, 633
Pujol, Joseph Dept. Chairperson
SOUTHEAST MISSOURI STATE UNIVERSITY,
435
Pujols, Luis Manager
NEW YORK-PENNSYLVANIA LEAGUE, 46
Pulaski, Peter Director
CONNECTICUT PGA SECTIONAL OFFICE,
104
Puleo, James Production, Marketing and Design
Manager
VIRGIL FILMS & ENTERTAINMENT, 1220
Puleri, Jeff Assistant Athletic Director for
Communic
MASSACHUSETTS COLLEGE OF LIBERAL
ARTS ATHLETICS(MCLA), 394
Pulford, David EVP
RCA GROUP EVENT MARKETING +
MANAGEMENT, 814
Puljan, Mark VP Central Region
INFOUSA, 797
Pullen, Elizabeth Paralegal
BOUTIN, DENTINO, GIBSON, DI GUISTO,
HODELL, INC., 876
Pulley, Brian Assistant Commissioner for External
Affa
OHIO VALLEY CONFERENCE, 300
Pullman, April Advertising Manager
CAPITAL JOURNAL, 470
Pullo, Frank Chair/Director
EAST STROUDSBURG UNIVERSITY OF, 419
Pullom, Wanda General Manager
FREMONT DIE CONSUMER PRODUCTS INC,
1145
Pulver, Ian Attorney
IAN C. PULVER, 894
Puma, Paul Executive Committee
AMERICAN MOTORCYCLIST ASSOCIATION,
143
Pumerantz, Richard President
IMPACT TRAINING SYSTEMS INC, 1157
Pumo, Matt Advertising Manager
WALA-TV, 707
Pump, Steve Director of Stadium Operations
EASTERN LEAGUE, 39, 970
Pund, Todd Director of Ticket Sales
INTERNATIONAL LEAGUE, 42
Puou, George Assistant Athletics Director
NOTRE DAME DE NAMUR
UNIVERSITY(NDNU), 368
Pupo, Mike Sports Producer
WJZ-TV, 713
Purcell, Greg Director Brand Strategy/Managing
Partner
REESE SPORTS, 814
Purcell, Jim President
TF PUBLISHING, 1212
Purcell, Kevin Executive Director
NEW JERSEY STATE GOLF ASSOCIATION,
113
Purcell, Tanya Secretary / Treasurer
SPORTIME, 1204
Purcell, Will Sports Information Director
MILLSAPS COLLEGE ATHLETICS (MCA), 395
Purdom, Larry Sports Editor
WAYCROSS JOURNAL-HERALD, 551
Purdum, David Sports Editor
SLIDELL SENTRY-NEWS, 536
Purdy, Jamie Assistant Director of Athletics
PIEDMONT COLLEGE ATHLETICS, 399
Purdy, Mark Sports Columnist
SAN JOSE MERCURY NEWS, 533

Purdy, Patience Director of Community Relations
SAMUEL J. PLUMERI FIELD AT MERCER
COUNTY WATERFRONT PARK, 1009
Puri, Ashwin Senior Associate AD/COO
VILLANOVA UNIVERSITY ATHLETICS, 348
Purks, Scott Sports Writer
ST. PETERSBURG TIMES, 538
Purnell, Jamie Associate Director of
Athletics/SWA
CALIFORNIA STATE
UNIVERSITY-DOMINGUEZ HILLS ATHLETICS,
353
Purnell, John Chief Executive Officer
BRUTE GROUP, 1121
Purpur, Ray Deputy AD
STANFORD UNIVERSITY ATHLETICS, 345
Purpura, Joe Territory Manager, Pennsylvania
HEARTLINE FITNESS PRODUCTS, INC., 1154
Purpura, Vinney Vice President
PIONEER BASEBALL LEAGUE (ADVANCED
ROOKIE LEVEL), 50
Pursell, Kris Director or Event Operations
PALM BEACH COUNTY SPORTS
COMMISSION, INC., 241
Pursell, Ronald Lawyer
NORTH, PURSELL, RAMOS & JAMESON,
PLC, 907
Purslow, Janice VP
LOG HOUSE DESIGNS, INC., 1168
Purtill, Jim Football Coach
SAINT NORBERT COLLEGE ATHLETICS, 401
Purvis, Judy Marketing
TERRAPLAS USA RENTALS, LLC, 1212
Puscavage, Carl Marketing Sales Manager
LACKAWANNA COUNTY CONVENTION &
VISITORS BUREAU, 236
Puska, Denis Director,
Broadcasting/Media/Community R
NORTH AMERICAN HOCKEY LEAGUE, 131
Puskar, Jay Weekend Sports Anchor
WICU-TV, 712
Putman, Garrett VP Online Marketing Internet
Marketing D
SPORTS ENDEAVORS, INC., 1250
Putnam, Bob Sports Writer
ST. PETERSBURG TIMES, 538
Putnam, Lou Vice President
UNITED STATES CORPORATE ATHLETICS
ASSOCIATION, 224
Putney, Kelly Management Committee Member
BASSFORD, LOCKHART, TRUESDELL &
BRIGGS, P.A., 873
Putter, Paul National Director Programming
VENUEWORKS, 1075
Putzel, Michelle Administrative
Assistant,Coordinator
U.S. HOCKEY HALL OF FAME, 257
Pyfrom, Shamika Associate AD
NORTH CAROLINA A&T STATE UNIVERSITY
ATHLETICS, 339
Pyle, Jeff Head Coach & General Manager,
Hockey Ope
EAST COAST HOCKEY LEAGUE/ECHL, 129
Pyle, Tim Sports Reporter
COLUMBIAN, 474
Pyle, Trevor Sports Reporter
SKAGIT VALLEY HERALD, 535
Pym, David Managing Director
CANADIAN SNOWSPORTS ASSOCIATION,
151
Pyne, George President IMG Sports &
Entertainment
IMG LOS ANGELES/IMG X SPORTS, 847

Q

Quade, Bruce Chairman
MARYLAND RACING COMMISSION, 81
Quade, Mike Manager
INTERNATIONAL LEAGUE, 43
Quagliariello, Ed Head of New York Sales
DIALGLOBAL, INC., 610
Quagliata, Erica Account Executive
SILVERMAN MEDIA & MARKETING GROUP,
816
Quaife, Steve Advertising Manager
DAILY NEWS (WA), 480

Qualls, Kent Director, Minor League Operations
AMERICAN LEAGUE OF PROFESSIONAL
BASEBALL CLUBS, THE, 29
Quan, Rick Sports Anchor
KPIX-TV, 701
Quandt, Dan Executive Director
AMARILLO CONVENTION & VISITOR
COUNCIL, 225
Quant, Larry Deputy Director of Athletics, Finance
&
CORNELL UNIVERSITY ATHLETICS, 327
Quaranta, Santino Head Coach
USL LEAGUE TWO, 160
Quarles, Shelton Director, Football Operations
NATIONAL FOOTBALL LEAGUE/NFL, 97
Quatraro, Matt Manager
ARIZONA FALL LEAGUE (ROOKIE), 34
Quatrocky, Sara Associate Athletics Director
LYNN UNIVERSITY ATHLETICS, 363
Quattlebaum, Gus VP, Professional Scouting
AMERICAN LEAGUE OF PROFESSIONAL
BASEBALL CLUBS, THE, 29
Quattlebaum, Julien Vice President
FOX SPORTS PRIME TICKET, 682, 683
Quattrone, Joel Senior Associate Athletics
Director
DICKINSON COLLEGE(DC) ATHLETICS, 384
Quave, Betty Secretary
SOUTH CAROLINA AAU ASSOCIATION, 214
Queally, Alicia Deputy AD/SWA
STETSON UNIVERSITY ATHLETICS, 345
Quebedeaux, Chris Sports Editor
CROWLEY POST-SIGNAL, 477
Queen, Debbie Secretary
COLORADO HILL CLIMB ASSOCIATION, 84
Queen, Marty Sports Editor
MCDOWELL NEWS, 509
Queeney, Tim Editor
OCEAN NAVIGATOR, 580
Queensland, Randy Vice-Chairperson
RIVERSIDE ARENA, 1006
Quel, Casey Advertising Director
GARDEN ISLAND, 493
Queliz, Kelvin Director of Sports Information
TEXAS A&M UNIVERSITY-KINGSVILLE
ATHLETICS, 373
Quenneville, Joel Head Coach
NATIONAL HOCKEY LEAGUE/NHL, 124
Quesada, Raul Vice President, Marketing
Communications
FOX SPORTS NETWORKS/FOX SPORTS
NET, 683
Quesnel, Donita Promotions Director
KOTV-TV, 701
Questa, Barb Deputy Director of Athletics
ST. BONAVENTURE UNIVERSITY
ATHLETICS, 345
Quevedo, Juan Director Market Intelligence
IMAGES USA, 797
Quezada, Luis Head Coach
WOMEN'S PREMIER SOCCER LEAGUE, 165
Quick, Glenn Associate Athletics Director -
Academic
UNIVERSITY OF KANSAS, 1022
Quick, Jason Sports Reporter
OREGONIAN, 520
Quick, Mike Host
HIGH SCHOOL WEEKLY, 691
Quick, Scott General Manager
BRAINARD INTERNATIONAL RACEWAY, 1032
Quick, Vic Sports Director
KTVZ-TV, 704
Quigley, Carl Assistant Athletic Director
ST. FRANCIS COLLEGE ATHLETICS (SFC),
372
Quigley, Rich Manager
PETRY MEDIA, 684
Quill, Eric Head Coach
USL LEAGUE ONE, 160
Quilley, Jason Executive VP, Finance
NATIONAL HOCKEY LEAGUE/NHL, 124
Quincey, James CEO
COCA-COLA COMPANY, 735
Quinlan, Joe Sr. Assoc. AD, Internal Operations
COLUMBIA UNIVERSITY ATHLETICS, 327
Quinlan, Keith Secretary, Racing
SANDOWN PARK, 1048, 1053

executive index

Rasizer, Lee Sports Reporter
ROCKY MOUNTAIN NEWS, 530

Raskin, Debra Partner
VLADECK WALDMAN ELIAS & ENGELHARD, P.C., 923

Raskopf, Dick Secretary/Treasurer
NATIONAL GOLF FOUNDATION, 103

Rasmussen, Bob Founder
VECTRA FITNESS CORPORATION, 1219

Rasmussen, Bruce Athletic Director
CREIGHTON UNIVERSITY ATHLETICS, 327, 964

Rasmussen, John Senior Associate AD, External Affairs
INDIANA UNIVERSITY-PURDUE UNIVERSITY INDIANAPOLIS, 332

Rasmussen, Stephen Chief Executive Officer
NATIONWIDE FINANCIAL SERVICES, 739

Raspino, Paul Military Sales - U.S. Army and National
POINT BLANK SOLUTIONS, 1186

Rassam, George VP Finance/Administration/CFO
SPONSORWISE, 770

Rassel, Richard Director, Global Client Relations
FELDMAN, OSCAR, 842

Ratcliff, Amy Operations Manager
BLUEGRASS STATE GAMES, 259

Ratcliff, Chris Director of Athletics
ARKANSAS-MONTICELLO ATHLETICS (UAM), 351

Ratcliff, J. Owner
WTON-AM, 676

Ratcliff, Jeff Sports Editor
NORTHWEST-SIGNAL, 518

Ratcliff, Kathy Advertising Manager
SENTINEL, 534

Ratcliffe, Jerry Sports Editor
DAILY PROGRESS, 481

Ratelle, Jay Vice President of Operations
NO FAULT SPORT GROUP, 1180

Rath, Charles EVP, Chief Marketing Officer
VALUE CITY DEPARTMENT STORES, 1251

Rathbun, Barbara President
WOMENS GOLFWORKS, 1223

Rathbun, Bonnie Executive Director
MIDWESTERN REPRESENTATIVES ASSOCIATION, 219

Rathbun, Jon Sports Editor
EVENING TIMES (NY), 490

Rathfon, Linda Assistant GM/Group Sales
CALIFORNIA LEAGUE (A-LEVEL), 36

Ratliff, Anita GM
THUNDER RIDGE RACING AND ENTERTAINMENT COMPLEX, 1044, 1054

Ratliff, Robert Executive Director
TUSCALOOSA CONVENTION & VISITORS BUREAU, 247

Ratner, Hank President, Chief Executive Officer
MADISON SQUARE GARDEN, 993

Ratner, Marc VP Regulatory Affairs
ULTIMATE FIGHTING CHAMPIONSHIP (UFC), 143

Ratoff, John SVP Corporate Partnerships
TD BANKNORTH GARDEN, 1017

Ratte, Mike Sports Director
WLVI-TV, 714

Ratushny, Ed Agent
FIDELIS COUNSEL ASSOCIATES, 889

Rau, Matthew Director of Corporate Sales
ROSENBLATT STADIUM, 1007

Rauber, Eric Director of Group Sales
JOHN THURMAN FIELD, 985

Rauch, Charles President
EMPIRE SPORTING GOODS MFG. COMPANY, INC., 1139

Rauch, Greg President
SOUTHERN LEAGUE OF PROFESSIONAL BASEBALL CLUBS, 53

Rauch, Matthew COO and CFO
FAGUE, TERENCE L., 888

Rauch, Mike Chief Financial Officer
NEW YORK-PENNSYLVANIA LEAGUE, 47

Rauch, Robert President
WORLD FLYING DISC FEDERATION, 98

Raupp, Gordon VP
KINSEY ASSOCIATES, 1070

Rausch, David Faculty Athletic Representative
WEST TEXAS A&M UNIVERSITY ATHLETICS (WTAMU), 376, 988

Rauscher, Bob Senior Coordinating Producer
NFL PRIMETIME, 691, 692

Rauscher, Nathan Assistant Director of Athletics
MOUNT ST. VINCENT ATHLETICS, COLLEGE OF, 396

Rautio, Trudy EVP and Chief Financial Officer
CARLSON TRAVEL NETWORK, 935

Ravech, Karl Anchor
ESPN, 690

Ravelo, Vania Media Manager
MEXICAN LEAGUE A.C., 44

Raven, Greg Technical Support &Webmaster
U.S. RACQUET STRINGERS ASSOCIATION, 172

Ravencraft, Michele Senior Director of Events
NATIONAL THOROUGHBRED RACING, 77

Rawak, Chrissi Director of Athletics
DELAWARE ATHLETICS, UNIVERSITY OF, 327

Rawitzer, Kasey Account Executive
LAKE ELSINORE STORM, 989

Rawlings, Andy Executive VP/COO
LEARFIELD SPORTS, 606

Rawlings, Guy Sports Anchor
WTVJ-TV, 689, 719

Rawlings, John Senior Vice President/Editorial Director
SPORTING NEWS, 590

Rawlings, William Lawyer
RAWLINGS, WILLIAM R., 911

Ray, Alan Technical Director
BANKSHOT SPORTS ORGANIZATION, 1229

Ray, Allan Technical
US CELLULAR ARENA, 1023

Ray, David Wrestling Head Coach
SOUTHERN ILLINOIS UNIVERSITY AT EDWARDSVILLE, 435, 572

Ray, Eric Operations Manager
KFNZ, 624

Ray, Kevin Sports Director
KMVP-AM, 631

Ray, Laura Senior Women Administrator
RIVIER UNIVERSITY ATHLETICS, 400

Ray, Logan Director Of Championship Operations
LOUISIANA GOLF ASSOCIATION, 102

Ray, Margie Treasurer
EVERGREEN REGIONAL COMMISSIONER/USA VOLLEYBALL, 209

Ray, Mike Executive Director
SOUTHERN TEXAS PGA SECTIONAL, 107

Ray, Patricia Chief Operating Officer
CANADIAN CURLING ASSOCIATION, 70

Ray, Radio Sports Director
KGAL-AM, 625

Ray, Rich Sports Director
KHUB-AM, 624, 626

Ray, Ricky Deputiy Director of Athletics
CAMPBELL UNIVERSITY ATHLETICS, 325

Ray, Rob News Director
WCDO-AM, 647

Ray, Sara Assoc. AD, Academic Services
UNIVERSITY OF WYOMING ARENA-AUDITORIUM, 1022

Ray, Tarlin Director ,Entreprenuer in Residence
PARK LANE - INVESTMENT BANKING SERVICES, 777

Ray, Tim General Manager
PIONEER BASEBALL LEAGUE, 50

Raya, Al Coordinator of Women's Basketball Offici
COLLEGE CONFERENCE OF ILLINOIS AND WISCONSIN, 292

Raybern, Jennifer Head Athletic Trainer
OTTAWA UNIVERSITY ATHLETICS, 316

Rayburn, Jimmy Chief Operating Officer
RAYCOM SPORTS, 606, 813

Rayburn, Sonya Sales & Community Affairs Director
SENIOR BOWL, 93

Rayfield, Marc Vice President/General Manager
WIP SPORTSRADIO 610, 658

Raymond, Eric Goaltending Coach
AMERICAN HOCKEY LEAGUE/AHL, 127

Raymond, Steve Program Director
WZXL-FM, 680

Rayne, Todd Faculty Athletics Representative
HAMILTON COLLEGE ATHLETICS, 388

Raynor, Mike Supervisor of Officials
NATIONAL PRO FASTPITCH, 168

Raynor, Tom Chairman / Chief Executive Officer
FLEET FEET, INC., 1239

Raythatha, Ashish Principal
TRITON SPORTS ASSOCIATES, 772

Raz, Michael Advertising Director
REGISTER-GUARD, 528

Razak, Brian Head Athletic Trainer
NEW ENGLAND ATHLETICS, UNIVERSITY OF, 397

Rea, Dan SVP/General Manager
INTERNATIONAL LEAGUE, 43, 994

Read, Bryan Sports Director
BROWNSVILLE HERALD, 469

Read, Dave Executive Vice-President
LEADING BRANDS, 1165

Read, Jeremy Advertising Manager
ST. ALBANS MESSENGER, 538

Read, Kirk General Manager
TBO (WFLA) NEWS CHANNEL 8, 706

Read, Kristian Sports Director
KECI-TV, 697

Read, Tim VP , Operations & Collective Bargain
DEL MAR THOROUGHBRED CLUB, 1046

Reade, Ian Director of Athletics
ALBERTA ATHLETICS, UNIVERSITY OF, 305

Readenour, Dustin President
NATIONAL VENTURING DIVISION, BOY SCOUTS OF AMERICA, 266

Reader, Bill Sports Assistant Editor
SEATTLE TIMES, 534

Reading, Tom Vice President of Ticketing
SOUTHERN PROFESSIONAL HOCKEY LEAGUE, 136

Ready, Danielle Secretary
NJCAA REGION XXIII WOMEN'S, 288

Ready, George Vice President
AMERICAN PAINT HORSE ASSOCIATION, 74

Ready, Keith Sports Director
WBRY-AM, 646

Reagins, Tony Chief Baseball Development Officer
NATIONAL LEAGUE OF PROFESSIONAL BASEBALL CLUBS, THE, 31

Reale, John Partner
DREW, ECKL & FARNHAM, LLP, 886

Reardon, Adam Sports Director
WMOP-AM, 664

Reardon, Jim President
ONE-ON-ONE SPORTS CONSULTANTS, 830

Reardon, Martine Chief Marketing Officer
BURDINE'S, 1232

Reardon, Thomas Esquire
HARBOUR, SMITH, HARRIS & MERRITT, 892

Reasoner, David Vice President
NEW JERSEY PGA SECTION, 106

Reasoner, Scott General Manager
PIONEER BASEBALL LEAGUE, 50, 964

Reasso, Bob Vice President for Athletics
PFEIFFER UNIVERSITY ATHLETICS, 368

Reasy, Justin Tournament Assistant
GOLF ASSOCIATION OF PHILADELPHIA, 110

Reaume, Josh Owner
NASCAR GANDER OUTDOORS TRUCK SERIES, 24

Reaves, Tammy Classified Manager
FLINT JOURNAL, 491

Reavlin, Paul Founder
REVGEAR SPORTS CO., 1193

Rebecca, Accounting - Administration
KAY RODGERS PARK, 987, 1050

Rebel, Nancy Director of Content Development
SPORT INFORMATION RESOURCE CENTER/SIRC, 257

Rebholz, Josh Senior Associate AD, External Relations
UC LOS ANGELES ATHLETICS, 348

Rebholz, Ryan Sports Information Director
INDIANA UNIVERSITY OF PENNSYLVANIA ATHLETICS, 361

Rebney, Bjorn Chief Executive Officer
SPIKE TV, 685

Rebolledo, Kevyn Crew Chief
NASCAR XFINITY SERIES, 24

Rebowe, Tim Head Coach, Football
MANNING FIELD AT JOHN L. GUIDRY STADIUM, 993

Rebstock, Dave Sports Information Director
MORNINGSIDE COLLEGE ATHLETICS, 315

Rockey, Joseph Chief Risk Officer
PNC FINANCIAL SERVICES, 740
Rockey, Robert President
DUCK HEAD APPAREL COMPANY, 1136
Rockoff, Clyde President
UNIVERSAL NUTRITION, 1218
Rockwell, David News Director
WTZN-AM, 677
Rodd, Donald Professor Exercise
SportScience/Physica
EVANSVILLE, UNIVERSITY OF, 420
Rodd, Linda Of Counsel
MEYER, SUOZZI, ENGLISH & KLEIN, 905
Roddick, Daniel Director
MATTEL SPORTS PROMOTION
DEPARTMENT, 803
Rodebaugh, Andrea Coach
WOMEN'S PREMIER SOCCER LEAGUE, 166
Rodenberg, Tom National Sales Manager
PARKER LABORATORIES, INC., 1183
Rodenburg, John Publisher
T & L GOLF, 594
Roderick, Lindsay Head Athletic Trainer
JOHN JAY COLLEGE OF CRIMINAL JUSTICE
ATHLETICS, 390
Rodewald, Chris Sales / Marketing VP
REDLINE PERFORMANCE PRODUCTS, INC.,
1192
Rodgers, Casey Chief Financial Officer
NATIONAL HOCKEY LEAGUE/NHL, 125
Rodgers, Charles Owner
WEPG-AM, 652
Rodgers, Dan Promoter
COMPETITION PARK MOTOCROSS, 1033
Rodgers, Janet President/CEO
ALPHARETTA CONVENTION & VISITORS
BUREAU, 225
Rodgers, Jill Fair Activities Assistant
YAKIMA VALLEY SUNDOME, 1030
Rodgers, John Sports Editor
PASADENA/SAN GABRIEL VALLEY
JOURNAL-NEWS, 522
Rodgers, Stephen Chief Executive Officer
PETER ROGERES, INC LTD, 608
Rodgers, Tammy News Director
KBEE-FM, 620
Rodgers, Travis Producer
THE JIM ROME SHOW, 616
Rodgers, Will News Director
WEPG-AM, 652
Rodman, Bill Executive Producer
GAMEDAY, 615
Rodman, Christopher Vice President and Group
Managing Direct
TOPPS COMPANY, INC., 1214
Rodowicz, Fran Regional Vice President
LIACOURAS CENTER, 991
Rodrigue, Sylvain Goaltending Coach
AMERICAN HOCKEY LEAGUE/AHL, 126
Rodrigues, M. Principal
ARCHITECTS DELAWIE WILKES RODRIGUES
BARKER, 1059
Rodrigues, Steve Secretary
U.S. HANG GLIDING AND PARAGLIDING
ASSOCIATION, 14
Rodriguez, Anita Co-Head Coach
WOMEN'S PREMIER SOCCER LEAGUE, 166
Rodriguez, Bert Maintenance Manager
PIMA COUNTY FAIR, 1052
Rodriguez, Carlos VP, Player Development &
International S
AMERICAN LEAGUE OF PROFESSIONAL
BASEBALL CLUBS, THE, 30
Rodriguez, Hector Executive of Sales and
Marketing
DYNASTY APPAREL INDUSTRIES, 1136
Rodriguez, Jeison Senior Art Director
SPIKE/DDB PRODUCTIONS, 817
Rodriguez, Jessica Executive Vice President of
Program Sche
GALAVISION, 683
Rodriguez, Johnny Manager
NEW YORK-PENNSYLVANIA LEAGUE, 47
Rodriguez, Jorge Sports Director
KWEX-TV, 705
Rodriguez, Juan Manager
MEXICAN LEAGUE A.C., 44, 536
Rodriguez, Justin Sports Reporter
TIMES HERALD RECORD, 544

Rodriguez, Mike VP, Ticket Operations
PACIFIC COAST LEAGUE OF
PROFESSIONAL BASEBALL CLUBS, 49
Rodriguez, Nathalie Chief Executive Officer
FEDERATION INTERNATIONALE D'ESCRIME
(FIE), 86, 202
Rodriguez, Raul Executive President
MEXICAN LEAGUE A.C., 44
Rodriguez, Robert Equity and Managing Partner
MILLER, KAGAN RODRIGUEZ AND SILVER,
P.A., 905
Rodriguez, Sam Sports Editor
DAILY JEFFERSON COUNTY UNION, 479
Rodriguez, Sophie Office Coordinator
NJCAA REGION I WOMEN'S, 284
Rodriguez, Stephen Chairman
NATIONAL SENIOR GAMES ASSOCIATION,
221
Rodriguez, Stephen Vice President
SUNSHINE STATE GAMES, 263
Rodriguez, Steven Vice President
FLORIDA SPORTS FOUNDATION, 232
Rodriguez, III, Luis President/General Manager
WOIZ-AM, 667
Rodriguez, Nelson President/General Manager
MAJOR LEAGUE SOCCER, 157
Roe, James SVP, Real Estate
FAMOUS FOOTWEAR, 1238
Roe, Scott Vice President
VF BRAND SOLUTIONS, 1219
Roe, Stephanie Director of Administration
BIG SOUTH CONFERENCE, 290
Roe, Tami President
ABSOLUTE FITNESS, INC, 1100
Roe, Tim Sports Editor
REPORTER, 528
Roebuck, Malcolm Chairman of the Board
BADGE-A-MINIT LTD., 1113
Roeder, Jesse Sports Turf Manager
VETERANS MEMORIAL STADIUM (CEDAR
RAPIDS), 1025
Roedl, Eric Deputy Athletic Director
OREGON ATHLETICS, UNIVERSITY OF, 341
Roegiers, Kelcey Senior Associate AD/SWA
GEORGIA STATE UNIVERSITY ATHLETICS,
331
Roehr, Dave Finance VP
CABELA'S, 1123, 1233
Roel, Gustave President/Executive Director
RESEAU DU SPORTETUDIANT DU QUEBEC,
201
Roenbeck, Clyde VP, Field Operations
HAT WORLD/LIDS CORP., 1241
Roesler, Mark Chairman/Chief Executive Officer
CURTIS MANAGEMENT GROUP, 838, 839
Roesler, Mark Chairman & CEO
CURTIS MANAGEMENT GROUP, 838, 839
Roest, Stacy General Manager
AMERICAN HOCKEY LEAGUE/AHL, 128
Roetert, E. CEO
SHAPE AMERICA SOCIETY OF HEALTH AND
PHYSICAL EDUCATORS, 222
Roetert, Paul CEO
SHAPE AMERICA SOCIETY OF HEALTH AND
PHYSICAL EDUCATORS, 85
Rog, Stewart Principal
DELOITTE & TOUCHE LLP, 1074
Rogalski, Dave Goaltending Coach
NATIONAL HOCKEY LEAGUE/NHL, 124
Rogan, Alan VP Eligibiity
CANADIAN COLLEGIATE ATHLETIC
ASSOCIATION, 281
Rogel, Malcolm VP, Ticket Operations & Event
Services
AMERICAN LEAGUE OF PROFESSIONAL
BASEBALL CLUBS, THE, 30
Rogen, Victoria Licensing
ARIZONA DEPARTMENT OF RACING, 79, 118
Rogers, Adeline Director, Marketing
SUNLAND PARK RACETRACK & CASINO,
1054
Rogers, Bart VP Sales/Marketing
FLEXCO, 136, 1144
Rogers, Carl CFO & Treasurer
EBONITE INTERNATIONAL, INC., 1138
Rogers, Chip Owner
WYXC-AM, 680
Rogers, Dawn Deputy Athletics Director
BAYLOR UNIVERSITY ATHLETICS, 324

Rogers, Dene EVP, Restructuring and Business
Improvem
KMART CORPORATION, 1243
Rogers, Edward Chairman, Toronto Blue Jays
AMERICAN LEAGUE OF PROFESSIONAL
BASEBALL CLUBS, THE, 31
Rogers, Felicia Customer Service
ALTUS ATHLETIC MFG. COMPANY, 1106
Rogers, Jack Sales VP
HUSSEY SEATING COMPANY, 1157
Rogers, Jackie Director of Athletic
Communications
DOWLING COLLEGE (DC) ATHLETICS, 357
Rogers, Jami Head Athletic Trainer
LAWRENCE UNIVERSITY ATHLETICS, 392
Rogers, Jane President, General Manager
NEW YORK-PENNSYLVANIA LEAGUE, 47,
1005
Rogers, John Secretary
PHILADELPHIA PGA SECTIONAL OFFICE,
106
Rogers, Kevin Director, Player Personnel
NATIONAL FOOTBALL LEAGUE/NFL, 95
Rogers, Mark General Manager
CESSNA STADIUM, 704, 964
Rogers, Matt Chairman
NATIONAL BASEBALL CONGRESS, 27
Rogers, Melanie Associate Principal/Director of
Human Re
DES ARCHITECTS/ENGINEERS, INC., 1063
Rogers, O President
STAGERIGHT CORP., 1207
Rogers, Paul Treasurer
SPECIAL OLYMPICS MISSISSIPPI, 193
Rogers, Phil Sports Writer
CHICAGO TRIBUNE, 472
Rogers, Randy General Manager
KOVO-AM, 632
Rogers, Rickey Promoter
ALASKA RACEWAY PARK, 1031
Rogers, Roland Chief Executive Officer
BLACK ATHLETE SPORTS NETWORK, 557
Rogers, Russell Director of Athletics
STEVENS INSTITUTE OF TECHNOLOGY
ATHLETICS, 404
Rogers, Stephen President, Chief Executive
Officer
SPORTS SPECIALISTS, LTD., 1250
Rogers, Stephen President & CEO
SPORTS SPECIALISTS, LTD., 1250
Rogers, Susan President
SPORTS HEALTH, 1205
Rogers, Thomas Governor
ARIZONA AAU ASSOCIATION, 212
Rogers, Tim Reporter
PLAIN DEALER, 524
Rogers, Tom General Manager
WPKY-AM, 668
Rogers, Tony Operations Manager
FLORENCE CIVIC CENTER, 974
Rogge, Jacques President
OLYMPIC MUSEUM, LIBRARY AND STUDIES
CENTRE, 204, 256
Rogge, Tom President / Chief Executive Officer
CRAMER PRODUCTS, INC., 1130
Roggin, Fred Sports Director/Anchor
KNBC-TV, 700
Roggow, Darby Assistant Athletic Director
TIFFIN UNIVERSITY ATHLETICS, 373
Roghaar, Brad Advertising Manager
STANDARD-EXAMINER, 538
Rogo, Gary Sports Editor
CONNECTICUT POST, 475
Rogol, Ian Head Athletic Trainer
MARY WASHINGTON UNIVERSITY
ATHLETICS, 394
Rogow, Mark Head Athletic Trainer
NATIONAL LEAGUE OF PROFESSIONAL
BASEBALL CLUBS, THE, 32
Rogowin, Adam Vice President, Communications
NATIONAL HOCKEY LEAGUE/NHL, 123
Rogus, Mike Chief Executive Officer
MOTORHEAD PRODUCTS, 1175
Roguska, Zsachlayne Head Athletc Trainer
LEES-MCRAE COLLEGE ATHLETICS, 362
Rohde, Heather Profile Products LLC - Exclusive
Distrib
COLBOND, INC., 1128

Rossman, Michael President & Chief Executive Officer
NEW TIER COMMUNICATIONS, 806, 830
Rossman, Mike Sports Director
WRCT-FM, 671
Rossman, Scott Sports Director
WJHG-TV, 713
Rosson, Judy Advertising Manager
TEXAS THOROUGHBRED, 595
Rossow, Jim Sports Editor
NEWS-GAZETTE, 516
Roswell, Jessica Assistant Athletic Director for Marketin
PACIFIC LUTHERAN UNIVERSITY ATHLETICS, 398
Rote, Rock Sports Director
WDJT-TV, 709
Rotert, Terry Arena Activities Director/Arena Manager
HURON ARENA, 981
Roth, Bill Promoter
MOBILE INTERNATIONAL SPEEDWAY, 1038
Roth, Chris Sports Director
WBAY-TV, 707
Roth, Ellen President
U.S. DEAF SKI & SNOWBOARD ASSOCIATION, 153
Roth, Garrett Head Coach/General Manager
NORTH AMERICAN HOCKEY LEAGUE, 132, 133
Roth, Hal Executive VP
NATIONAL LEAGUE OF PROFESSIONAL BASEBALL CLUBS, THE, 31
Roth, Jeff PRIORITY SPORTS & ENTERTAINMENT, 857, 858
Roth, Leo Sports Columnist
DEMOCRAT AND CHRONICLE, 485
Roth, Merianne Vice President Marketing & Communication
FORT WORTH CONVENTION & VISITORS BUREAU, 232
Roth, Mike Director of Athletics
GONZAGA UNIVERSITY ATHLETICS, 331
Roth, Scott Gymnastics Divisional Director
AMERICAN ATHLETIC INC., 1107
Rothamel, Paul SVP, Store Operations
PAMIDA, INC., 1246
Rothenberg, Alan Chairman
PREMIER PARTNERSHIPS, 810
Rothenberg, Alan Chairman
PREMIER PARTNERSHIPS, 810
Rothermel, Will Associate Athletic Director
ITHACA COLLEGE ATHLETICS, 390
Rothhammer, Dianne President
SPRINT AQUATICS, 1206
Rothman, Evan Executive Editor
GOLF MAGAZINE, 567
Rothman, Jennifer Sales Manager
LONG ISLAND CVB & SPORTS COMMISSION, 238
Rothman, Richard Founder
ROTHMAN INSTITUTE, 932
Rothrock, Ben Assistant General Manager of Operations
DIAMOND FIELD, 970
Rothschild, Philip Director
SOUTHWEST MISSOURI STATE UNIVERSITY, 436
Rothstein, Michael Sports Writer
JOURNAL GAZETTE, 501
Rotondi, Michael Vice President
E.B. ROTONDI & SONS, INC., 1137
Rottenberg, Paul Chair
DES MOINES AREA SPORTS COMMISSION, 230
Rotter, Merton Lawyer
WARSHAFSKY LAW FIRM, 923
Rottier, Bart Executive Director
DIXIE PGA SECTIONAL OFFICE, 104
Rotz, John Operations Manager
USL LEAGUE TWO, 159, 162
Rouge, Jean General Secretary
INTERNATIONAL JUDO FEDERATION, 203
Roughton, Keith Senior Associate AD, Compliance
GEORGIA SOUTHERN UNIVERSITY ATHLETICS, 330

Roundtree, Jim CFO
FIRST PLUS SPORTS MARKETING, 791
Rountree, Mark Deputy Director of Athletics
GEORGIA TECH ATHLETICS, 331, 489
Rourke, Jonathan Owner
CHAMPIONSHIP SPORTS GROUP, 760
Rouse, Jack Chief Executive Officer
JACK ROUSE ASSOCIATES, 798
Rouse, Nick Head Strength & Conditioning Coach
UNITED STATES HOCKEY LEAGUE, 136
Rouse, Scott Vice President, Senior Project Manager
FINK ROBERTS & PETRIE, 1066
Roussel, David Director of Athletics
THOMAS COLLEGE ATHLETICS, 405
Rousso, Doug CTO/CIO
CBS SPORTS, 681
Rousso, Nick Sports Editor
SEATTLE POST-INTELLIGENCER, 534
Roustan, W Owner
BURLEY'S, 1061
Roux, Antoine CEO, Internet Operations
M-NET TELEVISION, 686
Roux, Dennis News Director
KRJB-FM, 634
Roux, Jon Director
WESTERN PENNSYLVANIA ASSOCIATION, 215
Roux, Valerie S&E General Manager
HOFHEINZ PAVILION, 979
Rovine, David Director, Marketing
GULFSTREAM RACING & CASINO PARK, 1049
Rowan, Jennifer Publisher
SKI AREA MANAGEMENT, 586
Rowan, Olivia Associate Publisher
SKI AREA MANAGEMENT, 586
Rowan, Pat Sports Director
KDIN-TV, 696
Rowan, Russ Vice President of Sales and Marketing
SPYDER ACTIVE SPORTS, 1206
Rowat, Bill Director
CROQUET CANADA, 69
Rowdon, Andy Senior Associate AD, External Affairs
EASTERN MICHIGAN UNIVERSITY ATHLETICS, 329
Rowe, Chase Manager of Athletic Facilities
LA ROCHE COLLEGE ATHLETICS (LRC), 391
Rowe, Denis Director
ARTHRON, INC., 1110
Rowe, Doug Advertising Director
SANFORD HERALD, 533
Rowe, Howard Senior Editor
AMERICAN TURF MONTHLY, 555
Rowe, Kermit Sports Editor
SPRINGFIELD NEWS-SUN, 537
Rowe, Luke Vice President
FLEET FEET, INC., 1239
Rowe, Marty General Manager
KOHI-AM, 632
Rowe, Ray Facility Manager
ROBERTS STADIUM (IA), 1006
Rowe, Robert Executive Vice President
IRWIN BROH RESEARCH, 798
Rowek, Joseph Vice President
CONWAY, MICHAEL W., 838
Rowlett, Jim Marketing Director
NATIONAL STREET ROD ASSOCIATION, 18
Rowley, David News Director
WDOE-AM/FM, 650
Rowley, Jason CEO/President
NATIONAL BASKETBALL ASSOCIATION/NBA, 58
Rowley, Sandy Assistant Athletic Director
OHIO DOMINICAN UNIVERSITY ATHLETICS, 316
Roy, Ashley Communication Coordinator
NATIONAL DART ASSOCIATION, 72
Roy, Brian VP, Marketing
PROFESSIONAL SPORTS CONSULTANTS, INC., 859
Roy, Christine Promotions Manager
CAROLINA LEAGUE, 37
Roy, Derek Promotions Director
ESPN RADIO 920, 618
Roy, Fred President
WORLD ARMWRESTLING FEDERATION, 15

Roy, John Managing Director / Palm Beach Office
CHASE AMERICA, 837
Roy, Kate Associate Director of Athletics
LYNDON STATE COLLEGE ATHLETICS, 393
Roy, Patrick Head Coach & General Manager
QUEBEC MAJOR JUNIOR HOCKEY LEAGUE, 135
Roy, Ron General Manager
WTKT-AM, 675
Roy, Scott Assistant Athletic Director
RHODE ISLAND COLLEGE ATHLETICS, 382, 400
Roy, Sharon Executive Director of Human Resources
TRINITY MOTHER FRANCES ROSE STADIUM, 1020
Royal, David Sports Writer
DAILY TRIBUNE NEWS, 483
Royal, Paul Head Coach, Women's Soccer
MCCARTHY STADIUM, 994
Royce, Jody Sports Reporter
SARASOTA HERALD-TRIBUNE, 533
Roycroft, Jim Secretary
CANADIAN GYMNASTICS FEDERATION, 119
Royer, Dennis General Manager
WKLV-AM, 661
Royer, Don President
FLOATING SWIMWEAR INC, 1144
Royer, Jeff General Partner
NATIONAL LEAGUE OF PROFESSIONAL BASEBALL CLUBS, THE, 31
Royer, Richard Publisher
CHESAPEAKE BAY MAGAZINE, 559
Royer, Richard Publisher
OFFSHORE, 580
Roys, Josh Vice President, Tickets
AVISTA STADIUM, 956
Royster, Mike Executive Director
ATHLETIC EQUIPMENT MANAGERS ASSOCIATION, 216
Rozell, Marcia Tourism Sales Manager
MANHATTAN AREA SPORTS COMMISSION (CONVENTION AND VISITORS BUREAU), 238
Rozen, Eric Head Athletic Trainer
UNIVERSITY OF ROCHESTER ATHLETICS, 400
Rozich, Bill VP Marketing
BEST PORTABLE FENCE, 1116
Rozkov, Alex Head Coach
WOMEN'S PREMIER SOCCER LEAGUE, 166
Rubama, Larry Sports Writer
VIRGINIAN-PILOT, 549
Rubel, Matthew Chairman of the Board, President & CEO
KEDS CORPORATION, 1162
Rubendall, Joe Sport manager
CALIFORNIA STATE GAMES, 259
Rubenstein, Drew Sports Editor
DOMINION-POST, 487
Rubenstein, Lee President/COO
TBA ENTERTAINMENT CORPORATION, 809, 821
Rubenstein, Mark Member
RUBENSTEIN, MARK A., 913
Rubenstein, Mark Chairman & Co-Chief Executive Officer
PARAMOUNT HEADWEAR, INC., 1183
Rubin, Dan Sports Editor
WASHINGTON EXAMINER, 550
Rubin, Eric Esquire
RUBIN, ERIC M., 913
Rubin, Harvey Executive
iPAYATTENTION LLC, 610
Rubin, Kerry Classified Manager
HERALD NEWS, 496
Rubin, Michael Partner
RUBIN, MICHAEL D., 913
Rubin, R. Honorary Chairman
INTERNATIONAL JEWISH SPORTS HALL OF FAME, 252
Rubin, Rachel Deputy Director of Athletics/Chief of St
CONNECTICUT ATHLETICS, UNIVERSITY OF, 327
Rubino, Justin VP, Business Operations
NATIONAL LACROSSE LEAGUE, 141
Rubino, Robert Sports Reporter
PRESS DEMOCRAT, 526

Schneider, Nate Director of Partner Services
BB&T BALLPARK AT HISTORIC BOWMAN
FIELD, 957

Schneider, Paul Chairman of the Commission
IDAHO STATE POLICE, 80

Schneider, Peter President
ATHLETIC DEALERS OF AMERICA, 1228

Schneider, Roz Principal
BARKER RINKER SEACAT ARCHITECTURE,
1059

Schneider, Scott Chief Digital Officer
RUDER/FINN SPORTS, INC., 815

Schneider, Steve Athletic Director
PERU STATE COLLEGE ATHLETICS, 317, 706

Schneider, Suzy Administrative Assistant
NORTHERN CALIFORNIA SECTIONAL
OFFICE, 106

Schneider, Timothy Publisher
SPORTSTRAVEL MAGAZINE, 592

Schneiderer, Larry Director of Athletic Operations
DENISON UNIVERSITY(DU)ATHLETICS, 384

Schneider, Matthew Managing Director
GARVEY, SCHUBERT & BARER, 891

Schnelle, Lock Head Athletic Trainer
SOUTHWESTERN COLLEGE ATHLETICS, 319

Schnepf, Kevin Sports Editor
FORUM, 492

Schnitzer, Beth Vice President Strategic Alliance
PIER 39 MARKET DEVELOPMENT, 767

Schnitzer, Jenny Executive Director & Chief
Operating Off
USTA EASTERN, 172

Schnurbusch, Jim Contact
HUGHES SPORTS MARKETING, 796

Schoaf, Mike Director Media & Communications
ILLINOIS PGA SECTIONAL OFFICE, 104

Schoellkopf, Rosemary Editor
BULLPEN, 559

Schoen, Bill Publisher
CALIFORNIA HOCKEY & SKATING, 559

Schoen, Todd Senior Vice President Affiliate
FX NETWORKS, LLC, 683

Schoenadal, Tracy VP
TNS SPORT - NORTH AMERICA, 823

Schoenadel, Tracy Director, Center for Sports
Research
MASSACHUSETTS AMHERST, UNIVERSITY
OF, 428

Schoenbeck, James Operations / Advertising
SVP
DUCKWALL ALCO STORES, INC., 1237

Schoenbeck, Roger Vice President/Treasurer
VERMONT GOLF ASSOCIATION, 116

Schoenfeld, Gary President & Chief Executive
Officer
VANS, INC., 1251

Schoenfeld, Walter Chairman
VANS, INC., 1251

Schoeni, K. Partner
SCHOENI, K. ROGER, 914

Schoening, Bill General Manager
WFNZ-AM 610 SPORTS RADIO, 653

Schoenly, Karla Head Athletic Trainer
FROSTBURG STATE UNIVERSITY
ATHLETICS (FSU), 386

Schoenrock, Ashley Assistant General Manager
LEWIS AND CLARK PARK, 991

Schoenstein, Eric President
OREGON GOLF ASSOCIATION, 114

Schoenthaler, Todd Sports News Assistant
OKLAHOMAN, 519

Schoenwetter, Phil Head Athletic Trainer
MCPHERSON COLLEGE ATHLETICS, 314

Schoessel, Scott Sales VP/New Business
Development
GIGUNDA GROUP, 793

Schofield, Lawrence Engineer
E.B. ROTONDI & SONS, INC., 1137

Schoh, Eric Director of Athletics
WINONA STATE UNIVERSITY ATHLETICS,
376

Scholl, Bill Director of Athletics
MARQUETTE UNIVERSITY ATHLETICS, 336

Scholleart, Laurie Art Director
PRICE MEDIA, 582

Scholten, Bill President
SOUTH DAKOTA GOLF ASSOCIATION, 114

Scholvin, Cameron Senior VP & Chief Operating
Officer
NATIONAL HOCKEY LEAGUE/NHL, 123

Schon, Robyn Assistant Director
ROANOKE CIVIC CENTER, 1006

Schonter, Celeste Chief Administrative Officer
TAP, LLC, 62

Schonter, Loyd Founder/CEO
TAP, LLC, 62

Schoolfield, Hank Publisher
SOUTHERN MOTORACING, 588

Schoonmaker, Bill Chief Operating Officer
LACROSSE MUSEUM AND NATIONAL HALL
OF FAME MUSEUM, 253

Schoonmaker, Brink Manager of Athletic
Facilities
FLORIDA SOUTHERN COLLEGE ATHLETICS
(FSC), 359

Schoonmaker, Linda Associate Professor
WINTHROP UNIVERSITY, 430, 441

Schoonover, Matt Director, Stadium Operations
PIONEER BASEBALL LEAGUE, 50, 958

Schoonover, Paul Lawyer
SCHOONOVER, PAUL D., 914

Schoonveld, Tim Co-Athletic Director
HOPE COLLEGE ATHLETICS, 389

Schoppe, Dean President
HL BADMINTON, 1155

Schorg, Rick General Manager
KMNS-AM, 630

Schorling, William Shareholder
BUCHANAN INGERSOLL ROONEY, 878

Schott, Dean Jr. Olympic Vice President
NATIONAL GYMNASTICS JUDGES
ASSOCIATION, INC., 120

Schottenstein, Jay Chairman, Chief Executive
Officer
SCHOTTENSTEIN DEPARTMENT STORES,
1248

Schottenstein, Jay Chairman
VALUE CITY DEPARTMENT STORES, 1251

Schrader, Bud Sports Reporter
KIRKSVILLE DAILY EXPRESS & NEWS, 503

Schrader, Steve Sports Assistant Editor
DETROIT FREE PRESS, 486

Schrag, Jeff Publisher
THE FOOTBALL GREEN BOOK, 601, 603

Schram, Kendall President
USA SOUTH CONFERENCE, 304

Schram, Tim VP, Finance & Human Resources
BREEDERS' CUP, 75

Schramm, Chris Northeast Tournament Director
INTERNATIONAL JUNIOR GOLF TOUR/IJGT,
101

Schraufnagel, Gregg Marketing Manager
WTMJ-TV, 718

Schreckenberger, Charles
BRAUN & STEIDL ARCHITECTS INC, 1060

Schreiber, Franz Secretary General
INTERNATIONAL SHOOTING SPORT
FEDERATION (ISSF), 203

Schreiber, Greg National Sales Manager
TOMSED CORPORATION, 1213

Schreiber, Joe Senior Sports Producer
WRC-TV, 717

Schreiber, Jr., Robert VP/Shareholder
LINDNER & MARSACK, S.C., 900

Schreiner, Scott Co-Owner & VP
JOE FABER FIELD, 984

Schrempf, Detlef President
DETLEF SCHREMPF FOUNDATION, 189

Schrempf, Mari Vice President
DETLEF SCHREMPF FOUNDATION, 189

Schriber, Randy General Manager
WFSE-FM, 653

Schricker, Scott Marketing Director
METROPOLITAN RICHMOND SPORTS
BACKERS, 239

Schriefer, Mike President
SPEEDWAY GROUP, INC., 817

Schripsema, Jack President
GREATER LANSING CONVENTION &
VISITORS BUREAU, 233

Schrock, Lee Sports Director
WKAN-AM, 660

Schrock, Mark General Manager
USL LEAGUE TWO, 163

Schroeder, Barbara Vice President
HAWAII STATE WOMEN'S GOLF
ASSOCIATION, 110

Schroeder, Carrie Promotions Director
WTVT-TV, 719

Schroeder, Edward Product Development VP
PORTER ATHLETIC EQUIPMENT COMPANY,
1186

Schroeder, Jim Athletic Trainer
UNITED STATES HOCKEY LEAGUE, 137

Schroeder, Joshua Director of Athletic
Communications
THOMAS COLLEGE ATHLETICS, 314, 405

Schroeder, Paul Principal
ARCHITECTS DELAWIE WILKES RODRIGUES
BARKER, 1059

Schroeder-Barr, Mary News Director
WXDX-AM, 679

Schrom, Ken President
TEXAS BASEBALL LEAGUE, 53

Schroyer, Heath Director of Athletics
MCNEESE STATE UNIVERSITY ATHLETICS,
336

Schrum, Jake Senior Associate AD,
Facilities/Operatio
DELAWARE ATHLETICS, UNIVERSITY OF,
327

Schrupp, Wendy Associate Editor
SKI PATROL, 586

Schubert, Michael Chief Innovation Officer
RUDER/FINN SPORTS, INC., 815, 861

Schubert, Steven Treasurer
UNITED STATES DRESSAGE FOUNDATION,
78

Schuessler, Laura New Media & Marketing
Coordinator
INTERCOLLEGIATE TENNIS ASSOCIATION,
171

Schuessler, William President
WISSOTA MANUFACTURING COMPANY,
1222

Schuetz, Jon Sports Director
KETV-TV, 697

Schuldt, Tim COO & President
USL CHAMPIONSHIP, 159

Schulefand, Keith Esquire
SCHULEFAND, KEITH, 862

Schuler, Jeff Sports Reporter
MORNING CALL, 512

Schuler, Len Associate Athletic Director
NEUMANN UNIVERSITY ATHLETICS, 396

Schuler, Meredith Director of Operations
SOUTH FLORIDA PGA, 114

Schuler, Sarah Senior Manager, Marketing
NEW ERA PINSTRIPE BOWL, 92

Schuler, Tom Director
TEAM SPORTS, INC., 822

Schulist, Michael Associate Athletic Director
CARROLL UNIVERSITY ATHLETICS, 308

Schullenberg, Gene Sports Writer
HUNTSVILLE ITEM, 498

Schulman, Deb Associate Athletic Director
UNIVERSITY OF WISCONSIN-PLATTEVILLE
(UWP), 410

Schulman, Henry Sports Writer
SAN FRANCISCO CHRONICLE, 532

Schulman, Jeff Director of Athletics
VERMONT ATHLETICS, UNIVERSITY OF, 348

Schulman, Michael Chief Executive Officer
AMERICAN HOCKEY LEAGUE/AHL, 122, 128

Schulte, Chris Sports Editor
STEVENS POINT JOURNAL, 508, 540

Schulten, Carey Second Vice President
TEXAS GOLF ASSOCIATION, 115

Schulthess, Jay President
MERCURY SPORTS MANAGEMENT, 803

Schultz, Dave Sports Assistant Editor
PRESS & SUN-BULLETIN, 526

Schultz, Jeremy General Manager
WOMEN'S PREMIER SOCCER LEAGUE, 161,
165

Schultz, John President
FLORIDA COLLEGE SYSTEM ACTIVITIES
ASSOCIATION, 281

Schultz, Judy Instructor & Advisor
WASHINGTON STATE UNIVERSITY, 439

Schultz, Randy Chief Financial Officer
GOLD'S GYM INTERNATIONAL, INC., 1149

executive index

executive index

Smith, Miranda Volusia County Marketing & EventsManage
CENTRAL FLORIDA SPORTS COMMISSION, 259

Smith, Monica President/CEO
MACON-BIBB COUNTY CONVENTION AND VISITORS BUREAU, 238

Smith, Nancy Communication Account Representative
CLEVELAND STATE UNIVERSITY, 416

Smith, Neal Assistant Athletic Director, Facilities
HINKLE FIELDHOUSE, 979

Smith, Nick Director of Athletics
ASSUMPTION COLLEGE ATHLETICS, 331, 352, 827

Smith, O Chairman of the Board
NEW HAMPSHIRE MOTOR SPEEDWAY, 1039

Smith, O. Chairman of the Board
LAS VEGAS MOTOR SPEEDWAY/LVMS, 1036

Smith, O.Bruton Chairman
BRISTOL MOTOR SPEEDWAY & DRAGWAY, 1032

Smith, Pam Marketing / Advertising Manager
PVH CORP., 1190

Smith, Pat Station Manager
WLFN-AM, 662

Smith, Patricia Senior Vice President
NEW DIRECTIONS, 936

Smith, Paul Director of Athletic Communications
ARKANSAS TECH UNIVERSITY ATHLETICS, 351, 574, 936, 1042

Smith, Paula Director of Intercollegiate Athletics
UC IRVINE ATHLETICS, 348

Smith, Peter Director of Athletics
KENYON COLLEGE ATHLETICS, 391

Smith, Phil Director of Athletics Facilities
MCDANIEL COLLEGE ATHLETICS, 394

Smith, P draig Executive VP/General Manager
MAJOR LEAGUE SOCCER, 157

Smith, Randal VP Marketing
VIRCO MANUFACTURING CORPORATION, 1219

Smith, Randy Assistant Interim Athletic Director/Faci
TUCKER STADIUM, 717, 798, 1020

Smith, Ray Associate Athletic Director for Faciliti
MILLIGAN COLLEGE ATHLETICS, 33, 315

Smith, Rich Executive Director/CEO
NORTH FLORIDA PGA SECTIONAL OFFICE, 106

Smith, Richard Managing Partner
KIRKPATRICK, WILLIAMS & MEEKS, L.L.P., 897

Smith, Rick President, Team Operations & General Cou
PRIORITY SPORTS & ENTERTAINMENT, 857, 858

Smith, Rita Director of Athletic Training
LEES-MCRAE COLLEGE ATHLETICS, 362

Smith, Rob Sports Director
WFSE-FM, 653

Smith, Robert Athletic Director
FLORIDA MEMORIAL UNIVERSITY ATHLETICS, 311, 899

Smith, Robert Member
SMITH & SMITH ATTORNEYS AT LAW, 917

Smith, Rodney President/Founder
FUTURE FOR KIDS, 843

Smith, Roger Chairman / President
PAWLING CORPORATION/STANDARD PRODUCTS DIVISION, 1184

Smith, Ronald Secretary/National
JOURNAL OF SPORT HISTORY, 572

Smith, Ryan Director of Athletics Communications
MOUNT OLIVE COLLEGE ATHLETICS, 58, 366

Smith, Sam Assistant Sports Editor
RECORD (CA), 527

Smith, Sandra Sports Editor
CONCORD MONITOR, 111, 475

Smith, Sarah Administrative Assistant
WALTER J. ZABLE STADIUM AT CARY FIELD, 1026

Smith, Scott Sport Management Division Co-Director
CENTRAL MICHIGAN UNIVERSITY, 121, 228, 415, 593, 786

Smith, Sean Executive Director
SURF INDUSTRY MANUFACTURERS ASSOCIATION/SIMA, 169

Smith, Sekeia Administrative Coordinator
GEORGIA STATE UNIVERSITY, 421

Smith, Shannon Director, Finance & Administration
NORTH AMERICAN HOCKEY LEAGUE, 131

Smith, Shauna VP Client Relations
BDA SPORTS MANAGEMENT, 835

Smith, Shawn Sports Information Director
MINNESOTA-CROOKSTON ATHLETICS, UNIVERSITY OF (UMC), 365

Smith, Shirley Director of Sales
CENTRAL PENNSYLVANIA/PENN STATE COUNTRY CVB, 228

Smith, Stephanie Head Athletic Trainer
INDIANA UNIVERSITY NORTHWEST ATHLETICS, 312

Smith, Stephen First Vice Chairman
WEISMAN, PAUL, 925

Smith, Steve Chief Executive Officer
FITNESS COMPANY, 1239

Smith, Steven Equipment Manager
EAST COAST HOCKEY LEAGUE/ECHL, 131

Smith, Ted Founder
SMITHCO, 1201

Smith, Thomas Assistant VP-General Services
TRANS APPAREL, 315, 512, 1214

Smith, Tim Asst. Athletic Director for Internal Ope
ALCORN STATE UNIVERSITY ATHLETICS, 323, 512, 843

Smith, Todd Founder/President/Chief Executive Office
CLEAR BLUE MARKETING NETWORK, 580, 786

Smith, Tom Secretary/Treasurer
MINNESOTA GOLF ASSOCIATION, 112

Smith, Tom Chief Executive Officer
DYNAFLEX INTERNATIONAL, 908, 1136

Smith, Tony National Sales Manager -Golf Division
SLAZENGER GOLF PRODUCTS CO, 119, 1201

Smith, Tonya Membership Manager and Executive Assista
GREENWAY GROUP, THE, 1067

Smith, Tricia President
CANADIAN OLYMPIC COMMITTEE, 204

Smith, Tyrone President
FIRST AND GOAL, INC., 1074

Smith, Warren President/CEO
USL CHAMPIONSHIP, 159

Smith, Wayne Athletic Director
NJCAA REGION XV WOMEN'S, 287, 957, 1116

Smith, Wendy Director of Smith
HAVERFORD COLLEGE ATHLETICS, 388

Smith, Will Operating Partner
NEW YORK-PENNSYLVANIA LEAGUE, 47, 1009

Smith, William Executive Director
MARYLAND STATE GOLF ASSOCIATION, 111

Smith, William Executive Director
MARYLAND STATE GOLF ASSOCIATION - WOMEN'S DIVISION, 111

Smith CMP CASE CDME, Monica President and CEO
MACON-BIBB COUNTY CONVENTION AND VISITORS BUREAU, 238

Smith, Jr., Julious Chairman/Chief Executive Officer
MAUPIN, TAYLOR, P.A., 851

Smith-Brown, Stephanie Athletics Business Manager
GOLDEN LION STADIUM, 977

Smith-Everhard, Suzee Director Televideo
COX SPORTS/CHANNEL 9, 695

Smith-King, Branwen 2nd Vice President
NEW ENGLAND INTERCOLLEGIATE AMATEUR ATHLETIC ASSOCIATION, 284

Smithermanq, Rodger Senator
SMITHERMAN, RODGER, 864

Smitley, Brent Engineering Manager
LAFAYETTE INSTRUMENT COMPANY, 1165

Smits, Garry Sports Reporter
FLORIDA TIMES-UNION, 491

Smizik, Bob Sports Columnist
PITTSBURGH POST-GAZETTE, 524

Smoak, David Sports Director
KTBB-AM, 623, 636

Smoke, Matthew President
CUSTOM DECAL & EMBLEMS, INC., 1132

Smolen, Patti Director
TOURISM VANCOUVER, THE GREATER VANCOUVER CONVENTION & VISITORS BU, 247

Smolen, Rafal Slalom National Team Coach
USA CANOE/KAYAK, 206

Smolens, Amy Partner
CALAMARI VIDEO, 604

Smolenski, Don President
NATIONAL FOOTBALL LEAGUE/NFL, 96

Smolnycki, Dave Director, Media Relations
FEDERAL HOCKEY LEAGUE, 131

Smoltz, Michael Chief Operating Officer
TR GEAR/PROTONIC, 1214

Smoot, Donna Administrative Assistant & Collection Ma
OREGON SPORTS HALL OF FAME, 256

Smorol, Jason General Manager
INTERNATIONAL LEAGUE, 43

Smothers, Roderick President
PHILANDER SMITH COLLEGE ATHLETICS, 317

Smoyer, Mark Deputy Sports Editor
SAN FRANCISCO CHRONICLE, 532

Smtih, III, Fletcher Executive Vice President, Football
CSMG INTERNATIONAL, LTD, 788

Smucker, Luke Sports Editor
CLINTON JOURNAL, 474

Smucker, Michael Corporate Sales VP
AMERICAN NEEDLE & NOVELTY INC., 1108

Smulczenski, Scott VP, Baseball & Business Operations
TEXAS BASEBALL LEAGUE, 54

Smullen, Kate Assistant Athletic Director
UNIVERSITY OF BRIDGEPORT ATHLETICS, 374

Smyers, Steve Vice President
AMERICAN SOCIETY OF GOLF COURSE ARCHITECTS, 98

Smyrl, Stephanie Senior Women's Administrator
WHEELOCK COLLEGE ATHLETICS, 408

Smyrniotis, Bobby Head Coach/Technical Director
CANADIAN PREMIER LEAGUE, 156

Smyser, Jess Administrative Assistant
P.S. STARGAMES, 855

Smyth, Curt Sports Information Director
NEW ENGLAND ATHLETICS, UNIVERSITY OF, 397

Smyth, Darla Webmaster
NORTHERN NEVADA WOMEN'S GOLF ASSOCIATION, 113

Snarr, George Field Sales Representative
STALKER RADAR, 1207

Snead, Laura Senior Associate AD, Administration
LONGWOOD UNIVERSITY ATHLETICS, 334

Snead, Les General Manager
NATIONAL FOOTBALL LEAGUE/NFL, 96

Snead, Phil Associate AD, Business
LA SALLE UNIVERSITY ATHLETICS, 334

Snead, Sally Sr.Vp , Operations
CAREY WORLDWIDE CHAUFFERED SERVICES, 935

Snedden, Todd Associate Director of Athletics
CALIFORNIA STATE UNIVERSITY - SAN MARCOS ATHLETICS, 308

Snedecor, Casey Director of Media Relations
LONG ISLAND UNIVERSITY, C.W. POST ATHLETICS, 334, 363

Sneeringer, Tim Director of Recreation
UNIVERSITY OF PITTSBURGH AT BRADFORD ATHLETICS, 399

Snel, Alan Sports Business Writer
TAMPA TRIBUNE, 541

Snell, David President/Chief Executive Officer
IVRNET, 722

Snell, Debbie Director of Athletics
HOLY NAMES COLLEGE ATHLETICS, 361

Snelling, Mark President
BARRECRAFTERS, 1114

Snerson, Caryn Pricipal
MiCa SPORTS, 756

Snider, Dean Athletics Director
WHITMAN COLLEGE ATHLETICS, 408

Snider, Jay Chairman/Chief Executive Officer
VENUE 1, 832

Vitali, Peter President
SOUTH CENTRAL PGA SECTIONAL OFFICE, 107

Vitello, Tina Advertising Manager
COLLEGE & PRO FOOTBALL NEWSWEEKLY, 537, 561

Viteritti, Peter Volleyball Head Coach
SOUTHERN NEW HAMPSHIRE UNIVERSITY, 435

Vito, Marie Classified Manager
GLOUCESTER COUNTY TIMES, 493

Vitrano, Tony President
GAMEDAY MANAGEMENT GROUP, 763

Vitter, Jeffery Executive Vice Chancellor and Provost
POTTORFF, JAMES P. JR., 909

Vitter, Jeffrey EVP / Provost
KAISER, RONALD A., 896

Vitter, Jeffrey Executive Vice Chancellor, Provost
MCCLOUD, BARBARA, 903

Vitti, Anthony Director of Athletics
UNIVERSITY OF BRIDGEPORT ATHLETICS, 374

Vittone, Jason Director of Intercollegiate Athletics
WILLIAM WOODS UNIVERSITY ATHLETICS, 322

Vitu, Janet Publisher
TRACK & FIELD NEWS, 595

Viveiros, Manny Head Coach
AMERICAN HOCKEY LEAGUE/AHL, 127

Viverito, Frank President
ST. LOUIS SPORTS COMMISSION, 245

Viverito, Patty Senior Associate Commissioner
MISSOURI VALLEY CONFERENCE, 89, 298

Viviano, Mark Sports Director
WJZ-TV, 713

Vizaro, Connie Operations Manager
DYNOCOMM SPORTS TV, 605

Vizdai, Katy Special Projects Coordinator
MACOMB AREA CONVENTION AND VISITORS BUREAU, 238

Vizer, Marius President
INTERNATIONAL JUDO FEDERATION, 203

Vladeck, Anne Partner
VLADECK WALDMAN ELIAS & ENGELHARD, P.C., 923

Vlahos, Nick Sports Copy Editor
JOURNAL STAR, 501

Vlahov, Eric Dept. Chairperson
TAMPA, UNIVERSITY OF, 437

Vo, Daven Men's Basketball Head Coach
NJCAA REGION I WOMEN'S, 284

Vodden, David Chief Executive Officer/Promoter
THUNDERHILL RACEWAY PARK, 1044

Voden, Nick President
GLD PRODUCTS, 1148

Voe, Ben Sports Editor
DAVIS COUNTY CLIPPER, 484

Voegele, Corey Sports Editor
FARIBAULT DAILY NEWS, 491

Voeks, Keith Assistant Director
KELLY/SHORTS STADIUM, 987

Voepel, Mechelle Sports Reporter
KANSAS CITY STAR, 502

Voets, Keith Sales/Marketing Manager
HARTFORD SPORTS COMMISSION, GREATER (CONVENTION & VISITORS BUREAU, 234

Vogds, Ashley Head Athletic Trainer
MENLO COLLEGE ATHLETICS, 314

Vogel, Adam Senior VP, Ticketing Sales, Service & Op
AMERICAN HOCKEY LEAGUE/AHL, 129

Vogel, Frank Head Coach
NATIONAL BASKETBALL ASSOCIATION/NBA, 57

Vogel, George Sports Director
WLWT-TV, 714

Vogel, Rob President/Chief Operating Officer
BONHAM GROUP, INC., 784

Vogel, Tanya Director of Athletics
GEORGE WASHINGTON UNIVERSITY ATHLETICS, 330

Vogelsang, Steve Chief Marketing Officer
PORTER ATHLETIC EQUIPMENT COMPANY, 1186

Vogelsburg, Scott Editor
WOLFPACKER, 599

Vogl, John Sports Writer
BUFFALO NEWS, 469

Vogler, Bill Dept. Chairperson
SOUTHERN ILLINOIS UNIVERSITY AT EDWARDSVILLE, 435

Vohden, Danny Athletic Director for Communications and
STEVENS INSTITUTE OF TECHNOLOGY ATHLETICS, 404

Vohs, Jeff General Manager
POHLMAN FIELD, 1002

Voight, Bob Vice President
NATIONAL SPORTS FORUM, 805

Voight, Heather Vice President/Collegiate Initiatives
TEAMLINK.COM, INC, 723

Voigt, Darin Head Athletic Trainer
VANGUARD UNIVERSITY OF SOUTHERN CALIFORNIA ATHLETICS, 321

Voigt, Tom Advertising Manager
BRYAN TIMES, 469

Voinis, Nick Sr. Associate Athletics Director, Commun
DARRELL K ROYAL - TEXAS MEMORIAL STADIUM, 969

Voisin, Ailene Sports Senior Writer
SACRAMENTO BEE, 530

Vojtasek, Karen Advertising Manager
ROCHESTER SENTINEL, 529

Vojticek, Mike Assistant Director
VON BRAUN CENTER, 1026

Vojtisek, Michele Sales Manager
WENE, 652

Vokey, Mike Executive Director
FREDERICTON CAPITAL EXHIBIT CENTRE, 1048

Volk, Dustin Secretary
UTAH PGA SECTIONAL OFFICE, 107

Volkmann, Tim Director of Athletic Communications
STATE UNIVERSITY OF NEW YORK COLLEGE AT GENESEO ATHLETICS (SUNY), 404

Vollkommer-Lynch, Linda Vice President
NATIONAL INTERCOLLEGIATE WOMEN'S FENCING ASSOCIATION, 86

Vollmer, Natalie Executive Secretary
NATIONAL FIELD ARCHERY ASSOCIATION, 14

Volpe, Tom Vice President
CALIFORNIA LEAGUE (A-LEVEL), 36

Volpe, Vince Deputy Director of Athletics
TEXAS RIO GRANDE VALLEY ATHLETICS, UNIVERSITY OF, 346

Volts, Jane National Key Account Rep
MUELLER SPORTS MEDICINE, INC., 1176

Voltz, Don Sports Director
WDEL-AM, 649

Vomacka, Ed Racing Secretary
BEULAH PARK, 1045

VonHolle, Jeff Assistant GM & Director of Soccer Operat
USL LEAGUE TWO, 53, 162

Vonachen, Rocky President
MIDWEST LEAGUE, 45

Vonde-Harr, Bruce Sports Director
KODE-TV, 701

Vondenhuevel, Mark President
HOLLOWAY SPORTSWEAR, INC., 1156

Vonschwerin, Dagmar Director Marketing
CAMBRIDGE SEVEN ASSOCIATES INC., 1061

Voorhees, Peter Sports Director/ News Director
WNYY, 666

Voorheis, Jeff Tournament Director
METROPOLITAN PROFESSIONAL GOLFERS ASSOCIATION, 105

Voorhis, Amanda Director of Athletics
UMASS DARTMOUTH ATHLETIC DEPARTMENT, 394

Voorhis, Dave Director Business Development
HOPE-BECKHAM, INC., 796

Vora, Sunil Controller
UNIVISION TELEVISION NETWORK, 685

Vore, Todd President
SOF SOLE, 1201

Vorster, Justin Head Coach
WOMEN'S PREMIER SOCCER LEAGUE, 164

Vorwald, Bob Director Production
WGN-9 CHICAGO'S CW, 711

Vos, Ingmar President
FEDERATION EQUESTRE INTERNATIONALE (FEI), 75, 201

Vosburg, Craig President, North America
MASTERCARD, 738

Vosloo, Tom Chairman
M-NET TELEVISION, 686

Voss, Gary General Manager
WJCI-AM, 659

Voss, Holly League Administrator
MIDWEST LEAGUE (A LEVEL), 44

Voss, Wendy Chief of Administration
CALIFORNIA HORSE RACING BOARD, 80

Vot, Denis Chairman, Nissan North America
NISSAN NORTH AMERICA, 739

Votava, Kirstin Marketing Director
KXLY-AM, 639

Voutsinas, Mike General Manager
NEW YORK-PENNSYLVANIA LEAGUE, 46, 973

Vowels, Jr., Robert Director of Athletics
DETROIT MERCY ATHLETICS, UNIVERSITY OF, 328, 962

Voyles, Brad VP for Student Development
COVENANT COLLEGE ATHLETICS, 383

Vrabel, Mike Head Coach
NATIONAL FOOTBALL LEAGUE/NFL, 97

Vranjic, Dalibor Head Coach
CANADIAN SOCCER LEAGUE, 156

Vrentas, Jenny 1st Vice President
PRO FOOTBALL WRITERS OF AMERICA, 89

Vries, Brian Partner
SPLITSEASONTICKETS, LLC, 942

Vuch, John Director
APPALACHIAN LEAGUE, 34

Vuckovich, Miki Executive Director
TONY HAWK FOUNDATION, 191

Vught, Nick Athletic Trainer
NJCAA REGION XXI MEN'S, 288

Vujea, Mike Director of Group Sales
MIDWEST LEAGUE, 45

Vukovic, Sasa Coach
CANADIAN SOCCER LEAGUE, 156

Vuono, Ralph VP
16W MARKETING, LLC, 778

W

W C. Wiseman, Eric Chairman, Chief Executive Officer & Pres
VF CORPORATION, 1219

W Hicks Jr, Arthur President & COO
CYBEX INTERNATIONAL, INC., 1132

W. D. Lang, Scott Attorney
LANG, XIFARAS & BULLARD, 898

W. Holmes Johnson, Katheryn Director, media PR Communications
SOOY, KATHLEEN T., 917

W. Holmes Jr, Henry Counsel
GREENBERG TRAURIG, LLP, 892

W. Kazmaier Jr, Richard President / Chief Executive Officer
RUXIN, ROBERT H., 913

W. O'Doresio Jr, John Shareholder
ROBINSON, WATERS & E'DORISIO, 912

W. P Krueger, Blake Chairman of the Board, Chief Executive O
WOLVERINE WORLD WIDE, 1222

W. W. Behn, Robert President
MARLIN FIREARMS COMPANY, 1170

W. W. Hansen, Steven Attorney
HANSEN, STEVEN W., 892

W. W. Roberts, Jerry Member
LAMPROS & ROBERTS CONSULTING, 849

Waas-Russiyan, Cinthia President / Owner
GENERAL AWARDS, INC., 1147

Wach, Michael EVP, Advertising Sales
YANKEES ENTERTAINMENT & SPORTS NETWORK/YES, 685

Wachal, Mike Principal
DAVIS DESIGN, 1063

Wache, Pierre Technical Chief
FORMULA 1, 20

Wachler, Brad Vice President For Intercollegiate Athle
LINDENWOOD UNIVERSITY ATHLETICS, 363

Wachtel, Jeff EVP, Original Programming
USA NETWORK, 685

Walters, John Sports Director
WOI-TV, 716
Walters, Kyle General Manager
CANADIAN FOOTBALL LEAGUE/CFL, 94
Walters, Mitch Assistant Athletics Director
CUMBERLAND UNIVERSITY ATHLETICS, 310
Walters, Rex Men's Baskebtall Head Coach
SAN FRANCISCO, UNIVERSITY OF, 434
Walters, Roger Commissioner
NATIONAL INTERCOLLEGIATE RODEO
ASSOCIATION (NIRA), 146
Walters, W. Seed Production Manager
DLF INTERNATIONAL SEEDS, 1236
Walther, Chip Sales VP
RIDDELL ATHLETIC FOOTWEAR, 1193
Walther, Jim Chair
ALBUQUERQUE SPORTS COUNCIL, 225
Walton, Craig Advertising Manager
WQKT-FM, 661, 670
Walton, Glenn Vice President
NEW HAMPSHIRE GOLF ASSOCIATION, 113
Walton, Jamaal Associate AD, External
Operations
COLLEGE OF CHARLESTON ATHLETICS, 326
Walton, Karl Finance Executive
PRO ORTHOPEDIC DEVICES, INC., 1188
Walton, Luke Head Coach
NATIONAL BASKETBALL ASSOCIATION/NBA,
58
Walton, Peter President/Chief Executive Officer
INTERNATIONAL ASSOCIATION OF GOLF
TOUR OPERATORS, 101
Walton, Robson Chairman
WAL-MART STORES, INC., 1252
Walton, Ron General Manager
WFNR, 653
Walton, Tim Founder
INTEGRITY SPORTS PLAYER
MANAGEMENT, 847
Walts, Cory Fitness Center Director
HAVERFORD COLLEGE ATHLETICS, 388
Waltz, Aaron PGA Golf Management Director
FERRIS STATE UNIVERSITY/PROFESSIONAL
GOLF MANAGEMENT PROGRAM, 100
Waltz, Thomas President (F.J. Westcott Co.)
HAAS-JORDAN COMPANY, 1152
Waluszko, Laura News Director
WZVN-FM, 680
Walz, Bob Chief Operating Officer
FLAIR COMMUNICATIONS, 791
Walz, Gregor Director of Athletic Communications
UNIVERSITY OF PUGET SOUND, 399
Walz, Liz Executive Editor
BOATING INDUSTRY, 558
Walz, Ryan Physical Education/Religion
SIMMONS FIELD, 1011
Wampler, Karen Public Relations Director
HARA ARENA, 977
Wampler, Kimberly Event Coordinator
HARA ARENA, 977
Wan, Karen Manager, Financial Services
CANADIAN CURLING ASSOCIATION, 70
Wan, Tracey Vice Chairman / Chief Operating
Officer
SHARPER IMAGE, 1248
Wanat, Don President
FGX DIRECT LLC., 1142
Wandell, Chris Director, Business Development
PGA TOUR, 108
Wandishin, Michael Racing Secretary
ROSECROFT RACEWAY, 1053
Wandling, Gene EVP/Chief Financial Officer
LICENSING RESOURCE GROUP, INC., 802
Wandyes, Beth Sr. Assoc. AD, Compliance/SWA
BRYANT UNIVERSITY ATHLETICS, 325
Wang, Liwei Honorary Vice President
WORLD POOL BILLIARD ASSOCIATION, 63
Wang, Phil Senior Associate AD, External Affairs
UC IRVINE ATHLETICS, 348
Wang, Rich Director, Sales Analytics &
Engagement
NATIONAL FOOTBALL LEAGUE/NFL, 96
Wang, Rick Office Manager
PROPET USA INC., 1189
Wangemann, James Assistant Sports Editor
AUSTIN AMERICAN-STATESMAN, 464
Wangrin, Mark Sports Writer (College)
SAN ANTONIO EXPRESS-NEWS, 532

Wanless, Bill Vice President, Public Relations
INTERNATIONAL LEAGUE, 43
Wann, Tim Southern Regional Sales Manager
SOFFE COMPANY, INC., 1202
Wannemacher, Jim Vice President, Advertising
NEW ERA CAP, CO, 1178
Wanniger, Richard Sr. Assoc. Commissioner For
External Rel
PATRIOT LEAGUE, 301
Wansart, Terry Director of Athletics
HUNTER COLLEGE ATHLETICS, 389
Wanvig, Barbara 1st Vice President
COW PALACE, 968
Ward, Allen Administration - Director of Athletics
ROY STEWART STADIUM, 1003, 1008
Ward, Amy Manager
ADVANTAGE TENNIS SUPPLY, 680, 1104
Ward, Bob Athletics Director
ST. JOHN FISHER COLLEGE ATHLETICS
(SJFC), 396, 403
Ward, Chad Operations VP
BOB WARD & SONS, INC., 1231
Ward, Christie Associate Athletic Director for
Complian
GEORGIA SOUTHWESTERN STATE
UNIVERSITY ATHLETICS, 360
Ward, Cory Assistant Athletic Director for Operatio
GORDON COLLEGE ATHLETICS, 387
Ward, Dave President/CEO
NOBIS WORKS CENTER, 190
Ward, Deana Assistant Athletic Director
FARMINGDALE STATE UNIVERSITY (FSU)
ATHLETICS, 386
Ward, Dustin Sports Editor
DAILY DUNKLIN DEMOCRAT, 478
Ward, Everett President
ST. AUGUSTINE'S UNIVERSITY ATHLETICS,
372
Ward, Heidi Retail Advertising Manager
JOURNAL TIMES, 501
Ward, Jeff Head Trainer
CALIFORNIA MARITIME ACADEMY
ATHLETICS, 308
Ward, John President
BOSTON WHALER, INC., 118, 1103, 1119
Ward, John Chairman / Chief Executive Officer,
Russ
RUSSELL ATHLETIC, 1195
Ward, Jonathan Principal
NBBJ, 1071
Ward, Julia President
NATIONAL GREYHOUND ASSOCIATION, 119
Ward, Keith President
BOB WARD & SONS, INC., 1231
Ward, Lew President
LOUISIANA GOLF ASSOCIATION, 102
Ward, Mike Deputy Director of Athletics
ELON UNIVERSITY ATHLETICS, 329
Ward, Pete COO
NATIONAL FOOTBALL LEAGUE/NFL, 95
Ward, Reid President and COO
ADVOCARE INTERNATIONAL, 733
Ward, Robert Executive Director
RHODE ISLAND GOLF ASSOCIATION, 114
Ward, Roddy National Team Coach
BIATHLON CANADA, 61
Ward, Scott Director of Business Development
CASSEMCO, INC., 341, 975, 1124
Ward, William Chairman
SPORTGRASS, INC., 1204
Wardell, Peter Director, International Scouting
NATIONAL LEAGUE OF PROFESSIONAL
BASEBALL CLUBS, THE, 31
Wardell, Thomas Corporate
MCKENNA, LONG & ALDRIDGE, LLP, 904
Wardle, Janice Sports Management Program
Coordinator
WILMINGTON COLLEGE, 440
Wardle, Simon Chief Strategy Officer
OCTAGON SPORTS, 807, 842, 854
Wardltz, Josh Associate AD, Marketing & Sales
BELMONT UNIVERSITY ATHLETICS, 324
Ware, Rick Owner
NASCAR XFINITY SERIES, 23, 24
Ware, Robert Lawyer
WARE, R. DAVID, 923
Warech, Gary Managing VP, Media Services
SIMMONS MARKET RESEARCH
BUREAU/SMRB, 816

Warfel, Chet Chief Executive Officer
ARCOA INDUSTRIES, 1110
Warfield, Carmela Chairman
SPECIAL OLYMPICS ALASKA, 192
Warg, Dana Executive Director
TARGET CENTER, 1016
Warmke, Carolyn Advertising Manager
KWHI-AM, 638
Warner, Brenda Co-Founder
KURT WARNER FIRST THING'S FIRST
FOUNDATION, 190
Warner, Chris Head Athletic Trainer
UTICA COLLEGE ATHLETICS(UC), 406
Warner, Eric Director of Racing
MONTICELLO RACEWAY, 1051
Warner, Grant Sales Assistant/Account Executive
LINDBORG-CREGG FIELD, 991
Warner, Harvey President
ASSINIBOIA DOWNS, 1045
Warner, Jackie Public Relations
GREAT CANADIAN GAMING CORPORATION,
1048
Warner, Jon President
CANNON SPORTS INC., 1233
Warner, Kurt President/Founder
KURT WARNER FIRST THING'S FIRST
FOUNDATION, 190
Warner, Michael Director of Strategic Operations
CANNON SPORTS INC., 1233
Warner, Pat Fitness Director
SCHWINN CYCLING & FITNESS, 1197
Warner, R. Executive Director
MARYLAND PUBLIC SECONDARY SCHOOLS
ATHLETIC ASSOCIATION, 198
Warner, Robert Chairman of the Board
BROOME COUNTY VETERANS MEMORIAL
ARENA, 960
Warner, Tracie Executive Director
NORTHEASTERN NEW YORK PGA
SECTIONAL OFFICE, 106
Warnke, Marlene Athletic Business Manager
DAKOTA WESLEYAN UNIVERSITY
ATHLETICS, 310
Warnock, Elliott Sports Editor
CHAPEL HILL NEWS, 471
Warren, Betsy Co-Head Coach
WOMEN'S PREMIER SOCCER LEAGUE, 166
Warren, Cris Advertising Manager
DAILY NEWS TRIBUNE, 481
Warren, Debbie Director of Athletics
INDIANA INSTITUTE OF TECHNOLOGY
ATHLETICS, 312
Warren, Don Senior Pro Scout
NATIONAL FOOTBALL LEAGUE/NFL, 97
Warren, Jay Ballpark Operations Manager
FLORIDA STATE LEAGUE, 39
Warren, John General Manager, Sports Licensed
Divisio
REEBOK INTERNATIONAL LTD.-RETAIL,
1192, 1247
Warren, Kelly Executive Director
FLORIDA COLLEGE SYSTEM ACTIVITIES
ASSOCIATION, 281
Warren, Kenneth Managing Partner
GOWLING LAFLEUR HENDERSON, 844
Warren, Mark Assistant General Manager
INTERNATIONAL LEAGUE, 42
Warren, Matthew Executive Director
USTA PACIFIC NORTHWEST, 173
Warren, Otis Advertising Manager
KNZR-AM, 632
Warren, Phil Manager
FRONTIER LEAGUE, 41
Warren, Russell Deputy Director of Athletics
TEXAS AT ARLINGTON ATHLETICS,
UNIVERSITY OF, 346
Warren, Scott Director of Racing & Simulcasting
ROSECROFT RACEWAY, 1053
Warren, Ted President and Senior Partner
STRATEGIC RESOURCES, 757
Warren, Vivian General Manager
WMCR-FM, 664
Warshafsky, Ted Lawyer
WARSHAFSKY LAW FIRM, 923
Warshaw, Stuart Chief Financial Officer
E.P. PRO, 1137
Warsofsky, Ryan Head Coach
AMERICAN HOCKEY LEAGUE/AHL, 126

executive index

CALIFORNIA

geographic index

RUBENSTEIN, MARK A., 913
RUBIN, MICHAEL D., 913
RYKA, INC., 1196
SACRAMENTO BEE, 530
SACRAMENTO KINGS, 58
SACRAMENTO RACEWAY PARK
(DRAGSTRIP/MX), 1041
SACRAMENTO REPUBLIC FC, 159
SACRAMENTO RIVER CATS, 49
SACRAMENTO RUNNING ASSOCIATION, 148
SACRAMENTO SPORTS COMMISSION, 243
SALINAS CALIFORNIAN, 531
SAM LYNN BALLPARK, 1009
SAMSUNG ELECTRONICS NA, 740
SAN BERNARDINO AREA CONVENTION &
VISITORS BUREAU, 244
SAN BERNARDINO SUN, 532
SAN DIEGO ATHLETICS, UNIVERSITY OF, 343
SAN DIEGO AVIATORS, 174
SAN DIEGO CHRISTIAN COLLEGE ATHLETICS,
318
SAN DIEGO COUNTY WOMEN'S GOLF
ASSOCIATION, 114
SAN DIEGO GULLS, 128
SAN DIEGO HALL OF CHAMPIONS SPORTS
MUSEUM, THE, 257
SAN DIEGO PADRES, 32
SAN DIEGO STATE UNIVERSITY ATHLETICS,
343
SAN DIEGO STRIKE FORCE, 94
SAN DIEGO UNION-TRIBUNE, 532
SAN DIEGO WFC SEALIONS, 166
SAN FRANCISCO 49ERS, 97
SAN FRANCISCO ATHLETICS, UNIVERSITY OF,
343
SAN FRANCISCO CHRONICLE, 532
SAN FRANCISCO EXAMINER, 533
SAN FRANCISCO GIANTS, 32
SAN FRANCISCO NIGHTHAWKS, 166
SAN FRANCISCO STATE UNIVERSITY
ATHLETICS, 370
SAN FRANCISCO, UNIVERSITY OF, 434
SAN FRANSISCO GLENS SC, 162
SAN GABRIEL VALLEY DAILY TRIBUNE, 533
SAN JOAQUIN COUNTY FAIR, 1053
SAN JOSE BARRACUDA, 128
SAN JOSE EARTHQUAKES, 158
SAN JOSE GIANTS, 36
SAN JOSE MERCURY NEWS, 533
SAN JOSE MUNICIPAL STADIUM, 1009
SAN JOSE SHARKS, 125
SAN JOSE SPORTS AUTHORITY, 244
SAN JOSE STATE UNIVERSITY, 434
SAN JOSE STATE UNIVERSITY ATHLETICS,
343
SAN MATEO COUNTY TIMES, 533
SAN MATEO COUNTY/SILICON VALLEY
CONVENTION & VISITORS BUREAU, 244
SAND HILL RANCH, 1041
SAND SPORTS, 585
SANTA ANITA PARK, 1053
SANTA BARBARA NEWS-PRESS, 533
SANTA CLARA UNIVERSITY ATHLETICS, 343
SANTA CRUZ BREAKERS FC, 162
SANTA CRUZ SENTINEL, 533
SANTA CRUZ WARRIORS, 60
SANTA MARIA TIMES, 533
SANTANA, 585
SAUER, JR., RUSSELL F., 914
SCOTT BORAS CORPORATION, 862
SEA MAGAZINE, 585
SEALFLEX INDUSTRIES, INC., 1197
SEATS 3D, 816, 942
SEIRUS SPORTS ACCESSORIES, 1198
SELECT DISTRIBUTION/VISION STREET
WEAR, 1198
SENIOR SOFTBALL-USA, 167
SF WEEKLY, 535
SHANNON PROFESSIONAL MANAGEMENT,
863
SHAPIRO MANAGEMENT, 863
SHASTA DISTRICT FAIR, 1042
SHEN MILSON & WILKE, 1072
SHERMAN & NATHANSON, A PROFESSIONAL
CORPORATION, 915
SHERPA INC./DBA MOHN SKI RACK COMPANY,
1199
SHIMANO AMERICAN CORPORATION, 1199
SHOE CITY, 1249
SHOP, 816

SHOW CIRCUIT MAGAZINE, 586
SIDEOUT SPORT, INC., 1200
SIERRA MAGAZINE, 586
SIGNAL, 535
SIGNATURES NETWORK, 816
SILVER DOLLAR SPEEDWAY, 1042
SIMS, JR. JAMES A., 864
SISKAYOU MOTOR SPEEDWAY, 1042
SKATEBOARDER MAGAZINE, 586
SKECHERS USA, 1200
SKYWAY, 1201
SLAP MAGAZINE, 587
SLAUGHTER, FRED L., 916
SLEEP TRAIN ARENA, 1012
SLOTT, JEFFREY LAW OFFICE, 917
SMITH ASBURY, INC., 817
SMITH, FAUSE, MCDONALD, INC., 831
SNOWBOARDER MAGAZINE, 587
SOCAL FC, 166
SOCCER NOW, 588
SOL-EFFECT ENTERPRISE COMPANY LTD,
1202
SOLANO COUNTY FAIRGROUNDS, 1053
SONOMA COUNTY FAIRGROUNDS, 1054
SONOMA RACEWAY, 1042
SONY COMPUTER ENTERTAINMENT
AMERICA, INC., 1202
SOROY, H. MICHAEL, 917
SOURCE INTERLINK MEDIA, 588
SOUTH BAY LAKERS, 60
SOUTH COUNTY NEWS, 536
SOUTHERN CALIFORNIA ATHLETICS,
UNIVERSITY OF, 344
SOUTHERN CALIFORNIA GOLF ASSOCIATION,
115
SOUTHERN CALIFORNIA ORTHOPEDIC
INSTITUTE, 932
SOUTHERN CALIFORNIA PGA SECTIONAL
OFFICE, 107
SOUTHERN CALIFORNIA REGIONAL
COMMISSIONER/USA VOLLEYBALL, 211
SOUTHERN CALIFORNIA SEAHORSES, 163
SOUTHWIND KAYAK CENTER, 769
SPECIAL EVENTS MAGAZINE, 589
SPECIAL OLYMPICS NORTHERN CALIFORNIA,
194
SPECIAL OLYMPICS SOUTHERN CALIFORNIA,
195
SPECIALIZED BICYCLE COMPONENTS, INC.,
1203
SPECIALTY NETS, 1203
SPEED SKATELUBE, 1203
SPEEDPLAY, INC., 1203
SPIKE TV, 685
SPITZ, ROBERT J., 864
SPONSORVISION, 589
SPORT CHALET, INC., 1249
SPORT MANAGEMENT RESEARCH INSTITUTE,
818
SPORT PINS INTERNATIONAL, INC., 1204
SPORTCAP, INC., 1204
SPORTIME, 1204
SPORTRUST ASSOCIATES INTERNATIONAL,
864
SPORTS AFIELD, 590
SPORTS BUSINESS GROUP, 819
SPORTS BYLINE, 616
SPORTS BYLINE USA, 608
SPORTS BYLINE WEEKEND, 616
SPORTS CENTRAL, 688
SPORTS DISPLAY, 819
SPORTS FINAL, 688
SPORTS MARKETING & ENTERTAINMENT, INC,
819
SPORTS OVERNIGHT AMERICA WEEKEND,
616
SPORTS PLACEMENT SERVICE INC, 820
SPORTS TOUR CLASSICS, 937
SPORTS TUTOR INC, 1205
SPORTS WEST FOOTBALL, 865
SPORTS WEST SALES, INC., 1206
SPORTS XCHANGE, THE, 722
SPORTS ZONE, 689
SPORTS, ORTHOPEDIC & REHABILITATION
MEDICINE ASSOCIATES, 933
SPORTSBLAST, 608
SPORTSCAR, 592
SPORTSECONOMICS LLC, 770, 820
SPORTSMARK MANAGEMENT GROUP, 770

SPORTSPHONE 68 WITH LARRY KRUEGER,
613
SPORTSTRAVEL MAGAZINE, 592
SPORTSWIRE/BUSINESS WIRE, 723
SPORTSWRAP AT 10:45, 689
SPRINGCO, 1206
SPRINT AQUATICS, 1206
SPURS EAST BAY LADIES, 166
ST. MARY'S COLLEGE ATHLETICS, 345
STADIUM ROLL, 1207
STANFORD STADIUM, 1014
STANFORD UNIVERSITY ATHLETICS, 345
STAPLES CENTER/ANSCHUTZ
ENTERTAINMENT GROUP, 1014
STAR CREST ASSOCIATION, 13
STAR NEWS, 538
STARK EVENTS & ASSOCIATIONS, 771
STARTRAC BY UNISEN, INC., 1207
STEINBERG, LEIGH, 918
STELLARTV-SPORTS, 609
STEPHEN CAMERON RACING, 20
STEPHEN D. LINETT, ATTORNEY AT LAW, 918
STIMPERT & FORD, LLP, 918
STOCKTON CONVENTION & VISITORS
BUREAU, 246
STOCKTON HEAT, 128
STOCKTON KINGS, 60
STOCKTON PORTS, 37
THE STONE CLINIC, 934
STRATEGIC PLANNING CONCEPTS
INTERNATIONAL, 771
STRIVERS GROUP, 866
STUBHUB, 942
STUDENT SPORTS, 201, 593
STYLE EYES, INC., 1209
SUN (CA), 540
SUNDHEIM, GEORGE M., III, 866
SUNWEST SPORTS, 866
SUPERSTAR MANAGEMENT, INC., 866
SURF INDUSTRY MANUFACTURERS
ASSOCIATION/SIMA, 169
SURF NEWS, 593
SURFER, 593
SURFER TRAVEL REPORT, 593
SURFING, 593
SURFLINE.COM, 169
SWIM OUTLET, 1210
TABATA USA, INC., 1210
TAHOE DAILY TRIBUNE, 541
TAILWIND SPORTS/CYCLING DIVISION, 821
TAYLORMADE-ADIDAS GOLF, 1211
TENACIOUS LTD, 1212
TEVA BRAND, 1212
THOMAS & TEAFF, 921
THORSNES, BARTOLOTTA & MCGUIRE, 922
THRASHER SKATEBOARD MAGAZINE, 595
THUNDERBOATS UNLIMITED INC., 65
THUNDERBOWL RACEWAY, 1044
THUNDERHILL RACEWAY PARK, 1044
TICKETMASTER, 823, 943
TICKETS.COM, 943
TIDE-RIDER, INC., 1213
TIGER WOODS FOUNDATION, 191
TIMES-STANDARD, 545
TOMIC GOLF & SKI MFG., INC., 1213
TONIX, 1213
TONIX CORPORATION, 1213
TONY HAWK FOUNDATION, 191
TOOMEY FIELD, 1019
TOP OF THE THIRD, 1019
TRACK & FIELD NEWS, 595
TRACK COACH, 595
TRACK RECORD ENTERPRISES, 823
TRACKER TRUCKS, 1214
TRAILER BOATS, 595
TRANSWORLD BUSINESS, 595
TRANSWORLD SKATEBOARDING, 595
TRAVELERS CLUB LUGGAGE, 1214
TRI-VALLEY HERALD, 546
TRIBUNE (CA), 546
TRIMOTION, 1215
TROXEL, LLC, 1215
TRUEX GOLF, 1215
TUFF TOE, 1216
TULARE ADVANCE-REGISTER, 547
TURNER'S OUTDOORSMAN, 1251
TYR SPORT, INC., 1216
24 HOUR FITNESS CENTERS, 1227
U.S. BASE ASSOCIATION/PHOTO SHOOTING,
13

COLORADO

CONNECTICUT

DELAWARE

DISTRICT OF COLUMBIA

LEHMAN-SMITH-MCLEISH PLLC, 1070
MCAFEE, ARTHUR, 903
MYLAN WORLD TEAM TENNIS, 174
NATIONAL AERONAUTIC ASSOCIATION, 13
NATIONAL BASKETBALL ASSOCIATION/NBA, 56, 57, 58
NATIONAL CLUB ASSOCIATION, 220
NATIONAL LEAGUE OF PROFESSIONAL BASEBALL CLUBS, THE, 31, 32, 33
NATIONAL OUTDOOR SPORTS ADVERTISING, 805
NATIONALS PARK, 997
NFL PLAYERS ASSOCIATION, 89
OWENS, BRIGMAN, 855
PATTON BOGGS, 908
ROBERT F. KENNEDY MEMORIAL STADIUM, 1006
RUBIN, ERIC M., 913
SFX SPORTS GROUP, 863
SFX SPORTS GROUP, INC., 863
SOOY, KATHLEEN T., 917
SPECIAL OLYMPICS DC, 192
SPECIAL OLYMPICS INTERNATIONAL, 191
SPORTS EXTRA, 688
SWANSON COMMUNICATIONS, 821
UNIVERSITY OF DISTRICT OF COLUMBIA ATHLETICS, 357
UP AGAINST THE WALL, 1251
US SOCCER FOUNDATION, 156
VERIZON CENTER, 1024
WASHINGTON KASTLES, 174
WASHINGTON MYSTICS, 61
WASHINGTON NATIONALS, 33
WASHINGTON ORTHOPAEDICS & SPORTS MEDICINE, 934
WASHINGTON POST, 550
WASHINGTON SPORTS & ENTERTAINMENT, 825
WASHINGTON TIMES, 550
WASHINGTON WIZARDS, 58
WILLIAMS & CONNOLLY, 869
WOMEN'S NATIONAL BASKETBALL ASSOCIATION, 60, 61
WRC-TV, 717
WTOP-FM, 676
WTTG-TV, 719
WUSA-TV, 720
YWCA USA, 86

ENGLAND

ACTION IMAGES, 1102
BARC LIMITED, 1032
BRITISH TRIATHLON ASSOCIATION, 175
BSKYB, 617
CARLIN, 22
COMMONWEALTH GAMES FEDERATION, 260
COYLE & GREER AWARDS CANADA LTD., 1130
CROFT CLASSIC & HISTORIC MOTORSPORTS LTD (CCHM), 1033
DESTINET LIMITED, 941
FORMULA 1, 20
FOX SPORTS INTERNATIONAL, 682
HARDMAN COMPANY, 1153
IMPACT SPORTS MANAGEMENT, 847
INTERNATIONAL ASSOCIATION OF GOLF TOUR OPERATORS, 101
INTERNATIONAL COUNCIL OF MARINE INDUSTRY ASSOCIATIONS, 64
INTERNATIONAL SPORTS MARKETING CONSULTANTS, LTD., 798
INTERNATIONAL TENNIS FEDERATION, 171
ITV SPORT, 606
LOWE ALPINE SYSTEMS, 1168
MCLAREN, 20
MILLER & ASSOCIATES, CATHERINE, 766
N.E.C. ARENA BIRMINGHAM, 997
NETBALL ASSOCIATIONS, INTERNATIONAL FEDERATION OF, 144
OUTSIDE THE BOX MARKETING, INC, 855
PANASTADIA INTERNATIONAL, 581
PITCH PR, 809
PRINCE SPORTS, 1188
PRINCE SPORTS GROUP, INC., 1188
PROFESSIONAL SQUASH ASSOCIATION, 168
QUATRINI, JAY, 860
SPORTBUSINESS GROUP, 590
SPORTS PAGES, 592
STADIA MAGAZINE, 592
WILLIAMS, 20

WORLD SAILING, 178, 204
WORLD SQUASH FEDERATION/WSF, 169

FLORIDA

ABC ACTIVEWEAR LLC, 1100
ADVANCED CUTTING SYSTEMS, INC., 1103
ADVANCED PROMOTIONAL CONCEPTS, INC., 780
AGGRESSIVE SKATERS ASSOCIATION, 139
ALASKA AAU ASSOCIATION, 212
ALFRED LAWSON JR. MULTIPURPOSE CENTER, 954
ALL STAR FOWNES, 1105
ALL STAR INDUSTRIES, INC., 1105
ALLIED SPECIALTY INSURANCE, 775
AMATEUR ATHLETIC UNION KARATE PROGRAM, 142
AMATEUR ATHLETIC UNION OF THE UNITED STATES, INC./AAU, 211
AMERICAN ACADEMY OF PODIATRIC SPORTS MEDICINE, 83, 928
AMERICAN AIRLINES ARENA, 954
AMERICAN FOOTBALL MONTHLY, 554
AMERICAN SWIMMING COACHES ASSOCIATION, 170
AMERICAN WATER SKI EDUCATIONAL FOUNDATION/WATER SKI HALL OF FAME/MUSEUM, 250
AMERICAN YOUTH FOOTBALL, 264
ANDERSON & TUCKER, 871
ANDREWS INSTITUTE FOR ORTHOPAEDICS & SPORTS MEDICINE, 929
APPALACHIAN LEAGUE (ADVANCED ROOKIE), 33
AQUASPORT CORPORATION, 1109
ATHLETIC DEALERS OF AMERICA, 1228
ATHLETIC GUIDE PUBLISHING, 600
ATP WORLD TOUR, 171
AUTHENTIC SPORTS INVESTMENTS, 1229
AUTOMATIC RACING, 20
BARRY UNIVERSITY, 413
BARRY UNIVERSITY ATHLETICS, 352
BASEBALL GROUNDS OF JACKSONVILLE, 956
BASS IND INCORPORATED, 1115
BB&T CENTER, 957
BEALLS ENTERPRISES DEPARTMENT STORES, 1230
BECKER & POLIAKOFF, P.A., 874
BERGERON RODEO GROUNDS AND ENTERTAINMENT CENTER, 1045
BERNARD, PAMELA J., 874
BEST BET, 1055
BETHUNE-COOKMAN UNIVERSITY ATHLETICS, 324
BGB MOTORSPORTS, 20
BIG LEAGUE PROMOTIONS, 1116
BIOLIFE, LLC, 1117
BLUE DOLPHIN DISTRIBUTORS, 1231
BLUE FISH, 1118
BMK ARCHITECTS, 1060
BOATING, 558
BOATING LIFE, 558
BOBBY BOWDEN FIELD AT DOAK CAMPBELL STADIUM, 959
BOCA RATON BOWL, 90
BOSTON WHALER, INC., 1119
BOXEO TELEMUNDO, 690
BRADENTON HERALD, 468
BRADENTON MARAUDERS, 39
BRAGG MEMORIAL STADIUM, 960
BREVARD COUNTY MANATEES, 39
BRIGHT HOUSE NETWORKS STADIUM, 960
BUCS ZONE, 686
BURGER KING, 734
BURKE FIELD, 961
BVT PRODUCTS, LLC, 1122
C & H BASEBALL, 1122
CADDIE ASSOCIATION, 99
CALDER CASINO & RACE COURSE, 1046
CANVAS NURSERY INC, 1123
CAPE CORAL DAILY BREEZE, 470
CAPO INC./PANAMA JACK, 1124
CARD STUNTS BY KIVETT PRODUCTIONS, 760
CENTRAL FLORIDA ATHLETICS, 325
CENTRAL FLORIDA SPORTS COMMISSION, 228, 259
CENTRAL FLORIDA, UNIVERSITY OF, 415
CFE ARENA, 964
CHAMPION STADIUM, 964

CHAMPS SPORTS, 1234
CHARLOTTE STONE CRABS, 39
CHARLOTTE SUN HERALD, 471
CHECKERS DRIVE-IN RESTAURANTS, 1076
CHICAGO GOLF & SPORTS, 1234
CIRCLE TRACK & RACING TECHNOLOGY MAGAZINE, 560
CITRUS BOWL, 90
CITRUS COUNTY CHRONICLE, 473
CLEARWATER THRESHERS, 39
CMS SPORTS, 1235
COASTAL ORTHOPAEDIC & SPORTS MEDICINE CENTER, 930
COLLEGE SWIMMING COACHES ASSOCIATION OF AMERICA, 170
COMFORT LINE PRODUCTS, 1128
COMPETITOR MAGAZINE, 561
CORAL SPRINGS-PARKLAND FORUM, 476
CORPORATE SPORTS MARKETING GROUP/ATLANTA OFFICE, 787
CRANDON PARK TENNIS CENTER, 968
CRICHLOW DATA SCIENCES, 1225
CUSHEES, INC., 1131
DACON, 1132
DAILY COMMERCIAL, 478
DAN MARINO FOUNDATION, 189
DANIEL BLACKMAN CONSULTING, 788
DAYTONA BEACH KENNEL CLUB, 1055
DAYTONA BEACH LEISURE SERVICES, 969
DAYTONA BEACH NEWS-JOURNAL, 484
DAYTONA INTERNATIONAL SPEEDWAY, 1033
DAYTONA SC, 161
DAYTONA TORTUGAS, 39
DEE, PAUL T., 885
DERBY LANE, 1055
DeVOS SPORT BUSINESS MANAGEMENT, 419
DIARIO LAS AMERICAS, 486
DISCOVER ORANGE BOWL, 92
DIZZY DEAN BASEBALL, 27
DOLPHIN DIGEST, 562
DON GARLITS MUSEUM OF DRAG RACING AND INTERNATIONAL DRAG RACING HALL OF FAME, 251
DONALD L. TUCKER CIVIC CENTER, 970
DRAGONSPEED RACING, 21
DUNEDIN BLUE JAYS, 40
DYNASTY APPAREL INDUSTRIES, 1136
DYNOCOMM SPORTS TV, 605
EAGLES DIGEST, 562
EAGLES WINGS, 1137
EAST-WEST SHRINE GAME, 91
ECKERD COLLEGE ATHLETICS, 357
ED SMITH STADIUM/SPORTS COMPLEX, 972
EDWARD WATERS COLLEGE ATHLETICS, 310
EDWIN WATT'S GOLF SHOP, INC., 1238
EHRHARDT, CHARLES W., 887
EL NUEVO HERALD, 488
EL NUEVO PATRIA, 489
EMBRY-RIDDLE AERONAUTICAL UNIVERSITY ATHLETICS - (FL), 310, 358
ENTRY MEDIA, INC., 790
ESPN WIDE WORLD OF SPORTS COMPLEX, 972
ETCHASOFT, INC., 1140
EVENTNET USA, 790
EXCLUSIVE SPORTS MARKETING, INC., 791
EXECUTIVE RESTROOM TRAILERS, 1077
EXECUTIVE WOMEN'S GOLF ASSOCIATION, 99
FANATICS RETAIL GROUP, 1239
FC MIAMI CITY, 161
FC SURGE, 164
THE FEMALE ATHLETE, INC., 1251
FERGUSON, BRIG GEN/USA RET., MICHAEL L., 889
THE FERRARO LAW FIRM, 921
FIRST 4 SPORTS - SATURDAY, 687
FIRST 4 SPORTS - SUNDAY, 687
FIRST PLUS SPORTS MARKETING, 791
FLAGLER COLLEGE, 420
FLAGLER COLLEGE ATHLETICS, 359
FLAGLER DOG TRACK, 1055
FLORIDA A&M UNIVERSITY ATHLETICS, 329
FLORIDA A&M UNIVERSITY- DEPARTMENT OF HEALTH & PHYSICAL EDUCATION, 420
FLORIDA AAU ASSOCIATION, 212
FLORIDA ATHLETICS, UNIVERSITY OF, 329
FLORIDA ATLANTIC UNIVERSITY ATHLETICS, 329
FLORIDA ATLANTIC UNIVERSITY COLLEGE OF BUSINESS, 420

ORLANDO MAGIC, 58
ORLANDO PRIDE, 158
ORLANDO SENTINEL, 520
ORLANDO SOLAR BEARS, 130
OSCEOLA COUNTY STADIUM, 999
OUTBACK BOWL, 92
OVATION FOOD SERVICES LP, 1077
1320 WAMR, 617
PACKMAN, NEUWAHL & ROSENBERG, 908
PALM BEACH ATLANTIC UNIVERSITY, 433
PALM BEACH ATLANTIC UNIVERSITY
   ATHLETICS, 368
PALM BEACH ATLANTIC UNIVERSITY
   ATHLETICS(PBA), 368
PALM BEACH CARDINALS, 40
PALM BEACH COUNTY SPORTS COMMISSION,
   INC., 241
PALM BEACH DAILY NEWS, 521
PALM BEACH KENNEL CLUB, 1057
PALM BEACH POST, 521
PALM BEACH SUNS FC, 162
PALM CITY FC, 165
PANAMA CITY BEACH CHAMBER OF
   COMMERCE, 241
PANAMA CITY BEACH CONVENTION &
   VISITORS BUREAU, INC., 242
PANOZ/SANCHEZ GROUP, 767
PCA WORLDWIDE, INC., 809
PENSACOLA BAY CENTER, 1000
PENSACOLA BLUE WAHOOS, 53
PENSACOLA GREYHOUND TRACK, 1057
PENSACOLA ICE FLYERS, 136
PENSACOLA NEWS JOURNAL, 522
PENSACOLA SPORTS ASSOCIATION, 242
PERFORMANCE PROMOTIONS SPORT
   PROMOTIONS, 809
PERFORMANCE TECH MOTORSPORTS, 21
PERRY ELLIS INTERNATIONAL, 1184
PETER GLENN SKI & SPORT, 1246
PGA 20/20, 103, 856
PGA OF AMERICA/PROFESSIONAL GOLFERS'
   ASSOCIATION OF AMERICA, 103
PGA TOUR, 108
PGA WORLD GOLF HALL OF FAME, 256
PINELLAS COUNTY UNITED SC, 166
PLAYERS GOLF, 1185
POINT BLANK SOLUTIONS, 1186
POLK COUNTY SPORTS MARKETING, 242
POLO PLAYERS EDITION, 582
PORSCHE GT3 CUP CHALLENGE CANADA, 25
PORSCHE GT3 CUP CHALLENGE USA, 25
POWELL GOLF, INC., JOE, 1187
POWER IMAGES, 810
POWER SOURCE SPORTS INC, 1187
PRENSA GRAFICA, 526
PRO CYCLING MIAMI, 72
PROFESSIONAL BASEBALL UMPIRE
   CORPORATION, 28
PROFESSIONAL CADDIES ASSOCIATION
   WORLDWIDE, PCA, 108
PROFESSIONAL GOLFERS' ASSOCIATION
   HALL OF FAME, 256
PROJECT SPORTS MARKETING, 811
PROSTAR ENTERPRISES, INC., 859
PSC/ENCORE SELECT INC, 1189
PUERTO RICO AAU ASSOCIATION, 214
R.B. ROBERTSON & COMPANY, 813
RAUCH, JR., MARTIN W., 910
RAYMOND JAMES STADIUM, 1004
REBEL ROCK RACING, 20
RED MC EWEN BASEBALL FIELD, 1004
REPUBLICA DEPORTIVA, 692
RLS LIGHTING, INC., 1194
RMG3 EAST COAST, 814
RMY MANAGEMENT GROUP, 769
RODER USA, INC., 1075
ROGER DEAN STADIUM, 1006
ROLLINS COLLEGE ATHLETICS, 342, 369
RON JON SURF SHOP OF FLORIDA, 1248
ROSENHAUS SPORTS MANAGEMENT, 861
RUSSELL ATHLETIC BOWL, 93
SAINT LEO UNIVERSITY, 370
SAMMS, GREGORY A., 862
SANFORD-ORLANDO KENNEL CLUB, INC.,
   1057
SARASOTA HERALD-TRIBUNE, 533
SARASOTA KENNEL CLUB, INC., 1057
SARASOTA METROPOLIS FC, 163
SCHUTTS & BOWEN, 914
SCUBA SCHOOLS INTERNATIONAL (SSI), 149

SEBRING INTERNATIONAL RACEWAY, 1042
SEMINOLE COUNTY SPORTS TRAINING
   CENTER, 1017
SERVICE MERCHANDISE COMPANY, 1248
SHOWPROCO, LLC, 769
SICKING, RICHARD A., ESQ, 916
SKYDIVING, 587
SKYSIGNS UNLIMITED, 769
SMACK APPAREL, 1201, 1249
SOCCER MARKETING & PROMOTIONS, INC.,
   769, 817
SOLAR BLOC HATS, 1249
SOLAR TAN THRU SUITS, 1202
SOUTH ATLANTIC LEAGUE (A LEVEL), 51
SOUTH FLORIDA ATHLETICS, UNIVERSITY OF,
   344
SOUTH FLORIDA PGA, 114
SOUTH FLORIDA SUN-SENTINEL, 536
SOUTHERN BOATING MAGAZINE, 588
SOUTHERN PACIFIC AAU ASSOCIATION, 214
SPACE COAST STADIUM, 1013
SPECIAL OLYMPICS FLORIDA, 192
SPEEDLINE ATHLETIC WEAR, INC., 1203
SPL INTEGRATED SOLUTIONS, 831
SPORTS & SPONSORSHIPS, INC., 864
SPORTS CLUB OF TAMPA BAY, 246
SPORTS CONNECTION, 693
SPORTS IMMORTALS, 257
SPORTS IMMORTALS MUSEUM, 1205
SPORTS JAM, 688
SPORTS MARKETING SURVEYS USA, 819
SPORTS SPECIFIC SCIENCES, 1226
SPORTS TALK/THE TICKET, 613
SPORTS XTRA, 689
SPORTSLINE USA,
   INC./CBS.SPORTSLINE.COM, 939
ST. AUGUSTINE RECORD, 538
ST. AUGUSTINE, PONTE VEDRA & THE
   BEACHES VISITORS & CONVENTION
   BUREAU, 245
ST. LEO UNIVERSITY, 436
ST. LUCIE METS, 40
ST. PETERSBERG BOWL, 93
ST. PETERSBURG TIMES, 538
ST. PETERSBURG/CLEARWATER SPORTS
   COMMISSION, 246
ST. THOMAS UNIVERSITY, 436
STACKS OF PLAQUES, 1207
STADIUM JUMPING, INC., 77
STAR-BANNER, 539
STEARNS WEAVER MILLER, 918
STEELERS DIGEST, 592
STEPHEN C O'CONNELL CENTER, 1015
STETSON UNIVERSITY ATHLETICS, 345
STETSON UNIVESITY, 436
STOCK CAR RACING, 592
SUN LIFE STADIUM, 1016
SUN SHADER INTERNATIONAL,
   INC./WASHINGTON SQUARE GARDEN, INC,
   1209
SUN-SENTINEL, 541
SUNDAY SPORTS FINAL, 689
SUNSHINE STATE CONFERENCE, 304
SUNSHINE STATE GAMES, 263
SUNTEC PAINT, INC., 1209
SUNTIME/LINKSWALKER, 1209
SUPER BOAT INTERNATIONAL, 65
SUPERIOR UNIFORM GROUP INC., 1209
SW FLORIDA ADRENALINE, 163
SYMETRA TOUR, 108
T-BALL USA ASSOCIATION, 28
TALLAHASSEE DEMOCRAT, 541
TALLAHASSEE SPORTS COUNCIL, 246
TAMPA ATHLETICS, UNIVERSITY OF, 373
TAMPA BAY BUCCANEERS, 97
TAMPA BAY DOWNS, 1054
TAMPA BAY HELLENIC, 166
TAMPA BAY LIGHTNING, 125
TAMPA BAY RAYS, 30
TAMPA BAY ROWDIES, 160
TAMPA BAY ROWDIES U23, 163
TAMPA BAY SPORTS COMMISSION, 246
TAMPA BAY TIMES FORUM, 1016
TAMPA CONVENTION & VISITORS BUREAU,
   246
TAMPA SPORTS AUTHORITY, 246
TAMPA TRIBUNE, 541
TAMPA YANKEES, 40
TAMPA, UNIVERSITY OF, 437
TANGENT ASSOCIATES, INC., 1077

TASK INDUSTRIES, INC., 1211
TBO (WFLA) NEWS CHANNEL 8, 706
TBSA, 1072
TD WATERHOUSE CENTRE, 1017
TEAM BOCA BLAST, 166
TEAM FLORIDA MARKETING, 821
TECNIFIBRE USA, 1211
TELEMUNDO, 685
TERVIS TUMBLER COMPANY, 1212
THOMAS PILACEK & ASSOCIATES, 921
TIREPATCHEZ, 1213
TORPEDO SPORTS USA, INC., 1214
TRADITION FIELD SPORTS COMPLEX, 1019
TRANSMEDIA GROUP, 609
TREASURE COAST DYNAMITES, 166
TRIBUNE (FL), 546
TRIMAN TELE-GOAL, INC., 1215
TROPHY WORLD, 1215
TROPHYLAND USA, INC., 1215
TROPICANA FIELD, 1020
TRUSCO MFG. COMPANY, 1216
TV SPORTSFILE, 596
360 MANAGEMENT, LLC, 778
U.S. JUDO, INC/USA JUDO, 143
U.S. POLO ASSOCIATION, 145
U.S. TRAFFIC CORPORATION, 1217
U.S. WINDSURFING, 177
UHZ SPORTS MEDICINE INSTITUTE, 934
UNITED STATES CROQUET ASSOCIATION, 69
UNITED STATES GOLF TEACHERS
   FEDERATION, 117
UNITED STATES POLO ASSOCIATION, 79
UNITED STATES SPECIALTY SPORTS
   ASSOCATION, 168, 224
UNIVERSITY OF FLORIDA ORTHOPAEDICS &
   SPORT MEDICINE INSTITUTE, 934
UNIVERSITY OF WEST FLORIDA ATHLETICS
   (UWF), 375
UNIVISION TELEVISION NETWORK, 685
USA CRICKET ASSOCIATION, 69
USA WATER SKI, 177
USF SOCCER STADIUM, 1023
USF SUN DOME, 1023
USSSA FLORIDA PRIDE, 168
USTA FLORIDA, 173
VANTAGE SPORTS MANAGEMENT, 868
VENUS SWIMWEAR, 1219
THE VILLAGES SC, 163
VINTAGE MOTORSPORT, 597
VISION SPORTS, INC., 941
WAGENHEIM & WAGNER, P.A., 923
WAKE BOARDING MAGAZINE, 598
WAQI-AM, 643
WAR MEMORIAL AUDITORIUM, 1026
WARNER SOUTHERN COLLEGE, 439
WARNER UNIVERSITY ATHLETICS, 322
WATER SKI, 598
WATER SKIER, 598
WATER SPORTS INDUSTRY ASSOCIATION,
   224
WAVV-FM, 644
WBBH - NBC 2, 707
WBBH-TV, 707
WBFS-TV, 708
WBZE-FM / WGLF.FM/ WWLD.FM / WHBX.FM,
   647
WCJB-TV, 709
WDAE-AM 620, 649
WDBO-AM, 649
WEAR-TV, 710
WEBBER INTERNATIONAL UNIVERSITY, 439
WEBBER INTERNATIONAL UNIVERSITY
   ATHLETICS, 322
WENDEL, CHRITTON, PARKS, AND DEBARI
   CHARTERED, 925
WENG, 652
WESH-TV, 710
WEST FLORIDA ATHLETICS, UNIVERSITY OF,
   375
WEST TEXAS AAU ASSOCIATION, 215
WESTON FC, 164
WFLA-TV, 710
WFLF-AM, 653
WFTS-TV, 711
WFTV-TV, 711
WHTQ-FM, 657
WINDSURFING, 599
WINK-TV, 713
WITLIN PROFESSIONAL MANAGEMENT, 869
WJHG-TV, 713

1759

GERMANY

GEORGIA

HOLLAND

HUNGARY

HAWAII

ITALY

IDAHO

ILLINOIS

INDIANA

IOWA

ISRAEL

JAPAN

KOREA

KANSAS

KENTUCKY

LIECHTENSTEIN

LOUISIANA

geographic index

MASSACHUSETTS

geographic index

MICHIGAN

MINNESOTA

MISSISSIPPI

MISSOURI

geographic index

MONTANA

NEBRASKA

NEVADA

geographic index

geographic index

NORTH CAROLINA

WYRICK, ROBBINS, YATES & PONTON, L.L.P, 927
WZBO-AM, 680
YOUNG'S MOTORSPORTS, 24

NORTH DAKOTA

ALERUS CENTER, 953
BISMARCK BOBCATS, 132
BISMARCK BUCKS, 94
BISMARCK EVENT CENTER, 958
BISMARCK TRIBUNE, 467
BISMARCK-MANDAN CONVENTION & VISITORS BUREAU, 227
DAKOTA-10 ATHLETIC CONFERENCE, 293
DEVILS LAKE DAILY JOURNAL, 486
DICKINSON CONVENTION & VISITORS BUREAU, 231
DICKINSON PRESS, 487
DICKINSON STATE UNIVERSITY ATHLETICS, 310
FARGO FORCE, 136
FARGO-MOORHEAD CONVENTION & VISITOR BUREAU, 232
FARGODOME, 973
FORUM, 492
GRAND FORKS CONVENTION & VISITORS BUREAU, GREATER, 233
GRAND FORKS HERALD, 493
HYSLOP SPORTS CENTER, 981
INTERNATIONAL HANDGUN METALLIC SILHOUETTE ASSOCIATION, 149
JAMESTOWN CIVIC CENTER, 984
KDAK-AM, 622
KDDR-AM, 622
KDIX-AM, 622
KDLR-AM, 622
KFYR-TV, 698
KMAV-FM, 630
KMSR-AM, 631
KNDK-FM, 631
KNOX, 631
KOVC-AM, 632
KPOK-AM, 633
KVLY-TV, 705
KVOX-AM, 638
KXJB-TV, 706
MARY ATHLETICS, UNIVERSITY OF, 336
MAYVILLE STATE UNIVERSITY ATHLETICS, 314
MINOT DAILY NEWS, 511
MINOT MINOTAUROS, 132
MINOT STATE UNIVERSITY ATHLETICS, 365
NATIONAL HIGH SCHOOL ATHLETIC COACHES ASSOCIATION, 201
NEWMAN OUTDOOR FIELD, 997
NORTH DAKOTA AAU ASSOCIATION, 213
NORTH DAKOTA ATHLETICS, UNIVERSITY OF, 367
NORTH DAKOTA GOLF ASSOCIATION, 113
NORTH DAKOTA HS ACTIVITIES ASSOCIATION, 199
NORTH DAKOTA RACING COMMISSION, 82
NORTH DAKOTA STATE UNIVERSITY (NDSU), 367
NORTH DAKOTA STATE UNIVERSITY ATHLETICS, 367
PRAIRIE ROSE STATE GAMES, 262
RALPH ENGELSTAD ARENA, 1003
SCHEEL'S ALL SPORTS, INC., 1248
SPECIAL OLYMPICS NORTH DAKOTA, 194
SURE FOOT CORPORATION, 1209
UNIVERSITY OF JAMESTOWN ATHLETICS, 321
UNIVERSITY OF NORTH DAKOTA (UND), 367
VALLEY CITY TIMES-RECORD, 548
WDAZ-TV, 709

OHIO

ABERCROMBIE & FITCH CO., 1227
ACE MITCHELL BOWLERS MART, 1101
ACO POLYMER PRODUCTS, INC., 1101
ACOR, INC., 1101
ADVERTISER-TRIBUNE, 461
AKRON ATHLETICS, UNIVERSITY OF, 323
AKRON BEACON JOURNAL, 461
AKRON RACERS, 168
AKRON RUBBERDUCKS, 38

AKRON SUMMIT CONVENTION & VISITORS BUREAU, 225
ALCOX, PATRICK, 871
ALL AMERICAN AMATEUR BASEBALL ASSOCIATION, 938
ALL AMERICAN SPORTS CORP/RIDDELL ALL AMERICAN, 1105
ALL-AMERICAN SOAP BOX DERBY, 264
ALLIANCE REVIEW, 462
AMERICAN ELECTRIC LIGHTING, 1107
AMERICAN MOTORCYCLIST ASSOCIATION, 143
AMERICAN WHISTLE CORPORATION, 1108
ASHLAND TIMES-GAZETTE, 464
ASHLAND UNIVERSITY, 412
ASHLAND UNIVERSITY ATHLETICS, 352
ASSOCIATION OF LUXURY SUITE DIRECTORS, 216
ATH-ELITE MANAGEMENT SERVICES, 834
ATHENS MESSENGER, 464
ATHLETA, LLC, 1228
ATHLETES IN ACTION, 216
ATHLETIC & PERFORMANCE RIGGING/APR, 1111
ATHLETICS ADMINISTRATION, 555
BAILEY MANUFACTURING COMPANY, 1113
BALDWIN-WALLACE COLLEGE, 412
BALDWIN-WALLACE COLLEGE - LOU HIGGINS CENTER, 412
BALDWIN-WALLACE COLLEGE ATHLETICS, 378
BASIC COATINGS, INC., 1115
BEAVERCREEK NEWS CURRENT, 466
BEEGHLY GYM, 957
BELLEFONTAINE EXAMINER, 466
BELTERRA PARK, 1045
BETLIN INC., 1116
BEULAH PARK, 1045
BIGG'S HYPER SHOPPES, 1231
BLADE, 467
BLUFFTON COLLEGE ATHLETICS, 379
BLUFFTON UNIVERSITY ATHLETICS, 379
BLUNDEN BARCLAY ROBBIE ASSOCIATES ACHITECTS, 1060
BMW TEAM RLL, 21
BOWLING GREEN STATE UNIVERSITY, 413
BOWLING GREEN STATE UNIVERSITY ATHLETICS, 324
BRAUN & STEIDL ARCHITECTS INC, 1060
BRAZOS SPORTSWEAR, 1120
BRICKER & ECKLER, 877
BRYAN TIMES, 469
BRYENTON, GARY L., 878
BURDINE'S, 1232
CAMERA SPORTSEAT, INC., 1123
CAMOFACE, 1123
CAN-AM LEAGUE, 37
CANAL PARK, 963
CANTON CHARGE, 59
CANTON MEMORIAL CIVIC CENTER, 963
CANTON/STARK COUNTY CONVENTION & VISITORS BUREAU, 228, 259
CAPITAL UNIVERSITY, 415
CAPITAL UNIVERSITY ATHLETICS, 380
CARAVAN PROTECTIVE CASES, 1124
CASE WESTERN RESERVE UNIVERSITY ATHLETICS, 381
CEDARVILLE UNIVERSITY ATHLETICS, 308
CEDARVILLE UNIVERSITY- DEPARTMENT OF KINESIOLOGY AND ALLIED HEALTH, 415
CENTRAL STATE UNIVERSITY ATHLETICS, 309
CHERNESKY, RICHARD, 881
CHRONICLE-TELEGRAM, 472
CINCINNATI ATHLETICS, UNIVERSITY OF, 326
CINCINNATI BENGALS, 95
CINCINNATI CYCLONES, 129
CINCINNATI ENQUIRER, 472
CINCINNATI GAMES, 1126
CINCINNATI GARDENS, 966
CINCINNATI LADY SAINTS, 164
CINCINNATI POST, 473
CINCINNATI REDS, 31
CINCINNATI SPORTS CORPORATION, GREATER, 229
CINCINNATI SPORTSMEDICINE & ORTHOPAEDIC CENTER, 929
CIRCLEVILLE BIBLE COLLEGE, 355
CIRCLEVILLE HERALD, 473
CLASSIC PARK, 966
CLEVELAND BROWNS, 95

CLEVELAND CAVALIERS, 56
CLEVELAND CLINIC, 930
CLEVELAND INDIANS, 29
CLEVELAND MONSTERS, 127
CLEVELAND SPORTS COMMISSION, GREATER, 229
CLEVELAND STATE UNIVERSITY, 416
CLEVELAND STATE UNIVERSITY ATHLETICS, 326
THE COLLABORATIVE, INC., 1062
COLLEGE ATHLETIC BUSINESS MANAGEMENT ASSOCIATION/CABMA, 281
COLLEGE OF MOUNT ST. JOSEPH- SPORT MANAGEMENT DEPARTMENT, 416
COLLEGE PROSPECTS OF AMERICA, 940
COLUMBUA CLIPPERS, 42
COLUMBUS BLUE JACKETS, 123
COLUMBUS CREW SC, 157
COLUMBUS DISPATCH, 474
COLUMBUS DISTRICT GOLF ASSOCIATION, 109
COLUMBUS EAGLES, 164
COLUMBUS MARATHON, 148
COLUMBUS STATE COMMUNITY COLLEGE, 416
COLUMBUS WILD DOGS, 94
COMMUNICATOR NEWS, 475
COMMUNITY JOURNAL-CLERMONT, 475
COMODECA, JAMES A., 883
COSHOCTON TRIBUNE, 476
CRESCENT-NEWS, 477
CUYAHOGA FALLS NEWS-PRESS, 477
CYGNET TURF & EQUIPMENT, 1132
DAILY ADVOCATE, 477
DAILY GLOBE (OH), 479
DAILY JEFFERSONIAN, 480
DAILY RECORD (OH), 481
DAILY STANDARD, 483
DANDY PRODUCTS, INC., 1133
DAYTON ATHLETICS, UNIVERSITY OF, 327
DAYTON DAILY NEWS, 484
DAYTON DRAGONS, 45
DAYTON DUTCH LIONS, 161
DAYTON, UNIVERSITY OF, 418
DAYTON/MONTGOMERY COUNTY CONVENTION & VISITORS BUREAU, 230
DEFIANCE COLLEGE ATHLETICS, 384
DEFIANCE COLLEGE- BUSINESS & ALLIED HEALTH DIVISION, 418
DELAWARE COUNTY FAIR, 1046
DELAWARE GAZETTE, 484
DENISON UNIVERSITY ATHLETICS, 384
DENISON UNIVERSITY(DU)ATHLETICS, 384
DENUNE, III, RALPH, 885
DIEBOLD INCORPORATED, 1135
DOYT PERRY FIELD STADIUM, 970
DR. CHRIS STANKOVICH, 930
DRAG REVIEW, 562
DUBLIN CONVENTION & VISITOR BUREAU, 231
EDDIE BAUER, INC., 1238
ELECTRA TARP, 1138
ESPN990 SPORTS RADIO, 618
EXPRESS, 1238
FAGUE, TERENCE L., 888
FAIRBORN DAILY HERALD, 490
FANNING/HOWEY ASSOCIATES, INC., 1065
FC CINCINNATI, 157
FEDERATED DEPARTMENT STORES, INC., 1239
FERNO PERFORMANCE POOLS, 1142
FIFTH THIRD FIELD, 974
FINDLAY ATHLETICS, UNIVERSITY OF, 359
FINKELMEIER LAW FIRM, 889
FIRST ENERGY STADIUM, 974
FLAMBEAU OUTDOORS, 1144
FOX SPORTS OHIO, 683
FRANKEL, PAUL D., 890
GALION INQUIRER, 493
GAME DAY COMMUNICATIONS, 792
GANIM ENTERPRISES, 843
GEORGIA BOOT, 1148
GLASS BOWL STADIUM, 977
GOLDSMITH, JAMES A., 891
GOLF COURSE NEWS, 566
GOLFDOM, 567
GOLFWORKS, 1150
GOODYEAR TIRE & RUBBER CO., THE, 736
GRALAB, 1150
GREAT AMERICAN BALLPARK, 977

OKLAHOMA

ANAPOL, SCHWARTZ, WEISS, COHAN, FELDMAN & SMALLEY, P.C., 871
ARAMARK CORPORATION, 782, 1073, 1076
ARANDA GROUP, 833
ARCADIA UNIVERSITY ATHLETICS, 378
ARCADIA UNIVERSITY ATHLETICS DEPARTMENT-GLENSIDE, 378
ATLANTIC LEAGUE, 35, 36
ATLANTIC LEAGUE OF PROFESSIONAL BASEBALL, THE, 35
AUTO SPORTS MARKETING GROUP, 758, 782
BACKPACKER MAGAZINE, 556
BALAZS, INC., 1113
BB&T BALLPARK AT HISTORIC BOWMAN FIELD, 957
BEAUTYMAN ASSOCIATES, P.C., 874
BEAVER COUNTY TIMES, 466
BEAVER STADIUM, 957
BERNARD M. RESNICK, ESQ, P.C., 874
BERRY & HOMER, 783
BICYCLING, 557
BIKE LINE, 1231
BIKE USA INC., 1116
BIOFREEZE/PERFORMANCE HEALTH PRODUCTS, 1117
BIOFREEZE/PERFORMANCE HEALTHPRODUCTS, 1117
BLACK WOMEN IN SPORT FOUNDATION, 217
BLOOMSBURG UNIVERSITY ATHLETICS, 353
BOBBY JONES INTERNATIONAL, 1118
BON TON STORES, INC., 1232
BOSCH, GERARD R., 876
BOSCOV'S DEPARTMENT STORES, 1232
BRADFORD ERA, 468
BRESLIN, RIDYARD, FADERO ARCHITECTS, 1060
BRUTE GROUP, 1121
BRUTE WRESTLING, 1121
BRYCE JORDAN CENTER, 961
BUCHANAN INGERSOLL ROONEY, 878
BUCHANAN INGERSOLL ROONEY PC, 878
BUCKNELL UNIVERSITY ATHLETICS, 325
BUCKS COUNTY COMMUNITY COLLEGE - DEPT OF HEALTH, PE & NURSING, 414
BUCKS COUNTY COURIER TIMES, 469
BUTLER EAGLE, 470
BUXMONT TORCH FC, 164
CABRINI COLLEGE ATHLETICS, 380
CALIFORNIA UNIVERSITY OF PENNSYLVANIA, 414
CALIFORNIA UNIVERSITY OF PENNSYLVANIA ATHLETICS, 354
CAMBRIA COUNTY WAR MEMORIAL, 962
CARLOW COLLEGE ATHLETICS, 308
CARNEGIE MELLON UNIVERSITY ATHLETICS, 381
CBS PHILLY - SPORTSRADIO 94WIP, 611
CELLI & ASSOCIATES, 881
CENTENNIAL CONFERENCE, 291
CENTER CITY FILM & VIDEO, 604
CENTRAL PENNSYLVANIA/PENN STATE COUNTRY CVB, 228
CENTRE DAILY TIMES, 471
THE CHAPEL HILL NORTH GROUP, 822
CHESTNUT HILL COLLEGE ATHLETICS, 355
CHEYNEY UNIVERSITY ATHLETICS, 355
CHICK'S SPORTING GOODS, INC., 1234
CHOICE MARKETING SPORTSCARDS, 786
CHRISTIAN MOTORSPORTS ILLUSTRATED, 560
CINDRICH & COMPANY, 881
CITIZENS BANK PARK, 966
CITIZENS' VOICE, 473
CLARION UNIVERSITY OF PENNSYLVANIA ATHLETICS, 355
COLLEGE SPORTS INFORMATION DIRECTORS OF AMERICA/COSIDA, 281
COMCAST CORPORATION, 735
COMFORT PRODUCTS, INC., 1128
COMMUNITY PROFESSIONAL LOUDSPEAKERS, 829, 1129
CONSOL ENERGY CENTER, 967
CONTOUR SEATS, INC., 1129
COOPERSBURG SPORTS, 1235
COURIER-EXPRESS, 476
COVER SPORTS USA, 1130
CURRAN, RICHARD, 839
CWI PRODUCTIONS, INC., 605
DAD VAIL REGATTA, 146
DAILY AMERICAN, 477

DAILY COURIER (PA), 478
DAILY ITEM (PA), 479
DAILY LOCAL NEWS, 480
DAILY REVIEW (PA), 482
DANVILLE NEWS, 484
DE SALES UNIVERSITY, 418
DE SALES UNIVERSITY ATHLETICS, 384
DEKAI ENTERPRISES, 840
DELAWARE COUNTY DAILY TIMES, 484
DELAWARE VALLEY COLLEGE ATHLETICS, 384
DELAWARE VALLEY COLLEGE(DVC) ATHLETICS, 384
DERRICK, 485
DESALES UNIVERSITY- DIVISION OF BUSINESS, 418
DICK'S SPORTING GOODS INC., 1236
DICKINSON COLLEGE ATHLETICS, 384
DICKINSON COLLEGE(DC) ATHLETICS, 384
DIRT RAG, 562
DMI SPORTS INC, 1135
DREXEL UNIVERSITY, 418
DREXEL UNIVERSITY ATHLETICS, 328
DUQUESNE UNIVERSITY, 418
DUQUESNE UNIVERSITY ATHLETICS, 328
DYNAMIC TEAM SPORTS, 1136
EARTH & TURF, 1137
EAST STROUDSBURG UNIVERSITY (ESU) OF PENNSYLVANIA ATHLETICS, 357
EAST STROUDSBURG UNIVERSITY OF, 419
EAST STROUDSBURG UNIVERSITY OF PENNSYLVANIA ATHLETICS, 357
EASTERN INTERCOLLEGIATE WRESTLING ASSOCIATION, 178
EASTERN UNIVERSITY ATHLETICS, 385
EASTERN UNIVERSITY(EU) ATHLETICS, 385
ECKERT SEAMANS, 887
EDINBORO UNIVERSITY OF PENNSYLVANIA ATHLETICS, 358
ELITE SPORTSWEAR, L.P., 1139
ELIZABETHTOWN COLLEGE ATHLETICS, 385
ELLWOOD CITY LEDGER, 489
ENDLESS POOLS, INC., 1139
EPIC METALS, 1140
EQUIPTO, 1140
ERIE BAYHAWKS, 59
ERIE INSURANCE ARENA, 972
ERIE OTTERS, 133
ERIE SEAWOLVES, 38
ERNIE SAXTON'S MOTORSPORTS SPONSORSHIP MARKETING, 563
ESPN RADIO 1250 PITTSBURGH, 618
EVENING SUN (PA), 490
EVENING TIMES (PA), 490
EVENT STRATEGY GROUP, 790
EWING COLE CHERRY BROTT, 1065
EXECUTIVE DIVERSIONS, 1141
EXPRESS-TIMES, 490
FARREL STADIUM, 973
FC BUCKS, 164
FIRSTENERGY STADIUM, 974
FNB FIELD, 974
FOGDOG SPORTS, 1145
FOREMAN ARCHITECTS ENGINEERS INC., 1066
FORESITE SPORTS, 763
FOSTER, DON, 890
FRANKLIN & MARSHALL COLLEGE ATHLETICS, 386
FRANKLIN & MARSHALL COLLEGE ATHLETICS (FMC), 386
FRANKLIN FIELD, 975
THE FRED HONSBERGER SHOW, 613
GANNON UNIVERSITY ATHLETICS, 360
GANNON UNIVERSITY ATHLETICS (GU), 360
GEM GROUP, 844
GENEVA COLLEGE ATHLETICS, 311
GEORGI-SPORTS, 1148
GETTYSBURG COLLEGE ATHLETICS, 387
GETTYSBURG COLLEGE ATHLETICS (GC), 387
GETTYSBURG TIMES, 493
GIANT CENTER, 976
GLOBAL SPECTRUM, 764, 829, 1074
GNC CORPORATION, 1148, 1240
GOLD, KEVIN M., ESQUIRE, 891
GOLF ASSOCIATION OF PHILADELPHIA, 110
GOLF SOLUTIONS WORLDWIDE, 1149
GROVE CITY COLLEGE ATHLETICS, 387
GURWIN, DAVID A., 845
GWYNEDD MERCY COLLEGE ATHLETICS, 388

HARRISBURG SENATORS, 38
HAVERFORD COLLEGE ATHLETICS, 388
HAYES LARGE ARCHITECTS, 1068
HEAD DOWN TRAINERS.COM, 1153
HEINZ FIELD, 978
HERALD-STANDARD, 497
HERSHEY BEARS, 127
THE HERSHEY CO., 742
HERSHEY FC, 165
HOLLYWOOD CASINO AT PENN NATIONAL RACE COURSE, 1049
HOLMES, RICH, 894
HOLY FAMILY COLLEGE ATHLETICS, 361
HOLY FAMILY UNIVERSITY, 422
HOOK & HACKLE, 1156
HORSE OF DELAWARE VALLEY, 569
HOWARD J. LAMADE STADIUM, 980
HUMMER TURFGRASS SYSTEMS, INC., 1157
INDIANA GAZETTE, 499
INDIANA UNIVERSITY OF PENNSYLVANIA, 423
INDIANA UNIVERSITY OF PENNSYLVANIA ATHLETICS, 361
INTELLIGENCER JOURNAL, 499
INTERNATIONAL ASSOCIATION OF APPROVED BASKETBALL OFFICIALS, INC., 54
INTERNATIONAL INSTITUTE FOR SPORT HISTORY, 252
INTERNATIONAL MICRO SYSTEMS, INC., 941, 1074, 1077
INTROMARK INC, 798
JAMES CLIBANOFF BASKETBALL SERVICES, 848
JENNERSTOWN SPEEDWAY, 1036
JERRY UHT PARK, 984
JOHNSTOWN TOMAHAWKS, 132
JOURNAL OF SPORT HISTORY, 572
JUNIATA COLLEGE ATHLETICS, 390
KDKA-TV, 697
KEY SPORTZ-WEAR, 1163
KEYSTONE COLLEGE- SPORT AND RECREATION MANAGEMENT, 425
KEYSTONE REGIONAL COMMISSIONER/USA VOLLEYBALL, 210
KEYSTONE STATE GAMES, INC., 261
KING COBRA GAMING, 1163
KING'S COLLEGE ATHLETICS, 391
KIRBY SPORTS CENTER, 988
KUTZTOWN UNIVERSITY ATHLETICS, 362
KUTZTOWN UNIVERSITY ATHLETICS (KU ATHLETICS), 362
KUTZTOWN UNIVERSITY- DEPARTMENT OF SPORT MANAGEMENT, 425
KWIK GOAL LTD., 1164
KYW-TV, 706
L. ROBERT KIMBALL & ASSOCIATES, 1070
LA ROCHE COLLEGE ATHLETICS, 391
LA ROCHE COLLEGE ATHLETICS (LRC), 391
LA SALLE UNIVERSITY ATHLETICS, 334
LACKAWANNA COUNTY CONVENTION & VISITORS BUREAU, 236
LACKAWANNA COUNTY STADIUM, 989
LAFAYETE COLLEGE, 989
LAFAYETTE COLLEGE ATHLETICS, 334
LANCASTER BARNSTORMERS, 35
LANCASTER BIBLE COLLEGE-, 425
LANCASTER INFERNO, 165
LANCASTER NEW ERA, 504
LANGHORNE SKI & SPORT, 1243
LATROBE BULLETIN, 505
LATSHA DAVIS & MCKENNA, P.C., 898
LEADER-TIMES, 505
LEBANON VALLEY COLLEGE ATHLETICS, 392
LEBANON VALLEY COLLEGE ATHLETICS (LVC), 392
LEHIGH CARBON COMMUNITY COLLEGE, 425
LEHIGH UNIVERSITY ATHLETICS, 334
LEHIGH VALLEY IRON PIGS, 42
LEHIGH VALLEY PHANTOMS, 127
LEHIGH VALLEY SPORTS COMMISSION, 237
LEHIGH VALLEY UNITED, 162
LIACOURAS CENTER, 991
LINCOLN FINANCIAL FIELD, 991
LINCOLN UNIVERSITY ATHLETICS, 363
LITTLE LEAGUE BASEBALL, 27, 264
LITTLE LEAGUE BASEBALL MUSEUM, 253
LOCK HAVEN UNIVERSITY ATHLETICS (LHU), 363
LOCK HAVEN UNIVERSITY OF PENNSYLVANIA, 426
LOMMA GOLF, 1168

SOUTH DAKOTA

THE NETHERLANDS

TENNESSEE

TEXAS

UNITED ARAB EMIRATES

UTAH

ADP LEMCO, INC., 1103
BIG SKY CONFERENCE, 290
BLACK DIAMOND EQUIPMENT, LTD., 1117
BRENT BROWN BALLPARK, 960
BRIGHAM YOUNG UNIVERSITY ATHLETICS, 324
BROWNING, 1121
BYU COUGARS, 160
CLUB MARKETING AND MANAGEMENT SERVICES, 786
COBBLESTONES ACTIVEWEAR, 1127
CONCORD EXPO GROUP, 760
COURT COMPANY, 1130
DAILY HERALD (UT), 479
DALEBOOT U.S.A., 1133
DAVIS COUNTY CLIPPER, 484
DEE EVENTS CENTER, 969
DEE GLEN SMITH SPECTRUM, 969
DESCENTE NORTH AMERICA, INC., 1134
DESERET MORNING NEWS, 485
EASTON TECHNICAL PRODUCTS, 1137
ECCLES COLISEUM, 972
FAIRWAYS, 564
FFKR ARCHITECTS, 1065
FIELD GENERAL LLC, 1143
FOX 13 SPORTS PAGE, 687
FRANKLIN COVEY, 791
GAME FACE, INC., 755
GEAR.COM, INC., 1240
GOODE SKI TECHNOLOGIES, 1150
HAMMAKA, 1152
HERALD JOURNAL, 496
HOGGAN HEALTH INDUSTRIES, 1155
HOYT USA, 1156
HUGGER-MUGGER YOGA PRODUCTS, 1157
ICON HEALTH & FITNESS, INC., 1157
JON M. HUNTSMAN CENTER, 986
KAGJ-FM, 619
KBEE-FM, 620
KBER-FM, 620
KFNZ, 624
KOHS-FM, 632
KOVO-AM, 632
KSL-TV, 702
KSTU-TV, 703
KTVX-TV, 704
KUBL-FM, 637
KUTV-TV, 704
KWCR-FM, 638
LAVELL EDWARDS STADIUM, 990
LEGEND SPORTS, 1166
LIBERTY MOUNTAIN SPORTS, LLC., 1166
LIFETIME, 1166
LIFETIME PRODUCTS, INC., 1166
LINDQUIST FIELD, 992
MAGNUS RACING, 21
MARRIOTT CENTER, 994
MAX-AIR PRODUCTIONS, INC., 766, 851
MILLER SNOWBOARD SPECIALTIES, 1174
NEIGHBORHOOD BOX OFFICE, 941
NJCAA REGION XVIII MEN'S, 287
NJCAA REGION XVIII WOMEN'S, 287
NORDICTRACK, 1180
NORDICTRACK FITNESS STORES, 1245
OFF THE WALL PRODUCTS, LLC, 1181
OGDEN CITY SC, 162
OGDEN RAPTORS, 51
OREM OWLZ, 51
THE ORTHOPEDIC SPECIALTY HOSPITAL, 933
PINCKARD BASEBALL GLOVES, 1185
PIONEEER FAMILY BRANDS, INC., 1077
PIONEER BASEBALL LEAGUE, 50, 51
PORTAFLOOR, 1186
PRINCE YEATES, 910
PRO IMAGE, 1247
RAWLINGS, WILLIAM R., 911
REAL MONARCHS SLC, 159
REAL SALT LAKE, 158
REAL SALT LAKE WOMEN, 166
RICE-ECCLES STADIUM, 1005
ROSSIGNOL SKI COMPANY, INC., 1194
SALT LAKE BEES, 50
SALT LAKE CITY STARS, 60
SALT LAKE CONVENTION & VISITORS BUREAU, 244
SALT LAKE TRIBUNE, 532
SKIS DYNASTAR INC., 1200
SMITH'S BALLPARK, 1012

SMITH'S FOOD & DRUG, 1249
SNAPSPORTS, INC, 1226
SNOWMOBILE ADVENTURES BCD, LC, 936
SNOWSPORTS INDUSTRIES AMERICA, 153
SOUTHERN UTAH UNIVERSITY ATHLETICS, 345
SPECIAL OLYMPICS UTAH, 195
SPECTRUM, 537, 1013
SPORT COURT, INC., 1204
SPORTAMERICA, 818
SPORTSBEAT SATURDAY, 689
SPORTSBEAT SUNDAY, 689
SPORTSNUTS, INC., 723
STANDARD-EXAMINER, 538
TRANS-LUX SPORTS, 1214
TWIN LABORATORIES, INC., 1216
U.S. REPEATING ARMS COMPANY/WINCHESTER, 1217
U.S. SKI AND SNOWBOARD ASSOCIATION (USSA), 153, 205
U.S. SPEEDSKATING, 168
US SPEEDSKATING, 205
USA TEAM HANDBALL, 120
UTAH AAU ASSOCIATION, 215
UTAH ATHLETICS, UNIVERSITY OF, 348
UTAH GOLF ASSOCIATION, 115
UTAH GRIZZLIES, 130
UTAH HIGH SCHOOL ACTIVITIES ASSOCIATION, 200
UTAH JAZZ, 58
UTAH PGA SECTIONAL OFFICE, 107
UTAH SPORTS COMMISSION, 247
UTAH STATE UNIVERSITY ATHLETICS, 348
UTAH SUMMER GAMES, 263
UTAH VALLEY CONVENTION & VISITORS BUREAU, 247
UTAH WINTER GAMES, 263
VIVINT SMART HOME ARENA, 1025
VOILE MOUNTAIN EQUIPMENT, 1220
WASATCH TOURING, 1220
WEBER STATE UNIVERSITY ATHLETICS, 349
WESTMINSTER COLLEGE (UT) ATHLETICS, 376

VERMONT

AMERICAN MORGAN HORSE ASSOCIATION, 74
BACK COUNTRY MAGAZINE, 556
BENNINGTON BANNER, 466
BOGNER, 1119
BURLINGTON FREE PRESS, 470
BURTON SNOWBOARDS, 1122
CALEDONIAN RECORD, 470
CASTLETON STATE COLLEGE, 415
CASTLETON STATE UNIVERSITY ATHLETICS, 381
CONCEPT II, INC., 1129
DAMASCUS WORLDWIDE, INC., 1133
FUSE, 792
GARMONT USA, INC., 1147
GLOBAL REACH SPORTS, 722
GREEN MOUNTAIN COLLEGE ATHLETICS, 387
JOHNSON STATE COLLEGE ATHLETICS, 390
KARHU U.S.A. LIMITED, 1162
LYNDON STATE COLLEGE ATHLETICS, 393
MIDDLEBURY COLLEGE ATHLETICS, 395
MIDDLEBURY COLLEGE ATHLETICS (MCA), 395
MORGAN HORSE, 577
NEWPORT DAILY EXPRESS, 515
NORDIC NETWORK, 579
NORWICH UNIVERSITY ATHLETICS, 398
PROMOSPORT, 812
RUTLAND HERALD, 530
SOUTHERN VERMONT COLLEGE ATHLETICS, 403
SPECIAL OLYMPICS VERMONT, 195
ST. ALBANS MESSENGER, 538
ST. JOSEPH ATHLETICS, COLLEGE OF, 320
ST. MICHAEL'S COLLEGE ATHLETICS, 372
ST. MICHAEL'S COLLEGE ATHLETICS(SMC), 372
STOWE AREA ASSOCIATION, 771
TIMES ARGUS, 543
TRUE NORTH SPORTS MANAGEMENT, 868
VERMONT ATHLETICS, UNIVERSITY OF, 348
VERMONT GOLF ASSOCIATION, 116
VERMONT LAKE MONSTERS, 1025, 47
VERMONT ORIGINALS, 1219

VERMONT PRINCIPALS' ASSOCIATION, 200
VERMONT RACING COMMISSION, 83
VERMONT SPORTS & EVENTS COUNCIL, 248
VERMONT STATE WOMEN'S GOLF ASSOCIATION, 116
WCAX-TV, 708
WGLV-FM, 655

VIRGINIA

A&N STORES, 1227
ACOUSTICAL INTERIORS, 1102
ACTIVE ALERT, 828
ACUMEN, INC., 1102
ADVANTAGE TENNIS SUPPLY, 1104
ALUMNI FIELD STADIUM, VIRGINIA MILITARY INSTITUTE, 954
AMERICAN CANOE ASSOCIATION, 68
AMERICAN LIFEGUARD ASSOCIATION, 215
AMERICAN MILITARY UNIVERSITY, 411
AMERICAN PHYSICAL THERAPY ASSOCIATION, 84, 929
AMERICAN SPORTFISHING ASSOCIATION, 87
AMF BOWLING WORLDWIDE, 1108
APPALACHIAN LEAGUE, 33, 34
ARMSTRONG STADIUM, 955
ATLANTIC 10 CONFERENCE, 289
AVERETT COLLEGE SPORT MANAGEMENT PROGRAM, 412
AVERETT UNIVERSITY ATHLETICS, 378
AVERETT UNIVERSITY ATHLETICS (AU), 378
BABY FANATIC, LLC, 1113
BAG BOY COMPANY, 1113
BATTLE, MICHAEL RAY, 835
BICYCLE EXCHANGE, INC., 1230
BIMMERWORLD RACING, 20
BLUEFIELD COLLEGE ATHLETICS, 307, 353
BOAT OWNERS ASSOCIATION OF THE UNITED STATES (BOATUS), 64
BOAT U.S. MAGAZINE, 558
BRANDONBILT MOTORSPORTS, 24
BRIAN MITCHELL FOUNDATION, THE, 189
BRIDGEWATER COLLEGE ATHLETICS, 379
BRISTOL HERALD COURIER, 469
BRISTOL PIRATES, 33
BROTMAN WINTER FRIED COMMUNICATIONS, INC., 759
C M T SPECIALTY SPORTS, 1233
C. JAY ROBBINS, 880
CABLEFORM INC., 1123
CALFEE PARK, 962
CAMERON HALL, 962
CAPITAL ONE FINANCIAL, 735
CARDWELL, VICTOR, 880
CASSELL COLISEUM, 964
CENTRAL INTERCOLLEGIATE ATHLETIC ASSOCIATION, 292
CENTRAL VIRGINIA SPORTS MANAGEMENT, 837
CENTRE VIEW, 471
CHAMPIONSHIP SPORTS GROUP, 760
CHECKERED FLAG SPORTS, 1126
CHESAPEAKE REGIONAL COMMISSIONER/USA VOLLEYBALL, 209
CHESTERFIELD UNITED, 164
CHRISTOPHER NEWPORT UNIVERSITY ATHLETICS, 382
CHRONICLE OF THE HORSE, 560
CLUB MANAGERS ASSOCIATION OF AMERICA, 217
COLLEGE OF WILLIAM & MARY, 967
COLONIAL ATHLETIC ASSOCIATION, 293
COMMONWEALTH GAMES OF VIRGINIA, 260
CONNECTIONS CONSULTING, 787
CRADDOCK-CUNNINGHAM ARCHITECTURAL PARTNERS, 1063
CRAIGHILL, FRANCIS H., III, 839
CREATIVE URETHANES, 1131
CULPEPER STAR-EXPONENT, 477
DAILY NEWS-RECORD, 481
DAILY PRESS (VA), 481
DAILY PROGRESS, 481
DANVILLE BRAVES, 33
DANVILLE REGISTER AND BEE, 484
DATREK PROFESSIONAL BAG, 1134
DEVAULT MEMORIAL STADIUM, 970
DIAMOND FIELD, 970
DISCOVER LYNCHBURG, 231
DISSON SKATING, 788
DIXIE SPORTING GOODS, 1236

WPRZ-AM, 669
WRIC TV-8, 717
WRIC-TV, 717
WRNL-AM, 672
WRXL-FM, 672
WSIG-FM, 673
WSLS-TV, 718
WSNV-FM, 674
WTKR-TV, 718
WTON-AM, 676
WUVA-FM, 677
WVEC-TV, 720
WVGM-AM, 677
WWBT-TV, 720
WYTI-AM/FM, 679
WZBB-FM, 680
YACHTWORLD.COM, 179

WASHINGTON

ADVANTAGE SPORTS RACK, 1104
ALPHA SPORTSWEAR, INC., 1106
AMERICAN MEDICAL TENNIS ASSOCIATION,
171
ARC ARCHITECTS, 1059
AVISTA STADIUM, 956
BADEN SPORTS, INC., 1113
BAUM, ETENGOFF & BUCKLEY, 873
BELLINGHAM HERALD, 466
BELLINGHAM/WHATCOM CHAMBER OF
COMMERCE, 227
BETWEEN THE TOUCHLINES, 557
BROOKS, 1120
BUFFALO EXPORT, LLC, 1122
BUNKER JONES GOLF, INC, 1232
CANOE & KAYAK MAGAZINE, 559
CBS COLLEGIATE SPORT PROPERTIES, 785
CCI SOLUTIONS, 828
CENTRAL KITSAP REPORTER, 471
CENTRAL WASHINGTON UNIVERSITY, 415
CENTRAL WASHINGTON UNIVERSITY
ATHLETICS, 354
CENTRALIA KNITTING MILLS, INC., 1125
CHENEY STADIUM, 965
CHRONICLE (WA), 472
COLUMBIAN, 474
CONCESSION SOLUTIONS, INC., 1076
CONNELLY SKIS, 1129
CUTTER AND BUCK, INC., 1132
CYBERSPORTS, INC., 1236
DAILY NEWS (WA), 480
DAILY RECORD (WA), 482
DAILY WORLD, 483
DES MOINES NEWS AND HIGHLINE TIMES, 485
DETLEF SCHREMPF FOUNDATION, 189
DIADORA AMERICA, 1134
DIAMONDBACK BICYCLES, 1135
DON CAREY & ASSOCIATES, 1064
EASTERN WASHINGTON UNIVERSITY
ATHLETICS, 329
EBBETS FIELD FLANNELS, 1138
EMERALD DOWNS, 1047
ERICKSON MCGOVERN, 1065
ETTER, MCMAHON, LAMBERSON & CLARY,
P.C.A., 888
EVERETT AQUASOX, 48
EVERETT MEMORIAL STADIUM, 972
EVERETT SILVERTIPS, 138
EVERGREEN REGIONAL COMMISSIONER/USA
VOLLEYBALL, 209
EVERGREEN STATE UNIVERSITY ATHLETICS,
311
FAR POST, 564
FC TACOMA 253, 164
FEDERATION OF PETANQUE USA, 144
FIELDHOUSE, INC., 791
FOAMHEADS, LLC, 1145
FOSTER & EASLEY SPORTS MANAGEMENT
GROUP, 842
FUERZA FC, 165
48 DEGREES NORTH, 553
GLOBAL SPORTS PRODUCTIONS, 601
GLOBAL SPORTS PRODUCTIONS, LTD., 844
GONZAGA UNIVERSITY ATHLETICS, 331
HEC EDMUNDSON PAVILION, 978
HELLY HANSEN, (U.S.) INC., 1154
HERALD (WA), 496
HIGH 5 SPORTSWEAR, 1155
HIGHLINE TIMES, 497
HO SPORTS INC., 1155

HUSKY STADIUM, 981
IMPACT SPORTS, 606
IMPACT SPORTS, INC., 765
INLAND EMPIRE AAU ASSOCIATION, 212
INSTA-BENCH/CARRY GEAR SOLUTIONS, 1158
IRONMAN WETSUITS, 1159
ISC GUNNERS FC, 165
JOE ALBI STADIUM, 984
JOE MARTIN FIELD, 985
JUCKETT SPORTS & ENTERTAINMENT, 849
JUST SPORTS, 1242
K2 INC., 1162
KALE-AM, 619
KAPP-TV, 695
KCPQ-TV, 696
KEEPING IN TOUCH, 573
KELA, 623
KEYG-AM, 624
KEYLIN & ASSOCIATES, 766
KFLD, 624
KGRG-FM, 625
KHHO-AM, 626
KHTR-FM, 626
KIMA-TV, 699
KING COUNTY JOURNAL, 503
KING-TV, 699
KIRO-TV, 699
KIT, 627
KITSAP PUMAS, 161
KJR/KHHO SPORTS RADIO, 627
KLAY, 628
KLAY-AM, 628
KLCK-AM, 629
KLOG-AM, 629
KOMO 1000 AM RADIO, 632
KOMO-TV, 701
KONA-AM, 632
KPUG-AM, 633
KREM-TV, 702
KRKO-AM, 634
KTCV-FM, 636
KVAC-AM, 638
KVTI-FM, 638
KWIQ-AM, 638
KXLY-AM, 639
LAW OFFICE OF WILLIAM D HOCHBERG, 899
LEIGH STOWELL & COMPANY, 801
LEVINSON, FRIEDMAN, P.S., 899
LIGHTWEAR, 1167
LMN ARCHITECTS, 1070
LOCKED ON SPORTS, 612
LOPEZ & FANTEL, 900
MARYLAND SOCCER NEWS, 575
MATMAN WRESTLING COMPANY, 1171
MCNETT CORPORATION, 1172
MICHIGAN SOCCER, 576
MICROSOFT CORPORATION, 738
MINNESOTA SOCCER TIMES, 577
MISSISSIPPY IN TOUCH, 577
MORTON & MCGOLDRICK, P.S., 906
MOUNTAIN SAFETY RESEARCH, 1176
MOUNTAIN ZONE, 577
MOVING COMFORT, INC., 1176
NATIONAL INTERCOLLEGIATE RODEO
ASSOCIATION (NIRA), 146
NAUTILUS HPS, INC., 1177
NEWS TRIBUNE, 516
NOLIMITZ, 1180
NORTH CAROLINA YOUTH SOCCER, 579
NORTH SPORTS, INC., 1180
NORTHWEST CONFERENCE, 300
NORTHWEST VOLLEYBALL INC., 210
O'BRIEN INTERNATIONAL, 1181
OHIO SOCCER, 580
OL REIGN, 158
OLYMPIAN, 519
OLYMPIC FORCE, 165
OREGON GOAL LINES, 580
ORTHOPEDIC PHYSICIAN ASSOCIATES, 932
PACIFIC COAST LEAGUE OF PROFESSIONAL
BASEBALL CLUBS, 48, 49, 50
PACIFIC LUTHERAN UNIVERSITY ATHLETICS,
398
PACIFIC NORTHWEST AAU ASSOCIATION, 214
PACIFIC NORTHWEST GOLFER, 581
PACIFIC NORTHWEST PGA SECTIONAL
OFFICE, 106
PACIFIC NORTHWEST SKI ASSOCIATION, 152
PACIFIC TRAIL, 1183
PENINSULA DAILY NEWS, 522

PENINSULA GATEWAY/GATEWAY PLUS, 522
PERKINS COIE LAW FIRM, 909
PHILLIPS MARKETING, 809
PIONEER BASEBALL LEAGUE (ADVANCED
ROOKIE LEVEL), 50
PITCH, 582
PLAY ON: WASHINGTON STATE YOUTH
SOCCER NEWS, 582
PLAY VISIONS, 1185
POCOCK RACING SHELLS, 1186
PRECOR, INC, 1187
PRESTON, GATES & ELLIS, 910
PRICE COSTCO WHOLESALE, 1246
PRICE MEDIA, 582
PRO GOLF DISCOUNT, 1246
PROGEAR, INC., 1189
PROPET USA INC., 1189
PUGET SOUND ATHLETICS, UNIVERSITY OF,
399
PUGET SOUND REGIONAL
COMMISSIONER/USA VOLLEYBALL, 210
Q IT UP SPORTS, 688
QWEST FIELD, 1003
RACING WHEELS, 583
RALEIGH CYCLE, 768, 860, 1191
RECREATIONAL EQUIPMENT, INC./REI, 1247
REDDEN MARINE SUPPLY, INC., 1247
ROOT SPORTS NORTHWEST, 684
THE ROWERS' CODE, 822
SAFECO FIELD, 1009
SAINT MARTIN'S COLLEGE ATHLETICS, 370
SEA KAYAKER, 585
SEATTLE BIKE SUPPLY, 1198
SEATTLE KRAKEN, 125
SEATTLE MARINERS, 30
SEATTLE PACIFIC UNIVERSITY, 434
SEATTLE POST-INTELLIGENCER, 534
SEATTLE SEAHAWKS, 97
SEATTLE SOUNDERS FC, 158
SEATTLE STORM, 61
SEATTLE SYSTEMS/LENOX HILL BRACE
COMPANY, 1198
SEATTLE THUNDERBIRDS, 138
SEATTLE TIMES, 534
SEATTLE UNIVERSITY ATHLETICS, 318
SIMS SPORTS, INC., 1200
SKAGIT VALLEY HERALD, 535
SKI SKOOT INC, 1200
SMITH, PAYTON, 917
SOCCER CALIFORNIA, 588
SOCCER IN NEVADA, 588
SOCCER NEW JERSEY, 588
SOCCER OHIO SOUTH, 588
SOFTRIDE, 1202
SPECIAL OLYMPICS WASHINGTON, 195
SPOKANE CHIEFS, 139
SPOKANE HOOPFEST, 55
SPOKANE INDIANS, 48
SPOKANE REGIONAL SPORTS COMMISSION,
245
SPOKANE SHOCK, 94
SPOKANE VETERANS MEMORIAL ARENA, 1013
SPOKESMAN-REVIEW, 537
SPORTS AND EVENTS COUNCIL OF
SEATTLE/KING COUNTY, 245
SPORTS RADIO 1510 KGA, 641
SPORTS RADIO KJR, 612
SQUASH MAGAZINE, 592
STAIRMASTER HEALTH AND FITNESS
PRODUCTS, 1207
STRATEGIC RESOURCES, 757
STRIKER-WEST, 593
SUN (WA), 541
T-MOBILE USA, 741
TACOMA DEFIANCE, 159
TACOMA DOME, 1016
TACOMA RAINIERS, 50
TACOMA/PIERCE COUNTY SPORTS
COMMISSION, 246
TALON GROUP INTERNATIONAL
D/B/A/MANAGEMENT RECRUITERS OF
MERCER ISLAND, 757
TARSHES, DAVID C., 920
TEETER HAND UPS/STL INTERNATIONAL,
INCORPORATED, 1211
TITANIUM SPORTS TECHNOLOGIES, 1213
TM ATHLETICS, 1213
TOUCHLINE-EASTERN PENNSYLVANIA, 595
TRACE ATHLETIC CORPORATION, 1214
TRI-CITIES SPORTS COUNCIL, 247

WEST VIRGINIA

WISCONSIN

WYOMING

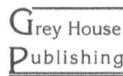

2021 Title List

Visit www.GreyHouse.com for Product Information, Table of Contents, and Sample Pages.

Opinions Throughout History

Opinions Throughout History: The Death Penalty
Opinions Throughout History: Diseases & Epidemics
Opinions Throughout History: Drug Use & Abuse
Opinions Throughout History: The Environment
Opinions Throughout History: Gender: Roles & Rights
Opinions Throughout History: Globalization
Opinions Throughout History: Guns in America
Opinions Throughout History: Immigration
Opinions Throughout History: Law Enforcement in America
Opinions Throughout History: National Security vs. Civil & Privacy Rights
Opinions Throughout History: Presidential Authority
Opinions Throughout History: Robotics & Artificial Intelligence
Opinions Throughout History: Social Media Issues
Opinions Throughout History: Sports & Games
Opinions Throughout History: Voters' Rights

This is Who We Were

This is Who We Were: Colonial America (1492-1775)
This is Who We Were: 1880-1899
This is Who We Were: In the 1900s
This is Who We Were: In the 1910s
This is Who We Were: In the 1920s
This is Who We Were: A Companion to the 1940 Census
This is Who We Were: In the 1940s (1940-1949)
This is Who We Were: In the 1950s
This is Who We Were: In the 1960s
This is Who We Were: In the 1970s
This is Who We Were: In the 1980s
This is Who We Were: In the 1990s
This is Who We Were: In the 2000s
This is Who We Were: In the 2010s

Working Americans

Working Americans—Vol. 1: The Working Class
Working Americans—Vol. 2: The Middle Class
Working Americans—Vol. 3: The Upper Class
Working Americans—Vol. 4: Children
Working Americans—Vol. 5: At War
Working Americans—Vol. 6: Working Women
Working Americans—Vol. 7: Social Movements
Working Americans—Vol. 8: Immigrants
Working Americans—Vol. 9: Revolutionary War to the Civil War
Working Americans—Vol. 10: Sports & Recreation
Working Americans—Vol. 11: Inventors & Entrepreneurs
Working Americans—Vol. 12: Our History through Music
Working Americans—Vol. 13: Education & Educators
Working Americans—Vol. 14: African Americans
Working Americans—Vol. 15: Politics & Politicians
Working Americans—Vol. 16: Farming & Ranching
Working Americans—Vol. 17: Teens in America

Education

Complete Learning Disabilities Resource Guide
Educators Resource Guide
The Comparative Guide to Elem. & Secondary Schools
Charter School Movement
Special Education: A Reference Book for Policy & Curriculum Development

Grey House Health & Wellness Guides

Autoimmune Disorders Handbook & Resource Guide
Cancer Handbook & Resource Guide
Cardiovascular Disease Handbook & Resource Guide
Dementia Handbook & Resource Guide

Consumer Health

Autoimmune Disorders Handbook & Resource Guide
Cancer Handbook & Resource Guide
Cardiovascular Disease Handbook & Resource Guide
Comparative Guide to American Hospitals
Complete Mental Health Resource Guide
Complete Resource Guide for Pediatric Disorders
Complete Resource Guide for People with Chronic Illness
Complete Resource Guide for People with Disabilities
Older Americans Information Resource

General Reference

African Biographical Dictionary
American Environmental Leaders
America's College Museums
Constitutional Amendments
Encyclopedia of African-American Writing
Encyclopedia of Invasions & Conquests
Encyclopedia of Prisoners of War & Internment
Encyclopedia of Rural America
Encyclopedia of the Continental Congresses
Encyclopedia of the United States Cabinet
Encyclopedia of War Journalism
The Environmental Debate
The Evolution Wars: A Guide to the Debates
Financial Literacy Starter Kit
From Suffrage to the Senate
The Gun Debate: Gun Rights & Gun Control in the U.S.
History of Canada
Historical Warrior Peoples & Modern Fighting Groups
Human Rights and the United States
Political Corruption in America
Privacy Rights in the Digital Age
The Religious Right and American Politics
Speakers of the House of Representatives, 1789-2021
US Land & Natural Resources Policy
The Value of a Dollar 1600-1865 Colonial to Civil War
The Value of a Dollar 1860-2019
World Cultural Leaders of the 20th Century

Business Information

Business Information Resources
The Complete Broadcasting Industry Guide: Television, Radio, Cable & Streaming
Directory of Mail Order Catalogs
Environmental Resource Handbook
Food & Beverage Market Place
The Grey House Guide to Homeland Security Resources
The Grey House Performing Arts Industry Guide
Guide to Healthcare Group Purchasing Organizations
Guide to U.S. HMOs and PPOs
Guide to Venture Capital & Private Equity Firms
Hudson's Washington News Media Contacts Guide
New York State Directory
Sports Market Place

Grey House Publishing | Salem Press | H.W. Wilson | 4919 Route, 22 PO Box 56, Amenia NY 12501-0056

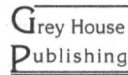

2021 Title List

Visit www.GreyHouse.com for Product Information, Table of Contents, and Sample Pages.

Statistics & Demographics

America's Top-Rated Cities
America's Top-Rated Smaller Cities
The Comparative Guide to American Suburbs
Profiles of America
Profiles of California
Profiles of Florida
Profiles of Illinois
Profiles of Indiana
Profiles of Massachusetts
Profiles of Michigan
Profiles of New Jersey
Profiles of New York
Profiles of North Carolina & South Carolina
Profiles of Ohio
Profiles of Pennsylvania
Profiles of Texas
Profiles of Virginia
Profiles of Wisconsin

Canadian Resources

Associations Canada
Canadian Almanac & Directory
Canadian Environmental Resource Guide
Canadian Parliamentary Guide
Canadian Venture Capital & Private Equity Firms
Canadian Who's Who
Cannabis Canada
Careers & Employment Canada
Financial Post: Directory of Directors
Financial Services Canada
FP Bonds: Corporate
FP Bonds: Government
FP Equities: Preferreds & Derivatives
FP Survey: Industrials
FP Survey: Mines & Energy
FP Survey: Predecessor & Defunct
Health Guide Canada
Libraries Canada
Major Canadian Cities: Compared & Ranked, First Edition

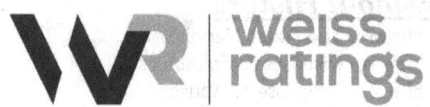

Weiss Financial Ratings

Financial Literacy Basics
Financial Literacy: How to Become an Investor
Financial Literacy: Planning for the Future
Weiss Ratings Consumer Guides
Weiss Ratings Guide to Banks
Weiss Ratings Guide to Credit Unions
Weiss Ratings Guide to Health Insurers
Weiss Ratings Guide to Life & Annuity Insurers
Weiss Ratings Guide to Property & Casualty Insurers
Weiss Ratings Investment Research Guide to Bond & Money
    Market Mutual Funds
Weiss Ratings Investment Research Guide to Exchange-Traded
    Funds
Weiss Ratings Investment Research Guide to Stock Mutual Funds
Weiss Ratings Investment Research Guide to Stocks

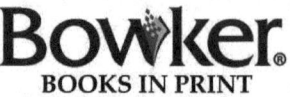

Books in Print Series

American Book Publishing Record® Annual
American Book Publishing Record® Monthly
Books In Print®
Books In Print® Supplement
Books Out Loud™
Bowker's Complete Video Directory™
Children's Books In Print®
El-Hi Textbooks & Serials In Print®
Forthcoming Books®
Law Books & Serials In Print™
Medical & Health Care Books In Print™
Publishers, Distributors & Wholesalers of the US™
Subject Guide to Books In Print®
Subject Guide to Children's Books In Print®

Grey House Publishing | Salem Press | H.W. Wilson | 4919 Route, 22 PO Box 56, Amenia NY 12501-0056

SALEM PRESS

2021 Title List

Visit www.SalemPress.com for Product Information, Table of Contents, and Sample Pages.

SALEM PRESS

LITERATURE

Critical Insights: Authors

Louisa May Alcott
Sherman Alexie
Isabel Allende
Maya Angelou
Isaac Asimov
Margaret Atwood
Jane Austen
James Baldwin
Saul Bellow
Roberto Bolano
Ray Bradbury
Gwendolyn Brooks
Albert Camus
Raymond Carver
Willa Cather
Geoffrey Chaucer
John Cheever
Joseph Conrad
Charles Dickens
Emily Dickinson
Frederick Douglass
T. S. Eliot
George Eliot
Harlan Ellison
Louise Erdrich
William Faulkner
F. Scott Fitzgerald
Gustave Flaubert
Horton Foote
Benjamin Franklin
Robert Frost
Neil Gaiman
Gabriel Garcia Marquez
Thomas Hardy
Nathaniel Hawthorne
Robert A. Heinlein
Lillian Hellman
Ernest Hemingway
Langston Hughes
Zora Neale Hurston
Henry James
Thomas Jefferson
James Joyce
Jamaica Kincaid
Stephen King
Martin Luther King, Jr.
Barbara Kingsolver
Abraham Lincoln
Mario Vargas Llosa
Jack London
James McBride
Cormac McCarthy
Herman Melville
Arthur Miller
Toni Morrison
Alice Munro
Tim O'Brien
Flannery O'Connor
Eugene O'Neill

George Orwell
Sylvia Plath
Philip Roth
Salman Rushdie
Mary Shelley
John Steinbeck
Amy Tan
Leo Tolstoy
Mark Twain
John Updike
Kurt Vonnegut
Alice Walker
David Foster Wallace
Edith Wharton
Walt Whitman
Oscar Wilde
Tennessee Williams
Richard Wright
Malcolm X

Critical Insights: Works

Absalom, Absalom!
Adventures of Huckleberry Finn
Aeneid
All Quiet on the Western Front
Animal Farm
Anna Karenina
The Awakening
The Bell Jar
Beloved
Billy Budd, Sailor
The Book Thief
Brave New World
The Canterbury Tales
Catch-22
The Catcher in the Rye
The Crucible
Death of a Salesman
The Diary of a Young Girl
Dracula
Fahrenheit 451
The Grapes of Wrath
Great Expectations
The Great Gatsby
Hamlet
The Handmaid's Tale
Harry Potter Series
Heart of Darkness
The Hobbit
The House on Mango Street
How the Garcia Girls Lost Their Accents
The Hunger Games Trilogy
I Know Why the Caged Bird Sings
In Cold Blood
The Inferno
Invisible Man
Jane Eyre
The Joy Luck Club
King Lear
The Kite Runner
Life of Pi
Little Women

Lolita
Lord of the Flies
Macbeth
The Metamorphosis
Midnight's Children
A Midsummer Night's Dream
Moby-Dick
Mrs. Dalloway
Nineteen Eighty-Four
The Odyssey
Of Mice and Men
One Flew Over the Cuckoo's Nest
One Hundred Years of Solitude
Othello
The Outsiders
Paradise Lost
The Pearl
The Poetry of Baudelaire
The Poetry of Edgar Allan Poe
A Portrait of the Artist as a Young Man
Pride and Prejudice
The Red Badge of Courage
Romeo and Juliet
The Scarlet Letter
Short Fiction of Flannery O'Connor
Slaughterhouse-Five
The Sound and the Fury
A Streetcar Named Desire
The Sun Also Rises
A Tale of Two Cities
The Tales of Edgar Allan Poe
Their Eyes Were Watching God
Things Fall Apart
To Kill a Mockingbird
War and Peace
The Woman Warrior

Critical Insights: Themes

The American Comic Book
American Creative Non-Fiction
The American Dream
American Multicultural Identity
American Road Literature
American Short Story
American Sports Fiction
The American Thriller
American Writers in Exile
Censored & Banned Literature
Civil Rights Literature, Past & Present
Coming of Age
Conspiracies
Contemporary Canadian Fiction
Contemporary Immigrant Short Fiction
Contemporary Latin American Fiction
Contemporary Speculative Fiction
Crime and Detective Fiction
Crisis of Faith
Cultural Encounters
Dystopia
Family
The Fantastic
Feminism

SALEM PRESS

2021 Title List

Visit www.SalemPress.com for Product Information, Table of Contents, and Sample Pages.

SALEM PRESS

Flash Fiction
Gender, Sex and Sexuality
Good & Evil
The Graphic Novel
Greed
Harlem Renaissance
The Hero's Quest
Historical Fiction
Holocaust Literature
The Immigrant Experience
Inequality
LGBTQ Literature
Literature in Times of Crisis
Literature of Protest
Magical Realism
Midwestern Literature
Modern Japanese Literature
Nature & the Environment
Paranoia, Fear & Alienation
Patriotism
Political Fiction
Postcolonial Literature
Pulp Fiction of the '20s and '30s
Rebellion
Russia's Golden Age
Satire
The Slave Narrative
Social Justice and American Literature
Southern Gothic Literature
Southwestern Literature
Survival
Technology & Humanity
Violence in Literature
Virginia Woolf & 20th Century Women Writers
War

Critical Insights: Film
Bonnie & Clyde
Casablanca
Alfred Hitchcock
Stanley Kubrick

Critical Approaches to Literature
Critical Approaches to Literature: Feminist
Critical Approaches to Literature: Moral
Critical Approaches to Literature: Multicultural
Critical Approaches to Literature: Psychological

Critical Surveys of Literature
Critical Survey of American Literature
Critical Survey of Drama
Critical Survey of Graphic Novels: Heroes & Superheroes
Critical Survey of Graphic Novels: History, Theme, and
    Technique
Critical Survey of Graphic Novels: Independents and
    Underground Classics
Critical Survey of Graphic Novels: Manga
Critical Survey of Long Fiction
Critical Survey of Mystery and Detective Fiction
Critical Survey of Mythology & Folklore: Gods & Goddesses
Critical Survey of Mythology & Folklore: Heroes and Heroines
Critical Survey of Mythology & Folklore: Love, Sexuality, and
    Desire
Critical Survey of Mythology & Folklore: World Mythology
Critical Survey of Poetry
Critical Survey of Poetry: Contemporary Poets
Critical Survey of Science Fiction & Fantasy Literature
Critical Survey of Shakespeare's Plays
Critical Survey of Shakespeare's Sonnets
Critical Survey of Short Fiction
Critical Survey of World Literature
Critical Survey of Young Adult Literature

Cyclopedia of Literary Characters & Places
Cyclopedia of Literary Characters
Cyclopedia of Literary Places

Introduction to Literary Context
American Poetry of the 20th Century
American Post-Modernist Novels
American Short Fiction
English Literature
Plays
World Literature

Magill's Literary Annual
Magill's Literary Annual, 2021
Magill's Literary Annual, 2020
Magill's Literary Annual, 2019

Masterplots
Masterplots, Fourth Edition
Masterplots, 2010-2018 Supplement

Notable Writers
Notable African American Writers
Notable American Women Writers
Notable Mystery & Detective Fiction Writers
Notable Native American Writers & Writers of the American West
Novels into Film: Adaptations & Interpretation
Recommended Reading: 600 Classics Reviewed

Grey House Publishing | Salem Press | H.W. Wilson | 4919 Route, 22 PO Box 56, Amenia NY 12501-0056

SALEM PRESS

SALEM PRESS

2021 Title List

Visit www.SalemPress.com for Product Information, Table of Contents, and Sample Pages.

HISTORY
The Decades
The 1910s in America
The Twenties in America
The Thirties in America
The Forties in America
The Fifties in America
The Sixties in America
The Seventies in America
The Eighties in America
The Nineties in America
The 2000s in America
The 2010s in America

Defining Documents in American History
Defining Documents: The 1900s
Defining Documents: The 1910s
Defining Documents: The 1920s
Defining Documents: The 1930s
Defining Documents: The 1950s
Defining Documents: The 1960s
Defining Documents: The 1970s
Defining Documents: American Citizenship
Defining Documents: The American Economy
Defining Documents: The American Revolution
Defining Documents: The American West
Defining Documents: Business Ethics
Defining Documents: Capital Punishment
Defining Documents: Civil Rights
Defining Documents: Civil War
Defining Documents: The Cold War
Defining Documents: Dissent & Protest
Defining Documents: Drug Policy
Defining Documents: The Emergence of Modern America
Defining Documents: Environment & Conservation
Defining Documents: Espionage & Intrigue
Defining Documents: Exploration and Colonial America
Defining Documents: The Formation of the States
Defining Documents: The Free Press
Defining Documents: The Gun Debate
Defining Documents: Immigration & Immigrant Communities
Defining Documents: The Legacy of 9/11
Defining Documents: LGBTQ+
Defining Documents: Manifest Destiny and the New Nation
Defining Documents: Native Americans
Defining Documents: Political Campaigns, Candidates & Discourse
Defining Documents: Postwar 1940s
Defining Documents: Prison Reform
Defining Documents: Secrets, Leaks & Scandals
Defining Documents: Slavery
Defining Documents: Supreme Court Decisions
Defining Documents: Reconstruction Era
Defining Documents: The Vietnam War
Defining Documents: U.S. Involvement in the Middle East
Defining Documents: World War I
Defining Documents: World War II

Defining Documents in World History
Defining Documents: The 17th Century
Defining Documents: The 18th Century
Defining Documents: The 19th Century
Defining Documents: The 20th Century (1900-1950)
Defining Documents: The Ancient World
Defining Documents: Asia
Defining Documents: Genocide & the Holocaust
Defining Documents: Nationalism & Populism
Defining Documents: Pandemics, Plagues & Public Health
Defining Documents: Renaissance & Early Modern Era
Defining Documents: The Middle Ages
Defining Documents: The Middle East
Defining Documents: Women's Rights

Great Events from History
Great Events from History: The Ancient World
Great Events from History: The Middle Ages
Great Events from History: The Renaissance & Early Modern Era
Great Events from History: The 17th Century
Great Events from History: The 18th Century
Great Events from History: The 19th Century
Great Events from History: The 20th Century, 1901-1940
Great Events from History: The 20th Century, 1941-1970
Great Events from History: The 20th Century, 1971-2000
Great Events from History: Modern Scandals
Great Events from History: African American History
Great Events from History: The 21st Century, 2000-2016
Great Events from History: LGBTQ Events
Great Events from History: Human Rights

Great Lives from History
Computer Technology Innovators
Fashion Innovators
Great Athletes
Great Athletes of the Twenty-First Century
Great Lives from History: African Americans
Great Lives from History: American Heroes
Great Lives from History: American Women
Great Lives from History: Asian and Pacific Islander Americans
Great Lives from History: Inventors & Inventions
Great Lives from History: Jewish Americans
Great Lives from History: Latinos
Great Lives from History: Scientists and Science
Great Lives from History: The 17th Century
Great Lives from History: The 18th Century
Great Lives from History: The 19th Century
Great Lives from History: The 20th Century
Great Lives from History: The 21st Century, 2000-2017
Great Lives from History: The Ancient World
Great Lives from History: The Incredibly Wealthy
Great Lives from History: The Middle Ages
Great Lives from History: The Renaissance & Early Modern Era
Human Rights Innovators
Internet Innovators
Music Innovators
Musicians and Composers of the 20th Century
World Political Innovators

Grey House Publishing | Salem Press | H.W. Wilson | 4919 Route, 22 PO Box 56, Amenia NY 12501-0056

2021 Title List

Visit www.SalemPress.com for Product Information, Table of Contents, and Sample Pages.

History & Government

American First Ladies
American Presidents
The 50 States
The Ancient World: Extraordinary People in Extraordinary
  Societies
The Bill of Rights
The Criminal Justice System
The U.S. Supreme Court

SOCIAL SCIENCES

Civil Rights Movements: Past & Present
Countries, Peoples and Cultures
Countries: Their Wars & Conflicts: A World Survey
Education Today: Issues, Policies & Practices
Encyclopedia of American Immigration
Ethics: Questions & Morality of Human Actions
Issues in U.S. Immigration
Principles of Sociology: Group Relationships & Behavior
Principles of Sociology: Personal Relationships & Behavior
Principles of Sociology: Societal Issues & Behavior
Racial & Ethnic Relations in America
World Geography

SCIENCE

Ancient Creatures
Applied Science
Applied Science: Engineering & Mathematics
Applied Science: Science & Medicine
Applied Science: Technology
Biomes and Ecosystems
Earth Science: Earth Materials and Resources
Earth Science: Earth's Surface and History
Earth Science: Earth's Weather, Water and Atmosphere
Earth Science: Physics and Chemistry of the Earth
Encyclopedia of Climate Change
Encyclopedia of Energy
Encyclopedia of Environmental Issues
Encyclopedia of Global Resources
Encyclopedia of Mathematics and Society
Forensic Science
Notable Natural Disasters
The Solar System
USA in Space

Principles of Science

Principles of Anatomy
Principles of Astronomy
Principles of Behavioral Science
Principles of Biology
Principles of Biotechnology
Principles of Botany
Principles of Chemistry
Principles of Climatology
Principles of Information Technology
Principles of Computer Science
Principles of Ecology
Principles of Energy
Principles of Geology

Principles of Marine Science
Principles of Mathematics
Principles of Modern Agriculture
Principles of Pharmacology
Principles of Physical Science
Principles of Physics
Principles of Programming & Coding
Principles of Robotics & Artificial Intelligence
Principles of Scientific Research
Principles of Sustainability
Principles of Zoology

HEALTH

Addictions, Substance Abuse & Alcoholism
Adolescent Health & Wellness
Aging
Cancer
Community & Family Health Issues
Integrative, Alternative & Complementary Medicine
Genetics and Inherited Conditions
Infectious Diseases and Conditions
Magill's Medical Guide
Nutrition
Psychology & Behavioral Health
Women's Health

Principles of Health

Principles of Health: Allergies & Immune Disorders
Principles of Health: Anxiety & Stress
Principles of Health: Depression
Principles of Health: Diabetes
Principles of Health: Nursing
Principles of Health: Obesity
Principles of Health: Pain Management
Principles of Health: Prescription Drug Abuse

Grey House Publishing | Salem Press | H.W. Wilson | 4919 Route, 22 PO Box 56, Amenia NY 12501-0056

SALEM PRESS

2021 Title List

SALEM PRESS

Visit www.SalemPress.com for Product Information, Table of Contents, and Sample Pages.

CAREERS

Careers: Paths to Entrepreneurship
Careers in the Arts: Fine, Performing & Visual
Careers in Building Construction
Careers in Business
Careers in Chemistry
Careers in Communications & Media
Careers in Education & Training
Careers in Environment & Conservation
Careers in Financial Services
Careers in Forensic Science
Careers in Gaming
Careers in Green Energy
Careers in Healthcare
Careers in Hospitality & Tourism
Careers in Human Services
Careers in Information Technology
Careers in Law, Criminal Justice & Emergency Services
Careers in the Music Industry
Careers in Manufacturing & Production
Careers in Nursing
Careers in Physics
Careers in Protective Services
Careers in Psychology & Behavioral Health
Careers in Public Administration
Careers in Sales, Insurance & Real Estate
Careers in Science & Engineering
Careers in Social Media
Careers in Sports & Fitness
Careers in Sports Medicine & Training
Careers in Technical Services & Equipment Repair
Careers in Transportation
Careers in Writing & Editing
Careers Outdoors
Careers Overseas
Careers Working with Infants & Children
Careers Working with Animals

BUSINESS

Principles of Business: Accounting
Principles of Business: Economics
Principles of Business: Entrepreneurship
Principles of Business: Finance
Principles of Business: Globalization
Principles of Business: Leadership
Principles of Business: Management
Principles of Business: Marketing

2021 Title List

Visit www.HWWilsonInPrint.com for Product Information, Table of Contents, and Sample Pages.

The Reference Shelf

Affordable Housing
Aging in America
Alternative Facts, Post-Truth and the Information War
The American Dream
American Military Presence Overseas
Arab Spring
Artificial Intelligence
The Business of Food
Campaign Trends & Election Law
College Sports
Conspiracy Theories
Democracy Evolving
The Digital Age
Dinosaurs
Embracing New Paradigms in Education
Faith & Science
Families - Traditional & New Structures
Food Insecurity & Hunger in the United States
Future of U.S. Economic Relations: Mexico, Cuba, & Venezuela
Global Climate Change
Graphic Novels and Comic Books
Guns in America
Hate Crimes
Immigration
Internet Abuses & Privacy Rights
Internet Law
LGBTQ in the 21st Century
Marijuana Reform
National Debate Topic 2014/2015: The Ocean
National Debate Topic 2015/2016: Surveillance
National Debate Topic 2016/2017: US/China Relations
National Debate Topic 2017/2018: Education Reform
National Debate Topic 2018/2019: Immigration
National Debate Topic 2019/2021: Arms Sales
National Debate Topic 2020/2021: Criminal Justice Reform
National Debate Topic 2021/2022
New Frontiers in Space
The News and its Future
Policing in 2020
Politics of the Oceans
Pollution
Prescription Drug Abuse
Propaganda and Misinformation
Racial Tension in a Postracial Age
Reality Television
Representative American Speeches, Annual Edition
Rethinking Work
Revisiting Gender
Robotics
Russia
Social Networking
The South China Sea Conflict
Space Exploration and Development
Sports in America
The Supreme Court
The Transformation of American Cities
The Two Koreas
U.S. Infrastructure
Vaccinations
Whistleblowers

Core Collections

Children's Core Collection
Fiction Core Collection
Graphic Novels Core Collection
Middle & Junior High School Core
Public Library Core Collection: Nonfiction
Senior High Core Collection
Young Adult Fiction Core Collection

Current Biography

Current Biography Cumulative Index 1946-2021
Current Biography Monthly Magazine
Current Biography Yearbook

Readers' Guide to Periodical Literature

Abridged Readers' Guide to Periodical Literature
Readers' Guide to Periodical Literature

Indexes

Index to Legal Periodicals & Books
Short Story Index
Book Review Digest

Sears List

Sears List of Subject Headings
Sears: Lista de Encabezamientos de Materia

History

American Game Changers: Invention, Innovation & Transformation
American Reformers
Speeches of the American Presidents

Facts About Series

Facts About the 20th Century
Facts About American Immigration
Facts About China
Facts About the Presidents
Facts About the World's Languages

Nobel Prize Winners

Nobel Prize Winners: 1901-1986
Nobel Prize Winners: 1987-1991
Nobel Prize Winners: 1992-1996
Nobel Prize Winners: 1997-2001
Nobel Prize Winners: 2002-2018

Famous First Facts

Famous First Facts
Famous First Facts About American Politics
Famous First Facts About Sports
Famous First Facts About the Environment
Famous First Facts: International Edition

American Book of Days

The American Book of Days
The International Book of Days

Grey House Publishing | Salem Press | H.W. Wilson | 4919 Route, 22 PO Box 56, Amenia NY 12501-0056